Encyclopedia
of
Human Rights

Encyclopedia
of
Human Rights

Edward Lawson

With a Foreword by
Jan Martenson
Under-Secretary-General for Human Rights
United Nations

Taylor & Francis Inc.
New York • Philadelphia • Washington • London

Published with the co-operation of the United Nations Centre for Human Rights as a contribution to the World Public Information Campaign for Human Rights.

UK Taylor & Francis Ltd., 4 John Street, London WC1N ZET

USA Taylor & Francis Inc., 1900 Frost Road, Suite 101, Bristol, Pennsylvania

All correspondence should be addressed to:
Encyclopedia of Human Rights
Taylor & Francis
1101 Vermont Avenue, N.W., Suite 200
Washington, DC 20005, USA

Encyclopedia of Human Rights

1 2 3 4 5 6 7 8 9 0   E B E B   9 8 7 6 5 4 3 2 1

This book was set in Baskerville by Creative Graphics Inc. The editor was M. L. Bertucci; the production supervisor was Jung Ra. Cover design by Berg Design.
Printing and binding by Edwards Brothers Inc.

A CIP catalog record for this book is available from the British Library.

Library of Congress Cataloging-in-Publication Data

Encyclopedia of human rights / Edward H. Lawson, editor.
   p.   cm.
   Includes bibliographies.
      1. Human rights—Dictionaries.   2. Civil rights—Dictionaries.
I. Lawson, Edward H.
JC571.E67   1989
323.4'03'21—de19   88-30643
                                                                                    CIP

ISBN 0-8002-8003-2

CONTENTS

FOREWORD

On 10 December 1988, the 40th anniversary of the Universal Declaration of Human Rights, the General Assembly of the United Nations launched a World Public Information Campaign for Human Rights, "under which the activities of the Organization in the field should be developed and strengthened in a global and practically oriented fashion, engaging the complementary activities of concerned bodies of the United Nations system, Member States and non-governmental organizations."

In so doing, the assembly affirmed "that activities to improve public knowledge in the field of human rights are essential to the fulfilment of the purposes of the United Nations set out in Article 1, paragraph 3, of the Charter of the United Nations and that carefully designed programs of teaching, education and information are essential to the achievement of lasting respect for human rights and fundamental freedoms."

The assembly called upon the United Nations Centre for Human Rights, which has primary responsibility within the United Nations system in the field of human rights, to coordinate the substantive activities of the world campaign and to serve as liaison with governments, regional and national institutions, non-governmental organizations, and concerned individuals in the development and implementation of the campaign's activities.

The fundamental aim of the world campaign is to create a universal culture of human rights, one that recognizes that human rights and fundamental freedoms are inherent in every human being without *any* distinction. The Centre for Human Rights considers the private publication of the *Encyclopedia of Human Rights,* as a most helpful contribution to the objectives of the World Public Information Campaign for Human Rights. It brings together in a single volume, and in an accessible form, documentation forming the basis of the myriad standard-setting and monitoring activities of many international organizations, including those of the United Nations and its specialized agencies such as the International Labor Organization, the United Nations Educational, Scientific and Cultural Organization, the Food and Agriculture Organization, and the World Health Organization; regional intergovernmental bodies such as the Council of Europe, the Organization of African Unity, and the Organization of American States; and independent organizations such as the International Committee of the Red Cross.

Compiled by Edward Lawson, a former officer of the then UN Division of Human Rights from 1946 until he retired as its deputy director in 1975, the encyclopedia demonstrates the same conscious effort to attain the fullest objectivity and impartiality as that which characterizes official publications of the United Nations. However, the selection and presentation of materials are solely the responsibility of Mr. Lawson.

I have no doubt that the *Encyclopedia of Human Rights* will serve as a useful tool in the complex but necessary process of coordinating and rationalizing the existing body of human rights instruments and activities—a task for which a world conference has been proposed. We at the Centre for Human Rights welcome this initiative and hope that the encyclopedia will prove of value to those engaged in the long and crucial struggle for the universal promotion and protection of human rights.

JAN MARTENSON
Under-Secretary-General for Human Rights
The United Nations

PREFACE

Half a century ago, in 1941, President Franklin D. Roosevelt of the United States of America and Prime Minister Winston Churchill of the United Kingdom expressed, in the Atlantic Charter, their fervent hope "to see established a peace which will afford to all nations the means of dwelling in safety within their own boundaries, and which will afford assurance that all the men in all the lands may live out their lives in freedom from want and fear."

One year later, 26 allied nations expressed, in the Declaration by United Nations, their firm conviction "that complete victory over their enemies is essential to defend life, liberty, independence and religious freedom, and to preserve human rights and justice in their own lands as well as in other lands." In so doing, they were the first to use the term "human rights" in an international instrument. Later, 21 additional nations joined in adherence to the declaration.

The United Nations Charter, which entered into force in 1945, provides that the UN promote (article 55) "universal respect for, and observance of, human rights and fundamental freedoms for all without distinction as to race, sex, language or religion," and that (article 56) "all Members pledge themselves to take joint and separate action in cooperation with the Organization for the achievement of the purposes set forth in Article 55."

In 1946, the Division of Human Rights was established as part of the United Nations Secretariat, then housed at Hunter College in the Bronx, New York; and I was one of the first to join its staff. I was then in no sense an expert on human rights—actually, there was none in those days because the term was new and undefined—but I had acquired a good record of success in placing members of various minorities in training programs and in employment, and in combatting prejudice and discrimination against them, first in the American federal emergency relief programs of the late 1930s and later in the employment programs of the War Production Board and the War Manpower Commission of the early 1940s.

The division's first assignment was to assist the newly established UN Commission on Human Rights—composed of the representatives of 18 UN member States under the chairmanship of Mrs. Franklin D. Roosevelt—to prepare an "international bill of rights." We did that primarily by studying the various draft bills which had been submitted by the delegations of Chile, Cuba, and Panama; by the American Federation of Labor; and by private individuals, including Dr. Lauterpacht of Cambridge University, Dr. Alvarez of the American Institute of International Law, the Rev. Parsons of the Catholic Association for International Peace, Mr. McNitt of the Faculty of Law of Southwestern University, and Mr. H.G. Wells. We prepared a mammoth analytical compilation of all the rights and freedoms mentioned in those draft bills, as well as those protected by the constitutions of UN member States; and on that basis formulated the "Secretariat Draft Outline of an International Bill of Human Rights" (UN Doc. E/CN.4/AC.1/3 and Add. 1). That draft outline, together with a few United States' proposals for the rewording of some of its items and a new draft International Bill of Human Rights submitted by the United Kingdom, provided the basis for the commission's work in this field.

It was at the second session of the commission, held at the European office of the United Nations in Geneva from 2 to 17 December 1947, that the conception of an international bill of human rights composed of three parts—a declaration, a convention, and measures for implementation—began to crystallize, as it became evident that many governments were prepared to support a declaration if it were to precede and not to replace a convention. The commission included in its report on that session (UN Doc. E/600) its views on measures of implementation, which served as a basis for all subsequent study in that field.

At its third session, held at Lake Success, New York, from 24 May to 18 June 1948, the commission redrafted the declaration, taking into account suggestions made by its drafting committee; by its Sub-Commission on Prevention of Discrimination and Protection of Minorities; by the Commission on the Status of Women; and by the United Nations Conference on Freedom of Information, which had met in Geneva in March 1948. It also took into account some provisions of the American Declaration of the Rights and Duties of Man which had been adopted by the Ninth International Conference of American States convened at Bogota in May 1948.

The UN General Assembly met in Paris that year and, after a general debate on the commission's draft declaration, referred it to its Third (Social, Humanitarian and Cultural) Committee for detailed consideration. The committee, composed then of the representatives of 56 member States, devoted 81 meetings to considering the draft and, in the process, examined and disposed of 168 proposals for amendments. As a result, the General Assembly was able to adopt and proclaim the Universal Declaration of Human Rights on 10 December 1948 by 48 votes in favor, none against, and eight abstentions.

Thus was born what Mrs. Roosevelt called the "Magna Carta of Mankind" and others termed the lodestar of the international community: a document that set out simply and clearly what was later described in the 1968 Proclamation of Teheran as "a common understanding of the peoples of the world concerning the inalienable and inviolable rights of all members of the human family."

Having lived through these eventful days, and having served as secretary of the Commission on Human Rights and of its Sub-Commission on Prevention of Discrimination and Protection of Minorities, and as deputy secretary of the United Nations Conference on Freedom of Information, I looked forward to a further whirlwind of activity which would rapidly make the enjoyment of human rights and fundamental freedoms a reality for all the peoples of the world. In particular, I hoped for the quick adoption of the remainder of the International Bill of Human Rights, for the preparation of some realistic measures which would protect suffering minorities throughout the world, and for the completion of a declaration or convention on freedom of information, which the General Assembly had designated as "a fundamental human right and the touchstone of all the freedoms to which the United Nations is consecrated."

But for many reasons—including political shifts which started when the change of government in Czechoslovakia in February 1948 cast its shadow over the Conference on Freedom of Information, intensified with the blockade of Berlin later the same year, and escalated finally into the long Cold War—my dreams were not fulfilled for many years, and then only in part.

The International Covenants on Human Rights were concluded only in 1966 and entered into force some ten years later. One of them—the Covenant on Civil and Political Rights—contains provisions on minorities (article 27) and on freedom of information (article 19). But the minorities provisions are so unsatisfactory that, in 1978, the Commission on Human Rights established an openended working group to draft a declaration on minority rights. That and similar working groups, established annually, were unable to produce a text suitable for consideration by the commission up to 1990. And the freedom of information provisions of the covenant clearly lack the precise definitions and the provisions for international supervision which had marked the draft convention prepared by the conference.

Another serious enthusiasm-damper stemmed from the curiously self-denying statement which the Commission on Human Rights adopted at its first session, in January 1947, to the effect that "the Commission recognizes that it has no power to take any action in regard to complaints concerning human rights." Such a statement had been formulated by some members who argued that, by drawing attention to the serious gap resulting from the absence of such power, the commission could stimulate its parent bodies to correct the situation; joined by other members who maintained that the commission should not be unduly taken up with the consideration of letters from individuals and organizations, and that, above all, it should not be turned into the "complaints bureau" of the United Nations. But, in practice, the statement, once approved by the Economic and Social Council, prevented the commission from dealing with the thousands of petitions, complaints, and other communications that flooded in to it from all parts of the world.

This incredible arrangement, almost impossible to explain to suffering victims of human rights violations, was maintained until 1970, when the council adopted a "Procedure for Dealing with Communications relating to Violations of Human Rights and Fundamental Freedoms" (resolution 1503 [XLVIII]). Many thousands of complaints have since been handled in accordance with that procedure, which authorizes the Sub-Commission on Prevention of Discrimination and Protection of Minorities to consider them together with other relevant information and to refer to the commission "particular situations which appear to reveal a consistent pattern of gross and reliably attested violations of human rights requiring attention by the Commission."

Earlier, the United Nations itself had undergone a slow but notable change; by the end of 1965, its original membership of 51 States had swelled to 119 with the addition of 68 new members: 36 from Africa, 16 from Asia, ten from western Europe, five from eastern Europe, and one from Latin America. The new majority, largely from the non-aligned third world, moved resolutely to put a stop to a broad range of violations of human rights:

—On 21 December 1965, the General Assembly concluded the International Convention on the Elimination of all Forms of Racial Discrimination, creating the first human rights monitoring machinery of global scope in the form of the Committee on the Elimination of Racial Discrimination;

—On 16 December 1966, the General Assembly adopted and opened for ratification or accession the International Covenant on Economic, Social and Cultural Rights; the International Covenant on Civil and Political Rights; and the Optional Protocol to the latter, creating additional monitoring machinery of global scope in the form of the Committee on Economic, Social and Cultural Rights and the Human Rights Committee; and

—On 13 May 1968, the International Conference on Human Rights consolidated a truly global concept by declaring, in the above-mentioned Proclamation of Teheran, that "the Universal Declaration of Human Rights states a common understanding of the peoples of the world concerning the inalienable and inviolable rights of all members of the human family and constitutes an obligation for the members of the international community."

The conference also gave new directions to the international human rights program. It observed, for example, that armed conflicts (resolution XXIII) continued to plague humanity; that the widespread violence and brutality of the times—including massacres, summary executions, tortures, inhuman treatment of prisoners, killing of civilians in armed conflicts, and the use of chemical and biological means of warfare—eroded human rights and engendered counter-brutality; and the conference expressed the conviction that humanitarian principles must prevail even during periods of armed conflict. It also pointed out in the Proclamation of Teheran (para. 18) that "while recent scientific discoveries and technological advances have opened vast prospects for economic, social and cultural progress, such developments may nevertheless endanger the rights and freedoms of individuals and will require continuing attention."

Thereafter, for some years, the Division of Human Rights prepared a series of studies, in consultation with the International Committee of the Red Cross, on steps which could be taken to secure the better application of existing humanitarian international conventions and rules in all armed conflicts and to address the need for additional instruments to ensure the better protection of civilians, prisoners, and combatants in such conflicts and to prohibit and limit the use of certain methods and means of warfare.

After examining the first and second of these reports, in 1969 and 1970, the General Assembly adopted (resolution 2675 [XXV]) a series of "Basic Principles for the Protection of Civilian Populations in Armed Conflicts." Seven further reports, prepared between 1971 and 1977, enabled the concerned United Nations organs to follow and to comment on the work of the Diplomatic Conference on the Reaffirmation and Development of International Humanitarian Law Applicable in Armed Conflicts, which had been convened by the Swiss Federal Council to consider draft additional protocols to the Geneva Conventions of 1949 prepared by the International Committee of the Red Cross. At its fourth and final session, held in Geneva in 1977, the diplomatic conference adopted and opened for ratification or accession two additional protocols to the Geneva Conventions, namely, Protocol I relating to the Protection of Victims of International Armed Conflicts and Protocol II relating to the Protection of Victims of Non-international Armed Conflicts. In addition, it proposed that a special conference be held to consider the prohibition of the use of certain conventional weapons for humanitarian reasons.

The Division of Human Rights also prepared a series of studies on the effect of various scientific and technological developments upon the enjoyment of human rights, dealing with such matters as the protection of the human personality and its physical and intellectual integrity in the light of advances in biology, medicine, and biochemistry (UN Docs. E/CN.4/1172 and Corr. 1 and Add. 1–3, and E/CN.4/1173); the balance which should be established between scientific and technological progress and the intellectual, spiritual, cultural, and moral advancement of humanity (UN Doc. E/CN.4/1199 and Add. 1); and the human rights implications of the genetic manipulation of microbes (UN Doc. E/CN.4/1235).

After examination of the studies, the General Assembly solemnly proclaimed, on 10 November 1975, the "Declaration on the Use of Scientific and Technological Progress in the Interests of Peace and for the Benefit of Mankind," which calls upon all States to ensure that the results of scientific and technological developments are used in the interests of strengthening international peace and security, freedom, and independence; for the economic and social development of peoples; and for the realization of human rights and fundamental freedoms in accordance with the United Nations Charter.

In 1974, the Division of Human Rights was transferred, except for a small liaison office, from the United Nations headquarters building in New York to its European office in Geneva, Switzerland, located in the Palais des Nations, which once had housed the League of Nations. While the shift may have been fully justified by those who proposed and supported it, its practical results were not always positive. For example, neither the Commission on

Human Rights nor its sub-commission—nor any of their sessional working groups—has since been convened in any city but Geneva. And Geneva—despite its beauty and charm, its inspiring history and perpetual neutrality, and its central location in the heart of Europe—still lacks the stimulating dynamism, the active information media, and the far-reaching communications networks of a city like New York. Getting the message of human rights out to all the peoples of the world is a bit more complicated from Geneva, and those of us who live in North America, for example, find it much harder to follow in detail significant human rights developments within the United Nations system.

The Division of Human Rights has since been strengthened and restructured into what is now known as the Centre for Human Rights. Its direction has been placed in the hands of the Under-Secretary-General for Human Rights, its mandate has been broadened to include new functions of coordination, its workload has increased tremendously, and its hard-working staff is being augmented.

Since 1977 activities of the Centre for Human Rights—and indeed all human rights activities within the United Nations system—have been based on a series of concepts formulated by the General Assembly as it prepared to commemorate the 30th anniversary (1978) of the Universal Declaration of Human Rights. These concepts, reaffirmed by the assembly at ten subsequent sessions, are as follows (resolution 32/130, para. 1 [a] to [h]:

> The General Assembly. . . .
>
> 1. Decides that the approach to the future work within the United Nations system with respect to human rights questions should take into account the following concepts:
>
> (a) All human rights and fundamental freedoms are indivisible and interdependent; equal attention and urgent consideration should be given to the implementation, promotion and protection of both civil and political, and economic, social and cultural rights;
>
> (b) "The full realization of civil and political rights without the enjoyment of economic, social and cultural rights is impossible; the achievement of lasting progress in the implementation of human rights is dependent upon sound and effective national and international policies of economic and social development" as recognized by the Proclamation of Teheran of 1968;
>
> (c) All human rights and fundamental freedoms of the human person and of peoples are inalienable;
>
> (d) Consequently, human rights questions should be examined globally, taking into account both the overall context of the various societies in which they present themselves, as well as the need for the promotion of the full dignity of the human person and the development and well-being of the society;
>
> (e) In approaching human rights questions within the United Nations system, the international community should accord, or continue to accord, priority to the search for solutions to the mass and flagrant violations of human rights of peoples and persons affected by situations such as those resulting from *apartheid,* from all forms of racial discrimination, from colonialism, from foreign domination and occupation, from aggression and threats against national sovereignty, national unity and territorial integrity, as well as from the refusal to recognize the fundamental rights of peoples to self-determination and of every nation to the exercise of full sovereignty over its wealth and natural resources;
>
> (f) The realization of the new international economic order is an essential element for the effective promotion of human rights and fundamental freedoms and should also be accorded priority;
>
> (g) It is of paramount importance for the promotion of human rights and fundamental freedoms that Member States undertake specific obligations through accession to or ratification of international instruments in this field; consequently, the standard-setting work within the United Nations system in the field of human rights and the universal acceptance and implementation of the relevant international instruments should be encouraged;
>
> (h) The experience and contribution of both developed and developing countries should be taken into account by all organs of the United Nations system in their work related to human rights and fundamental freedoms. . . .

Taking these directives into account, the work of the United Nations human rights organs has since expanded rapidly. Both the Commission on Human Rights and its sub-commission have learned to make the best use of qualified members either by appointing them as special rapporteurs to survey and report on situations existing in particular countries or to study controversial subjects such as religious intolerance, the use of torture, or the use of mercenaries as a means of violating human rights and impeding the exercise of the right of people to self-determination; or by assigning them to small working groups which handle complaints, seek to define the rights of minorities or indigenous peoples, endeavor to end slavery and other forms of servitude, or prepare the drafts of new international instruments. The result has been an incredibly rapid outpouring of resolutions, decisions, and instruments setting out new standards and rules designed to ensure to everyone on earth the full enjoyment of his human rights and fundamental freedoms.

Moreover, within the UN system, six independent treaty-monitoring bodies have become active and effective in their work: the Committee on the Elimination of Racial Discrimination; the Human Rights Committee; the Committee on Economic, Social and Cultural Rights; the Committee on the Elimination of Discrimination against Women; the Committee against Torture, and the Commission against *Apartheid* in Sports. A seventh, the Committee on the Rights of the Child, has been authorized by the Convention on the Rights of the Child, which entered into force on 2 September 1990.

In addition, several highly specialized organs are also active in the field, including the Special Committee to Investigate Israeli Practices Affecting the Human Rights of the Population of the Occupied Territories and the Committee on the Exercise of the Inalienable Rights of the Palestinian People, both of which report to the General Assembly; the *Ad Hoc* Working Group of Experts on Southern Africa, which reports to the Commission on Human Rights; and the Group of Three, composed of members of that commission, which monitors the implementation of the International Convention on the Suppression and Punishment of the Crime of *Apartheid*.

While most of these activities are funded out of the normal United Nations budget, several of the treaty-monitoring bodies are supported mainly by contributions assessed against the States parties to the conventions under which they were established. Some other work is financed, at least in part, by voluntary funds—for the victims of torture, for indigenous peoples, and for advisory services and technical assistance, for example—to which interested States, organizations, and individuals contribute.

Further intensive international activities to promote and protect the enjoyment of human rights are being carried on simultaneously by four of the specialized agencies within the United Nations system—the International Labor Organization; the United Nations Educational, Scientific and Cultural Organization; the Food and Agriculture Organization; and the World Health Organization—and by three major regional intergovernmental organizations outside the UN system—the Council of Europe, the Organization of African Unity, and the Organization of American States—as well as by specialized groups such as the International Committee of the Red Cross and the signers of the Helsinki Accord. Only by assessing all these efforts together can we see how widespread and intensive is the current World Campaign for Human Rights. Add on the thousands of active national and local campaigns directed to the same end, and it becomes all but impossible to keep track of them. All of these efforts inspire great hope for the future.

As a member of the UN Secretariat, one of my tasks was to organize and direct seminars and study groups on various aspects of human rights in such far-flung cities as Bangkok, Thailand; Bogota, Colombia; Budapest, Hungary; Dar-es-Salaam, Tanzania; Kandy, Sri Lanka; Lome, Togo; and Warsaw, Poland. After retiring in 1975, I taught courses in human rights to American undergraduate university students of political science and international affairs. These experiences made me realize that human rights had rapidly developed into a vast and important new subject—almost a new discipline—in which there was tremendous interest but a surprising paucity of relevant information available for intensive study or instruction.

That is why, several years ago, I set out to prepare a basic textbook for the teaching of human rights—a much-needed item which, although discussed in theory at great length in international conferences of educational experts, has yet to be produced.

At an early stage in that work I realized two things. First, there was an immediate prior need to identify and bring together in convenient form the unbelievably large bulk of documentation concerning human rights, including the 40-odd-year backlog and the continuing sizable output of the United Nations system and the equally large, if not larger, production of the regional intergovernmental and non-governmental organizations. Secondly, the ultimate requirement was not so much a single basic textbook suitable for use at every level and in every conceivable situation as a media blitz directed at a number of constituencies and designed to meet the unique human rights concerns of each: one campaign, for example, aimed at political leaders and legislators, another at religious leaders, and still another at students and teachers at various levels and in different disciplines. This trend of thought was confirmed by discussions, in the United Nations Seminar on the Teaching of Human Rights, held at Geneva from 5 to 9 December 1989. At its final meeting, the chairman summed up the major results of those discussions as follows (UN Doc. E/CN.4/1989/68, para. 121):

(b) What to teach? Human rights teaching should generally take a multidisciplinary approach in order to introduce different dimensions and perspectives of human life: historical, philosophical, religious, legal, social, cultural, political and economic. The main aim [is] to make known the basic facts about the universally accepted international human rights standards, including their intercultural background. The interrelationship between human rights and peace, development, environment and other international issues should also be emphasized in the process of human rights teaching.

(c) Whom to teach? It [is] very important to confirm that everyone [is] aware of his or her own rights, as human rights and fundamental freedoms should be guaranteed to everyone. Human rights teaching should thus be directed to every quarter. First of all, those in a position to directly affect the basic human rights of the individual, such as law enforcement personnel, lawyers and judges, as well as the military men when at war or when called upon to maintain security in times of emergency internal situations, should be well taught as regards human rights. It [is] also vital that legislators who are in charge of drafting laws should be educated about international human rights standards so that their legislation would be in conformity with their country's international obligations. Persons, be they in medicine, engineering, technology, media, data processing, political parties, civil service, municipalities and other centers of power, such as village councils, trade unions, etc., also [need] to be aware of human rights. Teaching and training of professionals should consist of not only the basic rules of the organization of their prospective profession, but also an ethical and legal code of conduct taking into account the impact of their activities on the basic human rights of others. School children and students at all institutions, be they civil, police or military, should also be the target of this process. . . .

With these views in mind, I temporarily put aside my plan for preparing a single basic human rights textbook, usable at all levels and in any circumstance, in favor of doing the necessary groundwork first. That groundwork is to be found in this encyclopedia, intended to serve as a standard reference work bringing together in a single volume everything important to know about the international, regional, and national activities so far undertaken with a view to promoting the enjoyment by everyone of his human rights and fundamental freedoms.

As will be seen, the encyclopedia deals with important developments in the field of human rights that occurred between 1945, when the United Nations Charter entered into force, and 30 June 1990, when the manuscript went to press. A few important instruments in force before 1945—for example, the Slavery Convention of 25 September 1926 and the ILO Forced Labor Convention of 28 June 1930—are included because they protected human rights both before and after 1945. And, in a few exceptional instances, it was possible to insert information concerning events which occurred after 30 June 1990 in the proofreading process, as for example in the case of the UN Security Council action immediately following the invasion of Kuwait by Iraq.

However, generally speaking, it was not possible to include in the body of the encyclopedia international decisions taken after mid-1990. I regret this shortcoming in the published edition, although it was beyond my control. It is due to the continuous and open-ended activity of the United Nations and other international organizations in the field of human rights. By its very nature, no encyclopedia can ever be totally up-to-date; and I hope to reduce the unavoidable time lag in subsequent editions.

These materials have been carefully selected and are presented objectively and with a minimum of editorial comment. They are arranged by title in letter-by-letter alphabetical sequence and are thoroughly cross-referenced and indexed. The entries include the complete official texts of some 200 international standard-setting instruments dealing with various aspects of human rights—covenants, conventions, protocols, agreements, declarations, recommendations, and statements of principle—of which 105 were prepared by organs of the United Nations; 34 by organs of the Council of Europe; 13 by organs of the Organization of American States; five by organs of the Organization of African Unity; four by diplomatic conferences convened by the Swiss Federal Council in cooperation with the International Committee of the Red Cross; and three by signers of the Helsinki Accord.

The material includes also information about the mandates and the work of 78 of the international governmental organs that normally deal with human rights questions, and about the activities of more than 125 international non-governmental organizations that participate actively in their proceedings. Information also is presented on the situation of human rights in each of 165 countries and territories, including all United Nations member States; and the human rights provisions of the constitutions of 25 of those countries are reproduced in full.

More than 200 entries deal with various aspects of particular rights and freedoms; they explain the concepts involved and indicate how the competent international organs have interpreted the scope and meaning of the relevant provisions. Others reproduce landmark international court decisions or provide information about studies, reports, or procedures still in the preliminary stages. Appendices include an extensive bibliography, compiled by Human Rights Internet, lists of the States that have ratified or acceded to major human rights conventions; a chronological list of international human rights instruments; a catalog of the numerous studies and reports on human rights prepared by or for United Nations bodies; and a list of the conventions adopted by the International Labor Conference between 1919 and 1989—sometimes referred to as the International Labor Code—each of which promotes the realization by working men and women of certain human rights and fundamental freedoms.

This mass of materials presents an impressive picture—particularly the numerous treaties, conventions, protocols, declarations, and statements of principle which set lofty standards with a view to protecting the status of the individual throughout the world. Their very existence has already brought about a radical change in the nature and the structure of world order: whereas the law of nations once regulated only the intercourse of independent States in peace and war, the new world order affirms that a primary aim of international cooperation in the field of human rights is for a life of freedom, dignity, and peace for all peoples and for every human being.

Formal international implementation of human rights standards, unfortunately, has not kept pace with the promulgation and acceptance of these standards. Treaty-monitoring bodies such as the Human Rights Committee, the Committee on Economic, Social and Cultural Rights, the Committee on the Elimination of Racial Discrimination, the Committee on the Elimination of Discrimination against Women, and the Committee against Torture are just beginning to make progress in their work; and their functioning is hampered by a continuing backlog of reports on implementation from States parties to the relevant conventions, by a shortage of financial resources, and by some overlapping of the issues dealt with in those conventions. These problems have been studied by an independent expert, whose recommendations on reporting and monitoring procedures, on servicing and financing of the supervisory bodies, and on long-term approaches to human rights standard-setting and implementation mechanisms are scheduled for early consideration by the General Assembly.

Meanwhile, the informal day-to-day realization of human rights proceeds irresistably and independently of such formal measures. Who would have thought, early in 1989, that revolutionary demands for civil and political rights, for free multi-party elections, and for free-market economics would have swept across such countries as Bulgaria, Czechoslovakia, East Germany, Hungary, Poland, Romania, and even portions of the Union of Soviet Socialist Republics; that the cold war would have ended; that the Berlin Wall would have come down; or that Germany would have been reunited, all within two years? And who would have imagined, early in 1990, that even these developments affecting the human rights and fundamental freedoms of millions of Europeans would so soon have been overshadowed by threats of war in the Middle East and the worldwide surge of concern about protection of the human rights and fundamental freedoms of civilians, hostages, prisoners of war, refugees, displaced persons, and women and children trapped in the areas of armed conflict?

However, intensification of international measures of implementation—primarily by treaty bodies competent to monitor applicable standards and to expose all who fail to live up to them—still appears to offer the most realistic possibility that, in due time, everyone will be able fully to enjoy his human rights and fundamental freedoms. The existing treaty-monitoring bodies should become increasingly effective as their problems are resolved, and new bodies undoubtedly will be added. At the same time, the Commission on Human Rights will be alerted whenever necessary to the existence of gross and systematic violations of human rights requiring urgent corrective action by its special rapporteurs and working groups which study and report on country-oriented and subject-oriented topics and on the complaints and other communications received.

Of course, if there ever is to develop a full balance between the lofty standards of the human rights instruments and their practical results, some more effective measures of enforcement eventually will be required. One possibility is the establishment of an international court of human rights, performing on a worldwide basis functions similar to those already performed in western Europe by the European Court of Human Rights and to those already performed in Latin America by the Inter-American Court of Human Rights. Another is the establishment of an international criminal court for the trial of persons charged with crimes against humanity and other crimes involving gross violations of human rights. A draft statute for such a court was prepared by two Committees on International Criminal Jurisdiction appointed by the General Assembly in 1951 and 1953, respectively; but such a statute was never concluded by the assembly.

As may be realized, the encyclopedia's substantive contents range well beyond the somewhat limited original concept of human rights and include a wide variety of closely interlinked social, humanitarian, and disarmament issues such as the advancement of women; the prevention of crime and the establishment of standards in criminal justice; the protection of refugees and displaced or stateless persons; the protection of civilians in time of armed conflict; the treatment of prisoners of war; and the prohibition of nuclear, chemical, bacteriological, or biological weapons.

Its basic function is to provide to all concerned—governments, regional and national organizations, research institutions, the media, public officials at all levels, students and interested individuals and groups throughout the world—easy access to the impressive wealth of documentation on human rights issues which the international community has developed and accumulated. A secondary aim is to make all those materials available also to those who teach and those who study in related disciplines such as political science and international affairs, as well as to those who provide and those who receive specialized training in such areas as law enforcement, military law, diplomacy, and medicine.

A third and most important goal is to distribute to all who suffer violations of their human rights or fundamental freedoms information on the scope and content of those rights and on the procedures available to them to put a stop to such violations and to remedy the wrongs that have been committed.

With a view to achieving these objectives, the encyclopedia is issued as a single, self-contained volume which does not require the use of any other publication. The selection of materials to be included has been impartial and objective in the sense that no single individual or national point of view; no social, economic, cultural or political system; and no academic discipline are stressed; and references to existing situations are always drawn from sources least likely to be biased: studies and reports prepared under the auspices of the competent international organizations and agencies.

Thus, while essentially a reference tool prepared to provide a factual and theoretical basis for serious high-level study of human rights principles and issues on a global scale, the encyclopedia may also appropriately serve as an interim manual for the teaching of those principles and issues. And hopefully it may contribute in some measure to eventual solution of some of the most pressing problems of the ongoing revolution for democracy and human rights that marks the 1990s as the "Decade for Democratization."

Unfortunately, even as that decade progresses, scourges such as foreign occupation and domination, racial and religious intolerance and discrimination, "disappearances," torture and mass poverty remain in place and must be extirpated. The spread of information and education about human rights principles and procedures is an imperative first step, and the uncompromising application of those principles and use of those procedures must immediately follow. For this to happen, both the past and future victims of human rights violations, as well as all entrusted with protecting the enjoyment of those rights, must become aware of the content and applicability of local, national and international human rights policies and procedures, and must not hesitate to use them.

The challenge of this decade is to realize by the year 2000, if not sooner, the full enjoyment by every living individual of his human rights and fundamental freedoms, guaranteed by a political order motivated by the conscience of the world. To promote and to assist in the achievement of that goal is the ultimate objective of this encyclopedia.

Finally, a personal word about the many individuals and organizations whose cooperation and contributions have helped to make *Encyclopedia of Human Rights* a compendium of basic knowledge and information on the subject of human rights and fundamental freedoms.

I am especially indebted to Jan Martenson, Under-Secretary-General for Human Rights of the United Nations, for his continuing encouragement and for his "Foreword" to this publication; and to all the staff of the Centre for Human Rights in Geneva and its Liaison Office at the UN headquarters in New York for the time and effort they have devoted to providing me with the voluminous but essential documentation which I have presented, summarized, or quoted here.

I am particularly grateful for the kind cooperation of so many governments for making available information on the human rights situation in their respective countries, either directly in response to my requests or indirectly through their reports to the competent treaty-monitoring bodies.

I am also grateful for the assistance provided by so many concerned international organizations, including such specialized agencies of the United Nations as the International Labor Organization; the United Nations Educational, Scientific and Cultural Organization; the Food and Agriculture Organization; and the World Health Organization; such regional bodies as the Council of Europe, the Organization of African Unity, and the Organization of American States; and such non-governmental bodies as the International Committee of the Red Cross and Amnesty International.

My sincere thanks go to Kate McKay, former president and publisher of Taylor and Francis, Inc., who first understood the need for such an encyclopedia; to Ted Crane who succeeded her; to Sharon Spina and Jung Ra who handled the production details; and to Human Rights Internet, which prepared the extensive bibliography, found in Appendix A.

And my very special thanks must go to Mary Lou Bertucci, the talented editor and human rights enthusiast who has, for several years, relieved me of the hardest part of my job—the organizing, the revising, the proofreading, the correcting, the ungarbling, the indexing, and the otherwise nursemaiding of a constantly expanding compilation of information—from her home in Philadelphia; and to my wife, Irene, without whose patience, understanding, and good humor I would not have finally been able to send this encyclopedia to press.

EDWARD LAWSON
Tampa, Florida

USER'S GUIDE

As detailed by the author in his preface, the *Encyclopedia of Human Rights* is a unique compendium that brings together material about international, regional, and national activities undertaken between the years 1945 and 1990 to promote and protect the enjoyment of human rights and fundamental freedoms by everyone without distinction. In its objective presentation of basic human rights documentation, the encyclopedia is comprehensive and carefully designed to make available in clear and accessible form a wealth of data that, so far, has not been adequately used and is already in danger of being neglected or lost.

Contents. Produced as a contribution to the World Public Information Campaign for Human Rights initiated by the UN General Assembly, this reference work includes a central core of information on:

—international instruments having a bearing on the enjoyment of human rights and fundamental freedoms;

—international organizations (both governmental and non-governmental) established to promote and protect those rights and freedoms;

—practical ways by which international, regional, and national bodies promote, monitor, and supervise the implementation of those rights and freedoms.

Information about the numerous intergovernmental and non-governmental organizations active in the human rights field is presented in entries bearing the names of those organizations. In addition, a number of national institutions concerned with human rights is listed in Appendix I.

In regard to continuing human rights situations in 165 countries and territories, reviews of existing conditions are presented in entries bearing the names of those States and areas. The information cited—culled from reports made available to the United Nations and other intergovernmental bodies by a variety of sources, including reports submitted to treaty-monitoring bodies by the individual governments; studies prepared by special rapporteurs, working groups, and experts; communications received from non-governmental organizations and interested individuals; and data available from previously published materials—provides an indication of prevailing conditions that may promote or inhibit the full enjoyment of rights and freedoms. In addition, the human rights provisions in the constitutions of a number of countries, as furnished by the governments at the author's request, are reproduced in full.

Finally, the composition and functions of each of the many international organizations, agencies, and bodies that deal with various aspects of human rights are set out in detail; and their activities and accomplishments are reviewed.

Alphabetical Order. The entries are presented in letter-by-letter alphabetical order. Documents are presented under their full official titles. Because the official title of UN-sponsored instruments (i.e., those adopted by the full General Assembly) may begin with words such as "Convention on. . ." or "Declaration concerning. . . ," the reader should refer to the Subject Index for the correct entry title. For example, a reader interested in a treaty addressing the subject of genocide will find an entry entitled "Genocide" but will not find the full treaty under that title. Instead, he will find the actual document listed alphabetically under its official title "Convention on the Prevention and Punishment of Genocide." Internal and external cross references, as explained further on, are used throughout the book to provide the reader with additional information on any subject.

In addition to UN conventions and declarations, documents concluded by the International Labor Organization are preceded by the acronym "ILO" and thus are grouped alphabetically together. Similarly, those concluded by the United Nations Educational, Scientific and Cultural Organization are preceded by "UNESCO"; those concluded by the Organization of American States, by the term "Inter-American"; those concluded by the Organization of African Unity, by "African"; and those concluded by the Council of Europe, by "European." The current status of many of these instruments is set out in Appendix C, while the composition of the concerned intergovernmental organizations is set out in Appendix H. In addition, a complete list of instruments comprising the International Labor Code—consisting of all documents adopted by the International Labor Organization, each having a bearing on the right to work— appears in Appendix E.

Finally the runners indicating the last entry to be found on the page repeat the full title of entry, as often as possible. However, due to the length of some official document titles, the runners for these entries have been shortened for convenience. These abbreviations do not break the alphabetical order of the entries.

Cross References. Entries may contain internal and external cross references to other entries within the encyclopedia. Internal cross references are set in small capitals, boldface type, and indicate material that is directly related to the entry. External cross references are set in italic type at the end of the entry, preceded by the words "**SEE ALSO**" and indicate material that supplements the primary entry. An example follows:

> **SAFEGUARDS GUARANTEEING THE PROTECTION OF THE RIGHTS OF THOSE FACING THE DEATH PENALTY (1984).** The UN Economic and Social Council, at its first regular session for 1984, acknowledged the work done by the UN COMMISSION ON HUMAN RIGHTS and its SUB-COMMISSION ON PREVENTION OF DISCRIMINATION AND PROTECTION OF MINORITIES in the areas of CAPITAL PUNISHMENT concerning summary or arbitrary executions, as well as the relevent views and comments of the HUMAN RIGHTS COMMITTEE, and strongly condemned and deplored (resolution 1984/50) the practice of arbitrary or summary executions in various parts of the world. It approved the "Safeguards Guaranteeing Protection of the Rights of those Facing the Death Penalty," which had been formulated and recommended by the COMMITTEE ON CRIME PREVENTION AND CONTROL, on the understanding that these safeguards would never be invoked to delay or to prevent the abolition of capital punishment. . . .
>
> **SEE ALSO** *Death Penalty: Safeguards; Executions: Report of Special Rapporteur; Principles on the Effective Prevention and Investigation of Extra-Legal, Arbitrary and Summary Executions.*

Citations. Many international instruments, national constitutions, official studies, and special rapporteur reports are reproduced, in full or in part. In all cases, the sources of these official documents are set directly in the body of the entry, as follows:

> . . . Such a text was adopted by the congress in Milan, Italy, on 5 September 1985. It was later endorsed by the UN General Assembly on 29 November 1985 (resolution 40/32) and on 13 December 1985 (resolution 40/146). The text (UN Doc. A/CONF.121/22, chap. I, sect. D.2) is as follows: . . .

Citations of documents issued by international organizations follow the system in use by those agencies. UN human rights documents, for example, usually bear symbols which indicate (1) the main issuing organ, for example, the General Assembly (A/), the Security Council (S/), the Economic and Social Council (E/), or the Secretariat (ST/); (2) the subsidiary organ, for example, the Commission on Human Rights (CN.4/),the Commission on the Status of Women (CN.6/), or the Sub-Commission on Prevention of Discrimination and Protection of Minorities (CN.4/Sub.2), or a specially convened conference (CONF.); (3) the year of issue (1990/); and (4) the number of the document in the year's series. Thus, a typical document numbered E/CN.4/Sub.2/1990/36 would be the 36th document issued for use by the sub-commission in 1990. The symbols are useful mainly in making a quick but precise reference to a particular document or in ordering copies of it from a source of supply, such as a UN repository library or Human Rights Internet.

Appendices. There are nine appendices in this work, some of which have already been referred to in this guide. The first is an extensive selected bibliography, prepared by Human Rights Internet, intended to supplement the information cited in the primary entries. HRI has provided references largely from independent, non-governmental studies published between 1985 and 1989. The second appendix is a glossary of terms often used in referring to human rights situations. These terms are defined in their international usage, irrespective of their applications in national laws or cultures. The glossary also includes selected Latin terms.

Appendix D offers a chronological list of the documents contained in this work. It is presented so that the student may see quickly and easily how human rights developed as an international field and how treaties address the changing nature of society and world concerns.

Appendix F presents an organizational chart of the UN's Centre for Human Rights, displaying the channels through which human rights concerns are addressed in that body.

Finally, Appendix G presents a list of past and on-going investigations and studies undertaken by those organs and agencies of the United Nations that are concerned with human rights.

Index. A subject index, the most expeditious method to provide access to the wealth of information contained in the encyclopedia, will be found at the end of the book. The method follows, as closely as possible, the subject-indexing terms employed by Human Rights Internet in its periodic comprehensive indexes, a method which will be familiar to students in the human rights field. The index is cross-referenced and provides the reader with the entry title and page number where he will find information on that subject.

The subject terms indicate one of two options. As shown in Example 1, the first option directs the reader to look under other terms for information on that subject:

Example 1: Abduction

      See: Detention; Disappearances; Hostages; Victims

As shown in Example 2, in which the term *is* employed in the index, the titles and page numbers of entries that address the topic follow:

Example 2: Adoption

      Declaration on Social and Legal Principles relating to the Protection and Welfare of Children, with Special Reference to Foster Placement Nationally and Internationally, 359

      European Convention on the Adoption of Children, 534

      Inter-American Convention on Conflict of Laws concerning the Adoption of Minors, 894

In addition, terms that are set in boldface indicate index titles that are also the title of an entry; these will be followed by a page number and possible further information:

Affirmative Action, 7

    See also: Indigenous Peoples; Minorities.

A

ABORTION. Abortion is defined as the intentional removal of a fetus from the mother's womb other than for the purpose of producing a live birth or removing a dead fetus. Neither accidental premature birth nor spontaneous expulsion of the fetus due to disease, malfunction, or trauma of the mother is normally considered as abortion.

Issues concerning the right to life of the mother and that of the unborn child were debated repeatedly in the course of the preparation of the INTERNATIONAL BILL OF HUMAN RIGHTS. When article 3 of the UNIVERSAL DECLARATION OF HUMAN RIGHTS was being drafted by the UN Commission on Human Rights and its drafting committee, it was proposed that the life of unborn children should be specifically protected by insertion of the words "from the moment of conception." The proposal was rejected after the representative of the COMMISSION ON THE STATUS OF WOMEN pointed out that this qualification of the right to life could not be reconciled with the legislation of many States which provides for abortion in cases specified by law, notably in order to preserve the life of a woman. The vote in each body was preceded by a discussion on the question as to whether or not the term "RIGHT TO LIFE" implied or contained the idea of life "from the moment of conception." While some participants in the drafting process considered the idea to be implicit in the term, others maintained that this was not necessarily the case.

Article 3 of the Universal Declaration of Human Rights, and later article 6 (1) of the INTERNATIONAL COVENANT ON CIVIL AND POLITICAL RIGHTS, was subsequently adopted by the General Assembly without the phrase "from the moment of conception."

In modern practice, abortion is prohibited in some countries and territories while available upon request in others. In a large number of countries, medical termination of pregnancy is permissible but only under specified conditions: for example, if continuation of the pregnancy would involve risk to the life of the pregnant woman or if there is a substantial risk that, if the child were born, it would suffer from such physical or mental abnormalities as to be seriously handicapped. In recent years, concern for the mental health of the prospective mother has begun to gain acceptance in national legislation as a justification for abortion, as in cases where pregnancy is the result of rape.

ACCEPTANCE OF INTERNATIONAL HUMAN RIGHTS INSTRUMENTS. International multi-lateral instruments concerned with human rights—usually designated as "treaties," "conventions," "covenants," or "protocols," are like other international multi-lateral instruments opened for signature and ratification or acceptance by States in accordance with the provisions of each particular instrument. Signature normally indicates only general approval of an instrument and the willingness of State authorities to consider definitive acceptance. Ratification or accession occurs when the head of State notifies the depository of the instrument—usually the UN Secretary-General, another State, or an intergovernmental organization designated as such in the instrument—that it accepts to be bound to apply the provisions of the instrument in territories under its control.

The question of the acceptance of human rights treaties, conventions, protocols, and other instruments is, therefore, of great importance; and several international bodies have concerned themselves with seeking out, and trying to correct, the most common causes of delay. Although these causes differ from State to State and from instrument to instrument, certain common factors have been identified. These factors were described in a paper (UN Doc. A/CONF.32/15) prepared by the UNITED NATIONS INSTITUTE FOR TRAINING AND RESEARCH (UNITAR) and presented to the INTERNATIONAL CONFERENCE ON HUMAN RIGHTS held in Teheran in 1968, as follows:

Lack of Expertise. The question of ratification of or accession to human rights treaties is far from a simple policy decision to be taken at the level of the foreign minister or head of State. It often involves investigation into the substantive scope of the treaties and the effects of the conventions upon existing law and policy of States. Not infrequently, ratification of treaties necessitates adoption of new legislation, and, consequently, the drafting of legislative bills. In addition, where the language of a State is not one of the official languages of the United Nations, the texts of conventions need to be translated into the official language or languages of the State. All this requires a machinery and personnel having the necessary expertise. In many States, and especially the newly independent States, there seems to be a shortage of administrative and legal expertise to carry out the necessary tasks.

Constitutional Questions. In some States, the executive is possessed of the power to ratify a treaty internationally, without the prior consent or approval of parliament; but, as some of the human rights treaties belong to the category of treaties which need to be implemented through national legislation, there is a need for legislative action. Seldom do States ratify or accede to a treaty internationally before the necessary legislation has been adopted. Preparation of new legislation entails time and is, in any case, conditioned by factors such as the business or agenda before the legislature, the items needing priority, and the policy of the government towards the subject-matter of a treaty.

Federal-State Questions. In some countries, arguments as to whether or not the balance between federal and state jurisdiction would be altered by acceptance of certain international human rights treaties have delayed or prevented the acceptance of such treaties.

Parallel Treaties. In some cases where there are a number of international treaties dealing with a single subject—such as, for example, the traffic in human beings—some States which are parties to the earlier treaties consider them to be adequate for the purpose and accordingly do not accept the newer ones. Similarly, in some cases where regional treaties cover either the same or similar questions as do the international treaties, States are reluctant to accept both.

Since 1979, the UN SUB-COMMISSION ON PREVENTION OF DISCRIMINATION AND PROTECTION OF MINORITIES has given concentrated attention to the task of encouraging all States which have not done so to ratify or accede to international human rights instruments. At its 1979 session, the sub-commission decided (resolution 1 B [XXXII]) that it would establish each year a sessional working group to assist it in this task and requested the Secretary-General to call upon the governments concerned to inform the sub-commission of the circumstances which have not enabled them to ratify or accede to the instruments in question and to explain any particular difficulties they might face. The working group was authorized to consider what forms of assistance could be provided to governments by the United Nations, with a view to assisting them to adhere to the conventions as soon as possible.

However, the activities of the working group did not produce the desired results, and its activities were suspended in 1984. At that time, the sub-commission requested its chairman to appoint one of its members to report to it on the basis of information obtained by the Secretary-General. Mr. Marc Bossuyt (Belgium) accordingly was appointed and presented a brief analysis of the information submitted by governments at the sub-commission's 1985 session (UN Doc. E/CN.4/Sub. 2/1985/27).

At its 1987 session, the sub-commission noted (in resolution 1987/1) that, as of 15 June of that year, only 90 States had accepted the International Covenant on Economic, Social and Cultural Rights; only 86 had accepted the International Covenant on Civil and Political Rights; and only 38 had accepted the optional protocol to the latter covenant, although more than 20 years had elapsed since the adoption of those instruments by the General Assembly; and that a substantial number of States parties to the covenants and related instruments had failed to produce the regular reports required by those instruments.

The sub-commission suggested that the General Assembly, recognizing that repeated exhortations had not brought the desired results and that more specific measures were required, should call upon all States which had not ratified the covenants to consider doing so and to call upon all States parties to the covenants and related instruments to file regularly and without delay the reports which they had undertaken to produce for submission to the bodies set up to supervise their implementation. It further suggested that a worldwide campaign should be launched, aimed at the universal acceptance of the international instruments relating to human rights.

The Secretary-General submitted to the sub-commission at its 1988 session a summary of new information on the subject he had received since 1985 (UN Doc. E/CN.4/Sub.2/1988/27). The sub-commission, while thanking the States that had supplied the information and calling upon the Secretary-General to continue collecting it, requested him further (a) to examine the idea of offering technical assistance, in the form of legal training of local staff or by providing human rights experts to assist in the drafting of appropriate national legislation and regulations, with a view to enabling States to ratify or accede to international human rights instruments; (b) to keep under review the idea of designating regional advisors on international human rights standards, whose function would include advising the States concerned on acceptance and implementation of such instruments; and (c) to continue holding informal discussions concerning prospects for ratification of human rights instruments with government delegations, giving priority to instruments drafted by the Commission on

Human Rights such as the International Covenants on Human Rights, the INTERNATIONAL CONVENTION ON THE ELIMINATION OF ALL FORMS OF RACIAL DISCRIMINATION, the INTERNATIONAL CONVENTION ON THE SUPPRESSION AND PUNISHMENT OF THE CRIME OF *APARTHEID,* and the CONVENTION AGAINST TORTURE AND OTHER CRUEL, INHUMAN OR DEGRADING TREATMENT OR PUNISHMENT.

ACCESS OF NEWS PERSONNEL TO UN MEETINGS.

The United Nations Conference on Freedom of Information, held at the European office of the United Nations, Geneva, from 23 March to 21 April 1948, recommended (resolution no. 9) that arrangements should be made for accredited news personnel of all countries to have free access to countries where UN meetings are held and to all sources of information connected with such meetings, except in cases where meetings are private.

On the recommendation of the conference and the Economic and Social Council, the General Assembly adopted a resolution on the subject on 21 October 1949 (resolution 314 [IV]), as follows:

The General Assembly,

Considering that the United Nations, in accordance with the aims and purposes of its Charter, should be prepared to grant all the necessary facilities for enabling media of information to function with full freedom and responsibility in following the course of its work and that of conferences called by it and by its specialized agencies,

Urges all States Members of the United Nations to grant news personnel of all countries who have been accredited to the United Nations or specialized agencies, as the case may be, free access:

(a) To countries where meetings of the United Nations or specialized agencies or any conferences convened by them take place, for the purpose of covering such meetings, in accordance with the terms and conditions of agreements made by the United Nations or its specialized agencies with the Governments of such countries, or, in the absence of such an agreement, on terms and conditions similar to those contained in agreements made by the United Nations or its specialized agencies with other Member States; and

(b) To all public information sources and services of the United Nations and the specialized agencies and to all meetings and conferences of the United Nations or of the specialized agencies which are open to the Press, equally and without discrimination.

SEE ALSO Convention on International Right of Correction; European Declaration on Mass Communication Media and Human Rights; Journalists: Protection of their Human Rights; UNESCO Declaration on Fundamental Principles concerning the Contribution of the Mass Media to Strengthening Peace and International Understanding, to the Promotion of Human Rights and to Countering Racialism, Apartheid and Incitement to War.

AD HOC WORKING GROUP OF EXPERTS ON SOUTHERN AFRICA.

Established on 6 March 1967 by the UN COMMISSION ON HUMAN RIGHTS (resolution 2 [XXIII]), the *Ad Hoc* Working Group of Experts was originally authorized by the commission to:

(1) investigate charges of torture and ill-treatment of prisoners, detainees, or persons in police custody in South Africa;

(2) receive communications, hear witnesses and use whatever procedures it deems appropriate;

(3) recommend action to be taken in concrete cases; and

(4) report to the commission at the earliest possible time.

These functions have since been extended. On 29 February 1988, the Commission on Human Rights decided "that the *Ad Hoc* Working Group of Experts should continue to investigate and study the policies and practices which violate human rights in South Africa and Namibia, as well as infringements of trade-union rights in South Africa in accordance with Economic and Social Council resolution 1987/63 of 29 May 1987." It requested the working group of experts, in cooperation with the SPECIAL COMMITTEE AGAINST *APARTHEID* and other investigatory and monitoring bodies, to continue to investigate cases of torture and ill-treatment of detainees and deaths of detainees in South Africa and called upon it "to continue to bring to the attention of the Chairman of the Commission on Human Rights, for whatever action he may deem appropriate, particularly serious violations of human rights in South Africa which may come to its attention during its studies." At the same time, it authorized the chairman of the working group to participate in conferences, symposia, seminars, and other events connected with action against *apartheid* organized under the auspices of the Special Committee against *Apartheid.*

The working group of experts normally follows a two-year schedule, submitting a final report to the commission biennially and an interim or progress report in alternate years. Occasionally, it prepares, in addition, special reports requested by the General Assembly, the Economic and Social Council, or the Commission on Human Rights.

The working group holds an organizational meeting of about one week early in the year to begin the gathering of new information, undertakes a field mission in July and August to cities in Europe and Africa where it can hear the testimony of witnesses on matters falling within its mandate, and meets later in the year to prepare its report. All meetings, except those on field missions, are held at the United Nations office in Geneva.

SEE ALSO Apartheid *entries.*

ADVANCEMENT OF WOMEN BRANCH. The Branch for the Advancement of Women, which forms part of the Center for Social Development and Humanitarian Affairs of the UNITED NATIONS SECRETARIAT, is located at the Vienna International Center, Austria. It provides executive direction, management, administrative and substantive services to all United Nations organs when they deal with questions relating to the advancement of women, including the GENERAL ASSEMBLY, the ECONOMIC AND SOCIAL COUNCIL, the COMMISSION ON THE STATUS OF WOMEN, the COMMITTEE ON THE ELIMINATION OF DISCRIMINATION AGAINST WOMEN, and their subsidiary bodies. In close collaboration with the Crime Prevention and Criminal Justice Branch of the Center, and with the intergovernmental and non-governmental organizations and research institutions concerned, it carries out research and prepares studies, reports, and other documentation at the request of these organs; assists in the implementation of their recommendations; and collects and disseminates information on their activities.

ADVISORY SERVICES IN THE FIELD OF HUMAN RIGHTS. In 1953 and 1954, the General Assembly of the United Nations first authorized the Secretary-General to assist governments, at their request, in promoting and safeguarding the rights of women, in eliminating racial discrimination, in protecting minorities, and in promoting freedom of information. In 1955, the assembly incorporated these provisions in a single program of advisory services in the field of human rights. Several forms of assistance are authorized under the program: seminars, regional training courses, fellowships, and the advisory services of experts. Such assistance may relate to any human rights question, provided that help is not otherwise available through a specialized agency or other organization. The program is designed to give governments an opportunity to share experiences and to exchange knowledge about the promotion and protection of human rights.

Seminars. As the program developed, emphasis was first placed on the holding of seminars for the discussion of various human rights problems and their possible solutions. The seminars, by bringing together for short periods of time key people nominated by their respective governments, are intended to stimulate thinking, provoke fresh ideas, elicit constructive suggestions, and make it possible to explore informally ways and means of dealing with matters relating to human rights that are of concern to the world community.

The first step in the organization of a seminar is the receipt of an invitation from a government offering to act as host. The secretary-general consults with that government, usually through its permanent mission, with regard to the subject-matter to be considered, the date and place of the seminar, and the list of governments to be invited to nominate participants. When these questions have been settled, an agreement is drawn up setting forth the responsibilities and services to be provided by the United Nations and by the host government. Generally speaking, the United Nations pays for the travel and subsistence of one participant from each country invited, for the preparation of background papers by expert consultants, and for assigning a team of officials from the UNITED NATIONS SECRETARIAT to organize and run the seminar. The host government is responsible for certain local costs and services, including the furnishing of appropriate conference facilities and personnel.

Invitations are then issued. In the case of world-wide seminars, 32 governments, in addition to the host government are invited on the basis of the geographical distribution of countries in the Commission on Human Rights: eight from western Europe and other States, four from eastern European States, six from Asian States, eight from African States, and six from Latin American States. For regional seminars, all member states of the region concerned are invited. Each invited government is asked to nominate a participant and up to three alternates to attend the seminar. The host government is invited to nominate up to five participants and five alternates or observers. Participants, although nominated by their governments, attend the seminar in their personal capacity at the invitation of the secretary-general and subject to confirmation by him, and do not speak on behalf of their government.

Specialized agencies and other intergovernmental organizations having an interest in the subject of the seminar are also invited to be represented. Non-governmental organizations in consultative status, whose aims and purposes are related to the subject of the seminar, are asked to send observers.

Expert consultants are called upon by the United Nations to prepare basic background papers to elucidate the topics on the agenda and to highlight problems with a view to stimulating their discussion at the seminar. These papers are translated, reproduced, and sent to those who will attend the seminar in advance of the opening date.

The United Nations pays for the air travel of one participant from each country invited, as well as a subsistence allowance for the duration of the seminar. Discussions at the seminar are conducted in an informal manner, no votes are taken, and no resolutions are adopted. There are no official records of the discussion; experience has shown that this results in a frank, friendly, and constructive exchange of opinions and experience. The report of the seminar, adopted at the last meeting, reflects the points of view expressed and summarizes the discussion. It may also include conclusions and recommendations if a consensus is achieved among participants as to their substance and formulation. Seminar reports are brought to the attention of competent United Nations organs, such as the General Assembly, the Commission on Human Rights, or the Commission on the Status of Women, in connection with their consideration of corresponding agenda items.

Training Courses. Training courses on various aspects of human rights were held in 1976 and 1977, respectively, the first at the Australian Institute of Criminology, Canberra, and the second at the United Nations Institute in Fuchu, Japan. Both were for candidates from countries members of the Economic and Social Commission for Asia and the Pacific.

Budgetary and administrative restraints reduced the number of training courses held in the following years. However, a sharp upturn occurred in 1977 after the Commission on Human Rights (resolution 1987/37) cited a course held in 1986 in La Paz, Bolivia, for persons involved in the preparation of reports under international human rights conventions as constituting "a particularly commendable example for future activities under the advisory services program" and requested the secretary-general to establish and administer a voluntary trust fund to provide additional financial support for practical activities focused on the implementation of international conventions and other international instruments on human rights promulgated by the United Nations, its specialized agencies, or regional organizations.

A training course on teaching human rights, for participants from the Asian Pacific region, was held at the headquarters of the Economic and Social Commission for Asia and the Pacific, Bangkok, from 12 to 23 October 1987. A course on the preparation of national reports under United Nations human rights conventions, for government officials from English-speaking African countries, was held at Lusaka from 9 to 20 November 1987. And a course on the latter subject, for participants from Spanish-speaking countries in Central America and the Caribbean, was held at San José, Costa Rica, from 23 November to 4 December 1987. The African course was organized jointly by the UN Centre for Human Rights, the UN Institute for Training and Research, and the Organization of African Unity. The Latin American course was organized by the UN Centre for Human Rights, the Inter-American Institute of Human Rights, and the Latin-American Institute for the Prevention of Crime and Treatment of Offenders.

Fellowships. Under the advisory services program, the secretary-general awards each year from 25 to 50 human rights fellowships to candidates nominated by their governments. The fellowships are intended to give persons entrusted with functions important to the promotion and protection of human rights in their respective countries an opportunity to broaden their professional knowledge and experience by acquainting themselves with advanced knowledge and techniques in this field already in use in other countries, so that their ability to understand and solve practical problems of human rights will be increased by the time they return to their own countries.

Most of the candidates nominated by governments are officials of high standing in national administration and have included judges, prosecutors, senior police officials, and officials responsible for drafting of national legislation. The greatest number of requests received has been for the study and observation of existing procedures of various aspects of the administration of justice, such as the use of writs of *habeas corpus,* techniques for ensuring the right of the accused to a speedy trial, and methods of interrogation of suspected or accused persons and their right to communicate with lawyers, family members, and friends. Fellowships have also been granted for the study of human rights questions which affect children and the family and for observation of the working of judicial and other remedies against the abuse of administrative authority.

The CENTER FOR HUMAN RIGHTS is responsible for the selection of fellows, for their placement—with the help of the host government concerned—with national institutions capable of providing the observation and training facilities required, and for evaluation of the success of each fellowship.

There is a continuing demand for fellowship awards from States at all stages of development, and the level of candidates proposed for such awards has been consistently high.

Advisory Services of Experts. Under the advisory services program, governments may request the services of an expert, or team of experts, to perform a specific task, such as drafting national legislation to promote and protect human rights or setting up national institutions for that purpose. However, only a few governments have so far availed themselves of such services; and, in 1987, the Commission on Human Rights (resolution 1987/38) encouraged them to do so, suggesting that they might use experts to draft basic legal texts in conformity with international human rights conventions.

Voluntary Trust Fund. The Commission on Human Rights, in the same resolution, requested the secretary-general "to establish and administer . . . a voluntary fund for advisory services and technical assistance in the field of human rights." The UNITED NATIONS VOLUNTARY FUND FOR VICTIMS OF TORTURE was, accordingly, established on 16 November 1987, and appeals for funds were sent to the governments and the intergovernmental and non-governmental organizations concerned. Resources pledged to the voluntary fund are expected to permit a wider, fuller, and more consistent implementation of United Nations' international human rights instruments through practical assistance.

Review of the Advisory Services Program. In 1988, the secretary-general presented to the Commission on Human Rights a comprehensive report (UN Doc. E/CN.4/1988/40 and Add. 1) on activities carried out within the framework of the advisory services program and on the establishment of the VOLUNTARY FUND FOR ADVISORY SERVICES AND TECHNICAL ASSISTANCE IN THE FIELD OF HUMAN RIGHTS. In the report, he outlined a new plan of activities for the program.

Under the proposed plan, the objectives of the program are (a) furthering knowledge and understanding of international human rights standards and their normative contents, with a view to promoting their widest application; (b) facilitating the implementation of international instruments (application of substantive provisions); and (c) practical assistance in the creation and development of national infrastructures for the promotion and protection of internationally recognized human rights norms and assistance to governments in this respect.

The developed program would include:

(1) regional seminars in those regions which could most benefit from such assistance, i.e., where a large number of States are not parties to human rights instruments;

(2) regional training courses, mainly for States parties to major human rights instruments, for government officials directly involved in the implementation of those instruments—legislators, judges, police and prison officials, and others responsible for the administration of justice;

(3) advisory services of experts and technical assistance in the field of human rights, with the aim of assisting governments in the development of the necessary infrastructures to meet international human rights standards;

(4) fellowships, to be awarded annually to official government nominees directly involved in functions affecting human rights, as well as members of national commissions on human rights and national non-governmental organizations involved;

(5) the establishment of regional arrangements for the promotion and protection of human rights in regions lacking them, including the establishment of regional depository centers for United Nations human rights materials and the establishment of regional institutes for training purposes; and

(6) the holding of regional seminars or training courses with a view to developing effective national institutions, including non-governmental organizations, for the promotion and protection of human rights in accordance with national legislation.

The Commission on Human Rights took note (resolution 1988/54) of the secretary-general's report, reaffirmed that the program of advisory services in the field of human rights should continue to provide practical assistance in the implementation of international conventions on human rights to those States which indicate a need for such assistance, and requested the secretary-general to pursue his efforts for an expanded program in which increasing emphasis would be placed on expert assistance and activities to assist governments in the development of the infrastructures necessary to meet international human rights standards.

The commission further called upon the secretary-general to ensure that the Center for Human Rights becomes a focal point to coordinate all UN advisory services activities and to ensure close cooperation between the activities of the regular program of advisory services and the activities undertaken by the voluntary fund.

In his 1990 report to the commission (UN Doc. E/CN.4/1990/43), the secretary-general summarized the steps taken to expand the program with increased emphasis on expert assistance and other activities to assist governments in developing the infrastructures necessary to meet international human rights standards. Highlights of the 1989 program included activities financed from the regular UN budget—such as an international seminar in Greece; a training course in the Union of Soviet Socialist Republics; advisory missions of experts to Equatorial Guinea, Guatemala, and Haiti; the awarding of fellowships; and activities financed under the Voluntary Fund for Advisory Services and Technical Assistance in the Field of Human Rights, such as assistance to the AFRICAN COMMISSION ON HUMAN AND PEOPLES' RIGHTS; country programs in Colombia, Guatemala, and the Gambia (including the provision of 21 fellowships and the advisory services of 17 experts); and the holding of training courses or workshops in Guinea, the Gambia, Ecuador, the Philippines, Italy, Peru, Argentina, and Guatemala.

After examining the report, the commission noted (resolution 1990/58) the secretary-general's enhanced efforts to coordinate system-wide advisory services and technical assistance in the field of human rights and to create a flexible interagency mechanism for human rights activities and supported the general thrust of the plan of future activities set out in the report. The operative paragraphs of the resolution were as follows (para. 1–18):

[The Commission on Human Rights]

1. Welcomes the increasing number of requests from governments for support and technical assistance in the field of human rights;

2. Reaffirms that the programme of advisory services in the field of human rights should continue to provide practical assistance in the implementation of international conventions on human rights to those States which indicate a need for such assistance;

3. Requests the Secretary-General to provide urgently more human and financial resources for the enlargement of advisory services, particularly from section 24 of the regular budget concerning technical co-operation, in order to meet the increased demand on this important instrument intended to invigorate the human rights spirit in the world;

4. Also requests the Secretary-General to pursue his efforts for a medium-term plan for advisory services and technical assistance in the field of human rights, taking into account the comments and views expressed by Governments at the forty-sixth session of the Commission on Human Rights;

5. Recommends to the Secretary-General that the provision of expert assistance and activities to assist Governments in the development of the necessary infrastructures to meet international human rights standards should continue to increase;

6. Welcomes the setting-up of an advisory group in the Centre for Human Rights to assist the Under-Secretary General for Human Rights in the identification and evaluation of projects, and requests the Secretary-General to further restructure the secretariat in this area aiming at even more effective management of these activities;

7. Requests the Secretary-General to enable the Centre for Human Rights to intensify co-ordination within the United Nations system of the activities for the provision of advisory services and technical assistance in the field of human rights in all their aspects;

8. Notes with appreciation the co-operation between the Centre for Human Rights and the United Nations Development Programme and encourages the leadership of both organizations to further enhance co-ordination and co-operation between them;

9. Requests the Secretary-General to explore yet further the possibilities offered by co-operation between the Centre for Human Rights and specialized bodies of the United Nations system, such as the United Nations Development Programme and the Office of the United Nations High Commissioner for Refugees, as well as the International Committee of the Red Cross, in the development of strategies for the setting up or the strengthening of national and regional infrastructures for the promotion and protection of human rights and fundamental freedoms and the planning, execution and evaluation of specific projects;

10. Also requests the Secretary-General to ensure close co-ordination between the activities of the regular programme of advisory services and those of the Voluntary Fund for Advisory Services and Technical Assistance in the Field of Human Rights;

11. Further requests the Secretary-General to bring the need for further technical assistance in the legal field that has been indicated by a number of States to the attention of the United Nations bodies and agencies that are active in providing assistance in the field of development with a view to promoting human rights in the development strategies and policies of the United Nations;

12. Invites competent United Nations bodies, such as the committees set up under the International Covenants on Human Rights, the Committee on the Elimination of Racial Discrimination and the Committee against Torture, to make suggestions and proposals for the implementation of advisory services;

13. Requests its special rapporteurs and representatives, as well as the Working Group on Enforced or Involuntary Disappearances, to inform Governments, whenever appropriate, of the possibility of availing themselves of the services provided for under the programme of advisory services and to include in their recommendations, whenever appropriate, proposals for specific projects to be realized under the programme of advisory services;

14. Also requests the Secretary-General to give special attention to such proposals of special rapporteurs and representatives;

15. Appeals to all Governments to consider making use of the possibility offered by the United Nations of organizing, under the programme of advisory services in the field of human rights, information and/or training courses at the national level for appropriate government personnel on the application of international human rights standards and the experience of relevant international organs;

16. Encourages Governments in need of technical assistance in the field of human rights to avail themselves of the advisory services of experts in the field of human rights, for example, for drafting basic legal texts in conformity with international conventions on human rights;

17. Expresses its appreciation to all Governments and intergovernmental and non-governmental organizations which have responded to the Secretary-General's call to provide assistance to States that indicated their need for technical assistance in the field of human rights, and requests the Secretary-General to pursue his efforts to coordinate and facilitate the flow of bilateral assistance in such cases;

18. Requests the Secretary-General to report to the Commission at its forty-seventh session on the progress made in the implementation of the programme of advisory services in the field of human rights.

AFFIRMATIVE ACTION. Several international instruments provide for action to be taken by States parties in order to remedy the effects of past discrimination on grounds such as race, sex, language, or religion. For example, the INTERNATIONAL COVENANT ON CIVIL AND POLITICAL RIGHTS provides:

Article 27. In those States in which ethnic, religious or linguistic minorities exist, persons belonging to such minorities shall not be denied the right, in community with the other members of their group, to enjoy their own culture, to profess and practice their own religion, or to use their own language.

The INTERNATIONAL CONVENTION ON THE ELIMINATION OF ALL FORMS OF RACIAL DISCRIMINATION contains the following provision:

Article 1 (4). Special measures taken for the sole purpose of securing adequate advancement of certain racial or ethnic groups or individuals requiring such protection as may be necessary to ensure such groups or individuals equal enjoyment or exercise of human rights and fundamental freedoms shall not be deemed racial discrimination, provided, however, that such measures do not, as a consequence, lead to the maintenance of separate rights for different racial groups and that they shall not be continued after the objectives for which they were taken have been achieved.

The CONVENTION ON THE ELIMINATION OF ALL FORMS OF DISCRIMINATION AGAINST WOMEN provides that:

Article 4. 1. Adoption by States Parties of temporary special measures aimed at accelerating *de facto* equality between men and women shall not be considered discrimination as defined in the present Convention, but shall in no way entail as a consequence the maintenance of unequal or separate standards; these measures shall be discontinued when the objectives of equality of opportunity and treatment have been achieved.
2. Adoption by States Parties of special measures, including those measures contained in the present Convention, aimed at protecting maternity shall not be considered discriminatory.

The Commission on the Status of Women has from time to time called for affirmative action to improve the status of women. On its recommendation, the UN Economic and Social Council, at its first 1989 session, urged governments (resolution 1989/36) "to give high priority to measures and temporary affirmative action programs that will more rapidly bring about equality in women's economic participation, in particular to programs that will ensure the following:

(a) women's access to the labor market and to education and training;
(b) elimination of sex segregation in the labor market and in education;
(c) women's participation in trade unions;
(d) equal pay for equal work;
(e) equal access to economic resources, including credit and membership in cooperatives; and
(f) improved conditions in the informal sector including, where desirable, the application of labor standards, and the development or improvement of sex-disaggregated statistics that accurately reflect women's work in the informal economic sector.

AFGHANISTAN. The Democratic Republic of Afghanistan is a country in Southern Asia. It has borders with Iran, Pakistan, and the Union of Soviet Socialist Republics. It achieved independence from Great Britain by the Treaty of Rawalpindi of 1919 and became a member of the United Nations in 1946. The population is estimated by the UN (1990) to be 21,033,000. Ethnic groups include Pathans, Hazaras, Tajiks, Turkomens, and Uzbeks. Languages commonly used include Dari and Pushtu. Islam (Sunni, 74%; Shi'ite, 25%) is the predominant religion. The courts follow the Hanafi jurisprudence of Islamic law in the absence of conflicting constitutional provisions.

The government (1990) took the form of a republic. Between 1964 and 1973, it had been governed in accordance with a constitution under which King Zahir Shah appointed one-third of the deputies, the people elected one-third, and one-third was chosen by the provincial assemblies. However, on 17 July 1973, Prime Minister Sardar Mohammed Daoud seized power, abrogated the constitution, and declared himself president and prime minister of the new republic.

In 1977, two factions of the People's Democratic Party of Afghanistan ended a 10-year disagreement, united, and organized a coup that overthrew Daoud and established the Democratic Republic of Afghanistan. The secretary-general of the People's Democratic Party (PDPA), Nur Mohammed Taraki, became president of the pro-Soviet Revolutionary Council, installed as the country's supreme governing body, and initiated a "reform" program which ran counter to many long-held traditions of the Afghan people. The dispute between the two factions of the PDPA led to further disagreement between two leaders. Taraki and Hafizullah Amin. In a September 1979 coup, Amin took over from Taraki.

On 24 December 1979, troops of the Union of Soviet Socialist Republics entered Afghanistan on the invitation of Hafizulla Amin and the Revolutionary Council under a "Treaty of Friendship, Good-Neighborliness and Co-operation," which had been negotiated during the presidency of Nur Mohammed Taraki. Amin died a few days later under mysterious circumstances; Pakistan later charged that he had been executed on 27 December by Soviet troops stationed in Kabul. He was replaced by Babrak Karmal, who, in turn, was succeeded in November 1986 by Lt. Gen. Mohammed Najibullah, a former head of the secret police who, since May of that year, had served as general secretary of the Central Committee of the People's Democratic Party.

In January 1980, with Soviet troop strength in Afghanistan reaching 85,000, the UN Security Council held an urgent meeting with a view to calling for the immediate withdrawal of Soviet troops but was unable to issue the call because of the negative vote cast by the Union of Soviet Socialist Republics. It then called for a special session of the General Assembly to consider the problem.

On 14 January 1980, the Assembly (resolution ES-6-1) expressed its grave concern about the developments in Afghanistan and their implications for international peace and security and called for the immediate, unconditional, and total withdrawal of foreign troops from that country in order to enable its people to determine their own form of government and to choose their economic, political, and social systems free from outside intervention, coercion, or restraint of any kind.

The Commission on Human Rights, in February 1980, condemned the Soviet military aggression against the Afghan people; denounced and deplored it as a flagrant violation of international laws, covenants, and norms; and called upon all peoples and governments to persist in condemning this aggression and denouncing it as a violation of human rights and of the freedoms of peoples.

For several years thereafter, the commission and the General Assembly repeatedly expressed the view that the withdrawal of foreign forces from Afghanistan was essential for restoring the enjoyment of human rights in that country and expressed their concern and anxiety at the continuing presence of the foreign troops and the reports of extensive human rights violations. On 15 March 1984, the commission proposed that the Economic and Social Council authorize the appointment of a special rapporteur to examine the human rights situation in Afghanistan, with a view to formulating proposals which could contribute to ensuring full protection of the human rights of all residents of the country before, during, and after the withdrawal of all foreign forces.

With the approval of the council, Mr. Felix Ermacora (Austria) was appointed as the commission's special rapporteur to examine the human rights situation in Afghanistan. In this capacity, he later submitted five reports to the commission (UN Docs. E/CN.4/1985/21, E/CN.4/1986/2, E/CN.4/1987 22, E/CN.4/1988 25, and E/CN.4/1990/25) and five to the General Assembly (UN Docs. A/40/843, A/41/778, A/42/667 and Corr. 1, A/43/742, and A/44/669). These reports were based upon his own observations following contacts and discussions with senior government officials, leaders of opposition movements, and other well-informed persons, the collection of a substantial body of documentation, and several visits to areas in Afghanistan and Pakistan.

In December 1987, the Secretary-General's personal representative, Diego Cordovez, visited Washington, D.C., and Moscow, where he held a number of meetings with senior officials of the United States of America and the Union of Soviet Socialist Republics. In Moscow, Foreign Minister Eduard Shevardnadze gave him assurance of his government's determination that negotiations towards the achievement of a comprehensive settlement of the situation relating to Afghanistan could be concluded. On the basis of these consultations, it was agreed that a round of talks would be held in Geneva beginning on 1 March 1988.

Following extended and intensive consultations in Geneva over a period of six weeks, it was possible to announce on 8 April 1988 that the instruments which would comprise the settlement were in final form and ready for signature. The "Agreements on the Settlement of the Situation Relating to Afghanistan" were signed on 14 April 1988 at the European office of the United Nations in Geneva. They comprised the following four instruments (the texts were issued as UN Doc. S/19835, annex):

(1) Bilateral Agreement between the Republic of Afghanistan and the Islamic Republic of Pakistan on the Principles of Mutual Relations, in Particular on Non-Interference and Non-Intervention;
(2) Declaration on International Guarantees;
(3) Bilateral Agreement between the Republic of Afghanistan and the Islamic Republic of Pakistan on the Voluntary Return of Refugees; and
(4) Agreement on the Interrelationships for the Settlement of the Situation Relating to Afghanistan (including the annexed Memorandum of Understanding on the monitoring arrangements to be provided by the United Nations).

The instruments were signed by Foreign Minister Abdul Wakil of Afghanistan and the Minister of State for Foreign Affairs Zain Noorani of the Islamic Republic of Pakistan on behalf of their respective governments as parties to the settlement, and by Foreign Minister Eduard Shevardnadze of the U.S.S.R. and Secretary of State George Shultz of the United States of America on behalf of their respective governments as states guarantors. At the signing ceremony, the UN Secretary-General noted that the arrangements laid the basis for the exercise by all Afghans of their right to self-determination and that the challenges facing the people of Afghanistan could and must be met by them alone. Later, he appointed Mr. Diego Cordovez as his representative on the Settlement of the Situation Relating to Afghanistan and established the Good Offices Mission, composed of 50 military officers temporarily detached from other United Nations operations, to monitor the implementation of the agreements, which called for the withdrawal of one-half of the foreign troops from Afghanistan by 15 August 1988 and the withdrawal of all troops within nine months.

The special rapporteur of the Commission on Human Rights, Felix Ermacora, welcomed signature of the so-called Geneva Agreements and agreed with the Secretary-General's statement that they represented "a major stride in the effort to bring peace to Afghanistan and to assure a reprieve for its people." However, he was not able to report any immediate improvement in the human rights situation within the country. "Acts of war are continuing," he stated in his report to the 1988 session of the General Assembly. "Violations of human rights are at least as frequent as in the past, affecting particularly the civilian population and endangering the lives and security of innocent men, women and children."

In this connection, he pointed out that the Geneva Agreements stipulated only the conditions for the exercise of the right of self-determination of the Afghan people; they were still to be implemented fully. The United Nations had established its Good Offices Mission, which had observed the withdrawal of Soviet troops, and had set up the Office of the Co-ordinator for United Nations Humanitarian and Economic Assistance Programs Relating to Afghanistan—both linked closely with human rights and humanitarian issues. However, the agreements were silent on several important human rights questions, such as the treatment of amnestied persons, investigation of the fate of persons who had "disappeared," the release of prisoners, and the dismantling of revolutionary or special tribunals, revolutionary or special prosecutors, and the special police. Moreover, he recalled that at the conclusion of the Geneva Agreements, the Alliance of the Opposition had indicated that its members did not feel bound by them because they had not been consulted or involved in the negotiations which produced the agreements.

In accordance with provisions of the Geneva Agreements, the Union of Soviet Socialist Republics began to withdraw its estimated 115,000 troops from Afghanistan on 15 May 1988. The withdrawal was completed on 15 February 1989.

After examining the report which the special rapporteur presented to its 1989 session (UN Doc. A/44/669, annex), the assembly recognized (resolution 44/161), with deep concern, that a situation of armed conflict continued to exist in Afghanistan, leaving large numbers of victims and causing enormous human suffering to the civilian population, that the treatment of prisoners detained in connection with that conflict did not conform to the internationally recognized principles of humanitarian law, and that more than five million refugees were living outside Afghanistan, with many others displaced within the country. The assembly noted that the main reasons given by the refugees for not returning to

Afghanistan, pending the achievement of a comprehensive political solution, were the continued fighting in some provinces, the use of very destructive arms in the conflict, and the minefields that had been laid in many parts of the country. It also noted that acts of terrorism had significantly increased.

The General Assembly, welcoming the cooperation which the Afghan authorities had accorded to the special rapporteur, urged all parties concerned to work for the achievement of a comprehensive political solution based on the right of self-determination and for the creation of a situation that would permit the return of refugees and the full enjoyment of human rights by all Afghans. It called upon all parties to the conflict, in order to alleviate the serious suffering of the Afghan people, strictly to respect human life and the principles and provisions of international humanitarian law and to cooperate fully and effectively with international humanitarian institutions, especially with the INTERNATIONAL COMMITTEE OF THE RED CROSS, in particular by granting it unrestricted access to all parts of the country.

At the same time, the assembly noted reports of the interrogation practices of the Afghan authorities, the large number of political prisoners, and the conditions of prisoners awaiting trial. It called upon the Afghan authorities to investigate thoroughly the fate of disappeared persons, to apply amnesty decrees equally to foreign detainees, to reduce the period during which prisoners await trial, to treat all prisoners—especially those awaiting trial or in custody in juvenile rehabilitation centers—in accordance with the STANDARD MINIMUM RULES FOR THE TREATMENT OF PRISONERS, and to allow the International Committee of the Red Cross to visit them regularly in accordance with its established criteria.

In the report which he presented to the 1990 session of the UN Commission on Human Rights (UN Doc. E/CN.4/1990/25), the special rapporteur summarized the conclusions he had reached after analyzing the information available to him in the following terms (para. 78):

A. Conclusions

The following conclusions are drawn in the light of the Special Rapporteur's scrupulous analysis of the information contained in the preceding chapters. They are his personal views on the overall situation of human rights in Afghanistan, and remain a matter of even deeper concern after the withdrawal of the Soviet troops:

1. The armed conflict in the country is still going on. The Afghan Government defends its authority against armed opposition movements whose goals are to break the present "non-religious" régime and replace it with another, more "fundamentalist", faction. The country has become

the theatre of a struggle between so-called "super powers" at the expense of the Afghan people.

2. These facts seriously compromise human rights and humanitarian law which is binding on all parties to the conflict. Due to the nature of the continuing hostilities, the problem of refugees remains unchanged.

3. The hope that, once the Soviet troops had withdrawn, the refugees would return, has not been fulfilled. The United Nations has only recently perceived the full role and influence of the opposition movements in organizing the five million refugees along party lines.

4. The Afghan Government claims to have allocated a large portion of its budget and considerable manpower to the needs of returning refugees. Despite the alleged return of about 235,000 persons, some five million refugees remain in exile. The Special Rapporteur has nevertheless been advised of certain moves towards their return. This fact is the subject of increasingly widespread rumours, but the Special Rapporteur has also received reports of various obstacles being placed in their way.

5. The obstacles to the return of refugees do not reside in the physical or economic instability of the country alone, or in the lack of an effective administration in provinces not under government control, but also in a growing pressure not to return. The refugees are thus placed in the desperate position of "collective hostages." This situation is contrary to international law and the spirit of the Geneva agreements.

6. As the refugee problem drags on, interest in their fate diminishes and their situation is gradually perceived as being normal. This has resulted in a sharp decrease of international aid, despite the efforts of international organizations, in particular the Office of the Co-ordinator for United Nations Humanitarian and Economic Assistance Programmes Relation to Afghanistan, to mobilize the international community.

7. The existence of minefields in many regions of the country is a further obstacle to the return of refugees. The Afghan Government is in possession of maps indicating the location of both Afghan and Soviet minefields, and has expressed its willingness to collaborate with international agencies in bringing a solution to the problem. It is also giving mine detection and disposal training. However, until a political settlement is reached between the parties concerned with a view to ending the conflict, there are little prospects for a solution to the minefield problem. The lack of maps indicating the location of minefields laid by the opposition movements is a further obstacle to carrying out a systematic mine detection policy. In the meantime, minefields endanger the lives of the population at large.

8. The hospitals in Pakistan and Afghanistan are still filled with war wounded and the statistics taken as a whole indicate that the conflict has not abated. No significant decrease in the numbers of wounded is foreseeable.

9. Far from ceasing, the armed conflict has intensified in particular around large towns and villages and strategic points. The Government is now conducting a defensive war, but this does not change the situation of the right to life and personal security which are constantly threatened.

10. There appears to be an increase in civilian targets, which is contrary to humanitarian law. Government forces endeavour to hit mainly military goals, whereas the opposition forces seem to fire indiscriminately, as well as committing acts of terrorism as defined by the First Additional Protocol to the Geneva Conventions. The shelling of cities and public places such as markets, bus stations, mosques and schools has caused the death of more than 1,000 civilians since September 1989. Other forms of terrorism have been reported, such as assassinations or the abuse of women and children. It has not been possible to trace the underlying responsibility for these acts.

11. Despite the alleged release of 17,000 prisoners from Afghan prisons since 1987, under various amnesty decrees, there is a constant of about 3,000 political prisoners, detained for crimes against State security. It is a matter of concern that a broad interpretation is given to the term "state security". The conviction of prominent figures on such charges and the flight of eminent political and scientific personalities tends to prove the general feeling of insecurity. The recent founding of the National Salvation Society, and its appeal to the Afghan people, are expressions of the evident concern felt by persons familiar with the situation in the country.

12. The improvements in psychological conditions for those under prison sentence must be welcomed. But the International Committee of the Red Cross, while benefiting from unrestricted access to those prisoners, should also be allowed to visit prisoners awaiting trial or verdict.

13. The opposition movements are also exercising jurisdiction and holding prisoners, but it is impossible to find out about their fate. Humanitarian law imposes the same criteria on both parties to a conflict: since the Afghan Government opens its prisons to international organizations, the opposition movements should not retain prisoners as virtual hostages.

14. The Special Rapporteur has been unable to visit areas not under government control, but it is alleged that such regions are seldom effectively administered and that many are considered to be no-man's-land. In addition, the Government has abandoned its policy of creating so-called "peace zones" or "peace regions".

15. An orderly educational system exists only in government-controlled areas, while in other areas the attempts at education are sporadic and not systematically followed through, giving rise to a generation of illiterates.

16. Economic rights are adversely affected by the war. When supply routes are open, the distribution of foodstuffs is guaranteed and goods reach the markets, and this leads to lower prices. However, in winter, inflation soars due to a deliberate blockading policy on the part of the opposition forces. It is doubtful whether such actions are in conformity with humanitarian law, inasmuch as they affect mainly the civil population and are aimed at political rather than military goals.

17. Full respect for human rights in Afghanistan will only result from a political solution to the conflict. Military action may enhance the personal honour and selfish goals of various groups and individuals but cannot serve the welfare of the country or its people.

18. An atmosphere which is conducive to negotiation between all parties involved must be created. The armed conflict, which is rejected by many persons with whom the Special Rapporteur spoke, does not contribute to building such an atmosphere. It is only through dialogue that the bloodshed, mine-laying and shelling will cease, and the refugees will be encouraged to return.

19. It is a matter of satisfaction to the Special Rapporteur that the General Assembly has adopted several of the recommendations contained in his reports.

B. Recommendations

1. The Special Rapporteur wishes to reiterate the recommendations contained of his report to the General Assembly (A/44/669, paras. 106 and 107).

2. The respective bodies of the United Nations should not hesitate to collaborate with both the Afghan Government and the opposition forces on the subject of mine detection. The conditions have been stated and, on the Government side, the maps of minefields are available.

3. All efforts must be made by both the opposition movements and the Afghan authorities detaining prisoners:

(a) to upgrade conditions of detention as well as treatment of prisoners to Standard Minimum Rules for the Treatment of Prisoners;

(b) to respect the right to life by all means.

4. The opposition movements should unconditionally open their prisons and detention centres for visits of prisoners by international humanitarian organizations such as the International Committee of the Red Cross.

5. Adequate conditions for the return of refugees should be created through international aid, regardless of the controlling faction in the areas concerned.

6. The mixed commissions provided for in article IV of the Geneva Agreements on the voluntary return of refugees should be set up. While the Government of the Islamic Republic of Iran is not a party to the agreements, it should none the less be invited to participate in the setting up of such mixed commissions.

7. No obstacles whatsoever should be placed in the way of refugees desirous of returning to Afghanistan. On the contrary, conditions conducive to their return should be created in order to encourage them to do so.

8. The Commission on Human Rights should appeal for the acceptance of unconditional dialogue between all parties to the conflict with a view to finding a peaceful solution.

9. The United Nations bodies concerned should continue to provide assistance to both belligerents in the conflict in a spirit of impartiality.

10. It is the Special Rapporteur's opinion that the Advisory Services of the United Nations should be called upon to assist in improving the respect of human rights to which all parties to the conflict adhered, whether under formally-taken obligations or under obligations resulting from the generally recognized standards of human rights and humanitarian law.

Having examined the special rapporteur's report, the Commission on Human Rights on 16 February 1990 noted (resolution 1990/5) the conclusion at Geneva, on 14 April 1988, of the Agreements on the Settlement of the Situation Relating to Afghanistan and welcomed the completion on 15 February 1989 of the withdrawal of foreign troops from Afghanistan in accordance with those agreements.

The commission expressed its grave concern at the situation in Afghanistan, which resulted from the violation of principles of the UNITED NATIONS CHARTER and of the recognized norms of inter-State conduct, and its awareness of the continuing concern of the international community over the suffering of the Afghan people and the magnitude of the social and economic problems posed to Pakistan and to the Islamic Republic of Iran by the presence on their soil of millions of Afghan refugees. Conscious of the urgent need for a comprehensive political settlement, of the Afghanistan situation it emphasized the importance of the Geneva Agreements, which constitute an important steps towards such a solution.

The commission called for respect for and implementation of the agreements by all parties concerned; reaffirmed the right of the Afghan people to self-determination and to determine their own form of government and to choose their economic, political, and social system free from outside intervention, subversion, coercion, or constraint of any kind whatsoever; and reiterated that the preservation of the sovereignty, territorial integrity, political independence, and non-aligned and Islamic character of Afghanistan is essential for a peaceful solution of the Afghanistan problem.

In particular, the commission called upon all parties concerned to work for the achievement of a comprehensive political solution and the creation of the necessary conditions of peace and normalcy which would enable Afghan refugees to return voluntarily to their homeland in safety and honor, and emphasized the need for an early start of the intra-Afghan dialogue for the establishment of a broad-based government to ensure the broadest support and immediate participation of all segments of the Afghan people.

A new approach to a comprehensive settlement emerged at a meeting of officials of the United States of America and the Union of Soviet Socialist Republics held in Helsinki, Finland, on 21 and 22 March 1990. At that meeting, the conclusion was reached that the conflict might best be ended by free elections, organized by an interim government and supervised by impartial observers including representatives of the United Nations and of the Organization of the Islamic Conference.

AFRICAN CHARTER ON HUMAN AND PEOPLES' RIGHTS (1981). The charter—which may be cited as the Banjul Charter on Human and Peoples' Rights because it was drafted in Banjul, Gambia—is unique in several ways: (1) it deals with civil and political rights as well as with economic, social, and cultural rights in a single document; (2) it sets out the obligations of human beings as well as their rights; and (3) it deals with the rights of peoples as well as those of individuals.

The charter was adopted on 28 June 1981 by the Heads of State and Government of the OAU (18th assembly) in Nairobi, Kenya, and entered into force on 21 October 1986 after being ratified by a majority of the OAU member States. The text (OAU Doc. CAB/ LEG/67/3/Rev. 5), is as follows:

Preamble

The African States members of the Organization of African Unity, parties to the present convention entitled "African Charter on Human and Peoples' Rights",

Recalling Decision 115 (XVI) of the Assembly of Heads of State and Government at its Sixteenth Ordinary Session held in Monrovia, Liberia, from 17 to 20 July 1979 on the preparation of a "preliminary draft on an African Charter on Human and Peoples' Rights providing *inter alia* for the establishment of bodies to promote and protect human and peoples' rights";

Considering the Charter of the Organization of African Unity, which stipulates that "freedom, equality, justice and dignity are essential objectives for the achievement of the legitimate aspirations of the African peoples";

Reaffirming the pledge they solemnly made in Article 2 of the said Charter to eradicate all forms of colonialism from Africa, to coordinate and intensify their cooperation and efforts to achieve a better life for the peoples of Africa and to promote international cooperation having due regard to the Charter of the United Nations and the Universal Declaration of Human Rights;

Taking into consideration the virtues of their historical tradition and the values of African civilization which should inspire and characterize their reflection on the concept of human and peoples' rights;

Recognizing on the one hand, that fundamental human rights stem from the attributes of human beings, which justifies their national and international protection and on the other hand that the reality and respect of peoples rights should necessarily guarantee human rights;

Considering that the enjoyment of rights and freedoms also implies the performance of duties on the part of everyone;

Convinced that it is henceforth essential to pay a particular attention to the right to development and that civil and political rights cannot be dissociated from economic, social and cultural rights in their conception as well as universality and that the satisfaction of economic, social and cultural rights is a guarantee for the enjoyment of civil and political rights;

Conscious of their duty to achieve the total liberation of Africa, the peoples of which are still struggling for their dignity and genuine independence, and undertaking to eliminate colonialism, neo-colonialism, apartheid, zionism and to dismantle aggressive foreign military bases and all forms of discrimination, particularly those based on race, ethnic group, color, sex, language, religion or political opinions;

Reaffirming their adherence to the principles of human and peoples' rights and freedoms contained in the declarations, conventions and other instruments adopted by the Organization of African Unity, the Movement of Non-Aligned Countries and the United Nations;

Firmly convinced of their duty to promote and protect human and peoples' rights and freedoms taking into account the importance traditionally attached to these rights and freedoms in Africa;

HAVE AGREED AS FOLLOWS:

Part I: Rights and Duties

Chapter I
Human and Peoples' Rights

Article 1. The Member States of the Organization of African Unity parties to the present Charter shall recognize the rights, duties and freedoms enshrined in this Charter and shall undertake to adopt legislative or other measures to give effect to them.

Article 2. Every individual shall be entitled to the enjoyment of the rights and freedoms recognized and guaranteed in the present Charter without distinction of any kind such as race, ethnic group, color, sex, language, religion, political or any other opinion, national and social origin, fortune, birth or other status.

Article 3. 1. Every individual shall be equal before the law.

2. Every individual shall be entitled to equal protection of the law.

Article 4. Human beings are inviolable. Every human being shall be entitled to respect for his life and the integrity of his person. No one may be arbitrarily deprived of this right.

Article 5. Every individual shall have the right to the respect of the dignity inherent in a human being and to the recognition of his legal status. All forms of exploitation and degradation of man particularly slavery, slave trade, torture, cruel, inhuman or degrading punishment and treatment shall be prohibited.

Article 6. Every individual shall have the right to liberty and to the security of his person. No one may be deprived of his freedom except for reasons and conditions previously laid down by law. In particular, no one may be arbitrarily arrested or detained.

Article 7. 1. Every individual shall have the right to have his cause heard. This comprises:

a) the right to an appeal to competent national organs against acts of violating his fundamental rights as recognized and guaranteed by conventions, laws, regulations and customs in force;

b) the right to be presumed innocent until proved guilty by a competent court or tribunal;

c) the right to defence, including the right to be defended by counsel of his choice;

d) the right to be tried within a reasonable time by an impartial court or tribunal.

2. No one may be condemned for an act or omission which did not constitute a legally punishable offence at the time it was committed. No penalty may be inflicted for an offence for which no provision was made at the time it was committed. Punishment is personal and can be imposed only on the offender.

Article 8. Freedom of conscience, the profession and free practice of religion shall be guaranteed. No one may, subject to law and order, be submitted to measures restricting the exercise of these freedoms.

Article 9. 1. Every individual shall have the right to receive information.

2. Every individual shall have the right to express and disseminate his opinions within the law.

Article 10. 1. Every individual shall have the right to free association provided that he abides by the law.

2. Subject to the obligation of solidarity provided for in Article 29 no one may be compelled to join an association.

Article 11. Every individual shall have the right to assemble freely with others. The exercise of this right shall be subject only to necessary restrictions provided for by law in particular those enacted in the interest of national security, the safety, health, ethics and rights and freedoms of others.

Article 12. 1. Every individual shall have the right to freedom of movement and residence within the borders of a State provided he abides by the law.

2. Every individual shall have the right to leave any country including his own, and to return to his country. This right may only be subject to restrictions, provided for by law for the protection of national security, law and order, public health or morality.

3. Every individual shall have the right, when persecuted, to seek and obtain asylum in other countries in accordance with laws of those countries and international conventions.

4. A non-national legally admitted in a territory of a State Party to the present Charter, may only be expelled from it by virtue of a decision taken in accordance with the law.

5. The mass expulsion of non-nationals shall be prohibited. Mass expulsion shall be that which is aimed at national, racial, ethnic or religious groups.

Article 13. 1. Every citizen shall have the right to participate freely in the government of his country, either directly or through freely chosen representatives in accordance with the provisions of the law.

2. Every citizen shall have the right of equal access to the public service of his country.

3. Every individual shall have the right of access to public property and services in strict equality of all persons before the law.

Article 14. The right to property shall be guaranteed. It may only be encroached upon in the interest of public need or in the general interest of the community and in accordance with the provisions of appropriate laws.

Article 15. Every individual shall have the right to work under equitable and satisfactory conditions, and shall receive equal pay for equal work.

Article 16. 1. Every individual shall have the right to enjoy the best attainable state of physical and mental health.

2. States parties to the present Charter shall take the necessary measures to protect the health of their people and to ensure that they receive medical attention when they are sick.

Article 17. 1. Every individual shall have the right to education.

2. Every individual may freely, take part in the cultural life of his community.

3. The promotion and protection of morals and traditional values recognized by the community shall be the duty of the State.

Article 18. 1. The family shall be the natural unit and basis of society. It shall be protected by the State which shall take care of its physical health and moral.

2. The State shall have the duty to assist the family which is the custodian of morals and traditional values recognized by the community.

3. The State shall ensure the elimination of every discrimination against women and also censure the protection of the rights of the woman and the child as stipulated in international declarations and conventions.

4. The aged and the disabled shall also have the right to special measures of protection in keeping with their physical or moral needs.

Article 19. All peoples shall be equal; they shall enjoy the same respect and shall have the same rights. Nothing shall justify the domination of a people by another.

Article 20. 1. All peoples shall have the right to existence.

They shall have the unquestionable and inalienable right to self-determination. They shall freely determine their political status and shall pursue their economic and social development according to the policy they have freely chosen.

2. Colonized or oppressed peoples shall have the right to free themselves from the bonds of domination by resorting to any means recognized by the international community.

3. All peoples shall have the right to the assistance of the States parties to the present Charter in their liberation struggle against foreign domination, be it political, economic or cultural.

Article 21. 1. All peoples shall freely dispose of their wealth and natural resources. This right shall be exercised in the exclusive interest of the people. In no case shall a people be deprived of it.

2. In case of spoliation the dispossessed people shall have the right to the lawful recovery of its property as well as to an adequate compensation.

3. The free disposal of wealth and natural resources shall be exercised without the prejudice to the obligation of promoting international economic cooperation based on mutual respect, equitable exchange and the principles of international law.

4. States parties to the present Charter shall individually and collectively exercise the right to free disposal of their wealth and natural resources with a view to strengthening African unity and solidarity.

5. States parties to the present Charter shall undertake to eliminate all forms of foreign economic exploitation particularly that practiced by international monopolies so as to enable their peoples to fully benefit from the advantages derived from their national resources.

Article 22. 1. All peoples shall have the right to their economic, social and cultural development with due regard to their freedom and identity and in the equal enjoyment of the common heritage of mankind.

2. States shall have the duty, individually or collectively, to ensure the exercise of the right to development.

Article 23. 1. All peoples shall have the right to national and international peace and security. The principles of solidarity and friendly relations implicitly affirmed by the Charter of the United Nations and reaffirmed by that of the Organization of African Unity shall govern relations between States.

2. For the purpose of strengthening peace, solidarity and friendly relations, States parties to the present Charter shall ensure that:

(a) any individual enjoying the right of asylum under Article 12 of the present Charter shall not engage in subversive activities against his country of origin or any other State party to the present Charter;

(b) their territories shall not be used as bases for subversive or terrorist activities against the people of any other State party to the present Charter.

Article 24. All peoples shall have the right to a general satisfactory environment favorable to their development.

Article 25. States parties to the present Charter shall have the duty to promote and ensure through teaching, education and publication, the respect of the rights and freedoms contained in the present Charter and to see to it that these freedoms and rights as well as corresponding obligations and duties are understood.

Article 26. States parties to the present Charter shall have the duty to guarantee the independence of the Courts and shall allow the establishment and improvement of appropriate national institutions entrusted with the promotion and protection of the rights and freedoms guaranteed by the present Charter.

Chapter II
Duties

Article 27. 1. Every individual shall have duties towards his family and society, the State and other legally recognized communities and the international community.

2. The rights and freedoms of each individual shall be exercised with due regard to the rights of others, collective security, morality and common interest.

Article 28. Every individual shall have the duty to respect and consider his fellow beings without discrimination, and to maintain relations aimed at promoting, safeguarding and reinforcing mutual respect and tolerance.

Article 29. The individual shall also have the duty:

1. To preserve the harmonious development of the family and to work for the cohesion and respect of the family; to respect his parents at all times, to maintain them in case of need;

2. To serve his national community by placing his physical and intellectual abilities at its service;

3. Not to compromise the security of the State whose national or resident he is;

4. To preserve and strengthen social and national solidarity, particularly when the latter is threatened;

5. To preserve and strengthen the national independence and the territorial integrity of his country and to contribute to its defence in accordance with the law;

6. To work to the best of his abilities and competence, and to pay taxes imposed by law in the interest of the society;

7. To preserve and strengthen positive African cultural values in his relations with other members of the society, in the spirit of tolerance, dialogue and consultation and, in general, to contribute to the promotion of the moral well being of society;

8. To contribute to the best of his abilities, at all times and at all levels, to the promotion and achievement of African unity.

Part II: Measures of Safeguard
Chapter I
Establishment and Organization of the African Commission on Human and Peoples' Rights

Article 30. An African Commission on Human and Peoples' Rights, hereinafter called "the Commission", shall be established within the Organization of African Unity to promote human and peoples' rights and ensure their protection in Africa.

Article 31. 1. The Commission shall consist of eleven members chosen from amongst African personalities of the highest reputation, known for their high morality, integrity, impartiality and competence in matters of human and peoples' rights; particular consideration being given to persons having legal experience.

2. The members of the Commission shall serve in their personal capacity.

Article 32. The Commission shall not include more than one national of the same State.

Article 33. The members of the Commission shall be elected by secret ballot by the Assembly of Heads of State and Government, from a list of persons nominated by the States parties to the present Charter.

Article 34. Each State party to the present Charter may not nominate more than two candidates. The candidates must have the nationality of one of the States parties to the present Charter. When two candidates are nominated by a State, one of them may not be a national of that State.

Article 35. 1. The Secretary General of the Organization of African Unity shall invite States parties to the present Charter at least four months before the elections to nominate candidates;

2. The Secretary General of the Organization of African Unity shall make an alphabetical list of the persons thus nominated and communicate it to the Heads of State and Government at least one month before the elections.

Article 36. The members of the Commission shall be elected for a six year period and shall be eligible for re-election. However, the term of office of four of the members elected at the first election shall terminate after two years and the term of office of the three others, at the end of four years.

Article 37. Immediately after the first election, the Chairman of the Assembly of Heads of State and Government of the Organization of African Unity shall draw lots to decide the names of those members referred to in Article 36.

Article 38. After their election, the members of the Commission shall make a solemn declaration to discharge their duties impartially and faithfully.

Article 39. 1. In case of death or resignation of a member of the Commission, the Chairman of the Commission shall immediately inform the Secretary General of the Organization of African Unity, who shall declare the seat vacant from the date of death or from the date on which the resignation takes effect.

2. If, in the unanimous opinion of other members of the Commission, a member has stopped discharging his duties for any reason other than a temporary absence, the Chairman of the Commission shall inform the Secretary General of the Organization of African Unity, who shall then declare the seat vacant.

3. In each of the cases anticipated above, the Assembly of Heads of State and Government shall replace the member whose seat became vacant for the remaining period of his term unless the period is less than six months.

Article 40. Every member of the Commission shall be in office until the date his successor assumes office.

Article 41. The Secretary General of the Organization of African Unity shall appoint the Secretary of the Commission. He shall also provide the staff and services necessary for the effective discharge of the duties of the Commission. The Organization of African Unity shall bear the costs of the staff and services.

Article 42. 1. The Commission shall elect its Chairman and Vice Chairman for a two year period. They shall be eligible for re-election.

2. The Commission shall lay down its rules of procedure.

3. Seven members shall form a quorum.

4. In case of an equality of votes, the Chairman shall have a casting vote.

5. The Secretary General may attend the meetings of the Commission. He shall neither participate in deliberations nor shall he be entitled to vote. The Chairman of the Commission may, however, invite him to speak.

Article 43. In discharging their duties, members of the Commission shall enjoy diplomatic privileges and immunities provided for in the General Convention on the Privileges and Immunities of the Organization of African Unity.

Article 44. Provision shall be made for the emoluments

and allowances of the members of the Commission in the Regular Budget of the Organization of African Unity.

Chapter II
Mandate of the Commission

Article 45. The functions of the Commission shall be:

1. To promote Human and Peoples' Rights and in particular:

    a) to collect documents, undertake studies and researches on African problems in the field of human and peoples' rights, organize seminars, symposia and conferences, disseminate information, encourage national and local institutions concerned with human and peoples' rights, and should the case arise, give its views or make recommendations to Governments.

    b) to formulate and lay down, principles and rules aimed at solving legal problems relating to human and peoples' rights and fundamental freedoms upon which African Governments may base their legislations.

    c) to co-operate with other African and international institutions concerned with the promotion and protection of human and peoples' rights.

2. Ensure the protection of human and peoples' rights under conditions laid down by the present Charter.

3. Interpret all the provisions of the present Charter at the request of a State party, an institution of the OAU or an African Organization recognized by the OAU.

4. Perform any other tasks which may be entrusted to it by the Assembly of Heads of State and Government.

Chapter III
Procedure of the Commission

Article 46. The Commission may resort to any appropriate method of investigation; it may hear from the Secretary General of the Organization of African Unity or any other person capable of enlightening it.

Communication From States

Article 47. If a State party to the present Charter has good reasons to believe that another State party to this Charter has violated the provisions of the Charter, it may draw, by written communication, the attention of that State to the matter. This communication shall also be addressed to the Secretary General of the OAU and to the Chairman of the Commission. Within three months of the receipt of the communication, the State to which the communication is addressed shall give the enquiring State, written explanation or statement elucidating the matter. This should include as much as possible relevant information relating to the laws and rules of procedure applied and applicable, and the redress already given or course of action available.

Article 48. If within three months from the date on which the original communication is received by the State to which it is addressed, the issue is not settled to the satisfaction of the two States involved through bilateral negotiation or by any other peaceful procedure, either State shall have the right to submit the matter to the Commission through the Chairman and shall notify the other States involved.

Article 49. Notwithstanding the provisions of Article 47, if a State party to the present Charter considers that another State party has violated the provisions of the Charter, it may refer the matter directly to the Commission by addressing a communication to the Chairman, to the Secretary General

of the Organization of African Unity and the State concerned.

Article 50. The Commission can only deal with a matter submitted to it after making sure that all local remedies, if they exist, have been exhausted, unless it is obvious to the Commission that the procedure of achieving these remedies would be unduly prolonged.

Article 51. 1. The Commission may ask the States concerned to provide it with all relevant information.

2. When the Commission is considering the matter, States concerned may be represented before it and submit written or oral representation.

Article 52. After having obtained from the States concerned and from other sources all the information it deems necessary and after having tried all appropriate means to reach an amicable solution based on the respect of Human and Peoples' Rights, the Commission shall prepare, within a reasonable period of time from the notification referred to in Article 48, a report stating the facts and its findings. This report shall be sent to the States concerned and communicated to the Assembly of Heads of States and Government.

Article 53. While transmitting its report, the Commission may make to the Assembly of Heads of State and Government such recommendations as it deems useful.

Article 54. The Commission shall submit to each ordinary Session of the Assembly of Heads of State and Government a report on its activities.

Other Communications

Article 55. 1. Before each Session, the Secretary of the Commission shall make a list of the communications other than those of States parties to the present Charter and transmit them to the members of the Commission, who shall indicate which communications should be considered by the Commission.

2. A communication shall be considered by the Commission if a simple majority of its members so decide.

Article 56. Communications relating to human and peoples' rights referred to in Article 55 received by the Commission, shall be considered if they:

1. indicate their authors even if the latter request anonymity;

2. are compatible with the Charter of the Organization of African Unity or with the present Charter;

3. are not written in disparaging or insulting language directed against the State concerned and its institutions or to the Organization of African Unity;

4. are not based exclusively on news discriminated through the mass media;

5. are sent after exhausting local remedies, if any, unless it is obvious that this procedure is unduly prolonged;

6. are submitted within a reasonable period from the time local remedies are exhausted or from the date the Commission is seized of the matter; and

7. do not deal with cases which have been settled by these States involved in accordance with the principles of the Charter of the United Nations, or the Charter of the Organization of African Unity or the provisions of the present Charter.

Article 57. Prior to any substantive consideration, all communications shall be brought to the knowledge of the State concerned by the Chairman of the Commission.

Article 58. 1. When it appears after deliberations of the Commission that one or more communications apparently relate to special cases which reveal the existence of a series of serious or massive violations of human and peoples' rights, the Commission shall draw the attention of the Assembly of Heads of State and Government to these special cases.

2. The Assembly of Heads of State and Government may then request the Commission to undertake an in-depth study of these cases and make a factual report, accompanied by its findings and recommendations.

3. A case of emergency duly noticed by the Commission shall be submitted by the latter to the Chairman of the Assembly of Heads of State and Government who may request an in-depth study.

Article 59. 1. All measures taken within the provisions of the present Chapter shall remain confidential until such a time as the Assembly of Heads of State and Government shall otherwise decide.

2. However, the report shall be published by the Chairman of the Commission upon the decision of the Assembly of Heads of State and Government.

3. The report on the activities of the Commission shall be published by its Chairman after it has been considered by the Assembly of Heads of State and Government.

Chapter IV
Applicable Principles

Article 60. The Commission shall draw inspiration from international law on human and peoples' rights, particularly from the provisions of various African instruments on human and peoples' rights, the Charter of the United Nations, the Charter of the Organization of African Unity, the Universal Declaration of Human Rights, other instruments adopted by the United Nations and by African countries in the field of human and peoples' rights as well as from the provisions of various instruments adopted within the Specialized Agencies of the United Nations of which the parties to the present Charter are members.

Article 61. The Commission shall also take into consideration, as subsidiary measures to determine the principles of law, other general or special international conventions, laying down rules expressly recognized by member states of the Organization of African Unity, African practices consistent with international norms on human and peoples' rights, customs generally accepted as law, general principles of law recognized by African states as well as legal precedents and doctrine.

Article 62. Each state party shall undertake to submit every two years, from the date the present Charter comes into force, a report on the legislative or other measures taken with a view to giving effect to the rights and freedoms recognized and guaranteed by the present Charter.

Article 63. 1. The present Charter shall be open to signature, ratification or adherence of the member states of the Organization of African Unity.

2. The instruments of ratification or adherence to the present Charter shall be deposited with the Secretary General of the Organization of African Unity.

3. The present Charter shall come into force three months after the reception by the Secretary General of the instruments of ratification or adherence of a simple majority of the member states of the Organization of African Unity.

Part III: General Provisions

Article 64. 1. After the coming into force of the present Charter, members of the Commission shall be elected in accordance with the relevant Articles of the present Charter.

2. The Secretary General of the Organization of African Unity shall convene the first meeting of the Commission at the Headquarters of the Organization within three months of the constitution of the Commission. Thereafter, the Commission shall be convened by its Chairman whenever necessary but at least once a year.

Article 65. For each of the States that will ratify or adhere to the present Charter after its coming into force, the Charter shall take effect three months after the date of the deposit by that State of its instrument of ratification or adherence.

Article 66. Special protocols or agreements may, if necessary, supplement the provisions of the present Charter.

Article 67. The Secretary General of the Organization of African Unity shall inform member states of the Organization of the deposit of each instrument of ratification or adherence.

Article 68. The present Charter may be amended if a State party makes a written request to that effect to the Secretary General of the Organization of African Unity. The Assembly of Heads of State and Government may only consider the draft amendment after all the States parties have been duly informed of it and the Commission has given its opinion on it at the request of the sponsoring State. The amendment shall be approved by a simple majority of the States parties. It shall come into force for each State which has accepted it in accordance with its constitutional procedure three months after the Secretary General has received notice of the acceptance.

SEE ALSO *American Convention on Human Rights and protocols; American Declaration on the Rights and Duties of Man; European Convention on Human Rights and protocols; International Covenant on Civil and Political Rights and protocols; International Covenant on Economic, Social and Cultural Rights; Universal Declaration of Human Rights.*

AFRICAN COMMISSION ON HUMAN AND PEOPLES' RIGHTS. The commission was established in accordance with Part II, chap. I, article 30 of the AFRICAN CHARTER ON HUMAN AND PEOPLES' RIGHTS (Banjul Charter), which provides that the purpose of the commission to "to promote human and peoples' rights and ensure their protection in Africa." The functions of the commission, as set out in article 45, are:

1. to promote Human and Peoples' Rights and in particular:

(a) to collect documents, undertake studies and researches on African problems in the field of human and peoples' rights, organize seminars, symposia and conferences, disseminate information, encourage national and local institutions concerned with human and peoples' rights, and, should the case arise, give its views or make recommendations to Governments;

(b) to formulate and lay down principles and rules

aimed at solving legal problems relating to human and peoples' rights and fundamental freedoms upon which African Governments may base their legislations;

(c) co-operate with other African and international institutions concerned with the promotion and protection of human and peoples' rights;

2. ensure the protection of human and peoples' rights under conditions laid down by the present Charter;

3. interpret all the provisions of the present Charter at the request of a State Party, an institution of the OAU or an African organization recognized by the OAU;

4. perform any other tasks which may be entrusted to it by the Assembly of Heads of State and Government.

The responsibilities of the Commission, as set out in articles 47 to 59 of the charter, may be summarized as follows:

Consideration of Communications from States Members. Under articles 47–49, a State party which believes that another State party has violated a provision of the charter may submit a written communication to that effect either to the State concerned or directly to the commission; in either case, the State concerned, the chairman of the commission and the secretary-general of the OAU are notified. If the issue is not settled within three months to the satisfaction of the two States involved, either State may submit it to the commission. After ascertaining that all domestic remedies have been exhausted, the commission examines such submissions with a view to securing a friendly settlement. If it fails to do so, it submits a report to the States concerned and to the OAU Assembly of Heads of State and Government stating the facts, its findings, and its recommendations if any.

Consideration of Other Communications. Under articles 55–59 of the charter, the commission receives before each session a list of communications other than those from States parties and decides which of them to consider. Such communications are considered if a simple majority of members of the commission decide to do so. Any communication to be considered is first brought to the knowledge of the State concerned. The procedure then followed is set out in articles 58 and 59 as follows:

Article 58. 1. When it appears after deliberations of the Commission that one or more communications apparently relate to special cases which reveal the existence of a series of serious or massive violations of human and peoples' rights, the Commission shall draw the attention of the Assembly of Heads of State and Government to these special cases.

2. The Assembly of Heads of State and Government may then request the Commission to undertake an in-depth study of these cases and make a factual report, accompanied by its findings and recommendations.

3. A case of emergency duly noticed by the Commission shall be submitted by the latter to the Chairman of the Assembly of Heads of State and Government, who may request an in-depth study;

Article 59. 1. All measures taken within the provisions of the present Chapter shall remain confidential until such a time as the Assembly of Heads of State and Government shall otherwise decide.

2. However, the report shall be published by the Chairman of the Commission upon the decision of the Assembly of Heads of State and Government.

3. The report on the activities of the Commission shall be published by its Chairman after it has been considered by the Assembly of Heads of State and Government.

In addition to the reports mentioned above, the commission submits a report on its activities to each ordinary session of the Assembly of Heads of State and Government, in accordance with article 54 of the charter.

Under articles 31–35 of the charter, the commission consists of 11 members "chosen from amongst African personalities of the highest reputation, known for their high morality, integrity, impartiality and competence in matters of human and peoples' rights, particular consideration being given to persons having legal experience." The members of the commission serve in their personal capacity. They are elected by secret ballot by the Assembly of Heads of State and Government from a list of persons nominated by the States parties to the charter.

Under article 64 of the charter, the commission is convened by its chairman whenever necessary, but at least once a year.

The first meeting of the commission was held in Addis Ababa on 2 November 1987. At that meeting, Mr. Isaac Nguema (Gabon) was elected chairman and Mr. Badawi Ibrahim El Sheikh (Egypt) was elected vice-chairman.

At its second session, convened in Dakar, Senegal, from 8 to 13 February 1988, the commission adopted its Rules of Procedure (Doc. AFR/COM/HPR.1). The rules provide that as a general principle sessions are closed, unless the commission decides otherwise, and that the reports of the commission to the OAU Assembly of Heads of State and Government are confidential. Reports submitted by States parties on measures they have taken to implement provisions of the charter are issued as public documents, and most decisions of the commission are made in open meetings by a show of hands.

The commission met in Libreville, Gabon, from 18 to 28 April 1988, to prepare its program of promotional activities; in Cairo, Egypt, from 17 to 26 October 1988, to draw up guidelines to be followed by States parties in preparing their reports; and in Benghazi, Libya, from 3 to 11 April 1989, to review communications.

During the first half of 1989, the commission organized, in cooperation with the UN CENTER FOR HUMAN RIGHTS, a training course on developing national strategies and mechanisms to promote and protect human rights in Africa. The course, held at Banjul, Gambia, from 24 April to 2 May 1989, sought to create awareness among participants from 26 countries of the need for adopting appropriate strategies and mechanisms to strengthen national infrastructures for the promotion and protection of human rights.

On 9 March 1990, Prof. U. O. Umozurike, chairman of the African Commission, addressed the United Nations Commission on Human Rights at a meeting of its 1990 session, held at the European office of the United Nations in Geneva, and provided the following account of the activities of the African Commission (UN Doc. E/CN.4/1990/SR. 55, para. 8–18):

Mr. Umozurike (Chairman, African Commission on Human and Peoples' Rights) said that the African Charter on Human and Peoples' Rights had entered into force on 21 October 1986, and had currently been ratified or acceded to by 39 African States. The Charter incorporated the usual civil and political rights. Some such as the rights to human dignity, inviolability of the person, equality before the law and freedom from discrimination and inhuman or degrading treatment, were unqualified. Others, such as the rights to liberty, freedom of conscience, expression, association and assembly, property and participation in government, were subject to the law of the land; unfortunately, there was no requirement that the law must be reasonably justifiable in a democratic society.

The Charter also incorporated rights of the type covered by the International Covenant on Economic, Social and Cultural Rights such as the right to work under satisfactory conditions and the right to education, health and medical attention. The African Charter provided for the immediate implementation of such rights, which, while they gave meaning to the first group, required efforts on the part of Governments.

The Charter also incorporated a so-called third generation of rights enjoyed by the group as a whole - the rights to self-determination, to national and international peace and security, to a satisfactory environment and to development. A United Nations study considered the last of those rights to be an individual one also. The achievement of such rights required international collaboration.

The Charter also spelt out individual duties such as those to the family, society, the State and the international community; in so doing, it combined legal, political and moral duties. Indeed, international morality was essential for a proper conduct of international relations, and the African Charter was unique in stressing that ingredient. In order to satisfy individual rights, moreover, national resources and potential must be put to maximum use.

The Charter was to be implemented mainly through the African Commission on Human and Peoples' Rights, which reported to the Assembly of OAU Heads of State and Government. The Commission consisted of 11 members chosen for their integrity and competence. It held two annual meetings, with the possibility of extraordinary sessions, and received communications on breaches by States parties from States members and from other entities or individuals, not necessarily African.

The Commission had so far granted observer status to 18 non-governmental organizations. No complaint had been hitherto received from a State member about another member; 90 percent of communications received had been against non-member States, some of them being non-African States. The Commission studied the situations reported and made recommendations to the parties, seeking traditional methods of settlement rather than the court system; situations which revealed a serious and consistent pattern of human rights denial were drawn to the attention of the OAU Assembly, which might in its turn call for studies or take other action which, in any case, could not preclude action at the international level. The Commission carried out its protective activities in sercrecy until the OAU Assembly authorized publication or its annual report was submitted.

The other major Commission activity was promotional, through research, documentation, dissemination of information and the organizing of seminars, symposia and conferences. Such activities covered a very wide field; but protective activity was circumscribed, although greater involvement was possible in the future.

What the African Charter had achieved was the clear internationalization, and in some respects the Africanization, of certain rights and duties not set forth in other international instruments or forming part of international customary laws.

The Commission, during its two and a half years of existence, had received support from the Centre for Human Rights, the European and American Commissions on Human Rights and elsewhere. It had had some moderate successes: its intervention had been enough to secure the release of certain detained persons, it had established guidelines relating to member States' biennial reports and it had made recommendations about human rights teaching. African States paid for the Commission's operations through their OAU contributions; those which had not yet ratified or acceded to the African Charter had been urged to do so in order to make it truly regional.

The Commission had yet to tackle certain issues. The reinforcement procedures were recommendatory and conciliatory; and certain rights, like the right to work, were currently beyond the capacity of African States to implement. Since the African system ruled out the court process, perhaps the incorporation of certain rights in a constitutional framework, fundamental laws and directive principles of States policy would suffice; the Indian and Nigerian Constitutions contained examples of that approach.

The Commission, conscious of the high expectations placed in it, appealed for support, and was anxious to contribute to the philosophy and practice of human rights. On the basis of the benefits it had already experienced, a comparable system could be recommended to regions which did not yet have a regional charter.

AFRICAN CONVENTION GOVERNING THE SPECIFIC ASPECTS OF REFUGEE PROBLEMS IN AFRICA (1969). The convention, complementing on a regional basis the CONVENTION RELATING TO THE STATUS OF REFUGEES, expressly defines in legal terms the principles set out in the DECLARATION ON TERRITORIAL ASYLUM.

The convention was adopted on 10 September 1969 by the Assembly of Heads of State and Government of the ORGANIZATION OF AFRICAN UNITY, convened at Addis Ababa, and entered into force on 20 June 1974. The text (UN Doc. MHCR/131 [1969]) is as follows:

Preamble

We, the Heads of State and Government assembled in the city of Addis Ababa, September 6–10, 1969

1. Noting with concern the constantly increasing numbers of refugees in Africa and desirous of finding ways and means of alleviating their misery and suffering as well as providing them with a better life and future,

2. Recognizing the need for an essentially humanitarian approach towards solving the problems of refugees,

3. Aware, however, that refugee problems are a source of friction among many Member States, and desirous of eliminating the source of such discord,

4. Anxious to make a distinction between a refugee who seeks a peaceful and normal life and a person fleeing his country for the sole purpose of fomenting subversion from outside,

5. Determined that the activities of such subversive elements should be discouraged, in accordance with the Declaration on the Problem of Subversion and Resolution on the Problem of Refugees adopted at Accra in 1965,

6. Bearing in mind that the Charter of the United Nations and the Universal Declaration of Human Rights have affirmed the principle that human beings shall enjoy fundamental rights and freedoms without discrimination,

7. Recalling Resolution 2312 (XXII) of 14 December 1967 of the United Nations General Assembly, relating to the Declaration on Territorial Asylum,

8. Convinced that all the problems of our continent must be solved in the spirit of the Charter of the Organization of African Unity and in the African context,

9. Recognizing that the United Nations Convention of 28 July 1951, as modified by the Protocol of 31 January 1967, constitutes the basic and universal instrument relating to the status of refugees and reflects the deep concern of States for refugees and their desire to establish common standards for their treatment,

10. Recalling Resolutions 26 and 104 of the OAU Assemblies of Heads of State and Government, calling upon Member States of the Organization who had not already done so to accede to the United Nations Convention of 1951 and to the Protocol of 1967 relating to the Status of Refugees, and meanwhile to apply their provisions to refugees in Africa,

11. Convinced that the efficiency of the measures recommended by the present Convention to solve the problem of refugees in Africa necessitates close and continuous collaboration between the Organization of African Unity and the Office of the United Nations High Commissioner for Refugees,

HAVE AGREED as follows:

Article 1. Definition of the Term "Refugee". 1. For the purposes of this Convention, the term "refugee" shall mean every person who, owing to well-founded fear of being persecuted for reasons of race, religion, nationality, membership of a particular social group or political opinion, is outside the country of his nationality and is unable or, owing to such fear, is unwilling to avail himself of the protection of that country, or who, not having a nationality and being outside the country of his former habitual residence as a result of such events is unable or, owing to such fear, is unwilling to return to it.

2. The term "refugee" shall also apply to every person who, owing to external aggression, occupation, foreign domination or events seriously disturbing public order in either part or the whole of his country of origin or nationality, is compelled to leave his place of habitual residence in order to seek refuge in another place outside his country of origin or nationality.

3. In the case of a person who has several nationalities, the term "a country of which he is a national" shall mean each of the countries of which he is a national, and a person shall not be deemed to be lacking the protection of the country of which he is a national if, without any valid reason based on well-founded fear, he has not availed himself of the protection of one of the countries of which he is a national.

4. This Convention shall cease to apply to any refugee if:

(a) he has voluntarily re-availed himself of the protection of the country of his nationality, or,

(b) having lost his nationality, he has voluntarily reacquired it, or,

(c) he has acquired a new nationality, and enjoys the protection of the country of his new nationality, or,

(d) he has voluntarily re-established himself in the country which he left or outside which he remained owing to fear of persecution, or,

(e) he can no longer, because the circumstances in connection with which he was recognized as a refugee have ceased to exist, continue to refuse to avail himself of the protection of the country of his nationality, or,

(f) he has committed a serious non-political crime outside his country of refuge after his admission to that country as a refugee, or,

(g) he has seriously infringed the purposes and objectives of this Convention.

5. The provisions of this Convention shall not apply to any person with respect to whom the country of asylum has serious reasons for considering that:

(a) he has committed a crime against peace, a war crime, or a crime against humanity, as defined in the international instruments drawn up to make provision in respect of such crimes;

(b) he committed a serious non-political crime outside the country of refuge prior to his admission to that country as a refugee;

(c) he has been guilty of acts contrary to the purposes and principles of the Organization of African Unity;

(d) he has been guilty of acts contrary to the purposes and principles of the United Nations.

6. For the purposes of this Convention, the Contracting State of Asylum shall determine whether an applicant is a refugee.

Article 2. Asylum. 1. Member States of the OAU shall use their best endeavours consistent with their respective legislations to receive refugees and to secure the settlement of those refugees who, for well-founded reasons, are unable or unwilling to return to their country of origin or nationality.

2. The grant of asylum to refugees is a peaceful and humanitarian act and shall not be regarded as an unfriendly act by any Member State.

3. No person shall be subjected by a Member State to measures such as rejection at the frontier, return or expulsion, which would compel him to return to or remain in a territory where his life, physical integrity or liberty would be threatened for the reasons set out in Article I, paragraphs 1 and 2.

4. Where a Member State finds difficulty in continuing to grant asylum to refugees, such Member State may appeal directly to other Member States and through the OAU, and such other Member States shall in the spirit of African solidarity and international co-operation take appropriate measures to lighten the burden of the Member State granting asylum.

5. Where a refugee has not received the right to reside in any country of asylum, he may be granted temporary residence in any country of asylum in which he first presented himself as a refugee pending arrangement for his resettlement in accordance with the proceeding paragraph.

6. For reasons of security, countries of asylum shall, as far as possible, settle refugees at a reasonable distance from the frontier of their country of origin.

Article 3. Prohibition of Subversive Activities. 1. Every refugee has duties to the country in which he finds himself, which require in particular that he conforms with its laws and regulations as well as with measures taken for the maintenance of public order. He shall also abstain from any subversive activities against any Member State of the OAU.

2. Signatory States undertake to prohibit refugees residing in their respective territories from attacking any State Member of the OAU, by any activity likely to cause tension between Member States, and in particular by use of arms, through the press, or by radio.

Article 4. Non-Discrimination. Member States undertake to apply the provisions of this Convention to all refugees without discrimination as to race, religion, nationality, membership of a particular social group or political opinions.

Article 5. Voluntary Repatriation. 1. The essentially voluntary character of repatriation shall be respected in all cases and no refugee shall be repatriated against his will.

2. The country of asylum, in collaboration with the country of origin, shall make adequate arrangements for the safe return of refugees who request repatriation.

3. The country of origin, on receiving back refugees, shall facilitate their resettlement and grant them the full rights and privileges of nationals of the country, and subject them to the same obligations.

4. Refugees who voluntarily return to their country shall in no way be penalized for having left it for any of the reasons giving rise to refugee situations. Whenever necessary, an appeal shall be made through national information media and through the Administrative Secretary-General of the OAU, inviting refugees to return home and giving assurance that the new circumstances prevailing in their country of origin will enable them to return without risk and to take up a normal and peaceful life without fear of being disturbed or punished, and that the text of such appeal should be given to refugees and clearly explained to them by their country of asylum.

5. Refugees who freely decide to return to their homeland, as a result of such assurances or on their own initiative, shall be given every possible assistance by the country of asylum, the country of origin, voluntary agencies and international and intergovernmental organizations, to facilitate their return.

Article 6. Travel Documents. 1. Subject to Article III, Member States shall issue to refugees lawfully staying in their territories documents in accordance with the United Nations Convention relating to the Status of Refugees and the Schedule and Annex thereto, for the purpose of travel outside their territory, unless compelling reasons of national security or public order otherwise require. Member States may issue such a travel document to any other refugee in their territory.

2. Where an African country of second asylum accepts a refugee from a country of first asylum, the country of first asylum may be dispensed from issuing a document with a return clause.

3. Travel documents issued to refugees under previous international agreements by States Parties thereto shall be recognized and treated by Member States in the same way as if they had been issued to refugees pursuant to this Article.

Article 7. Co-operation of the National Authorities With The Organization of African Unity. In order to enable the Administrative Secretary-General of the Organization of African Unity to make reports to the competent organs of the Organization of African Unity, Member States undertake to provide the Secretariat in the appropriate form with information and statistical data requested concerning:

(a) the condition of refugees;

(b) the implementation of this Convention, and

(c) laws, regulations and decrees which are, or may hereafter be, in force relating to refugees.

Article 8. Co-operation with the Office of the United Nations High Commissioner for Refugees. 1. Member States shall co-operate with the Office of the United Nations High Commissioner for Refugees.

2. The present Convention shall be the effective regional complement in Africa of the 1951 United Nations Convention on the Status of Refugees.

Article 9. Settlement of Disputes. Any dispute between States signatories to this Convention relating to its interpretation or application, which cannot be settled by other means, shall be referred to the Commission for Mediation, Conciliation and Arbitration of the Organization of African Unity, at the request of any one of the Parties to the dispute.

Article 10. Signature and Ratification. 1. This Convention is open for signature and accession by all Member States of the Organization of African Unity and shall be ratified by signatory States in accordance with their respective constitutional processes. The instruments of ratification shall be deposited with the Administrative Secretary-General of the Organization of African Unity.

2. The original instrument, done if possible in African languages, and in English and French, all texts being equally authentic, shall be deposited with the Administrative Secretary-General of the Organization of African Unity.

3. Any independent African State, Member of the Organization of African Unity, may at any time notify the Administrative Secretary-General of the Organization of African Unity of its accession to this Convention.

Article 11. Entry Into Force. This Convention shall come into force upon deposit of instruments of ratification by one-third of the Member States of the Organization of African Unity.

Article 12. Amendment. This Convention may be amended or revised if any member State makes a written request to the Administrative Secretary-General to that effect, provided however that the proposed amendment shall not be submitted to the Assembly of Heads of State and Government for consideration until all Member States have been duly notified of it and a period of one year has elapsed. Such an amendment shall not be effective unless approved by at least two-thirds of the Member States Parties to the present Convention.

Article 13. Denunciation. 1. Any Member State Party to this Convention may denounce its provisions by a written notification to the Administrative Secretary-General.

2. At the end of one year from the date of such notification, if not withdrawn, the Convention shall cease to apply with respect to the denouncing State. . . .

SEE ALSO *Convention relating to the Status of Refugees: Protocol; Refugees; Refugees: Students in Southern Africa; United Nations High Commissioner for Refugees.*

AFRICAN NATIONAL CONGRESS OF SOUTH AFRICA. A liberation movement recognized by the ORGANIZATION OF AFRICAN UNITY and invited by the UN General Assembly to participate in the work of UN bodies as an observer, the ANC is the largest and most powerful of several anti-*apartheid* organizations, representing the bulk of South Africa's 68% black majority. Competing movements include the PAN-AFRICANIST CONGRESS OF AZANIA and INKATHA.

Founded in 1912 to work for improvement in race relations in South Africa, the ANC in 1944 established its Youth League directed by three young men, Nelson Mandela, Walter Sisulu, and Oliver Tambo. By 1949, when the Africaner-dominated National Party came into power and introduced *apartheid* into the country's legal system, these three controlled the ANC. In 1952, as strict *apartheid* was extended into nearly every phase of daily life, Mandela, Sisulu, and Tambo organized a defiance campaign of civil disobedience. Despite the arrest of 8,500 of their supporters, they intensified the struggle; and in 1955, the ANC issued its "Freedom Charter," calling for a nonracial democratic organization of society, as follows:

Preamble

We, the people of South Africa, declare for all our country and the world to know:

That South Africa belongs to all who live in it, black and white, and that no government can justly claim authority unless it is based on the will of the people;

That our people have been robbed of their birthright to land, liberty and peace by a form of government founded on injustice and inequality;

That our country will never be prosperous or free until all our people live in brotherhood, enjoying equal rights and opportunities;

That only a democratic state, based on the will of the people can secure to all their birthright without distinction of colour, race, sex, or belief;

And therefore, we, the people of South Africa, black and white together—equals, countrymen and brothers—adopt this Freedom Charter. And we pledge ourselves to strive to-

gether, sparing nothing of our strength, and courage, until the democratic changes here set out have been won.

The People Shall Govern!

Every man and woman shall have the right to vote for and stand as a candidate for all bodies which make laws.

All the people shall be entitled to take part in administration of the country.

The rights of the people shall be the same regardless of race, colour or sex.

All bodies of minority rule, advisory boards, councils and authorities shall be replaced by democratic organs of self-government.

All National Groups Shall Have Equal Rights!

There shall be equal status in the bodies of state, in the courts and in the schools for all national groups and races;

All national groups shall be protected by law against insults to their race and national pride;

All people shall have equal rights to use their own language and to develop their own folk culture and customs;

The preaching and practice of national, race, or colour discrimination and contempt shall be a punishable crime;

All *apartheid* laws and practices shall be set aside.

The People Shall Share in the Country's Wealth!

The national wealth of our country, the heritage of all South Africans, shall be restored to the people;

The mineral wealth beneath the soil, the banks and monopoly industry shall be transferred to the ownership of the people as a whole;

All other industries and trade shall be controlled to assist the well-being of the people;

All people shall have equal rights to trade where they choose, to manufacture and to enter all trades, crafts and professions.

The Land Shall be Shared among Those Who Work It!

Restriction of land ownership on a racial basis shall be ended and all the land re-divided amongst those who work it, to banish famine and land hunger;

The state shall help the peasants with implements, seed, tractors and dams to save the soil and assist the tillers;

Freedom of movement shall be guaranteed to all who work on the land;

All shall have the right to occupy land wherever they choose;

People shall not be robbed of their cattle, and forced labour and farm prisons shall be abolished.

All Shall be Equal before the Law!

No one shall be imprisoned, deported or restricted without a fair trial;

No one shall be condemned by the order of any Government official;

The courts shall be representative of all the people;

Imprisonment shall be only for serious crimes against the people, and shall aim at re-education, not vengeance;

The police force and army shall be open to all on an equal basis and shall be the helpers and protectors of the people;

All laws which discriminate on grounds of race, colour or belief shall be repealed.

All Shall Enjoy Equal Human Rights!

The law shall guarantee to all their right to speak, to organise, to meet together, to publish, to preach, to worship, and to educate their children;

The privacy of the house from police raids shall be protected by law;

All shall be free to travel without restriction from countryside to town, from province to province and from South Africa abroad;

Pass laws, permits and all other laws restricting these freedoms shall be abolished.

There Shall be Work and Security!

All who work shall be free to form trade unions, to elect their officers and to make wage agreements with their employers;

The state shall recognise the right and duty of all to work, and to draw full unemployment benefits;

Men and women of all races shall receive equal pay for equal work;

There shall be a forty-hour working week, a national minimum wage, paid annual leave and sick leave for all workers and maternity leave on full pay for all working mothers;

Miners, domestic workers, farm workers and civil servants shall have the same rights as all others who work;

Child labour, compound labour, the tot system and contract labour shall be abolished.

The Doors of Learning and of Culture Shall be Opened!

The government shall discover, develop and encourage national talent for the enhancement of our cultural life;

All the cultural treasures of mankind shall be open to all, by free exchange of books, ideas, and contact with other lands;

The aim of education shall be to teach the youth to love their people and their culture, to honour human brotherhood, liberty and peace;

Education shall be free, compulsory, universal and equal for all children;

Higher education and technical training shall be opened to all by means of state allowances and scholarships awarded on the basis of merit;

Adult illiteracy shall be ended by a mass state education plan;

Teachers shall have all the rights of other citizens;

The colour bar in cultural life, in sport and in education shall be abolished.

There Shall be Houses, Security and Comfort!

All people shall have the right to live where they choose, to be decently housed, and to bring up their families in comfort and security;

Unused housing space is to be made available to the people;

Rent and prices shall be lowered, food plentiful and no one shall go hungry;

A preventive health scheme shall be run by the state;

Free medical care and hospitalisation shall be provided for all, with special care for mothers and young children;

Slums shall be demolished and new suburbs built where all have transport, roads, lighting, playing fields, creches and social centres;

The aged, the orphans, the disabled and the sick shall be cared for by the state;

Rest, leisure and recreation shall be the right of all;

Fenced locations and ghettos shall be abolished, and laws which break up families shall be repealed

There Shall be Peace and Friendship!

South Africa shall be a fully independent state, which respects the rights and sovereignty of all nations;

South Africa shall strive to maintain world peace and the settlement of all international disputes by negotiation— not war;

Peace and friendship amongst all our people shall be secured by upholding the equal rights, opportunities and status of all;

The people of the protectorates—Basutoland, Bechuanaland and Swaziland— shall be free to decide for themselves their own future;

The right of all the peoples of Africa to independence and self government shall be recognised, and shall be the basis of close cooperation.

Let all who love their people and their country now say, as we say here:

"These Freedoms We Will Fight for, Side by Side, Throughout Our Lives, until We Have Won Our Liberty."

In 1959, some ANC members, advocating greater militance, formed the rival Pan-Africanist Congress (PAC). Following the Sharpeville massacre of 21 March 1960—in which South African police killed 69 unarmed blacks—a state of emergency was declared by the government, and both the ANC and PAC were outlawed. Nevertheless, both launched guerilla movements in 1961. Nelson Mandela, who organized and commanded the ANC's new military wing, known as *Umkonto we Sizwe* (Spear of the People), was arrested in 1962 after returning from a trip abroad and charged with leaving the country illegally. In November of that year, he was convicted and sentenced to five years in prison.

While Mandela was in prison, the police raided ANC's underground headquarters in Rivonia, outside Johannesburg, and seized documents setting out plans for the proposed guerilla campaign. Accused of sabotage and conspiracy to overthrow the government, Mandela and eight co-defendants were convicted and sentenced to life imprisonment. Mandela spent the next 18 years in notorious Robben Island Prison, although the UN Security Council issued a call for his release in June 1980.

In 1985, South African President P.W. Botha offered to free Mandela if he would renounce violence. Mandela responded that he would not do so before the government took the initative in dismantling *apartheid* and granting full political rights to black South Africans.

By 1986, a new wave of black unrest had swept over the country and had become so violent that the government declared a nationwide state of emergency. However, by 1989, sanctions imposed by individual governments, and by the international community, began to take effect. In August 1989, Botha was replaced as president by F. W. de Klerk, a leader of the governing National Party who realized that white and black South Africans would have to share a single country, which he called "a new South Africa." Before the end of the year, President de Klerk had freed Mandela's colleagues and had conferred with Mandela at the presidential office in Cape Town.

On 2 February 1990, both the African National Congress and the Pan-Africanist Congress were legalized, and the government announced that those who had been imprisoned merely for belonging to those groups, or for other purely political reasons, would be released. At the same time, it put an end to the state of emergency in all but a small area of the country.

Nine days later, after 27 years in prison, Nelson Mandela was released and immediately began discussions, aimed at putting an end to *apartheid*, with President de Klerk. Visiting ANC headquarters-in-exile in Lusaka, Zambia, Mandela was designated as the organization's deputy president (President Oliver Tambo, seriously ill, was confined to a hospital in Sweden at the time), and discussed the ANC's approach to its first formal talks with government officials.

These talks, aimed at clearing the way for substantive future negotiations on ending white minority rule and abolishing the *apartheid* system, were held at Cape Town from 2 to 4 May 1990. When they concluded, the following joint communique was issued:

The government and the ANC agree on a common commitment toward the resolution of the existing climate of violence and intimidation from whatever quarter as well as a commitment to stability and to a peaceful process of negotiations. Flowing from this commitment, the following was agreed upon:

1. The establishment of a working group to make recommendations on a definition of political offenses in the South African situation; to discuss, in this regard, time scales; and to advise on norms and mechanisms for dealing with the release of political prisoners and the granting of immunity in respect of political offenses to those inside and outside South Africa. All persons who may be affected will be considered.

The working group will bear in mind experiences in Namibia and elsewhere. The working group will aim to complete its work before 21 May 1990. It is understood that the South African government, in its discretion, may consult other political parties and movements and other relevant bodies. The proceedings of the working group will be confidential.

In the meantime the following offenses will receive attention immediately: *(a)* The leaving of the country without a valid travel document. *(b)* Any offenses related merely to organizations which were previously prohibited.

2. In addition to the arrangements mentioned in Paragraph 1, temporary immunity from prosecution for political offenses committed before today will be considered on an urgent basis for members of the National Executive Committee and selected other members of the ANC from outside the country, to enable them to return and help with the establishment and management of political activities, to assist in bringing violence to an end and to take part in peaceful political negotiations.

3. The government undertakes to review existing security legislation to bring it into line with the new dynamic situation developing in South Africa in order to insure normal and free political activities.

4. The government reiterates its commitment to work toward the lifting of the state of emergency. In this context the ANC will exert itself to fulfill the objectives contained in the preamble.

5. Efficient channels of communication between the government and the ANC will be established in order to curb violence and intimidation from whatever quarter immediately.

The government and ANC agree that the objectives contained in this minute should be achieved as early as possible.

On 6 May 1990, Nelson Mandela and other ANC leaders briefed the heads of South Africa's black tribal "homelands" on the outcome of the Cape Town talks and sought to enlist them as allies. Chief Mangosuthu Gatsha Buthelezi of KwaZulu, whose Inkatha followers were at the time engaged in pitched battles with ANC supporters in Natal Province, was conspicuously absent.

Later in 1990, Mandela made an extensive tour of many countries, including Canada and the United States of America, in a highly successful campaign to publicize the work of the ANC and to raise funds to support its campaign to end *apartheid*. At every stop, he urged retention of sanctions against South Africa until the ideal of a democratic and free society in which all persons live together in harmony and with equal opportunities is realized.

AFRO-ASIAN PEOPLES' SOLIDARITY ORGANIZATION. An international non-governmental organization in consultative status (Category II) with the UN Economic and Social Council and UNESCO, and observer status with the Non-Aligned Movement, AAPSO is composed of 83 affiliated organizations located in approximately 75 countries of Africa, Asia, Europe, Latin and North America.

Founded in Egypt in 1957, and first known as the Organization for Afro-Asian Peoples' Solidarity, AAPSO endeavors to unite, coordinate and strengthen the struggle of the African and Asian people against imperialism and colonialism, to accelerate the independence of those peoples and to ensure their economic, social, and cultural development. It is mandated by its constitution "to safeguard, respect and uphold human rights and to support the struggle for democracy." It supports national liberation movements and cooperates with progressive and democratic organizations as part of the worldwide, anti-imperialist front of peoples.

AAPSO publishes, on a quarterly basis, *Development and Socio-Economic Progress,* the political magazine *Solidarity,* and the AAPSO *Bulletin.*

Afro-Asian Peoples' Solidarity Organization. Address: 89 Abdel Aziz al-Saoud Street, Manial, Cairo, Egypt. Telephone: 845014 or 845495. Cable: AFRO-ASIACO Cairo. Telex: 92627 APPSO UN. President: Nouri Abdul Razzak.

AGE OF CONSENT. The age at which persons are legally permitted to perform acts and undertake responsibilities prohibited to them earlier in life. Internationally, the CONVENTION ON CONSENT TO MARRIAGE, MINIMUM AGE FOR MARRIAGE AND REGISTRATION OF MARRIAGES, which is accepted as legally binding by States which have ratified or acceded to it, provides (in article 2) that:

States parties to the present Convention shall take legislative action to specify a minimum age for marriage. No marriage shall be legally entered into by any person under this age, except where a competent authority has granted a dispensation as to age, for serious reasons, in the interest of the intending spouses.

The RECOMMENDATION ON CONSENT TO MARRIAGE, MINIMUM AGE FOR MARRIAGE AND REGISTRATION OF MARRIAGES, which applies to all States, proposes a minimum age of 15 in Principle II, which provides that:

Member States shall take legislative action to specify a minimum age for marriage, which in any case shall not be less than fifteen years of age; no marriage shall be legally entered into by any person under this age, except where a competent authority has granted a dispensation as to age, for serious reasons, in the interest of the intending spouses.

AGGRESSION. The League of Nations attempted to define the term "aggression" in 1923 and 1924 but was unable to reach an agreement. The UN General Assembly assumed the task in 1950 and was able to complete it only in 1974, after numerous texts had been considered by the INTERNATIONAL LAW COMMISSION, the Sixth (Legal) Committee of the Assembly, and three special committees established by the Assembly in 1953, 1956, and 1967, respectively.

The definition was finalized by the third of the special committees and was adopted by the Assembly on 14 December 1974 (resolution 3314 [XXIX]). Its acceptance represented a resolution of many difficul-

ties which had divided member States up to that time, particularly regarding the meanings of the right to self-determination, freedom, and independence.

The text of the "Definition of Aggression," annexed to resolution 3314 (XXIX), is as follows:

The General Assembly,

Basing itself on the fact that one of the fundamental purposes of the United Nations is to maintain international peace and security and to take effective collective measures for the prevention and removal of threats to the peace, and for the suppression of acts of aggression or other breaches of the peace,

Recalling that the Security Council, in accordance with Article 39 of the Charter of the United Nations, shall determine the existence of any threat to the peace, breach of the peace or act of aggression and shall make recommendations, or decide what measures shall be taken in accordance with Articles 41 and 42, to maintain or restore international peace and security,

Recalling also the duty of States under the Charter to settle their international disputes by peaceful means in order not to endanger international peace, security and justice,

Bearing in mind that nothing in this Definition shall be interpreted as in any way affecting the scope of the provisions of the Charter with respect to the functions and powers of the organs of the United Nations,

Considering also that, since aggression is the most serious and dangerous form of the illegal use of force, being fraught, in the conditions created by the existence of all types of weapons of mass destruction, with the possible threat of a world conflict and all its catastrophic consequences, aggression should be defined at the present stage,

Reaffirming the duty of States not to use armed force to deprive peoples of their right to self-determination, freedom and independence, or to disrupt territorial integrity,

Reaffirming also that the territory of a State shall not be violated by being the object, even temporarily, of military occupation or of other measures of force taken by another State in contravention of the Charter, and that it shall not be the object of acquisition by another State resulting from such measures or the threat thereof,

Reaffirming also the provisions of the Declaration of Principles of International Law concerning Friendly Relations and Co-operation among States in accordance with the Charter of the United Nations,

Convinced that the adoption of a definition of aggression ought to have the effect of deterring a potential aggressor, would simplify the determination of acts of aggression and the implementation of measures to suppress them and would also facilitate the protection of the rights and lawful interests of, and the rendering of assistance to, the victim,

Believing that, although the question whether an act of aggression has been committed must be considered in the light of all the circumstances of each particular case, it is nevertheless desirable to formulate basic principles as guidance for such determination,

Adopts the following Definition of Aggression:

Article 1. Aggression is the use of armed force by a State against the sovereignty, territorial integrity or political independence of another State, or in any other manner inconsistent with the Charter of the United Nations, as set out in this Definition.

Explanatory note: In this Definition the term "State":

(a) Is used without prejudice to questions of recognition or to whether a State is a member of the United Nations;

(b) Includes the concept of a "group of States" where appropriate.

Article 2. The first use of armed force by a State in contravention of the Charter shall constitute *prima facie* evidence of an act of aggression although the Security Council may, in conformity with the Charter, conclude that a determination that an act of aggression has been committed would not be justified in the light of other relevant circumstances, including the fact that the acts concerned or their consequences are not of sufficient gravity.

Article 3. Any of the following acts, regardless of a declaration of war, shall, subject to and in accordance with the provisions of article 2, qualify as an act of aggression:

(a) The invasion or attack by the armed forces of a State of the territory of another State, or any military occupation, however temporary, resulting from such invasion or attack, or any annexation by the use of force of the territory of another State or part thereof;

(b) Bombardment by the armed forces of a State against the territory of another State or the use of any weapons by a State against the territory of another State;

(c) The blockade of the ports or coasts of a State by the armed forces of another State;

(d) An attack by the armed forces of a State on the land, sea or air forces, or marine and air fleets of another State;

(e) The use of armed forces of one State which are within the territory of another State with the agreement of the receiving State, in contravention of the conditions provided for in the agreement or any extension of their presence in such territory beyond the termination of the agreement;

(f) The action of a State in allowing its territory, which it has placed at the disposal of another State, to be used by that other State for perpetrating an act of aggression against a third State;

(g) The sending by or on behalf of a State of armed bands, groups, irregulars or mercenaries, which carry out acts of armed force against another State of such gravity as to amount to the acts listed above, or its substantial involvement therein.

Article 4. The acts enumerated above are not exhaustive and the Security Council may determine that other acts constitute aggression under the provisions of the Charter.

Article 5. 1. No consideration of whatever nature, whether political, economic, military or otherwise, may serve as a justification for aggression.

2. A war of aggression is a crime against international peace. Aggression gives rise to international responsibility.

3. No territorial acquisition or special advantage resulting from aggression is or shall be recognized as lawful.

Article 6. Nothing in this Definition shall be construed as in any way enlarging or diminishing the scope of the Charter, including its provisions concerning cases in which the use of force is lawful.

Article 7. Nothing in this Definition, and in particular article 3, could in any way prejudice the right to self-determination, freedom and independence, as derived from the Charter, of peoples forcibly deprived of that right and referred to in the Declaration on Principles of International Law concerning Friendly Relations and Co-operation among States in accordance with the Charter of the United Nations, particularly peoples under colonial and racist régimes or other forms of alien domination; nor the right of these peoples to struggle to that end and to seek and receive support, in accordance with the principles of the Charter and in conformity with the above-mentioned Declaration.

Article 8. In their interpretation and application the above provisions are interrelated and each provision should be construed in the context of the other provisions.

SEEL ALSO *Declaration on the Inadmissability of Intervention and Interference in the Internal Affairs of States.*

AGING. In 1948, Argentina submitted a draft Declaration of Old Age Rights to the UN General Assembly. The draft was referred to the Economic and Social Council, which called upon the Commission on Human Rights and the Social Commission to study the question. No definitive action resulted; and, in 1969, an item entitled "Question of the elderly and the aged" was put on the Assembly's agenda at the request of Malta.

In 1970 the Secretary-General issued a preliminary report (UN DOC. A/8364) to assist the Assembly in its discussion. The report pointed out that "the world is faced today with a paradoxical situation in which society is doing everything possible to increase the absolute and relative numbers of old people (through efforts to reduce death rates and birth rates respectively), but at the same time society is neglecting to utilize their vast potentials and very often creating socio-economic conditions which place a handicap on their physical and psycho-social adjustment."

The Assembly was unable to discuss the question at its 1970 session; but, on 18 December 1971, it requested the Secretary-General (resolution 2842 [XXVI]) to continue his study and to suggest guidelines for national policies and international action related to the needs and the role of the elderly and the aged in society.

In a further report on the subject presented to the General Assembly in 1973 (UN Doc. A/9126), the secretary-general pointed out (paras. 183–186) that:

In all areas of the world, but in particular in the more developed areas, major conditions of the aged, such as age discrimination, economic insecurity and the lack of the right to work, and failure of those responsible to provide for an equitable distribution of national income and wealth, require major redefinition of existing policies, such as social security, the right to work, the right to needed social and health services, housing, and educational and cultural and recreational opportunities. A policy on aging, therefore, is essential, as the world approaches the twenty-first century, in order to assure the increasing numbers and proportions of older persons their basic human rights—full participation and contribution to, as well as protection in, the society of which they are a part.

The report noted the demographic increase in the absolute and relative size of the aging populations of the world, a trend that was expected to continue because of medical advances and the decrease in birth and death rates. It states that, whereas in 1970, there were approximately 291 million persons 60 years of age or over throughout the world, this number was expected to increase to nearly 585 million by the year 2000, or by more than 100 per cent, whereas the world's population as a whole would increase from 3.6 to 6.5 billion, or by approximately 80 per cent. It was anticipated that the increase of the older populations would be proportionately higher in the less developed regions, where persons over 60 had numbered 5.4 per cent of the total population in 1970, as compared with 14.1 per cent in the more developed regions.

In 1978, the General Assembly decided (resolution 33/52) to organize a World Assembly on Aging in 1982 as a forum to launch an international program of action aimed at guaranteeing economic and social security to older persons, as well as opportunities for them to contribute to national development. In 1982, the World Assembly on Aging, held in Vienna, adopted by consensus the Vienna International Plan of Action on Aging, which the General Assembly subsequently endorsed (resolution 37/51). The endorsement was reaffirmed in 1987 (resolution 42/51), at which time the Assembly requested the Secretary-General, through the Commission for Social Development, to continue to monitor progress in the implementation of the plan of action and welcomed the establishment, in Malta, of the INTERNATIONAL INSTITUTE ON AGING, in pursuance of a recommendation made in the plan of action.

In his 1988 report on the subject to the General Assembly (UN Doc. A/43/583 para. 3), the secretary-general pointed out that:

The majority of the world's population aged 60 and over today are living in developing countries, and this proportion will increase from 58 per cent in 1990 to 62 per cent in 2000 and 71 per cent in 2025. The total global population of the elderly will increase from 487 million in 1990 to 612 million in 2000 and 1.2 billion in 2025. Simultaneously with the aging of populations, most countries are experiencing far-reaching technological changes and severe economic constraints. In such a climate, not every facet of aging can be dealt with; priorities need to be identified and resources pooled. Specific measures based on existing structures and activities, and more collaborative efforts encompassing Governments, intergovernmental and non-governmental organizations will not only achieve "more with less" but can tap the expanding awareness of the need and opportunities that exist for timely intervention.

In the light of these considerations, the Secretary-General suggested that the Assembly call for priority attention to be given to the following activities:

(a) At the national level, co-ordinating machineries or similar bodies with membership drawn from the Government, the non-governmental sector and the elderly themselves might be urged to draw up a national agenda on aging to 1992 and beyond; this process should also include the media, representatives of specialized educational institutions and the private sector, where appropriate.

(b) At the regional level, intergovernmental bodies should support national programmes on aging, devoting particular attention to expanding regional databases and instituting regional training courses on aging.

(c) At the international level, (i) the resources of the United Nations system-wide programme on aging should be increased, in the light of global demographic trends, for further implementation of the Plan of Action; (ii) an information exchange centre on aging should be established at UNOV/CSDHA, in its capacity as global focal point, to promote greater exchanges of knowledge and experience, particularly among developing countries.

At its 1988 session, the General Assembly (resolution 43/93) expressed satisfaction that the International Institute on Aging had been established in Malta and had been inaugurated by the Secretary-General on 15 April 1988; urged the Secretary-General to maintain and strengthen the existing international programs on aging, with the Centre for Social Development and Humanitarian Affairs in the United Nations office at Vienna continuing in its role as the focal point for activities in this field; requested the COMMISSION ON THE STATUS OF WOMEN to pay particular attention to the specific problems faced by elderly women and to the discrimination suffered by these women because of their gender and age; and strongly appealed to governments and to intergovernmental and non-governmental organizations to contribute generously to the United Nations Trust Fund for Aging.

In the report on implementation of the plan which he presented to the General Assembly at its 1989 session, the secretary-general included the following summary and recommendations (UN Doc. A/44/420, para. 3–7):

Implementation of the International Plan of Action on Aging is proceeding in stages. The first stage achieved was global awareness of the phenomenon of aging. Population aging is evident in most countries, incipient in the others. Between 1950 and 2025 the world's population will grow by a factor of a little more than three, the elderly population by a factor of six, and the "old" old - those 80 years and above - by a factor of 10. Every month about one million people cross the threshold of age 60. One billion elderly are projected for the year 2025, and more than 70 percent of them will be living in developing countries. The majority of the world's elderly population is already living in developing countries. The rate at which populations are aging has captured the attention of governments, institutions, communities and families throughout the world and presents a challenge to current ways of thinking, organization, distribution of resources and provision of services.

The second stage in the implementation of the Plan, now occurring, is infrastructural development. The General Assembly, in its resolution 43/93, supported several new structural initiatives to complement existing networks (see sects. IV and V).

The next and third stage of implementation has been identified in the second review and appraisal exercise recently completed, and relates to the participation of the elderly in development. There is sufficient time before the tenth anniversary of the adoption of the Plan of Action in 1992 for setting in motion a world-wide series of participation projects, including small-scale, integrated and self-help projects. The objective is to promote the participation of the elderly in their societies, thus diminishing their dependency together with its high social and financial costs. Governments, business, the professions, the voluntary sector, the family and the community all have roles to play in promoting the participation of the elderly in development.

The findings of the second review, annexed to Economic and Social Council resolution 1989/50 and the report of the Secretary-General (E/1989/13), address three broad areas: substantive priorities, new structural initiatives, and a draft programme of activities for 1992.

The General Assembly may wish to identify additional complementary measures to further the implementation of the Plan in practical ways, such as the following:

(a) The various networks on aging that co-operate with and within the United Nations system could identify and disseminate successful models of contributions by the elderly to society; effective care of the elderly as well as of their informal care-givers; integrated community development, encompassing participation and care strategies as well as intergenerational and inter-sectoral co-operation; Government support to the elderly, their families and communities, to encourage self-reliance and sharing; and census and other information gathering and processing for use in policy and programme formulation on aging.

(b) The major international non-governmental organizations and donor countries could join with the United Nations system in establishing a technical co-operation network. Such a network would design and support implementation of a series of self-help projects by the elderly, with a view to bridging the gap between major funding entities and local self-help initiatives as well as between globally espoused standards and the real living conditions of the elderly.

(c) The concerned specialized agencies and bodies of the United Nations system, together with donor organizations and countries, could support with available expertise and funds the emerging support structures for aging. These include national machineries on aging, self-help groups and organizations of the elderly, training institutes and centres, an African society of gerontology, and a world foundation on aging.

(d) Governments could support current efforts to launch an international fund-raising strategy for aging (including, for instance, the possible establishment of a world foundation on aging) and set a goal of resource mobilization by the year 1992 for the United Nations Trust Fund for Aging.

(e) National, regional and global planners could make aging a priority theme in development strategies for the 1990s and beyond.

(f) Governments could consider making a succinct formulation, in their respective countries and based on the Plan of Action, of the responsibilities and rights of the elderly in society for widespread distribution throughout 1992.

(g) The Centre for Social Development and Humanitarian Affairs of the United Nations Office at Vienna could elaborate for consideration of the General Assembly at its forty-fifth session a detailed global programme of activities for 1992, on the basis of the outline adopted by the Economic and Social Council (resolution 1989/50), which would guide the activities of the many participants in the global programme and serve as a model for national and regional level programmes.

(h) Member States having a special expertise or interest in aging could consider giving direct staff or extra-budgetary support to the Centre in its preparatory activities for 1992.

(i) Efforts could be continued within the inter-agency mechanism to further streamline activities within the United Nations programme on aging and to continue in the 1990s a unified approach to implementing the Plan of Action.

The secretary-general's conclusion, as set out in the report, was as follows (para. 73–74):

A timely and perceptive adjustment to aging requires global leadership and consultation. The General Assembly can provide the leadership, and to this end some initiatives are proposed for its consideration in section II; the United Nations system and its various collaborative networks can promote the necessary consultations. Global leadership and consultation serve to stimulate and support regional and national action in keeping with diverse needs, capacities, and cultures. Research into needs and capacities is needed to inform policies and programmes, but aging will not await the compilation of complete data. It proceeds apace and compels an immediate response. That response will vary widely from place to place, but two features seem constant: effective care requires the collaboration of the formal and informal systems, and participation of the elderly requires a series of small and diverse projects involving government, business, the professions, the community and the family.

More resources are needed at the national, regional, and international levels if we are to respond in time to aging. But even more important than financial resources is a co-operative and creative spirit in the many actors engaged in the implementation of the International Plan of Action on Aging. It is abundantly clear that the co-operative spirit is in place. What does seem lacking on a global scale is a sense of urgency and perhaps a vision of what the real capabilities of the elderly are. It is to be expected that this new perception will emerge in the next few years, building on the awareness and infrastructures now largely in place, and will materialize in a million small-scale projects that involve the elderly—as agents and beneficiaries—in the social, spiritual and economic development of their communities.

After examining and taking note of the report, the General Assembly on 8 December 1989 endorsed (resolution 44/67) the outline of a program of United Nations activities in the field of aging for 1992 and beyond, which the Economic and Social Council had formulated (council resolution 1989/50, annex II), and reiterated its appeal to the secretary-general to maintain and strengthen the existing programs on aging, with the Centre for Social Development and Humanitarian Affairs continuing in its role as focal point in the UN system for all such programs. It called upon him to prepare a system-wide plan on aging in order to ensure that all concerned organizations of the UN system address the problem in a coherent and effective manner.

In particular, the General Assembly requested the COMMISSION ON THE STATUS OF WOMEN to pay particular attention to the specific problems faced by elderly women and to the discrimination suffered by these women because of their gender and age and urged all UN agencies dealing with refugees to pay special attention to the plight of elderly refugees.

AGUDATH ISRAEL WORLD ORGANIZATION. An international non-governmental organization in consultative status (Category II) with the Economic and Social Council and with UNESCO, AIWO was founded in 1912 at a congress of orthodox Jewry convened in Katowice, Poland. Before World War II, it was represented in the parliaments of Poland, Romania, and Lithuania; in recent years, it has been represented in the Parliament of Israel.

Composed of national organizations in more than 25 countries, with a total membership above 500,000, Agudath Israel's function is to solve, by coordination of orthodox Jewish effort throughout the world, problems which periodically confront the Jewish people as a whole. To this end, it organizes frequent international conferences, furthers religious education, stimulates the development of a Jewish press and literature, and represents and protects the rights and interests of Jewish communities all over the world. It also contributes funds to a number of charities and provides funds for scholarships and religious activities.

AIWO publishes the daily *Hamodia* in Jerusalem; the weekly *Jewish Tribune* in London; and monthlies in Antwerp, Buenos Aires, New York, and Zurich.

Agudath Israel World Organization. Address: Hecherut Square, P.O.B. 326, Jerusalem, Israel. Telephone: 223357. Cable: Worldaguda, Jerusalem.

AIDS: GLOBAL PLAN. On 26 October 1987, the UN General Assembly expressed deep concern (resolution 42/8) that acquired immune deficiency syndrome (AIDS), caused by one or more naturally occurring retro-viruses of undetermined origin, had assumed pandemic proportions, affecting all regions of the world, and represented a threat to the attainment of health for all. The assembly commended the WORLD HEALTH ORGANIZATION (WHO) for its efforts towards global AIDS prevention and control, confirmed that WHO should continue to direct and coordinate the urgent global battle against AIDS, and invited that organization to facilitate the exchange of information on and the promotion of national and international research for the prevention and control of AIDS. The assembly, further, invited the Director-General of WHO to report to it in 1988, through the Economic and Social Council, on new developments in the global AIDS pandemic.

The report of the Director-General (UN Doc. A/43/341) included (1) an epidemiological overview (para. 14–15; 17–38), (2) a description of activities that WHO had undertaken to direct and coordinate the global AIDS strategy (para. 10–13), and (3) an indication of the collaboration within the United Nations system in the global fight against AIDS (para. 39–54). The text is as follows:

1. Epidemiology

World-wide AIDS surveillance is co-ordinated by the Global Programme on AIDS. Reports are received from WHO collaborating centres on AIDS as well as from individual ministries of health and WHO regional offices.

The number of AIDS cases reported to WHO continues to rise rapidly. As at 1 April 1988, 85,273 cases had been officially reported by 137 of 173 reporting countries. In the past four years, the cumulative number of AIDS cases reported to WHO increased over 15 fold. Nearly 100 more countries report AIDS cases today than four years ago. This not only illustrates the widespread awareness of AIDS, but also testifies to growing openness and international co-operation. . . .

The global AIDS surveillance data indicate that cases are distributed throughout the world. Large numbers have been reported from North America, Latin America, Oceania, Western Europe, and areas of central, eastern and southern Africa. A marked increasing trend is seen in all regions.

In 1985, a second human retrovirus, now called HIV-2, was identified and implicated as a cause of AIDS. The natural history of HIV-2 infection is not yet well defined. On the basis of preliminary serosurveys and the identification of cases, HIV-2 transmission appears to be occurring principally in West Africa.

Data suggest that HIV-2 infects populations similar to those infected by HIV-1, with heterosexual activity being the dominant mode of spread. Like HIV-1, HIV-2 has the potential to spread rapidly. Active surveillance of HIV-2 infection is necessary. Serosurveys are beginning to document the geographic scope of infection. The simultaneous occurrence of HIV-1 and HIV-2 will have implications for diagnostic services, blood donor screening programmes and vaccine development.

The official AIDS statistics are distributed widely and published in the *Weekly Epidemiological Record* and the journal *AIDS*. However, before any conclusions can be drawn from these data, the accuracy and completeness of reporting on AIDS needs to be evaluated. Under-recognition of AIDS and under-reporting to national health authorities, means that the number of reported cases is an underestimate of the total to date. The present world total may be closer to 150,000. Even these estimates do not adequately describe the current clinical burden caused by infection with the human immunodeficiency virus (HIV) because AIDS cases represent only the end-stage of severe or irreversible damage due to this severe viral infection.

Africa. As at 1 April 1988, a total of 10,995 cases (13 per cent of the world total) had been reported from 43 countries in Africa. Fourteen countries reported more than 50 cases each. More than 500 cases were reported by Burundi, Congo, Kenya, Malawi, Rwanda, Uganda, the United Republic of Tanzania and Zambia; Zaire and Zimbabwe each reported more than 300 cases. The highest number of cases have been reported from central, eastern and southern Africa. Although cases were first officially reported from Africa in the second half of 1982, over 70 per cent (7,914 of 10,995) were reported in the interval between July 1986 and December 1987.

Americas. Approximately 75 per cent of the world total of reported AIDS cases are from 42 countries in the Americas. As at 1 April 1988, the United States of America has reported a total of over 55,167 cases, representing close to 90 per cent of all cases in the region. Brazil had reported 2,325 cases, with the number increasing from 801 at the end of June 1986 to 1,695 at the end of June 1987. Canada had reported a total of 1,517. Other countries in the Americas reporting more than 100 cases include Haiti (912), Mexico (713), Dominican Republic (352), Trinidad and Tobago (206), Bahamas (163), Colombia (153), Argentina (120) and Venezuela (101).

Europe. A total of 10,667 cases (12.5 per cent of the world total) had been reported from 27 countries in Europe by 1 April 1988. Analysis of 10,181 cases reported (as at 31 December 1987) to the WHO Collaborating Centre on AIDS in Paris, France, shows that between December 1986 and December 1987 the number of European cases increased by 111 per cent. The greatest number of cases had been reported from France (3,073), the Federal Republic of Germany (1,669), Italy (1,411), the United Kingdom (1,227) and Spain (789). The highest rate per million population are in France, Switzerland and Denmark. Of countries with over 100 cases, six reported more than a 100 per cent increase between December 1986 and December 1987 (Austria, France, the Federal Republic of Germany, Italy, Spain and the United Kingdom). The lowest rates were reported from the Eastern European countries, with Albania reporting no cases.

Analysis of cases in Europe showed that the country of origin of the individual was European in 92 per cent of cases. Geographical origin for other adult cases was African (4 per cent), Caribbean (1 per cent) and other (3 per cent). The percentage of African cases reported from Europe had been decreasing over the past several years (12 per cent in June 1985, and 4 per cent in December 1987).

In Italy and Spain intravenous drug use accounts for 64 per cent and 53 per cent of adult cases, respectively. The two countries together reported 67 per cent of the cases in intravenous drug users in Europe.

Other Areas. The remaining 1 per cent of the world total, 834 cases, had been reported from Oceania (including 758 from Australia and 74 from New Zealand). Asia had reported 231 AIDS cases; the following countries reported more than 20 cases; Japan (59), Israel (47) and Turkey (21). From the eastern Mediterranean region, 100 cases had been reported.

Modes of Transmission. Epidemiological studies in Europe, the Americas, Africa and Australia repeatedly have documented only three modes of HIV transmission:

(1) Sexual intercourse (heterosexual or homosexual);

(2) Contact with blood, blood products, or donated organs and semen. Contacts with blood principally involve transfusion of unscreened blood or the use of unsterilized syringes and needles by IV drug abusers or in other settings;

(3) From infected mother to child—before, during or shortly after birth—(perinatal transmission).

Despite intense international scientific scrutiny, no evidence has emerged to suggest any change in these modes of transmission. There is no evidence to support any inherent racial or ethnic resistance to HIV infection or to the pathogenic effects of the virus.

Epidemiological and laboratory studies have established that, of the "body fluids", transmission seems limited to blood, semen, and vaginal/cervical secretions. Kissing has not been documented to pose a risk of HIV transmission. While unproven, some theoretical risk from vigorous "wet" kissing (deep kissing or tongue kissing) may exist.

There is no evidence to suggest that HIV can be transmitted by the respiratory or enteric routes or by casual person to person contact in any setting including household, social, work, school or prison settings. There is no evidence to suggest that HIV transmission involves insects, food, water, toilets, swimming pools, sweat, tears, shared eating and drinking utensils or other items such as second-hand clothing or telephones.

Global Epidemiological Patterns. Although the modes of HIV transmission are constant, three broad yet distinct epidemiological patterns can be recognized worldwide.

In the first (Pattern I), most cases occur among homosexual or bisexual males and intravenous drug users. Heterosexual transmission is responsible for only a small percentage of cases, but is increasing. Transmission due to blood and blood products occurred between the late 1970s and 1985, but has now been largely controlled through the self-deferral of persons with known risk factors or behaviour and by routine blood screening for the HIV antibody. Non-sterilized needles, other than those used by intravenous drug users, are not significant factors in HIV transmission. The male/female sex ratio ranges from 10:1 to 15:1. Perinatal transmission is occurring; the number of HIV-infected babies is low owing to the relatively low number of women currently infected. The prevalence of HIV infection in the overall population is estimated to be less than 1 per cent but it has been reported to exceed 50 per cent in persons practising high-risk behaviour, such as men with multiple male sex partners and intravenous drug users. This pattern is typical of industrialized countries with large numbers of reported AIDS cases, including North America, many western European countries, Australia and New Zealand, and parts of Latin America.

In the second (Pattern II), most cases occur among heterosexuals. The male/female ratio is approximately 1:1 and, as a result, perinatal transmission is common. Intravenous drug abuse and homosexual transmission are either non-existent or occur at a very low level. In a number of countries, overall population seroprevalence is estimated at more than 1 per cent, and in some urban areas, up to 25 per cent of the young and middle-aged adult population (15 to 49 years of age) are infected. Transmission through contaminated blood remains a significant problem in countries that have not yet implemented nation-wide blood donor screening. In addition, the use of non-sterilized needles and syringes for injection as well as instruments for other skin-piercing procedures is considered an important public health problem. This second pattern is observed in sub-Saharan Africa, and increasingly in Latin America, especially in some Caribbean countries.

In the third (Pattern III), HIV appears to have been introduced in the early to mid-1980s and only small numbers of cases have thus far been reported. Homosexual and heterosexual transmissions have been documented. Cases have generally occurred in persons who have travelled to endemic areas or who have had contact with individuals from endemic areas, such as homosexual men and female prostitutes. A small number of cases due to receipt of imported blood or blood products have been reported. This third pattern is found in Eastern Europe, North Africa, the eastern Mediterranean, Asia, and most of the Pacific.

Estimated Infection. WHO estimates that several million people have become infected with HIV from the mid-1970s to the present. Based on available information, between 5 to 10 million persons are estimated to be currently infected with HIV worldwide. For a more precise estimation, more valid national HIV prevalence data are required. It is not yet possible to determine the number of HIV-infected people in any individual country.

The WHO Global Data Bank is entering all available information from seroprevalence studies throughout the world. The data is required to assess, track and model the HIV pandemic. Increasing knowledge regarding the broad social, economic, cultural and political aspects of HIV and AIDS is also being obtained.

From the available data, WHO estimates that, during 1988, approximately 150,000 new cases of AIDS will occur. Therefore, the number of new AIDS cases during 1988 will equal the total number of cases that have thus far occurred worldwide. Adopting the conservative estimate that 5 million people are currently infected, a cumulative total of 1 million AIDS cases would be expected by 1991. The period 1988–1991 would therefore witness over 5 times more AIDS cases than have thus far occurred.

HIV infection is lifelong. The virus can survive in the human population if, during the lifetime of an infected person, it can spread to *one* other person. This suggests that, unless a curative treatment or a preventive vaccine is developed, HIV infection will perpetuate itself relatively easily. Neither cure nor vaccine are [sic] likely in the next several years. Despite considerable research a vaccine may be further away than was predicted a year ago.

2. Global Program on AIDS

In January 1988, at its 81st session, the WHO Executive Board noted the global support which the WHO Special Program on AIDS had provided in the preceding year and endorsed the proposal of the Director-General that the program be renamed "The Global Program on AIDS."

In accordance with the WHO Constitution definition of health as a state of complete physical, mental and social well-being and not merely the absence of disease or infirmity, WHO developed and issued a policy statement on the social aspects of AIDS prevention and control.

In view of the involvement of many disciplines and sectors in national AIDS control programmes, the Global Programme on AIDS is concerned with the biomedical, social and behavioural, informational and educational and health promotional aspects. Since information and education are the mainstay of prevention at this stage, WHO has been defining principles for proper information and education regarding AIDS, and is introducing these principles into national AIDS programmes. As these programmes are set up by national AIDS committees, it devolves on these committees to ensure the involvement of all sectors concerned. At the global level, WHO is ensuring the involvement of other sectors through bilateral and multilateral agencies.

To fulfil the mandate of the global AIDS strategy, WHO has taken the lead to issue policy statements of issues emerging from the world-wide epidemic of economic, social, cultural and political reaction to HIV infection and AIDS. WHO has developed policy on criteria for HIV screening programmes, international travel, AIDS in prisons, neuropsychiatric aspects of HIV infection, the effect of HIV on breast-feeding and routine childhood immunization, and on human rights.

Protection of human rights is a public health priority. There is no public health rationale to justify isolation, quarantine, or any discriminatory measures based solely on the fact that a person is suspected or known to be HIV-infected. Discrimination and other violations of human rights of HIV-infected persons will diminish the efficiency and effectiveness of national AIDS prevention programmes. WHO is organizing a meeting of all agencies with a major role in the human rights field to develop a common strategy to ensure protection of human rights in the fight against AIDS.

3. Collaboration Within the United Nations System

At the invitation of the Secretary-General of the United Nations, the Director-General of WHO and the Director of the Global Programme on AIDS presented the global AIDS problem and the Global AIDS Plan to a briefing of the United Nations General Assembly at its forty-second session, on 20 October 1987. After consideration of the report of the Economic and Social Council, the General Assembly adopted unanimously resolution 42/8 on the prevention and control of AIDS.

To ensure a well co-ordinated, multi-sectoral approach in the global fight against AIDS, the General Assembly confirmed WHO's directing and co-ordinating role and reiterated the call of the Economic and Social Council, urging bilateral and multilateral agencies, including those of the United Nations system, as well as non-governmental and voluntary organizations, to support national and international action against AIDS in conformity with WHO's Global Strategy on AIDS. The General Assembly further requested the Secretary-General in close co-operation with the Director-General of WHO, to ensure a co-ordinated response by the United Nations system.

In response to General Assembly resolution 42/8, the Secretary-General appointed the Under-Secretary-General for International Economic and Social Affairs as focal point at United Nations Headquarters for activities related to the prevention and control of AIDS. The Director-General welcomed the initiative of the Under-Secretary-General in establishing, under his chairmanshp, and in close co-operation with the Director-General of WHO, a United Nations Steering Committee to co-ordinate United Nations activities in support of WHO's Global Strategy for the prevention and control of AIDS, to identify possible joint activities and to develop linkage between individual programmes in this field. This co-ordination effort has already resulted in several new AIDS-related activities within the United Nations and with co-operating non-governmental organizations. A number of meetings have taken place between the Under-Secretary-General, the Director-General of WHO and the Director of the Global Programme on AIDS to facilitate co-operation. WHO is establishing an inter-agency advisory group, under its chairmanship, to facilitate the effective co-ordination of activities of the United Nations system in support of its Global Strategy on AIDS. The United Nations Steering Committee will provide a co-ordinated input to the work of the inter-agency advisory group.

In the spirit of General Assembly resolution 42/8, WHO has been working closely with many parts of the United Nations system to encourage and support active participation in AIDS control activities. Collaboration with organizations of the United Nations system is accelerating as these bodies analyse the effect of HIV on their programmes and develop their plans of action in concert with the Global Strategy. Initiatives from United Nations agencies have resulted in a wide variety of co-ordinated activities.

United Nations Development Programme—WHO/UNDP Alliance to Combat AIDS. The Director-General has been considering how best to ensure well co-ordinated action from all those concerned in the global combat against AIDS. The need for this has been reinforced by concern expressed by many countries about unco-ordinated, ill-timed or inappropriate offers of external assistance, as well as by the insistence of donor agencies on well co-ordinated activities in countries as a prerequisite for their support.

The Director-General reached the conclusion that the optimal solution is to combine the strengths of WHO as international leader in health policy and in scientific and technical matters related to health and as the lead agency in the fight against AIDS, and of the United Nations Development Programme (UNDP) as leader in socio-economic development and of each of its resident representatives as co-ordinator of United Nations operational activities for development in countries. He has now completed negotiations with the Administrator of UNDP. Attached (appendix II) is the policy framework of the WHO/UNDP alliance to combat AIDS, which came into force on 29 March 1988.

UNDP resident representatives are actively supporting the Global AIDS Programme to implement, monitor and evaluate national programme support activities. The alliance will ensure co-ordinated support for such national plans by all external partners, including those in the United Nations system.

United Nations Educational, Scientific and Cultural Organization. The Global Programme on AIDS and UNESCO have been actively collaborating in the promotion of AIDS education in schools. A joint UNESCO/WHO meeting of educational specialists was held in Paris from 29 June to 1 July 1987. The meeting formulated a plan of action on AIDS education in formal and informal educational settings, which was presented to the UNESCO General Conference held in Paris in October 1987. The Director of the Global

Programme on AIDS addressed the General Conference and Educational Section in support of this collaboration, on 28 October 1987. The Global Programme on AIDS will support the activity of UNESCO as an integral part of the Global AIDS Plan. To accelerate this process, WHO/UNESCO held joint briefing meetings of UNESCO field staff and UNESCO affiliated non-governmental organizations at Geneva from 14 to 22 April 1987.

United Nations Children's Fund. Co-operation with UNICEF continues and has been strengthened by the presentation of the Director of the Global Programme on AIDS before the Executive Board of UNICEF on 22 April of WHO's views on its agenda item entitled "Review of the impact of AIDS on women and children and the UNICEF response". WHO anticipates extensive collaboration with UNICEF in the examination of the significant impact of AIDS on women and children. The Global Programme on AIDS will make a presentation to the Regional Directors of UNICEF in New York, on 3 May 1988, on the activities of the Global Programme on AIDS at the country level. UNICEF is already involved in activities in several African countries in support of national AIDS programmes.

WHO and UNICEF have issued a Joint Statement on Immunization and AIDS and also issued updated information to field staff concerning the sterilization of syringes and needles. The statement reiterates that all injections should be given with a sterile syringe and a sterile needle. UNICEF participated in the consultation on HIV and routine childhood immunization and the consultation on breast-feeding/breast milk and HIV infection. UNICEF has participated in national donor meetings and other AIDS meetings.

United Nations Population Fund. UNFPA is collaborating with the Global Programme on AIDS in assessing the role of family planning and maternal and child health programmes in AIDS prevention and control activities. This co-operation will be strengthened through the appointment of a liaison officer between UNFPA and the Office of the Director of the Global Programme on AIDS. A representative of the Global Programme on AIDS addressed a meeting of national representatives of UNFPA in New York on 12 April 1988. UNFPA participated in the consultation on contraceptive methods and HIV infection and the consultation on breast-feeding/breast milk and HIV infection. A joint policy document is currently under consideration.

Food and Agriculture Organization of the United Nations. A meeting on nutrition and AIDS, co-sponsored by WHO and the Sub-Committee on Nutrition of the United Nations Administrative Committee on Co-ordination, was held at Geneva on 28 February 1988. Further discussions will be held with FAO on the potential interaction between nutrition and AIDS and the potential impact of AIDS on food production.

World Bank. The World Bank is collaborating with the Global Programme on AIDS in studies on the economic impact of AIDS in the developing world and on the demographic impact of AIDS. The initial phase of the development of a model for estimating the direct treatment-related costs and the indirect costs from the years of social and economic productivity lost due to HIV infections and AIDS has been completed in three central African countries during the first quarter of 1988. The initiative of the Director-General of WHO, launched at the Fourth Meeting of Participating Parties for the Prevention and Control of AIDS in November, 1987, to associate the World Bank more closely with the Global Strategy on AIDS has been welcomed by the

President of the World Bank and discussions are continuing.

International Labor Organization. The General Conference of the International Labour Organisation (ILO) passed a resolution on AIDS at its seventy-fourth (Maritime) session, held at Geneva in September 19;87. The Governing Board of the ILO is requested to consider, in close collaboration with WHO, undertaking a study on the health problems of seafarers.

In collaboration with ILO, WHO is planning a consultation for June 1988 to address the risks of HIV infection in the work-place and the appropriate policies for dealing with individuals who are infected with HIV. A joint WHO/ILO brochure on AIDS in the work-place will be released shortly.

World Tourism Organization. The Global Programme on AIDS released an "AIDS Information for Travellers" brochure at the General Conference of the World Tourism Organization (WTO) on 27 September 1987. WTO had endorsed the brochure and has involved travel agents, airlines and tourism organizations in its reproduction and distribution. Official translations exist in English, French and Spanish.

On 27 October 1988, the UN General Assembly noted with satisfaction (resolution 43/14) the development and implementation of the global strategy for the prevention and control of AIDS and recognized the urgent need to pursue multilateral efforts to promote and improve human health, control disease, and extend health care to achieve the objective of health for all by the year 2000. It took note of the WHO Global Program on AIDS and stressed the continuing need for adequate resources for its implementation and the corresponding need to continue to share the pool of worldwide medical and scientific knowledge and experience in the control and prevention of the disease. In addition, it called upon all States, in addressing the AIDS problem, to take into account the legitimate concerns of other countries and the interests of inter-State relations and invited the World Health Organization to continue to facilitate the exchange of information on and promotion of national and international research for the prevention and control of AIDS through the further development of collaborating centers for the WHO and similar existing mechanisms.

One year later, on 22 December 1989, the General Assembly took note (resolution 44/233) of a report by the Director-General of the World Health Organization of the global strategy for the prevention and control of AIDS and of the supplementary report on AIDS-related activities being carried out by the organizations of the United Nations system (UN Docs. A/44/274, annex, and A/44/274/Add. 1) and welcomed the arrangements which had been made to ensure a coordinated response by that system to the AIDS pandemic. It requested the Secretary-General,

in view of the potentially serious implications of that pandemic for socio-economic development in some developing countries, to mobilize all the technical and other relevant resources of the United Nations system to deal with this aspect of the problem. It urged member States to increase their efforts in combating AIDS and to encourage, support, and facilitate national efforts to prevent its further spread and called upon governments and all relevant intergovernmental and non-governmental organizations to promote greater awareness about the transmission of the pandemic in order to avoid misconceptions as much as possible and to increase the understanding of the general public towards people affected by the human immunodeficiency virus (HIV).

The assembly further requested the UN Secretary-General and the WHO Director-General to continue to develop and advance the global strategy for the prevention and control of AIDS, specifically,

(a) to promote the contribution of non-governmental organizations to the global AIDS strategy through support of national efforts;

(b) to collaborate, as appropriate, with the United Nations office at Vienna, the United Nations Children's Fund and other United Nations bodies, governments and non-governmental organizations in their efforts to develop:

(i) policies, programs, and research proposals to address the impact of AIDS, including issues affecting women, and to promote their vital role in preventing and controlling the pandemic;

(ii) policies and programs to alleviate the impact of AIDS, in all its aspects, on children;

(iii) policies and programs to combat the illicit traffic and abuse of drugs with a view to contributing to a reduction in the spread of the HIV infection;

(c) to promote access of all peoples to appropriate preventive, diagnostic, and therapeutic technologies and pharmaceuticals and to help make these technologies and pharmaceuticals available at an affordable cost; and

(d) to promote the active participation of public and private sector enterprises, including through financial contributions, in HIV/AIDS prevention and control efforts at the local, national, and international levels.

AIDS: NEUROPSYCHIATRIC ASPECTS. The neuropsychiatric aspects of HIV infection during the asymptomatic stage were examined during a consultation convened by the WORLD HEALTH ORGANIZATION in Geneva from 14 to 17 March 1988. The 48 participants, from 17 countries, included experts from the fields of clinical psychology, epidemiology, ethics, health economics, health policy, health service administration, law, neurology, occupational health, psychiatry, and public health. According to the report of the WHO director-general (UN Doc. A/43/341, para. 101–102),

The consultation reported that there is no evidence for an increase of clinically significant neurological or neuropsychological abnormalities in HIV-infected people who are healthy. Therefore, there is no justification for HIV screening as a strategy for detecting functional impairment in asymptomatic persons.

The most important outcome of these deliberations is that Governments, employers and the public can be assured that, based on the weight of available scientific evidence, otherwise healthy HIV-infected individuals are no more likely to be functionally impaired than uninfected persons. Thus, HIV screening would not be a useful strategy to identify functional impairment in otherwise healthy persons. Furthermore, there is no evidence that HIV screening of healthy persons would be useful in predicting the onset of functional impairment in persons who remain otherwise healthy.

AIDS: PREVENTION. The World Summit of Ministers of Health on Programs for AIDS Prevention, organized jointly by the WORLD HEALTH ORGANIZATION and the Government of the United Kingdom of Great Britain and Northern Ireland, was held in London from 26 to 28 January 1988. It was attended by 114 ministers of health, delegates from 149 States members of WHO, and representatives from UN agencies, intergovernmental organizations, and non-governmental organizations.

At the summit, the ministers declared the year 1988 as a "Year of Communication and Co-operation about AIDS," and the Director-General of WHO announced that 1 December 1988 would be observed as the first World AIDS Day, on which national governments and all organizations and institutions working on any aspect of AIDS research, prevention, control, and treatment would be encouraged to explain to their communities what they are doing about AIDS. Finally, on 28 January 1988, the summit adopted the "London Declaration on AIDS Prevention" (UN Doc. A/43/341, Appendix 1), which reads as follows:

The World Summit of Ministers of Health on Programmes for AIDS Prevention, involving delegates from 149 countries representing the vast majority of people of the world, makes the following declaration:

1. Since AIDS is a global problem that poses a serious threat to humanity, urgent action by all Governments and people the world over is needed to implement WHO's Global AIDS Strategy as defined by the Fortieth World Health Assembly and supported by the United Nations General Assembly.

2. We shall do all in our power to ensure that our Governments do indeed undertake such urgent action.

3. We undertake to devise national programmes to prevent and contain the spread of human immunodeficiency virus (HIV) infection as part of our countries' health systems. We commend to all Governments the value of a high level co-ordinating committee to bring together all government sectors, and we shall involve to the fullest extent possible all governmental sectors and relevant non-governmental organizations in the planning and implementation of such programmes in conformity with the Global AIDS Strategy.

4. We recognize that, particularly in the absence at present of a vaccine or cure for AIDS, the single most important component of national AIDS programmes is information and education because HIV transmission can be prevented through informed and responsible behaviour. In this respect, individuals, Governments, the media and other sectors all have major roles to play in preventing the spread of HIV infection.

5. We consider that information and education programmes should be aimed at the general public and should take full account of social and cultural patterns, different lifestyles, and human and spiritual values. The same principles should apply equally to programmes directed towards specific groups, involving these groups as appropriate. These include groups such as:
   —policy makers;
   —health and social service workers at all levels;
   —international travellers;
   —persons whose practices may place them at increased risk of infection;
   —the media;
   —youth and those that work with them, especially teachers;
   —community and religious leaders;
   —potential blood donors; and
   —those with HIV infections, their relatives and others concerned with their care, all of whom need appropriate counselling.

6. We emphasize the need in AIDS prevention programmes to protect human rights and human dignity. Discrimination against, and stigmatization of, HIV-infected people and people with AIDS and population groups undermine public health and must be avoided.

7. We urge the media to fulfil their important social responsibility to provide factual and balanced information to the general public on AIDS and on ways of preventing its spread.

8. We shall seek the involvement of all relevant governmental sectors and non-governmental organizations in creating the supportive social environment needed to ensure the effective implementation of AIDS prevention programmes and humane care of affected individuals.

9. We shall impress on our Governments the importance for national health of ensuring the availability of the human and financial resources, including health and social services with well-trained personnel, needed to carry out our national AIDS programmes, and in order to support informed and responsible behaviour.

10. In the spirit of United Nations General Assembly resolution 42/8, we appeal:
   —to all appropriate organizations of the United Nations system, including the specialized agencies;
   —to bilateral and multilateral agencies; and
   —to non-governmental and voluntary organizations

to support the world-wide struggle against AIDS in conformity with WHO's global strategy.

11. We appeal in particular to these bodies to provide well-co-ordinated support to developing countries in setting up and carrying out national AIDS programmes in the light of their needs. We recognize that these needs vary from country to country in the light of their epidemiological situation.

12. We also appeal to those involved in dealing with drug abuse to intensify their efforts in the spirit of the International Conference on Drug Abuse and Illicit Trafficking (Vienna, June 1987) with a view to contributing to the reduction in the spread of HIV infection.

13. We call upon the World Health Organization, through its Global Programme on AIDS, to continue to:

(a) Exercise its mandate to direct and co-ordinate the world-wide effort against AIDS;

(b) Promote, encourage and support the world-wide collection and dissemination of accurate information on AIDS;

(c) Develop and issue guidelines on the planning, implementation, monitoring and evaluation of information and education programmes, including the related research and development, and ensure that these guidelines are updated and revised in the light of evolving experiences;

(d) Support countries in monitoring and evaluating preventive programmes, including information and education activities, and encourage wide dissemination of the findings in order to help countries to learn from the experiences of others;

(e) Support and strengthen national programmes for the prevention and control of AIDS.

14. Following from this Summit, 1988 shall be a Year of Communication and Co-operation about AIDS, in which we shall:

—open fully the channels of communication in each society so as to inform and educate more widely, broadly and extensively;

—strengthen the exchange of information and experience among all countries; and

—forge, through information and education and social leadership, a spirit of social tolerance.

15. We are convinced that, by promoting responsible behaviour and through international co-operation, we can and will begin now to slow the spread of HIV infection.

AIDS: SCREENING PROGRAMS. The complexity of screening for human immunodeficiency virus (HIV) infection was considered at a meeting on "Criteria for HIV Screening Programs" convened by the Global Program on AIDS of the WORLD HEALTH ORGANIZATION in Geneva on 20 and 21 May 1987. Twenty-one participants from 17 countries attended the meeting, including epidemiologists, virologists, experts in legal medicine and ethics, social and behavioral scientists and disease control specialists. Concerning that meeting, the Director-General of WHO reported the following (UN Doc. A/43/341, para. 88–90):

The meeting developed a comprehensive list of criteria which should be explicitly addressed in the planning of any HIV screening programme. These criteria include: programme rationale; population selected; test methodology; location of laboratory testing; data management and confidentiality; plan for informing the person; counselling; social impact; legal and ethical considerations, including informed consent.

These criteria are designed to serve public health interest while protecting respect for human rights. Their application will help ensure the most effective outcome from screening programmes carried out as part of HIV prevention and control strategies.

Following consideration of the report of the above meeting and a meeting on international travel and HIV, the WHO Director-General issued the following directive for all WHO programme activities:

"The screening of international travellers for human immunodeficiency virus (HIV) has been carefully considered and WHO's technical guidance on this issue is that, at best and at great cost, such screening would only briefly retard the spread of HIV, whether regarded from the global or the national perspective. Serious logistic, epidemiological, economic, legal, political and ethical problems would be inherent in any such screening.

"However, one of the United Nations agencies, in organizing training seminars with participants from developing countries, has come under pressure from the host country government to request screening tests for HIV and a certificate of seronegativity for participants from aboard.

"Should this issue arise with respect to any programme activity organized by WHO, please ensure that it is dealt with in keeping with WHO's Global Strategy, including the above-mentioned technical guidance. Should Governments insist on such screening in spite of this guidance, WHO will have no alternative but to relocate the programme activity concerned."

AIDS AND HUMAN RIGHTS. At its 1988 session, the UN SUB-COMMISSION ON PREVENTION OF DISCRIMINATION AND PROTECTION OF MINORITIES decided (decision 1988/111) that information which it had received from the WORLD HEALTH ORGANIZATION and from the INTERNATIONAL COMMISSION OF JURISTS describing the problem of discrimination against persons with the HIV virus or suffering from AIDS justified consideration as to whether the sub-commission should make a study of that problem. The sub-commission accordingly requested one of its members, Mr. Luis Varela-Quirós (Costa Rica), to prepare a note proposing how such a study could be made.

At its 1989 session, the Commission on Human Rights considered a somewhat broader question, described under the heading HEALTH: DISCRIMINATORY PRACTICES. In resolution 1989/11 of 2 March 1989, it invited the sub-commission "to examine, using the opportunity provided by the study on discrimination against persons with the human immuno-deficiency virus (HIV) or suffering from acquired immuno-deficiency syndrome (AIDS) envisaged in its decision 1988/11 of 1 September 1988, the possibility of extending the scope of such a study to other kinds of discrimination against sick or disabled persons, in consultation with the World Health Organization and giving Governments that wish to express their views the opportunity to do so."

The special rapporteur's note, which he presented to the sub-commission at its 1989 session, set out (UN Doc. E/CN.4/Sub.2/1989/5) his proposals for a possible study on AIDS and human rights. In the note, he referred first to certain relevant medical and legal aspects of AIDS, as follows (sect. B, paras. 12–17):

AIDS has been described by the World Health Assembly as a disease caused by one or more naturally occurring retroviruses of undetermined geographical origin, which is affecting all regions of the world and represents a threat to the attainment of health for all. Furthermore, it has assumed the proportions of a pandemic, i.e. a general plague that knows no ethnic, geographical, cultural or social boundaries, and that as a result is continually spreading, especially in a society like todays, in which contacts among the various human groups are becoming increasingly easy, due to factors such as transport, and especially because long-standing discriminatory practices, which tended to isolate large segments of society, have been overcome. What makes the situation even more serious is the fact that for the time being there is no known cure for the disease or means of preventing its spread—nor, according to all the scientific forecasts, will such a cure be found in the near future.

However, unlike other plagues that affected mankind in the past, it has been scientifically proved that this disease can only be transmitted by one of the following means: (a) sexual relations that involve contact with the bodily fluids of a person already infected with the disease; (b) transmission by contact between the blood of an infected person and that of a healthy person, either by transfusion or by the use of needles or other items that may introduce the virus into the bloodstream; and (c) transmission by the mother to her child, either before, during or after birth (perinatal transmission).

Thus any other means of transmission of the disease have been rejected by medical science and are the product of groundless fears. Perhaps this fact, despite the medical establishment's repetitions, has not been clearly explained to the public at large, so that, while emphasizing the need to be cautious, panic and the resulting discriminatory behaviour, which have no positive effect on control of the disease, would be avoided. Perhaps the media, by stressing the negative aspect of the disease, have helped to form an equally negative backlash, this time not against the disease but against its victims, and this backlash has in some cases led to dehumanizing attitudes.

Some examples are the attitudes adopted against the children and relatives of the victims and even against close friends, the dismissal of a worker simply because he is suspected of being a carrier of the virus or the fear of sharing public transport with persons suspected of being HIV infected. Even more unjust and inhuman are measures such as denying AIDS victims medical treatment or care, evicting them from their apartments or houses and denying them access to social security, medical insurance and public or private educational establishments, which in nearly all societies today are considered to be rights or aspirations estab-

lished for the benefit of the entire community and which should be made available with the strictest adherence to the principles of non-discrimination on grounds of age, social origin, race, religion, or sex.

The occurrence of such practices, either with the express approval or unconcern of the State, entails violation of various rights, in particular the following: (a) the right to health; (b) the right to privacy; (c) the right to equality before the law; (d) the right to freedom and security; (e) the right to marry and found a family; (f) the right to education; (g) the right to life; (h) the right not to be subjected to cruel, inhuman or degrading treatment or punishment; (i) the right not to be discriminated against on grounds of sex, religion or ethnic origin; and (j) the right to education.

All the above-mentioned rights are duly recognized in all the basic human rights instruments, both universal and regional, and in one way or another are obligations of international law that States must respect.

After enumerating a series of questions which might conceivably be dealt with in a study on AIDS and human rights, the special rapporteur proposed that, should the sub-commission decide to undertake such a study, it should follow basically the following methods (sect. D, paras. 24–25):

(a) A descriptive study on the origin, current incidence and future prospects of AIDS;

(b) An interdisciplinary study on the medical, ethical, legal and social issues raised by the appearance of AIDS as the pandemic of the twentieth century;

(c) A study of the policies followed by States with regard to treatment of the illness and respect for human rights, through examination of the legislation and practices of States at four levels:

(i) negative measures or measures contravening the human rights of AIDS victims;

(ii) measures designed to guarantee and protect the essential rights of persons suffering from AIDS;

(iii) suggestions for bringing legislation into compliance with the international duties contracted by States in the area of protection of human rights, in the specific case of AIDS victims;

(iv) the organization of a world campaign to highlight the dangers to the health of all represented by any discriminatory measures or stigmatization directed at HIV-infected persons or AIDS sufferers, and to prevent and combat the disease.

We believe that any study undertaken by the Sub-Commission should avoid duplication of the excellent studies already conducted on the topic and should fit into the global strategy adopted by the World Health Organization and be prepared in close co-operation with that organization. In this context, we feel it would be appropriate for both the Centre for Human Rights and the World Health Organization, through its Global Programme on AIDS, to study the possibility, according to available resources, of holding special regional seminars on the topic, or of integrating the topic of AIDS and human rights into activities already programmed for 1989–1990. Such seminars would be primarily aimed at persons in charge of implementing and ensuring compliance with the law and would stress some of the major aspects relating to the need to avoid any acts violating the human rights of persons or groups of persons who are HIV-positive or suffer from AIDS.

The sub-commission, on 31 August 1989, expressed (resolution 1989/17) its appreciation to Mr. Varela-Quirós for the note and decided to entrust him with a study of problems and causes of discrimination against HIV-infected people or people with AIDS. It recommended that the special rapporteur take into consideration resolution 1989/11 of the Commission on Human Rights, the issues and guidelines contained in the International Consultation on HIV/AIDS and Human Rights convened in Geneva from 16 to 28 July 1989, as well as the view expressed by the members of the sub-commission. It recommended that he carry out his study in close cooperation with the World Health Organization and requested him to make a preliminary report to the sub-commission at its 1990 session.

ALBANIA. The People's Socialist Republic of Albania is a country in southern Europe, on the Adriatic Sea. It has borders with Greece and Yugoslavia. It achieved independence from Turkey in 1944 and became a member of the United Nations in 1955. Its population is estimated by the United Nations (1990) to be 3,338,000. Ethnic groups include Greeks, Vlachs, Bulgars, Serbs, and Gypsies. Languages commonly used include Albanian (official), Gheg in the north, and Tosk in the south. Religious observances are prohibited by the constitution; in 1967, the government closed all churches and mosques and declared Albania to be an atheist State. Religions practiced up to that time included Christianity (Albanian Orthodox, 20%; Roman Catholic, 10%) and Islam (70%). Literacy is estimated at 75%.

The government (1990) took the form of a republic. The Council of Ministers is the executive organ of government. However, policy decisions are taken by the Albanian Workers' (Communist) Party and its Politburo. The First Secretary of the Party is president of the Presidium and head of State.

On 29 August 1985, the UN SUB-COMMISSION ON PREVENTION OF DISCRIMINATION AND PROTECTION OF MINORITIES stated (resolution 1985/20) that it was deeply disturbed by the constitutional and legal measures adopted by the People's Socialist Republic of Albania to forbid the exercise of the right to freedom of conscience and religion to all individuals within its territory and that it believed that those measures constituted an affront to human dignity, a flagrant and systematic violation of human rights, a disavowal of the principles of the UN Charter, and an obstacle to friendly and peaceful relations between nations. It

requested the Commission on Human Rights to urge the Albanian government to provide adequate constitutional and legal measures consistent with the provisions of the UNIVERSAL DECLARATION OF HUMAN RIGHTS, the International Covenants on Human Rights, and the DECLARATION ON THE ELIMINATION OF ALL FORMS OF INTOLERANCE AND OF DISCRIMINATION BASED ON RELIGION OR BELIEF, with a view to ensuring freedom of religion or belief in a concrete manner, that discrimination on the ground of religion or belief is proscribed, and that adequate safeguards and remedies are provided against such discrimination. The commission, however, did not take the action requested by the sub-commission.

At its 44th session, in 1988, the Commission on Human Rights considered in closed session the item "Study of Situations which Appear to Reveal a Consistent Pattern of Gross Violations of Human Rights as provided in Commission Resolution 8 (XXIII) and Economic and Social Council Resolutions 1235 (XLII) and 1503 (XLVIII)," and examined the human rights situations in Albania, Benin, Brunei Darussalem, Grenada, Honduras, Iraq, Pakistan, Paraguay, and Zaire, as publicly announced by the chairman after the closed part of the 44th meeting. The chairman also announced that the situations in Albania, Benin, Grenada, Iraq, and Pakistan were no longer under consideration by the commission under council resolution 1503 (XLVIII), but that the decision taken by the commission in closed session concerning Albania would be made public.

Later in 1988, the Sub-Commission on Prevention of Discrimination and Protection of Minorities indicated (resolution 1988/15) that it was deeply disturbed by the continuing reports of grave violations of human rights and fundamental freedoms in Albania. Strongly disapproving the inhuman treatment of members of minorities living in Albania, the sub-commission requested the Commission on Human Rights (a) to urge the Albanian government to provide adequate constitutional and legal measures consistent with the international agreements it had cited in 1985, with a view to ensuring that freedom of religion or belief is assured in a concrete manner, that discrimination on grounds of religion or belief is proscribed, and that adequate safeguards and remedies are provided against such discrimination; and (b) to call upon that government to restore and guarantee all human rights and fundamental freedoms of the members of ethnic and religious minorities—in particular, of the Greek minority, the largest one—and to free all political prisoners.

At its 1989 session, the Commisssion on Human Rights recalled (resolution 1989/69) that the human rights situation in Albania had been under consideration since 1984 under confidential procedure and noted that the exhaustive efforts to solicit the cooperation of the government under that procedure, including the efforts of the UN secretary-general, had been in vain. The commisssion also noted that, for the second consecutive year, the Albanian government had failed to respond to the allegations transmitted to it by the commission's special rapporteur on the implementation of the Declaration on the Elimination of all Forms of Intolerance and of Discrimination based on Religion or Belief and called upon the government to respond to the allegations in question.

In January 1990, the UN secretary-general accepted in principle an invitation extended by the Albanian government to make an official visit to Albania. The invitation, widely considered as marking an extension of the gradual opening of Europe's most isolated country since the death in 1985 of its hard-line leader Enver Hoxha, was the first ever extended by Albania to a UN secretary-general and was scheduled to take place in May 1990.

The Commission on Human Rights considered, at its 1990 session, the human rights situation in Albania. A document containing the following information was circulated to the commission at the request of the Albanian government (UN Doc. E/CN.4/1990/74, annex):

A. Legal Protection in the Socialist People's Republic of Albania

1. The Constitution guarantees the protection of the individual in all its aspects. Specific provisions of the Criminal Code establish as a punishable offence any action directed against the life, health or dignity of the individual. The courts and the *Chambre d'accusation*, in applying the same rules for all, investigate each case in complete objectivity, in the fullest and most detailed manner possible, in order to protect every citizen against unjust prosecution or conviction and to determine the responsibility of the person genuinely guilty. Similarly, as regards the process of pre-trial investigation, the Code of Criminal Procedure categorically stipulates that "in the course of the investigation, the use of physical or psychological violence or other measures of the same kind are prohibited" (art.7).

2. The Ninth Plenum of the Central Committee of the Labour Party of Albania, which met on 22 and 23 January 1990, considered, *inter alia*, the question of the further improvement of the legislation of the Socialist People's Republic of Albania. The full text of a decision taken in this connection is reproduced below:

"III. *Let Us Perfect Socialist Legislation*. In this area, the achievements are already well known. Our legislation is fully constitutional, democratic and popular. Our laws, in their content and their application, express the interests of the people.

"Taking as its starting-point the need to improve this legislation still further in conformity with the improvement of the cultural level, conscience and legal training of the

workers, the Ninth Plenum recommended the following measures:

"(1) Measures should be devised to guarantee for citzens protection under the law, both during investigations and during the trial, in each case, at their request, in accordance with the rights recognized by the Constitution;

"(2) The institution of legal and juridicial rehabilitation and conditional pre-term release should be studied and implemented as forms of the application of justice, for a number of categories of ordinary offences and for convicted prisoners who later show evidence of good conduct within society;

"(3) It should be recommended to the organs of the State that, because of the broadening of the State's activity, the more difficult codification of legal activity and so on, it would be advisable to re-establish the Ministry of Law:

"(4) The Village, City and City District Courts Act should be revised and improved, the courts being classified as social organizations that do not have the right to pronounce sentences of a criminal nature;

All these questions must be prepared for the next meeting of the People's Assembly."

B. Travel by Foreign Visitors and Tourists in Albania and Albanians Abroad

3. In recent years, tourism has grown steadily in Albania. In 1989 alone, 14,435 persons from various countries stayed in Albania as tourists. The number of tourists from the neighboring countries increased appreciably: 3,830 were Greek, and there 633 from Yugoslavia in 1989.

4. Apart from tourists, many visitors with close relatives in Albania stayed in our country and many Albanian citizens visited their close relatives living abroad.

5. During the past year, 24 persons received a Yugoslav visa. The Yugoslav authorities refused entry visas to 610 persons. In the same period, the same authorities permitted 157 Yugoslav citizens to visit Albania, including 22 from Kosovo.

6. Travel by visitors from Greece, another neighbouring country, has grown in recent years: in 1989, 744 Greek visitors stayed in Albania and 643 Albanians travelled to Greece.

7. On 17 January 1990, in the town of Korçë (Albania), a regular passenger coach service between Korçë and Istanbul was inaugurated. This service will operate under the road transport agreement signed by the Socialist People's Republic of Albania and the Republic of Turkey. It will carry passengers and tourists from Albania to Turkey and in the opposite direction.

8. There have also been exchanges of visitors with other countries. In 1989, 1,600 foreign visitors came to Albania and 1,400 Albanians travelled abroad.

C. Alleged Imprisonment of Former Church Members

9. With regard to the allegations contained in the annex to the communication of 3 October 1988 from Mr. Angelo Vidal d'Almeida Ribeiro, Special Rapporteur, to the effect that former Bishop Nikolla Troshani and 13 former priests and church members mentioned by name had been imprisoned for religious reasons, we repeat that at present none of these persons is being held in Albanian prisons and that none of them has been convicted for purely religious reasons.

The commission took note (resolution 1990/49) of the invitation of the government to the UN secretary-general to visit the country but expressed concern about continuing reports which "in spite of reflecting some positive developments, continue to reveal violations of human rights, especially freedom of thought, conscience and religion, the right to leave a country and the right to a fair trial with all guarantees necessary for the defence." It once again called upon the Albanian government to provide information on the concrete manner in which constitutional and legal measures comply with provisions of the Universal Declaration on Human Rights and to respond to the specific allegations transmitted to the commission by its special rapporteur. The commission further requested the secretary-general to take its resolution into account when visiting the country and to bring the resolution to the attention of the government, inviting it to provide the requested information.

In April 1990, Albania took some steps away from its long-held policy of isolation when the leader of the Communist Party, Ramiz Alia, declared the willingness of the government to establish diplomatic relations with Moscow and Washington; for decades, the country had avoided any formal contact with either power. In May, Prime Minister Adil Carcani announced that Albania would joint the Conference on Security and Cooperation in Europe; Albania had refused to participate in the conference or to support the HELSINKI ACCORD, since 1975.

Also in May 1990, the Albanian parliament authorized the practice of religion—outlawed since 1967 when Albania became the world's first atheist country—and adopted laws ending internal exile and enabling Albanians to obtain passports for travel outside the country.

When the UN secretary-general visited Albania on 13 May 1990, Mr. Alia told foreign journalists that his policy of democratizing the country could not be stopped but that he intended to retain socialism and would not follow other Eastern European countries in dismantling communism altogether.

In a discussion of human rights with his Albanian host, the secretary-general was informed by Mr. Alia that his government was considering "reopening houses of worship." The secretary-general was also assured that six Albanians who had remained in the Italian embassy in Tirana as refugees since 1985 would be permitted to leave soon.

ALGERIA. The Democratic People's Republic of Algeria is a country in north Africa, on the Mediterranean Sea. It has borders with Libya, Mali, Mauritania, Morocco, Niger, Tunisia, and Western Sahara. It achieved independence from France in 1962 and became a member of the United Nations the same year.

Its total population is estimated by the UN (1990) to be 25,494,000. Ethnic groups include Arabs and Berbers, but national censuses have never indicated the ethnic or racial origin of inhabitants. Languages commonly used include Arabic (official), French, and Berber. Religions practiced include Islam (Sunni), the State religion, 99%; and Christianity (Roman Catholic), 1%. Literacy is estimated at about 52%.

The government (1990) took the form of a republic. Under its National Charter and Constitution of 1976, socialism is the political philosophy of the country. The president, elected for a five-year term, is head of State; the prime minister, representing the party or coalition given the majority in a popular election, is head of government. Legislative authority is in the hands of the 281-member National Popular Assembly, members of which are elected for five-year terms. The only political party is the National Liberation Front.

The National Commission of Legislation has conducted an extensive review of civil, criminal, public, commercial and family legislation which remained from the French colonial system. New codes have been, or are being, prepared, in many areas, and all French laws still on the books have been declared invalid. The new code which deals with family and personal status continues to be based on Muslim law but will be administered by the civil courts.

It is estimated that two-thirds of Algeria's population is under 30 years old. The government devotes more than half its budget to education and programs for young people, regarding them as a huge human potential. At independence, there were only 2,725 Algerian college students; in 1987, there were more than 100,000. Concerned about the lure of Islamic fundamentalism among the young, the government has tried to channel religious activity through State-supported mosques overseen by the Ministry of Religious Affairs.

Algeria played a key role in the release, on 20 January 1981, of 52 Americans who had been held captive for 444 days in the U.S. embassy in Teheran. Chosen by Iran to represent it in negotiations with the U.S. government, the Algerian government turned the hostages over to American authorities in Algiers.

In October 1988, economic and political unrest in Algeria gave rise to a series of riots that ended when President Chadli Benjdid announced a series of political changes, which included increasing the powers of the prime minister and broadening the base of representation by making changes in the ruling political party, the Front of National Liberation, which has governed Algeria without interruption since the end of the war of independence. However, demands for the institution of a multi-party system, and for putting an end to alleged official use of torture, have not produced the desired results.

ALIENS: EQUALITY WITH CITIZENS. After examining reports submitted by States Parties to the INTERNATIONAL COVENANT ON CIVIL AND POLITICAL RIGHTS in accordance with article 40 of that instrument, the HUMAN RIGHTS COMMITTEE in 1986 adopted a general comment setting out its view on the question of equality of aliens and citizens, as follows (UN Doc. A/41/40, Annex VI, para. 1–10):

Reports from States parties have often failed to take into account that each State party must ensure the rights in the Covenant to "all individuals within its territory and subject to its jurisdiction" (art. 2, para. 1). In general, the rights set forth in the Covenant apply to everyone, irrespective of reciprocity, and irrespective of his or her nationality or statelessness.

Thus, the general rule is that each one of the rights of the Covenant must be guaranteed without discrimination between citizens and aliens. Aliens receive the benefit of the general requirement of non-discrimination in respect of the rights guaranteed in the Covenant, as provided for in article 2 thereof. This guarantee applies to aliens and citizens alike. Exceptionally, some of the rights recognized in the Covenant are expressly applicable only to citizens (article 25), while article 13 applies only to aliens. However, the Committee's experience in examining reports shows that in a number of countries other rights that aliens should enjoy under the Covenant are denied to them or are subject to limitations that cannot always be justified under the Covenant.

A few constitutions provide for equality of aliens with citizens. Some constitutions adopted more recently carefully distinguish fundamental rights that apply to all and those granted to citizens only, and deal with each in detail. In many States, however, the constitutions are drafted in terms of citizens only when granting relevant rights. Legislation and case law may also play an important part in providing for the rights of aliens. The Committee has been informed that in some States fundamental rights, though not guaranteed to aliens by the Constitution or other legislation, will also be extended to them as required by the Covenant. In certain cases, however, there has clearly been a failure to implement Covenant rights without discrimination in respect of aliens.

The Committee considers that in their reports States parties should give attention to the position of aliens, both under their law and in actual practice. The Covenant gives aliens all the protection regarding rights guaranteed therein, and its requirements should be observed by States parties in their legislation and in practice as appropriate. The position of aliens would thus be considerably improved. States parties should ensure that the provisions of the Covenant and the rights under it are made known to aliens within their jurisdiction.

The Covenant does not recognize the right of aliens to enter or reside in the territory of a State party. It is in principle a matter for the State to decide who it will admit to its territory. However, in certain circumstances an alien may enjoy the protection of the Covenant even in relation to entry or residence, for example, when considerations of nondiscrimination, prohibition of inhuman treatment and respect for family life arise.

Consent for entry may be given subject to conditions relating, for example, to movement, residence and employment. A State may also impose general conditions upon an alien who is in transit. However, once aliens are allowed to enter the territory of a State party they are entitled to the rights set out in the Covenant.

Aliens thus have an inherent right to life, protected by law, and may not be arbitrarily deprived of life. They must not be subjected to torture or to cruel, inhuman or degrading treatment or punishment; nor may they be held in slavery or servitude. Aliens have the full right to liberty and security of the person. If lawfully deprived of their liberty, they shall be treated with humanity and with respect for the inherent dignity of their person. Aliens may not be imprisoned for failure to fulfil a contractual obligation. They have the right to liberty of movement and free choice of residence; they shall be free to leave the country. Aliens shall be equal before the courts and tribunals, and shall be entitled to a fair and public hearing by a competent, independent and impartial tribunal established by law in the determination of any criminal charge or of rights and obligations in a suit at law. Aliens shall not be subjected to retrospective penal legislation, and are entitled to recognition before the law. They may not be subjected to arbitrary or unlawful interference with their privacy, family, home or correspondence. They have the right to freedom of thought, conscience and religion, and the right to hold opinions and to express them. Aliens receive the benefit of the right of peaceful assembly and of freedom of association. They may marry when at marriageable age. Their children are entitled to those measures of protection required by their status as minors. In those cases where aliens constitute a minority within the meaning of article 27, they shall not be denied the right, in community with other members of their group, to enjoy their own culture, to profess and practise their own religion and to use their own language. Aliens are entitled to equal protection by the law. There shall be no discrimination between aliens and citizens in the application of these rights. These rights of aliens may be qualified only by such limitations as may be lawfully imposed under the Covenant.

Once an alien is lawfully within a territory, his freedom of movement within the territory and his right to leave that territory may only be restricted in accordance with article 12, paragraph 3. Differences in treatment in this regard between aliens and nationals, or between different categories of aliens, need to be justified under article 12, paragraph 3. Since such restrictions must, *inter alia*, be consistent with the other rights recognized in the Covenant, a State party cannot, by restraining an alien or deporting him to a third country, arbitrarily prevent his return to his own country (art. 12, para. 4).

Many reports have given insufficient information on matters relevant to article 13. That article is applicable to all procedures aimed at the obligatory departure of an alien, whether described in national law as expulsion or otherwise. If such procedures entail arrest, the safeguards of the Covenant relating to deprivation of liberty (arts. 9 and 10) may also be applicable. If the arrest is for the particular purpose of extradition, other provisions of national and international law may apply. Normally an alien who is expelled must be allowed to leave for any country that agrees to take him. The particular rights of article 13 only protect those aliens who are lawfully in the territory of a State party. This means that national law concerning the requirements for entry and stay must be taken into account in determining the scope of that protection, and that illegal entrants and aliens who have stayed longer than the law or their permits allow, in particular, are not covered by its provisions. However, if the legality of an alien's entry or stay is in dispute, any decision on this point leading to his expulsion or deportation ought to be taken in accordance with article 13. It is for the competent authorities of the State party, in good faith and in the exercise of their powers, to apply and interpret the domestic law, observing, however, such requirements under the Covenant as equality before the law (art. 26).

Article 13 directly regulates only the procedure and not the substantive grounds for expulsion. However, by allowing only those carried out "in pursuance of a decision reached in accordance with law", its purpose is clearly to prevent arbitrary expulsions. On the other hand, it entitles each alien to a decision in his own case and, hence, article 13 would not be satisfied with laws or decisions providing for collective or mass expulsions. This understanding, in the opinion of the Committee, is confirmed by further provisions concerning the right to submit reasons against expulsion and to have the decision reviewed by and to be represented before the competent authority or someone designated by it. An alien must be given full facilities for pursuing his remedy against expulsion so that this right will in all the circumstances of his case be an effective one. The principles of article 13 relating to appeal against expulsion and the entitlement to review by a competent authority may only be departed from when "compelling reasons of national security" so require. Discrimination may not be made between different categories of aliens in the application of article 13.

SEE ALSO Charter of Rights for Migrant Workers in Southern Africa; Declaration on the Human Rights of Individuals who are not Nationals of the Country in which They Live; European Code of Social Security and protocol; European Convention on Social Security; European Convention on the Legal Status of Migrant Workers; European Convention on Establishment and protocol; ILO Equality of Treatment (Social Security) Convention; ILO Migrant Workers (Supplementary Provisions) Convention; ILO Migration for Employment Convention; Migrant Workers.

ALIENS' RIGHTS. The subject of the *Study of International Provisions Protecting the Rights of Non-Citizens* (UN publication, Sales No. E.80.XIV.2) prepared by Baroness Diana Elles, special rapporteur of the UN SUB-COMMISSION ON PREVENTION OF DISCRIMINATION AND PROTECTION OF MINORITIES. The study was authorized by the sub-commission on 21 August 1974 (resolution 10 [XXVII]) and completed in 1979.

In initiating the study, the sub-commission recognized that, whereas human rights and fundamental freedoms are in principle applicable to every individual without distinction on the ground of nationality, some rights, nevertheless, are of such a nature that they can only be attributed to the nationals or citizens of the State. It called upon the special rapporteur to analyze contemporary international, regional, multilateral, and bilateral instruments concerning the human rights of non-citizens and to prepare a critical enumeration of the measures that might improve the situation. On the basis of her survey and analysis, the special rapporteur drew the following basic conclusions:

(1) The problem of the protection and treatment of aliens is not transient, temporary or local, but continuing and universal. It is not an isolated problem in point of time or of place, and therefore a universal approach is needed and an effort to reach universal consensus on this problem must be made.

(2) The many conditions attaching to the implementation and enforcement of provisions contained in international instruments have by no means been universally fulfilled.

(3) The wording of international instruments as they relate to aliens is unclear and imprecise, "nationality" not be included in the non-discrimination clauses. Both in the International Covenant on Economic, Social and Cultural Rights and in the International Convention on the Elimination of All Forms of Racial Discrimination, provision is made for distinction between nationals and aliens.

(4) Effective measures protecting the rights of individuals, including aliens, have so far been implemented at regional level. There has not so far been successful implementing machinery at international levels. The Human Rights Committee set up under the International Covenant on Civil and Political Rights and the obligation of the Economic and Social Council to receive reports under article 17 of the International Covenant on Economic, Social and Cultural Rights will now provide an opportunity to remedy this lacuna.

(5) Diplomatic protection available to citizens abroad by their State of nationality is discretionary and has some imperfections, but it remains for the time being the only effective form of protection available to the alien. A stateless person does not, of course, benefit from this form of protection.

(6) Instruments adopted to protect certain categories of aliens—the refugee, the stateless person and the migrant worker—are limited in their scope and effect. They cover a limited range of persons, they are ratified by only some States Members of the United Nations, and the rights recognized in these instruments are in some instances limited in their standard to a level below that available to nationals.

(7) Constitutions of international organizations proclaim concern for all individuals, but owing to the lack of resources and international co-operation, States are not always able at the present time to fully implement such policies.

(8) ILO Conventions, which play a considerable role in the improvement of the standard of living of all workers, have a flexible approach to the obligations of States, depending on the economic and social development of the area and the consequent possibility of applying benefits of economic progress to all individuals, alien as well as national.

(9) Regional organizations whose members have comparatively similar economic and social development may protect the rights of all individuals who are nationals of the

member States of the region. Aliens may benefit in particular with regard to conditions of employment, social security and other social benefits and educational opportunities, on a reciprocal basis.

(10) More favourable treatment may be given to the nationals of parties to bilateral agreements as compared with the treatment of other aliens. Refugees and stateless persons may, in some cases, also benefit from more favourable treatment under the relevant conventions.

(11) States usually recognize the right of aliens to have access to courts and tribunals and to a fair and public hearing on an equal basis with nationals, but there may be procedural and other formalities applicable to aliens which are not necessary or required in the case of nationals. Legal aid is not always available to aliens and may be the reason for an alien being unable to enforce the recognition of his rights or obtain redress for a violation of those rights.

(12) Political rights are usually reserved to nationals. There is evidence of one State giving voting rights to aliens for municipal elections and one State voting rights to aliens, on historical grounds, of one particular nationality.

(13) The requirements for an alien to acquire the nationality of a State of residence vary considerably from State to State even within the same region of the world.

(14) Reservations may be made on ratification of instruments, limitations and restrictions may be imposed by States on the rights and freedoms recognized in those instruments and derogations may be made in certain circumstances.

(15) Derogations may not be made from certain rights.

(16) Some limitations and restrictions are imposed on States in their treatment of aliens, both by international law and by treaty.

(17) Aliens have duties and obligations to the State in which they reside, although not precisely the same ones as those owed by citizens.

(18) Implementing machinery for the enforcement of human rights is inadequate and, in so far as it exists, not significantly effective. This applies to the protection of all individuals, nationals and aliens. Regional machinery is, in some areas, available to aliens as well as to nationals. It is effective, but it takes a long time for the individual to have redress.

(19) Overlapping of the competence of the European Court of Human Rights and the Human Rights Committee established under the International Covenant on Civil and Political Rights should not be allowed to impede any individual petition by an alien against a ratifying State party.

(20) Finally, it must be concluded that the rights of aliens are not universally protected. The application of the provisions of international human rights instruments to aliens is unclear and uncertain, and existing means of implementation are inadequate. The efforts made in certain regions of the world to protect the rights of all individuals, evidenced in multilateral and bilateral agreements, show that it is not impossible for States to guarantee protection for the rights of aliens as well as of their own citizens. This factor should be an encouragement to all States to seek to attain the standard set out in the Universal Declaration of Human Rights in accordance with the obligations laid down in the Charter of the United Nations.

On the basis of the above conclusions, the special rapporteur proposed the following recommendations for national and international action by States

and by regional and international organizations to ensure that the rights and freedoms of aliens receive more adequate protection. The report recommended that States should be urged:

National Action.

(1) To set up commissions to study their national laws with a view to ensuring that they correspond to the provisions for the protection and guarantee of all the human rights and fundamental freedoms contained in the Universal Declaration of Human Rights and the International Covenants on Human Rights in cases where these rights were heretofore protected by national legislation;

In relation to refugees and stateless persons:

(2) To ratify, if they have not already done so, the Convention relating to the Status of Refugees and the Protocol of 1967 to that Convention;

(3) In the case of member States of the Organization of African Unity, to ratify, if they have not already done so, the Convention Governing the Specific Aspects of Refugee Problems in Africa;

(4) To accede, in the case of member States of the Council of Europe which have not yet done so, to the European Agreement on the Abolition of Visas for Refugees of 20 April 1959;

(5) To study the matters of *refoulement*, expulsion and detention with a view to achieving a similar approach in the legislation and administrative procedures regarding the treatment of refugees;

(6) To make every effort to assist in the settlement of refugees who are for the time being receiving provisional shelter and so contribute to the integration of those refugees in the community of the host State on a permanent basis;

(7) To make every effort to accord to refugees as far as possible equal treatment to that of nationals;

(8) To make every effort to recognize the basic right of the refugee to retain the unity of his family;

(9) To give a liberal interpretation to the term "refugee";

(10) To give every moral, financial and practical support and assistance to the United Nations High Commissioner for Refugees in his humanitarian work;

(11) To ratify the Convention relating to the Status of Stateless Persons and the Convention on the Reduction of Statelessness. In particular, States are requested to make every effort to implement article 1 of the latter Convention and grant nationality to any child born within their territory who would otherwise be stateless;

(12) To recognize the rights of the stateless on the same basis, as far as possible, as nationals;

In relation to migrant workers:

(13) To ratify the Convention concerning Migrations in Abusive Conditions and the Promotion of Equality of Opportunity and Treatment of Migrant Workers, 1975, and to implement the recommendations contained in part II of that Convention with all possible speed;

(14) To support and encourage the work of the ILO in its efforts to promote the adoption of policies to improve the working and living conditions of all workers, especially migrant workers;

(15) To study the recommendations concerning the exploitation of labour through illicit and clandestine trafficking submitted by Mrs. Halima Warzazi (E/CN.4/Sub.2/L.636) with a view to implementing the measures proposed for host States and for the country of origin;

In relations with other States:

(16) To consider with other neighbouring States the formation of regional organizations for the improvement of the standard of living of all individuals within the region and the protection of the rights of all individuals within the jurisdiction of the States belonging to the region, on a basis of mutual assistance and reciprocity;

(17) To conclude bilateral and multilateral agreements for the protection of their nationals working in the territory of another State, in particular in relation to working conditions and social security benefits;

In relation to civil rights:

(18) To ensure that every facility is given through their administrative procedures and practices for aliens to be properly and adequately represented in courts and tribunals in order to obtain redress for violation of their rights;

(19) To grant legal aid, whenever necessary, to aliens on the same basis as to nationals;

(20) To be willing to exert their discretionary power of diplomatic protection for their citizens abroad whose rights have been violated;

Generally:

(21) To ratify the International Covenant on Economic, Social and Cultural Rights, the International Covenant on Civil and Political Rights and the Optional Protocol to the latter Covenant.

International Action.

(22) To consider extending the definition of the term "refugee" under the present Convention and Protocol to include all those categories of refugees who are not now covered, including displaced persons;

(23) To consider the inclusion of the term "nationality" as a ground for non-discrimination in future human rights instruments, taking into account the distinctions recognized in customary international law between a national and an alien;

(24) To request the International Institute for the Unification of Private Law (UNIDROIT) to study and make proposals on the approximation of laws relating to naturalization with a view to simplifying the legal and procedural requirements for aliens to acquire the citizenship of the country in which they live, especially as between countries within a geographical region;

(25) To consider the recommendations concerning the exploitation of labour through illicit and clandestine trafficking made by Mrs. Halima Warzazi (E/CN.4/Sub.2/L.636, p. 6), with a view to adopting them;

(26) To encourage, by the dissemination of information, Governments and non-governmental organizations in consultative status with the United Nations to report situations which reveal abuse or violation of the rights of aliens to the appropriate bodies within the United Nations;

(27) To request the Commission to propose to the Economic and Social Council to invite States parties to the International Covenant on Economic, Social and Cultural Rights, when submitting their reports in accordance with article 17 of the Covenant, to indicate where relevant the progress made in achieving protection for the rights of aliens;

(28) To request the Commission to propose to the Economic and Social Council to invite the Human Rights Committee to ask States parties to the International Covenant on Civil and Political Rights to include in their reports the measures taken to protect the rights of aliens;

(29) To make every effort to improve the legislation of Member States regarding the right of territorial asylum;

(30) To encourage by all means, particularly through the United Nations University, the teaching of the principles of the international law of human rights, using seminars, conferences and educational courses in order to inculcate respect and observance of the rights and freedoms of individuals under the law, including the rights of aliens;

(31) In recognition of the conclusions reached in chapter VIII of this report that there is no international instrument which is directed to the protection of the human rights of aliens and that those instruments that do exist are unclear, or are to be implemented progressively, or contain many limitations, restrictions and powers of derogation, to support the adoption of a declaration on this subject. Such a declaration:

(a) would be in accordance with the view expressed by the International Law Commission that a statement or re-statement of the law was required regarding the treatment of aliens;

(b) would be in line with the suggestions made by Mr. F. Garcia Amador, former Special Rapporteur of the International Law Commission, in his scholarly work on the recent codification of the law of State responsibility for injuries to aliens;

(c) would reflect and be evidence of State practice, resulting from bilateral and multilateral agreements, and be a source of encouragement to those States which do not so far recognize all economic, social, cultural and civil rights to aliens;

(d) would provide a clear statement seeking to maintain a just balance between the sovereignty of States and the protection of the rights and freedoms of all individuals;

(e) would draw the attention of States to the rights of aliens, who are not yet provided for as such in any international instrument in the field of human rights;

(f) may by custom become recognized as laying down rules binding upon States and serve as a first step towards the adoption of a Convention on the same subject-matter.

On the basis of the special rapporteur's study, the General Assembly was able to adopt, on 13 December 1985 (resolution 40/144), the DECLARATION ON THE HUMAN RIGHTS OF INDIVIDUALS WHO ARE NOT NATIONALS OF THE COUNTRY IN WHICH THEY LIVE.

SEE ALSO American Convention on Human Rights; American Declaration of the Rights and Duties of Man; Convention on the Reduction of Statelessness; Convention relating to the Status of Stateless Persons; European Convention on Establishment and protocol; European Convention on Human Rights: ILO Equality of Treatment (Social Security) Convention; International Covenant on Civil and Political Rights and protocol; Refugees.

ALL INDIA WOMEN'S CONFERENCE. An international non-governmental organization in consultative status with the UN Economic and Social Council (Category II), the All India Women's Conference is the largest women's organization in Southeast Asia, with over 500 centers in India and abroad; AIWC has 25 affiliated organizations throughout the world, with 1 million individual members. AIWC was established in 1945 and has since been active in promoting the status of women in Asia. Among its contributions, it has endeavored to ensure the equal status of women in society and law. The conference carries out an extensive program throughout Asia for the reestablishment of destitute women and the rehabilitation of drug addicts; it also conducts educational seminars on nutrition, family planning, environmental issues, and vocational training.

AIWC publishes the monthly journal *Roshni* (in English).

All India Women's Conference. Address: 6 Bhaghwan Das Road, New Delhi, India or 38 Ch. du Pont Ceard, 1290, Versoix/Geneva, Switzerland. Telephone: (022) 551152 (Geneva). President: Mrs. Ashoka Gupta.

AMERICAN CONVENTION ON HUMAN RIGHTS (1969).

The convention, also known as the Pact of San Jose, Costa Rica, provides protection of human rights on a regional basis by countries in North, Central, and South America, roughly comparable to that provided by countries in western Europe by the EUROPEAN CONVENTION ON HUMAN RIGHTS. It establishes two organs for this purpose: the INTER–AMERICAN COMMISSION ON HUMAN RIGHTS and the INTER–AMERICAN COURT OF HUMAN RIGHTS.

The functions of the commission include investigation, conciliation, the making of recommendations, and the issuance of reports setting out its findings and conclusions. The court, if its jurisdiction is accepted by the State concerned, may make definitive determinations of human rights violations by a State, award damages for the violations, and arrange for the consequences of the violations to be remedied.

The convention was adopted at San Jose on 22 November 1969 by the Inter-American Specialized Conference on Human Rights and entered into force on 18 July 1978.

Provisions adding certain economic, social, and cultural rights to the catalogue of matters with which the convention is concerned are set out in the AMERICAN CONVENTION ON HUMAN RIGHTS: ADDITIONAL PROTOCOL, also known as the Protocol of San Salvador, which will enter into force, in accordance with its article 74, "as soon as eleven States have deposited their instruments of ratification or accession." The additional protocol was approved unanimously by the OAS General Assembly on 17 November 1988 on the basis of a draft prepared by the Inter-American Commission on Human Rights.

The text of the convention, as adopted at San Jose in 1969, (OAS *Treaty Series* 36), is as follows:

Preamble

The American states signatory to the present Convention,

Reaffirming their intention to consolidate in this hemisphere, within the framework of democratic institutions, a system of personal liberty and social justice based on respect for the essential rights of man;

Recognizing that the essential rights of man are not derived from one's being a national of a certain state, but are based upon attributes of the human personality, and that they therefore justify international protection in the form of a convention reinforcing or complementing the protection provided by the domestic law of the American states;

Considering that these principles have been set forth in the Charter of the Organization of American States, in the American Declaration of the Rights and Duties of Man, and in the Universal Declaration of Human Rights, and that they have been reaffirmed and refined in other international instruments, worldwide as well as regional in scope;

Reiterating that, in accordance with the Universal Declaration of Human Rights, the ideal of free men enjoying freedom from fear and want can be achieved only if conditions are created whereby everyone may enjoy his economic, social, and cultural rights, as well as his civil and political rights; and

Considering that the Third Special Inter-American Conference (Buenos Aires, 1967) approved the incorporation into the Charter of the Organization itself of broader standards with respect to economic, social, and educational rights and resolved that an inter-American convention on human rights should determine the structure, competence, and procedure of the organs responsible for these matters,

Have agreed upon the following:

Part I
State Obligations and Rights Protected

Chapter I—General Obligations

Article 1. Obligation to Respect Rights. 1. The States Parties to this Convention undertake to respect the rights and freedoms recognized herein and to ensure to all persons subject to their jurisdiction the free and full exercise of those rights and freedoms, without any discrimination for reasons of race, color, sex, language, religion, political or other opinion, national or social origin, economic status, birth, or any other social condition.

2. For the purposes of this Convention, "person" means every human being.

Article 2. Domestic Legal Effects. Where the exercise of any of the rights or freedoms referred to in Article 1 is not already ensured by legislative or other provisions, the States Parties undertake to adopt, in accordance with their constitutional processes and the provisions of this Convention, such legislative or other measures as may be necessary to give effect to those rights or freedoms.

Chapter II—Civil and Political Rights

Article 3. Right to Juridical Personality. Every person has the right to recognition as a person before the law.

Article 4. Right to Life. 1. Every person has the right to have his life respected. This right shall be protected by law and, in general, from the moment of conception. No one shall be arbitrarily deprived of his life.

2. In countries that have not abolished the death penalty, it may be imposed only for the most serious crimes and pur-

suant to a final judgment rendered by a competent court and in accordance with a law establishing such punishment, enacted prior to the commission of the crime. The application of such punishment shall not be extended to crimes to which it does not presently apply.

3. The death penalty shall not be reestablished in states that have abolished it.

4. In no case shall capital punishment be inflicted for political offenses or related common crimes.

5. Capital punishment shall not be imposed upon persons who, at the time the crime was committed, were under 18 years of age or over 70 years of age; nor shall it be applied to pregnant women.

6. Every person condemned to death shall have the right to apply for amnesty, pardon, or commutation of sentence, which may be granted in all cases. Capital punishment shall not be imposed while such a petition is pending decision by the competent authority.

Article 5. Right to Humane Treatment. 1. Every person has the right to have his physical, mental, and moral integrity respected.

2. No one shall be subjected to torture or to cruel, inhuman, or degrading punishment or treatment. All persons deprived of their liberty shall be treated with respect for the inherent dignity of the human person.

3. Punishment shall not be extended to any person other than the criminal.

4. Accused persons shall, save in exceptional circumstances, be segregated from convicted persons, and shall be subject to separate treatment appropriate to their status as unconvicted persons.

5. Minors while subject to criminal proceedings shall be separated from adults and brought before specialized tribunals, as speedily as possible, so that they may be treated in accordance with their status as minors.

6. Punishments consisting of deprivation of liberty shall have as an essential aim the reform and social readaptation of the prisoners.

Article 6. Freedom from Slavery. 1. No one shall be subject to slavery or to involuntary servitude, which are prohibited in all their forms, as are the slave trade and traffic in women.

2. No one shall be required to perform forced or compulsory labor. This provision shall not be interpreted to mean that, in those countries in which the penalty established for certain crimes is deprivation of liberty at forced labor, the carrying out of such a sentence imposed by a competent court is prohibited. Forced labor shall not adversely affect the dignity or the physical or intellectual capacity of the prisoner.

3. For the purposes of this article, the following do not constitute forced or compulsory labor:

a. work or service normally required of a person imprisoned in execution of a sentence or formal decision passed by the competent judicial authority. Such work or service shall be carried out under the supervision and control of public authorities, and any persons performing such work or service shall not be placed at the disposal of any private party, company, or juridical person;

b. military service and, in countries in which conscientious objectors are recognized, national service that the law may provide for in lieu of military service;

c. service exacted in time of danger or calamity that threatens the existence or the well-being of the community; or

d. work or service that forms part of normal civic obligations.

Article 7. Right to Personal Liberty. 1. Every person has the right to personal liberty and security.

2. No one shall be deprived of his physical liberty except for the reasons and under the conditions established beforehand by the constitution of the State Party concerned or by a law established pursuant thereto.

3. No one shall be subject to arbitrary arrest or imprisonment.

4. Anyone who is detained shall be informed of the reasons for his detention and shall be promptly notified of the charge or charges against him.

5. Any person detained shall be brought promptly before a judge or other officer authorized by law to exercise judicial power and shall be entitled to trial within a reasonable time or to be released without prejudice to the continuation of the proceedings. His release may be subject to guarantees to assure his appearance for trial.

6. Anyone who is deprived of his liberty shall be entitled to recourse to a competent court, in order that the court may decide without delay on the lawfulness of his arrest or detention and order his release if the arrest or detention is unlawful. In States Parties whose laws provide that anyone who believes himself to be threatened with deprivation of his liberty is entitled to recourse to a competent court in order that it may decide on the lawfulness of such threat, this remedy may not be restricted or abolished. The interested party or another person in his behalf is entitled to seek these remedies.

7. No one shall be detained for debt. This principle shall not limit the orders of a competent judicial authority issued for nonfulfillment of duties of support.

Article 8. Right to a Fair Trial. 1. Every person has the right to a hearing, with due guarantees and within a reasonable time, by a competent, independent, and impartial tribunal, previously established by law, in the substantiation of any accusation of a criminal nature made against him or for the determination of his rights and obligations of a civil, labor, fiscal, or any other nature.

2. Every person accused of a criminal offense has the right to be presumed innocent so long as his guilt has not been proven according to law. During the proceedings, every person is entitled, with full equality, to the following minimum guarantees:

a. the right of the accused to be assisted without charge by a translator or interpreter, if he does not understand or does not speak the language of the tribunal or court;

b. prior notification in detail to the accused of the charges against him;

c. adequate time and means for the preparation of his defense;

d. the right of the accused to defend himself personally or to be assisted by legal counsel of his own choosing, and to communicate freely and privately with his counsel;

e. the inalienable right to be assisted by counsel provided by the state, paid or not as the domestic law provides, if the accused does not defend himself personally or engage his own counsel within the time period established by law;

f. the right of the defense to examine witnesses present in the court and to obtain the appearance, as witnesses, of experts or other persons who may throw light on the facts;

g. the right not to be compelled to be a witness against himself or to plead guilty; and

h. the right to appeal the judgment to a higher court.

3. A confession of guilt by the accused shall be valid only if it is made without coercion of any kind.

4. An accused person acquitted by a nonappealable judgment shall not be subjected to a new trial for the same cause.

5. Criminal proceedings shall be public, except insofar as may be necessary to protect the interests of justice.

Article 9. Freedom from Ex Post Facto Laws. No one shall be convicted of any act or omission that did not constitute a criminal offense, under the applicable law, at the time it was committed. A heavier penalty shall not be imposed than the one that was applicable at the time the criminal offense was committed. If subsequent to the commission of the offense the law provides for the imposition of a lighter punishment, the guilty person shall benefit therefrom.

Article 10. Right to Compensation. Every person has the right to be compensated in accordance with the law in the event he has been sentenced by a final judgment through a miscarriage of justice.

Article 11. Right to Privacy. 1. Everyone has the right to have his honor respected and his dignity recognized.

2. No one may be the object of arbitrary or abusive interference with his private life, his family, his home, or his correspondence, or of unlawful attacks on his honor or reputation.

3. Everyone has the right to the protection of the law against such interference or attacks.

Article 12. Freedom of Conscience and Religion. 1. Everyone has the right to freedom of conscience and of religion. This right includes freedom to maintain or to change one's religion or beliefs, and freedom to profess or disseminate one's religion or beliefs, either individually or together with others, in public or in private.

2. No one shall be subject to restrictions that might impair his freedom to maintain or to change his religion or beliefs.

3. Freedom to manifest one's religion and beliefs may be subject only to the limitations prescribed by law that are necessary to protect public safety, order, health, or morals, or the rights or freedoms of others.

4. Parents or guardians, as the case may be, have the right to provide for the religious and moral education of their children or wards that is in accord with their own convictions.

Article 13. Freedom of Thought and Expression. 1. Everyone has the right to freedom of thought and expression. This right includes freedom to seek, receive, and impart information and ideas of all kinds, regardless of frontiers, either orally, in writing, in print, in the form of art, or through any other medium of one's choice.

2. The exercise of the right provided for in the foregoing paragraph shall not be subject to prior censorship but shall be subject to subsequent imposition of liability, which shall be expressly established by law to the extent necessary to ensure:

    a. respect for the rights or reputations of others; or

    b. the protection of national security, public order, or public health or morals.

3. The right of expression may not be restricted by indirect methods or means, such as the abuse of government or private controls over newsprint, radio broadcasting frequencies, or equipment used in the dissemination of information, or by any other means tending to impede the communication and circulation of ideas and opinions.

4. Notwithstanding the provisions of paragraph 2 above, public entertainments may be subject by law to prior cen-

sorship for the sole purpose of regulating access to them for the moral protection of childhood and adolescence.

5. Any propaganda for war and any advocacy of national, racial, or religious hatred that constitute incitements to lawless violence or to any other similar action against any person or group of persons on any grounds including those of race, color, religion, language, or national origin shall be considered as offenses punishable by law.

Article 14. Right of Reply. 1. Anyone injured by inaccurate or offensive statements or ideas disseminated to the public in general by a legally regulated medium of communication has the right to reply or to make a correction using the same communications outlet, under such conditions as the law may establish.

2. The correction or reply shall not in any case remit other legal liabilities that may have been incurred.

3. For the effective protection of honor and reputation, every publisher, and every newspaper, motion picture, radio, and television company, shall have a person responsible who is not protected by immunities or special privileges.

Article 15. Right of Assembly. The right of peaceful assembly, without arms, is recognized. No restrictions may be placed on the exercise of this right other than those imposed in conformity with the law and necessary in a democratic society in the interest of national security, public safety or public order, or to protect public health or morals or the rights or freedom of others.

Article 16. Freedom of Association. 1. Everyone has the right to associate freely for ideological, religious, political, economic, labor, social, cultural, sports, or other purposes.

2. The exercise of this right shall be subject only to such restrictions established by law as may be necessary in a democratic society, in the interest of national security, public safety or public order, or to protect public health or morals or the rights and freedoms of others.

3. The provisions of this article do not bar the imposition of legal restrictions, including even deprivation of the exercise of the right of association, on members of the armed forces and the police.

Article 17. Rights of the Family. 1. The family is the natural and fundamental group unit of society and is entitled to protection by society and the state.

2. The right of men and women of marriageable age to marry and to raise a family shall be recognized, if they meet the conditions required by domestic law, insofar as such conditions do not affect the principle of nondiscrimination established in this Convention.

3. No marriage shall be entered into without the free and full consent of the intending spouses.

4. The States Parties shall take appropriate steps to ensure the equality of rights and the adequate balancing of responsibilities of the spouses as to marriage, during marriage, and in the event of its dissolution. In case of dissolution, provision shall be made for the necessary protection of any children solely on the basis of their own best interests.

5. The law shall recognize equal rights for children born out of wedlock and those born in wedlock.

Article 18. Right to a Name. Every person has the right to a given name and to the surnames of his parents or that of one of them. The law shall regulate the manner in which this right shall be ensured for all, by the use of assumed names if necessary.

Article 19. Rights of the Child. Every minor child has the right to the measures of protection required by his condition as a minor on the part of his family, society, and the state.

Article 20. Right to Nationality. 1. Every person has the right to a nationality.

2. Every person has the right to the nationality of the state in whose territory he was born if he does not have the right to any other nationality.

3. No one shall be arbitrarily deprived of his nationality or of the right to change it.

Article 21. Right to Property. 1. Everyone has the right to the use and enjoyment of his property. The law may subordinate such use and enjoyment to the interest of society.

2. No one shall be deprived of his property except upon payment of just compensation, for reasons of public utility or social interest, and in the cases and according to the forms established by law.

3. Usury and any other form of exploitation of man by man shall be prohibited by law.

Article 22. Freedom of Movement and Residence. 1. Every person lawfully in the territory of a State Party has the right to move about in it, and to reside in it subject to the provisions of the law.

2. Every person has the right to leave any country freely, including his own.

3. The exercise of the foregoing rights may be restricted only pursuant to a law to the extent necessary in a democratic society to prevent crime or to protect national security, public safety, public order, public morals, public health, or the rights or freedoms of others.

4. The exercise of the rights recognized in paragraph 1 may also be restricted by law in designated zones for reasons of public interest.

5. No one can be expelled from the territory of the state of which he is a national or be deprived of the right to enter it.

6. An alien lawfully in the territory of a State Party to this Convention may be expelled from it only pursuant to a decision reached in accordance with law.

7. Every person has the right to seek and be granted asylum in a foreign territory, in accordance with the legislation of the state and international conventions, in the event he is being pursued for political offenses or related common crimes.

8. In no case may an alien be deported or returned to a country, regardless of whether or not it is his country of origin, if in that country his right to life or personal freedom is in danger of being violated because of his race, nationality, religion, social status, or political opinions.

9. The collective expulsion of aliens is prohibited.

Article 23. Right to Participate in Government. 1. Every citizen shall enjoy the following rights and opportunities:

a. to take part in the conduct of public affairs, directly or through freely chosen representatives;

b. to vote and to be elected in genuine periodic elections, which shall be by universal and equal suffrage and by secret ballot that guarantees the free expression of the will of the voters; and

c. to have access, under general conditions of equality, to the public service of his country.

2. The law may regulate the exercise of the rights and opportunities referred to in the preceding paragraph only on the basis of age, nationality, residence, language, education, civil and mental capacity, or sentencing by a competent court in criminal proceedings.

Article 24. Right to Equal Protection. All persons are equal before the law. Consequently, they are entitled, without discrimination, to equal protection of the law.

Article 25. Right to Judicial Protection. 1. Everyone has the right to simple and prompt recourse, or any other effective recourse, to a competent court or tribunal for protection against acts that violate his fundamental rights recognized by the constitution or laws of the state concerned or by this Convention, even though such violation may have been committed by persons acting in the course of their official duties.

2. The States Parties undertake:

a. to ensure that any person claiming such remedy shall have his rights determined by the competent authority provided for by the legal system of the state;

b. to develop the possibilities of judicial remedy; and

c. to ensure that the competent authorities shall enforce such remedies when granted.

Chapter III—Economic, Social, and and Cultural Rights

Article 26. Progressive Development. The States Parties undertake to adopt measures, both internally and through international cooperation, especially those of an economic and technical nature, with a view to achieving progressively, by legislation or other appropriate means, the full realization of the rights implicit in the economic, social, educational, scientific, and cultural standards set forth in the Charter of the Organization of American States as amended by the Protocol of Buenos Aires.

Chapter IV—Suspension of Guarantees, Interpretation, and Application

Article 27. Suspension of Guarantees. 1. In time of war, public danger, or other emergency that threatens the independence or security of a State Party, it may take measures derogating from its obligations under the present Convention to the extent and for the period of time strictly required by the exigencies of the situation, provided that such measures are not inconsistent with its other obligations under international law and do not involve discrimination on the ground of race, color, sex, language, religion, or social origin.

2. The foregoing provision does not authorize any suspension of the following articles: Article 3 (Right to Juridical Personality), Article 4 (Right to Life), Article 5 (Right to Humane Treatment), Article 6 (Freedom from Slavery), Article 9 (Freedom from *Ex Post Facto* Laws), Article 12 (Freedom of Conscience and Religion), Article 17 (Rights of the Family), Article 18 (Right to a Name), Article 19 (Rights of the Child), Article 20 (Right to Nationality), and Article 23 (Right to Participate in Government), or of the judicial guarantees essential for the protection of such rights.

3. Any State Party availing itself of the right of suspension shall immediately inform the other States Parties, through the Secretary General of the Organization of American States, of the provisions the application of which it has suspended, the reasons that gave rise to the suspension, and the date set for the termination of such suspension.

Article 28. Federal Clause. 1. Where a State Party is constituted as a federal state, the national government of such State Party shall implement all the provisions of the Convention over whose subject matter it exercises legislative and judicial jurisdiction.

2. With respect to the provisions over whose subject matter the constituent units of the federal state have jurisdic-

tion, the national government shall immediately take suitable measures, in accordance with its constitution and its laws, to the end that the competent authorities of the constituent units may adopt appropriate provisions for the fulfillment of this Convention.

3. Whenever two or more States Parties agree to form a federation or other type of association, they shall take care that the resulting federal or other compact contains the provisions necessary for continuing and rendering effective the standards of this Convention in the new state that is organized.

Article 29. Restrictions Regarding Interpretation. No provision of this Convention shall be interpreted as:

a. permitting any State Party, group, or person to suppress the enjoyment or exercise of the rights and freedoms recognized in this Convention or to restrict them to a greater extent than is provided for herein;

b. restricting the enjoyment or exercise of any right or freedom recognized by virtue of the laws of any State Party or by virtue of another convention to which one of the said states is a party;

c. precluding other rights or guarantees that are inherent in the human personality or derived from representative democracy as a form of government; or

d. excluding or limiting the effect that the American Declaration of the Rights and Duties of Man and other international acts of the same nature may have.

Article 30. Scope of Restrictions. The restrictions that, pursuant to this Convention, may be placed on the enjoyment or exercise of the rights or freedoms recognized herein may not be applied except in accordance with laws enacted for reasons of general interest and in accordance with the purpose for which such restrictions have been established.

Article 31. Recognition of Other Rights. Other rights and freedoms recognized in accordance with the procedures established in Articles 76 and 77 may be included in the system of protection of this Convention.

Chapter V—Personal Responsibilities

Article 32. Relationship between Duties and Rights. 1. Every person has responsibilities to his family, his community, and mankind.

2. The rights of each person are limited by the rights of others, by the security of all, and by the just demands of the general welfare, in a democratic society.

Part II
Means of Protection

Chapter VI—Competent Organs

Article 33. The following organs shall have competence with respect to matters relating to the fulfillment of the commitments made by the States Parties to this Convention:

a. the Inter-American Commission on Human Rights, referred to as "The Commission;" and

b. the Inter-American Court of Human Rights, referred to as "The Court."

Chapter VII—Inter-American Commission on Human Rights

Section 1. Organization

Article 34. The Inter-American Commission on Human Rights shall be composed of seven members, who shall be persons of high moral character and recognized competence in the field of human rights.

Article 35. The Commission shall represent all the member countries of the Organization of American States.

Article 36. 1. The members of the Commission shall be elected in a personal capacity by the General Assembly of the Organization from a list of candidates proposed by the governments of the member states.

2. Each of those governments may propose up to three candidates, who may be nationals of the states proposing them or of any other member state of the Organization of American States. When a slate of three is proposed, at least one of the candidates shall be a national of a state other than the one proposing the slate.

Article 37. 1. The members of the Commission shall be elected for a term of four years and may be reelected only once, but the terms of three of the members chosen in the first election shall expire at the end of two years. Immediately following that election the General Assembly shall determine the names of those three members by lot.

2. No two nationals of the same state may be members of the Commission.

Article 38. Vacancies that may occur on the Commission for reasons other than the normal expiration of term shall be filled by the Permanent Council of the Organization in accordance with the provisions of the Statute of the Commission.

Article 39. The Commission shall prepare its Statute, which it shall submit to the General Assembly for approval. It shall establish its own Regulations.

Article 40. Secretariat services for the Commission shall be furnished by the appropriate specialized unit of the General Secretariat of the Organization. This unit shall be provided with the resources required to accomplish the tasks assigned to it by the Commission.

Section 2. Functions

Article 41. The main function of the Commission shall be to promote respect for and defense of human rights. In the exercise of its mandate, it shall have the following functions and powers:

a. to develop an awareness of human rights among the peoples of America;

b. to make recommendations to the governments of the member states, when it considers such action advisable, for the adoption of progressive measures in favor of human rights within the framework of their domestic law and constitutional provisions as well as appropriate measures to further the observance of those rights;

c. to prepare such studies or reports as it considers advisable in the performance of its duties;

d. to request the governments of the member states to supply it with information on the measures adopted by them in matters of human rights;

e. to respond, through the General Secretariat of the Organization of American States, to inquiries made by the member states on matters related to human rights and, within the limits of its possibilities, to provide those states with the advisory services they request;

f. to take action on petitions and other communications pursuant to its authority under the provisions of Articles 44 through 51 of this Convention; and

g. to submit an annual report to the General Assembly of the Organization of American States.

Article 42. The States Parties shall transmit to the Commission a copy of each of the reports and studies that they submit annually to the Executive Committees of the Inter-American Economic and Social Council and the Inter-American Council for Education, Science, and Culture, in their respective fields, so that the Commission may watch over the promotion of the rights implicit in the economic, social, educational, scientific, and cultural standards set forth in the Charter of the Organization of American States as amended by the Protocol of Buenos Aires.

Article 43. The States Parties undertake to provide the Commission with such information as it may request of them as to the manner in which their domestic law ensures the effective application of any provisions of this Convention.

Section 3. Competence

Article 44. Any person or group of persons, or any non-governmental entity legally recognized in one or more member states of the Organization, may lodge petitions with the Commission containing denunciations or complaints of violation of this Convention by a State Party.

Article 45. 1. Any State Party may, when it deposits its instrument of ratification of or adherence to this Convention, or at any later time, declare that it recognizes the competence of the Commission to receive and examine communications in which a State Party alleges that another State Party has committed a violation of a human right set forth in this Convention.

2. Communications presented by virtue of this article may be admitted and examined only if they are presented by a State Party that has made a declaration recognizing the aforementioned competence of the Commission. The Commission shall not admit any communication against a State Party that has not made such a declaration.

3. A declaration concerning recognition of competence may be made to be valid for an indefinite time, for a specified period, or for a specific case.

4. Declarations shall be deposited with the General Secretariat of the Organization of American States, which shall transmit copies thereof to the member states of that Organization.

Article 46. 1. Admission by the Commission of a petition or communication lodged in accordance with Articles 44 or 45 shall be subject to the following requirements:

a. that the remedies under domestic law have been pursued and exhausted in accordance with generally recognized principles of international law;

b. that the petition or communication is lodged within a period of six months from the date on which the party alleging violation of his rights was notified of the final judgment;

c. that the subject of the petition or communication is not pending in another international proceeding for settlement; and

d. that, in the case of Article 44, the petition contains the name, nationality, profession, domicile, and signature of the person or persons or of the legal representative of the entity lodging the petition.

2. The provisions of paragraphs 1.a and 1.b of this article shall not be applicable when:

a. the domestic legislation of the state concerned does not afford due process of law for the protection of the right or rights that have allegedly been violated;

b. the party alleging violation of his rights has been de-

nied access to the remedies under domestic law or has been prevented from exhausting them; or

c. there has been unwarranted delay in rendering a final judgment under the aforementioned remedies.

Article 47. The Commission shall consider inadmissible any petition or communication submitted under Articles 44 or 45 if:

a. any of the requirements indicated in Article 46 has not been met;

b. the petition or communication does not state facts that tend to establish a violation of the rights guaranteed by this Convention;

c. the statements of the petitioner or of the state indicate that the petition or communication is manifestly groundless or obviously out of order; or

d. the petition or communication is substantially the same as one previously studied by the Commission or by another international organization.

Section 4. Procedure

Article 48. 1. When the Commission receives a petition or communication alleging violation of any of the rights protected by this Convention, it shall proceed as follows:

a. If it considers the petition or communication admissible, it shall request information from the government of the state indicated as being responsible for the alleged violations and shall furnish that government a transcript of the pertinent portions of the petition or communication. This information shall be submitted within a reasonable period to be determined by the Commission in accordance with the circumstances of each case.

b. After the information has been received, or after the period established has elapsed and the information has not been received, the Commission shall ascertain whether the grounds for the petition or communication still exist. If they do not, the Commission shall order the record to be closed.

c. The Commision may also declare the petition or communication inadmissible or out of order on the basis of information or evidence subsequently received.

d. If the record has not been closed, the Commission shall, with the knowledge of the parties, examine the matter set forth in the petition or communication in order to verify the facts. If necessary and advisable, the Commission shall carry out an investigation, for the effective conduct of which it shall request, and the states concerned shall furnish to it, all necessary facilities.

e. The Commission may request the states concerned to furnish any pertinent information and, if so requested, shall hear oral statements or receive written statements from the parties concerned.

f. The Commission shall place itself at the disposal of the parties concerned with a view to reaching a friendly settlement of the matter on the basis of respect for the human rights recognized in this Convention.

2. However, in serious and urgent cases, only the presentation of a petition or communication that fulfills all the formal requirements of admissibility shall be necessary in order for the Commission to conduct an investigation with the prior consent of the state in whose territory a violation has allegedly been committed.

Article 49. If a friendly settlement has been reached in accordance with paragraph 1.f of Article 48, the Commission shall draw up a report, which shall be transmitted to the petitioner and to the States Parties to this Convention, and shall then be communicated to the Secretary General of the Organization of American States for publication. This report shall contain a brief statement of the facts and of the solution reached. If any party in the case so requests, the fullest possible information shall be provided to it.

Article 50. 1. If a settlement is not reached, the Commission shall, within the time limit established by its Statute, draw up a report setting forth the facts and stating its conclusions. If the report, in whole or in part, does not represent the unanimous agreement of the members of the Commission, any member may attach to it a separate opinion. The written and oral statements made by the parties in accordance with paragraph 1.e of Article 48 shall also be attached to the report.

2. The report shall be transmitted to the states concerned, which shall not be at liberty to publish it.

3. In transmitting the report, the Commission may make such proposals and recommendations as it sees fit.

Article 51. 1. If, within a period of three months from the date of the transmittal of the report of the Commission to the states concerned, the matter has not either been settled or submitted by the Commission or by the state concerned to the Court and its jurisdiction accepted, the Commission may, by the vote of an absolute majority of its members, set forth its opinion and conclusions concerning the question submitted for its consideration.

2. Where appropriate, the Commission shall make pertinent recommendations and shall prescribe a period within which the state is to take the measures that are incumbent upon it to remedy the situation examined.

3. When the prescribed period has expired, the Commission shall decide by the vote of an absolute majority of its members whether the state has taken adequate measures and whether to publish its report.

Chapter VIII—Inter-American Court of Human Rights

Section 1. Organization

Article 52. 1. The Court shall consist of seven judges, nationals of the member states of the Organization, elected in an individual capacity from among jurists of the highest moral authority and of recognized competence in the field of human rights, who possess the qualifications required for the exercise of the highest judicial functions in conformity with the law of the state of which they are nationals or of the state that proposes them as candidates.

2. No two judges may be nationals of the same state.

Article 53. 1. The judges of the Court shall be elected by secret ballot by an absolute majority vote of the States Parties to the Convention, in the General Assembly of the Organization, from a panel of candidates proposed by those states.

2. Each of the States Parties may propose up to three candidates, nationals of the state that proposes them or of any other member state of the Organization of American States. When a slate of three is proposed, at least one of the candidates shall be a national of a state other than the one proposing the slate.

Article 54. 1. The judges of the Court shall be elected for a term of six years and may be reelected only once. The term of three of the judges chosen in the first election shall expire at the end of three years. Immediately after the election, the names of the three judges shall be determined by lot in the General Assembly.

2. A judge elected to replace a judge whose term has not expired shall complete the term of the latter.

3. The judges shall continue in office until the expiration of their term. However, they shall continue to serve with regard to cases that they have begun to hear and that are still pending, for which purposes they shall not be replaced by the newly elected judges.

Article 55. 1. If a judge is a national of any of the States Parties to a case submitted to the Court, he shall retain his right to hear that case.

2. If one of the judges called upon to hear a case should be a national of one of the States Parties to the case, any other State Party in the case may appoint a person of its choice to serve on the Court as an *ad hoc* judge.

3. If among the judges called upon to hear a case none is a national of any of the States Parties to the case, each of the latter may appoint an *ad hoc* judge.

4. An *ad hoc* judge shall possess the qualifications indicated in Article 52.

5. If several States Parties to the Convention should have the same interest in a case, they shall be considered as a single party for purposes of the above provisions. In case of doubt, the Court shall decide.

Article 56. Five judges shall constitute a quorum for the transaction of business by the Court.

Article 57. The Commission shall appear in all cases before the Court.

Article 58. 1. The Court shall have its seat at the place determined by the States Parties to the Convention in the General Assembly of the Organization; however, it may convene in the territory of any member state of the Organization of American States when a majority of the Court considers it desirable, and with the prior consent of the state concerned. The seat of the Court may be changed by the States Parties to the Convention in the General Assembly by a two-thirds vote.

2. The Court shall appoint its own Secretary.

3. The Secretary shall have his office at the place where the Court has its seat and shall attend the meetings that the Court may hold away from its seat.

Article 59. The Court shall establish its Secretariat, which shall function under the direction of the Secretary of the Court, in accordance with the administrative standards of the General Secretariat of the Organization in all respects not incompatible with the independence of the Court. The staff of the Court's Secretariat shall be appointed by the Secretary General of the Organization, in consultation with the Secretary of the Court.

Article 60. The Court shall draw up its Statute which it shall submit to the General Assembly for approval. It shall adopt its own Rules of Procedure.

Section 2. Jurisdiction and Functions

Article 61. 1. Only the States Parties and the Commission shall have the right to submit a case to the Court.

2. In order for the Court to hear a case, it is necessary that the procedures set forth in Articles 48 and 50 shall have been completed.

Article 62. 1. A State Party may, upon depositing its instrument of ratification or adherence to this Convention, or at any subsequent time, declare that it recognizes as binding, *ipso facto,* and not requiring special agreement, the jurisdiction of the Court on all matters relating to the interpretation or application of this Convention.

2. Such declaration may be made unconditionally, on the

condition of reciprocity, for a specified period, or for specific cases. It shall be presented to the Secretary General of the Organization, who shall transmit copies thereof to the other member states of the Organization and to the Secretary of the Court.

3. The jurisdiction of the Court shall comprise all cases concerning the interpretation and application of the provisions of this Convention that are submitted to it, provided that the States Parties to the case recognize or have recognized such jurisdiction, whether by special declaration pursuant to the preceding paragraphs, or by a special agreement.

Article 63. 1. If the Court finds that there has been a violation of a right or freedom protected by this Convention, the Court shall rule that the injured party be ensured the enjoyment of his right or freedom that was violated. It shall also rule, if appropriate, that the consequences of the measure or situation that constituted the breach of such right or freedom be remedied and that fair compensation be paid to the injured party.

2. In cases of extreme gravity and urgency, and when necessary to avoid irreparable damage to persons, the Court shall adopt such provisional measures as it deems pertinent in matters it has under consideration. With respect to a case not yet submitted to the Court, it may act at the request of the Commission.

Article 64. 1. The member states of the Organization may consult the Court regarding the interpretation of this Convention or of other treaties concerning the protection of human rights in the American states. Within their spheres of competence, the organs listed in Chapter X of the Charter of the Organization of American States, as amended by the Protocol of Buenos Aires, may in like manner consult the Court.

2. The Court, at the request of a member state of the Organization, may provide that state with opinions regarding the compatibility of any of its domestic laws with the aforesaid international instruments.

Article 65. To each regular session of the General Assembly of the Organization of American States the Court shall submit, for the Assembly's consideration, a report on its work during the previous year. It shall specify, in particular, the cases in which a state has not complied with its judgments, making any pertinent recommendations.

Section 3. Procedure

Article 66. 1. Reasons shall be given for the judgment of the Court.

2. If the judgment does not represent in whole or in part the unanimous opinion of the judges, any judge shall be entitled to have his dissenting or separate opinion attached to the judgment.

Article 67. The judgment of the Court shall be final and not subject to appeal. In case of disagreement as to the meaning or scope of the judgment, the Court shall interpret it at the request of any of the parties, provided the request is made within ninety days from the date of notification of the judgment.

Article 68. 1. The States Parties to the Convention undertake to comply with the judgment of the Court in any case to which they are parties.

2. That part of a judgment that stipulates compensatory damages may be executed in the country concerned in accordance with domestic procedure governing the execution of judgments against the state.

Article 69. The parties to the case shall be notified of the judgment of the Court and it shall be transmitted to the States Parties to the Convention.

Chapter IX—Common Provisions

Article 70. 1. The judges of the Court and the members of the Commission shall enjoy, from the moment of their election and throughout their term of office, the immunities extended to diplomatic agents in accordance with international law. During the exercise of their official function they shall, in addition, enjoy the diplomatic privileges necessary for the performance of their duties.

2. At no time shall the judges of the Court or the members of the Commission be held liable for any decisions or opinions issued in the exercise of their functions.

Article 71. The position of judge of the Court or member of the Commission is incompatible with any other activity that might affect the independence or impartiality of such judge or member, as determined in the respective statutes.

Article 72. The judges of the Court and the members of the Commission shall receive emoluments and travel allowances in the form and under the conditions set forth in their statutes, with due regard for the importance and independence of their office. Such emoluments and travel allowances shall be determined in the budget of the Organization of American States, which shall also include the expenses of the Court and its Secretariat. To this end, the Court shall draw up its own budget and submit it for approval to the General Assembly through the General Secretariat. The latter may not introduce any changes in it.

Article 73. The General Assembly may, only at the request of the Commission or the Court, as the case may be, determine sanctions to be applied against members of the Commission or judges of the Court when there are justifiable grounds for such action as set forth in the respective statutes. A vote of a two-thirds majority of the member states of the Organization shall be required for a decision in the case of members of the Commission and, in the case of judges of the Court, a two-thirds majority vote of the States Parties to the Convention shall also be required.

Part III
General and Transitory Provisions

Chapter X—Signature, Ratification, Reservations, Amendments, Protocols, and Denunciation

Article 74. 1. This Convention shall be open for signature and ratification by or adherence of any member state of the Organization of American States.

2. Ratification of or adherence to this Convention shall be made by the deposit of an instrument of ratification or adherence with the General Secretariat of the Organization of American States. As soon as eleven states have deposited their instruments of ratification or adherence, the Convention shall enter into force. With respect to any state that ratifies or adheres thereafter, the Convention shall enter into force on the date of the deposit of its instrument of ratification or adherence.

3. The Secretary General shall inform all member states of the Organization of the entry into force of the Convention.

Article 75. This Convention shall be subject to reservations only in conformity with the provisions of the Vienna Convention on the Law of Treaties signed on May 23, 1969.

Article 76. 1. Proposals to amend this Convention may be

submitted to the General Assembly for the action it deems appropriate by any State Party directly, and by the Commission or the Court through the Secretary General.

2. Amendments shall enter into force for the state ratifying them on the date when two-thirds of the States Parties to this Convention have deposited their respective instruments of ratification. With respect to the other States Parties, the amendments shall enter into force on the dates on which they deposit their respective instruments of ratification.

Article 77. 1. In accordance with Article 31, any State Party and the Commission may submit proposed protocols to this Convention for consideration by the States Parties at the General Assembly with a view to gradually including other rights and freedoms within its system of protection.

2. Each protocol shall determine the manner of its entry into force and shall be applied only among the States Parties to it.

Article 78. 1. The States Parties may denounce this Convention at the expiration of a five-year period from the date of its entry into force and by means of notice given one year in advance. Notice of the denunciation shall be addressed to the Secretary General of the Organization, who shall inform the other States Parties.

2. Such a denunciation shall not have the effect of releasing the State Party concerned from the obligations contained in this Convention with respect to any act that may constitute a violation of those obligations and that has been taken by that state prior to the effective date of denunciation.

Chapter XI—Transitory Provisions

Section 1. Inter-American Commission on Human Rights

Article 79. Upon the entry into force of this Convention, the Secretary General shall, in writing, request each member state of the Organization to present, within ninety days, its candidates for membership on the Inter-American Commission on Human Rights. The Secretary General shall prepare a list in alphabetical order of the candidates presented, and transmit it to the member states of the Organization at least thirty days prior to the next session of the General Assembly.

Article 80. The members of the Commission shall be elected by secret ballot of the General Assembly from the list of candidates referred to in Article 79. The candidates who obtain the largest number of votes and an absolute majority of the votes of the representatives of the member states shall be declared elected. Should it become necessary to have several ballots in order to elect all the members of the Commission, the candidates who receive the smallest number of votes shall be eliminated successively, in the manner determined by the General Assembly.

Section 2. Inter-American Court of Human Rights

Article 81. Upon the entry into force of this Convention, the Secretary General shall, in writing, request each State Party to present, within ninety days, its candidates for membership on the Inter-American Court of Human Rights. The Secretary General shall prepare a list in alphabetical order of the candidates presented and transmit it to the States Parties at least thirty days prior to the next session of the General Assembly.

Article 82. The judges of the Court shall be elected from the list of candidates referred to in Article 81, by secret ballot of the States Parties to the Convention in the General Assembly. The candidates who obtain the largest number of votes and an absolute majority of the votes of the representatives of the States Parties shall be declared elected. Should it become necessary to have several ballots in order to elect all the judges of the Court, the candidates who receive the smallest number of votes shall be eliminated successively, in the manner determined by the States Parties.

SEE ALSO *African Charter on Human and Peoples' Rights; American Declaration on the Rights and Duties of Man; European Convention on Human Rights and Protocols I-VIII; European Social Charter and Protocol; Helsinki Accord; Inter-American Charter of Social Guarantees; International Covenant on Civil and Political Rights and Protocols; International Covenant on Economic, Social and Cultural Rights; Universal Declaration of Human Rights.*

AMERICAN CONVENTION ON HUMAN RIGHTS: ADDITIONAL PROTOCOL.

In its annual reports to the OAS GENERAL ASSEMBLY, the INTER-AMERICAN COMMISSION ON HUMAN RIGHTS highlighted, for a number of years, the importance of economic, social, and cultural rights and the need to establish institutional mechanisms to protect such rights effectively. Between 1980 and 1985, the commission—convinced that, as an organization specifically entrusted with the promotion and protection of human rights, it had the obligation to play as active a role in the protection of economic, social, and cultural rights as it was playing with regard to civil and political rights—studied all aspects of the subject.

In 1985, the OAS General Assembly requested the commission (resolution 778 [XV-]/85) to submit to it a draft additional protocol to the American Convention on Human Rights with regard to economic, social, and cultural rights. The assembly also directed the OAS PERMANENT COUNCIL to inform it of the views of member States and of the agencies and organizations interested in the content of the draft additional protocol, with respect to the rights to be protected and the institutional mechanisms that should be established for the appropriate protection of such rights.

In preparing the additional protocol, the commission coordinated its efforts with those of a working group established for that purpose by the Committee on Juridical and Political Affairs of the OAS Permanent Council. It sent its draft to the Permanent Council and submitted it to the OAS General Assembly.

The additional protocol, also known as the Protocol of San Salvador, was approved unanimously by the OAS General Assembly on 17 November 1988. It will enter into force, in accordance with its article 74, "as soon as eleven States have deposited their instruments of ratification or accession." The text is as follows:

Preamble

The States Parties to this Protocol Additional to the American Convention on Human Rights,

Reaffirming their intention to consolidate in this hemisphere, within the framework of democratic institutions, a system of personal liberty and social justice based on respect for the essential rights of man;

Recognizing that the essential rights of man are not derived from one's being a national of a certain State, but are based upon attributes of the human person, for which reason they merit international protection in the form of a convention reinforcing or complementing the protection provided by the domestic law of the American States;

Considering the close relationship that exists between economic, social, and cultural rights and civil and political rights, in that the two categories of rights constitute an indivisible whole based on the recognition of the dignity of the human person for which reason both require permanent protection and promotion if they are to be fully realized, although the violation of one group of rights in favor of the realization of the other group can never be justified;

Recognizing that, in accordance with the Universal Declaration of Human Rights and the American Convention on Human Rights, the ideal of free human beings enjoying freedom from fear and want can only be achieved if conditions are created whereby everyone may enjoy his economic, social and cultural rights as well as his civil and political rights;

Bearing in mind that, although fundamental economic, social and cultural rights have been embodied in earlier international instruments of both world and regional scope, it is essential that those rights be reaffirmed, developed and perfected in order to consolidate in America, on the basis of full respect for the rights of the individual, the democratic representative form of government as well as the right to its peoples to development, self-determination, and the free disposal, in accordance with international law, of their wealth and natural resources; and

Considering that the General Assembly of the Organization has repeatedly expressed its wish to draw up a protocol additional to the American Convention on Human Rights for the purpose of defining the economic, social, and cultural rights to be protected and to establish institutional arrangements for ensuring the appropriate protection of such rights; and

Considering that the American Convention on Human Rights provides that draft protocols additional to that Convention may be submitted for consideration to the States Parties, meeting together on the occasion of the General Assembly of the Organization of American States, for the purpose of gradually incorporating other rights and freedoms into the system for the protection thereof;

Have agreed upon the following Protocol Additional to the American Convention on Human Rights:

Article 1. Obligation to Adopt Measures. The States Parties to this Protocol Additional to the American Convention on Human Rights (Pact of San José, Costa Rica, 1969) undertake to adopt all the necessary measures within the extent of the resources available to them, to achieve the progressive realization of the rights recognized in this Protocol.

Article 2. Obligation of Non-discrimination. 1. The States Parties to this Protocol undertake to guarantee the exercise of the rights set forth herein without discrimination of any kind.

2. The States Parties to this Protocol undertake to invest men and women with equal title to the enjoyment of all the economic, social and cultural rights set forth in this Protocol.

Article 3. Obligation to Enact Domestic Legislation. If the exercise of the rights set forth in this Protocol is not already guaranteed by legislative or other provisions, the States Parties undertake to adopt, in accordance with their constitutional processes and the provisions of this Protocol, such legislative or other measures as may be necessary for making those rights a reality.

Article 4. Inadmissibility of Restrictions. Prohibited if any restriction or diminution of a right recognized or guaranteed in a state's internal legislation or by means of international treaties, on the pretext that the present Protocol does not recognize the right or recognizes it to a lesser degree.

Article 5. Scope of Restrictions and Limitations. The State Parties may only establish restrictions and limitations on the enjoyment and exercise of the rights established in the present Protocol by means of laws promulgated with the purpose of preserving the general welfare in a democratic society, to the extent that they are compatible with these rights, public health and morality.

Article 6. Right to Work. Everyone shall have the right to work, which includes the right of opportunity to lead a decent life by carrying out an activity which one freely chooses or accepts.

Article 7. Just and Satisfactory Conditions of Work. The right to work defined in the foregoing article presupposes that the same is carried out in just and satisfactory conditions, which the State Parties to the Present Protocol undertake to guarantee in their internal legislation:

a. Remuneration which guarantees, at a minimum, to all workers decent living conditions for them and their families and just and equal wages for work of equal value, without distinction. Women must be guaranteed working conditions equal to those of men.

b. Freedom to change employment, opportunities of promotion and mobility, work stability and the corresponding indemnization in the case of unjustified dismissal.

c. Safety and hygiene at work.

d. The prohibition of night work or unhealthy or dangerous working conditions for persons under the age of 18 and, in general, all work which could place in danger the youth's health, safety or morals. As regards minors under the age of 16, the work day will be subordinated to the provisions regarding compulsory education and in no case will it constitute an excused absence from classes or a limitation on benefitting from education received.

e. The limitation on the hours of work, both daily and weekly. The days will be of shorter duration if the work is dangerous or unhealthy.

f. Rest, leisure, reasonable limitation of working hours and paid vacations as well as remuneration for public holidays.

Article 8. Trade Union Rights. 1. The State Parties undertake to ensure the right of everyone to form trade unions and to join the trade union of his choice for the promotion and protection of his economic and social interests. As an extension of that right, the State Parties shall permit trade unions to establish national federations or confederations, or to join those that already exist, as well as to form international trade union organizations and to join that of their choice. The States Parties shall also permit trade unions, federations and confederations to function freely.

2. The exercise of the rights set forth above may be subject only to the restrictions stipulated by the law, provided that they are characteristic of a democratic society and necessary for safeguarding public order and protecting public health or morals and the rights and freedoms of other persons.

Article 9. Right to Strike. 1. The States Parties to the present Protocol recognize the right to strike of trade union organizations.

2. The right to strike recognized in the present Protocol must be exercised in conformity with the laws of the corresponding State.

3. The provision of the present article shall not prevent States from imposing legal restrictions on the right to strike as regards members of the armed forces, the police or other public service agents of the State.

Article 10. Right to Social Security. 1. Everyone shall have the right to social security that protects him against the consequences of unemployment, old age, and disability which, being the result of causes beyond his control, prevent him physically or mentally from earning the means for a decent living.

2. In the case of persons who are employed, the right to social security shall cover at least medical care and an allowance or retirement benefit in the case of occupational accidents or occupational disease and, in the case of women, paid maternity leave before and after childbirth.

Article 11. Right to Health. 1. Everyone shall have the right to health, which is understood to mean the enjoyment of the highest degree of physical, mental and social wellbeing.

2. To that end, the States Parties undertake to recognize health as a public good and in particular to guarantee this right by means of the following:

a. Primary health care, that is, essential health care made available to all individuals and families in the community;

b. To extend the benefits of health services to all individuals subject to the State's jurisdiction;

c. Universal immunization against the principal infectious diseases;

d. The prevention and treatment of endemic diseases;

e. The education of the population concerning the prevention and treatment of health problems;

f. The satisfaction of health needs of the highest risk groups, who because of their poverty are the most vulnerable.

Article 12. Right to a Healthy Enviroment. Everyone shall have the right to live in an environment free of pollution and to have access to basic urban services, especially a safe water supply and sewerage services.

Article 13. Right to Food. Everyone has the right to adequate nutrition which guarantees the possibility of enjoying the highest level of physical, emotional and intellectual development.

Article 14. Right to Education. 1. Everyone has the right to education.

2. The State Parties to the present Protocol agree that, in general, education should be directed towards the full development of the human personality and human dignity, and ought to strengthen respect for human rights, fundamental freedoms and peace. They agree, also, that education ought to equip all persons in the task of achieving a decent existence and enabling one to participate effectively in a democratic society.

3. The States Parties to the present Protocol recognize that, in order to achieve the complete exercise of the right to education:

a. Primary education shall be compulsory and accesible to all without cost;

b. Secondary education in its different forms, including technical and professional secondary education, shall be made generally available and accessible to all by every appropriate means, and in particular, by the progressive introduction of free education;

c. Higher education shall be made equally accessible to all, on the basis of capacity, by every appropriate means, and in particular, by the progressive introduction of free education;

d. Basic education shall be encouraged or intensified as far as possible for those persons who have not received or completed the whole cycle of primary instruction;

e. Programs of special education shall be established for the handicapped, so as to provide special instruction and training for persons with physical disabilities or mental deficiencies.

Article 15. Right to Freedom of Education. 1. The State Parties to this Protocol undertake to respect the liberty of parents and, where applicable, legal guardians to choose for their children schools other than those established by the public authorities, provided they conform to such minimum educational standards as which may be laid down or approved by the State, and to ensure the religious and moral education of their children in conformity with their own convictions.

2. No provision of this Article shall be construed so as to interfere with the freedom of individuals and organizations from establishing and directing educational institutions, subject to the observance of the principles set forth above and to the requirement that the education given in such institutions shall conform to such minimum standards as may be laid down by the State.

Article 16. Rights to the Benefits of Culture. 1. The States Parties to this Protocol recognize the right of everyone:

a. To take part in the cultural and artistic life of the community.

b. To enjoy the benefits of scientific progress and its applications.

2. The steps to be taken by the States Parties to this Protocol to ensure the full exercise of this right shall include those necessary for the conservation, the development and the diffusion of science, culture and art.

3. The States Parties to the present Protocol undertake to respect the freedom indispensable for scientific research and creative activity.

4. The States Parties to this Protocol recognize the benefits to be derived from the encouragement and development of international contacts and cooperation in the scientific and cultural fields.

Article 17. Right to the Founding and the Protection of Families. 1. The family is the natural and fundamental element of society and ought to be protected by the society and the State.

2. Everyone shall have the right to found a family, which he shall exercise in accordance with the provisions of the pertinent domestic legislation.

3. Without prejudice to the provisions of article 17 of the American Convention on Human Rights, the States Parties undertake, pursuant to the present Protocol, to accord special protection to the family group and in particular:

a. To accord special attention and assistance to mothers during a reasonable period before and after childbirth.

b. To guarantee children adequate nutrition both during nursing and while attending school.

c. To adopt special measures for the protection of adolescents in order to guarantee the full development of their physical, intellectual and moral capacities.

d. To undertake special programs of family training so as to help create a stable and positive environment in which children will receive and develop the values of understanding, solidarity, respect and responsibility.

Article 18. Rights of the Child. Every child has the right to the protection which the conditions of childhood requires as regards the family, society and the State. Every child has the right to grow under the protection and responsibility of its parents; except in exceptional circumstances, as defined by the courts, a child of young age ought not to be separated from its mother. Every child has the right to free and compulsory education, at least in its basic phase, and to continue at higher levels of the educational system.

Article 19. Protection of the Aged. Everyone shall have the right to special protection during his old age. To that end, the States Parties undertake to adopt the necessary measures for ensuring the realization of this right, and, in particular:

a. To provide appropriate facilities, such as specialized food and medical attention for persons of an advanced age who lack it and are unable to provide for themselves.

b. To undertake specific employment programs for providing the aged with an opportunity to engage in a productive activity appropriate to their ability and respectful of their vocation or wishes.

c. To promote the formation of social organizations designed to improve the quality of life of the aged.

Article 20. Protection of Disabled Persons. Everyone affected by a reduction in physical or mental capabilities shall have the right to receive special care to enable them to fully develop their personality. To that end, the States Parties undertake to adopt such measures as may be necessary for that purpose, and, in particular:

a. To undertake specific programs for providing disabled persons with the resources and necessary environment for achieving that objective, including employment programs adequate to their possibilities and which they shall be free to accept.

b. To include in urban development guidelines consideration of ways of solving the specific requirements generated by the necessities of this special group.

c. To promote the formation of social organizations in which disabled persons can develop a full life.

Article 21. Means of Protection. 1. The Inter-American Commission on Human Rights will monitor the observance of the economic, social and cultural rights set forth in the present Protocol by means of the preparation of special reports. The Commission's Regulations shall determine the nature of these reports.

2. The Commission shall take into consideration the progressive nature of the observance of the rights subject to protection by this Protocol.

3. The States Parties to the present Protocol undertake to supply the Inter-American Commission on Human Rights, at its request, with information on the measures which they have adopted at their own initiative or at the request of the latter and on the progress achieved as regards the goal of ensuring the observance of the rights recognized in this Protocol.

4. In the exercise of the function set forth in the above paragraphs, the Commission shall be able to count on the advice of experts and to establish the relations it considers appropriate with the organs and agencies of the inter-american and the UN Systems.

5. Without prejudice to the above, in the case of the rights set forth in Articles 8, 9 and 15 of this Protocol, in the case of a violation of these rights directly imputable to a State Party to this Protocol, such a situation shall give rise to the application of the individual petition procedure set forth in Articles 44 to 51 and 61 to 69 of the American Convention on Human Rights and the corresponding involvement of the Commission and where applicable, the Inter-American Court of Human Rights.

Article 22. Signature and Ratification or Accession Entry into Force. 1. This Protocol shall be open for signature and ratification or accession by any State Party to the American Convention on Human Rights.

2. Ratification or accession to this Protocol shall be effected through the deposit of an instrument of ratification or accession with the General Secretariat of the Organization of American States.

3. As soon as seven States have deposited their instruments of ratification or accession, the Protocol shall enter into force.

4. The Secretary General shall inform all the member States of the Organization of the entry into force of the Protocol.

Recommendations

On the basis of the background information and considerations set forth, the Commission requests the General Assembly of the Organization of American States, meeting at its sixteenth regular session, to adopt the following decisions:

1. That it reaffirm the urgent need for governments that have not yet reestablished representative democracy as their system of government to put in place the relevant institutional mechanisms for restoring that system in as short a period of time as possible free, secret and by means of informed elections, since democracy is the best guarantee for the observance of human rights and the basis of solidarity among the States of the Hemisphere.

2. That it recommend to the Member States that they provide all necessary guarantees to non-governmental human rights organizations so that they may continue to contribute to the promotion and defense of human rights and that the Member States respect the freedom and integrity of the leaders of said organizations.

3. That, with respect to the Additional Protocol to the American Convention on Human Rights on economic, social and cultural rights, it transmit the draft prepared by the Inter-American Commission on Human Rights to the Governments of the Member States so that they may make observations or comments on the draft and transmit them to the Permanent Council, which will enable the Council to submit them to the State Parties to the American Convention on Human Rights which will meet on the occasion of the seventeenth regular session of the General Assembly at which time they will be in a position to adopt the new version of the draft Protocol.

4. That it reiterate to the Member State which are not Parties to the American Convention on Human Rights (the 1969 Pact of San José, Costa Rica) that they ratify, or adhere to, said instrument, and in case they have not done so, to

recognize the competence of the Inter-American Commission on Human Rights to receive and examine inter-State communications in accordance with Article 45, paragraph 3 of the Convention as well as to accept the obligatory jurisdiction of the Inter-American Court on Human Rights, in conformity with Article 62, paragraph 2 of said Convention.

AMERICAN CONVENTION ON HUMAN RIGHTS: ADDITIONAL PROTOCOL ON THE ABOLITION OF THE DEATH PENALTY (DRAFT).

The INTER-AMERICAN COMMISSION ON HUMAN RIGHTS, in its 1986–1987 annual report, proposed to the States parties to the AMERICAN CONVENTION ON HUMAN RIGHTS, under the authority given it by article 77 of that convention, the following draft additional protocol to the convention (OAS Doc. OEA/Ser. L/V/II.71 Doc. 9/rev. 1, chap. V [I]):

Article 1. The States Parties to this Protocol shall not impose the death penalty on any person under their jurisdiction. Accordingly, no one may be punished by the death penalty nor executed.

Article 2. 1. Reservations may not be made to this Protocol except for the sole purpose of excluding from application of the Protocol especially severe military offenses that were committed during a foreign war.

2. A State making the reservation authorized by the previous paragraph may, at the time of deposition of its instrument of ratification or adhesion, inform the Secretary General of the Organization of American States as to what military offenses are subject to the death penalty under that country's domestic law.

Article 3. 1. This Protocol shall be open to the signature and to the ratification or adhesion of any State Party to the American Convention on Human Rights.

2. Ratification of this Protocol or adhesion to it shall be made through deposit of an instrument of ratification or adhesion at the General Secretariat of the Organization of American States.

In explanation of its proposal, the Commission included the following statement in the report:

The Inter-American Commission on Human Rights, concerned about the behavior of some States in extending the death penalty or applying it in a generalized manner, has appealed, on previous occasions, to all governments of the Americas to abolish the death penalty, in keeping with the spirit of Article 4 of the American Convention on Human Rights and in line with the universal trend toward abolition of the death penalty.

As is widely known, in order to facilitate adoption by the largest number of states, the American Convention on Human Rights did not abolish the death penalty but only restricted its application. Specifically, Article 4 of the Convention in five of its six paragraphs established various limitations on the imposition of the death penalty. These limitations are as follows: (1) the death penalty may be imposed only for the most serious crimes; (2) it may be imposed only pursuant to a sentence handed down by a court of competent jurisdiction; (3) also it may be imposed only under a law providing for such punishment, enacted prior to the commission of the crime; (4) it may not be re-established in States that have abolished it; (5) in no case shall capital punishment be inflicted for political offenses or related common crimes; (6) it may not be imposed upon persons who, at the time the crime was committed, were under 18 years of age or over 70 years of age; (7) nor may it be applied to pregnant women; and (8) every person condemned to death shall have the right to appeal for amnesty, pardon or commutation of sentence, which may be granted in all cases. Capital punishment shall not be imposed while such an appeal is pending decision by the authority of competent jurisdiction.

Although the Commission understands that in 1969, when the American Convention on Human Rights was adopted, prevailing conditions would have not permitted abolishing the death penalty through a convention, experience in the almost two decades since and the trend in the vast majority of the countries of the Americas to amend their criminal codes or even their constitutional provisions, as has occurred with Haiti and Nicaragua, in order to ban the death penalty, cause the Commission to consider that conditions are now ripe for adopting an instrument to abolish the death penalty.

In recent years, the Commission has observed that the purported purpose of capital punishment—that is, by imposing it, the State helps to save the lives of others by preventing the commission of the crimes for which the death penalty has been established—has not been achieved in practice, and on the contrary, the death penalty often has had a counterproductive effect by generating greater violence. In that regard, the Commission can only share the views set forth in numerous studies according to which it has not yet been shown that capital punishment has any impact on reducing criminality.

Moreover, there are a great many ethical and legal reasons and even reasons of civic harmony, which the Commission shares, requiring the abolition of the death penalty. From the ethical standpoint, one cannot justify defending an absolute value like human life by resorting to a strict application of the talionic principle of "an eye for an eye," which in this case becomes, "a life for a life." The foregoing involves a concept of law and punishment that is purely retributive, that is, one evil must be answered by another of a similar kind. In that sense, the State's right to punish certain criminal behavior cannot be absolute and must surely be limited by those rights of the human person that are inalienable, foremost among them being the right to life.

From the standpoint of criminal policy, the death penalty violates the principle of special prevention by denying the possibility of rehabilitation or reform of the offender, a rationale that constitutes one of the fundamental purposes of punishment.

The irreparable nature of the death penalty must also be kept in mind, that is, it does not admit of judicial errors. However, as unfortunately has occurred in the past, it has in hundreds of cases been shown later that the death penalty was imposed as a result of a judicial error.

It is also necessary to point out, as the Commission has, that the death penalty has been used by totalitarian regimes and military dictators as an instrument to eliminate dissidents or even to hide those really guilty of other crimes.

Finally, the Commission considers that the right to life, as has occurred with the right to humane treatment, should be protected in the most absolute manner possible under international law.

It is now possible to state that, thanks to the fact that the international community has become mindful of how intolerable the practice of torture is under any circumstances, the right not to suffer physical torment has become absolute. Consequently, how could it be accepted that the right to life, which is at the very basis of the other human rights, does not have similar protection? In this regard, the Commission considers that the death penalty is one of the most serious offenses against a human being that can be conceived of, because it terminates the person's very existence.

The above reasons, as well as the repugnance produced by the cruel, inhumane and degrading nature of this punishment, has led most American countries to abolish the death penalty, at least for common crimes. Thus, of the 19 countries that today are parties to the American Convention on Human Rights, only four retain the death penalty. It is also significant that those countries are not parties to the Pact of San José, Costa Rica—that is, they are States that have not shown an interest in undertaking international commitments to respect human rights. With the sole exception of Brazil, which is in the process of completing its internal procedures to be party to that instrument, all of them maintain the death penalty for all types of crimes.

Of the States that are parties to the American Convention on Human Rights, Bolivia, Colombia, Costa Rica, Dominican Republic, Ecuador, Haiti, Honduras, Nicaragua, Panama, Uruguay and Venezuela, have abolished the death penalty for all kinds of crimes. The domestic law of Argentina, El Salvador, Mexico, and Peru does not impose the death penalty for common crimes, and maintains it only for serious military offenses committed under exceptional circumstances, such as in time of war.

This trend to abolish the death penalty can also be seen in other regions. Thus, in April 1983, several States parties to the European Convention for the Protection of Human Rights and Fundamental Liberties—which, like the American Convention, allows the death penalty, under certain restrictions—adopted Protocol 6 to that Convention, abolishing the death penalty. Likewise, the United Nations is now considering, as a result of successive General Assembly resolutions, an Optional Protocol to the International Covenant on Civil and Political Rights, which declares the death penalty to be abolished.

All of these antecedents confirm to the Commission the desirability of proposing to the States parties to the American Convention on Human Rights that they take another step forward with respect to current Article 4 of that Convention, so that capital punishment will be banned through a new instrument.

The American Convention provides two possible ways to amend its provisions. Under Article 76, any State party to the Convention, the Commission or the Court can, through the OAS Secretary General, submit to the General Assembly proposed amendments to the Convention. Also, Article 77 empowers any State party and the Commission to submit "proposed protocols to this Convention for consideration by the States Parties at the General Assembly with a view to gradually including other rights and freedoms within its system of protection."

Which would be best—amending Article 4 or including the Additional Protocol to the Convention—should be carefully studied.

In the Commission's view, while the amendment to the current provision governing the right to life could be the best way to take a categorical stand against the death penalty, and, from the legal standpoint, regulate one subject under a single instrument, it might have the disadvantage that those States that are now parties to the Pact of San José, Costa Rica, or that in the future might become parties to it, and that still maintain the death penalty, would have to make an express reservation to that provision, if it is authorized, or if they do not accept the possibility of making a reservation, they would be prevented from participating in the Convention, which could cause even more difficulties from the standpoint of protecting human rights. In these circumstances, it would appear preferable to have on this topic two coexisting rules established by two successive treaties, a possibility allowed by the American Convention on Human Rights and authorized by general international law, as shown in Article 30 of the 1969 Vienna Convention on the Law of Treaties.

Thus the present Article 4 will remain in effect for countries that do not become parties to the additional protocol or that ratify it in the future or that are parties to the American Convention on Human Rights but not to the Additional Protocol on the Abolition of the Death Penalty.

Since the current Article 4 of the Convention coexists with the Additional Protocol, that will make it possible for the Convention to provide that reservations may not be made to the Protocol or that they will have a very limited and specific scope.

Another important problem to consider is whether the obligation the States parties to the Additional Protocol will acquire not to impose the death penalty will be absolute, that is, that under no circumstances may the death penalty be imposed, regardless of the offense committed, or, whether some exceptions might be accepted, particularly those that would make it possible to impose the death penalty for serious military crimes committed under exceptional circumstances, such as during a foreign war, a situation that the laws of a large number of States that are now parties to the Pact of San Jose, Costa Rica, now provide for.

If what is desired is to make, as the Commission seeks, significant progress regarding the present Article 4 of the American Convention on Human Rights, and also, to enable the new protocol to have the largest number of ratifications or adhesions possible, it would appear desirable that, as established in Protocol 6 of the European Convention on Human Rights and Basic Freedoms and provided for in the draft of the United Nations Special Rapporteur on abolition of the death penalty, the States might be authorized to impose the death penalty for specified military offenses committed in wartime.

Because of the exceptional character of such authorization, any statement made by a country on becoming party to the Protocol must expressly specify how it would be an express reservation to the general rule abolishing the death penalty.

Based on the above considerations, the Commission, under the authority given it by Article 77 of the American Convention on Human Rights, proposes to the States parties to the American Convention on Human Rights meeting on the occasion of the OAS General Assembly, the. . . . draft additional protocol to the Convention [reproduced above].

SEE ALSO *Capital Punishment; Capital Punishment: World Survey; Death Penalty: Applications to Persons under the Age of*

AMERICAN DECLARATION OF THE RIGHTS AND DUTIES OF MAN (1948). The declaration, drafted by the Inter-American Juridical Committee and completed and adopted by the Ninth International Conference of American States at Bogota, Colombia, on 2 May 1948, is unique in that it first recognized that States do not create or concede rights but only recognize rights that have always existed and that are inherent in the very nature of the individual human being. Adoption of the American Declaration preceded by only a few months the adoption of the UNIVERSAL DECLARATION OF HUMAN RIGHTS, based on the same principle. The text of the Declaration of the Rights and Duties of Man (OAS Doc. OEA/Ser. L/V/II.65, Doc. 6, pp. 19–25) is as follows:

WHEREAS:

The American peoples have acknowledged the dignity of the individual, and their national constitutions recognize that juridical and political institutions, which regulate life in human society, have as their principal aim the protection of the essential rights of man and the creation of circumstances that will permit him to achieve spiritual and material progress and attain happiness;

The American States have on repeated occasions recognized that the essential rights of man are not derived from the fact that he is a national of a certain state, but are based upon attributes of his human personality;

The international protection of the rights of man should be the principal guide of an evolving American law;

The affirmation of essential human rights by the American States together with the guarantees given by the internal regimes of the states establish the initial system of protection considered by the American States as being suited to the present social and juridical conditions, not without a recognition on their part that they should increasingly strengthen that system in the international field as conditions become more favorable,

The Ninth International Conference of American States

AGREES

To adopt the following

Preamble

All men are born free and equal, in dignity and in rights, and, being endowed by nature with reason and conscience, they should conduct themselves as brothers one to another.

The fulfillment of duty by each individual is a prerequisite to the rights of all. Rights and duties are interrelated in every social and political activity of man. While rights exalt individual liberty, duties express the dignity of that liberty.

Duties of a juridical nature presuppose others of a moral nature which support them in principle and constitute their basis.

Inasmuch as spiritual development is the supreme end of human existence and the highest expression thereof, it is the duty of man to serve that end with all his strength and resources.

Since culture is the highest social and historical expression of that spiritual development, it is the duty of man to preserve, practice and foster culture by every means within his power.

And, since moral conduct constitutes the noblest flowering of culture, it is the duty of every man always to hold it in high respect.

Chapter One: Rights

Article 1. Right to Life, Liberty and Personal Security. Every human being has the right to life, liberty and the security of his person.

Article 2. Right to Equality Before the Law. All persons are equal before the law and have the rights and duties established in this Declaration, without distinction as to race, sex, language, creed or any other factor.

Article 3. Right to Religious Freedom and Worship. Every person has the right freely to profess a religious faith, and to manifest and practice it both in public and in private.

Article 4. Right to Freedom of Investigation, Opinion, Expression and Dissemination. Every person has the right to freedom of investigation, of opinion, and of the expression and dissemination of ideas, by any medium whatsoever.

Article 5. Right to Protection of Honor, Personal Reputation and Private and Family Life. Every person has the right to the protection of the law and against abusive attacks upon his honor, his reputation, and his private and family life.

Article 6. Rights to a Family and to Protection thereof. Every person has the the right to establish a family, the basic element of society, and to receive protection therefor.

Article 7. Right to Protection for Mothers and Children. All women, during pregnancy and the nursing period, and all children have the right to special protection, care and aid.

Article 8. Right to Residence and Movement. Every person has the right to fix his residence within the territory of the state of which he is a national, to move about freely within such territory, and not to leave it except by his own will.

Article 9. Right to Inviolability of Home. Every person has the right to the inviolability of his home.

Article 10. Right to the Inviolability and Transmission of Correspondence. Every person has the right to the inviolability and transmission of his correspondence.

Article 11. Right to the Preservation of Health and to Wellbeing. Every person has the right to the preservation of his health through sanitary and social measures relating to food, clothing, housing and medical care, to the extent permitted by public and community resources.

Article 12. Right to Education. Every person has the right to an education, which should be based on the principles of liberty, morality and human solidarity.

Likewise every person has the right to an education that will prepare him to attain a decent life, to raise his standard of living, and to be a useful member of society.

The right to an education includes the right to equality of opportunity in every case, in accordance with natural talents, merit and the desire to utilize the resources that the state or the community is in a position to provide.

Every person has the right to receive, free, at least a primary education.

Article 13. Right to the Benefits of Culture. Every person has the right to take part in the cultural life of the community, to enjoy the arts, and to participate in the benefits that result from intellectual progress, especially scientific discoveries.

He likewise has the right to the protection of his moral and material interests as regards his inventions or any literary, scientific or artistic works of which he is the author.

Article 14. Right to Work and to Fair Remuneration. Every person has the right to work, under proper conditions, and to follow his vocation freely, in so far as existing conditions of employment permit.

Every person who works has the right to receive such remuneration as will, in proportion to his capacity and skill, assure him a standard of living suitable for himself and for his family.

Article 15. Right to Leisure Time and to the Use thereof. Every person has the right to leisure time, to wholesome recreation, and to the opportunity for advantageous use of his free time to his spiritual, cultural and physical benefit.

Article 16. Right to Social Security. Every person has the right to social security which will protect him from the consequences of unemployment, old age, and disabilities arising from causes beyond his control that make it physically or mentally impossible for him to earn a living.

Article 17. Right to Recognition of Juridical Personality and of Civil Rights. Every person has the right to be recognized everywhere as a person having rights and obligations, and to enjoy the basic civil rights.

Article 18. Right to a Fair Trial. Every person may resort to the courts to ensure respect for his legal rights. There should likewise be available to him a simple, brief procedure whereby the courts will protect him from acts of authority that, to his prejudice, violate any fundamental constitutional rights.

Article 19. Right to Nationality. Every person has the right to the nationality to which he is entitled by law and to change it, if he so wishes, for the nationality of any other country that is willing to grant it to him.

Article 20. Right to Vote and to Participate in Government. Every person having legal capacity is entitled to participate in the government of his country, directly or through his representatives, and to take part in popular elections, which shall be by secret ballot, and shall be honest, periodic and free.

Article 21. Right of Assembly. Every person has the right to assemble peaceably with others in a formal public meeting or an informal gathering, in connection with matters of common interest of any nature.

Article 22. Right of Association. Every person has the right to associate with others to promote, exercise and protect his legitimate interests of a political, economic, religious, social, cultural, professional, labor union or other nature.

Article 23. Right to Property. Every person has a right to own such private property as meets the essential needs of decent living and helps to maintain the dignity of the individual and of the home.

Article 24. Right of Petition. Every person has the right to submit respectful petitions to any competent authority, for reasons of either general or private interest, and the right to obtain a prompt decision thereon.

Article 25. Right of Protection from Arbitrary Arrest. No person may be deprived of his liberty except in the cases and according to the procedures established by pre-existing law.

No person may be deprived of liberty for nonfulfillment of obligations of a purely civil character.

Every individual who has been deprived of his liberty has the right to have the legality of his detention ascertained without delay by a court, and the right to be tried without due delay or, otherwise, to be released. He also has the right to humane treatment during the time he is in custody.

Article 26. Right to Due Process of Law. Every accused person is presumed to be innocent until proved guilty.

Every person accused of an offense has the right to be given an impartial and public hearing, and to be tried by courts previously established in accordance with pre- existing laws, and not to receive cruel, infamous or unusual punishment.

Article 27. Right of Asylum. Every person has the right, in case of pursuit not resulting from ordinary crimes, to seek and receive asylum in foreign territory, in accordance with the laws of each country and with international agreements.

Article 28. Scope of the Rights of Man. The rights of man are limited by the rights of others, by the security of all, and by the just demands of the general welfare and the advancement of democracy.

Chapter Two: Duties

Article 29. Duties to Society. It is the duty of the individual so to conduct himself in relation to others that each and every one man fully form and develop his personality.

Article 30. Duties toward Children and Parents. It is the duty of every person to aid, support, educate and protect his minor children, and it is the duty of children to honor their parents always and to aid, support and protect them when they need it.

Article 31. Duty to Receive Instructions. It is the duty of every person to acquire at least an elementary education.

Article 32. Duty to Vote. It is the duty of every person to vote in the popular elections of the country of which he is a national, when he is legally capable of doing so.

Article 33. Duty to Obey the Law. It is the duty of every person to obey the law and other legitimate commands of the authorities of his country and those of the country in which he may be.

Article 34. Duty to Serve the Community and the Nation. It is the duty of every able-bodied person to render whatever civil and military service his country may require for its defense and preservation, and, in case of public disaster, to render such services as may be in his power.

It is likewise his duty to hold any public office to which he may be elected by popular vote in the state of which he is a national.

Article 35. Duties with Respect to Social Security and Welfare. It is the duty of every person to cooperate with the state and the community with respect to social security and welfare, in accordance with his ability and with existing circumstances.

Article 36. Duty to Pay Taxes. It is the duty of every person to pay the taxes established by law for the support of public services.

Article 37. Duty to Work. It is the duty of every person to work, as far as his capacity and possibilities permit, in order to obtain the means of livelihood or to benefit his community.

Article 38. Duty to Refrain from Political Activities in a Foreign Country. It is the duty of every person to refrain from taking part in political activities that, according to law, are reserved exclusively to the citizens of the state in which he is an alien.

SEE ALSO *African Charter on Human and Peoples' Rights; American Convention on Human Rights and protocol; European Convention on Human Rights and protocols.*

AMERICAS WATCH. A human rights organization, established in 1981 to monitor human rights situations in the countries of South America, Central America, and the Caribbean, Americas Watch was founded, among other purposes, to counteract the approach to human rights espoused by some officials of the U.S. Reagan Administration (1980–1988), who allegedly advocated a "selective" approach in which human rights abuses by "hostile totalitarian" governments were treated differently from those committed by "friendly authoritarian" governments. Americas Watch opposes abuses of human rights regardless of the character or geopolitical alignment of the government committing the abuses. Americas Watch is affiliated with HUMAN RIGHTS WATCH.

Americas Watch has published a number of reports on human rights situations, among them: *Truth and Partial Justice in Argentina* (1987); *Human Rights Concerns in Chile* (1987); *The "MAS Case" in Colombia: Taking on the Death Squads* (1983); *Twenty Years and Forty Days: Life in a Cuban Prison* (1986); *Human Rights in El Salvador on the Eve of the Elections 1988* (1988); *Haiti Terror and the 1987 Elections* (1987); and *The Sumus in Nicaragua and Honduras: An Endangered People* (1987).

Americas Watch. Address: 522 K St., NW, No. 910, Washington, D.C. 20005–1202. Telephone: (202) 371-6592. Fax: (202) 371-0124. Executive Director: Juan Mendez.

AMNESTY INTERNATIONAL. An international nongovernmental organization in consultative status with the UN Economic and Social Council (Category II), and with UNESCO, OAS, OAU, and the Council of Europe, AI brought together 3,744 affiliated groups in 44 countries, and over 700,000 individual members in more than 150 countries as of 1988.

Amnesty International began in 1961 with a newspaper article by British lawyer Peter Benenson who urged people everywhere to begin working impartially and peacefully for the release of prisoners of conscience. Within months, thousands of people from various countries sent in offers of practical help—many were prepared to help collect information on cases, publicize them, and approach governments—and what started as a brief publicity effort has become one of the most influential and highly respected human rights organizations in the world.

As its primary mandate, AI seeks to release prisoners of conscience—those detained for their beliefs, color, sex, ethnic origin, language, or religion, who have not used or advocated violence. It works for fair and prompt trials for political prisoners and opposes the death penalty and torture of prisoners. Through its network of members and supporters, AI takes up individual cases, mobilizes public opinion, and seeks improved international standards for treatment of prisoners.

In 1977, for its contributions "to securing the ground for freedom, for justice and thereby for peace in the world," Amnesty International received the Nobel Peace Prize. On the occasion of the 30th anniversary of the Universal Declaration of Human Rights (1978), AI was awarded the UN Human Rights Prize.

To publicize its concerns and activities, Amnesty International supports a large-scale publication program. The most influential and widely disseminated of its many reports is the annually published *Amnesty International Report,* which provides a country-by-country survey of AI's work. The *Amnesty International Newsletter,* a bulletin issued monthly, updates reports of fact-finding missions, details of the arrest and release of political prisoners, and reliable reports of torture and executions. In addition, AI publishes *Amnesty International* (on microfiche), a collection of published and unpublished research materials, updated annually; *Voices for Freedom,* an anthology that relates the stories of AI prisoners of conscience; *Torture in the Eighties; Against Torture; Political Killings by Governments;* and numerous leaflets, booklets, individual accounts, and briefings on human rights situations in over 40 countries.

Amnesty International. Address: International Secretariat, 1 Easton Street, London WC1X 8DJ, UK. Telephone: (01) 833-1771. Cable: Amnesty London WC1. Fax: (01) 833-5100. Telex: 28502 Amnesty G. Secretary General: Ian Martin.

AMNESTY LAWS. At its 1983 session, the UN SUB-COMMISSION ON PREVENTION OF DISCRIMINATION AND PROTECTION OF MINORITIES approved (resolution 1983/34) the preparation of a study of amnesty laws and their role in the safeguard and promotion of human rights and appointed one of its members, Mr. Louis Joinet (France) as special rapporteur for the study.

The *Study on Amnesty Laws and their Role in the Safeguard and Promotion of Human Rights* (UN Doc. E/CN.4/Sub.2/1985/16) was presented to the sub-commission at its 1985 session. In the study, the special rapporteur reviewed the principal elements of amnesty laws, taking into account the specific characteristics of various legal systems, and explained the importance that the promulgation of such laws could have for the safeguard and promotion of human rights and fundamental freedoms.

In particular, the special rapporteur analyzed in some detail (para. 22–46) the various purposes of amnesty in the modern world, as follows:

1. Amnesty for Ordinary Offences

Amnesties covering ordinary offences must be clearly distinguished in their purposes from amnesties covering political offences.

In the field of human rights, amnesty for ordinary offences is an expression of the relatively broad power of civil society to grant every citizen the right of oblivion, if only to facilitate his reintegration into society.

Moreover, the constantly renewed hope of a future amnesty is a substantial contribution to the reduction of tension in prisons, especially when amnesty laws are promulgated at regular intervals.

Subsidiarily the authorities sometimes see in amnesty laws a means of dealing with the overcrowding of prisons, a situation which may prejudice the human rights of prisoners. The preambles of some amnesty laws explicitly refer to this consideration (e.g., Portugal, Decree Law No. 259/74 of 15 June 1974, providing for an amnesty for ordinary offences. See also the amnesty recently granted in the United Kingdom to reduce prison overcrowding).

In some cases, the purpose of an amnesty is strictly humanitarian. In Zaire, the act of 17 November 1981 covers disabled persons. In Syria, Act No. 26 of 12 March 1978 covers incurable or chronically ill prisoners. In the Eastern European countries, such humanitarian measures appear to be traditional, particularly in respect of children, women, the aged and the sick. In the USSR (Decrees of 19 October 1979 and 14 October 1981), in Bulgaria (1979) and in Hungary (Acts of 29 March 1975), measures of this kind have been adopted—in particular, to mark the International Year of the Child—for the benefit of minors, pregnant women and mothers of very young children.

2. Amnesty for Political Offences

As the aim of the authorities is directly linked to the current political situation, every amnesty can be described as being a "variable geometry measure." An analysis of the documents provided to the Rapporteur, shows that the goals most frequently sought are:

(a) *Amnesty and the Control of Tensions.* This is the role assigned to traditional amnesties granted at regular intervals to mark anniversaries, national holidays or elections. They are based largely on custom and are repetitive in nature, and their effectiveness lies in their regularity.

By the same token, as pointed out by the Inter American Commission on Human Rights (IACHR), the use of amnesty laws as a method of alleviating the consequences of emergency measures following the lifting of a state of emergency serves the same purpose. This point was highlighted in the Commission's report on Nicaragua (1981). (Doc. OEA/Ser. L/7/II/53, doc. 25, recommendations 3–5.

(b) *Amnesty and Transition to Democracy.* During the transition from an authoritarian régime to democracy, the scope of the amnesty is the tangible sign of the extent of the desire to open up the political process.

As the deadline for the establishment of democracy approaches, authoritarian régimes are tempted to grant themselves amnesty in order to escape the future rigours of democratic legislation. What is sought is not so much reconciliation as impunity. By promulgating an amnesty law known as the "pacification law" on 25 September 1983, the Argentine military junta attempted to obviate any possibility of criminal or civil proceedings being constituted against those responsible for serious violations of human rights committed during operations designed to restore public order. This law was based directly on Chilean Decree-Law No. 2191 of 18 April 1978, which benefited principally "those responsible for assassinations, torture and other offences committed during the administration of the Junta, rather than to grant a genuine amnesty to political opponents." (UN Doc. A/33/331, para. 273 and Annex XXVIII).

Like any amnesty granted unilaterally, the *"de facto"* Argentine law merely caused feelings to run higher. Consequently, one of the first acts of the new democratic régime was to repeal it and subsequently to introduce amendments to the criminal procedure enabling numerous persons detained on political grounds to be released. One example of a law which played a major role in the restoration and consolidation of democracy was the Uruguayan amnesty law of 8 March 1985. The reasons for this were both political and legal. Politically, it had been preceded by a large-scale propaganda campaign, even before the initiation of the democratic process. That campaign had facilitated the unification of the opposition—it is difficult to oppose a demand for a genuine amnesty—and enabled it to be used as a test of the political desire for openness. This was, so to speak, a "hard won" amnesty, which was ratified, after a broad exchange of views, by the newly elected parliament in a vote reflecting the diversity of opinions. A consensus, the prerequisite for the desired reconciliation, was thus achieved. Juridically, the amnesty enabled all political prisoners to be released, without granting impunity to those guilty of serious violations of human rights.

(c) *Amnesty and the Neutralization of Opposition Groups.* Here, the purpose of amnesty is to seek social tranquility less by consensus than by a reduction of tensions, and thus of the opposition's scope for action by forcing it to adopt a passive role. The aim is normalization rather than reconciliation through both persuasion and dissuasion.

Such was the aim of the Polish amnesty law of 20 September 1984, enacted after the lifting of martial law, whose effects it was designed to alleviate. The goal of reducing tensions was achieved given the large number of individuals benefiting from the amnesty. (According to the report submitted to Parliament by the Minister for Justice on 20 September 1984, 630 prisoners guilty of non-criminal offences against the State and public order were released, out of a total of 652 detainees. Proceedings against persons at liberty were discontinued in 1916 cases, of which 347 concerned social conflicts. Two hundred and twenty-five persons against whom action had not been taken presented themselves to the authorities to acknowledge their "anti-government acts" so as to benefit from the amnesty). From this standpoint, it was an excellent law, subsequently amended by two provisions which illustrate the exhortative approach involving the alternate use of persuasion and dissuasion. Persuasion: in order to benefit from the amnesty, offenders who have not been identified or against whom proceedings have not yet been taken, are encouraged under article 2 to present themselves within three months to the authorities to sign an undertaking to discontinue their activities and to disclose the nature, place and date of the reprehensible acts. Article 7 provides that, in the event of recidivism, any amnestied person forfeits entitlement to benefit from that measure. The sentence must be served or the proceedings re-opened. From this standpoint, it is not so much a law of amnesty as a measure employing the device of suspension.

In some cases, persuasion involves the reduction of sentences. In Syria, Act No. 49 of 17 July 1980 adopts this exhortative method in respect of a religious opposition group. As members of the group are liable to the death penalty the law provides that any convicted member who dissociates himself from the group in writing shall have his sentence commuted to forced labour or life imprisonment, with the possibility of a maximum reduction of five years. Other penalties may be reduced by from one to three years.

(d) Amnesty, Guerrillas and Dissociation. Clemency is used in anti-guerrilla campaigns to encourage combatants to leave their organizations.

Recent Guatemalan legislation provides a clear illustration of this method. Impunity is granted to guerrillas who give themselves up to the authorities, lay down their arms and sign a sworn undertaking to take no further part in guerrilla activities. The initial law of 27 March 1982, under which guerrillas were allowed 30 days "repentance period", has been extended by an impressive number of decree-laws with progressively longer time-limits—27 April 1983 (30 days), 11 August 1983 (90 days), 17 November 1983 (60 days), 17 January 1984 (60 days), 16 March 1984 (90 days), 15 June 1984 (90 days), 10 September 1984 (180 days) and 11 March 1985 (300 days).

(e) Amnesty, Guerrillas and Peace Strategies. In the case of international conflicts, the question of amnesty, when it arises, is in theory dealt with by peace agreements.

On the other hand, in the case of non-international armed conflicts governed by common article 3 of the 1949 Geneva Conventions and by the Additional Protocol II, peace agreements, which are by nature intergovernmental, are not applicable. The promulgation of an amnesty law designed to facilitate or confirm the cessation of the state of belligerence or rebellion, can to some extent play the role of an armistice.

The law may even be negotiated through neutral persons or institutions, or by means of any other mediation or good offices procedure, without the laying down of arms being a prerequisite, and with the promulgation of the amnesty law confirming the cessation of hostilities or the beginning of a truce. This is true of the talks currently being held in El Salvador between the Government and FDR-FMLN, with the help of the good offices of the Catholic Church. The first of the two proposals presented by the Government involves "a general and unconditional amnesty for all those who have participated directly or indirectly in offences related to the situation of political violence".

In the course of negotiations to end the Biafran war, item 11 of the negotiation plan provided for an amnesty of the same kind for participants in the rebellion. This law was finally promulgated on 14 January 1970.

Throughout the negotiations which preceded the Camp David accords, the Egyptian representatives continually urged upon the American and Israeli delegates the

"adoption of a new policy which could create a climate of confidence in the occupied territories". To this end, on 18 October 1978, the Minister for Foreign Affairs of Egypt sent a memorandum to the United States Secretary of State proposing, *inter alia,* "granting an amnesty to Palestinian political prisoners."

Colombian law No. 35 of 19 November 1982 "decreeing an amnesty and enacting other provisions for the restoration and preservation of peace" is a particularly good example of such measures. Firstly, the law was the mainspring of the "peace strategy" which was to culminate, initially, in the current truce. Secondly, taking into account the deep-rooted causes of the conflict, particularly the poverty of the most underprivileged segments, article 8 of the law provides that "the Government shall be authorized to make the necessary budgetary appropriations and transfers and to contract the domestic and external loans required to organize and carry out programmes of rehabilitation, land distribution, rural housing, credit, education, health and job creation for those who, under the amnesty granted by this act, become reintegrated in peaceful life under the protection of the institutions, together with all inhabitants of regions affected by the armed conflict."

It will be recalled that, in its resolution 1984/16, the Sub-Commission enthusiastically encouraged this initiative, considering that it constituted a valuable precedent "since it progressively transforms a process of conflict into a momentum for peace, creating conditions for national reconciliation, inasmuch as it takes into account not only the facts but also the economic and social causes of the situation." (UN Doc. E/CN.4/Sub.2/1984/43, p. 90.)

(f) Amnesty and Return of Exiles. "Return of exiles" and "amnesty" are closely linked. A comparative study of the 19 pieces of legislation intended specifically to encourage return which were communicated to the Rapporteur reveals the following characteristics:

The amnesty frequently becomes void if there is no actual return (or submission of applications) within a period determined by the law, and varying from one month (Zaire) to two years (Romania);

Either a limitative list of the beneficiaries is set forth in the act, or the text sets out a general measure (Ethiopia, with regard to the return of refugees from Djibouti), and, in some cases, lists the persons excluded from the scope of the amnesty (Chad). Perpetrators of war crimes are generally excluded (Hungary and Yugoslavia);

In some cases, exiles must confirm in writing that they wish to benefit from the amnesty (Hungary, Lesotho and Somalia);

Occasionally, provision is made for a monitoring authority (Chad and Somalia) or for a guaranteed appeal procedure (Yugoslavia).

In many cases, efforts to implement such legislation come up against three obstacles:

The obligation to return by, for example, imposing a time-limit, appears inconsistent with article 13 of the Universal Declaration of Human Rights and with article 12 of the International Covenant on Civil and Political Rights which guarantee the right of freedom of movement of individuals. The amnesty should be limited to restoring to the exile his full right to freedom of movement, without obliging him to exercise it;

The amnesty should lay down strict guarantees in order to ensure the safety of those benefiting from it. The effectiveness of such legislation is inversely proportional to the scope of the guarantees afforded. In the absence of such guarantees, the only effect of such legislation is to lend credence to the idea in world public opinion that a process of liberalization is in progress. In the case of Paraguay, for example, the authorization to return is based on a simple public statement by the authorities, and is not covered by the minimum guarantee afforded by the promulgation of a law. This omission, in addition to the continued state of siege, has deterred most of the very large number of exiles from returning;

The exercise of the right to return creates major reception and integration problems. Some laws contain provisions on that question. In Ghana, the amnesty law of 6 May 1962 provides for facilities for return and for reintegration procedures. The Uruguayan law referred to above contains a provision (article 24) setting up a national repatriation commission to assist refugees.

The conclusions of the special rapporteur, as set out in the final paragraphs (82–84) of the study, were as follows:

Amnesty deals only with the effects and not with the causes of national dissension, especially when article 21 of the Universal Declaration of Human Rights, which spells out the foundations of a democratic régime, is not respected and a state of emergency is instituted.

The same is true when serious and manifest violations of the most rudimentary cultural, social or economic rights are at the root of civil conflicts or dissension.

In such situations, the amnesty process can only be effective if it is coupled with social, economic or political measures permitting action to deal with the causes, viz.:

(a) In the short term, the repeal of emergency laws as a corollary of the amnesty: since like causes produce like effects, the release of political prisoners may come to nothing if the emergency laws which permitted massive arrests in violation of human rights subsist;

(b) In the medium term, the holding of elections in accordance with the stipulations of article 21 of the Universal Declaration of Human Rights;

(c) In the long term the implementation of economic and social measures attacking the root causes of national dissension.

After examining the study at its 1985 session, the sub-commission expressed its appreciation to the special rapporteur and recommended that the study should be published and disseminated as widely as possible, in all the official languages of the United Nations. The Commission on Human Rights and the Economic and Social Council approved this recommendation (Commission resolution 1986/51 and Council resolution 1986/38, respectively).

ANDEAN COMMISSION OF JURISTS.

An international non-governmental organization in consultative status with the UN Economic and Social Council (Category II), the commission has individual members in six South American countries.

Founded in 1980 in Bogota, Colombia, the commission promotes, defends, and publicizes the principles that constitute the rule of law and works for the protection of human rights in the Andean sub-region.

Andean Commission of Jurists. Address: Los Sauces 285, San Isidro, Lima 27, Peru. Telephone: (51-14) 407-79-07. Executive Secretary: Dr. Diego Garcia-Sayan.

Yearbook of International Organizations 1989/90 (K.G. Saur)

ANDORRA.

The Principality of Andorra is a country in western Europe and is not a member of the United Nations. It is situated in the eastern Pyrenees, on the border between France and Spain. One of the smallest countries in the world, it occupies a mountainous territory of only 185 square miles. Its total population is estimated at 45,000, scattered in seven villages. Ethnic groups include Catalan, Spanish, French, and Portuguese. Languages commonly used include Catalan (official), Spanish, and French. Literacy is estimated at 100%.

Andorra came into existence in 1278 when the French Count of Foix and the Spanish Bishop of Seo de Urgel agreed to recognize each other as co-princes of the Andorran valleys. Under this agreement, sovereignty is now exercised jointly by the president of the French Republic and the bishop of Urgel, who are charged with the conduct of foreign affairs, defense, and the judicial system. Every second year, the valleys pay the sum of 960 francs to France and 460 pesetas to the bishop.

The government (1990) took the form of a co-principality, ruled under the jurisdiction of the co-princes and their representatives by an Executive Council of 28 members, four from each of the seven parishes, elected for terms of four years. Since 1970, women have had equal suffrage with men. The council elects a *syndic* and a *sub-syndic* (managers) to implement its decisions.

The judicial system is handled jointly by the co-princes, who appoint two civil judges and alternately appoint an appeals judge. There are two supreme courts, the Perpignan Superior Court at Perpignan, France, and the Episcopal Superior Court of Seo de Urgel, Spain. Criminal law is administered by the *Tribunal de Corts,* consisting of two designated representatives of the co-princes and the judge of appeals.

There are no political parties in Andorra, and candidates for election run as independents.

ANGOLA.

The People's Republic of Angola is a country in middle Africa, on the Atlantic Ocean. It has borders with Congo, Namibia, Zaire, and Zambia. It achieved independence from Portugal in 1975 and became a member of the United Nations in 1976. Its population is estimated by the UN (1990) to be 10,002,000. Ethnic groups include the Ovimbundu (37%), Kimbundu (25%), Bakongo (13%), Chokwe and Lunda (8%), Ganguela (8%), and others (9%). Languages in common use include Bantu, Portuguese (official), and a number of African vernaculars. Religions practiced include Christianity (Roman Catholic, 70%; Protestant denominations, 20%) and Animism (10%). Angola is a secular State; its constitution calls for complete separation of religion and State and respect for all religious beliefs. Literacy is estimated at 25%.

The government (1990) took the form of a republic. However, elections called for by the constitution have not taken place and the officially recognized political party, the Popular Movement for the Liberation of Angola–Labor Party, makes most decisions concerning national policy. The head of that party is president of the country. After independence, certain portions of Angola, in the east and south, were controlled by the National Movement for the Total Independence of Angola, which sought to replace the existing government.

When Angola was granted independence by Portugal in 1974, it was understood that a constituent assembly would be elected immediately and that the difference between the three major political groups would be settled amicably. But after a brief period of conflict, the Popular Movement for the Liberation of Angola–Labor Party (MPLA) overrode its rivals, the National Front for the Liberation of Angola and the National Union for the Total Independence of Angola (UNITA), and an MPLA government was recognized by the Organization of African States. The struggle for political power did not end, however; and, late in 1987, some areas of Angola were not in the control of the government.

A one-party State ruled by the MPLA, Angola's political power is concentrated in the hands of President Jose Eduardo dos Santos, who is head of government and of the party. He is assisted by an 11-member Political Bureau, a 65-member Central Committee, and a Council of Ministers. There is a People's Assembly which meets annually, but policy decisions are normally made by the party. The constitution sets out the rights and duties of the citizen and provides for free elections and an independent judiciary. However in practice, opposition views and political parties are not tolerated, and all branches of the government tend to follow guidelines established by the party.

The National Union for the Total Independence of Angola (UNITA), led by Jonas Savimbi, established itself in the southeastern corner of Angola and, with assistance from the United States of America, steadily increased the area of its influence. However, its activities were confined to low-level guerrilla operations in the central highlands and eastern areas of the country. The National Front for the Liberation of Angola (FNLA) was less effective and its leader, Holden Roberto, left the country.

On 22 December 1988, after months of negotiation with the assistance of American mediators, two agreements were signed at UN headquarters in New York, the first a tri-partite agreement between Angola, Cuba, and South Africa providing for the independence of Namibia and the second an agreement between Angola and Cuba providing for the phased withdrawal of about 50,000 Cuban troops from Angola. The Cuban pullout was scheduled to begin on 1 April 1989 and to be completed by 1 July 1991. Earlier, towards the end of August 1988, South Africa had pulled its troops out of Angola after a 13-month offensive that had reached more than 180 miles into the country.

Angola's economic rehabilitation has since been a matter of concern for the international community. On 15 December 1989, the UN General Assembly, noting that the country's economy had been adversely affected by the acts of aggression and destabilization perpetrated by South Africa and expressing deep concern about the human suffering and the destruction of property which had resulted from those acts, expressed its solidarity with and support for the efforts of Angola to lessen those adverse effects and to cope with the economic and social problems, and appealed to the international community to render its substantial financial, material, and technical assistance necessary for the economic rehabilitation of Angola.

ANTIGUA AND BARBUDA. A country in the Caribbean comprising three islands of the Lesser Antilles: Antigua, Barbuda, and Redonda, it achieved independence from Great Britain in 1981 and became a member of the United Nations the same year. Its population is estimated by the UN (1990) to be 86,000. The bulk of the people are of African origin; the remainder are descendents of British, Portuguese, Lebanese, and Syrian settlers. The predominant religion is Christianity (Anglican and Roman Catholic). Literacy is estimated at 90%.

The government (1990) took the form of a monarchy and member of the Commonwealth of Nations, of which the British sovereign is the symbolic head. Executive power is vested in the governor-general, representing the crown, and a Cabinet headed by the prime minister, representing the party or coalition given a majority in popular elections. Legislation is prepared by the 17-member Parliament. The predominant political party is the Antigua Labour Party.

Originally inhabited by the "stone people," estimated to have lived there since 1775 B.C., Antigua became a slave-plantation colony after coming under British control in 1632, its trees being stripped away to permit sugarcane production. Although emancipated in 1934, the slaves—brought from the west coast of Africa—remained bound to their plantation owners until they formed trade unions in the early 1940s. The Antigua Trades and Labor Union (ALP) has dominated the political scene since that time and won its most recent victory in the general elections of 1984.

Antigua and Barbuda has an outstanding record in the field of human rights and a long history of fair elections, peaceful changes of government, and constitutional protection of freedom of opinion and expression and freedom from intolerance and discrimination on the ground of religion or belief.

ANTIGUA AND BARBUDA: CONSTITUTION. The Constitution of Antigua and Barbuda, which came into effect on 1 November 1981, includes the following provisions (Preamble and articles 1–21) specifically relating to human rights and fundamental freedoms:

WHEREAS the People of Antigua and Barbuda—

(a) proclaim that they are a sovereign nation founded upon principles that acknowledge the supremacy of God, the dignity and worth of the human person, the entitlement of all persons to the fundamental rights and freedoms of the individual, the position of the family in a society of free men and women and free institutions;

(b) respect the principles of social justice and, therefore, believe that the operation of their economic system should result in the material resources of their community being so distributed as to serve the common good, that there should be adequate means of livelihood for all, that labour should not be exploited or forced by economic necessity to operate in inhumane conditions but that there should be opportunity for advancement on the basis of recognition of merit, ability and integrity;

(c) assert their conviction that their happiness and prosperity can best be pursued in a democratic society in which all persons may, to the extent of their capacity, play some part in the national life;

(d) recognize that the law symbolises the public conscience, that every citizen owes to it an undivided allegiance not to be limited by any private views of justice or expediency and that the State is subject to the law;

(e) desire to establish a framework of supreme law within which to guarantee their inalienable human rights and freedoms, among them, the rights to liberty, property, security and legal redress of grievances, as well as freedom of speech, of the press and of assembly, subject only to the public interest:

NOW, THEREFORE, the following provisions shall have effect as the Constitution of Antigua and Barbuda:—

Chapter I
The State and the Constitution

1.—(1) Antigua and Barbuda shall be a unitary sovereign democratic State.

(2) The territory of Antigua and Barbuda shall comprise the islands of Antigua, Barbuda and Redonda and all other areas that were comprised in Antigua on 31st October 1981 together with such other areas as may be declared by Act of Parliament to form part of the territory of Antigua and Barbuda.

2. This Constitution is the supreme law of Antigua and Barbuda and, subject to the provisions of this Constitution, if any other laws is inconsistent with this Constitution, this Constitution shall prevail and the other law shall, to the extent of the inconsistency, be void.

Chapter II
Protection of Fundamental Rights and Freedoms of the Individual

3. Whereas every person in Antigua and Barbuda is entitled to the fundamental rights and freedoms of the individual, that is to say, the right, regardless of race, place of origin, political opinions or affiliations, colour, creed or sex, but subject to respect for the rights and freedoms of others and for the public interest, to each and all of the following, namely—

(a) life, liberty, security of the person, the enjoyment of property and the protection of the law;

(b) freedom of conscience, of expression (including freedom of the press) and of peaceful assembly and association; and

(c) protection for his family life, his personal privacy, the privacy of his home and other property and from deprivation of property without fair compensation,

the provisions of this Chapter shall have effect for the purpose of affording protection to the aforesaid rights and freedoms, subject to such limitations of that protection as are contained in those provisions, being limitations designed to ensure that the enjoyment of the said rights and freedoms by any individual does not prejudice the rights and freedoms of others or the public interest.

4.—(1) No person shall be deprived of his life intentionally save in execution of the sentence of a court in respect of a crime of treason or murder of which he has been convicted.

(2) A person shall not be regarded as having been deprived of his life in contravention of this section if he dies as the result of the use, to such extent and such circumstances as are permitted by law, of such force as is reasonably justifiable—

(a) for the defence of any person from violence or for the defence of property;

(b) in order to effect a lawful arrest or to prevent the escape of a person lawfully detained;

(c) for the purpose of suppressing a riot, insurrection or mutiny; or

(d) in order lawfully to prevent the commission by that person of a criminal offence,

or if he dies as the result of a lawful act of war.

5.—(1) No person shall be deprived of his personal liberty save as may be authorised by law in any of the following cases, that is to say—

(a) in consequence of his unfitness to plead to a criminal charge;

(b) in execution of the sentence or order of a court, whether established for Antigua and Barbuda or some other country, in respect of a criminal offence of which he has been convicted;

(c) in execution of an order of the High Court or of the Court of Appeal or such other court as may be prescribed by Parliament on the grounds of his contempt of any such court or of another court or tribunal;

(d) in execution of the order of a court made in order to secure the fulfilment of any obligation imposed on him by law;

(e) for the purpose of bringing him before a court in execution of the order of a court;

(f) upon reasonable suspicion of his having committed or of being about to commit a criminal offence under any law;

(g) under the order of a court or with the consent of his parent or guardian, for his education or welfare during any period ending not later than the date when he attains the age of eighteen years;

(h) for the purpose of preventing the spread of an infectious or contagious disease;

(i) in the case of a person who is, or is reasonably suspected to be, of unsound mind, addicted to drugs or alcohol, or a vagrant, for the purpose of his care or treatment or the protection of the community;

(j) for the purpose of preventing the unlawful entry of that person into Antigua and Barbuda, or for the purpose of effecting the expulsion, extradition or other lawful removal of that person from Antigua and Barbuda or for the purpose of restricting that person while he is being conveyed through Antigua and Barbuda in the course of his extradition or removal as a convicted prisoner from one country to another; or

(k) to such extent as may be necessary in the execution of a lawful order requiring that person to remain within a specified area within Antigua and Barbuda or prohibiting him from being within such an area or to such extent as may be reasonably justifiable for the taking of proceedings against that person relating to the making of any such order or relating to such an order after it has been made, or to such extent as may be reasonably justifiable for restraining that person during any visit that he is permitted to make to any part of Antigua and Barbuda in which, in consequence of any such order, his presence would otherwise be unlawful.

(2) Any person who is arrested or detained shall be informed orally and in writing as soon as reasonably practicable, in language that he understands, of the reason for his arrest or detention.

(3) Any person who is arrested or detained shall have the right, at any stage and at his own expense, to retain and instruct without delay a legal practitioner of his own choice, and to hold private communications with him, and in the case of a minor he shall also be afforded a reasonable opportunity for communication with his parent or guardian.

(4) When a person is arrested, excessive bail shall not be required in those cases where bail is being granted.

(5) Any person who is arrested or detained—

(a) for the purpose of bringing him before a court in execution of the order of a court; or

(b) upon reasonable suspicion of his having committed or being about to commit a criminal offence under any law,

and who is not released shall be brought before the court within forty-eight hours after his detention and, in computing time for the purposes of this subsection, Sundays and public holidays shall be excluded.

(6) If any person arrested or detained as mentioned in subsection (5)(b) of this section is not tried within a reasonable time, then, without prejudice to any further proceedings which may be brought against him, he shall be released either unconditionally or upon reasonable conditions, including in particular such conditions as are reasonably necessary to ensure that he appears at a later date for trial or for proceedings preliminary to trial and, subject to subsection (4) of this section, such conditions may include bail.

(7) Any person who is unlawfully arrested or detained by any other person shall, subject to such defences as may be provided by law, be entitled to compensation for such unlawful arrest or detention from the person who made the arrest or effected the detention, from any person or authority on whose behalf the person making the arrest or effecting the detention was acting or from them both:

Provided that a judge, a magistrate or a justice of the peace or an officer of a court of a police officer acting in pursuance of the order of a judge, a magistrate or a justice of the peace shall not be under any personal liability to pay compensation under this subsection in consequence of any act performed by him in good faith in the discharge of the functions of his office and any liability to pay any such compensation in consequence of any such act shall be a liability of the Crown.

(8) For the purposes of subsection (1)(b) of this section, a person charged with a criminal offence in respect of whom a special verdict has been returned that he was guilty of the act or omission charged but was insane when he did the act or made the omission shall be regarded as a person who has been convicted of a criminal offence and the detention of that person in consequence of such a verdict shall be regarded as detention in execution of the order of a court.

6.—(1) No person shall be held in slavery or servitude.

(2) No person shall be required to perform forced labour.

(3) For the purposes of this section, the expression "forced labour" does not include—

(a) any labour required in consequence of the sentence or order of a court;

(b) any labour required of any person while he is lawfully detained that, though not required in consequence of the sentence or order of a court, is reasonably necessary in the interests of hygiene or for the maintenance of the place at which he is detained;

(c) any labour required of a member of a disciplined force in pursuance of his duties as such or, in the case of a person who has conscientious objections to service as a member of a naval, military or air force, any labour that that person is required by law to perform in place of such service;

(d) any labour required during any period of public emergency or, in the event of any other emergency or calamity that threatens the life and well-being of the community, to the extent that the requiring of such labour is reasonably justifiable in the circumstances of any situation arising or existing during that period or as a result of that other emergency or calamity, for the purpose of dealing with that situation.

7.—(1) No person shall be subjected to torture or to inhuman or degrading punishment or other such treatment.

(2) Nothing contained in or done under the authority of any law shall be held to be inconsistent with or in contravention of this section to the extent that the law in question authorises the infliction of any description of punishment that was lawful in Antigua on 31st October 1981.

8.—(1) A person shall not be deprived of his freedom of movement, that is to say, the right to move freely throughout Antigua and Barbuda, the right to reside in any part of Antigua and Barbuda, the right to enter Antigua and Barbuda, the right to leave Antigua and Barbuda and immunity from expulsion from Antigua and Barbuda.

(2) Any restrictions on a person's freedom of movement that is involved in his lawful detention shall not be held to be inconsistent with or in contravention of this section.

(3) Nothing contained in or done under the authority of any law shall be held to be inconsistent with or in contravention of this section to the extent that the law in question makes provision—

(a) for the imposition of restrictions on the movements or residence within Antigua and Barbuda of any person or on any person's right to leave Antigua and Barbuda that are reasonably required in the interests of defence, public safety or public order;

(b) for the imposition of restrictions on the movements or residence within Antigua and Barbuda or on the right to leave Antigua and Barbuda of persons generally or any class of persons in the interests of defence, public safety, public order, public morality, or public health or, in respect of the right to leave Antigua and Barbuda, of securing compliance with any international obligation of Antigua and Barbuda particulars of which have been laid before the House and except so far as that provision or, as the case may be, the thing done under the authority thereof is shown not to be reasonably justifiable in a democratic society;

(c) for the imposition of restrictions, by order of a court, on the movement of residence within Antigua and Barbuda of any person or on any person's right to leave Antigua and Barbuda either in consequence of his having been found guilty of a criminal offence under a law or for the purpose of ensuring that he appears before a court at a later date for trial of such a criminal offence or for proceedings relating to his extradition or lawful removal from Antigua and Barbuda;

(d) for the imposition of restrictions on the freedom of movement of any person who is not a citizen;

(e) for the imposition of restrictions on the acquisition or use by any person of land or other property in Antigua and Barbuda;

(f) for the imposition of restrictions upon the movement or residence within Antigua and Barbuda or on the right to leave Antigua and Barbuda of any public officer that are reasonably required for the proper performance of his functions;

(g) for the removal of a person from Antigua and Barbuda to be tried or punished in some other country for a criminal offence under the law of that other country or to undergo imprisonment in some other country in execution of the sentence of a court in respect of a criminal offence under a law of which he has been convicted; or

(h) for the imposition of restrictions on the right of any person to leave Antigua and Barbuda that are reasonably required in order to secure the fulfilment of any obligations imposed on that person by law and except so far as

that provision or, as the case may be, the thing done under the authority thereof is shown not to be reasonably justifiable in a democratic society.

(4) If any person whose freedom of movement has been restricted by virtue of such a provision as is referred to in subsection (3)(a) of this section so requests at any time during the period of that restriction not earlier than two months after the restriction was imposed or two months after he last made such a request, as the case may be, his case shall be reviewed by an independent and impartial tribunal consisting of a president who shall be a legal practitioner of not less than seven years standing appointed by the Chief Justice and two other members appointed by the Governor-General acting in his discretion.

(5) On any review by a tribunal in pursuance of subsection (4) of this section of the case of any person whose freedom of movement has been restricted, the tribunal may make recommendations concerning the necessity for or expediency of the continuation of that restriction to the authority by whom it was ordered and, unless it is otherwise provided by law, that authority shall be obliged to act in accordance with any such recommendations.

9.—(1) No property of any description shall be compulsorily taken possession of, and no interest in or right to or over property of any description shall be compulsorily acquired, except for public use and except in accordance with the provisions of a law applicable to that taking of possession or acquisition and for the payment of fair compensation within a reasonable time.

(2) Every person having an interest in or right to or over property which is compulsorily taken possession of or whose interest in or right to or over any property is compulsorily acquired shall have the right of access to the High Court for—

(a) the determination of his interest or right, the legality of the taking of possession or acquisition of the property, interest or right and the amount of any compensation to which he is entitled; and

(b) the purpose of obtaining payment of that compensation:

Provided that if Parliament so provides in relation to any matter referred to in paragraph (a) of this subsection the right of access shall be by way of appeal (exercisable as of right at the instance of the person having the interest in or right to or over the property) from a tribunal or authority, other than the High Court, having jurisdiction under any law to determine that matter.

(3) The Chief Justice may make rules with respect to the practice and procedure of the High Court or any other tribunal or authority in relation to the jurisdiction conferred on the High Court by subsection (2) of this section or exercisable by the other tribunal or authority for the purposes of that subsection (including rules with respect to the time within which application or appeals to the High Court or applications to the other tribunals or authority may be brought).

(4) Nothing contained in or done under the authority of any law shall be held to be inconsistent with or in contravention of subsection (1) of this section—

(a) to the extent that the law in question makes provision for the taking of possession or acquisition of any property, interest or right—

(i) in satisfaction of any tax, rate or due;

(ii) by way of penalty for breach of the law or forfeiture in consequence of breach of the law;

(iii) as an incident of a lease, tenancy, mortgage, charge, bill of sale, pledge or contract;

(iv) in the execution of judgments or orders of a court in proceedings for the determination of civil rights or obligations;

(v) in circumstances where it is reasonably necessary so to do because the property is in a dangerous state or likely to be injurious to the health of human beings, animals or plants;

(vi) in consequence of any law with respect to the limitation of actions;

(vii) for so long as may be necessary for the purpose of any examination, investigation, trial or enquiry or, in the case of land, for the purposes of the carrying out thereon of work of soil conservation or the conservation of other natural resources or work relating to agricultural development or improvement (being work relating to such development or improvement that the owner or occupier of the land has been required, and has without reasonable excuse refused or failed, to carry out),

and except so far as the provision or, as the case may be, the thing done under the authority thereof is shown not to be reasonably justifiable in a democratic society;

(b) to the extent that the law in question makes provision for the taking of possession or acquisition of any of the following property (including and interest in or right to or over property), that is to say—

(i) enemy property;

(ii) property of a deceased person, a person of unsound mind or a person who had not attained the age of eighteen years, for the purpose of its administration for the benefit of the persons entitled to the beneficial interest therein;

(iii) the property of a person adjudged bankrupt or a body corporate in liquidation, for the purpose of its administration for the benefit of the creditors of the bankrupt or body corporate and, subject thereto, for the benefit of other persons entitled to the beneficial interest in the property; or

(iv) property subject to a trust, for the purpose of vesting the property in persons appointed as trustees under the instrument creating the trust or by a court or by order of a court for the purposes of giving effect to the trust.

(5) Nothing contained in or done under the authority of any law enacted by Parliament shall be held to be inconsistent with or in contravention of this section to the extent that the law in question makes provision for the compulsory taking of possession of any property, or the compulsory acquisition of any interest in or right to or over property, where that property, interest or right is held by a body corporate established by law for public purposes in which no monies have been invested other than monies provided by Parliament or any legislature established for the former colony or Associated State of Antigua.

(6) For the purposes of this section, "use" is "public" if it is intended to result or results in a benefit or advantage to the public and, without prejudice to its generality, includes any use affecting the physical, economic, social or aesthetic well-being of the public.

10.—(1) Except with his own consent, no person shall be subjected to the search of his person or his property or the entry by others on his premises.

(2) Nothing contained in or done under the authority of any laws shall be held to be inconsistent with or in contravention of this section to the extent that the law in question makes provision—

(a) that is reasonably required in the interests of defence, public safety, public order, public morality, public health, public revenue, town and country planning or the development and utilization of property in such a manner as to promote the public benefit;

(b) that authorises an office or agent of the Government, a local government authority or a body corporate established by law for public purposes to enter on the premises of any person in order to inspect those premises or anything thereon for the purpose of any tax, rate or due in order to carry out work connected with any property that is lawfully on those premises and that belongs to the Government, or to that authority or body corporate, as the case may be;

(c) that is reasonably required for the purpose of preventing or detecting crime;

(d) that is reasonably required for the purpose of protecting the rights or freedoms of other persons; or

(e) that authorises, for the purpose of enforcing the judgment or order of a court in any proceedings, the search of any person or property by order of a court of entry upon any premises by such order,

and except so far as that provision or, as the case may be, anything done under the authority thereof is shown not to be reasonably justifiable in a democratic society.

11.—(1) Except with his own consent, no person shall be hindered in the enjoyment of his freedom of conscience, and for the purposes of this section the said freedom includes freedom of thought and of religion, freedom to change his religion or belief, and freedom, either alone or in community with others, and both in public and in private, to manifest and propagate his religion or belief in worship, teaching, practice and observance.

(2) Except with his own consent (or, if he is under the age, of eighteen years, the consent of his parent or guardian) no person attending any place of education shall be required to receive religious instruction or to take part in or attend any religious ceremony or observance if that instruction, ceremony or observance relates to a religion other than his own.

(3) No person shall be compelled to take any oath which is contrary to his religion or belief or to take any oath in a manner which is contrary to his religion or belief.

(4) Nothing contained in or done under the authority of any law shall be held to be inconsistent with or in contravention of this section to the extent that the law in question makes provision that is reasonably required—

(a) in the interests of defence, public safety, public order, public morality or public health; or

(b) for the purpose of protecting the rights and freedoms of other persons, including the right to observe and practise any religion without the unsolicited intervention of members of any other religion,

and except so far as that provision or, as the case may be, the thing done under the authority thereof is shown not to be reasonably justifiable in a democratic society.

(5) Reference in this section to a religion shall be construed as including references to a religious denomination, and cognate expressions shall be construed accordingly.

12.—(1) Except with his own consent, no person shall be hindered in the enjoyment of his freedom of expression.

(2) For the purposes of this section the said freedom includes the freedom to hold opinions without interference, freedom to receive information and ideas without interference, freedom to disseminate information and ideas without interference (whether the dissemination be to the

public generally or to any person or class of persons) and freedom from interference with his correspondence or other means of communication.

(3) For the purposes of this section expression may be oral or written or by codes, signals, signs or symbols and includes recordings, broadcasts (whether on radio or television), printed publications, photographs (whether still or moving), drawings, carvings and sculptures or any other means of artistic expression.

(4) Nothing contained in or done under the authority of any law shall be held to be inconsistent with or in contravention of this section to the extent that the law in question makes provision—

(a) that is reasonably required—

(i) in the interests of defence, public safety, public order, public morality or public health; or

(ii) for the purpose of protecting the reputations, rights and freedoms of other persons, or the private lives of persons concerned in legal proceedings and proceedings before statutory tribunals, preventing the disclosure of information received in confidence, maintaining the authority and independence of Parliament and the courts, or regulating telephony, posts, broadcasting or other means of communication, public entertainments, public shows; or

(b) that imposes restrictions upon public officers that are reasonably required for the proper performance of their functions,

and except so far as that provision or, as the case may be, the thing done under the authority thereof is shown not to be reasonably justifiable in a democratic society.

13.—(1) Except with his own consent, no person shall be hindered in the enjoyment of his freedom of peaceful assembly and association, that is to say, his right peacefully to assemble freely and associate with other persons and in particular to form or belong to trade unions or other associations for the promotion and protection of his interests.

(2) Nothing contained in or done under the authority of any law shall be held to be inconsistent with or in contravention of this section to the extent that the law in question makes provision—

(a) that is reasonably required—

(i) in the interests of defence, public order, public morality or public health; or

(ii) for the purpose of protecting the rights or freedoms of other persons; or

(b) that imposes restrictions upon public officers that are reasonably required for the proper performance of their functions,

and except so far as that provision or, as the case may be, the thing done under the authority thereof is shown not to be reasonably justifiable in a democratic society.

14.—(1) Subject to the provisions of subsections (4), (5) and (7) of this section, no law shall make any provision that is discriminatory either of itself or in its effect.

(2) Subject to the provisions of subsections (6), (7) and (8) of this section, no person shall be treated in a discriminatory manner by any person acting by virtue of any law or in the performance of the functions of any public office or any public authority.

(3) In this section, the expression "discriminatory" means affording different treatment to different persons attributable wholly or mainly to their respective descriptions by race, place of origin, political opinions or affiliations, colour, creed, or sex whereby persons of one such description are subjected to disabilities or restrictions to which persons of another such description are not made

subject or are accorded privileges or advantages that are not accorded to persons of another such description.

(4) Subsection (1) of this section shall not apply to any law so far as the law makes provision—

(a) for the appropriation of public revenues or other public funds;

(b) with respect to persons who are not citizens; or

(c) whereby persons of any such description as is mentioned in subsection (3) of this section may be subjected to any disability or restriction or may be accorded any privilege or advantage that, having regard to its nature and to special circumstances pertaining to those persons or to persons of any other such description, is reasonably justifiable in a democratic society.

(5) Nothing contained in any law shall be held to be inconsistent with or in contravention of subsection (1) of this section to the extent that it makes provision with respect to qualifications (not being qualifications specifically relating to race, place of origin, political opinions or affiliations, colour, creed or sex) for service as a public officer or as a member of a disciplined force or for the service of a local government authority or a body corporate established by any law for public purposes.

(6) Subsection (2) of this section shall not apply to anything that is expressly or by necessary implication authorised to be done by any such provision of law as is referred to in subsection (4) or (5) of this section.

(7) Nothing contained in or done under the authority of any law shall be held to be inconsistent with or in contravention of this section to the extent that the law in question makes provision whereby persons of any such description as is mentioned in subsection (3) of this section may be subjected to any restriction on the rights and freedoms guaranteed by sections 8, 10, 11, 12, and 13 of this Constitution, being such a restriction as is authorised by paragraph (a) or (b) of subsection (3) of section 8, subsection (2) of section 10, subsection (4) of section 11, subsection (4) of section 12 or subsection (2) of section 13, as the case may be.

(8) Nothing in subsection (2) of this section shall affect any discretion relating to the institution, conduct or discontinuance of civil or criminal proceedings in any court that is vested in any person by or under this Constitution or any other law.

15.—(1) If any person is charged with a criminal offence then, unless the charge is withdrawn, he shall be afforded a fair hearing within a reasonable time by an independent and impartial court established by law.

(2) Every person who is charged with a criminal offence—

(a) shall be presumed to be innocent until he is proved or has pleaded guilty;

(b) shall be informed orally and in writing as soon as reasonably practicable, in language that he understands, of the nature of the offence with which he is charged;

(c) shall be given adequate time and facilities for the preparation of his defence;

(d) shall be permitted to defend himself before the court in person or by a legal practitioner of his own choice;

(e) shall be afforded facilities to examine in person or by his legal representative the witnesses called by the prosecution before the court and to obtain the attendance and carry out the examination of witnesses to testify on his behalf before the court on the same conditions as those applying to witnesses called by the prosecution; and

(f) shall be permitted to have without payment the

assistance of an interpreter if he cannot understand the language used at the trial of the charge,

and except with his own consent the trial shall not take place in his absence—

(i) except where, under the provisions of any law entitling him thereto, he is given adequate notice of the charge, the date, time and place of the trial or continuance thereof and afforded a reasonable opportunity of appearing before the court:

Provided that where the foregoing conditions have been compiled with, and the court is satisfied that owing to circumstances beyond his control he cannot appear, the trial shall not take place or continue in his absence; or

(ii) unless he so conducts himself as to render the continuance of the proceedings in his presence impracticable and the court has ordered him to be removed and the trial to proceed in his absence.

(3) When a person is tried for any criminal offence the accused person or any person authorised by him in that behalf shall, if he so requires and subject to payment of such reasonable fees as may be prescribed by law, be given within a reasonable time after judgment a copy of any record of the proceedings made by or on behalf of the court.

(4) No person shall be held to be guilty of a criminal offence on account of any act or omission that did not, at the time it took place, constitute such an offense, and no penalty shall be imposed for any criminal offence that is more severe in degree or description than the maximum penalty that might have been imposed for that offence at the time when it was committed.

(5) No person who shows that he has been tried by a competent court for a criminal offence and either convicted or acquitted shall again be tried for that offence or for any criminal offence of which he could have been convicted at the trial for the offence, save upon the order of a superior court in the course of appeal or review proceedings relating to the conviction or acquittal.

(6) No person shall be tried for a criminal offence if he shows that he has been pardoned for that offence.

(7) No person who is tried for a criminal offence shall be compelled to give evidence at the trial.

(8) Any court or other authority prescribed by law for the determination of the existence or extent of any civil right or obligation shall be established by law and shall be independent and impartial; and where proceedings for such a determination are instituted by any persons before such a court or other authority, the case shall be given a fair hearing within a reasonable time.

(9) Except with the agreement of all the parties thereto, all proceedings of every court and proceedings for the determination of the existence or extent of any civil right or obligation before any other authority, including the announcement of the decision of the court or other authority, shall be held in public.

(10) Nothing in subsection (9) of this section shall prevent the court or other authority from excluding from the proceedings persons other than the parties thereto and the legal practitioners representing them to such an extent as the court or other authority—

(a) may by law be empowered to do and may consider necessary or expedient in circumstances where publicity would prejudice the interests of justice or in interlocutory proceedings or in the interests of public morality, the welfare of persons under the age of eighteen years or the protection of the private lives of persons concerned in the proceedings; or

(b) may by law be empowered or required to do in the interests of defence, public safety, public order or public morality.

(11) Nothing contained in or done under the authority of any law shall be held to be inconsistent with or in contravention of—

(a) subsection (2) (a) of this section, to the extent that the law in question imposes upon any person charged with a criminal offence the burden of proving particular facts;

(b) subsection (2) (e) of this section, to the extent that the law in question imposes reasonable conditions that must be satisfied if witnesses called to testify on behalf of an accused person are to be paid their expenses out of public funds; or

(c) subsection (5) of this section, to the extent that the law in question authorises a court to try a member of a disciplined force for a criminal offence notwithstanding any trial and conviction or acquittal of that member under the disciplinary law of that force so however, that any court so trying such a member and convicting him shall in sentencing him to any punishment take into account any punishment awarded him under that disciplinary law.

(12) In the case of any person who is held in lawful detention, the provisions of subsection (1), paragraphs (d) and (e) of subsection (2), and subsection (3) of this section shall not apply in relation to his trial for a criminal offence under the law regulating the discipline of persons held in such detention.

(13) Nothing contained in or done under the authority of any law shall be held to be inconsistent with or in contravention of subsection (2) of this section to the extent that it authorises the trial of a defendant by a magistrate for a summary offence to take place in the defendant's absence.

(14) In this section "criminal offence" means a criminal offence under any law.

16. Nothing contained in or done under the authority of a law enacted by Parliament shall be held to be inconsistent with or in contravention of section 5 or section 14 of this Constitution to the extent that the law authorises the taking during any period of public emergency of measures that are reasonably justifiable, for dealing with the situation that exists in Antigua and Barbuda during that period.

17.—(1) When a person is detained by virtue of any such law as is referred to in section 16 of this Constitution the following provisions shall apply, that is to say—

(a) he shall, with reasonable promptitude and in any case not more than seven days after the commencement of his detention, be informed in a language that he understands and in detail of the grounds upon which he is detained and furnished with a written statement in English specifying those grounds in detail;

(b) not more than fourteen days after the commencement of his detention a notification shall be published in the Official Gazette stating that he has been detained and giving particulars of the provision of law under which his detention is authorised;

(c) not more than one month after the commencement of his detention and thereafter during the detention at intervals of not more than six months, his case shall be reviewed by an independent and impartial tribunal established by law and presided over by a suitably qualified legal practitioner of at least seven years standing appointed by the Chief Justice;

(d) he shall be afforded reasonable facilities to consult a legal representative of his own choice who shall be permitted to make representations to the tribunal appointed for the review of the case of the detained person; and

(e) at the hearing of his case by the tribunal appointed for the review of his case he shall be permitted to appear in person or by a legal practitioner of his own choice.

(2) On any review by a tribunal in pursuance of this section of the case of a detained person, the tribunal may make recommendations concerning the necessity or expediency of continuing his detention to the authority by which it was ordered but, unless it is otherwise provided by law, that authority shall not be obliged to act in accordance with any such recommendations.

(3) Nothing contained in subsection (1)(d) or subsection (1)(e) of this section shall be construed as entitling a person to legal representation at public expense.

18.—(1) If any person alleges that any of the provisions of sections 3 to 17 (inclusive) of this Constitution has been, is being or is likely to be contravened in relation to him (or, in the case of a person who is detained, if any other person alleges such a contravention in relation to the detained person), then, without prejudice to any other action with respect to the same matter that is lawfully available, that person (or that other person) may apply to the High Court for redress.

(2) The High Court shall have original jurisdiction—

(a) to hear and determine any application made by any person in pursuance of subsection (1) of this section; and

(b) to determine any question arising in the case of any person that is referred to it in pursuance of subsection (3) of this section,

and may make such declaration and orders, issue such writs and give such directions as it may consider appropriate for the purpose of enforcing or securing the enforcement of any of the provisions of sections 3 to 17 (inclusive) of this Constitution:

Provided that the High Court may decline to exercise its powers under this subsection if it is satisfied that adequate means of redress for the contravention alleged are or have been available to the person concerned under any other law.

(3) If in any proceedings in any court (other than the Court of Appeal, the High Court or a court-martial) any question arises as to the contravention of any of the provisions of sections 3 to 17 (inclusive) of this Constitution, the person presiding in that court may, and shall if any party to the proceedings so requests, refer the question to the High Court unless, in his opinion, the raising of the question is merely frivolous or vexatious.

(4) Where any question is referred to the High Court in pursuance of subsection (3) of this section, the High Court shall give its decision upon the question and the court in which the question arose shall dispose of the case in accordance with that decision of, if that decision is the subject of an appeal to the Court of Appeal or to Her Majesty in Council, in accordance with the decision of the Court of Appeal or, as the case may be, of Her Majesty in Council.

(5) There shall be such provision as may be made by Parliament for conferring upon the High Court such powers in addition to those conferred by this section as may appear to be necessary or desirable for the purpose of enabling that court more effectively to exercise the jurisdiction conferred upon it by this section.

(6) The Chief Justice may make rules with respect to the practice and procedure of the High Court in relation to the jurisdiction and powers conferred on it by or under this section (including rules with respect to the time within which applications may be brought and references shall be made to the High Court).

19. Except as is otherwise expressly provided in this Constitution, no law may abrogate, abridge or infringe or authorise the abrogation, abridgement or infringement of any of the fundamental rights and freedoms of the individual hereinbefore recognised and declared.

20.—(1) The Governor-General may, by Proclamation which shall be published in the Official Gazette, declare that a state of public emergency exists for the purposes of this Chapter.

(2) Every declaration shall lapse—

(a) in the case of a declaration made when Parliament is sitting, at the expiration of a period of seven days beginning with the date of publication of the declaration; and

(b) in any other case, at the expiration of a period of twenty-one days beginning with the date of publication of the declaration, unless it has in the meantime been approved by resolutions of both Houses of Parliament.

(3) A declaration of public emergency may at any time be revoked by the Governor-General by Proclamation which shall be published in the Official Gazette.

(4) A declaration of public emergency that has been approved of by resolutions of the Houses of Parliament in pursuance of subsection (2) of this section shall, subject to the provisions of subsection (3) of this section, remain in force so long as the resolutions of those Houses remain in force and no longer.

(5) A resolution of a House of Parliament passed for the purposes of this section shall remain in force for three months or such shorter period as may be specified therein:

Provided that any such resolution may be extended from time to time by a further such resolution each extension not exceeding three months from the date of the resolution effecting the extension and any such resolution may be revoked at any time by a resolution of that House.

(6) Any provision of this section that a declaration of emergency shall lapse or cease to be in force at any particular time is without prejudice to the making of a further such declaration whether before or after that time.

(7) A resolution of a House of Parliament for the purposes of subsection (2) of this section and a resolution extending any such resolution shall not be passed unless it is supported by the votes of a majority of all members of that House.

(8) The Governor-General may summon the Houses of Parliament to meet for the purpose of subsection (2) of this section notwithstanding that Parliament stands dissolved, and the persons who were members of the Senate and the House immediately before the dissolution shall be deemed, for those purposes, still to be members of those Houses, but, subject to the provisions of sections 33 and 42 of this Constitution (which relate to the election of the President, Vice-President, the Speaker, and the Deputy Speaker) a House of Parliament shall not, when summoned by virtue of this subsection, transact any business other than debating and voting upon a resolution for the purposes of subsection (2) of this section.

21.—(1) In this Chapter, unless the context otherwise requires—

"contravention", in relation to any requirement, includes a failure to comply with that requirement, and cognate expressions shall be construed accordingly;

"court" means any court of law having jurisdiction in Antigua and Barbuda other than a court established by a disciplinary law, and includes Her Majesty in Council and, in section 4 of this Constitution, a court established by a disciplinary law;

"disciplinary law" means a law regulating the discipline of any disciplined force;

"disciplined force" means—

(a) a naval, military or air force;

(b) the Police Force; or

(c) a prison service;

"member", in relation to a disciplined force, includes any person who, under the law regulating the discipline of that force, is subject to that discipline;

"legal practitioner" means a person entitled to practise as a barrister in Antigua and Barbuda or, except in relation to proceedings before a court in which a solicitor has no right of audience, entitled to practise as a solicitor in Antigua and Barbuda.

(2) In relation to any person who is a member of a disciplined force raised under any law, nothing contained in or done under the authority of the disciplinary law of that force shall be held to be inconsistent with or in contravention of any of the provisions of this Chapter other than sections 4, 6 and 7 of this Constitution.

(3) In relation to any person who is a member of a disciplined force raised otherwise than as aforesaid and lawfully present in Antigua and Barbuda, nothing contained in or done under the authority of the disciplinary law of that force shall be held to be inconsistent with or in contravention of any of the provisions of this Chapter.

(4) In this Chapter "public emergency" means any period during which—

(a) Her Majesty is at war; or

(b) there is in force a declaration of emergency under section 20 of this Constitution, or there are in force resolutions of both Houses of Parliament supported by the votes of not less than two-thirds of all the members of each House declaring that democratic institutions in Antigua and Barbuda are threatened by subversion.

(5) A Proclamation made by the Governor-General shall not be effective for the purpose of section 20 of this Constitution unless it contains a declaration that the Governor-General is satisfied—

(a) that a public emergency has arisen as a result of the imminence of a state of war between Her Majesty and a foreign State or as a result of the occurrence of any earthquake, hurricane, flood, fire, outbreak of pestilence, outbreak of infectious disease or other calamity whether similar to the foregoing or not; or

(b) that action has been taken or is immediately threatened by any person or body of persons of such a nature and on so extensive a scale as to be likely to endanger the public safety or to deprive the community, or any substantial portion of the community, of supplies or services essential to life.

ANTI-SLAVERY SOCIETY FOR THE PROTECTION OF HUMAN RIGHTS.

An international non-governmental organization in consultative status with the UN's Economic and Social Council (Category II), ILO, and UNESCO, the Anti-Slavery Society is affiliated with organizations in four countries and has 1,100 individual members worldwide.

Founded in 1839 as the British and Foreign Anti-Slavery Society, the organization was amalgamated in 1909 with the Aborigines Protection Society. The society works to eliminate all forms of slavery, including forced labor; to promote the well-being and defend the interests of oppressed and threatened indigenous and other peoples; and to promote human rights in accordance with the principles of the Universal Declaration of Human Rights. The society was active in activities which led to the adoption of the League of Nations Convention on Slavery (1926) and the UN Convention on Slavery (1956) and in the appointment of the Working Group on Contemporary Forms of Slavery.

At its 1989 session, the Sub-Commission on Prevention of Discrimination and Protection of Minorities (resolution 1989/1940) congratulated the Anti-Slavery Society, "the oldest human rights organization in the world," on the occasion of its 150th anniversary, noting "the great contribution that the Anti-Slavery Society has made to the cause of human rights over the last century-and-a-half by its tireless advocacy, research and concern for indigenous peoples as well as those suffering from the abuses of slavery and slavery-like practices," . . . "the important and continuing vital work the Society does in maintaining its global programs and providing information to the Sub-Commission," . . . and "the need for these valuable sources to be maintained."

The Anti-Slavery Society publishes the annual *Anti-Slavery Reporter,* the bi-annual *Newsletter,* and an annual report, as well as periodic research reports. The group has also issued special information series on such issues as human rights, child labor, and indigenous peoples.

Anti-Slavery Society for the Protection of Human Rights. Address: 180 Brixton Road, London SW9 6AT, UK. Telephone: 01-582-4040. Director: Peter Lowes.

APARTHEID. The first volume of the dictionary of the Afrikaans language, *Woordeboek van die Afrikaans Taal,* compiled under official auspices by a group of philologists and published in Pretoria, South Africa, in 1950, defines *apartheid* as

a political tendency or trend in South Africa based on the general principles (a) of a *differentiation* corresponding to differences of race and/or color and/or level of civilization, as opposed to *assimilation;* (b) of the maintenance and perpetuation of the individuality (identity) of the different color groups of which the population is composed, and of the separate development of these groups in accordance with their individual nature, traditions and capabilities, as opposed to *integration.* In its practical application this policy involves arrangements and endeavors including, *inter alia,* measures to effect a degree of purely local or spacial separation, e.g., with respect to residential zones, public utilities, transport, entertainments, etc.; measures concerning political rights, e.g., separate electoral lists, separate representation in Parliament and in the Provincial Councils; also a territorial segregation, e.g., the fact of reserving fairly extensive territories for the exclusive use of one population group, e.g., the Native territories.

When South Africa achieved independence in 1910, within the British Empire, it was composed of two formerly independent republics, Orange and Transvaal, and two former British colonies, Cape and Natal. A multi-ethnic State, it had a population of about 6,000,000 persons divided by the union authorities into four main groups: "Europeans," or persons of pure European descent; "natives," or persons of the Bantu race; "Asiatics," or natives of Asia and their descendents, mainly Indians; and "mixed or other coloured," or persons of mixed race, mainly Cape Coloured, Cape Malays, Bushmen, and Hottentots. These people were referred to collectively as "non-Europeans" and were generally relegated to an inferior position politically, economically, socially, and culturally.

The "Europeans" had two different origins. Some were descendents of Dutch colonists, speaking Afrikaans, whose families had lived in the country more than three centuries and who were concentrated in the rural agricultural areas; others were descendents of English-speaking immigrants whose families had lived in the country less than a century and who were concentrated in the cities of the Cape and Natal Province.

Even before independence, the Act of 1909, under which the Union of South Africa was organized, denied to non-Europeans the basic right of direct representation in Parliament, although they constituted more than three-quarters of the population. Discriminatory legislation adopted between 1910 and 1948 further limited their role in South African life but did not cut it off completely.

However, in 1948, the United Party, dominated by the English-speaking population, lost control of the government to the National Party of the Africaners, and policies of racial segregation and discrimination—*apartheid*—were installed. The new system effectively ensured Europeans a monopoly of economic power, while preventing non-Europeans from acquiring land in certain areas, reducing their productive capacity and earning ability, and training them, in segregated schools, to accept their inferior position.

The basic doctrine of *apartheid,* as expressed by South Africa's prime minister and minister of native affairs in the early 1950s, was summed up in a comprehensive *Report of the United Nations Commission on the Racial Situation in the Union of South Africa,* sub-mitted to the UN General Assembly in 1953 (UN Doc. A/2505 and Add. 1, Chap. V, para. 402–406) in the following terms:

One of the most striking phenomena of the world in which we live is the diversity of human races. They were created separate. This separation must be maintained even when economic or other circumstances have brought about a certain mingling of racial groups. With this aim in view, the sense of colour must be fostered and developed amongst the whites in such a way that the purity of the race is maintained.

As the heir to Western Christian civilization, the white race in South Africa has a twofold mission to fulfil: one with respect to the other members of the community of nations of Western Christian civilization, the other with respect to the coloured races with which events have brought it in contact and which are at a primitive or very backward stage of civilization.

Towards the former it owes a duty to maintain fully and to perpetuate its "character as a partner in the Western Christian civilization". It is the mission of the white race living in South Africa to protect that civilization "against attacks from outside and subversion from within". In other words, though representing a numerical minority, it must at any cost safeguard its position of domination over the coloured races. Naturally therefore it looks askance at any dogma of civic equality. This is why it cannot grant to the Natives, any more than to the Cape Coloured or the Indians, the same political rights which it itself enjoys. If the latter exercise the franchise as they do, for example, in Cape Province, they must vote on separate electoral lists and their representatives in Parliament and in the Provincial Councils must continue to be Europeans.

This position of domination imposes as a corollary a strict duty of justice and Christian "trusteeship" towards the non-White. This trusteeship must continue until the latter have reached a stage of maturity and responsibility that will justify an eventual process of emancipation.

On either side of the deep, wide gulf which, because of the difference in cultural levels, separates the White from the non-White, each race stands separated by characteristics which are permanent because they are hereditary. A race can only "fulfill itself" if it remains faithful to its inner law. This is especially true of the Bantu who have languages and their own distinct customs, rites and institutions. Mix them with the descendants of Europeans and they will be only pitiful imitators. They will lose the original qualities proper to their race without acquiring those of the superior group.

The best service, therefore, that the Whites can render to the non-Whites is to separate them from the white population, to consider them as distinct social and economic groups, and to see that, as far as possible, they live in territories, zones, or "locations" assigned to them as their own. In this way in their own communities they will enjoy all the rights of citizens for chief among those rights is the opportunity to develop to the maximum the distinct aptitudes of each member of the community.

Although aimed primarily at safeguarding the purity and the tutelary mission of the white race, *apartheid* is not in any way a negative policy of oppression or exploitation of the non-White by the White. On the contrary, it is a constructive policy, a policy of benevolence, protection and co-operation. In fact, according to this policy, "the supremacy *(baaskap)* of the European in his sphere" has a counterpart in the supremacy of the Bantu, the Cape Coloured or the Indian each in his own sphere.

The ideal situation for the *apartheid* policy would clearly have been that "the course of history had been different", that "there had arisen in South Africa a state in which only Bantu lived and worked, and another in which only Europeans lived and worked. This is not the situation today, however". As the result either of negligence or of a deliberate policy of *laissez-faire*, previous Governments have tolerated a sort of racial chaos in the country in which points and areas of contact and entanglement between different races have multiplied. The more numerous those points and areas of contact, however, the more chances are there of incidents, conflicts and outbursts. And unless energetic and concerted steps are taken to reverse the present trend towards a mixed development of races in the large urban centres, we may expect fearful clashes of interests and great suffering and bloodshed affecting all sections of the population.

The racist oppression of *apartheid* has caused enormous suffering among the non-European populations of South Africa by such devices as depriving them of rights of citizenship in their own country, crowding them into small barren areas where they cannot earn a living or practice a trade or profession, detaining them indefinitely without trial and torturing detainees held for interrogation, "banning" those who oppose the system, and even killing unarmed men, women, and children, as happened in Sharpeville in 1960 and Soweto in 1976.

In 1968 the INTERNATIONAL CONFERENCE ON HUMAN RIGHTS, in the PROCLAMATION OF TEHERAN, declared that:

Gross denials of human rights under the repugnant policy of *apartheid* are a matter of gravest concern to the international community. This policy of *apartheid*, condemned as a crime against humanity, continues seriously to disturb international peace and security. It is therefore imperative for the international community to use every possible means to eradicate this evil. The struggle against *apartheid* is recognized as legitimate.

General Assembly Actions against Apartheid. In 1970, the UN General Assembly, in the DECLARATION ON THE OCCASION OF THE TWENTY-FIFTH ANNIVERSARY OF THE UNITED NATIONS, declared that:

We strongly condemn the evil policy of *apartheid*, which is a crime against the conscience and dignity of mankind and, like nazism, is contrary to the principles of the Charter. We reaffirm our determination to spare no effort, including support to those who struggle against it, in accordance with the letter and the spirit of the Charter, to secure the elimination of *apartheid* in South Africa. We also condemn all forms of oppression and tyranny wherever they occur and racism and the practice of racial discrimination in all its manifestations.

In 1962, the General Assembly set up (resolution 1761 [XVII]) the SPECIAL COMMITTEE AGAINST APARTHEID, first known as the "Special Committee on the Policies of *Apartheid* of the Government of the Republic of South Africa," and assigned it to keep the racial policies of that government under review and to report as appropriate to the assembly, the Security Council, or both. The special committee has since reported regularly to both organs, and its conclusions and recommendations have provided a firm basis for their activities in this field.

In 1965, the assembly established (resolution 2054 B [XX]) the UNITED NATIONS TRUST FUND FOR SOUTH AFRICA to provide humanitarian assistance to victims of *apartheid* and racial discrimination in South Africa and Namibia. The trust fund is made up of voluntary contributions from governments, organizations, and individuals and provides grants for relief and legal aid to persons persecuted under repressive and discriminatory legislation. In 1967, it set up the United Nations EDUCATIONAL AND TRAINING PROGRAMME FOR SOUTHERN AFRICA to provide scholarships for nationals of South Africa and Namibia for study and training abroad; and, in 1975, it added the UNITED NATIONS TRUST FUND FOR PUBLICITY AGAINST APARTHEID to finance the printing and distribution of United Nations materials on *apartheid*.

In 1973, the General Assembly adopted and opened for ratification and accession (resolution 3068 [XXVIII]) the INTERNATIONAL CONVENTION ON THE SUPPRESSION AND PUNISHMENT OF THE CRIME OF APARTHEID, by which each State party agrees to declare that *apartheid* is a crime against humanity and to declare criminal those organizations, institutions, and individuals committing that crime. The convention entered into force on 18 July 1976.

In accordance with Article IX, the chairman of the Commission on Human Rights appointed a GROUP OF THREE members of the commission, who are also representatives of States parties to the convention, to meet immediately prior to each annual session of the commission to consider, and to adopt conclusions and recommendations concerning reports submitted by States parties on the legislative, judicial, administrative, or other measures that they have adopted and that give effect to the provisions of the convention. The Group of Three has also examined, at the request of the commission (resolution 1986/7), the nature and extent of the responsibility of transnational corporations for the continued existence of the system of *apartheid*, including legal actions that may be taken under the convention against such corporations whose operations in South Africa fall within the definition of the crime of *apartheid*.

In 1974, the General Assembly invited representatives of the South African liberation movements—the **AFRICAN NATIONAL CONGRESS OF SOUTH AFRICA** and the **PAN AFRICANIST CONGRESS OF AZANIA**—to participate as observers in the debates on *apartheid,* which were then held in its Special Political Committee. In 1976, the assembly began the practice of discussing *apartheid* in plenary rather than in committee meetings and again invited the two liberation movements to participate. At the 1976 session, it established (resolution 31/6 F) the Ad Hoc Committee on the Drafting of an International Convention against *Apartheid* and requested it to prepare both an international declaration and an international convention to put an end to *apartheid* in sports.

Also in 1976, the assembly prepared and adopted (resolution 31/6 J) a comprehensive Program of Action against *Apartheid,* "to be implemented by Governments, intergovernmental organizations, trade unions, churches, anti-*apartheid* and solidarity movements and other non-governmental organizations in order to assist the people of South Africa in their struggle for the total eradication of *apartheid* and the exercise of the right of self-determination by all the people of South Africa irrespective of race, color and creed." (See *APARTHEID:* **UN PROGRAM OF ACTION.**) In the introduction to the program, the assembly recalled that, for 30 years, the United Nations had made efforts to persuade the racist minority regimes in South Africa to abandon the bitter legacy of the past and to work for a peaceful solution in accordance with the principles of human equality and international cooperation, only to see those regimes meet the peaceful and just demands of the oppressed people by ruthless repression.

The assembly commended the program to all governments, organizations, and individuals; requested all United Nations organs and specialized agencies concerned to participate in its implementation; and requested the Special Committee against *Apartheid* and the **ORGANIZATION OF AFRICAN UNITY** to promote the realization of the program and to report on the progress achieved.

In 1976, the General Assembly received and welcomed (resolution 31/6 E) a proposal of the Special Committee against *Apartheid* that an international convention against *apartheid* in sports should be prepared and that, meanwhile, a declaration on the subject should be adopted. To draft these instruments, it established an ad hoc Committee on the Drafting of an International Convention against *Apartheid* in Sports, composed of the members of the special committee and seven additional members appointed by the assembly president with regard for equitable geographical distribution. The assembly urged all States, pending completion of these instruments, to imple-

ment the recommendations of the special committee on the subject, namely:

(a) to convey the United Nations resolutions on *apartheid* in sports to all national sports bodies with a request that necessary action be taken to implement those resolutions;

(b) to refuse any official sponsorship, assistance, or encouragement to sports contacts with South Africa, including official receptions to teams and payments of grants to sports bodies or teams or sportsmen involved in sporting competitions with South African teams or sportsmen;

(c) to refuse visas to South African sports bodies or teams or sportsmen, except for non-racial sports bodies endorsed by the special committee and the liberation movements;

(d) to deny facilities to sports bodies or teams or sportsmen for visits to South Africa; and

(e) to encourage national sports bodies concerned to support the exclusion of South Africa from international sports bodies and tournaments.

In 1977, the World Conference against *Apartheid,* held at Lagos from 22 to 26 August, adopted the **LAGOS DECLARATION FOR ACTION AGAINST** *APARTHEID* in which it set out its conclusion that

Apartheid, the policy of institutionalized racist domination and exploitation, imposed by a minority regime in South Africa, is a flagrant violation of the Charter of the United Nations and the Universal Declaration of Human Rights. It rests on the dispossession, plunder, exploitation and social deprivation of the African people since 1652 by colonial settlers and their descendents. It is a crime against the conscience and dignity of mankind. It has resulted in immense suffering and involved the forcible moving of millions of Africans under special laws restricting their freedom of movement; and the denial of elementary human rights to the great majority of the population as well as the violation of the inalienable right to self-determination of all of the people of South Africa. This inhuman policy has been enforced by ruthless measures of repression and has led to escalating tension and conflict.

Also in 1977, the UN General Assembly adopted and proclaimed (resolution 32/105 M) the **INTERNATIONAL DECLARATION AGAINST** *APARTHEID* **IN SPORTS.** And in 1985, it adopted and opened for ratification and acceptance the **INTERNATIONAL CONVENTION AGAINST** *APARTHEID* **IN SPORTS.** The convention entered into force on 3 April.

Both instruments recognize that participation in sports exchanges with teams selected on the basis of *apartheid* directly abets and encourages the commission of that crime and that sports contact with any country practicing *apartheid* condones and strengthens the system, in violation of the Olympic principle of non-discrimination on the grounds of race, religion, or political affiliation, and thereby becomes the legitimate concern of all governments. Both call for the adoption of all necessary measures to eradicate the practice of *apartheid* in sports and to promote international sports contacts based on the Olympic principle.

The convention defines *"apartheid,"* for its purposes, as meaning "a system of institutionalized racial segregation and discrimination for the purpose of establishing and maintaining domination by one racial group of persons over another racial group of persons and systematically oppressing them, such as that pursued in South Africa." It defines *"apartheid* in sports" as meaning "the application of the policies and practices of such a system in sports activities, whether organized on a professional or an amateur basis."

Under the convention, States parties undertake:

(a) to pursue immediately by all appropriate means the policy of eliminating the practice of *apartheid* in all its forms from sports;

(b) to take appropriate action to ensure that their sports bodies, teams, and individual sportsmen do not have such contact;

(c) to prevent sports contact with a country practicing *apartheid;* and

(d) to refuse to provide financial or other assistance to enable their sports bodies, teams, and individual sportsmen to participate in sports activities in a country practicing *apartheid* or with teams or individual sportsmen selected on the basis of *apartheid.*

Each State party also undertakes to take appropriate action against its sports bodies, teams, and individual sportsmen that participate in sports activities in a country practicing *apartheid* or with teams representing such a country; to deny visas and/or entry to representatives of sports bodies, teams, and individual sportsmen representing such a country; to take appropriate action to secure the expulsion of such a country from international and regional sports bodies; and to take measures to prevent international sports bodies from imposing financial or other penalties on affiliated bodies which refuse to participate in sports with a country practicing *apartheid.*

To monitor compliance with its provisions, the convention provides for the establishment (article 11) of the COMMISSION AGAINST *APARTHEID* IN SPORTS to review reports submitted by States parties on the legislative, judicial, administrative, or other measures which they have adopted to give effect to those provisions. In addition, a State party may at any time declare (article 13) that it recognizes the competence of the commission to receive and examine complaints concern-

ing breaches of the convention submitted by States parties which have also made such a declaration.

On the basis of the information available to it, the Special Committee against *Apartheid* included, in its 1988 report to the UN General Assembly, the following conclusions (UN Doc. A/43/22, chap. V, para. 183–193):

In the past year Pretoria escalated its repression in South Africa, trying to crush every form of opposition in the country and impose its political designs. At the same time, for a variety of reasons, the *apartheid* régime has recently become involved in diplomatic efforts aimed at a settlement in the conflict in southern Africa.

The renewal of the state of emergency and the series of repressive measures adopted against anti-*apartheid* organizations and domestic and foreign media suggest that the régime can advance its objectives only through the indiscriminate use of force and State-sponsored terrorism. The enactment of these repressive measures is designed to stifle opposition to the régime, to its "reforms" and to the scheduled elections for October 1988.

Pretoria's constitutional scheme excludes blacks from participation in Parliament and restricts it to the "homelands" and township councils. The reaction to that exclusion has contributed to the violence that has shaken South Africa since 1984. The régime's "reforms" give an appearance of power-sharing without substance. The centrepiece of the reformist scheme, the National Council soon to be called the Great Indaba, will be an advisory body. The scheme, among other things, preserves the fragmentation of the population and the limitation of black power to "own affairs", preserving as the domain for decision-making by whites those issues most critical to the national body politic. As long as the state of emergency is in effect, political prisoners and detainees remain imprisoned, anti-*apartheid* and political organizations continue to be banned, the prospects of a peaceful solution to the conflict in South Africa remain elusive and the country will continue its downward spiral into violence.

Recent negotiations in the southern African region give reason for cautious hope of the resolution of the war conflict in Angola and the independence of Namibia. The fact remains, however, that the root cause of the conflict in southern Africa is the maintenance of *apartheid* and as long as this system is in effect regional peace will be threatened constantly.

Apartheid is not only being aggressively maintained, but is also becoming the object of a disingenuous effort to camouflage it through "reforms". Thus the challenge to the international community remains as high as ever and the imposition of sanctions on the régime continues to be of crucial significance. In this respect, those sanctions imposed on South Africa by a number of countries significantly contributed to common efforts of international community and have had a considerable impact on the economy even if their implementation has been at times hesitant and on the whole unco-ordinated. Partly as a result of sanctions, the South African economy is experiencing slow rates of growth. The compound effects of disinvestment, the denial of long-term credit and the lack of new capital investment are beginning to be felt and show the vulnerability of South Africa's economy to sanctions.

In this context, the new measures adopted against South

Africa, and those being considered for adoption by the Commonwealth and the United States Congress are welcome. South Africa's trade with the Nordic countries has virtually ceased and that with the United States has decreased as a result of the measures they have undertaken in recent years.

It is regretful, however, that while some countries are gradually reducing their economic links with South Africa, others are filling that gap in defiance of United Nations resolutions calling for the complete isolation of the régime. Recent studies reveal a disturbing pattern: the traditional trade partners of South Africa are being replaced by new ones. Thus in 1987 the value of South African trade with Japan, the Federal Republic of Germany, Italy, Spain and Turkey has considerably increased over the 1983–1985 period. Japan, which has replaced the United States as the largest trading partner of South Africa, increased its imports of South African goods by 40 per cent while Switzerland increased by three times its imports from South Africa during this period. One of the most significant beneficiaries of trade restrictions against South Africa has been the Province of Taiwan which increased in 1987 its imports from South Africa by 150 per cent over the 1983–1985 average and has also invested in the "homelands". In addition, Israel's imports of iron and steel increased, as well as in commodities which are unclassified in Israel's trade statistics. The Federal Republic of Germany has become the largest exporter to South Africa followed by Japan, the United Kingdom and the United States. It is disturbing that some major industrialized countries still maintain significant trade, investment and military links with Pretoria. It is equally disturbing that some newly industrialized countries, particularly in the Far East, are seeking advantages by filling the economic gap created by the sanctions of those countries which have heeded the call of the international community to isolate South Africa. It is furthermore worrisome that some developments, admittedly in few African countries, suggest that the necessary vigilance is not being exercised; this allows Pretoria to evade sanctions.

Recent developments in South Africa proved once more that the régime cannot solve the conflict in the country by violence. Despite the régime's relentless attack on all fronts, the opposition is regrouping and its activities range from armed resistance to strikes and boycotts. It is imperative then that the international community exercise further economic and political pressure in order to induce the régime to introduce fundamental changes in the political system of the country amounting to the eradication of *apartheid*. There is strong evidence that economic sanctions can have a significant impact on the South African economy; they act as a catalyst on the domestic and international business community by affecting those economic sectors which have influence on the political decision-making process in the country. In the same vein other efforts to isolate South Africa, such as in the sports and the cultural field can exert a parallel pressure on the ruling white minority and, therefore, should be strengthened.

It is in that context that the Special Committee considers that the most effective sanctions, short of the imposition of comprehensive and mandatory sanctions, should be targeted at key areas of the economy, notably a ban on imports of coal and agricultural products, or supply of loans and credit, or transfer of technology and a ban on direct air flights to and from South Africa. A mandatory oil embargo still remains one of the most powerful ways of pressuring the régime. The effective monitoring of the arms embargo is also of extreme significance in the international campaign against *apartheid*. The EEC and Japan which, regarding the scope and implementation of sanctions, currently lag behind substantially the Nordic countries and the United States, are urgently invited to raise the level of their sanctions and close loopholes appearing within the context of their participation in the international action against *apartheid*.

Measures should also be considered to prevent countries from benefiting from the vacuum created by other States which have imposed sanctions. States, deciding to introduce sanctions, should adopt national legislative measures to penalize violators of sanctions, instead of merely relying on policy statements. Finally, experience so far has shown that the sanctions adopted against South Africa need strengthening, better co-ordination and standardization, improved implementation and a more effective centralized monitoring and reporting system.

While there are signs that the political climate in the region is improving, a development that the Special Committee welcomes, the international community should intensify its focus on the continuing deterioration of the internal situation in South Africa where *apartheid,* which has been the root cause of the regional conflict, remains virtually intact. The challenge to all the members of the international community is as urgent as ever.

On 5 December 1988, the General Assembly, having considered the report of the Special Committee against *Apartheid,* particularly the paragraphs reproduced above, expressed (resolution 43/50 A) its grave concern at the escalating repression of and State terror against opponents of *apartheid* and the increasing intransigience of the racist regime of South Africa, exemplified by the continuous extension of the state of emergency; the imposition of severe restrictions on peaceful anti-*apartheid* organizations and individuals; the increasing numbers of arbitrary detentions, trials, torture, and killings, including those of women and children; the increased use of vigilante groups; and the stifling of the press. It also took note with serious concern of the regime's continuing acts of aggression and destabilization against neighboring independent African States, including assassinations and abductions of freedom fighters in those States, and elsewhere, and the continuing illegal occupation of Namibia.

In the resolution, the assembly reaffirmed its full support to the majority of the South African people in their struggle—under the leadership of their national liberation movements, the African National Congress of South Africa and the Pan Africanist Congress of Azania—to eradicate *apartheid* totally, so that all the people of South Africa as a whole, irrespective of race, color, or creed, may enjoy equal and full political and other rights and participate freely in the determination of their destiny. It further reaffirmed the legitimacy of the struggle of the people of South Africa and their right to choose the necessary means, including armed struggle, to attain the eradication of *apartheid* and the establishment of a free, democratic, unfragmented, and non-racial South Africa.

In particular, the assembly demanded, as it had on past occasions:

(a) the lifting of the state of emergency;
(b) the immediate and unconditional release of Nelson Mandela and all other political prisoners and detainees;
(c) the lifting of the ban on all political organizations and opponents of *apartheid;*
(d) the safe return of all political exiles;
(e) the withdrawal of the régime's troops from black townships;
(f) the repeal of restrictions on the freedom of the press;
(g) the end of the policy of bantustanization and forced population removals; and
(h) the end of military and paramilitary activities aimed at the neighbouring countries.

It also demanded that the execution of political prisoners then on death row be stopped, that all detained children be unconditionally released, and that the abhorrent practice of applying repressive measures to children and minors cease immediately.

The assembly indicated that the implementation of the above demands would create the appropriate conditions for free consultations among all the people of South Africa with a view to negotiating a just and lasting solution to the conflict in that country. It appealed to all States, intergovernmental and non-governmental organizations, mass media, and city and other local authorities, as well as individuals, to increase urgently political, economic, educational, legal, humanitarian, and all other forms of necessary assistance to the people of South Africa and their national liberation movements; and also appealed to all States and intergovernmental and non-governmental organizations to step up material, financial, and other forms of support to the frontline and other neighboring independent States.

In 1989, the General Assembly held a special session on the question of *apartheid* at UN headquarters in New York, at which it reviewed developments relating to that question and unanimously adopted, on 14 December 1989, the DECLARATION ON *APARTHEID* AND ITS DESTRUCTIVE CONSEQUENCES IN SOUTHERN AFRICA. In the declaration, it urged that serious efforts should be made to put an end to *apartheid* through negotiations based on the principle of justice and peace for all.

Security Council Actions against Apartheid. The UN Security Council took up the question of race conflict in South Africa in 1960 and recognized (resolution 134 [1960]) that the situation, if continued, might endanger international peace and security. In 1963, the council instituted a voluntary embargo against the supply of arms to South Africa, calling upon all States (resolution 181 [1963]) to end the sale and shipment of arms, ammunition, and military vehicles to that country. This ban was reiterated and strengthened to include the sale of equipment and material for the maintenance and manufacture of arms and ammunition, in 1964, 1970, and 1972.

In 1974, the Security Council considered, at the request of the General Assembly, the relationship between the United Nations and South Africa "in the light of the constant violation by South Africa of the Charter and the Universal Declaration of Human Rights." A proposal for immediate expulsion of South Africa from the UN was considered but not adopted because of the negative vote—"veto"— of three permanent members: France, the United Kingdom, and the United States. Although it continued to be a UN member, South Africa was not represented at assembly sessions held in 1975, 1976, and 1977.

In 1975, the council considered a proposal to make the arms embargo mandatory but was unable to do so because of the negative votes of the same permanent members: France, the United Kingdom, and the United States. The General Assembly, which for ten years had been calling upon the council to take action against South Africa under chapter 7 of the UN Charter, expressed regret at its failure to do so and called the action of the permanent members "an abuse of their veto." Another attempt to make the embargo mandatory failed in 1976. However, in 1977, after a lengthy debate sparked by South Africa's resort to massive violence against African people, including the shooting of demonstrators at Soweto in June 1976, the council decided unanimously (resolution 418 [1977]) to impose a mandatory arms embargo. Its decision was that all States should cease any provision to South Africa of arms and related materiel of all types, including the sale or transfer of weapons and ammunition, military vehicles and equipment, paramilitary police equipment, and spare parts for them; and that all States should refrain from any cooperation with South Africa in the manufacture and development of nuclear weapons. The council further established a committee to monitor the progress of the implementation of the resolution and to study ways and means of making the embargo more effective.

In March 1985, the council called upon the South African authorities (resolution 560 [1985]) to release unconditionally and immediately all political prisoners and detainees, including Nelson Mandela and all other black leaders with whom it must deal in any meaningful discussion of the future of the country. In July of that year, it strongly condemned (resolution 569 [1985]) the *apartheid* system, the mass arrests and detentions carried out by the Pretoria government, and the murders that had been committed, as well as the establishment of a "state of emergency" in 36 districts. It demanded the immediate lifting of the state of emergency and reaffirmed its view that only the total elimination of *apartheid* and the establishment in South Africa of a free, united, and democratic society on the basis of universal suffrage could lead to a solution of the country's problems.

The council was unable, up to the end of 1988, to impose comprehensive and mandatory sanctions against South Africa as provided in chapter 7 of the UN Charter. In this connection, the General Assembly has for a number of years adopted resolutions (for example, resolutions 38/39 D, 39/72 A, 40/64 A, 41/35 B, and 42/23 C) urging the council to take such action and urging the governments of the United Kingdom, the United States of America, and others that are opposed to the application of such sanctions to reassess their policies and cease their opposition.

In June 1986, the president of the Security Council issued the following statement (UN Doc. S/18157) on behalf of the members of the council:

The members of the Security Council, on the occasion of the observance of the tenth anniversary of the wanton killings perpetrated by the *apartheid* régime in South Africa against the African people in Soweto, wish to recall Security Council resolution 392 (1976) of 19 June 1976 which strongly condemned the South African government for its resort to massive violence against and killings of the African people including schoolchildren and students and others opposing racial discrimination. They are convinced that a repetition of such tragic events would aggravate the already serious threat that the situation in South Africa poses to the security of the region and could have wider implications for international peace and security.

They condemn the policy and all the repressive measures which only serve to perpetuate the *apartheid* system, in particular the recent imposition of a nation-wide state of emergency and the arrest and detention of thousands of persons involved in the struggle against *apartheid*. They urge the immediate and unconditional release of all persons detained in this respect. In particular, they call for the immediate lifting of the state of emergency in order to allow the observance of the tenth anniversary of the Soweto massacre without any provocative interference or intimidation on the part of the police and military forces.

In this regard, the members of the Security Council, committed as they are to work for a just and equitable solution which will totally eradicate *apartheid* and avert further human suffering in South Africa, warn the South African Government that it will be held fully responsible for any violence, bloodshed, loss of life, injury and damage to property which may result from acts of repression and intimidation on the occasion of the observance of the tenth anniversary of the Soweto massacre.

The members of the Security Council reaffirm the legitimacy of the struggle of the oppressed people of South Africa for the total elimination of *apartheid* and recall previous resolutions calling upon the racist régime in South Africa to abolish *apartheid* and to establish a non-racial democratic society based on majority rule, through the full and free exercise of adult universal suffrage by all the people in a united and unfragmented South Africa.

In April 1987, the president of the council again issued a statement on behalf of members of the council (UN Doc. S/18808), as follows:

The members of the Security Council express their deep concern about the decree issued by the South African authorities on 10 April 1987, under which nearly all forms of protest against detentions without trial or support for those detained are prohibited. The members of the Council express their strong indignation at this latest measure, which is based on the June 1986 decree imposing the nation-wide state of emergency, the lifting of which was called for by the members of the Council in the statement made by the President on their behalf at the 2690th meeting of the Council, on 13 June 1986.

The members of the Council call upon the South African authorities to revoke the decree of 10 April 1987, which is contrary to fundamental human rights as envisaged in the Charter of the United Nations and to the relevant resolutions of the Security Council and can only aggravate the situation further, lead to an escalation of acts of violence and further intensify human suffering in South Africa.

The members of the Council, recognizing that the root cause of the situation in South Africa is *apartheid,* once again strongly condemn the *apartheid* system and all the policies and practices, including this latest decree, deriving therefrom. They again call upon the Government of South Africa to end the oppression and repression of the black majority by bringing *apartheid* to an end and to seek a peaceful, just and lasting solution in accordance with the principles of the Charter and the Universal Declaration of Human Rights. They also call upon the Government of South Africa to set free immediately and unconditionally all political prisoners and detainees, in order to avoid further aggravating the situation.

They urge the Government of South Africa to enter into negotiations with the genuine representatives of the South African people with a view to the establishment in South Africa of a free, united and democratic society on the basis of universal suffrage.

Commission on Human Rights Actions against Apartheid. After examining an interim report of its **AD HOC WORKING GROUP OF EXPERTS ON SOUTHERN AFRICA** (UN Doc. E/CN.4/1988/8) at its 1988 session, the UN Commission on Human Rights condemned the dramatic escalation of violations of human rights in South Africa since the imposition of the state of emergency in June 1986 and other subsequent regulations, as well as the widespread detention and incarceration of children under the inhuman *apartheid* penal system. It unequivocally rejected South Africa's so-called reforms, "which fall short of the termination of the existing state of emergency, the abolition of the *apartheid* laws, the dismantling of the bantustans, the lifting of the bans on all political organizations and parties, the return of all exiles and freedom fighters and the unconditional release of all political prisoners with whom the regime must deal in bringing about changes based on the 'one man-one vote' principle in a non-fragmented South Africa"; and demanded the unconditional and immediate release of Mr. Nelson Mandela, Mr. Zephania Mothopeng, and all other political prisoners and the cessation of the campaign of abduction and assassination of political refugees and members of the liberation movements based in neighboring States.

The commission called upon the Security Council to impose comprehensive and mandatory sanctions against the South African regime and endorsed, pending the adoption of such sanctions, the following measures that have been adopted by certain countries and organizations and commend them to the wider international community for urgent adoption and implementation:

(a) Prohibition of the transfer of technology to South Africa;

(b) Cessation of exports, sales or transport of oil and oil products to South Africa, and of any co-operation with South Africa's oil industry;

(c) Cessation of further investments in and financial loans to South Africa or Namibia and of any governmental insurance guarantee of credits to the racist régime;

(d) Cessation of all promotion of or support for trade with South Africa, including governmental assistance to trade missions;

(e) Prohibition of the sale of krugerrand and any other coins minted in South Africa;

(f) Prohibition of imports from South Africa of agricultural products, coal, uranium, iron and steel, etc.;

(g) Termination of any visa-free entry privileges and of the promotion of tourism to South Africa;

(h) Termination of air and shipping links with South Africa;

(i) Cessation of all academic, cultural, scientific and sports relations with South Africa, and of relations with individuals, institutions and other bodies endorsing or based on *apartheid;*

(j) Suspension or abrogation of agreements with South Africa, such as agreements on cultural and scientific co-operation;

(k) Termination of double taxation agreements with South Africa; and

(l) Ban on government contracts with majority-owned South African companies.

SEE ALSO Apartheid *entries ff.; Lagos Declaration for Action Against* Apartheid; *Slavery-Like Practices of* Apartheid *and Colonialism; South Africa; South Africa: UN Concern about* Apartheid.

APARTHEID: A COLLECTIVE FORM OF SLAVERY.
In 1980, the UN Secretary-General prepared and submitted to the SUB-COMMISSION ON PREVENTION OF DIS-CRIMINATION AND PROTECTION OF MINORITIES, at its request, a report entitled *"Apartheid* As a Collective Form of Slavery," in which he noted (UN Doc. E/CN.4/Sub.2/449, para. 231) that

.... the international community has recognized that the *apartheid* system in South Africa is not simply a racial discrimination problem to be solved through education and political and social reforms. Rather, it has been increasingly understood that the essence of *apartheid* lies in the dispossession of the black population through the imposition of quasi-colonial rule, and in the harnessing of the labor of the vanquished indigenous people through a variety of coercive measures for the benefit of white investors, both South African and foreign. The international community has therefore described the *apartheid* system as a slavery-like practice imposed on an entire collectivity, which can be eradicated only through a complete restructuring of the existing political and economic relationships.

After examining the report, the sub-commission referred it to the AD HOC WORKING GROUP OF EXPERTS ON SOUTHERN AFRICA, the SPECIAL COMMITTEE AGAINST APARTHEID, and the Director-General of the International Labor Organization for their consideration and such action as they may deem appropriate (resolution 8 [XXXIII]). At the same time, the sub-commission strongly rejected the labor practices of the Government of South Africa as constituting "a modern form of slavery."

SEE ALSO Apartheid: *An International Crime;* Apartheid: *Penal Tribunal; Declaration on* Apartheid *and its Destructive Consequences in Southern Africa; International Convention on the Suppression and Punishment of the Crime of* Apartheid; *Slavery-like Practices of* Apartheid *and Colonialism.*

APARTHEID: ADVERSE EFFECTS OF ASSISTANCE TO SOUTH AFRICA.
In 1974, the UN ECONOMIC AND SOCIAL COUNCIL condemned (resolution 1864 [LVI]) "the activities of States which continue to give political, military, economic and other assistance to the racist and colonial regimes in southern Africa or which refrain from taking any steps to prevent natural or juridical persons within their jurisdiction from assisting those regimes and thus encouraging them to continue violating fundamental human rights."

The Council authorized the appointment, by the Sub-Commission on Prevention of Discrimination and Protection of Minorities, of a special rapporteur to study the question; and, subsequently, Mr. Ahmed Khalifa (Egypt) was appointed as the special rapporteur. His reports—containing lists of banks, transnational corporations, and other organizations providing assistance to South Africa—have since been considered at regular intervals by the sub-commission, the Commission on Human Rights, the Economic and Social Council, and the General Assembly. Since 1980, these and other bodies concerned have regularly called upon the governments of countries where such organizations have their headquarters to take effective action to halt their activities constituting assistance to South Africa on the ground that all such activities are detrimental to the human rights of black residents of South Africa and Namibia.

A few positive developments were reflected in the special rapporteur's 1988 report (UN Doc. E/CN.4/Sub.2/1988/6), including the fact that, between 1984 and 1988, about 150 companies based in the United States of America had withdrawn from South Africa or had announced their intention to do so. However, more than 200 U.S.-based corporations continued to do business in that country or in Namibia; and, in some cases where such countries had reduced their operations in southern Africa, others from western Europe or Japan had stepped in to fill the gap.

After noting the report, the General Assembly, on 8 December 1988, reaffirmed (resolution 43/92) the inalienable right of the oppressed peoples of southern Africa to SELF-DETERMINATION, independence, and the enjoyment of the natural resources of their territories, and the right of those same peoples to dispose of those resources for their greater well-being and to obtain just reparation for the exploitation, depletion, loss, or depreciation of those natural resources, including reparation for the exploitation and abuse of their human resources.

The assembly vigorously condemned "the collaboration of certain Western States, Israel and other States, as well as the transnational corporations and other organizations, which maintain or continue to increase their collaboration with the racist and colonialist regime of South Africa, especially in the political, economic, military and nuclear fields, thus encouraging that regime to persist in its inhuman and criminal policy of brutal oppression of the peoples of southern Africa and denial of their human rights."

The assembly further expressed the view "that the updating of the report on the adverse consequences for the enjoyment of human rights of political, military, economic and other forms of assistance given to the racist and colonialist regime of South Africa is of the greatest importance to the cause of fighting *apartheid* and other violations of human rights in South Africa and Namibia" and invited the special rapporteur to continue the preparation of his reports.

Later both the Commission on Human Rights and the Economic and Social Council expressed their satisfaction with the report and their thanks to the

governments and organizations that had provided information to the special rapporteur. On recommendation of the commission, the council on 24 May 1989 (resolution 1989/73) invited the special rapporteur to continue to update the list of banks, transnational corporations, and other organizations assisting the racist regime of South Africa. The Secretary-General was requested to bring the special rapporteur's updated report to the attention of governments whose national financial institutions continue to deal with South Africa and to call upon them to provide the special rapporteur with information or comments on the matter.

The special rapporteur was called upon by the council to provide the sub-commission with a concise note on the feasibility of consolidating the lists maintained by United Nations organs of enterprises doing business with South Africa. He was also requested to provide the sub-commission with a brief analysis of the partial disinvestment of foreign enterprises in South Africa, enumerating the various techniques employed to avoid total withdrawal from participation in the South African economy.

***APARTHEID*: AN INTERNATIONAL CRIME.** In a number of resolutions and decisions adopted by the UN General Assembly between 1966 and 1970, the South African policy of *apartheid* was condemned as constituting a crime against humanity. In 1968, the International Conference on Human Rights declared, in resolution III, that "the policy of *apartheid* or other similar evils are a crime against humanity punishable in accordance with the provisions of relevant international instruments dealing with such crimes."

On 18 March 1970, the Commission on Human Rights called upon its AD HOC WORKING GROUP OF EXPERTS ON SOUTHERN AFRICA "to study, from the point of view of international penal law, the question of *apartheid*, which has been declared a crime against humanity" (resolution 8 [XXVI]). In 1972, the working group presented a "Study Concerning the Question of *Apartheid* from the Point of View of International Penal Law" (UN Doc. E./CN.4/1075) to the commission.

In the study, the working group analyzed the concept of international penal law in doctrine, then reviewed elements of the policy of *apartheid* brought to light in the work of the United Nations to which international penal law might be applied. The conclusions of the group were: (1) that ill-treatment of political prisoners and the like on racial grounds, the extermination of, or the attempt to exterminate, members of a racial group, the killing of persons, deportations, slavery-like practices and the ill-treatment inflicted upon freedom-fighters are acts resulting from the policies of *apartheid* and must be considered crimes under international law; (2) that South Africa is responsible for these acts either under international public law or under the Geneva Conventions and the peace treaties concluded at the end of the World War II to which South Africa is a party; (3) that no effective international machinery exists, however, for the judicial determination of the penal responsibility of States and individuals; and (4) that, besides alarming world public opinion regarding the fact that South Africa, by certain elements of its *apartheid* policies, is continuously committing crimes under international law, nothing can be done at this time to bring the State authorities in question to book.

The INTERNATIONAL CONVENTION ON THE SUPPRESSION AND PUNISHMENT OF THE CRIME OF *APARTHEID*, adopted by the General Assembly on 30 November 1973, opens with the statement that "the States parties to the present Convention declare that *apartheid* is a crime against humanity and that inhuman acts resulting from the policies and practices of *apartheid* and similar policies and practices of racial segregation and discrimination. . . . are crimes violating the principles of international law." After defining the term "the policy of *apartheid*," in Article II, the convention provides (article III) that

International criminal responsibility shall apply, irrespective of the motive involved, to individuals, members of organizations and institutions and representatives of the State, whether residing in the territory of the State in which the acts are perpetrated or in some other State, whenever they: (a) Commit, participate in, directly incite or conspire in the commission of the acts mentioned in article II of the Convention; (b) Directly abet, encourage or co-operate in the commission of the crime of *apartheid*.

Under article V of the convention, "persons charged with the acts enumerated in article II. . . . may be tried by a competent tribunal of any State party to the Convention which may acquire jurisdiction over the person of the accused or by an international penal tribunal having jurisdiction with respect to those States parties which shall have accepted its jurisdiction." It does not, however, go so far as to establish effective international machinery for the judicial determination of the States' penal responsibility toward individuals alleged to have committed the crime of *apartheid*.

APARTHEID: ILO DECLARATION AND PROGRAM OF ACTION. In 1964, 1981, and 1988, the International Labor Organization adopted its own Declaration and Program of Action against *Apartheid*.

The 1988 declaration and program of action, adopted by the International Labor Conference on 16 June 1988 (UN Doc. E/CN.4/1989/35, annex) is as follows:

The General Conference of the International Labour Organisation,

Recalling the Declaration concerning the Policy of Apartheid in South Africa unanimously adopted by the Conference on 8 July 1964 and the updated Declaration adopted by the Conference on 18 June 1981,

Considering that all Members of the ILO have by the Declaration of Philadelphia embodied in the Constitution as a statement of the aims and purposes of the Organization, solemnly affirmed that "all human beings, irrespective of race, creed or sex, have the right to pursue both their material well-being and their spiritual development in conditions of freedom and dignity, of economic security and equal opportunity",

Considering that according to its Constitution the ILO exists for the promotion of the objectives set forth in the Preamble thereto and in the Declaration of Philadelphia,

Considering that the Government of South Africa, having refused to promote the objectives set forth in the Preamble to the Constitution and in the Declaration of Philadelphia, adopted and is practising the inhuman policy of apartheid, which is wholly incompatible with the aims and principles of the Declaration of Philadelphia, thus creating an alarming situation, further aggravated by the extension of the apartheid system into Namibia through the illegal occupation of that territory by South Africa, incurred the condemnation of the International Labour Conference and withdrew from the Organisation by virtue of a communication dated 11 March 1964,

Considering that according to the Declaration of Philadelphia the principles set forth therein are fully applicable to all peoples everywhere and their implementation is a matter of concern to the whole world,

Considering that apartheid has been declared a crime against humanity by the General Assembly of the United Nations and that the Security Council, since its resolution 182 (1963) adopted unanimously on 4 December 1963, has affirmed the conviction that the situation in South Africa is seriously disturbing international peace and security,

Considering that the *apartheid* system in South Africa is the root cause of conflict in southern Africa as a whole and that the independence of Namibia, the freedom of the South African people and the peace and security in the region can only be attained through the elimination of apartheid,

Considering the programme for the elimination of apartheid in labour matters in South Africa adopted in 1964 and all subsequent measures to give effect to the ILO's determination to eradicate *apartheid*, including the annual Special Reports of the Director-General on apartheid in South Africa and the expansion of the activities of the International Labour Office in this field,

Considering especially the Report of the International Tripartite Meeting on Action against Apartheid held at Livingstone in May 1981, which recognized that the solution to the problem of apartheid must take into account the political implications of that system and went on to recommend specific action for the elimination of apartheid,

Considering also the reports of the Tripartite Conference on Action against Apartheid held in Lusaka in May 1984 and in Harare in May 1988,

Noting that the conclusions of these meetings were subsequently adopted by the International Labour Conference,

Sharing the growing concern of the international community at the deterioration of the situation in South Africa and Namibia under apartheid and the need for action thereon, as shown in the Programme of Action adopted at the United Nations General Assembly and in subsequent resolutions and instruments adopted by that Assembly (including the Convention on the Suppression and Punishment of the Crime of *Apartheid*) as well as the resolutions of the Security Council,

Reaffirming in addition the need to co-operate with all organisations in the campaign to eliminate apartheid, in particular the United Nations, the Organisation of African Unity and international and regional organisations of workers and employers,

Considering that developments which have taken place since the adoption of its Declaration and Programme for the elimination of Apartheid in 1964 have demonstrated that *apartheid* continues to deprive the Black population of employment and training, full enjoyment of freedom of association and the right to organise, and equality of opportunity and treatment in the field of labour, while recent events have shown that through the "Bantustan" policy and the use of repressive measures the South African Government still acts in a manner which violates international labour standards and which therefore requires urgent action by the international community to secure social justice, peace and freedom for all the peoples of South Africa and Namibia,

Reaffirming its determination to continue to fulfil its responsibility to promote and take its part in securing the freedom and dignity of the peoples of South Africa and Namibia and to fight the policy of apartheid practised by the Government of South Africa,

Faithful to its role as spokesman of the social conscience of mankind and affirming once again its conviction that a government which deliberately practises apartheid is unworthy of the community of nations,

Considering that only urgent and determined action by the international community, in particular the imposition of comprehensive and mandatory sanctions by the United Nations Security Council as the most effective and appropriate measure under the present circumstances, will bring the Government of South Africa to abandon its disastrous policy and to co-operate with employers' and workers' organisations in placing the relations between the various elements of the population of South Africa, and the relations between the people of South Africa and the rest of the world, on the basis of the equality of man, justice for all, good neighbourliness and mutual respect;

1. Solemnly reaffirms its fidelity to the fundamental principle of the Declaration of Philadelphia, according to which "all human beings, irrespective of race, creed or sex, have the right to pursue both their material well-being and their spiritual development in conditions of freedom and dignity, of economic security and equal opportunity".

2. Emphatically reaffirms its condemnation of the degrading, criminal and inhuman racial policies of the Government of South Africa and their extensions to Namibia, which policies are a violation of fundamental human rights and thus incompatible with the aims and purpose of the ILO.

3. Strongly reaffirms its determination to pursue its action until respect for the freedom and dignity of all human beings, irrespective of race, is fully assured in South Africa and Namibia and until, to this end, the following objectives have been attained:

- the total and final elimination of the policy of apartheid in South Africa and Namibia;
- the repeal of all legislative, administrative and other measures which are a violation of the principle of the equality and dignity of man and a direct negation of the inherent rights and freedoms of the peoples of South Africa and Namibia;
- the establishment and consistent pursuit of a policy of equal opportunity and treatment for all, in employment and occupation, irrespective of race, creed or sex;
- the cessation of all aggression, social and economic destabilisation of the front-line countries.

4. Urges the Committee on Action against Apartheid of the International Labour Conference to continue to monitor with increased vigour action against apartheid.

5. (a) Confirms the Director-General's mandate to monitor and follow the situation in South Africa and Namibia in respect of labour and social matters, and to submit every year for consideration by the Conference Committee on Action against Apartheid a Special Report on the subject; to this effect, to request governments, employers' and workers' organisations to provide individually information, in such form as the Governing Body may determine, on the action taken against apartheid in accordance with recommendations contained in the Programme of Action against Apartheid, including information on failure to take action and on the active promotion of relations which strengthen the apartheid system;

(b) invites the Governing Body's Committee on Discrimination to continue to consider the information described in subparagraph (a) above, and to submit a report to the Conference Committee on Action against Apartheid.

6. Invites the Governing Body and the Director-General to take the necessary steps:

(a) to increase the ILO's educational activities and technical assistance to the liberation movements, the Black workers and their independent trade unions as well as the Black entrepreneurs and their organisations in South Africa and Namibia in their fight against apartheid, in close co-operation with the Organisation of African Unity, the Special Committee against Apartheid, the Commission on Human Rights of the United Nations, and the United Nations Council for Namibia, the international and African workers' and employers' organisations and the front-line States and those States in the neighbourhood of South Africa which are seriously affected by the aggressive actions of South Africa, in particular by:

(i) an increase in the resources made available from the ILO regular budget, and from external sources on a bilateral or multilateral basis, for enlarging the ILO's capacity to combat apartheid and to provide assistance to its victims;

(ii) the establishment of a voluntary fund for the workers of South Africa and Namibia to which contributions should be made regularly by ILO member States as well as by employers' and workers' organisations;

(iii) the broadening of the scope of ILO assistance to liberation movements from southern Africa recognised by the Organisation of Africa Unity, in particular by the use of its technical services in the fields of vocational and management training, labour administration, occupational safety and health, rural development, workers' education, co-operative development, equality of treatment for women workers and advice on the elimination of discriminatory labour legislation;

(iv) the establishment of a training institute for South Africa, designed more specifically for the promotion of manpower training and development;

(v) assistance to the front-line and neighbouring States providing facilities for refugees from South Africa and Namibia at institutions of their own through the provision of equipment, expertise and fellowships;

(vi) the creation of training facilities and employment opportunities for refugees in their countries of refuge in such a way that their skills will be of immediate use and also of assistance to their countries of origin upon their return;

(vii) co-operation with the governments of the States in the immediate neighbourhood of South Africa, including the regional organisation, the Southern African Development Co-ordination Conference and the Southern African Labour Commission, in devising and implementing policies which will enable them to reduce their dependence on South Africa, and in particular the supply of migrant labour in South Africa;

(viii) providing the front-line and neighbouring States with assistance for infra-structural development to enhance their capacity for withstanding the effects of any retaliatory economic action by the apartheid regime and to develop human skills for the effective management of their national economies;

(ix) assistance in the establishment of long-term solutions to problems involving migrant labour including public works programmes and other labour intensive forms of job creation; the provision, over the short term, of assistance to migrant workers through advice on negotiations concerning their terms and conditions of employment, and through enabling migrant workers to be more fully informed of their rights;

(x) the expansion of the programme of the information on apartheid in labour matters and other questions of direct concern to the workers of southern Africa;

(b) to use existing ILO procedures, including those of the Committee on Discrimination of the Governing Body, to attain the objectives assigned to the ILO under its Programme for the Elimination of Apartheid;

(c) to encourage and extend financial support to workers' and employers' organisations in their programme of action against apartheid so that they can exert the maximum pressure for the implementation of various recommendations falling within their sphere of competence.

7. Renews its urgent appeal to governments, employers and workers of member States of the ILO to combine their efforts and put into application all appropriate measures to lead South Africa to heed the call of humanity and renounce its shameful policy of apartheid. In this respect, the basic guide-line should be the Programme of Action against Apartheid which is annexed to this updated Declaration.

8. Reaffirms its resolve to co-operate with the United Nations in seeking and guaranteeing freedom and dignity, economic security and equal opportunity for all the peoples of South Africa and Namibia and in particular with the United Nations Special Committee against Apartheid and the Council for Namibia and its desire to co-operate with the Organisation of African Unity in all fields related to the elimination of apartheid.

9. Requests the Governing Body and the Director-General to take the necessary steps to organise systematic consultations with a view to reinforcing ILO co-operation with the Organisation of African Unity, and with the United Nations, including its Special Committee against Apartheid, its Council for Namibia and its Commission on Human Rights, as well as with the other specialised agencies of the United Nations system and non-governmental organisations associated with them in order to intensify and co-ordinate all activities whose ultimate objective is to eliminate apartheid totally in all its facets in a more accelerated pace than hitherto.

Annex
Programme of Action against Apartheid

The General Conference of the International Labour Organisation, considering it appropriate to give effect to the updated Declaration concerning Action against Apartheid in South Africa adopted by the International Labour Conference in 1988, following the updated Declaration adopted by the Conference in 1981 and the initial Declaration adopted unanimously by the Conference in 1964,

Urging determined action by the international community to bring the Government of South Africa to abandon its disastrous policy of apartheid,

Taking into account the report of the Tripartite Meeting of Members of the Governing Body on apartheid in May 1980, the Report of the International Tripartite Meeting on Action against Apartheid held at Livingstone in 1981 and the conclusions on the Tripartite Conferences on Action against Apartheid held in Lusaka in 1984 and in Harare in 1988,

Further taking into account the resolutions adopted by the two International Trade Union Conferences against Apartheid in 1973 and 1977, and the Declaration adopted by the International Conference of Trade Unions on Sanctions and Other Actions against the Apartheid Regime in South Africa held in 1983,

Recalling also the ILO Programme for the Elimination of Apartheid in Labour Matters in the Republic of South Africa, which had been adopted in 1964, as well as subsequent measures undertaken by the ILO, in its determination to eradicate apartheid in the field of labour, including the Special Reports of the Director-General on the Application of the Declaration concerning the Policy of Apartheid in South Africa and Namibia, a wider range of education and promotional activities carried out by the International Labour Office in this field and the extension of technical assistance within its field of competence to the people of South Africa and Namibia and the national liberation movements and front-line and neighbouring States,

Reflecting on and sharing the growing concern of the international community at the deterioration of the situation in South Africa and Namibia under apartheid and calling for action thereon, as shown in the Programmes of Action adopted by the United Nations General Assembly and the Security Council,

Reaffirming the need to co-operate with all organisations in the campaign to eliminate apartheid, in particular the United Nations, the Organisation of African Unity and international and regional organisations of workers and employers,

Noting that it has become necessary to revise the Programme of Action of the ILO and its Members in the light of the failure by the Government of South Africa since 1981 to abandon its policy of apartheid, its intensified aggression in southern Africa including Namibia, its intransigence in the face of international pressure and the further polarisation of Blacks and Whites in South Africa resulting from the introduction of a new Constitution in 1984 which was further aggravated by the 1987 Whites-only election;

Recommends the following action:

I. Government Action through the United Nations

To take the measures necessary to give effect to the Programme of Action against Apartheid adopted by the United Nations General Assembly as well as the resolutions subsequently adopted by that body and other relevant United Nations bodies, in particular:

(a) To adopt comprehensive and mandatory sanctions against South Africa, in accordance with Chapter VII of the United Nations Charter.

(b) To establish a special monitoring unit, in co-operation with the International Maritime Organisation, Lloyds Register, the Shipping Research Bureau and other relevant organisations, to ensure that sanctions are strictly applied and to expose sanctions busters.

(c) To co-operate by all possible means in the implementation of United Nations resolution 435 for the independence of Namibia.

II. Government Action

1. To sever political, military, cultural, sporting and diplomatic relations with the South African Government, in so far as such relations with South Africa are maintained.

2. To stop trade and commercial relations with and to prohibit new public and private investment in South Africa, as well as the export of nuclear and other technology to the South African Government, parastatals and private enterprise in South Africa. In addition, to prohibit loans, trade credits and gold exchanges by banks to and with South Africa. Furthermore, to prohibit collaboration with South Africa in the operation of the international gold market, in particular to prevent the operation of the South African marketing company, the International Gold Corporation (INTERGOLD).

3. To adopt, through the appropriate government authorities, including regional and local authorities, stringent divestment/disinvestment measures, to prevent any new investments, and to withdraw all public funds from banks maintaining commercial relations with South Africa as well as to deny contracts for the provision of goods and services to all firms and enterprises having commercial relations with South Africa.

4. To deny the use of facilities intended to circumvent sanctions applied against South Africa.

5. To discourage emigration of their nationals and the promotion of tourism to South Africa, by such means as banning advertising and cutting air and sea links with South Africa.

6. To withhold recognition of Bantustans, deny the establishment of representative offices and the entry of representatives of Bantustans into their territories, to prohibit new investments in and to demand the withdrawal of existing investment from these areas.

7. To increase economic support, including development assistance and the development of alternative trade patterns, to those African countries which are forced through their geographical and economic situation to maintain links with South Africa, with particular emphasis on independent African States enclaved within South Africa and those in the immediate neighbourhood of South Africa.

8. To give material and moral support to the liberation movements, to the independent Black trade union movement and to popular movements struggling for the elimination of apartheid and the establishment of a non-racial democratic system and majority rule with respect for human rights and fundamental freedoms in South Africa and Namibia.

9. To lift all impediments preventing trade unions from participating in solidarity action with the workers engaged in the anti-apartheid struggle and in particular to ensure that the legal system does not prevent trade union action designed to oppose apartheid.

10. To encourage in line with the basic principles of the Constitution of the ILO initiatives which could lead to the elimination of apartheid and the achievement of durable peace in southern Africa.

11. To tighten the licensing procedures for the export and re-export of arms and related material as defined in Security Council Resolution 418 so as to ensure that none of it reaches South Africa and Namibia in violation of the United Nations Security Council decisions and resolutions.

III. Action by Employers' Organisations

1. To ensure that their members do not maintain trade, commercial or financial relations with South Africa and that economic and financial institutions do not extend loans to South Africa or collaborate with the apartheid regime in any way.

2. To disinvest from South Africa and to transfer these investments to other African countries, especially the front-line and SADCC States. In so doing, employers should ensure that early consultations are held with the appropriate union representing the Black workers in the enterprise on the conditions and terms of disinvestment. Such action should not circumvent the call for disinvestment by transferring the operation of their companies to local South African management whilst still maintaining the same commercial links.

3. To disinvest from and to cease all co-operation with the so-called Bantustans.

4. To refuse to co-operate with the South African authorities in the implementation of apartheid legislation or refrain from the exploitation of all advantages provided by the apartheid system particularly in labour relations and the so-called homelands and to make a firm commitment to the abolition of apartheid.

5. To urge banks and other financial institutions to refrain from making loans or providing credit for trade with South Africa and to urge governments to prohibit the activities of the International Gold Corporation (INTERGOLD) in their countries.

6. To provide technical and financial support for small business development and management training programmes for victims of *apartheid* in exile in the front-line and neighbouring States, and to organise subregional seminars for employers in such States for this purpose as well as sensitise employers about the plight of the victims of apartheid.

7. To ensure that members refrain from any form of victimisation of workers and their trade unions involved in

the defence of workers' basic rights in South Africa and Namibia and in solidarity action, outside the Republic, with the Black workers of South Africa.

IV. Action by Trade Unions the World Over

1. To exert maximum pressure on their respective governments for the adoption and the implementation of comprehensive and mandatory sanctions against South Africa by the United Nations Security Council, in accordance with Chapter VII of the United Nations Charter.

2. To place maximum pressure, including industrial action, on parent companies and their subsidiaries the world over in cases where their South African subsidiaries do not recognise the independent Black trade union movement and act in contradiction with internationally recognised labour standards.

3. To exert maximum pressure on the subsidiaries, outside South Africa, of South African multinational enterprises that are involved in the violation of internationally-recognised labour standards.

4. To increase mobilisation of workers and the public through information campaigns with a view to exerting the strongest possible pressure on their respective governments to adopt comprehensive sanctions against and to sever their links with South Africa, and on companies with interest in South Africa to oblige them to withdraw from that country.

5. To develop extensive educational activities to ensure that workers are informed of sanction measures in their own countries so that they can participate at all levels in the monitoring of such actions and be prepared for industrial action in cases of sanctions busting.

6. To organise consumer and other boycotts in order to promote sanctions against South Africa.

7. To give financial, material and moral support to the Black independent trade union movement inside South Africa and Namibia, including assistance in organising campaigns and educational programmes and legal and relief assistance to imprisoned and restricted trade unionists and their families, as well as organising solidarity action in support of the Black workers and their unions.

8. To organise campaigns to ensure that trade union members do not emigrate to South Africa or Namibia or visit these countries in the course of appropriate sanctions, to ban advertisements for jobs in South African recruitment offices abroad.

9. To withdraw all trade union funds from any company or investment scheme with interests in South Africa or Namibia, and to ensure that no pension funds are invested in such companies, banks or schemes.

10. To exercise the strongest possible pressure on banks and financial institutions to recall their existing loans to South Africa and to prevent the provision of new loans and trade credits to South Africa and Namibia, as well as gold exchanges to and with South Africa. In addition, trade unions should organise campaigns appealing to their members to close accounts with such banks.

11. To take all measures aimed at further isolating the South Africa regime and to support anti-apartheid activities.

12. To ensure trade union representation in delegations to the United Nations and the specialised agencies to press for the fullest implementation of the Programme of Action against Apartheid.

13. To co-ordinate trade union action against *apartheid* in

accordance with the Declaration adopted by the International Conference of Trade Unions on Sanctions and Other Actions against the *Apartheid* Regime, held in Geneva in 1983.

V. ILO Action

1. To give further impetus to the implementation of the Declaration concerning Action against Apartheid and the Programme of Action, with specific reference to operative paragraph 6 of the Declaration and to the following paragraphs of this section.

2. To increase enterpreneurial and management training and to encourage small business development programmes for the victims of apartheid in exile in neighbouring States and displaced persons as a means of creating self-employment for those deprived people and prepare them for business management responsibilities in a non-racial democratic South Africa and in an independent democratic Namibia.

3. To increase activities in the fields of workers' education, vocational training, assistance to migrant workers, improvements in infrastructures and in other fields of benefit to workers of southern Africa, including broader workers' education programmes for the trade unions of South Africa and Namibia. Such programmes should be conducted in conjunction with trade union organisations of the front-line States, particularly through the co-ordi- nation and co-operation of the Southern African Trade Union Co-ordination Council (SATUCC).

4. To ensure a wider dissemination of public information throughout all member States by all possible means, including ILO publications, about atrocities being perpetrated by the *apartheid* South African regime within South Africa and Namibia, as well as in front-line and neighbouring States, as a means of countering the news blackout imposed by the South African Government under its oppressive emergency measures and overcoming the silence of the mass media.

5. To address renewed appeals to the UNDP, international financial institutions and all multi-bilateral and bilateral donors to provide additional resources for the above-mentioned activities.

6. To request ILO constituents to provide a precise, itemised report on the Declaration, on each paragraph of the Programme of Action annexed to it and on the conclusions adopted at each session of the Conference.

VI. Other Action

1. The Conference calls upon governments, employers' and workers' organisations and the ILO to continue and re-inforce the campaign for the release of all trade unionists and political prisoners in South Africa and Namibia. In this connection the Conference deplores and denounces all measures which deny and violate civil and trade union rights in South Africa.

2. The Conference calls upon governments, employers' and workers' organisations, non-governmental bodies and individuals to make every possible contribution to the AFRICA (Action for Resisting Invasion, Colonialism and Apartheid) Fund, as well as to make contributions in order to ensure the early realisation of its objectives.

In 1989, the ILO set up a group of three independent experts to monitor sanctions and other actions against *apartheid* throughout the world, as provided in the ILO Declaration and Program of Action, with special attention to action taken to circumvent such measures. In addition, the ILO continued to monitor and disseminate information on recent developments in the social and labor fields in South Africa and Namibia, to provide technical cooperation assistance to the national liberation movements, black workers and their independent trade unions, and also to the frontline neighboring States.

The group of three independent experts was established in compliance with a recommendation to this effect made by the Committee on Action against *Apartheid* at the 1988 session of the INTERNATIONAL LABOR CONFERENCE. This recommendation also specified the tasks to be performed by the group, which included (a) investigating and evaluating the effects of present sanctions measures; (b) conducting feasibility and case studies on sanctions; (c) regularly surveying and updating the state of world trade with South Africa; (d) maintaining a register of investment and disinvestment in South Africa; and (e) publishing, three times a year, the results of the research. The group was requested to carry out its mandate in close cooperation with other United Nations bodies and international organizations in order to avoid duplication. At its first meeting, in October 1989, the group decided to place emphasis on studies relating to an embargo on South African coal, effective financial sanctions, and matters relating to the effective severance of air links with South Africa.

The director general's report on the application of the Declaration and Program of Action was examined by the International Labor Conference at its 1989 session. Chapter I of the report reviews recent developments in labor and social matters in South Africa and Namibia. Chapter II analyzes the information supplied by the ILO tripartite constituents concerning their action against *apartheid*. Chapter III provides information on international action against *apartheid*.

After considering the report, the Committee on Action against *Apartheid* adopted conclusions which, *inter alia*, expressed concern about the slowing down of the rate of disinvestment and the tendency of disinvesting multinationals to continue to maintain nonequity links with South Africa. The committee called upon the tripartite members and the ILO to intensify efforts to implement the recommendations contained in the updated Declaration and Program of Action, and specified some further measures to be taken in this area.

APARTHEID: PENAL TRIBUNAL. At its 1980 session, the COMMISSION ON HUMAN RIGHTS requested its AD HOC WORKING GROUP OF EXPERTS ON SOUTHERN AF-

RICA to undertake a study on ways and means of ensuring the implementation of international instruments such as the INTERNATIONAL CONVENTION ON THE SUPPRESSION AND PUNISHMENT OF THE CRIME OF *APARTHEID*, including the establishment of the international jurisdiction envisaged in that convention.

At the request of the working group, the study (UN Doc. E/CN.4/1426) was prepared by an expert consultant. It included (chapter 3) a draft "Convention on the Establishment of an International Penal Tribunal for the Suppression and Punishment of the Crime of *Apartheid* and other International Crimes," and (chapter 4) a draft "Additional Protocol for the Penal Enforcement of the International Convention on the Suppression and Punishment of the Crime of *Apartheid*." Both texts are based on article 5 of the *apartheid* convention. The draft convention contemplates the creation of a new international legal entity, the International Penal Tribunal, through a multilateral convention open to States parties to the *apartheid* convention and to other States. The draft additional protocol does not contemplate the creation of a new international entity but the use of existing United Nations structures with the addition of one new structure—an international panel of judges to adjudicate violations of article 2 of the convention.

After examining the study, the working group forwarded it to the Commission on Human Rights and requested the commission to invite States parties to the *apartheid* convention to submit their comments and views on its provisions.

Four years after the commission had complied with the request, the *ad hoc* working group included in its 1984 progress report to the commission a summary of the comments and views received from governments. The summary (UN Doc. E/CN.4/1984/8, part two, chapter 4) indicated that, of 24 States responding to the commission's invitation, nine either had no comments to make or were not in a position to submit substantive observations pending further study, while four saw no need for establishing such a tribunal. The views expressed by the remaining 11 States parties to the *apartheid* convention, and of two UN member States not parties to that convention, were inconclusive, some supporting the proposal in principle while others criticized technical aspects of the draft instruments.

The Commission on Human Rights, at the request of the working group, renewed its request that States parties to the convention submit their views on the working group's study. However, up to mid-1990, the question was not taken up again by the commission.

SEE ALSO South Africa: UN Concern about Apartheid.

APARTHEID: SOLIDARITY OBSERVANCES. Each year, opponents of *apartheid* throughout the world observe four "international days of solidarity" with victims of *apartheid*.

March 21 is observed as the International Day for the Elimination of Racial Discrimination, to commemorate the massacre in Sharpeville, South Africa, in which scores of unarmed people were killed while staging a peaceful demonstration of protest against the "pass laws" on 21 March 1960.

June 16 is observed as the International Day of Solidarity with the Struggling People of South Africa, to commemorate the massacre in Soweto, South Africa, on 16 June 1976, when hundreds of unarmed school children were brutalized and killed by the police as they demonstrated against the imposition of the Afrikaans language and the Bantu system of education.

August 9 is observed as the International Day of Solidarity with the Struggle of Women in South Africa and Namibia, to commemorate the demonstration by South African women on 9 August 1956, in Pretoria, to protest the extension of the "pass laws" to women.

October 11 is observed as the Day of Solidarity with South African Political Prisoners (all those imprisoned, interned, or otherwise restricted for opposing *apartheid*), to publicize their plight and to help bring about compliance by South Africa with United Nations decisions on the question.

In addition, many governments and organizations observe the anniversary of the death of Steve Biko, 12 September, to pay tribute to him and to all other martyrs in the struggle to end *apartheid*, including those killed while in prison; and the birthday of Nelson Mandela, 18 July, to pay tribute to him for his outstanding contribution to the struggle for liberation in South Africa as leader of the African National Congress and to publicize the heroic struggle of the liberation movement to which he dedicated his life.

APARTHEID: UN PROGRAM OF ACTION. On 9 November 1976, the UN General Assembly adopted (resolution 31/6 J) the following comprehensive program of international and national action "to be implemented by Governments, intergovernmental organizations, trade unions, churches, anti-*apartheid* and solidarity movements and other non-governmental organizations in order to assist the people of South Africa in their struggle for the total eradication of *apartheid* and the exercise of the right of self-determination by all the people of South Africa irrespective of race, color and creed."

Program of Action against Apartheid

1. The abolition of racist domination and exploitation in South Africa and assistance to the South African people to establish a non-racial society have become one of the primary concerns of the United Nations and the international community.

2. *Apartheid*, like slavery, must be eradicated because it is a crime against humanity.

3. *Apartheid* must be eradicated because it is an affront to human dignity and a grave threat to international peace and security.

4. *Apartheid* must be eradicated so that the continent of Africa may be finally emancipated, after all the miseries and tragedies to which it has been subjected for centuries, and enabled to play its rightful role in international affairs.

5. *Apartheid* must be eradicated because that is indispensable for the elimination of racism and for laying the basis for genuine international co-operation.

6. For thirty years the United Nations has been seized with the problem of racism in South Africa. It has made patient efforts to persuade the racist minority régimes to abandon the bitter legacy of the past and to work for a peaceful solution in accordance with the principles of human equality and international co-operation.

7. But these régimes have proved to be immune to persuasion. They have met the peaceful and just demands of the oppressed people by ruthless repression and have caused immense suffering in a desperate effort to preserve and consolidate racist domination.

8. The record of the *apartheid* régime which seized power in 1948 has few parallels in history for its inhumanity.

9. The black people, who constitute the overwhelming majority of the population of the country, have been constantly humiliated and brutally exploited. Millions of people have been forcibly moved from their homes to barren reserves or urban ghettos in an attempt to enforce racial segregation. Millions of Africans have been imprisoned under pass laws and other racist legislation. Thousands of patriots have been sentenced to long years in prison or tortured or banished. Hundreds of people have been massacred for peaceful demonstrations against racism.

10. The African workers have been denied elementary trade-union rights; they have been imprisoned or killed for nothing more than the "offence" of participating in strikes.

11. The struggle of the South African people against this racist monster has constituted a notable contribution to the struggle of humanity for the principles of the Charter of the United Nations and the Universal Declaration of Human Rights.

12. The General Assembly recalls that, in resolution 3411 C (XXX) of 28 November 1975, it proclaimed that the United Nations and the international community have a special responsibility towards the oppressed people of South Africa and their liberation movements, and towards those imprisoned, restricted or exiled for their struggle against *apartheid*, and reiterated its determination to devote increasing attention and all necessary resources to concert international efforts for the speedy eradication of *apartheid* in South Africa and the liberation of the South African people.

13. The General Assembly commends the courageous struggle of the oppressed people of South Africa, under the leadership of their national liberation movements recognized by the Organization of African Unity, to abolish racism. It reaffirms that their struggle for the total eradication

of *apartheid* and the exercise of the right to self- determination by all the inhabitants of South Africa is fully legitimate. It reiterates its solidarity with all South Africans struggling against *apartheid* and for the principles enshrined in the Charter of the United Nations and the Universal Declaration of Human Rights.

14. The General Assembly condemns the racist régime of South Africa for its repeated and flagrant defiance of United Nations resolutions. It denounces the manoeuvres of that régime to perpetuate and obtain acquiescence in its abhorrent *apartheid* policies. It denounces, in particular, the creation of bantustans as designed to deprive the African people of their inalienable rights in the country as a whole.

15. The General Assembly declares that the racist régime of South Africa is illegitimate and has no right to represent the people of South Africa. It recognizes that the national liberation movements are the authentic representatives of the great majority of the people of South Africa.

16. It is convinced that the collaboration by some Governments and vested interests with the racist régime of South Africa and their total disregard of United Nations resolutions and the legitimate demands of the South African people have impeded efforts for the eradication of *apartheid* and encouraged the racist régime to persist in its inhuman policies.

17. Those Governments and economic interests have enabled the racist régime of South Africa to build up a military machine for the suppression of the people and for aggression against neighbouring States. They have made profits, amounting to billions of dollars, through the exploitation of African labour in South Africa. They bear a grave responsibility for the sufferings of the South African people and for the threat to international peace resulting from the situation.

18. The General Assembly considers *apartheid* a matter of universal concern. Governments, organizations and peoples all over the world must increase their support to the righteous struggle of the South African people for justice and for their inalienable right to self-determination, under the leadership of their national liberation movements.

19. The General Assembly mandates the Special Committee against *Apartheid* to launch—in co-operation with Governments, specialized agencies and other intergovernmental organizations, trade unions, churches and other non-governmental organizations—an international campaign to assist the oppressed people of South Africa at this crucial and decisive stage of their struggle for liberation:

No arms to South Africa!

No profit from *apartheid*!

No compromise with racism!

I. Action by Government

20. The General Assembly calls upon all Governments, irrespective of any other differences, to unite in action against the crime of *apartheid* and to take vigorous and concerted measures in implementation of United Nations resolutions to isolate the *apartheid* régime and assist the oppressed people of South Africa and their liberation movements until they attain freedom.

21. The General Assembly calls upon all Governments, in particular:

A. Diplomatic, Consular and Other Official Relations. (a) To terminate diplomatic, consular and other official relations with the racist régime of South Africa, or to refrain from establishing such relations;

B. Military and Nuclear Collaboration. (b) To implement diplomatic, consular and other official relations with the racist régime of South Africa, or to refrain from establishing such relations;

(i) To refrain from the sale and shipment of arms, ammunition of all types and any vehicles or equipment for use of the armed forces and paramilitary organizations in South Africa;

(ii) To refrain from the sale and shipment of equipment and materials for the manufacture and maintenance of arms, ammunition and military vehicles and equipment in South Africa;

(iii) To refrain from the supply of spare parts for vehicles and equipment used by the armed forces and paramilitary organizations in South Africa;

(iv) To revoke any licences or patents granted to the racist régime of South Africa or to South African companies for the manufacture of arms, ammunition and military vehicles and equipment and to refrain from granting such licences and patents;

(v) To prohibit investment in, or technical assistance for, the manufacture of arms and ammunition, aircraft, naval craft and other military vehicles and equipment in South Africa;

(vi) To terminate any existing military arrangements with the racist régime of South Africa and to refrain from entering into any such arrangements;

(vii) To refrain from providing training for members of the South African armed forces;

(viii) To refrain from any joint military exercises with South Africa;

(ix) To prohibit warships or military aircraft from visiting South African ports and airports, and South African warships or military aircraft from visiting their territories;

(x) To prohibit visits of military personnel to South Africa and visits by South African military personnel to their countries;

(xi) To refrain from exchanges of military, naval or air attachés with South Africa;

(xii) To refrain from purchasing any military supplies manufactured by, or in collaboration with, South Africa;

(xiii) To refrain from any communications or contacts with the South African military establishment or installations;

(xiv) To refrain from any other form of military co-operation with South Africa;

(xv) To prohibit any violations of the arms embargo by corporations, institutions or individuals within their jurisdiction;

(xvi) To refrain from any collaboration with South Africa in the nuclear field;

(xvii) To prohibit any institutions, agencies or companies, within their national jurisdiction, from delivering to South Africa or placing at its disposal any equipment or fissionable material or technology that will enable the racist régime of South Africa to acquire nuclear-weapon technology;

C. Economic Collaboration. (c) To terminate all economic collaboration with South Africa and, in particular:

(i) To refrain from supplying petroleum, petroleum products or other strategic materials to South Africa;

(ii) To refrain from extending loans, investments

and technical assistance to the racist régime of South Africa and companies registered in South Africa;

(iii) To prohibit loans by banks or other financial institutions in their countries to the racist régime of South Africa or South African companies;

(iv) To prohibit economic and financial interests under their national jurisdiction from co-operating with the racist régime of South Africa and companies registered in South Africa;

(v) To deny tariff and other preferences to South African exports and any inducements or guarantees for investment in South Africa;

(vi) To take appropriate action in international agencies and organizations—such as the European Economic Community, the General Agreement on Tariffs and Trade, the International Monetary Fund and the International Bank for Reconstruction and Development—for denial by them of all assistance and commercial or other facilities to the South African régime;

(vii) To take appropriate action, separately or collectively, against transnational companies collaborating with South Africa;

D. Airlines and Shipping Lines. (d) To refuse landing and passage facilities to all aircraft belonging to the racist régime of South Africa and companies registered under the laws of South Africa;

(e) To close ports to all vessels flying the South African flag;

(f) To prohibit airlines and shipping lines registered in their countries from providing services to and from South Africa;

E. Emigration. (g) To prohibit or discourage the flow of immigrants, particularly skilled and technical personnel, to South Africa;

F. Cultural, Educational, Sporting and Other Collaboration with South Africa. (h) To suspend cultural, educational, sporting and other exchanges with the racist régime and with organizations or institutions in South Africa which practice *apartheid;*

(i) To implement United Nations resolutions on *apartheid* in sports and, in particular:

(i) To refrain from all contact with sports bodies established on the basis of *apartheid* or with racially selected sports teams from South Africa;

(ii) To withhold any support from sporting events which are organized in violation of the Olympic principle with the participation of racially selected teams from South Africa;

(iii) To encourage sports organizations to refrain from any exchanges with racially selected teams from South Africa;

G. Assistance to the Oppressed People of South Africa. (j) To provide financial and material assistance, directly or through the Organization of African Unity, to the South African liberation movements recognized by that organization;

(k) To encourage public collections in the country for assistance to the South African liberation movements;

(l) To contribute generously and regularly to the United Nations Trust Fund for South Africa, the United Nations Educational and Training Programme for Southern Africa, the United Nations Trust Fund for Publicity against *Apartheid* and other intergovernmental and nongovernmental funds for assistance to the oppressed people of South Africa and their liberation movements;

(m) To encourage judicial organizations, other appropriate bodies and the public in general to provide assistance to those persecuted by the racist régime of South Africa for their struggle against *apartheid;*

(n) To grant asylum and extend travel facilities and educational and employment opportunities to refugees from South Africa;

(o) To encourage the activities of anti-*apartheid* and solidarity movements and other organizations engaged in providing political and material assistance to the victims of *apartheid* and to the South African liberation movements;

H. Dissemination of Information on apartheid. (p) To ensure, in co-operation with the United Nations and the South African liberation movements, the widest possible dissemination of information on *apartheid* and on the struggle for liberation in South Africa;

(q) To encourage the establishment of national organizations for the purpose of enlightening public opinion on the evils of *apartheid;*

(r) To encourage the information media to contribute effectively to the international campaign against *apartheid;*

(s) To provide broadcasting facilities to South African liberation movements;

(t) To take all necessary measures against the operations of propaganda organizations of the racist régime of South Africa and of private organizations which advocate *apartheid;*

I. Other Measures. (u) To accede to the International Convention on the Suppression and Punishment of the Crime of *Apartheid;*

(v) To observe annually the International Day for the Elimination of Racial Discrimination, on 21 March, and the Day of Solidarity with South African Political Prisoners, on 11 October;

(w) To promote action by intergovernmental organizations in support of the struggle for liberation in South Africa;

(x) To provide, at their request, all necessary assistance to independent African States subjected to acts of aggression by the racist régime of South Africa in order to enable them to defend their sovereignty and territorial integrity.

II. Action by the Specialized Agencies and Other Intergovernmental Organizations

22. The General Assembly calls upon all specialized agencies and other intergovernmental organizations to contribute to the maximum to the international campaign against *apartheid.* It suggests in particular that they:

(a) Exclude the racist régime of South Africa from any participation in their organizations;

(b) Deny any assistance to the racist régime of South Africa;

(c) Invite representatives of the South African liberation movements recognized by the Organization of African Unity to attend, *inter alia,* their conferences and seminars and make financial provision for their participation;

(d) Provide appropriate assistance to the oppressed people of South Africa and to their liberation movements;

(e) Disseminate information against *apartheid* in co-operation with the United Nations;

(f) Provide employment within their secretariats and assistance for education and training to the oppressed people of South Africa.

III. Action by Trade Unions, Churches, Anti-*apartheid* and Solidarity Movements and Other Non-Governmental Organizations

23. The General Assembly commends the activities of all public organizations in denouncing the racist régime of South Africa, in supporting United Nations resolutions against *apartheid*, in assisting the oppressed people of South Africa and in mobilizing public opinion against *apartheid*.

24. The General Assembly encourages them to concert and redouble their efforts, in co-operation with the Special Committee against *Apartheid* and with the Centre against *Apartheid*, and, in particular:

(a) To exert their influence to persuade Governments which continue to collaborate with the racist régime of South Africa to desist from such collaboration;

(b) To press all Governments to implement United Nations resolutions against *apartheid;*

(c) To expand campaigns for the boycott of South African goods;

(d) To intensify campaigns against banks and other transnational companies which collaborate with South Africa;

(e) To establish solidarity funds and provide assistance to the South African liberation movements;

(f) To assist political refugees from South Africa;

(g) To publicize the struggle for liberation in South Africa;

(h) To observe annually the International Day for the Elimination of Racial Discrimination, on 21 March, and the Day of Solidarity with South African Political Prisoners, on 11 October.

25. The General Assembly calls upon trade unions, in particular:

(a) To organize rallies and information campaigns among the workers to make them fully aware of the problem of *apartheid* and to secure their collaboration in industrial action against South Africa;

(b) To support internationally co-ordinated boycotts of South African goods;

(c) To organize international trade-union action to ban the handling of goods going to and from South Africa;

(d) To investigate the operations of companies with subsidiaries inside South Africa;

(e) To undertake, in the countries concerned, industrial action against transnational companies which refuse to recognize African trade unions in South Africa and fail to comply with internationally recognized labour standards;

(f) To give moral and financial support to the African and non-racial trade unions in South Africa, including legal assistance to imprisoned and restricted trade unionists;

(g) To intensify the campaigns against the emigration of workers to South Africa;

(h) To request workers not to handle any arms orders to South Africa and to give full support to those workers who, on grounds of conscience, refuse to work on such orders.

26. The General Assembly appeals to churches and religious organizations, in particular:

(a) To exert all their influence and efforts to oppose any form of collaboration with the racist régime of South Africa;

(b) To expand campaigns against banks and transnational corporations collaborating with South Africa;

(c) To provide all forms of assistance to the oppressed people of South Africa and to their liberation movements;

(d) To disseminate information on the inhumanity of *apartheid* and on the righteous struggle of the oppressed people of South Africa.

27. The General Assembly appeals to sports bodies and sportsmen:

(a) To uphold the Olympic principle that no discrimination be allowed on the grounds of race, religion or political affiliation;

(b) To refrain from all contact with sports bodies established on the basis of *apartheid* or with racially selected sports teams from South Africa;

(c) To assist sportsmen and sports administrators persecuted in South Africa for their opposition to *apartheid* in sports;

(d) To take appropriate action to expel racist South African sports bodies from all international sports federations and competitions.

IV. Action by the Special Committee Against *Apartheid*

28. The General Assembly requests the Special Committee against *Apartheid*, with the assistance of the Centre against *Apartheid*, to take all appropriate measures to encourage concerted action against *apartheid* by Governments and intergovernmental and non-governmental organizations. It invites the Special Committee, in particular, to promote co-ordinated international campaigns:

(a) For assistance to the oppressed people of South Africa and their liberation movements;

(b) For an effective arms embargo against South Africa;

(c) Against all forms of nuclear co-operation with South Africa;

(d) Against all collaboration by Governments, banks and transnational corporations with South Africa;

(e) Against propaganda by the racist régime of South Africa and its collaborators;

(f) For the unconditional release of South African political prisoners;

(g) For the boycott of racially selected South African sports teams.

29. The General Assembly invites all specialized agencies, the Organization of African Unity and other intergovernmental organizations as well as trade unions, churches and other non-governmental organizations to co-operate with the Special Committee in the implementation of this Programme of Action.

SEE ALSO Ad Hoc *Working Group of Experts on Southern Africa; Declaration on* Apartheid *and its Destructive Consequences in Southern Africa; Group of Three; International Convention on the Suppression and Punishment of the Crime of* Apartheid; *South Africa: UN Concern about* Apartheid; *United Nations Trust Fund for Publicity against* Apartheid; *United Nations Trust Fund for South Africa.*

ARAB LAWYERS' UNION. An international non-governmental organization in consultative status with the UN Economic and Social Council (Category II), and with UNESCO, the union is affiliated with Bar associations in 15 countries.

Founded in Cairo in 1958, the Arab Lawyers' Union works to facilitate contacts between Arab lawyers, to assure the freedom of lawyers in their work and the independence of magistrates, and to allow all Arab lawyers to take cases in any Arab country. The union also seeks to safeguard and develop legislative and judiciary language and to harmonize the conditions of the legal profession. The union supports the Palestine Liberation Movement and the Defence of Palestinian Resistance Workers and is engaged in founding an Arab Organization for Human Rights.

The union publishes *Al Hakk (The Law)* in Arabic with French and English sections.

Arab Lawyers' Union. Address: 13 Arab Lawyers' Union Street, Garden City, Cairo, Egypt. Telephone: (202) 55-24-86. Cable: UNAVAR CAIRO. Secretary General : Farouk Abu Issa.

Yearbook of International Organizations 1989/90 (K. G. Saur).

ARBITRARY ARREST, DETENTION, OR EXILE.

Freedom from arbitrary arrest, detention, or exile is a fundamental freedom proclaimed in Article 9 of the UNIVERSAL DECLARATION OF HUMAN RIGHTS. The meaning and scope of this freedom is clarified in the INTERNATIONAL COVENANT ON CIVIL AND POLITICAL RIGHTS in the following provision:

Article 9. 1. Everyone has the right to liberty and security of person. No one shall be subjected to arbitrary arrest or detention. No one shall be deprived of his liberty except on such grounds and in accordance with such procedure as are established by law.

2. Anyone who is arrested shall be informed, at the time of arrest, of the reasons for his arrest and shall be promptly informed of any charges against him.

3. Anyone arrested or detained on a criminal charge shall be brought promptly before a judge or other officer authorized by law to exercise judicial power and shall be entitled to trial within a reasonable time or to release. It shall not be the general rule that persons awaiting trial shall be detained in custody, but release may be subject to guarantees to appear for trial, at any other stage of the judicial proceedings, and, should occasion arise, for execution of the judgement.

4. Anyone who is deprived of his liberty by arrest or detention shall be entitled to take proceedings before a court, in order that that court may decide without delay on the lawfulness of his detention and order his release if the detention is not lawful.

5. Anyone who has been the victim of unlawful arrest or detention shall have an enforceable right to compensation.

The AMERICAN CONVENTION ON HUMAN RIGHTS, open for acceptance by member States of the ORGANIZATION OF AMERICAN STATES, provides that:

1. Every person has the right to personal liberty and security.

2. No one shall be deprived of his physical liberty except for the reasons and under the conditions established beforehand by the constitution of the State Party concerned or by a law established pursuant thereto.

3. No one shall be subject to arbitrary arrest or imprisonment.

4. Anyone who is detained shall be informed of the reasons for his detention and shall be promptly notified of the charge or charges against him.

5. Any person detained shall be brought promptly before a judge or other officer authorized by law to exercise judicial power and shall be entitled to trial within a reasonable time or to be released without prejudice to the continuation of the proceedings. His release may be subject to guarantees to assure his appearance for trial.

6. Anyone who is deprived of his liberty shall be entitled to recourse to a competent court, in order that the court may decide without delay on the lawfulness of his arrest or detention and order his release if the arrest or detention is unlawful. In State Parties whose laws provide that anyone who believes himself to be threatened with deprivation of his liberty is entitled to recourse to a competent court in order that it may decide on the lawfulness of such threat, this remedy may not be restricted or abolished. The interested party or another person in his behalf is entitled to seek these remedies.

7. No one shall be detained for debt. This principle shall not limit the orders of a competent judicial authority issued for nonfulfillment of duties of support.

The AFRICAN CHARTER OF HUMAN AND PEOPLES' RIGHTS, open for acceptance by member States of the ORGANIZATION OF AFRICAN UNITY, provides that:

Every individual shall have the right to liberty and to the security of his person. No one may be deprived of his freedom except for reasons and conditions previously laid down by law. In particular, no one may be arbitrarily arrested or detained.

The EUROPEAN CONVENTION ON HUMAN RIGHTS, open for acceptance by members of the COUNCIL OF EUROPE, provides that:

1. Everyone has the right to liberty and security of person.

No one shall be deprived of his liberty save in the following cases and in accordance with a procedure prescribed by law;

a. the lawful detention of a person after conviction by a competent court;

b. the lawful arrest or detention of a person for noncompliance with the lawful order of a court or in order to secure the fulfilment of any obligation prescribed by law;

c. the lawful arrest or detention of a person effected for the purpose of bringing him before the competent legal authority on reasonable suspicion of having committed an offence or when it is reasonably considered necessary to prevent his committing an offence or fleeing after having done so;

d. the detention of a minor by lawful order for the purpose of educational supervision or his lawful detention for the purpose of bringing him before the competent legal authority;

e. the lawful detention of persons for the prevention of the spreading of infectious diseases, of persons of unsound mind, alcoholics or drug addicts or vagrants;

   f. the unlawful arrest or detention of a person to prevent his effecting an unauthorised entry into the country or of a person against whom action is being taken with a view to deportation or extradition.

2. Everyone who is arrested shall be informed promptly, in a language which he understands, of the reasons for his arrest and of any charge against him.

3. Everyone arrested or detained in accordance with the provisions of paragraph 1(c) of this Article shall be brought promptly before a judge or other officer authorised by law to exercise judicial power and shall be entitled to trial within a reasonable time or to release pending trial. Release may be conditioned by guarantees to appear for trial.

4. Everyone who is deprived of his liberty by arrest or detention shall be entitled to take proceedings by which the lawfulness of his detention shall be decided speedily by a court and his release ordered if the detention is not lawful.

5. Everyone who has been the victim of arrest or detention in contravention of the provisions of this Article shall have an enforceable right to compensation.

Comments on Article 9 of the International Covenant on Civil and Political Rights. In 1982, after examining reports submitted by States parties to the International Covenant on Civil and Political Rights in accordance with its article 40, the HUMAN RIGHTS COMMITTEE adopted the following general comments on article 9 (UN Doc. A/37/40, Annex V, para. 1 and 2):

Article 9, which deals with the right to liberty and security of persons, has often been somewhat narrowly understood in reports by States parties, and they have therefore given incomplete information. The Committee points out that paragraph 1 is applicable to all deprivations of liberty, whether in criminal cases or in other cases such as, for example, mental illness, vagrancy, drug addiction, educational purposes, immigration control, etc. It is true that some of the provisions of article 9 (part of paragraph 2 and the whole of paragraph 3) are only applicable to persons against whom criminal charges are brought. But the rest, and in particular the important guarantees laid down in paragraph 4, i.e. the right to control by a court of the legality of the detention, applies to all persons deprived of their liberty by arrest or detention. Furthermore, States parties have in accordance with article 2 (3) also to ensure that an effective remedy is provided in other cases in which an individual claims to be deprived of his liberty in violation of the Covenant.

Paragraph 3 of article 9 requires that in criminal cases any person arrested or detained has to be brought "promptly" before a judge or other officer authorized by law to exercise judicial power. More precise time limits are fixed by law in most States parties and, in the view of the Committee, delays must not exceed a few days. Many States have given insufficient information about the actual practices in this respect.

Study of the Right. In 1956, eight years after the Universal Declaration of Human Rights had proclaimed the right of everyone to LIBERTY and ten years before the International Covenant on Civil and Political Rights had been adopted, the UN COMMISSION ON HUMAN RIGHTS determined that no study of the practical effects of denial of the right to liberty had been undertaken on an international scale and decided that such a study was justified and necessary. It appointed a committee, composed of four of its members, to prepare the study.

The committee carried out its task on the basis of information provided by the Secretary-General, the governments of member States, and the competent intergovernmental and non-governmental organizations. It submitted the *Study of the Right of Everyone to be Free from Arbitrary Arrest, Detention and Exile* (UN publication, Sales No. 65.XIV.2) to the Commission on Human Rights in 1962.

The study concentrates largely on procedural laws governing deprivation of liberty prior to, or other than by, a final court sentence in criminal proceedings. For purposes of the study, the committee defined "arrest" to mean the act of taking a person into custody under the authority of the law or by compulsion of another kind and to include the period from the moment he is placed under restraint up to the time he is brought before an authority competent to order his continued custody or to release him. It defined "detention" to mean the act of confining a person to a certain place, whether or not in continuation of arrest, and under restraints which prevent him from living with his family or carrying out his normal occupational or social activities. "Exile" was applied to (a) the expulsion or exclusion of a person from the country of which he is a national and (b) the banishment of a person within the country by way of forcible removal from the place of residence.

Regarding the word "arbitrary," it was understood that one of the results of the study would be a definition of that word. For the purpose of the study, however, the committee adopted the following definition: An arrest or detention is arbitrary if it is (a) on grounds or in accordance with procedures other than those established by law or (b) under the provisions of a law the purpose of which is incompatible with respect for the right to liberty and security of person.

As requested by the Commission on Human Rights (resolution 2 [XVII]), the committee formulated its conclusions as a series of draft principles on freedom from arbitrary arrest and detention. As exile as a form of punishment appeared at that time to have virtually disappeared, the committee did not consider it necessary to include provisions regulating that situation; however, the committee refrained from proposing the complete abolition of exile on the ground that, in certain cases (e.g., voluntary exile in lieu of incarceration for political offenses), it may be more humane than incarceration or other more severe measures.

The Commission on Human Rights decided, at its 1962 session (resolution 2 [XVIII]), to transmit the draft principles to member States and to the specialized agencies for their comments. At the same time, it called upon the committee to proceed with a closely related study of the right of arrested persons to communicate with those whom it is necessary for them to consult in order to ensure their defense or to protect their essential interests.

Both studies were considered by the commission at its 1969 session. Noting that the second study (UN Doc. E/CN.4/996) proposed that certain modifications be made in the draft principles set out in the first, the commission again sought the comments of the governments and agencies concerned.

The commission did not consider the subject further until 1975, when it called upon the SUB-COMMISSION ON PREVENTION OF DISCRIMINATION AND PROTECTION OF MINORITIES (resolution 10 [XXXII]) to examine the relevant documentation and to draw up a body of principles for the protection of all persons under any form of detention or imprisonment.

The sub-commission completed the draft of such a body of principles in 1978, and the Economic and Social Council requested the Secretary-General (resolution 1979/34) to forward it to the General Assembly, together with the comments of governments thereon.

In 1980 the General Assembly referred the question to its Third (Social, Humanitarian and Cultural) Committee, in which an open-ended working group was set up to elaborate a final version of the principles. The working group was unable to complete its work in 1980; and, since 1981, the assembly has referred the question to its Sixth (Legal) Committee, where similar open-ended working groups have been set up at each annual session.

The working group which met during the 43d session (1988) of the assembly completed the elaboration of the draft Body of Principles for the Protection of All Persons Under any Form of Detention or Imprisonment. On its recommendation, and that of the Sixth Committee, the assembly approved on 9 December 1988 (resolution 43/173) the BODY OF PRINCIPLES FOR THE PROTECTION OF ALL PERSONS UNDER ANY FORM OF DETENTION OR IMPRISONMENT. It requested the Secretary-General to inform the members of the United Nations or members of specialized agencies of the adoption of the body of principles and urged that all efforts be made so that the principles becomes generally known and respected.

Meanwhile, the Sub-Commission on Prevention of Discrimination and Protection of Minorities continues the annual review of developments relating to the human rights of persons subjected to any form of detention or imprisonment, initiated in 1974 (resolution 7 [XXVII]). The review is conducted at each session of the sub-commission by its WORKING GROUP ON DETENTION. Issues given particular attention include (a) prolonged or indefinite detention of large numbers of unconvicted persons without formal charges brought against them; (b) the necessity of impartial judicial control over arrest and detention practices; (c) the lack of, or ineffectiveness of, judicial control over arrest and detention practices; (d) the role of secret police and paramilitary organizations; and (e) the position of the family and relatives of arrested and detained persons.

SEE ALSO Arrest, Detention, and Abduction of International Civil Servants; Arrested Person's Right to Communicate; Children: Detention; Detention: Administrative; Detention: UN Staff Members; Fair Trial; Imprisonment; Standard Minimum Rules for the Treatment of Prisoners.

ARGENTINA. The Argentine Republic is a country in temperate South America, on the Atlantic Ocean. It has borders with Bolivia, Brazil, Chile, Paraguay, and Uruguay. It achieved independence from Spain in 1816 and became a member of the United Nations in 1945. Its population is estimated by the UN (1990) to be 32,425,000. Ethnic groups include persons of Spanish, Italian, Lebanese, Syrian, and South American origin, and an indigenous population of about 50,000. Languages in common use include Spanish (official), English, Italian, Portuguese, and German. Religions practiced include Christianity (Roman Catholic, 92%; Protestant denominations, 2%), Judaism (2%), and others (2%). Under article 2 of the national constitution, the federal government supports the Roman Catholic Apostolic Church. Literacy is estimated at 95%.

The government (1990) took the form of a republic. It is a federal union of 22 provinces, one national territory, and one federal district. Under the constitution of 1853, the president and vice-president are elected by popular vote through an electoral college, each for a term of six years. The president and his cabinet together exercise executive authority. Legislation is prepared by the 254-member Chamber of Deputies and the 46-member Senate. Active political parties include the Radical Civic Union and the *Justicialista* (Peronist) Party.

Argentina experienced an extended period of violations of human rights under Juan Peron, the military dictator who absorbed many fascist ideas in the Italy of Mussolini and who collaborated with Germany through most of World War II. Overwhelmingly victorious in the election of February 1946, shortly after Argentina had belatedly entered the war on the side of the allies and had become a member of the United Nations, Peron established a regime based on the support of reactionaries, the army, nationalists, and clerical groups which curtailed all political and civil rights and created concentration camps for dissenters.

In 1960, Adolf Eichman was taken from Argentina, where he had found asylum, to Israel where he was put on trial for war crimes. At a meeting of the Security Council on 22 June, the foreign minister of Israel recognized that the persons who had captured Eichman had broken the laws of Argentina and apologized for this act, which Israel believed should be seen in the light of the "exceptional and unique character of the crimes attributed to Eichman." The council called for "appropriate reparation" on the part of Israel, to which the foreign minister replied that, in the view of his government, its expression of regret constituted adequate reparation.

During the period between 1976 and 1983, military regimes were responsible for a "dirty war" within the country that took the lives of nearly 9,000 people and included the torture of many more. Military rule was discredited and collapsed after an unsuccessful campaign to seize the Falkland Islands (Malvinas) from Great Britain. The civilian government that replaced it on 12 December 1983 has experienced difficulties in establishing and maintaining firm control over "the colonels" and in adopting the measures necessary to promote and protect the enjoyment of civil, political, economic, social and cultural rights.

Shortly after he assumed the presidency, in 1983, Raul Alfonsin defied the military to support the trial and conviction of five former armed forces commanders, two of them former presidents, on charges of human rights violations during the "dirty war." After these trials were over, however, the military and other elements called for a general AMNESTY which would prevent the trials from going deeper into the officer ranks. In December 1986, President Alfonsin, citing a desire for national reconciliation and a "military threat" to resume control of the country, supported passage of a law that set tight timetables for thousands of cases which had not reached the courts. The result was that fewer than 150 cases could be brought to trial, and no further charges or investigations were permitted. (See IMPUNITY: NGO REACTION).

President Alfonsin's successor, President Carlos Saul Menem, who took office in July 1989, announced in September of that year that 18 generals and admirals then facing trial on charges that they had committed human rights violations in the 1970s would be pardoned and that the cases of other former military leaders would be dealt with at a later date. In spite of widespread protests, the pardons were granted early in October 1989.

As regards the fate of the persons who "disappeared" between 1976 and 1987, the WORKING GROUP ON ENFORCED OR INVOLUNTARY DISAPPEARANCES reported to the 1990 session of the Commission on Human Rights (UN Doc. E/CN.4/1990/13) that, since 1981, it had transmitted 3,459 cases to the government of Argentina and had received 2,938 responses thereon. It considered only 41 of the cases to have been clarified by the government's responses (19 persons had been released from detention, six children had been located, the bodies of nine persons had been located and identified, and seven cases involved something other than a disappearance). Twenty-nine other cases had been clarified by non-governmental sources (seven persons had been released from detention, eight children had been found, and the bodies of 14 persons had been found and identified). Only one new case, however, was reported to have occurred in 1989.

ARGENTINA: DISAPPEARANCE OF CHILDREN. The situation of children who "disappeared" in Argentina during the period from 1974 to 1981 was drawn to the attention of the UN COMMISSION ON HUMAN RIGHTS by its WORKING GROUP ON ENFORCED OR INVOLUNTARY DISAPPEARANCES in the working group's first report, submitted to the commission in 1981 (UN Doc. E/CN.4/1435 and Add. 1) in the following terms (para. 171):

Most of the cases of the reported disappearance of children in Argentina relate to children born or presumed to be born of mothers who were themselves missing and reportedly held in secret detention centres at the time of their delivery. In a number of cases, information about the fact of delivery is provided by people who report having been themselves detained in such centres and to have direct knowledge of the birth. According to the information received, a large number of women—many of them pregnant—were held in one particular detention centre which reportedly had some facilities to attend to women in childbirth. In other cases, it is reported that women were taken to a military hospital for the birth. The reports in a number of cases, indicate that children born in the above circumstances were handed over to relatives, generally their grandparents. This information coincides with that provided by relatives of pregnant women reported missing to the effect that they were given new-born babies by members of the security forces or civilians who informed them that the person reported missing had given birth to the child; the relatives were warned not to make any inquiries or comments on the matter. In one case, the parent of a pregnant woman who had disappeared, reports that a group of unknown persons brought her home, where she left her child; then was taken away and is still missing. A report received from two people who state that they were detained in the same detention centre together with the pregnant woman in question confirms this. The Group also received reports relating to children who were abducted together with the parents and are still missing. Reports of cases of disappearance of minors who were reportedly arrested on their own were also received.

In 1984, the Argentine National Commission on the Disappearances of Persons, following its investigation into thousands of disappearances which had occurred in Argentina between 1974 and 1981, reported that:

(1) the forcible removal of a child from his legitimate family and his placement in another family environment chosen according to an ideological view of "what is needed to save him" is a treacherous usurpation of roles;
(2) the oppressors who removed the children from their homes or from their mothers at the time of birth decided the fate of those babies as coldly as someone dispensing of the spoils of war;
(3) the missing children, who have been stripped of their identity and taken away from their relatives, are, and will continue for a long time to be, a deep open wound in our society. A blow has been struck at the helpless, vulnerable and innocent, thus creating a new type of torture.

At the time the report was issued, the "Grandmothers of the Plaza de Mayo" (*Abuelas de Plaza de Mayo*) an organization established by the grandmothers of the missing children, knew of 172 children who had been detained together with their parents, or born during their mothers' captivity, and had not been returned to their families. A number of them were later located in Paraguay, Uruguay, Chile, and other South American countries, their identity being confirmed by hemogenetic tests.

In 1987, the SUB-COMMISSION ON PREVENTION OF DISCRIMINATION AND PROTECTION OF MINORITIES expressed deep concern (decision 1987/107) over reports concerning the critical situation of disappeared children in Argentina who had been located in Paraguay, sometimes living in the homes of military officers who had been involved in the torture or murder of their parents, and requested its chairman to appoint one of its members to establish and maintain contact with the competent authorities and institutions, including humanitarian organizations, which would report to him on the situation and ensure that there are no further risks of disappearances; and to request the authorities concerned to facilitate his task.

The Commission on Human Rights endorsed this request (resolution 1988/76) and Mr. Theo van Boven (Netherlands) was appointed to carry out the mandate of the sub-commission. He visited Argentina in July 1988 and received the cooperation of the authorities concerned and of the many interested orga-

nizations and individuals. He was unable, however, to visit Paraguay at that time because the Paraguayan government indicated that the question of the children was under examination by the courts and that, under these circumstances, such a visit could be considered as interference in the judicial process. In this connection, the government stated that, in all those cases in which extradiction had been requested by the Argentine government, there had been a ruling by the courts of first and second instance agreeing to the request. However, the cases had still to be examined by the supreme court.

In his report to the sub-commission (UN Doc. E/CN.4/Sub.2/1988/19), Mr. van Boven describes a number of cases of disappearance of children, and indicates how they were kidnapped, sometimes as a result of the collaboration and complicity of the security forces of more than one country. In this connection, he reports that:

During the proceedings instituted by the current Government of Argentina against the members of the three military juntas during whose term of office most of the 8,961 disappearances recorded by the National Commission on the Disappearance of Persons occurred, specific and concordant evidence was brought to the attention of the population of Argentina and of the world concerning the existence of repressive machinery operated by the military and designed systematically to eliminate not only the members of armed organizations, but also members of the opposition and their families and relatives, inasmuch as they might carry the possible seeds of the opposition's continuity. The eradication of a certain type of opposition in Argentine society was the objective that led to repressive practices of a genocidal nature based on the political ideas of the victims and on those of their families and close relatives.

The disappearances of very young children and of children born during their mothers' captivity was [sic] part of this scheme. The children of "subversive elements" should not be returned to their families, since they might then grow up in the same moral and political environment that had made their parents "subversive elements." It was therefore necessary "to hand them over" to other persons who would offer them an environment in keeping with the oppressors' ideology.

Mr. van Boven also described (para. 17–23) the activities of the group of Argentine women known as the Grandmothers of the Plaza de Mayo, organized to locate and facilitate the return of the "disappeared" children:

Like the Mothers of the Plaza de Mayo, the Grandmothers started looking for their children and grandchildren as soon as the disappearances began. Some of them knew that their children had been murdered and that only their grandchildren could give them back something of the lives that had been taken away from them. Others have so far been unable to find out exactly what happened to their children, but they do know that their grandchildren are in the hands of the persons responsible for the murder or disappearance of the parents or in the hands of officials, former officials and other persons involved in crimes connected with enforced or involuntary disappearances.

From the very beginning, the Grandmothers of the Plaza de Mayo worked with persistence and courage to find their grandchildren. Over the years and, as a result of their untiring efforts and appeals for national and international solidarity, the Grandmothers managed to set up an organization that has a computer system for the processing of information which is received from all types of sources inside and outside the country.

The Grandmothers also have teams of legal advisers, as well as teams of doctors and psychologists, which perform specific functions in connection with the search and recovery of missing children and the medical and psychological treatment required by the children who are returned to their legitimate families. The author of this report met during his mission with members of these teams and discussed with them the nature and the results of their work. He was also deeply moved by his meeting with some of the now eleven and twelve year old children who after their disappearance are reunited with their legitimate families.

With the assistance of the American Association for the Advancement of the Sciences, the Grandmothers of the Plaza de Mayo succeeded in introducing in Argentina the use of genetic analyses to determine kinship with the highest degree of certainty. This method, which was already being used in other countries to establish kinship, was used for the first time in Argentina to determine a child's relationship with its biological family in the absence of the parents. A team of Argentine doctors was trained to conduct genetic analyses to determine a child's real family.

As a result of their painstaking and untiring efforts, the Grandmothers of the Plaza de Mayo have acquired quite rightly considerable national and international prestige and have been able to find 42 children. The finding of the children is, however, not, as it should be, always the happy outcome of a difficult search; in some cases, as is also evident from the mandate given to the author of the present report, it marks the beginning of the arduous task of ensuring that the children are returned to their legitimate families.

The families of the children who were located had to institute and endure lengthy judicial proceedings during which they could not always count on the determination of the judges, some of whom were far too slow and did not use all the legal remedies available for the children's prompt return.

According to the Grandmothers of the Plaza de Mayo, delays in proceedings and the failure by the competent State agencies to keep watch on those who had appropriated the children enabled some of them to leave the country and take away the children being sought by their legitimate families.

The sub-commission examined Mr. van Boven's report and held a general debate on the question of "disappeared" children at its 1988 session, in the course of which the president of the Association of the Grandmothers of the Plaza de Mayo, Mrs. Chorobik de Mariani, urged the sub-commission to request the government of Argentina to initiate a speedy and active search for all disappeared children; to instruct the State apparatus to accelerate the formalities involved in the restoration of such children to their rightful families; and to order a review of adoptions authorized since 1976 because of the possibility that such adoptions had been fraudulent or designed to cover criminal acts, since many of the children concerned could have been victims of political abductions rather than abandoned, as her organization had continued to claim since 1977. However, the sub-commission did not adopt a resolution or other decision on the question at its 1988 session.

Study by Inter-American Commission on Human Rights. The INTER-AMERICAN COMMISSION ON HUMAN RIGHTS included in its annual report for 1987–1988, in accordance with resolution AG/RES. 890 (XVII-0/87) of the OAS General Assembly, a study on the situation of minors who are the children of disappeared persons and who have been separated from their parents and are being claimed by members of their legitimate families. The study attempts to summarize the problem as it has arisen in Latin America, particularly in Argentina. Cases cited by the commission occurred largely in that country during the counterinsurgency campaign called the "dirty war," under the military dictatorship that ruled that country between 1976 and 1983.

The conclusions and recommendations of the commission are as follows:

The Commission believes the objectives of the Abuelas de Plaza de Mayo and of other groups of relatives in other countries who share their aspirations to be worthy of support. The relatives of children who disappeared or were born in captivity have the right to insist on knowing the whereabouts of those infants and to participate in their education and upbringing, in the manner that is most conducive to the child's development and welfare.

The children victimized by this policy have a fundamental right to their identity as persons and to know that identity. They also have the right to recover the memory of their natural parents, and to know that those parents never abandoned them. They have the right to be in contact with their natural family so that they can nurture and provide continuity to that memory of affection.

The Commission believes that judges must have discretion to determine an appropriate custody arrangement, and where applicable, to regularize adoptions if the best familial environment for the healthy growth of the child is, in fact, the adoptive home. Even in these cases, however, judges must respect the exercise of the natural relatives to visitation rights and contacts with the child. In cases where the abduction was committed by a person who participated in the forced disappearance of the true parents, or in their torture or execution, or who became an accomplice to such atrocities, the Commission believes that the child's mental and physical health demands his immediate separation from that family group.

In light of the preceding observations, the Commission considers it necessary to point out and to support the measures adopted by the democratic government of Argentina as well as the actions taken by the Abuelas de Plaza de Mayo and similar groups which have attempted to solve the problem of minor children of disappeared persons who were separated from their parents and who are claimed by the members of their true families.

At the same time it recommends that other governments of the OAS offer all forms of scientific, judicial or investigatory cooperation available to them, to the Argentine Government and to all private associations interested in the topic.

In addition to the foregoing, and without prejudice to the specific measures which the Commission will propose in its draft Inter-American Convention on Forced Disappearance of Persons that is presently under consideration, the Commission requests that the General Assembly of the OAS, at its eighteenth regular meeting, recommend that all member states of the OAS:

(a) An increase in the penalties for the crimes of suppression and misrepresentation of civil status and abduction of minors, as well as the creation of a more serious form of the crime when it is committed under the protection of, or taking advantage of, the forced disappearance of the true parents;

(b) The review of procedural standards in each of the member states, in order to facilitate the introduction of scientific evidence to clarify these cases, to speed up processing of actions to establish familial relationships, and to allow magistrates to grant injunctive relief to prevent the flight of persons, the hiding of children or the destruction of evidence; and

(c) The review, and where necessary, the amendment, of substantive and procedural norms regarding adoption, in order to conform them to contemporary realities, thereby contributing to their increased observance in all countries.

SEE ALSO *Disappearances: UN Draft Declaration; Inter-American Convention on the Forced Disappearance of Persons (Draft).*

ARMED CONFLICTS. The question of protection of the human rights of civilians, prisoners, and combatants in international and non-international armed conflicts has been an important issue on the agenda of several United Nations organs since the International Conference on Human Rights, meeting in Teheran, pointed out on 12 May 1968 (resolution XXIII) "that the widespread violence and brutality of our times, including massacres, summary executions, tortures, inhuman treatment of prisoners, killing of civilians in armed conflicts and the use of chemical and biological means of warfare, including napalm bombing, erode human rights and engender counter-brutality." The conference called upon the Secretary-General to study "(a) the steps which could be taken to secure the better application of existing humanitarian conventions and rules in all armed conflicts and (b) the need for additional humanitarian international conventions or for possible revision of existing conventions to ensure the better protection of civilians, prisoners and com-

batants in all armed conflicts and the prohibition and limitation of the use of certain methods and means of warfare."

Later in 1968, the General Assembly affirmed (resolution 2444 [XXIII]), three basic principles to be observed by all governmental and other authorities responsible for action in armed conflicts which had been formulated by the International Conference of the Red Cross held in Vienna in 1965: "(a) that the right of the parties to a conflict to adopt means of injuring the enemy is not unlimited; (b) that it is prohibited to launch attacks against the civilian populations as such; and (c) that distinction must be made at all times between persons taking part in the hostilities and members of the civilian population to the effect that the latter be spared as much as possible."

In 1970, the General Assembly, while noting (resolution 2675 [XXV]) that a series of international instruments had been adopted for the alleviation of human suffering in any form and in particular in armed conflicts, including the Geneva Conventions of 1949, concluded that, nevertheless, there was a need for better protection of human rights in armed conflicts and that civilian populations were in special need of increased protection. The Assembly accordingly affirmed eight basic principles for the protection of civilian populations in armed conflicts, without prejudice to their future elaboration within the framework of progressive development of the international law of armed conflict:

1. Fundamental human rights, as accepted in international law and laid down in international instruments, continue to apply fully in situations of armed conflict.

2. In the conduct of military operations during armed conflicts, a distinction must be made at all times between persons actively taking part in the hostilities and civilian populations.

3. In the conduct of military operations, every effort should be made to spare civilian populations from the ravages of war, and all necessary precautions should be taken to avoid injury, loss or damage to civilian populations.

4. Civilian populations as such should not be the object of military operations.

5. Dwellings and other installations that are used only by civilian populations should not be the object of military operations.

6. Places or areas designated for the sole protection of civilians, such as hospital zones or similar refuges, should not be the object of military operations.

7. Civilian populations, or individual members thereof, should not be the object of reprisals, forcible transfers or other assaults on their integrity.

8. The provision of international relief to civilian populations is in conformity with the humanitarian principles of the Charter of the United Nations, the Universal Declaration of Human Rights and other international instruments in the field of human rights. The Declaration of Principles for International Humanitarian Relief to the Civilian Popu-

lation in Disaster Situations, as laid down in resolution XXVI adopted by the twenty-first International Conference of the Red Cross, shall apply in situations of armed conflict, and all parties to a conflict should make every effort to facilitate this application.

In 1973, the Assembly considered another aspect of the question: the legal status of the combatants struggling against colonial and alien domination and racist regimes. It noted that, despite its numerous appeals, compliance with universally recognized norms of modern international law had not yet been insured and that the treatment of combatants struggling against colonial and alien domination and racist regimes remained inhuman. As an interim measure it proclaimed (resolution 3103 [XXVIII]) six basic principles of the legal status of such combatants, again without prejudice to their elaboration in future within the framework of the development of international law applying to the protection of human rights in armed conflicts:

1. The struggle of peoples under colonial and alien domination and racist régimes for the implementation of their right to self-determination and independence is legitimate and in full accordance with the principles of international law.
2. Any attempt to suppress the struggle against colonial and alien domination and racist régimes is incompatible with the Charter of the United Nations, the Declaration on Principles of International Law concerning Friendly Relations with Co-operation among States in accordance with the Charter of the United Nations, the Universal Declaration of Human Rights and the Declaration on the Granting of Independence to Colonial Countries and Peoples and constitutes a threat to international peace and security.
3. The armed conflicts involving the struggle of people against colonial and alien domination and racist régimes are to be regarded as international armed conflicts in the sense of 1949 Geneva Conventions, and the legal status envisaged to apply to the combatants in the 1949 Geneva Conventions and other international instruments is to apply to the persons engaged in armed struggle against colonial and alien domination and racist régimes.
4. The combatants struggling against colonial and alien domination and racist régimes captured as prisoners are to be accorded the status of prisoners of war and their treatment should be in accordance with the provisions of the Geneva Convention relative to the Treatment of Prisoners of War, of 12 August 1949.
5. The use of mercenaries by colonial and racist régimes against the national liberation movements struggling for their freedom and independence from the yoke of colonialism and alien domination is considered to be a criminal act and the mercenaries should accordingly be punished as criminals.
6. The violation of the legal status of the combatants struggling against colonial and alien domination and racist régimes in the course of armed conflicts entails full responsibility in accordance with the norms of international law.

Also in 1973, the Assembly, noting that the Diplo-

matic Conference on the Reaffirmation and Development of International Humanitarian Law Applicable in Armed Conflicts was to be convened at Geneva in 1974 on the invitation of the Swiss Federal Council, invited the conference to examine the question of the use of napalm and other incendiary weapons, as well as other specific conventional weapons which may be deemed to cause unnecessary suffering or to have indiscriminate effects and to seek agreement on rules prohibiting or restricting the use of such weapons.

In 1974, the Assembly expressed its deep concern over the sufferings of women and children belonging to the civilian population who, in periods of emergency and armed conflict, are too often the victims of inhuman acts and suffer serious harm and proclaimed (resolution 3318 [XXIX]) the DECLARATION ON THE PROTECTION OF WOMEN AND CHILDREN IN EMERGENCY AND ARMED CONFLICT. The declaration calls for special efforts to be made by States involved in armed conflicts, military operations in foreign territories, or military operations in territories still under colonial domination to spare women and children from the ravages of war and to ensure that they not be deprived of food, shelter, medical care, and other inalienable rights.

The Diplomatic Conference on Reaffirmation and Development of International Humanitarian Law Applicable to Armed Conflicts met in Geneva in 1974, 1975, 1976, and 1977 and examined all of the questions mentioned above in the course of revising two draft additional protocols to the GENEVA CONVENTIONS of 12 August 1949 submitted by the INTERNATIONAL COMMITTEE OF THE RED CROSS. Both additional protocols were adopted by the Conference on 8 June 1977.

PROTOCOL I, ADDITIONAL TO THE GENEVA CONVENTIONS OF 12 AUGUST 1949, relating to the protection of victims of international armed conflicts, has six main parts. Part I sets out general principles and the scope of their application. Part II deals with the problems of the wounded, sick, and shipwrecked, with medical transportation and with missing or dead persons. Part III relates to methods and means of warfare and the status of combatants and prisoners of war. Part IV sets out methods for protection of the civilian population against the effects of hostilities and rules for the treatment of persons in the power of a party to the conflict. Part IV contains provisions for the execution of the Geneva Conventions and of the Protocol; and Part V sets out provisions for signature, ratification, acceptance, and amendment of the Protocol.

PROTOCOL II, ADDITIONAL TO THE GENEVA CONVENTIONS OF 12 AUGUST 1949, relating to the protection of victims of non-international armed conflicts, has five parts. Part I indicates the scope of the instrument, which is limited to conflicts that take place in the territory of a contracting party between its armed forces and dissident armed forces or other organized armed groups. Part II sets out rules for the humane treatment of all persons who do not take a direct part or who have ceased to take part in hostilities, whether or not their liberty has been restricted. Part III provides for the protection and care of the wounded, sick and shipwrecked; and Part IV, for the protection of the civilian population in general. Part V contains provisions for signature, ratification, and amendment of the Protocol.

Among the acts prohibited by the protocols are violence to the life, health, and physical or mental well-being of persons; collective punishments; the taking of hostages; acts of terrorism; outrages upon personal dignity; slavery and the slave trade in all their forms; pillage; and threats to commit any of these acts.

SEE ALSO Basic Principles for the Protection of Civilian Populations in Armed Conflicts; Basic Principles of the Legal Status of Combatants Struggling against Colonial and Alien Domination and Racist Regimes; Death Penalty in Armed Conflicts; Declaration on the Protection of Women and Children in Emergency and Armed Conflicts; UNESCO Convention for the Protection of Cultural Property in the Event of Armed Conflict and protocol.

ARMS SALES AND HUMAN RIGHTS. The Parliamentary Assembly of the COUNCIL OF EUROPE, in a resolution adopted on 27 September 1989 (resolution 928 [1989]), stated its conviction that then-existing levels of arms exports, while declining, clearly went beyond that required for legitimate self-defense and security purposes of many recipient nations and that purchases of arms often were pursued at the expense of the economic and social development of countries in the so-called third world countries. It also set out its view that many arms exports may be used for violations of human rights over which the exporting country has no control, except to refuse to export arms which could be used for domestic repression.

Concerned that the full facts and figures of international arms sales are not always revealed to parliaments or to the public of member countries and that the final destination of arms can be concealed, the Parliamentary Assembly called upon member States of the council:

a. to work in favor of reduced, better-controlled arms exports to third world countries, and to create, as a first step, control mechanisms, including at parliamentary level, to oversee hardware arms exports in particular;

b. to initiate the setting up of an open register on the production of and trade in conventional weapons, to which all members of the United Nations will be invited to adhere, such a register to be organized in co-operation with existing specialist organizations such as the Stockholm International Peace Research Institute (SIPRI) and the London International Institute-for Strategic Studies (IISS);

c. to establish common criteria and definitions for arms sales, including modernisation and maintenance of equipment already supplied, to draw attention to the risk of armed conflict in the regions of recipient states, and to pay particular regard to international obligations in the field of human rights;

d. to incorporate, where this is not already the case, such criteria in their national legislation while ensuring that they are scrupulously adhered to, and to establish parliamentary control bodies to this end;

e. to use their best endeavours to promote an international conference under the auspices of the United Nations, with the active participation of all the major arms-exporting countries, with a view to limiting, monitoring and controlling arms exports, bearing especially in mind the dangers to world peace of third world conflicts, and to create towards this end a co-ordinating body on North-South arms trade policies;

f. to promote, using where possible existing regional organisations, confidence-building and enhanced security measures for recipient countries consistent with programmes reducing levels of arms exports;

g. to urge third world countries to devote scarce resources primarily to civilian investment, rather than excessive armament, making this one of the factors to be considered when granting official development assistance and debt relief, and to promote democracy in third world societies aimed at the realisation of human rights and socially and environmentally sound policies, and hence help avoid their militarisation;

h. to build upon the 1982 United Nations' proposals and encourage national studies on the economics and practicalities of disarmament and development that can be implemented by exporting and recipient states alike;

i. to ask the Organisation for Economic Co-operation and Development (OECD) to study the problems, possibilities and consequences related to the conversion from military to civilian production, building on past experiences;

j. to give high priority to encouraging a level of harmonisation of national legislation controlling and licensing arms exports, and to take urgent steps to ensure the credibility of and compliance with end-user certificates for arms export sales with the maximum possible parliamentary scrutiny and contact.

ARREST, DETENTION AND ABDUCTION OF INTERNATIONAL CIVIL SERVANTS. The UN COMMISSION ON HUMAN RIGHTS, at its 1980 session, expressed its concern (resolution 31 [XXXVI]) at "infringements of the human rights of United Nations staff members" and appealed to member States to respect their obligations under the various international instruments they had undertaken to observe. A month later, the Administrative Committee on Coordination welcomed the commission's resolution and stated that "any infringement of the security and independence of staff members of organizations of the United Nations system by a member State is a serious threat to international co-operation."

Later that year, the General Assembly (resolution 35/212) took note of the statement of the administrative committee and requested the secretary-general to report to it on "any cases in which the international status of staff members of the United Nations or of the specialized agencies has not been fully respected."

Since then, the secretary-general has submitted a report annually to the assembly describing cases in which the privileges and immunities of international civil servants and their families have not been respected. The 1989 report (UN Doc. A/C.5/44/11), covering the period from 1 July 1988 to 30 June 1989, presents the following information (para. 3–25):

The reporting period has been marked by one particularly disturbing development, namely the report of the brutal murder of Lieutenant-Colonel William Richard Higgins. Colonel Higgins, an officer of the United States of America, was serving as the chief of a group of military observers assigned to the United Nations Interim Force in Lebanon (UNIFIL) when he was abducted on 17 February 1988. On 31 July 1989, an announcement at Beirut by his captors stated that he had been killed. The Security Council took note with great concern of the reports from Beirut that day, saying that, if true, the murder of Colonel Higgins was "a cruel and criminal act" (S/20758). On 1 August the Secretary-General sent Mr. Marrack Goulding, Under-Secretary-General for Special Political Affairs, to the area to ascertain, as far as was possible, what had happened to Colonel Higgins. Despite extensive conversations with various parties who may have been in a position to know the facts, Mr. Goulding could not obtain definitive proof of Colonel Higgins' fate. On 9 August, the Secretary-General, having received Mr. Goulding's report on his mission, announced that he had regretfully come to the conclusion that it was almost certain that Colonel Higgins was dead. He said he would continue to try to establish the facts and, if his fears were confirmed, to recover the body.

The Middle East continued to be an area of prime concern with the most cases of arrest, detention and abduction of officials. Efforts to improve the situation, however, have not produced encouraging results. The number of cases of arrest and detention without charge or trial of staff members of the United Nations Relief and Works Agency for Palestine Refugees in the Near East (UNRWA) remained very high. There have been regrettable cases of abuse of privileges and immunities in certain other regions that required, on a number of occasions, the personal intervention of the Secretary-General. At the same time, it should be noted that in the great majority of Member States, privileges and immunities of officials are scrupulously respected and any emerging cases are promptly resolved in a spirit of close co-operation between the parties concerned.

The Secretary-General, assisted by the United Nations Security Co-ordinator, his special representatives and the respective executive heads of the organizations concerned have continued, throughout the reporting period, to promote and ensure the observance of the privileges and immunities of officials of the United Nations and the specialized and related agencies, intervening, if required, with the Member States concerned on the basis of the relevant international legal instruments. In this endeavour, as in the past, they have enjoyed the full support of the representatives of the staff unions. While seeking the co-operation of Member States in fulfilling their obligations under the international instruments in force, the Secretary-General has also, as noted on several occasions in his previous reports, been conscious of the need to clarify for all officials the precise nature, scope and functional character of their privileges and immunities.

As was indicated in the report of the Secretary-General to the General Assembly at its forty-second session (A/C.5/42/14), when staff members of the United Nations and the specialized agencies and related organizations are arrested and detained, both legal and humanitarian considerations are taken into account by the Secretary-General or the executive head concerned in seeking access to them. The legal considerations derive from the relevant international instruments on privileges and immunities and relate principally to the determination of whether or not a staff member has been arrested or detained because of his or her official activities. This determination must be made by the organization concerned and, if the organization determines on the basis of visits to the detained or arrested staff members that the arrest or detention is related to official functions, then immunity is asserted. If, however, the visiting official is satisfied, both from an interview with the detainee and from the charges brought, that the matter is not related to official functions, there is no legal basis for asserting immunity and the legal as distinct from the humanitarian grounds for further intervention by the organization no longer exist.

The humanitarian considerations involved are much broader and, pursuant to such considerations, the Secretary-General or the executive head concerned seeks to ensure that any staff member who is arrested and detained is treated fairly, properly charged and promptly brought to trial.

I. Arrest, Detention and Abduction of Officials. While the majority of cases of arrest, detention or disappearance of officials are resolved to the satisfaction of the Secretary-General, a considerable amount of time is often spent both at Headquarters and at the duty station of the official concerned in obtaining such resolution. In particular, the arrest of locally recruited officials sometimes results in protracted negotiations with government officials on the rights of the organization *vis-à-vis* the official. It must be recalled that the term "official" in the context of the relevant conventions includes all members of the staff, with the exception of those who are both recruited locally and paid at hourly rates. To the great regret and disappointment of the Secretary-General, the number of cases of arrest, detention or disappearance of officials for which the organizations have not been able fully to exercise their rights has increased substantially in the reporting period. Particulars regarding these cases are contained in the reports submitted by individual organizations and agencies, which are summarized in annex II to the present report. With particular reference to the present reporting period the following should be added.

Despite the serious expression of concern voiced by the Secretary-General in his last report (A/C.5/43/18), the number of UNRWA staff arrested and detained has remained at the high level recorded for the previous year, and has, in fact, marginally increased. During the period 1 July 1988 to 30 June 1989, 157 UNRWA staff were arrested or detained. However, there was a decrease in the number of staff detained by one or other of the militia groups in Lebanon; this number fell from 24 last year, to 11. Nine of the 157 staff were arrested or detained and released without charge or trial, including 11 who had been held by militia groups. Eight were charged, tried and sentenced to various terms of imprisonment.

In no case has UNRWA received adequate and timely information on the reasons for the arrest and detention despite requests to the authorities. UNRWA has had access to 26 detained staff from the occupied West Bank and to 37 detained staff from the Gaza Strip. Several of these staff, however, were being held in prisons in Israel, having been transferred there from the occupied West Bank and the Gaza Strip.

As a result of the efforts undertaken by the Secretary-General, designated officials and officials in the field and with the strong support and activities of the staff unions, it has been possible to achieve the release of many staff members who were previously reported as being under arrest or detention. Mr. Shimelis Teklu, a staff member of the Office of the United Nations High Commissioner for Refugees (UNHCR), detained in Ethiopia since 2 January 1984, was released in June 1989. In Lebanon, Mr. Omar Mustafa Hussein, a staff member of UNRWA who had been listed as missing since 15 April 1987 was also released. Eleven other UNRWA staff members detained in Lebanon during the reporting period by militias or unknown elements were released. In Chad, active intervention assured the quick release on 24 May 1989 of Mr. Nassar Dandjita, local administrative assistant of the World Food Programme (WFP), who was arrested on 6 May 1989. In Jordan, Mr. Jibril Taher Mohammed Jibril, a staff member of UNRWA, detained since 31 December 1987, and whose case became a matter of strenuous efforts of the Administration and the Federation of International Civil Servants' Association (FICSA), was released on 21 February 1989. Of those arrested during the reporting period, 39 staff members of UNRWA in the occupied Gaza Strip and 35 in the occupied West Bank were released without charge or trial. Mr. Ahmad Mahmoud Lababidi, arrested in 1988 in the Syrian Arab Republic, Mr. Abdel Karim Keswamy and Mr. Jousef Juma'a, arrested by the Syrian armed forces in 1989 in Lebanon, all of whom are staff members of UNRWA, were released in the first half of 1989. Mr. Khalil Ahmad Abu Sleema, also a staff member of UNRWA, arrested in Egypt on 25 August 1988, was released without charge or trial on 20 December 1988.

The Secretary-General regrets to report that there have been negative developments in respect of some previously reported cases. Mr. Zeidan Jassin, a locally recruited UNRWA staff member who was listed in last year's report as detained in Lebanon by Syrian armed forces since 27 May 1987 (see A/C.5/43/18, annex I), died in prison on 17 December 1988. No additional information has been received regarding other staff members of UNRWA listed in the 1987 report (A/C.5/42/14) as detained in Lebanon by militias or unknown elements and the Syrian armed forces. There has been no further progress in the case of Mr. Tesfamariam Zeggae, a staff member of the United Nations Economic Commission for Africa (ECA). Despite the personal intervention of the Secretary-General of the United Nations and several interventions by the administration of ECA, Mr. Zeggae, who has been detained since 2 March 1982, was sentenced by the First Instance Court in March 1987 to life imprisonment. Details of his case are contained in annex II to the present report.

On 18 May 1988, Mr. Abdul Diallo and on 22 May 1988 Ms. Afton Ba Diallo, staff members of the United Nations Development Programme (UNDP), were detained by the Mauritanian authorities to ascertain their nationality. They were subsequently accused of fraudulently obtaining Mauritanian citizenship and expelled to Senegal. These actions were immediately protested by the resident representative of UNDP. Further to these representations, on 16 June 1989 the Administrator of UNDP sent to the Minister for Foreign Affairs of Mauritania an *aide-mémoire*, in which, *inter alia,* he stated that the actions of the Government of Mauritania not only impeded the proper functioning of the UNDP mission in Nouakchott, in contravention of the 1979 Basic Agreement between the United Nations and Mauritania, but also constituted a violation of the provisions of Article 105 of the Charter of the United Nations. It was pointed out that any expulsion of staff members from the UNDP mission in the country would, in the view of the Secretary-General, constitute a denial of the immunities guaranteed to United Nations officials by the Charter and considered necessary for the independent exercise of their functions in connection with the Organization. The Secretary-General felt obliged to intervene twice with regard to this matter. First, during his visit to Mauritania on 20 and 21 June 1989 and secondly, with the Minister for Foreign Affairs of Mauritania at the Assembly of Heads of State and Government of the Organization of African Unity (OAU) at Addis Ababa from 24 to 27 July 1989. Despite the assurance received by him that the situation would be corrected, these incidents are still pending resolution. It should also be noted with regret that representations made by the Food and Agriculture Organization of the United Nations (FAO) failed to prevent the arrest by Mauritanian authorities and expulsion to Senegal of the following five staff members of FAO: Mr. Abdoulaye Diaw, Mr. Ndiome Pouye, Mr. Demba Niang, Mr. Amadou Dieng and Mr. Mouhamedou Ba.

II. Restrictions on Official and Private Travel of Officials. UNRWA has continued to meet difficulties in the movement of staff into and out of the West Bank and the Gaza Strip. There has been substantial delay in the issue of entry permits and, in some cases, they have been refused. The movement of staff within the occupied territories was also seriously affected by frequent imposition of curfews and the designation of areas as closed military zones.

Restrictive regulations imposed by the United States authorities on travel beyond a 25-mile radius of Columbus Circle, New York, by staff members and their dependants who are nationals of particular countries, remained in force. On 26 January 1989, these restrictions were extended to non-official travel of staff members who are nationals of China. This measure was protested by the Secretary-General as another instance of discrimination in the treatment by the host country of staff members of the United Nations Secretariat solely on the basis of their nationality. The Secretary-General maintains the position he has expressed on previous occasions that, under the given circumstances, the compliance by individual staff members with such restrictive conditions cannot be considered to prejudice the legal position of the United Nations. In the reporting period, existing arrangements for official travel in the United States of the United Nations staff members have remained unchanged.

Some United Nations bodies that are not based in the United States have experienced delays in obtaining G-4 visas for entry into the United States by staff members of certain nationalities. On several occasions, such delays jeopardized the envisaged mission, or have rendered it impossible. In such circumstances, the management of United Nations bodies not based in the United States is severely constrained in sending staff members of certain nationalities on urgent business to United Nations Headquarters or to Washington-based institutions.

III. Taxation of Officials. Section 18 (b) of the Convention on the Privileges and Immunities of the United Nations provides that officials of the Organization shall be exempt from taxation on the salaries and emoluments paid to them by the United Nations. The rationale for this provision is to assure equality of treatment for all staff members, irrespective of their nationality, and to guarantee that funds contributed by Members of the Organization to its budget are not diverted to individual States by means of revenue-raising measures such as an income tax. The Convention on the Privileges and Immunities of the Specialized Agencies envisages in section 19 (b) that officials of the specialized agencies shall enjoy the same exemptions from taxation in respect of the salaries and emoluments paid to them by these agencies and on the same conditions as are enjoyed by officials of the United Nations. The Secretary-General regrets to report that, notwithstanding the above-mentioned provisions, as has been indicated in the previous reports to the forty-first and forty-third sessions (A/C.5/41/12 and Corr. 1 and A/C.5/43/18), a number of States, parties to both Conventions, have continued to impose taxes on the salaries of locally recruited officials.

Despite all efforts undertaken by the United Nations and some specialized agencies, there has been no change in Egypt in the recently enacted legislation concerning work permits. Under this legislation staff members of international organizations who are Egyptian nationals are required to obtain, for a considerable fee, work permits. Such a fee amounts to a direct tax on the emoluments of staff members of international organizations and as such is contrary to the provisions of the two Conventions referred to in the preceding paragraph. The Egyptian authorities have been requested to bring Egyptian legislation into conformity with these Conventions.

Early in 1988, the tax authorities of the Republic and Canton of Geneva decided to apply a global-rate system *(taux global)* to the taxable earnings of staff members of the United Nations and the specialized agencies at Geneva holding short-term contracts, thus taking into account the exempted income earned by such officials from their organizations in determining the rate of tax on earnings deriving from other sources. That decision seemed to be based on non-recognition of that category of employees as staff members (officials) of organizations in the United Nations common system. On behalf of the United Nations Office at Geneva and all the specialized agencies at Geneva, the Secretary-General took action on this question by sending a letter to the President of the Swiss Confederation, referring in particular to the right of the organizations to freely determine the categories of their personnel whom they considered to be officials, solely within the limits of the relevant charters, constitutions and staff regulations and subject to control only by Member States as collectively represented in the various governing bodies. In May 1989 the Head of the Federal Department for Foreign Affairs informed the Secretary-General that the Federal Council had requested the State Council of the Republic and Canton of Geneva to desist from applying the global-rate system to the taxable income of officials holding short-term contracts and that the Geneva Council of State had acceded to this request.

In Burundi, the Government adopted on 31 December 1988 a decree establishing a service tax on imported or exported articles, including "exempted articles". Such a tax represents a direct tax from payment of which the United Nations and specialized agencies are exempt under section 7 (a) of the Convention on the Privileges and Immunities of the United Nations and section 9 (a) of the Convention on the Privileges and Immunities of the Specialized Agencies respectively. Therefore, the adoption of the decree gave rise to concerted action on the part of the organizations of the United Nations system represented in Burundi, whereby they expressed their concern over the adoption of such a measure which contradicts the provisions of the above Conventions. The Government of Burundi admitted the legitimacy of such concern and on 29 March 1989 agreed to refrain from applying the aforementioned tax to the United Nations and specialized agencies.

The United Nations Truce Supervision Organization (UNTSO) reported problems experienced by it with regard to taxation. They are disclosed in detail in annex II to the present report. The 2 per cent ad valorem tax mentioned by UNTSO similarly affects the activities of the United Nations Interim Force in Lebanon (UNIFIL).

IV. Other Matters involving the Status, Privileges and Immunities of Officials. As was indicated in the previous report, the United States informed the Secretariat of the United Nations by note verbale dated 14 June 1988 about its policy with regard to the implementation of laws applicable to the employment of non-resident aliens in the United States (see A/C.5/43/18, paras. 25–27). The Secretariat of the United Nations in its response to this note expressed concern that the stringent application of the immigration regulations would substantially interfere with the authority of the Secretary-General to recruit staff under Article 101 of the Charter of the United Nations and would entail serious financial consequences for the Organization.

In order to resolve the difficulties, consultations were undertaken between officials of the United Nations and the United States. They resulted in the achievement in March 1989 of a working arrangement for visa conversion and local recruitment. It is understood that this arrangement is without prejudice to the position taken by the Secretary-General on the stringent application of immigration regulations by the United States authorities, or to any further discussions that may be held on the issue.

The Secretary-General deems it important to report recent developments relating to Mr. Dumitru Mazilu, a former member of the Sub-Commission on Prevention of Discrimination and Protection of Minorities, charged by the Sub-Commission in 1985 with the preparation of a report on the question of human rights and youth. Mr. Mazilu was not permitted by the Romanian authorities to travel to Geneva to present his report to the Sub-Commission and the Secretary-General was unable to establish personal contact with Mr. Mazilu.

In the circumstances, the Economic and Social Council of the United Nations adopted, on 24 May 1989, resolution 1989/75 entitled "Status of special rapporteurs." This resolution contained a request to the International Court of Justice to give its advisory opinion "on the legal question of the applicability of article VI, section 22, of the Convention on the Privileges and Immunities of the United Nations in the case of Mr. Dumitru Mazilu as Special Rapporteur of the Sub-Commission". In accordance with article 65 of the Statute of the Court, the Secretary-General transmitted to it a dossier of documents likely to throw light upon the question. In addition, the Legal Counsel of the United Nations, on behalf of the Secretary-General, submitted to the Court, on 28 July 1989, a detailed written statement outlining the legal position of the United Nations on the matter. Following oral hearings held on 4 and 5 October 1989, the Court is expected to give its advisory opinion before the end of the year. . . .

SEE ALSO Convention on the Prevention and Punishment of Crimes against Internationally Protected Persons; Detention: UN Staff Members; Special Rapporteurs: Privileges and Immunities.

ARRESTED PERSON'S RIGHT TO COMMUNICATE.

A study of the right of arrested persons to communicate with those with whom it is necessary for them to consult in order to ensure their defense or to protect their essential interests—first suggested at the 1960 Vienna Seminar on the Protection of Human Rights in Criminal Procedure—was initiated by the UN COMMISSION ON HUMAN RIGHTS in 1961 (resolution 2 [XVII]). The commission requested a committee of four of its members—which it had established in 1956 for the purpose of studying the right of everyone to be free from ARBITRARY ARREST, DETENTION, OR EXILE—to carry out the new study. That committee had already emphasized the need for a detailed study on the right to communicate and had emphasized that "the right is an important one. It safeguards the principle that a person is to be presumed innocent until proved guilty according to law and is therefore entitled to freedom of action necessary to defend himself. It helps him to protect his family or business interests and to make full use of his rights and remedies."

Using the same methods as for the earlier study, the committee submitted its report (UN Doc. E/CN.4/996) to the Commission on Human Rights in 1969. In the study, the committee summarized the available information on the arrested person's right to notify others of his arrest, to receive visits and to correspond; on the remedies available to him and on sanctions which may follow a wrongful denial of the right; on the institution of incommunicado or *mise au secret;* and on the rights of persons arrested under emergency legislation. In the light of this information, and mindful of comments which governments had submitted on the draft principles on freedom from arbitrary arrest and detention which it had prepared on the basis of the earlier study, the committee suggested a series of amendments to those draft principles. The proposed revisions were as follows:

Notification of the Fact of Arrest. Combine articles 18 and 19.2 of the draft principles on arbitrary arrest, detention, and exile and revise them to read:

1. Every arrested or detained person shall be entitled to request the arresting or detaining authority immediately to notify his family, legal counsel, or other person whom he may designate of his arrest or detention and of the place where he is kept in custody.

2. Where the arrested or detained person is a minor or otherwise under legal incapacity, the arresting or detaining authority shall immediately inform his family or legal representative even if not requested to do so.

Access to Counsel. Adjust Article 21 to read as follows:

1. The arrested or detained person and his counsel shall be allowed full opportunity for consultation.

2. Written messages between an arrested or detained person and his counsel shall not be censored or the transmittal thereof delayed by the authorities.

3. Interviews between the arrested or detained person and his counsel may be within sight, but not within the hearing, of a police or institution official.

4. The right of an arrested or detained person to be visited by and to communicate with his counsel may not be suspended or restricted on any grounds.

Visits and Correspondence. Restate these principles as follows:

1. The arrested or detained person shall be given ample opportunity to be visited by, and to communicate with, his family and friends, ministers of religion, medical practitioners, social workers and, if he is an alien, the diplomatic or consular representative of his country.

2. The right of the arrested or detained person to be visited by and to communicate with persons other than his counsel or the authorities shall be subject only to such restrictions as may be ordered by a judge or other officer authorized by law to exercise judicial powers for the purpose of preventing interference with witnesses or the suppression of evidence or the passing of information which may assist the detained person to escape or assist his accomplices.

Incommunicado. Replace article 19.1 by the following:

1. The arrested or detained person may not be held *incommunicado* or in solitary confinement except where the law expressly provides for such measure and recourse thereto is ordered for a specified period not exceeding three days by a judge or other officer authorized by law to exercise judicial power.

2. *Incommunicado* or solitary confinement shall not be ordered except when absolutely necessary for reasons of national security or as the sole means of preventing the destruction or distortion of evidence or the escape of suspects.

3. An order of *incommunicado* or solitary confinement shall be in writing and shall state the reasons on which it is based. Such order shall be immediately communicated to the arrested or detained person and his counsel.

4. An order of *incommunicado* or solitary confinement shall not affect the right of arrested or detained person to communicate with his counsel as hereinbefore provided.

Detention under Emergency Situations. Include the following additional paragraph in article 35:

The detained person shall enjoy the right of communication of a person arrested or detained under the ordinary criminal law, as set forth in the foregoing articles, except where compelling reasons of national security require stricter restrictions, provided that no restriction may be imposed on his right to be visited by and to communicate freely with his counsel for the purpose of making representations to the competent authorities.

Remedies and Sanctions. Add the following to the text of article 38:

Any arrested or detained person who believes that his right to communication, as set forth in the foregoing articles, has been arbitrarily denied or restricted, may seek relief by way of petition or request to the authority responsible for the supervision of the place where he is kept in custody or to any of other competent administrative authority.

The principles formulated by the committee on the basis of its study of arbitrary arrest, detention, and exile, and the amendments thereto which it formulated on the basis of its study of the right to arrested persons to communicate, were taken into account by the **SUB-COMMISSION ON PREVENTION OF DISCRIMINATION AND PROTECTION OF MINORITIES** when, in 1978, it completed the draft of a body of principles for the protection of all persons under any form of detention or imprisonment (See **BODY OF PRINCIPLES FOR THE PROTECTION OF ALL PERSONS UNDER ANY FORM OF DETENTION OR IMPRISONMENT**). The Economic and Social Council requested the Secretary-General to forward the draft body of principles to the General Assembly together with the comments of governments on its provisions (resolution 1979/34); and the assembly, in 1980, referred the question to its Third (Social, Humanitarian and Cultural) Committee, in which an open-ended working group was set up to elaborate a final version of the principles. Because this working group was unable to conclude the task in 1980, the assembly, since 1981, referred the question to its Sixth (Legal) Committee, in which similar open-ended working groups were set up at each annual session. The body of principles was finally adopted by the UN General Assembly on 9 December 1988 (resolution 43/173).

ASIA WATCH. A human rights organization, established in 1985 to respond to the human rights struggle taking place in countries in that region, Asia Watch monitors activities in Asian countries from Afghanistan to the east. Asia Watch is affiliated with **HUMAN RIGHTS WATCH.**

Asia Watch has published a number of reports on human rights situations, among them: *By Both Parties to the Conflict: Violations of the Laws of War in Afghanistan* (1988); *Intellectual Freedom in China: An Update* (1988); *Human Rights Concerns in Indonesia* (1986); *"A Stern, Steady Crackdown:" Legal Process and Human Rights in South Korea* (1987); and *Still Confined: Journalists in "Re-education" Camps and Prisons in Vietnam* (1987).

Asia Watch. Address: 45 Fifth Ave., New York, NY 10017. Telephone: (212) 972-8400. Fax: (212) 972-0905. Executive Director: Sidney Jones.

ASSEMBLY AND ASSOCIATION. The right of everyone to freedom of peaceful assembly and association is proclaimed in two articles of the **UNIVERSAL DECLARATION OF HUMAN RIGHTS**, as follows:

Article 20. 1. Everyone has the right to freedom of peaceful assembly and association
2. No one may be compelled to belong to an association. . . .
Article 23. 4. Everyone has the right to form and join trade unions for the protection of his interests.

Measures to promote and protect the right to freedom of peaceful assembly are set out in both International Covenants on Human Rights. The **INTERNATIONAL COVENANT ON ECONOMIC, SOCIAL AND CULTURAL RIGHTS** provides that:

Article 8. 1. The States Parties to the present Covenant undertake to ensure:
(a) The right of everyone to form trade unions and join the trade union of his choice, subject only to the rules of the organization concerned, for the promotion and protection of his economic and social interests. No restrictions may be placed on the exercise of this right other than those prescribed by law and which are necessary in a democratic society in the interests of national security or public order or for the protection of the rights and freedoms of others;
(b) The right of trade unions to establish national federations or confederations and the right of the latter to form or join international trade-union organizations;
(c) The right of trade unions to function freely subject to no limitations other than those prescribed by law and which are necessary in a democratic society in the interests of national security or public order or for the protection of the rights and freedoms of others;
(d) The right to strike, provided that it is exercised in conformity with the laws of the particular country.
2. This article shall not prevent the imposition of lawful restrictions on the exercise of these rights by members of the armed forces or of the police or of the administration of the State.
3. Nothing in this article shall authorize States Parties to the International Labour Organisation Convention of 1948 concerning Freedom of Association and Protection of the Right to Organize to take legislative measures which would prejudice, or apply the law in such a manner as would prejudice, the guarantees provided for in that Convention.

The **INTERNATIONAL COVENANT ON CIVIL AND POLITICAL RIGHTS** provides that:

Article 21. The right of peaceful assembly shall be recognized. No restrictions may be placed on the exercise of this right other than those imposed in conformity with the law and which are necessary in a democratic society in the interests of national security or public safety, public order *(ordre public)*, the protection of public health or morals or the protection of the rights and freedoms of others.
Article 22. 1. Everyone shall have the right to freedom of association with others, including the right to form and join trade unions for the protection of his interests.

2. No restrictions may be placed on the exercise of this right other than those which are prescribed by law and which are necessary in a democratic society in the interests of national security or public safety, public order *(ordre public)*, the protection of public health or morals or the protection of the rights and freedoms of others. This article shall not prevent the imposition of lawful restrictions on members of the armed forces and of the police in their exercise of this right.

3. Nothing in this article shall authorize States Parties to the International Labour Organisation Convention of 1948 concerning Freedom of Association and Protection of the Right to Organize to take legislative measures which would prejudice, or to apply the law in such a manner as to prejudice, the guarantees provided for in that Convention.

The **INTERNATIONAL CONVENTION ON THE ELIMINATION OF ALL FORMS OF RACIAL DISCRIMINATION** deals with freedom of peaceful assembly and association from a different perspective in articles 4 and 5, as follows:

Article 4. States Parties condemn all propaganda and all organizations which are based on ideas or theories of superiority and one race or group of persons of one colour or ethnic origin, or which attempt to justify or promote racial hatred and discrimination in any form, and undertake to adopt immediate and positive measures designed to eradicate all incitement to, or acts of, such discrimination, and to this end, with due regard to the principles embodied in the Universal Declaration of Human Rights and the rights expressly set forth in article 5 of this Convention, *inter alia:*

(a) Shall declare an offence punishable by law all dissemination of ideas based on racial superiority or hatred, incitement to racial discrimination, as well as all acts of violence or incitement to such acts against any race or group of persons of another colour or ethnic origin, and also the provision of any assistance to racist activities, including the financing thereof;

(b) Shall declare illegal and prohibit organizations, and also organized and all other propaganda activities, which promote and incite racial discrimination, and shall recognize participation in such organizations or activities as an offence punishable by law;

(c) Shall not permit public authorities or public institutions, national or local, to promote or incite racial discrimination.

Article 5. In compliance with the fundamental obligations laid down in article 2, States Parties undertake to prohibit and to eliminate racial discrimination in all its forms and to guarantee the right of everyone, without distinction as to race, colour, or national or ethnic origin, to equality before the law, notably in the enjoyment of the following rights:

(d) Other civil rights, in particular:. . . .

(ix) The right to peaceful assembly and association.

The **AMERICAN CONVENTION ON HUMAN RIGHTS,** open for acceptance by member States of the **ORGANIZATION OF AMERICAN STATES,** deals with the right to freedom of peaceful assembly and association in articles 15 and 16, as follows:

Article 15. The right of peaceful assembly, without arms, is recognized. No restrictions may be placed on the exercise of this right other than those imposed in conformity with the law necessary in a democratic society in the interest of national security, public safety or public order, or to protect public health or morals or the rights or freedoms of others.

Article 16. 1. Everyone has the right to associate freely for ideological, religious, political, economic, labor, social, cultural, sports, or other purposes.

2. The exercise of this right shall be subject only to such restrictions established by law as may be necessary in a democratic society, in the interest of national security, public safety or public order, or to protect public health or morals or the rights and freedoms of others.

3. The provisions of this article do not bar the imposition of legal restrictions, including even deprivation of the exercise of the right of association, on members of the armed forces and the police.

The **AFRICAN CHARTER ON HUMAN AND PEOPLE'S RIGHTS** also deals with the subject in two separate paragraphs, as follows:

Article 10. 1. Every individual shall have the right to free association provided that he abides by the law.

2. Subject to the obligation of solidarity provided for in Article 29 no one may be compelled to join an association.

Article 11. Every individual shall have the right to assemble freely with others. The exercise of this right shall be subject only to necessary restrictions provided for by law in particular those enacted in the interest of national security, the safety, health, ethics and rights and freedoms of others.

The **EUROPEAN CONVENTION ON HUMAN RIGHTS,** open for acceptance by member States of the **COUNCIL OF EUROPE,** contains the following provision:

Article 11. 1. Everyone has the right to freedom of peaceful assembly and to freedom of association with others, including the right to form and to join trade unions for the protection of his interests.

2. No restrictions shall be placed on the exercise of these rights other than such as are prescribed by law and are necessary in a democratic society in the interests of national security or public safety, for the prevention of disorder or crime, for the protection of health or morals or for the protection of the rights and freedoms of others. This Article shall not prevent the imposition of lawful restrictions on the exercise of these rights by members of the armed forces, of the police or of the administration of the State.

Article 6 of the **DECLARATION ON THE ELIMINATION OF ALL FORMS OF INTOLERANCE AND OF DISCRIMINATION BASED ON RELIGION OR BELIEF** provides that:

In accordance with article 1 of the present Declaration, and subject to the provisions of article 1, paragraph 3, the right to freedom of thought, conscience, religion or belief shall include, *inter alia,* the following freedoms:

(a) to worship or assemble in connection with a religion or belief, and to establish and maintain places for these purposes;. . .

(e) to teach a religion in places suitable for these purposes;. . .

(h) to observe days of rest and to celebrate holidays and ceremonies in accordance with the precepts of one's religion or belief;

(i) to establish and maintain communications with individuals and communities in matters of religion and belief at the national and international levels.

In the *Study of Discrimination in the Matter of Religious Rights and Practices,* prepared by Mr. Arcot Krishnaswami (India), special rapporteur of the Sub-Commission on Prevention of Discrimination and Protection of Minorities (United Nations publication, Sales No. 60. XIV.2), the following comments on article 20 of the Universal Declaration of Human Rights are presented:

In view of the generality of the terms of this article, there can be no doubt that it extends to the sphere of religion or belief. However, certain facts relating to the two freedoms here involved—freedom of assembly on the one hand and freedom of association and the right to organize on the other hand—must be pointed out.

History and contemporary practice show a remarkable difference in the attitude of public authorities towards these two freedoms when they are applied in the field of religion or belief, and when they are applied in other fields. In many fields freedom of association and the right to organize have been more readily conceded than freedom of assembly. But in the field of religion, freedom of association and the right to organize have often been, and still are, denied or severely curtailed, whereas freedom of assembly in houses of worship has been recognized first, at least for the dominant religion, and later for a number of recognized—or even all—religions or beliefs. The difference is not accidental; public authorities consider that, in fields other than religion, there is less of a threat to public order and security in the existence of permanent organizations than in the congregation in one place of a large number of people. In the religious field, on the other hand, a meeting held for purposes related purely to matters of religion or belief does not generally present a threat to public order and security, whereas the establishment of a new and permanent organization may be considered dangerous because of the considerable impact which a religion or belief normally has upon its followers. Moreover, freedom of association and the right to organize may have quite a different meaning in the field of religion from that which they have in other fields: such questions as the structure of the religious organization and the management of its religious affairs are often, to a large extent, questions of dogma and therefore not matters of voluntary choice.

Although freedom of assembly for individuals of a particular faith does not raise such complicated issues as freedom of association and the right to organize, conflicts may arise even here between freedom of assembly and considerations of morality, public order, the general welfare, or respect for the rights and freedoms of others.

With regard to articles 4 and 5 of the International Convention on the Elimination of All Forms of Racial Discrimination, the COMMITTEE ON THE ELIMINATION OF RACIAL DISCRIMINATION has adopted a series of general recommendations. The first, approved at its fifth session, held from 14 to 25 February 1972, was as follows (UN Doc. A/8718, Chap. IX A, general recommendation I);

On the basis of the consideration at its fifth session of reports submitted by States Parties under article 9 of the International Convention on the Elimination of All Forms of Racial Discrimination, the Committee found that the legislation of a number of States Parties did not include the provisions envisaged in article 4 (a) and (b) of the Convention, the implementation of which (with due regard to the principles embodied in the Universal Declaration of Human Rights and the rights expressly set forth in article 5 of the Convention) is obligatory under the Convention for all States Parties.

The Committee accordingly recommends that the States Parties whose legislation was deficient in this respect should consider, in accordance with their national legislative procedures, the question of supplementing their legislation with provisions conforming to the requirements of article 4 (a) and (b) of the Convention.

One year later, the committee at its seventh session, held from 16 April to 4 May 1973, reaffirmed the earlier recommendation and requested States parties to the convention (UN Doc. A/9018, chap. X, decision 3 [VII]):

1. to indicate what specific penal internal legislation designed to implement the provisions of article 4 (a) and (b) has been enacted in their respective countries and to transmit to the Secretary-General in one of the official languages the texts concerned as well as such provisions of general penal law as must be taken into account when applying such specific legislation;

2. where no such specific legislation has been enacted, to inform the Committee of the manner and the extent to which the provisions of the existing penal laws, as applied by the Courts, effectively implement their obligations under article 4 (a) and (b), and to transmit to the Secretary-General in one of the official languages the texts of those provisions;

3. to present such information by 31 December 1973.

At its 32d session, held from 5 to 23 August 1985, the committee again reaffirmed general recommendation I. Noting that, in a number of States parties, the necessary legislation to implement article 4 of the convention had not been enacted and that many States parties had not fulfilled all the requirements of article 4 (a) and (b) of the convention and recalling that, in accordance with the first paragraph of article 4, States parties "undertake to adopt immediate and positive measures designed to eradicate all incitement to, or acts of, such discrimination" with due regard to the principles embodied in the Universal Declaration of Human Rights and the rights expressly set forth in article 5 of the convention, the committee recommended (UN Doc. A/40/18, chap. VII B, general recommendation VII): (1) that those States parties whose legislation does not satisfy the provisions of article 4 (a) and (b) of the convention take the necessary steps with a view to satisfying the mandatory requirements of that article, and (2) that those States parties which had not done so inform the committee more fully in their periodic reports of the manner and extent to which the provisions of article 4 (a) and (b) are effectively implemented and quote the relevant parts of the texts in their reports. The committee further requested those States parties which had not done so to endeavour to provide in their periodic reports more information concerning decisions taken by the competent national tribunals and other State institutions regarding acts of racial discrimination and in particular those offences dealt with in article 4 (a) and (b).

Trade Union Rights. The right to form and join trade unions is dealt with in both International Covenants on Human Rights primarily because these rights, although clearly economic and social in nature, constitute an important aspect of the right to freedom of peaceful assembly and association. The International Covenant on Economic, Social and Cultural Rights recognizes (article 8.1 [d]) the right to strike, but only if that right is exercised "in conformity with the laws of the particular country"—an appreciable restriction. No ILO convention or recommendation recognizes the right to strike or defines the extent to which it may be exercised.

Within the United Nations system, the lead agency concerned with freedom of association and trade union rights is the INTERNATIONAL LABOR ORGANIZATION, which assumed major responsibilities in this field some five months before the proclamation of the Universal Declaration of Human Rights when its General Conference, on 9 July 1948, adopted the ILO FREEDOM OF ASSOCIATION AND PROTECTION OF THE RIGHT TO ORGANIZE CONVENTION. This instrument was followed closely by the ILO RIGHT TO ORGANIZE AND COLLECTIVE BARGAINING CONVENTION, 1949; and supplemented later by the ILO WORKERS' REPRESENTATIVES CONVENTION, 1971, the ILO RURAL WORKERS' ORGANIZATIONS CONVENTION, 1975, and the ILO LABOR RELATIONS (PUBLIC SERVICE) CONVENTION, 1978.

Under the Freedom of Association and Protection of the Right to Organize Convention, which entered into force on 4 July 1950, States Parties guarantee:

—that workers and employers, without any distinction whatsoever, shall have the right to establish and, subject only to the rules of the organization concerned, to join organizations of their own choosing without previous authorization;

—that workers' and employers' organizations shall have the right to draw up their constitutions and rules, to elect their representatives in full freedom, to organize their administration and activities, and to formulate their programs;

—that the public authorities shall refrain from any interferences which would restrict this right or impede the lawful exercise thereof;

—that workers' and employers' organizations shall not be liable to be dissolved or suspended by administrative authority; and

—that workers' and employers' organizations shall have the right to establish and join federations and confederations, and that any such organization, federation, or confederation shall have the right to affiliate with international organizations of workers and employers.

Under the Right to Organize and Collective Bargaining Convention, which entered into force on 18 July 1951, States parties undertake to provide protection for workers against acts of anti-union discrimination and for workers' and employers' organizations against mutual acts of interference in their establishment, to establish appropriate machinery for this purpose, and to encourage and promote voluntary collective negotiation between employers or employers' organizations and workers' organizations.

Under the Workers' Representatives Convention, which entered into force on 30 June 1973, the term "workers' representatives" is defined as meaning persons recognized as such under national law or practice, whether they be trade union representatives—namely representatives designated or elected by trade unions or by members of such unions— or elected representatives, namely representatives freely elected by the workers of the undertaking whose functions do not include activities recognized as the exclusive prerogative of trade unions in the country concerned. It provides that such representatives shall enjoy effective protection against any act prejudicial to them, including dismissal, based on their status or activities as a workers' representative or on union membership or participation in union activities, insofar as they act in conformity with existing laws or collective agreements or other jointly agreed arrangements. It further provides that they will be afforded such facilities as may be appropriate in order to enable them to carry out their functions promptly and efficiently, as long as the granting of such facilities does not impair the efficient functioning of the undertaking concerned. It further provides that, where there exist in the same undertaking both trade union representatives and elected representatives, appropriate measures shall be taken, wherever necessary, to ensure that the existence of elected representatives is not used to undermine the position of the trade unions concerned or of their representatives.

The standards set out in the instruments mentioned above have been reinforced by a number of recommendations and resolutions adopted by the ILO General Conference concerning various aspects of labor-management relations (negotiation of collective agreements, voluntary conciliation and arbitration, cooperation at the level of the undertaking, consultations between employers and workers, and the right to strike).

International Supervision. In 1949, the Economic and Social Council was informed, by the Director-General of the International Labor Organization, that the ILO Governing Body had approved the establishment of a fact-finding and conciliation commission to provide international supervision of the realization of freedom of association. The council (resolution 239 [IX]) called upon the UN Secretary-General and the ILO Director-General to work out a procedure for making the services of that commission available to the United Nations with respect to States members of the UN but not of the ILO. With their agreement, the council formulated, in 1950, a procedure for dealing with allegations concerning infringements of trade union rights; it decided (resolution 277 [X]) that it would forward to the ILO Governing Body, for its consideration for referral to the fact-finding and conciliation commission, all such allegations received from governments or trade union or employers' organizations against ILO States members; and invited the ILO to refer to the council any such allegations against a member of the United Nations which was not a member of ILO.

In 1951, the ILO Governing Body established its own Committee on Freedom of Association to make preliminary examinations of allegations concerning infringements of trade union rights and to advise it on the appropriateness of referring such allegations to the fact-finding and conciliation commission.

Since its establishment the Fact-Finding and Conciliation Commission on Freedom of Association has considered only a few complaints. It has been hampered by the need to obtain the consent of the governments concerned before it can act and also by the fact that the preliminary examination of complaints by the Governing Body Committee on Freedom of Association has been so effective that recourse to the Fact-Finding Commission was not necessary. The Governing Body Committee has dealt successfully with many hundreds of cases.

In light of the committee's proposals, the governing body has frequently urged countries to modify their legislation or their practice; as a result, the legislation in question has been repealed or amended and practices incompatible with the principle of freedom of association have been discontinued, imprisoned trade union leaders have been released, and death sentences for trade unionists have been commuted. The jurisprudence developed by the committee is largely based on standards set out in ILO conventions on freedom of association but also extends to certain matters not expressly dealt with in those conventions and to questions which, while involving human rights, also concern the effective exercise of trade union rights.

In 1967 and 1968, the Economic and Social Council received a number of allegations concerning violations of trade union rights in South Africa, which had ceased to be a member of the ILO. The council at that time authorized (resolutions 1216 [XLII] and 1302 [XLIV], respectively) the **AD HOC WORKING GROUP OF EXPERTS ON SOUTHERN AFRICA** of the Commission on Human Rights to deal with all such allegations relating to South Africa, Namibia, and Southern Rhodesia. The working group continues to monitor the situation of trade union rights in South Africa and Namibia, and reports to the commission and to the council thereon.

On the basis of these reports, the council has adopted a number of resolutions noting that dehumanizing conditions imposed on black workers by the government of South Africa continue and expressing concern at the escalation of the repression against the independent black trade union movement, in particular the severe restrictions placed on the Congress of South African Trade Unions and efforts to impose further restrictions on trade unions through legislative changes. On 27 May 1988, the council (resolution 1988/41) condemned the increased repression of the independent black trade union movement by the government of South Africa; demanded that the persecution of trade unionists and repression of the independent black trade union movement cease; requested immediate recognition of the right of the entire population of South Africa to exercise freedom of association and to form and join trade unions without impediment or discrimination of any kind; and demanded the immediate unconditional release of all trade unionists imprisoned for exercising their legitimate trade union rights.

ASSOCIATED COUNTRY WOMEN OF THE WORLD.

An international non-governmental organization in consultative status (Category II) with the UN Economic and Social Council, the organization consists of 179 constituent, 26 associate, and 100 corresponding societies in 64 countries and territories.

Founded in 1930 in Vienna as the "Liaison Committee of Rural Women's and Homemakers' Organizations," the Associated Country Women of the World promotes friendly relations and understanding among rural women and works to raise their standard of living. The group maintains a clearing house for information and collects information and compiles reports at the request of UN bodies, including the Commission on the Status of Women. The group has also established trust funds, such as the "Lady Aberdeen Scholarship Fund," the "Elsi Zimmern Memorial Fund" for leadership and organizational training, and the "Nutrition Education Fund" for aid to developing countries.

ACWW publishes the quarterly *The Countrywoman,* conference reports, pamphlets, and a 3H series of booklets for developing countries.

Associated Country Women of the World. Address: Vincent House, Vincent Square, London SW1P 2NB, UK. Telephone: (44–1) 534-86-35. Cable: Ascoworld London. Secretary-General: Jennifer Pearce.

Yearbook of International Organizations 1989/90 (K. G. Saur).

ATLANTIC CHARTER (1941). The charter, a joint declaration by Franklin D. Roosevelt, President of the United States of America, and Winston S. Churchill, Prime Minister of the United Kingdom, was issued on 14 August 1941. Although not technically an international instrument or even an official document, it set out a program of peace aims to which the signers of the DECLARATION BY UNITED NATIONS pledged adherence. The text follows:

The President of the United States of America and the Prime Minister, Mr. Churchill, representing His Majesty's Government in the United Kingdom, being met together, deem it right to make known certain common principles in the national policies of their respective countries on which they base their hopes for a better future for the world.

First, their countries seek no aggrandizement, territorial or other;

Second, they desire to see no territorial changes that do not accord with the freely expressed wishes of the peoples concerned;

Third, they respect the right of all peoples to choose the form of government under which they will live; and they wish to see sovereign rights and self-government restored to those who have been forcibly deprived of them;

Fourth, they will endeavor, with due respect for their existing obligations, to further the enjoyment by all states, great or small, victor or vanquished, of access, on equal terms, to the trade and to the raw materials of the world which are needed for their economic prosperity;

Fifth, they desire to bring about the fullest collaboration between all nations in the economic field with the object of securing, for all, improved labor standards, economic advancement, and social security;

Sixth, after the final destruction of the Nazi tyranny, they hope to see established a peace which will afford to all nations the means of dwelling in safety within their own boundaries, and which will afford assurance that all the men in all the lands may live out their lives in freedom from fear and want;

Seventh, such a peace should enable all men to traverse the high seas and oceans without hindrance;

Eighth, they believe that all the nations of the world, for realistic as well as spiritual reasons, must come to the abandonment of the use of force. Since no future peace can be maintained if land, sea, or air armaments continue to be employed by nations which threaten, or may threaten, aggression outside of their frontiers, they believe, pending the establishment of a wider and permanent system of general security, that the disarmament of such nations is essential. They will likewise aid and encourage all other practicable measures which will lighten for peace-loving peoples the crushing burden of armaments.

AUSTRALIA. The Commonwealth of Australia occupies an island continent in Oceania, between the Indian Ocean and the Coral and Tasmanian Seas. It includes five continental States and the island State of Tasmania and has jurisdiction over a number of island territories in the Indian Ocean and the sub-Antarctic, including the Australia Antarctic territory. It achieved independence from Great Britain in 1901, and became a member of the United Nations in 1945. Its population is estimated by the UN (1990) to be 16,708,000. The 1981 census counted 3,003,823 overseas-born persons, of whom nearly 54% were born in non-English-speaking countries. That census also counted 159,897 Australians identifying themselves as Aboriginals or Torres Strait Islanders. Members of these groups are entitled by law to the full range of fundamental rights and freedoms of other Australians but, in practice, remain in a disadvantaged position. English is the official language; aboriginal vernaculars are used by some of the indigenous peoples. Christianity (Anglican, 30%; Roman Catholic, 30%; Methodist/Presbyterian, 15%; and others, 25%) is the predominant religion. Literacy is estimated at 99%.

The government (1990) took the form of a monarchy and member of the Commonwealth of Nations, of which the British sovereign is the symbolic head. Executive power is exercised by the governor-general, representing the crown, and a cabinet headed by the prime minister, representing the party or coalition given the majority in a popular election. The federal Parliament consists of a 76-member Senate, members of which are elected for terms of six years, and a 148-member House of Representatives, members of which serve for terms of three years. Voting is compulsory for those 18 or over. Judicial authority is exercised by the High Court of Australia, federal courts, and state courts, each state having its own judicial system. Political parties include the Australian Labor Party, the Liberal Party, and the National Party.

From the early years of its independence, Australia has been noted for its legislation promoting the enjoyment of certain human rights: political rights for women were recognized in 1902, old-age pensions initiated in 1910, maternity allowances in 1912, subsidies to parents of more than one child in 1941, and unemployment and sickness benefits in 1944. At the same time, however, its "white Australia" immigration policy was known and condemned in most parts of the world. Although the policy was publicly discarded in 1973, European migrants are still favored; the criteria that prospective migrants must be "economically viable" and "have personal qualities that would enable them to fit into the Australian community" have been used to exclude millions of Asian and African candidates.

As regards Aboriginals, the Australian public was largely unaware of their condition until the Queen of England arrived in Canberra in 1974 to open Parliament and was confronted with an impressive demonstration protesting their deplorable situation. The resulting increased awareness of the problems which they faced led to the adoption on 10 December 1981 of the Human Rights Commission Act and the development of an attitude of "multiculturalism" in the country.

However, the situation of the aboriginal people was drawn to public attention forcibly in January 1988, when thousands of them gathered in Sydney to protest, rather than to join in, Australia's celebration of the bicentennial of the arrival of its first white settlers. Boycotting the festivities, the aboriginals pointed out that for them the two-century period had been one of annihilation, dispossession, and increasing poverty. Their population had been reduced to about 160,000—about half its total before the advent of the settlers—and they had become outcasts in their own land, living on reservations or in urban slums, suffering infant mortality three times the national rate and earning half the national average wage.

Australia's overall political structure was described by the government in its second periodic report submitted in 1987 to the **HUMAN RIGHTS COMMITTEE** under article 40 of the **INTERNATIONAL COVENANT ON CIVIL AND POLITICAL RIGHTS** (UN Doc. CCPR/C/42/Add. 2, para. 1–10) as follows:

I. Political Structure

Federal/State system. Australia is a federation in which legislative, executive and judicial powers are divided between the federal Parliament, executive and judiciary and the corresponding organs of the six constituent Australian States— New South Wales, Queensland, South Australia, Tasmania, Victoria and Western Australia. The structure of each of these political units is based on the United Kingdom Westminster system of government. In each unit there is a Par-

liament elected by the people, an executive responsible to that Parliament formed by the majority party or parties in Parliament, and an independent judiciary. The federal Government is also responsible for the Australian Territories which are those parts of Australia not comprised in a State.

Details of the area and population of Australia, together with statistics from the 1981 Census of Population and Housing, are set out in annex 1 to this report.

Northern Territory. One of the Territories, the Northern Territory, has in practice a degree of self-government so that it may be regarded, for the purposes of this report, as being in the same position as a State of Australia. Hereafter, references to the States include a reference to the Northern Territory, unless otherwise indicated.

Other Territories. In addition to the Northern Territory, Australia has nine other Territories. The inhabited Territories are: the Australian Capital Territory (which includes Canberra, the capital city of Australia and seat of the federal Government); and the Jervis Bay Territory (both of which are located on mainland Australia); and four Territories external to the mainland, namely the Australian Antarctic Territory; Norfolk Island; Cocos (Keeling) Islands; and Christmas Island.

Of the external Territories, the small Territory of Norfolk Island exercises a degree of self-government and its special position is dealt with in paragraph 17 below.

The uninhabited Territories which are all external to the mainland are: the Territory of Ashmore and Cartier Islands; the Coral Sea Islands Territory; and the Territory of Heard Island and McDonald Islands.

II. Legal Framework

The laws applying in Australia fall into two broad categories:

(a) Legislation in the form of statutes passes by a Parliament or subordinate legislation made by the executive, which is subject to disallowance by Parliament;

(b) Rules derived from decisions of courts of authority namely:

(i) The common law proper (that is, laws developed through judicial recognition, independent of any legislative enactment); and

(ii) Judicial interpretation of legislation.

In the Australian legal system every person, whether private citizen or government official, is equally subject to the law. Government must operate through and within the law. In particular, government officials must have legal authority for their actions and are subject to effective legal sanctions if they contravene the law.

A. Federal/State Legislative Powers. Under the Constitution of the Commonwealth of Australia the Commonwealth (i.e. federal) Parliament and executive are granted specified legislative and executive powers. The States, each of which has its own Constitution, and the Northern Territory, under the Northern Territory (Self-Government) Act 1978, as well as possessing the undefined residue of legislative powers, possess, concurrently with the Commonwealth, most of the legislative powers granted to the Commonwealth. However, pursuant to section 109 of the Constitution, a State law (not, in that context, including a Northern Territory law) which is inconsistent with a valid Commonwealth law, is to the extent of the inconsistency, invalid.

B. Laws in Australian Territories. Under section 122 of the Commonwealth Constitution, the Parliament has plenary power to make laws for any Australian Territories. The laws applying in the Territories are mainly a mixture of federal law and laws made by the Government or Administration of those Territories. As a general rule all Commonwealth laws apply in the Australian Capital Territory and Jervis Bay Territory. Commonwealth laws only apply in other Territories where it is expressly stated that they do so, or by necessary implication.

With regard to the elimination of racial discrimination, the government states in the report (para. 656–658) that:

The right to equality before the law in regard to the prohibition on racial discrimination is conferred by section 10 of the Racial Discrimination Act 1975. Section 10 provides:

"(1) If, by reason of, or of a provision of, a law of Australia or of a State or Territory, persons of a particular race, colour or national or ethnic origin do not enjoy a right that is enjoyed by persons of another race, colour or national or ethnic origin, or enjoy a right to a more limited extent than persons of another race, colour or national or ethnic origin, then, notwithstanding anything in that law, persons of the first-mentioned race, colour, or national or ethnic origin shall, by force of this section, enjoy that right to the same extent as persons of that other race, colour or national or ethnic origin.

"(2) A reference in subsection (1) to a right includes a reference to a right of a kind referred to in article 5 of the Convention."

The above provision does not apply to special measures to which paragraph 4 of article 1 of the International Convention on the Elimination of All Forms of Racial Discrimination applies. These are special measures taken for the sole purpose of securing adequate advancement of certain racial or ethnic groups or individuals requiring such protection to ensure equal enjoyment or exercise of human rights and fundamental freedoms. Such measures are not to lead to the maintenance of separate rights for different racial groups. The operation of these provisions was the subject of consideration by the High Court of *Gerhardy v. Brown.* The main issues and findings in that case are outlined in annex 4 to this report (see annex).

By the operation of the principle that a Parliament cannot bind its successors, later federal legislation which is inconsistent with the Sex Discrimination Act and Racial Discrimination Act will be valid. However the possibility of the enactment of such laws will to an extent be monitored by the Human Rights and Equal Opportunity Commission, which has the function of examining international instruments and federal laws to ensure that they contain nothing inconsistent with any human rights.

As to the rights of ethnic, religious, and other minorities in Australia, the government provides the following information in the report (para. 659–696):

Australia has a population composed of people drawn from many countries, in addition to the Aboriginals and Torres Strait Islanders who were already present when the first European settlers arrived in 1788. All Australian Governments are conscious of the need to recognize, support and protect minorities. In particular, for many years Australian Governments have actively pursued policies which encourage ethnic communities to participate fully in the mainstream of Australian Life. The resultant policies have tended to be divided into two main streams: those relating to the Aboriginal people and those relating to other ethnic minorities.

The basic position in Australia is that all persons and groups have full rights to pursue their own interests, provided these are consistent with the law. In general, laws are such that the minorities specified in the article can meet together to pursue activities related to their cultures, religions and languages.

The protection of the rights contained in this article is provided for under the general human rights machinery which exists in Australia, the most fundamental being the prohibition on racial discrimination. Increasingly, Governments in Australia have taken special measures to provide for the needs of ethnic minorities. These measures are contained in both legislation and administrative programmes. An outline of these measures appears below.

Ethnic Minorities

(a) Aborigines. As mentioned above, policies on ethnic minorities generally have developed in two streams: policies and legislation concerned with Australian Aboriginal people and those concerned with other ethnic minorities. Throughout Australia Aborigines live a variety of life-styles: as ordinary members of general urban or rural communities, on the fringes of towns or cities or in remote communities following a traditional life-style. There are different needs and problems facing Aboriginal people in each of these groupings. Government policies recognize these special needs in all jurisdictions by recognizing a basic right for Aborigines to retain, modify or develop their own cultures, customs, traditions and life-styles in their own way.

Aboriginal Cultural Heritage. The federal Government has taken a number of significant measures which provide protection for Aboriginal cultural heritage in the following ways:

(a) The Australian Heritage Commission Act has special provisions to protect places associated with Aboriginal history, culture or beliefs. Some 3,000 individual Aboriginal sites are now included on the Register of the National Estate. The Commission consults closely with Aboriginal bodies concerned with sites. Three of the five Australian areas on the World Heritage List are of great Aboriginal significance: Kakadu National Park, Willandra Lakes Region and the Western Tasmania Wilderness National Parks;

(b) The Aboriginal and Torres Strait Islander Heritage Protection Act 1984 provides a means for the Commonwealth to protect significant Aboriginal areas and objects. The Act complements existing State and Territory laws and is used only as a last resort where those laws do not provide effective protection of such areas and objects from injury or desecration. The Act also enables the Minister for Aboriginal Affairs to make declarations setting out what can or cannot be done in respect of those areas and objects. High penalties are provided for the breach of such declarations;

(c) The Museum of Australia Act provides that one of the Museum's three major components shall be a Gallery of Aboriginal Australia;

(d) The Aboriginal Arts Board plays a significant role in helping to conserve Aboriginal culture;

(e) The export of certain important Aboriginal materials is prohibited under the Customs (Prohibited Exports) Regulations;

(f) The Protection of Movable Cultural Heritage Act 1986 provides for the protection from export of objects which constitute the movable cultural heritage of Australia. This will include objects listed on a control list relating to members of the Aboriginal race of Australia and descendants of the indigenous inhabitants of the Torres Strait Islands.

The Australian Government is also currently investigating ways of involving Aboriginal people in the care and maintenance of collections of Aboriginal cultural material, both in the major museums and in Aboriginal holding places. This is seen as providing a basis for a more positive approach to the return of cultural material to communities. The legislation to establish the Museum of Australia is capable of facilitating the return of material relating to Aboriginals from the national collection to Aboriginal communities. The Act also provides for Aboriginals to be involved in the development and maintenance of the Museum's planned Gallery of Aboriginal Australia.

The federal Government also aims to finance programmes which develop Aboriginal self-sufficiency and which represent initiatives that Aboriginals themselves believe will enhance their dignity, self-respect and self-reliance. It also aims to promote cross-cultural understanding between Aboriginals and non-Aboriginals. These objectives are maintained in the funding of Aboriginal art and cultural activities. For example, the Aboriginal Arts Board (an all Aboriginal body which operates as part of the Australia Council) has stated its broad objectives in the following terms:

"To the Board, Aboriginal culture is not simply a remnant of the past, it is a living force, with its own dynamism and momentum. The Board aims to make this living force a part of the experience of all Aboriginals and a source of pride for all Australians".

Some protection of Aboriginal culture and designs is available through the Aboriginal Artists Agency Ltd., a non-profit company funded by the Aboriginal Arts Board. The Agency's role has expanded from the protection of Aboriginal tribal arts to copyright, publishing, promotional and entrepreneurial activities.

The States have had legislation in place since the 1970s which provides for the identification, registration and in some cases management of Aboriginal sites. There have been no major changes to such legislation in recent years although Western Australia does have amendments under consideration. In Victoria recent legislative amendments have already led to skeletal material being returned to the control of the museum, and the total restriction on the sale of Aboriginal artefacts and cultural material. Victoria is also considering further measures for the protection of the Aboriginal cultural heritage in that State.

In the Northern Territory, the Aboriginal Sacred Sites Act 1978 protects Aboriginal sacred sites. A significant number of sites have now been registered under the Act. There is also special legislation dealing with protection of Aboriginal artefacts. Under the Aboriginal Relics Preservation Act 1967–1976, provision is made to protect Aboriginal sites throughout Queensland. Any unauthorized interference with such sites and relics thereon is an offence. In Tasmania, the Aboriginal Relics Act 1975 provides protection for Aboriginal sites, artefacts and human remains. That Act is administered by the Director of the National Parks and Wildlife Service. The Act includes provisions enabling the Director to deal with artefacts and remains in a way which is approved by the Minister and an Advisory Council which includes representatives of the Aboriginal community.

In New South Wales the National Parks Act 1984 deals with Aboriginal artefacts and the use of Aboriginal areas within a series of by-laws. New South Wales has enacted the Land Rights Act 1983, pursuant to the Keen Committee report. This report also recommended new legislation to cover Aboriginal heritage and a working party is investigating these recommendations.

Aboriginal Studies. Alongside the growing interest in Australia in the preservation and diffusion of Aboriginal culture there is increasing acknowledgment that Aboriginal science and technology is of value. Bodies such as the Australian Institute of Aboriginal Studies, the National Parks and Wildlife Service and the Commonwealth Scientific and Industrial Research Organization have begun to investigate traditional Aboriginal knowledge and expertise in areas such as the use of fire (for regeneration of flora), concepts of sickness and health, and knowledge about plants and the processing of food. Application of Aboriginal scientific knowledge is occurring through the incorporation of Aboriginal techniques into environment conservation practice in Northern Territory National Parks. Traditional healers are being used in the delivery of health services in a number of tradition-oriented Aboriginal communities. Aboriginal knowledge of, and classification for, flora and fauna is also being incorporated into the curricula of various Northern Territory schools.

The Australian Institute of Aboriginal Studies is constituted by Act of Parliament to promote Aboriginal studies, to publish or assist in the publication of the results of Aboriginal studies, to encourage and assist co-operation among universities, museums and other institutions concerned with Aboriginal studies. It also assists these institutions in training research workers in fields relevant to Aboriginal studies.

Broadcasting. There have been a number of significant developments in Aboriginal broadcasting. In various parts of Australia, radio programmes are provided for and by Aboriginals in their own languages and in English. A number of public radio stations have provided broadcasting time so that Aboriginals can present their own programmes. The Aboriginal Media Association, as well as Aboriginal organizations using community broadcasting facilities, are assisted by the federal Government to undertake special workshop training in radio broadcasting techniques. An Aboriginal television company, Imparja Television, was recently awarded the Central Australian commercial television licence.

The Australian Broadcasting Corporation (the ABC) has a role, as a national broadcasting organization, in providing training for Aboriginal people in broadcasting skills both for careers in the ABC, and for broadcasting within the Aboriginal broadcasting organizations. With the advent of the satellite, and its potential to transmit television and radio to remote areas, the ABC is consulting with those Aboriginal communities on the impact of Western media on their cultures, and what control those communities should have on access of the media to those remote Aboriginal and Islander communities.

Education

Federal. The federal Government's policies in Aboriginal education seek to ensure that full educational opportunities are available to all persons of Aboriginal and Torres

Strait Islander descent and that they receive an education in harmony with their cultural values and chosen life-style which enables them to acquire the skills they desire. As most young Aboriginal children attend government primary schools, the major proportion of federal funding for this age group is made available to State Departments of Education to provide special educational support services designed to meet the distinct needs of Aboriginal students. Direct grants are also made available to Aboriginal and other independent schools.

A particular feature of the support services is the funding of Aboriginal teaching assistant positions in most States and Territories. This has enabled Aboriginal adults to enter paraprofessional roles undertaking such responsibilities as home-school liaison, teaching of Aboriginal studies and assisting in general teaching. Considerable emphasis is being given to funding programmes aimed at increasing the numbers of Aboriginal teachers who, in addition to usual teaching skills, will bring to Aboriginal and non-Aboriginal students a unique Aboriginal socio-cultural contribution to education philosophy and practice.

Government assistance is also available for Aboriginal students undertaking secondary school studies through programmes which provide financial assistance in the form of various allowances to enable Aboriginal students to take full advantage of the educational opportunities available to the wider community. Funds are available to provide academic and social support for Aboriginal students in tertiary institutions as well as financial assistance for other post-secondary school studies.

States. State programmes aimed at improving education services to Aboriginal primary school students include provision of advisory staff, in-service teacher education and curriculum development services in areas of language development, Aboriginal studies and bilingual materials in Aboriginal languages. The Northern Territory Bilingual Education Programme commenced by the federal Government in 1973 is being continued by the Northern Territory Government. It has introduced an assessment and accreditation programme aimed at placing the programme on a firmer footing. Continuing developments in bilingual education in government and Aboriginal independent schools have also occurred in Queensland, Western Australia and South Australia. The aims of such programmes involve maintenance of Aboriginal children's languages and cultures through programmes which include them as initial and continuing segments of the school curriculum as well as ensuring that Aboriginal children obtain the skills they will require to operate without disadvantage in the wider Australian community.

There are also difficulties in providing education services to isolated Aboriginal communities, particularly those family groups or clans which have moved away from larger communities to return to their traditional lands. In the Northern Territory the Department of Education has responded to requests for education services from such communities by providing a "homeland centre education programme". This involves provision of a basic curriculum taught by a literate member of the Aboriginal family group with support from a visiting teacher and utilizing special programmed materials and instruction tapes. The provision of appropriate educational services to children of Aboriginal communities living on the fringes of country towns presents a challenge to education authorities. While special programmes and approaches are being introduced, with Aboriginal people being involved to an increasing degree,

many students and schools have yet to be reached by these services. This is an area which will continue to receive close attention from Governments and education authorities.

The federal Government's Law Reform Commission, in its report on *The Recognition of Aboriginal Customary Laws* (Report No. 31), included the following observations on article 27:

"Aborigines may be taken to be members of an ethnic minority (or perhaps a number of such minorities): under article 27 they may not be denied the right 'to enjoy their own culture'. However, it is not clear to what extent article 27 imposes positive duties, as opposed to mere requirements of abstention, upon States parties. Under the Covenant, members of minority groups, in common with the other citizens, have individual rights to family life, to freedom of religion and association. Article 27 could be interpreted as merely precluding the State from interfering in the exercise of such rights by individuals 'in community with other members of their group'. But this minimal interpretation of article 27 does not seem satisfactory. It would make article 27 into a redundant commentary on the other provisions. The view that article 27 imposes substantive obligations has been adopted by the Human Rights Committee in a decision on a communication from a Canadian Indian under the Optional Protocol to the Covenant." (Para. 175 of the report.)

The Commission concluded that the scope of article 27 in regard to recognition of customary laws was as follows:

"The present position is that Australia is not precluded by its international obligations from an extensive recognition of Aboriginal customary laws (subject to protection of the 'human rights of individual Aborigines') ... However the only international obligation with respect to the granting of such recognition at present is article 27 of the International Covenant on Civil and Political Rights, which imposes only limited obligations in this context." (Para. 178 of the report.)

(b) Other Ethnic Groups. Government policy in all jurisdictions is to recognize the multicultural nature of Australian society and the existence within that society of many ethnic, religious and linguistic groups. The objective of this policy is a society with a high level of acceptance of different races and groups which offers security, well-being and equality of opportunity to all its members. Recognition and support is given to individuals or groups to preserve and develop their culture, languages, traditions and customs.

A major stimulus to improvements in the general standard of services to migrant and ethnic groups occurred with the federal Government's acceptance in full of the *Report of a Review of Post-Arrival Programmes and Services* (the Galbally Report) which was published in April 1978 in English and nine other languages. The Galbally measures were evaluated in 1982 by the Australian Institute of Multicultural Affairs, which recommended a continuation of the main thrust of migrant programmes and services on principles established by Galbally. In December 1985 the Minister for Immigration and Ethnic Affairs announced a Review of Migrant and Multicultural Programmes and Services (ROMAMPAS) to set directions for post-arrival services and programmes for immigrants over the next decade. The Review is designed to guide the federal Government in the development of its role and policies to assist overseas-born Australians and their families to achieve equitable participation in Australian society, and to refine the provision of programmes and services in line with this broad goal.

In 1978, after consideration of the Galbally Report the

federal Government formally accepted the following guidelines and principles in relation to programmes and services for migrants:

(a) All members of Australian society must have equal opportunity to realize their full potential and must have equal access to programme and services;

(b) Every person should be able to maintain his or her culture without prejudice or disadvantage and should be encouraged to understand and embrace other cultures;

(c) Needs of migrants should, in general, be met by programmes and services available to the whole community, but special services and programmes are necessary, at present, to ensure equality of access and provision;

(d) Services and programmes should be designed and operated in full consultation with clients, and self-help should be encouraged as much as possible, with a view to helping migrants to become self-reliant quickly.

In July 1985 the federal Government decided that each Minister whose portfolio had a significant impact on migrants should provide a statement on the adoption of measures to ensure access and equity in service delivery to migrants, together with measures planned to be adopted in the following year. In April 1986 the Minister for Immigration and Ethnic Affairs tabled in Parliament an overview of action taken and required to implement the Government's access and equity policy, based on the statements received from Government departments. The statements revealed the need for a coherent, service-wide strategy, to achieve access and equity objectives. Accordingly, the Government will adopt measures requiring all relevant departments and authorities to take steps to improve the effectiveness of their activities, and ensure that these are co-ordinated and monitored within the framework of progressive administrative reform.

In future, the Department of Immigration and Ethnic Affairs will issue federal departments and authorities with a statement of guidelines, which will require them to:

(a) Review at regular intervals, monitor and evaluate all services and programmes to ensure that they respond to the diverse linguistic and cultural needs in our society;

(b) Establish appropriate data collection systems;

(c) Deliver services and implement programmes in languages other than English, when that is necessary to provide effective service;

(d) Develop personnel practices which sensitize staff to cultural factors;

(e) Provide opportunities for participation by members of the ethnic communities in policy formulation and programme delivery;

(f) Develop appropriate programmes;

(g) Provide for legislative and administrative change where it is necessary to achieve access and equity objectives.

The Department of Immigration and Ethnic Affairs will assist Departments to develop three-year plans to give effect to these guidelines to the extent practicable, given current resource constraints. These plans, the first of which was due by 30 September 1986, for the triennium commencing 1 July 1987, will include groups to be targeted, proposed standards of service, and procedures and means of monitoring and evaluating performance. The needs of migrant women and their access to services and programmes will be specifically identified in these plans.

Departments and authorities will be required to integrate access and equity plans into their corporate planning and their financial programme budgeting. The plans will identify what goals and objectives could be achieved and

achievements put in place using existing resources within each relevant portfolio. Those departments which are key providers of services to migrants will be given priority attention.

National Population Council. The ethnic community has an input into immigration policy through its representatives on the National Population Council. Membership of the Council is drawn from a diverse range of community interests, including not only ethnic groups, but also voluntary organizations, trade unions, universities, industry and commerce. The Council's terms of reference are to advise the Minister for Immigration and Ethnic Affairs on, *inter alia,* the size and composition of the migrant intake, migration law and its application, citizenship laws, policy and practice, and post-arrival policies and programmes for migrants.

Office of Multicultural and Ethnic Affairs. In 1986 an Office of Multicultural and Ethnic Affairs was established within the Department of the Prime Minister and Cabinet. The new Office, which will come into being in January 1987, will have the responsibility of ensuring that relevant advice is available to the Government for day-to-day consideration. It will thus overtake and enhance some of the present functions of the Australian Institute of Multicultural Affairs (AIMA), which will cease to exist after the Office is set up. In transferring functions to the new Office, and through a review of the present advisory structures, the Government is committed to ensuring that the programme developed by AIMA is strengthened through the new arrangements. It is proposed that former AIMA Council members will be represented on an advisory body reporting directly to the Minister for Immigration and Ethnic Affairs.

States. Through the Ethnic Affairs Commission Act 1982, the Victorian Government has established a new Commission designed to promote the needs of all ethnic groups and monitor the development of government services for ethnic communities. Improved interpreter and translation services are being provided. Migrants will be protected against discrimination in employment, training and services of the law, and education services for migrants are being improved. Both New South Wales and South Australia also have Ethnic Affairs Commissions performing similar roles.

Ethnic media. Special programmes have been initiated by the federal Government designed to strengthen the place of ethnic minorities in all cultural areas, with those often seen to have the greatest impact being the initiation of ethnic radio and television services. Broadcasting in Australia is a federal responsibility and the Special Broadcasting Service (SBS) was established as a statutory authority to provide multicultural radio and television services. In addition to broadcasting, many newspapers and over 100 periodicals are published in Australia partly or wholly in languages other than English and are editorially and financially independent of the Government.

Cultural heritage. Cultural agreements entered into between Australia and foreign Governments provide a further means of promotion of mutual understanding and the maintenance of ethnic cultures. By early 1981, cultural agreements were current with the Governments of China, France, Greece, India, Indonesia, Italy, Japan, Malaysia, the Philippines, the Republic of Korea, Romania, Singapore, Thailand, the Union of Soviet Socialist Republics and Yugoslavia. Further agreements are under negotiation.

Australia Council. The Australia Council has also developed closer links with ethnic communities and works to ensure that ethnic arts receive an equitable proportion of funding for cultural activities. The Council's Community Arts Board discusses with ethnic communities and artists working in the field their perceived needs and exchanges information about new initiatives, developments and publicity. A directory of ethnic arts has been published. An Ethnic Artists' Service has been established and the Australia Council's Crafts Board, in conjunction with the Ethnic Affairs Commission of New South Wales, works towards development of opportunities for ethnic women to practise traditional crafts in a way which will result in rewarding employment and social contact. The Theatre Board of Australia also has a programme to provide professional service assistance to amateur ethnic dance groups.

Languages. Support is given in many jurisdictions to foster the use of ethnic community languages. English is the common language for social communication, and members of the community not fluent in English are encouraged to learn English. Special programmes of assistance are available for both children of school age and adults. It is recognized, however, that there will always be groups in the community who will not be able to communicate in English or whose English will not be fluent enough to enable them to function without some assistance. These groups include new arrivals, the elderly, and others. Interpreter services are therefore provided by most jurisdictions to assist migrants who have language difficulties in communicating their needs or advice and in obtaining access to services. There is a Commonwealth funded and operated Telephone Interpreter Service in Australia, covering most urban and regional centres where people whose first language is not English live, as well as a Translation Service to deal with written documents required for settlement. There are also active programmes of support for ethnic radio, multicultural television, ethnic newspapers, the use of universal signs and ethnic schools.

Education. Various government-funded schemes operate to assist schools to meet the language needs of children from ethnic minorities:

(a) Community-run ethnic schools engaged in teaching language and culture to ethnic children on a part-time basis are eligible for an annual federal government subsidy for each child. The report of a major review of ethnic schools is being considered at present by the Schools Commission and may lead to different funding arrangements in the future;

(b) The federal Government via the Schools Commission's Multicultural Education Programme provides funds for government and non-government schools which are coordinated at State level by State and Territory committees drawn from all school sectors (government, Catholic, independent and ethnic schools). Funds under the Programme are available for activities such as language teaching and inter-cultural studies.

There have also been additional burdens placed on Governments, in particular the State and Territory education systems, by the arrival of large numbers of refugees and their children. Special programmes exist to assist these families. In particular, the federal Government has made funds available for transitional services to help refugee children adjust to life in Australian schools. The funds have been allocated for a number of purposes, including the salaries of specialist language teachers and teachers' aides, assistance with teaching and learning materials and emergency class-room accommodation. The number of Indochinese refugees entering Australia has resulted in some

areas in increased facilities for people of Vietnamese and Chinese-speaking backgrounds.

In New South Wales the following measures have recently been introduced to help maintain relations between immigrant groups and the police:

(a) With regard to police training, there is a multicultural component in all training programmes for the police especially in the initial training at the Police Academy. Courses are conducted for senior police and seminars are held regularly. The police force conducts community education programmes with ethnic groups regarding the role and working of the police, and holds community consultative committees to provide a forum in which members of the community, leaders of specific ethnic groups, etc., may provide information to the police;

(b) There is now a pilot scheme under which a community relations section, including civilians, has been set up at Cabramatta in Sydney to deal with the specific problems of the Indochinese refugee communities of the area;

(c) The creation of the positions of police district community relations officers specifically to liaise with the community and government departments;

(d) The lowering of the height requirement for police recruits, which encourages people of other ethnic origins to join the police force.

Malay Ethnic Minority. There is a Malay ethnic minority in the Territory of the Cocos (Keeling) Islands. Section 18 of the Cocos (Keeling) Islands Act 1955 provides that the institutions, customs and usages of the Malay residents of the Territory shall, subject to any law in force in the Territory from time to time, be permitted to continue in existence.

Religious and Linguistic Minorities. Freedom of religion in Australia is discussed in detail in relation to article 18. Unlike linguistic minorities which are identified with the different Aboriginal and other ethnic groups existing in Australia, religious minorities are not necessarily so closely identified with these ethnic groups. As Australia does not have a particular recognized "State Church" or religion, it may well be inaccurate to think in terms of the existence of real religious minorities in this country. All religions are capable of existence and ethnic and religious communities are free to practise their religious beliefs. There is no restraint on any use of ethnic languages, including languages used by religious groups in their places or worship. There are few restrictions (as indicated in relation to article 21) on the right to assemble and such restrictions as do exist are considered not to impede the peaceful meeting for lawful purposes of members of groups which are the subject of article 27. As indicated above, Governments have instituted a number of programmes to assist groups to maintain their own languages.

AUSTRALIA: CONSTITUTION. The Australian Constitution, which took effect on 1 January 1901, includes the following provisions (articles 41, 51 [xxvi], 80, 116, and 117) specifically relating to human rights and fundamental freedoms:

41. No adult person who has or acquires a right to vote at elections for the more numerous House of the Parliament of a State shall, while the right continues, be prevented by any law of the Commonwealth from voting at elections for either House of the Parliament of the Commonwealth. . . .

51. The Parliament shall, subject to this Constitution, have power to make laws for the peace, order, and good government of the Commonwealth with respect to:

(xxiv). The people of any race for whom it is deemed necessary to make special laws. . . .

80. The trial on indictment of any offence against any law of the Commonwealth shall be by jury, and every such trial shall be held in the State where the offense was committed; and, if the offence was not committed within any State, the trial shall be held at such place or places as the Parliament prescribes. . . .

116. The Commonwealth shall not make any law for establishing any religion, or for imposing any religious observance, or for prohibiting the free exercise of any religion, and no religious test shall be required as a qualification for any office or public trust under the Commonwealth.

117. A subject of the Queen, resident in any State, shall not be subject in any other State to any disability or discrimination which would not be equally applicable to him if he were a subject of the Queen resident in such other State.

AUSTRIA. The Republic of Austria is a country in western Europe which has borders with Czechoslovakia, the Federal Republic of Germany, Hungary, Italy, Liechtenstein, Switzerland, and Yugoslavia. After occupation by German troops in 1938, it regained its independence in 1955 and became a member of the United Nations the same year. Its population was estimated by the UN (1990) to be 7,507,000.

In a report submitted to the **COMMITTEE ON THE ELIMINATION OF RACIAL DISCRIMINATION** on 19 June 1987, the government of Austria provided the following information concerning its population (UN Doc. CERD/C/158/Add. 1, para. 8–19):

As far as the demographic composition of Austria is concerned, the latest figures available are from the 1981 census.

If Austria's resident population is considered from the point of view of the language it commonly uses, the situation is as follows. Of the resident population of Austria (7,555,000 people), exactly 7,224,000 use no other language than German, i.e. 95.6 per cent of the population. If the 139,000 persons who indicated German as their second language are included, 97.5 per cent of the total population uses German.

The second most frequently used language in Austria is Serbo-Croat, spoken by 112,500 people (1.5 per cent of the resident population). It is followed by Turkish, which is used by 58,600 people (0.8 per cent of the resident population). These languages are primarily spoken by migrant workers.

The 1981 census also shows that 26,100 people (0.3 per cent) speak Croat, 15,900 (0.2 per cent) Magyar, 18,800 (0.2 per cent) Slovenian and 6,900 (0.1 per cent) Czech. These people are mostly Austrian nationals.

The Croat language is used mainly in the Burgenland. Of the population of the Burgenland with Austrian citizenship (267,800 people) 244,500 (91.3 per cent) speak only German as their everyday language. Croat was indicated by 18,600 people (7.0 per cent) as their everyday language, frequently together with German. The Croat-speaking Austrians living in the Burgenland account for 84.3 per cent of Austria's Croat-speaking population, the remaining Croats living mainly in Vienna. The Croat-speaking part of the Burgenland population lives in linguistic enclaves spread over the whole federal State. In selected communities, the percentage of Croat-speaking people is very high.

Of the 12,000 Austrians using Magyar as their everyday language, 4,000 (33.4 per cent) live in the Burgenland and 5,700 (47.2 per cent) in Vienna. In the Burgenland, the Magyars are concentrated in a few communities.

The Austrian population using Slovenian lives almost exclusively in the southern part of Carinthia. Of the Carinthian population with Austrian citizenship (528,000 people), 509,000 speak German only (95.5 per cent), 14,200 (2.7 per cent) use Slovenian usually together with German; 97.7 per cent of the Slovenian-speaking Austrians of Carinthia live in the southern part of Carinthia.

In Vienna, 3 out of 1,000 Viennese speak Czech and 4 out of 1,000 Viennese Magyar. The number of Czech-speaking people amounts to 4,100, those using Magyar to 5,700.

The 1981 census counted 290,000 aliens, i.e. persons not having Austrian citizenship. This represents 4.4 per cent of the resident population, of whom 113,000, or 40 per cent of all aliens, live in Vienna.

Most of the non-Austrians are Yugoslavs, who number 126,000 and account for 43 per cent of all aliens. The second biggest group of non-Austrians are the Turks, numbering 60,000 persons or 21 per cent of all aliens. Third are citizens of the Federal Republic of Germany amounting to 41,000 people, i.e. 14 per cent of all aliens. These three groups of non-Austrians taken together account for 78 per cent of all aliens living in Austria. The remaining 22 percent are people from more than 80 nations.

Most aliens, i.e. 69 per cent, are Europeans. If the Turks are included—for statistical purposes they are counted as Asians—the proportion of Europeans rises to approximately 90 per cent.

Finally, the predominant majority of the Austrian population, i.e. 84 per cent, is Roman Catholic, 6 per cent are Protestants, and 1 per cent are members of the Islamic religion.

The government (1990) took the form of a republic composed of nine provinces (*Bundesländer*). The president is elected by popular vote for a term of six years, and acts as head of State. The chancellor, representing the party or coalition given the majority in a popular election, is head of government. Legislation is prepared by the 58-member *Bundesrat,* members of which are elected by provincial assemblies, and the 183-member *Nationalrat,* members of which are elected by popular vote. The predominant political parties are the Social Democratic Party, the People's Party, and the *Freiheitliche* Party.

As regards the rules governing treatment of various elements of its population, the government furnished the following information in the previously mentioned report (UN Doc. CERD/C/158/Add. 1, para. 1–6):

The Constitution of the Austro-Hungarian Empire

of 1867 guaranteed all citizens equality before the law.

Under article 63 of the Treaty of Saint-Germain-en-Laye of 1919, Austria undertook "to assure full and complete protection of life and liberty to all inhabitants of Austria without distinction of birth, nationality, language, race or religion". Furthermore, article 66 of that Treaty stipulates that "all Austrian nationals shall be equal before the law and shall enjoy the same civil and political rights without distinction as to race, language or religion".

Article 7 of the State Treaty of Vienna of 1955 concedes special rights to the Slovene and Croat ethnic minorities of Burgenland, Carinthia and Styria, including the right to use their own language, also when dealing with the authorities, as well as rights in the fields of education, teaching and cultural life. The activities of organizations that aim at depriving the Croat or Slovenian population of their rights as minorities shall be outlawed. Those provisions of article 7 which were not directly applicable were compiled with by the passing of the Ethnic Groups Act of 1976 and by several implementing orders thereof.

Any discrimination in respect of one of the rights ensured under the European Convention on Human Rights and its eight additional protocols, which is part of Austria's constitutional law, is precluded on account of article 14 of that Convention. These rights are enjoyed by everybody in the same way.

A Constitutional Law on the Implementation of the International Convention on the Elimination of All Forms of Racial Discrimination was adopted on 3 July 1973. It contains a prohibition of any form of racial discrimination and puts the legislative and executive powers under an obligation to refrain from discriminatory measures. Article 1 of that law reads as follows:

"(1) Any form of racial discrimination—also if not already conflicting with article 7 of the Federal Constitution, as revised in 1929, and with article 14 of the Convention for the Protection of Human Rights and Fundamental Freedoms (*Fed. Law Gaz. 210/1958*)—shall be prohibited. The legislative and executive powers shall refrain from any discrimination on the sole ground of race, colour, descent or national or ethnic origin.

(2) Notwithstanding paragraph 1, particular rights may be granted to or particular obligations imposed upon Austrian nationals, in so far as this does not conflict with article 14 of the Convention for the Protection of Human Rights and Fundamental Freedoms."

In this connection, reference must also be made to the Civil Code, article 16 of which, drafted in 1812, reads: "It stands to reason that each human being has inborn rights and is accordingly to be regarded as an individual." Penal sanctions have effectively guaranteed respect for the prohibition of discrimination.

Austria has also established the institution of OM-BUDSMAN, similar to that functioning in a number of countries, for dealing with acts of maladministration by public authorities. Anyone may complain to the ombudsman regarding such acts, provided that the person is affected by the acts and has exhausted other legal remedies against them. The ombudsman is authorized to examine pertinent complaints and, if he considers them to be justified, to try to change the administrative measure in question. He may also recommend specific action in a certain case, or as a result of a certain case, to the competent federal minister. In addition, he is entitled to draw attention, in his annual reports, to grievances he has ascertained and, if necessary, to suggest changes in legal provisions.

With regard to the treatment of ethnic groups in particular, the Austrian Parliament on 7 July 1976 adopted the Act of Ethnic Groups (*Bundesgesetzblatt*, No. 396/1976) providing for the preservation, where warranted, of special assistance to such groups with a view to ensuring their continued existence and the preservation of their national characteristics. The act provides for the establishment of an Ethnic Group Advisory Board to propose methods of organizing assistance to such groups.

AUSTRIA: CONSTITUTION. The Austrian Federal Constitution includes the following provisions (articles 7, 8, 9, 9[a], and 87) specifically relating to human rights and fundamental freedoms:

Art. 7. (1) All Federal nationals are equal before the law. Privileges based upon birth, sex, estate, class or religion are excluded.

(2) Public employees, including members of the Federal Army, are guaranteed the unrestricted exercise of their political rights.

Art. 8. German is the official language of the Republic without prejudice to the rights provided by Federal law for linguistic minorities.

Art. 8a. (1) The colours of the Republic of Austria are red-white-red. The flag consists of three identically broad horizontal stripes of which the intermediate is white, the upper and the lower are red.

(2) The coat of arms of the Republic of Austria (the Federal coat of arms) consists of an unfettered, single-headed, black, gilt-armed and red-tongued eagle on whose breast is imposed a red shield intersected by a silver crosspiece. On its head the eagle bears a mural crown with three visible merlons. A sundered iron chain rings both talons. The right holds a golden sickle with inward turned blade, the left a golden hammer.

(3) Detailed provisions, in particular as to safeguard of the colours, the coat of arms, and the seal of the Republic, are settled by Federal law.

Art. 9. (1) The generally recognized rules of international law are regarded as integral parts of Federal law.

(2) Legislation or a treaty requiring sanction in accordance with Art. 50 para. 1 can transfer specific Federal competences to intergovernmental organizations and their authorities and can within the framework of international law regulate the activity of foreign states' agents inside Austria as well as the activity of Austrian agents abroad.

Art. 9a. (1) Austria subscribes to universal national defence. Its task is to preserve the Federal territory's outside independence as well as its inviolability and its unity, especially as regards the maintenance and defence of permanent neutrality. In this connection, too, the constitutional establishments and their capacity to function as well as the democratic freedoms of residents require to be safeguarded and defended against acts of armed attack from outside.

(2) Universal national defence comprises military, intellectual, civil and economic national defence.

(3) Every male Austrian national is liable for military service. Conscientious objectors who refuse the fulfilment of compulsory military service and are exonerated therefrom must perform an alternative service. The details are settled by law. . . .

Art. 87. (1) Judges are independent in the exercise of their judicial office.

(2) A judge is in the exercise of his judicial office during the performance of any judicial function properly his by law and the allocation of business, though to the exclusion of the judiciary's administrative business which in accordance with the provisions of the law shall not be discharged by tribunals or commissions.

(3) Business shall be allocated in advance among the judges of a court for the period provided by the law on the organization of the courts. A matter devolving upon a judge in accordance with this allocation may be removed from his jurisdiction by decree of the judiciary's administrative authorities only if he is prevented from the discharge of his responsibilities.

AZANIA. South Africa's name before its colonization, Azania is still used by many of its people and by its liberation movement, the PAN AFRICANIST CONGRESS OF AZANIA.

B

BAHÁ'Í INTERNATIONAL COMMUNITY. An international non-governmental organization in consultative status (Category II) with the UN Economic and Social Council, the Bahá'í community has four million members in 149 countries.

Founded in 1844, the community is a cross-section of peoples of the world, including almost all nationalities, classes trades, and professions, representing more than 1,600 ethnic groups. It comprises members of the Bahá'í faith, an independent world religion, founded in Persia (now Iran) by Mirza Husayn-Ali, known as Bahá'u'lláh, the Glory of God. The group participates in all UN activities related to human rights and strives, in particular, to eliminate prejudice and discrimination, based on the faith's fundamental belief in the organic oneness of humanity. The community also promotes the teachings of the Bahá'í religion and advocates equality of men and women, universal compulsory education, an international auxiliary language, a just solution to world economic problems, a universal tribunal, and a world commonwealth.

The community has an extensive publication program, including religious and children's publications and the periodic *Bahá'í World*, the monthly *Bahá'í News*, and the quarterlies *La pensee Baha'ie, Maailman-Kansalainen, Opinioni Bahá'í*, and *World Order*.

Bahá'í International Community. Address: 866 United Nations Plaza, Suite 120, New York, NY 10017 (USA). Telephone: (212) 486-0560. Cable: BAHAINTCOM. Fax: (212) 838-7027. Telex: 666363 BICNY. Secretary-General: Donald M. Barrett.

BAHAMAS. The Commonwealth of the Bahamas occupies an archipelago in the Caribbean consisting of more than 700 islands and islets, beginning 50 miles off the southeastern coast of the United States and extending 760 miles, almost to Haiti. The principal islands are New Providence, Grand Bahama, Eleuthera, and Long Island. It achieved independence from Great Britain in 1973 and became a member of the United Nations the same year. Its population is estimated by the UN (1990) to be 247,000. Ethnically, 85% of the population is descended from Africans imported as slaves and emancipated in 1838; the remainder are descendents of British and American residents. English is the only language in common use. Christianity (Anglican, 25%; Baptist, 30%; Methodist, 7%; and Roman Catholic, 22%) is the predominant religion. Literacy is estimated at 90%.

The government (1990) took the form of a monarchy and member of the Commonwealth of Nations, of which the British sovereign is the symbolic head. Executive power is exercised by the governor-general, representing the crown, and the prime minister, representing the party or coalition given a majority in a popular election. There is a bicameral legislature consisting of the Senate, appointed by the governor-general on advice of the prime minister and opposition party leader, and an Assembly elected by popular vote. The judiciary is organized along British lines. Political parties include the Progressive Liberal Party and the Free National Movement.

Up to 1968, the Bahamas were controlled by the predominantly white United Bahamians. The majority population has since retained full control by overwhelming victories in general elections. In 1987, the Progressive Liberal Party won 31 of the 49 seats in Parliament.

The rights of trade unions have occasionally been the subject of inquiry by international organizations. Allegations concerning the infringement of such rights were submitted to the Economic and Social Council in 1976 by unions in the Bahamas. Rejected as unfounded by the government, the allegations were forwarded to the International Labor Organization for consideration by its Fact-finding and Conciliation Commission on Freedom of Association.

BAHRAIN. The State of Bahrain is an Arab country in western Asia which occupies an archipelago consisting of 33 islands in the Persian Gulf, off the coast of Saudi Arabia. It achieved independence from Great Britain in 1971 and became a member of the United Nations the same year. Its population is estimated by the UN (1990) to be 520,000. Ethnic groups include Arabs, Iranians, Pakistanis, and Hindus. Arabic is the official language; Farsi and Urdu are commonly used. Islam (Shi'ite, 70%; Sunni, 30%) is the predominant religion. Literacy is estimated at 75%.

The government (1990) took the form of a monarchy. The emir is ruler and head of State; the prime minister, appointed by the emir, is head of government. There is a Council of Ministers, members of which are appointed by the emir. Judges are also appointed by the emir. The National Council, established by the constitution of 1973, was dissolved by the emir in 1975. In exercising his constitutional authority to close down the assembly, he reported to the people of Bahrain on the danger to national security stemming from the alleged subversive activity of some assembly members.

While it existed, the National Assembly, consisting of male citizens elected for four-year terms and about 16 Cabinet ministers, was the first elected Parliament in the country's history.

BANGLADESH. The People's Republic of Bangladesh is a country in southern Asia, located on the Bay of Bengal. It borders on India and Myanmar. Known as East Bengal until the British withdrew from the Indian sub-continent in 1947, and as East Pakistan for almost 25 years until the occupying Pakistani forces were driven out by Indian army units in 1971, Bangladesh achieved independence from Pakistan in 1974 and became a member of the United Nations the same year. Its population is estimated by the UN (1990) to be 15,244,000. Ethnic groups include the Bengalis (98%) and the Biharis (2%), the latter consisting of the descendents of about one million persons who migrated to East Bengal when the subcontinent was partitioned. Languages commonly used include Bengali (official), English, and Urdu. Religions practiced include Islam (83%), and Hinduism (17%). Literacy is estimated at 28%.

The government (1990) took the form of a monarchy and member of the Commonwealth of Nations, of which the British sovereign is the symbolic head. Political parties include the Jatita Party, the Awami League, the *Jamaat-i-Islami,* and the Bangladesh Nationalist Party.

Bangladesh was born of civil strife which broke out in East Pakistan in March 1971 and which resulted in the death of more than one million Bengalis and the flight to India of about 10 million Bengali refugees. The Secretary-General of the United Nations notified the Security Council that the situation constituted a threat to international peace and security, but the Council was unable to act because of the negative vote of the Union of Soviet Socialist Republics. The

General Assembly then called for a ceasefire and the withdrawal of troops.

In December 1971, India moved troops into East Pakistan and routed the West Pakistani occupation forces. A provisional government was formed in January 1972, with Justice Abu Sayeed Choudhury as president and Sheikh Mujibur Rahman as prime minister. Between 1975 and 1981, Bangladesh had four presidents: Kondakar Mushtaque Ahmed, founder of the Awami League, installed after the assassination of Mujibur by young army officers in a coup of 15 August 1975; Abu Sadat Mohammed Sayem, installed after a military coup had forced Ahmed from power on 6 November 1975; General Ziaur Rahman, army chief of staff, installed after Sayem's resignation on 21 April 1977; Vice President Abdus Sattar, installed after army officers had killed Ziaur in an attempted coup on 30 May 1981; and General Hossein Mohammed Ershad, army chief of staff, who took control after a bloodless coup of 24 March 1982 and assumed the office of president in 1983.

President Ershad committed himself to lifting martial law and restoring constitutional government. National elections were held in May 1986, filling the 300 elected seats of the National Assembly, and Ershad was elected president in October of that year, with 84% of the vote. Because the opposition contended that the election had been rigged, President Ershad dissolved Parliament and called for fresh elections to be held in March 1988. His party was again the overwhelming winner, but the elections were marred by widespread violence.

The country remains confronted with serious human rights problems, including the situation of the Biharis who consider themselves to be unwanted by India, Pakistan, or Bangladesh. To protect the rights and freedoms of this and other disadvantaged groups, the Bangladesh constitution aims at realizing, through democratic process, a society in which the rule of law, human rights, fundamental freedoms, and equality and justice is secured for all citizens without discrimination. The situation was described in a report submitted to the **COMMITTEE ON THE ELIMINATION OF RACIAL DISCRIMINATION** on 19 January 1988 as follows (UN Doc. CERD/C/144/Add. 3, para. 2–9).

Fundamental rights have been set out in Articles 26–47 of the Constitution. Under Article 26 any law inconsistent with the fundamental rights is void. Article 27 of the Constitution faithfully follows Article 7 of the Universal Declaration of Human Rights and provides that all citizens are equal before law and are entitled to equal protection of law. According to Article 31 it is the inalienable right of every citizen to enjoy the protection of law, and to be treated in accordance with law, and only in accordance with law, wherever he may be.

No sort of racial discrimination whatsoever is recognized in the country. Any discrimination against any citizen on grounds of only religion, race, caste, sex or place of birth is prohibited in the Constitution (Article 28). The Constitution provides further that no citizen shall, on grounds of religion, race, caste, sex or place of birth be subjected to any disability, liability, restriction or condition with regard to access to any place of public entertainment or resort, or admission to any educational institution.

In Bangladesh not only the equality of opportunity in public employment is guaranteed in the Constitution, but there is also a special provision in favour of backward sections of citizens for the purpose of securing their adequate representation in the service of the Republic. The provision finds manifestation in rules of recruitment of public servants as the said rules reserve a quota for the backward sections of people of different areas and races. The Constitution of the country provides for enjoyment or exercise on equal footing, of human rights and fundamental freedoms such as equality before law and right to protection of law, protection of right to life and personal liberty, safeguard as to arrest and detention, prohibition of forced labour, freedom of movement, freedom of assembly, freedom of association, freedom of thought, conscience and of speech and freedom of religion.

The government's policy of elimination of racial discrimination is further borne out in laws followed in the administration of criminal justice, namely the Penal Code. Injuring or defiling place of worship, with intent to insult the religion of any class, deliberate and malicious acts intended to outrage religious feelings of any class by insulting its religion or religious beliefs; disturbing religious assembly; trespassing on places of worship or any place of culture or any place set apart for the performance of funeral rites or as a depository for the remains of the dead, or offering any indignity to any human corpse, or causing disturbance to any persons assembled for the performance of funeral ceremonies, with the intention of wounding the feelings of any person or of insulting the religion of any person or with the knowledge that the feelings of any person are likely to be wounded or that the religion of any person is likely to be insulted thereby, have been made punishable under the Code in sections 295, 296, 297 and 298 respectively.

In Bangladesh religious and customary laws of different races, religions and ethnic groups are recognized as personal laws and are enforceable in courts of law.

In Bangladesh "the Convention" itself [International Convention on the Elimination of All Forms of Racial Discrimination] cannot be invoked and directly enforced by the courts, or tribunals.

The fundamental rights of the citizens in the Constitution encompass almost all the articles of the Universal Declaration of Human Rights which are all enforceable by the High Court Division of the Supreme Court under Articles 44 and 102.

It may, however, be mentioned here that during the period from March, 1982 to November 1986, the country was under Martial Law and the Constitution was under suspension. But nonetheless, no legislative or administrative measures were taken during this period which could be violative of the principles relating to prohibition of racial discrimination. Moreover, all the penal provisions of laws providing for protecting fundamental rights relating to religion remained undisturbed and enforceable. Any racial discrimination was emphatically condemned by the Government as a matter of national policy.

BARBADOS. Barbados is a country which occupies an island in the Caribbean, east of the Windward Islands. It achieved independence from Great Britain in 1966 and became a member of the United Nations the same year. Its population is estimated by the UN (1990) to be 263,000. Ethnic groups include blacks (92%), whites (3%), East Indians (0.5%), and others. (Chinese, Amerindians, Portuguese, and Syrian/Lebanese, 1.5%). The language in common use is English. Christianity (Anglican, 70%; R man Catholic, 4%; Methodist, 9%) is the predominant religion; 17% profess other faiths or none at all. Literacy is estimated at 99%.

The government (1990) took the form of a monarchy and member of the Commonwealth of Nations, of which the British sovereign is the symbolic head. Executive power is exercised by the governor-general, representing the crown, and the prime minister, representing the party or coalition given the majority in a popular election. Legislation is prepared by a bicameral legislature consisting of a 21-member Senate appointed by the governor-general after consultation with the prime minister, and a 27-member Assembly elected by the people. Political parties include the Barbados Labour Party and the Democratic Labour Party.

In Barbados, the population lives and co-exists in a liberal atmosphere generally free of the tensions which characterize race relations in some other parts of the world. Within the ethnic groups, there are cultural/religious associations, such as the Syrian Women's Association, the American Women's Group, and the Canadian Women's Group, the major aim of which is protection of the cultural traditions of their respective countries of origin.

In a report presented to the HUMAN RIGHTS COMMITTEE on 25 November 1987, the government of Barbados supplied the following information (UN Doc. CCPR/C/42/Add. 3, para. 1–9):

Barbados conforms to the Westminster model of a parliamentary democracy. It has adopted a written Constitution which is the supreme law of the land. The Constitution has incorporated a Bill of Rights which generally, and most times specifically, embodies the principles of the Covenant on Civil and Political Rights.

It is within this legal framework that the rights expressed in the Covenant are given effect or supported as the case may be.

Barbados subscribes to and supports the principles of the right of self-determination and free disposal of wealth and resources as embodied in article 1 of the Covenant. A review of Barbados' history at the United Nations will lend evidence of this.

Section 23 of the Constitution guarantees to a substantial degree protection against discrimination. The Barbados Constitution does not protect against discrimination based on the ground of sex. However the general laws do not embody the principle of sex discrimination and have progressively been updated to obviate any hardship which may previously have existed in common law. In this regard the Succession Act of 1975 makes it impossible for a husband to disinherit his wife. Women in Barbados have the same rights as men in respect of property, contracts and the family and this is supported by legislation, namely the Married Persons (formerly Married Women) Act, 1896, succeeded in some respects by the Property Act, 1979 and the Family Law Act, 1981.

Barbados recognizes that the problem is not simply one of legislation and has established a Women's Affairs Bureau further to advance the cause of women.

The Constitution does not provide for non-discrimination on the basis of language. The reason for its omission would seem to be that Barbados is essentially monocultural. This was so at the drafting of the Constitution and remains so today. A small section of the population comprises persons of Asian descent but there have been no expressions of having borne hardship on account of language.

The Constitution does provide for protection from discrimination on grounds of national origin though not social origin. The former would fall under the rubric of "place of origin" as provided in section 23. As regards social origin the area in which discrimination on this ground would be more operative would be in respect of children born out of wedlock. This problem has now been overcome by the Status of Children Reform Act, 1979 which equalizes the status of children born in Barbados and abolished the former common law distinctions of legitimate and illegitimate children.

The Constitution does not guarantee protection from discrimination to non-citizens of Barbados. In reality, however, there are no laws which impose restrictions on non-citizens in their enjoyment of the fundamental rights and freedoms guaranteed by the Constitution to citizens of Barbados. The exception is the protection of freedom of movement afforded by section 22 of the Constitution in so far as that section guarantees the right to enter Barbados and immunity from expulsion from Barbados. Restrictions are thought necessary in this regard to safeguard the integrity of its borders and immigration laws.

The Constitution excepts from its non-discrimination provision any law dealing with adoption, marriage, divorce, burial devolution of property on death or other matters of personal law. It is unclear what type of exceptions this provision of the Constitution anticipated. However, it is not possible to point to any rule or provision of personal law which but for this provision would have infringed the Constitution.

BASIC PRINCIPLES FOR THE PROTECTION OF CIVILIAN POPULATION IN ARMED CONFLICTS (1970).

As early as 1970, the UN General Assembly became convinced the civilian populations needed increased protection in time of armed conflicts and formulated basic principles to be applied for the protection of such populations. It, thus, set in motion machinery for updating the Geneva Conventions of 1949 by protocols thereto.

The basic principles document was adopted by the UN General Assembly on 9 December 1970 (GA resolution 2675 [XXV]). The text is as follows.

1. Fundamental human rights, as accepted in international law and laid down in international instruments, continue to apply fully in situations of armed conflict.
2. In the conduct of military operations during armed conflicts, a distinction must be made at all times between persons actively taking part in the hostilities and civilian populations.
3. In the conduct of military operations, every effort should be made to spare civilian populations from the ravages of war, and all necessary precautions should be taken to avoid injury, loss or damage to civilian populations.
4. Civilian populations as such should not be the object of military operations.
5. Dwellings and other installations that are used only by civilian populations should not be the object of military operations.
6. Places or areas designated for the sole protection of civilians, such as hospital zones or similar refuges, should not be the object of military operations.
7. Civilian populations, or individual members thereof, should not be the object of reprisals, forcible transfers or other assaults on their integrity.
8. The provision of international relief to civilian populations is in conformity with the humanitarian principles of the Charter of the United Nations, the Universal Declaration of Human Rights and other international instruments in the field of human rights. The Declaration of Principles for International Humanitarian Relief to the Civilian Population in Disaster Situations, as laid down in resolution XXVI adopted by the twenty-first International Conference of the Red Cross, shall apply in situations of armed conflict, and all parties to a conflict should make every effort to facilitate this application.

SEE ALSO Armed Conflicts; Declaration on the Protection of Women and Children in Emergency and Armed Conflicts; Geneva Convention relative to the Protection of Civilian Persons in Time of War and Protocols I and II.

BASIC PRINCIPLES OF THE LEGAL STATUS OF COMBATANTS STRUGGLING AGAINST COLONIAL AND ALIEN DOMINATION AND RACIST REGIMES (1973).

The basic principles were formulated and adopted by the UN General Assembly on 12 December 1973 (resolution 3103 [XXVIII]) because of its concern that many states were not complying with the GENEVA CONVENTIONS 12 August 1949 and other universally recognized norms of modern international law for the protection of human rights in armed conflicts and that, as a result, the treatment accorded to combatants struggling for independence and basic rights in their homeland tended to be inhumane. The text of the basic principles, annexed to resolution 3103 (XXVIII), is as follows:

1. The struggle of peoples under colonial and alien domination and racist régimes for the implementation of their

right to self-determination and independence is legitimate and in full accordance with the principles of international law.

2. Any attempt to suppress the struggle against colonial and alien domination and racist régimes is incompatible with the Charter of the United Nations, the Declaration of Principles of International Law concerning Friendly Relations and Co-operation among States in accordance with the Charter of the United Nations, the Universal Declaration of Human Rights and the Declaration on the Granting of Independence to Colonial Countries and Peoples and constitutes a threat to international peace and security.

3. The armed conflicts involving the struggle of peoples against colonial and alien domination and racist régimes are to be regarded as international armed conflicts in the sense of the 1949 Geneva Conventions, and the legal status envisaged to apply to the combatants in the 1949 Geneva Conventions and other international instruments is to apply to the persons engaged in armed struggle against colonial and alien domination and racist régimes.

4. The combatants struggling against colonial and alien domination and racist régimes captured as prisoners are to be accorded the status of prisoners of war and their treatment should be in accordance with the provisions of the Geneva Convention relative to the Treatment of Prisoners of War, of 12 August 1949.

5. The use of mercenaries by colonial and racist régimes against the national liberation movements struggling for their freedom and independence from the yoke of colonialism and alien domination is considered to be a criminal act and the mercenaries should accordingly be punished as criminals.

6. The violation of the legal status of the combatants struggling against colonial and alien domination and racist régimes in the course of armed conflicts entails full responsibility in accordance with the norms of international law.

SEE ALSO Armed Conflicts; Convention on Prohibitions or Restrictions on the Use of Certain Conventional Weapons which May be Deemed to be Excessively Injurious or to Have Indiscriminate Effects, and Protocol; Geneva Convention relative to the Treatment of Prisoners of War.

BASIC PRINCIPLES ON THE INDEPENDENCE OF THE JUDICIARY (1985). The basic principles are based upon draft guidelines concerning the independence of the judiciary elaborated by the COMMITTEE ON CRIME PREVENTION AND CONTROL, which the UN Economic and Social Council had submitted to the Seventh United Nations Congress on the Prevention of Crime and the Treatment of Offenders for consideration. Because of the complexity of the subject, in view of the many different judicial systems of the member States, the congress decided that an abbreviated text of the guidelines, setting out basic principles, would be more appropriate. Such a text was adopted by the congress in Milan, Italy, on 5 September 1985. It was later endorsed by the UN General Assembly on 29 November 1985 (resolution 40/32) and on 13 De-

cember 1985 (resolution 40/146). The text (UN Doc. A/CONF.121/22, chap. I, sect. D. 2) is as follows:

Whereas in the Charter of the United Nations the peoples of the world affirm, *inter alia,* their determination to establish conditions under which justice can be maintained to achieve international co-operation in promoting and encouraging respect for human rights and fundamental freedoms without any discrimination,

Whereas the Universal Declaration of Human Rights enshrines in particular the principles of equality before the law, of the presumption of innocence and of the right to a fair and public hearing by a competent, independent and impartial tribunal established by law,

Whereas the International Covenants on Economic, Social and Cultural Rights and on Civil and Political Rights both guarantee the exercise of those rights, and in addition, the Covenant on Civil and Political Rights further guarantees the right to be tried without undue delay,

Whereas frequently there still exists a gap between the vision underlying those principles and the actual situation,

Whereas the organization and administration of justice in every country should be inspired by those principles, and efforts should be undertaken to translate them fully into reality,

Whereas rules concerning the exercise of judicial office should aim at enabling judges to act in accordance with those principles,

Whereas judges are charged with the ultimate decision over life, freedom, rights, duties and property of citizens,

Whereas the Sixth United Nations Congress on the Prevention of Crime and the Treatment of Offenders, by its resolution 16, called upon the Committee on Crime Prevention and Control to include among its priorities the elaboration of guidelines relating to the independence of judges and the selection, professional training and status of judges and prosecutors,

Whereas it is, therefore, appropriate that consideration be first given to the role of judges in relation to the system of justice and to the importance of their selection, training and conduct,

The following basic principles, formulated to assist Member States in their task of securing and promoting the independence of the judiciary should be taken into account and respected by Governments within the framework of their national legislation and practice and be brought to the attention of judges, lawyers, members of the executive and the legislature and the public in general. The principles have been formulated principally with professional judges in mind, but they apply equally, as appropriate, to lay judges, where they exist.

Independence of the Judiciary. 1. The independence of the judiciary shall be guaranteed by the State and enshrined in the Constitution or the law of the country. It is the duty of all governmental and other institutions to respect and observe the independence of the judiciary.

2. The judiciary shall decide matters before them impartially, on the basis of facts and in accordance with the law, without any restrictions, improper influences, inducement, pressures, threats or interferences, direct or indirect, from any quarter or for any reason.

3. The judiciary shall have jurisdiction over all issues of a judicial nature and shall have exclusive authority to decide whether an issue submitted for its decision is within its competence as defined by law.

4. There shall not be any inappropriate or unwarranted interference with the judicial process, nor shall judicial decisions by the courts be subject to revision. This principle is without prejudice to judicial review or to mitigation or commutation by competent authorities of sentences imposed by the judiciary, in accordance with the law.

5. Everyone shall have the right to be tried by ordinary courts or tribunals using established legal procedures. Tribunals that do not use the duly established procedures of the legal process shall not be created to displace the jurisdiction belonging to the ordinary courts or judicial tribunals.

6. The principle of the independence of the judiciary entitles and requires the judiciary to ensure that judicial proceedings are conducted fairly and that the rights of the parties are respected.

7. It is the duty of each Member State to provide adequate resources to enable the judiciary to properly perform its functions.

Freedom of Expression and Association. 8. In accordance with the Universal Declaration of Human Rights, members of the judiciary are like other citizens entitled to freedom of expression, belief, association and assembly; provided, however, that in exercising such rights, judges shall always conduct themselves in such a manner as to preserve the dignity of their office and the impartiality and independence of the judiciary.

9. Judges shall be free to form and join association of judges or other organizations to represent their interests, to promote their professional training and to protect their judicial independence.

Qualifications, Selection and Training. 10. Persons selected for judicial office shall be individuals of integrity and ability with appropriate training or qualifications in law. Any method of judicial selection shall safeguard against judicial appointments for improper motives. In the selection of judges, there shall be no discrimination against a person on the grounds of race, colour, sex, religion, political or other opinion, national or social origin, property, birth or status, except that a requirement, that a candidate for judicial office must be a national of the country concerned, shall not be considered discriminatory.

Conditions of Service and Tenure. 11. The term of office of judges, their independence, security, adequate remuneration, conditions of service, pensions and the age of retirement shall be adequately secured by law.

12. Judges, whether appointed or elected, shall have guaranteed tenure until a mandatory retirement age or the expiry of their term of office, where such exists.

13. Promotion of judges, wherever such a system exists, should be based on objective factors, in particular ability, integrity and experience.

14. The assignment of cases to judges within the court to which they belong is an internal matter of judicial administration.

Professional Secrecy and Immunity. 15. The judiciary shall be bound by professional secrecy with regard to their deliberations and to confidential information acquired in the course of their duties other than in public proceedings, and shall not be compelled to testify on such matters.

16. Without prejudice to any disciplinary procedure or to any right of appeal or to compensation from the State, in accordance with national law, judges should enjoy personal immunity from civil suits for monetary damages for improper acts or omissions in the exercise of their judicial functions.

Discipline, Suspension and Removal. 17. A charge or complaint made against a judge in his/her judicial and professional capacity shall be processed expeditiously and fairly under an appropriate procedure. The judge shall have the right to a fair hearing. The examination of the matter at its initial stage shall be kept confidential, unless otherwise requested by the judge.

18. Judges shall be subject to suspension or removal only for reasons of incapacity or behaviour that renders them unfit to discharge their duties.

19. All disciplinary, suspension or removal proceedings shall be determined in accordance with established standards of judicial conduct.

20. Decisions in disciplinary, suspension or removal proceedings should be subject to an independent review. This principle may not apply to the decisions of the highest court and those of the legislature in impeachment or similar proceedings.

SEE ALSO *Judiciary; Judiciary: Study on Independence and Impartiality.*

BASIC PRINCIPLES ON THE INDEPENDENCE OF THE JUDICIARY: PROCEDURES FOR IMPLEMENTATION (1989).

The Seventh United Nations Congress on the Prevention of Crime and the Treatment of Offenders, when drafting the BASIC PRINCIPLES ON THE INDEPENDENCE OF THE JUDICIARY later endorsed by the UN General Assembly (resolutions 40/32 and 40/146), called upon the Committee on Crime Prevention and Control to consider, as a matter of priority, the implementation of those principles.

On recommendation of that committee, the UN Economic and Social Council adopted, on 24 May 1989, a series of Procedures for the Effective Implementation of the Basic Principles on the Independence of the Judiciary and invited the Eighth United Nations Congress on the Prevention of Crime and the Treatment of Offenders and its preparatory body to accord priority to ways and means of stimulating adherence to those procedures. The procedures adopted by the council (resolution 1989/60) are as follows:

Procedure 1. All States shall adopt and implement in their justice systems the Basic Principles on the Independence of the Judiciary in accordance with their constitutional process and domestic practice.

Procedure 2. No judge shall be appointed or elected for purposes, or be required to perform services, that are inconsistent with the Basic Principles. No judge shall accept judicial office on the basis of an appointment or election, or perform services, that are inconsistent with the Basic Principles.

Procedure 3. The Basic Principles shall apply to all judges, including, as appropriate, lay judges, where they exist.

Procedure 4. States shall ensure that the Basic Principles are widely publicized in at least the main or official language or languages of the respective country. Judges, lawyers, members of the executive, the legislature, and the public in general, shall be informed in the most appropriate manner of the content and the importance of the Basic Principles so that they may promote their application within the framework of the justice system. In particular, States shall make the text of the Basic Principles available to all members of the judiciary.

Procedure 5. In implementing principles 8 and 12 of the Basic Principles, States shall pay particular attention to the need for adequate resources for the functioning of the judicial system, including appointing a sufficient number of judges in relation to case-loads, providing the courts with necessary support staff and equipment, and offering judges appropriate personal security, remuneration and emoluments.

Procedure 6. States shall promote or encourage seminars and courses at the national and regional levels on the role of the judiciary in society and the necessity for its independence.

Procedure 7. In accordance with Economic and Social Council resolution 1986/10, section V, Member States shall inform the Secretary-General every five years, beginning in 1988, of the progress achieved in the implementation of the Basic Principles, including their dissemination, their incorporation into national legislation, the problems faced and difficulties or obstacles encountered in their implementation at the national level and the assistance that might be needed from the international community.

Procedure 8. The Secretary-General shall prepare independent quinquennial reports to the Committee on Crime Prevention and Control on progress made with respect to the implementation of the Basic Principles, on the basis of the information received from Governments under procedure 7, as well as other information available within the United Nations system, including information on the technical co-operation and training provided by institutes, experts and regional and interregional advisers. In the preparation of those reports the Secretary-General shall also enlist the co-operation of specialized agencies and the relevant intergovernmental organizations and non-governmental organizations, in particular professional associations of judges and lawyers, in consultative status with the Economic and Social Council, and take into account the information provided by such agencies and organizations.

Procedure 9. The Secretary-General shall disseminate the Basic Principles, the present implementing procedures and the periodic reports on their implementation referred to in procedures 7 and 8, in as many languages as possible, and make them available to all States and intergovernmental and non-governmental organizations concerned, in order to ensure the widest circulation of those documents.

Procedure 10. The Secretary-General shall ensure the widest possible reference to and use of the text of the Basic Principles and the present implementing procedures by the United Nations in all its relevant programmes and the inclusion of the Basic Principles as soon as possible in the United Nations publication entitled *Human Rights: A Compilation of International Instruments,* in accordance with Economic and Social Council resolution 1986/10, section V.

Procedure 11. As part of its technical co-operation programme, the United Nations, in particular the Department of Technical Co-operation for Development and the United Nations Development Programme, shall:

(a) Assist Governments, at their request, in setting up and strengthening independent and effective judicial systems;

(b) Make available to Governments requesting them, the services of experts and regional and interregional advisers on judicial matters to assist in implementing the Basic Principles;

(c) Enhance research concerning effective measures for implementing the Basic Principles, with emphasis on new developments in that area;

(d) Promote national and regional seminars, as well as other meetings at the professional and non-professional levels, on the role of the judiciary in society, the necessity for its independence, and the importance of implementing the Basic Principles to further those goals;

(e) Strengthen substantive support for the United Nations regional and interregional research and training institutes for crime prevention and criminal justice, as well as other entities within the United Nations system concerned with implementing the Basic Principles.

Procedure 12. The United Nations regional and interregional research and training institutes for crime prevention and criminal justice as well as other concerned entities within the United Nations system shall assist in the implementation process. They shall pay special attention to ways and means of enhancing the application of the Basic Principles in their research and training programmes, and to providing technical assistance upon the request of Member States. For this purpose, the United Nations institutes, in co-operation with national institutions and intergovernmental and non-governmental organizations concerned, shall develop curricula and training materials based on the Principles and the present implementing procedures, which are suitable for use in legal education programmes at all levels as well as in specialized courses on human rights and related subjects.

Procedure 13. The regional commissions, the specialized agencies and other entities within the United Nations system as well as other concerned intergovernmental organizations shall become actively involved in the implementation process. They shall inform the Secretary-General of the efforts made to disseminate the Basic Principles, the measures taken to give effect to them and any obstacles and shortcomings encountered. The Secretary-General shall also take steps to ensure that non-governmental organizations in consultative status with the Economic and Social Council become actively involved in the implementation process and the related reporting procedures.

Procedure 14. The Committee on Crime Prevention and Control shall assist the General Assembly and the Economic and Social Council in following up the present implementing procedures, including periodic reporting under procedures 6 and 7 above. To this end, the Committee shall identify existing obstacles to, or shortcomings in, the implementation of the Basic Principles and the reasons for them. The Committee shall make specific recommendations, as appropriate, to the Assembly and the Council and any other relevant United Nations human rights bodies on further action required for the effective implementation of the Basic Principles.

Procedure 15. The Committee on Crime Prevention and Control shall assist the General Assembly, the Economic and Social Council and any other relevant United Nations human rights bodies, as appropriate, with recommendations relating to reports of *ad hoc* inquiry commissions or bodies, with respect to matters pertaining to the application and implementation of the Basic Principles.

BEIJING RULES. A term applied to the UNITED NATIONS STANDARD MINIMUM RULES FOR THE ADMINISTRATION OF JUVENILE JUSTICE.

BELGIUM. The kingdom of Belgium is a country in western Europe, on the North Sea. It has borders with the Federal Republic of Germany, France, and the Netherlands. It achieved independence from the Netherlands in 1830 and became a member of the United Nations in 1945. Its population is estimated by the UN (1990) to be 9,949,000. Ethnic groups include persons of Italian, Moroccan, French, Dutch, Turkish, and Spanish origin. Languages spoken include Dutch (57%), French (32%), bi-lingual Dutch-French (9%), and others (2%). Dutch-speaking Belgians are commonly referred to as "Flemings;" French-speaking Belgians as "Walloons." Religions practiced include Christianity (mostly Roman Catholic), 98%; Islam, 1%; and others, 1%. Literacy is estimated at 98%.

The government (1990) took the form of a monarchy. The king is head of State. The prime minister, representing the party or coalition given the majority in a popular election, is head of government. The legislature consists of a 181-member Senate and a 212-member Chamber of Deputies. Of the Senate's members, 106 are chosen by popular vote, 50 by provincial authorities, and 25 by the Senate itself. Representatives are elected by proportional representation. Members of both houses serve for terms of four years. Suffrage is universal and those who fail to vote are fined. Political parties include Flemish-speaking Social Christians, French-speaking Social Christians, Flemish-speaking Socialists, French-speaking Socialists, French-speaking Liberals, Flemish-speaking Liberals, and the Flemish Peoples' Party.

Disagreement between French-speaking and Flemish-speaking elements of the population almost resulted in the downfall of the coalition government in 1985, 1986, and 1987. However, the coalition was retained by a small majority in elections held in December 1987.

In a report presented to the HUMAN RIGHTS COMMITTEE on 3 March 1988, the Belgian government provided the following information concerning the constitution of the country (UN Doc. CCPR/C/31/Add. 3, para. 1–2):

The Belgian Constitution is one of the oldest written constitutions currently in force. It was promulgated on 7 February 1831 and set up a constitutional monarchy based on three separate powers: the legislature, the executive and the judiciary. This separation of powers follows from the spirit of the Constitution and from the organization of Title III (Powers), which establishes a parliamentary régime and a system of checks and balances to ensure the autonomy and interdependence of the three powers,

thereby safeguarding citizens against any structural arbitrary act by any one of these powers. The Belgian Constitution of 1831 also defined the fundamental freedoms guaranteed to citizens to protect them against any arbitrary act by these powers.

Since then, the Belgian Constitution has been amended several times in order to adapt institutions to national and international political, economic, social and cultural changes. Over the years, these amendments have gradually extended the right to vote to the point of establishing universal suffrage and brought about far-reaching changes in government structures, not only by decentralizing political and administrative institutions, but also by providing for the autonomy of the country's cultural communities and regions. They have also led to the reform of the law courts and administrative tribunals, and rationalized the functioning of the legislature and the executive. Quite apart from any new needs that may arise as society changes, several problems still have to be solved in order to complete the institutional reform of government structures undertaken in the 1970s.

In the same report, the Belgian government described the general legal framework within which civil and political rights are protected in the country in the following terms (*Ibid.*, para. 3–12;14):

Belgium is a State subject to the rule of law and is based on a democracy elected by direct universal suffrage at the local level (communes and provinces) and at the regional and national levels (Community and Regional Councils and Parliament). It has a comprehensive judicial system for matters relating to civil, criminal and administrative law. Law enforcement is carried out: by the communal police under the authority of the burgomasters; by the national Gendarmerie under the authority of the Minister of the Interior and the Minister of Justice; and by the Judicial Police and Criminal Investigation Department under the authority of the Minister of Justice. Specialized units within various departments (finance, customs, agriculture, etc.) also have law-enforcement powers under the authority of the ministers concerned.

All these units are supervised by the Attorney-General's Offices and by the courts. Armed-forces combat units as such do not have law-enforcement powers.

The Constitution determines the powers and overall spheres of competence of the country's main institutions. Subsidiary powers and spheres of competence are in turn governed by laws, decrees and orders issued by the various authorities in accordance with the competence thus defined.

Human rights are protected by the Constitution and by various laws guaranteeing and governing such rights, including the laws ratifying the relevant international treaties, such as the European Convention for the Protection of Human Rights and Fundamental Freedoms and the Covenant. In this connection, however, it should be noted that Belgian legal opinion is divided on the distinctions to be made in connection with the self-executing nature of the provisions of an international convention in Belgian internal law, in other words, on whether a provision of such a convention may be invoked in court if the corresponding provision of internal law is not also invoked. Some writers thus draw a distinction between treaties whose overall structure would appear to exclude the interpretation that they contain directly applicable provisions, such as the Covenant, by which States *undertake* to respect and guarantee certain human rights, and treaties under which States automatically recognize obligations, such as the European Convention, by which States *recognize* those rights. The Belgian Government, and the Council of State, have followed this reasoning, excluding *a priori* the direct applicability of certain provisions of the Covenant.

A further distinction is made with regard to a treaty whose direct applicability has, in principle, been recognized. The only self-executing provisions are those which lend themselves to direct application by their very nature, i.e. essentially when no additional internal legislative provision is required for their implementation.

The Government has, however, always stated that a final decision on the direct applicability or otherwise of an international treaty provision lies with the courts.

Legal decisions have clearly opted for the view that the European Convention and several of its provisions are directly applicable.

The Court of Cassation does not appear to share the view of the Government and the Council of State concerning the Covenant, since in a judgement of 17 January 1984 it affirmed that article 9, paragraph 2, of the Covenant was directly applicable in internal Belgian law.

Even if this decision was not confirmed, the Government would nevertheless regard the question as being more theoretical than practical since, in its view, the substance of the rights guaranteed by the Covenant is in any event reflected in Belgian legislation as a whole for the benefit of the persons protected, as will be seen below.

The answer to the question whether some of the rights referred to in the Covenant are protected in the Constitution is, as we have already seen, affirmative. The rights guaranteed by the Constitution include:

(1) Equality before the law (art. 6) and enjoyment, without discrimination, of recognized rights and freedoms (art. 6 *bis*) (Covenants arts. 1, 2, 3 and 26);

(2) Liberty of person (art. 7) (Covenant arts. 8 and 9);

(3) The right to a judge assigned by law (art. 8) (Covenant art. 14);

(4) Lawfulness of penalties (art. 9) (Covenant art. 15);

(5) Inviolability of the home (art. 10) (Covenant art. 17);

(6) Legal personality (art. 13) (Covenant art. 16);

(7) Freedom of thought, conscience, religion and expression (art. 14) (Covenant arts. 18 and 19);

(8) Freedom of the press (art. 18) (Covenant art. 19);

(9) The right to assemble "peacefully and without arms" (art. 19) (Covenant art. 21);

(10) The right to freedom of association (art. 20) (Covenant art. 22);

(11) Freedom from interference with correspondence (art. 22) (Covenant art. 17);

(12) Political rights (arts. 32–59 *ter*) (Covenant art. 25);

(13) Proper administration of justice (arts. 92–107) (Covenant art. 14). . . .

As to other measures taken to ensure the implementation of the provisions of the Covenant, the Belgian Government's view, at the time of ratification, was that all the rights referred to in the Covenant were provided for in the existing Belgian legal system, with the exception of (a) internal-law provisions which it does not intend to amend, for which explicit interpretative declarations or formal reservations were deposited together with the instruments of ratification and which include constitutional rules on succession to the throne, and (b) internal-law provisions which it already intended to amend at a later date, including rules distinguishing between the status of legitimate and illegitimate children, which were under review by Parliament at the time when this report was being prepared. The Government therefore did not deem it necessary to take any special measures to implement the provisions of the Covenant since, as the Council of State noted during the ratification procedure, "as soon as the Covenants enter into force, the Belgian State will no longer be able to suppress or restrict any of the rights which are recognized by these instruments and are already provided for under Belgian law."

BELGIUM: CONSTITUTION. The Belgian Constitution of 1987 includes the following provisions (articles 3c to 24 and 59b and c) specifically relating to human rights and fundamental freedoms:

Concerning the Communities

Art. 3c. Belgium comprises three communities: the French Community, the Flemish Community, and the German-speaking Community.

Each community enjoys the powers vested in it by the Constitution or by such legislations as shall be enacted in terms thereof (rev. 24.12.1970 and 17.7.1980).

Concerning the Belgians and Their Rights

Art. 4. Belgian nationality is acquired, retained and withdrawn in accordance with the rules laid down by civil law.

The present Constitution and the other laws governing political rights determine which conditions, apart from nationality, are necessary for the exercise of those rights.

Art. 5. Naturalisation is granted by the Legislative power.

Only full naturalisation places the foreigner on an equal footing with the Belgian citizen where the exercise of political rights is concerned.

Art. 6. There is no distinction between orders in the State.

All Belgians are equal in the eyes of the law; they alone are acceptable for civil and military posts, with some exceptions which may be established by law in special cases.

Art. 6b. Enjoyment of the rights and liberties to which Belgians are entitled must be ensured without discrimination. To this end, laws and decrees shall guarantee amongst other things the rights and liberties of ideological and philosophical minorities (rev. 24.12.1970).

Art. 7. Individual liberty is guaranteed.

No person may be prosecuted except in cases laid down by the law and in the form it prescribes.

Apart from the case of *flagrante delicto,* no person may be arrested save on a motivated order by a judge, which must be signified at the time of the arrest or within twenty-four hours at the latest.

Art. 8. No person may be withdrawn from the judge assigned to him by the law, save with his consent.

Art. 9. No penalty may be decreed nor applied save in accordance with the law.

Art. 10. The home is inviolable; no entrance into a private house may be made save in those cases laid down by the law and in the manner it prescribes.

Art. 11. No persona may be deprived of his property save in the public interest, in cases laid down by the law and in the manner it prescribes, and on condition that just compensation is made previously.

Art. 12. The penalty consisting of confiscation of property may not be decreed.

Art. 13. The civilian death penalty is abolished and may not be reinstated.

Art. 14. Freedom of worship and its public exercise, together with freedom to manifest personal opinions in every way, are guaranteed save for the punishment of offences perpetrated in exercising those liberties.

Art. 15. No person may be constrained to assist in any way in the acts and ceremonies of any form of worship, nor to observe its days of rest.

Art. 16. The State has no right to intervene either in the appointment or the induction of ministers of any form of worship, nor to forbid them to correspond with their superiors and to publish their acts save, in the latter case, for the ordinary responsibility bound up with the press and publishing.

The civil wedding must always precede the nuptial benediction, save in exceptional cases to be established, where necessary, by law.

Art. 17. Education is free; any preventive measure is forbidden; the punishment of misdemeanours is regulated only by law.

Public education provided at the expense of the State, is also regulated by law.

Art. 18. The press is free; no form of censorship may ever be instituted: no cautionary deposit may be demanded from writers, publishers or printers.

When the author is known and is resident in Belgium, the publisher, printer or distributor may not be prosecuted.

Art. 19. Belgians have the right to hold peaceful, unarmed meetings; they must comply with the laws which may regulate the exercise of this right without, however, subjecting it to prior authorization.

This clause does not apply to open-air meetings which remain entirely subject to the police laws.

Art. 20. Belgians have the right to associate; this right may not be subjected to any preventive measure.

Art. 21. Every person has the right to address petitions signed by one or several people to the public authorities.

The constituted authorities alone have the right to send in collective petitions.

Art. 22. The secrecy of letters is inviolable. The law shall determine which agents are responsible for the violation of secrecy in the case of letters sent by post.

Art. 23. The use of the languages spoken in Belgium is optional; it may only be regulated by law and only in the case of acts by the public authorities and of legal matters.

Art. 24. No prior authorization is necessary to bring an action against civil servants with regard to their administrative acts, except as elsewhere specified for Ministers. . . .

Concerning the Community Councils

Art. 59b. § 1. There is a Council and an Executive of the French Community and a Council and an Executive of the Flemish Community, the composition and functioning of which are regulated by law. The Councils are composed of elected representatives.

With a view to the implementation of Article 107d, the Council of the French Community and the Council of the Flemish Community, together with their Executives, may exercise the forms of competence vested respectively in the Walloon Region and in the Flemish Region, in obedience to the conditions and methods laid down by the law.

The laws referred to in the preceding paragraphs must be enacted in terms of the majority vote specified in Article 1, last paragraph.

§ 2. The Community Councils, each in its own sphere, shall regulate by decree:

    1. cultural matters;

    2. education, excluding all matters appertaining to the Schools Covenant, compulsory education, teaching structures, diplomas, subsidies, salaries, and the standards governing the student population;

    3. co-operation between the Communities and international cultural co-operation.

A law enacted in terms of the majority vote specified in § 1, paragraph 3, shall define the cultural matters referred to in (1) and the forms of co-operation referred to in (3) of this paragraph.

§ 2b. The Community Councils, each for its own account, shall regulate by decree the personalised matters, as also co-operations between the Communities and international co-operation in such matters.

A law enacted in terms of the majority vote specified in Article 1, last paragraph, shall define these personalised matters and the forms such co-operation shall take.

§ 3. Furthermore, the Community Councils, each for its own account, shall regulate by decree, to the exclusion of the Legislative, the use of languages in the following area:

    1. administrative matters;

    2. the education provided in schools which are set up, subsidised or recognised by the public authorities;

    3. industrial relations between employers and their personnel, together with such business instruments and documents as are required by the law and the regulations.

§ 4. The decrees issued in terms of § 2 have the force of law respectively in the French language region and in the Dutch language region, and also with regard to institutions established in the bilingual region of Brussels-Capital which, by virtue of their activities, must be considered as belonging exclusively to one or other of the Communities.

Such decrees as are promulgated in pursuance of § 3 shall have the force of law respectively in the French-language region and in the Dutch-language region, except as regards:

—boroughs or groups of boroughs which are adjacent to another language region, and in which the law prescribes or permits the use of a language other than that of the region in which they are located;

—departments whose activities extend beyond the language region in which they are established;

—national and international institutions designated by law, whose activities are common to more than one community.

§ 4b. The decrees issued in terms of § 2b have the force of law respectively in the French language region and in the Dutch language region and also, except if a law passed on the basis of the majority vote specified in Article 1, last paragraph, shall provide otherwise, with regard to those institutions, established in the bilingual region of Brussels-Capital which, by virtue of their organisation, must be considered as belonging exclusively to one or other of the Communities.

§ 5. The right of initiative is vested in the Executive and in the members of the Council.

§ 6. The law determines the overall credit which is made

available to each Community Council, which controls the allocation thereof by decree.

This credit is calculated in the light of objective criteria laid down by the law. Equal endowments are established in matters which, of their very nature, do not lend themselves to objective criteria.

In obedience to the same rules, the law shall determine the proportion of this credit which must be set aside for the development of each Community within the territory of Brussels-Capital.

§ 7. The law defines those measures aimed at preventing any discrimination for ideological and philosophical reasons.

§ 8. The law sets up the procedure aimed at averting and settling any conflicts between laws and decrees, and between one decree and another (rev. 24.12.1970 and 17.7.1980).

Art. 59c. § 1. There is a Council and there is an Executive of the German-speaking Community, the composition and functioning of which are regulated by law.

The Council is composed of elected representatives.

Article 45 applies analogously to the members of the Council.

§ 2. The Council shall regulate by decree:

1. cultural matters;
2. personalized matters;
3. education, as far as for what is regulated under Article 59b, § 2, 2.
4. co-operation between the communities and international cultural co-operation as well as international co-operation in the matters referred to in 2.

These decrees have force of law in the German-speaking Region.

The law lays down the cultural and personalised matters referred to in 1 and 2, as well as the ways of the co-operation referred to in 4.

§ 3. On the motion of their respective Executives the Council of the German-speaking Community and the Walloon Regional Council may, by mutual consent and by separate decree, decide that the Council and the Executive of the German-speaking Community shall, within the German-speaking Region, exercise completely or partially the competence vested in the Walloon Region.

This competence shall, as the case may be, be exercised by means of decrees, orders or regulations.

§ 4. The Council and the Executive of the German-speaking Community exercise, by means of orders and regulations, any other competence vested in them by law.

Article 107 applies to these orders and regulations.

§ 5. The right of initiative is vested in the Executive and in the members of the Council.

§ 6. The law determines the overall credit which is made available to the Council, which controls the allocation thereof by decree.

§ 7. The law defines those measures aimed at preventing any discrimination for ideological and philosophical reasons.

BELIZE. A small country in central America, on the Caribbean Sea, formerly known as British Honduras, Belize achieved independence from Great Britain in 1974 and became a member of the United Nations in 1981. Its population is estimated by the UN (1990) to be 182,000. Ethnic groups include persons of African origin, Mestizos (mixed), and Amerindian Creoles. Languages commonly used include English (official), Spanish, and Mayan. Religions practiced include Christianity (Roman Catholic, 62%; Anglican, 12%; Methodist, 6%; and others, including Seventh Day Adventists, Mennonites, Jehovah's Witnesses, and Baptists, 17%) and the Bahá'í faith (3%).

The government (1990) took the form of a monarchy and member of the Commonwealth of Nations, of which the British sovereign is the symbolic head. Executive authority is exercised by the governor-general, representing the crown, and the prime minister, representing the party or coalition given the majority in a popular election. There is a 28-member Parliament elected by popular vote. The judiciary is organized along British lines. Political parties include the United Democratic Party, the People's United Party, and the Christian Democratic Party.

Belize is sparsely settled; and, up to 1972, its population diminished as workers migrated to the United States of America. However, since 1972, the population has grown because of an influx of settlers and refugees from neighboring Central American countries.

BENIN. The People's Republic of Benin is a country in western Africa, on the Gulf of Guinea. Formerly known as Dahomey, it has borders with Burkina Faso, Niger, Nigeria, and Togo. It achieved independence from France in 1960 and became a member of the United Nations the same year. Its population is estimated by the UN (1990) to be 4,585,000. Ethnic groups include the Fons, Adjas, Baribas, Yorubas, and Mahis. Languages commonly used include French (official), and several African vernaculars. Religions practiced include Animism (65%), Christianity (17%), and Islam (18%). Literacy is estimated at 20%.

The government (1990) took the form of a republic. However, since 1973, Benin has been under military rule, with all power in the hands of the president, a National Executive Council, a National Revolutionary Assembly, and a variety of People's Courts. Decisions relating to national policy are taken by the Party of the People's Revolution of Benin, the only political party.

During the 18th and 19th centuries, the kings of Dahomey sold thousands of slaves—mostly prisoners which they had taken in local welfare—to traders who shipped them to markets in Brazil and the Caribbean. France, which led the efforts to suppress the slave trade in west Africa, assumed control of the country in 1892 and organized it as a protectorate. It remained a French colony until 1960, when it became the independent Republic of Dahomey. Its name was changed to the People's Republic of Benin in 1975.

Since it achieved independence, Benin has been unstable politically and economically. There have been five coups, ten attempted coups, 12 governments and six constitutions. In the absence of exploitable natural resources, the economy has stagnated and the gross national product has been only slightly more than $300 per person. Government officials and students have complained of non-payment of salaries or allowances, and unemployment has increased dramatically.

On 8 December 1989 President Kerekou announced on national radio, after meetings of the government, of Parliament, and of the Central Committee of the Popular Revolution of Benin, that Marxism–Leninism no longer would be Benin's official ideology and that steps would be taken soon to introduce "a healthy political climate" in the country.

A few days later, large crowds demonstrated in the two major cities—Cotonou and Porto Novo—demanding the president's resignation because the promised reforms were not proceeding rapidly enough. They were dispersed by the police, and a ban was imposed on all public demonstrations "until further notice."

BHUTAN. The Kingdom of Bhutan is a country in southern Asia. It has borders with China and India. Always independent, Bhutan was occupied by the British and subsidized by them from 1910 until 1949, when India assumed control of its foreign affairs. Bhutan became a member of the United Nations in 1971. Its population is estimated by the UN (1990) to be 1,569,000. Ethnic groups include Nepalese (25%), Bhote (60%), and indigenous populations (15%). Languages in common use include Dzongkha, a Tibetan dialect (official), Nepali, and English. Religions practiced include Buddhism (70%), Hinduism (25%), and Islam (5%). Literacy is estimated at 15%.

The government (1990) took the form of a monarchy. The king is ruler, head of State and of government. He is advised by a Council of Ministers and a Royal Advisory Council. In addition, there is a National Assembly (*Tsongdu*), composed of not more than 150 members, 100 of whom are elected by the people, 10 by the organizations of lamas, and 40 appointed by the king. Heads of all government departments are required to subject themselves and their policies to the scrutiny of the National Assembly at least once a year. There are no political parties and suffrage, in voting for members of the National Assembly, is on the basis of one vote per family. Each family has a "headman," who either votes or designates someone to cast the family ballot.

B'NAI B'RITH INTERNATIONAL COUNCIL. Also referred to as B'nai B'rith International, BBI was established in New York City in 1843 as a national Jewish service organization. Now international in scope, with members in more than 50 countries, its activities are directed mainly towards uniting persons of the Jewish faith in the work of promoting the highest interests of humanity and in particular towards combatting discrimination on such grounds as race, religion, or origin.

Directed by a board of governors elected by its delegate conference, BBI is organized into lodges, chapters, and smaller units, most of which meet on a monthly basis. It is a member of the CONSULTATIVE COUNCIL OF JEWISH ORGANIZATIONS and works closely with other organizations in that council. Among its constituent organizations are the Anti-Defamation League of B'nai B'rith, which serves as a "watchdog" for Jewish people and acts to improve intergroup relations; B'nai B'rith Women; and the B'nai B'rith Youth Organization. Its main publication is the BBI *Jewish Monthly*.

B'nai B'rith International Council. Address: 1640 Rhode Island Avenue, N.W., Washington, D.C., 20036. Telephone: (202) 857-6600. Telex: 700-822-0068 BB WQH.

BODY OF PRINCIPLES FOR THE PROTECTION OF ALL PERSONS UNDER ANY FORM OF DETENTION OR IMPRISONMENT (1988). The Body of Principles was drafted by the UN SUB-COMMISSION ON PREVENTION OF DISCRIMINATION AND PROTECTION OF MINORITIES and by open-ended working groups established by the Third (Social, Humanitarian and Cultural) Committee and the Sixth (Legal) Committee of the UN General Assembly, and was approved by the assembly on 9 December 1988 (resolution 43/173).

The text of the Body of Principles, annexed to resolution 43/173, is as follows:

Scope of the Body of Principles

These Principles apply for the protection of all persons under any form of detention or imprisonment.

Use of Terms

For the purposes of the Body of Principles:
(a) "Arrest" means the act of apprehending a person for the alleged commission of an offence or by the action of an authority;
(b) "Detained person" means any person deprived of

131

personal liberty except as a result of conviction for an offence.

(c) "Imprisoned person" means any person deprived of personal liberty as a result of conviction for an offence;

(d) "Detention" means the condition of detained persons as defined above;

(e) "Imprisonment" means the condition of imprisoned persons as defined above;

(f) The words "a judicial or other authority" mean a judicial or other authority under the law whose status and tenure should afford the strongest possible guarantees of competence, impartiality and independence.

Principle 1. All persons under any form of detention or imprisonment shall be treated in a humane manner and with respect for the inherent dignity of the human person.

Principle 2. Arrest, detention or imprisonment shall only be carried out strictly in accordance with the provisions of the law and by competent officials or persons authorized for that purpose.

Principle 3. There shall be no restriction upon or derogation from any of the human rights of persons under any form of detention or imprisonment recognized or existing in any State pursuant to law, conventions, regulations or custom on the pretext that this Body of Principles does not recognize such rights or that it recognizes them to a lesser extent.

Principle 4. Any form of detention or imprisonment and all measures affecting the human rights of a person under any form of detention or imprisonment shall be offered by, or be subject to the effective control of, a judicial or other authority.

Principle 5. 1. These principals shall be applied to all persons within the territory of any given State, without distinction of any kind, such as race, colour, sex, language, religion or religious belief, political or other opinion, national ethnic or social origin, property, birth or other status.

2. Measures applied under the law and designed solely to protect the rights and special status of women, especially pregnant women and nursing mothers, children and juveniles, aged, sick or handicapped persons shall not be deemed to be discriminatory. The need for, and the application of, such measures shall always be subject to review by a judicial or other authority.

Principle 6. No person under any form of detention or imprisonment shall be subjected to torture or to cruel, inhuman or degrading treatment or punishment. (The term "cruel, inhuman or degrading treatment or punishment" should be interpreted so as to extend the widest possible protection against abuses, whether physical or mental, including the holding of a detained or imprisoned person in conditions which deprive him, temporarily or permanently, of the use of any of his natural senses, such as sight or hearing, or of his awareness of place and the passing of time.) No circumstance whatever may be invoked as a justification for torture or other cruel, inhuman or degrading treatment or punishment.

Principle 7. 1. States should prohibit by law any act contrary to the rights and duties contained in these Principles, make any such act subject to appropriate sanctions and conduct impartial investigations upon complaints.

2. Officials who have reason to believe that a violation of this Body of Principles has occurred or is about to occur shall report the matter to their superior authorities and, where necessary, to other appropriate authorities or organs vested with reviewing or remedial powers.

3. Any other person who has ground to believe that a violation of the Body of Principles has occurred or is about to occur shall have the right to report the matter to the superiors of the officials involved as well as to other appropriate authorities or organs vested with reviewing or remedial powers.

Principle 8. Persons in detention shall be subject to treatment appropriate to their unconvicted status. Accordingly, they shall, whenever possible, be kept separate from imprisoned persons.

Principle 9. The authorities which arrest a person, keep him under detentions or investigate the case shall exercise only the powers granted to them under the law and the exercise of these powers shall be subject to recourse to a judicial or other authority.

Principle 10. Anyone who is arrested shall be informed at the time of his arrest of the reason for his arrest and shall be promptly informed of any charges against him.

Principle 11. 1. A person shall not be kept in detention without being given an effective opportunity to be heard promptly by a judicial or other authority. A detained person shall have the right to defend himself or to be assisted by counsel as prescribed by law.

2. A detained person and his counsel, if any, shall receive prompt and full communication of any order of detention, together with the reasons therefor.

3. A judicial or other authority shall be empowered to review as appropriate the continuance of detention.

Principle 12. 1. There shall be duly recorded:

(a) The reasons for the arrest;

(b) The time of the arrest and the taking of the arrested person to a place of custody as well as that of his first appearance before a judicial or other authority;

(c) The identity of the law enforcement officials concerned;

(d) Precise information concerning the place of custody.

2. Such records shall be communicated to the detained person, or his counsel, if any, in the form prescribed by law.

Principle 13. Any person shall, at the moment of arrest and at the commencement of detention or imprisonment, or promptly thereafter, be provided by the authority responsible for his arrest, detention or imprisonment, respectively, with information on and an explanation of his rights and how to avail himself of such rights.

Principle 14. A person who does not adequately understand or speak the language used by the authorities responsible for his arrest, detention or imprisonment is entitled to receive promptly in a language which he understands the information referred to in principle 10, principle 11, paragraph 2, principle 12, paragraph 1, and principle 13 and to have the assistance, free of charge, if necessary, of an interpreter in connection with legal proceedings subsequent to his arrest.

Principle 15. Notwithstanding the exceptions contained in principle 16, paragraph 4, and principle 18, paragraph 3, communication of the detained or imprisoned person with the outside world, and in particular his family or counsel, shall not be denied for more than a matter of days.

Principle 16. 1. Promptly after arrest and after each transfer from one place of detention or imprisonment to another, a detained or imprisoned person shall be entitled to notify or to require the competent authority to notify members of his family or other appropriate persons of his choice of his arrest, detention or imprisonment or of the transfer and of the place where he is kept in custody.

2. If a detained or imprisoned person is a foreigner, he shall also be promptly informed of his right to communicate by appropriate means with a consular post or the diplomatic mission of the State of which he is a national or which is otherwise entitled to receive such communication in accordance with international law or with the representative of the competent international organization, if he is a refugee or is otherwise under the protection of an intergovernmental organization.

3. If a detained or imprisoned person is a juvenile or is incapable of understanding his entitlement, the competent authority shall on its own initiative undertake the notification referred to in this principle. Special attention shall be given to notifying parents or guardians.

4. Any notification referred to in this principle shall be made or permitted to be made without delay. The competent authority may however delay a notification for a reasonable period where exceptional needs of the investigation so require.

Principle 17. 1. A detained person shall be entitled to have the assistance of a legal counsel. He shall be informed of his right by the competent authority promptly after arrest and shall be provided with reasonable facilities for exercising it.

2. If a detained person does not have a legal counsel of his own choice, he shall be entitled to have a legal counsel assigned to him by a judicial or other authority in all cases where the interests of justice so require and without payment by him if he does not have sufficient means to pay.

Principle 18. 1. A detained or imprisoned person shall be entitled to communicate and consult with his legal counsel.

2. A detained or imprisoned person shall be allowed adequate time and facilities for consultations with his legal counsel.

3. The right of a detained or imprisoned person to be visited by and to consult and communicate, without delay or censorship and in full confidentiality, with his legal counsel may not be suspended or restricted save in exceptional circumstances, to be specified by law or lawful regulations, when it is considered indispensable by a judicial or other authority in order to maintain security and good order.

4. Interviews between a detained or imprisoned person and his legal counsel may be within sight, but not within the hearing, of a law enforcement official.

5. Communications between a detained or imprisoned person and his legal counsel mentioned in this principle shall be inadmissible as evidence against the detained or imprisoned person unless they are connected with a continuing or contemplated crime.

Principle 19. A detained or imprisoned person shall have the right to be visited by and to correspond with, in particular, members of his family and shall be given adequate opportunity to communicate with the outside world, subject to reasonable conditions and restrictions as specified by law or lawful regulations.

Principle 20. If a detained or imprisoned person so requests, he shall if possible be kept in a place of detention or imprisonment reasonably near his usual place of residence.

Principle 21. 1. It shall be prohibited to take undue advantage of the situation of a detained or imprisoned person for the purpose of compelling him to confess, to incriminate himself otherwise or to testify against any other person.

2. No detained person while being interrogated shall be subject to violence, threats or methods of interrogation which impair his capacity of decision or his judgment.

Principle 22. No detained or imprisoned person shall, even with his consent, be subjected to any medical or scientific experimentation which may be detrimental to his health.

Principle 23. 1. The duration of any interrogation of a detained or imprisoned person and of the intervals between interrogations as well as the identity of the officials who conducted the interrogation and other persons present shall be recorded and certified in such form as may be prescribed by law.

2. A detained or imprisoned person, or his counsel when provided by law, shall have access to the information described above.

Principle 24. A proper medical examination shall be offered to a detained or imprisoned person as promptly as possible after his admission to the place of detention or imprisonment, and thereafter medical care and treatment shall be provided whenever necessary. This care and treatment shall be provided free of charge.

Principle 25. A detained or imprisoned person or his counsel shall, subject only to reasonable conditions to ensure security and good order in the place of detention or imprisonment, have the right to request or petition a judicial or other authority for a second medical examination or opinion.

Principle 26. The fact that a detained or imprisoned person underwent a medical examination, the name of the physician and the results of such an examination shall be duly recorded. Access to such records shall be ensured. Modalities therefor shall be in accordance with relevant rules of domestic law.

Principle 27. Non-compliance with these Principles in obtaining evidence shall be taken into account in determining the admissibility of such evidence against a detained or imprisoned person.

Principle 28. A detained or imprisoned person shall have the right to obtain within the limits of available resources, if from public source, reasonable quantities of educational, cultural and informational material, subject to reasonable conditions to ensure security and good order in the place of detention or imprisonment.

Principle 29. 1. In order to supervise the strict observance of relevant laws and regulations, places of detention shall be visited regularly by qualified and experienced persons appointed by, and responsible to, a competent authority distinct from the authority directly in charge of the administration of the place of detention or imprisonment.

2. A detained or imprisoned person shall have the right to communicate freely and in full confidentiality with the persons who visit the places of detention or imprisonment in accordance with paragraph 1, subject to reasonable conditions to ensure security and good order in such places.

Principle 30. 1. The types of conduct of the detained or imprisoned person that constitute disciplinary offences during detention or imprisonment, the description and duration of disciplinary punishment that may be inflicted and the authorities competent to impose such punishment shall be specified by law or lawful regulations and duly published.

2. A detained or imprisoned person shall have the right to be heard before disciplinary action is taken. He shall have the right to bring such action to higher authorities for review.

Principle 31. The appropriate authorities shall endeavour to ensure, according to domestic law, assistance when needed to dependent and, in particular, minor members of the families of detained or imprisoned persons and shall devote a particular measure of care to the appropriate custody of children left without supervision.

Principle 32. 1. A detained person or his counsel shall be entitled at any time to take proceedings according to domestic law before a judicial or other authority to challenge the lawfulness of his detention in order to obtain his release without delay, if it is unlawful.

2. The proceedings referred to in paragraph 1 shall be simple and expeditious and at no cost for detained persons without adequate means. The detaining authority shall produce without reasonable delay the detained person before the reviewing authority.

Principle 33. 1. A detained or imprisoned person or his counsel shall have the right to make a request or complaint regarding his treatment, in particular in case of torture or other cruel, inhuman or degrading treatment, to the authorities responsible for the administration of the place of detention and to higher authorities and, when necessary, to appropriate authorities vested with reviewing or remedial powers.

2. In those cases where neither the detained or imprisoned person nor his counsel has the possibility to exercise his rights under paragraph 1, a member of the family of the detained or imprisoned person or any other person who has knowledge of the case may exercise such rights.

3. Confidentiality concerning the request or complaint shall be maintained if so requested by the complainant.

4. Every request or complaint shall be promptly dealt with and replied to without undue delay. If the request or complaint is rejected or, in case of inordinate delay, the complainant shall be entitled to bring it before a judicial or other authority. Neither the detained or imprisoned person nor any complaint under paragraph 1 shall suffer prejudice for making a request or complaint.

Principle 34. Whenever the death or disappearance of a detained or imprisoned person occurs during his detention or imprisonment, an inquiry into the cause of death or disappearance shall be held by a judicial or other authority, either on its own motion or at the instance of a member of the family of such a person or any person who has knowledge of the case. When circumstances so warrant, such an inquiry shall be held on the same procedural basis whenever the death or disappearance occurs shortly after the termination of the detention or imprisonment. The findings of such inquiry or a report thereon shall be made available upon request, unless doing so would jeopardize an ongoing criminal investigation.

Principle 35. 1. Damage incurred because of acts or omissions by a public official contrary to the rights contained in these Principles shall be compensated according to the applicable rules on liability provided by domestic law.

2. Information required to be recorded under these Principles shall be available in accordance with procedures provided by domestic law for use in claiming compensation under this principle.

Principle 36. 1. A detained person suspected of or charged with a criminal offence shall be presumed innocent and shall be treated as such until proved guilty according to law in a public trial at which he has had all the guarantees necessary for his defence.

2. The arrest or detention of such a person pending investigation and trial shall be carried out only for the purposes of the administration of justice on grounds and under conditions and procedures specified by law. The imposition of restrictions upon such a person which are not strictly required for the purpose of the detention or to prevent hindrance to the process of investigation or the administration of justice, or for the maintenance of security and good order in the place of detention shall be forbidden.

Principle 37. A person detained on a criminal charge shall be brought before a judicial or other authority provided by law promptly after his arrest. Such authority shall decide without delay upon the lawfulness and necessity of detention. No person shall be kept under detention pending investigation or trial except upon the written order of such an authority. A detained person shall, when brought before such an authority, have the right to make a statement on the treatment received by him while in custody.

Principle 38. A person detained on a criminal charge shall be entitled to trial within a reasonable time or to release pending trial.

Principle 39. Except in special cases provided for by law, a person detained on a criminal charge shall be entitled, unless a judicial or other authority decides otherwise in the interest of the administration of justice, to release pending trial subject to the conditions that may be imposed in accordance with the law. Such authority shall keep the necessity of detention under review.

General Clause. Nothing in the present Body of Principles shall be construed as restricting or derogating from any right defined in the International Covenant on Civil and Political Rights.

SEE ALSO *Arbitrary Arrest, Detention or Exile; Arrest, Detention, and Abduction of International Civil Servants; Arrested Person's Right to Communicate; Children: Detention; Convention against Torture and Other Cruel, Inhuman or Degrading Treatment or Punishment; Declaration on the Protection of all Persons from Being Subjected to Torture and Other Cruel, Inhuman or Degrading Treatment or Punishment; Detention: Administrative; Detention: UN Staff Members; European Convention for the Prevention of Torture and Inhuman or Degrading Treatment or Punishment; Imprisonment; Inter-American Convention to Prevent and Punish Torture; Liberty; Standard Minimum Rules for the Treatment of Prisoners; Working Group on Detention.*

BOLIVIA. The Republic of Bolivia is a landlocked country in tropical South America. It has borders with Argentina, Brazil, Chile, Paraguay, and Peru. It achieved independence from Spain in 1825 and became a member of the United Nations in 1945. Its population is estimated by the UN (1990) to be 7,314,000. Ethnic groups include the Aymara (25%) and Quecha (30%)—descendents of survivors of the once-predominant Amerindian population which was reduced to slavery by the Spanish colonists—European (20%), and mixed (25%). Languages commonly used include Spanish (official), Aymara, and Quecha. Religions practiced include Christianity (mostly Roman Catholic), 95%; the Bahá'í faith, 4%; and others, 1%. Literacy is estimated at 75%.

The (1990) government took the form of a republic. Under the 1967 constitution, the president is elected by popular vote and acts as head of State and government. However, in the event that no candidate receives 50% of the vote, a choice is made between the two top candidates by Congress. This, in fact, occurred in 1985, when the Nationalist Democratic Action Party (ADN), headed by General Hugo Banzer Suarez, won a narrow plurality of the popular vote (32.8%). The National Revolutionary Movement (MNR) came in second as its leader, former President Victor Paz Estenssoro, polled 30.4% of the vote, and the Movement of the Revolutionary Left (MIR) placed third with 10.2% of the vote for its candidate, Jaime Paz Zamora. In spite of the ADN plurality of some 37,000 votes—and because of the preference given to rural over urban votes in the apportionment of seats in Congress—the MNR won more legislative seats than the ADN. When, in the congressional run-off, the MIR cast its lot with the MNR, former President Victor Paz Estenssoro was elected to a fourth term in office.

A country naturally rich in minerals, the indifference of Bolivia's colonizers to the development of other resources gave rise in the 19th century to a system of social inequality in which the Amerindian indigenous peoples, although they constitute more than half the total population, were forced to work the mines and till the fields under duress and were ignored in society and in government.

In 1826, Simon Bolivar, then the most powerful man in South America after leading several successful revolutions, drew up a constitution for Bolivia. However, from that time onward, conflicting personal, military, and political aspirations plagued the country. Only in recent years did it begin to use its vast oil and mineral revenues to promote development. Frequent strikes have drawn attention to the lot of the Bolivian worker, while frequent revolts have dramatized the situation of the surviving Amerindian population.

Rich in natural resources but plagued by internal conflicts, strikes, inflation, and a wide variety of economic and social problems, Bolivia endured some 60 revolutions in 160 years and revised its Constitution more than 10 times. In one of the conflicts, which began in 1965, a Cuban-based revolutionary movement led by Major Ernesto (Che) Guevara was put down on 8 October 1967 by the Bolivian army with strong assistance from Bolivian peasants and U.S. military advisors, Guevara dying in the process.

On 17 July 1980, the government was taken over by Bolivian General Luis Garcia Tejada, and almost immediately rumors of serious violations of human rights began to circulate. In September 1980, the Sub-Commission on Prevention of Discrimination and Protection of Minorities, meeting in Geneva, called upon the Commission on Human Rights to study the situation and to take urgent steps to correct it.

The commission appointed one of its members,

Professor Hector Gros Espiell, as its special envoy for this purpose; and, in the three following years, he made three factfinding trips to Bolivia.

After the first trip, in 1981, he reported that he was convinced that, following 17 July 1980, grave, massive, and persistent violations of human rights were committed in Bolivia. He added, however, that "the situation has improved in recent months and the most serious and grave violations committed following 17 July 1980 have not recurred with the same intensity. It is to be hoped that the positive trend will continue, intensify and succeed in overcoming the obvious difficulties which restrict, hinder and affect it."

After the second trip, in 1982, he reported that he had found "an auspicious and positive situation of full respect for human rights and a total identification of the authorities with the idea that it is necessary to ensure, uphold and increase the promotion, defence and guarantee of those rights, and that their protection should be free from any kind of discrimination. This situation—which contrasts radically with that which existed after 17 July 1980—is however limited by the adverse economic and social conditions, which can only be overcome by political stability and economic and social development."

After the third trip, in 1983, he reported that "since 10 October 1982, when the constitutional government of President Hernan Siles Zuazo was established, the situation of human rights in Bolivia has improved notably. Not only have provisions which inherently affected the recognition and legal guarantees of human rights been repealed: there have, in actual fact, been no serious violations of human rights. . . . This assertion is based on and supported by the absence of fresh complaints and the direct personal conviction reached by the Special Envoy as a result of his visit."

The special envoy recommended that the United Nations should continue, "through advisory services and assistance, to support and promote the local effort—which is the irreplaceable and determining factor—to ensure the full observance of human rights and fundamental freedoms in Bolivia."

The Commission on Human Rights, at its 1983 session, noted the determination of the Bolivian government to ensure that a thorough investigation of all past violations of human rights would be undertaken with a view to establishing responsibility through due process or law, welcomed the accession by Bolivia to the International Covenants on Human Rights and the Optional Protocol to the International Covenant on Civil and Political Rights; and concluded its consideration of the matter after requesting the UN secretary-general to provide advisory services and other appropriate human rights assistance to the government of Bolivia upon its request.

BONDED LABOR. Information concerning the bonded labor system was drawn to the attention of the WORKING GROUP ON CONTEMPORARY FORMS OF SLAVERY at its 1989 session by a number of participants. As summarized in the report of the working group (UN Doc. E/CN.4/Sub.2/1989/39), the information related, on the one hand, to the exploitation of CHILD LABOR and, on the other, to the broader question of DEBT BONDAGE.

As regards the exploitation of child labor, the report stated (para. 61–69) that, in the course of the working group's deliberations,

The International Abolitionist Federation referred to ILO conventions on child labour. Some of these have been widely ratified by Member States, yet the children are exploited for their labour in agriculture, industry—factories, mines and at homes and on the street. In 1973 an ILO convention recommended the minimum age for employment at 15 years and made provisions for certain types of employment prohibited to those under 18 years of age. Yet the Member States of ILO often allow children as young as 12 or 13 to be exposed to hours of drudgery under appalling conditions jeopardizing their health and future.

The representative of Human Rights Internet reported on the progress made with respect to a project which was initiated after the Anti-Slavery Society investigated into the use of child labour in the carpet industry in India. Many of these children are children of bonded labourers and the project aims to establish school community centres in Pradesh for those who come from other provinces. It will provide basic education, vocational training, the teaching of personal and environmental hygiene and health care.

The representative of Pax Christi on behalf of the Centre for Child Labour, stated that, although India had enacted an Act proscribing the use of child labour, this Act did not provide for a minimum age. Therefore, several thousands of children are still reported to be working in health-hazardous industries.

The Observer for India informed the Working Group of the adoption by India of the Child Labour Act in December, 1986. This Act prohibits the employment of children below 14 years in certain specified processes and occupations and seeks to regulate the conditions in processes in which children are allowed to work. Besides this, other Acts like the Factories Act, 1948 and the Mines Act, 1952 also contain provisions prohibiting child labour. The implementation of these laws is mainly the responsibility of the State Governments which have been periodically directed to enforce them strictly.

India, in addition, formulated the Child Labour Policy in 1987 with the aim of suitably rehabilitating children who are withdrawn from the prohibited employments and to provide welfare inputs like education, health care, [and] skill development to the children working in permitted employments. The National Child Labour Policy envisaged the setting up of projects for the welfare of children in certain selected areas of concentration of child labour. A ma-jor component of these projects would be the setting up of special schools where educational, vocational training, supplementary nutrition, and health care were provided.

The Anti-Slavery Society reported on the use of child labour in Portugal, particularly in the shoe and textile industry. In 1989, Portugal had not yet ratified ILO Convention No. 138 on the Minimum Age for Admission to Employment, although Decree Law 49408 of 1969 proscribed the use of child labour under the age of 14 years.

The International Human Rights Internship Program reported on the alleged widespread use of young children in Haiti as servants, known locally as "restavek", involving children of poor, rural families who serve as domestics and servants for urban families. These children, who are reported to be as young as six years old, are, in essence, subjected to a system of involuntary servitude. According to the organization, the Government of Haiti does not regulate the practice of "restavek". Haitian child labour law specifically exempts children who work as domestics from their coverage.

The International Commission of Justice stated that on specific problems, such as child labour and debt bondage, identification of long-term and short-term measures is necessary in order to eradicate these problems.

The Anti-Slavery Society reported on the positive and constructive nature of the report of the Legal Committee of the Ghana National Commission on Children. This was in response to the Anti-Slavery Society's 1987 and 1988 submissions on the conditions of child workers in the Ashanti gold fields operations.

Regarding debt bondage, the report stated (para. 70–80) that, in the course of the working group's deliberations,

The Anti-Slavery Society recalled that debt bondage was recognized as one of the contemporary forms of slavery. For the past year the Anti-Slavery Society had been conducting research in the South Asian countries on the subject of child labour related to debt bondage. One important result of this research was the organization of a seminar arranged by an Indian non-governmental organization, the Bonded Labour Liberation Front, which was held at New Delhi from 30 June to 4 July and attended by representatives of non-governmental organizations from Bangladesh, India, Nepal, Pakistan and Sri Lanka.

The child bonded labour system could be broadly classified under two headings: (a) inherent bondage; (b) children subjected to bondage. The organization, quoting Indian governmental statistics of September 1988, stated that "about 235,670 bonded labourers were identified and freed up to 31.3.88" and that "children of these freed bonded labourers do not find a place in the list of released persons".

The Anti-Slavery Society proposed that the Working Group should draw up a definite programme for studying child bondage at its next session in 1990 and that, with that in mind, it should recommend that the International Labour Office should submit a report based on the documentation already at its disposal and organize a tripartite seminar on child servitude in South Asia.

Informing public opinion, especially in the South Asian countries, was a vital factor in the fight against child bondage. The non-governmental organizations attending the seminar in New Delhi had decided to commemorate a child bondage day on 18 September each year. In addition, a coalition of non-governmental organizations concerned with child servitude in South Asia has been set up, based in Delhi, but with a rotating secretariat.

The Observer for India replied that Indian Government's statistics cover all bonded labourers who are released, adults as well as children. He stated that the total number of bonded labourers identified and freed by 1 April 1989 was 242,532.

The Observer for India, in reply to the statement by the Anti-Slavery Society that the Bonded Labour Abolition Act of 1975 empowered only District Magistrates and Sub-Divisional Magistrates to identify and release bonded labourers, stated that, while the statutory power to identify and release bonded labourers rests with District Magistrates and Sub-Divisional Magistrates, other officials do in fact carry out the task of identifying bonded labourers with a view of obtaining their release. The Observer continued by stating that the system of debt bondage was not a creation of the Indian Government, but rather the outcome of certain categories of indebtedness which had prevailed for a long time involving certain economically exploited sections of society.

The Bonded Labour system had been abolished under the Bonded Labour Act and this Act envisages the release of all bonded labourers and the simultaneous liquidation of their debts. The World Labour Report, 1985, had noted that the Government of India stands out because of the action it had taken since 1975 to combat debt bondage. High priority continues to be given to this objective under the new 20 Point Programme announced in 1986 which stipulates that:

(1) there should be full implementation of the laws abolishing bonded labour; and

(2) there should be the involvement of voluntary agencies in the programme for bonded labour.

Another representative of the Anti-Slavery Society gave a report on the practice of bonded labour in Pakistan. It referred to the Brick-Kiln Labourers who are considered bonded labourers in a path-breaking verdict of the Pakistani Supreme Court on 18 September 1988. In order to abolish this practice in Pakistan it proposed, *inter alia*, the establishment of a commission to prepare a report about the misery, elimination and rehabilitation of bonded labourers, and the adoption by all the Governments of South Asia of effective laws for the abolition of Bonded Labour System from their countries as soon as possible.

The Observer for Pakistan underlined the strong commitment by the new democratic Government of his country to eliminate bonded labour in all its forms and reviewed steps taken for that purpose. Pakistan seeks to comply fully with the standards of the International Labour Organisation. In addition, under article 11 of the Constitution, child labour, forced labour and slavery in all its forms are prohibited, as well as traffic in human beings. Children under the age of 14 years shall not be employed in hazardous industries.

In case of violations of the Constitution and the laws of the country, the aggrieved have access to the Judiciary which is capable of delivering justice. The judgement of the Supreme Court of Pakistan of 18 September 1988 on Brick-Kiln workers fully substantiates this point.

At the conclusion of the discussion, the working group recommended that the information it had received should be studied at greater depth at its 1990 session, when the subject of child labor and bonded labor would be the main theme. At that time, specific recommendations could be prepared.

BOTSWANA. The Republic of Botswana is a country in southern Africa. It has borders with Namibia, South Africa, Zambia, and Zimbabwe. Formerly known as the Bechuanaland Protectorate, it achieved independence from Great Britain in 1966 and became a member of the United Nations the same year. Its population is estimated by the UN (1990) to be 1,332,000. The Batswana tribe, which makes up about 95% of the population, is divided into eight subgroups: Bamangwato, Bakwena, Batawana, Bangwaktse, Bakgatla, Bamalete, Barolong, and Batlokwa. Bushmen (Basarwa) and Kgalagadi constitute small minorities. In addition, there are about 5,500 British citizens and a increasingly large number of student refugees from South Africa and Namibia. The UN secretary-general, in cooperation with the UN high commissioner for refugees, has organized programs of assistance for such refugees, and the General Assembly has appealed to all States to contribute to such programs. Languages commonly spoken include English and Setswana. Religions practiced include Christianity (50%) and Animism (50%). Literacy is estimated at 24% (in English) and 35% (in Setswana).

The government (1990) took the form of a republic and member of the Commonwealth of Nations, of which the British monarch is the symbolic head. The president is head of State and government. There is a unicameral National Assembly consisting of 34 elected and six appointed members, which meets at least once every five years. There is also an advisory House of Chiefs, which considers any bill relating to a matter of tribal concern. Political parties include the Democratic Party, the National Front, the People's Party, and the Progressive Union.

Because of economic conditions in Botswana, about 40,000 residents are forced to work in neighboring African countries, mainly South Africa. Problems arise because wives and children normally are not allowed to accompany men to work areas in those countries.

Nevertheless, Bostwana has progressed from being one of the least developed African nations at the time of independence to one of the richest ex-colonies, mainly because it has effectively exploited its vast natural mineral resources, including diamonds, and has used the income wisely to provide roads, education, and health services. Moreover, because it has maintained good race relations, even though it borders with and is partly dependent upon South Africa, it has won broad political, economic, and moral support from democratic countries throughout the world.

BRAZIL. The Federative Republic of Brazil is the largest country in tropical South America, occupying nearly half the continent and having borders with every South American country except Chile and Ecuador. It achieved independence from Portugal in 1822 and became a member of the United Nations in 1945. Its population is estimated by the UN (1990) to be 150,368,000. Ethnic groups include descendents of slaves imported from Africa before 1888, as well as descendents of immigrants from Italy, Germany, Japan, Portugal, and Spain. Religions practiced include Christianity (Roman Catholic, 88%; Protestant, 6%) and others; social evolution in Brazil has been marked by the influence of many different religions and beliefs, which have often interchanged some of their elements and practices. Literacy is estimated at 75%.

The government (1990) took the form of a republic, consisting of 22 states, one federal district, and four territories. It is headed by the president, elected by the National Congress acting as an electoral college. That congress is composed of the Senate and the Chamber of Deputies. The president serves for a term of six years, members of the Senate for eight years, and members of the Chamber of Deputies for four years. Congressional elections are by equal, direct, and compulsory suffrage, and by proportional representation. The election of a civilian president under this procedure in 1985 ended 19 years of rule by military junta. Political parties include the Party of the Brazilian Democratic Movement, the Democratic Social Party, the Liberal Front Party, the Democratic Workers' Party, the Workers' Party, and the Brazilian Labor Party.

Slavery supported the Portuguese plantation structure until the slave trade was abolished in 1850; the slaves, of African origin, were emancipated gradually with complete abolition of slavery only in 1888. The modern population of Brazil is composed of three main racial elements—whites, blacks, and Amerindians—each made up of many ethnic groups. In recent years, a fourth element has been added: the largest community of Japanese immigrants outside Japan itself, clustered in Sao Paulo.

To deal with violations of human rights, the government in December 1985 re-organized the Brazilian Council for the Defence of Human Rights, which had been established in 1964, by creating within the council four sections, each placed under the responsibility of a "defender." These sections investigate, respectively, alleged abuses in respect of (1) electoral frauds, (2) violence resulting from land disputes in the countryside, (3) acts of discrimination on all grounds, and (4) abuse of power. The council's sessions, formerly closed, have been opened to the general public since it convened in its new form early in 1986.

As regards the Indian people who comprise about 1% of the total population, the main thrust of modern Brazilian policy is to preserve their culture while assuring their progressive integration into national life. A staff body within the Ministry of Culture coordinates and supports activities and initiatives of non-governmental organizations, private institutions, and individuals striving to enhance the Indians' role in national life by making their presence more visible while respecting their cultural identity. The new body plans to preserve Indian languages by printing books and preparing tapes in those languages, and, in general, to promote indigenous culture through all the media of communication.

On January 1985, after 21 years of military rule, Tancredo Neves, a civilian, was elected president by the 686-member electoral college. However, his untimely death just prior to the date on which he was to assume office, led to the inauguration of his running mate, Jose Sarney, as president.

In the arrangement through which the military yielded power to a civilian government, military leaders extracted promises that human rights abuses committed while they were in office would be overlooked. Accordingly, no investigations were made of a number of terrorist attacks or of many "disappearances" which had occurred between 1979 and 1985, in which the military were said to have been involved. President Sarney identified himself closely with the armed forces, which, in turn, supported his decision to serve for at least five years of the six-year term given him by the electoral college.

In Brazil's first direct presidential election since 1960, held in December 1989, Fernando Collor de Mello, a free-market advocate, was chosen to serve for a term of five years. The election—preceded by a national debate on Brazil's social and economic problems—was hailed by Brazilians as a step towards the return of full democracy.

A serious problem confronting the new president is the plight of Brazil's Yanomani Indians, described in a statement circulated to the 1990 session of the UN Commission on Human Rights by Survival International, a non-governmental organization in consultative status, as follows (UN Doc. E/CN.4/1990/NGO 63, para. 1–11):

Survival International, an organization for the protection of the rights of threatened tribal peoples in all regions of the world, has worked with and on behalf of the Yanomami in the Amazon Basin since Survival's establishment 20 years ago. We submit this statement to update the Commission on the urgent situation of the Yanomami in Brazil, who are faced with wholesale invasion of their land and their own physical destruction.

In the past several years, an estimated 45,000 Brazilian gold miners have invaded Yanomami territory, bringing with them disease, environmental degradation, and massive disruption of traditional Yanomami life. This invasion has been facilitated or tolerated by the Brazilian Government, despite domestic and international outcries.

The Brazilian Constitution states that Indians have a right to "their social organization customs, languages, beliefs and traditions, and aboriginal rights to the lands they traditionally occupy, it being the responsibility of the Union [the Brazilian federal government] to demarcate them, protect and guarantee respect for all their property". Traditional lands are defined as "those inhabited by them on a permanent basis, those utilized for their productive activities, those absolutely necessary for the preservation of environmental resources necessary to their well-being, and those necessary for their physical and cultural reproduction, according to their usages, customs and traditions".

While the Yanomami traditionally occupy and use 9.4 million hectares of land in Brazil, a presidential decree issued in February 1989 demarcated only 2.4 million hectares—in 19 separate and discontinuous areas—as Yanomami territory. The more than two-thirds of the Yanomami territory not demarcated is now considered "national forest" and is open to economic exploitation, including gold prospecting and mining.

There are a numerous reports of armed confrontations between the 45,000 miners and the 10,000 Yanomami, and miners have also unwittingly brought in much disease. A medical team comprised of human rights groups and the government Indian agency, FUNAI, completed a preliminary examination of the Yanomami in January 1990 and noted an alarming spread of a frequently fatal and resistant strain of malaria, falciparum. Of the Yanomami tested, almost one in four showed the presence of malaria and two-thirds of the malaria cases are of the falciparum type. In addition to malaria, 80 per cent of those examined were suffering from intestinal parasites, 20 per cent from severe malnutrition, and 12 per cent from respiratory infections. There were also numerous cases of conjunctivitis, gastroenteritis, hepatitis and tuberculosis.

In October 1989, a judge from the 7th Federal Court in Brasilia issued an injunction requiring the Government to evict the miners from all territory traditionally occupied by the Yanomami. However, on 11 January 1990, the Government issued a ruling effectively reversing the court order and halting the evictions.

In addition, Brazilian President Jose Sarney signed a decree on 25 January 1990 creating a "garimpeiro reserve" to house miners removed from Yanomami territory. The reserve is illegal under the terms of the October 1989 court injunction as some of the area lies within Yanomami territory.

Despite press reports that as many as 10,000 of the gold miners have left Yanomami territory for other areas in Brazil and Guyana, other observers have reported that any so-called evacuation of miners is proceeding at a "snail's pace". There are also reports that the miners will not move to the new reserve area as they claim its gold reserves are almost exhausted.

There has been much discussion within United Nations human rights bodies about the need for "early warning" systems which could alert bodies such as the Commission on Human Rights to situations in which action is urgently required. Such warnings of the possible destruction of the Yanomami as a people have been made to the Commission for years, yet no effective action has yet been taken.

Survival International recognizes that the Brazilian Government has taken some steps to protect the Yanomami, but developments in the past few months indicate that these measures are wholly inadequate and that the Yanomami are at even greater risk today that at this time last year. Survival understands the competing demands and desperate economic situation of many non-Indian Brazilians and is sympathetic to the Government's efforts to deal with this situation. However, economic development cannot be built upon the corpses of the Yanomami.

Survival International respectfully urges the Commission to request additional information from the Government of Brazil regarding the situation of the Yanomami and the guarantees promised them under the Brazilian Constitution and fundamental international human rights norms. In addition, we appeal to the Government of Brazil to abide by the decisions of its own courts and to demarcate and protect all the Yanomami lands from destructive exploitation and invasion.

BRUNEI DARUSSALAM. The State of Brunei Darussalam is a country in southeastern Asia, on the northwest coast of the island of Borneo, facing the South China Sea. It is split into two parts by the East Malaysian State of Sarawak. Formerly known as Brunei, it achieved independence from Great Britain on 1 January 1984 and became a member of the United Nations the same year. Its population is estimated by the UN (1990) to be 271,000. Ethnic groups include Malays (65%), Chinese (20%), indigenous populations, mainly Ibans, (8%) and others (7%). Languages in common use include Malay and English (both official), Chinese, Iban, and other indigenous vernaculars. Religions practiced include Islam (official), 66%; Buddhism, 14%; Christianity, 10%; and others, 10%. Literacy is estimated at 45% overall, 95% among the young.

The government (1990) took the form of a monarchy and member of the Commonwealth of Nations, of which the British sovereign is the symbolic head. The sultan rules, under a 1965 constitution, with the assistance of a six-member cabinet and a Council of Ministers, all appointed by himself. The constitution provides for an elected Legislative Council of 20 members; however, no elections were held after 1965. There is one political party: the Brunei National Democratic Party.

Because of its oil wealth, the people of Brunei Darussalam enjoy first-class schools and health systems. There are no universities in the country, but qualified students are given government scholarships to study in British institutions.

BULGARIA. The People's Republic of Bulgaria is a country in eastern Europe, on the Black Sea. It has borders with Greece, Romania, Turkey, and Yugoslavia. It achieved independence from Turkey in 1908 and became a member of the United Nations in 1955. Its population is estimated by the UN (1990) to be 9,246,000. Minority ethnic and national groups include persons of Armenian, Greek, Gypsy, Jewish, and Turkish descent, together making up about 9% of the population. Bulgarian is the only language in common use. Literacy is estimated at 95%.

The government (1990) took the form of a republic. Executive authority is vested in the chairman of the State Council and chairman of the Council of Ministers, who serves as prime minister. Legislation is prepared by the 400-member Great National Assembly, members of which are elected by popular vote and serve for a term of five years. In the elections of June 1986, more than 6.6 million voters participated, representing 99.9% of those registered and eligible to vote. Two political parties participated in the election: the Bulgarian Communist Party and the Agrarian Union. Of the deputies elected, 276 were members of the Bulgarian Communist Party, 99 were members of the Agrarian Union, and 25 were without party affiliation. The Agrarian Union, once Bulgaria's largest political party, does not compete with the Bulgarian Communist Party; and more than 99.9% of the votes cast were for candidates of a single, unified slate presented to the voters by the two parties. Bulgaria has been under communist rule since 9 September 1944, when a coalition known as the Fatherland Front seized power as Soviet troops marched into the country without resistance. Its 1971 constitution is modelled after the constitution of the Union of Soviet Socialist Republics and stipulates in its first article that "the leading force in society and in the State is the Bulgarian Communist Party."

Although the Bulgarian people were repeatedly subjected to discrimination and forced assimilation during periods of colonial occupation by the Ottoman Turks and although Bulgaria was an ally of Germany during the World Wars I and II, all strata of Bulgarian society firmly resisted attempts to hand over Bulgarian Jews to Nazi occupation forces during World War II, saving the lives of tens of thousands of people.

In recent years, Bulgaria adopted measures to overcome the backwardness of its Gypsy population, to improve their way of life and to raise their standard of living. These measures include the construction of housing, the establishment of children's homes, and the integration of Gypsy children into public educational institutions.

The government discourages the practice of religion, and there are no official statistics on the number of persons practicing a religion or belief. Most Bulgarians who practice a religion belong to the Bulgarian Orthodox Church; Roman Catholicism, Protestantism, Islam, and Judaism are also officially recognized. The State renders assistance to all faiths which it recognizes, supplements their budgets, provides relief from various taxes, and takes care of the protection and restoration of historical and cultural monuments of a religious nature.

Relations between Bulgaria's slavic majority and its large ethnic Turkish minority have been strained for many years. At the Sixteenth Islamic Conference of Foreign Ministers, held at Fez, Morocco, from 6 to 10 January 1986, a resolution on the plight of the Turkish–Muslim minority in Bulgaria was adopted, under which the secretary-general of the Organization of the Islamic Conference was entrusted with the task of appointing a three-member contact group composed of eminent personalities to examine the condition of the Muslim minority in Bulgaria. The contact group visited Bulgaria for this purpose in June 1987. In its report, submitted to the Seventeenth Islamic Conference of Foreign Ministers convened at Amman, Jordan, from 21 to 25 March 1988, the group summarized its conclusions as follows (UN Doc. A/ 43/230):

That the Muslims in Bulgaria have been subjected to official pressure and coercion in changing their Islamic names into Bulgarian/Slavic ones, which has the effect of destroying their Islamic identity;

That the Muslims in Bulgaria have been denied the right to follow their religion freely and that some of their religious rituals/rites, such as circumcision of young children, have been prohibited on pain of criminal prosecution;

That the Muslims in Bulgaria have been denied free use of their places of worship (mosques), and the restrictions on their use on a particular day in a week or on a particular time only is a negation of a basic religious right of Muslims;

That the Muslims in Bulgaria, the majority of whom are of Turkish origin, have been prohibited and denied the right to use their own language and to protect and preserve their cultural heritage, on pain of criminal prosecution and punishment for violation of such prohibition; and

That there are several cases of split families because of the migration of Muslims from Bulgaria to Turkey and that in some such cases, very close relations such as fathers, mothers, sons and daughters were separated from each other.

The circulation of excerpts from the contact group's report to the UN General Assembly at the request of the permanent representative of Turkey was protested by the permanent representative of Bulgaria, who stated (UN Doc. A/43/320):

The aforementioned report demonstrates that, in spite of its June 1987 visit to Bulgaria, the contact group has in fact elected to ignore its mandate and the truth about Bulgarian Muslims. In its own admission, the contact group did not take into consideration either what it had observed in Bulgaria or the information provided by the Bulgarian side. The report submitted on its behalf is written entirely on the basis of argumentation whose total mendacity and pronounced tendentiousness have been exposed time and again by the Bulgarian side, including by the Muslims of Bulgaria themselves.

The process of democratic reform proceeded at a slower pace in Bulgaria than in some other eastern European countries, reflecting perhaps Bulgaria's long history of Turkish domination and its 35 years of hardline Stalinist rule by Todor I. Zhivkov. A new party leadership replaced Zhivkov in November 1989 and the new president, Petar Mladenov, began talks with opposition groups—concentrated in the Union of Democratic Forces and in "Support," an independent trade union—after the communist party had undertaken to give up its guaranteed monopoly on power and Parliament had amended the constitution to make it lawful under certain circumstances to criticize the State. Free elections were scheduled to be held in May 1990, but some opposition groups pointed out that this did not give them time to make the necessary preparations, thus favoring continuation of the communist regime.

BURKINA FASO. A country in western Africa, formerly known as Upper Volta. It has borders with Benin, Ghana, Mali, Niger, and Togo. It achieved independence from France in 1960 and became a member of the United Nations the same year. Its population is estimated by the UN (1990) to be 7,923,000.

The Upper Volta, as it is still popularly called despite the official change of name in 1984, is a multinational State and a melting pot of peoples; more than 60 ethnic groups of varying size are included in its population. Among these groups are the Mossi, 48%; the Peul, 10%, the Lobi-Dagarai, 7%; the Mandé, 6.9%; the Bobo, 6.7%; the Sénoufo, 5.4%; the Gourounsi, 5.3%; the Bissa, 4.7%; and the Gourmantché, 4.5%. Each ethnic group has its own spoken language more or less widely used; the Mooré language, spoken by the Mossi, covers almost the entire central plateau of the Upper Volta and is increasingly spreading into many regions of the country. Bambara or Jula is widely spoken in large towns and other ur-

ban areas. The western Atlantic groups understand Poulon or Fulfuldé, a language spoken in the Sahel and by a few scattered groups of Peul. Religions practiced include Animism (67.8%), Islam (27.5%), and Christianity (Roman Catholic, 3.7%; and Protestant, .1%). Literacy is estimated at 10%.

The government (1990) took the form of a National Revolutionary Council, the president of which is head of State; the council acceded to power after the popular uprising of 4 August 1983 which followed a series of coups d'état (November 1980, November 1982, and May 1983).

Labor unrest and repeated allegations of government inefficiency have been major destabilizing factors in Burkina Faso since 1960, when the first constitution provided for the election of a president and members of a National Assembly by universal suffrage, for terms of five years.

A general strike and series of violent street demonstrations, organized by labor unions, forced the first president, Maurice Yameogo, to resign on 3 January 1966. The residency was taken over by Lt. Col. Aboubakar Sangoule Lamizana, chief of staff of the army, who suspended the constitution but announced that he intended to restore civilian rule after four years.

On 14 June 1970, the second constitution was adopted, establishing the four-year transition period. However, the government found itself paralyzed by a dispute between the prime minister and the National Assembly early in 1974, whereupon President Lamizana suspended the second constitution, dismissed the Cabinet and National Assembly, and postponed the return to civilian control.

A third constitution was adopted and a complete return to civilian government was carried out by late November 1977, and elections were held in April and May, 1978. President Lamizana, who had directed the transition, was returned to office. However, he found himself unable to resolve major differences with several labor unions; and, after a two-month teachers' strike, he was overthrown in a bloodless coup on 25 November 1980. Colonel Saye Zerbo, leader of the Military Committee for Reform and National Progress, assumed the presidency, suspended the third constitution, and dissolved the National Assembly.

A two-year period elapsed before still another coup ousted Col. Zerbo and established the People's Salvation Council, headed by Maj.-Dr. Jean-Baptiste Ouedraogo, as the supreme governing authority. The council, composed of 117 military personnel of various ranks and services, guaranteed the enjoyment of human rights so long as they did not threaten national security or public order, and promised a return to democratically elected civilian government by November 1984.

B

The People's Salvation Council was ousted, in turn, by a coup organized by Capt. Thomas Sankara—a follower of Libya Muammar Qadhafi—who had once served as prime minister in the Ouedraogo government, had been dismissed and imprisoned, and eventually had been released in an effort to end discord within the army leadership. Upon taking office, Sankara formed the National Council for the Revolution with himself as president, established a number of committees for the "Defense of the Revolution" to mobilize the masses and to carry out political education and restructuring functions, and announced the goal of the revolution to be a national, independent, self-sufficient planned economy. To signal the absence of any tie to its colonial past, the name of the country was changed to Burkina Faso ("Land of the Upright Men").

The National Council did not hesitate to discharge teachers who went on strike in March 1984, to imprison the leaders of the largest radical trade union, and to continue the ban on political activity. Its Popular Revolutionary Tribunals tried and sentenced a number of former government officials. Its policies with reference to human rights were announced on 2 October 1983 by President Sankara as follows:

One of the essential concerns of the National Revolutionary Council is to unite the various nationalities in the Upper Volta in the common struggle against the enemies of our revolution. In our country, there is a multitude of ethnic groups differing from one another in language and customs. All these groups together make up the Upper Voltan nation. Imperialism, with its policy of divide and rule, has done its utmost to exacerbate the differences between them to set them against each other. CNR policy will aim at joining together these different nationalities so that they can live in equality and enjoy the same opportunities. For this purpose, special stress will be laid on economic development of the various regions, the promotion of trade between them, combatting prejudices among ethnic groups and settling differences between them in a spirit of unity, and punishing those who sow dissention.

However, on 15 October 1989, President Sankara was overthrown by his second-in-command, Capt. Blaise Compaore. A unit of Capt. Compaore's commandos shot Sankara and 12 aides and buried their bodies in a common grave, supposedly to prevent President Sankara from carrying out a plot to kill Capt. Compaore. The new government, known as the Popular Front, has not been able to win either widespread civilian support or strong military backing.

BURMA. *SEE Myanmar.*

BURUNDI. The Republic of Burundi is a country in eastern Africa. It has borders with Rwanda, the United Republic of Tanzania, and Zaire. Burundi was originally part of a single United Nations trust territory known as Rwanda–Urundi, which was under Belgian administration. Its first national elections were held in January 1961 under UN supervision. On 1 July 1962, the General Assembly, in cooperation with Belgium, terminated the trusteeship agreement and recognized two independent States: Burundi and Rwanda. Burundi became a member of the United Nations the same year. Its population is estimated by the UN (1990) to be 5,443,000. Ethnic groups include the Hutu (85%), the Tutsi (14%), and the Twa (1%). Languages commonly used include Kirundi (official), French, and Swahili. Religions practiced include Christianity (Roman Catholic, 78%; Protestant denominations, 5%), Animism (17%), and Islam (1%). Literacy is estimated at 25%.

The government (1990) took the form of a republic. Under the 1974 constitution, Burundi is "a unitary, secular and democratic Republic," with no State religion and protection of the right of everyone to choose or not to choose a religious belief. The president is head of State and of government. Since 1976, the presidency has been filled by the head of the National Party of Unity and Progress, the only recognized political party. There is a 19-member Cabinet and a 65-member National Assembly, members of which are elected by universal adult suffrage.

Although the Hutu tribesmen, who are farmers of Bantu origin, comprise 85% of the country's population, and the Tutsi tribesmen, who are warrior-pastoralists of Nilotic origin, comprise less than 15%—and although both speak the same language and frequently intermarry—the minority Tutsis have controlled the government of Burundi since the day of independence. Their domination has deep roots but appears to be based, at least in part, on size: they are noticeably taller than the Hutus, and tower over the pygmy Twa (who average 5 feet, 1 inch, in height).

Serious intertribal conflicts broke out soon after independence. In 1965, and again in 1969, the Tutsis prevailed after killing hundreds of Hutus. Early in 1972, the Hutus attacked and killed about 2,000 Tutsis. The government retaliated with a countrywide massacre in which members of the police force and youth organizations methodically slaughtered some 150,000 Hutus, including most of that group's educated elite. About 100,000 more were forced to seek refuge in neighboring Rwanda, Tanzania, and Zaire.

A United Nations mission visited Burundi between 22 and 28 June 1972 and confirmed reports that between 80,000 and 200,000 had died in Burundi, that approximately 500,000 people were in need of assistance, that 40,000 refugees in Rwanda, Tanzania, and Zaire were also in need of assistance, and that a great number of houses, schools, hospitals, and other public buildings had been destroyed by the conflict.

New violence erupted in mid-May 1973 and continued through July of that year, in which further mass killings of Hutus were reported to be comparable in number to those of 1972. In this case, the ORGANIZATION OF AFRICAN UNITY assumed responsibility for dealing with the conflict, considering it a possible threat to African peace.

In their efforts to avoid involvement in the internal affairs of Burundi, the United Nations and most of its members, including the United States of America, dealt with the crisis in Burundi as a "humanitarian disaster" and a refugee problem, rather than as a series of gross violations of human rights or as a case of genocide. Their activities were confined for the most part to factfinding and to providing assistance to refugees and other displaced persons.

The Burundi Government headed by Col. Jean-Baptiste Bagaza—in which three-quarters of the Cabinet and the National Assembly and nearly all army officers were Tutsis—called for tribal reconciliation and national unity and arranged for many refugees to return to Burundi and to regain the possessions left behind when they fled from the country. Hutus, for their part, did not raise the issue of majority rule again. In 1984, President Bagaza was re-elected, receiving 99.63% of the vote; however, he was deposed on 3 September 1987, while attending a conference in Quebec, Canada. His successor, Maj. Pierre Buyoya, is also a member of the Tutsi tribe.

The tribal situation in Burundi erupted again in mid-1988 and was such that large numbers of people were forced to flee the country. Ethnic violence which erupted in mid-August between the ruling Tutsi tribe and the majority Hutus resulted in the massacre of more than 5,000 persons. Most of the deaths were attributed to Tutsi soldiers who turned their arms against the unarmed Hutu people. As a consequence, more than 35,000 Hutu refugees fled to nearby Rwanda.

At its 1988 session, the Sub-Commission on Prevention of Discrimination and Protection of Minorities, having received information on events which had caused mass exoduses of refugees from Burundi, requested the secretary-general (resolution 1988/1) to offer assistance to the government, under the program of UNITED NATIONS ADVISORY SERVICES IN THE FIELD OF HUMAN RIGHTS, needed for dealing with the situation and its causes.

Before his deposition, Col. Bagaza initiated a campaign aimed at the Catholic Church. Burundi's Catholic newspaper and radio station were shut down, religious gatherings without government approval were banned, and Catholic schools were closed. These activities, together with a shortage of priests and nuns, threatened to shut down most of Burundi's 1,144 Catholic parishes.

BYELORUSSIAN S.S.R. The Byelorussian Soviet Socialist Republic is a constituent unit of the UNION OF SOVIET SOCIALIST REPUBLICS. It has borders with Poland, the Latvian S.S.R., the Lithuanian S.S.R., the Russian Soviet Federated Socialist Republic, and the Ukrainian S.S.R. In accordance with an agreement reached before the preparation of the UNITED NATIONS CHARTER, the Byelorussian S.S.R. became a member of the United Nations in its own right in 1945. Ethnic and national groups include Byelorussians (80%), Russians (12%), Poles (4%), Ukrainians (2%), and Jews (2%). Languages in common use include Byelorussian and Russian; members of national minorities tend to use their own language in private discourse. Atheism predominates, and anti-religious propaganda and activity occurs. Among those who maintain a religious belief, Christianity (Roman Catholic and Russian Orthodox) and Judaism have the most adherents. The Church is separated from the State and the school from the Church.

The government (1990) took the form of a republic within the Union of Soviet Socialist Republics. Under article 78 of the Byelorussian constitution, the Soviets of People's Deputies—i.e., the Supreme Soviet; the Soviets of People's Deputies of regions; and the Soviets of People's Deputies of districts, cities, districts, settlements, and villages—constitute a single system of bodies of State authority. Members of the Supreme Soviet serve for a term of five years; those of local soviets for a term of two and one-half years. Soviets of People's Deputies direct all sectors of State economic, social, and cultural development; take decisions, ensure their execution, and verify their implementation.

For provisions of the constitution which relate to human rights, see BYELORUSSIAN S.S.R.: CONSTITUTION. For detailed information on changes in the law and practice of the Soviet Union as a whole affecting the realization of civil, political, and other human rights and fundamental freedoms, see UNION OF SOVIET SOCIALIST REPUBLICS: IMPLEMENTATION OF THE INTERNATIONAL COVENANT ON CIVIL AND POLITICAL RIGHTS.

Within the Byelorussian S.S.R., one important recent change was reflected in the adoption on 2 February 1988, by the Supreme Soviet, of the Act "On Popular Discussion of Important Problems of the State Life of the Byelorussian S.S.R." *(Collected Acts of the Byelorussian S.S.R.,* 1988, No. 4, p. 55). Under article 4 of the act, citizens are guaranteed free participation in the discussion of important problems of State and public life. The article forbids all direct or indirect restriction of the rights of citizens of the Byelorussian S.S.R. to participate in such discussion on the basis of their origin, social or property status, race or nationality, sex, education, language, attitude to religion, length of residence in a given locality, or type or nature of occupation. Article 10 provides important guarantees as regards citizens' free and equal participation in popular discussions. Officials of State or public bodies who permit the act to be violated and people who prevent citizens from freely exercising their right to participate in discussions are answerable for their actions as provided by law.

BYELORUSSIAN S.S.R.: CONSTITUTION. The Constitution (Fundamental Law) of the Byelorussian Soviet Socialist Republic, adopted at the Ninth Special Session of the Supreme Soviet of the Byelorussian S.S.R., includes the following provisions (articles 31–67) specifically relating to human rights and fundamental freedoms:

Part II
The State and the
Individual

Chapter 5
Citizenship of the Byelorussian SSR.
Equality of Citizens' Rights

Article 31. In accordance with the uniform federal citizenship established for the USSR, every citizen of the Byelorussian SSR is a citizen of the USSR.

The grounds and procedure for acquiring or forfeiting Soviet citizenship are defined by the Law on Citizenship of the USSR.

Citizens of the other Union Republics residing in the Byelorussian SSR enjoy equal rights with citizens of the Byelorussian SSR.

When abroad, citizens of the Byelorussian SSR enjoy the protection and assistance of the Soviet state.

Article 32. Citizens of the Byelorussian SSR are equal before the law, without distinction of origin, social or property status, race or nationality, sex, education, language, attitude to religion, type and nature of occupation, domicile or other status.

The equal rights of citizens of the Byelorussian SSR are guaranteed in all fields of economic, political, social and cultural life.

Article 33. Women and men have equal rights in the Byelorussian SSR.

Exercise of these rights is ensured by according women equal access with men to education and vocational and professional training, equal opportunities in employment, remuneration, and in social and political and cultural activity, and by special labour and health protection measures for women; by providing conditions enabling mothers to work; by legal protection and material and moral support for mothers and children, including paid leaves and other benefits for expectant mothers and mothers, and gradual reduction of working time for mothers with small children.

Article 34. Citizens of the Byelorussian SSR of different races and nationalities have equal rights.

Exercise of these rights is ensured by a policy of all-round development and drawing together of all the nations and nationalities of the USSR, by educating citizens in the spirit of Soviet patriotism and socialist internationalism, and by the possibility to use their native language and the languages of other peoples of the USSR.

Any direct or indirect limitation of the rights of citizens or establishment of direct or indirect privileges on grounds of race or nationality, and any advocacy of racial or national exclusiveness, hostility or contempt, are punishable by law.

Article 35. Citizens of other countries and stateless persons in the Byelorussian SSR are guaranteed the rights and freedoms provided by law, including the right to apply to a court and other state bodies for the protection of their personal, property, family and other rights.

Citizens of other countries and stateless persons, when in the Byelorussian SSR, are obliged to respect the Constitution of the USSR, the Constitution of the Byelorussian SSR and observe Soviet laws.

Article 36. The Byelorussian SSR grants the right of asylum to foreigners persecuted for defending the interests of the working people and the cause of peace, or for participation in the revolutionary and national-liberation movement, or for progressive social and political, scientific or other creative activity.

Chapter 6
The Basic Rights, Freedoms and Duties of
Citizens of the Byelorussian SSR

Article 37. Citizens of the Byelorussian SSR enjoy in full the social, economic, political and personal rights and freedoms proclaimed and guaranteed by the Constitution of the USSR, the Constitution of the Byelorussian SSR and by Soviet laws. The socialist system ensures enlargement of the rights and freedoms of citizens and continuous improvement of their living standards as social, economic and cultural development programmes are fulfilled.

Enjoyment by citizens of their rights and freedoms must not be to the detriment of the interests of society or the state, or infringe the rights of other citizens.

Article 38. Citizens of the Byelorussian SSR have the right to work (that is, to guaranteed employment and pay in accordance with the quantity and quality of their work, and not below the state-established minimum), including the right to choose their trade or profession, type of job and work in accordance with their inclinations, abilities, training and education, with due account of the needs of society.

This right is ensured by the socialist economic system, steady growth of the productive forces, free vocational and professional training, improvement of skills, training in new trades or professions, and development of the systems of vocational guidance and job placement.

Article 39. Citizens of the Byelorussian SSR have the right to rest and leisure.

This right is ensured by the establishment of a working week not exceeding 41 hours for workers and other employees, a shorter working day in a number of trades and industries, and shorter hours for night work; by the provision of paid annual holidays, weekly days of rest, extension of the network of cultural, educational and health-building institutions, and the development on a mass scale of sport, physical culture and camping and tourism; by the provision of neighbourhood recreational facilities and of other opportunities for rational use of free time.

The length of collective farmers' working and leisure time is established by their collective farms.

Article 40. Citizens of the Byelorussian SSR have the right to health protection.

This right is ensured by free, qualified medical care provided by state health institutions; by extension of the network of therapeutic and health-building institutions; by the development and improvement of safety and hygiene in industry; by carrying out broad prophylactic measures; by measures to improve the environment; by special care for the health of the rising generation, including prohibition of child labour, excluding the work done by children as part of the school curriculum; and by developing research to prevent and reduce the incidence of disease and ensure citizens a long and active life.

Article 41. Citizens of the Byelorussian SSR have the right to maintenance in old age, in sickness, and in the event of complete or partial disability or loss of the breadwinner.

This right is guaranteed by social insurance of workers and other employees and collective farmers; by allowances for temporary disability; by the provision by the state or by collective farms of retirement pensions, disability pensions, and pensions for loss of the breadwinner; by providing employment for the partially disabled; by care for the elderly and the disabled; and by other forms of social security.

Article 42. Citizens of the Byelorussian SSR have the right to housing.

This right is ensured by the development and upkeep of state and socially-owned housing; by assistance for cooperative and individual house building; by fair distribution, under public control, of the housing that becomes available through fulfilment of the programme of building well-appointed dwellings, and by low rents and low charges for utility services. Citizens of the Byelorussian SSR shall take good care of the housing allocated to them.

Article 43. Citizens of the Byelorussian SSR have the right to education.

This right is ensured by free provision of all forms of education, by the institution of universal, compulsory secondary education, and broad development of vocational, specialized secondary and higher education, in which instruction is oriented toward practical activity and production; by the development of extramural, correspondence and evening courses; by the provision of state scholarships and grants and privileges for students; by the free issue of school textbooks; by the opportunity to attend a school where teaching is in the native language; and by the provision of facilities for self-education.

Article 44. Citizens of the Byelorussian SSR have the right to enjoy cultural benefits.

This right is ensured by broad access to the cultural treasures of their own land and of the world that are preserved in state and other public collections; by the development and fair distribution of cultural and educational institutions throughout the country; by developing television and radio broadcasting and the publishing of books, newspapers and periodicals, and by extending the free library service; and by expanding cultural exchanges with other countries.

Article 45. Citizens of the Byelorussian SSR, in accordance with the aims of building communism, are guaranteed freedom of scientific, technical and artistic work. This freedom is ensured by broadening scientific research, encouraging invention and innovation, and developing literature and the arts. The state provides the necessary material conditions for this and support for voluntary societies and unions of workers in the arts, organizes introduction of inventions and innovations in production and other spheres of activity.

The rights of authors, inventors and innovators are protected by the state.

Article 46. Citizens of the Byelorussian SSR have the right to take part in the management and administration of state and public affairs and in the discussion and adoption of laws and measures of All-Union and local significance.

This right is ensured by the opportunity to vote and to be elected to Soviets of People's Deputies and other elective state bodies, to take part in nationwide discussions and referendums, in people's control, in the work of state bodies, public organizations and local community groups, and in meetings at places of work or residence.

Article 47. Every citizen of the Byelorussian SSR has the right to submit proposals to state bodies and public organizations for improving their activity, and to criticize shortcomings in their work.

Officials are obliged, within established time-limits, to examine citizens' proposals and requests, to reply to them and to take appropriate action.

Persecution for criticism is prohibited. Persons guilty of such persecution shall be called to account.

Article 48. In accordance with the interests of the people and in order to strengthen and develop the socialist system, citizens of the Byelorussian SSR are guaranteed freedom of speech, of the press and of assembly, meetings, street processions and demonstrations.

Exercise of these political freedoms is ensured by putting public buildings, streets and squares at the disposal of the working people and their organizations, by broad dissemination of information, and by the opportunity to use the press, television and radio.

Article 49. In accordance with the aims of building communism, citizens of the Byelorussian SSR have the right to associate in public organizations that promote their political activity and initiative and satisfaction of their various interests.

Public organizations are guaranteed conditions for successfully performing the functions defined in their rules.

Article 50. Citizens of the Byelorussian SSR are guaranteed freedom of conscience, that is, the right to profess or not to profess any religion, and to conduct religious worship or atheistic propaganda. Incitement of hostility or hatred on religious grounds is prohibited.

In the Byelorussian SSR the church is separated from the state and the school from the church.

Article 51. The family enjoys the protection of the state.

Marriage is based on the free consent of the woman and the man; the spouses are completely equal in their family relations.

The state helps the family by providing and developing a broad system of child-care institutions, by organizing and improving communal services and public catering, by paying grants on the birth of a child, by providing children's allowances and benefits for large families, and other forms of family allowances and assistance.

Article 52. Citizens of the Byelorussian SSR are guaranteed inviolability of the person. No one may be arrested except by a court decision or on the warrant of a procurator.

Article 53. Citizens of the Byelorussian SSR are guaranteed inviolability of the home. No one may, without lawful grounds, enter a home against the will of those residing in it.

Article 54. The privacy of citizens and of their correspondence, telephone conversations and telegraphic communications is protected by law.

Article 55. Respect for the individual and protection of the rights and freedoms of citizens are the duty of all state bodies, public organizations and officials.

Citizens of the Byelorussian SSR have the right to protection by the courts against encroachments on their honour and reputation, life and health, and personal freedom and property.

Article 56. Citizens of the Byelorussian SSR have the right to lodge a complaint against the actions of officials, state bodies and public bodies. Complaints shall be examined according to the procedure and within the time-limit established by law.

Actions by officials that contravene the law or exceed their powers and infringe the rights of citizens, may be appealed against in a court in the manner prescribed by law.

Citizens of the Byelorussian SSR have the right to compensation for damage resulting from unlawful actions by state organizations and public organizations, or by officials in the performance of their duties.

Article 57. Citizens' exercise of their rights and freedoms is inseparable from the performance of their duties and obligations.

Citizens of the Byelorussian SSR are obliged to observe the Constitution of the USSR, the Constitution of the Byelorussian SSR and Soviet laws, comply with the standards of socialist conduct, and uphold the honour and dignity of Soviet citizenship.

Article 58. It is the duty of, and a matter of honour for, every able-bodied citizen of the Byelorussian SSR to work conscientiously in his chosen, socially useful occupation, and strictly to observe labour discipline. Evasion of socially useful work is incompatible with the principles of socialist society.

Article 59. Citizens of the Byelorussian SSR are obliged to preserve and protect socialist property. It is the duty of a citizen of the Byelorussian SSR to combat misappropriation and squandering of state and socially-owned property and to make thrifty use of the people's wealth.

Persons encroaching in any way on socialist property shall be punished according to the law.

Article 60. Citizens of the Byelorussian SSR are obliged to safeguard the interests of the Soviet state, and to enhance its power and prestige.

Defence of the Socialist Motherland is the sacred duty of every citizen of the USSR.

Betrayal of the Motherland is the gravest of crimes against the people.

Article 61. Military service in the ranks of the Armed Forces of the USSR is an honourable duty of Byelorussian citizens.

Article 62. It is the duty of every citizen of the Byelorussian SSR to respect the national dignity of other citizens, and to strengthen friendship of the nations and nationalities of the multinational Soviet state.

Article 63. A citizen of the Byelorussian SSR is obliged to respect the rights and lawful interests of other persons, to be uncompromising toward anti-social behaviour, and to help maintain public order.

Article 64. Citizens of the Byelorussian SSR are obliged to concern themselves with the upbringing of children, to train them for socially useful work, and to raise them as worthy members of socialist society. Children are obliged to care for their parents and help them.

Article 65. Citizens of the Byelorussian SSR are obliged to protect nature and conserve its riches.

Article 66. Concern for the preservation of historical monuments and other cultural values is a duty and obligation of citizens of the Byelorussian SSR.

Article 67. It is the international duty of citizens of the Byelorussian SSR to promote friendship and cooperation with peoples of other lands and help maintain and strengthen world peace.

C

CAIRO DECLARATION: PROGRAM FOR PEACE AND INTERNATIONAL COOPERATION (1964).

The declaration, adopted by the Conference of Heads of State or Government of Non-Aligned Countries, in Cairo, on 10 October 1964, sets out a comprehensive program for peace and international cooperation covering a wide range of activity. Those portions of the declaration (conference document NAC-II/5) which relate to human rights concerns are reproduced below.

Introduction

. . . The Conference notes with satisfaction that the movements of national liberation are engaged in different regions of the world, in a heroic struggle against neo-colonialism, and the practices of apartheid and racial discrimination. This struggle forms part of the common striving towards freedom, justice and peace.

The Conference reaffirms that interference by economically developed foreign States in the internal affairs of newly independent, developing countries and the existence of territories which are still dependent constitute a standing threat to peace and security. . . .

I. Concerted Action for the Liberation of the Countries Still Dependent, Elimination of Colonialism, Neo-Colonialism and Imperialism

The Heads of State or Government of the Non-Aligned Countries declare that lasting world peace cannot be realized so long as unjust conditions prevail and peoples under foreign domination continue to be deprived of their fundamental right to freedom, independence and self-determination.

Imperialism, colonialism and neo-colonialism constitute a basic source of international tension and conflict because they endanger world peace and security. The participants in the Conference deplore that the Declaration of the United Nations on the granting of independence to colonial countries and peoples has not been implemented everywhere and call for the unconditional, complete and final abolition of colonialism now.

At present a particular cause of concern is the military or other assistance extended to certain countries to enable them to perpetuate by force colonialist and neo-colonialist situations which are contrary to the spirit of the Charter of the United Nations.

The exploitation by colonialist forces of the difficulties and problems of recently liberated or developing countries, interference in the internal affairs of these States, and colonialist attempts to maintain unequal relationships, particularly in the economic field, constitute serious dangers to these young countries. Colonialism and neo-colonialism have many forms and manifestations.

Imperialism uses many devices to impose its will on independent nations. Economic pressure and domination, interference, racial discrimination, subversion, intervention and the threat of force are neo-colonialist devices against which the newly independent nations have to defend themselves. The Conference condemns all colonialist, neo-colonialist and imperialist policies applied in various parts of the world. . . .

The newly independent countries have, like all other countries, the right of sovereign disposal in regard to their natural resources, and the right to utilize these resources as they deem appropriate in the interest of their peoples, without outside interference.

The process of liberation is irresistible and irreversible. Colonized peoples may legitimately resort to arms to secure the full exercise of their right to self-determination and independence if the colonial powers persist in opposing their natural aspirations.

The participants in the Conference undertake to work unremittingly to eradicate all vestiges of colonialism, and to combine all their efforts to render all necessary aid and support, whether moral, political or material, to the peoples struggling against colonialism and neo-colonialism. The participating countries recognize the nationalist movements of the peoples which are struggling to free themselves from colonial domination as being authentic representatives of the colonial peoples, and urgently call upon the colonial Powers to negotiate with their leaders. . . .

The Conference recommends that all necessary political, moral and material assistance be rendered to the liberation movements of these territories in their struggle against colonial rule. . . .

II. Respect for the Right of Peoples to Self-Determination and Condemnation of the Use of Force Against the Exercise of This Right

The Conference solemnly reaffirms the right of peoples to self-determination and to make their own destiny.

It stresses that this right constitutes one of the essential principles of the United Nations Charter, that it was laid down also in the Charter of the Organization of African Unity, and that the Conferences of Bandung and Belgrade demanded that it should be respected, and in particular insisted that it should be effectively exercised.

The Conference notes that this right is still violated or its exercise denied in many regions of the world and results in a continued increase of tension and the extension of the areas of war.

The Conference denounces the attitude of those Powers which oppose the exercise of the right of peoples to self-determination.

It condemns the use of force, and all forms of intimidation, interference and intervention which are aimed at preventing the exercise of this right.

III. Racial Discrimination and the Policy of Apartheid

The Heads of State or Government declare that racial discrimination—and particularly its most odious manifestation, apartheid—constitutes a violation of the Universal Declaration of Human Rights and of the principle of the equality of peoples. Accordingly, all Governments still persisting in the practice of racial discrimination should be completely ostracized until they have abandoned their unjust and inhuman policies. . . .

IV. Peaceful Coexistence and the Codification of the Principles by the United Nations

. . . Reaffirming their deep conviction that, in present circumstances, mankind must regard peaceful coexistence as the only way to strengthen world peace, which must be based on freedom, equality and justice between peoples within a new framework of peaceful and harmonious relations between the States and nations of the world;

Considering the fact that the principle of peaceful coexistence is based on the right of all peoples to be free and to choose their own political, economic and social systems according to their own national identity and their ideals, and is opposed to any form of foreign domination;

Convinced also that peaceful coexistence cannot be fully achieved throughout the world without the abolition of imperialism, colonialism and neo-colonialism;. . .

The Heads of State or Government solemnly proclaim the following fundamental principles of peaceful coexistence:

1. The right to complete independence, which is an inalienable right, must be recognized immediately and unconditionally as pertaining to all peoples, in conformity with the Charter and resolutions of the United Nations General Assembly; it is incumbent upon all States to respect this right and facilitate its exercise.

2. The right to self-determination, which is an inalienable right, must be recognized as pertaining to all peoples, accordingly, all nations and peoples have the right to determine their political status and freely pursue their economic, social and cultural development without intimidation or hindrance.

3. Peaceful coexistence between States with different social and political systems is both possible and necessary; it favours the creation of good-neighbourly relations between States with a view to the establishment of lasting peace and general well being, free from domination and exploitation.

4. The sovereign equality of States must be recognized and respected. It includes the right of all peoples to the free exploitation of their natural resources. . . .

6. All States shall respect the fundamental rights and freedoms of the human person and the equality of all nations and races. . . .

(3) The Conference solemnly reaffirms the right of all peoples to adopt the form of government they consider best suited to their development. . . .

IX. The United Nations: Its Role in International Affairs, Implementation of its Resolutions and Amendment of Its Charter

The participating countries declare:

The United Nations Organization was established to promote international peace and security, to develop international understanding and co-operation, to safeguard human rights and fundamental freedom and to achieve all the purposes of the Charter. In order to be an effective instrument, the United Nations Organization must be open to all the States of the world. It is particularly necessary that countries still under colonial domination should attain independence without delay and take their rightful place in the community of nations.

It is essential for the effective functioning of the United Nations that all nations should observe its fundamental principles of peaceful coexistence, co-operation, renunciation of the threat or the use of force, freedom and equality without discrimination on grounds of race, sex, language or religion. . . .

The Conference recognizes the paramount importance of the United Nations and the necessity of enabling it to carry out the functions entrusted to it to preserve international co-operation among States. . . .

XI. Cultural, Scientific and Educational Co-operation and Consolidation of the International and Regional Organizations Working for This Purpose

The Heads of State or Government participating in the Conference:

Considering that the political, economic, social and cultural problems of mankind are so interrelated as to demand concerted action;

Considering that co-operation in the fields of culture, education and science is necessary for the deepening of human understanding, for the consolidation of freedom, justice and peace, and for progress and development; . . .

Appreciating the work of the international and regional organizations in the promotion of educational, scientific and cultural co-operation among nations;

Believing that such co-operation among nations in the educational, scientific and cultural fields should be strengthened and expanded;

Recommend that international co-operation in education should be promoted in order to secure a fair opportunity for education to every person in every part of the world, to extend educational assistance to develop mutual understanding and appreciation of the different cultures and ways of life through the proper teaching of civics, and to promote international understanding through the teaching of the principles of the United Nations at various levels of education;

Propose that a free and more systematic exchange of scientific information be encouraged and intensified and, in particular, call on the advanced countries to share with developing countries their scientific knowledge and technical knowledge so that the advantages of scientific and technological advance can be applied to the promotion of economic development.

Urge all States to adopt in their legislation the principles embodied in the United Nations Declaration of Human Rights.

Agree that participating countries should adopt measures to strengthen their ties with one another in the fields of education, science and culture.

Express their determination to help, consolidate and strengthen the international and regional organizations working in this direction. . . .

CAMBODIA. This divided country is located in southeastern Asia, situated on the Indochinese Peninsula, facing the Gulf of Thailand. It has borders with Laos, Thailand, and Viet Nam. It achieved independence from France in 1949 and became a member of the United Nations in 1955 as Democratic Kampuchea. Its population is estimated by the UN (1990) to be 8,246,000. Ethnic groups include the Khmer (90%), Chinese (5%), and others including Chams, Vietnamese, and Burmese (5%). Languages commonly in use include Khmer (official), Chinese, French, and Vietnamese. Religions practiced include Buddhism (Theravada), Islam, and Animism. Literacy is estimated at 48%.

The government (1990) took the form of a republic. Under the 1975 constitution, executive authority is exercised by the president, legislation is prepared by a 250-member People's Assembly, and the judiciary is headed by a Supreme Judicial Tribunal. However, constitutional political processes were suspended in 1978, when the country was occupied by Vietnamese troops and a pro-Vietnamese government was installed.

No single government controls all of Cambodia. A coalition government in exile, formed in June 1982 and headed by Prince Samdech Norodom Sihanouk, is recognized by the United Nations; it represents an alliance which ex-President Sihanouk formed with his former prime minister, Son Sann, and Pol Pot's representative, Khieu Samphan, to oppose the regime installed in Phnom Penh by the Vietnamese. That regime, headed by President Heng Samrin, general secretary of the Kampuchean People's Revolutionary Party, administers the machinery of government and controls most of the territory of the country.

Once a part of the extensive Khmer Kingdom, which covered nearly all of Southeast Asia, Cambodia was in danger of being overrun by the neighboring Vietnamese until the French combined it with Laos and Vietnam to form French Indochina. After occupation by the Japanese during the World War II, Cambodia achieved independence within the French Union in 1949. As a result of the French–Indochinese war, the Cambodians, under Prince Sihanouk, won full military control of their country in 1953.

Incursions of Vietnamese into Cambodian territory, and anti-Vietnamese riots, provoked a coup which ended the Sihanouk regime in 1970. As the Vietnamese moved deeper into the country, the new government, headed by Lon Nol, was threatened until U.S. President Richard Nixon sent Vietnamese and American troops to clear them from the border areas. The Vietnam peace agreement of 1973 provided for the withdrawal of all foreign forces from Cambodia; however, sporadic fighting continued until 1975, when the Cambodian government collapsed.

The People's Republic of Kampuchea was established under a new constitution proclaimed in December 1975, under a State presidium headed by Pol Pot. Within the next two years, more than two million Cambodians died as a result of the brutality and other human rights violations of the new regime. On Christmas Day 1978, Vietnamese forces launched a full invasion of Cambodia, capturing Phnom Penh on 7 January and driving the remnants of Cambodia's army towards the Thai borders.

Between 1975 and 1980, thousands of Khmer fled first the terror of Pol Pot and then the attack and occupation by Vietnamese military forces. More than 200,000 were admitted to Thailand as refugees before the border was closed in 1980, more than 205,000 were accepted by third countries, and about 140,000 were admitted to the United States.

Since 1980, fleeing Cambodians have lived in camps along the Thai–Cambodian border. In 1984–85, a Vietnamese attack forced 225,000 of them into Thailand, where they were granted temporary asylum. Food, shelter, and medical care are provided to this population by joint efforts of the Royal Thai government, the United Nations Border Relief Operation, the **INTERNATIONAL COMMITTEE OF THE RED CROSS**, and private voluntary agencies.

The situation in Cambodia and related developments in southeast Asia were considered by the UN Security Council at a series of meetings held between January and March 1979, but the council was unable to reach a decision on action to be taken by the international community. The General Assembly, at its 1979 session, appealed to all States and national and international humanitarian organizations to render humanitarian relief to the civilian population involved, called for a cessation of hostilities and immediate withdrawal of all foreign forces, and resolved that the people of Cambodia should be enabled to choose their own government without outside interference, subversion, or coercion. In 1981, the assembly convened an international conference on Cambodia with the aim of working out a comprehensive settlement of the problem including the total withdrawal of foreign troops and United Nations-supervised free elections. The conference, held in New York from 13 to 17 July 1981, adopted a "Declaration on Kampuchea," in which it reaffirmed the basic principles for a political settlement in that nation and set out the elements of such a settlement. However, the declaration was not implemented.

The resulting human rights situation has been of great concern to the UN COMMISSION ON HUMAN RIGHTS since 1978. The commission has stated on several occasions that "the continued illegal occupation of Kampuchea by foreign forces deprives the people of Kampuchea of the exercise of their right to self-determination and constitutes the primary violation of human rights in Kampuchea. . . ." The commission has also pointed out that "the continuing illegal occupation of Kampuchea and the reported demographic changes imposed by foreign occupation forces in Kampuchea are a threat to the survival of the Kampuchean people and culture."

At its 1987, session the commission, in resolution 1987/6 of 19 February 1987, deplored the continued violations of fundamental human rights, the principles of international law, and the Charter of the United Nations—particularly the repeated military attacks and shelling by the occupying troops directed against Cambodian civilians, over 250,000 of whom had been forced to seek temporary refuge in UN-assisted evacuation sites along the Thai border—and further deplored the displacement of the Cambodian population. The commission reaffirmed its earlier calls to parties to the conflict "to cease all hostilities forthwith," and to withdraw immediately and unconditionally in order that:

(a) The Kampuchean people, free from any foreign interference, aggression and coercion, will be able to exercise their fundamental and inalienable human rights in their totality and indivisibility;

(b) The United Nations may be able to offer its services effectively in the field of human rights and fundamental freedoms in Kampuchea;

(c) In the exercise of their fundamental freedoms and inalienable rights, the Kampuchean people will then be able to choose and determine their own future through free and fair elections under United Nations supervision;

(d) The exercise of the right of all Kampuchean refugees to return to their homeland in safety may be made possible;

(e) Efforts towards a comprehensive political solution to the Kampuchean problem, within the framework of the Declaration on Kampuchea of 17 July 1981 and the relevant United Nations resolutions, may be pursued with a view to establishing an independent, free and non-aligned Kampuchea and thereby achieving durable peace in South-East Asia.

At its 1988 and 1989 sessions, the commission reiterated (resolutions 1988/6 and 1989/20) its condemnation of the persistent occurrence of gross and flagrant violations of human rights in Cambodia and emphasized that the Cambodian people should be enabled to exercise their inalienable right to self-determination through free, fair, and democratic elections under United Nations supervision.

In January 1990, a two-day meeting of the five permanent members of the UN Security Council—China, France, the United Kingdom of Great Britain and Northern Ireland, the United States of America, and the Union of Soviet Socialist Republic—was held in Paris to consider the situation in Cambodia. On 16 June 1990, they agreed that they would be guided by the following principles in working for a resolution of the problem:

No acceptable solution can be achieved by force of arms.

An enduring peace can only be achieved through a comprehensive political settlement including the verified withdrawal of foreign forces, a cease-fire and the cessation of outside military assistance.

The goal should be self-determination for the Cambodian people through free, fair and democratic elections.

All accept an enhanced U.N. role in the resolution of the Cambodian problem.

There is an urgent need to speed up diplomatic efforts to achieve a settlement.

The complete withdrawal of foreign forces must be verified by the United Nations.

The five would welcome an early resumption of a constructive dialogue among the Cambodian factions which is essential to facilitating the transition process and which should not be dominated by any one of them.

An effective U.N. presence will be required during the transition period in order to assure internal security.

A special representative of the U.N. Secretary General is needed in Cambodia to supervise U.N. activities during a transition period culminating in the inauguration of a democratically elected government.

The scale of the U.N. operation should be consistent with the successful implementation of a Cambodian settlement and its planning and execution should take account of the heavy financial burden that may be placed on member states.

Free and fair elections must be conducted under direct U.N. administration.

The elections must be conducted in a neutral political environment in which no party would be advantaged.

The five permanent members commit themselves to honouring the results of free and fair elections.

All Cambodians should enjoy the same rights, freedoms and opportunities to participate in the election process.

A supreme National Council might be the repository of Cambodian sovereignty during the transition process.

Questions involving Cambodian sovereignty should be resolved with the agreement of the Cambodian parties.

The five support all responsible efforts by regional parties to achieve a comprehensive political settlement and will remain in close touch with them, with the view to reconvening the Paris conference at an appropriate time. *Source: New York Times*, 17 Jan. 1990

At its 1990 session, the Commission on Human Rights reiterated its conviction (resolution 1990/9)

that the withdrawal of all foreign forces from Cambodia under supervision, control and verification of the United

Nations, the cessation of all outside military assistance, the creation of an interim administering authority, the promotion of national reconciliation among Cambodians under the leadership of Samdech Norodom Sihanouk, the non-return to the universally condemned policies and practices of a recent past, the restoration and preservation of the independence, sovereignty, territorial integrity and neutral and non-aligned status of Cambodia, the reaffirmation of the right of the Cambodian people to determine their own destiny and the commitment by all States to non-interference and non-intervention in the internal affairs of Cambodia, with effective guarantees, are the principal components of any just, lasting and comprehensive political settlement of the Cambodian problem.

The commission called upon all parties concerned to intensify urgently all efforts towards assuring that the Cambodian problem be resolved through a comprehensive political settlement in order to end human rights abuses inflicted upon Cambodians and enable the Cambodian people to determine their own future; to prevent further hostilities, subsequent loss of life, and the continued suffering of the Cambodian people; and to ensure the independence, sovereignty, territorial integrity, neutral and non-aligned status of Cambodia, and the non-return to the universally condemned policies and practices of a recent past. It expressed its conviction that the establishment and realization of a genuine and durable peace in Cambodia can be achieved only through the exercise by the Cambodian people of their inalienable rights and fundamental freedoms in conformity with the true intent, purpose, and spirit of the principles of human rights; and recommended that the UN Economic and Social Council continue to consider and undertake appropriate measures aimed at the early implementation of relevant recommendations with a view to achieving the full enjoyment of the fundamental human rights and freedoms of the Cambodian people, particularly the inalienable right to self-determination. The commission decided to review the situation in Cambodia again at its 1991 session.

In February 1990, the 12 countries of the European community passed a warning to the six countries of the South East Asian Nations Association that they would oppose what had become the normal practice of seating the coalition government headed by Prince Norodom Sihanouk at the September 1990 session of the UN General Assembly on the ground that it includes representatives of the Khmer Rouge. The United States of America and the European community countries have never recognized the coalition as the legitimate government of Cambodia but did not object to its participation in the work of the General Assembly while the country was occupied by the Vietnamese (The last of the Vietnamese forces left Cambodia in September 1989). Withdrawal of the Vietnamese, in their view, changed the conflict in Cambodia into a civil war in which the United Nations could not take sides. However, they encouraged all Cambodian factions to accept the peace plan of the Security Council's five permanent members as a means of ending the impasse.

CAMEROON. The Republic of Cameroon is a country in middle Africa, on the Gulf of Guinea. It has borders with Chad, the Central African Republic, the Congo, Equatorial Guinea, and Gabon. It achieved independence from France in 1960 and became a member of the United Nations the same year. Its population is estimated by the UN (1990) to be 11,359,000. The northern part of the country is inhabited by Sahelian nomadic peoples such as the Peul and the Fulbe, while the Bantu and Pygmies live in the south. Languages commonly used include English and French (both official) and more than 80 African vernaculars. Religions practiced include Christianity (Roman Catholic, 35%; Protestant, 18%), Islam (35%), and Animist (12%). Literacy is estimated at 65%.

The government (1990) took the form of a republic, uniting what were formly East and West Cameroon. Under the 1972 constitution, executive power is vested in the president, elected by popular vote with universal adult suffrage for a term of five years. There is no vice president or prime minister; should the presidency become vacant, its powers are assumed, until the election of a new president, by the president of the General Assembly. The president is assisted by a cabinet of 26 ministers which he appoints. Legislation is handled by the 150-member National Assembly, the members of which are elected for five-year terms which can be extended or shortened by the president. The only political party is the Cameroon National Union.

Unification of ethnic groups and harmozization of their development have always been among the priorities of the government. This desire to ensure national concord is clearly proclaimed in the preamble to the 1972 constitution, which reads:

Proud of its cultural and linguistic diversity, a feature of its national personality which it is helping to enrich, but profoundly aware of the imperative need to achieve complete unity, solemnly declares that it constitutes one and the same nation, committed to the same destiny, and affirms its unshakeable determination to construct the Cameroonian fatherland on the basis of the idea of fraternity, justice and progress.

Once a German colony, the Cameroons were occupied by French and British troops during World

War I. In 1919, the French and British zones became mandates under the League of Nations. In 1946, they were made trust territories of the United Nations. The territory administered by France became an autonomous State in 1957 and an independent country three years later.

Between 1955 and the mid-1960s, Cameroon suffered recurring waves of terrorist activity initiated by the outlawed Union of Cameroon Peoples and supported by radical regimes of nearby countries. Political conciliation was effected only after the last important rebel leader was captured in 1970. Since that time, the Cameroon People's Democratic Movement has dominated the political scene, with the cooperation of a unified labor movement and a variety of associations of women and youth. Traditional kingdoms and tribal organizations are permitted to exercise their customary functions of government among their followers, and the formal court system honors tribal laws and customs when they do not conflict with national law.

After serving four full five-year terms of office, President Ahmadou Ahidjo resigned in November 1982 and was succeded by Prime Minister Paul Biya. After Biya had received his own mandate as president on 25 January 1984, the position of prime minister was abolished. In 1984, the presidential security force attempted to overthrow the government, but the army remained loyal and ended the coup attempt. In March 1985, Biya presided at the Fourth Party Congress at which the party changed its name to the Cameroon People's Democratic Movement.

An act adopted by the National Assembly and promulgated by the president on 4 February 1984 modified the constitution, changing the name of the country from "United Republic of Cameroon" to "Republic of Cameroon," and providing that it be a unitary State, "one and indivisible, secular and devoted to social service."

All governments of the Cameroons have endeavored to re-educate Cameroonians in a spirit of ethnic co-existence so as to enable them to transcend the tribal framework and adjust to the new national dimension. Special social measures have been taken to protect women, youth, and the handicapped in recent years, and a program has been initiated to settle the Pygmies of the country's southeastern forests, an ethnic group estimated to number about 50,000, by regrouping them in village communities and establishing health centers and pilot schools.

CANADA. The second largest country in the world, Canada occupies the northern part of the North American continent. It has a border on the south with the United States of America, marked in part by the Great Lakes, and one in the far northwest, with Alaska. It fronts on the Atlantic, the Pacific, and the Arctic oceans. Canada achieved independence from Great Britain in 1867 and became a member of the United Nations in 1945. Its population is estimated by the UN (1990) to be 26,746,000.

The official census of Canada conducted in 1986 demonstrated that a wide range of ethnic groups make up the Canadian mosaic. Of a total of over 25,000,000 Canadians, 8.4 million (33.6%) were of British origin, 6.1 million (24.4%) of French origin, 6.2 million (24.8%) of origins neither British nor French, and 4.3 million (17.1%) of a multiple origin that included either British or French. Nearly three quarters of a million Canadians reported an aboriginal origin. Of all Canadians who reported having neither British nor French origins, 63% were of European background; 10%, Asian; 6%, South- or West-Asian (Middle Eastern); 6%, aboriginal; 3%, black; and 2%, other. Christianity is the religion practiced by the majority of the Canadian people (Roman Catholic, 46%; United Church, 18%; Anglican, 12%; and Eastern Orthodox, 1.5%). Many of the remainder report that they adhere to no religion.

The government (1990) took the form of a monarchy and member of the Commonwealth of Nations, of which the British sovereign is the symbolic head. However, all official acts of the sovereign and her representative, the governor-general, are determined by the Canadian authorities, who are responsible to the Canadian Parliament. The governor-general acts only with the agreement of the prime minister and his cabinet. The prime minister is the leader of the party or coalition holding the majority of seats in the House of Commons. Elections are normally held every five years but may be called earlier if the House of Commons so decides. Parliament is composed of a 104-member Senate, members of which are appointed for life, and a 282-member elected House of Commons, apportioned according to the provincial population. Political parties include the Progressive Conservative Party, the Liberal Party, and the New Democratic Party.

In December 1982, the Canadian House of Commons created a Special Committee on Indian Self-Government to review all legal and related institutional factors affecting the status, development, and responsibilities of tribal governments on Indian reserves and make recommendations in regard particularly to possible provisions of new legislation and improved administrative arrangements to apply to some or all of those governments, taking into account the various social, economic, administrative, political, and demographic situations of Indian bands and their views in regard to administrative or legal change. In its report, submitted to Parliament in November 1983, the committee recommended that the federal government establish a new relationship with Indian First Nations and that an essential element of this relationship be recognition of Indian self-government. The committee recommended that the right of the Indian people to self-government be explicitly stated and entrenched in the constitution of Canada. Indian First Nation governments would form a distinct order of government in Canada, with their jurisdiction being defined. Proposals to achieve such self-government were outlined in the report.

In June 1983, the Parliament established a special parliamentary committee to examine the problems related to the participation of "visible minorities" in Canadian society and to propose measures to increase such participation—"visible minorities" being defined as non-whites who are not participating fully in Canadian society. The committee's report, issued in March 1984 and entitled "Equality Now!", included 80 recommendations designed to increase the participation of such minorities in Canadian life and to facilitate their enjoyment of human rights and fundamental freedoms. The government has since been working on the implementation of those recommendations.

Also in June 1983, the Royal Commission of Inquiry on Equality in Employment was set up, by order-in-council. The commission was authorized to explore the most efficient, effective, and equitable means of promoting employment opportunities, eliminating systemic discrimination, and assisting all individuals to compete for employment opportunities on an equal basis. Four target groups were identified: women, native people, disabled persons, and "visible minorities."As the same time, the commission was requested to examine the employment practices of 11 designated crown and government-owned corporations. The commission's report, submitted in October 1984, contained 117 recommendations addressed to the government of Canada.

In March 1985, the government announced measures in response to the report, measures which touch the working lives of more than one million Canadians. They include mandatory employment equity reporting requirements in the private sector, an equity compliance policy for federal contractors, the integration of employment equity into all federal training and job development programs, and increased equity measures within the public service and federal crown corporations.

Changes were also made in the procedures for handling complaints under the Canadian Human Rights Act. A revamped complaints process, streamlining the system, has been adopted by the Canadian Human Rights Commission. The Human Rights Act, adopted in 1977, prohibits discrimination in employment and in the provision of goods, services, and accommodation on numerous grounds including race, color, and national or ethnic origin. As amended in 1983, it also prohibits harassment on any of those grounds and discrimination on the part of unions or employer's organizations.

The question of discrimination on the ground of language arose frequently in Canada because of the size and concentration of English-speaking and French-speaking elements of the population. In colonial days, the settlers, who were largely of French background, resented the influx of thousands of English-speaking immigrants from England and the United States, and had frequent disputes with them over the valuable fisheries and the fur trade. Gradually outnumbered, French-speaking Canadians began to fear that they had become second-class citizens and clashed with the newcomers over the issue of bilingualism in government, the courts, and the schools. This eventually led to the formation in the 1960s of a separatist movement in the predominantly French province of Quebec. However, Pierre Elliot Trudeau, a French Canadian who became prime minister in 1968, refused the idea of separation, although he supported programs for increased bilingualism and greater provincial autonomy. Separatism remained a national issue for some years, but the movement subsided after by-elections in 1977 produced easy victories for Trudeau's Liberals in four Quebec seats in the national legislature.

In 1984, the retirement of Trudeau led to the holding of a national election in which the Progressive Conservative Party won the largest political majority in Canadian history. As a result, the leader of that party, Brian Mulroney, was sworn in as prime minister on 17 September of that year.

CAPE VERDE. The Republic of Cape Verde is an archipelago in the Atlantic Ocean west of Dakar, Senegal; it consists of ten islands divided into two groups: Barlavento in the north and Sotavento in the south. It achieved independence from Portugal in 1975 and became a member of the United Nations the same year. Its population is estimated by the UN (1990) to be 367,000. A majority of its population are of mixed African and Portuguese origin. Languages commonly used include Portuguese (official) and Crioulo. Christianity (Roman Catholic, 80%; Protestant denominations, 20%) is the predominant religion. Literacy is estimated at 37%.

The government (1990) took the form of a republic, headed by a president and prime minister, both elected by the 56-member National Assembly. The president, as head of State, exercises executive authority in the country with the assistance of an appointed Council of Ministers.

One of the first acts of the National Assembly, after Cape Verde became independent, was to revoke and replace legislation inherited from the Portuguese occupation which was felt to be inconsistent with the real interests of the people. Besides replacing the colonial judicial system, it revised most of the laws regulating marriage, affiliation, and paternal-filial relations. Under the new laws, the exploitation of *contradados*—a form of FORCED LABOR—is forbidden, discrimination against persons born out of wedlock is abolished, and a network of people's tribunals is established to give the population greater facility of access to the organs of the judiciary and, incidentally, to open all positions in the judiciary to women.

Suffrage is universal. There is a single political party, the African Party for the Independence of Cape Verde.

CAPITAL PUNISHMENT. A subject of international concern since the second half of the 18th century, when it was drawn to public attention by Cesare Beccaria, the noted Italian jurist and criminologist, who in his *Essay on Crimes and Punishment* put forward a series of convincing arguments against capital punishment and the inhuman treatment of criminals.

In 1959, the UN General Assembly (resolution 1396 [XIV]) invited the Economic and Social Council to initiate a study of the question of capital punishment, of the laws and practices relating thereto, of the effects of capital punishment, and the abolition thereof, on the rate of criminality. The resulting study, entitled *Capital Punishment* (UN publication, Sales No. 62.IV.2), was prepared by Mr. Marc Ancel, a justice of the French Supreme Court and director of the Criminal Science Section of the Institute of Comparative Law in Paris.

In the study, the author summarized the two opposing views then being put forward for retaining or abolishing capital punishment, as follows (para. 213–230):

A theoretical controversy on the problem of capital punishment has been going on at least since Beccaria. George Fox had raised the issue as early as 1651 in his letters to the judges and in particular in his pamphlet *To the Parliament and Commonwealth of England* published in 1659, submitting 59 proposals for reforms, one of which was the proposal, then a very bold one, that henceforth the penalty of death should be applied only to murder. The British colonies of America had, before their independence, accepted the same ideas. There is no need to recall here the opinions expressed at the end of the eighteenth century and during the humanitarian and liberal period of the twentieth century. Whether one desires it or not, the controversy has once more become very topical in the last twenty years. Accordingly, in a comprehensive report on the problem as it stands today, one can hardly avoid giving an account of the two opposing views in the matter.

It is not the intention of the author to repeat here the reasons which were officially given in each of the countries concerned at the time of abolition or to analyse the respective positions of the various countries and national schools of thought; rather, he means to catalogue and briefly describe the reasons usually put forward today, for the guidance of public opinion, for retaining and for abolishing capital punishment.

In favour of the death penalty, the idea most commonly accepted is that of its deterrent effect—i.e., the protection of society from the risk of a second offence by a criminal who is not executed and who may subsequently be released or who may escape. Similarly, it is argued, the State has the right to protect itself. Many speak of the concept of self-defence and some even regard the death penalty as a necessity and the public authority as the representative in this regard of God on earth.

A related argument which is often advanced is that based on the idea of atonement: the death penalty (it is said) is the only just punishment for the gravest of crimes, or the only one capable of effacing an unpardonable crime. Some add that even if, from the philosophical point of view, the death penalty may be of doubtful legitimacy, it represents a political necessity for the protection not merely of society but of the social order itself. Similarly, it is contended that, since the death penalty is the only means of eliminating the offender altogether, this penalty is necessary, at least provisionally, when the public peace is endangered by certain particularly dangerous forms of crime. This view is based on concepts largely derived from the doctrine of *pericolosità* and of the irredeemability of certain offenders; on the basis of these ideas, capital punishment represents the extreme security measure of elimination. Some claim that, on this basis, it is legitimate to do away with "social monsters". This purely utilitarian idea is sometimes linked with the other idea that the State has a duty to impose inflexible rules of social conduct.

An analogous notion is that based on what is sometimes termed realism in the prevention of crime. The supporters of this view argue that a particularly potent weapon is needed for dealing with dangerous criminals and individuals. This is the reasoning of those who say that capital punishment is needed not only for the protection of human life and of certain cultural values but even to safeguard certain social property which is placed under the protection of the law.

Yet others argue that public opinion remains generally favourable to the death penalty and that the public as a whole, and particularly the police and prison officials, believe in its effectiveness. It is urged that this sincere belief should be respected and also that possible victims should be protected by maintaining the penalty of death. In the Middle East and in Africa, its value as a deterrent appears to be recognized in principle; even if its deterrent effect should be debatable, many claim that it ought to be regarded as genuine, or that, for reasons of public safety, those concerned ought to be encouraged to believe in it.

A somewhat similar idea is put forward by many who claim that the death penalty should be retained because it is virtually impossible to find another penalty to replace it; imprisonment, even for a long term, is said to be inadequate and its effects are moreover minimized by the practice of anticipated release. It is further argued that, if imprisonment in these cases were really to be a solitary confinement for life, it would be more cruel than death; and besides, imprisonment in perpetuity leaves no hope to the offender and does not encourage him to repentance in the same way as the immediate prospect of the supreme penalty.

Another, equally very utilitarian, view held in some countries is that the execution of the condemned person represents a saving of public funds and hence a saving for the taxpayer, who is not called upon to pay for the maintenance of anti-social criminals for an indefinite, or at least very long, period. And it is further said that an execution avoids certain popular reactions which must be expected in cases of heinous crimes if an over-excited public opinion were not aware that the criminal can be sentenced to death.

Against these arguments for the retention of the death penalty, the abolitionists advance the following considerations.

Their main argument is that based on the sanctity of human life; since it is wrong to kill, the State should set the example and should be the first to respect human life. Some go as far as to say that an execution is a self-mutilation of the State: though the State has admittedly the capacity to defend itself and to command, it is not empowered to eliminate a citizen, and in doing so the State does not erase the crime but repeats it.

It is further argued that the penalty of death can only be justified under the aspect of collective vengeance, of atonement, or of absolute retribution. But the modern tendency is to regard penalties as having no object other than prevention and punishment, and this object can be achieved by means other than the taking of life. The abolitionists refer in this connexion to the abuses frequently committed in the past, even in a recent past, when the death penalty was applied frequently and indiscriminately, and point out that its retention involves dangers of this kind. In Latin America, in particular, it is stressed that capital punishment might be used for political purposes.

Furthermore, it is said, the *lex talionis* is obsolete and hence an execution is a sort of judicial or legal murder; also, the existence of the penalty of death debases justice. For some years now, in America and Europe, it has been strenuously contended that the mere presence of capital punishment in the catalogue of penalties falsifies criminal proceedings, which take on the character of a sinister tragi-comedy; the existence of this penalty renders criminal justice uncertain. Recent works on sociology and judicial psychology indicate the extreme relatively of capital sentences.

Another argument used by the abolitionists is that the penalty of death rests in reality on a somewhat metaphysical concept of human freedom, whereas the social sciences show that an offender does not generally enjoy complete freedom. Absolute justice is therefore an illusion, and full atonement a fiction. Besides, how can human justice evaluate individual responsibility in absolute terms? The condemned person is in reality paying for other people or suffering for the sake of the example. His execution then appears to have no moral foundation.

Nor does the death penalty have the deterrent effect attributed to it: indeed, it is said, the statistics of crime show that its abolition does not lead to any increase in crime, and

consequently capital punishment loses its basic traditional justification.

Moreover, the penalty of death is a form of cruelty and inhumanity unworthy of a civilization which claims to be humane; doctors report that even the most efficient methods do not result in instantaneous and painless death. Above all, the chief defect of the death penalty is that it is irrevocable, and in spite of all the official statements, sometimes repeated with complacency, judicial error is always possible, and a few have certainly occurred recently. In such cases, the penalty of death appears as a unpardonable crime committed by society.

In any event, society can protect itself by other means, and the death penalty is no more than a lazy answer, which hinders the search for effective means of curbing crime and for a rational system of prevention. In addition, the death penalty is unjust in that, whatever may be claimed to the contrary, it affects not only the criminal himself but also his close relatives and brands the whole family with the mark of infamy. It is, moreover, paradoxical to claim that the death penalty alone makes repentance possible; it certainly totally precludes the rehabilitation of the human being concerned. The finality of the death penalty makes it impossible to adapt it to the gravity of the offence committed; all the attempts to draw a distinction between capital murder and other forms of homicide have proved arbitrary. In a progressive society, the death penalty appears on reflection as being the opposite of true atonement.

A further argument advanced by the abolitionists is that there is a contradiction in claiming that the death penalty has a deterrent effect and, at the same time, surrounding the execution with secrecy. The curiosity aroused by an execution is notoriously morbid, and it is increasingly realized that the penalty of death may itself have criminogenous effects, particularly upon those abnormal individuals who, in spite of all legal and judicial precautions, are often executed. And in some countries (it is added) the death penalty is applied most unequally, both from the social and from the radical points of view; some persons have not sufficient financial means to defend themselves or are morally unable to do so. The conclusion reached is, therefore, that this penalty, which should be the expression of absolute justice, often leads in practice to injustices against individuals.

These are the reasons generally given for and against capital punishment. Most of them have no doubt been stated over and over again. However, since the controversy has recently been revived and has even become heated, the author felt that he could hardly refrain from mentioning the arguments briefly in the present report.

In 1963, the study was examined by the *Ad Hoc* Committee of Experts on the Prevention of Crime and the Treatment of Offenders, the Economic and Social Council, and the General Assembly. The council and the assembly called upon the COMMISSION ON HUMAN RIGHTS to consider it from the point of view of human rights and requested the secretary-general to submit a report on new developments with respect to the law and practice concerning the death penalty and new contributions of the criminal sciences in the matter. This report, entitled *Capital Punishment— Developments 1961–1965* (UN publication, Sales No. E.67.IV.15, part II), was subsequently prepared by

Mr. Norval Morris, an expert appointed by the secretary-general.

After examining all the available information in 1968, the United Nations Consultative Group on the Prevention of Crime and the Treatment of Offenders summarized the situation then existing, with respect to capital punishment, in the following terms (UN Doc. A/7243, para. 11–30):

The Consultative Group, from the information made available to it and from experience of members with crime and its treatment in their own countries, was of the view that there is a strong trend in most countries towards the abolition of capital punishment or at least towards fewer executions. This tendency is particularly strong in relation to capital punishment for murder. This trend has legislative, judicial and executive aspects. A growing number of offenders who are sentenced to death is spared through processes of appeal or by executive clemency. Where it is used, capital punishment is increasingly a discretionary rather than a mandatory sanction. The Consultative Group also noted that a number of countries had abolished capital punishment for humanitarian reasons irrespective of any possible deterrent effect it might be thought to have.

There is a perceptible tendency in some countries, running contrary to what was noted in the previous paragraph, towards the legislative provision for, and actual application of, capital punishment for certain political and economic crimes. Times of political insecurity and attack have resulted, in some countries, in a larger recourse to capital punishment for statutory offences related to political or racial issues. The Consultative Group was of the view that in such cases it is of importance that if such a punishment is thought to be essential by the State it should not be mandatory.

Almost all countries provide for the exclusion of certain offenders from capital punishment because of their mental and physical condition, age, sex and extenuating circumstances. These exemptions are being gradually broadened at the legislative, judicial and executive levels.

The disparity between the legal provisions for capital punishment and the actual application of those provisions grows greater in those countries which have capital punishment in their laws.

Capital Punishment as an Exceptional Sanction. The capital punishment argument has changed. No member of the Consultative Group supported capital punishment other than as a temporary expendient or until the public should come to see the lack of need for this section. All looked with favour towards the day of abolition. Capital punishment thus becomes an "exceptional" not a routine sanction, which should be justified legislatively, judicially and by the executive: to be used as sparingly as social circumstances permit, so that the provisions of Article 3 of the Declaration of Human Rights may be implemented. Such a statement is not an interference with national autonomy; it simply recognizes that the burden of proof in relation to the need for capital punishment for any type of crime and for the execution of any individual criminal has shifted with the progress of social understanding and a larger recognition of the rights of man.

Legal Safeguards. The Consultative Group was of the opinion that in those States which retain capital punishment, it is essential that the normal judicial safeguards applicable to criminal trials be strictly observed in capital cases. There must always be a right of appeal to a superior, independent judicial tribunal composed of qualified and properly appointed judges. Further, there must be final recourse to the constitutional authority in the State empowered to commute the death sentence imposed.

The Consultative Group strongly endorsed the view in the Working Paper that an essential requirement of effective legal safeguards against error or abuse in capital cases is that the accused should have available at all stages (trial, appeal and petition for clemency) the services of competent, qualified and independent counsel. The Consultative Group recommended that no death sentence should be passed or carried out on a convicted person who had not been so assisted.

While free legal aid is practically universally accepted for an indigent accused in a capital case, problems sometimes arise as to the availability of competent, experienced and independent lawyers to undertake the defence in capital cases. It is therefore desirable that special provisions should be made in every jurisdiction to overcome this impediment to justice.

In all cases, the accused should be consulted as to the choice of counsel. Full facilities, immunities, and privileges must be extended to lawyers who appear for a person charged with a capital offence.

The Alternative Sanction. The Consultative Group noted the increasing tendency, with regard to offenders who are subject to capital punishment but who have been accorded another penalty, to confine them in conditions similar to those of other prisoners and to provide mechanisms for their eventual release. The question of the "alternative sanction" seemed to the Consultative Group to be of such importance as to merit comment beyond a mere noting of a trend.

The Consultative Group defined an "alternative sanction" as the punishment imposed on persons convicted of offences for which capital punishment might have been imposed by law, but who are not executed because either (a) the court or the jury has a discretion in imposing capital punishment and chooses a different penalty, or (b) the court or jury imposed a capital sentence which was subsequently commuted by executive clemency to a different penalty. The Consultative Group also included in its discussion under this heading the sentence imposed on those convicted of an offence which, until recently in the history of the jurisdiction in question, was punishable capitally.

The Consultative Group found itself in broad agreement with the recommendation of the *Ad Hoc* Advisory Committee of Experts on the Prevention of Crime and Treatment of Offenders as set out in paragraph 116 of *Capital Punishment: Developments 1961 to 1965,* but expanded those recommendations, as follows, in respect of the treatment of prisoners serving alternative sanctions.

Extended imprisonment is the generally accepted alternative sanction. The Consultative Group was of the view that, in principle, such prisoners should be treated neither more severely nor more leniently than other long-term prisoners. Their classification in terms of custody and training, the availability to them of placement in open institutions, and the circumstances of their imprisonment and correctional programmes, should be based on their dangerousness, their proclivity to escape, their training needs, and the available correctional resources; not on the fact that they are serving an alternative sanction.

The period of imprisonment should not be so long that

Earlier, at its 1982 session, the General Assembly had requested the Commission on Human Rights (resolution 37/192) to consider the idea of elaborating a draft of a second optional protocol to the International Covenant on Civil and Political Rights, aimed at the abolition of the death penalty, taking into account the available documentation on the subject. The request was passed on to the Sub-Commission on Prevention of Discrimination and Protection of Minorities, which in 1984 (resolution 1984/7) appointed one of its members, Mr. Marc Bossuyt, as special rapporteur and entrusted him with the preparation of a comparative analysis concerning the proposal to elaborate such an optional protocol. The report prepared by the special rapporteur (E/CN.4/Sub.2/1987/20) was examined by the subcommission in 1988 and transmitted to the Commission on Human Rights (resolution 1988/22).

The report analyzed the available information concerning the death penalty and the views on the subject expressed in the competent international bodies and presented the draft of a second optional protocol which envisaged the abolition of the death penalty for ordinary crimes with the possibility of retaining it for crimes under military law or crimes committed in exceptional circumstances such as in wartime.

The Commission on Human Rights forwarded the special rapporteur's report and the draft protocol to the General Assembly, which considered them in 1989 and adopted, on 15 December of that year, the INTERNATIONAL COVENANT ON CIVIL AND POLITICAL RIGHTS: SECOND OPTIONAL PROTOCOL, AIMING AT ABOLITION OF THE DEATH PENALTY.

SEE ALSO American Convention on Human Rights: Additional Protocol on the Death Penalty (Draft); Death Penalty entries; European Convention on Human Rights: Protocol VI; Executions: Report of Special Rapporteur; Principles on the Effective Prevention and Investigation of Extra-Legal, Arbitrary and Summary Executions; United States of America: Execution of Juvenile Offenders.

CAPITAL PUNISHMENT: WORLD SURVEY. Information on the status of capital punishment throughout the world, based on data supplied by governments or obtained from reliable nongovernmental sources, is summarized in the *Analysis Concerning the Proposition to Elaborate a Second Optional Protocol to the International Covenant on Civil and Political Rights* prepared by Mr. Marc Bossuyt (Belgium), special rapporteur of the SUB-COMMISSION ON PREVENTION OF DISCRIMINATION AND PROTECTION OF MINORITIES, in

1987 (UN Doc.E/CN.4/Sub.2/1987/20,para.73–75), as follows:

(a) Twenty-nine countries are abolitionist by law, which means that the country's laws do not provide for the death penalty: Austria, Bolivia, Cape Verde, Colombia, Costa Rica, Denmark, Dominican Republic, Ecuador, El Salvador, Finland, France, Federal Republic of Germany, Holy See, Honduras, Iceland, Kiribati, Luxembourg, Monaco, Netherlands, Nicaragua, Norway, Panama, Portugal, Solomon Islands, Sweden, Tuvalu, Uruguay, Vanuatu and Venezuela [according to information provided by Amnesty International, Australia abolished the death penalty for ordinary offences in 1984 and for all offences in 1985; the Philippines abolished the death penalty for all offences in 1987; according to Amnesty International, El Salvador and Monaco are abolitionist by law for ordinary crimes only];

(b) Twelve countries are abolitionist by law for ordinary crimes only, which means that the death penalty is imposed for exceptional crimes, that is, those subject to military law and/or committed in exceptional circumstances, for example in wartime: Brazil, Canada, Israel, Italy, Malta, Mexico, Nepal, Papua New Guinea, San Marino, Spain, Switzerland and the United Kingdom [according to information provided by Amnesty International, Argentina, Cyprus, El Salvador, Fiji, Monaco, New Zealand and Peru belong also to this category; according to Amnesty International, Nepal is retentionist];

(c) Two countries are abolitionist by custom for at least 40 years, which means that, although the country's laws provide for the death penalty for ordinary crimes, either nobody has been sentenced to death for the past 40 years or more, or nobody sentenced to death during that period has been executed: Belgium and Suriname [according to Amnesty International, both countries are retentionist; however, with one exception during the First World War, there have been no executions in Belgium for common crimes since 1863];

(d) Nine countries are abolitionist *de facto* at least for the past 10 years, which means that nobody has been reported executed for at least the last 10 years: Argentina, Brunei, Cyprus, Greece, Guyana, Ireland, Madagascar, Mauritius and New Zealand [according to Amnesty International those countries are retentionist, with the exception of Argentina, Cyprus and New Zealand which belong to the category of countries abolitionist for ordinary crimes only].

The other countries are reported retentionist:

(a) Nineteen belong to North Africa and the Middle East (Algeria, Bahrain, Democratic Yemen, Egypt, Islamic Republic of Iran, Iraq, Jordan, Kuwait, Lebanon, Libyan Arab Jamahiriya, Morocco, Oman, Qatar, Saudi Arabia, Syrian Arab Republic, Tunisia, Turkey, United Arab Emirates, Yemen);

(b) Forty-three belong to Africa south of the Sahara (Angola, Benin, Botswana, Burkina Faso, Burundi, Cameroon, Central African Republic, Chad, Comoros, Congo, Djibouti, Equatorial Guinea, Ethiopia, Gabon, Gambia, Ghana, Guinea, Guinea-Bissau, Ivory Coast, Kenya, Lesotho, Liberia, Malawi, Mali, Mauritania, Mozambique, Niger, Nigeria, Rwanda, Sao Tome and Principe, Senegal, Seychelles, Sierra Leone, Somalia, South Africa, Sudan, Swaziland, Togo, Uganda, United Republic of Tanzania, Zaire, Zambia, Zimbabwe);

(c) Twenty-three belong to Asia and the Pacific (Af-

C

ghanistan, Bangladesh, Bhutan, Burma, China, Democratic Kampuchea, Democratic People's Republic of Korea, Fiji, India, Indonesia, Japan, Lao People's Democratic Republic, Malaysia, Maldives, Mongolia, Pakistan, Republic of Korea, Samoa, Singapore, Sri Lanka, Thailand, Tonga, Viet Nam);

(d) Eleven belong to Eastern Europe (Albania, Bulgaria, Byelorussian Soviet Socialist Republic, Czechoslovakia, German Democratic Republic, Hungary, Poland, Romania, Ukrainian Soviet Socialist Republic, Union of Soviet Socialist Republics, Yugoslavia);

(e) Seventeen belong to Latin America and the Caribbean (Antigua and Barbuda, Bahamas, Barbados, Belize, Bermuda, Chile, Cuba, Dominica, Grenada, Guatemala, Haiti, Jamaica, Paraguay, Peru, Saint Lucia, Saint Vincent and the Grenadines, Trinidad and Tobago;

(f) In the Western group only Liechtenstein and certain States of the United States of America are retentionist [however, according to Amnesty International, there has been no execution in Liechtenstein since 1785].

According to information provided by Amnesty International, the following States have abolished the death penalty in recent years (1975–1987):

1975: Mexico abolished the death penalty for ordinary offences.

1976: Canada abolished the death penalty for ordinary offences.

1977: Portugal abolished the death penalty for all offences.

1978: Spain abolished the death penalty for ordinary offences; Denmark abolished the death penalty for all offences.

1979: Luxembourg, Nicaragua and Norway abolished the death penalty for all offences; Brazil and Fiji abolished the death penalty for ordinary offences.

1980: Peru abolished the death penalty for ordinary offences.

1981: France abolished the death penalty for all offences.

1982: The Netherlands abolished the death penalty for all offences.

1983: Cyprus and El Salvador abolished the death penalty for ordinary offences.

1984: Argentina and Australia abolished the death penalty for ordinary offences.

1985: Australia abolished the death penalty for all offences.

1987: Haiti and the Philippines abolished the death penalty for all offences.

SEE ALSO American Convention on Human Rights: Additional Protocol on the Abolition of the Death Penalty (Draft); Death Penalty: Application to persons under 18; Death Penalty: Safeguards; Death Penalty in Armed Conflicts; International Covenant on Civil and Political Rights, Second Optional Protocol Aiming at Abolition of the Death Penalty; Right to Life; Safeguards Guaranteeing the Rights of Those Facing the Death Penalty; and United States of America: Execution of Juvenile Offenders.

CARITAS INTERNATIONALIS. An international non-governmental organization in consultative status with the UN Economic and Social Council (Category II) and with ILO, UNESCO, FAO, UNICEF, and the Council of Europe, Caritas Internationalis is a member of the Conference of International Catholic Organizations and of the Pontifical Council CORUNUM.

Founded in 1951, CI is a confederation of 120 autonomous national Catholic organizations directed by its statutes "to spread charity and social justice in the world." Each national Caritas organization is independent, and its program differs according to local needs and conditions. The organization originated in 1947 when the Vatican's then-Substitute Secretary of State Archbishop Giovanni Montini (the future Pope Paul VI) faced with the problems of the post-war era, wanted to ensure a Catholic presence in the field of relief and social welfare. Thus conceived, CI aims to coordinate, inform, and represent the many charitable and social welfare efforts of the Catholic Church and works in particular for the powerless, refugees and exiles, and the homeless and hungry.

CI regularly publishes the periodical *Intercaritas*.

Caritas Internationalis. Address: Palazzo San Calisto, I-00120 Vatican City. Telephone: (39 6) 698.71.97. Cable: INTERCARITAS ROMA. Telex: (504) 2014 C.I.VA. Secretary General: Gerhard Meier.

CENTER FOR HUMAN RIGHTS. Formerly known as the Division of Human Rights, the center, which is the unit of the UNITED NATIONS SECRETARIAT most directly concerned with human rights, is a part of the United Nations office in Geneva. It is headed by Under-Secretary-General for Human Rights Jan Martenson, who is also the Director-General of that office.

The center provides executive direction, management, and administrative and substantive services to a number of United Nations organs when they deal with human rights matters, including the GENERAL ASSEMBLY, the ECONOMIC AND SOCIAL COUNCIL, the COMMISSION ON HUMAN RIGHTS, its SUB-COMMISSION ON PREVENTION OF DISCRIMINATION AND PROTECTION OF MINORITIES, the COMMITTEE ON THE ELIMINATION OF RACIAL DISCRIMINATION, the HUMAN RIGHTS COMMITTEE, the COMMITTEE ON ECONOMIC, SOCIAL AND CULTURAL RIGHTS, the COMMITTEE AGAINST TORTURE, and their subsidiary bodies. It carries out research and prepares studies at the request of these bodies, administers the program of ADVISORY SERVICES IN THE FIELD OF HUMAN RIGHTS, collects and disseminates information on questions related to human rights, and prepares publications on the subject.

The center includes the office of the Under-Secretary-General, within which there is an administrative support unit; the secretariat of the WORKING GROUP ON

ENFORCED OR INVOLUNTARY DISAPPEARANCES; the International Instrument Section; the Research, Studies and Prevention of Discrimination Section; the Advisory Services Section; and the External Relations, Publications and Documentation Section. There is also a liaison office located at the headquarters of the United Nations in New York City. (See Appendix F.)

The center endeavors to maintain and strengthen coordination with specialized agencies which are concerned with human rights questions, such as the INTERNATIONAL LABOR ORGANIZATION, the UNITED NATIONS EDUCATIONAL, SCIENTIFIC AND CULTURAL ORGANIZATION, the WORLD HEALTH ORGANIZATION, and the FOOD AND AGRICULTURAL ORGANIZATION OF THE UNITED NATIONS. Meetings to review ongoing programs and to explore cooperative endeavors are held at least once a year.

The center also cooperates closely with the human rights organs of regional intergovernmental organizations, such as those of the ORGANIZATION OF AMERICAN STATES, the ORGANIZATION OF AFRICAN UNITY and the COUNCIL OF EUROPE. For example, in July 1988, the center invited members of the AFRICAN COMMISSION ON HUMAN AND PEOPLES' RIGHTS to Geneva for briefings and participation in the work of United Nations human rights bodies.

In addition, the center maintains contact with interested governments in order to work out the details of advisory services and technical assistance projects for the promotion and protection of human rights. Such arrangements vary widely from country to country and include the training of officials, judges, police and military officers, the setting up of law faculties, the organization of law libraries, the drafting of legal texts in keeping with the provisions of international human rights instruments, the collection and circulation of relevant information and reference materials, and the publication of law journals.

On 7 March 1989, the Commission on Human Rights adopted without a vote a resolution entitled "Co-ordinating Role of the Center for Human Rights" (resolution 1989/54), in which it supported the efforts of the secretary-general to enhance the role and importance of the Center for Human Rights as a coordinating unit in the system of bodies dealing with the promotion and protection of human rights, and expressed the hope that the steps being taken in that direction, including the measures to promote the settlement of regional conflicts, will foster cooperation in upholding and protecting human rights and fundamental freedoms, better understanding, mutual respect, trust, and tolerance in relations between States and peoples.

The commission requested the secretary-general to request governments, United Nations specialized agencies, and intergovernmental and non-governmental bodies to express their views on the strengthening of the activities of the center, with special emphasis on new directions and forms, including increasing the representation of under-represented groups of States, notably the developing countries, in senior and policy-formulating posts in the center, while safeguarding the principle of equitable geographical distribution, and to submit a report setting out those views and opinions to the commission at its 1991 session, at which time, the commission will discuss the question of the coordinating role of the Center for Human Rights within the United Nations bodies and machinery dealing with the promotion and protection of human rights.

CENTER FOR THE STUDY OF HUMAN RIGHTS, COLUMBIA UNIVERSITY. The center was founded in 1978 to promote interdisciplinary research and teaching in human rights. A university-wide activity, it promotes research as a primary goal to elucidate the role that human rights considerations play in contemporary civilization. To that end, the center supports a number of programs, including the University Seminar on Human Rights, begun in 1978; dissertation fellowships, awarded to doctoral students whose dissertations concern or are related to human rights; an annual, week-long symposium, begun in 1979; the Gitleson/Meyerwitz Prize, awarded to a Columbia student for the best composition on human rights; and research projects. At the end of 1990, the center was sponsoring four research projects: (1) Rights and Constitutionalism in International Affairs; (2) the Protection of Children in War; (3) Religious Diversity and Human Rights; and (4) the Cambodia Project. In addition to its other activities, the center also sponsors the "Advocates Program," a four-month training program for human rights activists from third-world countries.

The document collection of the center is housed in Columbia's International Affairs Building and the Heyman Center. The collection comprises country-specific files, files on human rights organizations, offprints and pre-publication articles, human rights organization publications, and reports and bibliographic information.

The center offers summer internships enabling students to work with human rights groups in third world countries and has cooperated in the administration of the Law School's Summer Internship Human Rights Program. It publishes a periodic *Newsletter* and has published Louis Henkin's *The Rights of Man Today*, Adam Skryba's *Human Rights in Eastern Europe*,

C

and *Constitutionalism and Rights, American Ideas Overseas.*

Center for the Study of Human Rights. Address: Columbia University, 1108 International Affairs Building, 420 W. 118th Street, New York, NY 10027 (USA). Telephone: (212) 854-2479. Telex: 220094 COLU UR. Executive Director: Paul Martin.

CENTRAL AFRICAN REPUBLIC. The Central African Republic, formerly part of the colony of French Equatorial Africa, is a landlocked State in central Africa. It has borders with Cameroon, Chad (also formerly part of French Equatorial Africa), Congo, Sudan, and Zaire. It achieved independence from France in 1960 and became a member of the United Nations the same year. Its population is estimated by the UN (1990) to be 2,907,000. The population of the Central African Republic includes a large number of ethnic communities that form part of the following major ethnic groups: Banda, Baya, Mandjia, Yakoma, Ngbaka, Ali, Kaba, Karé, Baminga (Pygmies), Gbanou, Sango, Zandé, Nzakara, Mbati, Gbougou, Ngbakamandjia, Mboroco (Peuls), Hausa (of Arabized origin), etc. There are also groups from other African countries (Cameroon, Chad, Congo, Senegal, Sudan, and Zaire), as well as naturalized groups of French, Portuguese, and Lebanese origin. Languages commonly used include Sango and French (official) and a wide variety of African languages. Religions practiced include Christianity (Protestant faiths, 50%; Roman Catholic, 33%), Islam (5%), and Animism (12%). Literacy is estimated at 35%.

The government (1990) took the form of a republic under a constitution approved by more than 97% of the population on 5 February 1981, which guarantees the fundamental rights and freedoms of the people, the multiparty system, and the existence of trade unions. However, the constitution was suspended with the coming into power on 1 September 1981 of the Military Committee for National Recovery. The committee indicated that it would continue to respect and apply the provisions concerning the basic rights of citizens. Under committee rule, only its president, who is head of State, has discretionary power in the administrative sphere. The judicial system operates in a normal manner.

During the 14-year period between 1965 and 1979, the Central African Republic was ruled by an authoritarian and dictatorial regime headed by Jean–Bedel Bokassa, the army chief of staff who seized power in a military coup on 31 December 1965 and declared himself, successively, field marshal, president for life, and, on 4 December 1976, Emperor Bokassa I of the Central African Empire.

Although the constitution of the empire guaranteed the basic human rights and fundamental freedoms, it was ignored by the Bokassa regime, which became known for its gross violations of human rights, including arbitrary arrests, executions, and "disappearances," a massacre of schoolchildren, and the establishment of a military court system in which the accused had no right to a defense and no means of appeal.

Bokassa's initiatives and personal ambitions led him to spend more than $100 million on his coronation as emperor at a time when many of the country's three million people were without food or shelter. He sought and obtained assistance from the government of South Africa to build the "200-villas" complex in Bangui which he then used as his private property. And he ordered at least 20 of his real or imagined opponents to be put to death in Bangui's Ngaragba Prison. In 1979, he ordered the arrest of more than 100 schoolchildren when they protested against being forced to buy uniforms made in a factory owned by his wife, and soldiers called to quiet the disturbance opened fire and killed many of the children.

A French-backed coup under the leadership of former President David Dacko deposed Bokassa on 20 September 1979. A new constitution was prepared and was approved by 97% of the electorate on 5 February 1981. This constitution contained provisions guaranteeing fundamental human rights, including freedom of thought, freedom of expression, freedom to vote, and freedom of movement; established a multi-party system; and provided for the existence of trade unions. Unfortunately, serious differences soon arose based on varying interpretations of the idea of a multiparty system; and, as a result, the political, economic, and social life of the country was paralyzed. The army once again stepped in, on 1 September 1981, and assumed power under army General Andre Kolingba. The new regime suspended the constitution immediately but stated that it would respect and apply the provisions concerning the basic rights of citizens.

On 21 November 1986, a new constitution was enacted which provided for parliamentary elections to be held, in which only one party—the Centrafrican Democratic Assembly—would be eligible to participate. The new constitution also prolonged the term of office of President Kolingba by six years.

Jean-Bedel Bokassa, who had taken refuge in France, was sentenced to death in absentia in 1980. Nevertheless, he returned voluntarily to the Central African Republic in October 1986, saying he wanted to clear himself of all charges against him. He was tried by a nine-member court—three judges and six jurors—and found guilty of having ordered prisoners put to death by brutal means. He was also found guilty of the massacre of schoolchildren in September 1979. Acquitted on several of 14 charges, including cannibalism, he was sentenced to death in July 1987; however, in March 1988, his sentence was commuted to life in prison.

On 5 December 1980, the UN General Assembly affirmed (resolution 35/87) the need for international action to assist the government of the Central African Republic in its efforts to reconstruct, rehabilitate, and develop the country and requested the secretary-general to set up a program of financial, technical, and material assistance for this purpose. On 9 March 1981, the UN Commission on Human Rights requested the secretary-general (resolution 15 [XXXVII]) to provide advisory services to help the government in its efforts to guarantee the exercise of human rights and fundamental freedoms in the country; and invited all States, specialized agencies, UN organs, and humanitarian organizations to cooperate. The General Assembly noted, on 8 December 1986 (resolution 41/200) that, despite some progress and encouraging results, more external assistance was required and appealed for a generous response to the needs of the country. Again in 1988 (resolution 43/211), the assembly noted the persistence of the grave difficulties that the government of the Central African Republic continued to face in its efforts since 1982 to re-establish the economic stability of the country and reiterated its earlier appeals for assistance.

CHAD. The Republic of Chad, formerly part of the colony of French Equatorial Africa, is a landlocked State in central Africa. It has borders with Cameroon, Central African Republic (also formerly part of French Equatorial Africa), Libya, Niger, Nigeria, and Sudan. It achieved independence from France in 1960 and became a member of the United Nations the same year. Its population is estimated by the UN (1990) to be 5,668,000.

About 200 ethnic groups are included in the population. In the north the following groups may be distinguished: the Bouiala, the Arabs, the Khozam, the Djatne, the Kareda, the Amakaza, the Toubou, the Gorane, the Hadjarai, the Zakawa, the Kanembou, the Bornou, the Ouaddaiens, the Boudouna, the Niergue, the Kouka, the Dadjo, the Baguirmiens, and the Kotoko. This list is far from exhaustive. In the south the main groups are the Mboum, the Laka, the Kaba, the Soumou, the Gor, the Mongo, the Ngambave, the Goulaye, the Mbaye, the Sara, the Daye, the Ngama, the Sara-Kaba, the Boua, the Nyelim, the Mouroum, the Mberi, the Gabri, the Kabalaye the

Soumouraye, the Nanichere, the Marba, the Kim the Karo, the Massa, the Moudang, the Toupouri, the Falata, and the Goula. These are the principal ethnic groups of southern Chad. It should be noted that there is interpenetration between the different ethnic groups.

Languages commonly used include French and Arabic (both official) and Sara; in addition, more than 100 African languages and dialects are spoken. Religions practiced include Islam (45%), Christianity (30%), and Animism (25%). For the most part, Muslim groups, whose main activity is livestock breeding, live in the northern areas of the country, while Christian and animist groups, who engage in farming, live in the southern areas. Literacy is estimated at 20%.

The government (1990) took the form of a republic. However, the 1962 constitution, which provided an intrinsic guarantee of the human rights and public freedoms, as well as a guarantee of the rights of the citizen based on the principles of liberty, humanity, and equality, has been repealed. The Fundamental Act of the Third Republic, which replaced the constitution, provides, in article 18, for "the establishment of a political democracy which guarantees the fundamental freedoms and rights of the individual, of associations and of communities and the effective participation of all levels of society in the conduct of public affairs."

The president is head of State and of government and exercises administrative authority in the country. Legislation is dealt with by the National Consultative Assembly, constituted in 1982. The only political party is the National Union for Independence and Revolution.

A Libyan-financed rebel movement, the Chadian National Liberation Front, fomented and encouraged civil strife in northern Chad between 1975 and 1979. In March 1979, a number of rebel groups met at Lagos and formed a "provisional government" headed by Goukouni Oueddi. That government was challenged, after being in power for one year, by its own defense minister, Hissèn Habré, who ousted Goukouni Oueddi and set up a government of reconciliation with a cabinet which included the leaders of several earlier conflicts. His offer of a cabinet post to Goukouni Oueddi, who took refuge in Algiers, was turned down.

Libyan troops occupied much of northern Chad between 1980 and 1986. However, in March 1987, Hissèn Habré's Chadian forces took Libyan bases in Gouro and Ounianga, capturing an estimated half-billion dollars worth of weapons and supplies, including planes, tanks, artillery pieces, rocket launchers, trucks, and jeeps. As a result, Chad found itself with one of the best-equipped armies in Africa.

On 24 September 1987 Lybia and Chad agreed to let the ORGANIZATION OF AFRICAN UNITY mediate their territorial conflict over the Aozou border strip.

Tens of thousands of Chadians, who had been displaced in neighboring countries by drought and warfare, returned to Chad between 1986 and 1989. By the end of 1989, the UNITED NATIONS HIGH COMMISSIONER FOR REFUGEES had assisted the reintegration of several hundred thousand Chadian returnees who had repatriated mainly from the Central African Republic, Nigeria, and the Sudan.

On 15 December 1989, the UN General Assembly expressed (resolution 44/153) concern about the persistence of the harmful effects of the drought, desertification, floods, and infestations of locusts and grasshoppers—problems compounding the already precarious food and health situation in Chad—and concluded that the large mass of voluntary returnees and displaced persons would pose serious social and economic problems for the government of that country. It reiterated its earlier appeals to all States and intergovernmental and non-governmental organizations to support the efforts of the government of Chad to assist and resettle the returnees and displaced persons and again called upon the secretary-general and the United Nations High Commissioner for Refugees to mobilize emergency humanitarian assistance for this purpose.

CHARTER OF RIGHTS FOR MIGRANT WORKERS IN SOUTHERN AFRICA (1978). The charter, adopted by the Lusaka Conference on Migratory Labor in Southern Africa on 7 April 1978, was endorsed by the UN General Assembly on 20 December 1978 (resolution 33/162). In the resolution, the assembly urged all UN member States and all organizations of the United Nations system to extend to the African States affected by the migration of labor to South Africa all material, financial, technical, and political support for the initiation and implementation of specific development programs and projects aimed at enabling those States to utilize fully their available labor force for the development of their own economies and thereby eliminate the necessity to export such labor to the *apartheid* economy of South Africa. The text of the charter is as follows:

We the representatives of the States and peoples of southern Africa,

Noting that *apartheid* has been declared a crime against humanity by the United Nations General Assembly,

Noting the work done by the International Labour Organisation on the problems of migratory labour in southern Africa and recalling International Labour Organisation Conventions No. 87 of 9 July 1948 and Nos. 97 and 98 of 1 July 1949 concerning, respectively, the freedom of association and protection of the right to organize, migration for employment and the application of the principles of the right to organize and to bargain collectively,

Recognizing that the migratory labour system is one of the major instruments of *apartheid*,

Mindful of the gross indignities it inflicts on workers, who are denied many of their basic human rights,

Noting that it undermines family life and disrupts agrarian economies,

Hereby pledge ourselves to strive for the abolition of the migratory labour system practised in South Africa and, pending its elimination, agree to the present Charter of Rights for Migrant Workers in Southern Africa.

Chapter I
Rights of Association, Movement and Residence

Article 1. All workers shall have the right to:

(a) Form and join trade unions of their own choice;

(b) Participate in collective bargaining on equal terms with all other workers regardless of race, sex, political affiliation or religion;

(c) Withhold their labour by strike action in support of their demands.

Article 2. All workers shall have the right to freedom of movement and shall not be required to carry a pass or similar document.

Article 3. All workers shall have the right to be accommodated near their place of work with their families in suitable houses under home ownership schemes or to reside elsewhere if they choose so to do.

Article 4. All workers shall have the right of occupation free from colour bar, job reservation and all other forms of discrimination.

Article 5. Every worker regardless of race or sex, shall have the right to work, choose his occupation, and change from one employer to another without loss of accrued benefits and claims to promotion.

Article 6. All workers, without exception, shall have the right to equal pay for equal work.

Article 7. All workers shall have equal rights to vocational training and adult education for the purpose of acquiring skills and increasing their awareness.

Chapter II
Right to a Decent Standard of Living

Article 8. Every worker is entitled to a minimum basic wage sufficient for the maintenance of the health and well being of his family.

Article 9. All workers shall have the right to adequate protection against occupational accidents and diseases by means of approved safeguards and close supervision by an independent industrial and farming inspectorate operating in conjunction with workers' representatives.

Article 10. All workers and their families shall have an equal and absolute right to adequate, immediate and effective compensation for death or disability arising out of occupational diseases and accidents.

Article 11. All workers shall have a right to:

(a) Free medical services for themselves and their families;

(b) Sick leave and, where applicable, maternity leave with full pay;

(c) Annual paid holidays.

Article 12. All workers shall be entitled to retire on full pension or with a gratuity proportionate to their period of service.

Article 13. All workers shall have a right to determine their terms and conditions of employment through collective bargaining.

Article 14. All workers shall have a right to unemployment benefits.

Article 15. All women workers shall have the right to participate in all sectors of the economy without discrimination in respect of wages, training, job allocation or pension benefits.

SEE ALSO *European Convention on Legal Status of Migrant Workers; ILO Migrant Workers (Supplementary Provisions) Convention; ILO Migration for Employment Convention; Migrant Workers.*

CHEMICAL WEAPONS. On 1 September 1988, the UN Sub-Commission on Prevention of Discrimination and Protection of Minorities, referring to the PROTOCOL FOR THE PROHIBITION OF THE USE OF ASPHYXIATING, POISONOUS OR OTHER GASES, AND OF BACTERIOLOGICAL METHODS OF WARFARE, expressed deep concern (resolution 1988/27) about reports of the increased use of chemical weapons, especially against civilian populations, and stated that it was deeply shocked and saddened by the destruction of human life, life-long disabilities, and great suffering caused by such weapons.

Noting that negotiations were then under way, in the Conference on Disarmament, on the complete, effective, and verifiable prohibition of the development, production, stockpiling, and use of all chemical weapons and of their destruction, the sub-commission called upon all States that had not then done so to consider on a priority basis acceding to the protocol, and to observe strictly its principles and objectives. The sub-commission decised to study the subject further, and requested the Secretary-General to collect information on the use of chemical weapons, and on the danger they represent to life, physical security, and other human rights, and to submit a report to it at its 1989 session.

On 7 December 1988, the UN General Assembly called upon all States (resolution 43/74 A) to be guided by the need to curb the spread of chemical weapons pending the conclusion of a convention on the prohibition of all chemical weapons and on their destruction, and also requested the Secretary-General to investigate reports of the use of such weapons.

The Secretary-General's report to the 1989 session of the sub-commission (UN Doc. E/CN.4/Sub.2/1989/4) dealt with such issues as definition and de-

scription of chemical weapons; the use and allegations of the use of chemical weapons; the danger they represent to life, physical security, and other human rights; the importance and continuing validity of the Geneva Protocol of 1925; and relevant aspects of multilateral and national activities relating to the ban of chemical weapons. The Secretary-General then presented the following conclusions (paras. 109–112):

(a) recognizing that the use of chemical weapons agents may destroy human life and cause life-long disability and great suffering, the use of such weapons constitutes a violation of basic human rights, in particular the right to life and the right to liberty and security of person. Therefore, urgent and effective measures should be undertaken by the international community to prevent the future use of those kinds of weapons;

(b) efforts to achieve the complete and effective prohibition of the development, production and stockpiling of all chemical weapons and their destruction are of crucial importance and should be pursued by the international community as a matter of continuing urgency;

(c) the strict observance by all States of the principles and objectives of the 1925 Geneva Protocol could prevent the further use in military conflicts of asphyxiating, poisonous or other gases. The Secretary-General, in his statement at the Paris Conference, declared that "Sans respect du Protocole de Genève, il n'y aura pas d'élimination définitive de l'arme chimique;"

(d) the mobilization of the public opinion in favour of banning chemical weapons would also represent an important factor in that regard.

In almost all replies received the conviction was expressed that the only reliable and true way to eliminate the danger of future chemical war was the finalization and setting into force of a universal convention banning the development, production, stockpiling and use of chemical weapons, and obliging States parties to destroy their stockpiles of chemical weapons and their production facilities for these weapons.

Support was expressed for appropriate and effective steps taken by the United Nations in this field. It was affirmed that the United Nations provided a framework and an instrument enabling the international community to exercise vigilance with respect to the prohibition of the use of chemical weapons.

The initiative of the Sub-Commission in its resolution 1988/27 and its consideration of that issue were generally considered helpful in sensitizing public opinion for the work of the Conference on Disarmament towards the early conclusion of a global, universally adhered to chemical weapons ban, thereby eliminating any future use of chemical weapons.

Having examined the report, the sub-commission on 1 September 1989 took note of it (resolution 1989/39) and called upon all States to abide strictly by their international obligations in this field. In doing so, it endorsed Security Council resolutions 612 (1988) of 9 May 1988 and 620 (1988) of 26 August 1988, both on the need to consider appropriate and effective measures for eliminating the use of chemical weapons; and General Assembly resolution 43/74 A of 7 December 1988, in which the assembly called upon all States to be guided by the need to spread the curb of chemical weapons pending the conclusion of a convention on the complete, effective, and verifiable prohibition of the development, production, stockpiling, and use of all chemical weapons and on their destruction.

On 15 December 1989, the General Assembly renewed its call to all States (resolution 44/115 B) to observe strictly the principles and objectives of the Protocol for the Prohibition of the use in war of Asphyxiating, Poisonous or Other Gases, and of Bacteriological Methods of Warfare, and condemned vigorously all actions that violate that obligation. In that same resolution, the assembly requested the secretary-general to carry out promptly investigations in response to reports that may be brought to his attention by any member State concerning the possible use of chemical and bacteriological (biological) or toxic weapons that may constitute a violation of the 1925 general protocol or other relevant rules of customary international law in order to ascertain the facts of the matter, and to report promptly the results of any such investigation to all member States.

SEE ALSO Convention on the Prohibition of the Development, Production and Stockpiling of Bacteriological (Biological) and Toxin Weapons and on Their Destruction.

CHEMICAL WEAPONS: DECLARATION ON THEIR PROHIBITION.

The Conference on the Prohibition of Chemical Weapons, convened at Paris from 7 to 11 January 1989, adopted by consensus of the 149 participating States, on 11 January 1989, the following final declaration (UN Doc. A/44/88, Annex):

The Representatives of States participating in the conference on the Prohibition of Chemical Weapons, bringing together States Parties to the Geneva Protocol of 1925 and other interested States in Paris from 7 to 11 January 1989, solemnly declare the following:

1. The participating States are determined to promote international peace and security throughout the world in accordance with the Charter of the United Nations and to pursue effective disarmament measures. In this context, they are determined to prevent any recourse to chemical weapons by completely eliminating them. They solemnly affirm their commitments not to use chemical weapons and condemn such use. They recall their serious concern at recent violations as established and condemned by the competent organs of the United Nations. They support the humanitarian assistance given to the victims affected by chemical weapons.

2. The participating States recognize the importance and continuing validity of the Protocol for the prohibition of the use in war of asphyxiating, poisonous or other gases and bacteriological methods of warfare, signed on 17 June 1925 in Geneva. The States Parties to the Protocol solemnly reaffirm the prohibition as established in it. They call upon all States which have not yet done so to accede to the Protocol.

3. The participating States stress the necessity of concluding, at an early date, a Convention on the prohibition of the development, production, stockpiling and use of all chemical weapons, and on their destruction. This Convention shall be global and comprehensive and effectively verifiable. It should be of unlimited duration. To this end, they call on the Conference on Disarmament in Geneva to redouble its efforts, as a matter of urgency, to resolve expeditiously the remaining issues and to conclude the Convention at the earliest date. All States are requested to make, in an appropriate way, a significant contribution to the negotiations in Geneva by undertaking efforts in the relevant fields. The participating States therefore believe that any State wishing to contribute to these negotiations should be able to do so. In addition, in order to achieve as soon as possible the indispensable universal character of the Convention, they call upon all States to become parties thereto as soon as it is concluded.

4. The participating States are gravely concerned by the growing danger posed to international peace and security by the risk of the use of chemical weapons as long as such weapons remain and are spread. In this context, they stress the need for the early conclusion and entry into force of the Convention, which will be established on a nondiscriminatory basis. They deem it necessary, in the meantime, for each State to exercise restraint and to act responsibly in accordance with the purpose of the present declaration.

5. The participating States confirm their full support for the United Nations in the discharge of its indispensable role, in conformity with its Charter. They affirm that the United Nations provide a framework and an instrument enabling the international community to exercise vigilance with respect to the prohibition of the use of chemical weapons. They confirm their support for appropriate and effective steps taken by the United Nations in this respect in conformity with its Charter. They further reaffirm their full support for the Secretary-General in carrying out his responsibilities for investigations in the event of alleged violations of the Geneva Protocol. They express their wish for early completion of the work undertaken to strengthen the efficiency of existing procedures and call for the cooperation of all States, in order to facilitate the action of the Secretary-General.

6. The participating States, recalling the Final Document of the first Special Session of the United Nations General Assembly devoted to Disarmament in 1978, underline the need to pursue with determination their efforts to secure general and complete disarmament under effective international control, so as to ensure the right of all States to peace and security.

SEE ALSO Convention on the Prohibition of the Development, Production and Stockpiling of Bacteriological (Biological) and Toxin Weapons and on Their Destruction; Protocol for the Prohibition of the Use of Asphyxiating, Poisonous or Other Gases, and of Bacteriological Methods of Warfare.

CHILD LABOR. The exploitation of child labor is a practice which frequently gives rise to effects similar to those of slavery. At the request of the UN COMMISSION ON HUMAN RIGHTS, a "Seminar on Ways and Means of Achieving the Elimination of the Exploitation of Child Labor in All Parts of the World" was held at the European office of the United Nations, Geneva, from 28 October to 8 November 1984. Organized by the CENTER FOR HUMAN RIGHTS in close cooperation with the INTERNATIONAL LABOR OFFICE, under the program of advisory services in the field of human rights, the seminar was attended by experts nominated by the governments of 24 States and by the representatives of a number of intergovernmental and non- governmental organizations.

The conclusions of the seminar, as summarized in its report (UN Doc. ST/HR/SER. A/18, chap VI), are as follows:

(a) The exploitation of child labour is an intolerable evil which must be eliminated as a matter of the greatest urgency;

(b) The exact extent of the exploitation of child labour is not known, but it takes place in a very large number of countries throughout the world, and very many children, possibly over 100 million, are the victims of such exploitation;

(c) The exploitation of child labour takes many forms, and certain types of exploitation, for example, child prostitution and the employment of children in hazardous occupations including armed conflict, are particularly abhorrent;

(d) Certain categories of children, for example refugee or migrant children or children in countries with an *apartheid* régime, or territories under foreign occupation are particularly vulnerable to exploitation;

(e) The factors leading to the exploitation of child labour vary very widely, and include economic, social, cultural and other factors. Probably the most important causes of such exploitation are poverty and underdevelopment. For some children, work is at present an absolute necessity in order to survive;

(f) Other factors which have a bearing on the number of children at work include the general level of employment, the educational system of a country, and in particular whether, and up to what age school attendance is free and compulsory; the existence within a country of vocational training schemes, and of comprehensive legislation on the subject of child labour and the effectiveness of its enforcement; and the scope and adequacy for the needs of families of a country's social welfare and social security systems; the cultural changes that many countries are undergoing also constitute a factor influencing the number of children at work;

(g) The total elimination of all forms of exploitation of child labour throughout the world is endorsed unanimously as a long term objective. However, it will take many years to achieve. Success will depend on gradual progress in the achievement of a number of distinct short-term and medium-term programmes aimed at specific, clearly-defined, and realistic objectives;

(h) No one organization acting in isolation could hope to solve a problem of such magnitude. The elimination of the exploitation of child labour will require economic reforms aimed at a more equitable distribution of the world resources as well as the active co-operation of all those concerned with the problem, including international organizations, national Governments, local authorities, nongovernmental organizations at international, national and local levels, trade unions, employers, and the children themselves. Such co-operation is likely to depend on the effective mobilization of public opinion world-wide.

Bearing in mind the guiding principles set out in the above conclusions, the seminar prepared the following recommendations:

(a) The United Nations and specialized agencies should reinforce their programmes related to the elimination of the exploitation of child labour, and in particular to the study of the economic, social, legal and cultural factors which give rise to it;

(b) States, which have not already done so, should review their legislation in the field of child labour with a view to absolute prohibition of employment of children in the following cases:

Employment before the normal age of completion of primary schooling in the country concerned;

Sexual exploitation of children for personal gratification or financial gain;

Night work;

Work in dangerous or unhealthy conditions;

Work concerned with trafficking in and production of illicit drugs;

Work involving degrading or cruel treatment.

(c) States, which have not already done so, should take the appropriate steps to enable them to ratify ILO Convention No. 138. In this connection, greater assistance from ILO should be extended to the developing countries to facilitate their increased participation in standard setting activities and in the implementation of ratified conventions.

(d) States should, where necessary, undertake development programmes aimed at achieving equitable distribution of income, generating opportunities for employment, creation of small businesses, and agrarian reforms; and:

Abolish, wherever possible, primary school fees;

Introduce flexible school time-tables to enable children who work to receive education;

Adapt school curricula to the preparation of a child for a career;

Improve the training programmes of professional workers dealing with child labour, in particular labour inspectors, social workers, and magistrates, with a view, in particular, to making them more sensitive to the needs of children;

Establish or improve medical services for school children and children at work;

Arrange for research into the effect on children of exposure to pesticides and other dangerous substances.

(e) States should ensure the availability of a sufficient number of work inspectors, and train them systematically to deal with cases of exploitation of child labour. Particular attention should be given to national and regional plans for social and economic development to the occupational training of young people. National development plans should also include a section devoted particularly to the employment of young people, and to methods of ensuring that the most deprived have sufficient resources to be able to protect themselves from conditions leading to exploitation.

(f) Special attention should be paid to the most vulnerable categories of children: children of immigrants, street children, children of minority groups including indigenous minorities, children of refugees, children in occupied territories and in countries with a régime of *apartheid*.

(g) The United Nations and specialized agencies—having regard to their special responsibilities in the field of child labour—should pay special attention to the situation which is developing dangerously for children in South Africa and in occupied Arab territories.

(h) While the question of exploitation of child labour should primarily be dealt with in the ILO, the Centre for Human Rights should continue to be concerned with this question in the framework of the rights of the child in general. The Sub-Commission should continue to have responsibility also in this field and the Working Group on Slavery should present a periodical report on progress achieved.

(i) The United Nations should give consideration to organizing a World Year (or a World Day) for the Elimination of the Exploitation of Child Labour, the essential objective of which would be to alert world public opinion.

(j) The United Nations and the specialized agencies, including the University of the United Nations, should continue to incorporate in their programmes a series of interdisciplinary and multinational projects for comparative research into the various aspects of the exploitation of child labour throughout the world and in particular in the countries of Africa, Asia and Latin America.

(k) Agencies working with community-based organizations should identify those which are concerned with child labour, and should help them in all practical ways in their task of protecting working children from exploitation.

(l) The International Labour Office should arrange for information to be provided on a regular basis by Governments and non-governmental organizations concerning the exploitation of child labour and of their experiences to eliminate or reduce it; and should submit regularly a report which should be widely circulated.

(m) UNICEF, as the designated lead agency within the United Nations for children's affairs, should be invited to examine the contribution it could make to the elimination of exploitation of child labour, particularly when reviewing its policy on "children in especially difficult circumstances" at the 1986 session of its Executive Board.

(n) All practical steps should be taken by Governments, international organizations and non-governmental organizations to increase awareness amongst children, parents, workers and employers, of the causes and the adverse effects of child labour, and measures to combat its exploitation. Such steps could include the wider dissemination of relevant international instruments translated, where appropriate into other languages in addition to the official languages of the United Nations.

(o) Support should be given to non-governmental organizations concerned with the problems of child labour, particularly at the community level, and a constructive partnership should be evolved between Governments and non-governmental organizations.

(p) Particular priority should be given to the eradication of the most abhorrent forms of child exploitation, in particular prostitution and employment in hazardous activities.

(q) The International Labour Office should take steps to encourage the effective co-operation of all agencies concerned with the elimination of exploitation of child labour, and in particular establish a framework for improved liaison between Governments, voluntary organizations, trade unions, employers and families of working children. The establishment of an international training fund could help to redress the negative effects of the outflow of skilled labour on increasing the demand for child workers.

(r) In order to reach the core of one of the prime causes of exploitation of child labour, which is poverty, increased resources should be made available through bilateral and multilateral channels for the elimination of the exploitation of child labour.

In 1986, the UN Commission on Human Rights adopted a resolution on the exploitation of child labor (resolution 1986/34) in which it concluded that several issues, such as the sale of children, the exploitation of child labor, DEBT BONDAGE, the TRAFFIC IN PERSONS AND THE EXPLOITATION OF THE PROSTITUTION OF OTHERS, and practices similar to slavery such as *apartheid*, had not received sufficient attention. It recommended (a) that, in all societies, appropriate legislation be adopted; education facilities be made available at the place of work or elsewhere; a legal minimum age and minimum wage for children be introduced; and all competent national authorities should ensure that no children under the minimum age established by law are employed, either directly or through local sub-contractors; and (b) that all competent United Nations agencies, development banks, and intergovernmental bodies involved in development projects should encourage policies and measures to protect the human rights of children against abusive labor.

Child labor practices were examined in 1988 by the WORKING GROUP ON CONTEMPORARY FORMS OF SLAVERY of the SUB-COMMISSION ON PREVENTION OF DISCRIMINATION AND PROTECTION OF MINORITIES. The results of its review were summarized in the working group's 1988 report to the sub-commission (UN Doc. E/CN.4/Sub.2/1988/32, chap. III C, para. 41–55) as follows:

The representative of Defence for Children International reported the decision of the Pakistani Government to launch an inquiry into child exploitation. The representative stated that children were being kidnapped and disappeared to be sold into slavery by highly organized networks. Many were said to be sold into forced labour camps, patrolled by armed guards and dogs, in which they were kept under very bad conditions. The representative recommended that Pakistan request technical assistance from the International Labour Organisation in its efforts to combat the problem, that the Working Group should propose the appointment of a Special Rapporteur to report on the progress of the inquiry by the Pakistani Government and that the Pakistani Government should enlist the aid of local organizations in its inquiry.

With reference to the report by the Defence for Children International regarding Pakistan, the Observer for Pakistan indicated that the allegations contained in that report were unsubstantiated. The Observer went on to mention some of the laws in Pakistan outlawing the exploitation of child labour and stated that if the Government was informed of any instances of child labour exploitation, it would prosecute the offenders in accordance with the law. The Observer also indicated that Pakistan had ratified the United Nations Slavery Convention of 1926, the Supplementary Convention on the Abolition of Slavery, the Slave Trade, and Institutions and Practices Similar to Slavery as well as the Convention for the Suppression of the Traffic in Persons and of the Exploitation of Others.

The representative of the Anti-Slavery Society referred to a statement made by the Society to the Working Group at its twelfth session concerning the Ashanti Goldfields of Ghana. The representative reported that the authorities in Ghana had promised to mount an investigation and make known its findings but regretted that no such information had reached the Society. The representative reported that the Ghana National Commission on Children was to mount its own investigation into child labour and hoped that this would signal the end of hazardous child labour in the Ashanti Goldfields.

The representative of Pax Christi presented some information on child labour in India. A number of industries associated with child labour, including the carpet-weaving, pencil, glass bangles and diamond-cutting industries were examined. A review of Indian legislation related to child labour was also carried out. The question was raised whether the Government had taken enough action to ensure the effective implementation of the laws. Some loopholes in the laws were also pointed out regarding, for instance, the minimum age of children allowed to work and the definition of hazardous work which children were not allowed to perform. It was recommended, *inter alia,* that all such loopholes should be corrected, that an awareness campaign should be launched using the media to warn against child exploitation and that many industries should be modernized so as to reduce the need for child labour.

The Observer for India, while replying to the statement on India by Pax Christi, stated that the Government was aware that legislation alone could not bring an end to child labour, and, therefore, it had formulated the National Policy on Child Labour as a follow-up of the Child Labour Act of 1986. He indicated that this policy incorporated such ideas as the stringent enforcement of legislation, focusing of development programmes of different departments/ Ministries on child workers and their families in order to create socio-economic conditions in which the compulsion to send the children to work diminished and was taking steps to benefit child workers in areas of child labour concentration. Government action is targeted in the following areas: enforcement of legislation, employment generation programmes, formal and non-formal education programmes for working children as also for their parents, establishing special schools for child workers with provisions for vocational training, supplementary nutrition, health care as also stipends to compensate the children for their loss in earnings and general awareness programmes. Two pilot projects had already been launched in major concentrations of child labour, namely, the match industry of Sivakasi in Tamil Nadu and the carpet-weaving industry of Varanasi-Mirzapur in Uttar Pradesh. The Observer for India said that his Government's method for implementing the new law on the subject of child labour had received a favourable comment from the ILO.

The representative of the Anti-Slavery Society presented a report on Indian boy carpet-makers to the Working Group. The report highlighted the employment of children in the carpet-weaving industry in contravention of the law and under poor working conditions.

The representative of the Anti-Slavery Society announced the founding of Project Mala. This was aimed at providing more schools and better living conditions for children in affected areas. The project also sought to improve the working conditions of workers and to pay a stipend to the families of the children who would be encouraged to go to school, as compensation for lost income that the children might otherwise have brought into the family. The representative of the Anti-Slavery Society pointed out that the project brought together voluntary organizations, the State Government of Uttar Pradesh and representatives of the carpet industry in a collaborative effort which could serve as a model for similar schemes in other industries and countries.

With regard to the report on India by the Anti-Slavery Society, the Observer for India welcomed the announcement of Project Mala which is in keeping with the Government's National Policy on Child Labour. The schools being set up under this project had the same objectives as the special schools to be set up by the Government in the project areas under the National Child Labour Policy. The Indian Government is taking active steps to eradicate child labour by enforcing legal provisions, implementing poverty removal programmes and projects envisaged in the National Child Labour Policy.

The representative of the International Labour Organisation drew the attention of the Working Group to document E/CN.4/Sub.2/AC.2/1988/5/Add.2 regarding the International Labour Organisation's efforts in Pakistan.

The International Abolitionist Federation intervened to raise two principal issues. Firstly, the representative suggested that the authorities in France were lax in their treatment of violators of children. Secondly, the representative raised the issue of technological developments in the audio-visual field, for instance *Minitel Rose,* and indicated how these were being used for the sexual exploitation of children. It was also pointed out that any attempt to control the sale or use of this technology would be bound to be considered a violation of the freedom to buy and sell goods and the freedom to correspond privately between individuals.

The representative of the United Nations Children's Fund indicated that the United Nations Children's Fund was participating in the Working Group for the first time and intended to do so in the future. It had always worked closely with the International Labour Organisation in its efforts to improve the general conditions of children.

The representative of Defence for Children International gave examples of children forced to work for up to 14 hours a day enslaved on palm or rubber plantations in Asia. Not only were certain economic groups in Asia said to be responsible for this, but it was also suggested that the worldwide consumers of the products derived from the work of the children should be viewed as contributing to its continued existence.

The Observer for Venezuela stated that since it was established that children were being maltreated, it was important to take measures with a view to establishing institutions charged with defending the rights and interests of children and to provide assistance in rehabilitating victims and punishing the perpetrators of the crimes. It was emphasized that practical steps must be taken for and on behalf of the children as they were unable to articulate their problems and needs themselves. The attention of the Working Group was drawn to paragraph 5 (f) of a report on page 3 of document E/CN.4/Sub.2/AC.2/1988/5, in which similar sentiments were expressed by the United Nations Centre for Social Development and Humanitarian Affairs.

Mrs. Bautista reported that in the Philippines persons found to be engaging in child prostitution were being arrested, tried, convicted and, if foreigners, deported. It was stated that the laws of the Philippines banned child pornography. It was also reported that the laws on adoption had been severely tightened up so that abuses should be prevented. Street children were also reported to be better cared for by the combined efforts of the Government of the Philippines and non-governmental organizations. Among other measures, free schooling and child day-care centres for working mothers were to be provided. As an example of child exploitation in the Philippines, Mrs. Bautista gave the example of Japanese fishermen working in the Philippines using 8–16 year-old Filipino boys to dive under dangerous conditions as part of the fishing operations. Mrs. Bautista took the view that exploitation was an economic problem which could only be met by providing income-creating projects for families, a path which the authorities in the Philippines had already embarked upon. An extensive progress report covering many issues in the Philippines was also made available to the Working Group for consultation.

In response to Mrs. Bautista's statement, the Observer for Japan stated that the Japanese delegation had got the information that there were no Japanese fishing enterprises which were using as divers, exploiting or abusing Filipino children.

On the basis of the discussion summarized above, the working group made a number of recommendations, among them (a) that the United Nations agencies dedicated to child welfare, particularly UNICEF and the ILO, study the problem of child labor with a view to assisting countries to eradicate it; and (b) that all competent United Nations agencies, development banks and intergovernmental bodies involved in development projects should ensure that no children be employed, either directly or through local subcontractors. Recommendations along these lines were adopted by the sub-commission (resolution 1988/30) and forwarded to the Commission on Human Rights.

SEE ALSO ILO Minimum Age Convention.

CHILDREN: DETENTION. At its 1985 session, the UN SUB-COMMISSION ON PREVENTION OF DISCRIMINATION AND PROTECTION OF MINORITIES requested the Secretary-General (resolution 1985/19) to invite governments, United Nations organs, specialized agencies, intergovernmental organizations, the International Committee of the Red Cross, and other non-governmental organizations to submit information concerning the incarceration of children under the age of 18 with adult prisoners, and to solicit their views on ways and means of preventing this practice.

The Secretary-General was asked to compile the information received and to submit it in a report to the sub-commission at its 1986 session.

The information compiled by the Secretary-General (UN Doc. E/CN.4/Sub.2/1987/30 and Add. 1) was drawn to the attention of the sub-commission at its 1987 session, and was considered as background documentation by the sub-commission's WORKING GROUP ON CONTEMPORARY FORMS OF SLAVERY and its WORKING GROUP ON DETENTION. However, it was not examined in detail by the sub-commission or by either working group.

At its 1989 session, the sub-commission requested the Secretary-General (resolution 1989/31) to update his report by including in it further information made available to him on the question of children deprived of their liberty and to submit the new version to the sub-commission's 1990 session for consideration. At the same time, it appointed one of its members, Mrs. Mary Concepcion Bautista (Philippines), to prepare a report on the application of international standards concerning the human rights of detained juveniles, in particular the separation of jevenile and adult offenders in penal institutions, detention pending trial, least possible use of institutionalization, and the objectives of institutional treatment.

SEE ALSO United Nations Standard Minimum Rules for the Administration of Juvenile Justice.

CHILDREN: MILITARY SERVICE. The UN SUB-COMMISSION ON PREVENTION OF DISCRIMINATION AND PROTECTION OF MINORITIES at its 1989 session expressed deep concern (resolution 1989/41) that, in many parts of the world, children continue to take part in hostilities and are recruited into the armed forces. It recognized that children who have been trained to hate and have participated in war are often mentally and morally crippled for life and deplored the fact that many child soldiers have been killed or seriously injured, while others languish as prisoners of war.

The sub-commission decided to pursue the subject in subsequent sessions and called upon the Secretary-General to prepare for its examination a report dealing with the recruitment of children into government and non-governmental armed forces and their participation in hostilities.

CHILDREN: RIGHT TO PROTECTION. Article 24 of the INTERNATIONAL COVENANT ON CIVIL AND POLITICAL RIGHTS provides that:

1. Every child shall have, without any discrimination as to race, color, sex, language, religion, national or social origin, property, or birth, the right to such measures of protection as are required by his status as a minor, on the part of his family, society and the State.

2. Every child shall be registered immediately after birth and shall have a name.

3. Every child has the right to acquire a nationality.

With regard to article 24, the HUMAN RIGHTS COMMITTEE, at its 35th session, held at United Nations headquarters, New York, from 20 March to 7 April 1989, adopted the following comment (UN Doc. A/ 44/40, Annex VI, general comment 17 [35]):

1. Article 24 of the International Covenant on Civil and Political Rights recognizes the right of every child, without any discrimination, to receive from his family, society and the State the protection required by his status as a minor. Consequently, the implementation of this provision entails the adoption of special measures to protect children, in addition to the measures that States are required to take under article 2 to ensure that everyone enjoys the rights provided for in the Covenant. The reports submitted by States parties often seem to underestimate this obligation and supply inadequate information on the way in which children are afforded enjoyment of their right to a special protection.

2. In this connection, the Committee points out that the rights provided for in article 24 are not the only ones that the Covenant recognizes for children and that, as individuals, children benefit from all of the civil rights enunciated in the Covenant. In enunciating a right, some provisions of the Covenant expressly indicate to States measures to be adopted with a view to affording minors greater protection than adults. Thus, as far as the right to life is concerned, the death penalty cannot be imposed for crimes committed by persons under 18 years of age. Similarly, if lawfully deprived of their liberty, accused juvenile persons shall be separated from adults and are entitled to be brought as speedily as possible for adjudication; in turn, convicted juvenile offenders shall be subject to a penitentiary system that involves segregation from adults and is appropriate to their age and legal status, the aim being to foster reformation and social rehabilitation. In other instances, children are protected by the possibility of the restriction—provided that such restriction is warranted—of a right recognized by the Covenant, such as the right to publicize a judgement in a suit at law or a criminal case, from which an exception may be made when the interest of the minor so requires.

3. In most cases, however, the measures to be adopted are not specified in the Covenant and it is for each State to determine them in the light of the protection needs of children in its territory and within its jurisdiction. The Committee notes in this regard that such measures, although intended primarily to ensure that children fully enjoy the other rights enunciated in the Covenant, may also be economic, social and cultural. For example, every possible economic and social measure should be taken to reduce infant mortality and to eradicate malnutrition among children and to prevent them from being subjected to acts of violence and cruel and inhuman treatment or from being exploited by means of forced labour or prostitution, or by their use in the illicit trafficking of narcotic drugs, or by any other means. In the cultural field, every possible measure should be taken to foster the development of their personality and to provide them with a level of education that will enable them to enjoy the rights recognized in the Covenant, particularly the right to freedom of opinion and expression. Moreover, the Committee wishes to draw the attention of States parties to the need to include in their reports information on measures adopted to ensure that children do not take a direct part in armed conflicts.

4. The right to special measures of protection belongs to every child because of his status as a minor. Nevertheless, the Covenant does not indicate the age at which he attains his majority. This is to be determined by each State party in the light of the relevant social and cultural conditions. In this respect, States should indicate in their reports the age at which the child attains his majority in civil matters and assumes criminal responsibility. States should also indicate the age at which a child is legally entitled to work and the age at which he is treated as an adult under labour law. States should further indicate the age at which a child is considered adult for the purposes of article 10, paragraphs 2 and 3. However, the Committee notes that the age for the above purposes should not be set unreasonably low and that in any case a State party cannot absolve itself from its obligations under the Covenant regarding persons under the age of 18, notwithstanding that they have reached the age of majority under domestic law.

5. The Covenant requires that children should be protected against discrimination on any grounds such as race, colour, sex, language, religion, national or social origin, property or birth. In this connection, the Committee notes that, whereas non-discrimination in the enjoyment of the rights provided for in the Covenant also stems, in the case of children, from article 2 and their equality before the law from article 26, the non-discrimination clause contained in article 24 relates specifically to the measures of protection referred to in that provision. Reports by States parties should indicate how legislation and practice ensure that measures of protection are aimed at removing all discrimination in every field, including inheritance, particularly as between children who are nationals and children who are aliens or as between legitimate children and children born out of wedlock.

6. Responsibility for guaranteeing children the necessary protection lies with the family, society and the State. Although the Covenant does not indicate how such responsibility is to be apportioned, it is primarily incumbent on the family, which is interpreted broadly to include all persons composing it in the society of the State party concerned, and particularly on the parents, to create conditions to promote the harmonious development of the child's personality and his enjoyment of the rights recognized in the Covenant. However, since it is quite common for the father and mother to be gainfully employed outside the home, reports by States parties should indicate how society, social institutions and the State are discharging their responsibility to assist the family in ensuring the protection of the child. Moreover, in cases where the parents and the family seriously fail in their duties, ill-treat or neglect the child, the State should intervene to restrict parental authority and the child may be separated from his family when circumstances so require. If the marriage is dissolved, steps should be taken, keeping in view the paramount interest of the children, to give them necessary protection and, so far as is possible, to guarantee personal relations with both parents. The Committee considers it useful that re-

ports by States parties should provide information on the special measures of protection adopted to protect children who are abandoned or deprived of their family environment in order to enable them to develop in conditions that most closely resemble those characterizing the family environment.

7. Under article 24, paragraph 2, every child has the right to be registered immediately after birth and to have a name. In the Committee's opinion, this provision should be interpreted as being closely linked to the provision concerning the right to special measures of protection and it is designed to promote recognition of the child's legal personality. Providing for the right to have a name is of special importance in the case of children born out of wedlock. The main purpose of the obligation to register children after birth is to deduce the danger of abduction, sale of or traffic in children, or of other types of treatment that are incompatible with the enjoyment of the rights provided for in the Covenant. Reports by States parties should indicate in detail the measures that ensure the immediate registration of children born in their territory.

8. Special attention should also be paid, in the context of the protection to be granted to children, to the right of every child to acquire a nationality, as provided for in article 24, paragraph 3. While the purpose of this provision is to prevent a child from being afforded less protection by society and the State because he is stateless, it does not necessarily make it an obligation for States to give their nationality to every child born in their territory. However, States are required to adopt every appropriate measure, both internally and in co-operation with other States, to ensure that every child has a nationality when he is born. In this connection, no discrimination with regard to the acquisition of nationality should be admissible under internal law as between legitimate children and children born out of wedlock or of stateless parents or based on the nationality status of one or both of the parents. The measures adopted to ensure that children have a nationality should always be referred to in reports by States parties.

CHILDREN: SALE AND TRAFFICKING. A practice giving rise to effects similar to those of slavery or the slave trade. In 1983, the Economic and Social Council requested the CENTER FOR HUMAN RIGHTS (resolution 1983/30) to prepare, in liaison with the concerned United Nations agencies and with the competent non-governmental organizations, a study on the sale of children. The study (UN Doc. E/CN.4/Sub.2/28) was presented to the sub-commission at its 1987 session; but the sub-commission (resolution 1987/ 32) requested that it be put back on the drawing board and, with the help of United Nations agencies and non-governmental organizations, be given a deeper and broader accent, introducing matters relating to organ transplants and the foetus trade. The revised report on the sale of children (UN Doc. E/CN.4/Sub.2/1988/30) was submitted to the sub-commission at its 1988 session.

At that session, the WORKING GROUP ON CONTEMPO-RARY FORMS OF SLAVERY reviewed in detail develop-

ments relating to slavery and the slave trade. Its examination of the question of the sale of children was summarized in its report to the sub-commission (UN Doc. E/CN.4/Sub.2/1988/32, chap. III B, para. 17–28) as follows:

The attention of the Working Group was drawn by the representative of the Anti-Slavery Society to information alleging that babies were being kidnapped in Thailand and smuggled over the border into Malaysia. Although police on both sides of the frontier had recently become more active and had reportedly arrested some 60 kidnappers, no Thai government agency seemed to be officially charged with ending the trafficking. Credit for uncovering the infamous trade was due to the Bangkok-based Centre for the Protection of Children's Rights (CPCR), which was nearing the end of its investigation.

Minders were paid a small sum per day to keep each baby in a safe house until he or she was taken across the border. The Society joined the CPCR in calling for stricter observance of international law and for higher penalties than the 10 years in prison faced by convicted smugglers in Thailand. The Society also welcomed the Thai Government's intention to raise the minimum employment age from 13, and hoped that concern for child welfare would be extended to stopping the kidnapping and smuggling of babies, as well as avoidable deaths in the process.

Other instances of sale of children were brought to the attention of the Working Group by the representative of the Defence for Children International Movement, who made reference to an alleged traffic in children from Asian to Arab countries where they worked, *inter alia,* as jockeys in camel races in the desert.

The representative of the International Association of Democratic Lawyers described to the Working Group the different stages of an inquiry that Association had carried out in Haiti, along with the International Federation of Human Rights, to investigate the alleged kidnapping and sale of children for the purpose of organ transplants for the children of well-to-do families. The representative of the Association explained that the inquiry had provided no formal proof, although she stressed that organ transplants from poor and illiterate persons, and, in particular, children, were considered to be a sad reality by many of the people interviewed by the representatives of the Association. Allegedly, the children were kidnapped under the pretence of false adoption procedures and then disappeared (they were probably sent abroad); they were also subjected to all kinds of abuse. The Association underlined that these were the views of the persons interviewed but were not necessarily shared by the Association.

The Observer for Haiti, reviewing the report in detail, described it as unproven, unsubstantiated and maliciously motivated and rejected all the allegations made.

The Working Group noted that much more solid evidence would be required if the allegations on sale of children for organ transplants were to be substantiated.

The Observer for Venezuela drew the attention of the Working Group to the draft convention on the rights of the child being prepared by the Working Group of the Commission on Human Rights, and in particular to the draft articles (18, 18 *bis,* 18 *ter,* 18 *quater,* 18 *quinto* and 18 *sexto*) which attempted to protect the child from all forms of exploitation, including economic exploitation, narcotic and psychotropic substances, sexual exploitation, abduction, sale or traffic and to provide for the physical and psychological recovery and social reintegration of the children victims of exploitation. The Observer raised the issue as to whether the information and experience of the Working Group would reveal some form or forms of exploitation not covered by the draft convention; she invited the Working Group to review the articles of the draft convention for that purpose and to make its views known to the Sub-Commission.

Mrs. Bautista suggested accordingly that the concept of "mutilation" should be included in draft article 18 *sexto* of the draft convention as one of the practices that ought to be specifically forbidden. She added that an express prohibition of the use of children for medical experimentation should also be included in the draft convention.

One member of the Working Group wondered whether, at this late stage of the negotiations on the draft convention on the rights of the child, it was still possible to make any recommendations on that subject to the Working Group of the Commission on Human Rights.

The representative of Defence for Children International (DCI) informed the Working Group of a project undertaken by that organization at the request of the Government of Argentina. In 1987, the Argentine Government had asked DCI to make an investigation into certain questions affecting children in that country. An international commission of experts had accordingly been set up to make a full and independent investigation of trafficking in, and the sale of, children, among other matters, and a report had been produced analysing the causes of trafficking and making a number of interim recommendations, covering legislative reform, social policies and police practices.

The representative of DCI stated that the complexity and clandestine nature of the sale of and traffic in children inhibited the gathering of information; such information as had been obtained thus represented only the tip of the iceberg. Yet it was only by examining those practices that a framework could be established whereby an overview of the general situation could be obtained; this required co-ordinated action by Governments, international governmental organizations and non-governmental organizations as well as all other relevant sources. In particular, the help of groups and organizations at local and national levels, where these practices occurred was most relevant. At the same time, the co-operation of Governments was required both at the international and national levels. The different practices of the sale of and traffic in children needed to be distinguished within a socio-economic and cultural context in order to provide the basis for policy formulation; thus, judicious research programmes at the national level should be undertaken for this purpose.

In addition, the representative of DCI made reference to the revised report (E/CN.4/Sub.2/1988/30) on the question of the sale of children, noting that it had not taken account of the comments made by DCI and others in regard to the contents of the initial report. Finally, she requested the Working Group to consider the most effective way to deal with the above-mentioned practices, and explore the possibility of appointing a Special Rapporteur pursuant to the recommendation by the Commission on Human Rights. She further indicated that international co-operation between States was essential in the identification of networks of traffickers and also in the search for missing persons, underlining that the role of INTERPOL in that connection should be reinforced.

On the basis of the discussion summarized above, the working group made a number of recommendations, among them (a) that the Secretary-General should submit the information received on the alleged sale of children to governments for any comments that they may wish to make; (b) that the results of a symposium to be held by INTERPOL on traffic in persons, including the sale of children, as well as other information which INTERPOL may have on the sale of children, should be transmitted to the Secretary-General to facilitate the completion of his final report on this issue; (c) that the interested specialized agencies and non-governmental organizations should gather information on the sale of children, including their observations on ways and means of how to prevent the occurrence of this phenomenon, and send this information to the Secretary-General to facilitate the completion of his final report; and (d) that the Secretary-General's final report on the sale of children should be submitted to the working group at its 1989 session. Recommendations along these lines were adopted by the sub-commission and forwarded (resolution 1988/30) to the Commission on Human Rights.

On 6 March 1989, the Commission on Human Rights, having considered the recommendations of the sub-commission, expressed grave concern (resolution 1989/35) that slavery, the slave trade, slavery-like practices, and even modern manifestations of this phenomenon still exist, representing some of the gravest violations of human rights, and requested the Secretary-General to invite States parties to the SLAVERY CONVENTION SIGNED AT GENEVA ON 25 SEPTEMBER 1926, AS AMENDED, the SUPPLEMENTARY CONVENTION ON THE ABOLITION OF SLAVERY, THE SLAVE TRADE AND INSTITUTIONS AND PRACTICES SIMILAR TO SLAVERY of 1956 and the CONVENTION FOR THE SUPPRESSION OF THE TRAFFIC IN PERSONS AND OF THE EXPLOITATION OF THE PROSTITUTION OF OTHERS of 1949 to submit to the sub-commission regular reports on the situation in their countries, as provided for under the conventions and in Economic and Social Council decision 16 (LVI) of 17 May 1974. It further requested the Secretary-General to undertake a study of the ways and means by which an effective mechanism may be established for the implementation of those conventions.

The commission invited those eligible States which have not ratified the conventions to consider doing so as soon as possible and asked them to consider providing information regarding their national legislation and practices in this field; and requested the interested specialized agencies and non-governmental organizations to gather information on the sale of children, including their observations on ways and means of preventing the occurrence of this phenomenon, and to send this information to the Secretary-General for inclusion in his report.

The commission also urged member States to enact legislation, where they have not yet done so, making it a crime to produce, distribute, or possess pornographic material involving children; to take all appropriate action to protect children and promote their rights, including the possibility of establishing national bodies to achieve these objectives; and to take appropriate action for the protection of migrant women against exploitation by prostitution and other slavery-like practices.

In his report on the question to the 1989 session of the sub-commission (UN Doc. E/CN.4/Sub.2/1989/38), the Secretary-General indicated that, although he had addressed requests to governments, United Nations organs, specialized agencies, and competent intergovernmental and non-governmental organizations, only a few substantial replies had been received and that those communications did not add much in terms of reliably attested and substantiated facts to complement information previously available on the subject. He, therefore, suggested that the sub-commission consider recommending that a special rapporteur be appointed to undertake an overall study of the question of the sale of children, including commercially motivated (and especially transnational) adoptions.

At its 1989 session, the sub-commission, on recommendation of its Working Group on Contemporary Forms of Slavery, proposed (resolution 1989/42) the appointment of such a special rapporteur "to consider matters relating to the sale of children, child prostitution and child pornography, including the problem of the adoption of children for commercial purposes" and suggested that a person of international reputation should be appointed as special rapporteur by the chairman of the Commission on Human Rights following consultations with other officers of the commission.

At the same session, the sub-commission proposed (resolution 1989/43) that the Commission on Human Rights should call upon the Secretary-General to transmit to governments, specialized agencies, and the intergovernmental and non-governmental organizations concerned the draft of a Program of Action for Prevention of Sale of Children, Child Prostitution and Child Pornography contained in the report of its Working Group on Contemporary Forms of Slavery, to obtain their comments on the program and to present to the 1990 session of the sub-commission an analytical summary of the responses received. The draft program was as follows (UN Doc. E/CN.4/Sub.2/1989/39, chap. VII, annex A):

Draft Programme of Action for Prevention of Sale of Children, Child Prostitution and Child Pornography
A. General

1. To prevent the sale of children, child prostitution and child pornography, concerted measures are called for at the national and international level, including information, education, assistance and rehabilitation, legislative measures and a strengthening of law enforcement in this field. Co-ordinating agencies should be appointed or established at the national, regional and global level.

2. At the global level, co-ordination of the Programme of Action should be carried out by the Centre for Human Rights in co-operation with other sections of the United Nations Secretariat including the Centre for the Advancement of Women, and with concerned intergovernmental agencies, in particular UNICEF and UNESCO. Co-operation should also be established with INTERPOL.

Information and Education. 3. An international information campaign to raise public awareness of these abuses should form part of the Programme. Religious and lay organizations should be encouraged to participate. The media should also be called upon in order to help break the practice of silence surrounding these issues, while avoiding sensationalism. Law enforcement agencies should be given a significant role in this campaign.

4. To improve the sources of information, studies and investigations of these abuses should be undertaken by public and private institutions. The outcomes should, wherever possible, be made public and exchanged between governmental and non-governmental organizations at the national and international level.

5. To provide a focus for the campaign, a World Day for the Abolition of Contemporary Forms of Slavery might be proclaimed. One possibility is to use the date of 2 December, the anniversary of the adoption of the Convention for the Suppression of the Traffic in Persons and of the Exploitation of the Prostitution of Others.

6. Special educational measures should be adopted, to be directed both at the general public and to specific groups. The education should be based on universally agreed ethical principles including the recognition of every child's fundamental right to the integrity of its own body. Emphasis should be placed on the damaging effects which these abuses have on children, ways in which the abuses can be prevented, discovered and exposed, and ways to assist children who have suffered from such abuse.

7. Preventive educational programmes at the primary and secondary level should make the children understand the dangers of these abuses, including the health dangers such as AIDS, and make them aware of their own right to the integrity of their body and thereby strengthen their defence against abuses.

8. Such education must avoid underplaying the issues but should also avoid sensationalizing it. Great care must be taken in developing educational programmes on these subjects. The age of the children concerned and the culture in which the children are living must be taken into account.

9. For street children, who are particularly affected by these practices, alternative educational programmes should be developed.

10. Social workers, health workers, members of law enforcement agencies and of the judiciary should also receive education on the occurrence of such abuses and the ways in which they can be counteracted.

Social Measures, Development Assistance. 11. It is recognized that these practices are often linked to poverty, and that long-range structural reforms in the social and economic fields will be required for their prevention. In the shorter run, development activities of the United Nations and other international as well as national agencies should have a substantive and positive impact on children. Priority should be given to policies aimed at improving the social, economic and working conditions of women in general and of the poorest women in particular. Local community projects, including collective self-help projects by vulnerable mothers, should also be encouraged.

12. The needs of children exposed to sexual exploitation should be taken into account in development plans and assistance. Special attention should be given to certain groups of street children and children whose mothers are engaged in prostitution. Governments and non-governmental organizations should be encouraged to initiate projects designed to protect street children from sexual abuse (e.g. small-scale enterprise projects for children, "safe houses", emergency centres, etc.). Efforts should also be made to reunite street children in cities with their families in rural areas.

Legal Measures and Law Enforcement. 13. Preventive legislation aimed at protecting children should be strengthened and better enforced. Police, courts and treatment and support systems should focus more on children. Legal aid should be easily available to those who claim to have been sexually violated and to parents or legal guardians in cases of sale of children. Methods should be developed to obtain evidence from the child without further traumatization, and witnesses should be afforded protection.

14. Sexual abuse and traffic in children are serious crimes and must be treated as such. More severe penalties should be imposed on consumers and procurers.

15. Effective legislative and enforcement measures must also be directed against the middlemen and others who encourage and make a profit from the sale and sexual exploitation of children: agents, dealers, brothel-owners, and others involved. The proceeds from such activities should be confiscated.

16. The draft Convention on the Rights of the Child, when adopted, provides protection against sale of children and sexual exploitation. States are encouraged to become parties to the Convention at the earliest possible moment. For its implementation within States, national institutions, with representatives of public agencies and private organizations, might be established to co-ordinate action and to protect children and their rights.

Rehabilitation and Re-integration. 17. Programmes for rehabilitation and re-integration with an inter-disciplinary approach should be established to assist children who have been victims of sexual exploitation, and their families. Agencies implementing such programmes, whether public or non-governmental, should be given the necessary support and funding.

International Co-ordination. 18. Bilateral and multilateral co-operation among law enforcement agencies is essential. States should establish their own data base, improve their reporting at all levels, and report to INTERPOL to allow for a special data bank on suspects involved in such abuses across borders. The experience gained in international police co-operation in combating drug traffic should be made use of to prevent international traffic involving the sale and sexual exploitation of children.

B. Sale of Children

19. States should be encouraged to take effective legal and administrative measures to prevent the abduction and sale of children. Laws should be adopted or strengthened which impose penalties on parents and on all others knowingly involved in the traffic of children.

20. Measures should be taken to ensure that international adoptions do not involve the illicit removal of children from parents. Procedures for this purpose should be based on the 1986 United Nations Declaration on Social and Legal Principles relating to the Protection and Welfare of Children with Special Reference to Foster Placement and Adoption Nationally and Internationally, and the Convention on the Rights of the Child when adopted. Under no circumstances must adoption be allowed to involve financial gain for any of the parties involved.

21. States should adopt effective and urgent procedures at the national level and through international co-operation to find abducted, unlawfully removed or disappeared children and to reunite such children with their families.

C. Child Prostitution

22. Legislative and other measures should be taken to prevent sex tourism. Such measures should be adopted both in the countries from which the customer comes (most often the industrialized countries) and the countries to which they go (often to developing countries). Marketing tourism through the enticement of sex with women and children should be penalized on the same level as procurement.

23. The World Tourist Organization should be encouraged to convene a world conference on ways in which to prevent such practices.

24. States having military bases or troops on foreign territories, as well as host States, should take all the necessary measures to prevent such military personnel from being involved in child prostitution. The same applies to other categories of persons who for professional reasons are posted abroad.

25. Legislation should be adopted to prevent new forms of technology from being used for soliciting for prostitution.

D. Child Pornography

26. Taking into account, as stated at the INTERPOL symposium in September 1988, that child pornography is the permanent visual depiction of the sexual molestation and exploitation of a child, and that there is an international market for this material, law enforcement agencies should place a higher priority on the investigation of child pornography with particular emphasis placed on the welfare of the child.

27. States are urged to enact legislation, where they have not yet done so, making it a crime to produce, distribute or possess pornographic material involving children.

28. Postal and custom services should be required to detect and prevent the transmission of material containing child pornography. Special attention has to be paid to new technology for producing pornography, including video films.

29. States should be encouraged to protect children from exposure to adult pornography through suitable legislation and appropriate measures of control.

C

CHILDREN AND DRUGS. Alarmed by the fact that drug dealers' organizations are making use of children in their illicit production of and trafficking in drugs and by the increase in the number of drug-addicted children, and conscious of the physical and psychological damage inflicted on children by the illicit use of narcotic drugs and of its serious effects both on their potential for development and their relationships with their families and society, the UN General Assembly on 8 December 1988 (resolution 43/121) strongly condemned drug trafficking in all its forms, particularly those criminal activities which involve children in the use, production, and illicit sale of narcotic drugs and psychotropic substances; and urged all States to join together to promote the establishment of national and international programs to protect children from the illicit consumption of drugs and psychotropic substances and from involvement in illicit production and trafficking.

The assembly invited the governments of those States which are most affected by drug use among their child population to adopt urgent additional measures, as part of their national strategies, to prevent, reduce, and eliminate drug use by children, with the aim of ensuring for children a social and family environment that will preserve their health, physical fitness, and well-being. It also called upon all States to promote the adoption, by their legislative authorities, of measures providing for suitably severe punishment of drug-trafficking crimes that involve children.

Later, the Economic and Social Council, on 22 May 1989, appealed (resolution 1989/123) to the competent international agencies and the United Nations Fund for Drug Abuse Control to assign high priority to financial support for prevention campaigns and programs designed to rehabilitate drug-addicted minors and conducted by government bodies.

SEE ALSO Declaration on the Control of Drug Trafficking and Abuse; Drug Abuse.

CHILE. The Republic of Chile is a country in temperate South America, on the Pacific Ocean. It has borders with Argentina, Bolivia, and Peru; and a number of offshore islands are included in its territories. It achieved independence from Spain in 1818 and became a member of the United Nations in 1945. Its population is estimated by the UN (1990) to be 12,987,000. Over 92% of its people are of mixed Spanish and Amerindian descent, 2% are of European descent, and the remainder are indigenous Amerindians of the Araucanian, Fuegian, and Chango groups. Religions practiced include Christianity (Roman Catholic, 89%; Protestant denominations, 10%), and Judaism (1%). Languages in common use include Spanish (official) and Araucanian. Literacy is estimated at 94%.

The government (1990) took the form of a republic. The 1925 constitution provides for three branches of government: the executive under the president, the legislative in the form of a Congress, and the judicial with the Supreme Court as its authority. Under that constitution, the president is elected every five years. In 1970, President Salvador Allende Gossens was elected with 36% of the votes, defeating two other candidates, with the support of *Unidad Popular,* a combination of Socialists, Communists, and other leftist groups. His election was accepted in the international community as an example of a marxist elected to high office by the democratic process. However, the control of Congress remained in the hands of parties opposed to *Unidad Popular.* Although, in 1972, *Unidad Popular* won 44% of the popular vote, there was strong opposition to some parts of its program, which included nationalization of the banks and copper mines and acceleration of land reform.

On 11 September 1973, the government of President Allende was ousted by a *coup d'etat* engineered by a military junta, in which the president lost his life. The military chief, General Augusto Pinochet Ugarte, assumed the office of president on 17 December 1974. In the 16 years between that date and 15 December 1989—when Chile's voters elected Christian Democrat Patricio Aylwin to lead them back to civilian government—the situation in that country provoked innumerable complaints of gross violations of human rights, many of which proved valid upon investigation.

On 1 March 1974, the COMMISSION ON HUMAN RIGHTS received information alleging that violations of human rights had taken place in Chile and that the lives of many political, social, and educational figures were in danger. At that time, it called upon the government junta, for the first time, to cease activities contrary to the United Nations Charter and the International Covenants on Human Rights. Later, after receiving detailed and alarming studies of continuing widespread violations of human rights in Chile from such non-governmental organizations as AMNESTY INTERNATIONAL, the INTERNATIONAL COMMISSION OF JURISTS and the WORLD CONFEDERATION OF ORGANIZATIONS OF THE TEACHING PROFESSION, the commission established a working group to keep the situation under review. The working group was later replaced by a special rapporteur.

Several special rapporteurs have since kept the commission informed about the situation of human rights in Chile; they have been, successively, Judge Abdoulaye Dieye (Senegal), Judge Rajsoomer Lallah (Mauritius), and, most recently, Prof. Fernando Volio Jiminez (Costa Rica), who assumed his mandate on 1 February 1985. Each report, of each special rapporteur, clearly indicated the broad extent and serious nature of the violations of human rights which took place in Chile under the military regime of General Augusto Pinochet.

Prof. Fernando Volio Jiminez submitted ten reports on the subject either to the UN General Assembly or to the Commission on Human Rights between 1985 and 1990. The ninth report (UN Doc. A/44/635), submitted to the assembly's 1989 session, was a preliminary summary on the evolution of the human rights situation in Chile throughout 1989. The tenth report (UN Doc. E/CN.4/1990/5), submitted to the commission's 1990 session, covered the most significant developments during the second half of 1989.

The General Assembly took note of the ninth report and invited the commission (resolution 44/166) "to evaluate . . . the situation of human rights in Chile, bearing in mind the reports presented by the Special Rapporteur, to consider the mandate of the Special Rapporteur and also how the item is to be dealt with on the agenda in the light of developments in the situation, and to report to the General Assembly at its forty-fifth [1990] session."

The tenth report was examined in detail by the Commission on Human Rights at its 1990 session. In the report, the special rapporteur indicated that, while preparing it, he had not received any information from the Chilean government as had been the case in the past, that government having decided not to accept the renewal of his mandate due to the politically and ideologically based attitude that the Commission on Human Rights had maintained with respect to Chile. The report, accordingly, was based on information from other interested parties, which had provided him with testimony and documents of relevance to his mandate and which he had analyzed in the light of the norms set forth in the international treaties ratified by Chile and other norms of international human rights law recognized as universally applicable.

This information, on which the government of Chile declined to state its point of view or to permit an on-the-spot inquiry, led the special rapporteur to a series of conclusions and recommendations which he presented to the commission in the tenth report, as follows (UN Doc. E/CN.4/1990/5, chaps. IV and V):

Conclusions. In writing this report, the Special Rapporteur wishes to emphasize that the human rights situation in Chile is quite different from that in February 1985. During the last five years, the Special Rapporteur has witnessed a notable improvement in that field, in the direction of respect for freedom, in its various forms.

When he was appointed in February 1985, Chile was in the throes of deep social tensions, whose tragic repercussions took the form of very serious systematic breaches of fundamental rights. The Government had emerged out of a *coup d'état* in 1973 and was exercised by a Military Junta. Administrative internal banishment was widespread, torture and unlawful coercion abounded as part of a system of widespread repression, used mainly by the National Information Agency (CNI); the state of siege and two other states of emergency were in force; political parties were banned; the Government controlled the universities; the President of the Republic enjoyed excessive powers under the Constitution which conflicted with its democratic principles and lent themselves to abuses prejudicial to fundamental rights and in particular to the administration of justice; opponents of the régime were frequently subjected to intimidation, generally with serious results; thousands of Chileans were in exile; police, security forces and the armed forces acted violently, exceeding their functions to the detriment of Chileans' basic rights; and freedom of the press and freedom of assembly were tightly controlled by the exceptional powers of the President of the Republic.

Despite the situation described above (which merely summarizes the main contributory factors to the tension and the rifts characteristic of those five years), the Chilean people possessed the foresight, courage and wisdom needed to find a way out of the conflict. Individuals and groups emerged from all sectors and engaged in a quest for solutions, with the establishment of a democratic régime as their overriding objective.

The 1985 picture gradually changed. That of 1990 is very different. On two memorable occasions, principally, in October 1988 and December 1989, the Chilean people was able to exercise its right to decide on its political future by means of elections carried out in a conducive atmosphere since the obstacles mentioned above in paragraph 14 had been removed, and the way was open for representative democracy, the guardian of freedom.

In addition to the elections in December 1989, the following developments contributed to improve the human rights situation during the period covered in this report: (a) The adoption by the Government Junta (the current Legislative Power), of the National Congress Act, regulating the composition and powers of the Chamber of Deputies and the Senate, whose members were chosen in the aforementioned elections and who will take up their duties on 14 March 1990. This law has constitutional status and is the last of those laws which the Special Rapporteur worked to promote during his mandate, all of which were designed to protect fundamental rights, as a component of the new democratic structure; (b) The administrative internal banishment of two important trade-union leaders was ended; (c) The Government Junta adopted various amendments to the Penal Code and to the Code of Penal Procedure, to ensure better protection for the rights of persons facing trial in the civil courts; (d) The civil courts took a major step in the right direction when Judge Dobra Lusic of the Santiago Third Criminal Court sentenced four CNI agents, who had been among a group of 40 organized civilians who had attacked demonstrators on 1 May 1983 in the Plaza Venezuela in Santiago. The judgement observed that the attackers' purpose had been to "employ violence in order to repress acts through which the demonstrators indicated moral dissent"; (e) On 11 January 1990 the dissolution was announced of the CNI (the secret police).

The Special Rapporteur wishes to draw attention to two new and verified retrograde developments of particular importance:

(a) The call for the death penalty made by *Ad Hoc Military Prosecutor* Renato Gómez against 15 persons in the case concerning the attack on the presidential convoy and the attack on Los Queñes, and the call for the death penalty by Military Prosecutor Francisco Silva against two other persons in the case concerning the murder of *Carabinero* Miguel Vásquez Tobar, in 1986 in which two officials of the Vicaría de la Solidaridad also face charges.

(b) The final decision of the Supreme Court to terminate the investigation carried out by the Inspecting Magistrate Carlos Cerda. Not only did the Court fail to act on the investigations conducted by Judge Cerda, with admirable thoroughness and devotion to the cause of human dignity, which the Judiciary should guard with zeal, but it also prevented his work from achieving its ultimate objective in the case of 10 missing prisoners, as well as other similar investigations into the many unsolved cases involving the abhorrent offence of detention followed by disappearance, reported after the 1973 *coup d'état.*

The agreements concluded between the Government and the International Committee of the Red Cross (ICRC) remained in operation to prevent the practice of torture. The agreements, whose formulation the Special Rapporteur advocated, were the outcome of efforts by groups of Chileans who were opposed to the torture that had spread throughout the Chilean political system. During his four visits to Chile, the Special Rapporteur maintained close contacts with those groups and in the light of their experience and that of the Committee was able to indicate to high-ranking members of the Government his profound concern at the practice of torture generally employed by officials responsible for interrogating detained persons. The Government figures reacted in a positive manner and thus the current agreements which incorporate the main initiatives of the ICRC and which have been improved in the light of experience, were drawn up.

As a result of these developments, torture ceased to be practised systematically, although it has not yet been totally eliminated and remains a source of much concern to the Special Rapporteur.

The Special Rapporteur has given continuing and close attention to military justice. Its method, which run counter to the universal principles that regulate the administration of justice in general, as well as against the specific principles of the military régime, undermine the human rights of Chileans. Accordingly, the Special Rapporteur has energetically denounced, and continues to denounce, such methods. Unless there is a far-reaching reform of military justice, the human rights situation in Chile will always be precarious and a source of deep concern both for Chileans and for the democratic international community.

The death penalty called for by the military prosecutors against 17 persons casts a dark shadow over the human rights situation in Chile, on the eve of the establishment of a democratic political system. Article 6 of the International Covenant on Civil and Political Rights, ratified by Chile, states that "Every human being has the inherent right to life". Article 4 of the American Convention on Human Rights, also ratified by Chile, reiterates that "Every person has the right to have his life respected". The 17 applications

for the death penalty mentioned above should be viewed in the light of these legal provisions.

With the exception of the case of those persons who were burned (Rodrigo Rojas and Carmen Gloria Quintana), in the three other notorious cases, no significant progress has been made in investigating the facts and although in the case of those who were burned a ruling was handed down against the person found guilty, his penalty was light in relation to the seriousness of the acts, thereby depriving the ruling of any exemplary value.

Apart from the rebuttal issued by the Government of Chile (A/44/728), during the period covered by this report the Special Rapporteur has not found any fresh evidence that would allow him to form a view on the complaints concerning alleged human rights violations at *Colonia Dignidad,* most of whose residents are German subjects, to which he referred in his ninth report submitted to the General Assembly. However, the Special Rapporteur considers that the matter deserves careful and comprehensive investigation, without undermining the sovereignty of Chile, referred to by its Government.

The extremely disturbing case of the five detainees who disappeared at the end of 1987 has still not been clarified.

In preparing this report, the Special Rapporteur did not have official co-operation from the Government of Chile. He was only able to obtain, unofficially, some information on specific issues through the Ambassador of Chile to Costa Rica.

The task of continuing to restore the system of human rights protection will devolve upon the new Government of Chile, chosen in the December 1989 elections, to ensure that redress is made for the wrongs suffered by many individuals until March 1990, when the democratic Government will take office. That responsibility will obviously be an inherent component of the new political régime. Representative democracy was conceived in order to promote and ensure universal respect for freedom, and to use that essential and irreplaceable tool to make room for any activity that dignifies the human condition. The Special Rapporteur also feels that in those circumstances, the activities of a special rapporteur will not be necessary, although it might be desirable to have a new and specific form of international co-operation for the protection of human rights on the part of the United Nations. That would, of course, be left to the discretion of the Government of Chile and of the Commission on Human Rights.

Nevertheless, much remains to be done to ensure that Chilean society enjoys a reliable system of legal protection for freedom. The representative democracy that will take its place in March 1990 is without doubt an extraordinarily important starting-point from which to pursue the combat to ensure that freedom prevails in its manifold and prolific guises. However, this is no way overlooks the major obstacles that the men and institutions of the new régime will face in that sphere, as a result of the very nature of the system of Government and of democratic life, and on account of the deep rifts created within Chilean society over many years of acute political conflict, exacerbated by violence.

There is no need to underscore the difficulties that will confront the new Government, alien in nature to any form of dogmatism. It is sufficient to remember the famous words spoken by Winston Churchill in the House of Commons on 11 November 1947: "Many forms of Government have been tried and will be tried in this world of sin and woe. No one pretends that democracy is perfect or all-wise. Indeed, it has been said that democracy is the worst form of

Government except all those other forms that have been tried from time to time".

Neither is there any need to stress the repercussions of the grave and tragic events experienced by Chile in recent years. However, it is worth bearing in mind two quotations from "Troilus and Cressida" by William Shakespeare. According to the first of them, "Those wounds heal ill that men do give themselves" (Act III, 3,229), while the second reminds us that "The end crowns all; and that old common arbitrator, time, will one day end it" (Act IV, 5,224).

Moreover, the Chilean people has shown exemplary courage in overcoming every adversity in an unwavering quest for its inherent and essential rights. There is consequently no doubt that the cause of freedom and democracy will take root in Chile.

Recommendations. The Chilean Government should vigorously exert its influence, within the limits of its legal powers, to prevent the death penalty from being applied to the 17 persons accused in connection with the serious attack on the presidential convoy in September 1986, the attack on Los Queñes, and the death of the *Carabinero* Miguel Vásquez Tobar, in which connection two officials of the Vicaria de la Solidaridad also face charges.

As the Special Rapporteur has observed in previous reports, it is necessary to seek out a legal and political solution to allow Judge Carlos Cerda to continue his exemplary efforts to investigate all aspects of the 10 cases of detained and missing persons, as well as other similar cases reported since 1973.

It is important to prevent further cases of torture or unlawful coercion, even if cases occur sporadically and are not part of a repressive system. Accordingly, it is necessary to make an assessment of the current agreements with the International Committee of the Red Cross and to ensure that at all times they operate with maximum efficiency, providing protection for persons arrested on any grounds, including those held incommunicado, and above all political cases. It is also essential to carry out investigations into complaints of torture or unlawful coercion with the utmost diligence and to ensure that persons guilty of such serious and abhorrent breaches of fundamental rights are duly punished, in accordance with the law.

The system of military justice must be reviewed and reformed so as to avert those excesses that have been and still are the root causes of many of the most serious breaches of human rights, as the Special Rapporteur has indicated in his previous reports.

The Government should afford the maximum co-operation to inspecting or special magistrates entrusted with the notorious cases of the persons whose throats were cut, the "Corpus Christi" killings or "Albania operation" and the "September 1986 murder victims".

Proceedings connected with another famous case, that of those who were burned should also be concluded so as to afford the higher courts (the Military Appeal Court and the Supreme Court) the opportunity to review on impartial bases, the ruling by the Second Military Court, on 24 August 1989.

Chile should rapidly ratify the American Convention on Human Rights (Pact of San José) and subsequently recognize the jurisdiction of the Inter-American Court of Human Rights, which is one of the two bodies established by the Convention to protect those rights. Chile should also ratify the Optional Protocol to the International Covenant on Civil and Political Rights, thus enabling individual communications or complaints to be submitted to the United Nations Human Rights Committee, the body responsible for safeguarding the rights contained in the Covenant.

The archives of the recently disbanded National Information Agency (CNI) should be preserved and their integrity afforded adequate protection, so that they may assist the courts in their investigations on human rights issues.

Every effort should be made without further delay to complete the investigation into the serious attack against the staff and premises of the former Intergovernmental Committee for Migration (ICM) now called the International Organization for Migration (IOM). This attack took place in 1986. Failure to act as suggested by the Special Rapporteur would constitute a whitewashing of that outrage and encourage other similar attacks against international humanitarian organizations operating in Chile.

An evaluation should be made of the action taken on the recommendations put forward by the Special Rapporteur in his nine previous reports, so that the relevant measures may be taken to promote the effective protection of the human rights of the Chilean people.

The legal proceedings connected with offences allegedly committed by members of *Colonia Dignidad* should be pursued with the utmost diligence. Chilean Government authorities should provide all possible co-operation to the court dealing with the case.

The Special Rapporteur also wishes to emphasize the need to improve the circumstances of the indigenous peoples, and of the Mapuche people in particular, to ensure that the rights of their members are respected.

The Commission on Human Rights examined the special rapporteur's tenth report on the situation of human rights in Chile at its 1990 session. On 7 March 1990, it took note of the report (resolution 1990/78) also expressed its appreciation to the working group, the experts, and the other special rapporteurs who had contributed to the work done by the international community, for 16 years, to restore human rights in Chile.

The commission noted the improvement in the situation of human rights in that country, as described by the special rapporteur, but regretted that, despite the many recommendations by the international community to the military government of Chile, the following were still pending:

(a) judicial and administrative identification and punishment of the persons responsible for crimes, disappearances, torture, persecution, intimidation and other forms of cruel, inhuman and degrading treatment, as well as the situation of persons in custody on political grounds;

(b) a return to normal of the administration of justice, especially in regard to a reform of the system of military justice and a review of the decision by the military courts; and

(c) a review of the rules whereby persons committing serious violations of human rights are granted impunity.

The commission took note of the decision adopted

by the military government junta to disband the National Information Agency and expressed its trust that the agency's archives will be kept at the disposal of the courts of justice and the authorities of the government-elect.

In addition, the Commission noted the commitment made by the government-elect to carry out the efforts necessary to secure a full return to normal of the traditional democratic legal system which was affected, from 1973 onwards, as a result of an enforced system of institutions which made for more than 16 years of serious and systematic infringements of national and international standards on human rights. It also welcomed that government's commitment to bring Chile fully into the international human rights system established by the United Nations and thus to continue to follow up known unresolved cases and many others which emerge from inquiries conducted by bodies in the system.

In the belief that the Chilean democratic process and management by the government-elect will restore the rule of law based on full enjoyment of human rights and fundamental freedoms, the commission decided not to renew the mandate of the special rapporteur, as from the time the government-elect took office, and requested the government-elect of Chile to report to it, at its 1991 session, on the follow-up to the recommendations adopted by the United Nations up to 11 March 1990.

On 11 March 1990, when the special rapporteur's report was under consideration by the Commission on Human Rights, Chile's long period of military rule came to an end with the installation of a new president, Patricio Aylwin, as the elected successor to General Pinochet. The general, who had called for free elections after being defeated in a plebescite which could have extended his rule by eight years, urged his fellow Chileans to show a responsible attitude towards their new leader. He himself refused, however, to step aside as commander of the army; and it was assumed he felt he must retain that position in order to protect members of the armed forces from prosecution for the killings, "disappearances," and torture that had occurred during the period of his presidency.

President Aylwin indicated that he would not intentionally set out to prosecute General Pinochet or anyone who had served under him but that he would not block any congressional or judicial investigations that might lead to charges. On March 12, he announced that he had signed a decree freeing a number of political prisoners and would resolve other cases in a spirit of justice, with the exception of those accused of acts of violence. He also indicated that he would propose, as soon as possible, abolition of the death penalty in Chile.

CHINA. The People's Republic of China is a country in east Asia, on the Yellow Sea, the East China Sea and the South China Sea. It has borders with Afghanistan, Bhutan, India, Korea, Laos, Mongolia, Myanmar, Nepal, Pakistan, and the Union of Soviet Socialist Republics. Always independent, China became a member of the United Nations in 1945 and is one of the permanent members of the UN Security Council. Its population is estimated by the UN (1990) to be 1,123,875,000—the largest in the world.

China is a multinational country; 56 nationalities live on its 9.6 million sq. km. of land. All nationalities other than the Han, which has the largest population, are customarily called minority nationalities; however, in China the word "minority" does not have a political meaning. The census of 1982 showed a total of over 67,230,000 minority people, with 15 nationalities having populations of over one million each, 31 nationalities having populations of between 10,000 and one million each, and nine having populations of less than 10,000 each. The majority Han nationality accounts for 93.3% of the nation's total population, while the 55 minorities constitute 6.7%. The Zhuang are the largest minority with a population of 13 million, while the Hezhen are the smallest with only 1,400 people.

Languages in common use include modern standard Chinese (official), Mandarin, Cantonese, and many local languages and dialects. Although the practice of religion is discouraged, Confucianism, Buddhism, Christianity, and Islam are widely practiced. Literacy is estimated at 76.5%.

The government (1990) took the form of a republic. Under the 1982 constitution, China is governed by a State Council headed by the premier, who is elected by the main legislative organ, the 2,978-member National People's Congress. Deputies to the congress are elected by popular vote, with universal suffrage. The only political party is the Communist Party.

China has a long history of suffering, similar to that of other developing countries. Like them, China was the victim of colonialist aggression and oppression over a period of many years. Internally, it also was the victim of national oppression and discrimination.

By the end of the 19th century, Great Britain, France, Germany, and Russia had established "zones of influence" in China and had obtained valuable commercial "concesssions." The United States government tried to initiate an "open door" policy, under which all nations would enjoy equal access to China's trade; but Chinese fear and resentment of foreigners stood in the way, and the Boxer Rebellion of 1900 was aimed at expelling all foreign influence.

In 1911, Sun Yat-sen led a republican revolution which forced the abdication of China's emperor. Sun Yat-sen became China's first president but resigned within a year in favor of a military ruler who established a repressive regime. After World War I, which China entered on the allied side, the Nine-Power Treaty signed at the Washington Conference (1921–1922) guaranteed Chinese territorial integrity and the open door policy.

Civil war raged for some years between Sun Yat-sen's party, the Kuomintang, based in the south, and the "war lords" (semi-independent military commanders) based in the north. In 1928, the Kuomintang was able to establish a government in Nanking which won some foreign recognition. The Japanese, taking advantage of the dissention, occupied Manchuria in 1932. By 1937, the Kuomintang and the communists had reached a shaky agreement to cooperate against the Japanese.

While World War II eliminated the Japanese threat, the rift between the nationalists and the communists in China widened. After a period of civil war, a national assembly, boycotted by the communists, adopted a democratic constitution, under which the first elected legislature—composed largely of Kuomintang members and including no communists—met early in 1948 and selected Chiang Kai-shek as China's first constitutional president. Chiang's Executive Yuan (Cabinet) included Minority party members.

However, the Communists gained the upper hand in renewed internal warfare and, in August 1949, founded "New China" from their capital in Beijing (formerly Peking). They proceeded immediately to re-organize the country and to consolidate its territory; and, by April 1950, followers of Chiang Kai-Shek were forced to retreat to the offshore island of Formosa, which they renamed Taiwan.

The government of the United States refused to recognize the People's Republic of China for nearly 30 years. In the United Nations, China continued to be represented by the Chiang Kai-shek authorities for more than 20 years. However, the UN General Assembly, on 25 October 1971, decided "to restore all its rights to the People's Republic of China and to recognize the representatives of its Government as the only legitimate representatives of China to the United Nations, and to expel forthwith the representatives of Chiang Kai-Shek from the place which they unlawfully occupy at the United Nations and in all the organizations related to it." Chiang Kai-shek died of a heart attack on 5 April 1975, and the United States government recognized the People's Republic of China as of 1 January 1979.

In 1958, Mao Zedong, the communist party leader, organized the "Great Leap Forward" campaign of village industrialization and the establishment of rural communes. The campaign failed, and Mao and his supporters moved to Shanghai, from which they organized a "Cultural Revolution" in which Red Guard Units—composed mostly of students freed from the schools—campaigned against "old ideas, old culture, old habits and old customs." The campaign often involved mass brutality and gross violations of human rights by uncontrolled mobs of armed young people. Efforts to bring it under control were ineffective for several years.

Early in 1972 U.S. President Richard Nixon visited China and met with Mao as well as with President Zhou Enlai. This brought about a movement toward reconciliation. Mao died in 1976, after which his widow and three colleagues—known as the "Gang of Four"—were accused of having undermined the party, the government, and the economy. Later the Central Committee of the communist party found Mao Zedong responsible for the "grave blunders" of the Cultural Revolution.

For many years, the government of China has endeavored to eliminate the discrimination and oppression on the ground of "nationality" that has persistently divided the Chinese people. In a report presented to the **COMMITTEE ON THE ELIMINATION OF RACIAL DISCRIMINATION** on 7 March 1988, the government summarized its recent efforts in this field as follows (UN Doc. CERD/C.153/Add. 2, para. 3–22):

The People's Republic of China has always persisted in a policy of equality of all its nationalities and engaged in helping the minority nationalities develop their economy and culture. China has made new efforts in promoting national unity and common prosperity and has thereby achieved new results.

In the Seventh Five-Year Plan of the People's Republic of China for Economic and Social Development (1986–1990) there is a special provision on the development of areas inhabited by minority nationalities, "We should take full advantage of the abundant natural resources in these areas. We shall improve conditions for farming and animal husbandry, increase grain output, step up the development of pasture land by planting trees and grass, and gradually create a balanced ecological environment. We shall push forward the development of the energy and raw and semi-finished materials industries and improve transport facilities. We shall promote trade among different nationalities and encourage the production of articles of daily use to meet the special needs of minority peoples and accelerate the construction of culture in these areas."

The Chinese Government has adopted a series of economic, legal and administrative measures which are practical and effective to implement the economic and so-

181

cial development programme for the minority nationality areas and has scored notable results.

The central Government gives favourable consideration and assistance to the autonomous areas in finance. It is stipulated that revenues belonging to the autonomous areas in accordance with the State financial system can be disposed of by the autonomous organs. The State will also provide financial subsidies for their economic development when necessary. In 1985 and 1986 there is a 10% increase over the previous year in financial subsidy by the central Government to the five autonomous regions and Yunnan, Guizhou and Qinhai provinces where many minority nationalities inhabit. The central Government has given Tibet a total of more than 10 billion yuan RMB in the form of financial subsidy since 1952.

The State has established various forms of special funds to help economic construction in the areas inhabited by minority nationalities such as a subsidy for the construction of border areas, a subsidy for the areas inhabited by minority nationalities, a subsidy for border-region construction and a development fund for the economically underdeveloped areas. The central bank has since 1986, allocated each year 1 billion yuan in the form of discount interest loans to help the 271 counties that suffer a low economic growth. Forty-four per cent of them are autonomous counties and counties within the jurisdiction of autonomous prefectures, reaching a total number of 119.

From 1983 the State allocated special low interest loans to areas where economic growth is slow and where minority nationalities are inhabited, more than 50% of which were shared by the five autonomous regions and three multinational provinces of Yunnan, Guizhou and Qinhai.

In 1985 and 1986 State loans to the areas where minority nationalities are inhabited increased by an average of 61.61%, 11.04% higher than the average level enjoyed by the rest of the country.

In taxation all the autonomous areas of minority nationalities enjoy a certain level of exemption or reduction of taxes. For instance, village and township enterprises in these areas enjoy a certain level of preferential treatment of exemption or reduction of taxes within a certain period of time and special considerations are given in collecting the business tax and tax on value added. Special commodities needed by the minority nationalities enjoy exemption from or reduction of, taxes. Enterprises handling nationality trade enjoy a 50% reduction in income tax and exemption from regulation tax. The State has granted exemption from the agricultural tax as well as the income tax of the national industrial enterprises and the small and medium-sized collective or individual commercial enterprises throughout the Tibet Autonomous Region since 1980.

In order to develop commerce in the minority nationality areas, the Ministry of Commerce of the People's Republic of China made in July 1985 a special announcement that the State will exempt or reduce taxes of some of the commercial enterprises in these areas and continue to give price subsidies for some of the agricultural and special local products as well as those produced from animal husbandry.

The State encourages and helps the minority nationalities to develop their trade with foreign countries. The five autonomous regions and autonomous prefectures situated along the border have established foreign or border trading ports. Along the Sino-Nepolian border in the Tibet Autonomous Region, there have been established more than 20 border trade fairs. The Yanbian Korean Autonomous Prefecture of Jilin Province can engage in direct border trade with neighbouring Korea. Xinjiang Uygur Autonomous Region has established economic and trade relations with more than 50 countries and areas.

With regard to retention of foreign exchange income earned from foreign trade minority nationality areas are given special care. Tibet may keep all of its foreign exchange income while the other four autonomous regions and the three provinces of Yunnan, Guizhou and Qinhai can retain 50% compared with the average level of 25–30% enjoyed by the rest of the country.

In order to meet the living needs of people of minority nationalities and promote economic development in these areas the State has devoted a large amount of investment in the light industry of the five autonomous regions and the three provinces of Yunnan, Guizhou and Qinhai. The gross investment in 1985 and 1986 doubled that of 1983 and 1984. A relatively complete system of producing and supplying commodities used specially by the minority nationalities has been formed. Investment by the Ministry of Light Industry in the production of commodities used by the minority nationalities grew by 18.2 and 23.5% respectively over 1985. The annual gross product of commodities used by the minority nationalities increased 2.3 times over that of 1980.

There is a vast area inhabited by minority nationalities and the resources there are abundant. The State has enacted a series of laws to ensure and promote economic development in those areas.

The Grassland Law of the People's Republic of China, enacted in 1985, stipulates among other things that "the right to own or use grasslands shall be protected by law and may not be infringed upon by any unit or individual", "if grasslands in national autonomous areas are to be requisitioned or used for State construction, due consideration shall be given to the interest of the national autonomous areas and arrangements made in favour of the economic development of those areas".

The Mineral Resources Law of the People's Republic of China, enacted in 1986, stipulates that "in exploiting mineral resources in national autonomous areas, the State shall give due consideration to the interests of those areas and make arrangements favourable to the areas' economic construction and to the production and livelihood of the people of local minority nationalities", "the organs of self-government of national autonomous areas shall, in accordance with legal provisions and the unified State plan, have priority for rationally developing and utilizing the mineral resources that may be developed by local authorities".

In accordance with the above-mentioned legal provisions, the State geological departments have been making positive efforts to help the autonomous areas to explore and exploit minerals. More than 420 geological projects were arranged in 1986. The Ministry of Geology and Minerals has made a special decision on strengthening the geological work in Tibet and on Hainan Island. In order to solve the energy problem in Tibet, the geological department has focused its work in Tibet on the tapping of geothermal energy and accelerated the general survey of gold, placer tin, diamond, chromium and other minerals from which quick and better economic results can be achieved. Hainan Island, situated in the farthest south of China where minority nationalities are concentrated finds itself among the areas where mineral and geological work is to be focused.

In 1986 the geological departments of all provinces, autonomous regions and municipalities decided to pay special attention to helping the exploitation of natural resources in the 232 counties, two thirds of which are situated in areas inhabited by minority nationalities.

To help the minority nationality areas develop hydropower and electric power, the State has, since 1984, started a number of key hydro- and electric-power projects with a total investment of more than 40 billion RMB. The State has set up a special fund to subsidize the projects for tapping the Lhasa River in the Tibet Autonomous Region, the dam building and harnessing of rivers in Guangxi Zhuang Autonomous Region and the renovation of water conservation facilities in the Hetao irrigation area in the Inner Mongolian Autonomous region.

Counties in the minority nationality areas account for one third of the 100 electrification piloting counties in the country.

The State has also organized the economically developed provinces and municipalities to carry out economic and technical co-operation with, and provide assistance to, the minority nationality areas, organized and promoted activities such as economic and technical consultation and sending intellectuals to border regions, and encouraged and organized experts, scholars and technicians to give lectures, provide technical consultations and take part in the construction in the minority nationality areas.

A somewhat different aspect of the question of minorities was, however, revealed in a dispatch dated-lined Beijing, published in the *New York Times* on 20 February 1990, stating that, according to the official New China News Agency, Prime Minister Li Peng had warned against independence movements among China's ethnic minorities in a speech delivered a few days earlier and had warned that independence efforts would be crushed immediately. "We must not relax our vigilance," Mr. Li was quoted as saying; "We should wipe out all separatist activities while they are still in the embryonic stage."

In the course of the preceding year, 1989, Chinese authorities had summarily crushed both a major separatist movement and a major movement for democratic participation in government. In March, in Tibet, a peaceful demonstration calling for independence, led by monks and nuns, had led to the imposition of martial law after police had beaten and fired upon the demonstrators. In April, in Beijing, a peaceful demonstration calling for democracy, led by students, had again led to the imposition of martial law after the army had beaten, machine-gunned, and run over the demonstrators with trucks and armored vehicles.

The international community was strangely silent about these events for several months, and it was only in August 1989 that the UN SUB-COMMISSION ON PREVENTION OF DISCRIMINATION AND PROTECTION OF MINORITIES placed China on a list of countries accused of seriously violating the human rights of their citizens. By a secret ballot of 15 in favor and 9 against, the sub-

commission on 31 August expressed its concern (resolution 1989/5) about the events which had taken place in China and about their consequences in the field of human rights and requested the secretary-general to transmit to the Commission on Human Rights information provided by the government of China and by other reliable sources. At the same time, it made an appeal for clemency, in particular in favor of persons deprived of their liberty as a result of the above-mentioned events.

In accordance with the above-mentioned resolution, the secretary-general sent, on 30 October 1989, a *note verbale* to the minister of foreign affairs of China in which he referred to the resolution and requested the government of China, should it wish to submit information pursuant to operative paragraph 1, to do so before 1 January 1990.

On 1 December 1989, the permanent representative of the People's Republic of China to the United Nations office at Geneva replied as follows:

Last June, there occurred in Beijing a rebellion which was supported by hostile forces abroad and constituted an attempt to overthrow the legitimate Government of the People's Republic of China and subvert the socialist system set forth in the Constitution through violent means. The Chinese Government took resolute measures to quell the rebellion in the interests of the overwhelming majority of the Chinese people. This is entirely China's internal affairs and is a matter different in nature from the question of human rights. However, with the plotting and encouragement of some Western members, the Sub-Commission on Prevention of Discrimination and Protection of Minorities adopted resolution 1989/5 at its forty-first session. This is a brutal interference in China's internal affairs while hurting the feeling of the Chinese people. The Spokesman of the Foreign Ministry of the People's Republic of China issued a statement on 2 September 1989, solemnly declaring the firm objection of the Chinese Government to the resolution and deeming it to be illegal and null and void.

On 12 January 1990, the permanent representative of the People's Republic of China addressed a letter to the secretary-general with reference to sub-commission resolution 1989/5. At the request of the permanent representative, this letter was circulated as a document of the Commission on Human Rights. It was as follows (UN Doc. E/CN.4/1990/55, para. 1–16):

The United Nations Sub-Commission on Prevention of Discrimination and Protection of Minorities adopted a resolution (1989/5) entitled "Situation in China" on 31 August 1989. The Chinese Government's position on the resolution has already been put forth in the statement issued by the spokesman of the Ministry of Foreign Affairs of the People's Republic of China on 2 September 1989. I wish to reiterate here that the Chinese Government firmly re-

C

jects the resolution and any other possible action taken pursuant to it for the reasons set out below.

The Chinese Government showed the utmost tolerance and restraint in face of the illegal demonstrations.

In April and May 1989, illegal demonstrations took place in China's capital, Beijing, lasting for nearly 50 days, and even Tiananmen Square, centre of the nation's political activities, was illegally occupied for a long period of time. The demonstrations were illegal because their organizers, in total disregard of the laws of the State and the relevant regulations of the Beijing municipal government on demonstrations, refused to go through the procedures of application and approval. Those demonstrations had grave consequences, badly disrupting public order, communications and transportation in Beijing and its residents' normal life, and seriously interfering with the normal activities of the Government and even the activities of the official visit of an important State guest. In the mean time, the Chinese Government always exercised great restraint in an effort to solve the problem through persuasion and guidance. In mid-May, when some students staged a hunger strike at Tiananmen Square, the Chinese Government did its best to mobilize various departments to provide them with medical care, medicine, food and other materials, thus having protected their health and the safety of their life.

The imposition of martial law in Beijing was entirely necessary and in line with the provisions of the Constitution of the People's Republic of China.

The tolerance and restraint shown by the Chinese Government towards the above-mentioned illegal demonstrations failed to obtain a due response; the turmoil went from bad to worse, and ever more violent were the various activities hostile to the Chinese Government and aimed at subverting the Government of the People's Republic of China and the socialist system of China, activities supported and instigated by foreign forces. At such a critical moment, the Chinese Government could not but adopt the necessary measures. The State Council of the People's Republic of China decided, in accordance with clause 16, article 89, of the Constitution, to impose martial law in parts of Beijing, starting from 20 May. This decision, which was taken for the purpose of maintaining public order, protecting citizens' life and securing State property against any encroachment, was entirely necessary and legitimate.

The facts of the past period of over seven months have shown that the imposition of martial law in parts of Beijing was entirely justified. It quickly and effectively checked the turmoil and quelled the anti-Government rebellion in Beijing. It has not only maintained tranquillity in the capital, but has also safeguarded the security of the People's Republic of China. Now the situation in Beijing and the whole country has become stable, social order has returned to normal, production and life are in good order and the task of imposing martial law has been successfully fulfilled. Under such circumstances, the State Council of the People's Republic of China, in accordance with the provisions of clause 16, under article 89 of the Constitution, issued an order on 10 January 1990 lifting the martial law imposed in parts of Beijing as of 11 January 1990. This shows once again the determination of the Chinese Government to adopt timely measures to restore the normal life of society in accordance with the development of the situation.

The Chinese Government's actions to put an end to the turmoil and quell the rebellion were justified and legitimate.

After the declaration of martial law, the Chinese Government continued to use persuasion through various channels, expressing the hope that the trouble-makers would adopt a rational attitude, stop the turmoil and let public order be restored. However, far from diminishing, the anti-Government turmoil, instigated, incited and manipulated by hostile forces both at home and abroad, became all the more flagrant. On 3 June, the nearly two-month-long turmoil escalated abruptly into a rebellion designed to overthrow the Government by resorting to violence and terrorist means. Driven beyond forbearance, the Chinese Government could not but take decisive measures to quell the rebellion in order to maintain law and order and protect the life and property of the general public. This was absolutely necessary, justified and legitimate.

However, some people have gone so far as to describe the above-mentioned actions by the Chinese Government as armed suppression of a peaceful, pro-democracy movement. This is a slander which ignores facts, confounds right and wrong and involves ulterior motives. The fact is that, during the anti-Government rebellion on 3 and 4 June 1989, a handful of political conspirators gathered a group of hooligans to savagely use violence against the army and the public security personnel who were enforcing martial law under orders. Using sticks, daggers, Molotov cocktails, guns and other lethal weapons, they beat military personnel and burned military vehicles, thus causing serious casualties on the army and the destruction of many military vehicles. Moreover, the ruffians, in disregard of laws and regulations, attacked the headquarters of the Central Committee of the Communist Party of China, the State Council and some other important government institutions. This was by no means a "pro-democracy movement" or a "peaceful demonstration". Rather, it was a rebellion aimed at subverting the legal Government of China and the socialist system stipulated in the Chinese Constitution. It is an obligation of any responsible Government to quell rebellion, maintain public order and social stability and safeguard the sanctity of the Constitution. This is an indispensable and just action aimed at protecting the legal rights of citizens.

What needs to be pointed out is that, in the whole process of quelling the rebellion, a total of nearly 300 people died, including military personnel of the martial law enforcement troops. Besides ruffians, a small number of onlookers were shot accidentally, which is regrettable, and the Government has dealt appropriately with this matter.

The so-called "Tiananmen bloodbath" is sheer fabrication. After the quelling of the rebellion, such rumours as "Tiananmen bloodbath" or "Tiananmen massacre" were produced by some Western mass media. But these rumours have long been punctured by facts. Hou Dejian, a composer from China's Taiwan Province who was among the last to leave Tiananmen Square when troops began their clearing operation in the early morning of 4 June, later confirmed that, during the whole process of departure from the Square, he did not see any student, citizen or PLA soldier being killed or any tank or armoured vehicle rolling over crowds of people. Liu Xiaobo, Zhou Duo, Gao Xin and some students who were with Hou Dejian at the time also confirmed this fact to journalists. All this has forcefully shown that the so-called "Tiananmen bloodbath" was fabricated by people with ulterior motives.

It is entirely defensible to punish criminals who have violated the criminal law in accordance with the law.

Following the quelling of the rebellion, the Chinese Government has repeatedly stated that it will not inquire into the responsibilities of those students and citizens who were ordinary participants in marches, demonstrations and hunger strikes. However, during the turmoil and rebellion, a handful of people were engaged in organizing and plotting conspiracies or in such violent acts as beating, smashing, looting, burning and killing, thus violating the Chinese criminal law. Naturally, these criminals should be brought to justice, which is unobjectionable. Punishment of criminals in accordance with the law is a matter within the realm of a country's sovereignty, and no foreign country or international organization has the right to interfere in it.

The use of the United Nations forum by a small number of Western countries to interfere in China's internal affairs constitutes a complete violation of the purposes of the United Nations Charter and the norms governing international relations.

After the quelling of the rebellion by the Chinese Government, some Western countries, ignoring the facts and relying on nothing but distorted reports and misinformation, made arbitrary accusations against and applied pressures on the Chinese Government. They even went so far as to give open permission and support to criminals wanted by the Chinese public security organs in carrying out activities against the Chinese Government, and thereby interfered in China's internal affairs. To find a pretext for their unjust acts, they slandered China on the so-called human rights issue. This is the background against which members of some Western countries on the Sub-Commission on Prevention of Discrimination and Protection of Minorities plotted the adoption of the resolution on "Situation on China". They even altered the normal voting procedure of the Sub-Commission, thereby imposing their own will on the Sub-Commission to serve their political aims. This is a serious violation of the purposes and principles of the United Nations Charter. Such erroneous acts, if allowed to continue, will certainly cause even greater damage to the reputation of the United Nations and its human rights institution.

I am hereby instructed to request Your Excellency to distribute this letter as an official document of the United Nations Commission on Human Rights.

The secretary-general transmitted the information provided by the government of China to the Commission on Human Rights on 23 January 1990. On 30 January 1990, he transmitted to the commission certain information provided by "other reliable sources:" three non-governmental organizations in consultative status with the Economic and Social Council (UN Doc. E/CN.4/1990/52). The organizations were AMNESTY INTERNATIONAL (annex I), the INTERNATIONAL COMMISSION OF HEALTH PROFESSIONALS FOR HEALTH AND HUMAN RIGHTS (annex II), and the INTERNATIONAL LEAGUE FOR HUMAN RIGHTS (annex III). However, only the information provided by Amnesty International is presented here. That information was as follows (UN Doc. E/CN.4/1990/52, annex I):

Violations of Human Rights in China

Introduction. In this document Amnesty International describes its concerns about recent human rights violations in China. It believes it important that the recent events be considered in the light of the overall human rights situation in the country.

In August 1989, Amnesty International published a report entitled "Preliminary Findings on Killings of Unarmed Civilians, Arbitrary Arrests and Summary Executions since 3 June 1989" which described Amnesty International's concerns about human rights violations in China since early June 1989, when heavily armed troops moved into the centre of Beijing to suppress pro-democracy protests, killing many unarmed protesters and bystanders.

Serious violations of human rights continue to occur in China and Amnesty International has not recorded any significant improvement since August 1989. Though releases have occurred, thousands of people continue to be imprisoned throughout China for their participation in the pro-democracy protests of 1989. There have been further arbitrary arrests and prisoners continue to be detained incommunicado without charge or trial, imprisoned or executed after unfair trials. Martial law was lifted in Beijing on 10 January 1990, but no measures of clemency or redress have been announced for those imprisoned as prisoners of conscience, subjected to prolonged detention without charge or trial for political reasons, or sentenced to imprisonment or to death after unfair trials. Indeed, the laws which permit such violations to take place remain in force.

Amnesty International estimates that at least 1,000 people were killed and thousands more injured in Beijing in early June 1989 when troops fired into crowds of protesters and bystanders—the vast majority of them unarmed. Amnesty International believes that many of these killings were extrajudicial executions, the result of a deliberate decision by those in authority to suppress the peaceful protests even if this meant widespread killings. The atmosphere of terror which followed the military operation made it impossible to determine the true death toll. Thousands of people were subsequently detained throughout China in connection with the protests, including many prisoners of conscience, and most were held incommunicado for long periods. Some were reported to have been severely beaten or tortured by soldiers or police. Dozens were officially reported to have been sentenced to death or to terms of imprisonment after trials which were summary and unfair, and secret executions were also reported.

In March 1989, three months before the killings in Beijing, martial law was imposed in Lhasa, capital of the Tibet Autonomous Region (TAR). Over 1,000 people were subsequently reported to have been arrested there, including prisoners of conscience, and there were reports of torture and summary executions. Some protestors were brought to trial and sentenced. Others against whom no formal charges were brought were assigned to labour camps for up to three years without any form of trial under legislation providing for administrative detention.

Prisoners of conscience arrested in previous years continued to be imprisoned in China throughout 1989 and are still held. During 1989, other cases were reported of people arrested on account of their religious beliefs or political activities which were not connected with the pro-democracy protests. Torture and ill-treatment also continued to be reported in criminal cases and the death penalty continues to be used extensively.

Events in Beijing in Early June 1989. On 20 May 1989, following five weeks of peaceful student-led demonstrations, martial law was imposed in Beijing. The order was issued in the name of the State Council and signed by Prime Minister Li Peng. Its stated aim was to "firmly stop the unrest", to

C

safeguard public order and to "ensure the normal function" of government.

The student protests, which started in Beijing in mid-April 1989 and soon spread to most major cities, received wide popular support and developed into a pro-democracy movement. On 18 May 1989, an estimated one million people demonstrated in Beijing in support of students on hunger-strike and on 23 May 1989 a similar number again took to the streets to protest the imposition of martial law, the largest known popular demonstration of discontent in the history of the People's Republic of China.

On the night of 3 to 4 June 1989 hundreds of armoured military vehicles escorted by tens of thousands of troops moved into the centre of Beijing to enforce martial law, firing both at random and deliberately into crowds of protesters and bystanders—the vast majority of them unarmed. Further shootings of unarmed civilians occurred in the next few days. The numerous incidents in which civilians were deliberately shot by soldiers or crushed by military vehicles have been amply documented by the eyewitness testimonies and documents published or broadcast since then. Amnesty International described some of these incidents in its August 1989 report "Preliminary Findings on Killings of Unarmed Civilians, Arbitrary Arrests and Summary Executions Since 3 June 1989". Amnesty International concluded in that report that:

(a) From mid-April until the military operations of 3 and 4 June in Beijing, the popular protest movement started by Beijing students was peaceful. There is no indication that leaders of the protest movement at any point advocated violence or attempted to overthrow the Government by violent means.

(b) During the night of 3 to 4 June, some troops opened fire either at random or deliberately at crowds whenever they met obstructions or large groups of people. No warnings were given before troops opened fire. Conventional methods for the dispersal or control of crowds without resort to firearms or other use of lethal force were not used.

(c) The vast majority of civilians were unarmed. Some were killed in residential buildings due to random or intentional shooting by troops. Some were shot in the back among crowds of people running away from troops firing at them; some were crushed to death by military vehicles. Those killed included children and old people.

(d) After the army took control of central Beijing there were still, for several days, incidents during which troops opened fire on unarmed civilians without warning or provocation.

(e) Many of the killings of unarmed civilians were extrajudicial executions: deliberate killings by government forces acting outside the limits of the law. Troops deliberately shot and killed individuals even when there was no immediate threat of violence by them, in violation of international standards that lethal force should only be used when absolutely necessary and in direct proportion to the legitimate objective it is intended to achieve.

In the past few months, the Chinese authorities have publicized their official version of what happened in Beijing on 3 and 4 June. They have produced videotapes and testimonies from individuals suggesting that the army not only exercised "great restraint", but also that many soldiers were victims of violence provoked by ''rioters''. Testimonies have been used to support official claims that no one was killed during the final evacuation of Tianenmen Square, but these and other documentation provide only a partial version of what occurred. The authorities have failed to take account of the well-attested incidents in which civilians were deliberately shot by soldiers. They still have not explained why a decision was taken to use lethal force against unarmed civilians, and why conventional crowd control methods were not used to disperse protesters before 3 June. They continue to maintain that some 200 civilians only, as well as "several dozen" soldiers, were killed during the military operations in Beijing; but this represents a gross underestimate. Information received by Amnesty International indicated that at least a thousand civilians and, according to reports, about 16 soldiers were killed.

Amnesty International has continued to receive reports and eye witness testimonies about events in Beijing during the night of 3 to 4 June, which generally confirm the description given in its August 1989 report. Some contain new information. One eye witness who stayed in Tiananmen Square until dawn on 4 June reported to Amnesty International that he saw several young women crushed in a tent by an armoured personnel carrier (APC) during the final "clearing" of the square early that morning. Together with members of a medical team, he was one of the last civilians to leave the Square. Extracts from his testimony are given below:

"Meanwhile, I had gone to a tent northeast of the Monument to the People's Heroes where I met two friends. . . . By that time, soldiers had come right across to the Monument, students were leaving the Square by the southeast corner, and APCs were moving down slowly from the north. About half way between the Monument and the tent where I met my friends, a bit further to the north, was one of the temporary tents erected by students with posts and canvas over. The tent was open towards the south. There were about seven girls inside. The APCs were moving down very slowly but without stopping. I rushed to the tent and told the girls to leave, but they refused. I dragged one of them towards the west. I don't know what happened to her later. I rushed back to the tent. There were three other people trying to persuade the girls to leave. By that time, one of the APCs had come very close to the tent. I could see two soldiers sitting on the metal covering of the APC. I ran in front, shouting at them to stop. They told me to get out of the way. I was shouting and crying, but the APC continued to move ahead. The tent collapsed, trapping the girls inside. The APC went straight over it. I stood to one side, dazed. . . . I heard the medical team loudspeaker calling for evacuation. I ran towards them, at the edge of the APCs. Twenty to 30 APCs were coming down slowly, followed by soldiers and armed police. By that time, most of the students had left through the southeast. The medical team was still on the side of the History Museum. A large number of soldiers had been sitting for hours on the steps of the Museum and were still sitting there. They did not move. Fifteen to 20 wounded people had been brought in by students and were lying on the ground at the medical point. There were volleys of shots coming from the southwest side of the Monument. After one volley, three wounded students were brought to the medical point. They had been shot in the back. The soldiers on the steps of the Museum shouted their approval at each volley of firing. The medical team shouted back at them. It was by then impossible to get through to see whether anyone was wounded. A large number of armed police came from the north after the APCs. They picked up broken bricks on the ground and threw them towards the medical team who stood around the wounded. Some people were hurt by the bricks. One soldier ran from the west, stood on top of the metal railings on the side and shouted at police to stop. They stopped. Then a group of officers and soldiers came to the medical team and ordered us to evacuate. We took the wounded on stretchers and went down the Square towards the lane on the southeast side. As we went down the side of the Square, we saw soldiers with large plastic bags, north of the Monument. They were putting people in the bags. I could not tell how many people. . . . There were also people surrounded by soldiers, being kicked by them. I could hear shouts and the odd gun shot. I thought there were around 200 young people. They were pushed to the north side of the Square, towards the Forbidden City. . . . In early July, I heard from Public Security (police) sources that they had all been executed on 9 June in a rural district near Beijing. They included students and residents of Beijing."

Events in Chengdu on 4 and 5 June 1989. Killings of civilians are also reported to have occurred on 4 and 5 June 1989 in Chengdu, the capital of Sichuan province, where violent confrontations between security forces and protesters took place after news of the Beijing massacre spread. In Chengdu, as in many other cities, students had organized peaceful demonstrations and sit-ins in the centre of the city in May and early June. According to reports, on 4 June, as news of events in Beijing was received, crowds of people converged on the Sichuan Government Offices in central Chengdu and attacked the building with stones. Security forces then attacked the crowds with tear gas and truncheons, reportedly also using knives and bayonets. Gunfire was also heard intermittently during the violent confrontations which continued for two days, resulting in widespread damage to buildings in the centre of the city and many casualties.

According to official sources, eight civilians—including two students—were killed on 4 June during the clashes and 1,800 people were injured, including 700 civilians and 1,100 members of the security forces. Unofficial estimates of the number of civilian casualties are much higher, ranging from about 30 to over 300 for the number of those killed, with many more injured. One source reported that 27 people had died in one of Chengdu's four major hospitals as a result of the 4 June clashes. The total number of casualties recorded in hospitals is not known. Further violent confrontations occurred during the night of 5 and 6 June in various parts of central Chengdu.

While Amnesty International has been unable to ascertain the total number of people killed in Chengdu on 4 and 5 June 1989, it has received detailed testimonies indicating that the security forces used extreme brutality against unarmed protesters and bystanders. One foreigner who was in Chengdu at the time has described as follows the action of the security forces:

"Most of the action consisted of isolating groups of demonstrators and stabbing them and beating them to the ground. There is no question about the fact that none of the demonstrators were armed. The work of the security forces, on the other hand, was brutal in the extreme. Even after they had beaten demonstrators down, they would continue hitting them with truncheons and knives until they were motionless. There was a pattern to it: with males, the preferred area of attack was the head, with females it was the abdomen. Numerous individual acts of brutality occurred . . . The police and army violence was random. Even people who lay on the ground and pleaded for mercy were clubbed. There was no age discrimination."

An Italian businessman, interviewed in Hong Kong on 7 June after returning from Chengdu, stated that he saw a girl, 15 to 16 years old, being bayonetted in the stomach by a soldier in the morning of 4 June in central Chengdu. He said the girl was about 18 metres away from him at the time; the soldier then bayonetted her twice more in the chest and left the body in the street (*Reuter,* Hong Kong, 7 June 1989).

Several foreigners also saw a group of protesters being systematically beaten unconscious by soldiers in the grounds of the Jin Jiang Hotel during the night of 5 to 6 June. The attack reportedly left between 30 and 50 people critically wounded—some possibly dead. They were later thrown into trucks and taken away by soldiers. One of the foreigners who witnessed the incident has described it to Amnesty International as follows:

"The following was witnessed from an eighth floor room overlooking the front of the hotel and the main street between about 0145 hours and 0600 hours on Tuesday 6 June. A line of soldiers was drawn up outside the gate. Two army trucks were parked in the hotel grounds to the right of the gate. Captured protestors were being held in a small guard house to the left of the gate. The grounds of the hotel appeared to be empty of protesters. The street outside was largely empty, there were small groups of people standing round, doing nothing. One by one protestors were dragged out of the guard house. Soldiers formed a ring around them, linking arms. Several soldiers in the centre of the ring then beat the protesters, using clubs. After the beating, the protesters were carried/dragged back inside. It was not possible to ascertain whether protesters were alive or dead. This continued for some time. Then groups of soldiers went out of the hotel gates. They charged the very small groups of protesters standing in the middle of the road, seized several, dragged them back into the hotel grounds and beat them. The rest of the protesters disappeared.

"The soldiers then concealed themselves in the bushes. People were still drifting down the road from the direction of the People's Square. On several occasions, people wandered up to the gates. Soldiers leapt from hiding, seized them, beat them and carried them into the guard house. This continued until about 0400 hours. At about 0400 hours, all the people held in the guard house were dragged out—none was able to walk and most appeared unconscious. They were thrown into the backs of the two army trucks. Soldiers then mounted the trucks and formed a wall with the protesters in the middle. The trucks then left. This left only the private hotel security guards, all armed with clubs, patrolling the grounds. I do not know how many people were arrested and beaten as I was not watching continuously and I was also in despair."

Human rights Violations since June 1989. The Chinese authorities have not disclosed the total number of people detained, tried or executed throughout the country since the June crackdown on pro-democracy protesters. At least 6,000 arrests have been officially reported throughout China; but the real number of those detained is believed to run into tens of thousands. Between 8,000 and 10,000 people are said to have been detained in Beijing alone—the majority in June and July—although some sources suggest that around 4,000 were released after various periods in detention for interrogation. Arbitrary arrests, however, have continued. Since September, Amnesty International has received numerous reports about students, academics and others arrested in various places in China for their alleged activities in connection with the pro-democracy protests.

Few such arrests, however, have been confirmed by official sources.

The arbitrary detention or imprisonment of people involved in peaceful political or religious activities is facilitated by a number of provisions in Chinese law and by practices which, while contrary to the letter of the law, have become the norm in the People's Republic of China. It is common, for instance, for people to be detained by police for weeks or months without charge, in breach of the procedures for arrest and detention laid down in China's Criminal Procedure Law. A 1957 law, which was updated with new regulations in November 1979, also permits long-term detention without charge or trial: it provides for the detention of people considered to have "anti-socialist views" or to be "hooligans" in camps or prisons for up to four years for "re-education through labour". Detention orders for those subjected to "re-education through labour" are issued outside the judicial process by Public Security (police) officers. China's Criminal Law (1980) also includes provisions which are used to imprison people for the peaceful exercise of their basic human rights. Articles 98 and 102, in particular, provide punishments ranging from deprivation of political rights to life imprisonment for people charged with organizing or taking part in a "counter-revolutionary" group or with carrying out "counter-revolutionary propaganda and agitation". These two articles, as well as others, have often been used in the past to imprison people whom Amnesty International considers to be prisoners of conscience.

Those detained are believed to be held incommunicado. Chinese law does not permit access to lawyers until a few days before trial—or in some cases until the trial starts. It is also common for prisoners to be denied visits from their family until the trial. Some detainees are reported to have been severely beaten by soldiers or police after arrest, and many are feared to have been tortured or ill-treated to force them to confess to crimes or to denounce others.

Amnesty International has long been concerned about the occurrence of torture in China. In 1987 it published a report entitled "China: Torture and Ill-treatment of Prisoners", which documented the widespread use of torture in China and pointed out that the absence of sufficient safeguards for detainees' rights in Chinese law contributed to a pattern of abuse. It recommended the introduction of several safeguards, in particular that limits be placed on incommunicado detention, but none of these safeguards have yet been introduced in China.

Some of those arrested since June 1989 were sentenced to death or imprisonment after unfair trials. In June 1989, the Supreme People's Court called on local courts to "try quickly and punish severely" those involved in the "counter-revolutionary rebellion", using 1983 legislation that provides for swift and summary procedures with little opportunity for defence in the trials of "criminals who gravely endanger public security". This legislation allows the courts to bring defendants to trial without giving them a copy of the indictment in advance and without giving advance notice of the trial or issue summons in advance to all parties involved—including defence lawyers. Furthermore, trials are often a mere formality as the verdicts are usually decided in advance. The well-known practice of "verdict first, trial second" has been acknowledged by top Chinese legal officials in late 1988. This practice, as well as the use of torture to induce confessions and the extreme limitations on the role of defence lawyers, have been criticized by members of the Chinese legal profession in numerous articles published in the official legal press since 1987.

The following are a few examples of people officially reported to have been tried and sentenced in connection with the protests.

(a) Xiao Bin, a worker from Dalian in northeast China, was the first person known to be sentenced in connection with the protests for exercising his right to freedom of speech. He was arrested on 11 June 1989 after being shown on Chinese television speaking to an American ABC Television crew in Beijing earlier that month: on 13 July 1989 it was announced that he had been found guilty under Article 102 of the Criminal Law of "spreading rumours" and of "vilifying the righteous act of the martial law troops". He was sentenced to 10 years' imprisonment for "counter-revolutionary propaganda and incitement".

(b) In late August 1989 the first student officially reported to have been tried in connection with the demonstrations was sentenced to nine years' imprisonment on the same charge. Zhang Weiping, an art student in Hangzhou, was accused of telling Voice of America radio in June that students in Hangzhou had successfully asked provincial government officials to fly the flag at half mast to mourn those killed in Beijing.

(c) In a recent case, Chen Zhixiang, a 26-year-old teacher in Guangzhou (Canton), was sentenced to 10 years imprisonment on 11 January 1990 for displaying a poster attacking Chinese leaders three days after troops crushed the pro-democracy protests in Beijing on 4 June 1989.

Secret trials of students active in the protest movement were reported to have started in Beijing in November 1989. Four students from the Foreign Affairs college in Beijing were reported to have gone on trial that month for "counter-revolutionary" crimes, but their names and details of their cases were not known. The trials were reportedly held in secret and even the families of the accused were not allowed to attend. Trials of "counter-revolutionaries" are said to have continued, but only a few were officially reported. The fate, whereabouts and conditions of many intellectuals, students and workers involved in the protests remain unknown though they have now been imprisoned for several months. Leaders of the movement are known to be detained in Qincheng prison, north of Beijing, which has traditionally been used to hold prominent political prisoners.

Some of those arrested in connection with the protests were charged with ordinary criminal offences, such as blocking traffic, damaging vehicles, attacking soldiers or police, arson or looting—and faced summary trial and possible execution under the 1983 legislation. On 21 June three workers were shot in Shanghai after a "public sentencing rally" for allegedly setting fire to a train after it had ploughed through demonstrators blocking the track and killed at least six people. The next day seven "rioters" were executed in Beijing after being convicted of wounding troops and burning military vehicles in the capital on 4 June. Despite international appeals for clemency, all had their death sentences upheld by the courts.

Though only a few dozen executions have been publicly reported, some sources estimate that in Beijing alone several hundred people were executed secretly between June and August 1989. Various sources have reported that at least two execution grounds were used: one located in the north-west of Beijing, where groups of prisoners were reported to have been shot before dawn in June and July. One source said at least eight groups of up to 20 people had been shot near the bridge by mid-July 1989.

The Situation in Tibet. In Tibet, martial law was imposed in the capital, Lhasa, on 7 March 1989 following two days of violent confrontations after police attempted to stop a peaceful demonstration by a small group of Tibetan monks and nuns calling for Tibet's independence. Eye-witnesses described "ill-organized" police savagely beating Tibetans and "firing indiscriminately". By 9 March the official death toll was 16, but unofficial Tibetan sources estimated that over 60 people had died and more than 200 had been injured. Over 1,000 Tibetans were reportedly arrested, though the authorities acknowledged no more than a few hundred arrests, and there were reports of secret summary executions. Further arrests occurred in the following months.

Evidence of persistent human rights violations in Tibet since pro-independence demonstrations started in September 1987 includes reports of numerous arbitrary arrests, long-term detention without charge or trial and torture.

Amnesty International has received reports about the torture and ill-treatment of prisoners which include testimonies from political detainees who were released in late 1988 or early 1989 and others. They allege that many detainees were subjected to torture, including severe beatings, shocks with electric batons and prolonged suspension by the arms. Some detainees are said to have died as a result of torture. One detainee, Tseten Norgye, a married bookkeeper who was arrested in Lhasa in April or May 1989 reportedly suffered a severe eye injury as a result of torture. He was reported to have been arrested after police found a mimeograph machine in his house which they alleged was used to print literature advocating Tibetan independence. He is held in Lhasa's Chakpori detention centre and is not known to have been charged.

To Amnesty International's knowledge, the first trial of Tibetans involved in pro-independence activities since September 1987 took place in Lhasa in January 1989. The official New China News Agency announced at the time that 27 Tibetans had been publicly tried for offences related to demonstrations in 1987 and 1988. One of these—Yulo Dawa Tsering, a senior monk from Ganden monastery detained in December 1987—was sentenced to 10 years' imprisonment and three years' deprivation of political rights on charges of "collaborating with foreign reactionary elements".

In August 1989 the *People's Daily* announced that 10 Tibetans accused of offences related to the March 1988 protests in Lhasa had been sentenced. Others were tried and sentenced during the following months. One, named as Passang, was sentenced to life imprisonment for taking part in the protests.

Amnesty International has received other reports of arrests and trials of Tibetans in the past few months. At least 16 Tibetan nuns were reported to have been arrested for demonstrating in September and October 1989. Six of the nuns were subsequently sent to labour camps without charge or trial, after receiving administrative sentences of three years' "re-education through labour". Detention orders for "re-education through labour" are issued outside the judicial process by Public Security (police) officers and those thus punished cannot question the grounds for their detention or appeal against it in a court of law. Several other Tibetans, including four monks and one young student, were assigned to terms of up to three years' "re-education through labour" between September and

December 1989 for their alleged participation in demonstrations. Others, including 10 monks from Drepung monastery, were tried on "counter-revolutionary" charges for alleged pro-independence activities. Those arrested recently include five students from Lhasa No. 1 Middle School who were arrested on 8 December 1989 for allegedly setting up in March 1989 a "counter-revolutionary" group called the Gangchen (Mountain Range) Youth Association and putting up posters in various places in Lhasa. No punishment against them has yet been announced.

Other Concerns. Many prisoners of conscience arrested in previous years remain in detention throughout China and new arrests unrelated to the June crackdown were carried out during the past year. Xu Wenli is one of dozen of supporters of the democracy movement of the late 1970s who remain in prison. He was arrested in 1981 and later sentenced to 15 years' imprisonment for "counter-revolutionary activities". Since 1986, he has been held in solitary confinement in harsh conditions in Beijing and is reportedly in poor health. Song Yude is one of several Protestant evangelists who also remain in prison. He was sentenced to eight years' imprisonment in 1986 on charges of "counter-revolutionary propaganda and incitement".

Various charge groups continued to be harassed and some of their members were arrested during the past year for carrying out religious activities without official approval. Three Catholic seminarians detained in Hebei province in January 1989 were reportedly stripped naked, beaten, forced to lie on cold concrete and burned with cigarettes while in police custody.

In April 1989, several hundred Catholic villagers were severely beaten by police during a police raid on the village of Youtong, Luancheng district, Hebei province. Two youths were reported to have died as a result and over 300 villagers, including old people and children, were reportedly injured, 88 seriously. Police took away 32 people. Arrests of members of other religious groups were also reported during 1989. They included 165 Protestant leaders detained in Henan province in early October 1989 after police raided an "underground convention" of 500 church leaders in the province. By mid-October, all but 35 of those arrested had been released after paying fines. It is not known whether the 35 are still detained.

At least seven Catholic priests and bishops not affiliated to the officially recognized Patriotic Catholic Association are also reported to have been arrested between September and December 1989 in various places in North China. One of them is Joseph Li Side, Bishop of Tianjin Diocese, who is reported to have been arrested at his home during the night of 8 and 9 December 1989. According to information received, he was called to administer the last rites to a sick person in Hulu village, but as he opened the door of his house, he was met by a large contingent of Public Security personnel and arrested.

A large number of death sentences and executions of people charged with ordinary criminal offences unrelated to the pro-democracy protests were also reported during the second half of 1989. Many were executed for economic crimes such as corruption, fraud, smuggling or embezzlement. The number of executions recorded by Amnesty International in 1989 is the highest since 1983, when several thousand people are believed to have been executed after summary trials during the first few months of a campaign against crime launched in August that year. Amnesty International concerns about the use of the death penalty in

China are described in detail in two documents issued in 1989: "The Death Penalty in China" and "People's Republic of China: The Death Penalty Debate".

The Commission on Human Rights received, at its 1990 session, a draft resolution on the situation of human rights in China (UN Doc. E/CN.4/L. 47). However, at its 52d meeting, on 6 March 1990, the commission decided, under rule 65, para. 2, of the Rules of Procedure of Functional Commissions of the Economic and Social Council, to take no decision on the draft resolution.

CHRISTIAN DEMOCRATIC INTERNATIONAL.
An international non-governmental organization in consultative status with the UN Economic and Social Council (Category II), and with UNESCO and UNCTAD, the council draws together 55 national Christian Democratic organizations in 56 countries.

CDI conducts seminars on Christian Democratic ideology and has a Permanent Committee on Human Rights. It strives for world coordination of Christian Democratic organizations in the promotion of humanist values aimed at a communitarian, participatory, and pluralist society. One of its primary goals, as formulated in a resolution on human rights issued by its International Political Bureau in 1988, is "to work for the democratization of those countries where people are submitted to regimes which deny political, social, economic and cultural pluralism and are not generated by free elections." The resolution adds that "a respect for human rights means [1] a condition for citizens' participation. . . .in their country's affairs, [2] a guarantee for peace, as important as disarmament, [and 3] an assurance that the benefits of development will not be used by rulers. . . . to strengthen their position, but will be shared by all citizens in the framework of social justice."

CDI publishes its World Political Manifesto (1977) in seven languages and issues *CDI-IDC News* monthly in French, German, and Spanish.

Christian Democratic International. Address: Rue de la Victoire 16, Boite 1, B-1060 Brussels, Belgium. Telephone: (32-2) 537-13-22. Fax: 537-93-48. Telex: 61118 IDC. Secretary-General: Luis Herrera-Campins.

CHRISTIAN PEACE CONFERENCE.
An international non-governmental organization in consultative status (Category II) with the UN's Economic and Social Council, the Commission on Human Rights, and UNESCO, the conference is also a member of the CONGO Committee on Human Rights.

The Christian Peace Conference was founded in 1958 as an international movement of theologians, clergy, and laymen and grew out of their conviction of faith in a time of rising international tension. The CPC aims to be a forum in which Christians from all over the world can meet together and search for solutions to political, social, and economic problems. Through regional committees and member churches in 90 countries, CPC works for world peace through disarmament, human rights, international cooperation, and peaceful coexistence efforts. The conference promotes social and economic structures aimed toward eliminating oppression, exploitation, racial discrimination, hunger, and illiteracy and opposes imperialism.

The Christian Peace Conference publishes three journals: *CPC News from the United Nations* (monthly); *CPC Information* (bi-monthly); and *CPC Magazine* (quarterly).

Christian Peace Conference. Address: Jungmannova 9, 111 21 Prague 1, Czechoslovakia. Telephone: 2360289 or 2360290. Cable: EKUMRADA PRAHA. Telex: 12 33 63 cpr c. Secretary-General: Rev. Dr. Lubomir Mirejovsky.

CIVIL AND POLITICAL RIGHTS: HUMAN RIGHTS COMMITTEE'S VIEWS IN PARTICULAR CASES.
When considering particular communications received under the INTERNATIONAL COVENANT ON CIVIL AND POLITICAL RIGHTS: OPTIONAL PROTOCOL, under article 5 of that protocol, the HUMAN RIGHTS COMMITTEE, from time to time, adopts views which, in accordance with para. 4 of that article, are forwarded to the State party concerned and to the individual author of the communication. These views are made public in the reports of the committee and, together with the general comments adopted by the committee under article 40, para. 4, of the covenant itself, provide an authoritative commentary on the meaning and scope of various provisions of the covenant.

Substantive issues considered by the committee up to 1 January 1989 are presented below on an article-by-article basis, as summarized in the 1984 to 1988 annual reports of the committee to the General Assembly (UN Docs. A/39/40, para. 590–620; A/40/40 para. 697–700; A/41/40, para. 422–424; A/42/40, para. 406–410; and A/43/40, para. 590–620, respectively).

Article 6: The Right to Life. In case No. 45/1979 the Committee, commenting generally on article 6, stated *inter alia:* "The requirements that the right [to life] shall be protected by law and that no one shall be arbitrarily deprived of his life mean that the law must strictly control and limit the circumstances in which a person may be deprived of his life by the authorities of a State. In the present case it is evident from the fact that seven persons lost their lives as a result of the deliberate action of the police that the deprivation of life was intentional. Moreover, the police action was apparently taken without warning to the victims and without giving them any opportunity to surrender to the police patrol or to offer any explanation of their presence or intentions ...". In case No. 84/1981 the Committee observed that while it could not arrive at a definite conclusion as to whether the victim had committed suicide, was driven to suicide or was killed by others while in custody, "the inescapable conclusion is that in all the circumstances the [State party's] authorities either by act or by ommission were responsible for not taking adequate measures to protect his life, as required by article 6 (1) of the Covenant".

Article 6 of the Covenant protects the inherent right to life and provides that the right to life shall be protected by law and that no one shall be arbitrarily deprived of his life. At its twenty-fourth session, the Committee adopted views under article 5, paragraph 4, of the Optional Protocol in eight cases, Nos. 146/1983 and 148 to 154/1983 (Kanta Baboeram-Adhin *et al.* v. Suriname), concerning the right to life. Pursuant to rule 88, paragraph 2, of the Committee's provisional rule of procedure, the cases were dealt with jointly. In its views the Committee declared:

"The right enshrined in this article is the supreme right of the human being. It follows that the deprivation of life by the authorities of the State is a matter of the utmost gravity. This follows from the article as a whole and in particular is the reason why paragraph 2 of the article lays down that the death penalty may be imposed only for the most serious crimes. The requirements that the right shall be protected by law and that no one shall be arbitrarily deprived of his life mean that the law must strictly control and limit the circumstances in which a person may be deprived of his life by the authorities of a State. In the present case it is evident from the fact that 15 prominent persons lost their lives as a result of the deliberate action of the military police that the deprivation of life was intentional. The State party has failed to submit any evidence proving that these persons were shot while trying to escape.

"The Human Rights Committee, acting under article 5, paragraph 4, of the Optional Protocol to the International Covenant on Civil and Political Rights, is of the view that the victims were arbitrarily deprived of their lives contrary to article 6, paragraph 1, of the International Covenant on Civil and Political Rights. In the circumstances, the Committee does not find it necessary to consider assertions that other provisions of the Covenant were violated.

"The Committee therefore urges the State party to take effective steps: (i) to investigate the killings of December 1982; (ii) to bring to justice any persons found to be responsible for the death of the victims; (iii) to pay compensation to the surviving families; and (iv) to ensure that the right to life is duly protected in Suriname."

Article 7: The Right not to be Subjected to Torture or to Cruel, Inhuman or Degrading Treatment. In a number of cases (in particular Nos. 4/1977, 5/1977, 8/1977, 9/1977, 11/1977, 25/1978, 28/1978, 30/1978, 33/1978, 37/1978, 49/1979, 52/1979, 63/1979, 73/1980, 110/1981) concerning various forms of torture and other cruel treatment, the Committee has expressed the view that article 7 had been violated. A recurring theme in such cases has been the burden of proof. In this respect the Committee has established that it "cannot rest alone on the author of the communication, especially considering that the author and the State party do not always have equal access to the evidence and that frequently the State party alone has access to relevant information. It is implicit in article 4 (2) of the Optional Protocol that the State party has the duty to investigate in good faith all allegations of violation of the Covenant made against it and its authorities, especially when such allegations are corroborated by evidence submitted by the author of the communication, and to furnish to the Committee the information available to it. In cases where the author has submitted to the Committee allegations supported by substantial witness testimony, as in this case, and where further clarification of the case depends on information exclusively in the hands of the State party, the Committee may consider such allegations as substantiated in the absence of satisfactory evidence and explanations to the contrary submitted by the State party" (No. 30/1978). Furthermore, the Committee has repeatedly held that "a refutation of [the author's] allegations in general terms is not sufficient" (Nos. 11/1977, 37/1978).

Article 9 (1): Arbitrary Arrest and Detention. Although many communications submitted to the Committee claim that the victim has been subjected to arbitrary arrest, this allegation has proved to be difficult to establish, since State parties have been able to show in most cases that the arrest was carried out according to the law of the State concerned. In cases, however, where the facts showed that no arrest warrant had been issued or that the victim was not released from imprisonment after serving his term or after issuance of a release order, the Committee has found violations of article 9 (1).

In case No. 56/1979 the victim was abducted by agents of the State party in another country, brought across the border and charged with "subversive association". The Committee found a violation of article 9 (1), "because the act of abduction into [the State party's] territory constituted an arbitrary arrest and detention".

In case No. 37/1979 the Committee found a violation because the victim "was not released until one month after an order for her release was issued by the military court"; similarly, in case No. 33/1978, because the victim "was not released until approximately six or seven months after an order for his release was issued by the military court"; in case No. 25/1978 with respect to one victim, "because she continued to be detained after having served her prison sentence on 9 November 1977", and with respect to the other victim, "because she was subjected to arbitrary detention under the 'prompt security measures' until 12 August 1978 after having signed on 15 August 1974 the document for her provisional release".

In case No. 16/1977 the Committee found that the victim had been "arrested on 1 September 1977 in order to force him to disclose the whereabouts of [S.B] and that he was not released from detention until late in 1978 or early in 1979. The State party has not claimed that there was any criminal charge against him. In the view of the Committee, therefore, he was subject to arbitrary arrest and detention contrary to article 9 of the Covenant."

Article 9 (3): The Right to be Brought Promptly before a Judge and Tried within a Reasonable Time. One of the most fundamental rights of persons who have been arrested or detained on a criminal charge is the right to be brought "promptly" before a judicial officer and to "trial within a reasonable time". The Committee has received many communications concerning alleged violations of this right, but it has not yet established the precise meaning of the terms employed in article 9 (3) of the Covenant. The Committee

C

has, however, held that the article had been breached with respect to a victim who had been arrested on 24 March 1977 and detained until 9 January 1978 (i.e. over nine months) without having been brought before a judge (No. 90/1981). In another case of a breach the victim was arrested on 2 December 1980, was kept incommunicado and not brought before a judicial authority until 23 March 1981, i.e. over three months later (No. 84/1981). On the other hand, the Committee found no violation of article 9 (3) where the person was arrested on 28 September 1978 and charged before a military examining judge on 7 November 1978, i.e. six weeks later (No. 43/1979).

Article 9 (4): The Right to Challenge One's Arrest and Detention. The Committee has considered many communications in which the authors have alleged that the right to take proceedings before a court in order to challenge their arrest has been violated, in particular because they were denied the remedy of *habeas corpus*. The Committee has found violations of article 9 (4) in cases where it was established that the victims had no way of challenging their arrest, because the remedy of *habeas corpus* was not applicable to persons arrested under the so-called "prompt security measures" in the State party concerned (Nos. 4/1977, 5/1977, 6/1977, 8/1977, 9/1977, 10/1977, 11/1977, 25/1978, 28/1978, 32/1978, 33/1978, 37/1978, 43/1979, 44/1979).

In case No. 46/1979, involving another State party, the Committee noted: "As to the allegations of breaches of the provisions of article 9 of the Covenant, it has been established that the alleged victims did not have recourse to *habeas corpus*". The Committee concluded that the provision had been violated because the victims "could not themselves take proceedings in order that a court might decide without delay on the lawfulness of their detention".

Article 9 (5): The Right to Compensation for Unlawful Arrest or Detention. In a number of cases the Committee has expressed the view that the State party is under an obligation "to provide effective remedies to the victim, including compensation in accordance with article 9 (5) of the Covenant" (No. 9/1977; see also 8/1977, 25/1978, 30/1978, 90/1981, 107/1981).

Article 10: The Right to be Treated Humanely during Imprisonment. A violation of this article has been found in a number of cases, including case No. 49/1979, where the victim had been held "in a cell measuring 1 m × 2 m in the basement of the political police prison at . . . and has been held incommunicado ever since"; in case No. 109/1981 "because [the victim] was kept in solitary confinement for several months in conditions which failed to respect the inherent dignity of the human person"; in case No. 85/1981 "because [the victim] has not been treated with humanity and with respect for the inherent dignity of the human person, in particular because he was kept incommunicado at an unknown place of detention for several months (from November 1976 to the middle of 1977) during which time his fate and his whereabouts were unknown". (See also Nos. 4/1977, 5/1977, 8/1977, 10/1977, 11/1977, 25/1977, 27/1978, 28/1078, 30/1978, 33/1978, 37/1978, 44/1979, 56/1979, 63/1979, 70/1980 and 73/1980.)

Article 12: The Right to Freedom of Movement and to Leave any Country. While the Committee has not had the occasion to pronounce itself on alleged violations of the right of freedom of movement within a State (article 12 (1)), it has had a number of cases raising issues under article 12 (2) concerning the right to leave any country, including one's own, and, in particular, the question as to how a refusal to issue a passport to a citizen may affect the exercise of that right ("passport cases"). The first case involved a journalist living abroad, whose passport has not been renewed upon expiry on 27 September 1977; in response to the Committee's decision on admissibility (case No. 31/1978), the State party informed the Committee that it had instructed the relevant consulate to renew the claimant's passport, whereupon the Committee decided to discontinue consideration of the case. In another case the Committee found a violation of article 12 (2) of the Covenant, because the victim had been "refused the issuance of a passport without any justification therefore, thereby preventing her from leaving any country including her own" (No. 57/1979). In another case the Committee clarified further the content of article 12 (2): "As to the alleged violation of article 12 (2) of the Covenant, the Committee has observed that a passport is a means of enabling an individual 'to leave any country, including his own' as required by that provision: consequently, it follows from the very nature of that right that, in the case of a citizen resident abroad, article 12 (2) imposes obligations on the State of nationality as well as on the State of residence and, therefore, article 2 (1) of the Covenant cannot be interpreted as limiting the obligations of [the State party] under article 12 (2) to citizens within its own territory. The right recognized by article 12 (2) may, in accordance with article 12 (3), be subject to such restrictions as are 'provided by law, are necessary to protect national security, public order (*ordre public*), public health or morals or the rights and freedoms of others and are consistent with the other rights recognized in the Covenant'. There are, therefore, circumstances in which a State, if its law so provides, may refuse passport facilities to one of its citizens. However, in the present case, the State party has not, in its submissions to the Committee, put forward any such justification for refusing to renew the passport of [the victim]" (No. 106/1981, see also No. 108/1981).

Article 13: The Right of an Alien not to be Expelled Arbitrarily from his Country of Residence. The Covenant does not provide for a right to asylum, but "an alien lawfully in the territory of a State party . . . may be expelled therefrom only in pursuance of a decision reached in accordance with law." The application of this provision of article 13 was examined in case No. 58/1979, where the Committee underlined that "the article applies only to an alien 'lawfully in the territory' of a State party . . . The only question is whether the expulsion was 'in accordance with law' . . . The Committee takes the view that the interpretation of domestic law is essentially a matter for the courts and authorities of the State party concerned. It is not within the powers or functions of the Committee to evaluate whether the competent authorities of the State party in question have interpreted and applied the domestic law correctly in the case before it under the Optional Protocol, unless it is established that they have not interpreted and applied it in good faith or that it is evident that there has been an abuse of power." No violation was found.

At its twenty-seventh session, the Committee adopted the text of a general comment on the position of aliens under the Covenant. At its twenty-ninth session, the Committee concluded its examination of communication No. 155/1983 (Eric Hammel v. Madagascar). Maître Eric Hammel, a French national and resident of France, had been a practising attorney in Madagascar until his expulsion in February 1982. He had represented three persons before the Committee who alleged that they had been victims of violations of their rights by Madagascar. The Committee had adopted views in those three cases at its eighteenth and twenty-four sessions. In his own case, Maître Hammel claimed that his expulsion from Madagascar constituted a violation of article 13 of the Covenant. In its views under article 5, paragraph 4, of the Optional Protocol, the Committee elucidated the scope of article 13 of the Covenant, making express reference to its general comment:

"The Committee notes that, in the circumstances of the present case, the author was not given an effective remedy to challenge his expulsion and that the State party has not shown that there were compelling reasons of national security to deprive him of that remedy. In formulating its views the Human Rights Committee also takes into account its general comment 15 (27), on the position of aliens under the Covenant, and in particular points out that 'an alien must be given full facilities for pursuing his remedy against expulsion so that this right will in all the circumstances of his case be an effective one'.

"The Committee further notes with concern that, based on the information provided by the State party . . . , the decision to expel Eric Hammel would appear to have been linked to the fact that he had represented persons before the Human Rights Committee. Were that to be the case, the Committee observes that it would be both untenable and incompatible with the spirit of the International Covenant on Civil and Political Rights and the Optional Protocol thereto, if States parties to these instruments were to take exception to anyone acting as legal counsel for persons placing their communications before the Committee for consideration under the Optional Protocol."

Thus the Committee found that article 13 had been violated, "because, for grounds that were not those of compelling reasons of national security, he [Maître Hammel] was not allowed to submit the reasons against his expulsion and to have his case reviewed by a competent authority within a reasonable time."

At its thirty-third session, the Committee examined communication No. 236/1987 (V. M. R. B. v. Canada), which involved a number of issues related to asylum, immigration and deportation proceedings. In declaring that communication inadmissible, the Committee noted that a right of asylum was not protected by the Covenant and, with respect to article 13, observed:

"that one of the conditions for the application of this article is that the alien be lawfully in the territory of the State party, whereas Mr. R. has not been lawfully in the territory of Canada. Furthermore, the State party has pleaded reasons of national security in connection with the proceedings to deport him. It is not for the Committee to test a sovereign State's evaluation of an alien's security rating; moreover, on the basis of the information before the Committee, the procedures to deport Mr. R. have respected the safeguards provided for in article 13".

Article 14 (1): The Right to a Fair and Public Hearing by Competent, Independent and Impartial Tribunal. In case No. 70/1980 the Committee made findings of fact that the victim "was tried *in camera*, the trial was conducted without her presence and the judgement was not rendered in public" and held that these facts disclosed a violation of article 14 (1), "because she did not have a fair and public hearing". Similarly, in case No. 10/1977 the Committee found that article 14 (1) had been violated "because he did not have a fair and public hearing". In case No. 44/1979 the Committee made a finding of fact that the victim was sentenced "in a closed trial, conducted in writing and without his presence and the judgement of the Court was not made pub-

lic", and based thereon a finding of a violation of article 14 (1). (See also cases Nos. 28/1978, 32/1978.)

Article 14 (3) (b). The Right to Communicate with Counsel. Violations of article 14 (3) (b) have been found in numerous cases, e.g. No. 83/1981 "because the conditions of his detention from November 1980 to May 1981 effectively barred him from access to legal assistance", and No. 49/1979 "because he has been denied adequate opportunity to communicate with his counsel, [. . .], and because his right to the assistance of his counsel to represent him and prepare his defence has been interfered with by [the State party's] authorities".

Article 14 (3) (b). The Right to Have Adequate Time and Facilities for the Preparation of One's Defense. In case No. 158/1983 (O. F. v. Norway) the author had been convicted of driving his automobile at a speed exceeding that allowed by the traffic law and of failing to furnish information to an official register about a business firm that he operated. He claimed that he was not able adequately to prepare his defence because the Court did not provide him with copies of all relevant documents about the traffic violation. In declaring the case inadmissible, the Committee noted:

"that from 26 August to the date of the hearing on 21 October 1982 the author could have examined, personally or through his lawyer, documents relevant to his case at the police station. He chose not to do so, but requested that copies of all documents be sent to him. The Committee notes that the Covenant does not explicitly provide for a right of a charged person to be furnished with copies of all relevant documents in a criminal investigation, but does provide that he shall have adequate time and facilities for the preparation of his defence and to communicate with counsel of his own choosing. Even if all the allegations of the author were to be accepted as proven, there would be no ground for asserting that a violation of article 14, paragraph 3 (b), occurred."

Article 14 (3) (b) and (d). The Right to Legal Assistance of One's Own Choosing. In numerous cases the Committee found that the victims were denied the right to defend themselves through counsel of their own choosing and were compelled to accept *ex officio* counsel (Nos. 52/1979, 56/1979, 73/1980) in violation of article 14 (3) (b) and (d).

Article 14 (c). The Right to be Tried without Undue Delay. A violation of this provision of the Covenant is frequently accompanied by a violation of the right to be brought promptly before a judge and tried within a reasonable time (article 9 (c)). In neither case has the Committee defined the relevant terms, since the circumstances of each case must always be taken into account. In case No. 43/1979 a victim who had been arrested on 28 September 1978 and tried before a military court in July 1979 (10 months later) was deemed to have suffered a violation of his right to be tried without undue delay. The Committee has also found a violation of article 14 (3) (c) where the victim was arrested many years before the entry into force of the Covenant and the Optional Protocol and was not tried until some time after the entry into force of these instruments for the State party concerned. A violation was found in case No. 80/1980 where the victim had been arrested on 4 June 1972, the Covenant and Optional Protocol had entered into force on 23 March 1976 for the State party concerned and judgement was not pronounced by the court of first instance until 14 December 1977. (See also Nos. 4/1977, 5/1977, 6/

1977, 8/1977, 10/1977, 27/1978, 28/1978, 32/1978, 33/1978, 44/1979, 46/1979, 52/1979, 56/1979, 63/1979, 70/1980, 73/1980.)

Article 14 (3) (d). The Right to Free Legal Assistance. In case No. 158/1983 (O.F. v. Norway), the author claimed that his right to free legal assistance, . . . as provided for in article 14, paragraph 3 (d), of the Covenant, had been violated. The State party submitted that the fact that the author was not assigned free legal assistance must be seen in the light of the nature of the offences with which he was charged. Both charges, the State party argued, were trivial and ordinary and could in practice only lead to a light sentence. The author was sentenced to pay a fine of NKr. 1,000 or to serve 10 days' imprisonment if the fine was not paid. In declaring the communication inadmissible, the Committee noted that "The Covenant foresees free legal assistance to a charged person in any case where the interests of justice so require and without payment to him in any such case if he does not have sufficient means to pay for it. The author has failed to show that in his particular case the 'interests of justice' would have required the assignment of a lawyer at the expense of the State party."

Article 14 (3) (e): The Right to Examine Witnesses. In case No. 63/1979 the Committee found a violation of article 14 (3) (e) because the victim "was denied the opportunity to obtain the attendance and examination of witnesses on his behalf".

Article 14 (3) (g): The Right not to Incriminate Oneself. The use of forced confessions in order to convict accused persons has been found by the Committee to be in violation of article 14 (c) (g) in cases Nos. 52/1979 and 73/1980.

Article 14 (5): The Right to Review of Conviction and Sentence. In case No. 64/1979 the Committee noted "that the expression 'according to law' in article 14 (5) of the Covenant is not intended to leave the very existence of the right to review to the discretion of the States parties, since the rights are those recognized by the Covenant, and not merely those recognized by domestic law. Rather, what is to be determined 'according to law' is the modalities by which the review by a higher tribunal is to be carried out". The Committee found that the facts of the case disclosed a violation of article 14 (5), because the victim "was denied the right to review of her conviction by a higher tribunal".

In case No. 27/1977 the Committee observed "that the right under article 14 (3) (c) to be tried without undue delay should be applied in conjunction with the right under article 14 (5) to review by a higher tribunal, and that consequently there was in this case a violation of both of these provisions taken together".

Article 14 (7). Double Jeopardy. In communication No. 204/1986 (A. P. v. Italy), the author claimed a violation of article 14, paragraph 7, because he had been convicted in 1979 by the Criminal Court of Lugano, Switzerland, for complicity in the crime of conspiring to exchange currency notes, which came from the ransom paid for the release of a person who had been kidnapped, and because he was again convicted *in absentia* in 1983 by the Milan Court of Appeal for an offence arising out of the same kidnapping. In declaring the communication inadmissible *ratione materiae* under article 3 of the Optional Protocol, the Committee stated: ". . . article 14, paragraph 7, of the Covenant, which the author invokes, does not guarantee *non bis in idem* with regard to the national jurisdictions of two or more States. The Committee observes that this provision prohibits double jeopardy only with regard to an offence adjudicated in a given State".

Article 15: Nulla Poena Sine Lege. In case No. 28/1978 the Committee found that article 15 had been violated "because the penal law was applied retroactively against" the victim; the charge of conspiracy (*Asociación para delinquir*) was found to be tantamount to prosecution for membership in a political party, which had been lawful at the time when the victim was affiliated with it and which had been banned only afterwards. (See also Nos. 44/1979, 46/1979, 91/1981.)

The purpose of the main principle of article 15 is to protect individuals against *ex post facto* criminal laws operating to their detriment. The last sentence of paragraph 1 of article 15 departs from this safeguard when this purpose is absent; on the contrary, it not only allows, but prescribes the retroactive operation of a new law imposing a "lighter penalty". The Committee has been seized of two cases where it was claimed that a new law changing the conditions of parole should have been applied retroactively to two convicted criminals. In the specific circumstances of the cases, the Committee decided that no violation of the Covenant had taken place (Nos. 50/1979, 55/1979).

Articles 17 and 23: The Rights to Family Life and Protection of the Family; and Articles 2 (1), 3 and 26: Discrimination on the Ground of Sex. The Committee found a violation of these provisions taken together in a case where the State party's immigration law and deportation law subjected foreign husbands of native women to certain restrictions, whereas foreign wives of native men were not so subjected (No. 35/1978). The State party has subsequently informed the Committee that the laws in question have been amended, so as to remove the discriminatory provisions of those laws on the ground of sex.

Article 18: The Right to Freedom of Religion or Belief. The Committee has not been seized of cases concerning an alleged violation of the right to adopt and practise a religion, but it has examined the right of atheist parents to exempt their children from religious instruction pursuant to article 18 (4) of the Covenant, which provides that "States parties . . . undertake to have respect for the liberty of parents . . . to ensure the religious and moral education of their children in conformity with their own convictions". Although in case No. 40/1978 the Committee found that the author's submissions did not substantiate his allegation of a violation of article 18, the State party has taken action in response to the Committee's views by revising a law and charging the Board of Education with closer inspection of instruction of ethics and the history of religions.

Articles 18 and 19: The Right to Freedom of Thought, Conscience and Religion, and the Right to Hold Opinions. In case No. 185/1984 (L. T. K. v. Finland) the author claimed that the failure of the State party to recognize his status as a conscientious objector made him a victim of a breach by the State party of articles 18 and 19 of the Covenant. At its twenty-fifth session the Human Rights Committee declared the communication inadmissible on the ground that it was incompatible with the provisions of the Covenant, observing that "the Covenant does not provide for the right to conscientious objection; neither article 18 nor article 19 of the Covenant, especially taking into account paragraph 3 (c) (ii) of article 8, can be construed as implying that right".

Article 19: The Right to Hold Opinions; Freedom of Expression. In case No. 28/1978 the Committee found a violation of article 19 (2) because the victim "was detained for having disseminated information relating to trade union activities". In case No. 44/1979 the Committee similarly found a violation because the victim had been "arrested, detained and tried for his political and trade-union activities" and explained its finding as follows: "As regards article 19, the Covenant provides that everyone shall have the right to hold opinions without interference and that the freedom of expression set forth in paragraph 2 of that article shall be subject only to such restrictions as are necessary (a) for respect of the rights and reputations of others or (b) for the protection of national security or of public order (*ordre public*), or of public health or morals. The Government of [the State party] has submitted no evidence regarding the nature of the activities in which [the victim] was alleged to have been engaged and which led to his arrest, detention and committal for trial. Bare information from the State party that he was charged with subversive association and conspiracy to violate the Constitution, followed by preparatory acts thereto, is not in itself sufficient, without details of the alleged charges and copies of the court proceedings. The Committee is therefore unable to conclude on the information before it that the arrest, detention and trial of [the victim] was justified on any of the grounds mentioned in article 19 (3) of the Covenant". (See also Nos. 11/1977, 8/1977, 33/1978, 52/1979.)

This right has also been invoked in connection with alleged censorship in radio and television programmes dealing with homosexuality. In this connection the Committee had to look into the role of mass media and the application of the criteria of article 19 (3) to self-imposed restrictions. In its views in case No. 61/1979 the Committee noted "first, that public morals differ widely. There is no universally applicable common standard. Consequently, in this respect, a certain margin of discretion must be accorded to the responsible national authorities. The Committee finds that it cannot question the decision of the responsible organs of the [State party's] Broadcasting Corporation that radio and television are not the appropriate forums to discuss issues related to homosexuality, as far as a programme could be judged as encouraging homosexual behaviour. According to article 19 (3), the exercise of the rights provided for in article 19 (2) carries with it special duties and responsibilities for those organs. As far as radio and television programmes are concerned, the audience cannot be controlled. In particular, harmful effects on minors cannot be excluded." No violation was found.

Article 22: The Right to Strike. When discussing the question of admissibility of case No. 118/1982 (J.B. *et al.* v. Canada) the Committee had occasion to consider whether the prohibition of the right to strike for municipal employees (civil servants) amounts to a violation of article 22 of the International Covenant on Civil and Political Rights. In interpreting the scope of article 22 of the Covenant, the Committee first gave attention to the ordinary meaning of each element of the article in its context and in the light of its object and purpose, and also had recourse to supplementary means of interpretation by perusing the *travaux préparatoires* of the Covenant. The Committee could not deduce therefrom that the drafters of the Covenant on Civil and Political Rights intended to guarantee the right to strike.

"The conclusions to be drawn from the drafting history are corroborated by a comparative analysis of the International Covenant on Civil and Political Rights and the International Covenant on Economic, Social and Cultural Rights. Article 8, paragraph 1 (d), of the International Covenant on Economic, Social and Cultural Rights recognizes the right to strike, in addition to the right of everyone to

form and join trade unions for the promotion and protection of his economic and social interests, thereby making it clear that the right to strike cannot be considered as an implicit component of the right to form and join trade unions. Consequently, the fact that the International Covenant on Civil and Political Rights does not similarly provide expressly for the right to strike in article 22, paragraph 1, shows that this right is not included in the scope of this article, while it enjoys protection under the procedures and mechanisms of the International Covenant on Economic, Social and Cultural Rights, subject to the specific restrictions mentioned in article 8 of that instrument."

An individual opinion signed by five members of the Committee who could not agree with this analysis is also appended.

Article 23 (1) and (4). Protection of the Family, Protection of Children at the Dissolution of Marriage. Communication No. 201/1985 (Hendriks v. the Netherlands) concerned a divorced parent who claimed that the Netherlands courts' failure to grant him access to his son constituted a violation of article 23. The Committee found no violation, stating that, while the Netherlands courts recognized the right of children to permanent contacts with both parents and the right of access of the non-custodial parent, that right could be denied in the best interests of the child and that it was for the local court and not for the Committee to determine what constituted the best interests of the child in the particular case. The Committee also explained its understanding of the scope of article 23 as follows:

"In examining the communication, the Committee considers it important to stress that article 23, paragraphs 1 and 4, of the Covenant sets out three rules of equal importance, namely, that the family should be protected, that steps should be taken to ensure equality of rights of spouses upon the dissolution of the marriage and that provisions should be made for the necessary protection of any children. The words 'the family' in article 23, paragraph 1, do not refer solely to the family home as it exists during the marriage. The idea of the family must necessarily embrace the relation between parents and child. Although divorce legally ends a marriage, it cannot dissolve the bond uniting father—or mother—and child; this bond does not depend upon the continuation of the parents' marriage. It would seem that the priority given to the child's interests is compatible with this rule".

Article 25: The Right to Engage in Political Activity. Restrictions on the right to engage in political activity have been examined by the Committee in the light of State party contentions that such restrictions were necessary because of a state of emergency. In case No. 44/1979 the Committee found a violation of article 25, noting "that the sanction of deprivation of certain political rights is provided for in the legislation of some countries. Accordingly, article 25 of the Covenant prohibits 'unreasonable' restrictions. In no case, however, may a person be subjected to such sanctions solely because of his or her political opinion (articles 2 (1) and 26). Furthermore, the principle of proportionality would require that a measure as harsh as the deprivation of all political rights for a period of 15 years be specifically justified. No such attempt has been made in the present case."

In case No. 34/1978 the Committee found a violation, noting that "even on the assumption that there exists a situation of emergency in [the State party] the Human Rights Committee does not see what ground could be adduced to support the contention that, in order to restore peace and order, it was necessary to deprive all citizens, who as members of certain political groups had been candidates in the elections in 1966 and 1971, of any political right for a period as long as 15 years. This measure applies to every one, without distinction as to whether he sought to promote his political opinions by peaceful means or by resorting to, or advocating the use of, violent means. The Government of [the State party] has failed to show that the interdiction of any kind of political dissent is required in order to deal with the alleged emergency situation and pave the way back to political freedom."

Among the Committee's views under article 5, paragraph 4, of the Optional Protocol, two were adopted without the benefit of any submissions from the State party. In case No. 138/1983 (Nqalula Mpandanjila *et al.* v. Zaire) concerning 12 imprisoned Zairian parliamentarians, the Committee found, *inter alia*, violations of article 12, paragraph 1, of the Covenant, "because they were deprived of their freedom of movement during long periods of administrative banishment" and of article 25, "because they were deprived of the right equally to take part in the conduct of public affairs" (see annex VIII A). In case No. 157/1983 (André Alphonse Mpaka-Nsusu v. Zaire) the Committee found, *inter alia*, violations of article 12, paragraph 1, "because he was banished to his village of origin for an indefinite period" and of article 25, "because, notwithstanding the entitlement to stand for the presidency under Zairian law, he was not so permitted."

Article 26: Equality before the Law, Equal Protection of the Law. In the absence of a general comment on article 26 of the Covenant, the Committee has discussed the scope of this article extensively in connection with its examination of communications under the Optional Protocol. One of the unresolved questions before the Committee was whether the principle of non-discrimination enunciated in article 26 applied only with respect to the rights enshrined in the International Covenant on Civil and Political Rights, or whether non-discrimination constituted an autonomous right applicable to civil and political rights not protected in the Covenant or even to economic, social and cultural rights, which might be protected by other international instruments, such as the International Covenant on Economic, Social and Cultural Rights. While States parties have argued for a restrictive interpretation of article 26 on the basis that the two Covenants established two different monitoring systems and that provision was made for an individual complaints procedure only with respect to the International Covenant on Civil and Political Rights, the Committee decided at its twenty-ninth session with regard to communications Nos. 172/1984, 180/1984 and 182/1984 (see annex VIII B, C and D) that it could examine an allegation of discrimination with regard to economic, social and cultural rights. In all three cases, the Committee observed:

"For the purpose of determining the scope of article 26, the Committee has taken into account the 'ordinary meaning' of each element of the article in its context and in the light of its object and purpose (art. 31 of the Vienna Convention on the Law of Treaties). The Committee begins by noting that article 26 does not merely duplicate the guarantees already provided for in article 2. It derives from the principle of equal protection of the law without discrimination, as contained in article 7 of the Universal Declaration of Human Rights, which prohibits discrimination in law or in practice in any field regulated and protected by public authorities. Article 26 is thus concerned with the obliga-

tions imposed on States in regard to their legislation and the application thereof.

"Although article 26 requires that legislation should prohibit discrimination, it does not of itself contain any obligation with respect to the matters that may be provided for by legislation. Thus it does not, for example, require any State to enact legislation to provide for social security. However, when such legislation is adopted in the exercise of a State's sovereign power, then such legislation must comply with article 26 of the Covenant."

After deciding on its own competence to consider cases of alleged discrimination with regard to social security rights, the Committee examined whether certain facts constituted discrimination within the meaning of article 26 of the Covenant. In case No. 182/1984 (F.H. Zwaan-de Vries v. the Netherlands) the Committee found a violation of article 26:

"The right to equality before the law and to equal protection of the law without any discrimination does not make all differences of treatment discriminatory. A differentiation based on reasonable and objective criteria does not amount to prohibited discrimination within the meaning of article 26.

"It therefore remains for the Committee to determine whether the differentiation in Netherlands law at the time in question and as applied to Mrs. Zwaan-de Vries constituted discrimination within the meaning of article 26. The Committee notes that in Netherlands law the provisions of articles 84 and 85 of the Netherlands Civil Code imposes equal rights and obligations on both spouses with regard to their joint income. Under section 13, subsection 1 (1), of the Unemployment Benefits Act (WWV) a married woman, in order to receive WWV benefits, had to prove that she was a 'breadwinner'—a condition that did not apply to married men. Thus a differentiation which appears on one level to be one of status is in fact one of sex, placing married women at a disadvantage compared with married men. Such a differentiation is not reasonable, . . ."

Similarly, in case No. 172/1984 (S.W.M. Broeks v. the Netherlands), which involved the application of the same law in a comparable factual situation, the Committee also made a finding of a violation of article 26.

In case No. 180/1984 (L.G. Danning v. the Netherlands), the Committee found that the facts did not support a finding of a violation of article 26:

"In the light of the explanations given by the State party with respect to the differences made by Netherlands legislation between married and unmarried couples . . . , the Committee is persuaded that the differentiation complained of by Mr. Danning is based on objective and reasonable criteria. The Committee observes, in this connection, that the decision to enter into a legal status by marriage, which provides, in Netherlands law, both for certain benefits and for certain duties and responsibilities, lies entirely with the cohabiting persons. By choosing not to enter into marriage, Mr. Danning and his cohabitant have not, in law, assumed the full extent of the duties and responsibilities incumbent on married couples. Consequently, Mr. Danning does not receive the full benefits provided for in Netherlands law for married couples. The Committee concludes that the differentiation complained of by Mr. Danning does not constitute discrimination in the sense of article 26 of the Covenant."

Following the adoption of the Committee's views at its twenty-ninth session, in 1987, in cases Nos. 172/1984 (Broeks v. the Netherlands) and 182/1984 (Zwaan-de Vries

v. the Netherlands) recognizing that the scope of article 26 extends to rights not otherwise guaranteed by the Covenant, the Committee has received an increasing number of communications concerning alleged discrimination in contravention of article 26 of the Covenant.

As the Committee, however, observed in the Broeks and Zwaan-de Vries cases:

"The right to equality before the law and to equal protection of the law without any discrimination does not make all differences of treatment discriminatory. A differentiation based on reasonable and objective criteria does not amount to prohibited discrimination within the meaning of article 26."

A number of the communications received latterly have been declared inadmissible, since the authors failed to make at least a *prima facie* case of discrimination within the meaning of article 26.

In case No. 212/1986 (P. P. C. v. the Netherlands), the author had alleged discrimination because the application of a law providing for additional assistance to persons with a minimum income was linked to the person's income in the month of September. Since the author had not been unemployed in September, the annual calculation showed a figure higher than his real income for the year in question and he did not qualify for the desired additional assistance. In declaring the communication inadmissible, the Committee stated:

"The Committee has already had an opportunity to observe that the scope of article 26 can also cover cases of discrimination with regard to social security benefits (communications Nos. 172/1984, 180/1984, 182/1984). It considers, however, that the scope of article 26 does not extend to differences of results in the application of common rules in the allocation of benefits. In the case at issue, the author merely states that the determination of compensation benefits on the basis of a person's income in the month of September led to an unfavourable result in his case. Such determination is, however, uniform for all persons with a minimum income in the Netherlands. Thus, the Committee finds that the law in question is not *prima facie* discriminatory, and that the author does not, therefore, have a claim under article 2 of the Optional Protocol".

Two other cases concerned the different treatment of soldiers and civilians. In declaring communication No. 267/1987 (M. J. G. v. the Netherlands) inadmissible, the Committee stated:

"The Committee notes that the author claims that he is a victim of discrimination on the ground of 'other status' (Covenant, art. 26, *in fine*) because, being a soldier during the period of his military service, he could not appeal against a summons like a civilian. The Committee considers, however, that the scope of application of article 26 cannot be extended to cover situations such as the one encountered by the author. The Committee observes, as it did with respect to communication No. 245/1987 (R. T. Z.v. the Netherlands), that the Covenant does not preclude the institution of compulsory military service by States parties, even though this means that some rights of individuals may be restricted during military service, within the exigencies of such service. The Committee notes, in this connection, that the author has not claimed that the Netherlands military penal procedures are not being applied equally to all Netherlands citizens serving in the Netherlands armed forces. It therefore concludes that the author has no claim under article 2 of the Optional Protocol".

In case no. 191/1985 (Blom v. Sweden), which the Com-

mittee declared admissible and examined on the merits, the main issue was whether the author of the communication was the victim of a violation of article 26 of the Covenant because of the alleged incompatibility of the Swedish regulations on education allowances with that provision. In deciding that the State party had not violated article 26 by refusing to grant the author, as a pupil of a private school, an education allowance for the school year 1981/82, whereas pupils of public schools were entitled to education allowances for that period, the Committee stated:

"The State party's educational system provides for both private and public education. The State party cannot be deemed to act in a discriminatory fashion if it does not provide the same level of subsidy for the two types of establishments, when the private system is not subject to State supervision. As to the author's claim that the failure of the State party to grant an education allowance for the school year 1981/82 constituted discriminatory treatment, because the State party did not apply retroactively its decision of 17 June 1982 to place grades 10 and above under State supervision, the Committee notes that the granting of an allowance depended on actual exercise of State supervision; since State supervision could not be exercised prior to 1 July 1982 . . . , the Committee finds that consequently it could not be expected that the State party would grant an allowance for any prior period and that the question of discrimination does not arise. On the other hand, the question does arise whether the processing of the application of the Rudolf Steiner School to be placed under State supervision was unduly prolonged and whether this violated any of the author's rights under the Covenant. In this connection, the Committee notes that the evaluation of a school's curricula necessarily entails a certain period of time, as a result of a host of factors and imponderables, including the necessity of seeking advice from various governmental agencies. In the instant case the school's application was made in October 1981 and the decision was rendered eight months later, in June 1982. This lapse of time cannot be deemed to be discriminatory, as such."

Article 27: Protection of Minorities. Article 27 has been invoked before the Committee primarily in connection with the rights of North American Indians to their cultural heritage. In case No. 24/1977 a native Indian had been denied, by operation of the Indian Act, the legal right to reside on an Indian reserve because she had married a non-Indian. The Committee found a breach of article 27. The State party subsequently informed the Committee that the Indian Act is in process of amendment so as to remove therefrom any discriminatory provisions.

Communication No. 197/1985 (Kitok v. Sweden) concerned an ethnic Sami and reindeer breeder, who complained of an alleged violation of article 27 of the Covenant, because he had been excluded from membership in the Sami village (Sameby) by decision of the Sami community on the basis of the Reindeer Husbandry Act. Mr. Kitok's appeal to a Swedish court, under the same Act, was unsuccessful. One of the questions examined by the Committee was whether reindeer husbandry constituted a cultural activity. The Committee observed:

"The regulation of an economic activity is normally a matter for the State alone. However, where that activity is an essential element in the culture of an ethnic community, its application to an individual may fall under article 27 of the Covenant".

While the Committee found that the *ratio legis* of the Reindeer Husbandry Act was reasonable and consistent with article 27, it none the less expressed grave doubts as to whether certain provisions of the Act and their application to Mr. Kitok could be deemed compatible with article 27 of the Covenant:

"It can thus be seen that the Act provides certain criteria for participation in the life of an ethnic minority whereby a person who is ethnically a Sami can be held not to be a Sami for the purposes of the Act. The Committee has been concerned that the ignoring of objective ethnic criteria in determining membership of a minority, and the application to Mr. Kitok of the designated rules, may have been disproportionate to the legitimate ends sought by the legislation".

CIVIL AND POLITICAL RIGHTS: SIRACUSA PRINCIPLES. The "Siracusa Principles on the Limitation and Derogation Provisions of the International Covenant on Civil and Political Rights," set out below, were formulated by a group of 31 distinguished experts in international law, convened by the International Commission of Jurists, its American Association, the International Association of Penal Law, the Urban Morgan Institute of Human Rights, and the International Institute of Higher Studies in Criminal Sciences, meeting at Siracusa, Italy, from 30 April to 4 May 1984. Experts who participated came from Brazil, Canada, Chile, Egypt, France, Greece, Hungary, India, Ireland, Kuwait, the Netherlands, Norway, Poland, Switzerland, Turkey, the United Kingdom, the United States, the UN Center for Human Rights, the International Labor Organization, and the sponsoring organizations.

The participants agreed upon the need for a close examination of the conditions and grounds for permissible limitations and derogations enunciated in the covenant in order to achieve an effective implementation of the rule of law. As frequently emphasized by the UN General Assembly, a uniform interpretation of limitations on rights in the covenant is of great importance.

In examining these limitations and derogations, the participants sought to identify their legitimate objectives, the general principles of interpretation which govern their imposition and application, and some of the main features of the grounds for limitation or derogation. It was recognized that other criteria determined the scope of the rights in the covenant, e.g., the concept of arbitrariness, but time was not available to examine them.

Participants in the conference agreed that (a) there is a close relationship between respect for human rights and the maintenance of international peace and security; indeed, the systematic violation of human rights undermines national security and public order and may constitute a threat to international peace; and (b) notwithstanding the different stages of economic development reached in different States, the implementation of human rights is an essential requirement for development in the broadest sense.

The principles set out below were considered by participants in the conference to reflect the present state of international law, with the exception of certain recommendations indicated by the use of the verb "should," instead of "shall."

The principles, drawn to the attention of the Commission on Human Rights at its 1985 session by the permanent representative of the Netherlands to the UN office at Geneva, are as follows (UN Doc. E/-CN.4/1985/4):

Part I. The Limitation Clauses in the Covenant

A. *General Interpretative Principles relating to the Justification of Limitations.* (The term "limitations" in these principles includes the term "restrictions" as used in the Covenant.)

1. No limitations or grounds for applying them to rights guaranteed by the Covenant are permitted other than those contained in the terms of the Covenant itself.

2. The scope of a limitation referred to in the Covenant shall not be interpreted so as to jeopardize the essence of the right concerned.

3. All limitation clauses shall be interpreted strictly and in favour of the rights at issue.

4. All limitations shall be interpreted in the light and context of the particular right concerned.

5. All limitations on a right recognized by the Covenant shall be provided for by law and be compatible with the objects and purposes of the Covenant.

6. No limitation referred to in the Covenant shall be applied for any purpose other than that for which it has been prescribed.

7. No limitation shall be applied in an arbitrary manner.

8. Every limitation imposed shall be subject to the possibility of challenge to and remedy against its abusive application.

9. No limitation on a right recognized by the Covenant shall discriminate contrary to article 2, paragraph 1.

10. Whenever a limitation is required in the terms of the Covenant to be "necessary", this term implies that the limitation:

(a) Is based on one of the grounds justifying limitations recognized by the relevant article of the Covenant,

(b) Responds to a pressing public or social need,

(c) Pursues a legitimate aim, and

(d) Is proportionate to that aim.

Any assessment as to the necessity of a limitation shall be made on objective considerations.

11. In applying a limitation, a State shall use no more restrictive means than are required for the achievement of the purpose of the limitation.

12. The burden of justifying a limitation upon a right guaranteed under the Covenant lies with the State.

13. The requirement expressed in article 12 of the Covenant, that any restrictions be consistent with other rights recognized in the Covenant, is implicit in limitations to the other rights recognized in the Covenant.

14. The limitation clauses of the Covenant shall not be interpreted to restrict the exercise of any human rights protected to a greater extent by other international obligations binding on the State.

B. Interpretative Principles relating to Specific Limitation Clauses.

"Prescribed by law"

15. No limitation on the exercise of human rights shall be made unless provided for by national law of general application which is consistent with the Covenant and is in force at the time the limitation is applied.

16. Laws imposing limitations on the exercise of human rights shall not be arbitrary or unreasonable.

17. Legal rules limiting the exercise of human rights shall be clear and accessible to everyone.

18. Adequate safeguards and effective remedies shall be provided by law against illegal and abusive imposition or application of limitations on human rights.

"In a democratic society"

19. The expression "in a democratic society" shall be interpreted as imposing a further restriction on the limitation clauses it qualifies.

20. The burden is upon a State imposing limitations so qualified to demonstrate that the limitations do not impair the democratic functioning of the society.

21. While there is no single model of a democratic society, a society which recognizes, respects and protects the human rights set forth in the Charter of the United Nations and the Universal Declaration of Human Rights may be viewed as meeting this definition.

"Public order (ordre public)"

22. The expression "public order (*ordre public*)" as used in the Covenant may be defined as the sum of rules which ensure the functioning of society or the set of fundamental principles on which society is founded. Respect for human rights is part of public order (*ordre public*).

23. Public order (*ordre public*) shall be interpreted in the context of the purpose of the particular human right which is limited on this ground.

24. State organs or agents responsible for the maintenance of public order (*ordre public*) shall be subject to controls in the exercise of their power through the parliament, courts or other competent independent bodies.

"Public health"

25. Public health may be invoked as a ground for limiting certain rights in order to allow a State to take measures dealing with a serious threat to the health of the population or individual members of the population. These measures must be specifically aimed at preventing disease or injury or providing care for the sick and injured.

26. Due regard shall be had to the International Health Regulations of the World Health Organization.

"Public morals"

27. Since public morality varies over time and from one culture to another, a State which invokes public morality as a ground for restricting human rights, while enjoying a certain margin of discretion, shall demonstrate that the limitation in question is essential to the maintenance of respect for fundamental values of the community.

28. The margin of discretion left to States does not apply to the rule of non-discrimination as defined in the Covenant.

"National security"

29. National security may be invoked to justify measures limiting certain rights only when they are taken to protect the existence of the nation, its territorial integrity or political independence against force or threat of force.

30. National security cannot be invoked as a reason for imposing limitations to prevent merely local or relatively isolated threats to law and order.

31. National security cannot be used as a pretext for imposing vague or arbitrary limitations and may only be invoked when there exist adequate safeguards and effective remedies against abuse.

32. The systematic violation of human rights undermines national security and may jeopardize international peace and security. A State responsible for such violation shall not invoke national security as a justification for measures aimed at suppressing opposition to such violation or at perpetrating repressive practices against its population.

"Public safety"

33. Public safety means protection against danger to the safety of persons, to their life or physical integrity or serious damage to their property.

34. The need to protect public safety can justify limitations provided by law. It cannot be used for imposing vague or arbitrary limitations and may only be invoked when there exist adequate safeguards and effective remedies against abuse.

"Rights and freedoms of others" or the "Rights and reputations of others"

35. The scope of the rights and freedoms of others that may act as a limitation upon rights in the Covenant extends beyond the rights and freedoms recognized in the Covenant.

36. When a conflict exists between a right protected in the Covenant and one which is not, recognition and consideration should be given to the fact that the Covenant seeks to protect the most fundamental rights and freedoms. In this context especial weight should be afforded to the rights from which no derogation may be made under article 4 of the Covenant.

37. A limitation to a human right based upon the reputation of others shall not be used to protect the State and its officials from public opinion or criticism.

Restrictions on public trial

38. All trials shall be public unless the Court determines in accordance with law that:

The press or the public should be excluded from all or part of a trial on the basis of specific findings announced in open court showing that the interest of the private lives of the parties or their families or of juveniles so requires; or

The exclusion is strictly necessary to avoid publicity (a) prejudicial to the fairness of the trial or (b) endangering public morals, public order (*ordre public*) or national security in a democratic society.

Part II. Derogations in a Public Emergency

A. "Public Emergency which Threatens the Life of the Nation."

39. A State party may take measures derogating from its obligations under the International Covenant on Civil and Political Rights pursuant to article 4 (hereinafter called "derogation measures") only when faced with a situation of exceptional and actual or imminent danger which threatens the life of the nation. A threat to the life of the nation is one that:

(a) Affects the whole of the population and either the whole or part of the territory of the State, and

(b) Threatens the physical integrity of the population, the political independence or the territorial integrity of the State or the existence or basic functioning of institutions indispensable to ensure and protect the rights recognized in the Covenant.

40. Internal conflict and unrest that do not constitute a

grave and imminent threat to the life of the nation cannot justify derogations under article 4.

41. Economic difficulties *per se* cannot justify derogation measures.

B. Proclamation, Notification and Termination of a Public Emergency. 42. A State party derogating from its obligations under the Covenant shall make an official proclamation of the existence of a public emergency threatening the life of the nation.

43. Procedures under national law for the proclamation of a state of emergency shall be prescribed in advance of the emergency.

44. A State party derogating from its obligations under the Covenant shall immediately notify the other States parties to the Covenant, through the intermediary of the Secretary-General of the United Nations, of the provisions from which it has derogated and the reasons by which it was actuated.

45. The notification shall contain sufficient information to permit the States parties to exercise their rights and discharge their obligations under the Covenant. In particular it shall contain:

(a) The provisions of the Covenant from which it has derogated;

(b) A copy of the proclamation of emergency, together with the constitutional provisions, legislation, or decrees governing the state of emergency in order to assist the States parties to appreciate the scope of the derogation;

(c) The effective date of the imposition of the state of emergency and the period for which it has been proclaimed;

(d) An explanation of the reasons which actuated the Government's decision to derogate, including a brief description of the factual circumstances leading up to the proclamation of the state of emergency;

(e) A brief description of the anticipated effect of the derogation measures on the rights recognized by the Covenant, including copies of decrees derogating from these rights issued prior to the notification.

46. States parties may require that further information necessary to enable them to carry out their role under the Covenant be provided through the intermediary of the Secretary-General.

47. A State party which fails to make an immediate notification in due form of its derogation is in breach of its obligations to other States parties and may be deprived of the defences otherwise available to it in procedures under the Covenant.

48. A State party availing itself of the right of derogation pursuant to article 4 shall terminate such derogation in the shortest time required to bring to an end the public emergency which threatens the life of the nation.

49. The State party shall, on the date on which it terminates such derogation, inform the other States parties, through the intermediary of the Secretary-General of the United Nations, of the fact of the termination.

50. On the termination of a derogation pursuant to article 4, all rights and freedoms protected by the Covenant shall be restored in full. A review of the continuing consequences of derogation measures shall be made as soon as possible. Steps shall be taken to correct injustices and to compensate those who have suffered injustice during or in consequence of the derogation measures.

C. "Strictly Required by the Exigencies of the Situation."

51. The severity, duration and geographic scope of any derogation measure shall be such only as are strictly neces-

sary to deal with the threat to the life of the nation and are proportionate to its nature and extent.

52. The competent national authorities shall have a duty to assess individually the necessity of any derogation measure taken or proposed to deal with the specific dangers posed by the emergency.

53. A measure is not strictly required by the exigencies of the situation where ordinary measures permissible under the specific limitation clauses of the Covenant would be adequate to deal with the threat to the life of the nation.

54. The principle of strict necessity shall be applied in an objective manner. Each measure shall be directed to an actual, clear, present or imminent danger and may not be imposed merely because of an apprehension of potential danger.

55. The national constitution and laws governing states of emergency shall provide for prompt and periodic independent review by the legislature of the necessity for derogation measures.

56. Effective remedies shall be available to persons claiming that derogation measures affecting them are not strictly required by the exigencies of the situation.

57. In determining whether derogation measures are strictly required by the exigencies of the situation, the judgement of the national authorities cannot be accepted as conclusive.

D. Non-derogable Rights. 58. No State party shall, even in time of emergency threatening the life of the nation, derogate from the Covenant's guarantees of the right to life; freedom from torture, cruel, inhuman or degrading treatment or punishment, and from medical or scientific experimentation without free consent; freedom from slavery or involuntary servitude; the right not to be imprisoned for contractual debt; the right not to be convicted or sentenced to a heavier penalty by virtue of retroactive criminal legislation; the right to recognition as a person before the law; and freedom of thought, conscience and religion. These rights are not derogable under any conditions even for the asserted purpose of preserving the life of the nation.

59. States parties to the Covenant, as part of their obligation to ensure the enjoyment of these rights to all persons within their jurisdiction (article 3, paragraph 1), and to adopt measures to secure an effective remedy for violations (article 2, paragraph 3), shall take special precautions in time of public emergency to ensure that neither official nor semi-official groups engage in a practice of arbitrary and extrajudicial killings or involuntary disappearances, that persons in detention are protected against torture and other forms of cruel, inhuman or degrading treatment or punishment, and that no persons are convicted or punished under laws or decrees with retroactive effect.

60. The ordinary courts should maintain their jurisdiction, even in a time of public emergency, to adjudicate any complaint that a non-derogable right has been violated.

E. Some General Principles on the Introduction and Application of a Public Emergency and Consequent Derogation Measures.

61. Derogation from rights recognized under international law in order to respond to a threat to the life of the nation is not exercised in a legal vacuum. It is authorized by law and as such it is subject to several legal principles of general application.

62. A proclamation of a public emergency shall be made in good faith based upon an objective assessment of the situation in order to determine to what extent, if any, it poses a threat to the life of the nation. A proclamation of a public emergency, and consequent derogations from Covenant

obligations that are not made in good faith, are violations of international law.

63. The provisions of the Covenant allowing for certain derogations in a public emergency are to be interpreted restrictively.

64. In a public emergency the rule of law shall still prevail. Derogation is an authorized and limited prerogative to respond adequately to a threat to the life of the nation. The derogating State shall have the burden of justifying its actions under law.

65. The Covenant subordinates all procedures to the basic objectives of human rights. Article 5, paragraph 1, of the Covenant sets definite limits to actions taken under the Covenant:

"Nothing in the present Covenant may be interpreted as implying for any State, group or person any right to engage in any activity or perform any act aimed at the destruction of any of the rights and freedoms recognized herein or at their limitation to a greater extent than is provided for in the present Covenant."

Article 29, paragraph 2, of the Universal Declaration of Human Rights sets out the ultimate purpose of law:

"In the exercise of his rights and freedoms, everyone shall be subject only to such limitations as are determined by law solely for the purpose of securing due recognition and respect for the rights and freedoms of others and of meeting the just requirements of morality, public order and the general welfare in a democratic society."

These provisions apply with full force to claims that a situation constitutes a threat to the life of a nation and hence enables authorities to derogate.

66. A *bona fide* proclamation of a public emergency permits a derogation from specified obligations in the Covenant, but does not authorize a general departure from international obligations. The Covenant in articles 4, paragraph 1 and 5, paragraph 2, expressly prohibits derogations which are inconsistent with other obligations under international law. In this regard, particular note should be taken of international obligations which apply in a public emergency under the Geneva and ILO Conventions.

67. In a situation of a non-international armed conflict, a State party to the 1949 Geneva Conventions for the protection of war victims may not under any circumstances suspend the right to a trial by a court offering the essential guarantees of independence and impartiality (article 3 common to the 1949 Conventions). Under the 1977 additional Protocol II the following rights with respect to penal prosecution shall be respected under all circumstances by States parties to the Protocol:

(a) The duty to give notice of charges without delay and to grant the necessary rights and means of defence;

(b) Conviction only on the basis of individual penal responsibility;

(c) The right not to be convicted, or sentenced to a heavier penalty, by virtue of retroactive criminal legislation;

(d) Presumption of innocence;

(e) Trial in the presence of the accused;

(f) No obligation on the accused to testify against himself or to confess guilt;

(g) Duty to advise the convicted person on judicial and other remedies.

68. The ILO basic human rights conventions contain a number of rights dealing with such matters as forced labour, freedom of association, equality in employment and trade-union and workers' rights which are additional to those in the Covenant. Some of these are not subject to derogation during an emergency; others permit derogation, but only to the extent strictly necessary to meet the exigencies of the situation.

69. No State, including those that are not parties to the Covenant, may suspend or violate, even in times of public emergency:

—The right to life;

—Freedom from torture or cruel, inhuman or degrading treatment or punishment and from medical or scientific experimentation;

—The right not to be held in slavery or involuntary servitude; and

—The right not to be subjected to retroactive criminal penalties as defined in the Covenant.

Customary international law prohibits in all circumstances the denial of such fundamental rights.

70. Although protections against arbitrary arrest and detention (article 9) and the right to a fair and public hearing in the determination of a criminal charge (article 14) may be subject to legitimate limitations if strictly required by the exigencies of an emergency situation, the denial of certain rights fundamental to human dignity can never be strictly necessary in any conceivable emergency, and respect for them is essential in order to ensure enjoyment of non-derogable rights and to provide an effective remedy against their violation. In particular:

(a) All arrests and detention and the place of detention shall be recorded, if possible centrally, and made available to the public without delay;

(b) No person shall be detained for an indefinite period of time, whether detained pending judicial investigation or trial or detained without charge;

(c) No person shall be held in isolation without communication with his family, friend or lawyer for longer than a few days, e.g. three to seven days;

(d) Where persons are detained without charge, the need for their continued detention shall be considered periodically by an independent review tribunal;

(e) Any person charged with an offence shall be entitled to a fair trial by a competent, independent and impartial court established by law;

(f) Civilians shall normally be tried by the ordinary courts; where it is found strictly necessary to establish military tribunals or special courts to try civilians, their competence, independence and impartiality shall be ensured and the need for them reviewed periodically by the competent authority;

(g) Any person charged with a criminal offence shall be entitled to the presumption of innocence and to at least the following rights to ensure a fair trial:

—The right to be informed of the charges promptly, in detail and in a language he understands,

—The right to have adequate time and facilities to prepare the defence including the right to communicate confidentially with his lawyer,

—The right to a lawyer of his choice, with free legal assistance if he does not have the means to pay for it and to be informed of this right,

—The right to be present at the trial,

—The right not to be compelled to testify against himself or to make a confession,

—The right to obtain the attendance and examination of defence witnesses,

—The right to be tried in public save where the court orders otherwise on grounds of security with adequate safeguards to prevent abuse,

—The right to appeal to a higher court;

(h) An adequate record of the proceedings shall be kept in all cases;

(i) No person shall be tried or punished again for an offence for which he has already been convicted or acquitted.

F. Recommendations concerning the Functions and Duties of the Human Rights Committee and United Nations bodies.

71. In the exercise of its power to study, report and make general comments on States parties' reports under article 40 of the Covenant, the Human Rights Committee may and should examine the compliance of States parties with the provisions of article 4. Likewise it may and should do so when exercising its powers in relevant cases under article 41 and the Optional Protocol relating, respectively, to inter-State and individual communications.

72. In order to determine whether the requirements of article 4, paragraphs 1 and 2 have been met and for the purpose of supplementing information in States parties' reports, members of the Human Rights Committee, as persons of recognized competence in the field of human rights, may and should have regard to information they consider to be reliable provided by other intergovernmental bodies, nongovernmental organizations and communications by individuals.

73. The Human Rights Committee should develop a procedure for requesting additional reports under article 40, paragraph 1 (b), from States parties which have given notification of derogation under article 4, paragraph 3, or which are reasonably believed by the Committee to have imposed emergency measures subject to the constraints of article 4. Such additional reports should relate to questions concerning the emergency in so far as it affects the implementation of the Covenant and should be dealt with by the Committee at the earliest possible date.

74. In order to enable the Human Rights Committee to perform its fact-finding functions more effectively it should develop its procedures for the consideration of communications under the Optional Protocol in order to permit the hearing of oral submissions and evidence and visits to States parties alleged to be in violation of the Covenant. If necessary, the States parties to the Optional Protocol should consider amending it to this effect.

75. The United Nations Commission on Human Rights should request its Sub-Commission on Prevention of Discrimination and Protection of Minorities to prepare an annual list of States, whether parties to the Covenant or not, that proclaim, maintain or terminate a public emergency together with:

—In the case of a State party, the proclamation and notification; and

—In the case of other States, any available and apparently reliable information concerning the proclamation, threat to the life of the nation, derogation measures and their proportionality, non-discrimination and respect for non-derogable rights.

76. The United Nations Commission on Human Rights and its Sub-Commission should continue to utilize the technique of appointment of special rapporteurs and investigatory and fact-finding bodies in relation to prolonged public emergencies.

SEE ALSO *International Covenant on Civil and Political Rights and Optional Protocols.*

CLIMATE CONSERVATION. On the initiative of the government of Malta, the UN General Assembly considered at its regular 1988 session the item, "Conservation of Climate as Part of the Common Heritage of Mankind."

The assembly noted with concern (resolution 43/53) that the emerging evidence indicates that continued growth in atmospheric concentrations of "greenhouse" gases could produce global warming with eventual rise in sea levels, whose effects could be disastrous for mankind if timely steps are not taken at all levels, and that emissions of certain substances are depleting the ozone layer and thereby exposing the earth's surface to increased ultra-violet radiation which may pose a threat, *inter alia,* to human health, agricultural productivity, and animal and marine life.

Convinced that climate change affects humanity as a whole and should be confronted within a global framework so as to take into account the vital interests of all mankind, the assembly recognized that climate change is a common concern of mankind, since climate is an essential condition which sustains life on earth, and determined that necessary and timely action should be taken to deal with climate change within a global framework. It endorsed the action of the World Meteorological Organization and the UNITED NATIONS ENVIRONMENT PROGRAM in jointly establishing an "Intergovernmental Panel on Climate Change" to provide internationally coordinated scientific assessments of the magnitude, timing, and potential environmental and socio-economic impact of climate change and realistic response strategies; urged governments, intergovernmental, and nongovernmental organizations to treat climate change as a priority issue; and called upon all relevant organizations and programs of the United Nations system to support the work of the intergovernmental panel.

CODE OF CONDUCT FOR LAW ENFORCEMENT OFFICIALS (1979). This code sets out a series of principles aimed at ensuring the humane performance of law enforcement functions and at protecting the human rights of the men and women who must deal with them. Recognizing that the nature of the functions performed, and the manner in which they may be exercised, can at times produce serious negative effects upon the quality of life citizens enjoy, the code admonishes all law enforcement officials to perform their tasks diligently and with dignity, in full respect for and compliance with the principles of human rights.

The Code of Conduct was adopted by the UN General Assembly on 17 December 1979 (resolution 34/169). It contains, in addition to eight articles, a series of commentaries which provide information to facilitate the use of the code within the framework of national legislation or practice. The text of the code and commentaries is as follows:

The General Assembly,

Considering that the purposes proclaimed in the Charter of the United Nations include the achievement of international co-operation in promoting and encouraging respect for human rights and for fundamental freedoms for all without distinction as to race, sex, language or religion,

Recalling, in particular, the Universal Declaration of Human Rights and the International Covenants on Human Rights,

Recalling also the Declaration on the Protection of All Persons from Being Subjected to Torture and Other Cruel, Inhuman or Degrading Treatment or Punishment, adopted by the General Assembly in its resolution 3452 (XXX) of 9 December 1975,

Mindful that the nature of the functions of law enforcement in the defence of public order and the manner in which these functions are exercised have a direct impact on the quality of life of individuals as well as of society as a whole,

Conscious of the important task which law enforcement officials are performing diligently and with dignity, in compliance with the principles of human rights,

Aware, nevertheless, of the potential for abuse which the exercise of such duties entails,

Recognizing that the establishment of a code of conduct for law enforcement officials is only one of several important measures for providing the citizenry served by law enforcement officials with protection of all their rights and interests,

Aware that there are additional important principles and prerequisites for the humane performance of law enforcement functions, namely:

(a) That, like all agencies of the criminal justice system, every law enforcement agency should be representative of and responsive and accountable to the community as a whole,

(b) That the effective maintenance of ethical standards among law enforcement officials depends on the existence of a well-conceived, popularly accepted and humane system of laws,

(c) That every law enforcement official is part of the criminal justice system, the aim of which is to prevent and control crime, and that the conduct of every functionary within the system has an impact on the entire system,

(d) That every law enforcement agency, in fulfilment of the first premise of every profession, should be held to the duty of disciplining itself in complete conformity with the principles and standards herein provided and that the actions of law enforcement officials should be responsive to public scrutiny, whether exercised by a review board, a ministry, a procuracy, the judiciary, an ombudsman, a citizens' committee or any combination thereof, or any other reviewing agency,

(e) That standards as such lack practical value unless their content and meaning, through education and training and through monitoring, become part of the creed of every law enforcement official,

Adopts the Code of Conduct for Law Enforcement Officials set forth in the annex to the present resolution and decides to transmit it to Governments with the recommendation that favourable consideration should be given to its use within the framework of national legislation or practice as a body of principles for observance by law enforcement officials.

Code of Conduct for Law Enforcement Officials

Article 1. Law enforcement officials shall at all times fulfil the duty imposed upon them by law, by serving the community and by protecting all persons against illegal acts, consistent with the high degree of responsibility required by their profession.

Commentary. (a) The term "law enforcement officials" includes all officers of the law, whether appointed or elected, who exercise police powers, especially the powers of arrest or detention.

(b) In countries where police powers are exercised by military authorities, whether uniformed or not, or by state security forces, the definition of law enforcement officials shall be regarded as including officers of such services.

(c) Service to the community is intended to include particularly the rendition of services of assistance to those members of the community who by reason of personal, economic, social or other emergencies are in need of immediate aid.

(d) This provision is intended to cover not only all violent, predatory and harmful acts, but extends to the full range of prohibitions under penal statutes. It extends to conduct by persons not capable of incurring criminal liability.

Article 2. In the performance of their duty, law enforcement officials shall respect and protect human dignity and maintain and uphold the human rights of all persons.

Commentary. (a) The human rights in question are identified and protected by national and international law. Among the relevant international instruments are the Universal Declaration of Human Rights, the International Covenant on Civil and Political Rights, the Declaration on the Protection of All Persons from Being Subjected to Torture and Other Cruel, Inhuman or Degrading Treatment or Punishment, the United Nations Declaration on the Elimination of All Forms of Radial Discrimination, the International Convention on the Elimination of all Forms of Racial Discrimination, the International Convention on the Suppression and Punishment of the Crime of *Apartheid,* the Convention on the Prevention and Punishment of the Crime of Genocide, the Standard Minimum Rules for the Treatment of Prisoners and the Vienna Convention on Consular Relations.

(b) National commentaries to this provision should indicate regional or national provisions identifying and protecting these rights.

Article 3. Law enforcement officials may use force only when strictly necessary and to the extent required for the performance of their duty.

Commentary. (a) This provision emphasizes that the use of force by law enforcement officials should be exceptional; while it implies that law enforcement officials may be authorized to use force as is reasonably necessary under the circumstances for the prevention of crime or in effecting or assisting in the lawful arrest of offenders or suspected offenders, no force going beyond that may be used.

(b) National law ordinarily restricts the use of force by law enforcement officials in accordance with a principle of proportionality. It is to be understood that such national principles of proportionality are to be respected in the interpretation of this provision. In no case should this provision be interpreted to authorize the use of force which is disproportionate to the legitimate objective to be achieved.

(c) The use of firearms is considered an extreme measure. Every effort should be made to exclude the use of firearms, especially against children. In general, firearms should not be used except when a suspected offender offers armed resistance or otherwise jeopardizes the lives of others and less extreme measures are not sufficient to restrain or apprehend the suspected offender. In every instance in which a firearm is discharged, a report should be made promptly to the competent authorities.

Article 4. Matters of a confidential nature in the possession of law enforcement officials shall be kept confidential, unless the performance of duty, or the needs of justice, strictly require otherwise.

Commentary. By the nature of their duties, law enforcement officials obtain information which may relate to private lives or be potentially harmful to the interests, and especially the reputation, of others. Great care should be exercised in safeguarding and using such information, which should be disclosed only in the performance of duty or to serve the needs of justice. Any disclosure of such information for other purposes is wholly improper.

Article 5. No law enforcement official may inflict, instigate or tolerate any act of torture or other cruel, inhuman or degrading treatment or punishment, nor may any law enforcement official invoke superior orders or exceptional circumstances such as a state of war or a threat of war, a threat to national security, internal political instability or any other public emergency as a justification of torture or other cruel, inhuman or degrading treatment or punishment.

Commentary. (a) This prohibition derives from the Declaration on the Protection of All Persons from Being Subjected to Torture and Other Cruel, Inhuman or Degrading Treatment or Punishment, adopted by the General Assembly, according to which:

Such an act is "an offence to human dignity and shall be condemned as a denial of the purposes of the Charter of the United Nations and as a violation of the human rights and fundamental freedoms proclaimed in the Universal Declaration of Human Rights" and other international human rights instruments.

(b) The Declaration defines torture as follows:

". . . torture means any act by which severe pain or suffering, whether physical or mental, is intentionally inflicted by or at the instigation of a public official on a person for such purposes as obtaining from him or a third person information or confession, punishing him for an act he has committed or is suspected of having committed, or intimidating him or other persons. It does not include pain or suffering arising only from, inherent in or incidental to, lawful sanctions to the extent consistent with the Standard Minimum Rules for the Treatment of Prisoners."

(c) The term "cruel, inhuman or degrading treatment or punishment" has not been defined by the General Assembly, but should be interpreted so as to extend the widest possible protection against abuses, whether physical or mental.

Article 6. Law enforcement officials shall ensure the full protection of the health of persons in their custody and, in particular, take immediate action to secure medical attention whenever required.

Commentary. (a) "Medical attention", which refers to services rendered by any medical personnel, including certified medical practitioners and paramedics, shall be secured when needed or requested.

(b) While the medical personnel are likely to be attached to the law enforcement operation, law enforcement officials must take into account the judgement of such personnel when they recommend providing the person in custody with appropriate treatment through, or in consultation with, medical personnel from outside the law enforcement operation.

(c) It is understood that law enforcement officials shall also secure medical attention for victims of violations of law or of accidents occurring in the course of violations of law.

Article 7. Law enforcement officials shall not commit any act of corruption. They shall also rigorously oppose and combat all such acts.

Commentary. (a) Any act of corruption, in the same way as any other abuse of authority, is incompatible with the profession of law enforcement officials. The law must be enforced fully with respect to any law enforcement official who commits an act of corruption, as Governments cannot expect to enforce the law among their citizens if they cannot, or will not, enforce the law against their own agents and within their own agencies.

(b) While the definition of corruption must be subject to national law, it should be understood to encompass the commission or omission of an act in the performance of or in connexion with one's duties, in response to gifts, promises or incentives demanded or accepted, or the wrongful receipt of these once the act has been committed or omitted.

(c) The expression "act of corruption" referred to above should be understood to encompass attempted corruption.

Article 8. Law enforcement officials shall respect the law and the present Code. They shall also, to the best of their capability, prevent and rigorously oppose any violations of them.

Law enforcement officials who have reason to believe that a violation of this Code has occurred or is about to occur shall report the matter to their superior authorities and, where necessary, to other appropriate authorities or organs vested with reviewing or remedial power.

Commentary. (a) This Code shall be observed whenever it has been incorporated into national legislation or practice. If legislation or practice contains stricter provisions than those of the present Code, those stricter provisions shall be observed.

(b) The article seeks to preserve the balance between the need for internal discipline of the agency on which public safety is largely dependent, on the one hand, and the need for dealing with violations of basic human rights, on the other. Law enforcement officials shall report violations within the chain of command and take other lawful action outside the chain of command only when no other remedies are available or effective. It is understood that law enforcement officials shall not suffer administrative or other penalties because they have reported that a violation of this Code has occurred or is about to occur.

(c) The terms "appropriate authorities or organs vested with reviewing or remedial power" refer to any authority or organ existing under national law, whether internal to the law enforcement agency, or independent thereof, with statutory, customary or other power to review grievances and complaints arising out of violations within the purview of this Code.

(d) In some countries, the mass media may be regarded

as performing complaint review functions similar to those described in commentary (c). Law enforcement officials may, therefore, be justified if, as a last resort and in accordance with the laws and customs of their own countries and with the provisions of article 4 of the present Code, they bring violations to the attention of public opinion through the mass media.

(e) Law enforcement officials who comply with the provisions of this Code deserve the respect, the full support and the co-operation of the community and of the law enforcement agency in which they serve, as well as of the law enforcement profession.

CODE OF CONDUCT FOR LAW ENFORCEMENT OFFICIALS: GUIDELINES FOR IMPLEMENTATION (1989). With a view to promoting the implementation of the provisions of the CODE OF CONDUCT FOR LAW ENFORCEMENT OFFICIALS, which the UN General Assembly had adopted in 17 December 1979 (resolution 34/169), the Economic and Social Council on 24 May 1989 approved (resolution 1989/61) a series of Guidelines for the Effective Implementation of the Code of Conduct for Law Enforcement Officials which had been prepared at its request by the Committee on Crime Prevention and Control. The council at the same time invited the Eighth United Nations Congress on the Prevention of Crime and the Treatment of Offenders to explore ways and means of stimulating adherence to the guidelines.

The guidelines endorsed by the council (resolution 1989/61, Annex) are as follows:

I. Application of the Code

A. General Principles. 1. The principles embodied in the Code shall be reflected in national legislation and practice.

2. In order to achieve the aims and objectives set out in article 1 of the Code and its Commentaries, the definition of "law enforcement officials" shall be given the widest possible interpretation.

3. The Code shall be made applicable to all law enforcement officials, regardless of their jurisdiction.

4. Governments shall adopt the necessary measures to instruct, in basic training and all subsequent training and refresher courses, law enforcement officials in the provisions of national legislation that is connected with the Code as well as other basic texts on the issue of human rights.

B. Specific Issues. 1. Selection, education and training. The selection, education and training of law enforcement officials shall be given prime importance. Governments shall also promote education and training through a fruitful exchange of ideas at the regional and interregional levels.

2. Salary and working conditions. All law enforcement officials shall be adequately remunerated and shall be provided with appropriate working conditions.

3. Discipline and supervision. Effective mechanisms shall be established to ensure the internal discipline and external control as well as the supervision of law enforcement officials.

4. Complaints by members of the public. Particular provisions shall be made, within the mechanisms mentioned under paragraph 3 above, for the receipt and processing of complaints against law enforcement officials made by members of the public, and the existence of these provisions shall be made known to the public.

II. Implementation of the Code

A. At the National Level. 1. The Code shall be made available to all law enforcement officials and competent authorities in their own language.

2. Governments shall disseminate the Code and all domestic laws giving effect to it so as to ensure that the principles and rights contained therein become known to the public in general.

3. In considering measures to promote the application of the Code, Governments shall organize symposia on the role and functions of law enforcement officials in the protection of human rights and the prevention of crime.

B. At the International Level. 1. Governments shall inform the Secretary-General at appropriate intervals of at least five years on the extent of the implementation of the Code.

2. The Secretary-General shall prepare periodic reports on progress made with respect to the implementation of the Code, drawing also on observations and on the co-operation of specialized agencies and relevant intergovernmental organizations and non-governmental organizations in consultative status with the Economic and Social Council.

3. As part of the reports mentioned above, Governments shall provide to the Secretary-General copies of abstracts of laws, regulations and administrative measures concerning the application of the Code, any other relevant information on its implementation, as well as information on possible difficulties in its application.

4. The Secretary-General shall submit the above-mentioned reports to the Committee on Crime Prevention and Control for consideration and further action, as appropriate.

5. The Secretary-General shall make available the Code and the present guidelines to all States and intergovernmental and non-governmental organizations concerned, in all official languages of the United Nations.

6. The United Nations, as part of its advisory services and technical co-operation and development programmes, shall:

(a) Make available to Governments requesting them the services of experts and regional and interregional advisers to assist in implementing the provisions of the Code;

(b) Promote national and regional training seminars and other meetings on the Code and on the role and functions of law enforcement officials in the protection of human rights and the prevention of crime.

7. The United Nations regional institutes shall be encouraged to organize seminars and training courses on the Code and to carry out research on the extent to which the Code is implemented in the countries of the region as well as the difficulties encountered.

COLOMBIA. The Republic of Colombia is a country in tropical South America, on the Pacific Ocean and the Caribbean Sea. It has borders with Brazil, Ecuador, Panama, Peru, and Venezuela. It achieved independence from Spain in 1919 and became a member of the United Nations in 1945. Its population is estimated by the UN (1990) to be 31,820,000 including mestizos (57%), whites (20%), blacks (5%), mulattos (14%), and indigenous populations of Amerindian origin (4%). The language in common use is Spanish. The predominant religion is Christianity (Roman Catholic, 96%; Protestant denominations, 4%). Literacy is estimated at 85%.

The government (1990) took the form of a republic. The president is elected by popular vote, serves a four-year term of office, and appoints his own cabinet. The legislature is bicameral: a 199-member House of Representatives and a 114-member Senate. Members of both houses are elected by popular vote for terms of four years. Political parties include the Liberal Party, the Conservative Party, the National Popular Alliance, the National Opposition Union, the Front for the Unity of the People, the National Independent Labor Movement, the Communist Party, the Socialist Workers' Party, and the Patriotic Union of the Colombian Revolutionary Armed Forces.

The Colombian constitution establishes a general system of guarantees designed to make human rights effective in the country. These include the subordination of the power of the State to the rule of law (art. 2); the accountability of public officials for violation of the provisions of the constitution and for any conduct that encroaches upon the rights and freedoms recognized therein (arts. 20, 21, and 51); the functional distribution of public authority between branches which act separately but collaborate harmoniously in the attainment of the purposes of the State (art. 55); the existence of various types of control—participation, representation, and inspection—over the acts of persons in positions of authority (arts. 59, 118, 121, 122, and 143); the supremacy of the provisions of the constitution over the laws and acts of the administration (arts. 2 and 215); and the functioning of a widespread system of control of constitutionality (arts. 85–90, 214, and 215).

A further guarantee of freedom in Colombia is the establishment of *habeas corpus* in the Code of Criminal Procedure, under which any person deprived of his freedom for more than 48 hours is entitled, if he considers that a breach of the law has taken place, to request a criminal judge or a combined criminal/civil court judge or circuit judge to investigate whether he was arrested or detained in breach of legal formalities. If this was the case, the judge must order the immediate release of the aggrieved party and institute a criminal investigation of the arbitrary detention as effected by the responsible authorities.

Although Colombia has the reputation of being one of the most democratic countries in South America, it has experienced its share of human rights problems, due in large party to continuing rivalry between members of the Conservative Party, who favor centralism and participation by the Catholic Church in government and education, and those of the Liberal Party, who favor federalism, anticlericalism, and social reforms. This rivalry has given rise to serious disturbances, riots, and even civil war.

The country has been experiencing guerrilla and subversive movements since 1948. These forces, operating under various names, have periodically created violence and otherwise demonstrated their rejection of the policies of the government, recently with the support of gangs of drug traffickers.

Following the murder of Minister of Justice Rodrigo Lara Bonilla on 30 April 1984, the government declared a nationwide state of seige under which it assumed special powers authorized by the constitution, including the empowering of military criminal courts to try offenses defined in the "National Statute on Narcotic Drugs" and those relating to the carrying of, or traffic in, weapons exclusively used by the armed forces. During the four-year term of President Belisario Betancur Cuartas (1982–1986), the government made an extraordinary effort to secure peace in the country, including a proclamation of amnesty approved by Law No. 35 of 1982 and the establishment of a "Peace Committee" to mediate differences between the opposing factions.

At the time of the state-of-siege declaration, the government promulgated a series of decrees relating to the control of narcotic drugs. The National Statute on Narcotic Drugs was amended to embody these decrees by Law No. 30 of 31 January 1986; these decrees prohibited the unlawful trade in substances used in the production of narcotic drugs and empowered national and local officials to confiscate such substances. Subsequently, with technical assistance provided by the United Nations, the government formulated a national plan to combat the illicit traffic in and consumption of narcotic drugs and psychotropic substances and concluded an agreement under which the United Nations Fund for Drug Abuse finances the establishment of a data bank, a study of alternative possibilities for the treatment and rehabilitation of drug-dependent persons, and a plan whereby the coca lead crop in certain areas of the country is to be replaced by non-narcotic crops. In a number of international forums, Colombia has maintained that traffic in narcotic and psychotropic substances should be declared a crime against humanity.

As regards religion or belief, Colombia's constitution guarantees freedom of conscience (art. 53) and places only two limitations on the exercise of religious freedom: "Christian morality" and "the law."

The Penal Code punishes offences against the exercise of freedom of worship—compelling another person to perform a religious act or preventing him from participating in a religious rite—(art. 294), prevention or disruption of the celebration of a religious rite (art. 295), and damage or insults to persons engaged in, or objects intended for, religious worship (art. 296).

From 1888 to 1974, Colombia was bound by an agreement with the Holy See, known as the Valez–Rampolla Concordat, which was based on an extremely rigid and traditional concept of State religion. This agreement recognized Catholicism as the religion of Colombia, to be given protection and ensured respect by the public authorities; imposed canonical marriage on all who professed the Catholic faith (art. 17), and established a strict system of public religious education (arts. 12 and 13). It further stipulated that agreements between the Holy See and the Colombian government "for the promotion of Catholic missions among the barbarous tribes" would not require the prior approval of the Colombian Congress (art. 31).

An amended agreement, known as the Vasquez–Palmas Concordat, was signed in 1973 and entered into force the following year. Its main provisions were summarized by the government as follows:

(a) It does not proclaim an official religion. The State merely declares that it regards the Catholic religion as being of "fundamental importance to the public welfare and the full development of the community";

(b) The new concordat substantially retains the provisions of the 1887 Agreement concerning recognition by the State of the Church's spiritual authority, legal personality and capacity to collect offerings and contributions from its followers;

(c) The State accords Catholic marriage—i.e., "marriage celebrated in accordance with the norms of canonical law"—full recognition for civil purposes, but does not make it obligatory;

(d) Bishops—and persons canonically assimilated to them—are granted an immunity in criminal matters identical in scope to that extended to diplomatic agents;

(e) Members of the clergy and religious orders enjoy a degree of privilege in criminal proceedings instituted against them by the Commission on Non-Ecclesiastical Offences;

(f) The Church undertakes to give the President of the Republic advance confidential notice of episcopal appointments with a view to ascertaining whether he has "civil or political objections" to the candidates;

(g) The State acknowledges the Church's freedom of instruction and independence to organize and run faculties, institutes, seminaries and a training establishment for religious orders;

(h) The State undertakes to make a reasonable contribution to the maintenance of Catholic educational establishments and to include courses of religious instruction in its primary and secondary school curricula;

(i) Church and State undertake to co-operate in the social advancement of indigenous persons and other inhabitants of what were formerly known as "mission territories";

(j) The financial obligations acquired by the State by virtue of the Núñez Concordat and the Misiones Agreement of 1953 are consolidated."

The concordat regime is not considered to be inconsistent with effective recognition of freedom of conscience since the existence of a treaty between the civil and ecclesiastical authorities is not deemed to be prejudicial to the right of non-Catholic citizens to be exempt from compulsion in religious matters and since its maintenance does not affect adversely the equality of all citizens before the law. However, one effect of the concordat is that, in Colombia, all family law on matters normally within the public domain is in the hands of the Catholic Church.

The Indians of Colombia are considered to be an indigenous population, not an ethnic minority. The government respects their socio-cultural organization and their traditions, and they are considered to be Colombian citizens. They govern themselves in accordance with their own customs and traditions; in some communities, government is in the hands of an indigenous leader, while, in others, it is the responsibility of a governing council or similar body.

Lands originally held by the indigenous populations were plundered by settlers as they became more accessible by improved transport and communications. In an effort to alleviate the serious problem which was developing, the government established, first, a system of reservations and, subsequently, a number of indigenous reserves, designed to protect their land from encroachment. The Colombian Agrarian Reform Institute established 128 such reservations and reserves, on which more than 20,000 indigenous families are settled.

Each indigenous community, and each member who is of full age, has the right to participate actively in the political life of the country, with the corresponding rights and obligations of the exercise of citizenship authorized by the constitution and other legislation, including the right to vote and to stand in elections for all public or representative offices. Bilingual education is directed at providing education to young indigenous people in their own language, simultaneously with the teaching of Spanish; and the government has trained a number of young indigenous persons to promote education, health, etc., within their own communities.

The situation improved early in 1990 when the government recognized Indian land rights to half the Colombian Amazon—home to 55,000 Indians and 200 white settlers—covering 69,000 sq. mi. These traditional Indian lands now belong to the Indian communities in perpetuity and cannot be sold.

As an aftermath of the state of siege which prevailed in Colombia between 1984 and 1986, a number of complaints of "disappearances" were reported to inqternational bodies, including the Commissions on Human Rights of the United Nations and of the Organization of American States. In general, these complaints alleged that official violence was the consequence of a counter-insurgency strategy, in which the armed forces played the leading role. "Disappearances" were said to be a part of that strategy, in which military, security services, and the police were involved. Many of the "missing" persons had been taken to military, security, or police premises before "disappearing," according to a few who succeeded in escaping or were released.

The Colombian government responded by stating that, in fact, human rights violations resulting from excesses of government authorities had been markedly reduced in 1986 and that all complaints were being thoroughly investigated by the country's attorney-general. As of 8 September 1985, a State Human Rights Commission had been established in the attorney-general's office to deal with human rights matters in general and, in particular, such questions as disappearances, allegations of unlawful arrest, treatment of persons held by the authorities, and relations between the indigenous communities and the government.

However, the number of disappearances escalated markedly in 1987; and, in 1988, the WORKING GROUP ON ENFORCED OR INVOLUNTARY DISAPPEARANCES transmitted to the government of Colombia 123 new cases, of which 70 were reported to have occurred in 1987. Most of the victims were political or trade union leaders, university professors, or members of local human rights committees; and the campaign of violence apparently was aimed, at least in part, at preventing the development of a new political party, the Patriotic Union.

On 25 March 1988, the government of Colombia invited the working group to visit the country. The working group designated two of its members, Mr. Toine van Dongen (Netherlands) and Mr. Diego Garcia-Sayan (Peru), to make the visit on its behalf. During the visit, which took place from 24 October to 2 November 1988, the government provided new information with reference to many of the more than 500 outstanding cases. The remainder, it indicated, were under investigation either by the attorney-general, a judge, or the criminal police, or had been put aside for lack of information.

In its report to the 1990 session of the Commission on Human Rights (UN Doc. E/CN.4/1990/13), the working group cited 13 new cases reported to have occurred in 1989, bringing the overall total number of cases transmitted to the government to 692, of which 577 had not been fully clarified. Of 87 cases clarified by government responses, 14 persons were reported to be at liberty and eight in prison, 42 had been released from prison, one had escaped from prison, 21 were dead, and one had been abducted by rebels. Of 28 cases clarified by non-governmental sources, four were reported to be at liberty and three in prison, 14 had been released from prison, and seven were dead.

On 30 January 1989, the government of Colombia invited the commission's Special Rapporteur on Summary or Arbitrary Executions Mr. S. Amos Wako (Kenya) to visit the country. That visit took place from 11 to 20 October 1989. His report on the visit (UN Doc. E/CN.4/1990/22/Add.1), presented to the commission at its 1990 session, reflects the special rapporteur's conversations with governmental and non-governmental sources in Colombia and the oral and written information he received on the situation as regards summary or arbitrary executions.

In the report, he describes the context of violence in which the problem of summary or arbitrary executions in Colombia must be viewed (chap. II), presents the statistical data made available to him in the course of his visit (chap. III), describes briefly some of the cases of massacres reported to him while in Colombia (chap. IV), and summarizes the action taken by the government to deal with the problem (chap. V). Finally, he put forward his own conclusions and recommendations, as follows (chap. VI, para. 60–74):

The Special Rapporteur is grateful for the invitation extended to him to visit Colombia at a particularly critical period of its history. The Special Rapporteur appreciates the co-operation extended to him by the Government prior to and during the visit which made the visit worthwhile and useful.

Colombia has experienced a continuous and protracted period of violence of varying degrees and intensity since April 1948 following the assassination of the liberal leader Jorge Eliecer Gartan. There has been an increase in the type and number of actors in this climate of violence. For a similar period, Colombia has been under a state of siege. During the ten year period between 1948 and 1958, it is estimated that between 200,000 and 300,000 people died as a result of fighting between the supporters of the Liberal and Conservative Parties. The 1958 agreement between the two parties under which they agreed to share power alternatively for the next 16 years brought an end to this type of violence. However, sections of the population particularly those with a different ideology or political thinking from the Conservative and Liberal Parties felt excluded or marginalized from the political process.

A large number of poor Colombians felt excluded from participation in political life. Hence, the seeds of another source of violence, that of guerrilla movements, were planted. The peasant self-defence groups that had been promoted by the Liberal Party evolved into the Revolutionary Army Forces of Colombia (FARC) and the National Liberation Army (ELN). There are currently eight guerrilla movements including the "April 19" movement (M-19) which came into being after allegations of fraud during the 1970 presidential election. The main targets of the guerrilla action have been the armed forces and the police. To combat the guerillas, the civilian population was organized in civilian self-defence groups and this was regulated by Order No. 0005 of the High Command of the Armed Forces, 1969, and the Counter-Insurgency Regulations (Regulation EJC 3-10). As the drug trade became increasingly part of the Colombian society, another very important contribution to violence in Colombia was introduced. The drug barons engaged in wholesale purchasing of land by way of investment, often in guerrilla-controlled areas and this inevitably led to a conflict between them and the guerrillas. A number of killings have also occurred as a result of gang wars between the cartels over control of territory.

To achieve their aims, the drug traffickers set up paramilitary organizations. The first of such groups "Muerte a secuestradores" (M.A.S.) (Death to Kidnappers) was set up following the kidnapping of one of the daughters of a major drug baron by members of M-19. According to a DAS report, the hit men and drug dealers who operate in Puerto Boyaca use the Association of Farmers and Stock-Breeders of Central Magdalena (ACDEGAM) as a front for their illegal activities. In the course of time, many civilian self-defence groups were gradually taken over by the drug barons. It is estimated that there are currently over 140 paramilitary groups operating in Colombia today. The paramilitary groups are trained and financed by drug traffickers and possibly a few landowners. They operate very closely with elements in the armed forces and the police. Most of the killings and massacres carried out by the paramilitary groups occur in areas which are heavily militarized. The paramilitary groups are able to move easily in such areas and commit murders with impunity. As the report shows, in some cases, the military or police either turn a blind eye to what is being done by paramilitary groups or give support by offering safe conduct passes to members of the paramilitary or by impeding investigation. For example, the Director of the National Criminal Investigation Department at the time of the La Rochela massacre said that what worried him most was that inquiries for which he was responsible were turning up more and more evidence of indulgence, tolerance and backing of extreme right-wing groups by members of the police and the army. "We are carrying out very serious investigations and they have been harassing my men, who are being threatened by members of the National Police. The Judicial Technical Police is scared. It would be irresponsible of me to make any claim to the contrary."

Paramilitary groups are the greatest source of violations to the right to life in Colombian society today. Most of the killings and massacres have not only occurred at their hands but they have contributed to what has come to be known as impunity, that is the knowledge on the part of the perpetrators of these crimes that they will not be subject to the due process of law and punished for their misdeeds. Far reaching steps have to be taken to eliminate the prevailing climate of impunity and to curtail summary or arbitrary executions taking place as if they are part of everyday life. These policies will involve, not only strong political will but resources and technical expertise. It is for the latter, where

appropriate and with the agreement of Colombia, that the international community can provide assistance.

Any solution to the problem of violence in Colombian society today has to address itself to the problem posed by the paramilitary groups. The Government is aware of this and has taken steps against them. By Decree 813, an Advisory Commission was set up to combat paramilitary groups. The Commission's mandate is to create a plan of action to combat paramilitary groups. By Decree 814, a special force of up to 1,000 men was set up to combat these groups. The Special Rapporteur was informed that there had been some success in the war against such groups and that 17 of the groups had been disbanded. However, a lot more still needs to be done, bearing in mind that there are still 140 groups in existence. Decree 816 recognizes the role of properly instituted self-defence groups, but only at the initiative of the President by way of a decree which must be countersigned by the Ministers of Defence and the Government. The recruitment of civilians is only for defence purposes. The previous legislation which authorized the armed forces to give restricted weapons to self-defence groups has been revoked.

There should be an all out effort aimed at disbanding all the paramilitary groups not authorized and regulated by the law. The new Decree 1194/89 which aims at punishing those who promote, finance, train or take part in hired assassination (paramilitary) groups should be fully implemented. The enormity of this task should not be underestimated. There is bound to be resistance to such measures not only from within the military and the police but also from within the traditional political and economic élites who would rather have as priority the fight against the guerrillas. However if the violence is to be dealt with successfully then the problem of the existence of paramilitary groups has to be confronted.

Coupled with the disbanding of paramilitary groups, all persons in the armed forces and the police who have corroborated with or given support to such groups, hit men or drug traffickers, should be dismissed. The Government believes that the majority of the police and the military are not linked to the drug traffickers because otherwise the various actions aimed against them would not have been successful. It has been suggested that, through administrative action and the exercise of the constitutional powers vested in the President of the Republic to freely appoint and remove his agents, the Executive could and should remove members of the armed forces involved with such groups. Article 120, Ordinals 1 and 5 of the Constitution give the President power to do so, and Article 125, Ordinal 4 of Decree 095 of 1982, and Article III, Ordinal 4 of Decree 096 of 1989 give power to remove members of the armed forces from duty. Already, the Government has begun to do this. The Executive asserted its authority in the dismissal of four police officials guilty of causing the disappearance of persons and of committing torture and murders. There is also the example of Colonel Luis Bahorquez Montaya, Commander of the Puerto Boyaca who was relieved of his duty for his evident links with the paramilitary groups in the region. The same could possibly be said for Colonel Diego Hernan Velandia Postrana, Commander of the Santander Batallion of Ocána. However, there needs to be a more determined effort to remove such officers from the armed forces and police.

Another area which needs to be looked into as a matter of urgency is in the administration of justice. As can be seen from the report, very many judges, investigators and witnesses have either lost their lives or been threatened with death in the course of their duties. A climate of genuine fear exists among these groups of peoples which hampers the administration of justice and which contributes to the phenomena known as impunity. Witnesses cannot come forward to give evidence and even if they make statements, they are later retracted because of intimidation and fear of being killed. Proper investigations cannot be carried out and, therefore, many files are closed for lack of evidence. For those few files where there is evidence, a judge may not be able to mete out justice without fear or favour. The end result is that the guilty escape punishment because of lack of evidence. Adequate protection of all those involved in the administration of justice is, therefore, a matter of highest priority.

The Government is aware of this problem and on 18 August 1989, it issued a decree setting up a fund to pay for effective protection of judges and members of their families. Up to the time of the visit of the Special Rapporteur, however, no fund had been established because of lack of resources. Lack of funds is also the reason why witnesses are not given protection. DAS and the Department of Criminal Instruction have tried within their own limited resources to give protection to some of the witnesses but this has not on the whole been successful. The Special Rapporteur was told that in a few cases where the name, identity card and place of residence were changed, the witness was nevertheless killed. A fund for providing adequate security to those involved in the administration of justice is vital at this stage of Colombian history and it is an area in which the international community can assist.

The promotion of criminal investigation mechanisms particularly by the Judicial Police should be regarded as a matter of utmost priority. The Special Rapporteur visited the Department of Criminal Investigation which is the Technical Unit of the Judicial Police and was impressed by the high morale and determination of its officers in spite of the heavy odds against them. The investigators have to operate not only in a very precarious condition but they do not have sufficient infrastructure to guarantee an efficient operation, sufficient trained personnel, sufficient means of communication and the necessary technical expertise to be able to mount an effective investigation. A former director of the Department has said that the Government decrees requiring the police and the army to provide support and security for the judicial commissions of inquiry are not complied with, since the police and the army always say that they do not have enough staff, petrol or time or that their staff is on public order missions. This is a department that is pivotal in ensuring that people who commit crimes including crimes of murder do not escape prosecution. The Department should be considerably strengthened. The international community could, therefore, assist the Department in training, and by providing means of communication and technical expertise. It is vitally important that all cases of killings be properly investigated and the persons responsible whoever they are to be disciplined and punished according to the law.

The important role of the judiciary needs to be given more recognition and respect and this should be reflected in their terms and conditions of service. The Special Rapporteur was informed by the Judges Association that on average the salaries of judges and magistrates are less than those of civil servants of less educational level. Even lawyers in the Attorney-General's Office get on average at least $100 more than judges. Judges or magistrates have no social security, no housing and no libraries to enable them to carry out their work effectively. The terms and conditions of service of judges and magistrates need to be given consideration.

The worst hit groups of people have been peasants and workers. As somebody told the Special Rapporteur, every peasant is considered to be a potential guerrilla. The root causes giving rise to dissatisfaction among the peasants and workers have to be dealt with. It is therefore important that urgent programmes of action be taken to bring about social justice so that the economic and social conditions of peasants and workers can be considerably improved. The democratic reforms should be such that the peasant and the worker will not just be onlookers but active participants in the democratic and decision-making process. The role of groups which operate with peasants and workers, be they political parties, trade-unions, educators, non-governmental organizations dealing with economic, social, cultural and human rights issues, should be given due recognition and in a climate in which they can operate without intimidation from any quarter. There appears to be a systematic campaign by the paramilitary and extreme right-wing groups to eliminate or disrupt those organizations. The Government has already taken some steps to address the root causes: for example, dialogue with the guerrilla movements, programmes to ensure health and basic education for all, more jobs, agrarian reform and improving and rehabilitating sub-standard human settlement. The struggle against paramilitary groups and drug-traffickers will, it is hoped, eliminate or lessen the danger to these initiatives and thereby promote a healthy and constructive debate and discussion. This will, perhaps, lead to the accommodation of various sectors of the population and a consensus in the society that Colombia should be a society which belongs to all and in which there is peace, democracy, the rule of law, social justice and respect for human rights.

In a society which has been marked by such violence there is a need for a sustained campaign to promote human rights and the value of respecting them. Human rights need to be emphasized in the activities of the armed forces and police and whoever violates them should be disciplined and punished; the teaching of human rights should be compulsory to all public officials and in all educational establishments.

The efforts being made particularly by the Presidential Adviser on Human Rights in this regard are commendable and should be given support. Mention should also be made of the institution of Municipal Ombudsmen. The Special Rapporteur met a few of them. Some of them appeared to know their role but some did not. Some were operating not only under difficult conditions but also under threat to their lives. The Municipal Ombudsmen have a potential of really promoting and protecting human rights at the grass roots level. Their position should be strengthened and resources should be at their disposal so that they can function effectively.

The Commission on Human Rights examined the report of the special rapporteur at its 1990 session. On 6 March 1990, it strongly condemned once again (resolution 1990/51) the large number of summary or arbitrary executions, including extra-legal executions, which continue to take place in various parts of the world, and appealed urgently to governments,

United Nations bodies, specialized agencies, regional intergovernmental organizations, and non-governmental organizations to take effective action to combat and eliminate summary or arbitrary executions.

COMMISSION AGAINST *APARTHEID* IN SPORTS.

The commission was established in accordance with article 11 of the INTERNATIONAL CONVENTION AGAINST *APARTHEID* IN SPORTS, adopted and opened for signature and ratification or accession by the UN General Assembly on 10 December 1985 (resolution 40/64 G). The convention entered into force on 4 April 1988.

Under article 12 of the convention, each State party undertakes to submit to the UN secretary-general, for consideration by the commission, a report on the legislative, judicial, administrative, or other measures which it has adopted to give effect to the provisions of the convention within one year after its entry into force and thereafter every two years. The commission's function is to examine the information received, in particular, to examine the implementation of the provisions of article 10 of the convention; to request further information from the States parties, if necessary; and to make suggestions and recommendations based on its examination of the reports and information received. These suggestions and recommendations are to be set out in the commission's annual report to the General Assembly together with the comments, if any, of the States parties concerned.

At its 1989 session, the commission conducted consultations with the representatives of the International Olympic Committee, the World Boxing Council, and the South African Non-Racial Olympic Committee; authorized its chairman to cooperate with the SPECIAL COMMITTEE AGAINST *APARTHEID* in promoting the boycott of *apartheid* in sports and other activities for the realization of the objectives of the convention, and received reports from 13 States parties to the convention.

In its annual report to the General Assembly (UN Doc. A/44/47), the commission included the following conslusions and recommendations (para. 28–32):

The Commission recognized the progress achieved in the international boycott of *apartheid* sports. However, if felt that further action was needed on the national and international levels.

The Commission recognized the importance of the contribution of the International Olympic Committee in isolating South Africa from the Olympic Games and in persuading sporting federations recognized by the International Olympic Committee to expel South Africa from their membership and to terminate any sports contacts with South Africa. The Commission would continue to co-operate with the International Olympic Committee until *apartheid* is totally eradicated from South Africa.

Action was needed with regard to other non-Olympic sports, in particular concerning the continuing contacts with South Africa in golf, rugby and other sports.

The Commission took note of the fact that the World Boxing Council has since 1975 confirmed and reaffirmed its unequivocal stand against *apartheid* sports and has fully supported all the efforts of the Special Committee against *Apartheid* and the South African Non-Racial Olympic Committee. These efforts had been largely successful until the recent advent of splinter groups such as the International Boxing Federation and the World Boxing Organization. It is recommended, therefore, that both the International Boxing Federation and the World Boxing Organization be included in the Register of Sports contacts with South Africa. In the mean time, the Commission urges those organizations to terminate any contacts with South Africa.

The Commission recommended that the General Assembly:

(a) Urge all those States which have signed the Convention and not ratified it to ratify it, and all those States which have not signed the Convention to do so as soon as possible;

(b) Call on all States to extend co-operation to the Commission against *Apartheid* in Sports and to the Special Committee against *Apartheid* in matters relating to the boycott of *apartheid* sports;

(c) Urge States, organizations and individuals to take action to achieve the total isolation of *apartheid* in sports and to terminate any sports contacts with South Africa;

(d) Request the Secretary-General to provide the necessary services to the Commission to fulfil its mandate. Particular attention should be paid to publicity against *apartheid* sports.

On 22 November 1989, the General Assembly took note (resolution 44/27 L) of the commission's report, called upon States to ratify or to accede to it as soon as possible, and commended those governments, organizations, and individual sportsmen and sportswomen which have taken action in accordance with the "Register of Sports Contacts with South Africa" with a view to achieving a total isolation of *apartheid* in sports. It requested the Special Committee against *Apartheid* to continue issuing the register and called upon those international sports organizations and federations which have not expelled South Africa or suspended its membership to do so without further delay.

COMMISSION FOR SOCIAL DEVELOPMENT.

The commission, established in 1946 by the UN Economic and Social Council as the Social Commission (resolution 10 [II]) and given a new name and broader mandate in 1966 to act as the preparatory and advisory body in the whole range of social development (resolution 1139 [XLI]), is mandated to advise the council (1) on social policies of a general character, giving particular attention to policies designed to promote social progress, to establish social objectives, program priorities, and social research in areas affecting social and economic development; (2) on practical measures that may be needed in the social field, including questions of social welfare, community development, urbanization, housing, and social defense; (3) on measures needed for the coordination of activities in the social field; and (4) on such international agreements and conventions on any of these matters.

Before its change of name and mandate, the social commission, in 1950, prepared the draft of a declaration on the rights of the child, based on the Declaration of Geneva which had been adopted by the Assembly of the League of Nations in 1924. After the draft had been reviewed by the Commission on Human Rights and the Economic and Social Council, it was transmitted to the General Assembly which adopted and proclaimed the DECLARATION ON THE RIGHTS OF THE CHILD on 29 November 1959 (resolution 1386 [XIV]).

Later the Commission for Social Development prepared the draft of a declaration on social development, which the General Assembly adopted and proclaimed on 11 December 1969 (resolution 2542 [XXIV]) as the DECLARATION ON SOCIAL PROGRESS AND DEVELOPMENT. The declaration states that social progress and development shall aim at the continuous raising of the material and spiritual standards of living of all members of society, with respect for and compliance with human rights and fundamental freedoms, through the attainment of such goals as: (1) the assurance at all levels of the right to work and the right of everyone to form trade unions and workers' associations and to bargain collectively; (2) the elimination of hunger and malnutrition and the guarantee of the right to proper nutrition; (3) the achievement of the highest standards of health and the provision of health protection for all, if possible free of charge; (4) the eradication of illiteracy and the assurance of the right to universal access to culture, to free compulsory education at the elementary level, and to free education at all levels; and (5) the provision for all, particularly persons in low-income groups and large families, of adequate housing and community services. The declaration also calls for equitable sharing of scientific and technological advances by developed and developing countries and a steady increase in the use of science and technology for the benefit of the social development of society.

Originally set at 18, the membership of the commission was increased to 21 in 1961 and to 32 in 1966. The commission consists of one representative of each of the 32 States elected by the Economic and Social Council according to the following patterns:

eight members from African states, six from Asian states, six from Latin American states, eight from western European and other states, and four from socialist states of eastern Europe. The States elected to the commission are expected to nominate as their representatives nationals who hold key positions in the planning or execution of national social development policies or others qualified to discuss the formulation of such policies in more than one sector of development. With a view to securing a balanced representation in the various fields covered by the commission, the Secretary-General consults with the governments elected before they nominate their representatives. The representatives thus nominated are then confirmed by the council. They serve for a term of four years.

COMMISSION OF THE CHURCHES ON INTERNATIONAL AFFAIRS OF THE WORLD COUNCIL OF CHURCHES.

An international non-governmental organization in consultative status with the UN Economic and Social Council (Category II), and with ILO and UNESCO, the commission is an agency of the World Council of Churches and assists the constituency of WCC in dealing with questions of international scope. In this capacity, it studies world problems of international justice and world order, makes known the results of such studies to the churches and organizations affiliated with WCC, and represents WCC in its relations with international organs. The commission is composed of 30 commissioners and 40 commissioners-at-large, appointed by WCC upon nomination by its Executive Committee.

CCIA's primary human rights concerns are with the development, promotion and protection of religious liberty, the provision of assistance to dependent peoples, indigenous populations, refugees, migrants and other disadvantaged groups, and the operation of a broad program aimed at combating racism and racial discrimination. It also deals with questions related to conscientious objection to military service. In these functions, it is assisted by its Human Rights Advisory Group.

CCIA's extensive publications program includes the CCIA *Newsletter,* its background information papers and its annual reports.

Commission of the Churches on International Affairs of the World Council of Churches. Address: 150 route de Ferney, CH-1211 Geneva, Switzerland. Telephone: (41-22) 916111. Cable: OIKOUMENE GENEVA. Telex: 23 423 A OIK CH. FAX (41-22) 91-03-61. Director: Prof. Ninan Koshy.

COMMISSION ON HUMAN RIGHTS. The UN Commission on Human Rights was established by the UN Economic and Social Council on 16 February 1946 (resolution 5 [I]) in accordance with article 68 of the UNITED NATIONS CHARTER which authorizes the council to set up "commissions in economic and social fields and for the protection of human rights."

The commission's original mandate was to submit to the council proposals, recommendations, and reports regarding (1) an international bill of rights; (2) international declarations or conventions on civil liberties, the status of women, freedom of information and similar matters; (3) the protection of minorities; (4) the prevention of discrimination on grounds of race, sex, language, or religion; and (5) any other matter concerning human rights. In 1979, a new function was added: to assist the Economic and Social Council in the coordination of activities concerning human rights in the United Nations system (Council resolution 1979/36, approved in General Assembly resolution 34/25).

Since it first met in 1947, the commission has been at the forefront of international activity to define, promote, and protect human rights and fundamental freedoms. In addition to preparing a number of international treaties and declarations, the commission has considered many situations involving violations of those rights and freedoms; has sought, through persuasion and dialogue, to prevent and eliminate human rights violations; has recommended measures to ensure compliance with universally recognized norms of human rights; and has offered and provided, upon request, advisory services and other expert assistance to reduce the incidence of violations of human rights. In addition, it has monitored, through its GROUP OF THREE, governnments' implementation of the INTERNATIONAL CONVENTION ON THE SUPPRESSION AND PUNISHMENT OF THE CRIME OF *APARTHEID.*

The commission's most notable achievements include the initial drafting of the UNIVERSAL DECLARATION OF HUMAN RIGHTS; the INTERNATIONAL COVENANT ON ECONOMIC, SOCIAL AND CULTURAL RIGHTS; the INTERNATIONAL COVENANT ON CIVIL AND POLITICAL RIGHTS and OPTIONAL PROTOCOL thereto—instruments which together comprise the International Bill of Human Rights—and many other human rights treaties and declarations, including the INTERNATIONAL CONVENTION ON THE ELIMINATION OF ALL FORMS OF RACIAL DISCRIMINATION, the INTERNATIONAL CONVENTION ON THE SUPPRESSION AND PUNISHMENT OF THE CRIME OF *APARTHEID,* and the CONVENTION AGAINST TORTURE AND OTHER CRUEL, INHUMAN OR DEGRADING TREATMENT OR PUNISHMENT.

In addition to debating and taking action on items on the agenda of its annual sessions, the commission has developed a variety of mechanisms which enable it to carry out its work effectively. On many occasions, it has called upon one or more of its members, or other qualified experts, to perform fact-finding tasks, designating them as "SPECIAL RAPPORTEURS," "special representatives," or "special envoys." These experts, acting in their personal capacity, have examined questions relating to thematic human rights issues, such as summary and arbitrary executions, torture, intolerance based on religion or belief, and the use of mercenaries. They have also examined the human rights situations in particular countries. And, in a few cases, they have assisted governments to plan and take action to restore respect for human rights in territories under their jurisdiction. The commission has also made use of working groups to examine particular situations (such as the AD HOC WORKING GROUP OF EXPERTS ON SOUTHERN AFRICA), to consider broad categories of human rights violations (such as the WORKING GROUP ON ENFORCED OR INVOLUNTARY DISAPPEARANCES), to draft new international instruments (such as the Working Group on a Draft Convention of the Rights of the Child), or to consider the realization of specific rights (such as the WORKING GROUP OF GOVERNMENTAL EXPERTS ON THE RIGHT TO DEVELOPMENT).

The commission employs a special procedure, established by the Economic and Social Council in resolution 1503 (XLVIII) of 27 May 1970, in examining situations which appear to reveal a consistent pattern of violations of human rights. Under the procedure, communications alleging such situations received by the CENTER FOR HUMAN RIGHTS are forwarded first to the governments concerned for their comments, if any. The communications, together with the comments of governments, are first considered by a working group of the SUB-COMMISSION ON PREVENTION OF DISCRIMINATION AND PROTECTION OF MINORITIES. If the sub-commission, on recommendation of the working group, considers that a particular situation fulfills the criteria set out in council resolution 1503, it refers it to the commission, which decides what further action is to be taken. The commission reports on such action to the council. All activities under this procedure are confidential, and the results remain confidential, unless the council decides otherwise.

Originally 18, commission membership was increased to 21 in 1961, to 32 in 1966, and to 43 in 1979. The commission is composed of one representative from each of 43 member States, selected by the council on the basis of equitable geographical distribution according to the following pattern: eleven members from African States, nine from Asian States, eight from Latin American States, ten from Western European and other States, and five from socialist States of Eastern Europe. With a view to securing a balanced representation in the various fields covered by the commission, the Secretary-General consults with the governments elected by the council before those governments nominate their representatives. After nomination, the representatives are confirmed by the council. The term of office is three years. The commission meets for one session each year, usually at the United Nations office in Geneva, for a period of about six weeks between mid-February and late March. In recent years, the Economic and Social Council has authorized the commission to hold additional meetings beyond the period normally allotted, to enable it to complete its work.

COMMISSION ON THE STATUS OF WOMEN. The commission was established by the UN Economic and Social Council on 21 June 1946 (resolution 11 [II]) and is mandated to prepare reports and recommendations to the council on promoting women's rights in the political, economic, civic, social, and educational fields and to develop recommendations and proposals for action on urgent problems in the field of women's rights with the object of implementing the principle that men and women shall have equal rights. The commission also acts from time to time as the preparatory body for international conferences on the rights of women, and recently it has been assigned a major role in reviewing and coordinating all activities of the United Nations system relevant to women's issues. On 27 July 1988, the council expressed the view (resolution 1988/60) that the central substantive coordinating role of the commission in advancing the status of women and integrating women in development has three distinct aspects: (1) intergovernmental cooperation, regional, and sectoral intergovernmental bodies to achieve a coherent and complementary approach to implementing the NAIROBI FORWARD-LOOKING STRATEGIES FOR THE ADVANCEMENT OF WOMEN within the United Nations; (2) interagency coordination, which relates to measures taken by organizations of the United Nations system to coordinate the implementation of the forward-looking strategies; and (3) legislative linkage, which relates to action taken by the commission to link the implementation of the forward-looking strategies to all relevant United Nations intergovernmental decisions and other international strategies and plans and programs of action.

Originally 15, membership in the commission was increased to 18 in 1951; to 21 in 1961; to 32 in 1966; and, most recently, to 45 by resolution 1989/45 adopted by the Economic and Social Council on 24 May 1989. Under that resolution, the commission consists of one representative of each 45 States, elected by the council on the basis of equitable geographical distribution according to the following pattern: 13 members from African States, 11 members from Asian States, four members from Eastern European States, nine members from Latin American and Caribbean States, and eight members from western European and other States.

Council resolution 1989/45 provides for the enlargement of the commission to take effect from the beginning of 1990 and before the convening of the extended session of the commission to review and appraise progress in the implementation of the Nairobi Forward-looking Principles for the Advancement of Women. The additional seats resulting from the increase in membership would be filled by the council at its organizational session in May 1990.

The commission holds one session every two years, either at the International Conference Center in Vienna or at United Nations headquarters in New York. In 1983, 1984, and 1985, the commission, acting as the preparatory body for the World Conference to Review and Appraise the Achievements of the United Nations Decade for Women, held three sessions at the Vienna center and one at the United Nations headquarters in New York. The reports of those sessions (UN Docs. A/CONF. 116/PC/9 and Corr. 1; 19, 25 and 25/Add. 1) were submitted directly to the General Assembly. At those sessions, the commission dealt mainly with organizational aspects of the conference: initiating the necessary documentation, drafting provisional rules of procedure, and preparing the provisional agenda.

Although the commission has no permanent subsidiary bodies, it occasionally sets up temporary working groups or appoints special rapporteurs to assist it in its work.

At its 1988 session, the commission adopted (resolution 32/1) a statement on its structure and functions for consideration by the Special Commission of the Economic and Social Council on the In-depth Study of the United Nations Intergovernmental Structure and Functions in the Economic and Social Fields. The statement, annexed to the resolution, read in part as follows (para. 1–9):

The Commission on the Status of Women is the primary and central intergovernmental body of the United Nations system responsible for the advancement of women, an objective set out in the United Nations Charter, towards which the Commission has been working since the earliest years of the Organization. Member States have appreciated its work which included preparation of the Convention on the Elimination of All Forms of Discrimination against Women, preparations for International Women's Year, as well as the

United Nations Decade for Women and its three international conferences which lead to the adoption in July 1985, by consensus, of the Nairobi Forward-looking Strategies for the Advancement of Women. The importance attached by Governments to the Commission has been reflected in the high technical and political level of representation at its meetings, often at the ministerial level.

The endorsement of the Nairobi Forward-looking Strategies by the General Assembly in 1985 as the culmination of the United Nations Decade for Women was a milestone in the work of the Organization. The Strategies set an ambitious but realistic agenda for achieving full equality between men and women by the year 2000. The achievement of the objectives of the Nairobi Forward-looking Strategies is a priority of the Organizations over the next twelve years and beyond.

Tasks of the Commission. The General Assembly has given the Commission on the Status of Women the task of the monitoring, review and appraisal of the implementation of the Nairobi Forward-looking Strategies. This task is central to its work. In this connection, it has been assigned responsibility for reviewing the programming and co-ordination of activities related to the advancement of women in the United Nations system. Its role as the principal technical body in its field is to provide dynamic, creative and catalytic policy input to the work of the Economic and Social Council and the General Assembly.

The advancement of women is an objective which is relevant to a very broad range of United Nations activities and bodies. Its work is not limited to the social sectors but is rather multidisciplinary, cross-sectoral and cross-organizational. In performing its role as the only intergovernmental body dealing with the advancement of women in a comprehensive way, the Commission on the Status of Women must examine all aspects of the three objectives on which the Nairobi Forward-looking Strategies are built: equality, development and peace. The themes dealt with cut across traditional lines and include matters related to economic development, human rights, political conditions and cultural issues as well as social policy questions. The Commission's approach reflects the importance of mainstreaming women's issues, rather than viewing them in isolation. The conclusions drawn from its discussions are directly relevant to many of the themes dealt with by the Committee for Programme and Co-ordination, all three committees of the Economic and Social Council, the Second and Third Committees of the General Assembly and the specialized agencies.

Programme Planning and Co-ordination. The Commission on the Status of Women is the competent intergovernmental body responsible for substantive aspects of programming and co-ordination of activities related to the advancement of women. As such, it is responsible for overseeing the coherence, consistency and adequacy with which the Forward-looking Strategies are being implemented by the organizations of the United Nations system, who actively and regularly contribute to the work of the Commission. In this connection, it reviews programming and co-ordination documents such as the System-wide Medium-term Plan for Women and Development, the United Nations Medium-term Plan and the United Nations Programme Budget.

Policy Guidance for the Advancement of Women. More significantly, in its new stage of work, the Commission has a special responsibility for global leadership in the implementation of the Nairobi Forward-looking Strategies, in-cluding the development of substantive policy guidance on specific issues related to implementation of the Strategies. In those areas where they are not sufficiently specific, it is the task of the Commission to provide guidance based on global experience; in issues which have emerged since Nairobi, the task of the Commission is to suggest how the Nairobi Forward-looking Strategies should be applied in new situations. In support of the broader roles of the Economic and Social Council and the General Assembly, the Commission stands as the focal point in the intergovernmental structure necessary to implement the Nairobi Forward-looking Strategies.

Reforms Already Implemented. In order to undertake the above tasks successfully, the Commission on the Status of Women made significant progress at its session in 1987 at self-reform. It restructured its agenda along functional lines, developed a systematic long-term programme of work and urged improvements in the system of reporting, monitoring and appraising the implementation of the Forward-looking Strategies. Further, it strengthened and rationalized its role and functions in the moblization of the resources of the United Nations system as a whole towards the advancement of women, by integrating this objective in the programme planning and budgeting processes of the Organization. Since it agreed to hold annual sessions until the year 2000, implementation of the Nairobi Forward-looking Strategies requires continuity. Furthermore, the complexity of subjects to be considered did not admit to biennialization while the need to support the Economic and Social Council and the General Assembly on issues related to advancement of women remains constant. Biennial treatment of those issues would downgrade their importance and remove them from the central agenda at critical moments.

The Commission considers that, in coming to terms with these difficult and technical issues at its 1987 session, it has undertaken pioneering work which could be emulated by other bodies. It considers that the significant output of its 1987 session constitutes a substantive response to the concerns underlying Economic and Social Council decision 1987/112. The Commission should now be given the opportunity and resources to proceed with its work within the framework of reform agreed in 1987, and to implement further reforms as experience may show to be necessary.

A Continuing Process of Reform. The process of reform is not complete. The Commission is beginning to experiment with new means of preparing its work. An important innovation has been the use of expert meetings on the priority themes, such as those on violence in the family and on national machinery for the advancement of women, which helped prepare for the 1988 session of the Commission. Opportunities provided by Member States for informal consultations will also be used to expedite the work. The means by which a broader range of experience can be brought into play by enlarging the Commission, as was requested by Economic and Social Council resolution 1987/23, is being discussed at the present session. The Commission will keep its pattern of work under constant review and seek to improve it continually on the basis of experience gained....

Question of Enlargement of the Commission. On 26 May 1987, the UN Economic and Social Council accepted in principle the need for an increase in the membership of the commission and requested the commission to submit proposals to it in 1988. In taking this decision, the council reaffirmed the central role of the commission in promoting and monitoring the Nairobi Forward-looking Strategies for the Advancement of Women, as well as the normal responsibilities of the commission as the competent intergovernmental body on matters concerning the status of women.

Communications concerning the Status of Women. The WORKING GROUP ON COMMUNICATIONS, established by the commission at its 1988 session, examined a list of communications concerning the situation of women in specific countries and the replies received from a number of governments. It analyzed the substance of the communications and agreed that many of them dealt with very serious and extensive violations of human rights, including different forms of discrimination against women. Such discrimination took the form of unequal rights in economic and social life, inequality before the law, and continued physical and sexual violence against women in detention. In addition, a few reports concerned family relationships, educational rights and participation in political activities.

The working group expressed particular concern about sexual harassment of women at the workplace and urged continued monitoring of the problem. It was distressed at the lack of response from several governments to communications regarding violations of the education, employment, and political rights of women, as well as the safety of women in detention. It proposed that the Commission on the Status of Women urge the Economic and Social Council to recommend that member States take legislative and other appropriate measures to halt the current negative trends related to the status of women in their countries.

COMMISSIONS ON HUMAN RIGHTS. In addition to the UN Commission on Human Rights (see above), two other international organs bear the name "Commission on Human Rights." See EUROPEAN COMMISSION ON HUMAN RIGHTS and INTER-AMERICAN COMMISSION ON HUMAN RIGHTS. See also AFRICAN COMMISSION ON HUMAN AND PEOPLES' RIGHTS.

COMMITTEE AGAINST TORTURE. The committee was established in accordance with article 17 of the CONVENTION AGAINST TORTURE AND OTHER CRUEL, INHUMAN OR DEGRADING TREATMENT OR PUNISHMENT, adopted by the UN General Assembly on 10 December 1984 (resolution 39/46). Opened for signature and ratification or accession on 4 February 1985, the convention entered into force on 26 June 1987.

Each State party to the convention undertakes to take effective legislative, administrative, judicial, and other measures to prevent acts of torture in any territory under its jurisdiction, and to submit reports to the Committee against Torture on the measures it has taken to this end. The Committee against Torture is empowered to consider the reports, to make general comments on them which are forwarded to the State concerned, and to include its comments and observations in its annual report to the General Assembly.

States parties may, in addition, make declarations provided for in articles 21 and 22 of the convention. Under article 21, such a State may declare that it recognizes the competence of the committee to receive and consider communications to the effect that one State party claims that another is not fulfilling its obligations under the convention. The committee is authorized to deal with such a complaint only after it has ascertained that all domestic remedies have been invoked and exhausted. If that is the case, it may try to find a friendly solution, either directly or by setting up a conciliation commission for the purpose.

Under article 22, a State party may declare that it recognizes the competence of the committee to receive communications from or on behalf of individuals subject to its jurisdiction who claim to be victims of a violation by a State party of the provisions of the convention. The committee is authorized to deal with such a complaint after screening out communications which are anonymous or incompatible with the provisions of the convention. It may bring admissible communications to the State party concerned and consider them in the light of all the information made available by the individual and the State. It then forwards its views to both parties and reports annually on its activities to the General Assembly.

The provisions of articles 21 and 22 entered into force on 26 June 1987 after ten States had made the necessary declarations. At a meeting of the States parties, convened on that day at the United Nations office in Geneva, members of the Committee against Torture were elected.

At its first and second sessions, held in 1988 and 1989, respectively, the committee adopted its rules of procedure, including general rules (Part I, rules 1–63), rules relating to the functions of the committee (Part II, rules 64–112), and rules relating to interpretation and amendments (Part III, rules 113 and 144). The rules relating to the functions of the committee are as follows (UN Doc. CAT/C/3/Rev. 1):

XVI. Reports From States Parties Under Article 19 of the Convention

Rule 64. Submission of Reports. 1. The States parties shall submit to the Committee, through the Secretary-General, reports on the measures they have taken to give effect to their undertakings under the Convention, within one year after the entry into force of the Convention for the State party concerned. Thereafter the States parties shall submit supplementary reports every four years on any new measures taken and such other reports as the Committee may request.

2. The Committee may, through the Secretary-General, inform the States parties of its wishes regarding the form and contents of the reports to be submitted under article 19 of the Convention.

Rule 65. Non-Submission of Reports. 1. At each session, the Secretary-General shall notify the Committee of all cases of non-submission of reports under rules 64 and 67 of these rules. In such cases the Committee may transmit to the State party concerned, through the Secretary-General, a reminder concerning the submission of such report or reports.

2. If, after the reminder referred to in paragraph 1 of this rule, the State party does not submit the report required under rules 64 and 67 of these rules, the Committee shall so state in the annual report which it submits to the States parties and to the General Assembly of the United Nations.

Rule 66. Attendance by States Parties at Examination of Reports. The Committee shall, through the Secretary-General, notify the States parties, as early as possible, of the opening date, duration and place of the session at which their respective reports will be examined. Representatives of the States parties shall be invited to attend the meetings of the Committee when their reports are examined. The Committee may also inform a State party from which it decides to seek further information that it may authorize its representative to be present at a specified meeting. Such a representative should be able to answer questions which may be put to him by the Committee and make statements on reports already submitted by his State, and may also submit additional information from his State.

Rule 67. Request for Additional Reports. 1. When considering a report submitted by a State party under article 19 of the Convention, the Committee shall first determine whether the report provides all the information required under rule 64 of these rules.

2. If a report of a State party to the Convention, in the opinion of the Committee, does not contain sufficient information, the Committee may request that State to furnish an additional report, indicating by what date the said report should be submitted.

Rule 68. General Comments by the Committee. 1. After its consideration of each report, the Committee, in accordance with article 19, paragraph 3, of the Convention, may make such general comments on the report as it may consider appropriate and shall forward these, through the Secretary-General, to the State party concerned, which in reply may submit to the Committee any comment that it considers appropriate. The Committee may, in particular, indicate in its general comments whether, on the basis of its examination of the reports and information supplied by the State party, it appears that some of the obligations of that State under the Convention have not been discharged.

2. The Committee may, where necessary, indicate a time-limit within which observations from States parties are to be received.

3. The Committee may, at its discretion, decide to include any comments made by it in accordance with paragraph 1 of this rule, together with any observations thereon received from the State party concerned, in its annual re-

port made in accordance with article 24 of the Convention. If so requested by the State party concerned, the Committee may also include a copy of the report submitted under article 19, paragraph 1, of the Convention.

XVII. Proceedings Under Article 20 of the Convention

Rule 69. Transmission of Information to the Committee. 1. The Secretary-General shall bring to the attention of the Committee, in accordance with the present rules, information which is, or appears to be, submitted for the Committee's consideration under article 20, paragraph 1, of the Convention.

2. No information shall be received by the Committee if it concerns a State party which, in accordance with article 28, paragraph 1, of the Convention, declared at the time of ratification of or accession to the Convention that it did not recognize the competence of the Committee provided for in article 20, unless that State has subsequently withdrawn its reservation in accordance with article 28, paragraph 2, of the Convention.

Rule 70. Register of Information Submitted. The Secretary-General shall maintain a permanent register of information brought to the attention of the Committee in accordance with rule 69 above and shall make the information available to any member of the Committee upon request.

Rule 71. Summary of the Information. The Secretary-General, when necessary, shall prepare and circulate to the members of the Committee a brief summary of the information submitted in accordance with rule 69 above.

Rule 72. Confidentiality of Documents and Proceedings. All documents and proceedings of the Committee relating to its functions under article 20 of the Convention shall be confidential, until such time when the Committee decides, in accordance with the provisions of article 20, paragraph 5, of the Convention, to make them public.

Rule 73. Meetings. 1. Meetings of the Committee concerning its proceedings under article 20 of the Convention shall be closed.

2. Meetings during which the Committee considers general issues, such as procedures for the application of article 20 of the Convention, shall be public, unless the Committee decides otherwise.

Rule 74. Issue of Communiqués concerning Closed Meetings. The Committee may decide to issue communiqués, through the Secretary-General, for the use of the information media and the general public regarding its activities under article 20 of the Convention.

Rule 75. Preliminary Consideration of Information by the Committee. 1. The Committee, when necessary, may ascertain, through the Secretary-General, the reliability of the information and/or of the sources of the information brought to its attention under article 20 of the Convention or obtain additional relevant information substantiating the facts of the situation.

2. The Committee shall determine whether it appears to it that the information received contains well-founded indications that torture, as defined in article 1 of the Convention, is being systematically practised in the territory of the State party concerned.

Rule 76. Examination of the Information. 1. If it appears to the Committee that the information received is reliable and contains well-founded indications that torture is being systematically practised in the territory of a State party, the Committee shall invite the State party concerned, through the Secretary-General, to co-operate in its examination of the information and, to this end, to submit observations with regard to that information.

2. The Committee shall indicate a time-limit for the submission of observations by the State party concerned, with a view to avoiding undue delay in its proceedings.

3. In examining the information received, the Committee shall take into account any observations which may have been submitted by the State party concerned, as well as any other relevant information available to it.

4. The Committee may decide, if it deems it appropriate, to obtain from the representatives of the State party concerned, governmental and non-governmental organizations, as well as individuals, additional information or answers to questions relating to the information under examination.

5. The Committee shall decide, on its initiative and on the basis of its rules of procedure, the form and manner in which such additional information may be obtained.

Rule 77. Documentation from United Nations Bodies and Specialized Agencies. The Committee may at any time obtain, through the Secretary-General, any relevant documentation from United Nations bodies or specialized agencies that may assist it in the examination of the information received under article 20 of the Convention.

Rule 78. Establishment of an Inquiry. 1. The Committee may, if it decides that this is warranted, designate one or more of its members to make a confidential inquiry and to report to it within a time-limit which may be set by the Committee.

2. When the Committee decides to make an inquiry in accordance with paragraph 1 of this rule, it shall establish the modalities of the inquiry as it deems it appropriate.

3. The members designated by the Committee for the confidential inquiry shall determine their own methods of work in conformity with the provisions of the Convention and the rules of procedure of the Committee.

Rule 79. Co-operation of the State Party Concerned. The Committee shall invite the State party concerned, through the Secretary-General, to co-operate with it in the conduct of the inquiry. To this end, the Committee may request the State party concerned:

(a) To designate an accredited representative to meet with the members designated by the Committee;

(b) To provide its designated members with any information that they, or the State party, may consider useful for ascertaining the facts relating to the inquiry;

(c) To indicate any other form of co-operation that the State may wish to extend to the Committee and to its designated members with a view to facilitating the conduct of the inquiry.

Rule 80. Visiting Mission. If the Committee deems it necessary to include in its inquiry a visit of one or more of its members to the territory of the State party concerned, it shall request, through the Secretary-General, the agreement of that State party and shall inform the State party of its wishes regarding the timing of the mission and the facilities required to allow the designated members of the Committee to carry out their task.

Rule 81. Hearings in Connection with the Inquiry. 1. The designated members may decide to conduct hearings in connection with the inquiry as they deem it appropriate.

2. The designated members shall establish, in co-operation with the State party concerned, the conditions and guarantees required for conducting such hearings. They shall request the State party to ensure that no obstacles are placed in the way of witnesses and other individuals wishing to meet with the designated members of the Committee and that no retaliatory measure is taken against those individuals or their families.

3. Every person appearing before the designated members for the purpose of giving testimony shall be requested to take an oath or make a solemn declaration concerning the veracity of his/her testimony and the respect for confidentiality of the proceedings.

Rule 82. Assistance during the Inquiry. 1. In addition to the staff and facilities to be provided by the Secretary-General in connection with the inquiry and/or the visiting mission to the territory of the State party concerned, the designated members may invite, through the Secretary-General, persons with special competence in the medical field or in the treatment of prisoners as well as interpreters to provide assistance at all stages of the inquiry.

2. If the persons providing assistance during the inquiry are not bound by an oath of office to the United Nations, they shall be required to declare solemnly that they will perform their duties honestly, faithfully and impartially, and that they will respect the confidentiality of the proceedings.

3. The persons referred to in paragraphs 1 and 2 of the present rule shall be entitled to the same facilities, privileges and immunities provided for in respect of the members of the Committee, under article 23 of the Convention.

Rule 83. Transmission of Findings, Comments or Suggestions. 1. After examining the findings of its designated members submitted to it in accordance with rule 78, paragraph 1, the Committee shall transmit, through the Secretary-General, these findings to the State party concerned, together with any comments or suggestions that it deems appropriate.

2. The State party concerned shall be invited to inform the Committee within a reasonable delay of the action it takes with regard to the Committee's findings and in response to the Committee's comments or suggestions.

Rule 84. Summary Account of the Results of the Proceedings. 1. After all the proceedings of the Committee regarding an inquiry made under article 20 of the Convention have been completed, the Committee may decide, after consultations with the State party concerned, to include a summary account of the results of the proceedings in its annual report made in accordance with article 24 of the Convention.

2. The Committee shall invite the State party concerned, through the Secretary-General, to inform the Committee directly or through its designated representative of its view concerning the question referred to in paragraph 1 of this rule, and may indicate a time-limit within which the view of the State party should be communicated to the Committee.

XVIII. Procedure for the Consideration of Communications Received Under Article 21 of the Convention

Rule 85. Declarations by States Parties. 1. The Secretary-General shall transmit to the other States parties copies of the declarations deposited with him by States parties recognizing the competence of the Committee, in accordance with article 21 of the Convention.

2. The withdrawal of a declaration made under article 21 of the Convention shall not prejudice the consideration of any matter that is the subject of a communication already transmitted under that article; no further communication by any State party shall be received under that article after the notification of withdrawal of the declaration has been received by the Secretary-General, unless the State party has made a new declaration.

Rule 86. Notification by the State Parties Concerned. 1. A communication under article 21 of the Convention may be referred to the Committee by either State party concerned by notice given in accordance with paragraph 1 (b) of that article.

2. The notice referred to in paragraph 1 of this rule shall contain or be accompanied by information regarding:

(a) Steps taken to seek adjustment of the matter in accordance with article 21, paragraphs 1 (a) and (b), of the Convention, including the text of the initial communication and of any subsequent written explanations or statements by the States parties concerned which are pertinent to the matter;

(b) Steps taken to exhaust domestic remedies;

(c) Any other procedure of international investigation or settlement resorted to by the States parties concerned.

Rule 87. Register of Communications. The Secretary-General shall maintain a permanent register of all communications received by the Committee under article 21 of the Convention.

Rule 88. Information to the Members of the Committee. The Secretary-General shall inform the members of the Committee without delay of any notice given under rule 86 of these rules and shall transmit to them as soon as possible copies of the notice and relevant information.

Rule 89. Meetings. The Committee shall examine communications under article 21 of the Convention at closed meetings.

Rule 90. Issue of Communiqués concerning Closed Meetings. The Committee may, after consultation with the States parties concerned, issue communiqués, through the Secretary-General, for the use of the information media and the general public regarding the activities of the Committee under article 21 of the Convention.

Rule 91. Requirements for the Consideration of Communications. A communication shall not be considered by the Committee unless:

(a) Both States parties concerned have made declarations under article 21, paragraph 1, of the Convention;

(b) The time-limit prescribed in article 21, paragraph 1 (b), of the Convention has expired;

(c) The Committee has ascertained that all available domestic remedies have been invoked and exhausted in the matter, in conformity with the generally recognized principles of international law, or that the application of the remedies is unreasonably prolonged or is unlikely to bring effective relief to the person who is the victim of the violation of the Convention.

Rule 92. Good Offices. 1. Subject to the provisions of rule 91 of these rules, the Committee shall proceed to make its good offices available to the States parties concerned with a view to a friendly solution of the matter on the basis of respect for the obligations provided for in the Convention.

2. For the purpose indicated in paragraph 1 of this rule, the Committee may, when appropriate, set up an *ad hoc* conciliation commission.

Rule 93. Request for Information. The Committee may, through the Secretary-General, request the States parties concerned or either of them to submit additional information or observations orally or in writing. The Committee shall indicate a time-limit for the submission of such written information or observations.

Rule 94. Attendance by the States Parties Concerned. 1. The States parties concerned shall have the right to be represented when the matter is being considered in the Committee and to make submissions orally and/or in writing.

2. The Committee shall, through the Secretary-General, notify the States parties concerned as early as possible of the opening date, duration and place of the session at which the matter will be examined.

3. The procedure for making oral and/or written submissions shall be decided by the Committee, after consultation with the States parties concerned.

Rule 95. Report of the Committee. 1. Within 12 months after the date on which the Committee received the notice referred to in rule 86 of these rules, the Committee shall adopt a report in accordance with article 21, paragraph 1 (h), of the Convention.

2. The provisions of paragraph 1 of rule 94 of these rules shall not apply to the deliberations of the Committee concerning the adoption of the report.

3. The Committee's report shall be communicated, through the Secretary-General, to the States parties concerned.

XIX. Procedure for the Consideration of Communications Received Under Article 22 of the Convention
A. General Provisions

Rule 96. Declarations by States Parties. 1. The Secretary-General shall transmit to the other States parties copies of the declarations deposited with him by States parties recognizing the competence of the Committee, in accordance with article 22 of the Convention.

2. The withdrawal of a declaration made under article 22 of the Convention shall not prejudice the consideration of any matter which is the subject of a communication already transmitted under that article; no further communication by or on behalf of an individual shall be received under that article after the notification of withdrawal of the declaration has been received by the Secretary-General, unless the State party has made a new declaration.

Rule 97. Transmission of Communications to the Committee. 1. The Secretary-General shall bring to the attention of the Committee, in accordance with the present rules, communications which are or appear to be submitted for consideration by the Committee under paragraph 1 of article 22 of the Convention.

2. The Secretary-General, when necessary, may request clarification from the author of a communication as to his wish to have his communication submitted to the Committee for consideration under article 22 of the Convention. In case there is still doubt as to the wish of the author, the Committee shall be seized of the communication.

3. No communication shall be received by the Committee or included in a list under rule 98 if it concerns a State which has not made the declaration provided for in article 22, paragraph 1, of the Convention.

Rule 98. List and Register of Communications. 1. The Secretary-General shall prepare lists of the communications brought to the attention of the Committee in accordance with rule 97 above, with a brief summary of their contents, and shall circulate such lists to the members of the Committee at regular intervals. The Secretary-General shall also maintain a permanent register of all such communications.

2. The full text of any communication brought to the attention of the Committee shall be made available to any member of the Committee upon his request.

Rule 99. Request for Clarification or Additional Information.

1. The Secretary-General may request clarification from the author of a communication concerning the applicability of article 22 of the Convention to his communication, in particular regarding:

(a) The name, address, age and occupation of the author and the verification of his identity;

(b) The name of the State party against which the communication is directed;

(c) The object of the communication;

(d) The provision or provisions of the Convention alleged to have been violated;

(e) The facts of the claim;

(f) Steps taken by the author to exhaust domestic remedies;

(g) The extent to which the same matter is being examined under another procedure of international investigation or settlement.

2. When requesting clarification or information, the Secretary-General shall indicate an appropriate time-limit to the author of the communication with a view to avoiding undue delays in the procedure under article 22 of the Convention.

3. The Committee may approve a questionnaire for the purpose of requesting the above-mentioned information from the author of the communication.

4. The request for clarification referred to in paragraph 1 of the present rule shall not preclude the inclusion of the communication in the list provided for in rule 98, paragraph 1.

Rule 100. Summary of the Information. For each registered communication the Secretary-General shall, as soon as possible, prepare and circulate to the members of the Committee a summary of the relevant information obtained.

Rule 101. Meetings. 1. Meetings of the Committee or its subsidiary bodies during which communications under article 22 of the Convention will be examined shall be closed.

2. Meetings during which the Committee may consider general issues, such as procedures for the application of article 22 of the Convention, may be public if the Committee so decides.

Rule 102. Issue of Communiqués concerning Closed Meetings. The Committee may issue communiqués, through the Secretary-General, for the use of the information media and the general public regarding the activities of the Committee under article 22 of the Convention.

Rule 103. Inability of a Member to Take Part in the Examination of a Communication. 1. A member shall not take part in the examination of a communication by the Committee or its subsidiary body:

(a) If he has any personal interest in the case; or

(b) If he has participated in any capacity in the making of any decision on the case covered by the communication.

2. Any question which may arise under paragraph 1 above shall be decided by the Committee without the participation of the member concerned.

Rule 104. Withdrawal of a Member. If, for any reason, a member considers that he should not take part or continue to take part in the examination of a communication, he shall inform the Chairman of his withdrawal.

B. Procedure for Determining Admissibility of Communications

Rule 105. Method of Dealing with Communications. 1. In accordance with the following rules, the Committee shall decide as soon as possible whether or not a communication is admissible under article 22 of the Convention.

2. The Committee shall, unless it decides otherwise, deal with communications in the order in which they have been placed before it by the Secretariat.

3. The Committee may, if it deems it appropriate, decide to consider jointly two or more communications.

4. The Committee may, if it deems it appropriate, decide to join the consideration of the question of admissibility of a communication to the consideration of the communication on its merits.

Rule 106. Establishment of a Working Group. 1. The Committee may, in accordance with rule 61, set up a Working Group to meet shortly before its sessions, or at any other convenient time to be decided by the Committee in consultation with the Secretary-General, for the purpose of making recommendations to the Committee regarding the fulfilment of the conditions of admissibility of communications laid down in article 22 of the Convention and assisting the Committee in any manner which the Committee may decide.

2. The Working Group shall not comprise more than five members of the Committee. The Working Group shall elect its own officers, develop its own working methods, and apply as far as possible the rules of procedure of the Committee to its meetings.

Rule 107. Conditions for Admissibility of Communications. 1. With a view to reaching a decision on the admissibility of a communication, the Committee or its Working Group shall ascertain:

(a) That the communication is not anonymous and that it emanates from an individual subject to the jurisdiction of a State party recognizing the competence of the Committee under article 22 of the Convention;

(b) That the individual claims to be a victim of a violation by the State party concerned of the provisions of the Convention. The communication should be submitted by the individual himself or by his relatives or designated representatives or by others on behalf of an alleged victim when it appears that the victim is unable to submit the communication himself, and the author of the communication justifies his acting on the victim's behalf;

(c) That the communication is not an abuse of the right to submit a communication under article 22 of the Convention;

(d) That the communication is not incompatible with the provisions of the Convention;

(e) That the same matter has not been and is not being examined under another procedure of international investigation or settlement;

(f) That the individual has exhausted all available domestic remedies. However, this shall not be the rule where the application of the remedies is unreasonably prolonged or is unlikely to bring effective relief to the person who is the victim of the violation of this Convention.

2. The Committee shall consider a communication, which is otherwise admissible, whenever the conditions laid down in article 22, paragraph 5, are met.

Rule 108. Additional Information, Clarifications and Observations. 1. The Committee or the Working Group established under rule 106 may request, through the Secretary-General, the State party concerned or the author of the communication to submit additional written information, clarifications or observations relevant to the question of admissibility of the communication.

2. Requests referred to in paragraph 1 of this rule which

are addressed to the State party shall be accompanied by the text of the communication.

3. A communication may not be declared admissible unless the State party concerned has received the text of the communication and has been given an opportunity to furnish information or observations as provided in paragraph 1 of this rule, including information relating to the exhaustion of domestic remedies.

4. The Committee or the Working Group may adopt a questionnaire for requesting such additional information or clarifications.

5. The Committee or the Working Group shall indicate a time-limit for the submission of such additional information or clarification with a view to avoiding undue delay.

6. If the time-limit is not respected by the State party concerned or the author of a communication, the Committee or the Working Group may decide to consider the admissibility of the communication in the light of available information.

7. If the State party concerned disputes the contention of the author of a communication that all available domestic remedies have been exhausted, the State party is required to give details of the effective remedies available to the alleged victim in the particular circumstances of the case and in accordance with the provisions of article 22, paragraph 5 (b), of the Convention.

8. Within such time-limit as indicated by the Committee or the Working Group, the State party or the author of a communication may be afforded an opportunity to comment on any submission received from the other party pursuant to a request made under the present rule. Nonreceipt of such comments within the established time-limit should, as a rule, not delay the consideration of the admissibility of the communication.

9. In the course of the consideration of the question of the admissibility of a communication, the Committee or the Working Group may request the State party to take steps to avoid a possible irreparable damage to the person or persons who claim to be victim(s) of the alleged violation. Such a request addressed to the State party does not imply that any decision has been reached on the question of the admissibility of the communication.

Rule 109. Inadmissible Communications. 1. Where the Committee decides that a communication is inadmissible under article 22 of the Convention, or its consideration is suspended or discontinued, the Committee shall as soon as possible transmit its decision, through the Secretary-General, to the author of the communication and, where the communication has been transmitted to a State party concerned, to that State party.

2. If the Committee has declared a communication inadmissible under article 22, paragraph 5, of the Convention, this decision may be reviewed at a later date by the Committee upon a written request by or on behalf of the individual concerned. Such written request shall contain documentary evidence to the effect that the reasons for inadmissibility referred to in article 22, paragraph 5, of the Convention no longer apply.

C. Consideration of Communications on their Merits

Rule 110. Method of Dealing with Admissible Communications. 1. When it has decided that a communication is admissible under article 22 of the Convention, the Committee shall transmit to the State party, through the Secretary-General, the text of its decision together with any submission re-

ceived from the author of the communication not already transmitted to the State party under rule 108, paragraph 2. The Committee shall also inform the author of the communication, through the Secretary-General, of its decision.

2. Within six months, the State party concerned shall submit to the Committee written explanations or statements clarifying the case under consideration and the remedy, if any, that may have been taken by it. The Committee may indicate, if it deems it necessary, the type of information it wishes to receive from the State party concerned.

3. In the course of its consideration, the Committee may inform the State party of its views on the desirability, because of urgency, of taking interim measures to avoid possible irreparable damage to the person or persons who claim to be victim(s) of the alleged violation. In doing so, the Committee shall inform the State party concerned that such expression of its views on interim measures does not prejudge its final views on the merits of the communication.

4. Any explanations or statements submitted by a State party pursuant to this rule shall be transmitted, through the Secretary-General, to the author of the communication who may submit any additional written information or observations within such time-limit as the Committee shall decide.

5. The Committee may invite the author of the communication or his representative and representatives of the State party concerned to be present at specified closed meetings of the Committee in order to provide further clarifications or to answer questions on the merits of the communication.

6. The Committee may revoke its decision that a communication is admissible in the light of any explanations or statements submitted by the State party pursuant to this rule. However, before the Committee considers revoking that decision, the explanations or statements concerned must be transmitted to the author of the communication so that he may submit additional information or observations within a time-limit set by the Committee.

Rule 111. Views of the Committee on Admissible Communications. 1. Admissible communications shall be considered by the Committee in the light of all information made available to it by or on behalf of the individual and by the State party concerned. The Committee may refer the communication to the Working Group for assistance in this task.

2. The Committee or the Working Group may at any time, in the course of the examination, obtain through the Secretary-General any documentation that may assist in the disposal of the case from United Nations bodies or the specialized agencies.

3. After consideration of an admissible communication, the Committee shall formulate its views thereon. The views of the Committee shall be forwarded, through the Secretary-General, to the author of the communication and to the State party concerned.

4. Any member of the Committee may request that a summary of his individual opinion be appended to the views of the Committee when they are forwarded to the author of the communication and to the State party concerned.

5. The State party concerned shall be invited to inform the Committee in due course of the action it takes in conformity with the Committee's views.

Rule 112. Summaries in the Committee's Annual Report and Inclusion of Texts of Final Decisions. 1. The Committee shall include in its annual report a summary of the communications examined and, where appropriate, a summary of the explanations and statements of the States parties concerned and of its own views.

2. The Committee may decide to include in its annual report the text of its views under article 22, paragraph 7, of the Convention. It may also decide to include in its annual report the text of any decision declaring a communication inadmissible under article 22 of the Convention.

COMMITTEE OF MINISTERS OF THE COUNCIL OF EUROPE.

The committee performs two important functions within the framework of the EUROPEAN CONVENTION ON HUMAN RIGHTS, which is concerned primarily with the promotion and protection of civil 1and political rights: (1) it is required to decide whether the convention has been violated when a case has not been referred to the EUROPEAN COURT OF HUMAN RIGHTS by the EUROPEAN COMMISSION ON HUMAN RIGHTS within three months from the date of the commission's report on that case; and (2) it is required to supervise the execution of the judgment of the European Court of Human Rights when that court has made a final ruling on a case. Within the framework of the EUROPEAN SOCIAL CHARTER—which is concerned primarily with the promotion and protection of economic, social, and cultural rights—the committee directs a system of supervision based on the submission of biennial reports by the contracting parties on matters covered by those provisions of the charter which they have accepted. The supervision procedure in this case consists of examining reports and comments made thereon by the governmental committee consisting of representatives of the contracting States, on the basis of which the committee makes any necessary recommendations to either contracting party. In addition, the committee examines the machinery and application of the two conventions, preparing protocols as required and promoting the dissemination of informational and educational materials about them.

The committee is composed of members of the Council of Europe, represented either at the ministerial or at the deputy level. Its sessions, which are usually held at the headquarters of the Council of Europe in Strasbourg, are scheduled as required. It is assisted by the Steering Committee for Human Rights and occasionally by committees of experts appointed to perform particular tasks.

COMMITTEE ON CRIME PREVENTION AND CONTROL.

First established as an ad hoc advisory committee of experts by the UN General Assembly on 1 December 1950 (resolution 415 [V]), the committee was authorized by the UN Economic and Social Council in 1971 (resolution 1584 [L]) to advise the Secretary-General, the COMMISSION FOR SOCIAL DEVELOPMENT, the UN COMMISSION ON HUMAN RIGHTS, and other concerned bodies in devising and formulating programs for study on an international basis and policies for international action in the field of crime prevention and treatment of offenders. The committee was directed to report to the Commission for Social Development and, as appropriate, to the Commission on Human Rights, and the Commission on Narcotic Drugs.

Since 1978 the primary task of the committee has been to prepare United Nations Congresses on the Prevention of Crime and Treatment of Offenders, as authorized by the General Assembly (resolution 32/60) by submitting appropriate proposals to the Economic and Social Council concerning, *inter alia,* the place and time of the congresses, the provisional agenda, the participants, and the preparation of the necessary documentation.

The membership of the committee, originally 10, was increased to 15 and later to 27 in order to provide a variety of expertise on social defense questions. Members are elected by the Economic and Social Council for a term of four years, with half the membership being elected every two years, from among experts who possess the necessary qualifications and professional or scientific knowledge in the field and are nominated by member States. The committee normally meets in March of alternate years for a session of approximately eight days, at the International Conference Center in Vienna.

COMMITTEE ON ECONOMIC, SOCIAL AND CULTURAL RIGHTS.

The committee was established by the UN Economic and Social Council on 28 May 1985 (resolution 1985/17) to assist it in implementing the provisions of the INTERNATIONAL COVENANT ON ECONOMIC, SOCIAL AND CULTURAL RIGHTS, which entered into force on 3 January 1976. The committee replaced the council's Sessional Working Group of Governmental Experts on the Implementation of the Covenant, which had been established on 3 May 1978 (decision 1978/10).

States parties to the covenant agree to take steps, individually and through international assistance and cooperation, especially economic and technical, to the maximum of their available resources, with a view to achieving progressively the full realization of the rights recognized in the covenant by all appropriate means, particularly the adoption of legislative measures. They also undertake to guarantee that these rights will be exercised without discrimination of any kind and to ensure the equal right of men and women to their enjoyment.

States parties also undertake to submit to the Secretary-General, for consideration by the council, reports on the measures they have adopted and the progress made in achieving the observance of the rights recognized in the covenant. The council may also arrange to receive progress reports from the specialized agencies concerned. After considering all the information available to it, the council forwards to the General Assembly reports summarizing that information and presenting recommendations of a general character. The Committee on Economic, Social and Cultural Rights assists it in performing these tasks.

Under council resolution 1985/17, the committee consists of "eighteen members who shall be experts with recognized competence in the field of human rights, serving in their personal capacity, due consideration being given to equitable geographical distribution and to the representation of different forms of social and legal systems; to this end, fifteen seats will be equally distributed among the regional groups while the additional three seats will be allocated in accordance with the increase in the total number of States parties per regional group." Members of the committee are elected by the council by secret ballot for a term of four years, from a list of persons nominated by States parties to the covenant.

The committee holds one session per year, at the United Nations office in Geneva or at the United Nations headquarters in New York. The first session of the committee was held in Geneva from 9 to 27 March 1987.

As authorized by Economic and Social Council resolution 1988/4, each session is preceded by meetings of a pre-sessional working group composed of five of its members, appointed by the chairman in consultation with members of the committee. The principal purpose of the working group is to identify in advance the questions which might most usefully be discussed with representatives of the reporting States, with the aim of improving the efficiency of the system and facilitating the task of States' representatives by providing advance notice of the principal issues which might arise in the examination of the reports. The working group allocates to each of its members initial responsibility for undertaking a detailed review of a specific number of reports and of putting before the group a preliminary list of issues. The lists of issues, revised and supplemented on the basis of observations by the other members of the group, are transmitted to the permanent missions of the States concerned.

Rules relating to Functions of the Committee. The provisional rules of procedure adopted by the committee on 21 February 1989 include (Part II) the following rules (58–69) relating to the handling of reports received from States under articles 16 and 17 of the covenant, reports received from specialized agencies under article 18, and information and documentation received from other sources (UN Doc. E/1989/22, Annex IV):

XV. Reports from States Parties Under Articles 16 and 17 of the Covenant

Rule 58. Submission of Reports. 1. In accordance with article 16 of the Covenant, the States parties shall submit to the Council for consideration by the Committee reports on the measures which they have adopted and progress made in achieving the observance of the rights recognized in the Covenant.

2. In accordance with article 17 of the Covenant and Council resolution 1988/4, the States parties shall submit their initial reports within two years of the entry into force of the Covenant for the State party concerned and thereafter periodic reports at five-year intervals.

Rule 59. Non-Submission of Reports. 1. At each session, the Secretary-General shall notify the Committee of all cases of non-submission of reports under rule 58 of these rules. In such cases the Committee may recommend to the Council to transmit to the State party concerned, through the Secretary-General, a reminder concerning the submission of such reports.

2. If, after the reminder referred to in paragraph 1 of this rule, the State party does not submit the report required under rule 58 of these rules, the Committee shall so state in the annual report which it submits to the Council.

Rule 60. Form and Content of Reports. 1. Upon approval of the Council, the Committee may inform the States parties, through the Secretary-General, of its wishes regarding the form and contents of the reports to be submitted under article 16 of the Covenant and the programme established by Council resolution 1988/4.

2. The general guidelines for reports by the States parties may, when necessary, be considered by the Committee with a view to making suggestions for their improvement.

Rule 61. Consideration of Reports. 1. The Committee shall consider the reports submitted by States parties to the Covenant in accordance with the programme established by Council resolution 1988/4.

2. The Committee shall normally consider the reports submitted by States parties under article 16 of the Covenant in the order in which they have been received by the Secretary-General.

3. Reports of the States parties scheduled for consideration by the Committee shall be made available to the members of the Committee at least six weeks before the opening of the session of the Committee. Any reports by States parties received by the Secretary-General for processing less than 12 weeks before the opening of the session shall be made available to the Committee at its session in the following year.

Rule 62. Attendance by States Parties at Examination of Reports. 1. Representatives of the reporting States are entitled to be present at the meetings of the Committee when their reports are examined. Such representatives should be able to make statements on the reports submitted by their States and reply to questions which may be put to them by the members of the Committee.

2. The Secretary-General shall notify the States parties as early as possible of the opening date and duration of the

session of the Committee at which their respective reports are scheduled for consideration. For the meetings referred to in the preceding paragraph, representatives of the States parties concerned shall be specially invited to attend.

Rule 63. Request for Additional Information. 1. When considering a report submitted by a State party under article 16 of the Covenant, the Committee shall first satisfy itself that the report provides all the information required under existing guidelines.

2. If a report of a State party to the Covenant, in the opinion of the Committee, does not contain sufficient information, the Committee may request the State concerned to furnish the additional information which is required, indicating the manner as well as the time within which the said information should be submitted.

Rule 64. Suggestions and Recommendations. The Committee shall make suggestions and recommendations of a general nature on the basis of its consideration of reports submitted by States parties and of that reports submitted by the specialized agencies in order to assist the Council to fulfil, in particular, its responsibilities under articles 21 and 22 of the Covenant. The Committee may also make suggestions for the consideration by the Council with reference to articles 19 and 23 of the Covenant.

Rule 65. General Comments. The Committee may prepare general comments based on the various articles and provisions of the Covenant with a view to assisting States parties in fulfilling their reporting obligations.

XVI. Reports from Specialized Agencies Under Article 18 of the Covenant

Rule 66. Submission of Reports. In accordance with the provisions of article 18 of the Covenant and the arrangements made by the Council thereunder, the specialized agencies are called upon to submit reports on the progress made in achieving the observance of the provisions of the Covenant falling within the scope of their activities. These reports may include particulars of decisions and recommendations on such implementation adopted by their competent organs.

Rule 67. Consideration of Reports. The Committee is entrusted with the task of considering the reports of the specialized agencies, submitted to the Council in accordance with article 18 of the Covenant and the programme established under Council resolution 1988 (LX).

Rule 68. Participation of Specialized Agencies. The specialized agencies concerned shall be invited to designate representatives to participate at the meetings of the Committee. Such representatives may make general statements on matters falling within the scope of the activities of their respective organizations at the end of the discussion by the Committee of the report of each State party to the Covenant. The representatives of the States parties presenting reports to the Committee shall be free to respond to, or take into account, the statements made by the specialized agencies.

XVII. Other Sources of Information

Rule 69. Submission of Information, Documentation and Written Statements. 1. Non-governmental organizations in consultative status with the Council may submit to the Committee written statements that might contribute to full and universal recognition and realization of the rights contained in the Covenant.

2. The Committee may recommend to the Council to invite United Nations bodies concerned and regional intergovernmental organizations to submit to it information, documentation and written statements, as appropriate, relevant to its activities under the Covenant.

COMMITTEE ON NON-GOVERNMENTAL ORGANIZATIONS. The Economic and Social Council, as authorized by article 71 of the UNITED NATIONS CHARTER, has made arrangements for consultation with non-governmental organizations (NGOs) which are concerned with matters falling within its competence (council resolution 1296 [XLIV]). Under these arrangements the council's Committee on Non-Governmental Organizations divides such organizations into three groups: Category I, which is made of NGOs having a basic interest in most of the council's activities; Category II, which is made up of those having a special competence but are concerned with only a few of the council's activities; and the Roster, which contains the names of NGOs that can make occasional and useful contributions to the council's work.

All the organizations in "consultative status" may send observers to public meetings of the council and its subsidiary bodies. They can submit written statements for circulation and present their views orally. As regards human rights, more than 100 NGOs regularly attend and participate in meetings of the COMMISSION ON HUMAN RIGHTS, the SUB-COMMISSION ON PREVENTION OF DISCRIMINATION AND PROTECTION OF MINORITIES, and the COMMISSION ON THE STATUS OF WOMEN. The council, on 26 May 1987, invited all such organizations to submit to it written statements which might contribute to full and universal recognition and realization of the rights set out in the INTERNATIONAL COVENANT ON ECONOMIC, SOCIAL AND CULTURAL RIGHTS and requested the Secretary-General to make those statements available to the COMMITTEE ON ECONOMIC, SOCIAL AND CULTURAL RIGHTS.

In studying or dealing with human rights problems, UN organs often call upon NGOS in consultative status to supply information concerning situations which exist in various parts of the world. In addition, NGOS also supply information concerning allegations of violations of human rights to bodies authorized to supervise the application of various international instruments in the field.

As at 1 January 1990, the Committee on Non-Governmental Organizations consisted of representatives of the governments of 20 member States, as follows: Bulgaria, Burundi, Colombia, Costa Rica, Cuba, Cyprus, France, Greece, Kenya, Malawi, Nicaragua, Oman, Pakistan, Rwanda, Sao Tome and Principe, Sri Lanka, Sweden, Union of Social Soviet Republics, and the United States of America. Members were elected for a four-year term beginning on 1 January 1987.

COMMITTEE ON THE ELIMINATION OF DIS-CRIMINATION AGAINST WOMEN. The committee was established in accordance with article 17 of the CONVENTION ON THE ELIMINATION OF ALL FORMS OF DIS-CRIMINATION AGAINST WOMEN, adopted by the UN General Assembly on 18 December 1979 (resolution 34/180). States parties to the convention agree to pursue, by all appropriate means and without delay, a policy of elimination of discrimination against women, and to this end undertake:

(a) to embody the principle of equality of men and women in their national constitutions or other appropriate legislation if not yet incorporated therein and to ensure, through law and other appropriate means, the practical realization of this principle;

(b) to adopt appropriate legislative and other measures, including sanctions where appropriate, prohibiting all discrimination against women;

(c) to establish legal protection of the rights of women on an equal basis with men and to ensure through competent national tribunals and other public institutions the effective protection of women against any act of discrimination;

(d) to refrain from engaging in any or practice of discrimination against women and to ensure that public authorities and institutions shall act in conformity with this obligation;

(e) to take all appropriate measures to eliminate discrimination against women by any person, organization or enterprise;

(f) to take all appropriate measures, including legislation, to modify or abolish existing laws, regulations, customs and practices which constitute discrimination against women; and

(g) to repeal all national penal provisions which constitute discrimination against women.

The Committee on the Elimination of Discrimination against Women was established at a meeting of States parties to the convention. The committee consists of 23 members. They are nominated by States parties to the convention and elected at a meeting of those States, consideration being given to equitable geographical representation and to representation of different forms of civilization and the world's principal legal systems. The term of office is four years. The committee meets annually for a period of two weeks, normally at the Vienna International Centre or at United Nations headquarters in New York.

The responsibilities of the committee, set out in articles 18 to 22 of the convention, may be summarized as follows:

Consideration of Reports of States Parties. Under article 18 (1) of the convention, States parties undertake to submit to the secretary-general, for consideration by the committee, reports on the legislative, judicial, administrative, or other measures which they have adopted to give effect to the provisions of the convention and on the progress made in this respect. Under article 20, the committee may consider these reports to monitor the progress made in the implementation of the convention.

Making of Suggestions and General Recommendations. Under article 21, the committee may make suggestions and general recommendations based on its examination of the reports and information received from States.

The committee has no permanent subsidiary bodies but has set up standing working groups to expedite its work. At the 1988 session, two such working groups were formed: Working Group I to consider and suggest ways and means of expediting the work of the committee and Working Group II to consider ways and means of implementing article 21 of the convention, mentioned above.

Members of the committee are elected at meetings of the States parties convened by the UN secretary-general. The election is by secret ballot from a list of persons nominated by the State parties. Each State party may nominate one person from among its own nationals.

Rules relating to the Functions of the Committee. The committee's Rules of Procedure, adopted on 22 October 1982, the closing date of its first session and reproduced in the report of that session (UN Doc. A/35/45, Annex III), include the following provisions relating to the consideration of the periodic reports that the States parties are required to submit under article 18 of the convention:

Rule 46. Form of Reports. 1. The Committee may formulate suggestions and general recommendations as to the form, contents and dates of the periodic reports that the States parties are required to submit under article 18 of the Convention.

2. Such suggestions and general recommendations shall take into account the integrated reporting system on the status of women endorsed by the Economic and Social Council in its resolution 1980/38.

Rule 47. Non-receipt of Reports. 1. At each session the Secretary-General shall notify the Committee of the non-receipt of any report required from a State party under article 18 of the Convention.

2. The Committee may, through the Secretary-General, transmit to the States concerned reminders of any overdue reports.

3. If even after a reminder has been transmitted pursuant to paragraph 2 a State concerned does not submit the report required under the Convention, the Committee shall include a reference to this effect in its annual report to the General Assembly.

Rule 48. Suggestions and General Recommendations. 1. In

case the Committee finds that substantial improvement of its work is likely to be brought about by additional information on the part of a State party, concerning its report, the Committee may invite the State concerned to provide it with such additional information.

2. Suggestions and general recommendations made by the Committee based on the examination of the reports received from States parties under article 18 of the Convention shall be communicated by the Committee, through the Secretary-General, to the States parties for their comments.

3. The Committee may, where necessary, indicate a time-limit within which comments are to be received.

Rule 49. Attendance by States Parties. 1. Representatives of States parties shall be present at meetings of the Committee when the State's report is being examined and shall participate in discussions and answer questions concerning the said report.

2. The Committee shall, through the Secretary-General, notify the States parties at least six weeks in advance of the opening date, duration and place of the session at which their respective reports will be examined.

*Rule 50. Working Methods for Examining Reports.*The Committee may elaborate working methods to assist it in performing most efficiently its task of examining the reports of States parties and to consider the progress made since the entry into force of the Convention for them and since the submission of any previous reports.

At its 1988 session, the committee adopted four general recommendations. The first proposed that States parties to the convention make greater use of temporary special measures—such as positive action, preferential treatment, or quota systems to advance women's integration into education, the economy, politics, and employment. The second recommended that States parties to the convention establish and/or strengthen effective national machinery, institutions, and procedures to formulate and monitor the implementation of measures to eliminate discrimination against women. The third called for adequate resources and services to be made available to the committee to enable it to perform its functions under the convention. And the fourth proposed that States parties to the convention should ensure to women, on equal terms with men and without any discrimination, opportunities to represent their governments at the international level and to participate in the work of international organizations.

At its 1989 session, held at the United Nations office in Vienna from 20 February to 3 March 1989, the committee considered initial reports submitted by the governments of Belgium, Equatorial Guinea, Finland, Gabon, Ireland, and Nicaragua; and second periodic reports submitted by the governments of the Byelorussian S.S.R., the German Democratic Republic, and the Union of Soviet Socialist Republics. In addition, it adopted a number of general recommendations and suggestions on ways and means of implementing article 21 of the convention.

The recommendations and suggestions set out by the committee in its report to the General Assembly (UN Doc. A/44/38, chap. V) deal with questions such as the handling of statistical data concerning the situation of women, observance of the tenth anniversary of the adoption of the Convention on the Elimination of all Forms of Discrimination Against Women, the provision of technical advisory services to assist States on their request in fulfilling their reporting obligations under article 18 of the convention, the inclusion in the reports of States parties to the convention of information about measures taken to protect women against violence, and the adoption of measures to ensure the application of the principle of equal renumeration for work of equal value. The committee, in addition, suggested that the secretary-general should strengthen the UN secretariat services available to it in order to ensure its effective operation.

SEE ALSO *Advancement of Women Branch; Commission on the Status of Women; Convention on the Elimination of all Forms of Discrimination against Women; Declaration on the Elimination of Discrimination against Women; Women in the UN Secretariat.*

COMMITTEE ON THE ELIMINATION OF RACIAL DISCRIMINATION. The committee was established in accordance with articles 8 and 9 of the INTERNATIONAL CONVENTION ON THE ELIMINATION OF ALL FORMS OF RACIAL DISCRIMINATION, adopted by the UN General Assembly on 21 December 1965 (resolution 2106 A [XX]). The convention entered into force on 4 January 1969.

States parties to the convention undertake to pursue without delay a policy of eliminating racial discrimination in all its forms and of promoting understanding among races. Further, they undertake to guarantee equality before the law in the enjoyment of human rights, particularly in respect of the right of everyone to equal treatment before all organs administering justice; the right to security of persons and protection by the State against violence or bodily harm; and all the political, civil, economic, social and cultural rights that belong to every person. Racial discrimination is defined in the convention as "any distinction, exclusion, restriction or preference based on race, colour, descent, or national or ethnic origin which has the purpose or effect of nullifying or impairing the recognition, enjoyment or exercise, on an equal footing, of human rights and fundamental freedoms in the political, economic, social, cultural or any other field of public life."

The responsibilities of the Committee on the Elimination of Racial Discrimination, set out in articles 9 and 11–16 of the convention, include the following:

1. Consideration of Reports of States. Under Article 9, paragraph 1, States which have ratified or acceded to the convention undertake to submit to the Secretary-General for consideration by the committee reports on the legislative, judicial, administrative, or other measures that they have adopted and that give effect to the provisions of the convention, including its anti-discrimination provisions. The committee is empowered to examine these reports, to request further information from the States, to make suggestions and general recommendations based on consideration of the reports and information, and to report on those activities to the UN General Assembly.

2. Consideration of Complaints of One State against Another. Under Article 11, if a State party to the convention considers that another State party is not giving effect to the convention's provisions, it may bring the matter to the attention of the committee. With respect to such complaints, the committee is authorized (a) to transmit the communication to the concerned state; (b) to "deal with" the matter, after it has ascertained that all available domestic remedies have been invoked and exhausted, in conformity with the generally recognized principles of international law; (c) to appoint an ad hoc conciliation commission to attempt to find an amicable solution; (d) to communicate the report of the ad hoc commission to each of the disputing parties so that each may indicate whether or not it accepts the commission's recommendations; and (e) to communicate that report, together with the declarations of the concerned parties, to the other States parties to the convention and to report on the matter to the General Assembly.

3. Consideration of Communications from Individuals and Groups. Under article 14, and subject to the conditions and requirements set out there, the committee may receive and consider communications from individuals or groups of individuals, within its jurisdiction claiming to be victims of a violation by a State party to the convention of any of the rights set forth therein. With regard to such communications, the committee is authorized (a) to bring confidentially to the attention of the State alleged to be violating any provision of the convention and communication referred to it, but without revealing the identity of the individual or groups concerned without his or their express consent; (b) to consider the communication in light of all information made available to it by the concerned State and the petitioner; (c) to forward its suggestions and recommendations, if any, to the concerned State and the petitioner; and (d) to report on the matter to the General Assembly.

4. Consideration of Information relating to Trust and Non-Self-Governing Territories. Regarding racial discrimination in trust and non-self-governing territories, the committee is authorized, under article 15, (a) to receive from the competent UN bodies reports concerning measures taken by the administering powers within those territories and from the Secretary-General all relevant information available to him regarding those territories; (b) to express opinions and make recommendations addressed to the concerned UN bodies on the petitions and reports transmitted to it; and (c) to report on the matter to the General Assembly.

The committee submits an annual report to the General Assembly covering the matters mentioned above. If the committee has dealt with a complaint by one state against another, in accordance with articles 11–13 of the convention, there is no provision requiring that this be included in the annual report; instead, article 13, para. 3, provides that the chairman of the committee shall communicate the report of the ad hoc conciliation commission to the other States parties to the convention.

In its annual report to the General Assembly covering its activities in 1989, the committee reviewed the status of submission of reports by States parties to the convention as follows (UN Doc. A/44/18, chap. III [A], para. 27–30, 32):

From the establishment of the Committee on the Elimination of Racial Discrimination until the closing date of its thirty-seventh session (1 September 1989), a total of 979 reports under article 9, paragraph 1, of the Convention have been due from States parties as follows: 125 initial reports, 126 second periodic reports, 127 third periodic reports, 115 fourth periodic reports, 107 fifth periodic reports, 100 sixth periodic reports, 92 seventh periodic reports, 81 eighth periodic reports, 65 ninth periodic reports and 41 tenth periodic reports.

By the end of the thirty-seventh session, a total of 784 reports had been received by the Committee as follows: 121 initial reports, 111 second periodic reports, 106 third periodic reports, 98 fourth periodic reports, 88 fifth periodic reports, 79 sixth periodic reports, 69 seventh periodic reports, 55 eighth periodic reports, 38 ninth periodic reports and 19 tenth periodic reports.

In addition, 72 supplementary reports containing additional information were received from the States parties, submitted either on the initiative of the States parties concerned or at the request of the Committee following its examination of their respective initial or periodic reports under the Convention.

During the period under review, i.e., between the closing dates of the Committee's thirty-sixth and thirty-seventh sessions (12 August 1988 and 1 September 1989), 27 reports were received by the Committee: 1 initial report, 1 second periodic report, 1 third periodic report, 1 fourth periodic report, 2 sixth periodic reports, 3 seventh periodic reports, 3 eighth periodic reports, 6 ninth periodic reports and 9 tenth periodic reports. One supplementary report was also received during the period under review. . . .

As the information in table 1 shows, only 4 of the 27 reports received during the period under review were submitted on time or before the deadline provided for under article 9, paragraph 1, of the Convention. The rest were submitted after a delay, ranging from a few days to over four years.

As regards its consideration of communications under article 14 of the convention, the committee reported to the General Assembly (*Ibid.*, chap. IV, para. 444–449):

Under article 14 of the International Convention on the Elimination of All Forms of Racial Discrimination, individuals or groups of individuals who claim that any of their rights enumerated in the Convention have been violated by a State party and who have exhausted all available domestic remedies may submit written communications to the Committee on the Elimination of Racial Discrimination for consideration. Twelve of the 128 States that have ratified or acceded to the Convention have declared that they recognize the competence of the Committee to receive and consider communications under article 14 of the Convention. These States are Costa Rica, Denmark, Ecuador, France, Iceland, Italy, the Netherlands, Norway, Peru, Senegal, Sweden and Uruguay. No communication can be received by the Committee if it concerns a State party to the Convention which has not recognized the competence of the Committee to receive and consider communications.

Consideration of communications under article 14 of the Convention takes place in closed meetings (rule 88 of the Committee's rules of procedure). All documents pertaining to the work of the Committee under article 14 (submissions from the parties and other working documents of the Committee) are confidential.

In carrying out its work under article 14 of the Convention, the Committee may be assisted by a working group of not more than five of its members, which submits recommendations to the Committee regarding the fulfilment of the conditions of admissibility of communications (rule 87) or on the action to be taken in respect of communications which have been declared admissible (rule 95, para. 1).

The Committee began its work under article 14 of the Convention at its thirtieth session in 1984. It considered issues under article 14 at its thirty-first and thirty-second sessions in 1985, its thirty-fourth session in 1987, its thirty-sixth session in 1988, and its thirty-seventh session in 1989. At its thirty-sixth session, on 10 August 1988, the Committee adopted its opinion on communication No. 1/1984 (Yilmaz-Dogan v. The Netherlands).

At its thirty-seventh session, the Committee had before it communication No. 2/1989 (D. T. D. v. France). It decided to transmit the communication to the State party, pursuant to rule 92 of its rules of procedure, and to request information and observations relevant to the question of the admissibility of the communication.

Under article 14, paragraph 8, of the Convention, the Committee shall include in its annual report a summary of the communications considered by it and of the explanations and statements of the States parties concerned, together with the Committee's own suggestions and recommendations thereon. This reporting stage has not been reached yet in respect of communication No. 2/1989.

As regards its consideration of copies of petitions, copies of reports and other information relating to trust and non-self-governing territories and to all other territories to which General Assembly resolution 1514 (XV) on decolonization applies, the committee reported that, at its 1989 session, it had established three working groups to examine such documentation and had considered the reports of those working groups and that it had, as a result, decided to draw the attention of the General Assembly and the relevant United Nations bodies to the following observations:

The Committee has examined the information contained in the documents and relating to Trust and Non-Self-Governing Territories and to all other Territories to which General Assembly resolution 1514 (XV) applies, and transmitted to it by the Special Committee on the Situation with regard to the Implementation of the Declaration on the Granting of Independence to Colonial Countries and Peoples in accordance with the provisions of article 15, paragraph 2, of the International Convention on the Elimination of All Forms of Racial Discrimination.

The Committee once again finds it impossible to fulfil its functions under article 15 paragraph 2 (a) of the Convention, due to the total absence of any copies of petitions as provided therein. The Committee has studied the material furnished under article 15, paragraph 2 (b) and found that there was no valid information concerning legislative, judicial, administrative or other measures directly related to the principles and objectives of the Convention and, therefore, is unable to express any opinion and make any recommendation concerning the above-mentioned territories. The Committee therefore reiterates its request that it be furnished with the material expressly referred to in article 15 of the Convention to enable it to fulfill its functions.

Under article 8 of the convention, the committee is composed of "eighteen experts of high moral standing and acknowledged impartiality elected by States Parties from among their nationals, who shall serve in their personal capacity, consideration being given to equitable geographical distribution and to the representation of different forms of civilization as well as of the principal legal systems." The term of office is five years.

The committee normally holds two sessions each year, of from two to three weeks' duration, one at New York and the other at Geneva. However, due to non-payment of contributions by a number of States parties, it was unable to hold its spring session in 1989 and held only one extended session of four weeks' duration that year. That session was held at the United Nations office in Geneva from 7 August to 1 September 1989.

Rules relating to the Functions of the Committee. The committee's rules of procedure (UN Doc. CERD/C/35/Rev. 2) set out, in Part Two, rules (63–97) relating to the functions of the committee, which read in part as follows:

XV. Reports and Information from States Parties under Article 9 of the Convention

Rule 63. Form and Contents of Reports. The Committee may, through the Secretary-General, inform the States parties of its wishes regarding the form and contents of the periodic reports required to be submitted under article 9 of the Convention.

Rule 64. Attendance by States Parties at Examination of Reports. The Committee shall, through the Secretary-General, notify the States parties (as early as possible) of the opening date, duration and place of the session at which their respective reports will be examined. Representatives of the States parties may be present at the meetings of the Committee when their reports are examined. The Committee may also inform a State party from which it decides to seek further information that it may authorize its representative to be present at a specified meeting. Such a representative should be able to answer questions which may be put to him by the Committee and make statements on reports already submitted by his State, and may also submit additional information from his State.

Rule 65. Request for Additional Information. If the Committee decides to request an additional report or further information from a State party under the provisions of article 9, paragraph 1, of the Convention, it may indicate the manner as well as the time within which such additional report or further information shall be supplied and shall transmit its decision to the Secretary-General for communication, within two weeks, to the State party concerned.

Rule 66. Non-receipt of Reports. 1. At each session, the Secretary-General shall notify the Committee of all cases of non-receipt of reports or additional information, as the case may be, provided for under article 9 of the Convention. The Committee, in such cases, may transmit to the State party concerned, through the Secretary-General, a reminder concerning the submission of the report or additional information.

2. If even after the reminder, referred to in paragraph 1 of this rule, the State party does not submit the report or additional information required under article 9 of the Convention, the Committee shall include a reference to this effect in its annual report to the General Assembly.

Rule 67. Suggestions and General Recommendations. 1. When considering a report submitted by a State party under article 9, the Committee shall first determine whether the report provides the information referred to in the relevant communications of the Committee.

2. If a report of the State party to the Convention, in the opinion of the Committee, does not contain sufficient information, the Committee may request that State to furnish additional information.

3. If, on the basis of its examination of the reports and information supplied by the State party, the Committee determines that some of the obligations of that State under the Convention have not been discharged, it may make suggestions and general recommendations in accordance with article 9, paragraph 2, of the Convention.

Rule 68. Transmission of Suggestions and General Recommendations. 1. Suggestions and general recommendations made by the Committee based on the examination of the reports and information received from States parties under article 9, paragraph 2, of the Convention shall be communicated by the Committee through the Secretary-General to the State parties for their comments.

2. The Committee may, where necessary, indicate a time-limit within which comments from States parties are to be received.

3. Suggestions and general recommendations of the Committee, referred to in paragraph 1, shall be reported to the General Assembly, together with comments, if any, from States parties.

XVI. Communications from States Parties under Article 11 of the Convention

Rule 69. Method of Dealing with Communications from States Parties. 1. When a matter is brought to the attention of the Committee by a State party in accordance with article 11, paragraph 1, of the Convention, the Committee shall examine it at a private meeting and shall then transmit it to the State party concerned through the Secretary-General. The Committee in examining the communications shall not consider its substance. Any action at this stage by the Committee in respect of the communication shall in no way be construed as an expression of its views on the substance of the communication.

2. If the Committee is not in session, the Chairman shall bring the matter to the attention of its members by transmitting copies of the communication and requesting their consent to transmit such communication on behalf of the Committee, to the State party concerned in compliance with article 11, paragraph 1. The Chairman shall also specify a time-limit of three weeks for their replies.

3. Upon receipt of the consent of the majority of the members, or, if within the specified time-limit no replies are received, the Chairman shall transmit the communication to the State party concerned, through the Secretary-General, without delay.

4. In the event of any replies being received which represent the views of the majority of the Committee, the Chairman, while acting in accordance with such replies, shall bear in mind the requirement of urgency in transmitting the communication to the State party concerned on behalf of the Committee.

5. The Committee, or the Chairman on behalf of the Committee, shall remind the receiving State that the time-limit for submission of its written explanations or statement under the Convention is three months.

6. When the Committee receives the explanations or statements of the receiving State, the procedure laid down above shall be followed with respect to the transmission of those explanations or statements to the State party submitting the initial communication.

Rule 70. Request for Information. The Committee may call upon the States parties concerned to supply information relevant to the application of article 11 of the Convention. The Committee may indicate the manner as well as the time within which such information shall be supplied.

Rule 71. Notification to the States Parties Concerned. If any matter is submitted for consideration by the Committee under paragraph 2 of article 11 of the Convention, the Chairman, through the Secretary-General, shall inform the States parties concerned of the forthcoming consideration of this matter not later than 30 days in advance of the first meeting of the Committee, in the case of a regular session, and at least 18 days in advance of the first meeting of the Committee, in the case of a special session.

C

XVII. Establishment and Functions of the *Ad Hoc* Conciliation Commission under Articles 12 and 13 of the Convention

Rule 72. Consultations on the Composition of the Commission. After the Committee has obtained and collated all the information it thinks necessary as regards a dispute that has arisen under article 11, paragraph 2, of the Convention, the Chairman shall notify the States parties to the dispute and undertake consultations with them concerning the composition of the *Ad Hoc* Conciliation Commission (hereinafter referred to as "the Commission"), in accordance with article 12 of the Convention.

Rule 73. Appointment of Members of the Commission. Upon receiving the unanimous consent of the States parties to the dispute regarding the composition of the Commission, the Chairman shall proceed to the appointment of the members of the Commission and shall inform the States parties to the dispute of the composition of the Commission.

Rule 74. 1. If within three months of the Chairman's notification as provided in rule 72 above, the States parties to the dispute fail to reach agreement on all or part of the composition of the Commission, the Chairman shall then bring the situation to the attention of the Committee which shall proceed according to article 12, paragraph 1 (b), of the Convention at its next session.

2. Upon the completion of the election, the Chairman shall inform the States parties to the dispute of the composition of the Commission.

Rule 75. Solemn Declaration by Members of the Commission. Upon assuming his duties, each member of the Commission shall make the following solemn declaration at the first meeting of the Commission: "I solemnly declare that I will perform my duties and exercise my powers as a member of the *Ad Hoc* Conciliation Commission honourably, faithfully, impartially and conscientiously."

Rule 76. Filling of Vacancies in the Commission. Whenever a vacancy arises in the Commission, the Chairman of the Committee shall fill the vacancy as soon as possible in accordance with procedures laid down in rules 72 to 74. He shall proceed with filling such vacancy upon receipt of a report from the Commission or upon a notification by the Secretary-General.

Rule 77. Transmission of Information to Members of the Commission. The information obtained and collated by the Committee shall be made available by its Chairman, through the Secretary-General, to the members of the Commission at the time of notifying the members of the Commission of the date of the first meeting of the Commission.

Rule 78. Report of the Commission. 1. The Chairman of the Committee shall communicate the report of the Commission referred to in article 13 of the Convention as soon as possible after its receipt to each of the States parties to the dispute and to the members of the Committee.

2. The States parties to the dispute shall, within three months after the receipt of the Commission's report, inform the Chairman of the Committee whether or not they accept the recommendations contained in the report of the Commission. The Chairman shall transmit the information received from the States parties to the dispute to the members of the Committee.

3. After the expiry of the time-limit provided for in the preceding paragraph, the Chairman of the Committee shall communicate the report of the Commission and any declaration of States parties concerned to the other states parties to the Convention.

Rule 79. Keeping Members of the Committee Informed. The Chairman of the Committee shall keep the members of the Committee informed of his actions under rules 73 to 78.

XVIII. Procedure for Considering Communications from Individuals or Groups of Individuals under Article 14 of the Convention
A. General provisions

Rule 80. Competence of the Committee. 1. The Committee shall be competent to receive and consider communications and exercise the functions provided for in article 14 of the Convention only when at least 10 States parties are bound by declarations recognizing the competence of the Committee in conformity with paragraph 1 thereof.

2. The Secretary-General shall transmit to the other States parties copies of the declarations deposited with him by States parties recognizing the competence of the Committee.

3. Consideration of communications pending before the Committee shall not be affected by the withdrawal of a declaration made under article 14 of the Convention.

4. The Secretary-General shall inform the other States parties of the name, composition and functions of any national legal body which has been established or indicated by a State party, in conformity with paragraph 3 of article 14.

Rule 81. National Bodies. The Secretary-General shall keep the Committee informed of the name, composition and functions of any national legal body established or indicated under paragraph 2 of article 14 as competent to receive and consider petitions from individuals or groups of individuals claiming to be victims of a violation of any of the rights set forth in the Convention.

Rule 82. Certified Copies of Registers of Petitions. 1. The Secretary-General shall keep the Committee informed of the contents of all certified copies of the register of petitions filed with him in accordance with paragraph 4 of article 14.

2. The Secretary-General may request clarifications from the States parties concerning the certified copies of the registers of petitions emanating from the national legal bodies responsible for such registers.

3. The contents of the certified copies of the registers of petitions transmitted to the Secretary-General shall not be publicly disclosed.

Rule 83. Record of Communications Received by the Secretary-General. 1. The Secretary-General shall keep a record of all communications which are or appear to be submitted to the Committee by individuals or groups of individuals claiming to be victims of a violation of any of the rights set forth in the Convention and who are subject to the jurisdiction of a State party bound by a declaration under article 14.

2. The Secretary-General may, if he deems it necessary, request clarification of the author of a communication as to his wish to have his communication submitted to the Committee for consideration under article 14. In case of doubt as to the wish of the author, the Committee shall be seized of the communication.

3. No communication shall be received by the Committee or included in a list under rule 85 below if it concerns a State party which has not made a declaration as provided for in paragraph 1 of article 14.

Rule 84. Information to be Contained in a Communication. 1. The Secretary-General may request clarification from the author of a communication concerning the applicability of article 14 to his communication, in particular:

(a) The name, address, age and occupation of the author and the verification of his identity;

(b) The name(s) of the State party or States parties against which the communication is directed;

(c) The object of the communication;

(d) The provision or provisions of the Convention alleged to have been violated;

(e) The facts of the claim;

(f) Steps taken by the author to exhaust domestic remedies, including pertinent documents;

(g) The extent to which the same matter is being examined under another procedure of international investigation or settlement.

2. When requesting clarification or information, the Secretary-General shall indicate an appropriate time-limit to the author of the communication with a view to avoiding undue delays in the procedure.

3. The Committee may approve a questionnaire for the purpose of requesting the above-mentioned information from the author of the communication.

4. The request for clarification referred to in paragraph 1 of the present rule shall not preclude the inclusion of the communication in the list provided for in rule 85, paragraph 1, below.

5. The Secretary-General shall inform the author of a communication of the procedure that will be followed and that the text of his communication shall be transmitted confidentially to the State party concerned in accordance with paragraphs 6 (a) of article 14.

Rule 85. Transmission of Communications to the Committee. 1. The Secretary-General shall summarize each communication thus received and shall place the summaries, individually or in composite lists of communications, before the Committee at its next regular session, together with the relevant certified copies of the registers of petitions kept by the national legal body of the country concerned and filed with the Secretary-General in compliance with paragraph 4 of article 14.

2. The Secretary-General shall draw the attention of the Committee to those cases for which certified copies of the registers of petitions have not been received.

3. The contents of replies to requests for clarification and relevant subsequent submissions from either the author of the communication or the State party concerned shall be placed before the Committee in a suitable form.

4. An original case file shall be kept for each summarized communication. The full text of any communication brought to the attention of the Committee shall be made available to any member of the Committee upon request.

B. Procedure for Determining Admissibility of Communications

Rule 86. Method of Dealing with Communications. 1. In accordance with the following rules, the Committee shall decide as soon as possible whether or not a communication is admissible in conformity with article 14 of the Convention.

2. The Committee shall, unless it decides otherwise, deal with communications in the order in which they have been placed before it by the Secretariat. The Committee may, if it deems appropriate, decide to consider jointly two or more communications.

Rule 87. Establishment of a Working Group. 1. The Committee may, in accordance with rule 61, set up a Working Group to meet shortly before its sessions, or at any other convenient time to be decided by the Committee in consultation with the Secretary-General, for the purpose of making recommendations to the Committee regarding the fulfilment of the conditions of admissibility of communications laid down in article 14 of the Convention and assisting the Committee in any manner which the Committee may decide.

2. The Working Group shall not comprise more than five members of the Committee. The Working Group shall elect its own officers, develop its own working methods, and apply as far as possible the rules of procedure of the Committee to its meetings.

Rule 88. Meetings. Meetings of the Committee or its Working Group during which communications under article 14 of the Convention will be examined shall be closed. Meetings during which the Committee may consider general issues such as procedures for the application of article 14 may be public if the Committee so decides.

Rule 89. Inability of a Member to Take Part in the Examination of a Communication. 1. A member of the Committee shall not take part in the examination of a communication by the Committee or its Working Group:

(a) If he has any personal interest in the case; or

(b) If he has participated in any capacity in the making of any decision on the case covered by the communication.

2. Any question which may arise under paragraph 1 above shall be decided by the Committee without the participation of the member concerned.

Rule 90. Withdrawal of a Member. If, for any reason, a member considers that he should not take part or continue to take part in the examination of a communication, he shall inform the Chairman of his withdrawal.

Rule 91. Conditions for Admissibility of Communications. With a view to reaching a decision on the admissibility of a communication, the Committee or its Working Group shall ascertain:

(a) That the communication is not anonymous and that it emanates from an individual or group of individuals subject to the jurisdiction of a State party recognizing the competence of the Committee under article 14 of the Convention;

(b) That the individual claims to be a victim of a violation by the State party concerned of any of the rights set forth in the Convention. As a general rule, the communication should be submitted by the individual himself or by his relatives or designated representatives; the Committee may, however, in exceptional cases accept to consider a communication submitted by others on behalf of an alleged victim when it appears that the victim is unable to submit the communication himself, and the author of the communication justifies his acting on the victim's behalf;

(c) That the communication is compatible with the provisions of the Convention;

(d) That the communication is not an abuse of the right to submit a communication in conformity with article 14;

(e) That the individual has exhausted all available domestic remedies, including, when applicable, those mentioned in paragraph 2 of article 14. However, this shall not be the rule where the application of the remedies is unreasonably prolonged;

(f) That the communication is, except in the case of duly verified exceptional circumstances, submitted within six months after all available domestic remedies have been exhausted, including, when applicable, those indicated in paragraph 2 of article 14.

Rule 92. Additional Information, Classifications and Observations. 1. The Committee or the Working Group established under rule 87 may request, through the Secretary-General, the State party concerned or the author of the communication to submit additional written information or clarifications relevant to the question of admissibility of the communication.

2. Such requests shall contain a statement to the effect that the request does not imply that a decision has been reached on the question of admissibility of the communication by the Committee.

3. A communication may not be declared admissible unless the State party concerned has received the text of the communication and has been given an opportunity to furnish information or observations as provided in paragraph 1 of this rule, including information relating to the exhaustion of domestic remedies.

4. The Committee or the Working Group may adopt a questionnaire for requesting such additional information or clarifications.

5. The Committee or the Working Group shall indicate a deadline for the submission of such additional information or clarification.

6. If the deadline is not kept by the State party concerned or the author of a communication, the Committee or the Working Group may decide to consider the admissibility of the communication in the light of available information.

7. If the State party concerned disputes the contention of the author of a communication that all available domestic remedies have been exhausted, the State party is required to give details of the effective remedies available to the alleged victim in the particular circumstances of the case.

Rule 93. Inadmissible Communications. 1. When the Committee decides that a communication is inadmissible, or its consideration is suspended or discontinued, the Committee shall transmit its decisions as soon as possible, through the Secretary-General, to the petitioner and to the State party concerned.

2. A decision taken by the Committee, in conformity with paragraph 7 (a) of article 14, that a communication is inadmissible, may be reviewed at a later date by the Committee upon a written request by the petitioner concerned. Such written request shall contain documentary evidence to the effect that the reasons for inadmissibility referred to in paragraph 7 (a) of article 14 are no longer applicable.

C. Consideration of Communications on their Merits

Rule 94. Method of Dealing with Admissible Communications. 1. After it has been decided that a communication is admissible, in conformity with article 14, the Committee shall transmit, confidentially, through the Secretary-General, the text of the communication and other relevant information to the State party concerned without revealing the identity of the individual unless he has given his express consent. The Committee shall also inform, through the Secretary-General, the petitioner of the communication of its decision.

2. The State party concerned shall submit within three months to the Committee written explanations or statements clarifying the case under consideration and the remedy, if any, that may have been taken by that State party. The Committee may indicate, if it deems it necessary, the type of information it wishes to receive from the State party concerned.

3. In the course of its consideration, the Committee may inform the State party of its views on the desirability, because of urgency, of taking interim measures to avoid possible irreparable damage to the person or persons who claim to be victim(s) of the alleged violation. In doing so, the Committee shall inform the State party concerned that such expression of its views on interim measures does not prejudice either its final opinion on the merits of the communication or its eventual suggestions and recommendations.

4. Any explanations or statements submitted by a State party pursuant to this rule may be transmitted, through the Secretary-General, to the petitioner of the communication who may submit any additional written information or observations within such time-limit as the Committee shall decide.

5. The Committee may invite the presence of the petitioner or his representative and the presence of representatives of the State party concerned in order to provide additional information or to answer questions on the merits of the communication.

6. The Committee may revoke its decision that a communication is admissible in the light of any explanation or statements submitted by the State party. However, before the Committee considers revoking that decision, the explanations or statements concerned must be transmitted to the petitioner so that he may submit additional information or observations within the time-limit set by the Committee.

Rule 95. Opinion of the Committee on Admissible Communications and the Committee's Suggestions and Recommendations. 1. Admissible communications shall be considered by the Committee in the light of all information made available to it by the petitioner and the State party concerned. The Committee may refer the communication to the Working Group in order to be assisted in this task.

2. The Committee or the working group set up by it to consider a communication may at any time, in the course of the examination, obtain through the intermediary of the Secretary-General any documentation that may assist in the disposal of the case from United Nations bodies or the specialized agencies.

3. After consideration of an admissible communication, the Committee shall formulate its opinion thereon. The opinion of the Committee shall be forwarded, through the Secretary-General, to the petitioner and to the State party concerned, together with any suggestions and recommendations the Committee may wish to make.

4. Any member of the Committee may request that a summary of his individual opinion be appended to the opinion of the Committee when it is forwarded to the petitioner and to the State party concerned.

5. The State party concerned shall be invited to inform the Committee in due course of the action it takes in conformity with the Committee's suggestions and recommendations.

Rule 96. Summaries in the Committee's Annual Report. The Committee shall include in its annual report a summary of the communications examined and, where appropriate, a summary of the explanations and statements of the States parties concerned and of its own suggestions and recommendations.

Rule 97. Press Communiqués. The Committee may also issue communiqués, through the Secretary-General, for the use of information media and the general public regarding the activities of the Committee under article 14 of the Convention.

COMMITTEE ON THE EXERCISE OF THE INALIENABLE RIGHTS OF THE PALESTINIAN PEOPLE.

Established by the UN General Assembly on 10 November 1975 (resolution 3376 [XXX]), the committee's function is to recommend to the assembly a program designed to enable the Palestinian people to exercise (1) their right to self-determination without outside interference, (2) their right to national independence and sovereignty, and (3) their right to return to their homes and property from which they have been displaced and uprooted.

Originally composed of 20 UN member States, the committee was enlarged to 23 by the General Assembly (decision 31/318). The term of office of members is indeterminate. The commission holds one session each year.

COMOROS.

The Islamic Federal Republic of the Comoros is a country which occupies four islands in the Indian Ocean between the east African mainland and the Island of Madagascar; the islands are Grande-Comore, Anjouan, Moheli, and Mayotte. It achieved independence from France in 1975 and became a member of the United Nations the same year. However, Mayotte has since been the subject of contention, France having refused to withdraw from the island. The population of the Comoros is estimated by the UN (1990) to be 510,000. Ethnic groups include the Antalote, Cafre, Makoa, and Oimatsaha. Languages in common use include Shaafi Islam (a Swahili dialect), French, and Malagasy. Religions practiced include Islam (Shirazi Muslim), 80%; Christianity (Roman Catholic), 14%; and other faiths, 16%. The island of Mayotte has a Christian majority; the other islands are predominantly Islamic. Literacy is estimated at 15%.

The government (1990) took the form of a republic. The president is head of State; the premier, head of government. There is a Council of Government composed of nine ministers appointed by the president, on which each island's governor has a non-voting seat. There is also a 39-member unicameral Federal Assembly. Each island is administered by a governor nominated by the president and an elected Legislative Assembly. The judicial code is based on French and traditional Islamic law. The United Progress Party is the only political party.

The sovereignty of the Islamic Federal Republic of the Comoros over the island of Mayotte has been repeatedly reaffirmed by the UN General Assembly, the Organization of African Unity, the Movement of Non-Aligned Countries and the Organization of the Islamic Conference; but the government of France has not honored commitments, made prior to 1975, ensuring respect for the unity and territorial integrity of the Comoros.

In November 1989, President Ahmed Abdallah Abdermane—who had been elected first in 1972 when the Comoros was still a French possession and who had ruled since that time for all but three years—was assassinated by rebels shortly after winning a referendum that would have permitted him to seek another six-year term. He had survived earlier coup attempts in 1983, 1985, and 1987.

Replaced by an interim government headed by Supreme Court Justice Mohammed Djohar, the former president's authority actually was maintained for several weeks by Col. Bob Denard, a mercenary who had for many years controlled the 650-man presidential guard. Reluctant to return to France, where he faced legal action, he departed for South Africa on 15 December, together with 21 other mercenaries.

Elections held in February 1990—the first ever in independent Comoros—had to be suspended after widespread voting irregularities were reported and seven presidential candidates charged widespread fraud and demanded the immediate resignation of the interim president.

COMPENSATION FOR VICTIMS OF HUMAN RIGHTS VIOLATIONS.

International standards of compensation for those who are the victims of gross violations of human rights are clearly set out in several instruments.

The UNIVERSAL DECLARATION OF HUMAN RIGHTS proclaims that

Article 8. Everyone has the right to an effective remedy by the competent national tribunals for acts violating the fundamental rights granted him by the constitution or by law.

The INTERNATIONAL COVENANT ON CIVIL AND POLITICAL RIGHTS provides, in article 14 that

6. When a person has by a final decision been convicted of a criminal offence and when subsequently his conviction has been reversed or he has been pardoned on the ground that a new or newly discovered fact shows conclusively that there has been a miscarriage of justice, the person who has suffered punishment as a result of such conviction shall be compensated according to law, unless it is proved that the non-disclosure of the unknown fact in time is wholly or partly attributable to him.

Article 14 of the CONVENTION AGAINST TORTURE AND

OTHER CRUEL, INHUMAN OR DEGRADING TREATMENT OR PUNISHMENT reads as follows:

1. Each State Party shall ensure in its legal system that the victim of an act of torture obtains redress and has an enforceable right to fair and adequate compensation, including the means for as full rehabilitation as possible. In the event of the death of the victim as a result of an act of torture, his dependants shall be entitled to compensation.

2. Nothing in this article shall affect any right of the victim or other persons to compensation which may exist under national law.

Articles 8 to 21 of the DECLARATION OF BASIC PRINCIPLES OF JUSTICE FOR VICTIMS OF CRIME AND ABUSE OF POWER provide that

[*A. Victims of Crime.*] *Restitution.* 8. Offenders or third parties responsible for their behaviour should, where appropriate, make fair restitution to victims, their families or dependants. Such restitution should include the return of property or payment for the harm or loss suffered, reimbursement of expenses incurred as a result of the victimization, the provision of services and the restoration of rights.

9. Governments should review their practices, regulations and laws to consider restitution as an available sentencing option in criminal cases, in addition to other criminal sanctions.

10. In cases of substantial harm to the environment, restitution, if ordered, should include, as far as possible, restoration of the environment, reconstruction of the infrastructure, replacement of community facilities and reimbursement of the expenses of relocation, whenever such harm results in the dislocation of a community.

11. Where public officials or other agents acting in an official or quasi-official capacity have violated national criminal laws, the victims should receive restitution from the State whose officials or agents were responsible for the harm inflicted. In cases where the Government under whose authority the victimizing act or omission occurred is no longer in existence, the State or Government successor in title should provide restitution to the victims.

Compensation. 12. When compensation is not fully available from the offender or other sources, States should endeavour to provide financial compensation to:

(a) Victims who have sustained significant bodily injury or impairment of physical or mental health as a result of serious crimes;

(b) The family, in particular dependants of persons who have died or become physically or mentally incapacitated as a result of such victimization.

13. The establishment, strengthening and expansion of national funds for compensation to victims should be encouraged. Where appropriate, other funds may also be established for this purpose, including in those cases where the State of which the victim is a national is not in a position to compensate the victim for the harm.

Assistance. 14. Victims should receive the necessary material, medical, psychological and social assistance through governmental, voluntary, community-based and indigenous means.

15. Victims should be informed of the availability of health and social services and other relevant assistance and be readily afforded access to them.

16. Police, justice, health, social service and other personnel concerned should receive training to sensitize them to the needs of victims, and guidelines to ensure proper and prompt aid.

17. In providing services and assistance to victims, attention should be given to those who have special needs because of the nature of the harm inflicted. . .

[*B. Victims of Abuse of Power.*] 18. "Victims" means persons who, individually or collectively, have suffered harm, including physical or mental injury, emotional suffering, economic loss or substantial impairment of their fundamental rights, through acts or omissions that do not yet constitute violations of national criminal laws but of internationally recognized norms relating to human rights.

19. States should consider incorporating into the national law norms proscribing abuses of power and providing remedies to victims of such abuses. In particular, such remedies should include restitution and/or compensation, and necessary material, medical, psychological and social assistance and support.

20. States should consider negotiating multilateral international treaties relating to victims, as defined in paragraph 18.

21. States should periodically review existing legislation and practices to ensure their responsiveness to changing circumstances, should enact and enforce, if necessary, legislation proscribing acts that constitute serious abuses of political or economic power, as well as promoting policies and mechanisms for the prevention of such acts, and should develop and make readily available appropriate rights and remedies for victims of such acts.

Bearing these standards in mind, the SUB-COMMISSION ON PREVENTION OF DISCRIMINATION AND PROTECTION OF MINORITIES at its 1988 session recognized (resolution 1988/11) that all victims of gross violations of human rights and fundamental freedoms should be entitled to restitution; a fair and just compensation; and the means for as full a rehabilitation as possible for any damage suffered by them, either individually or collectively; and that, in the event of death of the victims as a result of such acts, their dependents should be entitled to fair and just compensation.

The sub-commission decided to examine the question further at its 1989 session with a view to considering the possibility of developing further basic principles and guidelines in this respect. At the 1989 session, the sub-commission decided (resolution 1989/13) to entrust one of its members, Mr. Theo van Boven (Netherlands) with the task of undertaking a study concerning the right to restitution, compensation and rehabilitation for victims of gross violations of human rights and fundamental freedoms, taking into account relevant existing international human rights norms on compensation and relevant decisions and views of international human rights organs, with a view to exploring the possibility of developing some basic principles and guidelines in this respect. Mr. van Boven was requested to submit a preliminary report to the sub-commission at its 1990 session.

SEE ALSO United Nations Voluntary Fund for Victims of Torture.

COMPLAINTS AND OTHER COMMUNICATIONS CONCERNING HUMAN RIGHTS. Many thousands of complaints and other communications concerning human rights reach the international organizations within the United Nations system every year, posted by individuals and groups in all parts of the world who appeal for help in realizing their human rights and fundamental freedoms or in obtaining redress for violations of those rights and freedoms.

A number of procedures have been established for dealing with different categories of complaints and communications, and their discreet handling has become a major function of several international organs including the UN COMMISSION ON HUMAN RIGHTS, its SUB-COMMISSION ON PREVENTION OF DISCRIMINATION AND PROTECTION OF MINORITIES, and the COMMISSION ON THE STATUS OF WOMEN. These procedures are summarized below. Procedures established by treaty-based monitoring bodies are summarized under the respective titles of such bodies: the COMMITTEE AGAINST TORTURE; the COMMITTEE ON ECONOMIC, SOCIAL AND CULTURAL RIGHTS; the COMMITTEE ON THE ELIMINATION OF DISCRIMINATION AGAINST WOMEN; the COMMITTEE ON THE ELIMINATION OF RACIAL DISCRIMINATION; the GROUP OF THREE; and the HUMAN RIGHTS COMMITTEE.

1. Procedures Provided by the UN Economic and Social Council

(a) Resolutions 75 (V) and 76 (V). In resolution 75 (V), adopted on 5 August 1947, the council approved a statement which had been adopted by the Commission on Human Rights at its first session, that "the Commission recognizes that it has no power to take any action in regard to any complaints concerning human rights," and requested the Secretary-General (i) to compile a confidential list of communications received concerning human rights, before each session of the commission, with a brief indication of the substance of each; (ii) to furnish this confidential list to the commission, in private meeting, without divulging the identity of the authors of the communications; (iii) to enable the members of the commission, upon request, to consult the originals of communications dealing with the principles involved in the promotion of universal respect for and observance of human rights; (iv) to inform the writers of all communications concerning human rights, however addressed, that their communications have been received and duly noted for consideration in accordance with the procedure laid down by the United Nations (where necessary, the Secretary-General should indicate that the commission has no power to take any action in regard to any complaint concerning human rights); and (v) to furnish each member State not represented on the commission with a brief indication of the substance of any communication concerning human rights which refers explicitly to that State or to territories under its jurisdiction, without divulging the name of the author. The council suggested to the commission that it should at each session appoint an ad hoc committee to meet shortly before its next session for the purpose of reviewing the confidential list of communications prepared by the Secretary-General and recommending which of these communications, in original, should, in accordance with (iii) above, be made available to members of the commission upon request.

In resolution 76 (V), the Economic and Social Council recognized that the Commission on the Status of Women, as in the case of the Commission on Human Rights, had no power to take any action in regard to any complaints concerning the status of women and requested the Secretary-General to follow a procedure identical to that which it had established in resolution 75 (V).

(b) Resolution 728 F (XXVIII). In this resolution, adopted on 30 July 1950, the council gave members of the Sub-Commission on Prevention of Discrimination and Protection of Minorities the same facilities, with respect to communications dealing with discrimination and minorities, as are enjoyed by members of the Commission on Human Rights.

(c) Resolution 1235 (XLII). In 1966, the General Assembly, now considerably enlarged by the admission of new member States, invited the Economic and Social Council and the Commission on Human Rights "to give urgent consideration to ways and means of improving the capacity of the United Nations to put an end to violations of human rights wherever they might occur." The council, on 6 June 1967, (resolution 1235 [XLII]) granted the commission and the sub-commission the authority "to examine information relevant to gross violations of human rights and fundamental freedoms. . . .contained in the communications listed by the Secretary-General pursuant to Council resolution 728 F (XXVIII)," and decided that the commission might, in appropriate cases and after careful consideration of the information made available to it, "make a thorough study of situations which reveal a consistent pattern of violations of human rights. . . .and report, with recommendations thereon, to the Economic and Social Council."

(d) Resolution 1503 (XLVIII). By this resolution, entitled "Procedure for Dealing with Communications relating to violations of Human Rights and Funda-

mental Freedoms," the Economic and Social Council on 27 May 1970 authorized the Sub-Commission on Prevention of Discrimination and Protection of Minorities to appoint a working group

... to consider all communications, including replies of Governments thereon, received by the Secretary-General under Council resolution 728 F (XXVIII) of 30 July 1959 with a view to bringing to the attention of the Sub-Commission those communications, together with replies of Governments, if any, which appear to reveal a consistent pattern of gross and reliably attested violations of human rights and fundamental freedoms within the terms of reference of the Sub-Commission." Communications received under Council resolution 728 F (XXVIII) are those concerning human rights (and also women's rights) "however addressed" that is, irrespective of the form or of the addressee of the communication. They may be addressed to the United Nations, the Secretary-General or to any office within the United Nations Secretariat.

On 13 August 1971, the sub-commission adopted (resolution 1 [XXIV])

provisional criteria for determining whether a communication is admissible under the procedure outlined in resolution 1503 (XLVIII). Those criteria have served during the 10 years of application of the procedure without change. They stipulate, *inter alia,* that the contents of the communication may not be in contradiction to the United Nations Charter, the Universal Declaration of Human Rights or other instruments on human rights; the examination of communications and replies by the Governments concerned must show that there are reasonable grounds to believe that they may reveal a consistent pattern of gross and reliably attested violations of human rights and fundamental freedoms. Such situations are considered not to be the exclusive internal affairs of a State and entitled United Nations organs to take action.

Resolution 1503 (XLVIII) sets the stage for a three-step procedure involving consideration of complaints by three bodies: a special working group of the Sub-Commission; the Sub-Commission itself; and the Commission on Human Rights. The working group, consisting of no more than five members, meets once a year in private meetings to consider all communications, including replies from Governments on them, received by the Secretary-General under Council resolution 728 F (XXVIII), in order to select by a majority vote those communications which appear to reveal a consistent pattern of gross and reliably attested violations of human rights and fundamental freedoms, in order to bring them to the attention of the Sub-Commission, together with the replies from Governments, if any.

The second stage of the procedure takes place in the Sub-Commission as a whole, which considers in private meetings the communications brought before it and any replies of Governments and other relevant information, in order to determine if particular situations which appear to reveal a consistent pattern of gross and reliably attested violations of human rights should be referred to the Commission on Human Rights.

The third step in the implementation of Council resolution 1503 (XLVIII) takes place at the Commission level. The Commission is called upon to determine whether a situation which has been referred to it by the Sub-Commission requires a thorough study by the Commission and a report and recommendations thereon to the Council in accordance with paragraph 3 of Council resolution 1235 (XLII), or whether it may be the subject of an investigation by an *ad hoc* committee, with the proviso that such an investigation can only be undertaken with the express consent of the State concerned, in constant co-operation with that State and under conditions agreed upon by it.

Paragraph 4 of Council resolution 1503 (XLVIII) contains specific instructions for the Secretary-General. The confidential lists of communications are to be prepared on a monthly basis for submission to the members of the Sub-Commission, together with the text of replies received from Governments. The Secretary-General is requested to make available to the members of the working group at their annual meetings the originals of such communications as they may request, and to circulate to the members of the Sub-Commission, in the working languages, the "originals" of those communications that have been referred to them by the working group.

At its 1989 session, the sub-commission adopted in closed meetings two decisions relating to the handling of communications. On 25 August 1989, it decided (decision 1989/101) to suspend rule 59 of the rules of procedure of the functional commissions of the council so as to allow for voting by secret ballot for decisions adopted at the 1989 session under resolution 1503 (XLVIII). On the same day, it decided (decision 1989/102) that thenceforth its Working Group on Communications should not consider a communication until the government concerned had been allowed five months in which to submit a reply, from the date on which the communication was transmitted to the government under council resolution 728 F (XXVIII).

(e) Resolutions 277 (X) and 474 A (XV), on Trade Union Rights. In accordance with these resolutions of 17 February 1950 and 9 April 1953, respectively, communications containing

allegations of infringements of trade union rights received from Governments or trade union or employers' organizations against States members of the International Labour Organisation (ILO) are forwarded to the Governing Body of the International Labour Office for its consideration as to referral to the Fact-Finding and Conciliation Commission on Freedom of Association. In regard to any Member of the United Nations which is not a member of the ILO, the Secretary-General, on behalf of the Council, will seek the consent of the Government concerned for the transmittal of a communication to the ILO. In the event that such consent is not forthcoming, the Council will decide on any appropriate alternative action designed to safeguard the rights relating to freedom of association involved in the case.

(f) Resolution 607 (XXI), on Forced Labor. In accordance with this resolution of 1 May 1956, the

Secretary-General transmits any information received on forced labour to the Director-General of the International Labour Office, notwithstanding the provisions of Council resolution 75 (V), as amended in resolution 116 A (V), 192 A (VIII) and 275 (X). The independent *Ad Hoc* Committee on Forced Labour of the International Labour Organisation seeks to obtain relevant information on the alleged existence of forced labour. The Council invited the International Labour Organisation, in resolution 607 (XXI) to include in its annual report to the Council an account of action taken in that field.

2. Procedures Adopted by Other United Nations Organs

(a) The General Assembly. The General Assembly does not as a rule deal with communications concerning human rights. However, a brief indication of communications from non-governmental organizations which relate to items on the agenda of the Assembly appears in lists distributed under the A/INF . . . series. Communications relating to human rights in non-self-governing territories are received and considered by the Special Committee on the Situation With Regard to the Implementation of the Declaration on the Granting of Independence to Colonial Countries and Peoples, and are issued in the A/AC.109 . . . series. The Special Committee has established a Sub-Committee which screens such communications. Communications relating to the racial policies of the Government of South Africa are received and considered by the Special Committee on *Apartheid.* That Committee has established a Sub-Committee which screens such communications and reports to the Special Committee with recommendations for appropriate action.

(b) The Security Council. A brief indication of communications which relate to matters of which the Security Council is seized appears in lists which are issued in the S/NC/ . . . series, and are circulated to the members of the Council. Copies are furnished, on request, to members of the Council.

(c) The Trusteeship Council. By Article 87 (b) of the Charter, the Trusteeship Council is empowered to accept petitions and to examine them in consultation with the administering authority. Communications relating to human rights in Trust Territories are issued in document series T/PET . . . and T/COM . . . The Economic and Social Council and the Trusteeship Council have agreed that those parts of the communications, dealt with by the latter, which are of concern to the Commission on Human Rights or the Commission on the Status of Women should be communicated to them. The Trusteeship Council may ask the Commission for such assistance as it may desire under Article 91 of the Charter.

3. Procedures Adopted by Specialized Agencies

(a) The International Labor Organization. The procedures on communications established by the International Labour Organisation (ILO) relate to problems in particular fields of social policy and legislation. None of them are confined to problems of particular categories of persons.

Articles 24 and 25 of the ILO Constitution provide for the examination of representations by employers' and workers' organizations concerning the observance of ratified ILO Conventions.

Under the Standing Orders (ILO Doc. GB 212/14/21)

concerning procedures for the examination of representations under articles 24 and 25 of the ILO Constitution, the Director-General shall acknowledge receipt when a representation is made to the International Labour Office under article 24 of the ILO Constitution and inform the Government against which the representation is made. The Director-General shall immediately bring the representation before the Officers of the governing body. If the governing body decides, on the basis of the report of its Officers, that a representation is receivable (the communication must be in written form, emanate from an industrial association of employers or workers, must concern a member of the ILO . . .), it shall set up a Committee for its examination, composed of members of the governing body chosen in equal numbers from the Government, employers' and workers' groups.

According to article 6 of the Standing Orders, the Committee, when it has completed its examination of the representation as regards substance, shall present a report to the governing body in which it shall describe the steps taken by it to examine the representation, present its conclusions on the issues raised therein and formulate its recommendations as to the decisions to be taken by the governing body.

The meetings of the governing body at which questions relating to a representation are considered, are to be held in private. The Governments concerned shall be invited to participate, without the right to vote.

Articles 26 to 34 of the ILO Constitution relate to complaints on the non-observance of ratified Conventions and the examination of such complaints by a Commission of Inquiry.

The procedures followed by Commissions of Inquiry are indicated in paragraph 85 of the Manual on Procedures Relating to International Labour Conventions and Recommendations (D.31.1965, Rev. 1980).

Paragraph 85 states that "there are no standing orders concerning the procedure of Commissions of Inquiry. In all cases in which complaints have been referred to a Commission of Inquiry, the governing body has left it to the Commission to determine its own procedures in accordance with the Constitution".

A special procedure for the examination of complaints of violations of trade union rights is provided in paragraphs 87 to 90 of the Manual. At the present time, there are three bodies which are competent to hear complaints lodged with the ILO alleging infringements of trade union rights: the Committee on Freedom of Association set up by the governing body, the governing body itself, and the Fact-Finding and Conciliation Commission on Freedom of Association.

Complaints lodged with ILO directly or via the United Nations must come either from organizations of workers or employers or from Governments. Allegations are receivable only if they are submitted by a national organization directly interested in the matter, by international organizations of employers or workers in consultative status with ILO, or other international organizations of employers or workers where the allegations relate to matters directly affecting their affiliated organizations.

Complaints must be presented in writing, duly signed by a representative of a body entitled to present them, and must be as fully supported as possible by proof of allegations relating to specific infringements of trade union rights.

Complaints originating from assemblies or gatherings

which are not permanent bodies, or even definitive entities with which it is impossible to correspond (either because they have only a temporary existence or because the complaints do not contain any addresses of the complainants), are not receivable.

The Committee does not take cognizance of complaints presented by persons who, through fear of reprisals, request that their names or the place and origin of the complaints should not be disclosed. An exception is made in cases where the Director-General, after examining the complaint in question, informs the Committee that it contains allegations of some degree of gravity which have not previously been examined by the Committee. The Committee can then decide what action, if any, should be taken with regard to such complaints.

Complaints which do not relate to specific infringements of trade union rights are referred by the Director-General to the Committee on Freedom of Association for an opinion, and the Committee decides whether any action should be taken.

The Committee consists of nine regular and nine substitute members, chosen from among the Government Group, the Employers' Group and the Workers' Group of the governing body, that is, three regular and three substitute members from each group. Each member sits in a personal capacity.

The Committee always endeavours to reach unanimous decisions. In the event of a vote, substitutes do not vote when all the regular members of the group are voting.

The responsibilities of the Committee are essentially to consider, for recommendation to the governing body, whether cases are worthy of examination.

It is open to the governing body to refer to the Fact-Finding and Conciliation Commission, for impartial examination, any allegation of infringements of trade union rights which the governing body, on the report of the Committee on Freedom of Association, or the Conference, acting on the report of its Credentials Committee, considers it appropriate to refer to the Commission for investigation. Any Government against which an allegation of infringements of trade union rights is made can refer such an allegation to the Commission for investigation.

The Fact-Finding and Conciliation Commission on Freedom of Association is appointed by the governing body and works in panels of not less than three nor more than five members. Its members are independent persons.

The Commission is essentially a fact-finding body, but it is authorized to discuss situations referred to it for investigation with the Government concerned, with a view to securing the adjustment of difficulties by agreement.

At its one-hundred-ninety-first session (November 1973) the governing body adopted a procedure for the examination of requests for "special surveys" which Governments or organizations of employers or workers may submit on questions concerning the elimination of discrimination in employment.

The possibility of undertaking such special surveys, with a view to evaluating facts and seeking solutions in certain situations, was provided for by the governing body at its one-hundred-eighty-eighth session (November 1972), on the proposal of its Committee on Discrimination.

It was understood that such special surveys might be based on criteria such as those laid down in the Discrimination (Employment and Occupation) Convention, 1958 (No. 111). However, this possibility is more general in

scope and is not limited to countries which have ratified the Convention.

The questions raised should concern the situation of groups of people defined, for example, according to race, religion, national extraction, social origin, member of a minority group, sex or age, but should not deal with individual cases unrelated to broader issues of policy.

The Director-General was entrusted with "examining the effect to be given to any request for a special survey submitted by a member State, or a workers' or employers' organization, on specific questions of concern to them, and, if the Government concerned agreed to such a survey, to settle the arrangements for carrying it out in agreement with the Government".

Provision is thus made for two different types of cases: those in which the request is directly submitted by the Government of a member State in connexion with questions arising in its own country, and those in which the request comes from an employers' or workers' organization or another member State.

Requests Submitted by the Government Concerned. The examination of the effect to be given to a request made in this circumstance raises no special procedural problems. The request may, for example, be aimed at obtaining a form of technical co-operation on question of evaluation or method in this field. In addition, recourse to outside observers, whose action would have an objective and impartial character, can help a Government to overcome difficulties arising inside the country in connexion with certain questions. In other circumstances, a Government may wish to clear up certain doubts to which its action in this field may have given rise at the international level. A special survey on the national situation can, in particular, help a Government to reach more precise conclusions regarding uncertainties which may have prevented it from ratifying the Discrimination (Employment and Occupation) Convention, 1958 (No. 111). The governing body felt that this possibility should be drawn to the special attention of Governments.

Requests Submitted by an Employers' or Workers' Organization or by Another Government

Receivability of Requests. As regards requests submitted by employers' or workers' organizations, the governing body laid down principles similar to those which apply in regard to freedom of association: the request must come either from a national organization directly concerned, or from international organizations in consultative status with ILO, or from other international or regional employers' or workers' organizations, provided the questions raised directly concern organizations affiliated to them.

In the case of a request submitted by the Government of a member State in connexion with questions arising in another country, the receivability of the request is strictly governed by the condition that the request must relate to "specific questions of concern to it". This presupposes a sufficiently close link between the interests of that Government and the questions raised; the governing body considered that this could be the case, for example, when such questions concerned the situation of its own nationals working in another country.

Communications with the Authors of Requests. The Director-General may, if necessary, ask the authors of requests to provide further details on the specific questions which they propose to raise, and to communicate additional information within a specified time-limit.

Communications with the Government of the Country in regard to which the Survey Would Be Requested. The Director-General will inform the Government concerned as soon as possible of any receivable and substantiated request, and will request the Government to communicate, within an appropriate time-limit, its observations on this question and its views concerning the possibility of carrying out a special survey under the auspices of ILO on the questions raised.

In cases where the Government requests or accepts such a survey, the Director-General will settle the arrangements for carrying it out in agreement with the Government, subject to the necessary safeguards, and in particular as regards the consultation of employers' and workers' circles concerned.

Reports to the Governing Body Committee on Discrimination. The Director-General will report to the Committee on requests received, replies from Governments, special surveys undertaken or planned, and on cases in which surveys could not be organized, including cases in which they have been refused or no replies have been communicated within a reasonable time-limit. On such questions, the Committee will, as necessary, be called upon regularly to make such recommendations as it deems appropriate.

List of Experts who Might be Called upon to Participate in Special Surveys. The Director-General was entrusted with examining the possibility of drawing up a list of experts and persons of acknowledged competence, selected from the different regions of the world, whose services could be called upon in appropriate cases. It was further understood that, depending on the circumstances, surveys could also be carried out directly by the International Labour Office.

The governing body considered that the guidelines set out above should be applied on an experimental basis, on the understanding that they could be re-examined or redefined at a later stage, in the light of their practical application.

(b) The United Nations Educational, Scientific and Cultural Organization. UNESCO's Committee on Conventions and Recommendations examines in private session communications received. It decides on their admissibility in accordance with the following conditions:

(i) the communication must not be anonymous;

(ii) the communication must originate from a person or a group of persons who, it can be reasonably presumed, are victims of an alleged violation of any of the human rights referred to in paragraph (iii) below. It may also originate from any person, group of persons or nongovernmental organization having reliable knowledge of those violations;

(iii) the communications must concern violations of human rights (women and men alike) falling within UNESCO's competence in the fields of education, science, culture and information and must not be motivated exclusively by other considerations;

(iv) the communication must be compatible with the principles of the Organization, the Charter of the United Nations, the Universal Declaration of Human Rights, the international covenants on human rights and other international instruments in the field of human rights;

(v) the communication must not be manifestly ill-founded and must appear to contain relevant evidence;

(vi) the communication must be neither offensive nor an abuse of the right to submit communications. However, such a communication may be considered if it meets all other criteria or admissibility, after the exclusion of the offensive or abusive parts;

(vii) the communication must not be based exclusively on information disseminated through the mass media;

(viii) the communication must be submitted within a reasonable time-limit following the facts which constitute its subject-matter or within a reasonable time-limit after the facts have become known;

(ix) the communication must indicate whether an attempt has been made to exhaust available domestic remedies with regard to the facts which constitute the subject-matter of the communication and the result of such an attempt, if any;

(x) communications relating to matters already settled by the States concerned in accordance with the human rights principles set forth in the Universal Declaration of Human Rights and the international covenants on human rights shall not be considered;

Under the Procedures contained in decision 104 EX/3.3:

(e) representatives of the governments concerned may attend meetings of the Committee in order to provide additional information or to answer questions from members of the Committee on either admissibility or the merits of the communication;

(f) The Committee may avail itself of the relevant information at the disposal of the Director-General;

(g) Communications which warrant further consideration shall be acted upon by the Committee with a view to helping to bring about a friendly solution designed to advance the promotion of the human rights falling with UNESCO's fields of competence.

Under paragraph 15 of decision 104 EX/3.3 the Committee is requested to submit confidential reports to the Executive Board at each session on the carrying out of its mandate under the present decision. These reports shall contain appropriate information arising from its examination of the communications which the Committee considers it useful to bring to the notice of the Executive Board. The reports shall also contain recommendations which the Committee may wish to make either generally or regarding the disposition of a communication under consideration.

Paragraph 18 of decision 104 EX/3.3 refers to questions of massive, systematic or flagrant violations of human rights and fundamental freedoms—including, for example, those perpetrated as a result of policies of aggression, interference in the internal affairs of States, occupation of foreign territory and implementation of a policy of colonialism, genocide, apartheid, racialism, or national and social oppression—falling within UNESCO fields of competence which should be considered by the Executive Board and the General Conference in public meetings.

CONGO. The People's Republic of the Congo is a country in middle Africa, on the Atlantic Ocean. It has borders with Angola, Cameroon, Central African Republic, Gabon, and Zaire. It achieved independence from France in 1960 and became a member of the United Nations the same year. Its population is estimated by the UN (1990) to be 1,994,000. More than 15 ethnic groups are included in the population, among them the Bacongo, the Bateke, the Bukongui, the M'bochi, and the Sangha. Languages commonly used include French (official), Lingala, and Kikongo. Religions practiced include Christianity (Roman Catholic, 54%); Protestant denominations, 24% Animism, 19%, and Islam 3%). Literacy is estimated at 56%.

The government (1990) took the form of "a single, indivisible and secular People's Republic." Under article 2 of the constitution of 8 July 1979 as amended in 1984, sovereignty resides in the people, and all authority emanates from the people through a single party, the Congolese Labour Party, "the highest form of political and social organization of the people." The constitution provides, specifically in Title II, entitled "Public Freedoms and the Individual," for the protection of the rights set out in the International Covenant on Civil and Political Rights, including the right to life; the right to freedom of the individual; the right to inviolability of the home; the right not to be subjected to searches, except in conditions laid down by law; the right to inviolability of correspondence; the right not to be imprisoned, except in cases provided for by law; and the right to non-discrimination. In addition, human rights are protected by provisions of the Penal Code, the Labor Code, the Nationality Code, the Family Code, and the Act of April 1983 reorganizing the system of justice.

CONSCIENTIOUS OBJECTION TO MILITARY SERVICE. The UN COMMISSION ON HUMAN RIGHTS took up the question of conscientious objection to military service, which had become a matter of great concern to young people in a number of countries, at its 1971 session. There was general agreement in the commission as to the duty of the individual national of a country to defend his family and society when that country was attacked and to contribute to the country's response to treaty obligations arising, for example, under the UNITED NATIONS CHARTER. But there were wide differences of opinion concerning the desirability of permitting any exceptions to bearing arms for active military duty on grounds such as conscientious objection, religious belief, or moral conviction.

To obtain up-to-date information on the subject, the commission requested the Secretary-General to prepare a report on national legislation and other measures relating to conscientious objection to military service and on alternative service. It received the report (UN Doc. E/CN.4/1118 and Corr. 1 and Add. 1–3) in 1972 but was unable to deal with the question further until 1980, when it authorized the SUB-COMMISSION ON PREVENTION OF DISCRIMINATION AND PROTECTION OF MINORITIES to prepare a compre-

hensive report. The sub-commission designated two of its members, Mr. Asbjørn Eide (Norway) and Mr. Chama Mubanga-Chipoya (Zambia) as special rapporteurs, and the report (UN Doc. E/CN.4/Sub.2/1982/24) was completed in 1982.

Meanwhile, the General Assembly had dealt with a closely related subject, the question of the status of persons refusing service in military or police forces recruited to enforce *APARTHEID*. In 1978, it had recognized (resolution 33/165) the right of all such persons to refuse that kind of service and had called upon member States to grant asylum or safe transit to another State to persons compelled to leave their country of nationality solely because of a conscientious objection to assisting in the enforcement of *apartheid* through service in military or police forces. And, in 1979, it had appealed (resolution 34/93 A) to the youth of South Africa to refrain from enlisting in the South African armed forces "designed to defend the inhuman system of *apartheid*, to repress the legitimate struggle of the oppressed people and to threaten, and commit, acts of aggression against neighboring States."

The report prepared by the special rapporteurs (subsequently issued as United Nations publication, Sales No. E.85.XIV.1) summarizes, in chapter I, the concept and dimensions of conscientious objection, the relevant international standards, and the action taken by international organizations to supervise the implementation of those standards. Chapter II contains an analysis of relevant information received from governments and the intergovernmental and non-governmental organizations concerned. In chapter III, the conclusions and recommendations of the special rapporteurs are set out. The conclusions are as follows (para. 139–152):

It seems appropriate to recall some basic contradictions encountered: on the one hand the need felt by almost every State for some degree of military strength and, on the other, the dual vocation of the United Nations to advance peace and international understanding as well as respect for the human being.

The contradictions reflect some fundamental dilemmas in the world today. One is between the assertion of national community and the search for a global community. Another is between the assertion of national authority and respect for those who dissent on grounds of conscience.

These dilemmas become more serious with the passage of time. The existence and the work of the United Nations and the specialized agencies, such as UNESCO, have provided young people everywhere with a vision of a world based on solidarity, justice and human dignity: 1985 has been declared International Youth Year, to be devoted to "participation, development and peace". In preparation for it, the General Assembly, in its resolution 37/48 of 3 December 1982, on International Youth Year, again considered it necessary to disseminate among youth the ideals of peace, respect for human rights and fundamental freedoms, human solidarity and dedication to the objectives of progress and development. UNESCO has for several years promoted education for human rights and international understanding, and is also now seeking to promote education on disarmament. These activities influence the thinking of young people and some respect should be shown for the dedication of youth to such ideals.

If the existing material is considered in the light of those dilemmas and the moral imperatives promoted by the United Nations and its specialized agencies, the following picture emerges.

1. Voluntarism or Compulsion in Performance of Military Service

State practice varies widely regarding the extent to which military service is voluntary or enforced. States can be divided into categories on this issue, as follows:

(a) A large number of States have no conscription, i.e. no compulsory military service. Available information indicates that 67 countries fall into this category (see annex II, list 1, below). The problem of conscientious objection is of less significance in such cases. Problems might emerge if objection developed in the mind of an enlisted person after joining the service. Provision should be made, in law or in the contract of enlistment, for withdrawal from service in such cases. Such provisions exist in some countries, but available material makes it difficult to ascertain their extent.

(b) A few countries have conscription in law, but do not enforce it. For practical purposes; the situation of the objector in such circumstances is similar to that under (a). Six countries fall into this category (see annex II, list 2, below). Legislation should be passed in the countries in this category to provide for recognition of conscientious objection in case conscription is enforced.

(c) The next category (see annex III, list 3, below) includes States which had conscription (compulsory service) and enforce it, but which mitigate that circumstance by formal and genuine recognition of conscientious objection, at least on some grounds. Fifteen countries fall into this category. Taken together, countries and territories belonging to categories (a), (b) and (c) grant freedom to the individual, to a greater or lesser extent, to decide whether or not to join the armed forces. Altogether, 88 countries appear to be included in this larger group.

(d) Then there are the countries which enforce compulsory service in the armed forces, and do not recognize the right of objectors to be exempted from military service, but which allow objectors, in certain circumstances, to be given non-combatant roles in the armed forces (see annex II, list 4, below). There are two subdivisions in this group: first, countries where the law provides for transfer to non-combatant roles (available material indicates that this is the situation in five countries); secondly, countries which in individual cases have allowed transfer to non-combatant roles on an *ad hoc* basis (information received indicates that this has happened in seven countries). It is difficult, however, to obtain reliable information on the extent to which this takes places, since it is an *ad hoc* decision by the relevant authorities to place a person in a non-combatant role and the reasons for it are not necessarily given.

(e) Finally, there is a group of 40 States with conscription which do not recognize conscientious objection in law and where there has been no indication that objectors have

been allowed, by administrative decision, to perform unarmed services within the armed forces (see annex II, list 5, below). It is possible that in some of these countries nobody has actually objected to military service. It should be noted that a few countries have been mentioned twice, for example Israel, which has obligatory military service for both men and women but which follows different practices with regard to the two sexes.

For the countries in category (c) above (those with conscription, which recognize conscientious objection), the range of grounds on which objection is considered valid requires consideration. Reference is often made to "religious", "moral" or "political" objection. The concept of "political" objection is particularly unfortunate, since it covers a wide range of different reasons for objecting—some of them laudable from a United Nations perspective, others less laudable.

The relevant distinction is between absolute and partial objection. Absolute objection is based on the conviction that it is wrong under all circumstances to take part in the killing of others. Partial objection is based on the acceptance of the use of armed force purely for defence, but refusal to serve in armed actions which are tantamount to aggression, occupation or repression of human rights, or where the means and methods of armed action are considered unacceptable. Both forms of objection are normally based on moral convictions of a religious or humanistic inspiration.

In practice, States that recognize conscientious objection normally do so only for those who hold an absolute, pacifist, position. In recent years there have been cases where partial objection has been recognized, in particular when the objection is based on refusal to serve in armed forces when the use of weapons of mass destruction is envisaged as a possibility.

One important reason why partial objection is not normally recognized is that State authorities probably never agree with the objector that their actual or contemplated use of force is or will be in contravention of international law.

As pointed out above (para. 92), the South African authorities do not agree that their use of armed force is illegal, even though universal opinion outside South Africa, as evidenced by decisions of the General Assembly and the Security Council, is that the continued occupation of Namibia is in contravention of international law and that armed force to maintain the occupation is clearly illegal. The fact that Governments will not accept that their use of force is illegal or illegitimate should not, however, prevent recognition of an objection to serve by individuals who disagree with the authorities. There have been in the past and will be in the future cases where public opinion (internationally and nationally) is split regarding the legitimacy of the use of force or the means used. It should be possible to accept that young persons called up for conscription may hold a justifiable position on a given issue which differs from that of the authorities. Therefore national authorities might recognize that some individuals, to the best of their conscience, hold a strong conviction which should be respected, even when it differs from the official position of the Government.

Where conscientious objection is recognized, differences exist regarding the way in which conscientious objector status can be obtained. Three sets of factors must be considered in this regard:

(a) How impartial are the institutions, or tribunals,

which decide whether or not such status shall be granted? Are the legal standards applied comparable to those applied in a fair trial?

(b) At what time must the request for objector status be made? Is it admitted at the time of call-up only, or also later, whenever the conscientious conviction develops?

(c) Does the Government disseminate information about the right to conscientious objection, and does it allow non-governmental organizations to do so?

The material collected indicates that some countries have developed impartial institutions or use the regular civilian courts, with the application of normal legal safeguards, to determine the issue. In other cases, military tribunals are used and may not be sufficiently impartial with regard to the issue of conscientious objection. In still other cases, the decision is left to the discretion of individuals within the military administration, with no possibility of appeal. It seems reasonable, if conscientious objection is recognized in some but not all cases, that an impartial tribunal should take the decision and that information on the right to objection should be available to all.

2. Alternative Service

Where conscientious objection is recognized, provision is normally made for alternative service, but there are also considerable differences in this connection. In some countries, the alternative service is such that it corresponds closely to the ideas expressed in the sixth preambular paragraph of General Assembly resolution 37/48, which states that the Assembly is

"Convinced of the imperative to harness the energies, enthusiasms and creative abilities of youth to the tasks of nation-building, the struggle for self-determination and national independence, in accordance with the Charter of the United Nations, and against foreign domination and occupation, for the economic, social and cultural advancement of peoples, the implementation of the new international economic order, the preservation of world peace and the promotion of international co-operation and understanding."

In some cases, therefore, objectors are assigned alternative service related to social improvement, development or promotion of international peace.

In other cases the alternative service seems to be considered more as a punishment for refusing military service, in that it consists in hard work without a meaningful content.

Recommendations of the special rapporteurs were presented in the form of a text by which the sub-commission would propose to the Commission on Human Rights the adoption of a resolution along the following lines:

The Commission of Human Rights, recalling its resolution 40 (XXXVII) of 12 March 1981 and General Assembly resolution 33/165 of 20 December 1978, as well as General Assembly resolutions 34/151 of 17 December 1979, 35/126 of 11 December 1980, 36/28 of 13 November 1981 and 37/48 of 3 December 1982 on International Youth Year: Participation, Development, Peace, recommends that the Economic and Social Council should request the General Assembly to make the following recommendations, preferably in connection with the preparations for International Youth Year, 1985:

1. Right to Conscientious Objection. (a) States should recognize by law the right of persons who, for reasons of conscience or profound conviction arising from religious, ethical, moral, humanitarian or similar motives, refuse to perform armed service, to be released from the obligation to perform military service.

(b) States should, as a minimum, extend the right of objection to persons whose conscience forbids them to take part in armed service under any circumstances (the pacifist position).

(c) States should recognize by law the right to be released from service in armed forces which the objector considers likely to be used to enforce *apartheid*.

(d) States should recognize by law the right to be released from service in armed forces which the objector considers likely to be used in action amounting to or approaching genocide.

(e) States should recognize by law the right to be released from service in armed forces which the objector considers likely to be used for illegal occupation of foreign territory.

(f) States should recognize the right of persons to be released from service in armed forces which the objector holds to be engaged in, or likely to be engaged in, gross violations of human rights.

(g) States should recognize the right of persons to be released from the obligation to perform service in armed forces which the objector considers likely to resort to the use of weapons of mass destruction or weapons which have been specifically outlawed by international law or to use means and methods which cause unnecessary suffering.

2. Procedural Aspects. (a) States should maintain or establish independent decision-making bodies to determine whether a conscientious objection is valid under national law in any specific case. There should always be a right of appeal to an independent, civilian judicial body.

(b) Applicants should be granted a hearing and be entitled to be represented by legal counsel and to call witnesses.

(c) States should disseminate information about the right of objection, and allow non-governmental organizations to do likewise.

3. Alternative Service. States should provide alternative service for the objector, which should be at least as long as the military service, but not excessively long so that it becomes in effect a punishment. States should, to the extent possible, seek to give the alternative service a meaningful content, including social work or work for peace, development and international understanding.

4. Trial and Penalties where the Objection is not Found Valid. Even when States give effect to the above recommendations, there will be some cases where the objection is not found valid, and where penalties will be imposed on persons who persist in their objection. In such cases:

(a) Imposition of such penalties should be decided upon by an impartial civilian court applying the normal criteria of fair trial;

(b) Penalties should not be excessively severe, and should take due account, as mitigating factors, of the conscience or conviction of the person concerned.

5. Asylum. Taking into account the existence of rules of international law, under which an individual retains the right and the duty to refuse illegal orders under national law, and the provisions of General Assembly resolution 33/165 as well as the basic right to freedom of conscience, international standards should be established which will ensure a favourable attitude towards conscientious objectors requesting asylum in conformity with obligations under international law. Furthermore, it appears to be the practice of many countries not to refuse asylum to conscientious objectors to military service. International legislation on this practice might clarify an area of human rights in which there are international and individual obligations.

6. Recruitment of Children and Minors. While the question of the use of children in war has not been dealt with as such in this report, it is nevertheless suggested that the Sub-Commission should consider how to follow up the concern expressed on this matter. In this connection, account should be taken of the provisions in Additional Protocol I of June 1977 to the Geneva Convention of 1949, article 77, paragraph 2, in which the parties to a conflict pledge themselves to take all feasible measures in order that children under 15 do not take a direct part in hostilities and, in particular, to refrain from recruiting them into their armed forces. A similar prohibition is found in Protocol II, article 4, paragraph 3 (c).

In 1983, the sub-commission received and examined the report, expressed its deep appreciation to the special rapporteurs, and transmitted the report (resolution 1983/22) to the Commission on Human Rights. The commission examined it in 1984; and, on its recommendation, the Economic and Social Council decided (resolution 1984/27) that it should be printed and given the widest possible distribution. The council also requested that it be transmitted to governments and to interested international organizations for their comments and that such comments should be drawn to the attention of the commission.

At its 1985 session, the commission, after reviewing the comments received by the Secretary-General (E/CN.4/1985/25 and Add. 1–4), considered a draft resolution on conscientious objection to military service (UN Doc. E/CN.4/1985/L.33/Rev. 1) and a number of amendments thereto. Unable to reach agreement in the time available, it adjourned the debate to its 1987 session.

On 10 March 1987, the commission, noting the comments and observations of governments and international organizations on the report, recognized (resolution 1987/46) that conscientious objection to military service derives from principles and reasons of conscience, including profound convictions arising from religious, ethical, moral, or similar motives, and appealed to States to recognize that conscientious objection to military service should be considered a legitimate exercise of the right to freedom of thought, conscience, and religion recognized by the UNIVERSAL DECLARATION OF HUMAN RIGHTS and the INTERNATIONAL COVENANT ON CIVIL AND POLITICAL RIGHTS.

The commission accordingly invited States to take measures aimed at exemption from military service on the basis of genuinely held conscientious objection to armed service; and recommended to States

with a system of compulsory military service, where such provision has not already been made, that they consider introducing various forms of alternative service for conscientious objectors which are compatible with the reasons for conscientious objection, bearing in mind the experience of some States in this respect, and that they refrain from subjecting such persons to imprisonment. It further recommended to member States, if they have not already done so, that they establish within the framework of their national legal system impartial decisionmaking procedures to determine whether a conscientious objection is valid in any specific case.

In resolution 1987/46, the commission also requested the Secretary-General to report to it at its 1989 session on the question of conscientious objection to military service, taking into account comments provided by governments and further information received by him. The Secretary-General accordingly invited all member States, United Nations bodies, specialized agencies, and intergovernmental and non-governmental organizations to supply any relevant information and comments for the report. The information and comments received were presented to the commission (UN Doc. E/CN.4/1989/30).

After considering the Secretary-General's report, and bearing in mind other relevant reports and decisions, the commission (resolution 1989/59) recognized that conscientious objection to military service derives from principles and reasons of conscience, including profound convictions, arising from religious or similar motives, and recognized further the right of everyone to have conscientious objections to military service as a legitimate exercise of the right to freedom of thought, conscience and religion as laid down in article 18 of the Universal Declaration of Human Rights as well as article 18 of the International Covenant on Civil and Political Rights.

Accordingly, the commission appealed to States to enact legislation and to take measures aimed at exemption from military service on the basis of genuinely held conscientious objection to armed service, and recommended to States with a system of compulsory military service, where such provision has not already been made, that they introduce for conscientious objectors various forms of alternative service which are compatible with the reasons for conscientious objection, bearing in mind the experience of some States in this respect, and that they refrain from subjecting such persons to imprisonment. It emphasized that such forms of alternative service should be in principle of a non-combatant or civilian character, in the public interest, and not of a punitive nature.

The commission further recommended to States members of the United Nations, if they have not al-

C

ready done so, that they establish within the framework of their national legal system independent and impartial decisionmaking bodies with the task of determining whether a conscientious objection is valid in a specific case.

The commission decided to consider the question further at its 1991 session.

CONSTITUTIONAL COUNCILS. Constitutional councils are organs established within the framework of the legislative system of many countries, having as one of their functions the protection and promotion of human rights. They are described in the UN Secretary-General's report entitled *National Institutions for the Protection and Promotion of Human Rights* (E/CN.4/1987/37, para. 16–18), prepared at the request of the General Assembly (resolution 42/123):

In many countries, organs have been established with a view to ensuring that laws adopted by parliament do not violate constitutional norms and principles.

For example, a 1983 amendment to the Hungarian Constitution called for the National Assembly to elect a Constitutional Council to exercise control over the constitutionality of legal rules and legal directives or guidelines. The Constitutional Council is empowered to suspend the enforcement of any legal provisions (except legislative enactments by the National and Presidential Council) and directives and rulings of the Supreme Court. The Constitutional Council also assists in the interpretation of the provisions of the Constitution.

Constitutional councils similarly charged with determining the constitutionality of legislative acts, may, in some countries, function as independent bodies outside the parliamentary sphere. For instance, in France, the Constitutional Council is neither a legislative nor a judicial organ. However, in accordance with article 61 of the French Constitution of 4 October 1958, the Constitutional Council is empowered to examine the constitutionality of acts referred to it, before they are promulgated. The Council may be seized by the President of the Republic, the Prime Minister, the President of the National Assembly, the President of the Senate or 60 deputies or senators.

CONSULTATIVE COUNCIL OF JEWISH ORGANIZATIONS. An international non-governmental organization in consultative status with the UN Economic and Social Council (Category II), the ILO, UNESCO, and the Council of Europe. Founded in 1946 in New York as the Coordinating Board of Jewish Organizations for Consultation with the Economic and Social Council of the United Nations, CCJO promotes respect for human rights and fundamental freedoms, cooperates and consults with the council and its subsidiary bodies on problems relating to human rights and economic, social, cultural, educational, and related matters. It has established a library in Paris (50,000 volumes) and one in New York (20,000 volumes).

CCJO publishes *AJA* (quarterly) and *Les nouveaux cahiers* (quarterly).

Consultative Council of Jewish Organizations. Address: 405 Lexington Ave., New York, NY 10170 (USA). Telephone: (212) 808-5437. Secretary General: Warren Green.

Yearbook of International Organizations 1989/90 (K. G. Saur).

CONVENTION AGAINST TORTURE AND OTHER CRUEL, INHUMAN OR DEGRADING TREATMENT OR PUNISHMENT (1984). The convention defines "torture" and obliges every State party to take effective legislative, administrative, judicial, and other measures to prevent acts of torture in any territory under its jurisdiction. It authorizes (article 17) the establishment of the COMMITTEE AGAINST TORTURE, consisting of ten experts elected by the States parties but serving in their personal capacity. The States parties undertake to submit to the committee every four years reports on the measures they have taken to give effect to the convention, and the committee is authorized to examine the reports and to make general comments on them.

The convention provides (article 20) for the handling by the committee of "reliable information which appears to contain well-founded indications that torture is being systematically practiced in the territory of a State Party." Under article 21, a State party may at any time declare that it recognizes the competence of the committee to receive and consider communications to the effect that a State party claims that another State party is not fulfilling its obligations under the convention. Special procedures are provided for the handling of such communications. Further, under article 22, a State party may at any time declare that it recognizes the competence of the committee to receive and consider communications from or on behalf of individuals subject to its jurisdiction who claim to be victims of a violation by a State party of the provisions of the convention, and special procedures are provided for the handling of those communications.

The convention, adopted by the UN General Assembly on 10 December 1984 (resolution 39/46), entered into force on 26 June 1987. The Committee against Torture was organized at a meeting of the States parties held on 26 June 1987.

The text of the convention, annexed to resolution 39/46, is as follows:

The States Parties to this Convention,
Considering that, in accordance with the principles proclaimed in the Charter of the United Nations, recognition

of the equal and inalienable rights of all members of the human family is the foundation of freedom, justice and peace in the world,

Recognizing that those rights derive from the inherent dignity of the human person,

Considering the obligation of States under the Charter, in particular Article 55, to promote universal respect for, and observance of, human rights and fundamental freedoms,

Having regard to article 5 of the Universal Declaration of Human Rights and article 7 of the International Covenant on Civil and Political Rights, both of which provide that no one shall be subjected to torture or to cruel, inhuman or degrading treatment or punishment,

Having regard also to the Declaration on the Protection of All Persons from Being Subjected to Torture and Other Cruel, Inhuman or Degrading Treatment or Punishment, adopted by the General Assembly on 9 December 1975,

Desiring to make more effective the struggle against torture and other cruel, inhuman or degrading treatment or punishment throughout the world,

Have agreed as follows:

Part I

Article 1. 1. For the purposes of this Convention, the term "torture" means any act by which severe pain or suffering, whether physical or mental, is intentionally inflicted on a person for such purposes as obtaining from him or a third person information or a confession, punishing him for an act he or a third person has committed or is suspected of having committed, or intimidating or coercing him or a third person, or for any reason based on discrimination of any kind, when such pain or suffering is inflicted by or at the instigation of or with the consent or acquiescence of a public official or other person acting in an official capacity. It does not include pain or suffering arising only from, inherent in or incidental to lawful sanctions.

2. This article is without prejudice to any international instrument or national legislation which does or may contain provisions of wider application.

Article 2. 1. Each State Party shall take effective legislative, administrative, judicial or other measures to prevent acts of torture in any territory under its jurisdiction.

2. No exceptional circumstances whatsoever, whether a state of war or a threat of war, internal political instability or any other public emergency, may be invoked as a justification of torture.

3. An order from a superior officer or a public authority may not be invoked as a justification of torture.

Article 3. 1. No State Party shall expel, return (*"refouler"*) or extradite a person to another State where there are substantial grounds for believing that he would be in danger of being subjected to torture.

2. For the purpose of determining whether there are such grounds, the competent authorities shall take into account all relevant considerations including, where applicable, the existence in the State concerned of a consistent pattern of gross, flagrant or mass violations of human rights.

Article 4. 1. Each State Party shall ensure that all acts of torture are offences under its criminal law. The same shall apply to an attempt to commit torture and to an act by any person which constitutes complicity or participation in torture.

2. Each State Party shall make these offences punishable by appropriate penalties which take into account their grave nature.

Article 5. 1. Each State Party shall take such measures as may be necessary to establish its jurisdiction over the offences referred to in article 4 in the following cases:

(a) When the offences are committed in any territory under its jurisdiction or on board a ship or aircraft registered in that State;

(b) When the alleged offender is a national of that State;

(c) When the victim is a national of that State if that State considers it appropriate.

2. Each State Party shall likewise take such measures as may be necessary to establish its jurisdiction over such offences in cases where the alleged offender is present in any territory under its jurisdiction and it does not extradite him pursuant to article 8 to any of the States mentioned in paragraph 1 of this article.

3. This Convention does not exclude any criminal jurisdiction exercised in accordance with internal law.

Article 6. 1. Upon being satisfied, after an examination of information available to it, that the circumstances so warrant, any State Party in whose territory a person alleged to have committed any offence referred to in article 4 is present shall take him into custody or take other legal measures to ensure his presence. The custody and other legal measures shall be as provided in the law of that State but may be continued only for such time as is necessary to enable any criminal or extradition proceedings to be instituted.

2. Such State shall immediately make a preliminary inquiry into the facts.

3. Any person in custody pursuant to paragraph 1 of this article shall be assisted in communicating immediately with the nearest appropriate representative of the State of which he is a national, or, if he is a stateless person, with the representative of the State where he usually resides.

4. When a State, pursuant to this article, has taken a person into custody, it shall immediately notify the States referred to in article 5, paragraph 1, of the fact that such person is in custody and of the circumstances which warrant his detention. The State which makes the preliminary inquiry contemplated in paragraph 2 of this article shall promptly report its findings to the said States and shall indicate whether it intends to exercise jurisdiction.

Article 7. 1. The State Party in the territory under whose jurisdiction a person alleged to have committed any offence referred to in article 4 is found shall in the cases contemplated in article 5, if it does not extradite him, submit the case to its competent authorities for the purpose of prosecution.

2. These authorities shall take their decision in the same manner as in the case of any ordinary offence of a serious nature under the law of that State. In the cases referred to in article 5, paragraph 2, the standards of evidence required for prosecution and conviction shall in no way be less stringent than those which apply in the cases referred to in article 5, paragraph 1.

3. Any person regarding whom proceedings are brought in connection with any of the offences referred to in article 4 shall be guaranteed fair treatment at all stages of the proceedings.

Article 8. 1. The offences referred to in article 4 shall be deemed to be included as extraditable offences in any extradition treaty existing between States Parties. States Parties undertake to include such offences as extraditable offences in every extradition treaty to be concluded between them.

2. If a State Party which makes extradition conditional on the existence of a treaty receives a request for extradition from another State Party with which it has no extradition treaty, it may consider this Convention as the legal basis for extradition in respect of such offences. Extradition shall be subject to the other conditions provided by the law of the requested State.

3. States Parties which do not make extradition conditional on the existence of a treaty shall recognize such offences as extraditable offences between themselves subject to the conditions provided by the law of the requested State.

4. Such offences shall be treated, for the purpose of extradition between States Parties, as if they had been committed not only in the place in which they occurred but also in the territories of the States required to establish their jurisdiction in accordance with article 5, paragraph 1.

Article 9. 1. States Parties shall afford one another the greatest measure of assistance in connection with criminal proceedings brought in respect of any of the offences referred to in article 4, including the supply of all evidence at their disposal necessary for the proceedings.

2. States Parties shall carry out their obligations under paragraph 1 of this article in conformity with any treaties on mutual judicial assistance that may exist between them.

Article 10. 1. Each State Party shall ensure that education and information regarding the prohibition against torture are fully included in the training of law enforcement personnel, civil or military, medical personnel, public officials and other persons who may be involved in the custody, interrogation or treatment of any individual subjected to any form of arrest, detention or imprisonment.

2. Each State Party shall include this prohibition in the rules or instructions issued in regard to the duties and functions of any such persons.

Article 11. Each State Party shall keep under systematic review interrogation rules, instructions, methods and practices as well as arrangements for the custody and treatment of persons subjected to any form of arrest, detention or imprisonment in any territory under its jurisdiction, with a view to preventing any cases of torture.

Article 12. Each State Party shall ensure that its competent authorities proceed to a prompt and impartial investigation, wherever there is reasonable ground to believe that an act of torture has been committed in any territory under its jurisdiction.

Article 13. Each State Party shall ensure that any individual who alleges he has been subjected to torture in any territory under its jurisdiction has the right to complain to, and to have his case promptly and impartially examined by, its competent authorities. Steps shall be taken to ensure that the complainant and witnesses are protected against all ill-treatment or intimidation as a consequence of his complaint or any evidence given.

Article 14. 1. Each State Party shall ensure in its legal system that the victim of an act of torture obtains redress and has an enforceable right to fair and adequate compensation, including the means for as full rehabilitation as possible. In the event of the death of the victim as a result of an act of torture, his dependants shall be entitled to compensation.

2. Nothing in this article shall affect any right of the victim or other persons to compensation which may exist under national law.

Article 15. Each State Party shall ensure that any statement which is established to have been made as a result of torture shall not be invoked as evidence in any proceedings, except against a person accused of torture as evidence that the statement was made.

Article 16. 1. Each State Party shall undertake to prevent in any territory under its jurisdiction other acts of cruel, inhuman or degrading treatment or punishment which do not amount to torture as defined in article 1, when such acts are committed by or at the instigation of or with the consent or acquiescence of a public official or other person acting in an official capacity. In particular, the obligations contained in articles 10, 11, 12 and 13 shall apply with the substitution for references to torture of references to other forms of cruel, inhuman or degrading treatment or punishment.

2. The provisions of this Convention are without prejudice to the provisions of any other international instrument or national law which prohibits cruel, inhuman or degrading treatment or punishment or which relates to extradition or expulsion.

Part II

Article 17. 1. There shall be established a Committee against Torture (hereinafter referred to as the Committee) which shall carry out the functions hereinafter provided. The Committee shall consist of ten experts of high moral standing and recognized competence in the field of human rights, who shall serve in their personal capacity. The experts shall be elected by the States Parties, consideration being given to equitable geographical distribution and to the usefulness of the participation of some persons having legal experience.

2. The members of the Committee shall be elected by secret ballot from a list of persons nominated by States Parties. Each State Party may nominate one person from among its own nationals. States Parties shall bear in mind the usefulness of nominating persons who are also members of the Human Rights Committee established under the International Covenant on Civil and Political Rights and who are willing to serve on the Committee against Torture.

3. Elections of the members of the Committee shall be held at biennial meetings of States Parties convened by the Secretary-General of the United Nations. At those meetings, for which two thirds of the States Parties shall constitute a quorum, the persons elected to the Committee shall be those who obtain the largest number of votes and an absolute majority of the votes of the representatives of States Parties present and voting.

4. The initial election shall be held no later than six months after the date of the entry into force of this Convention. At least four months before the date of each election, the Secretary-General of the United Nations shall address a letter to the States Parties inviting them to submit their nominations within three months. The Secretary-General shall prepare a list in alphabetical order of all persons thus nominated, indicating the States Parties which have nominated them, and shall submit it to the States Parties.

5. The members of the Committee shall be elected for a term of four years. They shall be eligible for re-election if renominated. However, the term of five of the members elected at the first election shall expire at the end of two years; immediately after the first election the names of

these five members shall be chosen by lot by the chairman of the meeting referred to in paragraph 3 of this article.

6. If a member of the Committee dies or resigns or for any other cause can no longer perform his Committee duties, the State Party which nominated him shall appoint another expert from among its nationals to serve for the remainder of his term, subject to the approval of the majority of the States Parties. The approval shall be considered given unless half or more of the States Parties respond negatively within six weeks after having been informed by the Secretary-General of the United Nations of the proposed appointment.

7. States Parties shall be responsible for the expenses of the members of the Committee while they are in performance of Committee duties.

Article 18. 1. The Committee shall elect its officers for a term of two years. They may be re-elected.

2. The Committee shall establish its own rules of procedure, but these rules shall provide, *inter alia,* that:

(a) Six members shall constitute a quorum;

(b) Decisions of the Committee shall be made by a majority vote of the members present.

3. The Secretary-General of the United Nations shall provide the necessary staff and facilities for the effective performance of the functions of the Committee under this Convention.

4. The Secretary-General of the United Nations shall convene the initial meeting of the Committee. After its initial meeting, the Committee shall meet at such times as shall be provided in its rules of procedure.

5. The States Parties shall be responsible for expenses incurred in connection with the holding of meetings of the States Parties and of the Committee, including reimbursement to the United Nations for any expenses, such as the cost of staff and facilities, incurred by the United Nations pursuant to paragraph 3 of this article.

Article 19. 1. The States Parties shall submit to the Committee, through the Secretary-General of the United Nations, reports on the measures they have taken to give effect to their undertakings under this Convention, within one year after the entry into force of the Convention for the State Party concerned. Thereafter, the States Parties shall submit supplementary reports every four years on any new measures taken and such other reports as the Committee may request.

2. The Secretary-General of the United Nations shall transmit the reports to all States Parties.

3. Each report shall be considered by the Committee which may make such general comments on the report as it may consider appropriate and shall forward these to the State Party concerned. That State Party may respond with any observations it chooses to the Committee.

4. The Committee may, at its discretion, decide to include any comments made by it in accordance with paragraph 3 of this article, together with the observations thereon received from the State Party concerned, in its annual report made in accordance with article 24. If so requested by the State Party concerned, the Committee may also include a copy of the report submitted under paragraph 1 of this article.

Article 20. 1. If the Committee receives reliable information which appears to it to contain well-founded indications that torture is being systematically practised in the territory of a State Party, the Committee shall invite that State Party to co-operate in the examination of the information and to

this end to submit observations with regard to the information concerned.

2. Taking into account any observations which may have been submitted by the State Party concerned, as well as any other relevant information available to it, the Committee may, if it decides that this is warranted, designate one or more of its members to make a confidential inquiry and to report to the Committee urgently.

3. If an inquiry is made in accordance with paragraph 2 of this article, the Committee shall seek the co-operation of the State Party concerned. In agreement with that State Party, such an inquiry may include a visit to its territory.

4. After examining the findings of its member or members submitted in accordance with paragraph 2 of this article, the Committee shall transmit these findings to the State Party concerned together with any comments or suggestions which seem appropriate in view of the situation.

5. All the proceedings of the Committee referred to in paragraphs 1 to 4 of this article shall be confidential, and at all stages of the proceedings the co-operation of the State Party shall be sought. After such proceedings have been completed with regard to an inquiry made in accordance with paragraph 2, the Committee may, after consultations with the State Party concerned, decide to include a summary account of the results of the proceedings in its annual report made in accordance with article 24.

Article 21. 1. A State Party to this Convention may at any time declare under this article that it recognizes the competence of the Committee to receive and consider communications to the effect that a State Party claims that another State Party is not fulfilling its obligations under this Convention. Such communications may be received and considered according to the procedures laid down in this article only if submitted by a State Party which has made a declaration recognizing in regard to itself the competence of the Committee. No communication shall be dealt with by the Committee under this article if it concerns a State Party which has not made such a declaration. Communications received under this article shall be dealt with in accordance with the following procedure:

(a) If a State Party considers that another State Party is not giving effect to the provisions of this Convention, it may, by written communication, bring the matter to the attention of that State Party. Within three months after the receipt of the communication the receiving State shall afford the State which sent the communication an explanation or any other statement in writing clarifying the matter, which should include, to the extent possible and pertinent, reference to domestic procedures and remedies taken, pending or available in the matter;

(b) If the matter is not adjusted to the satisfaction of both States Parties concerned within six months after the receipt by the receiving State of the initial communication, either State shall have the right to refer the matter to the Committee, by notice given to the Committee and to the other State;

(c) The Committee shall deal with a matter referred to it under this article only after it has ascertained that all domestic remedies have been invoked and exhausted in the matter, in conformity with the generally recognized principles of international law. This shall not be the rule where the application of the remedies is unreasonably prolonged or is unlikely to bring effective relief to the person who is the victim of the violation of this Convention;

(d) The Committee shall hold closed meetings when examining communications under this article;

(e) Subject to the provisions of subparagraph (c), the Committee shall make available its good offices to the States Parties concerned with a view to a friendly solution of the matter on the basis of respect for the obligations provided for in this Convention. For this purpose, the Committee may, when appropriate, set up an *ad hoc* conciliation commission;

(f) In any matter referred to it under this article, the Committee may call upon the States Parties concerned, referred to in subparagraph (b), to supply any relevant information;

(g) The States Parties concerned, referred to in subparagraph (b), shall have the right to be represented when the matter is being considered by the Committee and to make submissions orally and/or in writing;

(h) The Committee shall, within twelve months after the date of receipt of notice under subparagraph (b), submit a report:

(i) If a solution within the terms of subparagraph (e) is reached, the Committee shall confine its report to a brief statement of the facts and of the solution reached;

(ii) If a solution within the terms of subparagraph (e) is not reached, the Committee shall confine its report to a brief statement of the facts; the written submissions and record of the oral submissions made by the States Parties concerned shall be attached to the report.

In every matter, the report shall be communicated to the States Parties concerned.

2. The provisions of this article shall come into force when five States Parties to this Convention have made declarations under paragraph 1 of this article. Such declarations shall be deposited by the States Parties with the Secretary-General of the United Nations, who shall transmit copies thereof to the other States Parties. A declaration may be withdrawn at any time by notification to the Secretary-General. Such a withdrawal shall not prejudice the consideration of any matter which is the subject of a communication already transmitted under this article; no further communication by any State Party shall be received under this article after the notification of withdrawal of the declaration has been received by the Secretary-General, unless the State Party concerned has made a new declaration.

Article 22. 1. A State Party to this Convention may at any time declare under this article that it recognizes the competence of the Committee to receive and consider communications from or on behalf of individuals subject to its jurisdiction who claim to be victims of a violation by a State Party of the provisions of the Convention. No communication shall be received by the Committee if it concerns a State Party which has not made such a declaration.

2. The Committee shall consider inadmissible any communication under this article which is anonymous or which it considers to be an abuse of the right of submission of such communications or to be incompatible with the provisions of this Convention.

3. Subject to the provisions of paragraph 2, the Committee shall bring any communications submitted to it under this article to the attention of the State Party to this Convention which has made a declaration under paragraph 1 and is alleged to be violating any provisions of the Convention. Within six months, the receiving State shall submit to the Committee written explanations or statements clarifying the matter and the remedy, if any, that may have been taken by that State.

4. The Committee shall consider communications received under this article in the light of all information made available to it by or on behalf of the individual and by the State Party concerned.

5. The Committee shall not consider any communications from an individual under this article unless it has ascertained that:

(a) The same matter has not been, and is not being, examined under another procedure of international investigation or settlement;

(b) The individual has exhausted all available domestic remedies; this shall not be the rule where the application of the remedies is unreasonably prolonged or is unlikely to bring effective relief to the person who is the victim of the violation of this Convention.

6. The Committee shall hold closed meetings when examining communications under this article.

7. The Committee shall forward its views to the State Party concerned and to the individual.

8. The provisions of this article shall come into force when five States Parties to this Convention have made declarations under paragraph 1 of this article. Such declarations shall be deposited by the States Parties with the Secretary-General of the United Nations, who shall transmit copies thereof to the other States Parties. A declaration may be withdrawn at any time by notification to the Secretary-General. Such a withdrawal shall not prejudice the consideration of any matter which is the subject of a communication already transmitted under this article; no further communication by or on behalf of an individual shall be received under this article after the notification of withdrawal of the declaration has been received by the Secretary-General, unless the State Party has made a new declaration.

Article 23. The members of the Committee and of the *ad hoc* conciliation commissions which may be appointed under article 21, paragraph 1 (e), shall be entitled to the facilities, privileges and immunities of experts on mission for the United Nations as laid down in the relevant sections of the Convention on the Privileges and Immunities of the United Nations.

Article 24. The Committee shall submit an annual report on its activities under this Convention to the States Parties and to the General Assembly of the United Nations.

Part III

Article 25. 1. This Convention is open for signature by all States.

2. This Convention is subject to ratification. Instruments of ratification shall be deposited with the Secretary-General of the United Nations.

Article 26. This Convention is open to accession by all States. Accession shall be effected by the deposit of an instrument of accession with the Secretary-General of the United Nations.

Article 27. 1. This Convention shall enter into force on the thirtieth day after the date of the deposit with the Secretary-General of the United Nations of the twentieth instrument of ratification or accession.

2. For each State ratifying this Convention or acceding to it after the deposit of the twentieth instrument of ratification or accession, the Convention shall enter into force on the thirtieth day after the date of the deposit of its own instrument of ratification or accession.

Article 28. 1. Each State may, at the time of signature or ratification of this Convention or accession thereto, declare that it does not recognize the competence of the Committee provided for in article 20.

2. Any State Party having made a reservation in accordance with paragraph 1 of this article may, at any time, withdraw this reservation by notification to the Secretary-General of the United Nations.

Article 29. 1. Any State Party to this Convention may propose an amendment and file it with the Secretary-General of the United Nations. The Secretary-General shall thereupon communicate the proposed amendment to the States Parties with a request that they notify him whether they favour a conference of States Parties for the purpose of considering and voting upon the proposal. In the event that within four months from the date of such communication at least one third of the States Parties favours such a conference, the Secretary-General shall convene the conference under the auspices of the United Nations. Any amendment adopted by a majority of the States Parties present and voting at the conference shall be submitted by the Secretary-General to all the States Parties for acceptance.

2. An amendment adopted in accordance with paragraph 1 of this article shall enter into force when two thirds of the States Parties to this Convention have notified the Secretary-General of the United Nations that they have accepted it in accordance with their respective constitutional processes.

3. When amendments enter into force, they shall be binding on those States Parties which have accepted them, other States Parties still being bound by the provisions of this Convention and any earlier amendments which they have accepted.

Article 30. 1. Any dispute between two or more States Parties concerning the interpretation or application of this Convention which cannot be settled through negotiation shall, at the request of one of them, be submitted to arbitration. If within six months from the date of the request for arbitration the Parties are unable to agree on the organization of the arbitration, any one of those Parties may refer the dispute to the International Court of Justice by request in conformity with the Statute of the Court.

2. Each State may, at the time of signature or ratification of this Convention or accession thereto, declare that it does not consider itself bound by paragraph 1 of this article. The other States Parties shall not be bound by paragraph 1 of this article with respect to any State Party having made such a reservation.

3. Any State Party having made a reservation in accordance with paragraph 2 of this article may at any time withdraw this reservation by notification to the Secretary-General of the United Nations.

Article 31. 1. A State Party may denounce this Convention by written notification to the Secretary-General of the United Nations. Denunciation becomes effective one year after the date of receipt of the notification by the Secretary-General.

2. Such a denunciation shall not have the effect of releasing the State Party from its obligations under this Convention in regard to any act or omission which occurs prior to the date at which the denunciation becomes effective, nor shall denunciation prejudice in any way the continued consideration of any matter which is already under consideration by the Committee prior to the date at which the denunciation becomes effective.

3. Following the date at which the denunciation of a State Party becomes effective, the Committee shall not commence consideration of any new matter regarding that State.

Article 32. The Secretary-General of the United Nations shall inform all States Members of the United Nations and all States which have signed this Convention or acceded to it of the following:

(a) Signatures, ratifications and accessions under articles 25 and 26;

(b) The date of entry into force of this Convention under article 27 and the date of the entry into force of any amendments under article 29;

(c) Denunciations under article 31.

Article 33. 1. This Convention, of which the Arabic, Chinese, English, French, Russian and Spanish texts are equally authentic, shall be deposited with the Secretary-General of the United Nations.

2. The Secretary-General of the United Nations shall transmit certified copies of this Convention to all States.

SEE ALSO *Body of Principles for the Protection of All Persons under Any Form of Detention or Imprisonment; Declaration on the Protection of All Persons from Being Subjected to Torture, . . . ; Inter-American Convention to Prevent and Punish Torture; Torture; Torture: Special Rapporteur; United Nations Voluntary Fund for Victims of Torture.*

CONVENTION FOR THE SUPPRESSION OF THE TRAFFIC IN PERSONS AND OF THE EXPLOITATION OF THE PROSTITUTION OF OTHERS

(1949). The convention is based on a draft prepared by the UN Secretary-General in 1948, at the request of the Economic and Social Council, which unified four existing instruments for the suppression of the traffic in women and children (the International Agreement of 18 May 1904 for the Suppression of the White Slave Traffic; the International Convention of 4 May 1910 for the Suppression of the White Slave Traffic; the International Convention for 30 September 1921 for the Suppression of the Traffic in Women and Children; and the International Convention of 11 October 1933 for the Suppression of the Traffic in Women of Full Age) and also embodied the substance of a draft convention of the suppression of the exploitation of the prostitution of others prepared by the LEAGUE OF NATIONS in 1937. The convention was adopted by the UN General Assembly on 2 December 1949 (resolution 317 [IV]) and entered into force on 25 July 1951. The text (United Nations, *Treaty Series,* vol. 96, p. 271), is as follows:

Preamble

Whereas prostitution and the accompanying evil of the traffic in persons for the purpose of prostitution are incompatible with the dignity and worth of the human person and endanger the welfare of the individual, the family and the community,

Whereas, with respect to the suppression of the traffic in women and children, the following international instruments are in force:

1. International Agreement of 18 May 1904 for the Suppression of the White Slave Traffic, as amended by the Protocol approved by the General Assembly of the United Nations on 3 December 1948,

2. International Convention of 4 May 1910 for the Suppression of the White Slave Traffic, as amended by the above-mentioned Protocol,

3. International Convention of 30 September 1921 for the Suppression of the Traffic in Women and Children, as amended by the Protocol approved by the General Assembly of the United Nations of 20 October 1947,

4. International Convention of 11 October 1933 for the Suppression of the Traffic in Women of Full Age, as amended by the aforesaid Protocol,

Whereas the League of Nations in 1937 prepared a draft Convention extending the scope of the above-mentioned instruments, and

Whereas developments since 1937 make feasible the conclusion of a convention consolidating the above-mentioned instruments and embodying the substance of the 1937 draft Convention as well as desirable alterations therein:

Now therefore

The Contracting Parties

Hereby agree as hereinafter provided:

Article 1. The Parties to the present Convention agree to punish any person who, to gratify the passions of another:

1. Procures, entices or leads away, for purposes of prostitution, another person, even with the consent of that person;

2. Exploits the prostitution of another person, even with the consent of that person.

Article 2. The Parties to the present Convention further agree to punish any person who:

1. Keeps or manages, or knowingly finances or takes part in the financing of a brothel;

2. Knowingly lets or rents a building or other place or any part thereof for the purpose of the prostitution of others.

Article 3. To the extent permitted by domestic law, attempts to commit any of the offences referred to in articles 1 and 2, and acts preparatory to the commission thereof, shall also be punished.

Article 4. To the extent permitted by domestic law, intentional participation in the acts referred to in articles 1 and 2 above shall also be punishable.

To the extent permitted by domestic law, acts of participation shall be treated as separate offences whenever this is necessary to prevent impunity.

Article 5. In cases where injured persons are entitled under domestic law to be parties to proceedings in respect of any of the offences referred to in the present Convention, aliens shall be so entitled upon the same terms as nationals.

Article 6. Each Party to the present Convention agrees to take all the necessary measures to repeal or abolish any existing law, regulation or administrative provision by virtue of which persons who engage in or are suspected of engaging in prostitution are subject either to special registration or to the possession of a special document or to any exceptional requirement for supervision or notification.

Article 7. Previous convictions pronounced in foreign States for offences referred to in the present Convention shall, to the extent permitted by domestic law, be taken into account for the purpose of:

1. Establishing recidivism;

2. Disqualifying the offender from the exercise of civil rights.

Article 8. The offences referred to in articles 1 and 2 of the present Convention shall be regarded as extraditable offences in any extradition treaty which has been or may hereafter be concluded between any of the Parties to this Convention.

The Parties to the present Convention which do not make extradition conditional on the existence of a treaty shall henceforward recognize the offences referred to in articles 1 and 2 of the present Convention as cases for extradition between themselves.

Extradition shall be granted in accordance with the law of the State to which the request is made.

Article 9. In States where the extradition of nationals is not permitted by law, nationals who have returned to their own State after the commission abroad of any of the offences referred to in articles 1 and 2 of the present Convention shall be prosecuted in and punished by the courts of their own State.

This provision shall not apply if, in a similar case between the Parties to the present Convention, the extradition of an alien cannot be granted.

Article 10. The provisions of article 9 shall not apply when the person charged with the offence has been tried in a foreign State and, if convicted, has served his sentence or had it remitted or reduced in conformity with the laws of that foreign State.

Article 11. Nothing in the present Convention shall be interpreted as determining the attitude of a Party towards the general question of the limits of criminal jurisdiction under international law.

Article 12. The present Convention does not affect the principle that the offences to which it refers shall in each State be defined, prosecuted and punished in conformity with its domestic law.

Article 13. The Parties to the present Convention shall be bound to execute letters of request relating to offences referred to in the Convention in accordance with their domestic law and practice.

The transmission of letters of request shall be effected:

1. By direct communication between the judicial authorities; or

2. By direct communication between the Ministers of Justice of the two States, or by direct communication from another competent authority of the State making the request to the Minister of Justice of the State to which the request is made; or

3. Through the diplomatic or consular representative of the State making the request in the State to which the request is made; this representative shall send the letters of request direct to the competent judicial authority or to the authority indicated by the Government of the State to which the request is made, and shall receive direct from such authority the papers constituting the execution of the letters of request.

In cases 1 and 3 a copy of the letters of request shall always be sent to the superior authority of the State to which application is made.

Unless otherwise agreed, the letters of request shall be drawn up in the language of the authority making the request, provided always that the State to which the request is made may require a translation in its own language, certified correct by the authority making the request.

Each Party to the present Convention shall notify to each of the other Parties to the Convention the method or methods of transmission mentioned above which it will recognize for the letters of request of the latter State.

Until such notification is made by a State, its existing procedure in regard to letters of request shall remain in force.

Execution of letters of request shall not give rise to a claim for reimbursement of charges or expenses of any nature whatever other than expenses of experts.

Nothing in the present article shall be construed as an undertaking on the part of the Parties to the present Convention to adopt in criminal matters any form or methods of proof contrary to their own domestic laws.

Article 14. Each Party to the present Convention shall establish or maintain a service charged with the coordination and centralization of the results of the investigation of offences referred to in the present Convention.

Such services should compile all information calculated to facilitate the prevention and punishment of the offences referred to in the present Convention and should be in close contact with the corresponding services in other States.

Article 15. To the extent permitted by the domestic law and to the extent to which the authorities responsible for the services referred to in article 14 may judge desirable, they shall furnish to the authorities responsible for the corresponding services in other States the following information:

1. Particulars of any offence referred to in the present Convention or any attempt to commit such offence;

2. Particulars of any search for and any prosecution, arrest, conviction, refusal of admission or expulsion of persons guilty of any of the offences referred to in the present Convention, the movements of such persons and any other useful information with regard to them.

The information so furnished shall include descriptions of the offenders, their fingerprints, photographs, methods of operation, police records and records of conviction.

Article 16. The Parties to the present Convention agree to take or to encourage, through their public and private educational, health, social, economic and other related services, measures for the prevention of prostitution and for the rehabilitation and social adjustment of the victims of prostitution and of the offences referred to in the present Convention.

Article 17. The Parties to the present Convention undertake, in connexion with immigration and emigration, to adopt or maintain such measures as are required, in terms of their obligations under the present Convention, to check the traffic in persons of either sex for the purpose of prostitution.

In particular they undertake:

1. To make such regulations as are necessary for the protection of immigrants or emigrants, and in particular, women and children, both at the place of arrival and departure and while en route;

2. To arrange for appropriate publicity warning the public of the dangers of the aforesaid traffic;

3. To take appropriate measures to ensure supervision of railway stations, airports, seaports and en route, and of other public places, in order to prevent international traffic in persons for the purpose of prostitution;

4. To take appropriate measures in order that the appropriate authorities be informed of the arrival of persons who appear, *prima facie,* to be the principals and accomplices in or victims of such traffic.

Article 18. The Parties to the present Convention undertake, in accordance with the conditions laid down by domestic law, to have declarations taken from aliens who are prostitutes, in order to establish their identity and civil status and to discover who has caused them to leave their State. The information obtained shall be communicated to the authorities of the State of origin of the said persons with a view to their eventual repatriation.

Article 19. The Parties to the present Convention undertake, in accordance with the conditions laid down by domestic law and without prejudice to prosecution or other action for violations thereunder and so far as possible:

1. Pending the completion of arrangements for the repatriation of destitute victims of international traffic in persons for the purpose of prostitution, to make suitable provisions for their temporary care and maintenance;

2. To repatriate persons referred to in article 18 who desire to be repatriated or who may be claimed by persons exercising authority over them or whose expulsion is ordered in conformity with the law. Repatriation shall take place only after agreement is reached with the State of destination as to identity and nationality as well as to the place and date of arrival at frontiers. Each Party to the present Convention shall facilitate the passage of such persons through its territory.

Where the persons referred to in the preceding paragraph cannot themselves repay the cost of repatriation and have neither spouse, relatives nor guardian to pay for them, the cost of repatriation as far as the nearest frontier or port of embarkation or airport in the direction of the State of origin shall be borne by the State where they are in residence, and the cost of the remainder of the journey shall be borne by the State of origin.

Article 20. The Parties to the present Convention shall, if they have not already done so, take the necessary measures for the supervision of employment agencies in order to prevent persons seeking employment, in particular women and children, from being exposed to the danger of prostitution.

Article 21. The Parties to the present Convention shall communicate to the Secretary-General of the United Nations such laws and regulations as have already been promulgated in their States, and thereafter annually such laws and regulations as may be promulgated, relating to the subjects of the present Convention, a well as all measures taken by them concerning the application of the Convention. The information received shall be published periodically by the Secretary-General and sent to all Members of the United Nations and to non-member States to which the present Convention is officially communicated in accordance with article 23.

Article 22. If any dispute shall arise between the Parties to the present Convention relating to its interpretation or application and if such dispute cannot be settled by other means, the dispute shall, at the request of any one of the Parties to the dispute, be referred to the International Court of Justice.

Article 23. The present Convention shall be open for signature on behalf of any Member of the United Nations and also on behalf of any other State to which an invitation has been addressed by the Economic and Social Council.

The present Convention shall be ratified and the instruments of ratification shall be deposited with the Secretary-General of the United Nations.

The States mentioned in the first paragraph which have not signed the Convention may accede to it.

C

Accession shall be effected by deposit of an instrument of accession with the Secretary-General of the United Nations.

For the purposes of the present Convention the word "State" shall include all the colonies and Trust Territories of a State signatory or acceding to the Convention and all territories for which such State is internationally responsible.

Article 24. The present Convention shall come into force on the ninetieth day following the date of deposit of the second instrument of ratification or accession.

For each State ratifying or acceding to the Convention after the deposit of the second instrument of ratification or accession, the Convention shall enter into force ninety days after the deposit by such State of its instrument of ratification or accession.

Article 25. After the expiration of five years from the entry into force of the present Convention, any Party to the Convention may denounce it by a written notification addressed to the Secretary-General of the United Nations.

Such denunciation shall take effect for the Party making it one year from the date upon which it is received by the Secretary-General of the United Nations.

Article 26. The Secretary-General of the United Nations shall inform all Members of the United Nations and non-member States referred to in article 23:

(a) Of signatures, ratifications and accessions received in accordance with article 23;

(b) Of the date on which the present Convention will come into force in accordance with article 24;

(c) Of denunciations received in accordance with article 25.

Article 27. Each Party to the present Convention undertakes to adopt, in accordance with its Constitution, the legislative or other measures necessary to ensure the application of the Convention.

Article 28. The provisions of the present Convention shall supersede in the relations between the Parties thereto the provisions of the international instruments referred to in sub-paragraphs 1, 2, 3 and 4 of the second paragraph of the Preamble, each of which shall be deemed to be terminated when all the Parties thereto shall have become Parties to the present Convention.

Final Protocol

Nothing in the present Convention shall be deemed to prejudice any legislation which ensures, for the enforcement of the provisions for securing the suppression of the traffic in persons and of the exploitation of others for purposes of prostitution, stricter conditions than those provided by the present Convention.

The provisions of articles 23 to 26 inclusive of the Convention shall apply to the present Protocol.

SEE ALSO *Mauritania: Question of Slavery; Protocol amending the Slavery Convention; Slavery: Implementation of the International Conventions; Slavery and the Slave Trade; Slavery Convention Signed at Geneva on 25 September 1926, as Amended; Sudan: Question of Slavery; Supplementary Convention on the Abolition of Slavery, the Slave Trade and Institutions and Practices Similar to Slavery; Traffic in Persons and Exploitation of the Prostitution of Others; Working Group on Contemporary Forms of Slavery.*

CONVENTION FOR THE SUPPRESSION OF UNLAWFUL ACTS AGAINST THE SAFETY OF CIVIL AVIATION (1971).

Designed to protect the safety of civil aircraft and the right to life of those who travel in such aircraft, the convention provides for the prevention and punishment of certain offenses, described in article 1, which threaten the safety of civil aviation. Contracting States undertake to make such offenses punishable by severe penalties, to establish their jurisdiction over such offenses, and either to prosecute the offender or to arrange for his extradition. They also agree to report all the relevant facts to the International Civil Aviation Organization as promptly as possible. The convention contains rules supplementing those set out in earlier instruments protecting aircraft and their passengers, including the CONVENTION ON INTERNATIONAL CIVIL AVIATION (1944) and the PROTOCOL to that convention (1984), the CONVENTION ON OFFENSES AND CERTAIN OTHER ACTS COMMITTED ON BOARD AIRCRAFT (1963), and the CONVENTION FOR THE SUPPRESSION OR UNLAWFUL SEIZURE OF AIRCRAFT (1970).

The convention was adopted by the International Conference on Air Law, convened in Montreal under the auspices of the International Civil Aviation Organization, on 23 September 1971. The text of the convention (United Nations, *Juridical Yearbook for 1971*, p. 143), is as follows:

The States Parties to this Convention,

Considering that unlawful acts against the safety of civil aviation jeopardize the safety of persons and property, seriously affect the operation of air services, and undermine the confidence of the peoples of the world in the safety of civil aviation;

Considering that the occurrence of such acts is a matter of grave concern;

Considering that, for the purpose of deterring such acts, there is an urgent need to provide appropriate measures for punishment of offenders;

Have agreed as follows:

Article 1. 1. Any person commits an offence if he unlawfully and intentionally:

(a) performs an act of violence against a person on board an aircraft in flight if that act is likely to endanger the safety of that aircraft; or

(b) destroys an aircraft in service or causes damage to such an aircraft which renders it incapable of flight or which is likely to endanger its safety in flight; or

(c) places or causes to be placed on an aircraft in service, by any means whatsoever, a device or substance which is likely to destroy that aircraft, or to cause damage to it which renders it incapable of flight, or to cause damage to it which is likely to endanger its safety in flight; or

(d) destroys or damages air navigation facilities or interferes with their operation, if any such act is likely to endanger the safety of aircraft in flight; or

(e) communicates information which he knows to be false, thereby endangering the safety of an aircraft in flight.

2. Any person also commits an offence if he:

(a) attempts to commit any of the offences mentioned in paragraph 1 of this Article; or

(b) is an accomplice of a person who commits or attempts to commit any such offense.

Article 2. For the purpose of this Convention:

(a) an aircraft is considered to be in flight at any time from the moment when all its external doors are closed following embarkation until the moment when any such door is opened for disembarkation; in the case of a forced landing, the flight shall be deemed to continue until the competent authorities take over the responsibility for the aircraft and for persons and property on board;

(b) an aircraft is considered to be in service from the beginning of the preflight preparation of the aircraft by ground personnel or by the crew for a specific flight until twenty-four hours after any landing; the period of service shall, in any event, extend for the entire period during which the aircraft is in flight as defined in paragraph (a) of this Article.

Article 3. Each Contracting State undertakes to make the offences mentioned in Article 1 punishable by severe penalties.

Article 4. 1. This Convention shall not apply to aircraft used in military, customs or police services.

2. In the cases contemplated in subparagraphs (a), (b), (c) and (e) of paragraph 1 of Article 1, this Convention shall apply, irrespective of whether the aircraft is engaged in an international or domestic flight, only if:

(a) the place of take-off or landing, actual or intended, of the aircraft is situated outside the territory of the State of registration of that aircraft; or

(b) the offence is committed in the territory of a State other than the State of registration of the aircraft.

3. Notwithstanding paragraph 2 of this Article, in the cases contemplated in subparagraphs (a), (b), (c) and (e) of paragraph 1 of Article 1, this Convention shall also apply if the offender or the alleged offender is found in the territory of a State other than the State of registration of the aircraft.

4. With respect to the States mentioned in Article 9 and in the cases mentioned in subparagraphs (a), (b), (c) and (e) of paragraph 1 of Article 1, this Convention shall not apply if the places referred to in subparagraph (a) of paragraph 2 of this Article are situated within the territory of the same State where that State is one of those referred to in Article 9, unless the offence is committed or the offender or alleged offender is found in the territory of a State other than that State.

5. In the cases contemplated in subparagraph (d) of paragraph 1 of Article 1, this Convention shall apply only if the air navigation facilities are used in international air navigation.

6. The provisions of paragraphs 2, 3, 4 and 5 of this Article shall also apply in the cases contemplated in paragraph 2 of Article 1.

Article 5. 1. Each Contracting State shall take such measures as may be necessary to establish its jurisdiction over the offences in the following cases:

(a) when the offence is committed in the territory of that State;

(b) when the offence is committed against or on board an aircraft registered in that State;

(c) when the aircraft on board which the offence is committed lands in its territory with the alleged offender still on board;

(d) when the offence is committed against or on board

an aircraft leased without crew to a lessee who has his principal place of business or, if the lessee has no such place of business, his permanent residence, in that State.

2. Each Contracting State shall likewise take such measures as may be necessary to establish its jurisdiction over the offences mentioned in Article 1, paragraph 1 (a), (b) and (c), and in Article 1, paragraph 2, in so far as that paragraph relates to those offences, in the case where the alleged offender is present in its territory and it does not extradite him pursuant to Article 8 to any of the States mentioned in paragraph 1 of this Article.

3. This Convention does not exclude any criminal jurisdiction exercised in accordance with national law.

Article 6. 1. Upon being satisfied that the circumstances so warrant, any Contracting State in the territory of which the offender or the alleged offender is present, shall take him into custody or take other measures to ensure his presence. The custody and other measures shall be as provided in the law of that State but may only be continued for such time as is necessary to enable any criminal or extradition proceedings to be instituted.

2. Such State shall immediately make a preliminary enquiry into the facts.

3. Any person in custody pursuant to paragraph 1 of this Article shall be assisted in communicating immediately with the nearest appropriate representative of the State of which he is a national.

4. When a State, pursuant to this Article, has taken a person into custody, it shall immediately notify the States mentioned in Article 5, paragraph 1, the State of nationality of the detained person and, if it considers it advisable, any other interested States of the fact that such person is in custody and of the circumstances which warrant his detention. The State which makes the preliminary enquiry contemplated in paragraph 2 of this Article shall promptly report its findings to the said States and shall indicate whether it intends to exercise jurisdiction.

Article 7. The Contracting State in the territory of which the alleged offender is found shall, if it does not extradite him, be obliged, without exception whatsoever and whether or not the offence was committed in its territory, to submit the case to its competent authorities for the purpose of prosecution. Those authorities shall take their decision in the same manner as in the case of any ordinary offence of a serious nature under the law of that State.

Article 8. 1. The offences shall be deemed to be included as extraditable offences in any extradition treaty existing between Contracting States. Contracting States undertake to include the offences as extraditable offences in every extradition treaty to be concluded between them.

2. If a Contracting State which makes extradition conditional on the existence of a treaty receives a request for extradition from another Contracting State with which it has no extradition treaty, it may at its option consider this Convention as the legal basis for extradition in respect of the offences. Extradition shall be subject to the other conditions provided by the law of the requested State.

3. Contracting States which do not make extradition conditional on the existence of a treaty shall recognize the offences as extraditable offences between themselves subject to the conditions provided by the law of the requested State.

4. Each of the offences shall be treated, for the purpose of extradition between Contracting States, as if it had been committed not only in the place in which it occurred but also in the territories of the States required to establish

their jurisdiction in accordance with Article 5, paragraph 1 (b), (c) and (d).

Article 9. The Contracting States which establish joint air transport operating organizations or international operating agencies, which operate aircraft which are subject to joint or international registration shall, by appropriate means, designate for each aircraft the State among them which shall exercise the jurisdiction and have the attributes of the State of registration for the purpose of this Convention and shall give notice thereof to the International Civil Aviation Organization which shall communicate the notice to all States Parties to this Convention.

Article 10. 1. Contracting States shall, in accordance with international and national law, endeavour to take all practicable measures for the purpose of preventing the offences mentioned in Article 1.

2. When, due to the commission of one of the offences mentioned in Article 1, a flight has been delayed or interrupted, any Contracting State in whose territory the aircraft or passengers or crew are present shall facilitate the continuation of the journey of the passengers and crew as soon as practicable, and shall without delay return the aircraft and its cargo to the persons lawfully entitled to possession.

Article 11. 1. Contracting States shall afford one another the greatest measure of assistance in connection with criminal proceedings brought in respect of the offences. The law of the State requested shall apply in all cases.

2. The provisions of paragraph 1 of this Article shall not affect obligations under any other treaty, bilateral or multilateral, which governs or will govern, in whole or in part, mutual assistance in criminal matters.

Article 12. Any Contracting State having reason to believe that one of the offences mentioned in Article 1 will be committed shall, in accordance with its national law, furnish any relevant information in its possession to those States which it believes would be the States mentioned in Article 5, paragraph 1.

Article 13. Each Contracting State shall in accordance with its national law report to the Council of the International Civil Aviation Organization as promptly as possible any relevant information in its possession concerning:

(a) the circumstances of the offence;

(b) the action taken pursuant to Article 10, paragraph 2;

(c) the measures taken in relation to the offender or the alleged offender and, in particular, the results of any extradition proceedings or other legal proceedings.

Article 14. 1. Any dispute between two or more Contracting States concerning the interpretation or application of this Convention which cannot be settled through negotiation, shall, at the request of one of them, be submitted to arbitration. If within six months from the date of the request for arbitration the Parties are unable to agree on the organization of the arbitration, any one of those Parties may refer the dispute to the International Court of Justice by request in conformity with the Statute of the Court.

2. Each State may at the time of signature or ratification of this Convention or accession thereto, declare that it does not consider itself bound by the preceding paragraph. The other Contracting States shall not be bound by the preceding paragraph with respect to any Contracting State having made such a reservation.

3. Any Contracting State having made a reservation in accordance with the preceding paragraph may at any time withdraw this reservation by notification to the Depositary Governments.

Article 15. 1. This Convention shall be open for signature at Montreal on 23 September 1971, by States participating in the International Conference on Air Law held at Montreal from 8 to 23 September 1971 (hereinafter referred to as the Montreal Conference). After 10 October 1971, the Convention shall be open to all States for signature in Moscow, London and Washington. Any State which does not sign this Convention before its entry into force in accordance with paragraph 3 of this Article may accede to it at any time.

2. This Convention shall be subject to ratification by the signatory States. Instruments of ratification and instruments of accession shall be deposited with the Governments of the Union of Soviet Socialist Republics, the United Kingdom of Great Britain and Northern Ireland, and the United States of America, which are hereby designated the Depositary Governments.

3. This Convention shall enter into force thirty days following the date of the deposit of instruments of ratification by ten States signatory to this Convention which participated in the Montreal Conference.

4. For other States, this Convention shall enter into force on the date of entry into force of this Convention in accordance with paragraph 3 of this Article, or thirty days following the date of deposit of their instruments of ratification or accession, whichever is later.

5. The Depositary Governments shall promptly inform all signatory and acceding States of the date of each signature, the date of deposit of each instrument of ratification or accession, the date of entry into force of this Convention, and other notices.

6. As soon as this Convention comes into force, it shall be registered by the Depositary Governments pursuant to Article 102 of the Charter of the United Nations and pursuant to Article 83 of the Convention on International Civil Aviation (Chicago, 1944).

Article 16. 1. Any Contracting State may denounce this Convention by written notification to the Depositary Governments.

2. Denunciation shall take effect six months following the date on which notification is received by the Depositary Governments.

In witness whereof the undersigned Plenipotentiaries, being duly authorized thereto by their Governments, have signed this Convention.

Done at Montreal, this twenty-third day of September, one thousand nine hundred and seventy-one, in three originals, each being drawn up in four authentic texts in the English, French, Russian and Spanish languages.

CONVENTION FOR THE SUPPRESSION OF UNLAWFUL SEIZURE OF AIRCRAFT (1970).

With a view to protecting civil aircraft and the right to life of those who travel by this means, the convention deals with hijacking and related offenses which jeopardize the safety of persons and property, adversely affect the operation of air services, and undermine confidence in the safety of travel by air. It provides that each contracting state must establish its jurisdiction over such offenses, must detain the offenders, and must either submit the case to its competent authorities for prosecution or extradite the offenders in accordance with existing treaties. It must also take steps to restore control of the aircraft to its lawful commander, facilitate continuance of the journey of the passengers and crew as soon as practicable, and report the relevant information to the International Civil Aviation Organization. The convention supplements the provisions of the CONVENTION ON OFFENSES AND CERTAIN OTHER ACTS COMMITTED ON BOARD AIRCRAFT (1963).

Adopted at the Hague on 16 December 1970 by the Assembly of the International Civil Aviation Organization, the convention entered into force on 14 October 1971. The text of the convention (United Nations, *Treaty Series,* vol. 860, p. 105) is as follows:

The States, Parties to this Convention,

Considering that unlawful acts of seizure or exercise of control of aircraft in flight jeopardize the safety of persons and property, seriously affect the operation of air services, and undermine the confidence of the peoples of the world in the safety of civil aviation;

Considering that the occurrence of such acts is a matter of grave concern;

Considering that, for the purpose of deterring such acts, there is an urgent need to provide appropriate measures for punishment of offenders;

Have agreed as follows:

Article 1. Any person who on board an aircraft in flight:

(*a*) unlawfully, by force or threat thereof, or by any other form of intimidation, seizes, or exercises control of, that aircraft, or attempts to perform any such act, or

(*b*) is an accomplice of a person who performs or attempts to perform any such act

commits an offence (hereinafter referred to as "the offence").

Article 2. Each Contracting State undertakes to make the offence punishable by severe penalties.

Article 3. 1. For the purposes of this Convention, an aircraft is considered to be in flight as any time from the moment when all its external doors are closed following embarkation until the moment when any such door is opened for disembarkation. In the case of a forced landing, the flight shall be deemed to continue until the competent authorities take over the responsibility for the aircraft and for persons and property on board.

2. This Convention shall not apply to aircraft used in military, customs or police services.

3. This Convention shall apply only if the place of take-off or the place of actual landing of the aircraft on board which the offence is committed is situated outside the territory of the State of registration of that aircraft; it shall be immaterial whether the aircraft is engaged in an international or domestic flight.

4. In the cases mentioned in Article 5, this Convention shall not apply if the place of take-off and the place of actual landing of the aircraft on board which the offence is committed are situated within the territory of the same State where that State is one of those referred to in that Article.

5. Notwithstanding paragraphs 3 and 4 of this Article, Articles 6, 7, 8 and 10 shall apply whatever the place of take-off or the place of actual landing of the aircraft, if the offender or the alleged offender is found in the territory of a State other than the State of registration of that aircraft.

Article 4. 1. Each Contracting State shall take such measures as may be necessary to establish its jurisdiction over the offence and any other act of violence against passengers or crew committed by the alleged offender in connection with the offence, in the following cases:

(*a*) when the offence is committed on board an aircraft registered in that State;

(*b*) when the aircraft on board which the offence is committed lands in its territory with the alleged offender still on board;

(*c*) when the offence is committed on board an aircraft leased without crew to a lessee who has his principal place of business or, if the lessee has no such place of business, his permanent residence, in that State.

2. Each Contracting State shall likewise take such measures as may be necessary to establish its jurisdiction over the offence in the case where the alleged offender is present in its territory and it does not extradite him pursuant to Article 8 to any of the States mentioned in paragraph 1 of this Article.

3. This Convention does not exclude any criminal jurisdiction exercised in accordance with national law.

Article 5. The Contracting States which establish joint air transport operating organizations or international operating agencies, which operate aircraft which are subject to joint or international registration shall, by appropriate means, designate for each aircraft the State among them which shall exercise the jurisdiction and have the attributes of the State of registration for the purpose of this Convention and shall give notice thereof to the International Civil Aviation Organization which shall communicate the notice to all States Parties to this Convention.

Article 6. 1. Upon being satisfied that the circumstances so warrant, any Contracting State in the territory of which the offender or the alleged offender is present shall take him into custody or take other measures to ensure his presence. The custody and other measures shall be as provided in the law of that State but may only be continued for such time as is necessary to enable any criminal or extradition proceedings to be instituted.

2. Such State shall immediately make a preliminary enquiry into the facts.

3. Any person in custody pursuant to paragraph 1 of this Article shall be assisted in communicating immediately with the nearest appropriate representative of the State of which he is a national.

4. When a State, pursuant to this Article, has taken a person into custody, it shall immediately notify the State of registration of the aircraft, the State mentioned in Article 4, paragraph 1(*c*), the State of nationality of the detained person and, if it considers it advisable, any other interested States of the fact that such person is in custody and of the circumstances which warrant his detention. The State which makes the preliminary enquiry contemplated in paragraph 2 of this Article shall promptly report its findings to the said States and shall indicate whether it intends to exercise jurisdiction.

Article 7. The Contracting State in the territory of which the alleged offender is found shall, if it does not extradite him, be obliged, without exception whatsoever and whether or not the offence was committed in its territory, to submit the case to its competent authorities for the purpose of prosecution. Those authorities shall take their decision in the same manner as in the case of any ordinary offence of a serious nature under the law of that State.

Article 8. 1. The offence shall be deemed to be included as an extraditable offence in any extradition treaty existing between Contracting States. Contracting States undertake to include the offence as an extraditable offence in every extradition treaty to be concluded between them.

2. If a Contracting State which makes extradition conditional on the existence of a treaty receives a request for extradition from another Contracting State with which it has no extradition treaty, it may at its option consider this Convention as the legal basis for extradition in respect of the offence. Extradition shall be subject to the other conditions provided by the law of the requested State.

3. Contracting States which do not make extradition conditional on the existence of a treaty shall recognize the offence as an extraditable offence between themselves subject to the conditions provided by the law of the requested State.

4. The offence shall be treated, for the purpose of extradition between Contracting States, as if it had been committed not only in the place in which it occurred but also in the territories of the States required to establish their jurisdiction in accordance with Article 4, paragraph 1.

Article 9. 1. When any of the acts mentioned in Article 1(*a*) has occurred or is about to occur, Contracting States shall take all appropriate measures to restore control of the aircraft to its lawful commander or to preserve his control of the aircraft.

2. In the cases contemplated by the preceding paragraph, any Contracting State in which the aircraft or its passengers or crew are present shall facilitate the continuation of the journey of the passengers and crew as soon as practicable, and shall without delay return the aircraft and its cargo to the persons lawfully entitled to possession.

Article 10. 1. Contracting States shall afford one another the greatest measure of assistance in connection with criminal proceedings brought in respect of the offence and other acts mentioned in Article 4. The law of the State requested shall apply in all cases.

2. The provisions of paragraph 1 of this Article shall not affect obligations under any other treaty, bilateral or multilateral, which governs or will govern, in whole or in part, mutual assistance in criminal matters.

Article 11. Each Contracting State shall in accordance with its national law report to the Council of the International Civil Aviation Organization as promptly as possible any relevant information in its possession concerning:

    (*a*) the circumstances of the offence;

    (*b*) the action taken pursuant to Article 9;

    (*c*) the measures taken in relation to the offender or the alleged offender, and, in particular, the results of any extradition proceedings or other legal proceedings.

Article 12. 1. Any dispute between two or more Contracting States concerning the interpretation or application of this Convention which cannot be settled through negotiation, shall, at the request of one of them, be submitted to arbitration. If within six months from the date of the request for arbitration the Parties are unable to agree on the organization of the arbitration, any one of those Parties may refer the dispute to the International Court of Justice by request in conformity with the Statute of the Court.

2. Each State may at the time of signature or ratification of this Convention or accession thereto, declare that it does not consider itself bound by the preceding paragraph. The

other Contracting States shall not be bound by the preceding paragraph with respect to any Contracting State having made such a reservation.

3. Any Contracting State having made a reservation in accordance with the preceding paragraph may at any time withdraw this reservation by notification to the Depositary Governments.

Article 13. 1. This Convention shall be open for signature at The Hague on 16 December 1970, by States participating in the International Conference on Air Law held at The Hague from 1 to 16 December 1970 (hereinafter referred to as The Hague Conference). After 31 December 1970, the Convention shall be open to all States for signature in Moscow, London and Washington. Any State which does not sign this Convention before its entry into force in accordance with paragraph 3 of this Article may accede to it at any time.

2. This Convention shall be subject to ratification by the signatory States. Instruments of ratification and instruments of accession shall be deposited with the Governments of the Union of Soviet Socialist Republics, the United Kingdom of Great Britain and Northern Ireland, and the United States of America, which are hereby designated the Depositary Governments.

3. This Convention shall enter into force thirty days following the date of the deposit of instruments of ratification by ten States signatory to this Convention which participated in The Hague Conference.

4. For other States, this Convention shall enter into force on the date of entry into force on this Convention in accordance with paragraph 3 of this Article, or thirty days following the date of deposit of their instruments of ratification or accession, whichever is later.

5. The Depositary Governments shall promptly inform all signatory and acceding States of the date of each signature, the date of deposit of each instrument of ratification or accession, the date of entry into force of this Convention, and other notices.

6. As soon as this Convention comes into force, it shall be registered by the Depositary Governments pursuant to Article 102 of the Charter of the United Nations and pursuant to Article 83 of the Convention on International Civil Aviation (Chicago, 1944).

Article 14. 1. Any Contracting State may denounce this Convention by written notification to the Depositary Governments.

2. Denunciation shall take effect six months following the date on which notification is received by the Depositary Governments.

In witness whereof the undersigned Plenipotentiaries, being duly authorised thereto by their Governments, have signed this Convention.

Done at The Hague, this sixteenth day of December, one thousand nine hundred and seventy, in three originals, each being drawn up in four authentic texts in the English, French, Russian and Spanish languages.

CONVENTION ON CONSENT TO MARRIAGE, MINIMUM AGE FOR MARRIAGE AND REGISTRATION OF MARRIAGES (1962).

The convention resulted from an initiative taken by the COMMISSION ON THE STATUS OF WOMEN at the suggestion of the Diplomatic Conference which prepared the SUPPLEMEN-

TARY CONVENTION ON THE ABOLITION OF SLAVERY, THE SLAVE TRADE, AND INSTITUTIONS AND PRACTICES SIMILAR TO SLAVERY of 1956. The conference recommended that a study should be made "of the question of marriage, with the object of drawing attention to the desirability of free consent of both parties to a marriage and of the establishment of a minimum age for marriage, preferably of not less than fourteen years."

The convention, drafted by the commission at the request of the Economic and Social Council, provides (a) that consent to marriage must be expressed by the two intending spouses in person after due publicity and in the presence of the authority competent to solemnize the marriage and of witnesses as prescribed by law, (b) that State parties take legislative action to specify a minimum age for marriage, and (c) that all marriages shall be registered in an appropriate official register by the competent authority. It does not specify a minimum age for marriage but imposes upon States parties the obligation to do so. It may be noted that the RECOMMENDATION ON CONSENT TO MARRIAGE, MINIMUM AGE FOR MARRIAGE AND REGISTRATION OF MARRIAGES, adopted in 1965, expressly provides for a minimum age of not less than 15 to be specified by each State.

The convention was adopted by the General Assembly on 7 November 1962 (resolution 1763 A [XVII]) and entered into force on 9 December 1964. The text (United Nations *Treaty Series,* vol. 521, p. 231) is as follows:

The Contracting States,

Desiring, in conformity with the Charter of the United Nations, to promote universal respect for, and observance of, human rights and fundamental freedoms for all, without distinction as to race, sex, language or religion,

Recalling that article 16 of the Universal Declaration of Human Rights states that:

"(1) Men and women of full age, without any limitation due to race, nationality or religion, have the right to marry and to found a family. They are entitled to equal rights as to marriage, during marriage and at its dissolution.

"(2) Marriage shall be entered into only with the free and full consent of the intending spouses.",

Recalling further that the General Assembly of the United Nations declared, by resolution 843 (IX) of 17 December 1954, that certain customs, ancient laws and practices relating to marriage and the family were inconsistent with the principles set forth in the Charter of the United Nations and in the Universal Declaration of Human Rights.

Reaffirming that all States, including those which have or assume responsibility for the administration of Non-Self-Governing and Trust Territories until their achievement of independence, should take all appropriate measures with a view to abolishing such customs, ancient laws and practices by ensuring, *inter alia,* complete freedom in the choice of a spouse, eliminating completely child marriages and the betrothal of young girls before the age of puberty, establishing appropriate penalties where necessary and establishing a civil or other register in which all marriages will be recorded.

Hereby agree as hereinafter provided:

Article 1. 1. No marriage shall be legally entered into without the full and free consent of both parties, such consent to be expressed by them in person after due publicity and in the presence of the authority competent to solemnize the marriage and of witnesses, as prescribed by law.

2. Notwithstanding anything in paragraph 1 above, it shall not be necessary for one of the parties to be present when the competent authority is satisfied that the circumstances are exceptional and that the party has, before a competent authority and in such manner as may be prescribed by law, expressed and not withdrawn consent.

Article 2. States parties to the present Convention shall take legislative action to specify a minimum age for marriage. No marriage shall be legally entered into by any person under this age, except where a competent authority has granted a dispensation as to age, for serious reasons, in the interest of the intending spouses.

Article 3. All marriages shall be registered in an appropriate official register by the competent authority.

Article 4. 1. The present Convention shall, until 31 December 1963, be open for signature on behalf of all States Members of the United Nations or members of any of the specialized agencies, and of any other State invited by the General Assembly of the United Nations to become a party to the Convention.

2. The present Convention is subject to ratification. The instruments of ratification shall be deposited with the Secretary-General of the United Nations.

Article 5. 1. The present Convention shall be open for accession to all States referred to in article 4, paragraph 1.

2. Accession shall be effected by the deposit of an instrument of accession with the Secretary-General of the United Nations.

Article 6. 1. The present Convention shall come into force on the ninetieth day following the date of deposit of the eighth instrument of ratification or accession.

2. For each State ratifying or acceding to the Convention after the deposit of the eighth instrument of ratification or accession, the Convention shall enter into force on the ninetieth day after deposit by such State of its instrument of ratification or accession.

Article 7. 1. Any Contracting State may denounce the present Convention by written notification to the Secretary-General of the United Nations. Denunciation shall take effect one year after the date of receipt of the notification by the Secretary-General.

2. The present Convention shall cease to be in force as from the date when the denunciation which reduces the number of parties to less than eight becomes effective.

Article 8. Any dispute which may arise between any two or more Contracting States concerning the interpretation or application of the present Convention which is not settled by negotiation shall, at the request of all the parties to the dispute, be referred to the International Court of Justice for decision, unless the parties agree to another mode of settlement.

Article 9. The Secretary-General of the United Nations shall notify all States Members of the United Nations and the non-member States contemplated in article 4, paragraph 1, of the present Convention of the following:

(*a*) Signatures and instruments of ratification received in accordance with article 4;

C

(*b*) Instruments of accession received in accordance with article 5;

(*c*) The date upon which the Convention enters into force in accordance with article 6;

(*d*) Notifications of denunciation received in accordance with article 7, paragraph 1;

(*e*) Abrogation in accordance with article 7, paragraph 2.

Article 10. 1. The present Convention, of which the Chinese, English, French, Russian and Spanish texts shall be equally authentic, shall be deposited in the archives of the United Nations.

2. The Secretary-General of the United Nations shall transmit a certified copy of the Convention to all States Members of the United Nations and to the non-member States contemplated in article 4, paragraph 1.

CONVENTION ON INTERNATIONAL CIVIL AVIATION (1944).

The convention sets up the basic postwar international machinery for the control of international civil aviation, replacing the Paris Convention of 1919, which had established the International Commission for Air Navigation, and the Pan-American Convention on Air Navigation of 1928, by which contracting States had pledged to observe certain principles, including that of freedom of air passage, in their dealings with one another. The earlier conventions had been found to be inadequate to cope with the enormous development of air traffic during World War II.

The convention was adopted by the International Civil Aviation Conference, meeting in Chicago, on 7 December 1944, and entered into force on 4 April 1947, at which time the International Civil Aviation Organization was established. The text of the articles of the convention (United Nations, *Treaty Series,* vol. 15, p. 295) which have a direct bearing upon the enjoyment of human rights (articles 25, 26, and 35) is as follows:

Article 25. Aircraft in Distress. Each contracting State undertakes to provide such measures of assistance to aircraft in distress in its territory as it may find practicable, and to permit, subject to control by its own authorities, the owners of the aircraft or authorities of the State in which the aircraft is registered to provide such measures of assistance as may be necessitated by the circumstances. Each contracting State, when undertaking search for missing aircraft, will collaborate in coordinated measures which may be recommended from time to time pursuant to this Convention.

Article 26. Investigation of Accidents. In the event of an accident to an aircraft of a contracting State occurring in the territory of another contracting State, and involving death or serious injury, or indicating serious technical defect in the aircraft or air navigation facilities, the State in which the accident occurs will institute an inquiry into the circumstances of the accident, in accordance, so far as its laws permit, with the procedure which may be recommended by the International Civil Aviation Organization. The State in which the aircraft is registered shall be given the opportunity to appoint observers to be present at the inquiry and the State holding the inquiry shall communicate the report and findings in the matter to that State. . . .

Article 35. Cargo Restrictions. (a) No munitions of war or implements of war may be carried in or above the territory of a State in aircraft engaged in international navigation, except by permission of such State. Each State shall determine by regulations what constitutes munitions of war or implements of war for the purposes of this Article, giving due consideration, for the purposes of uniformity, to such recommendations as the International Civil Aviation Organization may from time to time make.

(b) Each contracting State reserves the right, for reasons of public order and safety, to regulate or prohibit the carriage in or above its territory of articles other than those enumerated in paragraph (a): provided that no distinction is made in this respect between its national aircraft engaged in international navigation and the aircraft of the other States so engaged; and provided further that no restriction shall be imposed which may interfere with the carriage and use on aircraft of apparatus necessary for the operation or navigation of the aircraft or the safety of the personnel or passengers.

CONVENTION ON INTERNATIONAL CIVIL AVIATION: PROTOCOL (1984).

The protocol, adopted in response to international reaction to the shooting down of a Korean Airlines civilian aircraft on 1 September 1983, adds a new article between articles 3 and 4 of the CONVENTION ON INTERNATIONAL CIVIL AVIATION. The protocol, while recognizing the right of every country to require the landing of civilian aircraft flying over its territory without authority, provides that the countries must refrain from using weapons against civilian aircraft in flight and must not endanger the lives of persons on board or the safety of the aircraft. The protocol was adopted by an extraordinary session of the Assembly of the International Civil Aviation Organization, meeting in Montreal on 10 May 1984. The text is as follows:

The Assembly of the International Civil Aviation Organization.

Having met in its Twenty-fifth Session (Extraordinary) at Montreal on 10 May 1984,

Having noted that international civil aviation can greatly help to create and preserve friendship and understanding among the nations and peoples of the world, yet its abuse can become a threat to general security,

Having noted that it is desirable to avoid friction and to promote that co-operation between nations and peoples upon which the peace of the world depends,

Having noted that it is necessary that international civil aviation may be developed in a safe and orderly manner,

Having noted that in keeping with elementary considerations of humanity the safety and the lives of persons on board civil aircraft must be assured,

Having noted that in the Convention on International Civil Aviation done at Chicago on the seventh day of December 1944 the contracting States

—recognize that every State has complete and exclusive sovereignty over the airspace above its territory,

—undertake, when issuing regulations for their state aircraft, that they will have due regard for the safety of navigation of civil aircraft, and

—agree not to use civil aviation for any purpose inconsistent with the aims of the Convention,

Having noted the resolve of the contracting States to take appropriate measures designed to prevent the violation of other States' airspace and the use of civil aviation for purposes inconsistent with the aims of the Convention and to enhance further the safety of international civil aviation,

Having noted the general desire of contracting States to reaffirm the principle of non-use of weapons against civil aircraft in flight,

1. Decides that it is desirable therefore to amend the Convention on International Civil Aviation done at Chicago on the seventh day of December 1944,

2. Approves, in accordance with the provision of article 94(a) of the Convention aforesaid, the following proposed amendment to the said Convention:

Insert, after article 3, a new article 3 *bis*:

"*Article 3 bis*. (a) The contracting States recognize that every State must refrain from resorting to the use of weapons against civil aircraft in flight and that, in case of interception, the lives of persons on board and the safety of aircraft must not be endangered. This provision shall not be interpreted as modifying in any way the rights and obligations of States set forth in the Charter of the United Nations.

(b) The contracting States recognize that every State, in the exercise of its sovereignty, is entitled to require the landing at some designated airport of a civil aircraft flying above its territory without authority or if there are reasonable grounds to conclude that it is being used for any purpose inconsistent with the aims of this Convention; it may also give such aircraft any other instructions to put an end to such violations. For this purpose, the contracting States may resort to any appropriate means consistent with relevant rules of international law, including the relevant provisions of this Convention, specifically paragraph (a) of this Article. Each contracting State agrees to publish its regulations in force regarding the interception of civil aircraft.

(c) Every civil aircraft shall comply with an order given in conformity with paragraph (b) of this Article. To this end each contracting State shall establish all necessary provisions in its national laws or regulations to make such compliance mandatory for any civil aircraft registered in that State or operated by a person having his principal place of business or permanent residence in that State. Each contracting State shall make any violation of such applicable laws or regulations punishable by severe penalties and shall submit the case to its competent authorities in accordance with its laws or regulations.

(d) Each contracting State shall take appropriate measures to prohibit the deliberate use of any civil aircraft registered in that State or operated by an operator who has his principal place of business or permanent residence in that State for any purpose inconsistent with the aims of this Convention. This provision shall not affect paragraph (a) or derogate from paragraphs (b) and (c) of this Article",

3. Specifies, pursuant to the provision of the said Article 94(a) of the said Convention, one hundred and two as the number of contracting States upon whose ratification the proposed amendment aforesaid shall come into force, and

4. Resolves that the Secretary General of the International Civil Aviation Organization draw up a Protocol, in the English, French, Russian and Spanish languages, each of which shall be of equal authenticity, embodying the proposed amendment above-mentioned and the matter hereinafter appearing:

(a) The Protocol shall be signed by the President of the Assembly and its Secretary General.

(b) The Protocol shall be open to ratification by any State which has ratified or adhered to the said Convention on International Civil Aviation.

(c) The instruments of ratification shall be deposited with the International Civil Aviation Organization.

(d) The Protocol shall come into force in respect of the States which have ratified it on the date on which the one hundred and second instrument of ratification is so deposited.

(e) The Secretary General shall immediately notify all contracting States of the date of deposit of each ratification of the Protocol.

(f) The Secretary General shall notify all States parties to the said Convention of the date on which the Protocol comes into force.

(g) With respect to any contracting State ratifying the Protocol after the date aforesaid, the Protocol shall come into force upon deposit of its instrument of ratification with the International Civil Aviation Organization.

CONVENTION ON OFFENSES AND CERTAIN OTHER ACTS COMMITTED ON BOARD AIRCRAFT (1963). This convention was the first international instrument to deal with crimes committed on board aircraft and in particular with the crime of hijacking an aircraft in flight. Its purpose is to protect the safety of aircraft and the right to life, liberty, and security of the person of air passengers.

The convention, adopted by the Assembly of the International Civil Aviation Organization, convened in Tokyo, on 14 September 1963, entered into force on 4 December 1969. Its terms were later updated in the CONVENTION FOR THE SUPPRESSION OF UNLAWFUL SEIZURE OF AIRCRAFT, adopted at the Hague in 1970; the CONVENTION FOR THE SUPPRESSION OF UNLAWFUL ACTS AGAINST THE SAFETY OF CIVIL AVIATION, adopted in Montreal in 1971; and the PROTOCOL to the CONVENTION ON INTERNATIONAL CIVIL AVIATION, adopted in Montreal in 1984.

The text of the Convention on Offenses and Certain Other Acts Committee on Board Aircraft (United Nations, *Treaty Series*, vol. 704, p. 219) is as follows:

The States Parties to this Convention
Have agreed as follows:

Chapter I—Scope of the Convention

Article 1. 1. This Convention shall apply in respect of:

(a) offences against penal law;

(b) acts which, whether or not they are offences, may or do jeopardize the safety of the aircraft or of persons or property therein or which jeopardize good order and discipline on board.

2. Except as provided in Chapter III, this Convention shall apply in respect of offences committed or acts done by a person on board any aircraft registered in a Contracting State, while that aircraft is in flight or on the surface of the high seas or of any other area outside the territory of any State.

3. For the purposes of this Convention, an aircraft is considered to be in flight from the moment when power is applied for the purpose of take-off until the moment when the landing run ends.

4. This Convention shall not apply to aircraft used in military, customs or police services.

Article 2. Without prejudice to the provisions of Article 4 and except when the safety of the aircraft or of persons or property on board so requires, no provision of this Convention shall be interpreted as authorizing or requiring any action in respect of offences against penal laws of a political nature or those based on racial or religious discrimination.

Chapter II—Jurisdiction

Article 3. 1. The State of registration of the aircraft is competent to exercise jurisdiction over offences and acts committed on board.

2. Each Contracting State shall take such measures as may be necessary to establish its jurisdiction as the State of registration over offences committed on board aircraft registered in such State.

3. This Convention does not exclude any criminal jurisdiction exercised in accordance with national law.

Article 4. A Contracting State which is not the State of registration may not interfere with an aircraft in flight in order to exercise its criminal jurisdiction over an offence committed on board except in the following cases:

(a) the offence has effect on the territory of such State;

(b) the offence has been committed by or against a national or permanent resident of such State;

(c) the offence is against the security of such State;

(d) the offence consists of a breach of any rules or regulations relating to the flight or manoeuvre of aircraft in force in such State;

(e) the exercise of jurisdiction is necessary to ensure the observance of any obligation of such State under a multilateral international agreement.

Chapter III—Powers of the Aircraft Commander

Article 5. 1. The provisions of this Chapter shall not apply to offences and acts committed or about to be committed by a person on board an aircraft in flight in the airspace of the State or registration or over the high seas or any other area outside the territory of any State unless the last point of take-off or the next point of intended landing is situated in a State other than that of registration, or the aircraft subsequently flies in the airspace of a State other than that of registration with such person still on board.

2. Notwithstanding the provisions of Article 1, paragraph 3, an aircraft shall for the purposes of this Chapter, be considered to be in flight at any time from the moment when all its external doors are closed following embarkation until the moment when any such door is opened for disembarkation. In the case of a forced landing, the provisions of this Chapter shall continue to apply with respect to offences and acts committed on board until competent au-

thorities of a State take over the responsibility for the aircraft and for the persons and property on board.

Article 6. 1. The aircraft commander may, when he has reasonable grounds to believe that a person has committed, or is about to commit, on board the aircraft, an offence or act contemplated in Article 1, paragraph 1, impose upon such person reasonable measures including restraint which are necessary:

(a) to protect the safety of the aircraft, or of persons or property therein; or

(b) to maintain good order and discipline on board; or

(c) to enable him to deliver such person to competent authorities or to disembark him in accordance with the provisions of this Chapter.

2. The aircraft commander may require or authorize the assistance of other crew members and may request or authorize, but not require, the assistance of passengers to restrain any person whom he is entitled to restrain. Any crew member or passenger may also take reasonable preventive measures without such authorization when he has reasonable grounds to believe that such action is immediately necessary to protect the safety of the aircraft, or of persons or property therein.

Article 7. 1. Measures of restraint imposed upon a person in accordance with Article 6 shall not be continued beyond any point at which the aircraft lands unless:

(a) such point is in the territory of a non-Contracting State and its authorities refuse to permit disembarkation of that person or those measures have been imposed in accordance with Article 6, paragraph 1 c) in order to enable his delivery to competent authorities;

(b) the aircraft makes a forced landing and the aircraft commander is unable to deliver that person to competent authorities; or

(c) that person agrees to onward carriage under restraint.

2. The aircraft commander shall as soon as practicable, and if possible before landing in the territory of a State with a person on board who has been placed under restraint in accordance with the provisions of Article 6, notify the authorities of such State of the fact that a person on board is under restraint and of the reasons for such restraint.

Article 8. 1. The aircraft commander may, in so far as it is necessary for the purpose of subparagraph a) or b) of paragraph 1 of Article 6, disembark in the territory of any State in which the aircraft lands any person who he has reasonable grounds to believe has committed, or is about to commit, on board the aircraft an act contemplated in Article 1, paragraph 1 b).

2. The aircraft commander shall report to the authorities of the State in which he disembarks any person pursuant to this Article, the fact of, and the reasons for, such disembarkation.

Article 9. 1. The aircraft commander may deliver to the competent authorities of any Contracting State in the territory of which the aircraft lands any person who he has reasonable grounds to believe has committed on board the aircraft an act which, in his opinion, is a serious offence according to the penal law of the State of registration of the aircraft.

2. The aircraft commander shall as soon as practicable and if possible before landing in the territory of a Contracting State with a person on board whom the aircraft commander intends to deliver in accordance with the pre-

ceding paragraph, notify the authorities of such State of his intention to deliver such person and the reasons therefor.

3. The aircraft commander shall furnish the authorities to whom any suspected offender is delivered in accordance with the provisions of this Article with evidence and information which, under the law of the State of registration of the aircraft, are lawfully in his possession.

Article 10. For actions taken in accordance with this Convention, neither the aircraft commander, any other member of the crew, any passenger, the owner or operator of the aircraft, nor the person on whose behalf the flight was performed shall be held responsible in any proceeding on account of the treatment undergone by the person against whom the actions were taken.

Chapter IV—Unlawful Seizure of Aircraft

Article 11. 1. When a person on board has unlawfully committed by force or threat thereof an act of interference, seizure, or other wrongful exercise of control of an aircraft in flight or when such an act is about to be committed, Contracting States shall take all appropriate measures to restore control of the aircraft to its lawful commander or to preserve his control of the aircraft.

2. In the cases contemplated in the preceding paragraph, the Contracting State in which the aircraft lands shall permit its passengers and crew to continue their journey as soon as practicable, and shall return the aircraft and its cargo to the persons lawfully entitled to possession.

Chapter V—Powers and Duties of States

Article 12. Any Contracting State shall allow the commander of an aircraft registered in another Contracting State to disembark any person pursuant to Article 8, paragraph 1.

Article 13. 1. Any Contracting State shall take delivery of any person whom the aircraft commander delivers pursuant to Article 9, paragraph 1.

2. Upon being satisfied that the circumstances so warrant, any Contracting State shall take custody or other measures to ensure the presence of any person suspected of an act contemplated in Article 11, paragraph 1 and of any person of whom it has taken delivery. The custody and other measures shall be as provided in the law of that State but may only be continued for such time as is reasonably necessary to enable any criminal or extradition proceedings to be instituted.

3. Any person in custody pursuant to the previous paragraph shall be assisted in communicating immediately with the nearest appropriate representative of the State of which he is a national.

4. Any Contracting State, to which a person is delivered pursuant to Article 9, paragraph 1, or in whose territory an aircraft lands following the commission of an act contemplated in Article 11, paragraph 1, shall immediately make a preliminary enquiry into the facts.

5. When a State, pursuant to this Article, has taken a person into custody, it shall immediately notify the State of registration of the aircraft and the State of nationality of the detained person and, if it considers it advisable, any other interested State of the fact that such person is in custody and of the circumstances which warrant his detention. The State which makes the preliminary enquiry contemplated in paragraph 4 of this Article shall promptly report its findings to the said States and shall indicate whether it intends to exercise jurisdiction.

Article 14. 1. When any person has been disembarked in accordance with Article 8, paragraph 1, or delivered in accordance with Article 9, paragraph 1, or has disembarked after committing an act contemplated in Article 11, paragraph 1, and when such person cannot or does not desire to continue his journey and the State of landing refuses to admit him, that State may, if the person in question is not a national or permanent resident of that State, return him to the territory of the State of which he is a national or permanent resident or to the territory of the State in which he began his journey by air.

2. Neither disembarkation, nor delivery, nor the taking of custody or other measures contemplated in Article 13, paragraph 2, nor return of the person concerned, shall be considered as admission to the territory of the Contracting State concerned for the purpose of its law relating to entry or admission of persons and nothing in this Convention shall affect the law of a Contracting State relating to the expulsion of persons from its territory.

Article 15. 1. Without prejudice to Article 14, any person who has been disembarked in accordance with Article 8, paragraph 1, or delivered in accordance with Article 9, paragraph 1, or has disembarked after committing an act contemplated in Article 11, paragraph 1, and who desires to continue his journey shall be at liberty as soon as practicable to proceed to any destination of his choice unless his presence is required by the law of the State of landing for the purpose of extradition or criminal proceedings.

2. Without prejudice to its law as to entry and admission to, and extradition and expulsion from its territory, a Contracting State in whose territory a person has been disembarked in accordance with Article 8, paragraph 1, or delivered in accordance with Article 9, paragraph 1 or has disembarked and is suspected of having committed an act contemplated in Article 11, paragraph 1, shall accord to such person treatment which is no less favourable for his protection and security than that accorded to nationals of such Contracting State in like circumstances.

Chapter VI—Other Provisions

Article 16. 1. Offences committed on aircraft registered in a Contracting State shall be treated, for the purpose of extradition, as if they had been committed not only in the place in which they have occurred but also in the territory of the State of registration of the aircraft.

2. Without prejudice to the provisions of the preceding paragraph, nothing in this Convention shall be deemed to create an obligation to grant extradition.

Article 17. In taking any measures for investigation or arrest or otherwise exercising jurisdiction in connection with any offence committed on board an aircraft the Contracting States shall pay due regard to the safety and other interests of air navigation and shall so act as to avoid unnecessary delay of the aircraft, passengers, crew or cargo.

Article 18. If Contracting States establish joint air transport operating organizations or international operating agencies, which operate aircraft not registered in any one State those States shall, according to the circumstances of the case, designate the State among them which, for the purposes of this Convention, shall be considered as the State of registration and shall give notice thereof to the International Civil Aviation Organization which shall communicate the notice to all States Parties to this Convention.

Chapter VII—Final Clauses

Article 19. Until the date on which this Convention comes into force in accordance with the provisions of Article 21, it shall remain open for signature on behalf of any State which at that date is a Member of the United Nations or of any of the Specialized Agencies.

Article 20. 1. This Convention shall be subject to ratification by the signatory States in accordance with their constitutional procedures.

2. The instruments of ratification shall be deposited with the International Civil Aviation Organization.

Article 21. 1. As soon as twelve of the signatory States have deposited their instruments of ratification of this Convention, it shall come into force between them on the nineteenth day after the date of the deposit of the twelfth instrument of ratification. It shall come into force for each State ratifying thereafter on the nineteenth day after the deposit of its instrument of ratification.

2. As soon as this Convention comes into force, it shall be registered with the Secretary-General of the United Nations by the International Civil Aviation Organization.

Article 22. 1. This Convention shall, after it has come into force, be open for accession by any State Member of the United Nations or of any of the Specialized Agencies.

2. The accession of a State shall be effected by the deposit of an instrument of accession with the International Civil Aviation Organization and shall take effect on the nineteenth day after the date of such deposit.

Article 23. 1. Any Contracting State may denounce this Convention by notification addressed to the International Civil Aviation Organization.

2. Denunciation shall take effect six months after the date of receipt by the International Civil Aviation Organization of the notification of denunciation.

Article 24. 1. Any dispute between two or more Contracting States concerning the interpretation or application of this Convention which cannot be settled through negotiation, shall, at the request of one of them, be submitted to arbitration. If within six months from the date of the request for arbitration the Parties are unable to agree on the organization of the arbitration, any one of those Parties may refer the dispute to the International Court of Justice by request in conformity with the Statute of the Court.

2. Each State may at the time of signature or ratification of this Convention or accession thereto, declare that it does not consider itself bound by the preceding paragraph. The other Contracting States shall not be bound by the preceding paragraph with respect to any Contracting State having made such a reservation.

3. Any Contracting State having made a reservation in accordance with the preceding paragraph may at any time withdraw this reservation by notification to the International Civil Aviation Organization.

Article 25. Except as provided in Article 24 no reservation may be made to this Convention.

Article 26. The International Civil Aviation Organization shall give notice to all States Members of the United Nations or of any of the Specialized Agencies:

    a) of any signature of this Convention and the date thereof;

    b) of the deposit of any instrument of ratification or accession and the date thereof;

    c) of the date on which this Convention comes into force in accordance with Article 21, paragraph 1;

    d) of the receipt of any notification of denunciation and the date thereof; and

    e) of the receipt of any declaration or notification made under Article 24 and the date thereof.

In witness whereof the undersigned Plenipotentiaries, having been duly authorized, have signed this Convention.

Done at Tokyo on the fourteenth day of September One Thousand Nine Hundred and Sixty-three in three authentic texts drawn up in the English, French and Spanish languages.

This Convention shall be deposited with the International Civil Aviation Organization with which, in accordance with Article 19, it shall remain open for signature and the said Organization shall send certified copies thereof to all States Members of the United Nations or of any Specialized Agency.

CONVENTION ON PROHIBITIONS OR RESTRICTIONS ON THE USE OF CERTAIN CONVENTIONAL WEAPONS WHICH MAY BE DEEMED TO BE EXCESSIVELY INJURIOUS OR TO HAVE INDISCRIMINATE EFFECTS, AND PROTOCOLS (1981). This convention and its annexed protocols I to III are significant recent additions to the body of international humanitarian law applicable in armed conflict, supplementing the GENEVA CONVENTION RELATIVE TO THE TREATMENT OF PRISONERS OF WAR, the GENEVA CONVENTION RELATIVE TO THE PROTECTION OF CIVILIAN PERSONS IN TIME OF WAR, the PROTOCOL ADDITIONAL TO THE GENEVA CONVENTIONS OF 12 AUGUST 1949, RELATING TO THE PROTECTION OF VICTIMS OF INTERNATIONAL ARMED CONFLICTS, and the PROTOCOL ADDITIONAL TO THE GENEVA CONVENTIONS OF 12 AUGUST 1949, RELATING TO THE PROTECTION OF VICTIMS OF NON-INTERNATIONAL CONFLICTS.

The convention and annexed protocols are based on the conviction that the suffering of victims of war would be significantly reduced by agreements prohibiting or restricting, on humanitarian grounds, the use of weapons which are excessively dangerous or which have indiscriminate effects. One of their purposes is to protect the right of everyone to live in peace and without being subjected to torture or to cruel, inhuman, or degrading treatment or punishment. Annexed Protocol I prohibits the use of any weapon the primary effect of which is to injure by fragments which, in the human body, escape detection by X-rays. Annexed Protocol II prohibits or restricts the use of mines, booby-traps, and other devices. Annexed Protocol III prohibits or restricts the use of incendiary weapons.

The convention and its protocols were prepared by the United Nations Conference on Prohibitions or Restrictions of Use of Certain Conventional Weapons Which May Be Deemed to be Excessively Injurious or to Have Indiscriminate Effects, convened at the European office of the United Nations, Geneva, and were adopted by the Conference on 10 October 1980. They were opened for signature and ratification or accession on 10 April 1981 and entered into force on 2 December 1983. The text of the convention and annexed protocols (UN Doc. A/CONF. 95/15 and Corr. 1, annex I) is as follows:

The High Contracting Parties,

Recalling that every State has the duty, in conformity with the Charter of the United Nations, to refrain in its international relations from the threat or use of force against the sovereignty, territorial integrity or political independence of any State, or in any other manner inconsistent with the purposes of the United Nations,

Further recalling the general principle of the protection of the civilian population against the effects of hostilities,

Basing themselves on the principle of international law that the right of the parties to an armed conflict to choose methods or means of warfare is not unlimited, and on the principle that prohibits the employment in armed conflicts of weapons, projectiles and material and methods of warfare of a nature to cause superfluous injury or unnecessary suffering,

Also recalling that it is prohibited to employ methods or means of warfare which are intended, or may be expected, to cause widespread, long-term and severe damage to the natural environment,

Confirming their determination that in cases not covered by this Convention and its annexed Protocols or by other international agreements, the civilian population and the combatants shall at all times remain under the protection and authority of the principles of international law derived from established custom, from the principles of humanity and from the dictates of public conscience,

Desiring to contribute to international détente, the ending of the arms race and the building of confidence among States, and hence to the realization of the aspiration of all peoples to live in peace,

Recognizing the importance of pursuing every effort which may contribute to progress towards general and complete disarmament under strict and effective international control,

Reaffirming the need to continue the codification and progressive development of the rules of international law applicable in armed conflict,

Wishing to prohibit or restrict further the use of certain conventional weapons and believing that the positive results achieved in this area may facilitate the main talks on disarmament with a view to putting an end to the production, stockpiling and proliferation of such weapons,

Emphasizing the desirability that all States become parties to this Convention and its annexed Protocols, especially the militarily significant States,

Bearing in mind that the General Assembly of the United Nations and the United Nations Disarmament Commission may decide to examine the question of a possible broadening of the scope of the prohibitions and restrictions contained in this Convention and its annexed Protocols,

Further bearing in mind that the Committee on Disarmament may decide to consider the question of adopting further measures to prohibit or restrict the use of certain conventional weapons,

Have agreed as follows:

Article 1. Scope of Application. This Convention and its annexed Protocols shall apply in the situations referred to in Article 2 common to the Geneva Conventions of 12 August 1949 for the Protection of War Victims, including any situation described in paragraph 4 of Article 1 of Additional Protocol I to these Conventions.

Article 2. Relations With Other International Agreements. Nothing in this Convention or its annexed Protocols shall be interpreted as detracting from other obligations imposed upon the High Contracting Parties by international humanitarian law applicable in armed conflict.

Article 3. Signature. This Convention shall be open for signature by all States at United Nations Headquarters in New York for a period of twelve months from 10 April 1981.

Article 4. Ratification, Acceptance, Approval or Accession.

1. This Convention is subject to ratification, acceptance or approval by the Signatories. Any State which has not signed this Convention may accede to it.

2. The instrument of ratification, acceptance, approval or accession shall be deposited with the Depositary.

3. Expressions of consent to be bound by any of the Protocols annexed to this Convention shall be optional for each State, provided that at the time of the deposit of its instrument of ratification, acceptance or approval of this Convention or of accession thereto, that State shall notify the Depositary of its consent to be bound by any two or more of these Protocols.

4. At any time after the deposit of its instrument of ratification, acceptance or approval of this Convention or of accession thereto, a State may notify the Depositary of its consent to be bound by any annexed Protocol by which it is not already bound.

5. Any Protocol by which a High Contracting Party is bound shall for that Party form an integral part of this Convention.

Article 5. Entry Into Force. 1. This Convention shall enter into force six months after the date of deposit of the twentieth instrument of ratification, acceptance, approval or accession.

2. For any State which deposits its instrument of ratification, acceptance, approval or accession after the date of the deposit of the twentieth instrument of ratification, acceptance, approval or accession, this Convention shall enter into force six months after the date on which that State has deposited its instrument of ratification, acceptance, approval or accession.

3. Each of the Protocols annexed to this Convention shall enter into force six months after the date by which twenty States have notified their consent to be bound by it in accordance with paragraph 3 or 4 of Article 4 of this Convention.

4. For any State which notifies its consent to be bound by a Protocol, annexed to this Convention after the date by which twenty States have notified their consent to be bound by it, the Protocol shall enter into force six months after the date on which that State has notified its consent so to be bound.

Article 6. Dissemination. The High Contracting Parties undertake, in time of peace as in time of armed conflict, to disseminate this Convention and those of its annexed Protocols by which they are bound as widely as possible in their respective countries and, in particular, to include the study thereof in their programmes of military instruction, so that those instruments may become known to their armed forces.

Article 7. Treaty Relations Upon Entry Into Force of This Con-

vention. 1. When one of the parties to a conflict is not bound by an annexed Protocol, the parties bound by this Convention and that annexed Protocol shall remain bound by them in their mutual relations.

2. Any High Contracting Party shall be bound by this Convention and any Protocol annexed thereto which is in force for it, in any situation contemplated by Article 1, in relation to any State which is not a party to this Convention or bound by the relevant annexed Protocol, if the latter accepts and applies this Convention or the relevant Protocol, and so notifies the Depositary.

3. The Depositary shall immediately inform the High Contracting Parties concerned of any notification received under paragraph 2 of this Article.

4. This Convention, and the annexed Protocols by which a High Contracting Party is bound, shall apply with respect to an armed conflict against that High Contracting Party of the type referred to in Article 1, paragraph 4, of Additional Protocol I to the Geneva Conventions of 12 August 1949 for the Protection of War Victims:

(*a*) where the High Contracting Party is also a party to Additional Protocol I and an authority referred to in Article 96, paragraph 3, of that Protocol has undertaken to apply the Geneva Conventions and Additional Protocol I in accordance with Article 96, paragraph 3, of the said Protocol, and undertakes to apply this Convention and the relevant annexed Protocols in relation to that conflict; or

(*b*) where the High Contracting Party is not a party to Additional Protocol I and an authority of the type referred to in subparagraph (*a*) above accepts and applies the obligations of the Geneva Conventions and of this Convention and the relevant annexed Protocols in relation to that conflict. Such an acceptance and application shall have in relation to that conflict the following effects:

(i) the Geneva Conventions and this Convention and its relevant annexed Protocols are brought into force for the parties to the conflict with immediate effect;

(ii) the said authority assumes the same rights and obligations as those which have been assumed by a High Contracting Party to the Geneva Conventions, this Convention and its relevant annexed Protocols; and

(iii) the Geneva Conventions, this Convention and its relevant annexed Protocols are equally binding upon all parties to the conflict.

The High Contracting Party and the authority may also agree to accept and apply the obligations of Additional Protocol I to the Geneva Conventions on a reciprocal basis.

Article 8. Review and Amendments. 1. (*a*) At any time after the entry into force of this Convention any High Contracting Party may propose amendments to this Convention or any annexed Protocol by which it is bound. Any proposal for an amendment shall be communicated to the Depositary, who shall notify it to all the High Contracting Parties and shall seek their views on whether a conference should be convened to consider the proposal. If a majority, that shall not be less than eighteen of the High Contracting Parties so agree, he shall promptly convene a conference to which all High Contracting Parties shall be invited. States not parties to this Convention shall be invited to the conference as observers.

(*b*) Such a conference may agree upon amendments which shall be adopted and shall enter into force in the same manner as this Convention and the annexed Protocols, provided that amendments to this Convention may be adopted only by the High Contracting Parties and that amendments to a specific annexed Protocol may be adopted only by the High Contracting Parties which are bound by that Protocol.

2. (*a*) At any time after the entry into force of this Convention any High Contracting Party may propose additional protocols relating to other categories of conventional weapons not covered by the existing annexed Protocols. Any such proposal for an additional protocol shall be communicated to the Depositary, who shall notify it to all the High Contracting Parties in accordance with subparagraph 1 (*a*) of this Article. If a majority, that shall not be less than eighteen of the High Contracting Parties so agree, the Depositary shall promptly convene a conference to which all States shall be invited.

(*b*) Such a conference may agree, with the full participation of all States represented at the conference, upon additional protocols which shall be adopted in the same manner as this Convention, shall be annexed thereto and shall enter into force as provided in paragraphs 3 and 4 of Article 5 of this Convention.

3. (*a*) If, after a period of ten years following the entry into force of this Convention, no conference has been convened in accordance with subparagraph 1 (*a*) or 2 (*a*) of this Article, any High Contracting Party may request the Depositary to convene a conference to which all High Contracting Parties shall be invited to review the scope and operation of this Convention and the Protocols annexed thereto and to consider any proposal for amendments of this Convention or of the existing Protocols. States not parties to this Convention shall be invited as observers to the conference. The conference may agree upon amendments which shall be adopted and enter into force in accordance with subparagraph 1 (*b*) above.

(*b*) At such conference consideration may also be given to any proposal for additional protocols relating to other categories of conventional weapons not covered by the existing annexed Protocols. All States represented at the conference may participate fully in such consideration. Any additional protocols shall be adopted in the same manner as this Convention, shall be annexed thereto and shall enter into force as provided in paragraphs 3 and 4 of Article 5 of this Convention.

(*c*) Such a conference may consider whether provision should be made for the convening of a further conference at the request of any High Contracting Party if, after a similar period to that referred to in subparagraph 3 (*a*) of this Article, no conference has been convened in accordance with subparagraph 1 (*a*) or 2 (*a*) of this Article.

Article 9. Denunciation. 1. Any High Contracting Party may denounce this Convention or any of its annexed Protocols by so notifying the Depositary.

2. Any such denunciation shall only take effect one year after receipt by the Depositary of the notification of denunciation. If, however, on the expiry of that year the denouncing High Contracting Party is engaged in one of the situations referred to in Article 1, the Party shall continue to be bound by the obligations of this Convention and of the relevant annexed Protocols until the end of the armed conflict or occupation and, in any case, until the termination of operations connected with the final release, repatriation or reestablishment of the person protected by the rules of international law applicable in armed conflict, and in the case of any annexed Protocol containing provisions concerning situations in which peace-keeping, observation or similar functions are performed by United Nations forces or missions in the area concerned, until the termination of those functions.

3. Any denunciation of this Convention shall be considered as also applying to all annexed Protocols by which the denouncing High Contracting Party is bound.

4. Any denunciation shall have effect only in respect of the denouncing High Contracting Party.

5. Any denunciation shall not affect the obligations already incurred, by reason of an armed conflict, under this Convention and its annexed Protocols by such denouncing High Contracting Party in respect of any act committed before this denunciation becomes effective.

Article 10. Depositary. 1. The Secretary-General of the United Nations shall be the Depositary of this Convention and of its annexed Protocols.

2. In addition to his usual functions, the Depositary shall inform all States of:

(*a*) signatures affixed to this Convention under Article 3;

(*b*) deposits of instruments of ratification, acceptance or approval of or accession to this Convention deposited under Article 4;

(*c*) notifications of consent to be bound by annexed Protocols under Article 4;

(*d*) the dates of entry into force of this Convention and of each of its annexed Protocols under Article 5; and

(*e*) notifications of denunciation received under article 9, and their effective date.

Article 11. Authentic Texts. The original of this Convention with the annexed Protocols, of which the Arabic, Chinese, English, French, Russian and Spanish texts are equally authentic, shall be deposited with the Depositary, who shall transmit certified true copies thereof to all States.

Protocol on Non-Detectable Fragments (Protocol I)

It is prohibited to use any weapon the primary effect of which is to injure by fragments which in the human body escape detection by X-rays.

Protocol on Prohibitions or Restrictions on the Use of Mines, Booby-Traps and Other Devices (Protocol II)

Article 1. Material Scope of Application. This Protocol relates to the use on land of the mines, booby-traps and other devices defined herein, including mines laid to interdict beaches, waterway crossings or river crossings, but does not apply to the use of anti-ship mines at sea or in inland waterways.

Article 2. Definitions. For the purpose of this Protocol:

1. "Mine" means any munition placed under, on or near the ground or other surface area and designed to be detonated or exploded by the presence, proximity or contact of a person or vehicle, and "remotely delivered mine" means any mine so defined delivered by artillery, rocket, mortar or similar means or dropped from an aircraft.

2. "Booby-trap" means any device or material which is designed, constructed or adapted to kill or injure and which functions unexpectedly when a person disturbs or approaches an apparently harmless object or performs an apparently safe act.

3. "Other devices" means manually-emplaced munitions and devices designed to kill, injure or damage and which are actuated by remote control or automatically after a lapse of time.

4. "Military objective" means, so far as objects are concerned, any object which by its nature, location, purpose or use makes an effective contribution to military action and whose total or partial destruction, capture or neutraliza-

tion, in the circumstances ruling at the time, offers a definite military advantage.

5. "Civilian objects" are all objects which are not military objectives as defined in paragraph 4.

6. "Recording" means a physical, administrative and technical operation designed to obtain, for the purpose of registration in the official records, all available information facilitating the location of minefields, mines and booby-traps.

Article 3. General Restrictions on the Use of Mines, Booby-Traps and Other Devices. 1. This Article applies to:

(*a*) mines;

(*b*) booby-traps; and

(*c*) other devices.

2. It is prohibited in all circumstances to direct weapons to which this Article applies, either in offence, defence or by way of reprisals, against the civilian population as such or against individual civilians.

3. The indiscriminate use of weapons to which this Article applies is prohibited. Indiscriminate use is any placement of such weapons:

(*a*) which is not on, or directed at, a military objective; or

(*b*) which employs a method or means of delivery which cannot be directed at a specific military objective; or

(*c*) which may be expected to cause incidental loss of civilian life, injury to civilians, damage to civilian objects, or a combination thereof, which would be excessive in relation to the concrete and direct military advantage anticipated.

4. All feasible precautions shall be taken to protect civilians from the effects of weapons to which this Article applies. Feasible precautions are those precautions which are practicable or practically possible taking into account all circumstances ruling at the time, including humanitarian and military considerations.

Article 4. Restrictions on the Use of Mines Other Than Remotely Delivered Mines, Booby-Traps and Other Devices in Populated Areas. 1. This Article applies to:

(*a*) mines other than remotely delivered mines;

(*b*) booby-traps; and

(*c*) other devices.

2. It is prohibited to use weapons to which this Article applies in any city, town, village or other area containing a similar concentration of civilians in which combat between ground forces is not taking place or does not appear to be imminent, unless either;

(*a*) they are placed on or in the close vicinity of a military objective belonging to or under the control of an adverse party; or

(*b*) measures are taken to protect civilians from their effects, for example, the posting of warning signs, the posting of sentries, the issue of warnings or the provision of fences.

Article 5. Restrictions on the Use of Remotely Delivered Mines. 1. The use of remotely delivered mines is prohibited unless such mines are only used within an area which is itself a military objective or which contains military objectives, and unless:

(*a*) their location can be accurately recorded in accordance with Article 7(1)(*a*); or

(*b*) an effective neutralizing mechanism is used on each such mine, that is to say, a self-actuating mechanism which is designed to render a mine harmless or cause it to destroy itself when it is anticipated that the mine will no longer serve the military purpose for which it was placed in position, or a remotely-controlled mechanism which is designed to render harmless or destroy a mine when the mine no longer serves the military purpose for which it was placed in position.

2. Effective advance warning shall be given of any delivery or dropping of remotely delivered mines which may affect the civilian population, unless circumstances do not permit.

Article 6. Prohibition on the Use of Certain Booby-Traps. 1. Without prejudice to the rules of international law applicable in armed conflict relating to treachery and perfidy, it is prohibited in all circumstances to use:

(*a*) any booby-trap in the form of an apparently harmless portable object which is specifically designed and constructed to contain explosive material and to detonate when it is disturbed or approached; or

(*b*) booby-traps which are in any way attached to or associated with:

(i) internationally recognized protective emblems, signs or signals;

(ii) sick, wounded or dead persons;

(iii) burial or cremation sites or graves;

(iv) medical facilities, medical equipment, medical supplies or medical transportation;

(v) children's toys or other portable objects or products specially designed for the feeding, health, hygiene, clothing or education of children;

(vi) food or drink

(vii) kitchen utensils or appliances except in military establishments, military locations or military supply depots;

(viii) objects clearly of a religious nature;

(ix) historic monuments, works of art or places of worship which constitute the cultural or spiritual heritage of peoples;

(x) animals or their carcasses.

2. It is prohibited in all circumstances to use any booby-trap which is designed to cause superfluous injury or unnecessary suffering.

Article 7. Recording and Publication of the Location of Minefields, Mines and Booby-traps. 1. The parties to a conflict shall record the location of:

(*a*) all pre-planned minefields laid by them; and

(*b*) all areas in which they have made large-scale and pre-planned use of booby-traps.

2. The parties shall endeavour to ensure the recording of the location of all other minefields, mines and booby-traps which they have laid or placed in position.

3. All such records shall be retained by the parties who shall:

(*a*) immediately after the cessation of active hostilities:

(i) take all necessary and appropriate measures, including the use of such records, to protect civilians from the effects of minefields, mines and booby-traps; and either

(ii) in cases where the forces of neither party are in the territory of the adverse party, make available to each other and to the Secretary-General of the United Nations all information in their possession concerning the location of minefields, mines and booby-traps in the territory of the adverse party; or

(iii) once complete withdrawal of the forces of the parties from the territory of the adverse party has taken place, make available to the adverse party and to the Secretary-General of the United Nations all information in

their possession concerning the location of minefields, mines and booby-traps in the territory of the adverse party;

(*b*) when a United Nations force or mission performs functions in any area, make available to the authority mentioned in Article 8 such information as is required by that Article;

(*c*) whenever possible, by mutual agreement, provide for the release of information concerning the location of minefields, mines and booby-traps, particularly in agreements governing the cessation of hostilities.

Article 8. Protection of United Nations Forces and Missions From the Effects of Minefields, Mines and Booby-traps. 1. When a United Nations force or mission performs functions of peace-keeping, observation or similar functions in any area, each party to the conflict shall, if requested by the head of the United Nations force or mission in that area, as far as it is able:

(*a*) remove or render harmless all mines or booby-traps in that area;

(*b*) take such measures as may be necessary to protect the force or mission from the effects of minefields, mines and booby-traps while carrying out its duties; and

(*c*) make available to the head of the United Nations force or mission in that area, all information in the party's possession concerning the location of minefields, mines and booby-traps in that area.

2. When a United Nations fact-finding mission performs functions in any area, any party to the conflict concerned shall provide protection to that mission except where, because of the size of such mission, it cannot adequately provide such protection. In that case it shall make available to the head of the mission the information in its possession concerning the location of minefields, mines and booby-traps in that area.

Article 9. International Co-operation in the Removal of Minefields, Mines and Booby-traps. After the cessation of active hostilities, the parties shall endeavour to reach agreement, both among themselves and, where appropriate, with other States and with international organizations, on the provision of information and technical and material assistance— including, in appropriate circumstances, joint operations—necessary to remove or otherwise render ineffective minefields, mines and booby-traps placed in position during the conflict.

Technical Annex to the Protocol on Prohibitions or Restrictions on the Use of Mines, Booby-Traps and Other Devices (Protocol II)

Guidelines on Recording. Whenever an obligation for the recording of the location of minefields, mines and booby-traps arises under the Protocol, the following guidelines shall be taken into account.

1. With regard to pre-planned minefields and large-scale and preplanned use of booby-traps:

(*a*) maps, diagrams or other records should be made in such a way as to indicate the extent of the minefield or booby-trapped area; and

(*b*) the location of the minefield or booby-trapped area should be specified by relation to the co-ordinates of a single reference point and by the estimated dimensions of the area containing mines and booby-traps in relation to that single reference point.

2. With regard to other minefields, mines and booby-traps laid or placed in position:

In so far as possible, the relevant information specified

in paragraph 1 above should be recorded so as to enable the areas containing minefields, mines and booby-traps to be identified.

Protocol on Prohibitions or Restrictions on the Use of Incendiary Weapons (Protocol III)

Article 1. Definitions. For the purpose of this Protocol:

1. "Incendiary weapon" means any weapon or munition which is primarily designed to set fire to objects or to cause burn injury to persons through the action of flame, heat, or a combination thereof, produced by a chemical reaction of a substance delivered on the target.

(*a*) Incendiary weapons can take the form of, for example, flame throwers, fougasses, shells, rockets, grenades, mines, bombs and other containers of incendiary substances.

(*b*) Incendiary weapons do not include:

(i) Munitions which may have incidental incendiary effects, such as illuminants, tracers, smoke or signalling systems;

(ii) Munitions designed to combine penetration, blast or fragmentation effects with an additional incendiary effect, such as armour-piercing projectiles, fragmentation shells, explosive bombs and similar combined-effects munitions in which the incendiary effect is not specifically designed to cause burn injury to persons, but to be used against military objectives, such as armoured vehicles, aircraft and installations or facilities.

2. "Concentration of civilians" means any concentration of civilians, be it permanent or temporary, such as in inhabited parts of cities, or inhabited towns or villages, or as in camps or columns of refugees or evacuees, or groups of nomads.

3. "Military objective" means, so far as objects are concerned, any object which by its nature, location, purpose or use makes an effective contribution to military action and whose total or partial destruction, capture or neutralization, in the circumstances ruling at the time, offers a definite military advantage.

4. "Civilian objects" are all objects which are not military objectives as defined in paragraph 3.

5. "Feasible precautions" are those precautions which are practicable or practically possible taking into account all circumstances ruling at the time, including humanitarian and military considerations.

Article 2. Protection of Civilians and Civilian Objects. 1. It is prohibited in all circumstances to make the civilian population as such, individual civilians or civilian objects the object of attack by incendiary weapons.

2. It is prohibited in all circumstances to make any military objective located within a concentration of civilians the object of attack by air-delivered incendiary weapons.

3. It is further prohibited to make any military objective located within a concentration of civilians the object of attack by means of incendiary weapons other than air-delivered incendiary weapons, except when such military objective is clearly separated from the concentration of civilians and all feasible precautions are taken with a view to limiting the incendiary effects to the military objective and to avoiding, and in any event to minimizing, incidental loss of civilian life, injury to civilians and damage to civilian objects.

4. It is prohibited to make forests or other kinds of plant cover the object of attack by incendiary weapons except when such natural elements are used to cover, conceal or camouflage combatants or other military objectives, or are themselves objectives. . . .

SEE ALSO Chemical Weapons: Declaration on their Prohibition; Convention on the Prohibition of the Development, Production and Stockpiling of Bacteriological (Biological) and Toxin Weapons and on their Destruction; Protocol for the Prohibition of the Use of Asphyxiating, Poisonous or Other Gases, and of Bacteriological Methods of Warfare.

CONVENTION ON THE ELIMINATION OF ALL FORMS OF DISCRIMINATION AGAINST WOMEN (1979).

The convention elaborates and puts into the form of a multilateral treaty the substantive provisions of the DECLARATION ON THE ELIMINATION OF DISCRIMINATION AGAINST WOMEN. It establishes international machinery for the implementation of its provisions along the lines of those established for implementation of the INTERNATIONAL COVENANT ON CIVIL AND POLITICAL RIGHTS, i.e., an 18-member COMMITTEE ON THE ELIMINATION OF DISCRIMINATION AGAINST WOMEN empowered to settle disputes between States parties concerning observance of the convention and to receive and examine information from them on measures taken to achieve its goals. The convention's underlying philosophy is that discrimination against women is incompatible with human dignity and constitutes an obstacle to the full realization of the potentialities of women; therefore, the right of women to share equally in improved conditions of life must be promoted and protected.

The convention was adopted by the UN General Assembly on 18 December 1979 (resolution 34/180) and entered into force on 3 September 1981; the text, annexed to the resolution, is as follows:

The States Parties to the present Convention,

Noting that the Charter of the United Nations reaffirms faith in fundamental human rights, in the dignity and worth of the human person and in the equal rights of men and women,

Noting that the Universal Declaration of Human Rights affirms the principle of the inadmissibility of discrimination and proclaims that all human beings are born free and equal in dignity and rights and that everyone is entitled to all the rights and freedoms set forth therein, without distinction of any kind, including distinction based on sex,

Noting that the States parties to the International Covenants on Human Rights have the obligation to ensure the equal right of men and women to enjoy all economic, social, cultural, civil and political rights,

Considering the international conventions concluded under the auspices of the United Nations and the specialized agencies promoting equality of rights of men and women,

Noting also the resolutions, declarations and recommendations adopted by the United Nations and the specialized agencies promoting equality of rights of men and women,

Concerned, however, that despite these various instruments extensive discrimination against women continues to exist,

Recalling that discrimination against women violates the principles of equality of rights and respect for human dignity, is an obstacle to the participation of women, on equal terms with men, in the political, social, economic and cultural life of their countries, hampers the growth of the prosperity of society and the family and makes more difficult the full development of the potentialities of women in the service of their countries and of humanity,

Concerned that in situations of poverty women have the least access to food, health, education, training and opportunities for employment and other needs,

Convinced that the establishment of the new international economic order based on equity and justice will contribute significantly towards the promotion of equality between men and women,

Emphasizing that the eradication of *apartheid*, all forms of racism, racial discrimination, colonialism, neo-colonialism, aggression, foreign occupation and domination and interference in the internal affairs of States is essential to the full enjoyment of the rights of men and women,

Affirming that the strengthening of international peace and security, the relaxation of international tension, mutual co-operation among all States irrespective of their social and economic systems, general and complete disarmament, in particular nuclear disarmament under strict and effective international control, the affirmation of the principles of justice, equality and mutual benefit in relations among countries and the realization of the right of peoples under alien and colonial domination and foreign occupation to self-determination and independence, as well as respect for national sovereignty and territorial integrity, will promote social progress and development and as a consequence will contribute to the attainment of full equality between men and women,

Convinced that the full and complete development of a country, the welfare of the world and the cause of peace require the maximum participation of women on equal terms with men in all fields,

Bearing in mind the great contribution of women to the welfare of the family and to the development of society, so far not fully recognized, the social significance of maternity and the role of both parents in the family and in the upbringing of children, and aware that the role of women in procreation should not be a basis for discrimination but that the upbringing of children requires a sharing of responsibility between men and women and society as a whole,

Aware that a change in the traditional role of men as well as the role of women in society and in the family is needed to achieve full equality between men and women,

Determined to implement the principles set forth in the Declaration on the Elimination of Discrimination against Women and, for that purpose, to adopt the measures required for the elimination of such discrimination in all its forms and manifestations,

Have agreed on the following:

Part I

Article 1. For the purposes of the present Convention, the term "discrimination against women" shall mean any distinction, exclusion or restriction made on the basis of sex which has the effect or purpose of impairing or nullifying the recognition, enjoyment or exercise by women, irrespective of their marital status, on a basis of equality of men and women, of human rights and fundamental freedoms in the political, economic, social, cultural, civil or any other field.

Article 2. States Parties condemn discrimination against women in all its forms, agree to pursue by all appropriate means and without delay a policy of eliminating discrimination against women and, to this end, undertake:

(a) To embody the principle of the equality of men and women in their national constitutions or other appropriate legislation if not yet incorporated therein and to ensure, through law and other appropriate means, the practical realization of this principle;

(b) To adopt appropriate legislative and other measures, including sanctions where appropriate, prohibiting all discrimination against women;

(c) To establish legal protection of the rights of women on an equal basis with men and to ensure through competent national tribunals and other public institutions the effective protection of women against any act of discrimination;

(d) To refrain from engaging in any act or practice of discrimination against women and to ensure that public authorities and institutions shall act in conformity with this obligation;

(e) To take all appropriate measures to eliminate discrimination against women by any person, organization or enterprise;

(f) To take all appropriate measures, including legislation, to modify or abolish existing laws, regulations, customs and practices which constitute discrimination against women;

(g) To repeal all national penal provisions which constitute discrimination against women.

Article 3. States Parties shall take in all fields, in particular in the political, social, economic and cultural fields, all appropriate measures, including legislation, to ensure the full development and advancement of women, for the purpose of guaranteeing them the exercise and enjoyment of human rights and fundamental freedoms on a basis of equality with men.

Article 4. 1. Adoption by States Parties of temporary special measures aimed at accelerating *de facto* equality between men and women shall not be considered discrimination as defined in the present Convention, but shall in no way entail as a consequence the maintenance of unequal or separate standards; these measures shall be discontinued when the objectives of equality of opportunity and treatment have been achieved.

2. Adoption by States Parties of special measures, including those measures contained in the present Convention, aimed at protecting maternity shall not be considered discriminatory.

Article 5. States Parties shall take all appropriate measures:

(a) To modify the social and cultural patterns of conduct of men and women, with a view to achieving the elimination of prejudices and customary and all other practices which are based on the idea of the inferiority or the superiority of either of the sexes or on stereotyped roles for men and women;

(b) To ensure that family education includes a proper understanding of maternity as a social function and the recognition of the common responsibility of men and women in the upbringing and development of their children, it being understood that the interest of the children is the primordial consideration in all cases.

Article 6. States Parties shall take all appropriate measures, including legislation, to suppress all forms of traffic in women and exploitation of prostitution of women.

Part II

Article 7. States Parties shall take all appropriate measures to eliminate discrimination against women in the political and public life of the country and, in particular, shall ensure to women, on equal terms with men, the right:

(a) To vote in all elections and public referenda and to be eligible for election to all publicly elected bodies;

(b) To participate in the formulation of government policy and the implementation thereof and to hold public office and perform all public functions at all levels of government;

(c) To participate in non-governmental organizations and associations concerned with the public and political life of the country.

Article 8. States Parties shall take all appropriate measures to ensure to women, on equal terms with men and without any discrimination, the opportunity to represent their Governments at the international level and to participate in the work of international organizations.

Article 9. 1. States Parties shall grant women equal rights with men to acquire, change or retain their nationality. They shall ensure in particular that neither marriage to an alien nor change of nationality by the husband during marriage shall automatically change the nationality of the wife, render her stateless or force upon her the nationality of the husband.

2. States Parties shall grant women equal rights with men with respect to the nationality of their children.

Part III

Article 10. States Parties shall take all appropriate measures to eliminate discrimination against women in order to ensure to them equal rights with men in the field of education and in particular to ensure, on a basis of equality of men and women:

(a) The same conditions for career and vocational guidance, for access to studies and for the achievement of diplomas in educational establishments of all categories in rural as well as in urban areas; this equality shall be ensured in pre-school, general, technical, professional and higher technical education, as well as in all types of vocational training;

(b) Access to the same curricula, the same examinations, teaching staff with qualifications of the same standard and school premises and equipment of the same quality;

(c) The elimination of any stereotyped concept of the roles of men and women at all levels and in all forms of education by encouraging coeducation and other types of education which will help to achieve this aim and, in particular, by the revision of textbooks and school programmes and the adaptation of teaching methods;

(d) The same opportunities to benefit from scholarships and other study grants;

(e) The same opportunities for access to programmes of continuing education, including adult and functional literacy programmes, particularly those aimed at reducing, at the earliest possible time, any gap in education existing between men and women;

(f) The reduction of female student drop-out rates and the organization of programmes for girls and women who have left school prematurely;

(g) The same opportunities to participate actively in sports and physical education;

(h) Access to specific educational information to help to ensure the health and well-being of families, including information and advice on family planning.

Article 11. 1. States Parties shall take all appropriate measures to eliminate discrimination against women in the field of employment in order to ensure, on a basis of equality of men and women, the same rights, in particular:

(a) The right to work as an inalienable right of all human beings;

(b) The right to the same employment opportunities, including the application of the same criteria for selection in matters of employment;

(c) The right to free choice of profession and employment, the right to promotion, job security and all benefits and conditions of service and the right to receive vocational training and retraining, including apprenticeships, advanced vocational training and recurrent training;

(d) The right to equal remuneration, including benefits, and to equal treatment in respect of work of equal value, as well as equality of treatment in the evaluation of the quality of work;

(e) The right to social security, particularly in cases of retirement, unemployment, sickness, invalidity and old age and other incapacity to work, as well as the right to paid leave;

(f) The right to protection of health and to safety in working conditions, including the safeguarding of the function of reproduction.

2. In order to prevent discrimination against women on the grounds of marriage or maternity and to ensure their effective right to work, States Parties shall take appropriate measures:

(a) To prohibit, subject to the imposition of sanctions, dismissal on the grounds of pregnancy or of maternity leave and discrimination in dismissals on the basis of marital status;

(b) To introduce maternity leave with pay or with comparable social benefits without loss of former employment, seniority or social allowances;

(c) To encourage the provision of the necessary supporting social services to enable parents to combine family obligations with work responsibilities and participation in public life, in particular through promoting the establishment and development of a network of child-care facilities;

(d) To provide special protection to women during pregnancy in types of work proved to be harmful to them.

3. Protective legislation relating to matters covered in this article shall be reviewed periodically in the light of scientific and technological knowledge and shall be revised, repealed or extended as necessary.

Article 12. 1. States Parties shall take all appropriate measures to eliminate discrimination against women in the field of health care in order to ensure, on a basis of equality of men and women, access to health care services, including those related to family planning.

2. Notwithstanding the provisions of paragraph 1 of this

article, States Parties shall ensure to women appropriate services in connexion with pregnancy, confinement and the post-natal period, granting free services where necessary, as well as adequate nutrition during pregnancy and lactation.

Article 13. States Parties shall take all appropriate measures to eliminate discrimination against women in other areas of economic and social life in order to ensure, on a basis of equality of men and women, the same rights, in particular:

(a) The right to family benefits;

(b) The right to bank loans, mortgages and other forms of financial credit;

(c) The right to participate in recreational activities, sports and all aspects of cultural life.

Article 14. 1. States Parties shall take into account the particular problems faced by rural women and the significant roles which rural women play in the economic survival of their families, including their work in the non-monetized sectors of the economy, and shall take all appropriate measures to ensure the application of the provisions of the present Convention to women in rural areas.

2. States Parties shall take all appropriate measures to eliminate discrimination against women in rural areas in order to ensure, on a basis of equality of men and women, that they participate in and benefit from rural development and, in particular, shall ensure to such women the right:

(a) To participate in the elaboration and implementation of development planning at all levels;

(b) To have access to adequate health care facilities, including information, counselling and services in family planning;

(c) To benefit directly from social security programmes;

(d) To obtain all types of training and education, formal and non-formal, including that relating to functional literacy, as well as, *inter alia,* the benefit of all community and extension services, in order to increase their technical proficiency;

(e) To organize self-help groups and co-operatives in order to obtain equal access to economic opportunities through employment or self-employment;

(f) To participate in all community activities;

(g) To have access to agricultural credit and loans, marketing facilities, appropriate technology and equal treatment in land and agrarian reform as well as in land resettlement schemes;

(h) To enjoy adequate living conditions, particularly in relation to housing, sanitation, electricity and water supply, transport and communications.

Part IV

Article 15. 1. States Parties shall accord to women equality with men before the law.

2. State Parties shall accord to women, in civil matters, a legal capacity identical to that of men and the same opportunities to exercise that capacity. In particular, they shall give women equal rights to conclude contracts and to administer property and shall treat them equally in all stages of procedure in courts and tribunals.

3. States Parties agree that all contracts and all other private instruments of any kind with a legal effect which is directed at restricting the legal capacity of women shall be deemed null and void.

4. States Parties shall accord to men and women the same rights with regard to the law relating to the movement of persons and the freedom to choose their residence and domicile.

Article 16. 1. States Parties shall take all appropriate measures to eliminate discrimination against women in all matters relating to marriage and family relations and in particular shall ensure, on a basis of equality of men and women:

(a) The same right to enter into marriage;

(b) The same right freely to choose a spouse and to enter into marriage only with their free and full consent;

(c) The same rights and responsibilities during marriage and at its dissolution;

(d) The same rights and responsibilities as parents, irrespective of their marital status, in matters relating to their children; in all cases the interests of the children shall be paramount;

(e) The same rights to decide freely and responsibly on the number and spacing of their children and to have access to the information, education and means to enable them to exercise these rights;

(f) The same rights and responsibilities with regard to guardianship, wardship, trusteeship and adoption of children, or similar institutions where these concepts exist in national legislation; in all cases the interests of the children shall be paramount;

(g) The same personal rights as husband and wife, including the right to choose a family name, a profession and an occupation;

(h) The same rights for both spouses in respect of the ownership, acquisition, management, administration, enjoyment and disposition of property, whether free of charge or for a valuable consideration.

2. The betrothal and the marriage of a child shall have no legal effect, and all necessary action, including legislation, shall be taken to specify a minimum age for marriage and to make the registration of marriages in an official registry compulsory.

Part V

Article 17. 1. For the purpose of considering the progress made in the implementation of the present Convention, there shall be established a Committee on the Elimination of Discrimination against Women (hereinafter referred to as the Committee) consisting, at the time of entry into force of the Convention, of eighteen and, after ratification of or accession to the Convention by the thirty-fifth State Party, of twenty-three experts of high moral standing and competence in the field covered by the Convention. The experts shall be elected by States Parties from among their nationals and shall serve in their personal capacity, consideration being given to equitable geographical distribution and to the representation of the different forms of civilization as well as the principal legal systems.

2. The members of the Committee shall be elected by secret ballot from a list of persons nominated by States Parties. Each State Party may nominate one person from among its own nationals.

3. The initial election shall be held six months after the date of the entry into force of the present Convention. At least three months before the date of each election the Secretary-General of the United Nations shall address a letter to the States Parties inviting them to submit their nominations within two months. The Secretary-General shall

prepare a list in alphabetical order of all persons thus nominated, indicating the States Parties which have nominated them, and shall submit it to the States Parties.

4. Elections of the members of the Committee shall be held at a meeting of States Parties convened by the Secretary-General at United Nations Headquarters. At that meeting, for which two thirds of the States Parties shall constitute a quorum, the persons elected to the Committee shall be those nominees who obtain the largest number of votes and an absolute majority of the votes of the representatives of States Parties present and voting.

5. The members of the Committee shall be elected for a term of four years. However, the terms of nine of the members elected at the first election shall expire at the end of two years; immediately after the first election the names of these nine members shall be chosen by lot by the Chairman of the Committee.

6. The election of the five additional members of the Committee shall be held in accordance with the provisions of paragraphs 2, 3 and 4 of this article, following the thirty-fifth ratification or accession. The terms of two of the additional members elected on this occasion shall expire at the end of two years, the names of these two members having been chosen by lot by the Chairman of the Committee.

7. For the filling of casual vacancies, the State Party whose expert has ceased to function as a member of the Committee shall appoint another expert from among its nationals, subject to the approval of the Committee.

8. The members of the Committee shall, with the approval of the General Assembly, receive emoluments from United Nations resources on such terms and conditions as the Assembly may decide, having regard to the importance of the Committee's responsibilities.

9. The Secretary-General of the United Nations shall provide the necessary staff and facilities for the effective performance of the functions of the Committee under the present Convention.

Article 18. 1. States Parties undertake to submit to the Secretary-General of the United Nations, for consideration by the Committee, a report on the legislative, judicial, administrative or other measures which they have adopted to give effect to the provisions of the present Convention and on the progress made in this respect:

(a) Within one year after the entry into force for the State concerned;

(b) Thereafter at least every four years and further whenever the Committee so requests.

2. Reports may indicate factors and difficulties affecting the degree of fulfilment of obligations under the present Convention.

Article 19. 1. The Committee shall adopt its own rules of procedure.

2. The Committee shall elect its officers for a term of two years.

Article 20. 1. The Committee shall normally meet for a period of not more than two weeks annually in order to consider the reports submitted in accordance with article 18 of the present Convention.

2. The meetings of the Committee shall normally be held at United Nations Headquarters or at any other convenient place as determined by the Committee.

Article 21. 1. The Committee shall, through the Economic and Social Council, report annually to the General Assembly of the United Nations on its activities and may make suggestions and general recommendations based on the examination of reports and information received from the States Parties. Such suggestions and general recommendations shall be included in the report of the Committee together with comments, if any, from States Parties.

2. The Secretary-General of the United Nations shall transmit the reports of the Committee to the Commission on the Status of Women for its information.

Article 22. The specialized agencies shall be entitled to be represented at the consideration of the implementation of such provisions of the present Convention as fall within the scope of their activities. The Committee may invite the specialized agencies to submit reports on the implementation of the Convention in areas falling within the scope of their activities.

Part VI

Article 23. Nothing in the present Convention shall affect any provisions that are more conducive to the achievement of equality between men and women which may be contained:

(a) In the legislation of a State Party; or

(b) In any other international convention, treaty or agreement in force for that State.

Article 24. States Parties undertake to adopt all necessary measures at the national level aimed at achieving the full realization of the rights recognized in the present Convention.

Article 25. 1. The present Convention shall be open for signature by all States.

2. The Secretary-General of the United Nations is designated as the depositary of the present Convention.

3. The present Convention is subject to ratification. Instruments of ratification shall be deposited with the Secretary-General of the United Nations.

4. The present Convention shall be open to accession by all States. Accession shall be effected by the deposit of an instrument of accession with the Secretary-General of the United Nations.

Article 26. 1. A request for the revision of the present Convention may be made at any time by any State Party by means of a notification in writing addressed to the Secretary-General of the United Nations.

2. The General Assembly of the United Nations shall decide upon the steps, if any, to be taken in respect of such a request.

Article 27. 1. The present Convention shall enter into force on the thirtieth day after the date of deposit with the Secretary-General of the United Nations of the twentieth instrument of ratification or accession.

2. For each State ratifying the present Convention or acceding to it after the deposit of the twentieth instrument of ratification or accession, the Convention shall enter into force on the thirtieth day after the date of the deposit of its own instrument of ratification or accession.

Article 28. 1. The Secretary-General of the United Nations shall receive and circulate to all States the text of reservations made by States at the time of ratification or accession.

2. A reservation incompatible with the object and purpose of the present Convention shall not be permitted.

3. Reservations may be withdrawn at any time by notification to this effect addressed to the Secretary-General of the United Nations, who shall then inform all States thereof. Such notification shall take effect on the date on which it is received.

Article 29. 1. Any dispute between two or more States Parties concerning the interpretation or application of the present Convention which is not settled by negotiation shall, at the request of one of them, be submitted to arbitration. If within six months from the date of the request for arbitration the parties are unable to agree on the organization of the arbitration, any one of those parties may refer the dispute to the International Court of Justice by request in conformity with the Statute of the Court.

2. Each State Party may at the time of signature or ratification of the present Convention or accession thereto declare that it does not consider itself bound by paragraph 1 of this article. The other States Parties shall not be bound by that paragraph with respect to any State Party which has made such a reservation.

3. Any State Party which has made a reservation in accordance with paragraph 2 of this article may at any time withdraw that reservation by notification to the Secretary-General of the United Nations.

Article 30. The present Convention, the Arabic, Chinese, English, French, Russian and Spanish texts of which are equally authentic, shall be deposited with the Secretary-General of the United Nations.

In witness whereof the undersigned, duly authorized, have signed the present Convention.

SEE ALSO Advancement of Women Branch; Commision on the Status of Women; Convention on the Political Rights of Women; Declaration of Mexico on the Equality of Women. . . ; Inter-American Convention on the Granting of Civil Rights to Women; Inter-American Convention on the Granting of Political Rights to Women; Nairobi Forward-Looking Strategies. . . ; Women Workers: ILO Plan of Action on Equality of Opportunity and Treatment of Men and Women in Employment.

CONVENTION ON THE HIGH SEAS (1958).

The convention sets out the conditions under which freedom of the high seas may be enjoyed. In particular, it contains provisions designed to prevent and punish slavery and piracy.

The convention was adopted by the United Nations Conference on the Law of the Sea, in Geneva, on 29 April 1958 and entered into force on 30 September 1962. Portions of the text (United Nations, *Treaty Series,* vol. 450, p. 82), which have a bearing upon the enjoyment of human rights, are as follows:

The States Parties to this Convention,
Desiring to codify the rules of international law relating to the high seas,
Recognizing that the United Nations Conference on the Law of the Sea, held at Geneva from 24 February to 27 April 1958, adopted the following provisions as generally declaratory of established principles of international law,
Have agreed as follows:
Article 1. The term "high seas" means all parts of the sea that are not included in the territorial sea or in the internal waters of a state.
Article 2. The high seas being open to all nations, no State may validly purport to subject any part of them to its sovereignty. Freedom of the high seas is exercised under the conditions laid down by these articles and by the other rules of international law. It comprises, *inter alia,* both for coastal and non-coastal States:
(1) Freedom of navigation;
(2) Freedom of fishing;
(3) Freedom to lay submarine cables and pipelines;
(4) Freedom to fly over the high seas.
These freedoms, and others which are recognized by the general principles of international law, shall be exercised by all States with reasonable regard to the interests of other States in their exercise of the freedom of the high seas. . . .
Article 13. Every State shall adopt effective measures to prevent and punish the transport of slaves in ships authorized to fly its flag, and to prevent the unlawful use of its flag for that purpose. Any slave taking refuge on board any ship, whatever its flag, shall *ipso facto,* be free.
Article 14. All States shall co-operate to the fullest possible extent in the repression of piracy on the high seas or in any other place outside the jurisdiction of any State.
Article 15. Piracy consists of any of the following acts:
(1) Any illegal acts of violence, detention or any act of depredation, committed for private ends by the crew or the passengers of a private ship or a private aircraft, and directed:
(*a*) On the high seas, against another ship or aircraft, or against persons or property on board such ship or aircraft;
(*b*) Against a ship, aircraft, persons or property in a place outside the jurisdiction of any State;
(2) Any act of voluntary participation in the operation of a ship or of an aircraft with knowledge of facts making it a pirate ship or aircraft;
(3) Any act of inciting or of intentionally facilitating an act described in sub-paragraph 1 or sub-paragraph 2 of this article. . . .

CONVENTION ON THE INTERNATIONAL RIGHT OF CORRECTION (1952).

The convention grew out of an amalgamation of two draft instruments, one relating to the gathering and international transmitting of news and the other to the institution of an "international right of correction." Both had been prepared by the UN Conference on Freedom of Information, held in Geneva in 1948. The combined drafts were adopted as a single instrument by the UN General Assembly in the belief that the establishment of the proposed right of correction would help to curb the dissemination of false or distorted news and thereby to strengthen peace.

The convention was adopted by the UN General Assembly on 16 December 1952 (resolution 630 [VII]), and entered into force on 24 August 1962. The text (United Nations, *Treaty Series,* vol. 435, p. 191) is as follows:

Preamble

The Contracting States,
Desiring to implement the right of their peoples to be fully and reliably informed,
Desiring to improve understanding between their peoples through the free flow of information and opinion,

Desiring thereby to protect mankind from the scourge of war, to prevent the recurrence of aggression from any source, and to combat all propaganda which is either designed or likely to provoke or encourage any threat to the peace, breach of the peace, or act of aggression,

Considering the danger to the maintenance of friendly relations between peoples and to the preservation of peace, arising from the publication of inaccurate reports,

Considering that at its second regular session the General Assembly of the United Nations recommended the adoption of measures designed to combat the dissemination of false or distorted reports likely to injure friendly relations between States,

Considering, however, that it is not at present practicable to institute, on the international level, a procedure for verifying the accuracy of a report which might lead to the imposition of penalties for the publication of false or distorted reports,

Considering, moreover, that to prevent the publication of reports of this nature or to reduce their pernicious effects, it is above all necessary to promote a wide circulation of news and to heighten the sense of responsibility of those regularly engaged in the dissemination of news,

Considering that an effective means to these ends is to give States directly affected by a report, which they consider false or distorted and which is disseminated by an information agency, the possibility of securing commensurate publicity for their corrections,

Considering that the legislation of certain States does not provide for a right of correction of which foreign governments may avail themselves, and that it is therefore desirable to institute such a right on the international level, and

Having resolved to conclude a Convention for these purposes,

Have agreed as follows:

Article 1. For the purposes of the present Convention:

1. "News dispatch" means news material transmitted in writing or by means of telecommunications, in the form customarily employed by information agencies in transmitting such news material, before publication, to newspapers, news periodicals and broadcasting organizations.

2. "Information agency" means a Press, broadcasting, film, television or facsimile organization, public or private, regularly engaged in the collection and dissemination of news material, created and organized under the laws and regulations of the Contracting State in which the central organization is domiciled and which, in each Contracting State where it operates, functions under the laws and regulations of that State.

3. "Correspondent" means a national of a Contracting State or an individual employed by an information agency of a Contracting State, who in either case is regularly engaged in the collection and the reporting of news material, and who when outside his State is identified as a correspondent by a valid passport or by a similar document internationally acceptable.

Article 2. 1. Recognizing that the professional responsibility of correspondents and information agencies requires them to report facts without discrimination and in their proper context and thereby to promote respect for human rights and fundamental freedoms, to further international understanding and co-operation and to contribute to the maintenance of international peace and security,

Considering also that, as a matter of professional ethics, all correspondents and information agencies should, in the case of news dispatches transmitted or published by them and which have been demonstrated to be false or distorted, follow the customary practice of transmitting through the same channels, or of publishing corrections of such dispatches,

The Contracting States agree that in cases where a Contracting State contends that a news dispatch capable of injuring its relations with other States or its national prestige or dignity transmitted from one country to another by correspondents or information agencies of a Contracting or non-Contracting State and published or disseminated abroad is false or distorted, if may submit its version of the facts (hereinafter called "communiqué") to the Contracting States within whose territories such dispatch has been published or disseminated.

A copy of the commuiqué shall be forwarded at the same time to the correspondent or information agency concerned to enable that correspondent or information agency to correct the news dispatch in question.

2. A communiqué may be issued only with respect to news dispatches and must be without comment or expression of opinion. It should not be longer than is necessary to correct the alleged inaccuracy or distortion and must be accompanied by a verbatim text of the dispatch as published or disseminated, and by evidence that the dispatch has been transmitted from abroad by a correspondent or an information agency.

Article 3. 1. With the least possible delay and in any case not later than five clear days from the date of receiving a communiqué transmitted in accordance with provisions of article II, a Contracting State, whatever be its opinion concerning the facts in question, shall:

(*a*) Release the communiqué to the correspondents and information agencies operating in its territory through the channels customarily used for the release of news concerning international affairs for publication; and

(*b*) Transmit the communiqué to the headquarters of the information agency whose correspondent was responsible for originating the dispatch in question, if such headquarters are within its territory.

2. In the event that a Contracting State does not discharge its obligation under this article, with respect to the communiqué of another Contracting State, the latter may accord, on the basis of reciprocity, similar treatment to a communiqué thereafter submitted to it by the defaulting State.

Article 4. 1. If any of the Contracting States to which a communiqué has been transmitted in accordance with article 2 fails to fulfil, within the prescribed time-limit, the obligations laid down in article 3, the Contracting State exercising the right of correction may submit the said communiqué, together with a verbatim text of the dispatch as published or disseminated, to the Secretary-General of the United Nations and shall at the same time notify the State complained against that it is doing so. The latter State, may, within five clear days after receiving such notice, submit its comments to the Secretary-General, which shall relate only to the allegation that it has not discharged its obligations under article 3.

2. The Secretary-General shall in any event, within ten clear days after receiving the communiqué, give appropriate publicity through the information channels at his disposal to the communiqué, together with the dispatch and the comments, if any, submitted to him by the State complained against.

Article 5. Any dispute between any two or more Contracting States concerning the interpretation or application of the present Convention which is not settled by negotiations shall be referred to the International Court of Justice for decision unless the Contracting States agree to another mode of settlement.

Article 6. 1. The present Convention shall be open for signature to all States Members of the United Nations, to every State invited to the United Nations Conference on Freedom of Information held at Geneva in 1948, and to every other State which the General Assembly may, by resolution, declare to be eligible.

2. The present Convention shall be ratified by the States signatory hereto in conformity with their respective constitutional processes. The instruments of ratification shall be deposited with the Secretary-General of the United Nations.

Article 7. 1. The present Convention shall be open for accession to the States referred to in article 6 (1).

2. Accession shall be effected by the deposit of an instrument of accession with the Secretary-General of the United Nations.

Article 8. When any six of the States referred to in article 6(1) have deposited their instruments of ratification or accession, the present Convention shall come into force among them on the thirtieth day after the date of the deposit of the sixth instrument of ratification or accession. It shall come into force for each State which ratifies or accedes after that date on the thirtieth day after the deposit of its instrument of ratification or accession.

Article 9. The provisions of the present Convention shall extend to or be applicable equally to a contracting metropolitan State and to all territories, be they Non-Self-Governing, Trust or Colonial Territories, which are being administered or governed by such metropolitan State.

Article 10. Any Contracting State may denounce the present Convention by notification to the Secretary-General of the United Nations. Denunciation shall take effect six months after the date of receipt of the notification by the Secretary-General.

Article 11. The present Convention shall cease to be in force as from the date when the denunciation which reduces the number of parties to less than six becomes effective.

Article 12. 1. A request for the revision of the present Convention may be made at any time by any Contracting State by means of a notification to the Secretary-General of the United Nations.

2. The General Assembly shall decide upon the steps, if any, to be taken in respect of such request.

Article 13. The Secretary-General of the United Nations shall notify the States referred to in article 6(1) of the following:

(*a*) Signatures, ratifications and accessions received in accordance with articles 6 and 7;

(*b*) The date upon which the present Convention comes into force in accordance with article 8;

(*c*) Denunciations received in accordance with article 10;

(*d*) Abrogation in accordance with article 11;

(*e*) Notifications received in accordance with article 12.

Article 14. 1. The present Convention, of which the Chinese, English, French, Russian and Spanish texts shall be equally authentic, shall be deposited in the archives of the United Nations.

2. The Secretary-General of the United Nations shall transmit a certified copy to each State referred to in article VI (1).

3. The present Convention shall be registered with the Secretariat of the United Nations on the date of its coming into force.

SEE ALSO *European Declaration on Mass Communication and Human Rights; Freedom of Information; Journalists: Protection of their Human Rights; UNESCO Declaration on Fundamental Principles concerning the Contribution of the Mass Media to Strengthening Peace and International Understanding, to the Promotion of Human Rights and to Countering Racialism,* Apartheid *and Incitement to War.*

CONVENTION ON THE NATIONALITY OF MARRIED WOMEN (1957).

At its 1948 session, the COMMISSION ON THE STATUS OF WOMEN took note of the many and varied forms of discrimination against women that could result from conflicts in nationality laws and requested the UN secretary-general to prepare a report on the subject, taking into account the Hague Convention on the Conflict of Nationality Laws (1930), the Montevideo Convention on the Nationality of Women (1933), and relevant studies which had been undertaken by the League of Nations.

On the basis of this and other documentation, the commission, in 1949, recommended that a convention on the nationality of married women should be prepared as promptly as possible, assuring women equality with men in the exercise of this right and preventing them from becoming stateless or otherwise suffering hardships arising out of conflicts of laws. The commission completed the preparation of a draft convention in 1955; and the Convention on the Nationality of Married Women was adopted by the General Assembly (resolution 1040 [XI]) on 29 January 1957, opened for signature and ratification or accession on 20 February of that year, and entered into force on 11 August 1958. The convention provides that neither the celebration nor the dissolution of a marriage between one of the nationals of a contracting State, nor the change of nationality by the husband during marriage, shall automatically affect the nationality of the wife (article 1); that each contracting State agrees that the alien wife of one of its nationals may, at her request, acquire the nationality of her husband (article 2); and that the convention shall not be construed as affecting any legislation or juridical practice by which the alien wife of one of its nationals may, at her request, acquire her husband's nationality as a matter of right (article 3).

The text of the convention (United Nations, *Treaty Series,* vol. 309, p.65) is as follows:

The Contracting States,

Recognizing that, conflicts in law in practice with reference to nationality arise as a result of provisions concerning the loss or acquisition of nationality by women as a result of marriage, of its dissolution or of the change of nationality by the husband during marriage,

Recognizing that, in article 15 of the Universal Declaration of Human Rights, the General Assembly of the United Nations has proclaimed that "everyone has the right to a nationality" and that "no one shall be arbitrarily deprived of his nationality nor denied the right to change his nationality",

Desiring to co-operate with the United Nations in promoting universal respect for, and observance of, human rights and fundamental freedoms for all without distinction as to sex,

Hereby agrees as hereinafter provided:

Article 1. Each Contracting State agrees that neither the celebration nor the dissolution of a marriage between one of its nationals and an alien, nor the change of nationality by the husband during marriage, shall automatically affect the nationality of the wife.

Article 2. Each Contracting State agrees that neither the voluntary acquisition of the nationality of another State nor the renunciation of its nationality by one of its nationals shall prevent the retention of its nationality by the wife of such national.

Article 3. 1. Each Contracting State agrees that the alien wife of one of its nationals may, at her request, acquire the nationality of her husband through specially privileged naturalization procedures; the grant of such nationality may be subject to such limitations as may be imposed in the interests of national security or public policy.

2. Each Contracting State agrees that the present Convention shall not be construed as affecting any legislation or judicial practice by which the alien wife of one of its nationals may, at her request, acquire her husband's nationality as a matter of right.

Article 4. 1. The present Convention shall be open for signature and ratification on behalf of any State Member of the United Nations and also on behalf of any other State which is or hereafter becomes a member of any specialized agency of the United Nations, or which is or hereafter becomes a Party to the Statute of the International Court of Justice, or any other State to which an invitation has been addressed by the General Assembly of the United Nations.

2. The present Convention shall be ratified and the instruments of ratification shall be deposited with the Secretary-General of the United Nations.

Article 5. 1. The present Convention shall be open for accession to all States referred to in paragraph 1 of article 4.

2. Accession shall be effected by the deposit of an instrument of accession with the Secretary-General of the United Nations.

Article 6. 1. The present Convention shall come into force on the ninetieth day following the date of deposit of the sixth instrument of ratification or accession.

2. For each State ratifying or acceding to the Convention after the deposit of the sixth instrument of ratification or accession, the Convention shall enter into force on the ninetieth day after deposit by such State of its instrument of ratification or accession.

Article 7. 1. The present Convention shall apply to all non-self-governing, trust, colonial and other non-metropolitan territories for the international relations of which any Contracting State is responsible; the Contracting State concerned shall, subject to the provisions of paragraph 2 of the present article, at the time of signature, ratification or accession declare the non-metropolitan territory or territories to which the Convention shall apply *ipso facto* as a result of such signature, ratification or accession.

2. In any case in which, for the purpose of nationality, a non-metropolitan territory is not treated as one with the metropolitan territory, or in any case in which the previous consent of a non-metropolitan territory is required by the constitutional laws or practices of the Contracting State or of the non-metropolitan territory for the application of the Convention to that territory, that Contracting State shall endeavour to secure the needed consent fo the non-metropolitan territory within the period of twelve months from the date of signature of the Convention by that Contracting State, and when such consent has been obtained the Contracting State shall notify the Secretary-General of the United Nations. The present Convention shall apply to the territory or territories named in such notification from the date of its receipt by the Secretary-General.

3. After the expiry of the twelve-month period mentioned in paragraph 2 of the present article, the Contracting States concerned shall inform the Secretary-General of the results of the consultations with those non-metropolitan territories for whose international relations they are responsible and whose consent to the application of the present Convention may have been withheld.

Article 8. 1. At the time of signature, ratification or accession, any State may make reservations to any article of the present Convention other than articles 1 and 2.

2. If any State makes a reservation in accordance with paragraph 1 of the present article, the Convention, with the exception of those provisions to which the reservation relates, shall have effect as between the reserving State and the other Parties. The Secretary-General of the United Nations shall communicate the text of the reservation to all States which are or may become Parties to the Convention. Any State Party to the Convention or which thereafter becomes a Party may notify the Secretary-General that it does not agree to consider itself bound by the Convention with respect to the State making the reservation. This notification must be made, in the case of a State already a Party, within ninety days from the date of the communication by the Secretary-General; and, in the case of a State subsequently becoming a Party, within ninety days from the date when the instrument of ratification or accession is deposited. In the event that such a notification is made, the Convention shall not be deemed to be in effect as between the State making the notification and the State making the reservation.

3. Any State making a reservation in accordance with paragraph 1 of the present article may at any time withdraw the reservation, in whole or in part, after it has been accepted, by a notification to this effect addressed to the Secretary-General of the United Nations. Such notification shall take effect on the date on which it is received.

Article 9. 1. Any Contracting State may denounce the present Convention by written notification to the Secretary-General of the United Nations. Denunciation shall take effect one year after the date of receipt of the notification of the Secretary-General.

2. The present Convention shall cease to be in force as from the date when the denunciation which reduces the number of Parties to less than six becomes effective.

Article 10. Any dispute which may arise between any two or more Contracting States concerning the interpretation or application of the present Convention which is not settled by negotiation, shall, at the request of any one of the Parties to the dispute, be referred to the International Court of Justice for decision, unless the Parties agree to another mode of settlement.

Article 11. The Secretary-General of the United Nations shall notify all States Members of the United Nations and the non-member States contemplated in paragraph 1 of article 4 of the present Convention of the following:

(*a*) Signatures and instruments of ratification received in accordance with article 4;

(*b*) Instruments of accession received in accordance with article 5;

(*c*) The date upon which the present Convention enters into force in accordance with article 6;

(*d*) Communications and notifications received in accordance with article 8;

(*e*) Notifications of denunciation received in accordance with paragraph 1 of article 9;

(*f*) Abrogation in accordance with paragraph 2 of article 9.

Article 12. 1. The present Convention, of which the Chinese, English, French, Russian and Spanish texts shall be equally authentic, shall be deposited in the archives of the United Nations.

2. The Secretary-General of the United Nations shall transmit a certified copy of the Convention to all States Members of the United Nations and to the non-member States contemplated in paragraph 1 of article 4.

SEE ALSO *Convention on Consent to Marriage, Minimum Age for Marriage and Registration of Marriages; Convention on the Elimination of all Forms of Discrimination against Women; Convention on the Political Rights of Women; Declaration on the Elimination of Discrimination against Women; ILO Maternity Protection Benefits; Inter-American Convention on the Granting of Civil Rights to Women; Inter-American Convention on the Granting of Political Rights to Women; Nairobi Forward-Looking Strategies for the Advancement of Women; Recommendation on Consent to Marriage, Minimum Age for Marriage and Registration of Marriages.*

CONVENTION ON THE NON-APPLICABILITY OF STATUTORY LIMITATIONS TO WAR CRIMES AND CRIMES AGAINST HUMANITY (1968).

The convention was prepared after studies by the UN secretary-general revealed that, in a number of countries, there were statutory limitations which would prevent the trial or punishment of certain war criminals after a specified date or period. The convention affirms in international law the principle that there is not, and cannot be, any period of limitation for the prosecution of perpetrators or war crimes or crimes against humanity.

The convention was adopted by the UN General Assembly on 26 November 1968 (resolution 2391 [XXIII]), and entered into force on 11 November 1970. The text (United Nations, *Treaty Series,* vol. 754, p.73) is as follows:

The States Parties to the present Convention,

Recalling resolutions of the General Assembly of the United Nations 3 (I) of 13 February 1946 and 170 (II) of 31 October 1947 on the extradition and punishment of war criminals, resolution 95 (I) of 11 December 1946 affirming the principles of international law recognized by the Charter of the International Military Tribunal, Nürnberg, and the judgement of the Tribunal, and resolutions 2184 (XXI) of 12 December 1966 and 2202 (XXI) of 16 December 1966 which expressly condemned as crimes against humanity the violation of the economic and political rights of the indigenous population on the one hand and the policies of *apartheid* on the other,

Recalling resolutions of the Economic and Social Council of the United Nations 1074 D (XXXIX) of 28 July 1965 and 1158 (XLI) of 5 August 1966 on the punishment of war criminals and of persons who have committed crimes against humanity,

Noting that none of the solemn declarations, instruments or conventions relating to the prosecution and punishment of war crimes and crimes against humanity made provision for a period of limitation,

Considering that war crimes and crimes against humanity are among the gravest crimes in international law,

Convinced that the effective punishment of war crimes and crimes against humanity is an important element in the prevention of such crimes, the protection of human rights and fundamental freedoms, the encouragement of confidence, the furtherance of co-operation among peoples and the promotion of international peace and security,

Noting that the application to war crimes and crimes against humanity of the rules of municipal law relating to the period of limitation for ordinary crimes is a matter of serious concern to world public opinion, since it prevents the prosecution and punishment of persons responsible for those crimes,

Recognizing that it is necessary and timely to affirm in international law, through this Convention, the principle that there is no period of limitation for war crimes and crimes against humanity, and to secure its universal application,

Have agreed as follows:

Article 1. No statutory limitation shall apply to the following crimes, irrespective of the date of their commission:

(*a*) War crimes as they are defined in the Charter of the International Military Tribunal, Nürnberg, of 8 August 1945 and confirmed by resolutions 3 (I) of 13 February 1946 and 95 (I) of 11 December 1946 of the General Assembly of the United Nations, particularly the "grave breaches" enumerated in the Geneva Conventions of 12 August 1949 for the protection of war victims;

(*b*) Crimes against humanity whether committed in time of war or in time of peace as they are defined in the Charter of the International Military Tribunal, Nürnberg, of 8 August 1945 and confirmed by resolutions 3 (I) of 13 February 1946 and 95 (I) of 11 December 1946 of the General Assembly of the United Nations, eviction by armed attack or occupation and inhuman acts resulting from the policy of *apartheid,* and the crime of genocide as defined in the 1948 Convention on the Prevention and Punishment of the Crime of Genocide, even if such acts do not constitute a violation of the domestic law of the country in which they were committed.

Article 2. If any of the crimes mentioned in article 1 is committed, the provisions of this Convention shall apply to representatives of the State authority and private individuals who, as principals or accomplices, participate in or who directly incite others to the commission of any of those crimes, or who conspire to commit them, irrespective of the degree of completion, and to representatives of the State authority who tolerate their commission.

Article 3. The States Parties to the present Convention undertake to adopt all necessary domestic measures, legislative or otherwise, with a view to making possible the extradition, in accordance with international law, of the persons referred to in article 2 of this Convention.

Article 4. The States Parties to the present Convention undertake to adopt, in accordance with their respective constitutional processes, any legislative or other measures necessary to ensure that statutory or other limitations shall not apply to the prosecution and punishment of the crimes referred to in articles 1 and 2 of this Convention and that, where they exist, such limitations shall be abolished.

Article 5. This Convention shall, until 31 December 1969, be open for signature by any State Member of the United Nations or member of any of its specialized agencies or of the International Atomic Energy Agency, by any State Party to the Statute of the International Court of Justice, and by any other State which has been invited by the General Assembly of the United Nations to become a Party to this Convention.

Article 6. This Convention is subject to ratification. Instruments of ratification shall be deposited with the Secretary-General of the United Nations.

Article 7. This Convention shall be open to accession by any State referred to in article 5. Instruments of accession shall be deposited with the Secretary-General of the United Nations.

Article 8. 1. This Convention shall enter into force on the ninetieth day after the date of the deposit with the Secretary-General of the United Nations of the tenth instrument of ratification or accession.

2. For each State ratifying this Convention or acceding to it after the deposit of the tenth instrument of ratification or accession, the Convention shall enter into force on the ninetieth day after the date of the deposit of its own instrument of ratification or accession.

Article 9. 1. After the expiry of a period of ten years from the date on which this Convention enters into force, a request for the revision of the Convention may be made at any time by any Contracting Party by means of a notification in writing addressed to the Secretary-General of the United Nations.

2. The General Assembly of the United Nations shall decide upon the steps, if any, to be taken in respect of such a request.

Article 10. 1. This Convention shall be deposited with the Secretary-General of the United Nations.

2. The Secretary-General of the United Nations shall transmit certified copies of this Convention to all States referred to in article 5.

3. The Secretary-General of the United Nations shall inform all States referred to in article 5 of the following particulars:

(*a*) Signatures of this Convention, and instruments of ratification and accession deposited under articles 5, 6 and 7;

(*b*) The date of entry into force of this Convention in accordance with article 8;

(*c*) Communications received under article 9.

Article 11. This Convention, of which the Chinese, English, French, Russian and Spanish texts are equally authentic, shall bear the date of 26 November 1968.

In witness whereof the undersigned, being duly authorized for that purpose, having signed this Convention.

SEE ALSO *Convention on the Prevention and Punishment of Genocide; Crimes against the Peace and Security of Mankind; Declaration on the Prevention of Nuclear Catastrophe; European Convention on the Non-Applicability of Statutory Limitations to Crimes against Humanity and War Crimes; Genocide; International Convention against Recruitment, Use, Financing and Training of Mercenaries; Mercenarism; Principles of International Co-operation in the Detection, Arrest, Extradition and Punishment of Persons Guilty of War Crimes; Principles of International Law Recognized in the Charter of the Nuremberg Tribunal and in the Judgment of the Tribunal; War Crimes File; War Criminals: Prosecution and Punishment.*

CONVENTION ON THE POLITICAL RIGHTS OF WOMEN (1952).

The convention is the first worldwide treaty by which States parties undertake a legal obligation concerning the exercise of political rights by their citizens and in which the UNITED NATIONS CHARTER principle of equal rights of men and women is applied to a concrete problem. It aims to insure that, in the territories of States parties, women shall have the rights, to vote, to be eligible for election, to hold public office, and to exercise all public functions on equal terms with men.

The convention was adopted by the UN General Assembly on 20 December 1952 (resolution 640 [VII]), and opened for signature and ratification or accession on 31 March 1953. It entered into force on 7 July 1954. The text (United Nations, *Treaty Series*, vol. 193, p. 135) is as follows:

The Contracting Parties,

Desiring to implement the principle of equality of rights for men and women contained in the Charter of the United Nations,

Recognizing that everyone has the right to take part in the government of his country directly or indirectly through freely chosen representatives, and has the right to equal access to public service in his country, and desiring to equalize the status of men and women in the enjoyment and exercise of political rights, in accordance with the provisions of the Charter of the United Nations and of the Universal Declaration of Human Rights.

Having resolved to conclude a Convention for this purpose,

Hereby agree as hereinafter provided:

Article 1. Women shall be entitled to vote in all elections on equal terms with men, without any discrimination.

Article 2. Women shall be eligible for election to all publicly elected bodies, established by national law, on equal terms with men, without any discrimination.

Article 3. Women shall be entitled to hold public office

and to exercise all public functions, established by national law, on equal terms with men, without any discrimination.

Article 4. 1. This Convention shall be open for signature on behalf of any Member of the United Nations and also on behalf of any other State to which an invitation has been addressed by the General Assembly.

2. This Convention shall be ratified and the instruments of ratification shall be deposited with the Secretary-General of the United Nations.

Article 5. 1. This Convention shall be open for accession to all States referred to in paragraph 1 of article 4.

2. Accession shall be effected by the deposit of an instrument of accession with the Secretary-General of the United Nations.

Article 6. 1. This Convention shall come into force on the ninetieth day following the date of deposit of the sixth instrument of ratification or accession.

2. For each State ratifying or acceding to the Convention after the deposit of the sixth instrument of ratification or accession the Convention shall enter into force on the ninetieth day after deposit by such State of its instrument of ratification or accession.

Article 7. In the event that any State submits a reservation to any of the articles of this Convention at the time of signature, ratification or accession, the Secretary-General shall communicate the text of the reservation to all States which are or may become parties to this Convention. Any State which objects to the reservation may, within a period of ninety days from the date of the said communication (or upon the date of its becoming a party to the Convention), notify the Secretary-General that it does not accept it. In such case, the Convention shall not enter into force as between such State and the State making the reservation.

Article 8. 1. Any State may denounce this Convention by written notification to the Secretary-General of the United Nations. Denunciation shall take effect one year after the date of receipt of the notification by the Secretary-General.

2. This Convention shall cease to be in force as from the date when the denunciation which reduces the number of parties to less than six becomes effective.

Article 9. Any dispute which may arise between any two or more Contracting States concerning the interpretation or application of this Convention, which is not settled by negotiation, shall at the request of any one of the parties to the dispute be referred to the International Court of Justice for decision, unless they agree to another mode of settlement.

Article 10. The Secretary-General of the United Nations shall notify all Members of the United Nations and the non-member States contemplated in paragraph 1 of article 4 of this Convention of the following:

(*a*) Signatures and instruments of ratification received in accordance with article 4;

(*b*) Instruments of accession received in accordance with article 5;

(*c*) The date upon which this Convention enters into force in accordance with article 6;

(*d*) Communications and notifications received in accordance with article 7;

(*e*) Notifications of denunciation received in accordance with paragraph 1 of article 8;

(*f*) Abrogation in accordance with paragraph 2 of article 8.

Article 11. 1. This Convention, of which the Chinese, English, French, Russian and Spanish texts shall be equally au-

thentic, shall be deposited in the archives of the United Nations.

2. The Secretary-General of the United Nations shall transmit a certified copy to all Members of the United Nations and to the non-member States contemplated in paragraph 1 of article 4.

SEE ALSO *Convention on the Elimination of all Forms of Discrimination against Women; Declaration on the Elimination of Discrimination against Women; Inter-American Convention on the Granting of Civil Rights to Women; Inter-American Convention on the Granting of Political Rights to Women.*

CONVENTION ON THE PREVENTION AND PUNISHMENT OF CRIMES AGAINST INTERNATIONALLY PROTECTED PERSONS, INCLUDING DIPLOMATIC AGENTS (1973).

In response to a request made by the General Assembly on 3 December 1971 (resolution 2780 [XXVI]), the INTERNATIONAL LAW COMMISSION studied the question of the protection and inviolability of diplomatic agents and other persons entitled to special protection under international law and prepared draft articles on the prevention and punishment of crimes against such persons. After considering the draft articles, the assembly, convinced of the importance of securing international agreement on appropriate and effective measures for dealing with crimes of this nature in view of the serious threat to the maintenance and promotion of friendly relations and cooperation among States, proceeded to elaborate and to adopt, on 14 December 1973 (resolution 3166 [XXVIII]), the Convention on the Prevention and Punishment of Crimes against Internationally Protected Persons, including Diplomatic Agents.

The convention defines "internationally protected persons" as including not only heads of state or of government and ministers for foreign affairs and accompanying members of their families, but also "any representative or official of a State or any official or other agent of an international organization of an intergovernmental character who. . . .is entitled pursuant to international law to special protection from any attack on his person, freedom or dignity, as well as members of his family forming part of his household." States parties undertake to make the murder, kidnapping, or other attack upon the person or liberty of such an individual a crime under their national law and to exercise jurisdiction over the offenders or to arrange for their extradition. Disputes concerning the interpretation or application of the convention are to be referred to the INTERNATIONAL COURT OF JUSTICE.

The text of the convention, annexed to General Assembly resolution 3166 [XXVIII]), is as follows:

The States Parties to this Convention,

Having in mind the purposes and principles of the Charter of the United Nations concerning the maintenance of international peace and the promotion of friendly relations and co-operation among States,

Considering that crimes against diplomatic agents and other internationally protected persons jeopardizing the safety of these persons create a serious threat to the maintenance of normal international relations which are necessary for co-operation among States,

Believing that the commission of such crimes is a matter of grave concern to the international community,

Convinced that there is an urgent need to adopt appropriate and effective measures for the prevention and punishment of such crimes,

Have agreed as follows:

Article 1. For the purposes of this Convention:

1. "Internationally protected person" means:

(*a*) A Head of State, including any member of a collegial body performing the functions of a Head of State under the constitution of the State concerned, a Head of Government or a Minister for Foreign Affairs, whenever any such person is in a foreign State, as well as members of his family who accompany him;

(*b*) Any representative or official of a State or any official or other agent of an international organization of an intergovernmental character who, at the time when and in the place where a crime against him, his official premises, his private accommodation or his means of transport is committed, is entitled pursuant to international law to special protection from any attack on his person, freedom or dignity, as well as members of his family forming part of his household;

2. "Alleged offender" means a person as to whom there is sufficient evidence to determine *prima facie* that he has committed or participated in one or more of the crimes set forth in article 2.

Article 2. 1. The intentional commission of:

(*a*) A murder, kidnapping or other attack upon the person or liberty of an internationally protected person;

(*b*) A violent attack upon the official premises, the private accommodation or the means of transport of an internationally protected person likely to endanger his person or liberty;

(*c*) A threat to commit any such attack;

(*d*) An attempt to commit any such attack; and

(*e*) An act constituting participation as an accomplice in any such attack shall be made by each State Party a crime under its internal law.

2. Each State Party shall make these crimes punishable by appropriate penalties which take into account their grave nature.

3. Paragraphs 1 and 2 of this article in no way derogate from the obligations of State Parties under international law to take all appropriate measures to prevent other attacks on the person, freedom or dignity of an internationally protected person.

Article 3. 1. Each State Party shall take such measures as may be necessary to establish its jurisdiction over the crimes set forth in article 2 in the following cases:

(*a*) When the crime is committed in the territory of that State or on board a shop or aircraft registered in that State;

(*b*) When the alleged offender is a national of that State;

(*c*) When the crime is committed against an internationally protected person as defined in article 1 who enjoys his status as such by virtue of functions which he exercises on behalf of that State.

2. Each State Party shall likewise take such measures as may be necessary to establish its jurisdiction over these crimes in cases where the alleged offender is present in its territory and it does not extradite him pursuant to article 8 to any of the States mentioned in paragraph 1 of this article.

3. This Convention does not exclude any criminal jurisdiction exercised in accordance with internal law.

Article 4. States Parties shall co-operate in the prevention of the crimes set forth in article 2, particularly by:

(*a*) Taking all practicable measures to prevent preparations in their respective territories for the commission of those crimes within or outside their territories;

(*b*) Exchanging information and co-ordinating the taking of administrative and other measures as appropriate to prevent the commission of those crimes.

Article 5. 1. The State Party in which any of the crimes set forth in article 2 has been committed shall, if it has reason to believe that an alleged offender has fled from its territory, communicate to all other States concerned, directly or through the Secretary-General of the United Nations, all the pertinent facts regarding the crime committed and all available information regarding the identity of the alleged offender.

2. Whenever any of the crimes set forth in article 2 has been committed against an internationally protected person, any State Party which has information concerning the victim and the circumstances of the crime shall endeavour to transmit it, under the conditions provided for in its internal law, fully and promptly to the State Party on whose behalf he was exercising his functions.

Article 6. 1. Upon being satisfied that the circumstances so warrant, the State Party in whose territory the alleged offender is present shall take the appropriate measures under its internal law so as to ensure his presence for the purpose of prosecution or extradition. Such measures shall be notified without delay directly or through the Secretary-General of the United Nations to:

(*a*) The State where the crime was committed;

(*b*) The State or States of which the alleged offender is a national or, if he is a stateless person, in whose territory he permanently resides;

(*c*) The State or States of which the internationally protected person concerned is a national or on whose behalf he was exercising his functions;

(*d*) All other States concerned; and

(*e*) The international organization of which the internationally protected person concerned is an official or an agent.

2. Any person regarding whom the measures referred to in paragraph 1 of this article are being taken shall be entitled:

(*a*) To communicate without delay with the nearest appropriate representative of the State of which he is a national or which is otherwise entitled to protect his rights or, if he is a stateless person, which he requests and which is willing to protect his rights; and

(*b*) To be visited by a representative of that State.

Article 7. The State Party in whose territory the alleged offender is present shall, if it does not extradite him, submit, without exception whatsoever and without undue delay, the case to its competent authorities for the purpose of prosecution, through proceedings in accordance with the laws of that State.

Article 8. 1. To the extent that the crimes set forth in article 2 are not listed as extraditable offences in any extradition treaty existing between States Parties, they shall be deemed to be included as such therein. States Parties undertake to include those crimes as extraditable offences in every future extradition treaty to be concluded between them.

2. If a State Party which makes extradition conditional on the existence of a treaty receives a request for extradition from another State Party with which it has no extradition treaty, it may, if it decides to extradite, consider this Convention as the legal basis for extradition in respect of those crimes. Extradition shall be subject to the procedural provisions and the other conditions of the law of the requested State.

3. States Parties which do not make extradition conditional on the existence of a treaty shall recognize those crimes as extraditable offences between themselves subject to the procedural provisions and the other conditions of the law of the requested State.

4. Each of the crimes shall be treated, for the purpose of extradition between States Parties, as if it had been committed not only in the place in which it occurred but also in the territories of the States required to establish their jurisdiction in accordance with paragraph 1 of article 3.

Article 9. Any person regarding whom proceedings are being carried out in connexion with any of the crimes set forth in article 2 shall be guaranteed fair treatment at all stages of the proceedings.

Article 10. 1. States Parties shall afford one another the greatest measure of assistance in connexion with criminal proceedings brought in respect of the crimes set forth in article 2, including the supply of all evidence at their disposal necessary for the proceedings.

2. The provision of paragraph 1 of this article shall not affect obligations concerning mutual assistance embodied in any other treaty.

Article 11. The State Party where an alleged offender is prosecuted shall communicate the final outcome of the proceedings to the Secretary-General of the United Nations, who shall transmit the information to the other States Parties.

Article 12. The provisions of this Convention shall not affect the application of the Treaties on Asylum, in force at the date of the adoption of this Convention, as between the States which are parties to those Treaties; but a State Party to this Convention may not invoke those Treaties with respect to another State Party to this Convention which is not a party to those Treaties.

Article 13. 1. Any dispute between two or more States Parties concerning the interpretation or application of this Convention which is not settled by negotiation shall, at the request of one of them, be submitted to arbitration. If within six months from the date of the request for arbitration the parties are unable to agree on the organization of the arbitration, any one of those parties may refer the dispute to the International Court of Justice by request in conformity with the Statute of the Court.

2. Each State Party may at the time of signature or ratification of this Convention or accession thereto declare that it does not consider itself bound by paragraph 1 of this article. The other States Parties shall not be bound by paragraph 1 of this article with respect to any State Party which has made such a reservation.

3. Any State Party which has made a reservation in accordance with paragraph 2 of this article may at any time withdraw that reservation by notification to the Secretary-General of the United Nations.

Article 14. This Convention shall be open for signature by all States, until 31 December 1974 at United Nations Headquarters in New York.

Article 15. This Convention is subject to ratification. The instruments of ratification shall be deposited with the Secretary-General of the United Nations.

Article 16. This Convention shall remain open for accession by any State. The instruments of accession shall be deposited with the Secretary-General of the United Nations.

Article 17. 1. This Convention shall enter into force on the thirtieth day following the date of deposit of the twenty-second instrument of ratification or accession with the Secretary-General of the United Nations.

2. For each State ratifying or acceding to the Convention after the deposit of the twenty-second instrument of ratification or accession, the Convention shall enter into force on the thirtieth day after deposit by such State of its instrument of ratification or accession.

Article 18. 1. Any State Party may denounce this Convention by written notification to the Secretary-General of the United Nations.

2. Denunciation shall take effect six months following the date on which notification is received by the Secretary-General of the United Nations.

Article 19. The Secretary-General of the United Nations shall inform all States, *inter alia:*

(*a*) Of signatures to this Convention, of the deposit of instruments of ratification or accession in accordance with articles 14, 15 and 16 and of notifications made under article 18;

(*b*) Of the date on which this Convention will enter into force in accordance with article 17.

Article 20. The original of this Convention, of which the Chinese, English, French, Russian and Spanish texts are equally authentic, shall be deposited with the Secretary-General of the United Nations, who shall send certified copies thereof to all States.

In witness whereof the undersigned, being duty authorized thereto by their respective Governments, have signed this Convention, opened for signature at New York on 14 December 1973.

SEE ALSO *Arrest, Detention, and Abduction of International Civil Servants; Detention: Administrative; Detention: UN Staff Members; Inter-American Convention on Diplomatic Asylum; Special Rappoteurs: Privileges and Immunities.*

CONVENTION ON THE PREVENTION AND PUNISHMENT OF THE CRIME OF GENOCIDE (1948). At the second part of its first session, on 11 December 1946, the UN General Assembly affirmed (resolution 96 [I]) that GENOCIDE is a crime under international law which the civilized world condemns and that those guilty of it, whoever they are and for whatever reason they committed it, are punishable. Recognizing the need to organize international cooperation for this purpose, the General Assembly called upon the UN Economic and Social Council to undertake the necessary studies for drawing up a draft convention on the crime of genocide. The council instructed the Secretary-General to prepare a preliminary draft with the assistance of three experts. On the basis of their work, and with the assistance of its *Ad Hoc* Committee on Genocide, the council was able to transmit the draft convention to the assembly in 1948. The assembly completed the convention and, on 9 December 1948, (resolution 260 A [III]) adopted it and opened it for signature and ratification or accession. It entered into force on 12 January 1951.

The text of the convention (United Nations, *Treaty Series,* vol. 78, p. 277) is as follows:

The Contracting Parties,

Having considered the declaration made by the General Assembly of the United Nations in its resolution 96 (I) dated 11 December 1946 that genocide is a crime under international law, contrary to the spirit and aims of the United Nations and condemned by the civilized world,

Recognizing that at all periods of history genocide has inflicted great losses on humanity, and

Being convinced that, in order to liberate mankind from such an odious scourge, international co-operation is required,

Hereby agree as hereinafter provided:

Article 1. The Contracting Parties confirm that genocide, whether committed in time of peace or in time of war, is a crime under international law which they undertake to prevent and to punish.

Article 2. In the present Convention, genocide means any of the following acts committed with intent to destroy, in whole or in part, a national, ethnical, racial or religious group, as such:

(a) Killing members of the group;

(b) Causing serious bodily or mental harm to members of the group;

(c) Deliberately inflicting on the group conditions of life calculated to bring about its physical destruction in whole or in part;

(d) Imposing measures intended to prevent births within the group;

(e) Forcibly transferring children of the group to another group.

Article 3. The following acts shall be punishable:

(a) Genocide;

(b) Conspiracy to commit genocide;

(c) Direct and public incitement to commit genocide;

(d) Attempt to commit genocide;

(e) Complicity in genocide.

Article 4. Persons committing genocide or any of the other acts enumerated in article 3 shall be punished, whether they are constitutionally responsible rulers, public officials or private individuals.

Article 5. The Contracting Parties undertake to enact, in accordance with their respective Constitutions, the necessary legislation to give effect to the provisions of the present Convention and, in particular, to provide effective penalties for persons guilty of genocide or any of the other acts enumerated in article 3.

Article 6. Persons charged with genocide or any of the other acts enumerated in article 3 shall be tried by a competent tribunal of the State in the territory of which the act was committed, or by such international penal tribunal as may have jurisdiction with respect to those Contracting Parties which shall have accepted its jurisdiction.

Article 7. Genocide and the other acts enumerated in article 3 shall not be considered as political crimes for the purpose of extradition.

The Contracting Parties pledge themselves in such cases to grant extradition in accordance with their laws and treaties in force.

Article 8. Any Contracting Party may call upon the competent organs of the United Nations to take such action under the Charter of the United Nations as they consider appropriate for the prevention and suppression of acts of genocide or any of the other acts enumerated in article 3.

Article 9. Disputes between the Contracting Parties relating to the interpretation, application or fulfilment of the present Convention, including those relating to the responsibility of a State for genocide or for any of the other acts enumerated in article 3, shall be submitted to the International Court of Justice at the request of any of the parties to the dispute.

Article 10. The present Convention, of which the Chinese, English, French, Russian and Spanish texts are equally authentic, shall bear the date of 9 December 1948.

Article 11. The present Convention shall be open until 31 December 1949 for signature on behalf of any Member of the United Nations and of any non-member State to which an invitation to sign has been addressed by the General Assembly.

The present Convention shall be ratified, and the instruments of ratification shall be deposited with the Secretary-General of the United Nations.

After 1 January 1950, the present Convention may be acceded to on behalf of any Member of the United Nations and of any non-member State which has received an invitation as aforesaid.

Instruments of accession shall be deposited with the Secretary-General of the United Nations.

Article 12. Any Contracting Party may at any time, by notification addressed to the Secretary-General of the United Nations, extend the application of the present Convention to all or any of the territories for the conduct of whose foreign relations that Contracting Party is responsible.

Article 13. On the day when the first twenty instruments of ratification or accession have been deposited, the Secretary-General shall draw up a *procès-verbal* and transmit a copy thereof to each Member of the United Nations and to each of the non-member States contemplated in article 11.

The present Convention shall come into force on the ninetieth day following the date of deposit of the twentieth instrument of ratification or accession.

Any ratification or accession effected, subsequent to the latter date shall become effective on the ninetieth day following the deposit of the instrument of ratification or accession.

Article 14. The present Convention shall remain in effect for a period of ten years as from the date of its coming into force.

It shall thereafter remain in force for successive periods of five years for such Contracting Parties as have not denounced it at least six months before the expiration of the current period.

Denunciation shall be effected by a written notification addressed to the Secretary-General of the United Nations.

Article 15. If, as a result of denunciations, the number of

Parties to the present Convention should become less than sixteen, the Convention shall cease to be in force as from the date on which the last of these denunciations shall become effective.

Article 16. A request for the revision of the present Convention may be made at any time by any Contracting Party by means of a notification in writing addressed to the Secretary-General.

The General Assembly shall decide upon the steps, if any, to be taken in respect of such request.

Article 17. The Secretary-General of the United Nations shall notify all Members of the United Nations and the non-member States contemplated in article 11 of the following:

(a) Signatures, ratifications and accessions received in accordance with article 11;

(b) Notifications received in accordance with article 12;

(c) The date upon which the present Convention comes into force in accordance with article 13;

(d) Denunciations received in accordance with article 14;

(e) The abrogation of the Convention in accordance with article 15;

(f) Notifications received in accordance with article 16.

Article 18. The original of the present Convention shall be deposited in the archives of the United Nations.

A certified copy of the Convention shall be transmitted to each Member of the United Nations and to each of the non-member States contemplated in article 11.

Article 19. The present Convention shall be registered by the Secretary-General of the United Nations on the date of its coming into force.

CONVENTION ON THE PROHIBITION OF THE DEVELOPMENT, PRODUCTION AND STOCKPILING OF BACTERIOLOGICAL (BIOLOGICAL) AND TOXIN WEAPONS AND ON THEIR DESTRUCTION.

Under the convention, States Parties undertake never to develop bacteriological or toxin weapons, to destroy or divert to peaceful uses all such weapons in their possession, and not to transfer such weapons to other States. A State party may, however, withdraw from the convention (article 13) "if it decides that extraordinary events, related to the subject matter of the Convention, have jeopardized the supreme interests of its country."

Opened for signature and ratification or accession simultaneously in London, Moscow, and Washington on 10 April 1972, the convention designates three depository governments: the United Kingdom of Great Britain and Northern Ireland, the United States of America, and the Union of Soviet Socialist Republics. It entered into force on 26 March 1975. The text of the convention (United Nations, *Juridical Yearbook,* 1971, p. 118) is as follows:

The States Parties to this Convention,

Determined to act with a view to achieving effective progress towards general and complete disarmament, including the prohibition and elimination of all types of weapons of mass destruction, and convinced that the prohibition of the development, production and stockpiling of chemical and bacteriological (biological) weapons and their elimination, through effective measures, will facilitate the achievement of general and complete disarmament under strict and effective international control,

Recognizing the important significance of the Protocol for the Prohibition of the Use in War of Asphyxiating, Poisonous or Other Gases, and of Bacteriological Methods of Warfare, signed at Geneva on June 17, 1925, and conscious also of the contribution which the said Protocol has already made, and continues to make, to mitigating the horrors of war,

Reaffirming their adherence to the principles and objectives of that Protocol and calling upon all States to comply strictly with them,

Recalling that the General Assembly of the United Nations has repeatedly condemned all actions contrary to the principles and objectives of the Geneva Protocol of June 17, 1925,

Desiring to contribute to the strengthening of confidence between peoples and the general improvement of the international atmosphere,

Desiring also to contribute to the realization of the purposes and principles of the Charter of the United Nations,

Convinced of the importance and urgency of eliminating from the arsenals of States, through effective measures, such dangerous weapons of mass destruction as those using chemical or bacteriological (biological) agents,

Recognizing that an agreement on the prohibition of bacteriological (biological) and toxin weapons represents a first possible step towards the achievement of agreement on effective measures also for the prohibition of the development, production and stockpiling of chemical weapons, and determined to continue negotiations to that end,

Determined, for the sake of all mankind, to exclude completely the possibility of bacteriological (biological) agents and toxins being used as weapons,

Convinced that such use would be repugnant to the conscience of mankind and that no effort should be spared to minimize this risk,

Have agreed as follows:

Article 1. Each State Party to this Convention undertakes never in any circumstances to develop, produce, stockpile or otherwise acquire or retain:

(1) Microbial or other biological agents, or toxins whatever their origin or method of production, of types and in quantities that have no justification for prophylactic, protective or other peaceful purposes;

(2) Weapons, equipment or means of delivery designed to use such agents or toxins for hostile purposes or in armed conflict.

Article 2. Each State Party to this Convention undertakes to destroy, or to divert to peaceful purposes, as soon as possible but not later than nine months after the entry into force of the Convention, all agents, toxins, weapons, equipment and means of delivery specified in article 1 of the Convention, which are in its possession or under its jurisdiction or control. In implementing the provisions of this article all necessary safety precautions shall be observed to protect populations and the environment.

Article 3. Each State Party to this Convention undertakes not to transfer to any recipient whatsoever, directly or indirectly, and not in any way to assist, encourage, or induce any State, group of States or international organizations to manufacture or otherwise acquire any of the agents, toxins, weapons, equipment or means of delivery specified in article 1 of the Convention.

Article 4. Each State Party to this Convention shall, in accordance with its constitutional processes, take any necessary measures to prohibit and prevent the development, production, stockpiling, acquisition or retention of the agents, toxins, weapons, equipment and means of delivery specified in article 1 of the Convention, within the territory of such State, under its jurisdiction or under its control anywhere.

Article 5. The States Parties to this Convention undertake to consult one another and to cooperate in solving any problems which may arise in relation to the objective of, or in the application of the provisions of, the Convention. Consultation and cooperation pursuant to this article may also be undertaken through appropriate international procedures within the framework of the United Nations and in accordance with its Charter.

Article 6. (1) Any State Party to this Convention which finds that any other State Party is acting in breach of obligations deriving from the provisions of the Convention may lodge a complaint with the Security Council of the United Nations. Such a complaint should include all possible evidence confirming its validity, as well as a request for its consideration by the Security Council.

(2) Each State Party to this Convention undertakes to cooperate in carrying out any investigation which the Security Council may initiate, in accordance with the provisions of the Charter of the United Nations, on the basis of the complaint received by the Council. The Security Council shall inform the States Parties to the Convention of the results of the investigation.

Article 7. Each State Party to this Convention undertakes to provide or support assistance, in accordance with the United Nations Charter, to any Party to the Convention which so requests, if the Security Council decides that such Party has been exposed to danger as a result of violation of the Convention.

Article 8. Nothing in this Convention shall be interpreted as in any way limiting or detracting from the obligations assumed by any State under the Protocol for the Prohibition of the Use in War of Asphyxiating, Poisonous or Other Gases, and of Bacteriological Methods of Warfare, signed at Geneva on June 17, 1925.

Article 9. Each State Party to this Convention affirms the recognized objective of effective prohibition of chemical weapons and, to this end, undertakes to continue negotiations in good faith with a view to reaching early agreement on effective measures for the prohibition of their development, production and stockpiling and for their destruction, and on appropriate measures concerning equipment and means of delivery specifically designed for the production or use of chemical agents for weapons purposes.

Article 10. (1) The States Parties to this Convention undertake to facilitate, and have the right to participate in, the fullest possible exchange of equipment, materials and scientific and technological information for the use of bacteriological (biological) agents and toxins for peaceful purposes. Parties to the Convention in a position to do so shall also cooperate in contributing individually or together with other States or international organizations to the further development and application of scientific discoveries in the field of bacteriology (biology) for prevention of disease, or for other peaceful purposes.

(2) This Convention shall be implemented in a manner designed to avoid hampering the economic or technological development of States Parties to the Convention or international cooperation in the field of peaceful bacteriological (biological) activities, including the international exchange of bacteriological (biological) agents and toxins and equipment for the processing, use or production of bacteriological (biological) agents and toxins for peaceful purposes in accordance with the provisions of the Convention.

Article 11. Any State Party may propose amendments to this Convention. Amendments shall enter into force for each State Party accepting the amendments upon their acceptance by a majority of the States Parties to the Convention and thereafter for each remaining State Party on the date of acceptance by it.

Article 12. Five years after the entry into force of this Convention, or earlier if it is requested by a majority of Parties to the Convention by submitting a proposal to this effect to the Depositary Governments, a conference of States Parties to the Convention shall be held at Geneva, Switzerland, to review the operation of the Convention, with a view to assuring that the purposes of the preamble and the provisions of the Convention, including the provisions concerning negotiations on chemical weapons, are being realized. Such review shall take into account any new scientific and technological developments relevant to the Convention.

Article 13. (1) This Convention shall be of unlimited duration.

(2) Each State Party to this Convention shall in exercising its national sovereignty have the right to withdraw from the Convention if it decides that extraordinary events, related to the subject matter of the Convention, have jeopardized the supreme interests of its country. It shall give notice of such withdrawal to all other States Parties to the Convention and to the United Nations Security Council three months in advance. Such notice shall include a statement of the extraordinary events it regards as having jeopardized its supreme interests.

Article 14. (1) This Convention shall be open to all States for signature. Any State which does not sign the Convention before its entry into force in accordance with paragraph (3) of this Article may accede to it at any time.

(2) This Convention shall be subject to ratification by Signatory States. Instruments of ratification and instruments of accession shall be deposited with the Governments of the United States of America, the United Kingdom of Great Britain and Northern Ireland and the Union of Soviet Socialist Republics, which are hereby designated the Depositary Governments.

(3) This Convention shall enter into force after the deposit of instruments of ratification by twenty-two Governments, including the Governments designated as Depositaries of the Convention.

(4) For States whose instruments of ratification or accession are deposited subsequent to the entry into force of this Convention, it shall enter into force on the date of the deposit of their instruments of ratification or accession.

(5) The Depositary Governments shall promptly inform all signatory and acceding States of the date of each signature, the date of deposit of each instrument of ratification or of accession and the date of the entry into force of this Convention, and of the receipt of other notices.

(6) This Convention shall be registered by the Depositary Governments pursuant to Article 102 of the Charter of the United Nations.

Article 15. This Convention, the English, Russian, French, Spanish and Chinese texts of which are equally authentic, shall be deposited in the archives of the Depositary Governments. Duly certified copies of the Convention shall be transmitted by the Depositary Governments to the Governments of the signatory and acceding States.

SEE ALSO *Chemical Weapons; Chemical Weapons: Declaration on Their Prohibition; Convention on Prohibitions or Restrictions on the Use of Certain Conventional Weapons which May be Deemed to Be Excessively Injurious or to Have Indiscriminate Effects, and Protocols; Declaration on the Prevention of Nuclear Catastrophe; Nuclear Disarmament; Protocol for the Prohibition of the Use of Asphyxiating, Poisonous or Other Gases, and of Bacteriological Methods of Warfare.*

CONVENTION ON THE REDUCTION OF STATELESSNESS (1961).

The convention was adopted and opened for signature by the United Nations Conference on the Elimination or Reduction of Future Statelessness, convened by the Secretary-General pursuant to General Assembly resolution 896 (IX) of 4 December 1954. The conference met at the UN European office in Geneva from 24 March-18 April 1959 and reconvened at UN headquarters in New York from 15–28 August 1961. The convention provides for the establishment, within the United Nations system, of a body to which a person claiming the benefit of the convention's provisions may apply for assistance. Since 1974, such assistance has been provided by the UNITED NATIONS HIGH COMMISSIONER FOR REFUGEES.

The text of the convention (A/Conf.9/15, 1961, annex) is as follows:

The Contracting States,

Acting in pursuance of resolution 896 (IX), adopted by the General Assembly of the United Nations on 4 December 1954,

Considering it desirable to reduce statelessness by international agreement,

Have agreed as follows:

Article 1. 1. A Contracting State shall grant its nationality to a person born in its territory who would otherwise be stateless. Such nationality shall be granted:

(*a*) At birth, by operation of law, or

(*b*) Upon an application being lodged with the appropriate authority, by or on behalf of the person concerned, in the manner prescribed by the national law. Subject to the provisions of paragraph 2 of this article, no such application may be rejected.

A Contracting State which provides for the grant of its nationality in accordance with sub-paragraph (*b*) of this paragraph may also provide for the grant of its nationality by operation of law at such age and subject to such conditions as may be prescribed by the national law.

2. A Contracting State may make the grant of its nationality in accordance with sub-paragraph (*b*) of paragraph 1 of this article subject to one or more of the following conditions:

(*a*) That the application is lodged during a period, fixed by the Contracting State, beginning not later than at the age of eighteen years and ending not earlier than at the age of twenty-one years, so, however, that the person concerned shall be allowed at least one year during which he may himself make the application without having to obtain legal authorization to do so;

(*b*) That the person concerned has habitually resided in the territory of the Contracting State for such period as may be fixed by that State, not exceeding five years immediately preceding the lodging of the application nor ten years in all;

(*c*) That the person concerned has neither been convicted of an offence against national security nor has been sentenced to imprisonment for a term of five years or more on a criminal charge,

(*d*) That the person concerned has always been stateless.

3. Notwithstanding the provisions of paragraphs 1 (*b*) and 2 of this article, a child born in wedlock in the territory of a Contracting State, whose mother has the nationality of that State, shall acquire at birth that nationality if it otherwise would be stateless.

4. A Contracting State shall grant its nationality to a person who would otherwise be stateless and who is unable to acquire the nationality of the Contracting State in whose territory he was born because he has passed the age for lodging his application or has not fulfilled the required residence conditions, if the nationality of one of his parents at the time of the person's birth was that of the Contracting State first above mentioned. If his parents did not possess the same nationality at the time of his birth, the question whether the nationality of the person concerned should follow that of the father or that of the mother shall be determined by the national law of such Contracting State. If application for such nationality is required, the application shall be made to the appropriate authority by or on behalf of the applicant in the manner prescribed by the national law. Subject to the provisions of paragraph 5 of this article, such application shall not be refused.

5. The Contracting State may make the grant of its nationality in accordance with the provisions of paragraph 4 of this article subject to one or more of the following conditions:

(*a*) That the application is lodged before the applicant reaches an age, being not less than twenty-three years, fixed by the Contracting State;

(*b*) That the person concerned has habitually resided in the territory of the Contracting State for such period immediately preceding the lodging of the application, not exceeding three years, as may be fixed by that State;

(*c*) That the person concerned has always been stateless.

Article 2. A foundling found in the territory of a Contracting State shall, in the absence of proof to the contrary, be considered to have been born within that territory of parents possessing the nationality of that State.

Article 3. For the purpose of determining the obligations of Contracting States under this Convention, birth on a ship or in an aircraft shall be deemed to have taken place in the territory of the State whose flag the ship flies or in the territory of the State in which the aircraft is registered, as the case may be.

Article 4. 1. A Contracting State shall grant its nationality to a person, not born in the territory of a Contracting State, who would otherwise be stateless, if the nationality of one of his parents at the time of the person's birth was that of that State. If his parents did not possess the same nationality at the time of his birth, the question whether the nationality of the person concerned should follow that of the father or that of the mother shall be determined by the national law of such Contracting State. Nationality granted in accordance with the provisions of this paragraph shall be granted:

(*a*) At birth, by operation of law, or

(*b*) Upon an application being lodged with the appropriate authority, by or on behalf of the person concerned, in the manner prescribed by the national law. Subject to the provisions of paragraph 2 of this article, no such application may be rejected.

2. A Contracting State may make the grant of its nationality in accordance with the provisions of paragraph 1 of this article subject to one or more of the following conditions:

(*a*) That the application is lodged before the applicant reaches an age, being not less than twenty-three years, fixed by the Contracting State;

(*b*) That the person concerned has habitually resided in the territory of the Contracting State for such period immediately preceding the lodging of the application, not exceeding three years, as may be fixed by that State;

(*c*) That the person concerned has not been convicted of an offence against national security;

(*d*) That the person concerned has always been stateless.

Article 5. 1. If the law of a Contracting State entails loss of nationality as a consequence of any change in the personal status of a person such as marriage, termination of marriage, legitimation, recognition or adoption, such loss shall be conditional upon possession or acquisition of another nationality.

2. If, under the law of a Contracting State, a child born out of wedlock loses the nationality of that State in consequence of a recognition of affiliation, he shall be given an opportunity to recover that nationality by written application to the appropriate authority, and the conditions governing such application shall not be more rigorous than those laid down in paragraph 2 of article 1 of this Convention.

Article 6. If the law of a Contracting State provides for loss of its nationality by a person's spouse or children as a consequence of that person losing or being deprived of that nationality, such loss shall be conditional upon their possession or acquisition of another nationality.

Article 7. 1. (*a*) If the law of a Contracting State entails loss or renunciation of nationality, such renunciation shall not result in loss of nationality unless the person concerned possesses or acquires another nationality.

(*b*) The provisions of sub-paragraph (*a*) of this paragraph shall not apply where their application would be inconsistent with the principles stated in articles 13 and 14 of the Universal Declaration of Human Rights approved on 10 December 1948 by the General Assembly of the United Nations.

2. A national of a Contracting State who seeks naturalization in a foreign country shall not lose his nationality unless he acquires or has been accorded assurance of acquiring the nationality of that foreign country.

3. Subject to the provisions of paragraphs 4 and 5 of this article, a national of a Contracting State shall not lose his nationality, so as to become stateless, on the ground of departure, residence abroad, failure to register or on any similar ground.

4. A naturalized person may lose his nationality on account of residence abroad for a period, not less than seven consecutive years, specified by the law of the Contracting State concerned if he fails to declare to the appropriate authority his intention to retain his nationality.

5. In the case of a national of a Contracting State, born outside its territory, the law of that State may make the retention of its nationality after the expiry of one year from his attaining his majority conditional upon residence at that time in the territory of the State or registration with the appropriate authority.

6. Except in the circumstances mentioned in this article, a person shall not lose the nationality of a Contracting State, if such loss would render him stateless, notwithstanding that such loss is not expressly prohibited by any other provision of this Convention.

Article 8. 1. A Contracting State shall not deprive a person of his nationality if such deprivation would render him stateless.

2. Notwithstanding the provisions of paragraph 1 of this article, a person may be deprived of the nationality of a Contracting State:

(*a*) In the circumstances in which, under paragraphs 4 and 5 of article 7, it is permissible that a person should lose his nationality;

(*b*) Where the nationality has been obtained by misrepresentation or fraud.

3. Notwithstanding the provisions of paragraph 1 of this article, a Contracting State may retain the right to deprive a person of his nationality, if at the time of signature, ratification or accession it specifies its retention of such right on one or more of the following grounds, being grounds existing in its national law at that time:

(*a*) That, inconsistently with his duty of loyalty to the Contracting State, the person:

(i) Has, in disregard of an express prohibition by the Contracting State rendered or continued to render services to, or received or continued to receive emoluments from, another State, or

(ii) Has conducted himself in a manner seriously prejudicial to the vital interests of the State;

(*b*) That the person has taken an oath, or made a formal declaration, of allegiance to another State, or given definite evidence of his determination to repudiate his allegiance to the Contracting State.

4. A Contracting State shall not exercise a power of deprivation permitted by paragraphs 2 or 3 of this article except in accordance with law, which shall provide for the person concerned the right to a fair hearing by a court or other independent body.

Article 9. A Contracting State may not deprive any person or group of persons of their nationality on racial, ethnic, religious or political grounds.

Article 10. 1. Every treaty between Contracting States providing for the transfer of territory shall include provisions designed to secure that no person shall become stateless as a result of the transfer. A Contracting State shall use its best endeavours to secure that any such treaty made by it with a State which is not a party to this Convention includes such provisions.

2. In the absence of such provisions a Contracting State to which territory is transferred or which otherwise acquires territory shall confer its nationality on such persons as would otherwise become stateless as a result of the transfer or acquisition.

Article 11. The Contracting States shall promote the establishment within the framework of the United Nations, as soon as may be after the deposit of the sixth instrument of ratification or accession, of a body to which a person claiming the benefit of this Convention may apply for the examination of his claim and for assistance in presenting it to the appropriate authority.

Article 12. 1. In relation to a Contracting State which does not, in accordance with the provisions of paragraph 1 of article 1 or of article 4 of this Convention, grant its nationality at birth by operation of law, the provisions of paragraph 1 of article 1 or of article 4, as the case may be, shall apply to persons born before as well as to persons born after the entry into force of this Convention.

2. The provisions of paragraph 4 of article 1 of this Convention shall apply to persons born before as well as to persons born after its entry into force.

3. The provisions of article 2 of this Convention shall apply only to foundlings found in the territory of a Contracting State after the entry into force of the Convention for that State.

Article 13. This Convention shall not be construed as affecting any provisions more conducive to the reduction of statelessness which may be contained in the law of any Contracting State now or hereafter in force, or may be contained in any other convention, treaty or agreement now or hereafter in force between two or more Contracting States.

Article 14. Any dispute between Contracting States concerning the interpretation or application of this Convention which cannot be settled by other means shall be submitted to the International Court of Justice at the request of any one of the parties to the dispute.

Article 15. 1. This Convention shall apply to all non-self-governing, trust, colonial and other non-metropolitan territories for the international relations of which any Contracting State is responsible; the Contracting State concerned shall, subject to the provisions of paragraph 2 of this article, at the time of signature, ratification or accession, declare the non-metropolitan territory or territories to which the Convention shall apply *ipso facto* as a result of such signature, ratification or accession.

2. In any case in which, for the purpose of nationality, a non-metropolitan territory is not treated as one with the metropolitan territory, or in any case in which the previous consent of a non-metropolitan territory is required by the constitutional laws or practices of the Contracting State or of the non-metropolitan territory for the application of the Convention to that territory, that Contracting State shall endeavour to secure the needed consent of the non-metropolitan territory within the period of twelve months from the date of signature of the Convention by that Contracting State, and when such consent has been obtained the Contracting State shall notify the Secretary-General of the United Nations. This Convention shall apply to the territory or territories named in such notification from the date of its receipt by the Secretary-General.

3. After the expiry of the twelve-month period mentioned in paragraph 2 of this article, the Contracting States concerned shall inform the Secretary-General of the results of the consultations with those non-metropolitan territories for whose international relations they are responsible and whose consent to the application of this Convention may have been withheld.

Article 16. 1. This Convention shall be open for signature at the Headquarters of the United Nations from 30 August 1961 to 31 May 1962.

2. This Convention shall be open for signature on behalf of:

(*a*) Any State Member of the United Nations;

(*b*) Any other State invited to attend the United Nations Conference on the Elimination or Reduction of Future Statelessness;

(*c*) Any State to which an invitation to sign or to accede may be addressed by the General Assembly of the United Nations.

3. This Convention shall be ratified and the instruments of ratification shall be deposited with the Secretary-General of the United Nations.

4. This Convention shall be open for accession by the States referred to in paragraph 2 of this article. Accession shall be effected by the deposit of an instrument of accession with the Secretary-General of the United Nations.

Article 17. 1. At the time of signature, ratification or accession any State may make a reservation in respect of articles 11, 14 or 15.

2. No other reservations to this Convention shall be admissible.

Article 18. 1. This Convention shall enter into force two years after the date of the deposit of the sixth instrument of ratification or accession.

2. For each State ratifying or acceding to this Convention after the deposit of the sixth instrument of ratification or accession, it shall enter into force on the ninetieth day after the deposit by such State of its instrument of ratification or accession or on the date on which this Convention enters into force in accordance with the provisions of paragraph 1 of this article, whichever is the later.

Article 19. 1. Any Contracting State may denounce this Convention at any time by a written notification addressed to the Secretary-General of the United Nations. Such denunciation shall take effect for the Contracting State concerned one year after the date of its receipt by the Secretary-General.

2. In cases where, in accordance with the provisions of article 15, this Convention has become applicable to a non-metropolitan territory of a Contracting State, that State may at any time thereafter, with the consent of the territory concerned, give notice to the Secretary-General of the United Nations denouncing this Convention separately in respect to that territory. The denunciation shall take effect one year after the date of the receipt of such notice by the Secretary-General, who shall notify all other Contracting States of such notice and the date of receipt thereof.

Article 20. 1. The Secretary-General of the United Nations shall notify all Members of the United Nations and the non-member States referred to in article 16 of the following particulars:

(*a*) Signatures, ratifications and accessions under article 16;

(*b*) Reservations under article 17;

(*c*) The date upon which this Convention enters into force in pursuance of article 18;

(*d*) Denunciations under article 19.

2. The Secretary-General of the United Nations shall, after the deposit of the sixth instrument of ratification or accession at the latest, bring to the attention of the General Assembly the question of the establishment, in accordance with article 11, of such a body as therein mentioned.

Article 21. This Convention shall be registered by the Secretary-General of the United Nations on the date of its entry into force.

In witness whereof the undersigned Plenipotentiaries have signed this Convention.

Done at New York, this thirtieth day of August, one thousand nine hundred and sixty-one, in a single copy, of which the Chinese, English, French, Russian and Spanish texts are equally authentic and which shall be deposited in the archives of the United Nations, and certified copies of which shall be delivered by the Secretary-General of the United Nations to all Members of the United Nations and to the non-member States referred to in article 16 of this Convention.

SEE ALSO *Convention Relating to the Status of Stateless Persons; Declaration on the Human Rights of Individuals who are not Nationals of the Country in which They Live; European Convention on Establishment and Protocol; Geneva Declaration on Palestine; Intifidah (Uprising) of the Palestinian People; Palestinian People's Rights.*

CONVENTION ON THE RIGHTS OF THE CHILD

(1989). The convention, concluded by the UN General Assembly on 20 November 1989 (resolution 44/25), affirms that children's rights require special protection and aims not only to provide such protection but also to ensure the continuous improvement in the situation of children all over the world, as well as their development and education in conditions of peace and security.

The convention establishes (article 43) a ten-member committee of experts on the rights of the child to examine the progress made by States parties in achieving its objectives. The experts are to be selected by the States parties from among their nationals.

A draft of the convention was submitted to the Commission on Human Rights, at its 1978 session, by Poland. Between 1979 and 1989, the commission elaborated the draft with the assistance of an open-ended working group. In 1988, the General Assembly requested the commission to give the highest priority to this task and to make every effort to complete the text in 1989, the year marking the 30th anniversary of the DECLARATION OF THE RIGHTS OF THE CHILD and the 10th anniversary of the INTERNATIONAL YEAR OF THE CHILD (1979).

The commission concluded its work on the convention at its 1989 session and forwarded it to the General Assembly through the Economic and Social Council. The assembly adopted it without a recorded vote and opened it for signature, ratification, and accession. The text of the Convention on the Rights of the Child, annexed to resolution 44/25, is as follows:

Preamble

The States Parties to the present Convention,

Considering that, in accordance with the principles proclaimed in the Charter of the United Nations, recognition of the inherent dignity and of the equal and inalienable rights of all members of the human family is the foundation of freedom, justice and peace in the world,

Bearing in mind that the peoples of the United Nations have, in the Charter, reaffirmed their faith in fundamental human rights and in the dignity and worth of the human person, and have determined to promote social progress and better standards of life in larger freedom,

Recognizing that the United Nations has, in the Universal Declaration of Human Rights and in the International Covenants on Human Rights, proclaimed and agreed that everyone is entitled to all the rights and freedoms set forth therein, without distinction of any kind, such as race, colour, sex, language, religion, political or other opinion, national or social origin, property, birth or other status,

Recalling that, in the Universal Declaration of Human Rights, the United Nations has proclaimed that childhood is entitled to special care and assistance,

Convinced that the family, as the fundamental group of society and the natural environment for the growth and well-being of all its members and particularly children, should be afforded the necessary protection and assistance so that it can fully assume its responsibilities within the community,

Recognizing that the child, for the full and harmonious development of his or her personality, should grow up in a family environment, in an atmosphere of happiness, love and understanding,

Considering that the child should be fully prepared to live an individual life in society, and brought up in the spirit of the ideals proclaimed in the Charter of the United Nations, and in particular in the spirit of peace, dignity, tolerance, freedom, equality and solidarity,

Bearing in mind that the need to extend particular care to the child has been stated in the Geneva Declaration of the Rights of the Child of 1924 and in the Declaration of the Rights of the Child adopted by the General Assembly on 20 November 1959 and recognized in the Universal Declaration of Human Rights, in the International Covenant on Civil and Political Rights (in particular in articles 23 and 24), in the International Covenant on Economic, Social and Cultural Rights (in particular in article 10) and in the statutes and relevant instruments of specialized agencies and international organizations concerned with the welfare of children,

Bearing in mind that, as indicated in the Declaration of the Rights of the Child, "the child, by reason of his physical and mental immaturity, needs special safeguards and care, including appropriate legal protection, before as well as after birth",

Recalling the provisions of the Declaration on Social and Legal Principles relating to the Protection and Welfare of Children, with Special Reference to Foster Placement and Adoption Nationally and Internationally; the United Nations Standard Minimum Rules for the Administration of Juvenile Justice (The Beijing Rules); and the Declaration on the Protection of Women and Children in Emergency and Armed Conflict,

Recognizing that, in all countries in the world, there are children living in exceptionally difficult conditions, and that such children need special consideration,

Taking due account of the importance of the traditions and cultural values of each people for the protection and harmonious development of the child,

Recognizing the importance of international co-operation for improving the living conditions of children in every country, in particular in the developing countries,

Have agreed as follows:

Part I

Article 1. For the purposes of the present Convention, a child means every human being below the age of eighteen years unless, under the law applicable to the child, majority is attained earlier.

Article 2. 1. States Parties shall respect and ensure the rights set forth in the present Convention to each child within their jurisdiction without discrimination of any kind, irrespective of the child's or his or her parent's or legal guardian's race, colour, sex, language, religion, political or other opinion, national, ethnic or social origin, property, disability, birth or other status.

2. States Parties shall take all appropriate measures to ensure that the child is protected against all forms of discrimination or punishment on the basis of the status, activities, expressed opinions, or beliefs of the child's parents, legal guardians, or family members.

Article 3. 1. In all actions concerning children, whether undertaken by public or private social welfare institutions, courts of law, administrative authorities or legislative bodies, the best interests of the child shall be a primary consideration.

2. States Parties undertake to ensure the child such protection and care as is necessary for his or her well-being, taking into account the rights and duties of his or her parents, legal guardians, or other individuals legally responsible for him or her, and, to this end, shall take all appropriate legislative and administrative measures.

3. States Parties shall ensure that the institutions, services and facilities responsible for the care or protection of children shall conform with the standards established by competent authorities, particularly in the areas of safety, health, in the number and suitability of their staff, as well as competent supervision.

Article 4. States Parties shall undertake all appropriate legislative, administrative, and other measures for the implementation of the rights recognized in the present Convention. With regard to economic, social and cultural rights, States Parties shall undertake such measures to the maximum extent of their available resources and, where needed, within the framework of international cooperation.

Article 5. States Parties shall respect the responsibilities, rights and duties of parents or, where applicable, the members of the extended family or community as provided for by local custom, legal guardians or other persons legally responsible for the child, to provide, in a manner consistent with the evolving capacities of the child, appropriate direction and guidance in the exercise by the child of the rights recognized in the present Convention.

Article 6. 1. States Parties recognize that every child has the inherent right to life.

2. States Parties shall ensure to the maximum extent possible the survival and development of the child.

Article 7. 1. The child shall be registered immediately after birth and shall have the right from birth to a name, the right to acquire a nationality and, as far as possible, the right to know and be cared for by his or her parents.

2. States Parties shall ensure the implementation of these rights in accordance with their national law and their obligations under the relevant international instruments in this field, in particular where the child would otherwise be stateless.

Article 8. 1. States Parties undertake to respect the right of the child to preserve his or her identity, including nationality, name and family relations as recognized by law without unlawful interference.

2. Where a child is illegally deprived of some or all of the elements of his or her identity, States Parties shall provide appropriate assistance and protection, with a view to speedily re-establishing his or her identity.

Article 9. 1. States Parties shall ensure that a child shall not be separated from his or her parents against their will, except when competent authorities subject to judicial review determine, in accordance with applicable law and procedures, that such separation is necessary for the best interests of the child. Such determination may be necessary in a particular case such as one involving abuse or neglect of the child by the parents, or one where the parents are living separately and a decision must be made as to the child's place of residence.

2. In any proceedings pursuant to paragraph 1 of the present article, all interested parties shall be given an opportunity to participate in the proceedings and make their views known.

3. States Parties shall respect the right of the child who is separated from one or both parents to maintain personal relations and direct contact with both parents on a regular basis, except if it is contrary to the child's best interests.

4. Where such separation results from any action initiated by a State Party, such as the detention, imprisonment, exile, deportation or death (including death arising from any cause while the person is in the custody of the State) of one or both parents or of the child, that State Party shall, upon request, provide the parents, the child or, if appropriate, another member of the family with the essential information concerning the whereabouts of the absent member(s) of the family unless the provision of the information would be detrimental to the well-being of the child. States Parties shall further ensure that the submission of such a request shall of itself entail no adverse consequences for the person(s) concerned.

Article 10. 1. In accordance with the obligation of States Parties under article 9, paragraph 1, applications by a child or his or her parents to enter or leave a State Party for the purpose of family reunification shall be dealt with by States Parties in a positive, humane and expeditious manner. States Parties shall further ensure that the submission of such a request shall entail no adverse consequences for the applicants and for the members of their family.

2. A child whose parents reside in different States shall have the right to maintain on a regular basis, save in exceptional circumstances personal relations and direct contacts with both parents. Towards that end and in accordance with the obligation of States Parties under article 9, paragraph 2, States Parties shall respect the right of the child and his or her parents to leave any country, including their own, and to enter their own country. The right to leave any country shall be subject only to such restrictions as are prescribed by law and which are necessary to protect the national security, public order (*ordre public*), public health or morals or the rights and freedoms of others and are consistent with the other rights recognized in the present Convention.

Article 11. 1. States Parties shall take measures to combat the illicit transfer and non-return of children abroad.

2. To this end, States Parties shall promote the conclu-

sion of bilateral or multilateral agreements or accession to existing agreements.

Article 12. 1. States Parties shall assure to the child who is capable of forming his or her own views the right to express those views freely in all matters affecting the child, the views of the child being given due weight in accordance with the age and maturity of the child.

2. For this purpose, the child shall in particular be provided the opportunity to be heard in any judicial and administrative proceedings affecting the child, either directly, or through a representative or an appropriate body, in a manner consistent with the procedural rules of national law.

Article 13. 1. The child shall have the right to freedom of expression; this right shall include freedom to seek, receive and impart information and ideas of all kinds, regardless of frontiers, either orally, in writing or in print, in the form of art, or through any other media of the child's choice.

2. The exercise of this right may be subject to certain restrictions, but these shall only be such as are provided by law and are necessary:

(a) For respect of the rights or reputations of others; or

(b) For the protection of national security or of public order (*ordre public*), or of public health or morals.

Article 14. 1. States Parties shall respect the right of the child to freedom of thought, conscience and religion.

2. States Parties shall respect the rights and duties of the parents and, when applicable, legal guardians, to provide direction to the child in the exercise of his or her right in a manner consistent with the evolving capacities of the child.

3. Freedom to manifest one's religion or beliefs may be subject only to such limitations as are prescribed by law and are necessary to protect public safety, order, health or morals, or the fundamental rights and freedoms of others.

Article 15. 1. States Parties recognize the rights of the child to freedom of association and to freedom of peaceful assembly.

2. No restrictions may be placed on the exercise of these rights other than those imposed in conformity with the law and which are necessary in a democratic society in the interests of national security or public safety, public order (*ordre public*), the protection of public health or morals or the protection of the rights and freedoms of others.

Article 16. 1. No child shall be subjected to arbitrary or unlawful interference with his or her privacy, family, home or correspondence, nor to unlawful attacks on his or her honour and reputation.

2. The child has the right to the protection of the law against such interference or attacks.

Article 17. States Parties recognize the important function performed by the mass media and shall ensure that the child has access to information and material from a diversity of national and international sources, especially those aimed at the promotion of his or her social, spiritual and moral well-being and physical and mental health. To this end, States Parties shall:

(a) Encourage the mass media to disseminate information and material of social and cultural benefit to the child and in accordance with the spirit of article 29;

(b) Encourage international co-operation in the production, exchange and dissemination of such information and material from a diversity of cultural, national and international sources;

(c) Encourage the production and dissemination of children's books;

(d) Encourage the mass media to have particular regard to the linguistic needs of the child who belongs to a minority group or who is indigenous;

(e) Encourage the development of appropriate guidelines for the protection of the child from information and material injurious to his or her well-being, bearing in mind the provisions of articles 13 and 18.

Article 18. 1. States Parties shall use their best efforts to ensure recognition of the principle that both parents have common responsibilities for the upbringing and development of the child. Parents or, as the case may be, legal guardians, have the primary responsibility for the upbringing and development of the child. The best interests of the child will be their basic concern.

2. For the purpose of guaranteeing and promoting the rights set forth in the present Convention, States Parties shall render appropriate assistance to parents and legal guardians in the performance of their child-rearing responsibilities and shall ensure the development of institutions, facilities and services for the care of children.

3. States Parties shall take all appropriate measures to ensure that children of working parents have the right to benefit from child-care services and facilities for which they are eligible.

Article 19. 1. States Parties shall take all appropriate legislative, administrative, social and educational measures to protect the child from all forms of physical or mental violence, injury or abuse, neglect or negligent treatment, maltreatment or exploitation, including sexual abuse, while in the care of parent(s), legal guardian(s), or any other person who has the care of the child.

2. Such protective measures should, as appropriate, include effective procedures for the establishment of social programmes to provide necessary support for the child and for those who have the care of the child, as well as for other forms of prevention and for identification, reporting, referral, investigation, treatment and follow-up of instances of child maltreatment described heretofore, and, as appropriate, for judicial involvement.

Article 20. 1. A child temporarily or permanently deprived of his or her family environment, or in whose own best interests cannot be allowed to remain in that environment, shall be entitled to special protection and assistance provided by the State.

2. States Parties shall in accordance with their national laws ensure alternative care for such a child.

3. Such care could include, *inter alia*, foster placement, *kafalah* of Islamic law, adoption or if necessary placement in suitable institutions for the care of children. When considering solutions, due regard shall be paid to the desirability of continuity in a child's upbringing and to the child's ethnic, religious, cultural and linguistic background.

Article 21. States Parties that recognize and/or permit the system of adoption shall ensure that the best interests of the child shall be the paramount consideration and they shall:

(a) Ensure that the adoption of a child is authorized only by competent authorities who determine, in accordance with applicable law and procedures and on the basis of all pertinent and reliable information, that the adoption is permissible in view of the child's status concerning parents, relatives and legal guardians and that, if required, the persons concerned have given their informed consent to the adoption on the basis of such counselling as may be necessary;

(b) Recognize that inter-country adoption may be

considered as an alternative means of child's care, if the child cannot be placed in a foster or an adoptive family or cannot in any suitable manner be cared for in the child's country of origin;

(c) Ensure that the child concerned by inter-country adoption enjoys safeguards and standards equivalent to those existing in the case of national adoption;

(d) Take all appropriate measures to ensure that, in inter-country adoption, the placement does not result in improper financial gain for those involved in it;

(e) Promote, where appropriate, the objectives of the present article by concluding bilateral or multilateral arrangements or agreements, and endeavour, within this framework, to ensure that the placement of the child in another country is carried out by competent authorities or organs.

Article 22. 1. States Parties shall take appropriate measures to ensure that a child who is seeking refugee status or who is considered a refugee in accordance with applicable international or domestic law and procedures shall, whether unaccompanied or accompanied by his or her parents or by any other person, receive appropriate protection and humanitarian assistance in the enjoyment of applicable rights set forth in the present Convention and in other international human rights or humanitarian instruments to which the said States are Parties.

2. For this purpose, States Parties shall provide, as they consider appropriate, co-operation in any efforts by the United Nations and other competent intergovernmental organizations or non-governmental organizations co-operating with the United Nations to protect and assist such a child and to trace the parents or other members of the family of any refugee child in order to obtain information necessary for reunification with his or her family. In cases where no parents or other members of the family can be found, the child shall be accorded the same protection as any other child permanently or temporarily deprived of his or her family environment for any reason, as set forth in the present Convention.

Article 23. 1. States Parties recognize that a mentally or physically disabled child should enjoy a full and decent life, in conditions which ensure dignity, promote self-reliance and facilitate the child's active participation in the community.

2. States Parties recognize the right of the disabled child to special care and shall encourage and ensure the extension, subject to available resources, to the eligible child and those responsible for his or her care, of assistance for which application is made and which is appropriate to the child's condition and to the circumstances of the parents or others caring for the child.

3. Recognizing the special needs of a disabled child, assistance extended in accordance with paragraph 2 of the present article shall be provided free of charge, whenever possible, taking into account the financial resources of the parents or others caring for the child, and shall be designed to ensure that the disabled child has effective access to and receives education, training, health care services, rehabilitation services, preparation for employment and recreation opportunities in a manner conducive to the child's achieving the fullest possible social integration and individual development, including his or her cultural and spiritual development.

4. States Parties shall promote, in the spirit of international co-operation, the exchange of appropriate information in the field of preventive health care and of medical, psychological and functional treatment of disabled children, including dissemination of and access to information concerning methods of rehabilitation, education and vocational services, with the aim of enabling States Parties to improve their capabilities and skills and to widen their experience in these areas. In this regard, particular account shall be taken of the needs of developing countries.

Article 24. 1. States Parties recognize the right of the child to the enjoyment of the highest attainable standard of health and to facilities for the treatment of illness and rehabilitation of health. States Parties shall strive to ensure that no child is deprived of his or her right of access to such health care services.

2. States Parties shall pursue full implementation of this right and, in particular, shall take appropriate measures:

(a) To diminish infant and child mortality;

(b) To ensure the provision of necessary medical assistance and health care to all children with emphasis on the development of primary health care;

(c) To combat disease and malnutrition, including within the framework of primary health care, through, *inter alia,* the application of readily available technology and through the provision of adequate nutritious foods and clean drinking-water, taking into consideration the dangers and risks of environmental pollution;

(d) To ensure appropriate pre-natal and post-natal health care for mothers;

(e) To ensure that all segments of society, in particular parents and children, are informed, have access to education and are supported in the use of basic knowledge of child health and nutrition, the advantages of breast-feeding, hygiene and environmental sanitation and the prevention of accidents;

(f) To develop preventive health care, guidance for parents and family planning education and services.

3. States Parties shall take all effective and appropriate measures with a view to abolishing traditional practices prejudicial to the health of children.

4. States Parties undertake to promote and encourage international co-operation with a view to achieving progressively the full realization of the right recognized in the present article. In this regard, particular account shall be taken of the needs of developing countries.

Article 25. States Parties recognize the right of a child who has been placed by the competent authorities for the purposes of care, protection or treatment of his or her physical or mental health, to a periodic review of the treatment provided to the child and all other circumstances relevant to his or her placement.

Article 26. 1. States Parties shall recognize for every child the right to benefit from social security, including social insurance, and shall take the necessary measures to achieve the full realization of this right in accordance with their national law.

2. The benefits should, where appropriate, be granted, taking into account the resources and the circumstances of the child and persons having responsibility for the maintenance of the child, as well as any other consideration relevant to an application for benefits made by or on behalf of the child.

Article 27. 1. States Parties recognize the right of every child to a standard of living adequate for the child's physical, mental, spiritual, moral and social development.

2. The parent(s) or others responsible for the child have the primary responsibility to secure, within their abilities

and financial capacities, the conditions of living necessary for the child's development.

3. States Parties, in accordance with national conditions and within their means, shall take appropriate measures to assist parents and others responsible for the child to implement this right and shall in case of need provide material assistance and support programmes, particularly with regard to nutrition, clothing and housing.

4. States Parties shall take all appropriate measures to secure the recovery of maintenance for the child from the parents or other persons having financial responsibility for the child, both within the State Party and from abroad. In particular, where the person having financial responsibility for the child lives in a State different from that of the child, States Parties shall promote the accession to international agreements or the conclusion of such agreements, as well as the making of other appropriate arrangements.

Article 28. 1. States Parties recognize the right of the child to education, and with a view to achieving this right progressively and on the basis of equal opportunity, they shall, in particular:

(a) Make primary education compulsory and available free to all;

(b) Encourage the development of different forms of secondary education, including general and vocational education, make them available and accessible to every child, and take appropriate measures such as the introduction of free education and offering financial assistance in case of need;

(c) Make higher education accessible to all on the basis of capacity by every appropriate means;

(d) Make educational and vocational information and guidance available and accessible to all children;

(e) Take measures to encourage regular attendance at schools and the reduction of drop-out rates.

2. States Parties shall take all appropriate measures to ensure that school discipline is administered in a manner consistent with the child's human dignity and in conformity with the present Convention.

3. States Parties shall promote and encourage international co-operation in matters relating to education, in particular with a view to contributing to the elimination of ignorance and illiteracy throughout the world and facilitating access to scientific and technical knowledge and modern teaching methods. In this regard, particular account shall be taken of the needs of developing countries.

Article 29. 1. States Parties agree that the education of the child shall be directed to:

(a) The development of the child's personality, talents and mental and physical abilities to their fullest potential;

(b) The development of respect for human rights and fundamental freedoms, and for the principle enshrined in the Charter of the United Nations;

(c) The development of respect for the child's parents, his or her own cultural identity, language and values, for the national values of the country in which the child is living, the country from which he or she may originate, and for civilizations different from his or her own;

(d) The preparation of the child for responsible life in a free society, in the spirit of understanding, peace, tolerance, equality of sexes, and friendship among all peoples, ethnic, national and religious groups and persons of indigenous origin;

(e) The development of respect for the natural environment.

2. No part of the present article or article 28 shall be construed so as to interfere with the liberty of individuals and bodies to establish and direct educational institutions, subject always to the observance of the principles set forth in paragraph 1 of the present article and to the requirements that the education given in such institutions shall conform to such minimum standards as may be laid down by the State.

Article 30. In those States in which ethnic, religious or linguistic minorities or persons of indigenous origin exist, a child belonging to such a minority or who is indigenous shall not be denied the right, in community with other members of his or her group, to enjoy his or her own culture, to profess and practise his or her own religion, or to use his or her own language.

Article 31. 1. States Parties recognize the right of the child to rest and leisure, to engage in play and recreational activities appropriate to the age of the child and to participate freely in cultural life and the arts.

2. States Parties shall respect and promote the right of the child to participate fully in cultural and artistic life and shall encourage the provision of appropriate and equal opportunities for cultural, artistic, recreational and leisure activity.

Article 32. 1. States Parties recognize the right of the child to be protected from economic exploitation and from performing any work that is likely to be hazardous or to interfere with the child's education, or to be harmful to the child's health or physical, mental, spiritual, moral or social development.

2. States Parties shall take legislative, administrative, social and educational measures to ensure the implementation of the present article. To this end, and having regard to the relevant provisions of other international instruments, States Parties shall in particular:

(a) Provide for a minimum age or minimum ages for admission to employment;

(b) Provide for appropriate regulation of the hours and conditions of employment;

(c) Provide for appropriate penalties or other sanctions to ensure the effective enforcement of the present article.

Article 33. States Parties shall take all appropriate measures, including legislative, administrative, social and educational measures, to protect children from the illicit use of narcotic drugs and psychotropic substances as defined in the relevant international treaties, and to prevent the use of children in the illicit production and trafficking of such substances.

Article 34. States Parties undertake to protect the child from all forms of sexual exploitation and sexual abuse. For these purposes, States Parties shall in particular take all appropriate national, bilateral and multilateral measures to prevent:

(a) The inducement or coercion of a child to engage in any unlawful sexual activity;

(b) The exploitative use of children in prostitution or other unlawful sexual practices;

(c) The exploitative use of children in pornographic performances and materials.

Article 35. States Parties shall take all appropriate national, bilateral and multilateral measures to prevent the abduction of, the sale of or traffic in children for any purpose or in any form.

Article 36. States Parties shall protect the child against all other forms of exploitation prejudicial to any aspects of the child's welfare.

Article 37. States Parties shall ensure that:

(a) No child shall be subjected to torture or other cruel, inhuman or degrading treatment or punishment. Neither capital punishment nor life imprisonment without possibility of release shall be imposed for offences committed by persons below eighteen years of age;

(b) No child shall be deprived of his or her liberty unlawfully or arbitrarily. The arrest, detention or imprisonment of a child shall be in conformity with the law and shall be used only as a measure of last resort and for the shortest appropriate period of time;

(c) Every child deprived of liberty shall be treated with humanity and respect for the inherent dignity of the human person, and in a manner which takes into account the needs of persons of his or her age. In particular, every child deprived of liberty shall be separated from adults unless it is considered in the child's best interest not to do so and shall have the right to maintain contact with his or her family through correspondence and visits, save in exceptional circumstances;

(d) Every child deprived of his or her liberty shall have the right to prompt access to legal and other appropriate assistance, as well as the right to challenge the legality of the deprivation of his or her liberty before a court or other competent, independent and impartial authority, and to a prompt decision on any such action.

Article 38. 1. States Parties undertake to respect and to ensure respect for rules of international humanitarian law applicable to them in armed conflicts which are relevant to the child.

2. States Parties shall take all feasible measures to ensure that persons who have not attained the age of fifteen years do not take a direct part in hostilities.

3. States Parties shall refrain from recruiting any person who has not attained the age of fifteen years into their armed forces. In recruiting among those persons who have attained the age of fifteen years but who have not attained the age of eighteen years, States Parties shall endeavour to give priority to those who are oldest.

4. In accordance with their obligations under international humanitarian law to protect the civilian population in armed conflicts, States Parties shall take all feasible measures to ensure protection and care of children who are affected by an armed conflict.

Article 39. States Parties shall take all appropriate measures to promote physical and psychological recovery and social reintegration of a child victim of: any form of neglect, exploitation, or abuse; torture or any other form of cruel, inhuman or degrading treatment or punishment; or armed conflicts. Such recovery and reintegration shall take place in an environment which fosters the health, self-respect and dignity of the child.

Article 40. 1. States Parties recognize the right of every child alleged as, accused of, or recognized as having infringed the penal law to be treated in a manner consistent with the promotion of the child's sense of dignity and worth, which reinforces the child's respect for the human rights and fundamental freedoms of others and which takes into account the child's age and the desirability of promoting the child's reintegration and the child's assuming a constructive role in society.

2. To this end, and having regard to the relevant provisions of international instruments, States Parties shall, in particular, ensure that:

(a) No child shall be alleged as, be accused of, or recognized as having infringed the penal law by reason of acts or omissions that were not prohibited by national or international law at the time they were committed;

(b) Every child alleged as or accused of having infringed the penal law has at least the following guarantees:

(i) To be presumed innocent until proven guilty according to law;

(ii) To be informed promptly and directly of the charges against him or her, and, if appropriate, through his or her parents or legal guardians, and to have legal or other appropriate assistance in the preparation and presentation of his or her defence;

(iii) To have the matter determined without delay by a competent, independent and impartial authority or judicial body in a fair hearing according to law, in the presence of legal or other appropriate assistance and, unless it is considered not to be in the best interest of the child, in particular, taking into account his or her age or situation, his or her parents or legal guardians;

(iv) Not to be compelled to give testimony or to confess guilt; to examine or have examined adverse witnesses and to obtain the participation and examination of witnesses on his or her behalf under conditions of equality;

(v) If considered to have infringed the penal law, to have this decision and any measures imposed in consequence thereof reviewed by a higher competent, independent and impartial authority or judicial body according to law;

(vi) To have the free assistance of an interpreter if the child cannot understand or speak the language used;

(vii) To have his or her privacy fully respected at all stages of the proceedings.

3. States Parties shall seek to promote the establishment of laws, procedures, authorities and institutions specifically applicable to children alleged as, accused of, or recognized as having infringed the penal law, and, in particular:

(a) The establishment of a minimum age below which children shall be presumed not to have the capacity to infringe the penal law;

(b) Whenever appropriate and desirable, measures for dealing with such children without resorting to judicial proceedings, providing that human rights and legal safeguards are fully respected.

4. A variety of dispositions, such as care, guidance and supervision orders; counselling; probation; foster care; education and vocational training programmes and other alternatives to institutional care shall be available to ensure that children are dealt with in a manner appropriate to their well-being and proportionate both to their circumstances and the offence.

Article 41. Nothing in the present Convention shall affect any provisions which are more conducive to the realization of the rights of the child and which may be contained in:

(a) The law of a State Party; or
(b) International law in force for that State.

Part II

Article 42. States Parties undertake to make the principles and provisions of the Convention widely known, by appropriate and active means, to adults and children alike.

Article 43. 1. For the purpose of examining the progress made by States Parties in achieving the realization of the obligations undertaken in the present Convention, there shall be established a Committee on the Rights of the

Child, which shall carry out the functions hereinafter provided.

2. The Committee shall consist of ten experts of high moral standing and recognized competence in the field covered by this Convention. The members of the Committee shall be elected by States Parties from among their nationals and shall serve in their personal capacity, consideration being given to equitable geographical distribution, as well as to the principal legal systems.

3. The members of the Committee shall be elected by secret ballot from a list of persons nominated by States Parties. Each State Party may nominate one person from among its own nationals.

4. The initial election to the Committee shall be held no later than six months after the date of the entry into force of the present Convention and thereafter every second year. At least four months before the date of each election, the Secretary-General of the United Nations shall address a letter to States Parties inviting them to submit their nominations within two months. The Secretary-General shall subsequently prepare a list in alphabetical order of all persons thus nominated, indicating States Parties which have nominated them, and shall submit it to the States Parties to the present Convention.

5. The elections shall be held at meetings of States Parties convened by the Secretary-General at United Nations Headquarters. At those meetings, for which two thirds of States Parties shall constitute a quorum, the persons elected to the Committee shall be those who obtain the largest number of votes and an absolute majority of the votes of the representatives of States Parties present and voting.

6. The members of the Committee shall be elected for a term of four years. They shall be eligible for re-election if renominated. The term of five of the members elected at the first election shall expire at the end of two years; immediately after the first election, the names of these five members shall be chosen by lot by the Chairman of the meeting.

7. If a member of the Committee dies or resigns or declares that for any other cause he or she can no longer perform the duties of the Committee, the State Party which nominated the member shall appoint another expert from among its nationals to serve for the remainder of the term, subject to the approval of the Committee.

8. The Committee shall establish its own rules of procedure.

9. The Committee shall elect its officers for a period of two years.

10. The meetings of the Committee shall normally be held at United Nations Headquarters or at any other convenient place as determined by the Committee. The Committee shall normally meet annually. The duration of the meetings of the Committee shall be determined, and reviewed, if necessary, by a meeting of the States Parties to the present Convention, subject to the approval of the General Assembly.

11. The Secretary-General of the United Nations shall provide the necessary staff and facilities for the effective performance of the functions of the Committee under the present Convention.

12. With the approval of the General Assembly, the members of the Committee established under the present Convention shall receive emoluments from United Nations resources on such terms and conditions as the Assembly may decide.

Article 44. 1. States Parties undertake to submit to the Committee, through the Secretary-General of the United Nations, reports on the measures they have adopted which give effect to the rights recognized herein and on the progress made on the enjoyment of those rights:

(a) Within two years of the entry into force of the Convention for the State Party concerned;

(b) Thereafter every five years.

2. Reports made under the present article shall indicate factors and difficulties, if any, affecting the degree of fulfilment of the obligations under the present Convention. Reports shall also contain sufficient information to provide the Committee with a comprehensive understanding of the implementation of the Convention in the country concerned.

3. A State Party which has submitted a comprehensive initial report to the Committee need not, in its subsequent reports submitted in accordance with paragraph 1 (b) of the present article, repeat basic information previously provided.

4. The Committee may request from States Parties further information relevant to the implementation of the Convention.

5. The Committee shall submit to the General Assembly, through the Economic and Social Council, every two years, reports on its activities.

6. States Parties shall make their reports widely available to the public in their own countries.

Article 45. In order to foster the effective implementation of the Convention and to encourage international co-operation in the field covered by the Convention:

(a) The specialized agencies, the United Nations Children's Fund, and other United Nations organs shall be entitled to be represented at the consideration of the implementation of such provisions of the present Convention as fall within the scope of their mandate. The Committee may invite the specialized agencies, the United Nations Children's Fund and other competent bodies as it may consider appropriate to provide expert advice on the implementation of the Convention in areas falling within the scope of their respective mandates. The Committee may invite the specialized agencies, the United Nations Children's Fund, and other United Nations organs to submit reports on the implementation of the Convention in areas falling within the scope of their activities;

(b) The Committee shall transmit, as it may consider appropriate, to the specialized agencies, the United Nations Children's Fund and other competent bodies, any reports from States Parties that contain a request, or indicate a need, for technical advice or assistance, along with the Committee's observations and suggestions, if any, on these requests or indications;

(c) The Committee may recommend to the General Assembly to request the Secretary-General to undertake on its behalf studies on specific issues relating to the rights of the child;

(d) The Committee may make suggestions and general recommendations based on information received pursuant to articles 44 and 45 of the present Convention. Such suggestions and general recommendations shall be transmitted to any State Party concerned and reported to the General Assembly, together with comments, if any, from States Parties.

Part III

Article 46. The present Convention shall be open for signature by all States.

Article 47. The present Convention is subject to ratification. Instruments of ratification shall be deposited with the Secretary-General of the United Nations.

Article 48. The present Convention shall remain open for accession by any State. The instruments of accession shall be deposited with the Secretary-General of the United Nations.

Article 49. 1. The present Convention shall enter into force on the thirtieth day following the date of deposit with the Secretary-General of the United Nations of the twentieth instrument of ratification or accession.

2. For each State ratifying or acceding to the Convention after the deposit of the twentieth instrument of ratification or accession, the Convention shall enter into force on the thirtieth day after the deposit by such State of its instrument of ratification or accession.

Article 50. 1. Any State Party may propose an amendment and file it with the Secretary-General of the United Nations. The Secretary-General shall thereupon communicate the proposed amendment to States Parties, with a request that they indicate whether they favour a conference of States Parties for the purpose of considering and voting upon the proposals. In the event that, within four months from the date of such communication, at least one third of the States Parties favour such a conference, the Secretary-General shall convene the conference under the auspices of the United Nations. Any amendment adopted by a majority of States Parties present and voting at the conference shall be submitted to the General Assembly for approval.

2. An amendment adopted in accordance with paragraph 1 of the present article shall enter into force when it has been approved by the General Assembly of the United Nations and accepted by a two-thirds majority of States Parties.

3. When an amendment enters into force, it shall be binding on those States Parties which have accepted it, other States Parties still being bound by the provisions of the present Convention and any earlier amendments which they have accepted.

Article 51. 1. The Secretary-General of the United Nations shall receive and circulate to all States the text of reservations made by States at the time of ratification or accession.

2. A reservation incompatible with the object and purpose of the present Convention shall not be permitted.

3. Reservations may be withdrawn at any time by notification to that effect addressed to the Secretary-General of the United Nations, who shall then inform all States. Such notification shall take effect on the date on which it is received by the Secretary-General.

Article 52. A State Party may denounce the present Convention by written notification to the Secretary-General of the United Nations. Denunciation becomes effective one year after the date of receipt of the notification by the Secretary-General.

Article 53. The Secretary-General of the United Nations is designated as the depositary of the present Convention.

Article 54. The original of the present Convention, of which the Arabic, Chinese, English, French, Russian and Spanish texts are equally authentic, shall be deposited with the Secretary-General of the United Nations.

In witness thereof the undersigned plenipotentiaries, being duly authorized thereto by their respective Governments, have signed the present Convention.

SEE ALSO *Children entries.*

CONVENTION RELATING TO THE STATUS OF REFUGEES (1951).

The convention was adopted on 28 July 1951 by the United Nations Conference of Plenipotentiaries on the Status of Refugees and stateless persons, convened at the European office of the United Nations in Geneva in accordance with a decision taken by the UN General Assembly (resolution 429 [V]) on 14 December 1950. It entered into force on 22 April 1954. The convention is the most far-reaching instrument relating to the protection of refugees adopted by the international community and has had the effect of encouraging governments to safeguard the basic human rights of refugees by instituting increasingly generous and liberal policies of asylum. The text of the convention (United Nations, *Treaty Series,* vol. 189, p. 150) is as follows:

Preamble

The High Contracting Parties,

Considering that the Charter of the United Nations and the Universal Declaration of Human Rights approved on 10 December 1948 by the General Assembly have affirmed the principle that human beings shall enjoy fundamental rights and freedoms without discrimination,

Considering that the United Nations has, on various occasions, manifested its profound concern for refugees and endeavoured to assure refugees the widest possible exercise of these fundamental rights and freedoms,

Considering that it is desirable to revise and consolidate previous international agreements relating to the status of refugees and to extend the scope of and the protection accorded by such instruments by means of a new agreement,

Considering that the grant of asylum may place unduly heavy burdens on certain countries, and that a satisfactory solution of a problem of which the United Nations has recognized the international scope and nature cannot therefore be achieved without international co-operation,

Expressing the wish that all States, recognizing the social and humanitarian nature of the problem of refugees, will do everything within their power to prevent this problem from becoming a cause of tension between States,

Noting that the United Nations High Commissioner for Refugees is charged with the task of supervising international conventions providing for the protection of refugees, and recognizing that the effective co-ordination of measures taken to deal with this problem will depend upon the co-operation of States with the High Commissioner,

Have agreed as follows:

Chapter I
General Provisions

Article 1. Definition of the Term "Refugee". **A.** For the purposes of the present Convention, the term "refugee" shall apply to any person who:

(1) Has been considered a refugee under the Arrange-

ments of 12 May 1926 and 30 June 1928 or under the Conventions of 28 October 1933 and 10 February 1938, the Protocol of 14 September 1939 or the Constitution of the International Refugee Organization;

Decisions of non-eligibility taken by the International Refugee Organization during the period of its activities shall not prevent the status of refugee being accorded to persons who fulfil the conditions of paragraph 2 of this section;

(2) As a result of events occurring before 1 January 1951 and owing to well-founded fear of being persecuted for reasons of race, religion, nationality, membership of a particular social group or political opinion, is outside the country of his nationality and is unable, or owing to such fear, is unwilling to avail himself of the protection of that country; or who, not having a nationality and being outside the country of his former habitual residence as a result of such events, is unable or, owing to such fear, is unwilling to return to it.

In the case of a person who has more than one nationality, the term "the country of his nationality" shall mean each of the countries of which he is a national, and a person shall not be deemed to be lacking the protection of the country of his nationality if, without any valid reason based on well-founded fear, he has not availed himself of the protection of one of the countries of which he is a national.

B. (1) For the purposes of this Convention, the words "events occurring before 1 January 1951" in article 1, section A, shall be understood to mean either (*a*) "events occurring in Europe before 1 January 1951"; or (*b*) "events occurring in Europe or elsewhere before 1 January 1951;" and each Contracting State shall make a declaration at the time of signature, ratification or accession, specifying which of these meanings it applies for the purpose of its obligations under this Convention.

(2) Any Contracting State which has adopted alternative (*a*) may at any time extend its obligations by adopting alternative (*b*) by means of a notification addressed to the Secretary-General of the United Nations.

C. This Convention shall cease to apply to any person falling under the terms of section A if:

(1) He has voluntarily re-availed himself of the protection of the country of his nationality; or

(2) Having lost his nationality, he has voluntarily reacquired it; or

(3) He has acquired a new nationality, and enjoys the protection of the country of his new nationality; or

(4) He has voluntarily re-established himself in the country which he left or outside which he remained owing to fear of persecution; or

(5) He can no longer, because the circumstances in connexion with which he has been recognized as a refugee have ceased to exist, continue to refuse to avail himself of the protection of the country of his nationality;

Provided that this paragraph shall not apply to a refugee falling under section A (1) of this article who is able to invoke compelling reasons arising out of previous persecution for refusing to avail himself of the protection of the country of nationality;

(6) Being a person who has no nationality he is, because the circumstances in connexion with which he has been recognized as a refugee have ceased to exist, able to return to the country of his former habitual residence;

Provided that this paragraph shall not apply to a refugee falling under section A (1) of this article who is able to invoke compelling reasons arising out of previous persecu-

tion for refusing to return to the country of his former habitual residence.

D. This Convention shall not apply to persons who are at present receiving from organs or agencies of the United Nations other than the United Nations High Commissioner for Refugees protection or assistance.

When such protection or assistance has ceased for any reason, without the position of such persons being definitively settled in accordance with the relevant resolutions adopted by the General Assembly of the United Nations, these persons shall *ipso facto* be entitled to the benefits of this Convention.

E. This Convention shall not apply to a person who is recognized by the competent authorities of the country in which he has taken residence as having the rights and obligations which are attached to the possession of the nationality of that country.

F. The provisions of this Convention shall not apply to any person with respect to whom there are serious reasons for considering that:

(*a*) He has committed a crime against peace, a war crime, or a crime against humanity, as defined in the international instruments drawn up to make provision in respect of such crimes;

(*b*) He has committed a serious non-political crime outside the country of refuge prior to his admission to that country as a refugee;

(*c*) He has been guilty of acts contrary to the purposes and principles of the United Nations.

Article 2. General Obligations. Every refugee has duties to the country in which he finds himself, which require in particular that he conform to its laws and regulations as well as to measures taken for the maintenance of public order.

Article 3. Non-discrimination. The Contracting States shall apply the provisions of this Convention to refugees without discrimination as to race, religion or country of origin.

Article 4. Religion. The Contracting States shall accord to refugees within their territories treatment at least as favourable as that accorded to their nationals with respect to freedom to practice their religion and freedom as regards the religious education of their children.

Article 5. Rights Granted Apart From This Convention. Nothing in this Convention shall be deemed to impair any rights and benefits granted by a Contracting State to refugees apart from this Convention.

Article 6. The Term "In the Same Circumstances." For the purpose of this Convention, the term "in the same circumstances" implies that any requirements (including requirements as to length and conditions of sojourn or residence) which the particular individual would have to fulfil for the enjoyment of the right in question, if he were not a refugee, must be fulfilled by him, with the exception of requirements which by their nature a refugee is incapable of fulfilling.

Article 7. Exemption From Reciprocity. 1. Except where this Convention contains more favourable provisions, a Contracting State shall accord to refugees the same treatment as is accorded to aliens generally.

2. After a period of three years' residence, all refugees shall enjoy exemption from legislative reciprocity in the territory of the Contracting States.

3. Each Contracting State shall continue to accord to refugees the rights and benefits to which they were already entitled, in the absence of reciprocity, at the date of entry into force of this Convention for that State.

4. The Contracting States shall consider favourably the

possibility of according to refugees, in the absence of reciprocity, rights and benefits beyond those to which they are entitled according to paragraphs 2 and 3, and to extending exemption from reciprocity to refugees who do not fulfil the conditions provided for in paragraphs 2 and 3.

5. The provisions of paragraphs 2 and 3 apply both to the rights and benefits referred to in articles 13, 18, 19, 21 and 22 of this Convention and to rights and benefits for which this Convention does not provide.

Article 8. Exemption From Exceptional Measures. With regard to exceptional measures which may be taken against the person, property or interests of nationals of a foreign State, the Contracting States shall not apply such measures to a refugee who is formally a national of the said State solely on account of such nationality. Contracting States which, under their legislation, are prevented from applying the general principle expressed in this article, shall, in appropriate cases, grant exemptions in favour of such refugees.

Article 9. Provisional Measures. Nothing in this Convention shall prevent a Contracting State, in time of war or other grave and exceptional circumstances, from taking provisionally measures which it considers to be essential to the national security in the case of a particular person, pending a determination by the Contracting State that that person is in fact a refugee and that the continuance of such measures is necessary in his case in the interests of national security.

Article 10. Continuity of Residence. 1. Where a refugee has been forcibly displaced during the Second World War and removed to the territory of a Contracting State, and is resident there, the period of such enforced sojourn shall be considered to have been lawful residence within that territory.

2. Where a refugee has been forcibly displaced during the Second World War from the territory of a Contracting State and has, prior to the date of entry into force of this Convention, returned there for the purpose of taking up residence, the period of residence before and after such enforced displacement shall be regarded as one uninterrupted period for any purposes for which uninterrupted residence is required.

Article 11. Refugee Seamen. In the case of refugees regularly serving as crew members on board a ship flying the flag of a Contracting State, that State shall give sympathetic consideration to their establishment on its territory and the issue of travel documents to them or their temporary admission to its territory particularly with a view to facilitating their establishment in another country.

Chapter II
Juridical Status

Article 12. Personal Status. 1. The personal status of a refugee shall be governed by the law of the country of his domicile or, if he has no domicile, by the law of the country of his residence.

2. Rights previously acquired by a refugee and dependent on personal status, more particularly rights attaching to marriage, shall be respected by a Contracting State, subject to compliance, if this be necessary, with the formalities required by the law of that State, provided that the right in question is one which would have been recognized by the law of that State had he not become a refugee.

Article 13. Movable and Immovable Property. The Contracting States shall accord to a refugee treatment as favourable as possible and, in any event, not less favourable than that accorded to aliens generally in the same circumstances, as regards the acquisition of movable and immovable property and other rights pertaining thereto, and to leases and other contracts relating to movable and immovable property.

Article 14. Artistic Rights and Industrial Property. In respect of the protection of industrial property, such as inventions, designs or models, trade marks, trade names, and of rights in literary, artistic and scientific works, a refugee shall be accorded in the country in which he has his habitual residence the same protection as is accorded to nationals of that country. In the territory of any other Contracting State, he shall be accorded the same protection as is accorded in that territory to nationals of the country in which he has his habitual residence.

Article 15. Right of Association. As regards non-political and non-profit-making associations and trade unions the Contracting States shall accord to refugees lawfully staying in their territory the most favourable treatment accorded to nationals of a foreign country, in the same circumstances.

Article 16. Access to Courts. 1. A refugee shall have free access to the courts of law on the territory of all Contracting States.

2. A refugee shall enjoy in the Contracting State in which he has his habitual residence the same treatment as a national in matters pertaining to access to the courts, including legal assistance and exemption from *cautio judicatum solvi*.

3. A refugee shall be accorded in the matters referred to in paragraph 2 in countries other than that in which he has his habitual residence the treatment granted to a national of the country of his habitual residence.

Chapter III
Gainful Employment

Article 17. Wage-earning Employment. 1. The Contracting States shall accord to refugees lawfully staying in their territory the most favourable treatment accorded to nationals of a foreign country in the same circumstances, as regards the right to engage in wage-earning employment.

2. In any case, restrictive measures imposed on aliens or the employment of aliens for the protection of the national labour market shall not be applied to a refugee who was already exempt from them at the date of entry into force of this Convention for the Contracting State concerned, or who fulfils one of the following conditions:

(*a*) He has completed three years' residence in the country;

(*b*) He has a spouse possessing the nationality of the country of residence. A refugee may not invoke the benefit of this provision if he has abandoned his spouse;

(*c*) He has one or more children possessing the nationality of the country of residence.

3. The Contracting States shall give sympathetic consideration to assimilating the rights of all refugees with regard to wage-earning employment to those of nationals, and in particular of those refugees who have entered their territory pursuant to programmes of labour recruitment or under immigration schemes.

Article 18. Self-employment. The Contracting States shall accord to a refugee lawfully in their territory treatment as favourable as possible and, in any event, not less favourable than that accorded to aliens generally in the same circumstances, as regards the right to engage on his own account in agriculture, industry, handicrafts and commerce and to establish commercial and industrial companies.

Article 19. Liberal Professions. 1. Each Contracting State shall accord to refugees lawfully staying in their territory who hold diplomas recognized by the competent authorities of that State, and who are desirous of practising a liberal profession, treatment as favourable as possible and, in any event, not less favourable than that accorded to aliens generally in the same circumstances.

2. The Contracting States shall use their best endeavours consistently with their laws and constitutions to secure the settlement of such refugees in the territories, other than the metropolitan territory, for whose international relations they are responsible.

Chapter IV
Welfare

Article 20. Rationing. Where a rationing system exists, which applies to the population at large and regulates the general distribution of products in short supply, refugees shall be accorded the same treatment as nationals.

Article 21. Housing. As regards housing, the Contracting States, in so far as the matter is regulated by laws or regulations or is subject to the control of public authorities, shall accord to refugees lawfully staying in their territory treatment as favourable as possible and, in any event, not less favourable than that accorded to aliens generally in the same circumstances.

Article 22. Public Education. 1. The Contracting States shall accord to refugees the same treatment as is accorded to nationals with respect to elementary education.

2. The Contracting States shall accord to refugees treatment as favourable as possible, and, in any event, not less favourable than that accorded to aliens generally in the same circumstances, with respect to education other than elementary education and, in particular, as regards access to studies, the recognition of foreign school certificates, diplomas and degrees, the remission of fees and charges and the award of scholarships.

Article 23. Public Relief. The Contracting States shall accord to refugees lawfully staying in their territory the same treatment with respect to public relief and assistance as is accorded to their nationals.

Article 24. Labour Legislation and Social Security. 1. The Contracting States shall accord to refugees lawfully staying in their territory the same treatment as is accorded to nationals in respect of the following matters:

(*a*) In so far as such matters are governed by laws or regulations or are subject to the control of administrative authorities: remuneration, including family allowances where these form part of remuneration, hours of work, overtime arrangements, holidays with pay, restrictions on home work, minimum age of employment, apprenticeship and training, women's work and the work of young persons, and the enjoyment of the benefits of collective bargaining;

(*b*) Social security (legal provisions in respect of employment injury, occupational diseases, maternity, sickness, disability, old age, death, unemployment, family responsibilities and any other contingency which, according to national laws or regulations, is covered by a social security scheme), subject to the following limitations:

(i) There may be appropriate arrangements for the maintenance of acquired rights and rights in course of acquisition;

(ii) National laws or regulations of the country of residence may prescribe special arrangements concerning benefits or portions of benefits which are payable wholly out of public funds, and concerning allowances paid to persons who do not fulfil the contribution conditions prescribed for the award of a normal pension.

2. The right to compensation for the death of a refugee resulting from employment injury or from occupational disease shall not be affected by the fact that the residence of the beneficiary is outside the territory of the Contracting State.

3. The Contracting States shall extend to refugees the benefits of agreements concluded between them, or which may be concluded between them in the future, concerning the maintenance of acquired rights and rights in the process of acquisition in regard to social security, subject only to the conditions which apply to nationals of the States signatory to the agreements in question.

4. The Contracting States will give sympathetic consideration to extending to refugees so far as possible the benefits of similar agreements which may at any time be in force between such Contracting States and non-contracting States.

Chapter V
Administrative Measures

Article 25. Administrative Assistance. 1. When the exercise of a right by a refugee would normally require the assistance of authorities of a foreign country to whom he cannot have recourse, the Contracting States in whose territory he is residing shall arrange that such assistance be afforded to him by their own authorities or by an international authority.

2. The authority or authorities mentioned in paragraph 1 shall deliver or cause to be delivered under their supervision to refugees such documents or certifications as would normally be delivered to aliens by or through their national authorities.

3. Documents or certifications so delivered shall stand in the stead of the official instruments delivered to aliens by or through their national authorities, and shall be given credence in the absence of proof to the contrary.

4. Subject to such exceptional treatment as may be granted to indigent persons, fees may be charged for the services mentioned herein, but such fees shall be moderate and commensurate with those charged to nationals for similar services.

5. The provisions of this article shall be without prejudice to articles 27 and 28.

Article 26. Freedom of Movement. Each Contracting State shall accord to refugees lawfully in its territory the right to choose their place of residence and to move freely within its territory subject to any regulations applicable to aliens generally in the same circumstances.

Article 27. Identity Papers. The Contracting States shall issue identity papers to any refugee in their territory who does not possess a valid travel document.

Article 28. Travel Documents. 1. The Contracting States shall issue to refugees lawfully staying in their territory travel documents for the purpose of travel outside their territory, unless compelling reasons of national security or public order otherwise require, and the provisions of the Schedule to this Convention shall apply with respect to such documents. The Contracting States may issue such a travel document to any other refugee in their territory; they shall in particular give sympathetic consideration to the issue of such a travel document to refugees in their territory who are unable to obtain a travel document from the country of their lawful residence.

2. Travel documents issued to refugees under previous international agreements by parties thereto shall be recognized and treated by the Contracting States in the same way as if they had been issued pursuant to this article.

Article 29. Fiscal Charges. 1. The Contracting States shall not impose upon refugees duties, charges or taxes, of any description whatsoever, other or higher than those which are or may be levied on their nationals in similar situations.

2. Nothing in the above paragraph shall prevent the application to refugees of the laws and regulations concerning charges in respect of the issue to aliens of administrative documents including identity papers.

Article 30. Transfer of Assets. 1. A Contracting State shall, in conformity with its laws and regulations, permit refugees to transfer assets which they have brought into its territory, to another country where they have been admitted for the purposes of resettlement.

2. A Contracting State shall give sympathetic consideration to the application of refugees for permission to transfer assets wherever they may be and which are necessary for their resettlement in another country to which they have been admitted.

Article 31. Refugees Unlawfully in the Country of Refuge. 1. The Contracting States shall not impose penalties, on account of their illegal entry or presence, on refugees who, coming directly from a territory where their life or freedom was threatened in the sense of article 1, enter or are present in their territory without authorization, provided they present themselves without delay to the authorities and show good cause for their illegal entry or presence.

2. The Contracting States shall not apply to the movements of such refugees restrictions other than those which are necessary and such restrictions shall only be applied until their status in the country is regularized or they obtain admission into another country. The Contracting States shall allow such refugees a reasonable period and all the necessary facilities to obtain admission into another country.

Article 32. Expulsion. 1. The Contracting States shall not expel a refugee lawfully in their territory save on grounds of national security or public order.

2. The expulsion of such a refugee shall be only in pursuance of a decision reached in accordance with due process of law. Except where compelling reasons of national security otherwise require, the refugee shall be allowed to submit evidence to clear himself, and to appeal to and be represented for the purpose before competent authority or a person or persons specially designated by the competent authority.

3. The Contracting States shall allow such a refugee a reasonable period within which to seek legal admission into another country. The Contracting States reserve the right to apply during that period such internal measures as they may deem necessary.

Article 33. Prohibition of Expulsion or Return ("Refoulement"). 1. No Contracting State shall expel or return ("refouler") a refugee in any manner whatsoever to the frontiers of territories where his life or freedom would be threatened on account of his race, religion, nationality, membership of a particular social group or political opinion.

2. The benefit of the present provision may not, however, be claimed by a refugee whom there are reasonable grounds for regarding as a danger to the security of the country in which he is, or who, having been convicted by a final judgment of a particularly serious crime, constitutes a danger to the community of that country.

Article 34. Naturalization. The Contracting States shall as far as possible facilitate the assimilation and naturalization of refugees. They shall in particular make every effort to expedite naturalization proceedings and to reduce as far as possible the charges and costs of such proceedings.

Chapter VI
Executory and Transitory Provisions

Article 35. Co-operation of the National Authorities With the United Nations. 1. The Contracting States undertake to co-operate with the Office of the United Nations High Commissioner for Refugees, or any other agency of the United Nations which may succeed it, in the exercise of its functions, and shall in particular facilitate its duty of supervising the application of the provisions of this Convention.

2. In order to enable the Office of the High Commissioner or any other agency of the United Nations which may succeed it, to make reports to the competent organs of the United Nations, the Contracting States undertake to provide them in the appropriate form with information and statistical data requested concerning:

(*a*) The condition of refugees,

(*b*) The implementation of this Convention, and

(*c*) Laws, regulations and decrees which are, or may hereafter be, in force relating to refugees.

Article 36. Information on National Legislation. The Contracting States shall communicate to the Secretary-General of the United Nations the laws and regulations which they may adopt to ensure the application of this Convention.

Article 37. Relation to Previous Conventions. Without prejudice to article 28, paragraph 2, of this Convention, this Convention replaces, as between parties to it, the Arrangements of 5 July 1922, 31 May 1924, 12 May 1926, 30 June 1928 and 30 July 1935, the Conventions of 28 October 1933 and 10 February 1938, the Protocol of 14 September 1939 and the Agreement of 15 October 1946.

Chapter VII
Final Clauses

Article 38. Settlement of Disputes. Any dispute between parties to this Convention relating to its interpretation or application, which cannot be settled by other means, shall be referred to the International Court of Justice at the request of any one of the parties to the dispute.

Article 39. Signature, Ratification and Accession. 1. This Convention shall be opened for signature at Geneva on 28 July 1951 and shall thereafter be deposited with the Secretary-General of the United Nations. It shall be open for signature at the European Office of the United Nations from 28 July to 31 August 1951 and shall be re-opened for signature at the Headquarters of the United Nations from 17 September 1951 to 31 December 1952.

2. This Convention shall be open for signature on behalf of all States Members of the United Nations, and also on behalf of any other State invited to attend the Conference of Plenipotentiaries on the Status of Refugees and Stateless Persons or to which an invitation to sign will have been addressed by the General Assembly. It shall be ratified and the instruments of ratification shall be deposited with the Secretary-General of the United Nations.

3. This Convention shall be open from 28 July 1951 for accession by the States referred to in paragraph 2 of this ar-

ticle. Accession shall be effected by the deposit of an instrument of accession with the Secretary-General of the United Nations.

Article 40. Territorial Application Clause. 1. Any State may, at the time of signature, ratification or accession, declare that this Convention shall extend to all or any of the territories for the international relations of which it is responsible. Such a declaration shall take effect when the Convention enters into force for the State concerned.

2. At any time thereafter any such extension shall be made by notification addressed to the Secretary-General of the United Nations and shall take effect as from the ninetieth day after the day of receipt by the Secretary-General of the United Nations of this notification, or as from the date of entry into force of the Convention for the State concerned, whichever is the later.

3. With respect to those territories to which this Convention is not extended at the time of signature, ratification or accession, each State concerned shall consider the possibility of taking the necessary steps in order to extend the application of this Convention to such territories, subject, where necessary for constitutional reasons, to the consent of the Governments of such territories.

Article 41. Federal Clause. In the case of a Federal or non-unitary State, the following provisions shall apply:

(*a*) With respect to those articles of this Convention that come within the legislative jurisdiction of the federal legislative authority, the obligations of the Federal Government shall to this extent be the same as those of Parties which are not Federal States;

(*b*) With respect to those articles of this Convention that come within the legislative jurisdiction of constituent states, provinces or cantons which are not, under the constitutional system of the Federation, bound to take legislative action, the Federal Government shall bring such articles with a favourable recommendation to the notice of the appropriate authorities of states, provinces or cantons at the earliest possible moment;

(*c*) A Federal State Party to this Convention shall, at the request of any other Contracting State transmitted through the Secretary-General of the United Nations, supply a statement of the law and practice of the Federation and its constituent units in regard to any particular provision of the Convention showing the extent to which effect has been given to that provision by legislative or other action.

Article 42. Reservations. 1. At the time of signature, ratification or accession, any State may make reservations to articles of the Convention other than to articles 1, 3, 4, 16 (1), 33, 36–46 inclusive.

2. Any State making a reservation in accordance with paragraph 1 of this article may at any time withdraw the reservation by a communication to that effect addressed to the Secretary-General of the United Nations.

Article 43. Entry Into Force. 1. This Convention shall come into force on the ninetieth day following the day of deposit of the sixth instrument of ratification or accession.

2. For each State ratifying or acceding to the Convention after the deposit of the sixth instrument of ratification or accession, the Convention shall enter into force on the ninetieth day following the date of deposit by such State of its instrument of ratification or accession.

Article 44. Denunciation. 1. Any Contracting State may denounce this Convention at any time by a notification addressed to the Secretary-General of the United Nations.

2. Such denunciation shall take effect for the Contrac-

ting State concerned one year from the date upon which it is received by the Secretary-General of the United Nations.

3. Any State which has made a declaration or notification under article 40 may, at any time thereafter, by a notification to the Secretary-General of the United Nations, declare that the Convention shall cease to extend to such territory one year after the date of receipt of the notification by the Secretary-General.

Article 45. Revision. 1. Any Contracting State may request revision of this Convention at any time by a notification addressed to the Secretary-General of the United Nations.

2. The General Assembly of the United Nations shall recommend the steps, if any, to be taken in respect of such request.

Article 46. Notifications by the Secretary-General of the United Nations. The Secretary-General of the United Nations shall inform all Members of the United Nations and non-member States referred to in article 39:

(*a*) Of declarations and notifications in accordance with section B of article 1;

(*b*) Of signatures, ratifications and accessions in accordance with article 39;

(*c*) Of declarations and notifications in accordance with article 40;

(*d*) Of reservations and withdrawals in accordance with article 42;

(*e*) Of the date on which this Convention will come into force in accordance with article 43;

(*f*) Of denunciations and notifications in accordance with article 44;

(*g*) Of requests for revision in accordance with article 45.

In faith whereof the undersigned, duly authorized, have signed this Convention on behalf of their respective Governments.

Done at Geneva, this twenty-eighth day of July, one thousand nine hundred and fifty-one, in a single copy, of which the English and French texts are equally authentic and which shall remain deposited in the archives of the United Nations, and certified true copies of which shall be delivered to all Members of the United Nations and to the non-member States referred to in article 39.

SEE ALSO *Declaration on the Human Rights of Individuals who are not Nationals of the Country in Which They Live; European Convention on Establishment and Protocol; Refugees; Refugees: Children; Refugees: Mass Exodus; Refugees: Security; Refugees: Students in Southern Africa; Refugees: Voluntary Repatriation; Refugees: Women and Children; United Nations High Commissioner for Refugees.*

CONVENTION RELATING TO THE STATUS OF REFUGEES: PROTOCOL (1967).

The purpose of the protocol is to remove the date contained in the "definition of refugees" (article 1) in the CONVENTION RELATING TO THE STATUS OF REFUGEES and thereby to make the convention applicable to refugee situations occurring after 1 January 1951. The protocol, recommended by the Executive Committee of the Program of the UNITED NATIONS HIGH COMMISSIONER FOR REFUGEES, was approved by the UN Economic and Social Council on 18 November 1966 (resolution 1186

[XLI]), and adopted by the UN General Assembly on 16 December 1966 (resolution 2198 [XXI]). It was opened for signature and ratification or accession on 31 January 1967 and entered into force on 4 October 1967. The text (United Nations, *Treaty Series,* vol. 606, p. 267) is as follows:

The States Parties to the present Protocol,

Considering that the Convention relating to the Status of Refugees done at Geneva on 28 July 1951 (hereinafter referred to as the Convention) covers only those persons who have become refugees as a result of events occurring before 1 January 1951,

Considering that new refugee situations have arisen since the Convention was adopted and that the refugees concerned may therefore not fall within the scope of the Convention.

Considering that it is desirable that equal status should be enjoyed by all refugees covered by the definition in the Convention irrespective of the dateline 1 January 1951,

Have agreed as follows:

Article 1. General Provision. 1. The States Parties to the present Protocol undertake to apply articles 2 to 34 inclusive of the Convention to refugees as hereinafter defined.

2. For the purpose of the present Protocol, the term "refugee" shall, except as regards the application of paragraph 3 of this article, mean any person within the definition of article 1 of the Convention as if the words "As a result of events occurring before 1 January 1951 and . . ." and the words ". . . as a result of such events," in article 1 A (2) were omitted.

3. The present Protocol shall be applied by the States Parties hereto without any geographic limitation, save that existing declarations made by States already Parties to the Convention in accordance with article 1 B (1) (*a*) of the Convention, shall, unless extended under article 1 B (2) thereof, apply also under the present Protocol.

Article 2. Co-operation of the National Authorities With the United Nations. 1. The States Parties to the present Protocol undertake to co-operate with the Office of the United Nations High Commissioner for Refugees, or any other agency of the United Nations which may succeed it, in the exercise of its functions, and shall in particular facilitate its duty of supervising the application of the provisions of the present Protocol.

2. In order to enable the Office of the High Commissioner or any other agency of the United Nations which may succeed it, to make reports to the competent organs of the United Nations, the States Parties to the present Protocol undertake to provide them with the information and statistical data requested, in the appropriate form, concerning:

(*a*) The condition of refugees;

(*b*) The implementation of the present Protocol;

(*c*) Laws, regulations and decrees which are, or may hereafter be, in force relating to refugees.

Article 3. Information on National Legislation. The States Parties to the present Protocol shall communicate to the Secretary-General of the United Nations the laws and regulations which they may adopt to ensure the application of the present Protocol.

Article 4. Settlement of Disputes. Any dispute between States Parties to the present Protocol which relates to its interpretation or application and which cannot be settled by other means shall be referred to the International Court of Justice at the request of any one of the parties to the dispute.

Article 5. Accession. The present Protocol shall be open for accession on behalf of all States Parties to the Convention and of any other State Member of the United Nations or member of any of the specialized agencies or to which an invitation to accede may have been addressed by the General Assembly of the United Nations. Accession shall be effected by the deposit of an instrument of accession with the Secretary-General of the United Nations.

Article 6. Federal Clause. In the case of a Federal or non-unitary State, the following provisions shall apply:

(*a*) With respect to those articles of the Convention to be applied in accordance with article 1, paragraph 1, of the present Protocol that come within the legislative jurisdiction of the federal legislative authority, the obligations of the Federal Government shall to this extent be the same as those of States Parties which are not Federal States;

(*b*) With respect to those articles of the Convention to be applied in accordance with article 1, paragraph 1, of the present Protocol that come within the legislative jurisdiction of constituent states, provinces or cantons which are not, under the constitutional system of the Federation, bound to take legislative action, the Federal Government shall bring such articles with a favourable recommendation to the notice of the appropriate authorities of states, provinces or cantons at the earliest possible moment;

(*c*) A Federal State Party to the present Protocol shall, at the request of any other State Party hereto transmitted through the Secretary-General of the United Nations, supply a statement of the law and practice of the Federation and its constituent units in regard to any particular provision of the Convention to be applied in accordance with article 1, paragraph 1, of the present Protocol, showing the extent to which effect has been given to that provision by legislative or other action.

Article 7. Reservations and Declarations. 1. At the time of accession, any State may make reservations in respect of article 4 of the present Protocol and in respect of the application in accordance with article 1 of the present Protocol of any provisions of the Convention other than those contained in articles 1, 3, 4, 16 (1) and 33 thereof, provided that in the case of a State Party to the Convention reservations made under this article shall not extend to refugees in respect of whom the Convention applies.

2. Reservations made by States Parties to the Convention in accordance with article 42 thereof shall, unless withdrawn, be applicable in relation to their obligations under the present Protocol.

3. Any State making a reservation in accordance with paragraph 1 of this article may at any time withdraw such reservation by a communication to that effect addressed to the Secretary-General of the United Nations.

4. Declarations made under article 40, paragraphs 1 and 2, of the Convention by a State Party thereto which accedes to the present Protocol, shall be deemed to apply in respect of the present Protocol, unless upon accession a notification to the contrary is addressed by the State Party concerned to the Secretary-General of the United Nations. The provisions of article 40, paragraphs 2 and 3, and of article 44, paragraph 3, of the Convention shall be deemed to apply *mutatis mutandis* to the present Protocol.

Article 8. Entry Into Force. 1. The present Protocol shall come into force on the day of deposit of the sixth instrument of accession.

2. For each State acceding to the Protocol after the de-

posit of the sixth instrument of accession, the Protocol shall come into force on the date of deposit by such State of its instrument of accession.

Article 9. Denunciation. 1. Any State Party hereto may denounce this Protocol at any time by a notification addressed to the Secretary-General of the United Nations.

2. Such denunciation shall take effect for the State Party concerned one year from the date on which it is received by the Secretary-General of the United Nations.

Article 10. Notifications by the Secretary-General of the United Nations. The Secretary-General of the United Nations shall inform the States referred to in article 5 above of the date of entry into force, accessions, reservations and withdrawals of reservations to and denunciations of the present Protocol, and of declarations and notifications relating hereto.

Article 11. Deposit in the Archives of the Secretary of the United Nations. A copy of the present Protocol, of which the Chinese, English, French, Russian and Spanish texts are equally authentic, signed by the President of the General Assembly and by the Secretary-General of the United Nations, shall be deposited in the archives of the Secretariat of the United Nations. The Secretary-General will transmit certified copies thereof to all States Members of the United Nations and to the other States referred to in article 5 above.

CONVENTION RELATING TO THE STATUS OF STATELESS PERSONS (1954).

The convention was adopted on 28 September 1954 by a Conference of Plenipotentiaries convened at the headquarters of the United Nations, New York, by the Economic and Social Council (resolution 526 A [XVII]). It entered into force on 6 June 1960. The convention defines a stateless person as "a person who is not considered as a national by any State under the operation of its law." States that ratify or accede to it undertake to grant to stateless persons approximately the same standard of treatment as is granted to refugees.

The text of the convention (United Nations, *Treaty Series,* vol. 360, p. 117) is as follows:

Preamble

The High Contracting Parties,

Considering that the Charter of the United Nations and the Universal Declaration of Human Rights approved on 10 December 1948 by the General Assembly of the United Nations have affirmed the principle that human beings shall enjoy fundamental rights and freedoms without discrimination,

Considering that the United Nations has, on various occasions, manifested its profound concern for stateless persons and endeavoured to assure stateless persons the widest possible exercise of these fundamental rights and freedoms,

Considering that only those stateless persons who are also refugees are covered by the Convention relating to the Status of Refugees of 28 July 1951, and that there are many stateless persons who are not covered by that Convention,

Considering that it is desirable to regulate and improve the status of stateless persons by an international agreement,

Have agreed as follows:

Chapter I
General Provisions

Article 1. Definition of the Term "Stateless Person." 1. For the purpose of this Convention, the term "stateless person" means a person who is not considered as a national by any State under the operation of its law.

2. This Convention shall not apply:

(i) To persons who are at present receiving from organs or agencies of the United Nations other than the United Nations High Commissioner for Refugees protection or assistance so long as they are receiving such protection or assistance;

(ii) To persons who are recognized by the competent authorities of the country in which they have taken residence as having the rights and obligations which are attached to the possession of the nationality of that country;

(iii) To persons with respect to whom there are serious reasons for considering that:

(*a*) They have committed a crime against peace, a war crime, or a crime against humanity, as defined in the international instruments drawn up to make provisions in respect of such crimes.

(*b*) They have committed a serious non-political crime outside the country of their residence prior to their admission to that country;

(*c*) They have been guilty of acts contrary to the purposes and principles of the United Nations.

Article 2. General Obligations. Every stateless person has duties to the country in which he finds himself, which require in particular that he conform to its laws and regulations as well as to measures taken for the maintenance of public order.

Article 3. Non-discrimination. The Contracting States shall apply the provisions of this Convention to stateless persons without discrimination as to race, religion or country of origin.

Article 4. Religion. The Contracting States shall accord to stateless persons within their territories treatment at least as favourable as that accorded to their nationals with respect to freedom to practise their religion and freedom as regards the religious education of their children.

Article 5. Rights Granted Apart From This Convention. Nothing in this Convention shall be deemed to impair any rights and benefits granted by a Contracting State to stateless persons apart from this Convention.

Article 6. The Term "In the Same Circumstances." For the purpose of this Convention, the term "in the same circumstances" implies that any requirements (including requirements as to length and conditions of sojourn or residence) which the particular individual would have to fulfil for the enjoyment of the right in question, if he were not a stateless person, must be fulfilled by him, with the exception of requirements which by their nature a stateless person is incapable of fulfilling.

Article 7. Exemption From Reciprocity. 1. Except where this Convention contains more favourable provisions, a Contracting State shall accord to stateless persons the same treatment as is accorded to aliens generally.

2. After a period of three years' residence, all stateless persons shall enjoy exemption from legislative reciprocity in the territory of the Contracting States.

3. Each Contracting State shall continue to accord to stateless persons the rights and benefits to which they were

already entitled, in the absence of reciprocity, at the date of entry into force of this Convention for that State.

4. The Contracting States shall consider favourably the possibility of according to stateless persons, in the absence of reciprocity, rights and benefits beyond those to which they are entitled according to paragraphs 2 and 3, and to extending exemption from reciprocity to stateless persons who do not fulfil the conditions provided for in paragraphs 2 and 3.

5. The provisions of paragraphs 2 and 3 apply both to the rights and benefits referred to in articles 13, 18, 19, 21 and 22 of this Convention and to rights and benefits for which this Convention does not provide.

Article 8. Exemption From Exceptional Measures. With regard to exceptional measures which may be taken against the person, property or interests of nationals or former nationals of a foreign State, the Contracting States shall not apply such measures to a stateless person solely on account of his having previously possessed the nationality of the foreign State in question. Contracting States which, under their legislation, are prevented from applying the general principle expressed in this article shall, in appropriate cases, grant exemptions in favour of such stateless persons.

Article 9. Provisional Measures. Nothing in this Convention shall prevent a Contracting State, in time of war or other grave and exceptional circumstances, from taking provisionally measures which it considers to be essential to the national security in the case of a particular person, pending a determination by the Contracting State that that person is in fact a stateless person and that the continuance of such measures is necessary in his case in the interests of national security.

Article 10. Continuity of Residence. 1. Where a stateless person has been forcibly displaced during the Second World War and removed to the territory of a Contracting State, and is resident there, the period of such enforced sojourn shall be considered to have been lawful residence within that territory.

2. Where a stateless person has been forcibly displaced during the Second World War from the territory of a Contracting State and has, prior to the date of entry into force of this Convention, returned there for the purpose of taking up residence, the period of residence before and after such enforced displacement shall be regarded as one uninterrupted period for any purposes for which uninterrupted residence is required.

Article 11. Stateless Seamen. In the case of stateless persons regularly serving as crew members on board a ship flying the flag of a Contracting State, that State shall give sympathetic consideration to their establishment on its territory and the issue of travel documents to them or their temporary admission to its territory particularly with a view to facilitating their establishment in another country.

Chapter II
Juridical Status

Article 12. Personal Status. 1. The personal status of a stateless person shall be governed by the law of the country of his domicile or, if he has no domicile, by the law of the country of his residence.

2. Rights previously acquired by a stateless person and dependent on personal status, more particularly rights attaching to marriage, shall be respected by a Contracting State, subject to compliance, if this be necessary, with the formalities required by the law of that State, provided that the right in question is one which would have been recognized by the law of that State had he not become stateless.

Article 13. Movable and Immovable Property. The Contracting States shall accord to a stateless person treatment as favourable as possible and, in any event, not less favourable than that accorded to aliens generally in the same circumstances, as regards the acquisition of movable and immovable property and other rights pertaining thereto, and to leases and other contracts relating to movable and immovable property.

Article 14. Artistic Rights and Industrial Property. In respect of the protection of industrial property, such as inventions, designs or models, trade marks, trade names, and of rights in literary, artistic and scientific works, a stateless person shall be accorded in the country in which he has his habitual residence the same protection as is accorded to nationals of that country. In the territory of any other Contracting State, he shall be accorded the same protection as is accorded in that territory to nationals of the country in which he has his habitual residence.

Article 15. Right of Association. As regards non-political and non-profit-making associations and trade unions the Contracting States shall accord to stateless persons lawfully staying in their territory treatment as favourable as possible, and in any event, not less favourable than that accorded to aliens generally in the same circumstances.

Article 16. Access to Courts. 1. A stateless person shall have free access to the courts of law on the territory of all Contracting States.

2. A stateless person shall enjoy in the Contracting State in which he has his habitual residence the same treatment as a national in matters pertaining to access to the courts, including legal assistance and exemption from *cautio judicatum solvi.*

3. A stateless person shall be accorded in the matters referred to in paragraph 2 in countries other than that in which he has his habitual residence the treatment granted to a national of the country of his habitual residence.

Chapter III
Gainful Employment

Article 17. Wage-earning Employment. 1. The Contracting States shall accord to stateless persons lawfully staying in their territory treatment as favourable as possible and, in any event, not less favourable that that accorded to aliens generally in the same circumstances, as regards the right to engage in wage-earning employment.

2. The Contracting States shall give sympathetic consideration to assimilating the rights of all stateless persons with regard to wage-earning employment to those of nationals, and in particular of those stateless persons who have entered their territory pursuant to programmes of labour recruitment or under immigration schemes.

Article 18. Self-employment. The Contracting States shall accord to a stateless person lawfully in their territory treatment as favourable as possible and, in any event, not less favourable than that accorded to aliens generally in the same circumstances, as regards the right to engage on his own account in agriculture, industry, handicrafts and commerce and to establish commercial and industrial companies.

Article 19. Liberal Professions. Each Contracting State shall accord to stateless persons lawfully staying in their territory who hold diplomas recognized by the competent authorities of that State, and who are desirous of practising a liberal profession, treatment as favourable as possible and, in any event, not less favourable than that accorded to aliens generally in the same circumstances.

Chapter IV
Welfare

Article 20. Rationing. Where a rationing system exists, which applies to the population at large and regulates the general distribution of products in short supply, stateless persons shall be accorded the same treatment as nationals.

Article 21. Housing. As regards housing, the Contracting States, in so far as the matter is regulated by laws or regulations or is subject to the control of public authorities, shall accord to stateless persons lawfully staying in their territory treatment as favourable as possible and, in any event, not less favourable than that accorded to aliens generally in the same circumstances.

Article 22. Public Education. 1. The Contracting States shall accord to stateless persons the same treatment as is accorded to nationals with respect to elementary education.

2. The Contracting States shall accord to stateless persons treatment as favourable as possible and, in any event, not less favourable than that accorded to aliens generally in the same circumstances, with respect to education other than elementary education and, in particular, as regards access to studies, the recognition of foreign school certificates, diplomas and degrees, the remission of fees and charges and the award of scholarships.

Article 23. Public Relief. The Contracting States shall accord to stateless persons lawfully staying in their territory the same treatment with respect to public relief and assistance as is accorded to their nationals.

Article 24. Labour Legislation and Social Security. 1. The Contracting States shall accord to stateless persons lawfully staying in their territory the same treatment as is accorded to nationals in respect of the following matters:

(*a*) In so far as such matters are governed by laws or regulations or are subject to the control of administrative authorities: remuneration, including family allowances where these form part of remuneration, hours of work, overtime arrangements, holidays with pay, restrictions on home work, minimum age of employment, apprenticeship and training, women's work and the work of young persons, and the enjoyment of the benefits of collective bargaining;

(*b*) Social security (legal provisions in respect of employment injury, occupational diseases, maternity, sickness, disability, old age, death, unemployment, family responsibilities and any other contingency which, according to national laws or regulations, is covered by a social security scheme), subject to the following limitations:

(i) There may be appropriate arrangements for the maintenance of acquired rights and rights in course of acquisition;

(ii) National laws or regulations of the country of residence may prescribe special arrangements concerning benefits or portions of benefits which are payable wholly out of public funds, and concerning allowances paid to persons who do not fulfil the contribution conditions prescribed for the award of a normal pension.

2. The right to compensation for the death of a stateless person resulting from employment injury or from occupational disease shall not be affected by the fact that the residence of the beneficiary is outside the territory of the Contracting State.

3. The Contracting States shall extend to stateless persons the benefits of agreements concluded between them, or which may be concluded between them in the future, concerning the maintenance of acquired rights and rights in the process of acquisition in regard to social security, subject only to the conditions which apply to nationals of the States signatory to the agreements in question.

4. The Contracting States will give sympathetic consideration to extending to stateless persons so far as possible the benefits of similar agreements which may at any time be in force between such Contracting States and non-contracting States.

Chapter V
Administrative Measures

Article 25. Administrative Assistance. 1. When the exercise of a right by a stateless person would normally require the assistance of authorities of a foreign country to whom he cannot have recourse, the Contracting State in whose territory he is residing shall arrange that such assistance be afforded to him by their own authorities.

2. The authority or authorities mentioned in paragraph 1 shall deliver or cause to be delivered under their supervision to stateless persons such documents or certifications as would normally be delivered to aliens by or through their national authorities.

3. Documents or certifications so delivered shall stand in the stead of the official instruments delivered to aliens by or through their national authorities and shall be given credence in the absence of proof to the contrary.

4. Subject to such exceptional treatment as may be granted to indigent persons, fees may be charged for the services mentioned herein, but such fees shall be moderate and commensurate with those charged to nationals for similar services.

5. The provisions of this article shall be without prejudice to articles 27 and 28.

Article 26. Freedom of Movement. Each Contracting State shall accord to stateless persons lawfully in its territory the right to choose their place of residence and to move freely within its territory, subject to any regulations applicable to aliens generally in the same circumstances.

Article 27. Identity Papers. The Contracting States shall issue identity papers to any stateless person in their territory who does not possess a valid travel document.

Article 28. Travel Documents. The Contracting States shall issue to stateless persons lawfully staying in their territory travel documents for the purpose of travel outside their territory, unless compelling reasons of national security or public order otherwise require, and the provisions of the Schedule to this Convention shall apply with respect to such documents. The Contracting States may issue such a travel document to any other stateless person in their territory; they shall in particular give sympathetic consideration to the issue of such a travel document to stateless persons in their territory who are unable to obtain a travel document from the country of their lawful residence.

Article 29. Fiscal Charges. 1. The Contracting States shall not impose upon stateless persons duties, charges or taxes, of any description whatsoever, other or higher than those which are or may be levied on their nationals in similar situations.

2. Nothing in the above paragraph shall prevent the application to stateless persons of the laws and regulations concerning charges in respect of the issue to aliens of administrative documents including identity papers.

Article 30. Transfer of Assets. 1. A Contracting State shall, in conformity with its laws and regulations, permit stateless persons to transfer assets which they have brought into its territory, to another country where they have been admitted for the purposes of resettlement.

2. A Contracting State shall give sympathetic consideration to the application of stateless persons for permission to transfer assets wherever they may be and which are necessary for their resettlement in another country to which they have been admitted.

Article 31. Expulsion. 1. The Contracting States shall not expel a stateless person lawfully in their territory save on grounds of national security or public order.

2. The expulsion of such a stateless person shall be only in pursuance of a decision reached in accordance with due process of law. Except where compelling reasons of national security otherwise require, the stateless person shall be allowed to submit evidence to clear himself, and to appeal to and be represented for the purpose before competent authority or a person or persons specially designated by the competent authority.

3. The Contracting States shall allow such a stateless person a reasonable period within which to seek legal admission into another country. The Contracting States reserve the right to apply during that period such internal measures as they may deem necessary.

Article 32. Naturalization. The Contracting States shall as far as possible facilitate the assimilation and naturalization of stateless persons. They shall in particular make every effort to expedite naturalization proceedings and to reduce as far as possible the charges and costs of such proceedings.

Chapter VI
Final Clauses

Article 33. Information on National Legislation. The Contracting States shall communicate to the Secretary-General of the United Nations the laws and regulations which they may adopt to ensure the application of this Convention.

Article 34. Settlement of Disputes. Any dispute between parties to this Convention relating to its interpretation or application, which cannot be settled by other means, shall be referred to the International Court of Justice at the request of any one of the parties to the dispute.

Article 35. Signature, Ratification and Accession. 1. This Convention shall be open for signature at the Headquarters of the United Nations until 31 December 1955.

2. It shall be open for signature on behalf of:

(*a*) Any State Member of the United Nations;

(*b*) Any other State invited to attend the United Nations Conference on the Status of Stateless Persons; and

(*c*) Any State to which an invitation to sign or to accede may be addressed by the General Assembly of the United Nations.

3. It shall be ratified and the instruments of ratification shall be deposited with the Secretary-General of the United Nations.

4. It shall be open for accession by the States referred to in paragraph 2 of this article. Accession shall be effected by the deposit of an instrument of accession with the Secretary-General of the United Nations.

Article 36. Territorial Application Clause. 1. Any State may, at the time of signature, ratification or accession, declare that this Convention shall extend to all or any of the territories for the international relations of which it is responsible. Such a declaration shall take effect when the Convention enters into force for the State concerned.

2. At any time thereafter any such extension shall be made by notification addressed to the Secretary-General of the United Nations and shall take effect as from the ninetieth day after the day of receipt by the Secretary-General of the United Nations of this notification, or as from the date of entry into force of the Convention for the State concerned, whichever is the later.

3. With respect to those territories to which this Convention is not extended at the time of signature, ratification or accession, each State concerned shall consider the possibility of taking the necessary steps in order to extend the application of this Convention to such territories, subject, where necessary for constitutional reasons, to the consent of the Governments of such territories.

Article 37. Federal Clause. In the case of a Federal or non-unitary State, the following provisions shall apply:

(*a*) With respect to those articles of this Convention that come within the legislative jurisdiction of the federal legislative authority, the obligations of the Federal Government shall to this extent be the same as those of Parties which are not Federal States;

(*b*) With respect to those articles of this Convention that come within the legislative jurisdiction of constituent states, provinces or cantons which are not, under the constitutional system of the Federation, bound to take legislative action, the Federal Government shall bring such articles with a favourable recommendation to the notice of the appropriate authorities of states, provinces or cantons at the earliest possible moment.

(*c*) A Federal State Party to this Convention shall, at the request of any other Contracting State transmitted through the Secretary-General of the United Nations, supply a statement of the law and practice of the Federation and its constituent units in regard to any particular provision of the Convention showing the extent to which effect has been given to that provision by legislative or other action.

Article 38. Reservations. 1. At the time of signature, ratification or accession, any State may make reservations to articles of the Convention other than to articles 1, 3, 4, 16 (1) and 33 to 42 inclusive.

2. Any State making a reservation in accordance with paragraph 1 of this article may at any time withdraw the reservation by a communication to that effect addressed to the Secretary-General of the United Nations.

Article 39. Entry Into Force. 1. This Convention shall come into force on the ninetieth day following the day of deposit of the sixth instrument of ratification or accession.

2. For each State ratifying or acceding to the Convention after the deposit of the sixth instrument of ratification or accession, the Convention shall enter into force on the ninetieth day following the date of deposit by such State of its instrument of ratification or accession.

Article 40. Denunciation. 1. Any Contracting State may denounce this Convention at any time by a notification addressed to the Secretary-General of the United Nations.

2. Such denunciation shall take effect for the Contracting State concerned one year from the date upon which it is received by the Secretary-General of the United Nations.

3. Any State which has made a declaration or notification under article 36 may, at any time thereafter, by a notification to the Secretary-General of the United Nations, declare that the Convention shall cease to extend to such

territory one year after the date of receipt of the notification by the Secretary-General.

Article 41. Revision. 1. Any Contracting State may request revision of this Convention at any time by a notification addressed to the Secretary-General of the United Nations.

2. The General Assembly of the United Nations shall recommend the steps, if any, to be taken in respect of such request.

Article 42. Notifications by the Secretary-General of the United Nations. The Secretary-General of the United Nations shall inform all Members of the United Nations and non-member States referred to in article 35:

(*a*) Of signatures, ratifications and accessions in accordance with article 35;

(*b*) Of declarations and notifications in accordance with article 36;

(*c*) Of reservations and withdrawals in accordance with article 38;

(*d*) Of the date on which this Convention will come into force in accordance with article 39;

(*e*) Of denunciations and notifications in accordance with article 40;

(*f*) Of requests for revision in accordance with article 41.

In faith whereof the undersigned, duly authorized, have signed this Convention on behalf of their respective Governments.

Done at New York, this twenty-eighth day of September, one thousand nine hundred and fifty-four, in a single copy, of which the English, French and Spanish texts are equally authentic and which shall remain deposited in the archives of the United Nations, and certified true copies of which shall be delivered to all Members of the United Nations and to the non-member States referred to in article 35.

SEE ALSO *Convention on the Reduction of Statelessness; Declaration on the Human Rights of Individuals who are not Nationals of the Country in which They Live; European Convention on Establishment and Protocol; Geneva Declaration on Palestine; Intifidah (Uprising) of the Palestinian People; Palestinian People's Rights.*

COORDINATING BOARD OF JEWISH ORGANIZATIONS.

An international non-governmental organization in consultative status (Category II) with the UN Economic and Social Council. Founded in New York in 1947, the board's function is to coordinate the United Nations work of its constituent organizations—which include the B'NAI B'RITH INTERNATIONAL COUNCIL and national bodies in South Africa and the United Kingdom—aimed at the promotion and protection of human rights, with special attention directed at combatting persecution and discrimination on grounds such as race, religion, and national or social origin.

CBJO publishes reports on its activities from time to time.

Coordinating Board of Jewish Organizations. Address: 1640 Rhode Island Avenue, N.W., Washington,

D.C., 20036 (USA). Telephone: (202) 857-6500. Executive Secretary: Thomas Neumann.

Yearbook of International Organizations 1989/90, (K.G. Saur).

COSTA RICA.

The Republic of Costa Rica is a country in Central America, between the Pacific Ocean and the Caribbean Sea. It has borders with Nicaragua and Panama. It achieved independence from Spain in 1821 and became a member of the United Nations in 1945. Its population is estimated by the UN (1990) to be 2,937,000. Ethnic groups include persons of European origin (96%), African origin (3%), and Amerindian origin (1%). Languages commonly used include Spanish and English. Christianity (Roman Catholic) is the State religion and the predominant faith. Literacy is estimated at 90%.

The government (1990) took the form of a republic. Under the 1949 constitution, the president is elected for a four-year term by popular vote and is not eligible for re-election. He exercises executive authority as head of State and government. Legislation is prepared by the 57-member unicameral Legislative Assembly, members of which also are elected for terms of four years. Political parties include the National Liberation Party, the Unity Party, the Communist Party, the *Pueblo Unido* Party, and the *Movimiento Nacional* Party.

Before the constitution of 1949 entered into force, an executive decree of 4 April 1942 prohibited entry into the country of aliens arriving as immigrants or temporary residents of "persons of the Negro race, Chinese, Arabs, Syrians, Turks, Armenians, Gypsies, coolies, etc." Restrictions against Chinese were abolished in 1943, and other restrictions were repealed in 1973. Article 33 of the 1949 constitution states: "All persons are equal before the law and no discrimination whatsoever may be practiced contrary to human dignity."

In order to promote the welfare of Costa Rica's indigenous populations, the National Indigenous Affairs Commission was established by Act No. 5251 of 19 June 1971.

COUNCIL OF EUROPE.

A regional intergovernmental organization composed of 21 States of western Europe, established in accordance with the COUNCIL OF EUROPE: STATUTE. The council endeavors to promote unity among its members for the purpose of safeguarding and realizing the ideals and principles which are their common heritage and facilitating their economic and social progress. It also works to improve living conditions and to develop human values; to uphold the principles of parliamentary democracy and human rights; and to demonstrate to Europeans that they live in a framework that goes beyond the individual State and that provides a "European dimension" to their lives.

The council's organizational structure includes the COMMITTEE OF MINISTERS OF THE COUNCIL OF EUROPE, composed of the foreign ministers of each member States or their alternates, which meets twice a year to take action on behalf of the council; the Consultative Assembly, composed of 170 members elected or appointed by their respective national parliaments, which meets three times a year to debate matters within its competence and to present its conclusions and recommendations to the Committee of Ministers; and the secretariat, consisting of the secretary-general, the deputy secretary-general, and such staff as may be required. The composition and functions of the Committee of Ministers are set out in detail in chapter IV of the statute of the council; those of the Consultative Assembly in chapter V; and those of the secretariat in chapter VI.

Since 1981, the council has awarded, every three years, the Council of Europe Human Rights Prize, consisting of a medal and a certificate, for outstanding work in the protection of human rights.

In addition to its human rights activities, the council is engaged in a broad range of activities, such as problems of the media in a democratic society; social and socio-economic matters; education, culture, and sport; youth; health; heritage and environment; local and regional government; and legal cooperation.

Among the council's publications are the *Yearbook of the European Convention on Human Rights,* issued annually; the *Human Rights Information Sheet,* issued twice a year; the *Digest of Strasbourg Case-law Relating to the European Convention on Human Rights,* issued annually in two series: Series A—*Judgements and Decisions,* and Series B—*Pleadings, Oral Arguments and Documents;* and the *European Treaty Series,* issued irregularly.

Council of Europe. Address: BP 431 R-6, F-67006 Strasbourg CEDEX, France. Telephone: (33) 88-61-49-61. Cable: EUROPA Strasbourg. Telex: EUR 870-943. Fax: 88-36-70-57. Secretary-General: Marcelino Oreja.

SEE ALSO "European" entries.

COUNCIL OF EUROPE: STATUTE (1949). The statute was prepared and adopted by representatives of Great Britain, France, Belgium, the Netherlands, Luxembourg, Norway, Sweden, Denmark, Ireland,

and Italy, who met in London, on 5 May 1949; it entered into force on 3 August of that year.

Under the statue, membership of the council is open to any European State invited to join by the COMMITTEE OF MINISTERS OF THE COUNCIL OF EUROPE on the ground that it is considered able and willing to fulfill the obligations set out in article 3 of the statue—i.e., to accept the principles of the rule of law and of the enjoyment by all persons within its jurisdiction of human rights and fundamental freedoms and to collaborate sincerely and effectively in the realization of the aims of the council.

The text of the statute *(European Treaty Series* No. 1), is as follows:

The Governments of the Kingdom of Belgium, the Kingdom of Denmark, the French Republic, the Irish Republic, the Italian Republic, the Grand Duchy of Luxembourg, the Kingdom of the Netherlands, the Kingdom of Norway, the Kingdom of Sweden and the United Kingdom of Great Britain and Northern Ireland;

Convinced that the pursuit of peace based upon justice and international co-operation is vital for the preservation of human society and civilisation;

Reaffirming their devotion to the spiritual and moral values which are the common heritage of their peoples and the true source of individual freedom, political liberty and the rule of law, principles which form the basis of all genuine democracy;

Believing that, for the maintenance and further realisation of these ideals and in the interests of economic and social progress, there is need of a closer unity between all like-minded countries of Europe;

Considering that, to respond to this need and to the expressed aspirations of their peoples in this regard, it is necessary forthwith to create an organisation which will bring European States into closer association,

Have in consequence decided to set up a Council of Europe consisting of a Committee of representatives of Governments and of a Consultative Assembly, and have for this purpose adopted the following Statute:

Chapter I
Aim of the Council of Europe

Article 1. (a) The aim of the Council of Europe is to achieve a greater unity between its Members for the purpose of safeguarding and realising the ideals and principles which are their common heritage and facilitating their economic and social progress.

(b) This aim shall be pursued through the organs of the Council by discussion of questions of common concern and by agreements and common action in economic, social, cultural, scientific, legal and administrative matters and in the maintenance and further realisation of human rights and fundamental freedoms.

(c) Participation in the Council of Europe shall not affect the collaboration of its Members in the work of the United Nations and of other international organisations or unions to which they are parties.

(d) Matters relating to National Defence do not fall within the scope of the Council of Europe.

Chapter II
Membership

Article 2. The Members of the Council of Europe are the Parties to this Statute.

Article 3. Every Member of the Council of Europe must accept the principles of the rule of law and of the enjoyment by all persons within its jurisdiction of human rights and fundamental freedoms, and collaborate sincerely and effectively in the realisation of the aim of the Council as specified in Chapter I.

Article 4. Any European State which is deemed to be able and willing to fulfil the provisions of Article 3 may be invited to become a Member of the Council of Europe by the Committee of Ministers. Any State so invited shall become a Member on the deposit on its behalf with the Secretary-General of an instrument of accession to the present Statute.

Article 5. (a) In special circumstances, a European country which is deemed to be able and willing to fulfil the provisions of Article 3 may be invited by the Committee of Ministers to become an Associate Member of the Council of Europe. Any country so invited shall become an Associate Member on the deposit on its behalf with the Secretary-General of an instrument accepting the present Statute. An associate Member shall be entitled to be represented in the Consultative Assembly only.

(b) The expression "Member" in this Statute includes an Associate Member except when used in connexion with representation on the Committee of Ministers.

Article 6. Before issuing invitations under Article 4 or 5 above, the Committee of Ministers shall determine the number of representatives on the Consultative Assembly to which the proposed Member shall be entitled and its proportionate financial contribution.

Article 7. Any Member of the Council of Europe may withdraw by formally notifying the Secretary-General of its intention to do so. Such withdrawal shall take effect at the end of the financial year in which it is notified, if the notification is given during the first nine months of that financial year. If the notification is given in the last three months of the financial year, it shall take effect at the end of the next financial year.

Article 8. Any Member of the Council of Europe which has seriously violated Article 3 may be suspended from its rights of representation and requested by the Committee of Ministers to withdraw under Article 7. If such Member does not comply with this request, the Committee may decide that it has ceased to be a Member of the Council as from such date as the Committee may determine.

Article 9. The Committee of Minsters may suspend the right of representation on the Committee and on the Consultative Assembly of a Member which has failed to fulfil its financial obligation during such period as the obligation remains unfulfilled.

Chapter III
General

Article 10. The organs of the Council of Europe are:

(i) the Committee of Ministers;

(ii) the Consultative Assembly.

Both these organs shall be served by the Secretariat of the Council of Europe.

Article 11. The seat of the Council of Europe is at Strasbourg.

Article 12. The official languages of the Council of Europe are English and French. The rules of procedure of the Committee of Ministers and of the Consultative Assembly shall determine in what circumstances and under what conditions other languages may be used.

Chapter IV
Committee of Ministers

Article 13. The Committee of Ministers is the organ which acts on behalf of the Council of Europe in accordance with Articles 15 and 16.

Article 14. Each Member shall be entitled to one representative on the Committee of Ministers, and each representative shall be entitled to one vote. Representatives on the Committee shall be the Ministers for Foreign Affairs. When a Minister for Foreign Affairs is unable to be present or in other circumstances where it may be desirable, an alternate may be nominated to act for him, who shall, whenever possible, be a member of his Government.

Article 15. (a) On the recommendation of the Consultative Assembly or on its own initiative, the Committee of Ministers shall consider the action required to further the aim of the Council of Europe, including the conclusion of conventions or agreements and the adoption by Governments of a common policy with regard to particular matters. Its conclusions shall be communicated to Members by the Secretary-General.

(b) In appropriate cases, the conclusions of the Committee may take the form of recommendations to the Governments of Members, and the Committee may request the Governments of Members to inform it of the action taken by them with regard to such recommendations.

Article 16. The Committee of Ministers shall, subject to the provisions of Articles 24, 28, 30, 32, 33 and 35, relating to the powers of the Consultative Assembly, decide with binding effect all matters relating to the internal organisation and arrangements of the Council of Europe. For this purpose the Committee of Ministers shall adopt such financial and administrative regulations as may be necessary.

Article 17. The Committee of Ministers may set up advisory and technical committees or commissions for such specific purposes as it may deem desirable.

Article 18. The Committee of Ministers shall adopt its rules of procedure, which shall determine amongst other things:

(i) the quorum;

(ii) the method of appointment and term of office of its President;

(iii) the procedure for the admission of items to its agenda, including the giving of notice of proposals for resolutions; and

(iv) the notifications required for the nomination of alternates under Article 14.

Article 19. At each session of the Consultative Assembly the Committee of Ministers shall furnish the Assembly with statements of its activities, accompanied by appropriate documentation.

Article 20. (a) Resolutions of the Committee of Ministers relating to the following important matters, namely:

(i) recommendations under Article 15 (b);

(ii) questions under Article 19;

(iii) questions under Article 21 (a) (i) and (b);

(iv) questions under Article 33;

(v) recommendations for the amendment of Articles I (d), 7, 15, 20 and 22; and

(vi) any other question which the Committee may, by a resolution passed under (d) below, decide should be subject to a unanimous vote on account of its importance require the unanimous vote of the representatives casting a vote, and of a majority of the representatives entitled to sit on the Committee.

(b) Questions arising under the rules of procedure or under the financial and administrative regulations may be decided by a simple majority vote of the representatives entitled to sit on the Committee.

(c) Resolutions of the Committee under Articles 4 and 5 require a two-thirds majority of all the representatives entitled to sit on the Committee.

(d) All other resolutions of the Committee, including the adoption of the Budget, of rules of procedure and of financial and administrative regulations, recommendations for the amendment of articles of this Statute, other than those mentioned in paragraph (a) (v) above, and deciding in case of doubt which paragraph of this Article applies, require a two-thirds majority of the representatives casting a vote and of a majority of the representatives entitled to sit on the Committee.

Article 21. (a) Unless the Committee decides otherwise, meetings of the Committee of Ministers shall be held:

    (i) in private, and

    (ii) at the seat of the Council.

(b) The Committee shall determine what information shall be published regarding the conclusions and discussions of a meeting held in private.

(c) The Committee shall meet before and during the beginning of every session of the Consultative Assembly and at such other times as it may decide.

Chapter V
Consultative Assembly

Article 22. The Consultative Assembly is the deliberative organ of the Council of Europe. It shall debate matters within its competence under this Statute and present its conclusions, in the form of recommendations, to the Committee of Ministers.

Article 23. (a) The Consultative Assembly may discuss and make recommendations upon any matter within the aim and scope of the Council of Europe as defined in Chapter I. It shall also discuss and may make recommendations upon any matter referred to it by the Committee of Ministers with a request for its opinion.

(b) The Assembly shall draw up its Agenda in accordance with the provisions of paragraph (a) above. In so doing, it shall have regard to the work of other European intergovernmental organisations to which some or all of the Members of the Council are parties.

(c) The President of the Assembly shall decide, in case of doubt, whether any question raised in the course of the Session is within the Agenda of the Assembly.

Article 24. The Consultative Assembly may, with due regard to the provisions of Article 38 (d), establish committees or commissions to consider and report to it on any matter which falls within its competence under Article 23, to examine and prepare questions on its agenda and to advise on all matters of procedure.

Article 25. (a) The Consultative Assembly shall consist of Representatives of each Member elected by its Parliament or appointed in such manner as that Parliament shall decide, subject, however, to the right of each Member Government to make any additional appointments necessary when the Parliament is not in session and has not laid down the procedure to be followed in that case. Each Representative must be a national of the Member whom he represents, but shall not at the same time be a member of the Committee of Ministers.

The term of office of Representatives thus appointed will date from the opening of the Ordinary Session following their appointment; it will expire at the opening of the next Ordinary Session except that, in the event of elections to their Parliaments having taken place, Members shall be entitled to make new appointments.

If a Member fills vacancies due to death or resignation, or proceeds to make new appointments as a result of elections to its Parliament, the term of office of the new Representatives shall date from the first Sitting of the Assembly following their appointment.

(b) No Representative shall be deprived of his position as such during a session of the Assembly without the agreement of the Assembly.

(c) Each Representative may have a substitute who may, in the absence of the Representative, sit, speak and vote in his place. The provisions of paragraph (a) above apply to the appointment of substitutes.

Article 26. Members shall be entitled to the number of Representatives given below:

Austria, 6; Belgium, 7; Denmark, 5; France, 18; Germany (Federal Republic), 18; Greece, 7; Iceland, 3; Ireland, 4; Italy, 18; Luxembourg, 3; Netherlands, 7; Norway, 5; Sweden, 6; Turkey, 10; United Kingdom of Great Britain and Northern Ireland, 18.

Article 27. The conditions under which the Committee of Ministers collectively may be represented in the debates of the Consultative Assembly, or individual representatives on the Committee or their alternates may address the Assembly, shall be determined by such rules of procedure on this subject as may be drawn up by the Committee after consultation with the Assembly.

Article 28. (a) The Consultative Assembly shall adopt its rules of procedure and shall elect from its members its President, who shall remain in office until the next ordinary session.

(b) The President shall control the proceedings but shall not take part in the debate or vote. The substitute of the Representative who is President may sit, speak and vote in his place.

(c) The rules of procedure shall determine *inter alia:*

    (i) the quorum;

    (ii) the manner of the election and terms of office of the President and other officers;

    (iii) the manner in which the agenda shall be drawn up and be communicated to Representatives; and

    (iv) the time and manner in which the names of Representatives and their Substitutes shall be notified.

Article 29. Subject to the provisions of Article 30, all resolutions of the Consultative Assembly, including resolutions:

    (i) embodying recommendations to the Committee of Ministers;

    (ii) proposing to the Committee matters for discussion in the Assembly;

    (iii) establishing committees or commissions;

    (iv) determining the date of commencement of its sessions;

    (v) determining what majority is required for resolutions in cases not covered by (i) to (iv) above or determining cases of doubt as to what majority is required, shall require a two-thirds majority of the Representatives casting a vote.

Article 30. On matters relating to its internal procedure, which includes the election of officers, the nomination of persons to serve on committees and commissions and the adoption of rules of procedure, resolutions of the Consultative Assembly shall be carried by such majorities as the Assembly may determine in accordance with Article 29 (v).

Article 31. Debates on proposals to be made to the Committee of Ministers that a matter should be placed on the Agenda of the Consultative Assembly shall be confined to an indication of the proposed subject-matter and the reasons for and against its inclusion in the Agenda.

Article 32. The Consultative Assembly shall meet in ordinary session once a year, the date and duration of which shall be determined by the Assembly so as to avoid as far as possible overlapping with parliamentary sessions of Members and with sessions of the General Assembly of the United Nations. In no circumstances shall the duration of an ordinary session exceed one month unless both the Assembly and the Committee of Ministers concur.

Article 33. Ordinary sessions of the Consultative Assembly shall be held at the seat of the Council unless both the Assembly and the Committee of Ministers concur that the session should be held elsewhere.

Article 34. The Consultative Assembly may be convened in extraordinary session, upon the initiative either of the Committee of Ministers or of the President of the Assembly after agreement between them, such agreement also to determine the date and place of the session.

Article 35. Unless the Consultative Assembly decides otherwise, its debates shall be conducted in public.

Chapter VI
Secretariat

Article 36. (a) The Secretariat shall consist of a Secretary-General, a Deputy Secretary-General and such other staff as may be required.

(b) The Secretary-General and Deputy Secretary-General shall be appointed by the Consultative Assembly on the recommendation of the Committee of Ministers.

(c) The remaining staff of the Secretariat shall be appointed by the Secretary-General, in accordance with the administrative regulations.

(d) No members of the Secretariat shall hold any salaried office from any Government or be a member of the Consultative Assembly or of any legislature or engage in any occupation incompatible with his duties.

(e) Every member of the staff of the Secretariat shall make a solemn declaration affirming that his duty is to the Council of Europe and that he will perform his duties conscientiously, uninfluenced by any national considerations, and that he will not seek or receive instructions in connexion with the performance of his duties from any Government or any authority external to the Council and will refrain from any action which might reflect on his position as an international official responsible only to the Council. In the case of the Secretary-General and the Deputy Secretary-General this declaration shall be made before the Committee, and in the case of all other members of the staff, before the Secretary-General.

(f) Every Members shall respect the exclusively international character of the responsibilities of the Secretary-General and the staff of the Secretariat and not seek to influence them in the discharge of their responsibilities.

Article 37. (a) The Secretariat shall be located at the seat of the Council.

(b) The Secretary-General is responsible to the Committee of Ministers for the work of the Secretariat. Amongst other things, he shall, subject to Article 38 (d), provide such secretariat and other assistance as the Consultative Assembly may require.

Chapter VII
Finance

Article 38. (a) Each Member shall bear the expenses of its own representation in the Committee of Ministers and in the Consultative Assembly.

(b) The expenses of the Secretariat and all other common expenses shall be shared between all Members in such proportions as shall be determined by the Committee on the basis of the population of Members.

The contributions of an Associate Member shall be determined by the Committee.

(c) In accordance with the financial regulations, the budget of the Council shall be submitted annually by the Secretary-General for adoption by the Committee.

(d) The Secretary-General shall refer to the Committee requests from the Assembly which involve expenditure exceeding the amount already allocated in the Budget for the Assembly and its activities.

(e) The Secretary-General shall also submit to the Committee of Ministers an estimate of the expenditure to which the implementation of each of the recommendations presented to the Committee would give rise. Any resolution the implementation of which requires additional expenditure shall not be considered as adopted by the Committee of Ministers unless the Committee has also approved the corresponding estimates for such additional expenditure.

Article 39. The Secretary-General shall each year notify the Government of each Member of the amount of its contribution, and each Member shall pay to the Secretary-General the amount of its contribution, which shall be deemed to be due on the date of its notification, not later than six months after that date.

Chapter VIII
Privileges and Immunities

Article 40. (a) The Council of Europe, representatives of Members and the Secretariat shall enjoy in the territories of its Members such privileges and immunities as are reasonably necessary for the fulfilment of their functions. These immunities shall include immunity for all Representatives to the Consultative Assembly from arrest and all legal proceedings in the territories of all Members, in respect of words spoken and votes cast in the debates of the Assembly or its committees or commissions.

(b) The Members undertake as soon as possible to enter into agreement for the purpose of fulfilling the provisions of paragraph (a) above. For this purpose the Committee of Ministers shall recommend to the Governments of Members the acceptance of an Agreement defining the privileges and immunities to be granted in the territories of all Members. In addition a special Agreement shall be concluded with the Government of the French Republic defining the privileges and immunities which the Council shall enjoy at its seat.

C

Chapter IX
Amendments

Article 41. (a) Proposals for the amendment of this Statute may be made in the Committee of Ministers or, in the conditions provided for in Article 23, in the Consultative Assembly.

(b) The Committee shall recommend and cause to be embodied in a Protocol those amendments which it considers to be desirable.

(c) An amending Protocol shall come into force when it has been signed and ratified on behalf of two-thirds of the Members.

(d) Notwithstanding the provisions of the preceding paragraphs of this Article, amendments to Articles 23—35, 38 and 39 which have been approved by the Committee and by the Assembly, shall come into force on the date of the certificate of the Secretary-General, transmitted to the Governments of Members, certifying that they have been so approved. This paragraph shall not operate until the conclusion of the second ordinary session of the Assembly.

Chapter X
Final Provisions

Article 42. (a) This Statute shall be ratified. Ratifications shall be deposited with the Government of the United Kingdom of Great Britain and Northern Ireland.

(b) The present Statute shall come into force as soon as seven instruments of ratification have been deposited. The Government of the United Kingdom shall transmit to all signatory Governments a certificate declaring that the Statute has entered into force and giving the names of the Members of the Council of Europe on that date.

(c) Thereafter each other signatory shall become a party to this Statute as from the date of the deposit of its instrument of ratification.

COURTS OF HUMAN RIGHTS. Two international courts of human rights have been established: the EUROPEAN COURT OF HUMAN RIGHTS and the INTER-AMERICAN COURT OF HUMAN RIGHTS.

CRIME PREVENTION, DEVELOPMENT, AND HUMAN RIGHTS. The seventh United Nations Congress on Prevention of Crime and the Treatment of Offenders, which met at Milan from 26 August to 6 September 1985, adopted a resolution (UN publication, sales no. E.86.IV.I, chap. E [22]) in which it emphasized that basic crime prevention strategy must seek to eliminate the causes and conditions that favor crime, bearing in mind that racial discrimination, including *apartheid,* unemployment, illiteracy, the deterioration of living conditions in certain regions of the world—in particular regarding grave economic situation confronting African and many other countries—and any form of violation of human rights and fundamental freedoms constitute especially negative factors in this respect.

The congress expressed the view that programs of crime prevention and treatment of offenders must be grounded in the political, economic, social, and cultural realities of each country and implemented in a climate of freedom and respect for human rights and that it is essential that UN member States develop an effective capacity for the formulation and planning of crime prevention policies in coordination with their strategies for economic, political, social, and cultural development. Deploring the increase and gravity of crime in different parts of the world, it called upon member States "to take all measures within their power to eliminate conditions of life that degrade human dignity and are factors relevant to crime, including unemployment, poverty, illiteracy, racial discrimination, *apartheid* and social injustice;" and recommended that all States promote the broadest possible participation of the people in political, social, and other measures designed to prevent crime.

SEE ALSO Milan Plan of Action.

CRIMES AGAINST THE PEACE AND SECURITY OF MANKIND. The UN General Assembly affirmed, at its 1946 session (resolution 94 [I]) the PRINCIPLES OF INTERNATIONAL LAW RECOGNIZED BY THE CHARTER OF THE NURMBERG TRIBUNAL AND THE JUDGMENT OF THE TRIBUNAL and directed its Committee on the Codification of International Law "to treat as a matter of primary importance plans for the formulation, in the context of a general codification of offenses against the peace and security of mankind, or of an International Criminal Code, of the principles recognized" in that charter and judgment. That committee did not undertake this task itself but recommended to the General Assembly the establishment of an international law commission, which the assembly established on 21 November 1947 (resolution 174 [II]). The assembly directed the new INTERNATIONAL LAW COMMISSION (resolution 177 [II]) to

(a) formulate the principles of international law recognized in the Charter of the Nurmberg Tribunal and in the Judgment of the Tribunal, and

(b) prepare a draft code of offenses against the peace and security of mankind, indicating clearly the place to be accorded to the principles mentioned in subparagraph (a) above.

On the basis of a report submitted by a special rapporteur, the commission completed its formulation of principles and submitted it to the General Assembly. The principles, in part, are as follows (UN Doc. A/1316, pt. three, para. 98–127):

Principle 1. Any person who commits an act which constitutes a crime under international law is responsible therefor and liable to punishment. . . .

Principle 6. The crimes hereinafter set out are punishable as crimes under international law:

(a) Crimes against peace:

(i) planning, preparation, initiation or waging a war of aggression or a war in violation of international treaties, agreements or assurances;

(ii) participation in a common plan or conspiracy for the accomplishment of any of the acts mentioned under (i).

(b) War crimes: Violations of the laws or customs of war which include, but are not limited to, murder, ill-treatment or deportation to slave-labor or for any other purpose of civilian population of or in occupied territory, murder or ill-treatment of prisoners of war, of persons on the seas, killing of hostages, plunder of public or private property, wanton destruction of cities, towns or villages, or devastation not justified by military necessity.

(c) Crimes against humanity: Murder, extermination, enslavement, deportation and other inhuman acts done against any civilian population, or persecutions on political, racial or religious grounds, when such acts are done or such persecutions are carried out in execution of or in connection with any crime against peace or any war crime.

Principle 7. Complicity in the commission of a crime against peace, a war crime, or a crime against humanity as set forth in Principle 6 is a crime under international law.

As regards the draft code of offenses, the commission's drafting sub-committee prepared a provisional draft code which was referred to the special rapporteur, who was requested to submit a further report.

The General Assembly, at its 1950 session, invited the governments of member States to furnish their observations on the formulation prepared by the commission and requested the commission, in preparing the draft code of offenses against the peace and security of mankind, to take account of any observations made on the formulation.

In 1951, the commission adopted a draft Code of Offenses against the Peace and Security of Mankind (UN Doc. A/1858, para. 57–58) and submitted it to the General Assembly. Three years later, in 1954, the commission made some changes in the previously adopted text and transmitted a revised version of the draft code to the assembly.

At its 1954 session, the General Assembly examined the draft code, found that it raised a number of problems closely related to the question of the definition of AGGRESSION, and decided (resolution 898 [IX]) to postpone further consideration of the code until its Special Committee on the Question of Defining Aggression had submitted its report.

There followed a long series of postponements and delays, even after the General Assembly had adopted by consensus the "Definition of Aggression" on 14 December 1974 (resolution 3314 [XXIX, annex]).

Finally, in 1981, the assembly resumed its invitation to the International Law Commission to proceed with its work on the draft Code of Offenses against the Peace and Security of Mankind. The commission did so; and, as the work progressed, it recommended that the title of the topic be changed to "Draft Code of Crimes against the Peace and Security of Mankind." The assembly expressed its agreement with this recommendation in 1987.

At the end of 1989, the commission had not completed the preparation of the draft code. However, in its 1989 annual report to the assembly, it presented the texts of all the draft articles which it had provisionally adopted up to that time (UN Doc. A/44/10, para. 217), as follows:

Chapter I—Introduction
Part I. Definition and Characterization

Article 1. Definition. The crimes [under international law] defined in this draft Code constitute crimes against the peace and security of mankind.

Article 2. Characterization. The characterization of an act or omission as a crime against the peace and security of mankind is independent of internal law. The fact that an act or omission is or is not punishable under internal law does not affect this characterization.

Part II. General Principles

Article 3. Responsibility and Punishment. 1. Any individual who commits a crime against the peace and security of mankind is responsible for such crime irrespective of any motives invoked by the accused that are not covered by the definition of the offence and is liable to punishment therefor.

2. Prosecution of an individual for a crime against the peace and security of mankind does not relieve a State of any responsibility under international law for an act or omission attributable to it.

Article 4. Obligation to Try or Extradite. 1. Any State in whose territory an individual alleged to have committed a crime against the peace and security of mankind is present shall either try or extradite him.

2. If extradition is requested by several States, special consideration shall be given to the request of the States in whose territory the crime was committed.

3. The provisions of paragraphs 1 and 2 of this article do not prejudge the establishment and the jurisdiction of an international criminal court. (This paragraph will be deleted if an international criminal court is established.)

Article 5. Non-applicability of Statutory Limitations. No statutory limitation shall apply to crimes against the peace and security of mankind.

Article 6. Judicial Guarantees. Any individual charged with a crime against the peace and security of mankind shall be entitled without discrimination to the minimum guarantees due to all human beings with regard to the law and the facts. In particular:

1. He shall have the right to be presumed innocent until proved guilty;

2. He shall have the rights:

(a) In the determination of any charge against him, to have a fair and public hearing by a competent, independent and impartial tribunal duly established by law or by treaty;

(b) To be informed promptly and in detail in a language which he understands of the nature and cause of the charge against him;

(c) To have adequate time and facilities for the preparation of his defence and to communicate with counsel of his own choosing;

(d) To be tried without undue delay;

(e) To be tried in his presence, and to defend himself in person or through legal assistance of his own choosing; to be informed, if he does not have legal assistance, of this right; and to have legal assistance assigned to him and without payment by him in any such case if he does not have sufficient means to pay for it;

(f) To examine, or have examined, the witnesses against him and to obtain the attendance and examination of witnesses on his behalf under the same conditions as witnesses against him;

(g) To have the free assistance of an interpreter if he cannot understand or speak the language used in court;

(h) Not to be compelled to testify against himself or to confess guilt.

Article 7. Non bis in idem. [1. No one shall be liable to be tried or punished for a crime under this Code for which he has already been finally convicted or acquitted by an international criminal court.]

2. Subject to paragraphs 3, 4 and 5 of this article, no one shall be liable to be tried or punished for a crime under this Code in respect of an act for which he has already been finally convicted or acquitted by a national court, provided that, if a punishment was imposed, it has been enforced or is in the process of being enforced.

3. Notwithstanding the provisions of paragraph 2, an individual may be tried and punished [by an international criminal court or] by a national court for a crime under this Code if the act which was the subject of a trial and judgement as an ordinary crime corresponds to one of the crimes characterized in this Code.

4. Notwithstanding the provisions of paragraph 2, an individual may be tried and punished by a national court of another State for a crime under this Code:

(a) if the act which was the subject of the previous judgement took place on the territory of that State;

(b) if that State has been the main victim of the crime.

5. In the case of a subsequent conviction under this Code, the court, in passing sentence, shall deduct any penalty imposed and implemented as a result of a previous conviction for the same act.

Article 8. Non-retroactivity. 1. No one shall be convicted under this Code for acts committed before its entry into force.

2. Nothing in this article shall preclude the trial and punishment of anyone for any act which, at the time when it was committed, was criminal in accordance with international law or domestic law applicable in conformity with international law. . . .

Article 10. Responsibility of the Superior. The fact that a crime against the peace and security of mankind was committed by a subordinate does not relieve his superiors of criminal responsibility, if they knew or had information enabling them to conclude, in the circumstances at the time, that the subordinate was committing or was going to commit such a crime and if they did not take all feasible measures within their power to prevent or repress the crime.

Article 11. Official Position and Criminal Responsibility. The official position of the individual who commits a crime against the peace and security of mankind, and particularly the fact that he acts as Head of State or Government, does not relieve him of criminal responsibility.

Chapter II—Acts Constituting Crimes Against the Peace and Security of Mankind
Part I. Crimes against Peace

Article 12. Aggression. 1. Any individual to whom responsibility for acts constituting aggression is attributed under this Code shall be liable to be tried and punished for a crime against peace.

2. Aggression is the use of armed force by a State against the sovereignty, territorial integrity or political independence of another State, or in any other manner inconsistent with the Charter of the United Nations.

3. The first use of armed force by a State in contravention of the Charter shall constitute *prima facie* evidence of an act of aggression although the Security Council may, in conformity with the Charter, conclude that a determination that an act of aggression has been committed would not be justified in the light of other relevant circumstances, including the fact that the acts concerned or their consequences are not of sufficient gravity.

4. [In particular] any of the following acts, regardless of a declaration of war, constitutes an act of aggression, due regard being paid to paragraphs 2 and 3 of this article:

(a) The invasion or attack by the armed forces of a State of the territory of another State, or any military occupation, however temporary, resulting from such invasion or attack, or any annexation by the use of force of the territory of another State or part thereof;

(b) Bombardment by the armed forces of a State against the territory of another State or the use of any weapons by a State against the territory of another State;

(c) The blockade of the ports or coasts of a State by the armed forces of another State;

(d) An attack by the armed forces of a State on the land, sea or air forces, or marine and air fleets of another State;

(e) The use of armed forces of one State which are within the territory of another State with the agreement of the receiving State, in contravention of the conditions provided for in the agreement, or any extension of their presence in such territory beyond the termination of the agreement;

(f) The action of a State in allowing its territory, which it has placed at the disposal of another State, to be used by that other State for perpetrating an act of aggression against a third State;

(g) The sending by or on behalf of a State of armed bands, groups, irregulars or mercenaries, which carry out acts of armed force against another State of such gravity as to amount to the acts listed above, or its substantial involvement therein;

(h) Any other acts determined by the Security Council as constituting acts of aggression under the provisions of the Charter.

[5. Any determination by the Security Council as to the existence of an act of aggression is binding on national courts.]

6. Nothing in this article shall be interpreted as in any way enlarging or diminishing the scope of the Charter of the United Nations including its provisions concerning cases in which the use of force is lawful.

7. Nothing in this article could in any way prejudice the right to self-determination, freedom and independence, as derived from the Charter, of peoples forcibly deprived of that right and referred to in the Declaration on Principles of International Law concerning Friendly Relations and Co-operation among States in accordance with the Charter of the United Nations, particularly peoples under colonial and racist regimes or other forms of alien domination; nor the right of these peoples to struggle to that end and to seek and receive support, in accordance with the principles of the Charter and in conformity with the above-mentioned Declaration.

Article 13. Threat of Aggression. Threat of aggression consisting of declarations, communications, demonstrations of force or any other measures which would give good reason to the Government of a State to believe that aggression is being seriously contemplated against that State.

Article 14. Intervention. 1. Intervention in the internal or external affairs of a State by fomenting [armed] subversive or terrorist activities or by organizing, assisting or financing such activities, or supplying arms for the purpose of such activities, thereby [seriously] undermining the free exercise by that State of its sovereign rights.

2. Nothing in this article shall in any way prejudice the right of peoples to self-determination as enshrined in the Charter of the United Nations.

Article 15. Colonial Domination and Other Forms of Alien Domination. Establishment or maintenance by force of colonial domination or any other form of alien domination contrary to the right of peoples to self-determination as enshrined in the Charter of the United Nations.

SEE ALSO *Convention on the Non-Applicability of Statutory Limitations to War Crimes and Crimes against Humanity; European Convention on the Non-Applicability of Statutory Limitations on Crimes against Humanity and War Crimes.*

CUBA. The Republic of Cuba is a country occupying the largest and westernmost of the West Indian Islands, situated at the point where the Atlantic Ocean, the Caribbean Sea, and the Gulf of Mexico converge. It achieved independence from Spain in 1899 and became a member of the United Nations in 1945. Its population is estimated by the UN (1990) to be 10,540,000. Ethnic groups include persons of Spanish, African, American, and mixed origins. The language in common use is Spanish. Literacy is estimated at 96%.

The government (1990) took the form of a republic. Executive authority is exercised by the president and 31-member Council of State, both elected by the National Assembly of People's Power. Members of the assembly are elected by popular vote, suffrage being universal for all citizens 16 years of age or older who have not applied for permanent emigration, and serve for terms of five years. The Communist Party of Cuba is the only recognized political party; the first secretary of the party is president of the Council of State and of the country. The judiciary is subordinate to the Council of State.

The Cuban Social Democratic Party is reported to function underground but is not recognized by the government and holds no group meetings. Its founder, Roberto Luque Escalona is its only known member. There, is, however, a small human rights movement, some members of which were reported to have been arrested for applauding international scrutiny of the human rights situation in the country.

Discovered by Columbus in 1492, Cuba served as a base for Spanish exploration of the Americas. The indigenous Arawak Indians were soon decimated by the colonists, who replaced them by slaves imported from Africa. After slavery was abolished in the 1880s, the freed black workers and their offspring contributed much to the social and political development of the island, if only by periodic revolts against their miserable lot. The colonial element was, however, constantly replenished by immigrants from Europe; and a wealthy, well-governed Cuba achieved representation in the Spanish *Cortes* in 1810. Withdrawal of this representation in 1848 led to a series of revolts against Spanish rule, some of which were supported by the United States of America.

After the sinking of the *Maine* in Havana Harbor, the forces of Cuba and the U.S.A. combined against the Spanish. The treaty that ended the Spanish–American War established Cuba as an independent republic but gave the United States government the right to intervene in Cuban affairs—an arrangement that was criticized as imperialism in Latin America and opposed by many in the United States. The United States' right to intervene was abandoned in 1934, when a new era of friendly relations with Cuba was inaugurated under the Franklin Roosevelt administration. This era ended, however, shortly after the Batista government was overthrown by the revolutionary government headed by Fidel Castro on 1 January 1959. A trade boycott of Cuba was imposed by the United States in 1960 and has since been tightened. In 1961, a band of anti-Castro immigrants, financed, trained, and supported by the U.S.A., attempted to invade Cuba but were routed in Cochinos Bay.

The nature and extent of human rights violations in Cuba is difficult to ascertain because of conflicting propaganda claims and the refusal of the Cuban government to cooperate with international organizations anxious to make on-the-spot investigations. However, allegations persist that a large number of political prisoners are being held in detention after arbitrary or summary trials and that some are subjected to systematic torture.

Thus, the **INTER-AMERICAN COMMISSION ON HUMAN**

C

RIGHTS, in its annual report for 1985–1986, emphasized that (OAS Doc. OEA/Ser. L/V/II.68, Doc. 8/Rev. 1, pp. 130–132) "the Government of Cuba has continued to deny it cooperation during the period. This prevents it from learning the opinion and point of view of that Government on the general state of human rights in that country and especially on the particular situations presented in the individual cases being processed."

Despite the lack of cooperation by Cuba, the OAS Commission on Human Rights stated, on the basis of information made available to it by other reliable sources,

that the situation of human rights in Cuba is not very different from that described in the evaluation contained in the 1983 Report and in its last Annual Report. Therefore, the two fundamental factors that have led to a lack of observance of civil and political rights persist: the concentration of power in the hands of a small group of persons since the beginning of the present political process, and the non-existence of a constitutional state since individuals are deprived of the remedies that protect them against acts of the state.

In its previous annual report, the commission had expressed the hope that domestic and international conditions would be created that would permit former political prisoners, who had been released by the government—and their family members—to leave Cuba and settle in the country of their choice, and added that:

this was the result of a series of efforts made by the U.S. Episcopal Conference and by the explorer Jacques Cousteau with the Cuban authorities. Senator Edward Kennedy succeeded in obtaining the release of Mr. Ricardo Montero Duque, one of the Commanders of the Bay of Pigs invasion. The Commission must reiterate this statement at this time, which refers especially to the entry facilities which ought to be provided by the immigration agencies of the United States, thereby to carry out the commitments adopted during the dialogue which resulted in the freeing of persons in 1979. Estimates provided to the Commission state that approximately 1,500 persons are affected by this situation.

The commission reported that 70 "*plantado*" (long-term) political prisoners had been freed and that 69 of them had departed from Cuba—one, unfortunately, died on the way to the airport—as well as 43 relatives of the released prisoners. It further reported that approximately 110 *plantado* political prisoners remained in detention.

As regards the situation of human rights advocacy groups, the committee drew attention to the case of Mr. Ricardo Bofil Pagés,

who was the President of the University of Havana and was released, after having been deprived of his freedom for

eight years on conviction for charges that were clearly of a political nature. Mr. Bofil had established an organization for the defense of human rights while in prison and was interested in continuing those activities after his release. In August however, Mr. Bofil had to seek asylum in the French Embassy in Cuba because of persistent threats to which he was subject. The IACHR hopes that a rapid solution will be found to the situation which affects Mr. Bofil.

The Commission has also learned that several days after Mr. Bofil sought asylum, the Cuban authorities arrested Messrs. Domingo Delgado Castro and Jose Luis Alvarado Delgado, both belonging to the human rights defense body presided over by Mr. Bofil. Pursuant to the information submitted both have been accused by the authorities of being "terrorists who are acting against the Cuban State," for which reason "they do not represent human rights." The Commission must profoundly regret this type of action on the part of the Cuban Government which impedes the activity of independent bodies to defend the elementary rights of the human person.

For some time, the OAS commission followed closely developments concerning relations between the government of Cuba and the Catholic Church. In its 1985–1986 report, it noted that the Cuban National Ecclesiastical Meeting had been held for the first time since 1959 and had been attended by Cardinal Eduardo Pironio as the representative of the Pope. The commission expressed the hope that this demonstration of the willingness of the government to enter into a dialogue with the Catholic community of Cuba would have a positive impact on religious freedom, and especially on the possibility of persons professing a religious belief to have access to decisionmaking positions, which will thus eliminate the monopoly so far held by members of the Communist Party. It also expressed the hope that this development may be translated into the grant of greater facilities for the dissemination of religious beliefs through the media and that this process will also have a positive impact on the Cuban educational system.

The UN **COMMISSION ON HUMAN RIGHTS,** at its 1988 session, considered a draft resolution submitted by the United States of America, entitled "Situation of Human Rights and Fundamental Freedoms in Cuba" (UN Doc. E/CN.4/1988/L.26) and a draft resolution submitted by Cuba entitled "Policy of Human Rights Violations of the Government of the United States of America" (UN Doc. E/CN.4/1988/L.35).

At a meeting of the commission held on 9 March 1988, the representative of Colombia announced that the delegations of Argentina, Mexico, Peru, and Colombia had held consultations with other members of the commission, and with the delegation of Cuba, in an effort to make a constructive contribution to the commission's work. Cuba had offered to invite the chairman of the commission, and the representatives of a number of member States designated regionally, to visit the country for the purpose of observing the human rights situation there. The observer for Cuba confirmed the invitation and stated that the Cuban government would facilitate access by the members of the commission to the competent authorities, to the officials dealing with prisons and penetentiaries, and to all documents of interest. The commission adopted without a vote the proposal submitted by Argentina, Colombia, Mexico, and Peru and decided that, under the circumstances, votes were no longer required on the proposals which had been submitted by the United States of America and by Cuba.

On 31 May 1988, the chairman of the commission announced the membership of the group which would visit Cuba. The group, under the chairmanship of Ambassador Alioune Sene, from Senegal, in his capacity as chairman of the Commission on Human Rights, was composed, after regional consultations, of the following members: Ambassador J. Sefi Attah, from Nigeria, representing the African group; Ambassador Todor Dichev, from Bulgaria, representing the eastern European group; Under-Secretary for Foreign Affairs Jose D. Ingles, from the Philippines, representing the Asian group; Ambassador Michael J. Lillis, from Ireland, representing the group of western European and other States; and Ambassador Rafael Rivas Posada, from Colombia, representing the Latin American group.

Accompanied by five members of the staff of the UN Centre for Human Rights, six interpreters, two sound engineers, and a press officer, the group arrived at Havana on 16 September 1988. During its stay in Cuba, it was received by senior government officials including Dr. Fidel Castro Ruz, president of the Council of State, scholars, and leaders of mass organizations. It visited numerous educational institutions, hospitals, and prisons, and received oral and written testimony from individuals and representatives of non-governmental organizations.

The group departed from Cuba on 25 September. It met again in Geneva from 5 to 9 December to review a preliminary draft of its report to the Commission on Human Rights and met there again from 16 to 20 January 1989 to complete and adopt the final text.

The "Report of the Mission which Took Place in Cuba in Accordance with Commission Decision 1988/106" (UN Doc. E/CN.4/1989/46 and Corr. 1) was presented to the Commission on Human Rights at its 1989 session. It included five chapters, entitled respectively: I. Mandate, Establishment and Activities of the Group; II. Constitutional and Legal Aspects of Human Rights in Cuba; III. Civil and Political Rights; IV. Economic, Social and Cultural Rights; and V. Final Considerations. It was followed by 32 annexes containing documentation forming an integral part of the report.

The report indicated that, in the course of its visit to Cuba, the group had received direct testimony from 87 persons it had interviewed, more than 30 of whom represented non-governmental organizations, and that the secretariat on behalf of the group had received written testimony from approximately 1,600 persons, whose names were given, with an indication of their complaints, in Annex VI.

On 25 September, the group was received separately by Dr. Fidel Castro Ruz, president of the Council of State, and by Mr. Carlos Rafael Rodriguez, vice president of that council. The latter answered the principal questions which had arisen during the group's visit concerning various aspects of human rights in Cuba and other questions the group wished to ask him.

On the afternoon of the same day, the group held a meeting in which it, *inter alia*, decided to send the following communications:

(1) a letter to the Cuban Ministry of the Interior requesting, on humanitarian grounds, a solution to the problems preventing the temporary or final entry or departure of approximately 65 persons (listed in annex IX);

(2) a list sent to the Cuban Deputy Minister for External Relations containing the names and addresses of all persons who contacted the group during its stay in Cuba. The letter, dated 11 October 1988, pointed out that the list was transmitted with the assurances given by the authorities that no difficulties would be created for any of those persons because they had contacted the group (text of the letter in annex X); and

(3) a letter to each of the persons who contacted the group in Cuba, together with the non-governmental organizations which offered to cooperate, dated 18 October 1988, in which the group indicated that it would do everything in its power to ensure that the cases in question were examined and dealt with by the competent authorities (text of the letter in annex XI).

During its third meeting, held in Geneva from 5 to 9 December, the group took note of the communications received after its return from Cuba and decided to transmit to the Cuban authorities the written testimony which it had received, except where persons submitting the testimony had requested that it should not be transmitted, together with the documents provided by non-governmental organizations and a transcription of the 87 interviews held by the group directly with individuals and representatives of Cuban non-government organizations (text of the letter in annex XII). It also took note of a communication from the Cuban government concerning persons who wished to leave the country (text of the letter in annex IX) and communicated orally to the permanent representative of Cuba in Geneva allegations of reprisals that the government was said to be taking against 14 persons who spoke with the group in Cuba (listed in annex XIII).

The report was first examined by the commission at that session. A *note verbale,* setting out certain preliminary comments by the Cuban Ministry of the Interior of the 1,648 communications received by the secretariat from private individuals was also circulated to the commission (UN Doc. E/CN.4/1988/75) which concluded with the following "general assessment:"

. . . Although the list prepared by the Secretariat includes 1,648 cases, the fact that some of these cases are submitted more than once under separate headings means that the total number of investigations concluded was much higher. This total includes:

(a) Complaints which could not be verified because of lack of information: 178;

(b) Cases where investigation has shown that the complainants lied or distorted the facts, or that they were ignorant of the law: 529;

(c) Under investigation by the competent authorities: 157;

(d) Cases not involving alleged violations of human rights in Cuba: 20;

(e) Cases not involving any complaint: 10.

It is significant that 65.7 per cent, or two out of every three, of the reports received concern entry into and departure from the country, rather than other alleged violations. Of the 1,075 cases in this category, 1,009 do not qualify as complaints.

On 9 March 1989, the Commission decided (decision 1989/113):

(a) to take note of the serious and comprehensive report (E/CN.4/1989/46 and Corr. 1) submitted by the Chairman of its forty-fourth session, together with the other members of the mission appointed under its decision 1988/106, as a result of their observation of human rights in Cuba;

(b) to thank the Government and people of Cuba for the co-operation extended to the mission in carrying out its visit and the reaffirmation of the desire of the Cuban authorities to continue co-operation in the human rights sphere and to keep the Secretary-General informed;

(c) also to bear in mind the willingness of the Government of Cuba to analyze the observations made by the mission in its report and to take into account the objective assessments formulated in the course of the debate with regard to the exercise and enjoyment of human rights in Cuba;

(d) to welcome the willingness of the Government of Cuba to co-operate with the Secretary-General in maintaining their direct contacts on the issues and questions contained in the report; these contacts and their results will be taken up by the Secretary-General in an appropriate manner;

(e) to emphasize the spirit of multilateral co-operation which characterized the fulfilment of the mission established by decision 1988/106.

The report was again drawn to the attention of the commission at its 1990 session. The representative of the United States of America, introducing a draft resolution entitled "Situation of Human Rights in Cuba," said that the report of the mission which had taken place in Cuba in accordance with commission decision 1988/106 contained the testimony of hundreds of individuals concerning the question of human rights in Cuba. In connection with that mission, the draft resolution called upon the government of Cuba to provide the commission, at its 1991 session, with a response to the unanswered questions put to the Cuban authorities by the commission's representatives (annex XVI of the report, reproduced below). The draft resolution also requested the secretary-general to inform the commission at its 1991 session of the results of his ongoing contacts with the government of Cuba.

Referring to reports of reprisals against witnesses, the American representative said that such harassment should be of concern to every member of the commission, particularly since the government of Cuba had promised that there would be no such reprisals, and added that it was because the sponsors were anxious that the commission's mechanisms should be able to function normally in every country, and not because of ideological concerns, that the resolution had been drafted.

The representative of Cuba responded that the draft resolution was completely unacceptable to his delegation on both substantive and procedural grounds. There was in his country no situation in the field of human rights which might justify the use of a procedure normally employed only in cases of mass and gross violations of human rights or of systematic policies of violation of human rights and fundamental freedoms. The Cuban representative further asserted that Cuba lagged behind no other country in the observance of human rights or willingness to abide by its obligations as a member of the United Nations. It had invited and received the mission which had visited Cuba in September 1988 and had consented to the mission's report being discussed in open session, and added that reports that individuals who had had contacts with the mission had been subjected to reprisals were a complete fabrication. Operative paragraph 1 of the draft resolution proceeded on an assumption of reprisals in the absence of any proof whatever.

As to the reference to annex XVI of the mission's report, the Cuban representative referred to the statement he had made in the commission on 28 February 1989 explaining that his government was under no obligation to submit its constitution and laws to the commission's scrutiny. As to annex III of the report, he contended it contained information sent to Geneva by counter-revolutionary and other groups concerning facts not observed by the mission during its visit to Cuba. Lastly, operative paragraph 3 prejudged the contents of the report requested from the Secretary-General and should likewise be rejected.

With regard to procedure, he recalled that commission decision 1989/113 left it with the secretary-general to determine the appropriate manner of maintaining contacts with the Cuban government on the issues and questions raised in the mission's report. The draft implied, *inter alia,* that the manner chosen by the secretary-general for dealing with the matter was not the appropriate one.

On a roll-call vote, the draft resolution was adopted on 6 March 1990, by 19 votes to 12, with 12 abstentions. Accordingly the commission, "aware of its responsibility to defend and support those who have put their faith in this body and its representatives in promoting and protecting human rights and fundamental freedoms," called upon the government of Cuba (resolution 1990/48) to honor its repeated guarantees to the representatives of the commission who visited Cuba pursuant to decision 1988/106 that individuals who attempted to present information to those representatives would not be subject to reprisals, detention, or negative consequences of any nature whatsoever; called upon the government of Cuba to provide the commission, at its 1991 session, with a response to the unanswered questions put to the Cuban authorities by representatives of the commission and to questions related to the documents listed in Annex III of the report; welcomed the willingness of the secretary-general to put himself at the disposal of the commission regarding his ongoing contacts with the government of Cuba as stated in a letter to the commission dated 29 January 1990 in which the secretary-general informed the commission that he had been maintaining ongoing contacts, both written and oral, with the government of Cuba on this matter—and expressed its appreciation to the secretary-general for his efforts in support of respect for human rights and fundamental freedoms, requesting that he provide the results of his contacts with the government of Cuba to the commission at its 1991 session.

Annexes III and XVI (UN Doc. E/CN.4/1989/46 and Corr. 1), appended to the report of the mission, are reproduced below:

List of Documents from Non-governmental Organizations Received by the Group and Sent to the Government of Cuba for Comment and List of Persons Particulars of Whose Cases Were Communicated to the Cuban Authorities on 29 August 1988.

— Decision expelling a medical student from the University of Havana.

— The student's record file from the Ministry of Education.

— "In Cuban Prisons," an article that appeared in *The New York Review of Books* on 30 June 1988.

— Preliminary report for the 1988 meeting of the United Nations Commission on Human Rights, by Ricardo Bofill Pagés.

— Form for opinion gathering.

— The situation of human rights in Cuba—seventh report, published by the Organization of American States.

— *La violación de los Derechos Humanos en Cuba: Una perspectiva vivencial* (The Violation of Human Rights in Cuba: an Experiential Perspective), by Juan M. Clark, preliminary version, February 1988.

— Amnesty International. Cuba—Political imprisonment—an update, January 1988.

— Human Rights in Cuba: Report of a Delegation of the Association of the Bar of the City of New York.

— List of [1,648] individual cases sent to the Cuban authorities on 29 August 1988.

Questions on Constitutional and Legal Matters Contained in the Note Sent by the Group on 29 August 1988 to the Government of Cuba and not Answered by the Government.

1. *Individual liberty* (articles 72, 73, 74, and 75 of the Penal Code and articles 3, 9, 11 and 12 of the Universal Declaration of Human Rights). With reference to dangerous states and individual liberty, the note sent to the Government of Cuba had the following to say:

A "dangerous state" is defined as "the special proclivity of a particular person to commit offences, as demonstrated by conduct clearly at variance with the standards of socialist morality" (art. 72). What are "the standards of socialist morality" and who is responsible for establishing them? Why is a person who merely maintains links or relations with persons who constitute a potential threat to the society, other persons and social, economic and political order of the socialist State officially warned "against engaging in socially dangerous or criminal activities" (art. 75)?

In connection with so-called "anti-social conduct" (art.73): (a) What is meant by habitual infringement of the rules of "social coexistence," who determines what these rules are and on the basis of what criteria are they established? (b) What is meant by "social parasite", who determines when a person is a social parasite and on the basis of what terms of reference? (c) What is meant by "socially reprehensible vices", who determines their existence and on the basis of what criteria? (d) Could not the pre-criminal security measure limiting the freedom of a person deemed to be in a "dangerous state" be used to restrict the freedom of persons whose relations with the Government are, for political reasons, not of the best? (e) Would a person's freedom be limited without recourse to judicial process and exclusively on the basis of a certain proclivity to so-called anti-social conduct?

2. *Administration of justice* (article 123 (a) and (b) of the Constitution and article 10 of the Universal Declaration of Human Rights). On the objectives of the courts, the note asked the following questions:

What is meant by "socialist legality" and by "safeguarding the economic, social and political régime established in this Constitution"? What would happen if the protection of these principles came into conflict with the citizens' rights provided for in the Constitution and the laws?

3. *Freedom of movement* (articles 215, 216 and 217 of the Penal Code and article 13 of the Universal Declaration of

Human Rights). On the question of illegal entry into and departure from the country, the note sent to the Government of Cuba read as follows:

"Although the Penal Code guarantees the right freely to enter and leave Cuban territory, it also establishes that the exercise of this right shall be regulated by law. What are the administrative and legal requirements for leaving and re-entering the country?"

4.*Freedom of religion, expression and the press* (articles 103, 109, 115 and 144 of the Penal Code and articles 2, 18 and 19 of the Universal Declaration of Human Rights). On the offence of enemy propaganda, the Group asked the following questions:

What is meant by incitement "against the social order, international solidarity or the socialist State"? Could this article be used to prevent the free exercise of political criticism and the control of the authorities by the people? Could it constitute a threat to persons who disagree with government policy, both in Cuba and abroad? Lastly, the fact of using the media to express opinions at variance with those of the Government constitutes, in accordance with article 103, paragraph (c), an aggravating circumstance as regards the offence defined as enemy propaganda. Would this article constitute a threat to persons who oppose the political régime in Cuba? Would this imply recognition by the criminal law of the prohibition of the use of the media to express opinions at variance with those of the Government?

With reference to the offence of causing alarm, the following questions were asked:

How is it determined when an act, because of the nature, means or occasion of its execution, "tends to cause public alarm with the aim of creating conditions affecting the security of the State"? What is meant by "security of the State" and by "causing alarm"?

On the dissemination of false information against international peace, the Group asked the following question:

On the basis of what criteria do the authorities determine the falsity of an item of information and the extent to which information which is indeed false may "disrupt international peace" or "endanger the prestige or credit of the Cuban State or its good relations with another State"?

On the offence of disrespect, the note contained the following questions:

What form of political criticism might be defined as not offensive and not insulting to the political authorities? Could this article constitute an obstacle to compliance with the constitutional provision granting the people the right to control its representatives and possibly revoke their mandate?

5. *Freedom of assembly, expression and association* (articles 7 and 53 of the Constitution, articles 34, para. 5, 57, paras. 3, 6 and 10, 58, paras. 5, 6 and 7, 98 and 99 of the Penal Code and article 20 of the Universal Declaration of Human Rights). With regard to the role of the mass organizations, the note read as follows:

Article 34, paragraph 5, article 57, paragraphs 3, 6 and 10, and article 58, paragraphs 5–7, confer certain functions on the mass organizations, such as supervising a number of penalties, and monitoring and guiding persons on whom penalties have been imposed and persons released on parole. Do these organizations have the necessary qualifications to perform these functions? What type of training guarantees the successful performance of these functions? Are there any appeal mechanisms against decisions taken by representatives of the mass organizations?

On the offence of rebellion, the note sent to the Government of Cuba asked the following questions:

What is meant by "or other unlawful means" (art.99)? Does it mean, for example, that members of any unregistered association that might seek partial changes in the Constitution or the economic, social or political régime in Cuba may be charged with rebellion for having used an unlawful means to achieve one of the objectives set forth in article 98, paragraph 1?

6. *Freedom of education and conscience* (article 38 (d) of the Constitution and article 26 of the Universal Declaration of Human Rights). *Article 38* (Constitution) The State orients, foments and promotes education, culture and science in all their manifestations.

Its educational and cultural policy is based on the following principles: . . .

(d) Artistic creativity is free as long as its content is not contrary to the Revolution. Forms of expression of art are free;

On artistic creativity, the note asked the following questions:

What is meant by the following in the context of this constitutional provision: "the Revolution", the Revolutionary Government; its principal institutions and leaders; its ideological and political bases? Who determines the substantive character of a work of art and who establishes when such a work is contrary to "the Revolution"?

CUBA: CONSTITUTION. The Constitution of the Republic of Cuba includes the following provisions (articles 8 [b], 20–27, 34–65, and 134–140 specifically relating to human rights and fundamental freedoms:

Article 8. The socialist state:

(b) as the power of the people and for the people, guarantees:

—that every man or woman, who is able to work, have the opportunity to have a job with which to contribute to the good of society and to the satisfaction of individual needs;

—that no disabled person be left without adequate means of subsistence;

—that no sick person be left without medical care;

—that no child be left without schooling, food and clothing;

—that no young person be left without the opportunity to study;

—that no one be left without access to studies, culture and sports. . . .

Article 20. The state recognizes the right of small farmers to own their lands and other means and implements of production, according to what the law stipulates.

Small farmers have the right to group themselves, in the way and following the requirements prescribed by law both for the purpose of agricultural production and for obtaining state loans and services.

The establishment of agricultural cooperatives in the instances and ways prescribed by law is authorized. Ownership of the cooperatives constitutes a form of collective ownership on the part of the peasants in those cooperatives.

The state supports the cooperative production of small

farmers as well as individual production which contribute to the growth of the national economy.

The state fosters the participation of small farmers, freely and voluntarily, in state projects and units of agricultural production.

Article 21. Small farmers have the right to sell their land with the previous authorization of the state agencies, as prescribed by law. In all cases, the state has preferential right to the purchase of the land while paying a fair price.

Land leases, share cropping, mortgages and all other forms which entail a lien on the land or partial cession to private individuals of the rights and title to the land which is the property of the small farmers are all prohibited.

Article 22. The state guarantees the right to personal ownership of earnings and savings derived from one's own work, of the dwelling to which one has legal title and of the other possessions and objects which serve to satisfy one's material and cultural needs.

Likewise, the state guarantees the right of citizens to ownership of their personal or family work tools, as long as these tools are not employed in exploiting the work of others.

Article 23. The state recognizes the right of political, social and mass organizations to ownership of the goods intended for the fulfillment of their objectives.

Article 24. The law regulates the right of citizens to inherit legal title to a place of residence and to other personal goods and chattels.

The land owned by a small farmer may only be inherited by the heirs who are personally involved in its cultivation, save for the exceptions prescribed by law.

With regard to goods which are part of cooperatives, the law prescribes the conditions under which said goods may be inherited.

Article 25. The expropriation of property for reasons of public benefit or social interest and with due compensation is authorized.

The law establishes the method for the expropriation and the bases on which the need for and usefulness of this action is to be determined as well as the form of compensation, taking into account the interest and the economic and social needs of the person whose property has been expropriated.

Article 26. Anybody who suffers damages, or injuries unjustly caused by a state official or employee while in the performance of his public functions has the right to claim and obtain the corresponding indemnification as prescribed by law.

Article 27. To ensure the well-being of citizens, the state and society are the protectors of nature. It falls within the jurisdiction of the legally qualified agencies and of each and every citizen to watch over the cleanliness of the waters and of the air, and to protect the soil, flora and fauna. . . .

Chapter III
The Family

Article 34. The state protects the family, motherhood and matrimony.

Article 35. Marriage is the voluntarily established union between a man and a woman, who are legally fit to marry, in order to live together. It is based on full equality of right and duties for the partners, who must see to the support of the home and the integral education of their children through a joint effort compatible with the social activities of both.

The law regulates the formalization, recognition and dissolution of marriage and the rights and obligations deriving from such acts.

Article 36. All children have the same rights, regardless of being born in or out of wedlock.

Any qualification concerning the nature of the relationship is abolished.

No statement shall be made either with regard to the difference in birth or the civil status of the parents in the registration of the children's birth of in any other documents that mention parenthood.

The state guarantees, through adequate legal means, the determination and recognition of paternity.

Article 37. The parents have the duty to provide nourishment for their children; to help them to defend their legitimate interests and in the realization of their just aspirations; and to contribute actively to their education and integral development as useful well-prepared citizens for life in a socialist society.

It is the children's duty, in turn, to respect and help their parents.

Chapter IV
Education and Culture

Article 38. The state orients foments and promotes education, culture and science in all their manifestations.

Its educational and cultural policy is based on the following principles:

a) the state bases its educational and cultural policy on the scientific world view, established and developed by Marxism-Leninism;

b) education is a function of the state. Consequently, educational institutions belong to the state. The fulfillment of the educational function constitutes a task in which all society participates and is based on the conclusions and contributions made by science and on the closest relationship between study and life, work and production;

c) the state must promote the communist education of the new generations and the training of children, young people and adults for social life. In order to make this principle a reality, general education and specialized scientific, technical or artistic education are combined with work, development research, physical education, sports, participation in political and social activities and military training;

d) education is provided free of charge. The state maintains a broad scholarship system for students and provides the workers with multiple opportunities to study, with a view to the universalization of education. The law establishes the integration and structure of the national system of education and the extent of compulsory education and defines the minimum level of general education that every citizen must acquire;

e) artistic creativity is free as long as its content is not contrary to the Revolution. Forms of expression of art are free;

f) in order to raise the level of culture of the people, the state foments and develops artistic education, the vocation for creation and the cultivation and appreciation of art;

g) creation and investigation in science are free. The state encourages and facilitates investigation and gives priority to that which is aimed at solving the problems related to the interests of the society and the well-being of the people;

h) the state makes it possible for the workers to engage

in scientific work and to contribute to the development of science;

  i) the state promotes, foments and develops all forms of physical education and sports as a means of education and of contribution to the integral development of the citizens;

  j) the state sees to the conservation of the nation's cultural heritage and artistic and historic wealth. The state protects national monuments and places known for their natural beauty or their artistic or historic value;

  k) the state promotes the participation of the citizens, through the country's social and mass organizations, in the development of its educational and cultural policy.

Article 39. The education of children and young people in the spirit of communism is the duty of all society.

The state and society give special protection to children and young people.

It is the duty of the family, the schools, the state agencies and the social and mass organizations to pay special attention to the integral development of children and young people.

Chapter V
Equality

Article 40. All citizens have equal rights and are subject to equal duties.

Article 41. Discrimination because of race, color, sex or national origin is forbidden and will be punished by law.

The institutions of the state educate everyone from the earliest possible age, in the principle of equality among human beings.

Article 42. The state consecrates the right achieved by the Revolution that all citizens, regardless of race, color or national origin:

  —have access, in keeping with their merits and abilities, to all positions and state and administrative jobs and of production and services;

  —can reach any rank of the Revolutionary Armed Forces and of Security and internal order, in keeping with their merits and abilities;

  —be given equal pay for equal work;

  —have a right to education at all national educational institutions, ranging from elementary schools to the universities, which are the same for all; be given medical care in all medical institutions;

  —live in any sector, zone or area and stay in any hotel;

  —be served at all restaurants and other public service establishments;

  —use, without any separations, all means of transportation by sea, land and air;

  —enjoy the same resorts, beaches, parks, social centers and other centers of culture, sports, recreation and rest.

Article 43. Women have the same rights as men in the economic, political and social fields as well as in the family.

In order to assure the exercise of these rights and especially the incorporation of women into socially organized work, the state sees to it that they are given jobs in keeping with their physical makeup; they are given paid maternity leave before and after giving birth; the state organizes such institutions as children's day-care centers, semiboarding schools and boarding schools; and it strives to create all the conditions which help to make real the principle of equality.

Chapter VI
Fundamental Rights, Duties and Guarantees

Article 44. Work in a socialist society is a right and duty and a source of pride for every citizen.

Work is remunerated according to its quality and quantity; when it is provided, the needs of the economy and of society, the decision of the worker and his skill and ability are taken into account; this is guaranteed by the socialist economic system, that facilitates social and economic development, without crises, and has thus eliminated unemployment and the dead season.

Nonpaid, voluntary work carried out for the benefit of all society in industrial, agricultural, technical, artistic and service arivities is recognized as playing an important role in the formation of our people's communist awareness.

Every worker has the duty to faithfully carry out tasks corresponding to him at his job.

Article 45. All those who work have the right to rest, which is guaranteed by the eight-hour work day, a weekly rest period and annual paid vacations.

The state contributes to the development of vacation plans and facilities.

Article 46. By means of the Social Security System the state assures adequate protection to every worker who is unable to work because of age, illness or disability.

If the worker dies this protection will be extended to his family.

Article 47. The state protects by means of social aid senior citizens lacking financial resources or anyone to take them in or care for them and anyone who is unable to work and has no relatives who can help him.

Article 48. The state guarantees the right to protection, safety and hygiene on the job by means of the adoption of adequate measures for the prevention of accidents at work and occupational diseases.

He who suffers an accident on the job or is affected by an occupational disease has the right to medical care and to compensation or retirement in those cases in which temporary or permanent work disability ensues.

Article 49. Everybody has the right to health protection and care. The state guarantees this right:

  —by providing free medical and hospital care by means of the installations of the rural medical service network, polyclinics, hospitals, preventive and specialized treatment centers;

  —by providing free dental care;

  —by promoting the health publicity campaigns, health education, regular medical examinations, general vaccinations and other measures to prevent the outbreak of disease. All the population cooperates in these activities and plans through the social and mass organizations.

Article 50. Everyone has the right to an education. This right is guaranteed by the free and widepsread system of schools, semiboarding and boarding schools and scholarships of all kinds and all levels of education, and because of the fact that all educational material is provided free of charge, which gives all children and young people, regardless of their family's economic position, the opportunity to study in keeping with their ability, social demands and the needs of socioeconomic development.

Adults are also guaranteed this right and education for them is free of charge with the specific facilities regulated by law, by means of the adult education program, technical and vocational education, training courses in state agencies and enterprises and the advanced courses for workers.

Article 51. Everyone has the right to physical education, sports and recreation.

Enjoyment of this right is assured by including the teaching and practice of physical education and sports in the curricula of the national educational system; and by the broad nature of the instruction and means placed at the service of the people, which makes possible the practice of sports and recreation on a mass basis.

Article 52. Citizens have freedom of speech and of the press in keeping with the objectives of socialist society. Material conditions for the exercise of that right are provided by the fact that the press, radio, television, movies, and other organs of the mass media are state or social property and can never be private property. This assures their use at the exclusive service of the working people and in the interests of society.

The law regulates the exercise of these freedoms.

Article 53. The rights to assembly, demonstration and association are exercised by workers, both manual and intellectual, peasants, women, students and other sectors of the working people, and they have the necessary means for this. The social and mass organizations have all the facilities they need to carry out those activities in which the members have full freedom of speech and opinion based on the unlimited right of initiative and criticism.

Article 54. The socialist state, which bases its activity and educates the people in the scientific materialist concept of the universe, recognizes and guarantees freedom of conscience and the right of everyone to profess any religious belief and to practice, within the framework of respect for the law, the belief of his preference.

The law regulates the activities of religious institutions.

It is illegal and punishable by law to oppose one's faith or religious belief to Revolution, education or the fulfillment of the duty to work, defend the homeland with arms, show reverence for its symbols and other duties established by the Constitution.

Article 55. The home is inviolable. Nobody can enter the home of another against his will, except in those cases foreseen by law.

Article 56. Mail is inviolable. It can only be seized, opened and examined in cases prescribed by law. Secrecy is maintained on matters other than those which led to the examination.

The same principle is to be applied in the case of cable, telegraph and telephone communication.

Article 57. Freedom and inviolability of persons is assured to all those who live in the country.

Nobody can be arrested, except in the manner, with the guarantees and in the cases indicated by law.

The person who has been arrested or the prisoner is inviolable in his personal integrity.

Article 58. Nobody can be tried or sentenced except by the competent tribunal by virtue of laws which existed prior to the crime and with the formalities and guarantees that the laws establish.

Every accused person has the right to a defense.

No violence or pressure of any kind can be used against people to force them to testify.

All statements obtained in violation of the above precept are null and void and those responsible for the violation will be punished as outlined by law.

Article 59. Confiscation of property is only applied as a punishment by the authorities in the cases and by the methods determined by law.

Article 60. Penal laws are retroactive when they benefit the accused or person who has been sentenced. Other laws are not retroactive unless the contrary is decided for reasons of social interest or because it is useful for public purposes.

Article 61. None of the freedoms which are recognized for citizens can be exercised contrary to what is established in the Constitution and the law, or contrary to the existence and objectives of the socialist state, or contrary to the decision of the Cuban people to build socialism and communism. Violations of this principle can be punished by law.

Article 62. Every citizen has the right to file complaints with and send petitions to the authorities and to be given the pertinent response or attention within a reasonable length of time, in keeping with the law.

Article 63. Every citizen has the duty of caring for public and social property, accepting work discipline, respecting the rights of others, observing standards of socialist living and fulfilling civic and social duties.

Article 64. Defense of the socialist homeland is the greatest honor and the supreme duty of every Cuban citizen.

The law regulates the military service which Cubans must do.

Treason against one's country is the most serious of crimes; those who commit it are subject to the most severe penalties.

Article 65. Strict fulfillment of the Constitution and the laws is an inexcusable duty of all. . . .

Chapter XI
Electoral System

Article 134. In all elections and in referendums, voting is free, equal and secret. Every voter has only one vote.

Article 135. All Cubans over 16 years of age, men and women alike, have the right to vote except those who:

a) are mentally disabled and have been declared so by court;

b) those who have committed a crime and because of this have lost the right to vote.

Article 136. All Cuban citizens, men and women alike, who have full political rights can be elected.

If the election is for deputies to the National Assemblies of People's Power they must be more than 18 years old.

Article 137. Members of the Revolutionary Armed Forces and other military institutions of the nation have the right to elect and be elected, just like any other citizen.

Article 138. The law determines the number of delegates that make up each of the assemblies in proportion to the number of people who live in each of the political-administrative regions into which the country is divided; it also regulates the form and manner of the election.

The delegates to the Municipal Assemblies are elected from previously determined electoral circumscriptions.

Article 139. The Municipal Assemblies elect, by means of secret balloting, the delegates to the provincial Assemblies of People's Power.

Article 140. In order for a delegate to be considered elected he must get more than half the number of votes cast in the circumscription.

If this does not happen the law stipulates the manner in which new elections will be held in order to decide who is elected from among those with the most votes.

CULTURE. The right of everyone to participate in cultural life is proclaimed in the UNIVERSAL DECLARATION OF HUMAN RIGHTS in the following terms:

Article 27. 1. Everyone has the right freely to participate in the cultural life of the community, to enjoy the arts and to share in scientific advancement and its benefits.
2. Everyone has the right to the protection of the moral and material interests resulting from any scientific, literary or artistic production of which he is the author.

The right is further elaborated in the INTERNATIONAL COVENANT ON ECONOMIC, SOCIAL AND CULTURAL RIGHTS, as follows:

Article 15. 1. The States Parties to the present Covenant recognize the right of everyone:
    (a) To take part in cultural life;
    (b) To enjoy the benefits of scientific progress and its applications;
    (c) To benefit from the protection of the moral and material interests resulting from any scientific, literary or artistic production of which he is the author.
2. The steps to be taken by the States Parties to the present Covenant to achieve the full realization of this right shall include those necessary for the conservation, the development and the diffusion of science and culture.
3. The States Parties to the present Covenant undertake to respect the freedom indispensable for scientific research and creative activity.
4. The States Parties to the present Covenant recognize the benefits to be derived from the encouragement and development of international contacts and co-operation in the scientific and cultural fields.

Non-discrimination on racial grounds in respect of the right to participate in culture is ensured by the INTERNATIONAL CONVENTION ON THE ELIMINATION OF ALL FORMS OF RACIAL DISCRIMINATION in the following provision:

Article 5. In compliance with the fundamental obligations laid down in article 2 of this Convention, States Parties undertake to prohibit and to eliminate racial discrimination in all its forms and to guarantee the right of everyone, without distinction as to race, colour, or national or ethnic origin, to equality before the law, notably in the enjoyment of the following rights:. . . .
    (e) Economic, social and cultural rights, in particular:. . . .
        (vi) The right to equal participation in cultural activities.

Non-discrimination on the ground of sex in respect of the right is ensured in the CONVENTION ON THE ELIMINATION OF ALL FORMS OF DISCRIMINATION AGAINST WOMEN in the following provision:

Article 13. States Parties shall take all appropriate measures to eliminate discrimination against women in other areas of economic and social life in order to ensure, on a basis of equality of men and women, the same rights, in particular:. . . .
    (c) The right to participate in recreational activities, sports and all aspects of cultural life.

Within the United Nations system, primary responsibility for the preparation and supervision of international measures to promote and protect enjoyment of the right to culture lies with the UNITED NATIONS EDUCATIONAL, SCIENTIFIC AND CULTURAL ORGANIZATION. Its basic tools in this endeavor are the UNESCO CONVENTION FOR THE PROTECTION OF CULTURAL PROPERTY IN THE EVENT OF ARMED CONFLICT, with regulations for the execution of the convention, of 14 May 1954 (known as the Hague Convention); the PROTOCOL of that convention, also of 14 May 1954; the UNESCO CONVENTION ON THE MEANS OF PROHIBITING AND PREVENTING THE ILLICIT IMPORT, EXPORT AND TRANSFER OF OWNERSHIP OF CULTURAL PROPERTY, of 14 November 1970; the UNESCO CONVENTION CONCERNING THE PROTECTION OF THE WORLD CULTURAL HERITAGE, of 16 November 1972; the UNESCO DECLARATION OF THE PRINCIPLES OF INTERNATIONAL CULTURAL CO-OPERATION, of 4 November 1966; the UNESCO DECLARATION ON THE GUIDING PRINCIPLES ON THE USE OF SATELLITE BROADCASTING FOR THE FREE FLOW OF INFORMATION, THE SPREAD OF EDUCATION AND GREATER CULTURAL EXCHANGE, of 15 November 1972; and the UNESCO DECLARATION ON FUNDAMENTAL PRINCIPLES CONCERNING THE CONTRIBUTION OF THE MASS MEDIA TO STRENGTHENING PEACE AND INTERNATIONAL UNDERSTANDING, TO THE PROMOTION OF HUMAN RIGHTS AND TO COUNTERING RACISM, *APARTHEID* AND INCITEMENT TO WAR, of 28 November 1978. Other normative instruments relating to the right to culture include the recommendation concerning the most effective means of rendering museums accessible to everyone, of 14 December 1960; the recommendation on the means of prohibiting and preventing the illicit import, export, and transfer of ownership of cultural property, of 19 November 1964; the recommendation concerning the protection, at the national level, of the cultural and natural heritage, of 16 November 1972; the recommendation concerning the safeguarding and contemporary role of historic areas, of 26 November 1976; the recommendation on the protection of moveable cultural property, of 28 November 1978; the UNESCO RECOMMENDATION CONCERNING THE STATUS OF THE ARTIST, of 27 October 1980; and the UNESCO RECOMMENDATION FOR THE SAFEGUARDING AND PRESERVATION OF MOVING IMAGES, of 27 October 1980.

In accordance with the procedures for implementation of the International Covenant on Economic, Social and Cultural Rights adopted by the Economic and Social Council on 11 May 1976 (resolution 1988 [LX]), UNESCO submits to the council, at regular intervals, reports on the progress made in achieving the observance of the provisions of the covenant falling within the scope of its activities, as provided under article 18 of the covenant. Information on the progress made in achieving the observance of the provisions of article 15 (1) of the covenant, on the right to take part in cultural life, are summarized under the heading ECONOMIC, SOCIAL AND CULTURAL RIGHTS: UNESCO ACTIVITIES.

CYPRUS. The Republic of Cyprus is a non-Arab country of western Asia, occupying an island in the eastern Mediterranean, 40 miles south of Turkey and 60 miles west of Syria. It achieved independence from Great Britain in 1960 and became a member of the United Nations the same year. Its population is estimated by the UN (1990) to be 704,000. Ethnic groups include persons of Greek origin (80%); and of Turkish origin (18%); the remaining 2% includes Armenians, Latins, Maronites, and others. Languages in common use include Greek and Turkish (both official) and English. Religions practiced include Christianity (Greek Orthodox, 75%; Roman Catholic, 3%; other faiths, 2%), and Islam (20%). Literacy is estimated at 90%.

The government (1990) took the form of a republic. Under the 1960 constitution, the president is of Greek origin and the vice president of Turkish origin; they are elected by the Greek and Turkish communities, respectively. Legislative authority is exercised by the House of Representatives, members of which also are elected by each community separately: 70% Greek Cypriotes and 30% Turkish Cypriotes. Each community is entitled to a communal chamber; however, the Greek communal chamber was abolished in 1965, while the Turkish communal chamber continued to function. Turkish members of the House of Representatives did not attend its sessions after 1964.

Since 1974, when the Cypriot National Guard ousted the president, Cyprus has been torn by communal tensions. The invasion of Cyprus by Turkey on 20 July 1974, explained as a necessity to protect the Turkish Cypriote minority, led to Turkish control of 40% of the island. Proclamation by Turkish Cypriot authorities of a "Turkish Republic of Northern Cyprus" was declared to be invalid by the UN Security Council, which requested the UN secretary-general to use his good offices in order to achieve progress towards a settlement of the problem.

In 1975, the UN COMMISSION ON HUMAN RIGHTS called on all parties concerned to undertake measures to facilitate the voluntary return of all refugees to their homes in safety and to settle all other aspects of the refugee problem. The general assembly re-

quested the secretary-general to exert every effort, in cooperation with the INTERNATIONAL COMMITTEE OF THE RED CROSS, to assist in tracing and accounting for missing persons. The secretary-general accordingly established the Committee on Missing Persons in Cyprus, which has since been engaged in investigating 168 individual cases on which it decided to concentrate its efforts.

At its 1987 session, the Commission on Human Rights received a report by the secretary-general on the progress of the committee's work. In resolution 1987/50 of 11 March 1987, the commission recommended that the interested parties do their utmost to find a solution to the Cyprus problem, based on respect for the sovereignty, independence, territorial integrity, and non-alignment of the Republic of Cyprus and on the restoration and safeguarding of the human rights of all Cypriots.

The commission received further reports from the secretary-general in 1988 and in 1989 (UN Docs. E/CN.4/1988 27 and 1989/27, respectively). The following information was included in the secretary-general's report to the 1990 session of the commission (UN Doc. E/CN.4/1990/21, para. 3–11):

As reflected in the Secretary-General's most recent reports (S/20663 and S/21010), the leaders of the two sides in Cyprus have, since August 1988, met for some 100 hours at the residence of the Secretary-General's Special Representative in Nicosia and have met with the Secretary-General on a number of occasions, jointly and separately, at United Nations Headquarters.

When the Secretary-General met the two leaders on 28 and 29 June 1989 he summarized in some detail the ideas which his colleagues had discussed with them in May and June and stated that those ideas offered a real possibility for bridging the positions of the two sides. He said that he had asked his Special Representative to bring them together in direct talks to complete the preparation of the outline of an overall agreement. Both leaders pledged their cooperation in completing that task and accepted the Secretary-General's invitation to meet him again in September to consider the completed outline and to launch the negotiation of an overall agreement.

From the latter part of June 1989, H.E. Mr. Denktash publicly expressed reservations about the process that had been followed in May and June. He subsequently indicated that because of tensions resulting from a demonstration in Nicosia on 19 July and because he had to seek guidance from other Turkish Cypriot authorities on the ideas referred to in paragraph 4 above he could not participate in the talks as scheduled.

As explained in his most recent report, the Secretary-General has since concentrated his efforts on finding a way to resume the talks. He remains of the view that a basis for effective negotiations does exist provided both leaders manifest the necessary goodwill and recognize that a viable solution must satisfy the legitimate interests of both communities. The discussions since last year have clearly brought out all the issues that need to be covered in an agreement, and have produced ideas that should facilitate the negotiating process. He therefore believes that it should be possible for the two leaders to proceed expeditiously to complete their work on an outline as they had agreed to do on 29 June.

On the occasion of the Security Council's meeting on 14 December 1989 on the renewal of the mandate of the United Nations Force in Cyprus (UNFICYP), the President issued a statement (S/21026) in which, on behalf of the members, he urged both leaders to proceed in the manner suggested by the Secretary-General and, as agreed in June, to co-operate with him and his Special Representative in completing work on the outline. They also urged the two parties to make a further determined effort to promote reconciliation and shared the Secretary-General's view that the adoption of goodwill measures could prove helpful in this regard. The members of the Council also requested the Secretary-General to report to the Council by 1 March 1990 on the progress made in resuming intensive talks and developing an agreed outline of an overall agreement.

Pending a settlement, the UNFICYP has continued, under its mandate, to discharge humanitarian functions on behalf of the Greek Cypriots, whose number stood at 611 at the beginning of December 1989, living in the northern part of the island. UNFICYP has also continued to make periodic visits to Turkish Cypriots living in the southern part and to help them maintain contact with their relatives in the northern part. UNFICYP officers have continued to interview, in private, Greek Cypriots who apply for permanent transfer to the southern part, in order to verify that all transfers take place voluntarily. Four such transfers took place during the period 1 December 1988 to 4 December 1989. UNFICYP has also continued to facilitate temporary visits by Greek Cypriots living in the northern part to the southern part for family and other reasons. During the period mentioned above, there were 1,304 such visits. Contacts between members of the Maronite community living on opposite sides of the ceasefire lines continued to be frequent.

Since the Secretary-General's last report to the Commission (E/CN.4/1989/28), the situation in Varosha has remained unchanged. Students continue to be accommodated in two hotels inside the fenced area and it has not yet been possible to obtain a date for their departure.

Between 1 December 1988 and 4 December 1989 the Committee on Missing Persons in Cyprus (CMP) held eight sessions, including 41 meetings, of which 25 were attended by the three Members and their assistants (formal meetings) and 16 by the three Members only (informal meetings).

The activities of UNFICYP, including those related to its humanitarian responsibilities, as well as a more detailed account of matters pertaining to the Secretary-General's mission of good offices, are described in the Secretary-General's most recent reports to the Security Council on the United Nations operation in Cyprus (S/20663 and S/21010).

After examining the question in some detail, the commission decided (decision 1990/104) that the debate should be postponed to its 1991 session, it being understood that action required by previous resolutions on the subject would remain operative,

including the request to the secretary to provide a report to the commission on their implementation.

CYPRUS: CONSTITUTION. The Constitution of the Republic of Cyprus includes the following provisions (articles 6–35) specifically relating to human rights and fundamental freedoms:

Part II—Fundamental Rights and Liberties

Article 6. Subject to the express provisions of this Constitution no law or decision of the House of Representatives or of any of the Communal Chambers, and no act or decision of any organ, authority or person in the Republic exercising executive power or administrative functions, shall discriminate against any of the two Communities or any person as a person or by virtue of being a member of a Community.

Article 7. 1. Every person has the right to life and corporal integrity.

2. No person shall be deprived of his life except in the execution of a sentence of a competent court following his conviction of an offence for which this penalty is provided by law. A law may provide for such penalty only in cases of premeditated murder, high treason, piracy jure gentium and capital offences under military law.

3. Deprivation of life shall not be regarded as inflicted in contravention of this Article when it results from the use of force which is no more than absolutely necessary—

(*a*) in defence of person or property against the infliction of a proportionate and otherwise unavoidable and irreparable evil;

(*b*) in order to effect an arrest or to prevent the escape of a person lawfully detained;

(*c*) in action taken for the purpose of quelling a riot or insurrection, when and as provided by law.

Article 8. No person shall be subjected to torture or to inhuman or degrading punishment or treatment.

Article 9. Every person has the right to a decent existence and to social security. A law shall provide for the protection of the workers, assistance to the poor and for a system of social insurance.

Article 10. 1. No person shall be held in slavery or servitude.

2. No person shall be required to perform forced or compulsory labour.

3. For the purposes of this Article the term "forced or compulsory labour" shall not include—

(*a*) any work required to be done in the ordinary course of detention imposed according to the provisions of Article 11 or during conditional release from such detention;

(*b*) any service of a military character if imposed or, in case of conscientious objectors, subject to their recognition by a law, service exacted instead of compulsory military service;

(*c*) any service exacted in case of an emergency or calamity threatening the life or well-being of the inhabitants.

Article 11. 1. Every person has the right to liberty and security of person.

2. No person shall be deprived of his liberty save in the following cases when and as provided by law:—

(*a*) the detention of a person after conviction by a competent court;

(*b*) the arrest or detention of a person for non-compliance with the lawful order of a court;

(*c*) the arrest or detention of a person effected for the purpose of bringing him before the competent legal authority on reasonable suspicion of having committed an offence or when it is reasonably considered necessary to prevent his committing an offence or fleeing after having done so;

(*d*) the detention of a minor by a lawful order for the purpose of educational supervision or his lawful detention for the purpose of bringing him before the competent legal authority;

(*e*) the detention of persons for the prevention of spreading of infectious diseases, of persons of unsound mind, alcoholics or drug addicts or vagrants;

(*f*) the arrest or detention of a person to prevent him effecting an unauthorised entry into the territory of the Republic or of an alien against whom action is being taken with a view to deportation or extradition.

3. Save when and as provided by law in case of a flagrant offence punishable with death or imprisonment, no person shall be arrested save under the authority of a reasoned judicial warrant issued according to the formalities prescribed by the law.

4. Every person arrested shall be informed at the time of his arrest in a language which he understands of the reasons of his arrest and shall be allowed to have the services of a lawyer of his own choosing.

5. The person arrested shall, as soon as is practicable after his arrest, and in any event not later than twenty-four hours after the arrest, be brought before a judge, if not earlier released.

6. The judge before whom the person arrested is brought shall promptly proceed to inquire into the grounds of the arrest in a language understandable by the person arrested and shall, as soon as possible and in any event not later than three days from such appearance, either release the person arrested on such terms as he may deem fit or where the investigation into the commission of the offence for which he has been arrested has not been completed remand him in custody and may remand him in custody from time to time for a period not exceeding eight days at any one time:

Provided that the total period of such remand in custody shall not exceed three months of the date of the arrest on the expiration of which every person or authority having the custody of the person arrested shall forthwith set him free.

Any decision of the judge under this paragraph shall be subject to appeal.

7. Every person who is deprived of his liberty by arrest or detention shall be entitled to take proceedings by which the lawfulness of his detention shall be decided speedily by a court and his release ordered if the detention is not lawful.

8. Every person who has been the victim of arrest or detention in contravention of the provisions of this Article shall have an enforceable right to compensation.

Article 12. 1. No person shall be held guilty of any offence on account of any act or omission which did not constitute an offence under the law at the time when it was committed; and no person shall have a heavier punishment imposed on him for an offence other than that expressly provided for it by law at the time when it was committed.

2. A person who has been acquitted or convicted of an offence shall not be tried again for the same offence. No person shall be punished twice for the same act or omission except where death ensues from such an act or omission.

3. No law shall provide for a punishment which is disproportionate to the gravity of the offence.

4. Every person charged with an offence shall be presumed innocent until proved guilty according to law.

5. Every person charged with an offence has the following minimum rights:—

(*a*) to be informed promptly and in a language which he understands and in detail of the nature and grounds of the charge preferred against him;

(*b*) to have adequate time and facilities for the preparation of his defence;

(*c*) to defend himself in person or through a lawyer of his own choosing or, if he has no sufficient means to pay for legal assistance, to be given free legal assistance when the interest of justice so require;

(*d*) to examine or have examined witnesses against him and to obtain the attendance and examination of witnesses on his behalf under the same conditions as witnesses against him;

(*e*) to have the free assistance of an interpreter if he cannot understand or speak the language used in court.

6. A punishment of general confiscation of property is prohibited.

Article 13. 1. Every person has the right to move freely throughout the territory of the Republic and to reside in any part thereof subject to any restrictions imposed by law and which are necessary only for the purposes of defence or public health or provided as punishment to be passed by a competent court.

2. Every person has the right to leave permanently or temporarily the territory of the Republic subject to reasonable restrictions imposed by law.

Article 14. No citizen shall be banished or excluded from the Republic under any circumstances.

Article 15. 1. Every person has the right to respect for his private and family life.

2. There shall be no interference with the exercise of this right except such as is in accordance with the law and is necessary only in the interests of the security of the Republic or the constitutional order or the public safety or the public order or the public health or the public morals or for the protection of the rights and liberties guaranteed by this Constitution to any person.

Article 16. 1. Every person's dwelling house is inviolable.

2. There shall be no entry in any dwelling house or any search therein except when and as provided by law and on a judicial warrant duly reasoned or when the entry is made with the express consent of its occupant or for the purpose of rescuing the victims of any offence of violence or of any disaster.

Article 17. 1. Every person has the right to respect for, and to the secrecy of, his correspondence and other communication if such other communication is made through means not prohibited by law.

2. There shall be no interference with the exercise of this right except in accordance with the law and only in cases of convicted and unconvicted prisoners and business correspondence and communication of bankrupts during the bankruptcy administration.

Article 18. 1. Every person has the right to freedom of thought, conscience and religion.

2. All religions whose doctrines or rites are not secret are free.

3. All religions are equal before the law. Without prejudice to the competence of the Communal Chambers under this Constitution, no legislative, executive or administrative act of the Republic shall discriminate against any religious institution or religion.

4. Every person is free and has the right to profess his faith and to manifest his religion or belief, in worship, teaching, practice or observance, either individually or collectively, in private or in public, and to change his religion or belief.

5. The use of physical or moral compulsion for the purpose of making a person change or preventing him from changing his religion is prohibited.

6. Freedom to manifest one's religion or belief shall be subject only to such limitations as are prescribed by law and are necessary in the interests of the security of the Republic or the constitutional order or the public safety or the public order or the public health or the public morals or for the protection of the rights and liberties guaranteed by this Constitution to any person.

7. Until a person attains the age of sixteen the decision as to the religion to be professed by him shall be taken by the person having the lawful guardianship of such person.

8. No person shall be compelled to pay any tax or duty the proceeds of which are specially allocated in whole or in part for the purposes of a religion other than his own.

Article 19. 1. Every person has the right to freedom of speech and expression in any form.

2. This right includes freedom to hold opinions and receive and impart information and ideas without interference by any public authority and regardless of frontiers.

3. The exercise of the rights provided in paragraphs 1 and 2 of this Article may be subject to such formalities, conditions, restrictions or penalties as are prescribed by law and are necessary only in the interests of the security of the Republic or the constitutional order or the public safety or the public order or the public health or the public morals or for the protection of the reputation or rights of others or for preventing the disclosure of information received in confidence or for maintaining the authority and impartiality of the judiciary.

4. Seizure of newspapers or other printed matter is not allowed without the written permission of the Attorney-General of the Republic, which must be confirmed by the decision of a competent court within a period not exceeding seventy-two hours, failing which the seizure shall be lifted.

5. Nothing in this Article contained shall prevent the Republic from requiring the licensing of sound and vision broadcasting or cinema enterprises.

Article 20. 1. Every person has the right to receive, and every person or institution has the right to give, instruction or education subject to such formalities, conditions or restrictions as are in accordance with the relevant communal law and are necessary only in the interests of the security of the Republic or the constitutional order or the public safety or the public order or the public health or the public morals or the standard and quality of education or for the protection of the rights and liberties of others including the right of the parents to secure for their children such education as is in conformity with their religious convictions.

2. Free primary education shall be made available by the Greek and the Turkish Communal Chambers in the respective communal primary schools.

3. Primary education shall be compulsory for all citizens of such school age as may be determined by a relevant communal law.

4. Education, other than primary education, shall be made available by the Greek and the Turkish Communal Chambers, in deserving and appropriate cases, on such terms and conditions as may be determined by a relevant communal law.

Article 21. 1. Every person has the right to freedom of peaceful assembly.

2. Every person has the right to freedom of association with others, including the right to form and to join trade unions for the protection of his interests. Notwithstanding any restriction under paragraph 3 of this Article, no person shall be compelled to join any association or to continue to be a member thereof.

3. No restrictions shall be placed on the exercise of these rights other than such as are prescribed by law and are absolutely necessary only in the interests of the security of the Republic or the constitutional order or the public safety or the public order or the public health or the public morals or for the protection of the rights and liberties guaranteed by this Constitution to any person, whether or not such person participates in such assembly or is a member of such association.

4. Any association the object or activities of which are contrary to the constitutional order is prohibited.

5. A law may provide for the imposition of restrictions on the exercise of these rights by members of the armed forces, the police or gendarmerie.

6. Subject to the provisions of any law regulating the establishment or incorporation, membership (including rights and obligations of members), management and administration, and winding up and dissolution, the provisions of this Article shall also apply to the formation of companies, societies and other associations functioning for profit.

Article 22. 1. Any person reaching nubile age is free to marry and to found a family according to the law relating to marriage, applicable to such person under the provisions of this Constitution.

2. The provisions of paragraph 1 of this Article shall, in the following cases, be applied as follows:—

(*a*) if the law relating to marriage applicable to the parties as provided under Article 111 is not the same, the parties may elect to have their marriage governed by the law applicable to either of them under such Article;

(*b*) if the provisions of Article 111 are not applicable to any of the parties to the marriage and neither of such parties is a member of the Turkish Community, the marriage shall be governed by a law of the Republic which the House of Representatives shall make and which shall not contain any restrictions other than those relating to age, health, proximity of relationship and prohibition of polygamy;

(*c*) if the provisions of Article 111 are applicable only to one of the parties to the marriage and the other party is not a member of the Turkish Community, the marriage shall be governed by the law of the Republic as in subparagraph (*b*) of this paragraph provided:

Provided that the parties may elect to have their marriage governed by the law applicable, under Article 111, to one of such parties in so far as such law allows such marriage.

3. Nothing in this Article contained shall, in any way, affect the rights, other than those on marriage, of the

Greek-Orthodox Church or of any religious group to which the provisions of paragraph 3 of Article 2 shall apply with regard to their respective members as provided in this Constitution.

Article 23. 1. Every person, alone or jointly with others, has the right to acquire, own, possess, enjoy or dispose of any movable or immovable property and has the right to respect for such right.

The right of the Republic to underground water, minerals and antiquities is reserved.

2. No deprivation or restriction or limitation of any such right shall be made except as provided in this Article.

3. Restrictions or limitations which are absolutely necessary in the interest of the public safety or the public health or the public morals or the town and country planning or the development and utilization of any property to the promotion of the public benefit or for the protection of the rights of others may be imposed by law on the exercise of such right.

Just compensation shall be promptly paid for any such restrictions or limitations which materially decrease the economic value of such property: such compensation to be determined in case of disagreement by a civil court.

4. Any movable or immovable property or any right over or interest in any such property may be compulsorily acquired by the Republic or by a municipal corporation or by a Communal Chamber for the educational, religious, charitable or sporting institutions, bodies or establishments within its competence and only from the persons belonging to its respective Community or by a public corporation or a public utility body on which such right has been conferred by law, and only

(*a*) for a purpose which is to the public benefit and shall be specially provided by a general law for compulsory acquisition which shall be enacted within a year from the date of the coming into operation of this Constitution; and

(*b*) when such purpose is established by a decision of the acquiring authority and made under the provisions of such law stating clearly the reasons for such acquisition; and

(*c*) upon the payment in cash and in advance of a just and equitable compensation to be determined in case of disagreement by a civil court.

5. Any immovable property or any right over or interest in any such property compulsorily acquired shall only be used for the purpose for which it has been acquired. If within three years of the acquisition such purpose has not been attained, the acquiring authority shall, immediately after the expiration of the said period of three years, offer the property at the price it has been acquired to the person from whom it has been acquired. Such person shall be entitled within three months of the receipt of such offer to signify his acceptance or non-acceptance of the offer, and if he signifies acceptance, such property shall be returned to him immediately after his returning such price within a further period of three months from such acceptance.

6. In the event of agricultural reform, lands shall be distributed only to persons belonging to the same Community as the owner from whom such land has been compulsorily acquired.

7. Nothing in paragraphs 3 and 4 of this Article contained shall affect the provisions of any law made for the purpose of levying execution in respect of any tax or penalty, executing any judgment, enforcing any contractual obligation or for the prevention of danger to life or property.

8. Any movable or immovable property may be requisi-

tioned by the Republic or by a Communal Chamber for the purposes of the educational, religious, charitable or sporting institutions, bodies or establishments within its competence and only where the owner and the person entitled to possession of such property belong to the respective Community, and only—

(*a*) for a purpose which is to the public benefit and shall be specially provided by a general law for requisitioning which shall be enacted within a year from the date of the coming into operation of this Constitution; and

(*b*) when such purpose is established by a decision of the requisitioning authority and made under the provisions of such law stating clearly the reasons for such requisitioning: and

(*c*) for a period not exceeding three years: and

(*d*) upon the prompt payment in cash of a just and equitable compensation to be determined in case of disagreement by a civil court.

9. Notwithstanding anything contained in this Article no deprivation, restriction or limitation of the right provided in paragraph 1 of this Article in respect of any movable or immovable property belonging to any See, monastery, church or any other ecclesiastical corporation or any right over it or interest therein shall be made except with the written consent of the appropriate ecclesiastical authority being in control of such property and the provisions of paragraphs 3, 4, 7 and 8 of this Article shall be subject to the provisions of this paragraph:

Provided that restrictions or limitations for the purposes of town and country planning under the provisions of paragraph 3 of this Article are exempted from the provisions of this paragraph.

10. Notwithstanding anything contained in this Article, no deprivation, restriction or limitation of any right provided in paragraph 1 of this Article in respect of any vakf movable or immovable property, including the objects and subjects of the vakfs and the properties belonging to the Mosques or to any other Moslem religious institutions, or any right thereon or interest therein shall be made except with the approval of the Turkish Communal Chamber and subject to the Laws and Principles of Vakfs and the provisions of paragraphs 3, 4, 7 and 8 of this Article shall be subject to the provisions of this paragraph:

Provided that restrictions or limitations for the purposes of town and country planning under the provisions of paragraph 3 of this Article are exempted from the provisions of this paragraph.

11. Any interested person shall have the right of recourse to the court in respect of or under any of the provisions of this Article, and such recourse shall act as a stay of proceedings for the compulsory acquisition; and in case of any restriction or limitation imposed upon paragraph 3 of this Article, the court shall have power to order stay of any proceedings in respect thereof.

Any decision of the court under this paragraph shall be subject to appeal.

Article 24. 1. Every person is bound to contribute according to his means towards the public burdens.

2. No such contribution by way of tax, duty or rate of any kind whatsoever shall be imposed save by or under the authority of a law.

3. No tax, duty or rate of any kind whatsoever shall be imposed with retrospective effect:

Provided that any import duty may be imposed as from the date of the introduction of the relevant Bill.

4. No tax, duty or rate of any kind whatsoever other than

customs duties shall be of a destructive or prohibitive nature.

Article 25. 1. Every person has the right to practise any profession or to carry on any occupation, trade or business.

2. The exercise of this right may be subject to such formalities, conditions or restrictions as are prescribed by law and relate exclusively to the qualifications usually required for the exercise of any profession or are necessary only in the interests of the security of the Republic or the constitutional order or the public safety or the public order or the public health or the public morals or for the protection of the rights and liberties guaranteed by this Constitution to any person or in the public interest:

Provided that no such formalities, conditions or restrictions purporting to be in the public interest shall be prescribed by a law if such formality, condition or restriction is contrary to the interests of either Community.

3. As an exception to the aforesaid provisions of this Article a law may provide, if it is in the public interest, that certain enterprises of the nature of an essential public service or relating to the exploitation of sources of energy or other natural resources shall be carried out exclusively by the Republic or a municipal corporation or by a public corporate body created for the purpose by such law and administered under the control of the Republic, and having a capital which may be derived from public and private funds or from either such source only:

Provided that, where such enterprise has been carried out by any person, other than a municipal corporation or a public corporate body, the installations used for such enterprise shall, at the request of such person, be acquired, on payment of a just price, by the Republic or such municipal corporation or such public corporate body, as the case may be.

Article 26. 1. Every person has the right to enter freely into any contract subject to such conditions, limitations or restrictions as are laid down by the general principles of the law of contract. A law shall provide for the prevention of exploitation by persons who are commanding economic power.

2. A law may provide for collective labour contracts of obligatory fulfilment by employers and workers with adequate protection of the rights of any person, whether or not represented at the conclusion of such contract.

Article 27. 1. The right to strike is recognised and its exercise may be regulated by law for the purposes only of safeguarding the security of the Republic or the constitutional order of the public order or the public safety or the maintenance of supplies and services essential to the life of the inhabitants or the protection of the rights and liberties guaranteed by this Constitution to any person.

2. The members of the armed forces, of the police and of the gendarmerie shall not have the right to strike. A law may extend such prohibition to the members of the public service.

Article 28. 1. All persons are equal before the law, the administration and justice and are entitled to equal protection thereof and treatment thereby.

2. Every person shall enjoy all the rights and liberties provided for in this Constitution without any direct or indirect discrimination against any person on the ground of his community, race, religion, language, sex, political or other convictions, national or social descent, birth, colour, wealth, social class, or on any ground whatsoever, unless there is express provision to the contrary in this Constitution.

3. No citizen shall be entitled to use or enjoy any privilege of any title of nobility or of social distinction within the territorial limits of the Republic.

4. No title or nobility or other social distinction shall be conferred by or recognised in the Republic.

Article 29. 1. Every person has the right individually or jointly with others to address written requests or complaints to any competent public authority and to have them attended to and decided expeditiously; an immediate notice of any such decision taken duly reasoned shall be given to the person making the request or complaint and in any event within a period not exceeding thirty days.

2. Where any interested person is aggrieved by any such decision or where no such decision is notified to such person within the period specified in paragraph 1 of this Article, such person may have recourse to a competent court in the matter of such request or complaint.

Article 30. 1. No person shall be denied access to the court assigned to him by or under this Constitution. The establishment of judicial committees or exceptional courts under any name whatsoever is prohibited.

2. In the determination of his civil rights and obligations or of any criminal charge against him, every person is entitled to a fair and public hearing within a reasonable time by an independent, impartial and competent court established by law. Judgment shall be reasoned and pronounced in public session, but the press and the public may be excluded from all or any part of the trial upon a decision of the court where it is in the interest of the security of the Republic or the constitutional order or the public order or the public safety or the public morals or where the interests of juveniles or the protection of the private life of the parties so require or, in special circumstances where, in the opinion of the court, publicity would prejudice the interests of justice.

3. Every person has the right—

(*a*) to be informed of the reasons why he is required to appear before the court;

(*b*) to present his case before the court and to have sufficient time necessary for its preparation;

(*c*) to adduce or cause to be adduced his evidence and to examine witnesses according to law;

(*d*) to have a lawyer of his own choice and to have free legal assistance where the interests of justice so require and as provided by law;

(*e*) to have free assistance of an interpreter if he cannot understand or speak the language used in court.

Article 31. Every citizen has, subject to the provisions of this Constitution and any electoral law of the Republic or of the relevant Communal Chamber made thereunder, the right to vote in any election held under this Constitution or any such law.

Article 32. Nothing in this Part contained shall preclude the Republic from regulating by law any matter relating to aliens in accordance with International Law.

Article 33. 1. Subject to the provisions of this Constitution relating to a state of emergency, the fundamental rights and liberties guaranteed by this Part shall not be subjected to any other limitations or restrictions than those in this Part provided.

2. The provisions of this Part relating to such limitations or restrictions shall be interpreted strictly and shall not be applied for any purpose other than those for which they have been prescribed.

Article 34. Nothing in this Part may be interpreted as implying for any Community, group or person any right to engage in any activity or perform any act aimed at the undermining or destruction of the constitutional order established by this Constitution or at the destruction of any of the rights and liberties set forth in this Part or at their limitation to a greater extent than is provided for therein.

Article 35. The legislative, executive and judicial authorities of the Republic shall be bound to secure, within the limits of their respective competence, the efficient application of the provisions of this Part.

CZECHOSLOVAKIA. The Czech and Slovak Federative Republic is a landlocked country in eastern Europe. It has borders with Austria, Hungary, the Federal Republic of Germany, the German Democratic Republic, and the Union of Soviet Socialist Republics. It achieved independence in 1918 as a result of the breakup of the Austro–Hungarian monarchy and became a member of the United Nations in 1945. Its population is estimated by the UN (1990) to be 15,829,000. Ethnic groups include Czechs, Slovaks, Ukrainians, Russians, Poles, Hungarians, Germans, and others. Languages commonly used include Czech, Slovak, and Hungarian. It is estimated that, for those who profess a religious faith, Christianity is predominant.

The government (1990) took the form of a republic. The Slovaks, who account for about one-third of the population, have often called for a separate State but have accepted the country's new name, Czech and Slovak Federated Republic, adopted by Parliament on 20 April 1989. Until the government is reorganized, the governing organ is the bicameral Federal Assembly, composed of a 200-member House of the People and a 150-member House of Nations (75 Czech and 75 Slovak deputies elected by their respective national councils). The president, elected by the Federal Assembly for a term of five years, is head of State and exercises executive authority. He appoints the premier and his cabinet, who are, however, responsible to the Federal Assembly. Political parties include the Communist Party, the Socialist Party, the Peoples Party (in the Czech region), and the Slovak Freedom Party (in Slovakia).

Although Czechoslovakia prospered after freeing itself from its Austrian rulers and was well-governed by its first presidents, T.G. Masaryk and Eduard Benes, it experienced serious political difficulties because of the presence within its borders of several antagonistic national minorities. A European crisis developed when the German minority, led by Konrad Henlein and backed by Adolph Hitler, demanded union of the country's predominantly German districts with Germany. Under threat of war, Hitler was given the Bohemian borderlands (*Sudetenland*) by the Munich Pact of September 1938.

During World War II, a provisional Czech government was set up in England, and Czech units fought against Nazi Germany. In April 1944, Russian and American forces moved into Czechoslovakia; and, in May 1945, European military operations ended with the fall of Prague. The Potsdam Conference of 1945 approved the expulsion of 3,000,000 Germans from Czechoslovakia, as well as an exchange of national minorities between Czechoslovakia and Hungary.

In the elections of 1946, the Communist Party emerged as the strongest political group. With Benes as president, a six-party coalition cabinet was formed with Clement Gottwald, head of the party, as premier. In February 1948, communist elements seized complete control of the State in a *coup d'etat.* Shortly thereafter, Benes resigned and Gottwald assumed the office of president. A new constitution was adopted which provided a measure of autonomy for Slovakia. Under its provisions, nearly every branch of Czech economic life was nationalized.

Czechoslovakia's transition to a multi-party political system may be said to have started in January 1977, when some 1,000 Czech "dissidents" signed a declaration of human rights known as Charter 77 (see CZECHOSLOVAKIA: CHARTER 77), based on provisions of the International Covenants on Human Rights and designed to enable all citizens "to live and work as free people."

Charter 77, and the loose organization which supported it, led the Czech government to tighten restrictions on the exercise of civil and political rights. Nevertheless, it gained strength over the years; and, in October 1989, Milos Jakes, chairman of the Communist Party of Czechoslovakia, found it necessary to send heavily armed police to crush a demonstration by some 10,000 people shouting "Freedom!" and "We want democracy!" after the arrest of Vaclav Havel, one of the originators of Charter 77, and other leading dissidents.

Demonstrators again thronged into the streets of Prague on 17 November after Mr. Jakes had asserted that such protests would not be tolerated and were brutally dispersed by the police. Two days later, they returned to protest the police actions, and elements of opposition formed an organization known as the Civic Forum to demand reforms.

On 24 November, Milos Jakes resigned; and, on 29 November, Parliament stripped the Czech constitution of the provision giving the Communist Party the dominant role in society. On 10 December, Czechoslovakia's first cabinet in 41 years without a Communist majority was sworn in.

On 28 December, Alexander Dubcek, who had led the ill-fated "Prague Spring" liberalization movement of 1968, was elected chairman of the Parliament. And on the next day, Vaclav Havel, playright and spokesman for Charter 77, was elected as Czechoslovakia's president.

With free elections scheduled for mid-1990 to create a State authority truly reflecting the will of the people, Parliament changed the country's name, on 20 April, from Czechoslovak Socialist Republic to Czech and Slovak Federative Republic.

CZECHOSLOVAKIA: CHARTER 77. In January 1977, a document signed by over 1,000 Czech citizens was circulated throughout the country, calling upon the government to live up to the obligations it had assumed in signing the International Covenants on Human Rights on 7 October 1968 and in ratifying them on 23 December 1975. It quoted extensively from texts contained in those covenants, which previously had been published only in obscure official publications not available to the general public, and pointed out that they were not being implemented.

Circulation of the document, which came to be known as "Charter 77," was met immediately by tighter government restrictions on the enjoyment of human rights and fundamental freedoms. But, in the long run, its appeal for justice and democracy prevailed.

The association of Czech citizens which drafted and circulated the document Charter 77 also called itself Charter 77. One of its spokesmen, Vaclav Havel, later was elected president of Czechoslovakia.

The text of Charter 77 is as follows:

On 13 October 1976 the Collection of Laws of the C.S.S.R. (No. 120) published the "International Covenant on Civil and Political Rights" and the "International Covenant on Economic, Social and Cultural Rights" which had been signed in the name of our Republic in 1968, confirmed in Helsinki in 1975, and which acquired validity here on 23 March 1976. From that day our citizens have the right, and our State the duty, to be guided by them.

The rights and freedoms of everyone, which are guaranteed by these Covenants, are important values of civilization for which the efforts of many progressive forces have been directed in history, and their statement in law can significantly assist human development in our society.

We therefore welcome the fact that the Czechoslovak Socialist Republic has ratified these Covenants.

Their publication, however, reminds us with new urgency how many fundamental civil rights remain, unfortunately, only on paper in our country. Countless citizens have to live in fear that, if they were to express themselves in accordance with their convictions, they or their children could be denied the right to education.

Exercising the right "to seek, receive and impart information and ideas of all kinds, regardless of frontiers, either orally, in writing or in print" or "in the form of art" (Article 19 [2] of the Covenant on Civil and Political Rights) is attacked not only extra-judicially, but also judicially, often in the guise of criminal prosecution (witness to this are, for example, the trials of young musicians now proceeding).

Freedom of expression is suppressed by the central control over all communications media and publishing and cultural facilities. No political, philosophical, scientific or artistic expression which however slightly deviates from the official ideological or aesthetic bounds can be published; public criticism of crisis symptoms in society is barred; there is no opportunity for public defense against false and offensive accusations by official propaganda (the legal protection against "attacks on honor and reputation," explicitly guaranteed by article 17 of the Covenant on Civil and Political Rights, does not exist in practice); false accusations cannot be refuted and every attempt to get restitution through the courts is in vain; open debate in the area of intellectual and cultural work is excluded. Many scholars and cultural workers and other citizens are discriminated against merely because in earlier years they legally or openly voiced opinions which are condemned by the present political power.

The right to thought, conscience and religion, explicitly guaranteed by article 18 of the Covenant on Civil and Political Rights, is systematically restricted by arbitrary authority: by curtailing the activities of priests, who are permanently threatened by the possibility that State consent to the performance of their office may be refused or withdrawn; by job or other sanctions against those who express their religious beliefs in word or deed; by suppressing religious teaching, etc.

As an instrument for restricting, and often completely suppressing, many civil rights we have the system whereby, in effect, all institutions and organizations of state are subordinated to the political directives from the apparatus of the ruling party and to the decisions of individuals influential in the power structure. The Constitution of the C.S.S.R. and the other laws and legal norms give no authority either for the content and form, nor for the making and application of such decisions; they are often purely verbal, entirely unknown to citizens, and uncontrollable by them; their originators are responsible to none but themselves and their hierarchy, yet they exert a decisive influence on the legislative and executive organs of state administration, the judiciary, the trade unions, organizations around special interests and other public organizations, other political parties, enterprises, factories institutes, offices, and other establishments, and their orders take precedence over the law. When an organization or individual comes into conflict with such an order in their interpretation of their rights and duties, they cannot turn to an impartial institution. All this gravely limits enjoyment of the rights deriving from articles 21 and 22 of the Covenant (the right to freedom of association and the prohibition of any restriction on the exercise of that right) and from article 25 (the equal right of everyone to take part in the conduct of public affairs), and 26 (prohibiting any discrimination before the law). The present situation also prevents workers and other employees from forming and joining the trade unions of their choice for the promotion and protection of their economic and social interests and from exercising the right to strike (article 8, para. 1 of the International Covenant on Economic, Social and Cultural Rights).

Other civil rights, including the explicit prohibition of "arbitrary or unlawful interference with privacy, family, home or correspondence" (article 17 of the Covenant on Civil and Political Rights) are also gravely infringed by the many ways in which the Ministry of the Interior controls citizens' lives, for instance by tapping telephones, by installing listening devices in homes, by checking on mail, by personal surveillance, by house searches, or by forming a network of informers from among the public (often won over by impermissable threats or promises), etc. The Ministry also frequently intervenes in employers' decisions, inspires discriminatory actions by official bodies and organizations, or campaigns in the media. This activity is not regulated by law; it is secret and the public has no defence against it.

In cases of politically motivated prosecution, the examining and judicial organs infringe the rights of the accused and of their defence, although these are guaranteed by article 14 of the International Covenant on Civil and Political Rights. People convicted in this manner are treated in prison in a way which denies them their human dignity, endangers their health and attempts to break them morally.

There is also a general infringement of paragraph 2 of article 2 of the Covenant on Civil and Political Rights, which guarantees the right of everyone to leave any country, including his own; under the pretext of "national security," mentioned in paragraph 3 of that article, the exercise of this right is tied to various impermissible conditions. Arbitrary procedure is also employed in issuing entry visas to foreign nationals, many of whom are unable to visit Czechoslovakia merely because they have had working or friendly contacts with people who are discriminated against here.

Some citizens call attention to the constant infringement of human rights and democratic freedoms—either privately at their places of work, or publicly, which is possible in practice only through the foreign media—and demand remedy in concrete cases; but their voices usually get no response, or they become the subjects of investigation.

The responsibility for maintaining civil rights in the land belongs, of course, to the political and State power. But not to it alone. Everyone bears his share of responsibility for public matters, and hence also for the observance of treaties valid in law, which are, in any case, binding not only upon governments but also on all citizens.

The sense of this responsibility, the belief in the meaning of citizens' commitment, the will for it, and the common need to seek a new and more effective expression of it, has led us to think of drawing up Charter 77, the origin of which we are publicly announcing today.

Charter 77 is a free, informal and open association of people of varied opinions, varied beliefs and professions, who are united by the will individually and jointly to work for the respecting of civil and human rights in our country and in the world—rights recognized for all men in both International Covenants on Human Rights, in the Final Act of the Helsinki Conference, in various other international documents against war, force and social and spiritual oppression, and which above all are set out in the Universal Declaration of Human Rights.

Charter 77 is rooted in the solidarity and friendship of people who share a concern for the ideals which they have seen, and still see, as part of their lives and work.

Charter 77 is not an organisation, it has no status, no permanent bodies or formally organised membership. Anyone who agrees with its ideas, takes part in its work, and supports it, belongs to it.

Charter 77 is not a basis for activity as a political opposition. It aims to serve the general interest as do many similar initiatives by citizens in various countries in the West and the East. Thus it is not intended to put forward its own programs of political or social reform or changes, but to conduct in its sphere a constructive dialogue with the political and State power, especially by calling attention to various cases where human and civil rights are infringed, to propose solutions, submit more general proposals aimed at strengthening these rights and their guarantees, to act as an intermediary in possible conflict situations which may be caused by the lack of political rights, etc.

By its symbolical name Charter 77 stresses its origin on the threshold of a year declared as the Year of Political Prisoners, and in which the Belgrade conference is to examine how the Helsinki undertakings have been implemented.

As signatories to this declaration, we empower Prof Dr. Jan Patocka, Dr. h.c. Vaclav Havel and Prof. Jiri Hajek DrSc to be spokesmen for Charter 77. These spokesmen are authorized to represent the Charter both in relation to State and other organisations, and to the public here and abroad, and they guarantee by their signatures the authenticity of the documents. In us, and in other citizens who join in, they will have their associates who will take part with them in any necessary negotiations, will undertake specific tasks and will share all responsibility with them.

We believe that Charter 77 will contribute to enabling all Czechoslovak citizens to live and work as free people.

D

DEATH PENALTY: APPLICATION TO PERSONS UNDER THE AGE OF 18. The UN SUB-COMMISSION ON PREVENTION OF DISCRIMINATION AND PROTECTION OF MINORITIES at its 1989 session, on recommendation of its WORKING GROUP ON DETENTION, urgently appealed (resolution 1989/32) to all member States that apply the death penalty to persons under the age of 18 to take the necessary legislative and administrative measures with a view to stopping this practice forthwith and requested States in which the death penalty is applicable to consider the possibility of enacting legislation specifically prohibiting its application to persons under 18 years of age, in accordance with existing international standards.

In support of this decision, the sub-commission pointed out that the non-applicability of the death penalty to persons under the age of 18 is stipulated by the INTERNATIONAL COVENANT ON CIVIL AND POLITICAL RIGHTS (article 6 [5]), the AMERICAN CONVENTION ON HUMAN RIGHTS (article 4 [5]), the CONVENTION ON THE RIGHTS OF THE CHILD (article 37 [a]), and the GENEVA CONVENTIONS and their PROTOCOLS I and II. It also recalled that the UN General Assembly had opposed the imposition of the death penalty on persons under the age of 18 (for example, in resolutions 35/172 of 15 December 1980 and 40/143 of 13 December 1985), indicating that the application of the death penalty for crimes committed by persons below that age violates minimum international standards for the protection of human rights applicable to all member States.

The sub-commission requested the Secretary-General to transmit its resolution to all governments and to specialized agencies and non-governmental organizations, requesting their comments on this issue and information on the relevant existing legislation.

SEE ALSO United States of America: Execution of Juvenile Offenders.

DEATH PENALTY: SAFEGUARDS. The following safeguards, guaranteeing protection of the rights of those facing the death penalty, were approved by the ECONOMIC AND SOCIAL COUNCIL of the United Nations on 25 May 1984 (resolution 1984/50):

1. In countries which have not abolished the death penalty, capital punishment may be imposed only for the most serious crimes, it being understood that their scope should not go beyond intentional crimes with lethal or other extremely grave consequences.

2. Capital punishment may be imposed only for a crime for which the death penalty is prescribed by law at the time of its commission, it being understood that if, subsequent to the commission of the crime, provision is made by law for the imposition of a lighter penalty, the offender shall benefit thereby.

3. Persons below 18 years of age at the time of the commission of the crime shall not be sentenced to death, nor shall the death sentence be carried out on pregnant women, or on new mothers, or on persons who have become insane.

4. Capital punishment may be imposed only when the guilt of the person charged is based upon clear and convincing evidence leaving no room for an alternative explanation of the facts.

5. Capital punishment may only be carried out pursuant to a final judgement rendered by a competent court after legal process which gives all possible safeguards to ensure a fair trial, at least equal to those contained in article 14 of the International Covenant on Civil and Political Rights, including the right of anyone suspected of or charged with a crime for which capital punishment may be imposed to adequate legal assistance at all stages of the proceedings.

6. Anyone sentenced to death shall have the right to appeal to a court of higher jurisdiction, and steps should be taken to ensure that such appeals shall become mandatory.

7. Anyone sentenced to death shall have the right to seek pardon, or commutation of sentence; pardon or commutation of sentence may be granted in all cases of capital punishment.

8. Capital punishment shall not be carried out pending any appeal or other recourse procedure or other proceeding relating to pardon or commutation of the sentence.

9. Where capital punishment occurs, it shall be carried out so as to inflict the minimum possible suffering.

SEE ALSO Safeguards Guaranteeing the Protection of the Rights of Those Facing the Death Penalty.

DEATH PENALTY IN ARMED CONFLICTS. The GENEVA CONVENTION RELATIVE TO THE TREATMENT OF PRISONERS OF WAR of 12 August 1949 provides safeguards against the arbitrary imposition of the death penalty on such prisoners in the following terms:

Article 100. Prisoners of war and the Protecting Powers shall be informed, as soon as possible, of the offences which are punishable by the death sentence under the laws of the Detaining Power.

Other offences shall not thereafter be made punishable by the death penalty without concurrence of the Power upon which the prisoners of war depend.

The death sentence cannot be pronounced on a prisoner of war unless the attention of the court has, in accordance with article 87, second paragraph been particularly called to the fact since the accused is not a national of the Detaining Power, he is not bound to it by any duty of allegiance, and that he is in its power as the result of circumstances independent of his own will.

Article 101. If the death penalty is pronounced on a prisoner of war, the sentence shall not be executed before the expiration of a period of at least six months from the date when the Protecting Power receives, at an indicated address, the detailed communication provided for in article 107.

Similarly, the GENEVA CONVENTION RELATIVE TO THE PROTECTION OF CIVILIAN PERSONS IN TIME OF WAR of 12 August 1949 restricts the freedom of the occupying power to impose capital punishment upon such persons, in the following terms:

Article 68 (2). The penal provisions promulgated by the Occupying Power in accordance with articles 64 and 65 may impose the death penalty on a protected person only in cases where the person is guilty of espionage, of serious acts of sabotage against the military installations of the Occupying Power or of international offences which caused the death of one or more persons, provided that such offences were punishable by death under the law of the occupied territory in force before the occupation began.

(3) The death penalty may not be pronounced on a protected person unless the attention of the court has been particularly called to the fact that since the accused is not a national of the Occupying Power, he is not bound to it by any duty of allegiance.

(4) In any case, the death penalty may not be pronounced on a protected person who was under 18 years of age at the time of the offence.

The same convention sets out procedural requirements to be met before the death penalty may be carried out, as follows:

In no case shall persons condemned to death be deprived of the right to petition for pardon or reprieve.

No death sentence shall be carried out before the expiration of a period of at least six months from the date of receipt by the Protecting Power of the notification of the final judgment confirming such death sentence, or of an order denying pardon or reprieve.

The six months' period of suspension of the death sentence herein prescribed may be reduced in individual cases in circumstances of grave emergency involving an organized threat to the security of the Occupying Power or its

forces, provided always that the Protecting Power is notified of such reduction and is given reasonable time and opportunity to make representations to the competent occupying authorities in respect of such death sentences.

Further, PROTOCOL I, ADDITIONAL TO THE GENEVA CONVENTIONS OF 12 AUGUST 1949, provides (article 76) that pregnant women shall not be executed and (article 77) that no one may be executed who was under 18 when the offense was committed.

SEE ALSO Armed Conflicts; Executions: Report of Special Rapporteur; Safeguards Guaranteeing the Protection of the Rights of Those Facing the Death Penalty.

DEATH THREATS. In his annual report to the UN Commission on Human Rights, the commission's Special Rapporteur on Summary and Arbitrary Executions S. Amos Wako (Kenya) indicated that he had received more appeals in 1989 than in previous years for urgent intervention in cases of death threats and had taken immediate action in every case where such a threat posed *prima facie* imminent danger to the life of those who had received such threats. In this connection, he informed the commission (UN Doc. E/CN.4/1990/22, chap. III, para. 448–454):

Reports of death threats and subsequent assassinations are still confined to a limited number of countries in certain regions. However, this heinous practice of terror is gradually spreading to countries where such practice had not been known to exist, but where the political and social situation has been markedly deteriorating.

According to the information received death threats are made against persons of various backgrounds and professions, in particular the following:

(a) Judges, lawyers, magistrates and prosecutors, etc., involved in trials, investigations or other legal proceedings;

(b) Human rights activists who collect and publicize cases of violation of human rights at the local, regional and/or national levels, and organize human rights activities;

(c) Public office holders, including legislators and community councillors, who publicly demand justice in cases of human rights violations;

(d) Trade unionists who organize workers and try to defend workers' rights;

(e) Educators who engage in adult education programmes and activities aimed at creating awareness of human rights in rural areas;

(f) Journalists who investigate and report cases of violation of human rights through the mass media;

(g) Eyewitnesses of crimes who are willing to testify in a trial or before a magistrate;

(h) Members of opposition groups, including political parties.

Judging by the information received on various cases of death threats, their aim appears to be to terrorize the persons concerned in order to prevent them from pursuing activities which are perceived as contrary to the interests of the authors of the threats.

The authors of death threats usually remain anonymous. However, they often use names of paramilitary or "vigilante" groups whose identify remains vague or unknown.

Threats are made by telephone, letters delivered to the homes of the victims, pamphlets, or "death lists" carrying the names of prospective targets of assassination.

According to the appeals made to the Special Rapporteur, in most cases the authorities had taken no effective measures to protect those who had received death threats or to undertake appropriate investigations. The appeals also indicated the involvement of the Government concerned, either directly, by orders given to officials or the employment of individuals or groups under the control of the Government, or indirectly by connivance in or collusion with such death threats by private individuals or groups. Absence of official investigation, prosecution and/or punishment of those responsible for such threats was the rule rather than the exception.

In certain countries where death threats are reported to be widespread, the majority of the victims of summary or arbitrary executions had in fact received death threats before they were assassinated.

SEE ALSO Terrorist Acts.

DEBT BONDAGE. A practice giving rise to effects similar to those of slavery or the slave trade, defined in the SUPPLEMENTARY CONVENTION ON THE ABOLITION OF SLAVERY, THE SLAVE TRADE AND INSTITUTIONS OR PRACTICES SIMILAR TO SLAVERY (article 1 [a]) as "the status or condition arising from a pledge by a debtor of his personal services or of those of a person under his control as security for debt, if the value of those services as reasonably assessed is not applied towards the liquidation of the debt or the length and nature of those services are not respectively limited and defined."

At its 1988 session, the WORKING GROUP ON CONTEMPORARY FORMS OF SLAVERY of the SUB-COMMISSION ON PREVENTION OF DISCRIMINATION AND PROTECTION OF MINORITIES reviewed recent developments relating to slavery and the slave trade. Its examination of the question of debt bondage was summarized in its report to the sub-commission (UN Doc. E/CN.4/Sub.2/1988/32, chap. III D, para. 58–64) as follows:

The representative of Defence for Children International reminded the Working Group that debt bondage existed in many countries in Africa, North and South America, Europe and the Middle East as well as in Asia, and that a general programme should be drawn up for its elimination.

The representative of the Anti-Slavery Society again raised the issue of bonded labour in India, maintaining the Society's position that there was cause for concern, because, although India was not the only country where debt bondage occurred, it was home to the largest number of bonded labourers in the world (the Society's sister organization, the Bonded Liberation Front, conservatively putting the number of chronic cases at 5 million).

The Working Group was informed that the Society had recently finished its own investigation into the nature of contemporary bonded labour, particularly as it affected the landless in, and migrants from, Bihar. Allegedly, thousands of Biharis migrated to economically more advanced areas every year. Frequently they were forced to do so by the village money-lender. Until the money was repaid in full, the debtor remained in bondage and his family formed a living surety for his return—if he left to work as a seasonal worker—or repayment. Reference was also made to sharecropping, which allegedly continued to be a means of entrapping borrowers into debt bondage; a poor peasant farmer might become a sharecropper and fall further into debt, in which case his land could be taken in lieu of unredeemed loans, causing him to join the ranks of the landless. In such a manner, a landless labourer or a poor peasant with insufficient land might be forced through the lack of alternative local employment to sharecrop for a large landlord or rich peasant; he became indebted to his "partner" through taking out loans in order to perform his role as a sharecropper. The eventual result was an increase in debt bondage.

In addition, it was suggested that the introduction of new technology in the more economically advanced States, particularly in Punjab and Haryana, had aggravated rather than relieved the age-old condition of debt bondage in India. That development, allied with traditional practices and obligations, had resulted in an increase in contemporary slavery. The Society repeated its pleas made in the Working Group in previous years, and urged the Government of India to take all measures not only to free its most vulnerable people, but to ensure that freed bonded labourers received the full rehabilitation sums due to them under the 1976 Bonded Labour (Abolition) Act.

Another representative of the Society suggested that a United Nations fact-finding mission could be sent to investigate the situation of bonded labour in South Asia. Extensively quoting from a committee of the Indian Parliament, he indicated that bonded labour was still a serious problem in India and pointed out that the problem also existed elsewhere, including Nepal, Pakistan and Bangladesh. He also urged that the Working Group's recommendation at its fifth session regarding the organization of a round table or symposium in order to study the problem in depth should be implemented, suggesting that its venue be New Delhi. He also called for the implementation of all other relevant recommendations adopted by the Working Group during its previous sessions.

The Observer for India stated that his Government was acutely conscious of the urgency of the problem of bonded labour and emphasized that attempts to tackle the problem were being made at various levels of the Indian Government. The Parliamentary Committee Report quoted in detail by a representative of the Anti-Slavery Society showed how much the Parliament was doing in this area. The press had also been giving a good deal of attention to the question and non-governmental organizations and voluntary agencies were also engaged in the struggle against bonded labour. In view of the fact that such awareness already existed in India and also because of the tremendous involvement of the Government in the efforts to end bonded labour, the Observer for India requested the Working Group to reject the suggestion made by one of the representatives of the Anti-Slavery Society that a United Nations investigative team should go to India for the purpose of examining the problem of bonded labour. Had the Government been turning a blind eye to the problem there would have been some justification for a visit by such a team but since this was not the case this suggestion did not merit consideration.

The Observer for India reiterated his Government's commitment to abolish the inhuman and degrading practice of bonded labour. The Bonded Labour (Abolition) Act in India had been amended in 1985 to clarify the definition of bonded labour, and it was hoped that the amendment would facilitate speedier and easier identification of bonded labourers. It had also been decided to secure the participation of voluntary agencies in the work of identification, and he explained that the procedure for the sanctioning of rehabilitation schemes for bonded labourers and the release of grants had been simplified and clarified. The sum allocated for rehabilitation assistance had been increased by more than 50 per cent in 1986, and measures had been taken to integrate the programmes for the rehabilitation of bonded labourers into other programmes. The principal idea underlying those measures was to ensure that the bonded labourers did not fall back into bondage; in certain States where government land was not available, land had been purchased and then allotted to released bonded labourers. In informing the Working Group of all those actions, the Observer for India said that they testified to his Government's determination to translate its commitment to eradicate bonded labour into action. The Observer for India answered some specific questions raised by the representative of the Anti-Slavery Society. However, he said that he would transmit them to his Government for information.

On the basis of the discussion summarized above, the working group made a number of recommendations, among them (1) that all competent United Nations agencies, development banks, and intergovernmental bodies involved in development projects ensure that their projects do not perpetuate or involve **BONDED LABOR** and that they contribute to its elimination; (2) that member States where the phenomenon of bonded labor exists be urged to take effective means, especially at the implementation level, to curtail such labor, e.g., (a) by seeking and encouraging the involvement of non-governmental organizations; (b) by effective dissemination of national legislation on labor rights and on the prohibition of bonded labor particularly directed towards victims of bonded labor; (c) by setting up vigilance committees under the law; and (d) by invoking to the fullest extent the constraining power of the law against violators; and (3) that ways and means be found so that transnational financial benefits be provided for liberated bonded laborers within the framework of rehabilitation measures.

Recommendations along these lines were adopted by the sub-commission (resolution 1988/30) and forwarded to the **COMMISSION ON HUMAN RIGHTS.**

SEE ALSO Forced Labor; Slavery and the Slave Trade; Traffic in Persons and Exploitation of the Prostitution of Others.

DECADES TO COMBAT RACISM AND RACIAL DISCRIMINATION. In 1972, the UN General Assembly launched (resolution 3057 [XXVIII]) the Decade to Combat Racism and Racial Discrimination, which was inaugurated on 10 December 1973, the 25th anniversary of the adoption of the UNIVERSAL DECLARATION OF HUMAN RIGHTS. The decade was designed as a period for intensified national, regional, and international action aimed at achieving the total and unconditional elimination of racism and racial discrimination in all its forms.

In 1983, the assembly, convinced of the need to take continuing and reinforced measures for the elimination of racism and racial discrimination, proclaimed the ten-year period beginning on 10 December 1983 as the Second Decade to Combat Racism and Racial Discrimination (resolution 38/14).

At its 1983 session, the SUB-COMMISSION ON PREVENTION OF DISCRIMINATION AND PROTECTION OF MINORITIES decided (resolution 1983/10) to appoint Mr. Asjbørn Eide (Norway) as its special rapporteur to prepare a comprehensive analysis of the achievements made and obstacles encountered during the first decade. Mr. Eide presented a progress report on the subject to the sub-commission in 1985 (UN Doc. E CN.4/Sub.2/1985/7), in which he reviewed the activities of the first decade. His final report, entitled *Study on the Achievements Made and Obstacles Encountered During the Decades to Combat Racism and Racial Discrimination* (UN Doc. E/CN.4/Sub.2/1989/8 and Add. 1) was presented to, and examined by, the sub-commission at its 1989 session.

The study endeavors to evaluate the achievements of the two decades. Chapter I highlights the main concerns of both decades as expressed in their respective programs of action. Chapter II describes the measures taken by the United Nations bodies and specialized agencies, by governments, and by regional and international organizations concerned. Chapter III reviews and assesses the wide variety of approaches adopted with a view to dealing with the manifold aspects of racism and racial discrimination in the modern world.

In Chapter IV, the special rapporteur presents the following conclusions and recommendations (UN Doc. E/CN.4/Sub.2/1989/8/Add. 1):

A. Conclusions

The main conclusion to be drawn for this study is that problems of racism occur in several different contexts. The United Nations has gradually recognized that they require different kinds of response. As a consequence, the need for co-ordination is great and the difficulties involved substantial. Many United Nations agencies deal with one or more aspects of racism without sufficient awareness of what others are doing, and with even less co-operation in implementation of measures adopted.

It is a great step forward that the task of co-ordination has been assigned to the Under-Secretary-General, Mr. Jan Martenson, with the assistance of the Centre for Human Rights. Significant steps have since been taken in the implementation of this task. More could be done to clarify the elements involved in this co-ordination.

As a minimum, it requires an improved exchange of information about steps taken and initiatives planned by different organs and agencies. Ideally, it should go beyond this to the formulation of a plan for concerted action where the different agencies undertake those parts of the plan for which they are functionally most qualified.

One significant victory has been won. It was largely achieved even before the launching of the Decades to Combat Racism and Racial Discrimination, but has been consolidated since: theories of superiority and inferiority on biological grounds have been utterly discredited. Very few participants in serious intellectual discourse make such assertions any more, since they fly in the face of scientific evidence, and the credibility of persons making such assertions would be lost. This victory is due to a large extent to the scientific community, the UNESCO has played a major role in encouraging science to focus on these fallacies of the past.

Today, the problems are more clearly faced as social conflicts and as cultural and ethnic exclusion and rejection. They have been shaped, however, by past pseudo-scientific theories and corresponding attitudes. The subconscious residues of these still need to be eradicated.

Apartheid continues to be the most serious problem, to which priority attention should be given. It has been shown that the alleged reforms are more formal than real. The distribution of South African land continues to be built on the assumption that the white minority shall continue its control over more than 80 per cent of it. Racist classifications of people continue as they have in the past; the apparent extensions of political rights continue to follow racial lines.

Nevertheless, there is a ferment of change also in South Africa. It is due in large part to the internal anti-*apartheid* movements, but also the external solidarity with these groups and the pressure directed against the Government. Changing attitudes can also be detected within the white community. Three groups can now be discerned: at one extreme are those who will cling to their established privileges at all cost. At the other end are those white groups which now join hands with the anti-*apartheid* movements; their numbers are increasing. Finally, there is the large middle group whose members are likely to make a rational cost/benefit analysis of the situation; when the cost of maintaining *apartheid* becomes higher than the privileges they gain from it, they will give it up.

For the international community, therefore, the response should be threefold. Sanctions, more concerted and comprehensive than today, should be directed against the South African economy to take away any benefit which the policy of *apartheid* gives it. Parallel with these sanctions, however, a systematic policy of co-operation should be developed with groups which, in one way or other, are active in the anti-*apartheid* struggle. Alternative contacts within sport, culture and even economy, under conditions laid down by the liberation movements and the internal anti-*apartheid* groups, would strengthen these in the titanic but largely non-violent struggle now going on in South Africa.

In Namibia, we will hopefully soon see an outcome where discrimination is brought to an end and democracy installed, but the international community must keep a close watch on the process.

As regards other situations of discrimination, substantial variations can be observed. While great steps forward have been made regarding awareness of the problems facing *indigenous* peoples and of ways in which these should be addressed—an awareness where the Sub-Commission, and the International Labour Organisation, have played major roles—the problems facing *minorities* have increased with the growing intensity of ethnic conflicts and nationalism. Undoubtedly, this will be a major challenge for the international community in the years to come. Finally, the problems facing *migrant workers* and *refugees* are substantial, and great efforts have to be made in order to face up to these problems.

The Sub-Commission should shoulder its part of the responsibility to find appropriate solutions. Hopefully, the analysis in the preceding sections and the recommendations which follow can be of some help for this.

B. Recommendations

The following recommendations concerning various aspects of racism are submitted by the Special Rapporteur.

1. General. In preparation for the completion of the Second Decade, the United Nations should start drafting now a plan for concerted actions to implement the many specific measures which have been recommended in the course of the Decades.

The function of co-ordination of the Under-Secretary-General for Human Rights should be strengthened. More resources should be made available for this purpose to the Centre for Human Rights. There should be more co-operation among the United Nations organs and agencies involved. The specialized agencies should be encouraged to develop more comprehensive plans within their functional field of competence. Contacts should be established or improved with regional organizations and non-governmental organizations, both international and national. This should include contacts with civil rights movements and the organizations of indigenous peoples and of migrant workers.

It might be desirable to update the study on racial discrimination prepared by Hernán Santa Cruz and presented in 1976. The main focus should be an assessment of the achievements made at the national level in different parts of the world in the elimination of racial discrimination. The assessment should examine the level of enjoyment by different ethnic and racial groups of all categories of human rights: civil, political, economic, social and cultural. It would be useful to divide the assessment according to the main contexts in which discrimination is likely to occur: *Apartheid*, discrimination against *indigenous peoples*, situations which originated in *slavery*, situations affecting *migrant workers and aliens,* and finally situations involving *members of ethnic groups.*

Particular attention should be given, in this assessment, to the scope and effectiveness of affirmative action undertaken within national jurisdictions in order to facilitate equal enjoyment of social and economic rights, as well as civil and political rights.

In order to bring about a complete elimination of the fallacious mythology of racial superiority and to foster the awareness of the fundamental unity of human kind, UNESCO should be encouraged, in co-operation with the Centre for Human Rights, to intensify its work. While biologists have already contributed significantly to this task, UNESCO should encourage social scientists to explore the hidden and subconscious elements of racism and ways in which it manifests itself. UNESCO should also intensify its efforts to bring these insights into education at all levels.

2. *South Africa.* United Nations agencies should reassess their approaches to the elimination of *apartheid.*

Sanctions should be continued and intensified. The United Nations should continue to call for global participation in these efforts. The sanctions should be directed against the South African economy, the South African military apparatus, and the South African administration, which is operating an illegitimate system. Sanctions and non-co-operation should be the main policy pursued by the international community directed against all elements of the South African society which operates under the *apartheid* system, including non-co-operation in all forms of sports and cultural activities which are based on *apartheid* regulations.

On the other hand, the United Nations should, in collaboration with liberation movements and with anti-*apartheid* movements inside South Africa, develop guidelines for international co-operation with those organizations and entities within South Africa which are actively struggling to change the system to bring about a democratic society. Alternative cultural movements, alternative sports networks, and other institutions explicitly declaring that they will not conform to *apartheid* regulations, should be encouraged.

Assistance to victims of *apartheid* should be intensified. In the process of transition through which South Africa will be going in the next decades, there is unfortunately a great risk that there will be more victims and the need for international solidarity to assist will become greater.

3. *Indigenous Peoples.* States should be encouraged to ratify as soon as possible the new ILO Convention on Tribal and Indigenous Peoples in Independent Countries.

ILO might consider the possibility of developing a procedure by which representatives of indigenous organizations can be associated with the monitoring of the implementation of the above-mentioned convention.

The Working Group of the Sub-Commission on Prevention of Discrimination and Protection of Minorities should complete as soon as possible the preparation of the Declaration of the Rights of Indigenous Peoples.

The Sub-Commission should recommend an appropriate procedure by which to monitor the implementation of that Declaration. In the meantime, the Working Group on Indigenous Peoples should continue to review developments affecting the rights of indigenous peoples in all parts of the world.

Governments should adopt legislative and administrative measures to prevent discrimination against members of indigenous peoples.

Relations between States and indigenous peoples living inside their territory should be based as far as possible on the principle of free and informed consent and co-operation.

States should, to the greatest extent possible, recognize the principle that indigenous peoples have a right to development based on their own preferences and cultural systems.

4. *Situations Originating in Slavery.* Research should be carried out in countries concerned to determine the degree to which descendants of persons held as slaves continue to suffer from social handicaps or deprivations.

Effective affirmative action should be carried out until such time as members of these groups experience no further handicaps or deprivations. Such affirmative action should not be construed to constitute discrimination against members of the dominant society.

In these, as in other contexts where past discrimination continues to cause social deprivation, precautions should be taken to avoid excessive use of force by law enforcement officials against such groups.

5. *Migrant Workers and Other Aliens.* The Convention on Migrant Workers and Their Families, now under negotiation, should be completed as soon as possible, and governments should be encouraged to ratify or accede to it as soon as possible.

Steps should be taken to reduce the tensions existing in many countries between the migrant workers and other inhabitants of the country concerned. It is therefore recommended that intensified efforts be made to advance cultural understanding between these groups. Migrant workers, on their side, should recognize the need to abide by the law and principles of the countries in which they live; members of the host country should accept and tolerate that migrant communities maintain their cultural traditions and practices as far as this is compatible with the laws of the host country and with internationally recognized human rights.

6. *Ethnic Discrimination, Conflicts and Protection of Minorities.* The United Nations should recognize the complexity of these issues and develop more functional responses to them.

It is recommended that efforts to define minorities be suspended, in order to give priority to the substantive issues involved.

Since ethnic conflicts often give rise to chauvenism and exclusiveness, on the one hand, and unacceptable national repression, on the other, it is essential to develop guidelines making it possible to harmonize the quest for separateness with the need for unity.

Priority should be given to the prevention of policies by which members of settled ethnic minorities are forced or pressured to leave their country of citizenship.

Policies of transmigration inside national borders should only be carried out with the free and informed consent both of the groups moved to new regions and of the people living in the region to which they are moved.

The United Nations might consider developing guidelines for the enjoyment of *linguistic* rights. While these, as a minimum, imply the right of every individual to use his or her mother tongue as well as to receive and disseminate information in that language, it remains unclear what the extent of the right is in regard to school education, in administration, and in other fields.

The United Nations might also consider developing guidelines for the enjoyment of one's own culture. While it obviously implies the right to manifest the formal aspects of one's culture, in so far as these are not incompatible with the respect for other human rights, it remains unclear whether the right includes a protection of the *material basis* of that culture.

Surrounded with much greater controversy is the issue of partial autonomy for minorities. The United Nations might consider examining the conditions under which minorities should be entitled to demand partial autonomy, and the scope which such autonomy should be given.

The United Nations might also consider the issue of the content of the right to development in so far as minorities and ethnic groups are concerned. While it seems reasonable that such groups to some extent should be entitled to determine their own priorities in development, this should not be carried out in ways which cause unjust deprivation for other peoples in the country concerned.

7. Elimination of Discrimination in General. The centrepiece in these endeavours will continue to be the International Convention on the Elimination of All Forms of Racial Discrimination as applied by CERD. States which have still not done so should be encouraged to become parties to the Convention, and those which have made reservations should be encouraged to withdraw these.

All States parties to the Convention should also be encouraged to make a declaration under its article 14, recognizing the competence of CERD to receive individual communications.

The activities of CERD should receive more support, and it should be given more time for its deliberations. Ways should be sought by which it could be funded under the regular United Nations budget. States should comply more fully with their reporting duties under the Convention.

Improved contacts and exchange of information should be developed between CERD and the Sub-Commission on Prevention of Discrimination and Protection of Minorities. Since both deal with similar issues, they should benefit from each other's experience, but full account must be taken of the fact that CERD is an entirely independent body.

Whether States are parties or not to the Convention, they should take the necessary steps to eliminate racial discrimination. This should include more stringent penal provisions against racist actions, and prosecution of those who engage in incitement of racial hatred.

Not infrequently, ghetto-like situations of poverty face some of the groups which have been discussed above: members of indigenous peoples who have migrated to urban centres, some of the descendants of persons which in earlier generations were held in slavery, and migrant workers. This raises a need for special precautions in law enforcement. Care should be taken to prevent excessive use of force by law enforcement agencies. In their education, members of the police and prison personnel, as well as other law enforcement officials, must be made aware and understand the social and psychological situation of these groups. It is also necessary that law enforcement officials are brought to accept and internalize the ethical principles and human rights requirements which should guide their work.

States should also ensure that law enforcement agencies give equal protection to all groups in society. There should be no less budgetary allocations per capita for legal protection, including policing functions, to the social groups which experience social handicaps and deprivations, than to other groups in society.

Effective recourse measures should exist at the national level in all countries for victims of racial discrimination.

To assist governments in the implementation of the preceding recommendations, the Centre for Human Rights should accelerate its efforts to develop model laws for the prevention of racial discrimination.

Education, both at informal and formal levels, is essential to the prevention of discrimination. Basic attitudes are often shaped at a very early stage in the life of human beings and transmitted from parents to children or through informal contacts in the immediate neighbourhood. Efforts within formal institutions of education to focus on the elimination of racial prejudice must therefore be com-

bined with measures which address the early socialization of children. In adopting the measures provided for under article 7 of the International Convention on the Elimination of All Forms of Racial Discrimination, States should cooperate with UNESCO and the Centre for Human Rights to develop better approaches in this area.

After considering the special rapporteur's report, the sub-commission decided on 31 August 1989 (resolution 1989/19) to refer it to the Commission on Human Rights for further consideration and to recommend strongly that it should be published and distributed on as wide a scale as possible.

SEE ALSO Apartheid *entries; Committee on the Elimination of Racial Discrimination; Declaration of the Second World Conference to Combat Racism and Racial Discrimination; Declaration on the Elimination of All Forms of Racial Discrimination; Inter-American Declaration on Racial Integration in the Americas; International Convention on the Elimination of All Forms of Racial Discrimination; Race: UNESCO Statement on Scientific Facts; Race and Racial Prejudice: Impact of the UNESCO Declaration; Racial Discrimination; Racial Discrimination: National and Local Recourses; Racial Prejudice: Prevention; Racial, Religious and National Hatred; Racism: Administration of Criminal Justice; Racism and Racial Discrimination: Second Decade Action Program; UNESCO Declaration on Race and Racial Prejudice.*

DECLARATION BY UNITED NATIONS (1942). On 1 January 1942, the representatives of 26 nations fighting against the Axis aggressors signed, in Washington, D.C., a document entitled "Declaration by United Nations." This is the first landmark in the evolution of the United Nations. The text of the declaration (*U.S. Department of State Bulletin,* 3 January 1942, p. 3) is as follows:

The Governments signatory hereto,

Having subscribed to a common program of purposes and principles embodied in the Joint Declaration of the President of the United States of America and the Prime Minister of the United Kingdom of Great Britain and Northern Ireland dated 14 August, 1941, known as the Atlantic Charter,

Being convinced that complete victory over their enemies is essential to defend life, liberty, independence and religious freedom, and to preserve human rights and justice in their own lands as well as in other lands, and that they are now engaged in a common struggle against savage and brutal forces seeking to subjugate the world,

Declare:

(1) Each Government pledges itself to employ its full resources, military or economic, against those members of the Tripartite Pact and its adherents with which such government is at war.

(2) Each Government pledges itself to co-operate with the Governments signatory hereto and not to make a separate armistice or peace with the enemies.

The foregoing declaration may be adhered to by other nations which are, or which may be, rendering material assistance and contributions in the struggle for victory over Hitlerism.

Done at Washington, January First, 1942.

The original signatories of the declaration were the United States, United Kingdom, Union of Soviet Socialist Republics, China, Australia, Belgium, Canada, Costa Rica, Cuba, Czechoslovakia, Dominican Republic, El Salvador, Greece, Guatemala, Haiti, Honduras, India, Luxembourg, Netherlands, New Zealand, Nicaragua, Norway, Panama, Poland, South Africa, and Yugoslavia. Later, 21 additional nations communicated their adherence to the declaration.

SEE ALSO *Atlantic Charter.*

DECLARATION CONCERNING ESSENTIALS OF PEACE (1949).

The declaration resulted from a lengthy and heated debate in the UN General Assembly over two proposals: one, by the Union of Soviet Socialist Republics, that the five permanent members of the Security Council conclude among themselves a "Pact for Strengthening the Peace"; and the second, by the United Kingdom and the United States of America, that the United Nations lay down the basic principles necessary to achieve an enduring peace. The Soviet proposal was criticized as an attempt to create a body superseding the Security Council, while that of the United Kingdom and United States was said to be "wholly unrealistic, inadequate, and composed of phrases culled from the UN Charter." The UK/USA proposal was adopted by 53 votes to 5.

The declaration was adopted by the UN General Assembly on 1 December 1949 (resolution 290 [IV]). The text is as follows.

The General Assembly

1. Declares that the Charter of the United Nations, the most solemn pact of peace in history, lays down basic principles necessary for an enduring peace; that disregard of these principles is primarily responsible for the continuance of international tension; and that it is urgently necessary for all Members to act in accordance with these principles in the spirit of co-operation on which the United Nations was founded;

Calls upon every nation

2. To refrain from threatening or using force contrary to the Charter;

3. To refrain from any threats or acts, direct or indirect, aimed at impairing the freedom, independence or integrity of any State, or at fomenting civil strife and subverting the will of the people in any State;

4. To carry out in good faith its international agreements;

5. To afford all United Nations bodies full co-operation and free access in the performance of the tasks assigned to them under the Charter;

6. To promote, in recognition of the paramount impor-

tance of preserving the dignity and worth of the human person, full freedom for the peaceful expression of political opposition, full opportunity for the exercise of religious freedom and full respect for all the other fundamental rights expressed in the Universal Declaration of Human Rights;

7. To promote nationally and through international co-operation, efforts to achieve and sustain higher standards of living for all peoples;

8. To remove the barriers which deny to peoples the free exchange of information and ideas essential to international understanding and peace;

Calls upon every Member

9. To participate fully in all the work of the United Nations:

Calls upon the five permanent members of the Security Council

10. To broaden progressively their co-operation and to exercise restraint in the use of the veto in order to make the Security Council a more effective instrument for maintaining peace;

Calls upon every nation

11. To settle international disputes by peaceful means and to co-operate in supporting United Nations efforts to resolve outstanding problems;

12. To co-operate to attain the effective international regulation of conventional armaments; and

13. To agree to the exercise of national sovereignty jointly with other nations to the extent necessary to attain international control of atomic energy which would make effective the prohibition of atomic weapons and assure the use of atomic energy for peaceful purposes only.

SEE ALSO *Cairo Declaration: Program for Peace and International Cooperation; Crimes against the Peace and Security of Mankind; Declaration on Principles of International Law concerning Friendly Relations and Co-operation among States in Accordance with the Charter of the United Nations; Declaration on the Preparation of Societies for Life in Peace; Declaration on the Right of Peoples to Peace; Human Rights and Peace; Proclamation of the International Year of Peace.*

DECLARATION OF ABIJAN (1976).

In the declaration, adopted by the UN Economic and Social Council at a meeting held in Abijan, the Ivory Coast, on 9 July 1976, the council directs attention to the problems of Africa and its many underdeveloped countries and calls for urgent action to put an end to the colonialism, *apartheid,* injustice, and inequality which has prevailed in that continent, with a view to accelerating the development of those countries. The text of the declaration, annexed to council resolution 2009 (LXI), is as follows:

The Economic and Social Council,

Meeting for the first time in Africa, from 30 June to 9 July 1976, at the invitation of the Government of the Republic of Ivory Coast,

1. Welcomes the important statement of His Excellency the President of the Republic of Ivory Coast before the Council at the opening meeting of its sixty-first session, in

which he eloquently analysed problems of developing countries in general and those of Africa in particular;

2. Remains mindful of the fundamental purposes of the United Nations, as laid down in the Charter of the United Nations, in particular the maintenance of international peace and security through, *inter alia,* effective collective measures for the prevention and removal of threats to peace and for the suppression of acts of aggression or other branches of the peace, the development of friendly relations among nations based on respect for the principle of equal rights and self-determination of peoples and the achievement of international co-operation in solving international problems of an economic, social, cultural or humanitarian character;

3. Welcomes the emergence to independence of States—the majority of which are in Africa—as a result of their struggle for self-determination and national liberation;

4. Calls for the speedy elimination of all forms of colonialism, neo-colonialism, foreign aggression and occupation, alien domination, racial discrimination and *apartheid* from the African continent and from wherever they exist and affirms that this should continue to receive very high priority among the major preoccupations of the international community;

5. Determines that there is an imperative need to eliminate injustice and inequality which afflict vast sections of humanity and to accelerate the development of developing countries;

6. Urges all countries and international organizations to give added impetus to the efforts of the international community towards the achievement of the goals, targets and objectives of the development of developing countries through individual or collective action, taking fully into account the Declaration and the Programme of Action on the Establishment of a New International Economic Order (General Assembly resolutions 3201 (S-VI) and 3202 (S-VI) of 1 May 1974), as well as the Charter of Economic Rights and Duties of States (General Assembly resolution 3281 (XXIX) of 12 December 1974), the International Development Strategy for the Second United Nations Development Decade (General Assembly resolution 2626 (XXV) of 24 October 1970) and General Assembly resolution 3362 (S-VII) of 16 September 1975 on development and international economic co-operation;

7. Further urges all countries and international organizations to pursue with the maximum sense of urgency the implementation of agreements reached within the United Nations system, including those reached at the fourth session of the United Nations Conference on Trade and Development and in other international conferences and fora, the search for further agreements and the widening of the existing ones where appropriate, bearing in mind the need to conduct negotiations and, where agreed, preparatory meetings for this purpose, so as to provide concrete solutions to the problems of developing countries;

8. Reaffirms the need to implement special measures or specific action adopted in favour of the most seriously affected, least developed, land-locked, and island developing countries;

9. Expresses its concern over the critical nature of the problems of development in Africa, reflected by the large number of African countries identified as least developed or most seriously affected countries, and urges developed countries, developing countries which are in a position to do so and the appropriate organs of the United Nations system to increase assistance to these countries;

10. Affirms the need to increase substantially the level of food production in developing countries, particularly those in Africa, and to extend adequate assistance to them for this purpose;

11. Urges all nations to display the necessary political will and place adequate resources at the disposal of the United Nations, in order to enable it to fulfil its role in the economic and social fields;

12. Finally declares that:

The objective of eliminating injustice and inequality and of achieving international co-operation for the promotion of economic progress and better standards of life, as well as social advancement and the encouragement of respect for human rights and for fundamental freedoms for all without distinction, has yet to be achieved in large areas of the world; to this end, the Council declares its adherence to the principles of national independence, sovereignty, and self-reliance and its faith in co-operation, dialogue and negotiation between developed and developing countries, based on a real political will to promote an equitable and just system of international economic relations in conformity with the principles of the United Nations Charter.

DECLARATION OF ALMA ATA (1978). The declaration was adopted by the International Conference on Primary Health Care, convened at Alma Ata, Union of Soviet Socialist Republics, from 6 to 12 September 1978, under the joint sponsorship of the WORLD HEALTH ORGANIZATION and the UNITED NATIONS CHILDREN'S FUND. It was endorsed by the UN General Assembly on 29 November 1979 (resolution 34/58), in which the assembly noted with approval the decision which the World Health Assembly had taken (resolution WHA 32.30) stating that the development of the programs of the World Health Organization and the allocation of its resources at the global, regional, and country levels should reflect the commitment of that organization to the priority of the achievement of health for all by the year 2000. The assembly called upon every competent United Nations body to coordinate with, and support, the efforts of the World Health Organization to achieve that goal.

The text of the declaration (UN Doc. E/ICEF/L. 1387, annex, sect. V) is as follows:

The International Conference on Primary Health Care, meeting in Alma-Ata this twelfth day of September in the year Nineteen hundred and seventy-eight, expressing the need for urgent action by all governments, all health and development workers, and the world community to protect and promote the health of all the people of the world, hereby makes the following Declaration:

I. The Conference strongly reaffirms that health, which is a state of complete physical, mental and social wellbeing, and not merely the absence of disease or infirmity, is a fundamental human right and that the attainment of the highest possible level of health is a most important world-wide social goal whose realization requires the action of many other social and economic sectors in addition to the health sector.

II. The existing gross inequality in the health status of the people particularly between developed and developing countries as well as within countries is politically, socially and economically unacceptable and is, therefore, of common concern to all countries.

III. Economic and social development, based on a New International Economic Order, is of basic importance to the fullest attainment of health for all and to the reduction of the gap between the health status of the developing and developed countries. The promotion and protection of the health of the people is essential to sustained economic and social development and contributes to a better quality of life and to world peace.

IV. The people have the right and duty to participate individually and collectively in the planning and implementation of their health care.

V. Governments have a responsibility for the health of their people which can be fulfilled only by the provision of adequate health and social measures. A main social target of governments, international organizations and the whole world community in the coming decades should be the attainment by all peoples of the world by the year 2000 of a level of health that will permit them to lead a socially and economically productive life. Primary health care is the key to attaining this target as part of development in the spirit of social justice.

VI. Primary health care is essential health care based on practical, scientifically sound and socially acceptable methods and technology made universally accessible to individuals and families in the community through their full participation and at a cost that the community and country can afford to maintain at every stage of their development in the spirit of self-reliance and self-determination. It forms an integral part both of the country's health system, of which it is the central function and main focus, and of the overall social and economic development of the community. It is the first level of contact of individuals, the family and community with the national health system bringing health care as close as possible to where people live and work, and constitutes the first element of a continuing health care process.

VII. Primary health care:

1. reflects and evolves from the economic conditions and socio-cultural and political characteristics of the country and its communities and is based on the application of the relevant results of social, biomedical and health services research and public health experience;

2. addresses the main health problems in the community, providing promotive, preventive, curative and rehabilitative services accordingly;

3. includes at least: education concerning prevailing health problems and the methods of preventing and controlling them; promotion of food supply and proper nutrition; an adequate supply of safe water and basic sanitation; maternal and child health care, including family planning; immunization against the major infectious diseases; prevention and control of locally endemic diseases; appropriate treatment of common diseases and injuries; and provision of essential drugs;

4. involves, in addition to the health sector, all related sectors and aspects of national and community development, in particular agriculture, animal husbandry, food, industry, education, housing, public works, communications and other sectors; and demands the coordinated efforts of all those sectors;

5. requires and promotes maximum community and individual self-reliance and participation in the planning, organization, operation and control of primary health care, making fullest use of local, national and other available resources; and to this end develops through appropriate education the ability of communities to participate;

6. should be sustained by integrated, functional and mutually-supportive referral systems, leading to the progressive improvement of comprehensive health care for all, and giving priority to those most in need;

7. relies, at local and referral levels, on health workers, including physicians, nurses, midwives, auxiliaries and community workers as applicable, as well as traditional practitioners as needed, suitably trained socially and technically to work as a health team and to respond to the expressed health needs of the community.

VIII. All governments should formulate national policies, strategies and plans of action to launch and sustain primary health care as part of a comprehensive national health system and in coordination with other sectors. To this end, it will be necessary to exercise political will, to mobilize the country's resources and to use available external resources rationally.

IX. All countries should cooperate in a spirit of partnership and service to ensure primary health care for all people since the attainment of health by people in any one country directly concerns and benefits every other country. In this context the joint WHO/UNICEF report on primary health care constitutes a solid basis for the further development and operation of primary health care throughout the world.

X. An acceptable level of health for all the people of the world by the year 2000 can be attained through a fuller and better use of the world's resources, a considerable part of which is now spent on armaments and military conflicts. A genuine policy of independence, peace, détente and disarmament could and should release additional resources that could well be devoted to peaceful aims and in particular to the acceleration of social and economic development of which primary health care, as an essential part, should be allotted its proper share.

The International Conference on Primary Health Care calls for urgent and effective national and international action to develop and implement primary health care throughout the world and particularly in developing countries in a spirit of technical cooperation and in keeping with a New International Economic Order. It urges governments, WHO and UNICEF, and other international organizations, as well as multilateral and bilateral agencies, non-governmental organizations, funding agencies, all health workers and the whole world community to support national and international commitment to primary health care and to channel increased technical and financial support to it, particularly in developing countries. The Conference calls on all the aforementioned to collaborate in introducing, developing and maintaining primary health care in accordance with the spirit and content of this Declaration.

SEE ALSO *Health; Health: Developments affecting the Enjoyment of Human Rights; Health: Discriminatory Practices.*

DECLARATION OF BASIC PRINCIPLES OF JUSTICE FOR VICTIMS OF CRIME AND ABUSE OF POWER (1985). The UN General Assembly formulated these basic principles on recommendation of the Sixth United Nations Congress on the Prevention of Crime and Treatment of Offenders because it realized that millions of people throughout the world suffer harm as a result of crime or the abuse of power and that the rights of these victims are not adequately recognized or protected: these victims, and also their families, witnesses and others who have aided them, are unjustly subjected to loss, damage, or injury and may, in addition, suffer hardship when assisting in the prosecution of offenders. The declaration is designed to assist governments and the international community in their efforts to secure justice and assistance for victims of crime or of abuse of power.

The declaration was adopted by the General Assembly on 29 November 1985 (resolution 40/34). The text is as follows:

A. Victims of Crime

1. "Victims" means persons who, individually or collectively, have suffered harm, including physical or mental injury, emotional suffering, economic loss or substantial impairment of their fundamental rights, through acts or omissions that are in violation of criminal laws operative within Member States, including those laws proscribing criminal abuse of power.

2. A person may be considered a victim, under this Declaration, regardless of whether the perpetrator is identified, apprehended, prosecuted or convicted and regardless of the familial relationship between the perpetrator and the victim. The term "victim" also includes, where appropriate, the immediate family or dependants of the direct victim and persons who have suffered harm in intervening to assist victims in distress or to prevent victimization.

3. The provisions contained herein shall be applicable to all, without distinction of any kind, such as race, colour, sex, age, language, religion, nationality, political or other opinion, cultural beliefs or practices, property, birth or family status, ethnic or social origin, and disability.

Access to Justice and Fair Treatment. 4. Victims should be treated with compassion and respect for their dignity. They are entitled to access to the mechanisms of justice and to prompt redress, as provided for by national legislation, for the harm that they have suffered.

5. Judicial and administrative mechanisms should be established and strengthened where necessary to enable victims to obtain redress through formal or informal procedures that are expeditious, fair, inexpensive and accessible. Victims should be informed of their rights in seeking redress through such mechanisms.

6. The responsiveness of judicial and administrative processes to the needs of victims should be facilitated by:

(a) Informing victims of their role and the scope, timing and progress of the proceedings and of the disposition of their cases, especially where serious crimes are involved and where they have requested such information;

(b) Allowing the views and concerns of victims to be presented and considered at appropriate stages of the proceedings where their personal interests are affected, without prejudice to the accused and consistent with the relevant national criminal justice system;

(c) Providing proper assistance to victims throughout the legal process.

(d) Taking measures to minimize inconvenience to victims, protect their privacy, when necessary, and ensure their safety, as well as that of their families and witnesses on their behalf, from intimidation and retaliation;

(e) Avoiding unnecessary delay in the disposition of cases and the execution of orders or decrees granting awards to victims.

7. Informal mechanisms for the resolution of disputes, including mediation, arbitration and customary justice or indigenous practices, should be utilized where appropriate to facilitate conciliation and redress for victims.

Restitution. 8. Offenders or third parties responsible for their behaviour should, where appropriate, make fair restitution to victims, their families or dependants. Such restitution should include the return of property or payment for the harm or loss suffered, reimbursement of expenses incurred as a result of the victimization, the provision of services and the restoration of rights.

9. Governments should review their practices, regulations and laws to consider restitution as an available sentencing option in criminal cases, in addition to other criminal sanctions.

10. In cases of substantial harm to the environment, restitution, if ordered, should include, as far as possible, restoration of the environment, reconstruction of the infrastructure, replacement of community facilities and reimbursement of the expenses of relocation, whenever such harm results in the dislocation of a community.

11. Where public officials or other agents acting in an official or quasi-official capacity have violated national criminal laws, the victims should receive restitution from the State whose officials or agents were responsible for the harm inflicted. In cases where the Government under whose authority the victimizing act or omission occurred is no longer in existence, the State or Government successor in title should provide restitution to the victims.

Compensation. 12. When compensation is not fully available from the offender or other sources, States should endeavour to provide financial compensation to:

(a) Victims who have sustained significant bodily injury or impairment of physical or mental health as a result of serious crimes;

(b) The family, in particular dependants of persons who have died or become physically or mentally incapacitated as a result of such victimization.

13. The establishment, strengthening and expansion of national funds for compensation to victims should be encouraged. Where appropriate, other funds may also be established for this purpose, including in those cases where the State of which the victim is a national is not in a position to compensate the victim for the harm.

Assistance. 14. Victims should receive the necessary material, medical, psychological and social assistance through governmental, voluntary, community-based and indigenous means.

15. Victims should be informed of the availability of health and social services and other relevant assistance and be readily afforded access to them.

16. Police, justice, health, social service and other personnel concerned should receive training to sensitize them

to the needs of victims, and guidelines to ensure proper and prompt aid.

17. In providing services and assistance to victims, attention should be given to those who have special needs because of the nature of the harm inflicted or because of factors such as those mentioned in paragraph 3 above.

B. Victims of Abuse of Power

18. "Victims" means persons who, individually or collectively, have suffered harm, including physical or mental injury, emotional suffering, economic loss or substantial impairment of their fundamental rights, through acts or omissions that do not yet constitute violations of national criminal laws but of internationally recognized norms relating to human rights.

19. States should consider incorporating into the national law norms proscribing abuses of power and providing remedies to victims of such abuses. In particular, such remedies should include restitution and/or compensation, and necessary material, medical, psychological and social assistance and support.

20. States should consider negotiating multilateral international treaties relating to victims, as defined in paragraph 18.

21. States should periodically review existing legislation and practices to ensure their responsiveness to changing circumstances, should enact and enforce, if necessary, legislation proscribing acts that constitute serious abuses of political or economic power, as well as promoting policies and mechanisms for the prevention of such acts, and should develop and make readily available appropriate rights and remedies for victims of such acts.

SEE ALSO Arbitrary Arrest, Detention, or Exile; Compensation for Victims of Human Rights Violations; United Nations Voluntary Fund for Victims of Torture.

DECLARATION OF MEXICO ON THE EQUALITY OF WOMEN AND THEIR CONTRIBUTION TO DEVELOPMENT AND PEACE (1975).
The year 1975, designated by the UN General Assembly as INTERNATIONAL WOMEN'S YEAR, was devoted to intensified international action to promote equality between men and women. The focus of the year was the World Conference of the International Women's Year, which convened in Mexico City from 19 June to 2 July 1975 as authorized by the General Assembly (resolution 3010 [XXVII]). The conference was attended by more than 1,000 delegates representing 133 States, about 70% of whom were women. The Declaration of Mexico, adopted by the conference, was later endorsed by the General Assembly (resolution 3520 [XXX]). The text of the declaration is as follows:

The World Conference of the International Women's Year,

Aware that the problems of women, who constitute half of the world's population, are the problems of society as a whole, and that changes in the present economic, political and social situation of women must become an integral part of efforts to transform the structures and attitudes that hinder the genuine satisfaction of their needs,

Recognizing that international co-operation based on the principles of the Charter of the United Nations should be developed and strengthened in order to find solutions to world problems and to build an international community based on equity and justice,

Recalling that in subscribing to the Charter, the peoples of the United Nations undertook specific commitments: "to save succeeding generations from the scourge of war . . . , to reaffirm faith in fundamental human rights, in the dignity and worth of the human person, in the equal rights of men and women and of nations large and small, and to promote social progress and better standards of life in larger freedom",

Taking note of the fact that since the creation of the United Nations very important instruments have been adopted, among which the following constitute landmarks: the Universal Declaration of Human Rights, the Declaration on the Granting of Independence to Colonial Countries and Peoples, the International Development Strategy for the Second United Nations Development Decade; and the Declaration and Programme of Action for the Establishment of a New International Economic Order based on the Charter of Economic Rights and Duties of States,

Taking into account that the United Nations Declaration on the Elimination of Discrimination against Women considers that: "discrimination against women is incompatible with human dignity and with the welfare of the family and of society, prevents their participation, on equal terms with men, in the political, social, economic and cultural life of their countries and is an obstacle to the full development of the potentialities of women in the service of their countries and of humanity",

Recalling that the General Assembly, in its resolution 3010 (XXVII) of 18 December 1972, proclaimed 1975 as International Women's Year and that the Year was to be devoted to intensified action with a view to: promoting equality between men and women, ensuring the integration of women in the total development effort, and increasing the contribution of women to the stregthening of world peace,

Recalling further that the Economic and Social Council, in its resolution 1849 (LVI) of 16 May 1974, adopted the programme for International Women's Year, and that the General Assembly, in its resolution 3275 (XXIX) of 10 December 1974, called for full implementation of the programme,

Taking into account the role played by women in the history of humanity, especially in the struggle for national liberation, the strengthening of international peace, and the elimination of imperialism, colonialism, neocolonialism, foreign occupation, zionism, alien domination, racism and *apartheid*,

Stressing that greater and equal participation of women at all levels of decision-making shall decisively contribute to accelerating the pace of development and the maintenance of peace,

Stressing also that women and men of all countries should have equal rights and duties and that it is the task of all States to create the necessary conditions for the attainment and the exercise thereof,

Recognizing that women of the entire world, whatever differences exist between them, share the painful experience of receiving or having received unequal treatment, and that as their awareness of this phenomenon increases they will become natural allies in the struggle against any form of oppression, such as is practised under colonialism, neo-colonialism, zionism, racial discrimination and *apartheid,* thereby constituting an enormous revolutionary potential for economic and social change in the world today,

Recognizing that changes in the social and economic structure of societies, even though they are among the prerequisites, cannot of themselves ensure an immediate improvement in the status of a group which has long been disadvantaged, and that urgent consideration must therefore be given to the full, immediate and early integration of women into national and international life,

Emphasizing that under-development imposes upon women a double burden of exploitation, which must be rapidly eliminated, and that full implementation of national development policies designed to fulfill this objective is seriously hindered by the existing inequitable system of international economic relations,

Aware that the role of women in child-bearing should not be the cause of inequality and discrimination, and that child-rearing demands shared responsibilities among women, men and society as a whole,

Recognizing also the urgency of improving the status of women and finding more effective methods and strategies which will enable them to have the same opportunities as men to participate actively in the development of their countries and to contribute to the attainment of world peace,

Convinced that women must play an important role in the promotion, achievement and maintenance of international peace, and that it is necessary to encourage their efforts towards peace, through their full participation in the national and international organizations that exist for this purpose,

Considering that it is necessary to promote national, regional and international action, in which the implementation of the World Plan of Action adopted by the World Conference of the International Women's Year should make a significant contribution, for the attainment of equality, development and peace,

Decides to promulgate the following principles:

1. Equality between women and men means equality in their dignity and worth as human beings as well as equality in their rights, opportunities and responsibilities.

2. All obstacles that stand in the way of enjoyment by women of equal status with men must be eliminated in order to ensure their full integration into national development and their participation in securing and in maintaining international peace.

3. It is the responsibility of the State to create the necessary facilities so that women may be integrated into society while their children receive adequate care.

4. National non-governmental organizations should contribute to the advancement of women by assisting women to take advantage of their opportunities, by promoting education and information about women's rights, and by co-operating with their respective Governments.

5. Women and men have equal rights and responsibilities in the family and in society. Equality between women and men should be guaranteed in the family, which is the basic unit of society and where human relations are nurtured. Men should participate more actively, creatively and responsibly in family life for its sound development in order to enable women to be more intensively involved in the activities of their communities and with a view to combining effectively home and work possibilities of both partners.

6. Women, like men, require opportunities for developing their intellectual potential to the maximum. National policies and programmes should therefore provide them with full and equal access to education and training at all levels, while ensuring that such programmes and policies consciously orient them towards new occupations and new roles consistent with their need for self-fulfillment and the needs of national development.

7. The right of women to work, to receive equal pay for work of equal value, to be provided with equal conditions and opportunities for advancement in work, and all other women's rights to full and satisfying economic activity are strongly reaffirmed. Review of these principles for their effective implementation is now urgently needed, considering the necessity of restructuring world economic relationships. This restructuring offers greater possibilities for women to be integrated into the stream of national economic, social, political and cultural life.

8. All means of communication and information as well as all cultural media should regard as a high priority their responsibility for helping to remove the attitudinal and cultural factors that still inhibit the development of women and for projecting in positive terms the value to society of the assumption by women of changing and expanding roles.

9. Necessary resources should be made available in order that women may be able to participate in the political life of their countries and of the international community since their active participation in national and world affairs at decision-making and other levels in the political field is a prerequisite of women's full exercise of equal rights as well as of their further development and of the national well-being.

10. Equality of rights carries with it corresponding responsibilities; it is therefore a duty of women to make full use of opportunities available to them and to perform their duties to the family, the country and humanity.

11. It should be one of the principal aims of social education to teach respect for physical integrity and its rightful place in human life. The human body, whether that of woman or man, is inviolable and respect for it is a fundamental element of human dignity and freedom.

12. Every couple and every individual has the right to decide freely and responsibly whether or not to have children as well as to determine their number and spacing, and to have information, education and means to do so.

13. Respect for human dignity encompasses the right of every woman to decide freely for herself whether or not to contract matrimonny.

14. The issue of inequality, as it affects the vast majority of the women of the world, is closely linked with the problem of under-development, which exists as a result not only of unsuitable internal structures but also of a profoundly unjust world economic system.

15. The full and complete development of any country requires the maximum participation of women as well as of men in all fields: the under-utilization of the potential of approximately half of the world's population is a serious obstacle to social and economic development.

16. The ultimate end of development is to achieve a better quality of life for all, which means not only the development of economic and other material resources but also the physical, moral, intellectual and cultural growth of the human person.

17. In order to integrate women into development, States should undertake the necessary changes in their economic and social policies because women have the right to participate and contribute to the total development effort.

18. The present state of international economic relations poses serious obstacles to a more efficient utilization of all human and material potential for accelerated development and for the improvement of living standards in developing countries aimed at the elimination of hunger, child mortality, unemployment, illiteracy, ignorance and backwardness, which concern all of humanity and women in particular. It is therefore essential to establish and implement with urgency the New International Economic Order, of which the Charter of Economic Rights and Duties of States constitutes a basic element, founded on equity, sovereign equality, interdependence, common interest, co-operation among all States irrespective of their social and economic systems, on the principles of peaceful coexistence and on the promotion by the entire international community of economic and social progress of all countries, especially developing countries, and on the progress of States comprising the international community.

19. The principle of the full and permanent sovereignty of every State over its natural resources, wealth and all economic activities, and its inalienable right of nationalization as an expression of this sovereignty constitute fundamental prerequisites in the process of economic and social development.

20. The attainment of economic and social goals, so basic to the realization of the rights of women, does not, however, of itself bring about the full integration of women in development on a basis of equality with men unless specific measures are undertaken for the elimination of all forms of discrimination against them. It is therefore important to formulate and implement models of development that will promote the participation and advancement of women in all fields of work and provide them with equal educational opportunities and such services as would facilitate housework.

21. Modernization of the agricultural sector of vast areas of the world is an indispensable element for progress, particularly as it creates opportunities for millions of rural women to participate in development. Governments, the United Nations, its specialized agencies and other competent regional and international organizations should support projects designed to utilize the maximum potential and develop the self-reliance of rural women.

22. It must be emphasized that, given the required economic, social and legal conditions as well as the appropriate attitudes conducive to the full and equal participation of women in society, efforts and measures aimed at a more intensified integration of women in development can be successfully implemented only if made an integral part of over-all social and economic growth. Full participation of women in the various economic, social, political and cultural sectors is an important indication of the dynamic progress of peoples and their development. Individual human rights can be realized only within the framework of total development.

23. The objectives considered in this Declaration can be achieved only in a world in which the relations between States are governed, *inter alia*, by the following principles: the sovereign equality of States, the free self-determination of peoples, the unacceptability of acquisition or attempted acquisition of territories by force and the prohibition of recognition of such acquisition, territorial integrity, and the right to defend it, and non-interference in the domestic affairs of States, in the same manner as relations between human beings should be governed by the supreme principle of the equality of rights of women and men.

24. International co-operation and peace require the achievement of national liberation and independence, the elimination of colonialism and neo-colonialism, foreign occupation, zionism, *apartheid,* and racial discrimination in all its forms as well as the recognition of the dignity of peoples and their right to self-determination.

25. Women have a vital role to play in the promotion of peace in all spheres of life: in the family, the community, the nation and the world. Women must participate equally with men in the decision-making processes which help to promote peace at all levels.

26. Women and men together should eliminate colonialism, neo-colonialism, imperialism, foreign domination and occupation, zionism, *apartheid,* racial discrimination, the acquisition of land by force and the recognition of such acquisition, since such practices inflict incalculable suffering on women, men and children.

27. The solidarity of women in all countries of the world should be supported in their protest against violations of human rights condemned by the United Nations. All forms of repression and inhuman treatment of women, men and children, including imprisonment, torture, massacres, collective punishment, destruction of homes, forced eviction and arbitrary restriction of movement shall be considered crimes against humanity and in violation of the Universal Declaration of Human Rights and other international instruments.

28. Women all over the world should unite to eliminate violations of human rights committed against women and girls such as: rape, prostitution, physical assault, mental cruelty, child marriage, forced marriage and marriage as a commercial transaction.

29. Peace requires that women as well as men should reject any type of intervention in the domestic affairs of States, whether it be openly or covertly carried on by other States or by transnational corporations. Peace also requires that women as well as men should also promote respect for the sovereign right of a State to establish its own economic, social and political system without undergoing political and economic pressures or coercion of any type.

30. Women as well as men should promote real, general and complete disarmament under effective international control, starting with nuclear disarmament. Until genuine disarmament is achieved, women and men throughout the world must maintain their vigilance and do their utmost to achieve and maintain international peace.

Wherefore,

The World Conference of the International Women's Year

1. Affirms its faith in the objectives of the International Women's Year, which are equality, development and peace;

2. Proclaims its commitment to the achievement of such objectives;

3. Strongly urges Governments, the entire United Nations system, regional and international intergovernmental organizations and the international community as a whole to dedicate themselves to the creation of a just society where women, men and children can live in dignity, freedom, justice and prosperity.

SEE ALSO *Declaration on the Participation of Women in Promoting International Peace and Co-operation; Nairobi Forward-Looking Strategies for the Advancement of Women; United Nations Development Fund for Women; Women and Peace.*

DECLARATION OF PRINCIPLES AND PROGRAM OF ACTION OF THE TRIPARTITE WORLD CONFERENCE ON EMPLOYMENT (1976).

The Tripartite World Conference on Employment, Income Distribution, Social Progress and the International Division of Labor, convened in Geneva from 4 to 17 June 1976 in accordance with a decision of the International Labor Conference (59th session), adopted on 14 June 1976 the Declaration of Principles and Program of Action aimed at the establishment of a more equitable international economic order in which neither poverty nor unemployment would subsist.

The declaration and program were noted with satisfaction by the UN General Assembly on 21 December 1976 (resolution 31/176), and the assembly called upon all competent UN specialized agencies and organizations to participate actively in their realization. The texts of the declaration and program (UN Doc. E/ 5857), are as follows:

Declaration of Principles

The Tripartite World Conference on Employment, Income Distribution and Social Progress, and the International Division of Labour held in Geneva from 4 to 17 June 1976 in accordance with the resolution adopted by the International Labour Conference during its 59th Session (1974):

Aware that past development strategies in most developing countries have not led to the eradication of poverty and unemployment; that the historical features of the development processes in these countries have produced an employment structure characterised by a large proportion of the labour force in rural areas with high levels of underemployment and unemployment; that underemployment and poverty in rural and urban informal sectors and open unemployment, especially in urban areas, has reached such critical dimensions that major shifts in development strategies at both national and international levels are urgently needed in order to ensure full employment and an adequate income to every inhabitant of this one world in the shortest possible time;

Aware that industrialised countries have not been able to maintain full employment and that economic recession has resulted in widespread unemployment;

Noting that the Conference is a major initiative on the part of the International Labour Organisation towards the efforts that many of the member countries are making to establish a more equitable international economic order, and that it is consistent with the deliberations of the important world conferences of recent years;

Recalling further the conclusions of the Sixth and Seventh Special Sessions of the United Nations General Assembly, in particular Resolution 3202 (S-VI) concerning the Establishment of a New International Economic Order, and Resolution 3362 (S-VII) concerning Development and International Economic Co-operation;

Noting that underemployment, unemployment, poverty, malnutrition and illiteracy are caused by both national and international factors; that at the national level they are caused by structural factors emanating from under-development and, at the international level, they are due mainly to the deteriorating situation in developing countries, which is partly the consequence of cyclical and structural imbalances in the world economic situation;

Recognising that one of the primary objectives of national development efforts and of international economic relations must be to achieve full employment and to satisfy the basic needs of all people throughout this one world;

Committed to the attainment of an equitable distribution of income and wealth through appropriate strategies to eradicate poverty and promote full, productive employment to satisfy basic needs;

Noting:

(a) that unemployment, underemployment and marginality are a universal concern and affect at least one-third of humanity at the present time, offending human dignity and preventing the exercise of the right to work;

(b) that the experience of the past two decades has shown that rapid growth of gross national product has not automatically reduced poverty and inequality in many countries, nor has it provided sufficient productive employment within acceptable periods of time;

(c) the current unsatisfactory international economic situation and the discussions of problems affecting unemployment and related issues in UNCTAD IV;

(d) that the existence of an informal urban sector which has grown out of proportion during the past decades in the developing countries and the chronic lack of jobs in rural areas burden the labour markets and hinder the sectoral and regional integration of national development policies;

(e) that it is necessary to replace the current international division of labour wherein the participation of developing countries in international trade is mainly the exportation of raw materials, semi-processed products and highly labour-intensive manufactured goods and the importation of highly capital-intensive industrial products, so as to enable all countries to engage in other types of production in accordance with their national priorities;

Recalling the Universal Declaration of Human Rights, in particular Article 23, adopted by the General Assembly of the United Nations in 1948;

Considering that only productive work and gainful employment, without discrimination, enable man to fulfil himself socially and as an individual, and reconfirming that the assured opportunity to work is a basic human right and freedom;

Considering that the growth of productive employment is one of the most effective means to ensure a just and equitable distribution of income and to raise the standard of living of the majority of the population;

Convinced that the establishment and modernisation of small and medium-sized enterprises in rural as well as in urban sectors will increase the volume of employment and therefore play an important part in a basic-needs strategy, and that the private sector has an important role to play in development and employment creation;

Considering that integrated development of developing countries can be achieved only in so far as equal priority is attached to the social, economic and political aspects of development;

Affirming that the problems of underemployment, unemployment and poverty must be attacked by means of direct, well co-ordinated measures at both national and international levels;

Recognising that in most developing countries, the government is the principal promoter of development and employment and the competent instrument to achieve a just and equitable distribution of income, with the effective participation of trade unions, rural workers' organisations and employers' associations;

Recognising that international relations should be based on co-operation, interdependence, national sovereignty, self-determination of peoples, and non-intervention in the internal affairs of countries;

Reconfirming the importance of regional and subregional co-operation as a major instrument to achieve the expansion of domestic markets, to facilitate the use of modern technologies, efficient industrialisation, better integration into the world economy, and to give greater weight to the positions of developing countries in international relations, with a view to accelerating the development of Third World countries;

Noting the firm commitment of the developing countries and of some developed countries to implement the New International Economic Order, based on the principles contained in the Charter of Economic Rights and Duties of States;

Noting that a review and appraisal of the strategy for the Second Development Decade (Resolution 3517 of the United Nations General Assembly) are taking place and that preparations for the Third Development Decade have commenced;

Convinced that the strategy for the Second Development Decade needs to be complemented by a programme of action to guide international and national development efforts towards fulfilling the basic needs of all the people and particularly the elementary needs of the lowest income groups;

Recalling that the ILO, particularly through its World Employment Programme, has a direct responsibility for elaborating such a strategy with regard to the achievement of full productive employment in decent working conditions, and ensuring respect for the freedoms and rights of association and collective bargaining laid down in Conventions Nos. 87, 98 and 135;

The Conference hereby adopts this Declaration of Principles and the Programme of Action and requests the Governing Body of the ILO to implement the Programme of Action where appropriate in co-operation with other international organisations.

Programme of Action
Basic Needs

1. Strategies and national development plans and policies should include explicitly as a priority objective the promotion of employment and the satisfaction of the basic needs of each country's population.

2. Basic needs, as understood in this Programme of Action, include two elements. First, they include certain minimum requirements of a family for private consumption: adequate food, shelter and clothing, as well as certain household equipment and furniture. Second, they include essential services provided by and for the community at large, such as safe drinking water, sanitation, public transport and health, educational and cultural facilities.

3. A basic-needs-oriented policy implies the participation of the people in making the decisions which affect them through organisations of their own choice.

4. In all countries freely chosen employment enters into a basic-needs policy both as a means and as an end. Employment yields an output. It provides an income to the employed, and gives the individual a feeling of self-respect, dignity and of being a worthy member of society.

5. It is important to recognise that the concept of basic needs is a country-specific and dynamic concept. The concept of basic needs should be placed within a context of a nation's over-all economic and social development. In no circumstances should it be taken to mean merely the minimum necessary for subsistence; it should be placed within a context of national independence, the dignity of individual and peoples and their freedom to chart their destiny without hindrance.

Strategies and Policies to Create Full Employment

6. In developing countries satisfaction of basic needs cannot be achieved without both acceleration in their economic growth and measures aimed at changing the pattern of growth and access to the use of productive resources by the lowest income groups. Often these measures will require a transformation of social structures, including an initial redistribution of assets, especially land, with adequate and timely compensation. Land reform should be supplemented by rural community development. In some countries, however, public ownership and control of other assets is an essential ingredient of their strategy. Obviously, each country must democratically and independently decide its policies in accordance with its needs and objectives.

7. Any national employment-centred development strategy aiming at satisfying the basic needs of the population as a whole should, however, include the following essential elements, to the extent that countries consider them to be desirable:

Macro-Economic Policies. (a) An increase in the volume and productivity of work in order to increase the incomes of the lowest income groups;

(b) strengthening the production and distribution system of essential goods and services to correspond with the new pattern of demand;

(c) an increase in resource mobilisation for investment; the introduction of progressive income and wealth taxation policies; the adoption of credit policies to ensure employment creation and increased production of basic goods and services;

(d) the control of the utilisation and processing of natural resources as well as the establishment of basic industries that would generate self-reliant and harmonious economic development;

(e) developing inter-regional trade, especially among the developing countries, in order to promote collective self-reliance and to ensure the satisfaction of basic import needs without depending permanently on external aid;

(f) a planned increase in investments in order to

achieve diversification of employment and technological progress and to overcome other regional and sectoral problems;

(g) reform of the price mechanism in order to achieve greater equity and efficiency in resource allocation and to ensure sufficient income to small producers;

(h) reform of the fiscal system to provide employment-linked incentives and more socially just patterns of income distribution;

(i) safe-guarding ecological and environmental balances;

(j) provision by the government of the policy framework to guide the private and public sectors towards meeting basic needs, and making its own industrial enterprises model employers; in many cases this can only be done in a national planning framework;

(k) the development of human resources through education and vocational training.

Employment Policy. 8. Member States should place prime emphasis on the generation of employment, in particular to meet the challenge of creating sufficient jobs in developing countries by the year 2000 and thereby achieve full employment. Specific targets should be set to reduce progressively unemployment and underemployment.

9. The following policies should be adopted to encourage employment creation:

(a) Member States should ratify ILO Convention No. 122 and should ratify, implement and safeguard fair labour standards, such as the right to organise and to engage in collective bargaining, as laid down in ILO Conventions Nos. 87, 98 and 135.

(b) In the criteria for project selection and appraisal, employment and income distribution aspects should have adequate emphasis in development planning and in the lending policies of international financial institutions.

(c) Member States should implement active labour market policies of the type set forth in the ILO Human Resources Development Convention, 1975 (No. 142), and the accompanying Human Resources Development Recommendation, 1975 (No. 150), and adjust enterprise-level policies, especially with regard to recruitment, work organisation, working conditions and work content, so as fully to absorb under-utilised labour resources.

(d) Wage policies should be such that:

(i) they ensure minimum levels of living;

(ii) the real wages of workers and the real incomes of self-employed producers are protected and progressively increased;

(iii) wage levels are equitable and reflect relative social productivity;

(iv) anti-inflationary incomes and price policies, where introduced, take these objectives into account.

(e) Equality of treatment and remuneration for women should be ensured.

Rural Sector Policies. 10. Governments should give high priority to rural development, and increase the effectiveness of their policies, including those to reorganise the agrarian structure. Rural development involves the modernisation of agriculture, the development of agro-based industries, and the provision of both physical and social infrastructure. It should encompass educational and vocational training facilities, the construction of main and feeder roads, the provision of credit facilities and technical assistance, especially to small farmers and agricultural labourers.

11. Co-operatives should be promoted in accordance with ILO Recommendation No. 127 and extend not only to the use of land, equipment and credit, but also to the fields of transportation, storage, marketing and the distribution network, processing and services generally. More emphasis should be placed on the development of co-operatives in national policies, especially when they can be implemented so as to involve the lowest income groups, through their own organisations.

12. In most of the developing countries, agrarian reform, land distribution and the provision of ancillary services are basic to rural development. A minimum requirement is to provide house sites for rural and plantation workers and other landless labourers so as to assist them in building their homes and making them independent, especially in case of loss of employment.

13. The main thrust of a basic-needs strategy must be to ensure that there is effective mass participation of the rural population in the political process in order to safeguard their interests. In view of the highly hierarchical social and economic structure of agrarian societies in some developing countries, measures of redistributive justice are likely to be thwarted unless backed by organisations of rural workers. A policy of active encouragement to small farmers and rural workers' organisations should be pursued to enable them to participate effectively in the implementation of:

(a) programmes of agrarian reforms, distribution of surplus lands and land settlement;

(b) programmes for developing ancillary services such as credit, supply of input and marketing; and

(c) programmes concerning other employment generation schemes, such as public works, agro-industries and rural crafts.

As specified in ILO Convention No. 141, Governments should create conditions for the development of effective organisations of rural workers.

Social Policies. 14. Social policies should be designed to increase the welfare of working people, especially women, the young and the aged.

Women. 15. Since women constitute the group on the bottom of the ladder in many developing countries in respect of employment, poverty, education, training and status, the Conference recommends that special emphasis be placed in developing countries on promoting the status, education, development and employment of women and on integrating women into the economic and civic life of the country.

16. Specifically, the Conference recommends:

(a) the abolition of every kind of discrimination as regards the right to work, pay, employment, vocational guidance and training (including in-service training promotion in employment and access to skilled jobs;

(b) that more favourable working conditions be ensured so that women may perform their other functions in society and married women may be able to return to either full-time or part-time productive employment;

(c) that the work burden and drudgery of women be relieved by improving their working and living conditions and by providing more resources for investment in favour of women in rural areas.

The Young, the Aged and the Handicapped. 17. In the implementation of basic-needs strategies, there should be no discrimination against the young, the aged or the handicapped. Every effort should be made to provide the young with productive employment, equal opportunity and equal pay for work of equal value, vocational training and working conditions suited to their age. Exploitation of child labour should be prohibited in accordance with the relevant ILO standards.

Participation of Organised Groups. 18. Governments must try to involve employers' organisations, trade unions and rural workers' and producers' organisations in decision-making procedures and in the process of implementation at all levels. These are the organisations which represent the vast majority of the population and, therefore, they must be the ones to help define the basic needs and apply the necessary strategies.

19. Employers' and producers' organisations, trade unions and other workers' organisations such as rural workers' organisations have an important role to play in the design and implementation of successful development strategies. They must be encouraged to participate effectively in the decision-making process. Workers' organisations are also of great importance in the search for a reform of the existing international economic structures and they have a major role to play in the achievement of a fairer distribution of income and wealth.

Education. 20. Education is itself a basic need, and equality of access to educational services, particularly in rural areas, is therefore an important ingredient of a basic-needs strategy. Lack of access to education denies many people, and particularly women, the opportunity to participate fully and meaningfully in the social, economic, cultural and political life of the community.

21. Educational and vocational training systems should be adapted to national development needs and should avoid an élitist bias; priority should be given to adult and primary education, especially in the rural areas.

Population Policy. 22. High birth rates in poverty-stricken areas are not the cause of under-development but a result of it. They may, however, jeopardise the satisfaction of basic needs. It is only through the fulfilment of these needs, with special emphasis on the development of the position and status of women, that couples will be in a better position to determine the size of their family in a manner compatible with the aims of their society. The Conference is of the view that population policies consistent with the culture and the societies involved, as recommended by the 1974 World Population Conference, should be strongly encouraged. It recommends that information on population programmes should be made available to people in a form and language that they can understand.

SEE ALSO *Employment: Anti-Discrimination Agencies; ILO Abolition of Forced Labor Convention and following ILO conventions; Unemployment; Work.*

DECLARATION OF THE RIGHTS OF THE CHILD (1959).

The declaration was adopted on 20 November 1959 by the UN General Assembly (resolution 1386 [XIV]). When it was under preparation, it was pointed out that many of the rights and freedoms which it dealt with had already been proclaimed for everyone, including children, in the UNIVERSAL DECLARATION OF HUMAN RIGHTS. The assembly decided, nevertheless, that the special needs of children justified a separate international instrument. The text of the declaration is as follows:

Preamble

Whereas the peoples of the United Nations have, in the Charter, reaffirmed their faith in fundamental human rights and in the dignity and worth of the human person, and have determined to promote social progress and better standards of life in larger freedom,

Whereas the United Nations has, in the Universal Declaration of Human Rights, proclaimed that everyone is entitled to all the rights and freedoms set forth therein, without distinction of any kind, such as race, colour, sex, language, religion, political or other opinion, national or social origin, property, birth or other status,

Whereas the child, by reason of his physical and mental immaturity, needs special safeguards and care, including appropriate legal protection, before as well as after birth,

Whereas the need for such special safeguards has been stated in the Geneva Declaration of the Rights of the Child of 1924, and recognized in the Universal Declaration of Human Rights and in the statutes of specialized agencies and international organizations concerned with the welfare of children,

Whereas mankind owes to the child the best it has to give,

Now therefore.

The General Assembly

Proclaims this Declaration of the Rights of the Child to the end that he may have a happy childhood and enjoy for his own good and for the good of society the rights and freedoms herein set forth, and calls upon parents, upon men and women as individuals, and upon voluntary organizations, local authorities and national Governments to recognize these rights and strive for their observance by legislative and other measures progressively taken in accordance with the following principles:

Principle 1. The child shall enjoy all the rights set forth in this Declaration. Every child, without any exception whatsoever, shall be entitled to these rights, without distinction or discrimination on account of race, colour, sex, language, religion, political or other opinion, national or social origin, property, birth or other status, whether of himself or of his family.

Principle 2. The child shall enjoy special protection, and shall be given opportunities and facilities, by law and by other means, to enable him to develop physically, mentally, morally, spiritually and socially in a healthy and normal manner and in conditions of freedom and dignity. In the enactment of laws for this purpose, the best interests of the child shall be the paramount consideration.

Principle 3. The child shall be entitled from his birth to a name and a nationality.

Principle 4. The child shall enjoy the benefits of social security. He shall be entitled to grow and develop in health; to this end, special care and protection shall be provided both to him and to his mother, including adequate pre-natal and post-natal care. The child shall have the right to adequate nutrition, housing, recreation and medical services.

Principle 5. The child who is physically, mentally or socially handicapped shall be given the special treatment, education and care required by his particular condition.

Principle 6. The child, for the full and harmonious development of his personality, needs love and understanding. He shall, wherever possible, grow up in the care and under the responsibility of his parents, and, in any case, in an atmosphere of affection and of moral and material security; a child of tender years shall not, save in exceptional circumstances, be separated from his mother. Society and the public authorities shall have the duty to extend particular care to children without a family and to those without adequate means of support. Payment of State and other assistance towards the maintenance of children of large families is desirable.

Principle 7. The child is entitled to receive education, which shall be free and compulsory, at least in the elementary stages. He shall be given an education which will promote his general culture and enable him, on a basis of equal opportunity, to develop his abilities, his individual judgement, and his sense of moral and social responsibility, and to become a useful member of society.

The best interests of the child shall be the guiding principle of those responsible for his education and guidance; that responsibility lies in the first place with his parents.

The child shall have full opportunity for play and recreation, which should be directed to the same purposes as education; society and the public authorities shall endeavour to promote the enjoyment of this right.

Principle 8. The child shall in all circumstances be among the first to receive protection and relief.

Principle 9. The child shall be protected against all forms of neglect, cruelty and exploitation. He shall not be the subject of traffic, in any form.

The child shall not be admitted to employment before an appropriate minimum age; he shall in no case be caused or permitted to engage in any occupation or employment which would prejudice his health or education, or interfere with his physical, mental or moral development.

Principle 10. The child shall be protected from practices, which may foster racial, religious and any other form of discrimination. He shall be brought up in a spirit of understanding, tolerance, friendship among peoples, peace and universal brotherhood, and in full consciousness that his energy and talents should be devoted to the service of his fellow men.

SEE ALSO *Children: Right to Protection; Convention on the Rights of the Child; International Year of the Child; United Nations Children Fund (UNICEF).*

DECLARATION OF THE SECOND WORLD CONFERENCE TO COMBAT RACISM AND RACIAL DISCRIMINATION (1983).

The declaration was adopted on 12 August 1983 by the Second World Conference to Combat Racism and Racial Discrimination, convened at the European Office of the United Nations, Geneva, from 1 to 12 August 1983, as authorized by the UN General Assembly (resolution 37/41).

The draft of the declaration, prepared in the First Committee of the conference, was approved by a majority of members of the committee although objections were raised to the inclusion of paragraphs 19 and 20. In plenary session, the conference adopted both paragraphs on separate votes. The declaration as a whole was adopted by 101 votes to 12, with 3 abstentions. Some governments later submitted written reservations or declarations concerning certain aspects of the declaration; these are set out in the report of the conference (United Nations publication, Sales No. E.84.XIV.4, chap. VII). The text of the declaration (chap. I) is as follows:

The Second World Conference to Combat Racism and Racial Discrimination

Solemnly reaffirms and declares that:

1. All human beings are born equal in dignity and rights. Any doctrine of racial superiority is, therefore, scientifically false, morally condemnable, socially unjust and dangerous, and has no justification whatsoever.

2. Racism and racial discrimination are continuing scourges which must be eradicated throughout the world;

3. Consequently, national, regional and international educational resources should be developed and used in ways which will promote mutual understanding between all human beings and demonstrate and teach the scientific basis of ethnic and racial equality and the value of cultural diversity with a view to destroying the basis of racist attitudes and practices;

4. All peoples and all human groups have contributed to the progress of civilization and cultures which constitute the common heritage of humanity;

5. All forms of discrimination are violations of fundamental human rights, and governmental policies which are based on the theory of racial superiority, exclusiveness or hatred also jeopardize friendly relations among peoples and co-operation between nations, and thereby jeopardize international peace and security;

6. *Apartheid* as an institutionalized form of racism is a deliberate and totally abhorrent affront to the conscience and dignity of mankind, a crime against humanity and a threat to international peace and security;

7. In South Africa the most extreme form of racism has led to a form of exploitation and degradation which is in clear contradiction to the principle of human rights and fundamental freedoms for all without distinction as provided for in the Charter of the United Nations;

8. The creation of bantustans is an inhuman policy designed to dispossess the African people of their land, deprive them of their citizenship and consolidate the political and economic domination of the minority white population of South Africa; this policy has been condemned by the international community, and should continue to be rejected and condemned;

9. United Nations sanctions against the racist South African régime must be implemented strictly and faithfully by all States in order to isolate it further. Assistance and collaboration in the economic, military, nuclear and other fields constitutes an impediment to the struggle against *apartheid.* It is the obligation of all Governments to develop appropriate legislation and regulations that would prevent transnational corporations from following those practices which assist and support the racist régime in Pretoria or which exploit the natural resources and people of South Africa and Namibia;

10. All those who contribute to the maintenance of the system of *apartheid* are accomplices in the perpetuation of this crime;

11. The Conference commends the selfless efforts of the people of South Africa and Namibia under the leadership of their national liberation movements for national independence and the establishment of a non-racial democratic society. It also reaffirms the legitimacy of the struggles and calls upon the international community to increase its moral, political and material support to these peoples;

12. Support should be provided to national liberation movements recognized by their respective regional organizations as a concrete form of international solidarity with all oppressed peoples and with all victims of racism and racial discrimination, colonialism and *apartheid;*

13. The Conference condemns the frequent and unjustified acts of aggression, destruction and sabotage, which the racist South African régime, directly and through the use of mercenaries and armed bandits, continues to perpetrate against the front-line States and other independent African States in the subregion because of their opposition to *apartheid,* assistance to refugees and support for the liberation movements. It therefore calls on all States to offer such assistance as would enable the front-line States and the other independent African States in the subregion to strengthen their defence capacity and peacefully rebuild their countries;

14. The Conference expresses its deep concern that many neo-Nazi and Fascist organizations have stepped up their activities which have encouraged tendencies towards racism and racial discrimination. Accordingly, measures should be taken against all ideologies and practices, such as *apartheid,* nazism, fascism and neo-fascism based on racial or ethnic exclusiveness or intolerance, hatred, terror or systematic denials of human rights and fundamental freedoms;

15. The proscription of racism and racial discrimination by law should be accompanied by vigorous efforts to ensure equality in the economic, social and cultural fields; and in particular special programmes, such as affirmative action programmes, should be developed to address the problem of racism and racial discrimination inherent in the system and institutionalized;

16. Education and information should provide an efficient means of action to combat racism and racial discrimination; the Conference supports the efforts of the United Nations Educational, Scientific and Cultural Organization for a more efficient utilization of education and information to combat racism and racial prejudice; it is also the responsibility of all Governments and all leaders of opinion within each society to educate people, especially children and youth, by all available means, to promote an awareness of the evils of racism, racial discrimination and *apartheid* and to ensure respect for the dignity and worth of all human beings. Information media should be encouraged to disseminate information on United Nations activities and programmes related to the elimination of racial discrimination;

17. *Apartheid,* racism and systematic racial discrimination are gross violations of human rights emanating from and leading to serious inequalities in the political and economic fields as well as in the fields of education, health, nutrition, housing, job opportunities and cultural development, and consequently the action required to combat such policies and practices should include measures at the national, regional and international levels, to improve the political, economic, social and cultural living conditions of men and women of all nations. International co-operation for development has an important role to play in securing the resources required by the developing countries to overcome these obstacles;

18. Governments should make clear their condemnation of all propaganda and all organizations which are based on ideas and theories of the superiority of one race or group of persons of one colour or ethnic origin, which attempt to justify or promote racial hatred and discrimination in any form, and should adopt measures designed to eradicate all incitement to, or acts of, such discrimination in accordance with article 4 of the International Convention on the Elimination of All Forms of Racial Discrimination;

19. The Conference condemns any form of co-operation with South Africa, notably the existing and increasing relations between Israel and the racist régime of South Africa, in particular those in the economic and military fields, and deplores and warns against co-operation between them in the nuclear fields; it particularly deplores the expansion and intensification of those relations at the time when the international community is exerting all its efforts towards the objective of completely isolating the racist régime of South Africa; the Conference views this co-operation as an act of deliberate choice and a hostile act against the oppressed people of South Africa, as well as a defiance of the resolutions of the United Nations and the efforts of the society of nations to ensure freedom and peace in southern Africa; the Conference also notes with concern the insidious propaganda by Israel against the United Nations and against Governments which are firmly opposed to *apartheid;*

20. The Conference recalls with deep regret the practices of racial discrimination against the Palestinians as well as other inhabitants of the Arab occupied territories which have such an impact on all aspects of their daily existence that they prevent the enjoyment of their fundamental rights; the Conference expresses its deep concern about this situation and calls for the cessation of all the practices of racial discrimination to which the Palestinians and the other inhabitants of the Arab territories occupied by Israel are subjected;

21. Persons belonging to national, ethnic and other minorities can play a significant role in the promotion of international co-operation and understanding, and the national protection of the rights of persons belonging to minorities in accordance with the International Convention on the Elimination of All Forms of Racial Discrimination, and the International Covenant on Civil and Political Rights, including its article 27, is essential to enable them to fulfil this role; the Conference stresses that granting persons belonging to minority groups the opportunity to participate fully in the political, economic and social life of their country can contribute to the promotion of understanding, co-operation and harmonious relations between persons belonging to the different groups living in a country; the Conference also recognizes that in certain cases special protection of the rights of persons belonging to minority groups may be called for, in particular by the adoption of effective measures in favour of persons belonging to particularly disadvantaged minority groups; the Conference endorses the action taken so far by the competent United Nations bodies to protect persons belonging to minorities, especially the present action of the Commission on Human Rights to elaborate a draft declaration on the protection of the rights of persons belonging to minorities, and is confident that future action currently envisaged will appropriately enhance the international protection of the rights of persons belonging to minorities; in promoting and guaranteeing the rights of persons belonging to minorities, there should be strict respect for the sovereignty, territorial integrity and political independence of the countries where they live and for non-interference in their internal affairs;

22. The rights of indigenous populations to maintain their traditional economic, social and cultural structures,

to pursue their own economic, social and cultural development and to use and further develop their own language, their special relationship to their land and its natural resources should not be taken away from them; the need for consultation with indigenous populations as regards proposals which concern them should be fully observed; the Conference welcomes the establishment of the United Nations Group on Indigenous Populations;

23. Whenever there is racial discrimination, women are often doubly discriminated against; consequently, further special efforts are called for to eliminate the effects of racial discrimination on the status and situation of women, and to ensure conditions promoting women's equal participation in the political, economic, social and cultural life of their societies. In this context, the implementation of the International Convention on the Elimination of All Forms of Discrimination against Women is of particular importance;

24. Relevant national and international bodies should consider specifically the psychological and physical consequences for children who are victims of racial discrimination, and should take care that special measures to counteract these effects are included in their future programmes;

25. The general principle of non-discrimination, with particular regard to refugees fleeing from *apartheid,* racism and racial discrimination, should be applied scrupulously in regard to refugees, particularly in respect of their admission, treatment and *non-refoulement* in countries providing refuge, including refuge on a temporary basis, and of international solidarity in providing assistance and in promoting durable solutions;

26. The urgent need to protect the rights of immigrants, migrant workers, as well as the human rights of those who are undocumented, and their families all over the world requires that States should ensure that their legislation, administration and other practices fully conform with international standards protecting the rights of migrant workers and their families, to mitigate and eliminate the social, economic and other causes of discriminatory measures or attitudes still existing to the detriment of migrant workers and their families; the Conference urges States Members of the United Nations to speed up the present work within the United Nations to elaborate a draft Convention on the Protection of the Rights of Migrant Workers and Members of their Families;

27. States, international organizations, governmental and non-governmental organizations, local and private institutions, religious institutions and trade unions should ensure the total and effective realization of the goals and objectives of the Decade for Action to Combat Racism and Racial Discrimination;

28. A Second Decade to Combat Racism and Racial Discrimination should be launched by the General Assembly with a view to achieving the total elimination of racism, racial discrimination and *apartheid.*

SEE ALSO *Decades to Combat Racism and Racial Discrimination; Declaration on the Elimination of all Forms of Racial Discrimination; Inter-American Declaration on Racial Integration in the Americas; International Convention on the Elimination of all Forms of Racial Discrimination; Race: UNESCO Statement on Scientific Facts; Race and Racial Prejudice: Impact of the UNESCO Declaration; Racial Discrimination; Racism and Racial Discrimination: Second Decade Action Program; UNESCO Declaration on Race and Racial Prejudice.*

DECLARATION OF THE UNITED NATIONS CONFERENCE ON THE HUMAN ENVIRONMENT (1972).

The declaration was adopted unanimously on 16 June 1972 by representatives of 112 nations attending the United Nations Conference on the Human Environment, convened in Stockholm from 5 to 16 June as authorized by the UN General Assembly (resolution 2398 [XXIII]). The assembly endorsed the declaration and drew it to the attention of all governments, on 15 December 1972 (resolution 2994 [XXVII]). The declaration was the first acknowledgement by the international community as a whole of the fact that new principles of behavior and responsibility must govern man's relations with his environment and influenced the establishment of the UNITED NATIONS ENVIRONMENT PROGRAM, based in Nairobi, to promote the acquisition, assessment, and exchange of environmental knowledge.

The text of the declaration is as follows:

The United Nations Conference on the Human Environment,

Having met at Stockholm from 5 to 16 June 1972,

Having considered the need for a common outlook and for common principles to inspire and guide the peoples of the world in the preservation and enhancement of the human environment,

I

Proclaims that:

1. Man is both creature and moulder of his environment, which gives him physical sustenance and affords him the opportunity for intellectual, moral, social and spiritual growth. In the long and tortuous evolution of the human race on this planet a stage has been reached when, through the rapid acceleration of science and technology, man has acquired the power to transform his environment in countless ways and on an unprecedented scale. Both aspects of man's environment, the natural and the man-made, are essential to his well-being and to the enjoyment of basic human rights—even the right to life itself.

2. The protection and improvement of the human environment is a major issue which affects the well-being of peoples and economic development throughout the world; it is the urgent desire of the peoples of the whole world and the duty of all Governments.

3. Man has constantly to sum up experience and go on discovering, inventing, creating and advancing. In our time, man's capability to transform his surroundings, if used wisely, can bring to all peoples the benefits of development and the opportunity to enhance the quality of life. Wrongly or heedlessly applied, the same power can do incalculable harm to human beings and the human environment. We see around us growing evidence of man-made harm in many regions of the earth: dangerous levels of pollution in water, air, earth and living beings; major and undesirable disturbances to the ecological balance of the biosphere; destruction and depletion of irreplaceable resources; and gross deficiences, harmful to the physical, mental and social health of man, in the man-made environment, particularly in the living and working environment.

4. In the developing countries most of the environmental problems are caused by under-development. Millions continue to live far below the minimum levels required for a decent human existence, deprived of adequate food and clothing, shelter and education, health and sanitation. Therefore, the developing countries must direct their efforts to development, bearing in mind their priorities and the need to safeguard and improve the environment. For the same purpose, the industrialized countries should make efforts to reduce the gap [between] themselves and the developing countries. In the industrialized countries, environmental problems are generally related to industrialization and technological development.

5. The natural growth of population continuously presents problems for the preservation of the environment, and adequate policies and measures should be adopted, as appropriate, to face these problems. Of all things in the world, people are the most precious. It is the people that propel social progress, create social wealth, develop science and technology and, through their hard work, continuously transform the human environment. Along with social progress and the advance of production, science and technology, the capability of man to improve the environment increases with each passing day.

6. A point has been reached in history when we must shape our actions throughout the world with a more prudent care for their environmental consequences. Through ignorance or indifference we can do massive and irreversible harm to the earthly environment on which our life and well-being depend. Conversely, through fuller knowledge and wiser action, we can achieve for ourselves and our posterity a better life in an environment more in keeping with human needs and hopes. There are broad vistas for the enhancement of environmental quality and the creation of a good life. What is needed is an enthusiastic but calm state of mind and intense but orderly work. For the purpose of attaining freedom in the world of nature, man must use knowledge to build, in collaboration with nature, a better environment. To defend and improve the human environment for present and future generations has become an imperative goal for mankind—a goal to be pursued together with, and in harmony with, the established and fundamental goals of peace and of worldwide economic and social development.

7. To achieve this environmental goal will demand the acceptance of responsibility by citizens and communities and by enterprises and institutions at every level, all sharing equitably in common efforts. Individuals in all walks of life as well as organizations in many fields, by their values and the sum of their actions, will shape the world environment of the future. Local and national governments will bear the greatest burden for large-scale environmental policy and action within their jurisdictions. International co-operation is also needed in order to raise resources to support the developing countries in carrying out their responsibilities in this field. A growing class of environmental problems, because they are regional or global in extent or because they affect the common international realm, will require extensive co-operation among nations and action by international organizations in the common interest. The Conference calls upon Governments and peoples to exert common efforts for the preservation and improvement of the human environment, for the benefit of all the people and for their posterity.

II—Principles

States the common conviction that:

Principle 1. Man has the fundamental right to freedom, equality and adequate conditions of life, in an environment of a quality that permits a life of dignity and well-being, and he bears a solemn responsibility to protect and improve the environment for present and future generations. In this respect, policies promoting or perpetuating *apartheid,* racial segregation, discrimination, colonial and other forms of oppression and foreign domination stand condemned and must be eliminated.

Principle 2. The natural resources of the earth, including the air, water, land, flora and fauna and especially representative samples of natural ecosystems, must be safeguarded for the benefit of present and future generations through careful planning or management, as appropriate.

Principle 3. The capacity of the earth to produce vital renewable resources must be maintained and, wherever practicable, restored or improved.

Principle 4. Man has a special responsibility to safeguard and wisely manage the heritage of wildlife and its habitat, which are now gravely imperilled by a combination of adverse factors. Nature conservation, including wildlife, must therefore receive importance in planning for economic development.

Principle 5. The non-renewable resources of the earth must be employed in such a way as to guard against the danger of their future exhaustion and to ensure that benefits from such employment are shared by all mankind.

Principle 6. The discharge of toxic substances or of other substances and the release of heat, in such quantities or concentrations as to exceed the capacity of the environment to render them harmless, must be halted in order to ensure that serious or irreversible damage is not inflicted upon ecosystems. The just struggle of the peoples of all countries against pollution should be supported.

Principle 7. States shall take all possible steps to prevent pollution of the seas by substances that are liable to create hazards to human health, to harm living resources and marine life, to damage amenities or to interfere with other legitimate uses of the sea.

Principle 8. Economic and social development is essential for ensuring a favourable living and working environment for man and for creating conditions on earth that are necessary for the improvement of the quality of life.

Principle 9. Environmental deficiencies generated by the conditions of under-development and natural disasters pose grave problems and can best be remedied by accelerated development through the transfer of substantial quantities of financial and technological assistance as a supplement to the domestic effort of the developing countries and such timely assistance as may be required.

Principle 10. For the developing countries, stability of prices and adequate earnings for primary commodities and raw materials are essential to environmental management since economic factors as well as ecological processes must be taken into account.

Principle 11. The environmental policies of all States should enhance and not adversely affect the present or future development potential of developing countries, nor should they hamper the attainment of better living conditions for all, and appropriate steps should be taken by States and international organizations with a view to reaching agreement on meeting the possible national and international economic consequences resulting from the application of environmental measures.

Principle 12. Resources should be made available to preserve and improve the environment, taking into account the circumstances and particular requirements of developing countries and any costs which may emanate from their incorporating environmental safeguards into their development planning and the need for making available to them, upon their request, additional international technical and financial assistance for this purpose.

Principle 13. In order to achieve a more rational management of resources and thus to improve the environment, States should adopt an integrated and co-ordinated approach to their development planning so as to ensure that development is compatible with the need to protect and improve environment for the benefit of their population.

Principle 14. Rational planning constitutes an essential tool for reconciling any conflict between the needs of development and the need to protect and improve the environment.

Principle 15. Planning must be applied to human settlements and urbanization with a view to avoiding adverse effects on the environment and obtaining maximum social, economic and environmental benefits for all. In this respect, projects which are designed for colonialist and racist domination must be abandoned.

Principle 16. Demographic policies which are without prejudice to basic human rights and which are deemed appropriate by Governments concerned should be applied in those regions where the rate of population growth or excessive population concentrations are likely to have adverse effects on the environment of the human environment and impede development.

Principle 17. Appropriate national institutions must be entrusted with the task of planning, managing or controlling the environmental resources of States with a view to enhancing environmental quality.

Principle 18. Science and technology, as part of their contribution to economic and social development, must be applied to the identification, avoidance and control of environmental risks and the solution of environmental problems and for the common good of mankind.

Principle 19. Education in environmental matters, for the younger generation as well as adults, giving due consideration to the underprivileged, is essential in order to broaden the basis for an enlightened opinion and responsible conduct by individuals, enterprises and communities in protecting and improving the environment in its full human dimension. It is also essential that mass media of communications avoid contributing to the deterioration of the environment, but, on the contrary, disseminate information of an educational nature on the need to protect and improve the environment in order to enable man to develop in every respect.

Principle 20. Scientific research and development in the context of environmental problems, both national and multi-national, must be promoted in all countries, especially the developing countries. In this connexion, the free flow of up-to-date scientific information and transfer of experience must be supported and assisted, to facilitate the solution of environmental problems; environmental technologies should be made available to developing countries on terms which would encourage their wide dissemination without constituting an economic burden on the developing countries.

Principle 21. States have, in accordance with the Charter of the United Nations and the principles of international law, the sovereign right to exploit their own resources pursuant to their own environmental policies, and the responsibility to ensure that activities within their jurisdiction or control do not cause damage to the environment of other States or of areas beyond the limits of national jurisdiction.

Principle 22. States shall co-operate to develop further the international law regarding liability and compensation for the victims of pollution and other environmental damage caused by activities within the jurisdiction or control of such States to areas beyond their jurisdiction.

Principle 23. Without prejudice to such criteria as may be agreed upon by the international community, or to standards which will have to be determined nationally, it will be essential in all cases to consider the systems of values prevailing in each country, and the extent of the applicability of standards which are valid for the most advanced countries but which may be inappropriate and of unwarranted social cost for the developing countries.

Principle 24. International matters concerning the protection and improvement of the environment should be handled in a co-operative spirit by all countries, big and small, on an equal footing. Co-operation through multilateral or bilateral arrangements or other appropriate means is essential to effectively control, prevent, reduce and eliminate adverse environmental effects resulting from activities conducted in all spheres, in such a way that due account is taken of the sovereignty and interests of all States.

Principle 25. States shall ensure that international organizations play a co-ordinated, efficient and dynamic role for the protection and improvement of the environment.

Principle 26. Man and his environment must be spared the effects of nuclear weapons and all other means of mass destruction. States must strive to reach prompt agreement, in the relevant international organs, on the elimination and complete destruction of such weapons.

SEE ALSO *Environment; Vancouver Declaration on Human Settlements.*

DECLARATION ON *APARTHEID* AND ITS DESTRUCTIVE CONSEQUENCES IN SOUTHERN AFRICA. The declaration, adopted unanimously by a special session of the UN General Assembly on 14 December 1989, sets out in detail the position of the international community with regard to the possibility of ending *apartheid* through negotiations.

At the special session, authorized by the General Assembly on 13 November 1989 (resolution 44/408) and held at the headquarters of the United Nations, New York, from 12 to 14 December 1989, an ad hoc committee of the assembly heard a number of nongovernmental organizations and individuals having a special interest in the question of *apartheid,* including the national liberation movements of South Africa recognized by the Organization of African Unity. The ad hoc committee, with the cooperation of representatives of the frontline States, reviewed a draft declaration prepared by officers of the Special Committee against *Apartheid* and put it into final form.

The text of the declaration (UN Doc. A/RES/S-16-1) is as follows:

We, the States Members of the United Nations,

Assembled at the sixteenth special session of the General Assembly, a special session on *apartheid* and its destructive consequences in southern Africa, guided by the fundamental and universal principles enshrined in the Charter of the United Nations and the Universal Declaration of Human Rights, in the context of our efforts to establish peace throughout the world by ending all conflicts through negotiations, and desirous of making serious efforts to bring an end to the unacceptable situation prevailing in southern Africa, which is a result of the policies and practices of *apartheid,* through negotiations based on the principle of justice and peace for all:

Reaffirming our conviction, which history confirms, that where colonial and racial domination or *apartheid* exist, there can be neither peace nor justice,

Reiterating, accordingly, that while the *apartheid* system in South Africa persists, the peoples of Africa as a whole cannot achieve the fundamental objectives of justice, human dignity and peace which are both crucial in themselves and fundamental to the stability and development of the continent,

Recognizing that, with regard to southern Africa, the entire world is vitally interested that the processes in which that region is involved, leading to the genuine national independence of Namibia and peace in Angola and Mozambique, should succeed in the shortest possible time, and equally recognizing that the world is deeply concerned that destabilization by South Africa of the countries of the region, whether through direct aggression, sponsorship of surrogates, economic subversion or other means, is unacceptable in all its forms and must not occur,

Also recognizing the reality that permanent peace and stability in southern Africa can only be achieved when the system of *apartheid* in South Africa has been eradicated and South Africa has been transformed into a united, democratic and non-racial country, and therefore reiterating that all the necessary measures should be adopted now to bring a speedy end to the *apartheid* system in the interest of all the people of southern Africa, the continent and the world at large,

Believing that, as a result of the legitimate struggle of the South African people for the elimination of *apartheid,* and of international pressure against that system, as well as global efforts to resolve regional conflicts, possibilities exist for further movement towards the resolution of the problems facing the people of South Africa,

Reaffirming the right of all peoples, including the people of South Africa, to determine their own destiny and to work out for themselves the institutions and the system of government under which they will, by general consent, live and work together to build a harmonious society, and remaining committed to doing everything possible and necessary to assist the people of South Africa, in such ways as they may, through their genuine representatives, determine to achieve this objective,

Making these commitments because we believe that all people are equal and have equal rights to human dignity and respect, regardless of colour, race, sex or creed, that all men and women have the right and duty to participate in their own government, as equal members of society, and that no individual or group of individuals has any right to govern others without their democratic consent, and reiterating that the *apartheid* system violates all these fundamental and universal principles,

Affirming that *apartheid*, characterized as a crime against the conscience and dignity of mankind, is responsible for the death of countless numbers of people in South Africa, has sought to dehumanize entire peoples, and has imposed a brutal war on the region of southern Africa, which has resulted in untold loss of life, destruction of property and massive displacement of innocent men, women and children and which is a scourge and affront to humanity that must be fought and eradicated in its totality,

Therefore we support and continue to support all those in South Africa who pursue this noble objective. We believe this to be our duty, carried out in the interest of all humanity,

While extending this support to those who strive for a non-racial and democratic society in South Africa, a point on which no compromise is possible, we have repeatedly expressed our objective of a solution arrived at by peaceful means; we note that the people of South Africa, and their liberation movements who felt compelled to take up arms, have also upheld their preference for this position for many decades and continue to do so,

Welcoming the Declaration of the *Ad-Hoc* Committee of the Organization of African Unity on Southern Africa on the question of South Africa, adopted at Harare on 21 August 1989, [UN Doc. A/44/697, annex], and subsequently endorsed by the Heads of State or Government of Non-Aligned Countries at their Ninth Conference, held at Belgrade from 4 to 7 September 1989, [UN Doc. A/44/551-S/20870], as a reaffirmation of readiness to resolve the problems of South Africa through negotiations. The Declaration is consistent with the positions contained in the Lusaka Manifesto [UN Doc. A/7754], of two decades ago, in particular regarding the preference of the African people for peaceful change, and takes into account the changes that have taken place in southern Africa since then. The Declaration constitutes a new challenge to the Pretoria régime to join in the noble efforts to end the *apartheid* system, an objective to which the United Nations has always been committed,

Noting with appreciation that the Commonwealth Heads of Government, at their meeting held at Kuala Lumpur from 18 to 24 October 1989, noted with satisfaction the strong preference for the path of negotiated and peaceful settlement inherent in the Declaration adopted at Harare on 21 August 1989, and considered what further steps they might take to advance the prospects for negotiations [UN Doc. A/44/672-S/20914],

Also noting with appreciation that the Third Francophone Conference of Heads of State and Government, held at Dakar from 24 to 26 May 1989, likewise called for negotiations between Pretoria and representatives of the majority of the people with a view to the establishment of a democratic and equalitarian system in South Africa,

Consequently, we shall continue to do everything in our power to increase support for the legitimate struggle of the South African people, including maintaining international pressure against the system of *apartheid* until that system is ended and South Africa is transformed into a united, democratic and non-racial country, with justice and security for all its citizens,

In keeping with this solemn resolve, and responding directly to the wishes of the majority of the people of South Africa, we publicly pledge ourselves to the positions contained hereunder, convinced that their implementation will lead to a speedy end of the *apartheid* system and heralding the dawn of a new era of peace for all the peoples of Africa, in a continent finally free from racism, white minority rule and colonial domination,

Declare as follows:

1. A conjuncture of circumstances exists, which, if there is a demonstrable readiness on the part of the South African régime to engage in negotiations genuinely and seriously, given the repeated expression of the majority of the people of South Africa of their long-standing preference to arrive at a political settlement, could create the possibility to end *apartheid* through negotiations.

2. We would therefore encourage the people of South Africa, as part of their legitimate struggle, to join together to negotiate an end to the *apartheid* system and agree on all the measures that are necessary to transform their country into a non-racial democracy. We support the position held by the majority of the people of South Africa that these objectives, and not the amendment or reform of the *apartheid* system, should be the goals of the negotiations.

3. We are at one with the people of South Africa that the outcome of such a process should be a new constitutional order determined by them and based on the Charter of the United Nations and the Universal Declaration of Human Rights. We therefore hold the following fundamental principles to be of importance:

(a) South Africa shall become a united, non-racial and democratic State;

(b) All its people shall enjoy common and equal citizenship and nationality, regardless of race, colour, sex or creed;

(c) All its people shall have the right to participate in the government and administration of the country on the basis of universal, equal suffrage, under a non-racial voters' roll, and by secret ballot, in a united and non-fragmented South Africa;

(d) All shall have the right to form and join any political party of their choice provided that this is not in furtherance of racism;

(e) All shall enjoy universally recognized human rights, freedoms and civil liberties, protected under an entrenched bill of rights;

(f) South Africa shall have a legal system that will guarantee equality of all before the law;

(g) South Africa shall have an independent and non-racial judiciary;

(h) There shall be created an economic order that will promote and advance the well-being of all South Africans;

(i) A democratic South Africa shall respect the rights, sovereignty and territorial integrity of all countries and pursue a policy of peace, friendship and mutually beneficial co-operation with all peoples.

4. We believe that acceptance of these fundamental principles could constitute the basis for an internationally acceptable solution that will enable South Africa to take its rightful place as an equal partner among the world community of nations.

A. Climate for Negotiations. 5. We believe that it is essential that the necessary climate be created for negotiations. There is an urgent need to respond positively to this universally acclaimed demand and thus create this climate.

6. Accordingly, the present South African régime should, at the least:

(a) Release all political prisoners and detainees un-

conditionally and refrain from imposing any restrictions on them;

(b) Lift all bans and restrictions on all proscribed and restricted organizations and persons;

(c) Remove all troops from the townships;

(d) End the state of emergency and repeal all legislation, such as the Internal Security Act, designed to circumscribe political activity;

(e) Cease all political trials and political executions.

7. These measures would help create the necessary climate in which free political discussion can take place—an essential condition to ensure that the people themselves participate in the process of remaking their country.

B. Guidelines to the Process of Negotiations. 8. We are of the view that the parties concerned should, in the context of the necessary climate, negotiate the future of their country and its people in good faith and in an atmosphere which, by mutual agreement between the liberation movements and the South African régime, would be free of violence. The process could commence along the following guidelines:

(a) Agreement on the mechanism for the drawing up of a new constitution, based on, among others, the principles enunciated above, and the basis for its adoption;

(b) Agreement on the role to be played by the international community in ensuring a successful transition to a democratic order;

(c) Agreed transitional arrangements and modalities for the process of the drawing up and adoption of a new constitution, and for the transition to a democratic order, including the holding of elections.

C. Programme of Action. 9. In pursuance of the objectives stated in this Declaration, we hereby decide:

(a) To remain seized of the issue of a political resolution of the South African question;

(b) To step up all-round support for the opponents of *apartheid* and to campaign internationally in pursuance of this objective;

(c) To use concerted and effective measures, including the full observance by all countries of the mandatory arms embargo, aimed at applying pressure to ensure a speedy end to *apartheid;*

(d) To ensure that the international community does not relax existing measures aimed at encouraging the South African régime to eradicate *apartheid* until there is clear evidence of profound and irreversible changes, bearing in mind the objectives of this Declaration;

(e) To render all possible assistance to the front-line and neighbouring States to enable them: to rebuild their economics, which have been adversely affected by South Africa's acts of aggression and destabilization; to withstand any further such acts; and to continue to support the peoples of Namibia and South Africa;

(f) To extend such assistance to the Governments of Angola and Mozambique as they may request in order to secure peace for their peoples, and to encourage and support peace initiatives undertaken by the Governments of Angola and Mozambique aimed at bringing about peace and normalization of life in their countries;

(g) The new South Africa shall, upon adoption of the new constitution, participate fully in relevant organs and specialized agencies of the United Nations.

10. We request the Secretary-General to transmit copies of the present Declaration to the South African Government and the representatives of the oppressed people of

South Africa and also request the Secretary-General to prepare a report and submit it to the General Assembly by 1 July 1990 on the progress made in the implementation of the present Declaration.

SEE ALSO "Apartheid" *entries; Group of Three; International Convention on the Suppression and Punishment of the Crime of* Apartheid*; Lagos Declaration for Action against* Apartheid*; Slavery-Like Practices of* Apartheid *and Colonialism; South Africa: UN Concern about* Apartheid*; Special Committee against* Apartheid.

DECLARATION ON PERMANENT SOVEREIGNTY OVER NATURAL RESOURCES (1962).

On 12 December 1958, the UN General Assembly established (resolution 1314 [XIII]) a commission to conduct a full survey of the status of the right of peoples and nations to permanent sovereignty over their natural wealth and resources, which it considered to be a basic constituent of the right of self-determination. On the basis of the work of the commission, the assembly was able, on 14 December 1962, to adopt (resolution 1803 [XVII]) a declaration setting out its views on the subject. The text of the declaration, annexed to the resolution, is as follows:

1. The right of peoples and nations to permanent sovereignty over their natural wealth and resources must be exercised in the interest of their national development and of the well-being of the people of the State concerned.

2. The exploration, development and disposition of such resources, as well as the import of the foreign capital required for these purposes, should be in conformity with the rules and conditions which the peoples and nations freely consider to be necessary or desirable with regard to the authorization, restriction or prohibition of such activities.

3. In cases where authorization is granted, the capital imported and the earnings on that capital shall be governed by the terms thereof, by the national legislation in force, and by international law. The profits derived must be shared in the proportions freely agreed upon, in each case, between the investors and the recipient State, due care being taken to ensure that there is no impairment, for any reason, of that State's sovereignty over its natural wealth and resources.

4. Nationalization, expropriation or requisitioning shall be based on grounds or reasons of public utility, security or the national interest which are recognized as overriding purely individual or private interests, both domestic and foreign. In such cases the owner shall be paid appropriate compensation, in accordance with the rules in force in the State taking such measures in the exercise of its sovereignty and in accordance with international law. In any case where the question of compensation gives rise to a controversy, the national jurisdiction of the State taking such measures shall be exhausted. However, upon agreement by sovereign States and other parties concerned, settlement of the dispute should be made through arbitration or international adjudication.

5. The free and beneficial exercise of the sovereignty of peoples and nations over their natural resources must be furthered by the mutual respect of States based on their sovereign equality.

6. International co-operation for the economic development of developing countries, whether in the form of public or private capital investments, exchange of goods and services, technical assistance, or exchange of scientific information, shall be such as to further their independent national development and shall be based upon respect for their sovereignty over their natural wealth and resources.

7. Violation of the rights of peoples and nations to sovereignty over their natural wealth and resources is contrary to the spirit and principles of the Charter of the United Nations and hinders the development of international co-operation and the maintenance of peace.

8. Foreign investment agreements freely entered into by or between sovereign States shall be observed in good faith; States and international organizations shall strictly and conscientiously respect the sovereignty of peoples and nations over their natural wealth and resources in accordance with the Charter and the principles set forth in the present resolution.

SEE ALSO Self-Determination entries; UNESCO Convention on the Means of Prohibiting and Preventing the Illicit Import, Export and Transfer of Ownership of Cultural Property; UNESCO Recommendation concerning the Preservation of Cultural Property Endangered by Public or Private Works.

DECLARATION ON PRINCIPLES OF INTERNATIONAL LAW CONCERNING FRIENDLY RELATIONS AND CO-OPERATION AMONG STATES IN ACCORDANCE WITH THE CHARTER OF THE UNITED NATIONS (1970).

In adopting this declaration, on the occasion of the 25th anniversary of the United Nations, the UN General Assembly expressed its strong conviction that the new instrument, by promoting the rule of law among nations and universal application of the principles of the UNITED NATIONS CHARTER, would strengthen world peace and constitute a landmark in the development of international law and of relations between States.

The declaration was adopted by the UN General Assembly on 24 October 1970 (resolution 2625 [XXV]). The text, annexed to the resolution, includes the following sections relevant to human rights concerns:

Preamble

The General Assembly,

Reaffirming in the terms of the Charter of the United Nations that the maintenance of international peace and security and the development of friendly relations and co-operation between nations are among the fundamental purposes of the United Nations,

Recalling that the peoples of the United Nations are determined to practise tolerance and live together in peace with one another as good neighbours,

Bearing in mind the importance of maintaining and strengthening international peace founded upon freedom, equality, justice and respect for fundamental human rights and of developing friendly relations among nations irrespective of their political, economic and social systems or the levels of their development.

Bearing in mind also the paramount importance of the Charter of the United Nations in the promotion of the rule of law among nations,

Considering that the faithful observance of the principles of international law concerning friendly relations and co-operation among States and the fulfilment in good faith of the obligations assumed by States, in accordance with the Charter, is of the greatest importance for the maintenance of international peace and security and for the implementation of the other purposes of the United Nations,

Noting that the great political, economic and social changes and scientific progress which have taken place in the world since the adoption of the Charter give increased importance to these principles and to the need for their more effective application in the conduct of States wherever carried on,

Recalling the established principle that outer space, including the Moon and other celestial bodies, is not subject to national appropriation by claim of sovereignty, by means of use or occupation, or by any other means, and mindful of the fact that consideration is being given in the United Nations to the question of establishing other appropriate provisions similarly inspired,

Convinced that the strict observance by States of the obligation not to intervene in the affairs of any other State is an essential condition to ensure that nations live together in peace with one another, since the practice of any form of intervention not only violates the spirit and letter of the Charter, but also leads to the creation of situations which threaten international peace and security,

Recalling the duty of States to refrain in their international relations from military, political, economic or any other form of coercion aimed against the political independence or territorial integrity of any State,

Considering it essential that all States shall refrain in their international relations from the threat or use of force against the territorial integrity or political independence of any State, or in any other manner inconsistent with the purposes of the United Nations,

Considering it equally essential that all States shall settle their international disputes by peaceful means in accordance with the Charter,

Reaffirming, in accordance with the Charter, the basic importance of sovereign equality and stressing that the purposes of the United Nations can be implemented only if States enjoy sovereign equality and comply fully with the requirements of this principle in their international relations,

Convinced that the subjection of peoples to alien subjugation, domination and exploitation constitutes a major obstacle to the promotion of international peace and security,

Convinced that the principle of equal rights and self-determination of peoples constitutes a significant contribution to contemporary international law, and that its effective application is of paramount importance for the promotion of friendly relations among States, based on respect for the principle of sovereign equality,

Convinced in consequence that any attempt aimed at the partial or total disruption of the national unity and territorial integrity of a State or country or at its political independence is incompatible with the purposes and principles of the Charter,

Considering the provisions of the Charter as a whole and taking into account the role of relevant resolutions adopted by the competent organs of the United Nations relating to the content of the principles,

Considering that the progressive development and codification of the following principles:

(a) The principle that States shall refrain in their international relations from the threat or use of force against the territorial integrity or political independence of any State, or in any other manner inconsistent with the purposes of the United Nations,

(b) The principle that States shall settle their international disputes by peaceful means in such a manner that international peace and security and justice are not endangered,

(c) The duty not to intervene in matters within the domestic jurisdiction of any State, in accordance with the Charter,

(d) The duty of States to co-operate with one another in accordance with the Charter,

(e) The principle of equal rights and self-determination of peoples,

(f) The principle of sovereign equality of States,

(g) The principle that States shall fulfil in good faith the obligations assumed by them in accordance with the Charter,

so as to secure their more effective application within the international community, would promote the realization of the purposes of the United Nations,

Having considered the principles of international law relating to friendly relations and co-operation among States,

1. Solemnly proclaims the following principles: . . .

The Principle Concerning the Duty not to Intervene in Matters Within the Domestic Jurisdiction of any State, in Accordance with the Charter. No State or group of States has the right to intervene, directly or indirectly, for any reason whatever, in the internal or external affairs of any other State. Consequently, armed intervention and all other forms of interference or attempted threats against the personality of the State or against its political, economic and cultural elements, are in violation of international law.

No State may use or encourage the use of economic, political or any other type of measures to coerce another State in order to obtain from it the subordination of the exercise of its sovereign rights and to secure from it advantages of any kind. Also, no State shall organize, assist, foment, finance, incite or tolerate subversive, terrorist or armed activities directed towards the violent overthrow of the régime of another State, or interfere in civil strife in another State.

The use of force to deprive peoples of their national identity constitutes a violation of their inalienable rights and of the principle of nonintervention.

Every State has an inalienable right to choose its political, economic, social and cultural systems, without interference in any form by another State.

Nothing in the foregoing paragraphs shall be construed as affecting the relevant provisions of the Charter relating to the maintenance of international peace and security.

The Principle of Equal Rights and Self-Determination of Peoples. By virtue of the principle of equal rights and self-determination of peoples enshrined in the Charter of the United Nations, all peoples have the right freely to determine, without external interference, their political status and to pursue their economic, social and cultural development, and every State has the duty to respect this right in accordance with the provisions of the Charter.

Every State has the duty to promote, through joint and separate action, realization of the principle of equal rights and self-determination of peoples, in accordance with the provisions of the Charter, and to render assistance to the United Nations in carrying out the responsibilities entrusted to it by the Charter regarding the implementation of the principle, in order:

(a) To promote friendly relations and cooperation among States; and

(b) To bring a speedy end to colonialism, having due regard to the freely expressed will of the peoples concerned;

and bearing in mind that subjection of peoples to alien subjugation, domination and exploitation constitutes a violation of the principle, as well as a denial of fundamental human rights, and is contrary to the Charter.

Every State has the duty to promote through joint and separate action universal respect for and observance of human rights and fundamental freedoms in accordance with the Charter.

The establishment of a sovereign and independent State, the free association or integration with an independent State or the emergence into any other political status freely determined by a people constitutes modes of implementing the right of self-determination by that people.

Every State has the duty to refrain from any forcible action which deprives peoples referred to above in the elaboration of the present principle of their right to self-determination and freedom and independence. In their actions against, and resistance to, such forcible action in pursuit of the exercise of their right to self-determination, such peoples are entitled to seek and to receive support in accordance with the purposes and principles of the Charter.

The territory of a colony or other Non-Self-Governing Territory has, under the Charter, a status separate and distinct from the territory of the State administering it; and such separate and distinct status under the Charter shall exist until the people of the colony or Non-Self-Governing Territory have exercised their right of self-determination in accordance with the Charter, and particularly its purposes and principles.

Nothing in the foregoing paragraphs shall be construed as authorizing or encouraging any action which would dismember or impair, totally or in part, the territorial integrity or political unity of sovereign and independent States conducting themselves in compliance with the principle of equal rights and self-determination of peoples as described above and thus possessed of a government representing the whole people belonging to the territory without distinction as to race, creed or colour.

Every State shall refrain from any action aimed at the partial or total disruption of the national unity and territorial integrity of any other State or country. . . .

2. Declares that:

In their interpretation and application the above principles are interrelated and each principle should be construed in the context of the other principles.

Nothing in this Declaration shall be construed as prejudicing in any manner the provisions of the Charter or the rights and duties of Member States under the Charter or the rights of peoples under the Charter, taking into account the elaboration of these rights in this Declaration.

3. Declares further that:

The principles of the Charter which are embodied in this Declaration constitute basic principles of international law,

and consequently appeals to all States to be guided by these principles in their international conduct and to develop their mutual relations on the basis of the strict observance of these principles.

SEE ALSO Declaration on the Occasion of the 25th Anniversary of the UN; Declaration on the Inadmissibility of Intervention and Interference in the Internal Affairs of States.

DECLARATION ON SOCIAL AND LEGAL PRINCIPLES RELATING TO THE PROTECTION AND WELFARE OF CHILDREN, WITH SPECIAL REFERENCE TO FOSTER PLACEMENT AND ADOPTION NATIONALLY AND INTERNATIONALLY (1986).

In 1979, the UN Economic and Social Council submitted to the General Assembly (resolution 1979/28) the text of a draft declaration on social and legal principles relating to the adoption and foster placement of children, for preliminary consideration and eventual adoption. The draft, prepared by an expert group, and the comments thereon submitted by governments, were considered in some detail over a period of years in the assembly's Third and Sixth Committees. In 1986, after extensive consultations of member States representing different legal systems, a satisfactory formulation was achieved. The declaration was adopted by the General Assembly on 3 December 1986 (resolution 41/85). The text of the declaration is as follows:

The General Assembly,

Recalling the Universal Declaration of Human Rights, the International Covenant on Economic, Social and Cultural Rights, the International Covenant on Civil and Political Discrimination and the Convention on the Elimination of All Forms of Discrimination against Women,

Recalling also the Declaration on the Rights of the Child, which it proclaimed by its resolution 1386 (XIV) of 20 November 1959,

Reaffirming principle 6 of that Declaration, which states that the child shall, wherever possible, grow up in the care and under the responsibility of his parents and, in any case, in an atmosphere of affection and of moral and material security,

Concerned at the large number of children who are abandoned or become orphans owing to violence, internal disturbance, armed conflicts, natural disasters, economic crises or social problems,

Bearing in mind that in all foster placement and adoption procedures the best interests of the child should be the paramount consideration.

Recognizing that under the principal legal systems of the world, various other alternative valuable institutions exist, such as the Kafala of Islamic Law, which provide substitute care to children who cannot be cared for by their own parents,

Recognizing further that only where a particular institution is recognized and regulated by the domestic law of a State would the provisions of this Declaration relating to that institution be relevant and that such provisions would in no way affect the existing alternative institutions in other legal systems,

Conscious of the need to proclaim universal principles to be taken into account in cases where procedures are instituted relating to foster placement or adoption of a child, either nationally or internationally,

Bearing in mind, however, that the principles set forth hereunder do not impose on States such legal institutions as foster placement or adoption,

Proclaims the following principles:

A. General Family and Child Welfare

Article 1. Every State should give a high priority to family and child welfare.

Article 2. Child welfare depends upon good family welfare.

Article 3. The first priority for a child is to be cared for by his or her own parents.

Article 4. When care by the child's own parents is unavailable or inappropriate, care by relatives of the child's parents, by another substitute—foster or adoptive—family or, if necessary, by an appropriate institution should be considered.

Article 5. In all matters relating to the placement of a child outside the care of the child's own parents, the best interests of the child, particularly his or her need for affection and right to security and continuing care, should be the paramount consideration.

Article 6. Persons responsible for foster placement or adoption procedures should have professional or other appropriate training.

Article 7. Governments should determine the adequacy of their national child welfare services and consider appropriate actions.

Article 8. The child should at all times have a name, a nationality and a legal representative. The child should not, as a result of foster placement, adoption or any alternative régime, be deprived of his or her name, nationality or legal representative unless the child thereby acquires a new name, nationality or legal representative.

Article 9. The need of a foster or an adopted child to know about his or her background should be recognized by persons responsible for the child's care, unless this is contrary to the child's best interests.

B. Foster Placement

Article 10. Foster placement of children should be regulated by law.

Article 11. Foster family care, though temporary in nature, may continue, if necessary, until adulthood but should not preclude either prior return to the child's own parents or adoption.

Article 12. In all matters of foster family care the prospective foster parents and, as appropriate, the child and his or her own parents should be properly involved. A competent authority or agency should be responsible for supervision to ensure the welfare of the child.

C. Adoption

Article 13. The primary aim of adoption is to provide the child who cannot be cared for by his or her own parents with a permanent family.

Article 14. In considering possible adoption placements, persons responsible for them should select the most appropriate environment for the child.

Article 15. Sufficient time and adequate counselling should be given to the child's own parents, the prospective adoptive parents and, as appropriate, the child in order to reach a decision on the child's future as early as possible.

Article 16. The relationship between the child to be adopted and the prospective adoptive parents should be observed by child welfare agencies or services prior to the adoption. Legislation should ensure that the child is recognized in law as a member of the adoptive family and enjoys all the rights pertinent thereto.

Article 17. If a child cannot be placed in a foster or an adoptive family or cannot in any suitable manner be cared for in the country of origin, intercountry adoption may be considered as an alternative means of providing the child with a family.

Article 18. Governments should establish policy, legislation and effective supervision for the protection of children involved in intercountry adoption. Intercountry adoption should, wherever possible, only be undertaken when such measures have been established in the States concerned.

Article 19. Policies should be established and laws enacted, where necessary, for the prohibition of abduction and of any other act for illicit placement of children.

Article 20. In intercountry adoption, placements should, as a rule, be made through competent authorities or agencies with application of safeguards and standards equivalent to those existing in respect of national adoption. In no case should the placement result in improper financial gain for those involved in it.

Article 21. In intercountry adoption through persons acting as agents for prospective adoptive parents special precautions should be taken in order to protect the child's legal and social interests.

Article 22. No intercountry adoption should be considered before it has been established that the child is legally free for adoption and that any pertinent documents necessary to complete the adoption, such as the consent of competent authorities, will become available. It must also be established that the child will be able to migrate and to join the prospective adoptive parents and may obtain their nationality.

Article 23. In intercountry adoption, as a rule, the legal validity of the adoption should be assured in each of the countries involved.

Article 24. Where the nationality of the child differs from that of the prospective adoptive parents, all due weight shall be given to both the law of the State of which the child is the national and the law of the prospective adoptive parents. In this connection due regard shall be given to the child's cultural and religious background and interests.

SEE ALSO *Children: Right to Protection; Convention on the Rights of the Child; Declaration on the Rights of the Child; European Convention on the Adoption of Children; Inter-American Convention on Conflict of Laws concerning the Adoption of Minors.*

DECLARATION ON SOCIAL PROGRESS AND DEVELOPMENT (1969). The declaration, drafted by the **COMMISSION FOR SOCIAL DEVELOPMENT,** defines the objectives of social development—so necessary for the realization of human rights and social justice—

and the means of attaining those objectives. Its message is that social development must aim at the continuous raising of the material and spiritual standards of living of all members of society with full respect for, and compliance with, all human rights and fundamental freedoms.

The declaration was adopted by the UN General Assembly on 11 December 1969 (resolution 2542 [XXIV]). The text, annexed to that resolution, is as follows:

The General Assembly,

Mindful of the pledge of Members of the United Nations under the Charter to take joint and separate action in co-operation with the Organization to promote higher standards of living, full employment and conditions of economic and social progress and development.

Reaffirming faith in human rights and fundamental freedoms and in the principles of peace, of the dignity and worth of the human person, and of social justice proclaimed in the Charter,

Recalling the principles of the Universal Declaration of Human Rights, the International Covenants on Human Rights, the Declaration of the Rights of the Child, the Declaration on the Granting of Independence to Colonial Countries and Peoples, the International Convention on the Elimination of All Forms of Racial Discrimination, the United Nations Declaration on the Elimination of All Forms of Racial Discrimination, the Declaration on the Promotion among Youth of the Ideals of Peace, Mutual Respect and Understanding between Peoples, the Declaration on the Elimination of Discrimination against Women and of resolutions of the United Nations,

Bearing in mind the standards already set for social progress in the constitutions, conventions, recommendations and resolutions of the International Labour Organisation, the Food and Agriculture Organization of the United Nations, the United Nations Educational, Scientific and Cultural Organization, the World Health Organization, the United Nations Children's Fund and of other organizations concerned,

Convinced that man can achieve complete fulfilment of his aspirations only within a just social order and that it is consequently of cardinal importance to accelerate social and economic progress everywhere, thus contributing to international peace and solidarity,

Convinced that international peace and security on the one hand, and social progress and economic development on the other, are closely interdependent and influence each other,

Persuaded that social development can be promoted by peaceful coexistence, friendly relations and co-operation among States with different social, economic or political systems,

Emphasizing the interdependence of economic and social development in the wider process of growth and change, as well as the importance of a strategy of integrated development which takes full account at all stages of its social aspects,

Regretting the inadequate progress achieved in the world social situation despite the efforts of States and the international community,

Recognizing that the primary responsibility for the development of the developing countries rests on those countries themselves and acknowledging the pressing need to narrow and eventually close the gap in the standards of living between economically more advanced and developing countries and, to that end, that Member States shall have the responsibility to pursue internal and external policies designed to promote social development throughout the world, and in particular to assist developing countries to accelerate their economic growth,

Recognizing the urgency of devoting to works of peace and social progress resources being expended on armaments and wasted on conflict and destruction,

Conscious of the contribution that science and technology can render towards meeting the needs common to all humanity,

Believing that the primary task of all States and international organizations is to eliminate from the life of society all evils and obstacles to social progress, particularly such evils as inequality, exploitation, war, colonialism and racism,

Desirous of promoting the progress of all mankind towards these goals and of overcoming all obstacles to their realization,

Solemnly proclaims this Declaration on Social Progress and Development and calls for national and international action for its use as a common basis for social development policies:

Part I—Principles

Article 1. All peoples and all human beings, without distinction as to race, colour, sex, language, religion, nationality, ethnic origin, family or social status, or political or other conviction, shall have the right to live in dignity and freedom and to enjoy the fruits of social progress and should, on their part, contribute to it.

Article 2. Social progress and development shall be founded on respect for the dignity and value of the human person and shall ensure the promotion of human rights and social justice, which requires:

(a) The immediate and final elimination of all forms of inequality, exploitation of peoples and individuals, colonialism and racism, including nazism and *apartheid,* and all other policies and ideologies opposed to the purposes and principles of the United Nations;

(b) The recognition and effective implementation of civil and political rights as well as of economic, social and cultural rights without any discrimination.

Article 3. The following are considered primary conditions of social progress and development:

(a) National independence based on the right of people to self-determination;

(b) The principle of non-interference in the internal affairs of States;

(c) Respect for the sovereignty and territorial integrity of States:

(d) Permanent sovereignty of each nation over its natural wealth and resources;

(e) The right and responsibility of each State and, as far as they are concerned, each nation and people to determine freely its own objectives of social development, to set its own priorities and to decide in conformity with the principles of the Charter of the United Nations the means and methods of their achievement without any external interference;

(f) Peaceful coexistence, peace, friendly relations and

co-operation among States irrespective of differences in their social, economic or political systems.

Article 4. The family as a basic unit of society and the natural environment for the growth and well-being of all its members, particularly children and youth, should be assisted and protected so that it may fully assume its responsibilities within the community. Parents have the exclusive right to determine freely and responsibly the number and spacing of their children.

Article 5. Social progress and development require the full utilization of human resources, including, in particular:

(a) The encouragement of creative initiative under conditions of enlightened public opinion;

(b) The dissemination of national and international information for the purpose of making individuals aware of changes occurring in society as a whole;

(c) The active participation of all elements of society, individually or through associations, in defining and in achieving the common goals of development with full respect for the fundamental freedoms embodied in the Universal Declaration of Human Rights;

(d) The assurance to disadvantaged or marginal sectors of the population of equal opportunities for social and economic advancement in order to achieve an effectively integrated society.

Article 6. Social development requires the assurance to everyone of the right to work and the free choice of employment.

Social progress and development require the participation of all members of society in productive and socially useful labour and the establishment, in conformity with human rights and fundamental freedoms and with the principles of justice and the social function of property, of forms of ownership of land and of the means of production which preclude any kind of exploitation of man, ensure equal rights to property for all and create conditions leading to genuine equality among people.

Article 7. The rapid expansion of national income and wealth and their equitable distribution among all members of society are fundamental to all social progress, and they should therefore be in the forefront of the preoccupations of every State and Government.

The improvement in the position of the developing countries in international trade resulting among other things from the achievement of favourable terms of trade and of equitable and remunerative prices at which developing countries market their products is necessary in order to make it possible to increase national income and in order to advance social development.

Article 8. Each Government has the primary role and ultimate responsibility of ensuring the social progress and well-being of its people, of planning social development measures as part of comprehensive development plans, of encouraging and co-ordinating or integrating all national efforts towards this end and of introducing necessary changes in the social structure. In planning social development measures, the diversity of the needs of developing and developed areas, and of urban and rural areas, within each country, shall be taken into due account.

Article 9. Social progress and development are the common concerns of the international community, which shall supplement, by concerted international action, national efforts to raise the living standards of peoples.

Social progress and economic growth require recognition of the common interest of all nations in the exploration, conservation, use and exploitation, exclusively for peaceful purposes and in the interests of all mankind, of those areas of the environment such as outer space and the sea-bed and ocean floor and the subsoil thereof, beyond the limits of national jurisdiction, in accordance with the Purposes and Principles of the Charter of the United Nations.

Part II—Objectives

Social progress and development shall aim at the continuous raising of the material and spiritual standards of living of all members of society, with respect for and in compliance with human rights and fundamental freedoms, through the attainment of the following main goals:

Article 10. (a) The assurance at all levels of the right to work and the right of everyone to form trade unions and workers' associations and to bargain collectively; promotion of full productive employment and elimination of unemployment and under-employment; establishment of equitable and favourable conditions of work for all, including the improvement of health and safety conditions; assurance of just remuneration for labour without any discrimination as well as a sufficiently high minimum wage to ensure a decent standard of living; the protection of the consumer;

(b) The elimination of hunger and malnutrition and the guarantee of the right to proper nutrition;

(c) The elimination of poverty; the assurance of a steady improvement in levels of living and of a just and equitable distribution of income;

(d) The achievement of the highest standards of health and the provision of health protection for the entire population, if possible free of charge;

(e) The eradication of illiteracy and the assurance of the right to universal access to culture, to free compulsory education at the elementary level and to free education at all levels; the raising of the general level of life-long education;

(f) The provision for all, particularly persons in low income groups and large families, of adequate housing and community services.

Social progress and development shall aim equally at the progressive attainment of the following main goals:

Article 11. (a) The provision of comprehensive social security schemes and social welfare services; the establishment and improvement of social security and insurance schemes for all persons who, because of illness, disability or old age, are temporarily or permanently unable to earn a living, with a view to ensuring a proper standard of living for such persons and for their families and dependants;

(b) The protection of the rights of the mother and child; concern for the upbringing and health of children; the provision of measures to safeguard the health and welfare of women and particularly of working mothers during pregnancy and the infancy of their children, as well as of mothers whose earnings are the sole source of livelihood for the family; the granting to women of pregnancy and maternity leave and allowances without loss of employment or wages;

(c) The protection of the rights and the assuring of the welfare of children, the aged and the disabled; the provision of protection for the physically or mentally disadvantaged;

(d) The education of youth in, and promotion among them of, the ideals of justice and peace, mutual respect and understanding among peoples; the promotion of full participation of youth in the process of national development;

(e) The provision of social defence measures and the

elimination of conditions leading to crime and delinquency, especially juvenile delinquency;

(f) The guarantee that all individuals, without discrimination of any kind, are made aware of their rights and obligations and receive the necessary aid in the exercise and safeguarding of their rights.

Social progress and development shall further aim at achieving the following main objectives:

Article 12. (a) The creation of conditions for rapid and sustained social and economic development, particularly in the developing countries; change in international economic relations; new and effective methods of international co-operation in which equality of opportunity should be as much a prerogative of nations as of individuals within a nation;

(b) The elimination of all forms of discrimination and exploitation and all other practices and ideologies contrary to the purposes and principles of the Charter of the United Nations;

(c) The elimination of all forms of foreign economic exploitation, particularly that practised by international monopolies, in order to enable the people of every country to enjoy in full the benefits of their national resources.

Social progress and development shall finally aim at the attainment of the following main goals:

Article 13. (a) Equitable sharing of scientific and technological advances by developed and developing countries, and a steady increase in the use of science and technology for the benefit of the social development of society;

(b) The establishment of a harmonious balance between scientific, technological and material progress and the intellectual, spiritual, cultural and moral advancement of humanity;

(c) The protection and improvement of the human environment.

Part III—Means and Methods

On the basis of the principles set forth in this Declaration, the achievement of the objectives of social progress and development requires the mobilization of the necessary resources by national and international action, with particular attention to such means and methods as:

Article 14. (a) Planning for social progress and development, as an integrated part of balanced over-all development planning;

(b) The establishment, where necessary, of national systems for framing and carrying out social policies and programmes, and the promotion by the countries concerned of planned regional development, taking into account differing regional conditions and needs, particularly the development of regions which are less favoured or under-developed by comparison with the rest of the country;

(c) The promotion of basic and applied social research, particularly comparative international research applied to the planning and execution of social development programmes.

Article 15. (a) The adoption of measures to ensure the effective participation, as appropriate, of all the elements of society in the preparation and execution of national plans and programmes of economic and social development:

(b) The adoption of measures for an increasing rate of popular participation in the economic, social, cultural and political life of countries through national governmental bodies, non-governmental organizations, cooperatives, rural associations, workers' and employers' organizations and

women's and youth organizations, by such methods as national and regional plans for social and economic progress and community development, with a view to achieving a fully integrated national society, accelerating the process of social mobility and consolidating the democratic system;

(c) Mobilization of public opinion, at both national and international levels, in support of the principles and objectives of social progress and development;

(d) The dissemination of social information, at the national and the international level, to make people aware of changing circumstances in society as a whole, and to educate the consumer.

Article 16. (a) Maximum mobilization of all national resources and their rational and efficient utilization; promotion of increased and accelerated productive investment in social and economic fields and of employment; orientation of society towards the development process;

(b) Progressively increasing provision of the necessary budgetary and other resources required for financing the social aspects of development;

(c) Achievement of equitable distribution of national income, utilizing, *inter alia,* the fiscal system and government spending as an instrument for the equitable distribution and redistribution of income in order to promote social progress;

(d) The adoption of measures aimed at prevention of such an outflow of capital from developing countries as would be detrimental to their economic and social development.

Article 17. (a) The adoption of measures to accelerate the process of industrialization, especially in developing countries, with due regard for its social aspects, in the interests of the entire population; development of an adequate organizational and legal framework conducive to an uninterrupted and diversified growth of the industrial sector; measures to overcome the adverse social effects which may result from urban development and industrialization, including automation; maintenance of a proper balance between rural and urban development, and in particular, measures designed to ensure healthier living conditions, especially in large industrial centres;

(b) Integrated planning to meet the problems of urbanization and urban development;

(c) Comprehensive rural development schemes to raise the levels of living of the rural populations and to facilitate such urban-rural relationships and population distribution as will promote balanced national development and social progress;

(d) Measures for appropriate supervision of the utilization of land in the interests of society.

The achievement of the objectives of social progress and development equally requires the implementation of the following means and methods:

Article 18. (a) The adoption of appropriate legislative, administrative and other measures ensuring to everyone not only political and civil rights, but also the full realization of economic, social and cultural rights without any discrimination;

(b) The promotion of democratically based social and institutional reforms and motivation for change basic to the elimination of all forms of discrimination and exploitation and conducive to high rates of economic and social progress, to include land reform, in which the ownership and use of land will be made to serve best the objective of social justice and economic development;

(c) The adoption of measures to boost and diversify agricultural production through, *inter alia,* the implementation of democratic agrarian reforms, to ensure an adequate and well-balanced supply of food, its equitable distribution among the whole population and the improvement of nutritional standards;

(d) The adoption of measures to introduce, with the participation of the Government, low-cost housing programmes in both rural and urban areas;

(e) Development and expansion of the system of transportation and communications, particularly in developing countries.

Article 19. (a) The provision of free health services to the whole population and of adequate preventive and curative facilities and welfare medical services accessible to all;

(b) The enactment and establishment of legislative measures and administrative regulations with a view to the implementation of comprehensive programmes of social security schemes and social welfare services and to the improvement and co-ordination of existing services;

(c) The adoption of measures and the provision of social welfare services to migrant workers and their families, in conformity with the provisions of Convention No. 97 of the International Labour Organisation (on migration for employment) and other international instruments relating to migrant workers;

(d) The institution of appropriate measures for the rehabilitation of mentally or physically disabled persons, especially children and youth, so as to enable them to the fullest possible extent to be useful members of society—these measures shall include the provision of treatment and technical appliances, education, vocational and social guidance, training and selective placement, and other assistance required—and the creation of social conditions in which the handicapped are not discriminated against because of their disabilities.

Article 20. (a) The provision of full democratic freedoms to trade unions; freedom of association for all workers, including the right to bargain collectively and to strike; recognition of the right to form other organizations of working people; the provision for the growing participation of trade unions in economic and social development; effective participation of all members of trade unions in the deciding of economic and social issues which affect their interests;

(b) The improvement of health and safety conditions for workers, by means of appropriate technological and legislative measures and the provision of the material prerequisites for the implementation of those measures, including the limitation of working hours;

(c) The adoption of appropriate measures for the development of harmonious industrial relations.

Article 21. (a) The training of national personnel and cadres, including administrative, executive, professional and technical personnel needed for social development and for over-all development plans and policies;

(b) The adoption of measures to accelerate the extension and improvement of general, vocational and technical education and of training and retraining, which should be provided free at all levels;

(c) Raising the general level of education; development and expansion of national information media, and their rational and full use towards continuing education of the whole population and towards encouraging its participation in social development activities; the constructive use of leisure, particularly that of children and adolescents;

(d) The formulation of national and international poli-

cies and measures to avoid the "brain drain" and obviate its adverse effects.

Article 22. (a) The development and co-ordination of policies and measures designed to strengthen the essential functions of the family as a basic unit of society;

(b) The formulation and establishment, as needed, of programmes in the field of population, within the framework of national demographic policies and as part of the welfare medical services, including education, training of personnel and the provision to families of the knowledge and means necessary to enable them to exercise their right to determine freely and responsibly the number and spacing of their children;

(c) The establishment of appropriate child-care facilities in the interest of children and working parents.

The achievement of the objectives of social progress and development finally requires the implementation of the following means and methods:

Article 23. (a) The laying down of economic growth rate targets for the developing countries within the United Nations policy for development, high enough to lead to a substantial acceleration of their rates of growth;

(b) The provision of greater assistance on better terms; the implementation of the aid volume target of a minimum of 1 per cent of the gross national product at market prices of economically advanced countries; the general easing of the terms of lending to the developing countries through low interest rates on loans and long grace periods for the repayment of loans, and the assurance that the allocation of such loans will be based strictly on socio-economic criteria free of any political considerations;

(c) The provision of technical, financial and material assistance, both bilateral and multilateral, to the fullest possible extent and on favourable terms, and improved co-ordination of international assistance for the achievement of the social objectives of national development plans;

(d) The provision to the developing countries of technical, financial and material assistance and of favourable conditions to facilitate the direct exploitation of their national resources and natural wealth by those countries with a view to enabling the peoples of those countries to benefit fully from their national resources;

(e) The expansion of international trade based on principles of equality and non-discrimination, the rectification of the position of developing countries in international trade by equitable terms of trade, a general non-reciprocal and non-discriminatory system of preferences for the exports of developing countries to the developed countries, the establishment and implementation of general and comprehensive commodity agreements, and the financing of reasonable buffer stocks by international institutions.

Article 24. (a) Intensification of international co-operation with a view to ensuring the international exchange of information, knowledge and experience concerning social progress and development;

(b) The broadest possible international technical, scientific and cultural co-operation and reciprocal utilization of the experience of countries with different economic and social systems and different levels of development, on the basis of mutual advantage and strict observance of and respect for national sovereignty;

(c) Increased utilization of science and technology for social and economic development; arrangements for the transfer and exchange of technology, including know-how and patents, to the developing countries.

Article 25. (a) The establishment of legal and administrative measures for the protection and improvement of the human environment, at both national and international level;

(b) The use and exploitation, in accordance with the appropriate international régimes, of the resources of areas of the environment such as outer space and the sea-bed and ocean floor and the subsoil thereof, beyond the limits of national jurisdiction, in order to supplement national resources available for the achievement of economic and social progress and development in every country, irrespective of its geographical location, special consideration being given to the interests and needs of the developing countries.

Article 26. Compensation for damages, be they social or economic in nature—including restitution and reparations— caused as a result of aggression and of illegal occupation of territory by the aggressor.

Article 27. (a) The achievement of general and complete disarmament and the channelling of the progressively released resources to be used for economic and social progress for the welfare of people everywhere and, in particular, for the benefit of developing countries;

(b) The adoption of measures contributing to disarmament, including, *inter alia,* the complete prohibition of tests of nuclear weapons, the prohibition of the development, production and stockpiling of chemical and bacteriological (biological) weapons and the prevention of the pollution of oceans and inland waters by nuclear wastes.

SEE ALSO *Declaration of Abijan; Declaration on the Right to Development; Khartoum Declaration; Right to Development; Working Group of Governmental Experts on the Right to Development.*

DECLARATION ON TERRITORIAL ASYLUM (1967).

Drawn up by the Sixth (Legal) Committee of the UN General Assembly, the declaration sets out principles relating to the granting or refusal of asylum by States and makes clear the continuing interest of the international community in the question of asylum. The declaration was adopted by the UN General Assembly on 14 December 1967 (resolution 2312 [XXII]). The text, annexed to that resolution, is as follows:

The General Assembly,

Noting that the purposes proclaimed in the Charter of the United Nations are to maintain international peace and security, to develop friendly relations among all nations and to achieve international co-operation in solving international problems of an economic, social, cultural or humanitarian character and in promoting and encouraging respect for human rights and for fundamental freedoms for all without distinction as to race, sex, language or religion,

Mindful of the Universal Declaration of Human Rights, which declares in article 14 that:

"1. Everyone has the right to seek and to enjoy in other countries asylum from persecution.

"2. This right may not be invoked in the case of prosecutions genuinely arising from non-political crimes or from acts contrary to the purposes and principles of the United Nations",

Recalling also article 13, paragraph 2, of the Universal Declaration of Human Rights, which states:

"Everyone has the right to leave any country, including his own, and to return to his country",

Recognizing that the grant of asylum by a State to persons entitled to invoke article 14 of the Universal Declaration of Human Rights is a peaceful and humanitarian act and that, as such, it cannot be regarded as unfriendly by any other State,

Recommends that, without prejudice to existing instruments dealing with asylum and the status of refugees and stateless persons, States should base themselves in their practices relating to territorial asylum on the following principles:

Article 1. 1. Asylum granted by a State, in the exercise of its sovereignty, to persons entitled to invoke article 14 of the Universal Declaration of Human Rights, including persons struggling against colonialism, shall be respected by all other States.

2. The right to seek and to enjoy asylum may not be invoked by any person with respect to whom there are serious reasons for considering that he has committed a crime against peace, a war crime or a crime against humanity, as defined in the international instruments drawn up to make provision in respect of such crimes.

3. It shall rest with the State granting asylum to evaluate the grounds for the grant of asylum.

Article 2. 1. The situation of persons referred to in article 1, paragraph 1, is, without prejudice to the sovereignty of States and the purposes and principles of the United Nations, of concern to the international community.

2. Where a State finds difficulty in granting or continuing to grant asylum, States individually or jointly or through the United Nations shall consider, in a spirit of international solidarity, appropriate measures to lighten the burden on that State.

Article 3. 1. No person referred to in article 1, paragraph 1, shall be subjected to measures such as rejection at the frontier or, if he has already entered the territory in which he seeks asylum, expulsion or compulsory return to any State where he may be subjected to persecution.

2. Exception may be made to the foregoing principle only for overriding reasons of national security or in order to safeguard the population, as in the case of a mass influx of persons.

3. Should a State decide in any case that exception to the principle stated in paragraph 1 of this article would be justified, it shall consider the possibility of granting to the person concerned, under such conditions as it may deem appropriate, an opportunity, whether by way of provisional asylum or otherwise, of going to another State.

Article 4. States granting asylum shall not permit persons who have received asylum to engage in activities contrary to the purposes and principles of the United Nations.

SEE ALSO *Inter-American Convention on Diplomatic Asylum; Inter-American Convention on Territorial Asylum.*

DECLARATION ON THE CONTROL OF DRUG TRAFFICKING AND DRUG ABUSE (1984). The

declaration reflects the view of the UN General Assembly that drug trafficking and drug abuse have become international criminal problems threatening the efforts of the international community to promote social progress and better standards of life for the peoples of the world. The text of the declaration, adopted by the assembly on 14 December 1984 (resolution 39/142), is as follows:

The General Assembly,

Bearing in mind that the purposes and principles of the Charter of the United Nations reaffirm faith in the dignity and worth of the human person and promote social progress and better standards of life in larger freedom and international co-operation in solving problems of an economic, social, cultural or humanitarian character,

Considering that Member States have undertaken in the Universal Declaration of Human Rights to promote social progress and better standards of life for the peoples of the world,

Considering that the international community has expressed grave concern at the fact that trafficking in narcotics and drug abuse constitute an obstacle to the physical and moral well-being of peoples and of youth in particular,

Desiring to heighten the awareness of the international community of the urgency of preventing and punishing the illicit demand for, abuse of and illicit production of and traffic in drugs,

Considering that the Quito Declaration against Traffic in Narcotic Drugs of 11 August 1984 and the New York Declaration against Drug Trafficking and the Illicit Use of Drugs of 1 October 1984 recognize the international nature of this problem and emphasize that it should be solved with the firm support of the entire international community,

Considering that the Commission on Narcotic Drugs, the International Narcotics Control Board and the United Nations Fund for Drug Abuse Control have made valuable contributions to the control and elimination of drug trafficking and drug abuse,

Recognizing that existing international instruments, including the Single Convention on Narcotic Drugs of 1961, as amended by the 1972 Protocol Amending the Single Convention on Narcotic Drugs of 1961, and the Convention on Psychotropic Substances of 1971, have created a legal framework for combating trafficking in narcotic drugs and drug abuse in their specialized fields.

Declares that:

1. Drug trafficking and drug abuse are extremely serious problems which, owing to their magnitude, scope and widespread pernicious effects, have become an international criminal activity demanding urgent attention and maximum priority.

2. The illegal production of, illicit demand for, abuse of and illicit trafficking in drugs impede economic and social progress, constitute a grave threat to the security and development of many countries and peoples and should be combated by all moral, legal and institutional means, at the national, regional and international levels.

3. The eradication of trafficking in narcotic drugs is the collective responsibility of all States, especially those affected by problems relating to illicit production, trafficking or abuse.

4. States Members shall utilize the legal instruments against the illicit production of and demand for, abuse of and illicit traffic in drugs and adopt additional measures to counter new manifestations of this shameful and heinous crime.

5. States Members undertake to intensify efforts and to co-ordinate strategies aimed at the control and eradication of the complex problem of drug trafficking and drug abuse through programmes including economic, social and cultural alternatives.

SEE ALSO Children and Drugs; Drug Abuse.

DECLARATION ON THE ELIMINATION OF ALL FORMS OF INTOLERANCE AND OF DISCRIMINATION BASED ON RELIGION OR BELIEF (1981).

The declaration elaborates upon the meaning of the principles of non-discrimination and equality before the law as applied to the right to freedom of THOUGHT, CONSCIENCE, RELIGION, and belief. It aims at promoting understanding, tolerance, and friendship for all religions or beliefs, whether theistic, nontheistic, or atheistic. It was adopted by the UN General Assembly on 25 November 1981 (resolution 36/55). The text is as follows:

The General Assembly,

Considering that one of the basic principles of the Charter of the United Nations is that of the dignity and equality inherent in all human beings, and that all Member States have pledged themselves to take joint and separate action in co-operation with the United Nations or promote and encourage universal respect for and observance of human rights and fundamental freedoms for all, without distinction as to race, sex, language or religion,

Considering that the Universal Declaration of Human Rights and the International Covenants on Human Rights proclaim the principles of non-discrimination and equality before the law and the right to freedom of thought, conscience, religion or belief,

Considering that the disregard and infringement of human rights and fundamental freedoms, in particular of the right to freedom of thought, conscience, religion or whatever belief, have brought, directly or indirectly, wars and great suffering to mankind, especially where they serve as a means of foreign interference in the internal affairs of other States and amount to kindling hatred between peoples and nations,

Considering that religion or belief, for anyone who professes either, is one of the fundamental elements in his conception of life and that freedom of religion or belief should be fully respected and guaranteed,

Considering that it is essential to promote understanding, tolerance and respect in matters relating to freedom of religion or belief and to ensure that the use of religion or belief for ends inconsistent with the Charter, other relevant instruments of the United Nations and the purposes and principles of the present Declaration is inadmissible,

Convinced that freedom of religion or belief should also contribute to the attainment of the goals of world peace, social justice and friendship among peoples and to the elimination of ideologies or practices of colonialism and racial discrimination,

Noting with satisfaction the adoption of several, and the

coming into force of some, conventions, under the aegis of the United Nations and of the specialized agencies, for the elimination of various forms of discrimination,

Concerned by manifestations of intolerance and by the existence of discrimination in matters of religion or belief still in evidence in some areas of the world,

Resolved to adopt all necessary measures for the speedy elimination of such intolerance in all its forms and manifestations and to prevent and combat discrimination on the grounds of religion or belief,

Proclaims this Declaration on the Elimination of All Forms of Intolerance and of Discrimination Based on Religion or Belief:

Article 1. 1. Everyone shall have the right to freedom of thought, conscience and religion. This right shall include freedom to have a religion or whatever belief of his choice, and freedom, either individually or in community with others and in public or private, to manifest his religion or belief in worship, observance, practice and teaching.

2. No one shall be subject to coercion which would impair his freedom to have a religion or belief of his choice.

3. Freedom to manifest one's religion or belief may be subject only to such limitations as are prescribed by law and are necessary to protect public safety, order, health or morals or the fundamental rights and freedoms of others.

Article 2. 1. No one shall be subject to discrimination by any State, institution, group of persons or person on the grounds of religion or belief.

2. For the purposes of the present Declaration, the expression "intolerance and discrimination based on religion or belief" means any distinction, exclusion, restriction or preference based on religion or belief and having as its purpose or as its effect nullification or impairment of the recognition, enjoyment or exercise of human rights and fundamental freedoms on an equal basis.

Article 3. Discrimination between human beings on the grounds of religion or belief constitutes an affront to human dignity and a disavowal of the principles of the Charter of the United Nations, and shall be condemned as a violation of the human rights and fundamental freedoms proclaimed in the Universal Declaration of Human Rights and enunciated in detail in the International Covenants on Human Rights, and as an obstacle to friendly and peaceful relations between nations.

Article 4. 1. All States shall take effective measures to prevent and eliminate discrimination on the grounds of religion or belief in the recognition, exercise and enjoyment of human rights and fundamental freedoms in all fields of civil, economic, political, social and cultural life.

2. All States shall make all efforts to enact or rescind legislation where necessary to prohibit any such discrimination, and to take all appropriate measures to combat intolerance on the grounds of religion or belief in this matter.

Article 5. 1. The parents or, as the case may be, the legal guardians of the child have the right to organize the life within the family in accordance with their religion or belief and bearing in mind the moral education in which they believe the child should be brought up.

2. Every child shall enjoy the right to have access to education in the matter of religion or belief in accordance with the wishes of his parents or, as the case may be, legal guardians, and shall not be compelled to receive teaching on religion or belief against the wishes of his parents or legal guardians, the best interests of the child being the guiding principle.

3. The child shall be protected from any form of discrimination on the grounds of religion or belief. He shall be brought up in a spirit of understanding, tolerance, friendship among peoples, peace and universal brotherhood, respect for freedom of religion or belief of others, and in full consciousness that his energy and talents should be devoted to the service of his fellow men.

4. In the case of a child who is not under the care either of his parents or of legal guardians, due account shall be taken of their expressed wishes or of any other proof of their wishes in the matter of religion or belief, the best interests of the child being the guiding principle.

5. Practices of a religion or belief in which a child is brought up must not be injurious to his physical or mental health or to his full development, taking into account article 1, paragraph 3, of the present Declaration.

Article 6. In accordance with article 1 of the present Declaration, and subject to the provisions of article 1, paragraph 3, the right to freedom of thought, conscience, religion or belief shall include, *inter alia,* the following freedoms:

(a) To worship or assemble in connection with a religion or belief, and to establish and maintain places for these purposes;

(b) To establish and maintain appropriate charitable or humanitarian institutions;

(c) To make, acquire and use to an adequate extent the necessary articles and materials related to the rites or customs of a religion or belief;

(d) To write, issue and disseminate relevant publications in these areas;

(e) To teach a religion or belief in places suitable for these purposes;

(f) To solicit and receive voluntary financial and other contributions from individuals and institutions;

(g) To train, appoint, elect or designate by succession appropriate leaders called for by the requirements and standards of any religion or belief;

(h) To observe days of rest and to celebrate holidays and ceremonies in accordance with the precepts of one's religion or belief;

(i) To establish and maintain communications with individuals and communities in matters of religion or belief at the national and international levels.

Article 7. The rights and freedoms set forth in the present Declaration shall be accorded in national legislations in such a manner that everyone shall be able to avail himself of such rights and freedoms in practice.

Article 8. Nothing in the present Declaration shall be construed as restricting or derogating from any right defined in the Universal Declaration of Human Rights and the International Covenants on Human Rights.

SEE ALSO *Racial, Religious, and National Hatred; Religious Intolerance and Discrimination: Special Rapporteur.*

DECLARATION ON THE ELIMINATION OF ALL FORMS OF RACIAL DISCRIMINATION (1963).

In January 1960, the SUB-COMMISSION ON PREVENTION OF DISCRIMINATION AND PROTECTION OF MINORITIES expressed deep concern over a series of manifestations of racial prejudice and religious intolerance which had occurred in several parts of western Europe. After studying the problem in some detail, at the request of the General Assembly, the sub-commission drafted first a declaration, and later a convention, on the subject. The assembly adopted both instruments unanimously.

The declaration was adopted by the assembly on 20 November 1963 (resolution 1904 [XVIII]). The text, annexed to that resolution, is as follows:

The General Assembly,

Considering that the Charter of the United Nations is based on the principles of the dignity and equality of all human beings and seeks, among other basic objectives, to achieve international co-operation in promoting and encouraging respect for human rights and fundamental freedoms for all without distinction as to race, sex, language or religion,

Considering that the Universal Declaration of Human Rights proclaims that all human beings are born free and equal in dignity and rights and that everyone is entitled to all the rights and freedoms set out in the Declaration, without distinction of any kind, in particular as to race, colour or national origin,

Considering that the Universal Declaration of Human Rights proclaims further that all are equal before the law and are entitled without any discrimination to equal protection of the law and that all are entitled to equal protection against any discrimination and against any incitement to such discrimination,

Considering that the United Nations has condemned colonialism and all practices of segregation and discrimination associated therewith, and that the Declaration on the Granting of Independence to Colonial Countries and Peoples proclaims in particular the necessity of bringing colonialism to a speedy and unconditional end,

Considering that any doctrine of racial differentiation of superiority is scientifically false, morally condemnable, socially unjust and dangerous, and that there is not justification for racial discrimination either in theory or in practice,

Taking into account the other resolutions adopted by the General Assembly and the international instruments adopted by the specialized agencies, in particular the International Labour Organisation and the United Nations Educational, Scientific and Cultural Organization, in the field of discrimination,

Taking into account the fact that, although international action and efforts in a number of countries have made it possible to achieve progress in that field, discrimination based on race, colour or ethnic origin in certain areas of the world continues none the less to give cause for serious concern,

Alarmed by the manifestations of racial discrimination still in evidence in some areas of the world, some of which are imposed by certain Governments by means of legislative, administrative or other measures, in the form, *inter alia*, of *apartheid*, segregation and separation, as well as by the promotion and dissemination of doctrines of racial superiority and expansionism in certain areas,

Convinced that all forms of racial discrimination and, still more so, governmental policies based on the prejudice of racial superiority or on racial hatred, besides constituting a violation of fundamental human rights, tend to jeopardize friendly relations among peoples, co-operation between nations and international peace and security,

Convinced also that racial discrimination harms not only those who are its objects but also those who practise it,

Convinced further that the building of a world society free from all forms of racial segregation and discrimination, factors which create hatred and division among men, is one of the fundamental objectives of the United Nations,

1. Solemnly affirms the necessity of speedily eliminating racial discrimination throughout the world, in all its forms and manifestations, and of securing understanding of and respect for the dignity of the human person;

2. Solemnly affirms the necessity of adopting national and international measures to that end, including teaching, education and information, in order to secure the universal and effective recognition and observance of the principles set forth below;

3. Proclaims this Declaration:

Article 1. Discrimination between human beings on the ground of race, colour or ethnic origin is an offence to human dignity and shall be condemned as a denial of the principles of the Charter of the United Nations, as a violation of the human rights and fundamental freedoms proclaimed in the Universal Declaration of Human Rights, as an obstacle to friendly and peaceful relations among nations and as a fact capable of disturbing peace and security among peoples.

Article 2. 1. No State, institution, group or individual shall make any discrimination whatsoever in matters of human rights and fundamental freedoms in the treatment of persons, groups of persons or institutions on the ground of race, colour or ethnic origin.

2. No State shall encourage, advocate or lend its support, through police action or otherwise, to any discrimination based on race, colour or ethnic origin by any group, institution or individual.

3. Special concrete measures shall be taken in appropriate circumstances in order to secure adequate development or protection of individuals belonging to certain racial groups with the object of ensuring the full enjoyment by such individuals of human rights and fundamental freedoms. These measures shall in no circumstances have as a consequence the maintenance of unequal or separate rights for different racial groups.

Article 3. 1. Particular efforts shall be made to prevent discrimination based on race, colour or ethnic origin, especially in the fields of civil rights, access to citizenship, education, religion, employment, occupation and housing.

2. Everyone shall have equal access to any place or facility intended for use by the general public, without distinction as to race, colour or ethnic origin.

Article 4. All States shall take effective measures to revise governmental and other public policies and to rescind laws and regulations which have the effect of creating and perpetuating racial discrimination wherever it still exists. They should pass legislation for prohibiting such discrimination and should take all appropriate measures to combat those prejudices which lead to racial discrimination.

Article 5. An end shall be put without delay to governmental and other public policies of racial segregation and especially policies of *apartheid*, as well as all forms of racial discrimination and separation resulting from such policies.

Article 6. No discrimination by reason of race, colour or ethnic origin shall be admitted in the enjoyment by any person of political and citizenship rights in his country, in particular the right to participate in elections through universal and equal suffrage and to take part in the government. Everyone has the right of equal access to public service in his country.

Article 7. 1. Everyone has the right to equality before the law and to equal justice under the law. Everyone, without distinction as to race, colour or ethnic origin, has the right to security of person and protection by the State against violence or bodily harm, whether inflicted by government officials or by any individual, group or institution.

2. Everyone shall have the right to an effective remedy and protection against any discrimination he may suffer on the ground of race, colour or ethnic origin with respect to his fundamental rights and freedoms through independent national tribunals competent to deal with such matters.

Article 8. All effective steps shall be taken immediately in the fields of teaching, education and information, with a view to eliminating racial discrimination and prejudice and promoting understanding, tolerance and friendship among nations and racial groups, as well as to propagating the purposes and principles of the Charter of the United Nations, of the Universal Declaration of Human Rights, and of the Declaration on the Granting of Independence to Colonial Countries and Peoples.

Article 9. 1. All propaganda and organizations based on ideas or theories of the superiority of one race or group of persons of one colour or ethnic origin with a view to justifying or promoting racial discrimination in any form shall be severely condemned.

2. All incitement to or acts of violence, whether by individuals or organizations against any race or group of persons of another colour or ethnic origin shall be considered an offence against society and punishable under law.

3. In order to put into effect the purposes and principles of the present Declaration, all States shall take immediate and positive measures, including legislative and other measures, to prosecute and/or outlaw organizations which promote or incite to racial discrimination, or incite to or use violence for purposes of discrimination based on race, colour or ethnic origin.

Article 10. The United Nations, the specialized agencies, States and non-governmental organizations shall do all in their power to promote energetic action which, by combining legal and other practical measures, will make possible the abolition of all forms of racial discrimination. They shall, in particular, study the causes of such discrimination with a view to recommending appropriate and effective measures to combat and eliminate it.

Article 11. Every State shall promote respect for and observance of human rights and fundamental freedoms in accordance with the Charter of the United Nations and shall fully and faithfully observe the provisions of the present Declaration, the Universal Declaration of Human Rights and the Declaration on the Granting of Independence to Colonial Countries and Peoples.

SEE ALSO *Committee on the Elimination of Racial Discrimination; Decades to Combat Racism and Racial Discrimination; Declaration of the Second World Conference to Combat Racism and Racial Discrimination; Inter-American Declaration on Racial Integration in the Americas; International Convention on the Elimination of All Forms of Racial Discrimination; Race: UNESCO Statement on Scientific Facts; Race and Racial Prejudice: Impact of the UNESCO Declaration; Racial Discrimination; Racial Discrimination: National and Local Recourses; Racism and Racial Discrimination: Second Decade Action Program; UNESCO Declaration on Race and Racial Prejudice.*

DECLARATION ON THE ELIMINATION OF DISCRIMINATION AGAINST WOMEN (1967). The declaration represents an important milestone in the work of the United Nations for the advancement of women. It terms discrimination against women "fundamentally unjust and . . . an offence against human dignity" and calls for measures to be taken to insure universal recognition of the principle of equality between men and women.

The declaration was adopted by the UN General Assembly on 7 November 1967 (resolution 2263 [XXII]). The text, annexed to that resolution, is as follows:

The General Assembly,

Considering that the peoples of the United Nations have, in the Charter, reaffirmed their faith in fundamental human rights, in the dignity and worth of the human person and in the equal rights of men and women,

Considering that the Universal Declaration on Human Rights asserts the principle of non-discrimination and proclaims that all human beings are born free and equal in dignity and rights and that everyone is entitled to all the rights and freedoms set forth therein without distinction of any kind, including any distinction as to sex,

Taking into account the resolutions, declarations, conventions and recommendations of the United Nations and the specialized agencies designed to eliminate all forms of discrimination and to promote equal rights for men and women,

Concerned that, despite the Charter of the United Nations, the Universal Declaration of Human Rights, the International Covenants on Human Rights and other instruments of the United Nations and the specialized agencies and despite the progress made in the matter of equality of rights, there continues to exist considerable discrimination against women,

Considering that discrimination against women is incompatible with human dignity and with the welfare of the family and of society, prevents their participation, on equal terms with men, in the political, social, economic and cultural life of their countries and is an obstacle to the full development of the potentialities of women in the service of their countries and of humanity,

Bearing in mind the great contribution made by women to social, political, economic and cultural life and the part they play in the family and particularly in the rearing of children,

Convinced that the full and complete development of a country, the welfare of the world and the cause of peace require the maximum participation of women as well as men in all fields,

Considering that it is necessary to ensure the universal recognition in law and in fact of the principle of equality of men and women,

Solemnly proclaims this Declaration:

Article 1. Discrimination against women, denying or limiting as it does their equality of rights with men, is fundamentally unjust and constitutes an offence against human dignity.

Article 2. All appropriate measures shall be taken to abolish existing laws, customs, regulations and practices which are discriminatory against women, and to establish adequate legal protection for equal rights of men and women, in particular:

(a) The principle of equality of rights shall be embodied in the constitution or otherwise guaranteed by law;

(b) The international instruments of the United Nations and the specialized agencies relating to the elimination of discrimination against women shall be ratified or acceded to and fully implemented as soon as practicable.

Article 3. All appropriate measures shall be taken to educate public opinion and to direct national aspirations towards the eradication of prejudice and the abolition of customary and all other practices which are based on the idea of the inferiority of women.

Article 4. All appropriate measures shall be taken to ensure to women on equal terms with men, without any discrimination:

(a) The right to vote in all elections and be eligible for election to all publicly elected bodies;

(b) The right to vote in all public referenda;

(c) The right to hold public office and to exercise all public functions.

Such rights shall be guaranteed by legislation.

Article 5. Women shall have the same rights as men to acquire, change or retain their nationality. Marriage to an alien shall not automatically affect the nationality of the wife either by rendering her stateless or by forcing upon her the nationality of her husband.

Article 6. 1. Without prejudice to the safeguarding of the unity and the harmony of the family, which remains the basic unit of any society, all appropriate measures, particularly legislative measures, shall be taken to ensure to women, married or unmarried, equal rights with men in the field of civil law, and in particular:

(a) The right to acquire, administer, enjoy, dispose of and inherit property, including property acquired during marriage;

(b) The right to equality in legal capacity and the exercise thereof;

(c) The same rights as men with regard to the law on the movement of persons.

2. All appropriate measures shall be taken to ensure the principle of equality of status of the husband and wife, and in particular:

(a) Women shall have the same right as men to free choice of a spouse and to enter into marriage only with their free and full consent;

(b) Women shall have equal rights with men during marriage and at its dissolution. In all cases the interest of the children shall be paramount;

(c) Parents shall have equal rights and duties in matters relating to their children. In all cases the interest of the children shall be paramount.

3. Child marriage and the betrothal of young girls before puberty shall be prohibited, and effective action, including legislation, shall be taken to specify a minimum age for marriage and to make the registration of marriages in an official registry compulsory.

Article 7. All provisions of penal codes which constitute discrimination against women shall be repealed.

Article 8. All appropriate measures, including legislation, shall be taken to combat all forms of traffic in women and exploitation of prostitution of women.

Article 9. All appropriate measures shall be taken to ensure to girls and women, married or unmarried, equal rights with men in education at all levels, and in particular:

(a) Equal conditions of access to, and study in, educational institutions of all types, including universities and vocational, technical and professional schools;

(b) The same choice of curricula, the same examinations, teaching staff with qualifications of the same standard, and school premises and equipment of the same quality, whether the institutions are co-educational or not;

(c) Equal opportunities to benefit from scholarships and other study grants;

(d) Equal opportunities for access to programmes of continuing education, including adult literacy programmes;

(e) Access to educational information to help in ensuring the health and well-being of families.

Article 10. 1. All appropriate measures shall be taken to ensure to women, married or unmarried, equal rights with men in the field of economic and social life, and in particular:

(a) The right, without discrimination on grounds of marital status or any other grounds, to receive vocational training, to work, to free choice of profession and employment, and to professional and vocational advancement;

(b) The right to equal remuneration with men and to equality of treatment in respect of work of equal value;

(c) The right to leave with pay, retirement privileges and provision for security in respect of unemployment, sickness, old age or other incapacity to work;

(d) The right to receive family allowances on equal terms with men.

2. In order to prevent discrimination against women on account of marriage or maternity and to ensure their effective right to work, measures shall be taken to prevent their dismissal in the event of marriage or maternity and to provide paid maternity leave, with the guarantee of returning to former employment, and to provide the necessary social services, including childcare facilities.

3. Measures taken to protect women in certain types of work, for reasons inherent in their physical nature, shall not be regarded as discriminatory.

Article 11. 1. The principle of equality of rights of men and women demands implementation in all States in accordance with the principles of the Charter of the United Nations and of the Universal Declaration of Human Rights.

2. Governments, non-governmental organizations and individuals are urged, therefore, to do all in their power to promote the implementation of the principles contained in this Declaration.

SEE ALSO *Commission on the Status of Women; Committee on the Elimination of Discrimination against Women; Convention on the Elimination of All Forms of Discrimination against Women; Convention on the Political Rights of Women; ILO Discrimination (Employment and Occupation) Convention; ILO Equal Remuneration Convention; ILO Equality of Treatment (Social Security) Convention; Inter-American Convention on the Granting of Civil Rights to Women; Inter-American Convention on the Granting of Political Rights to Women; Nairobi Forward-Looking Strategies for the Advancement of Women; Women Workers: ILO Plan of Action on Equality of Treatment of Men and Women in Employment.*

DECLARATION ON THE GRANTING OF INDE-PENDENCE TO COLONIAL COUNTRIES AND PEOPLES (1960). The proposal to adopt such a declaration was put forward by Nikita Krushchev, chairman of the Council of Ministers of the Union of Soviet Socialist Republics, in a statement which he made to the UN General Assembly in 1960. His proposal was that, in keeping with the principles of its charter, the United Nations should declare itself in favor of the "immediate and compete elimination of the colonial system in all its forms and manifestations." The assembly considered draft declarations to this effect proposed by the USSR and by 43 African and Asian nations and adopted the latter by 89 to 0, with nine abstentions.

The declaration was adopted by the UN General Assembly on 14 December 1960 (resolution 1514 [XV]). The text is as follows:

The General Assembly,

Mindful of the determination proclaimed by the peoples of the world in the Charter of the United Nations to reaffirm faith in fundamental human rights, in the dignity and worth of the human person, in the equal rights of men and women and of nations large and small and to promote social progress and better standards of life in larger freedom,

Conscious of the need for the creation of conditions of stability and well-being and peaceful and friendly relations based on respect for the principles of equal rights and self-determination of all peoples, and of universal respect for, and observance of, human rights and fundamental freedoms for all without distinction as to race, sex, language or religion,

Recognizing the passionate yearning for freedom in all dependent peoples and the decisive role of such peoples in the attainment of their independence,

Aware of the increasing conflicts resulting from the denial of or impediments in the way of the freedom of such peoples, which constitute a serious threat to world peace,

Considering the important role of the United Nations in assisting the movement for independence in Trust and Non-Self-Governing Territories,

Recognizing that the peoples of the world ardently desire the end of colonialism in all its manifestations,

Convinced that the continued existence of colonialism prevents the development of international economic co-operation, impedes the social, cultural and economic development of dependent peoples and militates against the United Nations ideal of universal peace,

Affirming that peoples may, for their own ends, freely dispose of their natural wealth and resources without prejudice to any obligations arising out of international economic co-operation, based upon the principle of mutual benefit, and international law,

Believing that the process of liberation is irresistible and irreversible and that, in order to avoid serious crises, an end must be put to colonialism and all practices of segregation and discrimination associated therewith,

Welcoming the emergence in recent years of a large number of dependent territories into freedom and inde-

pendence, and recognizing the increasingly powerful trends towards freedom in such territories which have not yet attained independence,

Convinced that all peoples have an inalienable right to complete freedom, the exercise of their sovereignty and the integrity of their national territory,

Solemnly proclaims the necessity of bringing to a speedy and unconditional end colonialism in all its forms and manifestations;

And to this end

Declares that:

1. The subjection of peoples to alien subjugation, domination and exploitation constitutes a denial of fundamental human rights, is contrary to the Charter of the United Nations and is an impediment to the promotion of world peace and co-operation.

2. All peoples have the right to self-determination; by virtue of that right they freely determine their political status and freely pursue their economic, social and cultural development.

3. Inadequacy of political, economic, social or educational preparedness should never serve as a pretext for delaying independence.

4. All armed action or repressive measures of all kinds directed against dependent peoples shall cease in order to enable them to exercise peacefully and freely their right to complete independence, and the integrity of their national territory shall be respected.

5. Immediate steps shall be taken, in Trust and Non-Self-Governing Territories or all other territories which have not yet attained independence, to transfer all powers to the peoples of those territories, without any conditions or reservations, in accordance with their freely expressed will and desire, without any distinction as to race, creed or colour, in order to enable them to enjoy complete independence and freedom.

6. Any attempt aimed at the partial or total disruption of the national unity and the territorial integrity of a country is incompatible with the purposes and principles of the Charter of the United Nations.

7. All States shall observe faithfully and strictly the provisions of the Charter of the United Nations, the Universal Declaration of Human Rights and the present Declaration on the basis of equality, non-interference in the internal affairs of all States, and respect for the sovereign rights of all peoples and their territorial integrity.

SEE ALSO *Self-Determination; Self-Determination: Definition and Implementation; Self-Determination: Universal Recognition of the Right; Slavery-like Practices of* Apartheid *and Colonialism.*

DECLARATION ON THE HUMAN RIGHTS OF IN-DIVIDUALS WHO ARE NOT NATIONALS OF THE COUNTRY IN WHICH THEY LIVE (1985). The declaration was the result of an extensive study of the applicability of existing international provisions on the protection of the human rights of aliens prepared by the Baroness Elles, a special rapporteur of the UN SUB-COMMISSION ON PREVENTION OF DISCRIMINATION AND PROTECTIONS OF MINORITIES. A draft declaration on ALIENS' RIGHTS was presented as part of the study and was considered in detail by the sub-commission and later by the Third Committee of the General Assembly.

The declaration was adopted by the UN General Assembly on 13 December 1985 (resolution 40/144). The text, annexed to that resolution, is as follows:

Article 1. For the purposes of this Declaration, the term "alien" shall apply, with due regard to qualifications made in subsequent articles, to any individual who is not a national of the State in which he or she is present.

Article 2. 1. Nothing in this Declaration shall be interpreted as legitimizing the illegal entry into and presence in a State of any alien, nor shall any provision be interpreted as restricting the right of any state to promulgate laws and regulations concerning the entry of aliens and the terms and conditions of their stay or to establish differences between nationals and aliens. However, such laws and regulations shall not be incompatible with the international legal obligations of that State, including those in the field of human rights.

2. This Declaration shall not prejudice the enjoyment of the rights accorded by domestic law and of the rights which under international law a State is obliged to accord to aliens, even where this Declaration does not recognize such rights or recognizes them to a lesser extent.

Article 3. Every State shall make public its national legislation or regulations affecting aliens.

Article 4. Aliens shall observe the laws of the State in which they reside or are present and regard with respect the customs and traditions of the people of that State.

Article 5. 1. Aliens shall enjoy, in accordance with domestic law and subject to the relevant international obligations of the State in which they are present, in particular the following rights:

(a) The right to life and security of person; no alien shall be subjected to arbitrary arrest or detention; no alien shall be deprived of his or her liberty except on such grounds and in accordance with such procedures as are established by law;

(b) The right to protection against arbitrary or unlawful interference with privacy, family, home or correspondence;

(c) The right to be equal before the courts, tribunals and all other organs and authorities administering justice and, when necessary, to free assistance of an interpreter in criminal proceedings and, when prescribed by law, other proceedings;

(d) The right to choose a spouse, to marry, to found a family;

(e) The right to freedom of thought, opinion, conscience and religion; the right to manifest their religion or beliefs, subject only to such limitations as are prescribed by law and are necessary to protect public safety, order, health or morals or the fundamental rights and freedoms of others;

(f) The right to retain their own language, culture and tradition;

(g) The right to transfer abroad earnings, savings or other personal monetary assets, subject to domestic currency regulations.

2. Subject to such restrictions as are prescribed by law and which are necessary in a democratic society to protect national security, public safety, public order, public health or morals or the rights and freedoms of others, and which are consistent with the other rights recognized in the relevant international instruments and those set forth in this Declaration, aliens shall enjoy the following rights:

(a) The right to leave the country;

(b) The right to freedom of expression;

(c) The right to peaceful assembly;

(d) The right to own property alone as well as in association with others, subject to domestic law.

3. Subject to the provisions referred to in paragraph 2, aliens lawfully in the territory of a State shall enjoy the right to liberty of movement and freedom to choose their residence within the borders of the State.

4. Subject to national legislation and due authorization, the spouse and minor or dependent children of an alien lawfully residing in the territory of a State shall be admitted to accompany, join and stay with the alien.

Article 6. No alien shall be subjected to torture or to cruel, inhuman or degrading treatment or punishment and, in particular, no alien shall be subjected without his or her free consent to medical or scientific experimentation.

Article 7. An alien lawfully in the territory of a State may be expelled therefrom only in pursuance of a decision reached in accordance with law and shall, except where compelling reasons of national security otherwise require, be allowed to submit the reasons why he or she should not be expelled and to have the case reviewed by, and be represented for the purpose before, the competent authority or a person or persons specially designated by the competent authority. Individual or collective expulsion of such aliens on grounds of race, colour, religion, culture, descent or national or ethnic origin is prohibited.

Article 8. 1. Aliens lawfully residing in the territory of a State shall also enjoy, in accordance with the national laws, the following rights, subject to their obligations under article 4:

(a) The right to safe and healthy working conditions, to fair wages and equal remuneration for work of equal value without distinction of any kind, in particular, women being guaranteed conditions of work not inferior to those enjoyed by men, with equal pay for equal work;

(b) The right to join trade unions and other organizations or associations of their choice and to participate in their activities. No restrictions may be placed on the exercise of this right other than those prescribed by law and which are necessary, in a democratic society, in the interests of national security or public order or for the protection of the rights and freedoms of others;

(c) The right to health protection, medical care, social security, social services, education, rest and leisure, provided that they fulfil the requirements under the relevant regulations for participation and that undue strain is not placed on the resources of the State.

2. With a view to protecting the rights of aliens carrying on lawful paid activities in the country in which they are present, such rights may be specified by the Governments concerned in multilateral or bilateral conventions.

Article 9. No alien shall be arbitrarily deprived of his or her lawfully acquired assets.

Article 10. Any alien shall be free at any time to communicate with the consulate or diplomatic mission of the State of which he or she is a national or, in the absence thereof, with the consulate or diplomatic mission of any other State entrusted with the protection of the interests of the State of which he or she is a national in the State where he or she resides.

SEE ALSO Aliens: Equality with Citizens; Convention relating to the Status of Refugees and protocol; European Convention on Establishment and Protocol; Refugees; Refugees: Voluntary Repatriation.

DECLARATION ON THE INADMISSIBILITY OF INTERVENTION AND INTERFERENCE IN THE INTERNAL AFFAIRS OF STATES (1981).

In adopting the declaration, the UN General Assembly expressed its deep concern at the gravity of the international situation and the increasing threat to international peace and security owing to frequent recourse to the threat or use of force, AGGRESSION, intimidation, military intervention and occupation, escalation of military presence, and all other forms of intervention or interference—direct or indirect, overt or covert—threatening the sovereignty and political independence of other States, with the aim of overthrowing their governments; and pointed out that such policies endanger the political independence of States, freedom of peoples, and permanent sovereignty over their natural resources, adversely affecting thereby the maintenance of international peace and security. In particular, it referred to "the imperative need for all foreign forces engaged in military occupation, intervention or interference to be completely withdrawn to their own territories, so that people under colonial domination, foreign occupation or racist regimes may freely and fully exercise their right to SELF-DETERMINATION, so as to enable the people of all States to administer their own affairs and determine their own political, economic and social system without external interference or control,"; and also to "the imperative need for any threat of aggression, any recruitment, any use of armed bands, in particular mercenaries, against sovereign States to be completely ended, so as to enable the peoples of all States to determine their own political, economic and social systems without external interference or control."

The declaration was approved by the UN General Assembly on 9 December 1981 (resolution 36/103). The text of the declaration, annexed to that resolution, is as follows:

The General Assembly,

Reaffirming, in accordance with the Charter of the United Nations, that no State has the right to intervene directly or indirectly for any reason whatsoever in the internal and external affairs of any other State,

Reaffirming further the fundamental principle of the Charter that all States have the duty not to threaten or use force against the sovereignty, political independence or territorial integrity of other States,

Bearing in mind that the establishment, maintenance and strengthening of international peace and security are founded upon freedom, equality, self-determination and independence, respect for the sovereignty of States, as well as permanent sovereignty of States over their natural resources, irrespective of their political, economic or social systems or the levels of their development,

Considering that full observance of the principle of non-intervention and non-interference in the internal and external affairs of States if of the greatest importance for the maintenance of international peace and security and for the fulfilment of the purposes and principles of the Charter,

Reaffirming, in accordance with the Charter, the right to self-determination and independence of peoples under colonial domination, foreign occupation or racist régimes,

Stressing that the purposes of the United Nations can be achieved only under conditions where peoples enjoy freedom and States enjoy sovereign equality and comply fully with the requirements of these principles in their international relations,

Considering that any violation of the principle of non-intervention and non-interference in the internal and external affairs of States poses a threat to the freedom of peoples, the sovereignty, political independence and territorial integrity of States and to their political, economic, social and cultural development, and also endangers international peace and security,

Considering that a declaration on the inadmissibility of intervention and interference in the internal affairs of States will contribute towards the fulfilment of the purposes and principles of the Charter,

Considering the provisions of the Charter as a whole and taking into account the resolutions adopted by the United Nations relating to that principle, in particular those containing the Declaration on the Strengthening of International Security, the Declaration on the Inadmissibility of Intervention in the Domestic Affairs of States and the Protection of Their Independence and Sovereignty, the Declaration on Principles of International Law concerning Friendly Relations and Co-operation among States in accordance with the Charter of the United Nations and the Definition of Aggression.

Solemnly declares that:

1. No State or group of States has the right to intervene or interfere in any form or for any reason whatsoever in the internal and external affairs of other States.

2. The principle of non-intervention and non-interference in the internal and external affairs of States comprehends the following rights and duties:

I. (a) Sovereignty, political independence, territorial integrity, national unity and security of all States, as well as national identity and cultural heritage of their peoples;

(b) The sovereign and inalienable right of a State freely to determine its own political, economic, cultural and social systems, to develop its international relations and to exercise permanent sovereignty over its natural resources, in accordance with the will of its people, without outside intervention, interference, subversion, coercion or threat in any form whatsoever;

(c) The right of States and peoples to have free access to information and to develop fully, without interference, their system of information and mass media and to use their information media in order to promote their political, social, economic and cultural interests and aspirations, based, *inter alia,* on the relevant articles of the Universal Declaration of Human Rights and the principles of the new international information order;

II. (a) The duty of States to refrain in their international relations from the threat or use of force in any form whatsoever to violate the existing internationally recognized boundaries of another State, to disrupt the political, social or economic order of other States, to overthrow or change the political system of another State or its Government, to cause tension between or among States or to deprive peoples of their national identity and cultural heritage;

(b) The duty of a State to ensure that its territory is not used in any manner which would violate the sovereignty, political independence, territorial integrity and national unity or disrupt the political, economic and social stability of another State; this obligation applies also to States entrusted with responsibility for territories yet to attain self-determination and national independence;

(c) The duty of a State to refrain from armed intervention, subversion, military occupation or any other form of intervention and interference, overt or covert, directed at another State or group of States, or any act of military, political or economic interference in the internal affairs of another State, including acts of reprisal involving the use of force;

(d) The duty of a State to refrain from any forcible action which deprives peoples under colonial domination or foreign occupation of their right to self-determination, freedom and independence;

(e) The duty of a State to refrain from any action or attempt in whatever form or under whatever pretext to destabilize or to undermine the stability of another State or of any of its institutions;

(f) The duty of a State to refrain from the promotion, encouragement or support, direct or indirect, of rebellious or secessionist activities within other States, under any pretext whatsoever, or any action which seeks to disrupt the unity or to undermine or subvert the political order of other States;

(g) The duty of a State to prevent on its territory the training, financing and recruitment of mercenaries, or the sending of such mercenaries into the territory of another State, and to deny facilities, including financing, for the equipping and transit of mercenaries;

(h) The duty of a State to refrain from concluding agreements with other States designed to intervene or interfere in the internal and external affairs of third States;

(i) The duty of States to refrain from any measure which would lead to the strengthening of existing military blocs or the creation or strengthening of new military alliances, interlocking arrangements, the deployment of interventionist forces or military bases and other related military installations conceived in the context of great-Power confrontation;

(j) The duty of a State to abstain from any defamatory campaign, vilification or hostile propaganda for the purpose of intervening or interfering in the internal affairs of other States;

(k) The duty of a State, in the conduct of its international relations in the economic, social, technical and trade fields, to refrain from measures which would constitute interference or intervention in the internal or external affairs of another State, thus preventing it from determining freely its political, economic and social development; this includes, *inter alia,* the duty of a State not to use its external economic assistance programme or adopt any multilateral or unilateral economic reprisal or blockade and to prevent the use of transnational and multinational corporations under its jurisdiction and control as instruments of political pressure or coercion against another State, in violation of the Charter of the United Nations;

(l) The duty of a State to refrain from the exploitation and the distortion of human rights issues as a means of interference in the internal affairs of States, of exerting pressure on other States or creating distrust and disorder within and among States or groups of States;

(m) The duty of a State to refrain from using terrorist practices as state policy against another State or against peoples under colonial domination, foreign occupation or racist régimes and to prevent any assistance to or use of or tolerant of terrorist groups, saboteurs or subversive agents against third States;

(n) The duty of a State to refrain from organizing, training, financing and arming political and ethnic groups on their territories or the territories of other States for the purpose of creating subversion, disorder or unrest in other countries;

(o) The duty of a State to refrain from any economic, political or military activity in the territory of another State without its consent;

III. (a) The right and duty of States to participate actively on the basis of equality in solving outstanding international issues, thus actively contributing to the removal of causes of conflict and interference;

(b) The right and duty of States fully to support the right to self-determination, freedom and independence of peoples under colonial domination, foreign occupation or racist régimes, as well as the right of these peoples to wage both political and armed struggle to that end, in accordance with the purposes and principles of the Charter;

(c) The right and duty of States to observe, promote and defend all human rights and fundamental freedoms within their own national territories and to work for the elimination of massive and flagrant violations of the rights of nations and peoples, and, in particular, for the elimination of *apartheid* and all forms of racism and racial discrimination;

(d) The right and duty of States to combat, within their constitutional prerogatives, the dissemination of false or distorted news which can be interpreted as interference in the internal affairs of other States or as being harmful to the promotion of peace, co-operation and friendly relations among States and nations;

(e) The right and duty of States not to recognize situations brought about by the threat or use of force or acts undertaken in contravention of the principle of non-intervention and non-interference.

3. The rights and duties set out in this Declaration are interrelated and are in accordance with the Charter.

4. Nothing in this Declaration shall prejudice in any manner the right to self-determination, freedom and independence of peoples under colonial domination, foreign occupation or racist régimes, and the right to seek and receive support in accordance with the purposes and principles of the Charter.

5. Nothing in this Declaration shall prejudice in any manner the provisions of the Charter.

6. Nothing in this Declaration shall prejudice action taken by the United Nations under Chapters VI and VII of the Charter.

SEE ALSO *Declaration on Permanent Sovereignty over Natural Resources; Declaration on Principles of International Law concerning Friendly Relations and Co-operation among States in Accordance with the Charter of the United Nations.*

DECLARATION ON THE OCCASION OF THE TWENTY-FIFTH ANNIVERSARY OF THE UNITED NATIONS (1970).

In this declaration, adopted 25 years after the UNITED NATIONS CHARTER entered into force, the General Assembly summed up *inter alia* progress achieved in liberating peoples of colonial, trust, and non-self-governing territories and in promoting respect for and observance of human rights and fundamental freedoms for all.

The declaration was adopted by the UN General Assembly on 24 October 1970 (resolution 2627 [XXV]). The text, annexed to that resolution, is as follows.

We, the representatives of the States Members of the United Nations, assembled at United Nations Headquarters on 24 October 1970 on the occasion of the twenty-fifth anniversary of the coming into force of the Charter of the United Nations, now solemnly declare that:

1. In furtherance of the anniversary objectives of peace, justice and progress, we reaffirm our dedication to the Charter of the United Nations and our will to carry out the obligations contained in the Charter.

2. The United Nations, despite its limitations, has, in its role as a centre for harmonizing the actions of nations in attaining the purposes mentioned in Article 1 of the Charter, made an important contribution to the maintenance of international peace and security, to developing friendly relations based on respect for the principle of equal rights and self-determination of peoples and to achieving international co-operation in economic, social, cultural and humanitarian fields. We reaffirm our deep conviction that the United Nations can provide a most effective means to strengthen the freedom and independence of nations.

3. In pursuance of the purposes of the Charter, we reaffirm our determination to respect the principles of international law concerning friendly relations and co-operation among States. We will exert our utmost efforts to develop such relations among all States, irrespective of their political, economic and social systems, on the basis of strict observance of the principles of the Charter, and in particular the principle of sovereign equality of States, the principle that States shall refrain in their international relations from the threat or use of force against the territorial integrity or political independence of any State, the principle that they shall settle their international disputes by peaceful means, the duty not to intervene in matters within the domestic jurisdiction of any State, the duty of States to co-operate with one another in accordance with the Charter, and the principle that States shall fulfil in good faith the ob-

ligations assumed by them in accordance with the Charter. The progressive development and codification of international law, in which important progress was made during the first twenty-five years of the United Nations, should be advanced in order to promote the rule of law among nations. In this connexion we particularly welcome the adoption today of the Declaration on Principles of International Law concerning Friendly Relations and Co-operation among States in accordance with the Charter of the United Nations.

4. Despite the achievements of the United Nations, a grave situation of insecurity still confronts the Organization and armed conflicts occur in various parts of the world, while at the same time the arms race and arms expenditure continue and a large part of humanity is suffering from economic under-development. We reaffirm our determination to take concrete steps to fulfil the central task of the United Nations—the preservation of international peace and security—since the solution to many other crucial problems, notably those of disarmament and economic development, is inseparably linked thereto, and to reach agreement on more effective procedures for carrying out United Nations peace-keeping consistent with the Charter. We invite all Member States to resort more often to the peaceful settlement of international disputes and conflicts by the means provided for in the Charter, notably through negotiation, inquiry, mediation, conciliation, arbitration and judicial settlement, making use as appropriate of the relevant organs of the United Nations, as well as through resort to regional agencies or arrangements or other peaceful means of their own choice.

5. On the threshold of the Disarmament Decade, we welcome the important international agreements which have already been achieved in the limitation of armaments, especially nuclear arms. Conscious of the long and difficult search for ways to halt and reverse the arms race and of the grave threat to international peace posed by the continuing development of sophisticated weapons, we look forward to the early conclusion of further agreements of this kind and to moving forward from arms limitation to a reduction of armaments and to disarmament everywhere, particularly in the nuclear field, with the participation of all nuclear Powers. We call upon all Governments to renew their determination to make concrete progress towards the elimination of the arms race and the achievement of the final goal—general and complete disarmament under effective international control.

6. We acclaim the role of the United Nations in the past twenty-five years in the process of the liberation of peoples of colonial, Trust and other Non-Self-Governing Territories. As a result of this welcome development, the number of sovereign States in the Organization has been greatly increased and colonial empires have virtually disappeared. Despite these achievements, many Territories and peoples continue to be denied their right to self-determination and independence, particularly in Namibia, Southern Rhodesia, Angola, Mozambique and Guinea (Bissau), in deliberate and deplorable defiance of the United Nations and world opinion by certain recalcitrant States and by the illegal régime of Southern Rhodesia. We reaffirm the inalienable right of all colonial peoples to self-determination, freedom and independence and condemn all actions which deprive any people of these rights. In recognizing the legitimacy of the struggle of colonial peoples for their freedom by all appropriate means at their disposal, we call upon all Governments to comply in this respect with the

provisions of the Charter, taking into account the Declaration on the Granting of Independence to Colonial Countries and Peoples adopted by the United Nations in 1960. We re-emphasize that these countries and peoples are entitled, in their just struggle, to seek and to receive all necessary moral and material help in accordance with the purposes and principles of the Charter.

7. We strongly condemn the evil policy of *apartheid,* which is a crime against the conscience and dignity of mankind and, like nazism, is contrary to the principles of the Charter. We reaffirm our determination to spare no effort, including support to those who struggle against it, in accordance with the letter and spirit of the Charter, to secure the elimination of *apartheid* in South Africa. We also condemn all forms of oppression and tyranny wherever they occur and racism and the practice of racial discrimination in all its manifestations.

8. The United Nations has endeavoured in its first twenty-five years to further the Charter objectives of promoting respect for, and observance of, human rights and fundamental freedoms for all. The international conventions and declarations concluded under its auspices give expression to the moral conscience of mankind and represent humanitarian standards for all members of the international community. The Universal Declaration of Human Rights, the International Covenants on Human Rights, the International Convention on the Elimination of All Forms of Racial Discrimination and the Convention on the Prevention and Punishment of the Crime of Genocide constitute a landmark in international co-operation and in the recognition and protection of the rights of every individual without any distinction. Although some progress has been achieved, serious violations of human rights are still being committed against individuals and groups in several regions of the world. We pledge ourselves to a continued and determined struggle against all violations of the rights and fundamental freedoms of human beings, by eliminating the basic causes of such violations, by promoting universal respect for the dignity of all people without regard to race, colour, sex, language or religion, and in particular through greater use of the facilities provided by the United Nations in accordance with the Charter.

9. During the past twenty-five years, efforts have been made, by adopting specific measures and by fashioning and employing new institutions, to give concrete substance to the fundamental objectives enshrined in the Charter, to create conditions of stability and well-being and to ensure a minimum standard of living consistent with human dignity. We are convinced that such economic and social development is essential to peace, international security and justice. The nations of the world have, therefore, resolved to seek a better and more effective system of international co-operation whereby the prevailing disparities may be banished and prosperity secured for all. International efforts for economic and technical co-operation whereby the prevailing disparities may be banished and prosperity secured for all. International efforts for economic and technical co-operation must be on a scale commensurate with that of the problem itself. In this context, the activities of the United Nations system designed to secure the economic and social progress of all countries, in particular the developing countries, which have grown significantly in the past twenty-five years, should be further strengthened and increased. Partial, sporadic and half-hearted measures will not suffice. On the occasion of this anniversary, we have proclaimed the 1970s to be the Second United Nations Development Dec-

ade, which coincides with and is linked to the Disarmament Decade, and have adopted the International Development Strategy for the Second United Nations Development Decade. We urge all Governments to give their full support to its most complete and effective implementation in order to realize the fundamental objectives of the Charter.

10. The new frontiers of science and technology demand greater international co-operation. We reaffirm our intention to make full use, *inter alia,* through the United Nations, of the unprecedented opportunities created by advances in science and technology for the benefit of peoples everywhere in such fields as outer space, the peaceful uses of the sea-bed beyond national jurisdiction and the improvement of the quality of the environment, so that the developed and developing countries can share equitably scientific and technical advances, thus contributing to the acceleration of economic development throughout the world.

11. The great increase in the membership of the Organization since 1945 testifies to its vitality; however, universality in terms of membership in the Organization has not yet been achieved. We express the hope that in the near future all other peace-loving States which accept and, in the judgement of the Organization, are able and willing to carry out the obligations of the Charter will become Members. It is furthermore desirable to find ways and means to strengthen the Organization's effectiveness in dealing with the growing volume and complexity of its work in all areas of its activities, and notably those relating to the strengthening of international peace and security, including a more rational division and coordination of work among the various agencies and organizations of the United Nations system.

12. Mankind is confronted today by a critical and urgent choice: either increased peaceful cooperation and progress or disunity and conflict, even annihilation. We, the representatives of the States Members of the United Nations, solemnly observing the twenty-fifth anniversary of the United Nations, reaffirm our determination to do our utmost to ensure a lasting peace on earth and to observe the purposes and principles embodied in the Charter, and express full confidence that the actions of the United Nations will be conducive to the advancement of mankind along the road to peace, justice and progress.

DECLARATION ON THE PARTICIPATION OF WOMEN IN PROMOTING INTERNATIONAL PEACE AND CO-OPERATION (1982). The declaration originated in a text (resolution 29) adopted by the World Conference of the INTERNATIONAL WOMEN'S YEAR (1975), which called upon women to intensify their forces in order to strengthen peace and to promote international cooperation. A draft declaration on the subject was discussed extensively in the Third Committee on the UN General Assembly in 1980 and 1981, and the declaration was adopted unanimously by the assembly on 3 December 1982 (resolution 37/63). The text, annexed to that resolution, is as follows:

Part I

Article 1. Women and men have an equal and vital interest in contributing to international peace and co-operation. To this end women must be enabled to exercise their right to participate in the economic, social, cultural, civil and political affairs of society on an equal footing with men.

Article 2. The full participation of women in the economic, social, cultural, civil and political affairs of society and in the endeavor to promote international peace and cooperation is dependent on a balanced and equitable distribution of roles between men and women in the family and in society as a whole.

Article 3. The increasing participation of women in the economic, social, cultural, civil and political affairs of society will contribute to international peace and co-operation.

Article 4. The full enjoyment of the rights of women and men and the full participation of women in promoting international peace and co-operation will contribute to the eradication of apartheid, of all forms of racism, racial discrimination, colonialism, neo-colonialism, aggression, foreign occupation and domination and interference in the internal affairs of States.

Article 5. Special national and international measures are necessary to increase the level of women's participation in the sphere of international relations so that women can contribute, on an equal basis, with men to national and international efforts to secure world peace and economic and social progress and to promote international cooperation.

Part II

Article 6. All appropriate measures shall be taken to intensify national and international efforts in respect of the participation of women in promoting international peace and cooperation by ensuring the equal participation of women in the economic, social, cultural, civil and political affairs of society through a balanced and equitable distribution of roles between men and women in the domestic sphere and in society as a whole, as well as by providing an equal opportunity for women to participate in the decision-making.

Article 7. All appropriate measures shall be taken to promote the exchange of experience at the national and international levels for the purpose of furthering the involvement of women in promoting international peace and cooperation and in solving other vital national and international problems.

Article 8. All appropriate measures shall be taken at the national and international levels to give effective publicity to the responsibility and active participation of women in promoting international peace and co-operation and in solving other vital national and international problems.

Article 9. All appropriate measures shall be taken to render solidarity and support to those women who are victims of mass and flagrant violations of human rights such as *apartheid*, all forms of racism, racial discrimination, colonialism, neo-colonialism, aggression, foreign occupation and domination and of all other violations of human rights.

Article 10. All appropriate measures shall be taken to pay tribute to the participation of women in promoting international peace and co-operation.

Article 11. All appropriate measures shall be taken to encourage women to participate in non-governmental and intergovernmental organizations aimed at the strengthening of international peace and security, the development of friendly relations among nations and the promotion of co-operation among States and, to that end, freedom of thought, conscience, expression, assembly, association, communication and movement, without distinction as to race, political or religious belief, language or ethnic origin, shall be effectively guaranteed.

Article 12. All appropriate measures shall be taken to provide practical opportunities for the effective participation of women in promoting international peace and cooperation, economic development and social progress and, to that end:

(a) To promote an equitable representation of women in governmental and non-governmental functions,

(b) To promote equality of opportunities for women to enter diplomatic service,

(c) To appoint or nominate women, on an equal basis with men, as members of delegations to national, regional or international meetings,

(d) To support increased employment of women at all levels in the secretariats of the United Nations and the specialized agencies, in conformity with Article 101 of the Charter of the United Nations.

Article 13. All appropriate measures shall be taken to establish adequate legal protection of the rights of women on an equal basis with men in order to ensure effective participation of women in the activities referred to above.

Article 14. Governments, non-governmental and international organizations, including the United Nations and the specialized agencies and individuals, are urged to do all in their power to promote the implementation of the principles contained in the present Declaration.

SEE ALSO *Declaration of Mexico. . . ; Women and Peace.*

DECLARATION ON THE PREPARATION OF SOCIETIES FOR LIFE IN PEACE (1978).

In this declaration, the UN General Assembly reaffirms the right of individuals, States, and all mankind to peace and points out that every State must accept certain duties and responsibilities as its contribution to insuring the enjoyment of that right.

The declaration was adopted by the General Assembly on 15 December 1978 (resolution 33/73). The text, annexed to that resolution, is as follows.

The General Assembly

I

Solemnly invites all States to guide themselves in their activities by the recognition of the supreme importance and necessity of establishing, maintaining and strengthening a just and durable peace for present and future generations and, in particular, to observe the following principles:

1. Every nation and every human being, regardless of race, conscience, language or sex, has the inherent right to life in peace. Respect for that right, as well as for the other human rights, is in the common interest of all mankind and an indispensable condition of advancement of all nations, large and small, in all fields.

2. A war of aggression, its planning, preparation or initiation are crimes against peace and are prohibited by international law.

3. In accordance with the purposes and principles of the United Nations, States have the duty to refrain from propaganda for wars of aggression.

4. Every State, acting in the spirit of friendship and good-neighbourly relations, has the duty to promote all-round, mutually advantageous and equitable political, economic, social and cultural co-operation with other States, notwithstanding their socio-economic systems, with a view to securing their common existence and co-operation in peace, in conditions of mutual understanding of and respect for the identity and diversity of all peoples, and the duty to take up actions conducive to the furtherance of the ideals of peace, humanism and freedom.

5. Every State has the duty to respect the right of all peoples to self-determination, independence, equality, sovereignty, the territorial integrity of States and the inviolability of their frontiers, including the right to determine the road of their development, without interference or intervention in their internal affairs.

6. A basic instrument of the maintenance of peace is the elimination of the threat inherent in the arms race, as well as efforts towards general and complete disarmament, under effective international control, including partial measures with that end in view, in accordance with the principles agreed upon within the United Nations and relevant international agreements.

7. Every State has the duty to discourage all manifestations and practices of colonialism, as well as racism, racial discrimination and *apartheid,* as contrary to the right of peoples to self-determination and to other human rights and fundamental freedoms.

8. Every State has the duty to discourage advocacy of hatred and prejudice against other peoples as contrary to the principles of peaceful coexistence and friendly co-operation.

II

Calls upon all States, in order to implement the above principles:

(a) To act perseveringly and consistently, with due regard for the constitutional rights and the role of the family, the institutions and the organizations concerned:

(i) To ensure that their policies relevant to the implementation of the present Declaration, including educational processes and teaching methods as well as media information activities, incorporate contents compatible with the task of the preparation for life in peace of entire societies and, in particular, the young generations;

(ii) Therefore, to discourage and eliminate incitement to racial hatred, national or other discrimination, injustice or advocacy of violence and war;

(b) To develop various forms of bilateral and multilateral co-operation, also in international, governmental and non-governmental organizations, with a view to enhancing preparation of societies to live in peace and, in particular, exchanging experiences on projects pursued with that end in view;

III

1. Recommends that the governmental and non-governmental organizations concerned should initiate appropriate action towards the implementation of the present Declaration;

2. States that a full implementation of the principles enshrined in the present Declaration calls for concerted action on the part of Governments, the United Nations and the specialized agencies, in particular the United Nations Educational, Scientific and Cultural Organization, as well as other interested international and national organizations, both governmental and non-governmental;

3. Requests the Secretary-General to follow the progress made in the implementation of the present Declaration and to submit periodic reports thereon to the General Assembly, the first such report to be submitted not later than at its thirty-sixth session.

SEE ALSO Declaration concerning Essentials of Peace; Declaration on Principles of International Law concerning Friendly Relations and Co-operation among States in Accordance with the Charter of the United Nations; Declaration on the Right of Peoples to Peace; Human Rights and Peace.

DECLARATION ON THE PREVENTION OF NUCLEAR CATASTROPHE (1981).

The declaration, outlawing the use of nuclear weapons and the waging of nuclear war, was adopted by the UN General Assembly on 9 December 1981 (resolution 36/100). The text of the declaration is as follows:

The General Assembly,

Bearing in mind that the foremost task of the United Nations, born in the flames of the Second World War, has been, is and will be to save present and succeeding generations from the scourge of war,

Recognizing that all the horrors of past wars and all other calamities that have befallen people would pale in comparison with what is inherent in the use of nuclear weapons capable of destroying civilization on earth,

Reaffirming that the universally accepted objective is to eliminate completely the possibility of the use of nuclear weapons through the cessation of their production, followed by the destruction of their stockpiles, and that, to this end, priority in disarmament negotiations should be given to nuclear disarmament,

Convinced that, as the first step in this direction, the use of nuclear weapons and the waging of nuclear war should be outlawed,

Solemnly proclaims, on behalf of the States Members of the United Nations:

1. States and statesmen that resort first to the use of nuclear weapons will be committing the gravest crime against humanity.

2. There will never be any justification or pardon for statesmen who take the decision to be the first to use nuclear weapons.

3. Any doctrines allowing the first use of nuclear weapons and any actions pushing the world towards a catastrophe are incompatible with human moral standards and the lofty ideals of the United Nations.

4. It is the supreme duty and direct obligation of the leaders of nuclear-weapon States to act in such a way as to eliminate the risk of the outbreak of a nuclear conflict. The nuclear-arms race must be stopped and reversed by joint efforts, through negotiations conducted in good faith and on the basis of equality, having as their ultimate goal the complete elimination of nuclear weapons.

5. Nuclear energy should be used exclusively for peaceful purposes and only for the benefit of mankind.

SEE ALSO Nuclear Disarmament.

DECLARATION ON THE PROMOTION AMONG YOUTH OF THE IDEALS OF PEACE, MUTUAL RESPECT AND UNDERSTANDING AMONG PEOPLES (1965).

The declaration echoes the conviction of the UN General Assembly that the education of the young—and exchanges of young people and ideas in a spirit of peace, mutual respect, and understanding—can help to improve international relations and to strengthen peace and security.

The declaration was adopted by the General Assembly on 7 December 1965 (resolution 2037 [XX]). The text, annexed to that resolution, is as follows:

The General Assembly,

Recalling that under the terms of the Charter of the United Nations the peoples have declared themselves determined to save succeeding generations from the scourge of war,

Recalling further that in the Charter the United Nations has affirmed its faith in fundamental human rights, in the dignity of the human person and in the equal rights of men and nations,

Reaffirming the principles embodied in the Universal Declaration of Human Rights, the Declaration on the Granting of Independence to Colonial Countries and Peoples, the United Nations Declaration on the Elimination of All Forms of Racial Discrimination, General Assembly resolution 110 (II) of 3 November 1947 condemning all forms of propaganda designed or likely to provoke or encourage any threat to the peace, the Declaration of the Rights of the Child, and General Assembly resolution 1572 (XV) of 18 December 1960, which have a particular bearing upon the upbringing of young people in a spirit of peace, mutual respect and understanding among peoples,

Recalling that the purpose of the United Nations Educational, Scientific and Cultural Organization is to contribute to peace and security by promoting collaboration among nations through education, science and culture, and recognizing the role and contributions of that organization towards the education of young people in the spirit of international understanding, co-operation and peace,

Taking into consideration the fact that in the conflagrations which have afflicted mankind it is the young people who have had to suffer most and who have had the greatest number of victims,

Convinced that young people wish to have an assured future and that peace, freedom and justice are among the chief guarantees that their desire for happiness will be fulfilled,

Bearing in mind the important part being played by young people in every field of human endeavour and the fact that they are destined to guide the fortunes of mankind,

Bearing in mind furthermore that, in this age of great scientific, technological and cultural achievements, the energies, enthusiasm and creative abilities of the young should be devoted to the material and spiritual advancement of all peoples,

Convinced that the young should know, respect and develop the cultural heritage of their own country and that of all mankind,

Convinced furthermore that the education of the young and exchanges of young people and of ideas in a spirit of peace, mutual respect and understanding between peoples can help to improve international relations and to strengthen peace and security,

Proclaims this Declaration on the Promotion among Youth of the Ideals of Peace, Mutual Respect and Understanding between Peoples and calls upon Governments, non-governmental organizations and youth movements to recognize the principles set forth therein and to ensure their observance by means of appropriate measures:

Principle 1. Young people shall be brought up in the spirit of peace, justice, freedom, mutual respect and understanding in order to promote equal rights for all human beings and all nations, economic and social progress, disarmament and the maintenance of international peace and security.

Principle 2. All means of education, including as of major importance the guidance given by parents or family, instruction and information intended for the young should foster among them the ideals of peace, humanity, liberty and international solidarity and all other ideals which help to bring peoples closer together, and acquaint them with the role entrusted to the United Nations as a means of preserving and maintaining peace and promoting international understanding and co-operation.

Principle 3. Young people shall be brought up in the knowledge of the dignity and equality of all men, without distinction as to race, colour, ethnic origins or beliefs, and in respect for fundamental human rights and for the right of peoples to self-determination.

Principle 4. Exchanges, travel, tourism, meetings, the study of foreign languages, the twinning of towns and universities without discrimination and similar activities should be encouraged and facilitated among young people of all countries in order to bring them together in educational, cultural and sporting activities in the spirit of this Declaration.

Principle 5. National and international associations of young people should be encouraged to promote the purposes of the United Nations, particularly international peace and security, friendly relations among nations based on respect for the equal sovereignty of States, the final abolition of colonialism and of racial discrimination and other violations of human rights.

Youth organizations in accordance with this Declaration should take all appropriate measures within their respective fields of activity in order to make their contribution without any discrimination to the work of educating the young generation in accordance with these ideals.

Such organizations, in conformity with the principle of freedom of association, should promote the free exchange of ideas in the spirit of the principles of this Declaration and of the purposes of the United Nations set forth in the Charter.

All youth organizations should conform to the principles set forth in this Declaration.

Principle 6. A major aim in educating the young shall be to develop all their faculties and to train them to acquire higher moral qualities, to be deeply attached to the noble ideals of peace, liberty, the dignity and equality of all men, and imbued with respect and love for humanity and its creative achievements. To this end the family has an important role to play.

Young people must become conscious of their responsibilities in the world they will be called upon to manage and should be inspired with confidence in a future of happiness for mankind.

SEE ALSO *Human Rights and Youth.*

DECLARATION ON THE PROTECTION OF ALL PERSONS FROM BEING SUBJECTED TO TORTURE AND OTHER CRUEL, INHUMAN, OR DEGRADING TREATMENT OR PUNISHMENT (1975).

After studying an analytical summary of information from UN member States indicating an urgent need for protecting individuals against torture and other cruel treatment or punishment, the Fifth United Nations Congress on the Prevention of Crime and the Treatment of Offenders drafted this declaration. In adopting it, the UN General Assembly called upon all member States not to wait until it entered into force but to make unilateral declarations against torture immediately and to adopt legislation prohibiting it.

The declaration was adopted by the General Assembly on 9 December 1975 (resolution 3452 [XXX]). The text, annexed to the resolution, is as follows:

Article 1. 1. For the purpose of this Declaration, torture means any act by which severe pain or suffering, whether physical or mental, is intentionally inflicted by or at the instigation of a public official on a person for such purposes as obtaining from him or a third person information or confession, punishing him for an act he has committed or is suspected of having committed, or intimidating him or other persons. It does not include pain or suffering arising only from, inherent in or incidental to, lawful sanctions to the extent consistent with the Standard Minimum Rules for the Treatment of Prisoners.

2. Torture constitutes an aggravated and deliberate form of cruel, inhuman or degrading treatment or punishment.

Article 2. Any act of torture or other cruel, inhuman or degrading treatment or punishment is an offence to human dignity and shall be condemned as a denial of the purposes of the Charter of the United Nations and as a violation of the human rights and fundamental freedoms proclaimed in the Universal Declaration of Human Rights.

Article 3. No State may permit or tolerate torture or other cruel, inhuman or degrading treatment or punishment. Exceptional circumstances such as a state of war or a threat of war, internal political instability or any other public emergency may not be invoked as a justification of torture or other cruel, inhuman or degrading treatment or punishment.

Article 4. Each State shall, in accordance with the provisions of this Declaration, take effective measures to prevent torture and other cruel, inhuman or degrading treatment or punishment from being practised within its jurisdiction.

Article 5. The training of law enforcement personnel and of other public officials who may be responsible for persons deprived of their liberty shall ensure that full account is taken of the prohibition against torture and other cruel, inhuman or degrading treatment or punishment. This prohibition shall also, where appropriate, be included in such general rules or instructions as are issued in regard to the duties and functions of anyone who may be involved in the custody or treatment of such persons.

Article 6. Each State shall keep under systematic review interrogation methods and practices as well as arrangements for the custody and treatment of persons deprived of their liberty in its territory, with a view to preventing any cases of torture or other cruel, inhuman or degrading treatment or punishment.

Article 7. Each State shall ensure that all acts of torture as defined in article 1 are offences under its criminal law. The same shall apply in regard to acts which constitute participation in, complicity in, incitement to or an attempt to commit torture.

Article 8. Any person who alleges that he has been subjected to torture or other cruel, inhuman or degrading treatment or punishment by or at the instigation of a public official shall have the right to complain to, and to have his case impartially examined by, the competent authorities of the State concerned.

Article 9. Wherever there is reasonable ground to believe that an act of torture as defined in article 1 has been committed, the competent authorities of the State concerned shall promptly proceed to an impartial investigation even if there has been no formal complaint.

Article 10. If an investigation under article 8 or article 9 establishes that an act of torture as defined in article 1 appears to have been committed, criminal proceedings shall be instituted against the alleged offender or offenders in accordance with national law. If an allegation of other forms of cruel, inhuman or degrading treatment or punishment is considered to be well founded, the alleged offender or offenders shall be subject to criminal, disciplinary or other appropriate proceedings.

Article 11. Where it is proved that an act of torture or other cruel, inhuman or degrading treatment or punishment has been committed by or at the instigation of a public official, the victim shall be afforded redress and compensation in accordance with national law.

Article 12. Any statement which is established to have been made as a result of torture or other cruel, inhuman or degrading treatment or punishment may not be invoked as evidence against the person concerned or against any other person in any proceedings.

SEE ALSO *Body of Principles for the Protection of All Persons under Any Form of Detention or Imprisonment; Committee against Torture; Convention against Torture and other Cruel, Inhuman or Degrading Treatment or Punishment; European Convention for the Prevention of Torture and Inhuman or Degrading Treatment or Punishment; Inter-American Convention to Prevent and Punish Torture; Torture: Special Rapporteur; United Nations Voluntary Fund for Victims of Torture.*

DECLARATION ON THE PROTECTION OF WOMEN AND CHILDREN IN EMERGENCY AND ARMED CONFLICT (1974).

In 1974, the UN General Assembly expressed concern over the suffering of women and children in periods of emergency and armed conflict. Aware that they too often were the victims of inhuman acts from which they suffered serious harm, and conscious of its responsibility for the destiny of the rising generation, the assembly adopted this declaration and called for its strict observance by all member States.

The declaration was adopted by the General Assembly on 14 December 1974 (resolution 3318 [XXIX]). The text, annexed to the resolution, is as follows:

The General Assembly,

Having considered the recommendation of the Economic and Social Council contained in its resolution 1861 (LVI) of 16 May 1974,

Expressing its deep concern over the sufferings of women and children belonging to the civilian population who in periods of emergency and armed conflict in the struggle for peace, self-determination, national liberation and independence are too often the victims of inhuman acts and consequently suffer serious harm,

Aware of the suffering of women and children in many areas of the world, especially in those areas subject to suppression, aggression, colonialism, racism, alien domination and foreign subjugation,

Deeply concerned by the fact that, despite general and unequivocal condemnation, colonialism, racism and alien and foreign domination continue to subject many peoples under their yoke, cruelly suppressing the national liberation movements and inflicting heavy losses and incalculable sufferings on the populations under their domination, including women and children,

Deploring the fact that grave attacks are still being made on fundamental freedoms and the dignity of the human person and that colonial and racist foreign domination Powers continue to violate international humanitarian law,

Recalling the relevant provisions contained in the instruments of international humanitarian law relative to the protection of women and children in time of peace and war,

Recalling, among other important documents, its resolutions 2444 (XXIII) of 19 December 1968, 2597 (XXIV) of 16 December 1969 and 2674 (XXV) and 2675 (XXV) of 9 December 1970, on respect for human rights and on basic principles for the protection of civilian populations in armed conflicts, as well as Economic and Social Council resolution 1515 (XLVIII) of 28 May 1970 in which the Council requested the General Assembly to consider the possibility of drafting a declaration on the protection of women and children in emergency or wartime,

Conscious of its responsibility for the destiny of the rising generation and for the destiny of mothers, who play an important role in society, in the family and particularly in the upbringing of children,

Bearing in mind the need to provide special protection of women and children belonging to the civilian population,

Solemnly proclaims this Declaration on the Protection of Women and Children in Emergency and Armed Conflict and calls for the strict observance of the Declaration by all Member States:

1. Attacks and bombings on the civilian population, inflicting incalculable suffering, especially on women and children, who are the most vulnerable members of the population, shall be prohibited, and such acts shall be condemned.

2. The use of chemical and bacteriological weapons in the course of military operations constitutes one of the most flagrant violations of the Geneva Protocol of 1925, the Geneva Conventions of 1949 and the principles of international humanitarian law and inflicts heavy losses on civilian populations, including defenceless women and children, and shall be severely condemned.

3. All States shall abide fully by their obligations under the Geneva Protocol of 1925 and the Geneva Conventions of 1949, as well as other instruments of international law relative to respect for human rights in armed conflicts, which offer important guarantees for the protection of women and children.

4. All efforts shall be made by States involved in armed conflicts, military operations in foreign territories or military operations in territories still under colonial domination to spare women and children from the ravages of war. All the necessary steps shall be taken to ensure the prohibition of measures such as persecution, torture, punitive measures, degrading treatment and violence, particularly against that part of the civilian population that consists of women and children.

5. All forms of repression and cruel and inhuman treatment of women and children, including imprisonment, torture, shooting, mass arrests, collective punishment, destruction of dwellings and forcible eviction, committed by belligerents in the course of military operations or in occupied territories shall be considered criminal.

6. Women and children belonging to the civilian population and finding themselves in circumstances of emergency and armed conflict in the struggle for peace, self-determination, national liberation and independence, or who live in occupied territories, shall not be deprived of shelter, food, medical aid or other inalienable rights, in accordance with the provisions of the Universal Declaration of Human Rights, the International Covenant on Civil and Political Rights, the International Covenant on Economic, Social and Cultural Rights, the Declaration of the Rights of the Child or other instruments of international law.

SEE ALSO *Armed Conflicts; Basic Principles for the Protection of Civilian Populations in Armed Conflicts; Geneva Convention relative to the Protection of Civilian Persons in Time of War and Protocols I and II.*

DECLARATION ON THE RIGHT OF PEOPLES TO PEACE (1984).

In this declaration, the UN General Assembly points out that recognition and enjoyment of the right of peoples to peace is essential to full implementation of the human rights and fundamental freedoms proclaimed by the United Nations. The declaration was adopted by the assembly on 12 November 1984 (resolution 39/11); the text, annexed to that resolution, is as follows:

The General Assembly,

Reaffirming that the principal aim of the United Nations is the maintenance of international peace and security,

Bearing in mind the fundamental principles of international law set forth in the Charter of the United Nations,

Expressing the will and the aspirations of all peoples to eradicate war from the life of mankind and, above all, to avert a world-wide nuclear catastrophe,

Convinced that life without war serves as the primary international prerequisite for the material well-being, development and progress of countries, and for the full implementation of the rights and fundamental human freedoms proclaimed by the United Nations,

Aware that in the nuclear age the establishment of a lasting peace on Earth represents the primary condition for the preservation of human civilization and the survival of mankind,

Recognizing that the maintenance of a peaceful life for peoples is the sacred duty of each State,

1. Solemnly proclaims that the peoples of our planet have a sacred right to peace;

2. Solemnly declares that the preservation of the right of peoples to peace and the promotion of its implementation constitute a fundamental obligation of each State;

3. Emphasizes that ensuring the exercise of the right of peoples to peace demands that the policies of States be directed towards the elimination of the threat of war, particularly nuclear war, the renunciation of the use of force in international relations and the settlement of international disputes by peaceful means on the basis of the Charter of the United Nations;

4. Appeals to all States and international organizations to do their utmost to assist in implementing the right of peoples to peace through the adoption of appropriate measures at both the national and the international level.

SEE ALSO Declaration concerning Essentials of Peace; Declaration on the Preparation of Societies for Life in Peace; Human Rights and Peace; Proclamation of the International Year of Peace.

DECLARATION ON THE RIGHTS OF DEAF-BLIND PERSONS (1977).

On 9 May 1979, the UN Economic and Social Council took note (resolution 1979/24) of the Declaration on the Rights of Deaf-Blind Persons, which had been adopted by the Helen Keller World Conference on Services to Deaf-Blind Youths and Adults on 16 September 1977, and drew it to the attention of the UN General Assembly as part of the documentation in connection with the International Year for Disabled Persons. The text, annexed to Council resolution 1979/24, is as follows:

Article 1. Every deaf-blind person is entitled to enjoy the universal rights that are guaranteed to all people by the Universal Declaration of Human Rights and the rights provided for all disabled persons by the Declaration on the Rights of Disabled Persons.

Article 2. Deaf-blind persons have the right to expect that their capabilities and their aspirations to lead a normal life within the community and their ability to do so shall be recognized and respected by all Governments, administrators, educational and rehabilitation personnel and the general public.

Article 3. Deaf-blind persons have the right to receive the best possible medical treatment and care for the restoration of sight and hearing and the services required to utilize remaining sight and hearing, including the provision of the most effective optical and hearing aids, speech training, when appropriate, and other forms of rehabilitation intended to secure maximum independence.

Article 4. Deaf-blind persons have the right to economic security to ensure a satisfactory standard of living and the

right to secure work commensurate with their capabilities and abilities or to engage in other meaningful tasks, for which the requisite education and training shall be provided.

Article 5. Deaf-blind persons shall have the right to lead independent lives as integrated members of the family and community, including the right to live on their own or to marry and raise a family. Where a deaf-blind person lives within a family, the greatest possible support shall be provided to the whole family unit by the appropriate authorities. If institutional care is advisable, it shall be provided in such surroundings and under such conditions that it resembles normal life as closely as possible.

Article 6. Deaf-blind persons shall have the right, and at no cost, to the services of an interpreter with whom they can communicate effectively to maintain contact with others and with the environment.

Article 7. Deaf-blind persons shall have the right to current news, information, reading matter and educational material in a medium and form which they can assimilate. Technical devices that could serve to this end shall be provided and research in this area shall be encouraged.

Article 8. Deaf-blind persons shall have the right to engage in leisure-time recreational activities, which shall be provided for their benefit, and the right and opportunity to organize their own clubs or associations for self-improvement and social betterment.

Article 9. Deaf-blind persons shall have the right to be consulted on all matters of direct concern to them and to legal advice and protection against improper abridgement of their rights due to their disabilities.

For purposes of implementation of the Declaration on the Rights of Deaf-Blind Persons, the definition of deaf-blind persons is as follows:

"Persons who have substantial visual and hearing losses such that the combination of the two causes extreme difficulty in pursuit of educational, vocational, avocational, or social skills."

SEE ALSO Tallinn Guidelines for Action on Human Resources. . . .

DECLARATION ON THE RIGHTS OF DISABLED PERSONS (1975).

In proclaiming the principles set out in this declaration, the UN General Assembly recommended that all member States bear them in mind in establishing their policies, plans, and programs. In 1976, the assembly proclaimed the year 1981 as the International Year of Disabled Persons; and in 1982, it adopted a World Programme for Action Concerning Disabled Persons.

The declaration was adopted by the General Assembly on 9 December 1975 (resolution 3447 [XXX]). The text, annexed to the resolution, is as follows:

The General Assembly,

Mindful of the pledge made by Member States, under the Charter of the United Nations; to take joint and separate action in co-operation with the Organization to promote higher standards of living, full employment and conditions of economic and social progress and development,

Reaffirming its faith in human rights and fundamental freedoms and in the principles of peace, of the dignity and worth of the human person and of social justice proclaimed in the Charter,

Recalling the principles of the Universal Declaration of Human Rights, the International Covenants on Human Rights, the Declaration of the Rights of the Child and the Declaration on the Rights of Mentally Retarded Persons, as well as the standards already set for social progress in the constitutions, conventions, recommendations and resolutions of the International Labour Organisation, the United Nations Educational, Scientific and Cultural Organization, the World Health Organization, the United Nations Children's Fund and other organizations concerned,

Recalling also Economic and Social Council resolution 1921 (LVIII) of 6 May 1975 on the prevention of disability and the rehabilitation of disabled persons,

Emphasizing that the Declaration on Social Progress and Development has proclaimed the necessity of protecting the rights and assuring the welfare and rehabilitation of the physically and mentally disadvantaged,

Bearing in mind the necessity of preventing physical and mental disabilities and of assisting disabled persons to develop their abilities in the most varied fields of activities and of promoting their integration as far as possible in normal life,

Aware that certain countries, at their present stage of development, can devote only limited efforts to this end,

Proclaims this Declaration on the Rights of Disabled Persons and calls for national and international action to ensure that it will be used as a common basis and frame of reference for the protection of these rights:

1. The term "disabled person" means any person unable to ensure by himself or herself, wholly or partly, the necessities of a normal individual and/or social life, as a result of a deficiency, either congenital or not, in his or her physical or mental capabilities.

2. Disabled persons shall enjoy all the rights set forth in this Declaration. These rights shall be granted to all disabled persons without any exception whatsoever and without distinction or discrimination on the basis of race, colour, sex, language, religion, political or other opinions, national or social origin, state of wealth, birth or any other situation applying either to the disabled person himself or herself or to his or her family.

3. Disabled persons have the inherent right to respect for their human dignity. Disabled persons, whatever the origin, nature and seriousness of their handicaps and disabilities, have the same fundamental rights as their fellow-citizens of the same age, which implies first and foremost the right to enjoy a decent life, as normal and full as possible.

4. Disabled persons have the same civil and political rights as other human beings; paragraph 7 of the Declaration on the Rights of Mentally Retarded Persons applies to any possible limitation or suppression of those rights for mentally disabled persons.

5. Disabled persons are entitled to the measures designed to enable them to become as self-reliant as possible.

6. Disabled persons have the right to medical, psychological and functional treatment, including prosthetic and orthetic appliances, to medical and social rehabilitation, education, vocational training and rehabilitation, aid, counselling, placement services and other services which will enable them to develop their capabilities and skills to the maximum and will hasten the process of their social integration or reintegration.

7. Disabled persons have the right to economic and social security and to a decent level of living. They have the right, according to their capabilities, to secure and retain employment or to engage in a useful, productive and remunerative occupation and to join trade unions.

8. Disabled persons are entitled to have their special needs taken into consideration at all stages of economic and social planning.

9. Disabled persons have the right to live with their families or with foster parents and to participate in all social, creative or recreational activities. No disabled person shall be subjected, as far as his or her residence is concerned, to differential treatment other than that required by his or her condition or by the improvement which he or she may derive therefrom. If the stay of a disabled person in a specialized establishment is indispensable, the environment and living conditions therein shall be as close as possible to those of the normal life of a person of his or her age.

10. Disabled persons shall be protected against all exploitation, all regulations and all treatment of a discriminatory, abusive or degrading nature.

11. Disabled persons shall be able to avail themselves of qualified legal aid when such aid proves indispensable for the protection of their persons and property. If judicial proceedings are instituted against them, the legal procedure applied shall take their physical and mental condition fully into account.

12. Organizations of disabled persons may be usefully consulted in all matters regarding the rights of disabled persons.

13. Disabled persons, their families and communities shall be fully informed, by all appropriate means, of the rights contained in this Declaration.

SEE ALSO *Disability; Tallinn Guidelines for Action on Human Resources. . . .*

DECLARATION ON THE RIGHTS OF MENTALLY RETARDED PERSONS (1971).

In adopting this declaration, the UN General Assembly drew international attention to the necessity of assisting mentally retarded persons to develop their abilities in various fields and to promote their integration as far as possible into normal life.

The declaration was adopted by the General Assembly on 20 December 1971 (resolution 2856 [XXVI]). The text, annexed to the resolution, is as follows:

The General Assembly,

Mindful of the pledge of the States Members of the United Nations under the Charter to take joint and separate action in co-operation with the Organization to promote higher standards of living, full employment and conditions of economic and social progress and development,

Reaffirming faith in human rights and fundamental freedoms and in the principles of peace, of the dignity and worth of the human person and of social justice proclaimed in the Charter,

Recalling the principles of the Universal Declaration of

Human Rights, the International Covenants on Human Rights, the Declaration of the Rights of the Child and the standards already set for social progress in the constitutions, conventions, recommendations and resolutions of the International Labour Organisation, the United Nations Educational, Scientific and Cultural Organization, the World Health Organization, the United Nations Children's Fund and other organizations concerned,

Emphasizing that the Declaration on Social Progress and Development has proclaimed the necessity of protecting the rights and assuring the welfare and rehabilitation of the physically and mentally disadvantaged,

Bearing in mind the necessity of assisting mentally retarded persons to develop their abilities in various fields of activities and of promoting their integration as far as possible in normal life,

Aware that certain countries, at their present stage of development, can devote only limited efforts to this end,

Proclaims this Declaration on the Rights of Mentally Retarded Persons and calls for national and international action to ensure that it will be used as a common basis and frame of reference for the protection of these rights:

1. The mentally retarded person has, to the maximum degree of feasibility, the same rights as other human beings.

2. The mentally retarded person has a right to proper medical care and physical therapy and to such education, training, rehabilitation and guidance as will enable him to develop his ability and maximum potential.

3. The mentally retarded person has a right to economic security and to a decent standard of living. He has a right to perform productive work or to engage in any other meaningful occupation to the fullest possible extent of his capabilities.

4. Whenever possible, the mentally retarded person should live with his own family or with foster parents and participate in different forms of community life. The family with which he lives should receive assistance. If care in an institution becomes necessary, it should be provided in surroundings and other circumstances as close as possible to those of normal life.

5. The mentally retarded person has a right to a qualified guardian when this is required to protect his personal well-being and interests.

6. The mentally retarded person has a right to protection from exploitation, abuse and degrading treatment. If prosecuted for any offence, he shall have a right to due process of law with full recognition being given to his degree of mental responsibility.

7. Whenever mentally retarded persons are unable, because of the severity of their handicap, to exercise all their rights in a meaningful way or it should become necessary to restrict or deny some or all of these rights, the procedure used for that restriction or denial of rights must contain proper legal safeguards against every form of abuse. This procedure must be based on an evaluation of the social capability of the mentally retarded person by qualified experts and must be subject to periodic review and to the right of appeal to higher authorities.

DECLARATION ON THE RIGHT TO DEVELOPMENT (1986).

Adopted after long study and some controversy, the declaration confirms the view of the international community that the RIGHT TO DEVELOPMENT is an inalienable human right "by virtue of which every human person and all peoples are entitled to participate in, contribute to and enjoy economic, social, cultural and political development, in which all human rights and fundamental freedoms can be fully realized."

The declaration was adopted by the UN General Assembly on 4 December 1986 (resolution 41/128). The text, annexed to that resolution, is as follows:

The General Assembly,

Bearing in mind the purposes and principles of the Charter of the United Nations relating to the achievement of international co-operation in solving international problems of an economic, social, cultural or humanitarian nature, and in promoting and encouraging respect for human rights and fundamental freedoms for all without distinction as to race, sex, language or religion,

Recognizing that development is a comprehensive economic, social, cultural and political process, which aims at the constant improvement of the well-being of the entire population and of all individuals on the basis of their active, free and meaningful participation in development and in the fair distribution of benefits resulting therefrom,

Considering that under the provisions of the Universal Declaration of Human Rights everyone is entitled to a social and international order in which the rights and freedoms set forth in that Declaration can be fully realized,

Recalling the provisions of the International Covenant on Economic, Social and Cultural Rights and the International Covenant on Civil and Political Rights,

Recalling further the relevant agreements, conventions, resolutions, recommendations and other instruments of the United Nations and its specialized agencies concerning the integral development of the human being, economic and social progress and development of all peoples, including those instruments concerning decolonization, the prevention of discrimination, respect for, and observance of, human rights and fundamental freedoms, the maintenance of international peace and security and the further promotion of friendly relations and co-operation among States in accordance with the Charter,

Recalling the right of peoples to self-determination, by virtue of which they have the right freely to determine their political status and to pursue their economic, social and cultural development,

Recalling further the right of peoples to exercise, subject to relevant provisions of both International Convenants on Human Rights, their full and complete sovereignty over all their natural wealth and resources,

Mindful of the obligation of States under the Charter to promote universal respect for, and observance of, human rights and fundamental freedoms for all without distinction of any kind such as race, colour, sex, language, religion, political or other opinion, national or social origin, property, birth or other status,

Considering that the elimination of the massive and flagrant violations of the human rights of the peoples and individuals affected by situations such as those resulting from colonialism, neo-colonialism, *apartheid*, all forms of racism and racial discrimination, foreign domination and occupation, aggression and threats against national sovereignty, national unity and territorial integrity and threats of war would contribute to the establishment of circumstances propitious to the development of a great part of mankind,

Concerned at the existence of serious obstacles to development, as well as to the complete fulfilment of human beings and of peoples, constituted, *inter alia,* by the denial of civil, political, economic, social and cultural rights, and considering that all human rights and fundamental freedoms are indivisible and interdependent and that, in order to promote development, equal attention and urgent consideration should be given to the implementation, promotion and protection of civil, political, economic, social and cultural rights and that, accordingly, the promotion of, respect for, and enjoyment of certain human rights and fundamental freedoms cannot justify the denial of other human rights and fundamental freedoms,

Considering that international peace and security are essential elements for the realization of the right to development,

Reaffirming that there is a close relationship between disarmament and development and that progress in the field of disarmament would considerably promote progress in the field of development and that resources released through disarmament measures should be devoted to the economic and social development and well-being of all peoples and, in particular, those of the developing countries,

Recognizing that the human person is the central subject of the development process and that development policy should therefore make the human being the main participant and beneficiary of development,

Recognizing that the creation of conditions favourable to the development of peoples and individuals is the primary responsibility of their States,

Aware that efforts to promote and protect human rights at the international level should be accompanied by efforts to establish a new international economic order,

Confirming that the right to development is an inalienable human right and that equality of opportunity for development is a prerogative both of nations and of individuals who make up nations,

Proclaims the following Declaration on the right to development:

Article 1. 1. The right to development is an inalienable human right by virtue of which every human person and all peoples are entitled to participate in, contribute to and enjoy economic, social, cultural and political development, in which all human rights and fundamental freedoms can be fully realized.

2. The human right to development also implies the full realization of the right of peoples to self-determination, which includes, subject to relevant provisions of both International Covenants on Human Rights, the exercise of their inalienable right to full sovereignty over all their natural wealth and resources.

Article 2. 1. The human person is the central subject of development and should be the active participant and beneficiary of the right to development.

2. All human beings have a responsibility for development, individually and collectively, taking into account the need for full respect of their human rights and fundamental freedoms as well as their duties to the community, which alone can ensure the free and complete fulfilment of the human being, and they should therefore promote and protect an appropriate political, social and economic order for development.

3. States have the right and the duty to formulate appropriate national development policies that aim at the constant improvement of the well-being of the entire population and of all individuals, on the basis of their active, free and meaningful participation in development and in the fair distribution of the benefits resulting therefrom.

Article 3. 1. States have the primary responsibility for the creation of national and international conditions favourable to the realization of the right to development.

2. The realization of the right to development requires full respect for the principles of international law concerning friendly relations and co-operation among States in accordance with the Charter of the United Nations.

3. States have the duty to co-operate with each other in ensuring development and eliminating obstacles to development. States should fulfil their rights and duties in such a manner as to promote a new international economic order based on sovereign equality, interdependence, mutual interest and co-operation among all States, as well as to encourage the observance and realization of human rights.

Article 4. 1. States have the duty to take steps, individually and collectively, to formulate international development policies with a view to facilitating the full realization of the right to development.

2. Sustained action is required to promote more rapid development of developing countries. As a complement to the efforts of developing countries effective international co-operation is essential in providing these countries with appropriate means and facilities to foster their comprehensive development.

Article 5. States shall take resolute steps to eliminate the massive and flagrant violations of the human rights of peoples and human beings affected by situations such as those resulting from *apartheid,* all forms of racism and racial discrimination, colonialism, foreign domination and occupation, aggression, foreign interference and threats against national sovereignty, national unity and territorial integrity, threats of war and refusal to recognize the fundamental right of peoples to self-determination.

Article 6. 1. All States should co-operate with a view to promoting, encouraging and strengthening universal respect for and observance of all human rights and fundamental freedoms for all without any distinction as to race, sex, language and religion.

2. All human rights and fundamental freedoms are indivisible and interdependent; equal attention and urgent consideration should be given to the implementation, promotion and protection of civil, political, economic, social and cultural rights.

3. States should take steps to eliminate obstacles to development resulting from failure to observe civil and political rights as well as economic, social and cultural rights.

Article 7. All States should promote the establishment, maintenance and strengthening of international peace and security and, to that end, should do their utmost to achieve general and complete disarmament under effective international control as well as to ensure that the resources released by effective disarmament measures are used for comprehensive development, in particular that of the developing countries.

Article 8. 1. States should undertake, at the national level, all necessary measures for the realization of the right to development and shall ensure, *inter alia,* equality of opportunity for all in their access to basic resources, education, health services, food, housing, employment and the fair distribution of income. Effective measures should be undertaken to ensure that women have an active role in the development process. Appropriate economic and social reforms should be made with a view to eradicating all social injustices.

2. States should encourage popular participation in all spheres as an important factor in development and in the full realization of all human rights.

Article 9. 1. All the aspects of the right to development set forth in this Declaration are indivisible and interdependent and each of them should be considered in the context of the whole.

2. Nothing in this Declaration shall be construed as being contrary to the purposes and principles of the United Nations, or as implying that any State, group or person has a right to engage in any activity or to perform any act aimed at the violation of the rights set forth in the Universal Declaration of Human Rights and in the International Covenants on Human Rights.

Article 10. Steps should be taken to ensure the full exercise and progressive enhancement of the right to development, including the formulation, adoption and implementation of policy, legislative and other measures at the national and international levels.

SEE ALSO *Declaration on Social Progress and Development.*

DECLARATION ON THE USE OF SCIENTIFIC AND TECHNOLOGICAL PROGRESS IN THE INTERESTS OF PEACE AND FOR THE BENEFIT OF MANKIND (1975).

The 1968 International Conference on Human Rights warned that new scientific discoveries and technological advances might soon endanger the enjoyment of certain human rights. In 1975, the UN General Assembly studied the impact of certain developments upon the right to health and the right to a clean environment and adopted the declaration reproduced below calling upon all States to prevent the use of scientific and technological developments from limiting or interfering with the enjoyment of human rights and fundamental freedoms.

The declaration was adopted by the General Assembly on 10 November 1975 (resolution 3384 [XXX]). The text, annexed to the resolution, is as follows:

The General Assembly,

Noting that scientific and technological progress has become one of the most important factors in the development of human society,

Taking into consideration that, while scientific and technological developments provide ever increasing opportunities to better the conditions of life of peoples and nations, in a number of instances they can give rise to social problems, as well as threaten the human rights and fundamental freedoms of the individual,

Noting with concern that scientific and technological achievements can be used to intensify the arms race, suppress national liberation movements and deprive individuals and peoples of their human rights and fundamental freedoms,

Also noting with concern that scientific and technological achievements can entail dangers for the civil and political rights of the individual or of the group and for human dignity,

Noting the urgent need to make full use of scientific and technological developments for the welfare of man and to neutralize the present and possible future harmful consequences of certain scientific and technological achievements,

Recognizing that scientific and technological progress is of great importance in accelerating the social and economic development of developing countries,

Aware that the transfer of science and technology is one of the principal ways of accelerating the economic development of developing countries,

Reaffirming the right of peoples to self-determination and the need to respect human rights and freedoms and the dignity of the human person in the conditions of scientific and technological progress,

Desiring to promote the realization of the principles which form the basis of the Charter of the United Nations, the Universal Declaration of Human Rights, the International Covenants on Human Rights, the Declaration on the Granting of Independence to Colonial Countries and Peoples, the Declaration on Principles of International Law concerning Friendly Relations and Co-operation among States in accordance with the Charter of the United Nations, the Declaration on Social Progress and Development, and the Charter of Economic Rights and Duties of States,

Solemnly proclaims that:

1. All States shall promote international co-operation to ensure that the results of scientific and technological developments are used in the interests of strengthening international peace and security, freedom and independence, and also for the purpose of the economic and social development of peoples and the realization of human rights and freedoms in accordance with the Charter of the United Nations.

2. All States shall take appropriate measures to prevent the use of scientific and technological developments, particularly by the State organs, to limit or interfere with the enjoyment of the human rights and fundamental freedoms of the individual as enshrined in the Universal Declaration of Human Rights, the International Covenants on Human Rights and other relevant international instruments.

3. All States shall take measures to ensure that scientific and technological achievements satisfy the material and spiritual needs of all sectors of the population.

4. All States shall refrain from any acts involving the use of scientific and technological achievements for the purposes of violating the sovereignty and territorial integrity of other States, interfering in their internal affairs, waging aggressive wars, suppressing national liberation movements or pursuing a policy of racial discrimination. Such acts are not only a flagrant violation of the Charter of the United Nations and principles of international law, but constitute an inadmissible distortion of the purposes that should guide scientific and technological developments for the benefit of mankind.

5. All States shall co-operate in the establishment, strengthening and development of the scientific and technological capacity of developing countries with a view to accelerating the realization of the social and economic rights of the peoples of those countries.

6. All States shall take measures to extend the benefits of

science and technology to all strata of the population and to protect them, both socially and materially, from possible harmful effects of the misuse of scientific and technological developments, including their misuse to infringe upon the rights of the individual or of the group, particularly with regard to respect for privacy and the protection of the human personality and its physical and intellectual integrity.

7. All States shall take the necessary measures, including legislative measures, to ensure that the utilization of scientific and technological achievements promotes the fullest realization of human rights and fundamental freedoms without any discrimination whatsoever on grounds of race, sex, language or religious beliefs.

8. All States shall take effective measures, including legislative measures, to prevent and preclude the utilization of scientific and technological achievements to the detriment of human rights and fundamental freedoms and the dignity of the human person.

9. All States shall, whenever necessary, take action to ensure compliance with legislation guaranteeing human rights and freedoms in the conditions of scientific and technological developments.

SEE ALSO Science and Technology; Scientific and Technological Developments: Effects on Human Rights; Scientific and Technological Developments: UN University Study; UNESCO Agreement on the Importation of Educational, Scientific and Cultural Materials and protocol.

DEFENSE FOR CHILDREN INTERNATIONAL. An international non-governmental organization in consultative status (Roster) with the UN Economic and Social Council and the Council of Europe, Defence for Children International was founded in Geneva, Switzerland, as one of the initiatives of the International Year of the Child (1979). DCI has grown to encompass 19 affiliated national sections, including sections in the United Kingdom, the United States of America, France, Finland, Mexico, Colombia, the Netherlands, Italy, and Argentina and has 3,000 indiavidual members in 51 countries. DCI fosters awareness about, and solidarity around, children's rights situations, issues, and initiatives throughout the world; seeks to promote and implement the most effective means of securing the protection of these rights in concrete situations, from both a preventative and a curative standpoint; and is one of the principal advocates of a proposed UN Convention on the Rights of the Child. Members of its staff assisted working groups drafting the standard minimum rules for the protection of juveniles deprived of their liberty. In recent years, DCI has submitted numerous statements on the violations of children's rights to the UN Center for Human Rights, paticularly concerning children in prison, child labor, child prostitution, and trafficking and sale of children. It has publicized specific cases of violations; has undertaken action-

oriented investigations and taken direct action in situations involving violations of the rights of specific groups of children; has monitored and evaluated the implementation of accepted children's rights; and has worked for improved international standards in this field.

DCI has an extensive publication program, with each national section publishing individual reports and studies on a national and international scope. Among the publications of the parent organization are *International Children's Rights Monitor; Children in Prison;* and *Child Labour: A Threat to Health and Development.*

Defense for Children International. Address: P.O. 88, CH–1211 Geneva 20, Switzerland. Telephone: 41–22–34–05–58. Telex: 289-925-dci-ch. Secretary-General: Per Tegmo.

DEMOCRATIC KAMPUCHEA. *SEE Cambodia.*

DEMOCRATIC YEMEN. *SEE Yemen.*

DENMARK. The Kingdom of Denmark is a country in northern Europe, between the North Sea and the Baltic. Jutland, the peninsular portion of the country, is joined to the European continent by a border with the Federal Republic of Germany. The country also includes the Faroe Islands, Greenland, and 406 smaller islands. Invaded and occupied by German forces in 1940, Denmark was liberated by British troops in May 1945 and became a member of the United Nations the same year. Its population is estimated by the UN (1990) to be 5,120,000. Ethnic groups include Danes, Eskimos, Faroese, and Germans; however, ethnicity is not registered by the government. Languages commonly used include Danish, English, German, Faroese, and Greenlandic. Christianity (Evangelical Lutheran, 97%) is the predominant religion, Literacy is estimated at 99%.

The government (1990) took the form of a monarchy. Under the 1953 constitution, the sovereign presides over the cabinet and appoints the prime minister. Legislative authority is exercised jointly by the sovereign and the 179-member *Folketing,* or Parliament, members of which are elected by popular vote for terms of four years. Political parties include the Conservative People's Party, the Socialist People's Party, the Liberal Party, the Radical Liberal Party, the Centre Democrats, the Progress Party, Common Cause, the Christian People's Party, and the Left-wing Socialists.

Serfdom was abolished in Denmark in 1788. During the 19th century, Denmark was transformed from a country of poor peasants to a nation of the most prosperous farmers in Europe, mainly because agricultural workers were taught in "folk schools" to specialize in dairy products. Economic recovery was more rapid in Denmark than in the rest of Europe after World War II, and thousands of immigrants flocked to the country in search of employment. By 1973, when a general recession and high unemployment reduced the need for foreign workers, Denmark imposed a ban on immigration. Since then, residence and work permits are issued only to aliens satisfying certain requirements established by law, with priority accorded to nationals of other Nordic countries and to those of member States of the European Economic Community. This practice has been characterized by some as a subtle form of discrimination against would-be immigrants from other countries.

Once admitted, immigrants enjoy largely the same rights as Danish citizens. After three years' residence, they may vote in local government elections. They are not, however, entitled to vote in elections for the *Folketing*. It is a main principle of immigration policy that problems encountered by immigrants should be dealt with, at both the central and the local government level, by the same authorities as those handling the rest of the population. At the central government level, elements of the immigration policy are coordinated by a special ministerial committee.

Demands for even stricter control of immigration were a factor in the general election held in 1981, which paved the way for Poul Schülter to become premier in 1982. Further disputes over immigration and general economic policies led to elections in 1988 in which Schülter's position was confirmed by a narrow margin.

Territories. Denmark administers two offshore territories: the Faeroe Islands and Greenland.

As regards the Faeroe Islands, there are 21 of them in the North Atlantic, near the Shetland Islands. They joined Denmark voluntarily in 1386 and, since 1948, have enjoyed home rule and send two members to the *Folketing*.

As regards Greenland, which became part of Denmark in 1953 and has enjoyed home rule since 1979, two human rights problems have caused concern.

Denmark's right to exploit Greenland's vast mineral resources has been challenged on the ground that the right to such exploitation is inherent in the right of the peoples of Greenland to self-determination as formulated in article 1 of both International Covenants on Human Rights. One point of view is that Greenlanders are not "people" in the legal sense

of the covenants; another is that they exercised their right to self-determination in 1953 by opting to make the island an integral part of Denmark.

The question of formal recognition by Denmark of the language of Greenland is another item of contention: Greenlanders conceive of their language as an integral part of their unique identity which deserves recognition and preservation; Danish authorities point out that Danish is the only linguistic link between Greenland's population and the rest of the world and that the major part of higher education can only take place in Danish-speaking universities. As a compromise, the Greenlandic Home Rule Act provides for thorough teaching of Danish as well as Greenlandic.

DENMARK: CONSTITUTION. The Danish Constitutional Act of 5 June 1953 includes the following provisions (articles 66–87) specifically relating to human rights and fundamental freedoms:

The Established Church; Other Religious Bodies
Part VII

Article 66. The constitution of the Established Church shall be laid down by statute.

Article 67. Citizens shall be at liberty to form congregations for the worship of God in a manner according with their convictions, provided that nothing contrary to good morals or public order shall be taught or done.

Article 68. No one shall be liable to make personal contributions to any denomination other then the one to which he adheres.

Article 69. Rules for religious bodies dissenting from the Established Church shall be laid down by statute.

Article 70. No person shall by reason of his creed or descent be deprived of access to the full enjoyment of civic and political rights, nor shall he for such reasons escape compliance with any common civic duty.

Right of Personal Liberty
Part VIII

Article 71. (1) Personal liberty shall be inviolable. No Danish subject shall, in any manner whatsoever, be deprived of his liberty because of his political or religious convictions or because of his descent.

(2) A person shall be deprived of his liberty only where this is warranted by law.

(3) Any person who is taken into custody shall be brought before a judge within twenty-four hours. Where the person taken into custody cannot be immediately released, the judge shall decide, in an order to be given as soon as possible and at the latest within three days, stating the grounds, whether the person taken into custody shall be committed to prison; and in cases where he can be released on bail, shall also determine the nature and amount of such bail. This provision may be departed from by statute as far as Greenland is concerned, if for local considerations such departure may be deemed necessary.

(4) The pronouncement of the judge may be at once sep-

arately appealed against to a higher court of justice by the person concerned.

(5) No person shall be remanded in custody for an offence which can involve only punishment by fine or mitigated imprisonment *(hæftet)*.

(6) Outside criminal procedure, the legality of deprivation of liberty not executed by order of a judicial authority, and not warranted by legislation relating to aliens, shall at the request of the person so deprived of his liberty, or the request of any person acting on his behalf, be brought before the ordinary courts of justice or other judicial authority for decision. Rules governing this procedure shall be provided by statute.

(7) The persons referred to in subsection (6) shall be under supervision by a board set up by the Folketing, to which board the persons concerned shall be permitted to apply.

Article 72. The dwelling shall be inviolable. House search, seizure and examination of letters and other papers, or any breach of the secrecy that shall be observed in postal, telegraph, and telephones matters, shall not take place except under a judicial order, unless particular exception is warranted by statue.

Private Property; Freedom of Business

Article 73. (1) The right of property shall be inviolable. No person shall be ordered to surrender his property except where required in the public interest. It shall be done only as provided by statue and against full compensation.

(2) Where a Bill has been passed relating to the expropriation of property, one-third of the members of the Folketing may, within three weekdays, from the final passing of such Bill, demand that it shall not be presented for the Royal Assent until new elections to the Folketing have been held and the Bill has again been passed by the Folketing assembling thereafter.

(3) Any question of the legality of an act of expropriation, and the amount of compensation, may be brought before the courts of justice. The hearing of issues relating to the amount of the compensation may by statute be referred to courts of justice established for such purpose.

Article 74. Any restraint on the free and equal access to trade, which is not based on the public interest, shall be abolished by statute.

Article 75. (1) In order to advance the public interest, efforts shall be made to guarantee work for every able-bodied citizen on terms that will secure his existence.

(2) Any person unable to support himself or his dependants shall, where no other person is responsible for his or their maintenance, be entitled to receive public assistance, provided that he shall comply with the obligations imposed by statute in such respect.

Article 76. All children of school age shall be entitled to free instruction in primary schools. Parents or guardians making their own arrangements for their children or wards to receive instruction equivalent to the general primary school standard shall not be obliged to have their children or wards taught in a publicly provided school.

Freedom of Speech, Association and Assembly

Article 77. Any person shall be at liberty to publish his ideas in print, in writing, and in speech, subject to his being held responsible in a court of law. Censorship and other preventive measures shall never again be introduced.

Article 78. (1) Citizens shall, without previous permission, be free to form associations for any lawful purpose.

(2) Associations employing violence, or aiming at the attainment of their object by violence, by instigation to violence, or by similar punishable influence on persons holding other views, shall be dissolved by court judgment.

(3) No association shall be dissolved by any government measure; but an association may be temporarily prohibited, provided that immediate proceedings be taken for its dissolution.

(4) Cases relating to the dissolution of political associations may, without special permission, be brought before the Supreme Court of Justice of the Realm.

(5) The legal effects of the dissolution shall be determined by statute.

Article 79. Citizens shall, without previous permission, be at liberty to assemble unarmed. The police shall be entitled to be present at public meetings. Open-air meetings may be prohibited when it is feared that they may constitute a danger to the public peace.

Article 80. In the event of riots the armed forces may not take action, unless attacked, until after the crowd has three times been called upon to disperse in the name of the King and the law and such warning has gone unheeded.

Military Service: Abolition of the Privileges of Rank

Article 81. Every male person able to bear arms shall be liable with his person to contribute to the defence of his country under such rules as are laid down by statute.

Article 82. The right of municipalities to manage their own affairs independently, under State supervision, shall be laid down by statute.

Article 83. All legislative privileges attaching to nobility, title, and rank shall be abolished.

Article 84. No fiefs, estates tail in land, or estates tail in personal property shall in future be created.

Article 85. The provisions of sections 71, 78, and 79 shall be applicable only to the defence forces, subject to such limitations as reconsequential to the provisions of military laws.

Part IX

Article 86. The age qualification for local government electors and congregational council electors shall be that applying at any time to Folketing electors. In respect of the Faroe Islands and Greenland, the age qualification for local government electors and congregational council electors shall be as may be provided for by statute, or determined in accordance with statute.

Article 87. Citizens of Iceland who enjoy equal rights with citizens of Denmark under the Danish-Icelandic Union (Abolition), etc., Act, shall continue to enjoy the rights of Danish citizenship under the provisions of the Constitutional Act.

DEROGATION. Article 4 of the INTERNATIONAL COVENANT ON CIVIL AND POLITICAL RIGHTS provides that:

1. In time of public emergency which threatens the life of the nation and the existence of which is officially proclaimed, the States Parties to the present Covenant may take measures derogating from their obligations under the present Covenant to the extent strictly required by the exi-

gencies of the situation, provided that such measures are not inconsistent with their other obligations under international law and do not involve discrimination solely on the ground of race, colour, sex, language, religion or social origin.

2. No derogation from articles 6, 7, 8 (paragraphs 1 and 2), 11, 15, 16 and 18 may be made under this provision.

3. Any State Party to the present Covenant availing itself of the right of derogation shall immediately inform the other States Parties to the present Covenant, through the intermediary of the Secretary-General of the United Nations, of the provisions from which it has derogated and of the reasons by which it was actuated. A further communication shall be made, through the same intermediary, on the date on which it terminates such derogation.

Some provisions of the covenant (for example, articles 19, 21, and 22) explicitly permit restrictions of particular rights or freedoms to be imposed by law when necessary for such purposes as the protection of national security, public safety, public order, public health or morals, or the rights and freedoms of others.

Under article 4, paragraph 1, the only situation in which a State party may legitimately impose further restrictions on the enjoyment of human rights and fundamental freedoms is the existence of a "state of public emergency which threatens the life of the nation and the existence of which has been publicly proclaimed."

Under article 4, paragraph 2, no derogations whatsoever may be made, even during a period of public emergency, with regard to the rights and freedoms set out in the following articles:

Article 6, on the right to life;
Article 7, on the prohibition of torture and cruel, inhuman or degrading treatment or punishment;
Article 8, para. 1 and 2, on the prohibition of slavery, the slave trade, and other forms of servitude;
Article 11, on contractual obligations;
Article 15, on the prohibition of retroactive application of penal law;
Article 16, on recognition as a person before the law; and
Article 18, on freedom of thought, conscience and religion.

The rights listed above are sometimes referred to as "basic" human rights.

Under article 4, paragraph 3, any State party availing itself of the right of derogation is required to inform other States parties immediately of the provisions from which it has abrogated and the reasons for its action and to inform them later of the date on which it terminates such derogation.

The HUMAN RIGHTS COMMITTEE adopted the following comment on article 4 at its 13th session, held at the United Nations office in Geneva from 13 to 31 July 1981 (UN Doc. A/36/40, chap. VII, general comment 5 [13], para. 1–3):

Article 4 of the Covenant has posed a number of problems for the Committee when considering reports from some states parties. When a public emergency which threatens the life of a nation arises and it is officially proclaimed, a State party may derogate from a number of rights to the extent strictly required by the situation. The State party, however, may not derogate from certain specific rights and may not take discriminatory measures on a number of grounds. The State party is also under no obligation to inform the other States parties immediately, through the Secretary-General, of the derogations it has made including the reasons therefor and the date on which the derogations are terminated.

States parties have generally indicated the mechanism provided in their legal systems for the declaration of a state of emergency and the applicable provisions of the law governing derogations. However, in the case of a few States which had apparently derogated from Covenant rights, it was unclear not only whether a state of emergency had been officially declared but also whether rights from which the Covenant allows no derogation had in fact not been derogated from and further whether the other States parties had been informed of the derogations and of the reasons for the derogations.

The Committee holds the view that measures taken under article 4 are of an exceptional and temporary nature and may only last as long as the life of the nation concerned is threatened and that, in times of emergency, the protection of human rights becomes all the more important, particularly those rights from which no derogations can be made. The Committee also considers that it is equally important for States parties, in times of public emergency, to inform the other States parties of the nature and extent of the derogations they have made and of the reasons therefor and, further, to fulfil their reporting obligations under article 40 of the Covenant by indicating the nature and extent of each right derogated from together with the relevant documentation.

In resolution 43/114 adopted on 8 December 1988, the UN General Assembly stressed the importance of avoiding the erosion of human rights by derogation and underlined the necessity of strict observance of the agreed conditions and procedures for derogation under article 4 of the International Covenant on Civil and Political Rights, bearing in mind the need for States parties to provide the fullest possible information during STATES OF EMERGENCY, so that the justification for and appropriateness of measures taken in these circumstances can be assessed.

DETENTION: ADMINISTRATIVE. This practice, whereby individuals may be detained or interned by the administrative authorities, without charge or trial by an independent judicial body and without any protection for their human rights, is in wide use in many countries, including some which regard themselves as democratic.

A preliminary examination of the situation relating to administrative detention was undertaken by the **SUB-COMMISSION ON PREVENTION OF DISCRIMINATION AND PROTECTION OF MINORITIES** at its 1985 session. At that time, it requested (decision 1985/110) one of its members, Mr. Louis Joinet (France), to prepare an explanatory paper on the subject. That paper (UN Doc. E/CN.4/Sub.2/1987/16) and an analysis of the legal features of administrative detention prepared later (UN Doc. E/CN.4/Sub.2/1988/12) were considered by the sub-commission at its 1988 session.

In the explanatory paper, Mr. Joinet listed the primary purposes of administrative detention as follows: (1) prevention (or suppression) of serious disturbances of public order and security of the State; (2) immigration control and expulsion of foreigners and surveillance of their political activities; (3) disciplinary measures; (4) medical-social measures (against drug addicts, the insane, etc.); (5) measures to combat social adjustment; and (6) measures to protect civilian populations in time of war.

In the analysis of legal issues, he proposed that the study should not deal with matters of detention already under consideration by the sub-commission, such as the situation of the mentally ill, the situation of "prisoners of opinion," or the question of administrative detention under a state of emergency, but should cover four categories of administrative detention as follows: (a) administrative detention connected with the prevention (or suppression) of serious disturbances of public order including, in case of war, internment in the interest of civilian populations pursuant to article 42 of the fourth **GENEVA CONVENTION;** (b) administrative detention connected with the status of **ALIENS,** *inter alia,* as it affects asylum-seekers and refugees; (c) administrative detention as a form of enforcement of certain disciplinary penalties; and (d) administrative detention affecting certain persons in a situation of great poverty or even social maladjustment.

The sub-commission requested Mr. Joinet (decision 1988/110) to prepare a final report for consideration at its 1989 session, based on replies to a questionnaire sent to all governments, specialized agencies, regional intergovernmental organizations, and concerned non-governmental organizations in consultative status.

The **COMMISSION ON HUMAN RIGHTS** also examined the explanatory paper, noted with concern (resolution 1988/45) that, in some cases, the administrative detention procedure is subject to abuse; and pointed out that, in order to prevent any abuse, such procedure must be applied in clearly defined conditions

laid down by national laws, in accordance with the norms of international law. It invited all governments, specialized agencies, and concerned international organizations to assist the special rapporteur in discharging his mandate by forwarding answers to the questionnaire sent them.

SEE ALSO *Arbitrary Arrest, Detention or Exile; Arrest, Detention and Abduction of International Civil Servants; Body of Principles for the Protection of All Persons under any Form of Detention or Imprisonment; Children: Detention; Imprisonment; Working Group on Detention.*

DETENTION: UN STAFF MEMBERS. At its 1980 session, the UN **COMMISSION ON HUMAN RIGHTS** expressed concern (resolution 31/XXXVI) at reports of infringements of the human rights of United Nations staff members and the abrogation of the rights conveyed to them under the Convention on the Privileges and Immunities of the United Nations. It appealed to member States to respect their obligations under that convention and under the **UNITED NATIONS CHARTER,** the **UNIVERSAL DECLARATION OF HUMAN RIGHTS** and the **INTERNATIONAL COVENANT ON CIVIL AND POLITICAL RIGHTS;** and requested the Secretary-General to use his good offices to ensure the full enjoyment of human rights and the enjoyment of the rights conveyed under the Convention on Privileges and Immunities, by United Nations staff members.

In 1986, the General Assembly deplored (resolution 41/205) the growing number of cases where the functioning, safety, and well-being of officials had been adversely affected, including cases of detention in Member States and abduction by armed groups and individuals, and the increasing number of cases in which the lives and well-being of officials had been placed in jeopardy during the exercise of their official functions.

In 1987, the **SUB-COMMISSION ON PREVENTION OF DISCRIMINATION AND PROTECTION OF MINORITIES** requested the Secretary-General (resolution 1987/21) to submit to it in 1988 "a detailed report on the situation of international civil servants and their families detained, imprisoned, missing or held in a country against their will, in order to enable the Sub-Commission to consider these cases in the light of the international instruments relating to human rights."

In response, the Secretary-General submitted to the sub-commission at its 1988 session a report (UN Doc. E/CN.4/Sub. 2/1988/17) in which he placed at the disposal of members of the sub-commission in his most recent report on the subject to the General Assembly (UN Doc. A/C.5/42/14), provided some additional information on recent developments, and analyzed the types of violations of human rights suffered by international civil servants. The analysis (Section III, para. 17–29) was as follows:

Types of Violations of Human Rights Suffered by International Civil Servants
A. Arbitrary Arrest and Detention

Most of the cases reported to the Secretary-General concern violations caused by the arrest and detention of staff members.

(a) *Legal Aspects.* When a staff member of the United Nations—whether internationally or locally recruited—is arrested or detained by government authorities, the Secretary-General has the right and the duty to find out the reasons for the arrest. Under the terms of the Charter of the United Nations (Article 105) and the Convention on the Privileges and Immunities of the United Nations (articles V and VI), all staff members are immune from legal process in respect of words spoken or written and all acts performed by them in their official capacity. As the Administrative Committee on Co-ordination pointed out in its report of 15 April 1980 (E/1980/34), on international co-operation and co-ordination in the United Nations system, "International organizations, which are the instrument of international co-operation, cannot fully discharge their duties unless they can count on a completely independent international civil service".

It follows that the United Nations is entitled to functional protection of its staff members. It is for the Secretary-General alone, and not for Member States, to determine whether or not an act by a staff member has been performed in his official capacity. To that end, he needs to learn the facts. He must be in a position to visit the staff member under arrest, to converse with him, to be apprised of the grounds for the arrest and the formal charges. He is entitled to assist the staff member in arranging legal counsel for his or her defence and to appear in legal proceedings to defend any United Nations interest affected by the arrest or detention. All these provisions are contained in a Memorandum on the United Nations legal rights when a staff member or other agent of the United Nations, or a member of their family, is arrested or detained (ST/AI/299, of 10 December 1982).

If it is established that the arrest or detention of a staff member is connected with his official duties, his right to immunity is invoked. If, on the other hand, it is found that the case is not connected with the person's official duties, the Secretary-General can and should waive immunity so that justice may take its course. In that case, the Secretary-General none the less ensures that the staff member under arrest and in detention is equitably treated and that due and proper procedures are followed.

(b) *Present Situation.* At the present time, for approximately 90 cases of detention the Secretary-General has still not been able fully to exercise his right of protection.

(c) *Conditions of Detention.* The Secretary-General's previous report (A/C.5/42/14) describes the ill-treatment inflicted on some staff members in the course of detention and the fact that, despite the Secretary-General's appeals, the authorities in the countries concerned have refused to allow the staff members to receive the necessary care.

All too often, the visiting rights, both of representatives of the Secretary-General and of the families, are refused, trials, if any, are held *in camera* and counsel appointed by the United Nations cannot take part in them. The report in question also states that "in many of the cases reported by UNRWA and UNIFIL . . . the staff members concerned are being detained not for the alleged commission of any offence but merely as part of large groups of persons who happen to live in a particular locality or village".

B. Killings, Executions, Deaths in Detention

Over the past 15 years, according to the report submitted by the staff representatives to the Fifth Committee of the General Assembly in 1987 (A/C.5/42/37), 10 staff members have been killed, executed, assassinated, have died—or are presumed to have died—in detention in conditions that have never been clarified.

C. Disappearances

According to report A/C.5/42/37 by the staff representatives, 11 staff members are still reported missing. The oldest case dates back to 1976.

D. Ban on Leaving a Country

Sometimes, officials sent on mission or coming back from home leave are no longer authorized to return to their duty station. In most cases, after some time a letter of resignation—signed or unsigned by the staff member—reaches the Secretary-General, who has no assurance that the resignation is an act freely decided on by the staff member, since he cannot talk openly and directly with the staff member.

E. Violation of the Rights of the Families

The arbitrary arrest, death or disappearance of a staff member, in itself means that the human rights of the families are violated. Moreover, the person in question is often the one who supports the family and therefore the families may experience serious financial difficulties. In cases of arbitrary arrest, the United Nations generally continues to pay the staff member's salary.

The family of a UNESCO staff member, Eugene Soloviev, has been held in the USSR for eight years and the steps taken by the Secretary-General, the Director-General of UNESCO and the Staff Associations have not been successful in securing authorization by the country concerned for this staff member's wife and daughter to join him at his duty station.

Three children of a local staff member of the United Nations Truce Supervision Organization in Palestine (UNTSO) were arrested by the Israeli authorities. One of them was released after 25 days without any charge being brought against him. The other two have been charged.

The sub-commission, after examining the report, expressed (resolution 1988/9) its appreciation of the efforts of the Secretary-General and the heads of specialized agencies to defend the fundamental rights of staff members of the United Nations system, ensure their security, and protect their independence; and noted that some cases had been successfully resolved. At the same time, it was concerned that violations of human rights of staff members and the threats against their security and independence had increased and that 100 cases remained unresolved, and expressed its belief "that these violations of the fundamental rights of the United Nations system and these threats against their security and independence can only have negative effects on the implementation of the mandates of the organs and agencies of the United Nations system."

The sub-commission appealed to member States to respect and to ensure respect for the rights of UN staff members, and requested the Secretary-General to redouble his efforts to ensure the full respect of the rights of staff members as well as experts in the service of the United Nations system.

In taking action on this problem, over the objection of several of its members who contended that it did not fall within the sub-commission's mandate, the sub-commission was concerned in particular about the fate of one of its special rapporteurs, Mr. Dumitru Mazilu (Romania), who had been appointed at its 1985 session to prepare a report on human rights and youth. Mr. Mazilu had not attended the 1987 session of the sub-commission (no session was held in 1986), and the sub-commission had not received his report or established any personal contact with him.

The sub-commission also was influenced by data submitted by international non-governmental organization which indicated that hundreds of UN staff members had been detained, imprisoned, or "disappeared" since the UN was formed, and that 120 staff members were at that time in this category.

The sub-commission entrusted one of its members, Ms. Mary Concepción Bautista (Philippines), with the task of undertaking an examination of such violations of the rights of UN staff members, their families, and experts, and the repercussions of those violations on the functioning of United Nations organs and agencies. At the same time, it decided (decision 1988/102) to request the Secretary-General to bring to the attention of the government of Romania the sub-commission's urgent need to establish personal contact with Mr. Mazilu and to request the government to assist in locating him and facilitating a visit to him by a member of the sub-commission and a member of the secretariat to assist him in completing his study on human rights and youth, if he so wished.

The Secretary-General submitted an updated version of his report to the sub-commission to the 1989 session of the Commission on Human Rights, following consideration by the 1988 General Assembly of the question of respect for the privileges and immunities of officials of the United Nations and its specialized agencies and related organizations. After examining the report, the commission, on 6 March 1989, welcomed (resolution 1989/28) the sub-commission's decision to entrust one of its members with the task of examining violations of human rights of United Na-

tions staff members, their families and experts, as well as the repercussions of those violations on the functioning of United Nations organs and agencies. The commission appealed to member States to respect and to ensure respect for the rights of UN staff members and others acting under the authority of the United Nations, and of their families.

The commission requested member States (a) to allow medical teams to investigate cases in which the health of staff members, experts, and their families who are being detained reportedly has suffered, and to permit the necessary medical treatment to be made available, and (b) to provide adequate and prompt information concerning the arrest or detention of United Nations staff members and their families, and to grant the representative of the competent international organizations access to them without delay.

A preliminary report entitled "Protection of the Human Rights of United Nations Staff Members, Experts and Their Families," prepared by the special rapporteur (UN Doc. E/CN.4/Sub.2/1989/28) was presented to the sub-commission at its 1989 session. The report explored the background of the concern of the United Nations with the question, surveyed the available information, and concluded with a series of preliminary observations and recommendations.

The special rapporteur summarized her observations as follows (para. 59–64):

It is clear to the Special Rapporteur that the issue of respect for the privileges and immunities and basic human rights of United Nations staff members, experts and their families is a matter of crucial importance to the ability of the United Nations to function effectively and thus achieve its objectives of promoting world peace and respect for human rights. Confidence by Member States and the international community at large in the objectivity and impartiality of United Nations staff members and experts is essential to the capacity of the United Nations to function and, in turn, the objectivity and impartiality of the staff and United Nations experts depends on their being free from the fear of intimidations, pressures, and reprisals. This is, therefore, an important issue which merits the continued consideration by the Sub-Commission, Commission on Human Rights, the Economic and Social Council and the General Assembly.

The United Nations is now being called upon increasingly to carry out very delicate missions connected with the promotion of peace and self-determination. These missions themselves require the Secretariat to demonstrate complete objectivity and impartiality in circumstances of danger to United Nations officials. These new missions require more than ever that States scrupulously respect the privileges and immunities and basic human rights of staff members, experts and their families and refrain from subjecting them to threats, intimidation or reprisals. These are obligations which flow from the United Nations Chamber itself.

The Special Rapporteur notes that, in most of the cases

reported to her, the United Nations staff member concerned was involved [in] peace keeping or missions of humanitarian assistance to populations in particular distress; such humanitarian missions should receive the priority protection from States and others concerned.

The Special Rapporteur notes with concern that in a large number of cases reported by the UNRWA Staff Association, the staff members arrested were teachers, school instructors or others in the teaching profession or connected with schools.

The Special Rapporteur is constrained to state that the information she has received indicates that in the large majority of cases of detention, death or the disappearance of staff members, the States concerned have not responded adequately to the requests for information by the Staff Member's Organization nor have they provided the necessary assistance to that Organization. This has prevented or seriously hampered the efforts of the Organization to fulfill its responsibility to the staff members.

The Special Rapporteur further notes that the cases reported to her have required and continue to require the use of United Nations resources which, at this time of budget any restriction, could best be used for productive endeavours.

Her recommendations were as follows (para. 65–78):

A review of the information received by the Special Rapporteur shows that there are numerous specific international norms relating to the privileges and immunities of United Nations staff members, experts and their families and to the basic human rights which they should enjoy. The first matter, therefore, is to achieve effective co-operation with States in order to ensure respect for those norms. The Special Rapporteur notes the detailed procedures established by the Secretary-General concerning the reporting of incidents and the rapid intervention called for in that regard. The Special Rapporteur also notes the personal involvement of the Secretary-General and the head of organizations in seeking to protect the rights of staff members and experts and believes that to be an important element in preventing new cases and resolving outstanding cases. Thus, the Special Rapporteur can only welcome the appeal of the Commission on Human Rights in its resolution 1989/28 to Member States to respect and to ensure respect for the rights of staff members and others acting under the authority of the United Nations, and their families.

Respect for the privileges and immunities and the basic human rights of United Nations staff members, experts and their families in cases of arrest and detention can be facilitated by establishing immediate contact between United Nations representatives, and the staff member, expert or family member concerned and the provision of full information on the case. The suggestion put forward by the United Nations Development Programme that in order to enhance the safety and protection of international civil servants in terms of their functional immunity Member States should agree that access by the designated official or his representative to detained United Nations staff be granted within 24 hours of their arrest, and that a formal explanation for the arrest and detention be furnished through the designated official to the Secretary-General within 48 hours would be a good step in this direction. In this regard the Special Rapporteur again notes Commission on Human Rights resolution 1981/28 and in particular para-

graph 4 in which the Commission urged Member States, in accordance with the Body of Principles for the Protection of All Persons under Any Form of Detention or Imprisonment adopted by the General Assembly in resolution 43/173 of 9 December 1988, to provide adequate and prompt information concerning the arrest or detention of United Nations staff members and their families, and to grant the representative of the competent international organization access to them without delay. In this regard, the Special Rapporteur believes that provision should also be made for observers from the respective Organization to attend any trial or other judicial proceeding.

The Special Rapporteur believes that it would greatly assist the solution of cases at an early stage if all States would inform the Secretary-General explicitly of their acceptance of the above procedures. In addition, the Secretary-General could consider seeking a specific agreement to the above procedures in connection with the implementation of any decision to send United Nations personnel on peace-keeping or humanitarian missions. All such agreements should also cover explicitly locally hired staff.

The Special Rapporteur notes that the list of information which, in accordance with the Bulletin of the United Nations Secretary-General, should be contained in the required report to Headquarters on the detention of a staff member. These elements are:

(a) The name and nationality of the person arrested or detained, his or her employment status with and official function for the United Nations; for family members the family relationship must be given;

(b) The time, place and other circumstances of the arrest or detention;

(c) The legal expression or term used by the applicable local law to describe the arrest or detention;

(d) The legal grounds for the arrest or detention, including any charges against the person concerned;

(e) The name of the governmental agency, such as a court or an administrative authority, under whose authority the measure was taken;

(f) Whether a representative of the United Nations has been or will be given access to the person arrested or detained; in the affirmative, any request or other reaction from the person concerned shall also be conveyed;

(g) Whether consular protection and/or legal counsel is or will be available to the person arrested or detained; in the affirmative, the identity of these services shall be conveyed.

In addition to these elements the Special Rapporteur would suggest that information be included on the health of the person or persons under detention and on any specific measures which should be taken in that regard.

The Special Rapporteur shares the concern expressed by staff representatives about the support which the families of staff members, victims of violations of their human rights often need in their distressing circumstances and recommends that consideration be given to ways that assistance and support can be provided.

The Special Rapporteur recommends that the Sub-Commission, the Commission on Human Rights, the Economic and Social Council and the General Assembly energetically draw the attention of all Governments to the need to respect the privileges and immunities and basic human rights of United Nations staff members, experts and their family members and to the very serious impediment to the functioning of the organizations that the failure to respect these obligations represents. The above-mentioned bodies should call on the Governments or authorities involved in the reported cases to immediately provide all the information requested, to allow the Secretary-General to establish contact with the persons concerned without delay, and to release persons held without any lawful charge filed against them. Should such a charge be filed, the staff member or experts, or as the case may be the family member, should have the right to a speedy trial held in accordance with international human rights standards. In those cases of death or disappearance, the circumstances should be fully explained and any penal procedures which are warranted by the evidence should be initiated.

While most of the information submitted to the Special Rapporteur deals with the detention of staff members, the Special Rapporteur cannot overlook the important role played by experts in the work of the Organizations of the United Nations system. The skills of such experts are indispensable and their ability to contribute successfully to the work of the Organizations of the United Nations system requires the same independence and impartiality demanded of staff members which in turn requires that their priviledges, immunities and human rights be respected. The Special Rapporteur thus expresses her deepest concern at the plight of Mr. Dumitru Mazilu, Special Rapporteur on Human Rights and Youth. The letter he addressed to the Chairman of the Sub-Commission at its fortieth session indicated that he is willing and able to prepare a report and present it personally to the Sub-Commission. However, from that letter we also learn that he and his family are the subject of threats precisely because of his United Nations mandate. In the view of the Special Rapporteur this matters merits the serious concern of the Sub-Commission.

The Special Rapporteur recognizes the efforts made by the Secretary-General and Heads of Agencies to ensure respect for the privileges and immunities and basic human rights of staff members, experts and their family members and recommends that they continue and strengthen their efforts. Closer co-operation between the Secretary-General and Heads of Agencies and the staff associations could be an important element in improving respect for the privileges and immunities and human rights of staff, experts and their families. A focal point within each organization should be established for information on cases and to give impetus to action.

In those cases where results are not forthcoming, as has been decided by the Secretary-General and Heads of Agencies in the Administrative Committee on Co-ordination, a careful review of any United Nations programmes, except humanitarian programmes, in the area concerned should be undertaken. Consideration should be given to any other measures which might be taken to encourage compliance with international obligations in the field.

It would be helpful, in the Special Rapporteur's view, if the General Assembly and other policy-making organs concerned could be provided with more detailed information on each case, the efforts made in that regard by the organization concerned and the response of the competent authorities. The information provided to the Special Rapporteur by the FAO (see annex I) is a good example in this regard.

A number of matters contained in the documents submitted in connection with the preliminary report require further reflection and the Special Rapporteur looks forward to the views and suggestions of the Sub-Commission's members and all others interested in this question.

In looking forward to the preparation of the final report,

the Special Rapporteur is conscious of the need for more ample information and has the intention of appealing again for further information. One specific suggestion is that the United Nations open individual files on each staff member, expert or family affected by what might be a breach of their privileges and immunities and that the file contain as much information as possible, including the matters set out in the Secretary-General's Bulletin.

In cases of arrest and detention, detailed international human rights norms exist and it might well be helpful if all United Nations staff members and, in particular, the designated security officer charged with handling cases of detention would have available in readily accessible form a compilation of such norms relating to arrest, detention and trial.

On 1 September 1989, the sub-commission examined and took note (resolution 1989/30) of the preliminary report and expressed grave concern that a significant number of personnel in the service of the United Nations continued to be held captive or were otherwise unaccounted for. Conscious that these violations of the fundamental rights of staff members of the United Nations system, and these threats against their security and independence, can only have negative effects on the implementation of the mandates of the organs and agencies of the United Nations system, the sub-commission appealed again to member States to respect, and to ensure respect for, the rights of staff members and others acting under the authority of the United Nations, and their families, and requested the Secretary-General to redouble his efforts to ensure that the human rights and privileges and immunities of the United Nations staff members and their families are respected. In particular, it urged member States to allow medical teams to investigate cases in which the health of staff members and experts and their families who are being detained is reported to have suffered and to permit the necessary medical treatment to be made available; and called upon those States to provide adequate and prompt information concerning the arrest or detention of United Nations staff members and their families, and to grant the representative of the competent international organization access to them without delay.

On 2 March 1990, the Commission on Human Rights adopted a similar resolution (resolution 1990/30), in which it urged member States, in accordance with the **BODY OF PRINCIPLES FOR THE PROTECTION OF ALL PERSONS UNDER ANY FORM OF DETENTION OR IMPRISONMENT,** to provide adequate and prompt imformation concerning the arrest or detention of United Nations staff members, experts, and their families and to grant the representative of the competent international organization access to them without delay.

The commission requested the secretary-general to submit to it, at its 1991 session, an updated version of his earlier report on the situation of UN staff members, experts, and their families detained, imprisoned, missing, or held in a country against their will, including those cases which have been successfully settled since the earlier report.

SEE ALSO *Arrest, Detention and Abduction of International Civil Servants; Convention on the Prevention and Punishment of Crimes against Internationally Protected Persons; Special Rapporteurs: Privileges and Immunities.*

DISABILITY. The United Nations has been continuously concerned, since its establishment, with the situation of disabled persons. In 1976, the UN General Assembly proclaimed (resolution 31/123) the year 1981 to be the International Year of Disabled Persons; and in 1982 it adopted (resolution 37/52) the World Programme of Action concerning Disabled Persons and proclaimed (resolution 37/53) the period 1983–1992 the United Nations Decade for Disabled Persons.

In 1984, the assembly requested the UN secretary-general to convene (resolution 39/26) a meeting of experts, consisting largely of disabled persons, to evaluate the progress achieved at the mid-point of the decade. At its 1987 session, it received and considered the secretary-general's report (UN Doc. A/42/561) and the report of the "Global Meeting of Experts to Review the World Programme of Action concerning Disabled Persons at the Midpoint of the United Nations Decade of Disabled Persons" (UN Doc. CSDHA/DDP/GME/7) and requested the secretary-general (resolution 42/58) to obtain the comments of governments and of the intergovernmental and non-governmental organizations concerned on the recommendations made by the experts.

At its 1988 session, the assembly examined the report of the secretary-general (UN Doc. A/43/634), reaffirmed (resolution 43/98) the validity of the World Programme of Action and directed that, during the second half of the United Nations Decade of Disabled Persons, special emphasis should be placed on the equalization of opportunities for disabled persons. It urged member States to develop and implement national plans of action for this purpose, using a multi-sectoral, interdisciplinary approach, in consultation with organizations of disabled persons. At the same time, it recognized the need to launch a special global awareness and fund-raising campaign to give added momentum to the decade and welcomed the appointment by the secretary-general of a Special Representative for the Promotion of the United Nations Decade of Disabled Persons.

The assembly further invited the secretary-general and member States to involve disabled persons to a greater extent in UN programs and activities, to consider alternative structures to ensure that the issue of disability is accorded high visibility, and to develop the Disabled Persons Unit of the Centre for Social Development and Humanitarian Affairs as a specialized facilitating agent engaging the available resources of the UN system and relevant networks outside the United Nations.

Study of Human Rights and Disabled Persons. At the request of the UN Economic and Social Council (resolution 1984/26), the SUB-COMMISSION ON PREVENTION OF DISCRIMINATION AND PROTECTION OF MINORITIES (resolution 1984/20) appointed one of its members, Mr. Leandro Despouy (Argentina), to undertake an in-depth study of the relationship between human rights and disability and to include in the study consideration of and recommendations regarding human rights and humanitarian law violations that result in disability or have a particular impact on disabled persons; all forms of discrimination against disabled persons; *apartheid* as it relates to disability; institutionalization and institutional abuse; and economic, social, and cultural rights as they relate to disability. The sub-commission also requested the special rapporteur to include, on a preliminary basis, an outline of the topic of scientific experimentation as it relates to disabled persons.

The special rapporteur presented a preliminary report (UN Doc. E/CN.4/Sub.2/1985/32) to the sub-commission at its 1985 session and a progress report (UN Doc. E/CN.4/Sub.2/1988/11) to it in 1988. Between 1985 and 1988, he obtained information and suggestions from governments, various UN bodies, specialized agencies, regional organizations, and interested non-governmental organizations, particularly organizations of disabled persons. On the basis of the replies received, he drew attention in the progress report to such issues as (a) the objectives and focus of the study, (b) multilateral activities relating to the disabled, (c) national legislation and practices, and (d) activities of non-governmental organizations.

In particular, the special rapporteur considered problems he had encountered in defining the terms "disability" and "disabled persons" and in avoiding the perjorative connotation of the terms used in everyday language and in legal texts to refer to disability and disabled persons. He pointed out in the progress report (para. 56–65) that:

The definition of a "disabled person" varies considerably from one country to another. Within the same State it differs from one legislative sector to another. The concept of total or partial incapacity for work due to illness or accident appears as a universal criterion in systems of disability insurance and workers' compensation for industrial accidents, and it also appears to constitute the basis of all the legislation on the disabled in a number of countries. A number of States have stated that they accept the WHO definition, which is taken up in the World Programme of Action, and is based essentially on the concept of the abnormal exercise of an identifiable function. Some of the replies reveal a tendency to adopt broader concepts, which take into account the possibility of participating on an equal footing and in an independent manner in all spheres of the life of society, including—as is sometimes expressly stated—leisure and recreational activities. It remains to be determined how far these new concepts have permeated into the law, administrative practice and judicial decisions.

The diversity of definitions, together with shortcomings in survey techniques and certain problems arising from social attitudes of embarrassment *vis-à-vis* the disabled, combine to make it very difficult to produce reliable statistics on the number of disabled persons, the origin of their problems and changes in their numbers over time. Certain developing countries consider that the proportion of disabled persons in their total population—between 6 and 10 per cent—will increase in coming years.

Among the probable causes of disability, a number of Governments mentioned certain factors which appear to be connected with non-respect for human rights in the broad sense, although the Governments making the replies disclaim all responsibility in that respect. These factors include: underdevelopment and its corollaries, namely poverty, malnutrition, inadequate housing and lack of public health facilities; national and international armed conflicts, including clashes between ethnic or religious groups; shortcomings in health education and information; and social attitudes (traditional or new) of indifference and even cruelty towards vulnerable groups such as women and children in certain circumstances, immigrants, refugees and persons whose behaviour is unorthodox in one way or another.

Most of the replies recognized—at least by implication—the existence of prejudice and discrimination against the disabled, but few Governments put forward an analysis of the causes and forms of those practices. With regard to the causes, however, several respondents had the courage to draw attention to traditional attitudes of shame, superstitious fear and rejection of which several categories of the disabled persons still suffer. The Governments concerned are endeavouring to eradicate such attitudes. In a variety of socio-economic contexts where resources and jobs are in short supply, these traditional attitudes combine with more concrete motivations to exclude the disabled from the educational system and from vocational training, thus religating them to subbordinate and underpaid jobs or to the mass of the unemployed.

In order to combat these prejudices, a number of Governments, in co-operation with the associations concerned, have organized campaigns to promote awareness of the problems of the disabled among children, teachers, enterprises and the public at large, for example by instituting "disabled people's days".

The enactment of legislation to punish acts of discrimination appears to raise certain problems. In most countries, the law condemns all forms of discrimination in general terms and could therefore, in principle, make it possible to punish the unjust distinctions of which disabled persons are the victims. In practice, however, difficulties are often experienced when trying to ensure that the authorities and the courts apply these general laws to specific cases of disabled persons. Special legislative provisions also exist on discrimination against disabled persons in various fields (pensions, education, employment, etc.), but they appear to lack consistency and undoubtedly leave many legal loopholes. The advisability of adopting a single body of legislation to suppress all forms of discrimination against the disabled has been the subject of discussion in a number of countries. As pointed out above, some recent constitutions expressly condemn violations of the human rights of the disabled.

The replies contain detailed information on policies aimed at providing the disabled with the necessary help and services to enable them to benefit from the fullest possible enjoyment of human rights on a footing of equality with other citizens. In this regard States must first take a fundamental decision: whether, and to what extent, to provide for treatment of the disabled in institutions. The great majority of government replies are firmly opposed to treating committal to institutions as a primary strategy. Emphasis is placed on rehabilitation in the family and in the community, in order to promote to the maximum the integration of the disabled in the life of society. Committed to an institution, however, remains a last resort in cases specified by law which appear to be of an extremely serious nature, as when a seriously mentally disturbed person is convicted of a crime or when a medical examination and a social enquiry duly establish that the person concerned cannot be guaranteed a minimum level of well-being outside an institution. The Governments of a few developing countries have stated that, in the present circumstances, extreme poverty, over-population and the inadequate health conditions of the family and local environment leave the public authorities no option but to favour committal of the disabled to institutions. A number of replies refer to the abuses to which such committal can give rise, in particular against mentally handicapped persons, for example in the form of sterilization or castration, and contain a declaration of resolve to eradicate such abuses.

With regard to education and vocational training, considerable efforts are being made in most countries in three broad areas: ensuring the fullest possible integration of the disabled in the ordinary school system; training specialized teachers and advisers and making sure that the necessary equipment is available to enable the disabled to achieve the same level of education as the other pupils; and setting up specialized educational centres when the nature or gravity of the disability—for example blindness or deaf-and-dumbness—prevent those concerned from following ordinary classes. Some of the replies mention the "right" of disabled persons to educational materials and specialist teachers.

In certain countries, the authorities and the trade unions ensure close co-ordination between training centres for the disabled, government and enterprises with a view to assuring maximum opportunities for employment for the disabled. Minimum quotas of posts or the earmarking of jobs for the disabled seem to be increasingly resorted to for the benefit of disabled persons, at least in the public sector. Subsidies or tax concessions are granted to employers who comply with these guidelines.

Significant progress has also been observed with regard to measures taken or planned to facilitate access by the disabled to buildings and transport facilities, at least in the public sector.

The sub-commission examined the progress report at its 1988 session and requested the special rapporteur (resolution 1988/8) to continue his work and to submit a final report to its 1990 session.

The secretary-general, in his report to the 1989 session of the General Assembly (UN Doc. A/44/ 406/ rev. 1), analyzed the situation as regards the United Nations Decade of Disabled Persons and the World Program of Action concerning Disabled Persons in the following terms (para. 3):

The decade already in its seventh year, has not met the expectations of the international community nor, most important, those of disabled persons themselves. The political commitment of Member States, who adopted the World Programme of Action and proclaimed the Decade, continues to be expressed mainly through annual resolutions at intergovernmental bodies. However, without more national-level action, including policy decisions, planning and allocation of sufficient resources, the Decade will soon end without having accomplished its purpose. Governments, public and private sectors must work together to ensure progress in the implementation of the World Programme of Action.

In the report, the secretary-general presented an overview of the relevant activities of the international community, governments, and organizations, indicating important activities and programs being planned and implemented at all levels; but pointed out that "the implementation of the World Program of Action still requires increased planning activities and resource allocations as evidence of the political will to promote action on behalf of disabled persons."

After considering the report, the General Assembly reaffirmed (resolution 44/70) the validity of the World Program of Action concerning Disabled Persons and reiterated that, for the second half of the United Nations Decade of Disabled Persons, emphasis should be placed on the equalization of opportunities for such persons. It urged member States, intergovernmental organizations, and non-governmental organizations to translate into action the priorities for global activities and programs during the second half of the decade, and invited governments to improve the living conditions of disabled persons by encouraging professional experts, in particular disabled persons, in various aspects of rehabilitation and the equalization of opportunity, including the expertise of retired persons.

The assembly, further, called upon the secretary-general to draw to the attention of member States, national coordinating bodies, and concerned intergovernmental and non-governmental bodies the TALLINN GUIDELINES FOR ACTION ON HUMAN RESOURCES DEVELOPMENT IN THE FIELD OF DISABILITY, adopted by the International Meeting on Human Resources in the Field of Disability which had been convened at Tallinn, Estonian Soviet Socialist Republic, U.S.S.R., from 14 to 22 August 1989.

SEE ALSO Declaration on the Rights of Disabled Persons.

DISABLED PEOPLE'S INTERNATIONAL. An international non-governmental organization in consultative status with the UN Economic and Social Council (Category II), and with ILO, UNESCO, and the Council of Europe, DPI brings together organizations of disabled persons in 70 countries.

Founded in 1981, Disabled Peoples' International has viewed "Equalization of Opportunities" as one of its fundamental concepts. The "DPI Manifesto" defines equalization of opportunities as full participation for the world's disabled in the rights to neducation, rehabilitation, employment, economic security, and independent living; to participation in social, cultural, and political activities; and to influence the development of society. DPI pursues its goals principally through its cooperation with other organizations of the disabled and through its world congress (held every three years) and world council meeting (held annually). DPI publishes *Vox Nostra*.

Disabled People's International. Address: P.O. 36033, Reimersholmsgatan 9, S-100 71 Stockholm, Sweden. Telephone: (46–8) 84-03-35. Cable: DISINT Stockholm, Sweden. Fax: (46–8) 84-78-13. Telex: 8106001 DPISEC. Head of Secretariat: Jan Johnson.

DISAPPEARANCE OF PERSONS. In December 1978, the UN General Assembly first expressed concern (resolution 33/173) about reports reaching it from various parts of the world relating to enforced or involuntary disappearances of persons and requested the Commission on Human Rights to consider the question of "disappeared" persons with a view to making appropriate recommendations. The assembly called upon governments, in the event of reports of enforced or involuntary disappearances, to devote appropriate resources to searching for such persons and to undertake speedy and impartial investigations; to ensure that law enforcement and security authorities or organizations are fully accountable, especially in law, in the discharge of their duties, such accountability to include legal responsibility for unjustifiable excesses which might lead to enforced or involuntary disappearances and to other violations of human rights; to ensure that the human rights of all persons, including those subjected to any form of detention or imprisonment, are fully respected; and to cooperate with other governments, relevant United

Nations organs, specialized agencies, intergovernmental organizations, and humanitarian bodies in a common effort to search for, locate, or account for such persons in the event of reports of enforced or involuntary disappearances.

The Commission on Human Rights, in 1980, decided (resolution 20 [XXVI]) to establish the WORKING GROUP ON ENFORCED OR INVOLUNTARY DISAPPEARANCES, consisting of five of its members serving as experts in their individual capacities, to examine questions relating to the disappearance of persons. The working group has presented reports to each session of the commission since 1981. Its report to the commission's 1990 session (UN Doc. E/CN.4/1990/13) covered its activities in 1989, in the course of which it held three sessions: the first in New York from 17 to 21 April, and the second and third in Geneva from 28 August to 1 September and from 6 to 15 December. At those meetings, the working group, as in previous years, examined information on enforced or involuntary disappearances received from governments, nongovernmental organizations, and individuals concerned and took decisions concerning clarification of the relevant cases.

The working group's report indicated that it had received, in 1989, some 2,700 reports on enforced and involuntary disappearances, and had transmitted 1,650 newly reported cases to the governments concerned. Of these cases, 721 were reported to have occurred in 1989, 515 were transmitted under the urgent action procedure, and 112 were clarified in the course of the year. The remaining cases were referred back to their sources as they lacked one or more of the elements required by the working group for transmission.

During the working group's August/September session, invitations for visits were extended to the group by the governments of El Salvador, the Philippines, and Sri Lanka. The working group expressed its gratitude for these invitations, which it considered representative of an increased degree of cooperation with the governments concerned; however, financial contraints prevented the group from any of the visits in the remaining months of 1989.

In its report to the commission, the working group summarized the information concerning enforced or involuntary disappearances in 41 countries which it had reviewed to date. Of these, there was only one in which all reported cases had been clarified: Cuba's single "disappeared" person was found to have been the victim of a common crime at sea en route to the United States of America. The remaining countries about which information was examined were Afghanistan, Angola, Argentina, Bolivia, Brazil, Chad, Chile, China, Colombia, Cyprus, Dominican Republic, Ec-uador, El Salvador, Ethiopia, Guatemala, Guinea, Haiti, Honduras, India, Indonesia, Iran, Iraq, Lebanon, Mexico, Morocco, Mozambique, Nepal, Nicaragua, Panama, Paraguay, Peru, Philippines, Seychelles, Sri Lanka, Syrian Arab Republic, Uganda, Uruguay, Viet Nam, Zaire, and Zimbabwe. The working group also reviewed information concerning enforced or involuntary disappearances in South Africa and Namibia.

The working group closed its report to the commission with a series of concluding observations, as follows (UN Doc. E/CN.4/1990/13, chap. V, para. 337–365):

Already a full decade ago, numerous reports of widespread disappearances had been perturbing world public opinion. In 1980—at the prompting of the General Assembly, the Economic and Social Council and the Sub-Commission—the Commission on Human Rights responded to these reports by setting up the Working Group on Enforced or Involuntary Disappearances. The present report to the Commission is therefore the Group's tenth. At this juncture, a brief review of its activities to date seems warranted. Such an examination will permit the Commission to remind itself of the Group's evolution over the years, and it may help to indicate new directions for the Group to take. The Group has chosen to do this by highlighting a number of aspects of disappearances, both as regards the problem itself, and as regards the approach taken by the Group. Some of these have already been discussed in previous reports to the Commission.

In different terms, the Working Group has consistently expressed the view that enforced or involuntary disappearances constitute the most comprehensive denial of human rights of our time. They are a gruesome form of human rights violation which, the Group believes, continue to warrant the unstinting attention of the international community and in particular that of the Commission on Human Rights.

In its first two reports, the Working Group specifically dwelt on the question of which human rights and fundamental freedoms are violated as a result of a disappearance. It pointed out that practically all basic human rights of a disappeared person are infringed in one way or another following an abduction. The same holds true, to a greater or lesser extent, for all economic, social and cultural rights guaranteed by the various international instruments. Likewise, the Working Group has drawn attention to the wide circle of victims caused by a disappearance. Family members and other relatives or dependants suffer the immediate consequences of a disappearance. Not only are they subjected to agonizing uncertainty about what happened to their parent, child or spouse, but in many cases also economic hardship and social alienation may be part of their sorry lot. The psychological effects on children are found to be severe, even devastating at times. Children born during the captivity of their disappeared mothers constitute a category all by themselves.

Making people disappear seems to be a convenient tactic for suppressing insurgence or stifling dissent, for it takes the victim out of the protective precinct of the law. People regarded as too militant in their quest for social justice or political reform may not be easily silenced by the process of law. The same may be true for people suspected of subversive activities. Yet, regardless of how sophisticated the protection of the individual citizen against abuse by his own Government provided by the law, all legal guarantees and procedural safeguards come to a grinding halt once a person is reported missing. Disappearances continue to manifest themselves in may ways. Yet, whatever form they take, the result is almost invariably the same: once the authorities disclaim any responsibility or knowledge of a particular case, prospects for finding the person alive become increasingly grim.

Several features may be emphasized which, in the Working Group's experience, are either contributing factors or corollaries to the incidence of disappearances. One striking relationship is that between the states of emergency and serious social or political turmoil or subversive activity. Situations such as these are common and often lead to human rights violations, including disappearances. One of the reasons is that the powers of the civil authorities are being curtailed and the military and security forces are accorded a staggering latitude in maintaining public order as they see fit. Also, the situation may be such that military operations are no longer or too little subject to ordinary democratic control or political guidance. This may be the result of the prevailing balance of power among the various branches of government, or of a deliberate policy of *laissez-aller.* In the most extreme form, of course, military and security personnel can be consciously used by civilian or military Government as an instrument of repression.

In many cases, paramilitary groups carry out disappearances. It is difficult in some situations to identify a direct link between those groups and certain military authorities or other branches of the executive; whilst in other situations the relationship may be all too clear, as evidenced by the absence of any real obstacles to or consequences of their operations.

Harassment of witnesses and of relatives is a profoundly disturbing consequence of disappearances. The increasing number of reports on incidents of this nature have prompted the Working Group to draw the Commission's attention to this issue. It is a practice which essentially adds insult to injury because it is directed at a group which is already vulnerable. The Working Group intends to intensify its contacts with Governments on this matter. The Commission, for its part, should continue to keep a close eye on developments in this regard.

Perhaps the single most important factor contributing to the phenomenon of disappearances may be that of impunity. The Working Group's experience over the past 10 years has confirmed the age-old adage that impunity breeds contempt for the law. Perpetrators of human rights violations, whether civilian or military, will become all the more brazen when they are not held to account before a court of law. Impunity can also induce victims of these practices to resort to a form of self-help and take the law into their own hands, which in turn exacerbates the spiral of violence.

Military courts contribute significantly to impunity, in the Working Group's experience. A recurrent theme in times of internal crisis or under the doctrine of national security is that military personnel attested to have engaged in gross misconduct, are almost invariably acquitted or given sentences that are disproportionate to the crime committed. Subsequent promotions are even commonplace.

One other cause of impunity, apart from the conduct induced by the State, is often institutional paralysis of the judicial system, in particular, the virtual or total lack of implementation of *habeas corpus.* Paralysis may be due either to overburdening of the judicial system on top of a long-standing lack of resources, or to assassination or systematic intimidation of judicial officers and other magistrates. Paralysis may also occur through lack of co-operation by the executive branch. *Habeas corpus,* for instance, is potentially one of the most powerful legal tools for unearthing the fate or whereabouts of a disappeared person. The most sophisticated rules governing this institution, however, are rendered inoperative in a situation where co-operation stops at the barrack's gate. In certain countries, *habeas corpus* laws have purposefully been subjected to severe restrictions.

On the question of impunity and responsibility, the Working Group's position, though clear and consistent from the very beginning, seems worth restating. In line with its non-accusatory approach, the Group does not engage in the attribution of responsibility of individual officers or agents of the State for individual cases of disappearances. More generally, the Group remains of the view that those responsible for disappearances should be prosecuted to the full extent of the law, a task that falls on the State. This concern was shared very early on by the General Assembly in resolution 33/173, which is one of the bases for the Group's mandate. The Group is primarily interested in the matter of responsibility from the perspective of prevention of disappearances.

Essentially, the mandate of the Working Group as described in Commission on Human Rights resolution 20 (XXXVI) is "to examine questions of enforced or involuntary disappearances". (The distinction between enforced and involuntary, incidentally, is one of historical value only and no longer plays any role in practice.) On the basis of its terms of reference, the Working Group has from its early days operated on three different levels. First of all, and for the most part, the Group has been concerned with individual cases, trying to assist relatives to ascertain the fate and whereabouts of their loved ones. On a second level, the Group has studied situations of disappearances in individual countries; it has recorded its observations in its general reports as well as in special reports following visits to certain countries. Thirdly, it has devoted attention to the phenomenon of disappearances *per se,* its dynamics and dimensions. This is evident from the conclusions and recommendations in each of its reports to the Commission, as well as from chapters on specific aspects of the problem.

It has been argued that the Working Group's approach to individual cases represents at the same time the strongest and the weakest point in its endeavours. Strong, in the sense that the Group opened a window—unique at the time—into the United Nations system, allowing private individuals whose rights have been violated to address the pertinent human rights body swiftly and directly. Weak, in the sense that the Group seeks to clarify cases of disappearances through co-operation with Governments which probably were responsible for them in the first place and who have little, if anything, to gain by strenuous investigations. Be that as it may, the Working Group has insisted repeatedly that its humanitarian approach, perhaps imperfect, is the only real option available to it, and that only through co-operation and dialogue with States can its primary objective—the elimination of disappearances—be achieved. That is still the Group's view today.

It is a matter of satisfaction to the Working Group that, through patient and persistent efforts over the years, it has been able increasingly to move Governments towards a more responsive attitude. Indeed, there are only a few countries that have never given substantive replies to the

Group's communications. On the other hand, when examining the substantive content of the co-operation received, one is struck by significant differences. Whereas some Governments have made efforts to comply with the Group's request by providing as much information as possible—Colombia is a case in point—others have, through written submissions and oral presentations and often by high-level delegations, tried to inform the Working Group about the political and other circumstances affecting the phenomenon in their countries or of the various problems encountered in the process of investigation. In the past year, this was the case for Argentina, Mexico, the Philippines and Sri Lanka. Although it is difficult to establish clear categories in this regard, the Working Group has attempted to reflect in each country subsection the degree of co-operation it is currently receiving from the Government concerned.

Very soon after its creation, the Working Group began to develop a mechanism to deal with the influx of a great many cases of disappearances in a matter that would allow a dynamic response to the needs of people looking for missing relatives and friends. Part of that mechanism was the so-called urgent action procedure, which requires the Chairman in between sessions of the Group to process cases submitted within three months after their alleged disappearance. Even though the overall clarification rate against all outstanding cases is not considerable—it hovers around 7 per cent—clarifications under the urgent action procedure are as high as 25 per cent. This suggests that when acting swiftly, the Group may in effect help to prevent irreparable damage. The urgent procedure was subsequently emulated by other thematic mechanisms of the Commission.

Almost from the beginning, the Working Group has relied on visits as a preferred option for assessing the overall situation of disappearances in a given country. Not only does a visit provide an opportunity to obtain first-hand information [on] the matter, it also puts the Group in direct contact with family members, witnesses and non-governmental groups, as well as with the competent authorities at different levels. Working relationships established in the course of a visit usually continue afterwards. A visit also enables the Group to get the views of people from different segments of society, in order to analyse properly the context of disappearances. In 1982, visits were made to Mexico and Cyprus. In 1984, the Group addressed a letter to eight Governments, requesting them to consider the possibility of such a visit. A similar request to five Governments was sent in 1988. The Group's first visit to a country where the phenomenon was still developing occurred in 1985, when two members of the Group went to Peru, following an invitation of the Government. Similar visits took place to Peru in 1986, Guatemala in 1987 and Colombia in 1988. At the moment, the Group has three invitations outstanding to visit El Salvador, Sri Lanka and the Philippines.

Since 1985, following reports on its various visits, the Working Group has been able to make headway in the further development of its methods of work. Two features are worth mentioning. The first one relates to the format of its reports: its account of the visit was published as a separate addendum to the main report, so that it might circulate independently. The second, more important one, had to do with the manner in which the Working Group expresses a position. As a rule, the Group never submits an evaluation of any given situation of disappearances. Under the various country sections of its general reports, the Group describes to the Commission what action it has taken, and gives a brief summary of the viewpoints submitted by both governmental and non-governmental sources. The conclusions and recommendations in its 10 general reports do not pertain to the situation in any country in particular, at least not explicitly so. In the four reports on its visits to various countries, however, the Group felt it was in a better position to offer its own analysis of the situation and provide specific recommendations.

On the question of country-specific recommendations, the Commission, in resolution 1989/27, asked Governments to give all necessary attention to them. Unfortunately, the Working Group has no information to present on the extent to which any follow-up is indeed being given to those recommendations. This is all the more disturbing as most recommendations are geared to such issues as guaranteeing the right to *habeas corpus,* setting up tracing mechanisms, strengthening the judicial system and improving the security of non-governmental organizations and human rights activists. Perhaps the Commission should henceforth take a more critical look at this matter and accord it due priority at its fourty-sixth session.

As to the format of its reports, the Group soon found a form of presentation which seemed to command the approval of the Commission. The introduction of statistical summaries, further refined in successive reports, as well as graphs, not only provided possibilities for easy reference but also constituted unique features in human rights reporting. Of course, these cannot take away a basic drawback, namely that the figures presented by the Group are based entirely on submissions from external sources, processed according to the Group's criteria. Consequently, they do not necessarily reflect the true dimensions of a given situation of disappearances, which in many cases may be considerably larger; nor do they allow for any comparison between countries or geographical regions.

Over the past 10 years, the Working Group has transmitted some 19,000 cases to a total of 41 Governments. It must be remembered that only those cases are being forwarded which conform to the criteria established by the Group. Therefore, the total number of cases examined by the Group, including the ones that did not qualify for transmission, is at least 50,000. Most Governments to which cases had been sent have made oral presentations to the Group at one time or another. Scores of non-governmental organizations, *ad-hoc* groups as well as individual witnesses have provided the group with pertinent information during its 29 meetings and its several missions. Some 20 Governments maintain more or less regular contact with the Group. A list of the non-governmental organizations that have addressed themselves to the Group over the years, is contained in annex I of the report.

In 1989, the Working Group dealt with some 700 cases said to have occurred in that very same year. This represents an alarming increase since 1988, when the corresponding number of cases totalled some 400. The Group is concerned about this development, in particular over the sharp rise in disappearances in certain countries, as reflected by the statistical summaries in the preceding pages.

For a number of years the Group has been stressing the importance of greater awareness of its aims and purpose as well as its *modus operandi.* Such awareness could, in its view, avoid erroneous ideas about what the Group was set up to do, prevent false expectations about what it could reasonably achieve and dispel misgivings about how it pursues its mandate. In the light of this, the Centre for Human Rights has recently published an information leaflet on the Working Group in its fact sheet series. Also, and more important for the Commission itself, the Working Group, in 1988, presented for the first time a comprehensive account of the methods of work it had developed over the previous eight years of operation. Since then it has continued to reflect on the development of its methods of work and kept the Commission informed accordingly.

The Working Group hopes that enhanced publicity may prompt organizations that have hitherto been unaware of the Group's existence to seek a working relationship with it. This, in turn, may lead to a more diversified flow of information, particularly from those corners of the world where the human rights infrastructure—in terms of grass-root organizations, national commissions and the like—is as yet rather frail.

In 1988, for the first time in history, an international judicial body rendered a judgement on cases of disappearances. The Inter-American Court of Human Rights, in deciding three cases that took place in Honduras, made a number of important observations which have a direct bearing on the Working Group's activities and methods of work. First, the Court made a detailed analysis of the internationally recognized principle of the State's responsibility for the human rights violations committed within its territory and its obligations to prevent such violations or to investigate them where they have occurred. It declared that such responsibility continued to exist, irrespective of changes of Government. Also, the Court submitted that the obligation of the State to investigate disappearances continued to exist for as long as uncertainty remained concerning the ultimate fate of the disappeared person.

These considerations have in different words been retained also by the Human Rights Committee in recent views expressed on cases brought before it under the Optional Protocol. These views are of direct relevance for the Working Group and reinforce the positions it has consistently taken. For in its dialogue with certain Governments arguments had been advanced first of all that cases stemming from a previous political period should not be ascribed to the Government in office and, hence, dropped from the Group's dossier. Secondly, it had been suggested rather strongly that the Working Group should declare inadmissible cases reported to it long after the alleged date of occurrence.

The Group, for its part, has always taken the view that a situation of disappearance does not come to an end once no new cases have been reported over a certain period of time. Under its terms of reference, the Group will continue to deal with cases as long as they have not been clarified. It believes that the need to insist on investigation of all cases of disappearances lies at the heart of its mandate. It does so bearing in mind the interest of those who will suffer anguish and bitterness as long as they cannot be assured of the fate or whereabouts of their loved ones. Furthermore, the Group has repeatedly stated that the advent of democracy or civil Government does not, in itself, imply that no new cases of disappearance will occur.

On three different occasions, the Working Group has recommended that the Commission on Human Rights, in one form or another, take action on the idea of an international instrument against disappearances. The Group feels gratified that the Sub-Commission is now in the process of elaborating a draft declaration on the subject, generously supported by a number of non-governmental organizations, and has offered some constructive comments. Hope-

fully, the Sub-Commission will pursue this exercise with all the necessary vigour.

The Working Group would like to commend the members of the Secretariat, whose unwavering dedication has allowed the Group to develop its methods of works and to deal with its case load. Particularly in the initial period, when the Group had to find its way through uncharted territory under sometimes trying circumstances, but also up to the present, innovative thinking as well as common sense have been the hallmarks of the Centre's support unit. Sifting through the thousands of communications, entering them into the computer, cross-checking data, correspondence with sources and Governments, preparing documentation, all of this is so labour-intensive that without the Secretariat, the Group would have been utterly helpless. Unfortunately, the Centre for Human Rights has, for several years already, been contending with a chronic shortage in financial and human resources. If immediate remedies are not applied, the level of service to the Working Group will no longer be sustainable. This will inevitably result in backlogs that would not be fair to the families concerned, nor to the respective Governments, for that matter. The Commission would be well-advised to give this question its most serious consideration; its agenda gives it ample occasion to do so.

Finally, the Working Group wishes to reiterate that the advisory services system would be of considerable benefit for many countries where the problem of disappearances has been endemic. It hopes that more and more Governments will avail themselves of the possibilities offered by the United Nations in this regard. As it is in the minds of people that human rights violations are conceived, it is in their minds, and hearts, that consciousness about the inherent dignity of the human person must be instilled. Failing that, it will be quite impossible to end disappearances for all time. In any event, given the difficulties, the road ahead will be long and arduous.

SEE ALSO *Argentina: Disappearance of Children; Guatemala: Disappearances; Honduras: Inter-American Court Hearings on Disappearances; Honduras: Velasquez Rodriguez Case entries; Inter-American Convention on the Forced Disappearance of Persons (Draft); Peru: Disappearances.*

DISAPPEARANCES: STATISTICAL SUMMARY. In the report on its 1989 activities, prepared at the close of that year for consideration by the UN Commission on Human Rights in 1990, the commission's WORKING GROUP ON ENFORCED OR INVOLUNTARY DISAPPEARANCES stated (UN Doc. E/CN.4/1990/13, para. 11) that, in the course of 1989, it had received some 2,700 reports on enforced or involuntary disappearances and had transmitted some 1,650 newly reported cases to the governments concerned; 721 of these cases were reported to have occurred in 1989. Among the new cases, 515 were transmitted under its urgent action procedure, and 112 were clarified the same year. The remaining cases were referred back to the sources as they lacked one or more elements required by the working group for their transmission. The working group also reminded governments of outstanding cases and, when requested, retransmitted summaries of those cases to them. Governments were also informed about the clarification of, or the receipt of new information on, previously transmitted cases.

The working group's report further indicated (para. 356) that, since its establishment in 1980, it had transmitted some 19,000 cases to a total of 41 governments and that the number of cases which it had examined, including the ones that did not qualify for transmission, was at least 50,000. In addition to maintaining contact with the governments concerned, the working group received pertinent information from scores of non-governmental organizations, ad hoc groups, and individual witnesses.

The activities of the working group up to 1 January 1990 may be summarized statistically, on a country-by-country basis, as follows:

Afghanistan. Four cases were transmitted to the government, none of which was reported to have occurred in 1989. None was clarified, leaving four outstanding.

Angola. Seven cases were transmitted to the government, none of which was reported to have occurred in 1989. None was clarified, leaving seven outstanding.

Argentina. 3,459 cases were transmitted to the government, one of which was reported to have occurred in 1989. Forty-one were clarified by government responses and 29 by non-governmental sources, leaving 3,389 outstanding.

Bolivia. Forty-eight cases were transmitted to the government, none of which was reported to have occurred in 1989. Twenty were clarified by government responses, leaving 28 outstanding.

Brazil. Forty-nine cases were transmitted to the government, of which none was reported to have occurred in 1989. Two were clarified by government responses, leaving 47 outstanding.

Chad. Two cases were transmitted to the government, neither of which was reported to have occurred in 1989. One was clarified by a government response, leaving one outstanding.

Chile. 464 cases were transmitted to the government, none of which was reported to have occurred in 1989. Two were clarified by government responses, leaving 462 outstanding.

China. Twenty-four cases were transmitted to the government, none of which was reported to have occurred in 1989. None was clarified by a government response, leaving 24 outstanding.

Colombia. 692 cases were transmitted to the government, of which 13 were reported to have occurred in 1989. Eighty-seven were clarified by government responses and 28 by non-governmental sources, leaving 577 outstanding.

Dominican Republic. Three cases were transmitted to the government, of which none was reported to have occurred in 1989. Two were clarified by government responses, leaving one outstanding.

Ecuador. Fourteen cases were transmitted to the government, of which none was reported to have occurred in 1989. Eight were clarified by government responses and one by a non-governmental source, leaving six outstanding.

El Salvador. 493 cases were transmitted to the government, of which 34 were reported to have occurred in 1989. 315 were clarified by government responses and 35 by non-governmental sources, leaving 2,161 outstanding.

Guatemala. 3,000 cases were transmitted to the government, of which 40 were reported to have occurred in 1989. Forty-one were clarified by government responses and 69 by non-governmental sources, leaving 2,890 outstanding.

Guinea. Twenty-eight cases were transmitted to the government, of which none was reported to have occurred in 1989. None was clarified by a government response, while seven were clarified by non-governmental sources, leaving 21 outstanding.

Haiti. Twenty-five cases were transmitted to the government, of which none was reported to have occurred in 1989. Thirteen were clarified by government responses and nine by non-governmental sources, leaving 16 outstanding.

Honduras. 188 cases were transmitted to the government, of which five were reported to have occurred in 1989. 122 were clarified by government responses and 22 by non-governmental sources, leaving 132 outstanding.

India. Ninety-two cases were transmitted to the government, of which 26 were reported to have occurred in 1989. Thirteen were clarified by government responses and 13 by non-governmental sources, leaving 79 outstanding.

Indonesia. Seventy-three cases were transmitted to the government, of which one was reported to have occurred in 1989. Twenty-seven were clarified by government responses and 11 by non-governmental sources, leaving 40 outstanding.

Iran. 393 cases were transmitted to the government, of which 121 were reported to have occurred in 1989. None was clarified, leaving 393 outstanding.

Iraq. 3,045 cases were transmitted to the government, of which none was reported to have occurred in 1989. Thirty-six were clarified by government responses and 17 by non-governmental sources, leaving 2,992 outstanding.

Lebanon. 247 cases were transmitted to the government, of which two were reported to have occurred in 1989. None was clarified by a government response, while five were clarified by non-governmental sources, leaving 242 outstanding.

Mexico. 252 cases were transmitted to the government, one of which was reported to have occurred in 1989. Thirty-seven were clarified by government responses, leaving 217 outstanding.

Morocco. Twenty-two cases were transmitted to the government, of which none was reported to have occurred in 1989. Five were clarified by non-governmental sources, leaving 17 outstanding.

Mozambique. One case was transmitted to the government, which was not reported to have occurred in 1989. It was not clarified by a government response, leaving one outstanding.

Nepal. Five cases were transmitted to the government, none of which was reported to have occurred in 1989. One was clarified by a non-governmental source, leaving four outstanding.

Nicaragua. 218 cases were transmitted to the government, of which none was reported to have occurred in 1989. 110 were clarified by government responses and 19 by non-governmental sources, leaving 88 outstanding.

Panama. One case was transmitted to the government, which was reported to have occurred in 1989. It was not clarified, leaving one outstanding.

Paraguay. Twenty-three cases were transmitted to the government, of which none was reported to have occurred in 1989. Twenty were clarified by government responses, leaving three outstanding.

Peru. 2,085 cases were transmitted to the government, of which 404 were reported to have occurred in 1989. Eighty-six were clarified by government responses and 265 by non-governmental sources, leaving 1,734 outstanding.

Philippines. 541 cases were transmitted to the government, of which 36 were reported to have occurred in 1989. Seventy-six were clarified by government responses and nine by non-governmental sources, leaving 456 outstanding.

Seychelles. Three cases were transmitted to the government, of which none was reported to have occurred in 1989. None was clarified, leaving three outstanding.

Sri Lanka. 936 cases were transmitted to the government, of which 33 were reported to have occurred in 1989. Fourteen were clarified by government responses and 21 by non-governmental sources, leaving 901 outstanding.

Syria. Five cases were transmitted to the government, of which none was reported to have occurred in 1989. Three were clarified by government responses and one by a non-governmental source, leaving one outstanding.

Uganda. Nineteen cases were transmitted to the government, of which none was reported to have occurred in 1989. One was clarified by a government response and five by non-governmental sources, leaving 13 outstanding.

Uruguay: Thirty-nine cases were transmitted to the government, of which none was reported to have occurred in 1989. Seven were clarified by government responses and one by a non-governmental source, leaving 31 outstanding.

Viet Nam. Seven cases were transmitted to the government, of which none was reported to have occurred in 1989. Two were clarified by government responses and four by non-governmental sources, leaving one outstanding.

Zaire. Eighteen cases were transmitted to the government, of which one was reported to have occurred in 1989. Six were clarified by government responses, leaving 12 outstanding.

Zimbabwe. One case was transmitted to the government, which was not reported to have occurred in 1989. It was not clarified, leaving one outstanding.

DISAPPEARANCES: UN DRAFT DECLARATION.

In 1983, the SUB-COMMISSION ON PREVENTION OF DISCRIMINATION AND PROTECTION OF MINORITIES requested its WORKING GROUP ON DETENTION (resolution 1983/23) to draft a declaration against the unacknowledged detention of persons. In 1984 and 1985, the sub-commission examined drafts which were not fully satisfactory. At the sub-commission's 1988 session, the working group produced a text which reflected a consensus on the subject (UN Doc. E/CN.4/Sub.2/1988/28, annex). The sub-commission requested the Secretary-General (resolution 1988/17) to transmit it to governments and to the competent intergovernmental and non-governmental organizations for their comments and suggestions and requested the working group, taking into account the comments and suggestions received, to complete the draft declaration and to submit it to the sub-commission for approval at its 1989 session.

The text of the draft Declaration on the Protection of All Persons from Enforced or Involuntary Disappearance prepared by the 1988 Working Group on Detention is as follows:

Article 1. Any enforced or involuntary disappearance inflicts severe suffering on the individual who is subject to the unacknowledged detention as well as on the individual's family and is an offence to human dignity. When practised or permitted directly or indirectly by public authorities, it violates the human rights and fundamental freedoms proclaimed in the Universal Declaration of Human Rights and, in particular, violates the prohibition of torture found, *inter alia,* in the Declaration on the Protection of All Persons from Being Subjected to Torture and Other Cruel, Inhuman or Degrading Treatment or Punishment and the Convention against Torture and Other Cruel, Inhuman or Degrading Treatment or Punishment.

Article 2. No State may permit or tolerate enforced or involuntary disappearances, even under such exceptional circumstances as a state of war, threat of war, internal instability or any other public emergency.

Article 3. Each State shall take effective legislative, administrative, judicial or other measures to prevent and terminate enforced or involuntary disappearances in any territory under its jurisdiction.

Article 4. Each State shall ensure that no individual is detained without prompt acknowledgement of the detention and notice of his or her whereabouts to the detained individual's family and any persons designated by him or her. Prolonged incommunicado detention shall not be permitted.

Article 5. No State shall expel, return ("refouler") or extradite an individual to any State where there are substantial grounds to believe that he or she would be in danger of enforced or involuntary disappearance.

Article 6. Each State shall ensure that all acts of enforced or involuntary disappearance by, or with the acquiescence of, a public official or anyone acting in an official capacity are offences of the gravest kind under its criminal law, including without limitation participation in, complicity in, incitement to or an attempt to cause enforced or involuntary disappearance. An order from a superior officer or a public authority may not be invoked as a justification for enforced or involuntary disappearances.

Article 7. Each State shall ensure that anyone who alleges that an individual has been subject to enforced or involuntary disappearances in any territory under its jurisdiction has the right to complain to, and to have the complaint promptly and impartially investigated by, its competent authorities. Steps shall be taken to ensure that the complainant and witnesses are protected against all ill-treatment or intimidation as a consequence of the complaint or any evidence given.

Article 8. Wherever there are reasonable grounds to believe that an enforced or involuntary disappearance has been committed, the competent authorities of the State concerned shall promptly proceed to an impartial investigation even if there has been no formal complaint.

Article 9. Each State shall ensure that persons identified pursuant to article 7 or article 8 as having committed an act referred to in article 6 are brought to justice either through prosecution or extradition regardless of their nationalities and regardless of where the offence was committed.

Article 10. Each State shall ensure in its legal system that the individual subject to an enforced or involuntary disappearance and the individual's family obtain redress and have an enforceable right to fair and adequate compensation. In the event of the death of an individual as a result of an enforced or involuntary disappearance, the individual's family shall be entitled to further compensation.

Article 11. Nothing in the present declaration shall be construed as restricting or derogating from any right defined in the Universal Declaration of Human Rights or in any other international instruments or in national legislation.

SEE ALSO *Inter-American Convention on the Forced Disappearance of Persons (Draft).*

DISARMAMENT AND DEVELOPMENT. A total of 150 States and 183 non-governmental organizations participated in the International Conference on the Relationship between Disarmament and Development, convened by the UN General Assembly (decision 41/422), which met at the headquarters of the United Nations in New York from 24 August to 11 September 1987, and concluded its work by adopting its report (UN publication, Sales No. E.87.IX.8) containing the final document of the conference (chap. II).

Many sections of the final document refer either to human rights in general, to particular rights and freedoms, or to matters bearing upon the realization of economic, social, cultural, civil, or political rights. Excerpts from these sections follow:

The States participating in the International Conference on the Relationship between Disarmament and Development,

Desirous of:

(a) Enhancing and strengthening the commitment of the international community to disarmament and development and giving impetus to renewed efforts in both these fields;

(b) Raising world consciousness that true and lasting peace and security in this interdependent world demands rapid progress in both disarmament and development;

(c) Directing global attention at a high political level on the implications of world-wide military spending against the sombre background of the present world economic situation;

(d) Looking at disarmament, development and security in their relationship in the context of the interdependence of nations, interrelationships among issues and mutuality of interests;

(e) Taking greater account of the relationship between disarmament and development in political decision-making;

(f) Furthering the international community's collective knowledge of the military and non-military threats to security;

Adopt the following Final Document:

In the Charter of the United Nations, Member States have undertaken to promote the establishment and maintenance of international peace and security with the least diversion for armaments of the world's human and economic resources. The Member States also express in the Charter their determination to employ international machinery for the promotion of the economic and social advancement of all peoples. The United Nations has thus a central role to play for the promotion of both disarmament and development.

Disarmament and development are two of the most urgent challenges facing the world today. They constitute priority concerns of the international community in which all nations—developed and developing, big and small, nuclear and non-nuclear—have a common and equal stake. Disarmament and development are two pillars on which enduring international peace and security can be built.

The continuing arms race is absorbing far too great a proportion of the world's human, financial, natural and technological resources, placing a heavy burden on the economies of all countries and affecting the international

405

D

flow of trade, finance and technology, in addition to hindering the process of confidence-building among States. The global military expenditures are in dramatic contrast to economic and social underdevelopment and to the misery and poverty afflicting more than two thirds of mankind. Thus, there is a commonality of interests in seeking security at lower levels of armaments and finding ways of reducing these expenditures.

The world can either continue to pursue the arms race with characteristic vigour or move consciously and with deliberate speed towards a more stable and balanced social and economic development within a more sustainable international economic and political order; it cannot do both.

Global interest in the relationship between disarmament and development is reflected in proposals by a politically and geographically broad spectrum of States since the early days of the United Nations. There is an increasing understanding of this relationship, in part due to the expert studies and reports prepared by the United Nations.

The contrast between the global military expenditures and the unmet socio-economic needs provides a compelling moral appeal for relating disarmament to development. There is also a growing recognition that both overarmament and underdevelopment constitute threats to international peace and security.

The convening under the aegis of the United Nations of the International Conference on the Relationship between Disarmament and Development is a landmark in the process of undertaking, at a political level, the multilateral consideration of the relationship between disarmament and development.

Relationship Between Disarmament and Development in all its Aspects and Dimensions. While disarmament and development both strengthen international peace and security and promote prosperity, they are distinct processes. Each should be pursued vigorously regardless of the pace of progress in the other; one should not be made a hostage to the other. Pursuit of development cannot wait for the release of resources from disarmament. Similarly, disarmament has its own imperative separate from the purpose of releasing resources for development.

However, disarmament and development have a close and multidimensional relationship. Each of them can have an impact at the national, regional and global levels in such a way as to create an environment conducive to the promotion of the other.

The relationship between disarmament and development in part derives from the fact that the continuing global arms race and development compete for the same finite resources at both the national and international levels. The allocation of massive resources for armaments impedes the pursuit of development to its optimal level.

Considering the present resource constraints of both developed and developing countries, reduced world military spending could contribute significantly to development. Disarmament can assist the process of development not only by releasing additional resources but also by positively affecting the global economy. It can create conditions conducive to promoting equitable economic and technological co-operation and to pursuing the objectives of a new international economic order.

Real economic growth as well as just and equitable development, and particularly the elimination of poverty, are necessary for a secure and stable environment at the na-

tional, regional and international levels. They can reduce tensions and conflicts and the need for armament.

In the relationship between disarmament and development, security plays a crucial role. Progress in any of these three areas would have a positive effect on the others.

Security is an overriding priority for all nations. It is also fundamental for both disarmament and development. Security consists of not only military, but also political, economic, social, humanitarian and human rights and ecological aspects. Enhanced security can, on the one hand, create conditions conducive to disarmament and, on the other, provide the environment and confidence for the successful pursuit of development. The development process, by overcoming non-military threats to security and contributing to a more stable and sustainable international system, can enhance security and thereby promote arms reduction and disarmament. Disarmament would enhance security both directly and indirectly. A process of disarmament that provides for undiminished security at progressively lower levels of armaments could allow additional resources to be devoted to addressing non-military challenges to security, and thus result in enhanced overall security.

An effective implementation of the collective security provisions of the Charter of the United Nations would enhance international peace and security and thus reduce the need of Member States to seek security by exercising their inherent right of individual or collective self-defence, also recognized by the Charter. The judgement as to the level of arms and military expenditures essential for its security rests with each nation. However, the pursuit of national security regardless of its impact on the security of others can create overall international insecurity, thereby undermining the very security it aims at promoting. This is even more so in the context of the catastrophic consequences of a nuclear war.

It is widely accepted that the world is overarmed and that security should be sought at substantially lower levels of armaments. The continued arms race in all its dimensions, and its spreading into new areas, pose a growing threat to international peace and security and even to the very survival of mankind. Moreover, global military spending on nuclear and conventional arms threatens to stall the efforts aimed at reaching the goals of development so necessary to overcome non-military threats to peace and security.

The use or threat of use of force in international relations, external intervention, armed aggression, foreign occupation, colonial domination, policies of *apartheid* and all forms of racial discrimination, violation of territorial integrity, of national sovereignty, of the right to self-determination, and the encroachment of the right of all nations to pursue their economic and social development free from outside interference constitute threats to international peace and security. International security will be guaranteed in turn to the extent that peaceful and negotiated solutions to regional conflicts are promoted.

Recently, non-military threats to security have moved to the forefront of global concern. Underdevelopment and declining prospects for development, as well as mismanagement and waste of resources, constitute challenges to security. The degradation of the environment presents a threat to sustainable development. The world can hardly be regarded as secure so long as there is polarization of wealth and poverty at the national and international levels. Gross and systematic violations of human rights retard genuine socio-economic development and create tensions which contribute to instability. Mass poverty, illiteracy, disease, squalor and malnutrition afflicting a large proportion of the world's population often become the cause of social strain, tension and strife.

Growing interdependence among nations, interrelationship among global issues, mutuality of interests, collective approach responding to the needs of humanity as a whole and multilateralism provide the international framework within which the relationship between disarmament, development and security should be shaped.

Implications of the Level and Magnitude of the Continuing Military Expenditures. The current level of global military spending in pursuit of security interests represents a real increase of between four and five times since the end of the Second World War. It also reflects approximately 6 per cent of the world gross domestic product and has been estimated to be more than 20 times as large as all official development assistance to developing countries. During the 1980s, global military expenditure has grown on an average at a faster rate than during the second half of the 1970s. . . .

In contrast to the current level and trends in global military expenditure, the state of the world economy in the 1980s has been characterized by a slow-down in growth of demand and output compared with the preceding two decades, generally lower rates of inflation, difficulties in many countries in adapting to structural changes, a mounting stock of debt, high real interest rates, inadequate net flows of financial resources, shifts in exchange rates, high and increasing levels of protection, commodity prices depressed to their lowest level in 50 years, terms-of-trade losses sustained by commodity exporting countries, and a generally insecure economic environment in which millions of people still lack the basic conditions for a decent life.

The use of resources for military purposes amounts to a reduction of resources for the civilian sector. Military spending provides little basis for future industrial civilian production. Military goods are generally destroyed or soon used up. While there are some civilian by-products of military research and training there are better direct, non-military routes to follow.

The opportunity cost of military expenditures over the past 40 years has been and continues to be borne by both developed and developing countries, as there is a pressing need for additional resources for development in both groups of countries. In developing countries, it has been estimated that close to 1 billion people are below the poverty line, 780 million people are undernourished, 850 million are illiterate, 1.5 billion have no access to medical facilities, an equally large number are unemployed, and 1 billion people are inadequately housed. In developed countries, resources are required, *inter alia,* for meeting the priority needs of urban renewal, the restoration of some of the infrastructures, the reduction of unemployment, the protection of the environment, the further development of welfare systems and the development of non-conventional sources of energy. The developing countries are doubly affected: (a) in proportion to the expenditure they incur themselves; and (b) because of the disturbing effect of military expenditure on the world economy.

The present world economic situation should also be seen in the context of the arms race. For certain countries the high deficits caused by military expenditures as well as the cumulative effect of subsequent rise in the interest rates have the effect of diverting substantial flows of capital away from development activities. In this sense, the whole world is affected by the arms race. . . .

Ways and Means of Releasing Additional Resources for Development Purposes. Apart from promoting international peace, security and co-operation, disarmament can improve the environment for the pursuit of development by:

(a) Releasing resources from the military to the civilian sector at the national level;

(b) Removing the distortions in the national and international economy induced by military expenditure;

(c) Creating favourable conditions for international economic, scientific and technological co-operation and for releasing resources for development at the regional and international levels, on both a bilateral and a multilateral basis.

Resources released as a result of disarmament measures should be devoted to the promotion of the well-being of all peoples, the improvement of the economic conditions of the developing countries and the bridging of the economic gap between developed and developing countries. These resources should be additional to those otherwise available for assistance to developing countries. . . .

The final document concludes with a comprehensive action program, designed with a view to fostering an interrelated perspective on disarmament, development, and security; to promoting multilateralism as providing the international framework for shaping the relationship between disarmament, development, and security based on interdependence among nations and mutuality of interests; and to strengthening the central role of the United Nations in the interrelated fields of disarmament and development.

In a resolution adopted on 7 December 1988 (resolution 43/75 B), the General Assembly requested the secretary-general to take action through the appropriate organs of the United Nations for the implementation of the action program adopted by the conference. In another resolution, adopted the following day (resolution 43/113), the assembly reaffirmed that there is a close and multi-dimensional relationship between disarmament and development, that progress in disarmament would considerably promote progress in development, and that resources released through disarmament measures could contribute to the economic and social development and well-being of all peoples; and recognized that the realization of the right to development may help to promote the enjoyment of all human rights and fundamental freedoms.

SEE ALSO *Right to Development.*

DJIBOUTI. The Republic of Djibouti is a country in eastern Africa, at the juncture of the Red Sea and the Gulf of Aden. It has borders with Ethiopia and Somalia. Formerly known as the territory of Afars and Issas, it achieved independence from France in 1977 and became a member of the United Nations the same year. Its population is estimated by the UN (1990) to be 436,000.

Ethnic groups include Somalis (48%), Afars (38%), Europeans (9%), and Arabs (5%). Languages commonly used include French (official), Somali, Afar, and Arabic. Religions practiced include Islam (94%), and Christianity (Roman Catholic) (6%). Literacy is estimated at 17%.

The government (1990) took the form of a republic. The president is head of State; the prime minister is head of government. Legislation is drafted by the 65-member Constituent Assembly. The only recognized political party is the People's Progress Assembly.

Djibouti is important as the terminal of the Djibouti–Addis Ababa railroad, which carries more than half of Ethiopia's foreign trade. It also serves as a base for ships and planes of the United States of America.

In 1988, the UN secretary-general reported to the General Assembly on the situation of refugees in Djibouti. As of the end of 1987, 11,356 refugees, mostly from Ethiopia, had entered the country. Approximately 11,000 lived in Dikhil and Ali-Sabieh camps, while the remainder resided in Djibouti-Ville. The voluntary repatriation of refugees to Ethiopia commenced in December 1986; and, by 30 June 1987, more than 3,000 had returned to their homes. However, the plight of the remaining refugees and the constantly increasing inflow of displaced persons severely affected the inadequate social services and the infrastructure of the country.

The refugee problem was still far from solution towards the end of 1989, when the General Assembly expressed its concern (resolution 44/150) about a new inflow of over 35,000 externally displaced persons, which had added considerably to the burden already carried by Djibouti.

Noting with satisfaction that over 6,000 refugees had already been granted settlement and integration in Djibouti, despite the physical, social, and economic obstacles that face the country, the assembly welcomed the steps the country had taken, in cooperation with the UNITED NATIONS HIGH COMMISSIONER FOR REFUGEES, and urged the high commissioner to mobilize, on an emergency basis, the necessary resources to provide assistance.

In another resolution, also adopted in 1989, the assembly declared (resolution 44/177) its solidarity with the government and people of Djbouti in the face of the devastating consequences of the torrential rains and floods that occurred in April 1989 and requested the secretary-general to arrange for the preparation of an urgent international program of rehabilitation and reconstruction.

DOMESTIC VIOLENCE. At its 1985 session, the UN General Assembly recognized (resolution 40/36) that abuse and battery in the family are critical problems that have serious physical and psychological effects on individual family members, especially the young, and jeopardize the health and survival of the family unit, and requested the Secretary-General to intensify research on the subject of domestic violence from a crimininological perspective and to formulate action-oriented strategies that could serve as a basis for policy formulation. All relevant United Nations bodies, agencies, and institutes were called upon to collaborate with the secretary-general in insuring a concerted and sustained effort to combat this problem, and UN member States were invited to adopt specific measures—including the following—with a view to making the criminal and civil justice system more sensitive in its response to domestic violence:

(a) To introduce, if not already in place, civil and criminal legislation in order to deal with particular problems of domestic violence, and to enact and enforce such laws in order to protect battered family members and punish the offender and to offer alternative ways of treatment for offenders, according to the type of violence;

(b) To respect, in all instances of the criminal proceeding, starting with the police investigation, the special and sometimes delicate position of the victim, in particular in the manner in which the victim is treated;

(c) To initiate preventive measures, such as providing support and counselling to families, in order to improve their ability to create a non-violent environment, emphasizing principles of education, equality of rights and equality of responsibilities between women and men, their partnership and the peaceful resolution of conflicts;

(d) To inform the public, as necessary, through all available channels, about serious acts of violence perpetrated against children, in order to create public awareness of this problem;

(e) To deliver appropriate, specialized assistance to victims of domestic violence, as an integral part of social policy;

(f) To provide, as a temporary solution, shelters and other facilities and services for the safety of victims of domestic violence;

(g) To provide specialized training and units for those who deal in some capacity with victims of domestic violence;

(h) To initiate or intensify research and collect data on the background, extent and types of domestic violence;

(i) To make legal remedies to domestic violence more accessible and, in view of the criminogenic effects of the phenomenon, in particular on young victims, to give due consideration to the interests of society by maintaining a balance between intervention and the protection of privacy;

(j) To ensure that social welfare and health administration systems are more intensely engaged in providing assistance to victims of familial violence and abuses, and to make all efforts to co-ordinate social welfare and criminal justice measures.

SEE ALSO *Marriage and the Family.*

DOMINICA. The Commonwealth of Dominica is a country occupying an island in the Windward Group of the West Indies, between Martinque and Guadeloupe. It achieved independence from Great Britain in 1978 and became a member of the United Nations the same year. Its population is estimated by the UN (1990) to be 81,000. Languages commonly used include English and a French *patois*. Christianity (Roman Catholic, 80%; Anglican, Methodist, and other Protestant denominations, 20%) is the predominant religion. Literacy is estimated at 80%.

The government (1990) took the form of a republic and member of the Commonwealth of Nations, of which the British sovereign is the symbolic head. The president, elected by the House of Assembly, is head of State; the prime minister, appointed by the president on advice of the assembly, is head of government. Legislation is prepared by the 21-member House of Assembly. Political parties include the Freedom Party, the Opposition Democratic Labor Party, and the United Dominica Labor Party.

Dominica is one of a small number of countries having a woman as prime minister. Mary Eugenia Charles became prime minister in July 1980 and was returned to office for a second five-year term in 1985.

DOMINICAN REPUBLIC. The Dominican Republic is a country occupying the eastern two-thirds of the island of Santo Domingo, formerly called Hispaniola, which it shares with Haiti. It achieved independence from Spain in 1844 and became a member of the United Nations in 1945. Its population is estimated by the UN (1990) to be 6,971,000. Languages commonly used include Spanish and Quech. Christianity (Roman Catholic) is the predominant religion. Literacy is estimated at 68%.

The government (1990) took the form of a republic. Under the 1962 constitution, national sovereignty is vested in the people, from whom emanate all powers of the State, which are exercised through representation. The president is elected by popular vote for a term of four years. Legislation is prepared by the Senate and the House of Deputies, members of which are also elected by popular vote for four-year terms. Suffrage is universal and mandatory for all over 18 years of age. Political parties include the Dominican Revolutionary Party, the Reformist Party, the Dominican Liberation Party, *Partido Quisquellana Demócrata,* and *Movimiento de Integración Democrática Anti-Relecccionista.*

Since 1981, the Dominican Republic has acted as host to the **INTERNATIONAL RESEARCH AND TRAINING INSTITUTE FOR THE ADVANCEMENT OF WOMEN,** an autonomous body under the auspices of the United Nations, functioning under guidelines established by the UN Economic and Social Council in resolution 1998 (LX) of 12 May 1976.

Because the part of the island of Santo Domingo now known as the Dominican Republic—the oldest European settlement in the western hemisphere—passed back and forth between Spain and France in the colonial days and was ruled by dictators for many years, its history is one of recurrent disorder and disregard for human rights.

In 1795, Spain ceded the colony to France. However, the area now known as the Dominican Republic was conquered by Haitians twice—once in 1801 by troops under the leadership of Toussaint L'Ouverture and again in 1822 by units commanded by Jean Pierre Boyer. On both occasions, the occupation was ended by Dominican revolts; the colonists, who were white and whose culture was predominantly Spanish, feared rule by the Haitians, who were black and of African origin. Uprising and disorder persisted under a series of dictators; and, in 1916, the United States Marines intervened to restore quiet, remaining in the country until 1934. They left after a Dominican sergeant who had been trained by the Marines, Rafael Leonides Trujillo, established a dictatorship which lasted until 1961.

After Trujillo's assassination, a new constitution was adopted and free elections were held. Juan Bosch, a leftist leader, was elevated to the presidency. But he was soon replaced by a military coup; and when Bosch's supporters rebelled, American marines and troops were again sent to the island to restore quiet. They were later replaced by a peacekeeping force composed of troops from a number of countries. In 1966, new elections were held, and the presidency was won by Joaquin Balaguer. The peacekeeping force withdrew, and President Balaguer was able to win three subsequent four-year terms in open, honest elections. He was defeated in 1978 by Antonio Guzman, who, in turn, was succeeded in 1982 by Salvador Jorge Blanco. However, former President Balauger was re-elected in 1986.

While enjoying comparative stability politically, the Dominican Republic has not been able to achieve economic stability because of the decling value of its main exports: gold, silver, and sugar. Fear of internal disturbances has caused the government to resist austerity measures proposed by the International Monetary Fund.

DRUG ABUSE. In the brief "Survey of Specific Humanitarian Issues in the Contemporary World" presented to the 1986 session of the UN General Assembly, the secretary-general included the following remarks on the subject of the drug problem (UN Doc. A/41/472, sect. U, para. 80–81):

The drug abuse phenomenon is increasingly recognized as having a negative impact in most regions of the world. Drug-related problems affect all social strata and age groups in developing countries as well as in the industrialized world. Despite national and international efforts, the world-wide production of illicit drugs continues to mount with devastating results. The scourge of illicit drug traffic and drug abuse has reached ever more dangerous proportions. The humanitarian dimensions of the drug abuse phenomenon are painfully clear, including the crippling of the drug-dependent person, the burden to family members, and the high social costs in terms of absenteeism, required medical care and, in growing numbers, drug-related deaths reflecting wasted lives. In addition, the siphoning of significant human and financial resources seriously affects economic and social development. One of the most tragic aspects is the devastation brought by drug abuse to the younger generation, as thousands of young lives are irreparably damaged or lost to this terrifying social blight.

In resolution 40/120 of 13 December 1985, the General Assembly expressed its deep concern at the constant upward trend in illicit traffic and drug abuse, which posed serious dangers for individual human rights and for the economic, cultural and political structures of society. In resolution 40/121 of the same date, it reaffirmed that maximum priority must be given to the fight against the illicit production of, demand for and traffic in illicit drugs and related international criminal activities, such as the illegal arms trade and terrorist practices, which also had an adverse effect not only on the well-being of peoples but also on the stability of institutions, as well as posing a threat to the sovereignty of States.

SEE ALSO *Children and Drugs; Declaration on the Control of Drug Trafficking and Abuse.*

E

ECONOMIC AND SOCIAL COUNCIL. Established in accordance with the UNITED NATIONS CHARTER (article 7) as a principal organ of the United Nations, the council's principal functions and powers are:

(a) to make or initiate studies and reports with respect to international economic, social, cultural, educational, health, and related matters, and to make recommendations with respect to any such matters to the General Assembly, to members of the United Nations and to the specialized agencies concerned;

(b) to make recommendations for the purpose of promoting respect for, and observance of, human rights and fundamental freedoms for all;

(c) to prepare draft conventions for submission to the General Assembly, with respect to matters falling within its competence; and

(d) to call, in accordance with the rules prescribed by the United Nations, international conferences on matters falling within its competence.

As regards the specialized agencies, the council may:

(a) enter into agreements with any of the specialized agencies, defining the terms on which the agencies shall be brought into relationship with the United Nations, such agreements being subject to approval by the General Assembly;

(b) coordinate the activities of the specialized agencies through consultation with and recommendations to such agencies and through recommendations to the General Assembly and to the members of the United Nations;

(c) take appropriate steps to obtain regular reports from the specialized agencies, and make arrangements with the members of the United Nations and with the specialized agencies, to obtain reports on the steps taken to give effect to its own recommendations and to recommendations on matters falling within its competence made by the General Assembly; and

(d) communicate its observations on these reports to the General Assembly.

The Economic and Social Council may furnish information to and assist the Security Council upon its request. It performs such functions as fall within its competence in connection with the carrying out of the recommendations of the General Assembly. It may, with the approval of the assembly, perform services at the request of members of the United Nations and at the request of specialized agencies.

Further, in accordance with the terms of the UN Charter, the council has been authorized by the General Assembly to request advisory opinions of the INTERNATIONAL COURT OF JUSTICE on legal questions arising within the scope of its activities.

As regards human rights, the council is empowered in article 55 of the UN Charter to promote "universal respect for, and observance of, human rights and fundamental freedoms for all without distinction as to to race, sex, language, or religion." States which are members of the United Nations pledge themselves, by article 56, "to take joint and separate action in cooperation with the Organization for the achievement of the purposes set forth in article 55."

Subsidiary organs reporting to the council include (a) functional commissions and sub-commissions; (b) regional commissions; (c) standing committees; (d) special bodies; and (e) ad hoc committees.

Of the functional commissions and sub-commissions, three are concerned exclusively with human rights matters: the COMMISSION ON HUMAN RIGHTS, the SUB-COMMISSION ON PREVENTION OF DISCRIMINATION AND PROTECTION OF MINORITIES, and the COMMISSION ON THE STATUS OF WOMEN. One other—the COMMISSION FOR SOCIAL DEVELOPMENT—is concerned with human rights occasionally when dealing with other questions within its mandate.

Of the standing committees, one—the COMMITTEE ON ECONOMIC, SOCIAL AND CULTURAL RIGHTS—is concerned exclusively with human rights. A second—the Social Committee—assists the council in dealing with human rights and other matters of a "social" nature. A third—the COMMITTEE ON NON-GOVERNMENTAL ORGANIZATIONS—serves as the council's link to non-governmental organizations active in the promotion and protection of human rights. Four special bodies—the HUMAN RIGHTS COMMITTEE, the COMMITTEE ON THE ELIMINATION OF DISCRIMINATION AGAINST WOMEN, the office of the UNITED NATIONS HIGH COMMISSIONER FOR

REFUGEES, and the UNITED NATIONS CHILDREN'S FUND—report to the General Assembly through the council.

The council was originally composed of 18 members in accordance with article 61 of the UN charter. The membership was increased to 27 by an amendment to that article which entered into force on 31 August 1965, and to 54 by an amendment which entered into force on 24 September 1973. Members of the council are elected by the General Assembly according to the following pattern established by assembly resolution 2847 (XXVI) of 20 December 1971: 14 from African States, 11 from Asian States, 10 from Latin American States, 13 from Western European and other States, and six from the socialist States of eastern Europe. Elections are held by secret ballot, and there are no nominations. Members are elected by a two-thirds' majority of the assembly; their term of office is three years. The council reports to the General Assembly.

The council normally holds three sessions each year. The first, an organizational session, is convened on the first Tuesday in February for approximately three days. The second is convened on the first Tuesday in May for approximately three weeks, and the third, on the first Wednesday in July, for approximately three weeks, in Geneva.

ECONOMIC, SOCIAL, AND CULTURAL RIGHTS.

The enjoyment of certain economic, social, and cultural rights, set out in articles 22 to 28 of the UNIVERSAL DECLARATION OF HUMAN RIGHTS and elaborated in the INTERNATIONAL COVENANT ON ECONOMIC, SOCIAL AND CULTURAL RIGHTS as well as in a number of international conventions adopted by specialized agencies and other intergovernmental organizations, cannot be adequately ensured merely by the enforcement of existing laws or the passage of new ones but can only be achieved progressively through gradual improvement of the economic, social, and cultural situations in which people live.

Accordingly, the covenant does not establish a complaint procedure but provides primarily (article 16) for States parties to report periodically on the measures they have adopted and the progress made in achieving the enjoyment of such rights. The rights involved include the right to work; the right to social security; the right to an adequate standard of living; the right to the enjoyment of the highest attainable standards of physical and mental health; the right of the family, motherhood, and childhood to protection and assistance; the right to education; the right to participate freely in cultural life; and the right to development.

The reports of States parties, and reports submitted by the specialized agencies concerned, are directed to the UN secretary-general, who transmits them to the Economic and Social Council. In monitoring the implementation of the covenant, the council is assisted by its COMMITTEE ON ECONOMIC, SOCIAL AND CULTURAL RIGHTS. The committee, established by the council on 25 May 1985 (resolution 1985/17), took over the functions of the sessional Working Group of Governmental Experts on the Implementation of the International Covenant on Economic, Social and Cultural Rights, which the council had established on a temporary basis in 1978 (resolution 1978/10).

The Committee on Economic, Social and Cultural Rights held its first annual session at the United Nations office in Geneva from 9 to 27 March 1987, and its second at the same location from 8 to 25 February 1988. The committee, and the sessional working group which preceded it, examined 124 initial reports and 44 second periodic reports concerning the rights covered by articles 6 to 9, 10 to 12, and 13 to 15 of the covenant up to the end of 1988. The reports were received from all regions of the world and included countries with widely differing socio-economic, cultural, political, and legal systems. They touched upon most of the problems which might arise in implementing the covenant, although they did not provide a reliable or complete picture on a worldwide basis of the situation of the enjoyment of economic, social and cultural rights.

In the report of its first session, the committee included the following general comments (UN Doc. E/1987/28, para. 301–304):

The Committee recognized that many States Members of the United Nations, in spite of all the efforts they were making, faced special difficulties in promoting the full enjoyment of economic, social and cultural rights. Among the sources of those difficulties was the insufficient level of socio-economic development in those States, the difficulties were often compounded by circumstances beyond their control.

In view of those special difficulties, the Committee reiterated that the progressive implementation of the Covenant was closely linked to the development process of each country, thus requiring a favourable international context. In that connection, the Committee expressed its serious concern at the widening gap between developed and developing countries, as well as at the heavy burden of external indebtedness suffered by the peoples of Latin America, Asia and Africa. In that respect, the Committee reiterated its deep concern about the negative impact of the current international economic situation, particularly on developing countries and, in that context, stressed the importance of further strengthening international co-operation for development and an equitable and just economic order.

The Committee considered that that negative economic context, as well as the level of development of each country, should be taken into account when considering the reports submitted by States parties to the Covenant. The Committee stressed that the presentation of a report should be viewed as an opportunity for dialogue between the Committee and the Governments of the States parties, directed to the better understanding of their efforts and achievements, as well as the obstacles and problems that many States parties faced in the progressive implementation of the Covenant, with a view to assisting them, if they wished, in overcoming those obstacles.

The Committee paid special attention to the fact that 1987 had been proclaimed the International Year of Shelter for the Homeless and considered that the objective was to improve the shelter and neighbourhoods of some of the poor and disadvantaged by the end of 1987, according to national priorities, and to demonstrate by the year 2000 ways and means of improving the shelter and neighbourhoods of the poor and disadvantaged. It expressed deep concern that millions of people did not enjoy the right to housing and reiterated the right of all persons to an adequate standard of living for themselves and their families, including adequate housing.

At its second session, the committee, in addition to examining the reports of a number of States parties to the covenant, prepared a series of recommendations relating to its methods of work and included them in its report to the council (UN Doc. E/1988/ 14, chap. IV). After examining and taking note of the report, the council (resolution 1988/4):

—endorsed the recommendation that States parties be requested to submit a single report within two years of the entry into force of the Covenant for the State party concerned and thereafter at five-year intervals;

—welcomed the decision of the committee to revise and simplify the guidelines for reports of States parties and to place limits on the time devoted to the consideration of the report of each State party;

—took note of the recommendation of the committee on its future sessions but considered that the provision for one annual session of three weeks' duration should be maintained for the time being;

—authorized the committee to establish a presessional working group to meet for a period of one week prior to each session;

—took note of the decision of the committee to devote one day during each session to a general discussion of one specific right or a particular article of the covenant in order to develop in greater depth its understanding of the relevant issues;

—welcomed the decision of the committee to prepare general comments, based on the various articles and provisions of the covenant, with a view to assisting States parties in fulfilling their reporting obligations; and

—urged the committee to encourage States parties, in conformity with article 2, paragraph 1, of the covenant, to consider identifying benchmarks for measuring achievements in the progressive realization of the rights recognized in the covenant and, in this context, to pay particular regard to the most vulnerable and disadvantaged persons.

The council also called upon the specialized agencies, the regional commissions, and other appropriate United Nations bodies, in particular the United Nations Development Program, to extend their full cooperation and support to the Committee on Economic, Social and Cultural Rights by, *inter alia,* enabling their representatives to attend meetings of the committee and submitting relevant information to it. It further invited non-governmental organizations in consultative status to submit to the committee written statements that might contribute to the full and universal recognition and realization of the rights set forth in the covenant.

ECONOMIC, SOCIAL AND CULTURAL RIGHTS: ILO ACTIVITIES. In its 1988 report to the Economic and Social Council under article 18 of the INTERNATIONAL COVENANT ON ECONOMIC, SOCIAL AND CULTURAL RIGHTS (UN Doc. E/1988/6), the International Labor Organization stated the following (para. 1–12):

By resolution 1988 (LX) of 11 May 1976, the United Nations Economic and Social Council called upon the specialized agencies to submit to it reports, in accordance with Article 18 of the International Covenant on Economic, Social and Cultural Rights, on the progress made in achieving the observance of the provisions of the Covenant falling within the scope of their activities. In November 1976, the Governing Body of the International Labour Office agreed, in response to this request, that the International Labour Organisation would present such reports to the Economic and Social Council. The Governing Body also decided, for that purpose, to entrust to the Committee of Experts on the Application of Conventions and Recommendations the task of examining reports and other available information on the implementation of the provisions of the Covenant falling within the scope of the ILO's activities.

In pursuance of the above-mentioned mandate, the Committee of Experts from 1978 to 1987 examined the situation in respect of the implementation of Articles 6 to 9 and of certain provisions of Article 10 of the Covenant by States Parties to the Covenant which have supplied reports in accordance with the reporting programme established by the Economic and Social Council. The Committee of Experts made nine reports on this subject which were transmitted to the Secretary-General of the United Nations and presented to the Council. . . .

In its last report in 1987, the Committee of Experts noted with particular interest that, by resolution 1985/17 of 28 May 1985, the United Nations Economic and Social Council had decided to set up a Committee on Economic, Social and Cultural Rights, composed of 18 experts serving in their personal capacity, and that this Committee should succeed in 1987 to the Sessional Working Group of governmental experts that the Council had set up in 1978 in order to assist it in its examination of the reports on the implementation of the Covenant.

Following the creation of the new Committee, the Committee of Experts re-examined the manner in which the ILO could best submit its reports in accordance with Article 18 of the Covenant. The Committee of Experts accordingly recommended that the ILO should no longer seek to evaluate separately the extent to which the Covenant was implemented, but that it should inform the new Committee of the results of the operation of the various ILO supervisory procedures in the fields covered by the Covenant and should entrust to the International Labour Office in future to communicate this information to the United Nations for presentation to the Committee on Economic, Social and Cultural Rights. It should remain open to the Committee of Experts to report on particular situations whenever it deemed this desirable or when specifically requested to do so by the new Committee. The Governing Body of the ILO, at its two hundred and thirty-sixth session (May 1987), approved this recommendation made by the Committee of Experts.

The present report has therefore been drawn up in accordance with the arrangements approved by the above decision of the Governing Body. It contains information concerning countries listed in the table of contents of which reports have been received by 1 December 1987.

The report will follow the approach adopted by the Committee of Experts for its reports since 1985, and will contain in Part II: (a) indications concerning the principal ILO Conventions relevant to Articles 6–10 of the Covenant; and (b) indications concerning ratifications of these Conventions and comments made by ILO supervisory bodies with regard to the application of these Conventions by the States concerned (in so far as the points at issue appear to have a bearing also on the provisions of the Covenant). The latter indications are based mainly on the comments of the Committee of Experts resulting from its examination of the reports on the Conventions in question. Account was also taken of the conclusions adopted under constitutional procedures for the examination of representations or complaints and, in the case of Article 8 of the Covenant, of the conclusions adopted by the Governing Body of the International Labour Office on the basis of the reports of its Committee on Freedom of Association following examination of complaints alleging violation of trade union rights.

In previous rights, the Committee of Experts has commented on several occasions on the relationship between the provisions of the Covenant and the standards laid down in international labour Conventions, the nature of the obligations resulting from them and the way in which the Committee of Experts consequently presented its comments on the implementation of the Covenant. Upon the completion of the first cycle of the reporting programme on the Covenant, the Committee of Experts, in its sixth report (E/1983/40), recalled these general observations which it hoped could be of use to the States Parties and would be of interest to the Economic and Social Council and its Sessional Working Group responsible for examining the implementation of the Covenant. It would therefore appear appropriate to recall briefly the main points of these observations.

The Committee of Experts noted that the provisions of Article 2, paragraph 1, of the Covenant, and the nature of a number of the rights recognized in the Covenant, rather than implying an immediate obligation to achieve a fixed standard, require continuing action for the mobilization of available resources in order to progressively implement and improve the exercise of these rights. This is the case,

for example, with the right to work, the right to the enjoyment of just and favourable conditions of work and the right to social security, which the States Parties undertake to recognize in accordance with Articles 6, 7 and 9 respectively of the Covenant. However, in respect of trade union rights, the States Parties undertake in accordance with Article 8 of the Covenant, not only to recognize, but also to ensure the rights in question. The nature of obligations under Article 8 of the Covenant is therefore similar to those under corresponding ILO Conventions. The Committee of Experts also noted that the achievement of union rights is not dependent on the availability of resources, but should represent an important contribution not only to a basic freedom but also to the effective participation of the productive forces in society in the development process.

With regard to the subjects dealt with in the various Articles of the Covenant, those covered by Articles 6–9 are all within the competence of the ILO. In respect of Articles 10–12, only two questions dealt with in paragraphs 2 and 3 of Article 10 fall directly within the scope of the ILO, namely maternity protection and the protection of children and young persons in relation to employment and work. However, of the matters dealt with within the framework of the application of Articles 6–9 of the Covenant, those in the fields of training and employment, remuneration and social security, affect the right to an adequate standard of living, within the meaning of Article 11. Similarly, questions concerning occupational safety and health and the provision of health care within the framework of social security also affect the right to health within the meaning of Article 12. Articles 13–15 deal with questions which fall principally within the scope of organizations other than the ILO.

Article 23 of the Covenant includes among the methods of international action for the achievement of the rights recognized in the Pact, the conclusion of Conventions and the adoption of Recommendations. In this respect, ILO standards that are relevant to Articles 6–10 of the Covenant, even if they have not been ratified, may provide a useful source of reference and guidance in the fields under consideration.

Mention may be made in this connection of the general surveys of the Committee of Experts that are undertaken each year on the application of instruments selected by the Governing Body of the ILO as the subject of reports on unratified Conventions and Recommendations and under article 19 of the Constitution of the International Labour Organisation. These general surveys in recent years have dealt with questions directly linked to the rights provided for under Articles 6–10 of the Covenant: abolition of forced labour (1979), minimum age (1981), freedom of association and collective bargaining (1983), working time (1984), equal remuneration (1986), protection of the working environment (1987). In 1988, the general survey of the Committee of Experts will be on the Discrimination (Employment and Occupation) Convention (No. 111) and Recommendation (No. 111), 1958. In 1989, the survey will deal with social security standards concerning old-age benefits.

In addition to standard-setting activities, other ILO activities may be of interest in view of their relevance to questions having a general influence on the recognition and achievement of the human rights provided for in the Covenant. Reference may be made by way of illustration to the High-Level Meeting on Employment and Structural Adjustment (Geneva, 23–25 November 1987), attended by representatives of the principal international institutions concerned, which examined the consequences of international trade and financial and monetary practices on employment and poverty. These questions are closely related to issues of the current, international economic situation in respect of which the Committee on Economic, Social and Cultural Rights has expressed its deep concern (Report on the First Session of the Committee, paragraph 302). Similarly, a number of the subjects discussed at the International Labour Conference or examined by the various bodies of the Governing Body of the ILO, would be of interest within the framework of the international measures likely to contribute to the effective implementation of the Covenant referred to under its Articles 22 and 23.

As Part II of the report, the ILO presented a list, for each of articles 6 to 10 of the covenant, of the principal relevant ILO conventions, as follows:

Article 6 of the Covenant

Unemployment Convention, 1919 (No. 2); Forced Labour Convention, 1930 (No. 29); Fee-Charging Employment Agencies Convention, 1933 (No. 34); Employment Service Convention, 1948 (No. 88); Fee-Charging Employment Agencies Convention (Revised), 1949 (No. 96); Abolition of Forced Labour Convention, 1957 (No. 105); Discrimination (Employment and Occupation) Convention, 1958 (No. 111); Social Policy (Basic Aims and Standards) Convention, 1962 (No. 117); Employment Policy Convention, 1964 (No. 122); Paid Educational Leave Convention, 1974 (No. 140); Human Resources Development Convention, 1975 (No. 142); Workers with Family Responsibilities Convention, 1981 (No. 156); Termination of Employment Convention, 1982 (No. 158); Vocational Rehabilitation and Employment (Disabled Persons) Convention, 1983 (No. 159).

Article 7 of the Covenant

Remuneration. Minimum Wage-Fixing Machinery Convention, 1928 (No. 26); Minimum Wage-Fixing Machinery (Agriculture) Convention, 1951 (No. 99); Minimum Wage-Fixing Convention, 1970 (No. 131).

Equal Remuneration. Equal Remuneration Convention, 1951 (No. 100).

Rest, limitation of working hours and holidays with pay. Hours of Work (Industry) Convention, 1919 (No. 1); Weekly Rest (Industry) Convention, 1921 (No. 14); Hours of Work (Commerce and Offices) Convention, 1930 (No. 30); Forty-Hour Week Convention, 1935 (No. 47); Holidays with Pay Convention, 1936 (No. 52); Holidays with Pay (Agriculture) Convention, 1952 (No. 101); Weekly Rest (Commerce and Offices) Convention, 1957 (No. 106); Holidays with Pay Convention (Revised), 1970 (No. 132).

Safe and Healthy Working Conditions. White Lead (Painting) Convention, 1921 (No. 13); Marking of Weight (Packages Transported by Vessels) Convention, 1929 (No. 27); Protection against Accidents (Dockers) Convention, 1929 (No. 28); Protection against Accidents (Dockers) Convention (Revised), 1932 (No. 32); Safety Provisions (Building) Convention, 1937 (No. 62); Labour Inspection Convention, 1947 (No. 81); Radiation Protection Convention, 1960 (No. 115); Guarding of Machinery Convention, 1963 (No. 119); Hygiene (Commerce and Offices) Convention, 1964 (No. 120); Maximum Weight Convention, 1967 (No. 127); Labour Inspection (Agriculture) Convention, 1969 (No. 129); Benzene Convention, 1971 (No. 136); Occupational Cancer Convention, 1974 (No. 139); Working Environment (Air Pollution, Noise and Vibration) Convention, 1977 (No. 148); Occupational Safety and Health (Dock Work) Convention, 1979 (No. 152); Occupational Safety and Health Convention, 1981 (No. 155); Occupational Health Services Convention, 1985 (No. 161); Asbestos Convention, 1986 (No. 162).

Article 8 of the Covenant

Right of Association (Agriculture) Convention, 1921 (No. 11); Freedom of Association and Protection of the Right to Organise Convention, 1948 (No. 87); Right to Organise and Collective Bargaining Convention, 1949 (No. 98); Workers' Representatives Convention, 1971 (No. 135); Rural Workers' Organisations Convention, 1975 (No. 141); Labour Relations (Public Service) Convention, 1978 (No. 151); Collective Bargaining Convention, 1981 (No. 154).

Article 9 of the Covenant

Workmen's Compensation (Agriculture) Convention, 1921 (No. 12); Workmen's Compensation (Accidents) Convention, 1925 (No. 17); Workmen's Compensation (Occupational Diseases) Convention, 1925 (No. 18); Equality of Treatment (Accident Compensation) Convention, 1925 (No. 19); Sickness Insurance (Industry) Convention, 1927 (No. 24); Sickness Insurance (Agriculture) Convention, 1927 (No. 25); Old-Age Insurance (Industry, etc.) Convention, 1933 (No. 35); Old-Age Insurance (Agriculture) Convention, 1933 (No. 36); Invalidity Insurance (Industry, etc.) Convention, 1933 (No. 37); Invalidity Insurance (Agriculture) Convention, 1933 (No. 38); Survivors' Insurance (Industry, etc.) Convention, 1933 (No. 39); Survivors' Insurance (Agriculture) Convention, 1933 (No. 40); Workmen's Compensation (Occupational Diseases) Convention (Revised), 1934 (No. 42); Unemployment Provisions Convention, 1934 (No. 44); Maintenance of Migrants' Pension Rights Convention, 1935 (No. 48); Social Security (Minimum Standards) Convention, 1952 (No. 102); Equality of Treatment (Social Security) Convention, 1962 (No. 118); Employment Injury Benefits Convention, 1964 (No. 121); Invalidity, Old-Age and Survivors' Benefits Convention, 1967 (No. 128); Medical Care and Sickness Benefits Convention, 1969 (No. 130); Maintenance of Social Security Rights Convention, 1982 (No. 157).

Article 10 of the Covenant

(a) Maternity Protection (re para. 2). Maternity Protection Convention, 1919 (No. 3); Maternity Protection Convention, (Revised), 1952 (No. 103).

(b) Protection of Children and Young Persons in Relation to Employment and Work (re para. 3). Minimum Age (Industry) Convention, 1919 (No. 5); Minimum Age (Sea) Convention, 1920 (No. 7); Minimum Age (Agriculture) Convention, 1921 (No. 10); Minimum Age (Trimmers and Stokers) Convention, 1921 (No. 15); Minimum Age (Non-Industrial Employment) Convention, 1932 (No. 33); Minimum Age (Sea) Convention (Revised), 1936 (No. 58); Minimum Age (Industry) Convention (Revised), 1937 (No. 59); Minimum Age (Non-Industrial Employment) Convention (Revised), 1937 (No. 60); Minimum Age (Fishermen) Convention, 1959 (No. 112); Social Policy (Basic Aims and Standards) Convention, 1952 (No. 117); Minimum Age (Underground

Work) Convention, 1965 (No. 123); Minimum Age Convention, 1973 (No. 138); Night Work of Young Persons (Industry) Convention, 1919 (No. 6); Night Work (Bakeries) Convention, 1925 (No. 20); Night Work of Young Persons (Non-Industrial Occupations) Convention, 1946 (No. 79); Night Work of Young Persons (Industry) Convention (Revised), 1948 (No. 90); White Lead (Painting) Convention, 1921 (No. 13) (Article 3); Radiation Protection Convention, 1960 (No. 115) (Article 7); Maximum Weight Convention, 1967 (No. 127) (Article 7); Benzene Convention, 1971 (No. 136) (Article 11); Medical Examination of Young Persons (Sea) Convention, 1921 (No. 16); Medical Examination (Seafarers) Convention, 1946 (No. 73); Medical Examination of Young Persons (Industry) Convention, 1946 (No. 77); Medical Examination of Young Persons (Non-Industrial Occupations) Convention, 1946 (No. 78); Medical Examination (Fishermen) Convention, 1959 (No. 113); Medical Examination of Young Persons (Underground Work) Convention, 1965 (No. 124).

ECONOMIC, SOCIAL, AND CULTURAL RIGHTS: LIMBURG PRINCIPLES.

The "Limburg Principles on the Implementation of the International Covenant on Economic, Social and Cultural Rights," set out below, were prepared by a group of independent experts in international law convened by the INTERNATIONAL COMMISSION OF JURISTS, the Faculty of Law of the University of Limburg (Maastricht, the Netherlands), and the Urban Morgan Institute for Human Rights of the University of Cincinnati, U.S.A.

The group met in Maastricht from 2 to 6 June 1986 to consider the nature and scope of the obligations of States parties to the covenant, the consideration of the reports of States parties by the COMMITTEE ON ECONOMIC, SOCIAL AND CULTURAL RIGHTS, and international cooperation under Part IV of the covenant. The principles were drawn to the attention of the UN COMMISSION ON HUMAN RIGHTS at its 1987 session at the request of the Permanent Mission of the Kingdom of the Netherlands (UN Doc. E/CN.4/1987/17).

The 29 experts comprising the group came from Australia, the Federal Republic of Germany, Hungary, Ireland, Mexico, the Netherlands, Norway, Senegal, Spain, the United Kingdom, the United States of America, Yugoslavia, the United Nations Centre for Human Rights, the International Labor Organization (ILO), the United Nations Educational, Scientific and Cultural Organization (UNESCO), the World Health Organization (WHO), the Commonwealth Secretariat, and the sponsoring organizations. Four of the participants were members of the Committee on Economic, Social and Cultural Rights.

The participants agreed unanimously on the following principles which they believe reflect the present state of international law, with the exception of certain recommendations indicated by the use of the verb "should" instead of "shall."

Part I: The Nature and Scope of States Parties' Obligations
A. General Observations

1. Economic, social and cultural rights are an integral part of international human rights law. They are the subject of specific treaty obligations in various international instruments, notably the International Covenant on Economic, Social and Cultural Rights.

2. The International Covenant on Economic, Social and Cultural Rights, together with the International Covenant on Civil and Political Rights and the Optional Protocol, entered into force in 1976. The Covenants serve to elaborate the Universal Declaration of Human Rights: these instruments constitute the International Bill of Human Rights.

3. As human rights and fundamental freedoms are indivisible and interdependent, equal attention and urgent consideration should be given to the implementation, promotion and protection of both civil and political, and economic, social and cultural rights.

4. The International Covenant on Economic, Social and Cultural Rights (hereinafter the Covenant) should, in accordance with the Vienna Convention on the Law of Treaties (Vienna, 1969), be interpreted in good faith, taking into account the object and purpose, the ordinary meaning, the preparatory work and the relevant practice.

5. The experience of the relevant specialized agencies as well as of United Nations bodies and intergovernmental organizations, including the United Nations working groups and special rapporteurs in the field of human rights, should be taken into account in the implementation of the Covenant and in monitoring States parties' achievements.

6. The achievement of economic, social and cultural rights may be realized in a variety of political settings. There is no single road to their full realization. Successes and failures have been registered in both market and non-market economies, in both centralized and decentralized political structures.

7. States parties must at all times act in good faith to fulfil the obligations they have accepted under the Covenant.

8. Although the full realization of the rights recognized in the Covenant is to be attained progressively, the application of some rights can be made justiciable immediately while other rights can become justiciable over time.

9. Non-governmental organizations can play an important role in promoting the implementation of the Covenant. This role should accordingly be facilitated at the national as well as the international level.

10. States parties are accountable both to the international community and to their own people for their compliance with the obligations under the Covenant.

11. A concerted national effort to invoke the full participation of all sectors of society is, therefore, indispensable to achieving progress in realizing economic, social and cultural rights. Popular participation is required at all stages, including the formulation, application and review of national policies.

12. The supervision of compliance with the Covenant should be approached in a spirit of co-operation and dialogue. To this end, in considering the reports of States parties, the Committee on Economic, Social and Cultural Rights, hereinafter called "the Committee", should analyse the causes and factors impeding the realization of the rights covered under the Covenant and, where possible, indicate solutions. This approach should not preclude a finding, where the information available warrants such a

conclusion, that a State party has failed to comply with its obligations under the Covenant.

13. All organs monitoring the Covenant should pay special attention to the principles of non-discrimination and equality before the law when assessing States parties' compliance with the Covenant.

14. Given the significance for development of the progressive realization of the rights set forth in the Covenant, particular attention should be given to measures to improve the standard of living of the poor and other disadvantaged groups, taking into account that special measures may be required to protect cultural rights of indigenous peoples and minorities.

15. Trends in international economic relations should be taken into account in assessing the efforts of the international community to achieve the Covenant's objectives.

B. Interpretative Principles Specifically Relating to Part II of the Covenant

Article 2 (1): "To Take Steps . . . by all Appropriate Means, Including Particularly the Adoption of Legislation." 16. All States parties have an obligation to begin immediately to take steps towards full realization of the rights contained in the Covenant.

17. At the national level States parties shall use all appropriate means, including legislative, administrative, judicial, economic, social and educational measures, consistent with the nature of the rights in order to fulfil their obligations under the Covenant.

18. Legislative measures alone are not sufficient to fulfil the obligations of the Covenant. It should be noted, however, that article 2 (1) would often require legislative action to be taken in cases where existing legislation is in violation of the obligations assumed under the Covenant.

19. States parties shall provide for effective remedies including, where appropriate, judicial remedies.

20. The appropriateness of the means to be applied in a particular State shall be determined by that State party, and shall be subject to review by the United Nations Economic and Social Council, with the assistance of the Committee. Such review shall be without prejudice to the competence of the other organs established pursuant to the Charter of the United Nations.

"To Achieve Progressively the Full Realization of the Rights." 21. The obligation "to achieve progressively the full realization of the rights" requires States parties to move as expeditiously as possible towards the realization of the rights. Under no circumstances shall this be interpreted as implying for States the right to defer indefinitely efforts to ensure full realization. On the contrary all States parties have the obligation to begin immediately to take steps to fulfil their obligations under the Covenant.

22. Some obligations under the Covenant requires immediate implementation in full by all States parties, such as the prohibition of discrimination in article 2 (2) of the Covenant.

23. The obligation of progressive achievement exists independently of the increase in resources; it requires effective use of resources available.

24. Progressive implementation can be effected not only by increasing resources, but also by the development of societal resources necessary for the realization by everyone of the rights recognized in the Covenant.

"To the Maximum of Its Available Resources." 25. States parties are obligated, regardless of the level of economic development, to ensure respect for minimum subsistence rights for all.

26. "Its available resources" refers to both the resources within a State and those available from the international community through international co-operation and assistance.

27. In determining whether adequate measures have been taken for the realization of the rights recognized in the Covenant attention shall be paid to equitable and effective use of and access to the available resources.

28. In the use of the available resources due priority shall be given to the realization of rights recognized in the Covenant, mindful of the need to assure to everyone the satisfaction of subsistence requirements as well as the provision of essential services.

"Individually and Through International Assistance and Co-operation, Especially Economic and Technical." 29. International co-operation and assistance pursuant to the Charter of the United Nations (arts. 55 and 56) and the Covenant shall have in view as a matter of priority the realization of all human rights and fundamental freedoms, economic, social and cultural as well as civil and political.

30. International co-operation and assistance must be directed towards the establishment of a social and international order in which the rights and freedoms set forth in the Covenant can be fully realized (cf. art. 28 Universal Declaration of Human Rights).

31. Irrespective of differences in their political, economic and social systems, States shall co-operate with one another to promote international social, economic and cultural progress, in particular the economic growth of developing countries, free from discrimination based on such differences.

32. States parties shall take steps by international means to assist and co-operate in the realization of the rights recognized by the Covenant.

33. International co-operation and assistance shall be based on the sovereign equality of States and be aimed at the realization of the rights contained in the Covenant.

34. In undertaking international co-operation and assistance pursuant to article 2 (1) the role of international organizations and the contribution of non-governmental organizations shall be kept in mind.

Article 2 (2): Non-discrimination. 35. Article 2 (2) calls for immediate application and involves and explicit guarantee on behalf of the States parties. It should, therefore, be made subject to judicial review and other recourse procedures.

36. The grounds of discrimination mentioned in article 2 (2) are not exhaustive.

37. Upon becoming a party to the Covenant States shall eliminate *de jure* discrimination by abolishing without delay any discriminatory laws, regulations and practices (including acts of omission as well as commission) affecting the enjoyment of economic, social and cultural rights.

38. *De facto* discrimination occurring as a result of the unequal enjoyment of economic, social and cultural rights, on account of a lack of resources or otherwise, should be brought to an end as speedily as possible.

39. Special measures taken for the sole purpose of securing adequate advancement of certain groups or individuals requiring such protection as may be necessary in order to ensure to such groups or individuals equal enjoyment of

economic, social and cultural rights shall not be deemed discrimination, provided, however, that such measures do not, as a consequence, lead to the maintenance of separate rights for different groups and that such measures shall not be continued after their intended objectives have been achieved.

40. Article 2 (2) demands from States parties that they prohibit private persons and bodies from practising discrimination in any field of public life.

41. In the application of article 2 (2) due regard should be paid to all relevant international instruments including the Declaration and Convention on the Elimination of all Forms of Racial Discrimination as well as to the activities of the supervisory committee (CERD) under the said Convention.

Article 2 (3): Non-nationals in Developing Countries. 42. As a general rule the Covenant applies equally to nationals and non-nationals.

43. The purpose of article 2 (3) was to end the domination of certain economic groups of non-nationals during colonial times. In the light of this the exception in article 2 (3) should be interpreted narrowly.

44. This narrow interpretation of article 2 (3) refers in particular to the notion of economic rights and to the notion of developing countries. The latter notion refers to those countries which have gained independence and which fall within the appropriate United Nations classifications of developing countries.

Article 3: Equal Rights for Men and Women. 45. In the application of article 3 due regard should be paid to the Declaration and Convention on the Elimination of All Forms of Discrimination against Women and other relevant instruments and the activities of the supervisory committee (CEDAW) under the said Convention.

Article 4: Limitations. 46. Article 4 was primarily intended to be protective of the rights of individuals rather than permissive of the imposition of limitations by the State.

47. The article was not meant to introduce limitations on rights affecting the subsistence or survival of the individual or integrity of the person.

"Determined by Law."

[The Limburg Principles 48–51 are derived from the Siracusa Principles 15–18, United Nations Doc. E/CN.4/1984/4, 28 September 1984 and 7 Human Rights Quarterly 3 (1985), at p. 5.]

48. No limitation on the exercise of economic, social and cultural rights shall be made unless provided for by national law of general application which is consistent with the Covenant and is in force at the time the limitation is applied.

49. Laws imposing limitations on the exercise of economic, social and cultural rights shall not be arbitrary or unreasonable or discriminatory.

50. Legal rules limiting the exercise of economic, social and cultural rights shall be clear and accessible to everyone.

51. Adequate safeguards and effective remedies shall be provided by law against illegal or abusive imposition on application of limitations on economic, social and cultural rights.

"Promoting the General Welfare." 52. This term shall be construed to mean furthering the well-being of the people as a whole.

"In a Democratic Society." 53. The expression "in a demo-

cratic society" shall be interpreted as imposing a further restriction on the application of limitations.

54. The burden is upon a State imposing limitations to demonstrate that the limitations do not impair the democratic functioning of the society.

55. While there is no single model of a democratic society, a society which recognizes and respects the human rights set forth in the United Nations Charter and the Universal Declaration of Human Rights may be viewed as meeting this definition.

"Compatible With the Nature of These Rights." 56. The restriction "compatible with the nature of these rights" requires that a limitation shall not be interpreted or applied so as to jeopardize the essence of the right concerned.

Article 5. 57. Article 5 (1) underlines the fact that there is no general, implied or residual right for a State to impose limitations beyond those which are specifically provided for in the law. None of the provisions in the law may be interpreted in such a way as to destroy "any of the rights or freedoms recognized". In addition article 5 is intended to ensure that nothing in the Covenant shall be interpreted as impairing the inherent right of all peoples to enjoy and utilize fully and freely their natural wealth and resources.

58. The purpose of article 5 (2) is to ensure that no provision in the Covenant shall be interpreted to prejudice the provisions of domestic law or any bilateral or multilateral treaties, conventions or agreements which are already in force, or may come into force, under which more favourable treatment would be accorded to the persons protected. Neither shall article 5 (2) be interpreted to restrict the exercise of any human right protected to a greater extent by national or international obligations accepted by the State party.

C. Interpretative Principles Specifically Relating to Part III of the Covenant

Article 8: "Prescribed by Law."

[The Limburg Principles 59–69 are derived from the Siracusa Principles 10, 15–26, 29–32 and 35–37, *ibid.*, at pp. 4–7.]

59. See the interpretative principles under the synonymous term "determined by law" in article 4.

"Necessary in a Democratic Society." 60. In addition to the interpretative principles listed under article 4 concerning the phrase "in a democratic society", article 8 imposes a greater restraint upon a State party which is exercising limitations on trade union rights. It requires that such a limitation is indeed necessary. The term "necessary" implies that the limitation:

(a) responds to a pressing public or social need;

(b) pursues a legitimate aim; and

(c) is proportional to that aim.

61. Any assessment as to the necessity of a limitation shall be based upon objective considerations.

"National Security." 62. National security may be invoked to justify measures limiting certain rights only when they are taken to protect the existence of the nation or its territorial integrity or political independence against force or threat of force.

63. National security cannot be invoked as a reason for imposing limitations to prevent merely local or relatively isolated threats to law and order.

64. National security cannot be used as a pretext for imposing vague or arbitrary limitations and may be invoked

only when there exist adequate safeguards and effective remedies against abuse.

65. The systematic violation of economic, social and cultural rights undermines true national security and may jeopardize international peace and security. A State responsible for such violation shall not invoke national security as a justification for measures aimed at suppressing opposition to such violation or at perpetrating repressive practices against its population.

"Public Order (Ordre Public)." 66. The expression "public order *(ordre public)"* as used in the Covenant may be defined as the sum of rules which ensures the functioning of society or the set of fundamental principles on which a society is founded. Respect for economic, social and cultural rights is part of public order *(ordre public)*.

67. Public order *(ordre public)* shall be interpreted in the context of the purpose of the particular economic, social and cultural rights which are limited on this ground.

68. State organs or agents responsible for the maintenance of public order *(ordre public)* shall be subject to controls in the exercise of their power through the parliament, courts, or other competent independent bodies.

"Rights and Freedoms of Others." 69. The scope of the rights and freedoms of others that may act as a limitation upon rights in the Covenant extends beyond the rights and freedoms recognized in the Covenant.

D. Violations of Economic, Social and Cultural Rights

70. A failure by a State party to comply with an obligation contained in the Covenant is, under international law, a violation of the Covenant.

71. In determining what amounts to a failure to comply, it must be borne in mind that the Covenant affords to a State party a margin of discretion in selecting the means for carrying out its objects, and that factors beyond its reasonable control may adversely affect its capacity to implement particular rights.

72. A State party will be in violation of the Covenant, *inter alia,* if:

—it fails to take a step which it is required to take by the Covenant;

—it fails to remove promptly obstacles which it is under a duty to remove to permit the immediate fulfilment of a right;

—it fails to implement without delay a right which it is required by the Covenant to provide immediately;

—it wilfully fails to meet a generally accepted international minimum standard of achievement, which is within its powers to meet;

—it applies a limitation to a right recognized in the Covenant other than in accordance with the Covenant;

—it deliberately retards or halts the progressive realization of a right, unless it is acting within a limitation permitted by the Covenant or it does so due to a lack of available resources or *force majeure;*

—it fails to submit reports as required under the Covenant.

73. In accordance with international law each State party to the Covenant has the right to express the view that another State party is not complying with its obligations under the Covenant and to bring this to the attention of that State party. Any dispute that may thus arise shall be settled in accordance with the relevant rules of international law relating to the peaceful settlement of disputes.

Part II. Consideration of States Parties' Reports and International Co-operation Under Part IV of the Covenant
A. Preparation and Submission of Reports by States Parties

74. The effectiveness of the supervisory machinery provided in Part IV of the Covenant depends largely upon the quality and timeliness of reports by States parties. Governments are therefore urged to make their reports as meaningful as possible. For this purpose they should develop adequate internal procedures for consultations with the competent government departments and agencies, compilation of relevant data, training of staff, acquisition of background documentation, and consultation with relevant non-governmental and international institutions.

75. The preparation of reports under article 16 of the Covenant could be facilitated by the implementation of elements of the programme of advisory services and technical assistance as proposed by the chairmen of the main human rights supervisory organs in their 1984 report to the General Assembly (United Nations Doc. A39/484).

76. States parties should view their reporting obligations as an opportunity for broad public discussion on goals and policies designed to realize economic, social and cultural rights. For this purpose wide publicity should be given to the reports, if possible in draft. The preparation of reports should also be an occasion to review the extent to which relevant national policies adequately reflect the scope and content of each right, and to specify the means by which it is to be realized.

77. States parties are encouraged to examine the possibility of involving non-governmental organizations in the preparation of their reports.

78. In reporting on legal steps taken to give effect to the Covenant, States parties should not merely describe any relevant legislative provisions. They should specify, as appropriate, the judicial remedies, administrative procedures and other measures they have adopted for enforcing those rights and the practice under those remedies and procedures.

79. Quantitative information should be included in the reports of States parties in order to indicate the extent to which the rights are protected in fact. Statistical information and information on budgetary allocations and expenditures should be presented in such a way as to facilitate the assessment of the compliance with Covenant obligations. States parties should, where possible, adopt clearly defined targets and indicators in implementing the Covenant. Such targets and indicators should, as appropriate, be based on criteria established through international cooperation in order to increase the relevance and comparability of data submitted by States parties in their reports.

80. Where necessary, governments should conduct or commission studies to enable them to fill gaps in information regarding progress made and difficulties encountered in achieving the observance of the Covenant rights.

81. Reports by States parties should indicate the areas where more progress could be achieved through international co-operation and suggest economic and technical co-operation programmes that might be helpful toward that end.

82. In order to ensure a meaningful dialogue between the States parties and the organs assessing their compliance with the provisions of the Covenant, States parties should

designate representatives who are fully familiar with the issues raised in the report.

B. Role of the Committee on Economic, Social and Cultural Rights

83. The Committee has been entrusted with assisting the Economic and Social Council in the substantive tasks assigned to it by the Covenant. In particular, its role is to consider States parties reports and to make suggestions and recommendations of a general nature, including suggestions and recommendations as to fuller compliance with the Covenant by States parties. The decision of the Economic and Social Council to replace its sessional Working Group by a Committee of independent experts should lead to a more effective supervision of the implementation by States parties.

84. In order to enable it to discharge fully its responsibilities the Economic and Social Council should ensure that sufficient sessions are provided to the Committee. It is imperative that the necessary staff and facilities for the effective performance of the Committee's functions be provided, in accordance with ECOSOC resolution 1985/17.

85. In order to address the complexity of the substantive issues covered by the Covenant, the Committee might consider delegating certain tasks to its members. For example, drafting groups could be established to prepare preliminary formulations or recommendations of a general nature or summaries of the information received. Rapporteurs could be appointed to assist the work of the Committee in particular to prepare reports on specific topics and for that purpose consult States parties, specialized agencies and relevant experts and to draw up proposals regarding economic and technical assistance projects that could help overcome difficulties States parties have encountered in fulfilling their Covenant obligations.

86. The Committee should, pursuant to articles 22 and 23 of the Covenant, explore with other organs of the United Nations, specialized agencies and other concerned organizations, the possibilities of taking additional international measures likely to contribute to the progressive implementation of the Covenant.

87. The Committee should reconsider the current six-year cycle of reporting in view of the delays which have led to simultaneous consideration of reports submitted under different phases of the cycle. The Committee should also review the guidelines for States parties to assist them in preparing reports and propose any necessary modifications.

88. The Committee should consider inviting States parties to comment on selected topics leading to a direct and sustained dialogue with the Committee.

89. The Committee should devote adequate attention to the methodological issues involved in assessing compliance with the obligations contained in the Covenant. Reference to indicators, in so far as they may help measure progress made in the achievement of certain rights, may be useful in evaluating reports submitted under the Covenant. The Committee should take due account of the indicators selected by or in the framework of the specialized agencies and draw upon or promote additional research, in consultation with the specialized agencies concerned, where gaps have been identified.

90. Whenever the Committee is not satisfied that the information provided by a State party is adequate for a meaningful assessment of progress achieved and difficulties encountered it should request supplementary information, specifying as necessary the precise issues or questions it would like the State party to address.

91. In preparing its reports under ECOSOC resolution 1985/17, the Committee should consider, in addition to the "summary of its consideration of the reports", highlighting thematic issues raised during its deliberations.

C. Relations between the Committee and Specialized Agencies, and Other International Organs

92. The establishment of the Committee should be seen as an opportunity to develop a positive and mutually beneficial relationship between the Committee and the specialized agencies and other international organs.

93. New arrangements under article 18 of the Covenant should be considered where they could enhance the contribution of the specialized agencies to the work of the Committee. Given that the working methods with regard to the implementation of economic, social and cultural rights vary from one specialized agency to another, flexibility is appropriate in making such arrangements under article 18.

94. It is essential for the proper supervision of the implementation of the Covenant under Part IV that a dialogue be developed between the specialized agencies and the Committee with respect to matters of common interest. In particular consultations should address the need for developing indicators for assessing compliance with the Covenant; drafting guidelines for the submission of reports by States parties; making arrangements for submission of reports by the specialized agencies under article 18. Consideration should also be given to any relevant procedures adopted in the agencies. Participation of their representatives in meetings of the Committee would be very valuable.

95. It would be useful if Committee members could visit specialized agencies concerned, learn through personal contact about programmes of the agencies relevant to the realization of the rights contained in the Covenant and discuss the possible areas of collaboration with those agencies.

96. Consultations should be initiated between the Committee and international financial institutions and development agencies to exchange information and share ideas on the distribution of available resources in relation to the realization of the rights recognized in the Covenant. These exchanges should consider the impact of international economic assistance on efforts by States parties to implement the Covenant and possibilities of technical and economic co-operation under article 22 of the Covenant.

97. The Commission on Human Rights, in addition to its responsibilities under article 19 of the Covenant, should take into account the work of the Committee in its consideration of items on its agenda relating to economic, social and cultural rights.

98. The Covenant on Economic, Social and Cultural Rights is related to the Covenant on Civil and Political Rights. Although most rights can clearly be delineated as falling within the framework of one or other Covenant, there are several rights and provisions referred to in both instruments which are not susceptible to clear differentiation. Both Covenants moreover share common provisions and articles. It is important that consultative arrangements be established between the Economic, Social and Cultural Rights Committee and the Human Rights Committee.

99. Given the relevance of other international legal instruments to the Covenant, early consideration should be given by the Economic and Social Council to the need for

developing effective consultative arrangements between the various supervisory bodies.

100. International and regional intergovernmental organizations concerned with the realization of economic, social and cultural rights are urged to develop measures, as appropriate, to promote the implementation of the Covenant.

101. As the Committee is a subsidiary organ of the Economic and Social Council, non-governmental organizations enjoying consultative status with the Economic and Social Council are urged to attend and follow the meetings of the Committee and, when appropriate, to submit information in accordance with ECOSOC resolution 1296 (XLIV).

102. The Committee should develop, in co-operation with intergovernmental organizations and non-governmental organizations as well as research institutes an agreed system for recording, storing and making accessible case law and other interpretative material relating to international instruments on economic, social and cultural rights.

103. As one of the measures recommended in article 23 it is recommended that seminars be held periodically to review the work of the Committee and the progress made in the realization of economic, social and cultural rights by States parties.

ECONOMIC, SOCIAL AND CULTURAL RIGHTS: STUDIES. An extensive study entitled *The Realization of Economic, Social and Cultural Rights: Problems, Policies, Progress,* prepared by Mr. Manouchehr Ganji (Iran) as special rapporteur of the UN COMMISSION ON HUMAN RIGHTS, was published by the United Nations in 1975 (United Nations publication, Sales No. E.75.XIV.2). The study reviewed and summarized the situation regarding national norms and standards relating to economic, social, and cultural rights in the less developed countries, in the socialist countries of eastern Europe, and in the developed market-economy countries. It also summarized the international action taken, up to the time of its publication, for the promotion and protection of economic, social, and cultural rights and concluded with a series of observations, conclusions, and recommendations.

On recommendation of the commission, the Economic and Social Council in 1974 drew the attention (resolution 1867 [LVI]) of all States and organizations within the United Nations system to the study and in particular to the observations, conclusions, and recommendations of the special rapporteur. Later the commission itself, having reviewed the report in greater detail, stressed at its 1977 session "the responsibility and duty of all members of the international community to create the necessary conditions for the full realization of economic, social and cultural rights as an essential means of ensuring the real and meaningful enjoyment of civil and political rights and fundamental freedoms," and called upon all States to take national and international measures to remove all obstacles to the full enjoyment of those rights.

The commission recommended that the Economic and Social Council invite the Secretary-General, in cooperation with UNESCO and other competent specialized agencies, to undertake a study on the subject "The International Dimensions of the Right to Development as a Human Right in Relation with Other Human Rights based on International Co-operation, Taking into Account the Requirements of the New International Economic Order and the Fundamental Human Needs." The council endorsed this proposal on 13 May 1977 (decision 229 [LXII]). The study prepared by the Secretary-General (UN Doc. E/CN.4/1988/9 and Add. 1 and 2) led eventually to the adoption of the DECLARATION ON THE RIGHT TO DEVELOPMENT and to the continuing activity of the commission's WORKING GROUP OF GOVERNMENTAL EXPERTS ON THE RIGHT TO DEVELOPMENT.

In 1987, the commission, mindful that the implementation and promotion of economic, social, and cultural rights had not received sufficient attention, requested the Sub-Commission on Prevention of Discrimination and Protection of Minorities (resolution 1987/19) to review the conclusions and recommendations of the report entitled *The Realization of Economic, Social and Cultural Rights: Problems, Policies Progress* and to propose a timetable for updating its conclusions and recommendations, many of which had been overtaken by events. The sub-commission was also asked to consider the preparation of a study on the impact on human rights of the policies and practices of the major international financial institutions, most notably the International Monetary Fund and the World Bank.

In response, the sub-commission requested authorization (resolution 1987/29) to appoint one of its members as special rapporteur to study problems, policies, and progressive measures relating to a more effective realization of economic, social, and cultural rights, which would take into account all available documentation on both subjects suggested by the commission and would pay special attention to the human rights aspects of such problems as the interrelationship between structural adjustment and food security, employment, health care, education, and cultural development.

Having received the authorization of the council, the sub-commission decided to entrust the study to one of its members, Mr. Danilo Türk (Yugoslavia), and called upon him to submit a preliminary report at its session in 1989.

A preliminary report entitled "Realization of Economic, Social and Cultural Rights" was presented to the sub-commission at its 1989 session (UN Doc. E/

CN.4/Sub2./1989/19). In the report, the special rapporteur outlined what he considered to be the main questions to be analyzed in the final version of his study with a view to providing a basis for discussion in the sub-commission. He then offered a series of tentative conclusions arising out of his preliminary work, and suggested that the study should be focused on the following problem areas (chap. IV, para. 94):

(a) The question of the evolution of a unified approach to the interpretation and realization of economic, social and cultural rights should be further discussed. This study should contribute to a more balanced approach to both major sets of human rights and to further elaboration of the concept of the interdependence and indivisibility of human rights;

(b) As regards the problem of the realization of economic, social and cultural rights at the national level, the study should focus on two questions: first, the question of extreme poverty and, secondly, the question of the effects of structural adjustment policies on the realization of economic, social and cultural rights. The basic reasons supporting this choice are explained in this preliminary report, while the analytical work will be done at subsequent stages;

(c) International co-operation constitutes a vital element in the realization of economic, social and cultural rights. Further analysis will focus on, first, questions relating to the future work of the specialized agencies which operate in the areas of economic, social and cultural rights (ILO, FAO, UNESCO and WHO) and, secondly, questions relating to the impact of the activities of the international financial institutions (notably IMF and IBRD) on the realization of economic, social and cultural rights;

(d) In the present preliminary report, the question of the possible role of United Nations development agencies, including UNDP, in the realization of economic, social and cultural rights has not been discussed. It is undeniable that this question should be addressed at an appropriate stage. However, it should be dealt with only after completion of the first round of analysis of the problems discussed in the present preliminary report. The same preliminary conclusion applies to the question of strengthening the co-ordinating role of the Economic and Social Council and the Commission on Human Rights in the field of realization of economic, social and cultural rights;

(e) The subsequent phase of preparation of the study on the realization of economic, social and cultural rights will be devoted to an analysis of the problems referred to in this preliminary report. The primary sources of information will be the relevant studies, reports and other documents prepared within the United Nations system as well as the relevant specialized literature and the information provided by non-governmental organizations. A further source of information will be the replies by States on the realization of economic, social and cultural rights under the relevant resolutions of the Commission on Human Rights and the reports of States under article 16 of the International Covenant on Economic, Social and Cultural Rights. The members of the Sub-Commission are invited to make their suggestions to the Special Rapporteur regarding the sources of information to be consulted;

(f) An additional method to be used at subsequent stages might be the attempt to collect information and to study particular experiences in the realization of economic, social and cultural rights in different States, particularly in those States that are experiencing the problems of implementation of structural adjustment programmes. The Special Rapporteur is ready to consult with the Governments that so wish in order to present their experience in subsequent reports on the realization of economic, social and cultural rights;

(g) Finally, the Special Rapporteur would appreciate it if the Sub-Commission would discuss, at its forty-first session, the possibility of considering the question of realization of economic, social and cultural rights under a separate item of its agenda. Consideration and a possible decision on this question will be important for the formulation of the methodology and timing of subsequent reports by the Special Rapporteur on the realization of economic, social and cultural rights.

The sub-commission examined the preliminary report, endorsed the special rapporteur's tentative conclusions, and requested him to prepare a report on the progress of his study for consideration at future sessions.

ECONOMIC, SOCIAL AND CULTURAL RIGHTS: UNESCO ACTIVITIES. In its 1988 report to the Economic and Social Council under article 18 of the INTERNATIONAL COVENANT ON ECONOMIC, SOCIAL AND CULTURAL RIGHTS (UN Doc. E/1988/7), the UNITED NATIONS EDUCATIONAL, SCIENTIFIC AND CULTURAL ORGANIZATION states that:

This report contains information on the progress made in achieving observance of the provisions of articles 13 to 15 of the International Covenant on Economic, Social and Cultural Rights. The last report was made in August 1981 in implementation of a decision of the Executive Board (109 EX/Decision 5.4.3) which instructed the Committee on Conventions and Recommendations "to prepare, pursuant to article 18 of the Covenant, a report on progress made in the enforcement of human rights that fall within the context of the Organization's activities, including *inter alia* information on the decisions and recommendations adopted by the General Conference and the Executive Board." Since the reporting period for specialized agencies is six years, this report is tabled for consideration by the Committee on Economic, Social and Cultural Rights at the spring 1988 session.

The normative instruments to which this report refers, and their state of ratification, are set out in annex I. The body of this report will deal with the implementation of some of these as well as, in some cases, programs of relevance to implementation.

Normative instruments, however, by their nature are only illustrative of the work UNESCO has done that is relevant to the subject of this document. Literacy for example is of importance not only to the right to education but to rights to culture, while copyright provisions, not mentioned in this document, are nevertheless crucial to the writer, actor or performer. General work on human rights or on discrimination has not been mentioned. This work is nevertheless crucial to the way in which the articles here dealt with are really implemented.

The report summarizes briefly (para. 8–10) UNESCO's system involving submission by member States of periodic reports, as follows:

Under the terms of Article VIII of UNESCO's Constitution, every Member State is required to submit to the Organization, at the request of the General Conference, a report on the action taken by it to give effect to recommendations and conventions it has adopted. In addition, under Article 7 of the Convention, States parties thereto must give information to the General Conference concerning the legislative and administrative provisions which they have adopted for the application of that Convention. A similar provision is included in the Recommendation in respect of all Member States. Moreover, the *Ad Hoc* Committee of Governmental Experts which drew up the Convention and the Recommendation stressed the decisive role that the reports would have to play in the conduct of a positive and continuous policy for which the Convention provides the essential basis. At its thirteenth session, in 1964, the General Conference decided that the time had come to give effect to the provisions of Article 7 of the Convention and to the similar provisions of the Recommendation, and it invited the Executive Board to take the necessary measures to put into effect by 1965 a procedure for the submission and examination of reports from Member States.

By a decision adopted in May 1965 (70 EX/Decision 5.2.1), the Executive Board stipulated that the reports of the Governments should be presented at regular intervals in a standardized form so as to cover all the provisions of both the Convention and the Recommendation and enable the General Conference to make an evaluation of their worth, as well as formulate proposals for new recommendations. The same decision also stated that, to ensure uniformity in the reports, clear, specific and simple questionnaires should be prepared to which Governments would be requested to reply within 10 months.

Lastly, the Executive Board decided that these reports, after analysis by the Secretariat, would be examined by a special committee of the Executive Board and transmitted with the Board's comments to the General Conference.

Article 13: Right to Education. The 1988 report lists eight UNESCO instruments as being of particular relevance to realization of the right to education. It does not, however, provide specific information on the significance of these instruments to the implementation of the provisions of article 13. The eight UNESCO instruments are as follows:

(a), (b) and (c) The Convention and Recommendation against Discrimination in Education, of 14 December 1960 and the Protocol instituting a Conciliation and Good Offices Commission to be responsible for seeking the settlement of any disputes which may arise between States Parties to the Convention against Discrimination in Education, of 10 December 1962;

(d) The Revised Recommendation concerning Technical and Vocational Education, of 19 November 1974;

(e) The Recommendation concerning the Status of Teachers, of 5 October 1966;

(f) The Recommendation concerning Education for International Understanding, Co-operation and Peace and Education Relating to Human Rights and Fundamental Freedoms, of 19 November 1974;

(g) The Recommendation on the Development of Adult Education, of 26 November 1976;

(h) The Declaration on Race and Racial Prejudice, of 27 November 1978;

(i) The International Charter of Physical Education and Sport, of 21 November 1978.

Implementation of the Convention and Recommendation against Discrimination in Education. In its 1988 report to the Economic and Social Council, UNESCO quotes, in para. 16–32, the following extracts from the report submitted to the UNESCO General Conference in Sofia in 1985 on the implementation of the UNESCO CONVENTION AGAINST DISCRIMINATION IN EDUCATION and the corresponding recommendation. The report was based on examination, by UNESCO's Committee on Conventions and Recommendations, of information supplied by the governments of 84 countries:

Discrimination. The Committee noted that with the sole exception of the report drawn up by the United Nations body responsible for Namibia all the replies received contained the assertion that there are no legal provisions or regulations providing for discrimination in education.

The Committee observed that certain situations described in some of the reports were of a discriminatory nature, although it was not always possible to determine whether such situations result from a deficiency in the law or from specific infringements of it.

Furthermore, the Committee noted that preferential measures were taken for the benefit of underprivileged groups in some countries. As it already indicated in its previous reports, it considers that the differences introduced for the purposes of protection and consisting, for example, in according preferential treatment to children from culturally underprivileged backgrounds are not discriminatory in the sense in which this term is used in the Convention and Recommendation, but on the contrary are some of the legitimate means of promoting equality of opportunity, in the spirit of the relevant provisions of the International Convention on the Elimination of all Forms of Racial Discrimination adopted by the United Nations General Assembly at its twentieth session.

Separate Educational Systems or Establishments for Students of the Two Sexes. The Committee was already of the opinion in its third report that it was possible to detect a gradual expansion of co-education, especially at the primary and higher levels. It would seem clear from the fourth consultation that this tendency has increased and that co-education has been introduced in some countries where, for traditional or pedagogical reasons, separate education was the rule. In these countries co-educational institutions have appeared alongside single sex establishments, which have continued in existence mainly at the secondary level.

The Committee has also noted with satisfaction the efforts made by some developing States to achieve not only equal opportunity of access to education for both sexes and an improvement in the enrolment ratio of girls (which nevertheless still remains considerably lower than that of boys), but also equality as regards the courses of study available, the equipment and the qualifications of the staff when education is provided in separate establishments.

Compulsory and Free Primary Education. Despite improvements in the enrolment ratios in the vast majority of the countries, primary education has not been made compulsory and provided free of charge in a number of Member States on account of a number of difficulties, which include not only the lack of financial resources, the shortage of teachers, shortages of educational equipment and facilities and the geographically scattered nature of the population, but also in some cases restrictions of a religious or traditional nature and even the opposition of parents who require the assistance of their children for agricultural or domestic work.

Generalization of Secondary Education. The Committee is pleased to note the progress which has been achieved by many Member States towards the generalization of secondary education. The extension of compulsory schooling to cover the first phase or all the various phases of such education has been achieved in several countries; such schooling has been provided free of charge and this principle has often been extended to cover textbooks, meals, clothing and even the provision of accommodation for pupils in some States. The considerable increase achieved over 10 years in enrolment ratios for the child population as a whole in the case of Benin or for the culturally underprivileged aboriginal groups in the case of Australia reveal the success of the efforts undertaken by the Governments concerned.

The Committee also noted with interest the attention given by many Member States to achieving a fair balance between general secondary education and vocational and professional training in order to create a better preparation for working life and take into account socio-economic conditions and the needs of the labour market.

The reports of several States mention the difficulties which they have encountered in their efforts to generalize secondary education: inadequacy of financial resources, shortages of teachers, lack of premises and equipment and the scattered nature of the population.

Access to Higher Education. New higher education establishments have been set up in several countries and a decentralization effort is under way in certain States with a view to making access to higher education easier for population groups far away from the metropolitan countries and major cities, through improved geographical distribution.

The Committee noted with satisfaction that this growth in higher education is accompanied in several countries by better access to this level of education for hitherto disadvantaged population categories. It noted the information contained in certain reports stressing that the proportion of minorities in the student population has improved considerably, or that the number of female students is about to reach, as in Poland, or even overtake, as in the United States, that of male students.

The Committee further noted that several Governments which had answered this part of the questionnaire were of the view that equality of access to higher education based on the abilities of each person had been achieved in their territories. Certain reports specify that higher education is in fact open to all according to individual abilities, merits and aptitudes.

The Committee must however observe that the concept of equality of opportunities and treatment is much wider and more complex than that of mere legal equality in the right of access: it also covers the differences existing between *de facto* situations and the resultant material difficulties, which national policies seeking to establish equality of opportunities, which the 1960 instruments require States to develop and implement, must strive to overcome.

Free education is an important factor in equality of opportunity and the Committee noted with satisfaction that it had been extended to higher education in many countries. It also noted, however, that the cost of registration and tuition fees in several States was too high and that it hampered access by many candidates to this level of education.

The granting of fellowships and loans to students offsets these difficulties to a certain extent and the Committee noted with interest information providing details, in the reports received, of financial assistance and other facilities granted to students in order to meet both their registration and tuition fees and their maintenance expenses.

Adult Education and Continuing Education. The Committee was happy to note the interest shown by all the 58 Governments who replied to this part of the questionnaire in the struggle against illiteracy. During the past 12 years, and particularly since the last consultation of Member States, major strides have been made in this field and the illiteracy rate has fallen markedly in many countries.

The Committee further noted that the efforts of the Governments concerned were not limited merely to providing literacy training for persons who had not received any primary education and that craft or vocational training taking employment needs into account had been organized in most cases.

In any case, adult education is not restricted to the primary level. Continuing education leading to or even including higher education has been organized in many countries.

Implementation of the Revised Recommendation concerning Technical and Vocational Education. According to the revised recommendation [para. 33–34], adopted by the UNESCO General Conference on 19 November 1974, member States should contribute to the achievement of society's goals of greater democratization and social, cultural, and economic development through technical and vocational education, which should aim at eliminating barriers between levels and areas of education, between education and employment and between school and society. The Revised Recommendation makes specific reference to equality of access for women and men to such education, special forms of education for disadvantaged and handicapped persons, participation of representatives of various segments of society in policy formulation on local and national levels, and equal standards of quality in different educational streams in order to exclude possible discrimination between them.

In accordance with resolution 25 adopted by the General Conference at its twenty-second session, a questionnaire for reporting on the implementation of the Revised Recommendation since its adoption in 1974 was sent to all Member States in December 1985 and a synoptic analysis of the 44 reports received was submitted to the Committee on Conventions and Recommendations of the Executive Board at its one hundred and twenty-second session. Also, in conformity with the above-cited resolution, the Committee's report, which contains the synoptic analysis as well as the Committee's conclusions and recommendations, including a proposed timetable for the second consultation of Member States on the application of the Revised Recommendation, will be submitted to the General Conference at its twenty-fourth session.

Implementation of the Recommendation concerning the Status of Teachers. The UNESCO General Conference, on the basis of the report [para. 35–37] on the application of the Recommendation submitted to it by the Joint ILO/UNESCO Committee of Experts on the Application of the Recommendation concerning the Status of Teachers, invited Member States to respond to the next questionnaire to be sent to them on the application of the Recommendation and also invited the Director-General, in consultation with the Director-General of the International Labour Office, to continue to examine the question of a possible revision of the Recommendation.

The fourth questionnaire relating to the implementation of the Recommendation on the Status of Teachers was sent to Member States in January 1987. The replies of Member States will be analysed by the Joint ILO/UNESCO Committee of Experts and a report presented to the General Conference in 1989.

The programme of activities undertaken during the 1984–1985 and 1986–1987 biennia has been based on the conclusions of the 1982 report of the Joint ILO/UNESCO Committee of Experts dealing notably with the need for the improvement of the quality of teachers through training. Studies concerning a possible convention were carried out in 1987 and consultations with ILO are in progress prior to the preparation of a technical report on the question for submission to the Executive Board and the General Conference.

Implementation of the Recommendation concerning Education for International Understanding, Co-operation and Peace and Education relating to Human Rights and Fundamental Freedoms [para. 38–39]. The Intergovernmental Conference on Education for International Understanding, Co-operation and Peace and Education Relating to Human Rights and Fundamental Freedoms, with a view to Developing a Climate of Opinion Favourable to the Strengthening of Security and Disarmament (April 1983) was convened by the Director-General of UNESCO, in pursuance of resolution 1/01 (paragraph 5 (d)) adopted by the General Conference at its twenty-first session; it took place at UNESCO Headquarters in Paris from 12 to 20 April 1983, and was considered by the speakers to occupy a special place in UNESCO's action in the development of international education, and to reflect increased awareness of the role played by education in the fields covered by the 1974 Recommendation.

The program for 1986–1987 included:

(i) The launching of a Plan for the Development of Education for International Understanding, Co-operation and Peace, which was adopted at the twenty-third session of the General Conference, and executed in 1986, which was proclaimed International Year of Peace by the United Nations General Assembly.

(ii) The establishment of a Consultative Committee on steps to promote the full and comprehensive implementation of the 1974 Recommendation.

(iii) The establishment of a permanent system of reporting on the steps taken by Member States to implement the 1974 Recommendation. . . .

Implementation of the Declaration on Race and Racial Prejudice [para. 41–42]. In accordance with paragraph 2 (a), (b) and (c) of the resolution for the implementation of that Declaration, the Director-General prepared "a comprehensive report on the world situation in the fields covered by the Declaration", which was submitted to the General

Conference at its twenty-first session, held in 1980, in the case of the first report (UNESCO Doc. 21 C/78). The second report (UNESCO Doc. 22 C/86) was submitted to the General Conference in 1983.

In pursuance of resolution 12.2 adopted at that session, which invites the Director-General "to increase to four years the periodicity of his comprehensive reports on the world situation in the fields covered by the Declaration on Race and Racial Prejudice", the third report will be submitted to the General Conference in 1987. . . .

Implementation of the Recommendation on the Development of Adult Education [para. 47–52]. The fourth International Conference on Adult Education was held in Paris from 19 to 29 March 1985. Among other topics, the Conference discussed the development of adult education as an essential prerequisite for lifelong education and an important factor in the democratization of education. The Conference also considered the contribution adult education could make to the development of active participation in economic, social and cultural life. A declaration on "the right to learn" was unanimously adopted.

The International Congress on Human Rights Teaching, Information and Documentation, nine years after the Vienna International Congress on the Teaching of Human Rights, was held in Malta from 31 August to 5 September 1987.

The programme covered the following themes: human rights education and teaching; human rights research in the social and human sciences, legal and political sciences, history and philosophy; human rights information and documentation.

After recalling the provisions of Article 13 (1) of the International Covenant on Economic, Social and Cultural Rights and Article 7 of the International Convention on the Elimination of all Forms of Racial Discrimination, the Congress recommended that in its periodic reports to the Committee of Experts on the International Covenant on Economic, Social and Cultural Rights and to the Committee on the Elimination of Racial Discrimination (CERD) respectively, UNESCO draw the attention of Member States to their obligation to ensure the human rights education requested in Article 13 (1) of the Covenant and Article 7 of the Convention, and particularly to the efforts made by the States parties to include human rights teaching in school and university curricula.

In the recommendations regarding priorities for research, the main emphasis was placed on economic, social and cultural rights and the exercise of individual rights. In addition, UNESCO was requested to further the debate on collective rights with a view to elucidating their various dimensions. Prominence was thus given to research on the interactions between individual human rights and the rights of ethnic, religious, political or other minorities. Furthermore, the participants in the Congress considered that UNESCO should contribute to analysing the different conceptual approaches to human rights in view of the fact that, despite appearances, they refer at present to different contexts.

In co-operation with the committee for research on the sociology of education of the International Sociological Association, a series of studies on the right to education were prepared and discussed at the World Congress of Sociology, held in New Delhi (India) in August 1986. The studies, relating in particular to Colombia, Ghana, Guyana, Nigeria, Pakistan and the Philippines, highlight the structural obstacles to the effective exercise of the right to education and the efforts made to overcome them. Special attention is paid to the question of access of girls and women to education.

In addition, in collaboration with the International Association for the Development of Cross-Cultural Communication (AIMAV) and in co-operation with the Faculty of Law of the Federal University of Pernambuco, UNESCO organized an international symposium in Recife (Brazil) from 7 to 9 October 1987 on human rights and cultural rights, particularly linguistic rights.

Implementation of the International Charter of Physical Education and Sport. In adopting this Charter on 21 November 1987, the UNESCO General Conference expressed its conviction "that one of the essential conditions for the effective exercise of human [para. 53–60] rights is that everyone should be free to develop and preserve his or her physical, intellectual and moral powers, and that access to physical education and sport should consequently be assured and guaranteed for all human beings". The Preamble also recalls the United Nations Charter, in which the peoples proclaim their faith in fundamental human rights, and the Universal Declaration of Human Rights. The purpose of the Charter, according to the final paragraph of the Preamble is "placing the development of physical education and sport at the service of human progress, promoting their development, and urging governments, competent non-governmental organizations, educators, families and individuals themselves to be guided thereby, to disseminate it and to put it into practice".

In accordance with Article 1 of the Charter, which stipulates that "every human being has a fundamental right of access to physical education and sport", considerable progress has been noted in respect of the training of personnel, the extension of the practice of sport for all and international co-operation.

With regard to training, concerning which the Charter states in Article 4, paragraph 4.1, that all personnel who assume professional responsibility for physical education and sport must be given preliminary as well as further training, two subregional seminars, one of which was to promote sport for women, and one national seminar were organized in Africa in 1986 and 1987, training courses were provided in Latin America (Brazil and Mexico) and a seminar was held in Asia in 1985 (Republic of Korea).

The practice of physical education and sport for all was in fact extended to girls and women as a result of pilot projects carried out in Egypt, Peru and the Philippines within the framework of the 1986–1987 biennium, along with a national seminar held in Africa.

Millions of people in all population groups participated in the first World Week of Physical Fitness and Sport for All, organized in the context of International Youth Year in 1985. A second such Week is planned during the 1988–1989 biennium.

The rehabilitation of certain traditional sports such as wushu in China has enabled thousands of people to rediscover and practise them. Studies and research have been undertaken on traditional games and dances, thereby opening up the possibilty of organizing world traditional games and dance festivals (document 24 C/5).

Agreements and a memorandum on co-operation have been signed with the Supreme Council for Sport in Africa (SCSA), the Conférence des ministres de la jeunesse et des sports des pays d'expression française (CONFEJES) and the International Olympic Committee (IOC).

Lastly, it is noteworthy that since the adoption of a recommendation concerning the difficulties involved in organizing and staging international sports competitions by the Intergovernmental Committee for Physical Education and Sport, which has held five sessions since it was set up (1979, 1981, 1983, 1984 and 1986), the Organization has hosted the second United Nations International Conference on Sports Boycott against South Africa (1986) and contributed to the preparation of the United Nations International Convention against *Apartheid* in Sports.

Article 15. Right to Take Part in Cultural Life and Enjoy the Benefits of Scientific Progress. The 1988 report lists 15 UNESCO instruments as being of general relevance to realization of the right to take part in cultural life and enjoy the benefits of scientific progress, as follows:

(a) Convention for the Protection of Cultural Property in the Event of Armed Conflict, with Regulations for the Execution of the Convention of 14 May 1954 (Hague Convention);

(b) Protocol for the Protection of Cultural Property in the Event of Armed Conflict, of 14 May 1954;

(c) Recommendation concerning the Most Effective Means of Rendering Museums Accessible to Everyone, of 14 December 1960;

(d) Recommendation on the Means of Prohibiting and Preventing the Illicit Export, Import and Transfer of Ownership of Cultural Property, of 19 November 1964;

(e) Declaration of the Principles of International Cultural Co-operation, of 4 November 1966;

(f) Convention on the Means of Prohibiting and Preventing the Illicit Import, Export and Transfer of Ownership of Cultural Property, of 14 November 1970;

(g) Declaration of Guiding Principles on the Use of Satellite Broadcasting for the Free Flow of Information, the Spread of Education and Greater Cultural Exchange, of 15 November 1972;

(h) Recommendation concerning the Protection, at National Level, of the Cultural and Natural Heritage, of 16 November 1972;

(i) Convention concerning the Protection of the World Cultural Heritage, of 16 November 1972;

(j) Recommendation concerning the Safeguarding and Contemporary Role of Historic Areas, of 26 November 1976;

(k) Recommendation on Participation by the People at Large in Cultural Life and Their Contribution to It, of 26 November 1976;

(l) Declaration on Fundamental Principles concerning the Contribution of the Mass Media to Strengthening Peace and International Understanding, to the Promotion of Human Rights and to Countering Racialism, *Apartheid* and Incitement to War, of 28 November 1978;

(m) Recommendation on the Protection of Movable Cultural Property, of 28 November 1978;

Of these, the report considers in detail only three of the more recently adopted instruments, pointing out that, while this approach is dictated by the need to avoid an unduly long report, the remaining instruments are all of considerable importance in terms of the implementation of the International Covenant on Economic, Social and Cultural Rights.

Implementation of the Recommendation on Participation by the People at Large in Cultural Life and Their Contribution to It (para. 62–69). This recommendation, adopted by the UNESCO General Conference on 26 November 1976, aims to promote cultural rights as human rights and

to ensure by appropriate legislation and regulations as well as by technical, administrative, economic and financial measures, access to culture and participation in cultural life by the population at large.

The recommendation specifies that "culture is an integral part of social life", that it is "at one and the same time the acquisition of knowledge, the demand for a way of life and the need to communicate" and that "participation by the greatest possible number of people and associations in a wide variety of cultural activities of their own free choice is essential to the development of basic human values and dignity of the individual".

In its preamble the recommendation makes reference to the obligations of States under a number of international instruments, including the International Covenant on Economic, Social and Cultural Rights. In addition the preamble notes that cultural action often involves only a minute proportion of the population and that existing organizations and means used do not always meet the needs of those who are in a particularly vulnerable position because of their inadequate education, low standard of living, poor housing conditions and economic and social dependence in general. It also notes that there is often a wide discrepancy between the reality and the proclaimed ideals, declared intentions, programmes or expected results, but observes that while it is essential and urgent to define objectives, contents and methods for a policy of participation by the people at large in cultural life, the solutions envisaged cannot be identical for all countries, in view of the current differences between the socio-economic and political situations in States.

The broad scope of the recommendation is indicated in its first Article which states that it concerns everything that should be done by Member States or the authorities to democratize the means and instruments of cultural activity, so as to enable all individuals to participate freely and fully in cultural creation and its benefits, in accordance with the requirements of social progress.

The recommendation also contains definitions of the phrases "access to culture", "participation in cultural life" and "communication" and provides that free participation in cultural life is related to policy in a wide range of other areas including development in general, lifelong education, science and technology, social progress, environment, communication and international co-operation. In general the recommendation provides, *inter alia,* that States should take appropriate action in order to: guarantee as human rights those rights bearing on access to and participation in cultural life; provide effective safeguards for free access to national and world cultures by all members of society without distinction or discrimination based on race, colour, sex, language, religion, political convictions, national or social origin, financial situation or any other consideration; pay special attention to women's full entitlement to access to culture and of effective participation in cultural life; create

appropriate conditions enabling the populations to play an increasingly active part in building the future of their society, to assume responsibilities and duties and exercise rights in that process; and to guarantee the recognition of the equality of cultures, including the cultures of national minorities and of foreign minorities if they exist, as forming part of the common heritage of all mankind, and ensure that they are promoted at all levels without discrimination.

A World Conference on Cultural Policies (MONDIACULT) was held in Mexico to take stock of the experience gained since the Venice Conference. Its purpose was to stimulate thinking on the fundamental problems of culture in the contemporary world and in the world of tomorrow and to formulate new guidelines (cf. paras. 17 to 22 of the Mexico City Declaration on Cultural Policies).

In accordance with Recommendation No. 27 adopted by the World Conference on Cultural Policies (MONDIACULT), the United Nations General Assembly, on the proposal of UNESCO, proclaimed, on 8 December 1986, the World Decade for Cultural Development for the period 1988–1997. Two of the four objectives to which the Plan of Action for the Decade are keyed bear explicitly upon (a) broadening participation in culture and (b) promotion of international cultural co-operation.

Mention should also be made of the studies undertaken on the rights and legislative provisions enshrined in the legal systems of some countries in respect of culture, in order to identify those of them that facilitate the application of the measures advocated in the Recommendation on Participation by the People at Large in Cultural Life and Their Contribution to It and the various MONDIACULT recommendations.

Implementation of the Declaration on Fundamental Principles concerning the Contribution of the Mass Media to Strengthening Peace and International Understanding, to the Promotion of Human Rights and to Countering Racialism, Apartheid and Incitement to War. This declaration, adopted by the UNESCO General Conference on 28 November 1978, is of major importance in the context of UNESCO's efforts to ensure, pursuant to article 2, para. 2, of the covenant that the rights with which it is concerned will be exercised without discrimination of any kind. The declaration is of particular relevance in relation to article 15, para. 4, of the covenant, whereby States parties recognize the benefits to be derived from the encouragement and development of international contacts and cooperation in the scientific and cultural fields (para. 72).

The principles on which the Declaration is based are clearly indicated in Article I, which states that:

"The strengthening of peace and international understanding, the promotion of human rights and the countering of racialism, *apartheid* and incitement to war demand a free flow and a wider and better balanced dissemination of information. To this end, the mass media have a leading contribution to make. This contribution will be the more effective to the extent that the information reflects the different aspects of the subject dealt with. . . ."

A new world information and communication order [para. 75–77]. Resolution 21 C/4.19 states a number of considerations

E

on which a new world information and communication order could be based, including:

respect for each people's cultural identity and for the right of each nation to inform the world public about its interests, its aspirations and its social and cultural values;

respect for the right of all peoples to participate in international exchanges of information on the basis of equality, justice and mutual benefit; and

respect for the right of the public, of ethnic and social groups and of individuals to have access to information sources and to participate actively in the communication process.

UNESCO's efforts in the past few years have concentrated mostly on the further elucidation of the notion of a new world information and communication order. Thus, the first roundtable on this subject was organized jointly with the United Nations Department of Public Information in Igls, Austria, September 1983, followed by a second roundtable, held in Copenhagen, Denmark, April 1986. The reports of both of these roundtables were submitted respectively to the United Nations General Assembly. Parallel to that, the General Conference at its twenty-second session (Paris, 1983) stressed that a new world information and communication order is to be seen as *an evolving and continuous process*, which has henceforth become part of the official term.

At the more operational level, the International Programme for the Development of Communication, created in 1980 and regarded as an important practical step towards the implementation of a new world information and communication order, seen as an evolving and continuous process, has been carrying out its mandate in assisting the developing countries in their efforts to develop their human and material potential for communication. Since its establishment IPDC has received requests for financing amounting to $US 79,210,000. Financing has been ensured through a Special Account amounting to $US 11,710,000, which covers only 14.7 per cent of expressed needs. In addition to this, it has to date awarded 470 fellowships under its training programme. These figures make it clear, however, that the response of the international community to the stated needs has not yet been such as to launch a process which would put an end to the imbalance existing worldwide in respect both of the means of communication and of the flow of information. The Intergovernmental Council asked the secretariat to make a detailed study of ways of improving the mobilization of IPDC's financial resources, and of its procedures and methods of work.

Implementation of the Recommendation concerning the Status of the Artist. In its preamble, the recommendation, adopted by the UNESCO General Conference on 27 October 1980, recalls (para. 78–82) a number of international instruments, including the International Covenant on Economic, Social and Cultural Rights; it recognizes *inter alia* that the arts in their fullest and broadest definition are and should be an integral part of life and that it is necessary and appropriate for governments to help create and sustain not only a climate encouraging freedom of artistic expression but also the material conditions facilitating the release of this creative talent.

The Recommendation sets forth a number of guiding principles for Member States in this field: they should ensure that the population as a whole, has access to art and encourage all activities designed to highlight the action of artists for cultural development; they have a duty to protect, defend and assist artists and their freedom of creation, and

ensure them of the right to establish trade unions and professional organizations of their choosing; they should make it possible for organizations representing artists to participate in the formulation of cultural policies and employment policies; they should define a policy for providing assistance and material and moral support for artists; they should see that artists are accorded the protection provided for in respect of freedom of expression and communication by international and national legislation concerning human rights; they should ensure that all individuals have the same opportunities to acquire and develop the skills necessary for the complete development and exercise of their artistic talents, to obtain employment and to exercise their profession without discrimination.

The Recommendation further invites Member States to take appropriate measures to encourage the vocation and training of artists; to promote and protect their social status; to improve employment, working and living conditions of artists, so as to enable them to benefit from all the legal, social and economic advantages pertaining to the status of workers; and closely to associate artists with decisions relating to cultural policies and their implementation.

This Recommendation is of particular relevance to Articles 6 and 15 of the Covenant—which are reproduced in the Annex to the Recommendation—whereby the States parties recognize *inter alia* "the right to work, which includes the right of everyone to the opportunity to gain his living by work which he freely chooses or accepts" and "the right of everyone to take part in cultural life" and "to benefit from the protection of the moral and material interests resulting from any scientific, literary or artistic production of which he is the author".

In order to measure the progress made in implementing this Recommendation, in December 1986 UNESCO sent a questionnaire to Member States and to the national committees of the non-governmental organizations concerned. It emerges from the replies received by August 1987 from 27 Member States representing five regions and 13 NGO national committees that a number of legislative and/or administrative measures have been adopted to improve the status of artists. These measures relate in particular to the protection of the moral and material rights of performing artists and the improvement of their economic and social status. However, considerable progress still needs to be made to give effect to all the provisions of the Recommendation. It should be noted that, with this in view, UNESCO proposes, during the 1988–1989 biennium, to draw up in consultation with government authorities and artists in different fields a 10-year plan for the systematic implementation of the Recommendation. The 10-year plan forms part of the activities envisaged by UNESCO as its contribution to implementation of the World Decade for Cultural Development.

Implementation of the Recommendation on the Status of Scientific Researchers. The Recommendation, adopted by the UNESCO General Conference on 24 November 1974, [para. 83–86] is noteworthy in respect both of the wide range of topics with which it deals, and of the fact of its having been adopted by governments with no votes against and with only four abstentions.

To assist UNESCO Member States in creating national legislation concerning the status of scientific researchers, whether members of the national civil service or personnel assimilated thereto, a model framework-law on the "National Cadre of Scientific Researchers" has been drawn up by the Division of Science and Technology Policies of UNESCO. This model is based on the text of the above-mentioned UNESCO 1974 Recommendation. The framework-law, which scrupulously respects the substance of the Recommendation aims at facilitating the practical application of the principles and norms which that standard-setting text sets forth.

Being aware of the importance of greater public awareness of the indispensable role that science and technology have to play in our contemporary world, and of the social, moral, [and] ethical problems that modern scientific and technological progress has introduced into the life of societies, UNESCO has published a book "Science and scientific researchers in modern society" written by Dr. John P. Dickinson.

It describes the socio-economic and cultural aspects of scientific research as well as the rights and responsibilities inherent in the researcher's work. The work contains examples of codes and standards concerning the ethics of scientific research and established precedents, together with various statements by international non-governmental and intergovernmental organizations. This information appears in an annex to the book, which makes it very useful for a wide readership.

Implementation of the Recommendation and Convention on the Means of Prohibiting and Preventing the Illicit Import, Export and Transfers of Ownership of Cultural Property. One of the major objectives of UNESCO is the promotion of international contacts and cooperation in all the spheres of its organizational competence. In pursuit of this objective, UNESCO has adopted a large range of normative instruments. Among these, the Recommendation (1964) and the Convention (1970) on the Means of Prohibiting and Preventing the Illicit Import, Export and Transfers of Ownership of Cultural Property are of particular importance (para. 88–94).

Article 1 of the Convention defines the term "cultural property" for the purposes of the Convention and in Article 2 the States Parties to the Convention recognize that the illicit import, export and transfer of ownership of cultural property is one of the main causes of the impoverishment of the cultural heritage of the countries of origin of such property and that international co-operation constitutes one of the most efficient means of protecting each country's cultural property against all the dangers resulting therefrom. To this end, the States Parties undertake to oppose such practices with the means at their disposal, and particularly by removing their causes, putting a stop to current practices, and by helping to make the necessary reparations.

For the purpose of promoting the attainment of these objectives, the States Parties to the Convention undertake to comply with a range of specific obligations contained in Articles 5 to 14. Article 16 provides that the States Parties shall in their periodic reports submitted to the General Conference of UNESCO, give information on the legislative and administrative provisions which they have adopted and other action which they have taken for the application of the Convention, together with details of the experience acquired in this field. Similarly, paragraph 15 of the Recommendation provides that "Member States should endeavour to assist each other by exchanging the fruits of their

experience in the fields covered by (the) Recommendation".

At its twentieth session in 1978, the General Conference of UNESCO examined reports from Member States on measures taken to implement these two instruments. It noted from the report of the Committee on Conventions and Recommendations on this question that certain problems had been raised by some States with respect to the implementation of the Convention which constituted obstacles to the ratification of this instrument (see paras. 204–205 of document 112 EX/CR/SS.1). The General Conference therefore requested the Director-General to seek further information on the problems raised by States as well as on the experience acquired by other States on these issues. It furthermore invited the Executive Board to "instruct its Committee on Conventions and Recommendations to formulate, on the basis of the additional and more comprehensive data referred to above, proposals for the implementation of the Convention, as foreseen in Article 17 thereof, and to submit these proposals in due course to the General Conference". It decided in addition, that Member States would be invited to forward a second report on implementation for examination by the General Conference at its twenty-fourth session.

In pursuance of the above resolution, the Director-General invited Member States to forward to the Secretariat a description of any difficulties that had arisen for the competent authorities in their countries with respect to the implementation of the Convention, asking them to refer not only to the legal but also to the administrative and practical aspects of the question. He also invited Member States to provide information on experience they had acquired in regard to the implementation of the Convention. Since the reports received from States provided very little information on the experience acquired by States concerning the problems of interpretation and implementation referred to by other States, the Director-General convened a group of experts to examine the problems raised by States and to give their views thereon.

The Committee on Convention and Recommendations reviewed in 1983 the information received from States on the problems encountered concerning the implementation of the Convention as well as information received on the experience acquired by other States with respect to these issues. The report of the meeting of experts referred to above was also brought to the attention of the Committee. On the basis of this information the Committee drew up proposals for the implementation of the Convention for consideration by the Executive Board and General Conference.

At its twenty-second session in 1983, the General Conference endorsed the proposals of the Committee on Conventions and Recommendations and by resolution 11.4 invited States to take a number of measures which, it considered, could improve the implementation of the Convention. In addition to inviting those States which had not already done so to become parties to the Convention, the General Conference invited States to strengthen regional co-operation in the fight against illicit traffic; to draw the attention of all persons benefiting from diplomatic immunities to the need to respect the laws of their host country governing the export of cultural property; to ensure that cultural property which has been the subject of illicit traffic is not provided with services of authentication, evaluation and conservation which may serve to legitimize such traffic; and to adopt the measures advocated in the Recommendation concerning the international exchange of cultural property, in order to develop the circulation of cultural property as a means of discouraging the spread of illicit traffic. The General Conference also called on those States to which illegally exported cultural property is often conveyed to offer assistance to those States which suffer from illicit export of cultural property, in the drawing up of national inventories of cultural property and in the training of specialized personnel.

In accordance with the request of the General Conference at its twentieth session, Member States were invited to submit a second report on action taken to implement the Convention for examination by the General Conference at its twenty-fourth session. Responses received from 25 States Parties to the Convention and 13 States not Parties were examined by the Committee on Conventions and Recommendations meeting during the one hundred and twenty-seventh session of the Executive Board. The reports received from States revealed that considerable importance was attached by States to the system of international co-operation established by the Convention and there was a general recognition that it was only through closer co-operation among States that effective action could be taken to combat the illicit international movement of cultural property and thus protect the cultural heritage of nations from the dangers of theft, clandestine excavations and illicit export of cultural property. The Committee noted that the main problem with respect to the implementation of the Convention stemmed from the fact that, of the 60 States parties to the Convention, most were victims of illicit traffic. To render the instrument more effective, it would be necessary for more States to participate in the system of international co-operation it established and furthermore, for countries victims of illicit traffic to strengthen the protection of their cultural heritage and, in particular, to reinforce export control and for the so-called "importing" countries to take complementary measures, in the name of international solidarity, to regulate the import of cultural property. It would also be necessary to develop a better circulation among States of all useful information which could contribute to the suppression of illicit traffic of cultural property and to strengthen bilateral as well as regional co-operation. The proposals made by the Committee to this end were endorsed by the Executive Board at its one hundred and twenty-seventh session and will be submitted to the General Conference at its twentyh-fourth session.

Article 14: Principle of Compulsory Education, Free of Charge for All. The 1988 report lists three UNESCO instruments as being of particular relevance to this principle: the CONVENTION AGAINST DISCRIMINATION IN EDUCATION, the recommendation on the same subject, and the PROTOCOL to convention instituting a Conciliation and Good Offices Commission to be responsible for seeking a settlement of any disputes which may arise between States parties to the convention. As regards these instruments, the report states that:

This Convention and this Recommendation are of particular significance in connection with the implementation of many of the provisions contained in both Articles 13 and 14 of the International Covenant on Economic, Social and Cultural Rights.

The purpose of the Convention and Recommendation is not only to eliminate and to prevent all discrimination, but also to promote equality of opportunity and treatment in education. These instruments thus correspond in two separate but complementary aims contained in UNESCO's Constitution. Indeed, in addition to forms of discrimination which result from legal provisions or administrative practices and thus are a deliberate denial of the right of certain members of the community to education, the injustices to be countered and eradicated include inequalities which are often the consequence not so much of a conscious intention as of a set of social, geographical, human, economic and historical circumstances. These inequalities have sometimes been called "passive" forms of discrimination, the better to distinguish them from "active" and wilful forms.

Under Article 3, States parties to the Convention pledge themselves to take a series of steps immediately. They must *inter alia* abrogate or modify any statutory provisions and discontinue any administrative practices which involve discrimination in education. They must also "not allow differences of treatment by the public authorities between nationals, except on the basis of merit or need, in the matter of school fees and the grant of scholarships or other forms of assistance to pupils . . .".

On the other hand, the measures to be taken to ensure equality of opportunity in education are, in many countries, of a complex character and are not restricted to the field of education. They also call for considerable expenditure which has to be spread out in time.

The Convention therefore stipulates that States undertake to formulate, develop and apply a national policy which, by methods appropriate to the circumstances and to national usage, will tend to promote equality of opportunity and of treatment in the matter of education.

ECUADOR. The Republic of Ecuador is a country in tropical South America, on the Pacific Ocean. It has borders with Colombia and Peru and includes the offshore Galapagos Islands. It achieved independence from Spain in 1822 when it became part of Greater Colombia, a union which dissolved in 1830 with Ecuador becoming an independent State; and became a member of the United Nations in 1945. Its population is estimated by the UN (1990) to be 10,782,000. Ethnic groups include *mestizos* (36%), whites (26.5%), Amerindians (18.5%), mulattos (14.5%), and Negroes (4.5%). Languages commonly used include Spanish, Quecha, Jibaro, and many Amerindian vernaculars. Christianity (Roman Catholic) is the predominant religion; since the revolution of 1895 replaced conservative by liberal party rule, the Roman Catholic Church is no longer established and freedom of worship is constitutionally guaranteed.

The government (1990) took the form of a republic. The 1978 constitution, which restored civilian rule after eight years of military government, provides (art. 2) that "the primary function of the State is to strengthen national unity, to secure the implementation of the fundamental human rights and to promote the economic, social and cultural development of its inhabitants." Title II, section VII, includes the following provisions:

Article 44. The State guarantees all individuals, men and women, who are subject to its jurisdiction, the free and effective exercise and enjoyment of the civil, political, economic, social and cultural rights set forth in the declarations covenants, agreements and other international instruments in force.

The president and members of the 71-member House of Representatives are elected by popular vote for terms of four years. All literate citizens over 18 years of age are compelled to vote; illiterates may vote if they wish. There are 17 legally recognized political parties, and elections normally are won by coalitions of two or more parties.

Because the country is scarcely populated—the main bulk of the people being Amerindians or *mestizos* living in the highlands or the forests—and because its natural resources do not compare with those of neighboring countries, Ecuador has consistently found it difficult to achieve a balanced economy. Exploitation of the indigenous peoples was reduced considerably by bloody revolts, but industrial development lagged in spite of adequate manpower.

The indigenous populations of Ecuador, who have preserved their ancient cultural traditions and ways of life for many centuries, have been of concern in recent years to the government and to human rights groups. The Political Constitution of 1978 guarantees equal rights and guarantees for all Eduadorans, but this goal is not easy to attain. Article 1 (3) of the constitution safeguards the linguistic values of the indigenous populations by providing that "the official language is Spanish. Quecha and other indigenous languages are recognized as elements of the national culture." Article 27 (6) provides that "the State shall . . . ensure the preservation of the cultural heritage and the artistic and historical wealth of the Nation," and article 27 (9) provides that ". . . in the schools situated in areas where the population is predominantly indigenous, Quechua or the appropriate indigenous language shall be used in addition to Spanish."

As a step towards meeting these standards, the Ministry of Education and Culture has introduced a system of intercultural bilingual education directed mainly towards the majority indigenous group, the Quechua-speaking population. It has also introduced didactic methods to achieve literacy in the vernacular of each region covered by its "National Literacy Plan." The success of that plan has helped raise the country's literacy rate to about 85%.

In a report presented to the **COMMITTEE ON THE ELIMINATION OF RACIAL DISCRIMINATION** on 5 February 1988, the government of Ecuador provided the following information in regard to the participation of women and of the indigenous population in the life of the country (UN Doc CERD/C/172/Add. 4, para. 2–13; 15–28):

The Constitution adopted on 10 August 1979 and amended on 10 August 1984 establishes a general rule in article 44, namely:
"The State guarantees all individuals subject to its jurisdiction, whether men or women, free and effective exercise and enjoyment of the civil, political, economic, social and cultural rights set forth in the declarations, covenants, conventions and other international instruments in force."

In other words, every inhabitant, whether an Ecuadorian or a foreigner, enjoys, in addition to the fundamental guarantees recognized by the Constitution and the laws of Ecuador, the rights enunciated in the more than 20 international human rights instruments to which Ecuador is a party. Consequently, in the event of a grievance, anyone may apply either to the courts of justice of the Republic or to the relevant international bodies: the Human Rights Committee established under the International Covenant on Civil and Political Rights, the Inter-American Commission on Human Rights and the Inter-American Court of Human Rights and the Committee on the Elimination of Racial Discrimination, for Ecuador is one of the few States which has voluntarily agreed to the competence of such bodies to consider any cases of disregard of the provisions of the relevant covenants or conventions.

The rights embodied in the various constitutions Ecuador has adopted in the past include equality before the law. The present Constitution stipulates in article 19, paragraph 5, that:
"Without prejudice to other rights necessary for the purpose of full moral and material development inherent in the nature of the individual, the State guarantees him equality before the law. Any discrimination based on race, colour, sex, language, religion, political or any other affiliation, social origin or financial position or birth is prohibited."

From the eight periodic reports submitted so far, it has been possible for the Committee to observe the spirit of cooperation Ecuador has always displayed and for it to gain the conviction that no kind of racial discrimination whatsoever exists or has existed in this country.

Indeed, since the Convention on the Elimination of All Forms of Racial Discrimination entered into force and Ecuador agreed to the Committee's competence to consider any complaint, no such complaint has been made to date. Nor has any inhabitant of the Republic made an application to the courts, to demand punishment for persons committing the offence of racial discrimination, under the terms of the Criminal Code that penalize such offences.

This is the most reliable proof that there is no racial discrimination in Ecuador, because there is no concept whatsoever of class superiority based on chromosomes. Actually, there is genuine and extensive miscegenation, a great movement of national integration in a country which itself, like a large part of South America, is a racial melting pot.

Consequently, Ecuador's efforts are aimed more at reducing cultural and economic differences, in a constant search for better distribution of incomes, new sources of employment and improved living conditions for the peas-

431

ants and the people in the disadvantaged areas of the towns and cities.

These efforts must necessarily have an impact in the field of education, which continues to be the solution to inequality. Accordingly, public education in our country is compulsory and free of charge at the primary and secondary levels and free of charge in higher education, since a student is only required to pay a sum equivalent to $5 for university enrolment. For the same reason, the Constitution also establishes that not less than 30 per cent of the national budget is to be allocated to the Ministry of Education.

The parts of this consolidated report that follow are intended to answer some comments and to clear up any concern expressed by various members of the Committee in regard to the participation of women and the indigenous population in the life of the country, and the progress achieved by agrarian reform in Ecuador.

Participation of Women. In the matter of the equality of the sexes, under article 19 of the Constitution, women, regardless of their civil status, are granted the same rights and opportunities as men in all aspects of public, private and family life.

While there has never been any restriction in law on women voting, the 1929 Constitution specifically stated that women could vote, if they wished. In 1967, the Constitution specified that it was compulsory for both men and women to vote, a duty which is also set out in article 33 of the present Constitution.

It should be noted that, before the Convention on the Political Rights of Women was ratified, Ecuador expressly established the right of women to vote and to exercise political rights, something which was affirmed by Congress in the preamble to the decree of ratification, published in *Registro Oficial* No. 120, of 26 January 1949. . . .

In regard to political rights, every Ecuadorian over 18 years of age, whether male or female, can elect and stand for election to public office and perform public duties. In the electioneering which has begun in Ecuador, many women figure as candidates for posts by election: Vice-President of the Republic, Deputies to Congress, Mayors and Provincial Prefects, Municipal and Provincial Counsellors. The elections are to be held on 31 January 1988.

In labour matters, the law prohibits discrimination against women and affords protection against arbitrary termination of employment, ensures equal pay for equal work without distinction as to sex, equal opportunity for promotion, and admission to public employment in terms of merit and qualification. An employee, whether a man or a woman, is entitled to form and join or withdraw from any occupational associations or trade unions he or she thinks fit.

In regard to education, the State guarantees free access for men and women to primary, secondary and university education, which is free of charge at all levels in the public system. In State universities, the sole contribution by students, men and women, is an annual enrolment fee equivalent to $5.

The number of professional women e.g. doctors, economists, lawyers, engineers, architects, chemists and so on, who bring their skills to the public and private sectors, is increasing every day.

In civil matters, some legal provisions still affect the position of married women. However, in order for the laws, as subsidiary rules, to be in conformity with the higher ranking precepts of the Constitution, the authorities have been bringing the laws up to date in order to guarantee absolute equality for women.

The Legislative Commission of Ecuador, in Act No. 256, published in *Registro Oficial* No. 446, of 4 June 1970, which is attached as an annex, amended the Civil Code so that man and woman, father and mother, and husband and wife are placed on an equal footing, thereby avoiding any discrimination against the individual on the grounds of sex.

Similarly, in the new text of the Code of Civil Procedure, all provision that previously affected the principle of the equality of the spouses in the eyes of the law have been eliminated. The codification, published in *Registo Oficial* No. 687, of 18 May 1987, eliminated the relevant paragraph of article 34, so that a married women can now appear in court as plaintiff or defendant. It also eliminates the sections of the Code on "proceedings to grant permission to married women requiring to enter into a contract or appear in court" and voluntary auction and sale of a married woman's property.

The Civil Code still contains some articles which will have to be brought into line with the provisions of the Constitution in order to guarantee the equality of husband and wife. For this purpose, Congress is considering a reform bill which, on adoption, will bring to an end the last remaining legal rules whereby the husband is given a privileged position in marriage.

Women have organized at the various national levels in associations and bodies intended to foster the integration of women at every stage in the process of social and economic development. The survey conducted by CIM and CECIM (1984) reported 176 women's organizations with legal personality and statutes approved by the Ministry of Labour and by the Ministry of Social Welfare between 1976 and 1984.

Participation of the Indigenous Population. In the 1970s, Ecuador's policy was based on new attitudes which called for revalorization of the national ethnic groups and their cultures. In 1983, the National Office of Indigenous Affairs was established as part of the Ministry of Social Welfare, in order to shape policies on Ecuador's indigenous problems. The Office's functions were, among others, to promote the organization of the indigenous population, to conduct research, to publicize the situation and to co-ordinate activities to assist indigenous population through other State bodies. At the present time, the unit has been given a higher status as the National Directorate of Indigenous Affairs.

The organization of the indigenous population and the State's new policy concepts have made it possible over the present decade to carry out a number of activities, such as further promotion of the literacy programme by incorporating indigenous persons as officials of the National Literacy Office, along with the participation of an appreciable number of such persons as literacy instructors; the implementation of various Integral Rural Development programmes for the indigenous inhabitants; the furtherance of initiatives to safeguard, re-enhance and spread the cultures of the various indigenous peoples by means of special institutes, including the Andean Institute of Popular Arts (IADAP) and the Inter-American Centre for Crafts and Popular Arts (CIDAP); and consolidation of the organization of the indigenous peoples.

The ECURANARI (Ecuador Runacapac Riccharimuri) Movement emerged in 1972 and the Napo Indigenous Organizations Federation (FOIN) was established in 1973. Large numbers of the Quechua-speaking population of the

Amazon region joined together in the Union of Natives of the Ecuadorian Amazon (UNAE). The Shuar Federation has been strengthened by creating a number of different centres and it is the first indigenous organization to have developed its own system of bilingual education (Spanish-Shuar). In the Amazon the process led to the formation of a regional organization combining the various local organizations (CONFENIAE) and a nationwide co-ordinating body for the indigenous peasant population has also been established, namely the Ecuadorian Indigenous Peoples Co-ordinating Council (CONACNIE).

Historically, the indigenous population in the Sierra has consisted of communes with a domestic economy based on socio-productive complementarity. With this situation as the point of departure, co-operatives, associations and community undertakings have been organized as socio-productive alternatives, sponsored by the indigenous federations and by the State. The indigenous population on the Coast and in Oriente have been nomadic, living from hunting, fishing and food gathering. Accordingly, the Ecuadorian State has embarked on the implementation of rural community development projects through the Ministry of Agriculture and the Ministry of Welfare and FODERUMA (Marginalized Rural Areas Development Fund), and their aims are to provide training, financial support for the construction of community works, and supply credit to *de facto* or *de jure* organizations for investment in productive projects. The organizations participate as a factor of paramount importance in these activities. The State allocated $37,600,000 for this purpose in 1986 and 1987.

Under the 1978 Constitution, persons who are illiterate, as are a high proportion of the indigenous inhabitants, may vote. Participation by the indigenous population in political activity is channelled through their organization, both regional and national. These organizations have succeeded in winning a number of demands. Access to land has been achieved in the inter-Andean region through agrarian reform. In the Amazon region, this has been done by granting communal ownership of the land traditionally occupied by the people in the region, and by keeping control over land settlement and the adjudication of land to enterprises. In regard to education and culture, it has been possible to protect indigenous cultures and their values, to respect the unhampered development of those cultures and to foster bilingual and bicultural education.

EDUCATION. The right of everyone to education is proclaimed in the UNIVERSAL DECLARATION OF HUMAN RIGHTS in the following terms:

Article 26 (1). Everyone has the right to education. Education shall be free, at least in the elementary and fundamental stages. Elementary education shall be compulsory. Technical and professional education shall be made generally available and higher education shall be equally accessible to all on the basis of merit.

(2) Education shall be directed to the full development of the human personality and to the strengthening of respect for human rights and fundamental freedoms. It shall promote understanding, tolerance and friendship among all nations, racial or religious groups, and shall further the activities of the United Nations for the maintenance of peace.

(3) Parents have a prior right to choose the kind of education that shall be given to their children.

The right to education is further elaborated in the INTERNATIONAL COVENANT ON ECONOMIC, SOCIAL AND CULTURAL RIGHTS in the following provisions:

Article 13. 1. The States Parties to the present Covenant recognize the right of everyone to education. They agree that education shall be directed to the full development of the human personality and the sense of its dignity, and shall strengthen the respect for human rights and fundamental freedoms. They further agree that education shall enable all persons to participate effectively in a free society, promote understanding, tolerance and friendship among all nations and all racial, ethnic or religious groups, and further the activities of the United Nations for the maintenance of peace.

2. The States Parties to the present Covenant recognize that, with a view to achieving the full realization of this right:

(a) Primary education shall be compulsory and available free to all;

(b) Secondary education in its different forms, including technical and vocational secondary education, shall be made generally available and accessible to all by every appropriate means, and in particular by the progressive introduction of free education;

(c) Higher education shall be made equally accessible to all, on the basis of capacity, by every appropriate means, and in particular by the progressive introduction of free education;

(d) Fundamental education shall be encouraged or intensified as far as possible for those persons who have not received or completed the whole period of their primary education;

(e) The development of a system of schools at all levels shall be actively pursued, an adequate fellowship system shall be established, and the material conditions of teaching staff shall be continuously improved.

3. The States Parties to the present Covenant undertake to have respect for the liberty of parents and, when applicable, legal guardians to choose for their children schools, other than those established by the public authorities, which conform to such minimum educational standards as may be laid down or approved by the State and to ensure the religious and moral education of their children in conformity with their own convictions.

4. No part of this article shall be construed so as to interfere with the liberty of individuals and bodies to establish and direct educational institutions, subject always to the observance of the principles set forth in paragraph 1 of this article and to the requirement that the education given in such institutions shall conform to such minimum standards as may be laid down by the State.

Article 14. Each State Party to the present Covenant which, at the time of becoming a Party, has not been able to secure in its metropolitan territory or other territories under its jurisdiction compulsory primary education, free of charge, undertakes, within two years, to work out and adopt a detailed plan of action for the progressive implementation, within a reasonable number of years, to be fixed in the plan, of the principle of compulsory education free of charge for all.

Non-discrimination on racial grounds is ensured by the INTERNATIONAL CONVENTION ON THE ELIMINATION OF ALL FORMS OF RACIAL DISCRIMINATION in the following provision:

Article 5. In compliance with the fundamental obligations laid down in article 2 of this Convention, States parties undertake to prohibit and to eliminate racial discrimination in all its forms and to guarantee the right of everyone, without distinction as to race, colour, or national or ethnic origin, to equality before the law, notably in the enjoyment of the following rights:. . . .
   (e) Economic, social and cultural rights, in particular:. . . .
      (vi) The right to education and training.

Non-discrimination on the ground of sex is ensured by the CONVENTION ON THE ELIMINATION OF ALL FORMS OF DISCRIMINATION AGAINST WOMEN in the following provision:

Article 10. States Parties shall take all appropriate measures to eliminate discrimination against women in order to ensure to them equal rights with men in the field of education and in particular to ensure, on a basis of equality of men and women:
   (a) The same conditions for career and vocational guidance, for access to studies and for the achievement of diplomas in educational establishments of all categories in rural as well as in urban areas; this equality shall be ensured in pre-school, general, technical, professional and higher technical education, as well as in all types of vocational training;
   (b) Access to the same curricula, the same examinations, teaching staff with qualifications of the same standard and school premises and equipment of the same quality;
   (c) The elimination of any stereotyped concept of the roles of men and women at all levels and in all forms of education by encouraging coeducation and other types of education which will help to achieve this aim and, in particular, by the revision of textbooks and school programmes and the adaptation of teaching methods;
   (d) The same opportunities to benefit from scholarships and other study grants;
   (e) The same opportunities for access to programmes of continuing education, including adult and functional literacy programmes, particularly those aimed at reducing, at the earliest possible time, any gap in education existing between men and women;
   (f) The reduction of female student drop-out rates and the organization of programmes for girls and women who have left school prematurely;
   (g) The same opportunities to participate actively in sports and physical education;
   (h) Access to specific educational information to help to ensure the health and well-being of families, including information and advice on family planning.

Finally, the AFRICAN CHARTER ON HUMAN AND PEOPLE'S RIGHTS provides, in article 17, that every individual shall have the right to education.

Within the United Nations system, primary responsibility for the preparation and supervision of international measures to promote and protect enjoyment of the right to education lies with the UNITED NATIONS EDUCATIONAL, SCIENTIFIC AND CULTURAL ORGANIZATION. Its basic tools in this endeavor are the UNESCO CONVENTION AGAINST DISCRIMINATION IN EDUCATION, adopted by its General Conference on 14 December 1960; the PROTOCOL INSTITUTING A CONCILIATION AND GOOD OFFICES COMMISSION to be responsible for seeking the settlement of any disputes which may arise between States parties to the Convention against Discrimination in Education, adopted by the conference on 10 December 1962; and the UNESCO RECOMMENDATION CONCERNING EDUCATION FOR INTERNATIONAL UNDERSTANDING, CO-OPERATION AND PEACE AND EDUCATION RELATING TO HUMAN RIGHTS AND FUNDAMENTAL FREEDOMS, adopted by the conference on 19 November 1974. Other normative UNESCO instruments relating to the right to education include the Recommendation against Discrimination in Education, or 14 December 1960; the UNESCO RECOMMENDATION CONCERNING THE STATUS OF TEACHERS, of 5 October 1966; the revised UNESCO RECOMMENDATION CONCERNING TECHNICAL AND VOCATIONAL EDUCATION, of 19 November 1974; the UNESCO INTERNATIONAL CHARTER OF PHYSICAL EDUCATION AND SPORT, of 21 November 1978; and the UNESCO DECLARATION ON RACE AND RACIAL PREJUDICE, of 27 November 1978.

In accordance with the procedures for the implementation of the International Covenant on Economic, Social and Cultural Rights adopted by the Economic and Social Council on 11 May 1976 (resolution 1988 [LX]), UNESCO submits to the council, at regular intervals, reports on the progress made in achieving the observance of the provisions of the covenant falling within the scope of its activities, as provided under article 18 of the covenant. Information on the progress made in achieving observance of the provisions of article 13 of the covenant, on the right to education, are summarized under the heading ECONOMIC, SOCIAL AND CULTURAL RIGHTS: UNESCO ACTIVITIES.

EDUCATIONAL AND TRAINING FUND FOR SOUTHERN AFRICA. The fund, made up of voluntary contributions, was established by the UN General Assembly on 19 December 1967 (resolution 2349 [XXI]). It provides scholarship assistance to inhabitants of South Africa and Namibia for study at senior, secondary, or university level, with preference for study in African institutions. When Angola, Cape Verde, Guinea-Bissau, Mozambique, and Sao Tome and Principe were under Portuguese administration, scholarship assistance was also provided to inhabitants of those territories.

The Advisory Committee on the Educational and Training Program for Southern Africa, established by the General Assembly in 1968, was enlarged from seven to 13 members in 1978 (resolution 33/42). Members are appointed by the Secretary-General after consultation with the regional groups and serve for an indeterminate term. Reports of the advisory committee are submitted to the assembly through the Secretary-General. The committee meets as required to perform its functions.

EGYPT. The Arab Republic of Egypt is a country in northern Africa fronting on the Mediterranean (north) and the Red Sea (east). It has borders with Israel, Libya, and Sudan. It achieved independence from Great Britain in 1922 and became a member of the United Nations in 1945. Its population is estimated by the UN (1990) to be 52,536,000. A single ethnic group, speaking the same language (Arabic) and professing the same religion (Islam) constitutes the vast majority of the population. However, there are other linguistic and religious groups, including the Copts, who form approximately 7% of the population, the Nubians, and the Bedouins. Languages commonly used include Arabic (official) and English; the Berbers and Nubians use their own language as well as Arabic. Islam is the State religion and the faith of the overwhelming majority of the population. Religious minorities include Christian Copts, a small number of Catholics and Protestants, and a Jewish community whose numbers dwindled after the World War II.

The government (1990) took the form of a republic, defined in the 1971 constitution as "an Arab Republic with a democratic, socialist system." Executive authority is exercised by the president as head of State and the premier as head of Government. Legislative matters are dealt with by the 448-member Parliament, elected by popular vote with universal suffrage. The president appoints his own cabinet and may appoint one or more vice presidents. Political parties include the National Democratic Party and the New *Wafd*.

There have been four Arab–Israeli wars since 1956. In that year, Egyptian President Gamal Abdel Nasser nationalized the Suez Canal, and Israel invaded the Gaza Strip and the Sinai Peninsula. After the canal had been protected by a United Nations emergency force, all troops were evacuated in 1957. In 1967, Israel invaded the Sinai Peninsula, the east bank of the Jordan River, and the area around the Gulf of Aqaba;

and stopped its advance only after the United Nations had arranged a ceasefire and established a peacekeeping force. In 1969, Nasser repudiated the ceasefire and re-opened the war but was forced in 1970 to accept an American peace plan under which Egypt recognized Israel's right to secure boundaries and Israel withdrew from part of the occupied Sinai territories.

Nasser died in 1970; and, under his successor, Anwar el-Sadat, Egypt in 1973 recaptured portions of the Sinai by an attack launched on the eve of Yom Kippur and coordinated with an attack by Syria on the Israeli-held Golan Heights. The 30 years of warfare ended with a truce sponsored by the United Nations in 1974, followed by a peace plan negotiated by U.S. Secretary of State Henry Kissinger. The Suez Canal was cleared and opened in 1975, and a new UN peacekeeping force was established in the Sinai. Anwar el-Sadat and Menachem Begin, after a series of meetings at Camp David sponsored by American President Jimmy Carter, signed a peace treaty on 26 March 1979 which settled many questions but left unresolved the problem of Arab autonomy in the Gaza Strip and the West Bank area. Assassinated in 1981, Sadat was succeeded by his vice president, former Air Force Chief of Staff Hosni Mubarak. After completing his first six-year term of office successfully, Mubarak was re-elected in October 1987, receiving a majority vote of 97.1% in a nationwide referendum approving his nomination by Parliament.

Aside from persistent human rights problems resulting from the poverty of its people and the inability of its economic structure to provide adequate standards of living and health care, Egypt has been torn by disputes between Islamic factions, with Muslim fundamentalists organizing politically to force a return to application of the ancient *Sharia* legal code, while the government responds by increasing its strict control of all religious activities. In 1977, the Political Parties Regulatory Act No. 40 prohibited the exploitation of religion for the establishment of political parties in an effort to prevent the nation from being split into conflicting religious groups organized on political lines.

EGYPT: CONSTITUTION. The 1980 Constitution of the Arab Republic of Egypt, after the amendments ratified in the referendum of 22 May 1980, includes the following provisions (articles 7-22, 40-63, and 206-211) relating specifically to human rights and fundamental freedoms:

Part Two: Basic Constituents of the Society
Chapter I: Social and Moral Constituents

Article 7. Social solidarity is the basis of the society.

Article 8. The State shall guarantee equality of opportunity to all citizens.

Article 9. The family is the basis of the society founded on religion, morality and patriotism.

The State is keen to preserve the genuine character of the Egyptian family—with what it embodies of values and traditions—while affirming and developing this character in the relations within the Egyptian society.

Article 10. The State shall guarantee the protection of motherhood and childhood, take care of children and youth and provide the suitable conditions for the development of their talents.

Article 11. The State shall guarantee the proper coordination between the duties of woman towards the family and her work in the society, considering her equal with man in the fields of political, social, cultural and economic life without violation of the rules of Islamic jurisprudence.

Article 12. The society shall be committed to safeguarding and protecting morals, promoting the genuine Egyptian traditions and abiding by the high standards of religious education, moral and national values, historical heritage of the people, scientific facts, socialist conduct and public morality within the limits of the law.

The State is committed to abiding by these principles and promoting them.

Article 13. Work is a right, a duty and an honour ensured by the State. Workers who excel in their field of work shall receive the appreciations of the State and the society.

No work shall be imposed on the citizens, except by virtue of the law, for the performance of a public service and in return for a fair remuneration.

Article 14. Public offices are the right of all citizens and an assignment for their occupants in the service of the people. The State guarantees their (the occupants) protection and the performance of their duties in safeguarding the interests of the people. They may not be dismissed by other than the disciplinary way, except in the cases specified by the law.

Article 15. The war veterans, those injured in war or because of it, and the wives and children of those killed shall have priority in work opportunities according to the law.

Article 16. The State shall guarantee cultural, social and health services, and work to ensure them for the villages in particular in an easy and regular manner in order to raise their standard.

Article 17. The State shall guarantee social and health insurance services and all the citizens have the right to pensions in cases of incapacity, unemployment and old-age, in accordance with the law.

Article 18. Education is a right guaranteed by the State. It is obligatory in the primary stage and the State shall work to extend obligation to other stages. The State shall supervise all branches of education and guarantee the independence of universities and scientific research centres, with a view to linking all this with the requirements of society and production.

Article 19. Religious education shall be a principal subject in the courses of general education.

Article 20. Education in the State educational institutions shall be free of charge in its various stages.

Article 21. Combating illiteracy shall be a national duty for which all the people's energies should be mobilized.

Article 22. The institution of civil titles shall be prohibited. . . .

Part Three: Public Freedoms, Rights and Duties

Article 40. All citizens are equal before the law. They have equal public rights and duties without discrimination between them due to race, ethnic origin, language, religion or creed.

Article 41. Individual freedom is a natural right and shall not be touched. Except in cases of *flagrante delicto* no person may be arrested, inspected, detained or his freedom restricted or prevented from free movement except by an order necessitated by investigations and preservation of the security of the society. This order shall be given by the competent judge or the Public Prosecution in accordance with the provisions of the law. The law shall determine the period of custody.

Article 42. Any person arrested, detained or his freedom restricted shall be treated in the manner concomitant with the preservation of his dignity. No physical or moral harm is to be inflicted upon him. He may not be detained or imprisoned except in places defined by laws organising prisons.

If a confession is proved to have been made by a person under any of the aforementioned forms of duress or coercion, it shall be considered invalid and futile.

Article 43. Any medical or scientific experiment may not be undergone on any person without his free consent.

Article 44. Homes shall have their sanctity and they may not be entered or inspected except by a causal judicial warrant prescribed by the law.

Article 45. The law shall protect the inviolability of the private life of citizens. Correspondence, wires, telephone calls and other means of communication shall have their own sanctity and secrecy and may not be confiscated or monitored except by a causal judicial warrant and for a definite period according to the provisions of the law.

Article 46. The State shall guarantee the freedom of belief and the freedom of practice of religious rites.

Article 47. Freedom of opinion is guaranteed. Every individual has the right to express his opinion and to publicise it verbally or in writing or by photography or by other means within the limits of the law. Self-criticism and constructive criticism is the guarantee for the safety of the national structure.

Article 48. Freedom of the press, printing, publication and mass media shall be guaranteed. Censorship on newspapers is forbidden as well as notifying, suspending or cancelling them by administrative methods. In a state of emergency or in time of war a limited censorship may be imposed on the newspapers, publications and mass media in matters related to public safety or purposes of national security in accordance with the law.

Article 49. The State shall guarantee the freedom of scientific research and literary, artistic and cultural invention and provide the necessary means for its realisation.

Article 50. No citizen may be prohibited from residing in any place and no citizen may be forced to reside in a particular place, except in the cases defined by the law.

Article 51. No citizen may be deported from the country or prevented from returning to it.

Article 52. Citizens shall have the right to permanent or temporary immigration.

The law shall regulate this right and the measures and conditions of immigration and leaving the country.

Article 53. The right to political asylum shall be guaranteed by the State for every foreigner persecuted for defending the peoples' interests, human rights, peace or justice.

The extradition of political refugees is prohibited.

Article 54. Citizens shall have the right to peaceable and unarmed private assembly, without the need for prior notice. Security men should not attend these private meetings.

Public meetings, processions and gatherings are allowed within the limits of the law.

Article 55. Citizens shall have the right to form societies as defined in the law. The establishment of societies whose activities are hostile to the social system, clandestine or have a military character is porhibited.

Article 56. The creation of syndicates and unions on a democratic basis is a right guaranteed by law, and should have a moral entity.

The law regulates the participation of syndicates and unions in carrying out the social programmes and plans, raising the standard of efficiency, consolidating the socialist behavior among their members, and safeguarding their funds.

They are responsible for questioning their members about their behaviour in exercising their activities according to certain codes of morals, and for defending the rights and liberties of their members as defined in the law.

Article 57. Any assault on individual freedom or on the inviolability of private life of citizens and any other public rights and liberties guaranteed by the Constitution and the law shall be considered a crime, whose criminal and civil lawsuit is not liable to prescription. The State shall grant a fair compensation to the victim of such an assault.

Article 58. The defence of the motherland is a sacred duty, and conscription is obligatory in accordance with the law.

Article 59. Safeguarding, consolidating and preserving the socialist gains is a national duty.

Article 60. Protecting national unity and keeping State secrets is the duty of every citizen.

Article 61. Payment of taxes and public imposts is a duty, in accordance with the law.

Article 62. Citizens shall have the right to vote, nominate and express their opinions in referendums according to the provisions of the law. Their participation in public life is a national duty.

Article 63. Every individual has the right to address public authorities in writing and with his own signature. Addressing public authorities should not be in the name of groups, with the exception of disciplinary organs and moral personalities. . . .

Chapter II: The Press

Article 206. The Press is a popular, independent authority exercising its ture vocation in accordance with the stipulations of the Constitution and the law.

Article 207. The Press shall exercise its true vocation freely and independently in the service of society through all means of expression. It shall thus interpret the trend of public opinion, while contributing to its formation and orientation within the framework of the basic components of society, the safeguard of the liberties, rights and public duties and respect of the sanctity of the private lives of citizens, as stipulated in the Constitution and defined by law.

Article 208. The freedom of the press is guaranteed and press censorship is forbidden. Also forbidden is to threaten, suppress, or foreclose a newspaper through administrative measures, as stipulated in the Constitution and defined by law.

Article 209. The freedom of body corporates, whether public or private, or political parties to publish or own newspapers is safeguarded in accordance with the law.

The financing and ownership of newspapers come under the supervision of the people, as stipulated in the Constitution and defined by law.

Article 210. Journalists have the right to obtain news and information according to the regulations set by law.

Their activities are not subject to any authority other than the law.

Article 211. A Supreme Press Council shall deal with matters concerning the press. The law shall define its composition, competences and its relationship with the State authorities.

The Supreme Press Council shall exercise its competences with a view to consolidate the freedom of the press and its independence, to uphold the basic foundations of society, and to guarantee the soundness of national unity and social peace as stipulated in the Constitution and defined by law.

EL SALVADOR. The Republic of El Salvador is a country in Central America, on the Pacific Ocean. It has borders with Guatemala and Honduras. It achieved independence from Spain in 1838 and became a member of the United Nations in 1945. Its population is estimated by the UN (1990) to be 6,484,000. The language commonly used is Spanish. The predominant religion is Christianity (Roman Catholic). Literacy is estimated at 65%.

The government (1990) took the form of a republic. Under the 1983 constitution, executive authority is exercised by the president, elected for a five-year, non-renewable, term. Legislative matters are dealt with by the 60-member National Assembly, elected by popular vote under a proportional representation scheme. There is a Supreme Court, members of which are elected by the assembly, and a series of lower courts.

The UN General Assembly, the UN COMMISSION ON HUMAN RIGHTS, the INTER-AMERICAN COMMISSION ON HUMAN RIGHTS, and other international bodies, governmental and non-governmental, have been deeply concerned about the human rights situation in El Salvador since 1980, when the UN General Assembly requested the commission to examine that question as soon as possible. Early in 1981, the commission appointed a special representative to investigate the reports about murders, abductions, disappearances, terrorist acts, and other grave violations of human rights, based on information from all available sources, and to report thereon.

The special representative, Mr. José Antonio Pastor Ridruejo, monitored the situation closely and reported both to the General Assembly and to the commission for a number of years. His first reports indicated that a state of siege was in effect in El Salvador and that all constitutional safeguards of freedom of movement, freedom of speech, and freedom of correspondence had been suspended.

Later reports indicated that, although serious violations of human rights continued to occur, primarily as a result of the ongoing state of war which persisted in El Salvador, the government had been increasingly effective in its efforts to suppress them.

In 1989, the special representative submitted a report on the situation of human rights in El Salvador (UN Doc. A/44/677). The assembly, on 15 December 1989, took note of that report (resolution 44/165), endorsed the recommendations contained therein, and requested the special representative to update them in the light of the serious events taking place in that country.

In January 1990, the special representative, who had visited El Salvador from 8 to 15 October 1989, submitted an updated report (UN Doc. E/CN.4/1990/26) to the Commission on Human Rights. In that report, he set out his conclusions as follows (chap. VI, para. 108–123):

The situation regarding economic, social and cultural rights of Salvadorians is still adversely affected by a combination of factors, more particularly the persistent and intensified conflict between the armed forces and the FMLN [Farabundo Marti National Liberation Front] and the consequent climate of widespread violence.

The FMLN's systematic attacks on El Salvador's economic infrastructure also do serious harm to the present and future enjoyment by Salvadorians of important economic, social and cultural rights.

This year there has been a disturbing increase in government actions of all kinds against trade union, peasant, humanitarian and other organizations. The Government contends that some of these organizations are submissive to the FMLN, a position which the organizations concerned deny but one which, if true, in no sense justifies violations of human rights.

Summary Executions. Members of the State apparatus, particularly the armed forces, have committed politically-motivated summary executions, including mass executions. It is difficult to determine their exact number but it is generally higher than the already disturbing level of last year. One point of interest is that judicial inquiries and proceedings have been undertaken in connection with some of these summary executions.

Many sources continue to attribute disturbing summary executions and other serious violations of human rights to the so-called "death squads", said to be connected with the armed forces or security forces or tolerated by them. The Special Representative finds these charges credible, but because of the difficulties involved in investigating claims of this type, he is unable to reach definite conclusions on specific cases. He does not, however, rule out the possibility that these activities are used to cover up ordinary offenses.

The FMLN, for its part, has continued to perpetrate summary executions of alleged collaborators with the armed forces, military personnel and senior civil servants, as well as people ideologically opposed to it. Such crimes could have been committed by squads of left-wing extremists independent of the FMLN. The Front has also carried out disturbing indiscriminate actions in towns and cities which have killed and wounded civilians.

Abductions and Disappearances. Disturbing cases of politically-motivated disappearances are still taking place. It is difficult to determine precisely the number of such disappearances and who the abductors are, although the Special Representative does not rule out the possibility that the "death squads" may have had a part in some of the cases.

In addition, the guerrilla organizations have carried out disturbing kidnappings of individuals.

Treatment of Political Prisoners. The number of arrests on political grounds rose in 1989 and, although the Special Representative does not deny that El Salvador's constitutional authorities are entitled to proceed against those who use violence to overthrow the constitutional system, he does think that in the past year more use has been made of physical and mental torture in police questioning of detainees. However, torture is not a widespread practice nor is it an instrument of government policy.

The Criminal Courts. In 1989, an army officer was convicted in a non-military case of homicide, and court action has continued in connection with a mass execution committed in the past year. Proceedings have also been initiated with regard to a number of summary executions which occurred in 1989. There is, however, no significant progress in previous cases pending nor court action of any kind regarding many summary executions and other abuses committed in 1988 and 1989, for which reason the Special Representative takes the view that the situation regarding the criminal courts is still highly unsatisfactory. The difficulties in the normal functioning of the courts, as well as the proposed judicial reforms, must none the less be taken into account.

The Armed Conflict. The armed forces' treatment of the civilian population in the areas of conflict has been harsh and distressing, and their military activities have caused civilian fatalities and injuries, particularly during the counter-attack against the general offensive by the FMLN. Casualties do not occur in a general and indiscriminate fashion, but they do happen occasionally, albeit in smaller numbers than summary executions unconnected with combat. In the course of the dismantling of FMLN health posts, army action has caused fatalities and other casualties among medical and health personnel.

The FMLN, for its part, has caused fatalities among civilians who have set off mines, although in some months in 1989 there were no reports of incidents of this type; guerrilla gunfire has caused other civilian casualties. There are also reports that guerrilla organizations have engaged in extortion against peasants in the areas of conflict.

Efforts to Enhance Respect for Human Rights. It should be noted that, despite harassment by the FMLN, the presidential elections were held on 19 March 1989, and that on 1 June 1989 the transfer of power took place normally, as provided for in the Constitution.

The Special Representative also wishes to place on record the fact that respect for human rights and dialogue for peace are fundamental components of the policy of Mr. Cristiani, the Constitutional President of the Republic. He considers that such policies, although they are not being reflected immediately and overtly in everyday life, are sincere. He expresses his hope and fervent desire that, through due constitutional control of all agencies of the State apparatus, it will prove possible to overcome the current difficulties in order that peace and respect for human rights in El Salvador may rapidly become an everyday reality.

As regards the process of dialogue between the Government and the FMLN, the Special Representative can only express his deep concern at the present deadlock and his hope that, once dialogue is resumed, it will rapidly lead to a negotiated solution of the conflict.

Lastly, the Special Representative wishes to place on record the FMLN's policy of not using contact mines in its military activities, even though in recent months civilians have been killed by guerrilla mines.

On the basis of these conclusions, the special representative puts forward the following recommendations (chap. VII, para. 124–128):

The Special Representative is deeply alarmed at the number and seriousness of human rights violations during 1989, which represent a worsening of the already disturbing situation in 1988. He again most emphatically urges the Government and all the authorities, agencies and political forces in El Salvador, including the guerrilla organizations, immediately to take all necessary steps to end once and for all attacks on human life, integrity and dignity, both in combat and in non-combat situations.

The Special Representative also appeals most emphatically to the Government and the FMLN to resume the process of dialogue and negotiation and to manifest in this process a spirit of political realism, generosity and imagination, in order that a negotiated and just peace and the subsequent rebuilding of the country may be achieved as early as possible.

The Special Representative particularly reiterates to the constitutional authorities of the Republic of El Salvador the recommendations contained in his previous report to the Commission on Human Rights (UN Doc. A/43/736), and more specifically recommends that:

(a) The necessary measures should immediately be adopted in order to ensure that police interrogation of detainees conforms to the standards embodied in the 1983 Constitution and in the international commitments undertaken by the Republic in the area of human rights;

(b) The encouragement of judicial reform should be maintained in order that the criminal courts may function in accordance with the above-mentioned standards;

(c) The judicial proceedings initiated in connection with the mass killings in the last three months of 1989 should be expedited in order that they may give rise to just and exemplary sentences as soon as possible;

(d) The agrarian reform and other structural reforms necessary for the greater well-being of the population should be continued.

To the FMLN and guerrilla organizations, the Special Representative reiterates the recommendations he made in the previous report to the Commission on Human Rights, and, in particular, further recommends that:

(a) They should continue to adhere firmly to the policy of not laying contact mines which may cause deaths or injuries among the civilian population;

(b) They should immediately refrain from any kind of indiscriminate urban action.

Lastly, the Special Representative again recommends to all States members of the international community, and particularly to the richest and most developed States, that they should increase the assistance necessary to alleviate and improve the living conditions of Salvadorian citizens who have been displaced, made refugees or resettled as a result of the hostilities.

After considering the updated report, the Commission on Human Rights adopted on 7 March 1990 a resolution on the situation of human rights in El Salvador (resolution 1990/77), the operative paragraphs of which are as follows (para. 1–17):

Commends the Special Representative for his report on the situation of human rights in El Salvador (E/CN.4/1990/26);

Expresses its serious concern at the increase in the number of grave, politically motivated violations of human rights, such as summary executions, torture and abductions, and at the persistence of enforced disappearances;

Also expresses its deepest concern at the worsening of the armed conflict, particularly in November 1989, which led to a fresh outbreak of violence, bombings and the indiscriminate use of heavy weapons in densely populated areas, causing numerous civilian casualties and substantial damage;

Also expresses its serious concern at the systematic attacks on the economic infrastructure, which severely impair the present and future enjoyment of important economic, social and cultural rights by the Salvadorian people;

Condemns the murder of the Rector and seven other members of the Central American University, acknowledges that the Government of El Salvador has brought several persons suspected of perpetrating this abominable crime before the courts and hopes that it will continue to investigate this crime in order that all the culprits may be punished;

Regrets the fact that the so-called death squads in El Salvador are continuing to commit serious human rights violations with impunity;

Expresses, furthermore, its deep concern with the indiscriminate actions by the Frente Farabundo Martí para la Liberación Nacional in towns and cities, as well as the actions by violent commandos independent of the FMLN, also represent serious and unpunished violations of human rights;

Also expresses its deep concern at the continued unsatisfactory capacity of the judicial system, despite the efforts of the Government of El Salvador to determine the responsibility of persons committing serious violations of human rights, and therefore urges the competent authorities to hasten the adoption of the reforms and measures necessary for ensuring its efficiency;

Calls upon the Government of El Salvador, the Frente Farabundo Martí para la Liberación Nacional and all the country's political powers, agencies and forces to take immediate measures, as recommended by the Special Representative, to put an end to attempts on human life, integrity and dignity, both in non-combat situations and in or as a result of combat;

Requests the parties to the conflict to guarantee respect

for the humanitarian standards applicable to non-international armed conflicts such as that in El Salvador, especially to protect the civilian population, the war-wounded and persons deprived of their freedom for reasons connected with the conflict and to co-operate with humanitarian organizations engaged in alleviating the suffering of the civilian population wherever such organizations operate in the country; and in no circumstances to penalize medical and health personnel for carrying out their activities;

Offers its full support to the good offices mission of the Secretary-General of the United Nations with a view to achieving the resumption and successful conclusion of the dialogue between the Government of El Salvador and the Frente Farabundo Martí para la Liberación Nacional, on the basis of Security Council resolution 637 (1989);

Strongly appeals to the Government of El Salvador and the Frente Farabundo Martí para la Liberación Nacional to use the good offices of the Secretary-General to endeavour to achieve, as rapidly as possible, a negotiated political solution to the armed conflict that will encourage the existence and strengthening of a democratic, pluralist and participatory process involving the promotion and respect of the human rights of the Salvadorian people, in particular the right freely to choose its own political, economic and social system without external interference of any kind;

Reiterates its appeal to all States to refrain from intervening in the internal situation in El Salvador and, instead of helping in any way to prolong and intensify the armed conflict, to encourage the conclusion of a just and lasting peace;

Repeats its request that the bodies and organizations of the United Nations system, on the basis of General Assembly resolution 44/165 and Commission on Human Rights resolution 1989/68, should provide such advice and assistance in the promotion and protection of human rights and fundamental freedoms as the Government of El Salvador may request from them;

Notes with satisfaction that, with the consent of the Government, there have been a number of mass returns of refugees who have decided of their own free will to resettle in rural areas of conflict, and urges the competent authorities to make every effort to ensure that such persons are assisted in respect of their most basic needs and to prevent acts of violence against them or their settlements;

Decides to consider at its forty-seventh session the situation of human rights in El Salvador and the mandate of the Special Representative, taking account of developments in the situation of human rights in that country;

Decides to extend the mandate of the Special Representative for another year and requests him to submit his report on further developments in the situation of human rights in El Salvador to the General Assembly at its forty-fifth session and to the Commission on Human Rights at its forty-seventh session.

EMPLOYMENT: ANTI-DISCRIMINATION AGENCIES. Established by national or local governments with a view to eliminating discrimination based on any ground such as race, sex, language, or religion, the role and functions of such agencies are described in the Secretary-General's report entitled *National Institutions for the Protection and Promotion of Human Rights* (UN Doc. E/CN.4/1987/37), prepared at the request of the General Assembly (resolution 40/123), in the following terms (para. 91–98):

The importance of fair labour practices and the availability of adequate redress for discrimination in the area of employment has been generally recognized throughout the world as an essential part of any comprehensive human rights protection programme. While Governments frequently include Ministers of Labour in their cabinets to deal with the many issues and problems which characterize the area of employment, an ever-increasing number of States consider that resources of a local and specialized nature are required to address the needs and demands of workers adequately. For instance, labour courts and tribunals, which conciliate, mediate and adjudicate disputes arising under labour agreements, or between workers' unions and employers, have been established in many countries.

States have also created administrative commissions or agencies, responsible for addressing specific problems in the labour market that may infringe on the rights of some groups and individuals in the community to equal work for fair and equal compensation and adequate working conditions. These commissions frequently operate under the Ministry of Labour. For example, to assist in eradicating unemployment, the Government of Zimbabwe created the Department of Employment and Employment Promotion, which functions under the Ministry of Labour and Social Services. The primary purpose of this body is to match persons seeking work with existing employment vacancies as quickly as possible, and to work closely with other governmental bodies in an attempt to create productive employment opportunities.

Many of the organizations created by States are established to deal primarily with sexual and racial discrimination in employment. The powers and duties of these commissions and agencies differ from country to country. Sometimes, they exist solely on the national level, but they are often organized on both the national and local level. For instance, in Australia National and Local Employment Discrimination Committees were established in 1973 to deal with cases of discrimination covered by the International Labour Organisation (ILO) Discrimination (Employment and Occupation) Convention (No. 111), 1958. Basically, the Australian Employment Discrimination Committees consider questions concerning possible discrimination in the remuneration of employees. The National Committee's primary functions are to:

". . . consider allegations of discrimination referred by the State (Local) Committees; consider allegations which involve the Federal Government as an employer and those which are of national significance; to advise the Federal Government on relevant matters of policy; and to develop and promote a community education programme."

The six State (Local) Committees investigate charges of discrimination against employers, and attempt to arrive at amicable settlements through conciliation. The membership of Australia's Employment Discrimination Committees is comprised of representatives of Government, national employers' organizations and the trade-union movement, as well as individuals with special expertise in the problems of employment regarding Aboriginals, migrants and women.

With some modifications, similar powers and duties characterize the United States Equal Employment Opportunity Commission (EEOC). Established by the Civil Rights

Act of 1964, EEOC was created to hear and investigate claims a discrimination in employment practices and procedures. When EEOC receives a complaint, it transfers that complaint to the competent State or local agency, which is required to act on the complaint within 60 days. If no such action takes place, EEOC then takes up the claim, investigates the complaint and attempts to arrive at an amicable settlement. If no settlement can be reached, EEOC is empowered to seize the United States District Court (federal court) for adjudication of the matter. This seizure of the court by EEOC does not preclude the victim in the case from initiating his own judicial action as well. Decisions or rulings by the court constitute legally binding precedents, which affect employment policy throughout the nation. Finally, State and local agencies of EEOC which investigate claims of discrimination in employment, are also empowered to investigate charges of unequal access to public facilities and housing as a result of discrimination.

Some equal employment agencies function as "watchdogs" to ensure that particular pieces of legislation concerning employment and labour are fully complied with. As an example of such an agency, mention may be made of the Vigilance Committees in India. These Committees were created under the Bonded Labour Systems Abolition Act of 1976. Vigilance Committees are comprised of officials, representatives of the locality, social workers and financial and credit institutions. Their basic functions are to advise the district authorities on the implementation of the Act forbidding the practice of bonded labour, to monitor offences under the Act, and to make recommendations on whether action should be taken regarding these offences. The Committee also defends suits instituted against bonded debts.

Often equal employment commissions and agencies also perform advisory services. As previously stated, the Australian National Employment Discrimination Committee advises the Federal Government on employment and labour policy. Similarly, the Tripartite Advisory Committees in India, comprised of government, employer and employee representatives, were established to advise the Government on the formulation of labour policy and to ensure the implementation of labour laws. The French Supreme Council for Professional Equality Between Men and Women, established in 1983 is also an advisory body. The Supreme Council is consulted by the Government on bills and draft decrees designed to ensure professional equality between men and women, as well as on texts dealing with the particular working conditions of the different sexes. The Council may also make proposals designed to improve professional equality between the sexes.

Equal employment agencies are also required, in most cases, to include activities aimed at promoting equality in the employment area as part of their basic functions. For example, both the Danish Equality Council and the Portuguese Commission on Women's Conditions are charged with promoting equality between the sexes in employment and vocational training. The United States EEOC proposes affirmative action hiring plans to employers and industries for voluntary undertaking. Once employers accept such plans, they become binding. In many countries, however, the promotion of equality in employment is the responsibility of human rights and civil rights commissions.

The role of equal employment commissions in safeguarding the workplace from discrimination is clearly an important factor in protecting the human and civil rights of the individual. Although it is often the responsibility of human rights commissions to address issues concerning dis-

crimination in employment, the existence of widespread discrimination in the field of labour relations seems to corroborate the idea that separate agencies, designed to deal solely with employment and labour issues are needed to protect the individual's right to work in an environment free from discrimination. Moreover, agencies comprised of employers and workers play an important role in advising Governments on the needs of the working community. Discrimination in employment is one of the most pernicious violations of human rights, since it undercuts the very livelihood of the individual and frequently triggers a chain reaction of financial and social circumstances which often expose the individual to further exploitation. Therefore, agencies which can address the problem of discrimination in the workplace exclusively, provide an essential service in the protection of human rights.

SEE ALSO *ILO Discrimination (Employment and Occupation) Convention.*

ENVIRONMENT. At its 1989 session, the UN SUB-COMMISSION ON PREVENTION OF DISCRIMINATION AND PROTECTION OF MINORITIES decided (decision 1989/108) to request one of its members, Ms. Fatma Ksentini (Algeria), to prepare a concise note setting forth methods by which a study of the problem of the environment and its relation to human rights could be made. The Secretary-General was called upon to obtain relevant information and observations from governments and intergovernmental and non-governmental organizations and to make them available to Ms. Ksentini for inclusion in her note.

SEE ALSO *Declaration of the United Nations Conference on the Human Environment; Right to Life: Disposal of Dangerous Products and Wastes; Toxic and Dangerous Products and Wastes; United Nations Environment Program; Vancouver Declaration on Human Settlements.*

ENVIRONMENT: TOXIC AND DANGEROUS WASTES. Concerned about the increase in illegal international traffic in, and the dumping and resulting accumulation of, toxic and dangerous wastes which jeopardize the right of everyone to a clean environment and adversely affect many countries—in particular, developing countries—the UN General Assembly on 20 December 1988 urged all States (resolution 43/212) to take the necessary legal and technical measures in order to halt such illegal traffic in toxic and dangerous products and wastes and, in particular, urged States generating such products and wastes to make every effort to treat and dispose of them in the country of origin to the maximum extent possible, consistent with environmentally sound disposal.

The assembly called upon all States to prohibit all

transboundary movement of toxic and dangerous wastes carried without prior consent of the competent authorities of the importing country or without full recognition of the sovereign rights of the transit countries and, in this connection, urged them to prohibit such movement without prior notification in writing of the competent authorities of all countries concerned, including the transit countries, and to provide all information required to ensure the proper management of the wastes and full disclosure of the nature of the substances to be received or transported.

SEE ALSO Declaration of the United Nations Conference on the Human Environment; Right to Life: Disposal of Dangerous Products and Wastes; Toxic and Dangerous Products and Wastes.

EQUALITY. A general principle of elementary justice applicable to all human rights, meaning that, whatever level may be reached in the realization of those rights in a particular country or territory, should apply to every individual residing there without discrimination of any kind, the principle is proclaimed in the UNIVERSAL DECLARATION OF HUMAN RIGHTS as follows:

Article 2. Everyone is entitled to all the rights and freedoms set forth in this Declaration, without distinction of an kind, such as race, colour, sex, language, religion, political or other opinion, national or social origin, property, birth or other status.

Furthermore, no distinction shall be made on the basis of the political, jurisdictional or international status of the country or territory to which a person belongs, whether it be independent, trust, non-self governing or under any other limitation of sovereignty. . . .

Article 7. All are equal before the law and are entitled without any discrimination to equal protection of the law. All are entitled to equal protection against any discrimination in violation of this Declaration and against any incitement to such discrimination.

The INTERNATIONAL COVENANT ON ECONOMIC, SOCIAL AND CULTURAL RIGHTS deals with the principle in the following provisions:

Article 2.2. The States Parties to the present Covenant undertake to guarantee that the rights enunciated in the present Covenant will be exercised without discrimination of any kind as to race, colour, sex, language, religion, political or other opinion, national or social origin, property, birth or other status.

Article 3. The States Parties to the present Covenant undertake to ensure the equal right of men and women to the enjoyment of all economic, social and cultural rights set forth in the present Covenant.

The INTERNATIONAL COVENANT ON CIVIL AND POLITICAL RIGHTS contains the following provisions:

Article 2.1. Each State Party to the present Covenant undertakes to respect and to ensure to all individuals within its territory and subject to its jurisdiction the rights recognized in the present Covenant, without distinction of any kind, such as race, colour, sex, language, religion, political or other opinion, national or social origin, property, birth or other status. . . .

Article 3. The States Parties to the present Covenant undertake to ensure the equal right of men and women to the enjoyment of all civil and political rights set forth in the present Covenant. . . .

Article 26. All persons are equal before the law and are entitled without any discrimination to the equal protection of the law. In this respect, the law shall prohibit any discrimination and guarantee to all persons equal and effective protection against discrimination on any ground such as race, colour, sex, language, religion, political or other opinion, national or social origin, property, birth or other status.

The INTERNATIONAL CONVENTION ON THE ELIMINATION OF ALL FORMS OF RACIAL DISCRIMINATION provides that:

Article 2.1. States Parties condemn racial discrimination and undertake to pursue by all appropriate means and without delay a policy of eliminating racial discrimination in all its forms, and promoting understanding among all races, and to this end:

(a) Each State Party undertakes to engage in no act or practise of racial discrimination against persons, groups of persons or institutions and to ensure that all public authorities and public institutions, national and local, shall act in conformity with this obligation;

(b) Each State Party undertakes not to sponsor, defend or support racial discrimination by any persons or organizations;

(c) Each State Party shall take effective measures to review governmental, national and local policies, and to amend, rescind or nullify any laws and regulations which have the effect of creating or perpetuating racial discrimination wherever it exists;

(d) Each State Party shall prohibit and bring to an end, by all appropriate means, including legislation as required by circumstances, racial discrimination by any persons, group or organization;

(e) Each State Party undertakes to encourage, where appropriate, integrationist multi-racial organizations and movements and other means of eliminating barriers between races, and to discourage anything which tends to strengthen racial division.

The CONVENTION OF THE ELIMINATION OF ALL FORMS OF DISCRIMINATION AGAINST WOMEN contains the following provisions:

Article 2. States Parties condemn discrimination against women in all its forms, agree to pursue by all appropriate means and without delay a policy of eliminating discrimination against women and, to this end, undertake:

(a) To embody the principle of the equality of men and women in their national constitutions or other appropriate legislation if not yet incorporated therein and to ensure, through law and other appropriate means, the practical realization of this principle;

(b) To adopt appropriate legislative and other measures, including sanctions where appropriate, prohibiting all discrimination against women;

(c) To establish legal protection of the rights of women on an equal basis with men and to ensure through competent national tribunals and other public institutions the effective protection of women against any act of discrimination;

(d) To refrain from engaging in any act or practice of discrimination against women and to ensure that public authorities and institutions shall act in conformity with this obligation;

(e) To take all appropriate measures to eliminate discrimination against women by any persons, organization or enterprise;

(f) To take all appropriate measures, including legislation, to modify or abolish existing laws, regulations, customs and practices which constitute discrimination against women;

(g) To repeal all national penal provisions which constitute discrimination against women. . . .

Article 15. 1. State Parties shall accord to women equality with men before the law.

2. State Parties shall accord to women, in civil matters, a legal capacity identical to that of men and the same opportunities to exercise that capacity. In particular, they shall give women equal rights to conclude contracts and to administer property and shall treat them equally in all stages of procedure in courts and tribunals.

3. States Parties agree that all contracts and all other private instruments of any kind with a legal effect which is directed at restricting the legal capacity of women shall be deemed null and void.

4. States Parties shall accord to men and women the same rights with regard to the law relating to the movement of persons and the freedom to choose their residence and domicile.

The **AMERICAN CONVENTION ON HUMAN RIGHTS,** open for acceptance by member States of the **ORGANIZATION OF AMERICAN STATES,** provides that:

Article 1. The States Parties to this Convention undertake to respect the rights and freedoms recognized herein and to ensure to all persons subject to their jurisdiction the free and full exercise of those rights and freedoms, without any discrimination for reasons of race, color, sex, language, religion, political or other opinion, national or social origin, economic status, birth, or any other social condition.

The **AFRICAN CHARTER ON HUMAN AND PEOPLE'S RIGHTS,** open for acceptance by member States of the **ORGANIZATION OF AFRICAN UNITY,** contains the following provisions:

Article 2. Every individual shall be entitled to the enjoyment of the rights and freedoms recognized and guaranteed in the present Charter without distinction of any

kind such as race, ethnic group, colour, sex, language, religion, political or any other opinion, national and social origin, fortune, birth or other status.

Article 3 (1). Every individual shall be equal before the law.

(2) Every individual shall be entitled to equal protection of the law.

The **EUROPEAN CONVENTION ON HUMAN RIGHTS,** open for acceptance by member States of the **COUNCIL OF EUROPE,** provides that:

Article 1. The High Contracting Parties shall secure to everyone within their jurisdiction the rights and freedoms defined in Section I of this Convention. . . .

Article 14. The enjoyment of the rights and freedoms set forth in this Convention shall be secured without discrimination on any ground such as sex, race, colour, language, religion, political or other opinion, national or social origin, association with a nationality minority, property, birth or other status.

After examining reports submitted by States parties to the International Covenant on Civil and Political Rights in accordance with article 40 of that instrument, the **HUMAN RIGHTS COMMITTEE** in 1981 adopted a general comment on article 3 setting out its views on the question of the equal right of men and women to the enjoyment of civil and political rights, as follows (UN Doc. A/36/40, Annex VII, para. 1–5):

Article 3 of the Covenant requiring, as it does, States parties to ensure the equal right of men and women to the enjoyment of all civil and political rights provided for in the Covenant, has been insufficiently dealt with in a considerable number of States reports and has raised a number of concerns, two of which may be highlighted.

First, article 3, as articles 2 (1) and 26 in so far as those articles primarily deal with the prevention of discrimination on a number of grounds, among which sex is one, requires not only measures of protection but also affirmative action designed to ensure the positive enjoyment of rights. This cannot be done simply by enacting laws. Hence more information has generally been required regarding the role of women in practice with a view to ascertaining what measures, in addition to purely legislative measures of protection, have been or are being taken to give effect to the precise and positive obligations under article 3 and to ascertain what progress is being made or what factors or difficulties are being met in this regard.

Secondly, the positive obligation undertaken by States parties under that article may itself have an inevitable impact on legislation or administrative measures specifically designed to regulate matters other than those dealt with in the Covenant but which may adversely affect rights recognized in the Covenant. One example, among others, is the degree to which immigration laws which distinguish between a male and a female citizen may or may not adversely affect the scope of the right of the woman to marriage to non-citizens or to hold public office.

The Committee, therefore, considers that it might assist States parties if special attention were given to a review by specially appointed bodies or institutions of laws or measures which inherently draw a distinction between men and women in so far as those laws or measures adversely affect the rights provided for in the Covenant and, secondly, that States parties should give specific information in their reports about all measures, legislative or otherwise, designed to implement their undertaking under this article.

The Committee considers that it might help the States parties in implementing this obligation, if more use could be made of existing means of international co-operation with a view to exchanging experience and organizing assistance in solving the practical problems connected with the ensurance of equal rights for men and women.

The COMMITTEE ON THE ELIMINATION OF RACIAL DISCRIMINATION has adopted several general recommendations to States parties to the International Convention of the Elimination of all Forms of Racial Discrimination after examining periodic reports submitted by those States. In one of these, adopted at its fifth session, held from 14 to 25 February 1972, the committee noted that some of the States parties had expressed or implied the belief that certain information on racial discrimination which the committee had requested in a circular communication need not be supplied by the States on whose territories such discrimination did not exist. The committee responded (UN Doc. A/8718, chap. IX, General Recommendation I) as follows:

However, inasmuch as, in accordance with article 9, paragraph 1, of the International Convention on the Elimination of All Forms of Racial Discrimination, all States Parties undertake to submit reports on the measures that they have adopted and that give effect to the provisions of the Convention and, since all the categories of information listed in the Committee's communication of 28 January 1970 refer to obligations undertaken by the States Parties under the Convention, that communication is addressed to all States Parties without distinction, whether or not racial discrimination exists in their respective territories. The Committee welcomes the inclusion in the reports from all States Parties, which have not done so, of the necessary information in conformity with all the headings set out in the aforementioned communication of the Committee.

In another general recommendation, approved at its sixth session, held from 7 to 25 August 1972, the committee indicated a willingness to receive information from States parties to the convention regarding the status of their relations with racist regimes in southern Africa (UN Doc. A/8718, Chap. IX, General Recommendation III) as follows:

The Committee has considered some reports from States Parties containing information about measures taken to implement resolutions of United Nations organs concerning relations with the racist régimes in southern Africa.

The Committee notes that, in the tenth paragraph of the preamble to the International Convention on the Elimination of All Forms of Racial Discrimination, States Parties

have "resolved", *inter alia,* "to build an international community free from all forms of racial segregation and racial discrimination".

It notes also that, in article 3 of the Convention, "States Parties particularly condemn racial segregation and *apartheid*".

Furthermore, the Committee notes that, in resolution 2784 (XXVI), section III, the General Assembly, immediately after taking note with appreciation of the Committee's second annual report and endorsing certain opinions and recommendations. submitted by it, proceeded to call upon "all the trading partners of South Africa to abstain from any action that constitutes an encouragement to the continued violation of the principles and objectives of the International Convention on the Elimination of All Forms of Racial Discrimination by South Africa and the illegal régime in Southern Rhodesia".

The Committee expresses the view that measures adopted on the national level to give effect to the provisions of the Convention are interrelated with measures taken on the international level to encourage respect everywhere for the principles of the Convention.

The Committee welcomes the inclusion in the reports submitted under article 9, paragraph 1, of the Convention, by any State Party which chooses to do so, of information regarding the status of its diplomatic, economic and other relations with the racist régimes in southern Africa.

Similarly, the COMMITTEE ON THE ELIMINATION OF DISCRIMINATION AGAINST WOMEN, after examining reports submitted by States parties to the Convention on the Elimination of all Forms of Discrimination against Women, adopted at its 1988 session two general recommendations on steps to be taken to give effect to the provisions of that instrument.

In the first (UN Doc. A/43/38, chap. V, general recommendation No. 5), the committee, noting that, while significant progress had been achieved in regard to repealing or modifying discriminatory laws, there was still a need for action to be taken to implement fully the convention by introducing measures to promote *de facto* equality between men and women, recommended that States parties make more use of temporary special measures such as positive action, preferential treatment, or quota systems to advance women's integration into education, the economy, politics, and employment.

In the second, (*Ibid.*, general recommendation No. 6), the committee recommended that States parties:

1. Establish and/or strengthen effective national machinery, institutions and procedures, at a high level of Government, and with adequate resources, commitment and authority to:
   (a) Advise on the impact on women of all government policies;
   (b) Monitor the situation of women comprehensively;
   (c) Help formulate new policies and effectively carry out strategies and measures to eliminate discrimination;
2. Take appropriate steps to ensure the dissemination of the Convention, the reports of the States parties under arti-

cle 18 and the reports of the Committee in the language of the States concerned;

3. Seek the assistance of the Secretary-General and the Department of Public Information in providing translations of the Convention and the reports of the Committee;

4. Include in their initial and periodic reports the action taken in respect of this recommendation.

SEE ALSO ILO *Equality of Treatment (Social Security) Convention.*

EQUALITY: ADMINISTRATION OF JUSTICE. At its 1963 session, the UN SUB-COMMISSION ON PREVENTION OF DISCRIMINATION AND PROTECTION OF MINORITIES decided (resolution 1 [XV]) to undertake a study of equality in the administration of justice, in accordance with article 10 of the UNIVERSAL DECLARATION OF HUMAN RIGHTS, and appointed one of its members, Mr. Mohammed A. Abu Rannat (Sudan), as special rapporteur for the study. The study was completed and presented to the sub-commission in 1969 and later was published under the title *Study of Equality in the Administration of Justice* (UN publication, Sales No. E.71.XIV.3).

The study, deriving as it does from article 10 of the Universal Declaration of Human Rights, deals not with substantive law but with equal entitlement to a fair hearing. It notes that, while many legal systems have recognized the importance of equal justice, not all have stressed the elaboration or formal statement of the necessary guarantees, and some have failed to provide the necessary judicial organization or procedures.

Chapter II of the study explores the implications of a fair hearing with a view to indicating the accepted norms so that departures from those norms may be accurately identified. In this connection, it is recognized that the general elements of a fair hearing, which can be derived from the text of article 10, are elaborated in articles 14 and 15 of the INTERNATIONAL COVENANT ON CIVIL AND POLITICAL RIGHTS.

In chapter III, the grounds on which discrimination operates in the administration of justice are described; they include race or colour, sex, language, religion, political or other opinion, national origin or nationality, property, birth or social origin or position, other status (such as that of minors, ministers of religion and diplomats), and the status of the territory to which an individual belongs.

In chapter IV, the wide variety of measures adopted by various States to combat such discrimination is described, including arrangements designed to encourage the total independence and impartiality of the courts, of judges, or jurors, and of members of the legal profession. A number of specific governmental institutions and procedures found in practice to promote equality in the administration of justice—for instance, by improving the working efficiency of the courts and reducing judicial delay—are also described.

Chapter V sets out the special rapporteur's conclusions and recommendations with regard to methods of dealing effectively with discrimination in the administration of justice: first, on the national level by the regulation of matters affecting the administration of justice by means of constitutional or statutory provisions or by rules of court and, second, on the international level by the preparation of a convention, a declaration, or both. With a view to facilitating decisions in the matter, the special rapporteur prepared a comprehensive series of draft principles on equality in the administration of justice for consideration by the Sub-Commission and its superior bodies.

The sub-commission, after examining the study as a whole, considered and amended the draft principles and forwarded them to the COMMISSION ON HUMAN RIGHTS (resolution 3 [XXIII]). However, the commission, for lack of time, was unable to consider them in detail for several years. In 1972, it decided to give them high priority at its 1973 session and requested the Secretary-General to obtain the views and comments of the governments of member States on them, and comments on the form in which they should be set forth. At its 1973 session, the commission was again unable to deal with them, and some members pointed out that there was a lack of consensus among governments as to their disposition.

Accordingly, on recommendation of the commission, the General Assembly on 14 December 1973 (resolution 3144 [XXVIII]) called upon member States "to give due consideration, in formulating legislation and taking other measures affecting equality in the administration of justice, to the draft principles, which may be regarded as setting forth valuable norms, with a view to arriving at the elaboration of an appropriate international declaration or instrument."

The draft principles, as formulated and adopted by the sub-commission on the basis of texts proposed by the special rapporteur, are as follows:

Draft Principles on Equality in the Administration of Justice

Whereas the peoples of the world have, in the Charter of the United Nations, proclaimed their determination to reaffirm faith in fundamental human rights, in the dignity and worth of the human person and in the equal rights of men and women, and to promote social progress and better standards of life in larger freedom,

Whereas the Charter sets forth, as one of the purposes of the United Nations, the promotion and encouragement of respect for human rights and fundamental freedoms for all without distinction as to race, sex, language or religion,

Whereas the Universal Declaration of Human Rights proclaims in its article 2 that everyone is entitled to all the rights and freedoms set forth in that Declaration without distinction of any kind, such as race, colour, sex, language, religion, political or other opinion, national or social origin, property, birth or other status, or the status of the territory to which he belongs,

Whereas the Universal Declaration proclaims in its article 10 that everyone is entitled in full equality to a fair and public hearing by an independent and impartial tribunal, in the determination of his rights and obligations and of any criminal charge against him,

Whereas the United Nations has already dealt with some aspects of the administration of justice in provisions of other international instruments, including articles 9, 10, 11, 14 and 15 of the International Covenant on Civil and Political Rights, article 5 (a) of the International Convention on the Elimination of All Forms of Racial Discrimination, article 16 of the Convention Relating to the Status of Refugees and article 16 of the Convention Relating to the Status of Stateless Persons,

Whereas sufficient national experience has been gained in various parts of the world concerning the methods and forms of combating the types of discrimination condemned by the Universal Declaration of Human Rights,

Whereas the types of discrimination in the administration of justice under consideration which still exist make it necessary to adopt an international instrument or instruments with a view to the elimination of discrimination in the administration of justice,

Whereas the attainment of the goal of equal rights in the administration of justice requires not only the recognition of the civil and political rights of the individual but also the establishment of the social, economic, educational and cultural conditions which are essential to the full development of the human potential and dignity,

Now therefore the following principles are proclaimed with a view to eliminating all forms of discrimination in the administration of justice:

1. General Principles

Principle 1. To the fullest extent consistent with the nature of the question, matters connected with the administration of justice shall be regulated by constitutional or statutory provisions or by rules of court, whichever may be appropriate, and not by executive decisions. Written constitutions, where they exist, shall lay down at least the basic general rules affecting the administration of justice.

Principle 2. The State shall have the exclusive power and obligation to administer justice to persons within its jurisdiction.

Principle 3. National laws concerning the rights to equal access to the courts and to equality before the law in general shall provide specifically that these rights shall be accorded to all, without distinction of any kind, such as race, colour, sex, language, religion, political or other opinion, national or social origin, property, birth or other status.

Principle 4. In the allocation of jurisdiction and determination of competence of tribunals of whatever characterization, no such allocation or determination shall be made upon the basis of race, colour, sex, language, religion, political or other opinion national or social origin, property, birth or other status.

Principle 5. Being essential requirements for promoting equality in the administration of justice, the independence and impartiality of members of all levels of the judiciary shall be ensured by the laws and practices governing their training, selection, jurisdiction, oath or affirmation, privileges and immunities, tenure of office, transfer, salaries and pensions, the limitations placed on their non-judicial activities, the circumstances disqualifying them from acting in particular cases, the protection against improper influences accorded to them by the criminal law and the sanctions applicable to them in the event of their failing to display independence and impartiality in performing their functions.

Principle 6. Being essential requirements for promoting equality in the administration of justice, the independence and impartiality of jurors and assessors, where they function, shall be ensured by the laws and practices affecting their selection and compensation, their oath or affirmation, their immunities, the incompatibility of certain activities with service as juror or assessor, the challenges which may be made to their acting in particular cases, the protection against improper influences accorded to them by the criminal law and the sanctions applicable to them in the event of their failing to display independence and impartiality in performing their functions.

Principle 7. Being essential requirements for promoting equality in the administration of justice, the independence of lawyers practising before courts and their impartiality in according their services to potential clients shall be ensured by the laws and practices affecting the relationship between such lawyers and their organizations, on the one hand, and the State, on the other, the incompatibility of certain activities with the profession of the law, the circumstances under which a practising lawyer may not accept a case, the grounds on which a practising lawyer mot not refuse his services to a client, the access of the individual to his lawyer and the privacy of communication between the two, the preservation of the secrecy of information received by lawyers during professional dealing with their clients, the immunities of lawyers and the sanctions applicable to them.

Principle 8. National laws shall ensure that no one shall be denied equal access to the judiciary and to the legal profession, without distinction based upon race, colour, sex, language, religion, political or other opinion, national or social origin, property, birth or other status.

Principle 9. Where the State or any other body subsidizes the training of judges, lawyers and court interpreters, they shall do so without distinction of any kind, such as race, colour, sex, language, religion, political or other opinion, national or social origin, property, birth or other status.

Principle 10. Judges, jurors, assessors, accused persons, other parties to judicial proceedings, lawyers, witnesses and interpreters shall be permitted to make an affirmation instead of taking an oath if they object to the religious character of any oath required of them in connexion with their roles in the administration of justice.

Principle 11. National laws concerning legal aid for the poor shall develop such aid to the utmost extent consistent with the economic resources of the country concerned. Needy persons shall be entitled to be relieved of all charges and expenses in judicial proceedings and to free aid for their defence.

Principle 12. Provisions shall be made through legal aid schemes or otherwise for ensuring adequate legal representation to persons whose political opinions may otherwise be a disadvantage to them in judicial proceedings.

Principle 13. Aliens in a country shall have the benefits of legal aid to the same extent as citizens.

Principle 14. National laws concerning appeals to higher courts shall include provision for appeals on grounds of the discriminatory application of laws relating to jurisdiction and procedure as well as of substantive law.

Principle 15. With a view to eliminating discrimination arising out of the status of the territory to which a person belongs, full application shall be given to the Declaration on the Granting of Independence to Colonial Countries and Peoples, proclaimed by the United Nations General Assembly in resolution 1514 (XV) of 14 December 1960, which proclaims the necessity of bringing to an end colonialism in all its forms.

2. Principles Relating to All Courts

Principle 16. Everyone, without distinction of any kind, such as race, colour, sex, language, religion, political or other opinion, national or social origin, property, birth or other status, shall be guaranteed the following rights in the examination of any criminal charge against him, whether it relates to a crime falling within ordinary jurisdiction or within military or special jurisdiction, or in the determination of his rights and responsibilities through civil, administrative or other judicial proceedings:

(i) The right to access to tribunals;

(ii) The right to be heard by his lawful judge, that is to say, by the competent tribunal previously established by law or established under pre-existing law and not by a tribunal assigned *ad hoc* or specially set up to hear his case;

(iii) The right to be heard by an independent and impartial tribunal;

(iv) The right to be assisted and represented by counsel of his own choosing;

(v) The right to a prompt and speedy hearing, subject to his being given adequate time to prepare his case;

(vi) The right, either in person or through counsel, to present his case and to produce and examine witnesses and other evidence, or to have such witnesses or other evidence produced and examined;

(vii) The right to a public hearing, subject to the possibility that the press and the public may be excluded from all or part of a hearing for reasons of morals, public order, or national security in a democratic society, or when the interest of the private lives of the parties so requires, or to the extent strictly necessary in the opinion of the court in special circumstances where publicity would prejudice the interests of justice;

(viii) The right to have the decision in his case based only on the evidence placed before the court and known to all the parties;

(ix) The right to have the decision on his case rendered in public, except where the interest of juveniles otherwise requires or the proceedings concern matrimonial disputes or the guardianship of children;

(x) The right to appeal to a higher court.

Principle 17. As regards the administration of justice, married women shall be ensured the right to an independent domicile.

Principle 18. The distribution of courts within a country and the movements of itinerant judges shall be determined by the distribution of population, subject to the special needs of persons living in isolated areas.

Principle 19. In view of the hardship caused in particular to poor persons by delays in judicial proceedings, measures shall be taken, appropriate to the circumstances prevailing in each country concerned, to reduce the delays facing the courts in reaching and dealing with cases to the minimum consistent with the right of accused or other parties parties to judicial proceedings adequately to prepare and present their cases.

Principle 20. National laws relating to the place of hearing or trial shall provide for the change of place of hearing or trial whenever such change is necessary to ensure a fair hearing or trial.

Principle 21. Measures taken for the special protection of minors in judicial proceedings shall not diminish their right to equality in the administration of justice.

Principle 22. Whatever the jurisdiction of such religious courts as may exist in a country, civil courts shall offer a forum for the settlement of all justifiable disputes. No person shall be without a court to resort to, due to his not belonging to any of the religions whose courts have exclusive jurisdiction over the matter at issue.

Principle 23. Interpretation shall be provided free for all accused persons and other parties to judicial proceedings if they do not have a command of the language of the Court. Analogous arrangements shall be made free for accused persons and other parties to judicial proceedings who are handicapped in speech or hearing.

Principle 24. The right to a public hearing may be restricted by laws framed so as to prohibit, prior to the final decision of the court, publicity prejudicial to accused persons or other parties to judicial proceedings.

Principle 25. Courts shall be required to give their reasons when rendering judgement.

3. Principles relating to Criminal Courts

Principle 26. Everyone against whom a criminal charge is preferred shall be guaranteed, in addition to the above-mentioned rights, the following rights, without distinction of any kind, such as race, colour, sex, language, religion, political or other opinion, national or social origin, property, birth or other status:

(i) The right to be presumed innocent until proved guilty according to law;

(ii) The right to be informed promptly and in detail in a language which he understands of the nature and cause of the charge against him;

(iii) The right to be informed of his right to defend himself either in person or through counsel of his choosing;

(iv) The right to have legal assistance assigned to him in any case, if the interests of justice and of the person involved in the judicial proceedings so require, without payment if he does not have sufficient means to pay for it;

(v) The right to compulsory representation by counsel in proceedings for crimes of a grave nature;

(vi) The right to examine, or have examined, the witnesses and documentary evidence against him and to obtain documentary evidence and the attendance and examination of witnesses on his behalf;

(vii) The right to have the free assistance of an interpreter if he cannot understand or speak the language used in court;

(viii) The right not to be compelled to testify against himself or to confess guilt.

Principle 27. Judges shall explain to accused persons their essential procedural rights during trial and their right of appeal.

Principle 28. National laws concerning provisional release from custody pending or during trial shall be so framed as to eliminate any requirement of pecuniary guarantees and shall be designed also so as to reduce detention pending or during trial to a minimum.

Principle 29. No one shall be compelled to incriminate himself. No accused person or witness shall be subject to physical or psychic pressure, including anything calculated to impair his will or violate his dignity. Evidence obtained in breach of this right shall not be admissible, and the extraction of purported confessions by means of such influences shall be an offence. No one shall be compelled to testify against his spouse, ascendants or descendants.

Resolutions of the Commission on Human Rights and the General Assembly. In 1988, both the UN Commission on Human Rights and the UN General Assembly considered, and adopted resolutions on, the question of human rights in the administration of justice.

The commission reiterated (resolution 1988 [33]) its earlier calls upon member States to spare no effort in providing for effective legislation and ither mechanisms and procedures and adequate resources to ensure more effective implementation of existing international standards relating to human rights in the administration of justice. It emphasized, as it had in the past, the importance of education and public information programs in the field of human rights for law students, the legal profession, and all those responsible for the administration of justice, and recognized the important role that non-governmental organizations, including professional associations of lawyers and judges, can play in promoting human rights in the administration of justice. It urged the Sub-Commission on Prevention of Discrimination and Protection of Minorities to pursue vigorously its consideration of the issue of the independence and impartiality of the judiciary, jurors, and assessors and the independence of lawyers, on the basis of the report of its special rapporteur on this subject; and to formulate, as a matter of priority, its concrete recommendations on this issue.

Towards the end of 1988, the General Assembly (resolution 43/153) recognized the important contribution of the Commission on Human Rights to the promotion of human rights in the administration of justice, and reaffirmed the importance of the full implementation of United Nations norms and standards in that field. It urged member States to develop strategies for the practical realization of those standards, in particular:

(a) To adopt in national legislation and practice existing international standards relating to human rights in the administration of justice, and to make them available to all persons concerned;

(b) To design realistic and effective mechanisms for the full implementation of these standards and provide the necessary administrative as well as judicial structures for their continuous monitoring;

(c) To devise measures to promote the observance of these standards, as well as public awareness about their importance role, in particular through their widespread dissemination and through educational and promotional activities;

(d) To include, where appropriate, references to the implementation of these standards in their reports under the various international human rights instruments;

(e) To increase, as far as possible, their support to technical co-operation and advisory services at all levels for the more effective implementation of these standards, either directly or through international funding agencies, such as the United Nations Development Programme, when developing countries include specific projects in their country programmes;

The General Assembly welcomed the steps initiated by the CENTER FOR HUMAN RIGHTS and the Crime Prevention and Criminal Justice Branch of the Centre for Social Development and Humanitarian Affairs of the United Nations office at Vienna to ensure closer cooperation on all matters of human rights in the administration of justice, especially with respect to criminal violations of human rights and mass victimization; and requested the Secretary-General to continue to provide all necessary support to United Nations bodies working on setting standards in this field and to develop further the newly created focal points within the two centers to monitor the human rights aspects of the administration of justice within the various elements of United Nations programs in this field, as well as the work of specialized agencies, regional organizations, and non-governmental organizations in consultative status, and to provide, as appropriate, advice on coordination and other relevant issues in this field.

Standards in Criminal Justice. In May 1977, the UN Economic and Social Council endorsed (resolution 2075 [LXII]) certain recommendations made by the COMMITTEE ON CRIME PREVENTION AND CONTROL in its report under the heading, "Human Rights in the Administration of Justice." The recommendations included:

(a) the development of standards that would ensure just, humane, and effective judicial proceedings, improved selection and training of judges and prosecutors, and the establishment of safeguards against the abuse of discretion in sentencing;

(b) the elaboration of a set of standard minimum rules for the treatment of offenders in the community;

(c) the strengthening of inmate grievance procedures by ensuring prisoners the right of recourse to an independent authority, both at the national and the international levels;

(d) the facilitating of the return of persons convicted of crime abroad to their domicile to serve their sentences; and

(e) the improvement of the situation of persons detained either in police custody or in prison custody before trial.

SEE ALSO *Body of Principles for the Protection of All Persons under any Form of Detention of Imprisonment; Equal Justice; Fair Trial; Racism: Administration of Criminal Justice.*

EQUALITY: MEN AND WOMEN. Although the principle of equality of men and women has won almost universal acceptance, full equality between men and women is far from being realized in practice.

The Copenhagen World Conference of the United Nations Decade for Women, in 1980, the mid-point of the decade, interpreted equality as meaning not only legal equality and the elimination of *de jure* discrimination but also equality of rights, responsibilities, and opportunities for the participation of women in development, both as beneficiaries and as active agents. Later, the NAIROBI FORWARD-LOOKING STRATEGIES FOR THE ADVANCEMENT OF WOMEN, adopted by the World Conference to Review and Appraise the Achievements of the United Nations Decade for Women, which met in Nairobi, Kenya, from 15 to 26 July 1985, further clarified the meaning of equality as "both a goal and a means whereby individuals are accorded equal treatment under the law and equal opportunities to enjoy their rights and to develop their potential talents and skills so that they can participate in national political, economic, social and cultural development and can benefit from its results. For women in particular, equality means the realization of rights that have been denied as a result of cultural, institutional, behavioral and attitudinal discrimination. Equality is important for development and peace because national and global inequities perpetuate themselves and increase tensions of all types."

The United Nations is committed by its charter to the principle of equality of men and women and has explored new ways of promoting and protecting that principle. In the preamble of the charter, the peoples of the United Nations proclaim their determination "to reaffirm faith in fundamental human rights, in the worth and dignity of the human person, in the equal rights of men and women and of nations large and small." One of the purposes of the United Nations, as set out in article 1 of the charter, is to achieve "international co-operation in solving international problems of an economic, social, cultural or humani-

tarian character, and in promoting and encouraging respect for human rights and fundamental freedoms for all without distinction." Article 8 provides that "the United Nations shall place no restrictions on the eligibility of men and women to participate in any capacity and under conditions of equality in its principal and subsidiary organs." Articles 13, 55, and 75 call for the realization of human rights and fundamental freedoms "for all without distinction as to race, sex, language or religion." Under article 56, member States have pledged themselves to take joint and separate action, in cooperation with the United Nations, to achieve these aims.

The principle of EQUALITY, and the prohibition of discrimination on the ground of sex, is reaffirmed and elaborated in a number of international instruments, including the UNIVERSAL DECLARATION OF HUMAN RIGHTS (articles 1, 2, and 7), the INTERNATIONAL COVENANT ON ECONOMIC, SOCIAL AND CULTURAL RIGHTS (articles 2 (2) and 3), the INTERNATIONAL CONVENTION ON THE ELIMINATION OF ALL FORMS OF RACIAL DISCRIMINATION (article 2), the AMERICAN CONVENTION ON HUMAN RIGHTS (article 1), the AFRICAN CHARTER ON HUMAN AND PEOPLES' RIGHTS (ARTICLES 2 AND 3), and the EUROPEAN CONVENTION ON HUMAN RIGHTS (articles 1 and 14). In addition, the DECLARATION ON THE ELIMINATION OF DISCRIMINATION AGAINST WOMEN and the CONVENTION ON THE ELIMINATION OF ALL FORMS OF DISCRIMINATION AGAINST WOMEN are devoted in their entirety to promotion and protection of the principle of equality of men and women.

Further, a number of specific problems confronting women in various parts of the world in their efforts to attain full equality with men have been dealt with in conventions and recommendations adopted and opened for ratification or accession by the United Nations or one of its specialized agencies, such as the CONVENTION FOR THE SUPPRESSION OF THE TRAFFIC IN PERSONS AND THE EXPLOITATION OF THE PROSTITUTION OF OTHERS, approved by the General Assembly in 1949; the SUPPLEMENTARY CONVENTION ON THE ABOLITION OF SLAVERY, THE SLAVE TRADE, AND INSTITUTIONS AND PRACTICES SIMILAR TO SLAVERY, approved by a conference of plenipotentiaries in 1956; the CONVENTION ON THE POLITICAL RIGHTS OF WOMEN, approved by the General Assembly in 1952; the CONVENTION ON THE NATIONALITY OF MARRIED WOMEN, approved by the General Assembly in 1957; the CONVENTION ON CONSENT TO MARRIAGE, MINIMUM AGE FOR MARRIAGE, AND REGISTRATION OF MARRIAGES, approved by the General Assembly in 1962; the ILO DISCRIMINATION (EMPLOYMENT AND OCCUPATION) CONVENTION, approved by the International Labor Conference in 1958; and the UNESCO CONVENTION AGAINST DISCRIMINATION IN EDU-

CATION, approved by the General Conference of UNESCO in 1958.

The NAIROBI FORWARD-LOOKING STRATEGIES FOR THE ADVANCEMENT OF WOMEN, proposes a number of concrete measures designed to overcome the many obstacles encountered in efforts to achieve the decade's goals and objectives for the advancement of women. These strategies reaffirm the international concern regarding the status of women and provide a framework for renewed commitment by the international community to the advancement of women and the elimination of gender-based discrimination.

On 24 May 1989, the UN Economic and Social Council recalled that the General Assembly had endorsed the Nairobi Forward-looking Strategies for the Advancement of Women in 1985 and noted that progress in achieving *de jure* equality between women and men had been steady. It welcomed the clear improvement in some indicators of equality in social participation in most regions but expressed concern that progress in other regions is slowing. It was particularly concerned that the pace of achieving *de facto* equality, particularly equality in economic participation, had evidently been slowing in most countries over the preceding decade.

Recognizing that equality for women is closely linked to their economic independence and noting that various affirmative action policies can accelerate the elimination of discrimination against women, the council urged governments to give high priority to measures and temporary affirmative action programs that will more rapidly bring about equality in women's economic participation, in particular to programs that will ensure the following:

(a) women's access to the labor market and to education and training;

(b) elimination of sex segregation in the labor market and in education;

(c) women's participation in trade unions;

(d) equal pay for equal work;

(e) equal access to economic resources, including credit and membership in cooperatives; and

(f) improved conditions in the informal sector including, where desirable, the application of labor standards and the development or improvement of sex-disaggregated statistics that accurately reflect women's work in the informal economic sector.

The council called upon the COMMISSION ON THE STATUS OF WOMEN, in carrying out its review and appraisal of the implementation of the Nairobi Forward-looking Strategies, to consider measures to accelerate the pace of achieving equality in economic and social participation, including the definition and compilation of benchmark statistical indicators that could be used for national, regional, and international reporting, as well as affirmative action programs.

As regards article 3 of the International Covenant on Civil and Political Rights, the HUMAN RIGHTS COMMITTEE adopted the following comment at its 13th session, held at the United Nations office in Geneva from 13 to 31 July 1981 (UN Doc. A/36/40, General comment 4/13, para. 1–5):

Article 3 of the Covenant requiring, as it does, States parties to ensure the equal right of men and women to the enjoyment of all civil and political rights provided for in the Covenant, has been insufficiently dealt with in a considerable number of States reports and has raised a number of concerns, two of which may be highlighted.

Firstly, article 3, as articles 2 (1) and 26 in so far as those articles primarily deal with the prevention of discrimination on a number of grounds, among which sex is one, requires not only measures of protection but also affirmative action designed to ensure the positive enjoyment of rights. This cannot be done simply by enacting laws. Hence, more information has generally been required regarding the role of women in practice with a view to ascertaining what measures, in addition to purely legislative measures of protection, have been or are being taken to give effect to the precise and positive obligations under article 3 and to ascertain what progress is being made or what factors or difficulties are being met in this regard.

Secondly, the positive obligation undertaken by States parties under that article may itself have an inevitable impact on legislation or administrative measures specifically designed to regulate matters other than those dealt with in the Covenant but which may adversely affect rights recognized in the Covenant. One example, among others, is the degree to which immigration laws which distinguish between a male and a female citizen may or may not adversely affect the scope of the right of the woman to marriage to non-citizens or to hold public office.

The Committee, therefore, considers that it might assist States parties if special attention were given to a review by specially appointed bodies or institutions of laws or measures which inherently draw a distinction between men and women in so far as those laws or measures adversely affect the rights provided for in the Covenant and, secondly, that States parties should give specific information in their reports about all measures, legislative or otherwise, designed to implement their undertaking under this article.

The Committee considers that it might help the States parties in implementing this obligation, if more use could be made of existing means of international co-operation with a view to exchanging experience and organizing assistance in solving the practical problems connected with the ensurance of equal rights for men and women.

SEE ALSO *Women Workers: ILO Plan of Action. . . .*

EQUALITY: NATIONAL CONSTITUTIONAL AND LEGISLATIVE PROVISIONS ON NON-DISCRIMINATION.

In the DECLARATION OF THE SECOND WORLD CONFERENCE TO COMBAT RACISM AND RACIAL DISCRIMINATION, adopted on 12 August 1983, that conference recognized the central importance of national legislation and judicial and administrative action to combat racial discrimination and the specific value of recourse procedures for the implementation of human rights norms.

In the Program for Action for the Second Decade to Combat Racism and Racial Discrimination, prepared by the conference and approved by the UN General Assembly on 22 November 1983 (resolution 38/14), the assembly recommended (para. 50) that:

(a) Governments, where necessary, should guarantee non-discrimination on grounds of race and equal rights for all individuals in their constitutions and legislation;

(b) Governments, where necessary, should undertake to review and update all national legislation and remove all discriminatory provisions;

(c) Legislation should be consistent with international standards embodied in international instruments;

(d) Victims of discrimination should be informed and advised of their rights, by all possible means, and given assistance in securing those rights;

(e) Governments should, where necessary, establish appropriate and effective machinery, including conciliation and mediation procedures and national commissions to ensure that such legislation is enforced effectively and thereby to promote equality of opportunity and good race relations.

The Program of Action further provided that a system of regular review and appraisal should be continued, to enable member States and all organizations of the United Nations system, including relevant regional bodies and non-governmental organizations, to assess the measures taken towards achieving the aims and objectives of the decade (See RACISM AND RACIAL DISCRIMINATION: SECOND DECADE ACTION PROGRAM).

At the request of the General Assembly, the Secretary-General submitted to it, in 1984, a plan of activities for implementing the program of action for the 1985–1989 period, in which the compilation and publication of a consolidated volume of national laws designed to combat racism and racial discrimination was suggested. The assembly approved the suggestion in 1984 (resolution 39/16), and in 1985 (resolution 40/22) called for the compilation to be submitted to it in 1988.

In order to prepare the compilation, the Secretary-General requested governments to supply the relevant information and received responses from 44 of them. The resulting compilation, in tentative form, was made available to the Assembly in 1988 for consultation. At the same time, an overview of the available texts (UN Doc. A/43/637) was presented to the assembly. The overview (para. 13–49) is reproduced below.

II. Overview of the Texts Submitted for the Global Compilation

The constitutional and legislative texts submitted reflect the concerns and recommendations of the Second World Conference and the General Assembly as outlined above. Each one of the elements for national action dealt with by the Conference and the Assembly found constitutional and legislative expressions in the texts submitted. Most States responding provided information and texts relating to the basic guarantees of equality in the enjoyment of human rights, either taken globally or with regard to specific human rights. They also, in many cases, supplied information on non-discrimination provisions relating to the exercise of specific rights. Information was also provided on the mechanisms established for protecting the enjoyment of human rights and on the sanctions provided for in cases of violation.

A few States submitted the text of legislation dealing specifically with race relations or the promotion of human rights, focusing on the issue of discrimination in many areas and establishing specific procedures in that regard. The following overview seeks to highlight the main points of the texts submitted. It is not exhaustive, and particular States are mentioned by way of example.

A. Equality and Non-discrimination in the Enjoyment of Human Rights. It is recognized by the overwhelming majority of States that individuals are entitled to equality of treatment before the law, and most States have passed legislation to this effect. The form and content of such legislation varies from one country to another. Many States do not raise distinctions as regards the class of persons protected by the law, thus ensuring universal equality of treatment. Examples of this would include the constitutions of Brazil—"all are equal before the law"; Canada—"every individual is equal before and under the law"; and El Salvador—"all men are equal before the law". In each of these examples, not only is the class of persons protected an infinite one but it is specifically emphasized that for the purposes of the law in question discrimination on the basis of race is not permitted.

Legislation passed has sometimes raised the distinction of citizenship as regards the class of persons protected. This distinction may be of little practical significance if, as in the case of the Union of Soviet Socialist Republics, another law guarantees non-citizens the rights and freedoms provided by law and specifically mentions that aliens have the right to apply to court to protect their various rights.

Even where it has been officially recognized that individuals are to be treated equally by the law, it has been acknowledged that there might be practical problems in the achievement of this policy. The Constitution of Austria draws attention to this by stating that nationals belonging to a minority should receive the same treatment "in law and in fact".

It is the view of some States that to realize *de facto* equality for all it may be necessary to take affirmative action in support of some groups in society that have already been victims of discrimination. In New Zealand and the United Kingdom of Great Britain and Northern Island, for example, the taking of such action is deemed not to be in breach of the laws against racial discrimination. This position is shared by Canada where, for instance, the law expressly obliges employers to examine situations in which employees might be suffering discrimination and to take steps to eradicate it.

In New Zealand, the State has taken the precaution of legislating against discrimination by subterfuge. Consequently, where a condition is imposed which is not apparently in contravention of a provision but which has a discriminatory effect in a situation that would otherwise be unlawful, then that condition will be deemed to be unlawful unless the person imposing it establishes good reason for its imposition and shows that its imposition is not a subterfuge to avoid complying with that provision.

Many States, such as El Salvador, have recognized the need to ensure that civil rights are enjoyed by all without discrimination. Although it could be argued that the general declarations of equality provided by most States are enough to ensure this, many of them have gone further in specifically listing at least some of the rights to be enjoyed free of discrimination. For example, some States seek to ensure that all persons are free to marry as they choose. In New Zealand, any condition in restraint of marriage that is based on race will be null and void. The Venezuelan constitution declares that no impediment imposed by another country will be recognized as a bar to an alien wishing to marry in Venezuela. There are some countries, such as Bulgaria, that go further in indicating that any person who takes measures to prevent mixed marriages shall be punished.

The right to own and transfer property is recognized for everyone by the constitutions of, for instance, Portugal and El Salvador. It is recognized in Mauritius that all, regardless of race, have the right to the protection of their property and to be free of deprivation thereof unless they are properly compensated. This sort of protection is also recognized in Tuvalu. In both States, however, the right to property is subject to the rights of others as well as to the national interest.

The right to security of person is one of the utmost importance in ensuring the dignity of human beings and, therefore, one that should be guaranteed by States to all persons, citizens and non-citizens alike. States have legislated on this issue in two principal ways. Some, as illustrated by the constitution of Trinidad and Tobago, have asserted the right of the individual to liberty and the security of the person. Others approach this issue differently, for example, the constitution of the United Arab Emirates seeks to secure the right by declaring that all persons should be free of arbitrary arrest, searches or restriction of liberty. In other States, the constitution also declares that no person should be subjected to torture or degrading treatment. Other examples would include Venezuela, which seeks to ensure this right by allowing asylum for anyone in danger for political reasons, subject to his satisfying the conditions established by law.

Equality and non-discrimination in the exercise of political rights is also important. States often provide that there should be equal and universal suffrage, thus implicitly barring the possibility of racial discrimination. Laws in Austria and Trinidad and Tobago, for example, make this explicit by specifically prohibiting the interference with an individual's rights, *inter alia*, on the ground of race.

Some States have adopted legislation in order to ensure that their political systems are generally free of racial discrimination. In Panama, for instance, the constitution makes it unlawful to form political parties, *inter alia*, on the ground of race. Moreover, the electoral code states that political parties should not discriminate on the ground of race in their admission of members. In Portugal, the constitution indicates that deputies convicted by a court of participating in organizations linked to Fascist ideology shall forfeit their mandate. The constitution also lists a number of principles governing the conduct of election campaigns, including freedom in canvassing votes, equal treatment and opportunity for all candidates and the impartial treatment of all candidates by the public authorities.

Freedom of association and the right to assembly are provided for all, without distinction of race, by such States as Trinidad and Tobago and Tuvalu. Some States seek to protect the rights of individuals as members of an association. In Panama, a law provides that the beliefs of members of peasant organizations must be respected, regardless, *inter alia*, of race. In the United Kingdom of Great Britain and Northern Ireland, associations may not discriminate in admitting applicants or in the terms on which they will admit them. It is also provided that associations may not discriminate in granting to members access to any benefits of the association, nor may any member be arbitrarily deprived of his membership or made subject to any other detriment simply on the ground of race.

On the other hand, some States take steps to prohibit associations that promote racial discrimination. In Spain, associations formed for the promotion of racial discrimination are viewed as illegal. Similarly, Portugal prohibits Fascist organizations and Panama does not permit associations based on the premise of the superiority of any race. States such as Bulgaria, France and Iran provide for the punishment of individuals who either form or participate in the activities of associations such as these. In France, these types of associations can be dissolved and become null and void.

Freedom of expression is guaranteed to every person in, for example, Cyprus and Nigeria, and certain States explicitly state that it shall be enjoyed without distinction as to race. However, steps are also taken to prohibit the use of freedom of expression to promote racism. In Australia and New Zealand, for example, it is prohibited to publish an advertisement that indicates an intention to perform an act in breach of the laws against racial discrimination. In the United Kingdom of Great Britain and Northern Ireland, no one may advertise an intention to perform an act of racial discrimination, whether such act be unlawful or not. In Portugal, advertisements must not encourage, *inter alia*, racial discrimination. In Mexico, the broadcast of anything racially discriminatory is prohibited, as is the broadcast of anything which might bring ridicule to any person.

Freedom from discrimination in employment is also specifically guaranteed in some texts. In Australia, France, New Zealand and the United Kingdom, one may not refuse to employ or dismiss another on the ground of race. In the United Kingdom, it is stipulated that professional bodies and training courses responsible for conferring the appropriate qualifications may not withhold them on the ground of race, and the laws of Australia, Canada, Finland, New Zealand and the United Kingdom indicate that discrimination as to the conditions of work of employees is prohibited. In Canada, legislation provides that companies should pinpoint and, if necessary, correct by special measures and accommodation of differences, any conditions of disadvantage in employment experienced by racial minority groups.

Access to housing is another area where discrimination is prohibited. In Australia, Canada, New Zealand and the United Kingdom, it is prohibited for individuals to be denied access to property or to be discriminated against regarding the terms on which property is offered simply on the ground of race. These countries also prohibit the ill-treatment of occupants such as by depriving them of benefits they might otherwise have had and arbitrarily evicting them on the ground of race. In Dominica, it is indicated that a landlord may not withhold his licence on the ground of race, nor may an individual be harassed in Canada on the same ground.

Education is another area where discrimination is often specifically prohibited. In Cuba and Panama, all educational establishments are open to all without distinction of race. In Brazil, Colombia, New Zealand and the United Kingdom, it is specifically prohibited to bar the entrance of a student to an educational establishment on the ground of race. As indicated by the laws of Venezuela, the only limitation to access to education should be aptitude. In order to ensure that language is not an impediment to education, students in the Union of Soviet Socialist Republics may choose their language of instruction. In Ecuador, it is stipulated that the indigenous population should be taught in its own language.

Education is an area where the fight against racial discrimination can be carried out. In Portugal, for example, the law states that education shall be used to eradicate all socio-economic prejudices. In Ecuador, the educational system is obliged to impart to children a greater understanding of their culture and society. Colombia shares this position and further stipulates that education should help forge greater links between the various groups in society. In Mexico, education is used to develop a sense of brotherhood in all citizens.

Many States have recognized the right of access to public services or facilities and have legislated in order to ensure that the right is enjoyed by all without discrimination. In Finland, for example, it is provided that anyone who does not serve another in the normal course of his employment, on the ground of racial discrimination, shall be punished. The laws of some other countries differ in two material respects. In Australia, Canada, New Zealand and the United Kingdom, for instance, even when the discrimination impeding an individual's enjoyment of this right is performed outside the normal course of the discriminator's employment, it is generally prohibited. Also, in these same countries, as in countries such as Brazil, Denmark and Norway, the sort of discrimination prohibited is more explicitly stated. They generally prohibit any person from barring another access to, or forcing another to cease the enjoyment of any services, facilities or places generally open to the public solely on the ground of race. Many of those countries also indicate that discrimination in the terms on which such access will be granted is prohibited. In an attempt to facilitate the application of these laws, the laws of New Zealand and the United Kingdom give examples of the sorts of facilities and places to which these laws shall be applicable.

B. Specific Institutions for the Promotion of Racial Tolerance and Harmony. Some States have legislated to provide protective measures and institutions so as to facilitate the investigation of problems before they become too acute. Such measures and institutions also provide a mechanism for the mitigation or correction of any situations of discrimination that may arise. Commissions of this nature have been established in Australia, Canada and the United Kingdom of Great Britain and Northern Ireland. They undertake a variety of programmes under the general objective of striving to improve racial relations and promoting equality for all people. They have the task of creating, conducting or supporting research and educational programmes; they monitor the implementation of anti-discriminatory laws and impart their specialized knowledge and advice to other persons interested in the eradication of discrimination. In Australia, the subsidiary Community Relations Council assists the Commission by making recommendations to it as regards various relevant issues, either at request of the Commission or Minister or of its own volition.

Institutions such as the Commissions are also mandated to accept, investigate and try to settle complaints of discrimination, which they often do with the aid of subsidiary conciliatory machinery. These institutions are not merely passive but are entitled to act *suo motu* if they think that the circumstances so warrant.

C. Recourse Procedures. Recourse procedures before the courts are available for the protection of the individual's human rights in general, and thus for violations based on racial discrimination (in Venezuela, for example), and they are provided for in some States with specific reference to racial discrimination. In Mauritius, complaints of racial discrimination may be taken to the Supreme Court; in the Federal Republic of Germany, they may be taken to the Federal Constitutional Court. In Nigeria access is provided via the High Courts and in the United Kingdom of Great Britain and Northern Ireland via the county courts, which, for the purposes of handling racial discrimination, are entitled to grant the same sorts of remedies as the High Courts.

Many informal avenues of recourse have also been provided by some States. These are often cheaper and quicker than the formal ones and are therefore essential to an individual already suffering disadvantage. The conciliatory machinery of Australia and New Zealand are examples of such avenues of recourse. Countries such as the Federal Republic of Germany, New Zealand and the United Kingdom also provide access via such specialized bodies as industrial or equal opportunity tribunals. The institution of the Ombudsman in countries such as Austria, Denmark and Portugal provides a further avenue of recourse, while countries such as Portugal and Venezuela preserve the right of the individual to petition anybody in order to protect his rights and freedoms.

A number of specific measures have been undertaken by some States to facilitate access to recourse procedures for all sectors of the population. In Venezuela, the constitution provides that there should be laws ensuring that even those without means will be able to enjoy access. In the United Kingdom an individual contemplating or having actually commenced proceedings may seek assistance from the Commission for Racial Equality, which will grant it only if the circumstances of the case so warrant. As a further aid to complainants in pursuit of a case, the Secretary of State of the United Kingdom is entitled to prescribe forms in which alleged discriminators should be questioned. With the same goal in mind, the Human Rights Commission of Australia and the Conciliator of New Zealand may undertake investigations, either on complaint or *suo moto,* if they feel it appropriate in the circumstances. The Human Rights Commission of Australia is also entitled to convene compulsory conferences in order to fully ascertain the facts of a disputed situation. Within the general intention of facilitating access for complainants, individuals in countries such as Mauritius, Nigeria and Tuvalu do not have to allege that they have been actual victims of discrimination; it is enough that they allege that they are "likely to be". In Australia, it is indicated that where civil proceedings are undertaken to seek a remedy the individual has to prove his case to the reasonable satisfaction of the court only.

D. Remedies. Remedies in most countries consist of the

possibility of obtaining redress for the violation of one's rights, as well as the possibility of ensuring that steps are taken to terminate ongoing infringements and to prohibit any potential infringements. In Mauritius and Nigeria, the courts are authorized to secure the enjoyment of rights by issuing such writs and making such orders and directions as they consider to be appropriate. Such wide discretion is also provided for in the United Kingdom of Great Britain and Northern Ireland, where complaint of racial discrimination may be pursued in court in the same manner as any claim in tort or for breach of statutory duty.

Some countries specify at least a few of the remedies available to individuals whose rights have been violated. In Hungary, for instance, an individual may apply to court to establish the commission of a wrong or for some other forms of satisfaction, such as a declaration by the wrong-doer. In Australia and Canada, specific performance may be sought in order to ensure that a person responsible for a discriminatory act takes measures to compensate for those actions. A variety of other measures may be applied for, some of which appear to be designed to restore the *status quo*. In Australia, for example, if the discrimination resulted in the making of a contract, such contract may be annulled or have its terms varied. In Canada, a complainant can ensure that opportunities and privileges one was formerly denied should be made available.

Financial compensation is a remedy that is often provided for. In Hungary, for instance, anyone offended in the enjoyment of his rights may apply to court for damages. Such recourse is most often used to cover material losses such as, in the case of Australia, loss of benefits. In Canada one may claim for lost wages and expenses incurred in obtaining alternative goods and services where such losses were brought about by acts of discrimination.

Other remedies exist which are more suited to the termination of ongoing breaches or prohibiting potential ones. In New Zealand, for example, one may seek that an assurance be given to the conciliator that all discriminatory practices will be discontinued and will not be resumed in the future. In Australia, Canada and Hungary, one may apply for an injunction to prevent future breaches of one's rights. Although similar in object and effect, the latter remedy differs from the former in that it is imposed on the discrimination by a judicial body.

E. Penalties. In addition to declaring that individuals are entitled to enjoy certain rights free of discrimination, and providing remedies for those whose rights have been violated, some States have sought to secure the enjoyment of rights by imposing various types of penalties for certain acts of racial discrimination. For instance, in Brazil it is a punishable offence to refuse lodging or goods to another person on account of his race. In France and Norway also, discrimination in the provision of services is punishable. Many States punish individuals not only for acts of racial discrimination, but also for advocating or promoting racial discrimination, for example by acts of incitement, agitation and propaganda aimed at arousing racial hatred. Threats of violence, provocation and defamation with the same intent are also punished. Some States impose punishments even in the absence of intent; in the United Kingdom of Great Britain and Northern Ireland, an individual is punished for his actions if, having regard to all the circumstances, racial hatred was likely to be aroused by such actions. A similar law exists in Hungary. In the Netherlands, acts of incitement are punished if done with reasonable cause to sus-

pect what their effect will be, if actual intent is proven, the punishment is doubled.

A wide variety of penalties are employed by States in their attempts to secure the general enjoyment of rights. In the Netherlands, for instance, if a person is convicted for discrimination in the course of his occupation twice within five years, such person may be barred from continuing the same occupation. Similarly, in Brazil, if it is found that discrimination is practised in allowing access to public service, the person in charge of the selection procedure is stripped of his functions. In Ecuador, where a public body is found to be engaging in acts of discrimination the director is imprisoned and loses his political rights for the duration of the prison term. The conviction of an individual in Turkey for using an association to promote discrimination, even if he is later pardoned, bars that individual from later forming another association. In Poland, if discriminatory views are expressed in a publication, the authorities are allowed to confiscate the instruments and objects employed in its production, even if they are not owned by the perpetrator.

However, the most widespread penalties for discrimination include prison sentences, such as may be imposed in Cyprus and Ecuador, or the payment of fines, as is provided for in countries like Finland and France. In Brazil, Denmark, Iran and New Zealand the imposition of either one of these penalties is provided for, and in countries like Dominica, the Federal Republic of Germany, Pakistan and the United Kingdom, the simultaneous imposition of both penalties for the same offence is allowed. In the Byelorussian Soviet Socialist Republic, for example, a term of either imprisonment or of exile may be imposed, and in Czechoslovakia, some other reformatory measure may be applied instead of imprisonment.

Certain factors are viewed by some States as aggravating the normal offence of discrimination and therefore warranting the imposition of stiffer penalties. The use of violence is viewed in this way by such States as Bulgaria, Czechoslovakia, Ecuador and Hungary. Also, in Bulgaria, any individual who instigates, sets up or leads a mob or association to acts of discrimination is punished more severely than the ordinary members of such a group. In Austria, Cyprus, Pakistan and Poland, the use of publications or some other media to promote discrimination attracts greater punishment than would otherwise be the case. In many countries severe punishment is provided for persons guilty of genocide. In Czechoslovakia, such a crime is punished by seven times the term of imprisonment than is normally imposed for discrimination. In Finland and the Federal Republic of Germany, individuals convicted for genocide may be punished with life imprisonment, and in the Bahamas, Bulgaria, Czechoslovakia and Hungary the death penalty is provided for.

F. Fight against Apartheid. Many States, in particular in their reports submitted under the International Convention on the Elimination of All Forms of Racial Discrimination, clearly stated their opposition to *apartheid* and referred to their legislation in that sense, including that establishing in national law the crime of *apartheid* and laws or decisions cutting off economic relations with South Africa. India provided the text of its Anti-*Apartheid* Act, which gives force of law to those provisions from the International Convention for the Suppression and Punishment of the Crime of *Apartheid* annexed to the Act, and Cuba submitted a text providing penalties for certain acts done for the purpose of instituting or maintaining the domination of one racial group over another. Bulgarian legislation provides penalties for the practice of *apartheid* and Venezuela reported that the International Convention on the Suppression and Punishment of the Crime of *Apartheid* had become part of Venezuelan internal law. Very severe penalties are imposed for the crime of *apartheid;* for example, the death penalty is provided for in Bulgaria and India and long prison sentences in Cuba.

Several States reported severing economic relations with South Africa in the context of their activities against racial discrimination. Denmark provided the text of a Parliamentary Resolution dated 20 May 1984 on tightening the policy of sanctions against South Africa, and of a bill on prohibition of new Danish investments in South Africa and Namibia. Qatar submitted legislation halting petroleum exports to South Africa and severing all economic, trade and commercial relations with that country.

III. Conclusions

The global compilation of legislation against racial discrimination is one element in the Second Decade's overall effort aimed at strengthening the protection against racial discrimination on the national level. Other elements, as mentioned above, include, on the one hand, the preparation of basic reference texts such as the "model legislation", a handbook on recourse procedures and the preparation of a manual of existing national institutions and, on the other hand, steps designed to encourage or facilitate the adoption of those measures, such as training courses for legislative draftsmen, regional workshops on the adoption of legislation, and seminars on community relations commissions and their functions.

The texts submitted for the global consultation, taken together with the reports of seminars and training courses held on these matters and the information submitted in relation to international instruments in this field, provide a good basis for the preparation of "model texts". It is the Secretary-General's intention to proceed as rapidly as resources permit with the preparation of the "model texts" and with the organization of the seminars or training courses designed to encourage their adoption.

EQUAL JUSTICE. The principle of equality for all in the administration of justice is set out in article 10 of the UNIVERSAL DECLARATION OF HUMAN RIGHTS as follows:

Article 10. Everyone is entitled in full equality to a fair and public hearing by an independent and impartial tribunal, in the determination of his rights and obligations and of any criminal charge against him.

Since the implementation of all human rights and fundamental freedoms depends upon the proper administration of justice, the principle is of great importance. Its meaning is elaborated further in articles 14 and 15 of the INTERNATIONAL COVENANT ON CIVIL AND POLITICAL RIGHTS, which respectively set out the elements of a fair trial and prohibit the retroactive application of penal law:

Article 14. 1. All persons shall be equal before the courts and tribunals. In the determination of any criminal charge against him, or of his rights and obligations in a suit at law, everyone shall be entitled to a fair and public hearing by a competent, independent and impartial tribunal established by law. The Press and the public may be excluded from all or part of a trial for reasons of morals, public order *(ordre public)* or national security in a democratic society, or when the interest of the private lives of the parties so requires, or to the extent strictly necessary in the opinion of the court in special circumstances where publicity would prejudice the interests of justice; but any judgment rendered in a criminal case or in a suit at law shall be made public except where the interest of juvenile persons otherwise requires or the proceedings concern matrimonial disputes or the guardianship of children.

2. Everyone charged with a criminal offence shall have the right to be presumed innocent until proved guilty according to law.

3. In the determination. of any criminal charge against him, everyone shall be entitled to the following minimum guarantees, in full equality:

(a) To be informed promptly and in detail in a language which he understands of the nature and cause of the charge against him

(b) To have adequate time and facilities for the preparation of his defence and to communicate with counsel of his own choosing;

(c) To be tried without undue delay;

(d) To be tried in his presence, and to defend himself in person or through legal assistance of his own choosing; to be informed, if he does not have legal assistance, of this right; and to have legal assistance, of this right; and to have legal assistance assigned to him, in any case where the interests of justice so require, and without payment by him in any such case if he does not have sufficient means to pay for it;

(e) To examine, or have examined, the witnesses against him and to obtain the attendance and examination of witnesses on his behalf under the same conditions as witnesses against him;

(f) To have the free assistance of an interpreter if he cannot understand or speak the language used in court;

(g) Not to be compelled to testify against himself or to confess guilt.

4. In the case of juvenile persons, the procedure shall be such as will take account of their age and the desirability of promoting their rehabilitation.

5. Everyone convicted of a crime shall have the right to his conviction and sentence being reviewed by a higher tribunal according to law.

6. When a person has by a final decision been convicted of a criminal offence and when subsequently his conviction had been reversed or he had been pardoned on the ground that a new or newly discovered fact shows conclusively that there has been a miscarriage of justice, the person who has suffered punishment as a result of such conviction shall be compensated according to law, unless it is proved that the non-disclosure of the unknown fact in time is wholly or partly attributable to him.

7. No one shall be liable to be tried or punished again for an offence for which he has already been finally convicted or acquitted in accordance with the law and penal procedure of each country.

Article 15. 1. No one shall be held guilty of any criminal offence on account of any act or omission which did not constitute a criminal offence, under national or international law, at the time when it was committed. Nor shall a heavier penalty be imposed than the one that was applicable at the time when the criminal offence was committed. If, subsequent to the commission of the offence, provision is made by law for the imposition of the lighter penalty, the offender shall benefit thereby.

2. Nothing in this article shall prejudice the trial and punishment of any person for any act or omission which, at the time when it was committed, was criminal according to the general principles of law recognized by the community of nations.

Article 5 of the **INTERNATIONAL CONVENTION ON THE ELIMINATION OF ALL FORMS OF RACIAL DISCRIMINATION** states:

In compliance with the fundamental obligations laid down in article 2 of this Convention, States Parties undertake to prohibit and to eliminate racial discrimination in all its forms and to guarantee the right of everyone, without distinction as to race, colour, or national or ethnic origin, to equality before the law, notably in the enjoyment of the following rights:

(a) The right to equal treatment before the tribunals and all other organs administering justice.

Article 16 of the **CONVENTION RELATING TO THE STATUS OF REFUGEES** provides that:

1. A refugee shall have free access to the courts of law on the territory of all Contracting States.

2. A refugee shall enjoy in the Contracting State in which he has his habitual residence the same treatment as a national in matters pertaining to access to the courts, including legal assistance and exemption from *cautio judicatum solvi*.

3. A refugee shall be accorded in the matters referred to in paragraph 2 in countries other than that in which he has his habitual residence the treatment granted to a national of the country of his habitual residence.

And the **CONVENTION RELATING TO THE STATUS OF STATELESS PERSONS** contains a corresponding article 16.

After examining reports submitted by States parties to the International Covenant on Civil and Political Rights in accordance with article 40 of that instrument, the **HUMAN RIGHTS COMMITTEE** in 1984 adopted a general comment on article 14 setting out its views on the meaning of certain provisions, as follows (UN Doc. A/39/40, Annex VI, para. 1–19):

The Committee notes that article 14 of the Covenant is of a complex nature and that different aspects of its provisions will need specific comments. All of these provisions are aimed at ensuring the proper administration of justice, and to this end uphold a series of individual rights such as equality before the courts and tribunals and the right to a fair and public hearing by a competent, independent and impartial tribunal established by law. Not all reports provided details on the legislative or other measures adopted specifically to implement each of the provisions of article 14.

In general, the reports of States parties fail to recognize that article 14 applies not only to procedures for the determination of criminal charges against individuals but also to procedures to determine their rights and obligations in a suit at law. Laws and practices dealing with these matters vary widely from State to State. This diversity makes it all the more necessary for States parties to provide all relevant information and to explain in greater detail how the concepts of "criminal charge" and "rights and obligations in a suit at law" are interpreted in relation to their respective legal systems.

The Committee would find it useful if, in their future reports, States parties could provide more detailed information on the steps taken to ensure that equality before the courts, including equal access to courts, fair and public hearings and competence, impartiality and independence of the judiciary are established by law and guaranteed in practice. In particular, States parties should specify the relevant constitutional and legislative texts which provide for the establishment of the courts and ensure that they are independent, impartial and competent, in particular with regard to the manner in which judges are appointed, the qualifications for appointment, and the duration of their terms of office; the conditions governing promotion, transfer and cessation of their functions and the actual independence of the judiciary from the executive branch and the legislature.

The provisions of article 14 apply to all courts and tribunals within the scope of that article whether ordinary or specialized. The Committee notes the existence, in many countries, of military or special courts which try civilians. This could present serious problems as far as the equitable, impartial and independent administration of justice is concerned. Quite often the reason for the establishment of such courts is to enable exceptional procedures to be applied which do not comply with normal standards of justice. While the Covenant does not prohibit such categories of courts, nevertheless the conditions which it lays down clearly indicate that the trying of civilians by such courts should be very exceptional and take place under conditions which genuinely afford the full guarantees stipulated in article 14. The Committee has noted a serious lack of information in this regard in the reports of some States parties whose judicial institutions include such courts for the trying of civilians. In some countries such military and special courts do not afford the strict guarantees of the proper administration of justice in accordance with the requirements of article 14 which are essential for the effective protection of human rights. If States parties decide in circumstances of a public emergency as contemplated by article 4 to derogate from normal procedures required under article 14, they should ensure that such derogations do not exceed those strictly required by the exigencies of the actual situation, and respect the other conditions in paragraph 1 of article 14.

The second sentence of article 14, paragraph 1, provides that "everyone shall be entitled to a fair and public hearing". Paragraph 3 of the article elaborates on the requirements of a "fair hearing" in regard to the determination of criminal charges. However, the requirements of paragraph 3 are minimum guarantees, the observance of which is not always sufficient to ensure the fairness of a hearing as required by paragraph 1.

The publicity of hearings is an important safeguard in the interest of the individual and of society at large. At the same time article 14, paragraph 1, acknowledges that courts have the power to exclude all or part of the public for reasons spelt out in that paragraph. It should be noted that, apart from such exceptional circumstances, the Committee considers that a hearing must be open to the public in general, including members of the press, and must not, for instance, be limited only to a particular category of persons. It should be noted that, even in cases in which the public is excluded from the trial, the judgment must, with certain strictly defined exceptions, be made public.

The Committee has noted a lack of information regarding article 14, paragraph 2, and, in some cases, has even observed that the presumption of innocence, which is fundamental to the protection of human rights, is expressed in very ambiguous terms or entails conditions which render it ineffective. By reason of the presumption of innocence, the burden of proof of the charge is on the prosecution and the accused has the benefit of doubt. No guilt can be presumed until the charge has been proved beyond reasonable doubt. Further, the presumption of innocence implies a right to be treated in accordance with this principle. It is therefore a duty for all public authorities to refrain from prejudging the outcome of a trial.

Among the minimum guarantees in criminal proceedings prescribed by paragraph 3, the first concerns the right of everyone to be informed in a language which he understands of the charge against him (subparagraph (a)). The Committee notes that State reports often do not explain how this right is respected and ensured. Article 14, subparagraph 3 (a) applies to all cases of criminal charges, including those of persons not in detention. The Committee notes further that the right to be informed of the charge "promptly" requires that information is given in the manner described as soon as the charge is first made by a competent authority. In the opinion of the Committee this right must arise when in the course of an investigation a court or an authority of the prosecution decides to take procedural steps against a person suspected of a crime or publicly names him as such. The specific requirements of subparagraph 3 (a) may be met by stating the charge either orally or in writing, provided that the information indicates both the law and the alleged facts on which it is based.

Subparagraph 3 (b) provides that the accused must have adequate time and facilities for the preparation of his defence and to communicate with counsel of his own choosing. What is "adequate time" depends on the circumstance of each case, but the facilities must include access to documents and other evidence which the accused requires to prepare his case, as well as the opportunity to engage and communicate with counsel. When the accused does not want to defend himself in person or request a person or an association of his choice, he should be able to have recourse to a lawyer. Furthermore, this subparagraph requires counsel to communicate with the accused in conditions giving full respect for the confidentiality of their communications. Lawyers should be able to counsel and to represent their clients in accordance with their established professional standards and judgement without any restrictions, influences, pressures or undue interference from any quarter.

Subparagraph 3 (c) provides that the accused shall be tried without undue delay. This guarantee relates not only to the time by which a trial should commence, but also the time by which it should end and judgement be rendered; all stages must take place "without undue delay". To make this right effective, a procedure must be available in order to ensure that the trial will proceed "without undue delay", both in first instance and on appeal.

Not all reports have dealt with all aspects of the right of defence as defined in subparagraph 3 (d). The Committee has not always received sufficient information concerning the protection of the right of the accused to be present during the determination of any charge against him nor how the legal system assures his right either to defend himself in person or to be assisted by counsel of his own choosing, or what arrangements are made if a person does not have sufficient means to pay for legal assistance. The accused or his lawyer must have the right to act diligently and fearlessly in pursuing all available defences and the right to challenge the conduct of the case if they believe it to be unfair. When exceptionally for justified reasons trials *in absentia* are held, strict observance of the rights of the defence is all the more necessary.

Subparagraph 3 (e) states that the accused shall be entitled to examine or have examined the witnesses against him and to obtain the attendance and examination of witnesses on his behalf under the same conditions as witnesses against him. This provision is designed to guarantee to the accused the same legal powers of compelling the attendance of witnesses and of examining or cross-examining any witnesses as are available to the prosecution.

Subparagraph 3 (f) provides that if the accused cannot understand or speak the language used in court he is entitled to the assistance of an interpreter free of any charge. This right is independent of the outcome of the proceedings and applies to aliens as well as to nationals. It is of basic importance in cases in which ignorance of the language used by a court or difficulty in understanding may constitute a major obstacle to the right of defence.

Subparagraph 3 (g) provides that the accused may not be compelled to testify against himself or to confess guilt. In considering this safeguard the provisions of article 7 and article 10, paragraph 1, should be borne in mind. In order to compel the accused to confess or to testify against himself frequently methods which violate these provisions are used. The law should require that evidence provided by means of such methods or any other form of compulsion is wholly unacceptable.

In order to safeguard the rights of the accused under paragraphs 1 and 3 of article 14, judges should have authority to consider any allegations made of violations of the rights of the accused during any stage of the prosecution.

Article 14, paragraph 4, provides that in the case of juvenile persons, the procedure shall be such as will take account of their age and the desirability of promoting their rehabilitation. Not many reports have furnished sufficient information concerning such relevant matters as the minimum age at which a juvenile may be charged with a criminal offence, the maximum age at which a person is still considered to be a juvenile, the existence of special courts and procedures, the laws governing procedures against juveniles and how all these special arrangements for juveniles take account of "the desirability of promoting their rehabilitation". Juveniles are to enjoy at least the same guarantees and protection as are accorded to adults under article 14.

Article 14, paragraph 5, provides that everyone convicted of a crime shall have the right to his conviction and sentence being reviewed by a higher tribunal according to law. Particular attention is drawn to the other language versions of the word "crime" *("infraction", "delito", "prestuplenie")* which show that the guarantee is not confined only to the most serious offences. In this connection, not enough information has been provided concerning the procedures of appeal, in particular the access to and the powers of reviewing tribunals, what requirements must be satisfied to appeal against a judgement and the way in which the procedures before review tribunals take account of the fair and public hearing requirements of paragraph 1 of article 14.

Article 14, paragraph 6, provides for compensation according to law in certain cases of a miscarriage of justice as described therein. It seems from many State reports that this right is often not observed or insufficiently guaranteed by domestic legislation. States should, where necessary, supplement their legislation in this area in order to bring it into line with the provisions of the Covenant.

In considering State reports differing views have often been expressed as to the scope of paragraph 7 of article 14. Some States parties have even felt the need to make reservations in relation to procedures for the resumption of criminal cases. It seems to the Committee that most States parties make a clear distinction between a resumption of a trial justified by exceptional circumstances and a retrial prohibited pursuant to the principal of *ne bis in idem* as contained in paragraph 7. This understanding of the meaning of *ne bis in idem* may encourage States parties to reconsider their reservations to article 14, paragraph 7.

SEE ALSO Equality:Administration of Justice.

EQUATORIAL GUINEA. The Republic of Equatorial Guinea is a country in middle Africa, on the Gulf of Guinea; it includes the mainland area of Rio Muni and several islands in the gulf, among them Bioko (formerly known as Fernando Po), Pagalu (formerly known as Annobon), Corisco, Elobey Grande, and Elobey Chico. It has borders with Cameroon and Gabon. Formerly known as Spanish Guinea, it achieved independence from Spain in 1968, and became a member of the United Nations the same year. Its population is estimated by the UN (1990) to be 430,000. Ethnics groups include the Fang and the Bubi. Languages commonly used include Spanish (official), Fang, Bubi, and several African vernaculars. Christianity (Roman Catholic, 83%; Protestant, 10%) is the predominant religion; 7% adhere to other faiths or have no religious beliefs. Literacy is estimated at 55%.

The government (1990) took the form of a republic. However, the 1973 constitution was suspended after a *coup d'etat* of 3 August 1979 resulted in a military regime. The Supreme Military Council has since exercised all power, with its chairman, Lieut. Col. Teodoro Obiang Nguema Mbasogo, as president and head of State. No political parties have been permitted.

At its 1979 session, the UN COMMISSION ON HUMAN RIGHTS appointed a special rapporteur to study the situation of human rights in Equatorial Guinea. At its 1980 session, the commission, after examining the special rapporteur's report, noted that the new government has expressed an interest in cooperating with the United Nations in order to ensure the effective enjoyment of human rights in that country. After lengthy negotiations, two jurists were sent to Equatorial Africa by the United Nations in 1986 to provide assistance in the drafting and codification of certain basic legal texts. Their mission was not successful because of difficulties caused by the absence of material conditions required to carry out their work: many of the applicable laws, for example, had not been published because of inadequate printing facilities. The jurists could only recommend a number of measures without which the work could not proceed satisfactorily. The report and recommendation of the jurists were transmitted to the government, and the Commission on Human Rights on 10 March 1987 expressed the hope (resolution 1987/36) that the government would give appropriate consideration to the plan of action proposed by the jurists.

At its 1980 session, the Commission decided (resolution 33 [XXXVI]), in response to the request of the government, to appoint an expert with wide experience of the situation in Equatorial Guinea to assist the government in taking the action necessary for the full restoration of human rights and fundamental freedoms; and requested the secretary-general to provide the assistance necessary to enable the government to take such action. Mr. Fernando Volio Jiménez (Costa Rica), the expert so appointed, drew up a comprehensive plan of action after studying the situation that existed. The plan was accepted by the government.

On 15 August 1982, a new constitution was drawn up under the supervision of the export and two consultant jurists designated by him. Since then, the expert has continued to provide advice in further implementation of the plan of action.

On 7 April 1987, the government of Equatorial Guinea communicated its observations on the report to the consultant jurists. After examining these documents, the expert informed the secretary-general that, in the circumstances, particularly in view of the length of time that had elapsed since the acceptance of the plan of action, steps should be taken to ensure as soon as possible that the protection of human rights in Equatorial Guinea is guaranteed by an adequate juridical system. For this purpose, he proposed that accelerated implementation of the plan of action be entrusted to the National Codification Commission, whose establishment the government had announced in its observations, with the assistance of further technical expertise to be provided within the UN advisory services program in consultation with the expert.

At its 1988 session, the UN Commission on Human

Rights (resolution 1988/52) requested the government of Equatorial Guinea to give appropriate consideration to the implementation of the plan of action and called upon Mr. Fernando Volio Jiminez to report to it on the manner in which the government intended to implement the plan and the progress achieved.

The secretary-general, in transmitting resolution 1988/52 to the government, requested its agreement to a visit to the country by the expert to make it possible for him to have direct contact with the authorities there. The government agreed in principle to the visit, which was scheduled for the last week in January 1989. However, Mr. Fernando Volio Jiminez fell ill; and, with the approval of the undersecretary-general for human rights and the agreement of the government, Mr. Arnaldo Ortiz Lopez (Costa Rica) visited Equatorial Guinea in his place, acting as a consultant.

The report presented to the 1990 session of the commission by the expert (UN Doc. E/CN.4/1990/42 and Add 1) includes an account of Mr. Ortiz's visit (para 1–40). The expert then summarizes his conclusions as follows (para. 41–52):

The work carried out in Equatorial Guinea by Mr. Arnaldo Ortiz López of Costa Rica in his capacity as Consultant was of the highest order. He made an orderly and detailed assessment of the Plan of Action proposed by the Expert at the thirty-seventh session of the Commission on Human Rights (E/CN.4/1439). The objective of the Plan was to develop a system for the protection of human rights that would be linked to the advisory services programmes of the Centre for Human Rights and to bilateral and multilateral technical and financial co-operation programmes for the development of the country in all spheres.

Although some of the measures provided for in the Plan of Action had already been implemented, such as the drafting and adoption of a Constitution, it was necessary to evaluate the process as a whole and to identify a new starting point in order to give the required impetus to the policy of human rights protection in Equatorial Guinea.

The work done by the Consultant clearly shows that the Government continues to support the Plan of Action and is prepared to adopt the necessary measures to speed up its implementation. This confirmation of political support for the objectives of the Plan is the most positive result of the Consultant's visit to Equatorial Guinea.

Mention should also be made of the following achievements made so far: (a) adoption and ratification of the International Covenants on Civil and Political and Economic, Social and Cultural Rights and of the Optional Protocol to the International Covenant on Civil and Political Rights; (b) the decision to issue a decree based on those Covenants and on the Universal Declaration of Human Rights; such a Decree would disseminate information on the fundamental rights of citizens, thereby enabling them to invoke those rights; (c) the decision to initiate the process of the approval and ratification of the Convention against Torture, the Convention on the Elimination of All Forms of Racial Discrimination, the Convention on the Rights of the Child, as well as to start considering the conventions on the rights of women and the family; (d) reassertion of political determination to complete the codification of modern civil and criminal legislation, together with the relevant codes of procedure, in keeping with the country's customs; the codification was discussed in the past, in accordance with the wishes of the Government and the Plan of Action, but it was delayed for a number of reasons, what is now required is fresh impetus to bring the initiative to completion; (e) the emphasis placed by the Government on improving the legal system, as provided for in the Plan of Action; in the Expert's opinion, this is one of the most important and pressing objectives for the achievement of effective human rights protection; (f) instruction in law for the people is being properly carried out in accordance with the Plan of Action; (g) a School of Public Administration already exists and the programme proposed in the Plan of Action is thus being implemented, although the main ideas require further development; (h) the development of educational programmes, as provided for in the Plan of Action, although the main ideas require further development; (i) the development of education programmes, as provided for in the Plan of Action, appears to have received adequate attention; (j) the same observation may be made in respect of labour relations; (k) the Government decision to develop an education programme to prepare citizens to consider and solve their communities' problems. Under the programme, local leaders are elected directly by the citizens. In the Expert's view, this would be a very positive step towards electoral processes for the democratic appointment of Government authorities, provided that it applies throughout the country.

The Associations Act proposed by the Plan of Action has not yet been adopted and there is no political pluralism. These two shortcomings are serious obstacles preventing citizens from fully defending their fundamental rights and living under a democratic régime.

The exile of Equatorial Guinean citizens jeopardizes the cause of human rights and hampers the country's economic and social development, as it is in dire need of human resources for its modernization, including in the political sphere.

Apart from a State television station and State radio station, which broadcast over a small area of the country, there are no media. This factor naturally jeopardizes the cause of human rights. The Government's willingness to comply with the proposals to this effect contained in the Plan of Action is a positive element, but improvements in the situation have to be made without delay. In this connection, it should be noted that the Government has emphasized the need for assistance with the installation of a printing press to enable it, *inter alia,* to publish a newspaper.

The Special Review Commission to ensure compliance with all aspects of the Plan of Action, which was one of the main recommendations made by the Expert in the Plan, has not yet been established. However, the Government has reaffirmed its intention to set up the Commission without further delay. The Commission would greatly stimulate the introduction of legal and political measures to protect fundamental rights.

The Government of Equatorial Guinea urgently requires international assistance in order to improve the living conditions of its citizens in all areas. Such assistance and the resulting improvements would greatly facilitate the programme for the promotion and protection of fundamental rights.

For the purposes of international assistance, it should be

borne in mind that Equatorial Guinea was devastated by the long, cruel dictatorship of Francisco Macías, as a result of which it was plunged into a catastrophic economic and social crisis that worsened the circumstances of a noble and intelligent people, as Equatorial Guinea is sparsely populated and had few natural resources.

The efforts made by the Government and citizens of Equatorial Guinea, together with multilateral and bilateral international co-operation, are still not adequate to tackle the extremely grave problems weighing down this small country that is admirable in so many respects. Further efforts to provide Equatorial Guinea with assistance therefor have to be made on the basis of the Plan of Action which was agreed on with the Government and which needs to be enriched by new initiatives that have emerged or may emerge from the country's most recent experience.

It is above all essential that international co-operation should be aimed at affirming Equatorial Guinea's right to self-determination and its right to defend its sovereignty against any form of bilateral assistance that might undermine its values.

The expert formulated his recommendations to the commission as follows (para. 53–64):

The Special Review Commission proposed in the Plan of Action should be established without further delay and the other measures suggested should be adopted for the purpose of promoting and protecting human rights.

The dissemination of the main human rights instruments should be continued with the support of information material provided by the Centre for Human Rights in Geneva. A batch of this material was sent to the Government in 1989 by the Advisory Services Section of the Centre for Human Rights, as ascertained by the Consultant, Mr. Ortiz López, during his visit to the country in November 1989.

The task of codifying the basic civil and criminal laws, as well as the procedural laws necessary for the operation of the courts, should be performed without delay in order to ensure the protection of citizens. The Advisory Services Section of the Centre for Human Rights could make a valuable contribution if it assigned at least two experts to co-operate with the Government in carrying out that task.

The Government should be given assistance in establishing working relations with the Central American Public Administration Institute in San José, Costa Rica. These links could be arranged by the Centre with the assistance of the Expert. It might also be possible to obtain scholarships from the Institute. This measure would enhance the praiseworthy efforts now being made by the School of Public Administration in Equatorial Guinea, with the assistance of UNDP.

It is essential to train lawyers in order to strengthen the administration of justice. To this end, the Centre should arrange for expanded Spanish co-operation to Equatorial Guinea through the *Universidad Estatal a Distancia,* which has an office in Malabo. A total of 15 scholarships has been suggested for this purpose. The Centre should also consider the possibility of other means of achieving this objective. The huge and pressing need for trained court personnel is a matter of great concern.

The consideration of amendments to the Constitution should begin as soon as possible. The Government requires the assistance of at least one expert and the recommenda-

tions made in 1982 by two experts sent by the Secretary-General pursuant to the Plan of Action and on the recommendation of the Expert should be borne in mind. During the Consultant's visit, the President of Equatorial Guinea confirmed the political resolve to undertake these reforms.

A printing press should be set up in the country so that a newspaper may be published once again and publications may be issued by citizens in the exercise of their freedom of expression. The press would also be used to disseminate Government decrees and other important information, as well as human rights material.

The exile of the régime's opponents should come to an end. They should be allowed to return to their country without delay and to resume their personal and public activities without reprisals. The Government should grant a broad amnesty to make this possible.

An Associations Act should be adopted to enable citizens to carry out their personal and civic activities, and to lay down the foundations for a system of political parties as a contribution to the establishment of representative democracy in all spheres. This important question is referred to in the Plan of Action.

The death penalty should be abolished in order to guarantee respect for the right to life and as a means of safeguarding fundamental rights, above all at the present time, when it is proving difficult to ensure that due process forms the basis for procedural rules. Reference has already been made to this important issue (see E/CN.4/1985/9, p. 20).

These recommendations are made without prejudice to any others included in this report or those contained in previous reports by the Expert and in the Plan of Action.

The Expert wishes to stress the need for the international community to provide the noble and intelligent people of Equatorial Guinea with generous and timely co-operation to allow it to tackle the serious challenges arising from oppressing economic and social circumstances and to improve its political system in a framework of representative democracy within which freedom may blossom and take root.

After examining the report, the commission on 7 March 1990, welcomed (resolution 1990/57) the news that the government of Equatorial Guinea was to ratify the **CONVENTION AGAINST TORTURE AND OTHER CRUEL, INHUMAN OR DEGRADING TREATMENT OR PUNISHMENT** and the **INTERNATIONAL CONVENTION ON THE ELIMINATION OF ALL FORMS OF RACIAL DISCRIMINATION.** It urged the government to establish a special review commission to monitor the implementation of the plan of action as soon as possible and to adopt other measures suggested by the expert for the purpose of promoting and protecting human rights.

The commission recommended that the government avail itself of the advisory services in the field of human rights to assist it in preparing reports called for under the International Covenants on Human Rights and to draw up a general associations act to facilitate the implementation of the rights recognized in those covenants. Also, on recommendation of the expert, the commission encouraged the government to facilitate the repatriation of all refugees and exiles by adopting measures permitting the full participations of all citizens in the country's political, economic, social and cultural affairs, thus helping to resolve the shortage of specialized personnel available in the country.

ETHIOPIA. A country in eastern Africa, on the Red Sea, the People's Democratic Republic of Ethiopia has borders with Djibouti, Kenya, Somalia, and Sudan. It achieved independence from Italy first in 1896 and again in 1941 and became a member of the United Nations in 1945. Its population is estimated by the UN (1990) to be 50,087,000. Ethnic groups include the Oromo, the Amhara, the Tigre, and the Sidama. Languages commonly used include Amharic (official), Arabic, English, Oromegna, Tegrina, Kunamigna, Sidamigna, Seltegna, Afar, Kefamocha, and Sahogna. Religions practiced include Islam (45%), Coptic Christianity (Ethiopian Orthodox) (40%), and other beliefs or none (15%). Literacy is estimated at 25%.

Once a monarchy under Emperor Haile Selassie, Ethiopia was taken over by its armed forces committee in August 1974 after a period of famine caused by drought had led to riots and mutinies. Haile Selassie's palace and estates were nationalized, and he was deposed, after nearly 58 years as emperor, on 12 September 1974. With Parliament dissolved and the constitution suspended, Lt. Col. Mengistu Haile Mariam was named head of State. A communist regime was proclaimed on 10 September 1984.

Ethiopia's recent large-scale human rights problems stem largely from drought, famine, and disease. Between 1974 and 1978, the country was threatened by Somali guerrillas—a conflict that ended only with the help of military aid supplied by Cuba and the Union of Soviet Socialist Republics. In 1986 and 1987, it was compelled to deal with secessionists from Eritrea.

In 1988, Ethiopia was confronted by two massive problems: assistance to refugees from Somalia and assistance to returnees from Djibouti, Somalia, and Sudan. On the first of these problems, the UN secretary-general reported to the General Assembly (UN Doc. A/43/595, para. 2–5):

Over the past few months, Somali refugees have been arriving in eastern Ethiopia at a rate that represents one of the highest sustained refugee influxes of recent years. By mid-August, UNHCR was assisting over 250,000 refugees. A further 60,000 were being assisted by the Ethiopian authorities pending transfer to a more accessible location. Although there are indications that the extraordinary high rate of arrival may now be declining some 2,000 more refugees are still being registered each day at one location alone. The refugees state that lack of security in north-west

Somalia as a result of events since the end of May is the reason for their flight. There was no prior warning of this massive influx and, therefore, no possibility of contingency planning.

At the same time, Sudanese refugees fleeing civil strife in the south of their country continue to arrive in the west of Ethiopia at an average rate of some 10,000 each month. Their numbers now exceed 300,000. A major relief operation has been mounted to respond to their needs. The long distances involved, problems with access to remote sites, particularly during the rains, and the severely malnourished state of many new arrivals have made this a complex and difficult operation. While much remains to be done and more resources in cash and food are needed in response to the High Commissioner's appeal on 18 May for $26.7 million, the situation of the Sudanese refugees has improved. Although this progress must not be compromised, the immediate priorities in these exceptional circumstances clearly lie with the needs of the Somali refugees in eastern Ethiopia.

The health of the Somali refugees is generally good on arrival, but the locations where they are gathered are very difficult of access and devoid of natural resources. The largest group is divided between Hartishiek and Harshin, some 75 km and 125 km respectively south-east of Jijiga. The second group is some 120 km east of Degeh Bur, a town 170 km south-east of Jijiga. A further 60,000 refugees are reported to be some 100 km east of the second group. The immediate priority is action to improve the access roads. This work is under way. There are no sources of ground water near the refugees and water is being trucked from distances of between 75 km and 125 km. Food and other supplies have to be moved over much longer distances. As the area lacks natural shelter, the sites are exposed, and it has been raining.

In close co-operation with the Ethiopian authorities, a great effort is under way to mobilize the necessary assistance. Much of what is immediately needed by way of food, medicaments and logistics is available within Ethiopia. Significant contributions have been made by the United Nations system, including the provision of two aircraft currently moving supplies from Djibouti, and non-governmental organizations. Food has also been lent, and the World Food Programme has approved an initial allocation covering 200,000 refugees for six months. Urgently needed supplies that are not available within the country, notably tents and water equipment, are being airlifted. Much remains to be done to bring the situation under control, and the major immediate constraint is the lack of financial resources.

As regards the second problem, the secretary-general reported (para. 9):

Since the inception of the special programme in December 1986, 4,940 Ethiopian refugees had returned home from Somalia and 3,591 from Djibouti under UNHCR auspices by the end of March 1988. In addition, some 11,000 refugees returned spontaneously from the Sudan. Assistance was provided to these returnees to reintegrate around their home areas in the form of food rations for up to 12 months, agricultural tools, seeds, materials for home construction and livestock. The programme has now been extended until the end of December 1988 and a new project has been established to cover the period. Based on experience gained in recent years, it has become clear that a review of the overall rehabilitation operations in favour of the population of the Ogaden should be carried out. A study to this end has, therefore, been commissioned. The results of this study will be the source of specific project ideas which will be developed jointly by UNHCR and UNDP. It had, however, been indicated that the Government would retain the initiative in attracting donor interest in such project ideas, it being understood that UNHCR will pursue those activities within its competence and mandate when appropriate, and thus play a supportive, catalytic and promotional role in relation to the Government's initiatives.

After examining the secretary-general's report, the UN General Assembly, on 8 December 1988, expressed its concern (resolution 43/144) at the massive flow of refugees and voluntary returnees into Ethiopia and the enormous burden thus placed on the country's infrastructure and meager resources and also at the grave consequences this had entailed for the country's capability to grapple with the effects of a prolonged drought. It commended the Office of the UNITED NATIONS HIGH COMMISSIONER FOR REFUGEES, as well as intergovernmental organizations and voluntary agencies, for their assistance in mitigating the plight of the high number of refugees and voluntary returnees and requested the high commissioner to continue his efforts to mobilize humanitarian assistance for the relief, rehabilitation, and resettlement of those persons.

The Secretary-General's report on the subject to the 1989 session of the General Assembly (UN Doc. A/44/482) also indicated that the number of refugees and voluntary returnees in Ethiopia had been increasing, and that this had placed an enormous burden on the country's resources. Deeply concerned, the Assembly appealed (resolution 44/154) to member States and to international organizations and voluntary bodies to provide adequate material, financial, and technical assistance to support relief and rehabilitation programs for the refugees and returnees.

ETHIOPIA: CONSTITUTION. The Constitution of the People's Democratic Republic of Ethiopia of 12 September 1987 includes the following provisions (articles 35–58) relating specifically to human rights and fundamental freedoms:

Chapter Seven
Fundamental Freedoms, Rights and Duties of Citizens

*Article 35.*1. Ethiopians are equal before the law, irrespective of nationality, sex, religion, occupation, social or other status.

2. Equality among Ethiopians shall be ensured through equal participation in political, economic, social and cultural affairs.

Article 36. 1. In the People's Democratic Republic of Ethiopia women and men have equal rights.

2. The state shall provide women with special support, particularly in education, training and employment so that they may participate in political, economic, social and cultural affairs on an equal basis with men.

3. The state shall ensure that appropriate measures are progressively taken for women to be provided with health services, suitable working conditions and adequate rest period during pregnancy and maternity.

Article 37. 1. Marriage is based on the consent of a man and a woman who have attained majority. Spouses have equal rights in their family relations. Marriage shall be protected by the state.

2. Children, whether born in or out of wedlock, have equal rights.

Article 38. 1. Ethiopians have the right to work.

2. The state shall, based on the development of the national economy, progressively ensure that employment opportunities are created and working conditions improved.

Article 39. 1. The right of the working people to rest is guaranteed.

2. The state shall determine working hours and rest periods and ensure that social services beneficial for the leisure of the working people are progressively expanded.

Article 40. 1. Ethiopians have the right to free education.

2. The state shall progressively ensure compulsory education for school-age children and expand schools and vocational institutions of various types and levels.

Article 41. 1. Ethiopians have the freedom to conduct research and engage in creative activities in science, technology and the arts.

2. The state shall encourage the research and creative activities of citizens, and provide special support for research and creative activities that contribute to the improvement of the living standard of the working people and the acceleration of socialist construction.

Article 42. 1. Ethiopians have the right to health care.

2. The state shall provide health services by progressively expanding health institutions.

Article 43. 1. Ethiopians are guaranteed inviolability of the person.

2. Ethiopians are guaranteed inviolability of the home. No one may enter the home of another against his will, except as prescribed by law.

Article 44. 1. No person may be arrested except in *flagrante delicto,* or by the order of procurator, or by a court decision, or as may be prescribed by law.

2. Any arrested person shall be produced in court within 48 hours, however, this period shall not include the time required to reach the nearest court.

Article 45. 1. No person criminally accused of violating the law shall be considered guilty unless it is so determined by a court.

2. The criminal law does not apply retroactively unless it favours the accused.

3. Any accused person has the right to defend himself or appoint a defence council. Where a person is charged with a serious offence and his inability to appoint a defence council is established, the state shall appoint one for him free of charge, as determined by law.

4. Everyone has the duty to give legal testimony except against himself or as may be prescribed by law; however, no violence or pressure may be applied to compel a person to testify. Any testimony obtained by violence or pressure shall be null and void.

Article 46. 1. Ethiopians are guaranteed freedom of conscience and religion.

2. The exercise of freedom of religion may not be in a manner contrary to the interest of the state and the revolution, public morality or the freedom of other citizens.

3. State and religion are separate. The legal status of religious institutions shall be determined by law.

Article 47. 1. Ethiopians are guaranteed freedom of speech, press, assembly, peaceful demonstration and association.

2. The state shall provide the necessary material and moral support for the exercise of these freedoms.

Article 48. 1. Ethiopians are guaranteed freedom of movement.

2. Every Ethiopian has the freedom to change his place of residence within the territory of the People's Democratic Republic of Ethiopia.

Article 49. Ethiopians are guaranteed secrecy of correspondence.

Article 50. 1. Ethiopians have the right to elect and be elected.

2. Every Ethiopian, except the insane and those deprived by law of the right to elect and be elected, has, irrespective of nationality, sex, religion, occupation, social or other status, the right to elect members of the organs of state power on attaining the age of eighteen and to be elected to same on attaining the age of twenty-one. Particulars shall be determined by law.

*Article 51.*1. Ethiopians have the right to submit proposals as well as criticisms supported by evidence concerning the functioning of state and mass organizations.

2. The officials and institutions concerned must examine and respond to the proposals and criticisms submitted and take appropriate action. Taking retaliatory measures against a citizen who submits proposals or criticisms shall be punishable by law.

Article 52. Ethiopians have the right to submit complaints against state organs and mass organizations or officials thereof. Such complaints must be examined and responded to.

Article 53. 1. Safeguarding the security of the Motherland, the revolution and the gains of the working people is a great honour, supreme duty and obligation of every Ethiopian.

2. Treason against the Motherland is the gravest crime committed against the people, entailing severe punishment.

3. National military service is the right and duty of every Ethiopian. Its implementation shall be determined by law.

Article 54. Ethiopians have the duty to work by respecting their responsibilities and work discipline, caring for property and raising productivity in their respective fields of endeavour, recognizing that labour is socially useful and is the basis of human life and that he who works benefits therefrom.

Article 55. 1. Ethiopians have the duty to safeguard and care for socialist property.

2. Ethiopians have the duty to participate in state and societal endeavours to safeguard, care for, collect and utilize historical memorabilia and cultural heritage.

3. Ethiopians have the duty to protect and conserve nature and natural resources, especially to develop forests and to protect and care for soil and water resources.

Article 56. Ethiopians have the duty to assist in the effort of ensuring the equality of the sexes and occupations, of strengthening the ties and mutual respect among the working people of the various nationalities, and of enhancing the culture of collective effort in the building of a socialist system.

Article 57. Every Ethiopian has the duty to observe the Constitution and laws of the People's Democratic Republic of Ethiopia, and to uphold the honour and dignity of Ethiopian citizenship.

Article 58. The exercise of freedoms and rights and the discharge of duties by citizens shall be determined by law. The exercise of freedoms and rights by citizens may be limited by law only in order to protect the interests of the state and society as well as the freedoms and rights of other individuals.

ETHNIC MINORITIES: WORLD GUIDE. The UNITED NATIONS UNIVERSITY, in its report to the 1988 session of the UN General Assembly, indicated (UN Doc. A/43/31, para. 95) that one of the products of its "Project on Ethnic Minorities and Human and Social Development" is a computerized *World Guide to Ethic Minorities,* centralized at *El Colegio de Mexico* in Mexico City. Data have been collected on more than 800 ethnic groups. Cooperating institutions around the world have provided input in return for access to the data bank. The *Guide* includes items on the principal social, economic, and cultural characteristics of each minority, as well as information on major economic and political problems arising from relations with other ethnic groups or with the State. Reference is also included to international dimensions, where they exist.

SEE ALSO ILO Indigenous and Tribal Peoples Convention; Minority Rights; Working Group on the Rights of Persons belonging to National, Ethnic, Religious and Linguistic Minorities.

EUROPEAN AGREEMENT ON REGULATIONS GOVERNING THE MOVEMENT OF PERSONS BETWEEN MEMBER STATES OF THE COUNCIL OF EUROPE (1957). The agreement aims at facilitating freedom of movement between the territories of contracting States by individuals holding recognized travel documents. Such documents are listed in an appendix to the agreement, which is not reproduced here. Some States revise, from time to time, the list of documents acceptable to them. The agreement was concluded in Paris on 13 December 1957 by the COMMITTEE OF MINISTERS OF THE COUNCIL OF EUROPE and entered into force on 1 January 1958. The text (*European Treaty Series* 25) is as follows:

The governments signatory hereto, being Members of the Council of Europe,

Desirous of facilitating personal travel between their countries,

Have agreed as follows:

Article 1. 1. Nationals of the Contracting Parties, whatever their country of residence, may enter or leave the territory of another Party by all frontiers on presentation of one of the documents listed in the Appendix to this Agreement, which is an integral part thereof.

2. The facilities mentioned in paragraph 1. above shall be available only for visits of not more than three months' duration.

3. Valid passports and visas may be required for all visits of more than three months' duration or whenever the territory of another Party is entered for the purpose of pursuing a gainful activity.

4. For the purposes of this Agreement, the term "territory" of a Contracting Party shall have the meaning assigned to it by such a Party in a declaration addressed to the Secretary General of the Council of Europe for communication to all other Contracting Parties.

Article 2. To the extent that one or more Contracting Parties deem necessary, the frontier shall be crossed only at authorised points.

Article 3. The foregoing provisions shall in no way prejudice the laws and regulations governing visits by aliens to the territory of any Contracting Party.

Article 4. This Agreement shall not prejudice the provisions of any domestic law and bilateral or multilateral treaties, conventions or agreements now in force or which may hereafter enter into force, whereby more favourable terms are applied to the nationals of other Contracting Parties in respect of the crossing of frontiers.

Article 5. Each Contracting Party shall allow the holder of any of the documents mentioned in the list drawn up by it and embodied in the Appendix to this Agreement to re-enter its territory without formality even if his nationality is under dispute.

Article 6. Each Contracting Party reserves the right to forbid nationals of another Party whom it considers undesirable to enter or stay in its territory.

Article 7. Each Contracting Party reserves the option, on grounds relating to *ordre public,* security or public health, to delay the entry into force of this Agreement or order the temporary suspension thereof in respect of all or some of the other Parties, except insofar as the provisions of Article 5 are concerned. This measure shall immediately be notified to the Secretary General of the Council of Europe, who shall inform the other Parties. The same procedure shall apply as soon as this measure ceases to be operative.

A Contracting Party which avails itself of either of the options mentioned in the preceding paragraph may not claim the application of this Agreement by another Party save insofar as it also applies it in respect of that Party.

Article 8. This Agreement shall be open to the signature of the Members of the Council of Europe, who may become Parties to it either by:

(a) signature without reservation in respect of ratification;

(b) signature with reservation in respect of ratification followed by ratification.

Instruments of ratification shall be deposited with the Secretary General of the Council of Europe.

Article 9. This Agreement shall enter into force on the first day of the month following the date on which three Members of the Council shall, in accordance with Article 8, have signed the Agreement without reservation in respect of ratification or shall have ratified it.

In the case of any Member who shall subsequently sign the Agreement without reservation in respect of ratification or shall ratify it, the Agreement shall enter into force

on the first day of the month following such signature or the deposit of the instrument of ratification.

Article 10. After entry into force of this Agreement, the Committee of Ministers of the Council of Europe may invite any non-member State to accede to it. Such accession shall take effect on the first day of the month following the deposit of the instrument of accession with the Secretary General of the Council of Europe.

Article 11. Any government wishing to sign or accede to this Agreement which has not yet drawn up its list of the documents mentioned in Article 1, paragraph 1, and appearing in the Appendix, shall submit a list of such documents to the Contracting Parties through the Secretary General of the Council of Europe. This list shall be considered to be approved by all the Contracting Parties and shall be added to the Appendix to this Agreement if no objection is raised within two months of its transmission by the Secretary General.

The same procedure shall apply if a signatory government wishes to alter the list of documents drawn up by it and embodied in the Appendix.

Article 12. The Secretary General of the Council of Europe shall notify Members of the Council and acceding States:

(a) of the date of entry into force of this Agreement and the names of any Members who have signed without reservation in respect of ratification or who have ratified it;

(b) of the deposit of any instrument of accession in accordance with Article 10;

(c) of any notification received in accordance with Article 13 and of its effective date.

Article 13. Any Contracting Party may terminate its own application of the Agreement by giving three months' notice to that effect to the Secretary General of the Council of Europe.

In witness whereof the undersigned, being duly authorised thereto, have signed this Agreement.

Done at Paris, this 13th day of December 1957, in English and French, both texts being equally authentic, in a single copy which shall remain deposited in the archives of the Council of Europe. The Secretary General of the Council of Europe shall transmit certified copies to the signatory governments.

SEE ALSO *European Convention on Human Rights: Protocol IV; Helsinki Accord entries; Movement and Residence; Right to Leave any Country, including One's Own, and to Return to One's Own Country.*

EUROPEAN AGREEMENT RELATING TO PERSONS PARTICIPATING IN PROCEEDINGS OF THE EUROPEAN COMMISSION AND COURT OF HUMAN RIGHTS (1969).

The agreement aims at protecting the freedom of movement and of correspondence of persons seeking to participate in the work of the EUROPEAN COMMISSION ON HUMAN RIGHTS of the EUROPEAN COURT OF HUMAN RIGHTS, or any of their subsidiary bodies. Contracting States undertake to grant such persons immunity in respect of oral or written statements they may make, or documents or evidence they may submit, to any of these bodies.

The agreement was concluded by the COMMITTEE OF MINISTERS OF THE COUNCIL OF EUROPE, convened in London, on 6 May 1969, and entered into force on 17 April 1971. The text (*European Treaty Series* 67) is as follows:

The member States of the Council of Europe, signatory hereto,

Having regard to the Convention for the Protection of Human Rights and Fundamental Freedoms, signed at Rome on 4 November 1950 (hereinafter referred to as "the Convention");

Considering that it is expedient for the better fulfilment of the purposes of the Convention that persons taking part in proceedings before the European Commission of Human Rights (hereinafter referred to as "the Commission") or the European Court of Human Rights (hereinafter referred to as "the Court") shall be accorded certain immunities and facilities;

Desiring to conclude an Agreement for this purpose,

Have agreed as follows:

Article 1. 1. The persons to whom this Agreement applies are:

(a) agents of the Contracting Parties and advisers and advocates assisting them;

(b) persons taking part in proceedings instituted before the Commission under Article 25 of the Convention, whether in their own name or as representatives of one of the applicants enumerated in the said Article 25;

(c) barristers, solicitors or professors of law, taking part in proceedings in order to assist one of the persons enumerated in sub-paragraph (b) above;

(d) persons chosen by the delegates of the Commission to assist them in proceedings before the Court;

(e) witnesses, experts and other persons called upon by the Commission or the Court to take part in proceedings before the Commission or the Court.

2. For the purpose of this Agreement, the terms "Commission" and "Court" shall include a sub-Commission or Chamber, or members of either body carrying out their duties under the terms of the Convention or of the rules of the Commission or of the Court, as the case may be; and the term "taking part in proceedings" shall include making communications with a view to a complaint against a State which has recognised the right of individual petition under Article 25 of the Convention.

3. If, in the course of the exercise by the Committee of Ministers of its functions under Article 32 of the Convention, any person mentioned in paragraph 1 of this article is called upon to appear before, or to submit written statements to the Committee of Ministers, the provisions of this Agreement shall apply in relation to him.

Article 2. 1. The persons referred to in paragraph 1 of Article 1 of this Agreement shall have immunity from legal process in respect of oral or written statements made, or documents or other evidence submitted by them before or to the Commission or the Court.

2. This immunity does not apply to the communication, outside the Commission or the Court, by or on behalf of any person entitled to immunity under the preceding paragraph, of any such statements, documents or evidence or any part thereof submitted by that person to the Commission or the Court.

Article 3. 1. The Contracting Parties shall respect the right of the persons referred to in paragraph 1 of Article 1 of this Agreement to correspond freely with the Commission and the Court.

2. As regards persons under detention, the exercise of this right shall in particular imply that:

(a) if their correspondence is examined by the competent authorities, its despatch and delivery shall nevertheless take place without undue delay and without alteration;

(b) such persons shall not be subject to disciplinary measures in any form on account of any communication sent through the proper channels to the Commission or the Court;

(c) such persons shall have the right to correspond, and consult out of hearing of other persons, with a lawyer qualified to appear before the courts of the country where they are detained in regard to an application to the Commission, or any proceedings resulting therefrom.

3. In application of the preceding paragraphs, there shall be no interference by a public authority except such as is in accordance with the law and is necessary in a democratic society in the interests of national security, for the detection or prosecution of a criminal offence or for the protection of health.

Article 4. 1. (a) The Contracting Parties undertake not to hinder the free movement and travel, for the purpose of attending and returning from proceedings before the Commission or the Court, of persons referred to in paragraph 1 of Article 1 of this Agreement whose presence has in advance been authorised by the Commission or the Court.

(b) No restrictions shall be placed on their movement and travel other than such as are in accordance with the law and necessary in a democratic society in the interests of national security or public safety, for the maintenance of *ordre public*, for the prevention of crime, for the protection of health or morals, or for the protection of the rights and freedoms of others.

2. (a) Such persons shall not, in countries of transit and in the country where the proceedings take place, be prosecuted or detained or be subjected to any other restriction of their personal liberty in respect of acts or convictions prior to the commencement of the journey.

(b) Any Contracting Party may at the time of signature or ratification of this Agreement declare that the provisions of this paragraph will not apply to its own nationals. Such a declaration may be withdrawn at any time by means of a notification addressed to the Secretary General of the Council of Europe.

3. The Contracting Parties undertake to re-admit on his return to their territory any such person who commenced his journey in the said territory.

4. The provisions of paragraphs 1 and 2 of this article shall cease to apply when the person concerned has had for a period of 15 consecutive days from the date when his presence is no longer required by the Commission or the Court the opportunity of returning to the country from which his journey commenced.

5. Where there is any conflict between the obligations of a Contracting Party resulting from paragraph 2 of this article and those resulting from a Council of Europe Convention or from an extradition treaty or other treaty concerning mutual assistance in criminal matters with other Contracting Parties, the provisions of paragraph 2 of this article shall prevail.

Article 5. 1. Immunities and facilities are accorded to the persons referred to in paragraph 1 of Article 1 of this Agreement solely in order to ensure for them the freedom of speech and the independence necessary for the discharge of their functions, tasks or duties, or the exercise of their rights in relation to the Commission and the Court.

2. (a) The Commission or the Court, as the case may be, shall alone be competent to waive, in whole or in part, the immunity provided for in paragraph 1 of Article 2 of this Agreement; they have not only the right but the duty to waive immunity in any case where, in their opinion, such immunity would impede the course of justice and waiver in whole or in part would not prejudice the purpose defined in paragraph 1 of this article.

(b) The immunity may be waived by the Commission or by the Court, either *ex officio* or at the request, addressed to the Secretary General of the Council of Europe, of any Contracting Party or of any person concerned.

(c) Decisions waiving immunity or refusing the waiver shall be accompanied by a statement of reasons.

3. If a Contracting Party certifies that waiver of the immunity provided for in paragraph 1 of Article 2 of this Agreement is necessary for the purpose of proceedings in respect of an offence against national security, the Commission or the Court shall waive immunity to the extent specified in the certificate.

4. In the event of the discovery of a fact which might, by its nature, have a decisive influence and which at the time of the decision refusing waiver of immunity was unknown to the author of the request, the latter may make a new request to the Commission or the Court.

Article 6. Nothing in this Agreement shall be construed as limiting or derogating from any of the obligations assumed by the Contracting Parties under the Convention.

Article 7. 1. This Agreement shall be open to signature by the member States of the Council of Europe, who may become Parties to it either by:

(a) signature without reservation in respect of ratification or acceptance, or

(b) signature with reservation in respect of ratification or acceptance, followed by ratification or acceptance.

2. Instruments of ratification or acceptance shall be deposited with the Secretary General of the Council of Europe.

Article 8. 1. This Agreement shall enter into force one month after the date on which five member States of the Council shall have become Parties to the Agreement, in accordance with the provisions of Article 7.

2. As regards any member States who shall subsequently sign the Agreement without reservation in respect of ratification or acceptance or who shall ratify or accept it, the Agreement shall enter into force one month after the date of such signature or after the date of deposit of the instrument of ratification or acceptance.

Article 9. 1. Any Contracting Party may, at the time of signature or when depositing its instrument of ratification or acceptance, specify the territory or territories to which this Agreement shall apply.

2. Any Contracting Party may, when depositing its instrument of ratification or acceptance or at any later date, by declaration addressed to the Secretary General of the Council of Europe, extend this Agreement to any other territory or territories specified in the declaration and for whose international relations it is responsible or on whose behalf it is authorised to give undertakings.

3. Any declaration made in pursuance of the preceding paragraph may, in respect of any territory mentioned in such declaration, be withdrawn according to the procedure laid down in Article 10 of this Agreement.

Article 10. 1. This Agreement shall remain in force indefinitely.

2. Any Contracting Party may, insofar as it is concerned, denounce this Agreement by means of a notification addressed to the Secretary General of the Council of Europe.

3. Such denunciation shall take effect six months after the date of receipt by the Secretary General of such notification. Such a denunciation shall not have the effect of releasing the Contracting Parties concerned from any obligation which may have arisen under this Agreement in relation to any person referred to in paragraph 1 of Article 1.

Article 11. The Secretary General of the Council of Europe shall notify the member States of the Council of:

(a) any signature without reservation in respect of ratification or acceptance;

(b) any signature with reservation in respect of ratification or acceptance;

(c) the deposit of any instrument of ratification or acceptance;

(d) any date of entry into force of this Agreement in accordance with Article 8 thereof;

(e) any declaration received in pursuance of the provisions of paragraph 2 of Article 4 and of paragraphs 2 and 3 of Article 9;

(f) any notification of withdrawal of a declaration in pursuance of the provisions of paragraph 2 of Article 4 and any notification received in pursuance of the provisions of Article 10 and the date on which any denunciation takes effect.

In witness whereof the undersigned, being duly authorised thereto, have signed this Agreement.

Done at London, this 6th day of May 1969, in the English and French languages, both texts being equally authoritative, in a single copy which shall remain deposited in the archives of the Council of Europe. The Secretary General of the Council of Europe shall transmit certified copies to each of the signatory States.

EUROPEAN CODE OF SOCIAL SECURITY AND PROTOCOL (1964). The code, including an annex and two addenda, and the protocol, were concluded by the COMMITTEE OF MINISTERS OF THE COUNCIL OF EUROPE, meeting in Strasbourg, on 16 April 1964, and entered into force on 17 March 1968. They spell out in detail the meaning of the right to social security by specifying benefits to be paid to workers in the event of sickness, unemployment, old age, or incapacity. The protocol sets, for States prepared to accept its provisions, a standard somewhat higher than does the basic code. Both instruments improve upon the minimum-standard level which have been embodied in the ILO SOCIAL SECURITY (MINIMUM STANDARDS) CONVENTION of 28 June 1952.

In the code, reference is made to the need for a special instrument to deal with questions relating to social security for foreigners and migrants in European countries; such an instrument, the EUROPEAN CONVENTION ON SOCIAL SECURITY, was concluded in 1972.

The texts of the code and of its protocol (*European Treaty Series* 48) are as follows:

Preamble

The member States of the Council of Europe, signatory hereto,

Considering that the aim of the Council of Europe is to achieve a greater unity between its Members for the purpose, among others, of facilitating their social progress;

Considering that one of the objects of the social programme of the Council of Europe is to encourage all Members to develop further their systems of social security;

Recognising the desirability of harmonising social charges in member countries;

Convinced that it is desirable to establish a European Code of Social Security at a higher level than the minimum standards embodied in International Labour Convention No. 102 concerning Minimum Standards of Social Security,

Have agreed on the following provisions, which have been prepared with the collaboration of the International Labour Office:

Part I
General Provisions

Article 1. 1. In this Code:

(a) the term "the Committee of Ministers" means the Committee of Ministers of the Council of Europe;

(b) the term "the committee" means the Committee of Experts on Social Security of the Council of Europe or such other committee as the Committee of Ministers may designate to carry out the duties laid down in Article 2, paragraph 3; Article 74, paragraph 4, and Article 78, paragraph 3;

(c) the term "Secretary General" means the Secretary General of the Council of Europe;

(d) the term "prescribed" means determined by or in virtue of national laws or regulations;

(e) the term "residence" means ordinary residence in the territory of the Contracting Party concerned and the term "resident" means a person ordinarily resident in the territory of the Contracting Party concerned;

(f) the term "wife" means a wife who is maintained by her husband;

(g) the term "widow" means a woman who was maintained by her husband at the time of his death;

(h) the term "child" means a child under school-leaving age or under 15 years of age, as may be prescribed;

(i) the term "qualifying period" means a period of contribution, or a period of employment, or a period of residence, or any combination thereof, as may be prescribed.

2. In Articles 10, 34 and 49 the term "benefit" means either direct benefit in the form of care or indirect benefit consisting of a reimbursement of the expenses borne by the person concerned.

Article 2. 1. Each Contracting Party shall comply with:

(a) Part I;

(b) at least six of Parts II to X, provided that Part II shall count as two Parts and Part V as three Parts;

(c) the relevant provisions of Parts XI and XII; and

(d) Part XIII.

2. The terms of sub-paragraph (b) of the foregoing paragraph can be regarded as fulfilled if:

(a) at least three of Parts II to X, including at least one of Parts IV, V, VI, IX and X are complied with; and

(b) in addition, proof is furnished that the social security legislation in force is equivalent to one of the combinations provided for in that sub-paragraph, taking into account:

(i) the fact that certain branches covered by sub-paragraph (a) of this paragraph exceed the standards of the Code in respect of their scope of protection or their level of benefits, or both;

(ii) the fact that certain branches covered by sub-paragraph (a) of this paragraph exceed the standards of the Code by granting supplementary services of advantages listed in Addendum 2; and

(iii) branches which do not attain the standards of the Code.

3. A Signatory desiring to avail itself of the provisions of paragraph 2 (b) of this article shall make a request to this effect in the report to the Secretary General submitted in accordance with the provisions of Article 78. The committee, basing itself on the principle of equivalence of cost, shall lay down rules co-ordinating and defining the conditions for taking into account the provisions of paragraph 2 (b) of this article. These provisions may only be taken into account in each case with the approval of the committee, the decision to be taken by a two-thirds majority.

Article 3. Each Contracting Party shall specify in its instrument of ratification those parts of Parts II to X in respect of which it accepts the obligations of this Code, and shall also state whether and to what extent it avails itself of the provisions of Article 2, paragraph 2.

Article 4. 1. Each Contracting Party may subsequently notify the Secretary General that it accepts the obligations of the Code in respect of one or more of Parts II to X not already specified in its ratification.

2. The undertakings referred to in paragraph 1 of this article shall be deemed to be an integral part of the ratification and to have the force of ratification as from the date of notification.

Article 5. Where, for the purpose of compliance with any of the Parts II to X of this Code which are to be covered by its ratification, a Contracting Party is required to protect prescribed classes of persons constituting not less than a specified percentage of employees or residents, that Contracting Party shall satisfy itself, before undertaking to comply with any such part, that the relevant percentage is attained.

Article 6. For the purpose of compliance with Parts II, III, IV, V, VIII (in so far as it relates to medical care), IX or X of this Code, a Contracting Party may take account of protection effected by means of insurance which, although not made compulsory by national laws or regulations for the persons to be protected,

(a) is subsidised by the public authorities or, where such insurance is complementary only, is supervised by the public authorities or administered, in accordance with prescribed standards, by joint operation of employers and workers;

(b) covers a substantial part of the persons whose earnings do not exceed those of the skilled manual male employer, determined in accordance with Article 65; and

(c) complies, in conjunction with other forms of protection, where appropriate, with the relevant provisions of the Code.

E

Part II
Medical Care

Article 7. Each Contracting Party for which this part of this Code is in force shall secure to the persons protected the provision of benefit in respect of a condition requiring medical care of a preventive or curative nature in accordance with the following articles of this part.

Article 8. The contingencies covered shall include any morbid condition, whatever its cause, and pregnancy and confinement and their consequences.

Article 9. The persons protected shall comprise:

(a) prescribed classes of employees, constituting not less than 50 per cent of all employees, and also their wives and children; or

(b) prescribed classes of the economically active population, constituting not less than 20 per cent of all residents, and also their wives and children; or

(c) prescribed classes of residents, constituting not less than 50 per cent of all residents.

Article 10. 1. The benefit shall include at least:

(a) in case of a morbid condition,

(i) general practitioner care, including domiciliary visiting;

(ii) specialist care at hospitals for in-patients and out-patients, and such specialist care as may be available outside hospitals;

(iii) the essential pharmaceutical supplies as prescribed by medical or other qualified practitioners; and

(iv) hospitalisation where necessary; and

(b) in case of pregnancy and confinement and their consequences,

(i) pre-natal, confinement and post-natal care either by medical practitioners or by qualified midwives; and

(ii) hospitalisation where necessary.

2. The beneficiary or his breadwinner may be required to share in the cost of the medical care the beneficiary receives in respect of a morbid condition; the rules concerning such cost-sharing shall be so designed as to avoid hardship.

3. The benefit provided in accordance with this article shall be afforded with a view to maintaining, restoring or improving the health of the person protected and his ability to work and to attend to his personal needs.

4. The institutions or government departments administering the benefit shall, by such means as may be deemed appropriate, encourage the persons protected to avail themselves of the general health services placed at their disposal by the public authorities or by other bodies recognised by the public authorities.

Article 11. The benefit specified in Article 10 shall, in a contingency covered, be secured at least to a person protected who has completed, or whose breadwinner has completed, such qualifying period as may be considered necessary to preclude abuse.

Article 12. The benefit specified in Article 10 shall be granted throughout the contingency covered, except that, in case of a morbid condition, its duration may be limited to 26 weeks in each case, but benefit shall not be suspended while a sickness benefit continues to be paid, and provision shall be made to enable the limit to be extended for prescribed diseases recognised as entailing prolonged care.

Part III
Sickness Benefit

Article 13. Each Contracting Party for which this part of the Code is in force shall secure to the persons protected the provision of sickness benefit in accordance with the following articles of this part.

Article 14. The contingency covered shall include incapacity for work resulting from a morbid condition and involving suspension of earnings, as defined by national laws or regulations.

Article 15. The persons protected shall comprise:

(a) prescribed classes of employees, constituting not less than 50 per cent of all employees; or

(b) prescribed classes of the economically active population, constituting not less than 20 per cent of all residents; or

(c) all residents whose means during the contingency do not exceed limits prescribed in such a manner as to comply with the requirements of Article 67.

Article 16. 1. Where classes of employees or classes of the economically active population are protected, the benefit shall be a periodical payment calculated in such a manner as to comply with the requirements of Article 65 or with the requirements of Article 66.

2. Where all residents whose means during the contingency do not exceed prescribed limits are protected, the benefit shall be a periodical payment calculated in such a manner as to comply with the requirements of Article 67; provided that a prescribed benefit shall be guaranteed, without means test, to the prescribed classes of persons determined in accordance with Article 15 (a) or (b).

Article 17. The benefit specified in Article 16 shall, in a contingency covered, be secured at least to a person protected who has completed such qualifying period as may be considered necessary to preclude abuse.

Article 18. The benefit specified in Article 16 shall be granted throughout the contingency, except that the benefit may be limited to 26 weeks in each case of sickness, and need not be paid for the first three days of suspension of earnings.

Part IV
Unemployment Benefit

Article 19. Each Contracting Party for which this part of the Code is in force shall secure to the persons protected the provision of unemployment benefit in accordance with the following articles of this part.

Article 20. The contingency covered shall include suspension of earnings, as defined by national laws or regulations, due to inability to obtain suitable employment in the case of a person protected who is capable of, and available for, work.

Article 21. The persons protected shall comprise:

(a) prescribed classes of employees, constituting not less than 50 per cent of all employees; or

(b) all residents whose means during the contingency do not exceed limits prescribed in such a manner as to comply with the requirements of Article 67.

Article 22. 1. Where classes of employees are protected, the benefit shall be a periodical payment calculated in such a manner as to comply either with the requirements of Article 65 or with the requirements of Article 66.

2. Where all residents whose means during the contingency do not exceed prescribed limits are protected, the benefit shall be a periodical payment calculated in such a manner as to comply with the requirements of Article 67; provided that a prescribed benefit shall be guaranteed, without means test, to the prescribed classes of employees determined in accordance with Article 21 (a).

Article 23. The benefit specified in Article 22 shall, in a contingency covered, be secured at least to a person protected who has completed such qualifying period as may be considered necessary to preclude abuse.

Article 24. 1. The benefit specified in Article 22 shall be granted throughout the contingency, except that its duration may be limited,

(a) where classes of employees are protected, to 13 weeks within a period of 12 months, or to 13 weeks in each case of suspension of earnings; or

(b) where all residents whose means during the contingency do not exceed prescribed limits are protected, to 26 weeks within a period of 12 months; provided that the duration of the prescribed benefit, guaranteed without means test, may be limited in accordance with subparagraph (a) of this paragraph.

2. Where national laws or regulations provide that the duration of the benefit shall vary with the length of the contribution period and/or the benefit previously received within a prescribed period, the provisions of paragraph 1 of this article shall be deemed to be fulfilled if the average duration of benefit is at least 13 weeks within a period of 12 months.

3. The benefit need not be paid for a waiting period of the first seven days in each case of suspension of earnings, counting days of unemployment before and after temporary employment lasting not more than a prescribed period as part of the same case of suspension of earnings.

4. In the case of seasonal workers the duration of the benefit and the waiting period may be adapted to their conditions of employment.

Part V
Old-age Benefit

Article 25. Each Contracting Party for which this part of the Code is in force shall secure to the persons protected the provision of old-age benefit in accordance with the following articles of this part.

Article 26. 1. The contingency covered shall be survival beyond a prescribed age.

2. The prescribed age shall be not more than 65 years or than such higher age that the number of residents having attained that age is not less than 10 per cent of the number of residents under that age but over 15 years of age.

3. National laws or regulations may provide that the benefit of a person otherwise entitled to it may be suspended if such person is engaged in any prescribed gainful activity or that the benefit, if contributory, may be reduced, where the earnings of the beneficiary exceed a prescribed amount and, if non-contributory, may be reduced where the earnings of the beneficiary or his other means or the two taken together exceed a prescribed amount.

Article 27. The persons protected shall compromise:

(a) prescribed classes of employees, constituting not less than 50 per cent of all employees; or

(b) prescribed classes of the economically active population, constituting not less than 20 per cent of all residents; or

(c) all residents whose means during the contingency do not exceed limits prescribed in such a manner as to comply with the requirements of Article 67.

Article 28. The benefit shall be a periodical payment calculated as follows:

(a) where classes of employees or classes of the economically active population are protected, in such a manner as to comply either with the requirements of Article 65 or with the requirements of Article 66;

(b) where all residents whose means during the contingency do not exceed prescribed limits are protected, in such a manner as to comply with the requirements of Article 67.

Article 29. 1. The benefit specified in Article 28 shall, in a contingency covered, be secured at least:

(a) to a person protected who has completed, prior to the contingency, in accordance with prescribed rules, a qualifying period which may be 30 years of contribution or employment, or 20 years of residence; or

(b) where, in principle, all economically active persons are protected, to a person protected who has completed a prescribed qualifying period of contribution and in respect of whom while he was of working age, the prescribed yearly average number of contributions has been paid.

2. Where the benefit referred to in paragraph 1 of this article is conditional upon a minimum period of contribution or employment, a reduced benefit shall be secured at least:

(a) to a person protected who has completed, prior to the contingency, in accordance with prescribed rules, a qualifying period of 15 years of contribution or employment; or

(b) where, in principle, all economically active persons are protected, to a person protected who has completed a prescribed qualifying period of contribution and in respect of whom, while he was of working age, half the yearly average number of contributions prescribed in accordance with paragraph 1 (b) of this article has been paid.

3. The requirements of paragraph 1 of this article shall be deemed to be satisfied where a benefit calculated in conformity with the requirements of Part XI but at a percentage of ten points lower than shown in the schedule appended to that part for the standard beneficiary concerned is secured at least to a person protected who has completed, in accordance with prescribed rules, ten years of contribution or employment, or five years of residence.

4. A proportional reduction of the percentage indicated in the schedule appended to Part XI may be effected where the qualifying period for the benefit corresponding to the reduced percentage exceeds ten years of contribution or employment but is less than 30 years of contribution or employment; if such qualifying period exceeds 15 years, a reduced benefit shall be payable in conformity with paragraph 2 of this article.

5. Where the benefit referred to in paragraphs 1, 3 or 4 of this article is conditional upon a minimum period of contribution or employment, a reduced benefit shall be payable under prescribed conditions to a person protected who, by reason only of his advanced age when the provisions concerned in the application of this part come into force, has not satisfied the conditions prescribed in accordance with paragraph 2 of this article, unless a benefit in conformity with the provisions of paragraphs 1, 3 or 4 of this article is secured to such person at an age higher than the normal age.

Article 30. The benefits specified in Articles 28 and 29 shall be granted throughout the contingency.

Part VI
Employment Injury Benefit

Article 31. Each Contracting Party for which this part of the Code is in force shall secure to the persons protected the provision of employment injury benefit in accordance with the following articles of this part.

Article 32. The contingencies covered shall include the following where the state of affairs described is due to accident or a prescribed disease resulting from employment:

(a) a morbid condition;

(b) incapacity for work resulting from such a condition and involving suspension of earnings, as defined by national laws or regulations;

(c) total loss of earning capacity or partial loss thereof in excess of a prescribed degree, likely to be permanent, or corresponding loss of faculty; and

(d) the loss of support suffered by the widow or child as the result of the death of the breadwinner; in the case of a widow, the right to benefit may be made conditional on her being presumed, in accordance with national laws or regulations, to be incapable of self-support.

Article 33. The persons protected shall comprise prescribed classes of employees, constituting not less than 50 per cent of all employees, and, for benefit in respect of death of the breadwinner, also their wives and children.

Article 34. 1. In respect of a morbid condition, the benefit shall be medical care as specified in paragraphs 2 and 3 of this article.

2. The medical care shall comprise:

(a) general practitioner and specialist in-patient care and out-patient care, including domiciliary visiting;

(b) dental care;

(c) nursing care at home or in hospital or other medical institutions;

(d) maintenance in hospitals, convalescent homes, sanatoria or other medical institutions;

(e) dental, pharmaceutical and other medical or surgical supplies, including prosthetic appliances, kept in repair, and eyeglasses; and

(f) the care furnished by members of such other professions as may at any time be legally recognised as allied to the medical profession, under the supervision of a medical or dental practitioner.

3. The medical care provided in accordance with the preceding paragraphs shall be afforded with a view to maintaining, restoring or improving the health of the person protected and his ability to work and to attend to his personal needs.

Article 35. 1. The institutions or government departments administering the medical care shall co-operate, wherever appropriate, with the general vocational rehabilitation services, with a view to the re-establishment of handicapped persons in suitable work.

2. National laws or regulations may authorise such institutions or departments to ensure provision for the vocational rehabilitation of handicapped persons.

Article 36. 1. In respect of incapacity for work, total loss of earning capacity likely to be permanent, or corresponding loss of faculty, or the death of the breadwinner, the benefit shall be a periodical payment calculated in such a manner as to comply either with the requirements of Article 65 or with the requirements of Article 66.

2. In case of partial loss of earning capacity likely to be permanent, or corresponding loss of faculty, the benefit, where payable, shall be a periodical payment representing a suitable proportion of that specified for total loss of earning capacity or corresponding loss of faculty.

3. The periodical payment may be commuted for a lump sum:

(a) where the degree of incapacity is slight; or

(b) where the competent authority is satisfied that the lump sum will be properly utilised.

Article 37. The benefit specified in Articles 34 and 36 shall, in a contingency covered, be secured at least to a person protected who was employed on the territory of the Contracting Party concerned at the time of the accident if the injury is due to accident or at the time of contracting the disease if the injury is due to a disease and, for periodical payments in respect of death of the breadwinner, to the widow and children of such person.

Article 38. The benefit specified in Articles 34 and 36 shall be granted throughout the contingency, except that, in respect of incapacity for work, the benefit need not be paid for the first three days in each case of suspension of earnings.

Part VII
Family Benefit

Article 39. Each Contracting Party for which this part of the Code is in force shall secure to the persons protected the provision of family benefit in accordance with the following articles of this part.

Article 40. The contingency covered shall be responsibility for the maintenance of children as prescribed.

Article 41. The persons protected shall comprise, as regards the periodical payments specified in Article 42:

(a) prescribed classes of employees, constituting not less than 50 per cent of all employees; or

(b) prescribed classes of the economically active population, constituting not less than 20 per cent of all residents.

Article 42. The benefit shall be:

(a) a periodical payment granted to any person protected having completed the prescribed qualifying period; or

(b) the provision to or in respect of children of food, clothing, housing, holidays or domestic help; or

(c) a combination of the benefits provided for in subparagraphs (a) and (b) of this article.

Article 43. The benefit specified in Article 42 shall be secured at least to a person protected who, within a prescribed period, has completed a qualifying period which may be one month of contribution or employment, or six months of residence, as may be prescribed.

Article 44. The total value of the benefits granted in accordance with Article 42 to the persons protected shall be such as to respect 1.5 per cent of the wage of an ordinary adult male labourer as determined in accordance with the rules laid down in Article 66, multiplied by the total number of children of all residents.

Article 45. Where the benefit consists of a periodical payment, it shall be granted throughout the contingency.

Part VIII
Maternity Benefit

Article 46. Each Contracting Party for which this part of the Code is in force shall secure to the persons protected the provision of maternity benefit in accordance with the following articles of this part.

Article 47. The contingencies covered shall include

pregnancy and confinement and their consequences, and suspension of earnings, as defined by national laws or regulations resulting therefrom.

Article 48. The persons protected shall comprise:

(a) all women in prescribed classes of employees, which classes constitute not less than 50 per cent of all employees, and, for maternity medical benefit, also the wives of men in these classes; or

(b) all women in prescribed classes of the economically active population, which classes constitute not less than 20 per cent of all residents, and, for maternity medical benefit, also the wives of men in these classes.

Article 49. 1. In respect of pregnancy and confinement and their consequences, the maternity medical benefit shall be medical care as specified in paragraphs 2 and 3 of this article.

2. The medical care shall include at least:

(a) pre-natal, confinement and post-natal care either by medical practitioners or by qualified midwives; and

(b) hospitalisation where necessary.

3. The medical care specified in paragraph 2 of this article shall be afforded with a view to maintaining, restoring or improving the health of the woman protected and her ability to work and to attend to her personal needs.

4. The institutions or government departments administering the maternity medical benefit shall, by such means as may be deemed appropriate, encourage the women protected to avail themselves of the general health services placed at their disposal by the public authorities or by other bodies recognised by the public authorities.

Article 50. In respect of suspension of earnings resulting from pregnancy and from confinement and their consequences, the benefit shall be a periodical payment calculated in such a manner as to comply either with the requirements of Article 65 or with the requirements of Article 66. The amount of the periodical payment may vary in the course of the contingency, subject to the average rate thereof complying with these requirements.

Article 51. The benefit specified in Articles 49 and 50 shall, in a contingency covered, be secured at least to a woman in the classes protected who has completed such qualifying period as may be considered necessary to preclude abuse, and the benefit specified in Article 49 shall also be secured to the wife of a man in the classes protected where the latter has completed such qualifying period.

Article 52. The benefit specified in Articles 49 and 50 shall be granted throughout the contingency, except that the periodical payment may be limited to 12 weeks, unless a longer period of abstention from work is required or authorised by national laws or regulations, in which event it may not be limited to a period less than such longer period.

Part IX
Invalidity Benefit

Article 53. Each Contracting Party for which this part of the Code is in force shall secure to the persons protected the provision of invalidity benefit in accordance with the following articles of this part.

Article 54. The contingency covered shall include inability to engage in any gainful activity, to an extent prescribed, which inability is likely to be permanent or persists after the exhaustion of sickness benefit.

Article 55. The persons protected shall comprise:

(a) prescribed classes of employees, constituting not less than 50 per cent of all employees; or

(b) prescribed classes of the economically active population, constituting not less than 20 per cent of all residents; or

(c) all residents whose means during the contingency do not exceed limits prescribed in such a way as to comply with the requirements of Article 67.

Article 56. The benefit shall be a periodical payment calculated as follows:

(a) where classes of employees or classes of the economically active population are protected, in such a manner as to comply either with the requirements of Article 65 or with the requirements of Article 66;

(b) where all residents whose means during the contingency do not exceed prescribed limits are protected, in such a manner as to comply with the requirements of Article 67.

Article 57. 1. The benefit specified in Article 56 shall, in a contingency covered, be secured at least:

(a) to a person protected who has completed, prior to the contingency, in accordance with prescribed rules, a qualifying period which may be 15 years of contribution or employment, or 10 years of residence; or

(b) where, in principle, all economically active persons are protected, to a person protected who has completed a qualifying period of three years of contribution and in respect of whom, while he was of working age, the prescribed yearly average number of contributions has been paid.

2. Where the benefit referred to in paragraph 1 of this article is conditional upon a minimum period of contribution or employment, a reduced benefit shall be secured at least:

(a) to a person protected who has completed, prior to the contingency, in accordance with prescribed rules, a qualifying period of five years of contribution or employment; or

(b) where, in principle, all economically active persons or protected, to a person protected who has completed a qualifying period of three years of contribution and in respect of whom, while he was of working age, half the yearly average number of contributions prescribed in accordance with paragraph 1 (b) of this article has been paid.

3. The requirements of paragraph 1 of this article shall be deemed to be satisfied where a benefit calculated in conformity with the requirements of Part XI but at a percentage of ten points lower than shown in the schedule appended to that part for the standard beneficiary concerned is secured at least to a person protected who has completed, in accordance with prescribed rules, five years of contribution, employment or residence.

4. A proportional reductional of the percentage indicated in the schedule appended to Part XI may be effected where the qualifying period for the pension corresponding to the reduced percentage exceeds five years of contribution or employment but is less than 15 years of contribution or employment; a reduced benefit shall be payable in conformity with paragraph 2 of this article.

Article 58. The benefit specified in Articles 56 and 57 shall be granted throughout the contingency or until an old-age benefit becomes payable.

Part X
Survivors' Benefit

Article 59. Each Contracting Party for which this part of the Code is in force shall secure to the persons protected the provision of survivor's benefit in accordance with the following articles of this part.

Article 60. 1. The contingency covered shall include the loss of support suffered by the widow or child as the result of the death of the breadwinner; in the case of a widow, the right to benefit may be made conditional on her being presumed, in accordance with national laws or regulations, to be incapable of self-support.

2. National laws or regulations may provide that the benefit of a person otherwise entitled to it may be suspended if such person is engaged in any prescribed gainful activity or that the benefit, if contributory, may be reduced where the earnings of the beneficiary exceed a prescribed amount, and, if non-contributory, may be reduced where the earnings of the beneficiary or his other means or the two taken together exceed a prescribed amount.

Article 61. The persons protected shall comprise:

(a) the wives and the children of breadwinners in prescribed classes of employees, which classes constitute not less than 50 per cent of all employees; or

(b) the wives and the children of breadwinners in prescribed classes of the economically active population, which classes constitute not less than 20 per cent of all residents; or

(c) all resident widows and resident children who have lost their breadwinner and whose means during the contingency do not exceed limits prescribed in such a manner as to comply with the requirements of Article 67.

Article 62. The benefit shall be a periodical payment calculated as follows:

(a) where the wives and children of breadwinners in classes of employees or classes of the economically active population are protected, in such manner as to comply either with the requirements of Article 65 or with the requirements of Article 66;

(b) where all resident widows and resident children whose means during the contingency do not exceed prescribed limits are protected, in such a manner as to comply with the requirements of Article 67.

Article 63. 1. The benefit specified in Article 62 shall, in a contingency covered, be secured at least:

(a) to a person protected whose breadwinner has completed, in accordance with prescribed rules, a qualifying period which may be 15 years of contribution or employment, or 10 years of residence; or

(b) where, in principle, the wives and children of all economically active persons are protected, to a person protected whose breadwinner has completed a qualifying period of three years of contribution and in respect of whose breadwinner, while he was of working age, the prescribed yearly average number of contributions has been paid.

2. Where the benefit referred to in paragraph 1 of this article is conditional upon a minimum period of contribution or employment, a reduced benefit shall be secured at least:

(a) to a person protected whose breadwinner has completed, in accordance with prescribed rules, a qualifying period of five years of contribution or employment; or

(b) where, in principles, the wives and children of all economically active persons are protected, to a person protected whose breadwinner has completed a qualifying period of three years of contribution and in respect of whose breadwinner, while he was of working age, half the yearly average number of contributions prescribed in accordance with paragraph 1 (b) of this article have been paid.

3. The requirements of paragraph 1 of this article shall be deemed to be satisfied where a benefit calculated in conformity with the requirements of Part XI but at a percentage of ten points lower than shown in the schedule appended to that part for the standard beneficiary concerned is secured at least to a person protected whose breadwinner has completed, in accordance with prescribed rules, five years of contribution, employment or residence.

4. A proportional reduction of the percentage indicated in the schedule appended to Part XI may be effected where the qualifying period for the benefit corresponding to the reduced percentage exceeds five years of contribution or employment but is less than 15 years of contribution or employment; a reduced benefit shall be payable in conformity with paragraph 2 of this article.

5. In order that a childless widow presumed to be incapable of self-support may be entitled to a survivor's benefit, a minimum duration of the marriage may be required.

Article 64. The benefit specified in Articles 62 and 63 shall be granted throughout the contingency.

Part XI
Standards to be Complied with by Periodical Payments

Article 65. 1. In the case of a periodical payment to which this article applies, the rate of the benefit, increased by the amount of any family allowances payable during the contingency, shall be such as to attain, in respect of the contingency in question, for the standard beneficiary indicated in the schedule appended to this part, at least the percentage indicated therein of the total of the previous earnings of the beneficiary or his breadwinner and of the amount of any family allowances payable to a person protected with the same family responsibilities as the standard beneficiary.

2. The previous earnings of the beneficiary or his breadwinner shall be calculated according to prescribed rules, and, where the persons protected or their breadwinners are arranged in classes according to their earnings, their previous earnings may be calculated from the basic earnings of the classes to which they belonged.

3. A maximum limit may be prescribed for the rate of the benefit or for earnings taken into account for the calculation of the benefit, provided that the maximum limit is fixed in such a way that the provisions of paragraph 1 of this article are complied with, where the previous earnings of the beneficiary or his breadwinner are equal to or lower than the wage of a skilled manual male employee.

4. The previous earnings of the beneficiary or his breadwinner, the wage of the skilled manual male employee, the benefit and any family allowances shall be calculated on the same time basis.

5. For the other beneficiaries, the benefit shall bear a reasonable relation to the benefit for the standard beneficiary.

6. For the purpose of this article, a skilled manual male employee shall be:

(a) a fitter or turner in the manufacture of machinery other than electrical machinery; or

(b) a person deemed typical of skilled labour selected in accordance with the provisions of paragraph 7 of this article; or

(c) a person whose earnings are equal to 125 per cent of the average earnings of all the persons protected.

7. The person deemed typical of skilled labour for the purposes of paragraph 6 (b) of this article shall be a person employed in the major group of economic activities with the largest number of economically active male persons

protected in the contingency in question, or of the breadwinners of the persons protected, as the case may be, in the division comprising the largest number of such persons or breadwinners; for this purpose, the international standard industrial classification of all economic activities, adopted by the Economic and Social Council of the United Nations at its Seventh Session on 27 August 1948, and reproduced in Addendum 1 to this Code, or such classification as at any time amended, shall be used.

8. Where the rate of benefit varies by region, the skilled manual male employee may be determined for each region in accordance with paragraphs 6 and 7 of this article.

9. The wage of the skilled manual male employee selected in accordance with paragraph 6 (a) and (b) of this article shall be determined on the basis of the rates of wages for normal hours of work fixed by collective agreements, by or in pursuance of national laws or regulations, where applicable, or by custom, including cost-of-living allowances if any; where such rates differ by region but paragraph 8 of this article is not applied, the median rate shall be taken.

10. The rates of current periodical payments in respect of old age, employment injury (except in case of incapacity for work), invalidity and death of breadwinner, shall be reviewed following substantial changes in the general level of earnings where these result from substantial changes in the cost of living.

Article 66. 1. In the case of a periodical payment to which this article applies, the rate of the benefit, increased by the amount of any family allowances payable during the contingency, shall be such as to attain, in respect of the contingency in question, for the standard beneficiary indicated in the schedule appended to this part, at least the percentage indicated therein of the total of the wage of an ordinary adult male labourer and of the amount of any family allowances payable to a person protected with the same family responsibilities as the standard beneficiary.

2. The wage of the ordinary adult male labourer, the benefit and any family allowances shall be calculated on the same time basis.

3. For the other beneficiaries, the benefit shall bear a reasonable relation to the benefit for the standard beneficiary.

4. For the purpose of this article, the ordinary adult male labourer shall be:

(a) a person deemed typical of unskilled labour in the manufacture of machinery other than electrical machinery; or

(b) a person deemed typical of unskilled labour selected in accordance with the provisions of the following paragraph.

5. The person deemed typical of unskilled labour for the purpose of paragraph 4 (b) of this article shall be a person employed in the major group of economic activities with the largest number of economically active male persons protected in the contingency in question, or of the breadwinners of the persons protected, as the case may be, in the division comprising the largest number of such persons or breadwinners; for this purpose the international standard industrial classification of all economic activities, adopted by the Economic and Social Council of the United Nations at its Seventh Session on 27 August 1948, and reproduced in Addendum 1 to this Code, or such classification as at any time amended, shall be used.

6. Where the rate of benefit varies by region, the ordinary adult male labourer may be determined for each region in accordance with paragraphs 4 and 5 of this article.

7. The wage of the ordinary adult male labourer shall be determined on the basis of the rates of wages for normal hours of work fixed by collective agreements, by or in pursuance of national laws or regulations, where applicable, or by custom, including cost-of-living allowances if any; where such rates differ by region but paragraph 6 of this article is not applied, the median rate shall be taken.

8. The rates of current periodical payments in respect of old age, employment injury (except in case of incapacity for work), invalidity and death of breadwinner, shall be reviewed following substantial changes in the general level of earnings where these result from substantial changes in the cost of living.

Article 67. In the case of a periodical payment to which this article applies:

(a) the rate of the benefit shall be determined according to a prescribed scale or a scale fixed by the competent public authority in conformity with prescribed rules;

(b) such rate may be reduced only to the extent by which the other means of the family of the beneficiary exceed prescribed substantial amounts or substantial amounts fixed by the competent public authority in conformity with prescribed rules;

(c) the total of the benefit and any other means, after deduction of the substantial amounts referred to in sub-paragraph (b) of this article, shall be sufficient to maintain the family of the beneficiary in health and decency, and shall be not less than the corresponding benefit calculated in accordance with the requirements of Article 66;

(d) the provisions of sub-paragraph (c) of this article shall be deemed to be satisfied if the total amount of benefits paid under the part concerned exceeds, by at least 30 per cent, the total amount of benefits which would be obtained by applying the provisions of Article 66 and the provisions of:

(i) Article 15 (b) for Part III;
(ii) Article 27 (b) for Part V;
(iii) Article 55 (b) for Part IX;
(iv) Article 61 (b) for Part X. . . .

Part XII
Common Provisions

Article 68. A benefit to which a person protected would otherwise be entitled in compliance with any of Parts II to X of this Code may be suspended to such extent as may be prescribed:

(a) as long as the person concerned is absent from the territory of the Contracting Party concerned;

(b) as long as the person concerned is maintained at public expense, or at the expense of a social security institution or service, subject to a portion of the benefit being granted to the dependents of the beneficiary;

(c) as long as the person concerned is in receipt of another social security cash benefit, other than a family benefit, and during any period in respect of which he is indemnified for the contingency by a third party, subject to the part of the benefit which is suspended not exceeding the other benefit or the indemnity by a third party;

(d) where the person concerned has made a fraudulent claim;

(e) where the contingency has been caused by a criminal offence committed by the person concerned;

(f) where the contingency has been caused by the wilful misconduct of the person concerned;

(g) in appropriate cases, where the person concerned neglects to make use of the medical or rehabilitation services placed at his disposal or fails to comply with rules prescribed for verifying the occurrence or continuance of the contingency or for the conduct of the beneficiaries;

(h) in the case of unemployment benefit, where the person concerned has failed to make use of the employment services placed at his disposal;

(i) in the case of unemployment benefit, where the person concerned has lost his employment as a direct result of a stoppage of work due to a trade dispute, or has left it voluntarily without just cause; and

(j) in the case of survivors' benefit, as long as the widow is living with a man as his wife.

Article 69. 1. Every claimant shall have a right of appeal in case of refusal of the benefit or complaint as to its quality or quantity.

2. Where in the application of this Code a government department responsible to a legislature is entrusted with the administration of medical care, the right of appeal provided for in paragraph 1 of this article may be replaced by a right to have a complaint concerning the refusal of medical care or the quality of the care received investigated by the appropriate authority.

3. Where a claim is settled by a special tribunal established to deal with social security questions and on which the persons protected are represented, no right of appeal shall be required.

Article 70. 1. The cost of the benefits provided in compliance with this Code and the cost of the administration of such benefits shall be borne collectively by way of insurance contributions or taxation or both in a manner which avoids hardship to persons of small means and takes into account the economic situation of the Contracting Party concerned and of the classes of persons protected.

2. The total of the insurance contributions borne by the employees protected shall not exceed 50 per cent of the total of the financial resources allocated to the protection of employees and their wives and children. For the purpose of ascertaining whether this condition is fulfilled, all the benefits provided by the Contracting Party concerned in compliance with this Code, except family benefit and, if provided by a special branch, employment injury benefit, may be taken together.

3. The Contracting Party concerned shall accept general responsibility for the due provision of the benefits provided in compliance with this Code, and shall take all measures required for this purpose; it shall ensure, where appropriate, that the necessary actuarial studies and calculations concerning financial equilibrium are made periodically and, in any event, prior to any change in benefits, the rate of insurance contributions, or the taxes allocated to covering the contingencies in question.

Article 71. 1. Where the administration is not entrusted to a government department responsible to a legislature, representatives of the persons protected shall participate in the management, or be associated therewith in a consultative capacity, under prescribed conditions; national laws or regulations may likewise decide as to the participation of representatives of employers and of the public authorities.

2. The Contracting Party concerned shall accept general responsibility for the proper administration of the institutions and services concerned in the application of this Code.

Part XIII
Miscellaneous Provisions

Article 72. This Code shall not apply to:

(a) contingencies which occurred before the coming into force of the relevant part of the Code for the Contracting Party concerned.

(b) benefits in contingencies occurring after the coming into force of the relevant part of the Code for the Contracting Party concerned in so far as the rights to such benefits are derived from periods preceding that date.

Article 73. The Contracting Parties shall endeavour to conclude a special instrument governing questions relating to social security for foreigners and migrants, particularly with regard to equality of treatment with their own nationals and to the maintenance of acquired rights and rights in course of acquisition.

Article 74. 1. Each Contracting Party shall submit to the Secretary General an annual report concerning the application of this Code. This report shall include:

(a) full information concerning the laws and regulations by which effect is given to the provisions of this Code covered by the ratification; and

(b) evidence of compliance with the statistical conditions specified in:

(i) Articles 9 (a),(b) or (c); 15 (a) or (b); 21 (a); 27 (a) or (b); 33; 41 (a) or (b); 48 (a) or (b); 55 (a) or (b); 61 (a) or (b); as regards the number of persons protected;

(ii) Articles 44, 65, 66, or 67, as regards the rates of benefit;

(iii) Article 24, paragraph 2, as regards duration of unemployment benefit; and

(iv) Article 70, paragraph 2, as regards the proportion of the financial resources constituted by the insurance contributions of employees protected.

Such evidence shall as far as possible be presented in such general order and manner as may be suggested by the committee.

2. Each Contracting Party shall furnish to the Secretary General, if so requested by him, further information of the manner in which it has implemented the provisions of the Code covered by its ratification.

3. The Committee of Ministers may authorise the Secretary General to transmit to the Consultative Assembly copies of the report and further information submitted in accordance with paragraphs 1 and 2 of this article respectively.

4. The Secretary General shall send to the Director General of the International Labour Office the report and further information submitted in accordance with paragraphs 1 and 2 of this article respectively, and shall request the latter to consult the appropriate body of the International Labour Organisation with regard to the said report and further information and to transmit to the Secretary General the conclusions reached by such body.

5. Such report and further information and the conclusions of the body of the International Labour Organisation referred to in paragraph 4 of this article shall be examined by the committee which shall submit to the Committee of Ministers a report containing its conclusions.

Article 75. 1. After consulting the Consultative Assembly, if it considers it appropriate, the Committee of Ministers shall, by a two-thirds majority in accordance with Article 20, paragraph (d) of the Statute of the Council of Europe, decide whether each Contracting Party has complied with the obligations of this Code which it has accepted.

2. If the Committee of Ministers considers that a Contracting Party is not complying with its obligations under this Code, it shall invite the said Contracting Party to take such measures as the Committee of Ministers considers necessary to ensure such compliance.

Article 76. Each Contracting Party shall report every two years to the Secretary General on the state of its law and practice in regard to any of Parts II to X of the Code which such Contracting Party has not specified in its ratification of the Code pursuant to Article 3 or in a notification made subsequently pursuant to Article 4.

Part XIV
Final Provisions

Article 77. 1. This Code shall be open to signature by the member States of the Council of Europe. It shall be subject to ratification. Instruments of ratification shall be deposited with the Secretary General, provided that the Committee of Ministers in appropriate cases has previously given an affirmative decision as provided for in Article 78, paragraph 4.

2. This Code shall enter into force one year after the date of the deposit of the third instrument of ratification.

3. As regards any Signatory ratifying subsequently, this Code shall enter into force one year after the date of deposit of its instruments of ratification.

Article 78. 1. Any Signatory wishing to avail itself of the provisions of Article 2, paragraph 2, shall, before ratification, submit to the Secretary General a report showing to what extent its system of Social Security is in conformity with the provisions of this Code.

Such report shall include a statement of:

(a) the relevant laws and regulations; and

(b) evidence of compliance with the statistical conditions specified in:

(i) Articles 9 (a), (b) or (c); 15 (a) or (b); 21 (a); 27 (a) or (b); 33; 41 (a) or (b); 48 (a) or (b); 55 (a) or (b); 61 (a) or (b), as regards the number of persons protected;

(ii) Articles 44, 65, 66 or 67, as regards the rates of benefits;

(iii) Article 24, paragraph 2, as regards duration of unemployment benefit; and

(iv) Article 70, paragraph 2, as regards the proportion of the financial resources constituted by the insurance contributions of employees protected; and

(c) all elements which the Signatory wishes to be taken into account, in accordance with Article 2, paragraphs 2 and 3.

Such evidence shall, as far as possible, be presented in such general order and manner as may be suggested by the committee.

2. The Signatory shall furnish to the Secretary General, if so requested by him, further information on the manner in which its system of Social Security is in conformity with the provisions of this Code.

3. Such report and further information shall be examined by the committee which shall take into account the provisions of Article 2, paragraph 3. The committee shall submit to the Committee of Ministers a report containing its conclusions.

4. The Committee of Ministers shall, by a two-thirds majority in accordance with Article 20, paragraph (d) of the Statute of the Council of Europe, decide whether the system of Social Security of such Signatory is in conformity with the requirements of this Code.

5. If the Committee of Ministers decides that the said Social Security scheme is not in conformity with the provisions of this Code, it shall so inform the Signatory concerned and may make recommendations as to how such conformity may be effected.

Article 79. 1. After the entry into force of this Code, the Committee of Ministers may invite any non-member State of the Council of Europe to accede to the Code. The accession of such State shall be subject to the same conditions and procedure as laid down in the Code with regard to ratification.

2. A State shall accede to this Code by depositing an instrument of accession with the Secretary General. The Code shall come into force for any State so acceding one year after the date of deposit of its instrument of accession.

3. The obligation and rights of an acceding State shall be the same as those provided for in this Code for a Signatory which has ratified the Code.

Article 80. 1. This Code shall apply to the metropolitan territory of each Contracting Party. Each Contracting Party may, at the time of signature or of the deposit of its instrument of ratification or accession, specify, by declaration addressed to the Secretary General, the territory which shall be considered to be its metropolitan territory for this purpose.

2. Each Contracting Party ratifying the Code or each acceding State may, at the time of deposit of its instrument of ratification or accession, or at any time thereafter, notify the Secretary General that this Code shall, in whole or in part and subject to any modifications specified in the notification, extend to any part of its metropolitan territory not specified under paragraph 1 of this article or to any of the other territories for whose international relations it is responsible. Modifications specified in such notification may be cancelled or amended by subsequent notification.

3. Any Contracting Party may, at such time as it can denounce the Code in accordance with Article 81, notify the Secretary General that the Code shall cease to apply to any part of its metropolitan territory or to any of the other territories to which the Code has been extended by it in accordance with paragraph 2 of this article.

Article 81. Each Contracting Party may denounce the Code or any one or more of Parts II to X thereof only at the end of a period of five years from the date on which the Code entered into force for such Contracting Party, or at the end of any successive period of five years, and in each case after giving one year's notice to the Secretary General. Such denunciation shall not affect the validity of the Code in respect of the other Contracting Parties, provided that at all times there are not less than three such Contracting Parties.

Article 82. The Secretary General shall notify the member States of the Council of Europe, the government of any acceding State and the Director General of the International Labour Office:

(i) of the date of entry into force of this Code and the names of any Members who ratify it;

(ii) of the deposit of any instrument of accession in accordance with Article 79 and of such notifications as are received with it;

(iii) of any notification received in accordance with Articles 4 and 80; or

(iv) of any notice received in accordance with Article 81.

Article 83. The Annex to this Code shall form a integral part of it.

In witness whereof the undersigned, being duly authorised thereto, have signed this Protocol.

Done at Strasbourg, this 16th day of April 1964, in French and English, both texts being equally authoritative, in a single copy which shall remain deposited in the archives of the Council of Europe, and of which the Secretary General shall send certified copies to each of the signatory and acceding States and to the Director General of the International Labour Office.

European Code of Social Security: Protocol

Preamble

The member States of the Council of Europe, signatory hereto,

Being resolved to establish a higher level of social security than that provided for in the provisions of the European Code of Social Security signed at Strasbourg on the 16th April 1964 (hereinafter referred to as "the Code");

Desirous that all member States of the Council should strive to achieve such higher level, with due regard to economic considerations in their respective countries,

Have agreed on the following provisions which have been prepared with the collaboration of the International Labour Office:

Section I

In respect of any member State of the Council of Europe which has ratified the Code and the Protocol thereto, and in respect of any State which has acceded to both these Acts, the following provisions shall replace the corresponding articles, paragraphs and sub-paragraphs of the Code:

Article 1, paragraph 1, sub-paragraph (h), shall read:
The term "child" means:

(i)) a child under 16 years of age; or

(ii) a child under school-leaving age or under 15 years of age, as may be prescribed, provided that in the case of a child continuing its education, apprenticed or invalid, it shall mean a child under 18 years of age;

Article 2, paragraph 1, sub-paragraph (b), shall read:

(b) At least eight of these Parts II to X for which the member State concerned has accepted the obligations of the Code in virtue of Article 3, provided that Part II shall count as two parts and Part V as three parts;

Article 2, paragraph 2, shall read:

2. The terms of sub-paragraph (b) of the foregoing paragraph can be regarded as fulfilled if:

(a) At least six of those Parts II to X for which the member State concerned has accepted the obligations of the Code in virtue of Article 3, including at least one of Parts IV, V, VI, IX, and X are complied with; and

(b) in addition, proof is furnished that the social security legislation in force is equivalent to one of the combinations provided for in that sub-paragraph, taking into account:

(i) the fact that certain branches covered by sub-paragraph (a) of this paragraph exceed the standards of the Code in respect of their scope of protection or their level of benefits, or both;

(ii) the fact that certain branches covered by sub-paragraph (a) of this paragraph exceed the standards of the Code by granting supplementary services of advantages listed in Addendum 2 to the Code as modified by the Protocol; and

(iii) branches which do not attain the standards of the Code.

Article 9 shall read:
The persons protected shall comprise:

(a) prescribed classes of employees, constituting not less than 80 per cent of all employees, and also their wives and children; or

(b) prescribed classes of the economically active population, constituting not less than 30 per cent of all residents, and also their wives and children; or

(c) prescribed classes of residents, constituting not less than 65 per cent of all residents.

Article 10, paragraphs 1 and 2, shall read:

1. The benefit shall include at least:

(a) in the case of a morbid condition:

(i) care by general practitioners, including domiciliary visiting, and care by specialists in accordance with prescribed conditions;

(ii) hospital care including maintenance, care by general practitioners or specialists as required, nursing and all auxiliary services required;

(iii) all necessary non-proprietary pharmaceutical supplies and proprietary preparations regarded as essential; and

(iv) conservative dental care for the children protected; and

(b) in the case of pregnancy, confinement and their consequences;

(i) pre-natal, confinement and post-natal care either by medical practitioners or by qualified midwives;

(ii) hospitalisation where necessary; and

(iii) pharmaceutical supplies.

2. The beneficiary or his breadwinner may be required to share in the costs of the medical care which the beneficiary receives:

(a) in case of morbid condition, provided that the rules concerning such cost-sharing shall be so designed as to avoid hardship, and that the part of the cost paid by the beneficiary or breadwinner shall not exceed:

(i) for care by general practitioners and specialists outside hospital wards: 25 per cent;

(ii) for hospital care: 25 per cent;

(iii) for pharmaceutical supplies: 25 per cent on the average;

(iv) for conservative dental care: 33 1/3 per cent;

(b) in case of pregnancy, confinement and their consequences, in respect of pharmaceutical supplies only for which the part of the cost paid by the patient or breadwinner shall not exceed 25 per cent on the average; the rules concerning such cost-sharing shall be so designed as to avoid hardship;

(c) where cost-sharing takes the form of a fixed sum is respect of each case or course of treatment or each prescription of pharmaceutical supplies, the total of such payments made by all persons protected in respect of any one of the types of care referred to in sub-paragraphs (a) or (b) shall not exceed the specified percentage of the total cost of that type of care within a given period.

Article 12 shall read:
The benefits specified in Article 10 shall be granted throughout the contingency covered, except that hospital care may be limited to 52 weeks in each case or to 78 weeks in any consecutive period of three years.

Article 15, paragraphs (a) and (b), shall read:
The persons protected shall comprise:

(a) prescribed classes of employees, constituting not less than 80 per cent of all employees; or

(b) prescribed classes of the economically active population constituting not less than 30 per cent of all residents; or

Article 18 shall read:

The benefit specified in Article 16 shall be granted throughout the contingency, except that it need not be paid for the first three days of suspension of earnings and may be limited to 52 weeks in each case of sickness or to 78 weeks in any consecutive period of three years.

Article 21, paragraph (a), shall read:

The persons protected shall comprise:

(a) prescribed classes of employees constituting not less than 55 per cent of all employees; or

Article 24 shall read:

1. Where classes of employees are protected, the duration of the benefits specified in Article 22 may be limited to 21 weeks within a period of 12 months, or to 21 weeks in each case of suspension of earnings.

2. Where all residents whose means during the contingency do not exceed prescribed limits are protected, the benefit specified in Article 22 shall be granted throughout the contingency. Provided that the duration of the prescribed benefit guaranteed without a means test may be limited in accordance with paragraph 1 of this article.

3. Where national laws or regulations provide that the duration of the benefit shall vary with the length of the contribution period and/or the benefit it previously received within a prescribed period, the provisions of paragraph 1 shall be deemed to be fulfilled if the average duration of benefit is at least 21 weeks within a period of 12 months.

4. The benefit need not be paid:

(a) for the first three days in each case of suspension of earnings, counting the days of unemployment before and after temporary employment lasting not more than a prescribed period as part of the same case of suspension of earnings; or

(b) for the first six days within a period of twelve months.

5. In the case of seasonal workers, the duration of the benefit and the waiting period may be adapted to their conditions of employment.

6. Measures shall be taken to maintain a high and stable level of employment in the country, and appropriate facilities shall be provided to assist unemployed persons to obtain suitable new work including placement services, vocational training courses, assistance in their transfer to another district when necessary to find suitable employment, and related services.

Article 26, paragraphs 2 and 3, shall read:

2. The prescribed age shall be not more than 65 years of age or than such higher age that the number of residents having attained that age is not less than 10 per cent of the number of residents under that age but over 15 years. Provided that, where prescribed classes of employees only are protected, the prescribed age shall be not more than 65 years.

3. National laws or regulations may provide that the benefit of a person otherwise entitled to it may be suspended if he is engaged in any prescribed gainful activity, or that the benefit, if contributory, may be reduced whenever the earnings of the beneficiary exceed a prescribed amount.

Article 27, paragraphs (a) and (b), shall read:

The persons protected shall comprise:

(a) prescribed classes of employees, constituting not less than 80 per cent of all employees; or

(b) prescribed classes of the economically active population, constituting not less than 30 per cent of all residents; or

Article 28, paragraph (b), shall read:

(b) where all residents whose means during the contingency do not exceed prescribed limits are protected, in such a manner as to comply with the requirements of Article 67. Provided that a prescribed benefit shall be guaranteed without means tests to the prescribed classes of persons determined in accordance with sub-paragraphs (a) or (b) of Article 27, subject to qualifying conditions not more stringent than those specified in paragraph 1 of Article 29.

Article 32, paragraph (d), shall read:

(d) the loss of support suffered by the widow or child as the result of the death of the breadwinner.

Article 33 shall read:

The persons protected shall comprise prescribed classes of employees constituting not less than 80 per cent of all employees and, for the benefit in respect of the death of the breadwinner, also their wives and children.

Article 41 shall read:

The persons protected shall comprise, in so far as periodical payments are concerned:

(a) prescribed classes of employees, constituting not less than 80 per cent of all employees; or

(b) prescribed classes of the economically active population, constituting not less than 30 per cent of all residents.

Article 44 shall read:

The total value of the benefits granted in accordance with Article 42 shall be such as to represent 2 per cent of the wage of an ordinary adult male labourer as determined in accordance with the rules laid down in Article 66 multiplied by the total number of children of all residents.

Article 48 shall read:

The persons protected shall comprise:

(a) all women in prescribed classes of employees, which classes constitute not less than 80 per cent of all employees, and, for maternity medical benefit, also the wives of men in these classes; or

(b) all women in prescribed classes of the economically active population, which classes constitute not less than 30 per cent of all residents, and, for maternity medical benefit, also the wives of men in these classes.

Article 49, paragraph 2, shall read:

2. The medical care shall include at least:

(a) pre-natal, confinement and post-natal care, either by medical practitioners or by qualified midwives;

(b) hospitalisation where necessary; and

(c) pharmaceutical supplies; the patient or her breadwinner may be required to share in the cost of the pharmaceutical supplies the beneficiary receives. The rules concerning such cost-sharing shall be so designed as to avoid hardship, and the part of the cost paid by the beneficiary or breadwinner shall not exceed 25 per cent on the average. Where cost-sharing takes the form of a fixed sum in respect of each prescription, the total of such payments made by all persons protected shall not exceed 25 per cent of the total cost within a given period.

Article 54 shall read:

The contingency covered shall include inability to engage in any gainful occupation to an extent prescribed, which inability is likely to be permanent or to persist after the exhaustion of sickness benefit. Provided that the prescribed extent of such inability shall not exceed two-thirds.

Article 55, paragraphs (a) and (b), shall read:

The persons protected shall comprise:

(a) prescribed classes of employees, constituting not less than 80 per cent of all employees; or

(b) prescribed classes of the economically active population, constituting not less than 30 per cent of all residents; or

Article 56 shall read:

1. The benefit shall be a periodical payment calculated as follows:

(a) where classes of employees or classes of the economically active population are protected, in such a manner as to comply either with the requirements of Article 65 or with the requirements of Article 66;

(b) where all residents whose means during the contingency do not exceed prescribed limits are protected, in such a manner as to comply with the requirements of Article 67. Provided that a prescribed benefit shall be guaranteed without a means test to the prescribed classes of persons determined in accordance with sub-paragraphs (a) or (b) of Article 55, subject to qualifying conditions not more stringent than those specified in paragraph 1 of Article 57.

2. Measures shall be taken to provide for functional and vocational rehabilitation services, and to maintain appropriate facilities to assist handicapped persons in obtaining suitable work, including placement services, assistance in helping them transfer to another district when necessary to find suitable employment, and related services.

Article 61, paragraphs (a) and (b), shall read:

The persons protected shall comprise:

(a) the wives and children of breadwinners in prescribed classes of employees, which classes constitute not less than 80 per cent of all employees; or

(b) the wives and children of breadwinners in prescribed classes of the economically active population, which classes constitute not less than 30 per cent of all residents; or

Article 62, paragraph (b), shall read:

(b) where all resident widows and resident children whose means during the contingency do not exceed prescribed limits are protected, in such a manner as to comply with the requirements of Article 67. Provided that a prescribed benefit shall be guaranteed without a means test to the wives and children of breadwinners in the prescribed classes of persons determined in accordance with sub-paragraphs (a) or (b) of Article 61, subject to qualifying conditions not more stringent than those specified in paragraph 1 of Article 63. . . .

Article 74, paragraphs 1 and 2, shall read:

1. Each member State which has ratified the Code and this Protocol shall submit to the Secretary General an annual report concerning the application of these Acts. This report shall include:

(a) full information concerning the laws and regulations by which effect is given to the provisions of these Acts covered by the ratification; and

(b) evidence of compliance with the statistical conditions specified in:

(i) Articles 9 (a), (b) or (c); 15 (a) or (b); 21 (a); 27 (a) or (b); 33; 41 (a) or (b); 48 (a) or (b); 55 (a) or (b); 61 (a) or (b); as regards the number of persons protected;

(ii) Articles 44, 65, 66 or 67, as regards the rates of benefit;

(iii) Article 24, paragraph 2, as regards duration of unemployment benefit; and

(iv) Article 70, paragraph 2, as regards the proportion of the financial resources constituted by the insurance contributions of employees protected.

Such evidence shall as far as possible be presented in such general order and manner as may be suggested by the committee.

2. Each member State which has ratified the Code and this Protocol shall furnish to the Secretary General, if so requested by him, further information of the manner in which it has implemented the provisions of these Acts covered by its ratification.

Article 75 shall read:

1. After consulting the Consultative Assembly, if it considers it appropriate, the Committee of Ministers shall, by a two-thirds majority in accordance with Article 20, paragraph (d) of the Statute of the Council of Europe, decide whether each member State which has ratified the Code and this Protocol has complied with the obligations of the Code and the Protocol that it has accepted.

2. If the Committee of Ministers considers that a member State which has ratified the Code and this Protocol is not complying with its obligations under these Acts, it shall invite the said member State to take such measures as the Committee of Ministers considers necessary to ensure such compliance.

Article 76 shall read:

Each member State which has ratified the Code and this Protocol shall report every two years to the Secretary General on the state of its law and practice in regard to any of Parts II to X of the Code and the Protocol thereto which such Member has not specified in its ratification of the Code and the Protocol in virtue of Article 3 or in a notification made subsequently in virtue of Article 4.

Article 79 shall read:

1. After the entry into force of this Protocol, the Committee of Ministers may invite any State not being a Member of the Council of Europe to accede to the Protocol. The accession of such State shall be subject to the same conditions and procedure as laid down in the Protocol with regard to ratification.

2. A State shall accede to this Protocol by depositing an instrument of accession with the Secretary General. This Protocol shall come into force for any State so acceding one year after the date of deposit of its instrument of accession.

3. The obligations and rights of an acceding State shall be the same as those provided for in this Protocol for member States which have ratified the Protocol.

Article 80 shall read:

1. The Code and/or this Protocol shall apply to the metropolitan territory of each member State for which it is in force and of each acceding State. Each member State or each acceding State may, at the time of signature or of the deposit of its instrument of ratification or accession, specify, by declaration addressed to the Secretary General, the territory which shall be considered to be its metropolitan territory for this purpose.

2. Each member State ratifying the Code and/or this

Protocol or each acceding State may, at the time of deposit of its instrument of ratification or accession, or at any time thereafter, notify the Secretary General that the Code and/or this Protocol shall, in whole or in part and subject to any modifications specified in the notification, extend to any part of its metropolitan territory not specified under paragraph 1 of this article or to any of the other territories for whose international relations it is responsible. Modifications specified in such notification may be cancelled or amended by subsequent notification.

3. Any member State for which the Code or the Code and this Protocol is in force or any acceding State may, at such time as it can denounce the Code and/or this Protocol in accordance with Article 81, notify the Secretary General that the Code and/or the Protocol shall cease to apply to any part of its metropolitan territory or to any of the other territories to which the Code and/or the Protocol has been extended by it in accordance with paragraph 2 of this article.

Article 81 shall read:

Each member State which has ratified the Code and this Protocol and each State which has acceded to them may denounce the Code and the Protocol or only the Protocol or any one or more of Parts II to X of these Acts only at the end of a period of five years from the date on which the Code and/or the Protocol thereto entered into force respectively for such a member State or acceding State, or at the end of any successive period of five years, and in each case after giving one year's notice to the Secretary General. Such denunciation shall not affect the validity of the Code and/or of the Protocol in respect of the other member States which have ratified them or in respect of the other States which have acceded to them, provided that at all times there are not less than three such member States or acceding States Parties to the Code and not less than three such member States or acceding States Parties to the Protocol.

Article 82 shall read:

The Secretary General shall notify the member States of the Council, the government of any acceding State and the Director General of the International Labour Office:

(i) of the date of entry into force of this Protocol and the names of any member States who ratify it;

(ii) of the deposit of any instrument of accession in accordance with Article 79 and of such notifications as are received with it;

(iii) of any notification received in accordance with Articles 4 and 80; and

(iv) of any notice received in accordance with Article 81.

Section II

1. No member State of the Council of Europe shall sign or ratify this Protocol without having simultaneously or previously signed or ratified the European Code of Social Security.

2. No State shall accede to this Protocol without having simultaneously or previously acceded to the European Code of Social Security.

Section III

1. This Protocol shall be open to signature by the member States. It shall be subject to ratification. Instruments of ratification shall be deposited with the Secretary General, provided that the Committee of Ministers in appropriate cases has previously given an affirmative decision as provided for in Section IV, paragraph 4.

2. This Protocol shall enter into force one year after the date of the deposit of the third instrument of ratification.

3. As regards any Signatory ratifying subsequently, this Protocol shall enter into force one year after the date of deposit of its instrument of ratification.

Section IV

1. Any Signatory wishing to avail itself of the provisions of Article 2, paragraph 2 of the Code as amended by the Protocol shall, before ratification, submit to the Secretary General a report showing to what extent its system of social security is in conformity with the provisions of this Protocol.

Such report shall include a statement of:

(a) the relevant laws and regulations; and

(b) evidence of compliance with the statistical conditions specified in the following provisions of the Code as amended by this Protocol:

(i) Articles 9 (a), (b) or (c); 15 (a) or (b); 21(a); 27(a) or (b); 33; 41 (a) or (b); 48 (a) or (b); 55 (a) or (b); 61 (a) or (b), as regards the number of persons protected;

(ii) Articles 44, 65, 66 or 67, as regards the rates of benefit;

(iii) Article 24, paragraph 2, as regards duration of unemployment benefit; and

(iv) Article 70, paragraph 2, as regards the proportion of the financial resources constituted by the insurance contributions of employees protected; and

(c) all elements which the Signatory wishes to be taken into account, in accordance with Article 2, paragraphs 2 and 3 of the Code as amended by this Protocol.

Such evidence shall, as far as possible, be presented in such general order and manner as may be suggested by the committee.

2. The Signatory shall furnish to the Secretary General, if so requested by him, further information on the manner in which its system of social security is in conformity with the provisions of this Protocol.

3. Such report and further information shall be examined by the committee which shall take into account the provisions of Article 2, paragraph 3 of the Code. The committee shall submit to the Committee of Ministers a report containing its conclusions.

4. The Committee of Ministers shall, by a two-thirds majority in accordance with Article 20, paragraph *(d)* of the Statute of the Council of Europe, decide whether the system of social security of such Signatory is in conformity with the requirements of this Protocol.

5. If the Committee of Ministers decides that the said social security scheme is not in conformity with the provisions of this Protocol, it shall so inform the Signatory concerned and may make recommendations as to how such conformity may be effected.

In witness whereof the undersigned, being duly authorised thereto, have signed this Protocol.

Done at Strasbourg, this 16th day of April 1964, in French and English, both texts being equally authoritative, in a single copy which shall remain deposited in the archives of the Council of Europe, and of which the Secretary General shall send certified copies to each of the signatory and acceding States and to the Director General of the International Labour Office.

Addendum 2

Addendum 2 Shall Read:

Supplementary Services or Advantages

Part II
Medical Care

1. Medical supervision or treatment as required, maintenance, nursing and other auxiliary services in convalescent homes, spas, and preventoria and similar institutions for the prevention of tuberculosis, provided that the beneficiary or his breadwinner may be required to share in the cost of the care received to the extent of one-third.

2. Conservative dental care for all persons protected, provided that the beneficiary or his breadwinner may be required to share in the cost of the care received to the extent of 25 per cent except in the case of children and expectant mothers.

3. Dental prostheses, provided that the beneficiary or his breadwinner may be required to share in the cost of the prostheses supplied to the extent of one-half.

4. Hospital care, including maintenance, care by general practitioners or specialists, as required, nursing and all auxiliary services required, without limit of duration.

5. Home nursing and domestic aid, provided that the beneficiary or his breadwinner may be required to share in the cost of the care received to an extent that will not involve hardship.

6. Eye-glasses, provided that the beneficiary or his breadwinner may be required to share in the cost of the eye-glasses supplied to the extent of one-half.

7. Hearing aids, provided that the beneficiary or his breadwinner may be required to share in the cost of the hearing aids supplied to the extent of one-half.

8. Artificial limbs and other major medical or surgical supplies, provided that the beneficiary or his breadwinner may be required to share in the cost of the supplies received to the extent of one-half.

9. Where cost-sharing takes the form of a fixed sum in respect of each case of treatment or each prescription of supplies, the total of such payments made by all persons protected in respect of any one of the types of care referred to in items 1, 2, 3, 5, 6, 7 or 8 shall not exceed the specified percentage of the total cost of that type of care within a given period.

10. The provision of medical care to the extent stipulated in Article 10 of the Code as amended by this Protocol, without qualifying period.

Part III
Sickness Benefit

11. Sickness benefit at a rate not lower than the specified in Article 16 of the Code, without limit of duration.

Part IV
Unemployment Benefit

12. Unemployment benefit at a rate not lower than that specified in Article 22 of the Code, without limit of duration, where recourse is had to Article 21 (a) of the Code as amended by the Protocol for the purpose of ratification.

13. Benefits for workers who are unable to claim the right to them under the normal provisions of the law or who have exceeded the period during which benefits are normally paid.

Part V
Old-age Benefit

14. Old-age benefit at a rate of at least 50 per cent of the benefit specified in Article 28 of the Code as amended by this Protocol:

(a) under paragraph 2 of Article 29 of the Code or where the benefit specified in Article 28 of the Code as amended by this Protocol is conditional upon a period of residence, and the Member does not avail itself of paragraph 3 of Article 29 of the Code, after ten years of residence; and

(b) under paragraph 5 of Article 29 of the Code, subject to prescribed conditions regarding the previous economic activity of the person protected.

Part VI
Employment Injury Benefit

15. Vocational rehabilitation for victims of employment injury.

16. Periodical payments to the ascendants of a breadwinner protected, in case of death due to employment injury of the breadwinner, amounting to not less than 20 per cent of the previous earnings of the breadwinner or of the wage of the ordinary adult male labourer, calculated in such a manner as to comply with the requirements of Article 65 or with the requirements of Article 66 of the Code, as the case may be, provided that the periodical payments need not exceed the amount that was contributed by the breadwinner towards the maintenance of the ascendants.

17. Periodical payments to the survivors of a breadwinner protected, in case of death not due to employment injury, where the breadwinner was in receipt of a pension in respect of total serious loss of earning capacity; such payments to survivors shall be in conformity with the requirements of the relevant provisions of the Code as amended by this Protocol.

Part VIII
Maternity Benefit

18. A birth grant or grants, or a periodical payment during the nursing of the child by the mother.

19. Periodical payments, in accordance with the relevant provisions of the Code as amended by this Protocol, for the dependent wives of men in the classes protected, amounting to at least 50 per cent of the benefit specified in Article 50 of the Code as amended by this Protocol.

20. Provision of maternity benefit without qualifying period.

Part IX
Invalidity Benefit

21. Invalidity benefit as a rate of at least 50 per cent of the benefit specified in Article 56 of the Code as amended by this Protocol:

(a) under paragraph 2 of Article 57 of the Code or, where the benefit specified in Article 56 of the Code as amended by this Protocol is conditional upon a period of residence, and the Member does not avail itself of paragraph 3 of Article 57 of the Code, after five years of residence; and

(b) for a person protected who, by reason only of his advanced age when the provisions concerned in the application of this part as amended by this Protocol come into force, has not satisfied the conditions prescribed in accordance with paragraph 2 of Article 57 of the Code, subject to prescribed conditions regarding the previous economic activity of the person protected.

22. Vocational rehabilitation for invalids.

Part X
Survivors' Benefit

23. Survivors' benefit at a rate of at least 30 per cent of the benefit specified in Article 62 of the Code as amended by this Protocol:

(a) under paragraph 2 of Article 63 of the Code or, where the benefit specified in Article 62 of the Code as amended by this Protocol is conditional upon a period of residence, and the Member does not avail itself of paragraph 3 of Article 63 of the Code, after five years of residence;

(b) to the persons protected whose breadwinner had not satisfied the conditions prescribed in accordance with paragraph 2 of Article 63 of the Code, by reason only of his advanced age when the provisions concerned in the application of this part as amended by this Protocol come into force, subject to prescribed conditions regarding the previous economic activity of the breadwinner.

24. Periodical payments to the invalid widower who is indigent of a woman breadwinner protected, amounting to not less than 20 per cent of the previous earnings of the breadwinner or of the wage of the ordinary adult male labourer, calculated in such a manner as to comply with the requirements of Article 65 or with the requirements of Article 66 of the Code, as the case may be.

Parts II, III, VI or X

25. Funeral benefit for economically active persons protected amounting to:

(i) thirty times the daily previous earnings of the person protected which serve, or would have served, for the calculation of the sickness, employment injury or survivors' benefit, as the case may be, provided that the total benefit need not exceed thirty times the daily wage of the skilled male manual employee determined in accordance with the provisions of Article 65 of the Code; or

(ii) thirty times the daily wage of the ordinary adult male labourer, determined in accordance with the provisions of Article 66 of the Code.

Parts II or III

26. Funeral benefit for the dependent wives and children protected or for the dependent wives and children of the persons protected, amounting to:

(i) fifteen times the daily previous earnings of the breadwinner protected which serve for the calculation of sickness benefit, provided that the total benefit need not exceed fifteen times the daily wage of the skilled male manual employee determined in accordance with the provisions of Article 65 of the Code; or

(ii) fifteen times the daily wage of the ordinary adult male labourer determined in accordance with the provisions of Article 66 of the Code.

EUROPEAN COMMISSION ON HUMAN RIGHTS.
The European Commission on Human Rights of the COUNCIL OF EUROPE was established in 1955 in accordance with article 19 of the EUROPEAN CONVENTION ON HUMAN RIGHTS in order to ensure the observance of the engagements undertaken by States parties to that convention.

Under article 21 of the convention, any State party may refer to the commission, through the Secretary-General of the Council of Europe, any alleged breach of the provisions of the convention by another State party. Moreover, under article 25, the commission may receive petitions from any person, non-governmental organization, or group of individuals claiming to be the victim of a violation by one of the States parties of the rights set forth in the convention, provided that the State against which the complaint is lodged has declared that it recognizes the competence of the commission to receive such petitions. The commission's first task is to determine whether or not the petition is admissible under the provisions of the convention, dismissing those that are anonymous, manifestly unfounded, or abusive of the right of petition and those involving situations in which national remedies have not been exhausted. It must then investigate and ascertain the facts and place itself at the disposal of the parties concerned with a view to securing a friendly settlement of the problem. If such a settlement is achieved, the commission draws up a report and sends it to the parties concerned, the Committee of Ministers, and the Secretary-General of the Council of Europe for publication. If no settlement is reached, the commission draws up a detailed report outlining the facts and stating its opinion as to whether or not they disclose a breach of any obligation assumed under the convention. This report is transmitted to the parties concerned and to the Committee of Ministers together with such proposals as the commission may consider appropriate. The commission may also refer the matter to the European Court of Human Rights.

The commission consists of 21 members, that being the number of States members of the Council of Europe, all of which are parties to the convention. Members are elected by the Committee of Ministers on the basis of nominations submitted by members of the Consultative Committee of the Council. No two members of the commission may be nationals of the same State. All serve in their personal capacity for a term of four years. The commission usually holds five or six sessions per year, totalling about 60 session days, all at the headquarters of the Council of Europe in Strasbourg.

The commission has no permanent subsidiary bodies but usually establishes a sub-commission, composed of seven of its members, to assist it in the performances of its fact-finding and conciliation functions.

E

EUROPEAN CONVENTION FOR THE PREVENTION OF TORTURE AND INHUMAN OR DEGRADING TREATMENT OR PUNISHMENT (1987). The convention was concluded by the COMMITTEE OF MINISTERS OF THE COUNCIL OF EUROPE on 26 June 1987 and entered into force on 1 February 1989. The text of the Convention (*European Treaty Series* 126) is as follows:

Preamble

The member States of the Council of Europe, signatory hereto,

Having regard to the provisions of the Convention for the Protection of Human Rights and Fundamental Freedoms,

Recalling that, under Article 3 of the same Convention, "no one shall be subjected to torture or to inhuman or degrading treatment or punishment";

Noting that the machinery provided for in that Convention operates in relation to persons who allege that they are victims of violations of Article 3;

Convinced that the protection of persons deprived of their liberty against torture and inhuman or degrading treatment or punishment could be strengthened by non-judicial means of a preventive character based on visits,

Have agreed as follows:

Section I

Article 1. There shall be established a European Committee for the Prevention of Torture and Inhuman or Degrading Treatment or Punishment (hereinafter referred to as "the Committee"). The Committee shall, by means of visits, examine the treatment of persons deprived of their liberty with a view to strengthening, if necessary, the protection of such persons from torture and from inhuman or degrading treatment or punishment.

Article 2. Each Party shall permit visits, in accordance with this Convention, to any place within its jurisdiction where persons are deprived of their liberty by a public authority.

Article 3. In the application of this Convention, the Committee and the competent national authorities of the Party concerned shall co-operate with each other.

Section II

Article 4. 1. The Committee shall consist of a number of members equal to that of the Parties.

2. The members of the Committee shall be chosen from among persons of high moral character, known for their competence in the field of human rights or having professional experience in the areas covered by this Convention.

3. No two members of the Committee may be nationals of the same State.

4. The members shall serve in their individual capacity, shall be independent and impartial, and shall be available to serve the Committee effectively.

Article 5. 1. The members of the Committee shall be elected by the Committee of Ministers by an absolute majority of votes, from a list of names drawn up by the Bureau of the Consultative Assembly; each national delegation of the Parties in the Consultative Assembly shall put forward three candidates, of whom two at least shall be its nationals.

2. The same procedure shall be followed in filling casual vacancies.

3. The members of the Committee shall be elected for a period of four years. They may only be re-elected once. However, among the members elected at the first election, the terms of three members shall expire at the end of two years. The members whose terms are to expire at the end of the initial period of two years shall be chosen by lot by the Secretary General of the Council of Europe immediately after the first election has been completed.

Article 6. 1. The Committee shall meet in camera. A quorum shall be equal to the majority of its members. The decisions of the Committee shall be taken by a majority of the members present, subject to Article 10, paragraph 2.

2. The Committee shall draw up its own rules of procedure.

3. The Secretariat of the Committee shall be provided by the Secretary General of the Council of Europe.

Section III

Article 7. 1. The Committee shall organise visits to places referred to in Article 2. Apart from periodic visits, the Committee may organise such other visits as appear to it to be required in the circumstances.

2. As a general rule, the visits shall be carried out by at least two members of the Committee. The Committee may, if it considers it necessary, be assisted by experts and interpreters.

Article 8. 1. The Committee shall notify the Government of the Party concerned of its intention to carry out a visit. After such notification, it may at any time visit any place referred to in Article 2.

2. A Party shall provide the Committee with the following facilities to carry out its task:

a. access to its territory and the right to travel without restriction;

b. full information on the places where persons deprived of their liberty are being held;

c. unlimited access to any place where persons are deprived of their liberty, including the right to move inside such places without restriction;

d. other information available to the Party which is necessary for the Committee to carry out its task. In seeking such information, the Committee shall have regard to applicable rules of national law and professional ethics.

3. The Committee may interview in private persons deprived of their liberty.

4. The Committee may communicate freely with any person whom it believes can supply relevant information.

5. If necessary, the Committee may immediately communicate observations to the competent authorities of the Party concerned.

Article 9. 1. In exceptional circumstances, the competent authorities of the Party concerned may make representations to the Committee against a visit at the time or to the particular place proposed by the Committee. Such representations may only be made on grounds of national defence, public safety, serious disorder in places where persons are deprived of their liberty, the medical condition of a person or that an urgent interrogation relating to a serious crime is in progress.

2. Following such representations, the Committee and the Party shall immediately enter into consultations in order to clarify the situation and seek agreement on arrangements to enable the Committee to exercise its functions expeditiously. Such arrangements may include the transfer to another place of any person whom the Committee pro-

posed to visit. Until the visit takes place, the Party shall provide information to the Committee about any person concerned.

Article 10. 1. After each visit, the Committee shall draw up a report on the facts found during the visit, taking account of any observations which may have been submitted by the Party concerned. It shall transmit to the latter its report containing any recommendations it considers necessary. The Committee may consult with the Party with a view to suggesting, if necessary, improvements in the protection of persons deprived of their liberty.

2. If the Party fails to co-operate or refuses to improve the situation in the light of the Committee's recommendations, the Committee may decide, after the Party has had an opportunity to make known its views, by a majority of two-thirds of its members to make a public statement on the matter.

Article 11. 1. The information gathered by the Committee in relation to a visit, its report and its consultations with the Party concerned shall be confidential.

2. The Committee shall publish its report, together with any comments of the Party concerned, whenever requested to do so by that Party.

3. However, no personal data shall be published without the express consent of the person concerned.

Article 12. Subject to the rules of confidentiality in Article 11, the Committee shall every year submit to the Committee of Ministers a general report on its activities which shall be transmitted to the Consultative Assembly and made public.

Article 13. The members of the Committee, experts and other persons assisting the Committee are required, during and after their terms of office, to maintain the confidentiality of the facts or information of which they have become aware during the discharge of their functions.

Article 14. 1. The names of persons assisting the Committee shall be specified in the notification under Article 8, paragraph 1.

2. Experts shall act on the instructions and under the authority of the Committee. They shall have particular knowledge and experience in the areas covered by this Convention and shall be bound by the same duties of independence, impartiality and availability as the members of the Committee.

3. A Party may exceptionally declare that an expert or other person assisting the Committee may not be allowed to take part in a visit to a place within its jurisdiction.

Section IV

Article 15. Each Party shall inform the Committee of the name and address of the authority competent to receive notifications to its Government, and of any liaison officer it may appoint.

Article 16. The Committee, its members and experts referred to in Article 7, paragraph 2 shall enjoy the privileges and immunities set out in the Annex to this Convention.

Article 17. 1. This Convention shall not prejudice the provisions of domestic law or any international agreement which provide greater protection for persons deprived of their liberty.

2. Nothing in this Convention shall be construed as limiting or derogating from the competence of the organs of the European Convention on Human Rights or from the obligations assumed by the Parties under that Convention.

3. The Committee shall not visit places which representa-

tives or delegates of Protecting Powers or the International Committee of the Red Cross effectively visit on a regular basis by virtue of the Geneva Conventions of 12 August 1949 and the Additional Protocols of 8 June 1977 thereto.

Section V

Article 18. This Convention shall be open for signature by the member States of the Council of Europe. It is subject to ratification, acceptance or approval. Instruments of ratification, acceptance or approval shall be deposited with the Secretary General of the Council of Europe.

Article 19. 1. This Convention shall enter into force on the first day of the month following the expiration of a period of three months after the date on which seven member States of the Council of Europe have expressed their consent to be bound by the Convention in accordance with the provisions of Article 18.

2. In respect of any member State which subsequently expresses its consent to be bound by it, the Convention shall enter into force on the first day of the month following the expiration of a period of three months after the date of the deposit of the instrument of ratification, acceptance or approval.

Article 20. 1. Any State may at the time of signature or when depositing its instrument of ratification, acceptance or approval, specify the territory or territories to which this Convention shall apply.

2. Any State may at any later date, by a declaration addressed to the Secretary General of the Council of Europe, extend the application of this Convention to any other territory specified in the declaration. In respect of such territory the Convention shall enter into force on the first day of the month following the expiration of a period of three months after the date of receipt of such declaration by the Secretary General.

3. Any declaration made under the two preceding paragraphs may, in respect of any territory specified in such declaration, be withdrawn by a notification addressed to the Secretary General. The withdrawal shall become effective on the first day of the month following the expiration of a period of three months after the date of receipt of such notification by the Secretary General.

Article 21. No reservation may be made in respect of the provisions of this Convention.

Article 22. 1. Any Party may, at any time, denounce this Convention by means of a notification addressed to the Secretary General of the Council of Europe.

2. Such denunciation shall become effective on the first day of the month following the expiration of a period of twelve months after the date of receipt of the notification by the Secretary General.

Article 23. The Secretary General of the Council of Europe shall notify the member States of the Council of Europe of:

a. any signature;

b. the deposit of any instrument of ratification, acceptance or approval;

c. any date of entry into force of this Convention in accordance with Articles 19 and 20;

d. any other act, notification or communication relating to this Convention, except for action taken in pursuance of Articles 8 and 10.

In witness whereof, the undersigned, being duly authorised thereto, have signed this Convention.

Done at Strasbourg, this 26th day of November, 1987, in

E

English and French, both texts being equally authentic, in a single copy which shall be deposited in the archives of the Council of Europe. The Secretary General of the Council of Europe shall transmit certified copies to each member State of the Council of Europe.

Annex

Privileges and Immunities
(Article 16)

1. For the purpose of this annex, references to members of the Committee shall be deemed to include references to experts mentioned in Article 7, paragraph 2.

2. The members of the Committee shall, while exercising their functions and during journeys made in the exercise of their functions, enjoy the following privileges and immunities:

   a. immunity from personal arrest or detention and from seizure of their personal baggage and, in respect of words spoken or written and all acts done by them in their official capacity, immunity from legal process of every kind;

   b. exemption from any restrictions on their freedom of movement on exit from and return to their country of residence, and entry into and exit from the country in which they exercise their functions, and from alien registration in the country which they are visiting or through which they are passing in the exercise of their functions.

3. In the course of journeys undertaken in the exercise of their functions, the members of the Committee shall, in the matter of customs and exchange control, be accorded:

   a. by their own Government, the same facilities as those accorded to senior officials travelling abroad on temporary official duty;

   b. by the Governments of other Parties, the same facilities as those accorded to representatives of foreign Governments on temporary official duty.

4. Documents and papers of the Committee, in so far as they relate to the business of the Committee, shall be inviolable.

The official correspondence and other official communications of the Committee may not be held up or subjected to censorship.

5. In order to secure for the members of the Committee complete freedom of speech and complete independence in the discharge of their duties, the immunity from legal process in respect of words spoken or written and all acts done by them in discharging their duties shall continue to be accorded, notwithstanding that the persons concerned are no longer engaged in the discharge of such duties.

6. Privileges and immunities are accorded to the members of the Committee, not for the personal benefit of the individuals themselves but in order to safeguard the independent exercise of their functions. The Committee alone shall be competent to waive the immunity of its members; it has not only the right, but is under a duty, to waive the immunity of one of its members in any case where, in its opinion, the immunity would impede the course of justice, and where it can be waived without prejudice to the purpose for which the immunity is accorded.

SEE ALSO *Body of Principles for the Protection of All Persons under Any Form of Detention or Imprisonment; Convention against Torture and Other Cruel, Inhuman or Degrading Treatment or Punishment; Declaration on the Protection of All Persons from being Subjected to Torture and Other Cruel, Inhuman or Degrading Treatment or Punishment; Inter-American Convention to Prevent and Punish Torture; Torture.*

EUROPEAN CONVENTION FOR THE PROTECTION OF INDIVIDUALS WITH REGARD TO AUTOMATIC PROCESSING OF PERSONAL DATA (1981). States parties to this convention undertake to enact legislation and to take other necessary measures to ensure that data contained in automated personal data files are not disclosed to unauthorized persons. The convention sets out a series of basic principles designed to protect the right of privacy of the individual whose personal data are fed into such files. The principles regulate the procedures by which such data are obtained, preserved, revised, or corrected, and made available to others. In particular, they prohibit the processing of data revealing racial origin, political opinions, religious or other beliefs, or information concerning health or sexual life, unless domestic laws provide adequate safeguards against the disclosure of such information.

The convention was adopted by the COMMITTEE OF MINISTERS OF THE COUNCIL OF EUROPE, convened in Strasbourg, on 28 January 1981, and entered into force on 1 October 1985. The text (*European Treaty Series* 108) is as follows:

Preamble

The member States of the Council of Europe, signatory hereto,

Considering that the aim of the Council of Europe is to achieve greater unity between its members, based in particular on respect for the rule of law, as well as human rights and fundamental freedoms;

Considering that it is desirable to extend the safeguards for everyone's rights and fundamental freedoms, and in particular the right to the respect for privacy, taking account of the increasing flow across frontiers of personal data undergoing automatic processing;

Reaffirming at the same time their commitment to freedom or information regardless of frontiers;

Recognising that it is necessary to reconcile the fundamental values of the respect for privacy and the free flow of information between peoples,

Have agreed as follows:

Chapter I—General Provisions

Article 1. Object and Purpose. The purpose of this Convention is to secure in the territory of each Party for every individual, whatever his nationality or residence, respect for his rights and fundamental freedoms, and in particular his right to privacy, with regard to automatic processing of personal data relating to him ("data protection").

Article 2. Definitions. For the purposes of this Convention:

   (a) "personal data" means any information relating to an identified or identifiable individual ("data subject");

   (b) "automated data file" means any set of data undergoing automatic processing;

   (c) "automatic processing" includes the following operations if carried out in whole or in part by automated means: storage of data, carrying out of logical and/or arithmetical operations on those data, their alteration, erasure, retrieval or dissemination;

(d) "controller of the file" means the natural or legal person, public authority, agency or any other body who is competent according to the national law to decide what should be the purpose of the automated data file, which categories of personal data should be stored and which operations should be applied to them.

Article 3. Scope. 1. The Parties undertake to apply this Convention to automated personal data files and automatic processing of personal data in the public and private sectors.

2. Any State may, at the time of signature or when depositing its instrument of ratification, acceptance, approval or accession, or at any later time, give notice by a declaration addressed to the Secretary General of the Council of Europe:

(a) that it will not apply this Convention to certain categories of automated personal data files, a list of which will be deposited. In this list it shall not include, however, categories of automated data files subject under its domestic law to data protection provisions. Consequently, it shall amend this list by a new declaration whenever additional categories of automated personal data files are subjected to data protection provisions under its domestic law;

(b) that it will also apply this Convention to information relating to groups of persons, associations, foundations, companies, corporations and any other bodies consisting directly or indirectly of individuals, whether or not such bodies possess legal personality;

(c) that it will also apply this Convention to personal data files which are not processed automatically.

3. Any State which has extended the scope of this Convention by any of the declarations provided for in sub-paragraph 2 (b) or (c) above may give notice in the said declaration that such extensions shall apply only to certain categories of personal data files, a list of which will be deposited.

4. Any Party which has excluded certain categories of automated personal data files by a declaration provided for in sub-paragraph 2 (a) above may not claim the application of this Convention to such categories by a Party which has not excluded them.

5. Likewise, a Party which has not made one or other of the extensions provided for in sub-paragraphs 2 (b) and (c) above may not claim the application of this Convention on these points with respect to a Party which has made such extensions.

6. The declarations provided for in paragraph 2 above shall take effect from the moment of the entry into force of the Convention with regard to the State which has made them if they have been made at the time of signature or deposit of its instrument of ratification, acceptance, approval or accession, or three months after their receipt by the Secretary General of the Council of Europe if they have been made at any later time. These declarations may be withdrawn, in whole or in part, by a notification addressed to the Secretary General of the Council of Europe. Such withdrawals shall take effect three months after the date of receipt of such notification.

Chapter II—Basic Principles for Data Protection

Article 4. Duties of the Parties. 1. Each Party shall take the necessary measures in its domestic law to give effect to the basic principles for data protection set out in this chapter.

2. These measures shall be taken at the latest at the time of entry into force of this Convention in respect of that Party.

Article 5. Quality of Data. Personal data undergoing automatic processing shall be:

(a) obtained and processed fairly and lawfully;

(b) stored for specified and legitimate purposes and not used in a way incompatible with those purposes;

(c) adequate, relevant and not excessive in relation to the purposes for which they are stored;

(d) accurate and, where necessary, kept up to date;

(e) preserved in a form which permits identification of the data subjects for no longer than is required for the purpose for which those data are stored.

Article 6. Special Categories of Data. Personal data revealing racial origin, political opinions or religious or other beliefs, as well as personal data concerning health or sexual life, may not be processed automatically unless domestic law provides appropriate safeguards. The same shall apply to personal data relating to criminal convictions.

Article 7. Data Security. Appropriate security measures shall be taken for the protection of personal data stored in automated data files against accidental or unauthorised destruction or accidental loss as well as against unauthorised access, alteration or dissemination.

Article 8. Additional Safeguards for the Data Subject. Any person shall be enabled:

(a) to establish the existence of an automated personal data file, its main purposes, as well as the identity and habitual residence or principal place of business of the controller of the file;

(b) to obtain at reasonable intervals and without excessive delay or expense confirmation of whether personal data relating to him are stored in the automated data file as well as communication to him of such data in an intelligible form;

(c) to obtain, as the case may be, rectification or erasure of such data if these have been processed contrary to the provisions of domestic law giving effect to the basic principles set out in Articles 5 and 6 of this Convention;

(d) to have a remedy if a request for confirmation or, as the case may be, communication, rectification or erasure as referred to in paragraphs (b) and (c) of this Article is not complied with.

Article 9. Exceptions and Restrictions. 1. No exception to the provisions of Articles 5, 6 and 8 of this convention shall be allowed except within the limits defined in this Article.

2. Derogation from the provisions of Articles 5, 6 and 8 of this Convention shall be allowed when such derogation is provided for by the law of the Party and constitutes a necessary measure in a democratic society in the interests of:

(a) protecting State security, public safety, the monetary interests of the State or the suppression of criminal offences;

(b) protecting the data subject or the rights and freedoms of others.

3. Restrictions on the exercise of the rights specified in Article 8, paragraphs (b), (c) and (d), may be provided by law with respects to automated personal data files used for statistics or for scientific research purposes when there is obviously no risk of an infringement of the privacy of the data subjects.

Article 10. Sanctions and Remedies. Each Party undertakes to establish appropriate sanctions and remedies for violations of provisions of domestic law giving effect to the basic principles for data protection set out in this chapter.

Article 11. Extended Protection. None of the provisions of this chapter shall be interpreted as limiting or otherwise affecting the possibility for a Party to grant data subjects a wider measure of protection than that stipulated in this Convention.

Chapter III—Transborder Data Flows

Article 12. Transborder Flows of Personal Data and Domestic Law. 1. The following provisions shall apply to the transfer across national borders, by whatever medium, or personal data undergoing automatic processing or collected with a view to their being automatically processed.

2. A Party shall not, for the sole purpose of the protection of privacy, prohibit or subject to special authorisation transborder flows of personal data going to the territory of another Party.

3. Nevertheless, each Party shall be entitled to derogate from the provisions of paragraph 2:

(a) insofar as its legislation includes specific regulations for certain categories of personal data or of automated personal data files, because of the nature of those data or those files, except where the regulations of the other Party provide an equivalent protection;

(b) when the transfer is made from its territory to the territory of a non-Contracting State through the intermediary of the territory of another Party, in order to avoid such transfers resulting in circumvention of the legislation of the Party referred to at the beginning of this paragraph.

Chapter IV—Mutual Assistance

Article 13. Co-operation Between Parties. 1. The Parties agree to render each other mutual assistance in order to implement this Convention.

2. For that purpose:

(a) each Party shall designate one or more authorities, the name and address of each of which it shall communicate to the Secretary General of the Council of Europe;

(b) each Party which has designated more than one authority shall specify in its communication referred to in the previous sub-paragraph the competence of each authority.

3. An authority designated by a Party shall at the request of an authority designated by another Party:

(a) furnish information on its law and administrative practice in the field of data protection;

(b) take, in conformity with its domestic law and for the sole purpose of protection of privacy, all appropriate measures for furnishing factual information relating to specific automatic processing carried out in its territory, with the exception however of the personal data being processed.

Article 14. Assistance to Data Subjects Resident Abroad. 1. Each Party shall assist any person resident abroad to exercise the rights conferred by its domestic law giving effect to the principles set out in Article 8 of this Convention.

2. When such a person resides in the territory of another Party he shall be given the option of submitting his request through the intermediary of the authority designated by that Party.

3. The request for assistance shall contain all the necessary particulars, relating *inter alia* to:

(a) the name, address and any other relevant particulars identifying the person making the request;

(b) the automated personal data file to which the request pertains, or its controller;

(c) the purpose of the request.

Article 15. Safeguards Concerning Assistance Rendered by Designated Authorities. 1. An authority designated by a Party which has received information from an authority designated by another Party either accompanying a request for assistance or in reply to its own request for assistance shall not use that information for purposes other than those specified in the request for assistance.

2. Each Party shall see to it that the persons belonging to or acting on behalf of the designated authority shall be bound by appropriate obligations of secrecy or confidentiality with regard to that information.

3. In no case may a designated authority be allowed to make under Article 14, paragraph 2, a request for assistance on behalf of a data subject resident abroad, of its own accord and without the express consent of the person concerned.

Article 16. Refusal of Requests for Assistance. A designated authority to which a request for assistance is addressed under Articles 13 or 14 of this Convention may not refuse to comply with it unless:

(a) the request is not compatible with the powers in the field of data protection of the authorities responsible for replying;

(b) the request does not comply with the provisions of this Convention;

(c) compliance with the request would be incompatible with the sovereignty, security or public policy (*ordre public*) of the Party by which it was designated, or with the rights and fundamental freedoms of persons under the jurisdiction of that Party.

Article 17. Costs and Procedures of Assistance. 1. Mutual assistance which the Parties render each other under Article 13 and assistance they render to data subjects abroad under Article 14 shall not give rise to the payment of any costs or fees other than those incurred for experts and interpreters. The latter costs or fees shall be borne by the Party which has designated the authority making the request for assistance.

2. The data subject may not be charged costs or fees in connection with the steps taken on his behalf in the territory of another Party other than those lawfully payable by residents of that Party.

3. Other details concerning the assistance relating in particular to the forms and procedures and the languages to be used, shall be established directly between the Parties concerned.

Chapter V—Consultative Committee

Article 18. Composition of the Committee. 1. A Consultative Committee shall be set up after the entry into force of this Convention.

2. Each Party shall appoint a representative to the committee and a deputy representative. Any member State of the Council of Europe which is not a Party to the Convention shall have the right to be represented on the committee by an observer.

3. The Consultative Committee may, by unanimous decision, invite any non-member State of the Council of Europe which is not a Party to the Convention to be represented by an observer at a given meeting.

Article 19. Functions of the Committee. The Consultative Committee:

(a) may make proposals with a view to facilitating or improving the application of the Convention;

(b) may make proposals for amendment of this Convention in accordance with Article 21;

(c) shall formulate its opinion on any proposal for amendment of this Convention which is referred to it in accordance with Article 21, paragraph 3;

(d) may, at the request of a Party, express an opinion on any question concerning the application of this Convention.

Article 20. Procedure. 1. The Consultative Committee shall be convened by the Secretary General of the Council of Europe. Its first meeting shall be held within twelve months of the entry into force of this Convention. It shall subsequently meet at least once every two years and in any case when one-third of the representatives of the Parties request its convocation.

2. A majority of representatives of the Parties shall constitute a quorum for a meeting of the Consultative Committee.

3. After each of its meetings, the Consultative Committee shall submit to the Committee of Ministers of the Council of Europe a report on its work and on the functioning of the Convention.

4. Subject to the provisions of this Convention, the Consultative Committee shall draw up its own Rules of Procedure.

Chapter VI—Amendments

Article 21. Amendments. 1. Amendments to this Convention may be proposed by a Party, the Committee of Ministers of the Council of Europe or the Consultative Committee.

2. Any proposal for amendment shall be communicated by the Secretary General of the Council of Europe to the member States of the Council of Europe and to every non-member State which has acceded to or has been invited to accede to this Convention in accordance with the provisions of Article 23.

3. Moreover, any amendment proposed by a Party or the Committee of Ministers shall be communicated to the Consultative Committee, which shall submit to the Committee of Ministers its opinion on that proposed amendment.

4. The Committee of Ministers shall consider the proposed amendment and any opinion submitted by the Consultative Committee and may approve the amendment.

5. The text of any amendment approved by the Committee of Ministers in accordance with paragraph 4 of this Article shall be forwarded to the Parties for acceptance.

6. Any amendment approved in accordance with paragraph 4 of this Article shall come into force on the thirtieth day after all Parties have informed the Secretary General of their acceptance thereof.

Chapter VII—Final Clauses

Article 22. Entry into Force. 1. This Convention shall be open for signature by the member States of the Council of Europe. It is subject to ratification, acceptance or approval. Instruments of ratification, acceptance or approval shall be deposited with the Secretary General of the Council of Europe.

2. This Convention shall enter into force on the first day of the month following the expiration of a period of three months after the date on which five member States of the Council of Europe have expressed their consent to be bound by the Convention in accordance with the provisions of the preceding paragraph.

3. In respect of any member State which subsequently expresses its consent to be bound by it, the Convention shall enter into force on the first day of the month following the expiration of a period of three months after the date of the deposit of the instrument of ratification, acceptance or approval.

Article 23. Accession by Non-member States. 1. After the entry into force of this Convention, the Committee of Ministers of the Council of Europe may invite any State not a member of the Council of Europe to accede to this Convention by a decision taken by the majority provided for in Article 20 (d) of the Statute of the Council of Europe and by the unanimous vote of the representatives of the Contracting States entitled to sit on the Committee.

2. In respect of any acceding State, the Convention shall enter into force on the first day of the month following the expiration of a period of three months after the date of deposit of the instrument of accession with the Secretary General of the Council of Europe.

Article 24. Territorial Clause. 1. Any State may at the time of signature or when depositing its instrument of ratification, acceptance, approval or accession, specify the territory or territories to which this Convention shall apply.

2. Any State may at any later date, by a declaration addressed to the Secretary General of the Council of Europe, extend the application of this Convention to any other territory specified in the declaration. In respect of such territory the Convention shall enter into force on the first day of the month following the expiration of a period of three months after the date of receipt of such declaration by the Secretary General.

3. Any declaration made under the two preceding paragraphs may, in respect of any territory specified in such declaration, be withdrawn by a notification addressed to the Secretary General. The withdrawal shall become effective on the first day of the month following the expiration of a period of six months after the date of receipt of such notification by the Secretary General.

Article 25. Reservations. No reservation may be made in respect of the provisions of this Convention.

Article 26. Denunciation. 1. Any Party may at any time denounce this Convention by means of a notification addressed to the Secretary General of the Council of Europe.

2. Such denunciation shall become effective on the first day of the month following the expiration of a period of six months after the date of receipt of the notification by the Secretary General.

Article 27. Notifications. The Secretary General of the Council of Europe shall notify the member States of the Council and any State which has acceded to this Convention of:

(a) any signature;

(b) the deposit of any instrument of ratification, acceptance, approval or accession;

(c) any date of entry into force of this Convention in accordance with Articles 22, 23 and 24;

(d) any other act, notification or communication relating to this Convention.

In witness whereof the undersigned, being duly authorised thereto, have signed this Convention.

Done at Strasbourg, the 28th day of January 1981, in English and in French, both texts being equally authoritative, in a single copy which shall remain deposited in the archives of the Council of Europe. The Secretary General of the Council of Europe shall transmit certified copies to each member State of the Council of Europe and to any State invited to accede to this Convention.

SEE ALSO *Privacy: Computerized Personal Data Files.*

EUROPEAN CONVENTION ON ESTABLISHMENT, AND PROTOCOL (1955). The convention, concluded at Paris on 13 December 1955 by the **COMMITTEE OF MINISTERS OF THE COUNCIL OF EUROPE,** regulates the legal and *de facto* treatment of nationals of the contracting States when they travel to territories under the jurisdiction of other contracting States. It has the effect of placing the nationals of the contracting States in a position more favorable than those of other States in such matters as admission, legal protection, taxation, public service benefits, and private and civil rights. It authorizes the establishment of an international standing committee, composed of one representative of each contracting State, monitor its practical application or, if necessary, to supplement its provisions.

The convention is followed by a protocol providing detailed explanations and qualifications of certain provisions. Both the convention and the protocol entered into force on 23 February 1965. Their texts (*European Treaty Series* 19) are as follows:

The governments signatory hereto, being Members of the Council of Europe,

Considering that the aim of the Council of Europe is to safeguard and to realise the ideals and principles which are the common heritage of its Members and to facilitate their economic and social progress;

Recognising the special character of the links between the member countries of the Council of Europe as affirmed in conventions and agreements already concluded within the framework of the Council such as the Convention for the Protection of Human Rights and Fundamental Freedoms signed on 4 November 1950, the Protocol to this Convention signed on 20 March 1952, the European Convention on Social and Medical Assistance and the two European Interim Agreements on Social Security signed on 11 December 1953;

Being convinced that, by the conclusion of a regional convention, the establishment of common rules for the treatment accorded to nationals of each member State in the territory of the others may further the achievement of greater unity;

Affirming that the rights and privileges which they grant to each other's nationals are conceded solely by virtue of the close association uniting the member countries of the Council of Europe by means of its Statute;

Noting that the general plan of the Convention fits into the framework of the organisation of the Council of Europe,

Have agreed as follows:

Chapter I
Entry, Residence and Expulsion

Article 1. Each Contracting Party shall facilitate the entry into its territory by nationals of the other Parties for the purpose of temporary visits and shall permit them to travel freely within its territory except when this would be contrary to *ordre public,* national security, public health or morality.

Article 2. Subject to the conditions set out in Article 1 of this Convention, each Contracting Party shall, to the extent permitted by its economic and social conditions, facilitate the prolonged or permanent residence in its territory of nationals of the other Parties.

Article 3. 1. Nationals of any Contracting Party lawfully residing in the territory of another Party may be expelled only if they endanger national security or offend against *ordre public* or morality.

2. Except where imperative considerations of national security otherwise require, a national of any Contracting Party who has been so lawfully residing for more than two years in the territory of any other Party shall not be expelled without first being allowed to submit reasons against his expulsion and to appeal to, and be represented for the purpose before, a competent authority or a person or persons specially designated by the competent authority.

3. Nationals of any Contracting Party who have been lawfully residing for more than ten years in the territory of any other Party may only be expelled for reasons of national security or if the other reasons mentioned in paragraph 1 of this article are of a particularly serious nature.

Chapter II
Exercise of Private Rights

Article 4. Nationals of any Contracting Party shall enjoy in the territory of any other Party treatment equal to that enjoyed by nationals of the latter Party in respect of the possession and exercise of private rights, whether personal rights or rights relating to property.

Article 5. Notwithstanding Article 4 of this Convention, any Contracting Party may, for reasons of national security or defence, reserve the acquisition, possession or use of any categories of property for its own nationals or subject nationals of other Parties to special conditions applicable to aliens in respect of such property.

Article 6. 1. Apart from cases relating to national security or defence,

(a) Any Contracting Party which has reserved for its nationals or, in the case of aliens including those who are nationals of other Parties, made subject to regulations the acquisition, possession or use of certain categories of property, or has made the acquisition, possession or use of such property conditional upon reciprocity, shall, at the time of the signature of this Convention, transmit a list of these restrictions to the Secretary General of the Council of Europe indicating which provisions of its municipal law are the basis of such restrictions. The Secretary General shall forward these lists to the other Signatories;

(b) After this Convention has entered into force in respect of any Contracting Party, that Contracting Party shall not introduce any further restrictions as to the acquisition, possession or use of any categories of property by nationals of the other Parties, unless it finds itself compelled to do so for imperative reasons of an economic or social character or in order to prevent monopolisation of the vital resources of the country. It shall in this event keep the Secretary General fully informed of the measures taken, the relevant provisions of municipal law and the reasons for such measures. The Secretary General shall communicate this information to the other Parties.

2. Each Contracting Party shall endeavour to reduce its list of restrictions for the benefit of nationals of the other Parties. It shall notify the Secretary General of any such changes and he shall communicate them to the other Parties.

Each Party shall also endeavour to grant to nationals of other Parties such exemptions from the general regulations concerning aliens as are provided for in its own legislation.

Chapter III
Judicial and Administrative Guarantees

Article 7. Nationals of any Contracting Party shall enjoy in the territory of any other Party, under the same conditions as nationals of the latter Party, full legal and judicial protection of their persons and property and of their rights and interests. In particular, they shall have, in the same manner as the nationals of the latter Party, the right of access to the competent judicial and administrative authorities and the right to obtain the assistance of any person of their choice who is qualified by the laws of the country.

Article 8. 1. Nationals of any Contracting Party shall be entitled in the territory of any other Party to obtain free legal assistance under the same conditions as nationals of the latter Party.

2. Indigent nationals of a Contracting Party shall be entitled to have copies of *actes de l'état civil* issued to them free of charge in the territory of another Contracting Party in so far as these are so issued to indigent nationals of the latter Contracting Party.

Article 9. 1. No security or deposit of any kind may be required, by reason of their status as aliens or of lack of domicile or residence in the country, from nationals of any Contracting Party, having their domicile or normal residence in the territory of a Party, who may be plaintiffs or third parties before the Courts of any other Party.

2. The same rule shall apply to the payment which may be required of plaintiffs or third parties to guarantee legal costs.

3. Orders to pay the costs and expenses of a trial imposed upon a plaintiff or third party who is exempted from such security, deposit or payment in pursuance either of the preceding paragraphs of this article or of the law of the country in which the proceedings are taken, shall without charge, upon a request made through the diplomatic channel, be rendered enforceable by the competent authority in the territory of any other Contracting Party.

Chapter IV
Gainful Occupations

Article 10. Each Contracting Party shall authorise nationals of the other Parties to engage in its territory in any gainful occupation on an equal footing with its own nationals, unless the said Contracting Party has cogent economic or social reasons for withholding the authorisation. This provision shall apply, but not be limited, to industrial, commercial, financial and agricultural occupations, skilled crafts and the professions, whether the person concerned is self-employed or is in the service of an employer.

Article 11. Nationals of any Contracting Party who have been allowed by another Party to engage in a gainful occupation for a certain period may not, during that period, be subjected to restrictions not provided for at the time the authorisation was granted to them unless such restrictions are equally applicable to nationals of the latter Party in similar circumstances.

Article 12. 1. Nationals of any Contracting Party lawfully residing in the territory of any other Party shall be authorised, without being made subject to the restrictions referred to in Article 10 of this Convention, to engage in any gainful occupation on an equal footing with nationals of the latter Party, provided they comply with one of the following conditions:

(a) they have been lawfully engaged in a gainful occupation in that territory for an uninterrupted period of five years;

(b) they have lawfully resided in that territory for an uninterrupted period of ten years;

(c) they have been admitted to permanent residence.

Any Contracting Party may, at the time of signature or of deposit of its instrument of ratification of this Convention, declare that it does not accept one or two of the conditions mentioned above.

2. Such Party may also, in accordance with the same procedure, increase the period laid down in paragraph 1 (a) of this article to a maximum of ten years, provided that after the first period of five years renewal of an authorisation may in no case be refused in respect of the occupation pursued up to that time nor may such renewal be conditional upon any change in that occupation. It may also declare that it will not in all cases automatically grant the right to change from a wage-earning occupation to an independent occupation.

Article 13. Any Contracting Party may reserve for its own nationals the exercise of public functions or of occupations connected with national security or defence, or make the exercise of these occupations by aliens subject to special conditions.

Article 14. 1. Apart from the functions or occupations mentioned in Article 13 of this Convention,

(a) any Contracting Party which has reserved certain occupations for its own nationals or made the exercise of them by aliens, including nationals of the other Parties, subject to regulations or reciprocity, shall at the time of signature of this Convention transmit a list of these restrictions to the Secretary General of the Council of Europe, indicating which provisions of its municipal law are the basis of such restrictions. The Secretary General shall forward these lists to the other Signatories;

(b) after this Convention has entered into force in respect of any Contracting Party, that Party shall not introduce any further restrictions as to the exercise of gainful occupations by the nationals of other Parties unless it finds itself compelled to do so for imperative reasons of an economic or social character. It shall in this event keep the Secretary General fully informed of the measures taken, the relevant provisions of municipal law and the reasons for such measures. The Secretary General shall communicate this information to the other Parties.

2. Each Contracting Party shall endeavour for the benefit of nationals of the other Parties:

—to reduce the list of occupations which are reserved for its own nationals or the exercise of which by aliens is subject to regulations or reciprocity; it shall notify the Secretary General of any such changes, and he shall communicate them to the other Parties;

—in so far as its laws permit, to allow individual exemptions from the provisions in force.

Article 15. The exercise by nationals of one Contracting Party in the territory of another Party of an occupation in respect of which nationals of the latter Party are required to possess professional or technical qualifications or to furnish guarantees shall be made subject to the production of the same guarantees or to the possession of the same qualifications or of others recognised as their equivalent by the competent national authority;

Provided that nationals of the Contracting Parties engaged in the lawful pursuit of their profession in the territory of any Party may be called into the territory of any other Party by one of their colleagues for the purpose of lending assistance in a particular case.

Article 16. Commercial travellers who are nationals of a Contracting Party and are employed by an undertaking whose principal place of business is situated in the territory of a Contracting Party shall not need any authorisation in order to exercise their occupation in the territory of any other Party, provided that they do not reside therein for more than two months during any half-year.

Article 17. 1. Nationals of any Contracting Party shall, in the territory of another Party, enjoy treatment no less favourable than nationals of the latter Party in respect of any statutory regulation by a public authority concerning wages and working conditions in general.

2. The provisions of this Chapter shall not be understood as requiring a Contracting Party to accord in its territory more favourable treatment as regards the exercise of a gainful occupation to the nationals of any other Party than that accorded to its own nationals.

Chapter V
Individual Rights

Article 18. No Contracting Party may forbid nationals of another Party who have been lawfully engaged for at least five years in an appropriate occupation in the territory of the former Party from taking part on an equal footing with its own nationals as electors in elections held by bodies or organisations of an economic or professional nature such as Chambers of Commerce or of Agricultural or Trade Associations, subject to the decisions which such bodies or organisations may take in this respect within the limits of their competence.

Article 19. Nationals of any Contracting Party in the territory of any other Party shall be permitted, without any restrictions other than those applicable to nationals of the latter Party, to act as arbitrators in arbitral proceedings in which the choice of arbitrators is left entirely to the parties concerned.

Article 20. In so far as access to education is under State control, nationals of school age of any Contracting Party lawfully residing in the territory of any other Party shall be admitted, on an equal footing with the nationals of the latter Party, to institutions for primary and secondary education and technical and vocational training. The application of this provision to the grant of scholarships shall be left to the discretion of individual Parties. School attendance shall be compulsory for nationals of school age residing in the territory of another Contracting Party if it is compulsory for the nationals of the latter Party.

Chapter VI
Taxation, Compulsory Civilian Services, Expropriation, Nationalisation

Article 21. 1. Subject to the provisions concerning double taxation contained in agreements already concluded or to be concluded, nationals of any Contracting Party shall not be liable in the territory of any other Party to duties, charges, taxes or contributions, of any description whatsoever, other, higher or more burdensome than those imposed on nationals of the latter Party in similar circumstances; in particular, they shall be entitled to deductions or exemptions from taxes or charges and to all allowances, including allowances for dependants.

2. A Contracting Party shall not impose on nationals of any other Party any residence charge not required of its own nationals. This provision shall not prevent the imposition in appropriate cases of charges connected with administrative formalities such as the issue of permits and authorisations which aliens are required to have, provided that the amount levied is not more than the expenditure incurred by such formalities.

Article 22. Nationals of a Contracting Party may in no case be obliged to perform in the territory of another Party any civilian services, whether of a personal nature or relating to property, other or more burdensome than those required of nationals of the latter Party.

Article 23. Without prejudice to the provision of Article 1 of the Protocol to the Convention for the Protection of Human Rights and Fundamental Freedoms, nationals of any Contracting Party shall be entitled, in the event of expropriation or nationalisation of their property by any other Party, to be treated at least as favourably as nationals of the latter Party.

Chapter VII
Standing Committee

Article 24. 1. A Standing Committee shall be set up within a year of the entry into force of this Convention. This committee may formulate proposals designed to improve the practical implementation of the Convention and, if necessary, to amend or supplement its provisions.

2. In the event of differences of opinion arising between the Parties over the interpretation or application of the provisions of Article 6, paragraph 1 (b), and Article 14, paragraph 1 (b), of this Convention, the committee shall at the request of any Party concerned endeavour to settle such differences.

3. The committee shall arrange for the publication of a periodical report containing all information regarding the laws and regulations in the territory of the Parties in respect of matters provided for in this Convention.

4. Each Member of the Council of Europe which has ratified this Convention shall appoint a representative to this committee. Any other Member of the Council may be represented by an observer with the right to speak.

5. The committee shall be convened by the Secretary General of the Council of Europe.

Its first session shall take place within three months of the date of its establishment. Subsequent sessions shall be held at least once every two years. The committee may also be convened whenever the Committee of Ministers of the Council considers it necessary. The period of two years shall run from the date of the end of the last session.

6. Opinions or recommendations of the Standing Committee shall be submitted to the Committee of Ministers.

7. The Standing Committee shall draw up its own Rules of Procedure.

Chapter VIII
General Provisions

Article 25. The provisions of this Convention shall not prejudice the provisions of municipal law, bilateral or multilateral treaties, conventions or agreements which are already in force or may come into force under which more favourable treatment would be accorded to nationals of one or more of the other Contracting Parties.

Article 26. 1. Any Member of the Council of Europe may, when signing this Convention or when depositing its instrument of ratification, make a reservation in respect of any particular provision of the Convention to the extent that any law then in force in its territory is not in conformity with the said provision. Reservations of a general nature shall not be permitted under this article.

2. Any reservation made under this article shall contain a brief statement of the law concerned.

3. Any Member of the Council which makes a reservation under this article shall withdraw the said reservation as soon as circumstances permit. Such withdrawal shall be made by notification addressed to the Secretary General of the Council and shall take effect from the date of the receipt of such notification. The Secretary General shall transmit the text of this notification to all the Signatories of the Convention.

Article 27. A Contracting Party which has made a reservation in respect of a particular provision of the Convention in accordance with Article 26 of this Convention may not claim application of the said provision by another Party save in so far as it has itself accepted the provision.

Article 28. 1. In time of war or other public emergency threatening the life of the nation, any Contracting Party may take measures derogating from its obligations under this Convention to the extent strictly required by the exigencies of the situation and provided that such measures are not inconsistent with its other obligations under international law.

2. Any Contracting Party availing itself of this right of derogation shall keep the Secretary General of the Council of Europe fully informed of the measures which it has taken and the reasons therefor. It shall also inform the Secretary General of the Council when such measures have ceased to operate and the provisions of the Convention are again being fully executed.

Chapter IX
Field of Application of the Convention

Article 29. 1. This Convention shall apply to the metropolitan territories of the Contracting Parties.

2. Any Member of the Council may, at the time of the signature or ratification of this Convention or at any later date, declare by notice addressed to the Secretary General of the Council of Europe that this Convention shall apply to the territory or territories mentioned in the said declaration and for whose international relations it is responsible.

3. Any declarations made in accordance with the preceding paragraph may, in respect of any territory mentioned in such declaration, be withdrawn according to the procedure laid down in Article 33 of this Convention.

4. The Secretary General shall communicate to the other Members of the Council any declaration transmitted to him in accordance with paragraph 2 or paragraph 3 of this article.

Article 30. 1. For the purpose of this Convention, "nationals" means physical persons possessing the nationality of one of the Contracting Parties.

2. No Contracting Party shall be obliged to grant the benefits of this Convention to nationals of another Contracting Party ordinarily resident in a non-metropolitan territory of the latter Party to which the Convention does not apply.

Chapter X
Settlement of Disputes

Article 31. 1. Any disputes which may arise between the Contracting Parties concerning the interpretation or the application of this Convention shall be submitted to the International Court of Justice by special agreement or by application by one of the parties to the dispute, unless the parties agree on a different method of peaceful settlement.

2. After the entry into force of the European Convention for the Peaceful Settlement of Disputes, the Parties to that Convention shall apply those of its provisions which are binding upon them to all disputes which may arise between them concerning the present Convention.

3. Any dispute subjected to a procedure referred to in the preceding paragraphs shall be immediately reported by the parties concerned to the Secretary General of the Council of Europe, who shall inform the other Contracting Parties without delay.

4. If one of the parties to a dispute fails to carry out its obligations laid down in a decision of the International Court of Justice or the award of an arbitral tribunal, the other party may appeal to the Committee of Ministers of the Council of Europe. The latter may, if it deems necessary, make recommendations by a majority of two thirds of the representatives entitled to sit on the Committee with a view to ensuring the execution of the said decision or award.

Chapter XI
Final Provisions

Article 32. The Protocol attached to this Convention shall form an integral part of it.

Article 33. 1. A Contracting Party may denounce this Convention only at the end of five years from the date on which it became a Party to it, having previously given six months' notice by notification addressed to the Secretary General of the Council of Europe, who shall inform the other Parties. A Party which does not so exercise the right of denunciation will remain bound for further successive periods of two years and may denounce this Convention only at the end any such period, having given notice six months previously.

2. Denunciation shall not have the effect of releasing the Contracting Party concerned from its obligations under this Convention in respect of any act which may have been performed by it before the date upon which the denunciation became effective.

3. Any Contracting Party which ceases to be a Member of the Council of Europe shall under the same conditions cease to be a Party to this Convention.

Article 34. 1. This Convention shall be open for signature by the Members of the Council of Europe. It shall be ratified. Instruments of ratification shall be deposited with the Secretary General of the Council of Europe.

2. This Convention shall come into force on the date of deposit of the fifth instrument of ratification.

3. As regards any Signatory ratifying subsequently, the Convention shall come into force on the date of deposit of its instrument of ratification.

4. The Secretary General shall notify all the Members of the Council of the entry into force of the Convention, the names of the Contracting Parties which have ratified it, any reservations made and the subsequent deposit of any instruments of ratification.

In witness whereof, the undersigned, being duly authorised thereto, have signed this Convention.

Done at Paris, this 13th day of December 1955, in English and in French, both texts being equally authoritative, in a single copy which shall remain deposited in the archives of the Council of Europe. The Secretary General

491

shall transmit certified true copies to each of the Signatories.

Protocol

Section I

Articles 1, 2, 3, 5, 6 paragraphs 1 (b), 10,13 and 14 paragraph 1 (b). (a) Each Contracting Party shall have the right to judge by national criteria:

1. the reasons of *"ordre public,* national security, public health or morality" which may provide grounds for the exclusion from its territory of nationals of other Parties;

2. "the economic and social conditions" which may prevent the admission of nationals of other Parties to prolonged or permanent residence or the exercise of gainful occupations in its territory;

3. the circumstances which constitute a threat to national security or an offence against *ordre public* or morality;

4. the reasons specified in the Convention for which a Contracting Party may reserve for its own nationals the acquisition, possession or use of any categories of property or the exercise of certain rights and occupations or may make the exercise thereof by nationals of the other Parties subject to special conditions.

(b) Each Contracting Party shall determine whether the reasons for expulsion are of a "particularly serious nature". In this connection account shall be taken of the behaviour of the individual concerned during his whole period of residence.

(c) A Contracting Party may only restrict the rights of nationals of other Parties for the reasons set forth in this Convention and to the extent compatible with the obligations assumed by the Parties.

Section II

Articles 1, 2, 3, 10, 11, 12, 13, 14, 15, 16, 17 and 20. (a) Regulations governing the admission, residence and movement of aliens and also their right to engage in gainful occupations shall be unaffected by this Convention in so far as they are not inconsistent with it.

(b) Nationals of a Contracting Party shall be considered as lawfully residing in the territory of another Party if they have conformed to the said regulations.

Section III

Articles 1, 2 and 3. (a) The concept of *"ordre public"* is to be understood in the wide sense generally accepted in continental countries. A Contracting Party may, for instance, exclude a national of another Party for political reasons, or if there are grounds for believing that he is unable to pay the expenses of his stay or that he intends to engage in a gainful occupation without the necessary permits.

(b) The Contracting Parties undertake, in the exercise of their established rights, to pay due regard to family ties.

(c) The right of expulsion may be exercised only in individual cases.

The Contracting Parties shall, in exercising their right of expulsion, act with consideration, having regard to the particular relations which exist between the Members of the Council of Europe. They shall in particular take due account of family ties and the period of residence in their territory of the person concerned.

Section IV

Articles 8 and 9. Articles 8 and 9 of this Convention in no way affect obligations contracted under the Hague Convention on Civil Procedure.

Section V

Articles 10, 11, 12, 13, 14, 15, 16 and 17. (a) The provisions of Articles 10, 11, 12, 13, 14, 15, 16 and 17 of this Convention shall be subject to the conditions governing entry and residence laid down in Articles 1 and 2.

(b) The husband or wife and dependent children of nationals of any Contracting Party lawfully residing in the territory of another Party who have been authorised to accompany or rejoin them shall as far as possible be allowed to take up employment in that territory in accordance with the conditions laid down in this Convention.

(c) The provisions of Article 12 of this Convention shall not apply to nationals of a Contracting Party residing in the territory of another Party in pursuance of special regulations or engaged in a gainful occupation therein in pursuance of special rules or agreements, including such persons as members, or staff not locally recruited, of diplomatic or consular missions; members of the staff of international organisations; student employees, apprentices, students and persons employed for the purpose of completing their vocational training; crews of ships and aircraft.

(d) For the purposes of Article 16 of this Convention, the Contracting Parties shall not, in their municipal legislation or regulations, treat the occupation of commercial traveller as an itinerant trade or form of hawking.

(e) It is understood that Article 16 applies only to commercial travellers acting under the orders of an undertaking situated outside the receiving country and remunerated solely by such undertaking.

(f) Article 17, paragraph 1, of this Convention shall not apply to the special case of student employees in respect of their remuneration.

Section VI

Articles 2, 11, 12, 13, 14, 15, 16, 17 and 25. (a) It is understood that this Convention shall not apply to industrial, literary and artistic property and new vegetable products, as these subjects are reserved for international conventions or other international agreements relating thereto which are already in force or will come into force.

(b) Those Contracting Parties to this Convention which are now or will be bound by the decisions of the Organisation for European Economic Co-operation governing the employment of nationals of its member countries shall, in their mutual relations and in respect of the exercise of wage-earning occupations, apply the provisions of this Convention or of the said decisions, whichever grant the more favourable treatment to wage-earners. In applying the provisions of Articles 2, 10, 11, 12, 13, 14, 15, 16 and 17 of this Convention and judging the economic or social reasons mentioned in Articles 10 and 14, they shall conform to the spirit and the letter of the said decisions in so far as the latter are more favourable to wage-earners than the provisions of this Convention.

Section VII

Article 26, paragraph 1. The Contracting Parties shall exercise their right to make reservations only in so far as they consider that essential provisions of their municipal law so require.

Section VIII

Article 29, paragraph 1. (a) This Convention shall, in respect of France, also apply to Algeria and the overseas Departments.

(b) The Federal Republic of Germany may extend the application of this Convention to the *Land* Berlin by a declaration addressed to the Secretary General of the Council of Europe who shall notify the other Contracting Parties thereof.

Article 29, paragraph 2. Any Member of the Council of Europe which makes a declaration in accordance with Article 29, paragraph 2 of this Convention shall, at the same time and in respect of any territory mentioned in such declaration, transmit to the Secretary General of the Council the lists of restrictions specified in Article 6, paragraph 1, and Article 14, paragraph 1, any declaration made in accordance with Article 12 and any reservation made in accordance with Article 26 of this Convention.

Article 30. The term "ordinarily resident" shall be defined according to the regulations applicable in the country of which the person concerned is a national.

Section IX

Article 31, paragraph 1. Contracting Parties not party to the Statute of the International Court of Justice shall take the necessary steps to obtain access to the Court.

SEE ALSO Aliens: Equality with Citizens; Aliens' Rights; Charter of Rights for Migrant Workers in Southern Africa; Declaration on the Human Rights of Individuals Who Are not Nationals of the Country in Which They Live.

EUROPEAN CONVENTION ON EXTRADITION
(1957). The convention, concluded by the COMMITTEE OF MINISTERS OF THE COUNCIL OF EUROPE meeting in Paris on 13 December 1957, aims at establishing uniform rules to govern the decisions of States parties when dealing with requests from other States for the surrender of persons sought either for prosecution or for the carrying out of a sentence or detention order. The convention entered into force on 18 April 1960. Its provisions were later supplemented by the EURO-PEAN CONVENTION ON EXTRADITION: ADDITIONAL PROTOCOL (1975) and by the EUROPEAN CONVENTION ON EXTRADITION: SECOND ADDITIONAL PROTOCOL (1978).

The text of the parent convention (*European Treaty Series* 24) is as follows:

The governments signatory hereto, being Members of the Council of Europe,

Considering that the aim of the Council of Europe is to achieve a greater unity between its Members;

Considering that this purpose can be attained by the conclusion of agreements and by common action in legal matters;

Considering that the acceptance of uniform rules with regard to extradition is likely to assist this work of unification,

Have agreed as follows:

Article 1. Obligation to Extradite. The Contracting Parties undertake to surrender to each other, subject to the provisions and conditions laid down in this Convention, all persons against whom the competent authorities of the requesting Party are proceeding for an offence or who are wanted by the said authorities for the carrying out of a sentence or detention order.

Article 2. Extraditable Offences. 1. Extradition shall be granted in respect of offences punishable under the laws of the requesting Party and of the requested Party by deprivation of liberty or under a detention order for a maximum period of at least one year or by a more severe penalty. Where a conviction and prison sentence have occurred or a detention order has been made in the territory of the requesting Party, the punishment awarded must have been for a period of at least four months.

2. If the request for extradition includes several separate offences each of which is punishable under the laws of the requesting Party and the requested Party by deprivation of liberty or under a detention order, but of which some do not fulfil the condition with regard to the amount of punishment which may be awarded, the requested Party shall also have the right to grant extradition for the latter offences.

3. Any Contracting Party whose law does not allow extradition for certain of the offences referred to in paragraph 1 of this article may, in so far as it is concerned, exclude such offences from the application of this Convention.

4. Any Contracting Party which wishes to avail itself of the right provided for in paragraph 3 of this article shall, at the time of the deposit of its instrument of ratification or accession, transmit to the Secretary General of the Council of Europe either a list of the offences for which extradition is allowed or a list of those for which it is excluded and shall at the same time indicate the legal provisions which allow or exclude extradition. The Secretary General of the Council shall forward these lists to the other Signatories.

5. If extradition is subsequently excluded in respect of other offences by the law of a Contracting Party, that Party shall notify the Secretary General. The Secretary General shall inform the other Signatories. Such notification shall not take effect until three months from the date of its receipt by the Secretary General.

6. Any Party which avails itself of the right provided for in paragraphs 4 or 5 of this article may at any time apply this Convention to offences which have been excluded from it. It shall inform the Secretary General of the Council of such changes, and the Secretary General shall inform the other Signatories.

7. Any Party may apply reciprocity in respect of any offences excluded from the application of the Convention under this article.

Article 3. Political Offences. 1. Extradition shall not be granted if the offence in respect of which it is requested is regarded by the requested Party as a political offence or as an offence connected with a political offence.

2. The same rule shall apply if the requested Party has substantial grounds for believing that a request for extradition for an ordinary criminal offence has been made for the purpose of prosecuting or punishing a person on account of his race, religion, nationality or political opinion, or that that person's position may be prejudiced for any of these reasons.

3. The taking or attempted taking of the life of a Head of State or a member of his family shall not be deemed to be a political offence for the purposes of this Convention.

4. This article shall not affect any obligations which the Contracting Parties may have undertaken or may undertake under any other international convention of a multilateral character.

Article 4. Military Offences. Extradition for offences under military law which are not offences under ordinary criminal law is excluded from the application of this Convention.

Article 5. Fiscal Offences. Extradition shall be granted, in accordance with the provisions of this Convention, for offences in connection with taxes, duties, customs and exchange only if the Contracting Parties have so decided in respect of any such offence or category of offences.

Article 6. Extradition of Nationals. 1. (a) A Contracting Party shall have the right to refuse extradition of its nationals.

(b) Each Contracting Party may, by a declaration made at the time of signature or of deposit of its instrument of ratification or accession, define as far as it is concerned the term "nationals" within the meaning of this Convention.

(c) Nationality shall be determined as at the time of the decision concerning extradition. If, however, the person claimed is first recognised as a national of the requested Party during the period between the time of the decision and the time contemplated for the surrender, the requested Party may avail itself of the provision contained in sub-paragraph (a) of this article.

2. If the requested Party does not extradite its national, it shall at the request of the requesting Party submit the case to its competent authorities in order that proceedings may be taken if they are considered appropriate. For this purpose, the files, information and exhibits relating to the offence shall be transmitted without charge by the means provided for in Article 12, paragraph 1. The requesting Party shall be informed of the result of its request.

Article 7. Place of Commission. 1. The requested Party may refuse to extradite a person claimed for an offence which is regarded by its law as having been committed in whole or in part in its territory or in a place treated as its territory.

2. When the offence for which extradition is requested has been committed outside the territory of the requesting Party, extradition may only be refused if the law of the requested Party does not allow prosecution for the same category of offence when committed outside the latter Party's territory or does not allow extradition for the offence concerned.

Article 8. Pending Proceedings for the Same Offences. The requested Party may refuse to extradite the person claimed if the competent authorities of such Party are proceeding against him in respect of the offence or offences for which extradition is requested.

Article 9. Non bis in idem. Extradition shall not be granted if final judgment has been passed by the competent authorities of the requested Party upon the person claimed in respect of the offence or offences for which extradition is requested. Extradition may be refused if the competent authorities of the requested Party have decided either not to institute or to terminate proceedings in respect of the same offence or offences.

Article 10. Lapse of Time. Extradition shall not be granted when the person claimed has, according to the law of either the requesting or the requested Party, become immune by reason of lapse of time from prosecution or punishment.

Article 11. Capital Punishment. If the offence for which extradition is requested is punishable by death under the law of the requesting Party, and if in respect of such offence the death-penalty is not provided for by the law of the requested Party or is not normally carried out, extradition may be refused unless the requesting Party gives such assurance as the requested Party considers sufficient that the death-penalty will not be carried out.

Article 12. The Request and Supporting Documents. 1. The request shall be in writing and shall be communicated through the diplomatic channel. Other means of communication may be arranged by direct agreement between two or more Parties.

2. The request shall be supported by:

(a) the original or an authenticated copy of the conviction and sentence or detention order immediately enforceable or of the warrant of arrest or other order having the same effect and issued in accordance with the procedure laid down in the law of the requesting Party;

(b) a statement of the offences for which extradition is requested. The time and place of their commission, their legal descriptions and a reference to the relevant legal provisions shall be set out as accurately as possible; and

(c) a copy of the relevant enactments or, where this is not possible, a statement of the relevant law and as accurate a description as possible of the person claimed, together with any other information which will help to establish his identity and nationality.

Article 13. Supplementary Information. If the information communicated by the requesting Party is found to be insufficient to allow the requested Party to make a decision in pursuance of this Convention, the latter Party shall request the necessary supplementary information and may fix a time-limit for the receipt thereof.

Article 14. Rule of Speciality. 1. A person who has been extradited shall not be proceeded against, sentenced or detained with a view to the carrying out of a sentence or detention order for any offence committed prior to his surrender other than that for which he was extradited, nor shall he be for any other reason restricted in his personal freedom, except in the following cases:

(a) When the Party which surrendered him consents. A request for consent shall be submitted, accompanied by the documents mentioned in Article 12 and a legal record of any statement made by the extradited person in respect of the offence concerned. Consent shall be given when the offence for which it is requested is itself subject to extradition in accordance with the provisions of this Convention;

(b) when that person, having had an opportunity to leave the territory of the Party to which he has been surrendered, has not done so within 45 days of his final discharge, or has returned to that territory after leaving it.

2. The requesting Party may, however, take any measures necessary to remove the person from its territory, or any measures necessary under its law, including proceedings by default, to prevent any legal effects of lapse of time.

3. When the description of the offence charged is altered in the course of proceedings, the extradited person shall only be proceeded against or sentenced in so far as the offence under its new description is shown by its constituent elements to be an offence which would allow extradition.

Article 15. Re-extradition to a Third State. Except as provided for in Article 14, paragraph 1 (b), the requesting Party shall not, without the consent of the requested Party, surrender to another Party or to a third State a person surrendered to the requesting Party and sought by the said other Party or third State in respect of offences committed before his surrender. The requested Party may request the production of the documents mentioned in Article 12, paragraph 2.

Article 16. Provisional Arrest. 1. In case of urgency the competent authorities of the requesting Party may request the provisional arrest of the person sought. The competent authorities of the requested Party shall decide the matter in accordance with its law.

2. The request for provisional arrest shall state that one of the documents mentioned in Article 12, paragraph 2 (a), exists and that it is intended to send a request for extradition. It shall also state for what offence extradition will be requested and when and where such offence was committed and shall so far as possible give a description of the person sought.

3. A request for provisional arrest shall be sent to the competent authorities of the requested Party either through the diplomatic channel or direct by post or telegraph or through the International Criminal Police Organisation (Interpol) or by any other means affording evidence in writing or accepted by the requested Party. The requesting authority shall be informed without delay of the result of its request.

4. Provisional arrest may be terminated if, within a period of 18 days after arrest, the requested Party has not received the request for extradition and the documents mentioned in Article 12. It shall not, in any event, exceed 40 days from the date of such arrest. The possibility of provisional release at any time is not excluded, but the requested Party shall take any measures which it considers necessary to prevent the escape of the person sought.

5. Release shall not prejudice re-arrest and extradition if a request for extradition is received subsequently.

Article 17. Conflicting Requests. If extradition is requested concurrently by more than one State, either for the same offence or for different offences, the requested Party shall make its decision having regard to all the circumstances and especially the relative seriousness and place of commission of the offences, the respective dates of the requests, the nationality of the person claimed and the possibility of subsequent extradition to another State.

Article 18. Surrender of the Person to be Extradited. 1. The requested Party shall inform the requesting Party by the means mentioned in Article 12, paragraph 1, of its decision with regard to the extradition.

2. Reasons shall be given for any complete or partial rejection.

3. If the request is agreed to, the requesting Party shall be informed of the place and date of surrender and of the length of time for which the person claimed was detained with a view to surrender.

4. Subject to the provisions of paragraph 5 of this article, if the person claimed has not been taken over on the appointed date, he may be released after the expiry of 15 days and shall in any case be released after the expiry of 30 days. The requested Party may refuse to extradite him for the same offence.

5. If circumstances beyond its control prevent a Party from surrendering or taking over the person to be extradited, it shall notify the other Party. The two Parties shall agree a new date for surrender and the provisions of paragraph 4 of this article shall apply.

Article 19. Postponed or Conditional Surrender. 1. The requested Party may, after making its decision on the request for extradition, postpone the surrender of the person

claimed in order that he may be proceeded against by that Party or, if he has already been convicted, in order that he may serve his sentence in the territory of that Party for an offence other than that for which extradition is requested.

2. The requested Party may, instead of postponing surrender, temporarily surrender the person claimed to the requesting Party in accordance with conditions to be determined by mutual agreement between the Parties.

Article 20. Handing over of Property. 1. The requested Party shall, in so far as its law permits and at the request of the requesting Party, seize and hand over property:

(a) which may be required as evidence or

(b) which has been acquired as a result of the offence and which, at the time of the arrest, is found in the possession of the person claimed or is discovered subsequently.

2. The property mentioned in paragraph 1 of this article shall be handed over even if extradition, having been agreed to, cannot be carried out owing to the death or escape of the person claimed.

3. When the said property is liable to seizure or confiscation in the territory of the requested Party, the latter may, in connection with pending criminal proceedings, temporarily retain it or hand it over on condition that it is returned.

4. Any rights which the requested Party or third parties may have acquired in the said property shall be preserved. Where these rights exist, the property shall be returned without charge to the requested Party as soon as possible after the trial.

Article 21. Transit. 1. Transit through the territory of one of the Contracting Parties shall be granted on submission of a request by the means mentioned in Article 12, paragraph 1, provided that the offence concerned is not considered by the Party requested to grant transit as an offence of a political or purely military character having regard to Articles 3 and 4 of this Convention.

2. Transit of a national, within the meaning of Article 6, of a country requested to grant transit may be refused.

3. Subject to the provisions of paragraph 4 of this article, it shall be necessary to produce the documents mentioned in Article 12, paragraph 2.

4. If air transport is used, the following provisions shall apply:

(a) when it is not intended to land, the requesting Party shall notify the Party over whose territory the flight is to be made and shall certify that one of the documents mentioned in Article 12, paragraph 2 (a) exists. In the case of an unscheduled landing, such notification shall have the effect of a request for provisional arrest as provided for in Article 16, and the requesting Party shall submit a formal request for transit;

(b) when it is intended to land, the requesting Party shall submit a formal request for transit.

5. A Party may, however, at the time of signature or of the deposit of its instrument of ratification of, or accession to, this Convention, declare that it will only grant transit of a person on some or all of the conditions on which it grants extradition. In that event, reciprocity may be applied.

6. The transit of the extradited person shall not be carried out through any territory where there is reason to believe that his life or his freedom may be threatened by reason of his race, religion, nationality or political opinion.

Article 22. Procedure. Except where this Convention otherwise provides, the procedure with regard to extradition and provisional arrest shall be governed solely by the law of the requested Party.

Article 23. Language to be Used. The documents to be produced shall be in the language of the requesting or requested Party. The requested Party may require a translation into one of the official languages of the Council of Europe to be chosen by it.

Article 24. Expenses. 1. Expenses incurred in the territory of the requested Party by reason of extradition shall be borne by that Party.

2. Expenses incurred by reason of transit through the territory of a Party requested to grant transit shall be borne by the requesting Party.

3. In the event of extradition from a non-metropolitan territory of the requested Party, the expenses occasioned by travel between that territory and the metropolitan territory of the requesting Party shall be borne by the latter. The same rule shall apply to expenses occasioned by travel between the non-metropolitan territory of the requested Party and its metropolitan territory.

Article 25. Definition of "Detention Order". For the purposes of this Convention, the expression "detention order" means any order involving deprivation of liberty which has been made by a criminal court in addition to or instead of a prison sentence.

Article 26. Reservations. 1. Any Contracting Party may, when signing this Convention or when depositing its instrument of ratification or accession, make a reservation in respect of any provision or provisions of the Convention.

2. Any Contracting Party which has made a reservation shall withdraw it as soon as circumstances permit. Such withdrawal shall be made by notification to the Secretary General of the Council of Europe.

3. A Contracting Party which has made a reservation in respect of a provision of the Convention may not claim application of the said provision by another Party save in so far as it has itself accepted the provision.

Article 27. Territorial Application. 1. This Convention shall apply to the metropolitan territories of the Contracting Parties.

2. In respect of France, it shall also apply to Algeria and to the overseas Departments and, in respect of the United Kingdom of Great Britain and Northern Ireland, to the Channel Islands and to the Isle of Man.

3. The Federal Republic of Germany may extend the application of this Convention to the *Land* of Berlin by notice addressed to the Secretary General of the Council of Europe, who shall notify the other Parties of such declaration.

4. By direct arrangement between two or more Contracting Parties, the application of this Convention may be extended, subject to the conditions laid down in the arrangement, to any territory of such Parties, other than the territories mentioned in paragraphs 1, 2 and 3 of this article, for whose international relations any such Party is responsible.

Article 28. Relations between this Convention and Bilateral Agreements. 1. This Convention shall, in respect of those countries to which it applies, supersede the provisions of any bilateral treaties, conventions or agreements governing extradition between any two Contracting Parties.

2. The Contracting Parties may conclude between themselves bilateral or multilateral agreements only in order to supplement the provisions of this Convention or to facilitate the application of the principles contained therein.

3. Where, as between two or more Contracting Parties, extradition takes place on the basis of a uniform law, the Parties shall be free to regulate their mutual relations in respect of extradition exclusively in accordance with such a system notwithstanding the provisions of this Convention. The same principle shall apply as between two or more Contracting Parties each of which has in force a law providing for the execution in its territory of warrants of arrest issued in the territory of the other Party or Parties. Contracting Parties which exclude or may in the future exclude the application of this Convention as between themselves in accordance with this paragraph shall notify the Secretary General of the Council of Europe accordingly. The Secretary General shall inform the other Contracting Parties of any notification received in accordance with this paragraph.

Article 29. Signature, Ratification and Entry into Force. 1. This Convention shall be open to signature by the Members of the Council of Europe. It shall be ratified. The instruments of ratification shall be deposited with the Secretary General of the Council.

2. The Convention shall come into force 90 days after the date of deposit of the third instrument of ratification.

3. As regards any signatory ratifying subsequently, the Convention shall come into force 90 days after the date of the deposit of its instrument of ratification.

Article 30. Accession. 1. The Committee of Ministers of the Council of Europe may invite any State not a Member of the Council to accede to this Convention, provided that the resolution containing such invitation receives the unanimous agreement of the Members of the Council who have ratified the Convention.

2. Accession shall be by deposit with the Secretary General of the Council of an instrument of accession, which shall take effect 90 days after the date of its deposit.

Article 31. Denunciation. Any Contracting Party may denounce this Convention in so far as it is concerned by giving notice to the Secretary General of the Council of Europe. Denunciation shall take effect six months after the date when the Secretary General of the Council received such notification.

Article 32. Notifications. The Secretary General of the Council of Europe shall notify the Members of the Council and the government of any State which has acceded to this Convention of:

(a) the deposit of any instrument of ratification or accession;

(b) the date of entry into force of this Convention;

(c) any declaration made in accordance with the provisions of Article 6, paragraph 1, and of Article 21, paragraph 5;

(d) any reservation made in accordance with Article 26, paragraph 1;

(e) the withdrawal of any reservation in accordance with Article 26, paragraph 2;

(f) any notification of denunciation received in accordance with the provisions of Article 31 and by the date on which such denunciation will take effect.

In witness whereof the undersigned, being duly authorised thereto, have signed this Convention.

Done at Paris, this 13th day of December 1957, in English and French, both texts being equally authentic, in a single copy which shall remain deposited in the archives of the Council of Europe. The Secretary General of the Council of Europe shall transmit certified copies to the signatory governments.

EUROPEAN CONVENTION ON EXTRADITION: ADDITIONAL PROTOCOL (1975). The first of two additional protocols to the European Convention on Extradition was concluded by the COMMITTEE OF MINISTERS OF THE COUNCIL OF EUROPE meeting in Strasbourg on 15 October 1975 and entered into force on 20 August 1979. It excludes war crimes and crimes against humanity from the category of political offences, set out in article 3 of the parent convention, to which extradition does not apply. It also authorizes States parties to refuse extradition if the offender has already been tried for the offence, or offences, in respect of which the request is made. The text of the additional protocol (*European Treaty Series* 86) is as follows:

The member States of the Council of Europe, signatory to this Protocol,

Having regard to the provisions of the European Convention on Extradition opened for signature in Paris on 13 December 1957 (hereinafter referred to as "the Convention") and in particular Articles 3 and 9 thereof;

Considering that it is desirable to supplement these Articles with a view to strengthening the protection of humanity and of individuals,

Have agreed as follows:

Chapter I

Article 1. For the application of Article 3 of the Convention, political offences shall not be considered to include the following:

(a) the crimes against humanity specified in the Convention on the Prevention and Punishment of the Crime of Genocide adopted on 9 December 1948 by the General Assembly of the United Nations;

(b) the violations specified in Article 50 of the 1949 Geneva Convention for the Amelioration of the Condition of the Wounded and Sick in Armed Forces in the Field, Article 51 of the 1949 Geneva Convention for the Amelioration of the Condition of Wounded, Sick and Shipwrecked Members of Armed Forces at Sea, Article 130 of the 1949 Geneva Convention relative to the Treatment of Prisoners of War and Article 147 of the 1949 Geneva Convention relative to the Protection of Civilian Persons in Time of War;

(c) any comparable violations of the laws of war having effect at the time when this Protocol enters into force and of customs of war existing at that time, which are not already provided for in the above-mentioned provisions of the Geneva Conventions.

Chapter II

Article 2. Article 9 of the Convention shall be supplemented by the following text, the original Article 9 of the Convention becoming paragraph 1 and the under-mentioned provisions becoming paragraphs 2, 3 and 4:

"2. The extradition of a person against whom a final judgment has been rendered in a third State, Contracting Party to the Convention, for the offence or offences in respect of which the claim was made, shall not be granted:

(a) if the afore-mentioned judgment resulted in his acquittal;

(b) if the term of imprisonment or other measure to which he was sentenced:

(i) has been completely enforced;

(ii) has been wholly, or with respect to the part not enforced, the subject of a pardon or an amnesty;

(c) if the court convicted the offender without imposing a sanction.

3. However, in the cases referred to in paragraph 2, extradition may be granted:

(a) if the offence in respect of which judgment has been rendered was committed against a person, an institution or any thing having public status in the requesting State;

(b) if the person on whom judgment was passed had himself a public status in the requesting State;

(c) if the offence in respect of which judgment was passed was committed completely or partly in the territory of the requesting State or in a place treated as its territory.

4. The provisions of paragraphs 2 and 3 shall not prevent the application of wider domestic provisions relating to the effect of *ne bis in idem* attached to foreign criminal judgments."

Chapter III

Article 3. 1. This Protocol shall be open to signature by the member States of the Council of Europe which have signed the Convention. It shall be subject to ratification, acceptance or approval. Instruments of ratification, acceptance or approval shall be deposited with the Secretary General of the Council of Europe.

2. The Protocol shall enter into force 90 days after the date of the deposit of the third instrument of ratification, acceptance or approval.

3. In respect of a signatory State ratifying, accepting or approving subsequently, the Protocol shall enter into force 90 days after the date of the deposit of its instruments of ratification, acceptance or approval.

4. A member State of the Council of Europe may not ratify, accept or approve this Protocol without having, simultaneously or previously, ratified the Convention.

Article 4. 1. Any State which has acceded to the Convention may accede to this Protocol after the Protocol has entered into force.

2. Such accession shall be effected by depositing with the Secretary General of the Council of Europe an instrument of accession which shall take effect 90 days after the date of its deposit.

Article 5. 1. Any State may, at the time of signature or when depositing its instrument of ratification, acceptance, approval or accession, specify the territory or territories to which this Protocol shall apply.

2. Any State may, when depositing its instrument of ratification, acceptance, approval or accession or at any later date, by declaration addressed to the Secretary General of the Council of Europe, extend this Protocol to any other territory or territories specified in the declaration and for whose international relations it is responsible or on whose behalf it is authorised to give undertakings.

3. Any declaration made in pursuance of the preceding paragraph may, in respect of any territory mentioned in such declaration, be withdrawn according to the procedure laid down in Article 8 of this Protocol.

Article 6. 1. Any State may, at the time of signature or when depositing its instrument of ratification, acceptance, approval or accession, declare that it does not accept one or the other of Chapters I or II.

2. Any Contracting Party may withdraw a declaration it has made in accordance with the foregoing paragraph by

means of a declaration addressed to the Secretary General of the Council of Europe which shall become effective as from the date of its receipt.

3. No reservation may be made to the provisions of this Protocol.

Article 7. The European Committee on Crime Problems of the Council of Europe shall be kept informed regarding the application of this Protocol and shall do whatever is needful to facilitate a friendly settlement of any difficulty which may arise out of its execution.

Article 8. 1. Any Contracting Party may, in so far as it is concerned, denounce this Protocol by means of a notification addressed to the Secretary General of the Council of Europe.

2. Such denunciation shall take effect six months after the date of receipt by the Secretary General of such notification.

3. Denunciation of the Convention entails automatically denunciation of this Protocol.

Article 9. The Secretary General of the Council of Europe shall notify the member States of the Council and any State which has acceded to the Convention of:

(a) any signature;

(b) any deposit of an instrument of ratification, acceptance, approval or accession;

(c) any date of entry into force of this Protocol in accordance with Article 3 thereof;

(d) any declaration received in pursuance of the provisions of Article 5 and any withdrawal of such a declaration;

(e) any declaration made in pursuance of the provisions of Article 6, paragraph 1;

(f) the withdrawal of any declaration carried out in pursuance of the provisions of Article 6, paragraph 2;

(g) any notification received in pursuance of the provisions of Article 8 and the date on which denunciation takes effect.

In witness whereof, the undersigned, being duly authorised thereto, have signed this Protocol.

Done at Strasbourg, this 15th day of October 1975, in English and in French, both texts being equally authoritative, in a single copy which shall remain deposited in the archives of the Council of Europe. The Secretary General of the Council of Europe shall transmit certified copies to each of the signatory and acceding States.

EUROPEAN CONVENTION ON EXTRADITION: SECOND ADDITIONAL PROTOCOL (1978). The

Second Additional Protocol to the European Convention on Extradition was concluded by the COMMITTEE OF MINISTERS OF THE COUNCIL OF EUROPE meeting in Strasbourg on 17 March 1978 and entered into force on 5 June 1983. It revises provisions of the parent convention relating to such matters as fiscal offences, judgements *in absentia,* and amnesty, with a view to facilitating the application of that convention. The text of the second additional protocol (*European Treaty Series* 98) is as follows:

The member States of the Council of Europe, signatory to this Protocol,

Desirous of facilitating the application of the European Convention on Extradition opened for signature in Paris on 13 December 1957 (hereinafter referred to as "the Convention") in the field of fiscal offences;

Considering it also desirable to supplement the Convention in certain other respects,

Have agreed as follows:

Chapter I

Article 1. Paragraph 2 of Article 2 of the Convention shall be supplemented by the following provision:

"This right shall also apply to offences which are subject only to pecuniary sanctions."

Chapter II

Article 2. Article 5 of the Convention shall be replaced by the following provisions:

"Fiscal Offences

1. For offences in connection with taxes, duties, customs and exchange extradition shall take place between the Contracting Parties in accordance with the provisions of the Convention if the offence, under the law of the requested Party, corresponds to an offence of the same nature.

2. Extradition may not be refused on the ground that the law of the requested Party does not impose the same kind of tax or duty or does not contain a tax, duty, customs or exchange regulation of the same kind as the law of the requesting Party."

Chapter III

Article 3. The Convention shall be supplemented by the following provisions;

"Judgments in absentia

1. When a Contracting Party requests from another Contracting Party the extradition of a person for the purpose of carrying out a sentence or detention order imposed by a decision rendered against him in absentia, the requested Party may refuse to extradite for this purpose if, in its opinion, the proceedings leading to the judgment did not satisfy the minimum rights of defence recognised as due to everyone charged with criminal offence. However, extradition shall be granted if the requesting Party gives an assurance considered sufficient to guarantee to the person claimed the right to a retrial which safeguards the rights of defence. This decision will authorise the requesting Party either to enforce the judgment in question if the convicted person does not make an opposition or, if he does, to take proceedings against the person extradited.

2. When the requested Party informs the person whose extradition has been requested of the judgment rendered against him in absentia, the requesting Party shall not regard this communication as a formal notification for the purposes of the criminal procedure in that State."

Chapter IV

Article 4. The Convention shall be supplemented by the following provisions:

"Amnesty

Extradition shall not be granted for an offence in respect of which an amnesty has been declared in the requested State and which that State had competence to prosecute under its own criminal law."

Chapter V

Article 5. Paragraph 1 of Article 12 of the Convention shall be replaced by the following provisions:

"The request shall be in writing and shall be addressed by the Ministry of Justice of the requesting Party to the Ministry of Justice of the requested Party; however, use of the diplomatic channel is not excluded. Other means of communication may be arranged by direct agreement between two or more Parties."

Chapter VI

Article 6. 1. This Protocol shall be open to signature by the member States of the Council of Europe which have signed the Convention. It shall be subject to ratification, acceptance or approval. Instruments of ratification, acceptance or approval shall be deposited with the Secretary General of the Council of Europe.

2. The Protocol shall enter into force 90 days after the date of the deposit of the third instrument of ratification, acceptance or approval.

3. In respect of a signatory State ratifying, accepting or approving subsequently, the Protocol shall enter into force 90 days after the date of the deposit of its instrument of ratification, acceptance or approval.

4. A member State of the Council of Europe may not ratify, accept or approve this Protocol without having, simultaneously or previously, ratified the Convention.

Article 7. 1. Any State which has acceded to the Convention may accede to this Protocol after the Protocol has entered into force.

2. Such accession shall be effected by depositing with the Secretary General of the Council of Europe an instrument of accession which shall take effect 90 days after the date of its deposit.

Article 8. 1. Any State may, at the time of signature or when depositing its instrument of ratification, acceptance, approval or accession, specify the territory or territories to which this Protocol shall apply.

2. Any State may, when depositing its instrument of ratification, acceptance, approval or accession or at any later date, by declaration addressed to the Secretary General of the Council of Europe, extend this Protocol to any other territory or territories specified in the declaration and for whose international relations it is responsible or on whose behalf it is authorised to give undertakings.

3. Any declaration made in pursuance of the preceding paragraph may, in respect of any territory mentioned in such declaration, be withdrawn by means of a notification addressed to the Secretary General of the Council of Europe. Such withdrawal shall take effect six months after the date of receipt by the Secretary General of the Council of Europe of the notification.

Article 9. 1. Reservations made by a State to a provision of the Convention shall be applicable also to this Protocol, unless that State otherwise declares at the time of signature or when depositing its instrument of ratification, acceptance, approval or accession.

2. Any State may, at the time of signature or when depositing its instrument of ratification, acceptance, approval or accession, declare that it reserves the right:

(a) not to accept Chapter I;

(b) not to accept Chapter II, or to accept it only in respect of certain offences or certain categories of the offences referred to in Article 2;

(c) not to accept Chapter III, or to accept only paragraph 1 of Article 3;

(d) not to accept Chapter IV;

(e) not to accept Chapter V.

3. Any Contracting Party may withdraw a reservation it has made in accordance with the foregoing paragraph by means of a declaration addressed to the Secretary General of the Council of Europe which shall become effective as from the date of its receipt.

4. A Contracting Party which has applied to this Protocol a reservation made in respect of a provision of the Convention or which has made a reservation in respect of a provision of this Protocol may not claim the application of that provision by another Contracting Party; it may, however, if its reservation is partial or conditional, claim the application of that provision in so far as it has itself accepted it.

5. No other reservation may be made to the provisions of this Protocol.

Article 10. The European Committee on Crime Problems of the Council of Europe shall be kept informed regarding the application of this Protocol and shall do whatever is needful to facilitate a friendly settlement of any difficulty which may arise out of its execution.

Article 11. 1. Any Contracting Party may, in so far as it is concerned, denounce this Protocol by means of a notification addressed to the Secretary General of the Council of Europe.

2. Such denunciation shall take effect six months after the date of receipt by the Secretary General of such notification.

3. Denunciation of the Convention entails automatically denunciation of this Protocol.

Article 12. The Secretary General of the Council of Europe shall notify the member States of the Council and any State which has acceded to the Convention of:

(a) any signature of this Protocol;

(b) any deposit of an instrument of ratification, acceptance, approval or accession;

(c) any date of entry into force of this Protocol in accordance with Articles 6 and 7;

(d) any declaration received in pursuance of the provisions of paragraphs 2 and 3 of Article 8;

(e) any declaration received in pursuance of the provisions of paragraph 1 of Article 9;

(f) any reservation made in pursuance of the provisions of paragraph 2 of Article 9;

(g) the withdrawal of any reservation carried out in pursuance of the provisions of paragraph 3 of Article 9;

(h) any notification received in pursuance of the provisions of Article 11 and the date on which denunciation takes effect.

In witness whereof the undersigned, being duly authorised thereto, have signed this Protocol.

Done at Strasbourg, this 17th day of March 1978, in English and in French, both texts being equally authoritative, in a single copy which shall remain deposited in the archives of the Council of Europe. The Secretary General of the Council of Europe shall transmit certified copies to each of the signatory and acceding States.

EUROPEAN CONVENTION ON HUMAN RIGHTS (1950). Formally entitled Convention for the Protection of Human Rights and Fundamental Freedoms, this is the first international treaty which provides for

the collective enforcement of a number of human rights and fundamental freedoms set out in the UNIVERSAL DECLARATION OF HUMAN RIGHTS. Prepared under the auspices of the COUNCIL OF EUROPE and open for signature and ratification by all members of the council, it defines the rights and freedoms with which it is concerned and their permissible restrictions and establishes the regional machinery to supervise their implementation: the EUROPEAN COMMISSION ON HUMAN RIGHTS and the EUROPEAN COURT OF HUMAN RIGHTS.

Under article 25, the commission may receive petitions from any person, non-governmental organization or group of individuals claiming to be the victim of a violation by one of the high contracting parties of the rights set forth in the convention, provided that the high contracting party against which the complaint has been lodged has declared that it recognizes the competence of the commission to receive such petitions. The commission may then deal with the petition with a view to effecting a friendly settlement of the complaint. If a solution is not reached, it must draw up a report and transmit it to the COMMITTEE OF MINISTERS OF THE COUNCIL OF EUROPE and to the States concerned.

Under article 46, any of the high contracting parties may at any time declare that it recognizes as compulsory *ipso facto* and without special agreement the jurisdiction of the court. Under article 48, a case may be brought before the court by the commission or by one of the high contracting Parties concerned. The high contracting parties undertake (article 53) to abide by the decision of the court in any case to which they are parties.

The European Convention on Human Rights has been supplemented by eight protocols: PROTOCOL I (1950), PROTOCOLS II, III AND IV (1963), PROTOCOL V (1966), PROTOCOL VI (1983), PROTOCOL VII (1984) and PROTOCOL VIII (1985).

The convention was concluded by the Committee of Ministers of the Council of Europe, convened in Rome, on 4 November 1950, and entered into force on 3 September 1953. Its text (*European Treaty Series* 5), amended in accordance with the provisions of Protocol III, is as follows:

The governments signatory hereto, being Members of the Council of Europe,

Considering the Universal Declaration of Human Rights proclaimed by the General Assembly of the United Nations on 10 December 1948;

Considering that this Declaration aims at securing the universal and effective recognition and observance of the rights therein declared;

Considering that the aim of the Council of Europe is the achievement of greater unity between its Members and that one of the methods by which that aim is to be pursued is the maintenance and further realisation of human rights and fundamental freedoms;

Reaffirming their profound belief in those fundamental freedoms which are the foundation of justice and peace in the world and are best maintained on the one hand by an effective political democracy and on the other by a common understanding and observance of the human rights upon which they depend;

Being resolved, as the governments of European countries which are like-minded and have a common heritage of political traditions, ideals, freedom and the rule of law, to take the first steps for the collective enforcement of certain of the rights stated in the Universal Declaration;

Have agreed as follows:

Article 1. The High Contracting Parties shall secure to everyone within their jurisdiction the rights and freedoms defined in Section I of this Convention.

Section I

Article 2. 1. Everyone's right to life shall be protected by law. No one shall be deprived of his life intentionally save in the execution of a sentence of a court following his conviction of a crime for which this penalty is provided by law.

2. Deprivation of life shall not be regarded as inflicted in contravention of this article when it results from the use of force which is no more than absolutely necessary;

(a) in defence of any person from unlawful violence;

(b) in order to effect a lawful arrest or to prevent the escape of a person lawfully detained;

(c) in action lawfully taken for the purpose of quelling a riot or insurrection.

Article 3. No one shall be subjected to torture or to inhuman or degrading treatment or punishment.

Article 4. 1. No one shall be held in slavery or servitude.

2. No one shall be required to perform forced or compulsory labour.

3. For the purpose of this article the term "forced or compulsory labour" shall not include:

(a) any work required to be done in the ordinary course of detention imposed according to the provisions of Article 5 of this Convention or during conditional release from such detention;

(b) any service of a military character or, in case of conscientious objectors in countries where they are recognised, service exacted instead of compulsory military service;

(c) any service exacted in case of an emergency or calamity threatening the life or well-being of the community;

(d) any work or service which forms part of normal civic obligations.

Article 5. 1. Everyone has the right to liberty and security of person.

No one shall be deprived of his liberty save in the following cases and in accordance with a procedure prescribed by law:

(a) the lawful detention of a person after conviction by a competent court;

(b) the lawful arrest or detention of a person for non-compliance with the lawful order of a court or in order to secure the fulfilment of any obligation prescribed by law;

(c) the lawful arrest or detention of a person effected for the purpose of bringing him before the competent legal authority on reasonable suspicion of having committed an offence or when it is reasonably considered necessary to prevent his committing an offence or fleeing after having done so;

(d) the detention of a minor by lawful order for the purpose of educational supervision or his lawful detention for the purpose of bringing him before the competent legal authority;

(e) the lawful detention of persons for the prevention of the spreading of infectious diseases, of persons of unsound mind, alcoholics or drug addicts or vagrants;

(f) the lawful arrest or detention of a person to prevent his effecting an unauthorised entry into the country or of a person against whom action is being taken with a view to deportation or extradition.

2. Everyone who is arrested shall be informed promptly, in a language which he understands, of the reasons for his arrest and of any charge against him.

3. Everyone arrested or detained in accordance with the provisions of paragraph 1 (c) of this article shall be brought promptly before a judge or other officer authorised by law to exercise judicial power and shall be entitled to trial within a reasonable time or to release pending trial. Release may be conditioned by guarantees to appear for trial.

4. Everyone who is deprived of his liberty by arrest or detention shall be entitled to take proceedings by which the lawfulness of his detention shall be decided speedily by a court and his release ordered if the detention is not lawful.

5. Everyone who has been the victim of arrest or detention in contravention of the provisions of this article shall have an enforceable right to compensation.

Article 6. 1. In the determination of his civil rights and obligations or of any criminal charge against him, everyone is entitled to a fair and public hearing within a reasonable time by an independent and impartial tribunal established by law. Judgment shall be pronounced publicly but the press and public may be excluded from all or part of the trial in the interests of morals, public order or national security in a democratic society, where the interests of juveniles or the protection of the private life of the parties so require, or to the extent strictly necessary in the opinion of the court in special circumstances where publicity would prejudice the interests of justice.

2. Everyone charged with a criminal offence shall be presumed innocent until proved guilty according to law.

3. Everyone charged with a criminal offence has the following minimum rights:

(a) to be informed promptly, in a language which he understands and in detail, of the nature and cause of the accusation against him;

(b) to have adequate time and facilities for the preparation of his defence;

(c) to defend himself in person or through legal assistance of his own choosing or, if he has not sufficient means to pay for legal assistance, to be given it free when the interests of justice so require;

(d) to examine or have examined witnesses against him and to obtain the attendance and examination of witnesses on his behalf under the same conditions as witnesses against him;

(e) to have the free assistance of an interpreter if he cannot understand or speak the language used in court.

Article 7. 1. No one shall be held guilty of any criminal offence on account of any act or omission which did not constitute a criminal offence under national or international law at the time when it was committed. Nor shall a heavier penalty be imposed than the one that was applicable at the time the criminal offence was committed.

2. This article shall not prejudice the trial and punishment of any person for any act or omission which, at the time when it was committed, was criminal according to the general principles of law recognised by civilised nations.

Article 8. 1. Everyone has the right to respect for his private and family life, his home and his correspondence.

2. There shall be no interference by a public authority with the exercise of this right except such as is in accordance with the law and is necessary in a democratic society in the interests of national security, public safety or the economic well-being of the country, for the prevention of disorder or crime, for the protection of health or morals, or for the protection of the rights and freedoms of others.

Article 9. 1. Everyone has the right to freedom of thought, conscience and religion; this right includes freedom to change his religion or belief and freedom, either alone or in community with others and in public or private, to manifest his religion or belief, in worship, teaching, practice and observance.

2. Freedom to manifest one's religion or beliefs shall be subject only to such limitations as are prescribed by law and are necessary in a democratic society in the interests of public safety, for the protection of public order, health or morals, or for the protection of the rights and freedoms of others.

Article 10. 1. Everyone has the right to freedom of expression. This right shall include freedom to hold opinions and to receive and impart information and ideas without interference by public authority and regardless of frontiers. This article shall not prevent States from requiring the licensing of broadcasting, television or cinema enterprises.

2. The exercise of these freedoms, since it carries with it duties and responsibilities, may be subject to such formalities, conditions, restrictions or penalties as are prescribed by law and are necessary in a democratic society, in the interests of national security, territorial integrity or public safety, for the prevention of disorder or crime, for the protection of health or morals, for the protection of the reputation or rights of others, for preventing the disclosure of information received in confidence, or for maintaining the authority and impartiality of the judiciary.

Article 11. 1. Everyone has the right to freedom of peaceful assembly and to freedom of association with others, including the right to form and to join trade unions for the protection of his interests.

2. No restrictions shall be placed on the exercise of these rights other than such as are prescribed by law and are necessary in a democratic society in the interests of national security or public safety, for the prevention of disorder or crime, for the protection of health or morals or for the protection of the rights and freedoms of others. This article shall not prevent the imposition of lawful restrictions on the exercise of these rights by members of the armed forces, of the police or of the administration of the State.

Article 12. Men and women of marriageable age have the right to marry and to found a family, according to the national laws governing the exercise of this right.

Article 13. Everyone whose rights and freedoms as set forth in this Convention are violated shall have an effective remedy before a national authority notwithstanding that the violation has been committed by persons acting in an official capacity.

Article 14. The enjoyment of the rights and freedoms set

forth in this Convention shall be secured without discrimination on any ground such as sex, race, colour, language, religion, political or other opinion, national or social origin, association with a national minority, property, birth or other status.

Article 15. 1. In time of war or other public emergency threatening the life of the nation any High Contracting Party may take measures derogating from its obligations under this Convention to the extent strictly required by the exigencies of the situation, provided that such measures are not inconsistent with its other obligations under international law.

2. No derogation from Article 2, except in respect of deaths resulting from lawful acts of war, or from Articles 3, 4 (paragraph 1) and 7 shall be made under this provision.

3. Any High Contracting Party availing itself of this right of derogation shall keep the Secretary General of the Council of Europe fully informed of the measures which it has taken and the reasons therefor. It shall also inform the Secretary General of the Council of Europe when such measures have ceased to operate and the provisions of the Convention are again being fully executed.

Article 16. Nothing in Articles 10, 11, and 14 shall be regarded as preventing the High Contracting Parties from imposing restrictions on the political activity of aliens.

Article 17. Nothing in this Convention may be interpreted as implying for any State, group or person any right to engage in any activity or perform any act aimed at the destruction of any of the rights and freedoms set forth herein or at their limitation to a greater extent than is provided for in the Convention.

Article 18. The restrictions permitted under this Convention to the said rights and freedoms shall not be applied for any purpose other than those for which they have been prescribed.

Section II

Article 19. To ensure the observance of the engagements undertaken by the High Contracting Parties in the present Convention, there shall be set up:

(a) A European Commission of Human Rights hereinafter referred to as "the Commission";

(b) A European Court of Human Rights, hereinafter referred to as "the Court".

Section III

Article 20. The Commission shall consist of a number of members equal to that of the High Contracting Parties. No two members of the Commission may be nationals of the same State.

Article 21. 1. The members of the Commission shall be elected by the Committee of Ministers by an absolute majority of votes, from a list of names drawn up by the Bureau of the Consultative Assembly; each group of the Representatives of the High Contracting Parties in the Consultative Assembly shall put forward three candidates, of whom two at least shall be its nationals.

2. As far as applicable, the same procedure shall be followed to complete the Commission in the event of other States subsequently becoming Parties to this Convention, and in filling casual vacancies.

Article 22. 1. The members of the Commission shall be elected for a period of six years. They may be re-elected. However, of the members elected at the first election, the terms of seven members shall expire at the end of three years.

2. The members whose terms are to expire at the end of the initial period of three years shall be chosen by lot by the Secretary General of the Council of Europe immediately after the first election has been completed.

3. A member of the Commission elected to replace a member whose term of office has not expired shall hold office for the remainder of his predecessor's term.

4. The members of the Commission shall hold office until replaced. After having been replaced, they shall continue to deal with such cases as they already have under consideration.

Article 23. The members of the Commission shall sit on the Commission in their individual capacity.

Article 24. Any High Contracting Party may refer to the Commission, through the Secretary General of the Council of Europe, any alleged breach of the provisions of the Convention by another High Contracting Party.

Article 25. 1. The Commission may receive petitions addressed to the Secretary General of the Council of Europe from any person, non-governmental organisation or group of individuals claiming to be the victim of a violation by one of the High Contracting Parties of the rights set forth in this Convention, provided that the High Contracting Party against which the complaint has been lodged has declared that it recognises the competence of the Commission to receive such petitions. Those of the High Contracting Parties who have made such a declaration undertake not to hinder in any way the effective exercise of this right.

2. Such declarations may be made for a specific period.

3. The declarations shall be deposited with the Secretary General of the Council of Europe who shall transmit copies thereof to the High Contracting Parties and publish them.

4. The Commission shall only exercise the powers provided for in this article when at least six High Contracting Parties are bound by declarations made in accordance with the preceding paragraphs.

Article 26. The Commission may only deal with the matter after all domestic remedies have been exhausted, according to the generally recognised rules of international law, and within a period of six months from the date on which the final decision was taken.

Article 27. 1. The Commission shall not deal with any petition submitted under Article 25 which:

(a) is anonymous, or

(b) is substantially the same as a matter which has already been examined by the Commission or has already been submitted to another procedure of international investigation or settlement and if it contains no relevant new information.

2. The Commission shall consider inadmissible any petition submitted under Article 25 which it considers incompatible with the provisions of the present Convention, manifestly ill-founded, or an abuse of the right of petition.

3. The Commission shall reject any petition referred to it which it considers inadmissible under Article 26.

Article 28. In the event of the Commission accepting a petition referred to it:

(a) it shall, with a view to ascertaining the facts, undertake together with the representatives of the parties an examination of the petition and, if need be, an investigation, for the effective conduct of which the States concerned shall furnish all necessary facilities, after an exchange of views with the Commission;

(b) it shall place itself at the disposal of the parties concerned with a view to securing a friendly settlement of the matter on the basis of respect for human rights as defined in this Convention.

Article 29. After it has accepted a petition submitted under Article 25, the Commission may nevertheless decide unanimously to reject the petition if, in the course of its examination, it finds that the existence of one of the grounds for non-acceptance provided for in Article 27 has been established.

In such a case, the decision shall be communicated to the Parties.

Article 30. If the Commission succeeds in effecting a friendly settlement in accordance with Article 28, it shall draw up a report which shall be sent to the States concerned, to the Committee of Ministers and to the Secretary General of the Council of Europe for publication. This report shall be confined to a brief statement of the facts and of the solution reached.

Article 31. 1. If a solution is not reached, the Commission shall draw up a report on the facts and state its opinion as to whether the facts found disclose a breach by the State concerned of its obligations under the Convention. The opinions of all the members of the Commission on this point may be stated in the report.

2. The report shall be transmitted to the Committee of Ministers. It shall also be transmitted to the States concerned, who shall not be at liberty to publish it.

3. In transmitting the report to the Committee of Ministers the Commission may make such proposals as it thinks fit.

Article 32. 1. If the question is not referred to the Court in accordance with Article 48 of this Convention within a period of three months from the date of the transmission of the report to the Committee of Ministers, the Committee of Ministers shall decide by a majority of two thirds of the members entitled to sit on the Committee whether there has been a violation of the Convention.

2. In the affirmative case the Committee of Ministers shall prescribe a period during which the High Contracting Party concerned must take the measures required by the decision of the Committee of Ministers.

3. If the High Contracting Party concerned has not taken satisfactory measures within the prescribed period, the Committee of Ministers shall decide by the majority provided for in paragraph 1 above what effect shall be given to its original decision and shall publish the report.

4. The High Contracting Parties undertake to regard as binding on them any decision which the Committee of Ministers may take in application of the preceding paragraphs.

Article 33. The Commission shall meet in camera.

Article 34. Subject to the provisions of Article 29, the Commission shall take its decisions by a majority of the members present and voting.

Article 35. The Commission shall meet as the circumstances require. The meetings shall be convened by the Secretary General of the Council of Europe.

Article 36. The Commission shall draw up its own rules of procedure.

Article 37. The secretariat of the Commission shall be provided by the Secretary General of the Council of Europe.

Section IV

Article 38. The European Court of Human Rights shall consist of a number of judges equal to that of the Members of the Council of Europe. No two judges may be nationals of the same State.

Article 39. 1. The members of the Court shall be elected by the Consultative Assembly by a majority of the votes cast from a list of persons nominated by the Members of the Council of Europe; each Member shall nominate three candidates, of whom two at least shall be its nationals.

2. As far as applicable, the same procedure shall be followed to complete the Court in the event of the admission of new Members of the Council of Europe, and in filling casual vacancies.

3. The candidates shall be of high moral character and must either possess the qualifications required for appointment to high judicial office or be jurisconsults of recognised competence.

Article 40. 1. The members of the Court shall be elected for a period of nine years. They may be re-elected. However, of the members elected at the first election the terms of four members shall expire at the end of three years, and the terms of four more members shall expire at the end of six years.

2. The members whose terms are to expire at the end of the initial periods of three and six years shall be chosen by lot by the Secretary General immediately after the first election has been completed.

3. A member of the Court elected to replace a member whose term of office has not expired shall hold office for the remainder of his predecessor's term.

4. The members of the Court shall hold office until replaced. After having been replaced, they shall continue to deal with such cases as they already have under consideration.

Article 41. The Court shall elect its President and Vice-President for a period of three years. They may be re-elected.

Article 42. The members of the Court shall receive for each day of duty a compensation to be determined by the Committee of Ministers.

Article 43. For the consideration of each case brought before it the Court shall consist of a Chamber composed of seven judges. There shall sit as an ex officio member of the Chamber the judge who is a national of any State party concerned, or, if there is none, a person of its choice who shall sit in the capacity of judge; the names of the other judges shall be chosen by lot by the President before the opening of the case.

Article 44. Only the High Contracting Parties and the Commission shall have the right to bring a case before the Court.

Article 45. The jurisdiction of the Court shall extend to all cases concerning the interpretation and application of the present Convention which the High Contracting Parties or the Commission shall refer to it in accordance with Article 48.

Article 46. 1. Any of the High Contracting Parties may at any time declare that it recognizes as compulsory ipso facto and without special agreement the jurisdiction of the Court in all matters concerning the interpretation and application of the present Convention.

2. The declarations referred to above may be made unconditionally or on condition of reciprocity on the part of several or certain other High Contracting Parties or for a specified period.

3. These declarations shall be deposited with the Secretary General of the Council of Europe who shall transmit copies thereof to the High Contracting Parties.

Article 47. The Court may only deal with a case after the Commission has acknowledged the failure of efforts for a friendly settlement and within the period of three months provided for in Article 32.

Article 48. The following may bring a case before the Court, provided that the High Contracting Party concerned, if there is only one, or the High Contracting Parties concerned, if there is more than one, are subject to the compulsory jurisdiction of the Court or, failing that, with the consent of the High Contracting Party concerned, if there is only one, or of the High Contracting Parties concerned if there is more than one:

(a) the Commission;

(b) a High Contracting Party whose national is alleged to be a victim;

(c) a High Contracting Party which referred the case to the Commission;

(d) a High Contracting Party against which the complaint has been lodged.

Article 49. In the event of dispute as to whether the Court has jurisdiction, the matter shall be settled by the decision of the Court.

Article 50. If the Court finds that a decision or a measure taken by a legal authority or any other authority of a High Contracting Party is completely or partially in conflict with the obligations arising from the present Convention, and if the internal law of the said Party allows only partial reparation to be made for the consequences of this decision or measure, the decision of the Court shall, if necessary, afford just satisfaction to the injured party.

Article 51. 1. Reasons shall be given for the judgment of the Court.

2. If the judgment does not represent in whole or in part the unanimous opinion of the judges, any judge shall be entitled to deliver a separate opinion.

Article 52. The judgment of the Court shall be final.

Article 53. The High Contracting Parties undertake to abide by the decision of the Court in any case to which they are Parties.

Article 54. The judgment of the Court shall be transmitted to the Committee of Ministers which shall supervise its execution.

Article 55. The Court shall draw up its own rules and shall determine its own procedure.

Article 56. 1. The first election of the members of the Court shall take place after the declarations by the High Contracting Parties mentioned in Article 46 have reached a total of eight.

2. No case can be brought before the Court before this election.

Section V

Article 57. On receipt of a request from the Secretary General of the Council of Europe any High Contracting Party shall furnish an explanation of the manner in which its internal law ensures the effective implementation of any of the provisions of this Convention.

Article 58. The expenses of the Commission and the Court shall be borne by the Council of Europe.

Article 59. The members of the Commission and of the Court shall be entitled, during the discharge of their functions, to the privileges and immunities provided for in Article 40 of the Statute of the Council of Europe and in the agreements made thereunder.

Article 60. Nothing in this Convention shall be construed as limiting or derogating from any of the human rights and fundamental freedoms which may be ensured under the laws of any High Contracting Party or under any other agreement to which it is a Party.

Article 61. Nothing in this Convention shall prejudice the powers conferred on the Committee of Ministers by the Statute of the Council of Europe.

Article 62. The High Contracting Parties agree that, except by special agreement, they will not avail themselves of treaties, conventions or declarations in force between them for the purpose of submitting, by way of petition, a dispute arising out of the interpretation or application of this Convention to a means of settlement other than those provided for in this Convention.

Article 63. 1. Any State may at the time of its ratification or at any time thereafter declare by notification addressed to the Secretary General of the Council of Europe that the present Convention shall extend to all or any of the territories for whose international relations it is responsible.

2. The Convention shall extend to the territory or territories named in the notification as from the thirtieth day after the receipt of this notification by the Secretary General of the Council of Europe.

3. The provisions of this Convention shall be applied in such territories with due regard, however, to local requirements.

4. Any State which has made a declaration in accordance with paragraph 1 of this article may at any time thereafter declare on behalf of one or more of the territories to which the declaration relates that it accepts the competence of the Commission to receive petitions from individuals, non-governmental organisations or groups of individuals in accordance with Article 25 of the present Convention.

Article 64. 1. Any State may, when signing this Convention or when depositing its instrument of ratification, make a reservation in respect of any particular provision of the Convention to the extent that any law then in force in its territory is not in conformity with the provision. Reservations of a general character shall not be permitted under this article.

2. Any reservation made under this article shall contain a brief statement of the law concerned.

Article 65. 1. A High Contracting Party may denounce the present Convention only after the expiry of five years from the date on which it became a Party to it and after six months' notice contained in a notification addressed to the Secretary General of the Council of Europe, who shall inform the other High Contracting Parties.

2. Such a denunciation shall not have the effect of releasing the High Contracting Party concerned from its obligations under this Convention in respect of any act which, being capable of constituting a violation of such obligations, may have been performed by it before the date at which the denunciation became effective.

3. Any High Contracting Party which shall cease to be a Member of the Council of Europe shall cease to be a Party to this Convention under the same conditions.

4. The Conventions may be denounced in accordance with the provisions of the preceding paragraphs in respect of any territory to which it has been declared to extend under the terms of Article 63.

Article 66. 1. This Convention shall be open to the signature of the Members of the Council of Europe. It shall be ratified. Ratifications shall be deposited with the Secretary General of the Council of Europe.

2. The present Convention shall come into force after the deposit of ten instruments of ratification.

3. As regards any signatory ratifying subsequently, the Convention shall come into force at the date of the deposit of its instrument of ratification.

4. The Secretary General of the Council of Europe shall notify all the Members of the Council of Europe of the entry into force of the Convention, the names of the High Contracting Parties who have ratified it, and the deposit of all instruments of ratification which may be effected subsequently.

Done at Rome this 4th day of November 1950 in English and French, both texts being equally authentic, in a single copy which shall remain deposited in the archives of the Council of Europe. The Secretary General shall transmit certified copies to each of the Signatories.

SEE ALSO *African Charter on Human and Peoples' Rights; American Convention on Human Rights and Protocol; Universal Declaration of Human Rights.*

EUROPEAN CONVENTION ON HUMAN RIGHTS: PROTOCOL I (1952).

The protocol adds three rights to those set out in the parent convention: the right to peaceful enjoyment of one's possessions, the right to education, and the right to participate in elections under conditions ensuring the free expression of the opinion of the people in the choice of the legislature.

The protocol was concluded by the COMMITTEE OF MINISTERS OF THE COUNCIL OF EUROPE, convened at Paris, on 20 March 1952, and entered into force on 18 May 1954. The text (*European Treaty Series* 9) is as follows:

The Governments signatory hereto, being Members of the Council of Europe,

Being resolved to take steps to ensure the collective enforcement of certain rights and freedoms other than those already included in section I of the Convention for the Protection of Human Rights and Fundamental Freedoms signed at Rome on 4 November 1950 (hereinafter referred to as "the Convention"),

Have agreed as follows:

Article 1. Every natural or legal person is entitled to the peaceful enjoyment of his possessions. No one shall be deprived of his possessions except in the public interest and subject to the conditions provided for by law and by the general principles of international law.

The preceding provisions shall not, however, in any way impair the right of a State to enforce such laws as it deems necessary to control the use of property in accordance with the general interest or to secure the payment of taxes or other contributions or penalties.

Article 2. No person shall be denied the right to education. In the exercise of any functions which it assumes in relation to education and to teaching, the State shall respect the right of parents to ensure such education and teaching in conformity with their own religious and philosophical convictions.

Article 3. The High Contracting Parties undertake to hold free elections at reasonable intervals by secret ballot, under conditions which will ensure the free expression of the opinion of the people in the choice of the legislature.

Article 4. Any High Contracting Party may at the time of signature or ratification or at any time thereafter communicate to the Secretary-General of the Council of Europe a declaration stating the extent to which it undertakes that the provisions of the present protocol shall apply to such of the territories for the international relations of which it is responsible as are named therein.

Any High Contracting Party which has communicated a declaration in virtue of the preceding paragraph may from time to time communicate a further declaration modifying the terms of any former declaration or terminating the application of the provisions of this protocol in respect of any territory.

A declaration made in accordance with this article shall be deemed to have been made in accordance with paragraph (1) of article 63 of the Convention.

Article 5. As between the High Contracting Parties the provisions of articles 1, 2, 3 and 4 of this protocol shall be regarded as additional articles to the Convention and all the provisions of the Convention shall apply accordingly.

Article 6. This protocol shall be open for signature by the members of the Council of Europe, who are the signatories of the Convention; it shall be ratified at the same time as or after the ratification of the Convention. It shall enter into force after the deposit of ten instruments of ratification. As regards any signatory ratifying subsequently, the protocol shall enter into force at the date of the deposit of its instrument of ratification.

The instruments of ratification shall be deposited with the Secretary-General of the Council of Europe, who will notify all members of the names of those who have ratified.

EUROPEAN CONVENTION ON HUMAN RIGHTS: PROTOCOL II (1963).

The protocol confers upon the EUROPEAN COURT OF HUMAN RIGHTS competence to give advisory opinions on legal questions concerning the parent convention and its protocols. Such advisory opinions may be requested only by the COMMITTEE OF MINISTERS OF THE COUNCIL OF EUROPE. The protocol was concluded by that committee, convened at Strasbourg, on 6 May 1963, and entered into force on 21 September 1970. The text (*European Treaty Series* 44) is as follows:

The member States of the Council of Europe signatory hereto:

Having regard to the provisions of the Convention for the Protection of Human Rights and Fundamental Freedoms signed at Rome on 4 November 1950 (hereinafter referred to as "the Convention") and, in particular, Article 19 instituting, among other bodies, a European Court of Human Rights (hereinafter referred to as "the Court");

Considering that it is expedient to confer upon the Court competence to give advisory opinions subject to certain conditions;

Have agreed as follows:

Article 1. 1. The Court may, at the request of the Committee of Ministers, give advisory opinions on legal questions concerning the interpretation of the Convention and the Protocols thereto.

2. Such opinions shall not deal with any question relating to the content or scope of the rights or freedoms defined in Section 1 of the Convention and in the Protocols thereto, or with any other question which the Commission, the Court or the Committee of Ministers might have to consider in consequence of any such proceedings as could be instituted in accordance with the Convention.

3. Decisions of the Committee of Ministers to request an advisory opinion of the Court shall require a two-thirds majority vote of the representatives entitled to sit on the Committee.

Article 2. The Court shall decide whether a request for an advisory opinion submitted by the Committee of Ministers is within its consultative competence as defined in Article 1 of this Protocol.

Article 3. 1. For the consideration of requests for an advisory opinion, the Court shall sit in plenary session.

2. Reasons shall be given for advisory opinions of the Court.

3. If the advisory opinion does not represent in whole or in part the unanimous opinion of the judges, any judge shall be entitled to deliver a separate opinion.

4. Advisory opinions of the Court shall be communicated to the Committee of Ministers.

Article 4. The powers of the Court under Article 55 of the Convention extend to the drawing up of such rules and the determination of such procedure as the Court may think necessary for the purposes of this Protocol.

Article 5. 1. This Protocol shall be open to signature by member States of the Council of Europe, signatories to the Convention, who may become Parties to it by:

(a) signature without reservation in respect of ratification or acceptance;

(b) signature with reservation in respect of ratification or acceptance, followed by ratification or acceptance.

Instruments of ratification or acceptance shall be deposited with the Secretary-General of the Council of Europe.

2. This Protocol shall enter into force as soon as all States Parties to the Convention shall have become Parties to the Protocol, in accordance with the provisions of paragraph 1 of this Article.

3. From the date of the entry into force of this Protocol, Articles 1 to 4 shall be considered an integral part of the Convention.

4. The Secretary-General of the Council of Europe shall notify the member States of the Council of:

(a) any signature without reservation in respect of ratification or acceptance;

(b) any signature with reservation in respect of ratification or acceptance;

(c) the deposit of any instrument of ratification or acceptance;

(d) the date of entry into force of this Protocol in accordance with paragraph 2 of this Article.

In witness whereof the undersigned, being duly authorised thereto, have signed this Protocol.

Done at Strasbourg, this 6th day of May 1963, in English and in French, both texts being equally authoritative, in a single copy which shall remain deposited in the archives of the Council of Europe. The Secretary General shall transmit certified copies to each of the signatory States.

EUROPEAN CONVENTION ON HUMAN RIGHTS: PROTOCOL III (1963). The protocol amends the parent convention, simplifying the procedure of the **EUROPEAN COMMISSION ON HUMAN RIGHTS** by abolishing the system of sub-commissions. The protocol was concluded by the **COMMITTEE OF MINISTERS OF THE COUNCIL OF EUROPE,** convened at Strasbourg, on 6 May 1963 and entered into force on 21 September 1970. The text *(European Treaty Series* 45) is as follows:

The member States of the Council of Europe, signatories to this Protocol,

Considering that it is advisable to amend certain provisions of the Convention for the Protection of Human Rights and Fundamental Freedoms signed at Rome on 4 November 1950 (hereinafter referred to as "the Convention") concerning the procedure of the European Commission of Human Rights,

Have agreed as follows:

Article 1. 1. Article 29 of the Convention is deleted.

2. The following provision shall be inserted in the Convention:

"Article 29

"After it has accepted a petition submitted under Article 25, the Commission may nevertheless decide unanimously to reject the petition if, in the course of its examination, it finds that the existence of one of the grounds for non-acceptance provided for in Article 27 has been established.

"In such a case, the decision shall be communicated to the parties."

Article 2. In Article 30 of the Convention, the word "Sub-Commission" shall be replaced by the word "Commission".

Article 3. 1. At the beginning of Article 34 of the Convention, the following shall be inserted:

"Subject to the provisions of Article 29 . . ."

2. At the end of the same Article, the sentence "the Sub-Commission shall take its decisions by a majority of its members" shall be deleted.

Article 4. 1. This Protocol shall be open to signature by the member States of the Council of Europe, who may become Parties to it either by:

(a) signature without reservation in respect of ratification or acceptance, or

(b) signature with reservation in respect of acceptance, followed by ratification or acceptance.

Instruments of ratification or acceptance shall be deposited with the Secretary-General of the Council of Europe.

2. This Protocol shall enter into force as soon as all States Parties to the Convention shall have become Parties to the Protocol, in accordance with the provisions of paragraph 1 of this Article.

3. The Secretary-General of the Council of Europe shall notify the member States of the Council of:

(a) any signature without reservation in respect of ratification or acceptance;

(b) any signature with reservation in respect of ratification or acceptance;

(c) the deposit of any instrument of ratification or acceptance;

(d) the date of entry into force of this Protocol in accordance with paragraph 2 of this Article.

In witness whereof the undersigned, being duly authorised thereto, have signed this Protocol.

Done at Strasbourg, this 6th day of May 1963, in English

and in French, both texts being equally authoritative, in a single copy which shall remain deposited in the archives of the Council of Europe. The Secretary General shall transmit certified copies to each of the signatory States.

EUROPEAN CONVENTION ON HUMAN RIGHTS: PROTOCOL IV (1963).

The protocol secures certain rights and freedoms other than those included in the parent convention and in Protocol I thereto: the right not to be deprived of one's liberty merely on the ground of inability to fulfill a contractural obligation; the right to liberty of movement and freedom to choose one's residence; the right to leave any country, including his own; and the right not to be expelled from the territory of the State of which one is a national. It also prohibits the collective expulsion of aliens.

The protocol was concluded by the COMMITTEE OF MINISTERS OF THE COUNCIL OF EUROPE, convened at Strasbourg, on 16 September 1963, and entered into force on 2 May 1968. The text *(European Treaty Series 46)* is as follows:

The Governments signatory hereto, being Members of the Council of Europe,

Being resolved to take steps to ensure the collective enforcement of certain rights and freedoms other than those already included in Section 1 of the Convention for the Protection of Human Rights and Fundamental Freedoms signed at Rome on 4 November 1950 (hereinafter referred to as "the Convention") and in Articles 1 to 3 of the First Protocol to the Convention, signed at Paris on 20 March 1952,

Have agreed as follows:

Article 1. No one shall be deprived of his liberty merely on the ground of inability to fulfil a contractual obligation.

Article 2. 1. Everyone lawfully within the territory of a State shall, within that territory, have the right to liberty of movement and freedom to choose his residence.

2. Everyone shall be free to leave any country, including his own.

3. No restrictions shall be placed on the exercise of these rights other than such as are in accordance with law and are necessary in a democratic society in the interests of national security or public safety, for the maintenance of *ordre public,* for the prevention of crime, for the protection of health or morals, or for the protection of the rights and freedoms of others.

4. The rights set forth in paragraph 1 may also be subject, in particular areas, to restrictions imposed in accordance with law and justified by the public interest in a democratic society.

Article 3. 1. No one shall be expelled, by means either of an individual or of a collective measure, from the territory of the State of which he is a national.

2. No one shall be deprived of the right to enter the territory of the State of which he is a national.

Article 4. Collective expulsion of aliens is prohibited.

Article 5. 1. Any High Contracting Party may, at the time of signature or ratification of this Protocol, or at any time thereafter, communicate to the Secretary-General of the Council of Europe a declaration stating the extent to which it undertakes that the provisions of this Protocol shall apply to such of the territories for the international relations of which it is responsible as are named therein.

2. Any High Contracting Party which has communicated a declaration in virtue of the preceding paragraph may, from time to time, communicate a further declaration modifying the terms of any former declaration or terminating the application of the provisions of this Protocol in respect of any territory.

3. A declaration made in accordance with this Article shall be deemed to have been made in accordance with paragraph 1 of Article 63 of the Convention.

4. The territory of any State to which this Protocol applies by virtue of ratification or acceptance by that State, and each territory to which this Protocol is applied by virtue of a declaration by that State under this Article, shall be treated as separate territories for the purpose of the references in Articles 2 and 3 to the territory of a State.

Article 6. 1. As between the High Contracting Parties the provisions of Articles 1 to 5 of this Protocol shall be regarded as additional Articles to the Convention, and all the provisions of the Convention shall apply accordingly.

2. Nevertheless, the right of individual recourse recognised by a declaration made under Article 25 of the Convention, or the acceptance of the compulsory jurisdiction of the Court by a declaration made under Article 46 of the Convention, shall not be effective in relation to this Protocol unless the High Contracting Party concerned has made a statement recognising such right, or accepting such jurisdiction, in respect of all or any of Articles 1 to 4 of the Protocol.

Article 7. 1. This Protocol shall be open for signature by the Members of the Council of Europe who are the signatories of the Convention; it shall be ratified at the same time as or after the ratification of the Convention. It shall enter into force after the deposit of five instruments of ratification. As regards any signatory ratifying subsequently, the Protocol shall enter into force at the date of the deposit of its instrument of ratification.

2. The instruments of ratification shall be deposited with the Secretary-General of the Council of Europe, who will notify all Members of the names of those who have ratified.

In witness whereof the undersigned, being duly authorised thereto, have signed this Protocol.

Done at Strasbourg, this 16th day of September 1963, in English and in French, both texts being equally authoritative, in a single copy which shall remain deposited in the archives of the Council of Europe. The Secretary General shall transmit certified copies to each of the signatory States.

SEE ALSO European Agreement on Regulations concerning the Movement of Persons between Member States of the Council of Europe; Helsinki Accord entries; Movement and Residence; Right to Leave Any Country, including One's Own, and to Return to One's Own Country.

EUROPEAN CONVENTION ON HUMAN RIGHTS: PROTOCOL V (1966).

The protocol amends articles 22 and 40 of the parent convention with a view to ensuring as far as possible a periodic turnover in the membership of the EUROPEAN COMMISSION ON HUMAN

RIGHTS and the EUROPEAN COURT OF HUMAN RIGHTS, respectively. The protocol was concluded by the COMMITTEE OF MINISTERS OF THE COUNCIL OF EUROPE, convened at Strasbourg, on 20 January 1966 and entered into force on 21 December 1971. The text *(European Treaty Series* 55), is as follows:

The Governments signatory hereto, being Members of the Council of Europe,

Considering that certain inconveniences have arisen in the application of the provisions of Articles 22 and 40 of the Convention for the Protection of Human Rights and Fundamental Freedoms signed at Rome on 4th November 1950 (hereinafter referred to as "the Convention") relating to the length of the terms of office of the members of the European Commission of Human Rights (hereinafter referred to as "the Commission") and of the European Court of Human Rights (hereinafter referred to as "the Court");

Considering that it is desirable to ensure as far as possible an election every three years of one half of the members of the Commission and of one third of the members of the Court;

Considering therefore that it is desirable to amend certain provisions of the Convention,

Have agreed as follows:

Article 1. In Article 22 of the Convention, the following two paragraphs shall be inserted after paragraph (2):

"(3) In order to ensure that, as far as possible, one half of the membership of the Commission shall be renewed every three years, the Committee of Ministers may decide, before proceeding to any subsequent election, that the term or terms of office of one or more members to be elected shall be for a period other than six years but not more than nine and not less than three years.

"(4) In cases where more than one term of office is involved and the Committee of Ministers applies the preceding paragraph, the allocation of the terms of office shall be effected by the drawing of lots by the Secretary General, immediately after the election."

Article 2. In Article 22 of the Convention, the former paragraphs (3) and (4) shall become respectively paragraphs (5) and (6).

Article 3. In Article 40 of the Convention, the following two paragraphs shall be inserted after paragraph (2):

"(3) In order to ensure that, as far as possible, one third of the membership of the Court shall be renewed every three years, the Consultative Assembly may decide, before proceeding to any subsequent election, that the term or terms of office of one or more members to be elected shall be for a period other than nine years but not more than twelve and not less than six years.

"(4) In cases where more than one term of office is involved and the Consultative Assembly applies the preceding paragraph, the allocation of the terms of office shall be effected by the drawing of lots by the Secretary General immediately after the election."

Article 4. In Article 40 of the Convention, the former paragraphs (3) and (4) shall become respectively paragraphs (5) and (6).

Article 5. 1. This Protocol shall be open to signature by Members of the Council of Europe, signatories to the Convention, who may become Parties to it by:

(a) Signature without reservation in respect of ratification or acceptance;

(b) Signature with reservation in respect of ratification or acceptance, followed by ratification or acceptance.

Instruments of ratification or acceptance shall be deposited with the Secretary General of the Council of Europe.

2. This Protocol shall enter into force as soon as all Contracting Parties to the Convention shall have become Parties to the Protocol, in accordance with the provisions of paragraph 1 of this Article.

3. The Secretary General of the Council of Europe shall notify the Members of the Council of:

(a) Any signature without reservation in respect of ratification or acceptance;

(b) Any signature with reservation in respect of ratification or acceptance;

(c) The deposit of any instrument of ratification or acceptance;

(d) The date of entry into force of this Protocol in accordance with paragraph 2 of this Article.

In witness whereof the undersigned, being duly authorised thereto, have signed this Protocol.

Done at Strasbourg, this 20th day of January 1966, in English and in French, both texts being equally authoritative, in a single copy which shall remain deposited in the archives of the Council of Europe. The Secretary General shall transmit certified copies to each of the signatory governments.

EUROPEAN CONVENTION ON HUMAN RIGHTS: PROTOCOL VI (1983).

In the protocol, member States of the COUNCIL OF EUROPE agree (article 1) that the death penalty shall be abolished and that no one shall be condemned to such penalty or executed. However, according to article 2, a State may make provision in its law for the death penalty in respect of acts committed in time of war or imminent threat of war, provided that such penalty is applied only in instances laid down in the law and in accordance with its provisions.

The protocol was concluded by the COMMITTEE OF MINISTERS OF THE COUNCIL OF EUROPE, convened in Strasbourg, on 28 April 1983 and entered into force on 1 March 1985. The text *(European Treaty Series* 114) is as follows:

The member States of the Council of Europe, signatory to this Protocol to the Convention for the Protection of Human Rights and Fundamental Freedoms, signed at Rome on 4 November 1950 (hereinafter referred to as "the Convention"),

Considering that the evolution that has occurred in several member States of the Council of Europe expresses a general tendency in favour of abolition of the death penalty;

Have agreed as follows:

Article 1. The death penalty shall be abolished. No one shall be condemned to such penalty or executed.

Article 2. A State may make provision in its law for the death penalty in respect of acts committed in time of war or of imminent threat of war; such penalty shall be applied only in the instances laid down in the law and in accordance with its provisions. The State shall communicate to the Secretary General of the Council of Europe the relevant provisions of that law.

Article 3. No derogation from the provisions of this Protocol shall be made under Article 15 of the Convention.

Article 4. No reservation may be made under Article 64 of the Convention in respect of the provisions of this Protocol.

Article 5. 1. Any State may at the time of signature or when depositing its instrument of ratification, acceptance or approval, specify the territory or territories to which this Protocol shall apply.

2. Any State may at any later date, by a declaration addressed to the Secretary General of the Council of Europe, extend the application of this Protocol to any other territory specified in the declaration. In respect of such territory the Protocol shall enter into force on the first day of the month following the date of receipt of such declaration by the Secretary General.

3. Any declaration made under the two preceding paragraphs may, in respect of any territory specified in such declaration, be withdrawn by a notification addressed to the Secretary General. The withdrawal shall become effective on the first day of the month following the date of receipt of such notification by the Secretary General.

Article 6. As between the States Parties the provisions of Articles 1 to 5 of this Protocol shall be regarded as additional articles to the Convention and all the provisions of the Convention shall apply accordingly.

Article 7. This Protocol shall be open for signature by the member States of the Council of Europe, signatories to the Convention. It shall be subject to ratification, acceptance or approval. A member State of the Council of Europe may not ratify, accept or approve this Protocol unless it has, simultaneously or previously, ratified the Convention. Instruments of ratification, acceptance or approval shall be deposited with the Secretary General of the Council of Europe.

Article 8. 1. This Protocol shall enter into force on the first day of the month following the date on which five member States of the Council of Europe have expressed their consent to be bound by the Protocol in accordance with the provisions of Article 7.

2. In respect of any member State which subsequently expresses its consent to be bound by it, the Protocol shall enter into force on the first day of the month following the date of the deposit of the instrument of ratification, acceptance or approval.

Article 9. The Secretary General of the Council of Europe shall notify the member States of the Council of:

(a) any signature;

(b) the deposit of any instrument of ratification, acceptance or approval;

(c) any date of entry into force of this Protocol in accordance with Articles 5 and 8;

(d) any other act, notification or communication relating to this Protocol.

In witness whereof the undersigned, being duly authorised thereto, have signed this Protocol.

Done at Strasbourg, the 28 April 1983, in English and French, both texts being equally authentic, in a single copy which shall be deposited in the archives of the Council of Europe. The Secretary General of the Council of Europe shall transmit certified copies to each member State of the Council of Europe.

SEE ALSO *American Convention on Human Rights: Additional Protocol on the Death Penalty (Draft); International Covenant on Civil and Political Rights: Second Optional Protocol Aiming at the Abolition of the Death Penalty.*

EUROPEAN CONVENTION ON HUMAN RIGHTS: PROTOCOL VII (1984).

The protocol supplements the provisions of the parent convention by the addition of six articles recognizing new rights (articles 1 to 6 of the protocol) with a view to ensuring the collective enforcement of those rights by means of the parent convention. The protocol was concluded by the COMMITTEE OF MINISTERS OF THE COUNCIL OF EUROPE, convened in Strasbourg, on 22 November 1984 and entered into force on 1 November 1988. The text *(European Treaty Series* 117) is as follows:

The member States of the Council of Europe signatory hereto,

Being resolved to take further steps to ensure the collective enforcement of certain rights and freedoms by means of the Convention for the Protection of Human Rights and Fundamental Freedoms signed at Rome on 4 November 1950 (hereinafter referred to as "the Convention");

Have agreed as follows:

Article 1. 1. An alien lawfully resident in the territory of a State shall not be expelled therefrom except in pursuance of a decision reached in accordance with law and shall be allowed:

a. to submit reasons against his expulsion,

b. to have his case reviewed, and

c. to be represented for these purposes before the competent authority or a person or persons designated by that authority.

2. An alien may be expelled before the exercise of his rights under paragraph 1(a), (b) and (c) of this Article, when such expulsion is necessary in the interests of public order or is grounded on reasons of national security.

Article 2. 1. Everyone convicted of a criminal offence by a tribunal shall have the right to have conviction or sentence reviewed by a higher tribunal. The exercise of this right, including the grounds on which it may be exercised, shall be governed by law.

2. This right may be subject to exceptions in regard to offences of a minor character, as prescribed by law, or in cases in which the person concerned was tried in the first instance by the highest tribunal or was convicted following an appeal against acquittal.

Article 3. When a person has by a final decision been convicted of a criminal offence and when subsequently his conviction has been reversed, or he has been pardoned, on the ground that a new or newly discovered fact shows conclusively that there has been a miscarriage of justice, the person who has suffered punishment as a result of such conviction shall be compensated according to the law or the practice of the State concerned, unless it is proved that the non-disclosure of the unknown fact in time is wholly or partly attributable to him.

Article 4. 1. No one shall be liable to be tried or punished again in criminal proceedings under the jurisdiction of the same State for an offence for which he has already been finally acquitted or convicted in accordance with the law and penal procedure of that State.

2. The provisions of the preceding paragraph shall not prevent the re-opening of the case in accordance with the law and penal procedure of the State concerned, if there is evidence of new or newly discovered facts, or if there has been a fundamental defect in the previous proceedings, which could affect the outcome of the case.

3. No derogation from this Article shall be made under Article 15 of the Convention.

Article 5. 1. Spouses shall enjoy equality of rights and responsibilities of a private law character between them, and in their relations with their children, as to marriage, during marriage and in the event of its dissolution. This Article shall not prevent States from taking such measures as are necessary in the interests of the children.

Article 6. 1. Any State may at the time of signature or when depositing its instrument of ratification, acceptance or approval, specify the territory or territories to which this Protocol shall apply and state the extent to which it undertakes that the provisions of this Protocol shall apply to this or these territories.

2. Any State may at any later date, by a declaration addressed to the Secretary-General of the Council of Europe, extend the application of this Protocol to any other territory specified in the declaration. In respect of such territory the Protocol shall enter into force on the first day of the month following the expiration of a period of two months after the date of receipt by the Secretary-General of such declaration.

3. Any declaration made under the two preceding paragraphs may, in respect of any territory specified in such declaration, be withdrawn or modified by a notification addressed to the Secretary-General. The withdrawal or modification shall become effective on the first day of the month following the expiration of a period of two months after the day of receipt of such notification by the Secretary-General.

4. A declaration made in accordance with this Article shall be deemed to have been made in accordance with paragraph 1 of Article 63 of the Convention.

5. The territory of any State to which this Protocol applies by virtue of ratification, acceptance or approval by that State, and each territory to which this Protocol is applied by virtue of a declaration by that State under this Article, may be treated as separate territories for the purpose of the reference in Article 1 to the territory of a State.

Article 7. 1. As between the State Parties, the provisions of Articles 1 to 6 of this Protocol shall be regarded as additional Articles to the Convention, and all the provisions of the Convention shall apply accordingly.

2. Nevertheless, the right of individual recourse recognised by a declaration made under Article 25 of the Convention, or the acceptance of the compulsory jurisdiction of the Court by a declaration made under Article 46 of the Convention, shall not be effective in relation to this Protocol unless the State concerned has made a statement recognising such right, or accepting such jurisdiction in respect of Articles 1 to 5 of this Protocol.

Article 8. This Protocol shall be open for signature by member States of the Council of Europe which have signed the Convention. It is subject to ratification, acceptance or approval. A member State of the Council of Europe may not ratify, accept or approve this Protocol without previously or simultaneously ratifying the Convention. Instruments of ratification, acceptance or approval shall be deposited with the Secretary General of the Council of Europe.

Article 9. 1. This Protocol shall enter into force on the first day of the month following the expiration of a period of two months after the date on which seven member States of the Council of Europe have expressed their consent to be bound by the Protocol in accordance with the provisions of Article 8.

2. In respect of any member State which subsequently expresses its consent to be bound by it, the Protocol shall enter into force on the first day of the month following the expiration of a period of two months after the date of the deposit of the instrument of ratification, acceptance or approval.

Article 10. The Secretary General of the Council of Europe shall notify all the member States of the Council of:

a. any signature;

b. the deposit of any instrument of ratification, acceptance or approval;

c. any date of entry into force of this Protocol in accordance with Articles 6 and 9;

d. any other act, notification or declaration relating to this Protocol.

In witness whereof the undersigned, being duly authorised thereto, have signed this Protocol.

Done at Strasbourg, the twenty-two November one thousand nine hundred and eighty four, in English and French, both texts being equally authentic, in a single copy which shall be deposited in the archives of the Council of Europe shall transmit certified copies to each member State of the Council.

EUROPEAN CONVENTION ON HUMAN RIGHTS: PROTOCOL VIII (1985). The protocol amends certain provisions of the parent convention with a view to expediting the functioning of the EUROPEAN COMMISSION ON HUMAN RIGHTS. It also amends certain provisions of the parent convention which relate to the procedures of the EUROPEAN COURT OF HUMAN RIGHTS. The protocol was concluded by the COMMITTEE OF MINISTERS OF THE COUNCIL OF EUROPE, convened in Vienna, on 19 March 1985. The text *(European Treaty Series* 118) is as follows:

The member States of the Council of Europe, signatories to this Protocol to the Convention for the Protection of Human Rights and Fundamental Freedoms, signed at Rome on 4 November 1950 (hereinafter referred to as "the Convention"),

Considering that it is desirable to amend certain provisions of the Convention with a view to improving and in particular to expediting the procedure of the European Commission of Human Rights,

Considering that it is also advisable to amend certain provisions of the Convention concerning the procedure of the European Court of Human Rights,

Have agreed as follows:

Article 1. The existing text of Article 20 of the Convention shall become paragraph 1 of that Article and shall be supplemented by the following four paragraphs:

"2. The Commission shall sit in plenary session. It may, however, set up Chambers, each composed of at least seven members. The Chambers may examine petitions submitted under Article 25 of this Convention which can be dealt with on the basis of established case law or which raise no serious question affecting the interpretation or application of the Convention. Subject to this restriction and to the provisions of paragraph 5 of this Article, the Chambers shall exercise all the powers conferred on the Commission by the Convention.

The member of the Commission elected in respect of a High Contracting Party against which a petition has been lodged shall have the right to sit on a Chamber to which that petition has been referred.

3. The Commission may set up committees, each composed of at least three members, with the power, exercisable by a unanimous vote, to declare inadmissible or strike from its list of cases a petition submitted under Article 25, when such a decision can be taken without further examination.

4. A Chamber or committee may at any time relinquish jurisdiction in favour of the plenary Commission, which may also order the transfer to it of any petition referred to a Chamber or committee.

5. Only the plenary Commission can exercise the following powers:

a. the examination of applications submitted under Article 24;

b. the bringing of a case before the Court in accordance with Article 48a;

c. the drawing up of rules of procedure in accordance with Article 36."

Article 2. Article 21 of the Convention shall be supplemented by the following third paragraph:

"3. The candidates shall be of high moral character and must either possess the qualifications required for appointment to high judicial office or be persons of recognised competence in national or international law."

Article 3. Article 23 of the Convention shall be supplemented by the following sentence:

"During their term of office they shall not hold any position which is incompatible with their independence and impartiality as members of the Commission or the demands of this office."

Article 4. The text, with modifications, of Article 28 of the Convention shall become paragraph 1 of that Article and the text, with modifications, of Article 30 shall become paragraph 2. The new text of Article 28 shall read as follows:

"*Article 28.* 1. In the event of the Commission accepting a petition referred to it:

a. it shall, with a view to ascertaining the facts, undertake together with the representatives of the parties an examination of the petition and, if need be, an investigation, for the effective conduct of which the States concerned shall furnish all necessary facilities, after an exchange of views with the Commission;

b. it shall at the same time place itself at the disposal of the parties concerned with a view to securing a friendly settlement of the matter on the basis of respect for Human Rights as defined in this Convention.

2. If the Commission succeeds in effecting a friendly settlement, it shall draw up a Report which shall be sent to the States concerned, to the Committee of Ministers and to the Secretary General of the Council of Europe for publication. This Report shall be confined to a brief statement of the facts and of the solution reached."

Article 5. In the first paragraph of Article 29 of the Convention, the word "unanimously" shall be replaced by the words "by a majority of two-thirds of its members."

Article 6. The following provision shall be inserted in the Convention:

"*Article 30.* 1. The Commission may at any stage of the proceedings decide to strike a petition out of its list of cases where the circumstances lead to the conclusion that:

a. the applicant does not intend to pursue his petition, or

b. the matter has been resolved, or

c. for any other reason established by the Commission, it is no longer justified to continue the examination of the petition.

However, the Commission shall continue the examination of a petition if respect for Human Rights as defined in this Convention so requires.

2. If the Commission decides to strike a petition out of its list after having accepted it, it shall draw up a Report which shall contain a statement of the facts and the decision striking out the petition together with the reasons therefor. The Report shall be transmitted to the parties, as well as to the Committee of Ministers for information. The Commission may publish it.

3. The Commission may decide to restore a petition to its list of cases if it considers that the circumstances justify such a course."

Article 7. In Article 31 of the Convention, paragraph 1 shall read as follows:

"1. If the examination of a petition has not been completed in accordance with Article 28 (paragraph 2), 29 or 30, the Commission shall draw up a Report on the facts and state its opinion as to whether the facts found disclose a breach by the State concerned of its obligations under the Convention. The individual opinions of members of the Commission on this point may be stated in the Report."

Article 8. Article 34 of the Convention shall read as follows:

"Subject to the provisions of Articles 20 (paragraph 3) and 29, the Commission shall take its decisions by a majority of the members present and voting."

Article 9. Article 40 of the Convention shall be supplemented by the following seventh paragraph:

"7. The members of the Court shall sit on the Court in their individual capacity. During their term of office they shall not hold any position which is incompatible with their independence and impartiality as members of the Court or the demands of this office."

Article 10. Article 41 of the Convention shall read as follows:

"The Court shall elects its President and one or two Vice-Presidents for a period of three years. They may be re-elected."

Article 11. In the first sentence of Article 43 of the Convention, the word "seven" shall be replaced by the word "nine".

Article 12. 1. This Protocol shall be open for signature by member States of the Council of Europe signatories to the Convention, which may express their consent to be bound by:

a. signature without reservation as to ratification, acceptance or approval, or

b. signature subject to ratification, acceptance or approval, followed by ratification, acceptance or approval.

2. Instruments of ratification, acceptance or approval shall be deposited with the Secretary General of the Council of Europe.

Article 13. This Protocol shall enter into force on the first day of the month following the expiration of a period of three months after the date on which all Parties to the Convention have expressed their consent to be bound by the Protocol in accordance with the provisions of Article 12.

Article 14. The Secretary General of the Council of Europe shall notify the member States of the Council of:

a. any signature;

b. the deposit of any instrument of ratification, acceptance or approval;

c. the date of entry into force of this Protocol in accordance with Article 13;

d. any other act, notification or communication relating to this Protocol.

In witness whereof the undersigned, being duly authorised thereto, have signed this Protocol.

Done at Vienna, this 19th day of March 1985, in English and French, both texts being equally authentic, in a single copy which shall be deposited in the archives of the Council of Europe. The Secretary General of the Council of Europe shall transmit certified copies to each member State of the Council of Europe.

EUROPEAN CONVENTION ON RECOGNITION AND ENFORCEMENT OF DECISIONS CONCERNING CUSTODY OF CHILDREN AND ON RESTORATION OF CUSTODY OF CHILDREN (1980).

The convention establishes procedures whereby a child improperly removed from a contracting State to another contracting State, in breach of an enforcable decision relating to its custody, can be returned to the person having custody. Each contracting State undertakes to appoint a central authority to deal with such matters, to whom any person who has obtained a decision in that State relating to the custody of a child and who wishes to have that decision recognized and enforced in another contracting State may submit an application. The central authorities cooperate in locating the child, in obtaining recognition or enforcement of custody decisions, and in restoring the child to the person having custody.

The convention was adopted by the COMMITTEE OF MINISTERS OF THE COUNCIL OF EUROPE, convened in Luxembourg, on 20 May 1980 and entered into force on 1 September 1983. The text *(European Treaty Series* 105) is as follows:

The member States of the Council of Europe, signatory hereto,

Recognising that in the member States of the Council of Europe the welfare of the child is of overriding importance in reaching decisions concerning his custody;

Considering that the making of arrangements to ensure that decisions concerning the custody of a child can be more widely recognised and enforced will provide greater protection of the welfare of children;

Considering it desirable, with this end in view, to emphasize that the right of access of parents is a normal corollary to the right of custody;

Noting the increasing number of cases where children have been improperly removed across an international frontier and the difficulties of securing adequate solutions to the problems caused by such cases;

Desirous of making suitable provision to enable the custody of children which has been arbitrarily interrupted to be restored;

Convinced of the desirability of making arrangements for this purpose answering to different needs and different circumstances;

Desiring to establish legal co-operation between their authorities,

Have agreed as follows:

Article 1. For the purposes of this Convention:

(a) *child* means a person of any nationality, so long as he is under 16 years of age and has not the right to decide on his own place of residence under the law of his habitual residence, the law of his nationality or the internal law of the State addressed;

(b) *authority* means a judicial or administrative authority;

(c) *decision relating to custody* means a decision of an authority in so far as it relates to the care of the person of the child, including the right to decide on the place of his residence, or to the right of access to him;

(d) *improper removal* means the removal of a child across an international frontier in breach of a decision relating to his custody which has been given in a Contracting State and which is enforceable in such a State; improper removal also includes:

(i) the failure to return a child across an international frontier at the end of a period of the exercise of the right of access to this child or at the end of any other temporary stay in a territory other than that where the custody is exercised;

(ii) a removal which is subsequently declared unlawful within the meaning of Article 12.

Part I
Central Authorities

Article 2. 1. Each Contracting State shall appoint a central authority to carry out the functions provided for by this Convention.

2. Federal States and States with more than one legal system shall be free to appoint more than one central authority and shall determine the extent of their competence.

3. The Secretary General of the Council of Europe shall be notified of any appointment under this Article.

Article 3. 1. The central authorities of the Contracting States shall co-operate with each other and promote co-operation between the competent authorities in their respective countries. They shall act with all necessary despatch.

2. With a view to facilitating the operation of this Convention, the central authorities of the Contracting States:

(a) shall secure the transmission of requests for information coming from competent authorities and relating to legal or factual matters concerning pending proceedings;

(b) shall provide each other on request with information about their law relating to the custody of children and any changes in that law;

(c) shall keep each other informed of any difficulties likely to arise in applying the Convention and, as far as possible, eliminate obstacles to its application.

Article 4. 1. Any person who has obtained in a Contracting State a decision relating to the custody of a child and who wishes to have that decision recognised or enforced in another Contracting State may submit an application for this purpose to the central authority in any Contracting State.

2. The application shall be accompanied by the documents mentioned in Article 13.

3. The central authority receiving the application, if it is not the central authority in the State addressed, shall send the documents directly and without delay to that central authority.

4. The central authority receiving the application may refuse to intervene where it is manifestly clear that the conditions laid down by this Convention are not satisfied.

5. The central authority receiving the application shall keep the applicant informed without delay of the progress of his application.

Article 5. 1. The central authority in the State addressed shall take or cause to be taken without delay all steps which it considers to be appropriate, if necessary by instituting proceedings before its competent authorities, in order:

(a) to discover the whereabouts of the child;

(b) to avoid, in particular by any necessary provisional measures, prejudice to the interests of the child or of the applicant;

(c) to secure the recognition or enforcement of the decision;

(d) to secure the delivery of the child to the applicant where enforcement is granted;

(e) to inform the requesting authority of the measures taken and their results.

2. Where the central authority in the State addressed has reason to believe that the child is in the territory of another Contracting State it shall send the documents directly and without delay to the central authority of that State.

3. With the exception of the cost of repatriation, each Contracting State undertakes not to claim any payment from an applicant in respect of any measures taken under paragraph 1 of this Article by the central authority of that State on the applicant's behalf, including the costs of proceedings and, where applicable, the costs incurred by the assistance of a lawyer.

4. If recognition or enforcement is refused, and if the central authority of the State addressed considers that it should comply with a request by the applicant to bring in that State proceedings concerning the substance of the case, that authority shall use its best endeavours to secure the representation of the applicant in the proceedings under conditions no less favourable than those available to a person who is resident in and a national of that State and for this purpose it may, in particular, institute proceedings before its competent authorities.

Article 6. 1. Subject to any special agreements made between the central authorities concerned and to the provisions of paragraph 3 of this Article:

(a) communications to the central authority of the State addressed shall be made in the official language or in one of the official languages of that State or be accompanied by a translation into that language;

(b) the central authority of the State addressed shall

nevertheless accept communications made in English or in French or accompanied by a translation into one of these languages.

2. Communications coming from the central authority of the State addressed, including the results of enquiries carried out, may be made in the official language or one of the official languages of that State or in English or French.

3. A Contracting State may exclude wholly or partly the provisions of paragraph 1 (b) of this Article. When a Contracting State has made this reservation any other Contracting State may also apply the reservation in respect of that State.

Part II
Recognition and Enforcement of Decisions and Restoration of Custody of Children

Article 7. A decision relating to custody given in a Contracting State shall be recognised and, where it is enforceable in the State of origin, made enforceable in every other Contracting State.

Article 8. 1. In the case of an improper removal, the central authority of the State addressed shall cause steps to be taken forthwith to restore the custody of the child where:

(a) at the time of the institution of the proceedings in the State where the decision was given or at the time of the improper removal, if earlier, the child and his parents had as their sole nationality the nationality of that State and the child had his habitual residence in the territory of that State, and

(b) a request for the restoration was made to a central authority within a period of six months from the date of the improper removal.

2. If, in accordance with the law of the State addressed, the requirements of paragraph 1 of this Article cannot be complied with without recourse to a judicial authority, none of the grounds of refusal specified in this Convention shall apply to the judicial proceedings.

3. Where there is an agreement officially confirmed by a competent authority between the person having the custody of the child and another person to allow the other person a right of access, and the child, having been taken abroad, has not been restored at the end of the agreed period to the person having the custody, custody of the child shall be restored in accordance with paragraphs 1 (b) and 2 of this Article. The same shall apply in the case of a decision of the competent authority granting such a right to a person who has not the custody of the child.

Article 9. 1. In cases of improper removal, other than those dealt with in Article 8, in which an application has been made to a central authority within a period of six months from the date of the removal, recognition and enforcement may be refused only if:

(a) in the case of a decision given in the absence of the defendant or his legal representative, the defendant was not duly served with the document which instituted the proceedings or an equivalent document in sufficient time to enable him to arrange his defence; but such a failure to effect service cannot constitute a ground for refusing recognition or enforcement where service was not effected because the defendant had concealed his whereabouts from the person who instituted the proceedings in the State of origin;

(b) in the case of a decision given in the absence of the defendant or his legal representative, the competence of the authority giving the decision was not founded:

(i) on the habitual residence of the defendant, or

(ii) on the last common habitual residence of the child's parents, at least one parent being still habitually resident there, or

(iii) on the habitual residence of the child;

(c) the decision is incompatible with a decision relating to custody which became enforceable in the State addressed before the removal of the child, unless the child has had his habitual residence in the territory of the requesting State for one year before his removal.

2. Where no application has been made to a central authority, the provisions of paragraph 1 of this Article shall apply equally, if recognition and enforcement are requested within six months from the date of the improper removal.

3. In no circumstances may the foreign decision be reviewed as to its substance.

Article 10. 1. In cases other than those covered by Articles 8 and 9, recognition and enforcement may be refused not only on the grounds provided for in Article 9 but also on any of the following grounds:

(a) if it is found that the effects of the decision are manifestly incompatible with the fundamental principles of the law relating to the family and children in the State addressed;

(b) if it is found that by reason of a change in the circumstances including the passage of time but not including a mere change in the residence of the child after an improper removal, the effects of the original decision are manifestly no longer in accordance with the welfare of the child;

(c) if at the time when the proceedings were instituted in the State of origin:

(i) the child was a national of the State addressed or was habitually resident there and no such connection existed with the State of origin;

(ii) the child was a national both of the State of origin and of the State addressed and was habitually resident in the State addressed;

(d) if the decision is incompatible with a decision given in the State addressed or enforceable in that State after being given in a third State, pursuant to proceedings begun before the submission of the request for recognition or enforcement, and if the refusal is in accordance with the welfare of the child.

2. In the same cases, proceedings for recognition or enforcement may be adjourned on any of the following grounds:

(a) if an ordinary form of review of the original decision has been commenced;

(b) if proceedings relating to the custody of the child, commenced before the proceedings in the State of origin were instituted, are pending in the State addressed;

(c) if another decision concerning the custody of the child is the subject of proceedings for enforcement or of any other proceedings concerning the recognition of the decision.

Article 11. 1. Decisions on rights of access and provisions of decisions relating to custody which deal with the right of access shall be recognised and enforced subject to the same conditions as other decisions relating to custody.

2. However, the competent authority of the State addressed may fix the conditions for the implementation and exercise of the right of access taking into account, in particular, undertakings given by the parties on this matter.

3. Where no decision on the right of access has been taken or where recognition or enforcement of the decision relating to custody is refused, the central authority of the State addressed may apply to its competent authorities for a decision on the right of access, if the person claiming a right of access so requests.

Article 12. Where, at the time of the removal of a child across an international frontier, there is no enforceable decision given in a Contracting State relating to his custody, the provisions of this Convention shall apply to any subsequent decision, relating to the custody of that child and declaring the removal to be unlawful, given in a Contracting State at the request of any interested person.

Part III—Procedure

Article 13. 1. A request for recognition or enforcement in another Contacting State of a decision relating to custody shall be accompanied by:

(a) a document authorising the central authority of the State addressed to act on behalf of the applicant or to designate another representative for that purpose;

(b) a copy of the decision which satisfies the necessary conditions of authenticity;

(c) in the case of a decision given in the absence of the defendant or his legal representative, a document which establishes that the defendant was duly served with the document which instituted the proceedings or an equivalent document;

(d) if applicable, any document which establishes that, in accordance with the law of the State of origin, the decision is enforceable;

(e) if possible, a statement indicating the whereabouts or likely whereabouts of the child in the State addressed;

(f) proposals as to how the custody of the child should be restored.

2. The documents mentioned above shall, where necessary, be accompanied by a translation according to the provisions laid down in Article 6.

Article 14. Each Contracting State shall apply a simple and expeditious procedure for recognition and enforcement of decisions relating to the custody of a child. To that end it shall ensure that a request for enforcement may be lodged by simple application.

Article 15. 1. Before reaching a decision under paragraph 1 (b) of Article 10, the authority concerned in the State addressed:

(a) shall ascertain the child's views unless this is impracticable having regard in particular to his age and understanding; and

(b) may request that any appropriate enquiries be carried out.

2. The cost of enquiries in any Contracting State shall be met by the authorities of the State where they are carried out.

3. Requests for enquiries and the results of enquiries may be sent to the authority concerned through the central authorities.

Article 16. For the purposes of this Convention, no legalisation or any like formality may be required.

Part IV—Reservations

Article 17. 1. A Contracting State may make a reservation that, in cases covered by Articles 8 and 9 or either of these Articles, recognition and enforcement of decisions relating to custody may be refused on such of the grounds provided under Article 10 as may be specified in the reservation.

2. Recognition and enforcement of decisions given in a Contracting State which has made the reservation provided for in paragraph 1 of this Article may be refused in any other Contracting State on any of the additional grounds referred to in that reservation.

Article 18. A Contracting State may make a reservation that it shall not be bound by the provisions of Article 12. The provisions of this Convention shall not apply to decisions referred to in Article 12 which have been given in a Contracting State which has made such a reservation.

Part V—Other Instruments

Article 19. This Convention shall not exclude the possibility of relying on any other international instrument in force between the State of origin and the State addressed or on any other law of the State addressed not derived from an international agreement for the purpose of obtaining recognition or enforcement of a decision.

Article 20. 1. This Convention shall not affect any obligations which a Contracting State may have towards a non-contracting State under an international instrument dealing with matters governed by this Convention.

2. When two or more Contracting States have enacted uniform laws in relation to custody of children or created a special system of recognition or enforcement of decisions in this field, or if they should do so in the future, they shall be free to apply, between themselves, those laws or that system in place of this Convention or any part of it. In order to avail themselves of this provision the States shall notify their decision to the Secretary General of the Council of Europe. Any alteration or revocation of this decision must also be notified.

Part VI
Final Clauses

Article 21. This Convention shall be open for signature by the member States of the Council of Europe. It is subject to ratification, acceptance or approval. Instruments of ratification, acceptance or approval shall be deposited with the Secretary General of the Council of Europe.

Article 22. 1. This Convention shall enter into force on the first day of the month following the expiration of a period of three months after the date on which three member States of the Council of Europe have expressed their consent to be bound by the Convention in accordance with the provisions of Article 21.

2. In respect of any member State which subsequently expresses its consent to be bound by it, the Convention shall enter into force on the first day of the month following the expiration of a period of three months after the date of the deposit of the instrument of ratification, acceptance or approval.

Article 23. 1. After the entry into force of this Convention, the Committee of Ministers of the Council of Europe may invite any State not a member of the Council to accede to this Convention, by a decision taken by the majority provided for by Article 20 (d) of the Statue and by the unanimous vote of the representatives of the Contracting States entitled to sit on the Committee.

2. In respect of any acceding State, the Convention shall enter into force on the first day of the month following the expiration of a period of three months after the date of deposit of the instrument of accession with the Secretary General of the Council of Europe.

Article 24. 1. Any State may at the time of signature or when depositing its instrument of ratification, acceptance, approval or accession, specify the territory or territories to which this Convention shall apply.

2. Any State may at any later date, by a declaration addressed to the Secretary General of the Council of Europe, extend the application of this Convention to any other territory specified in the declaration. In respect of such territory, the Convention shall enter into force on the first day of the month following the expiration of a period of three months after the date of receipt by the Secretary General of such declaration.

3. Any declaration made under the two preceding paragraphs may, in respect of any territory specified in such declaration, be withdrawn by a notification addressed to the Secretary General. The withdrawal shall become effective on the first day of the month following the expiration of a period of six months after the date of receipt of such notification by the Secretary General.

Article 25. 1. A State which has two or more territorial units in which different systems of law apply in matters of custody of children and of recognition and enforcement of decisions relating to custody may, at the time of signature or when depositing its instrument of ratification, acceptance, approval or accession, declare that this Convention shall apply to all its territorial units or to one or more of them.

2. Such a State may at any later date, by a declaration addressed to the Secretary General of the Council of Europe, extend the application of this Convention to any other territorial unit specified in the declaration. In respect of such territorial unit the Convention shall enter into force on the first day of the month following the expiration of a period of three months after the date of receipt by the Secretary General of such declaration.

3. Any declaration made under the two preceding paragraphs may, in respect of any territorial unit specified in such declaration, be withdrawn by notification addressed to the Secretary General. The withdrawal shall become effective on the first day of the month following the expiration of a period of six months after the date of receipt of such notification by the Secretary General.

Article 26. 1. In relation to a State which has in matters of custody two or more systems of law of territorial application:

(a) reference to the law of a person's habitual residence or to the law of a person's nationality shall be construed as referring to the system of law determined by the rules in force in that State or, if there are no such rules, to the system of law with which the person concerned is most closely connected;

(b) reference to the State of origin or to the State addressed shall be construed as referring, as the case may be, to the territorial unit where the decision was given or to the territorial unit where recognition or enforcement of the decision or restoration of custody is requested.

2. Paragraph 1(a) of this Article also applies *mutatis mutandis* to States which have in matters of custody two or more systems of law of personal application.

Article 27. 1. Any State may, at the time of signature or when depositing its instrument of ratification, acceptance, approval or accession, declare that it avails itself of one or more of the reservations provided for in paragraph 3 of Article 6, Article 17 and Article 18 of this Convention. No other reservation may be made.

2. Any Contracting State which has made a reservation under the preceding paragraph may wholly or partly with-

draw it by means of a notification addressed to the Secretary General of the Council of Europe. The withdrawal shall take effect on the date of receipt of such notification by the Secretary General.

Article 28. At the end of the third year following the date of the entry into force of this Convention and, on his own initiative, at any time after this date, the Secretary General of the Council of Europe shall invite the representatives of the central authorities appointed by the Contracting States to meet in order to study and to facilitate the functioning of the Convention. Any member State of the Council of Europe not being a party to the Convention may be represented by an observer. A report shall be prepared on the work of each of these meetings and forwarded to the Committee of Ministers of the Council of Europe for information.

Article 29. 1. Any Party may at any time denounce this Convention by means of a notification addressed to the Secretary General of the Council of Europe.

2. Such denunciation shall become effective on the first day of the month following the expiration of a period of six months after the date of receipt of the notification by the Secretary General.

Article 30. The Secretary General of the Council of Europe shall notify the member States of the Council and any State which has acceded to this Convention, of:

(a) any signature;

(b) the deposit of any instrument of ratification, acceptance, approval or accession;

(c) any date of entry into force of this Convention in accordance with Articles 22, 23, 24 and 25;

(d) any other act, notification or communication relating to this Convention.

In witness whereof the undersigned, being duly authorised thereto, have signed this Convention.

Done at Luxembourg, the 20th day of May 1980, in English and French, both texts being equally authentic, in a single copy which shall be deposited in the archives of the Council of Europe. The Secretary General of the Council of Europe shall transmit certified copies to each member State of the Council of Europe and to any State invited to accede to this Convention.

SEE ALSO *European Convention on the Repatriation of Minors.*

EUROPEAN CONVENTION ON SOCIAL SECURITY (1972).

The convention was concluded by the COMMITTEE OF MINISTERS OF THE COUNCIL OF EUROPE, meeting in Paris, on 14 December 1972 and entered into force on 1 March 1977. Prepared to meet the need for a special instrument to govern questions relating to SOCIAL SECURITY for foreigners and migrants in European countries, foreseen in article 73 of the EUROPEAN CODE OF SOCIAL SECURITY, the convention aims at ensuring that all persons resident in the territory of a contracting State—including nationals of other contracting parties, refugees, and stateless persons—enjoy equality of treatment with nationals as regards the benefits available to them under social security schemes. The convention was accompanied by a detailed agreement as to its application, not reproduced here.

The text of the convention *(European Treaty Series* 78) is as follows:

The member States of the Council of Europe signatory hereto,

Considering that the aim of the Council of Europe is to achieve greater unity between its Members, in particular for the purpose of facilitating their social progress;

Considering that multilateral co-ordination of social security legislation is one of the means of achieving that aim;

Considering that the European Code of Social Security, opened for signature on 16 April 1964, provides, in Article 73, that the Contracting Parties to the Code shall endeavour to conclude a special instrument governing questions relating to social security for foreigners and migrants, particularly with regard to equality of treatment with their own nationals and to the maintenance of acquired rights and rights in course of acquisition;

Affirming the principle of equality of treatment for nationals of the Contracting Parties, refugees and stateless persons, under the social security legislation of each Contracting Party, and the principle that the benefits under social security legislation should be maintained despite any change of residence by the protected persons within the territories of the Contracting Parties, principles which underlie not only certain provisions of the European Social Charter but also several conventions of the International Labour Organisation,

Have agreed as follows:

Title I
General Provisions

Article 1. For the purposes of this Convention:

(a) the term "Contracting Party" means any State which has deposited an instrument of ratification of acceptance or of accession, in accordance with the provisions of Article 75, paragraph 1, or of Article 77;

(b) the terms "territory of a Contracting Party" and "national of a Contracting Party" are defined in Annex I; each Contracting Party shall give notice, in accordance with the provisions of Article 81, paragraph 1, of any amendment to be made to Annex I;

(c) the term "legislation" means any laws, regulations and other statutory instruments which are in force at the time of signature of this Convention or may enter into force subsequently in the whole or any part of the territory of each Contracting Party and which relate to the social security branches and schemes specified in Article 2, paragraphs 1 and 2;

(d) the term "social security convention" means any bilateral or multilateral instrument by which two or more Contracting Parties are, or may subsequently be, bound exclusively, and any multilateral instrument by which at least two Contracting Parties and one or more other States are, or may subsequently be, bound in the field of social security in respect of all or of part of the social security branches and schemes specified in Article 2, paragraphs 1 and 2, as well as any agreements concluded pursuant to the said instruments;

(e) the term "competent authority" means the Minister, Ministers or other corresponding authority responsible for the social security schemes in all or any part of the territory of each Contracting Party;

(f) the term "institution" means the body or authority responsible for applying all or part of the legislation of each Contracting Party;

(g) the term "competent institution" means:

(i) in relation to a social insurance scheme, either the institution with which the person concerned is insured when he claims benefit, or the institution from which he is entitled to receive benefit or would be entitled to receive benefit if he were resident in the territory of the Contracting Party where that institution is situated, or the institution designated by the competent authority of the Contracting Party concerned;

(ii) in relation to a scheme other than a social insurance scheme, or in relation to a family benefits scheme, the institution designated by the competent authority of the Contracting Party concerned;

(iii) in relation to a scheme concerning an employer's liability in respect of benefits referred to in Article 2, paragraph 1, either the employer or his insurer or, in default thereof, the body or authority designated by the competent authority of the Contracting Party concerned;

(h) the term "competent State" means the Contracting Party in whose territory the competent institution is situated;

(i) the term "residence" means ordinary residence;

(j) the term "temporary residence" means a temporary stay;

(k) the term "institution of the place of residence" means the institution empowered, under the Contracting Party's legislation which it applies, to pay the benefits in question at the place of residence or, where no such institution exists, the institution designated by the competent authority of the Contracting Party concerned;

(l) the term "institution of the place of temporary residence" means the institution empowered, under the Contracting Party's legislation which it applies, to pay the benefits in question at the place of temporary residence or, where no such institution exists, the institution designated by the competent authority of the Contracting Party concerned;

(m) the term "worker" means an employed person or a self-employed person or a person treated as such under the legislation of the Contracting Party concerned, unless otherwise specified in this Convention;

(n) the term "frontier worker" means an employed person who is employed in the territory of one Contracting Party and resides in the territory of another Contracting Party where he returns in principle every day or at least once a week; provided that

(i) as regards relations between France and the Contracting Parties bordering France, the person concerned must, to be deemed a frontier worker, reside and be employed within a zone which does not, in principle, extend more than twenty kilometres on either side of the common frontier;

(ii) a frontier worker employed in the territory of one Contracting Party by an undertaking which is his normal employer, who is sent by that undertaking to work outside the frontier area, either in the territory of the same Contracting Party or in the territory of another Contracting Party, for a period not expected to exceed four months, shall retain the status of frontier worker during such employment for a period not exceeding four months;

(o) the term "refugee" has the meaning assigned to it in Article 1, Section A, of the Convention on the Status of Refugees, signed at Geneva on 28 July 1951, and in Article 1, paragraph 2, of the Protocol on the Status of Refugees of 31 January 1967, without any geographical limitation;

(p) the term "stateless person" has the meaning assigned to it in Article 1 of the Convention on the Status of Stateless Persons, done at New York on 28 September 1954;

(q) the term "members of the family" means the persons defined, or recognised as such, or designated as members of the household, by the legislation applied by the institution responsible for paying benefits, or, in the cases referred to in Article 21, paragraph 1, sub-paragraphs (a) and (c) and Article 24, paragraph 6, by the legislation of the Contracting Party in whose territory they reside; where, however, this legislation regards only persons living with the person concerned as members of the family or members of the household, this condition shall be deemed to be satisfied if such persons are mainly maintained by the person concerned;

(r) the term "survivors" means the persons defined or recognised as such by the legislation under which the benefits are granted; where, however, this legislation regards as survivors only persons who were living with the deceased, this condition shall be deemed to be satisfied, if the persons concerned were mainly maintained by the deceased;

(s) the term "periods of insurance" means periods of contributions, employment, occupational activity or residence as defined or recognised as periods of insurance by the legislation under which they were completed, and any other periods, in so far as they are regarded by this legislation as equivalent to periods of insurance;

(t) the terms "periods of employment" and "periods of occupational activity" means periods defined or recognised as such by the legislation under which they were completed, and any other periods, in so far as they are regarded by this legislation as equivalent to periods of employment or occupational activity;

(u) the term "periods of residence" means periods of residence as defined or recognised as such by the legislation under which they were completed;

(v) the terms "benefits" and "pensions" mean all benefits or pensions, including all components thereof provided out of public funds and all increases, revaluation allowances or supplementary allowances, unless otherwise specified in this Convention, and any benefits awarded for the purpose of maintaining or improving earning capacity, such lump sum benefits as are payable in lieu of pensions and, where applicable, any payments made by way of refund or contributions;

(w) the term "family allowances" means periodical cash benefits granted according to the number and age of children; the expression "family benefits" means any benefits in kind or in cash granted to offset family maintenance costs, except the special birth grants explicitly excluded in Annex II; each Contracting Party concerned shall give notice in accordance with the provisions of Article 81, paragraph 1, of any amendment to be made to Annex II in respect of any special birth grants provided by its legislation;

(x) term "death grant" means any lump sum payable in the event of death, other than the lump sum benefits mentioned in sub-paragraph (v) of this article;

(y) the term "contributory" applies to benefits, the award of which depends either on direct financial participation by the persons protected or by their employer, or on a qualifying period of occupational activity, and to legislation or schemes which provide for such benefits; benefits, the award of which does not depend on direct financial participation by the persons protected or by their employer, or on a qualifying period of occupational activity, and the legislation or schemes under which they are exclusively awarded, are said to be "non-contributory";

(z) the term "benefits granted under transitional arrangements" means benefits granted to persons who are over a given age on the date of entry into force of the legislation applicable, or benefits granted provisionally in consideration of events that have occurred or periods that have been completed outside the current frontiers of the territory of a Contracting Party.

Article 2. 1. This Convention applies to all legislation governing the following branches of social security:

(a) sickness and maternity benefits;

(b) invalidity benefits;

(c) old-age benefits;

(d) survivor's benefits;

(e) benefits in respect of occupational injuries and diseases;

(f) death grants;

(g) unemployment benefits;

(h) family benefits.

2. This Convention applies to all general social security schemes and special schemes, whether contributory or non-contributory, including employers' liability schemes in respect of the benefits referred to in the preceding paragraph. Bilateral or multilateral agreements between two or more Contracting Parties shall determine, as far as possible, the conditions in which this Convention shall apply to schemes established by means of collective agreements made compulsory be decision of the public authorities.

3. Where schemes relating to seafarers are concerned, the provisions of Title III of this Convention shall apply without prejudice to the legislation of any Contracting Party governing the liabilities of ship-owners, who shall be treated as the employers for the purpose of the application of this Convention.

4. This Convention does not apply to social or medical assistance schemes, to benefit schemes for victims of war or its consequences, or to special schemes for civil servants or persons treated as such.

5. This Convention does not apply to legislation designed to give effect to a social security convention concluded between a Contracting Party and one or more other States.

Article 3. 1. Annex II specifies, in respect of each Contracting Party, the legislation and schemes referred to in Article 2, paragraphs 1 and 2.

2. Each Contracting Party shall give notice, in accordance with the provisions of Article 81, paragraph 1, of any amendment to be made to Annex II as a result of the adoption of new legislation. Such notice shall be given within three months from the date of publication of such legislation or, in the case of legislation published before the date of ratification of this Convention, on the date of ratification.

Article 4. 1. The provisions of this Convention shall be applicable:

(a) to persons who are or have been subject to the legislation of one or more of the Contracting Parties and are nationals of a Contracting Party, or are refugees or stateless persons resident in the territory of a Contracting Party, as well as to the members of their families and their survivors;

(b) to the survivors of persons who were subject to the legislation of one or more of the Contracting Parties, irrespective of the nationality of such persons, where these survivors are nationals of a Contracting Party, or refugees or stateless persons resident in the territory of a Contracting Party;

(c) without prejudice to Article 2, paragraph 4, to civil servants and persons treated as such under the legislation of the Contracting Party concerned, in so far as they are subject to any legislation of that Contracting Party to which this Convention applies.

2. Notwithstanding the provisions of sub-paragraph (c) of the preceding paragraph, the categories of persons— other than members of the service staff of diplomatic missions or consular posts and persons employed in the private service of officials of such missions or posts—in respect of whom the Vienna Convention on Diplomatic Relations and the Vienna Convention on Consular Relations provide for exemption from the social security provisions which are in force in the receiving State, shall not benefit from the provisions of this Convention.

Article 5. 1. Subject to the provisions of Article 6, this Convention replaces, in respect of persons to whom it is applicable, any social security conventions binding:

(a) two or more Contracting Parties exclusively; or

(b) at least two Contracting Parties and one or more other States in respect of cases calling for no action on the party of an institution of one of the latter States.

2. However, where the application of certain provisions of this Convention is subject to the conclusion of bilateral or multilateral agreements, the provisions of the conventions referred to in sub-paragraphs (a) and (b) of the preceding paragraph shall remain applicable until the entry into force of such agreements.

Article 6. 1. The provisions of this Convention shall not affect obligations under any convention adopted by the International Labour Conference.

2. This Convention shall not affect the provisions on social security in the Treaty of 25 March 1957 establishing the European Economic Community nor the association agreements envisaged under that Treaty nor the measures taken in application of those provisions.

3. Notwithstanding the provisions of Article 5, paragraph 1, two or more Contracting Parties may keep in force, by mutual agreement and in respect of themselves, the provisions of social security conventions by which they are bound by specifying them in Annex II or, in the case of provisions relating to the application of these conventions, by specifying them in an annex to the Supplementary Agreement for the application of this Convention.

4. However, this Convention shall apply in all cases requiring action on the part of an institution of a Contracting Party other than those which are bound by the provisions referred to in paragraph 2 or in paragraph 3 of this article as well as in the case of persons who are entitled to benefits under this Convention and to whom the said provisions are not exclusively applicable.

5. Two or more Contracting Parties which are bound by the provisions specified in Annex III may, by mutual agreement and in respect of themselves, make appropriate amendments to this Annex by giving notice thereof in accordance with the provisions of Article 81, paragraph 1.

Article 7. 1. Two or more Contracting Parties may, if need be, conclude with each other social security conventions founded on the principles of this Convention.

2. Each Contracting Party shall give notice, in accordance with the provisions of Article 81, paragraph 1, of any convention which it concludes by virtue of the preceding paragraph, and of any subsequent amendment or denunciation of such a convention. Such notice shall be given within three months from the date of entry into force of that convention or its amendment, or from the date on which its denunciation takes effect.

Article 8. 1. Unless otherwise specified in this Convention, persons who are resident in the territory of a Contracting Party and to whom the Convention is applicable shall have the same rights and obligations under the legislation of every Contracting Party as the nationals of such Party.

2. However, entitlement to not-contributory benefits, the amount of which does not depend on the length of the periods of residence completed, may be made conditional on the beneficiary having resided in the territory of the Contracting Party concerned or, in the case of survivors' benefits, on the deceased having resided there for a period which may not be set:

(a) at more than six months immediately preceding the lodging of the claim, for maternity benefits and unemployment benefits;

(b) at more than five consecutive years immediately preceding the lodging of the claim, for invalidity benefits, or immediately preceding death, for survivors' benefits;

(c) at more than ten years between the age of sixteen and the pensionable age, of which it may be required that five years shall immediately precede the lodging of the claim, for old-age benefits.

3. If a person does not fulfil the conditions laid down in sub-paragraph (b) or sub-paragraph (c) of the preceding paragraph, but has been subject—or, in the case of survivors' benefits, if the deceased has been subject—to the legislation of the Contracting Party concerned for at least one year, that person or the survivors of the deceased shall nevertheless, without prejudice to the provisions of Article 27, be entitled to benefits calculated on the basis of the full benefit and up to an amount not exceeding it:

(a) in the case of invalidity or death benefits, in proportion to the ratio of the number of years of residence completed by the person concerned or the deceased under the said legislation between the date on which he reached the age of sixteen and the date of his incapacity for work followed by invalidity or death, to two-thirds of the number of years separating those two dates, disregarding any years subsequent to pensionable age;

(b) in the case of old-age pension, in proportion to the ratio of the number of years of residence completed by the person concerned under the said legislation between the date on which he reached the age of sixteen and the pensionable age, to thirty years.

4. Annex IV specifies, for each Contracting Party concerned, the benefits provided under its legislation to which the provisions of paragraph 2 or paragraph 3 of this article are applicable.

5. Each Contracting Party concerned shall give notice, in accordance with the provisions of Article 81, paragraph 1, of any amendment to be made to Annex IV. If such an amendment results from the adoption of new legislation, such notice shall be given within three months from the date of publication of that legislation or, in the case of legislation published before the date of ratification of this Convention, on the date of ratification.

6. The provisions of paragraph 1 of this article shall not affect the legislation of any Contracting Party in so far as it concerns participation in social security administration or membership of social security tribunals.

7. Special measures may be adopted concerning the participation in voluntary insurance or optional continued insurance of persons not resident in the territory of the Contracting Party concerned, or the entitlement to benefits under the transitional arrangements specified in Annex VII.

Article 9. 1. The benefit of the provisions of social security conventions which remain in force by virtue of Article 6, paragraph 3, and the provisions of social security conventions concluded by virtue of Article 7, paragraph 1, may be extended by agreement between the Parties bound thereby, to nationals of every Contracting Party.

2. Annex V specifies the provisions of social security conventions which remain in force by virtue of Article 6, paragraph 3, and whose application is to be extended, in accordance with paragraph 1 of the present article, to nationals of every Contracting Party.

3. The Contracting Parties concerned shall give notice, in accordance with the provisions of Article 81, paragraph 1, of the provisions of the social security conventions concluded by them by virtue of Article 7, paragraph 1, whose application is extended, in accordance with paragraph 1 of the present article, to nationals of every Contracting Party. The provisions of the said conventions shall be indicated in Annex V.

4. Two or more Contracting Parties which are bound by the provisions specified in Annex V may, by mutual agreement and in respect of themselves, make appropriate amendments to this Annex by giving notice thereof in accordance with the provisions of Article 81, paragraph 1.

Article 10. If the legislation of a Contracting Party makes admission to voluntary insurance or optional continued insurance conditional upon the completion of periods of insurance, the institution applying that legislation shall to that end, for the purpose of adding periods together, take account, to the extent necessary, of periods of insurance completed under the legislation of any other Contracting Party and, where appropriate, of periods of residence completed after the age of sixteen under the non-contributory scheme of any other Contracting Party, as if they had been periods of insurance completed under the legislation of the first Party.

Article 11. 1. Unless otherwise specified in this Convention, neither invalidity cash benefits, old-age or survivors' cash benefits, pensions in respect of occupational injuries or diseases, nor death grants, payable under the legislation of one or more Contracting Parties, shall be liable to reduction, modification, suspension, suppression or forfeiture by reason of the fact that the beneficiary is resident in the territory of a Contracting Party other than that in which the institution liable for payment is situated.

2. However, notwithstanding the provisions of Article 8, paragraphs 1 and 2, the invalidity, old-age or survivors' benefits specified in Annex IV shall be calculated in accordance with the provisions of sub-paragraph (a) or sub-paragraph (b) of paragraph 3 of the said Article 8, as the case may be, if the beneficiary is resident in the territory of

a Contracting Party other than that in which the institution liable for payment is situated.

3. The provisions of paragraphs 1 and 2 of the present article shall not apply to the following benefits, in so far as they are specified in Annex VI:

(a) special non-contributory benefits granted to invalids who are unable to earn a living;

(b) special non-contributory benefits granted to persons not entitled to normal benefits;

(c) benefits granted under transitional arrangements;

(d) special benefits granted as assistance or in case of need.

4. Each Contracting Party concerned shall give notice, in accordance with the provisions of Article 81, paragraph 1, of any amendment to be made to Annex VI. If such an amendment results from the adoption of new legislation, such notice shall be given within three months from the date of publication of that legislation or, in the case of legislation published before the date of ratification of this Convention, on the date of ratification.

5. Where the legislation of a Contracting Party makes the repayment of contributions conditional upon the person concerned having ceased to be subject to compulsory insurance, that condition shall not be regarded as fulfilled so long as that person is subject to compulsory insurance under the legislation of any other Contracting Party.

6. The Contracting Party shall determine by means of bilateral or multilateral agreements, the conditions of payment of benefits referred to in paragraph 1 of the present article due to persons enjoying rights under this Convention who are resident in the territory of a State which is not a Contracting Party.

Article 12. The rules governing changes in rates of benefit laid down in the legislation of a Contracting Party shall be applicable to benefits payable under such legislation in accordance with the provisions of this Convention.

Article 13. 1. Except for benefits in respect of invalidity, old age, survivors or occupational disease which are paid by the institutions of two or more Contracting Parties in accordance with the provisions of Article 29 or of Article 47, sub-paragraph (b), this Convention shall not confer or maintain entitlement to several benefits of the same nature or to several benefits relating to one and the same period of compulsory insurance.

2. Provisions in the legislation of a Contracting Party for the reduction, suspension or suppression of benefits where there is overlapping with other benefits or other income, or because of an occupational activity, shall apply also to a beneficiary in respect of benefits acquired under the legislation of another Contracting Party or in respect of income obtained, or occupation followed, in the territory of another Contracting Party. This rule shall not, however, apply to benefits of the same nature payable in respect of invalidity, old age, survivors or occupational disease by the institutions of two or more Contracting Parties in accordance with the provisions of Article 29 or of Article 47, sub-paragraph (b).

Title II
Provisions which Determine the Legislation Applicable

Article 14. In respect of persons coming within the scope of this Convention, the legislation applicable shall be determined in accordance with the following provisions:

(a) employed persons who are employed in the territory of a Contracting Party shall be subject to the legislation of that Party, even if they are resident in the territory of another Contracting Party or if the undertaking which employs them has its principal place of business, or their employer has his place of residence, in the territory of another Contracting Party;

(b) workers who follow their occupation on board a ship flying the flag of a Contracting Party shall be subject to the legislation of that Party;

(c) self-employed persons who follow their occupation in the territory of a Contracting Party shall be subject to the legislation of that Party, even if they reside in the territory of another Contracting Party;

(d) civil servants and persons treated as such shall be subject to the legislation of the Contracting Party in whose administration they are employed.

Article 15. 1. The rule stated in Article 14, sub-paragraph (a), shall apply subject to the following exceptions or modifications:

(a) (i) employed persons who are employed in the territory of a Contracting Party by an undertaking which is their regular employer and who are sent by that undertaking to work for it in the territory of another Contracting Party shall remain subject to the legislation of the first Party provided that the expected duration of the work does not exceed twelve months and that they are not sent to replace other employed persons who have completed their period of employment abroad;

(ii) if the work to be carried out continues because of unforeseeable circumstances for a period longer than originally intended and exceeding twelve months, the legislation of the first Party shall remain applicable until the work is completed, subject to the consent of the competent authority of the second Party or of the body designated by it;

(b) (i) employed persons who are employed in international transport in the territory of two or more Contracting Parties as travelling personnel in the service of an undertaking which has its principal place of business in the territory of a Contracting Party and which, on behalf of others or on its own account, transports passengers or goods by rail, road, air or inland waterway, shall be subject to the legislation of the latter Party;

(ii) however, if they are employed by a branch or permanent agency which the said undertaking has in the territory of a Contracting Party other than the Party in whose territory it has its principal place of business, they shall be subject to the legislation of the Contracting Party in whose territory the branch or permanent agency is situated;

(iii) if they are employed wholly or mainly in the territory of the Contracting Party where they are resident, they shall be subject to the legislation of that Party, even if the undertaking which employs them has neither its principal place of business nor a branch or permanent agency in that territory;

(c) (i) employed persons other than those in international transport who normally follow their occupation in the territory of two or more Contracting Parties shall be subject to the legislation of the Contracting Party in whose territory they reside if their occupation is carried on partly in that territory or if they are employed by several undertakings or by several employers having their principal places of business or their places of residence in the territory of different Contracting Parties;

(ii) in other cases, they shall be subject to the legislation of the Contracting Party in whose territory the undertaking which employes them has its principal place of business or their employer has his place of residence;

(d) employed persons who are employed in the territory of a Contracting Party by an undertaking which has its principal place of business in the territory of another Contracting Party and lies astride the common frontier of the Contracting Party concerned shall be subject to the legislation of the Contracting Party in whose territory the undertaking has its principal place of business.

2. The rule stated in Article 14, sub-paragraph (b), shall apply subject to the following exceptions:

(a) employed persons who are employed by an undertaking which is their regular employer, either in the territory of a Contracting Party or on board a ship flying the flag of a Contracting Party, and who are sent by that undertaking to work for it on board a ship flying the flag of another Contracting Party, shall remain subject to the legislation of the first Party, subject to the conditions laid down in paragraph 1, sub-paragraph (a), of the present article;

(b) workers who normally follow their occupation in the territorial waters or in a port of a Contracting Party on board a ship flying the flag of another Contracting Party but who are not members of the ship's crew, shall be subject to the legislation of the first Party; and

(c) employed persons who are employed on board a ship flying the flag of a Contracting Party and who are paid in respect of this occupation by an undertaking having its principal place of business, or by a person having his place of residence, in the territory of another Contracting Party, shall be subject to the legislation of the latter Party if they reside in its territory; the undertaking or person paying the remuneration shall be considered as the employer for the purpose of the application of the said legislation.

3. The rule stated in Article 14, sub-paragraph (c), shall apply subject to the following exceptions or modifications:

(a) self-employed persons who reside in the territory of one Contracting Party and follow their occupation in the territory of another Contracting Party shall be subject to the legislation of the first Party:

(i) if the second Party has no legislation applicable to them, or

(ii) if, under the legislation of the two Parties concerned, self-employed persons are subject to such legislation solely by reason of the fact that they are resident in the territory of those Parties;

(b) self-employed persons who normally follow their occupation in the territory of two or more Contracting Parties shall be subject to the legislation of the Contracting Party in whose territory they are resident, if they work partly in that territory or if, under that legislation, they are subject to it solely by reason of the fact that they are resident in the territory of that Party;

(c) where the self-employed persons referred to in the preceding sub-paragraph do not follow a part of their occupation in the territory of the Contracting where they are resident, or where, under the legislation of that Party, they are not subject to that legislation solely by reason of the fact that they are resident, or where that Party has no legislation applicable to them, they shall be subject to the legislation jointly agreed upon by the Contracting Parties concerned or by their competent authorities.

4. Where by virtue of the preceding paragraphs of this article, a worker is subject to the legislation of a Contracting Party in whose territory he does not work, that legislation shall be applicable to him as if he worked in the territory of that Party.

Article 16. 1. The provisions of Articles 14 and 15 shall not apply to voluntary insurance or optional continued insurance.

2. Where the application of the legislation of two or more Contracting Parties would result in affiliation to a compulsory insurance scheme and at the same time permit membership of one or more voluntary insurance or optional continued insurance schemes, the person concerned shall be subject exclusively to the compulsory insurance scheme. However, in respect of invalidity, old age, and death (pensions), this Convention shall not affect the provisions of legislation of any Contracting Party permitting simultaneous affiliation to a voluntary insurance or optional continued insurance scheme and to a compulsory insurance scheme.

3. Where the application of the legislation of two or more Contracting Parties would result in the possibility of membership of two or more voluntary insurance or optional continued insurance schemes, the person concerned shall be admitted solely to the voluntary insurance or optional continued insurance scheme of the Contracting Party in whose territory he is resident or, if he is not resident in the territory of one of these Contracting Parties, to the scheme of that Contracting Party for whose legislation he has opted.

Article 17. 1. The provisions of Article 14, sub-paragraph (a), shall apply to members of the service staff of diplomatic missions or consular posts, and also to persons employed in the private service of officials of such missions or posts.

2. However, workers referred to in the preceding paragraph, who are nationals of a Contracting Party which is the sending State, may opt for the application of the legislation of that Party. Such right of option may be exercised only once, within the three months following the entry into force of this Convention or on the date on which the person concerned is engaged by the diplomatic mission or consular post or enters the private service of an official of that mission or that post, as the case may be. The option shall take effect on the date on which it is exercised.

Article 18. 1. The competent authorities of two or more Contracting Parties may, by agreement, provide for exceptions to the provisions of Articles 14 to 17 in the interests of persons affected thereby.

2. The application of the provisions of the preceding paragraph shall, if need be, be subject to a request by the workers concerned and, where appropriate, by their employers. Moreover, such application shall be the subject of a decision by which the competent authority of the Contracting Party whose legislation is applicable confirms that the said workers are no longer subject to the aforesaid legislation and will henceforth be subject to the legislation of another Contracting Party.

Title III
Special Provisions Governing the Various Categories of Benefits

Chapter 1
Sickness and Maternity

Article 19. 1. Where the legislation of a Contracting Party makes the acquisition, maintenance or recovery of the entitlement to benefits conditional upon the completion of periods of insurance, the competent institution of that Party shall, to that end, for the purpose of adding periods together, take account, to the extent necessary, of periods of insurance completed under the legislation of any other Contracting Party and, where appropriate, of periods of residence completed after the age of sixteen under non-contributory schemes of any other Contracting Party, as if they were periods of insurance completed under the legislation of the first Party.

2. Where the legislation of a Contracting Party makes admission to compulsory insurance conditional upon the completion of periods of insurance, periods of insurance completed under the legislation of any other Contracting Party and, where appropriate, periods of residence completed after the age of sixteen under the non-contributory schemes of any other Contracting Party shall, to that end, for the purpose of adding periods together, be taken into account, to the extent necessary, as if they were periods of insurance completed under the legislation of the first Party.

Article 20. 1. Persons who reside in the territory of a Contracting Party other than the competent State and who satisfy the conditions for entitlement prescribed by the legislation of the latter State, regard being had, where appropriate, to the provisions of Article 19, shall receive in the territory of the Contracting Party in which they are resident:

(a) benefits in kind, provided at the expense of the competent institution by the institution of the place of residence in accordance with the provisions of the legislation which the latter institution applies, as if these persons were affiliated to it;

(b) cash benefits, paid by the competent institution in accordance with the provisions of the legislation which it applies, as if these persons were resident in the territory of the competent State. However, by agreement between the competent institution and the institution of the place of residence, cash benefits may also be paid through the later institution, on behalf of the competent institution.

2. The provisions of the preceding paragraph shall apply, *mutatis mutandis,* in respect of benefits in kind to members of the family who are resident in the territory of a Contracting Party other than the competent State.

3. Benefits may also be paid to frontier workers by the competent institution in the territory of the competent State, in accordance with the provisions of the legislation of that State, as if they were resident in its territory. However, members of their family shall be entitled to benefits in kind under the same conditions only if there is an agreement to that effect between the competent authorities of the Contracting Parties concerned, or failing that, except in case of emergency, if there is prior authorisation by the competent institution.

4. Persons to whom this article applies, other than frontier workers or members of their families, who are temporarily resident in the territory of the competent State, shall be entitled to benefits in accordance with the provisions of the legislation of that State as if they were resident in its territory even if they were already receiving benefits for the same case of sickness or maternity before taking up their temporary residence.

5. Persons to whom this article applies who transfer their residence to the territory of the competent State shall be entitled to benefits in accordance with the provisions of the legislation of that State, even if they were already receiving benefits for the same case of sickness or maternity before transferring their residence.

Article 21. 1. Persons who satisfy the conditions for entitlement to benefits under the legislation of the competent State, regard being had, where appropriate, to the provisions of Article 179 and:

(a) whose condition necessitates the immediate provision of benefits during temporary residence in the territory of a Contracting Party other than the competent State, or

(b) who, having become entitled to benefits payable by the competent institution, are authorised by that institution to return to the territory of a Contracting Party other than the competent State where they are resident or to transfer their residence to the territory of a Contracting Party other than the competent State, or

(c) who are authorised by the competent institution to go to the territory of a Contracting Party other than the competent State in order to receive the treatment required by their condition,
shall receive:

(i) benefits in kind, provided at the expense of the competent institution by the institution of the place of residence or temporary residence in accordance with the provisions of the legislation applied by the latter institution, as if these persons were affiliated to it, for a period not exceeding any period which may be prescribed by the legislation of the competent State;

(ii) cash benefits, paid by the competent institution in accordance with the provisions of the legislation which it applies, as if these persons were in the territory of the competent State. However, by agreement between the competent institution and the institution of the place of residence or temporary residence, cash benefits may be paid through the latter institution, on behalf of the competent institution.

2. (a) The authorisation referred to in sub-paragraph (b) of the preceding paragraph may be refused only if the move might prejudice the health or the course of medical treatment of the person concerned;

(b) the authorisation referred to in sub-paragraph (c) of the preceding paragraph shall not be refused when the requisite treatment cannot be given in the territory of the Contracting Party in which the person concerned resides.

3. The provisions of the preceding paragraphs of this article shall apply, *mutatis mutandis,* to members of the family in respect of benefits in kind.

Article 22. 1. Where the legislation of a Contracting Party makes the provisions of benefits in kind to members of the family conditional on their being personally insured, the provisions of Articles 20 and 21 shall apply to members of the family of a person subject to that legislation only if they are personally affiliated to the same institution of the said Party as that person, or to another institution of the said Party which provides corresponding benefits.

2. Where the legislation of a Contracting Party provides that the calculation of cash benefits shall be based on average earnings, the competent institution of that Party shall determine those average earnings exclusively on the basis of the earnings recorded during the periods completed under the said legislation.

3. Where the legislation of a Contracting Party provides that the calculation of cash benefits shall be based on fixed earnings, the competent institution of that Party shall take account exclusively of such fixed earnings or, where appropriate, of the average fixed earnings corresponding to the periods completed under the said legislation.

4. Where the legislation of a Contracting Party provides that the amount of cash benefits shall vary with the number

of members of the family, the competent institution of that Party shall take account also of members of the family resident in the territory of another Contracting Party, as if they were resident in the territory of the first Party.

Article 23. Unemployed persons who satisfy the conditions for entitlement to benefits in kind under the legislation of the Contracting Party responsible for providing unemployment benefit, regard being had, where appropriate, to provisions of Article 19, shall be entitled, together with the members of their families, to benefits in kind if they are resident in the territory of another Contracting Party. Such benefits in kind shall be provided by the institution of the place of residence in accordance with the provisions of the legislation which that institution applies, as if the persons concerned were entitled to the benefits by virtue of that legislation, but the cost shall be borne by the competent institution of the first-mentioned Party.

Article 24. 1. Where a person receiving a pension under the legislation of two or more Contracting Parties is entitled to benefits in kind under the legislation of the Contracting Party in whose territory he is resident, regard being had, where appropriate, to the provisions of Article 19, such benefits shall be provided for him and for the members of his family by the institution of the place of residence at its own cost, as if he were a pensioner under the legislation of the latter Party only.

2. Where a person receiving a pension under the legislation of a Contracting Party, or pensions under the legislation of two or more Contracting Parties, is not entitled to benefits in kind under the legislation of the Contracting Party in whose territory he is resident, he shall nevertheless be entitled to such benefits for himself, and for the members of his family, if he is entitled to them under the legislation of the former Party, or of one of the former Parties, regard being had, where appropriate, to the provisions of Article 19, or if he would be entitled to them if he were resident in the territory of one of those Parties. The benefits in kind shall be provided by the institution of the place of residence, in accordance with the provisions of the legislation which it applies, as if the pensioner were entitled to the said benefits under that legislation, but the cost shall be borne by the institution as determined under the rules laid down in the following paragraph.

3. In the cases referred to in the preceding paragraph, the institution which shall bear the cost of the benefits in kind shall be determined according to the following rules:

(a) where the pensioner is entitled to the said benefits under the legislation of one Contracting Party only, the cost shall be borne by the competent institution of that Party;

(b) where the pensioner is entitled to the said benefits under the legislation of two or more Contracting Parties, the cost shall be borne by the competent institution of the Contracting Party under whose legislation the pensioner completed the longest period of insurance or residence; if by virtue of this rule two or more institutions would be liable for the cost of the benefits, the cost shall be borne by the institution of the Contracting Party to whose legislation the pensioner was last subject.

4. Where the members of the family of a person receiving a pension under the legislation of a Contracting Party or pensions under the legislation of two or more Contracting Parties are resident in the territory of a Contracting Party other than that in which the pensioner himself resides, they shall receive benefits in kind as if the pensioner were resident in the same territory, provided that he is entitled to

such benefits under the legislation of a Contracting Party. The benefits in kind shall be provided by the institution of the place of residence of the members of the family under the provisions of the legislation which it applies, as if they were entitled to such benefits under that legislation, but their cost shall be borne by the institution of the pensioner's place of residence.

5. Members of the family to whom the preceding paragraph applies who transfer their residence to the territory of the Contracting Party in which the pensioner resides shall be entitled to benefits under the provisions of the legislation of that Party even if they have already received benefits for the same case of sickness or maternity before transferring their residence.

6. A person receiving a pension under the legislation of a Contracting Party, or pensions under the legislation of two or more Contracting Parties, who is entitled to benefits in kind under the legislation of one of these Parties, shall, together with the members of his family, be entitled to such benefits:

(a) during temporary residence in the territory of a Contracting Party other than that in which they are resident, where their condition requires the immediate provision of benefit; or

(b) where they have been authorised by the institution of the place of residence to go to the territory of a Contracting Party other than that in which they are resident in order to receive the treatment required by their condition.

7. In the cases referred to in the preceding paragraph, the benefits in kind shall be provided by the institution of the place of temporary residence in accordance with the provisions of the legislation which it applies, as if the persons concerned were entitled to such benefits under that legislation, but the cost shall be borne by the institution of the pensioner's place of residence.

8. Where the legislation of a Contracting Party provides for contributions to be deducted from the pension payable for the purpose of entitlement to benefits in kind, the institution of the Party which pays the pension shall be authorised to make such deductions if the cost of the benefits in kind is borne by an institution of that Party by virtue of this article.

Article 25. 1. Where the legislation applied by the institution of the place of residence or temporary residence provides for two or more sickness and maternity insurance schemes, the rules to be applied in respect of the provision of benefits in kind, in the cases covered by Article 20, paragraphs 1 and 2, Article 21, paragraphs 1 and 3, Article 23, and Article 24, paragraphs 2, 4 and 6, shall be those of the general scheme or, failing that, of the scheme for industrial workers.

2. Where the legislation of a Contracting Party makes the award of benefits dependent on the origin of the sickness, that condition shall not apply to persons covered by this Convention, irrespective of the territory of the Contracting Party in which they reside.

3. Where the legislation of a Contracting Party fixes a maximum period for the award of benefits, the institution which applies that legislation may, where appropriate, take account of any period during which benefits have already been provided by the institution of another Contracting Party for the same case of sickness or maternity.

Article 26. 1. The application of the provisions of Articles 20, 21, 23 and 24 as between two or more Contracting Parties shall be subject to the conclusion between those

Parties of bilateral or multilateral agreements which may also contain appropriate special arrangements.

2. The agreements referred to in the preceding paragraph shall specify in particular:

(a) the categories of persons to whom the provisions of Articles 20, 21, 23 and 24 shall apply;

(b) the period during which benefits in kind may be provided by the institution of one Contracting Party, the cost being borne by the institution of another Contracting Party;

(c) the special conditions governing the supply of prosthetic appliances, major aids and other major benefits in kind;

(d) rules to prevent the overlapping of benefits of the same kind;

(e) arrangements for the refund of benefits provided by the institution of one Contracting Party the cost being borne by the institution of another Contracting Party.

3. Two or more Contracting Parties may agree that there shall be no refunds between the institutions in their jurisdiction.

Chapter 2
Invalidity, Old Age and Death (Pensions)

Section 1: Common Provisions

Article 27. Where a person has been subject successively or alternatively to the legislation of two or more Contracting Parties, the said person or his survivors shall be entitled to benefits in accordance with the provisions of this Chapter, even if such persons would be entitled to claim benefits under the legislation of one or more Contracting Parties without these provisions being applied.

Article 28. 1. Where the legislation of a Contracting Party makes the acquisition, maintenance or recovery of entitlement to benefits conditional upon the completion of periods of insurance, the institution which applies that legislation shall, to that end, for the purpose of adding periods together, take account of periods of insurance completed under the legislation of any other Contracting Party and, where appropriate, of periods of residence completed after the age of sixteen under non-contributory schemes of any other Contracting Party, as if they were periods of insurance completed under the legislation of the first Party.

2. Where the legislation of a Contracting Party makes the acquisition, maintenance or recovery of entitlement to benefits conditional upon the completion of periods of residence, the institution which applies that legislation shall, to that end, for the purpose of adding periods together, take account of periods of insurance completed under the legislation of any other Contracting Party, and, where appropriate, of periods of residence completed after the age of sixteen under non-contributory schemes of any other Contracting Party, as if they were periods of residence completed under the legislation of the first Party.

3. Where, under the legislation of a Contracting Party, a person has been affiliated at the same time to a contributory scheme and to a non-contributory scheme for the same contingency, the institution of any other Contracting Party concerned shall have regard, in applying paragraphs 1 or 2 of this article, to the longest period of insurance or of residence completed under the legislation of the first Party.

4. Where the legislation of a Contracting Party makes the provision of certain benefits conditional upon the completion of periods of insurance in an occupation covered by a special scheme or in a specified occupation or employment, only periods completed under a corresponding scheme, or, failing that, in the same occupation or, where appropriate, in the same employment, under the legislation of other Contracting Parties, shall be taken into account for the award of such benefits. If, notwithstanding periods completed in this way, the person concerned does not satisfy the conditions for entitlement to the said benefits, the periods concerned shall be taken into account for the award of benefits under the general scheme or, failing that, the scheme applicable to wage-earners or to salaried employees, as appropriate.

5. Where the legislation of a Contracting Party, which does not make entitlement to benefits or the amount thereof subject to any specific period of insurance or employment but makes the provision of such benefits conditional on the person concerned or, in the case of survivors' benefits, the deceased having been subject to that legislation at the time at which the contingency arose, that condition shall be considered fulfilled if the person concerned or the deceased, as the case may be, was subject at that time to the legislation of another Contracting Party.

6. Where the legislation of a Contracting Party provides that the period of payment of a pension may be taken into consideration for the acquisition, maintenance or recovery of entitlement to benefits, the competent institution of that Party shall to that end take account of any period during which a pension was paid under the legislation of any other Contracting Party.

Article 29. 1. The institution of each Contracting Party to whose legislation the person concerned has been subject shall determine, in accordance with the legislation which it applies, whether such person satisfies the conditions for entitlement to benefits having regard, where appropriate, to the provisions of Article 28.

2. If the person concerned satisfies those conditions, the said institution shall calculate the theoretical amount of the benefit he could claim if all the periods of insurance and of residence completed under the legislation of the Contracting Parties concerned, and taken into account for determining entitlement, in accordance with the provisions of Article 28, had been completed exclusively under the legislation which that institution applies.

3. However,

(a) in the case of benefits the amount of which does not depend on the length of periods completed, that amount shall be taken to be the theoretical amount referred to in the preceding paragraph;

(b) in the case of benefits specified in Annex IV, the theoretical amount referred to in the preceding paragraph may be calculated on the basis of the full benefit and up to an amount not exceeding it:

(i) in the case of invalidity or death, in proportion to the ratio of the total periods of insurance and residence completed, before the contingency arose, by the person concerned or the deceased under the legislation of all Contracting Parties concerned and taken into account in accordance with the provisions of Article 28, to two-thirds the number of years which elapsed between the date on which the person concerned or the deceased reached the age of sixteen and the date on which occurred the incapacity for work followed by invalidity or the death, as the case may be, disregarding any years subsequent to pensionable age;

(ii) in the case of old age, in proportion to the ratio of the total periods of insurance and residence completed by the person concerned under the legislation of all the

Contracting Parties concerned, and taken into account in accordance with the provisions of Article 28, to thirty years, disregarding any years subsequent to pensionable age.

4. The said institution shall then calculate the actual amount of the benefit payable by it to the person concerned on the basis of the theoretical amount calculated in accordance with the provisions of paragraph 2 or of paragraph 3 of this article, as appropriate, and in proportion to the ratio of the periods of insurance or residence completed before the contingency arose under the legislation which it applies, to the total of the periods of insurance or residence completed before the contingency arose under the legislation of all the Contracting Parties concerned.

5. Where the legislation of a Contracting Party provides that the amount of benefits or certain parts thereof shall be in proportion to the periods of insurance or residence completed, the competent institution of that Party may calculate those benefits or parts thereof directly, solely on the basis of the periods completed under the legislation which it applies, notwithstanding the provisions of paragraphs 2 to 4 of this article.

Article 30. 1. For the calculation of the theoretical amount referred to in Article 29, paragraph 2:

(a) where the legislation of a Contracting Party provides that benefits shall be calculated on the basis of average earnings, an average contribution, an average increase or on the basis of the ratio of the claimant's gross earnings during the periods of insurance to the average gross earnings of all insured persons other than apprentices, such average figures or ratios shall be determined by the competent institution of that Party solely on the basis of the periods completed under the legislation of the said Party or of the gross earnings received by the person concerned during those periods only;

(b) where the legislation of a Contracting Party provides that benefits shall be calculated on the basis of the amount of earnings, contributions or increases, the earnings, contributions or increases to be taken into account by the competent institution of that Party in respect of periods completed under the legislation of other Contracting Parties shall be determined on the basis of the average earnings, contributions or increases recorded for the periods completed under the legislation of the first Party;

(c) where the legislation of a Contracting Party provides that benefits shall be calculated on the basis of fixed earnings or a fixed amount, the earnings or the amount to be taken into account by the competent institution of that Party in respect of periods completed under the legislation of other Contracting Parties shall be equal to the fixed earnings or the fixed amount or, where appropriate, the average fixed earnings or fixed amount corresponding to the periods completed under the legislation of the first Party;

(d) where the legislation of a Contracting Party provides that benefits shall be calculated, in respect of certain periods, on the basis of earnings and, in respect of other periods, on the basis of fixed earnings or a fixed amount, the competent institution of that Party shall take into account, in respect of periods completed under the legislation of other Contracting Parties, the earnings or amounts determined in accordance with the provisions of sub-paragraph (b) or sub-paragraph (c) of this paragraph, as appropriate; where in respect of all the periods completed under the legislation of the first Party, the benefits are calculated on the basis of fixed earnings or a fixed amount, the earnings to be taken into account by the competent institution of that Party, in respect of periods completed under the legislation

of other Contracting Parties, shall be equal to the national earnings corresponding to the said fixed earnings or fixed amount.

2. Where the legislation of a Contracting Party embodies rules providing for the revaluation of the factors taken into account for the calculation of benefits these rules shall apply, where appropriate, to the factors taken into account by the competent institution of that Party, in accordance with the provisions of the preceding paragraph, in respect of periods completed under the legislation of other Contracting Parties.

3. Where the legislation of a Contracting Party provides that the amount of benefits shall vary with the number of members of the family, the competent institution of that Party shall take account also of the members of the family resident in the territory of another Contracting Party, as if they were resident in the territory of the first Party.

Article 31. 1. Notwithstanding the provisions of Article 29, where the total duration of the periods of insurance or residence completed under the legislation of a Contracting Party is less than one year and where, taking into account only those periods, no entitlement to benefits exists under that legislation, the institution of the Party concerned shall not be bound to award benefits in respect of the said periods.

2. The periods referred to in the preceding paragraph shall be taken into account by the institution of each of the other Contracting Parties concerned for the purpose of applying Article 29, except paragraph 4 thereof.

3. However, where the application of the provisions of paragraph 1 of this article would have the effect of relieving all the institutions concerned of the obligation to award benefits, benefits shall be award exclusively under the legislation of the last Contracting Party whose conditions are fulfilled by the person concerned, regard being had to the provisions of Article 28, as if all the periods referred to in paragraph 1 of the present article had been completed under the legislation of that Party.

Article 32. 1. Notwithstanding the provisions of Article 29, where the total of all periods of insurance or residence completed under the legislation of a Contracting Party is at least one year but less than five years, the institution of that Party shall not be bound to award old-age benefits in respect of the said periods.

2. The periods referred to in the preceding paragraph shall be taken into account, for the purpose of applying Article 29, by the institution of the Contracting Party under whose legislation the person concerned completed the longest period of insurance or residence, as if the periods in question had been completed under the legislation of that Party. Where, under this rule, the said periods would have to be taken into account by more than one institution, they shall be taken into account only by the institution of the Contracting Party to whose legislation the person concerned was last subject.

3. The institution referred to in paragraph 1 of this article shall transfer to the institution mentioned in paragraph 2, in final settlement, a lump sum equal to ten times the annual amount of the part-benefit payable by the last-mentioned institution, in accordance with the provisions of Article 29, in respect of periods completed under the legislation applied by the first institution. The competent authorities of the Contracting Parties concerned may agree on different arrangements for settling their liabilities in respect of such periods.

4. However, where the application of the provisions of

paragraph 1 of this article would have the effect of relieving all the institutions concerned of the obligation of award benefits, benefits shall be awarded in accordance with the provision of Article 29.

5. Where the combined application of the provisions of Article 31, paragraph 1, and of paragraph 1 of this article would have the effect of relieving all the institutions concerned of the obligation to award benefits, benefits shall be awarded in accordance with the provisions of Article 29, without prejudice to the provisions of Article 31, paragraphs 1 and 2.

6. The application of the provisions of the preceding paragraphs of this article as between two or more Contracting Parties shall be subject to the conclusion of bilateral or multilateral agreements between those Parties and shall be limited to cases in which the persons concerned have been subject exclusively to the legislation of those Parties.

Article 33. 1. If the person concerned does not, at a given date, satisfy the conditions required by the legislation of all the Contracting Parties concerned, regard being had to the provisions of Article 28, but satisfies the conditions of the legislation of only one or more of them, the following provisions shall apply:

(a) the amount of the benefits payable shall be calculated in accordance with the provisions of paragraphs 2 to 4 or of paragraphs 5 of Article 29, as appropriate, by each of the competent institutions applying legislation the conditions of which are fulfilled;

(b) however,

(i) if the person concerned satisfies the conditions of at least two legislations, without any need to include periods of insurance or residence completed under legislations the conditions of which are not fulfilled, such periods shall not be taken into account for the purpose of applying the provisions of Article 29, paragraphs 2 to 4;

(ii) if the person concerned satisfies the conditions of one legislation only, without any need to invoke the provisions of Article 28, the amount of the benefit payable shall be calculated exclusively in accordance with the provisions of the legislation the conditions of which are fulfilled, taking account of periods completed under that legislation only.

2. Benefits awarded under one or more of the legislations concerned in the case covered by the preceding paragraph shall be recalculated *ex officio,* in accordance with the provisions of paragraphs 2 to 4 or of paragraph 5 of Article 29, as appropriate, as and when the conditions prescribed by the other legislation or legislations concerned are satisfied, regard being had, where appropriate, to the provisions of Article 28.

3. Benefits awarded under the legislation of two or more Contracting Parties shall be recalculated, in accordance with the provisions of paragraph 1 of this article, at the request of the beneficiary, when the conditions prescribed by one or more of the legislations concerned cease to be fulfilled.

Article 34. 1. Where the amount of the benefits a person would be entitled to claim under the legislation of a Contracting Party, disregarding the provisions of Articles 28 to 33, is greater than the total benefits payable in accordance with those provisions, the competent institution of that Party shall pay a supplement equal to the difference between the two amounts, and shall bear the whole cost thereof.

2. Where the application of the provisions of the preceding paragraph would have the effect of entitling the person

concerned to supplements from the institutions of two or more Contracting Parties, he shall receive only whichever is the largest, and the cost shall be apportioned among the competent institutions of the Contracting Parties concerned according to the ratio between the amount of the supplement which each of them would have to pay if it alone had been concerned and the amount of the combined supplement which all the said institutions would have had to pay.

3. The supplement referred to in the preceding paragraphs of this article shall be regarded as a component of the benefits provided by the institution liable for payment. Its amount shall be determined once and for all, except where it may be necessary to apply the provisions of paragraph 2 or paragraph 3 of Article 33.

Section 2: Special Provisions concerning Invalidity

Article 35. 1. In the event of an aggravation of any invalidity for which a person is receiving benefits under the legislation of one Contracting Party only, the following provisions shall apply:

(a) if the person concerned, since he began to receive benefits, has not been subject to the legislation of any other Contracting Party, the competent institution of the first Party shall be bound to award benefits, taking the aggravation into account, in accordance with the provisions of the legislation which that institution applies;

(b) if the person concerned, since he began to receive benefits, has been subject to the legislation of one or more other Contracting Parties, benefits shall be awarded, taking the aggravation into account, in accordance with the provisions of Articles 28 to 34;

(c) in the case referred to in the preceding subparagraph, the date on which the aggravation was established shall be regarded as the date on which the contingency arose;

(d) if in the case referred to in sub-paragraph (b) of this paragraph the person concerned is not entitled to benefits from the institution of another Contracting Party, the competent institution of the first Party shall be bound to award benefits, taking the aggravation into account, in accordance with the provisions of the legislation which that institution applies.

2. In the event of an aggravation of any invalidity for which a person is receiving benefits under the legislation of two or more Contracting Parties, benefits shall be awarded, taking the aggravation into account, in accordance with the provisions of Articles 28 to 34. The provisions of subparagraph (c) of the preceding paragraph shall apply, *mutatis mutandis.*

Article 36. 1. Where, after the suspension of benefits, payment thereof is to be resumed, this shall be done by the institution or institutions which were liable for payment of the benefits at the time of the suspension, without prejudice to the provisions of Article 37.

2. Where, after the suppression of benefits, the state of health of the person concerned justifies the award of further benefits, such benefits shall be awarded in accordance with the provisions of Article 28 to 34.

Article 37. 1. Invalidity benefits shall, where appropriate, be converted into old-age benefits, on the conditions prescribed by the legislation or legislations under which they have been awarded and in accordance with the provisions of Articles 28 to 34.

2. Where, in the case referred to in Article 33, a recipient

of invalidity benefits payable under the legislation of one or more Contracting Parties becomes entitled to old-age benefits, any institution liable for the payment of invalidity benefits shall continue to pay the recipient the benefits to which he is entitled under the legislation which it applies until such time as the provisions of the preceding paragraph become applicable in respect of that institution.

Chapter 3
Occupational Injuries and Diseases

Article 38. 1. Workers having sustained an occupational injury or contracted an occupational disease who reside in the territory of a Contracting Party other than the competent State shall be entitled to receive in the territory of the Contracting Party in which they are resident:

(a) benefits in kind, provided at the expense of the competent institution by the institution of the place of residence in accordance with the provisions of the legislation which the latter institution applies, as if these workers were affiliated to it;

(b) cash benefits, paid by the competent institution in accordance with the provisions of the legislation which it applies, as if these workers were resident in the territory of the competent State. However, by agreement between the competent institution and the institution of the place of residence, cash benefits may also be paid through the latter institution, on behalf of the competent institution.

2. Benefits may also be paid to frontier workers by the competent institution in the territory of the competent State, in accordance with the provisions of the legislation of that State, as if they were resident in its territory.

3. Workers to whom this article applies, other than frontier workers, who are temporarily resident in the territory of the competent State, shall be entitled to benefits in accordance with the provisions of the legislation of that State as if they were resident in its territory even if they were already receiving benefits before taking up their temporary residence.

4. Workers to whom this article applies who transfer their residence to the territory of the competent State shall be entitled to benefits in accordance with the provisions of the legislation of that State even if they were already receiving benefits before transferring their residence.

Article 39. An accident on the way to or from work, which happens in the territory of a Contracting Party other than the competent State, shall be regarded as having happened in the territory of the competent State.

Article 40. 1. Workers having sustained an occupational injury or contracted an occupational disease and:

(a) who are temporarily resident in the territory of a Contracting Party other than the competent State, or

(b) who, having become entitled to benefits payable by the competent institution, are authorised by that institution to return to the territory of a Contracting Party other than the competent State where they are resident, or to transfer their residence to the territory of a Contracting Party other than the competent State, or

(c) who are authorised by the competent institution to go to the territory of a Contracting Party other than the competent State in order to receive the treatment required by their condition,

shall receive:

(i) benefits in kind, provided at the expense of the competent institution by the institution of the place of residence or temporary residence in accordance with the provisions of the legislation applied by the latter institution, as if these workers were affiliated to it, for a period not exceeding any period which may be prescribed by the legislation of the competent State;

(ii) cash benefits, paid by the competent institution in accordance with the provisions of the legislation which it applies, as if these workers were in the territory of the competent State. However, by agreement between the competent institution and the institution of the place of residence or temporary residence, cash benefits may be paid through the latter institution, on behalf of the competent institution.

2. (a) The authorisation referred to in sub-paragraph (b) of the preceding paragraph may be refused only if the move might prejudice the health or the course of medical treatment of the worker;

(b) the authorisation referred to in sub-paragraph (c) of the preceding paragraph shall not be refused when the requisite treatment cannot be given in the territory of the Contracting Party in which the worker resides.

Article 41. In the cases mentioned in Article 38, paragraph 1, and in Article 40, paragraph 1, the competent authorities of two or more Contracting Parties may agree to make the provision of prosthetic appliances, major aids and other major benefits in kind conditional upon authorisation by the competent institution.

Article 42. 1. Where the legislation of the competent State provides for the payment of the cost of transporting the injured worker to his place or residence or to hospital, the cost of transport to the corresponding place in the territory of another Contracting Party where he is resident shall be borne by the competent institution, in accordance with the provisions of the legislation which it applies, provided that it has given prior authorisation for the said transport, due account being taken of the reasons justifying it.

2. Where the legislation of the competent State provides for the payment of the cost of transporting the body of a deceased worker to the place of burial, the cost of transport to the corresponding place in the territory of another Contracting Party where the deceased was resident shall be borne by the competent institution, in accordance with the provisions of the legislation which it applies.

3. The application of the provisions of the preceding paragraphs of this article as between two or more Contracting Parties shall be subject to the conclusion of bilateral or multilateral agreements between those Parties. Such agreements shall specify the categories of persons to whom the said provisions shall apply and the arrangements for apportioning the transport costs between the Contracting Parties concerned.

Article 43. 1. Where no insurance scheme covering occupational injuries or diseases exists in the territory of the Contracting Party where the worker happens to be or where an insurance scheme exists but has no institution responsible for the provisions of benefits in kind, such benefits shall be provided by the institution of the place of residence or temporary residence responsible for providing benefits in kind in the event of sickness.

2. Where the legislation of the competent State provides that benefits in kind shall not be completely free unless use is made of the medical service organised by the employer, the benefits in kind provided in the cases referred to in Article 38, paragraph 1, and in Article 40, paragraph 1, shall be deemed to have been provided by such medical service.

3. Where the legislation of the competent State embodies an employers' liability scheme, the benefits in kind

provided in the cases referred to in Article 38, paragraph 1, and in Article 40, paragraph 1, shall be deemed to have been provided at the request of the competent institution.

4. Where the legislation of one Contracting Party explicitly or implicitly provides that previous occupational injuries or diseases shall be taken into account in the assessment of the degree of incapacity, the competent institution of that Party shall also take into account for this purpose occupational injuries or diseases previously recognised in accordance with the legislation of any other Contracting Party, as if they had occurred under the legislation which that institution applies.

Article 44. 1. Where the legislation applied by the institution of the place of residence or temporary residence embodies two or more compensation schemes, the rules to be applied in respect of the provision of benefits in kind, in cases referred to in Article 38, paragraph 1, and in Article 40, paragraph 1, shall be those of the general scheme or, failing that, of the scheme for industrial workers.

2. Where the legislation of a Contracting Party fixes a maximum period for the provision of benefits, the institution which applies that legislation may, where appropriate, take account of any period during which benefits have already been provided by the institution of another Contracting Party for the same case of occupational injury or disease.

Article 45. 1. Where the legislation of a Contracting Party provides that the calculation of cash benefits shall be based on average earnings, the competent institution of that Party shall determine those average earnings exclusively on the basis of the earnings recorded during the period completed under the said legislation.

2. Where the legislation of a Contracting Party provides that the calculation of cash benefits shall be based on fixed earnings, the competent institution of that Party shall take account exclusively of such fixed earnings or, where appropriate, of the average fixed earnings corresponding to the periods completed under the said legislation.

3. Where the legislation of a Contracting Party provides that the amount of cash benefits shall vary with the number of members of the family, the competent institution of that Party shall take account also of members of the family resident in the territory of another Contracting Party, as if they were resident in the territory of the first Party.

Article 46. 1. If a worker having contracted an occupational disease has followed, under the legislation of two or more Contracting Parties, an occupation liable to cause such a disease, the benefits to which he or his survivors may be entitled shall be awarded exclusively under the legislation of the last of the said Parties the conditions of which they fulfil, regard being had, where appropriate, to the provisions of paragraphs 2, 3 and 4 of this article.

2. Where the legislation of a Contracting Party makes entitlement to benefits for occupational diseases conditional upon the disease in question being first diagnosed in its territory, that conditions shall be deemed to have been fulfilled if this disease was first diagnosed in the territory of another Contracting Party.

3. Where the legislation of a Contracting Party explicitly or implicitly makes entitlement to benefits for occupational diseases conditional upon the disease in question being diagnosed within a specified period after the termination of the last occupation liable to have caused it, the competent institution of that Party, when ascertaining the time at which the occupation in question was followed, shall take account to the extent necessary of any occupa-

tion of the same kind followed under the legislation of any other Contracting Party, as if it had been followed under the legislation of the first Party.

4. Where the legislation of a Contracting Party explicitly or implicitly makes entitlement to benefits for occupational diseases conditional upon an occupation liable to cause the disease in question having been followed for a specified period, the competent institution of that Party shall take account, to the extent necessary, for the purpose of adding periods together, of periods during which such an occupation was followed in the territory of any other Contracting Party.

5. The application of the provisions of paragraphs 3 and 4 of this article as between two or more Contracting Parties shall be subject to the conclusion of bilateral or multilateral agreements between those Parties. Such agreements shall specify the occupational diseases to which these provisions shall be applicable and the arrangements for apportioning the cost of the benefits between the Contracting Parties concerned.

Article 47. Where a worker having contracted an occupational disease has received or is receiving compensation paid by the institution of a Contracting Party, and, in the event of an aggravation of his condition, claims benefits from the institution of another Contracting Party, the following provisions shall apply:

(a) where the worker has not followed, under the legislation of the second Party, an occupation liable to cause or to aggravate the disease in question, the competent institution of the first Party shall bear the cost of the benefits, taking the aggravation into account, in accordance with the provisions of the legislation which that institution applies;

(b) where the worker followed such an occupation under the legislation of the second Party, the competent institution of the first Party shall bear the cost of the benefits, leaving the aggravation out of account, in accordance with the provisions of the legislation which it applies; the competent institution of the second Party shall award to the worker a supplementary benefit the amount of which shall be equal to the difference between the amount of the benefits due after the aggravation, in accordance with the provisions of the legislation which that institution applies, if the disease in question had been contracted under the legislation of that Party.

Article 48. 1. The competent institution shall be bound to refund the cost of benefits in kind provided on its behalf by virtue of Article 38, paragraph 1, and Article 40, paragraph 1.

2. The refund referred to in the preceding paragraph shall be determined and made under arrangements to be agreed between the competent authorities of the Contracting Parties.

3. Two or more Contracting Parties may agree that there shall be no refunds between the institutions in their jurisdiction.

Chapter 4
Death (Grants)

Article 49. 1. Where the legislation of a Contracting Party makes the acquisition, maintenance or recovery of entitlement to death grants conditional upon the completion of periods of insurance, the institution which applies that legislation shall, to that end, for the purpose of adding periods together, take account, to the extent necessary, of periods of insurance completed under the legislation of any other Contracting Party and, where appropriate, of periods of residence completed after the age of sixteen under non-contributory schemes of any other Contracting Party, as if they were periods of insurance completed under the legislation of the first Party.

2. Where the legislation of a Contracting Party makes the acquisition, maintenance or recovery of entitlement to death grants conditional upon the completion of periods of residence, the institution which applies that legislation shall, to that end, for the purpose of adding periods together, take account, to the extent necessary, of periods of insurance completed under the legislation of any other Contracting Party and, where appropriate, of periods of residence completed after the age of sixteen under non-contributory schemes of any other Contracting Party, as if they were periods of residence completed under the legislation of the first Party.

Article 50. 1. Where a person dies in the territory of a Contracting Party other than the competent State, the death shall be deemed to have occurred in the territory of the competent State.

2. The competent institution shall provide death grants due under the legislation which it applies, even if the beneficiary resides in the territory of a Contracting Party other than the competent State.

3. The provisions of the preceding paragraphs of this article shall apply also where death results from an occupational injury or disease.

Chapter 5
Unemployment

Article 51. 1. Where the legislation of a Contracting Party makes the acquisition, maintenance or recovery of entitlement to benefits conditional upon the completion of periods of insurance, the institution which applies that legislation shall, to that end, for the purpose of adding periods together, take account, to the extent necessary, of periods of insurance, employment or occupational activity completed under the legislation of any other Contracting Party, as if they were periods of insurance completed under the legislation of the first Party, provided however that, in the case of periods of employment or occupational activity, these periods would have been considered as periods of insurance if they had been completed under the last mentioned legislation.

2. Where the legislation of a Contracting Party makes the entitlement to benefits conditional upon the completion of periods of employment, occupational activity or residence, the institution which applies that legislation shall, to that end, for the purpose of adding periods together, take account, to the extent necessary, of periods of insurance, employment or occupational activity completed under the legislation of any other Contracting Party, as if they were periods of employment, occupational activity or residence completed under the legislation of the first Party.

3. Where the legislation of a Contracting Party makes the provision of certain benefits conditional upon the completion of periods of insurance in an occupation covered by a special scheme, only periods completed under a corresponding scheme, or, failing that, in the same occupation under the legislation of other Contracting Parties, shall be taken into account for the provision of such benefits. If, notwithstanding periods completed in this way, the person concerned does not satisfy the conditions for entitlement to the said benefits, the period concerned shall be taken into account for the provision of benefits under the general scheme.

4. The application of the provisions of the preceding paragraphs of this article is subject to the condition that the person concerned was last subject to the legislation of the Contracting Party under which the benefits are claimed, except in the cases referred to in Article 53, paragraph 2, sub-paragraphs (a) (ii) and (b) (ii).

Article 52. Unemployed workers who satisfy the conditions for entitlement to benefits prescribed by the legislation of one Contracting Party in respect of the completion of periods of insurance, employment, occupational activity or residence, regard being had, where appropriate, to the provisions of Article 51, and who transfer their residence to the territory of another Contracting Party, shall be deemed to satisfy also the conditions of entitlement to benefits prescribed by the legislation of the second Party in this respect, provided that they lodge a claim with the institution of their new place of residence within thirty days of their transfer of residence. The benefits shall be paid by the institution of the place of residence, in accordance with the provisions of the legislation which that institution applies, the cost being borne by the competent institution of the first Party.

Article 53. 1. Without prejudice to the provisions of Article 52, an unemployed worker who, during his last employment, was resident in the territory of a Contracting Party other than the competent State shall receive benefits in accordance with the following provisions:

(a) (i) a frontier worker, whose unemployment in the undertaking which employs him is partial or incidental, shall receive benefits in accordance with the provisions of the legislation of the competent State, as if he were resident in the territory of that State, regard being had, where appropriate, to the provisions of Article 51; such benefits shall be paid by the competent institution;

(ii) a frontier worker who is wholly unemployed shall receive benefits in accordance with the provisions of the legislation of the Contracting Party in whose territory he is resident, as if he had been subject to that legislation during his last employment, regard being had, where appropriate, to the provisions of Article 51; such benefits shall be paid by the institution of the place of residence;

(b) (i) a worker, other than a frontier worker, who become partially, incidentally or wholly unemployed and remains available to his employer or to the employment services in the territory of the competent State, shall receive benefits in accordance with the provisions of the legislation of the competent State, as if he were resident in the territory of the State, regard being had, where appropriate, to the provisions of Article 51; such benefits shall be paid by the competent institution;

(ii) a worker, other than a frontier worker, who becomes wholly unemployed and makes himself available to the employment services in the territory of the Contracting Party where he is resident, or returns to that territory, shall receive benefits in accordance with the provisions of the legislation of that Party, as if he had been subject to that legislation during his last employment, regard being had, where appropriate, to the provisions of Article 51; such benefits shall be paid by the institution of the place of residence;

(iii) however, if the worker referred to in sub-paragraph (b) (ii) of this paragraph has become entitled to benefits from the competent institution of the Contracting Party to whose legislation he was last subject, he shall receive benefits in accordance with the provisions of Article 52, as if he had transferred his residence to the territory of the Contracting Party referred to in sub-paragraph (b) (ii) of this paragraph.

2. As long as an unemployed worker is entitled to benefits by virtue of sub-paragraphs (a) (i) or (b) (i) of the preceding paragraph, he shall not be entitled to benefits under the legislation of the Contracting Party in whose territory he resides.

Article 54. Where, in the cases referred to in Article 52 and in Article 53, paragraph 1, sub-paragraph (b) (iii), the legislation applied by the institution of the place of residence prescribes a maximum period for the award of benefits, the said institution may, where appropriate, take account of any period during which benefits have already been paid by the institution of another Contracting Party since entitlement to benefits was last established.

Article 55. 1. Where the legislation of a Contracting Party provides that the calculation of benefits shall be based on the amount of previous earnings, the institution which applies that legislation shall take account exclusively of the earnings of the worker concerned in the last occupation which he followed in the territory of the said Party or, if he was not last employed in that territory for at least four weeks, of the corresponding normal wage at his place of residence, for work equivalent or similar to his last occupation in the territory of another Contracting Party.

2. Where the legislation of a Contracting Party provides that the amount of benefits shall vary with the number of members of the family, the institution which applies that legislation shall take account also of the members of the family resident in the territory of another Contracting Party, as if they were resident in the territory of the first Party.

3. Where the legislation applied by the institution of the place of residence provides that the time during which benefits are payable shall depend on the length of the periods completed, the time during which benefits are payable shall be determined with due regard, where appropriate, to the provisions of paragraph 1 or paragraph 2 of Article 51.

Article 56. 1. The application of the provisions of Articles 52 to 54 as between two or more Contracting Parties shall be subject to the conclusion between those Parties of bilateral or multilateral agreements which may also contain appropriate special arrangements.

2. The agreements referred to in the preceding paragraph shall specify in particular:

(a) the categories of persons to whom the provisions of Articles 52 to 54 shall apply;

(b) the period during which benefits may be paid by the institution of one Contracting Party, the cost being borne by the institution of another Contracting Party;

(c) arrangements for the refund of benefits provided by the institution of one Contracting Party where the cost is to be borne by the institution of another Contracting Party.

3. Two or more Contracting Parties may agree that there shall be no refunds between the institutions in their jurisdiction.

Chapter 6
Family Benefits

Article 57. Where the legislation of a Contracting Party makes the entitlement to benefits conditional upon the completion of periods of employment, occupational activity or residence, the institution which applies that legislation shall, to that end, for the purpose of adding periods

together, take account, to the extent necessary, of periods of employment, occupational activity or residence completed under the legislation of any other Contracting Party, as if they were periods of employment, occupational activity or residence completed under the legislation of the first Party.

Article 58. 1. The application of the provisions of Section 1 or Section 2 of this Chapter as between two or more Contracting Parties shall be subject to the conclusion between those Parties of bilateral or multilateral agreements which may also contain appropriate special arrangements.

2. The agreements referred to in the preceding paragraph shall specify in particular:

(a) the categories of persons to whom the provisions of Articles 59 to 62 shall apply;

(b) rules to prevent the overlapping of benefits of the same kind;

(c) where appropriate, the maintenance of rights acquired by virtue of social security conventions.

Section 1: Family Allowances

Article 59. 1. For the purpose of the application of this article and of Article 60, the term "children" shall, within the limits prescribed in the legislation of the Contracting Party concerned, mean:

(a) legitimate children, legitimised children, acknowledged illegitimate children, adopted children and orphaned grandchildren of the beneficiary;

(b) legitimate children, legitimised children, acknowledged illegitimate children, adopted children and orphaned grandchildren of the beneficiary's spouse, on condition that they are living in the beneficiary's household in the territory of a Contracting Party.

2. Persons subject to the legislation of one Contracting Party, having children who are resident or are being brought up in the territory of another Contracting Party, shall be entitled in respect of such children to the family allowances provided for by the legislation of the first Party, as if these children were permanently resident or were being brought up in the territory of that Party.

3. However, in the case referred to in the preceding paragraph, the amount of the family allowances may be limited to the amount of family allowances provided for by the legislation of the Contracting Party in whose territory the children are resident or are being brought up.

4. For the purpose of applying the provisions of the preceding paragraph the comparison of the amounts of family allowances payable under the two legislations concerned shall be made on the basis of the total number of children of the same beneficiary. Where the legislation of the Contracting Party in whose territory the children are resident or are being brought up provides for different family allowances rates for different categories of beneficiaries, regard shall be had to the amounts that would be payable if the beneficiary were subject to that legislation.

5. The provisions of paragraphs 3 and 4 of this article shall not be applicable to an employed person covered by Article 15, paragraph 1, sub-paragraph (a), in respect of such children as accompany him to the territory of the Contracting Party where he is sent to work.

6. Family allowances shall be paid in accordance with the provisions of the legislation of the Contracting Party to which the beneficiary is subject, even if the physical or legal person to whom the allowances are payable resides or is temporarily in the territory of another Contracting Party.

Article 60. 1. Unemployed workers drawing unemployment benefits at the expense of the institution of one Contracting Party, and having children who are resident or are being brought up in the territory of another Contracting Party, shall be entitled, in respect of such children, to the family allowances payable in that contingency under the legislation of the first Party, as if they were resident or were being brought up in the territory of this Party.

2. In the case referred to in the preceding paragraph, the provisions of Article 59, paragraphs 1, 3, 4 and 6 shall apply, *mutatis mutandis.*

Section 2: Family Benefits

Article 61. 1. Persons who are subject to the legislation of a Contracting Party shall be entitled, in respect of members of their family resident in the territory of another Contracting Party, to the benefits provided under the legislation of the latter Party, as if those persons were subject to that Party's legislation. Such benefits shall be paid to the members of the family by the institution of their place of residence, in accordance with the provisions of the legislation which that institution applies, and the cost shall be borne by the competent institutions.

2. Notwithstanding the provisions of the preceding paragraph, an employed person to whom Article 15, paragraph 1, sub-paragraph (a), refers shall be entitled, in respect of such members of his family as accompany him to the territory of the Contracting Party where he is sent to work, to the benefits provided under the legislation of the Contracting Party to which he remains subject. Such benefits shall be paid by the competent institution of the latter Party. However, by agreement between the competent institution and the institution of the place of residence, the benefits may also be paid through the latter institution, on behalf of the competent institution.

Article 62. Unemployed workers drawing unemployment benefits payable by an institution of a Contracting Party shall be entitled, in respect of members of their family resident in the territory of another Contracting Party, to the family benefits payable under the legislation of the latter Party provided that, under the legislation of the first Party, family benefits are payable in the event of unemployment. The family benefits shall be paid to the members of the family by the institution of their place of residence, in accordance with the provisions of the legislation which that institution applies, and the cost shall be borne the competent institution of the first Party.

Article 63. 1. In those cases where the provisions of this Section are applied between two or more Contracting Parties, the bilateral or multilateral agreements referred to in Article 58, paragraph 1, shall specify the arrangements for the refund of benefits provided by the institution of one Contracting Party where the cost is to be borne by the institution of another Contracting Party.

2. Two or more Contracting Parties may agree that there shall be no refunds between the institutions in their jurisdiction.

Title IV
Miscellaneous Provisions

Article 64. 1. The competent authorities of the Contracting Parties shall communicate to each other:

(a) all information regarding measures taken by them for the application of this Convention; and

(b) all information regarding changes made in their legislation which may affect the application of this Convention.

2. For the purpose of applying this Convention the authorities and institutions of the Contracting Parties shall assist one another as if it were a matter of applying their own legislation. In principle the administrative assistance furnished by the said authorities and institutions to one another shall be free of charge. However, the competent authorities of the Contracting Parties may agree to reimburse certain expenses.

3. The authorities and institutions of the Contracting Parties may, for the purpose of applying this Convention, communicate directly with one another and with the individuals concerned or their representatives.

4. The authorities, institutions and jurisdictions of one Contracting Party may not reject claims or other documents submitted to them by reason of the fact that they are written in an official language of another Contracting Party.

Article 65. 1. Any exemption from, or reduction of, taxes, stamp duty, legal dues or registration fees provided for in the legislation of one Contracting Party in connection with certificates or documents required to be produced for the purposes of the legislation of that Party shall be extended to similar certificates and documents required to be produced for the purposes of the legislation of another Contracting Party or of this Convention.

2. All official instruments, documents or certificates of any kind that are required to be produced for the purposes of this Convention shall be exempt from authentication or any similar formality.

Article 66. 1. Where a claimant is resident in the territory of a Contracting Party other than the competent State, he may validly present his claim to the institution of his place of residence, which shall refer it to the competent institution or institutions mentioned in the claim.

2. Any claim, declaration or appeal that should have been submitted, under the legislation of a Contracting Party, within a specified time to an authority, institution or jurisdiction of that Party shall be admissible if it is submitted within the same period to an authority, institution or jurisdiction of another Contracting Party. In such event the authority, institution or jurisdiction receiving the claim, declaration or appeal shall forward it without delay to the competent authority, institution or jurisdiction of the first Party, either directly or through the intermediary of the competent authorities of the Contracting Parties concerned. The date on which any claim, declaration or appeal was submitted to an authority, institution or jurisdiction of the second Contracting Party shall be deemed to be the date of its submission to the authority, institution or jurisdiction competent to deal with it.

Article 67. 1. Medical examinations prescribed by the legislation of one Contracting Party may be carried out, at the request of the institution which applies this legislation, in the territory of another Contracting Party, by the institution of the place of temporary residence or residence. In such event, they shall be deemed to have been carried out in the territory of the first Party.

2. The application of the provisions of the preceding paragraphs as between two or more Contracting Parties shall be subject to the conclusion of bilateral or multilateral agreements between those Parties.

Article 68. 1. Where, under this Convention, the institution of one Contracting Party is liable to pay cash benefits to a beneficiary who is in the territory of another Contracting Party, is liability shall be expressed in the currency of the first Party. That institution may validly discharge its liability in the currency of the second Party.

2. Where, under this Convention, the institution of one Contracting Party is liable to pay sums in refund of benefits provided by the institution of another Contracting Party, its liability shall be expressed in the currency of the second Party. The first institution may validly discharge its liability in that currency, unless the Contracting Parties concerned have agreed on other arrangements.

3. Transfers of funds which result from the application of this Convention shall be effected in accordance with the relevant agreements in force between the Contracting Parties concerned at the date of transfer. Failing such agreements, the arrangements for effecting such transfers shall be agreed between the said Parties.

Article 69. 1. For the calculation of the amount of contributions due to the institution of a Contracting Party, account shall be taken, where appropriate, of any income received in the territory of any other Contracting Party.

2. The recovery of contributions due to the institution of one Contracting Party may be effected in the territory of another Contracting Party in accordance with the administrative procedures and subject to the guarantees and privileges applicable to the recovery of contributions due to a corresponding institution of the latter Party.

3. The application of the provisions of paragraphs 1 and 2 of this article as between two or more Contracting Parties shall be subject to the conclusion of bilateral or multilateral agreements between those Parties. Such agreements may also deal with legal procedure for recovery.

Article 70. 1. Where a person is receiving benefits under the legislation of one Contracting Party in respect of an injury caused or sustained in the territory of another Contracting Party, the rights of the institution liable to pay benefits against the third party liable to pay damages shall be regulated in the following manner:

(a) where the said institution, under the legislation applicable to it, is substituted for the beneficiary in any rights which he may have against the third party, such substitution shall be recognised by every other Contracting Party; and

(b) where the said institution has a direct right against the third party, such right shall be recognised by every other Contracting Party.

2. The application of the provisions of the preceding paragraph as between two or more Contracting Parties shall be subject to the conclusion of bilateral or multilateral agreements between those Parties.

3. The rules governing the liability of employers or their agents in the case of occupational injuries or accidents on the way to or from work which happen in the territory of a Contracting Party other than the competent State shall be determined by agreement between the Contracting Parties concerned.

Article 71. 1. Any dispute arising between two or more Contracting Parties as to the interpretation or application of this Convention shall first of all be the subject of negotiations between the Parties to the dispute.

2. If one of the Parties to the dispute considers that there is a question likely to affect all the Contracting Parties, the Parties to the dispute jointly, or failing that, one of them, shall submit it to the Committee of Ministers of the Council of Europe, which shall give an opinion on the question within six months.

3. If it has not proved possible to settle the dispute either, as the case may be, within six months from the request for the opening of negotiations as prescribed by paragraph 1 of this article, or within three months from the communication to the Contracting Parties of the opinion given by the Committee of Ministers, the dispute may be the subject of arbitration proceedings before one arbitrator, at the request of any Party to the dispute. The requesting Party shall notify the other Party, through the Secretary General of the Council of Europe, of the subject matter of the request it intends to refer to arbitration and of the grounds on which the request is based.

4. Unless otherwise agreed by the Parties to the dispute, the arbitrator shall be appointed by the President of the European Court of Human Rights. The arbitrator shall not be a national of one of the Parties to the dispute, nor have his usual place of residence in the territory of these Parties, nor be employed by them, nor have dealt with the case in another capacity.

5. If, in the case referred to in the preceding paragraph, the President of the European Court of Human Rights is unable to act or is a national of one of the Parties to the dispute, the arbitrator shall be appointed by the Vice-President of the Court or by the most senior member of the Court who is not unable to act and is not a national of one of the Parties to the dispute.

6. Failing a special agreement between the Parties to the dispute, or failing a sufficiently precise agreement, the arbitrator shall give his decision on the basis of the provisions of this Convention, taking due account of the general principles of international law.

7. The arbitrator's decision shall be binding and final.

Article 72. 1. Annex VII specifies, for each Contracting Party concerned, the particular measures for the application of its legislation.

2. Each Contracting Party concerned shall give notice, in accordance with the provisions of Article 81, paragraph 1, of any amendment to be made to Annex VII. If such an amendment results from the adoption of new legislation, notice shall be given within three months from the date of publication of that legislation or, in the case of legislation published before the date of ratification of this Convention, on the date of ratification.

Article 73. 1. The Annexes referred to in Article 1, sub-paragraph (b), Article 3, paragraph 1, Article 6, paragraph 3, Article 8, paragraph 4, Article 9, paragraph 2, Article 11, paragraph 3, and Article 72, paragraph 1, and any subsequent amendments made to these Annexes, shall be an integral part of this Convention.

2. Any amendment to the Annexes referred to in the preceding paragraph shall be considered as adopted if, within the three months following the notification provided for in Article 81, paragraph 2, sub-paragraph (d), of this Convention, no Contracting Party or signatory State has opposed it by notification addressed to the Secretary General of the Council of Europe.

3. In the event of such opposition being notified to the Secretary General, the question shall be settled in accordance with a procedure to be established by the Committee of Ministers of the Council of Europe.

Title V
Transitional and Final Provisions

Article 74. 1. This Convention shall confer no rights for any period before its entry into force in respect of the Contracting Party or Parties concerned.

2. All periods of insurance and, where appropriate, of

employment, occupational activity or residence completed under the legislation of a Contracting Party before the date on which this Convention enters into force shall be taken into account for the purpose of determining rights arising from this Convention.

3. Subject to the provisions of paragraph 1 of this article, rights may arise under this Convention even in respect of a contingency which arose before its entry into force.

4. Any benefit which has not been provided or which has been suspended on account of the nationality of the person concerned or of his residence in the territory of the Contracting Party other than that in which the institution liable to pay the benefits is situated shall, at the request of the person concerned, be provided or resumed with effect from the date on which this Convention enters into force, unless the rights previously extinguished have given rise to the payment of a lump sum.

5. The rights of persons concerned who have been awarded a pension before the entry into force of this Convention shall be revised at their request, regard being had to the provisions of this Convention. These rights may also be served *ex officio*. In no circumstances shall such a revision operate to lessen the former rights of the person concerned.

6. Where the request referred to in paragraph 4 or in paragraph 5 of this article is submitted within two years of the date on which this Convention enters into force, the rights arising in accordance with the provisions of the Convention shall be acquired as from that date, and those provisions of the legislation of any Contracting Party which concern the loss of rights or the extinction of rights by lapse of time shall not be raised against the person concerned.

7. Where the request referred to in paragraph 4 or in paragraph 5 of this article is submitted more than two years after the date on which this Convention enters into force, such rights as have not lapsed or have not been extinguished by lapse of time shall be acquired only with reference to the date on which the request was submitted, unless there are more favourable provisions in the legislation of the Contracting Party concerned.

Article 75. 1. The Convention shall be open to signature by the member States of the Council of Europe. It shall be subject to ratification or acceptance. Instruments of ratification or acceptance shall be deposited with the Secretary General of the Council of Europe.

2. This Convention shall enter into force on the first day of the third month following that in which the third instrument of ratification or acceptance is deposited.

3. In respect of a signatory State ratifying or accepting subsequently, the Convention shall enter into force three months after the date of deposit of its instrument of ratification or acceptance.

Article 76. From the date of entry into force of this Convention, the provisions of the European Interim Agreement on Social Security other than Schemes for Old Age, Invalidity and Survivors and Protocol thereto, and European Interim Agreement on Social Security Schemes relating to Old Age, Invalidity and Survivors and Protocol thereto shall cease to be applicable in relations between Contracting Parties.

Article 77. 1. After the entry into force of this Convention, the Committee of Ministers of the Council of Europe may invite any State not a Member of the Council to accede to this Convention, provided that the resolution containing such invitation receives the unanimous agreement of the member States of the Council who have ratified or accepted the Convention.

2. Accession shall be effected by the deposit with the Secretary General of the Council of Europe of an instrument of accession which shall take effect three months after the date of its deposit.

Article 78. 1. This Convention shall remain in force indefinitely.

2. Any Contracting Party may, in so far as it is concerned, denounce this Convention after it has been in force for five years in respect of that Party, by means of a notification addressed to the Secretary General of the Council of Europe.

3. Such denunciation shall take effect six months after the date of receipt by the Secretary General of such notification.

Article 79. 1. In the event of denunciation of this Convention, all rights acquired under its provisions shall be maintained.

2. Rights in process of acquisition in respect of periods before the date on which the denunciation takes effect shall not lapse as a result of the denunciation; their subsequent continued recognition shall be determined by agreement, or failing such agreement, by the legislation which the institution concerned applies.

Article 80. 1. The application of this Convention shall be governed by a Supplementary Agreement which shall be open to signature by the member States of the Council of Europe.

2. The Contracting Parties or, in so far as the constitutional provisions of these Parties permit, their competent authorities, shall make all other arrangements necessary for the application of this Convention.

3. Any State signatory to this Convention which ratifies or accepts it must, at the same time, either ratify or accept the Supplementary Agreement or sign it without reservation in respect of ratification or acceptance, not later than the date of deposit of its instrument of ratification or acceptance of the Convention.

4. Any State which accedes to this Convention must at the same time accede to the Supplementary Agreement.

5. Any Contracting Party which denounces this Convention must at the same time denounce the Supplementary Agreement.

Article 81. 1. The notifications or declarations referred to in Article 1, sub-paragraph (b) and (w), Article 3, paragraph 2, Article 6, paragraph 5, Article 7, paragraph 2, Article 8, paragraph 5, Article 9, paragraphs 3 and 4, Article 11, paragraph 4 and Article 72, paragraph 2, shall be addressed to the Secretary General of the Council of Europe.

2. The Secretary General of the Council of Europe shall, within one month, notify the Contracting Parties, signatory States and the Director General of the International Labour Office of:

(a) any signature and any deposit of an instrument of ratification, acceptance or accession;

(b) any date of entry into force of this Convention in accordance with the provisions of Article 75 and Article 7;

(c) any notification of denunciation received in pursuance of the provisions of Article 78, paragraph 2, and the date on which denunciation takes effect;

(d) any notification or declaration received in pursuance of the provisions of paragraph 1 of this article.

In witness whereof, the undersigned, being duly authorised thereto, have signed this Convention.

Done at Paris, this 14th day of December 1972, in English and in French, both texts being equally authoritative, in a single copy which shall remain deposited in the archives of the Council of Europe. The Secretary General shall transmit certified copies to each of the signatory and acceding States.

EUROPEAN CONVENTION ON THE ADOPTION OF CHILDREN. The convention provides for the establishment of common principles and practices for the adoption of children in all contracting States. Those States agree to ensure that their laws are in accordance with the "Essential Provisions" set out in Part II and further agree to put into effect as soon as possible the "Supplementary Provisions" enumerated in Part III.

The convention was adopted at Strasbourg on 24 April 1967 by the COMMITTEE OF MINISTERS OF THE COUNCIL OF EUROPE and entered into force 26 April 1968. The text *(European Treaty Series* 58) is as follows:

Preamble

The member States of the Council of Europe, signatory hereto,

Considering that the aim of the Council of Europe is to achieve a greater unity between its Members for the purpose, among others, of facilitating their social progress;

Considering that, although the institution of the adoption of children exists in all member countries of the Council of Europe, there are in those countries differing views as to the principles which should govern adoption and differences in the procedure for effecting, and the legal consequences of, adoption; and

Considering that the acceptance of common principles and practices with respect to the adoption of children would help to reduce the difficulties caused by those differences and at the same time promote the welfare of children who are adopted,

Have agreed as follows:

Part I
Undertakings and Field of Application

Article 1. Each Contracting Party undertakes to ensure the conformity of its law with the provisions of Part II of this Convention and to notify the Secretary General of the Council of Europe of the measures taken for that purpose.

Article 2. Each Contracting Party undertakes to give consideration to the provisions set out in Part III of this Convention, and if it gives effect, or if, having given effect, it ceases to give effect to any of these provisions, it shall notify the Secretary General of the Council of Europe.

Article 3. This Convention applies only to legal adoption of a child who, at the time when the adopter applies to adopt him, has not attained the age of 18, is not and has not been married, and is not deemed in law to have come of age.

Part II
Essential Provisions

Article 4. An adoption shall be valid only if it is granted by a judicial or administrative authority (hereinafter referred to as "the competent authority").

Article 5. 1. Subject to paragraphs 2 to 4 of this article, an adoption shall not be granted unless at least the following consents to the adoption have been given and not withdrawn:

(a) the consent of the mother and, where the child is legitimate, the father; or if there is neither father nor mother to consent, the consent of any person or body who may be entitled in their place to exercise their parental rights in that respect;

(b) the consent of the spouse of the adopter.

2. The competent authority shall not:

(a) dispense with the consent of any person mentioned in paragraph 1 of this article, or

(b) overrule the refusal to consent of any person or body mentioned in the said paragraph 1,

save on exceptional grounds determined by law.

3. If the father or mother is deprived of his or her parental rights in respect of the child, or at least of the right to consent to an adoption, the law may provide that it shall not be necessary to obtain his or her consent.

4. A mother's consent to the adoption of her child shall not be accepted unless it is given at such time after the birth of the child, not being less than six weeks, as may be prescribed by law, or, if no such time has been prescribed, at such time as, in the opinion of the competent authority, will have enabled her to recover sufficiently from the effects of giving birth to the child.

5. For the purposes of this article "father" and "mother" mean the persons who are according to law the parents of the child.

Article 6. 1. The law shall not permit a child to be adopted by either two persons married to each other, whether they adopt simultaneously or successively, or by one person.

2. The law shall not permit a child to be again adopted save in one or more of the following circumstances:

(a) where the child is adopted by the spouse of the adopter;

(b) where the former adopter has died;

(c) where the former adoption has been annulled;

(d) where the former adoption has come to an end.

Article 7. 1. A child may be adopted only if the adopter has attained the minimum age prescribed for the purpose, this age being neither less than 21 nor more than 35 years.

2. The law may, however, permit the requirement as to the minimum age to be waived:

(a) when the adopter is the child's father or mother, or

(b) by reason of exceptional circumstances.

Article 8. 1. The competent authority shall not grant an adoption unless it is satisfied that the adoption will be in the interest of the child.

2. In each case the competent authority shall pay particular attention to the importance of the adoption providing the child with a stable and harmonious home.

3. As a general rule, the competent authority shall not be satisfied as aforesaid if the difference in age between the adopter and the child is less than the normal difference in age between parents and their children.

Article 9. 1. The competent authority shall not grant an adoption until appropriate enquiries have been made concerning the adopter, the child and his family.

2. The enquiries, to the extent appropriate in each case, shall concern, *inter alia,* the following matters:

(a) the personality, health and means of the adopter, particulars of his home and household and his ability to bring up the child;

(b) why the adopter wishes to adopt the child;

(c) where only one of two spouses of the same marriage applies to adopt a child, why the other spouse does not join in the application;

(d) the mutual suitability of the child and the adopter, and the length of time that the child has been in his care and possession;

(e) the personality and health of the child, and subject to any limitations imposed by law, his antecedents;

(f) the views of the child with respect to the proposed adoption;

(g) the religious persuasion, if any, of the adopter and of the child.

3. These enquiries shall be entrusted to a person or body recognised for that purpose by law or by a judicial or administrative body. They shall, as far as practicable, be made by social workers who are qualified in this field as a result of either their training or their experience.

4. The provisions of this article shall not affect the power or duty of the competent authority to obtain any information or evidence, whether or not within the scope of these enquiries, which it considers likely to be of assistance.

Article 10. 1. Adoption confers on the adopter in respect of the adopted person the rights and obligations of every kind that a father or mother has in respect of a child born in lawful wedlock.

Adoption confers on the adopted person in respect of the adopter the rights and obligations of every kind that a child born in lawful wedlock has in respect of his father or mother.

2. When the rights and obligations referred to in paragraph 1 of this article are created, any rights and obligations of the same kind existing between the adopted person and his father or mother or any other person or body shall cease to exist. Nevertheless, the law may provide that the spouse of the adopter retains his rights and obligations in respect of the adopted person if the latter is his legitimate, illegitimate or adopted child.

In addition the law may preserve the obligation of the parents to maintain (in the sense of *l'obligation d'entretenir* and *l'obligation alimentaire)* or set up in life or provide a dowry for the adopted person if the adopter does not discharge any such obligation.

3. As a general rule, means shall be provided to enable the adopted person to acquire the surname of the adopter either in substitution for, or in addition to, his own.

4. If the parent of a child born in lawful wedlock has a right to the enjoyment of that child's property, the adopter's right to the enjoyment of the adopted person's property may, notwithstanding paragraph 1 of this article, be restricted by law.

5. In matters of succession, in so far as the law of succession gives a child born in lawful wedlock a right to share in the estate of his father or mother, an adopted child shall, for the like purposes, be treated as if he were a child of the adopter born in lawful wedlock.

Article 11. 1. Where the adopted child does not have, in the case of an adoption by one person, the same nationality as the adopter, or in the case of an adoption by a married couple, their common nationality, the Contracting Party of which the adopter or adopters are nationals shall facilitate acquisition of its nationality by the child.

2. A loss of nationality which could result from an adoption shall be conditional upon possession or acquisition of another nationality.

Article 12. 1. The number of children who may be adopted by an adopter shall not be restricted by law.

2. A person who has, or is able to have, a child born in lawful wedlock, shall not on that account be prohibited by law from adopting a child.

3. If adoption improves the legal position of a child, a person shall not be prohibited by law from adopting his own child not born in lawful wedlock.

Article 13. 1. Before an adopted person comes of age the adoption may be revoked only by a decision of a judicial or administrative authority on serious grounds, and only if revocation on that ground is permitted by law.

2. The preceding paragraph shall not affect the case of:

(a) an adoption which is null and void;

(b) an adoption coming to an end where the adopted person becomes the legitimated child of the adopter.

Article 14. When the enquiries made pursuant to Articles 8 and 9 of this Convention relate to a person who lives or has lived in the territory of another Contracting Party, that Contracting Party shall, if a request for information is made, promptly endeavour to secure that the information requested is provided. The authorities may communicate directly with each other for this purpose.

Article 15. Provision shall be made to prohibit any improper financial advantage arising from a child being given up for adoption.

Article 16. Each Contracting Party shall retain the option of adopting provisions more favourable to the adopted child.

Part III
Supplementary Provisions

Article 17. An adoption shall not be granted until the child has been in the care of the adopters for a period long enough to enable a reasonable estimate to be made by the competent authority as to their future relations if the adoption were granted.

Article 18. The public authorities shall ensure the promotion and proper functioning of public or private agencies to which those who wish to adopt a child or to cause a child to be adopted may go for help and advice.

Article 19. The social and legal aspects of adoption shall be included in the curriculum for the training of social workers.

Article 20. 1. Provisions shall be made to enable an adoption to be completed without disclosing to the child's family the identity of the adopter.

2. Provision shall be made to require or permit adoption proceedings to take place *in camera.*

3. The adopter and the adopted person shall be able to obtain a document which contains extracts from the public records attesting the fact, date and place of birth of the adopted person, but not expressly revealing the fact of adoption or the identity of his former parents.

4. Public records shall be kept and, in any event, their contents reproduced in such a way as to prevent persons who do not have a legitimate interest from learning the fact that a person has been adopted if or, if that is disclosed, the identity of his former parents.

Part IV
Final Clauses

Article 21. 1. This Convention shall be open to signature by the member States of the Council of Europe. It shall be subject to ratification or acceptance. Instruments of ratification or acceptance shall be deposited with the Secretary General of the Council of Europe.

2. This Convention shall enter into force three months after the date of the deposit of the third instrument of ratification or acceptance.

3. In respect of a signatory State ratifying or accepting subsequently, the Convention shall come into force three months after the date of the deposit of its instrument of ratification or acceptance.

Article 22. 1. After the entry into force of this Convention, the Committee of Ministers of the Council of Europe may invite any non-member State to accede thereto.

2. Such accession shall be effected by depositing with the Secretary General of the Council of Europe an instrument of accession which shall take effect three months after the date of its deposit.

Article 23. 1. Any Contracting Party may, at the time of signature or when depositing its instrument of ratification, acceptance or accession, specify the territory or territories to which this Convention shall apply.

2. Any Contracting Party may, when depositing its instrument of ratification, acceptance or accession or at any later date, by declaration addressed to the Secretary General of the Council of Europe, extend this Convention to any other territory or territories specified in the declaration and for whose international relations it is responsible or on whose behalf it is authorised to give undertakings.

3. Any declaration made in pursuance of the preceding paragraph may, in respect of any territory mentioned in such declaration, be withdrawn according to the procedure laid down in Article 27 of this Convention.

Article 24. 1. Any Contracting Party whose law provides more than one form of adoption shall have the right to apply the provisions of Article 10, paragraphs 1, 2, 3 and 4, and Article 12, paragraphs 2 and 3, of this Convention to one only of such forms.

2. The Contracting Party exercising this right, shall, at the time of signature or when depositing its instrument of ratification, acceptance or accession, or when making a declaration in accordance with paragraph 2 of Article 23 of this Convention, notify the Secretary General of the Council of Europe thereof and indicate the way in which it has been exercised.

3. Such Contracting Party may terminate the exercise of this right and shall give notice thereof to the Secretary General of the Council of Europe.

Article 25. 1. Any Contracting Party may, at the time of signature or when depositing its instrument of ratification, acceptance or accession, or when making a declaration in accordance with paragraph 2 of Article 23 of this Convention, make not more than two reservations in respect of the provisions of Part II of the Convention.

Reservations of a general nature shall not be permitted; each reservation may not affect more than one provision.

A reservation shall be valid for five years from the entry into force of this Convention for the Contracting Party concerned. It may be renewed for successive periods of five years by means of a declaration addressed to the Secretary General of the Council of Europe before the expiration of each period.

2. Any Contracting Party may wholly or partly withdraw a reservation it has made in accordance with the foregoing paragraph by means of a declaration addressed to the Secretary General of the Council of Europe, which shall become effective as from the date of its receipt.

Article 26. Each Contracting Party shall notify the Secretary General of the Council of Europe of the names and addresses of the authorities to which requests under Article 14 may be addressed.

Article 27. 1. This Convention shall remain in force indefinitely.

2. Any Contracting Party may, in so far as it is concerned, denounce this Convention by means of a notification addressed to the Secretary General of the Council of Europe.

3. Such denunciation shall take effect six months after the date of receipt by the Secretary General of such notification.

Article 28. The Secretary General of the Council of Europe shall notify the member States of the Council and any state which has acceded to this Convention of:

(a) any signature;

(b) any deposit of an instrument of ratification, acceptance or accession;

(c) any date of entry into force of this Convention in accordance with Article 21 thereof;

(d) any notification received in pursuance of the provisions of Article 1;

(e) any notification received in pursuance of the provisions of Article 2;

(f) any declaration received in pursuance of the provisions of paragraphs 2 and 3 of Article 23;

(g) any information received in pursuance of the provisions of paragraphs 2 and 3 of Article 24;

(h) any reservation made in pursuance of the provisions of paragraph 1 of Article 25;

(i) the renewal of any reservation carried out in pursuance of the provisions of paragraph 1 of Article 25;

(j) the withdrawal of any reservation carried out in pursuance of the provisions of paragraph 2 of Article 25;

(k) any notification received in pursuance of the provisions of Article 26;

(l) any notification received in pursuance of the provisions of Article 27 and the date on which denunciation takes effect.

In witness whereof the undersigned, being duly authorised thereto, have signed this Convention.

Done at Strasbourg, this 24th day of April 1967, in English and in French, both texts being equally authoritative, in a single copy which shall remain deposited in the archives of the Council of Europe. The Secretary General of the Council of Europe shall transmit certified copies to each of the signatory and acceding States.

SEE ALSO *Declaration on Social and Legal Principles relating to the Protection and Welfare of Children, with Special Reference to Foster Placement Nationally and Internationally; Inter-American Convention on Conflicts of Laws concerning the Adoption of Minors.*

EUROPEAN CONVENTION ON THE LEGAL STATUS OF CHILDREN BORN OUT OF WEDLOCK (1975).

The convention aims at reducing the differences between the legal and social status of children born out of wedlock as compared to those of children born of married parents. It was concluded in Strasbourg on 15 October 1975 by the COMMITTEE OF MINISTERS OF THE COUNCIL OF EUROPE and entered into force on 11 August 1978. The text (*European Treaty Series* 85) is as follows:

The member States of the Council of Europe, signatory hereto,

Considering that the aim of the Council of Europe is to achieve a greater unity between its Members, in particular by the adoption of common rules in the field of law;

Noting that in a great number of member States efforts have been, or are being, made to improve the legal status of children born out of wedlock by reducing the differences between their legal status and that of children born in wedlock which are to the legal or social disadvantage of the former;

Recognising that wide disparities in the laws of member States in this field still exist;

Believing that the situation of children born out of wedlock should be improved and that the formulation of certain common rules concerning their legal status would assist this objective and at the same time would contribute to a harmonisation of the laws of the member States in this field;

Considering however that is necessary to allow progressive stages for those States which consider themselves unable to adopt immediately certain rules of this Convention,

Have agreed as follows:

Article 1. Each Contracting Party undertakes to ensure the conformity of its law with the provisions of this Convention and to notify the Secretary General of the Council of Europe of the measures taken for that purpose.

Article 2. Maternal affiliation of every child born out of wedlock shall be based solely on the fact of the birth of the child.

Article 3. Paternal affiliation of every child born out of wedlock may be evidenced or established by voluntary recognition or by judicial decision.

Article 4. The voluntary recognition of paternity may not be opposed or contested insofar as the internal law provides for these procedures unless the person seeking to recognise or having recognised the child is not the biological father.

Article 5. In actions relating to paternal affiliation scientific evidence which may help to establish or disprove paternity shall be admissible.

Article 6. 1. The father and mother of a child born out of wedlock shall have the same obligation to maintain the child as if it were born in wedlock.

2. Where a legal obligation to maintain a child born in wedlock falls on certain members of the family of the father or mother, this obligation shall also apply for the benefit of a child born out of wedlock.

Article 7. 1. Where the affiliation of a child born out of wedlock has been established as regards both parents, parental authority may not be attributed automatically to the father alone.

2. There shall be power to transfer parental authority; cases of transfer shall be governed by the internal law.

Article 8. Where the father or mother of a child born out of wedlock does not have parental authority over or the custody of the child, that parent may obtain a right of access to the child in appropriate cases.

Article 9. A child born out of wedlock shall have the same right of succession in the estate of its father and its mother and of a member of its father's or mother's family, as if it had been born in wedlock.

Article 10. The marriage between the father and mother of a child born out of wedlock shall confer on the child the legal status of a child born in wedlock.

Article 11. 1. This Convention shall be open to signature by the member States of the Council of Europe. It shall be subject to ratification, acceptance or approval. Instruments of ratification, acceptance or approval shall be deposited with the Secretary General of the Council of Europe.

2. This Convention shall enter into force three months after the date of the deposit of the third instrument of ratification, acceptance or approval.

3. In respect of a signatory State ratifying, accepting or approving subsequently, the Convention shall come into force three months after the date of the deposit of its instrument of ratification, acceptance or approval.

Article 12. 1. After the entry into force of this Convention, the Committee of Ministers of the Council of Europe may invite any non-member State to accede to this Convention.

2. Such accession shall be effected by depositing with the Secretary General of the Council of Europe an instrument of accession which shall take effect three months after the date of its deposit.

Article 13. 1. Any State may, at the time of signature, or when depositing its instrument of ratification, acceptance, approval or accession, specify the territory or territories to which this Convention shall apply.

2. Any State may, when depositing its instrument of ratification, acceptance, approval or accession or at any later date, by declaration addressed to the Secretary General of the Council of Europe, extend this Convention to any other territory or territories specified in the declaration and for whose international relations it is responsible or on whose behalf it is authorised to give undertakings.

3. Any declaration made in pursuance of the preceding paragraph may, in respect of any territory mentioned in such declaration, be withdrawn according to the procedure laid down in Article 15 of this Convention.

Article 14. 1. Any State may, at the time of signature, or when depositing its instrument of ratification, acceptance, approval or accession or when making a declaration in accordance with paragraph 2 of Article 13 of this Convention, make not more than three reservations in respect of the provisions of Articles 2 and 10 of the Convention.

Reservations of a general nature shall not be permitted; each reservation may not affect than one provision.

2. A reservation shall be valid for five years from the entry into force of this Convention for the Contracting Party concerned. It may be renewed for successive periods of five years by means of a declaration addressed to the Secretary General of the Council of Europe before the expiration of each period.

3. Any Contracting Party may wholly or partly withdraw a reservation it has made in accordance with the foregoing paragraphs by means of a declaration addressed to the Secretary General of the Council of Europe, which shall become effective as from the date of its receipt.

Article 15. 1. Any Contracting Party may, insofar as it is concerned, denounce this Convention by means of a notification addressed to the Secretary General of the Council of Europe.

2. Such denunciation shall take effect six months after the date of receipt by the Secretary General of such notification.

Article 16. The Secretary General of the Council of Europe shall notify the member States of the Council and any State which has acceded to this Convention of:

(a) any signature;

(b) any deposit of an instrument of ratification, acceptance, approval or accession;

(c) any date of entry into force of this Convention in accordance with Article 11 thereof;

(d) any notification received in pursuance of the provisions of Article 1;

(e) any declaration received in pursuance of the provisions of paragraphs 2 and 3 of Article 13;

(f) any reservation made in pursuance of the provisions of paragraph 1 of Article 14;

(g) the renewal of any reservation carried out in pursuance of the provisions of paragraph 2 of Article 14;

(h) the withdrawal of any reservation carried out in pursuance of the provisions of paragraph 3 of Article 14;

(i) any notification received in pursuance of the provisions of Article 15 and the date on which denunciation takes effect.

In witness whereof, the undersigned, being duly authorised thereto, have signed this Convention.

Done at Strasbourg, this 15th day of October 1975, in English and in French, both texts being equally authoritative, in a single copy, which shall remain deposited in the archives of the Council of Europe. The Secretary General of the Council of Europe shall transmit certified copies to each of the signatory and acceding States.

SEE ALSO Persons Born Out of Wedlock.

EUROPEAN CONVENTION ON THE LEGAL STATUS OF MIGRANT WORKERS (1977).

Concluded by the COMMITTEE OF MINISTERS OF THE COUNCIL OF EUROPE, meeting in Strasbourg, on 24 November 1977, the convention entered into force on 1 May 1983. Its primary purpose is to regulate the legal status of migrant workers in such a way as to ensure that they are treated no less favorably than workers who are nationals of the receiving State in all aspects of living and working conditions. The text of the convention *(European Treaty Series* 93) is as follows:

The member States of the Council of Europe, signatory hereto,

Considering that the aim of the Council of Europe is to achieve a greater unity between its Members for the purpose of safeguarding and realising the ideals and principles which are their common heritage and facilitating their economic and social progress while respecting human rights and fundamental freedoms;

Considering that the legal status of migrant workers who are nationals of Council of Europe member States should be regulated so as to ensure that as far as possible they are treated no less favourably than workers who are nationals of the receiving State in all aspects of living and working conditions;

Being resolved to facilitate the social advancement of migrant workers and members of their families;

Affirming that the rights and privileges which they grant to each other's nationals are conceded by virtue of the close association uniting the member States of the Council of Europe by means of its Statute,

Have agreed as follows:

Chapter 1

Article 1. Definition. 1. For the purpose of this Convention, the term "migrant worker" shall mean a national of a Contracting Party who has been authorised by another Contracting Party to reside in its territory in order to take up paid employment.

2. This Convention shall not apply to:

(a) frontier workers;

(b) artists, other entertainers and sportsmen engaged for a short period and members of a liberal profession;

(c) seamen;

(d) persons undergoing training;

(e) seasonal workers; seasonal migrant workers are those who, being nationals of a Contracting Party, are employed on the territory of another Contracting Party in an activity dependent on the rhythm of the seasons, on the basis of a contract for a specified period or for specified employment;

(f) workers, who are nationals of a Contracting Party, carrying out specific work in the territory of another Contracting Party on behalf of an undertaking having its registered office outside the territory of that Contracting Party.

Chapter II

Article 2. Forms of Recruitment. 1. The recruitment of prospective migrant workers may be carried out either by named or by unnamed request and in the latter case shall be effected through the intermediary of the official authority in the State of origin if such an authority exists and, where appropriate, through the intermediary of the official authority of the receiving State.

2. The administrative costs of recruitment, introduction and placing, when these operations are carried out by an official authority, shall not be borne by the prospective migrant worker.

Article 3. Medical Examination and Vocational Test. 1. Recruitment of prospective migrant workers may be preceded by a medical examination and a vocational test.

2. The medical examination and the vocational test are intended to establish whether the prospective migrant worker is physically and mentally fit and technically qualified for the job offered to him and to make certain that his state of health does not endanger public health.

3. Arrangements for the reimbursement of expenses connected with medical examination and vocational test shall be laid down when appropriate by bilateral agreements, so as to ensure that such expenses do not fall upon the prospective migrant worker.

4. A migrant worker to whom an individual offer of employment is made shall not be required, otherwise than on grounds of fraud, to undergo a vocational test except at the employer's request.

Article 4. Right of Exit—Right to Admission—Administrative Formalities. 1. Each Contracting Party shall guarantee the following rights to migrant workers:

—the right to leave the territory of the Contracting Party of which they are nationals;

—the right to admission to the territory of a Contracting Party in order to take up paid employment after being authorised to do so and obtaining the necessary papers.

2. These rights shall be subject to such limitations as are prescribed by legislation and are necessary for the protection of national security, public order, public health or morals.

3. The papers required of the migrant worker for emigra-

tion and immigration shall be issued as expeditiously as possible free of charge or on payment of an amount not exceeding their administrative cost.

Article 5. Formalities and Procedure relating to the Work Contract. Every migrant worker accepted for employment shall be provided prior to departure for the receiving State with a contract of employment or a definite offer of employment, either of which may be drawn up in one or more of the languages in use in the State of origin and in one or more of the languages in use in the receiving State. The use of at least one language of the State of origin and one language of the receiving State shall be compulsory in the case of recruitment by an official authority or an officially recognised employment bureau.

Article 6. Information. 1. The Contracting Parties shall exchange and provide for prospective migrants appropriate information on their residence, conditions of and opportunities for family reunion, the nature of the job, the possibility of a new work contract being concluded after the first has lapsed, the qualifications required, working and living conditions (including the cost of living), remuneration, social security, housing, food, the transfer of savings, travel, and on deductions made from wages in respect of contributions for social protection and social security, taxes and other charges. Information may also be provided on the cultural and religious conditions in the receiving State.

2. In the case of recruitment through an official authority of the receiving State, such information shall be provided, before his departure, in a language which the prospective migrant worker can understand, to enable him to take a decision in full knowledge of the facts. The translation, where necessary, of such information into a language that the prospective migrant worker can understand shall be provided as a general rule by the State of origin.

3. Each Contracting Party undertakes to adopt the appropriate steps to prevent misleading propaganda relating to emigration and immigration.

Article 7. Travel. 1. Each Contracting Party undertakes to ensure, in the case of official collective recruitment, that the cost of travel to the receiving State shall never be borne by the migrant worker. The arrangements for payment shall be determined under bilateral agreements, which may also extend these measures to families and to workers recruited individually.

2. In the case of migrant workers and their families in transit through the territory of one Contracting Party en route to the receiving State, or on their return journey to the State of origin, all steps shall be taken by the competent authorities of the transit State to expedite their journey and prevent administrative delays and difficulties.

3. Each Contracting Party shall exempt from import duties and taxes at the time of entry into the receiving State and of the final return of the State of origin and in transit:

(a) the personal effects and movable property of migrant workers and members of their family belonging to their household;

(b) a reasonable quantity of hand-tools and portable equipment necessary for the occupation to be engaged in.

The exemptions referred to above shall be granted in accordance with the laws or regulations in force in the States concerned.

Chapter III

Article 8. Work Permit. 1. Each Contracting Party which allows a migrant worker to enter its territory to take up paid employment shall issue or renew a work permit for him (unless he is exempt from this requirement), subject to the conditions laid down in its legislation.

2. However, a work permit issued for the first time may not as a rule bind the worker to the same employer or the same locality for a period longer than one year.

3. In case of renewal of the migrant worker's work permit, this should as a general rule be for a period of at least one year, insofar as the current state and development of the employment situation permits.

Article 9. Residence Permit. 1. Where required by national legislation, each Contracting Party shall issue residence permits to migrant workers who have been authorised to take up paid employment on their territory under conditions laid down in this Convention.

2. The residence permit shall in accordance with the provisions of national legislation be issued and, if necessary, renewed for a period as a general rule at least as long as that of the work permit. When the work permit is valid indefinitely, the residence permit shall as a general rule be issued and, if necessary, renewed for a period of at least one year. It shall be issued and renewed free of charge or for a sum covering administrative costs only.

3. The provisions of this Article shall also apply to members of the migrant worker's family who are authorised to join him in accordance with Article 12 of this Convention.

4. If a migrant worker is no longer in employment, either because he is temporarily incapable of work as a result of illness or accident or because he is involuntarily unemployed, this being duly confirmed by the competent authorities, he shall be allowed for the purpose of the application of Article 25 of this Convention to remain on the territory of the receiving State for a period which should not be less than five months.

Nevertheless, no Contracting Party shall be bound, in the case provided for in the above sub-paragraph, to allow a migrant worker to remain for a period exceeding the period of payment of the unemployment allowance.

5. The residence permit, issued in accordance with the provisions of paragraphs 1 to 3 of this Article, may be withdrawn:

(a) for reasons of national security, public policy or morals;

(b) if the holder refuses, after having been duly informed of the consequences of such refusal, to comply with the measures prescribed for him by an official medical authority with a view to the protection of public health;

(c) if a condition essential to its issue or validity is not fulfilled.

Each Contracting Party nevertheless undertakes to grant to migrant workers whose residence permits have been withdrawn, an effective right to appeal, in accordance with the procedure for which provision is made in its legislation, to a judicial or administrative authority.

Article 10. Reception. 1. After arrival in the receiving State, migrant workers and members of their families shall be given all appropriate information and advice as well as all necessary assistance for their settlement and adaptation.

2. For this purpose, migrant workers and members of their families shall be entitled to help and assistance from the social services of the receiving State or from bodies working in the public interest in the receiving State and to help from the consular authorities of their State of origin. Moreover, migrant workers shall be entitled, on the same basis as national workers, to help and assistance from the employment services. However, each Contracting Party

shall endeavour to ensure that special social services are available, whenever the situation so demands, to facilitate or co-ordinate the reception of migrant workers and their families.

3. Each Contracting Party undertakes to ensure that migrant workers and members of their families can worship freely, in accordance with their faith; each Contracting Party shall facilitate such worship, within the limit of available means.

Article 11. Recovery of Sums due in respect of Maintenance. 1. The status of migrant workers must not interfere with the recovery of sums due in respect of maintenance to persons in the State of origin to whom they have maintenance obligations arising from a family relationship, parentage, marriage or affinity, including a maintenance obligation in respect of a child who is not legitimate.

2. Each Contracting Party shall take the steps necessary to ensure the recovery of sums due in respect of such maintenance, making use as far as possible of the form adopted by the Committee of Ministers of the Council of Europe.

3. As far as possible, each Contracting Party shall take steps to appoint a single national or regional authority to receive and despatch applications for sums due in respect of maintenance provided for in paragraph 1 above.

4. This Article shall not affect existing or future bilateral or multilateral agreements.

Article 12. Family Reunion. 1. The spouse of a migrant worker who is lawfully employed in the territory of a Contracting Party and the unmarried children thereof, as long as they are considered to be minors by the relevant law of the receiving State, who are dependent on the migrant worker, are authorised on conditions analogous to those which this Convention applies to the admission of migrant workers and according to the admission procedure prescribed by such law or by international agreements to join the migrant worker in the territory of a Contracting Party, provided that the latter has available for the family housing considered as normal for national workers in the region where the migrant worker is employed. Each Contracting Party may make the giving of authorisation conditional upon a waiting period which shall not exceed twelve months.

2. Any State may, at any time, by declaration addressed to the Secretary General of the Council of Europe, which shall take effect one month after the date of its receipt, make the family reunion referred to in paragraph 1 above further conditional upon the migrant worker having steady resources sufficient to meet the needs of his family.

3. Any State may, at any time, by declaration addressed to the Secretary General of the Council of Europe, which shall take effect one month after the date of its receipt, derogate temporarily from the obligation to give the authorisation provided for in paragraph 1 above, for one or more parts of its territory which it shall designate in its declaration, on the condition that these measures do not conflict with obligations under other international instruments. The declaration shall state the special reasons justifying the derogation with regard to receiving capacity.

Any State availing itself of this possibility of derogation shall keep the Secretary General of the Council of Europe fully informed of the measures which it has taken and shall ensure that these measures are published as soon as possible. It shall also inform the Secretary General of the Council of Europe when such measures cease to operate and the provisions of the Convention are again being fully executed.

The derogation shall not, as a general rule, affect requests for family reunion submitted to the competent authorities, before the declaration is addressed to the Secretary General, by migrant workers already established in the part of the territory concerned.

Article 13. Housing. 1. Each Contracting Party shall accord to migrant workers, with regard to access to housing and rents, treatment not less favourable than that accorded to its own nationals, insofar as this matter is covered by domestic laws and regulations.

2. Each Contracting Party shall ensure that the competent national authorities carry out inspections in appropriate cases in collaboration with the respective consular authorities, acting within their competence, to ensure that standards of fitness of accommodations are kept up for migrant workers as for its own nationals.

3. Each Contracting Party undertakes to protect migrant workers against exploitation in respect of rents, in accordance with its laws and regulations on the matter.

4. Each Contracting Party shall ensure, by the means available to the competent national authorities, that the housing of the migrant worker shall be suitable.

Article 14. Pretraining—Schooling—Linguistic Training—Vocational Training and Retraining. 1. Migrant workers and members of their families officially admitted to the territory of a Contracting Party shall be entitled, on the same basis and under the same conditions as national workers, to general education and vocational training and retraining and shall be granted access to higher education according to the general regulations governing admission to respective institutions in the receiving State.

2. To promote access to general and vocational schools and to vocational training centres, the receiving State shall facilitate the teaching of its language or, if there are several, one of its languages to migrant workers and members of their families.

3. For the purpose of the application of paragraphs 1 and 2 above, the granting of scholarships shall be left to the discretion of each Contracting Party which shall make efforts to grant the children of migrant workers living with their families in the receiving State—in accordance with the provisions of Article 12 of this Convention—the same facilities in this respect as the receiving State's nationals.

4. The workers' previous attainments, as well as diplomas and vocational qualifications acquired in the State of origin, shall be recognised by each Contracting Party in accordance with arrangements laid down in bilateral and multilateral agreements.

5. The Contracting Parties concerned, acting in close co-operation, shall endeavour to ensure that the vocational training and retraining schemes, within the meaning of this Article, cater as far as possible for the needs of migrant workers with a view to their return to their State of origin.

Article 15. Teaching of the Migrant Worker's Mother Tongue. The Contracting Parties concerned shall take action by common accord to arrange, so far as practicable, for the migrant worker's children, special courses for the teaching of the migrant worker's mother tongue, to facilitate, inter alia, their return to their State of origin.

Article 16. Conditions of Work. 1. In the matter of conditions of work, migrant workers authorised to take up employment shall enjoy treatment not less favourable than that which applies to national workers by virtue of legislative or administrative provisions, collective labour agreements or custom.

2. It shall not be possible to derogate by individual con-

tract from the principle of equal treatment referred to in the foregoing paragraph.

Article 17. Transfer of Savings. 1. Each Contracting Party shall permit, according to the arrangements laid down by its legislation, the transfer of all or such parts of the earnings and savings of migrant workers as the latter may wish to transfer.

This provision shall apply also to the transfer of sums due by migrant workers in respect of maintenance. The transfer of sums due by migrant workers in respect of maintenance shall on no account be hindered or prevented.

2. Each Contracting Party shall permit, under bilateral agreements or by any other means, the transfer of such sums as remain due to migrant workers when they leave the territory of the receiving State.

Article 18. Social Security. 1. Each Contracting Party undertakes to grant within its territory, to migrant workers and members of their families, equality of treatment with its own nationals, in the matter of social security, subject to conditions required by national legislation and by bilateral and multilateral agreements already concluded or to be concluded between the Contracting Parties concerned.

2. The Contracting Parties shall moreover endeavour to secure to migrant workers and members of their families the conservation of rights in course of acquisition and acquired rights, as well as provision of benefits abroad, through bilateral and multilateral agreements.

Article 19. Social and Medical Assistance. Each Contracting Party undertakes to grant within its territory, to migrant workers and members of their families who are lawfully present in its territory, social and medical assistance on the same basis as nationals in accordance with the obligations it has assumed by virtue of other international agreements and in particular of the European Convention on Social and Medical Assistance of 1953.

Article 20. Industrial Accidents and Occupational Diseases— Industrial Hygiene. 1. With regard to the prevention of industrial accidents and occupational diseases and to industrial hygiene, migrant workers shall enjoy the same rights and protection as national workers, in application of the laws of a Contracting Party and collective agreements and having regard to their particular situation.

2. A migrant worker who is victim of an industrial accident or who has contracted an occupational disease in the territory of the receiving State shall benefit from occupational rehabilitation on the same basis as national workers.

Article 21. Inspection of Working Conditions. Each Contracting Party shall inspect or provide for inspection of the conditions of work of migrant workers in the same manner as for national workers. Such inspection shall be carried out by the competent bodies or institutions of the receiving State and by any other authority authorised by the receiving State.

Article 22. Death. Each Contracting Party shall take care, within the framework of its laws and, if need be, within the framework of bilateral agreements, that steps are taken to provide all help and assistance necessary for the transport to the State of origin of the bodies of migrant workers deceased as the result of an industrial accident.

Article 23. Taxation on Earnings. 1. In the matter of earnings and without prejudice to the provisions on double taxation contained in agreements already concluded or which may in future be concluded between Contracting Parties, migrant workers shall not be liable, in the territory of a Contracting Party, to duties, charges, taxes or contributions of any description whatsoever either higher or more burdensome

than those imposed on nationals in similar circumstances. In particular, they shall be entitled to deductions or exemptions from taxes or charges and to all allowances, including allowances for dependants.

2. The Contracting Parties shall decide between themselves, by bilateral or multilateral agreements on double taxation, what measures might be taken to avoid double taxation on the earnings of migrant workers.

Article 24. Expiry of Contract and Discharge. 1. On the expiry of a work contract concluded for a specified period at the end of the period agreed on and in the case of anticipated cancellation of such a contract or cancellation of a work contract for an unspecified period, migrant workers shall be accorded treatment not less favourable than that accorded to national workers under the provisions of national legislation or collective labour agreements.

2. In the event of individual or collective dismissal, migrant workers shall receive the treatment applicable to national workers under national legislation or collective labour agreements, particularly as regards the form and period of notice, the compensation provided for in legislation or agreements or such as may be due in cases of unwarranted cancellation of their work contracts.

Article 25. Re-employment. 1. If a migrant worker loses his job for reasons beyond his control, such as redundancy or prolonged illness, the competent authority of the receiving State shall facilitate his re-employment in accordance with the laws and regulations of that State.

2. To this end the receiving State shall promote the measures necessary to ensure, as far as possible, the vocational retraining and occupational rehabilitation of the migrant worker in question, provided that he intends to continue in employment in the State concerned afterwards.

Article 26. Right of Access to the Courts and Administrative Authorities in the Receiving State. 1. Each Contracting Party shall secure to migrant workers treatment not less favourable than that of its own nationals in respect of legal proceedings. Migrant workers shall be entitled, under the same conditions as nationals, to full legal and judicial protection of their persons and property and of their rights and interests; in particular, they shall have, in the same manner as nationals, the right of access to the competent courts and administrative authorities, in accordance with the law of the receiving State, and the right to obtain the assistance of any person of their choice who is qualified by the law of that State, for instance in disputes with employers, members of their families or third parties. The rules of private international law of the receiving State shall not be affected by this Article.

2. Each Contracting Party shall provide migrant workers with legal assistance on the same conditions as for their own nationals and, in the case of civil or criminal proceedings, the possibility of obtaining the assistance of an interpreter where they cannot understand or speak the language used in court.

Article 27. Use of Employment Services. Each Contracting Party recognises the right of migrant workers and of the members of their families officially admitted to its territory to make use of employment services under the same conditions as national workers subject to the legal provisions and regulations and administrative practice, including conditions of access, in force in that State.

Article 28. Exercise of the Right to Organise. Each Contracting Party shall allow to migrant workers the right to organise for the protection of their economic and social interests on the conditions provided for by national legislation for its own nationals.

Article 29. Participation in the Affairs of the Undertaking. Each Contracting Party shall facilitate as far as possible the participation of migrant workers in the affairs of the undertaking on the same conditions as national workers.

Chapter IV

Article 30. Return Home. 1. Each Contracting Party shall, as far as possible, take appropriate measures to assist migrant workers and their families on the occasion of their final return to their State of origin, and in particular the steps referred to in paragraphs 2 and 3 of Article 7 of this Convention. The provision of financial assistance shall be left to the discretion of each Contracting Party.

2. To enable migrant workers to know, before they set out on their return journey, the conditions on which they will be able to resettle in their State of origin, this State shall communicate to the receiving State, which shall keep available for those who request it, information regarding in particular:

—possibilities and conditions of employment in the State of origin;

—financial aid granted for economic reintegration;

—the maintenance of social security rights acquired abroad;

—steps to be taken to facilitate the finding of accommodation;

—equivalence accorded to occupational qualifications obtained abroad and any tests to be passed to secure their official recognition;

—equivalence accorded to educational qualifications, so that migrant workers' children can be admitted to schools without down-grading.

Chapter V

Article 31. Conservation of Acquired Rights. No provision of this Convention may be interpreted as justifying less favourable treatment than that enjoyed by migrant workers under the national legislation of the receiving State or under bilateral and multilateral agreements to which that State is a Contracting Party.

Article 32. Relations between this Convention and the Laws of the Contracting Parties or International Agreements. The provisions of this Convention shall not prejudice the provisions of the laws of the Contracting Parties or of any bilateral or multilateral treaties, conventions, agreements or arrangements, as well as the steps taken to implement them, which are already in force, or may come into force, and under which more favourable treatment has been, or would be, accorded to the persons protected by the Convention.

Article 33. Application of the Convention. 1. A Consultative Committee shall be set up within a year of the entry into force of this Convention.

2. Each Contracting Party shall appoint a representative to the Consultative Committee. Any other member State of the Council of Europe may be represented by an observer with the right to speak.

3. The Consultative Committee shall examine any proposals submitted to it by one of the Contracting Parties with a view to facilitating or improving the application of the Convention, as well as any proposal to amend it.

4. The opinions and recommendations of the Consultative Committee shall be adopted by a majority of the members of the Committee; however, proposals to amend the Convention shall be adopted unanimously by the members of the Committee.

5. The opinions, recommendations and proposals of the Consultative Committee referred to above shall be addressed to the Committee of Ministers of the Council of Europe, which shall decide on the action to be taken.

6. The Consultative Committee shall be convened by the Secretary General of the Council of Europe and shall meet, as a general rule, at least once every two years and, in addition, whenever at least two Contracting Parties or the Committee of Ministers so requests. The committee shall also meet at the request of one Contracting Party whenever the provisions of paragraph 3 of Article 12 are applied.

7. The Consultative Committee shall draw up periodically, for the attention of the Committee of Ministers, a report containing information regarding the laws and regulations in force in the territory of the Contracting Parties in respect of matters provided for in this Convention.

Chapter VI

Article 34. Signature, Ratification and Entry into Force. 1. This Convention shall be open to signature by the member States of the Council of Europe. It shall be subject to ratification, acceptance or approval. Instruments of ratification, acceptance or approval shall be deposited with the Secretary General of the Council of Europe.

2. This Convention shall enter into force on the first day of the third month following the date of the deposit of the fifth instrument of ratification, acceptance or approval.

3. In respect of a signatory State ratifying, approving or accepting subsequently, the Convention shall enter into force on the first day of the third month following the date of the deposit of its instrument of ratification, acceptance or approval.

Article 35. Territorial Scope. 1. Any State may, at the time of signature or when depositing its instrument of ratification, acceptance or approval or at any later date, by declaration addressed to the Secretary General of the Council of Europe, extend the application of this Convention to all or any of the territories for whose international relations it is responsible or on whose behalf it is authorised to give undertakings.

2. Any declaration made in pursuance of the preceding paragraph may, in respect of any territory mentioned in such declaration, be withdrawn. Such withdrawal shall take effect six months after receipt by the Secretary General of the Council of Europe of the declaration of withdrawal.

Article 36. Reservations. 1. Any State may, at the time of signature or when depositing its instrument of ratification, acceptance or approval, make one or more reservations which may relate to no more than nine articles of Chapters II to IV inclusive, other than Articles 4, 8, 9, 12, 16, 17, 20, 25, 26.

2. Any State may, at any time, wholly or partly withdraw a reservation it has made in accordance with the foregoing paragraph by means of a declaration addressed to the Secretary General of the Council of Europe, which shall become effective as from the date of its receipt.

Article 37. Denunciation of the Convention. 1. Each Contracting Party may denounce this Convention by notification addressed to the Secretary General of the Council of Europe, which shall take effect six months after the date of its receipt.

2. No denunciation may be made within five years of the

date of the entry into force of the Convention in respect of the Contracting Party concerned.

3. Each Contracting Party which ceases to be a Member of the Council of Europe shall cease to be a Party to this Convention six months after the date on which it loses its quality as a Member of the Council of Europe.

Article 38. Notifications. The Secretary General of the Council of Europe shall notify the member States of the Council of:

(a) any signature;

(b) the deposit of any instrument of ratification, acceptance or approval;

(c) any notification received in respect of paragraphs 2 and 3 of Article 12;

(d) any date of entry into force of this Convention in accordance with Article 34 thereof;

(e) any declaration received in pursuance of the provisions of Article 35;

(f) any reservation made in pursuance of the provisions of paragraph 1 of Article 36;

(g) withdrawal of any reservation carried out in pursuance of the provisions of paragraph 2 of Article 36;

(h) any notification received in pursuance of the provisions of Article 37 and the date on which denunciation takes place.

In witness whereof, the undersigned, being duly authorised thereto, have signed this Convention.

Done at Strasbourg, this 24th day of November 1977, in English and in French, both texts being equally authoritative, in a single copy which shall remain deposited in the archives of the Council of Europe. The Secretary General of the Council of Europe shall transmit certified copies to each of the signatory States.

SEE ALSO *Charter of Rights for Migrant Workers in Southern Africa; ILO Equality of Treatment (Social Security) Convention; ILO Migrant Workers (Supplementary Provisions) Convention; Migrant Workers.*

EUROPEAN CONVENTION ON THE NON-APPLICABILITY OF STATUTORY LIMITATIONS TO CRIMES AGAINST HUMANITY AND WAR CRIMES (1974).

The convention follows the general lines of the CONVENTION ON THE NON-APPLICABILITY OF STATUTORY LIMITATIONS TO WAR CRIMES AND CRIMES AGAINST HUMANITY adopted by the UN General Assembly on 26 November 1968. Under the European convention, member States of the COUNCIL OF EUROPE undertake to adopt any measures necessary to ensure that no statutory limitation shall apply to crimes against humanity or war crimes or to the enforcement of sentences imposed for such offenses insofar as they are punishable under its domestic law.

The convention was concluded by the COMMITTEE OF MINISTERS OF THE COUNCIL OF EUROPE, convened in Strasbourg, on 25 January 1974. The text of the convention *(European Treaty Series,* 82) is as follows:

The member States of the Council of Europe, signatory hereto,

Considering the necessity to safeguard human dignity in time of war and in time of peace;

Considering that crimes against humanity and the most serious violations of the laws and customs of war constitute a serious infraction of human dignity;

Concerned in consequence to ensure that the punishment of those crimes is not prevented by statutory limitations whether in relation to prosecution or to the enforcement of the punishment;

Considering the essential interest in promoting a common criminal policy in this field, the aim of the Council of Europe being to achieve a greater unity between its Members,

Have agreed as follows:

Article 1. Each Contracting State undertakes to adopt any necessary measures to secure that statutory limitations shall not apply to the prosecution of the following offences, or to the enforcement of the sentences imposed for such offences, in so far as they are punishable under its domestic law:

1. the crimes against humanity specified in the Convention on the Prevention and Punishment of the Crime of Genocide adopted on 9 December 1948 by the General Assembly of the United Nations;

2. (a) the violations specified in Article 50 of the 1949 Geneva Convention for the Amelioration of the Condition of the Wounded and Sick in Armed Forces in the Field, Article 51 of the 1949 Geneva Convention for the Amelioration of the Condition of Wounded, Sick and Shipwrecked Members of Armed Forces at Sea, Article 130 of the 1949 Geneva Convention relative to the Treatment of Prisoners of War and Article 147 of the 1949 Geneva Convention relative to the Protection of Civilian Persons in Time of War,

(b) any comparable violations of the laws of war having effect at the time when this Convention enters into force and of customs of war existing at that time, which are not already provided for in the above-mentioned provisions of the Geneva Conventions,

when the specific violation under consideration is of a particularly grave character by reason either of its factual and intentional elements or of the extent of its foreseeable consequences;

3. any other violation of a rule or custom of international law which may hereafter be established and which the Contracting State concerned considers according to a declaration under Article 6 as being of a comparable nature to those referred to in paragraph 1 or 2 of this article.

Article 2. 1. The present Convention applies to offences committed after its entry into force in respect of the Contracting State concerned.

2. It applies also to offences committed before such entry into force in those cases where the statutory limitation period had not expired at that time.

Article 3. 1. This Convention shall be open to signature by the member States of the Council of Europe. It shall be subject to ratification or acceptance. Instruments of ratification or acceptance shall be deposited with the Secretary General of the Council of Europe.

2. The Convention shall enter into force three months after the date of deposit of the third instrument of ratification or acceptance.

3. In respect of a signatory State ratifying or accepting subsequently, the Convention shall come into force three

months after the date of the deposit of its instrument of ratification or acceptance.

Article 4. 1. After the entry into force of this Convention, the Committee of Ministers of the Council of Europe may invite any non-member State to accede thereto, provided that the resolution containing such invitation receives the unanimous agreement of the Members of the Council who have ratified the Convention.

2. Such accession shall be effected by depositing with the Secretary General of the Council of Europe an instrument of accession which shall take effect three months after the date of its deposit.

Article 5. 1. Any State may, at the time of signature or when depositing its instrument of ratification, acceptance or accession, specify the territory or territories to which this Convention shall apply.

2. Any State may, when depositing its instrument of ratification, acceptance or accession or at any later date, be declaration addressed to the Secretary General of the Council of Europe, extend this Convention to any other territory or territories specified in the declaration and for whose international relations it is responsible or on whose behalf it is authorised to give undertakings.

3. Any declaration made in pursuance of the preceding paragraph may, in respect of any territory mentioned in such declaration, be withdrawn according to the procedure laid down in Article 7 of this Convention.

Article 6. 1. Any Contracting State may, at any time, by declaration addressed to the Secretary General of the Council of Europe, extend this Convention to any violations provided for in Article 1, paragraph 3, of this Convention.

2. Any declaration made in pursuance of the preceding paragraph may be withdrawn according to the procedure laid down in Article 7 of this Convention.

Article 7. 1. This Convention shall remain in force indefinitely.

2. Any Contracting State may, in so far as it is concerned, denounce this Convention by means of a notification addressed to the Secretary General of the Council of Europe.

3. Such denunciation shall take effect six months after the date of receipt by the Secretary General of such notification.

Article 8. The Secretary General of the Council of Europe shall notify the member States of the Council and any State which has acceded to this Convention of:

(a) any signature;

(b) any deposit of an instrument of ratification, acceptance or accession;

(c) any date of entry into force of this Convention in accordance with Article 3 thereof;

(d) any declaration received in pursuance of the provisions of Article 5 or Article 6;

(e) any notification received in pursuance of the provisions of Article 7 and the date on which the denunciation takes effect.

In witness whereof the undersigned, being duly authorised thereto, have signed this Convention.

Done at Strasbourg, this 25th day of January 1974, in the English and French languages, both texts being equally authoritative, in a single copy which shall remain deposited in the archives of the Council of Europe. The Secretary General of the Council of Europe shall transmit certified copies to each of the signatory and acceding States.

EUROPEAN CONVENTION ON THE REPATRIATION OF MINORS (1970). Under this convention, contracting states undertake to cooperate in the repatriation of minors who have been taken abroad against the wishes of their parents or guardians in contravention of the applicable laws. While providing that, in normal circumstances, requests for such cooperation should be considered favorably, the convention refers to circumstances in which favorable action may reasonably be denied or postponed.

The Convention was concluded by the COMMITTEE OF MINISTERS OF THE COUNCIL OF EUROPE, convened at the Hague, on 28 May 1970. The text of the convention (*European Treaty Series* 71) is as follows:

The member States of the Council of Europe, signatory hereto,

Considering that their close unity is manifested particularly in increased movements of persons;

Considering that although this generally has beneficial consequences, certain problems are nevertheless involved, in particular when a minor is in the territory of a State against the will of those responsible for protecting his interests or when his presence in the territory of a State is incompatible either with his own interests or those of that State;

Convinced of the necessity for mutual co-operation to enable such minors to be compulsorily transferred from one State to another,

Have agreed as follows:

Section I
General Information

Article 1. For the purpose of this Convention:

(a) the term "minor" shall mean any person not having attained his majority under the law applicable according to the rules of private international law of the requesting State and who under this same law has not the right himself to determine his own place of residence;

(b) the term "parental authority" shall mean the authority devolving upon natural or legal persons under the law or by a legal or administrative decision, to determine a minor's place of residence;

(c) the term "repatriation" shall mean the transfer, in implementation of this Convention, of a minor from one Contracting State to another Contracting State, whether or not the latter is the State of which he is a national.

Article 2. 1. This Convention shall apply to minors in the territory of a Contracting State whose repatriation is requested by another Contracting State for one of the following reasons:

(a) the presence of the minor in the territory of the requested State is against the will of the person or persons having parental authority in respect of him;

(b) the presence of the minor in the territory of the requested State is incompatible with a measure of protection or re-education taken in respect of him by the competent authorities of the requesting State;

(c) the presence of the minor is necessary in the territory of the requesting State because of the institution of proceedings there with a view to taking measures of protection and re-education in respect of him.

2. This Convention shall also apply to the repatriation of

minors whose presence in its territory a Contracting State deems to be incompatible with its own interests or with the interests of the minors concerned, provided that its legislation authorises removal of the minor from its territory.

Article 3. Each Contracting State shall designate a central authority to formulate, issue and receive requests for repatriation and notify the Secretary General of the Council of Europe of the authority so designated.

Section II
Repatriation of a Minor on the Request of a State other than the State of Sojourn

Article 4. 1. Applications for the repatriation of a minor for one of the reasons set out in Article 2, paragraph 1, shall be addressed to the central authority of the State to which the minor is to be repatriated.

2. If the competent authorities of that State consider that the application is well founded and reasonable, the central authority shall issue a request for repatriation to the central authority of the State of sojourn of the minor.

Article 5. 1. No decision shall be taken concerning a request for repatriation until the minor, if his capacity for discernment allows, has been heard in person by a competent authority in the requested State.

2. The said authority shall also endeavour to obtain the views of those persons having an interest in the decision, in particular, those having parental authority or those who, in the territory of the requested State, have *de facto* custody of the minor. This ascertainment of views shall not take place in so far as it is likely to prejudice the interests of the minor by reason of the delay which it may cause.

Article 6. The requested State shall grant any request for repatriation which is in conformity with the provisions of the present Convention and grounded on Article 2, paragraph 1, unless it exercises its right to refuse a request in accordance with Articles 7 and 8.

Article 7. A request may be refused:

(a) if the minor, according to the law applicable under the rules of private international law of the requested State, has the right himself to determine his place of residence, or if such a right follows from the national law of the requested State;

(b) if it is grounded on Article 2, paragraph 1 (a) and is designed to submit the minor to the authority of a person or persons who do not have parental authority according to the law applicable under the rules of private international law of the requested State or do not have parental authority under the national law of the requested State;

(c) if the requested State considers that the requesting State is not competent to take the measures referred to in Article 2, paragraph 1 (b) and (c);

(d) if the requested State considers that the repatriation of the minor would be contrary to *ordre public;*

(e) if the minor is a national of the requested State;

(f) if the minor in question is a national of a State which is not a Party to the Convention, and whose repatriation would not be compatible with the obligations existing between that State and the requested State.

Article 8. The requested State may, moreover, having regard to all the aspects of the case, refuse the request:

(a) if, being present in the territory of the requested State, the person or persons having parental authority or those having care of the minor, oppose repatriation;

(b) if the repatriation is considered by the requested State to be contrary to the interests of the minor, in particular when he has effective family or social ties in that State or when repatriation is incompatible with a measure of protection or re-education taken in the said State.

Article 9. The decision of the requested State on the request may be postponed:

(a) if the parental authority upon which the request is based is contested on serious grounds;

(b) if it considers it necessary to prosecute the minor for an offence or to require him to submit to a penal sanction involving deprivation of liberty.

Article 10. If the request is granted the competent authorities in the requesting State and the requested State shall agree as promptly as possible on the repatriation procedure.

Article 11. The requested State may take such provisional measures as seem necessary for the purpose of repatriation, in particular placing the minor in a home for juveniles. It may at any time terminate these measures which shall, in any case, be terminated after the expiration of a period of 30 days if the request has not been granted. The measures in question are governed by the domestic law of the requested State.

Article 12. In urgent cases, the central authority in the requesting State may ask that the provisional measures mentioned in Article 11 be taken before the requested State has received the request for repatriation. Such measures shall cease if the request for repatriation has not been received within ten days.

Article 13. 1. No prosecution may be initiated or continued in the requesting State against a person repatriated in accordance with the provisions of this section for offences committed prior to his repatriation, unless the requested State expressly consents to such prosecution. Such consent shall also be required in order to enforce a penal sanction involving deprivation of liberty or any more severe sentence passed in the requesting State before repatriation.

2. The consent referred to in paragraph 1 shall be governed by the rules regulating extradition in the requested State or by such other rules established there for the implementation of this article.

3. Consent may not be withheld in cases where the requested State would be obliged to grant extradition, were extradition to be requested.

Section III
Repatriation on the Request of the State of Sojourn

Article 14. 1. In the cases provided for in Article 2, paragraph 2, the State of sojourn of the minor may request another Contracting State to agree to the repatriation of such a minor as hereinafter provided:

(a) when the person or persons having parental authority are in another Contracting State, the request shall be addressed to that other State;

(b) when the person or persons having parental authority are in a State which is not a Party to this Convention, the request shall be addressed to the Contracting State where the minor has his habitual residence;

(c) when it is not known in what State the person or persons having parental authority are to be found or when no one has parental authority, the request shall be addressed to the Contracting State where the minor has his habitual residence or, if repatriation to that State is not agreed to or otherwise proves impossible, to the Contracting State of which the minor is a national.

2. The provisions of paragraph 1 shall not affect the

powers which Contracting States enjoy under their own legislation in respect of foreign nationals.

Article 15. 1. If the requested State agrees to receive the minor, the competent authorities in the requesting State and in the requested State shall agree as promptly as possible on the repatriation procedure.

2. The request relating to repatriation may be accompanied by a request that measures be taken which are deemed appropriate because of the conduct, or the situation, of the minor in the requesting State. The request may also specify all other conditions with which the repatriation must comply.

Section IV
Common Provisions

Article 16. 1. All requests relating to repatriation shall be submitted in writing and shall state, in particular:

(a) the name of the issuing central authority;

(b) the identity and nationality of the minor whose repatriation is requested and, if possible, his address in the requested State;

(c) the reasons invoked in support of the request;

(d) if applicable, the authority or person making the application for repatriation as well as their legal relations with the minor.

2. In cases grounds on Article 2, paragraph 1, the request shall be accompanied, where appropriate, by the original or a certified copy either of the document proving parental authority except where such authority derives directly from law, or of the decision ordering a measure of protection or re-education of the minor concerned or of the documents proving the necessity for the minor to appear at the proceedings in course in the requesting State and the purpose of such proceedings.

3. If the requested State considers that the information supplied by the requesting State is not sufficient to enable it to decide on the request, it shall ask for the necessary additional information. It may fix a time-limit for the receipt of such information.

Article 17. 1. Subject to paragraph 2 of this article, no translation of requests or of the supporting documents shall be required.

2. Any Contracting State may, when signing or depositing its instrument of ratification, acceptance or accession, by a declaration addressed to the Secretary General of the Council of Europe, reserve the right to stipulate that requests and supporting documents shall be accompanied by a translation into its own language or one of its languages or into one of the official languages of the Council of Europe or into such one of those languages as it shall indicate. The other Contracting States may apply reciprocity.

3. This article shall be without prejudice to any provision concerning translation of requests and supporting documents contained in agreements or arrangements now in force or which may be concluded between two or more Contracting States.

Article 18. Evidence and documents transmitted in connection with this Convention shall be exempt from all formalities of legislation.

Article 19. 1. The transit of a minor in process of repatriation, in pursuance of the present Convention, through the territory of a Contracting State, shall be authorised upon single notification, of which there shall be a written record by the State from which the repatriation is to be effected.

2. Transit may be refused when:

(a) the minor is the subject of a criminal prosecution in the State of transit or if he is required to submit to a penal sanction involving deprivation of liberty or a more severe penalty;

(b) the minor is a national of the State of transit.

3. If transit is not refused, the minor may neither be arrested nor detained in the State of transit for offences committed before his entry into that State.

4. The State of transit shall seek to ensure that the minor does not elude repatriation.

Article 20. Reasons shall be given for any refusal of repatriation or transit.

Article 21. Communications between central authorities in connection with the implementation of this Convention may be transmitted through the International Criminal Police Organisation (Interpol).

Article 22. 1. Any costs incurred in implementing this Convention shall be borne by:

(a) the requested State, if such costs are incurred in its territory;

(b) the requesting State, in all other cases.

2. This article shall not prevent the recovery of costs from the minor or other persons responsible for them.

Section V
Final Clauses

Article 23. 1. This Convention shall be open to signature by the member States represented on the Committee of Ministers of the Council of Europe. It shall be subject to ratification or acceptance. Instruments of ratification or acceptance shall be deposited with the Secretary General of the Council of Europe.

2. This Convention shall enter into force three months after the date of the deposit of the third instrument of ratification or acceptance.

3. In respect of a signatory State ratifying or accepting subsequently, the Convention shall come into force three months after the date of deposit of its instrument of ratification or acceptance.

Article 24. 1. After the entry into force of this Convention, the Committee of Ministers of the Council of Europe may invite any non-member State to accede thereto.

2. Such accession shall be effected by depositing with the Secretary General of the Council of Europe an instrument of accession which shall take effect three months after the date of its deposit.

Article 25. Any Contracting State may, at the time of signature or when depositing its instrument of ratification, acceptance or accession, make a declaration defining, as far as it is concerned, the term "nationals" as used in this Convention.

Article 26. 1. Any Contracting State may, at the time of signature or when depositing its instrument of ratification, acceptance or accession, specify the territory or territories to which this Convention shall apply.

2. Any Contracting State may, when depositing its instrument of ratification, acceptance or accession or at any later date, by declaration addressed to the Secretary General of the Council of Europe, extend this Convention to any other territory or territories specified in the declaration and for whose international relations it is responsible or on whose behalf it is authorised to give undertakings.

3. Any declaration made in pursuance of the preceding paragraph may, in respect of any territory mentioned in

such declaration, be withdrawn according to the procedure laid down in Article 29 of this Convention.

Article 27. 1. Subject to the provisions of paragraphs 3 and 4 of this article, this Convention shall, in respect of the territories to which it applies, supersede the provisions of any treaties, conventions or bilateral agreements between Contracting States governing the repatriation of minors for the reasons specified in Article 2, to the extent that the Contracting States may always avail themselves of the facilities for repatriation provided for in this Convention.

2. This Convention shall not prevent repatriations or extradition founded either on international agreements or conventions, or on the internal law of the State in question.

3. Contracting States may conclude between themselves bilateral or multilateral agreements on matters governed by this Convention; however, such agreements shall only be made in order to supplement the provisions of this Convention or to facilitate the application of the principles contained herein. Such bilateral or multilateral agreements or arrangements may provide, in particular, for direct relations between competent national authorities.

4. Furthermore, where two or more Contracting States have established or establish relations on the basis of uniform legislation or a special system, these States shall, notwithstanding the provisions of this Convention, be free to regulate their mutual relations in this field exclusively in accordance with such legislation or system. Contracting States which, in accordance with this paragraph, exclude, as between themselves, the application of this Convention, shall notify the Secretary General of the Council of Europe accordingly.

Article 28. The Council of Europe shall keep itself informed concerning the application of this Convention and shall do whatever is needful to facilitate a friendly settlement of any difficulty which may arise out of its execution.

Article 29. 1. This Convention shall remain in force indefinitely.

2. Any Contracting State may, in so far as it is concerned, denounce this Convention by means of a notification addressed to the Secretary General of the Council of Europe.

3. Such denunciation shall take effect six months after the date of receipt by the Secretary General of such notification.

Article 30. The Secretary General of the Council of Europe shall inform the member States represented on the Committee of Ministers of the Council and any State which has acceded to this Convention of:

(a) any signature;

(b) any deposit of an instrument of ratification, acceptance or accession;

(c) any notification received in accordance with Article 3 of this Convention;

(d) any date of entry into force of this Convention in accordance with Article 23 thereof;

(e) any declaration received in accordance with Article 25;

(f) any notification received in accordance with Article 26;

(g) any notification received in accordance with Article 27, paragraph 4;

(h) any notification received in pursuance of Article 29 and the date on which the denunciation takes effect.

In witness whereof the undersigned, being duly authorised thereto, have signed this Convention.

Done at The Hague this 28th May 1970, in English and in French, both texts being equally authoritative, in a single copy which shall remain deposited in the archives of the Council of Europe. The Secretary General shall transmit certified copies to each of the signatory and acceding States.

SEE ALSO European Convention on Recognition and Enforcement of Decisions concerning Custody of Children and on Restoration of Custody of Children.

EUROPEAN CONVENTION ON THE SUPPRESSION OF TERRORISM (1977).

Under the convention, contracting States undertake to extradite persons who have committed serious terrorist offenses, such as the taking of HOSTAGES, the hijacking of an aircraft, or the use of explosives, even though they seek to justify those actions on political grounds. However, the State may refuse to extradite a person if it has reasonable grounds to believe that the request for extradition has been made for the purpose of prosecuting or punishing a person on account of his race, religion, nationality, or political opinion.

The convention was concluded by the COMMITTEE OF MINISTERS OF THE COUNCIL OF EUROPE, convened in Strasbourg, on 27 January 1977 and entered into force on 4 August 1978. The text *(European Treaty Series* 90) is as follows:

The member States of the Council of Europe, signatory hereto,

Considering that the aim of the Council of Europe is to achieve a greater unity between its Members;

Aware of the growing concern caused by the increase in acts of terrorism;

Wishing to take effective measures to ensure that the perpetrators of such acts do not escape prosecution and punishment;

Convinced that extradition is a particularly effective measure for achieving this result,

Have agreed as follows:

Article 1. For the purposes of extradition between Contracting States, none of the following offences shall be regarded as a political offence or as an offence connected with a political offence or as an offence inspired by political motives:

(a) an offence within the scope of the Convention for the Suppression of Unlawful Seizure of Aircraft, signed at The Hague on 16 December 1970;

(b) an offence within the scope of the Convention for the Suppression of Unlawful Acts against the Safety of Civil Aviation, signed at Montreal on 23 September 1971;

(c) a serious offence involving an attack against the life, physical integrity or liberty of internationally protected persons, including diplomatic agents;

(d) an offence involving kidnapping, the taking of a hostage or serious unlawful detention;

(e) an offence involving the use of a bomb, grenade, rocket, automatic firearm or letter or parcel bomb if this use endangers persons;

(f) an attempt to commit any of the foregoing offences or participation as an accomplice of a person who commits or attempts to commit such an offence.

Article 2. 1. For the purposes of extradition between Contracting States, a Contracting State may decide not to regard as a political offence or as an offence connected with a political offence or as an offence inspired by political motives a serious offence involving an act of violence, other than one covered by Article 1, against the life, physical integrity or liberty of a person.

2. The same shall apply to a serious offence involving an act against property, other than one covered by Article 1, if the act created a collective danger for persons.

3. The same shall apply to an attempt to commit any of the foregoing offences or participation as an accomplice of a person who commits or attempts to commit such an offence.

Article 3. The provisions of all extradition treaties and arrangements applicable between Contracting States, including the European Convention on Extradition, are modified as between Contracting States to the extent that they are incompatible with this Convention.

Article 4. For the purposes of this Convention and to the extent that any offence mentioned in Article 1 or 2 is not listed as an extraditable offence in any extradition convention or treaty existing between Contracting States, it shall be deemed to be included as such therein.

Article 5. Nothing in this Convention shall be interpreted as imposing an obligation to extradite if the requested State has substantial grounds for believing that the request for extradition for an offence mentioned in Article 1 or 2 has been made for the purpose of prosecuting or punishing a person on account of his race, religion, nationality or political opinion, or that that person's position may be prejudiced for any of these reasons.

Article 6. 1. Each Contracting State shall take such measures as may be necessary to establish its jurisdiction over an offence mentioned in Article 1 in the case where the suspected offender is present in its territory and it does not extradite him after receiving a request for extradition from a Contracting State whose jurisdiction is based on a rule of jurisdiction existing equally in the law of the requested State.

2. This Convention does not exclude any criminal jurisdiction exercised in accordance with national law.

Article 7. A Contracting State in whose territory a person suspected to have committed an offence mentioned in Article 1 is found and which has received a request for extradition under the conditions mentioned in Article 6, paragraph 1, shall, if it does not extradite that person, submit the case, without exception whatsoever and without undue delay, to its competent authorities for the purpose of prosecution. Those authorities shall take their decision in the same manner as in the case of any offence of a serious nature under the law of that State.

Article 8. 1. Contracting States shall afford one another the widest measure of mutual assistance in criminal matters in connection with proceedings brought in respect of the offences mentioned in Article 1 or 2. The law of the requested State concerning mutual assistance in criminal matters shall apply in all cases. Nevertheless this assistance may not be refused on the sole ground that it concerns a political offence or an offence connected with a political offence or an offence inspired by political motives.

2. Nothing in this Convention shall be interpreted as imposing an obligation to afford mutual assistance if the requested State has substantial grounds for believing that the request for mutual assistance in respect of an offence mentioned in Article 1 or 2 has been made for the purpose of prosecuting or punishing a person on account of his race,

religion, nationality or political opinion or that that person's position may be prejudiced for any of these reasons.

3. The provisions of all treaties and arrangements concerning mutual assistance in criminal matters applicable between Contracting States, including the European Convention on Mutual Assistance in Criminal Matters, are modified as between Contracting States to the extent that they are incompatible with this Convention.

Article 9. 1. The European Committee on Crime Problems of the Council of Europe shall be kept informed regarding the application of this Convention.

2. It shall do whatever is needful to facilitate a friendly settlement of any difficulty which may arise out of its execution.

Article 10. 1. Any dispute between Contracting States concerning the interpretation or application of this Convention, which has not been settled in the framework of Article 9, paragraph 2, shall, at the request of any Party to the dispute, be referred to arbitration. Each Party shall nominate an arbitrator and the two arbitrators shall nominate a referee. If any Party has not nominated its arbitrator within the three months following the request for arbitration, he shall be nominated at the request of the other Party by the President of the European Court of Human Rights. If the latter should be a national of one of the Parties to the dispute, this duty shall be carried out by the Vice-President of the Court or, if the Vice-President is a national of one of the Parties to the dispute, by the most senior judge of the Court not being a national of one of the Parties to the dispute. The same procedure shall be observed if the arbitrators cannot agree on the choice of referee.

2. The arbitration tribunal shall lay down its own procedure. Its decisions shall be taken by majority vote. Its award shall be final.

Article 11. 1. This Convention shall be open to signature by the member States of the Council of Europe. It shall be subject to ratification, acceptance or approval. Instruments of ratification, acceptance or approval shall be deposited with the Secretary General of the Council of Europe.

2. The Convention shall enter into force three months after the date of the deposit of the third instrument of ratification, acceptance or approval.

3. In respect of a signatory State ratifying, accepting or approving subsequently, the Convention shall come into force three months after the date of the deposit of its instrument of ratification, acceptance or approval.

Article 12. 1. Any State may, at the time of signature or when depositing its instrument of ratification, acceptance or approval, specify the territory or territories to which this Convention shall apply.

2. Any State may, when depositing its instrument of ratification, acceptance or approval or at any later date, by declaration addressed to the Secretary General of the Council of Europe, extend this Convention to any other territory or territories specified in the declaration and for whose international relations it is responsible or on whose behalf it is authorised to give undertakings.

3. Any declaration made in pursuance of the preceding paragraph may, in respect of any territory mentioned in such declaration, be withdrawn by means of a notification addressed to the Secretary General of the Council of Europe. Such withdrawal shall take effect immediately or at such later date as may be specified in the notification.

Article 13. 1. Any State may, at the time of signature or when depositing its instrument of ratification, acceptance or approval, declare that it reserves the right to refuse extradition in respect of any offence mentioned in Article 1 which it considers to be a political offence, an offence connected with a political offence or an offence inspired by political motives, provided that it undertakes to take into due consideration, when evaluating the character of the offence, any particularly serious aspects of the offence, including:

(a) that it created a collective danger to the life, physical integrity or liberty of persons; or

(b) that it affected persons foreign to the motives behind it; or

(c) that cruel or vicious means have been used in the commission of the offence.

2. Any State may wholly or partly withdraw a reservation it has made in accordance with the foregoing paragraph by means of a declaration addressed to the Secretary General of the Council of Europe which shall become effective as from the date of its receipt.

3. A State which has made a reservation in accordance with paragraph 1 of this Article may not claim the application of Article 1 by any other State; it may, however, if its reservation is partial or conditional, claim the application of that article in so far as it has itself accepted it.

Article 14. Any Contracting State may denounce this Convention by means of a written notification addressed to the Secretary General of the Council of Europe. Any such denunciation shall take effect immediately or at such later date as may be specified in the notification.

Article 15. This Convention ceases to have effect in respect of any Contracting State which withdraws from or ceases to be a Member of the Council of Europe.

Article 16. The Secretary General of the Council of Europe shall notify the member States of the Council of:

(a) any signature;

(b) any deposit of an instrument of ratification, acceptance or approval;

(c) any date of entry into force of this Convention in accordance with Article 11 thereof;

(d) any declaration or notification received in pursuance of the provisions of Article 12;

(e) any reservation made in pursuance of the provisions of Article 13, paragraph 1;

(f) the withdrawal of any reservation effected in pursuance of the provisions of Article 13, paragraph 2;

(g) any notification received in pursuance of Article 14 and the date on which denunciation takes effect.

(h) any cessation of the effects of the Convention pursuant to Article 15.

In witness whereof, the undersigned, being duly authorised thereto, have signed this Convention.

Done at Strasbourg, this 27th day of January 1977, in English and in French, both texts being equally authoritative, in a single copy which shall remain deposited in the archives of the Council of Europe. The Secretary General of the Council of Europe shall transmit certified copies to each of the signatory States.

SEE ALSO *Convention for the Suppression of Unlawful Acts against the Safety of Civil Aviation; Convention for the Suppression of Unlawful Seizure of Aircraft; Convention on Offenses and Certain Other Acts Committed on Board Aircraft; Convention on the High Seas; Convention on the Prevention and Punishment of Crimes against Internationally Protected Persons; Death Threats; European Recommendation concerning International Cooperation in the Prosecution and Punishment of Terrorism; Terrorist Acts.*

EUROPEAN CONVENTION ON THE TRANSFER OF PROCEEDINGS IN CRIMINAL MATTERS (1972).

The convention provides that, when a person is suspected of having committed an offense under the law of a contracting State, that State may request another contracting State to take proceedings against him in certain cases and under certain conditions. Such cases arise, for example, when the suspected person is a national, or is ordinarily resident in, the requested State or is imprisoned there. Concluded by the COMMITTEE OF MINISTERS OF THE COUNCIL OF EUROPE, convened in Strasbourg, on 15 May 1972, the convention entered into force on 30 March 1978. Its text (*European Treaty Series* 73) is as follows:

The member States of the Council of Europe, signatory hereto,

Considering that the aim of the Council of Europe is the achievement of greater unity between its Members;

Desiring to supplement the work which they have already accomplished in the field of criminal law with a view to arriving at more just and efficient sanctions;

Considering it useful to this end to ensure, in a spirit of mutual confidence, the organisation of criminal proceedings on the international level, in particular, by avoiding the disadvantages resulting from conflicts of competence,

Have agreed as follows:

Part I
Definitions

Article 1. For the purposes of this Convention:

(a) "offence" comprises acts dealt with under the criminal law and those dealt with under the legal provisions listed in Appendix III to this Convention on condition that where an administrative authority is competent to deal with the offence it must be possible for the person concerned to have the case tried by a court;

(b) "sanction" means any punishment or other measure incurred or pronounced in respect of an offence or in respect of a violation of the legal provisions listed in Appendix III.

Part II
Competence

Article 2. 1. For the purposes of applying this Convention, any Contracting State shall have competence to prosecute under its own criminal law any offence to which the law of another Contracting State is applicable.

2. The competence conferred on a Contracting State exclusively by virtue of paragraph 1 of this article may be exercised only pursuant to a request for proceedings presented by another Contracting State.

Article 3. Any Contracting State having competence under its own law to prosecute an offence may, for the purposes of applying this Convention, waive or desist from proceedings against a suspected person who is being or will be prosecuted for the same offence by another Contracting State. Having regard to Article 21, paragraph 2, any such decision to waive or to desist from proceedings shall be provisional pending a final decision in the other Contracting State.

Article 4. The requested State shall discontinue proceedings exclusively grounded on Article 2 when to its knowledge the right of punishment is extinguished under the law of the requesting State for a reason other than time-limitation, to which Articles 10 (c), 11 (f) and (g), 22, 23, and 26 in particular apply.

Article 5. The provisions of Part III of this Convention do not limit the competence given to a requested State by its municipal law in regard to prosecutions.

Part III
Transfer of Proceedings

Section 1: Request for Proceedings

Article 6. 1. When a person is suspected of having committed an offence under the law of a Contracting State, that State may request another Contracting State to take proceedings in the cases and under the conditions provided for in this Convention.

2. If under the provisions of this Convention a Contracting State may request another Contracting State to take proceedings, the competent authorities of the first State shall take that possibility into consideration.

Article 7. 1. Proceedings may not be taken in the requested State unless the offence in respect of which the proceedings are requested would be an offence if committed in its territory and when, under these circumstances, the offender would be liable to sanction under its own law also.

2. If the offence was committed by a person of public status or against a person, an institution or any thing of public status in the requesting State, it shall be considered in the requested State as having been committed by a person of public status or against such a person, an institution or any thing corresponding, in the latter State, to that against which it was actually committed.

Article 8. 1. A Contracting State may request another Contracting State to take proceedings in any one or more of the following cases:

(a) if the suspected person is ordinarily resident in the requested State;

(b) if the suspected person is a national of the requested State or if that State is his State of origin;

(c) if the suspected person is undergoing or is to undergo a sentence involving deprivation of liberty in the requested State;

(d) if proceedings for the same or other offences are being taken against the suspected person in the requested State;

(e) if it considers that transfer of the proceedings is warranted in the interests of arriving at the truth and in particular that the most important items of evidence are located in the requested State;

(f) if it considers that the enforcement in the requested State of a sentence if one were passed is likely to improve the prospects for the social rehabilitation of the person sentenced;

(g) if it considers that the presence of the suspected person cannot be ensured at the hearing of proceedings in the requesting State and that his presence in person at the hearing of proceedings in the requested State can be ensured;

(h) if it considers that it could not itself enforce a sentence if one were passed, even by having recourse to ex-

tradition, and that the requested State could do so.

2. Where the suspected person has been finally sentenced in a Contracting State, that State may request the transfer of proceedings in one or more of the cases referred to in paragraph 1 of this article only if it cannot itself enforce the sentence, even by having recourse to extradition, and if the other Contracting State does not accept enforcement of a foreign judgment as a matter of principle or refuses to enforce such sentence.

Article 9. 1. The competent authorities in the requested State shall examine the request for proceedings made in pursuance of the preceding articles. They shall decide, in accordance with their own law, what action to take thereon.

2. Where the law of the requested State provides for the punishment of the offence by an administrative authority, that State shall, as soon as possible, so inform the requesting State unless the requested State has made a declaration under paragraph 3 of this article.

3. Any Contracting State may at the time of signature, or when depositing its instrument of ratification, acceptance or accession, or at any later date indicate, by declaration addressed to the Secretary General of the Council of Europe, the conditions under which its domestic law permits the punishment of certain offences by an administrative authority. Such a declaration shall replace the notification envisaged in paragraph 2 of this article.

Article 10. The requested State shall not take action on the request:

(a) if the request does not comply with the provisions of Articles 6, paragraph 1, and 7, paragraph 1;

(b) if the institution of proceedings is contrary to the provisions of Article 35;

(c) if, at the date on the request, the time-limit for criminal proceedings has already expired in the requesting State under the legislation of that State.

Article 11. Save as provided for in Article 10 the requested State may not refuse acceptance of the request in whole or in part, except in any one or more of the following cases:

(a) if it considers that the grounds on which the request is based under Article 8 are not justified;

(b) if the suspected person is not ordinarily resident in the requested State;

(c) if the suspected person is not a national of the requested State and was not ordinarily resident in the territory of that State at the time of the offence;

(d) if it considers that the offence for which proceedings are requested is an offence of a political nature or a purely military or fiscal one;

(e) if it considers that there are substantial grounds for believing that the request for proceedings was motivated by considerations of race, religion, nationality or political opinion;

(f) if its own law is already applicable to the offence and if at the time of the receipt of the request proceedings were precluded by lapse of time according to that law; Article 26, paragraph 2, shall not apply in such a case;

(g) if its competence is exclusively grounded on Article 2 and if at the time of the receipt of the request proceedings would be precluded by lapse of time according to its law, the prolongation of the time-limit by six months under the terms of Article 23 being taken into consideration;

(h) if the offence was committed outside the territory of the requesting State;

(i) if proceedings would be contrary to the international undertakings of the requested State;

(j) if proceedings would be contrary to the fundamental principles of the legal system of the requested State;

(k) if the requesting State has violated a rule of procedure laid down in this Convention.

Article 12. 1. The requested State shall withdraw its acceptance of the request if, subsequent to this acceptance, a ground mentioned in Article 10 of this Convention for not taking action on the request becomes apparent.

2. The requested State may withdraw its acceptance of the request:

(a) if it becomes apparent that the presence in person of the suspected person cannot be ensured at the hearing of proceedings in that State or that any sentence, which might be passed, could not be enforced in that State;

(b) if one of the grounds for refusal mentioned in Article 11 becomes apparent before the case is brought before a court; or

(c) in other cases, if the requesting State agrees.

Section 2: Transfer Procedure

Article 13. 1. All requests specified in this Convention shall be made in writing. They, and all communications necessary for the application of this Convention, shall be sent either by the Ministry of Justice of the requesting State to the Ministry of Justice of the requested State or, by virtue of special mutual arrangement, direct by the authorities of the requesting State to those of the requested State; they shall be returned by the same channel.

2. In urgent cases, requests and communications may be sent through the International Criminal Police Organisation (Interpol).

3. Any Contracting State may, by declaration addressed to the Secretary General of the Council of Europe, give notice to its intention to adopt in so far is it itself is concerned rules of transmission other than those laid down in paragraph 1 of this article.

Article 14. If a Contracting State considers that the information supplied by another Contracting State is not adequate to enable it to apply this Convention, it shall ask for the necessary additional information. It may prescribe a date for the receipt of such information.

Article 15. 1. A request for proceedings shall be accompanied by the original, or a certified copy, of the criminal file and all other necessary documents. However, if the suspected person is remanded in custody in accordance with the provisions of Section 5 and if the requesting State is unable to transmit these documents at the same time as the request for proceedings, the documents may be sent subsequently.

2. The requesting State shall also inform the requested State in writing of any procedural acts performed or measures taken in the requesting State after the transmission of the request which have a bearing on the proceedings. This communication shall be accompanied by any relevant documents.

Article 16. 1. The requested State shall promptly communicate its decision on the request for proceedings to the requesting State.

2. The requested State shall also inform the requesting State of a waiver of proceedings or of the decision taken as a result of proceedings. A certified copy of any written decision shall be transmitted to the requesting State.

Article 17. If the competence of the requested State is exclusively grounded on Article 2 that State shall inform the suspected person of the request for proceedings with a view to allowing him to present his views on the matter before that State has taken a decision on the request.

Article 18. 1. Subject to paragraph 2 of this article, no translation of the documents relating to the application of this Convention shall be required.

2. Any Contracting State may, at the time of signature or when depositing its instrument of ratification, acceptance or accession, by declaration addressed to the Secretary General of the Council of Europe, reserve the right to require that, with the exception of the copy of the written decision referred to in Article 16, paragraph 2, the said documents be accompanied by a translation. The other Contracting States shall send the translations in either the national language of the receiving State or such one of the official languages of the Council of Europe as the receiving State shall indicate. However, such an indication is not obligatory. The other Contracting States may claim reciprocity.

3. This article shall be without prejudice to any provisions concerning translation of requests and supporting documents that may be contained in agreements or arrangements now in force or that may be concluded between two or more Contracting States.

Article 19. Documents transmitted in application of this Convention need not be authenticated.

Article 20. Contracting Parties shall not claim from each other the refund of any expenses resulting from the application of this Convention.

Section 3: Effects in the Requesting State of a Request for Proceedings

Article 21. 1. When the requesting State has requested proceedings, it can no longer prosecute the suspected person for the offence in respect of which the proceedings have been requested or enforce a judgment which has been pronounced previously in that State against him for that offence. Until the requested State's decision on the request for proceedings has been received, the requesting State shall, however, retain its right to take all steps in respect of prosecution, short of bringing the case to trial, or, as the case may be, allowing the competent administrative authority to decide on the case.

2. The right of prosecution and of enforcement shall revert to the requesting State:

(a) if the requested State informs it of a decision in accordance with Article 10 not to take action on the request;

(b) if the requested State informs it of a decision in accordance with Article 11 to refuse acceptance of the request;

(c) if the requested State informs it of a decision in accordance with Article 12 to withdraw acceptance of the request;

(d) if the requested State informs it of a decision not to institute proceedings or discontinue them;

(e) if it withdraws its request before the requested State has informed it of a decision to take action on the request.

Article 22. A request for proceedings, made in accordance with the provisions of this Part, shall have the effect in the requesting State of prolonging the time-limit for proceedings by six months.

Section 4: Effects in the Requested State of a Request for Proceedings

Article 23. If the competence of the requested State is exclusively grounded on Article 2 the time-limit for proceedings in that State shall be prolonged by six months.

Article 24. 1. If proceedings are dependent on a complaint in both States the complaint brought in the requesting State shall have equal validity with that brought in the requested State.

2. If a complaint is necessary only in the requested State, that State may take proceedings even in the absence of a complaint if the person who is empowered to bring the complaint has not objected within a period of one month from the date of receipt by him of notice from the competent authority informing him of his right to object.

Article 25. In the requested State the sanction applicable to the offence shall be that prescribed by its own law unless that law provides otherwise. Where the competence of the requested State is exclusively grounded on Article 2, the sanction pronounced in that State shall not be more severe than that provided for in the law of the requesting State.

Article 26. 1. Any act with a view to proceedings, taken in the requesting State in accordance with its law and regulations, shall have the same validity in the requested State as if it had been taken by the authorities of that State, provided that assimilation does not give such act a greater evidential weight than it has in the requesting State.

2. Any act which interrupts time-limitation and which has been validly performed in the requesting State shall have the same effects in the requested State and vice versa.

Section 5: Provisional Measures in the Requested State

Article 27. 1. When the requesting State announces its intention to transmit a request for proceedings, and if the competence of the requested State would be exclusively grounded on Article 2, the requested State may, on application by the requesting State and by virtue of this Convention, provisionally arrest the suspected person:

(a) if the law of the requested State authorises remand in custody for the offence, and

(b) if there are reasons to fear that the suspected person will abscond or that he will cause evidence to be suppressed.

2. The application for provisional arrest shall state that there exists a warrant of arrest or other order having the same effect, issued in accordance with the procedure laid down in the law of the requesting State; it shall also state for what offence proceedings will be requested and when and where such offence was committed and it shall contain as accurate a description of the suspected person as possible. It shall also contain a brief statement of the circumstances of the case.

3. An application for provisional arrest shall be sent direct by the authorities in the requesting State mentioned in Article 13 to the corresponding authorities in the requested State, by post or telegram or by any other means affording evidence in writing or accepted by the requested State. The requesting State shall be informed without delay of the result of its application.

Article 28. Upon receipt of a request for proceedings accompanied by the documents referred to in Article 15, paragraph 1, the requested State shall have jurisdiction to apply all such provisional measures, including remand in custody of the suspected person and seizure of property, as could be applied under its own law if the offence in respect of which proceedings are requested had been committed in its territory.

Article 29. 1. The provisional measures provided in Articles 27 and 28 shall be governed by the provisions of this Convention and the law of the requested State. The law of that State, or the Convention shall also determine the conditions on which the measures may lapse.

2. These measures shall lapse in the cases referred to in Article 21, paragraph 2.

3. A person in custody shall in any event be released if he is arrested in pursuance of Article 27 and the requested State does not receive the request for proceedings within 18 days from the date of the arrest.

4. A person in custody shall in any event be released if he is arrested in pursuance of Article 27 and the documents which should accompany the request for proceedings have not been received by the requested State within 15 days from the receipt of the request for proceedings.

5. The period of custody applied exclusively by virtue of Article 27 shall not in any event exceed 40 days.

Part IV
Plurality of Criminal Proceedings

Article 30. 1. Any Contracting State which, before the institution or in the course of proceedings for an offence which it considers to be neither of a political nature nor a purely military one, is aware of proceedings pending in another Contracting State against the same person in respect of the same offence shall consider whether it can either waive or suspend its own proceedings, or transfer them to the other State.

2. If it deems it advisable in the circumstances not to waive or suspend its own proceedings it shall so notify the other State in good time and in any event before judgment is given on the merits.

Article 31. 1. In the eventuality referred to in Article 30, paragraph 2, the States concerned shall endeavour as far as possible to determine, after evaluation in each case of the circumstances mentioned in Article 8, which of them alone shall continue to conduct proceedings. During this consultative procedure the States concerned shall postpone judgment on the merits without however being obliged to prolong such postponement beyond a period of 30 days as from the despatch of the notification provided for in Article 30, paragraph 2.

2. The provisions of paragraph 1 shall not be binding:

(a) on the State despatching the notification provided for in Article 30, paragraph 2, if the main trial has been declared open there in the presence of the accused before despatch of the notification;

(b) on the State to which the notification is addressed, if the main trial has been declared open there in the presence of the accused before receipt of the notification.

Article 32. In the interests of arriving at the truth and with a view to the application of an appropriate sanction, the States concerned shall examine whether it is expedient that one of them alone shall conduct proceedings and, if so, endeavour to determine which one, when:

(a) several offences which are materially distinct and which fall under the criminal law of each of those States are ascribed either to a single person or to several persons having acted in unison;

(b) a single offence which falls under the criminal law of each of those States is ascribed to several persons having acted in unison.

Article 33. All decisions reached in accordance with Articles 31, paragraph 1, and 32 shall entail, as between the States concerned, all the consequences of a transfer of proceedings as provided for in this Convention. The State which waives its own proceedings shall be deemed to have transferred them to the other State.

Article 34. The transfer procedure provided for in Section 2 of Part III shall apply in so far as its provisions are compatible with those contained in the present Part.

Part V
Ne bis in idem

Article 35. 1. A person in respect of whom a final and enforceable criminal judgment has been rendered may for the same act neither be prosecuted nor sentenced nor subjected to enforcement of a sanction in another Contracting State:

(a) if he was acquitted;

(b) if the sanction imposed:

(i) has been completely enforced or is being enforced, or

(ii) has been wholly, or with respect to the part not enforced, the subject of a pardon or an amnesty, or

(iii) can no longer be enforced because of lapse of time;

(c) if the court convicted the offender without imposing a sanction.

2. Nevertheless, a Contracting State shall not, unless it has itself requested the proceedings, be obliged to recognise the effect of *ne bis in idem* if the act which gave rise to the judgment was directed against either a person or an institution or any thing having public status in that State, or if the subject of the judgment had himself a public status in that State.

3. Furthermore, a Contracting State where the act was committed or considered as such according to the law of that State shall not be obliged to recognise the effect of *ne bis in idem* unless that State has itself requested the proceedings.

Article 36. If new proceedings are instituted against a person who in another Contracting State has been sentenced for the same act, then any period of deprivation of liberty arising from the sentence enforced shall be deducted from the sanction which may be imposed.

Article 37. This Part shall not prevent the application of wider domestic provisions relating to the effect of *ne bis in idem* attached to foreign criminal judgments.

Part VI
Final Clauses

Article 38. 1. This Convention shall be open to signature by the member States of the Council of Europe. It shall be subject to ratification or acceptance. Instruments of ratification or acceptance shall be deposited with the Secretary General of the Council of Europe.

2. This Convention shall enter into force three months after the date of the deposit of the third instrument of ratification or acceptance.

3. In respect of a signatory State ratifying or accepting subsequently, the Convention shall come into force three months after the date of the deposit of its instrument of ratification or acceptance.

Article 39. 1. After the entry into force of this Convention, the Committee of Ministers of the Council of Europe may invite any non-member State to accede thereto provided that the resolution containing such invitation receives the unanimous agreement of the Members of the Council who have ratified the Convention.

2. Such accession shall be effected by depositing with the Secretary General of the Council of Europe an instrument of accession which shall take effect three months after the date of its deposit.

Article 40. 1. Any Contracting State may, at the time of signature or when depositing its instrument of ratification, acceptance or accession, specify the territory or territories to which this Convention shall apply.

2. Any Contracting State may, when depositing its instrument of ratification, acceptance or accession or at any later date, by declaration addressed to the Secretary General of the Council of Europe, extend this Convention to any other territory or territories specified in the declaration and for whose international relations it is responsible or on whose behalf it is authorised to give undertakings.

3. Any declaration made in pursuance of the preceding paragraph may, in respect of any territory mentioned in such declaration, be withdrawn according to the procedure laid down in Article 45 of this Convention.

Article 41. 1. Any Contracting State may, at the time of signature or when depositing its instrument of ratification, acceptance or accession, declare that it avails itself of one or more of the reservations provided for in Appendix I or make a declaration provided for in Appendix II to this Convention.

2. Any Contracting State may wholly or partly withdraw a reservation or declaration it has made in accordance with the foregoing paragraph by means of a declaration addressed to the Secretary General of the Council of Europe which shall become effective as from the date of its receipt.

3. A Contracting State which has made a reservation in respect of any provision of this Convention may not claim the application of that provision by any other Contracting State; it may, however, if its reservation is partial or conditional, claim the application of that provision in so far as it has itself accepted it.

Article 42. 1. Any Contracting State may at any time, by declaration addressed to the Secretary General of the Council of Europe, set out the legal provisions to be included in Appendix III to this Convention.

2. Any change of the national provisions listed in Appendix III shall be notified to the Secretary General of the Council of Europe if such a change renders the information in this Appendix incorrect.

3. Any changes made in Appendix III in application of the preceding paragraphs shall take effect in each Contracting State one month after the date of their notification by the Secretary General of the Council of Europe.

Article 43. 1. This Convention affects neither the rights and the undertakings derived from extradition treaties and international multilateral conventions concerning special matters, nor provisions concerning matters which are dealt with in the present Convention and which are contained in other existing conventions between Contracting States.

2. The Contracting States may not conclude bilateral or multilateral agreements with one another on the matters dealt with in this Convention, except in order to supplement its provisions or facilitate application of the principles embodied in it.

3. Should two or more Contracting States, however, have already established their relations in this matter on the ba-

sis of uniform legislation, or instituted a special system of their own, or should they in future do so, they shall be entitled to regulate those relations accordingly, notwithstanding the terms of this Convention.

4. Contracting States ceasing to apply the terms of this Convention to their mutual relations in this matter in accordance with the provisions of the preceding paragraph shall notify the Secretary General of the Council of Europe to that effect.

Article 44. The European Committee on Crime Problems of the Council of Europe shall be kept informed regarding the application of this Convention and shall do whatever is needful to facilitate a friendly settlement of any difficulty which may arise out of its execution.

Article 45. 1. This Convention shall remain in force indefinitely.

2. Any Contracting State may, in so far as it is concerned, denounce this Convention by means of a notification addressed to the Secretary General of the Council of Europe.

3. Such denunciation shall take effect six months after the date of receipt by the Secretary General of such notification.

Article 46. The Secretary General of the Council of Europe shall notify the member States of the Council and any State which has acceded to this Convention of:

(a) any signature;

(b) any deposit of an instrument of ratification, acceptance or accession;

(c) any date of entry into force of this Convention in accordance with Article 38 thereof;

(d) any declaration received in pursuance of the provision of Article 9, paragraph 3;

(e) any declaration received in pursuance of the provisions of Article 13, paragraph 3;

(f) any declaration received in pursuance of the provisions of Article 18, paragraph 2;

(g) any declaration received in pursuance of the provisions of Article 40, paragraphs 2 and 3;

(h) any reservation or declaration made in pursuance of the provisions of Article 41, paragraph 1;

(i) the withdrawal of any reservation or declaration carried out in pursuance of the provisions of Article 41, paragraph 2;

(j) any declaration received in pursuance of Article 42, paragraph 1, and any subsequent notification received in pursuance of paragraph 2 of that article;

(k) any notification received in pursuance of the provisions of Article 43, paragraph 4;

(l) any notification received in pursuance of the provisions of Article 45 and the date on which denunciation takes effect.

Article 47. This Convention and the notifications and declarations authorised there-under shall apply only to offences committed after the Convention comes into effect for the Contracting States involved.

In witness whereof, the undersigned, being duly authorised thereto, have signed this Convention.

Done at Strasbourg, this 15th day of May 1972, in English and in French, both texts being equally authoritative, in a single copy, which shall remain deposited in the archives of the Council of Europe. The Secretary General shall transmit certified copies to each of the signatory and acceding governments.

EUROPEAN CONVENTION ON TRANSFRONTIER TELEVISION (1989). The convention, concluded at Strasbourg on 5 May 1989 by member States of the Council of Europe and the other States party to the European Cultural Convention (i.e., the Holy See and Yugoslavia), will enter into force "on the first day of the month following the expiration of a period of three months after the date on which seven States, of which at least five are Member States of the Council of Europe, have expressed their consent" to be bound by it.

The convention reflects the conviction, expressed in article 10 of the EUROPEAN CONVENTION ON HUMAN RIGHTS, that freedom of expression and information constitutes one of the essential principles of a democratic society and one of the basic conditions for progress and for the development of every human being.

The text (*International Legal Materials* [1989], vol. 27, p. 859) is as follows:

Preamble

The member States of the Council of Europe and the other States party to the European Cultural Convention, signatory hereto,

Considering that the aim of the Council of Europe is to achieve a greater unity between its members, for the purpose of safeguarding and realising the ideals and principles which are their common heritage;

Considering that the dignity and equal worth of every human being constitute fundamental elements of those principles;

Considering that the freedom of expression and information, as embodied in Article 10 of the Convention for the Protection of Human Rights and Fundamental Freedoms, constitutes one of the essential principles of a democratic society and one of the basic conditions for its progress and for the development of every human being;

Reaffirming their commitment to the principles of the free flow of information and ideas and the independence of broadcasters, which constitute an indispensable basis for their broadcasting policy;

Affirming the importance of broadcasting for the development of culture and the free formation of opinions in conditions safeguarding pluralism and equality of opportunity among all democratic groups and political parties;

Convinced that the continued development of information and communication technology should serve to further the right, regardless of frontiers, to express, to seek, to receive and to impart information and ideas whatever their source;

Being desirous to present an increasing range of choice of programme services for the public, thereby enhancing Europe's heritage and developing its audiovisual creation, and being determined to achieve this cultural objective through efforts to increase the production and circulation of high-quality programmes, thereby responding to the public's expectations in the political, educational and cultural fields;

Recognising the need to consolidate the common broad framework of regulation;

Bearing in mind Resolution No. 2 and the Declaration of the 1st European Ministerial Conference on Mass Media Policy;

Being desirous to develop the principles embodied in the existing Council of Europe Recommendations on principles on television advertising, on equality between women and men in the media, on the use of satellite capacity for television and sound radio, and on the promotion of audiovisual production in Europe,

Have agreed as follows:

Chapter 1—General Provisions

Article 1. Object and Purpose. This Convention is concerned with programme services embodied in transmissions. The purpose is to facilitate, among the Parties, the transfrontier transmission and the retransmission of television programme services.

Article 2. Terms Employed. For the purposes of this Convention:

a. "Transmission" means the initial emission by terrestrial transmitter, by cable, or by satellite of whatever nature, in encoded or unencoded form, of television programme services for reception by the general public. It does not include communication services operating on individual demand;

b. "Retransmission" signifies the fact of receiving and simultaneously transmitting, irrespective of the technical means employed, complete and unchanged television programme services, or important parts of such services, transmitted by broadcasters for reception by the general public;

c. "Broadcaster" means the natural or legal person who composes television programme services for reception by the general public and transmits them or has them transmitted, complete and unchanged, by a third party;

d. "Programme service" means all the items within a single service provided by a given broadcaster within the meaning of the preceding paragraph;

e. "European audiovisual works" means creative works, the production or co-production of which is controlled by European natural or legal persons;

f. "Advertisement" means any public announcement intended to promote the sale, purchase or rental of a product or service, to advance a cause or idea or to bring about some other effect desired by the advertiser, for which transmission time has been given to the advertiser for remuneration or similar consideration;

g. "Sponsorship" means the participation of a natural or legal person, who is not engaged in broadcasting activities or in the production of audiovisual works, in the direct or indirect financing of a programme with a view to promoting the name, trademark or image of that person.

Article 3. Field of Application. This Convention shall apply to any programme service transmitted or retransmitted by entities or by technical means within the jurisdiction of a Party, whether by cable, terrestrial transmitter or satellite, and which can be received, directly or indirectly, in one or more other Parties.

Article 4. Freedom of Reception and Retransmission. The Parties shall ensure freedom of expression and information in accordance with Article 10 of the Convention for the Protection of Human Rights and Fundamental Freedoms and they shall guarantee freedom of reception and shall not restrict the retransmission on their territories of programme services which comply with the terms of this Convention.

Article 5. Duties of the Transmitting Parties. 1. Each transmitting Party shall ensure, by appropriate means and through its competent organs, that all programme services transmitted by entities or by technical means within its jurisdiction, within the meaning of Article 3, comply with the terms of this Convention.

2. For the purposes of this Convention, the transmitting Party shall be:

a. in the case of terrestrial transmissions, the Party in which the initial emission is effected;

b. in the case of satellite transmissions:

i. the Party in which the satellite up-link is situated;

ii. the Party which grants the use of the frequency or a satellite capacity when the up-link is situated in a State which is not a Party to this Convention;

iii. the Party in which the broadcaster has its seat when responsibility under the sub-paragraphs i and ii is not established.

3. When programme services transmitted from States which are not Parties to this Convention are retransmitted by entities or by technical means within the jurisdiction of a Party, within the meaning of Article 3, that Party, acting as transmitting Party, shall ensure, by appropriate means and through its competent organs, compliance with the terms of this Convention.

Article 6. Provision of Information. 1. The responsibilities of the broadcaster shall be clearly and adequately specified in the authorisation issued by, or contract concluded with, the competent authority of each Party, or by any other legal measure.

2. Information about the broadcaster shall be made available, upon request, by the competent authority of the transmitting Party. Such information shall include, as a minimum, the name or denomination, seat and status of the broadcaster, the name of the legal representative, the composition of the capital, the nature, purpose and mode of financing of the programme service the broadcaster is providing or intends providing.

Chapter II—Programming Matters

Article 7. Responsibilities of the Broadcaster. 1. All items of programme services, as concerns their presentation and content, shall respect the dignity of the human being and the fundamental rights of others.

In particular, they shall not:

a. be indecent and in particular contain pornography;

b. give undue prominence to violence or be likely to incite to racial hatred.

2. All items of programme services which are likely to impair the physical, mental or moral development of children and adolescents shall not be scheduled when, because of the time of transmission and reception, they are likely to watch them.

3. The broadcaster shall ensure that news fairly present facts and events and encourage the free formation of opinions.

Article 8. Right of Reply. 1. Each transmitting Party shall ensure that every natural or legal person, regardless of nationality or place of residence, shall have the opportunity to exercise a right of reply or to seek other comparable legal or administrative remedies relating to programmes transmitted or retransmitted by entities or by technical means within its jurisdiction, within the meaning of Article 3. In particular, it shall ensure that timing and other arrangements for the exercise of the right of reply are such that this right can be effectively exercised. The effective exercise of this right or other comparable legal or administrative remedies shall be ensured both as regards the timing and the modalities.

2. For this purpose, the name of the broadcaster responsible for the programme service shall be identified therein at regular intervals by appropriate means.

Article 9. Access of the Public to Major Events. Each Party shall examine the legal measures to avoid the right of the public to information being undermined due to the exercise by a broadcaster of exclusive rights for the transmission or retransmission, within the meaning of Article 3, of an event of high public interest and which has the effect of depriving a large part of the public in one or more other Parties of the opportunity to follow that event on television.

Article 10. Cultural Objectives. 1. Each transmitting Party shall ensure, where practicable and by appropriate means, that broadcasters reserve for European works a majority proportion of their transmission time, excluding the time appointed to news, sports events, games, advertising and teletext services. This proportion, having regard to the broadcaster's informational, educational, cultural and entertainment responsibilities to its viewing public, should be achieved progressively, on the basis of suitable criteria.

2. In case of disagreement between a receiving Party and a transmitting Party on the application of the preceding paragraph, recourse may be had, at the request of one of the Parties, to the Standing Committee with a view to its formulating an advisory opinion on the subject. Such a disagreement shall not be submitted to the arbitration procedure provided for in Article 26.

3. The Parties undertake to look together for the most appropriate instruments and procedures to support, without discrimination between broadcasters, the activity and development of European production, particularly in countries with a low audiovisual production capacity or restricted language area.

4. The Parties, in the spirit of co-operation and mutual assistance which underlies this Convention, shall endeavour to avoid that programme services transmitted or retransmitted by entities or by technical means within their jurisdiction, within the meaning of Article 3, endanger the pluralism of the press and the development of the cinema industries. No cinematographic work shall accordingly be transmitted in such services, unless otherwise agreed between its rights holders and the broadcaster, until two years have elapsed since the work was first shown in cinemas; in the case of cinematographic works co-produced by the broadcaster, this period shall be one year.

Chapter III—Advertising

Article 11. General Standards. 1. All advertisements shall be fair and honest.

2. Advertisements shall not be misleading and shall not prejudice the interests of consumers.

3. Advertisements addressed to or using children shall avoid anything likely to harm their interests and shall have regard to their special susceptibilities.

4. The advertiser shall not exercise any editorial influence over the content of programmes.

Article 12. Duration. 1. The amount of advertising shall not exceed 15% of the daily transmission time. However, this percentage may be increased to 20% to include forms of advertisements such as direct offers to the public for the sale, purchase or rental of products or for the provision of services, provided the amount of spot advertising does not exceed 15%.

2. The amount of spot advertising within a given one-hour period shall not exceed 20%.

3. Forms of advertisements such as direct offers to the public for the sale, purchase or rental of products or for the provision of services shall not exceed one hour per day.

Article 13. Form and Presentation. 1. Advertisements shall be clearly distinguishable as such and recognisably separate from the other items of the programme service by optical or acoustic means. In principle, they shall be transmitted in blocks.

2. Subliminal advertisements shall not be allowed.

3. Surreptitious advertisements shall not be allowed, in particular the presentation of products or services in programmes when it serves advertising purposes.

4. Advertisements shall not feature, visually or orally, persons regularly presenting news and current affairs programmes.

Article 14. Insertion of Advertisements. 1. Advertisements shall be inserted between programmes. Provided the conditions contained in paragraphs 2 to 5 of this Article are fulfilled, advertisements may also be inserted during programmes in such a way that the integrity and value of the programme and the rights of the rights holders are not prejudiced.

2. In programmes consisting of autonomous parts, or in sports programmes and similarly structured events and performances comprising intervals, advertisements shall only be inserted between the parts or in the intervals.

3. The transmission of audiovisual works such as feature films and films made for television (excluding series, serials, light entertainment programmes and documentaries), provided their duration is more than forty-five minutes, may be interrupted once for each complete period of forty-five minutes. A further interruption is allowed if their duration is at least twenty minutes longer than two or more complete periods of forty-five minutes.

4. Where programmes, other than those covered by paragraph 2, are interrupted by advertisements, a period of at least twenty minutes should elapse between each successive advertising break within the programme.

5. Advertisements shall not be inserted in any broadcast of a religious service. News and current affairs programmes, documentaries, religious programmes, and children's programmes, when they are less than thirty minutes of duration, shall not be interrupted by advertisements. If they last for thirty minutes or longer, the provisions of the previous paragraphs shall apply.

Article 15. Advertising of Particular Products. 1. Advertisements for tobacco products shall not be allowed.

2. Advertisements for alcoholic beverages of all varieties shall comply with the following rules:

    a. they shall not be addressed particularly to minors and no one associated with the consumption of alcoholic beverages in advertisements should seem to be a minor;

    b. they shall not link the consumption of alcohol to physical performance or driving;

    c. they shall not claim that alcohol has therapeutic qualities or that it is a stimulant, a sedative or a means of resolving personal problems;

    d. they shall not encourage immoderate consumption of alcohol or present abstinence or moderation in a negative light;

    e. they shall not place undue emphasis on the alcoholic content of beverages.

3. Advertisements for medicines and medical treatment which are only available on medical prescription in the transmitting Party shall not be allowed.

4. Advertisements for all other medicines and medical treatment shall be clearly distinguishable as such, honest, truthful and subject to verification and shall comply with the requirement of protection of the individual from harm.

Article 16. Advertising Directed Specifically at a Single Party. 1. In order to avoid distortions in competition and endangering the television system of a Party, advertisements which are specifically and with some frequency directed to audiences in a single Party other than the transmitting Party shall not circumvent the television advertising rules in that particular Party.

2. The provisions of the preceding paragraph shall not apply where:

a. the rules concerned establish a discrimination between advertisements transmitted by entities or by technical means within the jurisdiction of that Party and advertisements transmitted by entities or by technical means within the jurisdiction of another Party, or

b. the Parties concerned have concluded bilateral or multilateral agreements in this area.

Chapter IV—Sponsorship

Article 17. General Standards. 1. When a programme or series of programmes is sponsored in whole or in part, it shall clearly be identified as such by appropriate credits at the beginning and/or end of the programme.

2. The content and scheduling of sponsored programmes may in no circumstances be influenced by the sponsor in such a way as to affect the responsibility and editorial independence of the broadcaster in respect of programmes.

3. Sponsored programmes shall not encourage the sale, purchase or rental of the products or services of the sponsor or a third party, in particular by making special promotional references to those products or services in such programmes.

Article 18. Prohibited Sponsorship. 1. Programmes may not be sponsored by natural or legal persons whose principal activity is the manufacture or sale of products, or the provision of services, the advertising of which is prohibited by virtue of Article 15.

2. Sponsorship of news and current affairs programmes shall not be allowed.

Chapter V—Mutual Assistance

Article 19. Co-operation between the Parties. 1. The Parties undertake to render each other mutual assistance in order to implement this Convention.

2. For that purpose:

a. each Contracting State shall designate one or more authorities, the name and address of each of which it shall communicate to the Secretary General of the Council of Europe at the time of deposit of its instrument of ratification, acceptance, approval or accession;

b. each Contracting State which has designated more than one authority shall specify in its communication under sub-paragraph *a* the competence of each authority.

3. An authority designated by a Party shall:

a. furnish the information foreseen under Article 6, paragraph 2, of this Convention;

b. furnish information at the request of an authority designated by another Party on the domestic law and practices in the fields covered by this Convention;

c. co-operate with the authorities designated by the other Parties whenever useful, and notably where this would enhance the effectiveness of measures taken in implementation of this Convention;

d. consider any difficulty arising from the application of this Convention which is brought to its attention by an authority designated by another Party.

Chapter VI—Standing Committee

Article 20. Standing Committee. 1. For the purposes of this Convention, a Standing Committee shall be set up.

2. Each Party may be represented on the Standing Committee by one or more delegates. Each delegation shall have one vote. Within the areas of its competence, the European Economic Community shall exercise its right to vote with a number of votes equal to the number of its member States which are Parties to this Convention; the European Economic Community shall not exercise its right to vote in cases where the member States concerned exercise theirs, and conversely.

3. Any State referred to in Article 29, paragraph 1, which is not a Party to this Convention may be represented on the Standing Committee by an observer.

4. The Standing Committee may seek the advice of experts in order to discharge its functions. It may, on its own initiative or at the request of the body concerned, invite any international or national, governmental or non-governmental body technically qualified in the fields covered by this Convention to be represented by an observer at one or part of one of its meetings. The decision to invite such experts or bodies shall be taken by a majority of three-quarters of the members of the Standing Committee.

5. The Standing Committee shall be convened by the Secretary General of the Council of Europe. Its first meeting shall be held within six months of the date of entry into force of the Convention. It shall subsequently meet whenever one-third of the Parties or the Committee of Ministers of the Council of Europe so requests, or on the initiative of the Secretary General of the Council of Europe in accordance with the provisions of Article 23, paragraph 2, or at the request of one or more Parties in accordance with the provisions of Articles 21, sub-paragraph *c*, and 25, paragraph 2.

6. A majority of the Parties shall constitute a quorum for holding a meeting of the Standing Committee.

7. Subject to the provisions of paragraph 4 and Article 23, paragraph 3, the decisions of the Standing Committee shall be taken by a majority of three-quarters of the members present.

8. Subject to the provisions of this Convention, the Standing Committee shall draw up its own Rules of Procedure.

Article 21. Functions of the Standing Committee. The Standing Committee shall be responsible for following the application of this Convention. It may:

a. make recommendations to the Parties concerning the application of the Convention;

b. suggest any necessary modifications of the Convention and examine those proposed in accordance with the provisions of Article 23;

c. examine, at the request of one or more Parties, questions concerning the interpretation of the Convention;

d. use its best endeavours to secure a friendly settlement of any difficulty referred to it in accordance with the provision of Article 25;

e. make recommendations to the Committee of Ministers concerning States other than those referred to in Article 29, paragraph 1, to be invited to accede to this Convention.

Article 22. Reports of the Standing Committee. After each meeting, the Standing Committee shall forward to the Parties and the Committee of Ministers of the Council of Europe a report on its discussions and any decisions taken.

Chapter VII—Amendments

Article 23. Amendments. 1. Any Party may propose amendments to this Convention.

2. Any proposal for amendment shall be notified to the Secretary General of the Council of Europe who shall communicate it to the member States of the Council of Europe, to the other States party to the European Cultural Convention, to the European Economic Community and to any non-member State which has acceded to, or has been invited to accede to this Convention in accordance with the provisions of Article 30. The Secretary General of the Council of Europe shall convene a meeting of the Standing Committee at the earliest two months following the communication of the proposal.

3. The Standing Committee shall examine any amendment proposed and shall submit the text adopted by a majority of three-quarters of the members of the Standing Committee to the Committee of Ministers for approval. After its approval, the text shall be forwarded to the Parties for acceptance.

4. Any amendment shall enter into force on the thirtieth day after all the Parties have informed the Secretary General of their acceptance thereof.

Chapter VIII—Alleged Violations of this Convention

Article 24. Alleged Violations of this Convention. 1. When a Party finds a violation of this Convention, it shall communicate to the transmitting Party the alleged violation and the two Parties shall endeavour to overcome the difficulty on the basis of the provisions of Articles 19, 25 and 26.

2. If the alleged violation is of a manifest, serious and grave nature which raises important public issues and concerns Articles 7, paragraphs 1 or 2, 12, 13, paragraph 1, first sentence, 14 or 15, paragraphs 1 or 3, and if it persists within two weeks following the communication, the receiving Party may suspend provisionally the retransmission of the incriminated programme service.

3. In all other cases of alleged violation, with the exception of those provided for in paragraph 4, the receiving Party may suspend provisionally the retransmission of the incriminated programme service eight months following the communication, if the alleged violation persists.

4. The provisional suspension of retransmission shall not be allowed in the case of alleged violations of Articles 7, paragraph 3, 8, 9 or 10.

Chapter IX—Settlement of Disputes

Article 25. Conciliation. 1. In case of difficulty arising from the application of this Convention, the parties concerned shall endeavour to achieve a friendly settlement.

2. Unless one of the parties concerned objects, the Standing Committee may examine the question, by placing itself at the disposal of the parties concerned in order to reach a satisfactory solution as rapidly as possible and, where appropriate, to formulate an advisory opinion on the subject.

3. Each party concerned undertakes to accord the Standing Committee without delay all information and facilities necessary for the discharge of its functions under the preceding paragraph.

Article 26. Arbitration. 1. If the parties concerned cannot settle the dispute in accordance with the provisions of Article 25, they may, by common agreement, submit it to arbitration, the procedure of which is provided for in the appendix to this Convention. In the absence of such an agreement within six months following the first request to open the procedure of conciliation, the dispute may be submitted to arbitration at the request of one of the parties.

2. Any Party may, at any time, declare that it recognizes as compulsory *ipso facto* and without special agreement in respect of any other Party accepting the same obligation the application of the arbitration procedure provided for in the appendix to this Convention.

Chapter X—Other International Agreements and the Internal Law of the Parties

Article 27. Other International Agreements or Arrangements. 1. In their mutual relations, Parties which are members of the European Economic Community shall apply Community rules and shall not therefore apply the rules arising from this Convention except in so far as there is no Community rule governing the particular subject concerned.

2. Nothing in this Convention shall prevent the Parties from concluding international agreements completing or developing its provisions or extending their field of application.

3. In the case of bilateral agreements, this Convention shall not alter the rights and obligations of Parties which arise from such agreements and which do not affect the enjoyment of other Parties of their rights or the performance of their obligations under this Convention.

Article 28. Relations between the Convention and the Internal Law of the Parties. Nothing in this Convention shall prevent the Parties from applying stricter or more detailed rules than those provided for in this Convention to programme services transmitted by entities or by technical means within their jurisdiction, within the meaning of Article 3.

Chapter XI—Final Provisions

Article 29. Signature and Entry into Force. 1. This Convention shall be open for signature by the member States of the Council of Europe and the other States party to the European Cultural Convention, and by the European Economic Community. It is subject to ratification, acceptance or approval. Instruments of ratification, acceptance or approval shall be deposited with the Secretary General of the Council of Europe.

2. This Convention shall enter into force on the first day of the month following the expiration of a period of three months after the date on which seven States, of which at least five member States of the Council of Europe, have expressed their consent to be bound by the Convention in accordance with the provisions of the preceding paragraph.

3. A State may, at the time of signature or at any later date prior to the entry into force of this Convention in respect of that State, declare that it shall apply the Convention provisionally.

4. In respect of any State referred to in paragraph 1, or the European Economic Community, which subsequently express their consent to be bound by it, this Convention shall enter into force on the first day of the month follow-

ing the expiration of a period of three months after the date of deposit of the instrument of ratification, acceptance or approval.

Article 30. Accession by Non-member States. 1. After the entry into force of this Convention, the Committee of Ministers of the Council of Europe, after consulting the Contracting States may invite any other State to accede to this Convention by a decision taken by the majority provided for in Article 20.*d* of the Statute of the Council of Europe and by the unanimous vote of the representatives of the Contracting States entitled to sit on the Committee.

2. In respect of any acceding State, this Convention shall enter into force on the first day of the month following the expiration of a period of three months after the date of deposit of the instrument of accession with the Secretary General of the Council of Europe.

Article 31. Territorial Application. 1. Any State may, at the time of signature or when depositing its instrument of ratification, acceptance, approval or accession, specify the territory or territories to which this Convention shall apply.

2. Any State may, at any later date, by a declaration addressed to the Secretary General of the Council of Europe, extend the application of this Convention to any other territory specified in the declaration. In respect of such territory, the Convention shall enter into force on the first day of the month following the expiration of a period of three months after the date of receipt of such declaration by the Secretary General.

3. Any declaration made under the two preceding paragraphs may, in respect of any territory specified in such declaration, be withdrawn by a notification addressed to the Secretary General. The withdrawal shall become effective on the first day of the month following the expiration of a period of six months after the date of receipt of such notification by the Secretary General.

Article 32. Reservations. 1. At the time of signature or when depositing its instrument of ratification, acceptance, approval or accession:

a. any State may declare that it reserves the right to restrict the retransmission on its territory, solely to the extent that it does not comply with its domestic legislation, of programme services containing advertisements for alcoholic beverages according to the rules provided for in Article 15, paragraph 2, of this Convention;

b. the United Kingdom may declare that it reserves the right not to fulfil the obligation, set out in Article 15, paragraph 1, to prohibit advertisements for tobacco products, in respect of advertisements for cigars and pipe tobacco broadcast by the Independent Broadcasting Authority by terrestrial means on its territory.

No other reservation may be made.

2. A reservation made in accordance with the preceding paragraph may not be the subject of an objection.

3. Any Contracting State which has made a reservation under paragraph 1 may wholly or partly withdraw it by means of a notification addressed to the Secretary General of the Council of Europe. The withdrawal shall take effect on the date of receipt of such notification by the Secretary General.

4. A Party which has made a reservation in respect of a provision of this Convention may not claim the application of that provision by any other Party; it may, however, if its reservation is partial or conditional, claim the application of that provision in so far as it has itself accepted it.

Article 33. Denunciation. 1. Any Party may, at any time, de-nounce this Convention by means of a notification addressed to the Secretary General of the Council of Europe.

2. Such denunciation shall become effective on the first day of the month following the expiration of a period of six months after the date of receipt of the notification by the Secretary General.

Article 34. Notifications. The Secretary General of the Council of Europe shall notify the member States of the Council, the other States party to the European Cultural Convention, the European Economic Community and any State which has acceded to, or has been invited to accede to this Convention of:

a. any signature;

b. the deposit of any instrument of ratification, acceptance, approval or accession;

c. any date of entry into force of this Convention in accordance with the provisions of Articles 29, 30 and 31;

d. any report established in accordance with the provisions of Article 22;

e. any other act, declaration, notification or communication relating to this Convention.

In witness whereof the undersigned, being duly authorised thereto, have signed this Convention.

Done at ...., the ...., in English and French, both texts being equally authentic, in a single copy which shall be deposited in the archives of the Council of Europe. The Secretary General of the Council of Europe shall transmit certified copies to each member State of the Council of Europe, to the other States party to the European Cultural Convention, to the European Economic Community and to any State invited to accede to this Convention.

Appendix

Arbitration. 1. A request for arbitration shall be notified to the Secretary General of the Council of Europe. It shall include the name of the other party to the dispute and the subject matter of the dispute. The Secretary General shall communicate the information so received to all the Parties to this Convention.

2. In the event of a dispute between two Parties one of which is a member State of the European Economic Community, the latter itself being a Party, the request for arbitration shall be addressed both to the member State and to the Community, which jointly shall notify the Secretary General, within one month of receipt of the request, whether the member State or the Community, or the member State and the Community jointly, shall be party to the dispute. In the absence of such notification within the said time-limit, the member State and the Community shall be considered as being one and the same party to the dispute for the purposes of the application of the provisions governing the constitution and procedure of the arbitration tribunal. The same shall apply when the member State and the Community jointly present themselves as party to the dispute. In cases envisaged by this paragraph, the time-limit of one month foreseen in the first sentence of paragraph 4 hereafter shall be extended to two months.

3. The arbitration tribunal shall consist of three members: each of the parties to the dispute shall appoint one arbitrator; the two arbitrators so appointed shall designate by common agreement the third arbitrator who shall be the chairman of the tribunal. The latter shall not be a national of either of the parties to the dispute, nor have his usual place of residence in the territory of either of those parties,

nor be employed by either of them, nor have dealt with the case in another capacity.

4. If one of the parties has not appointed an arbitrator within one month following the communication of the request by the Secretary General of the Council of Europe, he shall be appointed at the request of the other party by the President of the European Court of Human Rights within a further one-month period. If the President of the Court is unable to act or is a national of one of the parties to the dispute, the appointment shall be made by the Vice-President of the Court or by the most senior judge to the Court who is available and is not a national of one of the parties to the dispute. The same procedure shall be observed if, within a period of one month following the appointment of the second arbitrator, the Chairman of the arbitration tribunal is not designated.

5. The provisions of paragraphs 3 and 4 shall apply, as the case may be, in order to fill any vacancy.

6. Two or more parties which determine by agreement that they are in the same interest shall appoint an arbitrator jointly.

7. The parties to the dispute and the Standing Committee shall provide the arbitration tribunal with all facilities necessary for the effective conduct of the proceedings.

8. The arbitration tribunal shall draw up its own Rules of Procedure. Its decisions shall be taken by majority vote of its members. Its award shall be final and binding.

9. The award of the arbitration tribunal shall be notified to the Secretary General of the Council of Europe who shall communicate it to all the Parties to this Convention.

10. Each party to the dispute shall bear the expenses of the arbitrator appointed by it; these parties shall share equally the expenses of the other arbitrator, as well as other costs entailed by the arbitration.

SEE ALSO European Declaration on Mass Communication Media and Human Rights; Principles Governing the Use by States of Artificial Earth Satellites for International Direct Television Broadcasting; UNESCO Declaration of Guiding Principles on the Use of Satellite Broadcasting for the Free Flow of Information, the Spread of Education and Greater Cultural Exchange.

EUROPEAN COURT OF HUMAN RIGHTS.

The Court of Human Rights of the COUNCIL OF EUROPE was established in accordance with article 19 of the EUROPEAN CONVENTION ON HUMAN RIGHTS in order to ensure observance of the engagements undertaken by States parties to that convention, and the court has jurisdiction in all cases concerning its interpretation and application.

Any State party may, at any time, declare that it recognizes as compulsory *ipso facto* and without special agreement the jurisdiction of the court in all matters concerning the interpretation and application of the convention (article 46). The court may deal with a case only after the EUROPEAN COMMISSION ON HUMAN RIGHTS has acknowledged the failure of its efforts for a friendly settlement and within a period of three months from the date of transmission of the commission's report to the Council of Ministers (article 47). A case may be brought before the court by (a) the

commission, (b) a party whose national is alleged to be a victim, (c) the party which referred the case to the commission, or (d) a party against which the complaint has been lodged (article 48). If the court finds that a decision or measure taken by a legal authority or any other authority of a party is completely or partially in conflict with the obligations arising from the convention, and if the international law of the said party allows only partial reparation to be made for the consequences of this decision or measure, the decision of the court shall, if necessary, afford just satisfaction to the injured party (article 50). Judgments of the court are final, and all parties undertake to abide by them. The judgments are transmitted to the COMMITTEE OF MINISTERS OF THE COUNCIL OF EUROPE, which is authorized to supervise their execution.

In accordance with article 38 of the convention, the court consists of 21 members, that being the number of members States of the Council of Europe, all of which are parties to the convention. Members are elected by the Consultative Assembly of the Council of Europe on the basis of nominations submitted by the members of the Council of Europe. Under article 39 (3), candidates "shall be of high moral character and must either possess the qualifications required for appointment to high judicial office or be juriconsults of recognized competence." They serve for a term of nine years.

The court schedules its sessions as required. All are held in Strasbourg.

For the consideration of each case brought before it, the court consists of a chamber composed of seven judges. The judge who is a national of any State party concerned sits as an *ex officio* member of the chamber or, if there is none, a person of its choice sits in the capacity as judge. Names of the other judges are chosen by lot by the president before the opening of a case.

EUROPEAN DECLARATION ON FREEDOM OF EXPRESSION AND INFORMATION (1982).

The declaration draws attention to the fact that freedom of expression and information, as proclaimed in article 19 of the UNIVERSAL DECLARATION OF HUMAN RIGHTS and in article 10 of the EUROPEAN CONVENTION ON HUMAN RIGHTS, is a basic element of a democratic and pluralist society. It establishes goals for States to aim at with a view to ensuring the full enjoyment of this fundamental freedom and indicates the willingness of European Sates to endeavor to achieve those goals.

The declaration was adopted by the COMMITTEE OF AMINISTERS OF THE COUNCIL OF EUROPE, convened at Strasbourg, on 29 April 1982. The text of the Declaration (Council of Europe Press Release C[82] 22) is as follows:

The member States of the Council of Europe,

1. Considering that the principles of genuine democracy, the rule of law and respect for human rights form the basis of their co-operation, and that the freedom of expression and information is a fundamental element of those principles;

2. Considering that this freedom has been proclaimed in national constitutions and international instruments, and in particular in Article 19 of the Universal Declaration of Human Rights and Article 10 of the European Convention on Human Rights;

3. Recalling that through that Convention they have taken steps for the collective enforcement of the freedom of expression and information by entrusting the supervision of its application to the organs provided for by the Convention;

4. Considering that the freedom of expression and information is necessary for the social, economic, cultural and political development of every human being, and constitutes a condition for the harmonious progress of social and cultural groups, nations and the international community;

5. Convinced that the continued development of information and communication technology should serve to further the right, regardless of frontiers, to express, to seek, to receive and to impart information and ideas, whatever their source;

6. Convinced that States have the duty to guard against infringements of the freedom of expression and information and should adopt policies designed to foster as much as possible a variety of media and a plurality of information sources, thereby allowing a plurality of ideas and opinions;

7. Noting that, in addition to the statutory measures referred to in the second paragraph of Article 10 of the European Convention on Human Rights, codes of ethics have been voluntarily established and are applied by professional organisations in the field of the mass media;

8. Aware that a free flow and wide circulation of information of all kinds across frontiers is an important factor for international understanding, for bringing peoples together and for the mutual enrichment of cultures,

I. Reiterate their firm attachment to the principles of freedom of expression and information as a basic element of democratic and pluralist society;

II. Declare that in the field of information and mass media they seek to achieve the following objectives:

(a) protection of the right of everyone, regardless of frontiers, to express himself, to seek and receive information and ideas, whatever their source, as well as to impart them under the conditions set out in Article 10 of the European Convention on Human Rights;

(b) absence of censorship or any arbitrary controls or constraints on participants in the information process, on media content or on the transmission and dissemination of information;

(c) the pursuit of an open information policy in the public sector, including access to information, in order to enhance the individual's understanding of, and his ability to discuss freely political, social, economic and cultural matters;

(d) the existence of a wide variety of independent and autonomous media, permitting the reflection of diversity of ideas and opinions;

(e) the availability and access on reasonable terms to adequate facilities for the domestic and international transmission and dissemination of information and ideas;

(f) the promotion of international co-operation and assistance, through public and private channels, with a view to fostering the free flow of information and improving communication infrastructures and expertise;

III. Resolve to intensify their co-operation in order:

(a) to defend the right of everyone to the exercise of the freedom of expression and information;

(b) to promote, through teaching and education, the effective exercise of the freedom of expression and information;

(c) to promote the free flow of information, thus contributing to international understanding, a better knowledge of convictions and traditions, respect for the diversity of opinions and the mutual enrichment of cultures;

(d) to share their experience and knowledge in the media field;

(e) to ensure that new information and communication techniques and services, where available, are effectively used to broaden the scope of freedom of expression and information.

SEE ALSO Freedom of Information; Freedom of Information: The Concept; Information and Communication; Opinion and Expression.

EUROPEAN DECLARATION ON MASS COMMUNICATION MEDIA AND HUMAN RIGHTS (1970).

The declaration defines the meaning of the right to freedom of expression when applied to mass communication media and sets out principles to be observed by those media. It calls for freedom of the press to seek, receive, impart, publish, and distribute information and ideas; for independence of the press from control by the State; and for no direct or indirect censorship of the media. At the same time, it indicates ways and means by which the press and other mass media may discharge their functions with a sense of responsibility and ways and means to protect the individual against interference with his right to privacy.

The declaration was adopted (resolution 428 [1970]) by the CONSTITUENT ASSEMBLY OF THE COUNCIL OF EUROPE, convened at Strasbourg, on 23 January 1970. The text is as follows:

A. Status and Independence of the Press and the Other Mass Media

1. The press and the other mass media, though generally not public institutions, perform an essential function for the general public. In order to enable them to discharge that function in the public interest, the following principles should be observed.

2. The right to freedom of expression shall apply to mass communication media.

3. This right shall include freedom to seek, receive, impart, publish and distribute information and ideas. There shall be a corresponding duty for the public authorities to make available information on matters of public interest within reasonable limits and a duty for mass communication media to give complete and general information on public affairs.

4. The independence of the press and other mass media

from control by the state should be established by law. Any infringement of this independence should be justifiable by courts and not be executive authorities.

5. There shall be no direct or indirect censorship of the press, or of the contents of radio and television programmes, or of news or information conveyed by other media such as news reels shown in cinemas. Restrictions may be imposed within the limits authorized by Article 10 of the European Convention on Human Rights. There shall be no control by the state of the contents of radio and television programmes, except on the grounds set out in paragraph 2 of that Article.

6. The internal organisation of mass media should guarantee the freedom of expression of the responsible editors. Their editorial independence should be preserved.

7. The independence of mass media should be protected against the dangers of monopolies. The effects of concentration in the press, and possible measures of economic assistance require further consideration.

8. Neither individual enterprises, nor financial groups should have the right to institute a monopoly in the fields of press, radio or television, nor should government-controlled monopoly be permitted. Individuals, social groups, regional or local authorities should have—as far as they comply with the established licensing provisions—the right to engage in these activities.

9. Special measures are necessary to ensure the freedom of foreign correspondents, including the staff of international press agencies, in order to permit the public to receive accurate information from abroad. These measures should cover the status, duties and privileges of foreign correspondents and should include protection from arbitrary expulsion. They impose a corresponding duty of accurate reporting.

B. Measures to Secure Responsibility of the Press and Other Mass Media

It is the duty of the press and other mass media to discharge their functions with a sense of responsibility towards the community and towards the individual citizens. For this purpose, it is desirable to institute (where not already done):

(a) Professional training for journalists under the responsibility of editors and journalists;

(b) A professional code of ethics for journalists; this should cover *inter alia* such matters as accurate and well balanced reporting, rectification of inaccurate information, clear distinction between reported information and comments, avoidance of calumny, respect for privacy, respect for the right to a fair trial as guaranteed by Article 6 of the European Convention on Human Rights;

(c) Press councils empowered to investigate and even to censure instances of unprofessional conduct with a view to the exercising of self-control by the press itself.

C. Measures to Protect the Individual Against Interference with his Right to Privacy

1. There is an area in which the exercise of the right of freedom of information and freedom of expression may conflict with the right to privacy protected by Article 8 of the Convention on Human Rights. The exercise of the former right must not be allowed to destroy the existence of the latter.

2. The right to privacy consists essentially in the right to live one's own life with a minimum of interference. It concerns private, family and home life, physical and moral integrity, honour and reputation, avoidance of being placed in a false light, non-relevation of irrelevant and embarrassing facts, unauthorized publication of private photographs, protection against misuse of private communications, protection from disclosure of information given or received by the individual confidentially. Those who, by their own actions, have encouraged indiscreet revelations about which they complain later on, cannot avail themselves of the right to privacy.

3. A particular problem arises as regards the privacy of persons in public life. The phrase "where public life begins, private life ends" is inadequate to cover this situation. The private lives of public figures are entitled to protection, save where they may have an impact upon public events. The fact that an individual figures in the news does not deprive him of a right to a private life.

4. Another particular problem arises from attempts to obtain information by modern technical devices (wiretapping, hidden microphones, the use of computers, etc.), which infringe the right to privacy. Further consideration of this problem is required.

5. Where regional, national or international computer-data banks are instituted the individual must not become completely exposed and transparent by the accumulation of information referring even to his private life. Data banks should be restricted to the necessary minimum of information required for the purposes of taxation, pension schemes, social security schemes and similar matters.

6. In order to counter these dangers, national law should provide a right of action enforceable at law against persons responsible for such infringements of the right to privacy.

7. The right to privacy afforded by Article 8 of the Convention on Human rights should not only protect an individual against interference by public authorities, but also against interference by private persons or institutions, including the mass media. National legislations should comprise provisions guaranteeing this protection.

SEE ALSO Convention on the International Right of Correction; UNESCO Declaration on Fundamental Principles concerning the Contribution of the Mass Media to Strengthening Peace and International Understanding . . . .

EUROPEAN HUMAN RIGHTS PRIZE. On the basis of proposals submitted by the Parliamentary Assembly of the Council of Europe, the Committee of Ministers of the Council awarded the European Human Rights Prize for 1989 jointly to Mr. Lech Walesa (Poland) and the **INTERNATIONAL HELSINKI FEDERATION OF HUMAN RIGHTS** (Vienna). The two prize winners were considered by the committee to have served the cause of human rights in an outstanding manner in conformity with the principles of individual liberty, political freedom, and the preeminence of law, which form the basis of a truly democratic society and which are guaranteed in particular by the **EUROPEAN CONVENTION ON HUMAN RIGHTS.**

**EUROPEAN RECOMMENDATION CONCERN-
ING INTERNATIONAL COOPERATION IN THE
PROSECUTION AND PUNISHMENT OF TER-
RORISM (1982).** The recommendation, directed to
all States members of the COUNCIL OF EUROPE, purposes measures to improve cooperation between
those States when acts of terrorism occur, including
measures for expediting exchanges of information
concerning suspects and measures for the prosecution of international offenders by a single competent
State best suited for conducting such proceedings.
The recommendation was adopted by the COMMITTEE
OF MINISTERS OF THE COUNCIL OF EUROPE at the 342d
meeting of the Ministers' Deputies, convened at
Strasbourg, on 15 January 1982. The text is as follows:

The committee of Ministers, under the terms of Article
15 (b) of the Statute of the Council of Europe.
Considering that the aim of the Council of Europe is to
achieve greater unity among its members;
Concerned at the increased number of acts of terrorism
committed in certain member States;
Considering the prevention and suppression of such acts
to be indispensable to the maintenance of the democratic
institutions of member States;
Having regard to Council of Europe initiatives in the
past aimed at the suppression of terrorism, which represent
important contributions to the fight against this threat to
society;
Convinced that it is necessary to develop further and to
strengthen international co-operation in this field;
Desirous of rendering existing procedures of international judicial co-operation simpler and more expeditious,
of improving the exchange of information between the
competent authorities of member States, particularly between those with a common border, and of facilitating the
prosecution and punishment of acts of terrorism;
Having regard to existing co-operation and channels of
communications between the police forces of member
States;
Recalling the Declaration on Terrorism adopted by the
Committee of Ministers on 23 November 1978;
Emphasising that any measure of international co-
operation must be fully compatible with the protection of
human rights and particularly with the principles contained in the Convention for the Protection of Human
Rights and Fundamental Freedoms signed in Rome on
4 November 1950,
Recommends the Governments of member States to give
effect, by the most appropriate means, to the following
measures aimed at improving international co-operation in
the prosecution and punishment of acts of terrorism
directed against the life, physical integrity or liberty of persons, or against property where they create a collective danger for persons, including, in accordance with domestic
law, attempts of or threats of or participation as an accomplice in these acts (referred to as "acts of terrorism" in the
present recommendation).

I. Channels of Communication for Mutual Judicial
Assistance in Criminal Matters

1. Direct communication between the authorities concerned in the requesting and requested State, of requests

for judicial assistance and the replies thereto should be encouraged in all cases where it is permitted by the law of
these States or by any treaty to which these States are Party,
if it is likely to render mutual judicial assistance more
expeditious.
2. Where direct transmission is permitted, cases involving acts of terrorism should be treated with urgency according to the procedure provided by Article 15 (2) of the
European Convention on Mutual Assistance in Criminal
Matters or by other treaties in force between member States
or by the law of these States, so that letters rogatory may be
addressed by the authority concerned in the requesting
State, it being understood that the requested State may require a copy to be sent to its Ministry of Justice or other
competent ministry.
3. Where requests for assistance and the replies thereto
may be communicated directly between the authorities
concerned in the requesting and the requested State, their
transmission should be effected as rapidly as possible, either through Interpol National Central Bureau, insofar as
this is not contrary to Interpol's Constitution, or by other
existing ways of transmission.
4. Where communication is effected between Ministries
of Justice or other competent ministries, the authority concerned in the requesting State should be allowed directly to
provide the authority concerned in the requested State
with an advance copy of the request. The authority concerned in the requested State should be advised that the
sole purpose of transmitting the copy is to enable it to prepare for the execution of the request.

II. Exchange of Information

5. Exchanges of information between member States
should be improved and reinforced. To that end, the competent authorities should, insofar as this is not contrary to
domestic law, be enabled to furnish, of their own accord, information in their possession on such matters as:
i. measures concerning the prosecution of the alleged
offender (e.g. arrest, indictment)
ii. the outcome of any judicial or administrative
proceedings (e.g. conviction, decision on extradition)
iii. the enforcement of any sentence (including pardon, conditional release)
iv. other relevant information relating to the whereabouts of the person concerned (e.g. expulsion, escape,
execution of an extradition decision)
to the authorities of any member State concerned, as for instance, the State where the act of terrorism was committed,
the State which has jurisdiction over the offence, the State
of which the offender is a national, the State where the offender has his habitual residence, or any other State likely
to have an interest in the particular element of information.
6. The exchange of this information should be effected
with all necessary expediency either through Interpol National Central Bureaux, insofar as this is not contrary to
Interpol's Constitution, or by other existing ways of transmission.

III. Prosecution and Trial of Offences of an
International Character

7. Where one or several acts of terrorism have been committed in the territory of two or several member States and
there is a link between those acts or their authors, the member States concerned should examine the possibility of

having the prosecution and the trial conducted in only one State. To that end, the States concerned should agree on the competent State, in accordance with existing international treaties and their internal law. The same should apply, if possible, where one or several acts of terrorism of an international character have been committed in the territory of a single State by several persons acting in unison who have been apprehended in various States. In negotiating such agreements on the competent State, the States concerned should, with a view to ensuring that prosecution and trial take place in the State best suited for conducting the proceedings, take into account the number of offences committed in each State, the seriousness of the offences, the availability of evidence, the personal circumstances of the alleged offender, in particular his nationality and residence, and the prospects of rehabilitation.

SEE ALSO European Convention on the Suppression of Terrorism.

EUROPEAN SOCIAL CHARTER (1961). The charter sets out measures to ensure the enjoyment of a number of economic and social rights without discrimination on grounds such as race, color, sex, religion, political opinion, national extraction, or social origin in States members of the **COUNCIL OF EUROPE.** It is, in effect, a counterpart to the **EUROPEAN CONVENTION ON HUMAN RIGHTS** but does not provide for comparable international machinery of implementation.

Under the charter, States parties undertake to ensure the effective exercise of the enumerated economic and social rights and to report to the council on the results of their endeavors. The reports are examined first by a committee of experts, then by a subcommittee of the Governmental Social Committee of the council, and, finally, by the council's Consultative Assembly. Eventually, the **COMMITTEE OF MINISTERS OF THE COUNCIL OF EUROPE,** after consultation with the Consultative Assembly, may make recommendations to the contracting parties.

An appendix, which forms an integral part of the charter (article 38), defines the scope of its provisions in terms of the persons protected.

The charter was concluded by the States members of the Council of Europe, convened in Turin, on 18 October 1961 and entered into force on 26 February 1965. Its text (*European Treaty Series* 35) is as follows:

The governments signatory hereto, being Members of the Council of Europe,

Considering that the aim of the Council of Europe is the achievement of greater unity between its Members for the purpose of safeguarding and realising the ideals and principles which are their common heritage and of facilitating their economic and social progress, in particular by the maintenance and further realisation of human rights and fundamental freedoms;

Considering that in the European Convention for the Protection of Human Rights and Fundamental Freedoms signed at Rome on 4 November 1950, and the Protocol thereto signed at Paris on 20 March 1952, the member States of the Council of Europe agreed to secure to their populations the civil and political rights and freedoms therein specified;

Considering that the enjoyment of social rights should be secured without discrimination on grounds of race, colour, sex, religion, political opinion, national extraction or social origin;

Being resolved to make every effort in common to improve the standard of living and to promote the social well-being of both their urban and rural populations by means of appropriate institutions and action,

Have agreed as follows:

Part I

The Contracting Parties accept as the aim of their policy, to be pursued by all appropriate means, both national and international in character, the attainment of conditions in which the following rights and principles may be effectively realised:

1. Everyone shall have the opportunity to earn his living in an occupation freely entered upon.

2. All workers have the right to just conditions of work.

3. All workers have the right to safe and healthy working conditions.

4. All workers have the right to a fair remuneration sufficient for a decent standard of living for themselves and their families.

5. All workers and employers have the right to freedom of association in national or international organisations for the protection of their economic and social interests.

6. All workers and employers have the right to bargain collectively.

7. Children and young persons have the right to a special protection against the physical and moral hazards to which they are exposed.

8. Employed women, in case of maternity, and other employed women as appropriate, have the right to a special protection in their work.

9. Everyone has the right to appropriate facilities for vocational guidance with a view to helping him choose an occupation suited to his personal aptitude and interests.

10. Everyone has the right to appropriate facilities for vocational training.

11. Everyone has the right to benefit from any measures enabling him to enjoy the highest possible standard of health attainable.

12. All workers and their dependents have the right to social security.

13. Anyone without adequate resources has the right to social and medical assistance.

14. Everyone has the right to benefit from social welfare services.

15. Disabled persons have the right to vocational training, rehabilitation and resettlement, whatever the origin and nature of their disability.

16. The family as a fundamental unit of society has the right to appropriate social, legal and economic protection to ensure its full development.

17. Mothers and children, irrespective of marital status and family relations, have the right to appropriate social and economic protection.

18. The nationals of any one of the Contracting Parties have the right to engage in any gainful occupation in the territory of any one of the others on a footing of equality with the nationals of the latter, subject to restrictions based on cogent economic or social reasons.

19. Migrant workers who are nationals of a Contracting Party and their families have the right to protection and assistance in the territory of any other Contracting Party.

Part II

The Contracting Parties undertake, as provided for in Part III, to consider themselves bound by the obligations laid down in the following articles and paragraphs.

Article 1. The Right to Work. With a view to ensuring the effective exercise of the right to work, the Contracting Parties undertake:

1. to accept as one of their primary aims and responsibilities the achievement and maintenance of as high and stable a level of employment as possible, with a view to the attainment of full employment;

2. to protect effectively the right of the worker to earn his living in an occupation freely entered upon;

3. to establish or maintain free employment services for all workers;

4. to provide or promote appropriate vocational guidance, training and rehabilitation.

Article 2. The Right to Just Conditions of Work. With a view to ensuring the effective exercise of the right to just conditions of work, the Contracting Parties undertake:

1. to provide for reasonable daily and weekly working hours, the working week to be progressively reduced to the extent that the increase of productivity and other relevant factors permit;

2. to provide for public holidays with pay;

3. to provide for a minimum of two weeks annual holiday with pay;

4. to provide for additional paid holidays or reduced working hours for workers engaged in dangerous or unhealthy occupations as prescribed;

5. to ensure a weekly rest period which shall, as far as possible, coincide with the day recognised by tradition or custom in the country or region concerned as a day of rest.

Article 3. The Right to Safe and Healthy Working Conditions. With a view to ensuring the effective exercise of the right to safe and healthy working conditions, the Contracting Parties undertake:

1. to issue safety and health regulations;

2. to provide for the enforcement of such regulations by measures of supervision;

3. to consult, as appropriate, employers' and working' organisations on measures intended to improve industrial safety and health.

Article 4. The Right to a Fair Remuneration. With a view to ensuring the effective exercise of the right to a fair remuneration, the Contracting Parties undertake:

1. to recognise the right of workers to a remuneration such as will give them and their families a decent standard of living;

2. to recognise the right of workers to an increased rate of remuneration for overtime work, subject to exceptions in particular cases;

3. to recognise the right of men and women workers to equal pay for work of equal value;

4. to recognise the right of all workers to a reasonable period of notice for termination of employment;

5. To permit deductions from wages only under conditions and to the extent prescribed by national laws or regulations or fixed by collective agreements or arbitration awards.

The exercise of these rights shall be achieved by freely concluded collective agreements, by statutory wage-fixing machinery, or by other means appropriate to national conditions.

Article 5. The Right to Organise. With a view to ensuring or promoting the freedom of workers and employers to form local or international organisations for the protection of their economic and social interests and to join those organisations, the Contracting Parties undertake that national law shall not be such as to impair, nor shall it be so applied as to impair, this freedom. The extent to which the guarantees provided for in this Article shall apply to the police shall be determined by national laws or regulations. The principle governing the application to the members of the armed forces of these guarantees and the extent to which they shall apply to persons in this category shall equally be determined by national laws or regulations.

Article 6. The Right to Bargain Collectively. With a view to ensuring the effective exercise of the right to bargain collectively, the Contracting Parties undertake:

1. to promote joint consultation between workers and employers;

2. to promote, where necessary and appropriate, machinery for voluntary negotiations between employers or employers' organisations and workers' organisations, with a view to the regulation of terms and conditions of employment by means of collective agreements;

3. to promote the establishment and use of appropriate machinery for conciliation and voluntary arbitration for the settlement of labour disputes;
and recognise:

4. the right of workers and employers to collective action in cases of conflicts of interest, including the right to strike, subject to obligations that might arise out of collective agreements previously entered into.

Article 7. The Right of Children and Young Persons to Protection. With a view to ensuring the effective exercise of the rights of children and young persons to protection, the Contracting Parties undertake:

1. to provide that the minimum age of admission to employment shall be 15 years, subject to exceptions for children employed in prescribed light work without harm to their health, morals or education;

2. to provide that a higher minimum age of admission to employment shall be fixed with respect to prescribed occupations regarded as dangerous or unhealthy;

3. to provide that persons who are still subject to compulsory education shall not be employed in such work as would deprive them of the full benefit of their education;

4. to provide that the working hours of persons under 16 years of age shall be limited in accordance with the needs of their development, and particularly with their need for vocational training;

5. to recognise the right of young workers and apprentices to a fair wage or other appropriate allowances;

6. to provide that the time spent by young persons in vocational training during the normal working hours with the consent of the employer shall be treated as forming part of the working day;

7. to provide that employed persons of under 18 years of age shall be entitled to not less than three weeks' annual holiday with pay;

8. to provide that persons under 18 years of age shall not be employed in night work with the exception of certain occupations provided for by national laws or regulations;

9. to provide that persons under 18 years of age employed in occupations prescribed by national laws or regulations shall be subject to regular medical control;

10. to ensure special protection against physical and moral dangers to which children and young persons are exposed, and particularly against those resulting directly or indirectly from their work.

Article 8. The Right of Employed Women to Protection. With a view to ensuring the effective exercise of the right of employed women to protection, the Contracting Parties undertake:

1. to provide either by paid leave, by adequate social security benefits or by benefits from public funds for women to take leave before and after childbirth up to a total of at least 12 weeks;

2. to consider it as unlawful for an employer to give a woman notice of dismissal during her absence on maternity leave or to give her notice of dismissal at such a time that the notice would expire during such absence;

3. to provide that mothers who are nursing their infants shall be entitled to sufficient time off for this purpose;

4. (a) to regulate the employment of women workers on night work in industrial employment;

(b) to prohibit the employment of women workers in underground mining, and, as appropriate, on all other work which is unsuitable for them by reason of its dangerous, unhealthy, or arduous nature.

Article 9. The Right to Vocational Guidance. With a view to ensuring the effective exercise of the right to vocational guidance, the Contracting Parties undertake to provide or promote, as necessary, a service which will assist all persons, including the handicapped, to solve problems related to occupational choice and progress, with due regard to the individual's characteristics and their relation to occupational opportunity: this assurance should be available free of charge, both to young persons, including school children, and to adults.

Article 10. The Right to Vocational Training. With a view to ensuring the effective exercise of the right to vocational training, the Contracting Parties undertake:

1. to provide or promote, as necessary, the technical and vocational training of all persons, including the handicapped, in consultation with employers' and workers' organisations, and to grant facilities for access to higher technical and university education, based solely on individual aptitude;

2. to provide or promote a system of apprenticeship and other systematic arrangements for training young boys and girls in their various employments;

3. to provide or promote, as necessary:

(a) adequate and readily available training facilities for adult workers;

(b) special facilities for the re-training of adult workers needed as a result of technological development or new trends in employment;

4. to encourage the full utilisation of the facilities provided by appropriate measures such as:

(a) reducing or abolishing any fees or charges;

(b) granting financial assistance in appropriate cases;

(c) including in the normal working hours time spent on supplementary training taken by the worker, at the request of his employer, during employment;

(d) ensuring, through adequate supervision, in consultation with the employers' and workers' organisations, the efficiency of apprenticeship and other training arrangements for young workers, and the adequate protection of young workers generally.

Article 11. The Right to Protection of Health. With a view to ensuring the effective exercise of the right to protection of health, the Contracting Parties undertake, either directly or in co-operation with public or private organisations, to take appropriate measures designed inter alia:

1. to remove as far as possible the causes of ill-health;

2. to provide advisory and educational facilities for the promotion of health and the encouragement of individual responsibility in matters of health;

3. to prevent as far as possible epidemic, endemic and other diseases.

Article 12. The Right to Social Security. With a view to ensuring the effective exercise of the right to social security, the Contracting Parties undertake:

1. to establish or maintain a system of social security;

2. to maintain the social security system at a satisfactory level at least equal to that required for ratification of International Labour Convention (No. 102) concerning Minimum Standards of Social Security;

3. to endeavour to raise progressively the system of social security to a higher level;

4. to take steps, by the conclusion of appropriate bilateral and multi-lateral agreements, or by other means, and subject to the conditions laid down in such agreements, in order to ensure:

(a) equal treatment with their own nationals of the nationals of other Contracting Parties in respect of social security rights, including the retention of benefits arising out of social security legislation, whatever movements the persons protected may undertake between the territories of the Contracting Parties;

(b) the granting, maintenance and resumption of social security rights by such means as the accumulation of insurance or employment periods completed under the legislation of each of the Contracting Parties.

Article 13. The Right to Social and Medical Assistance. With a view to ensuring the effective exercise of the right to social and medical assistance, the Contracting Parties undertake:

1. to ensure that any person who is without adequate resources and who is unable to secure such resources either by his own efforts or from other sources, in particular by benefits under a social security scheme, by granted adequate assistance, and, in case of sickness, the care necessitated by his condition;

2. to ensure that persons receiving such assistance shall not, for that reason, suffer from a diminution of their political or social rights;

3. to provide that everyone may receive by appropriate public or private services such advice and personal help as may be required to prevent, to remove, or to alleviate personal or family want;

4. to apply the provisions referred to in paragraph 1, 2 and 3 of this article on an equal footing with their nationals to nationals of other Contracting Parties lawfully within their territories, in accordance with their obligations under the European Convention of Social and Medical Assistance, signed at Paris on 11 December 1953.

Article 14. The Right to Benefit from Social Welfare Services. With a view to ensuring the effective exercise of the right to benefit from social welfare services, the Contracting Parties undertake:

1. to promote or provide services which, by using meth-

ods of social work, would contribute to the welfare and development of both individuals and groups in the community, and to their adjustment to the social environment;

2. to encourage the participation of individuals and voluntary or other organisations in the establishment and maintenance of such services.

Article 15. The Right of Physically or Mentally Disabled Persons to Vocational Training, Rehabilitation and Social Resettlement. With a view to ensuring the effective exercise of the right of the physically or mentally disabled to vocational training, rehabilitation and resettlement, the Contracting Parties undertake:

1. to take adequate measures for the provision of training facilities, including, where necessary, specialized institutions, public or private;

2. to take adequate measures for the placing of disabled persons in employment, such as specialised placing services, facilities for sheltered employment and measure to encourage employers to admit disabled persons to employment.

Article 16. The Right of the Family to Social, Legal and Economic Protection. With a view to ensuring the necessary conditions for the full development of the family, which is a fundamental unit of society, the Contracting Parties undertake to promote the economic, legal and social protection of family life by such means as social and family benefits, fiscal arrangements, provision of family housing, benefits for the newly married, and other appropriate means.

Article 17. The Right of Mothers and Children to Social and Economic Protection. With a view to ensuring the effective exercise of the right of mothers and children to social and economic protection, the Contracting Parties will take all appropriate and necessary measures to that end, including the establishment or maintenance of appropriate institutions or services.

Article 18. The Right to Engage in a Gainful Occupation in the Territory of other Contracting Parties. With a view to ensuring the effective exercise of the right to engage in a gainful occupation in the territory of any other Contracting Party, the Contracting Parties undertake:

1. to apply existing regulations in a spirit of liberality;

2. to simplify existing formalities and to reduce or abolish chancery dues and other charges payable by foreign workers or their employers;

3. to liberalise, individually or collectively, regulations governing the employment of foreign workers;
and recognise:

4. the right of their nationals to leave the country to engage in a gainful occupation in the territories of the other Contracting Parties.

Article 19. The Right of Migrant Workers and their Families to Protection and Assistance. With a view to ensuring the effective exercise of the right of migrant workers and their families to protection and assistance in the territory of any other Contracting Party, the Contracting Parties undertake:

1. to maintain or to satisfy themselves that there are maintained adequate and free services to assist such workers, particularly in obtaining accurate information, and to take all appropriate steps, so far as national laws and regulations permit, against misleading propaganda relating to emigration and immigration;

2. to adopt appropriate measures within their own jurisdiction to facilitate the departure, journey and reception of such workers and their families, and to provide, within their own jurisdiction, appropriate services for health,

medical attention and good hygienic conditions during the journey;

3. to promote co-operation, as appropriate, between social services, public and private, in emigration and immigration countries;

4. to secure for such workers lawfully within their territories, insofar as such matters are regulated by law or regulations or are subject to the control of administrative authorities, treatment not less favourable than that of their own nationals in respect of the following matters:

(a) remuneration and other employment and working conditions;

(b) membership of trade unions and enjoyment of the benefits of collective bargaining;

(c) accommodation;

5. to secure for such workers lawfully within their territories treatment not less favourable than that of their own nationals with regard to employment taxes, dues or contributions payable in respect of employed persons;

6. to facilitate as far as possible the reunion of the family of a foreign worker permitted to establish himself in the territory;

7. to secure for such workers lawfully within their territories treatment not less favourable than that of their own nationals in respect of legal proceedings relating to matters referred to in this Article;

8. to secure that such workers lawfully residing within their territories are not expelled unless they endanger national security or offend against public interest or morality;

9. to permit, within legal limits, the transfer of such parts of the earnings and savings of such workers as they may desire;

10. to extend the protection and assistance provided for in this Article to self-employed migrants insofar as such measures apply.

Part III

Article 20. Undertakings. 1. Each of the Contracting Parties undertakes:

(a) to consider Part I of this Charter as a declaration of the aims which it will pursue by all appropriate means, as stated in the introductory paragraph of that Part;

(b) to consider itself bound by at least five of the following Articles of Part II of this Charter: Articles 1, 5, 6, 12, 13, 16 and 19;

(c) in addition to the articles selected by it in accordance with the preceding sub-paragraph, to consider itself bound by such a number of articles or numbered paraygraphs of Part II of the Charter as it may select, provided that the total number of articles or numbered paragraphs by which it is bound is not less than 10 articles or 45 numbered paragraphs.

2. The articles or paragraphs selected in accordance with sub-paragraphs (b) and (c) of paragraph 1 of this article shall be notified to the Secretary General of the Council of Europe at the time when the instrument of ratification or approval of the Contracting Party concerned is deposited.

3. Any Contracting Party may, at a later date, declare by notification to the Secretary General that it considers itself bound by any articles or any numbered paragraphs of Part II of the Charter which it has not already accepted under the terms of paragraph 1 of this article. Such undertakings subsequently given shall be deemed to be an integral part of the ratification or approval, and shall have the

same effect as from the thirtieth day after the date of the notification.

4. The Secretary General shall communicate to all the signatory governments and to the Director-General of the International Labour Office any notification which he shall have received pursuant to this Part of the Charter.

5. Each Contracting Party shall maintain a system of labour inspection appropriate to national conditions.

Part IV

Article 21. Reports concerning Accepted Provisions. The Contracting Parties shall send to the Secretary General of the Council of Europe a report at two-yearly intervals, in a form to be determined by the Committee of Ministers, concerning the application of such provisions of Part II of the Charter as they have accepted.

Article 22. Reports concerning Provisions which are not Accepted. The Contracting Parties shall send to the Secretary General, at appropriate intervals as requested by the Committee of Ministers, reports relating to the provisions of Part II of the Charter which they did not accept at the time of their ratification or approval or in a subsequent notification. The Committee of Ministers shall determine from time to time in respect of which provisions such reports shall be requested and the form of the reports to be provided.

Article 23. Communication of Copies. 1. Each Contracting Party shall communicate copies of its reports referred to in Articles 21 and 22 to such of its national organisations as are members of the international organisations of employers and trade unions to be invited under Article 27, paragraph 2, to be represented at meetings of the Sub-committee of the Governmental Social Committee.

2. The Contracting Parties shall forward to the Secretary General any comments on the said reports received from these national organisations, if so requested by them.

Article 24. Examination of the Reports. The reports sent to the Secretary General in accordance with Articles 21 and 22 shall be examined by a committee of experts, who shall have also before them any comments forwarded to the Secretary General in accordance with paragraph 2 of Article 23.

Article 25. Committee of Experts. 1. The committee of experts shall consist of not more than seven members appointed by the Committee of Ministers from a list of independent experts of the highest integrity and of recognised competence in international social questions, nominated by the Contracting Parties.

2. The members of the committee shall be appointed for a period of six years. They may be reappointed. However, of the members first appointed, the terms of office of two members shall expire at the end of four years.

3. The members whose terms of office are to expire at the end of the initial period of four years shall be chosen by lot by the Committee of Ministers immediately after the first appointment has been made.

4. A member of the committee of experts appointed to replace a member whose term of office has not expired shall hold office for the remainder of his predecessor's term.

Article 26. Participation of the International Labour Organisation. The International Labour Organisation shall be invited to nominate a representative to participate in a consultative capacity in the deliberations of the committee of experts.

Article 27. Sub-committee of the Governmental Social Committee. 1. The reports of the Contracting Parties and the conclusions of the committee of experts shall be submitted for examination to a Sub-committee of the Governmental Social Committee of the Council of Europe.

2. The sub-committee shall be composed of one representative of each of the Contracting Parties. It shall invite no more than two international organisations of employers and no more than two international trade union organisations as it may designate to be represented as observers in a consultative capacity at its meetings. Moreover, it may consult no more than two representatives of international non-governmental organisations having consultative status with the Council of Europe, in respect of questions with which the organisations are particularly qualified to deal, such as social welfare, and the economic and social protection of the family.

3. The sub-committee shall present to the Committee of Ministers a report containing its conclusions and append the report of the committee of experts.

Article 28. Consultative Assembly. The Secretary General of the Council of Europe shall transmit to the Consultative Assembly the conclusions of the committee of experts. The Consultative Assembly shall communicate its views on these conclusions to the Committee of Ministers.

Article 29. Committee of Ministers. By a majority of two thirds of the members entitled to sit on the Committee of Ministers may, on the basis of the report of the sub-committee, and after consultation with the Consultative Assembly, make to each Contracting Party any necessary recommendations.

Part V.

Article 30. Derogations in Time of War or Public Emergency. 1. In time of war or other public emergency threatening the life of the nation any Contracting Party may take measures derogating from its obligations under this Charter to the extent strictly required by the exigencies of the situation, provided that such measures are not inconsistent with its other obligations under international law.

2. Any Contracting Party which had availed itself of this right of derogation shall, within a reasonable lapse of time, keep the Secretary General of the Council of Europe fully informed of the measures taken and of the reasons therefor. It shall likewise inform the Secretary General when such measures have ceased to operate and the provisions of the Charter which it has accepted are again being fully executed.

3. The Secretary General shall in turn inform other Contracting Parties and the Director-General of the International Labour Office of all communications received in accordance with paragraph 2 of this article.

Article 31. Restrictions. 1. The rights and principles set forth in Part I when effectively realised, and their effective exercise as provided for in Part II, shall not be subject to any restrictions or limitations not specified in those Parts, except such as are prescribed by law and are necessary in a democratic society for the protection of the rights and freedoms of others or for the protection of public interest, national security, public health, or morals.

2. The restrictions permitted under this Charter to the rights and obligations set forth herein shall not be applied for any purpose other than that for which they have been prescribed.

Article 32. Relations between the Charter and Domestic Law of International Agreements. The provisions of this Charter shall not prejudice the provisions of domestic law or of any bilateral or multilateral treaties, conventions or agreements which are already in force, or may come into force, under which more favourable treatment would be accorded to the persons protected.

Article 33. Implementation by Collective Agreements. 1. In member States where the provisions of paragraphs 1, 2, 3, 4 and 5 of Article 2, paragraphs 4, 6 and 7 of Article 7 and paragraphs 1, 2, 3 and 4 of Article 10 of Part II of this Charter are matters normally left to agreements between employers or employers' organisations and workers' organisations, or are normally carried out otherwise than by law, the undertakings of those paragraphs may be given and compliance with them shall be treated as effective if their provisions are applied through such agreements or other means to the great majority of the workers concerned.

2. In member States where these provisions are normally the subject of legislation, the undertakings concerned may likewise be given, and compliance with them shall be regarded as effective if the provisions are applied by law to the great majority of the workers concerned.

Article 34. Territorial Application. 1. This Charter shall apply to the metropolitan territory of each Contracting Party. Each signatory government may, at the time of signature or of the deposit of its instrument of ratification or approval, specify, by declaration addressed to the Secretary General of the Council of Europe, the territory which shall be considered to be its metropolitan territory for this purpose.

2. Any Contracting Party may, at the time of ratification or approval of this Charter or at any time thereafter, declare by notification addressed to the Secretary General of the Council of Europe, that the Charter shall extend in whole or in part to a non-metropolitan territory or territories specified in the said declaration for whose international relations it is responsible or for which it assumes international responsibility. It shall specify in the declaration the articles or paragraphs of Part II of the Charter which it accepts as binding in respect of the territories named in the declaration.

3. The Charter shall extend to the territory or territories named in the aforesaid declaration as from the thirtieth day after the date on which the Secretary General shall have received notification of such declaration.

4. Any Contracting Party may declare at a later date by notification addressed to the Secretary General of the Council of Europe, that, in respect of one or more of the territories to which the Charter has been extended in accordance with paragraph 2 of this article, it accepts as binding any articles or any numbered paragraphs which it has not already accepted in respect of that territory or territories. Such undertakings subsequently given shall be deemed to be an integral part of the original declaration in respect of the territory concerned, and shall have the same effect as from the thirtieth day after the date of the notification.

5. The Secretary General shall communicate to the other signatory governments and to the Director-General of the International Labour Office any notification transmitted to him in accordance with this article.

Article 35. Signature, Ratification and Entry into Force. 1. This Charter shall be open for signature by the Members of the Council of Europe. It shall be ratified or approved. Instruments of ratification or approval shall be deposited with the Secretary-General of the Council of Europe.

2. This Charter shall come into force as from the thirtieth day after the date of deposit of the fifth instrument of ratification or approval.

3. In respect of any signatory government ratifying subsequently, the Charter shall come into force as from the thirtieth day after the date of deposit of its instrument of ratification or approval.

4. The Secretary General shall notify all the Members of the Council of Europe and the Director-General of the International Labour Office, of the entry into force of the Charter, the names of the Contracting Parties which have ratified or approved it and the subsequent deposit of any instruments of ratification or approval.

Article 36. Amendments. Any Member of the Council of Europe may propose amendments to this Charter in a communication addressed to the Secretary General of the Council of Europe. The Secretary General shall transmit to the other Members of the Council of Europe any amendments so proposed, which shall then be considered by the Committee of Ministers and submitted to the Consultative Assembly for opinion. Any amendments approved by the Committee of Ministers shall enter into force as from the thirtieth day after all the Contracting Parties have informed the Secretary General of their acceptance. The Secretary General shall notify all the Members of the Council of Europe and the Director-General of the International Labour Office of the entry into force of such amendments.

Article 37. Denunciation. 1. Any Contracting Party may denounce this Charter only at the end of a period of five years from the date on which the Charter entered into force for it, or at the end of any successive period of two years, and, in each case, after giving six months notice to the Secretary General of the Council of Europe, who shall inform the other Parties and the Director-General of the International Labour Office accordingly. Such denunciation shall not affect the validity of the Charter in respect of the other Contracting Parties provided that at all times there are not less than five such Contracting Parties.

2. Any Contracting Party may, in accordance with the provisions set out in the preceding paragraph, denounce any article or paragraph of Part II of the Charter accepted by it provided that the number of articles or paragraphs by which this Contracting Party is bound shall never be less than 10 in the former case and 45 in the latter and that this number of articles or paragraphs shall continue to include the articles selected by the Contracting Party among those to which special reference is made in Article 20, paragraph 1, sub-paragraph *(b)*.

3. Any Contracting Party may denounce the present Charter or any of the articles or paragraphs of Part II of the Charter, under the conditions specified in paragraph 1 of this article in respect of any territory to which the said Charter is applicable by virtue of a declaration made in accordance with paragraph 2 of Article 34.

Article 38. Appendix. The Appendix to this Charter shall form an integral part of it.

In witness whereof, the undersigned, being duly authorised thereto, have signed this Charter.

Done at Turin, this 18th day of October 1961, in English and French, both texts being equally authoritative, in a single copy which shall be deposited within the archives of the Council of Europe. The Secretary General shall transmit certified copies to each of the Signatories.

Appendix to the Social Charter

Scope of the Social Charter in Terms of Persons Protected

1. Without prejudice to Article 12, paragraph 4 and Article 13, paragraph 4, the persons covered by Articles 1 to 17 include foreigners only insofar as they are nationals of other Contracting Parties lawfully resident or working regularly within the territory of the Contracting Party concerned, subject to the understanding that these Articles are to be interpreted in the light of the provisions of Articles 18 and 19.

This interpretation would not prejudice the extension of similar facilities to other persons by any of the Contracting Parties.

2. Each Contracting Party will grant to refugees as defined in the Convention relating to the Status of Refugees, signed at Geneva on 28 July 1951, and lawfully staying in its territory, treatment as favourable as possible, and in any case not less favourable than under the obligations accepted by the Contracting Party under the said Convention and under any other existing international instruments applicable to those refugees.

Part I—Paragraph 18
Part II—Article 18, paragraph 1

It is understood that these provisions are not concerned with the question of entry into the territories of the Contracting Parties and do not prejudice the provisions of the European Convention on Establishments, signed at Paris on 13 December 1955.

Part II

Article 1, paragraph 2. This provision shall not be interpreted as prohibiting or authorising any union security clause or practice.

Article 4, paragraph 4. This provision shall be so understood as not to prohibit immediate dismissal for any serious offence.

Article 4, paragraph 5. It is understood that a Contracting Party may give the undertaking required in this paragraph if the great majority of workers are not permitted to suffer deductions from wages either by law or through collective agreements or arbitration awards, the exceptions being those persons not so covered.

Article 6, paragraph 4. It is understood that each Contracting Party may, insofar as it is concerned, regulate the exercise of the right to strike by law, provided that any further restriction that this might place on the right can be justified under the terms of Article 31.

Article 7, paragraph 8. It is understood that a Contracting Party may give the undertaking required in this paragraph if it fulfils the spirit of the undertaking by providing by law that the great majority of persons under 18 years of age shall not be employed in night work.

Article 12, paragraph 4. The words "and subject to the conditions laid down in such agreements" in the introduction to this paragraph are taken to imply inter alia that with regard to benefits which are available independently of any insurance contribution a Contracting Party may require the completion of a prescribed period of residence before granting such benefits to nationals of other Contracting Parties.

Article 13, paragraph 4. Governments not Parties to the European Convention on Social and Medical Assistance may ratify the Social Charter in respect of this paragraph provided that they grant to nationals of other Contracting Parties a treatment which is in conformity with the provisions of the said Convention.

Article 19, paragraph 6. For the purpose of this provision, the term "family of a foreign worker" is understood to mean at least his wife and dependent children under the age of 21 years.

Part III

It is understood that the Charter contains legal obligations of an international character, the application of which is submitted solely to the supervision provided for in Part IV thereof.

Article 20, paragraph 1. It is only understood that the "numbered paragraphs" may include articles consisting of only one paragraph.

Part V

Article 30. The term "in time of war or other public emergency" shall be so understood as to cover also the *threat* of war.

EUROPEAN SOCIAL CHARTER: PROTOCOL (1987).

The first protocol to the European Social Charter was concluded by the member States of the Council of Europe in Strasbourg on 26 November 1987 and was opened for signature by member States of the council on 5 May 1988.

The protocol, which will enter into force one month after the deposit of the third instrument of ratification, adds the following rights to those set out in the charter:

(a) The right to equal opportunity and treatment in employment and occupation without discrimination on the ground of sex;

(b) The right of workers to information and to consultation within the workplace;

(c) The right of workers to participate in decisions relating to their working conditions and environment, such as those relating to the protection of their health and safety, and in the enforcement of regulations;

(d) The right of the aging to social protection and to appropriate services including adequate resources, suitable housing, and health care.

EXECUTIONS: REPORT OF SPECIAL RAPPORTEUR.

On 15 December 1980, the UN General Assembly expressed alarm (resolution 35/172) at the incidence in various parts of the world of summary executions, as well as arbitrary executions, and its concern about the occurrence of executions widely regarded as having been politically motivated. The assembly called upon the Secretary-General to use his endeavors in cases where the minimum standard of legal guarantees appeared not to have been respected and to seek the view of member States and international organizations on ways and means of dealing with the problem of summary or arbitrary executions.

The Sixth United Nations Congress on the Prevention of Crime and the Treatment of Offenders, convened at Caracas in 1981, adopted a resolution on "Extra-legal Executions" in which it affirmed as a particularly abhorrent crime the practice of executing political opponents or suspected offenders by armed forces, law enforcement or other governmental agencies, or by paramilitary or political groups acting with the tacit or open consent of such forces or agencies. It also called upon all governments to take effective measures to prevent such acts.

In September 1981, the UN SUB-COMMISSION ON PREVENTION OF DISCRIMINATION AND PROTECTION OF MINORITIES expressed concern (resolution 1 [XXXIV]) about the scale of executions in various parts of the world, particularly of political opponents and imprisoned or detained persons and also about the summary execution of persons who are subsequently reported to have "disappeared," and drew the attention of the UN COMMISSION ON HUMAN RIGHTS to the increasing scale of politically motivated executions. At the same time, it recommended that the Economic and Social Council should call upon governments to abolish capital punishment for political offenses.

On 11 March 1982, the Commission on Human Rights recommended the appointment of an individual of recognized international standing as special rapporteur, with the mandate to submit to the commission a comprehensive report on the occurrence and extent of the practice of summary or arbitrary executions. After approval by the Economic and Social Council (resolution 1982/35), the chairman of the commission, on 4 August 1982, appointed Mr. S. Amos Wako (Kenya) as special rapporteur.

In his 1983 report to the commission, the special rapporteur examined in some detail the basic concepts underlying his study, bearing in mind the fact that no international instrument defines either "summary" or "arbitrary" executions. For the purpose of his work, he adopted the following tentative definitions (UN Doc. E/CN.4/1983/16, para. 66):

—"Summary execution" is the arbitrary deprivation of life as a result of a sentence imposed by the means of summary procedure in which the due process of law and in particular the minimum procedural guarantees as set out in article 14 of the International Covenant on Civil and Political Rights are either curtailed, distorted, or not followed;

—"Arbitrary execution" is the arbitrary deprivation of life as the result of the killing of persons carried out by the order of a government or with its complicity or tolerance or acquiescence without any judicial or legal process;

—"Extra-legal execution" refers to killings committed outside the judicial or legal process, and at the time illegal under relevant national or international laws. Accordingly, in certain circumstances, an "arbitrary execution," as defined above, can be an extra-legal execution.

In this connection, he pointed out that the types of executions enumerated above do not include deaths resulting from the use of reasonable force in law enforcement or permitted under relevant national or international legal standards; nor do they include killings in armed conflict not forbidden under international humanitarian law. Further, he added that "although the resolutions leading to the mandate of the present study limit the concept of summary or arbitrary executions to acts of omissions attributable to governments or government agents, the Special Rapporteur considers that further thought should be given to responsibility of non-governmental groups for acts of omissions leading to the deprivation of life in a manner equaivalent to that resulting from summary or arbitrary execution."

In subsequent reports, the special rapporteur analyzed the information which reached him from various sources concerning a considerable number of alleged summary or arbitrary executions, while realizing that that information represented only a small part of the entire phenomenon of this violation of the right to life. He concluded that a considerable number of summary or arbitrary executions remained undetected or unknown, not only by the international community but also by the population in the countries concerned, and called for suggestions as to how the phenomenon might be more accurately monitored.

In these reports, he also indicated that summary or arbitrary executions take place in all parts of the world, most frequently as a result of internal armed conflict but also as the result of excessive or illegal use of force by law enforcement agencies in arresting or detaining suspects. In some cases, individuals were simply executed without a trial, or after a trial which lacked the safeguards to protect the rights of the defendent prescribed in article 14 of the INTERNATIONAL COVENANT ON CIVIL AND POLITICAL RIGHTS.

In his search for possible remedial or preventive measures for protection of the right to life, the special rapporteur pointed out in various reports that it was necessary to ensure strict safeguards for the rights of the accused in all judicial proceedings, especially in cases involving the death penalty. He also emphasized the need to develop international standards for the proper investigation of all cases of suspicious death— a procedure which he considered essential not only to bring those responsible to justice but also to prevent further summary or arbitrary executions. Further, noting the difficulties encountered by newly established governments in protecting the right to life, he suggested that they might explore the possibility of receiving international assistance for this purpose within the framework of the program of UN ADVISORY SERVICES IN THE FIELD OF HUMAN RIGHTS.

In the report covering his 1987 activities, the special rapporteur set out some further recommendations, as follows (UN Doc E/CN.4/1988/22, para. 207):

(a) As a matter of urgency, training programmes should be organized with a view of training or educating law enforcement officers in human rights issues connected with their work. Over the years it has been noticed that arbitrary deprivation of life most frequently takes place in connection with the activities of law enforcement officers. It is therefore imperative that attention be drawn urgently to the training of such officers. The United Nations Centre for Human Rights and the United Nations Institute for Training and Research have over the years organized regional seminars and workshops in which government officers have been trained to draft reports under the various international human rights Covenants. It is urged that similar seminars or workshops be started for law enforcement officers to train them to carry out their work with due respect for the human rights of the individual and to familiarize them with various international human rights instruments;

(b) Governments should ratify international human rights instruments and the Optional Protocol to the International Covenant on Civil and Political rights and review national laws and regulations with a view to embodying in their laws and regulations the minimum requirements stipulated in the international human rights instruments with regard to law enforcement activities, inquiry procedures, judicial procedures, etc;

(c) Governments should maintain the machinery for checking and controlling the practice of law enforcement organs, including military forces, with a view to ensuring that their activities conform to the relevant laws and regulations;

(d) Governments and international organizations should support the efforts made in United Nations forums towards the adoption of an international instrument which would incorporate international standards for proper investigation of all cases of death in suspicious circumstances;

(e) Governments and international organizations should strengthen their efforts to find ways and means to bring about peaceful and lasting solutions to the situations of conflict in which indiscriminate killings often take place;

(f) Governments and international organizations should strengthen their efforts to assist, either bilaterally or multilaterally, in an efficient and effective manner, those Governments which, in their struggle to restore or raise the level of respect for human rights, are in need of technical and other assistance.

After the report had been reviewed by the UN Commission on Human Rights and the Economic and Social Council, the latter, on 27 May 1988, endorsed the suggestions put forward by the special rapporteur, renewed his mandate for a period of two years, and requested him to respond effectively to the information reaching him, in particular when a summary or arbitrary execution is imminent or threatened or when such an execution has occurred.

The council encouraged governments, international organizations, and non-governmental organizations to organize training programs and to support projects with a view to providing training or education for law enforcement officers on human rights issues connected with their work and appealed to the international community to support such endeavors. Further, it invited governments, international organizations, and non-governmental organizations to support the efforts made in United Nations fora towards the adoption of an international instrument that would incorporate international standards for the proper investigation of all cases of death in suspicious circumstances, including provision for adequate autopsy.

In the report covering his activities in 1988, the special rapporteur summarizes his correspondence with 36 governments concerning alleged summary or arbitrary executions in their countries: Bangladesh, Benin, Brazil, Burma, Chad, China, Colombia, Czechoslovakia, the former Democratic Yemen, El Salvador, Ethiopia, Guatemala, Haiti, Honduras, India, Indonesia, Iran, Iraq, Israel, Mauritania, Nepal, Nicaragua, Nigeria, Pakistan, Peru, Philippines, Somalia, South Africa, Sri Lanka, Sudan, Syria, Thailand, Uganda, United Kingdom of Great Britain and Northern Ireland, Yemen, and Zaire. In addition, he held meetings with representatives of nine governments in connection with alleged summary or arbitrary executions in their countries: Algeria, Benin, Burma, China, Indonesia, Iraq, Nigeria, and Sri Lanka.

The conclusions and recommendations set out in that report, prepared at the end of 1988 for consideration by the UN Commission on Human Rights at its 1989 session, are as follows (UN Doc. E/CN.4/1989/25, para. 311–316):

As mentioned in previous reports, hundreds of thousands of people have died in situations of international and internal armed conflicts. In 1988, however, a number of positive initiatives were taken in various international conflicts leading to a creation of an atmosphere in which situations conducive to summary or arbitrary executions can be reduced. It is very much hoped that these efforts will give rise to definitive solutions so that international peace and security can be achieved. It is only in an atmosphere of peace that human rights, and in particular the right to life, can be guaranteed and that the national institutions established to protect human rights and enable persons to enjoy them can be strengthened and operate effectively. Therefore the efforts under way to resolve these conflicts are to be welcomed.

Unfortunately, the initiatives taken in dealing with international conflict areas have not so far been matched by similar initiatives to resolve internal armed conflicts or tensions. Consequently, thousands of lives still continue to be lost by civilians in such conflicts. In the period under review, there has been a lot of indiscriminate killing of unarmed civilians on the part of governmental forces. The groups opposing Governments have also been guilty of this practice. In fact, in some situations where Governments have genuinely tried to address the grievances giving rise to such groups and have tried to involve all persons in the democratic process, such groups have tried to sabotage those efforts and in so doing have wantonly killed people.

It is a matter of regret that, in some areas where peace negotiations have ended international armed conflict, reports are emerging which indicate that the governmental instruments of power have turned from the enemy across the border to civilians within the country, with the result that there has been a very noticeable increase in summary or arbitrary executions by the Governments concerned of their own civilians. In some cases, according to the allegations made, persons who had already been tried, without the proper procedural safeguards, and sentenced to a term of imprisonment have been executed without further due process of the law or trial.

In the period under review, the Special Rapporteur has received more reports than at any time during the period of his mandate, alleging increased use of chemical weapons. In at least three areas, there were allegations that chemical weapons had been used and that they had resulted in thousands of deaths. In this regard, the Special Rapporteur welcomes the determination of the international community as reflected in the Final Declaration of the representatives of States participating in the Conference on the Prohibition of Chemical Weapons which met in Paris from 7 to 11 January 1989 when they resolved to prevent any recourse to chemical weapons by completely eliminating them, and solemnly affirmed their commitment not to use chemical weapons and condemned such use.

A disturbing feature of the period under review is the increasing number of allegations which the Special Rapporteur has received to the effect that thousands of people have lost their lives at the hands of police or other law enforcement officials in demonstrations. It would appear that the law enforcement officials did not act with the restraint required in such cases according to the Code of Conduct for Law Enforcement Officials. The Special Rapporteur would therefore strongly reiterate the recommendation he made in his last report that the United Nations Centre for Human Rights should organize seminars or workshops for law enforcement officials to train them and inculcate in them the principle that they should carry out their work with due respect for the human rights of the individual, and to familiarize them with various international human rights instruments which are directly related to their work. There is also room for bilateral and multilateral technical assistance in this regard.

One of the problematic issues that has faced the Special Rapporteur is how to determine whether a "death squad" or an extreme right- or left-wing group which is responsible for killing people is acting independently or with the support, tolerance, connivance or encouragement of the Government. In some countries it is alleged that, although such groups are ostensibly independent, they are sponsored by the Government or the Government tolerates them or in fact they include police and military personnel in plain clothes and under orders from their superiors. The

Governments have said that such groups act independently of them. The Special Rapporteur would welcome the Commission's views on how to deal with this problem. Whatever the position, it is the primary duty and responsibility of the Government to ensure that the right to life is guaranteed and protected from anyone who attempts to violate it.

In the report covering his activities in 1989, the special rapporteur set out the following conclusions and recommendations (UN Doc. E/CN.4/1990/22, chap. IV, para. 469–477):

With his present report, the Special Rapporteur has completed his eighth year since the establishment of his mandate in 1982. By going through his past reports and the information he has received, he concludes that the phenomenon of summary or arbitrary executions is unfortunately still prevalent in many parts of the world. Armed conflicts causing the death of civilians, political assassinations, illegal and/or excessive use of force by law enforcement or security force personnel, deaths in custody and executions without trial, or with a trial but without the safeguards to protect the rights of the defendant—the whole pattern of summary or arbitrary executions has already been well-documented and analysed in the Special Rapporteur's reports. Up to the present, the picture has remained unchanged.

During the past several years, the activities of the Special Rapporteur have markedly increased. On the one hand, every year he has received more communications containing information on summary or arbitrary executions; on the other hand, he has taken more frequent action in regard to the Governments concerning which allegations of summary or arbitrary executions have been made. The Special Rapporteur is of the view that this may be indicative of the fact that his mandate is becoming better known.

The Special Rapporteur is aware that the information which has reached him represents only a part of the entire phenomenon of summary or arbitrary executions. He hopes that the efforts and co-operation of various international and national organizations directed at establishing a better information network will continue to improve the transmission of information both in quantity and in speed.

In the present report, the Special Rapporteur has taken note of a particularly alarming trend, which is rapidly spreading, namely, the practice of "death threats" deliberately directed, in particular, against persons who play key roles in defending human rights and achieving social and criminal justice in a society. Rigorous measures must be taken to protect this group of persons.

On the other hand, the Special Rapporteur is happy to note the considerable achievements made by the General Assembly and the Economic and Social Council during the past year in areas directly or indirectly related to his mandate.

The General Assembly adopted, on 9 December 1988, resolution 43/173 entitled "Body of Principles for the Protection of All Persons under Any Form of Detention or Imprisonment". The Economic and Social Council adopted, on 24 May 1989, several resolutions concerning the administration of justice, and in particular resolution 1989/65, entitled "Effective prevention and investigation of extralegal, arbitrary and summary executions". This resolution has set the standards which the Special Rapporteur will apply when he examines alleged cases of summary or arbitrary executions. It should also help Governments to improve and/or maintain the level of protection of the right to life of those under their jurisdiction.

Furthermore, the Special Rapporteur takes special note of General Assembly resolution 44/159 of 15 December 1989, in which he was requested "to promote exchanges of views between Governments and those who provide reliable information to the Special Rapporteur, where the Special Rapporteur considers that such exchanges of information might be useful" (para. 7). The Special Rapporteur is willing to assume this task in order to facilitate constructive co-operation between the parties concerned and to seek more effective ways of combating the practice of summary or arbitrary executions.

With regard to the advisory services and technical assistance envisaged in Commission on Human Rights resolution 1989/72 of 8 March 1989, the Special Rapporteur is willing to explore further how best such programmes and projects of advisory services and technical assistance could be formulated and proposed in the context of his mandate. In chapter III, D, above, he has tried to elaborate the necessary conditions and elements for the effective implementation of such programmes and projects. He welcomes any suggestions in this regard.

In view of these conclusions, the Special Rapporteur would like to make a number of recommendations, as follows:

(a) Governments:

(i) Review national laws and regulations, as well as the practice of the judicial and law enforcement authorities, with a view to securing effective implementation of the standards set by Economic and Social Council resolution 1989/65 of 24 May 1989;

(ii) As a matter of priority, take measures to ensure the effective protection of persons who play key roles in defending human rights and promoting social justice from death threats and assassination attempts;

(iii) Include a thorough curriculum of human rights in the training of all law enforcement and military personnel;

(iv) Establish an office within the Government in order to improve co-operation with the United Nations and other international organizations in human rights matters.

(b) International organizations:

(i) Emphasize the importance of the implementation of international human rights norms and principles as set forth in international human rights instruments and resolutions, in particular by the General Assembly and the Economic and Social Council;

(ii) Organize at the regional and national levels human rights seminars and training courses, utilizing the manual on the effective prevention and investigation of extra-legal, arbitrary and summary executions;

(iii) Strengthen the United Nations Centre for Human Rights with a view to meeting the ever-growing requirements in the monitoring of human rights protection and advisory services;

(iv) Promote information activities in order to disseminate as widely as possible the latest achievements in the field of human rights, so that the international community may be aware of the ways in which human rights can be protected and promoted.

After examining the special rapporteur's report, the Commission on Human Rights, on 6 March 1990, took note of the report with appreciation (resolution 1990/51), welcomed the recommendations, and extended his mandate for two years.

The commission, further, encouraged governments, international organizations and non-governmental organizations to set up training programs and to support projects with a view to training or educating law enforcement officers in human rights issues concerned with their work, and appealed to the international community to support endeavors to that end; and urged all governments to co-operate with and assist the special rapporteur so that he might carry out his mandate effectively. It called upon the secretary-general to consider ways of publicizing the work of the special rapporteur as well as his recommendations, and to continue to use his best endeavors in cases where the minimum standard of legal safeguards provided for in articles 6, 14, and 15 of the International Covenant on Civil and Political Rights appears not to be respected.

SEE ALSO *Death Threats; Principles on the Effective Prevention and Investigation of Extra-Legal, Arbitrary and Summary Executions.*

F

FAIR TRIAL. The UN SUB-COMMISSION ON PREVENTION OF DISCRIMINATION AND PROTECTION OF MINORITIES, at its 1989 session, noted (resolution 1989/27) that, although article 10 of the UNIVERSAL DECLARATION OF HUMAN RIGHTS and article 14 of the INTERNATIONAL COVENANT ON CIVIL AND POLITICAL RIGHTS deal with various aspects of a "fair and public hearing," no comprehensive study has been made of recent developments concerning standards guaranteeing the right to a fair trial. The sub-commission also noted that, under the covenant, the right to a fair trial is considered to be a derogable right which may be suspended in certain circumstances, such as in time of public emergency. (See DEROGATION.)

The sub-commission appointed two of its members, Mr. Stanislav Chernichenko (U.S.S.R.) and Mr. William Treat (U.S.A.) as rapporteurs to prepare a report on existing international norms and standards pertaining to the right to a fair trial. The study is to be submitted to the sub-commission through its WORKING GROUP ON DETENTION.

FEDERATION OF ASSOCIATIONS OF FORMER INTERNATIONAL CIVIL SERVANTS.

An international non-governmental organization in consultative status (Category II) with the UN Economic and Social Council, the federation consists of nine associations, representing 6,000 individuals.

Founded in 1975, in Geneva, to link associations of former employees of organizations within the UN system, the federation protects and represents the common interests of former international civil servants, particularly in matters of pensions and health insurance. The group supports the work of UN organizations and bodies, especially regarding health, aging, and housing problems.

Federation of Associations of Former International Civil Servants. Address: Room C-542-1, Palais des Nations, CH-1211, Geneva 10, Switzerland. Telephone: (41–22) 34-60-11. Secretary: Angela Butler.

Yearbook of International Organizations 1989/90 (K. G. Saur).

FIJI. A country consisting of 332 islands in the southwestern Pacific Ocean, including the islands of Viti Levu, Vanua Levu, and Rotuma, Fiji achieved independence from Great Britain in 1970 and became a member of the United Nations the same year. About 110 of the islands are inhabited, the total population being estimated by the UN (1990) to be 748,000. Ethnic groups include Fijians (45%), Indians (50%), and Chinese and others (5%). Religions practiced include Christianity (50%), Hinduism (42%), and Islam (8%).

Under the constitution which took effect when Fiji became independent in 1970, the country's government took the form of a parliamentary democracy and a member of the Commonwealth of Nations, of which the British sovereign is the symbolic head. However, on 6 October 1987, Lieut. Col. Sitiveni Rabuka, the leader of a military coup, formally declared Fiji a republic and proclaimed the right of the "indigenous Fijian race" to govern themselves for their advancement and welfare. Britain rejected these actions and announced that it still regarded the governor-general as Fiji's sole authority holding executive power as the representative of the British monarch. Sitiveni Rabuka later served as minister for home affairs in a government headed by President Penaia Ganilau.

FINLAND. The Republic of Finland is a country in northern Europe, on the Gulf of Bothnia (part of the Baltic Sea) and the Gulf of Finland. It has borders with Norway, Sweden, and the Union of Soviet Socialist Republics. It achieved independence from Russia in 1917 and became a member of the United Nations in 1955. Its population is estimated by the UN (1990) to be 4,966,000. Ethnic groups include the Sami (about 5,300) and the Romany (Gypsy) populations; the latter numbers between 6,000 and 9,000. Languages commonly used include Finnish and Swedish (both official), Sami, and Romany. Christianity (Lutheran National Church, 90%; Greek Orthodox of Finland, 2%) is the predominant religion; 8% reports no religious affiliation. Literacy is estimated at 99%.

The government (1990) took the form of a republic. The president, selected by a popularly elected 301-member electoral college for a term of six years, is head of State; the premier, representing the party or coalition given the majority in the election, is head of government. Legislation is prepared by the unicameral 200-member Diet, known as the *Eduskunta,* members of which are elected for four-year terms by proportional representation. The chancellor of justice (*Oikeuskansleri*) and the solicitor-general (*Oikeusasiamies)* exercise control over the administration of justice. Political parties include the Social Democratic Party, the National Coalition Party, the Centre Party, the People's Democratic League, the Finnish Rural Party, the Swedish People's Party, and the Christian League.

Human rights problems arise infrequently for Finnish citizens, but the situation of aliens in Finland—and of its ethnic minorities, i.e., the Sami and Romany populations—have been a subject of concern.

As regards aliens, the fundamental rights laid down in chapter II of the Finnish Constitution Act apply as such to Finnish citizens only. However, the INTERNATIONAL COVENANT ON CIVIL AND POLITICAL RIGHTS, which Finland has ratified and incorporated into its domestic law, applies to all persons subjected to Finnish jurisdiction. Aliens thus enjoy the same procedural rights as Finnish citizens; however, some restrictions on their political rights still apply. They may not become members of political parties and may not vote to be elected in general elections. Aliens from Nordic countries have, however, been accorded the right to vote and to be elected in municipal elections since 1976.

As regards the Sami and Romany populations, the Government provided the following information in a report to the COMMITTEE ON THE ELIMINATION OF RACIAL DISCRIMINATION on 19 January 1988 (UN Doc. CERD/C/159/Add. 1, para. 5–60):

A. The Samis

There are 5,700 Samis in Finland of whom 3,900 live in their native area of Utsjoki, Inari or Enontekiö, or the Vuotso area of the Sodankylä municipality. More than one third of the population of the native Sami areas is Sami (Utsjoki 72 per cent, Inari 30 per cent, Enontekiö 16 per cent).

In Finland a person is considered Sami if he, or at least one of his parents or grandparents spoke Sami as the first language. The language has always been the main criterion in determining whether or not a person is Sami. Problems in the Sami culture are the dominance of the Finnish language and the mainstream culture in Sami language and culture in addition to the weak legal safeguards for the rights in respect of land and waterways which the Samis hold on the basis of tenure since time immemorial.

Researchers do not agree about the ethnic origin of the Samis. The Samis themselves, and current anthropological research, include them in the original peoples of the Arcticum. Parallels to them and to their culture can be found in other circumpolar areas of the globe.

The Sami population in Finland, Sweden and Norway is an authochthonous population and constitutes an ethnic group with its own background, language and traditional means of subsistence. They also are the only ethnic group in Finland indigenous to the present areas of habitation. Their historical existence is traced back by archeologists to the beginning of the post-glacial period. It is suggested that from the oldest archeological findings in Northern Fennoscandia one can see continuity to the times when the Samis *ipso facto* inhabited the area. The theory states that the present-day Samis descend from the population following the retreating edge of the continental glacier from Europe up to Scandinavia. Their contacts with the proto-Sami population of Finland and East Karelia resulted in the beginnings of the Sami culture at the beginning of the first millenium B.C.

The Samis' Livelihood and Rights to Land and Water Resources. The structure of the Samis' means of livelihood is increasingly similar to that of the main population. Nevertheless the Samis are still characterized by mixed economy where a household draws its income from several sources. Nearly 30 per cent of the Samis gain their main livelihood from agriculture, forestry and fishing, and only 10 per cent currently have reindeer husbandry as their main occupation. Still one half of all those whose main occupation is reindeer husbandry live in the traditionally Sami areas. South of those areas, reindeer husbandry usually constitutes a secondary source of income. Hunting and berrypicking are another important source of income for the Samis.

The economic condition of the Samis are considerably furthered by the new Scolt Act (the Scolts are a Sami community displaced as consequence of the war 1939–1944), the Reindeer Husbandry Act and the Act on Marginal Lands Subsistence Livelihood, although they do not exclusively apply to the Samis. These Acts enable subsistence farmers and other nature-dependent persons to obtain land rights, credit and subsidies.

Regional price subsidies are also essential for Sami type agriculture. For the diversification of the income structure, regional legislation on entrepreneurial subsidies, the provincial development fund (since the beginning of 1985) for development of projects to the means of livelihood, and the Rural Development Act (a of 1987) concerning subsidies for secondary agricultural activities, are of vital importance.

For the Samis private land or real estate ownership has traditionally been alien as to many nomadic or semi-nomadic peoples. Sami villages have, however, for centuries paid tax to the State for their land rights. In recent research, attempted legislative measures and land reforms the State's ownership of land traditionally occupied by Samis has been challenged. The Parliamentary Constitution Committee, too, has established that the Samis have a constitutional right to the lands currently in State ownership. As these rights have not been recorded in the law, areas of reindeer grazing, hunting, berry-picking and fishing have been subjected to such measures of utilizing the forest and water resources that the Samis livelihood has been jeopardized.

In 1985 a bill was submitted to Parliament to reform the

laws governing reindeer husbandry which would have safeguarded the right to reindeer husbandry to everyone living in the traditional Sami areas. The bill has not been passed, however, one reason being that the Samis were not content with a general right. Similar problems were encountered with the new Fishing Act (as of 1983) which excluded the three northernmost municipalities. The Negotiating Team for Sami Affairs, established in 1978, and consisting of Sami and Government representatives continues its research on Sami rights in respect of the land and water resources in the traditional Sami areas. The purpose of the research is to provide laws governing Sami land rights.

Linguistic and Educational Rights, and Social Services for the Samis. For preserving Sami culture and safeguarding their linguistic rights, the Sami Delegation which is an officially elected representative body has drawn up a bill (1987) for the utilization of the Sami language with authorities. The intention is to guarantee the Samis the same right to use their mother-tongue in courts of justice and with the authorities in general as Finnish citizens with Finnish or Swedish mother-tongue. The right would apply to all State, municipal and church authorities in the traditional Sami areas in addition to a few central authorities in the country. The bill does not propose that civil servants be required to know the Sami language, but that the Samis' right to use their own language be guaranteed through translating and interpreting services. Knowledge of the Sami language is not currently required for any Government position in the Sami municipalities excepting those of the Secretary-General and the jurist for the Sami Delegation (Parlamenta).

For translating and interpreting services it is suggested that a Sami language office be established in connection with the Sami Delegation. Furthermore, it is suggested that the translators' (eight in number have been suggested) salaries in the Sami municipalities be paid out of central Government funds.

The Sami Language Act would not cover the Samis' right to schools and instruction in the Sami language. This would be provided for elsewhere in the law. In current legislation the most important provisions on the Sami language are found in the laws governing education.

Both under the Comprehensive Schools Act and the High Schools Act the language of instruction in the Sami municipalities may be Sami. The Comprehensive Schools Decree provides that Sami mother-tongue pupils in the Sami municipalities are entitled to instruction in Sami. The High Schools Decree provides that Sami be an optional subject in the curriculum in the Sami municipalities. The Act Governing Occupational Training for the Samis stipulates that the languages of instruction are Finnish and Sami.

Teaching of the Sami language has increased in comprehensive schools. In the academic year of 1986–1987 the language of general instruction was Sami for 93 pupils, and 361 pupils had Sami as one of their school subjects. The three high schools of the area included the Sami language in the curriculum of 25 pupils.

Progress in the teaching of or in the Sami language is slowed down by the shortage of teachers and teaching material. This is one reason why parents are not always eager to put their child in a Sami school or section despite the Sami mother-language.

The Sami language is taught at university level in Helsinki, Oulu and Rovaniemi. The University of Oulu and the Lapland Institute of Higher Education (Rovaniemi) have a joint quota of five Sami mother-tongue students in their comprehensive school teachers' training programmes. Furthermore, Sami is taught in for instance at Lapland Summer University and folk academies.

The University of Lapland has a quota of one for Sami mother-tongue students in the Faculty of Law. At the Research Institute for Domestic Languages there is one position for research in Sami.

In Inari there is a Sami training centre which provides elementary, and intermediate occupational training as well as complementary or retraining courses. The study streams are Sami crafts, forestry, agriculture and co-existence with wildlife. Subjects cannot be taught in Sami on account of the shortage of teachers with a knowledge of the language. Retraining for the unemployed is provided throughout the Sami area.

The Inari Institute, owned by the Sami Promotion Society, is an adult education centre specialized in general and voluntary leisure time courses. In addition, the folk academies of the area annually arrange leisure time courses in nearly every village.

The lack of day-care centers with Sami-speaking staff renders the Sami children increasingly Finnish-speaking. In the Oulu Institute for Training Pre-school Teachers there is a quota of two Sami mother-tongue students. In the municipality of Utsjoki there is an experimental mobile Sami-language day-care centre.

A committee to investigate the availability of social services in the native language (1985) recommends that social services in Sami be increased by training a sufficient number of social workers familiar with Sami language and culture. Furthermore, the committee finds that a knowledge of the Sami language should be a requirement for the social service staff in the Sami areas.

The Sami culture committee (1986) proposed that the position of the Sami language be safeguarded through legislation, and that knowledge of the Sami language should be deemed a special merit in the appointment of administrative, educational and other positions in the Sami areas.

Sami Cultural Activities. Both the Lutheran and the Orthodox Church have programmes in the Sami language. In church services interpreters are used at least during the major church holidays, and recently church services have even been run entirely in the Sami language. An abundance of religious literature has been translated into dialects of Sami.

The radio broadcasts just over three hours of Sami programmes a week; educational Sami programmes take just under one hour a week in the Sami areas. In fact only the news and current events are adequately covered in Sami. The television has broadcast programmes on the national network only occasionally.

The committee to develop Sami radio broadcasting (1987) has proposed that the National Broadcasting Corporation aim at offering own equal choice in Sami as in Finnish and Swedish.

A Sami periodical Sápmelás is published every second month. A Norwegian Sami-language periodical Sámi Aigi which is published twice a week also deals with Finnish Sami matters. A periodical called Sáá'm Oddaz is published in Scolt Sami. In addition to these, the Finnish-language newspapers in Lapland have a weekly column in Sami.

The major problem with Sami literature is the limited spread of the language and the unprofitable and scattered publishing activities. Sami music has recently spread to nearly all fields of musical expression. The only Sami-language theatre group in non-professional and is called Rávgoš. The problems with drama activities are the lack of facilities, funds and training. Traditional crafts have known an upsurge, and the Samis have agreed on a pan-Nordic trademark to protect genuine Sami crafts.

The Sami culture committee (1986) proposed to introduce a special Sami allocation in the national budget to be administered by a Permanent Sami Culture Council under the Ministry of Education. The funds thus reserved to promote Sami arts and culture could be granted as subsidy for publishing, translating, reporting, drama activities, artists and groups of artists, and the recording of music, production of films and video-tapes.

There have been no changes in the status of the Sami language in education since the eighth periodic report (Chapters 11–13).

The previous report (Chapter 14) stated that the Sami syllabus was being drawn up. In 1985 the National Board of General Education confirmed the following syllabi:

1. Sami and Finnish taught as mother tongue in the comprehensive school (Comprehensive School Act, art. 27 [2]);

2. Sami and Finnish as voluntary subjects on the lower level of the comprehensive school (Comprehensive School Decree, art. 34 [2]);

3. Sami as an optional subject on the upper level of the comprehensive school (Comprehensive School Decree, art. 35 [3]);

4. Sami as a voluntary subject in the upper secondary school (Upper Secondary School Decree, art. 32 [5]).

The National Board of General Education, together with the Government Printing Centre, will continue to publish educational material for the teaching of Sami on the basis of the approved syllabi. Likewise, translation of other material into Sami will continue.

Under a decree given in April 1986 (321/86), a Council for Sami Education Affairs was established on 30 October 1986. The Council assists the Ministry of Education and deals with larger matters of principle pertaining to the development of the education of the Sami language as well as takes initiative and gives statements in these matters. The Council works in connection with the Lapland Provincial Office. According to the Decree, the Sami Education Council will take special account of the preservation and development of the Sami language and culture and of securing instruction of and in Sami for Sami children as prescribed in the school legislation. The Council should also take into account international co-operation connected with Sami education and culture. The Decree also states that the Ministry of Education and the National Boards of General and Vocational Education must consult the Sami Education Council on matters pertaining to general development of Sami education, questions of principle connected with it and annual budgets, before taking relevant decisions.

A major principle in the development of social welfare is to provide services for Finnish citizens irrespective of their race or religion. In Finland social welfare is responsible also for child care and pre-school education which focuses on educational questions so as to make it possible for the children to grow up into adults who accept the differences in others and learn to respect persons representing other cultures as a source of wealth in their own living environment.

Under the section concerning educational objectives in the Child Day Care Act, the physical, social and emotional development of the child should be promoted and esthetic, intellectual, moral and religious education should be supported in agreement with the child's age and individual needs. In supporting religious education, the conviction of the child's parents and guardian should be respected. While promoting the development of the child, day care should support the growth of the child into joint responsibility and peace, and the protection of the living environment.

According to the same Act the day care of children must be provided in the mother tongue of the child, either in Finnish, Swedish or the Sami language.

Within social welfare, special attention has during recent years been paid to the minority groups living in Finland: the Romanies and the Samis. On 30 November 1984, the Ministry of Social Affairs and Health set up a working group for investigating the availability of social services in everyone's own language.

Since 1973, a Sami delegation has functioned subordinate to the office of the Council of State, being in charge of the social affairs of the Lapps. The social position of the Lapps has been promoted e.g. by a project financed by the National Board of Social Welfare and completed in 1985, examining the conditions of development of the Lapps. Also the National Board of Social Welfare has proposed the inclusion of an appropriation in the State budget for the establishment of a day nursery, guidance and cultural centre for Lapp children and their parents. Moreover, efforts have been made to Sami-speaking social welfare personnel to take part in social welfare training.

In connection with our co-operation with Norway and Sweden, Sami affairs have held a central position. It should be possible for the Sami population to use services in their own language flexibly, irrespective of the country where the services are provided.

B. The Romany Population

The first written mention of Gypsies or the Romany people in Finland is from the 1500s. From that date until 1809 the same special laws concerning the Romany governed both the Finnish and Swedish Romanies. The ancestors of today's 6,000–9,000 Romanies in Finland first came to Finland in the middle of the sixteenth century. Their history in Finland, as elsewhere, is one of hostility and contempt. The general attitude towards them was formalized in the laws of the seventeenth, eighteenth and nineteenth centuries, which aimed variously at assimilation, expulsion and control. The effect of these laws was quite minimal on the Romanies, and their enforcement not effective, mainly because the Romanies lived in the most sparsely populated rural provinces until well into this century.

So far as the State is concerned, the improvement of Romany housing conditions has been considered the first priority. In 1975 an Act on Improving the Housing of the Romanies was passed. Under this Act, it is the local municipalities' responsibility to improve the housing of the Romanies within their area. The State gave special finance for this purpose to the municipalities.

The Romany economic structure has suffered hard knocks in the wake of general societal change in Finland. Presently the main income for the Finnish Romanies comes from occasional trading, of which the handwork hold by Romany women forms the largest part, and from various social welfare benefits. It must be pointed out here that in Finland there are some third and fourth generation Romany farmers as well, who have retained their Romany cultural characteristics.

In the last few years a large proportion of Finnish Romanies have moved to Sweden, and according to the estimates by social welfare authorities and Romany organizations about 2,000 Finnish Romanies live more or less permanently in Sweden. The migration has been caused by the better standard of living in Sweden.

The Romanies can be understood to form a common and distinct ethnic group mainly on the basis of their clothing. The clothing of Romany women, especially, differs entirely from Finnish clothing, in terms of materials and styles as well as in terms of colours used.

The Finnish Romanies speak Finnish as their mother tongue these days, and this is also their main language of communication with each other. The majority of the Finnish Romanies can speak Romany to some extent, but its usage can be said to be diminishing and is limited to the expression of ideas or feelings which no Finnish equivalent can convey adequately, or when it is desired that communication is limited to those present who can speak Romany. Attempts to retain and develop the Romany language are hampered by the lack of written material, and also by the resistance from the Romanies in allowing the language to be put within reach of non-Romanies.

In 1967, the Romanies organized themselves into a pressure group as the Finnish Gypsy Association. The Association was instrumental in getting some important laws onto the statute books, such as the Law Prohibiting Discrimination on the Basis of Racial or Ethnic Origin (1970), and a law aimed at improving the Romany housing conditions. (1975). Under the latter law, the country's Romanies were to have been adequately housed by 1980, but only a small portion were housed with the aid of this law by the decreed time. The work of the Gypsy Association has at least temporarily ceased, owing to some rather serious disagreements on a number of issues—the main problems centre around whether the Association should be run by a reasonably well-known "elite", or by "ordinary" Romanies.

Since the submission of the eighth periodic report (1985) the following developments can be reported as regards promotion of general education among the Romany people:

In order to fulfil the needs of special groups, such as the Romany people, the National Board of General Education published a guidebook called *Erilainen oppilas* (A Different Pupil) in 1981. The book gives information about Romany culture and traditions and advice on how to take account of the demands stemming from the different cultural and social background of the Romany people.

Since 1973 the annual State budget has included an appropriation for adult education of the Romany people to supplement the deficient basic education among the Romany. These funds were used to arrange small group and individual tuition in four civic and workers' institutes, with the following syllabi:

— reading and writing, civics, Romany culture (in Helsinki);

— reading and writing (in Hämeenlinna)

— Finnish language and literature, biology, civics and art education, mathematics, Romany culture and language (in Joutseno);

— reading, writing and arithmetics, civics, Romany culture (in Sonkajärvi).

The total number of students was 36 and lesson hours 744.

In the opinion of the National Board of General Education, it is necessary to organize special education for the Romany people. Efforts are being made to produce teaching material that fulfils the needs of the Romany population. The National Boards of General and Vocational Education produced a primary of the Romany language in 1982. A user's guide is being published by the National Boards and the State Printing Centre.

Likewise, the National Board will soon publish teaching material in mathematics for basic education in civic and workers' institutes and special education in the comprehensive schools for population groups that need immediate, efficient and practical training.

In addition, the National Board of General Education and the Swedish National Board of Education, in collaboration, have published a primary of reading and writing for adults and a reader for adults.

As regards vocational education, training of unemployed Romany people has continued in the traditional Romany trades in 1984–1987: a course for close-range educators in children's and adolescents' institutes was terminated at the end of 1985; a few courses on Romany dressmaking have been arranged annually; a nine-month horse-keeping course was arranged in 1986 on a horse farm owned by Romany people.

On the initiative of the Romany Association, a working group was set up by the Ministry of Education to:

— gauge the quantitative and qualitative need for vocational education among Romany youth;

— plan vocational education of the Romany population on the basis of the present education system and the possibilities offered by the educational unit serving the special needs of Romany people, and

— prepare a proposal for the establishment of a vocational education centre for the Romany people with detailed cost calculation as well as draft enactments and eventual further measures.

Further, the working group was to gauge possibilities for arranging supplementary general education and teaching of the Romany language in connection with vocational education. The working group published its report on 31 March 1987.

The National Board of Vocational Education has continued to disseminate information on special Romany features on in-service education courses for headmasters and teachers to prevent any inter-racial conflicts.

The Advisory Board for Romany Affairs set up by the Council of State functions within the Ministry of Social Affairs and Health, its members consisting of central authorities and representatives of the Romany population. The task of this Advisory Board is to follow and supervise the development and improvement of the social conditions of the Romany population, to make necessary proposals to this end, and to give statements to the authorities.

In 1986 a report by the Advisory Board for Romany Affairs financed by the National Board of Housing and the National Board of Social Welfare was completed concerning the housing conditions of the Romanies. ("The housing condition of Romanies—report on Romanies with inadequate or no housing", 1985, by Riikka Tanner, Report Series No. 5/1986 of the National Board of Social Welfare). As a result of the research, the Advisory Board for Romany Affairs has consulted the National Board of Housing concerning measures to be taken in order to improve the housing conditions of the Romanies. Moreover, the Advisory Board for Romany affairs has made several proposals to various authorities concerning e.g. occupational education and certain issues related to health care.

The Advisory Board for Romany Affairs has also maintained extensive contacts for exchanging information and experiences in order to improve the living conditions of the Romany population. The Advisory Board arranged, on 24–25 April 1986, a Swedish-Finnish co-operation conference on Romany affairs in Helsinki. Also a Swedish-Finnish working group on the social welfare and health care of immigrants has drawn attention to Romany affairs by establishing a two-year section for dealing with the issue.

FOOD. The right of everyone to an adequate standard of living for himself and his family, including adequate food, is proclaimed in the UNIVERSAL DECLARATION OF HUMAN RIGHTS as follows:

Article 25.1. Everyone has the right to a standard of living adequate for the health and well-being of himself and of his family, including food, clothing, housing and medical care and necessary social services. . . .

The INTERNATIONAL COVENANT ON ECONOMIC, SOCIAL AND CULTURAL RIGHTS contains the following provision:

Article 11. 1. The States Parties to the present Covenant recognize the right of everyone to an adequate standard of living for himself and his family, including adequate food, clothing and housing, and to the continuous improvement of living conditions. The States Parties will take appropriate steps to ensure the realization of this right, recognizing to this effect the essential importance of international co-operation based on free consent.

2. The States Parties to the present Covenant, recognizing the fundamental right of everyone to be free from hunger, shall take, individually and through international co-operation, the measures, including specific programmes, which are needed:

(a) To improve methods of production, conservation and distribution of food by making full use of technical and scientific knowledge, by disseminating knowledge of the principles of nutrition and by developing or reforming agrarian systems in such a way as to achieve the most efficient development and utilization of natural resources;

(b) Taking into account the problems of both food-importing and food-exporting countries, to ensure an equitable distribution of world food supplies in relation to need.

It may be noted that States parties to the covenant specifically accept to undertake the measures specified there with a view to ensuring the supply of adequate food to everyone.

The WORLD HEALTH ORGANIZATION, both independently and in association with such other United Nations agencies as FAO, UNESCO, and UNICEF, has been active in seeking to attain the objectives set out in the provisions cited above together with and on behalf of governments. Nevertheless, despite great im-

provements in agricultural techniques and extension of knowledge of nutritional physiology and pathology, it is probable that at least one half of the world's population still suffers from undernourishment or malnutrition.

In 1983, the UN Economic and Social Council (decision 1983/140) authorized the SUB-COMMISSION ON PREVENTION OF DISCRIMINATION AND PROTECTION OF MINORITIES to entrust one of its members, Mr. Asbjørn Eide (Norway), with the preparation of a study on the right to adequate food as a human right. It instructed the special rapporteur to take account of all relevant work being done within the United Nations system and to consult with organs and agencies such as the WORLD FOOD COUNCIL, the FOOD AND AGRICULTURE ORGANIZATION OF THE UNITED NATIONS, the UNITED NATIONS CONFERENCE ON TRADE AND DEVELOPMENT and relevant non-governmental organizations in the field. He was further instructed "to give special attention to the normative content of the right to food and its significance in relation to the establishment of the new international economic order."

The special rapporteur's report (UN Doc. E/CN.4/Sub.2/1987/23) was presented to the subcommission at its 1987 session. In clarifying the issues involved, he quoted estimates made by competent international organizations indicating that:

—more than one billion people are chronically hungry;

—every year, 13 to 18 million people die as a result of hunger and starvation;

—every 24 hours, 35,000 human beings die as a direct or indirect result of hunger and starvation: 24 every minute, 18 of whom are children under five years of age;

—more people have died from hunger in the last two years than were killed in World War I and World War II together;

—340 million people in developing countries (China excluded) did not have enough income to attain a minimum food energy standard (calories) that would prevent serious health problems and stunted growth in children, while 730 million fell below a standard that would allow an active working life.

At the same time, the world output of major food crops reached 1,830 million metric tons. The average amount produced per capita was calculated from this to be, given the world population of 4,605 million, more than 400 kilograms, or well over one kilogram per person per day the world over. Thus, if the total amount of food could have been equally distributed to all inhabitants of the earth, there would be more than enough for all.

The conclusions (para. 274–284) of the special rapporteur—after examining the existing situation, the state of recognition of the right to food in international law, and the situation as regards State obligations, international obligations, and the problems involved in monitoring and supervising activities for ensuring the enjoyment by everyone of the right to food—are as follows:

This study has shown that the right to food is widely recognized in international law, both in general and in more specific terms. In its most general formulation, it is found in the Universal Declaration of Human Rights, to which all members of the international community subscribe, whatever legal consequences they draw from it; in more unequivocal terms it is found also in the international Covenant on Economic, Social and Cultural Rights to which at present 85 States are parties.

In more specific terms, it is found in a great variety of contexts which have been listed above. They attest to a widely accepted view that access to food is an essential right which should be respected and protected under all circumstances.

The corresponding obligations, however, are less developed. In particular, the obligations found in the more general provisions are vague, diverse and found in many different instruments. In view of the urgent need to respond to hunger and malnutrition in the world today, it is necessary to consolidate and further develop existing law through the drafting of an appropriate instrument on the right to food. It might contain declaratory and obligatory parts. As a contribution by a non-governmental organization, the International Law Association has established a working group for this purpose.

At the national level, plans for national food security have obtained increasing attention. Properly approached, with a particular focus on the conditions necessary to promote food security at household and community level according to the principles in the "food security matrix" suggested in this report, such plans could constitute the agenda for the implementation of the right to food nationwide. Country-specific application could then be made of the otherwise general and vague international obligations. This agenda accommodates a wide range of approaches.

There exists in many States the beginning of national arrangements for the monitoring of the progressive realization of the right to food; such efforts should be encouraged in all States where access to food for some groups presents particular problems, and where special attention therefore must be given to the situation of such groups.

It remains the primary responsibility of States to ensure enjoyment of the right to food by all within their jurisdiction. But States have obligations also to the peoples of other States and to the international community. These can be derived from provisions found within human rights law and from a set of principles of international law, as outlined in chapter V.

For the organized international community to be able to enhance the compliance with internal and external obligations of States, there is also a need for international monitoring and supervision. This should be carried out in order to supplement and strengthen the national efforts and to assist in the elimination of obstacles to the realization of the right to food.

It has been argued above that the functions served by international agencies and organs should be to encourage and promote the national efforts, to assist in overcoming obstacles and difficulties, and to react to gross neglect of these obligations wherever such occurs.

International monitoring may be of help in encouraging and promoting national food security efforts. Through international monitoring it may also become feasible to organize adequate international support and assistance, and to create awareness of situations where actions by other States are detrimental to the progressive realization of the right to food inside a State.

At present, however, such international monitoring and supervision is rather weak, as pointed out in chapter VI. The specialized agencies concerned have not approached the issue of food from the perspective of human rights.

The relevant body within the human rights field is the new Committee on Economic, Social and Cultural Rights, which started its work in March 1987, and which will have substantial difficulties to overcome in its important work. Five of the major difficulties have been outlined in chapter VI: (a) the lack of clarity of obligations; (b) the lack of guidance for State reporting (c) the limited co-operation from the specialized agencies, (d) the non-involvement of non-governmental organizations and (e) the limited time and capacity of the Committee itself.

On the basis of these conclusions, the special rapporteur submitted to the sub-commission an extensive series of recommendations, as follows:

States should:
Draw up plans for national food security according to the overall framework suggested in this study, focusing on household and community food security and building on a nation-wide system of identifying local needs and opportunities for achieving such food security;

Identify in particular within such plans the needs of groups which have the greatest difficulties in achieving food security, and set specific goals to ensure sustainable access to adequate food for those groups.

Ensure popular participation in periodically assessing and analysing local needs and opportunities, and facilitate inputs by the least privileged groups in society into the action plans that should follow from such assessment and analysis;

Indicate specifically the areas in which international assistance is required and spell out details of the assistance needed;

Ensure that an adequate system for monitoring the right to food is developed and put into action, guided by the principles of food security as suggested in this study (enough and adequate food in terms of nutrition and cultural acceptability, viable patterns of procurement of food, and a sustainable food resource base); such a system may build on and integrate information from different systems (e.g. Timely Warning, Nutritional Surveillance, etc., and national data bases in general), if necessary with appropriate assistance from international agencies;

Provide details of the national food security plans and of progress made and obstacles encountered in the implementation of these plans in their reports for States parties to the Covenant;

Recognize and comply with their obligations in regard to the peoples of other States arising from the right to food and from principles of general international law, as outlined in Chapter VI of this study.

National non-governmental organizations, universities and research institutions dealing with development and human rights issues should:

Participate in the elaboration of local needs and opportunities for food security and in the formulation and implementation of food security action plans;

Disseminate information about international human rights standards and stimulate local and national debate on the implementation of the right to food.

The specialized agencies should:

Examine their mandates for their relevance and relationship to food as a human right, *inter alia* through establishing as needed interdivisional working groups or task forces for this purpose;

Pay increased attention to the food-related work of the human rights organs and be prepared to co-operate with them in setting up the overall framework for promoting the right to food in given national situations and to develop subsequent action plans;

Develop further, advise on and assist in establishing appropriate systems for monitoring aspects of food security within their domains according to the framework suggested in this study, and consider how relevant information from such systems may be utilized and integrated with that of other systems for the purpose of monitoring the realization of the right to food;

Explore the possibility of developing for such co-operation special mechanisms for inter-agency co-operation in this field under the Administrative Committee on Co-ordination or other existing co-ordinating mechanisms.

The Economic and Social Council should:

Consider requesting the Committee on Economic, Social and Cultural Rights to designate one or two of its members to pay particular attention to the right to food dimensions of the work of the Committee. These members could, from time to time, draft general comments for consideration by the Committee with a view to developing greater understanding of the normative and practical implications of the right to food;

Consider requesting a Working Group of the Committee on Economic, Social and Cultural Rights to undertake a series of hearings at which experts from relevant international agencies would make submissions and respond to questions with a view to developing a more sophisticated an mutually rewarding understanding of the best ways by which the international community could promote more effectively implementation of the right to food.

Consider the establishment of relevant intersecretariat and inter-agency co-operative arrangements that would facilitate closer working relations between the Centre for Human Rights and other relevant parts of the Secretariat as well as the specialized agencies, to ensure the best performance of the United Nations in promoting the right to food.

The Committee on Economic, Social and Cultural Rights should:

Improve its guidelines for States parties' reports so that more meaningful data are generated on the extent to which the right to food is not presently enjoyed and on the obstacles which block its enjoyment;

Encourage States parties to the Covenant to involve community groups and non-governmental organizations in the preparation of reports under the Covenant;

Improve the links with the relevant specialized agencies in order to obtain access to information which could be used to make the supervision process more meaningful;

Take measures to implement articles 22 and 23 of the Covenant by encouraging the provision of technical assistance to States parties which have encountered difficulties in realizing the right to food;

Emphasize to States that the obligation contained in article 2 (1) of the Covenant to "take steps" is of immediate application and does not necessarily depend on the availability of extra resources; the most appropriate step under article 2 (1) being the establishment of a system for the preparation of national food security action plans;

Reorganize the periodicity of the handling of reports in order to obtain shorter intervals; for this purpose, more time might need to be allocated to the Committee;

Indicate also, in its comments on State reports, the required compliance with external obligations of States necessary in order to facilitate a satisfactory realization of the right to food;

Make suggestions for further and improved co-operation between States on a voluntary basis, aimed at better worldwide realization of the right to food.

International non-governmental organizations should:

Support the efforts to realize the right to food worldwide, through information, awareness-formation and action as appropriate;

Base their food-related efforts on the right to food rather than on policy statements which are often vague and contentious;

Develop or strengthen their co-operation, on the basis of the right to food, with the relevant parts of the Secretariat and the specialized agencies, the Economic and Social Council, and the Committee on Economic, Social and Cultural Rights.

The Sub-Commission on the Prevention of Discrimination and Protection of Minorities should:

Seek authorization, through the Commission on Human Rights, from the Economic and Social Council to initiate an effort to consolidate and further develop existing law through the drafting of an appropriate instrument on the right to food. Such an instrument might contain declaratory and obligatory parts, and should give due account also to methods for monitoring and implementation.

In this endeavour, account should be taken of the efforts currently made within the International Law Association to prepare a model draft instrument on the right to food.

Action Taken on the Study. At its 1987 session, the sub-commission, having examined the special rapporteur's study, expressed its appreciation and thanks to Mr. Eide and submitted the study, together with the relevant documentation, to the COMMISSION ON HUMAN RIGHTS. Having noted a need for further information in the status of the right to food in domestic law, it called upon the Secretary-General to obtain such information from States and from the Food and Agriculture Organization of the United Nations. It decided that it would return to a debate on the normative content of the right to food at a subsequent session, taking into account the information obtained by the Secretary-General as well as the draft model instrument on the right to food then under elaboration by the International Law Association.

The Economic and Social Council, at its first regular session, in 1988, noted (resolution 1988/33) the study with satisfaction, decided that it should be published by the United Nations and given the widest possible circulation, and drew it to the attention of the COMMITTEE ON ECONOMIC, SOCIAL AND CULTURAL RIGHTS, inviting the committee to submit its observations thereon to the council. Further, the council decided to take steps to ensure better coordination between specialized agencies and organs dealing with food-related matters and human rights bodies of the United Nations, if possible through interagency cooperative arrangements.

The Committee on Economic, Social and Cultural Rights devoted two meetings at its third session, held at the United Nations office in Geneva from 6 to 24 February 1989, to a general discussion on article 11 of the International Covenant on Economic, Social and Cultural Rights and in particular to the study on the right to adequate food as a human right prepared by Mr. Eide. On invitation of the committee, Mr. Eide analyzed the contents of his study and participated in a free exchange of views with members of the committee.

The essential features of Mr. Eide's analysis are summarized in the 1989 report of the committee as follows (E/1989/22, chap. IV, sect. B):

(a) that the concept of freedom from want lies at the very heart of economic, social and cultural rights;

(b) that the right to food must be seen in the wider context of civil and political rights and economic, social and cultural rights, all such rights being indivisible and interdependent, and forming part of the overall framework of development, environment and peace;

(c) that the right to food involves not only food production globally and nationally but differential access to food within countries (food entitlements);

(d) that food is a basic need for all human beings and everyone requires access to food which is (i) sufficient, balanced and safe so as to satisfy nutritional requirements, (ii) culturally acceptable and (iii) accessible in a manner that does not destroy one's dignity as a human being;

(e) that the argument as to whether the right to food proclaimed in article 11 of the Covenant was an individual human right or a broadly formulated programme for governmental policies in the economic and social field; or that the rights were not justiciable so as to entitle the individual to have recourse to the Courts for their enforcement—all these arguments were sterile and a pragmatic approach was required for the understanding and realization of the right to food;

(f) that apart from whether human rights, including the right to food, are classified jurisprudentially as constituting legal relations between the individual and the State and the individual as a subject of international law, there were three (3) basic obligations, namely: (i) *the obligation to respect* the freedom of the individual to provide for his well being; (ii) *the obligation to protect* the individual against the action of others and (iii) *the obligation to fulfil* by securing the right to food for those individuals who are marginalized and afflicted by poverty;

(g) that the three basic obligations to *respect, protect* and *fulfil,* arose at both the national and international level; that despite the somewhat vague nature of the language in which the right to food is formulated, the State's obligations clearly emerged from a number of provisions in the Covenant, including articles 2, 11, 22 and 25; and the obligations under international law were founded upon the Charter of the United Nations (especially Article 1, para 3 and Article 55 (a), (b), (c)), the Universal Declaration of Human Rights (especially article 25, para. 1 as well as articles 2, 3, 22, 28, 29), the Covenant on Economic, Social and Cultural Rights (especially article 11, as well as article 2, paras. 1 and 2 and articles 6, 9, 10, and 12) as well as various resolutions and instruments of international organizations;

(h) that the right to food is of particular importance in the context of poverty since poverty was a global problem which permeated both the industrialized and developing countries;

(i) that the right to food was particularly critical in times of famine and disasters (natural and artificial) and posed serious problems in relation to distribution and access to food;

(j) that although it is the primary responsibility of the State to secure the enjoyment of the right to food to all within its jurisdiction, all States had international obligations to ensure humanity's survival by the guarantee of adequate food for all;

(k) that there was a need for a Global Food Security System to complement and strengthen national systems; such a system would recognize the need to guarantee access to food at (i) the household level, (ii) the national level and (iii) the global level; and that it was important to recognize the significance of access to food at the *household level* since "for those who do not have the purchasing power or other entitlements to food, it does not help much that enough food is being produced". At the national level there was the need for States to draw up plans for food security, identify needs and goals, ensure popular participation in the elaboration of these plans, indicate areas of international assistance, recognize its international obligations and establish an adequate system for monitoring the right to food;

(l) that monitoring at the international level was rather weak and there was need for a co-ordinated approach among international agencies in seeing the issue of food from the perspective of human rights. In this regard it was necessary to provide a greater amount of advice and assistance and was desirable to establish an inter-agency consultative mechanism;

(m) that the Committee seek to clarify the obligations of States, provide guidance for State Reporting in respect of their obligations under article 11 of the Covenant and be provided with more time and support for carrying out its monitoring and supervisory responsibility under the Covenant.

In a related statement to the committee, the representative of the Food and Agriculture Organization of the United Nations (FAO) fully supported the concept of States having

international obligations in guaranteeing the right to food, although he considered that whether that duty was owed to the individual or to the State was an open question.

Issues of sovereignty were involved. He was of the view that if the recommendation of FAO regarding World Food Security and the Principles and Plan of Action of the World Conference on Agrarian Reform and Rural Development were more fully implemented, this would go a long way towards the realization of the right to food. But it was first necessary for three elements to be in place, namely (a) the political will (b) the allocation of necessary resources and (c) the full use of the programme and mechanisms of FAO, WFP and IFAD.

The FAO representative submitted that the right to be free from hunger was proclaimed to be a fundamental right in article 11 (2) of the Covenant and this clearly related to the right to life recognized by the Universal Declaration of Human Rights. In this context any discretionary power of States, both developed and developing, in securing the right to food would be limited by the fundamental nature of the right to be free from hunger as an integral part of the right to life.

The observations put forward by various members of the committee in the course of the exchange of views are summarized in the committee's report as follows (*Ibid.*, sect. C, para. 319–326):

The observations made by members of the Committee were varied and far-reaching. Some members noted the lack of clarity in the formulation of the right to food and the obligations of States and pointed out the difficulty of the provisions of article 11 fitting into traditional concepts of rights and obligations. It was not clear in the view of these members whether the individual had an international legal right or merely a moral or social right. Other members considered that the legal foundation of the right to food was established by treaty law under the Covenant and other international instruments and that the obligations of States flowed directly from these provisions; that since the individual was clearly intended to be the beneficiary of those rights, it was within the power of the individual, increasingly recognized as a subject of international law, to demand respect for the obligations of the Covenant.

It was generally agreed that the right to food was much more extensive than the right to stand in line for food and that the individual should have the right to receive food not simply as an act of mercy; that the right to receive food was not simply a question of calories but adequate nutrition; and it had to be culturally acceptable. It was also suggested that all members of the population should receive an adequate income so as to make food affordable by all.

Some members of the Committee considered that every country should take immediate steps to ensure the realization of the right to food; that ultimate realization at the fullest acceptable level may in the circumstances of some countries be achieved progressively but the national and international obligations arising under the Covenant meant that with co-ordinated efforts a meaningful start could be made immediately in all States, whilst it was generally agreed that the primary responsibility for ensuring the right to food rested with the individual. Some members felt that there was a point at which the denial of the human need for food constituted a violation of a human right; that such a right was analogous to a right in public law; that such a right was important to the protection of the disadvantaged and marginalized affected by poverty; that there should be a common law right of action against the State where (a) there was a systematic deprivation of access to food for individuals or the community and (b) the State by its action or inaction had behaved so outrageously as to offend the dignity of the human personality.

It was further contended by some members that the obligations of States at the international level in relation to the right to food supported the thesis that there was an obligation on the part of all States to make food available so as to guarantee the fundamental right of freedom from hunger, that accordingly it could be said that the excess world food resources were the common heritage of mankind's hungry and impoverished and that it would be a denial of justice to refuse access to such resources by the hungry and the starving. This was not to be seen in terms of charity but in terms of human rights. The international obligations of States should be reflected in the reports by states, indicating the extent to which they participate in food aid programmes, multilaterally or bilaterally.

It was the widespread view among members that many of the problems relating to the production and distribution of food, particularly in developing countries dependent upon agriculture, related to the inequitable terms of trade between the primary producers of agricultural products and producers of manufactured products; that the prices received for the primary agricultural products did not keep pace with the prices of manufactured products which producing countries had to import with their limited export earnings from primary agricultural products. It was therefore an important part of the solution of the problem of the right to food that there should be an adjustment in the terms of trade as called for by the new international economic and social order. The role of transnationals would also have to receive attention.

Considerable emphasis was placed by some members on the need to see the right to food not as an isolated phenomenon but as part of the right to life. It was generally agreed that the right to food was necessary for human life and that without adequate food other human rights may be non-existent or meaningless. There was an interdependence and indivisibility between civil and political rights and economic, social and cultural rights.

There was considerable discussion in the Committee as to whether the right to humanitarian assistance transcended sovereignty so as to give the victim the right to require assistance directly rather than through the State. It was recognized that it was important to guarantee the individuals access to food.

Members examined the role of the Committee in making recommendations to States on compliance with the obligations arising under article 11 of the Covenant. The question was asked as to how far the Committee could go in this direction. It was recognized that the position was an evolving one and that by constructive dialogue with States, greater clarity could be achieved as to the extent of the obligation of States and the development of those obligations. Our understanding of human rights evolved with the development and evolution of the human personality and the Committee was a part of this process. Members of the Committee considered that the monitoring and supervisory mechanism was an important part of the Committee's function and that it was necessary to establish, through constructive dialogue, the guidelines for reporting and the bench marks for assessing compliance. It was said that the Committee had a choice between adopting a "positivist" and a "possibilist" approach. In this context it was necessary to continuously improve the co-operation between the Committee and States. It was also necessary to recognize that the Committee constituted an important means of recourse for the fulfilment of the right to food and that the Committee, in co-ordination with other United Nations agencies and non-governmental organizations, would need to intensify its efforts, which in turn would require the provision of adequate time and resources for the Council and the Committee to fulfil their obligations with respect to the Covenant. It was important that the Economic and Social Council bear this is mind in the allocation of resources to the Committee.

SEE ALSO *Hunger and Malnutrition; Standard of Living.*

FOOD AND AGRICULTURE ORGANIZATION OF THE UNITED NATIONS. By its constitution of 1945, the UN Food and Agriculture Organization was established as an autonomous permanent intergovernmental organization with a basic purpose of contributing towards an expanding world economy and ensuring humanity's freedom from hunger. Article 1 of that constitution mandates the FAO to collect, analyse, interpret, and disseminate information relating to nutrition, food, and agriculture; and to promote and recommend national and international action with respect to (1) conducting scientific, technological, social, and economic research relating to nutrition, food, and agriculture; (2) improving education and administration relating to nutrition, food, and agriculture, and spreading public knowledge of nutritional and agricultural science and practice; (3) conserving natural resources and adopting improved methods of agricultural production; (4) improving the processing, marketing, and distribution of food and agricultural products; (5) adopting national and international policies for the provision of adequate agricultural credit; and (6) adopting international policies with respect to agricultural commodity arrangements. The FAO is also authorized to furnish such technical assistance in its field of competence as governments may request.

As regards human rights, the FAO through its "Freedom from Hunger" campaign, launched in 1960, has distributed hundreds of thousands of tons of food to persons throughout the world who suffered from malnutrition. More recently, it joined the United Nations in establishing the World Food Programme which has carried out a far-reaching and highly successful campaign of development assistance through the supply of food.

A total of 156 States are members of the FAO; they include all UN Members States, with a few exceptions (Brunei, Byelorussian S.S.R., German Democratic Republic [before its re-unification with West Germany], Singapore, Solomon Islands, South Africa,

and Ukrainian S.S.R.), and five non-member States: the Democratic Republic of Korea, the Republic of Korea, Namibia (represented by the United Nations Council for Namibia), Switzerland, and Tonga. The main organs of the FAO are the General Conference, the Council, and the Secretariat. All members are represented in the General Conference, which determines policy and approves work programs and budgets. The Council, which supervises the day-to-day activities of the organization, is composed of representatives of 49 member States. The Director-General is appointed by the Council and supervises the work of the Secretariat.

The General Conference meets every two years, for a period of about three weeks, usually at FAO headquarters in Rome. The Council usually holds two annual sessions of approximately ten days each, one in June and one in November, also in Rome.

Under the terms of its agreement with the United Nations, the Food and Agriculture Organization transmits reports to UN organs on its activities and complies to the fullest extent possible with requests from those organs for special reports, studies, or information.

SEE ALSO *World Food Council.*

FORCED LABOR. Forced or compulsory labor is a practice which produces effects similar to slavery or develops into conditions analogous to slavery.

International problems resulting from forced or compulsory labor were studied by the INTERNATIONAL LABOR OFFICE from 1922 onwards; and, in 1929, the office issued a report (International Labor Conference, 12th session, Geneva, 1929: *Forced Labour: Report and Draft Questionnaire*) surveying the law and practice in this field. The report distinguished between three "purposes for which compulsion is employed:" (1) forced labour for general public purposes, such as the requisitioning of labor for public works, compulsory porterage, and compulsory cultivation of the land; (2) forced labor for local public purposes, such as the cleaning of village streets, disposal of refuse, or the construction and maintenance of government buildings and schools; and (3) forced labor for private employers, such as the labor which landowners sometimes may exact by law or custom from the population on their lands or the provision of convict labor to work for private employers.

The report indicated that, over a period of years, there had been a tendency both in law and in practice to eliminate the most brutal and unfair forms of forced labor and that the stage was set for international regulations banning the most reprehensible practices while making them subject to restrictive regulations in order to avoid abuses. This was the purpose of the ILO FORCED LABOR CONVENTION (ILO Convention No. 29), adopted by the International Labor Conference on 28 June 1930.

The convention defines "forced or compulsory labor" as "all work or service which is exacted from any person under the menace of any penalty and for which the said person has not offered himself voluntarily." However, article 2 (2) lists a number of forms of forced or compulsory labor which are excluded from the general definition and consequently are not banned or regulated by the Convention, among them:

(a) any work or service exacted in virtue of compulsory military service laws for work of a purely military character;

(b) any work or service which forms part of normal civic obligations of citizens of a fully self-governing country;

(c) any work or service exacted from any person as a consequence of a conviction in a court of law, provided that the said work or service is carried out under the supervision and control of a public authority and that the said person is not hired to or placed at the disposal of private individuals, companies or associations;

(d) any work or services exacted in cases of emergency, that is to say, in the event of war or of a calamity or threatened calamity, such as fire, flood, famine, earthquake, violent epidemic or epizootic diseases, invasion by animal, insect or vegetable pests, and in general any circumstance that would endanger the existence or the well-being of the whole or part of the population;

(e) minor communal services of a kind which, being performed by the members of the community in the direct interest of the said community, can therefore be considered as a normal civic obligations incumbent upon the members of the community, provided that the members of the community or their direct representatives shall have the right to be consulted in regard to the need for such services.

Under article 8, the power to exact forced or compulsory labor is vested in the highest civil authority of the territory concerned, which may, in certain cases, delegate that power to the highest local authorities. Article 9 provides that, before deciding to have recourse to forced or compulsory labor, the competent authority must satisfy itself (a) that the work to be done or the service to be rendered is of important direct interest for the community called upon to do the work or render the service; (b) that the work or service is of present or imminent necessity; (c) that it has been impossible to obtain voluntary labor for carrying out the work or rendering the service by the offer of rates for wages and conditions of work not less favorable than those prevailing in the area concerned for similar work or service; and (d) that the work or service will not lay too heavy a burden upon the present population, having regard to the labor available and its capacity to undertake the work.

Article 11 sets out conditions limiting the persons or types of persons who may be called upon for forced or compulsory labor, and article 12 limits the period for which a person may be taken for such labor to 60 days in any one period of 12 months. Under article 23, the competent authority is required to issue complete and precise regulations governing the use of forced or compulsory labor in order to give effect to the Convention.

The 1930 Forced Labor Convention was applied primarily by the colonial powers with respect to the territories which they administered. In such territories, it considerably strengthened the movement towards full freedom of employment. However, circumstances created by World War II gave rise to a revival of forced or compulsory labor, not only in the dependent territories but in some independent countries as well; and the ILO Committee of Experts on the Application of Conventions and Recommendations found it necessary to draw the attention of governments to the fact that the 1930 convention applied to independent as well as to dependent countries and territories.

After the establishment of the United Nations, an item entitled "Survey of Forced Labor and Measures for its Abolition" was placed on the agenda of the Economic and Social Council at the request of the American Federation of Labor. Subsequently, in 1951, the United Nations and the International Labor Organization jointly established the temporary Committee on Forced Labor, which received and investigated numerous allegations that such labor existed in various parts of the world.

The committee finished its work in 1953. The report which it submitted to the Economic and Social Council of the United Nations and the Governing Body of the International Labor Office (UN Doc. E/2431, para. 548–555; 557–561) set out the following general observations:

The Committee's enquiry has revealed the existence in the world of two principal systems of forced labour, the first being employed as a means of political coercion or punishment for holding or expressing political views, the second being employed for important economic purposes.

A system of forced labour as a means of political coercion was found by the Committee to be established in certain countries, to be probably in existence in several other countries, and to be possible of establishment in others. Such a system was found to exist in its fullest form and in the form which most endangers human rights where it is expressly directed against people of a particular "class" (or social origin) and even against political "ideas" or "attitudes" in men's minds; where a person may be sentenced to forced labour for the offence of having in some way expressed his ideological opposition to the established political order, or even because he is only suspected of such hostility; when he may be sentenced by procedures which do not afford him full rights of defence, often by a purely administrative order; and when, in addition, the penalty of forced labour to which he is condemned is intended for his political "correction" or "re-education", that is, to alter his political convictions to the satisfaction of the government in power. Such a system is, by its very nature and attributes, a violation of the fundamental rights of the human person as guaranteed by the Charter of the United Nations and proclaimed in the Universal Declaration of Human Rights. Apart from the physical suffering and hardship involved, what makes the system most dangerous to human freedom and dignity is that it trespasses on the inner convictions and ideas of persons to the extent of forcing them to change their opinions, convictions and even mental attitudes to the satisfaction of the State.

The Committee has also found that the systems of forced labour as a means of political coercion are applied with varying degrees of intensity in a number of countries, but it has observed in the trend of the laws and the aims and purposes of legislative enactments and administrative practices a tendency for countries which have less severe systems to approximate them to the more severe described above. The possibility of the extension of this system of forced labour as a means of political coercion to other countries or territories where unsettled conditions may prevail cannot be ignored.

While less seriously jeopardising the fundamental rights of the human person, *systems of forced labour for economic purposes* are no less a violation of the Charter of the United Nations and the Universal Declaration of Human Rights. Although such systems may be found in different parts of the world, their nature and scope are not everywhere the same.

These systems—still found to exist in some countries or territories where a large indigenous population lives side by side with a population of another origin—most often result from a combination of various practices or institutions affecting only the indigenous populations, and involving direct or indirect compulsion to work, such as compulsory labour properly so-called, various coercive methods of recruiting, the infliction of heavy penalties for breaches of contracts of employment, the abusive use of vagrancy legislation, restrictions on freedom of movement, restrictions on the possession and use of land, and other similar measures.

For nearly 25 years the International Labour Organisation has been striving to bring about the abolition of such practices and to improve the situation of indigenous workers. Conventions Nos. 29, 50, 64 and 65, and a number of supplementary Recommendations adopted by this Organisation, have shown the way of advance. The Committee's investigation has revealed that many of the countries concerned have ratified these Conventions and accepted the Recommendations, and in several of these countries or territories progress is commendable inasmuch as many of these practices have either been eliminated or are gradually declining. But progress has not been as rapid elsewhere. . . .

The Committee's enquiry has revealed that, while the forms of forced labour contemplated in the Conventions of the International Labour Organisation were virtually in relation to "indigenous" inhabitants of dependent territories, the systems of forced labour for economic purposes found to exist in some fully self-governing countries (where there is no "indigenous" population) raise new problems and call for action either by the countries concerned or at the international level.

Such systems of forced labour affecting the working population of fully self-governing countries result from various general measures involving compulsion in the recruitment, mobilisation or direction of labour. The Committee finds that these measures, taken in conjunction with other restrictions on the freedom of employment and stringent rules of labour discipline—coupled with severe penalties for any failure to observe them—go beyond the "general obligation to work" embodied in several modern Constitutions, as well as the "normal civic obligations" and "emergency" regulations contemplated in international labour Convention No. 29. They often deprive the individual of the free choice of employment and freedom of movement, and in this and other ways are contrary to the principles of the Universal Declaration of Human Rights.

In view of these findings, the Committee is of the opinion that the problems of compulsory labour, labour recruiting, the length of contracts of employment, penal sanctions for breaches of such contracts and other measures which have been examined in greater detail in regard to individual countries in Section IV, and which the International Labour Organisation has so far considered mainly in connection with indigenous workers, should now be examined also in connection with workers in fully self-governing countries.

The Committee has come to the conclusion that, however attractive the idea of using such methods with a view to promoting the economic progress of a country may seem to be, the result is a system of forced labour which not only subjects a section of the population to conditions of serious hardship and indignity, but which must gradually lower the status and dignity of even the free workers in such countries. The Committee suggests that, wherever necessary, international action be taken, either by framing new Conventions or by amending existing Conventions, so that they may be applicable to the position regarding forced labour conditions found to exist among the workers of fully self-governing countries.

The Committee undertook its work as a fact-finding body; its enquiry has revealed the existence of facts relating to systems of forced labour of so grave a nature that they seriously threaten fundamental human rights and jeopardise the freedom and status of workers in contravention of the obligations and provisions of the Charter of the United Nations. The Committee feels, therefore, that these systems of forced labour, in any of their forms, should be abolished, to ensure universal respect for, and observance of, human rights and fundamental freedoms.

In 1954, both the UN Economic and Social Council and the General Assembly condemned such systems of forced labor and appealed to all governments to re-examine their laws and administrative practices with a view to eliminating them. In 1957, the International Labor Conference adopted the **ILO ABOLITION OF FORCED LABOR CONVENTION** (**ILO** convention 105) under which States parties undertake to suppress and not to make use of any form of forced or compulsory labor (a) as a means of political coercion or education or as a punishment for holding or expressing political views or views ideologically opposed to the established political, social, or economic system; (b) as a method of mobilizing and using labor for purposes of economic development; (c) as a means of labor discipline; (d) as a punishment for having participated in strikes; or (e) as a means of racial, social, national, or religious discrimination.

The implementation of the 1930 and the 1957 conventions is monitored by the ILO Committee of Experts and the Conference Committee on the Application of Conventions and Recommendations, in accordance with a regular procedure based on the examination of reports from ratifying States.

SEE ALSO Bonded Labor.

FOREIGN DEBT: EFFECTS ON THE ENJOYMENT OF HUMAN RIGHTS. On 2 March 1989, the UN Commission on Human Rights stated its conclusion (resolution 1989/15) that social progress and economic development in all countries are key factors in the full promotion of human rights and fundamental freedoms and, accordingly, decided to include in the agenda of its 1990 session, under the item "Problems relating to the Right to Enjoy an Adequate Standard of Living: the Right to Development," a specific point entitled "Foreign Debt, Economic Adjustment Policies and Their Effects on the Full Enjoyment of Human Rights and, in particular, on the Implementation of the Declaration on the Right to Development."

FRANCE. The French Republic is a country in western Europe, on the Atlantic Ocean, the Mediterranean Sea, and the English Channel. It has borders with Belgium, the Federal Republic of Germany, Italy, Luxembourg, Spain, and Switzerland. It became a member of the United Nations in 1945. Its population is estimated by the UN (1990) to be 55,475,000. In addition, 1982 census statistics indicated that 1,252,000 persons lived at that time in French overseas departments (Guadeloupe, French Guyana, Martinique, Reunion, and *St. Pierre-et-Miquelon),* and 330,000 in French overseas territories (Mayotte, New Caledonia, French Polynesia, *Wallis-et-Fortuna,* and the southern and Antarctic territories). Ethnic groups in metropolitan France include persons of Celtic, Latin, Teutonic, Slavic, North African, Indochinese, and Basque origins. Languages commonly used are French (official), Arabic, German, and English. Religions practiced include Christianity (Roman Catholic, 90%; Protestant denominations, 5%), Islam (3%), and Judaism (2%). Literacy is estimated at 99%.

The government (1990) took the form of a republic. The president, elected by popular vote for a term of seven years, is head of State. He appoints the premier, who together with the cabinet is responsible to Parliament. The bi-cameral Parliament includes a 577-member National Assembly and a senate. The president has the right to dissolve the National Assembly or to ask Parliament to reconsider a law. The judicial system includes the Court of Cassation (civil and criminal law), Council of State (administrative law), and Constitutional Council (constitutional law). Political parties include the Socialist Party, the Rally for the Republic, the Union for French Democracy, the National Front, and the Communist Party. Francois Mitterrand, a socialist, was elected to a second seven-year term as president on 8 May 1988.

For some time, the increasing number of aliens in France has been a matter of concern. Between 31 December 1981 and 31 December 1982, for example, the increase amounted to 235,000 persons, including 120,000 illegal aliens whose status was regularized and 30,000 persons who benefitted from family unification measures. The largest national groups included Portuguese, 866,000; Algerians, 805,000; Moroccans, 492,000; Italians, 441,000; Spaniards, 395,000; Tunisians, 212,000; and Turks, 135,000. In addition, there were 139,000 refugees from other countries.

French policy provides for extra French language courses to be provided for children who need them, in order to raise foreign children's knowledge of the language to a minimum level required to integrate them into normal classes. Education also is provided in the language and culture of origin with the aim of facilitating both the integration of foreign students and, if necessary, their return to their country of origin.

In recent years, resentment has mounted in France against an estimated three million Muslim Arab immigrants now living in the country, and the extremist right-wing National Front has called for the eviction of all of France's total of about five million immigrants. In March 1990, after a bomb destroyed a mosque in western France, President Mitterrand denounced racism and added that "what is not acceptable is a crime that has its origin in the rejection of others and that is inspired by instinctive hatred." Jean Marie Le Pen, head of the National Front, responded that "these declarations by some political leaders are indecent when we know that these incidents are directly tied to social phenomena which are the direct results of the policy of immigration about which they are directly responsible."

The desecration in mid-May 1990 of 34 graves in a Jewish cemetery in Carpentras, north of Marseilles, was also blamed on racism incited by the National Front, although both the Front itself and Mr. Le Pen condemned the acts. Thousands of outraged French citizens and religious leaders from all parts of France participated in a pilgrimage of penitence and protest to the cemetery on 13 May; and thousands more, led by President Mitterrand, joined in a solemn mass protest demonstration in central Paris on the following day.

Territories. The government of France retained, or undertook, responsibility for the administration of a number of overseas departments and territories after the establishment of the United Nations, among them, overseas departments in French Guiana, Guadeloupe, Martinique, and Reunion; overseas territories in French Polynesia, New Caledonia and dependencies, St. Pierre and Miquelon, the southern and Atlantic lands and the Wallis and Fortuna Islands; and the island of Mayotte, which for some years has been the subject of a dispute. In 1974, and again in 1976, the largely Christian population of Mayotte voted against joining the Federal Islamic Republic of the COMOROS and declared its independence, retaining its close ties to France.

As regards the islands of New Caledonia, which are part of the chain of Melanesian islands spreading east and southeast from Papua New Guinea, Solomon Islands, and Vanuatu to Fiji, the territory was annexed by France on 24 September 1953. The colonization was resisted by the indigenous Melanesian Kanaks, resulting in bloody uprisings in which the Kanak population was decimated. By 1983, when the Kanaks had been reduced to 61,870—42.6% of the total population of 145,368—there was mounting pressure for independence for New Caledonia, which has rich mineral deposits including 40% of the world's known reserves of nickel. After a round-table conference between France and all parties in New Caledonia was held in July 1983, the French government recognized "the territory, including their innate and active right to independence. . . ."

In May 1984, France proposed, under the so-called Lemoine Statute, internal self-government for five years and a referendum in 1989 to choose between maintaining the status quo or independence. The statute, however, enfranchised any French citizen resident in New Caledonia for more than six months and failed to recognize demands of pro-independence parties for electoral reform and an earlier date for the proposed referendum. It was abandoned in 1985 in favor of a new concept—independence in association with France, to be the subject of a referendum in 1987. However, up to the end of 1988, the referendum had not been held.

France has consistently maintained that New Caledonia is an overseas territory of the French republic, not a colonial territory of which France is the administering power; and has claimed that it was the "sole judge of the state of emancipation reached by peoples under its administration." The majority of UN member States held, however, that it was for the United Nations to decide when a territory ceased to be non-self-governing.

On 22 November 1988, the UN General Assembly noted (resolution 43/34) that a dialogue with the peoples of New Caledonia had been initiated under the auspices of the French authorities on the status of the territory and noted that those authorities were taking positive measures to promote political, economic, and social development in New Caledonia to provide a framework for the peaceful progress of that territory to self-determination. The assembly urged all the parties involved, in the interest of all the people of New Caledonia, to continue that dialogue and to refrain from acts of violence.

A year later, on 11 December 1989, the assembly noted (resolution 44/89) "the positive measures being pursued in New Caledonia by the French authorities, in co-operation with all sectors of the population, to promote political, economic and social development in the Territory, in order to provide a framework for its peaceful progress to self-determination." Further, it invited all the parties involved to continue promoting a framework for the peaceful progress of the territory towards an act of self-determination in which all options are open and which would safeguard the rights of all New Caledonians.

As regards the question of the Comorian island of Mayotte, a dispute between France and the Comoros has persisted since December 1974, when the latter acceded to independence as the result of a referendum in which the peoples of the islands of Anjouan, Grande-Comore, and Moheli voted for self-government, while those of the island of Mayotte voted to retain close ties with France. The government of the Comoros, maintaining that the results of the referendum were to be considered on a global basis and not island-by-island under the terms of an agreement with France, has repeatedly expressed a wish to initiate as soon as possible a frank and serious dialogue with the French government with a view to accelerating the return to the Comorian island of Mayotte to the Islamic Federal Republic of the Comoros. The position of the government of the Comoros is supported by the United Nations, the Organization of African Unity, the Movement of Non-Aligned Countries, and the Organization of the Islamic Conference.

On 18 October 1989, the General Assembly, bearing in mind decisions on the subject taken by the aforementioned international organizations, reaffirmed the sovereignty of the Islamic Federal Republic of the Comoros over the island of Mayotte and invited the government of France to honor the commitments entered into prior to the referendum on the self-determination of the Comoro archipelago of 22 December 1974 concerning respect for the unity and territorial integrity of the Comoros. It urged the government of France to accelerate the process of negotiations with the government of the Comoros with a view to ensuring the return of Mayotte to the Comoros.

FRANCE: CONSTITUTION. The French Constitution, adopted by the referendum of 28 September 1958 and promulgated on 4 October 1958, as ammended (articles 6 and 7), includes the following provisions (Preamble and articles 1–7 and 64–66) relating specifically to human rights and fundamental freedoms:

Preamble

The French people hereby solemnly proclaims its attachment to the Rights of Man and the principles of national sovereignty as defined by the Declaration of 1789, reaffirmed and complemented by the Preamble of the Constitution of 1946.

By virtue of these principles and that of the free determination of peoples, the Republic hereby offers to the Overseas Territories that express the desire to adhere to them new institutions based on the common ideal of liberty, equality, and fraternity and conceived with a view to their democratic evolution.

Article 1. The Republic and the peoples of the Overseas Territories who, by an act of free determination, adopt the present Constitution thereby institute a Community.

The Community shall be based on the equality and the solidarity of the peoples composing it.

Title I—On Sovereignty

Article 2. France is a Republic, indivisible, secular, democratic and social. It shall ensure the equality of all citizens before the law, without distinction of origin, race or religion. It shall respect all beliefs.

The national emblem is the tricolor flag, blue, white and red.

The national anthem is the "Marseillaise."

The motto of the Republic is "Liberty, Equality, Fraternity."

Its principle is government of the people, by the people and for the people.

Article 3. National sovereignty belongs to the people, which shall exercise this sovereignty through its representatives and by means of referendums.

No section of the people, nor any individual, may attribute to themselves or himself the exercise thereof.

Suffrage may be direct or indirect under the conditions stipulated by the Constitution. It shall always be universal, equal and secret.

All French citizens of both sexes who have reached their majority and who enjoy civil and political rights may vote under the conditions to be determined by law.

Article 4. Political parties and groups shall be instrumental in the expression of the suffrage. They shall be formed freely and shall carry on their activities freely. They must respect the principles of national sovereignty and democracy.

Title II—The President of the Republic

Article 5. The President of the Republic shall see that the Constitution is respected. He shall ensure, by his arbitration, the regular functioning of the governmental authorities, as well as the continuance of the State.

He shall be the guarantor of national independence, of the integrity of the territory, and of respect for Community agreements and treaties.

Article 6. The President of the Republic shall be elected for seven years by direct universal suffrage.

The procedures implementing the present article shall be determined by an organic law.

Article 7. The President of the Republic shall be elected by an absolute majority of the votes cast. If this is not obtained on the first ballot, there shall be a second ballot on the second Sunday following. Only the two candidates who have received the greatest number of votes on the first ballot shall present themselves, taking into account the possible withdrawal of more favored candidates.

The voting shall begin at the formal summons of the Government.

The election of the new President shall take place twenty days at the least and thirty-five days at the most before the expiration of the powers of the President in office.

In the event that the Presidency of the Republic has been vacated, for any cause whatsoever, or impeded in its functioning as officially noted by the Constitutional Council, to which the matter has been referred by the Government, and which shall rule by an absolute majority of its members, the functions of the President of the Republic, with the exception of those provided for by Articles 11 and 12 below, shall be temporarily exercised by the President of the Senate and, if the latter is in his turn impeded in the exercise of these functions, by the Government.

In case of a vacancy, or when the impediment is declared definitive by the Constitutional Council, the voting for the election of a new President shall take place, except in case of an emergency officially noted by the Constitutional Council, twenty days at the least and thirty-five days at the most after the beginning of the vacancy or the declaration of the definitive character of the impediment.

There may be no application of either Articles 49 and 50 or of Article 89 of the Constitution during the vacancy of the Presidency of the Republic or during the period that elapses between the declaration of a definitive character of the impediment of the President of the Republic and the election of his successor. . . .

Title VIII—On Judicial Authority

Article 64. The President of the Republic shall be the guarantor of the independence of the judicial authority.

He shall be assisted by the High Council of the Judiciary.

An organic law shall determine the status of magistrates.

Magistrates may not be removed from office.

Article 65. The High Council of the Judiciary shall be presided over by the President of the Republic. The Minister of

Justice shall be its Vice President ex officio. He may preside in place of the President of the Republic.

The High Council shall, in addition, include nine members appointed by the President of the Republic in conformity with the conditions to be determined by an organic law.

The High Council of the Judiciary shall present nominations for judges of the Court of Cassation [Supreme Court of Appeal] and for First Presidents of Courts of Appeal. It shall give its opinion, under the conditions to be determined by an organic law, on proposals of the Minister of Justice relative to the nomination of the other judges. It shall be consulted on questions of pardon under conditions to be determined by an organic law.

The High Council of the Judiciary shall act as a disciplinary council for judges. In such cases, it shall be presided over by the First President of the Court of Cassation.

Article 66. No one may be arbitrarily detained.

The judicial authority, guardian of individual liberty, shall ensure respect for this principle under the conditions stipulated by law.

FRANCE: DECLARATION OF THE RIGHTS OF MAN AND OF THE CITIZEN.

Inspired by the American Declaration of Independence (SEE UNITED STATES OF AMERICA: DECLARATION OF INDEPENDENCE), the Declaration of the Rights of Man and of the Citizen was drafted by the French revolutionary clergyman, pamphleteer, and statesman Emmanuel Joseph (Abbé) Sieyes and decreed by the French National Assembly in morning sessions held on 20, 21, 22, 23, 24, and 26 August 1789. It was signed by Louis XVI on 5 October 1789 and was later embodied as a preamble in the French constitution of 1791.

The English translation below appeared in *The Constitution and Other Select Documents Illustrative of the History of France* (pp. 58–60), published by H. W. Wilson and Company, New York, 1904, and was reproduced in *Birthright of Man* (pp. 200–203), published by UNESCO, Paris, 1969.

Preamble

The representatives of the French people, organized in the National Assembly, considering that ignorance, forgetfulness or contempt of the rights of man are the sole causes of the public miseries and of the corruption of governments, have resolved to set forth in a solemn declaration the natural, inalienable, and sacred rights of man, in order that this declaration, being ever present to all the members of the social body, may unceasingly remind them of their rights and duties; in order that the acts of the legislative power and those of the executive power may be each moment compared with the aim of every political institution and thereby may be more respected; and in order that the demands of the citizens, grounded henceforth upon simple and incontestable principles, may always take the direction of maintaining the constitution and the welfare of all.

In consequence, the National Assembly recognizes and declares in the presence and under the auspices of the Supreme Being, the following rights of man and of the citizen:

I. Men are born and remain free and equal in rights. Social distinctions can be based only upon public utility.

II. The aim of every political association is the preservation of the natural and imprescriptible rights of man. These rights are liberty, property, security and resistance to oppression.

III. The source of all sovereignty is essentially in the nation; no body, no individual can exercise authority that does not proceed from it in plain terms.

Session of Thursday, 20 August

IV. Liberty consists in the power to do anything that does not injure others; accordingly, the exercise of the natural rights of each man has for its only limits those that secure to the other members of society the enjoyment of these same rights. These limits can be determined only by law.

V. The law has the right to forbid only such actions as are injurious to society. Nothing can be forbidden that is not interdicted by the law, and no one can be constrained to do that which it does not order.

VI. Law is the expression of the general will. All citizens have the right to take part personally or by their representatives in its formation. It must be the same for all, whether it protects or punishes. All citizens being equal in its eyes, are equally eligible to all public dignities, places employments, according to their capacities, and without other distinction than that of their virtues and their talents.

Session of Friday, 21 August

VII. No man can be accused, arrested or detained except in the cases determined by the law and according to the forms that it has prescribed. Those who procure, expedite, execute or cause to be executed arbitrary orders ought to be punished; but every citizen summoned or seized in virtue of the law ought to render instant obedience; he makes himself guilty by resistance.

VIII. The law ought to establish only penalties that are strictly and obviously necessary and no one can be punished except in virtue of a law established and promulgated prior to the offence and legally applied.

IX. Every man being presumed innocent until he has been pronounced guilty, if it is thought indispensable to arrest him, all severity that may not be necessary to secure his person ought to be strictly suppressed by law.

Session of Saturday, 22 August

X. No one ought to be disturbed on account of his opinions, even religious, provided their manifestation does not derange the public order established by law.

Session of Sunday, 23 August

XI. The free communication of ideas and opinions is one of the most precious of the rights of man; every citizen can freely speak, write, and print, subject to responsibility for the abuse of this freedom in the cases determined by law.

XII. The guarantee of the rights of man and of the citizen requires a public force; this force then is instituted for the advantage of all and not for the personal benefit of those to whom it is entrusted.

XIII. For the maintenance of the public force and for the expenses of administration a general tax is indispensable; it ought to be equally apportioned among all the citizens according to their means.

Session of Monday, 24 August

XIV. All the citizens have the right to ascertain, by themselves or by their representatives, the necessity of the public tax, to consent to it freely, to follow the employment of it, and to determine the quota, the assessment, the collection and the duration of it.

XV. Society has the right to call for an account from every public agent of its administration.

XVI. Any society in which the guarantee of the rights is not secured or the separation of powers not determined has no constitution at all.

XVII. Property being a sacred and inviolable right, no one can be deprived of it unless a legal established public necessity evidently demands it, under the condition of a just and prior indemnity.

Session of Wednesday, 26 August

FREEDOM OF INFORMATION. A most important element of freedom of expression and opinion is the right to freedom of information. While this right appears to enjoy almost universal acceptance in broad principle, a precise definition of its meaning and scope has eluded the international community for more than 40 years.

The General Assembly of the United Nations, at the first part of its first session, held in London in 1946, discussed a Philippine proposal to call an International Press Conference to ensure the establishment, operation, and movement of a free press throughout the world. On 9 February 1946, the assembly instructed the secretary-general (resolution 59 [I]) to place the question of the organization of such a conference on the agenda of the second part of that session.

In the resolution, the General Assembly declared that "freedom of information is a fundamental right and is the touchstone of all the freedoms to which the United Nations is consecrated," and resolved "to authorize the holding of a conference of all Members of the United Nations on freedom of information." The Economic and Social Council was instructed to undertake the convocation of such a conference, the purpose of which would be to formulate views concerning the rights, obligations, and practices that should be included in the concept of freedom of information. The assembly specified that delegations to the conference should include, in each instance, persons actually engaged or experienced in press, radio, motion pictures, and other media for the dissemination of information.

Accordingly, the council convened (resolution 74 [V]) the United Nations Conference on Freedom of Information, which met in Geneva in March-April 1948. The conference prepared three draft conventions—on the gathering and international transmission of news, on the institution of an international right of correction, and on freedom of information, as well as draft articles for inclusion in the Universal Declaration of Human Rights and the proposed Covenant on Human Rights. In addition, the conference adopted a series of general principles to be applied in the promotion and protection of freedom of information. These general principles are as follows:

Whereas

Freedom of information is a fundamental right of the people, and is the touchstone of all the freedoms to which the United Nations is dedicated, without which world peace cannot well be preserved; and

Freedom of information carries the right to gather, transmit, and disseminate news anywhere and everywhere without fetters; and

Freedom of information depends for its validity upon the availability to the people of a diversity of sources of news and of opinion; and

Freedom of information further depends upon the willingness of the Press and other agencies of information to employ the privileges derived from the people without abuse, and to accept and comply with the obligation to seek the facts without prejudice and to spread knowledge without malicious intent; and

Freedom of information further depends upon the effective enforcement of recognized responsibilities,

The United Nations Conference on Freedom of Information Resolves, therefore,

1. That everyone shall have the right to freedom of thought and expression: this shall include freedom to hold opinions without interference; and to seek, receive and impart information and ideas by any means and regardless of frontiers;

2. That the right of news personnel to have the widest possible access to the sources of information, to travel unhampered in pursuit thereof, and to transmit copy without unreasonable or discriminatory limitations, should be guaranteed by action on the national and international plane;

3. That the exercise of these rights should be limited only by recognition of and respect for the rights of others, and the protection afforded by law to the freedom, welfare, and security of all;

4. That in order to prevent abuses of freedom of information, Governments in so far as they are able should support measures which will help to improve the quality of information and to make a diversity of news and opinion available to the people;

5. That it is the moral obligation of the Press and other agencies of information to seek the truth and report the facts, thereby contributing to the solution of the world's problems through free interchange of information bearing on them, promoting respect for human rights and fundamental freedoms without discrimination, fostering understanding and co-operation between peoples, and helping maintain international peace and security;

6. That this moral obligation, under the spur of public opinion, can be advanced through organizations and associations of journalists and through individual news personnel;

7. That encouragement should be given to the establishment and to the functioning within the territory of a State of one or more non-official organizations of persons employed in the collection and dissemination of information to the public, and that such organization or organizations should encourage the fulfilment *inter alia* of the following obligations by all individuals or organizations engaged in the collection and dissemination of information;

(*a*) To report facts without prejudice and in their

proper context and to make comment without malicious intent;

(*b*) To facilitate the solution of the economic, social and humanitarian problems of the world as a whole through the free interchange of information bearing on such problems;

(*c*) To help promote respect for human rights and fundamental freedoms without discrimination;

(*d*) To help maintain international peace and security;

(*e*) To counteract the spreading of intentionally false or distorted reports which promote hatred or prejudice against States, persons or groups of different race, language, religion or philosophical conviction;

8. That observance of the obligations of the Press and other agencies of information, except those of a recognized legal nature, can also be effectively advanced by the people served by these instrumentalists, provided that news and opinion reach them through a diversity of sources and that the people have adequate means of obtaining and promoting a better performance from the Press and other agencies of information.

At the same time, the conference recognized (resolution No. 2) that the attainment of a just and lasting peace depends in great degree upon the free flow of true and honest information to all peoples and upon the spirit of responsibility with which all personnel of the press and other agencies of information seek the truth and report the facts; and that peoples have been misled and their mutual understanding seriously endangered by inaccurate reports, by defective or distorted presentation, and by deliberate or malicious misinterpretation of facts in various parts of the world. It condemned all propaganda either designed or likely to provoke or encourage any threat to the peace, breach of the peace, or act of aggression, and all distortion and falsification of news through whatever channels, private or governmental, since such activities can only promote misunderstanding and mistrust between the peoples of the world and thereby endanger the lasting peace which the United Nations is consecrated to maintain.

The conference also noted that there are, in some countries, media of information which disseminate racial and national hatred and recommended that the governments of such countries should encourage the widest possible dissemination of free information through a diversity of sources as the best safeguard against the creation of racial and national hatred and prejudice, encourage suitable and effective non-legislative measures against the dissemination of such hatred and prejudice, and encourage dissemination of information promoting friendly relations between races and nations based upon the purposes and principles of the United Nations.

On 13 May 1949, the assembly adopted the draft Convention on the International Transmission of News and Right of Correction, which consisted of an amalgamation of the provisions of the draft Convention on the Gathering and International Transmission of News and Convention on the Institution of an International Right of Correction. The assembly, however, decided that the convention it had approved should not be open for signature until the assembly had taken definite action on the draft Convention on Freedom of Information.

On 16 December 1952, the General Assembly decided to open for signature the substantive provisions of the convention that it had approved in 1949. Consequently, it adopted and opened for signature the CONVENTION ON THE INTERNATIONAL RIGHT OF CORRECTION (resolution 630 [VII]). The convention has been in force since 24 August 1962.

The "definite action" on the draft Convention on Freedom of Information which the General Assembly contemplated in 1949 had not been taken by the assembly up to the end of 1989. However, a committee established by the assembly in 1950 prepared a new version of the draft convention (Annex I), and on the basis of its work the assembly's Third Committee approved the preamble and four operative paragraphs (Annex II). These texts are reproduced below. Up to the end of 1989, they had not been approved by the assembly in plenary session.

In 1960, the Economic and Social Council prepared a draft Declaration on Freedom of Information and transmitted it to the assembly for consideration. The draft declaration is reproduced below (Annex III). Up to the end of 1989, it had not been considered or approved by the assembly.

Annex I
Preamble and Articles 1 to 4 of the Draft Convention on Freedom of Information, as Adopted by the Third Committee of the General Assembly
Preamble

The States Parties to this Convention,

Bearing in mind the Charter of the United Nations and the Universal Declaration of Human Rights,

Considering that freedom of expression, information and opinions are fundamental human rights,

Considering that the free interchange of accurate, objective and comprehensive information and of opinions, both in the national and in the international spheres, is essential to the causes of democracy and peace and for the achievement of political, social, cultural and economic progress,

Considering that freedom of information implies respect for the right of everyone to form an opinion through the fullest possible knowledge of the facts,

Desiring to co-operate fully with one another to guarantee these freedoms and to promote democratic institutions, friendly relations between States and peoples and the peace and welfare of mankind, and

Recognizing that in order to achieve these aims the media of information should be free from pressure or dictation, but that these media, by virtue of their power for influencing public opinion, bear to the peoples of the world a great responsibility, and have the duty to respect the truth and to promote understanding among nations,

Have accepted the following provisions:

Article 1. Subject to the provisions of this Convention,

(a) Each Contracting State undertakes to respect and protect the right of every person to have at his disposal diverse sources of information;

(b) Each Contracting State shall secure to its own nationals, and to such of the nationals of every other Contracting State as are lawfully within its territory, freedom to gather, receive and impart without governmental interference, save as provided in article 2, and regardless of frontiers, information and opinions orally, in writing or in print, in the form of art or by duly licensed visual or auditory devices;

(c) No Contracting State shall regulate or control the use or availability of any of the means of communication referred to in the preceding paragraph in any manner discriminating against any of its own nationals or of such of the nationals of any other Contracting State as are lawfully within its territory on political grounds or on the basis of their race, sex, language or religion.

Article 2. (a) The exercise of the freedom referred to in article 1 carries with it duties and responsibilities. It may, however, by subject only to such necessary restrictions as are clearly defined by law and applied in accordance with the law in respect of: national security and public order *(ordre public);* systematic dissemination of false reports harmful to friendly relations among nations and of expressions inciting to war or to national, racial or religious hatred; attacks on founders of religions; incitement to violence and crime; public health and morals; the rights, honour and reputation of others; and the fair administration of justice.

(b) The restrictions specified in the preceding paragraph shall not be deemed to justify the imposition by any State of prior censorship on news, comments and political opinions and may not be used as grounds for restricting the right to criticize the Government.

Article 3. Nothing in the present Convention may be interpreted as limiting or derogating from any of the rights and freedoms to which the present Convention refers which may be guaranteed under the laws of any Contracting State or any convention to which it is a party.

Article 4. The Contracting States recognize that the right of reply is a corollary of freedom of information and may establish appropriate means for safeguarding that right.

Annex II
Articles 5 to 19 of the Draft Convention on Freedom of Information, not yet Considered by the Third Committee of the General Assembly

Article 5. Each Contracting State shall encourage the establishment and functioning within its territory of one or more non-official organizations of persons employed in the dissemination of information and opinions to the public, so that such persons may thus be encouraged to observe high standards of professional conduct and, in particular, the moral obligations to report facts without prejudice and in their proper context and to make comments without malicious intent, and thereby to:

(a) Facilitate the solution of the economic, social and humanitarian problems of the world as a whole, by the free exchange of information bearing on them;

(b) Help to promote respect for human rights and fundamental freedoms without discrimination;

(c) Help to maintain international peace and security;

(d) Counteract the dissemination of false or distorted reports which offend the national dignity of peoples or promote hatred or prejudice against other States, or against persons or groups of different race, language, religion or philosophical conviction; or

(e) Combat any form of propaganda for war.

Article 6. Nothing in the present Convention shall affect the right of any Contracting State to take measures which it deems necessary in order to safeguard its external financial position and balance of payments.

Article 7. Nothing in the present Convention shall affect the right of any Contracting State to take measures which it deems necessary in order:

(a) To develop and protect its national news enterprises until such time as they are fully developed;

(b) To prevent restrictive or monopolistic practices or agreements in restraint of the free flow of information and opinions;

(c) To control international broadcasting originating within its territory, provided that such measures may not be used as a means of preventing the entry, movement or residence of nationals of other Contracting States engaged in the gathering and transmission of information and opinions for dissemination to the public.

Article 8. Nothing in the present Convention shall prevent a Contracting State from reserving under its legislation to its own nationals the right to edit newspapers or news periodicals produced within its territory, or the right to own or operate telecommunication facilities, including radio broadcasting stations, within its territory.

Article 9. (a) Nothing in the present Convention shall limit the discretion of any Contracting State to refuse entry into its territory to any particular person, or to restrict the period of his residence therein.

(b) The present Convention shall not apply to any national of a Contracting State who, while not otherwise admissible into the territory or another Contracting State, is nevertheless admitted conditionally, in accordance with an agreement between that other Contracting State and the United Nations or a specialized agency thereof, or pursuant to a special arrangement made by that other Contracting State in order to facilitate the entry of such national.

Article 10. As between the Contracting States which become parties to any general agreement on human rights sponsored by the United Nations and containing provisions relating to the freedom of information, in so far as any provision of the general agreement relates to the same subject matter, the two provisions shall, whenever possible, be treated as complementary so that both provisions shall be applicable and neither shall narrow the effect of the other; but in any case of incompatibility the provisions of the general agreement shall prevail.

Article 11. (a) In time of war or other public emergency, a Contracting State may take measures derogating from its obligations under the present Convention to the extent strictly limited by the exigencies of the situation.

(b) Any Contracting State availing itself of this right of derogation shall promptly inform the Secretary-General of the United Nations of the measures which it has thus adopted and of the reasons therefor. It shall also inform him as and when the measures cease to operate.

Article 12. Any dispute between any two or more Contracting States concerning the interpretation or application of the present Convention which is not settled by negotiations shall be referred to the International Court of Justice for decision unless the Contracting States agree to another mode of settlement.

Article 13. (a) The present Convention shall be open for signature to all States Members of the United Nations, to every State invited to the United Nations Conference on Freedom of Information held at Geneva in 1948, and to every other State which the General Assembly may declare to be eligible.

(b) The present Convention shall be ratified by the States signatory hereto in conformity with their respective constitutional processes. The instruments of ratification shall be deposited with the Secretary-General of the United Nations.

Article 14. (a) The present Convention shall be open for accession to the States referred to in paragraph (a) of article 13.

(b) Accession shall be effected by the deposit of an instrument of accession with the Secretary-General of the United Nations.

Article 15. (a) The present Convention shall come into force on the thirtieth day following the date of deposit of the sixth instrument of ratification or accession.

(b) For each State ratifying or acceding to the Convention after the deposit of the sixth instrument of ratification or accession, the Convention shall enter into force thirty days after the deposit by such State of it instrument of ratification or accession.

Article 16. The provisions of the present Convention shall extend to or be applicable equally to a signatory metropolitan State and to all the territories, be they non-self-governing, trust or colonial territories, which are being administered or governed by such metropolitan State.

Article 17. (a) Any Contracting State may denounce the present Convention by notification of denunciation to the Secretary-General of the United Nations.

(b) Denunciation shall take effect six months after the date of receipt by the Secretary-General of the United Nations of the notification of denunciation.

Article 18. The Secretary-General of the United Nations shall notify the States referred to in paragraph (a) of article 13 of the following:

(a) Information received in accordance with article 11;

(b) Signatures, ratifications and accessions received in accordance with articles 13 and 14;

(c) The date upon which the present Convention comes into force in accordance with article 15;

(d) Notifications received in accordance with article 17.

Article 19. (a) The present Convention, of which the Chinese, English, French, Russian and Spanish texts shall be equally authentic, shall be deposited in the archives of the United Nations.

(b) The Secretary-General of the United Nations shall transmit a certified copy to each State referred to in paragraph (a) of article 13.

Annex III
Draft Declaration on Freedom of Information as Adopted by the Economic and Social Council
Preamble

Whereas the development of friendly relations among nations and the promotion of respect for human rights and fundamental freedoms for all are basic purposes of the United Nations,

Whereas the Universal Declaration of Human Rights affirms: "Everyone has the right to freedom of opinion and expression; this right includes freedom to hold opinions without interference and to seek, receive and impart information and ideas through any media and regardless of frontiers",

Whereas freedom of information is essential to the respect for other human rights and fundamental freedoms, since no other liberty is secure if information cannot be freely sought, received and imparted,

Whereas freedom of information is also fundamental to peaceful and friendly relations between peoples and nations, since the erection of barriers to the free flow of information obstructs international understanding and thus impairs prospects for world peace,

Whereas newspapers, periodicals, books, radio, television, films and other media of information play an important role in enabling people to acquire the knowledge of public affairs necessary for the discharge of their responsibilities as citizens, and in shaping the attitudes of peoples and nations to each other, and therefore bear a great responsibility for conveying accurate information,

Now, therefore, the General Assembly,

Desiring to reaffirm the principles which should be upheld and observed and which domestic law and international conventions and other instruments for the protection of freedom of information should support and endeavour to promote,

Proclaim this Declaration on Freedom of Information in proof of its determination that all peoples should fully enjoy free interchange of information and access to all media of expression:

Article 1. The right to know and the right freely to seek the truth are inalienable and fundamental rights of man. Everyone has the right, individually and collectively, to seek, receive and impart information.

Article 2. All Governments should pursue policies under which the free flow of information, within countries and across frontiers, will be protected. The right to seek and transmit information should be assured in order to enable the public to ascertain facts and appraise events.

Article 3. Media of information should be employed in the service of the people. No Government or public or private body or interests should exercise such control over media for disseminating information as to prevent the existence of a diversity of sources of information or to deprive the individual of free access to such sources. The development of independent national media of information should be encouraged.

Article 4. The exercise of these rights and freedoms entails special responsibilities and duties. Those who disseminate information must strive in good faith to ensure the accuracy of the facts reported and respect the rights and the dignity of nations, and of groups and individuals without distinction as to race, nationality or creed.

Article 5. The rights and freedoms proclaimed above should be universally recognized and respected, and may in no case be exercised contrary to the purposes and principles of the United Nations. They should be subject only to such limitations as are determined by law solely for the purpose of securing due recognition and respect for the rights and freedoms of others and of meeting the just requirements of national security, public order, morality and the general welfare in a democratic society.

F

FREEDOM OF INFORMATION: THE CONCEPT.
In 1952, the UN Economic and Social Council (resolution 442 C [XIV]) appointed, for an experimental period of one year, and in a personal capacity, a special rapporteur on freedom of information, Mr. Salvador P. Lopez of the Philippines. In the report on contemporary problems and developments relating to freedom of information which he presented to the council in 1953 (UN Doc. E/2426), the special rapporteur analyzed the concept of freedom of information as follows:

The term "freedom of information" is a relatively new one. The concept, however, is old, being little more than the aggregate of the more familiar antecedent principles of freedom of thought, freedom of expression and freedom of the Press. Where freedom of information involves freedom of thought, it has deep roots in man's inborn thirst for knowledge, in his first struggles against ignorance and superstition, and in his earliest strivings after truth; where, on the other hand, it involves freedom of expression, its mainspring lies in the emergent political consciousness of man, his growing realization that this freedom is an indispensable weapon in the struggle against arbitrary and oppressive authority. Freedom of information is freedom of the Press by extension; it takes into account the other powerful media of mass communications which modern technology has placed in the service of ideas, as well as the rights and interests of the consumer of news.

Reverence for truth is age-old. An ancient Hebrew prophet proclaimed that "truth abideth and is strong for ever: she liveth and conquereth for everyone." In the Upanishads of India the supremacy of truth is declared: "Truth wins ever, not falsehood. With truth is paved the road to the divine."

In Athens, freedom of speech was recognized as a right of citizens. However, the trial and death of Socrates shows that this right did not necessarily include the absolute freedom to question all popular beliefs. Socrates preferred death to surrender of his convictions: "If you propose to acquit me", he said, "on condition that I abandon my search for truth, I will say: I thank you, O Athenians, but I will obey God, who, as I believe, set me this task, rather than you and so long as I have breath and strength I will never cease from my occupation with philosophy". Of free discussion he spoke in words which are still timely: "In me you have a stimulating critic, persistently testing your opinions and trying to show you that you are really ignorant of what you suppose you know. Daily discussion of the matters about which you hear me conversing is the highest good for man. Life that is not tested by such discussion is not worth living".

Similarly, in the later Roman Republic and the early Empire, no restrictions were imposed on opinion. There was general tolerance throughout the Empire of all religions and all opinions. The principle was expressed in the maxim of Emperor Tiberius: "If the gods are insulted, let them see to it themselves". An exception to the rule of tolerance was made in the case of the Christian sect which the state sought to extirpate by means of periodic bloody persecutions.

In the Middle Ages, the Church kept a firm hand on the expression of opinion, spoken or written, and when printing was discovered it co-operated with the secular authority in maintaining an even more stringent control of the printed word. Although freedom of belief and freedom of expression were reasserted by the religious leaders of the Reformation and the secular leaders of the Renaissance, censorship as an institution was firmly established under a bull issue by Pope Alexander VI in 1501 against unlicensed printing. In 1535 Francis I issued an edict prescribing the death penalty for the unauthorized printing of books, and soon afterwards the Sorbonne became the licensing authority and remained so until the French Revolution.

In England under Henry VIII the power of censorship passed from the ecclesiastical authorities to the Crown, which began to grant by letters patent the privilege of printing or selling books as a monopoly. Under subsequent rulers, limitations were placed on the number of printers and presses. Under an ordinance adopted by the Long Parliament, the licensing authority devolved primarily on the Archbishop of Canterbury and the chancellors or vice-chancellors of the universities.

It was this ordinance which called forth, in 1644, what is now recognised as the most famous defence of freedom of publication, John Milton's "Areopagitica, a Speech for the Liberty of Unlicensed Printing". Though it apparently received little notice when it was written, it has become, together with John Stuart Mill's essay "On Liberty", the classic argument in the English language for free speech:

"And though all the winds of doctrine were let loose to play upon the earth, so truth be in the field, we do injuriously by licensing and prohibiting to misdoubt her strength. Let her and falsehood grapple; who ever knew truth put to the worse, in a free and open encounter . . . For who knows not that truth is strong next to the Almighty; she needs no policies, nor stratagems, nor licensings to make her victorious, those are the shifts and defenses that error uses against her power."

In his essay "On Liberty" published two centuries later (1859), John Stuart Mill went beyond a merely utilitarian defence of liberty. When he said that all mankind has no right to silence one dissenter, he was proclaiming freedom of thought and expression as an ultimate value and as a moral attribute inseparable from the dignity of man.

In England, following the lapse of the Licensing Act in 1695, various court decisions clearly established the principle of the liberty of the Press. A succinct statement of this principle was made by Lord Mansfield in 1784:

"The liberty of the Press consists in printing without any previous license, subject to the consequences of the law."

The First Amendment of the United States Constitution adopted in 1791, provides:

"Congress shall make no law respecting an establishment of religion, or prohibiting the free exercise thereof; or abridging the freedom of speech, or of the Press; or the right of the people to assemble, and to petition the Government for a redress of grievances."

In varying phraseology, the constitution of the different states declare that every citizen may freely speak, write and publish his sentiments, on all subjects, being responsible for the abuse of that right; and no law shall be passed to restrain, or abridge, the liberty of speech, or of the Press.

While the First Amendment merely imposes a limitation upon action by Congress, the constitutions of virtually all the states contain, in addition, the concept of individual responsibility for abuse. Thus, the First Amendment as such did nothing to protect freedom of speech and of the Press against state action, and even when, after the Civil War, the Fourteenth Amendment appeared to extend the protection of the First Amendment to all "privileges or immunities of citizens of the United States" against abridgment through the states, the Supreme Court blocked, for a long time, the achievement of this broad purpose. It was not until 1925 that the Supreme Court, reversing earlier doctrines, began to make parts of the federal Bill of Rights applicable to the states.

In France, ecclesiastical control and licensing of publication remained effective until the French Revolution. During the first half of the eighteenth century, however, oppressive censorship both of religious and political opinion had already made freedom of publication a vital issue, and in this cause no one laboured so tirelessly as Voltaire. Of all the arguments for freedom of expression, none is more eloquent than the simple declaration attributed to him: "I wholly disapprove of what you say but will defend to the death your right to say it."

The principle of freedom of information in France is still that which was stated in article 11 of the Declaration of the Rights of Man and of the Citizen of 1789: "The unrestrained communication of thoughts or opinions being one of the most precious rights of man, every citizen may speak, write and publish freely, provided he be responsible for the abuse of this liberty in the cases determined by law."

Like other provisions of the Declaration, this was "reaffirmed" by the preamble of the Constitution of 27 October 1946. The Press Law of 29 July 1881, which embodies this principle, prohibits administrative intervention preceding publication, and precisely defines those cases where penalties may subsequently be imposed in accordance with law.

A similar provision is to be found in the constitutions of many modern States.

Soviet theorists consider freedom of speech and of the Press to be "among the most important political freedoms". However, their approach to securing freedom of information is conditioned by the basic Marxist opposition to private ownership of the means of production, distribution and exchange. Thus, according to Lenin, "the freedom of the Press is a delusion so long as capitalists commandeer the better printing establishments and the largest stores of paper, and capital retains its power over the Press". The technical and material facilities for publication are regarded as elements of socialist property which must be handed over to the working class and poorer peasantry for the purpose "of assuring in behalf of the toilers actual freedom to express their opinions".

In accordance with this doctrine, article 125 of the 1936 Constitution of the Union of Soviet Socialist Republics provides:

"In conformity with the interests of the working people, and in order to strengthen the socialist system, the citizens of the USSR are guaranteed by law:

"(*a*) Freedom of speech;

"(*b*) Freedom of the Press;

"(*c*) Freedom of assembly, including the holding of mass meetings;

"(*d*) Freedom of street processions and demonstrations.

"These civil rights are ensured by placing at the disposal of the working people and their organizations printing presses, stocks of paper, public buildings, the streets, communications facilities and other material requisites for the exercise of these rights."

Interpreting this principle, Mr. Andrei Vyshinsky has stated that "freedom of speech, of the Press . . . are the property of all the citizens in the USSR, fully guaranteed by the State upon which the sole condition that they be uti-

lized in accord with the interests of the toilers and to the end of strengthening the socialist social order". Freedom of speech and of the Press are denied to the foes of socialism, and "every sort of attempt on their part to utilize to the detriment of the State—that is to say, to the detriment of all the toilers—these freedoms granted to the toilers must be classified as a counter-revolutionary crime to which article 58, paragraph 10, or one of the corresponding articles of the Criminal Code is applicable . . ."

It may be argued, however, that the Soviet theory and practice is not necessarily inherent in socialist philosophy, since there are socialist governments which do not draw from the Marxist doctrine the same conclusion that the Press and other media of information are elements of socialist property. Moreover, though the same words are used, it is obvious that the Soviet interpretation of freedom of information has little in common with that which has evolved under the liberal individualist philosophy of the West.

Although the Soviet theory and practice in this field does represent a significant exception, freedom of information in the traditional Western concept has received widespread recognition as a fundamental human right. Both in theory and in law the essence of the principle is the recognition of complete freedom of expression, by writing or by other means, without prior restraint, but subject to the consequences of the law. The limitations relate to a number of strictly defined matters, principally libel, slander, obscenity, sedition and national security.

By analogy with the older concepts of freedom of thought and freedom of expression, freedom of information should be regarded as a fundamental right which must be defended at all times against infringement or denial by governmental authority. But, in accordance with the principle that every human right is necessarily limited by respect for the equal rights of others, freedom of information has unavoidable social implications. A man's right to impart information has no meaning of itself except in relation to the right of others to receive information.

To the extent that every new invention in mass communications has augmented the reach and impact of ideas, it has served to enhance also the social or collective aspect of freedom of information. Indeed, since ideas can now girdle the earth instantaneously through the ether, freedom of information has given rise to problems of a definitely international character. Consequently, the protection of the right to impart and to receive information has become a legitimate concern of governments acting individually in the interest of their respective peoples or jointly in the interest of all.

Moreover, the Press, film, radio and television have become highly organized institutions requiring considerable financial and technical resources for their operation. The right of a man to harangue a small group of persons at a street corner is one thing, but the right of a man or group to establish a newspaper, a radio or television state is another matter altogether. Gigantic systems of information present organized society with problems of a different order, quantitatively as well as qualitatively speaking. There is need for effective guarantees to ensure their successful operation, as well as for measures to minimize the possibilities of abuse and to prevent tendencies which would sacrifice the general welfare in the interests of private economic power.

The degree of freedom of information varies from country to country and technological advances are rapidly changing the nature of the problems everywhere. The important thing is to determine, in the light of existing conditions, how the principle—the right to impart information as well as the right to receive information—can be most effectively guaranteed. . . .

Dr. Hilding Eek of the University of Stockholm, Sweden, an expert consultant appointed by the secretary-general at the request of the Economic and Social Council, further elaborated on the concept of freedom of information in the *Report on Developments in the Field of Freedom of Information Since 1954* (UN Doc. E/3443), which he submitted to the council in 1960. Dr. Eek pointed out (para. 315–317) that:

This report has not sought for a definition of the concept of freedom of information. One main difficulty in dealing with "freedom of information" in connexion with the activities and aims of the United Nations is, in fact, that in the language of the United Nations "freedom of information" means nothing definite, constant and uncontroversial. Nor has the United Nations today a clear-cut programme which can be referred to as the United Nations programme in the field of freedom of information. "Freedom of information" means only an item on the agendas of various organs of the United Nations or one or several "projects", in the language of UNESCO.

Historical developments explain this situation. The term "freedom of information" and even more the traditional term "freedom of the Press" or "liberty of the press" is generally used and understood in an ideological sense. It refers to the struggle for the freedom of the Press and the arguments used in this struggle. A study of the text of the constitutions of States, where broad principles of government are laid down, would give the impression that there is general agreement amongst all or most States on what freedom of information means. But this is not the case. The explanation is that from the ideological and, as far as verbal formulation is concerned, common concepts of freedom, divergent legal concepts have evolved in the various countries. In many countries, legislation or judge-made laws is based on the ideal that the gathering and dissemination of news and opinions form an occupation which, because of its usefulness to society, should be granted special privileges and be protected against governmental interference. In other countries, however, the idea that information activities are a social function has led to the conclusion that, from the point of view of the law, no distinction in principle should be made between those activities and other activities within society, for instance sanitation or education, and that they may all, when it is thought necessary, be subject to administrative regulations and even severe governmental control.

The United Nations Conference on Freedom of Information (1948) was confronted with this basic difference of opinion. Although, since the Conference, freedom of information has been defined, in "ideological" terms, in the Universal Declaration of Human Rights, it has not been possible for the organs of the United Nations, i.e., for its Member States, to develop on the basis of the Declaration a common legal concept of freedom of information. Just as the political concepts vary from country to country, so do legal concepts diverge and with respect to freedom of information it has not been possible to bridge the gaps. At the same time the difficulties which the Conference had to face

and which the United Nations still is facing are augmented by the fact that in the contemporary world the basic problems are not the same as were encountered a hundred years ago when the battle for the freedom of the Press was fought and won. As a result of the technological revolution of the last century, the Press of today is a big industry in every country of the world where industrial development has taken place. There is in many countries a tendency towards concentration of ownership in the field of news media and a decrease of the numbers of competing newspapers. Dissatisfaction is sometimes shown by the public with the performance of the Press and other media; this performance is to a large extent the result of the professional work of professional men and women, while in the old days the printer, the publisher, the editor and the journalist were often the same man and his qualifications those of an *homme de lettres*. The growth of news agencies with a world-wide sphere of action and the development of such media as films, radio and television have also changed the picture, and created new and difficult problems which concern Governments and the public at large as well as those who direct information media or earn their living as information personnel.

SEE ALSO *Access of News Personnel to UN Meetings; Convention on International Right of Correction; European Convention on Transfrontier Television; European Declaration on Mass Communication Media and Human Rights; Journalists: Protection of Their Human Rights; UNESCO Declaration of Guiding Principles on the Use of Sattellite Broadcasting for the Free Flow of Information, the Spread of Education and Greater Cultural Exchange; UNESCO International Program for the Development of Communications.*

FRIENDS WORLD COMMITTEE FOR CONSULTATION. An international non-governmental organization in consultative status with the UN Economic and Social Council (Category II), and with UNESCO, UNICEF, and UNCTAD, the committee coordinates the work of Quaker organizations in 56 countries with a total individual membership of 241,000.

The committee was established in September 1937 in Swarthmore, Pennsylvania (U.S.A.), at a worldwide conference of the Religious Society of Friends, to encourage the spiritual life and solidarity of Quakers everywhere and to promote understanding between Friends and members of other faiths. It works to ensure human rights, disarmament, and resolution of conflicts, with an emphasis on the rights of minority peoples, the welfare of refugees, the promotion of conscientious objection, and education in disarmament and world peace.

FWCC's publications include the *Quaker Information Network* (issued six times a year) and *Friends World News* (issued two times a year). In addition, individual national Peace and Service organizations issue their own publications concerning human rights' issues.

Friends World Committee for Consultation. Address: Drayton House, 30 Gordon Street, London, WC1H OAX, England. Telephone: 44-01-388-0497. General Secretary: Val Ferguson.

G

GABON. The Gabonese Republic is a country in western Africa, on the Atlantic Ocean. It has borders with Cameroon, Congo, and Equatorial Guinea. It achieved independence from France in 1960 and became a member of the United Nations the same year. Its population is estimated by the UN (1990) to be 1,245,000. Ethnic groups include the Fang people, who constitute one-third of its population, and numerous tribal groups. Languages commonly used are French (official) and a variety of Bantu tongues. Christianity (Roman Catholic, 64%; Protestant faiths, 19%) is the prodominant religion; Animism and other faiths make up the remaining 17%. Literacy is estimated at 65%.

The government (1990) took the form of a republic. The president, elected by popular vote for a term of seven years, is head of State; the premier, appointed by him, is head of government. Legislation is prepared by the 120-member unicameral National Assembly. The predominant political party is the Gabonese Democratic Party.

An abundance of natural resources and an influx of foreign investment capital have made Gabon one of the most prosperous countries in western Africa.

GAMBIA. The Republic of Gambia is a country in western Africa, on the Atlantic Ocean. It is surrounded on three sides by Senegal. It achieved independence from Great Britain in 1965 and became a member of the United Nations the same year. Its population is estimated by the UN (1990) to be 715,000. Ethnic groups include a number of tribal populations. Languages in common use include English (official) and tribal vernaculars. Religions practiced include Islam (85%), Animism (13%), and Christianity (2%). Literacy is estimated at 20%.

The government (1990) took the form of a republic and member of the Commonwealth of Nations, of which the British sovereign is the symbolic head. In the Gambia, executive authority is exercised by the president, who is elected by popular vote and serves for a term of five years. Legislation is prepared by the 35-member unicameral House of Representatives;

the president selects his vice president and cabinet from among its members. The predominant political party is the People's Progressive Party.

Questions have been raised concerning the provisions of section 26 of the Gambian constitution, which permit DEROGATION from the right to non-discrimination during a period of public emergency. The government has explained to the HUMAN RIGHTS COMMITTEE that

what article 26 is designed to do is to enable the Government to deal effectively with any threat to the security or the integrity of the nation that may be posed by the actions of any particular religious, tribal or racial group. Such situations have arisen before in several countries. Where there is such a threat from any such group it is obvious that any action taken by the Government to remedy the situation will be directed at that particular group, not out of any desire to discrimination against that group, but in fulfilment of the duty of the State to preserve order, security and the integrity of the nation. Furthermore such action by the State can only be of a temporary nature and is only authorized during a period of public emergency. . . .

GENERAL ASSEMBLY. The General Assembly of the United Nations was established in accordance with article 7 of the UNITED NATIONS CHARTER. Its principal functions and powers are (1) to discuss any questions or any matters within the scope of the charter or relating to the powers and functions of any organs provided for in the charter, and to make recommendations to member States or to the Security Council, or both, on any such questions and matters; (2) to consider the general principles of cooperation in the maintenance of international peace and security, and to make recommendations with regard to such principles; (3) to discuss any questions relating to the maintenance of international peace and security brought before it by any member State, or by the Security Council, or by a non-member State, unless the Security Council is dealing with the question; and (4) to call the attention of the Security Council to situations which are likely to endanger international peace and security. Article 13 of the charter empowers the assembly to initiate studies and make recommendations for the purpose of "promoting international co-operation in the economic, social, cultural, educational and health fields, and assisting in the realization of human rights and fundamental freedoms for all without distinction as to race, sex, language or religion." Under article 14, it may recommend measures for the peaceful adjustment of any situation, regardless of origin, which it deems likely to impair the general welfare or friendly relations among nations. Under article 15, it receives and considers reports from the other UN organs, including the Security Council. Under article 16, it performs certain functions with respect to the international trusteeship system, including the approval of trusteeship agreements for the areas not designated as strategic. Under article 17, it considers and approves the budget of the United Nations and its financial and budgetary arrangements with the specialized agencies.

All members of the United Nations, which is open to every state which accepts the obligations set out in the UN Charter and is judged able and willing to carry out those obligations, are members of the General Assembly. The assembly admits them to membership on recommendation of the Security Council. In a few cases, states have been suspended or expelled by a decision of the assembly on recommendation of the Security Council, and in a few cases states have withdrawn from membership.

The General Assembly has three procedural committees: (1) the General Committee, which deals with the organization of its work; (2) the Committee on Conferences, which deals with the scheduling of sessions of subsidiary bodies; and (3) the Credentials Committee, which examines and reports on the credentials of representatives. In addition, it establishes seven main committees at each session: the First (Political and Security) Committee; the Special Political Committee; the Second (Economic and Financial) Committee; the Third (Social, Humanitarian and Cultural) Committee; the Fourth (Decolonization) Committee; the Fifth (Administrative and Budgetary) Committee; and the Sixth (Legal) Committee. It also sets up temporary committees and working groups as required. The main committees correspond to the major fields of responsibility of the General Assembly. On each of them, each member State has one vote. The role of the committees is to consider in detail agenda items referred to them and to prepare draft resolutions or decisions for final decision by the assembly in plenary session. The majority of items relating to human rights are usually considered by the Third Committee. However, such times are sometimes referred to and dealt with by the First Committee, the Special Political Committee, the Second Committee, the Fourth Committee, or the Sixth Committee. The financial implications of all draft resolutions and decisions are considered by the Fifth Committee before final action is taken by the assembly.

GENEVA CONVENTION RELATIVE TO THE PROTECTION OF CIVILIAN PERSONS IN TIME OF WAR (1949).

The convention (No. IV of the Geneva Red Cross Conventions for the Protection of Victims of War) was adopted on 12 August 1949 by the Diplomatic Conference for the Establishment of International Conventions for the Protection of Victims of War, convened in Geneva by the Swiss Federal Council with the cooperation of the International Committee of the Red Cross. The convention entered into force on 21 October 1950. Switzerland serves as the depository.

The convention was later revised and supplemented by PROTOCOL I, ADDITIONAL TO THE 1949 GENEVA CONVENTIONS AND RELATING TO THE PROTECTION OF VICTIMS OF INTERNATIONAL ARMED CONFLICTS, and by PROTOCOL II, ADDITIONAL TO THE 1949 GENEVA CONVENTIONS AND RELATING TO THE PROTECTION OF VICTIMS OF NON-INTERNATIONAL ARMED CONFLICTS. Both protocols entered into force on 7 December 1978.

The text of the convention is as follows:

The undersigned Plenipotentiaries of the Governments represented at the Diplomatic Conference held at Geneva from April 21 to August 12, 1949, for the purpose of establishing a Convention for the Protection of Civilian Persons in Time of War, have agreed as follows:

Part I
General Provisions

Article 1. The High Contracting Parties undertake to respect and to ensure respect for the present Convention in all circumstances.

Article 2. In addition to the provisions which shall be implemented in peacetime, the present Convention shall apply to all cases of declared war or of any other armed conflict which may arise between two or more of the High Contracting Parties, even if the state of war is not recognized by one of them.

The Convention shall also apply to all cases of partial or total occupation of the territory of a High Contracting Party, even if the said occupation meets with no armed resistance.

Although one of the Powers in conflict may not be a party to the present Convention, the Powers who are parties thereto shall remain bound by it in their mutual relations. They shall furthermore be bound by the Convention in relation to the said Power, if the latter accepts and applies the provisions thereof.

Article 3. In the case of armed conflict not of an international character occurring in the territory of one of the High Contracting Parties, each Party to the conflict shall be bound to apply, as a minimum, the following provisions:

(1) Persons taking no active part in the hostilities, in-

cluding members of armed forces who have laid down their arms and those placed *hors de combat* by sickness, wounds, detention, or any other cause, shall in all circumstances be treated humanely, without any adverse distinction founded on race, colour, religion or faith, sex, birth or wealth, or any other similar criteria.

To this end, the following acts are and shall remain prohibited at any time and in any place whatsoever with respect to the above-mentioned persons:

(*a*) violence to life and person, in particular murder of all kinds, mutilation, cruel treatment and torture;

(*b*) taking of hostages;

(*c*) outrages upon personal dignity, in particular humiliating and degrading treatment;

(*d*) the passing of sentences and the carrying out of executions without previous judgment pronounced by a regularly constituted court, affording all the judicial guarantees which are recognized as indispensable by civilized peoples.

(2) The wounded and sick shall be collected and cared for.

An impartial humanitarian body, such as the International Committee of the Red Cross, may offer its services to the Parties to the conflict.

The Parties to the conflict should further endeavour to bring into force, by means of special agreements, all or part of the other provisions of the present Convention.

The application of the preceding provisions shall not affect the legal status of the Parties to the conflict.

Article 4. Persons protected by the Convention are those who, at a given moment and in any manner whatsoever, find themselves, in case of a conflict or occupation, in the hands of a Party to the conflict or Occupying Power of which they are not nationals.

Nationals of a State which is not bound by the Convention are not protected by it. Nationals of a neutral State who find themselves in the territory of a belligerent State, and nationals of a co-belligerent State, shall not be regarded as protected persons while the State of which they are nationals has normal diplomatic representation in the State in whose hands they are.

The provisions of Part II are, however, wider in application, as defined in Article 13.

Persons protected by the Geneva Convention for the Amelioration of the Condition of the Wounded and Sick in Armed Forces in the Field of August 12, 1949, or by the Geneva Convention for the Amelioration of the Condition of Wounded, Sick and Shipwrecked Members of Armed Forces at Sea of August 12, 1949, or by the Geneva Convention relative to the Treatment of Prisoners of War of August 12, 1949 shall not be considered as protected persons within the meaning of the present Convention.

Article 5. Where, in the territory of a Party to the conflict, the latter is satisfied that an individual protected person is definitely suspected of or engaged in activities hostile to the security of the State, such individual person shall not be entitled to claim such rights and privileges under the present Convention as would, if exercised in the favour of such individual person, be prejudicial to the security of such State.

Where in occupied territory an individual protected person is detained as a spy or saboteur, or as a person under definite suspicion of activity hostile to the security of the Occupying Power, such person shall, in those cases where absolute military security so requires, be regarded as having forfeited rights of communication under the present Convention.

In each case, such persons shall nevertheless be treated with humanity, and in case of trial, shall not be deprived of the rights of fair and regular trial prescribed by the present Convention. They shall also be granted the full rights and privileges of a protected person under the present Convention at the earliest date consistent with the security of the State or Occupying Power, as the case may be.

Article 6. The present Convention shall apply from the outset of any conflict or occupation mentioned in Article 2.

In the territory of Parties to the conflict, the application of the present Convention shall cease on the general close of military operations.

In the case of occupied territory, the application of the present Convention shall cease one year after the general close of military operations; however, the Occupying Power shall be bound, for the duration of the occupation, to the extent that such Power exercises the functions of government in such territory, by the provisions of the following Articles of the present Convention: 1 to 12, 27, 29 to 34, 47, 49, 51, 52, 53, 59, 61 to 77, 143.

Protected persons whose release, repatriation or reestablishment may take place after such dates shall meanwhile continue to benefit by the present Convention.

Article 7. In addition to the agreements expressly provided for in Articles 11, 14, 15, 17, 36, 108, 109, 132, 133 and 149, the High Contracting Parties may conclude other special agreements for all matters concerning which they may deem it suitable to make separate provision. No special agreement shall adversely affect the situation of protected persons, as defined by the present Convention, nor restrict the rights which it confers upon them.

Protected persons shall continue to have the benefit of such agreements as long as the Convention is applicable to them, except where express provisions to the contrary are contained in the aforesaid or in subsequent agreements, or where more favourable measures have been taken with regard to them by one or other of the Parties to the conflict.

Article 8. Protected persons may in no circumstances renounce in part or in entirety the rights secured to them by the present Convention, and by the special agreements referred to in the foregoing Article, if such there be.

Article 9. The present Convention shall be applied with the cooperation and under the scrutiny of the Protecting Powers whose duty it is to safeguard the interests of the Parties to the conflict. For this purpose, the Protecting Powers may appoint, apart from their diplomatic or consular staff, delegates from amongst their own nationals or the nationals of other neutral Powers. The said delegates shall be subject to the approval of the Power with which they are to carry out their duties.

The Parties to the conflict shall facilitate to the greatest extent possible the task of the representatives or delegates of the Protecting Powers.

The representatives or delegates of the Protecting Powers shall not in any case exceed their mission under the present Convention. They shall, in particular, take account of the imperative necessities of security of the State wherein they carry out their duties.

Article 10. The provisions of the present Convention constitute no obstacle to the humanitarian activities which the International Committee of the Red Cross or any other impartial humanitarian organization may, subject to the consent of the Parties to the conflict concerned, undertake for the protection of civilian persons and for their relief.

Article 11. The High Contracting Parties may at any time agree to entrust to an organization which offers all guarantees of impartiality and efficacy the duties incumbent on the Protecting Powers by virtue of the present Convention.

When persons protected by the present Convention do not benefit or cease to benefit, no matter for what reason, by the activities of a Protecting Power or of an organization provided for in the first paragraph above, the Detaining Power shall request a neutral State, or such an organization, to undertake the functions performed under the present Convention by a Protecting Power designated by the Parties to a conflict.

If protection cannot be arranged accordingly, the Detaining Power shall request or shall accept, subject to the provisions of this Article, the offer of the services of a humanitarian organization, such as the International Committee of the Red Cross, to assume the humanitarian functions performed by Protecting Powers under the present Convention.

Any neutral Power, or any organization invited by the Power concerned or offering itself for these purposes, shall be required to act with a sense of responsibility towards the Party to the conflict on which persons protected by the present Convention depend, and shall be required to furnish sufficient assurances that it is in a position to undertake the appropriate functions and to discharge them impartially.

No derogation from the preceding provisions shall be made by special agreements between Powers one of which is restricted, even temporarily, in its freedom to negotiate with the other Power or its allies by reason of military events, more particularly where the whole, or a substantial part, of the territory of the said Power is occupied.

Whenever in the present Convention mention is made of a Protecting Power, such mention applies to substitute organizations in the sense of the present Article.

The provisions of this Article shall extend and be adapted to cases of nationals of a neutral State who are in occupied territory or who find themselves in the territory of a belligerent State in which the State of which they are nationals has not normal diplomatic representation.

Article 12. In cases where they deem it advisable in the interest of protected persons, particularly in cases of disagreement between the Parties to the conflict as to the application or interpretation of the provisions of the present Convention, the Protecting Powers shall lend their good offices with a view to settling the disagreement.

For this purpose, each of the Protecting Powers may, either at the invitation of one Party or on its own initiative, propose to the Parties to the conflict a meeting of their representatives, and in particular of the authorities responsible for protected persons, possibly on neutral territory suitably chosen. The Parties to the conflict shall be bound to give effect to the proposals made to them for this purpose. The Protecting Powers may, if necessary, propose for approval by the Parties to the conflict, a person belonging to a neutral Power or delegated by the International Committee of the Red Cross, who shall be invited to take part in such a meeting.

Part II
General Protection of Populations Against Certain Consequences of War

Article 13. The provisions of Part II cover the whole of the populations of the countries in conflict, without any adverse distinction based, in particular, on race, nationality, religion or political opinion, and are intended to alleviate the sufferings caused by war.

Article 14. In time of peace, the High Contracting Parties and, after the outbreak of hostilities, the Parties thereto, may establish in their own territory and, if the need arises, in occupied areas, hospital and safety zones and localities so organized as to protect from the effects of war, wounded, sick and aged persons, children under fifteen, expectant-mothers and mothers of children under seven.

Upon the outbreak and during the course of hostilities, the Parties concerned may conclude agreements on mutual recognition of the zones and localities they have created. They may for this purpose implement the provisions of the Draft Agreement annexed to the present Convention, with such amendments as they may consider necessary.

The Protecting Powers and the International Committee of the Red Cross are invited to lend their good offices in order to facilitate the institution and recognition of these hospital and safety zones and localities.

Article 15. Any Party to the conflict may, either direct or through a neutral State or some humanitarian organization, propose to the adverse Party to establish, in the regions where fighting is taking place, neutralized zones intended to shelter from the effects of war the following persons, without distinction:

(*a*) wounded and sick combatants or non-combatants;

(*b*) civilian persons who take no part in hostilities, and who, while they reside in the zones, perform no work of a military character.

When the Parties concerned have agreed upon the geographical position, administration, food supply and supervision of the proposed neutralized zone, a written agreement shall be concluded and signed by the representatives of the Parties to the conflict. The agreement shall fix the beginning and the duration of the neutralization of the zone.

Article 16. The wounded and sick, as well as the infirm, and expectant mothers, shall be the object of particular protection and respect.

As far as military considerations allow, each Party to the conflict shall facilitate the steps taken to search for the killed and wounded, to assist the shipwrecked and other persons exposed to grave danger, and to protect them against pillage and ill-treatment.

Article 17. The Parties to the conflict shall endeavour to conclude local agreements for the removal from besieged or encircled areas, of wounded, sick, infirm, and aged persons, children and maternity cases, and for the passage of ministers of all religions, medical personnel and medical equipment on their way to such areas.

Article 18. Civilian hospitals organized to give care to the wounded and sick, the infirm and maternity cases, may in no circumstances be the object of attack, but shall at all times be respected and protected by the Parties to the conflict.

States which are Parties to a conflict shall provide all civilian hospitals with certificates showing that they are civilian hospitals and that the buildings which they occupy are not used for any purpose which would deprive these hospitals of protection in accordance with Article 19.

Civilian hospitals shall be marked by means of the emblem provided for in Article 38 of the Geneva Convention for the Amelioration of the Condition of the Wounded and Sick in Armed Forces in the Field of August 12, 1949, but only if so authorized by the State.

The Parties to the conflict shall, in so far as military considerations permit, take the necessary steps to make the distinctive emblems indicating civilian hospitals clearly visible to the enemy land, air and naval forces in order to obviate the possibility of any hostile action.

In view of the dangers to which hospitals may be exposed by being close to military objectives, it is recommended that such hospitals be situated as far as possible from such objectives.

Article 19. The protection to which civilian hospitals are entitled shall not cease unless they are used to commit, outside their humanitarian duties, acts harmful to the enemy. Protection may, however, cease only after due warning has been given, naming, in all appropriate cases, a reasonable time limit, and after such warning has remained unheeded.

The fact that sick or wounded members of the armed forces are nursed in these hospitals, or the presence of small arms and ammunition taken from such combatants and not yet handed to the proper service, shall not be considered to be acts harmful to the enemy.

Article 20. Persons regularly and solely engaged in the operation and administration of civilian hospitals, including the personnel engaged in the search for, removal and transporting of and caring for wounded and sick civilians, the infirm and maternity cases, shall be respected and protected.

In occupied territory and in zones of military operations, the above personnel shall be recognizable by means of an identity card certifying their status, bearing the photograph of the holder and embossed with the stamp of the responsible authority, and also by means of a stamped, water-resistant armlet which they shall wear on the left arm while carrying out their duties. This armlet shall be issued by the State and shall bear the emblem provided for in Article 38 of the Geneva Convention for the Amelioration of the Condition of the Wounded and Sick in Armed Forces in the Field of August 12, 1949.

Other personnel who are engaged in the operation and administration of civilian hospitals shall be entitled to respect and protection and to wear the armlet, as provided in and under the conditions prescribed in this Article, while they are employed on such duties. The identity card shall state the duties on which they are employed.

The management of each hospital shall at all times hold at the disposal of the competent national or occupying authorities an up-to-date list of such personnel.

Article 21. Convoys of vehicles or hospital trains on land or specially provided vessels on sea, conveying wounded and sick civilians, the infirm and maternity cases, shall be respected and protected in the same manner as the hospitals provided for in Article 18, and shall be marked, with the consent of the State, by the display of the distinctive emblem provided for in Article 38 of the Geneva Convention for the Amelioration of the Condition of the Wounded and Sick in Armed Forces in the Field of August 12, 1949,[1]

Article 22. Aircraft exclusively employed for the removal of wounded and sick civilians, the infirm and maternity cases, or for the transport of medical personnel and equipment, shall not be attacked, but shall be respected while flying at heights, times and on routes specifically agreed upon between all the Parties to the conflict concerned.

They may be marked with the distinctive emblem provided for in Article 38 of the Geneva Convention for the Amelioration of the Condition of the Wounded and Sick in Armed Forces in the Field of August 12, 1949.

Unless agreed otherwise, flights over enemy or enemy-occupied territory are prohibited.

Such aircraft shall obey every summons to land. In the event of a landing thus imposed, the aircraft with its occupants may continue its flight after examination, if any.

Article 23. Each High Contracting Party shall allow the free passage of all consignments of medical and hospital stores and objects necessary for religious worship intended only for civilians of another High Contracting Party, even if the latter is its adversary. It shall likewise permit the free passage of all consignments of essential foodstuffs, clothing and tonics intended for children under fifteen, expectant mothers and maternity cases.

The obligation of a High Contracting Party to allow the free passage of the consignments indicated in the preceding paragraph is subject to the condition that this Party is satisfied that there are no serious reasons for fearing:

(*a*) that the consignments may be diverted from their destination.

(*b*) that the control may not be effective, or

(*c*) that a definite advantage may accrue to the military efforts or economy of the enemy through the substitution of the above-mentioned consignments for goods which would otherwise be provided or produced by the enemy or through the release of such material, services or facilities as would otherwise be required for the production of such goods.

The Power which allows the passage of the consignments indicated in the first paragraph of this Article may make such permission conditional on the distribution to the persons benefited thereby being made under the local supervision of the Protecting Powers.

Such consignments shall be forwarded as rapidly as possible, and the Power which permits their free passage shall have the right to prescribe the technical arrangements under which such passage is allowed.

Article 24. The Parties to the conflict shall take the necessary measures to ensure that children under fifteen, who are orphaned or are separated from their families as a result of the war, are not left to their own resources, and that their maintenance, the exercise of their religion and their education are facilitated in all circumstances. Their education shall, as far as possible, be entrusted to persons of a similar cultural tradition.

The Parties to the conflict shall facilitate the reception of such children in a neutral country for the duration of the conflict with the consent of the Protecting Power, if any, and under due safeguards for the observance of the principles stated in the first paragraph.

They shall, furthermore, endeavour to arrange for all children under twelve to be identified by the wearing of identity discs, or by some other means.

Article 25. All persons in the territory of a Party to the conflict, or in a territory occupied by it, shall be enabled to give news of a strictly personal nature to members of their families, wherever they may be, and to receive news from them. This correspondence shall be forwarded speedily and without undue delay.

If, as a result of circumstances, it becomes difficult or impossible to exchange family correspondence by the ordinary post, the Parties to the conflict concerned shall apply to a neutral intermediary, such as the Central Agency provided for in Article 140, and shall decide in consultation with it how to ensure the fulfilment of their obligations under the best possible conditions, in particular with the cooperation of the National Red Cross (Red Crescent, Red Lion and Sun) Societies.

If the Parties to the conflict deem it necessary to restrict family correspondence, such restrictions shall be confined to the compulsory use of standard forms containing twenty-five freely chosen words, and to the limitation of the number of these forms despatched to one each month.

Article 26. Each Party to the conflict shall facilitate enquiries made by members of families dispersed owing to the war, with the object of renewing contact with one another and of meeting, if possible. It shall encourage, in particular, the work of organizations engaged on this task provided they are acceptable to it and conform to its security regulations.

Part III
Status and Treatment of Protected Persons
Section I—Provisions Common to the Territories of the Parties to the Conflict and to Occupied Territories

Article 27. Protected persons are entitled, in all circumstances, to respect for their persons, their honour, their family rights, their religious convictions and practices, and their manners and customs. They shall at all times be humanely treated, and shall be protected especially against all acts of violence or threats thereof and against insults and public curiosity.

Women shall be especially protected against any attack on their honour, in particular against rape, enforced prostitution, or any form of indecent assault.

Without prejudice to the provisions relating to their state of health, age and sex, all protected persons shall be treated with the same consideration by the Party to the conflict in whose power they are, without any adverse distinction based, in particular, on race, religion or political opinion.

However, the Parties to the conflict may take such measures of control and security in regard to protected persons as may be necessary as a result of the war.

Article 28. The presence of a protected person may not be used to render certain points or areas immune from military operations.

Article 29. The Party to the conflict in whose hands protected persons may be, is responsible for the treatment accorded to them by its agents, irrespective of any individual responsibility which may be incurred.

Article 30. Protected persons shall have every facility for making application to the Protecting Powers, the International Committee of the Red Cross, the National Red Cross (Red Crescent, Red Lion and Sun) Society of the country where they may be, as well as to any organization that might assist them.

These several organizations shall be granted all facilities for that purpose by the authorities, within the bounds set by military or security considerations.

Apart from the visits of the delegates of the Protecting Powers and of the International Committee of the Red Cross, provided for by Article 143, the Detaining or Occupying Powers shall facilitate as much as possible visits to protected persons by the representatives of other organizations whose object is to give spiritual aid or material relief to such persons.

Article 31. No physical or moral coercion shall be exercised against protected persons, in particular to obtain information from them or from third parties.

Article 32. The High Contracting Parties specifically agree that each of them is prohibited from taking any measure of such a character as to cause the physical suffering or extermination of protected persons in their hands. This prohibition applies not only to murder, torture, corporal punishment, mutilation and medical or scientific experiments not necessitated by the medical treatment of a protected person, but also to any other measures of brutality whether applied by civilian or military agents.

Article 33. No protected person may be punished for an offence he or she has not personally committed. Collective penalties and likewise all measures of intimidation or of terrorism are prohibited.

Pillage is prohibited.

Reprisals against protected persons and their property are prohibited.

Article 34. The taking of hostages is prohibited.

Section II
Aliens in the Territory of a Party to the Conflict

Article 35. All protected persons who may desire to leave the territory at the outset of, or during a conflict, shall be entitled to do so, unless their departure is contrary to the national interests of the State. The applications of such persons to leave shall be decided in accordance with regularly established procedures and the decision shall be taken as rapidly as possible. Those persons permitted to leave may provide themselves with the necessary funds for their journey and take with them a reasonable amount of their effects and articles of personal use.

If any such person is refused permission to leave the territory, he shall be entitled to have such refusal reconsidered as soon as possible by an appropriate court or administrative board designated by the Detaining Power for that purpose.

Upon request, representatives of the Protecting Power shall, unless reasons of security prevent it, or the persons concerned object, be furnished with the reasons for refusal of any request for permission to leave the territory and be given, as expeditiously as possible, the names of all persons who have been denied permission to leave.

Article 36. Departures permitted under the foregoing Article shall be carried out in satisfactory conditions as regards safety, hygiene, sanitation and food. All costs in connection therewith, from the point of exit in the territory of the Detaining Power, shall be borne by the country of destination, or, in the case of accommodation in a neutral country, by the Power whose nationals are benefited. The practical details of such movements may, if necessary, be settled by special agreements between the Powers concerned.

The foregoing shall not prejudice such special agreements as may be concluded between Parties to the conflict concerning the exchange and repatriation of their nationals in enemy hands.

Article 37. Protected persons who are confined pending proceedings or serving a sentence involving loss of liberty, shall during their confinement be humanely treated.

As soon as they are released, they may ask to leave the territory in conformity with the foregoing Articles.

Article 38. With the exception of special measures authorized by the present Convention, in particular by Articles 27 and 41 thereof, the situation of protected persons shall continue to be regulated, in principle, by the provisions concerning aliens in time of peace. In any case, the following rights shall be granted to them:

(1) They shall be enabled to receive the individual or collective relief that may be sent to them.

(2) They shall, if their state of health so requires, receive

medical attention and hospital treatment to the same extent as the nationals of the State concerned.

(3) They shall be allowed to practise their religion and to receive spiritual assistance from ministers of their faith.

(4) If they reside in an area particularly exposed to the dangers of war, they shall be authorised to move from that area to the same extent as the nationals of the State concerned.

(5) Children under fifteen years, pregnant women and mothers of children under seven years shall benefit by any preferential treatment to the same extent as the nationals of the State concerned.

Article 39. Protected persons who, as a result of the war, have lost their gainful employment, shall be granted the opportunity to find paid employment. That opportunity shall, subject to security considerations and to the provisions of Article 40, be equal to that enjoyed by the nationals of the Power in whose territory they are.

Where a Party to the conflict applies to a protected person methods of control which result in his being unable to support himself, and especially if such a person is prevented for reasons of security from finding paid employment on reasonable conditions, the said Party shall ensure his support and that of his dependents.

Protected persons may in any case receive allowances from their home country, the Protecting Power, or the relief societies referred to in Article 30.

Article 40. Protected persons may be compelled to work only to the same extent as nationals of the Party to the conflict in whose territory they are.

If protected persons are of enemy nationality, they may only be compelled to do work which is normally necessary to ensure the feeding, sheltering, clothing, transport and health of human beings and which is not directly related to the conduct of military operations.

In the cases mentioned in the two preceding paragraphs, protected persons compelled to work shall have the benefit of the same working conditions and of the same safeguards as national workers, in particular as regards wages, hours of labour, clothing and equipment, previous training and compensation for occupational accidents and diseases.

If the above provisions are infringed, protected persons shall be allowed to exercise their right of complaint in accordance with Article 30.

Article 41. Should the Power in whose hands protected persons may be consider the measures of control mentioned in the present Convention to be inadequate, it may not have recourse to any other measure of control more severe than that of assigned residence or internment, in accordance with the provisions of Articles 42 and 43.

In applying the provisions of Article 39, second paragraph, to the cases of persons required to leave their usual places of residence by virtue of a decision placing them in assigned residence elsewhere, the Detaining Power shall be guided as closely as possible by the standards of welfare set forth in Part III, Section IV of this Convention.

Article 42. The internment or placing in assigned residence of protected persons may be ordered only if the security of the Detaining Power makes it absolutely necessary.

If any person, acting through the representatives of the Protecting Power, voluntarily demands internment, and if his situation renders this step necessary, he shall be interned by the Power in whose hands he may be.

Article 43. Any protected person who has been interned or placed in assigned residence shall be entitled to have such action reconsidered as soon as possible by an appro-priate court or administrative board designated by the Detaining Power for that purpose. If the internment or placing in assigned residence is maintained, the court or administrative board shall periodically, and at least twice yearly, give consideration to his or her case with a view to the favourable amendment of the initial decision, if circumstances permit.

Unless the protected persons concerned object, the Detaining Power shall, as rapidly as possible, give the Protecting Power the names of any protected persons who have been interned or subjected to assigned residence, or who have been released from internment or assigned residence. The decisions of the courts or boards mentioned in the first paragraph of the present Article shall also, subject to the same conditions, be notified as rapidly as possible to the Protecting Power.

Article 44. In applying the measures of control mentioned in the present Convention, the Detaining Power shall not treat as enemy aliens exclusively on the basis of their nationality *de jure* of an enemy State, refugees who do not, in fact, enjoy the protection of any government.

Article 45. Protected persons shall not be transferred to a Power which is not a party to the Convention.

This provision shall in no way constitute an obstacle to the repatriation of protected persons, or to their return to their country of residence after the cessation of hostilities.

Protected persons may be transferred by the Detaining Power only to a Power which is a party to the present Convention and after the Detaining Power has satisfied itself of the willingness and ability of such transferee Power to apply the present Convention. If protected persons are transferred under such circumstances, responsibility for the application of the present Convention rests on the Power accepting them, while they are in its custody. Nevertheless, if that Power fails to carry out the provisions of the present Convention in any important respect, the Power by which the protected persons were transferred shall, upon being so notified by the Protecting Power, take effective measures to correct the situation or shall request the return of the protected persons. Such request must be complied with.

In no circumstances shall a protected person be transferred to a country where he or she may have reason to fear persecution for his or her political opinions or religious beliefs.

The provisions of this Article do not constitute an obstacle to the extradition, in pursuance of extradition treaties concluded before the outbreak of hostilities, of protected persons accused of offences against ordinary criminal law.

Article 46. In so far as they have not been previously withdrawn, restrictive measures taken regarding protected persons shall be cancelled as soon as possible after the close of hostilities.

Restrictive measures affecting their property shall be cancelled, in accordance with the law of the Detaining Power, as soon as possible after the close of hostilities.

Section III—Occupied Territories

Article 47. Protected persons who are in occupied territory shall not be deprived, in any case or in any manner whatsoever, of the benefits of the present Convention by any change introduced, as the result of the occupation of a territory, into the institutions or government of the said territory, nor by any agreement concluded between the authorities of the occupied territories and the Occupying

Power, nor by any annexation by the latter of the whole or part of the occupied territory.

Article 48. Protected persons who are not nationals of the Power whose territory is occupied, may avail themselves of the right to leave the territory subject to the provisions of Article 35, and decisions thereon shall be taken according to the procedure which the Occupying Power shall establish in accordance with the said Article.

Article 49. Individual or mass forcible transfers, as well as deportations of protected persons from occupied territory to the territory of the Occupying Power or to that of any other country, occupied or not, are prohibited, regardless of their motive.

Nevertheless, the Occupying Power may undertake total or partial evacuation of a given area if the security of the population or imperative military reasons so demand. Such evacuations may not involve the displacement of protected persons outside the bounds of the occupied territory except when for material reasons it is impossible to avoid such displacement. Persons thus evacuated shall be transferred back to their homes as soon as hostilities in the area in question have ceased.

The Occupying Power undertaking such transfers or evacuations shall ensure, to the greatest practicable extent, that proper accommodation is provided to receive the protected persons, that the removals are effected in satisfactory conditions of hygiene, health, safety and nutrition, and that members of the same family are not separated.

The Protecting Power shall be informed of any transfers and evacuations as soon as they have taken place.

The Occupying Power shall not detain protected persons in an area particularly exposed to the dangers of war unless the security of the population or imperative military reasons so demand.

The Occupying Power shall not deport or transfer parts of its own civilian population into the territory it occupies.

Article 50. The Occupying Power shall, with the cooperation of the national and local authorities, facilitate the proper working of all institutions devoted to the care and education of children.

The Occupying Power shall take all necessary steps to facilitate the identification of children and the registration of their parentage. It may not, in any case, change their personal status, nor enlist them in formations or organizations subordinate to it.

Should the local institutions be inadequate for the purpose, the Occupying Power shall make arrangements for the maintenance and education, if possible by persons of their own nationality, language and religion, of children who are orphaned or separated from their parents as a result of the war and who cannot be adequately cared for by a near relative or friend.

A special section of the Bureau set up in accordance with Article 136 shall be responsible for taking all necessary steps to identify children whose identity is in doubt. Particulars of their parents or other near relative should always be recorded if available.

The Occupying Power shall not hinder the application of any preferential measures in regard to food, medical care and protection against the effects of war, which may have been adopted prior to the occupation in favour of children under fifteen years, expectant mothers, and mothers of children under seven years.

Article 51. The Occupying Power may not compel protected persons to serve in its armed or auxiliary forces. No pressure or propaganda which aims at securing voluntary enlistment is permitted.

The Occupying Power may not compel protected persons to work unless they are over eighteen years of age, and then only on work which is necessary either for the needs of the army of occupation, or for the public utility services, or for the feeding, sheltering, clothing, transportation or health of the population of the occupied country. Protected persons may not be compelled to undertake any work which would involve them in the obligation of taking part in military operations. The Occupying Power may not compel protected persons to employ forcible means to ensure the security of the installations where they are performing compulsory labour.

The work shall be carried out only in the occupied territory where the persons whose services have been requisitioned are. Every such person shall, so far as possible, be kept in his usual place of employment. Workers shall be paid a fair wage and the work shall be proportionate to their physical and intellectual capacities. The legislation in force in the occupied country concerning working conditions, and safeguards as regards, in particular, such matters as wages, hours of work, equipment, preliminary training and compensation for occupational accidents and diseases, shall be applicable to the protected persons assigned to the work referred to in this Article.

In no case shall requisition of labour lead to a mobilization of workers in an organization of a military or semi-military character.

Article 52. No contract, agreement or regulation shall impair the right of any worker, whether voluntary or not and wherever he may be, to apply to the representatives of the Protecting Power in order to request the said Power's intervention.

All measures aiming at creating unemployment or at restricting the opportunities offered to workers in an occupied territory, in order to induce them to work for the Occupying Power, are prohibited.

Article 53. Any destruction by the Occupying Power of real or personal property belonging individually or collectively to private persons, or to the State, or to other public authorities, or to social or cooperative organizations, is prohibited, except where such destruction is rendered absolutely necessary by military operations.

Article 54. The Occupying Power may not alter the status of public officials or judges in the occupied territories, or in any way apply sanctions to or take any measures of coercion or discrimination against them, should they abstain from fulfilling their functions for reasons of conscience.

This prohibition does not prejudice the application of the second paragraph of Article 51. It does not affect the right of the Occupying Power to remove public officials from their posts.

Article 55. To the fullest extent of the means available to it, the Occupying Power has the duty of ensuring the food and medical supplies of the population; it should, in particular, bring in the necessary foodstuffs, medical stores and other articles if the resources of the occupied territory are inadequate.

The Occupying Power may not requisition foodstuffs, articles or medical supplies available in the occupied territory, except for use by the occupation forces and administration personnel, and then only if the requirements of the civilian population have been taken into account. Subject to the provisions of other international Conventions, the Occupying Power shall make arrangements to ensure that fair value is paid for any requisitioned goods.

The Protecting Power shall, at any time, be at liberty to verify the state of the food and medical supplies in occupied territories, except where temporary restrictions are made necessary by imperative military requirements.

Article 56. To the fullest extent of the means available to it, the Occupying Power has the duty of ensuring and maintaining, with the cooperation of national and local authorities, the medical and hospital establishments and services, public health and hygiene in the occupied territory, with particular reference to the adoption and application of the prophylactic and preventive measures necessary to combat the spread of contagious diseases and epidemics. Medical personnel of all categories shall be allowed to carry out their duties.

If new hospitals are set up in occupied territory and if the competent organs of the occupied State are not operating there, the occupying authorities shall, if necessary, grant them the recognition provided for in Article 18. In similar circumstances, the occupying authorities shall also grant recognition to hospital personnel and transport vehicles under the provisions of Articles 20 and 21.

In adopting measures of health and hygiene and in their implementation, the Occupying Power shall take into consideration the moral and ethical susceptibilities of the population of the occupied territory.

Article 57. The Occupying Power may requisition civilian hospitals only temporarily and only in cases of urgent necessity for the care of military wounded and sick, and then on condition that suitable arrangements are made in due time for the care and treatment of the patients and for the needs of the civilian population for hospital accommodation.

The material and stores of civilian hospitals cannot be requisitioned so long as they are necessary for the needs of the civilian population.

Article 58. The Occupying Power shall permit ministers of religion to give spiritual assistance to the members of their religious communities.

The Occupying Power shall also accept consignments of books and articles required for religious needs and shall facilitate their distribution in occupied territory.

Article 59. If the whole or part of the population of an occupied territory is inadequately supplied, the Occupying Power shall agree to relief schemes on behalf of the said population, and shall facilitate them by all the means at its disposal.

Such schemes, which may be undertaken either by States or by impartial humanitarian organizations such as the International Committee of the Red Cross, shall consist, in particular, of the provision of consignments of foodstuffs, medical supplies and clothing.

All Contracting Parties shall permit the free passage of these consignments and shall guarantee their protection.

A Power granting free passage to consignments on their way to territory occupied by an adverse Party to the conflict shall, however, have the right to search the consignments, to regulate their passage according to prescribed times and routes, and to be reasonably satisfied through the Protecting Power that these consignments are to be used for the relief of the needy population and are not to be used for the benefit of the Occupying Power.

Article 60. Relief consignments shall in no way relieve the Occupying Power of any of its responsibilities under Articles 55, 56 and 59. The Occupying Power shall in no way

whatsoever divert relief consignments from the purpose for which they are intended, except in cases of urgent necessity, in the interests of the population of the occupied territory and with the consent of the Protecting Power.

Article 61. The distribution of the relief consignments referred to in the foregoing Articles shall be carried out with the cooperation and under the supervision of the Protecting Power. This duty may also be delegated, by agreement between the Occupying Power and the Protecting Power, to a neutral Power, to the International Committee of the Red Cross or to any other impartial humanitarian body.

Such consignments shall be exempt in occupied territory from all charges, taxes or customs duties unless these are necessary in the interests of the economy of the territory. The Occupying Power shall facilitate the rapid distribution of these consignments.

All Contracting Parties shall endeavour to permit the transit and transport, free of charge, of such relief consignments on their way to occupied territories.

Article 62. Subject to imperative reasons of security, protected persons in occupied territories shall be permitted to receive the individual relief consignments sent to them.

Article 63. Subject to temporary and exceptional measures imposed for urgent reasons of security by the Occupying Power:

(*a*) recognized National Red Cross (Red Crescent, Red Lion and Sun) Societies shall be able to pursue their activities in accordance with Red Cross principles, as defined by the International Red Cross Conferences. Other relief societies shall be permitted to continue their humanitarian activities under similar conditions;

(*b*) the Occupying Power may not require any changes in the personnel or structure of these societies, which would prejudice the aforesaid activities.

The same principles shall apply to the activities and personnel of special organizations of a non-military character, which already exist or which may be established, for the purpose of ensuring the living conditions of the civilian population by the maintenance of the essential public utility services, by the distribution of relief and by the organization of rescues.

Article 64. The penal laws of the occupied territory shall remain in force, with the exception that they may be repealed or suspended by the Occupying Power in cases where they constitute a threat to its security or an obstacle to the application of the present Convention. Subject to the latter consideration and to the necessity for ensuring the effective administration of justice, the tribunals of the occupied territory shall continue to function in respect of all offences covered by the said laws.

The Occupying Power may, however, subject the population of the occupied territory to provisions which are essential to enable the Occupying Power to fulfill its obligations under the present Convention, to maintain the orderly government of the territory, and to ensure the security of the Occupying Power, of the members and property of the occupying forces or administration, and likewise of the establishments and lines of communication used by them.

Article 65. The penal provisions enacted by the Occupying Power shall not come into force before they have been published and brought to the knowledge of the inhabitants in their own language. The effect of these penal provisions shall not be retroactive.

Article 66. In case of a breach of the penal provisions promulgated by it by virtue of the second paragraph of Article 64, the Occupying Power may hand over the accused to its properly constituted, non-political military courts, on condition that the said courts sit in the occupied country. Courts of appeal shall preferably sit in the occupied country.

Article 67. The courts shall apply only those provisions of law which were applicable prior to the offence, and which are in accordance with general principles of law, in particular the principle that the penalty shall be proportionate to the offence. They shall take into consideration the fact that the accused is not a national of the Occupying Power.

Article 68. Protected persons who commit an offence which is solely intended to harm the Occupying Power, but which does not constitute an attempt on the life or limb of members of the occupying forces or administration, nor a grave collective danger, nor seriously damage the property of the occupying forces or administration or the installations used by them, shall be liable to internment or simple imprisonment, provided the duration of such internment or imprisonment is proportionate to the offence committed. Furthermore, internment or imprisonment shall, for such offences, be the only measure adopted for depriving protected persons of liberty. The courts provided for under Article 66 of the present Convention may at their discretion convert a sentence of imprisonment to one of internment for the same period.

The penal provisions promulgated by the Occupying Power in accordance with Articles 64 and 65 may impose the death penalty on a protected person only in cases where the person is guilty of espionage, of serious acts of sabotage against the military installations of the Occupying Power or of intentional offences which have caused the death of one or more persons, provided that such offences were punishable by death under the law of the occupied territory in force before the occupation began.

The death penalty may not be pronounced against a protected person unless the attention of the court has been particularly called to the fact that since the accused is not a national of the Occupying Power, he is not bound to it by any duty of allegiance.

In any case, the death penalty may not be pronounced against a protected person who was under eighteen years of age at the time of the offence.

Article 69. In all cases, the duration of the period during which a protected person accused of an offence is under arrest awaiting trial or punishment shall be deducted from any period of imprisonment awarded.

Article 70. Protected persons shall not be arrested, prosecuted or convicted by the Occupying Power for acts committed or for opinions expressed before the occupation, or during a temporary interruption thereof, with the exception of breaches of the laws and customs of war.

Nationals of the occupying Power who, before the outbreak of hostilities, have sought refuge in the territory of the occupied State, shall not be arrested, prosecuted, convicted or deported from the occupied territory, except for offences committed after the outbreak of hostilities, or for offences under common law committed before the outbreak of hostilities which, according to the law of the occupied State, would have justified extradition in time of peace.

Article 71. No sentence shall be pronounced by the competent courts of the Occupying Power except after a regular trial.

Accused persons who are prosecuted by the Occupying Power shall be promptly informed, in writing, in a language which they understand, of the particulars of the charges preferred against them, and shall be brought to trial as rapidly as possible. The Protecting Power shall be informed of all proceedings instituted by the Occupying Power against protected persons in respect of charges involving the death penalty or imprisonment for two years or more; it shall be enabled, at any time, to obtain information regarding the state of such proceedings. Furthermore, the Protecting Power shall be entitled, on request, to be furnished with all particulars of these and of any other proceedings instituted by the Occupying Power against protected persons.

The notification to the Protecting Power, as provided for in the second paragraph above, shall be sent immediately, and shall in any case reach the Protecting Power three weeks before the date of the first hearing. Unless, at the opening of the trial, evidence is submitted that the provisions of this Article are fully complied with, the trial shall not proceed. The notification shall include the following particulars:

(*a*) description of the accused;

(*b*) place of residence or detention;

(*c*) specification of the charge or charges (with mention of the penal provisions under which it is brought);

(*d*) designation of the court which will hear the case;

(*e*) place and date of the first hearing.

Article 72. Accused persons shall have the right to present evidence necessary to their defence and may in particular, call witnesses. They shall have the right to be assisted by a qualified advocate or counsel of their own choice, who shall be able to visit them freely, and shall enjoy the necessary facilities for preparing the defence.

Failing a choice by the accused, the Protecting Power may provide him with an advocate or counsel. When an accused person has to meet a serious charge and the Protecting Power is not functioning, the Occupying Power, subject to the consent of the accused, shall provide an advocate or counsel.

Accused persons shall, unless they freely waive such assistance, be aided by an interpreter, both during preliminary investigation and during the hearing in court. They shall have the right at any time to object to the interpreter and to ask for his replacement.

Article 73. A convicted person shall have the right of appeal provided for by the laws applied by the court. He shall be fully informed of his right to appeal or petition and of the time limit within which he may do so.

The penal procedure provided in the present Section shall apply, as far as it is applicable, to appeals. Where the laws applied by the Court make no provision for appeals, the convicted person shall have the right to petition against the finding and sentence to the competent authority of the Occupying Power.

Article 74. Representatives of the Protecting Power shall have the right to attend the trial of any protected person, unless the hearing has, as an exceptional measure, to be held *in camera* in the interests of the security of the Occupying Power, which shall then notify the Protecting Power. A notification in respect of the date and place of trial shall be sent to the Protecting Power.

Any judgment involving a sentence of death, or imprisonment for two years or more, shall be communicated, with the relevant grounds, as rapidly as possible to the Protecting Power. The notification shall contain a reference to the notification made under Article 71, and, in the case of sentences of imprisonment, the name of the place where the sentence is to be served. A record of judgments other than those referred to above shall be kept by the court and shall be open to inspection by representatives of the Protecting Power. Any period allowed for appeal in the case of sentences involving the death penalty, or imprisonment of two years or more, shall not run until notification of judgment has been received by the Protecting Power.

Article 75. In no case shall persons condemned to death be deprived of the right of petition for pardon or reprieve.

No death sentence shall be carried out before the expiration of a period of at least six months from the date of receipt by the Protecting Power of the notification of the final judgment confirming such death sentence, or of an order denying pardon or reprieve.

The six months period of suspension of the death sentence herein prescribed may be reduced in individual cases in circumstances of grave emergency involving an organized threat to the security of the Occupying Power or its forces, provided always that the Protecting Power is notified of such reduction and is given reasonable time and opportunity to make representations to the competent occupying authorities in respect of such death sentences.

Article 76. Protected persons accused of offences shall be detained in the occupied country, and if convicted they shall serve their sentences therein. They shall, if possible, be separated from other detainees and shall enjoy conditions of food and hygiene which will be sufficient to keep them in good health, and which will be at least equal to those obtaining in prisons in the occupied country.

They shall receive the medical attention required by their state of health.

They shall also have the right to receive any spiritual assistance which they may require.

Women shall be confined in separate quarters and shall be under the direct supervision of women.

Proper regard shall be paid to the special treatment due to minors.

Protected persons who are detained shall have the right to be visited by delegates of the Protecting Power and of the International Committee of the Red Cross, in accordance with the provisions of Article 143.

Such persons shall have the right to receive at least one relief parcel monthly.

Article 77. Protected persons who have been accused of offences or convicted by the courts in occupied territory, shall be handed over at the close of occupation, with the relevant records, to the authorities of the liberated territory.

Article 78. If the Occupying Power considers it necessary, for imperative reasons of security, to take safety measures concerning protected persons, it may, at the most, subject them to assigned residence or to internment.

Decisions regarding such assigned residence or internment shall be made according to a regular procedure to be prescribed by the Occupying Power in accordance with the provisions of the present Convention. This procedure shall include the right of appeal for the parties concerned. Appeals shall be decided with the least possible delay. In the event of the decision being upheld, it shall be subject to periodical review, if possible every six months, by a competent body set up by the said Power.

Protected persons made subject to assigned residence and thus required to leave their homes shall enjoy the full benefit of Article 39 of the present Convention.

Section IV—Regulations for the Treatment of Internees
Chapter I—General Provisions

Article 79. The Parties to the conflict shall not intern protected persons, except in accordance with the provisions of Articles 41, 42, 43, 68 and 78.

Article 80. Internees shall retain their full civil capacity and shall exercise such attendant rights as may be compatible with their status.

Article 81. Parties to the conflict who intern protected persons shall be bound to provide free of charge for their maintenance, and to grant them also the medical attention required by their state of health.

No deduction from the allowances, salaries or credits due to the internees shall be made for the repayment of these costs.

The Detaining Power shall provide for the support of those dependent on the internees, if such dependents are without adequate means of support or are unable to earn a living.

Article 82. The Detaining Power shall, as far as possible, accommodate the internees according to their nationality, language and customs. Internees who are nationals of the same country shall not be separated merely because they have different languages.

Throughout the duration of their internment, members of the same family, and in particular parents and children, shall be lodged together in the same place of internment, except when separation of a temporary nature is necessitated for reasons of employment or health or for the purposes of enforcement of the provisions of Chapter IX of the present Section. Internees may request that their children who are left at liberty without parental care shall be interned with them.

Wherever possible, interned member of the same family shall be housed in the same premises and given separate accommodation from other internees, together with facilities for leading a proper family life.

Chapter II—Places of Internment

Article 83. The Detaining Power shall not set up places of internment in areas particularly exposed to the dangers of war.

The Detaining Power shall give the enemy Powers, through the intermediary of the Protecting Powers, all useful information regarding the geographical location of places of internment.

Whenever military considerations permit, internment camps shall be indicated by the letters IC, placed so as to be clearly visible in the daytime from the air. The Powers concerned may, however, agree upon any other system of marking. No place other than an internment camp shall be marked as such.

Article 84. Internees shall be accommodated and administered separately from prisoners of war and from persons deprived of liberty for any other reason.

Article 85. The Detaining Power is bound to take all necessary and possible measures to ensure that protected persons shall, from the outset of their internment, be accommodated in buildings or quarters which afford every possible safeguard as regards hygiene and health, and provide efficient protection against the rigours of the climate and the effects of the war. In no case shall permanent places of internment be situated in unhealthy areas, or in districts the climate of which is injurious to the internees. In all cases where the district, in which a protected person is temporarily interned, is in an unhealthy area or has a climate which is harmful to his health, he shall be removed to a more suitable place of internment as rapidly as circumstances permit.

The premises shall be fully protected from dampness, adequately heated and lighted, in particular between dusk and lights out. The sleeping quarters shall be sufficiently spacious and well ventilated, and the internees shall have suitable bedding and sufficient blankets, account being taken of the climate, and the age, sex, and state of health of the internees.

Internees shall have for their use, day and night, sanitary conveniences which conform to the rules of hygiene and are constantly maintained in a state of cleanliness. They shall be provided with sufficient water and soap for their daily personal toilet and for washing their personal laundry; installations and facilities necessary for this purpose shall be granted to them. Showers or baths shall also be available. The necessary time shall be set aside for washing and for cleaning.

Whenever it is necessary, as an exceptional and temporary measure, to accommodate women internees who are not members of a family unit in the same place of internment as men, the provision of separate sleeping quarters and sanitary conveniences for the use of such women internees shall be obligatory.

Article 86. The Detaining Power shall place at the disposal of interned persons, of whatever denomination, premises suitable for the holding of their religious services.

Article 87. Canteens shall be installed in every place of internment, except where other suitable facilities are available. Their purpose shall be to ensure internees to make purchases, at prices not higher than local market prices, of foodstuffs and articles of everyday use, including soap and tobacco, such as would increase their personal well-being and comfort.

Profits made by canteens shall be credited to a welfare fund to be set up for each place of internment, and administered for the benefit of the internees attached to such place of internment. The Internee Committee provided for in Article 102 shall have the right to check the management of the canteen and of the said fund.

When a place of internment is closed down, the balance of the welfare fund shall be transferred to the welfare fund of a place of internment for internees of the same nationality, or, if such a place does not exist, to a central welfare fund which shall be administered for the benefit of all internees remaining in the custody of the Detaining Power. In case of a general release, the said profits shall be kept by the Detaining Power, subject to any agreement to the contrary between the Powers concerned.

Article 88. In all places of internment exposed to air raids and other hazards of war, shelters adequate in number and structure to ensure the necessary protection shall be installed. In case of alarms, the internees shall be free to enter such shelters as quickly as possible, excepting those who remain for the protection of their quarters against the aforesaid hazards. Any protective measures taken in favour of the population shall also apply to them.

All due precautions must be taken in places of internment against the danger of fire.

Chapter III—Food and Clothing

Article 89. Daily food rations for internees shall be sufficient in quantity, quality and variety to keep internees in a good state of health and prevent the development of nutritional deficiencies. Account shall also be taken of the customary diet of the internees.

Internees shall also be given the means by which they can prepare for themselves any additional food in their possession.

Sufficient drinking water shall be supplied to internees. The use of tobacco shall be permitted.

Internees who work shall receive additional rations in proportion to the kind of labour which they perform.

Expectant and nursing mothers, and children under fifteen years of age, shall be given additional food, in proportion to their physiological needs.

Article 90. When taken into custody, internees shall be given all facilities to provide themselves with the necessary clothing, footwear and change of underwear, and later on, to procure further supplies if required. Should any internees not have sufficient clothing, account being taken of the climate, and be unable to procure any, it shall be provided free of charge to them by the Detaining Power.

The clothing supplied by the Detaining Power to internees and the outward markings placed on their own clothes shall not be ignominious nor expose them to ridicule.

Workers shall receive suitable working outfits, including protective clothing, whenever the nature of their work so requires.

Chapter IV—Hygiene and Medical Attention

Article 91. Every place of internment shall have an adequate infirmary, under the direction of a qualified doctor, where internees may have the attention they require, as well as an appropriate diet. Isolation wards shall be set aside for cases of contagious or mental diseases.

Maternity cases and internees suffering from serious diseases, or whose condition requires special treatment, a surgical operation or hospital care, must be admitted to any institution where adequate treatment can be given and shall receive care not inferior to that provided for the general population.

Internees shall, for preference, have the attention of medical personnel of their own nationality.

Internees may not be prevented from presenting themselves to the medical authorities for examination. The medical authorities of the Detaining Power shall, upon request, issue to every internee who has undergone treatment an official certificate showing the nature of his illness or injury, and the duration and nature of the treatment given. A duplicate of this certificate shall be forwarded to the Central Agency provided for in Article 140.

Treatment, including the provision of any apparatus necessary for the maintenance of internees in good health, particularly dentures and other artificial appliances and spectacles, shall be free of charge to the internee.

Article 92. Medical inspections of internees shall be made at least once a month. Their purpose shall be, in particular, to supervise the general state of health, nutrition and cleanliness of internees, and to detect contagious diseases, especially tuberculosis, malaria, and venereal diseases. Such inspections shall include, in particular, the checking of weight of each internee and, at least once a year, radioscopic examination.

Chapter V—Religious, Intellectual and Physical Activities

Article 93. Internees shall enjoy complete latitude in the exercise of their religious duties, including attendance at the services of their faith, on condition that they comply with the disciplinary routine prescribed by the detaining authorities.

Ministers of religion who are interned shall be allowed to minister freely to the members of their community. For this purpose, the Detaining Power shall ensure their equitable allocation amongst the various places of internment in which there are internees speaking the same language and belonging to the same religion. Should such ministers be too few in number, the Detaining Power shall provide them with the necessary facilities, including means of transport, for moving from one place to another, and they shall be authorized to visit any internees who are in hospital. Ministers of religion shall be at liberty to correspond on matters concerning their ministry with the religious authorities in the country of detention and, as far as possible, with the international religious organizations of their faith. Such correspondence shall not be considered as forming a part of the quota mentioned in Article 107. It shall, however, be subject to the provisions of Article 112.

When internees do not have at their disposal the assistance of ministers of their faith, or should these latter be too few in number, the local religious authorities of the same faith may appoint, in agreement with the Detaining Power, a minister of the internees' faith or, if such a course is feasible from a denominational point of view, a minister of similar religion or a qualified layman. The latter shall enjoy the facilities granted to the ministry he has assumed. Persons so appointed shall comply with all regulations laid down by the Detaining Power in the interests of discipline and security.

Article 94. The Detaining Power shall encourage intellectual, educational and recreational pursuits, sports and games amongst internees, whilst leaving them free to take part in them or not. It shall take all practicable measures to ensure the exercise thereof, in particular by providing suitable premises.

All possible facilities shall be granted to internees to continue their studies or to take up new subjects. The education of children and young people shall be ensured; they shall be allowed to attend schools either within the place of internment or outside.

Internees shall be given opportunities for physical exercise, sports and outdoor games. For this purpose, sufficient open spaces shall be set aside in all places of internment. Special playgrounds shall be reserved for children and young people.

Article 95. The Detaining Power shall not employ internees as workers, unless they so desire. Employment which, if undertaken under compulsion by a protected person not in internment, would involve a breach of Articles 40 or 51 of the present Convention, and employment on work which is of a degrading or humiliating character are in any case prohibited.

After a working period of six weeks, internees shall be free to give up work at any moment, subject to eight days' notice.

These provisions constitute no obstacle to the right of the Detaining Power to employ interned doctors, dentists and other medical personnel in their professional capacity on behalf of their fellow internees, or to employ internees for administrative and maintenance work in places of internment and to detail such persons for work in the kitchens or for other domestic tasks, or to require such persons to undertake duties connected with the protection of internees against aerial bombardment or other war risks. No

internee may, however, be required to perform tasks for which he is, in the opinion of a medical officer, physically unsuited.

The Detaining Power shall take entire responsibility for all working conditions, for medical attention, for the payment of wages, and for ensuring that all employed internees receive compensation for occupational accidents and diseases. The standards prescribed for the said working conditions and for compensation shall be in accordance with the national laws and regulations, and with the existing practice; they shall in no case be inferior to those obtaining for work of the same nature in the same district. Wages for work done shall be determined on an equitable basis by special agreements between the internees, the Detaining Power, and, if the case arises, employers other than the Detaining Power, due regard being paid to the obligation of the Detaining Power to provide for free maintenance of internees and for the medical attention which their state of health may require. Internees permanently detailed for categories of work mentioned in the third paragraph of this Article, shall be paid fair wages by the Detaining Power. The working conditions and the scale of compensation for occupational accidents and diseases to internees thus detailed, shall not be inferior to those applicable to work of the same nature in the same district.

Article 96. All labour detachments shall remain part of and dependent upon a place of internment. The competent authorities of the Detaining Power and the commandant of a place of internment shall be responsible for the observance in a labour detachment of the provisions of the present Convention. The commandant shall keep an up-to-date list of the labour detachments subordinate to him and shall communicate it to the delegates of the Protecting Power, of the International Committee of the Red Cross and of other humanitarian organizations who may visit the places of internment.

Chapter VI—Personal Property and Financial Resources

Article 97. Internees shall be permitted to retain articles of personal use. Monies, cheques, bonds, etc., and valuables in their possession may not be taken from them except in accordance with established procedure. Detailed receipts shall be given therefor.

The amounts shall be paid into the account of every internee as provided for in Article 98. Such amounts may not be converted into any other currency unless legislation in force in the territory in which the owner is interned so requires or the internee gives his consent.

Articles which have above all a personal or sentimental value may not be taken away.

A woman internee shall not be searched except by a woman.

On release or repatriation, internees shall be given all articles, monies or other valuables taken from them during internment and shall receive in currency the balance of any credit to their accounts kept in accordance with Article 98, with the exception of any articles or amounts withheld by the Detaining Power by virtue of its legislation in force. If the property of an internee is so withheld, the owner shall receive a detailed receipt.

Family or identity documents in the possession of internees may not be taken away without a receipt being given. At no time shall internees be left without identity documents. If they have none, they shall be issued with special documents drawn up by the detaining authorities, which will serve as their identity papers until the end of their internment.

Internees may keep on their persons a certain amount of money, in cash or in the shape of purchase coupons, to enable them to make purchases.

Article 98. All internees shall receive regular allowances, sufficient to enable them to purchase goods and articles, such as tobacco, toilet requisites, etc. Such allowances may take the form of credits or purchase coupons.

Furthermore, internees may receive allowances from the Power to which they owe allegiance, the Protecting Powers, the organizations which may assist them, or their families, as well as the income on their property in accordance with the law of the Detaining Power. The amount of allowances granted by the Power to which they owe allegiance shall be the same for each category of internees (infirm, sick, pregnant women, etc.), but may not be allocated by that Power or distributed by the Detaining Power on the basis of discriminations between internees which are prohibited by Article 27 of the present Convention.

The Detaining Power shall open a regular account for every internee, to which shall be credited the allowances named in the present Article, the wages earned and the remittances received, together with such sums taken from him as may be available under the legislation in force in the territory in which he is interned. Internees shall be granted all facilities consistent with the legislation in force in such territory to make remittances to their families and to other dependants. They may draw from their accounts the amounts necessary for their personal expenses, within the limits fixed by the Detaining Power. They shall at all times be afforded reasonable facilities for consulting and obtaining copies of their accounts. A statement of accounts shall be furnished to the Protecting Power on request, and shall accompany the internee in case of transfer.

Chapter VII—Administration and Discipline

Article 99. Every place of internment shall be put under the authority of a responsible officer, chosen from the regular military forces or the regular civil administration of the Detaining Power. The officer in charge of the place of internment must have in his possession a copy of the present Convention in the official language, or one of the official languages, of his country and shall be responsible for its application. The staff in control of internees shall be instructed in the provisions of the present Convention and of the administrative measures adopted to ensure its application.

The text of the present Convention and the texts of special agreements concluded under the said Convention shall be posted inside the place of internment, in a language which the internees understand, or shall be in the possession of the Internee Committee.

Regulations, orders, notices and publications of every kind shall be communicated to the internees and posted inside the places of internment, in a language which they understand.

Every order and command addressed to internees individually, must likewise, be given in a language which they understand.

Article 100. The disciplinary regime in places of internment shall be consistent with humanitarian principles, and shall in no circumstances include regulations imposing on internees any physical exertion dangerous to their health or involving physical or moral victimization. Identification by tattooing or imprinting signs or markings on the body, is prohibited.

In particular, prolonged standing and roll-calls, punishment drill, military drill and manoeuvres, or the reduction of food rations, are prohibited.

Article 101. Internees shall have the right to present to the authorities in whose power they are, any petition with regard to the conditions of internment to which they are subjected.

They shall also have the right to apply without restriction through the Internee Committee or, if they consider it necessary, direct to the representatives of the Protecting Power, in order to indicate to them any points on which they may have complaints to make with regard to the conditions of internment.

Such petitions and complaints shall be transmitted forthwith and without alteration, and even if the latter are recognized to be unfounded, they may not occasion any punishment.

Periodic reports on the situation in places of internment and as to the needs of the internees, may be sent by the Internee Committees to the representatives of the Protecting Powers.

Article 102. In every place of internment, the internees shall freely elect by secret ballot every six months, the members of a Committee empowered to represent them before the Detaining and the Protecting Powers, the International Committee of the Red Cross and any other organization which may assist them. The members of the committee shall be eligible for re-election.

Internees so elected shall enter upon their duties after their election has been approved by the detaining authorities. The reasons for any refusals or dismissals shall be communicated to the Protecting Powers concerned.

Article 103. The Internee Committees shall further the physical, spiritual and intellectual well-being of the internees.

In case the internees decide, in particular, to organize a system of mutual assistance amongst themselves, this organization would be within the competence of the Committees in addition to the special duties entrusted to them under other provisions of the present Convention.

Article 104. Members of Internee Committees shall not be required to perform any other work, if the accomplishment of their duties is rendered more difficult thereby.

Members of Internee Committees may appoint from amongst the internees such assistants as they may require. All material facilities shall be granted to them, particularly a certain freedom of movement necessary for the accomplishment of their duties (visits to labour detachments, receipt of supplies, etc.).

All facilities shall likewise be accorded to members of Internee Committees for communication by post and telegraph with the detaining authorities, the Protecting Powers, the International Committee of the Red Cross and their delegates, and with the organizations which give assistance to internees. Committee members in labour detachments shall enjoy similar facilities for communication with their Internee Committee in the principal place of internment. Such communications shall not be limited, nor considered as forming a part of the quota mentioned in Article 107.

Members of Internee Committees who are transferred shall be allowed a reasonable time to acquaint their successors with current affairs.

Chapter VIII—Relations with the Exterior

Article 105. Immediately upon interning protected persons, the Detaining Powers shall inform them, the Power to which they owe allegiance and their Protecting Power of the measures taken for executing the provisions of the present Chapter. The Detaining Powers shall likewise inform the Parties concerned of any subsequent modifications of such measures.

Article 106. As soon as he is interned, or at the latest not more than one week after his arrival in a place of internment, and likewise in cases of sickness or transfer to another place of internment or to a hospital, every internee shall be enabled to send direct to his family, on the one hand, and to the Central Agency provided for by Article 140, on the other, an internment card similar, if possible, to the model annexed to the present Convention, informing his relatives of his detention, address and state of health. The said cards shall be forwarded as rapidly as possible and may not be delayed in any way.

Article 107. Internees shall be allowed to send and receive letters and cards. If the Detaining Power deems it necessary to limit the number of letters and cards sent by each internee, the said number shall not be less than two letters and four cards monthly; these shall be drawn up so as to conform as closely as possible to the models annexed to the present Convention. If limitations must be placed on the correspondence addressed to internees, they may be ordered only by the Power to which such internees owe allegiance, possibly at the request of the Detaining Power. Such letters and cards must be conveyed with reasonable despatch; they may not be delayed or retained for disciplinary reasons.

Internees who have been a long time without news, or who find it impossible to receive news from their relatives, or to give them news by the ordinary postal route, as well as those who are at a considerable distance from their homes, shall be allowed to send telegrams, the charges being paid by them in the currency at their disposal. They shall likewise benefit by this provision in cases which are recognized to be urgent.

As a rule, internees' mail shall be written in their own language. The Parties to the conflict may authorize correspondence in other languages.

Article 108. Internees shall be allowed to receive, by post or by any other means, individual parcels or collective shipments containing in particular foodstuffs, clothing, medical supplies, as well as books and objects of a devotional, educational or recreational character which may meet their needs. Such shipments shall in no way free the Detaining Power from the obligations imposed upon it by virtue of the present Convention.

Should military necessity require the quantity of such shipments to be limited, due notice thereof shall be given to the Protecting Power and to the International Committee of the Red Cross, or to any other organization giving assistance to the internees and responsible for the forwarding of such shipments.

The conditions for the sending of individual parcels and collective shipments shall, if necessary, be the subject of special agreements between the Powers concerned, which may in no case delay the receipt by the internees of relief supplies. Parcels of clothing and foodstuffs may not include books. Medical relief supplies shall, as a rule, be sent in collective parcels.

Article 109. In the absence of special agreements between Parties to the conflict regarding the conditions for the receipt and distribution of collective relief shipments, the regulations concerning collective relief which are annexed to the present Convention shall be applied.

The special agreements provided for above shall in no case restrict the right of Internee Committees to take possession of collective relief shipments intended for internees, to undertake their distribution and to dispose of them in the interests of the recipients.

Nor shall such agreements restrict the right of representatives of the Protecting Powers, the International Committee of the Red Cross, or any other organization giving assistance to internees and responsible for the forwarding of collective shipments, to supervise their distribution to the recipients.

Article 110. All relief shipments for internees shall be exempt from import, customs and other dues.

All matter sent by mail, including relief parcels sent by parcel post and remittances of money, addressed from other countries to internees or despatched by them through the post office, either direct or through the Information Bureaux provided for in Article 136 and the Central Information Agency provided for in Article 140, shall be exempt from all postal dues both in the countries of origin and destination and in intermediate countries. To this end, in particular, the exemption provided by the Universal Postal Convention of 1947 and by the agreements of the Universal Postal Union in favour of civilians of enemy nationality detained in camps or civilian prisons, shall be extended to the other interned persons protected by the present Convention. The countries not signatory to the above-mentioned agreements shall be bound to grant freedom from charges in the same circumstances.

The cost of transporting relief shipments which are intended for internees and which, by reason of their weight or any other cause, cannot be sent through the post office, shall be borne by the Detaining Power in all the territories under its control. Other Powers which are Parties to the present Convention shall bear the cost of transport in their respective territories.

Costs connected with the transport of such shipments, which are not covered by the above paragraphs, shall be charged to the senders.

The High Contracting Parties shall endeavour to reduce, so far as possible, the charges for telegrams sent by internees, or addressed to them.

Article 111. Should military operations prevent the Powers concerned from fulfilling their obligation to ensure the conveyance of the mail and relief shipments provided for in Articles 106, 107, 108 and 113, the Protecting Powers concerned, the International Committee of the Red Cross or any other organization duly approved by the Parties to the conflict may undertake the conveyance of such shipments by suitable means (rail, motor vehicles, vessels or aircraft, etc.). For this purpose, the High Contracting Parties shall endeavour to supply them with such transport, and to allow its circulation, especially by granting the necessary safe-conducts.

Such transport may also be used to convey:

(a) correspondence, lists and reports exchanged between the Central Information Agency referred to in Article 140 and the National Bureaux referred to in Article 136;

(b) correspondence and reports relating to internees which the Protecting Powers, the International Committee of the Red Cross or any other organization assisting the in-

ternees exchange either with their own delegates or with the Parties to the conflict.

These provisions in no way detract from the right of any Party to the conflict to arrange other means of transport if it should so prefer, nor preclude the granting of safe-conducts, under mutually agreed conditions, to such means of transport.

The costs occasioned by the use of such means of transport shall be borne, in proportion to the importance of the shipments, by the Parties to the conflict whose nationals are benefited thereby.

Article 112. The censoring of correspondence addressed to internees or despatched by them shall be done as quickly as possible.

The examination of consignments intended for internees shall not be carried out under conditions that will expose the goods contained in them to deterioration. It shall be done in the presence of the addressee, or of a fellow-internee duly delegated by him. The delivery to internees of individual or collective consignments shall not be delayed under the pretext of difficulties of censorship.

Any prohibition of correspondence ordered by the Parties to the conflict either for military or political reasons, shall be only temporary and its duration shall be as short as possible.

Article 113. The Detaining Powers shall provide all reasonable facilities for the transmission, through the Protecting Power or the Central Agency provided for in Article 140, or as otherwise required, of wills, powers of attorney, letters of authority, or any other documents intended for internees or despatched by them.

In all cases the Detaining Powers shall facilitate the execution and authentication in due legal form of such documents on behalf of internees, in particular by allowing them to consult a lawyer.

Article 114. The Detaining Power shall afford internees all facilities to enable them to manage their property, provided this is not incompatible with the conditions of internment and the law which is applicable. For this purpose, the said Power may give them permission to leave the place of internment in urgent cases and if circumstances allow.

Article 115. In all cases where an internee is a party to proceedings in any court, the Detaining Power shall, if he so requests, cause the court to be informed of his detention and shall, within legal limits, ensure that all necessary steps are taken to prevent him from being in any way prejudiced, by reason of his internment, as regards the preparation and conduct of his case or as regards the execution of any judgment of the court.

Article 116. Every internee shall be allowed to receive visitors, especially near relatives, at regular intervals and as frequently as possible.

As far as is possible, internees shall be permitted to visit their homes in urgent cases, particularly in cases of death or serious illness of relatives.

Chapter IX—Penal and Disciplinary Sanctions

Article 117. Subject to the provisions of the present Chapter, the laws in force in the territory in which they are detained will continue to apply to internees who commit offences during internment.

If general laws, regulations or orders declare acts committed by internees to be punishable, whereas the same acts are not punishable when committed by persons who are not internees, such acts shall entail disciplinary punishments only.

No internee may be punished more than once for the same act, or on the same count.

Article 118. The courts or authorities shall in passing sentence take as far as possible into account the fact that the defendant is not a national of the Detaining Power. They shall be free to reduce the penalty prescribed for the offence with which the internee is charged and shall not be obliged, to this end, to apply the minimum sentence prescribed.

Imprisonment in premises without daylight and, in general, all forms of cruelty without exception are forbidden.

Internees who have served disciplinary or judicial sentences shall not be treated differently from other internees.

The duration of preventive detention undergone by an internee shall be deducted from any disciplinary or judicial penalty involving confinement to which he may be sentenced.

Internee Committees shall be informed of all judicial proceedings instituted against internees whom they represent, and of their result.

Article 119. The disciplinary punishments applicable to internees shall be the following:

(1) A fine which shall not exceed 50 per cent of the wages which the internee would otherwise receive under the provisions of Article 95 during a period of not more than thirty days.

(2) Discontinuance of privileges granted over and above the treatment provided for by the present Convention.

(3) Fatigue duties, not exceeding two hours daily, in connection with the maintenance of the place of internment.

(4) Confinement.

In no case shall disciplinary penalties be inhuman, brutal or dangerous for the health of internees. Account shall be taken of the internee's age, sex and state of health.

The duration of any single punishment shall in no case exceed a maximum of thirty consecutive days, even if the internee is answerable for several breaches of discipline when his case is dealt with, whether such breaches are connected or not.

Article 120. Internees who are recaptured after having escaped or when attempting to escape, shall be liable only to disciplinary punishment in respect of this act, even if it is a repeated offence.

Article 118, paragraph 3, notwithstanding, internees punished as a result of escape or attempt to escape, may be subjected to special surveillance, on condition that such surveillance does not affect the state of their health, that it is exercised in a place of internment and that it does not entail the abolition of any of the safeguards granted by the present Convention.

Internees who aid and abet an escape or attempt to escape, shall be liable on this count to disciplinary punishment only.

Article 121. Escape, or attempt to escape, even if it is a repeated offence, shall not be deemed an aggravating circumstance in cases where an internee is prosecuted for offences committed during his escape.

The Parties to the conflict shall ensure that the competent authorities exercise leniency in deciding whether punishment inflicted for an offence shall be of a disciplinary or judicial nature, especially in respect of acts committed in connection with an escape, whether successful or not.

Article 122. Acts which constitute offences against discipline shall be investigated immediately. This rule shall be applied, in particular, in cases of escape or attempt to escape. Recaptured internees shall be handed over to the competent authorities as soon as possible.

In case of offences against discipline, confinement awaiting trial shall be reduced to an absolute minimum for all internees, and shall not exceed fourteen days. Its duration shall in any case be deducted from any sentence of confinement.

The provisions of Articles 124 and 125 shall apply to internees who are in confinement awaiting trial for offences against discipline.

Article 123. Without prejudice to the competence of courts and higher authorities, disciplinary punishment may be ordered only by the commandant of the place of internment, or by a responsible officer or official who replaces him, or to whom he has delegated his disciplinary powers.

Before any disciplinary punishment is awarded, the accused internee shall be given precise information regarding the offences of which he is accused, and given an opportunity of explaining his conduct and of defending himself. He shall be permitted, in particular, to call witnesses and to have recourse, if necessary, to the services of a qualified interpreter. The decision shall be announced in the presence of the accused and of a member of the Internee Committee.

The period elapsing between the time of award of a disciplinary punishment and its execution shall not exceed one month.

When an internee is awarded a further disciplinary punishment, a period of at least three days shall elapse between the execution of any two of the punishments, if the duration of one of these is ten days or more.

A record of disciplinary punishments shall be maintained by the commandant of the place of internment and shall be open to inspection by representatives of the Protecting Power.

Article 124. Internees shall not in any case be transferred to penitentiary establishments (prisons, penitentiaries, convict prisons, etc.) to undergo disciplinary punishment therein.

The premises in which disciplinary punishments are undergone shall conform to sanitary requirements; they shall in particular be provided with adequate bedding. Internees undergoing punishment shall be enabled to keep themselves in a state of cleanliness.

Women internees undergoing disciplinary punishment shall be confined in separate quarters from male internees and shall be under the immediate supervision of women.

Article 125. Internees awarded disciplinary punishment shall be allowed to exercise and to stay in the open air at least two hours daily.

They shall be allowed, if they so request, to be present at the daily medical inspections. They shall receive the attention which their state of health requires and, if necessary, shall be removed to the infirmary of the place of internment or to a hospital.

They shall have permission to read and write, likewise to send and receive letters. Parcels and remittances of money, however, may be withheld from them until the completion of their punishment; such consignments shall meanwhile be entrusted to the Internee Committee, who will hand over to the infirmary the perishable goods contained in the parcels.

No internee given a disciplinary punishment may be deprived of the benefit of the provisions of Articles 107 and 143 of the present Convention.

Article 126. The provisions of Articles 71 to 76 inclusive shall apply, by analogy, to proceedings against internees who are in the national territory of the Detaining Power.

Chapter X—Transfers of Internees

Article 127. The transfer of internees shall always be effected humanely. As a general rule, it shall be carried out by rail or other means of transport, and under conditions at least equal to those obtaining for the forces of the Detaining Power in their changes of station. If, as an exceptional measure, such removals have to be effected on foot, they may not take place unless the internees are in a fit state of health, and may not in any case expose them to excessive fatigue.

The Detaining Power shall supply internees during transfer with drinking water and food sufficient in quantity, quality and variety to maintain them in good health, and also with the necessary clothing, adequate shelter and the necessary medical attention. The Detaining Power shall take all suitable precautions to ensure their safety during transfer, and shall establish before their departure a complete list of all internees transferred.

Sick, wounded or infirm internees and maternity cases shall not be transferred if the journey would be seriously detrimental to them, unless their safety imperatively so demands.

If the combat zone draws close to a place of internment, the internees in the said place shall not be transferred unless their removal can be carried out in adequate conditions of safety, or unless they are exposed to greater risks by remaining on the spot than by being transferred.

When making decisions regarding the transfer of internees, the Detaining Power shall take their interests into account and, in particular, shall not do anything to increase the difficulties of repatriating them or returning them to their own homes.

Article 128. In the event of transfer, internees shall be officially advised of their departure and of their new postal address. Such notification shall be given in time for them to pack their luggage and inform their next of kin.

They shall be allowed to take with them their personal effects, and the correspondence and parcels which have arrived for them. The weight of such baggage may be limited if the conditions of transfer so require, but in no case to less than twenty-five kilograms per internee.

Mail and parcels addressed to their former place of internment shall be forwarded to them without delay.

The commandant of the place of internment shall take, in agreement with the Internee Committee, any measures needed to ensure the transport of the internees' community property and of the luggage the internees are unable to take with them in consequence of restrictions imposed by virtue of the second paragraph.

Chapter XI—Deaths

Article 129. The wills of internees shall be received for safekeeping by the responsible authorities; and in the event of the death of an internee his will shall be transmitted without delay to a person whom he has previously designated.

Deaths of internees shall be certified in every case by a doctor, and a death certificate shall be made out, showing the causes of death and the conditions under which it occurred.

An official record of the death, duly registered, shall be drawn up in accordance with the procedure relating thereto in force in the territory where the place of internment is situated, and a duly certified copy of such record shall be transmitted without delay to the Protecting Power as well as to the Central Agency referred to in Article 140.

Article 130. The detaining authorities shall ensure that internees who die while interned are honourably buried, if possible according to the rites of the religion to which they belonged, and that their graves are respected, properly maintained, and marked in such a way that they can always be recognized.

Deceased internees shall be buried in individual graves unless unavoidable circumstances require the use of collective graves. Bodies may be cremated only for imperative reasons of hygiene, on account of the religion of the deceased or in accordance with his expressed wish to this effect. In case of cremation, the fact shall be stated and the reasons given in the death certificate of the deceased. The ashes shall be retained for safe-keeping by the detaining authorities and shall be transferred as soon as possible to the next of kin on their request.

As soon as circumstances permit, and not later then the close of hostilities, the Detaining Power shall forward lists of graves of deceased internees to the Powers on whom the deceased internees depended, through the Information Bureaux provided for in Article 136. Such lists shall include all particulars necessary for the identification of the deceased internees, as well as the exact location of their graves.

Article 131. Every death or serious injury of an internee, caused or suspected to have been caused by a sentry, another internee or any other person, as well as any death the cause of which is unknown, shall be immediately followed by an official enquiry by the Detaining Power.

A communication on this subject shall be sent immediately to the Protecting Power. The evidence of any witnesses shall be taken, and a report including such evidence shall be prepared and forwarded to the said Protecting Power.

If the enquiry indicates the guilt of one or more persons, the Detaining Power shall take all necessary steps to ensure the prosecution of the person or persons responsible.

Chapter XII—Release Repatriation and Accommodation in Neutral Countries

Article 132. Each interned person shall be released by the Detaining Power as soon as the reasons which necessitated his internment no longer exist.

The Parties to the conflict shall, moreover, endeavour during the course of hostilities, to conclude agreements for the release, the repatriation, the return to places of residence or the accommodation in a neutral country of certain classes of internees, in particular children, pregnant women and mothers with infants and young children, wounded and sick, and internees who have been detained for a long time.

Article 133. Internment shall cease as soon as possible after the close of hostilities.

Internees in the territory of a Party to the conflict against whom penal proceedings are pending for offences not exclusively subject to disciplinary penalties, may be detained until the close of such proceedings and, if circumstances require, until the completion of the penalty. The same shall apply to internees who have been previously sentenced to a punishment depriving them of liberty.

By agreement between the Detaining Power and the Powers concerned, committees may be set up after the close of hostilities, or of the occupation of territories, to search for dispersed internees.

Article 134. The High Contracting Parties shall endeavour, upon the close of hostilities or occupation, to ensure the return of all internees to their last place of residence, or to facilitate their repatriation.

Article 135. The Detaining Power shall bear the expense of returning released internees to the places where they were residing when interned, or, if it took them into custody while they were in transit or on the high seas, the cost of completing their journey or of their return to their point of departure.

Where a Detaining Power refuses permission to reside in its territory to a released internee who previously had his permanent domicile therein, such Detaining Power shall pay the cost of the said internee's repatriation. If, however, the internee elects to return to his country on his own responsibility or in obedience to the Government of the Power to which he owes allegiance, the Detaining Power need not pay the expenses of his journey beyond the point of his departure from its territory. The Detaining Power need not pay the costs of repatriation of an internee who was interned at his own request.

If internees are transferred in accordance with Article 45, the transferring and receiving Powers shall agree on the portion of the above costs to be borne by each.

The foregoing shall not prejudice such special agreements as may be concluded between Parties to the conflict concerning the exchange and repatriation of their nationals in enemy hands.

Section V—Information Bureaux and Central Agency

Article 136. Upon the outbreak of a conflict and in all cases of occupation, each of the Parties to the conflict shall establish an official Information Bureau responsible for receiving and transmitting information in respect of the protected persons who are in its power.

Each of the Parties to the conflict shall, within the shortest possible period, give its Bureau information of any measure taken by it concerning any protected persons who are kept in custody for more than two weeks, who are subjected to assigned residence or who are interned. It shall, furthermore, require its various departments concerned with such matters to provide the aforesaid Bureau promptly with information concerning all changes pertaining to these protected persons, as, for example, transfers, releases, repatriations, escapes, admittances to hospitals, births and deaths.

Article 137. Each national Bureau shall immediately forward information concerning protected persons by the most rapid means to the Powers of whom the aforesaid persons are nationals, or to Powers in whose territory they resided, through the intermediary of the Protecting Powers and likewise through the Central Agency provided for in Article 140. The Bureaux shall also reply to all enquiries which may be received regarding protected persons.

Information Bureaux shall transmit information concerning a protected person unless its transmission might be detrimental to the person concerned or to his or her relatives. Even in such a case, the information may not be withheld from the Central Agency which, upon being notified of the circumstances, will take the necessary precautions indicated in Article 140.

All communications in writing made by any Bureau shall be authenticated by a signature or a seal.

Article 138. The information received by the national Bureau and transmitted by it shall be of such a character as to make it possible to identify the protected person exactly and to advise his next of kin quickly. The information in respect of each person shall include at least his surname, first names, place and date of birth, nationality, last residence and distinguishing characteristics, the first name of the father and the maiden name of the mother, the date, place and nature of the action taken with regard to the individual, the address at which correspondence may be sent to him and the name and address of the person to be informed.

Likewise, information regarding the state of health of internees who are seriously ill or seriously wounded shall be supplied regularly and if possible every week.

Article 139. Each national Information Bureau shall, furthermore, be responsible for collecting all personal valuables left by protected persons mentioned in Article 136, in particular those who have been repatriated or released, or who have escaped or died; it shall forward the said valuables to those concerned, either direct, or, if necessary, through the Central Agency. Such articles shall be sent by the Bureau in sealed packets which shall be accompanied by statements giving clear and full identity particulars of the person to whom the articles belonged, and by a complete list of the contents of the parcel. Detailed records shall be maintained of the receipt and despatch of all such valuables.

Article 140. A Central Information Agency for protected persons, in particular for internees, shall be created in a neutral country. The International Committee of the Red Cross shall, if it deems necessary, propose to the Powers concerned the organization of such an Agency, which may be the same as that provided for in Article 123 of the Geneva Convention relative to the Treatment of Prisoners of War of August 12, 1949.

The function of the Agency shall be to collect all information of the type set forth in Article 136 which it may obtain through official or private channels and to transmit it as rapidly as possible to the countries of origin or of residence of the persons concerned, except in cases where such transmissions might be detrimental to the persons whom the said information concerns, or to their relatives. It shall receive from the Parties to the conflict all reasonable facilities for effecting such transmissions.

The High Contracting Parties, and in particular those whose nationals benefit by the services of the Central Agency, are requested to give the said Agency the financial aid it may require.

The foregoing provisions shall in no way be interpreted as restricting the humanitarian activities of the International Committee of the Red Cross and of the relief societies described in Article 142.

Article 141. The national Information Bureaux and the Central Information Agency shall enjoy free postage for all mail, likewise the exemptions provided for in Article 110, and further, so far as possible, exemption from telegraphic charges or, at least, greatly reduced rates.

**Part IV
Execution of the Convention
Section I—General Provisions**

Article 142. Subject to the measures which the Detaining Powers may consider essential to ensure their security or to meet any other reasonable need, the representatives of religious organizations, relief societies, or any other organizations assisting the protected persons, shall receive from these Powers, for themselves or their duly accredited agents, all facilities for visiting the protected persons, for distributing relief supplies and material from any source, intended for educational, recreational or religious purposes, or for assisting them in organizing their leisure time within the places of internment. Such societies or organizations may be constituted in the territory of the Detaining Power, or in any other country, or they may have an international character.

The Detaining Power may limit the number of societies and organizations whose delegates are allowed to carry out their activities in its territory and under its supervision, on condition, however, that such limitation shall not hinder the supply of effective and adequate relief to all protected persons.

The special position of the International Committee of the Red Cross in this field shall be recognized and respected at all times.

Article 143. Representatives or delegates of the Protecting Powers shall have permission to go to all places where protected persons are, particularly to places of internment, detention and work.

They shall have access to all premises occupied by protected persons and shall be able to interview the latter without witnesses, personally or through an interpreter.

Such visits may not be prohibited except for reasons of imperative military necessity, and then only as an exceptional and temporary measure. Their duration and frequency shall not be restricted.

Such representatives and delegates shall have full liberty to select the places they wish to visit. The Detaining or Occupying Power, the Protecting Power and when occasion arises the Power of origin of the persons to be visited, may agree that compatriots of the internees shall be permitted to participate in the visits.

The delegates of the International Committee of the Red Cross shall also enjoy the above prerogatives. The appointment of such delegates shall be submitted to the approval of the Power governing the territories where they will carry out their duties.

Article 144. The High Contracting Parties undertake, in time of peace as in time of war, to disseminate the text of the present Convention as widely as possible in their respective countries, and, in particular, to include the study thereof in their programmes of military and, if possible, civil instruction, so that the principles thereof may become known to the entire population.

Any civilian, military, police or other authorities, who in time of war assume responsibilities in respect of protected persons, must possess the text of the Convention and be specially instructed as to its provisions.

Article 145. The High Contracting Parties shall communicate to one another through the Swiss Federal Council and, during hostilities, through the Protecting Powers, the official translations of the present Convention, as well as the laws and regulations which they may adopt to ensure the application thereof.

Article 146. The High Contracting Parties undertake to enact any legislation necessary to provide effective penal sanctions for persons committing, or ordering to be committed any of the grave breaches of the present Convention defined in the following Article.

Each High Contracting Party shall be under the obligation to search for persons alleged to have committed, or to have ordered to be committed, such grave breaches, and shall bring such persons, regardless of their nationality, before its own courts. It may also, if it prefers, and in accordance with the provisions of its own legislation, hand such persons over for trial to another High Contracting Party concerned, provided such High Contracting Party has made out a *prima facie* case.

Each High Contracting Party shall take measures necessary for the suppression of all acts contrary to the provisions of the present Convention other than the grave breaches defined in the following Article.

In all circumstances, the accused persons shall benefit by safeguards of proper trial and defence, which shall not be less favourable than those provided by Article 105 and those following of the Geneva Convention relative to the Treatment of Prisoners of War of August 12, 1949.

Article 147. Grave breaches to which the preceding Article relates shall be those involving any of the following acts, if committed against persons or property protected by the present Convention: wilful killing, torture or inhuman treatment, including biological experiments, wilfully causing great suffering or serious injury to body or health, unlawful deportation or transfer or unlawful confinement of a protected person, compelling a protected person to serve in the forces of a hostile Power, or wilfully depriving a protected person of the rights of fair and regular trial prescribed in the present Convention, taking of hostages and extensive destruction and appropriation of property, not justified by military necessity and carried out unlawfully and wantonly.

Article 148. No High Contracting Party shall be allowed to absolve itself or any other High Contracting Party of any liability incurred by itself or by another High Contracting Party in respect of breaches referred to in the preceding Article.

Article 149. At the request of a Party to the conflict, an enquiry shall be instituted, in a manner to be decided between the interested Parties, concerning any alleged violation of the Convention.

If agreement has not been reached concerning the procedure for the enquiry, the Parties should agree on the choice of an umpire who will decide upon the procedure to be followed.

Once the violation has been established, the Parties to the conflict shall put an end to it and shall repress it with the least possible delay.

Section II—Final Provisions

Article 150. The present Convention is established in English and in French. Both texts are equally authentic.

The Swiss Federal Council shall arrange for official translations of the Convention to be made in the Russian and Spanish languages.

Article 151. The present Convention, which bears the date of this day, is open to signature until February 12, 1950, in the name of the Powers represented at the Conference which opened at Geneva on April 21, 1949.

Article 152. The present Convention shall be ratified as soon as possible and the ratifications shall be deposited at Berne.

A record shall be drawn up of the deposit of each instrument of ratification and certified copies of this record shall be transmitted by the Swiss Federal Council to all the Powers in whose name the Convention has been signed, or whose accession has been notified.

Article 153. The present Convention shall come into force six months after not less than two instruments of ratification have been deposited.

Thereafter, it shall come into force for each High Contracting Party six months after the deposit of the instrument of ratification.

Article 154. In the relations between the Powers who are bound by The Hague Conventions respecting the Laws and Customs of War on Land, whether that of July 29, 1899, or that of October 18, 1907, and who are parties to the present Convention, this last Convention shall be supplementary to Sections II and III of the Regulations annexed to the above mentioned Conventions of The Hague.

Article 155. From the date of its coming into force, it shall be open to any Power in whose name the present Convention has not been signed, to accede to this Convention.

Article 156. Accessions shall be notified in writing to the Swiss Federal Council, and shall take effect six months after the date on which they are received.

The Swiss Federal Council shall communicate the accessions to all the Powers in whose name the Convention has been signed, or whose accession has been notified.

Article 157. The situations provided for in Articles 2 and 3 shall give immediate effect to ratifications deposited and accessions notified by the Parties to the conflict before or after the beginning of hostilities or occupation. The Swiss Federal Council shall communicate by the quickest method any ratifications or accessions received from Parties to the conflict.

Article 158. Each of the High Contracting Parties shall be at liberty to denounce the present Convention.

The denunciation shall be notified in writing to the Swiss Federal Council, which shall transmit it to the Governments of all the High Contracting Parties.

The denunciation shall take effect one year after the notification thereof has been made to the Swiss Federal Council. However, a denunciation of which notification has been made at a time when the denouncing Power is involved in a conflict shall not take effect until peace has been concluded, and until after operations connected with the release, repatriation and re-establishment of the persons protected by the present Convention have been terminated.

The denunciation shall have effect only in respect of the denouncing Power. It shall in no way impair the obligations which the Parties to the conflict shall remain bound to fulfil by virtue of the principles of the law of nations, as they result from the usages established among civilized peoples, from the laws of humanity and the dictates of the public conscience.

Article 159. The Swiss Federal Council shall register the present Convention with the Secretariat of the United Nations. The Swiss Federal council shall also inform the Secretariat of the United Nations of all ratifications, accessions and denunciations received by it with respect to the present Convention.

In witness whereof the undersigned, having deposited their respective full powers, have signed the present Convention.

Done at Geneva this twelfth day of August, 1949, in the English and French languages. The original shall be deposited in the Archives of the Swiss Confederation. The Swiss Federal Council shall transmit certified copies thereof to each of the signatory and acceding States.

SEE ALSO Basic Principles for the Protection of Civilian Populations in Armed Conflicts; Declaration on the Protection of Women and Children in Emergency and Armed Conflict; Geneva Conventions, Protocols I and II.

GENEVA CONVENTION RELATIVE TO THE TREATMENT OF PRISONERS OF WAR (1949).

The convention (No. III of the Geneva Red Cross Conventions for the Protection of Victims of War) was adopted on 12 August 1949 by the Diplomatic Conference for the Establishment of International Conventions for the Protection of Victims of War, convened in Geneva by the Swiss Federal Council with the cooperation of the International Committee of the Red Cross. The convention entered into force on 21 October 1950. Switzerland serves as the depository.

The convention replaced, for the parties thereto, the 1929 Geneva Convention Relative to the Treatment of Prisoners of War and was accepted by all States parties to that earlier convention.

The 1949 convention was later revised and supplemented by PROTOCOL I, ADDITIONAL TO THE 1949 GENEVA CONVENTIONS AND RELATING TO THE PROTECTION OF VICTIMS OF INTERNATIONAL ARMED CONFLICTS, and by PROTOCOL II, ADDITIONAL TO THE 1949 GENEVA CONVENTIONS AND RELATING TO THE PROTECTION OF VICTIMS OF NON-INTERNATIONAL ARMED CONFLICTS. Both protocols entered into force on 7 December 1978.

The text of the convention is as follows:

Preamble

The undersigned, Plenipotentiaries of the Governments represented at the Diplomatic Conference held at Geneva from April 21 to August 12, 1949, for the purpose of revising the Convention concluded at Geneva on July 27, 1929, relative to the Treatment of Prisoners of War, have agreed as follows:

Article 1. The High Contracting Parties undertake to respect and to ensure respect for the present Convention in all circumstances.

Article 2. In addition to the provisions which shall be implemented in peace-time, the present Convention shall apply to all cases of declared war or of any other armed conflict which may rise between two or more of the High Contracting Parties, even if the state of war is not recognized by one of them.

The Convention shall also apply to all cases of partial or total occupation of the territory of a High Contracting Party, even if the said occupation meets with no armed resistance.

Although one of the Powers in conflict may not be a party to the present Convention, the Powers who are parties thereto shall remain bound by it in their mutual rela-tions. They shall furthermore be bound by the Convention in relation to the said Power, if the latter accepts and applies the provisions thereof.

Article 3. In the case of armed conflict not of an international character occurring in the territory of one of the High Contracting Parties, each Party to the conflict shall be bound to apply, as a minimum, the following provisions:

(1) Persons taking no active part in the hostilities, including members of armed forces who have laid down their arms and those placed *hors de combat* by sickness, wounds, detention, or any other cause, shall in all circumstances be treated humanely, without any adverse distinction founded on race, colour, religion or faith, sex, birth or wealth, or any other similar criteria.

To this end, the following acts are and shall remain prohibited at any time and in any place whatsoever with respect to the above-mentioned persons:

(*a*) violence to life and person, in particular murder of all kinds, mutilation, cruel treatment and torture;

(*b*) taking of hostages;

(*c*) outrages upon personal dignity, in particular, humiliating and degrading treatment;

(*d*) the passing of sentences and the carrying out of executions without previous judgment pronounced by a regularly constituted court affording all the judicial guarantees which are recognized as indispensable by civilized peoples.

(2) The wounded and sick shall be collected and cared for.

An impartial humanitarian body, such as the International Committee of the Red Cross, may offer its services to the Parties to the conflict.

The Parties to the conflict should further endeavour to bring into force, by means of special agreements, all or part of the other provisions of the present Convention.

The application of the preceding provisions shall not affect the legal status of the Parties to the conflict.

Article 4. A. Prisoners of war, in the sense of the present Convention, are persons belonging to one of the following categories, who have fallen into the power of the enemy:

(1) Members of the armed forces of a Party to the conflict as well as members of militias or volunteer corps forming part of such armed forces.

(2) Members of other militias and members of other volunteer corps, including those or organized resistance movements, belonging to a Party to the conflict and operating in or outside their own territory, even if this territory is occupied, provided that such militias or volunteer corps, including such organized resistance movements, fulfill the following conditions:

(*a*) that of being commanded by a person responsible for his subordinates;

(*b*) that of having a fixed distinctive sign recognizable at a distance;

(*c*) that of carrying arms openly;

(*d*) that of conducting their operations in accordance with the laws and customs of war.

(3) Members of regular armed forces who profess allegiance to a government or an authority not recognized by the Detaining Power.

(4) Persons who accompany the armed forces without actually being members thereof, such as civilian members of military aircraft crews, war correspondents, supply contractors, members of labour units or of services responsible for the welfare of the armed forces, provided that they have received authorization from the armed forces which they ac-

company, who shall provide them for that purpose with an identity card similar to the annexed model.

(5) Members of crews, including masters, pilots and apprentices, of the merchant marine and the crews of civil aircraft of the Parties to the conflict, who do not benefit by more favourable treatment under any other provisions of international law.

(6) Inhabitants of a non-occupied territory, who on the approach of the enemy spontaneously take up arms to resist the invading forces, without having had time to form themselves into regular armed units, provided they carry arms openly and respect the laws and customs of war.

B. The following shall likewise be treated as prisoners of war under the present Convention:

(1) Persons belonging, or having belonged, to the armed forces of the occupied country, if the occupying Power considers it necessary by reason of such allegiance to intern them, even though it has originally liberated them while hostilities were going on outside the territory it occupies, in particular where such persons have made an unsuccessful attempt to rejoin the armed forces to which they belong and which are engaged in combat, or where they fail to comply with a summons made to them with a view to internment.

(2) The persons belonging to one of the categories enumerated in the present Article, who have been received by neutral or non-belligerent Powers on their territory and whom these Powers are required to intern under international law, without prejudice to any more favourable treatment which these Powers may choose to give and with the exception of Articles 8, 10, 15, 30, fifth paragraph, 58–67, 92, 126 and, where diplomatic relations exist between the Parties to the conflict and the neutral or non-belligerent Power concerned, those Articles concerning the Protecting Power. Where such diplomatic relations exist, the Parties to a conflict on whom these persons depend shall be allowed to perform towards them the functions of a Protecting Power as provided in the present Convention, without prejudice to the functions which these Parties normally exercise in conformity with diplomatic and consular usage and treaties.

C. This Article shall in no way affect the status of medical personnel and chaplains as provided for in Article 33 of the present Convention.

Article 5. The present Convention shall apply to the persons referred to in Article 4 from the time they fall into the power of the enemy and until their final release and repatriation.

Should any doubt arise as to whether persons, having committed a belligerent act and having fallen into the hands of the enemy, belong to any of the categories enumerated in Article 4, such persons shall enjoy the protection of the present Convention until such time as their status has been determined by a competent tribunal.

Article 6. In addition to the agreements expressly provided for in Articles 10, 23, 28, 33, 60, 65, 66, 67, 72, 73, 75, 109, 110, 118, 119, 122 and 132, the High Contracting Parties may conclude other special agreements for all matters concerning which they may deem it suitable to make separate provision. No special agreement shall adversely affect the situation of prisoners of war, as defined by the present Convention, nor restrict the rights which it confers upon them.

Prisoners of war shall continue to have the benefit of such agreements as long as the Convention is applicable to them, except where express provisions to the contrary are contained in the aforesaid or in subsequent agreements, or where more favourable measures have been taken with regard to them by one or other of the Parties to the conflict.

Article 7. Prisoners of war may in no circumstances renounce in part or in entirety the rights secured to them by the present Convention, and by the special agreements referred to in the foregoing Article, if such there be.

Article 8. The present Convention shall be applied with the co-operation and under the scrutiny of the Protecting Powers whose duty it is to safeguard the interests of the Parties to the conflict. For this purpose, the Protecting Powers may appoint, apart from their diplomatic or consular staff, delegates from amongst their own nationals or the nationals of other neutral Powers. The said delegates shall be subject to the approval of the Power with which they are to carry out their duties.

The Parties to the conflict shall facilitate to the greater extent possible the task of the representatives or delegates of the Protecting Powers.

The representatives or delegates of the Protecting Powers shall not in any case exceed their mission under the present Convention. They shall, in particular, take account of the imperative necessities of security of the State wherein they carry out their duties.

Article 9. The provisions of the present Convention constitute no obstacle to the humanitarian activities which the International Committee of the Red Cross or any other impartial humanitarian organization may, subject to the consent of the Parties to the conflict concerned, undertake for the protection of prisoners of war and for their relief.

Article 10. The High Contracting Parties may at any time agree to entrust to an organization which offers all guarantees of impartiality and efficacy the duties incumbent on the Protecting Powers by virtue of the present Convention.

When prisoners of war do not benefit or cease to benefit, no matter for what reason, by the activities of a Protecting Power or of an organization provided for in the first paragraph above, the Detaining Power shall request a neutral State, or such an organization, to undertake the functions performed under the present Convention by a Protecting Power designated by the Parties to a conflict.

If protection cannot be arranged accordingly, the Detaining Power shall request or shall accept, subject to the provisions of this Article, the offer of the services of a humanitarian organization, such as the International Committee of the Red Cross, to assume the humanitarian functions performed by Protecting Powers under the present Convention.

Any neutral Power or any organization invited by the Power concerned or offering itself for these purposes, shall be required to act with a sense of responsibility towards the Party to the conflict on which persons protected by the present Convention depend, and shall be required to furnish sufficient assurances that it is in a position to undertake the appropriate functions and to discharge them impartially.

No derogation from the preceding provisions shall be made by special agreements between Powers one of which is restricted, even temporarily, in its freedom to negotiate with the other Power or its allies by reason of military events, more particularly where the whole, or a substantial part, of the territory of the said Power is occupied.

Whenever in the present Convention mention is made of a Protecting Power, such mention applies to substitute organizations in the sense of the present Article.

Article 11. In cases where they deem it advisable in the interest of protected persons, particularly in cases of disagreement between the Parties to the conflict as to the application or interpretation of the provisions of the present Convention, the Protecting Powers shall lend their good offices with a view to settling the disagreement.

For this purpose, each of the Protecting Powers may, either at the invitation of one Party or on its own initiative, propose to the Parties to the conflict a meeting of their representatives, and in particular of the authorities responsible for prisoners of war, possibly on neutral territory suitably chosen. The Parties to the conflict shall be bound to give effect to the proposals made to them for this purpose. The Protecting Powers may, if necessary, propose for approval by the Parties to the conflict a person belonging to a neutral Power, or delegated by the International Committee of the Red Cross, who shall be invited to take part in such a meeting.

Part II
General Protection of Prisoners of War

Article 12. Prisoners of war are in the hands of the enemy Power, but not of the individuals or military units who have captured them. Irrespective of the individual responsibilities that may exist, the Detaining Power is responsible for the treatment given them.

Prisoners of war may only be transferred by the Detaining Power to a Power which is a party to the Convention and after the Detaining Power has satisfied itself of the willingness and ability of such transferee Power to apply the Convention. When prisoners of war are transferred under such circumstances, responsibility for the application of the Convention rests on the Power accepting them while they are in its custody.

Nevertheless if that Power fails to carry out the provisions of the Convention in any important respect the Power by whom the prisoners of war were transferred shall, upon being notified by the Protecting Power, take effective measures to correct the situation or shall request the return of the prisoners of war. Such requests must be complied with.

Article 13. Prisoners of war must at all times be humanely treated. Any unlawful act or omission by the Detaining Power causing death or seriously endangering the health of a prisoner of war in its custody is prohibited and will be regarded as a serious breach of the present Convention. In particular, no prisoner of war may be subjected to physical mutilation or to medical or scientific experiments of any kind which are not justified by the medical, dental or hospital treatment of the prisoner concerned and carried out in his interest.

Likewise, prisoners of war must at all times be protected, particularly against acts of violence or intimidation and against insults and public curiosity.

Measures of reprisal against prisoners of war are prohibited.

Article 14. Prisoners of war are entitled in all circumstances to respect for their persons and their honour.

Women shall be treated with all the regard due to their sex and shall in all cases benefit by treatment as favourable as that granted to men.

Prisoners of war shall retain the full civil capacity which they enjoyed at the time of their capture. The Detaining Power may not restrict the exercise, either within or without its own territory, of the rights such capacity confers except in so far as the captivity requires.

Article 15. The Power detaining prisoners of war shall be bound to provide free of charge for their maintenance and for the medical attention required by their state of health.

Article 16. Taking into consideration the provisions of the present Convention relating to rank and sex, and subject to any privileged treatment which may be accorded to them by reason of their state of health, age or professional qualifications, all prisoners of war shall be treated alike by the Detaining Power, without any adverse distinction based on race, nationality, religious belief or political opinions, or any other distinction founded on similar criteria.

Part III—Captivity
Section I—Beginning of Captivity

Article 17. Every prisoner of war, when questioned on the subject is bound to give only his surname, first names and rank, date of birth, and army, regimental, personal or serial number, or failing this, equivalent information.

If he wilfully infringes this rule he may render himself liable to a restriction of the privileges accorded to his rank or status.

Each Party to a conflict is required to furnish the persons under its jurisdiction who are liable to become prisoners of war, with an identity card showing the owner's surname, first names, rank, army, regimental, personal or serial number or equivalent information, and date of birth. The identity card may, furthermore, bear the signature or the fingerprints, or both, of the owner, and may bear, as well, any other information the Party to the conflict may wish to add concerning persons belonging to its armed forces. As far as possible the card shall measure 6.5 x 10 cm. and shall be issued in duplicate. The identity card shall be shown by the prisoner of war upon demand, but may in no case be taken away from him.

No physical or mental torture, nor any other form of coercion may be inflicted on prisoners of war to secure from them information of any kind whatever. Prisoners of war who refuse to answer may not be threatened, insulted, or exposed to any unpleasant or disadvantageous treatment of any kind.

Prisoners of war who, owing to their physical or mental condition, are unable to state their identity shall be handed over to the medical service. The identity of such prisoners shall be established by all possible means, subject to the provisions of the preceding paragraph.

The questioning of prisoners of war shall be carried out in a language which they understand.

Article 18. All effects and articles of personal use, except arms, horses, military equipment and military documents, shall remain in the possession of prisoners of war, likewise their metal helmets and gas masks and like articles issued for personal protection. Effects and articles used for their clothing or feeding shall likewise remain in their possession, even if such effects and articles belong to their regulation military equipment.

At no time should prisoners of war be without identity documents. The Detaining Power shall supply such documents to prisoners of war who possess none.

Badges of rank and nationality, decorations and articles having above all a personal or sentimental value may not be taken from prisoners of war.

Sums of money carried by prisoners of war may not be taken away from them except by order of an officer, and after the amount and particulars of the owner have been recorded in a special register and an itemized receipt has been given, legibly inscribed with the name, rank and unit of the person issuing the said receipt. Sums in the currency of the Detaining Power, or which are changed into such currency at the prisoner's request, shall be placed to the credit of the prisoner's account as provided in Article 64.

The Detaining Power may withdraw articles of value from prisoners of war only for reasons of security; when such articles are withdrawn, the procedure laid down for sums of money impounded shall apply.

Such objects, likewise the sums taken away in any currency other than that of the Detaining Power, and the conversion of which has not been asked for by the owners, shall be kept in the custody of the Detaining Power and shall be returned in their initial shape to prisoners of war at the end of their captivity.

Article 19. Prisoners of war shall be evacuated as soon as possible after their capture, to camps situated in an area far enough from the combat zone for them to be out of danger.

Only those prisoners of war who, owing to wounds or sickness, would run greater risks by being evacuated than by remaining where they are, may be temporarily kept back in a danger zone.

Prisoners of war shall not be unnecessarily exposed to danger while awaiting evacuation from a fighting zone.

Article 20. The evacuation of prisoners of war shall always be effected humanely and in conditions similar to those for the forces of the Detaining Power in their changes of station.

The Detaining Power shall supply prisoners of war who are being evacuated with sufficient food and potable water, and with the necessary clothing and medical attention. The Detaining Power shall take all suitable precautions to ensure their safety during evacuation, and shall establish as soon as possible a list of the prisoners of war who are evacuated.

If prisoners of war must, during evacuation, pass through transit camps, their stay in such camps shall be as brief as possible.

Section II—Internment of Prisoners of War
Chapter I—General Observations

Article 21. The Detaining Power may subject prisoners of war to internment. It may impose on them the obligation of not leaving, beyond certain limits, the camp where they are interned, or if the said camp is fenced in, of not going outside its perimeter. Subject to the provisions of the present Convention relative to penal and disciplinary sanctions, prisoners of war may not be held in close confinement except where necessary to safeguard their health and then only during the continuation of the circumstances which make such confinement necessary.

Prisoners of war may be partially or wholly released on parole or promise, in so far as is allowed by the laws of the Power on which they depend. Such measures shall be taken particularly in cases where this may contribute to the improvement of their state of health. No prisoner of war shall be compelled to accept liberty on parole or promise.

Upon the outbreak of hostilities, each Party to the conflict shall notify the adverse Party of the laws and regulations allowing or forbidding its own nationals to accept liberty on parole or promise. Prisoners of war who are paroled or who have given their promise in conformity with the laws and regulations so notified, are bound on their personal honour scrupulously to fulfil, both towards the Power on which they depend and the Power which has captured them, the engagements of their paroles or promises.

In such cases, the Power on which they depend is bound neither to require nor to accept from them any service incompatible with the parole or promise given.

Article 22. Prisoners of war may be interned only in premises located on land and affording every guarantee of hygiene and healthfulness. Except in particular cases which are justified by the interest of the prisoners themselves, they shall not be interned in penitentiaries.

Prisoners of war interned in unhealthy areas, or where the climate is injurious for them, shall be removed as soon as possible to a more favourable climate.

The Detaining Power shall assemble prisoners of war in camps or camp compounds according to their nationality, language and customs, provided that such prisoners shall not be separated from prisoners of war belonging to the armed forces with which they were serving at the time of their capture, except with their consent.

Article 23. No prisoner of war may at any time be sent to, or detained in areas where he may be exposed to the fire of the combat zone, nor may his presence be used to render certain points or areas immune from military operations.

Prisoners of war shall have shelters against air bombardment and other hazards of war, to the same extent as the local civilian population. With the exception of those engaged in the protection of their quarters against the aforesaid hazards, they may enter such shelters as soon as possible after the giving of the alarm. Any other protective measure taken in favour of the population shall also apply to them.

Detaining Powers shall give the Powers concerned, through the intermediary of the Protecting Powers, all useful information regarding the geographical location of prisoner-of-war camps.

Whenever military considerations permit, prisoner-of-war camps shall be indicated in the daytime by the letters PW or PG, placed so as to be clearly visible from the air. The Powers concerned may, however, agree upon any other system of marking. Only prisoner-of-war camps shall be marked as such.

Article 24. Transit or screening camps of a permanent kind shall be fitted out under conditions similar to those described in the present Section, and the prisoners therein shall have the same treatment as in other camps.

Chapter II
Quarters, Food and Clothing of Prisoners of War

Article 25. Prisoners of war shall be quartered under conditions as favourable as those for the forces of the Detaining Power who are billeted in the same area. The said conditions shall make allowance for the habits and customs of the prisoners and shall in no case be prejudicial to their health.

The foregoing provisions shall apply in particular to the dormitories of prisoners of war as regards both total surface and minimum cubic space, and the general installations, bedding and blankets.

The premises provided for the use of prisoners of war individually or collectively, shall be entirely protected from dampness and adequately heated and lighted, in particular between dusk and lights out. All precautions must be taken against the danger of fire.

In any camps in which women prisoners of war, as well as men, are accommodated, separate dormitories shall be provided for them.

Article 26. The basic daily food rations shall be sufficient in quantity, quality and variety to keep prisoners of war in good health and to prevent loss of weight or the development of nutritional deficiencies. Account shall also be taken of the habitual diet of the prisoners.

The Detaining Power shall supply prisoners of war who work with such additional rations as are necessary for the labour on which they are employed.

Sufficient drinking water shall be supplied to prisoners of war. The use of tobacco shall be permitted.

Prisoners of war shall, as far as possible, be associated with the preparation of their meals; they may be employed for that purpose in the kitchens. Furthermore, they shall be given the means of preparing, themselves, the additional food in their possession.

Adequate premises shall be provided for messing.

Collective disciplinary measures affecting food are prohibited.

Article 27. Clothing, underwear and footwear shall be supplied to prisoners of war in sufficient quantities by the Detaining Power, which shall make allowance for the climate of the region where the prisoners are detained. Uniforms of enemy armed forces captured by the Detaining Power should, if suitable for the climate, be made available to clothe prisoners of war.

The regular replacement and repair of the above articles shall be assured by the Detaining Power. In addition, prisoners of war who work shall receive appropriate clothing, wherever the nature of the work demands.

Article 28. Canteens shall be installed in all camps, where prisoners of war may procure foodstuffs, soap and tobacco and ordinary articles in daily use. The tariff shall never be in excess of local market prices.

The profits made by camp canteens shall be used for the benefit of the prisoners; a special fund shall be created for this purpose. The prisoners' representative shall have the right to collaborate in the management of the canteen and of this fund.

When a camp is closed down, the credit balance of the special fund shall be handed to an international welfare organization, to be employed for the benefit of prisoners of war of the same nationality as those who have contributed to the fund. In case of a general repatriation, such profits shall be kept by the Detaining Power, subject to any agreement to the contrary between the Powers concerned.

Chapter III—Hygiene and Medical Attention

Article 29. The Detaining Power shall be bound to take all sanitary measures necessary to ensure the cleanliness and healthfulness of camps, and to prevent epidemics.

Prisoners of war shall have for their use, day and night, conveniences which conform to the rules of hygiene and are maintained in a constant state of cleanliness. In any camps in which women prisoners of war are accommodated, separate conveniences shall be provided for them.

Also, apart from the baths and showers with which the camps shall be furnished, prisoners of war shall be provided with sufficient water and soap for their personal toilet and for washing their personal laundry; the necessary installations, facilities and time shall be granted them for that purpose.

Article 30. Every camp shall have an adequate infirmary where prisoners of war may have the attention they require, as well as appropriate diet. Isolation wards shall, if necessary, be set aside for cases of contagious or mental disease. Prisoners of war suffering from serious disease, or whose

condition necessitates special treatment, a surgical operation or hospital care, must be admitted to any military or civil medical unit where such treatment can be given, even if their repatriation is contemplated in the near future. Special facilities shall be afforded for the care to be given to the disabled, in particular to the blind, and for their rehabilitation, pending repatriation.

Prisoners of war shall have the attention, preferably, of medical personnel of the Power on which they depend and, if possible, of their nationality.

Prisoners of war may not be prevented from presenting themselves to the medical authorities for examination. The detaining authorities shall, upon request, issue to every prisoner who has undergone treatment an official certificate indicating the nature of his illness or injury, and the duration and kind of treatment received. A duplicate of this certificate shall be forwarded to the Central Prisoners of War Agency.

The costs of treatment, including those of any apparatus necessary for the maintenance of prisoners of war in good health, particularly dentures and other artificial appliances, and spectacles, shall be borne by the Detaining Power.

Article 31. Medical inspections of prisoners of war shall be made at least once a month. They shall include the checking and the recording of the weight of each prisoner of war. Their purpose shall be, in particular, to supervise the general state of health, nutrition and cleanliness of prisoners and to detect contagious diseases, especially tuberculosis, malaria and venereal disease. For this purpose the most efficient methods available shall be employed, e.g. periodic mass miniature radiography for the early detection of tuberculosis.

Article 32. Prisoners of war who, though not attached to the medical service of their armed forces, are physicians, surgeons, dentists, nurses or medical orderlies, may be required by the Detaining Power to exercise their medical functions in the interests of prisoners or war dependent on the same Power. In that case they shall continue to be prisoners of war, but shall receive the same treatment as corresponding medical personnel retained by the Detaining Power. They shall be exempted from any other work under Article 49.

Chapter IV
Medical Personnel and Chaplains Retained to Assist Prisoners of War

Article 33. Members of the medical personnel and chaplains while retained by the Detaining Power with a view to assisting prisoners of war, shall not be considered as prisoners of war. They shall, however, receive as a minimum the benefits and protection of the present Convention, and shall also be granted all facilities necessary to provide for the medical care of, and religious ministration to prisoners of war.

They shall continue to exercise their medical and spiritual functions for the benefit of prisoners of war, preferably those belonging to the armed forces upon which they depend, within the scope of the military laws and regulations of the Detaining Power and under the control of its competent services, in accordance with their professional etiquette. They shall also benefit by the following facilities in the exercise of their medical or spiritual functions:

(*a*) They shall be authorized to visit periodically prisoners of war situated in working detachments or in hospitals outside the camp. For this purpose, the Detaining Power shall place at their disposal the necessary means of transport.

(b) The senior medical officer in each camp shall be responsible to the camp military authorities for everything connected with the activities of retained medical personnel. For this purpose, Parties to the conflict shall agree at the outbreak of hostilities on the subject of the corresponding ranks of the medical personnel, including that of societies mentioned in Article 26 of the Geneva Convention for the Amelioration of the Condition of the Wounded and Sick in Armed Forces in the Field of August 12, 1949. This senior medical officer, as well as chaplains, shall have the right to deal with the competent authorities of the camp on all questions relating to their duties. Such authorities shall afford them all necessary facilities for correspondence relating to these questions.

(c) Although they shall be subject to the internal discipline of the camp in which they are retained, such personnel may not be compelled to carry out any work other than that concerned with their medical or religious duties.

During hostilities, the Parties to the conflict shall agree concerning the possible relief of retained personnel and shall settle the procedure to be followed.

None of the preceding provisions shall relieve the Detaining Power of its obligations with regard to prisoners of war from the medical or spiritual point of view.

Chapter V
Religious, Intellectual and Physical Activities

Article 34. Prisoners of war shall enjoy complete latitude in the exercise of their religious duties, including attendance at the service of their faith, on condition that they comply with the disciplinary routine prescribed by the military authorities.

Adequate premises shall be provided where religious services may be held.

Article 35. Chaplains who fall into the hands of the enemy Power and who remain or are retained with a view to assisting prisoners of war, shall be allowed to minister to them and to exercise freely their ministry amongst prisoners of war of the same religion, in accordance with their religious conscience. They shall be allocated among the various camps and labour detachments containing prisoners of war belonging to the same forces, speaking the same language or practicing the same religion. They shall enjoy the necessary facilities, including the means of transport provided for in Article 33, for visiting the prisoners of war outside their camp. They shall be free to correspond, subject to censorship, on matters concerning their religious duties with the ecclesiastical authorities in the country of detention and with the international religious organizations. Letters and cards which they may send for this purpose shall be in addition to the quota provided for in Article 71.

Article 36. Prisoners of war who are ministers of religion, without having officiated as chaplains to their own forces, shall be at liberty, whatever their denomination, to minister freely to the members of their community. For this purpose, they shall receive the same treatment as the chaplains retained by the Detaining Power. They shall not be obliged to do any other work.

Article 37. When prisoners of war have not the assistance of a retained chaplain or of a prisoner of war minister of their faith, a minister belonging to the prisoners' or a similar denomination, or in his absence a qualified layman, if such a course is feasible from a confessional point of view, shall be appointed at the request of the prisoners concerned to fill this office. This appointment, subject to the approval of the Detaining Power, shall take place with the agreement of the community of prisoners concerned and, wherever necessary, with the approval of the local religious authorities of the same faith. The person thus appointed shall comply with all regulations established by the Detaining Power in the interests of discipline and military security.

Article 38. While respecting the individual preferences of every prisoner, the Detaining Power shall encourage the practice of intellectual, educational and recreational pursuits, sports and games amongst prisoners, and shall take the measures necessary to ensure the exercise thereof by providing them with adequate premises and necessary equipment.

Prisoners shall have opportunities for taking physical exercise including sports and games and for being out of doors. Sufficient open spaces shall be provided for this purpose in all camps.

Chapter VI—Discipline

Article 39. Every prisoner-of-war camp shall be put under the immediate authority of a responsible commissioned officer belonging to the regular armed forces of the Detaining Power. Such officer shall have in his possession a copy of the present Convention; he shall ensure that its provisions are known to the camp staff and the guard and shall be responsible, under the direction of his government, for its application.

Prisoners of war, with the exception of officers, must salute and show to all officers of the Detaining Power the external marks of respect provided for by the regulations applying in their own forces.

Officer prisoners of war are bound to salute only officers of a higher rank of the Detaining Power; they must, however, salute the camp commander regardless of his rank.

Article 40. The wearing of badges of rank and nationality, as well as of decorations, shall be permitted.

Article 41. In every camp the text of the present Convention and its Annexes and the contents of any special agreement provided for in Article 6, shall be posted, in the prisoners' own language, at places where all may read them. Copies shall be supplied, on request, to the prisoners who cannot have access to the copy which has been posted.

Regulations, orders, notices and publications of every kind relating to the conduct of prisoners of war shall be issued to them in a language which they understand. Such regulations, orders and publications shall be posted in the manner described above and copies shall be handed to the prisoners' representative. Every order and command addressed to prisoners of war individually must likewise be given in a language which they understand.

Article 42. The use of weapons against prisoners of war, especially against those who are escaping or attempting to escape, shall constitute an extreme measure, which shall always be preceded by warnings appropriate to the circumstances.

Chapter VII—Rank of Prisoners of War

Article 43. Upon the outbreak of hostilities, the Parties to the conflict shall communicate to one another the titles and ranks of all the persons mentioned in Article 4 of the present Convention, in order to ensure equality of treatment between prisoners of equivalent rank. Titles and ranks which are subsequently created shall form the subject of similar communications.

The Detaining Power shall recognize promotions in rank which have been accorded to prisoners of war and which have been duly notified by the Power on which these prisoners depend.

Article 44. Officers and prisoners of equivalent status shall be treated with the regard due to their rank and age.

In order to ensure service in officers' camps, other ranks of the same armed forces who, as far as possible, speak the same language, shall be assigned in sufficient numbers, account being taken of the rank of officers and prisoners of equivalent status. Such orderlies shall not be required to perform any other work.

Supervision of the mess by the officers themselves shall be facilitated in every way.

Article 45. Prisoners of war other than officers and prisoners of equivalent status shall be treated with the regard due to their rank and age.

Supervision of the mess by the prisoners themselves shall be facilitated in every way.

Chapter VIII
Transfer of Prisoners of War After Their Arrival in Camp

Article 46. The Detaining Power, when deciding upon the transfer of prisoners of war, shall take into account the interests of the prisoners themselves, more especially so as not to increase the difficulty of their repatriation.

The transfer of prisoners of war shall always be effected humanely and in conditions not less favourable than those under which the forces of the Detaining Power are transferred. Account shall always be taken of the climatic conditions to which the prisoners of war are accustomed and the conditions of transfer shall in no case be prejudicial to their health.

The Detaining Power shall supply prisoners of war during transfer with sufficient food and drinking-water to keep them in good health, likewise with the necessary clothing, shelter and medical attention. The Detaining Power shall take adequate precautions especially in case of transport by sea or by air, to ensure their safety during transfer, and shall draw up a complete list of all transferred prisoners before their departure.

Article 47. Sick or wounded prisoners of war shall not be transferred as long as their recovery may be endangered by the journey, unless their safety imperatively demands it.

If the combat zone draws closer to a camp, the prisoners of war in the said camp shall not be transferred unless their transfer can be carried out in adequate conditions of safety, or if they are exposed to greater risks by remaining on the spot than by being transferred.

Article 48. In the event of transfer, prisoners of war shall be officially advised of their departure and of their new postal address. Such notifications shall be given in time for them to pack their luggage and inform their next of kin.

They shall be allowed to take with them their personal effects, and the correspondence and parcels which have arrived for them. The weight of such baggage may be limited, if the conditions of transfer so require, to what each prisoner can reasonably carry, which shall in no case be more than twenty-five kilograms per head.

Mail and parcels addressed to their former camp shall be forwarded to them without delay. The camp commander shall take, in agreement with the prisoners' representative,

any measures needed to ensure the transport of the prisoners' community property and of the luggage they are unable to take with them in consequence of restrictions imposed by virtue of the second paragraph of this Article.

The costs of transfers shall be borne by the Detaining Power.

Section III
Labour of Prisoners of War

Article 49. The Detaining Power may utilize the labour of prisoners of war who are physically fit, taking into account their age, sex, rank and physical aptitude, and with a view particularly to maintaining them in a good state of physical and mental health.

Non-commissioned officers who are prisoners of war shall only be required to do supervisory work. Those not so required may ask for other suitable work which shall, so far as possible, be found for them.

If officers or persons of equivalent status ask for suitable work, it shall be found for them, so far as possible, but they may in no circumstances be compelled to work.

Article 50. Besides work connected with camp administration, installation or maintenance, prisoners of war may be compelled to do only such work as is included in the following classes:

(*a*) agriculture;

(*b*) industries connected with the production or the extraction of raw materials, and manufacturing industries, with the exception of metallurgical, machinery and chemical industries; public works and building operations which have no military character or purpose;

(*c*) transport and handling of stores which are not military in character or purpose;

(*d*) commercial business, and arts and crafts;

(*e*) domestic service;

(*f*) public utility services having no military character or purpose.

Should the above provisions be infringed, prisoners of war shall be allowed to exercise their right of complaint, in conformity with Article 78.

Article 51. Prisoners of war must be granted suitable working conditions, especially as regards accommodation, food, clothing and equipment; such conditions shall not be inferior to those enjoyed by nationals of the Detaining Power employed in similar work; account shall also be taken of climatic conditions.

The Detaining Power, in utilizing the labour of prisoners of war, shall ensure that in areas in which prisoners are employed, the national legislation concerning the protection of labour and, more particularly, the regulations for the safety of workers, are duly applied.

Prisoners of war shall receive training and be provided with the means of protection suitable to the work they will have to do and similar to those accorded to the nationals of the Detaining Power. Subject to the provisions of Article 52, prisoners may be submitted to the normal risks run by these civilian workers.

Conditions of labour shall in no case be rendered more arduous by disciplinary measures.

Article 52. Unless he be a volunteer, no prisoner of war may be employed on labour which is of an unhealthy or dangerous nature.

No prisoner of war shall be assigned to labour which would be looked upon as humiliating for a member of the Detaining Power's own forces.

The removal of mines or similar devices shall be considered as dangerous labour.

Article 53. The duration of the daily labour of prisoners of war, including the time of the journey to and fro, shall not be excessive, and must in no case exceed that permitted for civilian workers in the district, who are nationals of the Detaining Power and employed on the same work.

Prisoners of war must be allowed, in the middle of the day's work, a rest of not less than one hour. This rest will be the same as that to which workers of the Detaining Power are entitled, if the latter is of longer duration. They shall be allowed, in addition, a rest of twenty-four consecutive hours every week, preferably on Sunday or the day of rest in their country of origin. Furthermore, every prisoner who has worked for one year shall be granted a rest of eight consecutive days, during which his working pay shall be paid him.

If methods of labour such as piece work are employed, the length of the working period shall not be rendered excessive thereby.

Article 54. The working pay due to prisoners of war shall be fixed in accordance with the provisions of Article 62 of the present Convention.

Prisoners of war who sustain accidents in connection with work, or who contract a disease in the course, or in consequence of their work, shall receive all the care their condition may require. The Detaining Power shall furthermore deliver to such prisoners of war a medical certificate enabling them to submit their claims to the Power on which they depend, and shall send a duplicate to the Central Prisoners of War Agency provided for in Article 123.

Article 55. The fitness of prisoners of war for work shall be periodically verified by medical examinations, at least once a month. The examinations shall have particular regard to the nature of the work which prisoners of war are required to do.

If any prisoner of war considers himself incapable of working, he shall be permitted to appear before the medical authorities of his camp. Physicians or surgeons may recommend that the prisoners who are, in their opinion, unfit for work be exempted therefrom.

Article 56. The organization and administration of labour detachments shall be similar to those of prisoner-of-war camps.

Every labour detachment shall remain under the control of and administratively part of a prisoner-of-war camp. The military authorities and the commander of the said camp shall be responsible, under the direction of their government, for the observance of the provisions of the present Convention in labour detachments.

The camp commander shall keep an up-to-date record of the labour detachments dependent on his camp, and shall communicate it to the delegates of the Protecting Power, of the International Committee of the Red Cross, or of other agencies giving relief to prisoners of war, who may visit the camp.

Article 57. The treatment of prisoners of war who work for private persons, even if the latter are responsible for guarding and protecting them, shall not be inferior to that which is provided for by the present Convention. The Detaining Power, the military authorities and the commander of the camp to which such prisoners belong shall be entirely responsible for the maintenance, care, treatment, and payment of the working pay of such prisoners of war.

Such prisoners of war shall have the right to remain in communication with the prisoners' representatives in the camps on which they depend.

Section IV
Financial Resources of Prisoners of War

Article 58. Upon the outbreak of hostilities, and pending an arrangement on this matter with the Protecting Power, the Detaining Power may determine the maximum amount of money in cash or in any similar form, that prisoners may have in their possession. Any amount in excess, which was properly in their possession and which has been taken or withheld from them, shall be placed to their account, together with any monies deposited by them, and shall not be converted into any other currency without their consent.

If prisoners of war are permitted to purchase services or commodities outside the camp against payment in cash, such payments shall be made by the prisoner himself or the camp administration who will charge them to the accounts of the prisoners concerned. The Detaining Power will establish the necessary rules in this respect.

Article 59. Cash which was taken from prisoners of war, in accordance with Article 18, at the time of their capture, and which is in the currency of the Detaining Power, shall be placed to their separate accounts, in accordance with the provisions of Article 64 of the present Section.

The amounts, in the currency of the Detaining Power, due to the conversion of sums in other currencies that are taken from the prisoners of war at the same time, shall also be credited to their separate accounts.

Article 60. The Detaining Power shall grant all prisoners of war a monthly advance of pay, the amount of which shall be fixed by conversion, into the currency of the said Power, of the following amounts:

Category I: Prisoner ranking below sergeants: eight Swiss francs.

Category II: Sergeants and other non-commissioned officers, or prisoners of equivalent rank: twelve Swiss francs.

Category III: Warrant officers and commissioned officers below the rank of major or prisoners of equivalent rank: fifty Swiss francs.

Category IV: Majors, lieutenant-colonels, colonels or prisoners of equivalent rank: sixty Swiss francs.

Category V: General officers or prisoners of war of equivalent rank: seventy-five Swiss francs.

However, the Parties to the conflict concerned may by special agreement modify the amount of advances of pay due to prisoners of the preceding categories.

Furthermore, if the amounts indicated in the first paragraph above would be unduly high compared with the pay of the Detaining Power's armed forces or would, for any reason, seriously embarrass the Detaining Power, then, pending the conclusion of a special agreement with the Power on which the prisoners depend to vary the amounts indicated above, the Detaining Power:

(a) shall continue to credit the accounts of the prisoners with the amounts indicated in the first paragraph above;

(b) may temporarily limit the amount made available from these advances of pay to prisoners of war for their own use, to sums which are reasonable, but which, for Category I, shall never be inferior to the amount that the Detaining Power gives to the members of its own armed forces.

The reasons for any limitations will be given without delay to the Protecting Power.

Article 61. The Detaining Power shall accept for distribution as supplementary pay to prisoners of war sums which the Power on which the prisoners depend may forward to them, on condition that the sums to be paid shall be the same for each prisoner of the same category, shall be payable to all prisoners of that category depending on that Power, and shall be placed in their separate accounts, at the earliest opportunity, in accordance with the provisions of Article 64. Such supplementary pay shall not relieve the Detaining Power of any obligation under this Convention.

Article 62. Prisoners of war shall be paid a fair working rate of pay by the detaining authorities direct. The rate shall be fixed by the said authorities, but shall at no time be less than one-fourth of one Swiss franc for a full working day. The Detaining Power shall inform prisoners of war, as well as the Power on which they depend, through the intermediary of the Protecting Power, of the rate of daily working pay that it has fixed.

Working pay shall likewise be paid by the detaining authorities to prisoners of war permanently detailed to duties or to a skilled or semi-skilled occupation in connection with the administration, installation or maintenance of camps, and to the prisoners who are required to carry out spiritual or medical duties on behalf of their comrades.

The working pay of the prisoners' representative, of his advisers, if any, and of his assistants, shall be paid out of the fund maintained by canteen profits. The scale of this working pay shall be fixed by the prisoners' representative and approved by the camp commander. If there is no such fund, the detaining authorities shall pay these prisoners a fair working rate of pay.

Article 63. Prisoners of war shall be permitted to receive remittances of money addressed to them individually or collectively.

Every prisoner of war shall have at his disposal the credit balance of his account as provided for in the following Article, within the limits fixed by the Detaining Power, which shall make such payments as are requested. Subject to financial or monetary restrictions which the Detaining Power regards as essential, prisoners of war may also have payments made abroad. In this case payments addressed by prisoners of war to dependents shall be given priority.

In any event, and subject to the consent of the Power on which they depend, prisoners may have payments made in their own country, as follows: the Detaining Power shall send to the aforesaid Power through the Protecting Power, a notification giving all the necessary particulars concerning the prisoners of war, the beneficiaries of the payments, and the amount of the sums to be paid, expressed in the Detaining Power's currency. The said notification shall be signed by the prisoners and countersigned by the camp commander. The Detaining Power shall debit the prisoners' account by a corresponding amount; the sums thus debited shall be placed by it to the credit of the Power on which the prisoners depend.

To apply the foregoing provisions, the Detaining Power may usefully consult the Model Regulations in Annex V of the present Convention.

Article 64. The Detaining Power shall hold an account for each prisoner of war, showing at least the following:

(1) The amounts due to the prisoner or received by him as advances of pay, as working pay or derived from any other source; the sums in the currency of the Detaining Power which were taken from him; the sums taken from him and converted at his request into the currency of the said Power.

(2) The payments made to the prisoner in cash, or in any other similar form; the payments made on his behalf and at his request; the sums transferred under Article 63, third paragraph.

Article 65. Every item entered in the account of a prisoner of war shall be countersigned or initialled by him, or by the prisoners' representative acting on his behalf.

Prisoners of war shall at all times be afforded reasonable facilities for consulting and obtaining copies of their accounts, which may likewise be inspected by the representatives of the Protecting Powers at the time of visits to the camp.

When prisoners of war are transferred from one camp to another, their personal accounts will follow them. In case of transfer from one Detaining Power to another, the monies which are their property and are not in the currency of the Detaining Power will follow them. They shall be given certificates for any other monies standing to the credit of their accounts.

The Parties to the conflict concerned may agree to notify to each other at specific intervals through the Protecting Power, the amount of the accounts of the prisoners of war.

Article 66. On the termination of captivity, through the release of a prisoner of war or his repatriation, the Detaining Power shall give him a statement, signed by an authorized officer of that Power, showing the credit balance then due to him. The Detaining Power shall also send through the Protecting Power to the government upon which the prisoner of war depends, lists giving all appropriate particulars of all prisoners of war whose captivity has been terminated by repatriation, release, escape, death or any other means, and showing the amount of their credit balances. Such lists shall be certified on each sheet by an authorized representative of the Detaining Power.

Any of the above provisions of this Article may be varied by mutual agreement between any two Parties to the conflict.

The Power on which the prisoner of war depends shall be responsible for settling with him any credit balance due to him from the Detaining Power on the termination of his captivity.

Article 67. Advances of pay, issued to prisoners of war in conformity with Article 60, shall be considered as made on behalf of the Power on which they depend. Such advances of pay, as well as all payments made by the said Power under Article 63, third paragraph, and Article 68, shall form the subject of arrangements between the Powers concerned, at the close of hostilities.

Article 68. Any claim by a prisoner of war for compensation in respect of any injury or other disability arising out of work shall be referred to the Power on which he depends, through the Protecting Power. In accordance with Article 54, the Detaining Power will, in all cases, provide the prisoner of war concerned with a statement showing the nature of the injury or disability, the circumstances in which it arose and particulars of medical or hospital treatment given for it. This statement will be signed by a responsible officer of the Detaining Power and the medical particulars certified by a medical officer.

Any claim from a prisoner of war for compensation in respect of personal effects, monies or valuables impounded by the Detaining Power under Article 18 and not forthcoming on his repatriation, or in respect of loss alleged to be due to the fault of the Detaining Power or any of its servants, shall likewise be referred to the Power on which he depends. Nevertheless, any such personal effects required for use by the prisoners of war whilst in captivity shall be replaced at the expense of the Detaining Power. The Detaining Power will, in all cases, provide the prisoner of war with a statement, signed by a responsible officer, showing all available information regarding the reasons why such effects, monies or valuable have not been restored to him. A copy of this statement will be forwarded to the Power on which he depends through the Central Agency for Prisoners of War provided for in Article 123.

Section V—Relations of Prisoners of War With the Exterior

Article 69. Immediately upon prisoners of war falling into its power, the Detaining Power shall inform them and the Powers on which they depend, through the Protecting Power, of the measures taken to carry out the provisions of the present Section. They shall likewise inform the parties concerned of any subsequent modifications of such measures.

Article 70. Immediately upon capture, or not more than one week after arrival at a camp, even if it is a transit camp, likewise in case of sickness or transfer to hospital or another camp, every prisoner of war shall be enabled to write direct to his family, on the one hand, and to the Central Prisoners of War Agency provided for in Article 123, on the other hand, a card similar, if possible, to the model annexed to the present Convention, informing his relatives of his capture, address and state of health. The said cards shall be forwarded as rapidly as possible and may not be delayed in any manner.

Article 71. Prisoners of war shall be allowed to send and receive letters and cards. If the Detaining Power deems it necessary to limit the number of letters and cards sent by each prisoner of war, the said number shall not be less than two letters and four cards monthly, exclusive of the capture cards provided for in Article 70, and conforming as closely as possible to the models annexed to the present Convention. Further limitations may be imposed only if the Protecting Power is satisfied that it would be in the interests of the prisoners of war concerned to do so owing to difficulties of translation caused by the Detaining Power's inability to find sufficient qualified linguists to carry out the necessary censorship. If limitations must be placed on the correspondence addressed to prisoners of war, they may be ordered only by the Power on which the prisoners depend, possibly at the request of the Detaining Power. Such letters and cards must be conveyed by the most rapid method at the disposal of the Detaining Power; they may not be delayed or retained for disciplinary reasons.

Prisoners of war who have been without news for a long period, or who are unable to receive news from their next of kin or to give them news by the ordinary postal route, as well as those who are at a great distance from their homes, shall be permitted to send telegrams, the fees being charged against the prisoners of war's accounts with the Detaining Power or paid in the currency at their disposal. They shall likewise benefit by this measure in cases of urgency.

As a general rule, the correspondence of prisoners of war shall be written in their native language. The Parties to the conflict may allow correspondence in other languages.

Sacks containing prisoner-of-war mail must be securely sealed and labelled so as clearly to indicate their contents, and must be addressed to offices of destination.

Article 72. Prisoners of war shall be allowed to receive by post or by any other means individual parcels or collective shipments containing, in particular, foodstuffs, clothing, medical supplies and articles of a religious, educational or recreational character which may meet their needs, including books, devotional articles, scientific equipment, exami-

nation papers, musical instruments, sports outfits and materials allowing prisoners of war to pursue their studies or their cultural activities.

Such shipments shall in no way free the Detaining Power from the obligations imposed upon it by the virtue of the present Convention.

The only limits which may be placed on these shipments shall be those proposed by the Protecting Power in the interest of the prisoners themselves, or by the International Committee of the Red Cross or any other organization giving assistance to the prisoners, in respect of their own shipments only, on account of exceptional strain on transport or communications.

The conditions for the sending of individual parcels and collective relief shall, if necessary, be the subject of special agreements between the Powers concerned, which may in no case delay the receipt by the prisoners of relief supplies. Books may not be included in parcels of clothing and foodstuffs. Medical supplies shall, as a rule, be sent in collective parcels.

Article 73. In the absence of special agreements between the Powers concerned on the conditions for the receipt and distribution of collective relief shipments, the rules and regulations concerning collective shipments, which are annexed to the present Convention, shall be applied.

The special agreements referred to above shall in no case restrict the right of prisoners' representatives to take possession of collective relief shipments intended for prisoners of war, to proceed to their distribution or to dispose of them in the interest of the prisoners.

Nor shall such agreements restrict the right of representatives of the Protecting Power, the International Committee of the Red Cross or any other organization giving assistance to prisoners of war and responsible for the forwarding of collective shipments, to supervise their distribution to the recipients.

Article 74. All relief shipments for prisoners of war shall be exempt from import, customs and other dues.

Correspondence, relief shipments and authorized remittances of money addressed to prisoners of war or despatched by them through the post office, either direct or through the Information Bureaux provided for in Article 122 and the Central Prisoners of War Agency provided in Article 123, shall be exempt from any postal dues, both in the countries of origin and destination, and in intermediate countries.

If relief shipments intended for prisoners of war cannot be sent through the post office by reason of weight or for any other cause, the cost of transportation shall be borne by the Detaining Power in all the territories under its control. The other Powers party to the Convention shall bear the cost of transport in their respective territories.

In the absence of special agreements between the Parties concerned, the costs connected with transport of such shipments, other than costs covered by the above exemption, shall be charged to the senders.

The High Contracting Parties shall endeavour to reduce, so far as possible, the rates charged for telegrams sent by prisoners of war, or addressed to them.

Article 75. Should military operations prevent the Powers concerned from fulfilling their obligation to assure the transport of the shipments referred to in Articles 70, 71, 72 and 77, the Protecting Powers concerned, the International Committee of the Red Cross or any other organization duly approved by the Parties to the conflict may undertake to ensure the conveyance of such shipments by suitable means (railway wagons, motor vehicles, vessels or aircraft, etc.). For this purpose, the High Contracting Parties shall endeavour to supply them with such transport and to allow its circulation, especially by granting the necessary safe-conducts.

Such transport may also be used to convey:

(*a*) correspondence, lists and reports exchanged between the Central Information Agency referred to in Article 123 and the National Bureaux referred to in Article 122;

(*b*) correspondence and reports relating to prisoners of war which the Protecting Powers, the International Committee of the Red Cross or any other body assisting the prisoners, exchange either with their own delegates or with the Parties to the conflict.

These provisions in no way detract from the right of any Party to the conflict to arrange other means of transport, if it should so prefer, nor preclude the granting of safe-conducts, under mutually agreed conditions, to such means of transport.

In the absence of special agreements, the costs occasioned by the use of such means of transport shall be borne proportionally by the Parties to the conflict whose nationals are benefited thereby.

Article 76. The censoring of correspondence addressed to prisoners of war or despatched by them shall be done as quickly as possible. Mail shall be censored only by the despatching State and the receiving State, and once only by each.

The examination of consignments intended for prisoners of war shall not be carried out under conditions that will expose the goods contained in them to deterioration; except in the case of written or printed matter, it shall be done in the presence of the addressee, or of a fellow-prisoner duly delegated by him. The delivery to prisoners of individual or collective consignments shall not be delayed under the pretext of difficulties of censorship.

Any prohibition of correspondence ordered by Parties to the conflict, either for military or political reasons, shall be only temporary and its duration shall be as short as possible.

Article 77. The Detaining Powers shall provide all facilities for the transmission, through the Protecting Power or the Central Prisoners of War Agency provided for in Article 123, of instruments, papers or documents intended for prisoners of war or despatched by them, especially powers of attorney and wills.

In all cases they shall facilitate the preparation and execution of such documents on behalf of prisoners of war; in particular, they shall allow them to consult a lawyer and shall take what measures are necessary for the authentication of their signatures.

Section VI—Relations Between Prisoners of War and the Authorities
Chapter I—Complaints of Prisoners of War Respecting the Conditions of Captivity

Article 78. Prisoners of war shall have the right to make known to the military authorities in whose power they are, their requests regarding the conditions of captivity to which they are subjected.

They shall also have the unrestricted right to apply to the representatives of the Protecting Powers either through their prisoners' representative or, if they consider it necessary, direct, in order to draw their attention to any points on which they may have complaints to make regarding their conditions of captivity.

These requests and complaints shall not be limited nor considered to be a part of the correspondence quota referred to in Article 71. They must be transmitted immediately. Even if they are recognized to be unfounded, they may not give rise to any punishment.

Prisoners' representatives may send periodic reports on the situation in the camps and the needs of the prisoners of war to the representatives of the Protecting Powers.

Chapter II—Prisoners of War Representatives

Article 79. In all places where there are prisoners of war, except in those where there are officers, the prisoners shall freely elect by secret ballot, every six months, and also in case of vacancies, prisoners' representatives entrusted with representing them before the military authorities, the Protecting Powers, the International Committee of the Red Cross and any other organization which may assist them. These prisoners' representatives shall be eligible for re-election.

In camps for officers and persons of equivalent status or in mixed camps, the senior officer among the prisoners of war shall be recognised as the camp prisoners' representative. In camps for officers, he shall be assisted by one or more advisers chosen by the officers; in mixed camps, his assistant shall be chosen from among the prisoners of war who are not officers and shall be elected by them.

Officer prisoners of war of the same nationality shall be stationed in labour camps for prisoners of war, for the purpose of carrying out the camp administration duties for which the prisoners of war are responsible. These officers may be elected as prisoners' representatives under the first paragraph of this Article. In such a case the assistants to the prisoners' representatives shall be chosen from among those prisoners of war who are not officers.

Every representative elected must be approved by the Detaining Power before he has the right to commence his duties. Where the Detaining Power refuses to approve a prisoner of war elected by his fellow prisoners of war, it must inform the Protecting Power of the reason for such refusal.

In all cases the prisoners' representative must have the same nationality, language and customs as the prisoners of war whom he represents. Thus, prisoners of war distributed in different sections of a camp, according to their nationality, language or customs, shall have for each section their own prisoners' representative, in accordance with the foregoing paragraphs.

Article 80. Prisoners' representatives shall further the physical, spiritual and intellectual well-being of prisoners of war.

In particular, where the prisoners decide to organize amongst themselves a system of mutual assistance, this organization will be within the province of the prisoners' representative, in addition to the special duties entrusted to him by other provisions of the present Convention.

Prisoners' representatives shall not be held responsible, simply by reason of their duties, for any offences committed by prisoners of war.

Article 81. Prisoners' representatives shall not be required to perform any other work, if the accomplishment of their duties is thereby made more difficult.

Prisoners' representatives may appoint from amongst the prisoners such assistants as they may require. All material facilities shall be granted them, particularly a certain freedom of movement necessary for the accomplishment of their duties (inspections of labour detachments, receipt of supplies, etc.).

Prisoners' representatives shall be permitted to visit premises where prisoners of war are detained, and every prisoner of war shall have the right to consult freely his prisoners' representative.

All facilities shall likewise be accorded to the prisoners' representatives for communication by post and telegraph with the detaining authorities, the Protecting Powers, the International Committee of the Red Cross and their delegates, the Mixed Medical Commission and with the bodies which give assistance to prisoners of war. Prisoners' representatives of labour detachments shall enjoy the same facilities for communication with the prisoners' representatives of the principal camp. Such communications shall not be restricted, nor considered as forming a part of the quota mentioned in Article 71.

Prisoners' representatives who are transferred shall be allowed a reasonable time to acquaint their successors with current affairs.

In case of dismissal, the reasons therefor shall be communicated to the Protecting Power.

Chapter III—Penal and Disciplinary Sanctions
(I) General Provisions

Article 82. A prisoner of war shall be subject to the laws, regulations and orders in force in the armed forces of the Detaining Power; the Detaining Power shall be justified in taking judicial or disciplinary measures in respect of any offence committed by a prisoner of war against such laws, regulations or orders. However, no proceedings or punishments contrary to the provisions of this Chapter shall be allowed.

If any law, regulation or order of the Detaining Power shall declare acts committed by a prisoner of war to be punishable, whereas the same acts would not be punishable if committed by a member of the forces of the Detaining Power, such acts shall entail disciplinary punishments only.

Article 83. In deciding whether proceedings in respect of an offence alleged to have been committed by a prisoner of war shall be judicial or disciplinary, the Detaining Power shall ensure that the competent authorities exercise the greatest leniency and adopt, wherever possible, disciplinary rather than judicial measures.

Article 84. A prisoner of war shall be tried only by a military court, unless the existing laws of the Detaining Power expressly permit the civil courts to try a member of the armed forces of the Detaining Power in respect of the particular offence alleged to have been committed by the prisoner of war.

In no circumstances whatever shall a prisoner of war be tried by a court of any kind which does not offer the essential guarantees of independence and impartiality as generally recognized, and, in particular, the procedure of which does not afford the accused the rights and means of defence provided for in Article 105.

Article 85. Prisoners of war prosecuted under the laws of the Detaining Power for acts committed prior to capture shall retain, even if convicted, the benefits of the present Convention.

Article 86. No prisoner of war may be punished more than once for the same act or on the same charge.

Article 87. Prisoners of war may not be sentenced by the military authorities and courts of the Detaining Power to any penalties except those provided for in respect of members of the armed forces of the said Power who have committed the same acts.

When fixing the penalty, the courts or authorities of the Detaining Power shall take into consideration, to the widest extent possible, the fact that the accused, not being a national of the Detaining Power, is not bound to it by any duty of allegiance, and that he is in its power as the result of circumstances independent of his own will. The said courts or authorities shall be at liberty to reduce the penalty provided for the violation of which the prisoner of war is accused, and shall therefore not be bound to apply the minimum penalty prescribed.

Collective punishment for individual acts, corporal punishments, imprisonment in premises without daylight and, in general, any form of torture or cruelty, are forbidden.

No prisoner of war may be deprived of his rank by the Detaining Power, or prevented from wearing his badges.

Article 88. Officers, non-commissioned officers and men who are prisoners of war undergoing a disciplinary or judicial punishment, shall not be subjected to more severe treatment than that applied in respect of the same punishment to members of the armed forces of the Detaining Power of equivalent rank.

A woman prisoner of war shall not be awarded or sentenced to a punishment more severe, or treated whilst undergoing punishment more severely, than a woman member of the armed forces of the Detaining Power dealt with for a similar offence.

In no case may a woman prisoner of war be awarded or sentenced to a punishment more severe, or treated whilst undergoing punishment more severely, than a male member of the armed forces of the Detaining Power dealt with for a similar offence.

Prisoners of war who have served disciplinary or judicial sentences may not be treated differently from other prisoners of war.

(II) Disciplinary Sanctions

Article 89. The disciplinary punishments applicable to prisoners of war are the following:

(1) a fine which shall not exceed 50 per cent of the advances of pay and working pay which the prisoner of war would otherwise receive under the provisions of Articles 60 and 62 during a period of not more than thirty days.

(2) Discontinuance of privileges granted over and above the treatment provided for by the present Convention.

(3) Fatigue duties not exceeding two hours daily.

(4) Confinement.

The punishment referred to under (3) shall not be applied to officers.

In no case shall disciplinary punishments be inhuman, brutal or dangerous to the health of prisoners of war.

Article 90. The duration of any single punishment shall in no case exceed thirty days. Any period of confinement awaiting the hearing of a disciplinary offence or the award of disciplinary punishment shall be deducted from an award pronounced against a prisoner of war.

The maximum of thirty days provided above may not be exceeded, even if the prisoner of war is answerable for several acts at the same time when he is awarded punishment, whether such acts are related or not.

The period between the pronouncing of an award of disciplinary punishment and its execution shall not exceed one month.

When a prisoner of war is awarded a further disciplinary punishment, a period of at least three days shall elapse between the execution of any two of the punishments, if the duration of one of these is ten days or more.

Article 91. The escape of a prisoner of war shall be deemed to have succeeded when:

(1) he has joined the armed forces of the Power on which he depends, or those of an allied Power;

(2) he has left the territory under the control of the Detaining Power, or of an ally of the said Power;

(3) he has joined a ship flying the flag of the Power on which he depends, or of an allied Power, in the territorial waters of the Detaining Power, the said ship not being under the control of the last named Power.

Prisoners of war who have made good their escape in the sense of this Article and who are recaptured, shall not be liable to any punishment in respect of their previous escape.

Article 92. A prisoner of war who attempts to escape and is recaptured before having made good his escape in the sense of Article 91 shall be liable only to a disciplinary punishment in respect of this act, even if it is a repeated offence.

A prisoner of war who is recaptured shall be handed over without delay to the competent military authority.

Article 88, fourth paragraph, notwithstanding, prisoners of war punished as a result of an unsuccessful escape may be subjected to special surveillance. Such surveillance must not affect the state of their health, must be undergone in a prisoner of war camp, and must not entail the suppression of any of the safeguards granted them by the present Convention.

Article 93. Escape or attempt to escape, even if it is a repeated offence, shall not be deemed an aggravating circumstance if the prisoner of war is subjected to trial by judicial proceedings in respect of an offence committed during his escape or attempt to escape.

In conformity with the principle stated in Article 83, offences committed by prisoners of war with the sole intention of facilitating their escape and which do not entail any violence against life or limb, such as offences against public property, theft without intention of self-enrichment, the drawing up or use of false papers, the wearing of civilian clothing, shall occasion disciplinary punishment only.

Prisoners of war who aid or abet an escape or an attempt to escape shall be liable on this count to disciplinary punishment only.

Article 94. If an escaped prisoner of war is recaptured, the Power on which he depends shall be notified thereof in the manner defined in Article 122, provided notification of his escape has been made.

Article 95. A prisoner of war accused of an offence against discipline shall not be kept in confinement pending the hearing unless a member of the armed forces of the Detaining Power would be so kept if he were accused of a similar offence, or if it is essential in the interests of camp order and discipline.

Any period spent by a prisoner of war in confinement awaiting the disposal of an offence against discipline shall be reduced to an absolute minimum and shall not exceed fourteen days.

The provisions of Articles 97 and 98 of this Chapter shall apply to prisoners of war who are in confinement awaiting the disposal of offences against discipline.

Article 96. Acts which constitute offences against discipline shall be investigated immediately.

Without prejudice to the competence of courts and superior military authorities, disciplinary punishment may be ordered only by an officer having disciplinary powers in his capacity as camp commander, or by a responsible officer who replaces him or to whom he has delegated his disciplinary powers.

In no case may such powers be delegated to a prisoner of war or be exercised by a prisoner of war.

Before any disciplinary award is pronounced, the accused shall be given precise information regarding the offences of which he is accused, and given an opportunity of explaining his conduct and of defending himself. He shall be permitted, in particular, to call witnesses and to have recourse, if necessary, to the services of a qualified interpreter. The decision shall be announced to the accused prisoner of war and to the prisoners' representative.

A record of disciplinary punishments shall be maintained by the camp commander and shall be open to inspection by representatives of the Protecting Power.

Article 97. Prisoners of war shall not in any case be transferred to penitentiary establishments (prisons, penitentiaries, convict prisons, etc.) to undergo disciplinary punishment therein.

All premises in which disciplinary punishments are undergone shall conform to the sanitary requirements set forth in Article 25. A prisoner of war undergoing punishment shall be enabled to keep himself in a state of cleanliness, in conformity with Article 29.

Officers and persons of equivalent status shall not be lodged in the same quarters as non-commissioned officers or men.

Women prisoners of war undergoing disciplinary punishment shall be confined in separate quarters from male prisoners of war and shall be under the immediate supervision of women.

Article 98. A prisoner of war undergoing confinement as a disciplinary punishment, shall continue to enjoy the benefits of the provisions of this Convention except in so far as these are necessarily rendered inapplicable by the mere fact that he is confined. In no case may he be deprived of the benefits of the provisions of Articles 78 and 126.

A prisoner of war awarded disciplinary punishment may not be deprived of the prerogatives attached to his rank.

Prisoners of war awarded disciplinary punishment shall be allowed to exercise and to stay in the open air at least two hours daily.

They shall be allowed, on their request, to be present at the daily medical inspections. They shall receive the attention which their state of health requires and, if necessary, shall be removed to the camp infirmary or to a hospital.

They shall have permission to read and write, likewise to send and receive letters. Parcels and remittances of money, however, may be withheld from them until the completion of the punishment; they shall meanwhile be entrusted to the prisoners' representative, who will hand over to the infirmary the perishable goods contained in such parcels.

(III) Judicial Proceedings

Article 99. No prisoner of war may be tried or sentenced for an act which is not forbidden by the law of the Detaining Power or by International Law, in force at the time the said act was committed.

No moral or physical coercion may be exerted on a prisoner of war in order to induce him to admit himself guilty of the act of which he is accused.

No prisoner of war may be convicted without having had an opportunity to present his defence and the assistance of a qualified advocate or counsel.

Article 100. Prisoners of war and the Protecting Powers shall be informed, as soon as possible, of the offences which are punishable by the death sentence under the laws of the Detaining Power.

Other offences shall not thereafter be made punishable by the death penalty without the concurrence of the Power upon which the prisoners of war depend.

The death sentence cannot be pronounced on a prisoner of war unless the attention of the court has, in accordance with Article 87, second paragraph, been particularly called to the fact that since the accused is not a national of the Detaining Power, he is not bound to it by any duty of allegiance, and that he is in its power as the result of circumstances independent of his own will.

Article 101. If the death penalty is pronounced on a prisoner of war, the sentence shall not be executed before the expiration of a period of at least six months from the date when the Protecting Power receives, at an indicated address, the detailed communication provided for in Article 107.

Article 102. A prisoner of war can be validly sentenced only if the sentence has been pronounced by the same courts according to the same procedure as in the case of members of the armed forces of the Detaining Power, and if, furthermore, the provisions of the present Chapter have been observed.

Article 103. Judicial investigations relating to a prisoner of war shall be conducted as rapidly as circumstances permit and so that his trial shall take place as soon as possible. A prisoner of war shall not be confined while awaiting trial unless a member of the armed forces of the Detaining Power would be so confined if he were accused of a similar offence, or if it is essential to do so in the interests of national security. In no circumstances shall this confinement exceed three months.

Any period spent by a prisoner of war in confinement awaiting trial shall be deducted from any sentence of imprisonment passed upon him and taken into account in fixing any penalty.

The provisions of Articles 97 and 98 of this Chapter shall apply to a prisoner of war whilst in confinement awaiting trial.

Article 104. In any case in which the Detaining Power has decided to institute judicial proceedings against a prisoner of war, it shall notify the Protecting Power as soon as possible and at least three weeks before the opening of the trial. This period of three weeks shall run as from the day on which such notification reaches the Protecting Power at the address previously indicated by the latter to the Detaining Power.

The said notification shall contain the following information:

(1) Surname and first names of the prisoner of war, his rank, his army, regimental, personal or serial number, his date of birth, and his profession or trade, if any.

(2) Place of internment or confinement.

(3) Specification of the charge or charges on which the prisoner of war is to be arraigned, giving the legal provisions applicable.

(4) Designation of the court which will try the case, likewise the date and place fixed for the opening of the trial.

The same communication shall be made by the Detaining Power to the prisoners' representative.

If no evidence is submitted, at the opening of a trial, that the notification referred to above was received by the Protecting Power, by the prisoner of war and by the prisoners' representative concerned, at least three weeks before the opening of the trial, then the latter cannot take place and must be adjourned.

Article 105. The prisoner of war shall be entitled to assistance by one of his prisoner comrades, to defence by a qualified advocate or counsel of his own choice, to the calling of witnesses and, if he deems necessary, to the services of a competent interpreter. He shall be advised of these rights by the Detaining Power in due time before the trial.

Failing a choice by the prisoner of war, the Protecting Power shall find him an advocate or counsel, and shall have at least one week at its disposal for the purpose. The Detaining Power shall deliver to the said Power, on request, a list of persons qualified to present the defence. Failing a choice of an advocate or counsel by the prisoner of war or the Protecting Power, the Detaining Power shall appoint a competent advocate or counsel to conduct the defence.

The advocate or counsel conducting the defence on behalf of the prisoner of war shall have at his disposal a period of two weeks at least before the opening of the trial, as well as the necessary facilities to prepare the defence of the accused. He may, in particular, freely visit the accused and interview him in private. He may also confer with any witnesses for the defence, including prisoners of war. He shall have the benefit of these facilities until the term of appeal or petition has expired.

Particulars of the charge or charges on which the prisoner of war is to be arraigned, as well as the documents which are generally communicated to the accused by virtue of the laws in force in the armed forces of the Detaining Power, shall be communicated to the accused prisoner of war in a language which he understands, and in good time before the opening of the trial. The same communication in the same circumstances shall be made to the advocate or counsel conducting the defence on behalf of the prisoner of war.

The representatives of the Protecting Power shall be entitled to attend the trial of the case, unless, exceptionally, this is held *in camera* in the interest of State security. In such a case the Detaining Power shall advise the Protecting Power accordingly.

Article 106. Every prisoner of war shall have, in the same manner as the members of the armed forces of the Detaining Power, the right of appeal or petition from any sentence pronounced upon him, with a view to the quashing or revising of the sentence or the reopening of the trial. He shall be fully informed of his right to appeal or petition and of the time limit within which he may do so.

Article 107. Any judgment and sentence pronounced upon a prisoner of war shall be immediately reported to the Protecting Power in the form of a summary communication, which shall also indicate whether he has the right of appeal with a view to the quashing of the sentence or the reopening of the trial. This communication shall likewise be sent to the prisoners' representative concerned. It shall also be sent to the accused prisoner of war in a language he understands, if the sentence was not pronounced in his presence. The Detaining Power shall also immediately communicate to the Protecting Power the decision of the prisoner of war to use or to waive his right of appeal.

Furthermore, if a prisoner of war is finally convicted or if a sentence pronounced against a prisoner of war in the first instance is a death sentence, the Detaining Power shall as soon as possible address to the Protecting Power a detailed communication containing:

(1) the precise wording of the finding and sentence;

(2) a summarized report of any preliminary investigation and of the trial, emphasizing in particular the elements of the prosecution and the defence;

(3) notification, where applicable, of the establishment where the sentence will be served.

The communications provided for in the forgoing subparagraphs shall be sent to the Protecting Power at the address previously made known to the Detaining Power.

Article 108. Sentences pronounced on prisoners of war after a conviction has become duly enforceable shall be served in the same establishments and under the same conditions as in the case of members of the armed forces of the Detaining Power. These conditions shall in all cases conform to the requirements of health and humanity.

A woman prisoner of war on whom such a sentence has been pronounced shall be confined in separate quarters and shall be under the supervision of women.

In any case, prisoners of war sentenced to a penalty depriving them of their liberty shall retain the benefit of the provisions of Articles 78 and 126 of the present Convention. Furthermore, they shall be entitled to receive and despatch correspondence, to receive at least one relief parcel monthly, to take regular exercise in the open air, to have the medical care required by their state of health, and the spiritual assistance they may desire. Penalties to which they may be subjected shall be in accordance with the provisions of Article 87, third paragraph.

Part IV
Termination of Captivity
Section I—Direct Repatriation and Accommodation in Neutral Countries

Article 109. Subject to the provisions of the third paragraph of this Article, Parties to the conflict are bound to send back to their own country, regardless of number or rank, seriously wounded and seriously sick prisoners of war, after having cared for them until they are fit to travel, in accordance with the first paragraph of the following Article.

Throughout the duration of hostilities, Parties to the conflict shall endeavour, with the co-operation of the neutral Powers concerned, to make arrangements for the accommodation in neutral countries of the sick and wounded prisoners of war referred to in the second paragraph of the following Article. They may, in addition, conclude agreements with a view to the direct repatriation or internment in a neutral country of able-bodied prisoners of war who have undergone a long period of captivity.

No sick or injured prisoner of war who is eligible for repatriation under the first paragraph of this Article, may be repatriated against his will during hostilities.

Article 110. The following shall be repatriated direct:

(1) Incurably wounded and sick whose mental or physical fitness seems to have been gravely diminished.

(2) Wounded and sick who, according to medical opinion, are not likely to recover within one year, whose condition requires treatment and whose mental or physical fitness seems to have been gravely diminished.

(3) Wounded and sick who have recovered, but whose mental or physical fitness seems to have gravely and permanently diminished.

The following may be accommodated in a neutral country:

(1) Wounded and sick whose recovery may be expected within one year of the date of the wound or the beginning of the illness, if treatment in a neutral country might increase the prospects of a more certain and speedy recovery.

(2) Prisoners of war whose mental or physical health, according to medical opinion, is seriously threatened by continued captivity, but whose accommodation in a neutral country might remove such a threat.

The conditions which prisoners of war accommodated in a neutral country must fulfil in order to permit their repatriation shall be fixed, as shall likewise their status, by agreement between the Powers concerned. In general, prisoners of war who have been accommodated in a neutral country, and who belong to the following categories, should be repatriated:

(1) Those whose state of health has deteriorated so as to fulfil the conditions laid down for direct repatriation;

(2) Those whose mental or physical powers remain, even after treatment, considerably impaired.

If no special agreements are concluded between the Parties to the conflict concerned, to determine the cases of disablement or sickness entailing direct repatriation or accommodation in a neutral country, such cases shall be settled in accordance with the principles laid down in the Model Agreement concerning direct repatriation and accommodation in neutral countries of wounded and sick prisoners of war and in the Regulations concerning Mixed Medical Commissions annexed to the present Convention.

Article 111. The Detaining Power, the Power on which the prisoners of war depend, and a neutral Power agreed upon by these two Powers, shall endeavour to conclude agreements which will enable prisoners of war to be interned in the territory of the said neutral Power until the close of hostilities.

Article 112. Upon the outbreak of hostilities, Mixed Medical Commissions shall be appointed to examine sick and wounded prisoners of war, and to make all appropriate decisions regarding them. The appointment, duties and functioning of these Commissions shall be in conformity with the provisions of the Regulations annexed to the present Convention.

However, prisoners of war who, in the opinion of the medical authorities of the Detaining Power, are manifestly seriously injured or seriously sick, may be repatriated without having to be examined by a Mixed Medical Commission.

Article 113. Besides those who are designated by the medical authorities of the Detaining Power, wounded or sick prisoners of war belonging to the categories listed below shall be entitled to present themselves for examination by the Mixed Medical Commissions provided for in the forgoing Article:

(1) Wounded and sick proposed by a physician or surgeon who is of the same nationality, or a national of a Party to the conflict allied with the Power on which the said prisoners depend, and who exercises his functions in the camp.

(2) Wounded and sick proposed by their prisoners' representative.

(3) Wounded and sick proposed by the Power on which they depend, or by an organization duly recognized by the said Power and giving assistance to the prisoners.

Prisoners of war who do not belong to one of the three foregoing categories may nevertheless present themselves for examination by Mixed Medical Commissions, but shall be examined only after those belonging to the said categories.

The physician or surgeon of the same nationality as the prisoners who present themselves for examination by the Mixed Medical Commission, likewise the prisoners' representative of the said prisoners, shall have permission to be present at the examination.

Article 114. Prisoners of war who meet with accidents shall, unless the injury is self-inflicted, have the benefit of the provisions of this Convention as regards repatriation or accommodation in a neutral country.

Article 115. No prisoner of war on whom a disciplinary punishment has been imposed and who is eligible for repatriation or for accommodation in a neutral country, may be kept back on the plea that he has not undergone his punishment.

Prisoners of war detained in connection with a judicial prosecution or conviction and who are designated for repatriation or accommodation in a neutral country, may benefit by such measures before the end of the proceedings or the completion of the punishment, if the Detaining Power consents.

Parties to the conflict shall communicate to each other the names of those who will be detained until the end of the proceedings or the completion of the punishment.

Article 116. The costs of repatriating prisoners of war or of transporting them to a neutral country shall be borne, from the frontiers of the Detaining Power, by the Power on which the said prisoners depend.

Article 117. No repatriated person may be employed on active military service.

Section II—Release and Repatriation of Prisoners of War at the Close of Hostilities

Article 118. Prisoners of war shall be released and repatriated without delay after the cessation of active hostilities.

In the absence of stipulations to the above effect in any agreement concluded between the Parties to the conflict with a view to the cessation of hostilities, or failing any such agreement, each of the Detaining Powers shall itself establish and execute without delay a plan of repatriation in conformity with the principle laid down in the foregoing paragraph.

In either case, the measures adopted shall be brought to the knowledge of the prisoners of war.

The costs of repatriation of prisoners of war shall in all cases be equitably apportioned between the Detaining Power and the Power on which the prisoners depend. This apportionment shall be carried out on the following basis:

(a) If the two Powers are contiguous, the Power on which the prisoners of war depend shall bear the costs of repatriation from the frontiers of the Detaining Power.

(b) If the two Powers are not contiguous, the Detaining Power shall bear the costs of transport of prisoners of war over its own territory as far as its frontier or its port of embarkation nearest to the territory of the Power on which the prisoners of war depend. The Parties concerned shall agree between themselves as to the equitable apportionment of the remaining costs of the repatriation. The conclusion of this agreement shall in no circumstances justify any delay in the repatriation of the prisoners of war.

Article 119. Repatriation shall be effected in conditions similar to those laid down in Articles 46 to 48 inclusive of the present Convention for the transfer of prisoners of war, having regard to the provisions of Article 118 and to those of the following paragraphs.

On repatriation, any articles of value impounded from prisoners of war under Article 18, and any foreign currency which has not been converted into the currency of the Detaining Power, shall be restored to them. Articles of value and foreign currency which, for any reason whatever, are not restored to prisoners of war on repatriation, shall be despatched to the Information Bureau set up under Article 122.

Prisoners of war shall be allowed to take with them their personal effects, and any correspondence and parcels which have arrived for them. The weight of such baggage may be limited, if the conditions of repatriation so require, to what each prisoner can reasonably carry. Each prisoner shall in all cases be authorized to carry at least twenty-five kilograms.

The other personal effects of the repatriated prisoner shall be left in the charge of the Detaining Power which shall have them forwarded to him as soon as it has concluded an agreement to this effect, regulating the conditions of transport and the payment of the costs involved, with the Power on which the prisoner depends.

Prisoners of war against whom criminal proceedings for an indictable offence are pending may be detained until the end of such proceedings, and, if necessary, until the completion of the punishment. The same shall apply to prisoners of war already convicted for an indictable offence.

Parties to the conflict shall communicate to each other the names of any prisoners of war who are detained until the end of proceedings or until punishment has been completed.

By agreement between the Parties to the conflict, commissions shall be established for the purpose of searching for dispersed prisoners of war and of assuring their repatriation with the least possible delay.

Section III—Death of Prisoners of War

Article 120. Wills of prisoners of war shall be drawn up so as to satisfy the conditions of validity required by the legislation of their country of origin, which will take steps to inform the Detaining Power of its requirements in this respect. At the request of the prisoner of war and, in all cases, after death, the will shall be transmitted without delay to the Protecting Power; a certified copy shall be sent to the Central Agency.

Death certificates, in the form annexed to the present Convention, or lists certified by a responsible officer, of all persons who die as prisoners of war shall be forwarded as rapidly as possible to the Prisoner of War Information Bureau established in accordance with Article 122. The death certificates or certified lists shall show particulars of identity as set out in the third paragraph of Article 17, and also the date and place of death, the cause of death, the date and place of burial and all particulars necessary to identify the graves.

The burial or cremation of a prisoner of war shall be preceded by a medical examination of the body with a view to confirming death and enabling a report to be made and, where necessary, establishing identity.

The detaining authorities shall ensure that prisoners of war who have died in captivity are honourably buried, if possible according to the rites of the religion to which they belonged, and that their graves are respected, suitably maintained and marked so as to be found at any time. Wherever possible, deceased prisoners of war who depended on the same Power shall be interred in the same place.

Deceased prisoners of war shall be buried in individual graves unless unavoidable circumstances require the use of collective graves. Bodies may be cremated only for imperative reasons of hygiene, on account of the religion of the deceased or in accordance with his express wish to this effect. In case of cremation, the fact shall be stated and the reasons given in the death certificate of the deceased.

In order that graves may always be found, all particulars of burials and graves shall be recorded with a Graves Registration Service established by the Detaining Power. Lists of graves and particulars of the prisoners of war interred in cemeteries and elsewhere shall be transmitted to the Power on which such prisoners of war depended. Responsibility for the care of these graves and for records of any subsequent moves of the bodies shall rest on the Power controlling the territory, if a party to the present Convention. These provisions shall also apply to the ashes which shall be kept by the Graves Registration Service until proper disposal thereof in accordance with the wishes of the home country.

Article 121. Every death or serious injury of a prisoner of war caused or suspected to have been caused by a sentry, another prisoner of war, or any other person, as well as any death the cause of which is unknown, shall be immediately followed by an official enquiry by the Detaining Power.

A communication on this subject shall be sent immediately to the Protecting Power. Statements shall be taken from witnesses, especially from those who are prisoners of war, and a report including such statements shall be forwarded to the Protecting Power.

If the enquiry indicates the guilt of one or more persons, the Detaining Power shall take all measures for the prosecution of the person or persons responsible.

Part V
Information Bureaux and Relief Societies
for Prisoners of War

Article 122. Upon the outbreak of a conflict and in all cases of occupation, each of the Parties to the conflict shall institute an official Information Bureau for prisoners of war who are in its power. Neutral or non-belligerent Powers who may have received within their territory persons belonging to one of the categories referred to in Article 4, shall take the same action with respect to such persons. The Power concerned shall ensure that the Prisoners of War Information Bureau is provided with the necessary accommodation, equipment and staff to ensure its efficient working. It shall be at liberty to employ prisoners of war in such a Bureau under the conditions laid down in the Section of the present Convention dealing with work by prisoners of war.

Within the shortest possible period, each of the Parties to the conflict shall give its Bureau the information referred to in the fourth, fifth and sixth paragraphs of this Article regarding any enemy person belonging to one of the categories referred to in Article 4, who has fallen into its power. Neutral or non-belligerent Powers shall take the same action with regard to persons belonging to such categories whom they have received within their territory.

The Bureau shall immediately forward such information by the most rapid means to the Powers concerned through the intermediary of the Protecting Powers and likewise of the Central Agency provided for in Article 123.

This information shall make it possible quickly to advise the next of kin concerned. Subject to the provisions of Article 17, the information shall include, in so far as available to the Information Bureau, in respect of each prisoner of war, his surname, first names, rank, army, regimental, personal or serial number, place and full date of birth, indication of the Power on which he depends, first name of the father and maiden name of the mother, name and address of the person to be informed and the address to which correspondence for the prisoner may be sent.

The Information Bureau shall receive from the various departments concerned information regarding transfers, releases, repatriations, escapes, admissions to hospital, and deaths, and shall transmit such information in the manner described in the third paragraph above.

Likewise, information regarding the state of health of prisoners of war who are seriously ill or seriously wounded shall be supplied regularly, every week if possible.

The Information Bureau shall also be responsible for replying to all enquiries sent to it concerning prisoners of war, including those who have died in captivity; it will make any enquiries necessary to obtain the information which is asked for if this is not in its possession.

All written communications made by the Bureau shall be authenticated by a signature or a seal.

The Information Bureau shall furthermore be charged with collecting all personal valuables, including sums in currencies other than that of the Detaining Power and documents of importance to the next of kin, left by prisoners of war who have been repatriated or released, or who have escaped or died, and shall forward the said valuables to the Powers concerned. Such articles shall be sent by the Bureau in sealed packets which shall be accompanied by statements giving clear and full particulars of the identity of the person to whom the articles belonged, and by a complete list of the contents of the parcel. Other personal effects of such prisoners of war shall be transmitted under arrangements agreed upon between the Parties to the conflict concerned.

Article 123. A Central Prisoners of War Information Agency shall be created in a neutral country. The International Committee of the Red Cross shall, if it deems necessary, propose to the Powers concerned the organization of such an Agency.

The function of the Agency shall be to collect all the information it may obtain through official or private channels respecting prisoners of war, and to transmit it as rapidly as possible to the country of origin of the prisoners of war or to the Power on which they depend. It shall receive from the Parties to the conflict all facilities for effecting such transmissions.

The High Contracting Parties, and in particular those whose nationals benefit by the services of the Central Agency, are requested to give the said Agency the financial aid it may require.

The foregoing provisions shall in no way be interpreted as restricting the humanitarian activities of the International Committee of the Red Cross, or of the relief Societies provided for in Article 125.

Article 124. The national Information Bureaux and the Central Information Agency shall enjoy free postage for mail, likewise all the exemptions provided for in Article 74, and further, so far as possible, exemption from telegraphic charges or, at least, greatly reduced rates.

Article 125. Subject to the measures which the Detaining Powers may consider essential to ensure their security or to meet any other reasonable need, the representatives of religious organizations, relief societies, or any other organization assisting prisoners of war, shall receive from the said Powers, for themselves and their duly accredited agents, all necessary facilities for visiting the prisoners, distributing relief supplies and material, from any source, intended for religious, educational or recreative purposes, and for assisting them in organizing their leisure time within the camps. Such societies or organizations may be constituted in the territory of the Detaining Power or in any other country, or they may have an international character.

The Detaining Power may limit the number of societies and organizations whose delegates are allowed to carry out their activities in its territory and under its supervision, on condition, however, that such limitation shall not hinder the effective operation of adequate relief to all prisoners of war.

The special position of the International Committee of the Red Cross in this field shall be recognized and respected at all times.

As soon as relief supplies or material intended for the above-mentioned purposes are handed over to prisoners of war, or very shortly afterwards, receipts for each consignment, signed by the prisoners' representative, shall be forwarded to the relief society or organization making the shipment. At the same time, receipts for these consignments shall be supplied by the administrative authorities responsible for guarding the prisoners.

Part VI
Execution of the Convention
Section I—General Provisions

Article 126. Representatives or delegates of the Protecting Powers shall have permission to go to all places where prisoners of war may be, particularly to places of internment, imprisonment and labour, and shall have access to all premises occupied by prisoners of war; they shall also be allowed to go to the places of departure, passage and arrival of prisoners who are being transferred. They shall be able to interview the prisoners, and in particular the prisoners' representatives, without witnesses, either personally or through an interpreter.

Representatives and delegates of the Protecting Powers shall have full liberty to select the places they wish to visit. The duration and frequency of these visits shall not be restricted. Visits may not be prohibited except for reasons of imperative military necessity, and then only as an exceptional and temporary measure.

The Detaining Power and the Power on which the said prisoners of war depend may agree, if necessary, that compatriots of these prisoners of war be permitted to participate in the visits.

The delegates of the International Committee of the Red Cross shall enjoy the same prerogatives. The appointment of such delegates shall be submitted to the approval of the Power detaining the prisoners of war to be visited.

Article 127. The High Contracting Parties undertake, in time of peace as in time of war, to disseminate the text of the present Convention as widely as possible in their respective countries, and, in particular, to include the study thereof in their programmes of military and, if possible, civil instruction, so that the principles thereof may become known to all their armed forces and to the entire population.

Any military or other authorities, who in time of war assume responsibilities in respect of prisoners of war, must possess the text of the Convention and be specially instructed as to its provisions.

Article 128. The High Contracting Parties shall communicate to one another through the Swiss Federal Council and, during hostilities, through the Protecting Powers, the official translations of the present Convention, as well as the laws and regulations which they may adopt to ensure the application thereof.

Article 129. The High Contracting Parties undertake to enact any legislation necessary to provide effective penal sanctions for persons committing, or ordering to be committed, any of the grave breaches of the present Convention defined in the following Article.

Each High Contracting Party shall be under the obligation to search for persons alleged to have committed, or to have ordered to be committed, such grave breaches, and shall bring such persons, regardless of their nationality, before its own courts. It may also, if it prefers, and in accordance with the provisions of its own legislation, hand such persons over for trial to another High Contracting Party concerned, provided such High Contracting Party has made out a *prima facie* case.

Each High Contracting Party shall take measures necessary for the suppression of all acts contrary to the provisions of the present Convention other than the grave breaches defined in the following Article.

In all circumstances, the accused persons shall benefit by safeguards of proper trial and defence, which shall not be less favourable than those provided by Article 105 and those following of the present Convention.

Article 130. Grave breaches to which the preceding Article relates shall be those involving any of the following acts, if committed against persons or property protected by the Convention: wilful killing, torture or inhuman treatment, including biological experiments, wilfully causing great suffering or serious injury to body or health, compelling a prisoner of war to serve in the forces of the hostile Power, or wilfully depriving a prisoner of war of the rights of fair and regular trial prescribed in this Convention.

Article 131. No High Contracting Party shall be allowed to absolve itself or any other High Contracting Party of any liability incurred by itself or by another High Contracting Party in respect of breaches referred to in the preceding Article.

Article 132. At the request of a Party to the conflict, an enquiry shall be instituted, in a manner to be decided between the interested Parties, concerning any alleged violation of the Convention.

If agreement has not been reached concerning the procedure for the enquiry, the Parties should agree on the choice of an umpire who will decide upon the procedure to be followed.

Once the violation has been established, the Parties to the conflict shall put an end to it and shall repress it with the least possible delay.

Section II—Final Provisions

Article 133. The present Convention is established in English and in French. Both texts are equally authentic.

The Swiss Federal Council shall arrange for official translations of the Convention to be made in the Russian and Spanish languages.

Article 134. The present Convention replaces the Convention of July 27, 1929, in relations between the High Contracting Parties.

Article 135. In the relations between the Powers which are bound by the Hague Convention respecting the Laws and Customs of War on Land, whether that of July 29, 1899, or that of October 18, 1907, and which are parties to the present Convention, this last Convention shall be complementary to Chapter II of the Regulations annexed to the above-mentioned Conventions of The Hague.

Article 136. The present Convention, which bears the date of this day, is open to signature until February 12, 1950, in the name of the Powers represented at the Conference which opened at Geneva on April 21, 1949; furthermore, by Powers not represented at that Conference, but which are parties to the Convention of July 27, 1929.

Article 137. The present Convention shall be ratified as soon as possible and the ratifications shall be deposited at Berne.

A record shall be drawn up of the deposit of each instrument of ratification and certified copies of this record shall be transmitted by the Swiss Federal Council to all the Powers in whose name the Convention has been signed, or whose accession has been notified.

Article 138. The present Convention shall come into force six months after not less than two instruments of ratification have been deposited.

Thereafter, it shall come into force for each High Contracting Party six months after the deposit of the instrument of ratification.

Article 139. From the date of its coming into force, it shall be open to any Power in whose name the present Convention has not been signed, to accede to this Convention.

Article 140. Accessions shall be notified in writing to the Swiss Federal Council, and shall take effect six months after the date on which they are received.

The Swiss Federal Council shall communicate the accessions to all the Powers in whose name the Convention has been signed or whose accession has been notified.

Article 141. The situations provided for in Articles 2 and 3 shall give immediate effect to ratifications deposited and accessions notified by the Parties to the conflict before or after the beginning of hostilities or occupation. The Swiss Federal Council shall communicate by the quickest method any ratifications or accessions received from Parties to the conflict.

Article 142. Each of the High Contracting Parties shall be at liberty to denounce the present Convention.

The denunciation shall be notified in writing to the Swiss Federal Council which shall transmit it to the Governments of all the High Contracting Parties.

The denunciation shall take effect one year after the notification thereof has been made to the Swiss Federal Council. However, a denunciation of which notification has been made at a time when the denouncing Power is involved in a conflict shall not take effect until peace has been concluded, and until after operations connected with release and repatriation of the persons protected by the present Convention have been terminated.

The denunciation shall have effect only in respect of the denouncing Power. It shall in no way impair the obligations which the Parties to the conflict shall remain bound to fulfil by virtue of the principles of the law of nations, as they result from the usages established among civilized peoples, from the laws of humanity and the dictates of the public conscience.

Article 143. The Swiss Federal Council shall register the present Convention with the Secretariat of the United Nations. The Swiss Federal Council shall also inform the Secretariat of the United Nations of all ratifications, accessions and denunciations received by it with respect to the present Convention.

SEE ALSO *Armed Conflicts; Basic Principles of the Legal Status of Combatants Struggling against Colonial and Alien Domination and Racist Regimes; Death Penalty in Armed Conflicts; International Convention against Recruitment, Use, Financing and Training of Mercenaries; Mercenarism.*

GENEVA CONVENTIONS: PROTOCOL I, ADDITIONAL TO THE GENEVA CONVENTIONS OF 12 AUGUST 1949, RELATING TO THE PROTECTION OF VICTIMS OF INTERNATIONAL ARMED CONFLICTS (1977).

The protocol revises and supplements the Geneva Conventions of 12 August 1949, broadening the scope of their protection of victims or armed conflicts in many respects. In particular, article 1 (4) of the protocol clarifies the definition of ARMED CONFLICTS which appears in article 2 common to each of the four Geneva Conventions so as to include "armed conflicts in which people are fighting against colonial domination and alien occupation and against racist regimes in the exercise of their right of self-determination as enshrined in the Charter of the United Nations and the Declaration on Principles of International Law concerning Friendly Relations and Co-operation among States in accordance with the Charter of the United Nations."

The protocol also authorizes the establishment (article 90) of an international fact-finding commission, consisting of 15 members of high moral standing elected by the high contracting parties, with competence to (1) inquire into any facts alleged to be a grave breach as defined in the conventions and in this protocol or other serious violation of the conventions or of the protocol; and (2) facilitate, through its good offices, the restoration of an attitude of respect for the conventions and the protocol.

The protocol was prepared by the Diplomatic Conference on the Reaffirmation and Development of International Humanitarian Law, convened in 1974, 1975, 1976, and 1977 by the Swiss Federal Council with the cooperation of the INTERNATIONAL COMMITTEE OF THE RED CROSS. It was adopted by the conference on 8 June 1977 and entered into force on 7 December 1978. The text (UN Doc. A/32/144, annex I) is as follows:

Preamble

The High Contracting Parties,

Proclaiming their earnest wish to see peace prevail among peoples,

Recalling that every State has the duty, in conformity with the Charter of the United Nations, to refrain in its international relations from the threat or use of force against the sovereignty, territorial integrity or political independence of any State, or in any other manner inconsistent with the purposes of the United Nations,

Believing it necessary nevertheless to reaffirm and develop the provisions protecting the victims of armed conflicts and to supplement measures intended to reinforce their application,

Expressing their conviction that nothing in this Protocol or in the Geneva Conventions of 12 August 1949 can be construed as legitimizing or authorizing any act of aggression or any other use of force inconsistent with the Charter of the United Nations,

Reaffirming further that the provisions of the Geneva Conventions of 12 August 1949 and of this Protocol must be fully applied in all circumstances to all persons who are protected by those instruments, without any adverse distinction based on the nature or origin of the armed conflict or on the causes espoused by or attributed to the Parties to the conflict,

Have agreed on the following:

Part I
General Provisions

Article 1. General Principles and Scope of Application. 1. The High Contracting Parties undertake to respect and to ensure respect for this Protocol in all circumstances.

2. In cases not covered by this Protocol or by other international agreements, civilians and combatants remain under the protection and authority of the principles of international law derived from established custom, from the principles of humanity and from dictates of public conscience.

3. This Protocol, which supplements the Geneva Conventions of 12 August 1949 for the protection of war victims, shall apply in the situations referred to in Article 2 common to those Conventions.

4. The situations referred to in the preceding paragraph include armed conflicts in which peoples are fighting against colonial domination and alien occupation and against racist régimes in the exercise of their right of self-determination, as enshrined in the Charter of the United Nations and the Declaration on Principles of International Law concerning Friendly Relations and Co-operation among States in accordance with the Charter of the United Nations.

Article 2. Definitions. For the purposes of this Protocol:

(a) "First Convention", "Second Convention", "Third Convention" and "Fourth Convention" mean, respectively, the Geneva Convention for the Amelioration of the Condition of the Wounded and Sick in Armed Forces in the Field of 12 August 1949; the Geneva Convention for the Amelioration of the Condition of Wounded, Sick and Shipwrecked Members of Armed Forces at Sea of 12 August 1949; the Geneva Convention relative to the Treatment of Prisoners of War of 12 August 1949; the Geneva Convention relative to the Protection of Civilian Persons in Time of War of 12 August 1949; "the Conventions" means the four Geneva Conventions of 12 August 1949 for the protection of war victims;

(b) "Rules of international law applicable in armed conflict" means the rules applicable in armed conflict set forth in international agreements to which the Parties to the conflict are Parties and the generally recognized principles and rules of international law which are applicable to armed conflict;

(c) "Protecting Power" means a neutral or other State not a Party to the conflict which has been designated by a Party to the conflict and accepted by the adverse Party and has agreed to carry out the functions assigned to a Protecting Power under the Conventions and this Protocol;

(d) "Substitute" means an organization acting in place of a Protecting Power in accordance with Article 5.

Article 3. Beginning and End of Application. Without prejudice to the provisions which are applicable at all times:

(a) the Conventions and this Protocol shall apply from the beginning of any situation referred to in Article 1 of this Protocol;

(b) the application of the Conventions and of this Protocol shall cease, in the territory of Parties to the conflict, on the general close of military operations and, in the case of occupied territories, on the termination of the occupation, except, in either circumstance, for those persons whose final release, repatriation or re-establishment takes place thereafter. These persons shall continue to benefit from the relevant provisions of the Conventions and of this Protocol until their final release repatriation or re-establishment.

Article 4. Legal Status of the Parties to the Conflict. The application of the Conventions and of this Protocol, as well as the conclusion of the agreements provided for therein, shall not affect the legal status of the Parties to the conflict. Neither the occupation of a territory nor the application of the Conventions and this Protocol shall affect the legal status of the territory in question.

Article 5. Appointment of Protecting Powers and of their Substitute. 1. It is the duty of the Parties to a conflict from the beginning of that conflict to secure the supervision and implementation of the Conventions and of this Protocol by the application of the system of Protecting Powers, including *inter alia* the designation and acceptance of those Powers, in accordance with the following paragraphs. Protecting Powers shall have the duty of safeguarding the interests of the Parties to the conflict.

2. From the beginning of a situation referred to in Article 1, each Party to the conflict shall without delay designate a Protecting Power for the purpose of applying the Conventions and this Protocol and shall, likewise without delay and for the same purpose, permit the activities of a Protecting Power which has been accepted by it as such after designation by the adverse Party.

3. If a Protecting Power has not been designated or accepted from the beginning of a situation referred to in Article 1, the International Committee of the Red Cross, without prejudice to the right of any other impartial humanitarian organization to do likewise, shall offer its good offices to the Parties to the conflict with a view to the designation without delay of a Protecting Power to which the Parties to the conflict consent. For that purpose it may *inter alia* ask each Party to provide it with a list of at least five States which that Party considers acceptable to act as Protecting Power on its behalf in relation to an adverse Party and ask each adverse Party to provide a list of at least five States which it would accept as the Protecting Power of the first

Party; these lists shall be communicated to the Committee within two weeks after the receipt of the request; it shall compare them and seek the agreement of any proposed State named on both lists.

4. If, despite the foregoing, there is no Protecting Power, the Parties to the conflict shall accept without delay an offer which may be made by the International Committee of the Red Cross or by any other organization which offers all guarantees of impartiality and efficacy, after due consultations with the said Parties and taking into account the result of these consultations, to act as a substitute. The functioning of such a substitute is subject to the consent of the Parties to the conflict; every effort shall be made by the Parties to the conflict to facilitate the operations of the substitute in the performance of its tasks under the Conventions and this Protocol.

5. In accordance with Article 4, the designation and acceptance of Protecting Powers for the purpose of applying the Conventions and this Protocol shall not affect the legal status of the Parties to the conflict or of any territory, including occupied territory.

6. The maintenance of diplomatic relations between Parties to the conflict or the entrusting of the protection of a Party's interests and those of its nationals to a third State in accordance with the rules of international law relating to diplomatic relations is no obstacle to the designation of Protecting Powers for the purpose of applying the Conventions and this Protocol.

7. Any subsequent mention in this Protocol of a Protecting Power includes also a substitute.

Article 6. Qualified Persons. 1. The High Contracting Parties shall, also in peacetime, endeavour, with the assistance of the national Red Cross (Red Crescent, Red Lion and Sun) Societies, to train qualified personnel to facilitate the application of the Conventions and of this Protocol, and in particular the activities of the Protecting Powers.

2. The recruitment and training of such personnel are within domestic jurisdiction.

3. The International Committee of the Red Cross shall hold at the disposal of the High Contracting Parties the lists of persons so trained which the High Contracting Parties may have established and may have transmitted to it for that purpose.

4. The conditions governing the employment of such personnel outside the national territory shall, in each case, be the subject of special agreements between the Parties concerned.

Article 7. Meetings. The depositary of this Protocol shall convene a meeting of the High Contracting Parties, at the request of one or more of the said Parties and upon the approval of the majority of the said Parties, to consider general problems concerning the application of the Conventions and of the Protocol.

Part II
Wounded, Sick and Shipwrecked

Section I
General Protection

Article 8. Terminology. For the purposes of this Protocol:

1. "Wounded" and "sick" mean persons, whether military or civilian, who, because of trauma, disease or other physical or mental disorder or disability, are in need of medical assistance or care and who refrain from any act of hostility. These terms also cover maternity cases, new-born babies and other persons who may be in need of immediate medical assistance or care, such as the infirm or expectant mothers, and who refrain from any act of hostility;

2. "Shipwrecked" means persons, whether military or civilian, who are in peril at sea or in other waters as a result of misfortune affecting them or the vessel or aircraft carrying them and who refrain from any act of hostility. These persons, provided that they continue to refrain from any act of hostility, shall continue to be considered shipwrecked during their rescue until they acquire another status under the Conventions or this Protocol;

3. "Medical personnel" means those persons assigned, by a Party to the conflict, exclusively to the medical purposes enumerated under (5) or to the administration of medical units or to the operation or administration of medical transports. Such assignments may be either permanent or temporary. The term includes:

(a) medical personnel of a Party to the conflict, whether military or civilian, including those described in the First and Second Conventions, and those assigned to civil defence organizations;

(b) medical personnel of national Red Cross (Red Crescent, Red Lion and Sun) Societies and other national voluntary aid societies duly recognized and authorized by a Party to the conflict;

(c) medical personnel of medical units or medical transports described in Article 9, paragraph 2.

4. "Religious personnel" means military or civilian persons, such as chaplains, who are exclusively engaged in the work of their ministry and attached:

(a) to the armed forces of a Party to the conflict;

(b) to medical units or medical transports of a Party to the conflict;

(c) to medical units or medical transports described in Article 9, paragraph 2; or

(d) to civil defence organizations of a Party to the conflict.

The attachment of religious personnel may be either permanent or temporary, and the relevant provisions mentioned under (11) apply to them;

5. "Medical units" means establishments and other units, whether military or civilian, organized for medical purposes, namely the search for, collection, transportation, diagnosis or treatment—including first-aid treatment—of the wounded, sick and shipwrecked, or for the prevention of disease. The term includes, for example, hospitals and other similar units, blood transfusion centres, preventive medicine centres and institutes, medical depots and the medical and pharmaceutical stores of such units. Medical units may be fixed or mobile, permanent or temporary;

6. "Medical transportation" means the conveyance by land, water or air of the wounded, sick, shipwrecked, medical personnel, religious personnel, medical equipment or medical supplies protected by the Conventions and by this Protocol;

7. "Medical transports" means any means of transportation, whether military or civilian, permanent or temporary, assigned exclusively to medical transportation and under the control of a competent authority of a Party to the conflict;

8. "Medical vehicles" means any medical transports by land;

9. "Medical ships and craft" means any medical transports by water;

10. "Medical aircraft" means any medical transports by air;

11. "Permanent medical personnel", "permanent medical units" and "permanent medical transports" mean those assigned exclusively to medical purposes for an indeterminate period. "Temporary medical personnel", "temporary medical units" and "temporary medical transports" mean those devoted exclusively to medical purposes for limited periods during the whole of such periods. Unless otherwise specified, the terms "medical personnel", "medical units" and "medical transports" cover both permanent and temporary categories;

12. "Distinctive emblem" means the distinctive emblem of the red cross, red crescent or red lion and sun on a white ground when used for the protection of medical units and transports, or medical and religious personnel, equipment or supplies;

13. "Distinctive signal" means any signal or message specified for the identification exclusively of medical units or transports in Chapter III of Annex I to this Protocol.

Article 9. Field of Application. 1. This Part, the provisions of which are intended to ameliorate the condition of the wounded, sick and shipwrecked, shall apply to all those affected by a situation referred to in Article 1, without any adverse distinction founded on race, colour, sex, language, religion or belief, political or other opinion, national or social origin, wealth, birth or other status, or on any other similar criteria.

2. The relevant provisions of Articles 27 and 32 of the First Convention shall apply to permanent medical units and transports (other than hospital ships, to which Article 25 of the Second Convention applies) and their personnel made available to a Party to the conflict for humanitarian purposes:

(a) by a neutral or other State which is not a Party to that conflict;

(b) by a recognized and authorized aid society of such a State;

(c) by an impartial international humanitarian organization.

Article 10. Protection and Care. 1. All the wounded, sick and shipwrecked, to whichever Party they belong, shall be respected and protected.

2. In all circumstances they shall be treated humanely and shall receive, to the fullest extent practicable and with the least possible delay, the medical care and attention required by their condition. There shall be no distinction among them founded on any grounds other than medical ones.

Article 11. Protection of Persons. 1. The physical or mental health and integrity of persons who are in the power of the adverse Party or who are interned, detained or otherwise deprived of liberty as a result of a situation referred to in Article 1 shall not be endangered by any unjustified act or omission. Accordingly, it is prohibited to subject the persons described in this Article to any medical procedure which is not indicated by the state of health of the person concerned and which is not consistent with generally medical standards which would be applied under similar medical circumstances to persons who are nationals of the Party conducting the procedure and who are in no way deprived of liberty.

2. It is, in particular, prohibited to carry out on such persons, even with their consent:

(a) physical mutilations;

(b) medical or scientific experiments;

(c) removal of tissue or organs for transplantation, ex-

cept where these acts are justified in conformity with the conditions provided for in paragraph 1.

3. Exceptions to the prohibition in paragraph 2 (c) may be made only in the case of donations of blood for transfusion or of skin for grafting, provided that they are given voluntarily and without any coercion or inducement, and then only for therapeutic purposes, under conditions consistent with generally accepted medical standards and controls designed for the benefit of both the donor and the recipient.

4. Any wilful act or omission which seriously endangers the physical or mental health or integrity of any person who is in the power of a Party other than the one on which he depends and which either violates any of the prohibitions in paragraphs 1 and 2 or fails to comply with the requirements of paragraph 3 shall be a grave breach of this Protocol.

5. The persons described in paragraph 1 have the right to refuse any surgical operation. In case of refusal, medical personnel shall endeavour to obtain a written statement to that effect, signed or acknowledged by the patient.

6. Each Party to the conflict shall keep a medical record for every donation of blood for transfusion or skin for grafting by persons referred to in paragraph 1, if that donation is made under the responsibility of that Party. In addition, each Party to the conflict shall endeavour to keep a record of all medical procedures undertaken with respect to any person who is interned, detained or otherwise deprived of liberty as a result of a situation referred to in Article 1. These records shall be available at all times for inspection by the Protecting Power.

Article 12. Protection of Medical Units. 1. Medical units shall be respected and protected at all times and shall not be the object of attack.

2. Paragraph 1 shall apply to civilian medical units, provided that they:

(a) belong to one of the Parties to the conflict;

(b) are recognized and authorized by the competent authority of one of the Parties to the conflict; or

(c) are authorized in conformity with Article 9, paragraph 2, of this Protocol or Article 27 of the First Convention.

3. The Parties to the conflict are invited to notify each other of the location of their fixed medical units. The absence of such notification shall not exempt any of the Parties from the obligation to comply with the provisions of paragraph 1.

4. Under no circumstances shall medical units be used in an attempt to shield military objectives from attack. Whenever possible, the Parties to the conflict shall ensure that medical units are so sited that attacks against military objectives do not imperil their safety.

Article 13. Discontinuance of Protection of Civilian Medical Units. 1. The protection to which civilian medical units are entitled shall not cease unless they are used to commit, outside their humanitarian function, acts harmful to the enemy. Protection may, however, cease only after a warning has been given setting, whenever appropriate, a reasonable time-limit, and after such warning has remained unheeded.

2. The following shall not be considered as acts harmful to the enemy:

(a) that the personnel of the unit are equipped with light individual weapons for their own defence or for that of the wounded and sick in their charge;

(b) that the unit is guarded by a picket or by sentries or by an escort;

(c) that small arms and ammunition taken from the

wounded and sick, and not yet handed to the proper service, are found in the units;

(d) that members of the armed forces or other combatants are in the unit for medical reasons.

Article 14. Limitations on Requisition of Civilian Medical Units. 1. The Occupying Power has the duty to ensure that the medical needs of the civilian population in occupied territory continue to be satisfied.

2. The Occupying Power shall not, therefore, requisition civilian medical units, their equipment, their *matériel* or the services of their personnel, so long as these resources are necessary for the provision of adequate medical services for the civilian population and for the continuing medical care of any wounded and sick already under treatment.

3. Provided that the general rule in paragraph 2 continues to be observed, the Occupying Power may requisition the said resources, subject to the following particular conditions:

(a) that the resources are necessary for the adequate and immediate medical treatment of the wounded and sick members of the armed forces of the Occupying Power or of prisoners of war;

(b) that the requisition continues only while such necessity exists; and

(c) that immediate arrangements are made to ensure that the medical needs of the civilian population, as well as those of any wounded and sick under treatment who are affected by the requisition, continue to be satisfied.

Article 15. Protection of Civilian Medical and Religious Personnel. 1. Civilian medical personnel shall be respected and protected.

2. If needed, all available help shall be afforded to civilian medical personnel in an area where civilian medical services are disrupted by reason of combat activity.

3. The Occupying Power shall afford civilian medical personnel in occupied territories every assistance to enable them to perform, to the best of their ability, their humanitarian functions. The Occupying Power may not require that, in the performance of those functions, such personnel shall give priority to the treatment of any person except on medical grounds. They shall not be compelled to carry out tasks which are not compatible with their humanitarian mission.

4. Civilian medical personnel shall have access to any place where their services are essential, subject to such supervisory and safety measures as the relevant Party to the conflict may deem necessary.

5. Civilian religious personnel shall be respected and protected. The provisions of the Conventions and of this Protocol concerning the protection and identification of medical personnel shall apply equally to such persons.

Article 16. General Protection of Medical Duties. 1. Under no circumstances shall any person be punished for carrying out medical activities compatible with medical ethics, regardless of the person benefiting therefrom.

2. Persons engaged in medical activities shall not be compelled to perform acts or to carry out work contrary to the rules of medical ethics or to other medical rules designed for the benefit of the wounded and sick or to the provisions of the Conventions or of this Protocol, or to refrain from performing acts or from carrying out work required by those rules and provisions.

3. No person engaged in medical activities shall be compelled to give to anyone belonging either to an adverse Party, or to his own Party except as required by the law of the latter Party, any information concerning the wounded and sick who are, or who have been, under his care, if such information would, in his opinion, prove harmful to the patients concerned or to their families. Regulations for the compulsory notification of communicable diseases shall, however, be respected.

Article 17. Role of the Civilian Population and of Aid Societies. 1. The civilian population shall respect the wounded, sick and shipwrecked, even if they belong to the adverse Party, and shall commit no act of violence against them. The civilian population and aid societies, such as national Red Cross (Red Crescent, Red Lion and Sun) Societies, shall be permitted, even on their own initiative, to collect and care for the wounded, sick and shipwrecked, even in invaded or occupied areas. No one shall be harmed, prosecuted, convicted or punished for such humanitarian acts.

2. The Parties to the conflict may appeal to the civilian population and the aid societies referred to in paragraph 1 to collect and care for the wounded, sick and shipwrecked, and to search for the dead and report their location; they shall grant both protection and the necessary facilities to those who respond to this appeal. If the adverse Party gains or regains control of the area, that Party also shall afford the same protection and facilities for so long as they are needed.

Article 18. Identification. 1. Each Party to the conflict shall endeavour to ensure that medical and religious personnel and medical units and transports are identifiable.

2. Each Party to the conflict shall also endeavour to adopt and to implement methods and procedures which will make it possible to recognize medical units and transports which use the distinctive emblem and distinctive signals.

3. In occupied territory and in areas where fighting is taking place or is likely to take place, civilian medical personnel and civilian religious personnel should be recognizable by the distinctive emblem and an identity card certifying their status.

4. With the consent of the competent authority, medical units and transports shall be marked by the distinctive emblem. The ships and craft referred to in Article 22 of this Protocol shall be marked in accordance with the provisions of the Second Convention.

5. In addition to the distinctive emblem, a Party to the conflict may, as provided in Chapter III of Annex I to this Protocol, authorize the use of distinctive signals to identify medical units and transports. Exceptionally, in the special cases covered in that Chapter, medical transports may use distinctive signals without displaying the distinctive emblem.

6. The application of the provisions of paragraphs 1 to 5 of this article is governed by Chapters I to III of Annex I to this Protocol. Signals designated in Chapter III of the Annex for the exclusive use of medical units and transports shall not, except as provided therein, be used for any purpose other than to identify the medical units and transports specified in that Chapter.

7. This article does not authorize any wider use of the distinctive emblem in peacetime than is prescribed in Article 44 of the First Convention.

8. The provisions of the Conventions and of this Protocol relating to supervision of the use of the distinctive emblem and to the prevention and repression of any misuse thereof shall be applicable to distinctive signals.

Article 19. Neutral and Other States not Parties to the Conflict. Neutral and other States not Parties to the conflict shall apply the relevant provisions of this Protocol to persons protected by this Part who may be received or interned within their territory, and to any dead of the Parties to that conflict whom they may find.

Article 20. Prohibition of Reprisals. Reprisals against the persons and objects protected by this Part are prohibited.

Section II
Medical Transportation

Article 21. Medical Vehicles. Medical vehicles shall be respected and protected in the same way as mobile medical units under the Conventions and this Protocol.

Article 22. Hospital Ships and Coastal Rescue Craft. 1. The provisions of the Conventions relating to:

(a) vessels described in Articles 22, 24, 25 and 27 of the Second Convention.

(b) their lifeboats and small craft,

(c) their personnel and crews, and

(d) the wounded, sick and shipwrecked on board,

shall also apply where these vessels carry civilian wounded, sick and shipwrecked who do not belong to any of the categories mentioned in Article 13 of the Second Convention. Such civilians shall not, however, be subject to surrender to any Party which is not their own, or to capture at sea. If they find themselves in the power of a Party to the conflict other than their own they shall be covered by the Fourth Convention and by this Protocol.

2. The protection provided by the Conventions to vessels described in Article 25 of the Second Convention shall extend to hospital ships made available for humanitarian purposes to a Party to the conflict:

(a) by a neutral or other State which is not a Party to that conflict; or

(b) by an impartial international humanitarian organization,

provided that, in either case, the requirements set out in that Article are complied with.

3. Small craft described in Article 27 of the Second Convention shall be protected even if the notification envisaged by that Article has not been made. The Parties to the conflict are, nevertheless, invited to inform each other of any details of such craft which will facilitate their identification and recognition.

Article 23. Other Medical Ships and Craft. 1. Medical ships and craft other than those referred to in Article 22 of this Protocol and Article 38 of the Second Convention shall, whether at sea or in other waters, be respected and protected in the same way as mobile medical units under the Conventions and this Protocol. Since this protection can only be effective if they can be identified and recognized as medical ships or craft, such vessels should be marked with the distinctive emblem and as far as possible comply with the second paragraph of Article 43 of the Second Convention.

2. The ships and craft referred to in paragraph 1 shall remain subject to the laws of war. Any warship on the surface able immediately to enforce its command may order them to stop, order them off, or make them take a certain course, and they shall obey every such command. Such ships and craft may not in any other way be diverted from their medical mission so long as they are needed for the wounded, sick and shipwrecked on board.

3. The protection provided in paragraph 1 shall cease only under the conditions set out in Articles 34 and 35 of the Second Convention. A clear refusal to obey a command given in accordance with paragraph 2 shall be an act harm-

ful to the enemy under Article 34 of the Second Convention.

4. A Party to the conflict may notify any adverse Party as far in advance of sailing as possible of the name, description, expected time of sailing, course and estimated speed of the medical ship or craft, particularly in the case of ships of over 2,000 gross tons, and may provide any other information which would facilitate identification and recognition. The adverse Party shall acknowledge receipt of such information.

5. The provisions of Article 37 of the Second Convention shall apply to medical and religious personnel in such ships and craft.

6. The provisions of the Second Convention shall apply to the wounded, sick and shipwrecked belonging to the categories referred to in Article 13 of the Second Convention and in Article 44 of this Protocol who may be on board such medical ships and craft. Wounded, sick and shipwrecked civilians who do not belong to any of the categories mentioned in Article 13 of the Second Convention shall not be subject, at sea, either to surrender to any Party which is not their own, or to removal from such ships or craft; if they find themselves in the power of a Party to the conflict other than their own, they shall be covered by the Fourth Convention and by this Protocol.

Article 24. Protection of Medical Aircraft. Medical aircraft shall be respected and protected, subject to the provisions of this Part.

Article 25. Medical Aircraft in Areas not Controlled by an Adverse Party. In and over land areas physically controlled by friendly forces, or in and over sea areas not physically controlled by an adverse Party, the respect and protection of medical aircraft of a Party to the conflict is not dependent on any agreement with an adverse Party. For greater safety, however, a Party to the conflict operating its medical aircraft in these areas may notify the adverse Party, as provided in Article 29, in particular when such aircraft are making flights bringing them within range of surface-to-air weapons systems of the adverse Party.

Article 26. Medical Aircraft in Contact or Similar Zones. 1. In and over those parts of the contact zone which are physically controlled by friendly forces and in and over those areas the physical control of which is not clearly established, protection for medical aircraft can be fully effective only by prior agreement between the competent military authorities of the Parties to the conflict, as provided for in Article 29. Although, in the absence of such an agreement, medical aircraft operate at their own risk, they shall nevertheless be respected after they have been recognized as such.

2. "Contact zone" means any area on land where the forward elements of opposing forces are in contact with each other, especially where they are exposed to direct fire from the ground.

Article 27. Medical Aircraft in Areas Controlled by an Adverse Party. 1. The medical aircraft of a Party to the conflict shall continue to be protected while flying over land or sea areas physically controlled by an adverse Party, provided that prior agreement to such flights has been obtained from the competent authority of that adverse Party.

2. A medical aircraft which flies over an area physically controlled by an adverse Party without, or in deviation from, the terms of, an agreement provided for in paragraph 1, either through navigational error or because of an emergency affecting the safety of the flight, shall make every effort to identify itself and to inform the adverse Party of

the circumstances. As soon as such medical aircraft has been recognized by the adverse Party, that Party shall make all reasonable efforts to give the order to land or to alight on water, referred to in Article 30, paragraph 1, or to take other measures to safeguard its own interests, and, in either case, to allow the aircraft time for compliance, before resorting to an attack against the aircraft.

Article 28. Restrictions on Operations of Medical Aircraft.
1. The Parties to the conflict are prohibited from using their medical aircraft to attempt to acquire any military advantage over an adverse Party. The presence of medical aircraft shall not be used in an attempt to render military objectives immune from attack.

2. Medical aircraft shall not be used to collect or transmit intelligence data and shall not carry any equipment intended for such purposes. They are prohibited from carrying any persons or cargo not included within the definition in Article 8 (6). The carrying on board of the personal effects of the occupants or of equipment intended solely to facilitate navigation, communication or identification shall not be considered as prohibited.

3. Medical aircraft shall not carry any armament except small arms and ammunition taken from the wounded, sick and shipwrecked on board and not yet handed to the proper service, and such light individual weapons as may be necessary to enable the medical personnel on board to defend themselves and the wounded, sick and shipwrecked in their charge,

4. While carrying out the flights referred to in Article 26 and 27, medical aircraft shall not, except by prior agreement with the adverse Party, be used to search for the wounded, sick and shipwrecked.

Article 29. Notifications and Agreements concerning Medical Aircraft. 1. Notifications under Article 25, or requests for prior agreement under Articles 26, 27, 28, paragraph 4, or 31 shall state the proposed number of medical aircraft, their flight plans and means of identification, and shall be understood to mean that every flight will be carried out in compliance with Article 28.

2. A Party which receives a notification given under Article 25 shall at once acknowledge receipt of such notification.

3. A Party which receives a request for prior agreement under Articles 26, 27, 28, paragraph 4, or 31 shall, as rapidly as possible, notify the requesting Party:

(a) that the request is agreed to;

(b) that the request is denied; or

(c) of reasonable alternative proposals to the request. It may also propose a prohibition or restriction of other flights in the area during the time involved. If the Party which submitted the request accepts the alternative proposals, it shall notify the other Party of such acceptance.

4. The Parties shall take the necessary measures to ensure that notifications and agreements can be made rapidly.

5. The Parties shall also take the necessary measures to disseminate rapidly the substance of any such notifications and agreements to the military units concerned and shall instruct those units regarding the means of identification that will be used by the medical aircraft in question.

Article 30. Landing and Inspection of Medical Aircraft.
1. Medical aircraft flying over areas which are physically controlled by an adverse Party, or over areas the physical control of which is not clearly established, may be ordered to land or to alight on water, as appropriate, to permit inspection in accordance with the following paragraphs. Medical aircraft shall obey any such order.

2. If such an aircraft lands or alights on water, whether ordered to do so or for other reasons, it may be subjected to inspection solely to determine the matters referred to in paragraphs 3 and 4. Any such inspection shall be commenced without delay and shall be conducted expeditiously. The inspecting Party shall not require the wounded and sick to be removed from the aircraft unless their removal is essential for the inspection. That Party shall in any event ensure that the condition of the wounded and sick is not adversely affected by the inspection or by the removal.

3. If the inspection discloses that the aircraft:

(a) is a medical aircraft within the meaning of Article 8 (10),

(b) is not in violation of the conditions prescribed in Article 28, and

(c) has not flown without or in breach of a prior agreement where such agreement is required,
the aircraft and those of its occupants who belong to the adverse Party or to a neutral or other State not a Party to the conflict shall be authorized to continue the flight without delay.

4. If the inspection discloses that the aircraft:

(a) is not a medical aircraft within the meaning of Article 8 (10),

(b) is in violation of the conditions prescribed in Article 28, or

(c) has flown without or in breach of a prior agreement where such agreement is required,
the aircraft may be seized. Its occupants shall be treated in conformity with the relevant provisions of the Conventions and of this Protocol. Any aircraft seized which had been assigned as a permanent medical aircraft may be used thereafter only as a medical aircraft.

Article 31. Neutral or Other States not Parties to the Conflict.
1. Except by prior agreement, medical aircraft shall not fly over or land in the territory of a neutral or other State not a Party to the conflict. However, with such an agreement, they shall be respected throughout their flight and also for the duration of any calls in the territory. Nevertheless they shall obey any summons to land or to alight on water, as appropriate.

2. Should a medical aircraft, in the absence of an agreement or in deviation from the terms of an agreement, fly over the territory of a neutral or other State not a Party to the conflict, either through navigational error or because of an emergency affecting the safety of the flight, it shall make every effort to give notice of the flight and to identify itself. As soon as such medical aircraft is recognized, that State shall make all reasonable efforts to give the order to land or to alight on water referred to in Article 30, paragraph 1, or to take other measures to safeguard its own interests, and, in either case, to allow the aircraft time for compliance, before resorting to an attack against the aircraft.

3. If a medical aircraft, either by agreement or in the circumstances mentioned in paragraph 2, lands or alights on water in the territory of a neutral or other State not Party to the conflict, whether ordered to do so or for other reasons, the aircraft shall be subject to inspection for the purposes of determining whether it is in fact a medical aircraft. The inspection shall be commenced without delay and shall be conducted expeditiously. The inspecting Party shall not require the wounded and sick of the Party operating the aircraft to be removed from it unless their removal is essential

for the inspection. The inspecting Party shall in any event ensure that the condition of the wounded and sick is not adversely affected by the inspection or the removal. If the inspection discloses that the aircraft is in fact a medical aircraft, the aircraft with its occupants, other than those who must be detained in accordance with the rules of international law applicable in armed conflict, shall be allowed to resume its flight, and reasonable facilities shall be given for the continuation of the flight. If the inspection discloses that the aircraft is not a medical aircraft, it shall be seized and the occupants treated in accordance with paragraph 4.

4. The wounded, sick and shipwrecked disembarked, otherwise than temporarily, from a medical aircraft with the consent of the local authorities in the territory of a neutral or other State not a Party to the conflict shall, unless agreed otherwise between that State and the Parties to the conflict, be detained by that State where so required by the rules of international law applicable in armed conflict, in such a manner that they cannot again take part in the hostilities. The cost of hospital treatment and internment shall be borne by the State to which those persons belong.

5. Neutral or other States not Parties to the conflict shall apply any conditions and restrictions on the passage of medical aircraft over, or on the landing of medical aircraft in, their territory equally to all Parties to the conflict.

Section III
Missing and Dead Persons

Article 32. General Principle. In the implementation of this Section, the activities of the High Contracting Parties, of the Parties to the conflict and of the international humanitarian organizations mentioned in the Conventions and in this Protocol shall be prompted mainly by the right of families to know the fate of their relatives.

Article 33. Missing Persons. 1. As soon as circumstances permit, and at the latest from the end of active hostilities, each Party to the conflict shall search for the persons who have been reported missing by an adverse Party. Such adverse Party shall transmit all relevant information concerning such persons in order to facilitate such searches.

2. In order to facilitate the gathering of information pursuant to the preceding paragraph, each Party to the conflict shall, with respect to persons who would not receive more favourable consideration under the Conventions and this Protocol:

(a) record the information specified in Article 138 of the Fourth Convention in respect of such persons who have been detained, imprisoned or otherwise held in captivity for more than two weeks as a result of hostilities or occupation, or who have died during any period of detention;

(b) to the fullest extent possible, facilitate and, if need be, carry out the search for and the recording of information concerning such persons if they have died in other circumstances as a result of hostilities or occupation.

3. Information concerning persons reported missing pursuant to paragraph 1 and requests for such information shall be transmitted either directly or through the Protecting Power or the Central Tracing Agency of the International Committee of the Red Cross or national Red Cross (Red Crescent, Red Lion and Sun) Societies. Where the information is not transmitted through the International Committee of the Red Cross and its Central Tracing Agency, each Party to the conflict shall ensure that such information is also supplied to the Central Tracing Agency.

4. The Parties to the conflict shall endeavour to agree on arrangements for teams to search for, identify and recover the dead from battlefield areas, including arrangements, if appropriate, for such teams to be accompanied by personnel of the adverse Party while carrying out these missions in areas controlled by the adverse Party. Personnel of such teams shall be respected and protected while exclusively carrying out these duties.

Article 34. Remains of Deceased. 1. The remains of persons who have died for reasons related to occupation or in detention resulting from occupation or hostilities and those of persons not nationals of the country in which they have died as a result of hostilities shall be respected, and the gravesites of all such persons shall be respected, maintained and marked as provided for in Article 130 of the Fourth Convention, where their remains or gravesites would not receive more favourable consideration under the Conventions and this Protocol.

2. As soon as circumstances and the relations between the adverse Parties permit, the High Contracting Parties in whose territories graves and, as the case may be, other locations of the remains of persons who have died as a result of hostilities or during occupation or in detention are situated, shall conclude agreements in order:

(a) to facilitate access to the gravesites by relatives of the deceased and by representatives of official graves registration services and to regulate the practical arrangements for such access;

(b) to protect and maintain such gravesites permanently;

(c) to facilitate the return of the remains of the deceased and of personal effects to the home country upon its request or, unless that country objects, upon the request of the next of kin.

3. In the absence of the agreements provided for in paragraph 2 (b) or (c) and if the home country of such deceased is not willing to arrange at its expense for the maintenance of such gravesites, the High Contracting Party in whose territory the gravesites are situated may offer to facilitate the return of the remains of the deceased to the home country. Where such an offer has not been accepted the High Contracting Party may, after the expiry of five years from the date of the offer and upon due notice to the home country, adopt the arrangements laid down in its own laws relating to cemeteries and graves.

4. A High Contracting Party in whose territory the gravesites referred to in this Article are situated shall be permitted to exhume the remains only:

(a) in accordance with paragraphs 2 (c) and 3, or

(b) where exhumation is a matter of overriding public necessity, including cases of medical and investigative necessity, in which case the High Contracting Party shall at all times respect the remains, and shall give notice to the home country of its intention to exhume the remains together with details of the intended place of reinterment.

Part III
Methods and Means of Warfare
Combatant and Prisoner-of-War Status

Section I
Methods and Means of Warfare

Article 35. Basic rules. 1. In any armed conflict, the right of the Parties to the conflict to choose methods or means of warfare is not unlimited.

2. It is prohibited to employ weapons, projectiles and

material and methods of warfare of a nature to cause superfluous injury or unnecessary suffering.

3. It is prohibited to employ methods or means of warfare which are intended, or may be expected, to cause widespread, long-term and severe damage to the natural environment.

Article 36. New Weapons. In the study, development, acquisition or adoption of a new weapon, means or method of warfare, a High Contracting Party is under an obligation to determine whether its employment would, in some or all circumstances, be prohibited by this Protocol or by any other rule of international law applicable to the High Contracting Party.

Article 37. Prohibition of Perfidy. 1. It is prohibited to kill, injure or capture an adversary by resort to perfidy. Acts inviting the confidence of an adversary to lead him to believe that he is entitled to, or is obliged to accord, protection under the rules of international law applicable in armed conflict, with intent to betray that confidence, shall constitute perfidy. The following acts are examples of perfidy:

(a) the feigning of an intent to negotiate under a flag of truce or of a surrender;

(b) the feigning of an incapacitation by wounds or sickness;

(c) the feigning of civilian, non-combatant status; and

(d) the feigning of protected status by the use of signs, emblems or uniforms of the United Nations or of neutral or other States not Parties to the Conflict.

2. Ruses of war are not prohibited. Such ruses are acts which are intended to mislead an adversary or to induce him to act recklessly but which infringe no rule of international law applicable in armed conflict and which are not perfidious because they do not invite the confidence of an adversary with respect to protection under that law. The following are examples of such ruses: the use of camouflage, decoys, mock operations and misinformation.

Article 38. Recognized Emblems. 1. It is prohibited to make improper use of the distinctive emblem of the red cross, red crescent or red lion and sun or of other emblems, signs or signals provided for by the Conventions or by this Protocol. It is also prohibited to misuse deliberately in an armed conflict other internationally recognized protective emblems, signs or signals, including the flag of truce, and the protective emblem of cultural property.

2. It is prohibited to make use of the distinctive emblem of the United Nations, except as authorized by that Organization.

Article 39. Emblems of Nationality. 1. It is prohibited to make use in an armed conflict of the flags or military emblems, insignia or uniforms of neutral or other States not Parties to the conflict.

2. It is prohibited to make use of the flags or military emblems, insignia or uniforms of adverse Parties while engaging in attacks or in order to shield, favour, protect or impede military operations.

3. Nothing in this Article or in Article 37, paragraph 1 (d), shall affect the existing generally recognized rules of international law applicable to espionage or to the use of flags in the conduct of armed conflict at sea.

Article 40. Quarter. It is prohibited to order that there shall be no survivors, to threaten an adversary therewith or to conduct hostilities on this basis.

Article 41. Safeguard of an Enemy Hors de Combat. 1. A person who is recognized or who, in the circumstances should be recognized to be *hors de combat* shall not be made the object of attack.

2. A person is *hors de combat* if:

(a) he is in the power of an adverse Party;

(b) he clearly expresses an intention to surrender; or

(c) he has been rendered unconscious or is otherwise incapacitated by wounds or sickness, and therefore is incapable of defending himself;

provided that in any of these cases he abstains from any hostile act and does not attempt to escape.

3. When persons entitled to protection as prisoners of war have fallen into the power of an adverse Party under unusual conditions of combat which prevent their evacuation as provided for in Part III, Section I, of the Third Convention, they shall be released and all feasible precautions shall be taken to ensure their safety.

Article 42. Occupants of Aircraft. 1. No person parachuting from an aircraft in distress shall be made the object of attack during his descent.

2. Upon reaching the ground in territory controlled by an adverse Party, a person who has parachuted from an aircraft in distress shall be given an opportunity to surrender before being made the object of attack, unless it is apparent that he is engaging in a hostile act.

3. Airborne troops are not protected by this Article.

Section II
Combatant and Prisoner-of-War Status

Article 43. Armed Forces. 1. The armed forces of a Party to a conflict consist of all organized armed forces, groups and units which are under a command responsible to that Party for the conduct of its subordinates, even if that Party is represented by a government or an authority not recognized by an adverse Party. Such armed forces shall be subject to an internal disciplinary system which, *inter alia,* shall enforce compliance with the rules of international law applicable in armed conflict.

2. Members of the armed forces of a Party to a conflict (other than medical personnel and chaplains covered by Article 33 of the Third Convention) are combatants, that is to say, they have the right to participate directly in hostilities.

3. Whenever a Party to a conflict incorporates a paramilitary or armed law enforcement agency into its armed forces it shall so notify the other Parties to the conflict.

Article 44. Combatants and Prisoners of War. 1. Any combatant, as defined in Article 43, who falls into the power of an adverse Party shall be a prisoner of war.

2. While all combatants are obliged to comply with the rules of international law applicable in armed conflict, violations of these rules shall not deprive a combatant of his right to be a combatant or, if he falls into the power of an adverse Party, of his right to be a prisoner of war, except as provided in paragraphs 3 and 4.

3. In order to promote the protection of the civilian population from the effects of hostilities, combatants are obliged to distinguish themselves from the civilian population while they are engaged in an attack or in a military operation preparatory to an attack. Recognizing, however, that there are situations in armed conflicts where, owing to the nature of the hostilities an armed combatant cannot so distinguish himself, he shall retain his status as a combatant, provided that, in such situations, he carries his arms openly:

(a) during each military engagement, and

(b) during such time as he is visible to the adversary

while he is engaged in a military deployment preceding the launching of an attack in which he is to participate.

Acts which comply with the requirements of this paragraph shall not be considered as perfidious within the meaning of Article 37, paragraph 1 (c).

4. A combatant who falls into the power of an adverse Party while failing to meet the requirements set forth in the second sentence of paragraph 3 shall forfeit his right to be a prisoner of war, but he shall, nevertheless, be given protections equivalent in all respects to those accorded to prisoners of war by the Third Convention and by this Protocol. This protection includes protections equivalent to those accorded to prisoners of war by the Third Convention in the case where such a person is tried and punished for any offences he has committed.

5. Any combatant who falls into the power of an adverse Party while not engaged in an attack or in a military operation preparatory to an attack shall not forfeit his rights to be a combatant and a prisoner of war by virtue of his prior activities.

6. This Article is without prejudice to the right of any person to be a prisoner of war pursuant to Article 4 of the Third Convention.

7. This Article is not intended to change the generally accepted practice of States with respect to the wearing of the uniform by combatants assigned to the regular, uniformed armed units of a Party to the conflict.

8. In addition to the categories of persons mentioned in Article 13 of the First and Second Conventions, all members of the armed forces of a Party to the conflict, as defined in Article 43 of this Protocol, shall be entitled to protection under those Conventions if they are wounded or sick or, in the case of the Second Convention, shipwrecked at sea or in other waters.

Article 45. Protection of Persons Who Have Taken Part in Hostilities. 1. A person who takes part in hostilities and falls into the power of an adverse Party shall be presumed to be a prisoner of war, and therefore shall be protected by the Third Convention, if he claims the status of prisoner of war, or if he appears to be entitled to such status, or if the Party on which he depends claims such status on his behalf by notification to the detaining Power or to the Protecting Power. Should any doubt arise as to whether any such person is entitled to the status of prisoner of war, he shall continue to have such status and, therefore, to be protected by the Third Convention and this Protocol until such time as his status has been determined by a competent tribunal.

2. If a person who has fallen into the power of an adverse Party is not held as a prisoner of war and is to be tried by that Party for an offence arising out of the hostilities, he shall have the right to assert his entitlement to prisoner-of-war status before a judicial tribunal and to have that question adjudicated. Whenever possible under the applicable procedure, this adjudication shall occur before the trial for the offence. The representatives of the Protecting Power shall be entitled to attend the proceedings in which that question is adjudicated, unless, exceptionally, the proceedings are held *in camera* in the interest of State security. In such a case the detaining Power shall advise the Protecting Power accordingly.

3. Any person who has taken part in hostilities, who is not entitled to prisoner-of-war status and who does not benefit from more favourable treatment in accordance with the Fourth Convention shall have the right at all times to the protection of Article 75 of this Protocol. In occupied territory, any such person, unless he is held as a spy, shall also be entitled, notwithstanding Article 5 of the Fourth Convention, to his rights of communication under that Convention.

Article 46. Spies. 1. Notwithstanding any other provision of the Conventions or of this Protocol, any member of the armed forces of a Party to the conflict who falls into the power of an adverse Party while engaging in espionage shall not have the right to the status of prisoner of war and may be treated as a spy.

2. A member of the armed forces of a Party to the conflict who, on behalf of that Party and in territory controlled by an adverse Party, gathers or attempts to gather information shall not be considered as engaging in espionage if, while so acting, he is in the uniform of his armed forces.

3. A member of the armed forces of a Party to the conflict who is a resident of territory occupied by an adverse Party and who, on behalf of the Party on which he depends, gathers or attempts to gather information of military value within that territory shall not be considered as engaging in espionage unless he does so through an act of false pretences or deliberately in a clandestine manner. Moreover, such a resident shall not lose his right to the status of prisoner of war and may not be treated as a spy unless he is captured while engaging in espionage.

4. A member of the armed forces of a Party to the conflict who is not a resident of territory occupied by an adverse Party and who has engaged in espionage in that territory shall not lose his right to the status of prisoner of war and may not be treated as a spy unless he is captured before he has rejoined the armed forces to which he belongs.

Article 47. Mercenaries. 1. A mercenary shall not have the right to be a combatant or a prisoner of war.

2. A mercenary is any person who:

(a) is specially recruited locally or abroad in order to fight in an armed conflict;

(b) does, in fact, take a direct part in the hostilities;

(c) is motivated to take part in the hostilities essentially by the desire for private gain and, in fact, is promised, by or on behalf of a Party to the conflict, material compensation substantially in excess of that promised or paid to combatants of similar ranks and functions in the armed forces of that Party;

(d) is neither a national of a Party to the conflict nor a resident of territory controlled by a Party to the conflict;

(e) is not a member of the armed forces of a Party to the conflict; and

(f) has not been sent by a State which is not a Party to the conflict on official duty as a member of its armed forces.

Part IV
Civilian Population

Section I
General Protection Against Effects of Hostilities

Chapter I
Basic Rule and Field of Application

Article 48. Basic Rule. In order to ensure respect for and protection of the civilian population and civilian objects, the Parties to the conflict shall at all times distinguish between the civilian population and combatants and between civilian objects and military objectives and accordingly shall direct their operations only against military objectives.

Article 49. Definition of Attacks and Scope of Application.

1. "Attacks" means acts of violence against the adversary, whether in offence or in defence.

2. The provisions of this Protocol with respect to attacks apply to all attacks in whatever territory conducted, including the national territory belonging to a Party to the conflict but under the control of an adverse Party.

3. The provisions of this section apply to any land, air or sea warfare which may affect the civilian population, individual civilians or civilian objects on land. They further apply to all attacks from the sea or from the air against objectives on land but do not otherwise affect the rules of international law applicable in armed conflict at sea or in the air.

4. The provisions of this section are additional to the rules concerning humanitarian protection contained in the Fourth Convention, particularly in part II thereof, and in other international agreements binding upon the High Contracting Parties, as well as to other rules of international law relating to the protection of civilians and civilian objects on land, at sea or in the air against the effects of hostilities.

Chapter II
Civilians and Civilian Population

Article 50. Definition of Civilians and Civilian Population. 1. A civilian is any person who does not belong to one of the categories of persons referred to in Article 4 (A) (1), (2), (3) and (6) of the Third Convention and in Article 43 of this Protocol. In case of doubt whether a person is a civilian, that person shall be considered to be a civilian.

2. The civilian population comprises all persons who are civilians.

3. The presence within the civilian population of individuals who do not come within the definition of civilians does not deprive the population of its civilian character.

Article 51. Protection of the Civilian Population. 1. The civilian population and individual civilians shall enjoy general protection against dangers arising from military operations. To give effect to this protection, the following rules, which are additional to other applicable rules of international law, shall be observed in all circumstances.

2. The civilian population as such, as well as individual civilians, shall not be the object of attack. Acts or threats of violence the primary purpose of which is to spread terror among the civilian population are prohibited.

3. Civilians shall enjoy the protection afforded by this section, unless and for such time as they take a direct part in hostilities.

4. Indiscriminate attacks are prohibited. Indiscriminate attacks are:

(a) those which are not directed at a specific military objective;

(b) those which employ a method or means of combat which cannot be directed at a specific military objective; or

(c) those which employ a method or means of combat the effects of which cannot be limited as required by this Protocol;

and consequently, in each such case, are of a nature to strike military objectives and civilians or civilian objects without distinction.

5. Among others, the following types of attacks are to be considered as indiscriminate:

(a) an attack by bombardment by any methods or means which treats as a single military objective a number of clearly separated and distinct military objectives located in a city, town, village or other area containing a similar concentration of civilians or civilian objects; and

(b) an attack which may be expected to cause incidental loss of civilian life, injury to civilians, damage to civilian objects, or a combination thereof, which would be excessive in relation to the concrete and direct military advantage anticipated.

6. Attacks against the civilian population or civilians by way of reprisals are prohibited.

7. The presence or movements of the civilian population or individual civilians shall not be used to render certain points or areas immune from military operations, in particular in attempts to shield military objectives from attacks or to shield, favour or impede military operations. The Parties to the conflict shall not direct the movement of the civilian population or individual civilians in order to attempt to shield military objectives from attacks or to shield military operations.

8. Any violation of these prohibitions shall not release the Parties to the conflict from their legal obligations with respect to the civilian population and civilians, including the obligation to take the precautionary measures provided for in Article 57.

Chapter III
Civilian Objects

Article 52. General Protection of Civilian Objects. 1. Civilian objects shall not be the object of attack or of reprisals. Civilian objects are all objects which are not military objectives as defined in paragraph 2.

2. Attacks shall be limited strictly to military objectives. In so far as objects are concerned, military objectives are limited to those objects which by their nature, location, purpose or use make an effective contribution to military action and whose total or partial destruction, capture or neutralization, in the circumstances ruling at the time, offers a definite military advantage.

3. In case of doubt whether an object which is normally dedicated to civilian purposes, such as a place of worship, a house or other dwelling or a school, is being used to make an effective contribution to military action, it shall be presumed not to be so used.

Article 53. Protection of Cultural Objects and of Places of Worship. Without prejudice to the provisions of the Hague Convention for the Protection of Cultural Property in the Event of Armed Conflict of 14 May 1954, and of other relevant international instruments, it is prohibited:

(a) to commit any acts of hostility directed against the historic monuments, works of art or places of worship which constitute the cultural or spiritual heritage of peoples;

(b) to use such objects in support of the military effort;

(c) to make such objects the object of reprisals.

Article 54. Protection of Objects Indispensable to the Survival of the Civilian Population. 1. Starvation of civilians as a method of warfare is prohibited.

2. It is prohibited to attack, destroy, remove or render useless objects indispensable to the survival of the civilian population, such as food-stuffs, agricultural areas for the production of food-stuffs, crops, livestock, drinking water installations and supplies and irrigation works, for the specific purpose of denying them for their sustenance value to the civilian population or to the adverse Party, whatever the

motive, whether in order to starve out civilians, to cause them to move away, or for any other motive.

3. The prohibitions in paragraph 2 shall not apply to such of the objects covered by it as are used by an adverse Party:

(a) as sustenance solely for the members of its armed forces; or

(b) if not as sustenance, then in direct support of military action, provided, however, that in no event shall actions against these objects be taken which may be expected to leave the civilian population with such inadequate food or water as to cause its starvation or force its movement.

4. These objects shall not be made the object of reprisals.

5. In recognition of the vital requirements of any Party to the Conflict in the defence of its national territory against invasion, derogation from the prohibitions contained in paragraph 2 may be made by a Party to the conflict within such territory under its own control where required by imperative military necessity.

Article 55. Protection of the Natural Environment. 1. Care shall be taken in warfare to protect the natural environment against widespread, long-term and severe damage. This protection includes a prohibition of the use of methods or means of warfare which are intended or may be expected to cause such damage to the natural environment and thereby to prejudice the health or survival of the population.

2. Attacks against the natural environment by way of reprisals are prohibited.

Article 56. Protection of Works and Installations containing Dangerous Forces. 1. Works or installations containing dangerous forces, namely dams, dykes and nuclear electrical generating stations, shall not be made the object of attack, even where these objects are military objectives, if such attack may cause the release of dangerous forces and consequent severe losses among the civilian population. Other military objectives located at or in the vicinity of these works or installations shall not be made the object of attack if such attack may cause the release of dangerous forces from the works or installations and consequent severe losses among the civilian population.

2. The special protection against attack provided by paragraph 1 shall cease:

(a) for a dam or a dyke only if it is used for other than its normal function and in regular, significant and direct support of military operations and if such attack is the only feasible way to terminate such support;

(b) for a nuclear electrical generating station only if it provides electric power in regular, significant and direct support of military operations and if such attack is the only feasible way to terminate such support;

(c) for other military objectives located at or in the vicinity of these works or installations only if they are used in regular, significant and direct support of military operations and if such attack is the only feasible way to terminate such support.

3. In all cases, the civilian population and individual civilians shall remain entitled to all the protection accorded them by international law, including the protection of the precautionary measures provided for in Article 57. If the protection ceases and any of the works, installations or military objectives mentioned in paragraph 1 is attacked, all practical precautions shall be taken to avoid the release of the dangerous forces.

4. It is prohibited to make any of the works, installations

or military objectives mentioned in paragraph 1 the object of reprisals.

5. The Parties to the conflict shall endeavour to avoid locating any military objectives in the vicinity of the works or installations mentioned in paragraph 1. Nevertheless, installations erected for the sole purpose of defending the protected works or installations from attack are permissible and shall not themselves be made the object of attack, provided that they are not used in hostilities except for defensive actions necessary to respond to attacks against the protected works or installations and that their armament is limited to weapons capable only of repelling hostile action against the protected works or installations.

6. The High Contracting Parties and the Parties to the conflict are urged to conclude further agreements among themselves to provide additional protection for objects containing dangerous forces.

7. In order to facilitate the identification of the objects protected by this article, the Parties to the conflict may mark them with a special sign consisting of a group of three bright orange circles placed on the same axis, as specified in Article 16 of Annex I to this Protocol. The absence of such marking in no way relieves any Party to the conflict of its obligations under this Article.

Chapter IV
Precautionary Measures

Article 57. Precautions in Attack. 1. In the conduct of military operations, constant care shall be taken to spare the civilian population, civilians and civilian objects.

2. With respect to attacks, the following precautions shall be taken:

(a) those who plan or decide upon an attack shall:

(i) do everything feasible to verify that the objectives to be attacked are neither civilians nor civilian objects and are not subject to special protection but are military objectives within the meaning of paragraph 2 of Article 52 and that it is not prohibited by the provisions of this Protocol to attack them;

(ii) take all feasible precautions in the choice of means and methods of attack with a view to avoiding, and in any event to minimizing, incidental loss of civilian life, injury to civilians and damage to civilian objects;

(iii) refrain from deciding to launch any attack which may be expected to cause incidental loss of civilian life, injury to civilians, damage to civilian objects, or a combination thereof, which would be excessive in relation to the concrete and direct military advantage anticipated;

(b) an attack shall be cancelled or suspended if it becomes apparent that the objective is not a military one or is subject to special protection or that the attack may be expected to cause incidental loss of civilian life, injury to civilians, damage to civilian objects, or a combination thereof, which would be excessive in relation to the concrete and direct military advantage anticipated;

(c) effective advance warning shall be given of attacks which may affect the civilian population, unless circumstances do not permit.

3. When a choice is possible between several military objectives for obtaining a similar military advantage, the objective to be selected shall be that the attack on which may be expected to cause the least danger to civilian lives and to civilian objects.

4. In the conduct of military operations at sea or in the air, each Party to the conflict shall, in conformity with its

rights and duties under the rules of international law applicable in armed conflict, take all reasonable precautions to avoid losses of civilian lives and damage to civilian objects.

5. No provision of this article may be construed as authorizing any attacks against the civilian population, civilians or civilian objects.

Article 58. Precautions Against the Effects of Attacks. The Parties to the conflict shall, to the maximum extent feasible:

    (a) without prejudice to Article 49 of the Fourth Convention, endeavour to remove the civilian population, individual civilians and civilian objects under their control from the vicinity of military objectives;

    (b) avoid locating military objectives within or near densely populated areas;

    (c) take the other necessary precautions to protect the civilian population, individual civilians and civilian objects under their control against the dangers resulting from military operations.

Chapter V
Localities and Zones Under Special Protection

Article 59. Non-defended localities. 1. It is prohibited for the Parties to the conflict to attack, by any means whatsoever, non-defended localities.

2. The appropriate authorities of a Party to the conflict may declare as a non-defended locality any inhabited place near or in a zone where armed forces are in contact which is open for occupation by an adverse Party. Such a locality shall fulfil the following conditions:

    (a) all combatants, as well as mobile weapons and mobile military equipment must have been evacuated;

    (b) no hostile use shall be made of fixed military installations or establishments;

    (c) no acts of hostility shall be committed by the authorities or by the population; and

    (d) no activities in support of military operations shall be undertaken.

3. The presence, in this locality, of persons specially protected under the Conventions and this Protocol, and of police forces retained for the sole purpose of maintaining law and order, is not contrary to the conditions laid down in paragraph 2.

4. The declaration made under paragraph 2 shall be addressed to the adverse Party and shall define and describe, as precisely as possible, the limits of the non-defended locality. The Party to the conflict to which the declaration is addressed shall acknowledge its receipt and shall treat the locality as a non-defended locality unless the conditions laid down in paragraph 2 are not in fact fulfilled, in which event it shall immediately so inform the Party making the declaration. Even if the conditions laid down in paragraph 2 are not fulfilled, the locality shall continue to enjoy the protection provided by the other provisions of this Protocol and the other rules of international law applicable in armed conflict.

5. The Parties to the conflict may agree on the establishment of non-defended localities even if such localities do not fulfil the conditions laid down in paragraph 2. The agreement should define and describe, as precisely as possible, the limits of the non-defended locality; if necessary, it may lay down the methods of supervision.

6. The Party which is in control of a locality governed by such an agreement shall mark it, so far as possible, by such signs as may be agreed upon with the other Party, which

shall be displayed where they are clearly visible, especially on its perimeter and limits and on highways.

7. A locality loses its status as a non-defended locality when its ceases to fulfil the conditions laid down in paragraph 2 or in the agreement referred to in paragraph 5. In such an eventuality, the locality shall continue to enjoy the protection provided by the other provisions of this Protocol and the other rules of international law applicable in armed conflict.

Article 60. Demilitarized Zones. 1. It is prohibited for the Parties to the conflict to extend their military operations to zones on which they have conferred by agreement the status of demilitarized zone, if such extension is contrary to the terms of this agreement.

2. The agreement shall be an express agreement, may be concluded verbally or in writing, either directly or through a Protecting Power or any impartial humanitarian organization, and may consist of reciprocal and concordant declarations. The agreement may be concluded in peacetime, as well as after the outbreak of hostilities, and should define and describe, as precisely as possible, the limits of the demilitarized zone and, if necessary, lay down the methods of supervision.

3. The subject of such an agreement shall normally be any zone which fulfils the following conditions:

    (a) all combatants, as well as mobile weapons and mobile military equipment, must have been evacuated;

    (b) no hostile use shall be made of fixed military installations or establishments;

    (c) no acts of hostility shall be committed by the authorities or by the population; and

    (d) any activity linked to the military effort must have ceased.

The Parties to the conflict shall agree upon the interpretation to be given to the condition laid down in subparagraph (d) and upon persons to be admitted to the demilitarized zone other than those mentioned in paragraph 4.

4. The presence, in this zone, of persons specially protected under the Conventions and this Protocol, and of police forces retained for the sole purpose of maintaining law and order, is not contrary to the conditions laid down in paragraph 3.

5. The Party which is in control of such a zone shall mark it, so far as possible, by such signs as may be agreed upon with the other Party, which shall be displayed where they are clearly visible, especially on its perimeter and limits and on highways.

6. If the fighting draws near to a demilitarized zone, and if the Parties to the conflict have so agreed, none of them may use the zone for purposes related to the conduct of military operations or unilaterally revoke its status.

7. If one of the Parties to the conflict commits a material breach of the provisions of paragraphs 3 or 6, the other Party shall be released from its obligations under the agreement conferring upon the zone the status of demilitarized zone. In such an eventuality, the zone loses its status but shall continue to enjoy the protection provided by the other provisions of this Protocol and the other rules of international law applicable in armed conflict.

Chapter VI
Civil Defence

Article 61. Definitions and Scope. For the purpose of this Protocol:

1. "Civil defence" means the performance of some or all

of the undermentioned humanitarian tasks intended to protect the civilian population against the dangers, and to help it to recover from the immediate effects, of hostilities or disasters and also to provide the conditions necessary for its survival. These tasks are:

(a) warning;

(b) evacuation;

(c) management of shelters;

(d) management of blackout measures;

(e) rescue;

(f) medical services, including first aid, and religious assistance;

(g) fire-fighting;

(h) detection and marking of danger areas;

(i) decontamination and similar protective measures;

(j) provision of emergency accommodation and supplies;

(k) emergency assistance in the restoration and maintenance of order in distressed areas;

(l) emergency repair of indispensable public utilities;

(m) emergency disposal of the dead;

(n) assistance in the preservation of objects essential for survival;

(o) complementary activities necessary to carry out any of the tasks mentioned above, including, but not limited to, planning and organization;

2. "Civil defence organizations" means those establishments and other units which are organized or authorized by the competent authorities of a Party to the conflict to perform any of the tasks mentioned under 1, and which are assigned and devoted exclusively to such tasks;

3. "Personnel" of civil defence organizations means those persons assigned by a Party to the conflict exclusively to the performance of the tasks mentioned under 1, including personnel assigned by the competent authority of that Party exclusively to the administration of these organizations;

4. "Matériel" of civil defence organizations means equipment, supplies and transports used by these organizations for the performance of the tasks mentioned under 1.

Article 62. General Protection. 1. Civilian civil defence organizations and their personnel shall be respected and protected, subject to the provisions of this Protocol, particularly the provisions of this section. They shall be entitled to perform their civil defence tasks except in case of imperative military necessity.

2. The provisions of paragraph 1 shall also apply to civilians who, although not members of civilian civil defence organizations, respond to an appeal from the competent authorities and perform civil defence tasks under their control.

3. Buildings and *matériel* used for civil defence purposes and shelters provided for the civilian population are covered by Article 52. Objects used for civil defence purposes may not be destroyed or diverted from their proper use except by the Party to which they belong.

Article 63. Civil Defence in Occupied Territories. 1. In occupied territories, civilian civil defence organizations shall receive from the authorities the facilities necessary for the performance of their tasks. In no circumstances shall their personnel be compelled to perform activities which would interfere with the proper performance of these tasks. The Occupying Power shall not change the structure or personnel of such organizations in any way which might jeopardize the efficient performance of their mission. These

organizations shall not be required to give priority to the nationals or interests of that Power.

2. The Occupying Power shall not compel, coerce or induce civilian civil defence organizations to perform their tasks in any manner prejudicial to the interests of the civilian population.

3. The Occupying Power may disarm civil defence personnel for reasons of security.

4. The Occupying Power shall neither divert from their proper use nor requisition buildings or *matériel* belonging to or used by civil defence organizations if such diversion or requisition would be harmful to the civilian population.

5. Provided that the general rule in paragraph 4 continues to be observed, the Occupying Power may requisition or divert these resources, subject to the following particular conditions:

(a) that the buildings or *matériel* are necessary for other needs of the civilian population; and

(b) that the requisition or diversion continues only while such necessity exists.

6. The Occupying Power shall neither divert nor requisition shelters provided for the use of the civilian population or needed by such population.

Article 64. Civilian Civil Defence Organizations of Neutral or Other States not Parties to the Conflict and International Coordinating Organizations. 1. Articles 62, 63, 65 and 66 shall also apply to the personnel and *matériel* of civilian civil defence organizations of neutral or other States not Parties to the conflict which perform civil defence tasks mentioned in Article 61 in the territory of a Party to the conflict, with the consent and under the control of that Party. Notification of such assistance shall be given as soon as possible to any adverse Party concerned. In no circumstances shall this activity be deemed to be an interference in the conflict. This activity should, however, be performed with due regard to the security interests of the Parties to the conflict concerned.

2. The Parties to the conflict receiving the assistance referred to in paragraph 1 and the High Contracting Parties granting it should facilitate international co-ordination of such civil defence actions when appropriate. In such cases the relevant international organizations are covered by the provisions of this Chapter.

3. In occupied territories, the Occupying Power may only exclude or restrict the activities of civilian civil defence organizations of neutral or other States not Parties to the conflict and of international co-ordinating organizations if it can ensure the adequate performance of civil defence tasks from its own resources or those of the occupied territory.

Article 65. Cessation of Protection. 1. The protection to which civilian civil defence organizations, their personnel, buildings, shelters and *matériel* are entitled shall not cease unless they commit or are used to commit, outside their proper tasks, acts harmful to the enemy. Protection may, however, cease only after a warning has been given setting, whenever appropriate, a reasonable time-limit, and after such warning has remained unheeded.

2. The following shall not be considered as acts harmful to the enemy:

(a) that civil defence tasks are carried out under the direction or control of military authorities;

(b) that civilian civil defence personnel co-operate with military personnel in the performance of civil defence tasks, or that some military personnel are attached to civilian civil defence organizations;

(c) that the performance of civil defence tasks may incidentally benefit military victims, particularly those who are *hors de combat.*

3. It shall also not be considered as an act harmful to the enemy that civilian civil defence personnel bear light individual weapons for the purpose of maintaining order or for self-defence. However, in areas where land fighting is taking place or is likely to take place, the Parties to the conflict shall undertake the appropriate measures to limit these weapons to handguns, such as pistols or revolvers, in order to assist in distinguishing between civil defence personnel and combatants. Although civil defence personnel bear other light individual weapons in such areas, they shall nevertheless be respected and protected as soon as they have been recognized as such.

4. The formation of civilian civil defence organizations along military lines, and compulsory service in them, shall also not deprive them of the protection conferred by this Chapter.

Article 66. Identification. 1. Each Party to the conflict shall endeavour to ensure that its civil defence organizations, their personnel, buildings and *matériel,* are identifiable while they are exclusively devoted to the performance of civil defence tasks. Shelters provided for the civilian population should be similarly identifiable.

2. Each Party to the conflict shall also endeavour to adopt and implement methods and procedures which will make it possible to recognize civilian shelters as well as civil defence personnel, buildings and *matériel* on which the international distinctive sign of civil defence is displayed.

3. In occupied territories and in areas where fighting is taking place or is likely to take place, civilian civil defence personnel should be recognizable by the international distinctive sign of civil defence and by an identity card certifying their status.

4. The international distinctive sign of civil defence is an equilateral blue triangle on an orange ground when used for the protection of civil defence organizations, their personnel, buildings and *matériel* and for civilian shelters.

5. In addition to the distinctive sign, Parties to the conflict may agree upon the use of distinctive signals for civil defence identification purposes.

6. The application of the provisions of paragraphs 1 to 4 is governed by Chapter V of Annex I to this Protocol.

7. In time of peace, the sign described in paragraph 4 may, with the consent of the competent national authorities, be used for civil defence identification purposes.

8. The High Contracting Parties and the Parties to the conflict shall take the measures necessary to supervise the display of the international distinctive sign of civil defence and to prevent and repress any misuse thereof.

9. The identification of civil defence medical and religious personnel, medical units and medical transports is also governed by Article 18.

Article 67. Members of the Armed Forces and Military Units Assigned to Civil Defence Organizations. 1. Members of the armed forces and military units assigned to civil defence organizations shall be respected and protected, provided that:

(a) such personnel and such units are permanently assigned and exclusively devoted to the performance of any of the tasks mentioned in Article 61;

(b) if so assigned, such personnel do not perform any other military duties during the conflict;

(c) such personnel are clearly distinguishable from the other members of the armed forces by prominently dis-

playing the international distinctive sign of civil defence, which shall be as large as appropriate, and such personnel are provided with the identity card referred to in Chapter V of Annex I to this Protocol certifying their status;

(d) such personnel and such units are equipped only with light individual weapons for the purpose of maintaining order or for self-defence. The provisions of Article 65, paragraph 3 shall also apply in this case;

(e) such personnel do not participate directly in hostilities, and do not commit, or are not used to commit, outside their civil defence tasks, acts harmful to the adverse Party.

(f) such personnel and such units perform their civil defence tasks only within the national territory of their Party.

The non-observance of the conditions stated in (e) above by any member of the armed forces who is bound by the conditions prescribed in (a) and (b) above is prohibited.

2. Military personnel serving within civil defence organizations shall, if they fall into the power of an adverse Party, be prisoners of war. In occupied territory they may, but only in the interest of the civilian population of that territory, be employed on civil defence tasks in so far as the need arises, provided however that, if such work is dangerous, they volunteer for such tasks.

3. The buildings and major items of equipment and transports of military units assigned to civil defence organizations shall be clearly marked with the international distinctive sign of civil defence. This distinctive sign shall be as large as appropriate.

4. The matériel and buildings of military units permanently assigned to civil defence organizations and exclusively devoted to the performance of civil defence tasks shall, if they fall into the hands of an adverse Party, remain subject to the laws of war. They may not be diverted from their civil defence tasks, except in case of imperative military necessity, unless previous arrangements have been made for adequate provision for the needs of the civilian population.

Section II
Relief in Favour of the Civilian Population

Article 68. Field of Application. The provisions of this Section apply to the civilian population as defined in this Protocol and are supplementary to Articles 23, 55, 59, 60, 61 and 62 and other relevant provisions of the Fourth Convention.

Article 69. Basic Needs in Occupied Territories. 1. In addition to the duties specified in Article 55 of the Fourth Convention concerning food and medical supplies, the Occupying Power shall, to the fullest extent of the means available to it and without any adverse distinction, also ensure the provision of clothing, bedding, means of shelter, other supplies essential to the survival of the civilian population of the occupied territory and objects necessary for religious worship.

2. Relief actions for the benefit of the civilian population of occupied territories are governed by Articles 59, 60, 61, 62, 108, 109, 110 and 111 of the Fourth Convention, and by Article 71 of this Protocol, and shall be implemented without delay.

Article 70. Relief Actions. 1. If the civilian population of any territory under the control of a Party to the conflict, other than occupied territory, is not adequately provided with the supplies mentioned in Article 69, relief actions which are humanitarian and impartial in character and conducted without any adverse distinction shall be undertaken, subject to the agreement of the Parties concerned in such relief actions. Offers of such relief shall not be regarded as interference in the armed conflict or as unfriendly acts. In the distribution of relief consignments, priority shall be given to those persons, such as children, expectant mothers, maternity cases and nursing mothers, who, under the Fourth Convention or under this Protocol, are to be accorded privileged treatment or special protection.

2. The Parties to the conflict and each High Contracting Party shall allow and facilitate rapid and unimpeded passage of all relief consignments, equipment and personnel provided in accordance with this Section, even if such assistance is destined for the civilian population of the adverse Party.

3. The Parties to the conflict and each High Contracting Party which allows the passage of relief consignments, equipment and personnel in accordance with paragraph 2:

(a) shall have the right to prescribe the technical arrangements, including search, under which such passage is permitted;

(b) may make such permission conditional on the distribution of this assistance being made under the local supervision of a Protecting Power;

(c) shall, in no way whatsoever, divert relief consignments from the purpose for which they are intended nor delay their forwarding, except in cases of urgent necessity in the interest of the civilian population concerned.

4. The Parties to the conflict shall protect relief consignments and facilitate their rapid distribution.

5. The Parties to the conflict and each High Contracting Party concerned shall encourage and facilitate effective international co-ordination of the relief actions referred to in paragraph 1.

Article 71. Personnel Participating in Relief Actions. 1. Where necessary, relief personnel may form part of the assistance provided in any relief action, in particular for the transportation and distribution of relief consignments; the participation of such personnel shall be subject to the approval of the Party in whose territory they will carry out their duties.

2. Such personnel shall be respected and protected.

3. Each Party in receipt of relief consignments shall, to the fullest extent practicable, assist the relief personnel referred to in paragraph 1 in carrying out their relief mission. Only in case of imperative military necessity may the activities of the relief personnel be limited or their movements temporarily restricted.

4. Under no circumstances may relief personnel exceed the terms of their mission under this Protocol. In particular they shall take account of the security requirements of the Party in whose territory they are carrying out their duties. The mission of any of the personnel who do not respect these conditions may be terminated.

Section III
Treatment of Persons in the Power of a
Party to the Conflict

Chapter I
Field of Application and Protection of
Persons and Objects

Article 72. Field of Application. The provisions of this Section are additional to the rules concerning humanitarian protection of civilians and civilian objects in the power of a Party to the conflict contained in the Fourth Convention, particularly Parts I and III thereof, as well as to other applicable rules of international law relating to the protection of fundamental human rights during international armed conflict.

Article 73. Refugees and Stateless Persons. Persons who, before the beginning of hostilities, were considered as stateless persons or refugees under the relevant international instruments accepted by the Parties concerned or under the national legislation of the State of refuge or State of residence shall be protected persons within the meaning of Parts I and III of the Fourth Convention, in all circumstances and without any adverse distinction.

Article 74. Reunion of Dispersed Families. The High Contracting Parties and the Parties to the conflict shall facilitate in every possible way the reunion of families dispersed as a result of armed conflicts and shall encourage in particular the work of the humanitarian organizations engaged in this task in accordance with the provisions of the Conventions and of this Protocol and in conformity with their respective security regulations.

Article 75. Fundamental Guarantees. 1. In so far as they are affected by a situation referred to in Article 1 of this Protocol, persons who are in the power of a Party to the conflict and who do not benefit from more favourable treatment under the Conventions or under this Protocol shall be treated humanely in all circumstances and shall enjoy, as a minimum, the protection provided by this Article without any adverse distinction based upon race, colour, sex, language, religion or belief, political or other opinion, national or social origin, wealth, birth or other status, or on any other similar criteria. Each Party shall respect the person, honour, convictions and religious practices of all such persons.

2. The following acts are and shall remain prohibited at any time and in any place whatsoever, whether committed by civilian or by military agents:

(a) violence to the life, health, or physical or mental well-being of persons, in particular:

(i) murder;

(ii) torture of all kinds, whether physical or mental;

(iii) corporal punishment; and

(iv) mutilation;

(b) outrages upon personal dignity, in particular humiliating and degrading treatment, enforced prostitution and any form of indecent assault;

(c) the taking of hostages;

(d) collective punishments; and

(e) threats to commit any of the foregoing acts.

3. Any person arrested, detained or interned for actions related to the armed conflict shall be informed promptly, in a language he understands, of the reasons why these measures have been taken. Except in cases of arrest or detention for penal offences, such persons shall be released with the minimum delay possible and in any event as soon as the circumstances justifying the arrest, detention or internment have ceased to exist.

4. No sentence may be passed and no penalty may be executed on a person found guilty of a penal offence related to the armed conflict except pursuant to a conviction pronounced by an impartial and regularly constituted court respecting the generally recognized principles of regular judicial procedure, which include the following:

(a) the procedure shall provide for an accused to be informed without delay of the particulars of the offence alleged against him and shall afford the accused before and during his trial all necessary rights and means of defence;

(b) no one shall be convicted of an offence except on the basis of individual penal responsibility;

(c) no shall be accused or convicted of a criminal offence on account of any act or omission which did not constitute a criminal offence under the national or international law to which he was subject at the time when it was committed; nor shall a heavier penalty be imposed than that which was applicable at the time when the criminal offence was committed; if, after the commission of the offence, provision is made by law for the imposition of a lighter penalty, the offender shall benefit thereby;

(d) anyone charged with an offence is presumed innocent until proved guilty according to law;

(e) anyone charged with an offence shall have the right to be tried in his presence;

(f) no one shall be compelled to testify against himself or to confess guilt;

(g) anyone charged with an offence shall have the right to examine, or have examined, the witnesses against him and to obtain the attendance and examination of witnesses on his behalf under the same conditions as witnesses against him;

(h) no one shall be prosecuted or punished by the same Party for an offence in respect of which a final judgement acquitting or convicting that person has been previously pronounced under the same law and judicial procedure;

(i) anyone prosecuted for an offence shall have the right to have the judgement pronounced publicly; and

(j) a convicted person shall be advised on conviction of his judicial and other remedies and of the time-limits within which they may be exercised.

5. Women whose liberty has been restricted for reasons related to the armed conflict shall be held in quarters separated from men's quarters. They shall be under the immediate supervision of women. Nevertheless, in cases where families are detained or interned, they shall, whenever possible, be held in the same place and accommodated as family units.

6. Persons who are arrested, detained or interned for reasons related to the armed conflict shall enjoy the protection provided by this Article until their final release, repatriation or re-establishment, even after the end of the armed conflict.

7. In order to avoid any doubt concerning the prosecution and trial of persons accused of war crimes or crimes against humanity, the following principles shall apply:

(a) persons who are accused of such crimes should be submitted for the purpose of prosecution and trial in accordance with the applicable rules of international law; and

(b) any such persons who do not benefit from more favourable treatment under the Conventions of this Protocol shall be accorded the treatment provided by this Article, whether or not the crimes of which they are accused constitute grave breaches of the Conventions or of this Protocol.

8. No provision of this Article may be construed as limiting or infringing any other more favourable provision granting greater protection, under any applicable rules of international law, to persons covered by paragraph 1.

Chapter II
Measures in Favour of Women and Children

Article 76. Protection of Women. 1. Women shall be the object of special request and shall be protected in particular against rape, forced prostitution and any other form of indecent assault.

2. Pregnant women and mothers having dependent infants who are arrested, detained or interned for reasons related to the armed conflict, shall have their cases considered with the utmost priority.

3. To the maximum extent feasible, the Parties to the conflict shall endeavour to avoid the pronouncement of the death penalty on pregnant women or mothers having dependent infants, for an offence related to the armed conflict. The death penalty for such offences shall not be executed on such women.

Article 77. Protection of Children. 1. Children shall be the object of special respect and shall be protected against any form of indecent assault. The Parties to the conflict shall provide them with the care and aid they require, whether because of their age or for any other reason.

2. The Parties to the conflict shall take all feasible measures in order that children who have not attained the age of fifteen years do not take a direct part in hostilities and, in particular, they shall refrain from recruiting them into their armed forces. In recruiting among those persons who have attained the age of fifteen years but who have not attained the age of eighteen years the Parties to the conflict shall endeavour to give priority to those who are oldest.

3. If, in exceptional cases, despite the provisions of paragraph 2, children who have not attained the age of fifteen years take a direct part in hostilities and fall into the power of an adverse Party, they shall continue to benefit from the special protection accorded by this Article, whether or not they are prisoners of war.

4. If arrested, detained or interned for reasons related to the armed conflict, children shall be held in quarters separate from the quarters of adults, except where families are accommodated as family units as provided in Article 75, paragraph 5.

5. The death penalty for an offence related to the armed conflict shall not be executed on persons who had not attained the age of eighteen years at the time the offence was committed.

Article 78. Evacuation of Children. 1. No Party to the conflict shall arrange for the evacuation of children, other than its own nationals, to a foreign country except for a temporary evacuation where compelling reasons of the health or medical treatment of the children or, except in occupied territory, their safety, so require. Where the parents or legal guardians can be found, their written consent to such evacuation is required. If these persons cannot be found, the written consent to such evacuation of the persons who by law or custom are primarily responsible for the care of the children is required. Any such evacuation shall be supervised by the Protecting Power in agreement with the Parties concerned, namely, the Party arranging for the evacuation, the Party receiving the children and any Parties whose nationals are being evacuated. In each case, all Parties to the conflict shall take all feasible precautions to avoid endangering the evacuation.

2. Whenever an evacuation occurs pursuant to paragraph 1, each child's education, including his religious and

moral education as his parents desire, shall be provided while he is away with the greatest possible continuity.

3. With a view to facilitating the return to their families and country of children evacuated pursuant to this Article, the authorities of the Party arranging for the evacuation and, as appropriate, the authorities of the receiving country shall establish for each child a card with photographs, which they shall send to the Central Tracing Agency of the International Committee of the Red Cross. Each card shall bear, whenever possible, and whenever it involves no risk of harm to the child, the following information:

(a) surname(s) of the child;

(b) the child's first name(s);

(c) the child's sex;

(d) the place and date of birth (or, if that date is not known, the approximate age);

(e) the father's full name;

(f) the mother's full name and her maiden name;

(g) the child's next-of-kin;

(h) the child's nationality;

(i) the child's native language, and any other languages he speaks;

(j) the address of the child's family;

(k) any identification number for the child;

(l) the child's state of health;

(m) the child's blood group;

(n) any distinguishing features;

(o) the date on which and the place where the child was found;

(p) the date on which and the place from which the child left the country;

(q) the child's religion, if any;

(r) the child's present address in the receiving country;

(s) should the child die before his return, the date, place and circumstances of death and place of interment.

Chapter III
Journalists

Article 79. Measures of Protection for Journalists. 1. Journalists engaged in dangerous professional missions in areas of armed conflict shall be considered as civilians within the meaning of Article 50, paragraph 1.

2. They shall be protected as such under the Conventions and this Protocol, provided that they take no action adversely affecting their status as civilians, and without prejudice to the right of war correspondents accredited to the armed forces to the status provided for in Article 4 (A) (4) of the Third Convention.

3. They may obtain an identity card similar to the model in Annex II of this Protocol. This card, which shall be issued by the government of the State of which the journalist is a national or in whose territory he resides or in which the news medium employing him is located, shall attest to his status as a journalist.

Part V
Execution of the Conventions and of This Protocol
Section I
General Provisions

Article 80. Measures for Execution. 1. The High Contracting Parties and the Parties to the conflict shall without delay take all necessary measures for the execution of their obligations under the Conventions and this Protocol.

2. The High Contracting Parties and the Parties to the conflict shall give orders and instructions to ensure observance of the Conventions and this Protocol, and shall supervise their execution.

Article 81. Activities of the Red Cross and Other Humanitarian Organizations. 1. The Parties to the conflict shall grant to the International Committee of the Red Cross all facilities within their power so as to enable it to carry out the humanitarian functions assigned to it by the Conventions and this Protocol in order to ensure protection and assistance to the victims of conflicts; the International Committee of the Red Cross may also carry out any other humanitarian activities in favour of these victims, subject to the consent of the Parties to the conflict concerned.

2. The Parties to the conflict shall grant to their respective Red Cross (Red Crescent, Red Lion and Sun) organizations the facilities necessary for carrying out their humanitarian activities in favour of the victims of the conflict, in accordance with the provisions of the Conventions and this Protocol and the fundamental principles of the Red Cross as formulated by the International Conferences of the Red Cross.

3. The High Contracting Parties and the Parties to the conflict shall facilitate in every possible way the assistance which Red Cross (Red Crescent, Red Lion and Sun) organizations and the League of Red Cross Societies extend to the victims of conflicts in accordance with the provisions of the Conventions and this Protocol and with the fundamental principles of the Red Cross as formulated by the International Conferences of the Red Cross.

4. The High Contracting Parties and the Parties to the conflict shall, as far as possible, make facilities similar to those mentioned in paragraphs 2 and 3 available to the other humanitarian organizations referred to in the Conventions and this Protocol which are duly authorized by the respective Parties to the conflict and which perform their humanitarian activities in accordance with the provisions of the Conventions and this Protocol.

Article 82. Legal Advisers in Armed Forces. The High Contracting Parties at all times, and the Parties to the conflict in time of armed conflict, shall ensure that legal advisers are available, when necessary, to advise military commanders at the appropriate level on the application of the Conventions and this Protocol and on the appropriate instruction to be given to the armed forces on this subject.

Article 83. Dissemination. 1. The High Contracting Parties undertake, in time of peace as in time of armed conflict, to disseminate the Conventions and this Protocol as widely as possible in their respective countries and, in particular, to include the study thereof in their programmes of military instruction and to encourage the study thereof by the civilian population, so that those instruments may become known to the armed forces and to the civilian population.

2. Any military or civilian authorities who, in time of armed conflict, assume responsibilities in respect of the application of the Conventions and this Protocol shall be fully acquainted with the text thereof.

Article 84. Rules of Application. The High Contracting Parties shall communicate to one another, as soon as possible, through the depositary and, as appropriate, through the Protecting Powers, their official translations of this Protocol, as well as the laws and regulations which they may adopt to ensure its application.

Section II
Repression of Breaches of the Conventions
and of This Protocol

Article 85. Repression of Breaches of this Protocol. 1. The provisions of the Conventions relating to the repression of breaches and grave breaches, supplemented by this Section, shall apply to the repression of breaches and grave breaches of this Protocol.

2. Acts described as grave breaches in the Conventions are grave breaches of this Protocol if committed against persons in the power of an adverse Party protected by Articles 44, 45 and 73 of this Protocol, or against the wounded, sick and shipwrecked of the adverse Party who are protected by this Protocol, or against those medical or religious personnel, medical units or medical transports which are under the control of the adverse Party and are protected by this Protocol.

3. In addition to the grave breaches defined in Article 11, the following acts shall be regarded as grave breaches of this Protocol, when committed wilfully, in violation of the relevant provisions of this Protocol, and causing death or serious injury to body or health:

(a) making the civilian population or individual civilians the object of attack;

(b) launching an indiscriminate attack affecting the civilian population or civilian objects in the knowledge that such attack will cause excessive loss of life, injury to civilians or damage to civilian objects, as defined in Article 57, paragraph 2 (a) (iii);

(c) launching an attack against works or installations containing dangerous forces in the knowledge that such attack will cause excessive loss of life, injury to civilians or damage to civilian objects, as defined in Article 57, paragraph 2 (a) (iii);

(d) making non-defended localities and demilitarized zones the object of attack;

(e) making a person the object of attack in the knowledge that he is *hors de combat;*

(f) the perfidious use, in violation of Article 37, of the distinctive emblem of the red cross, red crescent or red lion and sun or of other protective signs recognized by the Conventions or this Protocol.

4. In addition to the grave breaches defined in the preceding paragraphs and in the Conventions, the following shall be regarded as grave breaches of this Protocol, when committed wilfully and in violation of the Conventions or the Protocol:

(a) the transfer by the occupying Power of parts of its own civilian population into the territory it occupies, or the deportation or transfer of all or parts of the population of the occupied territory within or outside this territory, in violation of Article 49 of the Fourth Convention;

(b) unjustifiable delay in the repatriation of prisoners of war or civilians;

(c) practices of *apartheid* and other inhuman and degrading practices involving outrages upon personal dignity, based on racial discrimination;

(d) making the clearly-recognized historic monuments, works of art or places of worship which constitute the cultural or spiritual heritage of peoples and to which special protection has been given by special arrangement, for example, within the framework of a competent international organization, the object of attack, causing as a result extensive destruction thereof, where there is no evidence of the violation by the adverse Party of Article 53, subparagraph (b), and when such historic monuments, works of art and places of worship are not located in the immediate proximity of military objectives;

(e) depriving a person protected by the Conventions or referred to in paragraph 2 of this Article of the rights of fair and regular trial.

5. Without prejudice to the application of the Conventions and of this Protocol, grave breaches of these instruments shall be regarded as war crimes.

Article 86. Failure to Act. 1. The High Contracting Parties and the Parties to the conflict shall repress grave breaches, and take measures necessary to suppress all other breaches, of the Conventions or of this Protocol which result from a failure to act when under a duty to do so.

2. The fact that a breach of the Conventions or of this Protocol was committed by a subordinate does not absolve his superiors from penal disciplinary responsibility, as the case may be, if they knew, or had information which should have enabled them to conclude in the circumstances at the time, that he was committing or was going to commit such a breach and if they did not take all feasible measures within their power to prevent or repress the breach.

Article 87. Duty of Commanders. 1. The High Contracting Parties and the Parties to the conflict shall require military commanders, with respect to members of the armed forces under their command and other persons under their control, to prevent and, where necessary, to suppress and to report to competent authorities breaches of the Conventions and of this Protocol.

2. In order to prevent and suppress breaches, High Contracting Parties and Parties to the conflict shall require that, commensurate with their level of responsibility, commanders ensure that members of the armed forces under their command are aware of their obligations under the Conventions and this Protocol.

3. The High Contracting Parties and Parties to the conflict shall require any commander who is aware that subordinates or other persons under his control are going to commit or have committed a breach of the Conventions or of this Protocol, to initiate such steps as are necessary to prevent such violations of the Conventions or this Protocol, and, where appropriate, to initiate disciplinary or penal action against violators thereof.

Article 88. Mutual Assistance in Criminal Matters. 1. The High Contracting Parties shall afford one another the greatest measure of assistance in connexion with criminal proceedings brought in respect of grave breaches of the Conventions or of this Protocol.

2. Subject to the rights and obligations established in the Conventions and in Article 85, paragraph 1 of this Protocol, and when circumstances permit, the High Contracting Parties shall co-operate in the matter of extradition. They shall give due consideration to the request of the State in whose territory the alleged offence has occurred.

3. The law of the High Contracting Party requested shall apply in all cases. The provisions of the preceding paragraphs shall not, however, affect the obligations arising from the provisions of any other treaty of a bilateral or multilateral nature which governs or will govern the whole or part of the subject of mutual assistance in criminal matters.

Article 89. Co-operation. In situations of serious violations of the Conventions or of this Protocol, the High Contracting Parties undertake to act jointly or individually, in co-operation with the United Nations and in conformity with the United Nations Charter.

Article 90. International Fact-Finding Commission. 1. (a) An

International Fact-Finding Commission (hereinafter referred to as "the Commission") consisting of 15 members of high moral standing and acknowledged impartiality shall be established;

(b) When not less than 20 High Contracting Parties have agreed to accept the competence of the Commission pursuant to paragraph 2, the depositary shall then, and at intervals of five years thereafter, convene a meeting of representatives of those High Contracting Parties for the purpose of electing the members of the Commission. At the meeting, the representatives shall elect the members of the Commission by secret ballot from a list of persons to which each of those High Contracting Parties may nominate one person;

(c) The members of the Commission shall serve in their personal capacity and shall hold office until the election of new members at the ensuing meeting;

(d) At the election, the High Contracting Parties shall ensure that the persons to be elected to the Commission individually possess the qualifications required and that, in the Commission as a whole, equitable geographical representation is assured;

(e) In the case of a casual vacancy, the Commission itself shall fill the vacancy, having due regard to the provisions of the preceding subparagraphs;

(f) The depositary shall make available to the Commission the necessary administrative facilities for the performance of its functions.

2. (a) The High Contracting Parties may at the time of signing, ratifying or acceding to the Protocol, or at any other subsequent time, declare that they recognize *ipso facto* and without special agreement, in relation to any other High Contracting Party accepting the same obligation, the competence of the Commission to inquire into allegations by such other Party, as authorized by this Article;

(b) The declaration referred to above shall be deposited with the depositary, which shall transmit copies thereof to the High Contracting Parties;

(c) The Commission shall be competent to:

(i) inquire into any facts alleged to be a grave breach as defined in the Conventions and this Protocol or other serious violation of the Conventions or of this Protocol;

(ii) facilitate, through its good offices, the restoration of an attitude of respect for the Conventions and this Protocol;

(d) In other situations, the Commission shall institute an inquiry at the request of a Party to the conflict only with the consent of the other Party or Parties concerned;

(e) Subject to the foregoing provisions of this paragraph, the provisions of Article 52 of the First Convention, Article 53 of the Second Convention, Article 132 of the Third Convention and Article 149 of the Fourth Convention shall continue to apply to any alleged violation of the Conventions and shall extend to any alleged violation of this Protocol.

3. (a) Unless otherwise agreed by the Parties concerned, all inquiries shall be undertaken by a Chamber consisting of seven members appointed as follows:

(i) five members of the Commission, not nationals of any Party to the conflict, appointed by the President of the Commission on the basis of equitable representation of the geographical areas, after consultation with the Parties to the conflict;

(ii) two *ad hoc* members, not nationals of any Party to the conflict, one to be appointed by each side;

(b) Upon receipt of the request for an inquiry, the President of the Commission shall specify an appropriate time-limit for setting up a Chamber. If any *ad hoc* member has not been appointed within the time-limit, the President shall immediately appoint such additional member or members of the Commission as may be necessary to complete the membership of the Chamber.

4. (a) The Chamber set up under paragraph 3 to undertake an inquiry shall invite the Parties to the conflict to assist it and to present evidence. The Chamber may also seek such other evidence as it deems appropriate and may carry out an investigation of the situation *in loco;*

(b) All evidence shall be fully disclosed to the Parties, which shall have the right to comment on it to the Commission;

(c) Each Party shall have the right to challenge such evidence.

5. (a) The Commission shall submit to the Parties a report on the findings of fact of the Chamber, with such recommendations as it may deem appropriate;

(b) If the Chamber is unable to secure sufficient evidence for factual and impartial findings, the Commission shall state the reasons for that inability;

(c) The Commission shall not report its findings publicly, unless all the Parties to the conflict have requested the Commission to do so.

6. The Commission shall establish its own rules, including rules for the presidency of the Commission and the presidency of the Chamber. Those rules shall ensure that the functions of the President of the Commission are exercised at all times and that, in the case of an inquiry, they are exercised by a person who is not a national of a Party to the conflict.

7. The administrative expenses of the Commission shall be met by contributions from the High Contracting Parties which made declarations under paragraph 2, and by voluntary contributions. The Party or Parties to the conflict requesting an inquiry shall advance the necessary funds for expenses incurred by a Chamber and shall be reimbursed by the Party or Parties against which the allegations are made to the extent of 50 per cent of the costs of the Chamber. Where there are counter-allegations before the Chamber each side shall advance 50 per cent of the necessary funds.

Article 91. Responsibility. A Party to the conflict which violates the provisions of the Conventions or of this Protocol shall, if the case demands, be liable to pay compensation. It shall be responsible for all acts committed by persons forming part of its armed forces.

Part VI
Final Provisions

Article 92. Signature. This Protocol shall be open for signature by the Parties to the Conventions six months after the signing of the Final Act and will remain open for a period of twelve months.

Article 93. Ratification. This Protocol shall be ratified as soon as possible. The instruments of ratification shall be deposited with the Swiss Federal Council, depositary of the Conventions.

Article 94. Accession. This Protocol shall be open for accession by any Party to the Conventions which has not signed it. The instruments of accession shall be deposited with the depositary.

Article 95. Entry into Force. 1. This Protocol shall enter into force six months after two instruments of ratification or accession have been deposited.

2. For each Party to the Conventions thereafter ratifying or acceding to this Protocol, it shall enter into force six months after the deposit by such Party of its instrument of ratification or accession.

Article 96. Treaty Relations upon Entry into Force of This Protocol. 1. When the Parties to the Conventions are also Parties to this Protocol, the Conventions shall apply as supplemented by this Protocol.

2. When one of the Parties to the conflict is not bound by this Protocol, the Parties to the Protocol shall remain bound by it in their mutual relations. They shall furthermore be bound by this Protocol in relation to each of the Parties which are not bound by it, if the latter accepts and applies the provisions thereof.

3. The authority representing a people engaged against a High Contracting Party in an armed conflict of the type referred to in Article 1, paragraph 4, may undertake to apply the Conventions and this Protocol in relation to that conflict by means of a unilateral declaration addressed to the depositary. Such declaration shall, upon its receipt by the depositary, have in relation to that conflict the following effects:

(a) the Conventions and this Protocol are brought into force for the said authority as a Party to the conflict with immediate effect;

(b) the said authority assumes the same rights and obligations as those which have been assumed by a High Contracting Party to the Conventions and this Protocol; and

(c) the Conventions and this Protocol are equally binding upon all Parties to the conflict.

Article 97. Amendment. 1. Any High Contracting Party may propose amendments to this Protocol. The text of any proposed amendment shall be communicated to the depositary, which shall decide, after consultation with all the High Contracting Parties and the International Committee of the Red Cross, whether a conference should be convened to consider the proposed amendment.

2. The depositary shall invite to that conference all the High Contracting Parties as well as the Parties to the Conventions, whether or not they are signatories of this Protocol.

Article 98. Revision of Annex I. 1. Not later than four years after the entry into force of this Protocol and thereafter at intervals of not less than four years, the International Committee of the Red Cross shall consult the High Contracting Parties concerning Annex I to this Protocol and, if it considers it necessary, may propose a meeting of technical experts to review Annex I and to propose such amendments to it as may appear to be desirable. Unless, within six months of the communication of a proposal for such a meeting to the High Contracting Parties, one third of them object, the International Committee of the Red Cross shall convene the meeting, inviting also observers of appropriate international organizations. Such a meeting shall also be convened by the International Committee of the Red Cross at any time at the request of one third of the High Contracting Parties.

2. The depositary shall convene a conference of the High Contracting Parties and the Parties to the Conventions to consider amendments proposed by the meeting of technical experts if, after that meeting, the International Committee of the Red Cross or one third of the High Contracting Parties so request.

3. Amendments to Annex I may be adopted at such a

conference by a two-thirds majority of the High Contracting Parties present and voting.

4. The depositary shall communicate any amendment so adopted to the High Contracting Parties and to the Parties to the Conventions. The amendment shall be considered to have been accepted at the end of a period of one year after it has been so communicated, unless within that period a declaration of non-acceptance of the amendment has been communicated to the depositary by not less than one third of the High Contracting Parties.

5. An amendment considered to have been accepted in accordance with paragraph 4 shall enter into force three months after its acceptance for all High Contracting Parties other than those which have made a declaration of non-acceptance in accordance with that paragraph. Any Party making such a declaration may at any time withdraw it and the amendment shall then enter into force for that Party three months thereafter.

6. The depositary shall notify the High Contracting Parties and the Parties to the Conventions of the entry into force of any amendment, of the Parties bound thereby, of the date of its entry into force in relation to each Party, of declarations of non-acceptance made in accordance with paragraph 4, and of withdrawals of such declarations.

Article 99. Denunciation. 1. In case a High Contracting Party should denounce this Protocol, the denunciation shall only take effect one year after receipt of the instrument of denunciation. If, however, on the expiry of that year the denouncing Party is engaged in one of the situations referred to in Article I, the denunciation shall not take effect before the end of the armed conflict or occupation and not, in any case, before operations connected with the final release, repatriation or re-establishment of the persons protected by the Convention or this Protocol have been terminated.

2. The denunciation shall be notified in writing to the depositary, which shall transmit it to all the High Contracting Parties.

3. The denunciation shall have effect only in respect of the denouncing Party.

4. Any denunciation under paragraph 1 shall not affect the obligations already incurred, by reason of the armed conflict, under this Protocol by such denouncing Party in respect of any act committed before this denunciation becomes effective.

Article 100. Notifications. The depositary shall inform the High Contracting Parties as well as the Parties to the Conventions, whether or not they are signatories of this Protocol, of:

(a) signatures affixed to this Protocol and the deposit of instruments of ratification and accession under Articles 93 and 94;

(b) the date of entry into force of this Protocol under Article 95;

(c) communications and declarations received under Articles 84, 90 and 97;

(d) declarations received under Article 96, paragraph 3, which shall be communicated by the quickest methods; and

(e) denunciations under Article 99.

Article 101. Registration. 1. After its entry into force, this Protocol shall be transmitted by the depositary to the Secretariat of the United Nations for registration and publication, in accordance with Article 102 of the Charter of the United Nations.

2. The depositary shall also inform the Secretariat of the

United Nations of all ratifications, accessions and denunciations received by it with respect to this Protocol.

Article 102. Authentic texts. The original of this Protocol, of which the Arabic, Chinese, English, French, Russian and Spanish texts are equally authentic, shall be deposited with the depositary, which shall transmit certified true copies thereof to all the Parties to the Conventions.

Annex I to Protocol I
Regulations Concerning Identification

Chapter I
Identity Cards

Article 1. Identity Card for Permanent Civilian Medical and Religious Personnel. 1. The identity card for permanent civilian medical and religious personnel referred to in Article 18, paragraph 3, of the Protocol should:

(a) bear the distinctive emblem and be of such size that it can be carried in the pocket;

(b) be as durable as practicable;

(c) be worded in the national or official language (and may in addition be worded in other languages);

(d) mention the name, the date of birth (or, if that date is not available, the age at the time of issue) and the identity number, if any, of the holder;

(e) state in what capacity the holder is entitled to the protection of the Conventions and of the Protocol;

(f) bear the photograph of the holder as well as his signature or his thumbprint, or both;

(g) bear the stamp and signature of the competent authority;

(h) state the date of issue and date of expiry of the card.

2. The identity card shall be uniform throughout the territory of each High Contracting Party and, as far as possible, of the same type for all Parties to the conflict. The Parties to the conflict may be guided by [a] single-language model . . . At the outbreak of hostilities, they shall transmit to each other a specimen of the model they are using. The identity card shall be made out, if possible, in duplicate, one copy being kept by the issuing authority, which should maintain control of the cards which it has issued.

3. In no circumstances may permanent civilian medical and religious personnel by deprived of their identity cards. In the event of the loss of a card, they shall be entitled to obtain a duplicate copy.

Article 2. Identity Card for Temporary Civilian Medical and Religious Personnel. 1. The identity card for temporary civilian medical and religious personnel should, whenever possible, be similar to that provided for in Article 1 of these Regulations.

2. When circumstances preclude the provision to temporary civilian medical and religious personnel of identity cards similar to those described in Article 1 of these Regulations, the said personnel may be provided with a certificate signed by the competent authority certifying that the person to whom it is issued is assigned to duty as temporary personnel and stating, if possible, the duration of such assignment and his right to wear the distinctive emblem. The certificate should mention the holder's name and date of birth (or if that date is not available, his age at the time when the certificate was issued), his function and identity number, if any. It shall bear his signature or his thumbprint, or both. . .

Chapter II
The Distinctive Emblem

Article 3. Shape and Nature. 1. The distinctive emblem (red on a white ground) shall be as large as appropriate under the circumstances [in the] shapes of the cross, the crescent or the lion and sun. . . .

2. At night or when visibility is reduced, the distinctive emblem may be lighted or illuminated; it may also be made of materials rendering it recognizable by technical means of detection.

Article 4. Use. 1. The distinctive emblem shall, whenever possible, be displayed on a flat surface or on flags visible from as many directions and from as far away as possible.

2. Subject to the instructions of the competent authority, medical and religious personnel carrying out their duties in the battle area shall, as far as possible, wear headgear and clothing bearing the distinctive emblem.

Chapter III
Distinctive Signals

Article 5. Optional Use. 1. Subject to the provisions of Article 6 of these Regulations, the signals specified in this Chapter for exclusive use by medical units and transports shall not be used for any other purpose. The use of all signals referred to in this Chapter is optional.

2. Temporary medical aircraft which cannot, either for lack of time or because of their characteristics, be marked with the distinctive emblem, may use the distinctive signals authorized in this Chapter. The best method of effective identification are recognition of medical aircraft is, however, the use of a visual signal, either the distinctive emblem or the light signal specified in Article 6, or both, supplemented by the other signals referred to in Articles 7 and 8 of these Regulations.

Article 6. Light Signal. 1. The light signal, consisting of a flashing blue light, is established for the use of medical aircraft to signal their identity. No other aircraft shall use this signal. The recommended blue colour is obtained by using, as trichromatic co-ordinates:

green boundary—$y = 0.065 + 0.805x$
white boundary—$y = 0.400 - x$
purple boundary—$x = 0.133 + 0.600y$

The recommended flashing rate of the blue light is between 60 and 100 flashes per minute.

2. Medical aircraft should be equipped with such lights as may be necessary to make the light signal visible in as many directions as possible.

3. In the absence of a special agreement between the Parties to the conflict reserving the use of flashing blue lights for the identification of medical vehicles and ships and craft, the use of such signals for other vehicles or ships is not prohibited.

Article 7. Radio Signal. 1. The radio signal shall consist of a radiotelephonic or radiotelegraphic message preceded by a distinctive priority signal to be designated and approved by a World Administrative Radio Conference of the International Telecommunication Union. It shall be transmitted three times before the call sign of the medical transport involved. This message shall be transmitted in English at appropriate intervals on a frequency or frequencies specified pursuant to paragraph 3. The use of the priority signal shall be restricted exclusively to medical units and transports.

2. The radio message preceded by the distinctive priority signal mentioned in paragraph 1 shall convey the following data:

(a) call sign of the medical transport;
(b) position of the medical transport;
(c) number and type of medical transports;
(d) intended route;
(e) estimated time en route and of departure and arrival, as appropriate;
(f) any other information such as flight altitude, radio frequencies guarded, languages and secondary surveillance, radar modes and codes.

3. In order to facilitate the communications referred to in paragraphs 1 and 2, as well as the communications referred to in Articles 22, 23, 25, 26, 27, 28, 29, 30 and 31 of the Protocol, the High Contracting Parties, the Parties to a conflict, or one of the Parties to a conflict, acting in agreement or alone, may designate, in accordance with the Table of Frequency Allocations in the Radio Regulations annexed to the International Telecommunication Convention, and publish selected national frequencies to be used by them for such communications. These frequencies shall be notified to the International Telecommunication Union in accordance with procedures to be approved by a World Administrative Radio Conference.

Article 8. Electronic Identification. 1. The Secondary Surveillance Radar (SSR) system, as specified in Annex 10 to the Chicago Convention on International Civil Aviation of 7 December 1944, as amended from time to time, may be used to identify and to follow the course of medical aircraft. The SSR mode and code to be reserved for the exclusive use of medical aircraft shall be established by the High Contracting Parties, the Parties to a conflict, or one of the Parties to a conflict, acting in agreement or alone, in accordance with procedures to be recommended by the International Civil Aviation Organization.

2. Parties to a conflict may, by special agreement between them, establish for their use a similar electronic system for the identification of medical vehicles, and medical ships and craft.

Chapter IV
Communications

Article 9. Radiocommunications. The priority signal provided for in Article 7 of these Regulations may precede appropriate radiocommunications by medical units and transports in the application of the procedures carried out under Articles 22, 23, 25, 26, 27, 28, 29, 30 and 31 of the Protocol.

Article 10. Use of International Codes. Medical units and transports may also use the codes and signals laid down by the International Telecommunication Union, the International Civil Aviation Organization and the Inter-Governmental Maritime Consultative Organization. These codes and signals shall be used in accordance with the standards, practices and procedures established by these Organizations.

Article 11. Other Means of Communication. When two-way radiocommunication is not possible, the signals provided for the International Code of Signals adopted by the Inter-Governmental Maritime Consultative Organization or in the appropriate Annex to the Chicago Convention on International Civil Aviation of 7 December 1944, as amended from time to time, may be used.

Article 12. Flight plans. The agreements and notifications relating to flight plans provided for in Article 29 of the Protocol shall as far as possible be formulated in accordance with procedures laid down by the International Civil Aviation Organization.

Article 13. Signals and Procedures for the Interception of Medical Aircraft. If an intercepting aircraft is used to verify the identity of a medical aircraft in flight or to require it to land in accordance with Articles 30 and 31 of the Protocol, the standard visual and radio interception procedures prescribed by Annex 2 to the Chicago Convention on International Civil Aviation of 7 December 1944, as amended from time to time, should be used by the intercepting and the medical aircraft.

Chapter V
Civil Defence

Article 14. Identity card. 1. The identity card of the civil defence personnel provided for in Article 66, paragraph 3, of the Protocol is governed by the relevant provisions of Article 1 of these Regulations. . . .

3. If civil defence personnel are permitted to carry light individual weapons, an entry to that effect should be made on the card mentioned.

Article 15. International Distinctive Sign. 1. The international distinctive sign of civil defence provided for in Article 66, paragraph 4, of the Protocol is an equilateral blue triangle on an orange ground. . . .

2. It is recommended that:
(a) if the blue triangle is on a flag or armlet or tabard, the ground to the triangle be the orange flag, armlet or tabard;
(b) one of the angles of the triangle be pointed vertically upwards;
(c) no angle of the triangle touch the edge of the orange ground.

3. The international distinctive sign shall be as large as appropriate under the circumstances. The distinctive sign shall, whenever possible, be displayed on flat surfaces or on flags visible from as many directions and from as far away as possible. Subject to the instructions of the competent authority, civil defence personnel shall, as far as possible, wear headgear and clothing bearing the international distinctive sign. At night or when visibility is reduced, the sign may be lighted or illuminated; it may also be made of materials rendering it recognizable by technical means of detection.

Chapter VI
Works and Installations Containing Dangerous Forces

Article 16. International Special Sign. 1. The international special sign for works and installations containing dangerous forces, as provided for in Article 56, paragraph 7, of the Protocol, shall be a group of three bright orange circles of equal size, placed on the same axis, the distance between each circle being one radius . . .

2. The sign shall be as large as appropriate under the circumstances. When displayed over an extended surface it may be repeated as often as appropriate under the circumstances. It shall, whenever possible, be displayed on flat surfaces or on flags so as to be visible from as many directions and from as far away as possible.

3. On a flag, the distance between the outer limits of the sign and the adjacent sides of the flag shall be one radius of a circle. The flag shall be rectangular and shall have a white ground.

4. At night or when visibility is reduced, the sign may be lighted or illuminated. It may also be made of materials rendering it recognizable by technical means of detection . . .

[Annex II presents sample figures of identity cards for journalists.]

GENEVA CONVENTIONS: PROTOCOL II, ADDITIONAL TO THE GENEVA CONVENTIONS OF 12 AUGUST 1949, RELATING TO THE PROTECTION OF VICTIMS OF NON-INTERNATIONAL ARMED CONFLICTS (1977).

The protocol revises and supplements the Geneva Conventions of 12 August 1949, providing protection for victims of non-international armed conflicts such as civil wars, which had not been mentioned in the 1949 conventions. The broadened material and personal fields of application are set out in articles 1 and 2 of the protocol.

The protocol was prepared by the Diplomatic Conference on the Reaffirmation and Development of International Humanitarian Law, convened in 1974, 1975, 1976, and 1977 by the Swiss Federal Council with the cooperation of the International Committee of the Red Cross. It was adopted by the conference on 8 June 1977 and entered into force on 7 December 1978. The text (UN Doc. A/32/144, annex II) is as follows:

The High Contracting Parties,

Recalling that the humanitarian principles enshrined in Article 3 common to the Geneva Conventions of 12 August 1949, constitute the foundation of respect for the human person in cases of armed conflict not of an international character,

Recalling furthermore that international instruments relating to human rights offer a basic protection to the human person,

Emphasizing the need to ensure a better protection for the victims of those armed conflicts,

Recalling that, in cases not covered by the law in force, the human person remains under the protection of the principles of humanity and the dictates of the public conscience,

Have agreed on the following:

Part I
Scope of This Protocol

Article 1. Material Field of Application. 1. This Protocol, which develops and supplements Article 3 common to the Geneva Conventions of 12 August 1949 without modifying its existing conditions of application, shall apply to all armed conflicts which are not covered by Article 1 of the Protocol Additional to the Geneva Conventions of 12 August 1949, and relating to the Protection of Victims of International Armed Conflicts (Protocol I) and which take place in the territory of a High Contracting Party between its armed forces and dissident armed forces or other organized armed groups which, under responsible command, exercise such control over a part of its territory as to enable them to carry out sustained and concerted military operations and to implement this Protocol.

2. This Protocol shall not apply to situations of internal disturbances and tensions, such as riots, isolated and sporadic acts of violence and other acts of a similar nature, as not being armed conflicts.

Article 2. Personal Field of Application. 1. This Protocol shall be applied without any adverse distinction founded on race, colour, sex, language, religion or belief, political or other opinion, national or social origin, wealth, birth or other status, or on any other similar criteria (hereinafter referred to as "adverse distinction") to all persons affected by an armed conflict as defined in Article 1.

2. At the end of the armed conflict, all the persons who have been deprived of their liberty or whose liberty has been restricted for reasons related to such conflict, as well as those deprived of their liberty or whose liberty is restricted after the conflict for the same reasons, shall enjoy the protection of Articles 5 and 6 until the end of such deprivation or restriction of liberty.

Article 3. Non-intervention. 1. Nothing in this Protocol shall be invoked for the purpose of affecting the sovereignty of a State or the responsibility of the government, by all legitimate means, to maintain or re-establish law and order in the State or to defend the national unity and territorial integrity of the State.

2. Nothing in this Protocol shall be invoked as a justification for intervening, directly or indirectly, for any reason whatever, in the armed conflict or in the internal or external affairs of the High Contracting Party in the territory of which that conflict occurs.

Part II
Humane Treatment

Article 4. Fundamental Guarantees. 1. All persons who do not take a direct part or who have ceased to take part in hostilities, whether or not their liberty has been restricted, are entitled to respect for their person, honour and convictions and religious practices. They shall in all circumstances by treated humanely, without any adverse distinction. It it prohibited to order that there shall be no survivors.

2. Without prejudice to the generality of the foregoing, the following acts against the persons referred to in paragraph 1 are and shall remain prohibited at any time and in any place whatsoever:

(a) violence to the life, health and physical or mental well-being of persons, in particular murder as well as cruel treatment such as torture, mutilation or any form of corporal punishment;

(b) collective punishments;

(c) taking of hostages;

(d) acts of terrorism;

(e) outrages upon personal dignity, in particular humiliating and degrading treatment, rage, enforced prostitution and any form of indecent assault;

(f) slavery and the slave trade in all their forms;

(g) pillage;

(h) threats to commit any of the foregoing acts.

3. Children shall be provided with the care and aid they require, and in particular:

(a) they shall receive an education, including religious and moral education, in keeping with the wishes of their parents, or in the absence of parents, of those responsible for their care;

(b) all appropriate steps shall be taken to facilitate the reunion of families temporarily separated;

(c) children who have not attained the age of fifteen years shall neither be recruited in the armed forces or groups nor allowed to take part in hostilities;

(d) the special protection provided by this Article to children who have not attained the age of fifteen years shall remain applicable to them if they take a direct part in hostilities despite the provisions of subparagraph (c) and are captured;

(e) measures shall be taken, if necessary, and whenever possible with the consent of their parents or persons who by law or custom are primarily responsible for their care, to remove children temporarily from the area in which hostilities are taking place to a safer area within the country and ensure that they are accompanied by persons responsible for their safety and well-being.

Article 5. Persons whose Liberty has been Restricted. 1. In addition to the provisions of Article 4 the following provisions shall be respected as a minimum with regard to persons deprived of their liberty for reasons related to the armed conflict, whether they are interned or detained:

(a) the wounded and the sick shall be treated in accordance with Article 7;

(b) the persons referred to in this paragraph shall, to the same extent as the local civilian population, be provided with food and drinking water and be afforded safeguards as regards health and hygiene and protection against the rigours of the climate and the dangers of the armed conflict;

(c) they shall be allowed to receive individual or collective relief;

(d) they shall be allowed to practise their religion and, if requested and appropriate, to receive spiritual assistance from persons, such as chaplains, performing religious functions;

(e) they shall, if made to work, have the benefit of working conditions and safeguards similar to those enjoyed by the local civilian population.

2. Those who are responsible for the internment or detention of the persons referred to in paragraph 1 shall also, within the limits of their capabilities, respect the following provisions relating to such persons:

(a) except when men and women of a family are accommodated together, women shall be held in quarters separated from those of men and shall be under the immediate supervision of women;

(b) they shall be allowed to send and receive letters and cards, the number of which may be limited by competent authority if it deems necessary;

(c) places of internment and detention shall not be located close to the combat zone. The persons referred to in paragraph 1 shall be evacuated when the places where they are interned or detained become particularly exposed to danger arising out of the armed conflict, if their evacuation can be carried out under adequate conditions of safety;

(d) they shall have the benefit of medical examinations;

(e) their physical or mental health and integrity shall not be endangered by any unjustified act or omission. Accordingly, it is prohibited to subject the persons described in this Article to any medical procedure which is not indicated by the state of health of the person concerned, and which is not consistent with the generally accepted medical standards applied to free persons under similar medical circumstances.

3. Persons who are not covered by paragraph 1 but whose liberty has been restricted in any way whatsoever for reasons related to the armed conflict shall be treated humanely in accordance with Article 4 and with paragraphs 1 (a), (c) and (d), and 2 (b) of this Article.

4. If it is decided to release persons deprived of their liberty, necessary measures to ensure their safety shall be taken by those so deciding.

Article 6. Penal Prosecutions. 1. This Article applies to the prosecution and punishment of criminal offences related to the armed conflict.

2. No sentence shall be passed and no penalty shall be executed on a person found guilty of an offence except pursuant to a conviction pronounced by a court offering the essential guarantees of independence and impartiality. In particular:

(a) the procedure shall provide for an accused to be informed without delay of the particulars of the offence alleged against him and shall afford the accused before and during his trial all necessary rights and means of defence;

(b) no one shall be convicted of an offence except on the basis of individual penal responsibility;

(c) no one shall be held guilty of any criminal offence on account of any act or omission which did not constitute a criminal offence, under the law, at the time when it was committed; nor shall a heavier penalty be imposed than that which was applicable at the time when the criminal offence was committed; if, after the commission of the offence, provision is made by law for the imposition of a lighter penalty, the offender shall benefit thereby;

(d) anyone charged with an offence is presumed innocent until proved guilty according to law;

(e) anyone charged with an offence shall have the right to be tried in his presence;

(f) no one shall be compelled to testify against himself or to confess guilt.

3. A convicted person shall be advised on conviction of his judicial and other remedies and of the time-limits within which they may be exercised.

4. The death penalty shall not be pronounced on persons who were under the age of eighteen years at the time of the offence and shall not be carried out on pregnant women or mothers of young children.

5. At the end of hostilities, the authorities in power shall endeavour to grant the broadest possible amnesty to persons who have participated in the armed conflict, or those deprived of their liberty for reasons related to the armed conflict, whether they are interned or detained.

Part III
Wounded, Sick and Shipwrecked

Article 7. Protection and Care. 1. All the wounded, sick and shipwrecked, whether or not they have taken part in the armed conflict, shall be respected and protected.

2. In all circumstances they shall be treated humanely and shall receive to the fullest extent practicable and with the least possible delay, the medical care and attention required by their condition. There shall be no distinction among them founded on any grounds other than medical ones.

Article 8. Search. Whenever circumstances permit and particularly after an engagement, all possible measures shall be taken, without delay, to search for and collect the wounded, sick and shipwrecked, to protect them against pillage and ill-treatment, to ensure their adequate care,

G

and to search for the dead, prevent their being despoiled, and decently dispose of them.

Article 9. Protection of Medical and Religious Personnel. 1. Medical and religious personnel shall be respected and protected and shall be granted all available help for the performance of their duties. They shall not be compelled to carry out tasks which are not compatible with their humanitarian mission.

2. In the performance of their duties medical personnel may not be required to give priority to any person except on medical grounds.

Article 10. General Protection of Medical Duties. 1. Under no circumstances shall any person be punished for having carried out medical activities compatible with medical ethics, regardless of the person benefiting therefrom.

2. Persons engaged in medical activities shall neither be compelled to perform acts or to carry out work contrary to, nor be compelled to refrain from acts required by, the rules of medical ethics or other rules designed for the benefit of the wounded and sick, or this Protocol.

3. The professional obligations of persons engaged in medical activities regarding information which they may acquire concerning the wounded and sick under their care shall, subject to national law, be respected.

4. Subject to national law, no person engaged in medical activities may be penalized in any way for refusing or failing to give information concerning the wounded and sick who are, or who have been, under his care.

Article 11. Protection of Medical Units and Transports. 1. Medical units and transports shall be respected and protected at all times and shall not be the object of attack.

2. The protection to which medical units and transports are entitled shall not cease unless they are used to commit hostile acts, outside their humanitarian function. Protection may, however, cease only after a warning has been given setting, whenever appropriate, a reasonable time-limit, and after such warning has remained unheeded.

Article 12. The Distinctive Emblem. Under the direction of the competent authority concerned, the distinctive emblem of the red cross, red crescent or red lion and sun on a white ground shall be displayed by medical and religious personnel and medical units, and on medical transports. It shall be respected in all circumstances. It shall not be used improperly.

Part IV
Civilian Population

Article 13. Protection of the Civilian Population. 1. The civilian population and individual civilians shall enjoy general protection against the dangers arising from military operations. To give effect to this protection, the following rules shall be observed in all circumstances.

2. The civilian population as such, as well as individual civilians, shall not be the object of attack. Acts or threats of violence the primary purpose of which is to spread terror among the civilian population are prohibited.

3. Civilians shall enjoy the protection afforded by this part, unless and for such time as they take a direct part in hostilities.

Article 14. Protection of Objects Indispensable to the Survival of the Civilian Population. Starvation of civilians as a method of combat is prohibited. It is therefore prohibited to attack, destroy, remove or render useless, for that purpose, objects indispensable to the survival of the civilian population such as food-stuffs, agricultural areas for the production of food-stuffs, crops, livestock, drinking water installations and supplies and irrigation works.

Article 15. Protection of Works and Installations containing Dangerous Forces. Works or installations containing dangerous forces, namely dams, dykes and nuclear electrical generating stations, shall not be made the object of attack, even where these objects are military objectives, if such attack may cause the release of dangerous forces and consequent severe losses among the civilian population.

Article 16. Protection of Cultural Objects and of Places of Worship. Without prejudice to the provisions of the Hague Convention for the Protection of Cultural Property in the Event of Armed Conflict of 14 May 1954, it is prohibited to commit any acts of hostility directed against historic monuments, works of art or places of worship which constitute the cultural or spiritual heritage of peoples, and to use them in support of the military effort.

Article 17. Prohibition of Forced Movement of Civilians. 1. The displacement of the civilian population shall not be ordered for reasons related to the conflict unless the security of the civilians involved or imperative military reasons so demand. Should such displacements have to be carried out, all possible measures shall be taken in order that the civilian population may be received under satisfactory conditions of shelter, hygiene, health, safety and nutrition.

2. Civilians shall not be compelled to leave their own territory for reasons connected with the conflict.

Article 18. Relief Societies and Relief Actions. 1. Relief societies located in the territory of the High Contracting Party, such as Red Cross (Red Crescent, Red Lion and Sun) organizations, may offer their services for the performance of their traditional functions in relation to the victims of the armed conflict. The civilian population may, even on its own initiative, offer to collect and care for the wounded, sick and shipwrecked.

2. If the civilian population is suffering undue hardship owing to a lack of the supplies essential for its survival, such as food-stuffs and medical supplies, relief actions for the civilian population which are of an exclusively humanitarian and impartial nature and which are conducted without any adverse distinction shall be undertaken subject to the consent of the High Contracting Party concerned.

Part V
Final Provisions

Article 19. Dissemination. This Protocol shall be disseminated as widely as possible.

Article 20. Signature. This Protocol shall be open for signature by the Parties to the Conventions six months after the signing of the Final Act and will remain open for a period of twelve months.

Article 21. Ratification. This Protocol shall be ratified as soon as possible. The instruments of ratification shall be deposited with the Swiss Federal Council, depositary of the Conventions.

Article 22. Accession. This Protocol shall be open for accession by any Party to the Conventions which has not signed it. The instruments of accession shall be deposited with the depositary.

Article 23. Entry into Force. 1. This Protocol shall enter into force six months after two instruments of ratification and accession have been deposited.

2. For each Party to the Conventions thereafter ratifying or acceding to this Protocol, it shall enter into force six

months after the deposit by such Party of its instrument of ratification or accession.

Article 24. Amendment. 1. Any High Contracting Party may propose amendments to this Protocol. The text of any proposed amendment shall be communicated to the depositary which shall decide, after consultation with all the High Contracting Parties and the International Committee of the Red Cross, whether a conference should be convened to consider the proposed amendment.

2. The depositary shall invite to that conference all the High Contracting Parties as well as the Parties to the Conventions, whether or not they are signatories of this Protocol.

Article 25. Denunciation. 1. In case a High Contracting Party should denounce this Protocol, the denunciation shall only take effect six months after receipt of the instrument of denunciation. If, however, on the expiry of six months, the denouncing Party is engaged in the situation referred to in Article 1, the denunciation shall not take effect before the end of the armed conflict. Persons who have been deprived of liberty, or whose liberty has been restricted, for reasons related to the conflict shall nevertheless continue to benefit from the provisions of this Protocol until their final release.

2. The denunciation shall be notified in writing to the depositary, which shall transmit it to all the High Contracting Parties.

Article 26. Notifications. The depositary shall inform the High Contracting Parties as well as the Parties to the Conventions, whether or not they are signatories of this Protocol, of:

(a) signatures affixed to this Protocol and the deposit of instruments of ratification and accession under Articles 21 and 22;

(b) the date of entry into force of this Protocol under Article 23; and

(c) communications and declarations received under Article 24.

Article 27. Registration. 1. After its entry into force, this Protocol shall be transmitted by the depositary to the Secretariat of the United Nations for registration and publication, in accordance with Article 102 of the Charter of the United Nations.

2. The depositary shall also inform the Secretariat of the United Nations of all ratifications, accessions and denunciations received by it with respect to this Protocol.

Article 28. Authentic Texts. The original of this Protocol, of which the Arabic, Chinese, English, French, Russian and Spanish texts are equally authentic shall be deposited with the depositary, which shall transmit true copies thereof to all the Parties to the Conventions.

GENEVA DECLARATION ON PALESTINE. The International Conference on the Question of Palestine was held at the United Nations Office in Geneva from 29 August to 7 September 1983, in conformity with decisions of the UN General Assembly (resolutions 36/120 C of 10 December 1981, ES-7/7 of 10 August 1982, and 37/86 C of 10 December 1982) and with the subsequent recommendations of the Preparatory Committee.

Representation at the conference included 111 States, Namibia (represented by the United Nations council for Namibia); four national liberation movements, including the Palestine Liberation Organization; eight United Nations bodies and programs; five United Nations committees and commissions; eight intergovernmental organizations; and 104 nongovernmental organizations.

The Geneva Declaration on Palestine, adopted by the conference by acclamation on 7 September 1983, reads as follows:

1. The Conference, having thoroughly considered the question of Palestine in all its aspects, expresses the grave concern of all nations and peoples regarding the international tension that has persisted for several decades in the Middle East, the principal cause of which is the denial by Israel, and those supporting its expansionist policies, of the inalienable legitimate rights of the Palestinian people. The Conference reaffirms and stresses that a just solution of the question of Palestine, the core of the problem, is the crucial element in a comprehensive, just and lasting political settlement in the Middle East.

2. The Conference recognizes that, as one of the most acute and complex problems of our time, the question of Palestine—inherited by the United Nations at the time of its establishment—requires a comprehensive, just and lasting political settlement. This settlement must be based on the implementation of the relevant United Nations resolutions concerning the question of Palestine and the attainment of the legitimate, inalienable rights of the Palestinian people, including the right to self-determination and the right to the establishment of its own independent State in Palestine and should also be based on the provision by the Security Council of guarantees for peace and security among all States in the region, including the independent Palestinian State, within secure and internationally recognized boundaries. The Conference is convinced that the attainment by the Palestinian people of their inalienable rights, as defined by General Assembly resolution 3236 (XXIX) of 22 November 1974, will contribute substantially to the achievement of peace and stability in the Middle East.

3. The Conference considers the role of the United Nations in the achievement of a comprehensive, just and lasting peace in the Middle East to be essential and paramount. It emphasizes the need for respect for, and applications of the provisions of the Charter of the United Nations, the resolutions of the United Nations relevant to the question of Palestine and the observance of the principles of international law.

4. The Conference considers that the various proposals, consistent with the principles of international law, which have been presented on this question, such as the Arab peace plan adopted unanimously at the twelfth Arab Summit Conference held at Fez, Morocco, in September 1982, should serve as guidelines for concerted international effort to resolve the question of Palestine. These guidelines include the following:

(a) The attainment by the Palestinian people of its legitimate inalienable rights, including the right to return, the right to self-determination and the right to establish its own independent State in Palestine;

(b) The right of the Palestine Liberation Organization, the representative of the Palestinian people, to participate on an equal footing with other parties in all efforts, deliberations and conferences on the Middle East;

(c) The need to put an end to Israel's occupation of the Arab territories, in accordance with the principle of the inadmissibility of the acquisition of territory by force, and, consequently, the need to secure Israeli withdrawal from the territories occupied since 1967, including Jerusalem;

(d) The need to oppose and reject such Israeli policies and practices in the occupied territories, including Jerusalem, and any *de facto* situation created by Israel as are contrary to international law and relevant United Nations resolutions, particularly the establishment of settlements, as these policies and practices constitute major obstacles to the achievement of peace in the Middle East;

(e) The need to reaffirm as null and void all legislative and administrative measures and actions taken by Israel, the occupying Power, which have altered or purported to alter the character and status of the Holy City of Jerusalem, including the expropriation of land and property situated thereon, and in particular the so-called "Basic Law" on Jerusalem and the proclamation of Jerusalem as the capital of Israel;

(f) The right of all States in the region to existence within secure and internationally recognized boundaries, with justice and security for all the people, the *sine qua non* of which is the recognition and attainment of the legitimate, inalienable rights of the Palestinian people as stated in paragraph (a) above.

5. In order to give effect to these guidelines, the Conference considers it essential that an international peace conference on the Middle East be convened on the basis of the principles of the Charter of the United Nations and the relevant resolutions of the United Nations, with the aim of achieving a comprehensive, just and lasting solution to the Arab-Israeli conflict, an essential element of which would be the establishment of an independent Palestinian State in Palestine. This peace conference should be convened under the auspices of the United Nations, with the participation of all parties to the Arab-Israeli conflict, including the Palestine Liberation Organization, as well as the United States of America, the Union of Soviet Socialist Republics, and other concerned States, on an equal footing. In this context the Security Council has a primary responsibility to create appropriate institutional arrangements on the basis of relevant United Nations resolutions in order to guarantee and to carry out the accords of the international peace conference.

6. The International Conference on the Question of Palestine emphasizes the importance of the time factor in achieving a just solution to the problem of Palestine. The Conference is convinced that partial solutions are inadequate and delays in seeking a comprehensive solution do not eliminate tensions in the region.

SEE ALSO *Committee on the Exercise of the Inalienable Rights of the Palestinian People; Israel: Application of the Fourth Geneva Convention to the Territories Occupied since 1967; Israel: Detention and Deportation of Palestinians; Israel: Harassment of Educational Institutions in Occupied Palestinian Territory; Palestinian People's Rights.*

GENOCIDE. In the first multilateral human rights treaty adopted and opened for ratification or accession by the UN General Assembly, the CONVENTION ON THE PREVENTION AND PUNISHMENT OF THE CRIME OF GENOCIDE, contracting parties confirm that "genocide" is a crime under international law which they undertake to prevent and punish. Genocide is defined there as meaning

any of the following acts committed with intent to destroy, in whole or in part, a national, ethnical, racial or religious group, as such:
(a) killing members of the group;
(b) causing serious bodily or mental harm to members of the group;
(c) deliberately inflicting on the group conditions of life calculated to bring about its physical destruction in whole or in part;
(d) imposing measures intended to prevent births within the group; and
(e) forcibly transferring children of the group to another group.

In the convention, states parties placed it beyond doubt that genocide (and conspiracy, incitement, and attempts to commit it and complicity in it), even if perpetrated by a government in its own territory against its own citizens, is not a matter essentially within the domestic jurisdiction of States but a matter of international concern. When genocide occurs, any contracting party can call upon the appropriate United Nations organs to intervene.

Under the convention, genocide is a crime whether committed in time of peace or in time of war. Persons committing genocide, or conspiring, inciting, or attempting to commit it, are to be punished, whether they are constitutionally responsible rulers, public officials, or private citizens. Persons charged with this crime are to be tried by a competent tribunal of the State in the territory of which the act was committed or by such international penal tribunals as may have jurisdiction with respect to those contracting parties which will have accepted its jurisdiction.

Although the convention has achieved almost universal acceptance by members of the United Nations, its effectiveness has often been questioned. It is clear that, as long as an international criminal court has not been established, the convention can have only a limited scope. A trial of persons accused of genocide before the courts of the State on whose territory the act was committed is hardly likely to produce a finding of guilt.

Periodically, reports reach the United Nations of actual or potential situations involving genocide in the contemporary world. The COMMISSION ON HUMAN RIGHTS has on several occasions been presented with clear evidence that, in some of these situations, entire groups of persons have been liquidated or threatened with liquidation. In one case, the commission was advised that more than a million persons had died.

A comprehensive study of the prevention and punishment of the crime of genocide was completed in 1978 (UN Doc. E/CN.4/Sub.2/416) by Mr. Nicodeme Ruhashyankiko (Rwanda), a special rapporteur of the SUB-COMMISSION ON PREVENTION OF DISCRIMINATION AND PROTECTION OF MINORITIES. One of the special rapporteur's conclusions was that:

A number of allegations of genocide have been made since the adoption of the 1948 Convention. In the absence of a prompt investigation of these allegations by an impartial body, it has not been possible to determine whether they are well-founded. Either they have given rise to sterile controversy or, because of the political circumstances, nothing further has been heard of them. For these reasons, the Special Rapporteur feels that the Commission on Human Rights should consider the setting up of *ad hoc* committees to inquire into allegations of genocide brought to the knowledge of the Commission by a member State or an international organization and supported by sufficient *prima facie* evidence.

The study concluded with the following recommendation:

. . . since no international criminal court has yet been established, the question of universal punishment should be considered again if it is decided to prepare new international instruments for the prevention and punishment of genocide, since in practice, even if a Government were to commit serious acts of genocide there would be, as there has always been, some doubt as to the possibility of indicting it, unless it were replaced by a régime that would take the necessary legal action. While recognizing the political implications of the application of the principle of universal punishment for the crime of genocide, the Special Rapporteur remains convinced that the adoption of this principle would help to make the Genocide Convention more effective. Moreover, the adoption of the principle should not automatically entail the obligation to prosecute persons guilty of genocide. It would merely be an option that could be used, particularly in the case of Governments, in the light of all the circumstances and of the advisability of taking appropriate action. Moreover, a new international instrument on genocide, establishing the principle of universal jurisdiction, would offer the choice between extradition and the punishment of the crime by the State on whose territory the guilty person was found.

Continuing concern about the question of genocide led the Economic and Social Council, in 1983, to request the sub-commission (resolution 1983/33) to appoint a new special rapporteur to revise and update the study which had been prepared by Mr. Ruhashyankiko. The sub-commission designated one of its members, Mr. Benjamin C. G. Whitaker (United Kingdom of Great Britain and Northern Ireland), as special rapporteur for this purpose. The revised and updated study (UN Doc. E/CN.4/Sub.2/1985/6) was presented to the sub-commission at its 1985 session.

In the study, Mr. Whitaker describes the development of the concept of genocide in the following paragraphs (14–22; 24):

Genocide is the ultimate crime and the gravest violation of human rights it is possible to commit. Consequently, it is difficult to conceive of a heavier responsibility for the international community and the Human Rights bodies of the United Nations than to undertake any effective steps possible to prevent and punish genocide in order to deter its recurrence.

It has rightly been said that those people who do not learn from history, are condemned to repeat it. This belief underpins much of the Human Rights work of the United Nations. In order to prescribe the optimal remedies to prevent future genocide, it can be of positive assistance to diagnose past cases in order to analyse their causation together with such lessons as the international community may learn from the history of these events.

Genocide is a constant threat to peace, and it is essential to exercise the greatest responsibility when discussing a subject so emotive. It is certainly not the intention of this Study in any way to comment on politics or to awaken bitterness or feelings of revenge. The purpose and hope of this Study is exactly the opposite: to deter future violence by strengthening collective international responsibility and remedies. It would undermine this purpose, besides violating historical truth as well as the integrity of United Nations Studies, were anybody guilty of genocide to believe that international concern might be averted or historical records changed because of political or other pressure. If such an attempt were to succeed, that would serve to encourage those in the future who may be contemplating similar crimes. Equally, it is necessary to warn that nothing in these historical events should be used to provide an excuse for further violence or vendettas: this Study is a warning directed against violence. Its object is to deter terrorism or killing of whatever scale, and to encourage understanding and reconciliation. The scrutiny of world opinion and an honest recognition of the truth about painful past events have been the starting-point for a foundation of reconciliation, with, for example, post-war Germany, which will help to make the future more secure for humanity.

Amongst all human rights, the primacy of the right to life is unanimously agreed to be pre-eminent and essential: it is the *sine qua non,* for all other human rights (apart from that to one's posthumous reputation) depend for their potential existence on the preservation of human life. Every right can also only survive as a consequence of the exercise of responsibilities. The right of a person or people not to be killed or avoidably left to die depends upon the reciprocal duty of other people to render protection and help to avert this. The concept of this moral responsibility and interdependence in human society has in recent times received increasing international recognition and affirmation. In cases of famine in other countries, for example, the States parties to the International Covenant on Economic, Social and Cultural Rights in "recognizing the fundamental right of everyone to be free from hunger" have assumed responsibility to take "individually and through international cooperation" the measures required "to ensure an equitable distribution of world food supplies in relation to need".

The core of the right not to starve to death is a corollary of the right not to be killed, concerning which the duty of safeguarding life is recognized to extend not just to the individual's or group's own Government but to the international community as well.

More serious problems arise when the body responsible for threatening and causing death is—or is in complicity with—a State itself. The potential victims in such cases need to turn individually and collectively for protection not to, but from, their own Government. Groups subject to extermination have a right to receive something more helpful than tears and condolences from the rest of the world. Action under the Charter of the United Nations is indeed specifically authorized by the Convention on the Prevention and Protection of the Crime of Genocide, and might as appropriate be directed for example to the introduction of United Nations trusteeship. States have an obligation, besides not to commit genocide, in addition to prevent and punish violations of the crime by others; and in cases of failure in this respect too, the 1948 Convention recognizes that intervention may be justified to prevent or suppress such acts and to punish those responsible "whether they are constitutionally responsible rulers, public officials or private individuals".

The Convention on Genocide was unanimously adopted by the United Nations General Assembly on 9 December 1948, and therefore preceded—albeit by one day—the Universal Declaration of Human Rights itself. While the word "genocide" is a comparatively recent neologism for an old crime, the Convention's preamble notes that "at all periods of history genocide has inflicted great losses on humanity, and being convinced that, in order to liberate mankind from such an odious scourge, international co-operation is required".

Throughout recorded human history, war has been the predominant cause or pretext for massacres of national, ethnic, racial or religious groups. Wars in ancient and classical eras frequently aimed to exterminate if not enslave other peoples. Religious intolerance could also be a predisposing factor: in religious wars of the Middle Ages as well as in places in the Old Testament, some genocide was sanctioned by Holy Writ. The twentieth century equally has seen examples of "total wars" involving the destruction of civilian populations and which the development of nuclear weapons makes an almost inevitable matrix for future major conflicts. In the nuclear era, indeed the logical conclusion of this may be "omnicide".

Genocide, particularly of indigenous peoples, has also often occurred as a consequence of colonialism, with racism and ethnic prejudice commonly being predisposing factors. In some cases occupying forces maintained their authority by the terror of a perpetual threat of massacre. Examples could occur either at home or overseas: the English for example massacred native populations in Ireland, Scotland and Wales in order to deter resistance and to "clear" land for seizure, and the British also almost wholly exterminated the indigenous people when colonizing Tasmania as late as the start of the nineteenth century. Africa, Australasia and the Americas witnessed numerous other examples. The effect of genocide can be achieved in different ways: today, insensitive economic exploitation can threaten the extinction of some surviving indigenous peoples.

But genocide, far from being only a matter of historical study, is an aberration which also is a modern danger to civilization. No stronger evidence that the problem of genocide has—far from receding—grown in contemporary relevance is required than the fact that the gravest documented example of this crime is among the most recent, and furthermore occurred in the so-called developed world. Successive advances in killing-power underline that the need for international action against genocide is now more urgent than ever. It has been estimated that the Nazi holocaust in Europe slaughtered some 6 million Jews, 5 million Protestants, 3 million Catholics and half a million Gypsies. This was the product not of international warfare, but a calculated State political policy of mass murder that has been termed "a structural and systematic destruction of innocent people by a State bureaucratic apparatus". The Nazi intention to destroy particular human nations, races, religions, sexual groups, classes and political opponents as a premeditated plan was manifested before the Second World War. The war later offered the Nazi German leaders an opportunity to extend this policy from their own country to the peoples of occupied Poland, parts of the Soviet Union and elsewhere, with an intention of Germanizing their territories. The "final solution" included (as evidenced at the Nuremberg trial), "delayed-action genocide" aimed at destroying groups' biological future through sterilization, castration, abortion, and the forcible transfer of their children. . . .

The Nazi aberration has unfortunately not been the only case of genocide in the twentieth century. Among other examples which can be cited as qualifying are the German massacre of Hereros in 1904, the Ottoman massacre of Armenians in 1915–16, the Ukrainian pogrom of Jews in 1919, the Tutsi massacre of the Ache Indians prior to 1974, the Khmer Rouge massacre in Kampuchea between 1975 and 1978, and the contemporary Iranian killings of Baha'is. . . .

As regards future progress in the prevention and punishment of genocide, the special rapporteur presents the following suggestions (para. 71–72; 74–77):

The fact remains that although the Convention has been in force since 12 January 1951, any ascertainable effect of it is difficult to quantify, whereas all too much evidence continues to accumulate that acts of genocide are still being committed in various parts of the world. Certainly in its present form, the Convention therefore must be judged to be not enough. Further evolution of international measures against genocide are necessary and indeed overdue.

It is important that the historic momentum of the spirit of international unity against genocide displayed by Nuremberg and the Convention should not be allowed to falter or lapse. Failure to make effective international legal provisions is likely to threaten peace, to drive nations to desperate unilateral measures (such as the abduction of Adolf Eichmann in Argentina to bring him to trial in Israel for genocidal acts of 1961), or to open excuses for the deplorable violence of terrorist reprisals. For too many centuries war and violence have been the standard method of avenging grievances, or of creating new ones. Now in the era of atomic weapons, human society depends for its future survival upon establishing in time alternative international legal means to resolve such disputes peacefully. Despite the problems in doing so, the size of the risk permits little further time for any more delay. . . .

Although a historic impetus of international agreement achieved the unprecedented establishment of the Nuremberg and Tokyo Tribunals, these were open to the accusation that they were set up *ad hoc* to enable victors to pass judgement on vanquished. It would be a preferable concept to have instead an impartial but respected international body with permanent authority. None the less the final Count in the Nuremberg Charter broke new ground by charging defendants with "Crimes against Humanity", a term used to cover the persecution of racial and religious groups and the wholesale exploitation of peoples. Doenitz suggested in his memoirs that the acts the Tribunal had examined were a purely German affair: Germans, he said, should have been allowed to "investigate and then bring to justice those who had been responsible for the inhuman enormities that had taken place". But what some of the international lawyers at Nuremberg hoped was that the trial would be the foundation of a new legal order. They wanted international law to be advanced and to govern the future conduct of nations. Robert Jackson reported to President Truman subsequently that the London agreement, prior to Nuremberg, had for the first time made explicit that:

> "to persecute, oppress, or do violence to individuals or minorities on political, racial, or religious grounds in connection with such a war; or to exterminate, enslave or deport civilian populations is an international crime and that for the commission of such crimes individuals are responsible."

However once the International Military Tribunal at Nuremberg finished its work, there was no international criminal court. President Truman welcomed Biddle's recommendation that the United Nations be invited to draft a code of international criminal law. It has not yet been drafted. As historians of the Nuremberg cases observe, "it is in the broadest sense of political question whether nations prefer to have some objective body of law and an impartial institution to administer it or whether they prefer to settle disputes and fulfil their ambitions by force".

It has equally been suggested that the influence of historical events also caused the character of the Convention to constitute more of a protest against immediate past crimes than to create an effective instrument for the prevention or repression of genocide. Critics have in fact alleged that the Convention represents at best almost a dead letter, and at worst has been perverted into a weapon of political warfare, instead of being an instrument to liberate, unite and reconcile mankind. What should, and can be done?

One basic difficulty is that although the Convention concentrates on punishment of the crime, this is nearly meaningless at the international level in the absence of an International Penal Tribunal. Hence, it is only the Governments of States in the territories of which the crime was committed, that can institute proceedings for its punishment. However, in the case of "domestic" genocides, these are generally committed by or with the complicity of Governments, with the bizarre consequence that the Governments would be required to prosecute themselves. In actual practice, mass murderers are protected by their own Governments, save in exceptional cases, where these Governments have been overthrown. Thus in Equatorial Guinea, Macias was found guilty of a number of crimes, including genocide, and executed. In Kampuchea, however, Pol Pot is still at large, protected by his own army, and presumably also in some measure, by the continued international recognition of his régime.

There exists support for a Supplementary Convention or Protocols to improve the Convention, though consensus would be hard to achieve amongst all Governments. It is possible, and indeed to be hoped, though improvable, that the existence of the Convention may have deterred more genocide from being committed. But as in attitudes to improving United Nations human rights' effectiveness generally, too often respect for State sovereignty, domestic jurisdiction and territorial integrity can, and does, take precedence over the wider human concern for protection against genocide. In these circumstances, there is a need for some new ideas or for institutions, relatively independent of the deliberations of the delegations of member States, such as an International Penal Court, and a High Commissioner for Human Rights, or else for forms of organized action outside the United Nations by, for example, the international non-governmental organizations. The recent United Nations support for the new Convention on Torture (reproduced as an appendix to this study) may afford fresh grounds for optimism, as well as some useful parallels. It is important to be practical and realistic, but also to work hard and without delay in view of the gravity of the subject.

The special rapporteur's proposals call for (1) anticipation of potential genocide through the systematic study of up-to-date information, (2) the setting up of a system to provide an "early warning" of impending genocide, and (3) the establishment of an international body competent to deal with genocide when it occurs. These proposals are elaborated in the following paragraphs (78–87) of the study:

1. Prevention. Punishment after the event does not meet the priority problem of preventing great loss of life. Those personalities who are psychologically prepared to commit genocide are not always likely to be deterred by retribution, at least in this world. Perhaps, the Convention's most conspicuous weakness is that it insufficiently formulates preventive measures. Such international short-term and long-term action would need to relate to different stages in the evolution of a genocidal process—anticipation of its happening; early warning of its commencement; and action to be taken at the outset of or during a genocide itself to stop it.

Intelligent anticipation of potential cases could be based on a data bank of continuously updated information, which might enable remedial, deterrent or averting measures to be planned ahead. Reliable information is the essential oxygen for human rights: this could be facilitated by the development of a United Nations satellite communications network. Comparisons could be made with the lessons, both positive and negative, of previous cases. Experience international conciliators and mediators, from the United Nations and its agencies or other bodies such as the International Committee of the Red Cross, could serve to defuse tension.

H. G. Wells rightly stated that "Human history becomes more and more a race between education and catastrophe". Another highly important area of study is interdisciplinary research (to be co-ordinated perhaps by the United Nations University) into the psychological character and motivation of individuals and groups who commit genocide or racism, or the psychopathic dehumanizing of vulnerable minorities or scapegoats. In all human rights work, it is essential to go beyond condemnation of violations to analysing their causation.

The results of such research could help form one part

of a wide educational programme throughout the world against such aberrations, starting at an early age in schools. Without a strong basis of international public support, even the most perfectly redrafted Convention will be of little value. Conventions and good Governments can give a lead, but the mobilization of public awareness and vigilance is essential to guard against any recurrence of genocide and other crimes against humanity and human rights. There has recently occurred an encouraging change from preoccupation with particular genocides to wider concern for effective measures to deal with the general phenomenon itself.

As a further safeguard, public awareness should be developed internationally to reinforce the individual's responsibility, based on the knowledge that it is illegal to obey a superior order or law that violates human rights. Although some Governments may be reluctant to agree, such a concept has been an honoured tradition in many different parts of the world. Gandhi's and Martin Luther King's ideas on civil disobedience to unjust laws were developments of the earlier thinking of people such as Thoreau, who went to prison rather than acquiesce in the forced return of runaway slaves to their owners. (Thoreau in turn based his philosophy on the ideas of Granville Sharp who in the 1770's resigned from the London War Office rather than authorize arms to put down the American revolution; Sharp's ideas in turn helped to inspire Jefferson and others who drafted the Declaration of Independence.) All these people followed their conscience, at personal danger; the safeguarding of human rights in the final resort will always need to depend upon such integrity and courage.

2. Early Warning. In cases where evidence appears of an impending genocidal conflict, mounting repression, increasing polarization or the first indications of an unexpected case, an effective early warning system could help save several thousands of lives. This requires an efficient co-ordinating network, maintained in a state of permanent readiness, which could possibly also watch for early indications of mass famine and exoduses of refugees in conjunction with bodies such as the Office of the United Nations Disaster Relief Co-ordinator and the International Committee of the Red Cross.

On an early warning alert being received, the steps to be taken could include: the investigation of allegations; activating different organs of the United Nations and related organizations, both directly and through national delegations, and making representations to national Governments and to interregional organizations for active involvement; seeking support of the international press in providing information; enlisting the aid of other media to call public attention to the threat, or actuality, of genocidal massacre; asking relevant racial, communal and religious leaders, in appropriate cases, to intercede, and arranging the immediate involvement of suitable mediators and conciliators at the outset. Finally, there are the possibility of sanctions which could be applied with public support, by means of economic boycotts, the refusal to handle goods to or from offending States, and selective exclusion from participation in international activities and events. Representations would also be made to Governments to enlist their support in the application of sanctions.

3. An International Body to Deal with Genocide. Cogent support has been expressed for the establishment of a new impartial and respected international body whose special concern would be to deal over-all with genocide. Such a body could perhaps be created under the "competent organs" Article VIII of the Convention. Support for such a body has been expressed, *inter alia,* by the Government of Spain. A constructive possible formulation for such a body has been proposed by a non-governmental organization, the Baha'i International:

"We believe that, at the present time, the most effective means of preventing and controlling genocide is through the establishment by the United Nations of a new international body dealing exclusively with genocide and charged with responsibility for considering allegations of genocide, carrying out investigations in connection with those allegations and taking urgent steps to put a stop to genocide wherever it is known to be taking place. Since secrecy is the greatest ally of any Government that seeks to engage in genocide, and international publicity and condemnation the greatest enemy, it might be expected that the opprobrium that would attach to any Government which was identified as a violator of the Convention by a high-level international body of known competence and impartiality would, on its own, act as a deterrent to that Government, quite apart from any action that the international body itself was able to generate. We accordingly suggest that consideration be given to revising the existing Convention by adding to it appropriate provisions for the creation of a Committee on Genocide whose existence would derive directly from the Convention and which would concern itself exclusively with the subject-matter contained in its parent Convention.

"We envisaged that this Committee would concern itself primarily with questions of fact rather than with questions of law. It would, we envisage, hold a 'watching brief' on genocide: it would be the body to which any allegations of genocide were automatically referred and it would be responsible for investigating those allegations. In order to enable it to react effectively in cases where there were strong and reliable indications that genocide was, in fact, taking place, the Committee should, we suggest, be empowered to (a) invite the State party concerned to submit its observations with regard to the allegations of genocide; and (b) if it decided that the situation warranted it, designate one or more of its members to make a confidential inquiry and to report to the Committee urgently. In short, we envisage the Committee being given powers in this regard similar to those proposed for the Torture Committee in the Convention against torture and other cruel, inhuman or degrading treatment or punishment.

"We envisage that the Committee on Genocide, in common with other bodies created under the provisions of international human rights instruments (which it would very closely resemble in membership and procedures), would report annually to the General Assembly, but we suggest that the Committee should also be empowered to bring any situations of urgency to the immediate attention of the Secretary-General of the United Nations. We believe that the advantages of establishing a Committee under the provisions of the Convention would be:

"(a) To remove the subject of genocide as far as possible from the political arena;

"(b) To attract a high-calibre 'independent expert' membership;

"(c) To speed the international response to genocidal situations by obviating the necessity for cases of genocide to proceed through the hierarchical mechanisms of the United Nations human rights system;

"(d) To provide the high-profile, international focus for genocide that is currently lacking.

"We are, of course, aware that any proposed revision of the existing Convention must be requested by a State party and must then win the approval of the United Nations General Assembly and we are fully conscious of the difficulties attendant upon obtaining such approval. Nevertheless, we feel that it is appropriate to consider this course of action, bearing in mind the status of genocide as the major 'crime against humanity', the disturbing fact that genocide persists in the contemporary world, and the urgent need for determined international action to combat it. Failing agreement on the creation of a Committee on Genocide under the provisions of the Convention, we would suggest that a Working Group on Genocide be established under the aegis of the Commission on Human Rights."

4. An International Human Rights Tribunal or Court. Support has been expressed by, *inter alia,* the Government of El Salvador that:

"Regarding the possibility of setting up an international penal tribunal as proposed in article VI of the Convention on the Prevention and Punishment of the Crime of Genocide, the Government of El Salvador considers that, in view of the international importance of this crime, it would be appropriate to set up an international penal court competent to judge this and similar crimes. However, the binding and enforceable character of the decisions of such a court would require to be formally stated in the international instrument establishing it."

The Government of Morocco also suggests "the establishment of a full-scale international court with a prosecutor's office and an investigating arm". The Government of Chad likewise supports the idea of an international penal tribunal and an international body entrusted with carrying out investigations. It might obviate much argument about which massacres technically are, or are not, genocide, if such a Tribunal or Court dealt with all major crimes against humanity.

Other opinion and replies indicate a preference for instituting universality of jurisdiction, or for both proposals to provide a "fail-safe" or double system of safeguard.

The special rapporteur concluded his study by pointing out that "the reforms recommended will, like most things worthwhile in human progress, not be easy. They would, however, be the best living memorial to all the past victims of genocide. To do nothing, by contrast, would be to invite responsibility for helping cause future victims."

The special rapporteur's study was considered and debated by the Sub-Commission on Prevention of Discrimination and Protection of Minorities at its 1985 session. The sub-commission (resolution 1985/9), noting that divergent views had been expressed about the content and proposals of the study, limited itself to recommending "that the United Nations renew its efforts so as to make ratification by States Members of the Convention on the Prevention and Punishment of the Crime of Genocide universal as soon as possible."

GERMANY, EAST. The German Democratic Republic, formerly a country in eastern Europe, had borders with Czechoslovakia, the Federal Republic of Germany, and Poland. Recognized as a sovereign State in 1973, it became a member of the United Nations the same year but lost that privilege as a sovereign nation when it re-united with West Germany in October 1990. Its population is estimated by the UN (1990) to be 16,889,000. A community of Sorbs constitutes its only significant minority; about 100,000 Sorbs live in the counties of Dresden and Cottbus and, for centuries, were oppressed socially, politically, and economically. Languages in common use include German and among the Sorbs, the Sorb language. For those who profess a religious belief, Christianity (Protestant denominations, 53%; Roman Catholics, 8%), is predominant. A large percentage of the population registers its faith as atheism. Literacy is estimated at 99%.

Prior to re-unification with West Germany, the government (1990) took the form of a republic. Deputies to the 400-member *Volkskammer* (parliament) were elected by popular vote and served for terms of five years. The prime minister, representing the party or coalition winning a majority of parliamentary seats, formed a government and presented it to the *Volkskammer* for approval.

In the elections of 18 March 1990—the first multiparty free elections in the country since 1932—the Alliance for Germany—a coalition composed of the Christian Democratic Union, the German Social Union, and the Democratic Awakening—received 48.1% of the vote and took 193 seats in parliament. The Social Democratic Party was second, winning 21.8% of the vote and 87 seats, while the Party of Democratic Socialism (successor to the Communist Party) was third, winning 16.3% of the vote and 65 seats.

At the end of World War II, the Allied Plan for Germany, which called for Germany to be divided into four zones of occupation (American, British, French, and Russian) under a unified control commission in Berlin, and for reparations in kind to be collected from Germany for two years after surrender in order to destroy Germany military power, was implemented by the Potsdam Agreement. Under that agreement, the allies undertook to abolish all German armed forces and all organizations of the National Socialist Party; to abolish Nazi legislation; to punish all German war criminals; to remove all former Nazis from public or semi-public office; to control education in order to eliminate Nazi ideology and to foster democratic ideals; to restore local self-government; to allow and encourage all "democratic political parties"; to introduce representative and elective principles of government into regional, provincial, and state administration; and to establish no central German government "for the time being" but to establish certain German central administrative departments under allied supervision.

Rarely was any agreement honored so consistently in the breach as was the Potsdam Agreement. The work of the Allied Control Council for Germany was first blocked by France, which had not been represented at the Potsdam Conference. The council had not even begun to function when a dispute between the Soviet Union and the western democracies, mainly about the question of reparations, prevented it from taking any action. Thereafter, the eastern and the western powers proceeded to act unilaterally, each placing on the other the blame for failing to put the agreement into operation.

At Potsdam, some parts of Germany were transferred to Poland and others to the Soviet Union. The remainder was divided into four zones, to be occupied by Great Britain, France, the Soviet Union, and the United States, respectively. Berlin was also divided into four zones, each to be occupied by one of the victorious powers.

On 31 May 1948, the western powers merged their zones economically and introduced a separate currency. In retaliation, Soviet authorities blocked all ground access to the western sectors of Berlin. The western powers countered by organizing a gigantic airlift, requiring more than 60,000 men to operate, which flew supplies into the beleaguered city. The blockade continued until 12 May 1949.

On 23 May 1949, the Federal Republic of Germany was proclaimed, with its capital in Bonn. Free multi-party elections were held, and the Christian Democrats headed by Konrad Adenauer won the majority in the Constituent Assembly.

On 7 October of the same year, the Democratic Republic of Germany was proclaimed. It was recognized within the Soviet bloc but not by the western Powers. In 1961, the East German authorities built a fortified wall across Berlin to stop a large-scale exodus of citizens.

Conciliatory talks between the two States began in 1970; and, by 1973, formal relations were established, and both were admitted to the United Nations. Both prospered economically, but East Germany continued to challenge the access of the western powers to West Berlin.

Late in 1989, as East Germany prepared to celebrate its 40th anniversary, more than 13,000 East Germans who had travelled to Hungary either as refugees or as tourists found a way to leave that country and to proceed through Austria to West Germany, where they were warmly welcomed. Soon 8,000 more rushed to Hungary from Romania and 5,000 more from Czechoslovakia, all seeking to enter West Germany. Embarrassed by the mass migration, East Germany's leaders called Hungary's action "a clear violation of legal treaties" and accused West Germany of breaching international law by providing the East Germans with travel documents while they were in Hungary.

However, by the end of September 1989, the urge to leave East Germany was so contagious that the East German authorities were obliged to provide special trains to transport 5,000 refugees who had reached Prague and 800 who had reached Warsaw, through East Germany, to the West German cities of Hof and Helmstadt, respectively. The East German press explained the strange movement as an expulsion of "irresponsible anti-social traitors and criminals."

On 2 October 1989, as many as 5,000 East Germans crossed into Czechoslovakia by car. On 4 October, East German trains transported some 11,000 refugees from Prague to Hof.

On 25 September and 2 October, pro-democracy demonstrations followed evening prayer meetings at Nicholas Church in Leipzig, with more than 10,000 taking part. About the same time, East Germany's first nationwide opposition movement made its presence felt, demanding democratic reforms including the establishment of a multi-party political system.

On 9 November, after more than half a million people had staged a pro-democracy demonstration in East Berlin, the East German government resigned and a reformist, Egon Krenz, succeeded the ailing Erich Honecker. Within hours of the announcement, thousands of jubilant East Germans met at the Berlin wall for an all-night celebration. On 10 November, some 40,000 East Germans poured into West Berlin, and a holiday atmosphere prevailed on both sides.

By the end of 1989, approximately 210,000 East German refugees had made their way into West Germany. Because most of them were young, well-educated and highly skilled, their exodus was expected to have a serious adverse effect on East Germany.

In January 1990, three opposition groups—New Forum, Democratic Awakening, and the Initiative for Peace and Human Rights—formed a coalition to challenge the Communist Party in East Germany's general elections. The coalition, with support from West German Chancellor Helmut Kohl, won 48.1% of the vote, while the Social Democratic Party was second, with 21.8%.

Thus, on 12 April 1990, the East German parliament formally installed that country's first freely elected government, headed by Prime Minister Lothar de Maizière.

At the same time, it issued a statement accepting responsibility and apologizing for the actions of Germans in the past and expressing its wish "to integrate

Germany in a pan-European security system in such a way that our people are guaranteed peace and security."

Excerpts from the statement, as translated by Reuters and published in the *New York Times* of 13 April 1990, are as follows:

We, the first freely-elected parliamentarians of East Germany, admit our responsibility as Germans in East Germany for their history and their future and declare unanimously before the world:

Immeasurable suffering was inflicted on the peoples of the world by Germans during the time of National Socialism. Nationalism and racial madness led to genocide, particularly of the Jews in all European countries, of the people of the Soviet Union, the Polish people and the Gypsy people . . .

Parliament admits joint responsibility on behalf of the people for the humiliation, expulsion and murder of Jewish women, men and children. We feel sad and ashamed and acknowledge this burden of German history.

We ask the Jews of the world to forgive us. We ask the people of Israel to forgive us for the hypocrisy and hostility of official East German policies toward Israel and for the persecution and degradation of Jewish citizens also after 1945 in our country.

We declare our willingness to contribute as much as possible to the healing of mental and physical sufferings of survivors and to provide just compensation for material losses.

The Prague Spring. We are for giving persecuted Jews asylum in East Germany.

We wish to integrate Germany in a pan-European security system in such a way that our people are guaranteed peace and security.

We are aware that the changes in our country would not have been possible without new thinking and restructuring in the Soviet Union.

The East German Volkskammer acknowledges that East Germany shares guilt for the crushing of the Prague Spring of 1968 by Warsaw Pact troops.

Because of angst and faintheartedness, we failed to hinder this violation of international law. . . .

The Parliament of East Germany asks the people of Czechoslovakia to forgive us for the injustice done.

The East German people, through their peaceful revolution in the autumn of 1989, removed the dividing effects of the inhuman inter-German border.

Now the two parts of Germany should grow together and thus promote the creation of a pan-European peace order within the framework of the C.S.C.E. process.

World War II Borders. We declare solemnly once more our unequivocal recognition of the German borders with neighboring states, that resulted from World War II.

The Polish people in particular should know that their right to live within safe borders will not be questioned by territorial claims from us Germans, either now or in the future.

We confirm the inviolability of the Oder-Neisse border with the Republic of Poland as a foundation for the peaceful co-existence of our peoples in a common European house.

This should be confirmed by treaty by a future pan-German parliament.

On 3 October 1990, the German Democratic Republic, formerly known as East Germany, merged with the Federal Republic of Germany, formerly known as West Germany, to form one, re-united nation

GERMANY, WEST. The Federal Republic of Germany is a country in western Europe, on the North Sea. It has borders with Austria, Belgium, Czechoslovakia, Denmark, East Germany, France, Luxembourg, the Netherlands, and Switzerland, and, since re-unification with East Germany, a border with Poland. Under agreements reached by the western powers in Paris in 1954, West Germany attained full independence and sovereignty and became a member of NATO, on 5 May 1955. Under a separate agreement between France and West Germany, a plebescite was held in the Saar territory, which voted to rejoin West Germany. West Germany's population is estimated by the UN (1990) to be 60,332,000; however, it was enlarged by approximately 17 million people when East Germans became part of the Federal Republic. Minorities include the Danish population in Schleswig-Holstein, the Jewish population, and the Sinti and Romany Gypsies. German is the official language and the one in common use; Danish and Romany are used primarily by members of the respective population groups. Christianity is the predominant religion.

The government (1990) took the form of a republic. The president is elected by the entire parliament for a term of five years and serves as head of State. The chancellor, or prime minister, is elected by the lower house of parliament for a similar term and serves as head of government. Parliament includes the upper house, or *Bundesrat,* composed of representatives of the ten *Lander,* or states, and West Berlin; and the lower house, or *Bundestag,* composed of members elected by popular vote. Non-voting representatives of West Berlin participate in the work of both houses. Major political parties include the Christian Democratic Union/Christian Social Union, with 223 of 497 seats in the *Bundestag,* led by Chancellor Helmut Kohl; the Social Democratic Party (186 seats), the Free Democratic Party (46 seats), and the Greens (42 seats).

When, at the end of World War II, the European area known historically as Germany was divided into two zones of occupation, its western portion was converted by its occupying powers—France, the United Kingdom, and the United States of America—into the Federal Republic of Germany; and a program was instituted to return that territory to a constitutional system of government based on respect for human rights.

The Basic Law of the Federal Republic of Germany

was drafted in 1948/49, using as a model the Republic Constitution of Germany of 1919, which had contained the first catalog of basic rights applicable to Germany as a whole but which, unfortunately, had not included measures sufficiently effective to safeguard the free and democratic form of the State in times of crises; and, as an inspiration, the UNIVERSAL DECLARATION OF HUMAN RIGHTS, which had been adopted and proclaimed on 10 December 1948 by the UN General Assembly.

Provisions of the Basic Law relating to human rights and fundamental freedoms were described by the government of the Federal Republic in its third periodic report, presented to the UN HUMAN RIGHTS COMMITTEE on 7 March 1989, as follows (UN Doc. CCPR/C/52/Add. 3, para. 4–6):

The Basic Law of the Federal Republic of Germany was drafted in 1948–49 at a time of very severe material privation in the country following the Second World War. Nevertheless those responsible for drafting the Basic Law viewed the reconstitution of the State system idealistically and also allowed themselves to be influenced by impulses emanating from the United Nations Universal Declaration of Human Rights proclaimed on 10 December 1948. The constitutional system of the Federal Republic of Germany attaches paramount importance to human dignity. That is why paragraph 1 of Article 1 of the Basic Law reads as follows: "The dignity of man shall be inviolable. To respect and protect it shall be the duty of all State authority." This acknowledgement of the inviolable intrinsic value of the individual human being is allied with a firm rejection of totalitarian concepts, where the law is simply an instrument of politics and can be used in any way desired. German experience of such doctrines and practices tell us that they carry the seeds of a continuous and serious violation of human rights. This applies right across the board. In paragraph 2 of Article 1 of the Basic Law therefore, the German people acknowledges "inviolable and inalienable human rights as the basis of *every* community, of peace and of justice in the world".

The Basic Law contains a comprehensive catalogue of basic rights which are guaranteed partly as universal human rights for everyone, and partly as civil rights for Germans alone. General human rights cover in particular the right to the free development of the personality (paragraph 1 of Article 2 of the Basic Law), the right to life and to inviolability of the person and the right of liberty of the individual (paragraph 2 of Article 2 of the Basic Law), the right to equality before the law, which includes equal treatment for men and women in all fields of law (Article 3 of the Basic Law), the right to freedom of faith, conscience and creed (Article 4 of the Basic Law), including the right to conscientious objection, and the right to freedom of speech and freedom of information, including a guaranteed freedom of the press (Article 5 of the Basic Law). Articles 6 and 7 of the Basic Law contain special guarantees for the family and education. Paragraph 3 of Article 9 of the Basic Law guarantees "to everyone and to all professions" freedom of coalition, i.e. "the right to form associations to safeguard and improve working and economic conditions". Freedom of assembly and freedom of association

outside the sectors governed by paragraph 3 of Article 9—supplemented by the right to found political parties—are guaranteed under Article 8 and paragraph 1 of Article 9 and paragraph 1, sentence 2, of Article 21 of the Basic Law for all Germans, likewise the right to freedom of movement under Article 11 of the Basic Law and the basic right to a free choice of profession and place of work under Article 12 of the Basic Law. Article 10 of the Basic Law safeguards the privacy of correspondence, posts and telecommunications, Article 13 of the Basic Law the inviolability of the home.

Property is protected under Articles 14 and 15 of the Basic Law. Under Article 16 of the Basic Law no German may be deprived of his or her citizenship or extradited to a foreign country. Persons persecuted on political grounds are entitled to asylum under paragraph 2, sentence 2, of Article 16 of the Basic Law. Article 17 of the Basic Law also allows all persons the right to bring complaints before the competent authorities and before Parliament. Aside from those standardized in Section I, Articles 1 to 19, under the heading "Basic Rights", a number of other rights are also protected as basic. In particular they cover the right to resist attacks on the constitutional system (paragraph 4 of Article 20 of the Basic Law), the enjoyment of rights of citizenship under Article 33 of the Basic Law, the right to vote and the right to stand for election (Article 38 of the Basic Law) and elementary guarantees with respect to legal proceedings: the right to a lawful judge (Article 101 of the Basic Law), the entitlement to a hearing in accordance with the law, the ban on retrospective punishments and on double punishment (Article 103 of the Basic Law), and legal guarantees in the event of deprivation of liberty (Article 104 of the Basic Law). A number of these rights find parallels only in the Universal Declaration of Human Rights, not in the Covenant (e.g. the protection of property); others— e.g. the right to conscientious objection and the right to asylum—go further than the Covenant and the Universal Declaration of Human Rights.

Measures taken to protect the basic rights are described by the government, in the same report, as follows (para. 7–14):

The basic rights of the Basic Law have been specified and expanded in the rulings of our national courts, especially the Federal Constitutional Court (s. paragraphs 12 to 14), particular attention being paid to judgements passed by the European Commission of Human Rights and the European Court of Human Rights (s. paragraphs 23 to 25). One example of how basic rights are being expanded in court rulings is found in the right to informational self-determination (Federal Constitution Court decision 65, 1 ff.) derived from the right to free development of the personality in the light of modern data processing requirements.

To the extent that, on the basis of paragraph 1 of Article 24 of the Basic Law, the Federal Republic of Germany has transferred sovereign power to the European Community, basic rights are protected in relation to legal acts on the part of the Community by the judicial decisions of the European Court in Luxembourg.

The basic rights of the Basic Law are directly enforceable law and are binding on the legislature, the executive and the judiciary. This is provided specifically in paragraph 3 of Article 1 of the Basic Law. As a result of this commitment, basic rights have a direct effect in law also on the daily life of the Federal Republic of Germany. The protection of human rights is safeguarded by independent courts. According to paragraph 4 of Article 19 of the Basic Law, anyone whose rights are violated by public authority is entitled to have recourse to a court of law.

Basic rights are first of all rights to freedoms which protect the citizen from unauthorized interventions by public authorities. They also have a considerable effect on the application of law in that the legal provisions, if they leave any room for interpretation, are to be interpreted in the light of the basic rights protected by the Constitution. As this applies to all laws, the courts and authorities are constantly and directly involved in the protection of basic rights when applying the regulations. Respect for basic rights is therefore central not only to the written Constitution, but also to acts done by the State. Consequently basic rights in the Federal Republic of Germany have reached an unusually high degree of effectiveness. The judicial decisions of the Federal Constitutional Court contribute to this in that they adhere to the standard of the Basic Law and develop the Constitution by interpreting it. The Federal Constitutional Court's decisions are binding on the constitutional bodies of the Federal Government and Laender and on all courts and authorities, and after more specific legislative provision they gain force of law.

The Federal Constitutional Court thus plays a central part in the protection of basic rights.

The Basic Law can only be amended by a qualified majority. Bearing in mind the experiences made with the Hitler régime, those who drafted the Basic Law of the Federal Republic of Germany have also taken care to prevent our legislators from themselves abolishing the basic free and democratic order. Any amendment of the Basic Law is therefore declared inadmissible under paragraph 3 of Article 79 of the Basic Law in so far as "the basic principles set out in Articles 1 and 20" are affected. These basic principles also include a declaration of "inviolable and inalienable human rights as the basis of every community, of peace and of justice in the world" in paragraph 3 of Article 1 of the Basic Law. Another part of the unalterable content of the Basic Law which cannot be amended under the Constitution is the basic decision taken in Article 20 in favour of a republican, democratic and social constitutional order.

In addition, basic rights can only be restricted where and to the extent specifically admitted under the Basic Law. Even in such cases restrictions under Article 19 of the Basic Law are only admissible by or pursuant to a law. Under paragraph 2 of Article 19 of the Basic Law the legislator may never encroach upon the essential content of basic right.

The citizens of the Federal Republic of Germany have declared themselves for as long as the Republic has existed in countless ballots both free and secret, and by overwhelming majorities, in favour of a free constitutional order based on the respect for basic rights. Radical groups on the right or left of the political spectrum who call this order into question have been relegated by the electorate to the ranks of insignificant splinter groups. This stable and peaceful democratic order, unparalleled in German history, is based on the fact that respect for human rights is a reality in the Federal Republic of Germany: in the daily life of the individual citizen as much as in politics, which in the pursuit of its aims under paragraph 3 of Article 1 of the Basic Law is subject to the basic and human rights.

Measures by which the basic rights are implemented, on the national level, are described in the report as follows (para. 15–22):

Anyone holding office in the legislature, the executive or the judiciary is directly committed to the basic rights (paragraph 3 of Article 1 of the Basic Law). One particular consequence of this is that a judge is obliged *ex officio* to establish whether the legal provisions he is to apply are in conformity with the basic rights protected under the Basic Law.

If a court considers a regulation unconstitutional, the validity of which is relevant to its decision, it is obliged under Article 100 of the Basic Law to stay the proceedings and to obtain a decision from the Federal Constitutional Court.

As paragraph 3 of Article 1 of the Basic Law is also binding on the legislature, all those involved in the legislature must establish whether a draft law is compatible with the Constitution and stands up to scrutiny by the Federal Constitutional Court.

In case of differences of opinion or doubts regarding the compatibility of statutory regulations with the Basic Law, the Federal Constitutional Court will rule after the law is passed, provided the Federal Government, the Government of a constituent State ("Land") or one third of the members of the German Bundestag request this to be done.

Judicial reviews were either instituted or conducted, at the request of the above parties or on the basis of a submission by a court, in 143 cases in 1986, in 80 cases in 1987, and in an overall total of 2,505 cases by 1987. The Federal Constitutional Court has full legal powers in such proceedings to rule that a legal norm is unconstitutional and therefore null and void. This happened in 75 proceedings between 1973 and 1987.

An important instrument for the protection of basic rights is also the complaint of unconstitutionality under paragraph 1 (4) (a) of Article 93 of the Basic Law. If all other remedies are exhausted, it may be entered by any person who claims that one of his or her basic rights, guaranteed under the Constitution, or one of his or her rights under paragraph 4 of Article 20, under Articles 33, 38, 101, 103 or 104 of the Basic Law has been violated by public authority. Increasing use is being made of the option to enter a complaint of unconstitutionality. From the time the Federal Constitutional Court was constituted (1952) up to the end of 1987, 67,834 such complaints had been instituted; the figure for 1986 was 2,935 and for 1987, 3,358. A total of 65,859 such complaints had been dealt with by the end of 1987. Of that total 917 (1.39 per cent) had been successful. This has had some far-reaching consequences for the legislation.

The Federal Constitutional Court also decides on certain disputes between organs of the State—e.g. the Federal President, the Federal Government and the Bundestag—(paragraph 1 (1) and (4) of Article 93 of the Basic Law) and on matters relating to the ban on parties which, by reasons of their aims or the behaviour of their adherents, seek to impair or abolish the free democratic order or to endanger the existence of the Federal Republic of Germany (paragraph 2 of Article 21 of the Basic Law). The observance of the human rights which form an integral part of the constitutional order of the Federal Republic of Germany is only guaranteed if those persons and parties performing public functions consider themselves bound by this order. The Basic Law therefore provides the means of banning parties which are opposed to the Constitution, thereby preventing them from influencing public matters and calling the observance of human rights into question. For the same reason the obligation to be loyal, which has its basis in paragraph 4 of Article 33 of the Basic Law, obliges civil servants actively to support the free democratic order, in particular by observing the existing regulations under constitutional and other laws, and to perform their functions in the spirit of these regulations (Federal Constitutional Court decisions 39, 334, 347 ff.). Appointment to the civil service therefore presupposes that the applicant is making a commitment to support the free democratic order at all times (Federal Constitutional Court decisions 39, 334, 352).

Implementation of the law is supervised by the courts, and not only by the Federal courts (the Federal Court of Justice, the Federal Labour Court, the Federal Administrative Court, the Federal Social Court, the Federal Fiscal Court, the Federal Patents Court, the Federal Disciplinary Court, Military Service Courts), but also directly by the 801 courts of the Federal Laender, including courts of ordinary jurisdiction (604), the labour courts (96), the administrative courts (36), the social courts (51) and the fiscal courts (14). Basic rights directly affect the practice of the some 17,000 judges in the Federal service and the service of the Laender, as well as of the more than three and a half thousand public prosecutors and the more than 40,000 attorneys licensed in the Federal Republic of Germany. To protect the rights of citizens against acts by the State is an essential task of the administrative, fiscal and social courts. If none of these courts has jurisdiction, recourse is to the ordinary courts under paragraph 4, sentence 2, of Article 19 of the Basic Law.

International control of the protection of human rights in the Federal Republic of Germany is summarized by the government, in the report, as follows (para. 23–25):

Protection of human rights is not only a matter of national concern but it rather, as set out in paragraph 2 of Article 1 of the Basic Law in accordance with the Charter of the United Nations, the Universal Declaration of Human Rights and the International Covenants on Human Rights forms the basis for peace and justice throughout the world. It follows that peace and justice are dependent on effective international control of human rights protection. The Federal Republic of Germany was one of the first States to ratify the European Convention for the Protection of Human Rights and Fundamental Freedoms as early as 1952 and to subject its implementation to international control, which in accordance with the provisions of the Convention is exercised by the European Commission on Human Rights and the European Court of Human Rights in Strasbourg. The Federal Republic of Germany has also made a declaration under Article 25 of the Convention that it recognizes the competence of the Commission to deal with individual complaints which (after all domestic remedies have been exhausted) can be brought before the Commission against the Federal Republic of Germany by an individual who considers that his or her rights as protected by the Convention have been violated. In making a declaration under Article 46 of the Convention, the Federal Republic of Germany has also recognized as binding the jurisdiction of the European Court of Human Rights.

Since the Commission was set up, 13,457 complaints have been registered with it—up to the end of 1987—of which

about one third (4,701) were directed against the Federal Republic of Germany. In recent years this proportion has been reduced; of 706 new complaints registered in 1986, 106 (15 per cent) were directed against the Federal Republic of Germany, and in 1987 (108) (12.3 per cent) out of 860. The majority of complaints were rejected. Only in 16 cases of those brought against the Federal Republic of Germany on grounds of a violation of the Convention were proceedings instituted before the European Court of Human Rights. Only in seven cases did the Court find that the Convention had been violated. Of these seven cases, three related to the inordinately long time taken for proceedings before an administrative court (Koenig case), for criminal proceedings (Eckle case) and for proceedings before a social court (Deumeland case). Two cases involved interpreter's costs charged to a foreign national without knowledge of the language, in criminal proceedings (Luedicke/Belkacem/Koc case) and in fines proceedings (Ozturk case). A further case involved the non-assignment of a counsel for the defence appointed by the court for the oral hearing in proceedings on appeal (Pakelli case), and, another, the restriction of freedom of opinion of a veterinary surgeon, accused of a breach of professional rules on grounds of inadmissible advertising for his practice (Barthold case).

In line with its policy of advocacy of human rights at international level, the Federal Republic of Germany in 1973 also ratified the International Covenants on Human Rights. By making a declaration under article 41 of the International Covenant on Civil and Political Rights, it also recognized in regard to itself international control by way of the procedure for State complaints. It also subjects itself to international control of human rights practices by providing the Human Rights Committee established under the Covenant with information relating to the protection of human rights in the Federal Republic of Germany, by submitting the present report—as well as the two earlier reports submitted under article 40 of the Covenant; it further complies with other similar reporting obligations under article 16 ff. of the International Covenant on Economic, Social and Cultural Rights, under article 9 of the International Convention on the Elimination of All Forms of Racial Discrimination and under article 18 of the Convention on the Elimination of All Forms of Discrimination against Women.

Under the Basic Law, the Federal Republic of Germany proceeded to develop a prosperous free-market economy, embodying innovative ideas for increasing the participation of workers in the management of industry, and to improve its political situation in Europe. Its civil status was restored by the occupying powers in 1949. It was recognized by the United States of America in 1951 and by the Soviet Union in 1955. In 1957, the Saar territory rejoined West Germany as the result of a plebescite conducted under an agreement with France. In 1970, Chancellor Willy Brandt, who had succeeded Konrad Adenauer in 1969, signed a friendship treaty with the Union of Soviet Socialist Republics which renounced the use of force and declared respect for the territorial integrity of existing European States and a similar treaty with Poland setting its western border at the Oder–Neisse line. Later, a treaty with Czechoslovakia normalized relations with that country and "voided" the notorious Munich Agreement of 1938, by which the Sudetenland had been turned over to Nazi Germany.

Over the years, the governments of the Federal Republic took steps to improve the situation of its Danish minority in Schleswig-Holstein, the Jewish section of its population, and its Sinti and Romany Gypsies. Developments affecting those groups were described in the government's periodic report submitted to the UN COMMITTEE ON THE ELIMINATION OF RACIAL DISCRIMINATION on 3 January 1989 (UN Doc. CERD/C/172/Add. 13).

As regards the Danish minority, the report provides the following information (para. 7–9; 11–21);

After the end of the Second World War the Government of the Land of Schleswig-Holstein was determined to implement a minorities policy committed to the observation of human rights in relation to the Danish section of the population in Schleswig-Holstein. This policy was reflected in the "Declaration of Kiel" of 16 September 1949, the central statement of which is:

"The declaration of loyalty to Danish national characteristics and Danish culture is unrestricted. It may not be disputed or reviewed *ex officio.*"

This declaration was subsequently safeguarded by the German and Danish Governments under international law in the "Bonn-Copenhagen Declaration" of 29 March 1955 on the situation of the minorities on both sides. These declarations essentially state the following:

"The declaration of loyalty to Danish national characteristics and Danish culture is unrestricted and may not be disputed or reviewed *ex officio.*"

"Members of the Danish minority and its organizations may not be impeded in the verbal and written use of the desired language. The use of the Danish language before the courts and administrative authorities is governed by the statutory provisions.

"In relation to assistance and other benefits financed from public funds on which decisions are taken on a discretionary basis, members of the Danish minority may not be treated differently from other citizens.

"The special interest of the Danish minority in maintaining its religious, cultural and professional links with Denmark is recognized."

Mainly with a view to enabling the Danish minority to be represented politically, the Federal Electoral Act of 1953 for the first time exempted the parties of national minorities from application of the so-called "5% blocking clause", according to which a political party must obtain at least 5% of the valid votes cast in order to be represented in parliament. Sine 1955, the parties of the Danish minority have also been exempted from the application of a blocking clause in elections to the Landtag of the Land of Schleswig-Holstein. In Bundestag electoral law, additional alleviations in relation to the submission of nominations have applied for parties of national minorities since 1956. . . .

The South Schleswig Voters' Association has not stood for national (Bundestag) elections since 1965, since it sees no way of reaching the number of votes required to win a seat in the Bundestag.

Currently, therefore, some 23,000 persons profess membership of the Danish minority in Elections in Schleswig-

Holstein. The total number of members of the Danish minority is estimated at 50,000. It is not possible to determine the number more exactly, as professions of membership of a minority are not scrutinized (Declaration of Bonn). The cultural organization is the South Schleswig Association (*Sydslesvigsk Forening*—SSF), which had almost 19,000 members in 1987.

The Danish minority runs 54 schools with a total of roughly 5,200 pupils in South Schleswig. The Danish School Association runs 62 Danish kindergartens which are attended by roughly 1,880 children (1987). The minority also runs the Duborg Grammar School in Flensburg, an Adult Education Centre in Jarplund near Flensburg and a boarding school in Ladelund.

In 1986, the Danish schools in Schleswig necessitated total expenditure of some DM 80 million, roughly DM 39 million of which was provided by the Danish Government. The Land of Schleswig-Holstein spent approximately DM 36 million for the Danish schools system in 1986. In 1985, the Land subsidy was raised to 100% of the costs incurred by the Land for the education of a pupil at a public German school. The Danish schools are private schools whose final examinations are recognized both in Denmark and in the Federal Republic of Germany.

The Danish minority has its own central library (*Danske Centralbibliotek*) in Flensburg, which has been expanded with considerable financial assistance from the Federation and the Land of Schleswig-Holstein.

In 1987, the Land of Schleswig-Holstein spent more than DM 41 million on promoting the work of the Danish minority. In addition to the school system, financial support is given to cultural and youth work, adult education, the Danish Health Service, the Federation of Agricultural Associations and the political work of the SSW in the Landtag. On top of this, the administrative districts, towns and communities pay out some DM 3 million per year for the work of the Danish minority. In addition, projects of the Danish minority in the zonal border area of Schleswig-Holstein are promoted with Zonal Border Area Promotion Funds of the Federal Ministry for Intra-German Relations.

The central organization for youth work is the South Schleswig Youth Association (*Sydslesvigs Danske Ungdomsforeninger*—SDU), comprising 63 associations with roughly 11,600 members. It supports leisure centres and sports facilities. The amateur theatre company "Det lille Teater" in Flensburg is one of its affiliates.

The religious life of the Danish minority is supported by the Protestant Lutheran Danish Church in South Schleswig, an association with a total of 23 parishes. It is independent of the Protestant Lutheran Church of the North Elbe and of the Danish established church.

The Danish Health Service for South Schleswig operates its own social wards in Flensburg and Schleswig, as well as care centres for the ill in Husum and Leck. It additionally maintains senior citizens' homes in Flensburg and Leck, as well as a children's home in Glücksburg. Recreational holidays in Denmark are arranged for children and adults.

The costs of the cultural and social work of the Danish minority are covered by the Danish Government, the Danish Border Association (a central organization comprising numerous individual associations with roughly 50,000 members in all) and the Land of Schleswig-Holstein. The newspaper for the Danish minority is the bilingual *Flensborg Avis*, which is published daily. A newspaper for members of the SFF, "Kontakt", was published until 1985 and has now been replaced by a weekly special page in the Flensborg Avis.

The Federal Ministry of the Interior has maintained a Consultative Committee for Affairs Relating to the Danish Minority since 1965. The Committee is currently made up of seven members of the German Bundestag (two representatives each from the CDU/CSU, SPD and F.D.P. parliamentary parties and one representative of the Die Grünen (The Greens) parliamentary party), three representatives of the Danish minority, the Minister of the Interior of the Land of Schleswig-Holstein and the State Secretary in the Federal Ministry for Intra-German Relations. The Committee meets annually to deal with questions of Federal domestic policy affecting the Danish minority. In each case, an attempt is made to find appropriate solutions in coordination with the departments involved.

As regards the Jewish population, the report provides the following information (para. 22–25):

The Federal Republic of Germany has from the outset recognized its moral responsibility towards the victims of racial and political persecution under the Hitler régime and, in its constitutional and legal system based on the observation of human dignity, created the prerequisites for the Jewish population in the Federal Republic of Germany today to enjoy the same rights and the same protection as the other Germans living in the Federal Republic of Germany. It has expended over DM 80,000 million on reparation payments since 1950.

Within the framework of official statistics, the number of Jews was last established in the 1970 census. At that time, there were 31,700 members of the Jewish religious community living in the Federal Republic of Germany. Of these, 11,300 did not have German nationality. The corresponding results of the 1987 census are not yet available. According to the 1987 data of the "Central Welfare Office of the Jews in Germany" (Frankfurt/Main) and of the "Central Committee of the Jews in Germany" (Bonn), currently available to the Government of the Federal Republic of Germany, the Jewish communities in the Federal Republic of Germany have a total of 27,533 members professing the Jewish faith. The largest communities are in West Berlin (6,002), Munich (5,501) and Frankfurt am Main (4,909). There is a total of 65 communities with 14 rabbis. The communities have 53 synagogues, 22 oratories, 22 ritual baths and 55 community libraries. The interests of the Jewish population in the Federal Republic of Germany are for the most part looked after by the aforementioned "Central Committee of the Jews in Germany". This organization also publishes the German-language *General Jewish Weekly (Allgemeine jüdische Wochenzeitung)*, which has a weekly circulation of between 20,000 and 30,000 copies. The "Central Committee of the Jews in Germany" also voices the opinions of the section of the population which it represents in the Jewish Press Service *(Jüdischer Pressedienst)*, which appears at irregular intervals, about four times per year. Also published are newspapers of various Jewish communities (in Frankfurt, Munich and Aachen), as well as the *Annual Reports* of the Jewish Community in Berlin, these mainly being aimed at the members of the Jewish community.

One of the main problems of the Jewish population in the Federal Republic of Germany is doubtless the recollection of the horrors of the "holocaust". The German population is still moved and shocked by the fate of the Jews under the Hitler régime. The German public thus reacts negatively and highly sensitively to all statements which are meant to strengthen anti-Jewish prejudices or could be interpreted as doing so. Should anti-Jewish prejudices still exist, the Government of the Federal Republic of Germany is convinced that such prejudices will be broken down under the educational and enlightening influence of the mass media, which have always devoted considerable attention to the subject of the persecution of the Jews under the Hitler régime. In addition, a "Week of Brotherhood" (*Woche der Brüderlichkeit*) is held each year under the auspices of the President of the Federal Republic of Germany, the aim of which is to promote understanding between Jews and Christians and which attracts much public attention through reports on German television and in other mass media.

In view of the persecution to which the German Jews were subjected under the Hitler régime, the Government of the Federal Republic of Germany also pays particular attention to guaranteeing Jewish citizens the legal protection they require in order to live in the Federal Republic of Germany without discrimination. In this context, reference is made to the section of the Report relating to article 6 of the Convention.

[That section of the report is as follows (para. 56–60):]

To supplement the statements made in the past, particularly in the previous report, the Government of the Federal Republic of Germany points out that the Federal Republic of Germany has also complied with its obligations under article 6 of the Convention by issuing the 21st Criminal Law Amendment Act, dated 13 June 1985 (Federal Law Gazette I, p. 965). This Act is an attempt to improve the effective protection of the Jewish section of the population against racially discriminating acts—that is to say against the propagation of the so-called "Auschwitz lie"—and also aims at more effective control of racist propaganda.

The following can be stated with regard to the reasons for the 21st Criminal Law Amendment Act. Even before 1985, the distribution of publications serving as Neo-Nazi propaganda was punishable, as was the use of symbols of former Nazi organizations. The open assertion that the Jews had only invented the "holocaust" in order wrongfully to obtain compensation was also regarded as incitement of the people before 1985; this offence is punishable by up to five years' imprisonment.

Furthermore, the German courts considered the denial of the genocide committed against the Jews under the Hitler régime as an insult to every Jew living in the Federal Republic of Germany. Other derisory statements concerning the Jewish victims of persecution under the Hitler régime were also punished as insults or, where appropriate, as defamation of the remembrance of the dead.

However, problems arose from the fact that, under the legal situation prevailing before 1985, an insult was only subject to prosecution if the insulted person submitted a demand for prosecution. In this legal situation, therefore, anyone wanting to make the "Auschwitz lie" or a similar defamation the subject of prosecution was forced not only to submit a demand for prosecution personally in order to defend himself against the defamatory denial of the genocide, but also to prove that he was of Jewish origin as proof of his right of application. This could not be expected of Jewish citizens—especially in view of the particular fate which they had suffered. This is why the requirement for an application for offences relating to insults and defamation was restricted accordingly by the 21st Amendment Act of Criminal Law. Since this Act came into effect (1 August 1985), the "Auschwitz lie" has been liable to *ex officio* prosecution as defamation. A personal demand for prosecution is no longer necessary. Prosecution is only forgone if the insulted person objects. Furthermore, the Act even makes the importation, production or storage of the symbols of Neo-Nazi organizations punishable, also clearly stipulating that publications with a punishable content, particularly of a Neo-Nazi nature, can still be confiscated even after expiry of the time limit on criminal prosecution.

In the press statement on 30 April 1987, the Federal Minister of Justice, Mr. Engelhard, took the experience gained with the 21st Amendment Act to Criminal Law as an occasion for the following appraisal:

"The practical experience with the law to combat the so-called 'Auschwitz lie' proves that there are, unfortunately, still isolated right-wing radical scatterbrains in the Federal Republic who deny the historical fact of the genocide committed against the Jews. On the other hand, the fact that this law only had to be applied in a small number of cases also proves that National Socialist ideas have no chance in this country today and that the newly created instruments of criminal law offer adequate handle against the agitation and propaganda of the die-hards."

As regards the Sinti and Romany Gypsies, the report provides the following information (para. 26–30):

Like the Jewish section of the population, the Sinti and Romany Gypsies were also persecuted for racial reasons under the Hitler régime. Even before then, they had always suffered under the prejudices against their independent way of life with its special cultural and social traditions. Only in the last few decades has the understanding of their particular characteristics and their problems grown. The Government of the Federal Republic of Germany has given constant support to this development.

The number of Sinti and Romany Gypsies living in the Federal Republic of Germany today is estimated at some 50,000 to 70,000. Since there are no specific records within the framework of official statistics, it is not possible to give more accurate data. The same also applies to the question as to how many of these Sinti and Romany Gypsies have German nationality. In so far as they are not German nationals, the relatives of Sinti and Romany Gypsies are subject to the same general regulations under the law on aliens as all other foreigners. No special statutory regulations exist either for Sinti and Romany Gypsies or for other ethnic groups.

In relations to the laws on identification documentation and the residence of aliens, the following should be noted as regards the treatment of Sinti and Romany Gypsies with or without German nationality, or whose nationality is unclear and cannot be proven by way of a foreign passport or a document serving as a passport.

(a) Stateless Sinti and Romany Gypsies who have legally settled in the Federal Republic of Germany have a claim to a stateless person's travel document pursuant to article 28 of the United Nations Convention Relating to the Status of Stateless Persons of 28 September 1954, which came into effect for the Federal Republic of Germany on 24 January 1977.

(b) Politically persecuted Sinti and Romany Gypsies who have been recognized as entitled to asylum have a claim to a travel document as per article 28 of the United Nations Convention Relating to the Status of Refugees of 28 July 1951.

(c) Sinti and Romany Gypsies who fall under the Act on the Status of Homeless Foreigners in the Territory of the Federal Republic of Germany (HAG), dated 25 April 1951 (Federal Law Gazette I, p. 269), enjoy the status specified in this Act. Homeless foreigners are by law (Art. 12 HAG) entitled to reside in the territory of the Federal Republic of Germany; they are issued with refugees' travel documents.

(d) Sinti and Romany Gypsies who do not fulfil the conditions for owning one of the above-mentioned travel documents may be issued with an alien's passport.

Apart from a small minority, the Sinti and Romany Gypsies living in the Federal Republic of Germany have a fixed abode, from where in many cases they pursue their traditional occupations as peddlers, showmen, fortune-tellers, musicians, basket-makers, tinkers, etc. However, economic developments in the Federal Republic of Germany have led to a constant decline in the demand for the traditional services of the Sinti and Romany Gypsies. This has meant that the majority of this section of the population lost the economic basis for an independent existence. The problems of the Sinti and Romany Gypsies, which relate to the preservation of their own cultural and social identity, have attracted growing public attention in the Federal Republic of Germany in recent years. The German Bundestag has also dealt with the subject on several occasions.

The most important prerequisites for improving the social situation of the Sinti and Romany Gypsies are the furtherance of their self-responsibility and independence, as well as their schooling and vocational training, in order to restore the basis for an independent economic existence. . . .

The possibility of unification of the two Germanys improved considerably in the latter half of 1989 as a result of the massive exodus from East Germany to the west. By mid–1990, more than three million people had braved hardship and even death to flee from East Germany since 1949, and its remaining residents had put an end to Communist Party domination of their political system by their votes in free multi-party national and local elections.

The complicated and controversial unification process got under way on 18 May 1990 when the two finance ministers signed a state treaty making the West German mark the sole legal tender in both nations. The treaty was approved on 21 June 1990 by matching measures in the two parliaments: by 445 in favor, 60 against, and 1 abstention in Bonn; and by 302 in favor and 82 against in East Berlin.

On the same day, both parliaments adopted resolutions affirming the existing border with Poland along the Oder and Neisse Rivers and calling upon a unified Germany to confirm them in a treaty. The vote in West Germany was 487 in favor, 15 against, and 3 abstentions; in East Germany, 361 in favor, 6 against, and 18 abstentions.

On 22 June 1990, the foreign ministers of the United States, Great Britain, France, and the Soviet Union met in Berlin to begin negotiations that, it was hoped, would end the limitations on German sovereignty left from World War II. Among the problems faced were those of extricating East Germany from its military and economic links to the Soviet Union, arranging for the withdrawal of the occupation forces, and settling the security problems arising from the changeover, including the question of Germany's membership in the North Atlantic Treaty Organization (NATO). On 12 September, the four World War II allies agreed to end their occupation of Berlin, officially signing the document relinquishing all rights on 2 October.

On the next day, 3 October 1990, the two Germanys reunited for the first time in 44 years.

GHANA. The Republic of Ghana is a country in western Africa, on the Gulf of Guinea. It has borders with Burkina Faso, the Ivory Coast, and Togo. It achieved independence from Great Britain in 1957 and became a member of the United Nations the same year. Its population is estimated by the UN (1990) to be 36,072,000. Under a government directive of 21 March 1972, it is illegal for anyone to collect or disseminate information on the ethnic composition of Ghana's population. Languages commonly used include English (official), Twi, Fanti, Ga, Ewe, Dagbani, and other African vernaculars. Religions practiced include Christianity (65%), Islam (15%), and Animism (20%). Literacy is estimated at 45%.

The government (1990) took the form of a republic and member of the Commonwealth of Nations, of which the British sovereign is the symbolic head. However, since 31 December 1981, the constitution has been suspended, and all executive and legislative powers have been exercised by the Provisional National Defence Council, composed of six members of the military. The chairman of the council is head of State and government. A National Commission for Democracy has been established to formulate a program for a more effective realization of democracy based on Ghanian traditions and experience. The judicial system remains as it was before the imposition of military rule; but public tribunals have been established to try specified offenses such as economic crimes, sedition, corruption, and mismanagement by public officials. These courts operate side-by-side with the regular ones. There are no political parties.

Ghana's head of State, Flight Lt. Jerry Rawlings, first seized power on 4 June 1979, charging the military government then headed by Lt. Gen. Frederick Akuffo with repression and corruption. Rawlings then stepped aside to permit the election and installa-

tion of a civilian government headed by Hilla Limann. Two years later, however, he staged a second coup, again charging repression and corruption. Shortly after he took over as chairman of the Provisional National Defense Council, the council abrogated Ghana's 1979 constitution and replaced it by "Directive Principles of State Policy" designed to provide the basic framework for the exercise of all powers of government. These principles envisage that:

(a) a basis of social justice is to be established, particular attention being paid to the deprived sections of the community and to the reconstruction of the society in a revolutionary process directed against the previous structures of injustice and exploitation;

(b) respect for fundamental human rights and for the dignity of the human person are to be cultivated among all sections of the society and established as part of the basis of social justice;

(c) corrupt practices, exploitation in all its forms, as well as abuse of power are to be eradicated;

(d) national integration is to be encouraged and discrimination on grounds of ethnic origin discouraged. A spirit of loyalty to Ghana overriding sectional, ethnic or other loyalties, is to be cultivated among the people of Ghana. . . .

GOOD OFFICES, MEDIATION, OR CONCILIATION COMMISSION. On 4 December 1989, the UN General Assembly, on recommendation of its Sixth (Legal) Committee, commended (decision 44/415) the Special Committee on the Charter of the United Nations and on the Strengthening of the Role of the Organization for completing its work on a document on the resort to a commission of good offices, mediation, or conciliation within the United Nations and decided that the document should be drawn to the attention of States so that it may become generally known. The document, annexed to the assembly's decision, is as follows:

Resort to a Commission of Good Offices, Mediation or Conciliation Within the United Nations

States parties to disputes may wish to avail themselves of the possibility to resort to third-party assistance in the form of a commission of good offices, mediation or conciliation in order to settle their disputes by peaceful means. In doing so, they may be guided by the following:

1. Resort to a commission of good offices, mediation or conciliation within the United Nations may be considered by States as a procedure at their disposal for the peaceful settlement of international disputes in accordance with the provisions of the Charter of the United Nations.

2. Such a commission may be established for each particular case, in accordance with modalities described below, through the agreement of the States parties to a dispute, or, with their agreement, on the basis of a recommendation of the Security Council, or of the General Assembly or following the contacts of the States parties to a dispute with the

Secretary-General. Other modalities and conditions may also be agreed upon by the States parties to a dispute for the establishment of such a commission.

3. When the States parties to a dispute accept to resort to a commission of good offices, mediation or conciliation as described in paragraph 2 above, the designation of members of the commission is proceeded with.

4. For each particular case the commission of good offices, mediation or conciliation may be constituted of persons nominated by up to three States, which are not parties to the dispute concerned.

Such States will be designated by the States parties to the dispute or, with their agreement, as the case may be, by the President of the Security Council or by the President of the General Assembly or by the Secretary-General.

5. Each designated State will appoint, upon approval by the States parties to the dispute, a highly qualified person, with adequate experience, who will act in the commission in his individual capacity.

The chairman of the commission will be selected from among its members by the States parties to the dispute. They may also agree in a particular case that the chairman be appointed by the Secretary-General.

6. The proceedings of the commission may take place at United Nations Headquarters in New York, or in any other place agreed upon by the States parties to the dispute.

7. After taking note of the elements of the respective dispute, on the basis of submissions made by the States parties and, as appropriate, of information provided by the Secretary-General, the commission in performing its good offices functions will seek to bring the parties to enter immediately into direct negotiations for the settlement of the dispute, or to resume such negotiations or to resort to another means of peaceful settlement.

If the States parties to the dispute so request, the commission will seek to establish the aspects on which the States parties agree, as well as their differences of opinion and perception, and to elucidate the elements related to the dispute with a view to making suggestions for the beginning or the resuming of negotiations including their framework and stages as well as problems to solve.

8. If the States parties to the dispute request the commission, at any time, to mediate, the commission will offer to the parties proposals which it deems adequate for facilitating the negotiations and seeking through mediation to bring closer their positions until an agreement is reached.

9. The States parties to the dispute may agree at any moment of the procedure to entrust the commission with functions of conciliation. The States parties to the dispute determine the legal basis on which the commission should perform its functions. If such a basis is not determined, the commission should be guided mainly by the rights and duties of States resulting from the Charter of the United Nations and by the applicable principles of international law. In performing its functions the commission formulates the terms which it deems adequate for the amicable settlement of the dispute and submits them to the parties.

The States parties to the dispute will be requested to pronounce themselves on these terms within a period of time established by the commission, which may be prolonged if the States parties to the dispute deem it necessary.

10. A period of time during which the commission should discharge its mission may be established by the States parties to the dispute or, where appropriate, following their contacts with the Secretary-General.

11. The States parties to the dispute may wish that the commission work in confidentiality. As long as the commission continues its efforts, no statement will be made public on its activity without the agreement of the States parties to the dispute.

12. The States parties to the dispute may wish that, upon conclusion of the commission's activity, the commission prepare a report and communicate it to them. The States parties to the dispute will decide if the report is to be made public.

Where appropriate, the commission may submit a report to the United Nations organ concerned in the form accepted by the States parties to the dispute.

13. Unless otherwise provided, any expenses of the commission shall be borne by the States parties to the dispute. They may request the Secretary-General to provide the commission with reasonable assistance and facilities as it may require.

14. The States parties to the dispute, as well as other States, shall act in accordance with the purposes and principles of the United Nations and shall refrain from any action whatsoever which may aggravate the situation, endanger the maintenance of international peace and security or make more difficult or impede the peaceful settlement of the dispute.

15. Nothing in the present document shall be construed as prejudicing in any manner the provisions of the Charter, in particular those relating to the peaceful settlement of disputes.

SEE ALSO ILO Freedom of Association Fact-Finding and Conciliation Commission; Organization of African Unity: Protocol. . . Establishing the Commission of Mediation, Conciliation, and Arbitration; Permanent Court of Arbitration; UNESCO Convention against Discrimination in Education: Protocol Instituting a Conciliation and Good Offices Commission.

GREECE. The Hellenic Republic is a country on the Balkan Peninsula in southern Europe, on the Mediterranean between the Aegean and Ionian Seas. It has borders with Albania, Bulgaria, Turkey, and Yugoslavia and includes a number of islands, among them Crete, Rhodes, and numerous islets of the Ionian, Cyclades, and Dodecanese groups. It achieved independence in 1827 and became a member of the United Nations in 1945. Its population is estimated by the UN (1990) to be 10,085,000. There are a large number of ethnic groups, the Greeks having mingled through many centuries with invaders from the Balkans, Africa, and Asia. Languages commonly used include Greek, French, English, and Turkish. Christianity (Greek Orthodox) is the predominant religion. Literacy is estimated at 95%.

The government (1990) took the form of a republic, established by a referendum of December 1974 which ended the monarchy. The president, elected by popular vote, is head of state. The premier, representing the party or coalition given a majority in an election, is head of government and exercises executive authority; he is responsible directly to Parliament, which is a unicameral body of 300 members. Political parties include the Panhellenic Socialist Movement, the New Democratic Party, the Communist Party, the Democratic Renewal, and the Communist Part of the Interior.

King Constantine II was forced into exile in 1967 by a coup d'etat staged by rightist officers led by Col. George Papadopoulos. The new regime—which came to be known as "the colonels"—suspended Parliament and replaced the 1952 constitution by one which established a "crown parliamentary democracy," under which royal authority was exercised by a regent and Papadopoulos became premier. This became a "presidential parliamentary democracy" in 1973, with Papadopoulos as president. However, efforts by the colonels "to restore democracy" by suspending civil rights and resorting to torture and arbitrary detention backfired when parliamentary elections were postponed indefinitely, and they were forced out by another military coup. General Phaidon Gizikis, who became president, returned the government to civilian control in 1974. The 1952 civilian constitution and its guarantees of civil rights were restored on 1 August 1974, martial law was lifted in October of that year, and the monarchy was abolished by a referendum held on 8 December. On 18 October 1981, the first socialist government in Greek history was elected, and Andreas Papandreou became premier. The socialist victory in parliamentary elections was repeated on 1 June 1985. However, in April 1990, Constantine Mitsotakis was sworn in as premier as a result of an electoral victory by the center-right forces after nearly a decade of socialist rule. Mr. Mitsotakis's New Democratic Party won the elections with 46.9% of the vote and 150 seats, after failing by a few seats in elections held in June and November 1989.

A problem relating to the enjoyment of freedom of religion or belief continues to be of concern to human rights groups as well as to Greeks who are not members of the Eastern Orthodox Church. Article 13 of the constitution guarantees the freedom of "known" religions. This formula, which is primarily historical in origin, has been interpreted in legal decisions as establishing freedom to practice all religions whose beliefs are "known" as opposed to "secret." However, the constitution also qualifies the Eastern Orthodox Church as the "predominant Church" and prohibits proselytism. In the course of 1983 and 1984, more than 160 lawsuits were brought for proselytism, and none of the requests for authorization to open new places of worship was granted. Under a 1939 law still in force, such authorization cannot be given without the prior agreement of the Orthodox Church.

GRENADA. The State of Grenada is a country which occupies the southernmost portion of the Windward Islands, in the Caribbean Sea, 120 miles north of South America. Grenada achieved independence from Great Britain in 1974 and became a member of the United Nations in the same year. Its population is estimated by the UN (1990) to be 120,000. Ethnic groups include Amerindians and Caribs. Languages commonly used include English (official) and a French *patois*. Christianity (Roman Catholic, 64%; Anglican and other Protestant denominations, 25%) is the predominant religion.

The government (1990) took the form of a monarchy and member of the Commonwealth of Nations, of which the British sovereign is the symbolic head. Executive power is vested in the governor-general, who represents the crown. He appoints the Prime Minister, who represents the party or coalition given the majority in a popular election. There is a 15–member parliament and a judiciary organized along British lines. Political parties include the New National Party, the Grenada Unity Labor Party, the New Jewel Movement, the Democratic Labor Party, and the Christian Democratic Labor Party.

Abuses of power by the Prime Minister Sir Eric Gairy led to a marxist takeover in 1979 and the installation of Maurice Bishop as prime minister. Bishop was killed by radical elements in his New Jewel Movement in 1983, prompting an invasion on 25 October by 1,900 American marines and rangers and small military contingents from Antigua, Barbados, Dominica, Jamaica, St. Lucia, and St. Vincent. Resistance by Cuban military personnel on the island ended after one day when Pearls Airport was re-opened, and 1,000 American citizens were evacuated. After subsequent elections, Herbert Augustus Blaize, leader of the New Nationalist Party, was sworn in as prime minister on 4 December 1984.

GROUP OF THREE. In accordance with article 9 of the INTERNATIONAL CONVENTION ON THE SUPPRESSION AND PUNISHMENT OF THE CRIME OF *APARTHEID,* the chairman of the UN Commission on Human Rights is authorized to appoint a group consisting of three members of the commission, who are also representatives of States parties to the convention, to consider reports submitted by States parties in accordance with article 7. The group, which has been constituted at each annual session of the commission since 1977, meets for a period of not more than five days, either before the opening or after the closing of the commission's session, to consider the reports submitted in accordance with article 7.

The Group of Three held its 13th session at the

United Nations office in Geneva from 22 to 26 January 1990. The membership of the group was as follows: Mr. Scott Oguma E. Omene (Nigeria), Mr. Lourdes C. Vallarino (Panama), and Mr. Volodymyr Vassilenko (Ukrainian Soviet Socialist Republic). The group elected Mr. Vassilenko as chairman/rapporteur. In the course of the session, the group considered reports submitted by States parties to the convention in the presence of representatives of the reporting States who accepted its invitation to attend. In addition, it considered, in accordance with a request by the Commission on Human Rights (resolution 1989/8), whether the actions of transnational corporations operating in South Africa and Namibia came under the definition of the crime of APARTHEID and whether legal action could be taken against them under the convention. The group endorsed the conclusion that, by their complicity, the transnational corporations operating in South Africa, in conformity with article 3 (b) of the convention, must be considered accomplices in the crime of *apartheid* and must be prosecuted for their responsibility in the continuation of that crime. The group called upon all States parties to the convention to incorporate in their legislation provisions to that effect.

GUATEMALA. The Republic of Guatemala is a country in Central America. It has borders with Belize, El Salvador, Honduras, and Mexico. Once a Mayan Indian empire, it became a colony of Spain in 1524 and achieved independence from that country in 1821. The republic was established in 1839. It became a member of the United Nations in 1945. Its population is estimated by the UN (1989) to be 8,935,000. Ethnic groups include Maya (55%), Mestizos (42%), and descendants of Spanish and other European settlers (3%). Languages commonly used include Spanish, English, and Amerindian vernaculars. Christianity (Roman Catholic, 80%; and various Protestant denominations, 10%) and Mayan (10%) are the predominant religions. Literacy is estimated at 50%.

The government (1990) took the form of a republic. After the first civilian government of recent years was ousted by the army in 1982, there was a period of political violence which caused more than 200,000 Guatemalans to seek refuge in Mexico and Central American countries. A second military coup occurred in 1983, ending the reign of terror and promising to restore power to an elected civilian president. A Constituent Assembly was elected on 1 July 1984 and proceeded to prepare a new constitution. Elections for president, vice president and members of Congress took place in November and December 1985; and, on 14 January 1986, the new civilian government assumed power. Active political parties included the Christian Democrats, the *Union del Centro Nacional,* and the Social Democratic Party.

During the period of transition, the UN COMMISSION ON HUMAN RIGHTS continued to receive reports of continuing, serious violations of human rights in Guatemala, including reports of violence against non-combatants, widespread repression, and the killing and massive displacement of rural and indigenous peoples. On 8 March 1983, it appointed (resolution 1983/37) one of its members, Viscount Colville of Culross (United Kingdom) as its special representative to study and report on the situation. The special representative subsequently submitted a number of reports to the commission and to the General Assembly (UN Docs. A/38/485, E/CN.4/1984/30, A/39/635, E/CN.4/1985/19, A/40/865, E/CN.4/1986/23 and E/CN.4/1987/24). In the final report, the special representative summed up his general impressions in the following terms (UN Doc. E/CN.4/1987/24, para. 7–8):

. . . In the course of seven visits since the summer of 1983, the Special Representative has been observing the situation as it can only be perceived (however imperfectly) in the country itself. Whatever the past criticisms, which have been many and justified, there is now a democratically elected President and Congress. The President's attitude is that the country should by governed under civilian control, through himself (including his role as Commander-in-Chief of the armed forces), the Minister of Interior and other Ministers. Even the briefest visit to Congress indicates a lively, urgent parliamentary activity. The media seem now to be all persuasive, increasingly well-informed and, so far as the Special Representative is concerned, responsible in their reporting. Trade union protests and placards opposite the National Palace are new. The Special Representative is much indebted to the Army on earlier occasions for their safe-keeping and their transport, with many other kindnesses and facilities; nevertheless the 1986 visit was in civilian hands throughout and the differences were significant.

The Government faces huge political, practical and economic problems. The scale of crime is unacceptable to everyone, within and without the country. The poverty, especially when you see it at first hand, is hard to comprehend. Yet the dignity and friendliness of the people, in city or rural hamlet, cannot fail to impress. The Special Representative has noted the tributes paid, often in publications which are generally critical of the human rights situation in Guatemala, to the quality of the country's present leaders; he has attempted to describe the policies where they are pursuing. The Special Representative ventures to suggest that the efforts they are making to implement the new legal order for the protection of human rights and to guarantee the full enjoyment of fundamental freedoms, even if not yet perfect or complete, should receive the support of the international community. . . .

After considering the report at its 1987 session, the Commission on Human Rights noted (resolution

1987/53) the measures that had been taken by the government to guarantee the protection of human rights and fundamental freedoms, expressed the hope that the appropriate authorities would investigate human rights violations reported to them and would make all possible efforts to clarify the fate of the disappeared persons, expressed its gratitude to Viscount Colville of Culross and terminated his mandate, and requested the secretary-general to appoint an expert to formulate recommendations for the further restoration of human rights in Guatemala. Accordingly the secretary-general appointed Mr. Hector Gros Espiell (Uruguay) as the expert "with a view to assisting the Government of Guatemala, through direct contacts, in taking the necessary action for the further restoration of human rights."

Mr. Gros Espiell, in his first report to the commission (UN Doc. E/CN.4/1988/42, para. 16) stated that he believed that his mandate was to deal with the possibility offered to the constitutional government of Guatemala of requesting advisory services and other forms of assistance with a view to fostering advances in democracy and strengthening respect for human rights. After considering the report, the commission noted (resolution 1988/50) that the government of Guatemala was prepared "to guarantee the protection of human rights and fundamental freedoms in that country. However, after the expert submitted his second report (UN Doc.E/CN.4/1989/39) to the commission at its 1989 session, the commission expressed (in resolution 1989/74), "its serious concern at the harmful conditions that still exist and that place severe limitations on any genuine process of improving the human rights situation in Guatemala" and urged the government "to intensify its efforts to ensure that all its authorities and security forces fully respect the human rights and fundamental freedoms of all its citizens."

In his report to the 1990 session of the Commission (UN Doc. E/CN.4/1990/45 and Add. 1), Mr. Gros Espiell reviewed the situation of human rights in Guatemala on the basis of his visits to that country in May and October–November 1989 and reported on a technical assistance program on human rights questions carried out in 1988 and 1989 as a result of a request made by Guatemalan authorities to the UN CENTER FOR HUMAN RIGHTS. The program was financed in its entirety ($US 222,000) by the UNITED NATIONS VOLUNTARY FUND FOR ADVISORY SERVICES AND TECHNICAL ASSISTANCE IN THE FIELD OF HUMAN RIGHTS.

The expert's general conclusions from the study of the human rights situation in Guatemala, as summarized in the report, were as follows (UN Doc.E/CN.4/1990/45, chap. VI, para. 66–70):

(a) The development and progress in the legal framework for recognizing, guaranteeing and protecting human rights in Guatemala are undeniable;

(b) The Government's political will to ensure respect for these rights is definite. In the view of the Expert, its efforts in this regard cannot be doubted. But it lacked the firm and unrelenting determination to carry out a human rights policy at the proper time and, most important, at present it has no possibility to act with all the constitutional and political authority that is needed to achieve the desired goals;

(c) Virtually nothing has been done either by the Government or by the judiciary to investigate and punish earlier human rights violations;

(d) Major *de facto* harmful conditions still exist and place severe limitations on any genuine process of improving the human rights situation in Guatemala;

(e) A climate of social violence continues to exist. What is more, it has grown and become worse. A human rights culture will have to be developed in which tolerance takes the place of the present contempt for pluralism and opposing views among many sections of the population;

(f) Violations of civil and political rights, especially deaths and disappearances, are still taking place and have increased in number. These are apparently the outcome not of government orders on policy but of factors, of acts committed by power circles and a persistent climate of violence that are still beyond effective government control. The Government has proved powerless and incapable of remedying this situation. Its scope for action has lessened as the violence and violations have increased;

(g) It is necessary to make sure that people are not compelled to join civilian self-defence patrols and do not suffer reprisals for not doing so;

(h) Serious deficiencies remain in the situation regarding respect for economic, social and cultural rights. Society as a whole is still conditioned by injustice and discrimination;

(i) The situation of the indigenous populations continues to be a crucial problem. The habitual discrimination and exploitation of these populations has been a constant source of human rights violations. The Government is aware of this difficult problem and an examination and comprehensive plan of the political, economic, social and cultural aspects of the question is under way (see the conclusions of consultant Willemsen Diaz, especially on the legislation which is being drafted);

(j) If the democratic process grows stronger and takes root and if it is maintained without any institutional breakdowns, the slow process of improvement initiated by the constitutional Government can be expected to continue;

(k) For this to happen, aside from the essential political will and the commitment that the Guatemalan people and their freely elected authorities alone can provide, continued international assistance and support are required;

(l) The dialogue for national reconciliation should be encouraged whole-heartedly and there should be no unjustified exclusions from it. The Government should participate actively, demonstrating total political will in continuing this dialogue;

(m) The technical capability and efficiency of the police should be upgraded in accordance with the conclusions of the report by the consultant, J. Maier;

(n) The operation of the Judiciary should be improved as recommended by the consultant, J. Maier, in his conclusions;

(o) The Procurator for Human Rights should be given greater support to enable him to continue, extend and complete the work he has begun. (In this connection, see the conclusions of the experts from the Parliamentary High Commissioner of Spain);

(p) More emphasis should be placed on training in civics and democracy, in an atmosphere of respect for human rights, for senior officers of the armed forces;

(q) The total subordination in matters of jurisdiction of members of the armed forces to the ordinary system of justice should be studied;

(r) With reference to the problem of refugees (paras. 34–39), since repatriation depends on political, economic, and social conditions and the level of violence, efforts must be continued to encourage, freely the speeding up of the repatriation process which has experienced some vicissitudes.

These conclusions coincide in general with those the Expert put forward in his previous reports to the Commission. Political difficulties, the continuing climate of violence and the influence of the negative factors referred to above have prevented the Government, in its weakened state, from ensuring full safeguards and respect for human rights.

Events have not justified the relative and cautious optimism felt in 1987 and 1988. This is serious, disturbing and unfortunate.

International assistance and co-operation are essential if this process is to continue, through the application of the provisions of the international instruments ratified by Guatemala and through the promotion of human rights in the manner indicated in paragraph 71 (c) and (d).

Only in a pluralistic and representative democracy, with a fully operative Constitution, with free elections and with everyone subject to a single and legitimate civil authority, can the future be contemplated and can there be an improvement in the human rights situation in Guatemala. The present constitutional Government, notwithstanding its shortcomings and omissions should, therefore, be supported, as should future democratic Governments.

The Expert's recommendations to the Commission were as follows: (chap. VII, para. 71–72):

(a) It is necessary for the Commission to continue to observe the situation of human rights in whatever way it deems appropriate, bearing in mind the present situation in Guatemala;

(b) Conclusions (l) to (p) should be borne in mind;

(c) It is essential to continue the broad programme of assistance to the Government to help the democratic process, since this institutional framework is a necessary but not the only prerequisite for the future improvement of the situation which is undeniably tied in with the maintenance of democracy;

(d) In keeping with what has already been done, this programme should, *inter alia,* continue to consist of:

(i) Assistance to introduce human rights courses at all levels of education. This should include not only State education but also education in private schools, colleges and universities;

(ii) Assistance for courses and seminars intended for judges and officials of the Judiciary;

(iii) Assistance for courses and seminars for police officials. It must be ensured that human rights are included as a subject in the continuous training of senior police officials;

(iv) Assistance for courses and seminars intended for officers in the armed forces. Human rights must be included at all times as a subject in the courses in the Military College and in the courses for officers on the General Staff. Such courses should not be confined to international humanitarian law but should cover the overall topic of human rights.

Without prejudice to these specific recommendations, the Expert would also like to draw the attention to the value of:

(a) Continuing to provide suitable advice and assistance for the organization and activities of the Office of the Procurator for Human Rights;

(b) Continuing to provide multidisciplinary and sectoral support to help in devising an overall policy on development, assistance and non-discrimination in regard to the indigenous populations;

(c) Supporting and complementing bilateral aid, already negotiated and in the process of being furnished, for technical reform and material improvement of the police force, so that it will become an effective democratic organization protecting and guaranteeing law and order and everyone's rights and freedoms.

The expert ended his report to the commission with the following concluding remarks (chap. VIII, para. 74–83):

In the course of monitoring the situation in Guatemala for almost four years, the Expert has ascertained that extensive sections of Guatemalan society have begun to understand the problem of human rights, its conception and the limitations and obligations involved. Previously, it was a problem that did not impinge on the social conscience, one which was alien to a "culture", that had other components. But today, the start of a process of change can be glimpsed. It is a difficult and complex process and cannot be expected to come about automatically or rapidly. However, it is the only one that can bring about a legal situation, in the context of which the present and future democratic governments can work more effectively and efficiently than they have been able to do so far. This beginning of a change in thinking and a new awareness of the need to respect human rights—seen as deriving directly from the dignity of all human beings without any kind of discrimination—is perhaps the most important progress achieved in Guatemala in recent years and gives some ground for optimism about the future. Human rights violations are not confined to the Government or public officials acting in an official capacity. Human rights are also violated by terrorists and the guerrilla—especially in a democratic State, which, because it is pluralistic, guarantees the free expression of opposing political views by legitimate means—by armed fringe groups which act outside the control of the army or the police, or which are in the pay of private interests, by common criminals and by all who resort to violence in order to settle any kind of conflict or to express hatred, and to indicate the inability to conceive that there can be divergent views in freedom. But the many and varied causes of human rights violations in Guatemala as well as the injustice of placing the blame solely at the door of the Government must be borne in mind. it is equally true and should always be remembered that the Government has a legal, political and moral obligation both nationally and internationally, to guarantee the enjoyment of human rights to all persons under its jurisdiction.

For personal reasons, the Expert is unable to continue the mandate which the Commission had assigned him, and this report is therefore his last. He wishes to thank the Commission for the confidence shown him and the support which he received and to say that the case of Guatemala and the changes which occurred in the human rights situation during the years in which he was required to observe the process at firsthand enabled him to study a complex and difficult situation, which raises serious doubts and questions.

First of all, there is an apparently insurmountable gulf between law and reality, between what should be and what is and between the rule and what is actually done. This is a particularly serious matter in Guatemala and has already been referred to by the Expert in other reports. Until this gulf is bridged, until this breach begins to close, the human rights situation will not improve. The traditional legal approach, the belief that problems can be solved because a rule, full of fine-sounding words exists, but is not applied is one of the worst obstacles to progress on human rights issues. However, one should not think that the law does not play an extremely important role in the overall process of improvement. Legal standards are absolutely essential. Without the law, there can be no progress in human rights but if the law is not applies and no serious attempt is made to enforce it, maintain it and keep it alive and effective it is of little use. The law should be applied and should serve as a means of forcing a change in the situation and it is one's bounden duty to use it and not keep it there as an ethereal, distant, unattainable realization, divorced from reality.

Second, if material, economic, social and cultural conditions do not change, if there is no movement away from a society of exploitation, of immutable privileges and of entrenched injustice towards a society which is supportive, tolerant and fair, human rights cannot become a living reality, available to all, the basis for peace and progress.

Third, without democracy, without free elections, without constitutional Governments, it is not possible to contemplate an improvement in the human rights situation. However, one must recognize that the democratic Governments in Latin America which have succeeded military dictatorships have managed to achieve very little. This is not due only to the economic and social situation but to other real factors of power. These factors, which are outside the government apparatus, but which sometimes infiltrate the Government, the police and the armed forces, have proven to be stronger than even the Government itself, which is unable to dominate them.

The Government itself may respect human rights, but it lacks the ability, power or authority to ensure that they are fully and freely exercised and is unable to punish violations and guarantee peace and order based on freedom. It lives in fear, a prisoner of forces which it cannot control. This is a tragedy, a formidable problem, which has not been solved and with no prospect of an immediate solution. It has a negative and decisive impact on the situation in Guatemala which cannot be understood or tackled if it is not taken into account.

It should be acknowledged, with modesty and relativism, that it will not be possible to achieve any significant improvement in the human rights situation in the short term. A strengthened democratic Government, which is a genuine source of authority, based on the Constitution, public order safeguarded by the law, illegal centres of power brought under control or eliminated outright, a society that believes and trusts in the law, violence eschewed and tolerance embraced, an understanding of the need for pluralism and co-existence for all ideologies in a context of freedom, an acceptance, intellectually and at the practical level of the "human rights culture" are the conditions that must be met in order to improve the human rights situation in what can only be a lengthy and arduous process.

In order to advance in this process, democracy must perforce continue, there must be elections and the Constitution must be maintained. If there is any interruption of this process, the Government would not even be able to do what it has done so far despite its shortcomings, limitations and adverse conditions, but with sincerity and conviction, and there would be a backsliding into a maelstrom of unconfined violence and the horror of widespread and continued human rights violations, perpetrated, fanned and encouraged by governmental authority. This would be unacceptable. The Expert, therefore, believes that the maintenance of constitutional democracy in Guatemala, despite its limitations, shortcomings and weaknesses, is vital in order to envisage the protection of human rights in the future.

The Expert wished to make these comments as this will be his last report to the Commission. He considered that it was his duty to state his views in complete frankness, and without reticence of any kind.

During these years of contacts with the situation in Guatemala he has come to love the country and its people as if they were his own. That is why he is confident that Guatemala is capable of overcoming the anti-democratic violence and of securing respect for human rights, based on a fully effective Constitution and on the far-reaching changes needed in the present economic and social situation.

After examining the expert's final report, the Commission on Human Rights adopted on 7 March 1990 a resolution entitled "Assistance to Guatemala in the Field of Human Rights" (resolution 1990/80), the operative paragraphs of which are as follows (para. 1–15):

Expresses its gratitude to the Expert for the work done during his term of office and thanks him for his report and recommendations;

Expresses its appreciation also to the Government of Guatemala for its collaboration with the Commission on Human Rights in carrying out its advisory activities, as well as for the facilities and co-operation afforded to the Expert;

Recognizes that, while the Government of Guatemala has upheld its commitment to guaranteeing the protection of fundamental rights and freedoms, it has been unable to implement the decision with sufficient authority, so that the social violence and violations of human rights have continued;

Supports therefore the recommendations contained in the Expert's report (E/CN.4/1990/45) that the programme of assistance and advisory services in the field of human rights should be continued and strengthened;

Urgently appeals to the Government of Guatemala to continue to accord priority to its undertaking under the Esquipulas II Agreements and to promote and participate more actively in the national reconciliation dialogue, as one of the ways of consolidating the democratic process;

Deeply deplores the increase in murders, kidnappings and attacks on and threats against persons involved in political activities as jeopardizing the democratization process;

Expresses its profound concern at the resurgence of the criminal activities of the "death squads", as indicated in the report of the Special Rapporteur to examine questions relevant to torture (E/CN.4/1990/17);

Deplores, in particular, the recent murders of a member of the National Revolutionary Movement Party (MNR) of El Salvador, Secretary for Latin America of the Socialist International, and of a Guatemalan lawyer, on 12 January 1990 in Guatemala, and requests the Government of Guatemala to continue and strengthen the investigation already under way, with a view to identifying and punishing the culprits;

Requests the Government of Guatemala to intensify its efforts to ensure that all its authorities and security forces fully respect the human rights and fundamental freedoms of the Guatemalan people;

Urges the Government of Guatemala to initiate or intensify, as the case may be, investigations aimed at identifying and bringing to justice those responsible for acts of torture, disappearance, murders and extra-legal executions;

Further urges the Government of Guatemala to promote any measures necessary to identify and punish members of "death squads";

Encourages the Government of Guatemala to strengthen policies and programmes relating to the situation of the indigenous populations, taking into account their proposals and aspirations, to enable them to enjoy fully their fundamental rights and freedoms;

Requests the Secretary-General to continue to provide the Government of Guatemala with such advisory services and other forms of assistance in the field of human rights as may be necessary to foster and strengthen the consolidation of the democratic process, and to promote a human rights culture;

Requests the Secretary-General to appoint an independent expert as his representative to examine the human rights situation in Guatemala and continue assistance to the Government in the field of human rights who, within the framework of his mandate, shall prepare a report with appropriate recommendations for submission to the Commission at its forty-seventh session;

Decides to consider this matter at its forty-seventh session under an item of the agency to be determined in the light of the above-mentioned report and of the situation of human rights and fundamental freedoms in Guatemala.

GUATEMALA: DISAPPEARANCES. The 1987 report of the **WORKING GROUP ON ENFORCED OR INVOLUNTARY DISAPPEARANCES** includes an addendum (UN Doc. E/CN.4/1988/19/Add. 1) which reflects the results of a visit to Guatemala, from 5 to 9 October 1987, carried out by two members on behalf of the working group. The visit was made on invitation of the government of Guatemala, the working group acting in a purely humanitarian spirit with the sole object of assisting the families of the missing persons to determine the whereabouts of their relatives.

The circumstances leading up to the visit are described by the working group, in the addendum (para. 1–2), as follows:

As of its establishment in 1980, the Working Group on Enforced or Involuntary Disappearances was seized of an alarmingly high number of reports about the disappearance of persons in Guatemala. It was widely asserted that disappearances had begun to occur on a massive scale in the second half of the 1960s during the Government of Mr. Méndez Montenegro which had preceeded a decade and a half of military rule under which the number of reported cases had reached disquieting proportions. In the light of the reports received and in accordance with Commission on Human Rights resolution 1984/23—in paragraph 7 of which the Commission encouraged the Governments concerned to consider with special attention any wish expressed by the Working Group to visit their countries—in 1984 the Group stated that it would like to visit Guatemala. However, its request remained without response until the present constitutional Government took power in January 1986.

At the specific invitation of the new Government, the Working Group, represented by Mr. Jonas K.D. Foli [Ghana] and Mr. Luis Varela Quirós [Costa Rica], visited Guatemala from 5 to 9 October 1987. During the visit the two members of the Working Group were received by the President of the Republic, the Ministers of Defence and Foreign Affairs, the Vice-Ministers for Foreign Affairs and the Interior, the Human Rights Commission of the Guatemalan Congress and other Congressman, the President of the Supreme Court, the Procurador de Derechos Humanos (Attorney for Human Rights), the Director of the National Police and other officials of the executive, the judiciary and local authorities. The members also met many relatives of missing persons, witnesses and representatives of organizations concerned with the problem of disappearances or human rights questions in general. Furthermore, they heard the views of dignitaries of the Roman Catholic Church, representatives of various political parties and the media as well as other personalities from different segments of Guatemalan society.

The reports on disappearances received by the working group before and during the visit to Guatemala clearly indicated the existence of a problem in that country. They are summarized by the working group, in the addendum (para. 18–20) in the following paragraphs:

A variety of testimony received both in Guatemala City and away from the capital indicated that disappearances were not a recent phenomenon in Guatemala, but had been occurring since the mid-1960s. According to these testimonies, disappearances started to occur in areas where there was organized armed opposition to the Government, but then spread to all parts of the country, affecting all segments of the population. In particular, citizens involved in trade-union, student, political or community activities, even if they were openly and legitimately so involved, were suspected of supporting the subversive movement. A number of persons related that many villages fell victim to massacres, disappearances and reprisals of all kinds solely because the subversives had operated in neighbouring areas and the armed forces had assumed that they had enjoyed the support of those villages. All non-government sources consulted coincided in the view that the majority of disappearances which had taken place during that period were part of the anti-subversive policy of successive military Governments.

Up to the end of 1985 the Working Group had forwarded to the Government of Guatemala 2,156 reports of enforced or involuntary disappearances, of which 39 had been clarified (see E/CN.4/1986/18, para. 121, statistical summary). Many reports on disappearances which occurred between 1978 and 1985 asserted that the missing person had been detained by one of the security services or by the regular armed forces; the military personnel involved were generally said to be in uniform or to belong to local detachments known to the population. Other arrests were attributed to the National Police, the Judicial Police, the Treasury Police and the National Guard, or to specialized services such as the Dirección de Investigaciones Técnicas (DIT) (Directorate for Technical Investigations), the Brigada de Operaciones Especiales (BROE) (Brigade for Special Operations), the Corps of Detectives and the Army Intelligence Service (G-2). A number of reports attributed responsibility to unidentified heavily armed persons using vehicles without number-plates or vehicles with tinted windows. The authors of such reports frequently stressed that those characteristics indicated that the abduction was committed by forces connected with or condoned by the Government, as the abductors frequently acted in broad daylight and with complete impunity. In some such cases, mention was made of the presence near the scene of the incident of military or police personnel who did not intervene to prevent the abduction. Some reports indicated the registration numbers of the vehicles used.

During their visit, the members of the Working Group heard many testimonies from relatives of persons who had disappeared in the early 1980s. A great number of those cases had not been reported to the authorities until the democratic Government came to power. In all cases the relatives attributed responsibility for the disappearances to the armed forces or the security services. They said that, although the abductors often wore masks to conceal their identity, there was no doubt that they were members of those forces. Relatives mentioned as reasons for their allegations that other persons who had disappeared in similar circumstances had later been found killed and that cartridge cases from weapons possessed only by the armed forces had been found next to the victims' bodies.

On the basis of all the information available to it, including the data collected by its members on their fact-finding visit, the working group submitted to the **COMMISSION ON HUMAN RIGHTS** the following concluding observations (para. 75–86):

During the two decades preceding the advent of the present Government, Guatemala endured sustained and pervasive violence. Thousands of people disappeared. Indeed, it was in Guatemala, under the presidency of Mr. Méndez Montenegro, that the phenomenon of disappearances as a systematic method of repression emerged. In subsequent years, it set a sorry standard for repressive régimes elsewhere.

Against this background, the Working Group felt that it

would be particularly pertinent, in view of its mandate, if it were to pay a visit to Guatemala. As early as 1984, the Group asked the then military Government whether there were any prospects of such a visit taking place, but to no avail. A renewed approach to the Government of President Vinicio Cerezo brought a positive response. The Group is indebted to his Government for inviting it to undertake that mission and for the large measure of co-operation extended to its members. Their visit took place in an atmosphere of openness and a genuine desire to explain the exigencies of the present situation.

In an undoubtedly difficult context, the new democratic system has made great strides towards re-establishing the rule of law and respect for basic rights. The Constitution now guarantees all basic human rights. Conceptually the *habeas corpus* procedure is exemplary. The Office of the Attorney for Human Rights has been created, a Commission on Human Rights is about to be established and a special judge was appointed to expedite the handling of countless *habeas corpus* petitions. A modernization of the police force, with proper training schemes on human rights issues, is well under way. Violations of human rights are diminishing overall and disappearances have decreased notably compared with the years of military Government, particularly in urban areas.

Yet, despite these accomplishments, formidable obstacles remain. Disappearances still occur in substantial numbers, generally attributed to continued repressive action on the part of the military and groups acting in connivance with them. This is particularly true in the countryside; in areas where the situation is fully controlled by the armed forces, disappearances cannot be credibly attributed to members of the guerrilla. Since President Cerezo took power 203 cases have reportedly taken place, 50 in 1987, as compared with 294 in 1985.

Clearly, well-designed institutions alone cannot suffice. For instance, *habeas corpus* proceedings come to a stop at the barracks gate, military authorities being unwilling to co-operate beyond that point and the judiciary not being strong enough to pursue its aims with the necessary vigour; proceedings are further hampered by the fact that witnesses fail to give testimony for fear of reprisals, if not out of despondency.

The key problem, of course, remains the question of investigations of individual cases of disappearances and the prevention of their future occurrence. In accordance with its mandate, the Working Groups must insist that the authorities of a given country investigate the disappearances reported to it, with a view to alleviating the plight of relatives who have had to live in anguish and paralysing uncertainty for too long. General Assembly resolution 33/173 calls upon all Governments in unequivocal terms to undertake such investigations in a speedy and impartial manner.

It is against this background that, in the case of Guatemala, the Group, in the humanitarian spirit that permeates all its endeavours, will continue to encourage genuine efforts on the part of the Government to take convincing measures to prevent and clarify disappearances. This is an immediate task for the Government. The necessary political will seems to exist and the people are aware of and support the need for change.

On the subject of prevention, the members of the Group feel that a permanent presence of the International Committee of the Red Cross, apart from other merits, may well reduce the level of violence, particularly as regards detainees, and prevent the disappearance of those held incommunicado.

The members of the Group have not been in a position to study the extent to which indigenous Guatemalans, who make up the majority of the population, were and are affected by the practice of disappearances. Thus so far it has taken up only those cases that were channeled through human rights organizations in the city and abroad. During the limited time spent in the countryside, the members heard testimony relating to many cases which had never been submitted to the Group before, raising concern about the real magnitude of the problem.

For non-governmental organizations, conditions have been arduous in Guatemala. Kidnapping and assassination have been the lot of many human rights protagonists, particularly those who, in the eyes of some, were being too strident in their demands for justice. Harassment remains and bitterness, if not despair, abound. Given the role of non-governmental organizations in raising the level of public consciousness on human rights issues and in re-establishing trust in the democratic system and the rule of law, efforts should be made to encourage them in their endeavours and protect them effectively against abuse.

It would seem appropriate, as part of the Government's overall policy to stem the tide of violence, if Guatemala became a party to all international instruments in the field of human rights which would guarantee to its people the enjoyment of international protection in this field.

Any nation emerging from 20 years of carnage cannot be expected to change radically overnight. The heritage of protracted military rule presents the present Government with a Herculean task. Not surprisingly, a climate of fear still prevails in the country, with little confidence left in the State institutions. There is apprehension that the repressive machinery of past years, may still be firmly in place, ready for use again in moments of crisis. For so long violence was generated by subversion and by the armed forces or by groups acting with or without the approval of successive Governments. All segments of Guatemalan society are keenly aware of this. At the same time people seem to share the desire that such violence, disappearances included, should not be repeated. That desire has guided efforts by the present administration to avoid repetition. These efforts should be supported by the international community, enabling the Government to implement programmes of prevention and protection of human rights and to establish the legal and organizational structure which the country needs for the realization of that objective.

At its 1990 session, the Commission on Human Rights examined four reports in which reference was made to the question of disappearances in Guatemala: the report of its expert, Mr. Hector Gros Espiell (UN Doc. E/CN.4/1990/45 and Add.1), the report of the Working Group on Enforced or Involuntary Disappearances (UN Doc. E/CN.4/1990/13), and the reports of the special rapporteur on summary or arbitrary executions (UN Doc. E/CN.4/1990/22 and Corr.1) and of the special rapporteur on torture (UN Doc. E/CN.4/1990/17).

On 7 March 1990, the commission (resolution 1990/80) noted that the constitutional government of Guatemala had made considerable efforts to guarantee the full application of human rights and fundamental freedoms and to promote the process of democratic consolidation and that general elections were scheduled to be held October 1990. It also noted that Guatemala's Procurator for Human Rights has decided, with the support of the government, to expand and strengthen his functions by, *inter alia*, establishing an investigative department and departmental offices throughout Guatemala and expanding his procuratorial functions before the courts. The commission expressed serious concern, however, that the government had not been able to control the persistent climate of violence in the country, which had worsened and in which serious violations of human rights was still occurring. It also expressed concern about the serious situation faced by Guatemala's indigenous populations, who had been subjected to discrimination, exploitation, and other violations of their human rights and fundamental freedoms.

GUINEA. The Republic of Guinea is a country in western Africa, on the Atlantic Ocean. It has borders with Guinea-Bissau, the Ivory Coast, Liberia, Mali, Senegal, and Sierra Leone. It achieved independence from France in 1958 and became a member of the United Nations the same year. Its population is estimated by the UN (1990) to be 6,876,000. Ethnic groups include the Foulani (40%), Malinke (26%), Susu (11%), Kissi (5%) and many others. Languages commonly used include French (official), Malinke, Susu, and Fulani. Religions practiced include Islam (70%), Animism (29%), and Christianity (1%). Literacy is estimated at 30%.

The Government (1990) took the form of a republic. However, following a military *coup d'etat* in March 1984, the constitution was suspended. All State power was assumed by the *Comite Militaire de Redressement National*, the chairman of which became president of the republic. He assisted by a vice president and council of ministers appointed by himself. One of the first acts of the military government was to release all political prisoners, to declare the observance of human rights to be one of its primary objectives, and to reorganize the judiciary to increase its independence.

President Lansana Conté, who promoted himself from colonel to brigadier-general after the 1984 coup, succeeded Sékou Touré, who had made Guinea Africa's first marxist State and who had ruled with scant regard for human rights for 26 years. Touré died in the United States following surgery.

Guinea became independent by overwhelmingly rejecting the proposal that it should remain voluntarily as part of French West Africa under the Fifth Republic constitution drafted in 1958 by Gen. Charles de Gaulle. Angered by the 95% "no" vote, de Gaulle withdrew more than 4,000 French administrators, doctors, judges, technicians, and teachers from the territory with a view to teaching a lesson to other colonies considering total independence. The departing French civil servants burned their records, files, blueprints, and operating manuals, and left the country in an administrative shambles.

The efforts of Guinea's first president, Ahmed Sékou Touré, to replace French workers with substitutes from eastern-bloc nations was unsuccessful. Although Guinea was the first marxist State in Africa, the Soviet Union and other eastern countries provided little administrative help or guidance. Guinea's capital, Conakry, became the K.G.B. centre for West Africa, and its airstrip was used to ferry Cuban soldiers into the area. Once considered the "pearl of West Africa" because of its wealth in gold, diamonds, and bauxite, Guinea saw its mining industries disintegrate from neglect and its people reduced to famine by collectivist farm policies.

President Lansana Conté's first official act was to send a mission to Paris, seeking assistance in rebuilding the nation's railroads, highways and buildings, in paving its' streets, and in restoring its public transportation. Since that time, French has been reintroduced in Guinean primary schools, and French instructors have retrained Guinean soldiers, policemen, journalists, teachers, and members of the medical professions. French entrepreneurs have opened stores, beauty parlors, restaurants, and discotheques.

President Conté's opposition maintains that the French are trampling Guinea's dignity and national independence. The reply of the government is to express the hope that Americans, Germans, and Italians will join the French in aiding Guinea' reconstruction.

The President has promised the people of Guinea a new constitution, including a bill of rights, an independent judiciary, periodic multi-party elections, and a government that functions by majority rule. He has also introduced a program of economic rehabilitation meeting the free-market requirements of the World Bank and has eliminated State-operated collective farms.

GUINEA–BISSAU. The Republic of Guinea–Bissau is a country in western Africa, on the Atlantic Ocean; its territory includes about 25 islands off the coast. It has borders with Guinea and Senegal. It achieved independence from Portugal in 1974 and became a member of the United Nations the same year. Its population is estimated by the UN (1990) to be 987,000.

Ethnic groups include the Balante (27%), Fulani (23%), Malinke (12%), Mandjako (11%), and Pepel (10%). Languages commonly used include Portuguese (official) and Crioulo. Religions practiced include Animism (65%), Islam (30%), and Christianity (5%). Literacy is estimated at 10%.

The government (1990) took the form of a republic. However, the constitution was suspended in 1980 when a military *coup d'etat* deposed the president, and all State power was assumed by the nine-member Council of the Revolution. The president of the council, Brig. General Joao Bernardo Vieira, is president of the republic and head of State and government; he is assisted by a 15-member Council of Ministers and five State secretaries. The only political party is the African Party for the Independence of Guinea-Bissau and Cape Verde.

GUYANA. The Cooperative Republic of Guyana is a country in tropical South America, on the Atlantic Ocean. It has borders with Brazil Suriname, and Venezuela. Formerly known as British Guiana, it achieved independence from Great Britain in 1966 and became a member of the United Nations the same year. Its population is estimated by the UN (1990) to be 1,040,000. Ethnic groups include persons of East Indian (51%), African (30%), and Amerindian (6%) descent. Languages commonly used include English (official), Hindi, and Urdu. Religions practiced include Christianity (Roman Catholic, 18%; Anglican 16%; other Protestant denominations, 18%), Hinduism (34%), and Islam (14%). Literacy is estimated at 86%.

The government (1990) took the form of a republic and member of the Commonwealth of Nations, of which the British sovereign is the symbolic head. In Guyana, executive power is exercised by the president, Hugh Desmond Hoyte, who is head of State and of government and leader of a 24-member cabinet. Legislation is dealt with by the unicameral National Assembly, composed of 53 members elected by popular vote and 12 elected by local councils, all for five-year terms. Elections are held under a single-list system with proportional representation. Political parties include the People's National Congress, the People's Progressive Party, the United Force, and the Working People's Alliance.

GUYANA: CONSTITUTION. The constitution of the Co-operative Republic of Guyana includes the following provisions (articles 40 and 138 to 154) specifically relating to human rights and fundamental freedoms:

Chapter III
Fundamental Rights and Freedoms of The Individual

40.(1) Every person in Guyana is entitled to the basic right to a happy, creative and productive life, free from hunger, disease, ignorance and want. That right includes the fundamental rights and freedoms of the individual, that is to say, the right, whatever his race, place of origin, political opinions, colour, creed or sex, but subject to respect for the rights and freedoms of others and for the public interest to each and all of the following, namely—

(a) life, liberty, security of the person and the protection of the law;

(b) freedom of conscience, of expression and of assembly and association; and

(c) protection for the privacy of his home and other property and from deprivation of property without compensation.

(2) The provisions of Title 1 of Part 2 shall have effect for the purpose of affording protection to the aforesaid fundamental rights and freedoms of the individual subject to such limitations of that protection as are contained in those provisions being limitations designed to ensure that the enjoyment of the said rights and freedoms by any individual does not prejudice the rights and freedoms of others or the public interest. . . .

Part 2—Specific Rules
Title 1
Protection of Fundamental Rights and Freedoms of the Individual

138.(1) No person shall be deprived of his life intentionally save in execution of the sentence of a court in respect of an offence under the law of Guyana of which he has been convicted.

(2) Without prejudice to any liability for a contravention of any other law with respect to the use of force in such cases as are hereinafter mentioned, a person shall not be regarded as having been deprived of his life in contravention of this article if he dies as the result of the use of force to such extent as is reasonably justifiable in the circumstances of the case—

(a) for the defence of any person from violence or for the defence of property;

(b) in order to effect a lawful arrest or to prevent the escape of a person lawfully detained;

(c) for the purpose of suppressing a riot, insurrection or mutiny; or

(d) in order to prevent the commission by that person of a criminal offence.

or if he dies as the result of a lawful act of war.

139.(1) No person shall be deprived of his personal liberty save as may be authorised by law in any of the following cases, that is to say—

(a) in execution of the sentence or order of a court, whether established for Guyana or some other country, in respect of a criminal offence of which he has been convicted;

(b) in execution of an order of the High Court or the Court of Appeal or such other court as may be prescribed by Parliament punishing him for contempt of any such court or of another court or tribunal;

(c) in execution of the order of a court made to secure the fulfilment of any obligation imposed on him by law;

(d) for the purpose of bringing him before a court in execution of the order of a court;

(e) upon reasonable suspicion of his having committed, or being about to commit, a criminal offence under the law of Guyana;

(f) in the case of a person who has not attained the age of eighteen years, under the order of a court or with the consent of his parent or guardian, for the purpose of his education or welfare;

(g) for the purpose of preventing the spread of an infectious or contagious disease;

(h) in the case of a person who is, or is reasonably suspected to be, of unsound mind, addicted to drugs or alcohol, or a vagrant, for the purpose of his care or treatment or the protection of the community;

(i) for the purpose of preventing the unlawful entry of that person into Guyana, or for the purpose of effecting the expulsion, extradition or other lawful removal of that person from Guyana or for the purpose of restricting that person while he is being conveyed through Guyana in the course of his extradition or removal as a convicted prisoner from one country to another;

(j) to such extent as may be necessary in the execution of a lawful order requiring that person to remain within a specified area within Guyana or prohibiting him from being within such an area, or to such extent as may be reasonably justifiable for the taking of proceedings against that person with a view to the making of any such order or relating to such an order after it has been made or to such extent as may be reasonably justifiable for restraining that person during any visit that he is permitted to make to any part of Guyana in which, in consequence of any such order his presence would otherwise by unlawful.

(k) subject to the provisions of the next following paragraph, for the purpose of his preventive detention;

(l) for the purpose of his being called up for national service.

(2) (a) No law providing for preventive detention shall authorise the detention of a person for a longer period than three months unless a tribunal established for the purposes of this paragraph has reported before the expiration of the said period of three months that there is, in its opinion, sufficient cause for such detention.

(b) The references in subparagraph (a) to a period of three months include references to any lesser periods that amount in the aggregate to three months:

Provided that no two such lesser periods shall be aggregated for this purpose if the period between the expiration of the first and the commencement of the second is more than one month.

(c) A person who has been detained by virtue of the provisions of any law providing for preventive detention and who has been released from detention in consequence of a report of a tribunal established for the purposes of this paragraph that there is, in its opinion, insufficient cause for his detention shall not be again detained by virtue of such provisions within the period of six months from his release on the same grounds as he was originally detained.

(d) For the purposes of subparagraph (c) a person shall be deemed to have been detained on the same grounds as he was originally detained unless a tribunal established as aforesaid has reported that, in its opinion, there appear, *prima facie,* to be new and reasonable grounds for the detention (but the giving of any such report shall be without prejudice to the provisions of subparagraph (a)).

(e) A tribunal established for the purposes of this paragraph shall be established by law and shall consist of persons who are Judges of the Supreme Court of Judicature or who are qualified to be appointed as Puisne Judges of the High Court.

(3) Any person who is arrested or detained shall be informed as soon as reasonably practicable, in a language that he understands, of the reasons for his arrest or detention and shall be permitted, at his own expense, to retain and instruct without delay a legal adviser of his own choice, being a person entitled to practise in Guyana as an attorney-at-law, and to hold communication with him.

(4) Any person who is arrested or detained—

(a) for the purpose of bringing him before a court in execution of the order of a court; or

(b) upon reasonable suspicion of his having committed or being about to commit a criminal offence,

and who is not released, shall be brought before a court as soon as is reasonably practicable; and if any person arrested or detained upon reasonable suspicion of his having committed or being about to commit a criminal offence is not tried within a reasonable time, then, without prejudice to any further proceedings which may be brought against him, he shall be released either unconditionally or upon reasonable conditions, including in particular such conditions as are reasonably necessary to ensure that he appears at a later date for trial or for proceedings preliminary to trial.

(5) Any person who is unlawfully arrested or detained by any other person shall be entitled to compensation therefor from that other person.

(6) Nothing in the provisions of paragraphs (3) and (4) shall apply to any person arrested or detained by virtue of the provisions of any law providing for preventive detention except in so far as the provisions of the said paragraph (3) require that he shall be permitted to retain and instruct a legal adviser and to hold communication with him.

140.(1) No person shall be held in slavery or servitude.

(2) No person shall be required to perform forced labour.

(3) For the purposes of this article, the expression "forced labour" does not include—

(a) any labour required in consequence of the sentence or order of a court;

(b) any labour required of any person while he is lawfully detained that, though not required in consequence of the sentence or order of a court, is reasonably necessary in the interests of hygiene or for the maintenance of the place at which he is detained;

(c) any labour required of a member of a disciplined force in pursuance of his duties as such or, in the case of a person who has conscientious objections to service as a member of a naval, military or air force, any labour that that person is required by law to perform in place of such service; or

(d) any labour required during any period when Guyana is at war or in the event of any hurricane, earthquake, flood, fire or other like calamity that threatens the life or well-being of the community to the extent that the requiring of such labour is reasonably justifiable, in the circumstances of any situation arising or existing during that period or as a result of that calamity, for the purpose of dealing with that situation.

141.(1) No person shall be subjected to torture or to inhuman or degrading punishment or other treatment.

(2) Nothing contained in or done under the authority of any law shall be held to be inconsistent with or in contravention of this article to the extent that the law in question authorises the infliction of any punishment or the administration of any treatment that was lawful in Guyana immediately before the commencement of this Constitution.

142.(1) No property of any description shall be compulsorily taken possession of, and no interest in or right over property of any description shall be compulsorily acquired, except by or under the authority of a written law which provides for compensation for the property of any interest in or right over property so possessed or acquired and either fixes the amount of compensation or specifies the principles on which the compensation is to be determined and given and no such law shall be called in question in any court on the ground that the compensation provided by that law is not adequate.

(2) Nothing contained in or done under the authority of any law shall be held to be inconsistent with or in contravention of the preceding paragraph—

(a) to the extent that the law in question makes provision for the taking of possession or acquisition of any property—

(i) in satisfaction of any tax, duty, rate, cess or other impost;

(ii) by way of penalty for breach of the law, whether under civil process or after conviction of a criminal offence under the law of Guyana;

(iii) as an incident of a lease, tenancy, mortgage, charge, bill of sale, pledge, contract, grant, permission or licence;

(iv) in the execution of judgments or orders of a court in proceedings for the determination of civil rights or obligations;

(v) in circumstances where it is reasonably necessary so to do because the property is in a dangerous state or injurious to the health of human beings, animals or plants;

(vi) in consequence of any law with respect to the limitation of actions;

(vii) for so long only as may be necessary for the purposes of any examination, investigation, trial or inquiry or, in the case of land, for the purposes of the carrying out thereon of work of soil conservation or the conservation of other natural resources or work relating to agricultural development or improvement;

(viii) which is not beneficially occupied or which, if it is beneficially occupied, is not so occupied by the holder of the title to the land or by any member of his family; or

(ix) in consequence of any law requiring an employer to remunerate his employee during any period of compulsory national service which the employee has undertaken; or

(b) to the extent that the law in question makes provision for the taking of possession or acquisition of—

(i) property of the Amerindians of Guyana for the purpose of its care, protection and management or any right, title or interest held by any person in or over any lands situate in an Amerindian District, Area or Village established under the Amerindian Act for the purpose of effecting the termination or transfer thereof for the benefit of an Amerindian community;

(ii) enemy property;

(iii) property of a deceased person, a person of unsound mind or a person who has not attained the age of eighteen years, for the purpose of its administration for the benefit of the persons entitled to the beneficial interest therein;

(iv) property of a person adjudged insolvent or a body corporate in liquidation, for the purpose of its administration for the benefit of the creditors of the insolvent person or body corporate and, subject thereto for the benefit of other persons entitled to the beneficial interest in the property;

(v) property subject to a trust, for the purpose of vesting the property in persons appointed as trustees under the instrument creating the trust or by a court, or, by order of a court, for the purpose of giving effect to the trust; or

(vi) property to be used by the State for the purpose of providing, maintaining and managing any place of education, where the property was being used as a place of education at any time during 1976 and prior to the coming into operation of the law in question.

(3) Nothing in this article shall be construed as affecting the making or operation of any law—

(i) so far as it provides for the orderly marketing or production or growth or extraction of any agricultural product or mineral or any article or thing prepared for market or manufactured therefor or for the reasonable restriction of the use of any property in the interest of safeguarding the interests of others or the protection of tenants, licensees or others having rights in or over such property;

(ii) so far as it provides for the making of contributions compulsorily by workers to any industrial scheme or workers' organisation intended to work or provide for the benefit or welfare of such workers or of their fellow workers or of any relatives and dependants of any of them; or

(iii) for the compulsory taking of possession in the public interest of any property, or the compulsory acquisition in the public interest of any interest in or right over property, where that property, interest or right is held by a body corporate established directly by law for public purposes in which moneys provided by Parliament or by any Legislature previously established for the territory of Guyana have been invested.

143.(1) Except with his own consent, no person shall be subjected to the search of his person or his property or the entry by others on his premises.

(2) Nothing contained in or done under the authority of any law shall be held to be inconsistent with or in contravention of this article to the extent that the law in question makes provisions—

(a) that is reasonably required in the interests of defence, public safety, public order, public morality, public health, town or country planning, the development or utilisation of any other property in such manner as to promote the public benefit;

(b) that is reasonably required for the purpose of protecting the rights or freedoms of other persons;

(c) that authorises an officer or agent of the Government of Guyana, or of a local democratic organ or of a body corporate established directly by law for public purposes to enter on the premises of any person in order to inspect those premises or anything thereon for the purpose of any tax, duty, rate, cess or other impost or in order to carry out work connected with any property that is lawfully on those premises and that belongs to that Government, local democratic organ or body corporate, as the case may be, or for the purpose of obtaining or verifying information required for compiling national statistics or required for the purposes of planning, management and development of the national economy; or

(d) that authorises, for the purpose of enforcing the judgment or order of a court in any proceedings, the entry upon any premises by order of a court.

144.(1) If any person is charged with a criminal offence, then, unless the charge is withdrawn, the case shall be afforded a fair hearing within a reasonable time by an independent and impartial court established by law.

(2) It shall be the duty of a court to ascertain the truth in every case provided that every persons who is charged with a criminal offence—

(a) shall be presumed to be innocent until he is proved or has pleaded guilty;

(b) shall be informed as soon as reasonably practicable, in a language that he understands and in detail, of the nature of the offence charge;

(c) shall be given adequate time and facilities for the preparation of his defence;

(d) shall be permitted to defend himself before the court in person or by a legal representative of his own choice;

(e) shall be afforded facilities to examine in person or by his legal representative the witnesses called by the prosecution before the court and to obtain the attendance and carry out the examination of witnesses to testify on his behalf before the court on the same conditions as those applying to witnesses called by the prosecution; and

(f) shall be permitted to have without payment the assistance of an interpreter if he cannot understand the language used at the trial of the charge,

and, except with his consent, the trial shall not take place in his absence unless he so conducts himself as to render the continuance of the proceedings in his presence impracticable and the court has ordered him to be removed and the trial to proceed in his absence or he fails without reasonable excuse (the proof whereof shall lie on him) to attend court.

(3) When a person is tried for any criminal offence, the accused person or any person authorised by him in that behalf shall, if he so requires and subject to payment of such reasonable fee as may be prescribed by law, be given within a reasonable time after judgment a copy for the use of the accused person of any record of the proceedings made by or on behalf of the court.

(4) No person shall be held to be guilty of a criminal offence on account of any act or omission that did not, at the time it took place, constitute such an offence, and no penalty shall be imposed for any criminal offence that is more severe in degree or nature than the most severe penalty that might have been imposed for that offence at the time when it was committed.

(5) No person who shows that he has been tried by a competent court for a criminal offence and either convicted or acquitted shall again be tried for that offence or for any other criminal offence of which he could have been convicted at the trial for that offence, save upon the order of a superior court in the course of appeal proceedings relating to the conviction or acquittal.

(6) No person shall be tried for a criminal offence if he shows that he has been granted a pardon for that offence.

(7) No person who is tried for a criminal offence shall be compelled to give evidence at the trial.

(8) Any court or other tribunal prescribed by law for the determination of the existence or extent of any civil right or obligation shall be established by law and shall be independent and impartial; and where proceedings for such a determination are instituted by any person before such a court or other tribunal, the case shall be given a fair hearing within a reasonable time.

(9) Except with the agreement of all the parties thereto,

all proceedings of every court and proceedings for the determination of the existence or extent of any civil right or obligation before any other tribunal, including the announcement of the decision of the court or other tribunal, shall be held in public.

(10) Nothing in the preceding paragraph shall prevent the court or other tribunal from excluding from the proceedings persons other than the parties thereto and their legal representatives to such extent as the court or other tribunal

(a) may by law be empowered so to do and may consider necessary or expedient in circumstances where publicity would prejudice the interests of justice or in interlocutory proceedings or in the interests of decency, public morality, the welfare of persons under the age of eighteen years or the protection of the private lives of persons concerned in the proceedings; or

(b) may by law be empowered or required so to do in the interests of defence, public safety or public order.

(11) Nothing contained in or done under the authority of any law shall be held to be inconsistent with or in contravention of—

(a) paragraph (2)(a) to the extent that the law in question imposes upon any person charged with a criminal offence the burden of proving particular facts;

(b) paragraph (2)(e) to the extent that the law in question imposes conditions that must be satisfied if witnesses called to testify on behalf of an accused person are to be paid their expenses out of public funds; or

(c) paragraph (5) to the extent that the law in question authorises a court to try a member of a disciplined force for a criminal offence notwithstanding any trial and conviction or acquittal of that member under the disciplinary law of that force, so, however, that any court so trying such a member and convicting him shall, in sentencing him to any punishment, take into account any punishment awarded him under that disciplinary law.

(12) In the case of any person who is held in lawful detention, the provisions of paragraph (1), paragraph (2)(d) and (e) and paragraph (3) shall not apply in relation to his trial for a criminal offence under the law regulating the discipline of persons held in such detention.

(13) Nothing contained in paragraph (2)(d) shall be construed as entitling a person to legal representation at public expense but, subject thereto, it shall be the duty of the State to ensure that every person charged with a criminal offence is given a fair trial and accordingly to make provision for legal aid to be given in suitable cases.

(14) In this article "criminal offence" means a criminal offence under the law of Guyana.

145.(1) Except with his own consent, no person shall be hindered in the enjoyment of his freedom of conscience, and for the purposes of this article the said freedom includes freedom of thought and of religion, freedom to change his religion or belief, and freedom, either alone or in community with others, and both in public and in private, to manifest and propagate his religion or belief in worship, teaching, practice and observance.

(2) No religious community shall be prevented from providing religious instruction for persons of that community.

(3) Except with his own consent (or, if he is a person who has not attained the age of eighteen years, the consent of his guardian), no person attending any place of education shall be required to receive religious instruction or to take part in or attend any religious ceremony or observance of that instruction, ceremony or observance relates to a religion which is not his own.

(4) No person shall be compelled to take any oath which is contrary to his religion or belief or to take any oath in a manner which is contrary to his religion or belief.

(5) Nothing contained in or done under the authority of any law shall be held to be inconsistent with or in contravention of this article to the extent that the law in question makes provision—

(a) which is reasonably required—

(i) in the interests of defence, public safety, public order, public morality or public health; or

(ii) for the purpose of protecting the rights and freedoms of other persons, including the right to observe and practise any religion without the unsolicited intervention of members of any other religion; or

(b) with respect to standards or qualifications to be required in relation to places of education including any instruction (not being religious instruction) given at such places.

(6) References in this article to a religion shall be construed as including references to a religious denomination, and cognate expressions shall be construed accordingly.

146.(1) Except with his own consent, no person shall be hindered in the enjoyment of his freedom of expression, that is to say, freedom to hold opinions without interference, freedom to receive ideas and information without interference, freedom to communicate ideas and information without interference and freedom from interference with his correspondence.

(2) Nothing contained in or done under the authority of any law shall be held to be inconsistent with or in contravention of this article to the extent that the law in question makes provision—

(a) that is reasonably required in the interests of defence, public safety, public order, public morality or public health;

(b) that is reasonably required for the purpose of protecting the reputations, rights, and freedoms of other persons or the private lives of persons concerned in legal proceedings, preventing the disclosure of information received in confidence, maintaining the authority and independence of the courts, regulating the technical administration or the technical operation of telephony, telegraphy, posts, wireless broadcasting or television, or ensuring fairness and balance in the dissemination of information to the public; or

(c) that imposes restrictions upon public officers or officers of any corporate body established on behalf of the public or owned by or on behalf of the Government of Guyana.

147.(1) Except with his own consent, no person shall be hindered in the enjoyment of his freedom of assembly and association, that is to say, his right to assemble freely and associate with other persons and in particular to form or belong to political parties or to form or belong to trade unions or other associations for the protection of his interests.

(2) Nothing contained in or done under the authority of any law shall be held to be inconsistent with or in contravention of this article to the extent that the law in question makes provision—

(a) that is reasonably required in the interests of defence, public safety, public order, public morality or public health; or

(b) that is reasonably required for the purpose of protecting the rights or freedoms of other persons; or

(c) that imposes restrictions upon public officers; or

(d) that imposes an obligation on workers to become contributors to any industrial scheme or workers' organisation intended to work or provide for the benefit or welfare of such workers or of their fellow workers or of any relatives and dependants of any of them.

148.(1) No person shall be deprived of his freedom of movement, that is to say, the right to move freely throughout Guyana, the right to reside in any part of Guyana, the right to enter Guyana, the right to leave Guyana and immunity from expulsion from Guyana.

(2) Any restriction on a person's freedom of movement that is involved in his lawful detention shall not be held to be inconsistent with or in contravention of this article.

(3) Nothing contained in or done under the authority of any law shall be held to be inconsistent with or in contravention of this article to the extent that the law in question makes provision—

(a) for the imposition of restrictions on the movement or residence within Guyana of any person or on any person's right to leave Guyana that are reasonably required in the interests of defence, public safety or public order or for the purpose of preventing the subversion of democratic institutions in Guyana;

(b) for the imposition of restrictions on the movement or residence within Guyana or on the right to leave Guyana of persons generally or any class of persons that are reasonably required in the interests of defence, public safety, public order, public morality or public health or for the purpose of preventing the subversion of democratic institutions in Guyana;

(c) for the imposition of restrictions on the acquisition or use of land or other property in Guyana;

(d) for the imposition of restrictions, by order of a court on the movement or residence within Guyana of any person or on any person's right to leave Guyana either in consequence of his having been found guilty of a criminal offence under the law of Guyana or for the purpose of ensuring that he appears before a court at a later date for trial for such a criminal offence or for proceedings preliminary to trial or for proceedings relating to his extradition or lawful removal from Guyana;

(e) for the imposition of restrictions on the freedom of movement of persons who are not citizens of Guyana;

(f) for the imposition of restrictions upon the movement or residence within Guyana or on the right to leave Guyana of public officers;

(g) for the removal of persons from Guyana—

(i) to be tried or punished in some other country for a criminal offence under the law of that country; or

(ii) to undergo imprisonment in some other country in execution of the sentence of a court in respect of a criminal offence under the law of Guyana of which he has been convicted; or

(iii) to be detained in an institution in some other country for the purpose of giving effect to the order of a court made in pursuance of a law of Guyana relating to the treatment of offenders under a specified age; or

(iv) to be detained for care or treatment in a hospital or other institution in pursuance of a law of Guyana relating to persons suffering from defect or disease of the mind; or

(h) for the imposition of restrictions on the right of any person to leave Guyana that are reasonably required in order to secure the fulfilment of any obligations imposed on that person by law.

(4) The provisions of article 151 shall apply in relation to a person whose freedom of movement is restricted by virtue of such a provision as is referred to in paragraph (3)(a) as they apply in relation to a person whose freedom of movement is restricted by virtue of such a provision as is referred to in article 150(2).

149.(1) Subject to the provisions of this article—

(a) no law shall make any provision that is discriminatory either of itself or in its effect; and

(b) no person shall be treated in a discriminatory manner by any persons acting by virtue of any written law or in the performance of the functions of any public office or any public authority.

(2) In this article the expression "discriminatory" means affording different treatment to different persons attributable wholly or mainly to their respective descriptions by race, place of origin, political opinion, colour or creed whereby persons of one such description are subjected to disabilities or restrictions to which persons of another such description are not made subject or are accorded privileges or advantages which are not afforded to persons of another such description.

(3) Paragraph (1)(a) shall not apply to any law so far as that law makes provision—

(a) with respect to persons who are not citizens of Guyana;

(b) with respect to adoption, marriage, divorce, burial, devolution of property on death or other matters of personal law; or

(c) whereby persons of any such description as is mentioned in the preceding paragraph may be subjected to any disability or restriction or may be accorded any privilege or advantage which, having regard to its nature and to special circumstances pertaining to those persons or to persons of any other such description, is reasonably justifiable.

(4) Nothing contained in any law shall be held to be inconsistent with or in contravention of paragraph (1)(a) to the extent that it makes provision with respect to standards or qualifications (not being standards or qualifications specifically relating to race, place of origin, political opinion, colour or creed) to be required of any person who is appointed to any office in the public service, any office in a disciplined force, or any office in the service of a local democratic organ or of a body corporate established by any law for public purposes.

(5) Paragraph (1)(b) shall not apply to anything which is expressly or by necessary implication authorised to be done by any such provision of law as is referred to in either of the two preceding paragraphs.

(6) Nothing contained in or done under the authority of any law shall be held to be inconsistent with or in contravention of this article to the extent that the law in question makes provision—

(a) whereby persons of any such description as is mentioned in paragraph (2) may be subjected to any restriction on the rights and freedoms guaranteed by articles 143, 145, 146, 147 and 148, being such a restriction as is authorised by article 143 (2), article 145(5), article 146(2), article 147(2), or article 148(3), other than subparagraph (c) thereof, as the case may be;

(b) for the appropriation of revenue or other funds of Guyana; or

(c) for the protection, well-being or advancement of the Amerindians of Guyana.

(7) Paragraph (1)(b) shall not affect any discretion relating to the institution, conduct or discontinuance of civil or criminal proceedings in any court that is vested in any person by or under this Constitution or any other law.

150.(1) This article applies to any period when—

(a) Guyana is at war; or

(b) there is in force a proclamation (in this article referred to as a "proclamation of emergency") made by the President declaring that a state of public emergency exists for the purposes of this article; or

(c) there is in force a resolution of the National Assembly, in favour of which there were cast the votes of not fewer than two-thirds of all the elected members, declaring that democratic institutions in Guyana are threatened by subversion.

(2) Nothing contained in or done under the authority of any law shall be held to be inconsistent with or in contravention of article 139, 140(2) or 143, any provision of article 144 other than paragraph (4) thereof, or any provision of articles 145 to 149 (inclusive) to the extent that the law in question makes in relation to any period to which this article applies provision, or authorizes the doing during any such period of anything, which is reasonably justifiable in the circumstances of any situation arising or existing during that period for the purpose of dealing with that situation.

(3) (a) Where any proclamation of emergency has been made, copies thereof shall as soon as practicable be laid before the National Assembly, and if, by reason of its adjournment or the prorogation of Parliament, the Assembly is not due to meet within five days the President shall, by proclamation, summon the Assembly to meet within five days, and the Assembly shall accordingly meet and sit upon the day appointed by the proclamation and shall continue to sit and act as if it had stood adjourned or Parliament had stood prorogued to that day.

(b) A proclamation of emergency shall, unless it is sooner revoked by the President, cease to be in force at the expiration of a period of fourteen days beginning on the date on which it was made or such longer period as may be provided under the next following subparagraph, but without prejudice to the making of another proclamation of emergency at or before the end of that period.

(c) If at any time while a proclamation of emergency is in force (including any time while it is in force by virtue of the provisions of this subparagraph) a resolution is passed by the Assembly approving its continuance in force for a further period, not exceeding six months, beginning on the date on which it would otherwise expire, the proclamation shall, if not sooner revoked, continue in force for that further period.

(4) A resolution such as is referred to in paragraph (1)(c) shall, unless it is sooner revoked by a resolution of the Assembly, cease to be in force at the expiration of two years beginning on the date on which it was passed or such shorter period as may be specified therein, but without prejudice to the passing of another resolution by the Assembly in the manner prescribed by that paragraph at or before the end of that period.

151.(1) Where any person is lawfully detained by virtue of such a provision as is referred to in article 150(2), or the movement or residence within Guyana of any person or any person's right to leave Guyana is (otherwise than by order of a court) lawfully restricted by virtue of such a provision as aforesaid, his case shall be reviewed by a tribunal established for the purposes of this article not later than three months from the commencement of the detention or restriction and thereafter not later than six months from the date on which his case was last reviewed as aforesaid.

(2) On any review by a tribunal in pursuance of the preceding paragraph of the case of any person the tribunal may make recommendations concerning the necessity or expedience of continuing the detention or restriction to the authority by whom it was ordered but, unless it is otherwise provided by law, that authority shall not be obliged to act in accordance with any such recommendation.

(3) A tribunal established for the purpose of this article shall be so established by law and constituted in such manner as to secure its independence and impartiality and presided over by a person appointed by the Chancellor from among persons entitled to practise in Guyana as attorneys-at-law

152.(1) Except in proceedings commenced before the expiration of a period of six months from the commencement of this Constitution, with respect to a law made under the Guyana Independence Order 1966 and the Constitution annexed thereto, nothing contained in or done under the authority of any written law shall be held to be inconsistent with or in contravention of any provision of articles 138 to 149 (inclusive) to the extent that the law in question—

(a) is a law (in this article referred to as "an existing law") that had effect as part of the law of Guyana immediately before the commencement of this Constitution, and has continued to have effect as part of the law of Guyana at all times since that day;

(b) repeals or re-enacts an existing law without alteration; or

(c) alters an existing law and does not thereby render that law inconsistent with any provision of the said articles 138 to 149 in a manner in which, or to an extent to which, it was not previously so inconsistent.

(2) In subparagraph (c) of the preceding paragraph the reference to altering an existing law includes references to repealing it and re-enacting it with modifications or making different provisions in lieu thereof, and to modifying it; and in the preceding paragraph "written law" includes any instrument having the force of law and in this and the preceding paragraph references to the repeal and re-enactment of an existing law shall be construed accordingly.

(3) In relation to any person who is a member of a disciplined force raised under a law in force in Guyana, nothing contained in or done under the authority of the disciplinary law of that force shall be held to be inconsistent with or in contravention of any of the provisions of this Title, other than articles 138, 140 and 141.

(4) In relation to any person who is a member of a disciplined force raised otherwise than as aforesaid and lawfully present in Guyana, nothing contained in or done under the authority of the disciplinary law of that force shall be held to be inconsistent with or in contravention of any of the provisions of this Title.

153.(1) Subject to the provisions of paragraph (6), if any person alleges that any of the provisions of articles 138 to 151 (inclusive) has been, is being or is likely to be contravened in relation to him (or, in the case of a person who is detained, if any other person alleges such a contravention in relation to the detained person), then, without prejudice to any other action with respect to the same matter which is lawfully available, that person (or that other person; may apply to the High Court for redress.

(2) The High Court shall have original jurisdiction—

(a) to hear and determine any application made by any person in pursuance of the preceding paragraph;

(b) to determine any question arising in the case of any person which is referred to it in pursuance of the next following paragraph,

and may make such orders, issue such writs and give such directions as it may consider appropriate for the purpose of enforcing or securing the enforcement of any of the provisions of articles 138 to 151 (inclusive):

Provided that the High Court shall not exercise its powers under this paragraph if it is satisfied that adequate means of redress are or have been available to the person concerned under any other law.

(3) If in any proceedings in any court subordinate to the High Court any question arises as to the contravention of any of the provisions of article 138 to 151 (inclusive), the person presiding in that court shall refer the question to the High Court unless, in his opinion, the raising of the question is merely frivolous or vexatious.

(4) Where any question is referred to the High Court in pursuance of paragraph (3), the High Court shall give its decision upon the question and the court in which the question arose shall dispose of the case in accordance with that decision or, if that decision is the subject of an appeal under this Constitution to the Court of Appeal, in accordance with the decision of the Court of Appeal

(5) Parliament may confer upon the High Court such powers in addition to those conferred by this article as may appear to Parliament to be necessary or desirable for the purpose of enabling the High Court more effectively to exercise the jurisdiction conferred upon by this article.

(6) Parliament may make provision with respect to the practice and procedure—

(a) of the High Court in relation to the jurisdiction and powers conferred upon it by or under this article;

(b) of the High Court and the Court of Appeal in relation to appeals to the Court of Appeal from decisions of the High Court in the exercise of such jurisdiction;

(c) of subordinate courts in relation to references to the High Court under paragraph (3),

including provision with respect to the time within which any application, reference or appeal shall or may be made or brought; and, subject to any provision so made, provision may be made with respect to the matters aforesaid by rules of court.

154. In this Title, unless the context otherwise requires—

"contravention", in relation to any requirement, includes a failure to comply with that requirement, and cognate expressions shall be construed accordingly;

"court" means any court of law having jurisdiction in Guyana other than a court established by a disciplinary law and, in articles 138 and 140, a court established by a disciplinary law;

"disciplinary law" means a law regulating the discipline of any disciplined force;

"disciplined force" means—

(a) any group of persons functioning whether wholly or partially as a naval, military, paramilitary or air force;

(b) a police force;

(c) a prison service; or

(d) a fire service;

"legal representative", in relation to any court or other tribunal, means a person entitled to practise as an attorney-at-law before such court or tribunal;

"member", in relation to a disciplined force, includes any person who, under the law regulating the discipline of that force, is subject to that discipline; and

"national service" means service in any disciplined force a principal purpose of which is the training of people with a view to advancing the economic development of Guyana.

H

HAITI. The Republic of Haiti is a country which occupies the western third of the island of Hispaniola, in the West Indies. It has a border with the Dominican Republic, which occupies the remainder of the island. It achieved independence from France in 1804 and became a member of the United Nations in 1945. Its population is estimated by the UN (1990) to be 7,509,000. Ethnic groups include persons of African (90%), French (5%), and mixed (5%) descent. Languages commonly used are French (official) and Creole. Religions practiced include Christianity (Roman Catholic and several Protestant denominations) and a variety of folk beliefs. Literacy is estimated at 20%.

The government (1990) took the form of a republic. However, following the abrupt departure from the country of "President for Life" Jean-Claude Duvalier, military rule prevailed, with Army Chief of Staff Lt. Gen. Henri Namphy as president and head of the Governing Council.

Duvalier, the son of a former dictator Francois Duvalier, who had seized power and established a regime based on the use of secret police in 1957, was no less ruthless than his father in suppressing any hint of opposition. After succeeding his father—known as "Papa Doc"—in 1971, Jean-Claude—known as "Baby Doc"—ruled over the poorest and most densely populated country in the western hemisphere, until forced to flee the country in 1985 in the face of public protests and the threat of an uprising.

Between 1981 and 1986, the COMMISSION ON HUMAN RIGHTS examined materials relating to the human rights situation in Haiti within the framework of its confidential "communications" procedure, under which neither the allegations nor the response of the government are made public. These materials showed that the basic civil rights of Haitian citizens, including freedoms of expression, opinion, press, assembly, and association in trade unions, had been arbitrarily suspended or suppressed. Haitians were alleged to be regularly arrested without charge, detained without trial, and denied fair hearings and due process of law. Haitian lawyers were said to be fearful of representing their clients and of being subjected to intimidation in cases of political trial. The courts and the administra-

tion of justice were reported to be run by judges appointed by the "President for Life," who lacked the independence to make judgments against abuses of human rights.

The special security officers or militia, known as the *Tontons Macoutes,* were said to be responsible for large-scale corruption, violence, and harassment, including illegal arrests, detention in unknown places, interrogation under torture, and killings; they also engaged in activities of extortion and raids on public meetings. Human rights activists, political opponents, independent journalists, radio broadcasters, trade union leaders, and priests were reported to have been imprisoned without charge.

Unable to pursue a dialogue on these matters with representatives of the government of Haiti, the Commission on Human Rights sent a representative to undertake on-the-spot direct contacts. On request of the commission, an expert designated by the secretary-general also visited Haiti to discuss the possibility that the United Nations might provide advisory services and technical assistance to the government with a view to improving recognition and observance of human rights.

In March 1986, the commission adopted a confidential decision under which its chairman appointed a special representative "to collect any information concerning the human rights situation in Haiti and to evaluate the development of the situation as regards political, civil, economic, social and cultural rights and freedoms, including the holding of free elections;" and "to study, with the Government of Haiti, any assistance that might be given as part of the advisory services in the field of human rights."

On 12 August 1986, the chairman of the Commission on Human Rights appointed Ambassador Michel Gauvin (Canada) as the commission's special representative. Following prior discussions with the government of Haiti, and with its agreement, the special representative visited that country from 1 to 15 December 1986 and talked there with Council President Lt. Gen. Henri Namphy, members of the Governing Council, other government officials, and representatives of the legal profession, trade unions, churches, political parties, and non-governmental human rights organizations. In his report to the 1987 session of the commission, he summed up the situation of human rights in Haiti in the following terms (UN Doc. E/CN. 4/1987/61, para. 87):

Haiti is a country that has passed through nearly 30 years of a brutal and self-serving dictatorship. Its illiterate population has suffered from large-scale poverty, neglect and misery. Under Duvalier the enforcement of law and order was left to the VSN numbering between 250,000 to 300,000 according to estimates offered to the Special Representative while the armed forces numbering between 7,000 to 8,000 were confined to the defence of the country. With the end of the dictatorship and the abolition of the VSN the army has become the sole institution responsible for maintaining law and order, for steering the country to democratic elections and for laying the bases for observance of human rights in the future. The good faith of the Head of the Army and Chief of State, Lieutenant General Namphy, has been acknowledged by most of the leaders and dignitaries the Special Representative met in Haiti. It has to be recognized, however, that the army is very small in number to undertake the tasks which face it, with only about 1,000 soldiers trained in police duties. Furthermore a significant part of the lower ranks of the armed forces is illiterate. The Special Representative received a number of complaints about individual acts of misconduct on the part of members of the armed forces. Incidents reported to the Special Representative included arrests without warrants, intimidation of citizens by individual members of the army, particularly in the rural areas, acts of maltreatment during detention, two cases of disappearances of persons and reported incidents of torture. Having regard to the nature and size of the armed forces, its lack of experience in policing functions and its past role in Haitian society, it would seem that many incidents have taken place which do not result as much from policy as from ineptitude and breach of discipline. In view of the situation described above the Government would need to increase training of the armed forces in order to improve respect for human rights and fundamental freedoms. The need for a trained and more efficient police force is a priority need and the Special Representative was pleased to learn that the Government had sought outside help in the training of its police and armed forces.

In his discussions with members of the Governing Council, the special representative was assured that (Ibid., para. 90–92) it was

the firm determination of the Government to implement its declared course of leading the country towards the path of democracy and respect for human rights. They pointed to various positive measures that had been undertaken by the Government, including total freedom of expression, of assembly and of strikes, the freeing of all political prisoners, the liberty for former exiles to return, the prosecution of some past offenders against human rights, the abolition of repressive laws and the enactment of new laws such as those on political parties and the press, as well as the signing of new international conventions such as the Inter-American Convention Against Torture. Refer-

ence was also made to measures undertaken to improve the administration of justice to investigate past abuses and to train the armed forces to abide by the rules of a democracy. As far as the latter was concerned, seminars had been organized for the armed forces and training was being sought from countries such as France and Canada. With regard to investigations it was explained that one difficulty facing the Government was that people were often reluctant to come forward to testify owing to their experience with the past Government.

Difficulties encountered in bringing about reform during a period of transition were also explained. For example, the people were clamouring for the "de-Duvalierization" of the Government and especially of the foreign service. Efforts had been made to get rid of those whose association with the Duvalier régime was objectionable. However it was impossible to eliminate all persons who had served under that régime without bringing the Government to a halt. It was also essential in the foreign service to provide for continuity of service. A good number of diplomats had entered the foreign service through examinations and had been promoted on the basis of their qualifications. Furthermore, the removal *en masse* and the replacement of diplomats abroad was a costly operation that the Government could not afford at the moment.

Some Ministers mentioned a particular difficulty encountered by the Government. They said that a number of political leaders and groups failed to play a constructive role in the process of political organization and debate and consequently were not assisting the Government to consolidate stability in the country. It may be noted, however, that while the Special Representative was in Haiti a spokesman on behalf of 10 political parties met with the CNG to suggest to the Government the formation of a Conseil Electoral Permanent (CEP) in preparation for the election. The CNG promised to respond soon to their request.

Having examined the report and all information available relating to the situation of human rights in Haiti, the Commission on Human Rights recognized that the situation had improved considerably in 1986 and that the government was fully committed to the restoration of human rights and fundamental freedoms. In resolution 1987/13 of 2 March 1987, the commission recommended to the government the adoption of several concrete measures to be taken: (a) the training of the police, military, and prison personnel in respect for human rights and fundamental freedoms, (b) the strengthening of the independence of the judiciary, (c) the absolute prohibition of torture, (d) the establishment of a panel of eminent Haitians to investigate and report on past human rights abuses in the country, and (e) the invitation of international observers to future legislative and presidential elections.

The commission requested the UN secretary-general to appoint an expert who could assist the government of Haiti, through direct contacts, in taking the action necessary for the full restoration of human rights and authorized the expert to formulate recommendations for the full restoration of human rights in Haiti.

On 8 October 1987, the UN secretary-general entrusted Mr. Andre Braunschweig (France), an honorary divisional president of the French Court of Cassation and a member of the Committee on the Elimination of Racial Discrimination, with the mission of "assisting the Government of Haiti in taking the necessary action for the full restoration of human rights in Haiti." The Haitian authorities were informed of the appointment, and the government was requested to receive the expert for a visit in Haiti from 2 to 7 November 1987. However, for various reasons, it was necessary to postpone the proposed visit on several occasions, and Mr. Braunschweig was unable to carry out his mandate before reporting to the Commission on Human Rights in January 1988.

While the report (UN Doc. E/CN.4/1988/38) was under consideration by the commission, elections held on 17 and 24 January resulted in the installation of a civilian government headed by Leslie Manigat as president of the republic. That government indicated an intense desire to restore the enjoyment of human rights and fundamental freedoms to the Haitian people. However, it was later overthrown, on 20 June 1988, as the result of a military coup led by Lt. Gen. Henri Namphy, who resumed the presidency which he had previously occupied.

After examining Mr. Braunschweig's report, the Commission on Human Rights, on 8 March 1988, expressed the view (resolution 1988/51) that the obligation to promote and protect human rights and fundamental freedoms calls not only for measures to guarantee the protection of those rights and freedoms but also for measures intended effectively to prevent any violation of them. It invited the government of Haiti to give priority to the implementation of such measures, took note of the attitude displayed by the civil government towards continued cooperation with the commission, and requested the secretary-general to provide such advisory services and other appropriate forms of assistance in the field of human rights as the constitutional government of Haiti might request, in order to encourage democratic development and the strengthening of the institutions responsible for ensuring respect for human rights.

The Commission requested Mr. Braunschweig to establish direct contacts with the government of Haiti with a view to taking any action that might be necessary for the full restoration of human rights in that country and called upon the government to extend its cooperation to him.

Mr. Philippe Texier (France), who took over the expert mission in 1988, submitted a report to the com-

mission at its 1989 session (UN Doc. E/CN.4/1989/40), in which he described the cooperation extended by the authorities of Haiti during his visit to the country from 15 to 22 December 1988 and the readiness of those authorities to continue their cooperation with the commission. However, he also observed that, although there had been some improvement in the human rights situation, the basic causes of the violations had not been eliminated and might give rise to further outbreaks of violence at any time.

The commission (resolution 1989/73) Haiti's accession to a number of human rights conventions and the declared intention of the authorities to comply with the provisions of those instruments but urged them to take measures without delay to ensure that serious violations of human rights did not recur and that the culprits would be singled out for arrest and trial. The commission expressed the hope that the government would, as it had pledged, be able to restore as soon as possible a constitutional regime freely chosen by the Haitian people and encouraged it to pursue the contacts which it had established with the various democratic forces in the country in order to expedite the resumption of the electoral process and, *inter alia,* to take measures to ensure the physical safety of citizens and their freedom to vote. Further, it appealed to the international community to provide all possible assistance to Haiti in order to help it in the implementation of human rights.

On 13 March 1989, five days after the commission had adopted resolution 1989/73, General Prosper Avril partially restored the 1987 constitution through a decree "subject to temporary suspension of a number of articles which are incompatible with the nature of the present Government." The 36 articles provisionally set aside dealt principally with (a) the trial of members of the military before the ordinary courts, military courts only retaining their prerogative for cases of violations of military regulations; (b) the prerogatives and duties of the legislative power, exercised by two chambers (the Chamber of Deputies and the Senate); (c) the sharing of executive power between a president (the head of state) and a prime minister (the head of government); the replacement of the head of state, should the presidency fall vacant, by the president of the Court of Cassation; (d) the arrangements for state financing of procedures for consulting the electorate; and (e) the ban on amending the constitution by referendum.

The events that followed were described by the expert in his report (para. 24–51) as follows:

In March 1989, the Head of State dismissed several members of the military, mostly officers, accusing them of having links with drug-trafficking and of making money through illicit means. However, it seems that a number of dismissals, involving privates or non-commissioned officers, were for other reasons which have never been made public.

On 13 March, General Prosper Avril sent a letter to his Minister of Justice requesting him to undertake a thorough reform of the Haitian justice system, including the transfer of responsibility for the prison system to the Ministry of Justice.

The Provisional Electoral Council was formed, and had to be sworn in twice because of an attempted *coup d'état*. The Chairman was Louis Antoine Auguste, the Vice-Chairman—Gabriel H. Augustin, the Secretary-General in charge of public relations—Jean-Gérard Pierre, the Treasurer—Jacques Jovin and the Councillors—Archange Léon Joseph Lespérance, Rony Durand and Max Lélio Joseph. It also included Archange Léon and Pastor Jean-Baptiste Pauris.

In April there was an abortive *coup d'état* which came close enough to success to cause world-wide concern. In the night of 1–2 April 1989, at 2 A.M., General Prosper Avril was taken prisoner by members of the élite Leopard Corps. The intention was to take the President to the airport at around 10 A.M., and then on to an unknown destination, but the convoy escorting him was intercepted by troops from the Presidential Guard. After a short battle, they freed General Avril and took him back to the Palais National. The apparent instigators of the *coup d'état* were immediately arrested. These were: Lieutenant-Colonel Himmler Rébu, Commander of the Leopard Corps, Lieutenant-Colonel Philippe Biamby, Commander of the Presidential Guard, and Lieutenant-General Léonce Qualo from the General Headquarters. Hostages had been taken on both sides, including one of General Avril's sons. Talks took place throughout the day and, at 4 P.M., the Minister of Information announced that President Avril was in control of the situation.

During the night of 2–3 April, at 12.20 A.M., General Avril addressed the nation in Creole and French, surrounded by heavily armed troops. He did not mention the drug traffic, but the need, with our "foreign partners" in mind, for support to maintain the programme intended to lead to elections and the restoration of full democracy. The organizers of the *coup d'état* then released the President's mother-in-law and son and son of Colonel Acédius Saint-Louis, and the three arrested officers were taken to the Dominican Republic that evening.

Meanwhile, several clashes were taking place at Delmas and Petionville, and barricades were set up. In the next few days, schools, banks and department stores were closed; the situation seemed to be settling down when on 5 April the Dessalines barracks battalion rose up against the Government and went on the radio to demand that General Avril should step down and be replaced by a civilian. The Minister of the Interior then declared a state of emergency and imposed a curfew. Censorship of radio and television was also instituted.

On 6 April, members of the military sabotaged several radio transmitters, and on 7 April there was a direct confrontation between the Presidential Guard and the soldiers from the Dessalines barracks. On 8 April, the Dessalines barracks, abandoned by their occupants, were taken over by soldiers of the Presidential Guard. The shooting continued until 10 April. On that day, General Avril gave a press conference, at which he explained that there were no winners or losers and that only a military man like himself could handle such a situation. He also stated that the *coup d'état* was connected with the appointment of the members of the Provisional Electoral Council, that democracy was a long-term process, that the date of the elections was not the main priority and that he had the political will to guarantee the population's physical safety and right to be informed.

On 14 April, six soldiers killed during the clashes were buried, and the curfew was lifted. The schools did not start operating again properly until 17 April. The exact number of military killed during these clashes will never be known: the official figure is six; some have claimed the real figure is as many as several dozen. Several sources of information indicate that Duvalier supporters inside the country, and perhaps even outside, planned or participated in this takeover attempt.

One of the consequences of the failed *coup détat* was the disbandment of the two élite units of the Haitian army: the Dessalines barracks battalion and the Leopard Corps. Most of the officers and soldiers of these two units were transferred to the provinces by decision of the Military Government and the General Staff. Some resigned, but others were also appointed to other posts in Port-au-Prince. Since then, the Dessalines barracks have been occupied by the Presidential Guard, and the only access to them is through the National Palace.

The only operational military force for the Head of State is now the Presidential Guard, numbering 1,100 men. It is a sort of army within the army and, according to various sources, receives extra pay in comparison with the rest of the military. It is said to have repeatedly been guilty of acts of extortion against the civilian population and humiliation of senior officers of the ordinary army. As a result of these incidents, an Information and Security Service (SRS) is said to have been established under the direction of the Commander of the Presidential Guard, Colonel Christophe Dardompré.

As the months passed, insecurity continued to be a factor of serious concern for the Haitian population; on 16 May, for example, a bomb exploded on the Champ-de-Mars, within a hundred yards of the Presidential Palace, during a demonstration commemorating the one hundred and eighty sixth anniversary of Haitian Flag Day. Assaults, thefts, rapes, intimidation, kidnapping and murders in various parts of the country were reported in the press daily. Shopkeepers were visited by men in military fatigue dress demanding money; self-defence squads were established both in residential areas and in the shanty towns. It is difficult to establish the dividing line between ordinary crime and political acts, but there were so many cases of lawlessness and terrorism that some saw them as evidence of a deliberate intention to establish a climate unfavourable to the setting-up of a peaceful electoral process.

On 12 May, General Avril carried out a new cabinet reshuffle, appointing Mrs. Rose-Marie Nazon, one of his relatives, as Minister of Information, and replacing Mr. Serge Elie Charles by Mr. Yvon Perrier at the Ministry of Foreign Affairs.

In May–June, some serious events occurred in the Department of Artibonite, more specifically in the towns of Grand Bois, Ti Bois, third section of the Marchand Dessalines Commune. Peasants attempted to recover land that had been taken away from them during the Duvalier period, and a succession of violent incidents took place throughout the month of May. Despite legal proceedings, it was not possible to find a solution. Mr. Charidieu Joseph, who had grabbed dozens of hectares in that way, even managed to have several peasants arrested and tortured.

On 16 May 1989, 13 soldiers proceeded to make arrests

without warrants, shooting straight at people with heavy weapons. Two peasants were wounded in the legs, and another, Regis Charlot, was shot dead at point-blank range, while returning from his garden. The crowd, estimated at 2,000 persons, then went to Charidieu Joseph's house, lynched his 80-year-old mother and set the house on fire. Regis Charlot's family was unable to get the police to make a report and had to bury him without one. After the funeral, the family had to flee when military personnel arrived from several barracks, blew up one house and set fire to five others. Specific threats were then made against the peasants of the entire area, terrorizing them, in particular the young people, who were especially singled out.

On 2 June, the Military Government brought back into effect article 267-3 of the March 1987 Constitution, which made it possible for military personnel to be tried for offences in the ordinary courts. On 16 June, it enacted the Permanent Electoral Council (CEP) Organization Act. According to the Act, the CEP, a financially autonomous independent public-law institution with legal status, would be made up of a board of directors, a bureau comprising the general inspection and electoral disputes services and a general directorate co-ordinating the activities of an electoral operations office, a data-processing office and an administrative office. The same day, in a message to the nation, General Avril denounced the people who were fomenting insecurity and made an appeal for dialogue and solidarity. He blamed his Government's problems on "professional agitators who have seen fit to make insecurity our poor people's daily bread".

It was at that point that Grégory Delpé, a young student, and Ronald Jean Michel were murdered on 5 July 1989. This case, discussed in detail in chapter III on human rights (paras. 69 to 79), aroused the indignation of Haitian public opinion, especially because of the attitude of the police, who attempted to throw suspicion on one of the victim's brothers, Turneb Delpé, a leader of the National Progressive Democratic Party of Haiti (PNDPH). During that month of July, insecurity increased, and, in addition to the death of Grégory Delpé there were the murders of Joanis Malvoisin and the Exantus brothers, accompanied by arson in several villages in Artibonite.

During this entire period, the political parties were organizing and holding congresses. At their respective national congresses, the Movement for the Institution of Democracy in Haiti (MIDH), the National Progressive Revolutionary Party of Haiti (PANPRA) and the National Patriotic Movement of 28 November (MNP28) merged into a National Alliance for Democracy and Progress. The National Committee of the Congress of Democratic Movements (KONAKOM), for its part, held several regional congresses leading to a national congress, and turned itself into a political party.

On the anniversary of General Avril's takeover, 11 September 1989, the members of the military who had been removed from the army formed a People's Organization of 17 September (OP17), accusing the Head of State of having betrayed them. Meanwhile, in his anniversary speech, the General declared himself to be "satisfied with the results of this first year" and called on Haitians "to show tolerance and discipline during the elections to be held in 1990". By a decree of 14 September 1989, he established an Office for the Protection of the Citizenry, which would be headed by an official with the title "Citizens' Protector", and whose mission would be to consider cases of human rights violations submitted to him.

On 23 September 1989, the Electoral Council submitted the electoral timetable to the Head of State; it was officially published on 24 September. The following were the main stages:

(a) October–December 1989: Setting-up of CEP machinery at the national, departmental and communal levels;

(b) January–March 1990: Census and voter registration;

(c) April 1990: Elections to the Administrative Councils of the Community Sections (CASCE) in three stages;

(d) July 1990: Municipal and legislative elections;

(e) 17 October 1990: First round of presidential elections;

(f) 11 November 1990: Second round of presidential elections.

On 27 September, a general strike began, called by 33 political and trade-union organizations. It was well supported in Port-au-Prince, where the principal sectors of activity were paralysed, but to a lesser degree in the provinces. The point was to protest against the insecurity and high cost of living and to demand that the International Monetary Fund measures should be postponed. The 33 organizations formed a "national movement".

The representative of the Military Government in the CEP, Joseph Lespérance, sent his colleagues a memorandum indicating a difference of opinion on certain points, in particular the gradual move towards a new dictatorship, the CEP's lack of openness and credibility and the unsatisfactory nature of the electoral timetable. The different political forces expressed their views on the proposed schedule, which a majority of them found too long and too complex. The General Headquarters of the armed forces for its part, distributed a copy of the timetable to all the country's commanders and asked them to provide aid and protection for recognized parties involved in the electoral process and to ensure freedom of assembly and expression, as provided for in the 1987 Constitution.

On 5 October, a decree was published with the purpose of limiting "the uncontrolled proliferation of non-governmental development assistance organizations" and "to safeguard national sovereignty and maintain the economic and financial stability of the nation"; it prohibited NGOs from acting "as executing agencies of foreign Governments on the national territory or working with cooperatives without prior authorizations": the decree has been strongly criticized by the Association of Haitian Voluntary Organizations (HAVA), which accuses it of not encouraging the formation of Haitian non-governmental organizations and equating non-governmental organizations with government executing agencies.

Repression took a very serious turn at the beginning of November with the arrest of three trade-union and political leaders, Jean-Auguste Merzieux, Executive Secretary of the Autonomous Confederation of Haitian Workers (CATH), Evans Paul, leader of the Democratic Unity Confederation (KID) and Marino Etienne, leader of the People's Organization of 17 September (OP17). On 2 November 1989, Major Leopold Clairjeune showed these three men on national television with swollen faces and heads bandaged, showing visible marks of torture. The same day, the house of Mr. Joseph Maxi, President of the Haitian League for Human Rights, was searched; the Presidential Guard was looking for Sergeant Patrick Beauchard. The following day, the army came back and surrounded the house.

According to the Ministry of Information, the arrest of the three trade-union and political leaders on 1 November at 5.45 A.M. was associated with "a plan to unleash terrorist activities in order to kill the President of the Military Government, physically eliminate all the officers in the Haitian armed forces, physically eliminate certain prominent civilians and establish a peoples militia". It was reported that arms had been found in their possession. Immediately, a "wanted" notice was issued against Sergeant Beauchard which read as follows:

"The Criminal Investigation and Anti-gang Service presents its compliments and requests you to give wide publicity, among all citizens of the country to the fact that Franck Patrick Beauchard, former Sergeant in the Presidential Guard, is wanted by the police for 'a crime against the security of the State', an offence punishable under article 63, 64 *et seq* of the decree of 23 September 1985. Accordingly, all those who have seen the aforesaid Franck Beauchard in any part of the national territory are requested to notify the police. *Signed* Leopold Clairjeune, Haitian Armed Forces, Head of the Criminal Investigation and Anti-gang Service."

Haitian public opinion, particularly all the human rights organizations, reacted strongly to the evident marks of torture seen on television. To quote Mr. Maxi, President of the Haitian League for Human Rights: "What happened that evening is an escalation of human rights violations. It is intimidation which clearly reveals the contradiction between the theory advanced by a Government that has just established a body for the protection of citizens' rights and its practice. The Government is intimidating everyone who is prominent in efforts to protect human rights. If such people remain silent, the Government will then turn its attention to all sectors". The protests reached their height with the general strike launched by CATH "against the return to fascism". Supported by a large number of organizations, it is estimated to have caused a nearly 80 per cent stoppage in the country on 7 and 8 November 1989. Mr. Maxi has been in hiding since 2 November, the date on which his home was searched and pressure put on his family. Similarly, Jean-Baptiste Chavanne, leader of the Papaye Peasant Movement (MPP) was forced to go into hiding after his home at Hinche had been sacked. In spite of action by their lawyers, Jean-Claude Nord and Moise Senatus, the three accused were still being detained on 15 November; on 16 November, they decided to resume a hunger strike in order to draw attention to their state of health and demand their release.

On 30 November 1989, three activists of the Union of Progressive Nationalist Democrats (RDNP), Auguste Lorméus, Israel Isophe and Verelt Isophe were murdered at Drouillard, north of Port-au-Prince. The first two were shot and the third was tied to the rear bumper of a car and dragged along until he died. They were preparing posters advocating the return of Leslie Manigat.

There were widespread protests, and the response of the Head of State caused surprise. In a speech on 18 November 1989, he stated: "Suddenly a new way of showing one's love for the people consists in keeping the streets of our towns under permanent occupation or forcing people into a routine of weekly strikes, planned not to further anyone's claims but to foster a spirit of strife in a country which so greatly needs hours of work to improve its economy". On 27 November, during his tour in the south of the country, he said that "to stop those who have money from buying the majority of votes, the Haitian people must be able to eat before they go to the polls". During this time, the Provisional Electoral Council was debating the question of a possible change in the electoral timetable and estimated the assistance that the international community should provide at $5 million. At the end of November, the strikes protesting against the detention of Jean-Auguste Mézieux, Evans Paul and Etienne Marino were continuing in Port-au-Prince and in the provinces.

The hunger strike by the three political prisoners continuing, support movements multiplied, particularly in the form of a solidarity chain, a symbolic hunger strike of one day. Repression also grew worse. Thus 14 members of the Haitian League of Former Political Prisoners (LAPPH) were arrested on 22 November and charged with "subversion by inciting the population to go on hunger strike in support of three dissidents in detention since 1 November 1989". They were released six days later, the Jacmel Court having declared them innocent of the alleged offences.

Other events having a bearing upon the enjoyment of human rights, which took place in Haiti early in 1990, were described by the expert in an addendum to his report to the Commission on Human Rights (UN Doc. E/CN.4/1990/44/Add. 1) as follows (para. 1–25):

On 20 January 1990, public opinion throughout the world learned that General Prosper Avril had just issued two decrees suspending several articles of the 1987 Constitution, introducing a 30-day state of siege and requiring Haitians who wished to leave or enter the country to obtain a visa.

Shortly before these measures were announced, information was also received concerning a series of extremely brutal arrests. Censorship of the radio and press was immediately imposed, and only television was allowed to broadcast news.

The democratic sector as a whole, opposition parties and certain human rights bodies were affected by a wave of mostly unlawful arrests, whose clear objective was to terrorize the country's democratic forces.

The following persons were arrested: Serge Gilles, Georges Verleigh, Philippe Stephenson and Yves Duval, leaders of the Haitian Progressive Revolutionary Nationalist Party (PAMPRA), a member of the Socialist International, together with a pastor, Jackson Noël, all of whom were at the home of Serge Gilles. The circumstances of these arrests are described below.

On 20 January 1990 six heavily armed persons in civilian clothes entered the home of Serge Gilles without a warrant but with weapons drawn, threw him to the ground and kicked him several times in the stomach while insulting him, in front of his wife and two young children. They then ransacked several rooms in the house before again kicking Mr. Gilles, handcuffing him and dragging him out, while threatening all the members of PAMPRA.

All those present were thrown to the ground, hit with an ashtray and kicked. They were then handcuffed and taken to vehicles belonging to the Inland Revenue, parked in front of the house. Haby Brun, a leader of KONAKOM and Gesner Prudent, who had also been ill-treated, were already in one of the vehicles. (It should be mentioned that Haby Brun, who had clearly been tortured, had undergone an operation a few days previously and was already in poor physical condition.)

During the journey the perpetrators of these acts asked Serge Gilles to take them to the homes of Duly Brutus and Arnold Antonin, members of PAMPRA's Executive Secretariat, but he refused to do so.

These political figures were then taken to the presidential

...ere they were beaten and insulted by a number of ...who mocked their determination to organize dem... elections. Serge Gilles received a violent blow to the ear which burst his left ear-drum. Georges Verleigh was wounded in the head by a blow from a rifle butt; a corporal then intervened to stop the violence.

All the persons concerned were then taken to the premises of the anti-gang brigade where they were treated properly and where Major Clerjeune apologized to them. Apologies were also offered by Colonel Romulus, the police chief, and they were then taken back to their homes.

Dozens of political opponents were arrested: some of them were released quite quickly, others were imprisoned and yet others expelled from Haiti against their will. For example, Hubert de Ronceray, President of the centrist Mobilization for National Development party (MDN) was expelled to Miami. On Sunday 21 January, Max Bourjolly, deputy leader of the Unified Haitian Communist Party (PUC) was arrested and immediately expelled to Guadeloupe.

In all approximately 40 political figures were arrested on 20 and 21 January, including 74-year old Dr. Louis Roy, a person greatly respected by all Haitians and regarded as the father of the 1987 Constitution, who was expelled to the United States of America.

E. Prudent, a leader of the Movement for the Establishment of Haitian Democracy (MIDH) was also arrested, as was Dr. Sylvain Jolibois (a member of Rockefeller Guerre's UPN) who refused to allow himself to be expelled and has remained in detention. Similarly, Dr. Robert Jean-Louis, President of the Association of Haitian Doctors and his wife and Robert Duval, leader of the Association of Former Political Prisoners and his wife fled after military personnel failed to find them at home. Gérald Emile Brun, a member of the National Committee of the Congress of Democratic Movements (KONAKOM) and an official of the Ecumenical Centre for Human Rights, was arrested, tortured and deported. Twenty-eight members of KONAKOM were arrested and tortured before being released.

Most leaders of political parties, even the most moderate, have had to leave their homes and are still in hiding.

The pretext for these exceptional measures and the wave of arrests was the assassination, on 20 January at dawn, of Lieutenant Colonel André Neptune, an officer in the Presidential Guard responsible for distributing bonuses to soldiers, who was killed together with his wife and a domestic employee, in still unelucidated circumstances.

Political leaders who were abroad, such as Victor Benoit (KONAKOM), Louis Dejoie and Jean-Claude Bajeux, are uncertain whether they can return to Haiti. It should be stressed that all democratic political elements were affected by the arrests, including Marc Bazin's party, the MIDH, considered to be a centrist party. Violence was employed as a matter of course in all the arrests. For example, Hubert de Ronceray declared on arrival at Miami that he had been kicked and struck with rifle butts and asserted that a cigarette had been stubbed out in one of his eyes.

Once again, General Avril used the pretext of an attempted *coup d'état* within the Presidential Guard, which allegedly took place on Friday, 19 January, when he decided to dismiss Sergeant Heubreux, spokesman of the rank and file who had brought him to power in September 1988 and subsequently saved him at the time of the April 1989 *coup d'état.*. The sergeant had been promoted to the rank of lieutenant, and transferred away from the inner circle of power.

The violence sparked off unanimous protest. The ambassadors of the member countries of the European Economic Community represented in Haiti issued the following joint communiqué which they transmitted to their respective ministers:

"The Twelve deplore the declaration of a state of siege in Haiti, the suspension of certain articles of the Constitution relating to fundamental freedoms and the arrest, torture and deportation of political opponents as flagrant violations of human rights and a setback for the democratic process.

"When the EEC recently welcomed Haiti into the Lomé Convention, it expressed its interest in the economic development and the consolidation of democracy in the country.

"The Twelve request the Haitian Military Government rapidly to end the state of emergency and to guarantee the renewal of the electoral process to facilitate a smooth transition to democracy."

The United States also protested, and the State Department decided not to resume economic assistance; the State Department's spokeswoman, Mrs. Margaret Tutwiler, said in particular that the action taken by the Haitian Government was scandalous and totally indefensible, that it damaged relations between the United States and Haiti and undermined the prospects of future assistance. France also decided to suspend co-operation with Haiti "owing to the extent of human rights violations and the suspension of public freedoms". It cancelled a visit that the Minister of Co-operation was to have made to Haiti during the week beginning 22 January. A protest was also made by Canada.

Mr. Franqis Benoit, Haitian Ambassador to the United States, announced his resignation. The Haitian Chamber of Commerce and Industry denounced the "rule of arbitrariness" and the Association of Haitian Industrialists demanded an end to the state of siege and "the return of citizens forced into exile". Lastly, the Haitian church officially protested against the violations of human rights. Mgr. Willy Romelus, Bishop of Jérémie when interviewed by *Radio Soleil*, the Catholic Church radio station stated: "We protest against the wave of arbitrary arrests, of unlawful imprisonment, against the exile of several political leaders and the ill-treatment meted out to others" and invited the population to pray for "the deliverance of Haiti".

On Friday, 26 January 1990, General Avril announced that the state of siege would be lifted on the following Tuesday, i.e. on 30 January, and declared on television that it would be possible to end the "necessary evil that the short-lived state of emergency represented 'in view of' the positive results already achieved by efforts to curb the terrorist onslaught". However, he failed to indicate whether the seven public figures exiled the previous week would be allowed to return, whether the detainees would be released and whether press freedom, the only genuine achievement since February 1986, would be restored.

Attention should nevertheless be drawn to the tone of this speech in which political opponents were described as "enemies of the people" or as "anarchists challenging the authority of the State". Even if the state of siege were to be lifted in a few days, which seems likely, the desired objective of intimidation and fear has been achieved, and such an attitude leaves no room for optimism regarding the holding of genuinely democratic elections in normal conditions.

For several weeks General Avril has issued declarations in which he expressed a certain amount of reluctance to organize elections as long as the Haitian people was hungry, or as long as insecurity prevailed. At public meetings increasing numbers of individuals have been brandishing—with a questionable degree of spontaneity—banners with slogans such as "Avril for five years" or "Without Avril the country is done for"—disturbing omens for the future of a genuine transition.

This was particularly apparent when the Head of State returned from a trip to Taiwan. In a speech at the airport, the President described Haitians who had returned to the country after being exiled as "Stateless". It should be mentioned that, during his trip to Taiwan, part of the opposition had organized a week of protests, and on 12 January the National Rally had put out a call for a general strike to ensure that "the President remained abroad and did not return to Haiti". Those protests had considerably irritated the Head of State, although they had not been followed by the population.

It is quite likely that the state of siege will indeed be lifted within a few days; however, the arrests, torture, ill-treatment and expulsions that have occurred are particularly serious, as they were directed at the non-violent democratic sector as a whole, as well as some human rights organizations, in an attempt to assimilate them to terrorist groups and discredit them should elections be organized.

These facts confirm the pessimistic conclusions reached in the report by the Expert (E/CN.4/1990/44) and further support his recommendations, in particular the recommendation that a special rapporteur should be appointed or an effective system of electoral control established, should elections be held.

The conclusions of the expert set out in his 1990 report to the commission were as follows (UN Doc. E/CN.4/1990/44, para. 106):

(a) The effort, apparent in the early months of General Avril's Government, to give the international community an indication of its awareness of the need to ensure respect for human rights remains inadequate, and has even dwindled since July 1989;

(b) The commitment of December 1988 to ratify the international human rights conventions has not so far been honoured;

(c) The Government and the judicial authorities have still not taken effective measures to investigate past and present violations of human rights and to bring those responsible to justice;

(d) They have still not succeeded in preventing further frequent violations in the towns and, still more so in rural areas, where the section heads often commit abuses of authority with impunity;

(e) The obstacles hindering the process of real improvement in the human rights situation in Haiti have not been removed; these obstacles are as follows: (i) an ineffective judicial system; (ii) the militarization of the rural areas; (iii) the failure to separate the army and the police forces; and (iv) the fact that those responsible for the principal massacres, in particular those on 29 November 1987 and 11 September 1988, have not been put on trial;

(f) The military and economic power of the paramilitary forces has undoubtedly diminished inside the country, but not all have been disarmed, and many have taken refuge in the Dominican Republic, from which they are in a position to make incursions into Haiti with impunity;

(g) The Government still has no basis in law, although it has restored the 1987 Constitution in part, and still cannot rely on lasting support from the country's democratic forces. It should restore the Constitution *in toto;*

(h) The electoral process should now be speedily organized, with measures to safeguard citizens' physical safety and freedom to vote as they wish, so that they can take their country's future in hand forthwith;

(i) The situation as regards respect for economic, social and cultural rights is becoming more alarming day by day, and no serious effort has been made to remedy it;

(j) The improvement that followed in the first few months after 17 September 1988 seems to have come to a halt, and the extremely negative factors which remain lead me to take a pessimistic view of the situation, which cannot change without a more positive and consistent will to ensure respect for the minimum standards of the rule of law.

The recommendations of the expert set out in the 1990 report were as follows (para. 107–108):

(a) It is essential for the Commission to continue to monitor the human rights situation in Haiti, with a view to fostering a real process of improvement;

(b) It is advisable for the Commission to express deep concern at the continued deterioration in the situation regarding human rights and fundamental freedoms;

(c) In view of the events that have occurred since its forty-fifth session, it is desirable for the Commission to take note of the fact that no advisory service has been requested by the Haitian Government, despite the specific proposals made to it; and for it accordingly to consider the possibility of appointing a special rapporteur to study the situation of human rights and fundamental freedoms in Haiti and report on the subject;

(d) In addition, the Commission should consider whether it is appropriate to go on offering advisory services through the Secretary-General when the Haitian Government does not submit any specific request and when there has been no notable progress in the current situation in Haiti since the forty-fifth session:

(e) If the Commission were to consider extending the Expert's mission, it would have to establish a scheme to provide technical assistance in connection with the electoral process by sending observers before and during the elections, if they are to be held;

(f) The other recommendations submitted in the 1989 report (E/CN.4/1989/40, para. 139), which are reproduced below, should only be considered if the Haitian Government is prepared to make specific requests. The recommendations relate to: strengthening and improving the judiciary to enable it to fulfil its mission with complete independence; support for planning a general policy regarding development and assistance for the poorest communities; and specific technical assistance in matters pertaining to the police, so as to foster the organization of civilian police services trained in human rights and in the minimum standards for maintaining order.

These are the recommendations submitted by the Expert as a result of his second mission to Haiti. He considers it worthwhile to pursue the dialogue with the present Government of Haiti, provided that it is prepared to accept genuine advisory services, primarily for the purpose of organizing the elections. If such a wish is not expressed, it would seem preferable to appoint a special rapporteur, since no real progress can be said to have been achieved over the year, and there is no certainty that elections will be held.

The Commission on Human Rights, on 9 March 1990, noted (Resolution 1990/56) that the Haitian authorities had not acted upon the assistance proposals which he had submitted to them under the advisory services program. It expressed the hope that they would ensure that elections would be held as scheduled and in appropriate conditions of honesty and security, under the supervision of impartial observers, and requested them to take the necessary measures to enable exiled opponents to return and to ensure their security, so that they could participate in preparing the elections.

The commission, further, invited the Haitian government to bring back into force the full constitution of 29 March 1987, which was adopted in a referendum by an overwhelming majority; to expedite the investigation into the principal massacres, particularly those of 29 November 1987 and 11 September 1988, and to bring those responsible to trial; and to ratify the International Covenants on Human Rights and other international human rights conventions in accordance with its undertaking of December 1988.

Finally, the commission requested its chairman to appoint an independent expert to examine developments in the human rights situation in Haiti and to help to devise measures capable of making the necessary improvements.

On 12 March 1990, General Prosper Avril left Haiti aboard a military aircraft provided by the government of the United States of America. Justice Ertha Pascal-Trouillot, the only woman on Haiti's Supreme Court, was nominated as provisional president after civilian political leaders had rejected Chief Justice of the Supreme Court Gilbert Austin because of his closeness to General Avril despite a constitutional provision that put him first in line to succeed. Mrs. Pascal-Trouillot announced that her principal task would be to lead the country to early elections.

HARVARD LAW SCHOOL HUMAN RIGHTS PROGRAM. Established in 1984, the Human Rights Program offered by Harvard Law School, Cambridge, MA, U.S.A., supplies impetus and direction to the school's concern for the universal realization of human rights and fundamental freedoms. By making work in the field of human rights a significant part of legal education, the program complements domestic law courses by stressing the international and comparative dimensions of human rights.

The courses, conducted by Harvard Law faculty and visiting lecturers in human rights, explore political and civil rights and topics such as torture and arbitrary detention, race and gender discrimination, conflicts between religious and secular order, freedom of expression and modes of political participation, the organization and protection of labor, the provision of food and health care, and ethnic conflict and self-determination. The program also encourages independent advocacy and policy-oriented research that may be pursued in the academic environment or that may involve field work in the U.S. or abroad, and invites visiting fellows for varying periods.

In addition to regular courses and independent research, HRP offers Harvard law students summer internships to work for two months with public interest groups or international organizations concerned with human rights; some positions are in the U.S.A., but most are abroad. HRP has also supported compensated work at HUMAN RIGHTS INTERNET by students who assist in summarizing and classifying documentation.

In the spring of 1988, the Human Rights Program published the inaugural issue of the *Harvard Human Rights Journal*. This student-edited publication includes articles of general interest written by scholars, student-written notes reviewing human rights aspects of U.S. foreign policy, personal reflections of Harvard interns on their experiences, and reviews of books on human rights.

Human Rights Program, Harvard Law School. Address: Pound Hall 401, Harvard Law School, Cambridge, MA 02138 (USA). Telephone: (617) 495-9362. Fax: (617) 495-1110. Administrative Director: Jack Tobin.

HEALTH The UNIVERSAL DECLARATION OF HUMAN RIGHTS provides that:

Article 25. 1. Everyone has the right to a standard of living adequate for the health and well-being of himself and of his family, including food, clothing, housing and medical care and necessary social services, and the right to security in the event of unemployment, sickness, disability, widowhood, old age or other lack of livelihood in circumstances beyond his control. . . .

The INTERNATIONAL COVENANT ON ECONOMIC, SOCIAL AND CULTURAL RIGHTS contains the following provision:

Article 12. 1. The States Parties to the present Covenant recognize the right of everyone to the enjoyment of the highest attainable standard of physical and mental health.
2. The steps to be taken by the States Parties to the present Covenant to achieve the full realization of this right shall include those necessary for:
(a) The provision for the reduction of the stillbirth-

rate and of infant mortality and for the healthy development of the child;

(b) The improvement of all aspects of environmental and industrial hygiene;

(c) The prevention, treatment and control of epidemic, endemic, occupational and other diseases;

(d) The creation of conditions which would assure to all medical service and medical attention in the event of sickness.

Non-discrimination on the ground of sex is ensured by the CONVENTION ON THE ELIMINATION OF DISCRIMINATION AGAINST WOMEN in the following article:

Article 12. 1. States Parties shall take all appropriate measures to eliminate discrimination against women in the field of health care in order to ensure, on a basis of equality of men and women, access to health care services, including those related to family planning.

2. Notwithstanding the provisions of paragraph 1 of this article, States Parties shall ensure to women appropriate services in connection with pregnancy, confinement and the post-natal period, granting free services where necessary, as well as adequate nutrition during pregnancy and lactation.

The AFRICAN CHARTER ON HUMAN AND PEOPLES' RIGHTS provides that:

Article 16. 1. Every individual shall have the right to enjoy the best attainable state of physical and mental health.

2. States Parties to the present Charter shall take the necessary measures to protect the health of their people and to ensure that they receive medical attention when they are sick.

Within the United Nations system, primary responsibility for the preparation and supervision of international measures relating to the right to health lies with the WORLD HEALTH ORGANIZATION. Before the World Health Organization was established in 1948, international instruments having a bearing upon the right to health were prepared mainly by the International Labor Organization, which, as early as 1921, concluded a convention calling for annual health examinations of seamen under the age of 16 and the provision of medical certificates to them; or by regional organizations such as the Pan American Union, which in 1924 promulgated the Pan American Sanitary Code with a view to preventing the international spread of communicable diseases. That code, and many similar regional agreements, was replaced by the comprehensive International Health Regulations adopted in Boston on 25 July 1969 by the World Health Assembly.

From its inception the World Health Organization (WHO) has devoted all its efforts and available resources to the realization of the basic principle stated in the preamble to its constitution: "The enjoyment of the highest attainable standard of health is one of the fundamental rights of every human being without distinction of race, religion, political belief, economic and social conditions." WHO's definition of health includes "physical, mental and social well being." WHO has declared (UN Doc. A/CONF. 32/8):

Without health, other rights have little meaning. The right to health, however, cannot be exercised by the people unless the conditions which make a health life possible are provided and unless health services and health facilities are available. WHO considers that the basic health services essential for the provision of adequate health protection to the community should cover:

—care of mothers and children including midwifery;

—nutrition;

—prevention and control of communicable diseases;

—sanitation and water supply;

—health education;

—occupational health.

These also, in the main, are the fields of WHO's activity and since 1948 have received an increasingly greater share of the Organization's efforts. The study of WHO's current programme reveals that they are still among its major concerns. But there have been significant changes of method in approaching these problems, as a result of accumulated experience.

Care of Mothers and Children, Including Midwifery. Health is a fundamental right of the child and the mother. This means a right to special care and protection and the ability to live and develop in a healthy and normal manner. Without care and education at home and at school, all acquired rights of adults may be limited or unattainable. Increased value is placed on health and well-being of women and children. Recent years have witnessed a widening in demand for maternal and child health services throughout the world and a new awareness of the importance of health and the fact that children need not suffer and die.

The services needed to protect and promote the health of mothers and children are closely interrelated. They include pre-natal supervision, including treatment of important infections and other diseases, correction of anaemia and malnutrition, natal and post-natal care, the very important education of pregnant women in mothercraft, continuing health supervision, and total medical care of all children from birth through childhood and adolescence.

WHO advocates integration of originally separate maternal and child health services into the basic health services, as it is a suitable arrangement for countries short of staff and funds and as it is an instrument for widening the health coverage given to the child population.

Nutrition. It is alarming to record that about two-thirds of the world's population is still suffering from under-nutrition or malnutrition, in spite of a tremendous improvement in techniques and possibilities for increasing the food crops of the earth. The most important and widespread disorders of malnutrition are protein-calorie deficiency diseases, lack of vitamin A, nutritional anaemias and endemic goitre. Of these, protein-calorie deficiency disease and hypovitaminosis A principally affect weaning infants and pre-school children, while nutritional anaemias, particularly of the iron deficiency type, are widespread among women of child-bearing age.

Experience has shown that improved nutrition lowers infant mortality and the mortality of children under five years of age, in which malnutrition or undernutrition are clearly among the main factors. The devastating interaction of malnutrition and the ordinary infectious diseases of childhood is now well known.

WHO's efforts to relieve malnutrition and to promote good nutrition include the implementation of applied nutrition programmes with the assistance of FAO and UNICEF, and assistance in organizing nutritional rehabilitation centres in areas where malnutrition of young children is prevalent. The Organization also supports research into nutritional diseases and methods for their control, and into protein requirements of children.

Control of Communicable Diseases. It is becoming increasingly clear that the improvement of the people's health depends largely on the extent to which the developing countries can rid themselves of communicable diseases, which are responsible for an enormous amount of sickness, disability and loss of working time.

Much has already been accomplished, but very much remains to be done. The experience of recent years has shown that the communicable diseases still continue to be a most important challenge to the health, welfare and happiness of mankind. Cholera, small pox and tuberculosis are still currently and potentially major causes of death and morbidity. Malaria is still far from being eradicated. Governments express general concern at the increased incidence of such diseases as venereal diseases, infectious hepatitis, bilharziasis, etc. It is WHO's task to assist them in their efforts to bring the communicable diseases under control.

It is now generally recognized that eradication of the major communicable diseases can be achieved, provided that the following conditions are fulfilled: strengthening of the basic health services, systematic expansion of health facilities, establishment of priorities and the synchronization of efforts in neighbouring countries. Experience in the field has shown that the control of communicable diseases can only be carried out through a comprehensive network of health centres. The WHO-assisted control programmes today tend to put more emphasis on the development of rural health services, improvement in sanitation and health education, and integration of specialized programmes into the general public health services.

Sanitation and Water Supply. The need for clean and abundant water supplies is a primary one for all living creatures. Of almost equal importance to the health of man is the need for efficient and adequate disposal of human and other wastes. Population growth, urbanization and industrialization are causing an increase in the scope and complexity of environmental health problems. Contaminated water and insanitary conditions play a major role in the spread of cholera and other enteric diseases. Water-borne diseases are one of the causes of the high infant mortality in developing countries. These diseases also place a heavy burden on families and communities. It has however long been recognized that health conditions are bound to improve greatly with the introduction of satisfactory sanitation conditions.

These considerations have led WHO to assign major importance to the improvement of environmental hygiene. The Organization's present programme aims at strengthening national community water supply and waste disposal programmes, development of country projects and training of sanitary engineers and sanitarians.

Health Education. The attainment of the highest standard of health is not only the right of every human being, it is also his duty to use his own resources to improve his health and standard of living. Improvement in health conditions depends, to a large extent, upon action by the community and therefore education of the public is an important factor. The main aim of health education is to help people achieve health by their own actions and efforts and to stimulate them to take an active and responsible part in support of various efforts designed to strengthen and promote health services.

WHO's programme in health education includes assistance in the planning and organization of the education services in the national health programmes, integration of the health education services into the general public health administration, training of health workers in health education, and assistance to health education in schools.

Occupational Health. The protection and promotion of the health of people at work is an increasingly important element of every health programme. This is particularly the case in developing countries where many classes of skilled labour are in short supply and where there is a direct, and major, relationship between health and productivity.

The scope of occupational health has been defined by the Joint ILO/WHO Committee on Occupational Health as "the promotion and maintenance of the highest degree of physical, mental and social well-being of workers in all occupations; the prevention among workers of departures from health caused by their working conditions, the protection of workers in their employment from risks resulting from factors adverse to health; the placing and maintenance of the worker in an occupational environment adapted to his physiological and psychological equipment and to summarize: the adaptation of work to man and of each man to his job."

Apart from giving advice on specific toxicological matters and supporting certain research WHO, since 1950, has played a direct part in enabling Governments to evaluate what type of occupational health programme is needed, to train nationals, to assist in the formulation of control measures, including legislation and in-plant programmes, and in the establishment of occupational health institutes. These activities have been carried out mainly with respect to manufacturing industries and agriculture. In all such matters there is close liaison with the International Labour Office.

In 1978, the International Conference on Primary Health Care, held at Alma Ata, Union of Soviet Socialist Republics, under the auspices of the WHO, adopted the DECLARATION OF ALMA ATA calling for an integrated approach to the solution of health care problems. In 1981, the World Health Assembly unanimously adopted (resolution WHA 34.36) the "Global Strategy for Health for All by the Year 2000," based on the principles of the Alma Ata Declaration and designed to assist all people in achieving a level of health that will permit them to lead socially and economically productive lives. The strategy's implementation requires the combined efforts of governments and people using a primary health care model. The eight essential elements of primary health are education on prevailing health problems; proper food supply and nutrition; safe water and sanitation; maternal and child health, including family planning; immunization against major infectious diseases; prevention and control of local diseases; appropriate treatment of common diseases and injuries; and provision of essential drugs. The General Assembly endorsed the global strategy on 19 November 1981 (resolution 36/43) and urged all member States and appropriate international organizations to cooperate fully with WHO in implementing its provisions.

The UN Commission on Human Rights has from time to time dealt with problems relating to deprivation of the right to enjoy the best attainable standard of physical and mental health. In 1988, for example, it called upon its SUB-COMMISSION ON PREVENTION OF DISCRIMINATION AND PROTECTION OF MINORITIES (resolution 1988/57) to consider measures to be taken at the national and international levels to eliminate traditional practices affecting the health of women and children. (see HEALTH: EFFECTS OF TRADITIONAL PRACTICES ON WOMEN AND CHILDREN). And at the same session it requested the sub-commission, as a matter of urgency, to complete its work (resolution 1988/62) on the draft Body of Guidelines, Principles and Guarantees of the Rights of Persons Detained on Grounds of Mental Ill-health or Suffering from Mental Disorder. (see MENTALLY ILL PERSONS: DRAFT PRINCIPLES FOR THEIR PROTECTION; WORKING GROUP ON THE DRAFT BODY OF PRINCIPLES AND GUARANTEES FOR. . . MENTAL HEALTH).

In the latter case, the commission pointed to the urgent need for principles and guidelines to prevent the misuse of psychiatry and to safeguard the rights of all individuals and invited UN member States to adhere meanwhile to the existing standards set out in the Universal Declaration of Human Rights and the International Covenants on Human Rights.

At its 1989 session, the commission considered the question of non-discrimination in the field of health. Deeply concerned that it is not uncommon to observe discriminatory practices that are incompatible with medical ethics and human rights, and convinced that the permanent and deep-rooted struggle against unwarranted discriminatory practices in health matters must be based on full, accessible and effective information, the commission reaffirmed (resolution 1989/11) the right of everyone to the enjoyment of the highest attainable standard of physical and mental health, recalled that all human rights must apply to all patients without exception and that non-discrimination in the field of health should apply to all people and in all circumstances, and recognized the importance of the principle of non-discrimination concerning access to health care.

The commission encouraged the World Health Organization to continue its activities in this field. At the same time, it invited its Sub-Commission on Prevention of Discrimination and Protection of Minorities to examine, using the opportunity provided by the study on discrimination against persons with the human immunodeficiency virus (HIV) or suffering from acquired immunodeficiency syndrome (AIDS) (see AIDS AND HUMAN RIGHTS), the possibility of extending the scope of such a study to other kinds of discrimination against sick or disabled persons, in consultation with the World Health Organization.

HEALTH: DEVELOPMENTS AFFECTING THE ENJOYMENT OF HUMAN RIGHTS. An analysis of the effect of certain scientific and technological developments in the field of health on the enjoyment of human rights and fundamental freedoms (UN Doc. A/8055/Add. 1) was presented to the UN General Assembly at its 1970 session by the WORLD HEALTH ORGANIZATION. The analysis indicated that such developments had both positive and negative consequences, some of the latter tending to give rise to serious infringements of human rights. WHO pointed out that, in considering the effect of such advances, it is important to emphasize the great advantages which have accrued to millions of people by reason of the application of new health techniques rather than to concentrate upon any concomitant disadvantages or on the occasional abuse which may occur.

Among the developments dealt with in the analysis are the following (para. 34–90):

Protection of the Human Personality and Its Physical and Intellectual Integrity

(a) *Developments in Genetics.* A number of discoveries in biology have prompted writers to probe into the future, even though it is not yet certain whether these innovations are applicable to human beings.

Changes in the hereditary endowment have been achieved in such organisms as viruses and bacteria, where the processes of "transformation" and "transduction" often result in the acquisition of new genetic specifities by the organisms involved. Similar hereditary changes have been obtained also in mammalian cells cultured *in vitro* but, at present, they seem to be unstable.

The possibility of inducing desired changes in the genotype of human cells exists, but it seems quite remote at this stage of development of molecular genetics. The concern of some writers, that gene-manipulation is potentially capable of changing the human species and jeopardizing the integrity of human beings would seem to be premature, but thought given to future implications would be desirable.

(b) *Tissue or Organ Transplantations.* Many people die as the result of disease or injury of a particular organ or pair of organs, or from burns associated with excessive loss of skin. Others are incapacitated by loss of limbs, eyes, teeth and other structures. In many cases lives would be saved, or the disability alleviated if a diseased or injured organ or tissue could be replaced by a functionally effective substitute. The types of substitute which are available are of two kinds—mechanical substitutes (prostheses) and transplants.

Transplantation of skin, cartilage or bone from one site to another in the same person requires only skill in plastic surgery and since there is no tissue-incompatibility, there is no immunological reaction leading to rejection of the transplant. Transplants from a donor to another recipient may often be successful in special sites—e.g. corneal transplantation. On the other hand, the commonest form of tissue transplant, blood transfusion, requires tissue compatability between donor and recipient, and this is achieved by red blood cell typing. In more complex tissues, like the skin or in organs such as the kidney, tissue incompatibility leading to rejection of the transplant by the recipient, is always a major problem, except in the case of transplants between identical twins.

Although there has recently been some success in minimizing tissue-incompatibility by the use of tissue typing to select appropriate donors, and considerable progress had been made in overcoming graft rejection by the use of immunosuppressive drugs and sera, the best transplants are still those which are provided by blood relatives.

Transplants from cadavers are less successful (unless by chance there is better compatibility than with a blood relative) though they are the only source of unpaired organs such as the heart and liver. Transplants from animal species are so far not feasible because the immunological reaction to tissue of a foreign species is different to suppress.

The many problems in human rights arising in organ-transplantations are best seen by a study of kidney transplantations of which several thousand have now been carried out in various parts of the world.

Foremost amongst these problems is the question of consent by the donor in case a living donor is used. He is required to undergo a major operation and in addition loses the factor of safety and reserve provided by a second kidney in the event of accident to the remaining kidney.

It is therefore essential that the donor should be fully informed of the risks and that his or her consent to the sacrifice of the kidney should be absolutely voluntary. Since the potential donor of the most suitable kidney is usually a member of the family it is sometimes difficult to avoid the problem of whether moral pressure is being brought to bear on suitable individuals. It is recognized by transplantation surgeons that persuasion must be avoided.

With regard to the ordinary donor, there can be no question of a violation of human rights if care is taken to ensure that the consent is personal, informed, understanding and voluntary. It is doubtful whether a parent or guardian should give consent on behalf of a young dependent, not of legal age. It is now accepted that it is an infringement of human rights to take advantage of prisoners as donors of organs, even if no special privileges are involved.

At the present time most kidney transplantations are made from cadaver donors. The removal of the kidney can be effected if the deceased person has given his consent, or in the absence of his consent, with the authorization of close relatives. In many countries, legal measures have been taken in this respect.

There remains the ethical question of "triage"—the selection of patients to receive "transplants" when transplant material, technical personnel and supporting services are in short supply. This problem does not raise any question of human rights. In the case of the individual patient the selection is usually made by the medical head of the transplantation service, though in some centres it has become the practice to delegate this responsibility to a small committee.

(c) Heart Transplantations. Despite their rarity, heart transplantations create their own problems of which the time of death of the donor has caused the most discussion and controversy. Modern methods of resuscitation involving the use of artificial respirators enable cardiac and respiratory functions to be maintained even though the patient has sustained irreversible brain damage resulting in " brain death". Nevertheless the viability of the donor's heart and his artificially continued respiration are facts which conflict with the traditional criteria of death, namely the inability to maintain cardiac and respiratory function.

Fear undoubtedly exists in lay circles that some over-zealous transplantation surgeon may operate before the donor actually dies. To eliminate this problem the decision as to death should be made by two or more physicians not concerned with the performance of the transplantation.

The question of a new definition of death has therefore been extensively discussed at conferences held under the auspices of the CIBA Foundation (London 1966), the Council for International Organization of Medical Sciences (CIOMS, Geneva 1968), and the World Medical Association (Sydney, 1968). As a result new series of criteria have been prepared.

Certain governments are considering legislation establishing new criteria for the definition of death, but legal opinion on the subject still tends to await further medical action. It is felt that the criteria must first be endorsed by the medical associations representative of the profession as being ethically correct as well as pragmatic.

(d) Radical Medical Techniques in General. Human lives can be prolonged in certain cases by sophisticated and expensive techniques of which Renal Dialysis or the Artificial Kidney is a typical example. Because of their present cost and heavy demands for trained personnel, these techniques are not available for everyone who can benefit from them.

Renal dialysis is to some extent an alternative to renal transplantation and is applicable to the same type of patient, namely persons suffering from chronic uraemia.

Apart from the question of who should benefit from the technique, the fundamental questions are those of cost, effort and personnel, and whether it is justifiable to allocate funds for this purpose which, if applied to the development and extension of less sophisticated therapeutic or preventive procedures, could benefit many more people.

There is nothing quite comparable to renal dialysis. The intensive treatment of certain types of cancer, involving multiple operations, irradiation and powerful cytotoxic drugs, is not nearly as expensive. Questions, however, have been raised as to whether the effort and cost of these procedures is justifiable in incurably ill or very elderly patients. But, failure to provide these types of service could be regarded as a denial of human rights. From the medical point of view, long term medical care of the elderly and incurable cases must continue on humanitarian grounds.

The choice of patients to receive special forms of treatment such as renal dialysis may raise difficult ethical problems. Wherever possible appropriate criteria for determining choice should be drawn up by the professional groups most intimately concerned.

Experiments on Human Subjects

In one sense a great deal of modern therapy is experimental. Standard courses of treatment do not always apply and the physician with a wide range of powerful drugs available will adjust the treatment of his patient in accordance with the development of his illness. But in other circumstances, the human being is often used as a experimental subject. And it is these situations which have caused public concern. In brief, there is a feeling that certain experiments on human subjects are infringements of human rights. Article 7 of the International Covenant on Civil and Political Rights states, *inter alia*: "In particular no one shall be subjected without his consent to medical or scientific experimentation".

In the present context, "experiments on human subjects" will be considered very briefly under the three heads, which however are not intended to cover all the possibilities.

(*a*) *Experiments on Human Subjects in Physiology, Pathology and Psychology.* There are many examples of the use of human beings to advance knowledge of human physiology, the subjects concerned being often the experimenter himself, medical students, nurses, soldiers, etc. Recorded experiments have involved almost all physiological systems—cardiovascular, respiratory, nervous, muscular and metabolic.

Pathological studies have also been made particularly in the field of the communicable diseases. One heroic example was the ingestion of a culture of cholera vibrio; another was the use of conscientious objectors to military service to demonstrate the ecology of the scabies mite, and to compare methods of treating the infestation.

If any of these experiments has been undertaken without the knowledge and consent of the subjects, it would have constituted a definite violation of their human rights. But in the great majority of cases the subjects were genuine volunteers, many of whom had a personal scientific interest in the experiment. In such circumstances, no question of a violation of human rights or of ethical misconduct could arise.

(*b*) *Clinical Testing of Drugs.* In recent years, there has been world-wide interest in ensuring the safety of the increasing number of powerful drugs.

The World Health Organization has been especially active in encouraging and supporting these developments, and the Director-General was requested by the 17th World Health Assembly in 1964 "to undertake with the assistance of the (WHO) Advisory Committee on Medical Research, the formulation of generally accepted principles and requirements for the evaluation of the safety and efficacy of drugs". In compliance with this request, several meetings of leading experts were convened, and their reports have been the basis of much subsequent activity by national governments and the pharmaceutical industry.

For the investigation of drugs, planned scientific studies involving both animals and man are essential. It is not always recognized that it is unethical to introduce into general use a drug that has been inadequately tested. Adherence to ethical and humanitarian principles as well as economic and technical considerations limit the number of subjects and the number and quality of organized studies on man as compared with animals. It is therefore important not to waste human and economic resources. The prerequisites of a schema for effective drug control involves the following:

—pre-clinical testing in animals
—clinical evaluation on human subjects
—a monitoring system to collect and report adverse reactions to drugs in use.

The World Health Organization, through its advisory machinery, has formulated two sets of principles for the pre-clinical testing of drugs and for their clinical evaluation which have obtained a large measure of acceptance. Following upon a resolution of the Twenty-third World Health Assembly in May 1970, it has also accepted financial responsibility for the establishment of a monitoring service at WHO headquarters in Geneva.

With regard to clinical evaluation on human subjects, it is suggested that this should be done on healthy adults, patients suffering from the disease against which the drug is going to be used, and patients suffering from other diseases. Even when this recommendation is strictly followed there still remains the question of formal therapeutic trial to determine the usefulness of the drug and to compare it with existing therapy. In formulating rules for the organization of these trials, the outstanding consideration is to obtain the personal, informed, understanding and voluntary consent of the participants.

In some countries, these trials are operated by the pharmaceutical industry, with varying degrees of governmental surveillance and legal regulation. In others, governmental supervision and control operates primarily and throughout.

(*c*) *The Use of Chemical Additives in Foods and Potable Fluids.* The use of simple chemical substances such as salt to preserve foods, and of colouring materials (usually of vegetable origin) to improve their appearance is of very long standing. In recent years, many new synthetic chemicals have been developed for use as food additives. They serve to prevent spoilage, to stop food from becoming rancid, to improve the colour, flavour or texture of a food, to render food more amenable to mass production and processing, etc. The increased use of food additives stems from such social and technological changes as urbanization, development of long-distance food transport, and the demand for ready-to-serve foods.

The fact that additives are present in most processed and many semi-processed foods narrows the choice of foods for those who wish to avoid eating all or certain food additives. In this sense the wide-spread use of food additives is an encroachment on one aspect of human rights. However, this consideration must be balanced against the technological value of these additives as well as their contribution towards an abundant supply of wholesome and easy-to-serve food. (The addition of iodine and antimalarial drugs to salt is easily justified on health gounds and, in these cases, there is no infringement of human rights because medicaments-free salt is also available to the public.)

The main reason that some individuals consider the addition of chemicals to foods or drinks as undersirable is that they are not convinced that all these chemicals are absolutely free from health hazards. In fact, certain additives which were in use have since been found to possess potential health hazards.

Realizing this problem, many governments have legal means to control the use of food additives. Furthermore, the World Health Assembly also expressed concern at its Sixth Session in 1953, and subsequently a series of meetings of the Expert Committee on Food Additives were convened by WHO in conjunction with FAO to provide toxicological evaluations of food additives. These evaluations were transmitted to governmental agencies for information. More recently these have been made use of in the elaboration of food standards in the framework of the Joint FAO/WHO Food Standards Programme.

Deterioration of the Human Environment

Several human rights are prejudiced by the many prevailing manifestations of the deterioration of the environment. They include at least two accepted rights—the right to life, and the right to a standard of life adequate for the health of the individual and his family, which implies the right to enjoy life. Environmental deterioration also derogates from the highest attainable standard of health. The manifestations of deterioration are almost universal wherever human beings settle, live and work, and the causal factors have increased *pari passu* with technological developments.

To the traditional factors of air, soil and water pollution, and urbanization have been added noise, traffic congestion, the accumulation of wastes, soil erosion, oil pollution of the sea, and the waste products of nuclear energy plants. Urbanization and the trend towards urban industrial societies are manifest increasingly in both developed and developing countries. Together with bad housing they create physical, social and psychological problems which have impacts on health and infringe the human rights referred to.

To all these detrimental factors there has been added in recent years the all-pervading pesticides. Certain pesticides which have shown themselves as great benefactors in the control of such vector borne diseases as malaria, and in agriculture, if used improperly or unrestrictedly, are capable of producing detrimental effects on many forms of life—because of their indestructibility and toxicity. Certain governments have been so alarmed by the extent of the invasion of soil, water and sea by some persistent pesticides that they have restricted or forbidden the use of these substances. But universal prohibition of the use of certain insecticides would need to be balanced against the inevitable recrudescence of such diseases as malaria; this is unthinkable unless effective and economic substitute control methods are developed.

Against this recital of the negative developments, attention should be drawn to the technological advances in water supply which have so improved that the provision of water to all people as a health measure is now technically feasible.

Action against the deterioration of the environment postulates a recognition of the modes of pollution, public education as to their importance, legislative control and intensive research. Some countries have already achieved considerable success in the control of smoke pollution, and in the purification of effluent wastes, but much remains to be done.

In its own field, WHO had instituted or is associated with a large number of research projects, which can be summarized as follows:

Environmental pollution studies of water, air, soil and radioactive pollution in an effort to prevent pollution from reaching levels which interfere with the health and wellbeing of individuals.

Wastes disposal—research and establishment of scientific technical information and wastes management and control.

Vector biology and control—research and development on ecology, vector surveillance, insecticide resistance, genetics and genetic control, biological control, the development

and evaluation of alternative insecticides, rodent control and methods of aircraft disinfection.

Pesticides—assessment of hazards of pesticides and promotion of their safe use.

In addition, the Twenty-third World Health Assembly in 1970 expressed its growing concern that the consequences of factors in the environment are adversely affecting the condition of human health. It further requested the Director-General to develop and submit to the Twenty-fourth World Health Assembly a long-term programme for environmental health, including, in so far as might be found practicable, a programme for a world-wide system of surveillance and monitoring in close collaboration with national and international efforts. Attention was also directed to the need for the establishment of environmental health criteria, guidelines for preventive measures, and methods of determining priorities and allocating resources based on the health problems and needs in both developing and developed countries.

The organization has also co-operated with other members of the United Nations system, and in particular with FAO and UNESCO, on these problems. It is also participating in the preparations for the United Nations Conference on the Human Environment which is to be held in Stockholm, Sweden, in 1972.

Human Rights Aspects of the Delivery of Health Services

The right to health and medical care is widely accepted in the basic documents of the United Nations and WHO.

Prevention, treatment and control of disease constitute the *raison d'être* for the provision of health services and medical care. The components of this human right have been frequently identified by WHO in various official documents and can be summarized as follows: general medical services for prevention, treatment and rehabilitation; maternal and child care, including family planning advice and services; control of communicable disease; mental health; occupational health; health education and nutrition.

These services, other than occupation health services, but including certain aspects of environmental control, are commonly provided through what are described as the basic or community health services.

(a) Methods of Provision and Administration of Health and Medical Services. The systems of provision and administration of these services vary from country to country, and are entirely matters for the national government to determine. The pattern of provision is to some extent influenced by the financial situation of the country, and the sources from which the cost of providing the services is met. There are three main patterns. The first is where the government itself organizes and runs the health services and where it is the exclusive source of finance.

The second comprises health and medical care services which are provided to a certain extent by the State and partly under a compulsory insurance scheme.

Under the third arrangement, the cost of medical care is met from individual private funds and/or voluntary private insurance. Sometimes the cost of preventive services is borne by the State.

No question of an infringement of human rights would appear to arise by the imposition of any of these forms of provision, but the range and coverage of the services provided may give rise to certain questions relevant to human rights.

Obviously financial resources can determine the range

of the services provided. Some developing countries can give no more than the barely essential services. Certain developed countries may provide a comprehensive range of services, elaborately equipped hospitals, and access to costly methods of treatment. If a government is offering to all its citizens the best possible it can provide within its powers and resources, there can be no question of any deprivation of human rights.

On the other hand, if services are not evenly distributed, and if certain groups appear to benefit more than others without due reason, complaints will undoubtedly arise and may indicate an infringement. It may be reasonable, however, to give certain groups special consideration as, for example, expectant and nursing mothers and young children.

(b) Cost of Health Services and Medical Care. There is universal anxiety about the rising cost of health and medical care services as they exist at present, but the future is even more ominous. The development of other expensive techniques comparable to those now available for the intensive care of patients or for renal dialysis, together with further advances in the transplantation of kidneys, livers, hearts and skin (in the treatment of major burns) will all add to the financial burden, and to the manpower requirements.

The question may then arise as to who shall receive the full treatment and who shall be denied. But this question has already arisen in respect of transplantations and renal dialysis (paragraphs 45 and 51) at any rate for individual hospitals. The responsibility for the decision is usually accepted by the head of the services, with or without the assistance of a small committee.

At the national level, the decision *on principle* must be taken by the government, preferably with guidance from representatives of the medical and associated professions.

SEE ALSO *Environment: Toxic and Dangerous Wastes; Right to Life: Disposal of Dangerous Products and Wastes: Scientific and Technological Developments: Effects on Human Rights; Toxic and Dangerous Products and Wastes.*

HEALTH: DISCRIMINATORY PRACTICES. At its 1988 session, the UN Commission on Human Rights adopted two resolutions referring to certain discriminatory practices in the field of health. In resolution 1988/57, it requested its Sub-Commission on Prevention of Discrimination and Protection of Minorities to consider measures to be taken to eliminate traditional practices affecting the health of women and children; and, in resolution 1989/62, it called upon the sub-commission to complete as soon as possible its work on the draft Body of Guidelines, Principles and Guarantees of the Rights of Persons Detained on Grounds of Mental Ill-health or Suffering from Mental Disorder (see **MENTALLY ILL PERSONS: DRAFT PRINCIPLES FOR THEIR PROTECTION**).

In 1989, the commission expressed its deep concern (resolution 1989/11) that it is not uncommon to observe discriminatory practices that are incompatible with medical ethics and human rights and its conviction that the development of national cooperation

in the field of health could help to diminish discrimination among human beings in health matters. It reaffirmed the right of everyone to the enjoyment of the highest attainable standard of physical and mental care and recalled that all human rights must apply to all patients without exception and that non-discrimination in the field of health should apply to all people and in all circumstances.

The commission accordingly invited the sub-commission to examine, using the opportunity provided by its proposed study on AIDS AND HUMAN RIGHTS, the possibility of extending the scope of such a study to other kinds of discrimination against sick and disabled persons, in consultation with the WORLD HEALTH ORGANIZATION and giving governments that wish to express their views the opportunity to do so.

HEALTH: EFFECTS OF TRADITIONAL PRACTICES ON WOMEN AND CHILDREN. On 24 May 1984, the UN Economic and Social Council requested the Secretary-General (resolution 1984/34) to entrust to a working group composed of experts designated by the Sub-Commission on Prevention of Discrimination and Protection of Minorities; the United Nations Educational, Scientific and Cultural Organization; and the World Health Organization the task of conducting a comprehensive study on the phenomenon of traditional practices affecting the health of women and children; and requested all interested non-governmental organizations to cooperate in the study.

The Working Group on Traditional Practices Affecting the Health of Women and Children held three sessions at the European office of the United Nations in Geneva, the first in March 1985, the second in September of that year, and the third in January 1986. On the basis of the documentation available to it, the working group submitted a report to the Commission on Human Rights (UN Doc. E/CN.4/1986/42) in which it accorded priority consideration to such practices as (a) female circumcision, (b) preferential treatment for male children, and (c) traditional birth practices. The working group also submitted a list of traditional practices affecting the health of women and children, including both beneficial and adverse practices, together with an indication of the areas where such practices occur; the list is reproduced below.

A. Female Circumcision.

The term, as used by the working group, refers to the traditional practice which consists in cutting away all, or part, of the external female genital organs. Although in most countries where it is practiced it is an integral part of the "initiation rite," the operation has been shown to involve significant risks of damage to the mental and physical health of girls and women.

The conclusions reached by the working group, with regard to this practice (para. 108–120), are as follows:

A. Functions. Female circumcision is a practice that has complex social, ethnic, religious, economic and psychological aspects which vary from one social group to another.

As a social phenomenon, circumcision has an evolutionary aspect which can be understood and evaluated only in the context of the societies in which it is practiced.

In some societies, female circumcision has had and continues to have an initiatory function which varies from one social group to another. Moreover, there is a perceptible evolution of the role and function of female circumcision from the rural environment to the urban environment. Traditional practices have a more symbolic and ritual character, and their social and economic functions are easier to determine. These practices continue to have significant relationships with other aspects of social and cultural life.

The function of social integration is stronger and more instrumental within populations confronted with situations comprising contradictions and conflicts of values.

Generally speaking, attachment to traditions which have lost some of their significance is to a certain extent the consequence of the basic problem which these societies are facing. This function of the social integration of young girls is strengthened by the image which women and the community have of themselves and by the difference between the roles of men and women in society and the forms of discrimination resulting therefrom.

B. Evolution. There has been an evolution in the functions inherent in female circumcision and the methods and forms employed. In urban environments, in particular, a change of attitude has been noted in relation to certain variables (education, sex, age). This evolution may even go as far as the simulation of circumcision in the practice of the most benign form. Despite the positive evolution of these practices, it must not be forgotten that this evolution is often felt to be insufficient by certain population groups within which new models of societies have emerged.

C. Consequences. Female circumcision has consequences on the mental and physical health of women and children, the gravity of which increases with the degree of mutilation.

The consequences of these practices continue to be significant regardless of forms and procedures, in particular in groups of women or populations confronted with changing life patterns, whether in urban or other areas. The seriousness of the consequences cannot be diminished by evolution extending to the medicalization of the act. Medicalization entailing normalization and institutionalization of these practices would have particularly adverse consequences since it would deprive these acts of any ritual content and, in most cases, would not diminish the effects of mutilation on the physiological functioning of the genital organs of women and young girls.

It is interesting to note that some traditional practices were aimed, in traditional societies, at the closer incorporation of the individual within his social environment in order to enable him to benefit from all the rights of the individual which these societies recognized.

Today, because of the evolution in traditional societies due to various factors, these traditional practices are at variance with new standards defined by various international instruments relating to human rights.

In the light of these principles which today have the force of law, all countries which have ratified the International Covenants on Human Rights and the Convention on the Elimination of All Forms of Discrimination Against Women and which have morally endorsed the principles enunciated in the Universal Declaration of Human Rights and the United Nations Declaration on the Rights of the Child are currently confronted with the incompatibility which exists between these principles and the obligations they assume as States parties to the above-mentioned instruments, and the maintenance of certain traditional practices, especially since these practices have proved prejudicial to the physical and mental health of women and children.

During their consideration of this question, the members of the Working Group have been unable to avoid noting this incompatibility.

In conclusion, the Working Group, wishing to facilitate the work of the members of the Commission on Human Rights, makes the following suggestions relating to the study of this problem.

The working group offers the following suggestions for action (para. 121–138):

The legislative efforts to abolish female circumcision by the Government of Egypt should be noted with satisfaction and an appeal should be made to other Governments, which had not yet had the possibility of adopting clear-cut policies and appropriate legislation to abolish female circumcision, to take such action.

These measures should be preceded and followed up by public education.

To ensure the implementation of such legislation there is a need to set up an effective mechanism.

Note could be taken of the important action by African women in efforts to combat practices which are prejudicial to the health and well-being of women and children and which impede the full realization of their fundamental rights.

It would be desirable for Governments to support and reinforce this action: (a) decision-makers and professionals, professional bodies and non-governmental organizations, as well as the mass media, should be alerted with a view to obtaining their co-operation in order to implement attitudes to obtain their co-operation in order to influence attitudes towards the eradication of female circumcision; (b) opinion-builders at grass-root levels, such as village leaders and community health and development workers which should also be altered.

The Working Group further suggests that Governments should encourage and support by all available means the associations and organizations engaged in the process of eradicating female circumcision.

Specific Action. With a view to attaining the goal of health for all by the year 2000, national health policies should include among their priorities strategies aimed at the eradication of female circumcision in their primary health care programmes. The Working Group recommends that the competent public services should describe the adverse effects of female circumcision to birth attendants, nurses, mobile health teams, social workers, rural teachers and community auxiliaries at the beginning of their courses, not forgetting vocational health personnel and any other socio-vocational category concerned.

The Working Group further considers that information should also be given in health centres, pre-natal centres, women's development centres, handicraft centres and governmental-run social institutions.

Appropriate pedagogical material should be prepared for the training of educational, medical and paramedical personnel and even psychologists in order to enable them to tackle this problem adequately within the populations concerned.

Alternative training should be provided for the traditional practitioners whose main source of income derives from female circumcision.

In the area of education, sex education should be given in schools, including information on female circumcision and its eradication. This question should also be included in literacy campaigns. Moreover, the problem of female circumcision should be included in teacher-training programmes and curricula at all levels, and in all the disciplines concerned, not forgetting civic or religious education programmes.

In countries with an Islamic majority or which have a large Muslim population, stress must be laid on the importance accorded to women, on the condemnation of ill-treatment, and on the fact that female circumcision is not mentioned in the Koran and is in no way a religious obligation.

Education. In view of the limited amount of study and research on the socio-cultural aspects of the problem, multidiscipliniary research programmes should be established and supported, taking account of the complex and multiple aspects of this practice with a view to formulating action programmes.

Effective evaluation mechanisms should be instituted at the national level in order to build on the progress achieved in the area of the eradication of female circumcision.

Meetings should be organized at the international, regional and national levels enabling men and women from the countries concerned to exchange their views and experiences on female circumcision and means of achieving its eradication.

It would be appropriate to congratulate the international organizations on the efforts made and support extended by them and to call upon them to renew and reinforce such support.

The action and support provided so far by the international non-governmental organizations to national efforts for eradicating female circumcision and continuation of such international collaboration on a large scale for the realization of programmes to eliminate female circumcision should be noted with satisfaction.

It should be noted with satisfaction that progress has been made in work against female circumcision through the creation of the Inter-African Committee and its national bodies. Such national and regional efforts should be encouraged and supported.

B. Son Preference

Preference of parents for male children is a tradition in many parts of the world and often manifests itself in neglect, deprivation, or discriminatory treatment of girls to the detriment of their mental and physical health. According to the report of the working group,

"it refers to a whole range of values and attitudes that are manifested in many different practices whose common feature is preference for the male child with daughter neglect often a concomitant result. It may mean that a female child is disadvantaged since its birth, and may determine the quality and quantity of parental care and extent of investment on the child's development. It may lead to acute discrimination, particularly in settings where resources are scarce. Although neglect is the rule, in extreme cases son preference may lead to selective abortion or female infanticide—but more often it involves neglect."

The areas most affected by the practice, the working group found, "seem to be South Asia (Bangladesh, India, Nepal, and Pakistan), the Middle East (Algeria, Egypt, Jordan, Libya, Morocco, Syria, Tunisia, and Turkey), and parts of Africa (Cameroon, Liberia, Madagascar, and Senegal). In Latin America, there is evidence of abnormal sex ratios in mortality in Ecuador, Mexico, Peru, and Uruguay."

The reasons for this practice are set out by the working group as follows:

Those who have studied the low value accorded to daughters in several societies argue that: (a) where women's economic productivity is high or where there is a high demand for female labor in agriculture, discrimination against girls is less prevalent, but where women are economically dependent upon men they are put at a disadvantage since they have no control over their own lives; (b) sons are economic assets to their family and bring in an extra pair of hands for work when they marry; (c) parents view sons as having far greater obligations towards them in their old age whereas daughters are lost to the family after marriage; (d) sons are needed to carry on the family lineage; (e) most religious beliefs seem to consider women as inferior and so unfit to perform sacred duties and rituals; and (f) in certain societies, the lack of understanding and the misinterpretation of the female physiology results in the devalorization of the female person.

The main conclusion of the working group with regard to son preference is that "sex favoritism does affect the self-esteem and self-image of the less preferred female children and socializes them to be dependent upon men." Other conclusions include the following (para. 173–177):

Son preference is not necessarily a danger for daughters, but when it is often accompanied by neglect and discrimination towards female children it leads to serious health consequences which account for between 500,000 to 1 million deaths among female children.

In particular, such discrimination is reflected in food distribution, in which female children are disadvantaged and thus particularly suffer from malnutrition.

Likewise, an explicit manifestation of neglect towards girls is lack of care, in comparison with boys, in case of illness.

The following conclusions should be highlighted.

—There is an interdependence between the economic system and the family system. Where women's productivity is high or women are much in demand as agricultural workers, there is less discrimination against and undervaluation of women and girls.

—Food distribution on the basis of sex is heightened in times of shortage, whether resulting from seasonal scarcity, famine or chronic poverty. This discrimination on grounds of sex occurs in both poor and less poor families, which would appear to indicate that a better food supply would be a necessary but not a sufficient condition for eliminating food discrimination against female members of the family.

—Underinvestment in the education of girls seriously affects the health of future generations, since maternal education has a decisive influence on child health mortality.

—Excess female mortality in childhood is an indicator of serious external influences against the normal biological advantages with which nature has endowed the female.

—The neglect of daughters because of son preference affects both the health and the status of women directly and through each other.

Higher female than male infant and/or child mortality or even more female than male deaths among infants and children are a sure indicator of the existence of serious discrimination against girls.

The working group's recommendations on the question of son preference are as follows (para. 178–190):

Even where they have taken up the question of son preference, the World Fertility Survey and other demographic studies have unfortunately focused on the influence of that preference on fertility and not on the ensuing consequences for female children.

The same is true of the many studies carried out (a bibliography of which is attached to this report) whose concern was the nutritional status of children rather than nutritional differences on grounds of sex. It is, however, worthy to note that although these studies were not carried out with the principal aim of exploring male and female discrimination, nevertheless they all indicate without any doubt that the problems outlined above exist and are acute in many parts of the world.

Consequently, the first recommendation must be:

(a) To identify the problem of son preference,

(b) An essential prerequisite for action, in the short term, is information that helps to identify whether the problem exists in a given country. Most countries have at least some sources of information that can provide valuable data without having to initiate additional data collection.

There are a number of indicators which can be used as a signalling device to alert those responsible for planning and implementing health and development interventions.

(a) The mortality rates of female infants and children between 1 and 4 years of age is perhaps *the most crucial indicator*. Higher female than male infant and/or child mortality, or even more female than male deaths among infants and children are a sure indicator of the existence of serious discrimination against girls. Where civic registration is poor or non-existent sex specific mortality data may not exist, although community surveys carried out for other purposes, may yield useful data. The absence of a female excess in mortality does not however mean the absence of neglect of female children. It is necessary, therefore, to examine other indicators, such as sex differentials in nutritional status of children.

(b) An analysis by sex of *anthropometric data* collected in child-health clinics, school health records, child growth records maintained by health programmes etc. can reveal significant differences between the nutritional status of boys and girls. Community nutritional and/or health surveys are however more reliable sources of data, since clinic data could reflect an inherent sex-bias in clinic attendance—more malnourished boys than girls may be brought to clinics even if more girls than boys were malnourished in the child population as a whole.

(c) *Analysis by sex of clinic and hospital records and immunization records* would show if there is systematic bias against girls in seeking medical care—preventive or curative. In the case of curative care this would be true if in addition to there being a greater number of boys than girls attending the clinic, the girls who are brought show more advanced symptoms. This implies that there was a greater delay in seeking medical care for girls.

On-going Monitoring. It should become common practice for future demographic surveys and censuses to record and analyse infant and child mortality rates and to calculate life expectancies by sex in order to bring about sex differentials. Analysis by sex of community health surveys, hospital and immunization records and nutritional surveys should also become routine; such on-going monitoring will not only alert planners to sex-differential treatment of children, but also serve as a useful device to measure the impact of preventive action.

Preventive Action. If an examination on the basis of indicators such as the above shows the existence of widespread and systematic discrimination against female children, corrective measures will need to be planned and implemented without delay.

Combating Existing Practices. Although the elimination of undervaluation of daughters implies long-term and protracted action to change entrenched attitudes and values, several short-term measures can be initiated to prevent and compensate for the serious health consequences that result from it.

For example, all countries with excess female and child mortality may gear all health interventions towards the attainment of at least equal female and male infant and child mortality rates and, ultimately, the more normal 5–10 per cent higher male than female mortality rate in infancy and childhood. Feeding and other nutritional intervention programmes and immunization campaigns may need to include targets as to the minimal proportion of female children to be covered.

Another measure that may help improve the access to medical care of female infants and children is provision of services to all children on a compulsory basis and even free-of-charge.

(a) Health planners and practitioners, women's organizations, development agencies, community workers and all others concerned including legislators should be made aware of the gravity of the problems and encouraged to re-examine the situation in their countries, to document existing practices, and to plan corrective action.

(b) It would be necessary to sensitize the health staff about this discrimination and its effects.

(c) An information campaign should be launched through the mass media and health education programmes set up with a view to changing attitudes as regards discriminatory practices against female children, particularly in nutrition and access to health care.

Eliminating the Underlying Causes. Long-term measures to deal with the phenomenon of son preference and its implications would include enactment and implementation of legislation against discrimination on the grounds of sex.

Provision of free and compulsory primary education to all children may not be adequate to ensure girls' access to education, and suitable social support measures may have to be introduced in an attempt to minimize the disadvantages to the family due to the girls' schooling, adequate social security when possible for older people so that a son is no longer a must for security in old age. The social and economic status of women should be enhanced. Parents should be encouraged by incentives to send their girl children to school.

At the International Level. The specialized agencies concerned, such as WHO, UNESCO and UNICEF, should provide technical and other assistance to Governments which so request in order to eliminate this practice:

(a) Seminars should be organized under the auspices of the regional economic commissions, in particular to exchange information and experience in this field.

(b) The organs responsible for the implementation of conventions concerning the elimination of discrimination against women and equality of access of girls to education, should give special attention to this problem when studying reports submitted by States parties.

Finally, it is worth ending on an optimistic note. Some Asian countries are not indifferent to the enormous problems arising from son preference to the detriment of female children. Although their efforts remain limited, they should be supported in order to encourage more dynamic action.

C. Traditional Childbirth Practices

In its consideration of traditional childbirth practices, the working group points out in its report that not all of them are harmful, and some are either beneficial or at least harmless.

Among the beneficial practices, it lists breastfeeding, especially traditional "on demand" 12-month breastfeeding, which results in protection from infections and better nutrition and prolongs the intervals between births, and other traditional methods of birth spacing.

Among the harmful practices, it describes some of those considered to be the most harmful, including culturally prescribed dietary practices during pregnancy and puerperium, such as restrictions, in various localities, on the eating of meat, eggs, green vegetables, fruit, rice, milk, potatoes, and other nourishing foods; childbirth attended only by traditional birth attendants (TBA's), relatives, or no one at all in dark, secluded, and unsterile hideaways; unhygienic examinations, procedures, and operations; and improper treatment of complications, especially when TBA's delay recourse to trained medical assistance.

The working group puts forward the following recommendations for dealing with traditional childbirth practices (para. 222–229):

At the National Level. Since not all traditional childbirth practices are harmful, but on the contrary some are beneficial or at least harmless, it is recommended that each country should examine these practices in its own context, to identify those which are harmful and need to be eliminated, those which are beneficial and should be encouraged, and those which need no action at all.

Believing that in most cases the persistence of harmful traditional practices is largely due to the unavailability of trained assistance in pregnancy and childbirth, it is strongly recommended that Governments recall the commitments universally undertaken at the Alma Ata Conference on Primary Health Care and the subsequent adoption by the World Health Assembly and the United Nations General Assembly of the Strategy for Health for All by the Year 2000, and recall also the recommendations of the International Population Conference in Mexico in 1984 and the World Conference to Review and Appraise the Achievements of the United Nations Decade for Women: Equality, Development and Peace of 1985 about ensuring the availability of trained assistance in pregnancy and childbirth for all women who need it, and that Governments redouble their efforts to achieve this aim by elevating the level of priority which is given to maternity care in national development plans and budget allocations.

Aware that the registration of, training and supervision of Traditional Birth Attendants (TBAs) has been historically one of the means by which most countries who today provide adequate maternity care have achieved this, and aware also that this approach is in tune with both the development philosophy and practical possibilities of most developing countries, it is recommended that determined efforts should be made in the next few years to apply this approach nationwide wherever appropriate, and to provide adequate support to the TBAs in the form of training, supervision and support.

Countries are recommended to carry out campaigns of public education:

(a) Specifically to combat harmful traditional practices and to promote beneficial practices,

(b) To encourage women to use fully such opportunities as do exist for trained help in pregnancy and childbirth.

In public education and in collaboration with Governments in making available adequate maternity care, the non-government organizations of developing countries have a major role to play.

At the Regional Level. The Working Group noted with interest the creation of the Inter-African Committee on Traditional Practices Affecting the Health of Women and Children and the setting up so far of 12 national committees with the approval of Governments. An appeal should be made to all Governments concerned to support the Inter-African Committee which deals with the various practices studied at the Dakar Seminar. It should be also recommended, in appealing to Governments, to give higher priority to national action in this field, it is believed that at this early stage of action small regional meetings between countries might be useful.

At the International Level. The Commission on Human Rights should call upon all appropriate regional economic commissions and international agencies, such as WHO,

UNICEF, UNESCO, UNFPA, UNDP and the World Bank and the regional development banks again to take cognizance that still today over 50 per cent of women in developing countries have no trained assistance in childbirth, and therefore to give a very high priority to collaboration with and support to countries in improving their provision of maternal health care at primary and secondary levels.

The group also recommends to bilateral aid donors and to international NGOs who wish to assist health development to give particular emphasis to the provision of maternity care in order to resolve the gross discrepancies and inequities which prevail at present in this regard. [See chart at right.]

Action Taken on the Report. After examining the working group's report, the UN Commission on Human Rights requested the Sub-Commission on Prevention of Discrimination and Protection of Minorities (resolution 1988/57) to consider at its 1988 session, measures to be taken at the national and international levels to eliminate the practices described therein. The sub-commission, responding to that request, called upon Mrs. Halima Embarek Warzazi (Morocco), who had acted as chairman-rapporteur of the working group, to study, on the basis of information to be gathered from governments, specialized agencies, other intergovernmental and non-governmental organizations concerned, recent developments with regard to traditional practices affecting the health of women and children and to bring the results of her study to the attention of the sub-commission at its 1989 session.

In the preliminary report presented to the sub-commission at its 1989 session (UN Doc. E/CN.4/Sub.2/1989/42 and Add. 1), the special rapporteur summarized the information she had gathered from 16 governments, two United Nations organs, one specialized agency, and 12 non-governmental organizations and stated (chap. V) that the consultations had led her to make the following recommendations:

(a) The mandate given by the Sub-Commission should be extended by two years to make it possible to obtain the information needed in order appropriately to strengthen the report requested by the Sub-Commission;

(b) Study visits should be envisaged to selected countries in certain regions where traditional practices affecting women and children are prevalent and whose Governments have not yet sent a reply. The purpose of these visits would be to prepare for the holding of international seminars organized by the Centre for Human Rights; these seminars would study the effect of traditional practices on human rights and ways of eradicating traditional practices that adversely affect families and the community and of encouraging practices that are beneficial. The visits would also have the purpose of demonstrating the importance of holding such international seminars, aimed at government officials and national and international NGOs, and of mobilizing the NGO community at the national and international levels in support of such seminars;

(c) Sources of financing for holding these seminars

Traditional Practices Affecting the Health of Women and Children

Subject	Areas Affected	Sources of Information, Data
ADVERSE PRACTICES		
Female circumcision	In more than 20 countries of Africa (75 million women and children affected) and in some Asian countries	WHO publications and studies, including the report of the Khartoum seminar UNICEF supported studies and publications NGO studies and materials, including the report of the Dakar seminar Books and papers on anthropology
Other forms of mutilation	Rather rare Sudan (facial marks) some tribes	Anthropologists
Forced feeding	Mauritania, Other	Dakar seminar papers
Early marriage and adolescent child-bearing	Africa and Asia—also (outside marriage sometimes) America, Europe	WHO and other medical publications Some papers at Dakar seminar
Other taboos or practices or attitudes which prevent women from controling their own fertility	Most continents	Numerous, including INSTRAW, WHO
Nutritional taboos and differential feeding patterns—withholding certain nutritious foods from women and children	All continents	Nutritional, anthropological literature
Traditional birth practices including work of untrained traditional birth attendants (Note: some adverse, some beneficial), e.g.		
1. Application of contaminated substances to cord site resulting in neonatal tetanus	All continents	WHO and other medical literature
2. Dangerous medicaments to hasten labour resulting in ruptured uterus, etc.	Africa	Medical literature
Preference for male children Resulting in high female mortality, delay in care, higher female malnutrition, lower female literacy	Especially in Asia and North Africa	WHO (Divisions of Family Health and Epidemiological Surveillance and Health Situation and Trend Assesssment) UNICEF paper by Goldstein Other medical and anthropological literature
BENEFICIAL PRACTICES		
Breastfeeding, especially traditional "on demand" 12-month + breastfeeding, resulting in protection from infections, better nutrition, prolonging intervals between births	All countries	WHO and other medical literature
Other traditional methods of birth-spacing	All continents	WHO and many other sources

should be sought in the Centre for Human Rights and other United Nations agencies, particularly UNDP. The Centre for Human Rights should provide Mrs. Halima Embarek Warzazi with all possible support to enable her to fulfill the mandate entrusted to her;

(d) United Nations agencies, regional economic and social commissions of the United Nations and other interested bodies should be asked to provide any information they have collected on traditional practices and on measures taken to eradicate traditional practices affecting the health of women and children;

(e) There should be greater co-operation between the Centre for Human Rights and the Inter-African Committee and national NGOs, and with Governments and international NGOs, including their national branches, in order to ensure implementation of the recommendations contained in the report of the Working Group on Traditional Practices affecting the health of women and children;

(f) The Sub-Commission should recommend to WHO to invite Mrs. Halima Embarek Warzazi to address the Ministers of Health at the next World Health Assembly, at Geneva, on the subject of traditional practices affecting the health of women and children.

At that same session, the sub-commission took note (resolution 1989/16) of the special rapporteur's report, shared the concern she had expressed about the lack of information on the subject made available to her, and expressed the view that the issue of traditional practices is a matter of serious concern to the international community because of its human rights implications.

The sub-commission recommended (resolution 1989/16) that its parent bodies, the Commission on Human Rights and the Economic and Social Council, review the question in 1990 and arrange (a) for the mandate of the special rapporteur to be extended for two years to enable her to present a more complete report, (b) for her to undertake field missions if possible in two countries where harmful traditional practices are prevalent, and (c) for international regional seminars to be organized in Africa and Asia to consider the subject of harmful traditional practices.

HELSINKI ACCORD: COOPERATION IN HUMANITARIAN AND OTHER FIELDS. The Concluding Document of the Meeting of States Participating in the Conference on Security and Cooperation in Europe, convened in Vienna from 4 November 1986 to 17 January 1989 in accordance with the provisions of the Helsinki Accord, includes the following section relating to "Cooperation in Humanitarian and Other Fields:"

The participating States,
Considering that co-operation in humanitarian and

other fields is an essential factor for the development of their relations,

Agreeing that their co-operation in these fields should take place in full respect for the principles guiding relations between participating States as set forth in the Final Act as well as for the provisions in the Madrid Concluding Document and in the present Document pertaining to those principles,

Confirming that, in implementing the provisions concerning co-operation in humanitarian and other fields in the framework of their laws and regulations, they will ensure that those laws and regulations conform with their obligations under international law and are brought into harmony with their CSCE commitments,

Recognizing that the implementation of the relevant provisions of the Final Act of the Madrid Concluding Document requires continuous and intensified efforts,

Have adopted and will implement the following:

Human Contacts

1. In implementing the human contacts provisions of the Final Act, the Madrid Concluding Document and the present Document, they will fully respect their obligations under international law as referred to in the subchapter of the present Document devoted to principles, in particular that everyone shall be free to leave any country, including his own, and to return to his country, as well as their international commitments in this field.

2. They will ensure that their policies concerning entry into their territories are fully consistent with the aims set out in the relevant provisions of the Final Act, the Madrid Concluding Document and the present Document.

3. They will take the necessary steps to find solutions as expeditiously as possible, but in any case within six months, to all applications based on the human contacts provisions of the Final Act and the Madrid Concluding Document, outstanding at the conclusion of the Vienna Follow-up Meeting.

4. Thereafter they will conduct regular reviews in order to ensure that all applications based on the human contacts provisions of the Final Act and of the other afore-mentioned CSCE documents are being dealt with in a manner consistent with those provisions.

5. They will decide upon applications relating to family meetings in accordance with the Final Act and the other afore-mentioned CSCE documents in as short a time as possible and in normal practice within one month.

6. In the same manner they will decide upon applications relating to family reunification or marriage between citizens of different States, in normal practice within three months.

7. In dealing favourably with applications relating to family meetings, they will take due account of the wishes of the applicant, in particular on the timing and sufficiently long duration of such meetings, and on travelling together with other members of his family for joint family meetings.

8. In dealing favourably with applications relating to family meetings, they will also allow visits to and from more distant relatives.

9. In dealing favourably with applications relating to family reunification or marriage between citizens of different States, they will respect the wishes of the applicants on the country of destination ready to accept them.

10. They will pay particular attention to the solution of problems involving the reunification of minor children

717

with their parents. In this context and on the basis of the relevant provisions of the Final Act and of the other afore-mentioned CSCE documents, they will ensure

—that an application in this regard submitted while the child is a minor will be dealt with favourably and expeditiously in order to effect the reunification without delay; and

—that adequate arrangements are made to protect the interests and welfare of the children concerned.

11. They will consider the scope for gradually reducing and eventually eliminating any requirement which might exist for travellers to obtain local currency in excess of actual expenditure, giving priority to persons travelling for the purpose of family meetings. They will accord such persons the opportunity in practice to bring in or to take out with them personal possessions or gifts.

12. They will pay immediate attention to applications for travel of an urgent humanitarian nature and deal with them favourably as follows:

—they will decide within three working days upon applications relating to visits to a seriously ill or dying family member, travel to attend the funeral of a family member or travel by those who have a proven need of urgent medical treatment or who can be shown to be critically or terminally ill.

—they will decide as expeditiously as possible upon applications relating to travel by those who are seriously ill or by the elderly, and other travel of an urgent humanitarian nature.

They will intensify efforts by their local, regional and central authorities concerned with the implementation of the above, and ensure that charges for giving priority treatment to such applications do not exceed costs actually incurred.

13. In dealing with applications for travel for family meetings, family reunification or marriage between citizens of different States, they will ensure that acts or omissions by members of the applicant's family do not adversely affect the rights of the applicant as set forth in the relevant international instruments.

14. They will ensure that all documents necessary for applications based on the human contacts provisions of the Final Act and of the other afore-mentioned CSCE documents are easily accessible to the applicant. The documents will remain valid throughout the application procedure. In the event of a renewed application the documents already submitted by the applicant in connection with previous applications will be taken into consideration.

15. They will simplify practices and gradually reduce administrative requirements for applications based on the human contacts provisions of the Final Act and of the other afore-mentioned CSCE documents.

16. They will ensure that, when applications based on the human contacts provisions of the Final Act and of the other afore-mentioned CSCE documents are refused for reasons specified in the relevant international instruments, the applicant is promptly provided in writing with an official notification of the grounds on which the decision was based. As a rule and in all cases where the applicant so requests, he will be given the necessary information about the procedure for making use of any effective administrative or judicial remedies against the decision available to him as envisaged in the abovementioned international instruments. In cases where exit for permanent settlement abroad is involved, this information will be provided as part of the official notification foreseen above.

17. If in this context an individual's application for travel abroad has been refused for reasons of national security, they will ensure that, within strictly warranted time limits, any restriction on that individual's travel is as short as possible and is not applied in an arbitrary manner. They will also ensure that the applicant can have the refusal reviewed within six months and, should the need arise, at regular intervals thereafter so that any changes in the circumstances surrounding the refusal, such as the time elapsed since the applicant was last engaged in work or duties involving national security, are taken into account. Before individuals take up work or duties involving national security, they will be formally notified if and how this could affect applications they might submit for such travel.

18. Within one year of the conclusion of the Vienna Follow-up Meeting they will publish and make easily accessible, where this has not already been done, all their laws and statutory regulations concerning movement by individuals within their territory and travel between States.

19. In dealing favourably with applications based on the human contacts provisions of the Final Act and of the other afore-mentioned CSCE documents, they will ensure that these are dealt with in good time in order, *inter alia*, to take due account of important family, personal or professional considerations significant for the applicant.

20. They will deal favourably with applications for travel abroad without distinction of any kind, such as race, colour, sex, language, religion, political or other opinion, national or social origin, property, birth, age or other status. They will ensure that any refusal does not affect applications submitted by other persons.

21. They will further facilitate travel on an individual or collective basis for personal or professional reasons and for tourism, such as travel by delegations, groups and individuals. To this end they will reduce the time for the consideration of applications for such travel to a minimum.

22. They will give serious consideration to proposals for concluding agreements on the issuing of multiple entry visas and the reciprocal easing of visa processing formalities, and consider possibilities for the reciprocal abolition of entry visas on the basis of agreements between them.

23. They will consider adhering to the relevant multilateral instruments as well as concluding complementary or other bilateral agreements, if necessary, in order to improve arrangements for ensuring effective consular, legal and medical assistance for citizens of other participating States temporarily on their territory.

24. They will take any necessary measures to ensure that citizens of other participating States temporarily on their territory for personal or professional reasons, *inter alia* for the purpose of participating in cultural, scientific and educational activities, are afforded appropriate personal safety, where this is not already the case.

25. They will facilitate and encourage the establishment and maintenance of direct personal contacts between their citizens as well as between representatives of their institutions and organizations through travel between States and other means of communication.

26. They will facilitate such contacts and co-operation among their peoples through such measures as direct sports exchanges on a local and regional level, the unimpeded establishment and implementation of town-twinning arrangements, as well as student and teacher exchanges.

27. They will encourage the further development of direct contacts between young people, as well as between

governmental and non-governmental youth and student organizations and institutions; the conclusion between such organizations and institutions of bilateral and multilateral arrangements and programmes; and the holding on a bilateral and multilateral basis of educational, cultural and other events and activities by and for young people.

28. They will make further efforts to facilitate travel and tourism by young people, *inter alia,* by recommending to those of their railway authorities which are members of the International Union of Railways (UIC) that they expand the Inter-Rail system to cover all their European networks and by recommending to those of their railway authorities which are not members of the UIC that they consider establishing similar facilities.

29. In accordance with the Universal Postal Convention and the International Telecommunication Convention, they will

—guarantee the freedom of transit of postal communication;

—ensure the rapid and unhindered delivery of correspondence, including personal mail and parcels;

—respect the privacy and integrity of postal and telephone communications; and

—ensure the conditions necessary for rapid and uninterrupted telephone calls, including the use of international direct dialling systems, where they exist, and their development.

30. They will encourage direct personal contacts between the citizens of their States, *inter alia* by facilitating individual travel within their countries and by allowing foreigners to meet their citizens as well as, when invited to do so, to stay in private homes.

31. They will ensure that the status of persons belonging to national minorities or regional cultures on their territories is equal to that of other citizens with regard to human contacts under the Final Act and the other aforementioned CSCE documents and that these persons can establish and maintain such contacts through travel and other means of communication, including contacts with citizens of other States with whom they share a common national origin or cultural heritage.

32. They will allow believers, religious faiths and their representatives, in groups or on an individual basis, to establish and maintain direct personal contacts and communication with each other, in their own and other countries, *inter alia* through travel, pilgrimages and participation in assemblies and other religious events. In this context and commensurate with such contacts and events, those concerned will be allowed to acquire, receive and carry with them religious publications and objects related to the practice of their religion or belief.

33. They heard accounts of the Meeting of Experts on Human Contacts held in Bern from 15 April to 26 May 1986. Noting that no conclusions had been agreed upon at the Meeting, they regarded both the frankness of the discussion and the greater degree of openness in the exchanges as welcome developments. In this respect they noted the particular importance of the fact that proposals made at the Meeting had received further consideration at the Vienna Follow-up Meeting.

Information

34. They will continue efforts to contribute to an ever wider knowledge and understanding of life in their States, thus promoting confidence between peoples.

They will make further efforts to facilitate the freer and wider dissemination of information of all kinds, to encourage co-operation in the field of information and to improve the working conditions for journalists.

In this connection and in accordance with the International Covenant on Civil and Political Rights, the Universal Declaration of Human Rights and their relevant international commitments concerning seeking, receiving and imparting information of all kinds, they will ensure that individuals can freely choose their sources of information. In this context they will

—ensure that radio services operating in accordance with the ITU Radio Regulations can be directly and normally received in their states; and

—allow individuals, institutions and organizations, while respecting intellectual property rights, including copyright, to obtain, possess, reproduce and distribute information material of all kinds.

To these ends they will remove any restrictions inconsistent with the above-mentioned obligations and commitments.

35. They will take every opportunity offered by modern means of communication, including cable and satellites, to increase the freer and wider dissemination of information of all kinds. They will also encourage co-operation and exchanges between their relevant institutions, organizations and technical experts, and work towards the harmonization of technical standards and norms. They will bear in mind the effects of these modern means of communication on their mass media.

36. They will ensure in practice that official information bulletins can be freely distributed on their territory by the diplomatic and other official missions and consular posts of the other participating States.

37. They will encourage radio and television organizations, on the basis of arrangements between them, to broadcast live, especially in the organizing countries, programmes and discussions with participants from different States and to broadcast statements of and interviews with political and other personalities from the participating States.

38. They will encourage radio and television organizations to report on different aspects of life in other participating States and to increase the number of telebridges between their countries.

39. Recalling that the legitimate pursuit of journalists' professional activity will neither render them liable to expulsion nor otherwise penalize them, they will refrain from taking restrictive measures such as withdrawing a journalist's accreditation or expelling him because of the content of the reporting of the journalist or of his information media.

40. They will ensure that, in pursuing this activity, journalists, including those representing media from other participating States, are free to seek access to and maintain contacts with public and private sources of information and that their need for professional confidentiality is respected.

41. They will respect the copyright of journalists.

42. On the basis of arrangements between them, where necessary, and for the purpose of regular reporting, they will grant accreditation, where it is required, and multiple entry visas to journalists from other participating States, regardless of their domicile. On this basis they will reduce to a maximum of two months the period for issuing both accreditation and multiple entry visas to journalists.

43. They will facilitate the work of foreign journalists by providing relevant information, on request, on matters of

practical concern, such as import regulations, taxation and accommodation.

44. They will ensure that official press conferences and, as appropriate, other similar official press events are also open to foreign journalists, upon accreditation, where this is required.

45. They will ensure in practice that persons belonging to national minorities or regional cultures on their territories can disseminate, have access to, and exchange information in their mother tongue.

46. They agree to convene an Information Forum to discuss improvement of the circulation of, access to and exchange of information; co-operation in the field of information; and the improvement of working conditions for journalists. The Forum will be held in London from 18 April to 12 May 1989. It will be attended by personalities from the participating States in the field of information. The agenda, time-table and other organizational modalities are set out in Annex VIII.

Co-operation and Exchanges in the Field of Culture

47. They will promote and give full effect to their cultural co-operation, *inter alia* through the implementation of any relevant bilateral and multilateral agreements concluded among them in the various fields of culture.

48. They will encourage non-governmental organizations interested in the field of culture, to participate, together with state institutions, in the elaboration and implementation of these agreements and specific projects, as well as in the elaboration of practical measures concerning cultural exchange and co-operation.

49. They will favour the establishment, by mutual agreement, of cultural institutes or centres of other participating States on their territory. Unhindered access by the public to such institutes or centres as well as their normal functioning will be assured.

50. They will assure unhindered access by the public to cultural events organized on their territory by persons or institutions from other participating States and ensure that the organizers can use all means available in the host country to publicize such events.

51. They will facilitate and encourage direct personal contacts in the field of culture, on both an individual and a collective basis, as well as contacts between cultural institutions, associations of creative and performing artists and other organizations in order to increase the opportunities for their citizens to acquaint themselves directly with the creative work in and from other participating States.

52. They will ensure the unimpeded circulation of works of art and other cultural objects, subject only to those restrictions aimed at preserving their cultural heritage which are based on respect for intellectual and artistic property rights or derive from their international commitments on the circulation of cultural property.

53. They will encourage co-operation between and joint artistic endeavours of persons from different participating states who are engaged in cultural activities; as appropriate, facilitate specific initiatives to this end by such persons, institutions and organizations and encourage the participation of young people in such initiatives. In this context they will encourage meetings and symposia, exhibitions, festivals and tours by ensembles or companies, and research and training programmes in which persons from the other participating States may also freely take part and make their contribution.

54. The replacement of persons or groups invited to participate in a cultural activity will be exceptional and subject to prior agreement by the inviting party.

55. They will encourage the holding of film weeks including, as appropriate, meetings of artists and experts as well as lectures on cinematographic art; facilitate and encourage direct contacts between film directors and producers with a view to co-producing films; and encourage co-operation in the protection of film material and the exchange of technical information and publications about the cinema.

56. They will explore the scope for computerizing bibliographies and catalogues of cultural works and productions in a standard form and disseminating them.

57. They will encourage museums and art galleries to develop direct contacts, *inter alia* with a view to organizing exhibitions, including loans of works of art, and exchanging catalogues.

58. They will renew their efforts to give effect to the provisions of the Final Act and the Madrid Concluding Document relating to less widely spoken languages. They will also encourage initiatives aimed at increasing the number of translations of literature from and into these languages and improving their quality, in particular by the holding of workshops involving translators, authors and publishers, by the publication of dictionaries and, where appropriate, by the exchange of translators through scholarships.

59. They will ensure that persons belonging to national minorities or regional cultures on their territories can maintain and develop their own culture in all its aspects, including language, literature and religion; and that they can preserve their cultural and historical monuments and objects.

60. They heard accounts of the work done and the ideas advanced during the Cultural Forum held in Budapest from 15 October to 25 November 1985. Noting that no conclusions had been agreed upon at the Forum, they welcomed the fact that many of the useful ideas and proposals put forward there had received renewed consideration at the Vienna Follow-up Meeting and that institutions and organizations in the participating States have based many activities on these ideas. They expressed their appreciation of the significant contributions made to the event by leading personalities in the field of culture, and noted, in the light of the experience gained, the importance of securing, both inside and outside future meetings of this nature, arrangements which would permit a freer and more spontaneous discussion.

61. Taking duly into account the originality and diversity of their respective cultures, they will encourage efforts to explore common features and to foster greater awareness of their cultural heritage. Accordingly they will encourage initiatives which may contribute to a better knowledge of the cultural heritage of the other participating States in all its forms, including regional aspects and folk art.

62. They agree to convene a Symposium on the Cultural Heritage of the CSCE participating States. The symposium will take place in Cracow from 28 May to 7 June 1991. It will be attended by scholars and other personalities from the participating States who are engaged in cultural activities. The agenda, timetable and other organizational modalities are set out in Annex IX.

Co-operation and Exchanges in the Field of Education

63. They will ensure access by all to the various types and levels of education without discrimination as to race, colour, sex, language, religion, political or other opinion, national or social origin, property, birth or other status.

64. In order to encourage wider co-operation in science and education, they will facilitate unimpeded communication between universities and other institutions of higher education and research. They will also facilitate direct personal contacts, including contacts through travel, between scholars, scientists and other persons active in these fields.

65. In this context they will also ensure unimpeded access by scholars, teachers and students from the other participating States to open information material available in public archives, libraries, research institutes and similar bodies.

66. They will facilitate exchanges of schoolchildren between their countries on the basis of bilateral arrangements, where necessary, including meeting and staying with families of the host country in their homes, with the aim of acquainting schoolchildren with life, traditions and education in other participating States.

67. They will encourage their relevant government agencies or educational institutions to include, as appropriate, the Final Act as a whole in the curricula of schools and universities.

68. They will ensure that persons belonging to national minorities or regional cultures on their territories can give and receive instruction on their own culture, including instruction through parental transmission of language, religion and cultural identity to their children.

69. They will encourage their radio and television organizations to inform each other of the educational programmes they produce and to consider exchanging such programmes.

70. They will encourage direct contacts and co-operation between relevant governmental institutions or organizations in the field of education and science.

71. They will encourage further co-operation and contacts between specialized institutions and experts in the field of education and rehabilitation of handicapped children.

HELSINKI ACCORD: FINAL ACT OF THE CONFERENCE ON SECURITY AND CO-OPERATION IN EUROPE (1975). The Final Act of the Conference, adopted by the high representatives of the 35 participating States convened in Helsinki, on 1 August 1975, contains a number of references to the promotion and protection of human rights and fundamental freedoms in those portions of Part I which set out the *Declaration on Principles Guiding Relations Between the Participating States* and those—informally referred to as "Basket III"—which appear under the heading "Co-operation in Humanitarian and Other Fields." These portions of the final act, and the relevant introductory paragraphs, are as follows:

Conference on Security and Co-operation in Europe
Final Act

The Conference on Security and Co-operation in Europe, which opened at Helsinki on 3 July 1973 and continued at Geneva from 18 September 1973 to 21 July 1975, was concluded at Helsinki on 1 August 1975 by the High Representatives of Austria, Belgium, Bulgaria, Canada, Cyprus, Czechoslovakia, Denmark, Finland, France, the German Democratic Republic, the Federal Republic of Germany, Greece, the Holy See, Hungary, Iceland, Ireland, Italy, Liechtenstein, Luxembourg, Malta, Monaco, the Netherlands, Norway, Poland, Portugal, Romania, San Marino, Spain, Sweden, Switzerland, Turkey, the Union of Soviet Socialist Republics, the United Kingdom, the United States of America and Yugoslavia.

During the opening and closing stages of the Conference the participants were addressed by the Secretary-General of the United Nations as their guest of honour. The Director-General of UNESCO and the Executive Secretary of the United Nations Economic Commission for Europe addressed the Conference during its second stage.

During the meetings of the second stage of the Conference, contributions were received, and statements heard, from the following nonparticipating Mediterranean States on various agenda items: the Democratic and Popular Republic of Algeria, the Arab Republic of Egypt, Israel, the Kingdom of Morocco, the Syrian Arab Republic, Tunisia.

Motivated by the political will, in the interest of peoples, to improve and intensify their relations and to contribute in Europe to peace, security, justice and co-operation as well as to rapprochement among themselves and with the other States of the world,

Determined, in consequence, to give full effect to the results of the Conference and to assure, among their States and throughout Europe, the benefits deriving from those results and thus to broaden, deepen and make continuing and lasting the process of détente,

The High Representatives of the participating States have solemnly adopted the following:

Questions Relating to Security in Europe

The States participating in the Conference on Security and Co-operation in Europe,

Reaffirming their objective of promoting better relations among themselves and ensuring conditions in which their people can live in true and lasting peace free from any threat to or attempt against their security;

Convinced of the need to exert efforts to make détente both a continuing and an increasingly viable and comprehensive process, universal in scope, and that the implementation of the results of the Conference on Security and Co-operation in Europe will be a major contribution to this process;

Considering that solidarity among peoples, as well as the common purpose of the participating States in achieving the aims as set forth by the Conference on Security and Co-operation in Europe, should lead to the development of better and closer relations among them in all fields and thus to overcoming the confrontation stemming from the character of their past relations, and to better mutual understanding;

Mindful of their common history and recognizing that the existence of elements common to their traditions and values can assist them in developing their relations, and desiring to search, fully taking into account the individuality

...y of their positions and views, for possibilities of ...ir efforts with a view to overcoming distrust and ...ing confidence, solving the problems that separate them and co-operating in the interest of mankind;

Recognizing the indivisibility of security in Europe as well as their common interest in the development of co-operation throughout Europe and among themselves and expressing their intention to pursue efforts accordingly;

Recognizing the close link between peace and security in Europe and in the world as a whole and conscious of the need for each of them to make its contribution to the strengthening of world peace and security and to the promotion of fundamental rights, economic and social progress and well-being for all peoples;

Have adopted the following:

(a) Declaration on Principles Guiding Relations between Participating States

The participating States,

Reaffirming their commitment to peace, security and justice and the continuing development of friendly relations and co-operation;

Recognizing that this commitment, which reflects the interest and aspirations of peoples, constitutes for each participating State a present and future responsibility, heightened by experience of the past;

Reaffirming, in conformity with their membership in the United Nations and in accordance with the purposes and principles of the United Nations, their full and active support for the United Nations and for the enhancement of its role and effectiveness in strengthening international peace, security and justice, and in promoting the solution of international problems, as well as the development of friendly relations and co-operation among States;

Expressing their common adherence to the principles which are set forth below and are in conformity with the Charter of the United Nations, as well as their common will to act, in the application of these principles, in conformity with the purposes and principles of the Charter of the United Nations;

Declare their determination to respect and put into practice, each of them in its relations with all other participating States, irrespective of their political, economic or social systems as well as of their size, geographical location or level of economic development, the following principles, which are all of primary significance, guiding their mutual relations:

I. Sovereign Equality, Respect for the Rights Inherent in Sovereignty. . . .

II. Refraining from the Threat or Use of Force. . . .

III. Inviolability of Frontiers. . . .

IV. Territorial Integrity of States.

V. Peaceful Settlement of Disputes.

VI. Non-intervention in Internal Affairs. The participating States will refrain from any intervention, direct or indirect, individual or collective, in the internal or external affairs falling within the domestic jurisdiction of another participating State, regardless of their mutual relations.

They will accordingly refrain from any form of armed intervention or threat of such intervention against another participating State.

They will likewise in all circumstances refrain from any other act of military, or of political, economic or other coercion designed to subordinate to their own interest the exercise by another participating State of the rights inherent in its sovereignty and thus to secure advantage of any kind.

Accordingly, they will, inter alia, refrain from direct or indirect assistance to terrorist activities, or to subversive or other activities directed towards the violent overthrow of the regime of another participating State.

VII. Respect for Human Rights and Fundamental Freedoms, including the Freedom of Thought, Conscience, Religion or Belief. The participating States will respect human rights and fundamental freedoms, including the freedom of thought, conscience, religion or belief, for all without distinction as to race, sex, language or religion.

They will promote and encourage the effective exercise of civil, political, economic, social, cultural and other rights and freedoms all of which derive from the inherent dignity of the human person and are essential for his free and full development.

Within this framework the participating States will recognize and respect the freedom of the individual to profess and practise, alone or in community with others, religion or belief acting in accordance with the dictates of his own conscience.

The participating States on whose territory national minorities exist will respect the right of persons belonging to such minorities to equality before the law, will afford them the full opportunity for the actual enjoyment of human rights and fundamental freedoms and will, in this manner, protect their legitimate interests in this sphere.

The participating States recognize the universal significance of human rights and fundamental freedoms, respect for which is an essential factor for the peace, justice and well-being necessary to ensure the development of friendly relations and cooperation among themselves as among all States.

They will constantly respect these rights and freedoms in their mutual relations and will endeavour jointly and separately, including in co-operation with the United Nations, to promote universal and effective respect for them.

They confirm the right of the individual to know and act upon his rights and duties in this field.

In the field of human rights and fundamental freedoms, the participating States will act in conformity with the purposes and principles of the Charter of the United Nations and with the Universal Declaration of Human Rights. They will also fulfill their obligations as set forth in the international declarations and agreements in this field, including inter alia the International Covenants on Human Rights, by which they may be bound.

VIII. Equal Rights and Self-Determination of Peoples. The participating States will respect the equal rights of peoples and their right to self-determination, acting at all times in conformity with the purposes and principles of the Charter of the United Nations and with the relevant norms of international law, including those relating to territorial integrity of States.

By virtue of the principle of equal rights and self-determination of peoples, all peoples always have the right, in full freedom, to determine, when and as they wish, their internal and external political status, without external interference, and to pursue as they wish their political, economic, social and cultural development.

The participating States reaffirm the universal significance of respect for an effective exercise of equal rights and self-determination of peoples for the development of friendly relations among themselves or among all States; they also recall the importance of the elimination of any form of violation of this principle.

IX. Co-operation among States. The participating States will develop their co-operation with one another and with all

722

States in all fields in accordance with the purposes and principles of the Charter of the United Nations. In developing their co-operation the participating States will place special emphasis on the fields as set forth within the framework of the Conference on Security and Co-operation in Europe, with each of them making its contribution in conditions of full equality.

They will endeavour, in developing their co-operation as equals, to promote mutual understanding and confidence, friendly and good-neighbourly relations among themselves, international peace, security and justice. They will equally endeavour, in developing their co-operation, to improve the well-being of peoples and contribute to the fulfilment of their aspirations through, inter alia, the benefits resulting from increased mutual knowledge and from progress and achievement in the economic, scientific, technological, social, cultural and humanitarian fields. They will take steps to promote conditions favourable to making these benefits available to all; they will take into account the interest of all in the narrowing of differences in the levels of economic development, and in particular the interest of developing countries throughout the world.

They confirm that governments, institutions, organizations and persons have a relevant and positive role to play in contributing toward the achievement of these aims of their co-operation.

They will strive, in increasing their co-operation as set forth above, to develop closer relations among themselves on an improved and more enduring basis for the benefit of peoples.

X. Fulfilment in Good Faith of Obligations under International Law. . . .

Co-operation in Humanitarian and Other Fields

The participating States,

Desiring to contribute to the strengthening of peace and understanding among peoples and to the spiritual enrichment of the human personality without distinction as to race, sex, language or religion,

Conscious that increased cultural and educational exchanges, broader dissemination of information, contacts between people, and the solution of humanitarian problems will contribute to the attainment of these aims,

Determined therefore to co-operate among themselves, irrespective of their political, economic and social systems, in order to create better conditions in the above fields, to develop and strengthen existing forms of co-operation and to work out new ways and means appropriate to these aims,

Convinced that this co-operation should take place in full respect for the principles guiding relations among participating States as set forth in the relevant document,

Have adopted the following:

1. Human Contacts

The participating States,

Considering the development of contacts to be an important element in the strengthening of friendly relations and trust among peoples,

Affirming, in relation to their present effort to improve conditions in this area, the importance they attach to humanitarian considerations,

Desiring in this spirit to develop, with the continuance of détente, further efforts to achieve continuing progress in this field

And conscious that the questions relevant hereto must be settled by the States concerned under mutually acceptable conditions,

Make it their aim to facilitate freer movement and contacts, individually and collectively, whether privately or officially, among persons, institutions and organizations of the participating States, and to contribute to the solution of the humanitarian problems that arise in that connexion,

Declare their readiness to these ends to take measures which they consider appropriate and to conclude agreements or arrangements among themselves, as may be needed, and

Express their intention now to proceed to the implementation of the following:

(a)Contacts and Regular Meetings on the Basis of Family Ties. In order to promote further development of contacts on the basis of family ties the participating States will favourably consider applications for travel with the purpose of allowing persons to enter or leave their territory temporarily, and on a regular basis if desired, in order to visit members of their families.

Applications for temporary visits to meet members of their families will be dealt with without distinction as to the country of origin or destination: existing requirements for travel documents and visas will be applied in this spirit. The preparation and issue of such documents and visas will be effected within reasonable time limits: cases of urgent necessity—such as serious illness or death—will be given priority treatment. They will take such steps as may be necessary to ensure that the fees for official travel documents and visas are acceptable.

They confirm that the presentation of an application concerning contacts on the basis of family ties will not modify the rights and obligations of the applicant or of members of his family.

(b) Reunification of Families. The participating States will deal in a positive and humanitarian spirit with the applications of persons who wish to be reunited with members of their family, with special attention being given to requests of an urgent character—such as requests submitted by persons who are ill or old.

They will deal with applications in this field as expeditiously as possible.

They will lower where necessary the fees charged in connexion with these applications to ensure that they are at a moderate level.

Applications for the purpose of family reunification which are not granted may be renewed at the appropriate level and will be reconsidered at reasonably short intervals by the authorities of the country of residence, or destination, whichever is concerned; under such circumstances fees will be charged only when applications are granted.

Persons whose applications for family reunification are granted may bring with them or ship their household and personal effects; to this end the participating States will use all possibilities provided by existing regulations.

Until members of the same family are reunited meetings and contacts between them may take place in accordance with the modalities for contacts on the basis of family ties.

The participating States will support the efforts of Red Cross and Red Crescent Societies concerned with the problems of family reunification.

They confirm that the presentation of an application concerning family reunification will not modify the rights and obligations of the applicant or of members of his family.

The receiving participating State will take appropriate

care with regard to employment for persons from other participating States who take up permanent residence in that State in connexion with family reunification with its citizens and see that they are afforded opportunities equal to those enjoyed by its own citizens for education, medical assistance and social security.

(c) *Marriage between Citizens of Different States.* The participating States will examine favourably and on the basis of humanitarian considerations requests for exit or entry permits from persons who have decided to marry a citizen from another participating State.

The processing and issuing of the documents required for the above purposes and for the marriage will be in accordance with the provisions accepted for family reunification.

In dealing with requests from couples from different participating States, once married, to enable them and the minor children of their marriage to transfer their permanent residence to a State in which either one is normally a resident, the participating States will also apply the provisions accepted for family reunification.

(d) *Travel for Personal or Professional Reasons.* The participating States intend to facilitate wider travel by their citizens for personal or professional reasons and to this end they intend in particular:

—gradually to simplify and to administer flexibly the procedures for exit and entry;

—to ease regulations concerning movement of citizens from the other participating States in their territory, with due regard to security requirements.

They will endeavour gradually to lower, where necessary, the fees for visas and official travel documents.

They intend to consider, as necessary, means—including, in so far as appropriate, the conclusion of multilateral or bilateral consular conventions or other relevant agreements or understandings—for the improvement of arrangements to provide consular services, including legal and consular assistance.

They confirm that religious faiths, institutions and organizations, practising within the constitutional framework of the participating States, and their representatives can, in the field of their activities, have contacts and meetings among themselves and exchange information.

(e) *Improvement of Conditions for Tourism on an Individual or Collective Basis.* The participating States consider that tourism contributes to a fuller knowledge of the life, culture and history of other countries, to the growth of understanding among peoples, to the improvement of contacts and to the broader use of leisure. They intend to promote the development of tourism, on an individual or collective basis, and, in particular, they intend:

—to promote visits to their respective countries by encouraging the provision of appropriate facilities and the simplification and expediting of necessary formalities relating to such visits;

—to increase, on the basis of appropriate agreements or arrangements where necessary, co-operation in the development of tourism, in particular by considering bilaterally possible ways to increase information relating to travel to other countries and to the reception and service of tourists, and other related questions of mutual interest.

(f) *Meetings among Young People.* The participating States intend to further the development of contacts and exchanges among young people by encouraging:

—increased exchanges and contacts on a short or long term basis among young people working, training or un-

dergoing education through bilateral or multilateral agreements or regular programmes in all cases where it is possible;

—study by their youth organizations of the question of possible agreements relating to frameworks of multilateral youth co-operation;

—agreements or regular programmes relating to the organization of exchanges of students, of international youth seminars, of courses of professional training and foreign language study;

—the further development of youth tourism and the provision to this end of appropriate facilities;

—the development, where possible, of exchanges, contacts and co-operation on a bilateral or multilateral basis between their organizations which represent wide circles of young people working, training or undergoing education;

—awareness among youth of the importance of developing mutual understanding and of strengthening friendly relations and confidence among peoples.

(g) *Sport.* In order to expand existing links and co-operation in the field of sport the participating States will encourage contacts and exchanges of this kind, including sports meetings and competitions of all sorts, on the basis of the established international rules, regulations and practice.

(h) *Expansion of Contacts.* By way of further developing contacts among governmental institutions and non-governmental organizations and associations, including women's organizations, the participating States will facilitate the convening of meetings as well as travel by delegations, groups and individuals.

2. Information

The participating States,

Conscious of the need for an ever wider knowledge and understanding of the various aspects of life in other participating States,

Acknowledging the contribution of this process to the growth of confidence between peoples,

Desiring, with the development of mutual understanding between the participating States and with the further improvement of their relations, to continue further efforts towards progress in this field,

Recognizing the importance of the dissemination of information from the other participating States and of a better acquaintance with such information,

Emphasizing therefore the essential and influential role of the press, radio, television, cinema and news agencies and of the journalists working in these fields,

Make it their aim to facilitate the freer and wider dissemination of information of all kinds, to encourage co-operation in the field of information and the exchange of information with other countries, and to improve the conditions under which journalists from one participating State exercise their profession in another participating State, and

Express their intention in particular:

(a) *Improvement of the Circulation of, Access to, and Exchange of Information.*

(i) *Oral Information*

—To facilitate the dissemination of oral information through the encouragement of lectures and lecture tours by personalities and specialists from the other participating States, as well as exchanges of opinions at round table meetings, seminars, symposia, summer schools, congresses and other bilateral and multilateral meetings.

(ii) *Printed Information*

—To facilitate the improvement of the dissemination, on their territory, of newspapers and printed publications, periodical and non-periodical, from the other participating States. For this purpose: (1) they will encourage their competent firms and organizations to conclude agreements and contracts designed gradually to increase the quantities and the number of titles of newspapers and publications imported from the other participating States. These agreements and contracts should in particular mention the speediest conditions of delivery and the use of the normal channels existing in each country for the distribution of its own publications and newspapers, as well as forms and means of payment agreed between the parties making it possible to achieve the objectives aimed at by these agreements and contracts; [and] (2) where necessary, they will take appropriate measures to achieve the above objectives and to implement the provisions contained in the agreements and contracts.

—To contribute to the improvement of access by the public to periodical and non-periodical printed publications imported on the bases indicated above. In particular: (1) they will encourage an increase in the number of places where these publications are on sale; (2) they will facilitate the availability of these periodical publications during congresses, conferences, official visits and other international events and to tourists during the season; (3) they will develop the possibilities for taking out subscriptions according to the modalities particular to each country; [and] (4) they will improve the opportunities for reading and borrowing these publications in large public libraries and their reading rooms as well as in university libraries.

They intend to improve the possibilities for acquaintance with bulletins of official information issued by diplomatic missions and distributed by those missions on the basis of arrangements acceptable to the interested parties.

(iii) *Filmed and Broadcast Information*

—To promote the improvement of the dissemination of filmed and broadcast information. To this end: (1) they will encourage the wider showing and broadcasting of a greater variety of recorded and filmed information from the other participating States, illustrating the various aspects of life in their countries and received on the basis of such agreements or arrangements as may be necessary between the organizations and firms directly concerned; [and] (2) they will facilitate the import by competent organizations and firms of recorded audio-visual material from other participating States.

The participating States note the expansion in the dissemination of information broadcast by radio, and express the hope for the continuation of this process, so as to meet the interest of mutual understanding among peoples and the aims set forth by this Conference.

(*b*) *Co-operation in the Field of Information.* To encourage co-operation in the field of information on the basis of short or long term agreements or arrangements. In particular: (1) they will favour increased co-operation among mass media organizations including press agencies, as well as among publishing houses and organizations; (2) they will favour co-operation among public or private, national or international radio and television organizations, in particular through the exchange of both live and recorded radio and television programmes, and through the joint production and the broadcasting and distribution of such

programmes; (3) they will encourage meetings and contacts both between journalists' organizations and between journalists from the participating States; (4) they will view favourably the possibilities of arrangements between periodical publications as well as between newspapers from the participating States, for the purpose of exchanging and publishing articles; [and] (5) they will encourage the exchange of technical information as well as the organization of joint research and meetings devoted to the exchange of experience and views between experts in the field of the press, radio and television.

(*c*) *Improvement of Working Conditions for Journalists.* The participating States, desiring to improve the conditions under which journalists from one participating State exercise their profession in another participating State, intend in particular to:

—examine in a favourable spirit and within a suitable and reasonable time scale requests from journalists for visas;

—grant to permanently accredited journalists of the participating States, on the basis of arrangements, multiple entry and exit visas for specified periods;

—facilitate the issue to accredited journalists of the participating States of permits for stay in their country of temporary residence and, if and when these are necessary, of other official papers which it is appropriate for them to have;

—ease, on a basis of reciprocity, procedures for arranging travel by journalists of the participating States in the country where they are exercising their profession, and to provide progressively greater opportunities for such travel, subject to the observance of regulations relating to the existence of areas closed for security reasons;

—ensure that requests by such journalists for such travel receive, in so far as is possible, an expeditious response, taking into account the time scale of the request;

—increase the opportunities for journalists of the participating States to communicate personally with their sources, including organizations and official institutions;

—grant to journalists of the participating States the right to import, subject only to its being taken out again, the technical equipment (photographic, cinematographic, tape recorder, radio and television) necessary for the exercise of their profession;

—enable journalists of the other participating States, whether permanently or temporarily accredited, to transmit completely, normally and rapidly by means recognized by the participating States to the information organs which they represent, the results of their professional activity, including tape recordings and undeveloped film, for the purpose of publication or of broadcasting on the radio or television.

The participating States reaffirm that the legitimate pursuit of their professional activity will neither render journalists liable to expulsion nor otherwise penalize them. If an accredited journalist is expelled, he will be informed of the reasons for this act and may submit an application for re-examination of his case.

3. Co-operation and Exchanges in the Field of Culture

The participating States,

Considering that cultural exchanges and co-operation contribute to a better comprehension among people and among peoples, and thus promote a lasting understanding among States,

ing the conclusions already formulated in this
ne multilateral level, particularly at the Intergov-
nental Conference on Cultural Policies in Europe, organized by UNESCO in Helsinki in June 1972, where
interest was manifested in the active participation of the
broadest possible social groups in an increasingly diversified cultural life,

Desiring, with the development of mutual confidence
and the further improvement of relations between the participating States, to continue further efforts toward progress in this field,

Disposed in this spirit to increase substantially their
cultural exchanges, with regard both to persons and to
cultural works, and to develop among them an active co-
operation, both at the bilateral and the multilateral level, in
all the fields of culture,

Convinced that such a development of their mutual relations will contribute to the enrichment of the respective
cultures, while respecting the originality of each, as well as
to the reinforcement among them of a consciousness of
common values, while continuing to develop cultural co-
operation with other countries of the world,

Declare that they jointly set themselves the following objectives:

(a) to develop the mutual exchange of information
with a view to a better knowledge of respective cultural
achievements,

(b) to improve the facilities for the exchange and for
the dissemination of cultural property,

(c) to promote access by all to respective cultural
achievements,

(d) to develop contacts and co-operation among
persons active in the field of culture,

(e) to seek new fields and forms of cultural co-
operation,

Thus give expression to their common will to take progressive, coherent and long-term action in order to achieve
the objectives of the present declaration; and

Express their intention now to proceed to the implementation of the following:

(a) *Extension of Relations.* To expand, and improve at the
various levels co-operation and links in the field of culture,
in particular by:

—concluding, where appropriate, agreements on a bilateral or multilateral basis, providing for the extension of
relations among competent State institutions and non-
governmental organizations in the field of culture, as well
as among people engaged in cultural activities, taking into
account the need both for flexibility and the fullest possible
use of existing agreements, and bearing in mind that agreements and also other arrangements constitute important
means of developing cultural co-operation and exchanges;

—contributing to the development of direct communication and co-operation among relevant State institutions
and non-governmental organizations, including, where
necessary, such communication and co-operation carried
out on the basis of special agreements and arrangements;

—encouraging direct contacts and communications
among persons engaged in cultural activities, including,
where necessary, such contacts and communications carried out on the basis of special agreements and arrangements.

(b) *Mutual Knowledge.* Within their competence to adopt,
on a bilateral and multilateral level, appropriate measures
which would give their peoples a more comprehensive and
complete mutual knowledge of their achievements in the
various fields of culture, and among them:

—to examine jointly, if necessary with the assistance of
appropriate international organizations, the possible creation in Europe and the structure of a bank of cultural data,
which would collect information from the participating
countries and make it available to its correspondents on
their request, and to convene for this purpose a meeting of
experts from interested States;

—to consider, if necessary in conjunction with appropriate international organizations, ways of compiling in Europe an inventory of documentary films of a cultural or
scientific nature from the participating States;

—to encourage more frequent book exhibitions and to
examine the possibility of organizing periodically in Europe a large-scale exhibition of books from the participating States;

—to promote the systematic exchange, between the
institutions concerned and publishing houses, of catalogues of available books as well as of pre-publication material which will include, as far as possible, all forthcoming
publications; and also to promote the exchange of material between firms publishing encyclopaedias, with a view
to improving the presentation of each country;

—to examine jointly questions of expanding and improving exchanges of information in the various fields of
culture, such as theatre, music, library work as well as the
conservation and restoration of cultural property.

(c) *Exchanges and Dissemination.* To contribute to the
improvement of facilities for exchanges and the dissemination of cultural property, by appropriate means, in
particular by:

—studying the possibilities for harmonizing and reducing the charges relating to international commercial exchanges of books and other cultural materials, and also for
new means of insuring works of art in foreign exhibitions
and for reducing the risks of damage or loss to which these
works are exposed by their movement;

—facilitating the formalities of customs clearance, in
good time for programmes of artistic events, of the works
of art, materials and accessories appearing on lists agreed
upon by the organizers of these events;

—encouraging meetings among representatives of
competent organizations and relevant firms to examine
measures within their field of activity—such as the simplification of orders, time limits for sending supplies and modalities of payment—which might facilitate international
commercial exchanges of books;

—promoting the loan and exchange of films among
their film institutes and film libraries;

—encouraging the exchange of information among interested parties concerning events of a cultural character
foreseen in the participating States, in fields where this is
most appropriate, such as music, theatre and the plastic
and graphic arts, with a view to contributing to the compilation and publication of a calendar of such events, with
the assistance, where necessary, of the appropriate international organizations;

—encouraging a study of the impact which the foreseeable development, and a possible harmonization among
interested parties, of the technical means used for the dissemination of culture might have on the development of
cultural co-operation and exchanges, while keeping in
view the preservation of the diversity and originality of
their respective cultures;

—encouraging, in the way they deem appropriate,

within their cultural policies, the further development of interest in the cultural heritage of the other participating States, conscious of the merits and the value of each culture;

—endeavouring to ensure the full and effective application of the international agreements and conventions on copyrights and on circulation of cultural property to which they are party or to which they may decide in the future to become party.

(d) Access. To promote fuller mutual access by all to the achievements—works, experiences and performing arts—in the various fields of culture of their countries, and to that end to make the best possible efforts, in accordance with their competence, more particularly:

—to promote wider dissemination of books and artistic works, in particular by such means as: (1) facilitating, while taking full account of the international copyright conventions to which they are party, international contacts and recommendations between authors and publishing houses as well as other cultural institutions, with a view to a more complete mutual access to cultural achievements; (2) recommending that, in determining the size of editions, publishing houses take into account also the demand from the other participating States, and that rights of sale in other participating States be granted, where possible, to several sales organizations of the importing countries, by agreement between interested partners; (3) encouraging competent organizations and relevant firms to conclude agreements and contracts and contributing, by this means, to a gradual increase in the number and diversity of works by authors from the other participating States available in the original and in translation in their libraries and bookshops; (4) promoting, where deemed appropriate, an increase in the number of sales outlets where books by authors from the other participating States, imported in the original on the basis of agreements and contracts, and in translation, are for sale; [and] (5) promoting, on a wider scale, the translation of works in the sphere of literature and other fields of cultural activity, produced in the languages of the other participating States, especially from the less widely-spoken languages, and the publication and dissemination of the translated works by such measures as:

(a) encouraging more regular contacts between interested publishing houses;

(b) developing their efforts in the basic and advanced training of translators;

(c) encouraging, by appropriate means, the publishing houses of their countries to publish translations;

(d) facilitating the exchange between publishers and interested institutions of lists of books which might be translated;

(e) promoting between their countries the professional activity and co-operation of translators;

(f) carrying out joint studies on ways of further promoting translations and their dissemination; [and]

(g) improving and expanding exchanges of books, bibliographies and catalogue cards between libraries;

—to envisage other appropriate measures which would permit, where necessary by mutual agreement among interested parties, the facilitation of access to their respective cultural achievements, in particular in the field of books;

—to contribute by appropriate means to the wider use of the mass media in order to improve mutual acquaintance with the cultural life of each;

—to seek to develop the necessary conditions for migrant workers and their families to preserve their links with their national culture, and also to adapt themselves to their new cultural environment;

—to encourage the competent bodies and enterprises to make a wider choice and effect wider distribution of full-length and documentary films from the other participating States, and to promote more frequent non-commercial showings, such as premieres, film weeks and festivals, giving due consideration to films from countries whose cinematographic works are less well known;

—to promote, by appropriate means, the extension of opportunities for specialists from the other participating States to work with materials of a cultural character from film and audio-visual archives, within the framework of the existing rules for work on such archival materials;

—to encourage a joint study by interested bodies, where appropriate with the assistance of the competent international organizations, of the expediency and the conditions for the establishment of a repertory of their recorded television programmes of a cultural nature, as well as of the means of viewing them rapidly in order to facilitate their selection and possible acquisition.

(e) Contacts and Co-operation. To contribute, by appropriate means, to the development of contacts and co-operation in the various fields of culture, especially among creative artists and people engaged in cultural activities, in particular by making efforts to:

—to promote for persons active in the field of culture, travel and meetings including, where necessary, those carried out on the basis of agreements, contracts or other special arrangements and which are relevant to their cultural co-operation;

—encourage in this way contacts among creative and performing artists and artistic groups with a view to their working together, making known their works in other participating States or exchanging view on topics relevant to their common activity;

—encourage, where necessary through appropriate arrangements, exchanges of trainees and specialists and the granting of scholarships for basic and advanced training in various fields of culture such as the arts and architecture, museums and libraries, literary studies and translation, and contribute to the creation of favourable conditions of reception in their respective institutions;

—encourage the exchange of experience in the training of organizers of cultural activities as well as of teachers and specialists in fields such as theatre, opera, ballet, and music and fine arts;

—continue to encourage the organization of international meetings among creative artists, especially young creative artists, on current questions of artistic and literary creation which are of interest for joint study;

—study other possibilities for developing exchanges and co-operation among persons active in the field of culture, with a view to a better mutual knowledge of the cultural life of the participating States.

(f) Fields and Forms of Co-operation. To encourage the search for new fields and forms of cultural co-operation, to these ends contributing to the conclusion among interested parties, where necessary, of appropriate agreements and arrangements, and in this context to promote:

—joint studies regarding cultural policies, in particular in their social aspects, and as they relate to planning, town-planning, educational and environmental policies, and the cultural aspects of tourism;

—the exchange of knowledge in the realm of cultural diversity, with a view to contributing thus to a better under-

...anding by interested parties of such diversity where it occurs;

—the exchange of information, and as may be appropriate, meetings of experts, the elaboration and the execution of research programmes and projects, as well as their joint evaluation, and the dissemination of the results, on the subjects indicated above;

—such forms of cultural co-operation and the development of such joint projects as: (1) international events in the fields of the plastic and graphic arts, cinema, theatre, ballet, music, folklore, etc.; book fairs and exhibitions, joint performances of operatic and dramatic works, as well as performances given by soloists; (2) instrumental ensembles, orchestras, choirs and other artistic groups, including those composed of amateurs, paying due attention to the organization of international cultural youth events and the exchange of young artists; (3) the inclusion of works by writers and composers from the other participating States in the repertoires of soloists and artistic ensembles; (4) the preparation, translation and publication of articles, studies and monographs, as well as of low-cost books and of artistic and literary collections, suited to making better known respective cultural achievements, envisaging for this purpose meetings among experts and representatives of publishing houses; (5) the co-production and the exchange of films and of radio and television programmes, by promoting, in particular, meetings among producers, technicians and representatives of the public authorities with a view to working out favourable conditions for the execution of specific joint projects and by encouraging, in the field of co-production, the establishment of international filming teams; (6) the organization of competitions for architects and town-planners, bearing in mind the possible implementation of the best projects and the formation, where possible, of international teams; [and] (7) the implementation of joint projects for conserving, restoring and showing to advantage works of art, historical and archaeological monuments and sites of cultural interest, with the help, in appropriate cases, of international organizations of a governmental or non-governmental character as well as of private institutions—competent and active in these fields—envisaging for this purpose:

(a) periodic meetings of experts of the interested parties to elaborate the necessary proposals, while bearing in mind the need to consider these questions in a wider social and economic context;

(b) the publication in appropriate periodicals of articles designed to make known and to compare, among the participating States, the most significant achievements and innovations;

(c) a joint study with a view to the improvement and possible harmonization of the different systems used to inventory and catalogue the historical monuments and places of cultural interest in their countries;

(d) the study of the possibilities for organizing international courses for the training of specialists in different disciplines relating to restoration.

National minorities or regional cultures. The participating States, recognizing the contribution that national minorities or regional cultures can make to co-operation among them in various fields of culture, intend, when such minorities or cultures exist within their territory, to facilitate this contribution, taking into account the legitimate interests of their members.

4. Co-operation and Exchanges in the Field of Education

The participating States,

Conscious that the development of relations of an international character in the fields of education and science contributes to a better mutual understanding and is to the advantage of all peoples as well as to the benefit of future generations,

Prepared to facilitate, between organizations, institutions and persons engaged in education and science, the further development of exchanges of knowledge and experience as well as of contacts, on the basis of special arrangements where these are necessary,

Desiring to strengthen the links among educational and scientific establishments and also to encourage their co-operation in sectors of common interest, particularly where the levels of knowledge and resources require efforts to be concerted internationally, and

Convinced that progress in these fields should be accompanied and supported by a wider knowledge of foreign languages,

Express to these ends their intention in particular:

(a) *Extension of Relations.* To expand and improve at the various levels co-operation and links in the fields of education and science, in particular by:

—concluding, where appropriate, bilateral or multilateral agreements providing for co-operation and exchanges among State institutions, non-governmental bodies and persons engaged in activities in education and science, bearing in mind the need both for flexibility and the fuller use of existing agreements and arrangements;

—promoting the conclusion of direct arrangements between universities and other institutions of higher education and research, in the framework of agreements between governments where appropriate;

—encouraging among persons engaged in education and science direct contacts and communications, including those based on special agreements or arrangements where these are appropriate.

(b) *Access and Exchanges.* To improve access, under mutually acceptable conditions, for students, teachers and scholars of the participating States to each other's educational, cultural and scientific institutions, and to intensify exchanges among these institutions in all areas of common interest, in particular by:

—increasing the exchange of information on facilities for study and courses open to foreign participants, as well as on the conditions under which they will be admitted and received;

—facilitating travel between the participating States by scholars, teachers and students for purposes of study, teaching and research as well as for improving knowledge of each other's educational, cultural and scientific achievements;

—encouraging the award of scholarships for study, teaching and research in their countries to scholars, teachers and students of other participating States;

—establishing, developing or encouraging programmes providing for the broader exchange of scholars, teachers and students, including the organization of symposia, seminars and collaborative projects, and the exchanges of educational and scholarly information such as university publications and materials from libraries;

—promoting the efficient implementation of such arrangements and programmes by providing scholars, teachers and students in good time with more detailed information about their placing in universities and institutes and the programmes envisaged for them, by granting them the opportunity to use relevant scholarly, scientific and open archival materials; and by facilitating their travel within the receiving State for the purpose of study or research as well as in the form of vacation tours on the basis of the usual procedures;

—promoting a more exact assessment of the problems of comparison and equivalence of academic degrees and diplomas by fostering the exchange of information on the organization, duration and content of studies, the comparison of methods of assessing levels of knowledge and academic qualifications, and, where feasible, arriving at the mutual recognition of academic degrees and diplomas either through governmental agreements, where necessary, or direct arrangements between universities and other institutions of higher learning and research,

—recommending, moreover, to the appropriate international organizations that they should intensify their efforts to reach a generally acceptable solution to the problems of comparison and equivalence between academic degrees and diplomas.

(c) Science. Within their competence to broaden and improve co-operation and exchanges in the field of science, in particular:

To increase, on a bilateral or multilateral basis, the exchange and dissemination of scientific information and documentation by such means as:

—making this information more widely available to scientists and research workers of the other participating States through, for instance, participation in international information-sharing programmes or through other appropriate arrangements;

—broadening and facilitating the exchange of samples and other scientific materials used particularly for fundamental research in the fields of natural sciences and medicine;

—inviting scientific institutions and universities to keep each other more fully and regularly informed about their current and contemplated research work in fields of common interest.

To facilitate the extension of communications and direct contacts between universities, scientific institutions and associations as well as among scientists and research workers, including those based where necessary on special agreements or arrangements, by such means as:

—further developing exchanges of scientists and research workers and encouraging the organization of preparatory meetings or working groups on research topics of common interest;

—encouraging the creation of joint teams of scientists to pursue research projects under arrangements made by the scientific institutions of several countries;

—assisting the organization and successful functioning of international conferences and seminars and participation in them by their scientists and research workers;

—furthermore envisaging, in the near future, a "Scientific Forum" in the form of a meeting of leading personalities in science from the participating State to discuss interrelated problems of common interest concerning current and future developments in science, and to promote the expansion of contacts, communications and the exchange of information between scientific institutions and among scientists;

—foreseeing, at an early date, a meeting of experts representing the participating States and their national scientific institutions, in order to prepare such a "Scientific

Forum" in consultation with appropriate international organizations, such as UNESCO and the ECE;

—considering in due course what further steps might be taken with respect to the "Scientific Forum".

To develop in the field of scientific research, on a bilateral or multilateral basis, the co-ordination of programmes carried out in the participating States and the organization of joint programmes, especially in the areas mentioned below, which may involve the combined efforts of scientists and in certain cases the use of costly or unique equipment. The list of subjects in these areas is illustrative; and specific projects would have to be determined subsequently by the potential partners in the participating States, taking account of the contribution which could be made by appropriate international organizations and scientific institutions:

—*exact and natural sciences,* in particular fundamental research in such fields as mathematics, physics, theoretical physics, geophysics, chemistry, biology, ecology and astronomy;

—*medicine,* in particular basic research into cancer and cardiovascular diseases, studies on the diseases endemic in the developing countries, as well as medico-social research with special emphasis on occupational diseases, the rehabilitation of the handicapped and the care of mothers, children and the elderly;

—*the humanities and social sciences,* such as history, geography, philosophy, psychology, pedagogical research, linguistics, sociology, the legal, political and economic sciences, comparative studies on social, socio-economic and cultural phenomena which are of common interest to the participating States, especially the problems of human environment and urban development; and scientific studies on the methods of conserving and restoring monuments and works of art.

(d) Foreign Languages and Civilizations. To encourage the study of foreign languages and civilizations as an important means of expanding communication among peoples for their better acquaintance with the culture of each country, as well as for the strengthening of international co-operation; to this end to stimulate, within their competence, the further development and improvement of foreign language teaching and the diversification of choice of languages taught at various levels, paying due attention to less widely-spread or studied languages, and in particular:

—to intensify co-operation aimed at improving the teaching of foreign languages through exchanges of information and experience concerning the development and application of effective modern teaching methods and technical aids, adapted to the needs of different categories of students, including methods of accelerated teaching; and to consider the possibility of conducting, on a bilateral or multilateral basis, studies of new methods of foreign language teaching;

—to encourage co-operation between institutions concerned, on a bilateral or multilateral basis, aimed at exploiting more fully the resources of modern educational technology in language teaching, for example through comparative studies by their specialists and, where agreed, through exchanges or transfers of audio-visual materials, of materials used for preparing textbooks, as well as of information about new types of technical equipment used for teaching languages;

—to promote the exchange of information on the experience acquired in the training of language teachers and to

...sify exchanges on a bilateral basis of language teachers and students as well as to facilitate their participation in summer courses in language and civilizations, wherever these are organized;

—to encourage co-operation among experts in the field of lexicography with the aim of defining the necessary terminological equivalents, particularly in the scientific and technical disciplines, in order to facilitate relations among scientific institutions and specialists;

—to promote the wider spread of foreign language study among the different types of secondary education establishments and greater possibilities of choice between an increased number of European languages; and in this context to consider, wherever appropriate, the possibilities for developing the recruitment and training of teachers as well as the organization of the student groups required;

—to favour, in higher education, a wider choice in the languages offered to language students and greater opportunities for other students to study various foreign languages; also to facilitate, where desirable, the organization of courses in languages and civilizations, on the basis of special arrangements as necessary, to be given by foreign lecturers, particularly from European countries having less widely-spread or studied languages;

—to promote, within the framework of adult education, the further development of specialized programmes, adapted to various needs and interests, for teaching foreign languages to their own inhabitants and the languages of host countries to interested adults from other countries; in this context to encourage interested institutions to co-operate, for example, in the elaboration of programmes for teaching by radio and television and by accelerated methods, and also, where desirable, in the definition of study objectives for such programmes, with a view to arriving at comparable levels of language proficiency;

—to encourage the association, where appropriate, of the teaching of foreign languages with the study of the corresponding civilizations and also to make further efforts to stimulate interest in the study of foreign languages, including relevant out-of-class activities.

(e) Teaching Methods. To promote the exchange of experience, on a bilateral or multilateral basis, in teaching methods at all levels of education, including those used in permanent and adult education, as well as the exchange of teaching materials, in particular by:

—further developing various forms of contacts and co-operation in the different fields of pedagogical science, for example through comparative or joint studies carried out by interested institutions or through exchanges of information on the results of teaching experiments;

—intensifying exchanges of information on teaching methods used in various educational systems and on results of research into the processes by which pupils and students acquire knowledge, taking account of relevant experience in different types of specialized education;

—facilitating exchanges of experience concerning the organization and functioning of education intended for adults and recurrent education, the relationships between these and other forms and levels of education, as well as concerning the means of adapting education, including vocational and technical training, to the needs of economic and social development in their countries;

—encouraging exchanges of experience in the education of youth and adults in international understanding, with particular reference to those major problems of mankind whose solution calls for a common approach and wider international co-operation;

—encouraging exchanges of teaching materials—including school textbooks, having in mind the possibility of promoting mutual knowledge and facilitating the presentation of each country in such books—as well as exchanges of information on technical innovations in the field of education. . . .

National minorities or regional cultures. The participating States, recognizing the contribution that national minorities or regional cultures can make to co-operation among them in various fields of education, intend, when such minorities or cultures exist within their territory, to facilitate this contribution, taking into account the legitimate interests of their members. . . .

HELSINKI ACCORD: HUMAN DIMENSION OF THE CONFERENCE ON SECURITY AND CO-OPERATION IN EUROPE.

The attention of the 1990 session of the UN Commission on Human Rights was drawn to the final document of the Vienna meeting of the Conference on Security and Co-operation in Europe (CSCE), in particular the part which relates the "Human Dimension of the CSCE", reproduced below (UN Doc. E/CN.4/1990/84, Annex):

The participating States,

Recalling the undertakings entered into in the Final Act and in other CSCE documents concerning respect for all human rights and fundamental freedoms, human contacts and other issues of a related humanitarian character,

Recognizing the need to improve the implementation of their CSCE commitments and their co-operation in these areas which are hereafter referred to as the human dimension of the CSCE,

Have, on the basis of the principles and provisions of the Final Act and of other relevant CSCE documents, decided:

1. to exchange information and respond to requests for information and to representations made to them by other participating States on questions relating to the human dimension of the CSCE. Such communications may be forwarded through diplomatic channels or be addressed to any agency designated for these purposes;

2. to hold bilateral meetings with other participating States that so request, in order to examine questions relating to the human dimension of the CSCE, including situations and specific cases, with a view to resolving them. The date and place of such meetings will be arranged by mutual agreement through diplomatic channels;

3. that any participating State which deems it necessary may bring situations and cases in the human dimension of the CSCE, including those which have been raised at the bilateral meetings described in paragraph 2, to the attention of other participating States through diplomatic channels;

4. that any participating State which deems it necessary may provide information on the exchanges of information and the responses to its requests for information and to representations (paragraph 1) and on the results of the bilateral meetings (paragraph 2), including information concerning situations and specific cases, at the meetings of the

Conference on the Human Dimension as well as at the main CSCE Follow-up Meetings.

The participating States decide further to convene a Conference on the Human Dimension of the CSCE in order to achieve further progress concerning respect for all human rights and fundamental freedoms, human contacts and other issues of a related humanitarian character. The Conference will hold three meetings before the next CSCE Follow-up Meeting.

The Conference will:

—review developments in the human dimension of the CSCE including the implementation of the relevant CSCE commitments;

—evaluate the functioning of the procedures described in paragraphs 1 to 4 and discuss the information provided according to paragraph 4;

—consider practical proposals for new measures aimed at improving the implementation of the commitments relating to the human dimension of the CSCE and enhancing the effectiveness of the procedures described in paragraphs 1 to 4.

On the basis of these proposals, the Conference will consider adopting new measures.

The first Meeting of the Conference will be held in Paris from 30 May to 23 June 1989. The second Meeting of the Conference will be held in Copenhagen from 5 to 29 June 1990. The third Meeting of the Conference will be held in Moscow from 10 September to 4 October 1991.

The agenda, timetable and other organizational modalities are set out in Annex X [not included].

The next main CSCE Follow-up Meeting, to be held in Helsinki, commencing on 24 March 1992, will assess the functioning of the procedures set out in paragraphs 1 to 4 above and the progress made at the Meetings of the Conference on the Human Dimension of the CSCE. It will consider ways of further strengthening and improving these procedures and will take appropriate decisions.

HELSINKI WATCH. A human rights organization, affiliated with HUMAN RIGHTS WATCH, which was established in 1979 in response to the persecution of citizens in the Soviet Union and Czechoslovakia for their attempts to organize Helsinki Accord monitoring groups in their countries. Helsinki Watch focuses on the 35 governments in Eastern and Western Europe and North America that signed the 1975 Helsinki Accords, but its efforts have centered primarily on Warsaw Pact countries, Turkey, and Yugoslavia.

In 1982, Helsinki Watch organized the INTERNATIONAL HELSINKI FEDERATION FOR HUMAN RIGHTS to link existing Helsinki Watch committees in signatory countries and to organize additional committees in non-signatory countries to promote compliance with the human rights provisions of the Helsinki Accords. Helsinki Watch now has 13 national Helsinki committees affiliated with the International Helsinki Federation for Human Rights. The federation has its headquarters in Vienna, Austria.

The U.S. Helsinki Watch Committee has published a number of reports on human rights situations,

among them: *To Win the Children: Afghanistan's Other War* (1986); *Destroying Ethnic Identity: The Turks of Bulgaria* (1986); *Prague Winter: Charter 77 and the Movement for Human Rights in Czechoslovakia* (1980); *Prisons in Poland* (1988); *Bleak Reality: Human Rights in Romania* (1985); and *Soviet Abuse of Psychiatry for Political Purposes* (1988). In addition, the group publishers updated reports on violations of the Helsinki Accords in countries under its mandate.

Helsinki Watch. Address: 45 Fifth Ave., New York, NY 10017. Telephone: (212) 972-8400. Fax: (212) 972-0905.

HOLY SEE. The Vatican City State occupies a small territory within the city of Rome, on the right bank of the Tiber River, and is the site of the central administration of the Catholic Church throughout the world. It is sovereign and independent, and the Roman Catholic Pope exercises temporal as well as spiritual authority over it. Its religious functions are carried on by 11 congregations, three tribunals, three secretariats, and a number of councils, commissions, and committees, while its external relations are in the hands of the Papal Secretary of State.

Although not a member of the United Nations, the Holy See has observer status there. Its population is estimated by the UN (1990) to be 1,000, of whom about 85% are of Italian origin. Languages in common use include Italian and Latin.

Pope John Paul II—Polish Cardinal Karol Wojtyla—was chosen by the College of Cardinals in 1978 to succeed Pope John Paul I, who died only 34 days after his election. The first non-Italian to be elected Pope in 456 years, John Paul II has since established himself as "the people's Pope" largely by visiting many nations with large Catholic populations.

A Church-State treaty between Italy and the Holy See, which entered into force in 1985, affirmed the independence of the Vatican but ended the status of Catholicism as Italy's State religion and the designation of Rome as a "sacred city." A ban on diplomatic relations with the Vatican adopted by the Congress of the United States of America in 1867 was repealed in 1984.

HOMELESSNESS. In 1980, the UN General Assembly first expressed the view (resolution 35/76) that an international year devoted to the problems of homeless people in urban and rural areas of the developing countries could be an appropriate occasion to focus attention of the international community on those problems. Two years later, the assembly proclaimed lution 37/221) the year 1987 International Year of Shelter for the Homeless.

In so doing, the assembly expressed its concern that, despite the efforts of governments at the national and local levels and of international organizations, the living conditions of the majority of the people in slums and squatter areas and rural settlements, especially in developing countries, continue to deteriorate in both relative and absolute terms; and its conviction that a special effort to address this fundamental issue will strengthen overall national economic and social development.

At the close of the international year, the assembly welcomed (resolution 43/180) the success achieved in attaining the objectives of the year and took note with appreciation of the numerous and encouraging reports received from a total of 130 countries as at 31 December 1987, on activities, policies, programs, and projects undertaken by those countries within the context of the year and towards the successful attainment of its objectives. It requested governments to sustain the momentum generated during the program for the year and to continue implementing concrete and innovative activities aimed at improving the shelter and neighborhoods of the poor and the disadvantaged and requested the Secretary-General to keep it informed periodically on the progress achieved.

SEE ALSO Housing; Shelter.

HOMOSEXUALITY: DISCRIMINATION.

In 1982, the UN HUMAN RIGHTS COMMITTEE examined a communication which it had received under article 5, para. 4, of the INTERNATIONAL COVENANT ON CIVIL AND POLITICAL RIGHTS: OPTIONAL PROTOCOL, which contained allegations concerning discrimination on the ground of homosexuality. The action taken by the committee is summarized in its 1982 report to the General Assembly as follows (UN Doc. A/37/40, Annex XIV, para. 18–24):

The authors of this communication claimed that the authorities of their country, including organs of the State-controlled broadcasting company, had interfered with their right of freedom of expression and information, as laid down in article 19 of the International Covenant on Civil and Political Rights, by imposing sanctions against participants in, or censuring, radio and television programmes dealing with homosexuality. According to the communication, it was extremely difficult, if not impossible, for a journalist to prepare a programme in which homosexuals were portrayed as anything other than sick, disturbed, criminal or wanting to change their sex.

The State party concerned, while rejecting the allegation that it was in breach of article 19 of the Covenant, stressed that the purpose of the prohibition of public encouragement to indecent behaviour between persons of the same sex was to reflect the prevailing moral conceptions in the country as interpreted by parliament and by large groups of the population. It further contended that discussions in the parliament indicated that the word "encouragement" was to be interpreted in a narrow sense. Moreover, the Legislation Committee of the parliament expressly provided that the law should not hinder the presentation of factual information on homosexuality. As to the decision of the broadcasting company concerning the programmes referred to by the authors, the State party contended that it did not involve the application of censorship but was based on "general considerations of programme policy in accordance with the internal rules of the company".

In an additional submission the authors argued that article 19 of the Covenant, when read in connection with article 2, paragraph 1, required the State party to ensure that its broadcasting company "not only deals with the subject of homosexuality in its programmes but also that it affords a reasonable and, in so far as is possible, an impartial coverage of information and ideas on the subject, in accordance with its own programme regulations".

In its examination of the communication, the Committee pointed out that its task was confined to clarifying whether the restrictions applied against the alleged victims, irrespective of the scope of penal prohibitions under the State party's penal law, revealed a breach of any of the rights under the Covenant. In addition, the Committee stressed that it was limited to examining whether an individual had suffered an actual violation of his rights. It could not review in the abstract whether national legislation contravened the Covenant. With regard to the claim of one of the authors, the Committee observed that the sole fact that he took a personal interest in the dissemination of information about homosexuality did not make him a victim in the sense required by the Optional Protocol. The Committee accepted, however, the contention of two of the authors that their rights under article 19, paragraph 2, of the Covenant had been restricted. On the other hand, the Committee observed that article 19, paragraph 3, permitted certain restrictions on the exercise of the rights protected by article 19, paragraph 2, as were provided by law and were necessary for the protection of public order or of public health or morals. Concerning the communication under consideration, the Government of the State party had specifically invoked public morals as justifying the actions complained of.

In formulating its views, the Committee emphasized that public morals differed widely. There was no universally applicable common standard. Consequently, in that respect, a certain margin of discretion had to be accorded to national authorities. The Committee found that it could not question the decision of those authorities that radio and television were not the appropriate forums to discuss issues related to homosexuality, as far as a programme could be judged as encouraging homosexual behaviour. According to article 19, paragraph 3, the exercise of the rights provided for in article 19, paragraph 2, carried with it special duties and responsibilities for those organs. As far as radio and television programmes were concerned, the audience could not be controlled, and, in particular, harmful effects on minors could not be excluded. Accordingly, the Committee was of the view that there had been no violation of the rights of the authors of the communication under article 19, paragraph 2, of the Covenant.

In an individual opinion appended to the Committee's views, one member of the Committee, although he agreed with the conclusion of the Committee, wished to clarify the following points:

"This conclusion prejudges neither the right to be different and live accordingly, protected by article 17 of the Covenant, nor the right to have general freedom of expression in this respect, protected by article 19. Under article 19, paragraph 2, and subject to article 19, paragraph 3, everyone must in principle have the right to impart information and ideas—positive or negative—about homosexuality and discuss any problem relating to it freely, through any media of his choice and on his own responsibility.

"Moreover, in my view the conception and contents of 'public morals' referred to in article 19, paragraph 3, are relative and changing. State-imposed restrictions on freedom of expression must allow for this fact and should not be applied so as to perpetuate prejudice or promote intolerance. It is of special importance to protect freedom of expression as regards minority views, including those that offend, shock or disturb the majority. Therefore, even if . . . laws . . . may reflect prevailing moral conceptions, this is in itself not sufficient to justify it under article 19, paragraph 3. It must also be shown that the application of the restriction is 'necessary'.

"However, as the Committee has noted, this law has not been directly applied to any of the alleged victims. The question remains whether they have been more indirectly affected by it in a way which can be said to interfere with their freedom of expression, and if so, whether the grounds were justifiable.

"It is clear that nobody—and in particular no State—has any duty under the Covenant to promote publicity for information and ideas of all kinds. Access to media operated by others is always and necessarily more limited than the general freedom of expression. It follows that such access may be controlled on grounds which do not have to be justified under article 19, paragraph 3.

"It is true that self-imposed restrictions on publishing, or the internal programme policy of the media, may threaten the spirit of freedom of expression. Nevertheless, it is a matter of common sense that such decisions either entirely escape control by the Committee or must be accepted to a larger extent than externally imposed restrictions such as enforcement of criminal law or official censorship, neither of which took place in the present case. Not even media controlled by the State can under the Covenant be under an obligation to publish all that may be published. It is not possible to apply the criteria of article 19, paragraph 3, to self-imposed restrictions: quite apart from the 'public morals' issue, one cannot require that they shall be only such as are 'provided by law and are necessary' for the particular purpose. Therefore I prefer not to express any opinion on the possible reasons for the decisions complained of in the present case.

"The role of mass media in public debate depends on the relationship between journalists and their superiors who decide what to publish. I agree with the authors of the communication that the freedom of journalists is important, but the issues arising here can only partly be examined under article 19 of the Covenant."

Two other members of the Human Rights Committee associated themselves with the individual opinion expressed above.

SEE ALSO Minorities: Sexual; Transsexualism.

HONDURAS. The Republic of Honduras is a country in Central America, on the Pacific Ocean and the Caribbean Sea. It has borders with El Salvador, Guatemala, and Nicaragua. It achieved independence from Spain in 1921 and became a member of the United Nations in 1945. Its population is estimated by the UN (1990) to be 5,105,000. Ethnic groups include Mestizos (mixed European and Amerindian ancestry), 90%; Europeans, 10%; and Amerindians, 10%. Languages commonly used include Spanish and a number of Amerindian vernaculars. Christianity is the predominant religion. Literacy is estimated at 56%.

The government (1990) took the form of a republic. In 1982, Honduras returned to civilian government after 18 years of military rule. The president, elected by popular vote for a term of four years, is head of State and of government. Political parties include the Liberal Party, the National Party, the Innovation and Unity Party, and the Christian Democratic Party.

Up to 1982, Honduras, the least-developed country in Central America, was frequently the victim of internal conflicts and border disputes. American marines quelled serious disorders in 1903 and 1923, and government forces suppressed revolutions in 1931, 1932, and 1937. El Salvador invaded the country in 1969, charging that Honduras had unfairly deported migrant workers of Salvadoran nationality and left only after intervention by the Organization of American States.

Military rule prevailed, except for brief intervals, between 1955 and 1978, when the ruling *junta* organized open elections for members of the Constituent Assembly. After the assembly had prepared a new constitution and electoral law, general elections were held in 1981, and Roberto Suazo Cordova was inaugurated as president. A new president, Jose Azcona Hoyo, was elected in 1985, and the change of government represented the first peaceful transfer of power from one democratically elected head of State to another in 50 years.

On 16 February 1987, the government of Honduras forwarded to the Commission on Human Rights a copy of press communique No. 014-87 of 6 February 1987 from the office of the director for information and the press of the secretariat for foreign affairs, which reads as follows (UN Doc. E/CN.4/1987/54):

On 29 January, on the instructions of the President of the Republic, José Azcona H., the Interagency Commission on Human Rights entered into operation, for the purpose of furnishing a proper response to reports which may be made at both the national and the international level concerning violations of human rights.

The Commission is chaired by the Attorney-General,

Rubén D. Zepeda. Reports presented at the international level on alleged human rights violations will be accepted by the Secretariat for Foreign Affairs, which will forward them to the Attorney-General, who, in addition to undertaking appropriate investigations, will bring them to the attention of the members of the Commission. On the basis of any reports supplied by the members of the Commission, and the results of the steps taken by the Attorney-General, the Secretariat for Foreign Affairs will communicate with international organizations as appropriate concerning the reported facts. Domestically, any person who considers that his rights have been violated may present a report to the Attorney-General, upon which appropriate action will be taken immediately.

It should be pointed out that Honduras is one of the few countries in Latin America which has voluntarily accepted the mandatory jurisdiction of the Inter-American Court of Human Rights.

The Commission is composed of representatives of the Office of the Attorney-General, the Supreme Court, the armed forces, the National Congress, the Ministry of the Interior and Justice and the Secretariat for Foreign Affairs.

In recent years, Honduras sheltered units of the U.S. army and of the U.S.-backed opponents of the Sandinista regime in Nicaragua known as the "contras." In March 1988, more than 3,000 American combat troops were rushed to Palmerola Air Base, near Tegucigalpa, following reports that Nicaraguan troops had cross into Honduras in pursuit of contras and engaged in "military exercises" for a period of ten weeks. In September of that year, when talks between the contras and the Sandinistas broke down after a five-month truce, thousands of contras began moving out of Nicaragua into base camps in Honduras.

In February 1989, five Central American presidents agreed that the contras should be demobilized, and Nicaraguan President Daniel Ortega Saavedra agreed to free elections in 1990. In those elections, the Sandinistas were defeated, and the contras, after some delay, agreed to disband 12,000 troops then in Honduran base camps.

HONDURAS: INTER-AMERICAN COURT HEARINGS ON DISAPPEARANCES. A series of public hearings was held by the INTER-AMERICAN COURT OF HUMAN RIGHTS between 30 September and 7 October 1987 with respect to cases involving the forced disappearances of Alfredo Manfredo Velasquez Rodríguez, Saul Godinez, Francisco Fairen, and Yolanda Solis. At the headings, the court received evidence submitted to it by the INTER-AMERICAN COMMISSION ON HUMAN RIGHTS and heard statements by representatives of the commission and of the Government of Honduras.

On 15 January 1988, the court rendered its decision in the case of Angel Manfredo Velasquez Rodriguez (See HONDURAS: VELASQUEZ RODRIGUEZ CASE).

The hearings before the court were summarized in the commission's *Annual Report for 1987/1988* (OAS Doc. OEA/Ser. 1/V/II.74, Doc. 10 rev. 1, pp. 22–25) as follows:

The witnesses were interrogated about the following points of evidence. The first sought to prove that between 1981 and 1984 (the period in which Francisco Fairen Garbi, Yolanda Solis Corrales, Saul Godinez Cruz, and Manfredo Velasquez Rodríguez disappeared) numerous kidnappings and disappearances in Honduras had been perpetrated by the Honduran Armed Forces, or at least with the consent of the Government. The second point was designed to show that there had been no effective domestic remedy to protect the kidnap victims, who then disappeared as a result of action ascribed to the Honduran Armed Forces.

The Commission's delegates presented their oral arguments during the second stage of the hearings, on October 6 and 7. At that time President Gilda Russomano presented a general introduction and evidence that the domestic remedies had been exhausted or that such requirement was not applicable under international law. The other delegate, Mr. Edmundo Vargas Carreño presented an analysis of the IACHR evidence and documents, as well as some comments on the forced disappearances and the criteria that should guide the Court in regard to that practice.

Later on, the Court ordered further hearings, this time of a private nature. They took place on January 18, 19 and 20, 1988, and their purpose was to hear the testimony of Elsa Rosa Escoto, Francisco Fairen Almengor, Col. Roberto Nuñez Montes, Lt. Col. Alexander Hernandez, and Lt. Marco Tulio Regalado Hernandez (the last three being officers of the Honduran Armed Forces). These witnesses had been unable to appear at the previous hearings or, because of new developments, had been ordered to attend by the Court or at the request of the Government of Honduras, which had not presented any witnesses at the earlier hearings.

The witnesses were interrogated by IACHR delegate Edmundo Vargas Carreño and counselors Grossman, Mendez and Vivanco.

Some extraordinarily serious events transpired after the Court had ordered the closed hearings. On January 5, witness Jose Isaias Viloria—who was to appear before the Court a few days later—was murdered. On January 14, 1988, the same fate befell Miguel Angel Pavon, Vice Chairman of the Honduran Human Rights Committee and Alternate Deputy to Congress, who had testified at the October 1987 hearings.

Given these alarming incidents and after having requested the pertinent facts in the case from the Government of Honduras, the Commission asked the Court, pursuant to Art. 63, paragraph two of the American Convention on Human Rights, to take all pertinent and provisional measures in its power to protect the persons who had appeared as witnesses before the Court—or would do so in the future—from bodily harm and ensure their safety and that of everyone in any way connected with the trial.

On January 15, 1988, using the powers conferred on it by Art. 63 of its Regulations, the Court resolved:

1. To urge the Government of Honduras to adopt, without delay, such measures as might be necessary to prevent new attacks on the fundamental rights of persons who had appeared or were summoned to appear before this Court in

connection with the Velasquez Rodríguez, Fairen Garbi and Solis Corrales, and Godinez Cruz cases, complying punctiliously with the obligation to respect and guarantee human rights which that Government contracted pursuant to Article 1.1 of the Convention.

2. Similarly, to urge the Government of Honduras to take every measure within its power to investigate these reprehensible crimes, identify the perpetrators, and subject them to the penalties prescribed by Honduran domestic law.

Since the measures adopted by the Court had been very general, on January 18, 1988 the Commission's delegate, Mr. Edmundo Vargas Carreño, asked the Court to take specific and concrete steps in this regard and to request the Government of Honduras to inform the Court, within a period of 15 days, of the concrete measures it had adopted to ensure the physical safety of the persons who had testified before the Court or were in any way involved with those cases; and to report on the judicial investigation instituted and the results of the autopsies and ballistics tests conducted regarding the murders of Jose Isaias Vilorio and Miguel Angel Pavon.

On January 19, 1988, invoking the powers conferred on it by Articles 63.2, 33 and 62.3 of the American Convention on Human Rights, the Court acceded in every detail to the requests made by the IACHR delegate.

On February 3, 1988, the Government of Honduras complied in part with the Court's requests and requested an extension of the deadline, which was denied by the President of the Court.

In a public hearing held in San Jose, Costa Rica on July 29, 1988, the Court read out the sentence handed down in case N° 7920 involving the forced disappearance of Angel Manfredo Velásquez Rodríguez, leaving pending the other two decisions on the cases presented by the Commission.

The Court, after considering the arguments of the parties, delivered the following judgment:

1. Reject the preliminary objection interposed by the Government of Honduras alleging the inadmissibility of the case for the failure to exhaust domestic legal remedies.

2. Declare that Honduras has violated, in the case of Angel Manfredo Velásquez Rodríguez, its obligations to respect and to ensure the right to personal liberty set forth in Article 7 of the Convention, read in conjunction with Article 1(1) thereof.

3. Declare that Honduras has violated, in the case of Angel Manfredo Velásquez Rodríguez, its obligations to respect and to ensure the right to humane treatment set forth in Article 5 of the Convention, read in conjunction with Article 1(1) thereof.

4. Declare that Honduras has violated, in the case of Angel Manfredo Velásquez Rodríguez, its obligations to ensure the right to life set forth in Article 4 of the Convention, read in conjunction with Article 1(1) thereof.

5. Decide that Honduras is hereby required to pay fair compensation to the families of the victim.

6. Decide that the form and amount of such compensation, failing agreement between Honduras and the Commission within six months of the date of this judgment, shall be settled by the Court, and reserves for this purpose the subsequent procedure in the case.

7. Decide that the agreement on the form and amount of the compensation shall be approved by the Court.

8. Did not find it necessary to render a decision concerning costs.

The judgment was unanimous except for the dissent of Judge Piza on the sixth point.

SEE ALSO *Disappearance of Persons; Disappearances: Statistical Summary; Disappearances: UN Draft Declaration; Inter-American Convention on the Forced Disappearance of Persons (Draft).*

HONDURAS: VELASQUEZ RODRIGUEZ CASE.

In a landmark judgment of 29 July 1988, the INTER-AMERICAN COURT OF HUMAN RIGHTS decided unanimously that Honduras had failed, in the case of a young student who had been detained by government authorities and had later disappeared, to ensure that student's right to personal liberty, his right to humane treatment, and his right to life. The court further decided unanimously that Honduras should pay fair compensation to the victim's next-of-kin.

The text of the court's judgment (OAS *Decisions and Judgements,* Series C, No. 4) is as follows:

In the Velásquez Rodríguez case,
The Inter-American Court of Human Rights, composed of the following judges: Rafael Nieto-Navia, President; Héctor Gros Espiell, Vice President; Rodolfo E. Piza E., Judge; Thomas Buergenthal, Judge; Pedro Nikken, Judge; Héctor Fix-Zamudio, Judge; Rigoberto Espinal Irías, Judge ad hoc;

Also present: Charles Moyer, Secretary; Manuel Ventura, Deputy Secretary delivers the following judgment pursuant to Article 44(1) of its Rules of Procedure (hereinafter "the Rules of Procedure") in the instant case submitted by the Inter-American Commission on Human Rights against the State of Honduras.

1. The Inter-American Commission on Human Rights (hereinafter "the Commission") submitted the instant case to the Inter-American Court of Human Rights (hereinafter the "Court") on April 24, 1986. It originated in a petition (No. 7920) against the State of Honduras (hereinafter "Honduras" or "the Government"), which the Secretariat of the Commission received on October 7, 1981.

2. In submitting the case, the Commission invoked Articles 50 and 51 of the American Convention on Human Rights (hereinafter "the Convention" or "the American Convention") and requested that the Court determine whether the State in question had violated Articles 4 (Right to Life), 5 (Right to Human Treatment) and 7 (Right to Personal Liberty) of the Convention in the case of Angel Manfredo Velásquez Rodríguez (also known as Manfredo Velásquez). In addition, the Commission asked the Court to rule that "the consequences of the situation that constituted the breach of such right or freedom be remedied and that fair compensation be paid to the injured party or parties."

3. According to the petition filed with the Commission, and the supplementary information received subsequently, Manfredo Velásquez, a student at the National Autonomous University of Honduras, "was violently detained without a warrant for his arrest by members of the National Office of Investigations (DNI) and G-2 of the Armed Forces

of Honduras." The detention took place in Tegucigalpa on the afternoon of September 12, 1981. According to the petitioners, several eyewitnesses reported that Manfredo Velásquez and others were detained and taken to the cells of Public Security Forces Station No. 2 located in the Barrio El Manchén of Tegucigalpa, where he was "accused of alleged political crimes and subjected to harsh interrogation and cruel torture." The petition added that on September 17, 1981, Manfredo Velásquez was moved to the First Infantry Battalion, where the interrogation continued, but that the police and security forces denied that he had been detained.

4. After transmitting the relevant parts of the petition to the Government, the Commission, on various occasions, requested information on the matter. Since the Commission received no reply, it applied Article 42 (formerly 39) of its Regulations and presumed "as true the allegations contained in the communication of October 7, 1981, concerning the detention and disappearance of Angel Manfredo Velásquez Rodríguez in the Republic of Honduras" and pointed out to the Government "that such acts are most serious violations of the right to life (Art. 4) and the right to personal liberty (Art. 7) of the American Convention" (Resolution 30/83 of October 4, 1983).

5. On November 18, 1983, the Government requested the reconsideration of Resolution 30/83 on the grounds that domestic remedies had not been exhausted, that the National Office of Investigations had no knowledge of the whereabouts of Manfredo Velásquez, that the Government was making every effort to find him, and that there were rumors that Manfredo Velásquez was "with Salvadoran guerrilla groups."

6. On May 30, 1984, the Commission informed the Government that it had decided, "in light of the information submitted by the Honorable Government, to reconsider Resolution 30/83 and to continue its study of the case." The Commission also asked the Government to provide information on the exhaustion of domestic legal remedies.

7. On January 29, 1985, the Commission repeated its request of May 30, 1984 and notified the Government that it would render a final decision on the case at its meeting in March 1985. On March 1 of that year, the Government asked for a postponement of the final decision and reported that it had set up an Investigatory Commission to study the matter. The Commission agreed to the Government's request on March 11, granting it thirty days in which to present the information requested.

8. On October 17, 1985, the Government presented to the Commission the Report of the Investigatory Commission.

9. On April 7, 1986, the Government provided information about the outcome of the proceeding brought in the First Criminal Court against those persons supposedly responsible for the disappearance of Manfredo Velásquez and others. That Court dismissed the complaints "except as they applied to General Gustavo Alvarez Martínez, because he had left the country and had not given testimony." This decision was later affirmed by the First Court of Appeals.

10. By Resolution 22/86 of April 18, 1986, the Commission deemed the new information presented by the Government insufficient to warrant reconsideration of Resolution 30/83 and found, to the contrary, that "all evidence shows that Angel Manfredo Velásquez Rodríguez is still missing and that the Government of Honduras . . . has not offered convincing proof that would allow the Commission to determine that the allegations are not true." In that same Resolution, the Commission confirmed Resolution 30/83 and referred the matter to the Court.

I

11. The Court has jurisdiction to hear the instant case. Honduras ratified the Convention on September 8, 1977 and recognized the contentious jurisdiction of the Court, as set out in Article 62 of the Convention, on September 9, 1981. The case was submitted to the Court by the Commission pursuant to Article 61 of the Convention and Article 50(1) and 50(2) of the Regulations of the Commission.

II

12. The instant case was submitted to the Court on April 24, 1986. On May 13, 1986, the Secretariat of the Court transmitted the application to the Government, pursuant to Article 26(1) of the Rules of Procedure.

13. On July 23, 1986, Judge Jorge R. Hernández Alcerro informed the President of the Court (hereinafter "the President") that, pursuant to Article 19(2) of the Statute of the Court (hereinafter "the Statute"), he had "decided to recuse (him) self from hearing the three cases that . . . were submitted to the Inter-American Court." The President accepted the disqualification and, by note of that same date, informed the Government of its right to appoint a judge ad hoc under Article 10(3) of the Statute. The Government named Rigoberto Espinal Irías to that position by note of August 21, 1986.

14. In a note of July 23, 1986, the President confirmed a preliminary agreement that the Government present its submission by the end of August 1986. On August 21, 1986, the Government requested the extension of this deadline to November 1986.

15. By his Order of August 29, 1986, having heard the views of the parties, the President set October 31, 1986 as the deadline for the Government's presentation of its submissions. The President also fixed the deadlines of January 15, 1987 for the filing of the Commission's submissions and March 1, 1987 for the Government's response.

16. In its submissions of October 31, 1986, the Government objected to the admissibility of the application filed by the Commission.

17. On December 11, 1986, the President granted the Commission's request for an extension of the deadline for the presentation of its submissions to March 20, 1987 and extended the deadline for the Government's response to May 25, 1987.

18. In his Order of January 30, 1987, the President made clear that the application which gave rise to the instant proceeding should be deemed to be the Memorial provided for in Article 30(3) of the Rules of Procedure. He also specified that the deadline of March 20, 1987 granted to the Commission was the time limit set forth in Article 27(3) of the Rules for the presentation of its observations and conclusions on the preliminary objections raised by the Government. The President, after consulting the parties, ordered a public hearing on June 15, 1987 for the presentation of oral arguments on the preliminary objections and left open the time limits for submission on the merits, pursuant to the above-mentioned article of the Rules of Procedure.

19. By note of March 13, 1987, the Government informed the Court that because the Order of January 30, 1987 is not restricted to matters of mere procedure nor to the determination of deadlines, but rather involves the in-

terpretation and classification of the submissions, (the Government) considers it advisable, pursuant to Article 25 of the Statute of the Court and Article 44(2) of its Rules of Procedure, for the Court to affirm the terms of the President's Order of January 30, 1987, in order to avoid further confusion between the parties. As these are the first contentious cases submitted to the Court, it is especially important to ensure strict compliance with and the correct application of the procedural rules of the Court.

20. In a motion contained in its observations of March 20, 1987, the Commission asked the President to rescind paragraph 3 of his Order of January 30, 1987 in which he had set the date for the public hearing. The Commission also observed that "in no part of its Memorial had the Government of Honduras presented its objections as preliminary objections." In its note of June 11, 1987, the Government did however refer to its objections as "preliminary objections."

21. By Resolution of June 8, 1987, the Court affirmed the President's Order of January 30, 1987, in its entirety.

22. The hearing on the preliminary objections raised by the Government took place on June 15, 1987. Representatives of the Government and the Commission participated in this hearing.

23. On June 26, 1987, the Court delivered its judgment on the preliminary objections. In this unanimous decision, the Court:

1. Reject(ed) the preliminary objections interposed by the Government of Honduras, except for the issues relating to the exhaustion of the domestic legal remedies, which (were) ordered joined to the merits of the case.

2. Decide(d) to proceed with the consideration of the instant case.

3. Postpone(d) its decision on the costs until such time as it renders judgment on the merits.

(Velásquez Rodríguez Case, Preliminary Objections, Judgment of June 26, 1987. Series C No. 1).

24. On that same date, the Court adopted the following decision:

1. To instruct the President, in consultation with the parties, to set a deadline no later than August 27, 1987 for the Government to submit its Counter-Memorial on the merits and offer its evidence, with an indication of the facts that each item of evidence is intended to prove. In its offer of proof, the Government should show how, when and under what circumstances it wishes to present the evidence.

2. Within thirty days of the receipt of the submission of the Government, the Commission must ratify in writing the request of proof already made, without prejudice to the possibility of amending or supplementing what has been offered. The Commission should indicate the facts that each item of evidence is intended to prove and how, when and under what circumstances it wishes to present the evidence. As soon as possible after receiving the Government's submission referred to in paragraph one, the Commission may also supplement or amend its offer of proof.

3. To instruct the President, without prejudice to a final decision being taken by the Court, to decide preliminary matters that might arise, to admit or exclude evidence that has been offered or may be offered, to order the filing of expert or other documentary evidence that may be received and, in consultation with the parties, to set the date of the hearing or hearings on the merits at which evidence shall be presented, the testimony of witnesses and any experts shall be received, and at which the final arguments shall be heard.

4. To instruct the President to arrange with the respec-

tive authorities for the necessary guarantees of immunity and participation of the Agents and other representatives of the parties, witnesses and experts, and, if necessary, the delegates of the Court.

25. In its submission of July 20, 1987, the Commission ratified and supplemented its request for oral testimony and offered documentary evidence.

26. On August 27, 1987, the Government filed its Counter-Memorial and documentary evidence. In its prayer, the Government asked the Court to dismiss "the suit against the State of Honduras on the grounds that it does not find the allegations to be true and that the domestic remedies of the State of Honduras have not yet been exhausted."

27. In his Order of September 1, 1987, the President admitted the testimonial and documentary evidence offered by the Commission. On September 14, 1987, he also admitted the documentary evidence offered by the Government.

28. The Court held hearings on the merits and heard the final arguments of the parties from September 30 to October 7, 1987.

There appeared before the Court

a) for the Government of Honduras: Edgardo Sevilla Idiáquez, Agent; Ramón Pérez Zúñiga, Representative; Juan Arnaldo Hernández, Representative; Enrique Gómez, Representative; Rubén Darío Zepeda, Adviser; Angel Augusto Morales, Adviser; Olmeda Rivera, Adviser; Mario Alberto Fortín, Adviser; Ramón Rufino Mejía, Adviser.

b) for the Inter-American Commission on Human Rights: Gilda M.C.M. de Russomano, President, Delegate; Edmundo Vargas Carreño, Executive Secretary, Delegate; Claudio Grossman, Adviser; Juan Méndez, Adviser; Hugo A. Muñoz, Adviser; José Miguel Vivanco, Adviser.

c) Witnesses presented by the Commission to testify as to "whether between the years 1981 and 1984 (the period in which Manfredo Velásquez disappeared) there were numerous cases of persons who were kidnapped and who then disappeared, and whether these actions were imputable to the Armed Forces of Honduras and enjoyed the acquiescence of the Government of Honduras:" Miguel Angel Pavón Salazar, Alternate Deputy; Ramón Custodio López, surgeon; Virgilio Carías, economist; Inés Consuelo Murillo, student; Efraín Díaz Arrivillaga, Deputy; Florencio Caballero, former member of the Armed Forces.

d) Witnesses presented by the Commission to testify as to "whether between the years 1981 and 1984 effective domestic remedies existed in Honduras to protect those persons who were kidnapped and who then disappeared in actions imputable to the Armed Forces of Honduras:" Ramón Custodio López, surgeon; Virgilio Carías, economist; Milton Jiménez Puerto, lawyer; Inés Consuelo Murillo, student; René Velásquez Díaz, lawyer; César Augusto Murillo, lawyer; José Gonzalo Flores Trejo, shoemaker.

e) Witnesses presented by the Commission to testify on specific facts related to this case: Leopoldo Aguilar Villalobos, advertising agent; Zenaida Velásquez Rodríguez, social worker.

f) The following witnesses offered by the Commission did not appear at these hearings: Leónidas Tores Arias, former member of the Armed Forces; Linda Drucker, reporter; José María Palacios, lawyer; Mauricio Villeda Bermúdez, lawyer; José Isías Vilorio, policeman.

29. After having heard the witnesses, the Court directed the submission of additional evidence to assist it in its deliberations. Its Order of October 7, 1987 reads as follows:

A. Documentary Evidence. 1. To request the Government of

Honduras to provide the organizational chart showing the structure of Battalion 316 and its position within the Armed Forces of Honduras.

B. Testimony. 1. To call as witnesses, Marco Tulio Regalado and Alexander Hernández, members of the Armed Forces of Honduras.

C. Reiteration of a Request. 1. To the Government of Honduras to establish the whereabouts of José Isaías Vilorio and, once located, to call him as a witness.

30. By the same Order, the Court set December 15, 1987 as the deadline for the submission of documentary evidence and decided to hear the oral testimony at its January session.

31. In response to that Order, on December 14, 1987 the Government: a) with respect to the organizational structure of Battalion 316, requested that the Court receive the testimony of its Commandant in a closed hearing "because of strict security reasons of the State of Honduras"; b) requested that the Court hear the testimony of Alexander Hernández and Marco Tulio Regalado "in the Republic of Honduras, in a manner to be decided by the Court and in a closed hearing to be set at an opportune time . . . because of security reasons and because both persons are on active duty in the Armed Forces of Honduras"; and c) reported that José Isaías Vilorio was "working as an administrative employee of the National Office of Investigations, a branch of the Public Security Forces, in the city of Tegucigalpa."

32. By note of December 24, 1987, the Commission objected to hearing the testimony of members of the Honduran military in closed session. This position was reiterated by note on January 11, 1988.

33. On the latter date, the Court decided to receive the testimony of the members of the Honduran military at a closed hearing in the presence of the parties.

34. Pursuant to its Order of October 7, 1987 and its decision of January 11, 1988, the court held a closed hearing on January 20, 1988, which both parties attended, at which it received the testimony of persons who identified themselves as Lt. Col. Alexander Hernández and Lt. Marco Tulio Regalado Hernández. The Court also heard the testimony of Col. Roberto Núñez Montes, Head of the Intelligence Services of Honduras.

35. On January 22, 1988, the Government submitted a brief prepared by the Honduran Bar Association on the legal remedies available in cases of disappeared persons. The Court had asked for this document in response to the Government's request of August 26, 1987.

36. On July 7, 1988, the Commission responded to a request of the Court concerning another case before the Court (Fairén Garbi and Solís Corrales Case). In its response, the Commission included some "final observations" on the instant case.

37. By decision of July 14, 1988, the President refused to admit the "final observations" because they were untimely and because "reopening the period for submissions would violate the procedure opportunely established and, moreover, would seriously affect the procedural equilibrium and equality of the parties."

38. The following non-governmental organizations submitted briefs as **amici curiae:** Amnesty International, Association of the Bar of the City of New York, Lawyers Committee for Human Rights and Minnesota Lawyers International Human Rights Committee.

III

39. By note of November 4, 1987, addressed to the President of the Court, the Commission asked the Court to take provisional measures under Article 63(2) of the Convention in view of the threats against the witnesses Milton Jiménez Puerto and Ramón Custodio López. Upon forwarding this information to the Government of Honduras, the President stated that he "does not have enough proof to ascertain which persons or entities might be responsible for the threats, but he strongly wishes to request that the Government of Honduras take all measures necessary to guarantee the safety of the lives and property of Milton Jiménez and Ramón Custodio and the property of the Committee for the Defense of Human Rights in Honduras (CODEH) . . ." The President also stated that he was prepared to consult with the Permanent Commission of the Court and, if necessary, to convoke the Court for an emergency meeting "for taking the appropriate measures, if that abnormal situation continues." By communications of November 11 and 18, 1987, the Agent of the Government informed the Court that the Honduran government would guarantee Ramón Custodio and Milton Jiménez "the respect of their physical and moral integrity . . . and the faithful compliance with the Convention. . . ."

40. By note of January 11, 1988, the Commission informed the Court of the death of José Isaías Vilorio, which occurred on January 5, 1988 at 7:15 A.M. The Court had summoned him to appear as a witness on January 18, 1988. He was killed "on a public thoroughfare in Colonia San Miguel, Comayaguela, Tegucigalpa, by a group of armed men who placed the insignia of a Honduran guerrilla movement known as Cinchonero on his body and fled in a vehicle at high speed."

41. On January 15, 1988, the Court was informed of the assassinations of Moisés Landaverde and Miguel Angel Pavón which had occurred the previous evening in San Pedro Sula. Mr. Pavón had testified before the Court on September 30, 1987 as a witness in this case. Also on January 15, the Court adopted the following provisional measures under Article 63(2) of the Convention:

1. That the Government of Honduras adopt, without delay, such measures as are necessary to prevent further infringements on the basic rights of those who have appeared or have been summoned to do so before this Court in the "Velásquez Rodríguez," "Fairén Garbi and Solís Corrales" and "Godínez Cruz" cases, in strict compliance with the obligation of respect for and observance of human rights, under the terms of Article 1(1) of the Convention.

2. That the Government of Honduras also employ all means within its power to investigate these reprehensible crimes, to identify the perpetrators and to impose the punishment provided for by the domestic law of Honduras.

42. After it had adopted the above Order of January 15, the Court received a request from the Commission, dated the same day, that the Court take the necessary measures to protect the integrity and security of those persons who had appeared or would appear before the Court.

43. On January 18, 1988, the Commission asked the Court to adopt the following complementary provisional measures:

1. That the Government of Honduras inform the Court, within 15 days, of the specific measures it has adopted to protect the physical integrity of witnesses who testified before the Court as well as those persons in any way

involved in these proceedings, such as representatives of human rights organizations.

2. That the Government of Honduras report, within that same period, on the judicial investigations of the assassinations of José Isaías Vilorio, Miguel Angel Pavón and Moisés Landaverde.

3. That the Government of Honduras provide the Court, within that same period, the public statements made regarding the aforementioned assassinations and indicate where those statements appeared.

4. That the Government of Honduras inform the Court, within the same period, on the criminal investigations of threats against Ramón Custodio and Milton Jiménez, who are witnesses in this case.

5. That it inform the Court whether it has ordered police protection to ensure the personal integrity of the witnesses who have testified and the protection of the property of CODEH.

6. That the Court request the Government of Honduras to send it immediately a copy of the autopsies and ballistic tests carried out regarding the assassinations of Messrs. Vilorio, Pavón and Landaverde.

44. That same day the Government submitted a copy of the death certificate and the autopsy report of José Isaías Vilorio, both dated January 5, 1988.

45. On January 18, 1988, the Court decided, by a vote of six to one, to hear the parties in a public session the following day regarding the measures requested by the Commission. After the hearing, taking into account "Articles 63(2), 33 and 62(3) of the American Convention on Human Rights, Articles 1 and 2 of the Statute of the Court and Article 23 of its Rules of Procedure and its character as a judicial body and the powers which derive therefrom," the Court unanimously decided, by Order of January 19, 1988, on the following additional provisional measures:

1. That the Government of Honduras, within a period of two weeks, inform this Court on the following points:

a. the measures that have been adopted or will be adopted to protect the physical integrity of, and to avoid irreparable harm to, those witnesses who have testified or have been summoned to do so in these cases.

b. the judicial investigations that have been or will be undertaken with respect to threats against the aforementioned individuals.

c. the investigations of the assassinations, including forensic reports, and the actions that are proposed to be taken within the judicial system of Honduras to punish those responsible.

2. That the Government of Honduras adopt concrete measures to make clear that the appearance of an individual before the Inter-American Commission or Court of Human Rights, under conditions authorized by the American Convention and by the rules of procedure of both bodies, is a right enjoyed by every individual and is recognized as such by Honduras as a party to the Convention.

This decision was delivered to the parties in Court.

46. Pursuant to the Court's decision of January 19, 1988, the Government submitted the following documents on February 3, 1988:

1. A copy of the autopsy report on the death of Professor Miguel Angel Pavón Salazar, certified by the Third Criminal Court of San Pedro Sula, Department of Cortés, on January 27, 1988 and prepared by forensic specialist Rolando Tábora, of that same Court.

2. A copy of the autopsy report on the death of Professor Moisés Landaverde Recarte, certified by the above Court on the same date and prepared by the same forensic specialist.

3. A copy of a statement made by Dr. Rolando Tábora, forensic specialist, as part of the inquiry undertaken by the above Court into the deaths of Miguel Angel Pavón and Moisés Landaverde Recarte, and certified by that Court on January 27, 1988. . . .

4. A copy of the inquiry into threats against the lives of Ramón Custodio and Milton Jiménez, conducted by the First Criminal Court of Tegucigalpa, Central District, and certified by that Court on February 2, 1988.

In the same submission, the Government stated that:

The content of the above documents shows that the Government of Honduras has initiated a judicial inquiry into the assassinations of Miguel Angel Pavón Salazar and Moisés Landaverde Recarte, under the procedures provided for by Honduran law.

Those same documents show, moreover, that the projectiles were not removed from the bodies for ballistic study because of the opposition of family members, which is why no ballistic report was submitted as requested.

47. The Government also requested an extension of the deadline ordered above "because, for justifiable reasons, it has been impossible to obtain some of the information." Upon instructions from the President, the Secretariat informed the Government on the following day that it was not possible to extend the deadline because it had been set by the full Court.

48. By communication of March 10, 1988, the Inter-Institutional Commission of Human Rights of Honduras, a governmental body, made several observations regarding the Court's decision of January 15, 1988. On the threats that have been made against some witnesses, it reported that Ramón Custodio "refused to bring a complaint before the proper courts and that the First Criminal Court of Tegucigalpa, Department of Morazán, had initiated an inquiry to determine whether there were threats, intimidations or conspiracies against the lives of Dr. Custodio and Milton Jiménez and had duly summoned them to testify and to submit any evidence," but they failed to appear. It added that no Honduran official "has attempted to intimidate, threaten or restrict the liberty of any of the persons who testified before the Court . . . who enjoy the same guarantees as other citizens."

49. On March 23, 1988 the Government submitted the following documents:

1. Copies of the autopsies performed on the bodies of Miguel Angel Pavón Salazar and Moisés Landaverde, certified by the Secretariat of the Third Criminal Court of the Judicial District of San Pedro Sula.

2. The ballistic report on the shrapnel removed from the bodies of those persons, signed by the Director of the Medical-Legal Department of the Supreme Court of Justice.

IV

50. The Government raised several preliminary objections that the Court ruled upon in its Judgment of June 26, 1987 (supra 16–23). There the Court ordered the joining of the merits and the preliminary objection regarding the failure to exhaust domestic remedies, and gave the Government and the Commission another opportunity to "substantiate their contentions" on the matter (Velásquez Rodríguez Case, Preliminary Objections, supra 23, para. 90).

51. The Court will first rule upon this preliminary objec-

tion. In so doing, it will make use of all the evidence before it, including that presented during the proceedings on the merits.

52. The Commission presented witnesses and documentary evidence on this point. The Government, in turn, submitted some documentary evidence, including examples of writs of habeas corpus successfully brought on behalf of some individuals (infra 120(c)). The Government also stated that this remedy requires identification of the place of detention and of the authority under which the person is detained.

53. In addition to the writ of habeas corpus, the Government mentioned various remedies that might possibly be invoked, such as appeal, cassation, extraordinary writ of amparo, ad effectum videndi, criminal complaints against those ultimately responsible and a presumptive finding of death.

54. The Honduran Bar Association in its brief (supra 35) expressly mentioned the writ of habeas corpus, set out in the Law of Amparo, and the suit before a competent court "for it to investigate the whereabouts of the person allegedly disappeared."

55. The Commission argued that the remedies mentioned by the Government were ineffective because of the internal conditions in the country during that period. It presented documentation of three writs of habeas corpus brought on behalf of Manfredo Velásquez that did not produce results. It also cited two criminal complaints that failed to lead to the identification and punishment of those responsible. In the Commission's opinion, those legal proceedings exhausted domestic remedies as required by Article 46 (1) (a) of the Convention.

56. The Court will first consider the legal arguments relevant to the question of exhaustion of domestic remedies and then apply them to the case.

57. Article 46 (1) (a) of the Convention provides that, in order for a petition or communication lodged with the Commission in accordance with Articles 44 or 45 to be admissible, it is necessary that the remedies under domestic law have been pursued and exhausted in accordance with generally recognized principles of international law.

58. The same article, in the second paragraph, provides that this requirement shall not be applicable when

a. the domestic legislation of the state concerned does not afford due process of law for the protection of the right or rights that have allegedly been violated;

b. the party alleging violation of his rights has been denied access to the remedies under domestic law or has been prevented from exhausting them; or

c. there has been unwarranted delay in rendering a final judgment under the aforementioned remedies.

59. In its Judgment of June 26, 1987, the Court decided, inter alia, that "the State claiming non-exhaustion has an obligation to prove that domestic remedies remain to be exhausted and that they are effective" (Velásquez Rodríguez Case, Preliminary Objections, supra 23, para. 88).

60. Concerning the burden of proof, the Court did not go beyond the conclusion cited in the preceding paragraph. The Court now affirms that if a State which alleges non-exhaustion proves the existence of specific domestic remedies that should have been utilized, the opposing party has the burden of showing that those remedies were exhausted or that the case comes within the exceptions of Article 46 (2). It must not be rashly presumed that a State Party to the Convention has failed to comply with its obligation to provide effective domestic remedies.

61. The rule of prior exhaustion of domestic remedies allows the State to resolve the problem under its internal law before being confronted with an international proceeding. This is particularly true in the international jurisdiction of human rights, because the latter reinforces or complements the domestic jurisdiction (American Convention, Preamble).

62. It is a legal duty of the States to provide such remedies, as this Court indicated in its Judgment of June 26, 1987, when it stated:

The rule of prior exhaustion of domestic remedies under the international law of human rights has certain implications that are present in the Convention. Under the Convention, States Parties have an obligation to provide effective judicial remedies to victims of human rights violations (Art. 25), remedies that must be substantiated in accordance with the rules of due process of law (Art. 8(1)), all in keeping with the general obligation of such States to guarantee the free and full exercise of the rights recognized by the Convention to all persons subject to their jurisdiction (Art. 1). (Velásquez Rodríguez Case, Preliminary Objections, supra 23, para. 91).

63. Article 46 (1) (a) of the Convention speaks of "generally recognized principles of international law." Those principles refer not only to the formal existence of such remedies, but also to their adequacy and effectiveness, as shown by the exceptions set out in Article 46 (2).

64. Adequate domestic remedies are those which are suitable to address an infringement of a legal right. A number of remedies exist in the legal system of every country, but not all are applicable in every circumstance. If a remedy is not adequate in a specific case, it obviously need not be exhausted. A norm is meant to have an effect and should not be interpreted in such a way as to negate its effect or lead to a result that is manifestly absurd or unreasonable. For example, a civil proceeding specifically cited by the Government, such as a presumptive finding of death based on disappearance, the purpose of which is to allow heirs to dispose of the estate of the person presumed deceased or to allow the spouse to remarry, is not an adequate remedy for finding a person or for obtaining his liberty.

65. Of the remedies cited by the Government, habeas corpus would be the normal means of finding a person presumably detained by the authorities, of ascertaining whether he is legally detained and, given the case, of obtaining his liberty. The other remedies cited by the Government are either for reviewing a decision within an inchoate proceeding (such as those of appeal or cassation) or are addressed to other objectives. If, however, as the Government has stated, the writ of habeas corpus requires the identification of the place of detention and the authority ordering the detention, it would not be adequate for finding a person clandestinely held by State officials, since in such cases there is only hearsay evidence of the detention, and the whereabouts of the victim is unknown.

66. A remedy must also be effective—that is, capable of producing the result for which it was designed. Procedural requirements can make the remedy of habeas corpus ineffective: if it is powerless to compel the authorities; if it presents a danger to those who invoke it; or if it is not impartially applied.

67. On the other hand, contrary to the Commission's argument, the mere fact that a domestic remedy does not produce a result favorable to the petitioner does not in and of itself demonstrate the inexistence or exhaustion of all effective domestic remedies. For example, the petitioner may

not have invoked the appropriate remedy in a timely fashion.

68. It is a different matter, however, when it is shown that remedies are denied for trivial reasons or without an examination of the merits, or if there is proof of the existence of a practice or policy ordered or tolerated by the government, the effect of which is to impede certain persons from invoking internal remedies that would normally be available to others. In such cases, resort to those remedies becomes a senseless formality. The exceptions of Article 46 (2) would be fully applicable in those situations and would discharge the obligation to exhaust internal remedies since they cannot fulfill their objective in that case.

69. In the Government's opinion, a writ of habeas corpus does not exhaust the remedies of the Honduran legal system because there are other remedies, both ordinary and extraordinary, such as appeal, cassation, and extraordinary writ of amparo, as well as the civil remedy of a presumptive finding of death. In addition, in criminal procedures parties may use whatever evidence they choose. With respect to the cases of disappearances mentioned by the Commission, the Government stated that it had initiated some investigations and had opened others on the basis of complaints, and that the proceedings remain pending until those presumed responsible, either as principals or accomplices, are identified or apprehended.

70. In its conclusions, the Government stated that some writs of habeas corpus were granted from 1981 to 1984, which would prove that this remedy was not ineffective during that period. It submitted various documents to support its argument.

71. In response, the Commission argued that the practice of disappearances made exhaustion of domestic remedies impossible because such remedies were ineffective in correcting abuses imputed to the authorities or in causing kidnapped persons to reappear.

72. The Commission maintained that, in cases of disappearances, the fact that a writ of habeas corpus or amparo has been brought without success is sufficient to support a finding of exhaustion of domestic remedies as long as the person does not appear, because that is the most appropriate remedy in such a situation. It emphasized that neither writs of habeas corpus nor criminal complaints were effective in the case of Manfredo Velásquez. The Commission maintained that exhaustion should not be understood to require mechanical attempts at formal procedures; but rather to require a case-by-case analysis of the reasonable possibility of obtaining a remedy.

73. The Commission asserted that, because of the structure of the international system for the protection of human rights, the Government bears the burden of proof with respect to the exhaustion of domestic remedies. The objection of failure to exhaust presupposes the existence of an effective remedy. It stated that a criminal complaint is not an effective means to find a disappeared person, but only serves to establish individual responsibility.

74. The record before the Court shows that the following remedies were pursued on behalf of Manfredo Velásquez:

a. Habeas Corpus

i. Brought by Zenaida Velásquez against the Public Security Forces on September 17, 1981. No result.

ii. Brought by Zenaida Velásquez on February 6, 1982. No result.

iii. Brought by various relatives of disappeared persons on behalf of Manfredo Velásquez and others on July 4, 1983. Denied on September 11, 1984.

b. Criminal Complaints

i. Brought by the father and sister of Manfredo Velásquez before the First Criminal Court of Tegucigalpa on November 9, 1982. No result.

ii. Brought by Gertrudis Lanza González, joined by Zenaida Velásquez, before the First Criminal Court of Tegucigalpa against various members of the Armed Forces on April 5, 1984. The court dismissed this proceeding and the First Court of Appeals affirmed on January 16, 1986, although it left open the complaint with regard to General Gustavo Alvarez Martínez, who was declared a defendant in absence (supra 9).

75. Although the Government did not dispute that the above remedies had been brought, it maintained that the Commission should not have found the petition admissible, much less submitted it to the Court, because of the failure to exhaust the remedies provided by Honduran law, given that there are no final decisions in the record that show the contrary. It stated that the first writ of habeas corpus was declared void because the person bringing it did not follow through; regarding the second and third, the Government explained that additional writs cannot be brought on the same subject, the same facts, and based on the same legal provisions. As to the criminal complaints, the Government stated that no evidence had been submitted and, although presumptions had been raised, no proof had been offered and that the proceeding was still before Honduran courts until those guilty were specifically identified. It stated that one of the proceedings was dismissed for lack of evidence with respect to those accused who appeared before the court, but not with regard to General Alvarez Martínez, who was out of the country. Moreover, the Government maintained that dismissal does not exhaust domestic remedies because the extraordinary remedies of amparo, rehearing and cassation may be invoked and, in the instant case, the statute of limitations has not yet run, so the proceeding is pending.

76. The record (infra Chapter V) contains testimony of members of the Legislative Assembly of Honduras, Honduran lawyers, persons who were at one time disappeared, and relatives of disappeared persons, which purports to show that in the period in which the events took place, the legal remedies in Honduras were ineffective in obtaining the liberty of victims of a practice of enforced or involuntary disappearances (hereinafter "disappearance" or "disappearances"), ordered or tolerated by the Government. The record also contains dozens of newspaper clippings which allude to the same practice. According to that evidence, from 1981 to 1984 more than one hundred persons were illegally detained, many of whom never reappeared, and, in general, the legal remedies which the Government claimed were available to the victims were ineffective.

77. That evidence also shows that some individuals were captured and detained without due process and subsequently reappeared. However, in some of those cases, the reappearances were not the result of any of the legal remedies which, according to the Government, would have been effective, but rather the result of other circumstances, such as the intervention of diplomatic missions or actions of human rights organizations.

78. The evidence offered shows that lawyers who filed writs of habeas corpus were intimidated, that those who were responsible for executing the writs were frequently prevented from entering or inspecting the places of detention, and that occasional criminal complaints against military or police officials were ineffective, either because

certain procedural steps were not taken or because the complaints were dismissed without further proceedings.

79. The Government had the opportunity to call its own witnesses to refute the evidence presented by the Commission, but failed to do so. Although the Government's attorneys contested some of the points urged by the Commission, they did not offer convincing evidence to support their arguments. The Court summoned as witnesses some members of the armed forces mentioned during the proceeding, but their testimony was insufficient to overcome the weight of the evidence offered by the Commission to show that the judicial and governmental authorities did not act with due diligence in cases of disappearances. The instant case is such an example.

80. The testimony and other evidence received and not refuted leads to the conclusion that, during the period under consideration, although there may have been legal remedies in Honduras that theoretically allowed a person detained by the authorities to be found, those remedies were ineffective in cases of disappearances because the imprisonment was clandestine; formal requirements made them inapplicable in practice; the authorities against whom they were brought simply ignored them, or because attorneys and judges were threatened and intimidated by those authorities.

81. Aside from the question of whether between 1981 and 1984 there was a governmental policy of carrying out or tolerating the disappearance of certain persons, the Commission has shown that although writs of habeas corpus and criminal complaints were filed, they were ineffective or were mere formalities. The evidence offered by the Commission was not refuted and is sufficient to reject the Government's preliminary objection that the case is inadmissible because domestic remedies were not exhausted.

V

82. The Commission presented testimony and documentary evidence to show that there were many kidnappings and disappearances in Honduras from 1981 to 1984 and that those acts were attributable to the Armed Forces of Honduras (hereinafter "Armed Forces"), which was able to rely at least on the tolerance of the Government. Three officers of the Armed Forces testified on this subject at the request of the Court.

83. Various witnesses testified that they were kidnapped, imprisoned in clandestine jails and tortured by members of the Armed Forces (testimony of Inés Consuelo Murillo, José Gonzalo Flores Trejo, Virgilio Carías, Milton Jiménez Puerto, René Velásquez Díaz and Leopoldo Aguilar Villalobos).

84. Inés Consuelo Murillo testified that she was secretly held for approximately three months. According to her testimony, she and José Gonzalo Flores Trejo, whom she knew casually, were captured on March 13, 1983 by men who got out of a car, shouted that they were from Immigration and hit her with their weapons. Behind them was another car which assisted in the capture. She said she was blindfolded, bound, and driven presumably to San Pedro Sula, where she was taken to a secret detention center. There she was tied up, beaten, kept nude most of the time, not fed for many days, and subjected to electrical shocks, hanging, attempts to asphyxiate her, threats of burning her eyes, threats with weapons, burns on the legs, punctures of the skin with needles, drugs and sexual abuse. She admitted carrying false identification when detained, but ten days

later she gave them her real name. She stated that thirty-six days after her detention she was moved to a place near Tegucigalpa, where she saw military officers (one of whom was Second Lt. Marco Tulio Regalado Hernández), papers with an Army letterhead, and Armed Forces graduation rings. This witness added that she was finally turned over to the police and was brought before a court. She was accused of some twenty crimes, but her attorney was not allowed to present evidence and there was no trial (testimony of Inés Consuelo Murillo).

85. Lt. Regalado Hernández said that he had no knowledge of the case of Inés Consuelo Murillo, except for what he had read in the newspaper (testimony of Marco Tulio Regalado Hernández).

86. The Government stated that it was unable to inform Ms. Murillo's relatives of her detention because she was carrying false identification, a fact which also showed, in the Government's opinion, that she was not involved in lawful activities and was, therefore, not telling the whole truth. It added that her testimony of a casual relationship with José Gonzalo Flores Trejo was not credible because both were clearly involved in criminal activities.

87. José Gonzalo Flores Trejo testified that he and Inés Consuelo Murillo were kidnapped together and taken to a house presumably located in San Pedro Sula, where his captors repeatedly forced his head into a trough of water until he almost drowned, kept his hands and feet tied, and hung him so that only his stomach touched the ground. He also declared that, subsequently, in a place where he was held near Tegucigalpa, his captors covered his head with a "capucha" (a piece of rubber cut from an inner tube, which prevents a person from breathing through the mouth and nose), almost asphyxiating him, and subjected him to electric shocks. He said he knew he was in the hands of the military because when his blindfold was removed in order to take some pictures of him, he saw a Honduran military officer and on one occasion when they took him to bathe, he saw a military barracks. He also heard a trumpet sound, orders being given and the report of a cannon (testimony of José Gonzalo Flores Trejo).

88. The Government argued that the testimony of the witness, a Salvadoran national, was not credible because he attempted to convince the Court that his encounters with Inés Consuelo Murillo were of a casual nature. The Government added that both individuals were involved in illicit activities.

89. Virgilio Carías, who was President of the Socialist Party of Honduras, testified that he was kidnapped in broad daylight on September 12, 1981, when 12 or 13 persons, armed with pistols, carbines and automatic rifles, surrounded his automobile. He stated that he was taken to a secret jail, threatened and beaten, and had no food, water or bathroom facilities for four or five days. On the tenth day, his captors gave him an injection in the arm and threw him, bound, in the back of a pick-up truck. Subsequently, they draped him over the back of a mule and set it walking through the mountains near the Nicaraguan border, where he regained his liberty (testimony of Virgilio Carías).

90. The Government indicated that this witness expressly admitted that he opposed the Honduran government. The Government also maintained that his answers were imprecise or evasive and argued that, because the witness said he could not identify his captors, his testimony was hearsay and of no evidentiary value since, in the Government's view, he had no personal knowledge of the events and only knew of them through others.

91. A Honduran attorney, who stated that he defended political prisoners, testified that Honduran security forces detained him without due process in 1982. He was held for ten days in a clandestine jail, without charges, and was beaten and tortured before he was brought before the court (testimony of Milton Jiménez Puerto).

92. The Government affirmed that the witness was charged with the crimes of threatening national security and possession of arms that only the Armed Forces were authorized to carry and, therefore, had a personal interest in discrediting Honduras with his testimony.

93. Another lawyer, who also said that he defended political detainees and who testified on Honduran law, stated that personnel of the Department of Special Investigations detained him in broad daylight in Tegucigalpa on June 1, 1982, blindfolded him, took him to a place he was unable to recognize and kept him without food or water for four days. He was beaten and insulted. He said that he could see through the blindfold that he was in a military installation (testimony of René Velásquez Díaz).

94. The Government claimed that this witness made several false statements regarding the law in force in Honduras and that his testimony "lacks truth or force because it is not impartial and his interest is to discredit the State of Honduras."

95. The Court received testimony which indicated that somewhere between 112 and 130 individuals were disappeared from 1981 to 1984. A former member of the Armed Forces testified that, according to a list in the files of Battalion 316, the number might be 140 or 150 (testimony of Miguel Angel Pavón Salazar, Ramón Custodio López, Efraín Díaz Arrivillaga and Florencio Caballero).

96. The Court heard testimony from the President of the Committee for the Defense of Human Rights in Honduras regarding the existence of a unit within the Armed Forces which carried out disappearances. According to his testimony, in 1980 there was a group called "the fourteen" under the command of Major Adolfo Díaz, attached to the General Staff of the Armed Forces. Subsequently, this group was replaced by "the ten," commanded by Capt. Alexander Hernández, and finally by Battalion 316, a special operations group, with separate units trained in surveillance, kidnapping, execution, telephone tapping, etc. The existence of this group had always been denied until it was mentioned in a communiqué of the Armed Forces in September 1986 (testimony of Ramón Custodio López. See also the testimony of Florencio Caballero).

97. Alexander Hernández, now a Lieutenant Colonel, denied having participated in the group "the ten," having been a part of Battalion 316, or having had any type of contact with it (testimony of Alexander Hernández).

98. The current Director of Honduran Intelligence testified that he learned from the files of his department that in 1984 an intelligence battalion called 316 was created, the purpose of which was to provide combat intelligence to the 101st, 105th and 110th Brigades. He added that this battalion initially functioned as a training unit, until the creation of the Intelligence School, to which all its training functions were gradually transferred, and that the Battalion was finally disbanded in September 1987. He stated that there was never any group called "the fourteen" or "the ten" in the Armed Forces or security forces (testimony of Roberto Núñez Montes).

99. According to testimony on the modus operandi of the practice of disappearances, the kidnappers followed a pattern: they used automobiles with tinted glass (which re-quires a special permit from the Traffic Division), without license plates or with false plates, and sometimes used special disguises, such as wigs, false mustaches, masks, etc. The kidnappings were selective. The victims were first placed under surveillance, then the kidnapping was planned. Microbuses or vans were used. Some victims were taken from their homes; others were picked up in public streets. On one occasion, when a patrol car intervened, the kidnappers identified themselves as members of a special group of the Armed Forces and were permitted to leave with the victim (testimony of Ramón Custodio López, Miguel Angel Pavón Salazar, Efraín Díaz Arrivillaga and Florencio Caballero).

100. A former member of the Armed Forces, who said that he belonged to Battalion 316 (the group charged with carrying out the kidnappings) and that he had participated in some kidnappings, testified that the starting point was an order given by the chief of the unit to investigate an individual and place him under surveillance. According to this witness, if a decision was made to take further steps, the kidnapping was carried out by persons in civilian clothes using pseudonyms and disguises and carrying arms. The unit had four double-cabin Toyota pick-up trucks without police markings for use in kidnappings. Two of the pick-ups had tinted glass (testimony of Florencio Caballero. See also testimony of Virgilio Carías).

101. The Government objected, under Article 37 of the Rules of Procedure, to the testimony of Florencio Caballero because he had deserted from the Armed Forces and had violated his military oath. By unanimous decision of October 6, 1987, the Court rejected the challenge and reserved the right to consider his testimony.

102. The current Director of Intelligence of the Armed Forces testified that intelligence units do not carry out detentions because they "get burned" (are discovered) and do not use pseudonyms or automobiles without license plates. He added that Florencio Caballero never worked in the intelligence services and that he was a driver for the Army General Headquarters in Tegucigalpa (testimony of Roberto Núñez Montes).

103. The former member of the Armed Forces confirmed the existence of secret jails and of specially chosen places for the burial of those executed. He also related that there was a torture group and an interrogation group in his unit, and that he belonged to the latter. The torture group used electric shock, the water barrel and the "capucha." They kept the victims nude, without food, and threw cold water on them. He added that those selected for execution were handed over to a group of former prisoners, released from jail for carrying out executions, who used firearms at first and then knives and machetes (testimony of Florencio Caballero).

104. The current Director of Intelligence denied that the Armed Forces had secret jails, stating that it was not its modus operandi. He claimed that it was subversive elements who do have such jails, which they call "the peoples' prisons." He added that the function of an intelligence service is not to eliminate or disappear people, but rather to obtain and process information to allow the highest levels of government to make informed decisions (testimony of Roberto Núñez Montes).

105. A Honduran officer, called as a witness by the Court, testified that the use of violence or psychological means to force a detainee to give information is prohibited (testimony of Marco Tulio Regalado Hernández).

106. The Commission submitted many clippings from the Honduran press from 1981 to 1984 which contain infor-

mation on at least 64 disappearances, which were apparently carried out against ideological or political opponents or trade union members. Six of those individuals, after their release, complained of torture and other cruel, inhuman and degrading treatment. These clippings mention secret cemeteries where 17 bodies had been found.

107. According to the testimony of his sister, eyewitnesses to the kidnapping of Manfredo Velásquez told her that he was detained on September 12, 1981, between 4:30 and 5:00 P.M., in a parking lot in downtown Tegucigalpa by seven heavily-armed men dressed in civilian clothes (one of them being First Sgt. José Isaías Vilorio), who used a white Ford without license plates (testimony of Zenaida Velásquez. See also testimony of Ramón Custodio López).

108. This witness informed the Court that Col. Leónidas Torres Arias, who had been head of Honduran military intelligence, announced in a press conference in Mexico City that Manfredo Velásquez was kidnapped by a special squadron commanded by Capt. Alexander Hernández, who was carrying out the direct orders of General Gustavo Alvarez Martínez (testimony of Zenaida Velásquez).

109. Lt. Col. Hernández testified that he never received any order to detain Manfredo Velásquez and had never worked in police operations (testimony of Alexander Hernández).

110. The Government objected, under Article 37 of the Rules of Procedure, to the testimony of Zenaida Velásquez because, as sister of the victim, she was a party interested in the outcome of the case.

111. The Court unanimously rejected the objection because it considered the fact that the witness was the victim's sister to be insufficient to disqualify her. The Court reserved the right to consider her testimony.

112. The Government asserted that her testimony was irrelevant because it did not refer to the case before the Court and that what she related about the kidnapping of her brother was not her personal knowledge but rather hearsay.

113. The former member of the Armed Forces who claimed to have belonged to the group that carried out kidnappings told the Court that, although he did not take part in the kidnapping of Manfredo Velásquez, Lt. Flores Murillo had told him what had happened. According to this testimony, Manfredo Velásquez was kidnapped in downtown Tegucigalpa in an operation in which Sgt. José Isaías Vilorio, men using the pseudonyms Ezequiel and Titanio, and Lt. Flores Murillo himself, took part. The Lieutenant told him that during the struggle Ezequiel's gun went off and wounded Manfredo in the leg. They took the victim to INDUMIL (Military Industries) where they tortured him. They then turned him over to those in charge of carrying out executions who, at the orders of General Alvarez, Chief of the Armed Forces, took him out of Tegucigalpa and killed him with a knife and machete. They dismembered his body and buried the remains in different places (testimony of Florencio Caballero).

114. The current Director of Intelligence testified that José Isaías Vilorio was a file clerk of the DNI. He said he did not know Lt. Flores Murillo and stated that INDUMIL had never been used as a detention center (testimony of Roberto Núñez Montes).

115. One witness testified that he was taken prisoner on September 29, 1981 by five or six persons who identified themselves as members of the Armed Forces and took him to the offices of DNI. They blindfolded him and took him in a car to an unknown place, where they tortured him. On Octo-

ber 1, 1981, while he was being held, he heard a moaning and pained voice through a hole in the door to an adjoining room. The person identified himself as Manfredo Velásquez and asked for help. According to the testimony of the witness, at that moment Lt. Ramón Mejía came in and hit him because he found him standing up, although the witness told the Lieutenant that he had gotten up because he was tired. He added that, subsequently, Sgt. Carlos Alfredo Martínez, whom he had met at the bar where he worked, told him they had turned Manfredo Velásquez over to members of Battalion 316 (testimony of Leopoldo Aguilar Villalobos).

116. The Government asserted that the testimony of this witness "is not completely trustworthy because of discrepancies that should not be overlooked, such as the fact that he had testified that he had only been arrested once, in 1981, for trafficking in arms and hijacking a plane, when the truth was that Honduran police had arrested him on several occasions because of his unenviable record."

117. The Commission also presented evidence to show that from 1981 to 1984 domestic judicial remedies in Honduras were ineffective in protecting human rights, especially the rights of disappeared persons to life, liberty and personal integrity.

118. The Court heard the following testimony with respect to this point:

a. The legal procedures of Honduras were ineffective in ascertaining the whereabouts of detainees and ensuring respect for their physical and moral integrity. When writs of habeas corpus were brought, the courts were slow to name judges to execute them and, once named, those judges were often ignored by police authorities. On several occasions, the authorities denied the detentions, even in cases in which the prisoners were later released. There were no judicial orders for the arrests and the places of detention were unknown. When writs of habeas corpus were formalized, the police authorities did not present the persons named in the writs (testimony of Miguel Angel Pavón Salazar, Ramón Custodio López, Milton Jiménez Puerto and Efraín Díaz Arrivillaga).

b. The judges named by the Courts of Justice to execute the writs did not enjoy all the necessary guarantees. Moreover, they feared reprisals because they were often threatened. Judges were imprisoned on more than one occasion and some of them were physically mistreated by the authorities. Law professors and lawyers who defended political prisoners were pressured not to act in cases of human rights violations. Only two dared bring writs of habeas corpus on behalf of disappeared persons and one of those was arrested while he was filling a writ (testimony of Milton Jiménez Puerto, Miguel Angel Pavón Salazar, Ramón Custodio López, César Augusto Murillo, René Velásquez Díaz and Zenaida Velásquez).

c. In no case between 1981 and 1984 did a writ of habeas corpus on behalf of a disappeared person prove effective. If some individuals did reappear, this was not the result of such a legal remedy (testimony of Miguel Angel Pavón Salazar, Inés Consuelo Murillo, César Augusto Murillo, Milton Jiménez Puerto, René Velásquez Díaz and Virgilio Carías).

VI

119. The testimony and documentary evidence, corroborated by press clippings, presented by the Commission, tend to show:

a. That there existed in Honduras from 1981 to 1984 a

systematic and selective practice of disappearances carried out with the assistance or tolerance of the government;

b. That Manfredo Velásquez was a victim of that practice and was kidnapped and presumably tortured, executed and clandestinely buried by agents of the Armed Forces of Honduras, and

c. That in the period in which those acts occurred, the legal remedies available in Honduras were not appropriate or effective to guarantee his rights to life, liberty and personal integrity.

120. The Government, in turn, submitted documents and based its argument on the testimony of three members of the Honduran Armed Forces, two of whom were summoned by the Court because they had been identified in the proceedings as directly involved in the general practice referred to and in the disappearance of Manfredo Velásquez. This evidence may be summarized as follows:

a. The testimony purports to explain the organization and functioning of the security forces accused of carrying out the specific acts and denies any knowledge of or personal involvement in the acts of the officers who testified;

b. Some documents purport to show that no civil suit had been brought to establish a presumption of the death of Manfredo Velásquez, and

c. Other documents purport to prove that the Supreme Court of Honduras received and acted upon some writs of habeas corpus and that some of those writs resulted in the release of the persons on whose behalf they were brought.

121. The record contains no other direct evidence, such as expert opinion, inspections or reports.

VII

122. Before weighing the evidence, the Court must address some questions regarding the burden of proof and the general criteria considered in its evaluation and finding of the facts in the instant proceeding.

123. Because the Commission is accusing the Government of the disappearance of Manfredo Velásquez, it, in principle, should bear the burden of proving the facts underlying its petition.

124. The Commission's argument relies upon the proposition that the policy of disappearances, supported or tolerated by the Government, is designed to conceal and destroy evidence of disappearances. When the existence of such a policy or practice has been shown, the disappearance of a particular individual may be proved through circumstantial or indirect evidence or by logical inference. Otherwise, it would be impossible to prove that an individual has been disappeared.

125. The Government did not object to the Commission's approach. Nevertheless, it argued that neither the existence of a practice of disappearances in Honduras nor the participation of Honduran officials in the alleged disappearance of Manfredo Velásquez had been proven.

126. The Court finds no reason to consider the Commission's argument inadmissible. If it can be shown that there was an official practice of disappearances in Honduras, carried out by the Government or at least tolerated by it, and if the disappearance of Manfredo Velásquez can be linked to that practice, the Commission's allegations will have been proven to the Court's satisfaction, so long as the evidence presented on both points meets the standard of proof required in cases such as this.

127. The Court must determine what the standards of proof should be in the instant case. Neither the Convention, the Statute of the Court nor its Rules of Procedure speak to this matter. Nevertheless, international jurisprudence has recognized the power of the courts to weigh the evidence freely, although it has always avoided a rigid rule regarding the amount of proof necessary to support the judgment (Cfr. Corfu Channel, Merits, Judgment, I.C.J. Reports 1949; Military and Paramilitary Activities in and against Nicaragua (Nicaragua v. United States of America), Merits, Judgment, I.C.J. Reports 1986, paras. 29–30 and 59–60).

128. The standards of proof are less formal in an international legal proceeding than in a domestic one. The latter recognize different burdens of proof, depending upon the nature, character and seriousness of the case.

129. The Court cannot ignore the special seriousness of finding that a State Party to the Convention has carried out or has tolerated a practice of disappearances in its territory. This requires the Court to apply a standard of proof which considers the seriousness of the charge and which, notwithstanding what has already been said, is capable of establishing the truth of the allegations in a convincing manner.

130. The practice of international and domestic courts shows that direct evidence, whether testimonial or documentary, is not the only type of evidence that may be legitimately considered in reaching a decision. Circumstantial evidence, indicia, and presumptions may be considered, so long as they lead to conclusions consistent with the facts.

131. Circumstantial or presumptive evidence is especially important in allegations of disappearances, because this type of repression is characterized by an attempt to suppress all information about the kidnapping or the whereabouts and fate of the victim.

132. Since this Court is an international tribunal, it has its own specialized procedures. All the elements of domestic legal procedures are therefore not automatically applicable.

133. The above principle is generally valid in international proceedings, but is particularly applicable in human rights cases.

134. The international protection of human rights should not be confused with criminal justice. States do not appear before the Court as defendants in a criminal action. The objective of international human rights law is not to punish those individuals who are guilty of violations, but rather to protect the victims and to provide for the reparation of damages resulting from the acts of the States responsible.

135. In contrast to domestic criminal law, in proceedings to determine human rights violations the State cannot rely on the defense that the complainant has failed to present evidence when it cannot be obtained without the State's cooperation.

136. The State controls the means to verify acts occurring within its territory. Although the Commission has investigatory powers, it cannot exercise them within a State's jurisdiction unless it has the cooperation of that State.

137. Since the Government only offered some documentary evidence in support of its preliminary objections, but none on the merits, the Court must reach its decision without the valuable assistance of a more active participation by Honduras, which might otherwise have resulted in a more adequate presentation of its case.

138. The manner in which the Government conducted its defense would have sufficed to prove many of the Commission's allegations by virtue of the principle that the si-

lence of the accused or elusive or ambiguous answers on its part may be interpreted as an acknowledgment of the truth of the allegations, so long as the contrary is not indicated by the record or is not compelled as a matter of law. This result would not hold under criminal law, which does not apply in the instant case (supra 134 and 135). The Court tried to compensate for this procedural principle by admitting all the evidence offered, even if it was untimely, and by ordering the presentation of additional evidence. This was done, of course, without prejudice to its discretion to consider the silence or inaction of Honduras or to its duty to evaluate the evidence as a whole.

139. In its own proceedings and without prejudice to its having considered other elements of proof, the Commission invoked Article 42 of its Regulations, which reads as follows:

The facts reported in the petition whose pertinent parts have been transmitted to the government of the State in reference shall be presumed to be true if, during the maximum period set by the Commission under the provisions of Article 34 paragraph 5, the government has not provided the pertinent information, as long as other evidence does not lead to a different conclusion.

Because the Government did not object here to the use of this legal presumption in the proceedings before the Commission and since the Government fully participated in these proceedings, Article 42 is irrelevant here.

VIII

140. In the instant case, the Court accepts the validity of the documents presented by the Commission and by Honduras, particularly because the parties did not oppose or object to those documents nor did they question their authenticity or veracity.

141. During the hearings, the Government objected, under Article 37 of the Rules of Procedure, to the testimony of witnesses called by the Commission. By decision of October 6, 1987, the Court rejected the challenge, holding as follows:

a. The objection refers to circumstances under which, according to the Government, the testimony of these witnesses might not be objective.

b. It is within the Court's discretion, when rendering judgment, to weigh the evidence.

c. A violation of the human rights set out in the Convention is established by facts found by the Court, not by the method of proof.

d. When testimony is questioned, the challenging party has the burden of refuting that testimony.

142. During cross-examination, the Government's attorneys attempted to show that some witnesses were not impartial because of ideological reasons, origin or nationality, family relations, or a desire to discredit Honduras. They even insinuated that testifying against the State in these proceedings was disloyal to the nation. Likewise, they cited criminal records or pending charges to show that some witnesses were not competent to testify (supra 86, 88, 90, 92, 101, 110 and 116).

143. It is true, of course, that certain factors may clearly influence a witness' truthfulness. However, the Government did not present any concrete evidence to show that the witnesses had not told the truth, but rather limited itself to making general observations regarding their alleged incompetency or lack of impartiality. This is insufficient to rebut testimony which is fundamentally consistent with that of other witnesses. The Court cannot ignore such testimony.

144. Moreover, some of the Government's arguments are unfounded within the context of human rights law. The insinuation that persons who, for any reason, resort to the inter-American system for the protection of human rights are disloyal to their country is unacceptable and cannot constitute a basis for any penalty or negative consequence. Human rights are higher values that "are not derived from the fact that (an individual) is a national of a certain state, but are based upon attributes of his human personality" (American Declaration of the Rights and Duties of Man, Whereas clauses and American Convention, Preamble).

145. Neither is it sustainable that having a criminal record or charges pending is sufficient in and of itself to find that a witness is not competent to testify in Court. As the Court ruled, in its decision of October 6, 1987, in the instant case: [U]nder the American Convention on Human Rights, it is impermissible to deny a witness, a priori, the possibility of testifying to facts relevant to a matter before the Court, even if he has an interest in that proceeding, because he has been prosecuted or even convicted under internal laws.

146. Many of the press clippings offered by the Commission cannot be considered as documentary evidence as such. However, many of them contain public and well-known facts which, as such, do not require proof; others are of evidentiary value, as has been recognized in international jurisprudence (Military and Paramilitary Activities in and against Nicaragua, supra 127, paras. 62–64), insofar as they textually reproduce public statements, especially those of high-ranking members of the Armed Forces, of the Government, or even of the Supreme Court of Honduras, such as some of those made by the President of the latter. Finally, others are important as a whole insofar as they corroborate testimony regarding the responsibility of the Honduran military and police for disappearances.

IX

147. The Court now turns to the relevant facts that it finds to have been proven. They are as follows:

a. During the period 1981 to 1984, 100 to 150 persons disappeared in the Republic of Honduras, and many were never heard from again (testimony of Miguel Angel Pavón Salazar, Ramón Custodio López, Efraín Díaz Arrivillaga, Florencio Caballero and press clippings).

b. Those disappearances followed a similar pattern, beginning with the kidnapping of the victims by force, often in broad daylight and in public places, by armed men in civilian clothes and disguises, who acted with apparent immunity and who used vehicles without any official identification, with tinted windows and with false license plates or no plates (testimony of Miguel Angel Pavón Salazar, Ramón Custodio López, Efraín Díaz Arrivillaga, Florencio Caballero and press clippings).

c. It was public and notorious knowledge in Honduras that the kidnappings were carried out by military personnel or the police, or persons acting under their orders (testimony of Miguel Angel Pavón Salazar, Ramón Custodio López, Efraín Díaz Arrivillaga, Florencio Caballero and press clippings).

d. The disappearances were carried out in a systematic manner, regarding which the Court considers the following circumstances particularly relevant:

i. The victims were usually persons whom Honduran

officials considered dangerous to State security (testimony of Miguel Angel Pavón Salazar, Ramón Custodio López, Efraín Díaz Arrivillaga, Florencio Caballero, Virgilio Carías, Milton Jiménez Puerto, René Velásquez Díaz, Inés Consuelo Murillo, José Gonzalo Flores Trejo, Zenaida Velásquez, César Augusto Murillo and press clippings). In addition, the victims had usually been under surveillance for long periods of time (testimony of Ramón Custodio López and Florencio Caballero);

    ii. the arms employed were reserved for the official use of the military and police, and the vehicles used had tinted glass, which requires special official authorization. In some cases, Government agents carried out the detentions openly and without any pretense or disguise; in others, government agents had cleared the areas where the kidnappings were to take place and, on at least one occasion, when government agents stopped the kidnappers they were allowed to continue freely on their way after showing their identification (testimony of Miguel Angel Pavón Salazar, Ramón Custodio López and Florencio Caballero);

    iii. The kidnappers blindfolded the victims, took them to secret, unofficial detention centers and moved them from one center to another. They interrogated the victims and subjected them to cruel and humiliating treatment and torture. Some were ultimately murdered and their bodies were buried in clandestine cemeteries (testimony of Miguel Angel Pavón Salazar, Ramón Custodio López, Florencio Caballero, René Velásquez Díaz, Inés Consuelo Murillo and José Gonzalo Flores Trejo);

    iv. When queried by relatives, lawyers and persons or entities interested in the protection of human rights, or by judges charged with executing writs of habeas corpus, the authorities systematically denied any knowledge of the detentions or the whereabouts or fate of the victims. That attitude was seen even in the cases of persons who later reappeared in the hands of the same authorities who had systematically denied holding them or knowing their fate (testimony of Inés Consuelo Murillo, José Gonzalo Flores Trejo, Efraín Díaz Arrivillaga, Florencio Caballero, Virgilio Carías, Milton Jiménez Puerto, René Velásquez Díaz, Zenaida Velásquez, César Augusto Murillo and press clippings);

    v. Military and police officials as well as those from the Executive and Judicial Branches either denied the disappearances or were incapable of preventing or investigating them, punishing those responsible, or helping those interested discover the whereabouts and fate of the victims or the location of their remains. The investigative committees created by the Government and the Armed Forces did not produce any results. The judicial proceedings brought were processed slowly with a clear lack of interest and some were ultimately dismissed (testimony of Inés Consuelo Murillo, José Gonzalo Flores Trejo, Efraín Díaz Arrivillaga, Florencio Caballero, Virgilio Carías, Milton Jiménez Puerto, René Velásquez Díaz, Zenaida Velásquez, César Augusto Murillo and press clippings);

    e. On September 12, 1981, between 4:30 and 5:00 P.M., several heavily-armed men in civilian clothes driving a white Ford without license plates kidnapped Manfredo Velásquez from a parking lot in downtown Tegucigalpa. Today, nearly seven years later, he remains disappeared, which creates a reasonable presumption that he is dead (testimony of Miguel Angel Pavón Salazar, Ramón Custodio López, Zenaida Velásquez, Florencio Caballero, Leopoldo Aguilar Villalobos and press clippings).

    f. Persons connected with the Armed Forces or under its direction carried out that kidnapping (testimony of Ramón Custodio López, Zenaida Velásquez, Florencio Caballero, Leopoldo Aguilar Villalobos and press clippings).

    g. The kidnapping and disappearance of Manfredo Velásquez falls within the systematic practice of disappearances referred to by the facts deemed proved in paragraphs a–d. To wit:

    i. Manfredo Velásquez was a student who was involved in activities the authorities considered "dangerous" to national security (testimony of Miguel Angel Pavón Salazar, Ramón Custodio López and Zenaida Velásquez).

    ii. The kidnapping of Manfredo Velásquez was carried out in broad daylight by men in civilian clothes who used a vehicle without license plates.

    iii. In the case of Manfredo Velásquez, there were the same type of denials by his captors and the Armed Forces, the same omissions of the latter and of the Government in investigating and revealing his whereabouts, and the same ineffectiveness of the courts where three writs of habeas corpus and two criminal complaints were brought (testimony of Miguel Angel Pavón Salazar, Ramón Custodio López, Zenaida Velásquez, press clippings and documentary evidence).

    h. There is no evidence in the record that Manfredo Velásquez had disappeared in order to join subversive groups, other than a letter from the Mayor of Langue, which contained rumors to that effect. The letter itself shows that the Government associated him with activities it considered a threat to national security. However, the Government did not corroborate the view expressed in the letter with any other evidence. Nor is there any evidence that he was kidnapped by common criminals or other persons unrelated to the practice of disappearances existing at that time.

148. Based upon the above, the Court finds that the following facts have been proven in this proceeding: (1) a practice of disappearances carried out or tolerated by Honduran officials existed between 1981 and 1984; (2) Manfredo Velásquez disappeared at the hands of or with the acquiescence of those officials within the framework of that practice; and (3) the Government of Honduras failed to guarantee the human rights affected by that practice.

X

149. Disappearances are not new in the history of human rights violations. However, their systematic and repeated nature and their use not only for causing certain individuals to disappear, either briefly or permanently, but also as a means of creating a general state of anguish, insecurity and fear, is a recent phenomenon. Although this practice exists virtually worldwide, it has occurred with exceptional intensity in Latin America in the last few years.

150. The phenomenon of disappearances is a complex form of human rights violation that must be understood and confronted in an integral fashion.

151. The establishment of a Working Group on Enforced or Involuntary Disappearances of the United Nations Commission on Human Rights, by Resolution 20 (XXXVI) of February 29, 1980, is a clear demonstration of general censure and repudiation of the practice of disappearances, which had already received world attention at the UN General Assembly (Resolution 33/173 of December 20, 1978), the Economic and Social Council (Resolution 1979/38 of May 10, 1979) and the Subcommission for the Prevention of Discrimination and Protection of Minorities (Resolu-

tion 5B (XXXII) of September 5, 1979). The reports of the rapporteurs or special envoys of the Commission on Human Rights show concern that the practice of disappearances be stopped, the victims reappear and that those responsible be punished.

152. Within the inter-American system, the General Assembly of the Organization of American States (OAS) and the Commission have repeatedly referred to the practice of disappearances and have urged that disappearances be investigated and that the practice be stopped (AG/RES.443 (IX-0/79) of October 31, 1979; AG/RES.510 (X-0/80) of November 27, 1980; AG/RES.618 (XII-0/82) of November 20, 1982; AG/RES.666 (XIII-0/83) of November 18, 1983; AG/RES.742 (XIV-0/84) of November 17, 1984 and AG/RES.890 (XVII-0/87) of November 14, 1987; Inter-American Commission on Human Rights: Annual Report 1978, pp. 24–27; Annual Report, 1980–1981, pp. 113–114; Annual Report, 1982–1983, pp. 46–47; Annual Report, 1985–1986, pp. 37–40; Annual Report, 1986–1987, pp. 277–284 and in many of its Country Reports, such as OEA/Ser.L/V/II.49, doc. 19, 1980 (Argentina); OEA/Ser.L/V/II.66, doc. 17, 1985 (Chile) and OEA/Ser.L/V/II.66, doc. 16, 1985 (Guatemala)).

153. International practice and doctrine have often categorized disappearances as a crime against humanity, although there is no treaty in force which is applicable to the States Parties to the Convention and which uses this terminology (Inter-American Yearbook on Human Rights, 1985, pp. 368, 686 and 1102). The General Assembly of the OAS has resolved that it "is an affront to the conscience of the hemisphere and constitutes a crime against humanity" (AG/RES.666, supra) and that "this practice is cruel and inhuman, mocks the rule of law, and undermines those norms which guarantee protection against arbitrary detention and the right to personal security and safety" (AG/RES.742, supra).

154. Without question, the State has the right and duty to guarantee its security. It is also indisputable that all societies suffer some deficiencies in their legal orders. However, regardless of the seriousness of certain actions and the culpability of the perpetrators of certain crimes, the power of the State is not unlimited, nor may the State resort to any means to attain its ends. The State is subject to law and morality. Disrespect for human dignity cannot serve as the basis for any State action.

155. The forced disappearance of human beings is a multiple and continuous violation of many rights under the Convention that the States Parties are obligated to respect and guarantee. The kidnapping of a person is an arbitrary deprivation of liberty, an infringement of a detainee's right to be taken without delay before a judge and to invoke the appropriate procedures to review the legality of the arrest, all in violation of Article 7 of the Convention which recognizes the right to personal liberty by providing that:

1. Every person has the right to personal liberty and security.

2. No one shall be deprived of his physical liberty except for the reasons and under the conditions established beforehand by the constitution of the State Party concerned or by a law established pursuant thereto.

3. No one shall be subject to arbitrary arrest or imprisonment.

4. Anyone who is detained shall be informed of the reasons for his detention and shall be promptly notified of the charge or charges against him.

5. Any person detained shall be brought promptly before a judge or other officer authorized by law to exercise judicial power and shall be entitled to trial within a reasonable time or to be released without prejudice to the continuation of the proceedings. His release may be subject to guarantees to assure his appearance for trial.

6. Anyone who is deprived of his liberty shall be entitled to recourse to a competent court, in order that the court may decide without delay on the lawfulness of his arrest or detention and order his release if the arrest or detention is unlawful. In States Parties whose laws provide that anyone who believes himself to be threatened with deprivation of his liberty is entitled to recourse to a competent court in order that it may decide on the lawfulness of such threat, this remedy may not be restricted or abolished. The interested party or another person in his behalf is entitled to seek these remedies.

156. Moreover, prolonged isolation and deprivation of communication are in themselves cruel and inhuman treatment, harmful to the psychological and moral integrity of the person and a violation of the right of any detainee to respect for his inherent dignity as a human being. Such treatment, therefore, violates Article 5 of the Convention, which recognizes the right to the integrity of the person by providing that:

1. Every person has the right to have his physical, mental, and moral integrity respected.

2. No one shall be subjected to torture or to cruel, inhuman, or degrading punishment or treatment. All persons deprived of their liberty shall be treated with respect for the inherent dignity of the human person.

In addition, investigations into the practice of disappearances and the testimony of victims who have regained their liberty show that those who are disappeared are often subjected to merciless treatment, including all types of indignities, torture and other cruel, inhuman and degrading treatment, in violation of the right to physical integrity recognized in Article 5 of the Convention.

157. The practice of disappearances often involves secret execution without trial, followed by concealment of the body to eliminate any material evidence of the crime and to ensure the impunity of those responsible. This is a flagrant violation of the right to life, recognized in Article 4 of the Convention, the first clause of which reads as follows:

1. Every person has the right to have his life respected. This right shall be protected by law and, in general, from the moment of conception. No one shall be arbitrarily deprived of his life.

158. The practice of disappearances, in addition to directly violating many provisions of the Convention, such as those noted above, constitutes a radical breach of the treaty in that it shows a crass abandonment of the values which emanate from the concept of human dignity and of the most basic principles of the inter-American system and the Convention. The existence of this practice, moreover, evinces a disregard of the duty to organize the State in such a manner as to guarantee the rights recognized in the Convention, as set out below.

XI

159. The Commission has asked the Court to find that Honduras has violated the rights guaranteed to Manfredo Velásquez by Articles 4, 5 and 7 of the Convention. The Government has denied the charges and seeks to be absolved.

160. This requires the Court to examine the conditions

under which a particular act, which violates one of the rights recognized by the Convention, can be imputed to a State Party thereby establishing its international responsibility.

161. Article 1 (1) of the Convention provides:

"Article 1. Obligation to Respect Rights. 1. The States Parties to this Convention undertake to respect the rights and freedoms recognized herein and to ensure to all persons subject to their jurisdiction the free and full exercise of those rights and freedoms, without any discrimination for reasons of race, color, sex, language, religion, political or other opinion, national or social origin, economic status, birth, or any other social condition."

162. This article specifies the obligation assumed by the States Parties in relation to each of the rights protected. Each claim alleging that one of those rights has been infringed necessarily implies that Article 1 (1) of the Convention has also been violated.

163. The Commission did not specifically allege the violation of Article 1 (1) of the Convention, but that does not preclude the Court from applying it. The precept contained therein constitutes the generic basis of the protection of the rights recognized by the Convention and would be applicable, in any case, by virtue of a general principle of law, iura novit curia, on which international jurisprudence has repeatedly relied and under which a court has the power and the duty to apply the juridical provisions relevant to a proceeding, even when the parties do not expressly invoke them ("Lotus", Judgment No. 9, 1927, P.C.I.J., Series A No. 10, p. 31 and Eur. Court H.R., Handyside Case, Judgment of 7 December 1976, Series A No. 24, para. 41).

164. Article 1(1) is essential in determining whether a violation of the human rights recognized by the Convention can be imputed to a State Party. In effect, that article charges the States Parties with the fundamental duty to respect and guarantee the rights recognized in the Convention. Any impairment of those rights which can be attributed under the rules of international law to the action or omission of any public authority constitutes an act imputable to the State, which assumes responsibility in the terms provided by the Convention.

165. The first obligation assumed by the States Parties under Article 1(1) is "to respect the rights and freedoms" recognized by the Convention. The exercise of public authority has certain limits which derive from the fact that human rights are inherent attributes of human dignity and are, therefore, superior to the power of the State. On another occasion, this Court stated:

> The protection of human rights, particularly the civil and political rights set forth in the Convention, is in effect based on the affirmation of the existence of certain inviolable attributes of the individual that cannot be legitimately restricted through the exercise of governmental power. These are individual domains that are beyond the reach of the State or to which the State has but limited access. Thus, the protection of human rights must necessarily comprise the concept of the restriction of the exercise of state power (The Word "Laws" in Article 30 of the American Convention on Human Rights, Advisory Opinion OC-6/86 of May 9, 1986. Series A No. 6, para. 21).

166. The second obligation of the States Parties is to "ensure" the free and full exercise of the rights recognized by the Convention to every person subject to its jurisdiction. This obligation implies the duty of the States Parties to organize the governmental apparatus and, in general, all the structures through which public power is exercised, so that they are capable of juridically ensuring the free and full enjoyment of human rights. As a consequence of this obligation, the States must prevent, investigate and punish any violation of the rights recognized by the Convention and, moreover, if possible attempt to restore the right violated and provide compensation as warranted for damages resulting from the violation.

167. The obligation to ensure the free and full exercise of human rights is not fulfilled by the existence of a legal system designed to make it possible to comply with this obligation—it also requires the government to conduct itself so as to effectively ensure the free and full exercise of human rights.

168. The obligation of the States is, thus, much more direct than that contained in Article 2, which reads:

"Article 2. Domestic Legal Effects. Where the exercise of any of the rights or freedoms referred to in Article 1 is not already ensured by legislative or other provisions, the States Parties undertake to adopt, in accordance with their constitutional processes and the provisions of this Convention, such legislative or other measures as may be necessary to give effect to those rights or freedoms."

169. According to Article 1(1), any exercise of public power that violates the rights recognized by the Convention is illegal. Whenever a State organ, official or public entity violates one of those rights, this constitutes a failure of the duty to respect the rights and freedoms set forth in the Convention.

170. This conclusion is independent of whether the organ or official has contravened provisions of internal law or overstepped the limits of his authority: under international law a State is responsible for the acts of its agents undertaken in their official capacity and for their omissions, even when those agents act outside the sphere of their authority or violate internal law.

171. This principle suits perfectly the nature of the Convention, which is violated whenever public power is used to infringe the rights recognized therein. If acts of public power that exceed the State's authority or are illegal under its own laws were not considered to compromise that State's obligations under the treaty, the system of protection provided for in the Convention would be illusory.

172. Thus, in principle, any violation of rights recognized by the Convention carried out by an act of public authority or by persons who use their position of authority is imputable to the State. However, this does not define all the circumstances in which a State is obligated to prevent, investigate and punish human rights violations, nor all the cases in which the State might be found responsible for an infringement of those rights. An illegal act which violates human rights and which is initially not directly imputable to a State (for example, because it is the act of a private person or because the person responsible has not been identified) can lead to international responsibility of the State, not because of the act itself, but because of the lack of due diligence to prevent the violation or to respond to it as required by the Convention.

173. Violations of the Convention cannot be founded upon rules that take psychological factors into account in establishing individual culpability. For the purposes of analysis, the intent or motivation of the agent who has violated the rights recognized by the Convention is irrelevant—the violation can be established even if the identity of the individual perpetrator is unknown. What is decisive is whether a violation of the rights recognized by the Convention has occurred with the support or the acquiescence of the govern-

ment, or whether the State has allowed the act to take place without taking measures to prevent it or to punish those responsible. Thus, the court's task is to determine whether the violation is the result of a State's failure to fulfill its duty to respect and guarantee those rights, as required by Article 1(1) of the Convention.

174. The State has a legal duty to take reasonable steps to prevent human rights violations and to use the means at its disposal to carry out a serious investigation of violations committed within its jurisdiction, to identify those responsible, to impose the appropriate punishment and to ensure the victim adequate compensation.

175. This duty to prevent includes all those means of a legal, political, administrative and cultural nature that promote the protection of human rights and ensure that any violations are considered and treated as illegal acts, which, as such, may lead to the punishment of those responsible and the obligation to indemnify the victims for damages. It is not possible to make a detailed list of all such measures, since they vary with the law and the conditions of each State Party. Of course, while the State is obligated to prevent human rights abuses, the existence of a particular violation does not, in itself, prove the failure to take preventive measures. On the other hand, subjecting a person to official, repressive bodies that practice torture and assassination with immunity is itself a breach of the duty to prevent violations of the rights to life and physical integrity of the person, even if that particular person is not tortured or assassinated, or if those facts cannot be proven in a concrete case.

176. The State is obligated to investigate every situation involving a violation of the rights protected by the Convention. If the State apparatus acts in such a way that the violation goes unpunished and the victim's full enjoyment of such rights is not restored as soon as possible, the State has failed to comply with its duty to ensure the free and full exercise of those rights to the persons within its jurisdiction. The same is true when the State allows private persons or groups to act freely and with impunity to the detriment of the rights recognized by the Convention.

177. In certain circumstances, it may be difficult to investigate acts that violate an individual's rights. The duty to investigate, like the duty to prevent, is not breached merely because the investigation does not produce a satisfactory result. Nevertheless, it must be undertaken in a serious manner and not as a mere formality preordained to be ineffective. An investigation must have an objective and be assumed by the State as its own legal duty, not as a step taken by private interests that depends upon the initiative of the victim or his family or upon their offer of proof, without an effective search for the truth by the government. This is true regardless of what agent is eventually found responsible for the violation. Where the acts of private parties that violate the Convention are not seriously investigated, those parties are aided in a sense by the government, thereby making the State responsible on the international plane.

178. In the instant case, the evidence shows a complete inability of the procedures of the State of Honduras, which were theoretically adequate, to carry out an investigation into the disappearance of Manfredo Velásquez, and of the fulfillment of its duties to pay compensation and punish those responsible, as set out in Article 1(1) of the Convention.

179. As the Court has verified above, the failure of the judicial system to act upon the writs brought before various tribunals in the instant case has been proven. Not one writ of habeas corpus was processed. No judge had access to the places where Manfredo Velásquez might have been detained. The criminal complaint was dismissed.

180. Nor did the organs of the Executive Branch carry out a serious investigation to establish the fate of Manfredo Velásquez. There was no investigation of public allegations of a practice of disappearances nor a determination of whether Manfredo Velásquez had been a victim of that practice. The Commission's requests for information were ignored to the point that the Commission had to presume, under Article 42 of its Regulations, that the allegations were true. The offer of an investigation in accord with Resolution 30/83 of the Commission resulted in an investigation by the Armed Forces, the same body accused of direct responsibility for the disappearances. This raises grave questions regarding the seriousness of the investigation. The government often resorted to asking relatives of the victims to present conclusive proof of their allegations even though those allegations, because they involved crimes against the person, should have been investigated on the Government's own initiative in fulfillment of the State's duty to ensure public order. This is especially true when the allegations refer to a practice carried out within the Armed Forces, which, because of its nature, is not subject to private investigations. No proceeding was initiated to establish responsibility for the disappearance of Manfredo Velásquez and apply punishment under international law. All of the above leads to the conclusion that the Honduran authorities did not take effective action to ensure respect for human rights within the jurisdiction of that State as required by Article 1(1) of the Convention.

181. The duty to investigate facts of this type continues as long as there is uncertainty about the fate of the person who has disappeared. Even in the hypothetical case that those individually responsible for crimes of this type cannot be legally punished under certain circumstances, the State is obligated to use the means at its disposal to inform the relatives of the fate of the victims and, if they have been killed, the location of their remains.

182. The Court is convinced, and has so found, that the disappearance of Manfredo Velásquez was carried out by agents who acted under cover of public authority. However, even had that fact not been proven, the failure of the State apparatus to act, which is clearly proven, is a failure on the part of Honduras to fulfill the duties it assumed under Article 1(1) of the Convention, which obligated it it to ensure Manfredo Velásquez the free and full exercise of his human rights.

183. The Court notes that the legal order of Honduras does not authorize such acts and that internal law defines them as crimes. The Court also recognizes that not all levels of the Government of Honduras were necessarily aware of those acts, nor is there any evidence that such acts were the result of official orders. Nevertheless, those circumstances are irrelevant for the purposes of establishing whether Honduras is responsible under international law for the violations of human rights perpetrated within the practice of disappearances.

184. According to the principle of the continuity of the State in international law, responsibility exists both independently of changes of government over a period of time and continuously from the time of the act that creates responsibility to the time when the act is declared illegal. The foregoing is also valid in the area of human rights although, from an ethical or political point of view, the attitude of the new government may be much more respectful of those

rights than that of the government in power when the violations occurred.

185. The Court, therefore, concludes that the facts found in this proceeding show that the State of Honduras is responsible for the involuntary disappearance of Angel Manfredo Velásquez Rodríguez. Thus, Honduras has violated Articles 7, 5 and 4 of the Convention.

186. As a result of the disappearance, Manfredo Velásquez was the victim of an arbitrary detention, which deprived him of his physical liberty without legal cause and without a determination of the lawfulness of his detention by a judge or competent tribunal. Those acts directly violate the right to personal liberty recognized by Article 7 of the Convention (supra 155) and are a violation imputable to Honduras of the duties to respect and ensure that right under Article 1(1).

187. The disappearance of Manfredo Velásquez violates the right to personal integrity recognized by Article 5 of the Convention (supra 156). First, the mere subjection of an individual to prolonged isolation and deprivation of communication is in itself cruel and inhuman treatment which harms the psychological and moral integrity of the person, and violates the right of every detainee under Article 5(1) and 5(2) to treatment respectful of his dignity. Second, although it has not been directly shown that Manfredo Velásquez was physically tortured, his kidnapping and imprisonment by governmental authorities, who have been shown to subject detainees to indignities, cruelty and torture, constitute a failure of Honduras to fulfill the duty imposed by Article 1(1) to ensure the rights under Article 5(1) and 5(2) of the Convention. The guarantee of physical integrity and the right of detainees to treatment respectful of their human dignity require States Parties to take reasonable steps to prevent situations which are truly harmful to the rights protected.

188. The above reasoning is applicable to the right to life recognized by Article 4 of the Convention (supra 157). The context in which the disappearance of Manfredo Velásquez occurred and the lack of knowledge seven years later about his fate create a reasonable presumption that he was killed. Even if there is a minimal margin of doubt in this respect, it must be presumed that his fate was decided by authorities who systematically executed detainees without trial and concealed their bodies in order to avoid punishment. This, together with the failure to investigate, is a violation by Honduras of a legal duty under Article 1(1) of the Convention to ensure the rights recognized by Article 4(1). That duty is to ensure to every person subject to its jurisdiction the inviolability of the right to life and the right not to have one's life taken arbitrarily. These rights imply an obligation on the part of States Parties to take reasonable steps to prevent situations that could result in the violation of that right.

XII

189. Article 63(1) of the Convention provides:

"If the Court finds that there has been a violation of a right or freedom protected by this Convention, the Court shall rule that the injured part be ensured the enjoyment of his right or freedom that was violated. It shall also rule, if appropriate, that the consequences of the measure or situation that constituted the breach of such right or freedom be remedied and that fair compensation be paid to the injured party."

Clearly, in the instant case the Court cannot order that the victim be guaranteed the enjoyment of the rights or freedoms violated. The Court, however, can rule that the consequences of the breach of the rights be remedied and that just compensation be paid.

190. During this proceeding the Commission requested the payment of compensation, but did not offer evidence regarding the amount of damages or the manner of payment. Neither did the parties discuss these matters.

191. The Court believes that the parties can agree on the damages. If an agreement cannot be reached, the Court shall award an amount. The case shall, therefore, remain open for that purpose. The Court reserves the right to approve the agreement and, in the event no agreement is reached, to set the amount and order the manner of payment.

192. The Rules of Procedure establish the legal procedural relations among the Commission, the State or States Parties in the case and the Court itself, which continue in effect until the case is no longer before the Court. As the case is still before the Court, the Government and the Commission should negotiate the agreement referred to in the preceding paragraph. The recipients of the award of damages will be the next-of-kin of the victim. This does not in any way imply a ruling on the meaning of the word "parties" in any other context under the Convention or the rules pursuant thereto.

XIII

193. With no pleading to support an award of costs, it is not proper for the Court to rule on them (Art. 45(1), Rules of Procedure).

XIV

194. THEREFORE,
THE COURT:
Unanimously

1. Rejects the preliminary objection interposed by the Government of Honduras alleging the inadmissibility of the case for the failure to exhaust domestic legal remedies.
Unanimously

2. Declares that Honduras has violated, in the case of Angel Manfredo Velásquez Rodríguez, its obligations to respect and to ensure the right to personal liberty set forth in Article 7 of the Convention, read in conjunction with Article 1(1) thereof.
Unanimously

3. Declares that Honduras has violated, in the case of Angel Manfredo Velásquez Rodríguez, its obligations to respect and to ensure the right to humane treatment set forth in Article 5 of the Convention, read in conjunction with Article 1(1) thereof.
Unanimously

4. Declares that Honduras has violated, in the case of Angel Manfredo Velásquez Rodríguez, its obligation to ensure the right to life set forth in Article 4 of the Convention, read in conjunction with Article 1(1) thereof.
Unanimously

5. Decides that Honduras is hereby required to pay fair compensation to the next-of-kin of the victim.
By six votes to one

6. Decides that the form and amount of such compensation, failing agreement between Honduras and the Commission within six months of the date of this judgment, shall be settled by the Court and, or that purpose, retains jurisdiction of the case. Judge Rodolfo E. Piza E. dissenting.

H

Unanimously

7. Decides that the agreement on the form and amount of the compensation shall be approved by the Court.

Unanimously

8. Does not find it necessary to render a decision concerning costs.

Done in Spanish and in English, the Spanish text being authentic, at the seat of the Court in San José, Costa Rica, this twenty-ninth day of July, 1988.

Dissenting Opinion of Judge Piza Escalante

1. I would have had no reservation in approving the Judgment in its entirety had point 6 been drafted as follows:

"6. Decides that the form and amount of such compensation, failing agreement between *the parties, with the intervention of the Commission,* within six months of the date of this judgment, shall be settled by the Court and, for that purpose, retains jurisdiction of the case."

I would even have concurred with a less definitive decision to remit the agreement *to the parties,* without referring to the Commission, as the Court concluded in paragraph 191; but not with the conclusions of paragraph 192, to which I also dissent.

2. My dissent is not on the merits or the basic sense of that provision, insofar as it reserves to the Court the final decision on the compensation awarded in the abstract and leaves to the parties the initiative to reach an agreement within the time period stipulated, but only to the granting of the status of parties for that purpose, which the majority vote gives the Commission, but not the assignees of the victim.

3. I dissent, therefore, in order to be consistent in my interpretation of the Convention and of the Regulations of the Commission and Rules of Procedure of the Court, according to which the only active party in the proceeding before the Court, in a substantive sense, is the victim and his assignees, who possess the rights in question and are the beneficiaries of the provisions contained in the Judgment, in keeping with Article 63(1) of the Convention, which specifically provides that ". . . fair compensation to be paid *to the injured party.*"

The Commission, an impartial and instrumental party comparable to a public prosecutor (Ministerio Público) in the inter-American system of protection of human rights, is a party only in a procedural sense, as the prosecution, and not in a substantive or material sense, as beneficiary of the judgment (Arts. 57 and 61, Convention; 19.b of the Regulations of the Commission; and 28 of the Statute of the Court).

4. This thesis regarding the parties in the proceeding before the Court is the same that I have consistently urged, beginning with my Separate Opinions on the decisions of 1981 and 1983 in the Matter of Viviana Gallardo et al. (see, e.g., Decision of November 13, 1981, "Explanation of Vote" by Judge Piza, para. 8, and Decision of September 8, 1983, "Separate Vote" of Judge Piza, paras. 36, 39 and operative point No. 8, where I argued, inter alia:

"39. . . . in my judgment, the parties in the substantial sense are . . . : a) the State of Costa Rica as the 'passive party,' which is charged with the violations and is the eventual debtor of its reparation . . . and b) *as the 'active party,' the person entitled to the rights claimed and, therefore, the creditor of any eventual estimatory sentence, the victims. . . . The Commission is not a party in any substantial sense because it is not the*

holder of the rights or the duties that might be or can be declared or constituted by the verdict)."

5. Although valid, the majority opinion is deficient because it does not recognize the assignees of Manfredo Velásquez as a party, in conformity with Article 63(1) of the Convention, and, also, insofar as what must be contained in the Judgment according to Article 45(2) and 45(3) of the Rules of Procedure, which read as follows:

"2. Where the Court finds that there is a breach of the Convention, it shall give in the same judgment a decision on the application of Article 63(1) of the Convention if that question, after being raised under Article 43 of these Rules, is ready for decision; if the question is not ready for decision, the Court shall decide on the procedure to follow. If, on the other hand, the matter has not been raised under Article 43, the Court shall determine the period within which it may be presented *by a party or by the Commission.*

"3. If the Court is informed that *an agreement has been reached between the victim of the violation and the State Party concerned,* it shall verify the equitable nature of such agreement."

6. In those Separate Opinions, I also explained my position regarding the procedural relationship of the parties, that is, not as beneficiary and debtor, but rather as plaintiff and respondent in the proceeding, as follows:

"40. . . . there is no valid reason to refuse to the victims, the substantial 'active party,' their independent condition of 'active party' in the proceedings. . . . in my judgment, the Convention only bars the individual from submitting a case to the Court (Art. 61(1)). This limitation, as such, is, in the light of the principles, a 'repugnant matter' (materia odiosa) and should thus be interpreted restrictively. Therefore, one cannot draw from that limitation the conclusion that the individual is also barred from his autonomous condition of 'party' in the procedures once they have begun . . . . (A)s concerns the Inter-American Commission, which must appear in all cases before the Court . . . this is clearly a sui generis role, purely procedural, as an auxiliary of the judiciary, like that of a 'Ministerio Público' of the inter-American system for the protection of human rights (Decision of September 8, 1983).

"As I have said (supra 1), the foregoing forces me to dissent to paragraph 192, insofar as it recognizes the Commission as the sole procedural party other than the State or States that participate in a case before the Court, without recognizing the legal standing, even in a purely procedural sense, of the victims or their assignees, among others."

7. In addition, I believe that if the Convention and the Rules of the Commission and the Court generally authorize a friendly settlement both before and after the case is brought to the Court, and this process is always controlled directly by the victim with only the mediation or oversight of the Commission, it makes no sense to authorize a direct agreement after the Court has ordered, in the abstract, the payment of an indemnization, naming the Commission as the only party to deal with the State concerned rather than the assignees of Manfredo Velásquez to whom the indemnization is owed. The following provisions are self-explanatory:

"Convention

Article 48. 1. When the Commission receives a petition or communication alleging violation of any of the rights protected by this Convention, . . .

f. (It) shall place itself *at the disposal of the parties con-*

cerned with a view to reaching a friendly settlement of the matter on the basis of respect for the human rights recognized in this Convention."

"Regulations of the Commission

Article 45. Friendly Settlement. 1. At the request of any of the parties, or on its own initiative, the Commission shall place itself at the disposal of the parties concerned, at any stage of the examination of a petition, with a view to reaching a friendly settlement of the matter on the basis of respect for the human rights recognized in the American Convention on Human Rights."

"Rules of Procedure of the Court

Article 42. Discontinuance. 2. When, in a case brought before the Court by the Commission, the Court *is informed of a friendly settlement,* arrangement or other fact of a kind to provide a solution of the matter, it may, *after having obtained the opinion, if necessary, of the delegates of the Commission,* strike the case off its list."

With respect to this last provision, it is obvious that if the "party" in the friendly settlement were the Commission, it would be absurd that the Court would later have to obtain the opinion of the Commission in order to strike the case off its list.

8. Nothing in the foregoing means that I do not understand or share the concern that the majority decision appears to reveal, in the sense that the Commission, possibly, is in a better condition to oversee the interests of the assignees of Manfredo Velásquez, or that a specific agreement between the Government and the Commission could have the greater standing of an international agreement. Nevertheless, I hold as follows:

a. Regarding the first point, that the Court is required to apply the norms of the Convention and its Rules in conformity with their ordinary meaning. In my opinion, the text of those norms does not support the interpretation adopted.

b. I did not mean to suggest at any time that the Commission should not actively participate in the negotiation of an agreement with the Government concerning the compensation ordered by the judgment. My draft specifically recognized that and my willingness to accept a simple reference to "the parties" implied the Commission's participation. Of course, the Court has reserved the right to confirm that agreement anyway (operative point 7, adopted unanimously).

c. Regarding the effectiveness of the agreement, I am not concerned whether the legal framework is national or international. In either case the validity and force of that agreement would derive from the Convention by virtue of the judgment itself and the confirmation or formal approval of the Court, which would be subject to execution at the international and the domestic level, as expressly provided by Article 68(2) of the Convention in the sense that

"2. That part of a judgment that stipulates compensatory damage may be executed in the country concerned *in accordance with domestic procedure governing the execution of judgments* against the state."

d. In addition, it must be kept in mind that the period established in the judgment is only six months, after which the Court shall hear the matter, either to confirm the agreement of the parties (operative point 7) or to set the amount of compensation and manner of payment (operative point 6) on the motion of the Commission or the inter-

ested parties, as provided by Article 45(2) and 45(3) of the Rules cited above, according to which

"2. . . . the Court shall determine the period within which it may be presented *by a party or by the Commission.*

3. If the Court is informed that an agreement has been reached between *the victim of the violation and the State Party concerned,* it shall verify the equitable nature of such agreement."

SEE ALSO *Compensation for Victims of Human Rights Violations; Declaration of Basic Principles of Justice for Victims of Crime and Abuse of Power.*

HONDURAS: VELASQUEZ RODRIGUEZ CASE—COMPENSATORY DAMAGES.

In a second landmark judgment adopted unanimously by the INTER-AMERICAN COURT OF HUMAN RIGHTS in the case of Angel Manfredo Velasquez Rodríguez, a young Honduran student who was detained by government authorities and later disappeared, the court, on 21 July 1989, awarded compensatory damages to be paid by Honduras to the family of the victim and decided "that the Court shall supervise the indemnification ordered and shall close the file only when the compensation has been paid." This judgment represents the first time an international court of human rights, in effect, found a government guilty in the disappearance of a citizen.

The text of the court's judgment (*Annual Report of the Inter-American Court of Human Rights, 1989,* pp. 123–139) is as follows:

In the Velásquez Rodríguez case,
The Inter-American Court of Human Rights, composed of the following judges: Héctor Gros-Espiell, President; Héctor Fix-Zamudio, Vice-President; Rodolfo E. Piza E., Judge; Pedro Nikken, Judge; Rafael Nieto-Navia, Judge; [and] Rigoberto Espinal-Irías, Judge ad hoc.
Also present: Manuel E. Ventura-Robles, interim Secretary.

Pursuant to Article 63 (1) of the American Convention on Human Rights (hereinafter "the Convention" or "the American Convention"), Article 44 (1) of the Court's Rules, and in accord with the judgment on the merits of July 29, 1988, the Court enters the following judgment in the instant case brought by the Inter-American Commission on Human Rights against the State of Honduras.

1. The Inter-American Commission on Human Rights (hereinafter "the Commission") submitted this case to the Inter-American Court of Human Rights (hereinafter "the Court") on April 24, 1986. It originated in a complaint (No. 7920), against the State of Honduras (hereinafter "Honduras" or "the Government"), lodged with the Secretariat of the Commission on October 7, 1981.

2. In its Judgment on the Merits of July 29, 1988, the Court
"5. Decides that Honduras is hereby required to pay fair compensation to the next of kin of the victim.
"6. Decides that the form and amount of such compensation, failing agreement between Honduras and the Com-

mission within six months of the date of this judgment, shall be settle by the Court and, for that purpose, retains jurisdiction of the case." (Velásquez Rodríguez Case, Judgment of July 29, 1988. Series C No. 4, para. 194).

I

3. The Court has jurisdiction to order the payment of fair compensation to the injured party in the instant case. Honduras ratified the Convention on September 8, 1977, and recognized the contentious jurisdiction of the Court on September 9, 1981, by depositing the instrument referred to in Article 62 of the Convention. The Commission submitted the case to the Court pursuant to Articles 61 of the Convention and 50 (1) and 50 (2) of their Regulations, and the Court decided the case on July 29, 1988.

II

4. By Resolution of January 20, 1989, the Court decided:

1. To authorize the President, should the State and the Commission fail to submit an agreement within the allotted time period, to consult with the Permanent Commission of the Court, to initiate whatever studies and name whatever experts might be convenient, so the Court will have the elements of judgment necessary to set the means and quantity of compensation.

2. To authorize the President, should it be necessary, to obtain the opinion of the victim's family, the Inter-American Commission on Human Rights, and the Government of Honduras.

3. To authorize the President, should it be necessary, and following consultation with the Permanent Commission of the Court, to set a hearing in this matter.

5. On January 24, 1989, the Agent gave the Secretariat a copy of the agreement signed by the Government and the Commission on the previous day in Honduras, and according to which:

First: The Government of Honduras reiterates its decision to implement fully the judgment entered by the Illustrious Inter-American Court of Human Rights, in conformity with the terms of that judgment.

Second: The Government of Honduras and the Commission recognize that the only beneficiaries of the compensation fixed by the Court are the wife of Manfredo Velásquez, Mrs. Emma Guzmán Urbina, and the children of the marriage, Héctor Ricardo Velásquez Guzmán, Nadia Waleska Velásquez Guzmán, and Herling Lizett Velásquez Guzmán. The children shall be recognized as beneficiaries as soon as they fulfill the prerequisites of Honduran law to be considered the legal heirs of Manfredo Velásquez.

Third: The Government of Honduras believes that the best way to carry out the Court's "order to pay just compensation to the next of kin of the victim" is by granting them the most favorable benefits that Honduran legislation provides for Hondurans in the case of accidental death.

Fourth: The Commission recognizes the Government's offer as an important step toward the just compensation of the victim's family, but believes that it should also create for the benefit of the heirs a fund whose amount and form of payment should be determined by the Inter-American Court of Human Rights, taking into account the requirements of international law and those of Honduran legislation.

6. The attorneys recognized as counselors or advisers to the Commission (hereinafter "the attorneys") asked the Court for a public hearing to listen to a psychiatric report on the moral damages suffered by the victim's family and the testimony of one of the experts on the methods and conclusions of the report.

7. Citing paragraph 2 of the Resolution of January 20, 1989, Mrs. Emma Guzmán de Velásquez, the wife of Angel Manfredo Velásquez Rodríguez (also known as Manfredo Velásquez), submitted a pleading of February 26, 1989, in which she asked the Court to order the Government to comply with the following points:

(1) An end to forced disappearances in Honduras.

(2) An investigation of each of the 150 cases.

(3) A complete and truthful public report on what happened to the disappeared persons.

(4) The trial and punishment of those responsible for this practice.

(5) A public undertaking to respect human rights, especially the rights to life, liberty, and integrity of the person.

(6) A public act to honor and dignify the memory of the disappeared. A street, park, school, high school, or hospital could be named for the victims of disappearances.

(7) The demobilization and disbanding of the repressive bodies especially created to kidnap, torture, make disappear and assassinate.

(8) Guarantees to respect the work of humanitarian and family organizations and public recognition of their social function.

(9) An end to all forms of overt or indirect aggression or pressure against the family of the disappeared and public recognition of their honor.

(10) The establishment of a fund for the primary, secondary, and university education of the children of the disappeared.

(11) Guaranteed employment for the children of the disappeared who are of working age.

(12) The establishment of a retirement fund for the parents of the disappeared.

8. As required by the Resolution of January 20, 1989, the Commission submitted its opinion on March 1, 1989. It asserted that the just compensation to be paid by Honduras to the family of Manfredo Velásquez should include the following:

1. The adoption of measures by the State of Honduras which express its emphatic condemnation of the facts that gave rise to the Court's judgment. In particular, it should be established that the Government has an obligation to carry out an exhaustive investigation of the circumstances of the disappearance of Manfredo Velásquez and bring charges against anyone responsible for the disappearance.

2. The granting to the wife and children of Manfredo Velásquez of the following benefits:

(a) Payment to the wife of Manfredo Valásquez, Mrs. Emma Guzmán Urbina, of the highest pension recognized by Honduran law.

(b) Payment to the children of Manfredo Velásquez, Héctor Ricardo, Nadia Waleska and Herling Lizzett Velásquez Guzmán, of a pension or subsidy until they complete their university education, and

(c) Title to an adequate house, equivalent to the house of a middle class professional family.

3. Payment to the wife and children of Manfredo Velásquez of a cash amount corresponding to the resultant damages, loss of earnings, and emotional harm suffered by the family of Manfredo Velásquez, to be determined by that Illustrious Court based upon the expert opinion offered by the victim's family.

9. On March 10, 1989, the attorneys submitted a pleading in which they assert that, in conformity with Article 63 of the Convention, reparation should be moral as well as monetary.

The measures they request as moral reparation are the following:

—A public condemnation of the practice of involuntary disappearances carried out between 1981 and 1984;

—An expression of solidarity with the victims of that practice, including Manfredo Velásquez. Public homage to those victims by naming a street, thoroughfare, school or other public places after them;

—An exhaustive investigation of the phenomenon of involuntary disappearances in Honduras, with special attention to the fate of each of the disappeared. The resulting information should be made known to the family and the public;

—Prosecution and appropriate punishment of those responsible of inciting, planning, implementing or covering up disappearances, in accord with the laws and procedures of Honduras.

In their opinion, the cash indemnity paid to the family of Manfredo Velásquez should include the following: damages, two hundred thousand lempiras; loss of earnings, two million four hundred and twenty-two thousand four hundred and twenty lempiras; emotional damages, four million eight hundred and forty-five thousand lempiras; and punitive damages, two million four hundred and twenty-two thousand lempiras.

They especially request, that Emma Guzmán de Velásquez and her minor children, Héctor Ricardo, Nadia and Herling Velásquez Guzmán, they recognized as the beneficiaries, and that the Government of Honduras be ordered to adopt special legislation making that determination, in order to facilitate the payment of indemnity without the need for judicial proceedings for a declaration of absence, presumed death or declaration of heirship. For that purpose, we formally state on behalf of those persons that there are no other persons with a superior claim to inherit from Manfredo Velásquez.

Moreover, they ask the Court to establish deadlines within which the Government should make moral reparation, and to reserve the right to see that they are met. Regarding the monetary reparation, they ask the Court to set "a deadline of 90 days for the execution of the judgment, and that a lump sum payment be made prior to that date to Emma Guzmán de Velásquez."

10. On March 10, 1989, the Delegate of the Commission submitted a clinical report prepared by a team of psychiatrists on the state of health of the family of Manfredo Velásquez.

11. The Agent informed the Court on March 14, 1989, that in payment of the indemnity, his Government was willing to apply the Honduran law of the National Social Security Institute for Teachers (Instituto Nacional de Previsión del Magisterio), which it considered the most favorable law in this case because it establishes the right to payment of thirty-seven thousand and eighty lempiras in life insurance, and four thousand one hundred and twenty lempiras as a severance benefit. In addition, the Government offered a voluntary contribution toward the indemnity to bring the total to one hundred and fifty thousand lempiras.

12. On March 15, 1989, the Court held a public audience to hear the parties regarding the indemnity to be awarded. The following persons were present:

(a) in representation of the Government of Honduras, Ambassador Edgardo Sevilla Idiáquez, Agent.

(b) in representation of the Inter-American Commission on Human Rights, Dr. Edmundo Vargas Carreño, Delegate; Dr. Claudio Grossman, Adviser.

(c) Called by the Commission, Dr. Federico Allodi, a psychiatrist, testified to the emotional harm suffered by the family of the victim.

13. As instructed by its President, the Secretariat of the Court addressed the Government on April 3, 1989, to request the following information to be duly certified by the appropriate officials:

1. The dates of birth of Manfredo Velásquez Rodríguez and Saúl Godínez Cruz, with their civil status at the time of disappearance as established by Honduran law;

2. The position or positions they held and the salaries or other income they received, either from the government, government entities or private institutions, together with their social security status or equivalent, and their income tax statements, if any;

3. Academic or professional degrees or special qualifications relevant to their financial and social situation at the time of disappearance, and the title to any property in their name;

4. The names and status of their wives; and those of any concubines recognized in any official document; the age of the former and the latter at the time of the disappearances; any property in their name or other sources of income, and the conjugal property rights of the wives (joint property and others);

5. The names and civil status of their children, those of the marriage and any outside the marriage; their ages at the time of the disappearances; whether they were students, and whether any is physically or mentally handicapped;

6. The names and civil status of their parents, their ages at the time of the disappearances; whether they had or have property or income of their own, and whether they were or are dependents of the disappeared;

7. The names, civil status, ages and situation of any other possible claimants under Honduran law at the time of the disappearances, or any other person recognized as a dependent in social security documents, tax statements or other documents which might contain that information;

8. Whether the disappeared had life insurance or other personal insurance, in what amount, the period of coverage, and the names of the beneficiaries;

9. Mortuary tables for men and women and commutation schedules (the latter are used for future tax discounts in return for prompt payment) effective in Honduras at the time of the disappearances;

10. Certified copies of Honduran legislation regarding: a) legal heirs as defined by civil and labor law; b) spousal property rights (joint property or other); c) beneficiaries with rights to support payments, showing the criteria used to determine support; d) beneficiaries of any government pensions based upon death or permanent disability; e) Honduran legislative and jurisprudential criteria for indemnification for death, accidental or nonaccidental.

14. On April 26, 1989, the Government submitted its response to the Commission's submission of March 1, 1989 (supra 8). The pleading also refers to matters that, in its opinion, should be taken into account in the indemnification of the family of Manfredo Velásquez. Regarding measures to express its condemnation of the facts that gave rise to the judgment and its obligation to investigate the disap-

pearance of Manfredo Velásquez and prosecute those responsible, the Government believes the Court's judgment on July 29, 1988, "is very clear and precise regarding the obligation of Honduras to pay damages, which is to pay *just compensation to the family of the victim, and nothing more*" (underlined in the original). Insofar as the benefits the Commission believes should be paid to the wife of Manfredo Velásquez, the Government believes that such payment "is only admissible insofar as whatever may be provided for by the system to which Mr. VELASQUEZ RODRÍGUEZ may have been affiliated." It asserts that damages, loss of earnings, and emotional harm are inadmissible because their purpose "is not merely to compensate the VELASQUEZ RODRÍGUEZ family but . . . to pay the expenses of the intense media campaign waged against Honduras within and without the country by national and foreign associations, and to pay the fees of lawyers and other professionals who cooperated with the Commission in this case."

15. In reply to point 2 of the Court's communication of April 3, 1989 (supra 13), the Government submitted on May 19, 1989, various documents and resolutions containing the information requested.

16. In response to points 2 and 9, the Government submitted the following information on May 26, 1989:

(a) Certification by the Secretary of the General Tax Office (Dirección General de Tributación) according to which Mssrs. MANFREDO VELASQUEZ RODRÍGUEZ and SAUL GODINEZ CRUZ did not file tax returns in 1979, 1980 and 1981.

(b) Mortuary Tables CSO 1958 commutation values at 7%, used by the Superintendent of Banks and Insurance (Superintendencia de Bancos y Seguros).

17. On that same date, in compliance with point 10, the Government submitted the following documentation:

1. Provisions on inheritance upon death and inter vivos gifts, contained in Book III of the 1906 Civil Code of Honduras.

2. Regulatory provisions of the Social Security Law applicable in Honduras when an insured person dies (Resolution No. 193, December 17, 1971).

3. Provisions of the Family Code: Duties and Rights arising from Marriage, Informal Unions, Economic Relationship, Family Patrimony, Paternity and Parent-Child Relationship (Decree No. 76–84).

4. Provisions of the Law of Military Social Security (Decree No. 905).

5. Retirement Law for the Judicial Branch (Decree No. 114 of the National Congress, May 5, 1954).

6. Law of Retirement and Pensions for Employees and Officials of the Executive Branch.

7. Law of the National Institute of Social Security for Teachers.

18. In reference to information requested but not yet submitted, the Government stated on June 13, 1989 that it

". . . has sent notes to various institutions and only a few have replied; nevertheless, despite the difficulties, the documents we have requested will be sent opportunely as they arrive.

"Likewise, I also inform you that in regard to numbers 4, 5, and 6 of the note of the Honorable Court, my Government believes it will be impossible to send certain documents which are very personal, and, therefore, suggests that this information should be presented by the Inter-American Commission or by the legal representatives of the plaintiffs against the State of Honduras."

19. *Amici curiae* pleadings were submitted by the Central American Association of Relatives of the Detained-Disappeared (Asociación Centroamericana de Familiares de Detenidos-Desaparecidos) and the following twelve jurists: Jean-Denis Archambault, Alejandro Artucio, Alfredo Etcheberry, Gustavo Gallón Giraldo, Diego García Sayán, Alejandro M. Garro, Robert K. Goldman, Jorge Mera, Denis Racicot, Joaquín Ruiz Giménez, Arturo Valencia Zea and Eugenio Raúl Zaffaroni.

III

20. The first question the Court must resolve is related to the implementation of resolutory point number 6 of the judgment on the merits, according to which it gave Honduras and the Commission six months from the date of the judgment of July 29, 1988, to reach an agreement on the form and amount of just compensation to be paid to the family of Manfredo Velásquez (*Velásquez Rodríguez Case, supra 2*).

21. In its pleading of March 1, 1989, the Commission reported on its attempts to reach an agreement with the Government. According to the Commission, only at the end of the six month period was it possible to meet in the city of Tegucigalpa with a Commission named by the President of the Republic of Honduras "to negotiate and determine the amount and form of payment of the compensation awarded in the Inter-American Court's judgment of July 29, 1988."

22. According to the record of that meeting (*supra 5*), the parties agreed only on the recognition of the beneficiaries of the compensation. The remaining points are simple declarations which establish no criteria for fixing the amount of the compensation and, even less, for payment. Therefore, resolutory point number 6 of the judgment on the merits of July 29, 1988, was not carried out.

IV

23. The written and oral arguments made to the Court show substantial differences of opinion insofar as the scope, bases and amount of the compensation. Some arguments refer to the need to rely upon the internal law of Honduras, or part of it, in determining or paying the indemnity.

24. Because of those disagreements and in order to implement the judgment on the merits of July 29, 1988, the Court must now define the scope and content of the just compensation to be paid by the Government to the family of Manfredo Velásquez.

25. It is a principle of international law, which jurisprudence has considered "even a general concept of law," that every violation of an international obligation which results in harm creates a duty to make adequate reparation. Compensation, on the other hand, is the most usual way of doing so (*Factory at Chorzów*, Jurisdiction, Judgment No. 8, 1927, P.C.I.J., Series A, No. 9, p. 21, and *Factory at Chorzów*, Merits, Judgment No. 13, 1928, P.C.I.J., Series A, No. 17, p. 29; *Reparation for Injuries Suffered in the Service of the United Nations*, Advisory Opinion, I.C.J. Reports 1949, p. 184).

26. Reparation of harm brought about by the violation of an international obligation consists in full restitution (restitutio in integrum), which includes the restoration of the prior situation, the reparation of the consequences of the violation, and indemnification for patrimonial and nonpatrimonial damages, including emotional harm.

27. As to emotional harm, the Court holds that indemnity may be awarded under international law and, in

particular, in the case of human rights violations. Indemnification must be based upon the principles of equity.

28. Indemnification for human rights violations is supported by international instruments of a universal and regional character. The Human Rights Committee, created by the International Covenant of Civil and Political Rights of the United Nations, has repeatedly called for, based on the Optional Protocol, indemnification for the violation of human rights recognized in the Covenant (see, for example, communications 4/1977; 6/1977; 11/1977; 138/1983; 147/1983; 132/1982; 161/1983; 188/1984; 194/1985; etc., Reports of the Human Rights Committee, United Nations). The European Court of Human Rights has reached the same conclusion based upon Article 50 of the Convention for the Protection of Human Rights and Fundamental Freedoms.

29. Article 63 (1) of the American Convention provides as follows:

1. If the Court finds that there has been a violation of a right or freedom protected by this Convention, the Court shall rule that the injured party be ensured the enjoyment of his right or freedom that was violated. It shall also rule, if appropriate, that the consequences of the measure or situation that constituted the breach of such right or freedom be remedied and that fair compensation be paid to the injured party.

30. This article does not refer to or limit the ability to ensure the effectiveness of the means of reparation available under the internal law of the State Party responsible for the violation, so it is not limited by the defects, imperfections or deficiencies of national law, but functions independently of it.

31. This implies that, in order to fix the corresponding indemnity, the Court must rely upon the American Convention and the applicable principles of international law.

V

32. The Commission and the attorneys maintain that, in implementing the judgment, the Court should order the Government to take some measures, such as the investigation of the facts related to the involuntary disappearance of Manfredo Velásquez; the punishment of those responsible; a public statement condemning that practice; the revindication of the victim, and other similar measures.

33. Measures of this type would constitute a part of the reparation of the consequences of the violation of rights or freedoms and not a part of the indemnity, in accordance with Article 63 (1) of the Convention.

34. However, in its judgment on the merits (*Velásquez Rodríguez Case, supra* 2, para. 181), the Court has already pointed out the Government's continuing duty to investigate so long as the fate of a disappeared person is known (supra 32). The duty to investigate is in addition to the duties to prevent involuntary disappearances and to punish those directly responsible (*Velásquez Rodríguez Case, supra* 2, para. 174).

35. Although these obligations were not expressly incorporated into the resolutory part of the judgment on the merits, it is a principle of procedural law that the bases of a judicial decision are a part of the same. Consequently, the Court declares that those obligations on the part of Honduras continue until they are fully carried out.

36. Otherwise, the Court understands that the judgment on the merits of July 29, 1988, is in itself a type of reparation and moral satisfaction of significance and importance for the families of the victims.

37. The attorneys also request the payment of punitive damages as part of the indemnity, because this case involved extremely serious violations of human rights.

38. The expression "fair compensation," used in Article 63 (1) of the Convention to refer to a part of the reparation and to the "injured party," is compensatory and not punitive. Although some domestic courts, particularly the Anglo-American, award damages in amounts meant to deter or to serve as an example, this principle is not applicable in international law at this time.

39. Because of the foregoing, the Court believes, then, that the fair compensation, described as "compensatory" in the judgment on the merits of July 29, 1988, includes reparation to the family of the victim of the material and moral damages they suffered because of the involuntary disappearance of Manfredo Velásquez.

VI

40. Having defined the scope and limitations of the fair compensation referred to in resolutory point number 6 of the judgment on the merits, the Court now turns to the bases for the payment of the same.

41. In this regard, the attorneys ask for compensation for patrimonial damages within the concept of damages and include in the latter the expenses of the family related to the investigation of the whereabouts of Manfredo Velásquez.

42. The Court cannot grant that request in the present case. Though it is theoretically correct that those expenses come within the definition of damages, they cannot be awarded in the instant case because they were not plead or proven up opportunely. No estimate or proof of expenses related to the investigation of the whereabouts of the victim was submitted during the trial. Likewise, with regard to litigation expenses in bringing the matter before the Court, the judgment on the merits already denied an award of costs because there was no pleading to support the request (Velásquez Rodríguez Case, supra 2, para. 193).

43. The Government argues that the compensation should be on the basis of the most favorable treatment possible for the family of Manfredo Velásquez under Honduran law, which is that provided by the Law of the National Institute of Social Security for Teachers in the case of accidental death. According to the Government, the family would be entitled to a total of forty-one thousand two hundred lempiras, to which it would contribute an additional amount to bring the compensation to one hundred and fifty thousand lempiras.

44. The Commission does not propose an amount, but rather asserts that the compensation should include two elements: (a) the greatest benefits that Honduran legislation allows nationals in cases of this type and which, according to the Commission, are those granted by the Institute of Military Pensions and (b) a cash amount which should be set according to what is provided for by Honduran and international law.

45. The attorneys believe that the basis should be the loss of earnings, calculated according to the income that Manfredo Velásquez received at the time of his kidnapping, at the age of 35, his studies toward a degree as an economist, which would have allowed him to work as a professional, and the possible promotions, Christmas bonuses, allowances and other benefits he would have been entitled

to at retirement. They calculate an amount which in thirty years would be one million six hundred and fifty-one thousand six hundred and fifty lempiras. They add to that the retirement benefits for ten years, according to life expectancy in Honduras for a person of that social class, calculated at seven hundred and seventy thousand seven hundred and sixty lempiras, which gives a total amount of two million four hundred and twenty-two thousand four hundred and twenty lempiras.

46. The Court notes that the disappearance of Manfredo Velásquez cannot be considered an accidental death for the purposes of compensation, given that it is the result of serious acts imputable to Honduras. The amount of compensation cannot, therefore, be based upon guidelines such as life insurance, but must be calculated as a loss of earnings based upon the income the victim would have received up to the time of his possible natural death. In that sense, one can take as a point of departure the salary that, according to the certification of the Honduran Vice-Minister of Planning on October 19, 1988, Manfredo Velásquez was receiving at the time of his disappearance (1,030 lempiras per month) and calculate the amount he would have received at the time of his obligatory retirement at the age of sixty, as provided by Article 69 of the Law of the National Institute of Social Security for Teachers and which the Government itself considers the most favorable. At retirement, he would have been entitled to a pension until his death.

47. However, the calculation of the loss of earnings must consider two distinct situations. When the beneficiary of the indemnity is a victim who is totally and permanently disabled, the compensation should include all he failed to receive, together with appropriate adjustments based upon his probable life expectancy. In that circumstance, the only income for the victim is what he would have received, but will not receive as earnings.

48. If the beneficiaries of the compensation are the family members, the situation is another. In principle, the family has an actual or future possibility of working or receiving income on their own. The children, who should be guaranteed the possibility of an education which might extend to the age of twenty five, could, for example, begin to work at that time. It is not correct, then, in these cases, to adhere to rigid criteria, more appropriate to the situation described in the above paragraph, but rather to arrive at a prudent estimate of the damages, given the circumstances of each case.

49. Based upon a prudent estimate of the possible income of the victim for the rest of his probable life and on the fact that, in this case, the compensation is for the exclusive benefit of the family of Manfredo Velásquez identified at trial, the Court sets the loss of earnings in the amount of five hundred thousand lempiras to be paid to the wife and to the children of Manfredo Velásquez as set out below.

50. The Court must now consider the question of the indemnification of the moral damages (supra 27), which is primarily the result of the psychological impact suffered by the family of Manfredo Velásquez because of the violation of the rights and freedoms guaranteed by the American Convention, especially by the dramatic characteristics of the involuntary disappearance of persons.

51. The moral damages are demonstrated by expert documentary evidence and the testimony of Dr. Federico Allodi (supra 12), psychiatrist and Professor of Psychology at the University of Toronto, Canada. According to his testimony, the above doctor examined the wife of Manfredo Velásquez, Mrs. Emma Guzmán Urbina de Velásquez and

his children, Héctor Ricardo, Herling Lizzett and Nadia Waleska Velásquez. According to those examinations, they had symptoms of fright, anguish, depression and withdrawal, all because of the disappearance of the head of the family. The Government could not disprove the existence of psychological problems that affect the family of the victim. The Court finds that the disappearance of Manfredo Velásquez produced harmful psychological impacts among his immediate family which should be indemnified as moral damages.

52. The Court believes the Government should pay compensation for moral damages in the amount of two hundred and fifty thousand lempiras, to be paid to the wife and children of Manfredo Velásquez as specified below.

VII

53. With regard to entitlement to receive the compensation, the representative of the Government and of the Commission, in the document they signed on January 23, 1989, recognized as the sole beneficiaries of that compensation the wife of Manfredo Velásquez, Mrs. Emma Guzmán Urbina and the children of that marriage, Héctor Ricardo, Nadia Waleska and Herling Lizzett Velásquez Guzmán. They added that their right could only be enforced once they had fulfilled the requirements of Honduran law to be recognized as heirs of the victim.

54. As previously stated, the obligation to indemnify is not derived from internal law, but from violation of the American Convention. It is the result of an international obligation. To demand indemnification, the family members of Manfredo Velásquez need only show their family relationship. They are not required to follow the procedure of Honduran inheritance law.

55. At the hearing of October 2, 1987, Zenaida Velásquez Rodríguez, referred to four children of her brother, Manfredo Velásquez, but in the document signed by the Commission and the Government on January 23, 1989, only three children are mentioned. Nor was any proof of the existence of a fourth child found in the Government's reply to point 5 of the request made by the Secretariat of the Court on April 3, 1989 (supra 13). Should there be a fourth child, he would be entitled to a proportionate share of the indemnity the Court has awarded to the children of the victim.

VIII

56. The Court now determines how the Government is to pay compensation to the family of Manfredo Velásquez.

57. Payment of the seven hundred and fifty thousand lempiras awarded by the Court must be carried out within ninety days from the date of notification of the judgment, free from any tax that might eventually be considered applicable. Nevertheless, the Government may pay in six equal monthly installments, the first being payable within ninety days and the reminder in successive months. In this case, the balance shall be incremented by the appropriate interest, which shall be at the interest rates current at that moment in Honduras.

58. One-fourth of the indemnity is awarded to the wife who shall receive that sum directly. The remaining three-fourths shall be distributed among the children. With the funds from the award to the children, a trust fund shall be set up in the Central Bank of Honduras under the most favorable conditions permitted by Honduran banking practice. The children shall receive monthly payments from this

trust fund, and at the age of twenty-five shall receive their proportionate part.

59. The Court shall supervise the implementation of the compensatory damages at all of its stages. The case shall be closed when the Government has fully complied with the instant judgment.

IX

60. THEREFORE,
THE COURT,
Unanimously

1. Awards seven hundred and fifty thousand lempiras in compensatory damages to be paid to the family of Angel Manfredo Velásquez Rodríguez by the State of Honduras.
Unanimously

2. Decides that the amount of the award corresponding to the wife of Angel Manfredo Velásquez Rodríguez shall be one hundred and eighty-seven thousand five hundred lempiras.
Unanimously

3. Decides that the amount of the award corresponding to the children of Angel Manfredo Velásquez Rodríguez shall be five hundred and sixty two thousand five hundred lempiras.
Unanimously

4. Orders that the form and means of payment of the indemnity shall be those specified in paragraphs 57 and 58 of this judgment.
Unanimously

5. Decides that the Court shall supervise the indemnification ordered and shall close the file only when the compensation has been paid.

Done in Spanish and in English, the Spanish text being authentic, at the seat of the Court in San José, Costa Rica, this twenty-first day of July, 1989.

HOSTAGES. Acts of hostage-taking and abduction have been recognized by the competent international organs as grave violations of human rights, exposing the hostages to privation, hardship, anguish, and danger to life and health. They are contrary to the principles set out in the UNIVERSAL DECLARATION OF HUMAN RIGHTS, which proclaims the right to life, liberty, and security of person; freedom from torture and other degrading treatment; freedom of movement; and protection against arbitrary detention. They are prohibited by the INTERNATIONAL CONVENTION AGAINST THE TAKING OF HOSTAGES, adopted and opened for ratification and accession by the UN General Assembly in 1979 (resolution 34/146, annex), which recognizes the taking of hostages as an offence of grave concern to the international community and provides for its punishment by the State having jurisdiction over that offence. Recently such acts were unequivocally condemned in a resolution adopted unanimously by the UN Security Council (resolution 579 [1985]), in which the council called for the immediate safe release of all hostages and abducted persons, wherever and by whomever they are being held, and affirmed the obligation of all States in whose territory hostages or abducted persons are held urgently to take all appropriate measures to secure their safe release and to prevent the commission of acts of hostage-taking and abduction in the future. In this connection the council called for the further development of international cooperation among States in devising and adopting effective measures which are in accordance with the rules of international law to facilitate the prevention, prosecution, and punishment of all acts of hostage-taking and abduction as manifestations of international terrorism.

The UN Commission on Human Rights and the Sub-Commission on Prevention of Discrimination and Protection of Minorities have repeatedly pointed out that the taking of hostages constitutes a grave violation of human rights. At its 1989 session, the commission, alarmed by the number of cases of hostage-taking throughout the world, expressed its distress at these unacceptable displays of violence towards innocent victims and at the anxiety and suffering of the families concerned; strongly condemned the taking of any person hostage, whoever is responsible and whatever the circumstances, whether or not the hostage is chosen at random and whatever his nationality; censured the actions of all persons responsible for taking hostages, whatever their motives, and demanded that they should immediately release those they are holding; and called upon States to take any measures necessary to prevent and punish the taking of hostages and to put an immediate end to cases of abduction and unlawful restraint on their territory.

Likewise, the Sub-Commission on Prevention of Discrimination and Protection of Minorities, on 1 September 1989, condemned (resolution 1989/26) hostage-taking and the torture and murder which frequently accompany such practices; condemned all who actively participate in or implicitly tolerate such activities by failing to take the appropriate corrective steps; specifically condemned the abduction and murder of United Nations personnel as exemplified by the brutal murder of the Commander of the United Nations Truce Supervision Organization in Lebanon, Lt. Col. William R. Higgins; and expressed its deepest sympathy and grief to the families of United Nations personnel whose members have been abducted and/or murdered.

The sub-commission called upon all States to take steps to prevent hostage-taking and bring to trial, in conformity with international standards, any who may participate in such an undertaking; and called upon all governments to become parties to the International Convention Against the Taking of Hostages and to observe faithfully its terms, in particular, the obligation to prosecute or extradite hostage-takers without exception. Further, it urged the Secretary-General to take all possible measures to stop hostage-taking and to seek the release of all hostages being unlawfully detained and to provide the sub-commission with a complete list of all United Nations personnel held in captivity with all available information concerning the names and whereabouts of the captors, if known.

SEE ALSO Arrest, Detention, and Abduction of International Civil Servants; Detention: UN Staff Members.

HOUSING. Having proclaimed the year 1987 International Year of Shelter for the Homeless, the UN General Assembly in 1986 expressed its deep concern (resolution 41/146) that millions of people do not enjoy the right to adequate housing and reiterated the need to take, at the national and international levels, measures for promoting the right of all persons to an adequate standard of living for themselves and their families, including adequate housing. It requested the Commission on Human Rights and the Economic and Social Council to give special attention to the question of the realization of the right to adequate housing during the International Year of Shelter for the Homeless and requested the Secretary-General to pay appropriate attention to that question in providing information to the Assembly on the results of the international year.

The COMMISSION ON HUMAN RIGHTS at its 1988 session decided (resolution 1988/24) to keep the question of the right to adequate housing under periodic review in accordance with the Assembly's request. The Economic and Social Council, on 27 May 1988, noted (resolution 1988/43) the measures and action taken and the renewed commitments made during the International Year of Shelter for the Homeless by member States, specialized agencies, and intergovernmental and non-governmental organizations to advance the realization of the right to adequate housing and recognized the importance of sustaining the momentum generated by the international year. It expressed its concern that millions of people do not enjoy the right to adequate housing and called upon all states and international organizations concerned to pay special attention to the realization of that right in carrying out measures to develop national shelter strategies and settlement improvement programs within the framework of the "Global Strategy for Shelter to the Year 2000." Further, it requested the Secretary-General to submit a report on the social aspects of the situation of homeless people to the General Assembly at its 1990 session.

A written statement on the right to housing (UN Doc. E/CN.4/Sub.2/1988/NGO11) was circulated to the SUB-COMMISSION ON PREVENTION OF DISCRIMINATION AND PROTECTION OF MINORITIES at its session in August 1988, at the request of Habitat International Coalition, an alliance of more than 200 non-governmental organizations and scientific and educational institutions organized with a view to obtaining recognition and implementation of the right of everyone to secure a place in which to live in dignity and peace. The coalition called upon the sub-commission to pay special attention, in the study it plans to make on the realization of economic, social and cultural rights, to the need to elaborate the right to adequate housing into implementable legal provisions and specific obligations of governments. The statement added that (para. 4–7):

The right to housing is a complex one. It needs to be analysed and disaggregated into a range of different elements such as the right to land; security of tenure; access to infrastructure and services; building codes; credit facilities; the right to form associations and to participate in the planning, construction and maintenance of houses and neighbourhoods; etc. This will require the adaptation of existing and the drafting of new legal instruments, both at the national and international level.

In this connection, Habitat International Coalition is of the opinion that the drafting of international rules of conduct concerning evictions is a subject of special urgency. It feels impelled to make this observation because of the cases of forced mass evictions which continue to occur in several countries.

HIC is aware of the fact that the Sub-Committee is already dealing with evictions in the context of its activities for the prevention of discrimination and when evictions take place in occupied territories and HIC hopes that the Sub-Commission will continue and intensify its action against evictions in all its manifestations.

Habitat International Coalition would like to inform the Sub-Commission that it has decided to launch an international campaign against forced evictions. It has also started to draft an international Charter of Housing Rights, which will be the subject of a workshop it intends to hold in Mexico on 14, 15 and 16 January 1989. In these and other activities Habitat International Coalition would be glad to co-operate closely with the Sub-Commission.

SEE ALSO Declaration of the UN Conference on Human Environment; Homelessness; Shelter; Vancouver Declaration on Human Settlements.

HUMAN RIGHTS: APPROACH TO FUTURE WORK. Each year, the UN General Assembly and Commission on Human Rights intensively review recent activities within the United Nations system aimed at the promotion and protection of human rights and fundamental freedoms and consider the approach to be taken to future work in this field.

The operative part of General Assembly resolution 44/63, entitled "Alternative Approaches and Ways and Means within the United Nations System for Improving the Effective Enjoyment of Human Rights and Fundamental Freedoms," adopted on 8 December 1989, provides an indication of the approach to future work recommended to organs and agencies within the United Nations system. It reads:

The General Assembly,

1. Reiterates its request that the Commission on Human Rights continue its current work on overall analysis with a view to further promoting and strengthening human rights and fundamental freedoms, including the question of the programme and working methods of the Commission, and on the overall analysis of the alternative approaches and ways and means for improving the effective enjoyment of human rights and fundamental freedoms, in accordance with the provisions and concepts of General Assembly resolution 32/130 and other relevant texts;

2. Affirms that a primary aim of international co-operation in the field of human rights is a life of freedom, dignity and peace for all peoples and for every human being, that all human rights and fundamental freedoms are indivisible and interrelated and that the promotion and protection of one category of rights should never exempt or excuse States from promoting and protecting the others;

3. Reaffirms that equal attention and urgent consideration should be given to the implementation, promotion and protection of civil and political rights and of economic, social and cultural rights;

4. Reaffirms that it is of paramount importance for the promotion of human rights and fundamental freedoms that Member States should assume specific obligations by acceding to or ratifying international instruments in this field, and, consequently, that the work within the United Nations system of setting standards in the field of human rights and universal acceptance and implementation of the relevant international instruments should be encouraged;

5. Reiterates once again that the international community should accord, or continue to accord, priority to the search for solutions to mass and flagrant violations of human rights of peoples and individuals affected by situations such as those mentioned in paragraph 1 (e) of General Assembly resolution 32/130, paying due attention also to other situations of violations of human rights;

6. Reaffirms its responsibility for achieving international co-operation in promoting and encouraging respect for human rights and fundamental freedoms for all, and expresses its concern at serious violations of human rights, in particular mass and flagrant violations of these rights, wherever they occur;

7. Expresses concern at the present situation as regards the achievement of the objectives and goals for the establishment of the new international economic order, and at its adverse effects on the full realization of human rights, in particular the right to development;

8. Reaffirms that the right to development is an inalienable human right;

9. Reaffirms also that international peace and security are essential elements for achieving full realization of the right to development;

10. Recognizes that all human rights and fundamental freedoms are indivisible and interdependent;

11. Considers that all Member States must promote inter-national co-operation on the basis of respect for the independence, sovereignty and territorial integrity of each State, including the right of every people to choose freely its own socio-economic and political system, with a view to solving international economic, social and humanitarian problems;

12. Expresses concern at the disparity existing between established norms and principles and the actual situation of all human rights and fundamental freedoms in the world;

13. Urges all States to co-operate with the Commission on Human Rights in the promotion and protection of human rights and fundamental freedoms;

14. Reiterates the need to create, at the national and international levels, conditions for the full promotion and protection of the human rights of individuals and peoples;

15. Reaffirms once again that, in order to facilitate the full enjoyment of all human rights without diminishing personal dignity, it is necessary to promote the rights to education, work, health and proper nourishment through the adoption of measures at the national level, including those that provide for the right of workers to participate in management, as well as the adoption of measures at the international level, including the establishment of the new international economic order;

16. Decides that the approach to future work within the United Nations system on human rights matters should also take into account the content of the Declaration on the Right to Development and the need for the implementation thereof;

17. Decides to include in the provisional agenda of its forty-fifth session the item entitled "Alternative approaches and ways and means within the United Nations system for improving the effective enjoyment of human rights and fundamental freedoms".

HUMAN RIGHTS: PROMOTION AND PROTECTION.

On 11 March 1982, the UN COMMISSION ON HUMAN RIGHTS restated (resolution 1982/30) a view which it had adopted on earlier occasions—that individuals, groups, and organs of society have a right and a responsibility to promote and protect the rights recognized in the UNIVERSAL DECLARATION OF HUMAN RIGHTS, the International Covenants on Human Rights, and all other relevant international instruments, without prejudice to articles 29 and 30 of the Universal Declaration. In this connection, the commission emphasized that, in the exercise of these rights and freedoms, the individual shall be subject only to such limitations as are determined in the UNITED NATIONS CHARTER, the Universal Declaration, and other relevant instruments; and that the imposition of other limitations or the persecution or punishment of anyone exercising, individually or collectively, his universally recognized human rights and fundamental freedoms is at variance with the obligations of States under these instruments to work for the full and effective enjoyment of those rights and freedoms.

The commission called upon the Secretary-General

761

to prepare, for consideration by the SUB-COMMISSION ON PREVENTION OF DISCRIMINATION AND PROTECTION OF MINORITIES, elements for a draft body of principles on the right and responsibility of individuals, groups, and organs of society to promote and protect human rights and fundamental freedoms; and requested the sub-commission to prepare, taking these elements into account, a report containing a draft of such a body of principles.

The sub-commission received and noted, at its 1982 session, the Secretary-General's report (UN Doc. E/CN.4/Sub.2/1982/12) setting out elements for a draft body of principles as requested. Recalling that the proposal for such a body of principles had initially been put forward in the study prepared by one of its members, Mrs. Erica-Irene A. Daes (Greece), entitled *Study of the Individual's Duties to the Community and the Limitations on Human Rights and Freedoms under Article 29 of the Universal Declaration of Human Rights—A Contribution to the Freedom of the Individual under Law* (United Nations publication, Sales. No. E.82.XIV.1), the sub-commission requested Mrs. Daes (resolution 1982/24) to prepare the draft principles. It received her report (UN Doc. E/CN.4/Sub.2/1985/30) at its 1985 session and referred it (resolution 1985/30) and other relevant documentation to the Commission on Human Rights for consideration by an open-ended working group which the commission had already established for the purpose (decision 1985/112).

The working group met before or during the 1986, 1987, 1988, and 1989 sessions of the commission but was not able to complete the preparation of the proposed declaration. The commission accordingly decided (resolution 1989/60) to consider the question further at its 1990 and future sessions.

SEE ALSO *Working Group on a Draft Declaration on the Right and Responsibility to Promote and Protect Human Rights.*

HUMAN RIGHTS: PUBLICITY.

The following general comment on article 2 of the INTERNATIONAL COVENANT ON CIVIL AND POLITICAL RIGHTS was adopted by the UN HUMAN RIGHTS COMMITTEE on 28 July 1981:

The Committee notes that article 2 of the Covenant generally leaves it to the States parties concerned to choose their method of implementation in their territories within the framework set out in that article. It recognizes, in particular, that the implementation does not depend solely on constitutional or legislative enactments, which in themselves are often not *per se* sufficient. The Committee considers it necessary to draw the attention of States parties to the fact that the obligation under the Covenant is not confined to the respect of human rights, but that States parties have also undertaken to ensure the enjoyment of these rights to all individuals under their jurisdiction. This aspect calls for specific activities by the States parties to enable individuals to enjoy their rights. This is obvious in a number of articles, but in principle this undertaking relates to all rights set forth in the Covenant.

In this connexion, it is very important that individuals should know what their rights under the Covenant (and the Optional Protocol, as the case may be) are and also that all administrative and judicial authorities should be aware of the obligations which the State party has assumed under the Covenant. To this end, the Covenant should be publicized in all official languages of the State and steps should be taken to familiarize the authorities concerned with its contents as part of their training. It is desirable also to give publicity to the State party's co-operation with the Committee.

HUMAN RIGHTS: TEACHING.

At its 1971 session, the UN COMMISSION ON HUMAN RIGHTS examined a report prepared by the UNITED NATIONS EDUCATIONAL, SCIENTIFIC AND CULTURAL ORGANIZATION (UN Doc. E/CN.4/1027) which drew attention to the difficulties encountered by educators in the teaching of human rights in schools and universities, and requested UNESCO (resolution 11 C [XXVII]) "to consider the desirability of envisaging the systematic study and the development of an independent scientific discipline of human rights, taking into account the principal legal systems of the world with a view to facilitating the understanding, comprehension, study and teaching of human rights at the university level, and subsequently at other educational levels. . . ." The UNESCO General Conference later invited the Director-General to carry out a feasibility study on the "creation of an international clearing-house for the teaching of human rights and for exchange of information on the curricula and on existing courses at all levels, as well as on specialized research."

Generally speaking, according to a report of the Director-General transmitted to the UN General Assembly in November 1988 (UN Doc. A/43/96), UNESCO's action with regard to human rights education has developed on the following five lines:

(a) cooperation with institutions specializing in human rights teaching, including universities;

(b) preparation of educational and teaching materials;

(c) development of human rights teaching methods;

(d) training at the primary, secondary, and higher levels, including teacher training; and

(e) knowledge of the basic texts on the protection and promotion of human rights, notably the INTERNATIONAL BILL OF HUMAN RIGHTS.

In the report (para. 7; 12–14), the Director-General pointed out that:

These five lines of approach are interconnected in many ways and cannot be completely dissociated in practice. They should, however, be distinguished according to the main objective sought by a given activity. The experience of co-operating with bodies specializing in human rights teaching, and with universities, shows that as an agency for international intellectual co-operation, UNESCO has a very important role to play in diversifying educational projects and in promoting exchanges of experience, both successful and unsuccessful. . . .

While at the pre-school and primary levels classroom life and relations within the school are vital for human rights teaching, at the level of secondary education equally great importance is given to knowledge of international human rights instruments and the 1974 UNESCO Recommendation on Education for International Understanding, Co-operation and Peace and Education relating to Human Rights and Fundamental Freedoms.

It is obvious that teacher-training institutions have a particularly vital role to play in human rights education. Admittedly in certain cases this education is part of their curricula. However, many examples attest that it is often on the initiative of a few teachers or a school principal that this subject is included in the curriculum of a teacher-training school. In this connection it should be noted that the International Days proclaimed by the United Nations General Assembly (for example, United Nations Day, Human Rights Day or the International Day of Peace) all provide opportunities for a school to launch educational activities concerning human rights.

Generally speaking, while it is recognized that in human rights teaching there is a conceptual aspect of the acquisition of knowledge (definitions, ideas and theories), it is nevertheless a fact that in this field emphasis should be placed on forming the intellectual and moral aptitudes required for observance of human rights. Care should therefore be taken not to overlook the aspect of the transmission of values by teachers. UNESCO has accordingly encouraged exchanges of teachers from different cultures and countries in order to make them aware of the importance of culture in education and to strengthen their vigilance with regard to prejudice, intolerance and racism so that they in turn can communicate their own experience of respect for other peoples. A workshop on teacher training for combating prejudice, intolerance and racism in the field of education was held in Chad in 1985. A practical guide for secondary school teachers, containing suggestions on ways of combating all forms of discrimination, was prepared for publication in 1989. In parallel with these exchanges, UNESCO encourages Member States to revise their textbooks so as to eliminate any references of a discriminatory nature.

The feasibility study authorized by the UNESCO General Conference was entrusted in 1985 to the Netherlands Institute of Human Rights in Utrecht. Its purpose is to examine the different possibilities for coordinating the dissemination and circulation of human rights information and documentation on the basis of knowledge gained by efforts in this field by other intergovernmental and non-governmental organizations.

UNESCO has organized two major international conferences on the teaching of human rights: the International Congress on the Teaching of Human Rights, held at Vienna in 1978, and the International Congress on Human Rights Teaching, Information and Documentation, held at Malta in 1987. Both were preceded by a number of regional meetings, and both made assessments of the progress achieved in the field. Recommendations of the congresses, and of the regional preparatory meetings, were summed up as follows in the Director-General's report (para. 62–89):

Universality of Human Rights. The universality of the human rights proclaimed by the Universal Declaration of Human Rights and recognized by the International Covenants of 1966 is reiterated. UNESCO's action should be placed within this framework. However, as regards international co-operation, the methodological approach to human rights education and teaching and the priorities given to research, information and documentation may vary from one region to another.

All of UNESCO's programme activities in the field of human rights should continue to draw on the guiding principles affirmed in resolution 34/46 of 23 November 1979, in which the United Nations General Assembly reaffirmed its conviction that all human rights are indivisible and interdependent, and that equal attention should be given to the implementation, promotion and protection of both civil and political, and economic, social and cultural rights.

Human Rights Education. Instruction in human rights should be given at all levels and in all forms of education, integrated into the different disciplines and reflected in the curricula.

For such education to be effective, the very atmosphere of social and cultural institutions must reflect respect for human rights; such education should be founded on a basis of reciprocity, solidarity and justice.

Educational action should take into account cultural diversity throughout the world, and be based on the cultural identity, social values, language, socialization and communication systems, etc. specific to each country.

The training of trainers is essential in the field of human rights. A particular effort should be made to encourage innovations and pilot projects in teacher-training colleges.

Teaching methods in human rights education should be active, with the maximum possible recourse to discovery and creative work by pupils or students. Data collection, interviews, exhibitions, etc. promote an in-depth understanding of human rights problems.

At present, there is a dearth of teaching materials in this area. It is therefore necessary to encourage the production and distribution of materials which have been tested and evaluated in practice. Particular attention should be paid to audiovisual aids, a teaching medium that has been little exploited so far.

Human rights education should be the basis of non-formal or mass education programmes, particularly in adult education. Innovative experiments carried out in many regions, particularly in rural areas, deserve support and encouragement. Education should take into account the situation of disadvantaged groups such as refugees, ethnic, linguistic and religious minorities, and so on. It should also be noted that non-formal education is one of the responsibility of, for example, trade unions, professional associations and learned societies.

In the context of lifelong or continuing education, specific teaching should be designed for the professionals most directly concerned with human rights, such as magistrates, lawyers, civil servants, policemen, members of the armed forces, journalists, trade unionists, social workers, health personnel, etc., with due regard for the type of problems with which they have to deal.

Human rights education and teaching should be provided in the language(s) used by those concerned, and be accessible to them in that/those language(s).

Research in the Social and Human Sciences. Since the rapid development of human rights education and teaching depends to a great extent on pedagogical research, such research should be encouraged, particularly from a comparative viewpoint and with a view to valuating the results of this education.

The introduction of human rights curricula should be encouraged, not only in law faculties but in faculties of literature, human sciences, social and economic sciences and also in faculties of science, medicine, pharmacy, etc., adopting the approach specific to each discipline.

The establishment of specialized human rights training, research and documentation centres or institutes, and their strengthening in countries where they already exist, should be promoted on multidisciplinary lines.

Interregional and regional research and researcher-training programmes should be encouraged, particularly with a view to co-operation among developing countries, together with exchanges of experience and of teachers and researchers.

Publications should be used to disseminate research findings and to contribute to a knowledge of the institutions specializing in training, research and documentation in the field of human rights.

The relationship between ethics, human rights and recent progress in the biological sciences and technology should be studied more deeply. For example, a study should be made of the links between professional ethics and human rights, especially with a view to training the professionals most directly concerned with human rights.

Human rights research should help to bring out the connection with the highly topical problems facing different societies and the international community as a whole (development, peace, discrimination, intolerance, etc.). Research should also take into account the radical changes at work in society and the emergence of new social movements, new patterns of social organization, etc.

Human Rights Information and Documentation. The mass media play a predominant role in disseminating knowledge about human rights to the general public. Experiments and innovations in this field, particularly in information programmes, deserve to be encouraged.

It is possible that insufficient recourse has been had to non-conventional communication media in disseminating knowledge of human rights. Here also greater use should be made of the theatre, painting, the cinema, songs or even educational or social games.

Documentation centres should be established or strengthened in order to support educational work and research. A network of documentation centres should gradually be established with a view to improved dissemination at the international level.

Special attention should be paid to educational docu-

mentation, with a view not only to production but also to improved dissemination.

Training should be provided in documentation (collection, processing, storage, circulation) which will take account of the specific nature of the human rights field.

The possibility of preparing a human rights thesaurus should be studied in collaboration with the relevant international and regional organizations.

Whenever possible and wherever the need is most keenly felt, encouragement and support should be given to the creation of a liaison or information newsletters and their circulation to universities, teachers and organizations concerned with human rights in different geographical, linguistic or cultural regions.

Role of Non-governmental Organizations. Co-operation with non-governmental organizations at the national, regional and international levels is equally vital. The leading role that they play in the fields of education and training, research, information and documentation deserves to be emphasized.

Dissemination by Member States of Basic Human Rights Texts. Resolution 217 (III) D, adopted by the United Nations General Assembly on 10 December 1948, appealed to all Member States to give due publicity to the text of the Universal Declaration of Human Rights and to "cause it to be disseminated, displayed, read and expounded principally in schools and other educational institutions". The dissemination of basic human rights texts is thus a long-standing commitment for all Governments.

It is therefore necessary to seek funds and request the cooperation of Member States in order to ensure the dissemination of basic human rights texts such as the Universal Declaration of Human Rights, the International Covenants of 1966, international conventions and other standards and procedures approved at the international level. It is recognized that Member States will not be in a position to meet their international commitments as long as there is no access to the basic texts in the languages required for the teaching and training activities which are carried out, in either a formal or a non-formal context.

HUMAN RIGHTS ADVOCATES. An international non-governmental organization in consultative status (Category II) with the UN Economic and Social Council, HRA has submitted briefs to and participated in the work of the UN Commission on Human Rights, its Sub-Commission on Prevention of Discrimination and Protection of Minorities, and the Organization of American States. The organization has members in 15 countries.

Founded in 1978, HRA is composed mainly of lawyers and human rights specialists who perform legal services (free of charge) to protect the rights of such persons as migrant workers, the mentally retarded, and the destitute. It also works closely with freedom fighters and liberation movements and provides technical assistance in the preparation of constitutions, bills of rights, and human rights legislation.

HRA publishes *Human Rights Advocates Newsletter*

triannually and has published numerous articles on human rights laws and their application.

Human Rights Advocates. Address: 2918 Florence Street, Berkeley, CA 94705 (USA). Telephone: (415) 841-2928. Executive Director: Rita Maran.

HUMAN RIGHTS AGENCIES: AID TO PARTICULAR GROUPS.

Institutions have been established by national or local governments with a view to protecting and promoting the rights of members of particular groups, such as ethnic and linguistic minorities, indigenous populations, aliens, migrants and immigrants, children and minors, and women. The role and functions of such institutions are described by the UN Secretary-General's report entitled *National Institutions for the Protection and Promotion of Human Rights* (UN Doc. E/CN.4/1987/37, para, 72–90), prepared at the request of the General Assembly (resolution 40/123), as follows:

In recognition of the fact that particular groups in the community are often subject to an inordinately high incidence of discrimination, many States have established institutions designed to protect and promote the rights of individuals in such groups. Members of the community who are most often recognized by Governments as needed specialized human rights agencies to protect their interests are persons belonging to ethnic and linguistic minorities, aliens, refugees, indigenous populations, women and children, as well as members of religious minority groups. For the most part, these agencies are designed to promote government and social policy which protects the rights of these groups, to investigate instances and patterns of discrimination and against individuals in the group and against the group as a whole; and to provide materials and consultative assistance to members of the group.

Such agencies are generally not empowered to make binding decisions or to initiate legal action. Most often, agencies for the protection of the rights of specific groups are consultative and advisory commissions to the parliament and executive branch of government, and are required to examine the status of human rights violations as regards the group concerned. These agencies are also generally responsible for monitoring the effectiveness of existing statutory and constitutional safeguards aimed at protecting the rights of specific groups in the community, and are additionally empowered to investigate claims of discrimination brought by members of the community against State and local authorities.

Agencies for the protection of minorities have been established in many States over the past several decades to protect the rights of members of ethnic and linguistic minority groups, who are traditionally subject to discrimination. For instance, in Yugoslavia, commissions have been established to address the specific problems faced by minorities and to promote the principle of equality and collective rights. Other organizations of a similar nature are designed primarily to investigate the grievances of minority group members charging State or local authorities with engaging in discriminatory practices. In Pakistan, for example, District Minority Committees have been organized under the chairmanship of Minority Officers to redress, at the local level, the grievances of the minority communities expressed by their representatives.

A broad mandate was contemplated when the Indian Minorities Commission was created in 1978. The functions of the Commission are:

(1) To evaluate the working of the various safeguards provided for in the Constitution and in laws passed by the Union and State Governments for the protection of minorities;

(2) To make recommendations with a view to ensuring the effective implementation and enforcement of all the safeguards and laws;

(3) To undertake a review of the implementation of the policies pursued by the Union and the State Governments with respect to minorities;

(4) To look into specific complaints regarding deprivation of rights and safeguards of minorities;

(5) To conduct studies, research and analysis on the question of avoidance of discrimination against minorities;

(6) To suggest appropriate legal and welfare measures in respect of any minority to be undertaken by the central or State Governments;

(7) To serve as a national clearing-house for information in respect of the conditions of minorities;

(8) To make periodical reports at prescribed intervals to the Government.

Such a body can clearly have a great impact on human rights policy in the country, as well as on the immediate problems facing minorities with regard to discrimination in the community.

In accordance with its Constitution, Singapore has established a Presidential Council for Minority Rights. The Council considers and reports on information received from Parliament or the Government on matters concerning persons belonging to racial and religious minorities. The Council is especially requested to report on any proposed legislation or regulation which may result in discriminatory or unequal treatment of persons in particular communities. For the protection of the rights of linguistic minorities, India has established a Commissioner for Linguistic Minorities. In accordance with article 350A of the Indian Constitution, all States must provide adequate facilities for instruction in the mother tongue at the primary school level of education. The Indian Commissioner for Linguistic Minorities investigates all matters relating to the safeguards provided for in the Constitution regarding the rights of linguistic minorities. The Commissioner is also required to report directly to the President on these matters. Another example of an organ established for the protection of linguistic minorities is the Austrian system of contact committees for the Slovene-speaking and Croatian-speaking minorities, organized within the Austrian Federal Chancellery. The contact committees meet at regular intervals and are comprised of members of the Federal Government, the provincial government concerned, the political parties represented in parliament and the provincial legislative assemblies concerned. Representatives of the minority groups also serve on these committees. The primary function of the committees is to consider measures for the implementation of the provisions of the State treaty of 1955 regarding minority rights. The committees are also charged with the consideration of all action relating to the peaceful cohabitation of the various ethnic groups and may deal with problems concerning individual members of the various ethnic groups or the groups as a whole.

Concerning ethnic groups more specifically, countries with an ethnically diverse population often create special commissions designed to ensure that the rights of the various ethnic groups in the community will be protected. For instance, in India, the Commissioner for Scheduled Castes and Tribes was empowered to investigate all matters relating to the safeguards provided for the scheduled castes and tribes under the Constitution. The Commissioner was responsible for submitting an annual report to the President, which was subsequently presented to both Houses of Parliament. Because of the magnitude of the problem however, a Commission for Scheduled Castes and Tribes—composed of a Chairman and four members—was organized to address the issues concerned in the protection of the rights of scheduled castes and tribes more effectively.

It has also been suggested that such commissions may be even more needed in ethnically homogeneous countries, in which small ethnic groups are virtually without representation at the State and local level and may be subject to a high incidence of discrimination in the community. Organizations established to protect the rights of such ethnic groups are often additionally charged with promoting respect for the various cultures present in the community. In Finland, for example, the Advisory Board for Gypsy Affairs has developed projects for the teaching of the Gypsy language, culture and history.

Agencies for the Protection of Indigenous Populations. Increasingly, the countries concerned have created organs to protect and promote the rights of indigenous populations, which are often subject to discrimination, dispossession of land and other human rights abuses.

In New Zealand for example, the Department of Maori and Island Affairs and the New Zealand Maori Council have been established to address the concerns of the Maori population. The Department of Maori and Island Affairs is responsible for co-ordinating and implementing government policy with respect to Maoris. The New Zealand Maori Council is a consultative body, which expresses its views on all proposed legislation affecting the Maori population. Norway, Finland and Sweden have all created independent commissions to deal with the concerns and problems of their respective Sami (formerly referred to as Lappish) populations. The Finnish Commission for Lappish Affairs is composed of representatives of the Ministries of Justice, Education and Agriculture, and of representatives of various Sami organizations. The main function of the Commission is to advise the Council of State on proposed measures designed to promote the culture of the Sami. The Commission is also consulted by State and local authorities on all matters concerning the Sami population. The Swedish Commission on Sami Affairs, created in 1970, is designed to examine the various problems confronting the Sami in Swedish society. The Commission is particularly concerned with addressing the needs of those Sami who have left reindeer husbandry and moved away from the breeding areas. Norway has created two organs to deal with Sami issues and concerns. The first, the Norwegian Lapp Council, is comprised of eight members, who are all Sami. The Council is primarily an advisory body, which may make recommendations on matters concerning the economic, social and cultural situation of the Sami. Norway has also established a Select Committee, comprised of government and Sami representatives. The Committee, organized under the Minis-

try of Church and Education, examines questions relating to the educational development of the Sami.

Another example of an organ created to address the concerns of indigenous populations is the Mexican Instituto Nacional Indigenista (National Institute for Indigenous Affairs), which was established to study issues concerning the indigenous populations, and to report on the implementation of measures taken to improve the situation of Mexico's indigenous populations.

Agencies for the Protection of Aliens, Migrants and Immigrants. To address the problems of discrimination against foreign migrants and refugees, many countries have created agencies to protect these individuals against discrimination and other obstacles which may obstruct the full exercise of their rights in the community. The Australian Ethnic Affairs Council, for example, advises the Minister for Immigration and Ethnic Affairs on matters relating to the integrations of migrants into the Australian community, particularly in the area of community services. In addition, the Australian Government has opened two Multi-Cultural Resource Centres established to provide an information and advisory service to meet the special needs of immigrants, and to provide information on the availability of benefits and services at the State and local level. The Centres are designed to provide premises for the centralized distribution of multilingual information material, such as pamphlets on social security benefits and other relevant information.

In Belgium in 1952, the Aliens Advisory Commission was created. This Commission must be consulted by the King in all cases in which an alien can only be removed from the country by an expulsion order. The Belgian Minister of Justice may seek the Commission's opinion before making a decision concerning an alien. If the Commission is not consulted prior to a decision which is the subject of an application for review, the Minister of Justice must obtain the Commission's views before ruling on that application. Similarly, concern with protecting the rights of immigrants resulted in the creation of the Norwegian Foreign Workers' Association, which is aimed at safeguarding the economic, social and cultural interests of Norway's many new immigrant groups. The Association receives substantial financial assistance from the Norwegian Government, and emphasis is placed on an increased commitment to permitting immigrant groups to exercise greater influence on matters which particularly concern them. In Sweden, the Commission on Ethnic Prejudice and Discrimination may propose to the Government, measures concerning the improvement of the situation of aliens. Finally, it was recently reported that, in an effort to address the needs of its growing refugee population, Denmark has created a Directorate for Aliens and a Refugee Board. The Directorate is the authority of first instance for decisions concerning refugee status. Such decisions are appealable to the Refugee Board, which functions procedurally like a court.

Agencies for the Protection of Children and Minors. Although in most countries protection of children's rights is primarily the responsibility of parents and legal guardians, mechanisms have been established by States for the protection of children whose parents do not fulfil their recognized duties, or who may be particularly vulnerable to exploitation. One of the primary concerns of such agencies is the exploitation of children in the labour market. Examples of institutions concerned with the prevention of child labour include the Egyptian Supreme Council for the Child, the Indian National Children's Board, the National Council for Children's Affairs in Bangladesh, the Chinese People's

National Committee for the Defence of Children, the National Council for the Child in the Dominican Republic, and the United States Federal Inter-Agency Committee for Children and Youth.

In some states, these agencies function as subsidiary organs of the legislative body. For instance, in the USSR, the Ukrainian SSR and the Byelorussian SSR, Commissions of the Supreme Soviet on Women's Working and Living Conditions, Maternity and Child Welfare, deal in a co-ordinated manner with all questions concerning the rights of the child. Similar functions are carried out by the Juvenile Welfare Board in Norway, the Commission on Children's Rights in Sweden, and the Child Care Board in Barbados. In India, the National Children's Board, established in accordance with the National Policy for the Children Resolution adopted by the Legislature in 1974, is headed by the Prime Minister. This Children's Board was designed to provide "a focus and a forum to plan and review and properly co-ordinate the multiplicity of services, striving to meet the needs of children."

Many agencies for the protection of children are increasingly concerned with the social protection of homeless and abandoned children. In Poland, for example, the Society of the Friends for Children renders special assistance to children's homes and day-care centres. Also concerned with the social protection of children, the Minors' Association of Mexico provides both moral and material assistance to young persons who have committed offences or who are socially abandoned.

Agencies for the Protection of Women. States have increasingly recognized the need for agencies which are equipped to deal with the problem of discrimination against and exploitation of women. Many of these organizations are concerned with the high incidence of discrimination against women in the area of employment. Several of these agencies have already been discussed in the section of the report on equal employment agencies (see sect. C below). However, other organs for the protection of women are more broadly designed to promote the rights of women, and to protect women from discrimination, not only in the workplace, but in all areas. One such organization is the Australian National Women's Advisory Council, which was created to give all Australian women a consultative voice at the federal level with a view to protecting the interests of women in the national sphere. This Council advises the Federal Government on issues affecting women through the Minister for Home Affairs. The women who serve on the Council are selected from different parts of the country and are of diverse backgrounds and interests. To eliminate discrimination against women in the federal sphere, and to monitor potential discrimination inherent in proposed federal laws and practices, Australia also has established the Office of Women's Affairs. This Office is additionally responsible for co-ordinating the work of women's affairs units in other departments. Another example of an agency designed to monitor potential discrimination in the law is the Commission on Women's Rights, created by the Government of Barbados in 1977. This Commission was established to examine all aspects of the law relating to women. The Commission presents reports, containing the results of its ongoing examination, to the Attorney-General, whose Ministry has a Department of Women's Affairs. In India, both the Committee on the Status of Women and the National Committee on Women are designed to promote the rights of women. The Committee on the Status of Women

in India is concerned primarily with emphasizing the need to co-ordinate agencies and communication in the implementation of measures to improve the status of women. The National Committee on Women is responsible for an ongoing review of the progress of programmes for women. The National Committee on Women is chaired by the Prime Minister of India, and the position of Vice-Chairman is held by the Minister of Education, Social Welfare and Culture. Other members of the National Committee are generally leading public figures in the field of women's issues.

Agencies created to protect groups in the community from the deleterious effects of discrimination and exploitation would seem to be an essential part of any comprehensive national programme for the protection and promotion of human rights. In all countries, groups characterized by race, ethnicity, national origin, religion or sex, may be, in varying degrees, subject to instances and practices of discrimination. When there is a tradition of bias or long-standing discrimination in a community, such groups are often underrepresented at the State and local official level, and subsequently may have little or no readily accessible means of alerting the proper authorities to redress such acts of discrimination. Moreover, when acts of discrimination are perpetrated by State or local authorities, the recourse available to members of particular groups in the community may be non-existent. Organizations which deal solely with the protection of these groups can offer an accessible and effective recourse to members of the community who traditionally lack responsive administrative machinery at the State and local level.

Finally, the high incidence of refugee and migratory movement, the continued abuse of the land rights of indigenous populations, and the pervasive level of racial and sexual discrimination which exist in countries throughout the world, overwhelmingly heighten the need for special agencies to address the problems and concerns which face particular groups of the community, which often suffer from inordinately high levels of discrimination.

SEE ALSO *Human Rights Commissions: National and Local.*

HUMAN RIGHTS AND PEACE. The UN SUB-COMMISSION ON PREVENTION OF DISCRIMINATION AND PROTECTION OF MINORITIES continued at its 1989 session its periodic consideration of the question of the interrelationship between human rights and international peace as it had been requested to do by the Commission on Human Rights in 1982 (resolution 1982/7).

The sub-commission based its work on a study prepared in 1988 by the Secretary-General (UN Doc. E/CN.4/Sub.2/1988/2) which reviewed the efforts of UN bodies and other organizations to focus attention on this question, pointed out that a number of international instruments made reference to the interrelationship between the realization of human rights and peace and drew attention to a special category of violations of human rights—terms "gross and flagrant violations"—that presented the most serious threat to peace.

After examining the report, the sub-commission agreed (resolution 1989/47) that the strengthening of international peace and security, as well as the reduction of expenditure for arms, are important conditions for economic and social development and for the materialization of all human rights and that, conversely, the effective realization of human rights in all parts of the world would contribute to the achievement of international peace and security.

As a basis for its further study of the question, the sub-commission invited one of its members, Mr. Murlidhar Bhandare (India), to prepare a working paper on the problem of the interrelationship between international peace and the effective materialization of all human rights for consideration at future sessions.

HUMAN RIGHTS AND YOUTH. At its 1985 session, the UN Commission on Human Rights emphasized (resolution 1985/13) the necessity to ensure full enjoyment by youth of the rights stipulated in all relevant international instruments as indispensible for human dignity and for the free development of the human personality, and requested its Sub-Commission on Prevention of Discrimination and Protection of Minorities to pay due attention to the role of youth in the field of human rights, particularly in achieving the objectives of the International Youth Year (1985).

In response the sub-commission, later in 1985, requested one of its members, Mr. Dumitru Mazilu (Romania), to prepare a report on human rights and youth analyzing the efforts and measures for securing the implementation and enjoyment by youth of human rights, particularly the right to life, the right to education, and the right to work. This decision was later endorsed by the Commission on Human Rights and the Economic and Social Council.

The report was originally scheduled to be presented by Mr. Mazilu at the 1986 session of the Sub-Commission. That session was, however, postponed until 1987 due to the financial situation of the United Nations. When Mr. Mazilu failed to submit his report or to appear in Geneva for the 1987 session of the sub-commission, consideration of the question was postponed to 1988. After the session, the Secretary-General, with a view to assisting Mr. Mazilu in the preparation and presentation of his report, invited him to visit Geneva for consultation with the staff of the Center for Human Rights and, at the same time, contacted the Permanent Mission to the United Nations in Geneva with a view to facilitating the visit. However, Mr. Mazilu at that time informed the Secretary-General that the proposed visit to Geneva had not been authorized by the competent Romanian authorities.

In April 1988, the Secretary-General received from Mr. Mazilu five chapters of his report, prepared partly in English and partly in Romanian, and sought unsuccessfully to contact the special rapporteur for an exchange of views on the presentation and editing of those chapters. In May 1989, the Secretary-General received from Mr. Mazilu the introduction, two further chapters of the report, a bibliography of sources consulted, and a separate text entitled "A Special View of the Romanian case."

After again endeavoring, without success, to contact the special rapporteur, the Secretary-General issued the report on 10 July 1989 in two parts: (1) the report entitled "Human Rights and Youth" (UN Doc. E/CN.4/Sub.2/1989/41) and (2) the addendum to that report sub-titled "A Special View on the Romanian case" (UN Doc. E/CN.4/Sub.2/1989/41/ Add. 1) (see ROMANIA: "A SPECIAL VIEW OF THE ROMANIAN CASE").

The sub-commission considered the report at its 1989 session, and decided (resolution 1989/45) to request Mr. Mazilu to update it and to present his updated report in person to the sub-commission at its 1990 session.

On 24 May 1989, the Economic and Social Council, on recommendation of the Commission on Human Rights and the sub-commission, concluded (resolution 1989/75) that a difference had arisen between the United Nations and the Government of Romania as to the applicability of the Convention on Privileges and Immunities of the United Nations to Mr. Dumitru Mazilu as special rapporteur of the sub-commission and requested, on a priority basis, an advisory opinion from the International Court of Justice on the legal question involved. The Court's advisory opinion, delivered on 15 December 1989, is reproduced in the entry entitled SPECIAL RAPPORTEURS: PRIVILEGES AND IMMUNITIES.

As regards the report on human rights and youth, the tentative conclusions and recommendations of the special rapporteur—which are to be updated in his final report to the sub-commission—are as follows (UN Doc. E/CN.4/Sub.2/1989/41), chap. VIII, para. 371–387):

A. Conclusions. Developments in the contemporary world convincingly demonstrate that young people have a more and more important role to play in attaining the objectives of progress and development set by all peoples. Their right to life, to education and to work and their freedoms are of particular importance and significance.

Consideration of these rights and freedoms in a special report is a mark of the real interest taken by the United Nations in alerting Governments and world public opinion and in giving impetus to concern already felt in this respect.

Millions of young people continue to be exposed to great

sufferings caused by lack of the resources needed for their informal physical and intellectual development, as is happening in Romania. In some countries, governed by tyrannical regimes, young people endure unimagined forms of coercion, a veritable aggression against their rights and freedoms. Through starvation, terror and cold, the rulers of those countries strive to reduce them to silence, to prevent them from concerning themselves with the major problems of their respective societies, and to transform them into an amorphous, easily manipulated mass. Many young people gain an education by great efforts, and when the teaching process is over they are disappointed not to find jobs in which to apply their knowledge, talent and characteristic enthusiasm. In other countries, the process of instruction and education is passing through an especially critical period owing to the absence of professionalism and the presence of a superfluity of doctrinaire, politicizing elements of no practical utility. The jobs young people get in those countries do not allow their skills to be encouraged or use to be made of their intelligence and characteristic energy, so that they lapse into indifference and uniformity.

Again, there are countries—including Romania—in which the lives of millions of young people are in jeopardy. The absence of the most elementary rights and freedoms, their arrest, conviction and execution on political grounds, bring to mind the darkest years of the oppression practised by maniacal despotic régimes. Threats of every kind, daily dangers directed against young people who have the courage to express critical opinions, maintain an atmosphere of tension and terror that is hard to bear.

The positive changes of recent years have rekindled the torch of freedom and dignity. The hopes of millions upon millions of young people for the elimination of repressive anachronisms and the possibility of a real restructuring of society on the principles of democracy and freedom have been reborn.

"No" is being said, with increasing determination, to policies of economic and cultural stagnation, of oppression and repression of ethnic and religious discrimination. There is a demand for the institution of political and economic structures which are consistently democratic and which preclude the monopoly of power of life and the imposition of maniacal despots. The fixing of precise terms of office in all public posts and election by secret ballot of all those who are to occupy them are major guarantees of democracy and freedom. The separation of powers in a State is the surest way to the normal conduct of legislative, judicial and executive business and to the elimination of abuses of power. The closing down of the concentration camps and the final elimination of ethnic and social genocide are priority objectives of the reinstatement of right and justice in human society.

The experiences of the past few decades have furnished compelling proof of the importance that attaches to economic and political pluralism and to diversity of opinion as prerequisites for effective progress in all spheres and as the expression of the level of culture and civilization attained in the development of human communities.

The young people of the world, including the young people of Romania, regard the refusal of reforms, the rejection of the process of democratic restructuring of society, as a reactionary attitude, as confirmation of the contempt for the human being, the disdain for human rights and freedoms, shown by some dictatorial cliques that have difficulty in parting with the regal privileges conferred by doctrinaire

ideas and structures of government which have long since fallen into disuse and been roundly condemned by the entire civilized world.

The young generation insistently demands the abandonment of out-of-date doctrines, the elimination of dogmas that run counter to human progress and to the happiness and well-being of man, and the removal of the oppressors, of the dictators who in the name of a few reactionary slogans oppose the increasingly powerful trend towards democracy and freedom. The voice of reason must carry the day. "Peoples are not herds of subjects that despots can drive where they choose with a whip!" "The people is the true sovereign and the maker of its own history!" "Any leader must subordinate himself to the will and interests of the people!" "The peoples are not in the service of the rulers; the rulers are the servants of human communities, which must be given an accounting of their actions and must be asked for approval regarding all government measures!" "Truth and right sometimes come tardily, but they come surely!"

Youth is the fiercest fighter for the rebuilding of the world on criteria of progress, well-being, democracy and freedom.

Orders based on terror, dictatorship and tyranny are repudiated and condemned by history.

The dark age of terror, dictatorship and tyranny is gradually passing away. A new age of freedom and human dignity can be glimpsed on the horizon. We are drawing closer as quickly as possible to giving back to young people the confidence they need in order to build a future of enlightenment and freedom.

B. Recommendations. Recognizing that young people have an important role in the life of society for the achievement of social justice and the attainment of the objectives of economic and social progress and the maintenance of international peace and security, and mindful of the grave political, economic, social and cultural problems facing youth and the need to ensure the full exercise of youth's fundamental rights to life, education, vocational training, work, social assistance, the elimination of all forms of social and racial discrimination, so that youth can participate actively in the decision-making process, we consider the following necessary:

(a) At the national and international levels, effective measures should be taken to put an immediate end to the flagrant violations of the fundamental right to life of young people. The right to life is sacrosanct. Deprivation of life is irrevocable. Respect for the right to life transcends all social, national, racial, political, religious, ethnic and other differences. Summary or arbitrary executions of young people opposed to, or perceived or imagined to be opposed to those who wield political or economic power in the State or government, or perceived to be opposed to certain aspects of their political, economic, social and cultural policies, as well as enforced or involuntary disappearances, torture and mistreatment of prisoners and detainees, are continuing on a large scale throughout the international community. These flagrant violations of the fundamental right to life of young people show a serious erosion in the level of acknowledgement of and respect for the right to life of young people.

(b) The international community must, as a matter of extreme urgency, act collectively to halt this erosion by adopting effective measures and means through which to react speedily to threatened or imminent summary of arbitrary executions, enforced or involuntary disappearances.

(c) All States should adopt effective measures for a healthier environment of young people and the containment and reduction of such afflictions as disease, famine, war, corruption, criminality and social breakdown.

(d) All States should attack on a priority basis every aspect of the illicit drug business, including the production, possession, trafficking, demand, consumption, and financing of illicit drugs, which must be recognized as a crime against humanity, and launch objective informational, educational and orientation programmes to make young people aware of the risks to health, security and other implications of illicit drug use, thus eliminating the demand for illicit drugs.

(e) At the national and international levels, effective measures should be taken for the elimination of illiteracy and for the promotion of education and vocational training for youth based upon both formal and informal learning and designed to link theoretical learning and practical training, on the one hand, with productive and creative work, on the other.

(f) Young people shall be brought up in a spirit of peace, justice, freedom, mutual respect and understanding in order to promote equal rights for all human beings and all nations, economic and social progress, and the maintenance of international peace and security. All means of education, including as of major importance the guidance given by parents or family, instruction and information intended for young people should foster the ideals of peace, humanity, liberty and international solidarity and all other ideals which help to bring peoples closer together, and acquaint young people with the role entrusted to the United Nations as a means of preserving and maintaining peace and promoting international understanding and co-operation.

(g) Young people should be brought up in the knowledge of the dignity and equality of all men, without distinction as to race, colour, ethnic origins or beliefs, and in respect for fundamental rights and for the right of peoples to self-determination. All States shall take the necessary measures, including legislative measures, to ensure that the utilization of scientific and technological achievements promotes the fullest realization of rights and fundamental freedoms of young people without any discrimination whatsoever on grounds of race, sex, language or religious beliefs.

(h) All States should take the necessary measures to implement large-scale national employment programmes, in conformity with the actual situation and priorities of every country, which would include legislative, educational, economic and social measures designed to eliminate all forms of discrimination, guarantee that young people participate actively in economic and social development and in the process of drawing up and taking decisions, and encourage adequate representation of youth in Parliament, in government, and in other decision-making bodies. All Government shall take every possible step to ensure appropriate education and employment opportunities for children of refugees, foreign nationals and peoples displaced from their country of origin.

(i) All States should take the necessary measures to ensure that, in the pursuit of balanced economic growth, industrialization and highest productivity, the application of new technologies will enhance the situation of young people in order to provide them with a productive, satisfying and secure future. All Governments shall give special attention to the problem of rapid demographic growth, especially in developing countries, and give high priority to achieving an appropriate relationship between resources, productivity, population levels and population distribution.

(j) Taking into account the fact that the relatively weak position of young workers in the labour market may at times render them vulnerable to exploitation and may oblige them to accept substandard wages and jobs, Governments, employers and workers should take action when necessary to prevent these situations from arising. Working conditions should be such as not to discriminate between various categories of workers. It should be recognized, at the same time, that young people in their formative years require clearly determined and defined hours and conditions, taking into account the need to limit working time in order to allow for sufficient time for education, rest and leisure activities. This policy is to aim at ensuring the fullest possible opportunity for each young worker to qualify for, and to use his skills and endowments in, a job for which he is well suited.

(k) At the national and international levels, encouragement and facilities should be given for exchanges, travel, tourism, meetings, the study of foreign languages, the twinning of towns and universities without discrimination and similar activities, to be organized for young people of all countries in order to bring them together in educational, cultural and sporting activities in a spirit of mutual respect, understanding and co-operation.

(l) All States, the United Nations, the specialized agencies, international intergovernmental and non-governmental organizations, as well as youth organizations, shall stimulate debates and convene seminars and conferences which could serve to mobilize efforts to promote the best educational, professional and living conditions for young people, to ensure their active participation in the overall development of society and to encourage the preparation of new local, national and international programmes in accordance with the ideals of peace, security, justice and dignity of human person.

Taking into account the fact that massive and flagrant violations of the rights and fundamental freedoms of young people and, in general, of every human being are continuing on a large scale throughout the international community, on the grounds that the individuals concerned are in opposition to, or are perceived or imagined to be in opposition to, those who wield political, economic, or social power in the State or government, or to certain aspects of their political, economic, social or cultural policies, and because life, liberty, justice, well-being and the dignity of the human person, human rights and fundamental freedoms, are universally recognized values transcending all social, national, racial, political, religious, ethnic and other differences, the international community must, as a matter of extreme urgency, act collectively to halt such massive and flagrant violations of the rights and fundamental freedoms of young people and, in general, of every human being, by adopting effective means such as setting up a mechanism that will react speedily to threatened or imminent flagrant violations of human rights. This mechanism should monitor this phenomenon and suggest ways and means of eliminating it altogether. High priority shall be given to the preventive measures and the involvement of Governments in this process.

Words of deploration and condemnation are by far not enough. Young people have asked us to give them real guarantees that massive and flagrant violations of human rights will be eliminated forever.

There are no international rules or principles that could be invoked by those who are violating human rights and fundamental freedoms. No one who really respects life, liberty and the dignity of human beings could ever oppose such urgent measures.

Taking into account the tragic experience of Romania and of other countries, I strongly suggest the setting up of a special body of the United Nations with full powers to supervise the situation of human rights in every country and to adopt recommendations and efficient measures in order to restore the liberty and dignity of man, where and when they are violated.

After the government of Romania was overthrown in December 1989 and President Ceacescu was executed, Mr. Dumitru Mazilu wrote to the UN Secretary-General, praising his "courage and determination under adverse conditions," for publishing the report on Human Rights and Youth and for the efforts of the United Nations in securing his release.

HUMAN RIGHTS BASED ON SOLIDARITY. The UN General Assembly decided on 15 December 1989 (resolution 44/148) to include in the provisional agenda of its 1990 session an item entitled "Human Rights Based on Solidarity" and requested the Commission on Human Rights to study the question after obtaining the views of States and of intergovernmental and non-governmental organizations. In doing so, the assembly stressed that respect for the inherent dignity and for the equal and inalienable rights of all members of the human family is the foundation of freedom, justice, and peace in the world and expressed its conviction that the severe suffering of innumerable people throughout the world, particularly those in conditions of extreme poverty, calls for the strengthening of a perceived sense of human solidarity.

HUMAN RIGHTS COMMISSIONS: NATIONAL AND LOCAL. Organs have been established by national or local governments with a view to ensuring that laws and regulations concerning the protection of human rights are effectively applied and to educating the public about the purpose and operation of such legislation. The role and functions of such commissions are described in general terms in the UN Secretary-General's report entitled *National Institutions for the Protection and Promotion of Human Rights* (UN Doc. E/CN.4/1987/37, para. 59–71), prepared at the request of the General Assembly (resolution 40/123), as follows:

Human rights commissions are concerned primarily with the protection of citizens against discrimination as well as with the protection of civil and other human rights. These commissions and similar public bodies at the national level are generally designed to hear and investigate individual charges of human rights violations or discriminatory acts committed in violation of existing law. Most human rights commissions are collegial bodies, comprised of members who, in most cases, are selected by the Executive. In many cases the commissions enjoy statutory independence, and are responsible for reporting on a regular basis, to the legislative body. In some cases, as in Canada and Japan, the human rights commissions are organized within the Ministry of Justice. Similarly, the Ministry of Foreign Affairs is responsible for the selection of the members of the Norwegian Human Rights Committee, and the same is true in Denmark.

Commission members may be selected from a number of fields, but preference is generally given to person having prior experience in the field of human rights. For instance, in Denmark, the members of the Human Rights Committee include representatives from the Foreign Ministry, other ministries and various non-governmental organizations concerned with human rights. In some cases, restrictions are place on selection of commission members. For example, in the United States, members of the Civil Rights Commission are selected by the President and must be confirmed by the Senate, with the requirement that not more than half of the Commission's members belong to the same political party. In Japan, the Ministry of Justice selects the members of the Civil Liberties Bureau from among citizens in each locality of the Bureau's eight offices across the country. The citizens chosen as Commissioners include social workers, schoolteachers, attorneys, media personnel and manual workers in agriculture and forestry.

Generally the laws or statutes which create a human rights commission define its jurisdiction, since they codify the range of discriminatory or violative conduct that the Commission is empowered to investigate. For example, the Australian Human Rights Commission (established in 1981) is authorized to hear and investigate complaints of violations of any rights defined in the Racial Discrimination Act and the Human Rights Commission Act. The United States Civil Rights Commission, may hear and investigate complaints alleging discrimination on the grounds of race, colour, religion, sex or national origin. An even broader range of rights is protected in Canada, in accordance with the Canadian Human Rights Act which empowers the Human Rights Commission to investigate allegations of discrimination based on race, national or ethnic origin, colour, religion, age, sex, marital status, conviction for an offence for which a pardon has been issued, and discriminatory employment practices against physically handicapped persons.

The procedures followed by human rights commissions in the investigation and resolution of complaints vary from country to country. It is true however, that in almost all countries the human rights commission does not have the power to make binding decisions itself in resolving a complaint. In most cases, the human rights commission attempts to arrive at settlements between parties. If the settlement or appropriate remedial steps suggested by the commission are not implemented, it frequently has the authority to seize the Courts or the Prosecutor's Office for adjudication or prosecution of the matter. The commission may, as in Australia, merely submit the matter to the Attorney-General with a recommendation as to the appropriate legal action.

771

In cases in which no settlement can be reached, the law often provides the procedures to be followed. In Canada, for example, the Provincial Minister of Justice concerned, may, upon the recommendation of the Human Rights Commission, set up a Board of Inquiry. The Board's membership is entirely independent of the Commission. If the Board decides that a human rights violation has indeed been committed, it may determine the appropriate remedial action to be taken, including the payment of damages. When the Board's recommendation is not implemented, it may be enforced by the courts, or in some Provinces, by the Human Rights Commission itself. In one Canadian Province, in which no Board of Inquiry exists, the Human Rights Commission may, with the plaintiff's consent, seek an injunction from the Court, in the event that its recommendation has not been implemented.

In some cases, a human rights commission may hear and investigate complaints, but may not be empowered to act upon them. This is true of the United States Civil Rights Commission. The Commission's function is, primarily, to review the status of compliance with civil rights law and to study the situation concerning respect for human rights. The Commission is empowered, however, to hear complaints and to receive information regarding those complaints. In fulfilling its responsibilities, the United States Civil Rights Commission may issue subpoenas and hold formal hearings.

One of the most important functions of a human rights commission is its power to review systematically existing government policy toward human rights and to suggest improvements. For instance, in addition to its competence to hear, investigate and apply remedies to cases involving human rights violations, the National Commission for the Promotion and Protection of Human Rights in Nicaragua conducts periodic reviews of the legislative and administrative systems and recommends to the Government ways in which these systems might be improved. Similarly, the Standing Advisory Commission on Human Rights for Northern Ireland advises Parliament on the adequacy and effectiveness of existing laws in preventing discrimination based on religious belief and political opinion.

Many human rights commissions engage in monitoring State legislative compliance with existing human rights law. In its review of every newly enacted State law, the Senate Legal Committee of Zimbabwe, for example, seeks to ensure that all new legislation complies with the Declaration of Rights embodied in the Zimbabwean Constitution. The Committee also advises the Government on whether any provisions in the new legislation would be in violation of the Declaration of Rights. Similarly, the Italian Interministerial Committee on Human Rights engages in a systematic review of legislative and administrative measures in an effort to ensure that Italy meets its obligations under international conventions on human rights. Also, in New Zealand, the Human Rights Commission is responsible for advising the Prime Minister on the acceptance by New Zealand of any international instruments on human rights. It may, in addition, give advice on the human rights implications of any policy or legislation proposed by the Government.

Most human rights commissions are also actively engaged in educating the public about their function and purpose, as well as about various important issues in the field of human rights. This has been referred to in previous reports as the "promotional role" of human rights commissions. They generally fulfil this function through seminars, counselling services and meetings, as well as through the distribution of periodic repots, studies and bulletins prepared by the commission or other human rights institutions. In fact recently, the Australian Human Rights Commission published its own handbook on human rights. Frequently, responsibility for educating the public on human rights issues is part of a human rights commission's statutory mandate. For example, part of the mandate of the Japanese Civil Liberties Bureau is to provide educational activities and to encourage community campaigns and nongovernmental organization activities, which promote respect for human rights. Even more specifically, the Canadian Human Rights Act requires its Human Rights Commission to provide assistance and advice with respect to special programmes; to institute information programmes to foster public understanding of the Canadian Human Rights Act; to carry out research programmes and undertake studies concerning discrimination, to consider recommendations received concerning human rights and individual freedoms; to take steps and encourage others to ensure that the physically handicapped have access to goods, services, facilities and accommodation that are customarily available to other people; to provide assistance and advice directed at ensuring compliance with the Act; and to maintain close liaison with bodies or authorities in the Provinces that are working against discrimination.

In some cases, commissions are created for the sole purpose of carrying out promotional and educational human rights duties. In fact, in 1984, Suriname reported that it had established a Commission for Information and Guidance regarding Human Rights in Suriname. Such a commission would, ostensibly, be solely devoted to providing promotional services to the community in heightening an awareness of human rights issues. Suriname later expressed its intention to broaden the scope of this Commission beyond its merely promotional duties, and eventually to establish a national institution for the promotion and protection of human rights pursuant to General Assembly resolution 38/123.

What appears to be the most essential ingredient for an effective human rights commission, is a strong connection between the law, the commission and the courts. First, the human rights commission requires a broad and clearly codified mandate (as part of the Constitution or of the law) to establish its jurisdiction, and to ensure its statutory independence from the Executive or parliamentary control. An effective human rights commission further requires recourse to the courts or the Prosecutor's Office, to enforce the results and recommendations of its investigations. Without this important connection (between the law, the commission and the court), a human rights commission would be largely impotent. The power to investigate complaints without the power to enforce the recommendations resulting from such investigations, may render a human rights commission powerless, and may ultimately discourage citizens from seeking recourse to such organs. The purpose and role of a human rights commission is highly questionable if a citizen must initiate another action, either in the courts or with another agency, after utilizing the offices of the commission, particularly since many individuals who have suffered some form of discrimination or a violation of their rights may be unwilling to initiate a second action after the first had produced an unenforceable decision and no actual relief.

In order to maintain low administrative costs (by eliminating the need for citizens to take their complaints to more than one agency), to ease the burden on the courts (by settling matters without the high cost of an independent adjudicative investigation), and most of all, to encourage citizens to seek redress for violations of their civil and human rights, human rights commissions must be empowered to enforce compliance with their recommendations, either by seizing the court or the Prosecutor's Office, or through an independent grant of power, enabling the human rights commissions to make binding decisions.

Another very important consideration to bear in mind in the development of a human rights commission is a mechanism for the equitable selection of commission members, as problems may arise if the selection procedure is unfair. Moreover, maintaining close ties with the community, and dispelling the image of human rights commissions as lofty government agencies, can only benefit the standing of human rights commissions as effective institutions for the protection of the human and civil rights of the ordinary citizen.

SEE ALSO Human Rights Agencies: Aid to Particular Groups.

HUMAN RIGHTS COMMISSIONS: UNIVERSAL AND REGIONAL.

There are four international human rights commissions which operate on a universal or a regional basis: (1) the COMMISSION ON HUMAN RIGHTS of the United Nations, authorized by article 68 of the UNITED NATIONS CHARTER, which is universal in the scope of its operations; (2) the EUROPEAN COMMISSION ON HUMAN RIGHTS, which functions on a regional basis within the framework of the COUNCIL OF EUROPE; (3) the INTER-AMERICAN COMMISSION ON HUMAN RIGHTS, which functions on a regional basis within the framework of the ORGANIZATION OF AMERICAN STATES; (4) and the AFRICAN COMMISSION ON HUMAN AND PEOPLES' RIGHTS, which functions on a regional basis within the framework of the ORGANIZATION OF AFRICAN UNITY.

HUMAN RIGHTS COMMITTEE.

The committee was established in accordance with article 28 of the INTERNATIONAL COVENANT ON CIVIL AND POLITICAL RIGHTS, adopted by the UN General Assembly on 16 December 1966 (resolution 2200 A [XXI]. The covenant entered into force on 23 March 1976.

Each State party to the covenant undertakes to respect and ensure to all individuals within its territory and subject to its jurisdiction the rights recognized therein, to adopt such legislative and other measures as may be necessary to give effect to those rights, to ensure that any person whose rights are violated shall have an effective remedy, to ensure that any person claiming such a remedy shall have his right thereto determined by competent authorities, and to ensure that those authorities enforce such remedies when granted. In addition, each State party undertakes to ensure the equal right of men and women to the enjoyment of all the rights set forth in the covenant.

The responsibilities of the committee, set out in articles 40 to 45 of the covenant, may be summarized as follows:

Consideration of Reports of States Parties. Under article 40, para. 1, States parties to the covenant undertake to submit to the Secretary-General for consideration by the committee reports on the measures they have adopted which give effect to the rights recognized therein and on the progress made in the enjoyment of those rights. The committee is empowered to study the reports and to transmit them, and such general comments as it may consider appropriate, to the States parties and to the Economic and Social Council.

Consideration of Complaints of States Parties against other States Parties. Under article 41, a State party to the covenant may declare that it recognizes the competence of the committee to receive and consider communications to the effect that another State party is not fulfilling its obligations under the covenant. With respect to such complaints, the committee is authorized (1) to deal with the matter when referred to it by either State after it has ascertained that all domestic remedies have been invoked and exhausted; (2) if the matter is not thus resolved to the satisfaction of the States parties concerned, to appoint an ad hoc conciliation commission which shall make its good offices available to those States with a view to an amicable solution of the matter; (3) to communicate the report of the ad hoc commission to the States parties concerned so that they may indicate whether or not they accept its contents; and (4) to report on the matter to the General Assembly.

Consideration of Communications from Individuals. Under articles 1 to 3 of the Optional Protocol to the International Covenant on Civil and Political Rights, and subject to the conditions set out there, the committee may receive and consider communications from individuals who claim that any of their rights enumerated in the covenant have been violated and who indicate that they have exhausted all available domestic remedies. With respect to such complaints, the committee is authorized (1) to consider their admissibility, screening out communications which are anonymous or which it considers to be an abuse of the right of submission or to be incompatible with the provisions of the covenant; (2) to bring them to the attention of the State party alleged to be violating any provision of the covenant; (3) to consider them in the light of all written information made available to it by the individual and by the State party concerned; (4) to forward its views to the State party concerned and to the individual; and (5) to report on these activities to the General Assembly through the Economic and Social Council.

The Committee normally holds three sessions each year, of from two to three weeks' duration. Most of the sessions are held at the United Nations office in Geneva, but occasionally one is held at the headquarters of the United Nations in New York. The committee submits an annual report to the General Assembly through the Economic and Social Council, covering its activities under the covenant and its optional protocol.

The committee's practice has been to establish two working groups, which meet prior to each of its sessions. The first makes recommendations regarding communications received under the optional protocol; the second makes suggestions concerning the committee's work program and prepares draft texts for consideration by the committee.

Under article 3 of the second optional protocol, aiming at the abolition of the death penalty, States parties to that protocol are to include in the reports they submit to the Human Rights Committee information on the measures they have adopted to give effect to the second optional protocol. Under article 4, which applies with respect to States parties to the covenant that have made a declaration under article 41, the competence of the Human Rights Committee to receive and consider communications when a State party claims that another State party is not fulfilling its obligations shall extend to the provisions of the protocol, unless the State party concerned has made a statement to the contrary at the moment of ratification or accession.

Rules relating to the Functions of the Committee. The committee adopted provisional rules of procedure at its first and second sessions, and subsequently amended them at the third, seventh, and 36th sessions. The rules relating to the functions of the committee, as amended at the committee's 918th meeting, on 26 July 1989, are as follows (UN Doc. CCPR/C/3/Rev. 2):

XV. Reports from States Parties under Article 40 of the Covenant

Rule 66. 1. The States parties to the Covenant shall submit reports on the measures they have adopted which give effect to the rights recognized in the Covenant and on the progress made in the enjoyment of those rights. Reports shall indicate the factors and difficulties, if any, affecting the implementation of the Covenant.

2. Whenever the Committee requests States parties to submit reports under article 40, paragraph 1 (b), of the Covenant, it shall determine the dates by which such reports shall be submitted.

3. The Committee may, through the Secretary-General, inform the States parties of its wishes regarding the form and contents of the reports to be submitted under article 40 of the Covenant.

Rule 67. 1. The Secretary-General may, after consultation with the Committee, transmit to the specialized agencies concerned copies of such parts of the reports from States members of those agencies as may fall within their field of competence.

2. The Committee may invite the specialized agencies to which the Secretary-General has transmitted parts of the reports to submit comments on those parts within such time-limits as it may specify.

Rule 68. The Committee shall, through the Secretary-General, notify the States parties as early as possible of the opening date, duration and place of the session at which their respective reports will be examined. Representatives of the States parties may be present at the meetings of the Committee when their reports are examined. The Committee may also inform a State party from which it decides to seek further information that it may authorize its representative to be present at a specified meeting. Such a representative should be able to answer questions which may be put to him by the Committee and make statements on reports already submitted by his State, and may also submit additional information from his State.

Rule 69. 1. At each session the Secretary-General shall notify the Committee of all cases of non-submission of reports or additional information requested under rules 66 and 70 of these rules. In such cases the Committee may transmit to the State party concerned, through the Secretary-General, a reminder concerning the submission of the report or additional information.

2. If, after the reminder referred to in paragraph 1 of this rule, the State party does not submit the report or additional information required under rules 66 and 70 of these rules, the Committee shall so state in the annual report which it submits to the General Assembly of the United Nations through the Economic and Social Council.

Rule 70. 1. When considering a report submitted by a State party under article 40 of the Covenant, the Committee shall first satisfy itself that the report provides all the information required under rule 66 of these rules.

2. If a report of a State party to the Covenant, in the opinion of the Committee, does not contain sufficient information, the Committee may request that State to furnish the additional information which is required, indicating by what date the said information should be submitted.

3. If, on the basis of its examination of the reports and information supplied by a State party, the Committee determines that some of the obligations of that State party under the Covenant have not been discharged, it may, in accordance with article 40, paragraph 4, of the covenant, make such general comments as it may consider appropriate.

Rule 71. 1. The Committee shall, through the Secretary-General, communicate to the States parties for their observations the general comments it has made under article 40, paragraph 4, of the Covenant on the basis of its examination of the reports and information furnished by States parties. The Committee may, where necessary, indicate a time-limit for the receipt of observations from States parties.

2. The Committee may also transmit to the Economic and Social Council the comments referred to in paragraph 1 of this rule, together with copies of the reports it has received from the States parties to the Covenant and the observations, if any, submitted by them.

XVI. Procedure for the Consideration of Communications Received under Article 41 of the Covenant

Rule 72. 1. A communication under article 41 of the Covenant may be referred to the Committee by either State party concerned by notice given in accordance with paragraph 1 (b) of that article.

2. The notice referred to in paragraph 1 of this rule shall contain or be accompanied by information regarding:

(a) Steps taken to seek adjustment of the matter in accordance with article 41, paragraphs 1 (a) and (b), of the Covenant, including the text of the initial communication and of any subsequent written explanations or statements by the States parties concerned which are pertinent to the matter;

(b) Steps taken to exhaust domestic remedies;

(c) Any other procedure of international investigation or settlement resorted to by the States parties concerned.

Rule 73. The Secretary-General shall maintain a permanent register of all communications received by the Committee under article 41 of the Covenant.

Rule 74. The Secretary-General shall inform the members of the Committee without delay of any notice given under rule 72 of these rules and shall transmit to them as soon as possible copies of the notice and relevant information.

Rule 75. 1. The Committee shall examine communications under article 41 of the Covenant at closed meetings.

2. The Committee may, after consultation with the States parties concerned, issue communiqués, through the Secretary-General, for the use of the information media and the general public regarding the activities of the Committee at its closed meetings.

Rule 76. A communication shall not be considered by the Committee unless:

(a) Both States parties concerned have made declarations under article 41, paragraph 1, of the Covenant which are applicable to the communication;

(b) The time-limit prescribed in article 41, paragraph 1 (b), of the Covenant has expired;

(c) The Committee has ascertained that all available domestic remedies have been invoked and exhausted in the matter in conformity with the generally recognized principles of international law, or that the application of the remedies is unreasonably prolonged.

Rule 77A. Subject to the provisions of rule 76 of these rules, the Committee shall proceed to make its good offices available to the States parties concerned with a view to a friendly solution of the matter on the basis of respect for human rights and fundamental freedoms as recognized in the Covenant.

Rule 77B. The Committee may, through the Secretary-General, request the States parties concerned or either of them to submit additional information or observations orally or in writing. The committee shall indicate a time-limit for the submission of such written information or observations.

Rule 77C. 1. The States parties concerned shall have the right to be represented when the matter is being considered in the Committee and to make submissions orally and/or in writing.

2. The Committee shall, through the Secretary-General, notify the States parties concerned as early as possible of the opening date, duration and place of the session at which the matter will be examined.

3. The procedure for making oral and/or written sub-mission shall be decided by the Committee, after consultation with the States parties concerned.

Rule 77D. 1. Within 12 months after the date on which the Committee received the notice referred to in rule 72 of these rules, the Committee shall adopt a report in accordance with article 41, paragraph 1 (h), of the Covenant.

2. The provisions of paragraph 1 of rule 77C of these rules shall not apply to the deliberations of the Committee concerning the adoption of the report.

3. The Committee's report shall be communicated, through the Secretary-General, to the States parties concerned.

Rule 77E. If a matter referred to the Committee in accordance with article 41 of the Covenant is not resolved to the satisfaction of the States parties concerned, the Committee may, with their prior consent, proceed to apply the procedure prescribed in article 42 of the Covenant.

XVII. Procedure for the Consideration of Communications Received under the Optional Protocol
A. Transmission of Communications to the Committee

Rule 78. 1. The Secretary-General shall bring to the attention of the Committee, in accordance with the present rules, communications which are or appear to be submitted for consideration by the Committee under article 1 of the Protocol.

2. The Secretary-General, when necessary, may request clarification from the author of a communication as to his wish to have his communication submitted to the Committee for consideration under the Protocol. In case there is still doubt as to the wish of the author, the Committee shall be seized of the communication.

3. No communication shall be received by the Committee or included in a list under rule 79 if it concerns a State which is not a party to the Protocol.

Rule 79. 1. The Secretary-General shall prepare lists of the communications submitted to the Committee in accordance with rule 78 above, with a brief summary of their contents, and shall circulate such lists to the members of the Committee at regular intervals. The Secretary-General shall also maintain a permanent register of all such communications.

2. The full text of any communication brought to the attention of the Committee shall be made available to any member of the Committee upon his request.

Rule 80. 1. The Secretary-General may request clarification from the author of a communication concerning the applicability of the Protocol to his communication, in particular regarding:

(a) The name, address, age and occupation of the author and the verification of his identity;

(b) The name of the State party against which the communication is directed;

(c) The object of the communication;

(d) The provision or provisions of the Covenant alleged to have been violated;

(e) The facts of the claim;

(f) Steps taken by the author to exhaust domestic remedies;

(g) The extent to which the same matter is being examined under another procedure of international investigation or settlement.

2. When requesting clarification or information, the Secretary-General shall indicate an appropriate time-limit

to the author of the communication with a view to avoiding undue delays in the procedure under the Protocol.

3. The Committee may approve a questionnaire for the purpose of requesting the above-mentioned information from the author of the communication.

4. The request for clarification referred to in paragraph 1 of the present rule shall not preclude the inclusion of the communication in the list provided for in rule 79, paragraph 1, above.

Rule 81. For each registered communication the Secretary-General shall as soon as possible prepare and circulate to the members of the Committee a summary of the relevant information obtained.

B. General Provisions Regarding the Consideration of Communications by the Committee or its Subsidiary Bodies

Rule 82. Meetings of the Committee or its subsidiary bodies during which communications under the Protocol will be examined shall be closed. Meetings during which the Committee may consider general issues such as procedures for the application of the Protocol may be public if the Committee so decides.

Rule 83. The Committee may issue communiqués, through the Secretary-General, for the use of the information media and the general public regarding the activities of the Committee at its closed meetings.

Rule 84. 1. A member shall not take part in the examination of a communication by the Committee:

(a) If he has any personal interest in the case; or

(b) If he has participated in any capacity in the making of any decision on the case covered by the communication.

2. Any question which may arise under paragraph 1 above shall be decided by the Committee.

Rule 85. If, for any reason, a member considers that he should not take part or continue to take part in the examination of a communication, he shall inform the Chairman of his withdrawal.

Rule 86. The Committee may, prior to forwarding its final views on the communication to the State party concerned, inform that State of its views whether interim measures may be desirable to avoid irreparable damage to the victim of the alleged violation. In doing so, the Committee shall inform the State party concerned that such expression of its views on interim measures does not imply a determination on the merits of the communication.

C. Procedure to Determine Admissibility

Rule 87. 1. The Committee shall decide as soon as possible and in accordance with the following rules whether the communication is admissible or is inadmissible under the Protocol.

2. A Working Group established under rule 89, paragraph 1, may also declare a communication admissible when it is composed of five members and all the members so decide.

Rule 88. 1. Communications shall be dealt with in the order in which they are received by the Secretariat, unless the Committee or a Working Group established under rule 89, paragraph 1, decides otherwise.

2. Two or more communications may be dealt with jointly if deemed appropriate by the Committee or a Working Group established under rule 89, paragraph 1.

Rule 89. 1. The Committee may establish one or more Working Groups of no more than five of its members to make recommendations to the Committee regarding the fulfilment of the conditions of admissibility laid down in articles 1, 2, 3 and 5 (2) of the Protocol.

2. The rules of procedure of the Committee shall apply as far as possible to the meetings of the Working Group.

3. The Committee may designate Special Rapporteurs from among its members to assist in the handling of communications.

Rule 90. With a view to reaching a decision on the admissibility of a communication, the Committee, or a Working Group established under rule 89, paragraph 1, shall ascertain:

(a) That the communication is not anonymous and that it emanates from an individual, or individuals, subject to the jurisdiction of a State party to the Protocol;

(b) That the individual claims, in a manner sufficiently substantiated, to be a victim of a violation by that State party of any of the rights set forth in the Covenant. Normally, the communication should be submitted by the individual himself or by his representative; a communication submitted on behalf of an alleged victim may, however, be accepted when it appears that he is unable to submit the communication himself;

(c) That the communication is not an abuse of the right to submit a communication under the Protocol;

(d) That the communication is not incompatible with the provisions of the Covenant;

(e) That the same matter is not being examined under another procedure of international investigation or settlement;

(f) That the individual has exhausted all available domestic remedies.

Rule 91. 1. The Committee or a Working Group established under rule 89, paragraph 1, or a Special Rapporteur designated under rule 89, paragraph 3, may request the State party concerned or the author of the communication to submit additional written information or observations relevant to the question of the admissibility of the communication. To avoid undue delays, a time-limit for the submission of such information or observations shall be indicated.

2. A communication may not be declared admissible unless the State party concerned has received the text of the communication and has been given an opportunity to furnish information or observations as provided in paragraph 1 of this rule.

3. A request addressed to a State party under paragraph 1 of this rule shall include a statement of the fact that such a request does not imply that any decision has been reached on the question of admissibility.

4. Within fixed time-limits, each party may be afforded an opportunity to comment on submissions made by the other party pursuant to this rule.

Rule 92. 1. Where the Committee decides that a communication is inadmissible under the Protocol it shall as soon as possible communicate its decision, through the Secretary-General, to the author of the communication and, where the communication has been transmitted to a State party concerned, to that State party.

2. If the Committee has declared a communication inadmissible under article 5, paragraph 2, of the protocol, this decision may be reviewed at a later date by the Committee upon a written request by or on behalf of the individual concerned containing information to the effect that the reasons for inadmissibility referred to in article 5, paragraph 2, no longer apply.

3. Any member of the Committee may request that a

summary of his individual opinion shall be appended to the Committee's decision declaring a communication inadmissible under the Optional Protocol.

D. Procedure for the Consideration of Communications on the Merits

Rule 93. 1. As soon as possible after the Committee or a Working Group acting under rule 87, paragraph 2, has taken a decision that a communication is admissible under the Protocol, that decision and the text of the relevant documents shall be submitted, through the Secretary-General, to the State party concerned. The author of the communication shall also be informed, through the Secretary-General, of the decision.

2. Within six months, the State party concerned shall submit to the Committee written explanation or statements clarifying the matter under consideration and the remedy, if any, that may have been taken by that State.

3. Any explanations or statements submitted by a State party pursuant to this rule shall be communicated, through the Secretary-General, to the author of the communication who may submit any additional written information or observations within fixed time-limits.

4. Upon consideration of the merits, the Committee may review a decision that a communication is admissible in the light of any explanation or statements submitted by the State party pursuant to this rule.

Rule 94. 1. If the communication is admissible, the Committee shall consider it in the light of all written information made available to it by the individuals and by the State party concerned and shall formulate its reviews thereon. For this purpose the Committee may refer the communication to a Working Group of not more than five of its members or to a Special Rapporteur to make recommendations to the Committee.

2. The views of the Committee shall be communicated to the individual and to the State party concerned.

3. Any member of the Committee may request that a summary of his individual opinion shall be appended to the views of the Committee.

HUMAN RIGHTS COMMITTEE: HANDLING OF COMMUNICATIONS. Under the INTERNATIONAL COVENANT ON CIVIL AND POLITICAL RIGHTS: OPTIONAL PROTOCOL, the HUMAN RIGHTS COMMITTEE may receive and consider written communications from individuals who claim that any of their rights enumerated in the covenant have been violated and who have exhausted all available domestic remedies. Of the 87 States that had acceded to or ratified the covenant up to the end of 1989, 45 accepted the competence of the committee to deal with such individual complaints by ratifying or acceding to the optional protocol. No communication can be received by the committee if it concerns a State party to the covenant that is not also a party to the optional protocol.

In its report to the UN General Assembly on its work in 1989, the committee pointed out (UN Doc. A/44/40, chap. V) that, since it started its work under the op-

tional protocol in 1977, 371 communications concerning 28 States parties had been placed before it for consideration. Of these, 96 had been concluded by views under article 5, para. 4, of the optional protocol, 85 had been declared inadmissible, 59 had been discontinued or withdrawn, 33 had been declared admissible but had not been concluded, and 98 were pending at the pre-admissibility stage.

In 1989, the committee concluded consideration of 11 cases by adopting its views thereon and concluded consideration of 14 cases by declaring them inadmissible. The texts of the views adopted on the 11 cases, as well as the decisions on the 14 cases declared inadmissible, are reproduced in annexes X and XI of its report.

At its 35th session, held at the United Nations headquarters, New York, from 20 March to 7 April 1989, the committee decided to designate a special rapporteur to process new communications under rule 91 of its rules of procedure as they are received, i.e., between sessions of the committee. Mrs. Rosalyn Higgins was so designated for a period of one year, and subsequently she transmitted a number of communications to the States parties concerned, under rule 91, requesting information or observations relevant to the question of the admissibility of the communication.

At its 36th session held at the United Nations office in Geneva from 10 to 28 July 1989, the committee authorized its Working Group on Communications, consisting of five members, to adopt decisions to declare communications admissible when all the members so agree. Failing an agreement among the five members, the working group refers the matter to the committee. The working group, however, is not competent to adopt decisions declaring communications inadmissible.

The committee's decisions on the merits are nonbinding recommendations and, as such, are referred to as "views under article 5, para. 4, of the Optional Protocol." After the committee has made a finding of a violation of a provision of the covenant, it proceeds to ask the State party involved to take appropriate steps to remedy the violation.

Violations were found by the committee in 82 of the 96 communications concluded, up to the end of 1989, with the adoption of views.

The committee's procedures for the handling of communications are spelled out in detail in its provisional rules of procedure. They are summarized briefly below. In addition, some of the procedural issues resolved by the committee are set out in extracts from its recent reports to the General Assembly.

Procedures for the Handling of Communications

Communications received under the optional protocol are examined in closed meetings of the committee, as prescribed in article 5 (3) of the protocol. All documents pertaining to the work of the committee in handling such communications are confidential, except the texts of final decisions of the committee, which are made public. As regards decisions declaring a communication inadmissible, which are also final, the committee has decided that it will normally make these decisions public, substituting initials for the names of the alleged victims or authors.

(a) Registration of Communications. Communications are received by the UN Secretariat and are registered in accordance with the committee's rules. They are numbered consecutively, indicating the year of registration (e.g., No. 1/ 1988). For each session of the committee, the Center for Human Rights prepares a list of the communications registered since the most recent session which contains summaries of new cases. An annex to the list contains summaries of communications which, although they relate to alleged violations of human rights by States parties to the Optional Protocol, have not yet been registered as cases by the Secretariat, but which are brought to the attention of the Committee as borderline cases. The Secretariat may also, when necessary, request clarification from the author concerning the applicability of the Protocol to his communication.

(b) Admissibility of Communication. Once a communication has been registered, the Committee must decide whether it is admissible under the Optional Protocol. The requirements for admissibility, which are contained in articles 1, 2, 3 and 5 (2) of the Optional Protocol, are listed in rule 90 of the Committee's provisional rules of procedure. Under rule 91 (1) the Committee or a Working Group may request the State party concerned or the author of the communication to submit, within a time-limit which is indicated in each such decision (normally between six weeks and two months), additional written information or observations relevant to the question of admissibility of the communication. Such a request does not imply that any decision has been taken on the question of admissibility (rule 91 (3)). The decision to declare a communication admissible or inadmissible rests with the Committee. The Committee may also decide to terminate or suspend consideration of a communication if its author indicates that he wants to withdraw the case or if the Secretariat has lost contact with the author. A decision to declare a communication inadmissible or otherwise to terminate or suspend consideration of it may, in a clear case, be taken without referring the case to the State party for its observations.

(c) Consideration on the Merits. If a communication is declared admissible, the Committee proceeds to consider the substance of the complaint. In accordance with article 4 of the Optional Protocol, it requests the State party concerned to submit to the Committee explanations or statements clarifying the matter. Under article 4 (2), the State party has a time-limit of six months in which to submit its observations. When they are received, the author is given an opportunity to comment on the observations of the State party. The Committee then normally formulates its views and fowards them to the State party and to the author of the communication, in accordance with article 5 (4) of the Optional Protocol. The State party may be requested to transmit a copy of the views to an imprisoned victim. In exceptional cases, further information may be sought from the State party or the author by means of an interm decision before the Committee finally adopts its views. A Committee member may also write an individual opinion, which is appended to the Committee's views.

Since the Committee, which meets three times a year, must allow both the author and the State party sufficient time to prepare their submissions, a decision on admissibility can only be taken between six months and a year after the initial submission; views under article 5 (4) may follow one year later. The entire procedure normally may be completed within two to three years. The Committee tries to deal expeditiously with all communications.

1. Procedural Issues

A number of questions relating to the admissibility of communications have been dealt with in the Committee's reports to the General Assembly or in the Committee's decisions on particular communications. These issues always depend, directly or indirectly, on the terms of the Optional Protocol, and concern, *inter alia,* the following matters.

(a) The Standing of the Author. Normally, a communication should be submitted by the individual himself or by his representative; the Committee may, however, accept to consider a communication submitted on behalf of an alleged victim when it appears that he is unable to submit the communication himself (rule 90 (1) (b)). In practice, the Committee has accepted communications not only from a duly authorized legal representative, but also from a close family member acting on behalf of an alleged victim, but in other cases the Committee has found that the author of a communication lacked standing. In case No. 128/1982, the author was a member of a non-governmental organization and had taken interest in the alleged victim's situation. He claimed to have authority to act because he believed "that every prisoner treated unjustly would appreciate further investigation of his case by the Human Rights Committee". The Committee decided that the author lacked standing and declared the communication inadmissible. The Human Rights Committee has thus established through a number of decisions on admissibility that a communication submitted by a third party on behalf of an alleged victim can only be considered if the author justifies his authority to submit the communication.

The Committee has also held that an organization as such cannot submit a communication. In case No. 163/1984 (see annex XV below) it stated: "According to article I of the Optional Protocol, only individuals have the right to submit a communication. To the extent, therefore, that the communication originates from the [organization], it has to be declared inadmissible because of lack of personal standing". Similarly, in case No. 104/1981, the Committee declared a communication inadmissible, partly because "the W.G. Party is an association and not an individual, and as such cannot submit a communication to the Committee under the Optional Protocol".

(b) The Victim. The Committee has clarified in case No. 35/1978 that "a person can only claim to be a victim in the sense of article 1 of the Optional Protocol if he or she is actually affected. It is a matter of degree how concretely this requirement should be taken. However, no individual can in the abstract, by way of an *actio popularis,* challenge a law or practice claimed to be contrary to the Covenant. If the law or practice has not already been concretely applied to the detriment of that individual, it must in any event be

applicable in such a way that the alleged victim's risk of being affected is more than a theoretical possibility". That is, a person is not a victim unless he has personally suffered a violation of his rights. In case No. 61/1979 the Committee stressed "that it has only been entrusted with the mandate of examining whether an individual has suffered an actual violation of his rights. It cannot review in the abstract whether national legislation contravenes the Covenant, although such legislation may, in particular circumstances, produce adverse effects which directly affect the individual, making him thus a victim in the sense contemplated by articles 1 and 2 of the Optional Protocol".

(c) Date of Entry into Force of the Covenant and the Optional Protocol. The Committee has indicated frequently that it "can consider only an alleged violation of human rights occurring on or after 23 March 1976 (the date of entry into force of the Covenant and the Protocol) for [the State party] unless it is an alleged violation which, although occurring before that date, continues or has effects which themselves constitute a violation after that date". The Committee has declared a number of communications inadmissible *ratione temporis* (or parts of said communications) when the alleged violations occurred prior to the entry into force of the Covenant and the Optional Protocol for the State party concerned. Although this issue is mostly disposed of at the admissibility stage, the Committee may indicate in its views that "the facts as found by the Committee, in so far as they continued or occurred after [the date of entry into force of the Covenant and the Optional Protocol for the State party concerned] disclose violations . . ." etc. (No. 123/1982, see annex XII below).

(d) Individuals Subject to a State Party's Jurisdiction. In several cases the Committee has had to address the question whether an alleged victim is "subject to the jurisdiction" of the State party for the purposes of article 1 of the Optional Protocol. In case No. 110/1981 (see annex XI below), the State Party contended that the communication was inadmissible because the alleged victim had been released from imprisonment and "he left the country to live abroad and he was therefore not subject to the jurisdiction" of the State party. The Committee noted in its views that "by virtue of article 2, paragraph 1 of the Covenant, each State party undertakes to respect and to ensure to 'all individuals within its territory and subject to its jurisdiction' the rights recognized in the Covenant. Article 1 of the Optional Protocol was clearly intended to apply to individuals subject to the jurisdiction of the State party concerned at the time of the alleged violation of the Covenant. This was manifestly the object and purpose of article 1". The same question was dealt with in case No. 25/1978.

A related issue arises when the alleged violation of the human rights of a national of a State party occurs when that person is not residing in his country at the time of the alleged violation. This was the situation in case No. 57/1979 where the author, while living abroad, requested the renewal of her passport. It was the Committee's view that "the issue of a passport to a [State party's] citizen is clearly a matter within the jurisdiction of the [State party's] authorities and he is 'subject to the jurisdiction' of [the State party] for that purpose. Moreover a passport is a means of enabling him 'to leave any country, including his own', as required by article 12 (2) of the Covenant. It therefore follows from the very nature of the right that, in the case of a citizen resident abroad it imposes obligations both on the State of residence and on the State of nationality". The Committee expressed a similar view at its twenty-first session when it declared communication No. 125/1982 admissible. It stated: "The question of the issue of a passport by [the State party] to a national [of the State party] wherever he may be, is clearly a matter within the jurisdiction of the [State party's] authorities and he is 'subject to jurisdiction' of [State party] for that purpose".

(e) Preclusion under Article 5 (2) (a) of the Optional Protocol if the Same Matter is Being Examined under Another Procedure of International Investigation or Settlement. The Optional Protocol precludes the competence of the Committee to consider cases which are simultaneously being examined under other procedures of international investigation or settlement, such as the procedures of the Inter-American Commission on Human Rights (IACHR) and the European Commission of Human Rights. When this situation arises, the practice of the Committee has been to instruct the Secretariat to explain to the author that consideration by the Committee is precluded under article 5 (2) (a) of the Optional Protocol. In the majority of such cases (which have concerned examination of the same matter by the Inter-American Commission on Human Rights) the authors have then withdrawn their communications from the IACHR in order to enable the Committee to proceed with their examination. In one case the author preferred to withdraw the case from the Human Rights Committee in order to have it considered by the European Commission of Human Rights.

In case No. 10/1977 the Committee concluded "that it is not prevented from considering the communication submitted to it by the authors on 10 March 1977 by reason of the subsequent complaint made by an unrelated third party under the procedures of the IACHR". The rationale for this decision was explained in case No. 74/1979 where the Committee observed that the provision of article 5 (2) (a) "cannot be so interpreted as to imply that an unrelated third party, acting without the knowledge and consent of the alleged victim, can preclude the latter from having access to the Human Rights Committee".

As to what constitutes the "same matter", the Committee decided in case No. 6/1977 that a two-line reference to the person concerned in a case before the Inter-American Commission on Human Rights, which listed in a similar manner the names of hundreds of other persons allegedly detained in the State party, "did not constitute the same matter as that described in detail by the author in his communication to the Human Rights Committee".

The Committee has also held that the submission of a similar case concerning a third party to another international procedure does not constitute the "same matter". Thus in case No. 75/1980 the Committee explained: ". . . the concept of the 'same matter' within the meaning of article 5 (2) (a) of the Optional Protocol must be understood as including the same claim concerning the same individual, submitted by him or someone else who has the standing to act on his behalf before the other international body".

In the first case placed before it under the Optional Protocol, the Committee had occasion to determine that the examination of a particular human rights situation in a given country under Economic and Social Council resolution 1503 (XLVIII), which governs a procedure for the examination of situations which appear to reveal "a consistent pattern of gross and reliably attested violations of human rights and fundamental freedoms", does not within the meaning of article 5 (2) (a) of the Optional Protocol constitute an examination of the "same matter" as a claim by an individual submitted to the Human Rights Committee under the Optional Protocol. The procedure governed by Economic and Social Council resolution 1503 (XLVIII) therefore does not bar the Human Rights Committee from considering an individual case. Also in one of the early cases considered, the Human Rights Committee determined that a procedure established by a non-governmental organization (such as the Inter-Parliamentary Council of the Inter-Parliamentary Union) does not constitute a procedure of international investigation or settlement within the meaning of article 5 (2) (a) of the Optional Protocol.

At its twenty-first session, the Committee also observed, when declaring admissible a number of similar and related cases concerning the same country, "that a study by an intergovernmental organization either of the human rights situation in a given country (such as that by the IACHR) or a study of the trade union rights situation in a given country (such as the issues examined by the Committee on Freedom of Association of the ILO), or of a human rights problem of a more global character (such as that of the Special Rapporteur of the Commission on Human Rights on summary or arbitrary executions), although such studies might refer to or draw on information concerning individuals, cannot be seen as being the same matter as the examination of individual cases within the meaning of article 5 (2) (a) of the Optional Protocol. Secondly, a procedure established by non-governmental organizations (such as Amnesty International, the International Commission of Jurists or the International Committee of the Red Cross, irrespective of the latter's standing in international law), does not constitute a procedure of international investigation or settlement within the meaning of article 5 (2) (a) of the Optional Protocol".

(f)Reservations by States Parties. Several States parties have further limited the competence of the Human Rights Committee to deal with communications under the Optional Protocol. With reference to article 5 (2) (a) the Governments of Denmark, Iceland, Italy, Norway and Sweden made reservations upon ratification of the Optional Protocol, precluding the competence of the Committee to consider a communication from an individual if the matter had already been examined under another procedure of international investigation or settlement. This reservation goes beyond the provision in the Optional Protocol which only precludes consideration with respect to cases which are simultaneously being considered elsewhere but not with respect to cases the consideration of which has been concluded under another procedure. In case No. 121/1982, the author had first submitted his communication to the European Commission of Human Rights, which had declared it inadmissible as manifestly ill-founded. The Committee at its sixteenth session concluded that it was not competent to consider the communication in the light of the State party's reservation. In a subsequent case concerning another State party, the author approached the European Commission of Human Rights but was informed that it was already too late to submit an application. The State party itself informed the Committee that it would not object to the admissibility of the communication on the basis of its reservation, because the case had not been examined by the European Commission of Human Rights.

(g) Exhaustion of Domestic Remedies. Under article 5 (2) (a) of the Optional Protocol, the Committee shall not consider any communication unless it has ascertained that the author has exhausted all available domestic remedies. Numerous communications before the Committee have been declared inadmissible on this ground. In its decisions on admissibility, the Committee has clarified the meaning of article 5 (2) (b) of the Optional Protocol, explaining, *inter alia,* that "exhaustion of domestic remedies can be required only to the extent that these remedies are effective and available" and further clarified that "an extraordinary remedy, such as seeking the annulment of decision(s) of the Ministry of Justice" does not constitute an effective remedy within the meaning of article 5 (2) (b) of the Optional Protocol.

In a number of early cases a State party had contended that the authors had failed to exhaust domestic remedies and submitted to the Committee a general description of remedies provided under the law of that State, without, however, linking these remedies to the specific circumstances of each case. The Committee considered that this was insufficient and informed the State party that it would be necessary to give "details of the remedies which it submitted had been available to the author in the circumstances of his case, together with evidence that there would be a reasonable prospect that such remedies would be effective" (No. 4/1977).

The Rules of Procedure also provide that a decision on admissibility may be reviewed in the light of any explanations or statements submitted by the State party under article 4 (2) of the Optional Protocol (rule 93 (4)). Such review requires that the State party give "specific details of domestic remedies which it claims to have been available to the alleged victim, together with evidence that there would be a reasonable prospect that such remedies would be effective".

(h) Inadmissibility Ratione Materiae. The Committee can consider communications only in so far as they relate to alleged violations of rights contained in the International Covenant on Civil and Political Rights. Communications relating to alleged violations of other rights must therefore be declared inadmissible *ratione materiae.* For instance, the Committee at its seventh session had to declare inadmissible communication No. 53/1979 because "the right to dispose of property, as such, is not protected by any provision of the International Covenant on Civil and Political Rights". Similarly, in its eighteenth session, the Committee declared communication No. 129/1982 inadmissible because "the assessment of taxable income and allocation of houses are not in themselves matters to which the Covenant applies".

(i) Substantiation of Allegations. Although at the stage of admissibility an author of a communication need not prove his case, he must submit sufficient evidence in substantiation of his allegations as will constitute a *prima facie* case. The Committee has declared a number of communications inadmissible on the grounds of non-substantiation of allegations.

(j) Abuse of the Right of Submission. Under article 3 of the Optional Protocol, the Committee shall declare inadmissible a communication which it considers to be an abuse of the right of submission. In case No. 72/1980, where the author had alleged violations of rights not protected in the Covenant, had failed to substantiate in fact or law other allegations which pertained to rights protected by the Covenant and had himself indicated that he still intended to pursue further domestic remedies, the Committee concluded that "in these circumstances, the submission of the communication must be regarded as an abuse of the right of submission under article 3 of the Optional Protocol".

(k) The "Claim" under Article 2 of the Optional Protocol. Arti-

cle 2 of the Optional Protocol requires that a claim of a violation must relate to a right enumerated in the Covenant. In case No. 174/1984 (J. K. v. Canada) the author, who had allegedly been injustly convicted of a criminal offence several years before the Covenant and the Optional Protocol entered into force for the State party, claimed that the stigma of the allegedly unjust conviction and the social and legal consequences thereof made him a victim today of violations of a number of articles of the Covenant. He asked the Committee to request the State party to annul the conviction and to pay him equitable indemnity. After noting that the communication was inadmissible, *ratione temporis,* in so far as it related to events said to have taken place prior to the entry into force of the Covenant and the Optional Protocol for the State party and that it was also beyond the Committee's competence to review findings of fact made by national tribunals or to determine whether national tribunals properly evaluated new evidence submitted on appeal, the Committee observed that the consequences of the conviction, as described by the author, "do not themselves raise issues under the International Covenant on Civil and Political Rights in his case. The Committee, accordingly, concludes that the author has no claim under article 2 of the Optional Protocol". The Human Rights Committee decided, therefore, that the communication was inadmissible.

In case No. 173/1984 (M. F. v. the Netherlands) the author, a national of Chile, filed an application for political asylum in the Netherlands. His request was turned down and an order was issued for his expulsion. The author claimed to be a victim of violations by the State party of a number of articles of the Covenant. The Human Rights Committee declared the communication inadmissible and stated as follows:

"A thorough examination of the communication has not revealed any facts in substantiation of the author's claim that he is a victim of a breach by the State party of any rights protected by the Covenant. In particular, it emerges from the author's own submission that he was given ample opportunity, in formal proceedings including oral hearings, to present his case for sojourn in the Netherlands. The Committee, accordingly, concludes that the author has no claim under article 2 of the Optional Protocol."

(l) Reservations by States Parties. The question of the Committee's competence in the light of State party reservations was the subject of its decision in case No. 168/1984 (V. O. v. Norway). At its twenty-fifth session, the Committee, in declaring the communication inadmissible, shed further light on the meaning of the term "the same matter", as applied to communications submitted both to the Committee and to another international procedure. In this regard the Committee stated:

"The Committee notes that the Norwegian reservation to article 5, paragraph 2, of the Optional Protocol stipulates that the Committee shall lack competence to consider a communication if 'the same matter' has already been examined under other international procedures. This phrase in the view of the Committee refers, with regard to identical parties, to the complaints advanced and facts adduced in support of them. Thus the Committee finds that the matter that is before the Committee now is in fact the same matter that was examined by the European Commission. While fully understanding the circumstances which have led the author to make a communication under the Covenant, the Committee finds that the State party's reservation operates to preclude it from examining the communication."

(m) Review of Decision on Admissibility. Rule 93, para-

graph 4, of the Committee's provisional rules of procedure permits the Committee to review a decision declaring a communication admissible in the light of explanations or statements submitted by the State party under article 4, paragraph 2, of the Optional Protocol. This rule was applied for the first time at the Committee's twenty-fourth session. Case No. 113/1981 (C. F. *et al.* v. Canada) had been declared admissible by the Committee at its nineteenth session. At its twenty-fourth session in April 1985, the Committee revised its prior decision as follows:

"Pursuant to rule 93, paragraph 4, of its provisional rules of procedure the Human Rights Committee has reviewed its decision on admissibility of 25 July 1983. On the basis of the additional information provided by the Canadian Government, the Committee concludes that the authors could have obtained redress for the violation complained of by seeking a declaratory judgement. The Committee has stressed in other cases that remedies the availability of which is not reasonably evident cannot be invoked by the Government to the detriment of the author in proceedings under the Optional Protocol. According to the detailed explanations contained in the submission of 17 February 1984, however, the legal position appears to be sufficiently clear in that the specific remedy of a declaratory judgement was available and, if granted, would have been an effective remedy against the authorities concerned. . . .

"In the light of the above considerations, the Committee finds that it is precluded under article 5, paragraph 2 (b), of the Optional Protocol from considering the merits of the case and *decides:*

"1. The decision of 25 July 1983 is set aside.

"2. The communication is inadmissible."

(n) Substantiation of Allegations. A number of communications have been declared inadmissible on the ground of non-substantiation of allegations. In case No. 178/1984 (J. D. B. v. the Netherlands) the author complained that he had suffered discrimination in the field of employment and referred to article 6 of the International Covenant on Economic, Social and Cultural Rights, which protects the right to work. The author claimed that the discrimination which he had allegedly suffered made him a victim of a violation of article 26 of the International Covenant on Civil and Political Rights. Concluding that no facts had been submitted in substantiation of the author's claim that he was a victim of a violation of any of the rights guaranteed by the International Covenant on Civil and Political Rights, the Human Rights Committee declared the communication inadmissible.

(o) The Requirement that a Communication be Declared Admissible before it is Examined on the Merits (rule 93). Although under rule 91 of the Committee's provisional rules of procedure States parties are requested to furnish information and observations only with regard to the question of the admissibility of a communication, frequently they also make extensive submissions at that stage on the merits of the case. Submissions from States parties under rule 91 are transmitted to the authors for comments, who sometimes make further extensive submissions on matters of substance. Thus, even before the adoption of a decision on the admissibility of a communication, the Committee may have before it all the information it needs in order to adopt a final decision on the merits. Under the rules of procedure, however, the Committee cannot adopt views under article 5, paragraph 4 of the Optional Protocol, until it has declared the case admissible and given the State party, pursuant to article 4, paragraph 2, of the Optional Protocol, six

months to submit "written explanations or statements clarifying the matter and the remedy, if any, that may have been taken by that State". In order to expedite the procedure when appropriate, the Committee has developed a new practice. Thus, in the admissibility decision concerning communication No. 198/1985 (R. Stalla Costa v. Uruguay), adopted at the Committee's twenty-ninth session in April 1987, the Committee noted:

". . . that the facts of the case, as already set out by the author and the State party, are sufficiently clear to permit an examination on the merits. At this stage the Committee must, however, limit itself to the procedural requirement of deciding on the admissibility of the communication. Should the State party, nevertheless, wish to add to its earlier submissions within six months of the transmittal to it of the present decision, the author of the communication will be given an opportunity to comment thereon. If no further explanations or statements are received from the State party under article 4, paragraph 2, of the Optional Protocol, the Committee will proceed to adopt its final views in the light of the written information already submitted by the parties."

The Committee therefore decided:

"That any further explanations or statements which the State party may wish to submit to clarify the matter and the measures taken by it, should, in accordance with article 4, paragraph 2, of the Optional Protocol, reach the Human Rights Committee within six months of the date of transmittal to it of this decision. Should the State party not intend to make a further submission in the case, it is requested to so inform the Committee as soon as possible to permit an early decision on the merits."

The State party responded, accordingly, that it would make no further submission in the case, thus enabling the Committee, at its thirtieth session in July 1987, to proceed to the adoption of views under article 5, paragraph 4, of the Optional Protocol.

(p) *The Standing of the Author under Article 2 of the Optional Protocol.* With respect to the standing of authors who have submitted communications to the Committee claiming to be victims of a violation of the right of self-determination enshrined in article 1 of the Covenant, the Committee held in an admissibility decision adopted at its twenty-ninth session:

". . . that the author, as an individual, cannot claim to be a victim of a violation of the right of self-determination enshrined in article 1 of the Covenant. Whereas the Optional Protocol provides a recourse procedure for individuals claiming that their rights have been violated, article 1 of the Covenant deals with rights conferred upon peoples, as such."

Similarly, in a decision adopted at its thirtieth session in respect of a communication submitted by an individual acting on his own behalf and claiming to act on behalf of others, the Committee reaffirmed

". . . that the Covenant recognizes and protects in most resolute terms a people's right of self-determination and its right to dispose of its natural resources, as an essential condition for the effective guarantee and observance of individual human rights and for the promotion and strengthening of those rights. However, the Committee observes . . . that the author, as an individual, cannot claim under the Optional Protocol to be a victim of a violation of the right of self-determination enshrined in article 1 of the Covenant, which deals with rights conferred upon peoples, as such."

The Committee decided, however, that the communication could be considered, in so far as it might raise issues under article 27 and other articles of the Covenant.

(q) *The Requirement of State Jurisdiction under Article 1 of the Optional Protocol.* The requirement in article 1 of the Optional Protocol that an individual be subject to the jurisdiction of the State party was further elucidated by the Committee in its decision declaring communication No. 217/1986 (H.v.d.P. v. the Netherlands) inadmissible. In that case the author, an international civil servant with the European Patent Office, had claimed to be a victim of discrimination in the promotion practices of that organization. He contended that the Human Rights Committee was competent to consider the case, since five States parties to the European Patent Convention (France, Italy, Luxembourg, the Netherlands and Sweden) were also parties to the Optional Protocol to the International Covenant on Civil and Political Rights. The author, a national of the Netherlands, submitted his communication against the Netherlands. The Committee observed, however:

". . . that it can only receive and consider communications in respect of claims that come under the jurisdiction of a State party to the Covenant. The author's grievances, however, concern the recruitment policies of an international organization, which cannot, in any way, be construed as coming within the jurisdiction of the Netherlands or of any other State party to the International Covenant on Civil and Political Rights and the Optional Protocol thereto. Accordingly, the author has no claim under the Optional Protocol."

(r) *Interim Measures under Rule 86.* The authors of a number of cases currently before the Committee are convicted persons who have been sentenced to death and are awaiting execution. These authors claim to be innocent of the crimes of which they were convicted and further allege that they were denied a fair hearing. In view of the urgency of the communications, the Committee has requested the two States parties concerned, under rule 86 of the Committee's provisional rules of procedure, not to carry out the death sentences until "the Committee has had the opportunity to render a final decision in this case" or "the Committee has had an opportunity to consider further . . . the question of admissibility of the present communication." Stays of execution have been granted in this connection.

Rule 86 was also invoked by the Committee at its thirtieth session in a case concerning a group of persons, in respect of whom the State party was requested to take steps to avoid irreparable damage.

(s) *The Requirement of Exhaustion of Domestic Remedies (Optional Protocol, article 5, para. 2 [b].* Pursuant to article 5, paragraph 2 (b), of the Optional Protocol, the Committee shall not consider any communication unless it has ascertained that the author has exhausted all available domestic remedies. However, the Committee has already established that the rule of exhaustion applies only to the extent that these remedies are effective and available and the State Party is required to give "details of the remedies which it submitted had been available to the author in the circumstances of his case, together with evidence that there would be a reasonable prospect that such remedies would be effective" (case No. 4/1977, Torres Ramírez v. Uruguay). The rule also provides that the Committee is not precluded from examining a communication if it is established that the application of the remedies in question is unreasonably prolonged.

In case No. 224/1987 (A. and S. N. v. Norway) the authors did not bring their case before any judicial or administrative instance in Norway, arguing that remedies would not have been effective, because the practice they were challenging was legal in Norway and because the Covenant could not be directly applied by Norwegian courts. Moreover, the authors decided to appeal directly to the Committee, arguing that the exhaustion of domestic remedies would be prolonged and be "a waste of time and money". The Committee asked the State party to explain the remedies available to the authors, in particular to clarify whether there was a competent tribunal or constitutional court in Norway, in which the authors could test the legality of the Day Nurseries Act as amended in 1983. In an extensive reply, the State party submitted that "Norwegian courts have given considerable weight to international treaties and conventions in the interpretation of domestic rules, even if these instruments have not been formally incorporated into domestic law", adding that "the possibility of setting aside a national statute altogether on the grounds of conflict with the Covenant cannot be disregarded". Moreover, the State party indicated that the authors could have argued that the Act in question was in conflict with article 2 (1) of the Norwegian Constitution, under which "all inhabitants of the Kingdom shall have the right to free exercise of their religion". In the light of the State party's explanations and the author's comments thereon, the Committee observed:

"that the authors have not pursued the domestic remedies which the State party has submitted were available to them. It notes the authors' doubts whether the International Covenant on Civil and Political Rights would be taken into account by Norwegian courts, and their belief that the matter could not be satisfactorily settled by Norwegian court. The State party, however, has submitted that the Covenant would be a source of law of considerable weight in interpreting the scope of the Christian object clause and that the authors would have stood a reasonable chance of challenging the christian object clause of the Day Nurseries Act and the prevailing practice as to their compatibility with the Covenant had they submitted the case to the Norwegian courts; the Committee notes further that there was a possibility for an expeditious handling of the authors' case before the local courts. The Committee finds, accordingly, that the pursuit of the authors' case before Norwegian courts could not be deemed *a priori* futile and that the authors' doubts about the effectiveness of domestic remedies did not absolve them from exhausting them. Thus, the requirements of article 5, paragraph 2 (b), of the Optional Protocol have not been met".

(t) No Claim under Article 2 of the Optional Protocol. Article 2 of the Optional Protocol provides that "individuals who claim that any of their rights enumerated in the Covenant have been violated and who have exhausted all available domestic remedies may submit a written communication to the Committee for consideration."

Although at the stage of admissibility an author need not prove the alleged violation, he must submit sufficient evidence in substantiation of his allegation to constitute a *prima facie* case. A "claim" is therefore not just any allegation, but an allegation supported by a certain amount of substantiating evidence. Thus, in cases where the Committee finds that the author has failed to make at least a *prima facie* case before the Committee, justifying further examination on the merits, the Committee has held the communication inadmissible, declaring that the author "has no claim under article 2 of the Optional Protocol". During the period covered by the present report the Committee has used this formula in declaring four communications inadmissible (see annex VIII, sects. B, F, H and K).

(u) Interim Measures under Rule 86. The authors of a number of cases currently before the Committee are convicted persons who have been sentenced to death and are awaiting execution. These authors claim to be innocent of the crimes of which they were convicted and further allege that they were denied a fair hearing. In view of the urgency of the communications, the Committee has requested the two States parties concerned, under rule 86 of the Committee's provisional rules of procedure, not to carry out the death sentences until "the Committee has had an opportunity to render a final decision in this case" or "the Committee has had an opportunity to consider further . . . the question of admissibility of the present communication". Stays of execution have been granted in this connection.

In view of the growing number of communications from persons awaiting execution, the Committee appointed one of its members, Mr. Andreas Mavrommatis, Special Rapporteur on death penalty cases, and authorized him to take rule 86 decisions on behalf of the Committee.

SEE ALSO Complaints and Other Communications concerning Human Rights.

HUMAN RIGHTS DAY. On 10 December 1948, the UN General Assembly adopted and proclaimed (resolution 217 A [III] the UNIVERSAL DECLARATION OF HUMAN RIGHTS. Two years later, on 4 December 1950, it invited (resolution 423 [V] all States and interested organizations to adopt December 10 of each year as "Human Rights Day," to observe this day to celebrate the proclamation of the declaration, and to exert increasing efforts in this field of human progress. The assembly expressed the view that the anniversary should be appropriately commemorated in all countries as part of the common effort to bring the principles set out in the declaration to the attention of all the peoples of the world and expressed its appreciation to those countries that had already begun to observe the anniversary.

Up to the end of 1989, Human Rights Day had been celebrated for 39 years in all parts of the world, with the most extensive celebrations occurring on the 10th anniversary of the declaration (1958), the 20th (1968), the 30th (1978), and the 40th (1988).

The 20th anniversary, 1968, was designated by the General Assembly as the INTERNATIONAL YEAR FOR HUMAN RIGHTS and was marked by the convening of the International Conference on Human Rights. The assembly decided (resolution 2081 [XX]) on 20 December 1965:

to promote further the principles contained in the Universal Declaration of Human Rights, to develop and guarantee political, civil, economic, social and cultural rights and to end all discrimination and denial of human rights and fundamental freedoms on grounds of race, colour, sex, language or religion, and in particular to permit the elimination of *apartheid,* an International Conference on Human Rights should be convened during 1968 in order to:

(a) Review the progress which has been made in the field of human rights since the adoption of the Universal Declaration of Human Rights;

(b) Evaluate the effectiveness of the methods used by the United Nations in the field of human rights, especially with respect to the elimination of all forms of racial discrimination and the practice of the policy of *apartheid;*

(c) Formulate and prepare a programme of further measures to be taken subsequent to the celebrations of the International Year for Human Rights.

The program approved by the General Assembly (resolution 2081 [XX], annex) gave first priority to the elimination of certain practices constituting some of the grosser forms of the denial of human rights. It then called for further study by United Nations bodies of international measures for the guarantee or protection of human rights and for the establishment of programs designed to promote the full enjoyment by all of human rights and fundamental freedoms. The national programs envisaged by the assembly called upon governments, *inter alia,* to embark upon a complementary program of education, including both adult and child education, designed to produce new thinking on the part of many people in regard to human rights, this program to aim at mobilizing some of the energies of:

(a) universities, colleges, and other institutions of higher learning, both private and public, within member States;

(b) the teaching staff of primary and secondary schools;

(c) foundations and charitable, scientific and research institutions; and

(d) media of information and mass communication, including the press, radio and television.

A further program approved by the General Assembly on 19 December 1966 (resolution 2217 A [XXI], annex), called upon the Secretary-General to do all in his power to publicize the 20th anniversary of the Universal Declaration and the observance of the International Year for Human Rights, recommended a long list of activities to be undertaken during 1968 by governments and interested organizations, and proposed that all the commemorative activities be coordinated by the Secretary-General.

The International Conference on Human Rights, convened at Teheran from 22 April to 13 May 1968, adopted the **PROCLAMATION OF TEHERAN,** by which it "affirmed its faith in the principles of the Universal Declaration of Human Rights and other international instruments in this field" and urged all peoples and governments to dedicate themselves to those principles and "to redouble their efforts to provide for all human beings a life consonant with freedom and dignity and conducive to physical, mental, social and spiritual welfare." The conference adopted 29 resolutions on various aspects of human rights.

After reviewing the final act of the conference, the assembly on 19 December 1968 expressed satisfaction (resolution 2442 [XXIII]) with the conference's work, endorsed the Proclamation of Teheran, and urged all States and concerned organizations to encourage and assist all media of mass communication in giving widespread publicity to the proclamation and to the work of the conference. The assembly also called upon all States and concerned organizations to take further action with a view to the full realization of human rights in the light of the recommendations of the conference.

In 1977, the UN COMMISSION ON HUMAN RIGHTS expressed the view (resolution 2442 [XXIII]) that the 30th anniversary of the Universal Declaration of Human Rights (10 December 1978) should afford an opportunity for Member States and their peoples, and particularly teachers and the parents of children, to comply fully with the request of the General Assembly that all peoples and every organ of society should strive in every possible way to promote respect for human rights and fundamental freedoms. In this connection, the Commission decided, *inter alia,*

to recommend to Member States, the specialized agencies and all international organizations, governmental and non-governmental, concerned with the protection and promotion of human rights, to take appropriate measures to ensure that the thirtieth anniversary of the Universal Declaration of Human Rights is the occasion of special efforts to promote international understanding, co-operation and peace and the universal and effective respect for human rights, more particularly by laying stress on the educational approach both within and outside formal school systems.

Both the Economic and Social council and the General Assembly endorsed the commission's resolution and the assembly requested the Secretary-General (resolution 32/123) to initiate appropriate activities. The assembly itself held a special commemorative meeting on 10 December 1978 to celebrate the anniversary.

The General Assembly decided on 4 December 1986 (resolution 41/150) to celebrate the 40th anniversary of the Universal Declaration of Human Rights (10 December 1988) and invited member States, specialized agencies, regional intergovernmental organizations, and non-governmental organizations throughout the world to take appropriate measures and to support appropriate activities aimed at encouraging the promotion and universal observance of human rights and fundamental freedoms. On 7 December 1987 (resolution 42/131), it reiterated that decision and resolved further that the 1988 celebration should be used as an occasion to highlight the achievements of the United Nations in its efforts to promote and protect human rights universally, to renew the commitment of the organization in this area and to encourage member States to ensure the promotion and protection of the rights enshrined in the Universal Declaration. The assembly again held a special commemorative meeting, on 8 December 1988, to observe the anniversary.

A worldwide program of activities for the observance of the 40th anniversary of the declaration was coordinated by the UN CENTER FOR HUMAN RIGHTS and the Department of Public Information. Activities began on World AIDS Day, 1 December, and ended on Human Rights Day. At UN headquarters in New York, a series of daily seminars was held dealing with various aspects of human rights, such as economic and social rights; human rights aspects of AIDS; human rights writers; the right to education as reflected in the proposed convention on the rights of the child; women and human rights; the role of non-governmental organizations in the work of the United Nations in the field of human rights; and the situation of United Nations staff members whose human rights have been violated. Film screenings and musical, cultural, and social events were also held.

In addition, on Human Rights Day 1988, the UN Secretary-General accepted the Nobel Peace Prize at Oslo on behalf of the United Nations peacekeeping forces, and ceremonies were held in Paris at the *Palais de Chaillot*, the site of the Universal Declaration of Human Rights by the General Assembly on 10 December 1948.

In a decision adopted on 8 December 1988 (resolution 43/90) the General Assembly reaffirmed the significance of the Universal Declaration of Human Rights as a source of inspiration for national and international efforts to promote and protect human rights and fundamental freedoms. Underlining the importance of the teaching of human rights at all levels, it noted the progress made up to that time in the field of human rights, including standard-setting and codification, but expressed its concern at mass and flagrant violations of human rights, including those stemming from racism and all forms of racial discrimination and *apartheid,* and at all violations of human rights that continue to take place in many parts of the world. Further, it affirmed the responsibility of the United Nations in protecting and promoting human

rights and fundamental freedoms and expressed the determination of the United Nations to deal, through appropriate United Nations bodies, with violations of human rights and fundamental freedoms.

Reaffirming the importance of the observance and effective implementation of universally recognized standards in the field of human rights contained in international human rights instruments, the assembly invited the UN Commission on Human Rights to consider a program of action which would include:

(a) measures to promote the universal ratification of or accession to United Nations instruments in the field of human rights and to strengthen United Nations machinery for the promotion and protection of human rights and fundamental freedoms enshrined in the Declaration;

(b) activities to develop human rights institutions and infrastructures, drawing upon the assistance of the United Nations Program for Advisory Services in the Field of Human Rights, including the Voluntary Fund for Technical Assistance and Advisory Services, and drawing also upon the relevant capabilities of the specialized agencies in this field, and other available multilateral and bilateral assistance;

(c) activities in the area of public information as may be determined by the commission in considering the world campaign for human rights; and

(d) measures to enhance national and existing regional institutions for the promotion of human rights, through appropriate educational, judicial, legal, and other channels, including direct contact among them.

HUMAN RIGHTS DEFENDERS. The protection of persons who participate in proceedings before international organs competent to deal with allegations concerning violations of human rights has been a matter of concern for some years. It has been proposed that standardized rules setting out the immunities of such persons, and of their lawyers, witnesses, and experts called upon to assist them, should be adopted. Such rules are already in effect in Europe.

In 1969, the COMMITTEE OF MINISTERS OF THE COUNCIL OF EUROPE adopted the EUROPEAN AGREEMENT RELATING TO PERSONS PARTICIPATING IN PROCEEDINGS OF THE EUROPEAN COMMISSION AND COURT OF HUMAN RIGHTS. The agreement applies to (a) agents of the contracting parties and advisors and advocates assisting them; (b) persons taking part in proceedings instituted before the commission under article 25 of the convention, whether in their own names or as representatives of one of the applicants enumerated in article 25; (c) barristers, solicitors, or professors of law, taking part in proceedings in order to assist one of the persons enumerated in (b) above; (d) persons chosen by the delegates of the commission to assist them in proceedings before the court; and (e) witnesses, experts, and other persons called upon by the commission or the court to take part in proceedings before the commission or the court. Article 2 states that these persons "shall have immunity from legal process in respect of oral or written statements made, or documents or other evidence submitted by them before or to the Commission or the Court." Under article 3, the contracting parties undertake to respect the right of these persons to correspond freely with the commission and the court; and, under article 4, they undertake not to hinder the free movement and travel, for the purpose of attending and returning from proceedings before the commission or the court, the above-mentioned persons whose presence has in advance been authorized by the commission or the court.

In 1970, the UN Secretary-General, at the request of the **COMMISSION ON HUMAN RIGHTS,** prepared draft model rules for United Nations bodies dealing with violations of human rights (UN Doc. E/CN.4/1020), in which it was proposed that all United Nations bodies investigating such violations should make the arrangements necessary with the State concerned to ensure that no obstacle provented representative or witnesses from attending meetings of the body and assuring any witness or any individual appearing before the body due protection against any acts of violence or intimidation, any threats or reprisals, or any discriminatory measures which might be directed against them because they attend the meetings or give their testimony, and against any legal proceedings which might be instituted against them because of their testimony. However, these proposals were not adopted; and it has since been the practice of UN bodies assigned to make on-the-spot fact-finding investigations of human rights violations to work out individual agreements with the governments concerned in which the government assures the group of its assistance in the protection of the persons the group desires to meet.

The **INTERNATIONAL FEDERATION OF HUMAN RIGHTS,** a non-governmental organization in consultative status, has been studying various aspects of the problem. In a written statement submitted to the **SUB-COMMISSION ON PREVENTION OF DISCRIMINATION AND PROTECTION OF MINORITIES** at its 1988 session (UN Doc. E/CN.4/Sub.2/1988/NGO/6), the federation pointed out that

. . .United Nations human rights agencies have increased the number of organs and procedures for direct access, thus enabling them to deal with individual communica-

tions and complaints and, on that basis, to report on the various situations involving violations of human rights. There has thus been steady progress towards a regular system for reporting violations and for monitoring offending States, although no specific measure to protect those individuals who have recourse to those procedures has been adopted. The duty of protecting human rights is becoming a particularly dangerous responsibility for persons who are denied the guarantees of the law. For régimes based on force, the affirmation of the primacy of the law becomes a subversive activity.

Usually the mere fact of alerting, informing or attempting, either through us or directly, to contact United Nations agencies causes those who are helping the victims to become victims in their turn. The various organs of the Commission have been able to verify on a number of occasions that a more selective repression is now directed particularly against human rights activists. The threat overthrowing the future of human rights through the persecution of their champions is very serious and the time and energy devoted to adopting a declaration by the General Assembly is too precious. Such a declaration should not merely confine itself to an abstract reaffirmation of rights but should, if it is to be effective, reaffirm and strengthen the freedom of association and propose universal rules for its exercise. In the interests of effectiveness, it is vital to have a prior knowledge of the status of the law in that regard. The FIDH requests the Sub-Commission to instruct one of its experts:

(a) To conduct a study on the national legislation regulating the protection of Human Rights advocates; [and]

(b) To prepare model rules for the use of those countries that do not yet provide measures of protection for these persons in their domestic law.

The **INTER-AMERICAN COMMISSION ON HUMAN RIGHTS** commented on the difficulties faced by human rights activists and their organizations in its annual report for 1985–1986 (OAS Ser. L/V/II.68, Doc. 8 rev. 1, pp. 194–195) as follows:

Limitations or weakness of the judiciary have led human rights organizations, particularly non-governmental ones, to play an active role in the protection of human rights, the denunciation of violations, and the movement to investigate such violations.

In some cases, the activities carried out by these organizations have helped to correct abuses; in other cases, as the Commission has regrettably found in examining the situation of human rights in various states, these organizations or their leaders have been persecuted by government authorities, which has enormously hampered their valuable work.

Several cases of such persecution can be cited. In some instances, human rights organizations have been denied legal status or juridical personality. In others, their offices have been raided and their property confiscated. Moreover, in at least three countries, their leaders have been subjected to threats, smear campaigns, harassment and even detention, in which the flimsiest pretexts have been used to block their functions and activities.

Since many of these methods have regrettably been used more intensively in recent years in some member states, the Commission feels obligated to reiterate to those member states where such organizations are carrying out their important functions under such precarious conditions, their obligation to guarantee the autonomy and freedom of activity of such human rights organizations, as well as the integrity and full freedom of their leaders.

The UN Commission on Human Rights, at its 1988 session, adopted a resolution (resolution 1988/39) in which it expressed its concern that, in many parts of the world, numerous persons are detained for seeking to exercise peacefully their human rights and fundamental freedoms, in particular the rights to freedom of expression, of assembly, and of association, or to promote and defend those rights and freedoms; and that these persons are often exposed to special dangers as regards the protection of their human rights and fundamental freedoms.

The commission requested all governments to release all persons deprived of their liberty for seeking peacefully to exercise these rights and freedoms or to promote and defend them; and called on all governments, pending such release, to take effective measures to safeguard the human rights and fundamental freedoms of such persons.

The Sub-Commission on Prevention of Discrimination and Protection of Minorities also adopted a resolution in 1988 (resolution 1988/38) in which it expressed its concern at the incidence of detention, torture, disappearances, and extra-legal executions of individuals, in particular those within their own countries who are working to promote and protect universally recognized human rights and fundamental freedoms, including lawyers complying with their professional ethical obligations to defend the legal rights of their clients.

The sub-commission called for the release of all persons detained, in violation of the rights to freedom of speech, association, and assembly; for defending the human rights of others; and for publicizing alleged violations of human rights. It further called for effective measures of protection for those working to promote and protect the human rights of others, as well as the rights of complainants, witnesses, and those who are threatened with violations of their own rights, particularly intimidation or threats to life or limb. It decided that, where relevant, studies being carried out by the sub-commission should pay particular attention to the rights of persons promoting and protecting the human rights of others and their violation; and urged the Commission on Human Rights to finalize as soon as possible its work on the drafting of a declaration on the right and responsibility of individuals, groups, and organs of society to promote and protect universally recognized human rights and fundamental freedoms.

In spite of the activities summarized above, 68 men and women who monitored human rights abuses were killed in 1989, and ten others disappeared after being seized by security forces, according to the 1989 annual report of HUMAN RIGHTS WATCH, a non-governmental organization in consultative status with the Economic and Social Council. The number of persons involved was considerably higher in 1989 than it had been in 1988, when 34 persons who testified to abuses were reported killed and four others disappeared.

HUMAN RIGHTS INFORMATION AND DOCUMENTATION SYSTEM (HURIDOCS). A non-profit participatory international communications network founded in Strasbourg, France, in 1979, HURIDOCS provides a worldwide clearinghouse for information and documentation relating to human rights. Established by human rights organizations and interested individuals from more than 50 countries, the organization reviews, analyzes, and systematizes the information it receives and makes it available for use in the promotion and protection of human rights. In addition, it conducts conferences and seminars on questions relating to human rights and issues their reports, as well as its periodical *HURIDOCS News*.

Human Rights Information and Documentation System, International. Address: Domplein 24, 3512 JE Utrecht, Netherlands. Telephone: (31-30) 39 40 33. Cable: SIMCABLE. Telex: 70779. Chairman: K. Rupesinghe.

Yearbook of International Organizations 1989/90. (K.G. Saur).

HUMAN RIGHTS INTERNET. A non-profit participatory international communications network founded in 1976 to provide a worldwide clearinghouse on matters related to human rights, Human Rights Internet is a non-partisan independent organization that is open to everyone who subscribes to the principles set out in the UNIVERSAL DECLARATION OF HUMAN RIGHTS.

Internet's constituency is a broad one, including non-governmental organizations concerned with human rights, international and national officials, lawyers, journalists, students, and the general public. Its main objectives are (1) to gather and disseminate information relating to the status of human rights in various parts of the world, the work of human rights organizations, and relevant developments international law and organization; (2) to promote research and teaching in the human rights field; and (3) to stimulate communication and coordination within the human rights community.

Internet's program includes the following activities:

(1) Human Rights Internet Reporter. Published quarterly, the *Reporter* systematically describes publication of human rights organizations on all continents; the work of governmental, non-governmental, and intergovernmental organizations; developments in international law; and resources for teaching and research. Each issue provides subject, geographic, and organizational indices, generated directly from HRI's computerized databases.

(2) HRI Directories. In 1979, Internet published its first directory on the work of U.S.-based human rights organizations; this has been expanded to a *North American Human Rights Directory (1984).* In 1981, HRI published the *Human Rights Directory: Latin America, Africa and Asia.* The third volume, on Western Europe, was published in 1982, and a fourth, on Eastern Europe and the USSR, was issued in 1987. Volumes followed on Africa (1989) and Latin America and the Caribbean (1990). Future directories are planned for Asia and the Middle East.

(3) HRI Documentation Center. In 1980, Internet began systematically to collect the publications—and unpublished documentation—produced by human rights organizations on all continents; HRI is now the unofficial depository for such documentation. The material is abstracted in the *Reporter,* maintained as the core of HRI's documentation center, and made available to those who come to HRI's library or who request copies of specific documents.

(4) HRI/Microfiche Project. To aid in the preservation and dissemination of documentation, Internet edits a comprehensive microfiche collection. Filming is completed for material from 1980 to 1988 of nearly 300 major non-governmental human rights organizations.

(5) HRI Databases. In 1985, Internet designed and implemented a computer database program to facilitate the retrieval of information and the production of the *Reporter.* Since Vol. 11, No. 1 (December 1985), the contents of the *Reporter* have been maintained in a computer database, and Internet's directories have been entered into another database for rapid updating and retrieval. HRI is exploring the possibility of transforming the database into an on-line system, making it available via telephone, to those with access to computer terminals. HRI also assists other human rights documentation centers in North America, Western Europe, and the third worlds in computerization.

(6) Documentation Assistance. Internet has provided technical assistance on library, acquisition, and bibliographic policies to a number of intergovernmental organizations, including UNESCO, OAS, and UNITAR, and to many non-governmental organizations including the African Centre for Democracy and Human Rights Studies (Banjul) and the Inter-American Institute of Human Rights (San Jose).

(7) Support for Teaching and Research. Internet produces specialized resources, such as *Teaching Human Rights* (1981) to facilitate research in the humanities, the social sciences, and the law. In addition, it sponsors an intern program to provide students with an opportunity to become familiar with human rights documentation and to gain exposure to the work and concerns of human rights organizations in all parts of the world.

Human Rights Internet. Address: Human Rights Centre, University of Ottawa, 57 Louis Pasteur, Ottawa, Ontario K1N GN5 (Canada). Telephone: (613) 564-3492. Fax: (613) 564-4054. Cable: INTERNET. Executive Director: Laurie S. Wiseberg.

HUMAN RIGHTS TEACHING PRIZE. In alternate years, since 1984, the UNITED NATIONS EDUCATIONAL, SCIENTIFIC AND CULTURAL ORGANIZATION has awarded the UNESCO Prize for Human Rights Teaching, created by the Executive Board at its 104th session. In 1984, the prize was awarded to Mr. Felix Ermacora (Austria) with an honorable mention to Mr. Kadir Asmal (Ireland); in 1986, to Mr. Hector Fix Zamudio (Mexico), with an honorable mention to Mr. Ralph Pettman (Australia); and in 1988, to the *Asamblea Permanente de los Derechos Humanos* (Bolivia), with honorable mention to Mr. Fred and Mrs. Bonnie Cappucino (Canada), Mrs. Jeanne Hersch (Switzerland), and Mr. Alfredo Bravo (Argentina).

HUMAN RIGHTS WATCH. A non-governmental organization which was established to link together the "Watch" organizations—HELSINKI WATCH, AMERICAS WATCH, and ASIA WATCH—and to establish new Watch groups (Middle East Watch and Africa Watch are anticipated by the 1990s). Human Rights Watch monitors the human rights practices of governments: murder, "disappearances," kidnapping, torture, imprisonment for non-violent expression or association, exile, psychiatric abuse, censorship, and deprivations of political freedom. The group sends missions to countries where abuses have been reported. The mission meets with government officials, opposition leaders, local human rights groups, church officials, labor leaders, journalists, college faculty members, lawyers, relief groups, doctors, and others to gather information on human rights practices. Where possible, the mission interviews victims, members of their families, and witnesses to abuses; the group also attends court proceedings and examines court records.

Human Rights Watch's membership is based in the United States. The group devotes much of its effort to shaping U.S. foreign policy towards countries that violate human rights, frequently testifying at congressional hearings; publishing an annual review of the administration's policy and an annual critique of the State Department's human rights reports; and generating pressure on the State Department and other federal agencies.

Human Rights Watch is affiliated with the Fund for Free Expression, which was established in 1975.

HRW publishes *Human Rights Watch,* a periodic newsletter that reports the activities of the Watch groups and the Fund for Free Expression.

Human Rights Watch. Address: 45 Fifth Ave., New York, NY 10017. Telephone: (212) 972-8400. Fax: 972-8400. Executive Director: Aryeh Neier.

HUNGARY. The Hungarian People's Republic is a country in eastern Europe. It has borders with Austria, Czechoslovakia, Romania, the Union of Soviet Socialist Republics, and Yugoslavia. It achieved independence in 1949 and became a member of the United Nations in 1955. Its population is estimated by the UN (1990) to be 10,658,000. Ethnic groups include Bulgarians who immigrated at the beginning of the 20th century, Poles and Greeks who settled during and after World War II, and Gypsies. The language most commonly used is Hungarian; however, the Bulgarians, Poles, Greeks, and Gypsies tend to use their own languages, as do members of the linguistic minorities: Southern Slavs (Croatians, Serbs, and Slovenes), Germans, Romanians, and Slovaks.

Under the Hungarian constitution (article 63), the State guarantees freedom of conscience and religious worship for all citizens and separates the Church from the State. Considering religion to be a private affair of citizens, the State keeps no statistics on religious affiliation. It does, however, recognize about 20 religious denominations and provides financial support for the protection of their buildings and institutes, as well as annual subsidies; and the functioning of churches is governed by various laws and regulations and by agreements concluded between the State and particular churches. It is privately estimated that between one and 1.5 million Hungarians are active church members, with Christianity as the predominant religion. Literacy is estimated at 98%.

The government (1990) took the form of a republic. Under the constitution, the supreme body of State power is the 21-member Presidential Council, elected by the National Assembly and headed by the president. Administrative power is exercised by the Council of Ministers, headed by the prime minister. The 352-member unicameral People's Assembly, whose members are elected by popular vote for terms of four years, is the national legislature. The administration of justice is the responsibility of the procurator-general, who is elected by the National Assembly.

Hungary's transition from a single-party State to a multi-party democracy was a gradual one which followed a sharp decline in the membership of the Communist Party and the emergency of numerous informal groups of dissidents which developed into full-fledged opposition parties.

In mid-March 1986, a group of Hungarian citizens attempted to march through Budapest to mark the anniversary of the 1956 uprising which had been crushed by Soviet tanks; the march was broken up by police using truncheons and tear gas. In mid-March 1987, about 3,000 Hungarians attempted such a march again; this time the march was tolerated by the communist authorities. In mid-March 1988, more than 10,000 people paraded through the center of Budapest after several members of the growing opposition had been arrested for "subversion" in a series of dawn raids; they chanted "Democracy!" and carried banners that demanded "press freedom," "real reforms," and "freedom of assembly." This time the police did not attempt to block the march.

In September 1989, the government, after months of negotiations, reached agreement with leaders of the opposition calling for the enactment of a more democratic electoral law, the creation of a stronger presidency, the legalization of political parties, and the liberalization of the penal code and rules of criminal procedure.

In October, a three-member body of the Communist Party took office and adopted a social democratic program in the hope of attracting aid from the West; at that time, it changed its name to the Socialist Party. In a referendum held on 26 November—the first free national vote in 42 years—voters rejected the party's plan for election of the president in January 1990, when it would still control Parliament. Instead, a timetable was established for multi-party elections to Parliament to be held on 25 March 1990, with the president to be elected by members of the new Parliament at a later date.

Twelve major political parties participated in the parliamentary elections: the Hungarian Socialist Party, the Hungarian Democratic Reform, the Alliance of Free Democrats, the Independent Smallholders' Party, the Federation of Young Democrats, the Social Democratic Party of Hungary, the Christian Democratic People's Party, the Hungarian People's

Party, the Hungarian Socialist Workers Party, the Entrepreneurs Party, the Patriotic Election Coalition, and the Agrarian Federation.

Arpad Goncz, a leading writer who had spent six months in jail after receiving a life sentence for the part he played in the 1956 uprising, was selected as head of Parliament and, thus, interim president of Hungary on 2 May 1990, receiving 339 of the 370 votes cast in the first freely elected Parliament convened in that country in four decades. On the same day, by agreement between the center-right Hungarian Democratic Forum and his own liberal opposition party, the Free Democrats, Mr. Goncz was selected to serve as Hungary's president.

A monarchy for more than 1,000 years and part of the of the Austro–Hungary monarchy from 1867 until its collapse in 1918, Hungary fought in World War II as an ally of Germany but, nevertheless, fell under German occupation. German forces were driven out by Soviet armies early in 1945, but the Soviet troops remained until 1949. In 1947, a new constitution was promulgated proclaiming Hungary a People's Republic.

Open criticism of the regime by Hungarian writers, students, and intellectuals led to demonstrations and street fighting in Budapest. The trial and sentencing of Jozsef Cardinal Mindszenty, the Roman Catholic primate of Hungary, aroused further angry demonstrations, and Soviet troops temporarily withdrew from Budapest. Premier Nagy, assenting to popular demand, proclaimed Hungary's neutrality and its withdrawal from the Warsaw Pact and announced the government's intention to hold free, multi-party elections.

Three days after these announcements, Soviet armed forces crushed the national uprising on 3 November 1956. Three decades later, Hungary has developed the reputation of being somewhat freer than most Eastern European States; however, its economic development is reported to have deteriorated slightly.

As regards human rights, Hungary is bound by article 2 of the Peace Treaty with the Allied and Associated Powers at Paris on 10 February 1947, which provides that:

1. Hungary shall take all measures necessary to secure to all persons under Hungarian jurisdiction, without distinction as to race, sex, language or religion, the enjoyment of human rights and of the fundamental freedoms, including freedom of expression, of press and publication, of religious worship, of political opinion and of public meeting.
2. Hungary further undertakes that the laws in force in Hungary shall not, either in their content or in their application, discriminate or entail any discrimination between persons of Hungarian nationality on the ground of their race, sex, language or religion, whether in reference to their persons, prosperity, business, professional or finan-

cial interests, status, political or civil rights or any other matter.

The "nationalities" situation in Hungary is a complex one. The Hungarian government, in a report submitted to the COMMITTEE ON THE ELIMINATION OF RACIAL DISCRIMINATION on 2 June 1986, stated that (UN Doc. CERD/C/149/Add. 9, para. 13–20):

To understand the situation of nationalities in Hungary one should be aware of the fact that none of the national minorities live in close settlements, in ethnically homogeneous areas, but are largely mingled with Hungarians in both urban and rural areas. Their scattered settlements or diaspora are partly a result of the accelerated mobility and migration of the population over the past decades, and partly an indication of the specific features of their original immigration or settlement. Most of the nationality populations settled in the present territory of Hungary at the turn of the seventeenth and eighteenth centuries. The period and historical circumstances of their settlement are also reflected in their current ethnic features, including the state of their native tongues (which are in general archaic vernaculars lacking in uniformity and palpably different from literary language).

In creating conditions for the enjoyment by nationalities of social, economic and cultural rights, the Hungarian Government has always kept in mind that the actual number of non-Hungarians is larger than that shown by census data.

According to the latest census data (1980), 101,000 citizens stated their mother tongue to be other than Hungarian, the breakdown being 38,800 Southern Slavs (Croatians, Serbs and Slovenes), 25,000 Germans, 14,200 Romanians and 16,100 Slovaks. It should also be noted that, in addition to the six largest nationalities with historical traditions, small ethnic groups totalling some 6,500 live in Hungary, including Bulgarians who immigrated at the beginning of this century and Poles and Greeks who settled during and after the Second World War.

Since earlier experience showed that the need for education in native tongues and for the cultivation of national cultures was greater than indicated by census figures, the census questionnaires of 1980 requested citizens to indicate their command of a language or languages other than their mother tongue. On the basis of replies an additional 95,800 citizens were found to speak one of the national idioms, namely Southern Slav (11,000), German (53,900), Romanian (3,000) and Slovak (26,900).

Parallel to the 1980 census, the Ministry of Education and Culture conducted a survey of 509 settlements with a view to facilitating more accurate planning for the satisfaction of educational and cultural needs. The survey showed 252,200 citizens interested in the cultivation of national cultures (132,400 for German, 39,700 for Southern Slav, 12,100 for Romanian and 68,000 for Slovak). These figures should be supplemented by the number of those who live in towns not covered by the survey for methodological reasons, and thus the total number of members of nationalities is estimated to be between 300,000 and 330,000 citizens who amount to 3.2 per cent of the total population.

The federations of nationalities have their own estimates which show that some 200,000 to 220,000 Germans, 80,000 to 100,000 Southern Slavs, 100,000 to 110,000 Slovaks and 20,000 to 25,000 Romanians live in Hungary.

In the preparation of development plans the Hungarian Government relies on data supplied by the federations of nationalities and revealed by scientific surveys. The basic principle of its policy is to ensure the conditions for nationalities to enjoy equal rights and to preserve their collective identities irrespective of their ratio to the country's population.

The foregoing shows that the Government endeavours to obtain a differentiated and accurate picture of the demographic pattern of nationalities and to rely on the most favourable data in ensuring the conditions of existence for the nationalities. While the Government does not expect citizens as individuals to declare themselves as belonging to a nationality against their will, it seeks to adopt measures to create natural conditions for them to preserve their identity as members of a nationality group, and its policy is supportive and practically designed to act against the process of assimilation.

As regards Hungary's Gypsy population, the Government stated in the same report that (*Ibid.*, para. 21 and 62–70):

There are currently between 370,000 and 380,000 Gypsies, amounting to some 3.6% of the total population.

Recent decades have seen a considerable improvement in the material conditions of a significant part of that population by comparison with the previously prevailing conditions of historical backwardness and marginality. While economic disadvantages were partially overcome, this ethnic group did not benefit from the process of development equally: some of them experienced further differentiation and there were consequential shifts of emphasis in the tasks concerning their integration into society.

Up to the late 1970s, the process of integration implied in the first place the elimination of segregation (living outside the norms of society), notably the acceptance of laws, participation in the social division of labour and creation of conditions for life in human dignity. The policy of the socialist State towards the Gypsy population in that period was based primarily on the effort to have them exercise the same rights and comply with the same duties as those of the rest of citizens.

From 1980 onwards, the process of integration imposes longer-term tasks on the Gypsy population, the Government and the social organizations. Now and in the years ahead, parallel to the general process of integration, more attention and support should be given to the Gypsy population for the attainment of a more favourable position in the socio-economic structure.

The Hungarian Government keeps the situation of Gypsies under review and adopts appropriate measures to improve their conditions of life.

The government programmes and measures cover a wide range of issues, such as employment, improved housing (liquidation of Gypsy shanties, easy-term credit for housing), education, higher cultural standards, health care, family planning and numerous other social problems.

The success of these efforts is reflected by the figures for the socio-economic situation of the Gypsy population. For nearly 20 years the ratio of able-bodied males employed has been about 85 per cent, conforming to that of non-Gypsy males. Significant progress is observed in the employment of Gypsy females, with some 53 per cent of them having permanent jobs or taking up seasonal or casual work on a regular basis. This ratio was 30 per cent at the end of the 1970s. (The national average ratio of women employed is 78 per cent at present).

Since the late 1970s vigorous progress has been made in improving the housing situation of Gypsies. The number of Gypsies living in shanties fell to less than 30,000 in 1985 from 81,000 in 1979. Some of them enlarged their dwellings, built larger ones, or moved into flats with modern conveniences.

Since the early 1980s, the ratio of Gypsy children accommodated in nursery schools has ranged between 50 and 60 per cent, while children not accommodated attend preschool courses. The primary school attendance of Gypsy children is a significant achievement, but many of them repeat classes and are over-age, which is often due to their unfavourable family circumstances. The ratio of those continuing studies after completion of primary schooling is likewise low (37 per cent compared with 94 per cent of non-Gypsy children). The Government is making considerable efforts to reduce the disadvantage of Gypsy children, assisting them with scholarships and other means to pursue secondary and higher studies.

Better living conditions resulted in an improvement of the Gypsies' health conditions as well. During the past 10 years, the infantile mortality rate fell by half and the average age increased somewhat. However, some groups of the Gypsy population still live in centuries-old backwardness, continue this heritage, and feel no need for change. This has led local councils to bring about, on a self-help basis and with government support, a family-care network to assist those groups with social enlightenment and education.

In a later report, presented to the same committee on 29 November 1988, the government supplied additional information on the subject, as follows (UN Doc. CERD/C/172/Add. 7, para. 24–31):

The facts and figures furnished for nationalities and Gypsies in Hungary are still valid. Additional information for the period 1986-1987 follows below.

No new comprehensive measures affecting the situation of nationalities in Hungary were introduced during the reporting period. The democratic associations of Germans, Southern Slavs, Slovaks and Romanians are to hold their congresses in 1988. It is to be expected that in the light of the positions and resolutions of those congresses the Government will subject the situation of nationalities to a comprehensive review and will determine the future tasks of the government organs in this respect.

During the past two years, however, the Government has introduced some measures in certain aspects of its policy towards the nationalities:

Act I of 1985 on Education, which entered into force in September 1986, laid down as one of its basic principles that "the language of education at kindergartens and of education and instruction at schools shall be Hungarian as well as all national idioms spoken in the Hungarian People's Republic" (art. 7, chap. I). The significance of this rule consists in that a legal guarantee for equality of language as recognized by the Constitution has now been provided in the field of education.

In 1986 the Government reviewed the contacts of nationalities with the countries of their language and stated its case for asserting the role of members of nationalities as subjects in international relations and emphasized the need for them to develop and widen their contacts with the nations of their tongue.

The reporting period has witnessed a continuing process of differentiation in the life of Gypsies living in Hungary. There is a considerable number of settlements where the living standards and the way of life of Gypsies have come close to those of the local population, or where Gypsies live and work as other Hungarian citizens do. It remains a fact, however, that the ratio is still high for those who, for one reason or another (lack of skill, low income, number of dependents per earner, unfavourable housing conditions, etc.), are disadvantaged in comparison with the social average. Nevertheless it should be stressed that this no longer means some sort of a general "disadvantage of Gypsies". The changes in the life of Gypsies link them to the different segments and groups of society, and the socio-economic situation of groups of Gypsies can also be characterized by that of those segments and groups (e.g. place in the division of labour, type of settlement, small and large families).

The formation by a small group of Gypsies of the Cultural Association of Hungarian Gypsies can be seen as a significant development in 1986. The Association as a cultural representative organization aims to cultivate the language and the progressive cultural traditions of Gypsies, their family customs and other habits promotive of development. The activity of the Association extends to the entire territory of the country and to all segments of Gypsies as an ethnic group in Hungary. A most significant achievement is the Association's foundation of a bi-weekly periodical entitled *Romano Nyevipe,* which publishes writings in Hungarian and Romany.

In 1986 the National Council of Gypsies was likewise reorganized within the framework of the National Council of the Patriotic People's Front. The Council is an organ composed of voluntary workers and carrying out its activity through the county councils of Gypsies, using the means of the Patriotic People's Front as a movement. It functions to promote the social integration of Gypsies.

Naturally the Government committee concerned with the improvement of the situation of Gypsies continues to keep under review and to assist the related activities of State and social organs.

HUNGER AND MALNUTRITION. The WORLD FOOD COUNCIL, meeting in Nicosia, Republic of Cyprus, from 23 to 26 May 1988, reviewed recent food and hunger trends in the world, examined the situation of global food-stocks and possible ways for their utilization as a means of development assistance, and addressed ecological issues vital to ensuring the food security of the present and future generations. In its report to the General Assembly, the council evaluated the situation at that time as follows (UN Doc. A/43/19, part I):

Global State of Hunger and Malnutrition. The untenable trends of growing hunger and malnutrition, to which the Council's Beijing Declaration drew the world's attention, are continuing. Famine again threatens large numbers of people in Africa, and millions of people in Asia and Latin America face extraordinary food shortages, in the wake of natural calamities or civil strife. Food consumption per person, which has been declining in a large number of developing countries throughout this decade, decreased further in all developing regions in 1987—indicating a tragic rise in the number of hungry people. More children are now suffering from malnutrition than a decade ago. According to United Nations estimates, over 14 million children under the age of five die needlessly every year from malnutrition and disease in the developing countries.

The living conditions of the poorest people continue to deteriorate in the difficult national and international economic conditions. Despite some slight improvements in 1987, the developing regions' economies continue to suffer from depressed international commodity prices, protectionism and worsening terms of trade, growing debt-service obligations, and reduced and—in many cases—negative net resource transfer abroad. It was recognized that a more equitable income distribution could contribute to the alleviation of hunger, malnutrition and poverty.

However, our review should also give rise to some hope. Social concern is growing. Many countries are seeking to protect the food security and well-being of their low-income people in the economic difficulties of this decade. International agencies are asked to continue to better respond to the assistance needs of these countries, for which purpose the agencies should have the necessary resources available.

We note with satisfaction that some progress has been made since the Beijing session with regard to disarmament, detente and regional peace efforts. Peace is a prerequisite for sound development, which should have the well-being of all people as its central objective.

The current imbalances that characterize the world economy challenge the entire international community to halt and reverse the trend of growing hunger and malnutrition. We reiterate our Beijing call for fundamental policy changes to improve the human condition. Specifically, we call for a joint effort by all countries and international agencies to improve the food condition and protect the nutritional levels of low-income groups during economic adjustment. We request the WFC secretariat to provide us regularly at future Council sessions with comprehensive analyses on policy options, country experiences and progress in the fight against hunger.

We emphasize that the alleviation of hunger and malnutrition requires that more resources be channelled, nationally and internationally, to the world's poor. Equitable economic development is essential to the alleviation of hunger and poverty and requires greater resource flows to developing countries through improved international trade conditions, feasible approaches to the debt problem and stepped-up development assistance.

Potential for Hunger Reduction through Food-Surplus-Based Development Assistance. Growing hunger admist food surpluses is a cruel fact of our times. As follow-up to the Council's Beijing (thirteenth) session, we have sought to put this problem into perspective by assessing the current and prospective food-stock situation, reviewing the developing countries' food needs and examining possible ways for surplus utilization in support of accelerated food-security focused development in developing countries.

Global cereal stocks increased during most of the 1980s, reaching record levels in 1987. They are expected to decline over the next two years. But in any event, stocks are likely to fluctuate above the levels considered "safe" for global food security and surpluses will persist in the medium term. While some developed countries are trying to draw down their stocks, developing nations are finding it increasingly difficult to feed their people. In many developing countries, food production has not kept pace with population growth, financial constraints have reduced food imports per person, non-emergency food aid has remained stagnant, and food consumption levels have been declining.

Against this background, we examined a proposal by the WFC secretariat for an international hunger initiative based on a combination of concessional food transfers from food-surplus countries, financial assistance from non-food-surplus developed countries and the efforts by developing countries to alleviate hunger and poverty. While the proposal met with widespread interest and drew wide support, it was observed that food "surpluses" and hunger were separate problems. The Council's primary concern is the solution of the problems of hunger.

From this perspective, the secretariat's proposal represented a limited contribution to the much broader efforts required to address hunger problems. Our discussions brought to the fore that past policies and programmes had not succeeded in reducing hunger and malnutrition. Future progress will critically hinge on a better understanding of why efforts of the international community have proved insufficient. At the same time, we emphasize that more studies will not feed hungry people. Rather, immediate and more effective action is required, which draws upon the lessons of the past. In this spirit, we have decided to launch the following:

Cyprus Initiative against Hunger in the World. They Cyprus Initiative calls for an urgent review and assessment of the efforts made to date in hunger reduction and for the identification of ways for improving current policies and programmes and of pragmatic, feasible and potentially effective new initiatives towards meeting the Council's fundamental objective: the elimination of hunger and malnutrition. We call on the Council's President to present a full, action-oriented report to the Council at its fifteenth ministerial session in mid-1989. In order to assist the President in this complex task, we have agreed to establish an informal *ad hoc* consultative group along the following lines:

Composition. Representatives of States Members of the United Nations convened by the regional Vice-Presidents of WFC, relevant international organizations and the President, thus constituting a small group.

Mandate. The group should, in particular:

(a) Review and assess the policies and instruments at present available to combat chronic hunger and malnutrition in developing countries, particularly in low-income food-deficit countries, and identify the reasons and obstacles that may have hindered their greater impact;

(b) Consider concrete and realistic measures that could make existing policies and instruments more effective;

(c) Identify workable initiatives;

(d) Recommend a course of action to combat hunger more effectively.

Implementation. The proposals of the group should be examined first in a meeting of the bureau of WFC before the end of 1988. They shall thereafter be presented to the fifteenth ministerial session of the Council.

Action by the General Assembly. On 20 December 1988, the UN General Assembly reaffirmed (resolution 43/191) the UNIVERSAL DECLARATION ON THE ERADICATION OF HUNGER AND MALNUTRITION and noted with concern that hunger and malnutrition had been increasing since the World Food Conference in 1974, that the number of people suffering from hunger and malnutrition had increased since the 1980's, and that the central objective of the World Food Conference remained largely unfulfilled. It welcomed the conclusions and recommendations of the World Food Council, in particular the Cyprus Initiative against Hunger in the World, and called upon governments and international and non-governmental organizations to assist the Council fully in implementing that objective.

The Assembly stressed, in particular, the need for coordinated international action to tackle the long-term problems of migratory pest control, particularly in Africa, and, expressing gratitude for the support of donors and recognizing the efforts made by the affected countries in the fight against the grasshopper and locust infection, called upon donors to continue to give high priority to the implementation and continued coordination by the FAO of emergency control programs, as well as longer-term measures, against grasshoppers and locusts currently affecting vast areas of Africa, as well as other regions of the developing world, and to remain prepared to provide financial and technical assistance to affected countries at short notice.

The Assembly urged the World Food Council to continue to assess the overall impact of structural adjustment programs in developing countries on the nutritional levels of their populations, especially among children and low-income groups, and to suggest remedial measures in that area, including ways of stimulating the provision of resources to eliminate the suffering of those groups.

SEE ALSO *Food; Food and Agriculture Organization of the United Nations; Standard of Living.*

I

ICELAND. The Republic of Iceland is a country which occupies an island in the north Atlantic Ocean, east of Greenland. It achieved independence in 1944 and became a member of the United Nations in 1946. Its population is estimated by the UN (1990) to be 254,000. Ethnic groups include descendents of the Norse and Celtic settlers. Languages commonly used include Icelandic, Danish, and English. Christianity is the predominant religion; the Evangelical Lutheran Church is the established church of Iceland. Literacy is estimated at 99.9%.

The government (1990) took the form of a republic. The president, elected by universal suffrage for a term of four years, is head of State. The prime minister, appointed by the president, represents the party or coalition obtaining the majority in a popular election and exercises executive authority with the assistance of the cabinet. The 60-member bicameral elected *Althing* is the National Parliament. The 60 members who are elected select 20 of themselves to constitute the Upper House; the remaining 40 sit in the Lower House. The judiciary is protected by the constitution against interference by other branches of government. Political parties include the Independence Party, the Progressive Party, the Social Democratic Party, the Social Democratic Alliance, and the Women's League.

Iceland's *Althing*, established in 930 A.D., is the oldest parliament in the world. It did not function during the period when Norway, and later Denmark, assumed control over Iceland; but when Denmark granted Iceland a constitution in 1843, it was re-established as a consultative assembly. When home rule was granted in 1903, the danish minister for Icelandic affairs was made responsible to the *Althing*.

Iceland was neutral in World War II but cooperated with the Allied powers. Following German occupation from 1940 to 1944, the country was established as an independent republic on 17 June 1944. It became a charter member of the North American Treaty Alliance—the only NATO Member without military forces of its own. Under a treaty between Iceland and the United States of America signed in 1951, the United States assumed responsibility for Iceland's defense,

and, since that time, U.S. forces have been stationed at the NATO base in Keflavik.

ILLITERACY. In a report to the 1986 session of the UN General Assembly (UN Doc. A/41/472), transmitting the views of governments regarding the proposal to promote a new international humanitarian order, the Secretary-General included a "Survey on Specific Humanitarian Issues in the Contemporary World" based on information solicited or collected from specialized agencies and other bodies within the United Nations system. The survey was prepared at the request of the assembly (resolution 40/126) within the United Nations Secretariat and, in appropriate instances, in consultation with the organizations directly concerned.

Section E of the survey, entitled "Massive Illiteracy," (para. 28–33) reads as follows:

Endeavours to establish a new international humanitarian order must address the problem of illiteracy that in 1985 afflicted an estimated 889 million adults or 27.7 per cent of the population (15 years and older) of the planet. The persistence of illiteracy, which is a consequence of underdevelopment but also a major impediment to development, makes it impossible for millions of men and women to play an effective part in the shaping of their own destinies: it condemns to failure the battle against poverty, the elimination of inequalities and any attempts to establish relations of equality between individuals and nations. As a problem of world-wide scope, illiteracy is of concern to all countries, even those not directly affected by it. Hence, an intensification of the struggle against illiteracy appears an indispensable part of the quest to create a new humanitarian order.

Illiteracy is not a random phenomenon. The geography of illiteracy closely corresponds to that of poverty and destitution. There is a strong correlation between illiteracy, on the one hand, and malnutrition, poor health, short life expectancy, inadequate shelter, lack of access to safe drinking water and related symptoms and consequences of poverty, on the other. Whereas the illiteracy rate averages 2.1 per cent in the developed countries, the average is 38.2 per cent in the developing countries and, in some cases, it is nearly 90 per cent. These high rates of adult illiteracy are paralled by unsatisfactory access of children to school as well as by high drop-out and repetition rates that reduce the effectiveness of investments in education. In 1980, an estimated 114 million children aged 6 to 11 years in the developing countries were not enrolled in school and, unless urgent remedial action is taken, they will become the illiterate adults of tomorrow.

It must be emphasized first of all that the promotion of literacy is a task that primarily involves the countries concerned since its success depends on the will of Governments and citizens to mobilize energies and resources. The United Nations organizations and agencies, particularly the United Nations Educational, Scientific and Cultural Organization (UNESCO), and the international community as a whole have, however, an important supportive role to play.

Viewing illiteracy as a major humanitarian problem that requires the solidarity of the international community with those countries most seriously affected, UNESCO has sought to mobilize world opinion in support of literacy work by making decision-makers and the public at large more aware of the nature, magnitude and implications of illiteracy.

UNESCO has also accorded literacy priority within its Regular Programme and budget. The funding thus provided is devoted primarily to co-operation with Governments in formulating and implementing literacy and post-literacy strategies and to the training of key national personnel needed to plan and carry out literacy activities. In recent years, UNESCO has assisted its member States in launching regional programmes and projects to accelerate the eradication of illiteracy through the advancement of technical co-operation between developing countries. These regional programmes and projects have taken a global approach in which literacy instruction for adults and out-of-school youth is co-ordinated with measures to generalize the coverage and upgrade the quality and relevance of primary education.

The promotion of literacy in the developing world calls not so much for new initiatives—although appropriate ones would be welcome—but for more intensive and systematic support to ongoing national efforts. Literacy work is a labour-intensive, not a capital-intensive, activity. Yet, there are irreducible material requirements that the Governments of developing nations, particularly the least developed among them, afflicted by a decade of economic crisis, are often unable to meet. Enhanced international co-operation to assist developing countries to ensure to all citizens the right to education could contribute to the creation of a more just, equitable and humanitarian world.

ILO. *SEE International Labor Organization.*

ILO ABOLITION OF FORCED LABOR CONVENTION (1957).

Formally entitled Convention (No. 105) concerning the Abolition of Forced Labor, this instrument provides for States parties to undertake to suppress, and refrain from using, any form of FORCED LABOR or compulsory labor for any of the purposes set out in article 1. The convention was adopted by the INTERNATIONAL LABOR CONFERENCE (40th session) on 25 June 1957 and entered into force on 17 January 1959. The text of the convention (*International Labour Con-*

ventions and Recommendations, 1919–1981, p. 39), with the exception of the ILO STANDARD FINAL PROVISIONS (articles 3–10), is as follows:

The General Conference of the International Labour Organisation,

Having been convened at Geneva by the Governing Body of the International Labour Office, and having met in its Fortieth Session on 5 June 1957, and

Having considered the question of forced labour, which is the fourth item on the agenda of the session, and

Having noted the provisions of the Forced Labour Convention, 1930, and

Having noted that the Slavery Convention, 1926, provides that all necessary measure shall be taken to prevent compulsory or forced labour from developing into conditions analogous to slavery and that the Supplementary Convention on the Abolition of Slavery, the Slave Trade and Institutions and Practices Similar to Slavery, 1956, provides for the complete abolition of debt bondage and serfdom, and

Having noted that the Protection of Wages Convention, 1949, provides that wages shall be paid regularly and prohibits methods of payment which deprive the worker of a genuine possibility of terminating his employment, and

Having decided upon the adoption of further proposals with regard to the abolition of certain forms of forced or compulsory labour constituting a violation of the rights of man referred to in the Charter of the United Nations and enunciated by the Universal Declaration of Human Rights, and

Having determined that these proposals shall take the form of an international Convention,

adopts this twenty-fifth day of June of the year one thousand nine hundred and fifty-seven the following Convention, which may be cited as the Abolition of Forced Labour Convention, 1957:

Article 1. Each Member of the International Labour Organisation which ratifies this Convention undertakes to suppress and not to make use of any form of forced or compulsory labour—

(a) as a means of political coercion or education or as a punishment for holding or expressing political views or views ideologically opposed to the established political, social or economic system;

(b) as a method of mobilising and using labour for purposes of economic development;

(c) as a means of labour discipline;

(d) as a punishment for having participated in strikes;

(e) as a means of racial, social, national or religious discrimination.

Article 2. Each Member of the International Labour Organisation which ratifies this Convention undertakes to take effective measures to secure the immediate and complete abolition of forced or compulsory labour as specified in Article 1 of this Convention....

SEE ALSO ILO Forced Labor Convention.

ILO COLLECTIVE BARGAINING CONVENTION (1981).

Formally entitled Convention (No. 154) concerning the Promotion of Collective Bargaining, the convention was adopted on 19 June 1981 by the INTER-

NATIONAL LABOR CONFERENCE (67th session) and entered into force on 11 August 1983. It complements and updated provisions of earlier conventions concerning collective bargaining between employers and employees, including the ILO FREEDOM OF ASSOCIATION AND RIGHT TO ORGANIZE CONVENTION (1948) and the ILO RIGHT TO ORGANIZE AND COLLECTIVE BARGAINING CONVENTION (1949).

The text of the convention (*International Labour Conventions and Recommendations, 1919–1981*, p. 218), with the exception of the ILO STANDARD FINAL PROVISIONS (articles 10–17), is as follows:

The General Conference of the International Labour Organisation,

Having been convened at Geneva by the Governing Body of the International Labour Office, and having met in its Sixty-seventh Session on 3 June 1981, and

Reaffirming the provision of the Declaration of Philadelphia recognising "the solemn obligation of the International Labour Organisation to further among the nations of the world programmes which will achieve . . . the effective recognition of the right of collective bargaining", and noting that this principle is "fully applicable to all people everywhere", and

Having regard to the key importance of existing international standards contained in the Freedom of Association and Protection of the Right to Organise Convention, 1948, the Right to Organise and Collective Bargaining Convention, 1949, the Collection Agreements Recommendation, 1951, the Voluntary Conciliation and Arbitration Recommendation, 1951, the Labour Relations (Public Service) Convention and Recommendation, 1978, and the Labour Administration Convention and Recommendation, 1978, and

Considering that it is desirable to make greater efforts to achieve the objectives of these standards and, particularly, the general principles set out in Article 4 of the Right to Organise and Collective Bargaining Convention, 1949, and in Paragraph 1 of the Collective Agreements Recommendation, 1951, and

Considering accordingly that these standards should be complemented by appropriate measures based on them and aimed at promoting free and voluntary collective bargaining, and

Having decided upon the adoption of certain proposals with regard to the promotion of collective bargaining, which is the fourth item on the agenda of the session, and

Having determined that these proposals shall take the form of an international Convention,
adopts this nineteenth day of June of the year one thousand nine hundred and eighty-one the following Convention, which may be cited as the Collective Bargaining Convention, 1981:

Part I. Scope and Definitions

Article 1. 1. This Convention applies to all branches of economic activity.

2. The extent to which the guarantees provided for in this Convention apply to the armed forces and the police may be determined by national laws or regulations or national practice.

3. As regards the public service, special modalities of application of this Convention may be fixed by national laws or regulations or national practice.

Article 2. For the purpose of this Convention the term "collective bargaining" extends to all negotiations which take place between an employer, a group of employers or one or more employers' organisations, on the one hand, and one or more workers' organisations, on the other, for—

(a) determining working conditions and terms of employment; and/or

(b) regulating relations between employers and workers; and/or

(c) regulating relations between employers or their organisations and a workers' organisation or workers' organisations.

Article 3. 1. Where national law or practice recognises the existence of workers' representatives as defined in Article 3, subparagraph (b), of the Workers' Representatives Convention, 1971, national law or practice may determine the extent to which the term "collective bargaining" shall also extend, for the purpose of this Convention, to negotiations with these representatives.

2. Where, in pursuance of paragraph 1 of this Article, the term "collective bargaining" also includes negotiations with the workers' representatives referred to in that paragraph, appropriate measures shall be taken, wherever necessary, to ensure that the existence of these representatives is not used to undermine the position of the workers' organisations concerned.

Part II. Methods of Application

Article 4. The provisions of this Convention shall, in so far as they are not otherwise made effective by means of collective agreements, arbitration awards or in such other manner as may be consistent with national practice, be given effect by national laws or regulations.

Part III. Promotion of Collective Bargaining

Article 5. 1. Measure adapted to national conditions shall be taken to promote collective bargaining.

2. The aims of the measures referred to in paragraph 1 of this Article shall be the following:

(a) collective bargaining should be made possible for all employers and all groups of workers in the branches of activity covered by this Convention;

(b) collective bargaining should be progressively extended to all matters covered by subparagraphs (a), (b) and (c) of Article 2 of this Convention;

(c) the establishment of rules of procedure agreed between employers' and workers' organisations should be encouraged;

(d) collective bargaining should not be hampered by the absence of rules governing the procedure to be used or by the inadequacy or inappropriateness of such rules;

(e) bodies and procedures for the settlement of labour dispute should be so conceived as to contribute to the promotion of collective bargaining.

Article 6. The provisions of this Convention do not preclude the operation of industrial relations systems in which collective bargaining takes place within the framework of conciliation and/or arbitration machinery or institutions, in which machinery or institutions the parties to the collective bargaining process voluntarily participate.

Article 7. Measures taken by public authorities to encourage and promote the development of collective bargaining shall be the subject of prior consultation and, whenever possible, agreement between public authorities and employers' and workers' organisations.

Article 8. The measures taken with a view to promoting collective bargaining shall not be so conceived or applied as to hamper the freedom of collective bargaining.

Part IV. Final Provisions

Article 9. This Convention does not revise any existing Convention or Recommendation. . . .

ILO COMMITTEE OF EXPERTS ON THE APPLICATION OF CONVENTIONS AND RECOMMENDATIONS.

Established by the ILO Governing Body in 1926, the committee's function is to determine and to point out, in complete independence, the extent to which each State member of the International Labor Organization applies the provisions of ILO conventions and recommendations and lives up to the obligations undertaken by its acceptance of the INTERNATIONAL LABOR ORGANIZATION CONSTITUTION. Each convention is a formal legal instrument regulating some aspect of labor administration, social welfare, or human rights and is binding upon all States that have ratified or acceded to it. Recommendations are more informal but apply equally to all member States. More than 250 conventions and recommendations have been adopted since the ILO was established in 1919, and together they constitute the International Labor Code (see Appendix E).

Member States are not bound to ratify a particular convention, even though they may have voted for its adoption. However, under the ILO constitution, they are required as a minimum to bring all conventions adopted by the International Labor Conference to the attention of their legislative authorities. If a convention is ratified, the ratifying State undertakes to report periodically to the ILO on the measures taken for the implementation of its provisions. Similarly, member States are expected to report from time to time on their position with respect to conventions that they have not ratified and recommendations that they have not accepted. It is on these reports that the Committee of Experts bases its conclusions and recommendations to the governing body.

Originally composed of six members, the committee has since been enlarged progressively to 20, four of whom are from Asian countries, three from African countries, three from eastern European countries, five from western European countries, three from South American countries, and two from countries in North and Central America. In establishing the committee, the governing body decided that its members should be selected from among persons of recognized technical competence whose complete impartiality could not be challenged; that they should, in no sense, be considered as representatives of governments; and that, therefore, they must be persons of independent standing, not directly connected with a government service or a trade organization. The experts accordingly are drawn from the judiciary, from academic circles, and from persons with considerable experience in public administration. They are appointed in their personal capacity by the governing body, on the proposal of the Director-General, and serve for a term of three years.

The Committee of Experts schedules its meetings as required; usually it convenes at least once a year at ILO headquarters in Geneva.

ILO DISCRIMINATION (EMPLOYMENT AND OCCUPATION) CONVENTION (1958).

Formally entitled Convention (No. 111) concerning Discrimination in Respect of Employment and Occupation, 1958, the convention was adopted on 25 June 1958 by the INTERNATIONAL LABOR CONFERENCE (42d session) and entered into force on 15 June 1960. It was the first human rights instrument prepared by the ILO at the request of the United Nations. Between 1952 and 1954, the SUB-COMMISSION ON PREVENTION OF DISCRIMINATION AND PROTECTION OF MINORITIES decided to undertake preliminary studies on the question of discrimination in employment. After the ECONOMIC AND SOCIAL COUNCIL had indicated (resolution 502 H[XVI]) that such a study should be undertaken by the specialized agency concerned, the sub-commission was advised that the ILO was willing to prepare the study. At its 1958 session, the sub-commission, after examining provisional drafts of a convention and a recommendation on the subject prepared by the ILO, discontinued its own studies. Later that year, both the draft convention and the draft recommendation were adopted by the International Labor Conference. Although the substantive provisions of both are similar, the convention is legally binding only upon its contracting States, whereas the recommendation is morally binding upon all States.

The text of the convention (*International Labour Conventions and Recommendations, 1919–1981*, p. 47), with the exception of the ILO STANDARD FINAL PROVISIONS (articles 7–14), is as follows:

The General Conference of the International Labour Organisation,

Having been convened at Geneva by the Governing Body of the International Labour Office, and having met in its forty-second session on 4 June 1958, and

Having decided upon the adoption of certain proposals with regard to discrimination in the field of employment and occupation, which is the fourth item on the agenda of the session, and

Having determined that these proposals shall take the form of an international Convention, and

Considering that the Declaration of Philadelphia affirms that all human beings, irrespective of race, creed or sex, have the right to pursue both their material well-being and their spiritual development in conditions of freedom and dignity, of economic security and equal opportunity, and

Considering further that discrimination constitutes a violation of rights enunciated by the Universal Declaration of Human Rights,

Adopts this twenty-fifth day of the year one thousand nine hundred and fifty-eight the following Convention, which may be cited as the Discrimination (Employment and Occupation) Convention, 1958:

Article 1. For the purpose of this Convention the term "discrimination" includes:

(a) Any distinction, exclusion or reference made on the basis of race, colour, sex, religion, political opinion, national extraction or social origin, which has the effect of nullifying or impairing equality of opportunity or treatment in employment or occupation;

(b) Such other distinction, exclusion or preference which has the effect of nullifying or impairing equality of opportunity or treatment in employment or occupation as may be determined by the Member concerned after consultation with representative employers; and workers' organisations, where such exist, and with other appropriate bodies.

2. Any distinction, exclusion or preference in respect of a particular job based on the inherent requirements thereof shall not be deemed to be discrimination.

3. For the purpose of this Convention the terms "employment" and "occupation" include access to vocational training, access to employment and to particular occupations, and terms and conditions of employment.

Article 2. Each Member for which this Convention is in force undertakes to declare and pursue a national policy designed to promote, by methods appropriate to national conditions and practice, equality of opportunity and treatment in respect of employment and occupation, with a view to eliminating any discrimination in respect thereof.

Article 3. Each Member for which the Convention is in force undertakes, by methods appropriate to national conditions and practice:

(a) To seek the co-operation of employers' and workers' organisations and other appropriate bodies in promoting the acceptance and observance of this policy;

(b) To enact such legislation and to promote such educational programmes as may be calculated to secure the acceptance and observance of the policy;

(c) To repeal any statutory provisions and modify any administrative instructions or practices which are inconsistent with the policy;

(d) To pursue the policy in respect of employment under the direct control of a national authority;

(e) To ensure observance of the policy in the activities of vocational guidance, vocational training and placement services under the direction of a national authority;

(f) To indicate in its annual reports on the application of the Convention the action taken in pursuance of the policy and the results secured by such action.

Article 4. Any measure affecting an individual who is justifiably suspected of, or engaged in, activities prejudicial to the security of the State shall not be deemed to be discrimination, provided that the individual concerned shall have the right to appeal to a competent body established in accordance with national practice.

Article 5. 1. Special measures of protection or assistance provided in other Conventions or Recommendations adopted by the International Labour Conference shall not be deemed to be discrimination.

2. Any Member may, after consultation with representative employers' and workers' organisations, where such exist, determine that other special measures designed to meet the particular requirements of persons who, for reasons such as sex, age, disablement, family responsibilities or social or cultural status, are generally recognised to require special protection or assistance, shall not be deemed to be discrimination.

Article 6. Each Member which ratifies this Convention undertakes to apply it to non-metropolitan territories in accordance with the provisions of the Constitution of the International Labour Organisation. . . .

SEE ALSO *Employment: Anti-Discrimination Agencies.*

ILO EMPLOYMENT POLICY CONVENTION (1964).
Formally entitled Convention (No. 122) concerning Employment Policy, this instrument was adopted on 9 July 1964 by the INTERNATIONAL LABOR CONFERENCE (48th session) and entered into force on 15 July 1966. Recognizing that employment is normally the first concern of every worker, the convention provides that each contracting State undertake to pursue, as a major goal, an active policy designed to promote full, productive and freely chosen employment. The text of the convention (*International Labour Conventions and Recommendations, 1919–1981,* p. 67), with the exception of the ILO STANDARD FINAL PROVISIONS (articles 4–11), is as follows:

The General Conference of the International Labour Organisation,

Having been convened at Geneva by the Governing Body of the International Labour Office, and having met in its forty-eighth session on 17 June 1964, and

Considering that the Declaration of Philadelphia recognises the solemn obligation of the International Labour Organisation to further among the nations of the world programmes which will achieve full employment and the raising of standards of living, and that the Preamble to the Constitution of the International Labour Organisation provides for the prevention of unemployment and the provision of an adequate living wage, and

Considering further that under the terms of the Declaration of Philadelphia it is the responsibility of the International Labour Organisation to examine and consider the bearing of economic and financial policies upon employment policy in the light of the fundamental objective that "all human beings, irrespective of race, creed or sex, have the right to pursue both their material well-being and their spiritual development in conditions of freedom and dignity, of economic security and equal opportunity", and

Considering that the Universal Declaration of Human

Rights provides that "everyone has the right to work, to free choice of employment, to just and favourable conditions of work and to protection against unemployment", and

Noting the terms of existing international labour Conventions and Recommendations of direct relevance to employment policy, and in particular of the Employment Service Convention and Recommendation, 1948, the Vocational Guidance Recommendation, 1949, the Vocational Training Recommendation, 1962, and the Discrimination (Employment and Occupation) Convention and Recommendation, 1958, and

Considering that these instruments should be placed in the wider framework of an international programme for economic expansion on the basis of full, productive and freely chosen employment, and

Having decided upon the adoption of certain proposals with regard to employment policy, which are included in the eighth item on the agenda of the session, and

Having determined that these proposals shall take the form of an international Convention,

Adopts this ninth day of July of the year one thousand nine hundred and sixty-four the following Convention, which may be cited as the Employment Policy Convention, 1964:

Article 1. 1. With a view to stimulating economic growth and development, raising levels of living, meeting manpower requirements and overcoming unemployment and underemployment, each Member shall declare and pursue, as a major goal, an active policy designed to promote full, protective and freely chosen employment.

2. The said policy shall aim at ensuring that:

(a) There is work for all who are available for and seeking work;

(b) Such work is as productive as possible;

(c) There is freedom of choice of employment and the fullest possible opportunity for each worker to qualify for, and to use his skills and endowments in, a job for which he is well suited, irrespective of race, colour, sex, religion, political opinion, national extraction or social origin.

3. The said policy shall take due account of the stage and level of economic development and the mutual relationships between employment objectives and other economic and social objectives, and shall be pursued by methods that are appropriate to national conditions and practices.

Article 2. Each Member shall, by such methods and to such extent as may be appropriate under national conditions:

(a) Decide on and keep under review, within the framework of a co-ordinated economic and social policy, the measures to be adopted for attaining the objectives specified in article 1;

(b) Take such steps as may be needed, including when appropriate the establishment of programmes, for the application of these measures.

Article 3. In the application of this Convention, representatives of the persons affected by the measures to be taken, and in particular representatives of employers and workers, shall be consulted concerning employment policies, with a view to taking fully into account their experience and views and securing their full co-operation in formulating and enlisting support for such policies.

SEE ALSO *Work; Youth: Education and Work.*

ILO EQUALITY OF TREATMENT (SOCIAL SECURITY) CONVENTION (1962). Formally entitled Convention (No. 118) Concerning Equality of Treatment of Nationals and Non-nationals in Social Security, the convention provides that nationals and non-nationals shall be treated equally in all matters relating to social security. It was adopted by the IN-TERNATIONAL LABOR CONFERENCE (46th session) on 28 June 1962 and entered into force on 25 April 1964. The text of the convention (*International Labour Conventions and Recommendations, 1919–1981*, p. 554), with the exception of the ILO STANDARD FINAL PROVISIONS (articles 14–21), is as follows:

The General Conference of the International Labor Organisation,

Having been convened at Geneva by the Governing Body of the International Labour Office, and having met in its Forty-sixth Session on 6 June 1962, and

Having decided upon the adoption of certain proposals with regard to equality of treatment of nationals and non-nationals in social security, which is the fifth item on the agenda of the session, and

Having determined that these proposals shall take the form of an international Convention.

adopts this twenty-eighth day of June of the year one thousand nine hundred and sixty-two the following Convention, which may be cited as the Equality of Treatment (Social Security) Convention, 1962:

Article 1. In this Convention—

(a) the term "legislation" includes any social security rules as well as laws and regulations;

(b) the term "benefits" refers to all benefits, grants and pensions, including any supplements or increments;

(c) the term "benefits granted under transitional schemes" means either benefits granted to persons who have exceeded a prescribed age at the date when the legislation applicable came into force, or benefits granted as a transitional measure in consideration of events occurring or periods completed outside the present boundaries of the territory of a Member;

(d) the term "death grant" means any lump sum payable in the event of death;

(e) the term "residence" means ordinary residence;

(f) the term "prescribed" means determined by or in virtue of national legislation as defined in subparagraph *(a)* above;

(g) the term "refugee" has the meaning assigned to it in Article 1 of the Convention relating to the Status of Refugees of 28 July 1951;

(h) the term "stateless person" has the meaning assigned to it in Article 1 of the Convention relating to the Status of Stateless Persons of 28 September 1954.

Article 2. 1. Each Member may accept the obligations of this Convention in respect of any one or more of the following branches of social security for which it has in effective operation legislation covering its own nationals within its own territory:

(a) medical care;

(b) sickness benefit;

(c) maternity benefit;

(d) invalidity benefit;

(e) old-age benefit;

(f) survivors' benefit;

(g) employment injury benefit;

(h) unemployment benefit; and

(i) family benefit.

2. Each Member for which this Convention is in force shall comply with its provisions in respect of the branch or branches of social security for which it has accepted the obligations of the Convention.

3. Each Member shall specify in its ratification in respect of which branch or branches of social security it accepts the obligations of this Convention.

4. Each Member which has ratified this Convention may subsequently notify the Director-General of the International Labour Office that it accepts the obligations of the Convention in respect of one or more branches of social security not already specified in its ratification.

5. The undertakings referred to in paragraph 4 of this Article shall be deemed to be an integral part of the ratification and to have the force of ratification as from the date of notification.

6. For the purpose of the application of this Convention, each Member accepting the obligations thereof in respect of any branch of social security which has legislation providing for benefits of the type indicated in clause (a) or (b) below shall communicate to the Director-General of the International Labour Office a statement indicating the benefits provided for by its legislation which it considers to be—

(a) benefits other than those the grant of which depends either on direct financial participation by the persons protected or their employer, or on a qualifying period of occupational activity; or

(b) benefits granted under transitional schemes.

7. The communication referred to in paragraph 6 of this Article shall be made at the time of ratification or at the time of notification in accordance with paragraph 4 of this Article; as regards any legislation adopted subsequently, the communication shall be made within three months of the date of the adoption of such legislation.

Article 3. 1. Each Member for which this Convention is in force shall grant within its territory to the nationals of any other Member for which the Convention is in force equality of treatment under its legislation with its own nationals, both as regards coverage and as regards the right to benefits, in respect of every branch of social security for which it has accepted the obligations of the Convention.

2. In the case of survivors' benefits, such equality of treatment shall also be granted to the survivors of the nationals of a Member for which the Convention is in force, irrespective of the nationality of such survivors.

3. Nothing in the preceding paragraphs of this Article shall require a Member to apply the provisions of these paragraphs, in respect of the benefits of a specified branch of social security, to the nationals of another Member which has legislation relating to that branch but does not grant equality of treatment in respect thereof to the nationals of the first Member.

Article 4. 1. Equality of treatment as regards the grant of benefits shall be accorded without any condition of residence: Provided that equality of treatment in respect of the benefits of a specified branch of social security may be made conditional on residence in the case of nationals of any Member the legislation of which makes the grant of benefits under that branch conditional on residence on its territory.

2. Notwithstanding the provisions of paragraph 1 of this

Article, the grant of the benefits referred to in paragraph 6 (a) of Article 2—other than medical care, sickness benefit, employment injury benefit and family benefit—may be made subject to the condition that the beneficiary has resided on the territory of the Member in virtue of the legislation of which the benefit is due, or, in the case of a survivor, that the deceased had resided there, for a period which shall not exceed—

(a) six months immediately preceding the filing of claim, for grant of maternity benefit and unemployment benefit;

(b) five consecutive years immediately preceding the filing of claim, for grant of invalidity benefit, or immediately preceding death, for grant of survivors' benefit;

(c) ten years after the age of 18, which may include five consecutive years immediately preceding the filing of claim, for grant of old-age benefit.

3. Special provisions may be prescribed in respect of benefits granted under transitional schemes.

4. The measures necessary to prevent the cumulation of benefits shall be determined, as necessary, by special arrangements between the Members concerned.

Article 5. 1. In addition to the provisions of Article 4, each Member which has accepted the obligations of this Convention in respect of the branch or branches of social security concerned shall guarantee both to its own nationals and to the nationals of any other Member which has accepted the obligations of the Convention in respect of the branch or branches in question, when they are resident abroad, provision of invalidity benefits, old-age benefits, survivors' benefits and death grants, and employment injury pensions, subject to measures for this purpose being taken, where necessary, in accordance with Article 8.

2. In case of residence abroad, the provision of invalidity, old-age and survivors' benefits of the type referred to in paragraph 6 (a) of Article 2 may be made subject to the participation of the Members concerned in schemes for the maintenance of rights provided for in Article 7.

3. The provisions of this Article do not apply to benefits granted under transitional schemes.

Article 6. In addition to the provisions of Article 4, each Member which has accepted the obligations of this Convention in respect of family benefit shall guarantee the grant of family allowances both to its own nationals and to the nationals of any other Member which has accepted the obligations of this Convention for that branch, in respect of children who reside on the territory of any such Member, under conditions and within limits to be agreed upon by the Members concerned.

Article 7. 1. Members for which this Convention is in force shall, upon terms being agreed between the Members concerned in accordance with Article 8, endeavour to participate in schemes for the maintenance of the acquired rights and rights in course of acquisition under their legislation of the nationals of Members for which the Convention is in force, for all branches of social security in respect of which the Members concerned have accepted the obligations of the Convention.

2. Such schemes shall provide, in particular, for the totalisation of periods of insurance, employment or residence and of assimilated periods for the purpose of the acquisition, maintenance or recovery of rights and for the calculation of benefits.

3. The cost of invalidity, old-age and survivors' benefits as so determined shall either be shared among the Members concerned, or be borne by the Member on whose territory

the beneficiaries reside, as may be agreed upon by the Members concerned.

Article 8. The Members for which this Convention is in force may give effect to their obligations under the provisions of Articles 5 and 7 by ratification of the Maintenance of Migrants' Pension Rights Convention, 1935, by the application of the provisions of that Convention as between particular Members by mutual agreement, or by any multilateral or bilateral agreement giving effect to these obligations.

Article 9. The provisions of this Convention may be derogated from by agreements between Members which do not affect the rights and duties of other Members and which make provision for the maintenance of rights in course of acquisition and of acquired rights under conditions at least as favourable on the whole as those provided for in this Convention.

Article 10. 1. The provisions of this Convention apply to refugees and stateless persons without any condition of reciprocity.

2. This Convention does not apply to special schemes for civil servants, special schemes for war victims, or public assistance.

3. This Convention does not require any Member to apply the provisions thereof to persons who, in accordance with the provisions of international instruments, are exempted from its national social security legislation.

Article 11. The Members for which this Convention is in force shall afford each other administrative assistance free of charge with a view to facilitating the application of the Convention and the execution of their respective social security legislation.

Article 12. 1. This Convention does not apply to benefits payable prior to the coming into force of the Convention for the Member concerned in respect of the branch of social security under which the benefit is payable.

2. The extent to which the Convention applies to benefits attributable to contingencies occurring before its coming into force for the Member concerned in respect of the branch of social security under which the benefit is payable thereafter shall be determined by multilateral or bilateral agreement or in default thereof by the legislation of the Member concerned.

Article 13. This Convention shall not be regarded as revising any existing Convention. . . .

SEE ALSO *ILO Migrant Workers (Supplementary Provisions) Convention; Migrant Workers.*

ILO EQUAL REMUNERATION CONVENTION (1951).
Formally entitled Convention (No. 100) concerning Equal Remuneration for Men and Women Workers for Work of Equal Value, the convention was adopted on 29 June 1951 by the INTERNATIONAL LABOR CONFERENCE (34th session) and entered into force on 23 May 1953. Under the convention, contracting States agree to enforce the basic principle—embodied in the Preamble to the INTERNATIONAL LABOR ORGANIZATION: CONSTITUTION—that men and women shall receive equal remuneration for work of equal value. This principle is to be applied, under the convention, either by national laws and regulations, by legally estab-

lished or recognized machinery for wage negotiation, by collective agreements between workers and employers, or by a combination of those methods. The text of the convention (*International Labour Conventions and Recommendations, 1919–1981*, p. 42), with the exception of the ILO STANDARD FINAL PROVISIONS (articles 5, 6, and 9–14), and the provisions relating to declarations of application to non-metropolitan territories made in accordance with article 35 of the ILO Constitution (articles 7 and 8), is as follows:

The General Conference of the International Labour Organisation,

Having been convened at Geneva by the Governing Body of the International Labour Office, and having met in its thirty-fourth session on 6 June 1951, and

Having decided upon the adoption of certain proposals with regard to the principle of equal remuneration for men and women workers for work of equal value, which is the seventh item on the agenda of the session, and

Having determined that these proposals shall take the form of an international Convention,

Adopts this twenty-ninth day of June of the year one thousand nine hundred and fifty-one the following Convention, which may be cited as the Equal Remuneration Convention, 1951:

Article 1. For the purpose of this Convention:

(a) the term "remuneration" includes the ordinary, basic or minimum wage or salary and any additional emoluments whatsoever payable directly or indirectly, whether in cash or in kind, by the employer to the worker and arising out of the worker's employment;

(b) The term "equal remuneration for men and women workers for work of equal value" refers to rates of remuneration established without discrimination based on sex.

Article 2. 1. Each Member shall, by means appropriate to the methods in operation for determining rates of remuneration, promote and, in so far as is consistent with such methods, ensure the application to all workers of the principle of equal remuneration for men and women workers for work of equal value.

2. This principle may be applied by means of:

(a) National laws or regulations;

(b) Legally established or recognised machinery for wage determination;

(c) Collective agreements between employers and workers; or

(d) A combination of these various means.

Article 3. 1. Where such action will assist in giving effect to the provisions of this Convention, measures shall be taken to promote objective appraisal of jobs on the basis of the work to be performed.

2. The methods to be followed in this appraisal may be decided upon by the authorities responsible for the determination of rates of remuneration, or, where such rates are determined by collective agreements, by the parties thereto.

3. Differential rates between workers, which correspond, without regard to sex, to differences, as determined by such objective appraisal, in the work to be performed, shall not be considered as being contrary to the principle of equal

remuneration for men and women workers for work of equal value.

Article 4. Each Member shall co-operate as appropriate with the employers' and workers' organisations concerned for the purpose of giving effect to the provisions of this Convention. . . .

SEE ALSO Women Workers: ILO Plan of Action on Equality of Opportunity and Treatment of Men and Women in Employment.

ILO FORCED LABOR CONVENTION (1930).

Formally entitled Convention (No. 29) Concerning Forced or Compulsory Labor, the convention was prepared first as a temporary transitional agreement aimed at suppressing FORCED LABOR or compulsory labor exacted of citizens by their own governments. Its provisions were later broadened and updated in the ILO ABOLITION OF FORCED LABOR CONVENTION (1957).

The Forced Labor Convention was adopted by the INTERNATIONAL LABOR CONFERENCE (14th session) on 28 June 1930, and entered into force on 1 May 1932. The text of the convention (*International Labour Conventions and Recommendations, 1919–1981,* p. 29), with the exception of the ILO STANDARD FINAL PROVISIONS (articles 26–29 and 31–33) and an article relating to denunciation (article 30), is as follows:

The General Conference of the International Labour Organisation,

Having been convened at Geneva by the Governing Body of the International Labour Office, and having met in its fourteenth session on 10 June 1930, and

Having decided upon the adoption of certain proposals with regard to forced or compulsory labour, which is included in the first item on the agenda of the session, and

Having determined that these proposals shall take the form of an international Convention,

Adopts this twenty-eighth day of June of the year one thousand nine hundred and thirty the following Convention, which may be cited as the Forced Labour Convention, 1930, for ratification by the Members of the International Labour Organisation in accordance with the provisions of the Constitution of the International Labour Organisation:

Article 1. Each Member of the International Labour Organisation which ratifies this Convention undertakes to suppress the use of forced or compulsory labour in all its forms within the shortest possible period.

2. With a view to this complete suppression, recourse to forced or compulsory labour may be had, during the transitional period, for public purposes only and as an exceptional measure, subject to the conditions and guarantees hereinafter provided.

3. At the expiration of a period of five years after the coming into force of this Convention, and when the Governing Body of the International Labour Office prepares the report provided for in article 31 below, the said Governing Body shall consider the possibility of the suppression of forced or compulsory labour in all its forms without a further transitional period and the desirability of placing this question on the agenda of the Conference.

Article 2. 1. For the purposes of this Convention the term "forced or compulsory labour" shall mean all work or service which is exacted from any person under the menace of any penalty and for which the said person has not offered himself voluntarily.

2. Nevertheless, for the purposes of this Convention, the term "forced or compulsory labour" shall not include:

(a) Any work or service exacted in virtue of compulsory military service laws for work of a purely military character;

(b) Any work or service which forms part of the normal civic obligations of the citizens of a fully self-governing country;

(c) Any work or service exacted from any person as a consequence of a conviction in a court of law, provided that the said work or service is carried out under the supervision and control of a public authority and that the said person is not hired to or placed at the disposal of private individuals, companies or associations;

(d) Any work or service exacted in cases of emergency, that is to say, in the event of war or of a calamity or threatened calamity, such as fire, flood, famine, earthquake, violent epidemic or epizootic diseases, invasion by animal, insect or vegetable pests, and in general any circumstance that would endanger the existence or the well-being of the whole or part of the population;

(e) Minor communal services of a kind which, being performed by the members of the community in the direct interest of the said community, can therefore be considered as normal civic obligations incumbent upon the members of the community, provided that the members of the community or their direct representatives shall have the right to be consulted in regard to the need for such services.

Article 3. For the purposes of this Convention the term "competent authority" shall mean either an authority of the metropolitan country or the highest central authority in the territory concerned.

Article 4. 1. The competent authority shall not impose or permit the imposition of forced or compulsory labour for the benefit of private individuals, companies or associations.

2. Where such forced or compulsory labour for the benefit of private individuals, companies or associations exist at the date on which a Member's ratification of this Convention is registered by the Director-General of the International Labour Office, the Member shall completely suppress such forced or compulsory labour from the date on which this Convention comes into force for that Member.

Article 5. 1. No concession granted to private individuals, companies or associations shall involve any form of forced or compulsory labour for the production or the collection of products which such private individuals, companies or associations utilise or in which they trade.

2. Where concessions exist containing provisions involving such forced or compulsory labour, such provisions shall be rescinded as soon as possible, in order to comply with article 1 of this Convention.

Article 6. Officials of the administration, even when they have the duty of encouraging the population under their charge to engage in some form of labour, shall not put constraint upon the said populations or upon any individual members thereof to work for private individuals, companies or associations.

Article 7. 1. Chiefs who do not exercise administrative functions shall not have recourse to forced or compulsory labour.

2. Chiefs who exercise administrative functions may, with the express permission of the competent authority, have recourse to forced or compulsory labour, subject to the provisions of article 10 of this Convention.

3. Chiefs who are duly recognised and who do not receive adequate remuneration in other forms may have the enjoyment of personal services, subject to due regulation and provided that all necessary measures are taken to prevent abuses.

Article 8. 1. The responsibility for every decision to have recourse to forced or compulsory labour shall rest with the highest civil authority in the territory concerned.

2. Nevertheless, that authority may delegate powers to the highest local authorities to exact forced or compulsory labour which does not involve the removal of the workers from their place of habitual residence. That authority may also delegate, for such periods and subject to such conditions as may be laid down in the regulations provided for in article 23 of this Convention, powers to the highest local authorities to exact forced or compulsory labour which involves the removal of the workers from their place of habitual residence for the purpose of facilitating the movement of officials of the administration, when on duty, and for the transport of Government stores.

Article 9. Except as otherwise provided for in Article 10 of this Convention, any authority competent to exact forced or compulsory labour shall, before deciding to have recourse to such labour, satisfy itself:

(a) That the work to be done or the service to be rendered is of important direct interest for the community called upon to do the work or render the service;

(b) That the work or service is of present or imminent necessity;

(c) That it has been impossible to obtain voluntary labour for carrying out the work or rendering the service by the offer of rates of wages and conditions of labour not less favourable than those prevailing in the area concerned for similar work or service; and

(d) That the work or service will not lay too heavy a burden upon the present population, having regard to the labour available and its capacity to undertake the work.

Article 10. 1. Forced or compulsory labour exacted as a tax and forced or compulsory labour to which recourse is had for the execution of public works by chiefs who exercise administrative functions shall be progressively abolished.

2. Meanwhile, where forced or compulsory labour is exacted as a tax, and where recourse is had to forced or compulsory labour for the execution of public works by chiefs who exercise administrative functions, the authority concerned shall first satisfy itself:

(a) That the work to be done or the service to be rendered is of important direct interest for the community called upon to do the work or render the service;

(b) That the work or the service is of present or imminent necessity;

(c) That the work or service will not lay too heavy a burden upon the present population, having regard to the labour available and its capacity to undertake the work;

(d) That the work or service will not entail the removal of the workers from their place of habitual residence;

(e) That the execution of the work or the rendering of the service will be directed in accordance with the exigencies of religion, social life and agriculture.

Article 11. 1. Only adult able-bodied males who are of an apparent age of not less than 18 and not more than 45 years may be called upon for forced or compulsory labour. Except in respect of the kinds of labour provided for in Article 10 of this Convention, the following limitations and conditions shall apply:

(a) Whenever possible prior determination by a medical officer appointed by the administration that the persons concerned are not suffering from any infectious or contagious disease and that they are physically fit for the work required and for the conditions under which it is to be carried out;

(b) Exemption of school teachers and pupils and of officials of the administration in general;

(c) The maintenance in each community of the number of adult able-bodied men indispensable for family and social life;

(d) Respect for conjugal and family ties.

2. For the purposes of sub-paragraph (c) of the preceding paragraph, the regulations provided for in article 23 of this Convention shall fix the proportion of the resident adult able-bodied males who may be taken at any one time for forced or compulsory labour, provided always that this proportion shall in no case exceed 25 per cent. In fixing this proportion the competent authority shall take account of the density of the population, of its social and physical development, of the seasons, and of the work which must be done by the persons concerned on their own behalf in their locality, and, generally, shall have regard to the economic and social necessities of the normal life of the community concerned.

Article 12. 1. The maximum period for which any person may be taken for forced or compulsory labour of all kinds in any one period of twelve months shall not exceed sixty days, including the time spent in going to and from the place of work.

2. Every person from whom forced or compulsory labour is exacted shall be furnished with a certificate indicating the periods of such labour which he has completed.

Article 13. 1. The normal working hours of any person from whom forced or compulsory labour is exacted shall be the same as those prevailing in the case of voluntary labour, and the hours worked in excess of the normal working hours shall be remunerated at the rates prevailing in the case of overtime for voluntary labour.

2. A weekly day of rest shall be granted to all persons from whom forced or compulsory labour of any kind is exacted and this day shall coincide as far as possible with the day fixed by tradition or custom in the territories or regions concerned.

Article 14. 1. With the exception of the forced or compulsory labour provided for in article 10 of this Convention, forced or compulsory labour of all kinds shall be remunerated in each at rates not less than those prevailing for similar kinds of work either in the district in which the labour is employed or in the district from which the labour is recruited, whichever may be the higher.

2. In the case of labour to which recourse is had by chiefs in the exercise of their administrative functions, payment of wages in accordance with the provisions of the preceding paragraph shall be introduced as soon as possible.

3. The wages shall be paid to each worker individually and not to his tribal chief or to any other authority.

4. For the purpose of payment of wages the days spent in travelling to and from the place of work shall be counted as working days.

5. Nothing in this article shall prevent ordinary rations being given as a part of wages, such rations to be at least eq-

uivalent in value to the money payment they are taken to represent, but deductions from wages shall not be made either for the payment of taxes or for special food, clothing or accommodation supplied to a worker for the purpose of maintaining him in a fit condition to carry on his work under the special conditions of any employment, or for the supply of tools.

Article 15. 1. Any laws or regulations relating to workmen's compensation for accidents or sickness arising out of the employment of the worker and any laws or regulations providing compensation for the dependants of deceased or incapacitated workers which are or shall be in force in the territory concerned shall be equally applicable to persons from whom forced or compulsory labour is exacted and to voluntary workers.

2. In any case it shall be an obligation on any authority employing any worker on forced or compulsory labour to ensure the subsistence of any such worker who, by accident or sickness arising out of his employment, is rendered wholly or partially incapable of providing for himself, and to take measures to ensure the maintenance of any persons actually dependent upon such a worker in the event of his incapacity or decrease arising out of his employment.

Article 16. 1. Except in cases of special necessity, persons from whom forced or compulsory labour is exacted shall not be transferred to districts where the food and climate differ so considerably from those to which they have been accustomed as to endanger their health.

2. In no case shall the transfer of such workers be permitted unless all measures relating to hygiene and accommodation which are necessary to adapt such workers to the conditions and to safeguard their health can be strictly applied.

3. When such transfer cannot be avoided, measures of gradual habituation to the new conditions of diet and of climate shall be adopted on competent medical advice.

4. In cases where such workers are required to perform regular work to which they are not accustomed, measures shall be taken to ensure their habituation to it, especially as regards progressive training, the hours of work and the provision of rest intervals, and any increase or amelioration of diet which may be necessary.

Article 17. Before permitting recourse to forced or compulsory labour for works of construction or maintenance which entail the workers remaining at the workplaces for considerable periods, the competent authority shall satisfy itself:

(1) That all necessary measures are taken to safeguard the health of the workers and to guarantee the necessary medical care, and, in particular, *(a)* that the workers are medically examined before commencing the work and at fixed intervals during the period of service, *(b)* that there is an adequate medical staff, provided with the dispensaries, infirmaries, hospitals and equipment necessary to meet all requirements, and *(c)* that the sanitary conditions of the workplaces, the supply of drinking water, food, fuel, and cooking utensils, and, where necessary, of housing and clothing, are satisfactory;

(2) That definite arrangements are made to ensure the subsistence of the families of the workers, in particular by facilitating the remittance, by a safe method, of part of the wages to the family, at the request or with the consent of the workers;

(3) That the journeys of the workers to and from the workplaces are made at the expense and under the responsibility of the administration, which shall facilitate such journeys by making the fullest use of all available means of transport;

(4) That, in case of illness or accident causing incapacity to work of a certain duration, the worker is repatriated at the expense of the administration;

(5) That any worker who may wish to remain as a voluntary worker at the end of his period of forced or compulsory labour is permitted to do so without, for a period of two years, losing his right to repatriation free of expense to himself.

Article 18. 1. Forced or compulsory labour for the transport of persons or goods, such as the labour of porters or boatmen, shall be abolished within the shortest possible period. Meanwhile the competent authority shall promulgate regulations determining, *inter alia, (a)* that such labour shall only be employed for the purpose of facilitating the movement of officials of the administration, when on duty, or for the transport of Government stores, or, in cases of very urgent necessity, the transport of persons other than officials, *(b)* that the workers so employed shall be medically certified to by physically fit, where medical examination is possible, and that where such medical examination is not practicable the person employing such workers shall be held responsible for ensuring that they are physically fit and not suffering from any infectious or contagious disease, *(c)* the maximum load which these workers may carry, *(d)* the maximum distance from their homes to which they may be taken, *(e)* the maximum number of days per month or other period for which they may be taken, including the days spent in returning to their homes, and *(f)* the persons entitled to demand this form of forced or compulsory labour and the extent to which they are entitled to demand it.

2. In fixing the maxima referred to under *(c), (d)* and *(e)* in the foregoing paragraph, the competent authority shall have regard to all relevant factors, including the physical development of the population from which the workers are recruited, the nature of the country through which they must travel and the climatic conditions.

3. The competent authority shall further provide that the normal daily journey of such workers shall not exceed a distance corresponding to an average working day of eight hours, it being understood that account shall be taken not only of the weight to be carried and the distance to be covered, but also of the nature of the road, the season and all other relevant factors, and that, where hours of journey in excess of the normal daily journey are exacted, they shall be remunerated at rates higher than the normal rates.

Article 19. 1. The competent authority shall only authorise recourse to compulsory cultivation as a method of precaution against famine or a deficiency of food supplies and always under the condition that the food or produce shall remain the property of the individuals or the community producing it.

2. Nothing in this article shall be construed as abrogating the obligation on members of a community, where production is organised on a communal basis by virtue of law or custom and where the produce or any profit accruing from the sale thereof remain the property of the community, to perform the work demanded by the community by virtue of law or custom.

Article 20. Collective punishment laws under which a community may be punished for crimes committed by any of its members shall not contain provisions for forced or compulsory labour by the community as one of the methods of punishment.

Article 21. Forced or compulsory labour shall not be used for work underground in mines.

Article 22. The annual reports that Members which ratify this Convention agree to make to the International Labour Office, pursuant to the provisions of article 22 of the Constitution of the International Labour Organisation, on the measure they have taken to give effect to the provisions of this Convention, shall contain as full information as possible, in respect of each territory concerned, regarding the extent to which recourse has been had to forced or compulsory labour in that territory, the purposes for which it has been employed, the sickness and death rates, hours of work, methods of payment of wages and rates of wages, and any other relevant information.

Article 23. 1. To give effect to the provisions of this Convention the competent authority shall issue complete and precise regulations governing the use of forced or compulsory labour.

2. These regulations shall contain, *inter alia,* rules permitting any person from whom forced or compulsory labour is exacted to forward all complaints relative to the conditions of labour to the authorities and ensuring that such complaints will be examined and taken into consideration.

Article 24. Adequate measures shall in all cases be taken to ensure that the regulations governing the employment of forced or compulsory labour are strictly applied, either by extending the duties of any existing labour inspectorate which has been established for the inspection of voluntary labour to cover the inspection of forced or compulsory labour or in some other appropriate manner. Measures shall also be taken to ensure that the regulations are brought to the knowledge of persons from whom such labour is exacted.

Article 25. The illegal exaction of forced or compulsory labour shall be punishable as a penal offence, and it shall be an obligation on any Member ratifying this Convention to ensure that the penalties imposed by law are really adequate and are strictly enforced. . . .

ILO FREEDOM OF ASSOCIATION AND PROTECTION OF THE RIGHT TO ORGANIZE CONVENTION. (1948).

Formally entitled Convention (No. 87) concerning Freedom of Association and Protection of the Right to Organize, the convention was adopted on 9 July 1948 by the INTERNATIONAL LABOR CONFERENCE (31st session) and entered into force on 4 July 1950. It is the first ILO convention on freedom of association applicable to non-agricultural workers and employers. The text of the convention, (*International Labour Conventions and Recommendations. 1919–1981,* p. 4), with the exception of the ILO STANDARD FINAL PROVISIONS (articles 14–21) and certain miscellaneous final provisions (articles 12 and 13), is as follows:

Part I
Freedom of Association

Article 1. Each Member of the International Labour Organisation for which this Convention is in force undertakes to give effect to the following provisions.

Article 2. Workers and employers, without distinction whatsoever, shall have the right to establish and, subject, only to the rules of the organisation concerned, to join organisations of their own choosing without previous authorisation.

Article 3. 1. Workers' and employers' organisations shall have the right to draw up their constitutions and rules, to elect their representatives in full freedom, to organise their administration and activities and to formulate their programmes.

2. The public authorities shall refrain from any interference which would restrict this right or impede the lawful exercise thereof.

Article 4. Workers' and employers' organisations shall not be liable to be dissolved or suspended by administrative authority.

Article 5. Workers' and employers' organisations shall have the right to establish and join federations and confederations and any such organisation, federation or confederation shall have the right to affiliate with international organisations of workers and employers.

Article 6. The provisions of articles 2, 3 and 4 hereof apply to federations and confederations of workers' and employers' organisations.

Article 7. The acquisition of legal personality by workers' and employers' organisations, federations and confederations shall not be made subject to conditions of such a character as to restrict the application of the provisions of articles 2, 3 and 4 hereof.

Article 8. 1. In exercising the rights provided for in this Convention workers and employers and their respective organisations, like other persons or organised collectivities, shall respect the law of the land.

2. The law of the land shall not be such as to impair, nor shall it be so applied as to impair, the guarantees provided for in this Convention.

Article 9. 1. The extent to which the guarantees provided for in this Convention shall apply to the armed forces and the police shall be determined by national laws or regulations.

2. In accordance with the principle set forth in paragraph 8 of article 19 of the Constitution of the International Labour Organisation the ratification of this Convention by any Member shall not be deemed to affect any existing law, award, custom or agreement in virtue of which members of the armed forces or the police enjoy any right guaranteed by this Convention.

Article 10. In this Convention the term "organisation" means any organisation of workers or of employers for furthering and defending the interests of workers or of employers.

Part II
Protection of the Right to Organise

Article 11. Each Member of the International Labour Organisation for which this Convention is in force undertakes to take all necessary and appropriate measures to ensure that workers and employers may exercise freely the right to organise. . . .

SEE ALSO *Assembly and Association; ILO Right of Association (Agricultural) Convention; ILO Right to Organize and Collective Bargaining Convention; ILO Rural Workers' Organization Convention; State of Emergency: Freedom of Association.*

ILO FREEDOM OF ASSOCIATION COMMITTEE OF THE GOVERNING BODY. The ILO Governing Body's Committee on Freedom of Association was established in 1951 for the preliminary examination of complaints of infringements of trade union rights. Its main function is to consider the appropriateness of referring particular complaints to the ILO FREEDOM OF ASSOCIATION FACT-FINDING AND CONCILIATION COMMISSION and to make recommendations concerning such action to the governing body.

The committee has established its own rules and procedures for dealing with such complaints, particularly regarding their receivability and regarding communication with the complainants on the one hand and with the governments concerned on the other. It is composed of nine members of the governing body: three government representatives, three employers' representatives, and three workers' representatives. Members are appointed by the governing body on proposal of the Director-General.

The committee has no subsidiary bodies; but, in urgent cases, the Director-General may, with the prior consent of the committee and of the government concerned, send a representative to the country named in a complaint with a view to ascertaining relevant facts.

Since its establishment, the committee has considered many hundreds of allegations concerning infringements of trade union rights. In only a few cases was it necessary to refer such cases to the Fact-Finding and Conciliation Commission.

ILO FREEDOM OF ASSOCIATION FACT-FINDING AND CONCILIATION COMMISSION. The Fact-Finding and Conciliation Commission on Freedom of Association of the International Labor Organization was established by the ILO Governing Body in 1950. Its primary function is to secure, by fact-finding and conciliation, a friendly settlement of complaints alleging infringements of trade union rights submitted by governments or by workers' or employers' organizations and referred to it either by the ILO Governing Body or by the UN Economic and Social Council, the latter of which decided, on 17 February 1950 (resolutions 277 [X]):

(a) to accept on behalf of the United Nations the services of the International Labour Organisation and the Fact-finding and Conciliation Commission as established by the International Labour Organisation;

(b) to forward to the Governing Body of the International Labour Office, for its consideration as to referral to the Commission, all allegations regarding infringements of trade union rights received from Governments or trade-union or employers' organizations against member States of the International Labour Organisation;

(c) (i) that, before acting on such allegations regarding any Member of the United Nations which is not a member of the International Labour Organisation the Secretary-General, on behalf of the Council, will seek the consent of the Government concerned; (ii) that upon receiving such consent, the Council will transmit to the Fact-finding and Conciliation Commission, through the Governing Body of the International Labour Office, any allegations regarding infringements of trade-union rights by Members of the United Nations which are not members of the International Labour Organisation, received from Governments or trade-union or employers' organizations, which it considers suitable for transmittal; (iii) that if such consent is not forthcoming, the Council will give consideration to such refusal with a view to taking any appropriate alternative action designed to safeguard the rights relating to freedom of information involved in the case.

Reports of the commission are submitted to the ILO Governing Body. In addition, the ILO Director-General includes in the ILO's annual report to the UN General Assembly an account of the work of the Fact-Finding and Conciliation Commission.

The commission is composed of nine independent members appointed by the ILO Governing Body on proposal of the Director-General. They serve for an indeterminate term and meet as required to perform their functions. The commission sometimes works in panels consisting of not less than three or more than five members.

ILO HOLIDAYS WITH PAY CONVENTION (REVISED) (1970). Formally entitled Convention (No. 132) concerning Annual Holidays with Pay (Revised), 1970, the convention provides that all employed persons in a contracting State—seafarers are the only exception specifically mentioned—are entitled to annual paid holidays of not less than three working weeks for one year of service. Public or customary holidays are not counted as part of the minimum annual holiday, and a worker on holiday must be paid at least his normal or average remuneration.

The Holidays with Pay Convention was adopted by the INTERNATIONAL LABOR CONFERENCE on 24 June 1970 (54th session) and entered into force on 30 June 1973. It revises and updates the earlier Holidays with Pay Convention (No. 52) of 24 June 1936 and the ILO Holidays with Pay (Agriculture) Convention (No. 101) of 26 June 1952.

The text of the convention (*International Labour Conventions and Recommendations, 1919–1981*, p. 323) is as follows:

The General Conference of the International Labour Organisation,

Having been convened at Geneva by the Governing Body

of the International Labour Office, and having met in its Fifty-fourth Session on 3 June 1970, and

Having decided upon the adoption of certain proposals with regard to holidays with pay, which is the fourth item on the agenda of the session, and

Having determined that these proposals shall take the form of an international Convention,

adopts this twenty-fourth day of June of the year one thousand nine hundred and seventy the following Convention, which may be cited as the Holidays with Pay Convention (Revised), 1970:

Article 1. The provisions of this Convention, in so far as they are not otherwise made effective by means of collective agreements, arbitration awards, court decisions, statutory wage fixing machinery, or in such other manner consistent with national practice as may be appropriate under national conditions, shall be given effect by national laws or regulations.

Article 2. 1. This Convention applies to all employed persons, with the exception of seafarers.

2. In so far as necessary, measures may be taken by the competent authority or through the appropriate machinery in a country, after consultation with the organisations of employers and workers concerned, where such exist, to exclude from the application of this Convention limited categories of employed persons in respect of whose employment special problems of a substantial nature, relating to enforcement or to legislative or constitutional matters, arise.

3. Each Member which ratifies this Convention shall list in the first report on the application of the Convention submitted under article 22 of the Constitution of the International Labour Organisation any categories which may have been excluded in pursuance of paragraph 2 of this Article, giving the reasons for such exclusion, and shall state in subsequent reports the position of its law and practice in respect of the categories excluded, and the extent to which effect has been given or is proposed to be given to the Convention in respect of such categories.

Article 3. 1. Every person to whom this Convention applies shall be entitled to an annual paid holiday of a specified minimum length.

2. Each Member which ratifies this Convention shall specify the length of the holiday in a declaration appended to its ratification.

3. The holiday shall in no case be less than three working weeks for one year of service.

4. Each Member which has ratified this Convention may subsequently notify the Director-General of the International Labour Office, by a further declaration, that it specifies a holiday longer than that specified at the time of ratification.

Article 4. 1. A person whose length of service in any year is less than that required for the full entitlement prescribed in the preceding Article shall be entitled in respect of that year to a holiday with pay proportionate to his length of service during that year.

2. The expression "year" in paragraph 1 of this Article shall mean the calendar year or any other period of the same length determined by the competent authority or through the appropriate machinery in the country concerned.

Article 5. 1. A minimum period of service may be required for entitlement to any annual holiday with pay.

2. The length of any such qualifying period shall be determined by the competent authority or through the appropri-

ate machinery in the country concerned but shall not exceed six months.

3. The manner in which length of service is calculated for the purpose of holiday entitlement shall be determined by the competent authority or through the appropriate machinery in each country.

4. Under conditions to be determined by the competent authority or through the appropriate machinery in each country, absence from work for such reasons beyond the control of the employed person concerned as illness, injury or maternity shall be counted as part of the period of service.

Article 6. 1. Public and customary holidays, whether or not they fall during the annual holiday, shall not be counted as part of the minimum annual holiday with pay prescribed in Article 3, paragraph 3, of this Convention.

2. Under conditions to be determined by the competent authority or through the appropriate machinery in each country, periods of incapacity for work resulting from sickness or injury may not be counted as part of the minimum annual holiday with pay prescribed in Article 3, paragraph 3, of this Convention.

Article 7. 1. Every person taking the holiday envisaged in this Convention shall receive in respect of the full period of that holiday at least his normal or average remuneration (including the cash equivalent of any part of that remuneration which is paid in kind and which is not a permanent benefit continuing whether or not the person concerned is on holiday), calculated in a manner to be determined by the competent authority or through the appropriate machinery in each country.

2. The amounts due in pursuance of paragraph 1 of this Article shall be paid to the person concerned in advance of the holiday, unless otherwise provided in an agreement applicable to him and the employer.

Article 8. 1. The division of the annual holiday with pay into parts may be authorized by the competent authority or through the appropriate machinery in each country.

2. Unless otherwise provided in an agreement applicable to the employer and the employed person concerned, and on condition that the length of service of the person concerned entitles him to such a period, one of the parts shall consist of at least two uninterrupted working weeks.

Article 9. 1. The uninterrupted part of the annual holiday with pay referred to in Article 8, paragraph 2, of this Convention shall be granted and taken no later than one year, and the remainder of the annual holiday with pay no later than eighteen months, from the end of the year in respect of which the holiday entitlement has arisen.

2. Any part of the annual holiday which exceeds a stated minimum may be postponed, with the consent of the employed person concerned, beyond the period specified in paragraph 1 of this Article and up to a further specified time limit.

3. The minimum and the time limit referred to in paragraph 2 of this Article shall be determined by the competent authority after consultation with the organisations of employers and workers concerned, or through collective bargaining, or in such other manner consistent with national practice as may be appropriate under national conditions.

Article 10. 1. The time at which the holiday is to be taken shall, unless it is fixed by regulation, collective agreement, arbitration award or other means consistent with national practice, be determined by the employer after consultation with the employed person concerned or his representatives.

2. In fixing the time at which the holiday is to be taken, work requirements and the opportunities for rest and relaxation available to the employed person shall be taken into account.

Article 11. An employed person who has completed a minimum period of service corresponding to that which may be required under Article 5, paragraph 1, of this Convention shall receive, upon termination of employment, a holiday with pay proportionate to the length of service for which he has not received such a holiday, or compensation in lieu thereof, or the equivalent holiday credit.

Article 12. Agreements to relinquish the right to the minimum annual holiday with pay prescribed in Article 3, paragraph 3, of this Convention or to forgo such a holiday, for compensation or otherwise, shall, as appropriate to national conditions, be null and void or be prohibited.

Article 13. Special rules may be laid down by the competent authority or through the appropriate machinery in each country in respect of cases in which the employed person engages, during the holiday, in a gainful activity conflicting with the purpose of the holiday.

Article 14. Effective measures appropriate to the manner in which effect is given to the provisions of this Convention shall be taken to ensure the proper application and enforcement of regulations or provisions concerning holidays with pay, by means of adequate inspection or otherwise.

Article 15. 1. Each Member may accept the obligations of this Convention separately:

(a) In respect of employed persons in economic sectors other than agriculture;

(b) In respect of employed persons in agriculture.

2. Each member shall specify in its ratification whether it accepts the obligations of the Convention in respect of the persons covered by subparagraph (a) of paragraph 1 of this Article, in respect of the persons covered by subparagraph (b) of paragraph 1 of this Article, or in respect of both.

3. Each Member which has on ratification accepted the obligations of this Convention only in respect either of the persons covered by subparagraph (a) of paragraph 1 of this Article or of the persons covered by subparagraph (b) of paragraph 1 of this Article may subsequently notify the Director-General of the International Labour Office that it accepts the obligations of the Convention in respect of all persons to whom this Convention applies.

Article 16. This Convention revises the Holidays with Pay Convention, 1936. and the Holidays with Pay (Agriculture) Convention, 1952, on the following terms:

(a) Acceptance of the obligations of this Convention in respect of employed persons in economic sectors other than agriculture by a Member which is a party to the Holidays with Pay Convention, 1936, shall *ipso jure* involve the immediate denunciation of that Convention;

(b) Acceptance of the obligations of this Convention in respect of employed persons in agriculture by a Member which is a party to the Holidays with Pay (Agriculture) Convention, 1952, shall *ipso jure* involve the immediate denunciation of that Convention;

(c) The coming into force of this Convention shall not close the Holidays with Pay (Agriculture) Convention, 1952, to further ratification.

Article 17. The formal ratifications of this Convention shall be communicated to the Director-General of the International Labour Office for registration.

Article 18. 1. This Convention shall be binding only upon those Members of the International Labour Organisation whose ratifications have been registered with the Director-General.

2. It shall come into force twelve months after the date on which the ratifications of two Members have been registered with the Director-General.

3. Thereafter, this Convention shall come into force for any Member twelve months after the date on which its ratification has been registered.

Article 19. 1. A Member which has ratified this Convention may denounce it after the expiration of ten years from the date on which the Convention first comes into force, by an act communicated to the Director-General of the International Labour Office for registration. Such denunciation shall not take effect until one year after the date on which it is registered.

2. Each Member which has ratified this Convention and which does not, within the year following the expiration of the period of ten years mentioned in the receding paragraph, exercise the right of denunciation provided for in this Article, will be bound for another period of ten years and, thereafter, may denounce this Convention at the expiration of each period of ten years under the terms provided for in this Article.

Article 20. 1. The Director-General of the International Labour Office shall notify all Members of the International Labour Organisation of the registration of all ratifications and denunciations communicated to him by the Members of the Organisation.

2. When notifying the Members of the Organisation of the registration of the second ratification communicated to him, the Director-General shall draw the attention of the Members of the Organisation to the date upon which the Convention will come into force.

Article 21. The Director-General of the International Labour Office shall communicate to the Secretary-General of the United Nations for registration in accordance with Article 102 of the Charter of the United Nations full particulars of all ratifications and acts of denunciation registered by him in accordance with the provisions of the preceding Articles.

Article 22. At such times as it may consider necessary the Governing Body of the International Labour Office shall present to the General Conference a report on the working of this Convention and shall examine the desirability of placing on the agenda of the Conference the question of its revision in whole or in part.

Article 23. 1. Should the Conference adopt a new Convention revising this Convention in whole or in part, then, unless the new Convention otherwise provides:

(a) The ratification by a Member of the new revising Convention shall *ipso jure* involve the immediate denunciation of this Convention, notwithstanding the provisions of Article 19 above, if and when the new revising Convention shall have come into force;

(b) As from the date when the new revising Convention comes into force this Convention shall cease to be open to ratification by the Members.

2. This Convention shall in any case remain in force in its actual form and content for those Members which have ratified it but have not ratified the revising Convention.

Article 24. The English and French versions of the text of this Convention are equally authoritative.

ILO HUMAN RESOURCES DEVELOPMENT CONVENTION (1975). Formally entitled Convention (No. 142) concerning Vocational Guidance and Vocational Training in the Development of Human Resources, the convention was adopted by the INTERNATIONAL LABOR CONFERENCE on 23 June 1975 (60th session) and entered into force on 19 July 1977. The text of the convention (*International Labour Conventions and Recommendations, 1919–1981*, p. 114), with the exception of the ILO STANDARD FINAL PROVISIONS (articles 6–13), is as follows:

The General Conference of the International Labour Organisation,

Having been convened at Geneva by the Governing Body of the International Labour Office, and having met in its Sixtieth Session on 4 June 1970, and

Having decided upon the adoption of certain proposals with regard to human resources development: vocational guidance and vocational training, which is the sixth item on the agenda of the session, and

Having determined that these proposals shall take the form of an international Convention,

adopts this twenty-third day of June of the year one thousand nine hundred and seventy-five the following Convention, which may be cited as the Human Resources Development Convention, 1975:

Article 1. 1. Each Member shall adopt and develop comprehensive and co-ordinated policies and programmes of vocational guidance and vocational training, closely linked with employment, in particular through public employment services.

2. These policies and programmes shall take due account of—

(a) employment needs, opportunities and problems, both regional and national;

(b) the stage and level of economic, social and cultural development; and

(c) the mutual relationships between human resources development and other economic, social and cultural objectives.

3. The policies and programmes shall be pursued by methods that are appropriate to national conditions.

4. The policies and programmes shall be designed to improve the ability of the individual to understand and, individually or collectively, to influence the working and social environment.

5. The policies and programmes shall encourage and enable all persons, on an equal basis and without any discrimination whatsoever, to develop and use their capabilities for work in their own best interests and in accordance with their own aspirations, account being taken of the needs of society.

Article 2. With the above ends in view, each Member shall establish and develop open, flexible and complementary systems of general, technical and vocational education, educational and vocational guidance and vocational training, whether these activities take place within the system of formal education or outside it.

Article 3. 1. Each Member shall gradually extend its systems of vocational guidance, including continuing employment information, with a view to ensuring that comprehensive information and the broadcast possible guidance are available

to all children, young persons and adults, including appropriate programmes for all handicapped and disabled persons.

2. Such information and guidance shall cover the choice of an occupation, vocational training and related educational opportunities, the employment situation and employment prospects, promotion prospects, conditions of work, safety and hygiene at work, and other aspects of working life in the various sectors of economic, social and cultural activity and at all levels of responsibility.

3. The information and guidance shall be supplemented by information on general aspects of collective agreements and of the rights and obligations of all concerned under labour law; this information shall be provided in accordance with national law and practice, taking into account the respective functions and tasks of the workers' and employers' organisations concerned.

Article 4. Each Member shall gradually extend, adapt and harmonise its vocational training systems to meet the needs for vocational training throughout life of both young persons and adults in all sectors of the economy and branches of economic activity and at all levels of skill and responsibility.

Article 5. Policies and programmes of vocational guidance and vocational training shall be formulated and implemented in co-operation with employers' and workers' organisations and, as appropriate and in accordance with national law and practice, with other interested bodies. . . .

SEE ALSO *UNESCO Convention on Technical and Vocational Education; UNESCO Recommendation concerning Technical and Vocational Education (Revised); UNESCO Recommendation on the Development of Adult Education.*

ILO INDIGENOUS AND TRIBAL PEOPLES CONVENTION (1989). Formally entitled *Convention (No. 169) concerning Indigenous and Tribal Peoples in Independent Countries,* the 1989 convention revises the ILO Indigenous and Tribal Populations Convention No. 107 of 1957. Whereas the earlier instrument had been oriented towards the integration and assimilation of indigenous peoples, the revision is based on the assumption that they would continue to exist as distinct elements within national societies. Accordingly, the revised document reaffirms the principle of respect for the cultures and traditions of indigenous peoples everywhere and their right to a voice in consultations and decisions about any measures which might affect them.

The convention was adopted by the INTERNATIONAL LABOR CONFERENCE (76th session) on 27 June 1989. The text of the convention is as follows:

The General Conference of the International Labour Organisation,

Having been convened at Geneva by the Governing Body of the International Labour Office, and having met in its 76th Session on 7 June 1989, and

Noting that the international standards contained in the Indigenous and Tribal Populations Convention and Recommendation, 1957, and

Recalling the terms of the Universal Declaration of Human Rights, the International Covenant on Economic, Social and Cultural Rights, the International Covenant on Civil and Political Rights, and the many international instruments on the prevention of discrimination, and

Considering that the developments which have taken place in international law since 1957, as well as developments in the situation of indigenous and tribal peoples in all regions of the world, have made it appropriate to adopt new international standards on the subject with a view to removing the assimilationist orientation of the earlier standards, and

Recognising the aspirations of these peoples to exercise control over their own institutions, ways of life and economic development and to maintain and develop their identities, languages and religions, within the framework of the States in which they live, and

Noting that in many parts of the world these peoples are unable to enjoy their fundamental human rights to the same degree as the rest of the population of the States within which they live, and that their laws, values, customs and perspectives have often been eroded, and

Calling attention to the distinctive contributions of indigenous and tribal peoples to the cultural diversity and social and ecological harmony of humankind and to international co-operation and understanding, and

Noting that the following provisions have been framed with the co-operation of the United Nations, the Food and Agriculture Organisation of the United Nations, the United Nations Educational, Scientific and Cultural Organisation and the World Health Organisation, as well as of the Inter-American Indian Institute, at appropriate levels and in their respective fields, and that it is proposed to continue this co-operation in promoting and securing the application of these provisions, and

Having decided upon the adoption of certain proposals with regard to the partial revision of the Indigenous and Tribal Populations Convention, 1957, (No. 107), which is the fourth item on the agenda of the session, and

Having determined that these proposals shall take the form of an international Convention revising the Indigenous and Tribal Populations Convention, 1957;

adopts this twenty-seventh day of June of the year one thousand nine hundred and eighty-nine the following Convention, which may be cited as the Indigenous and Tribal Peoples Convention, 1989:

Part I. General Policy

Article 1. 1. This Convention applies to:

(a) tribal peoples in independent countries whose social, cultural and economic conditions distinguish them from other sections of the national community, and whose status is regulated wholly or partially by their own customs or traditions or by special laws or regulations;

(b) peoples in independent countries who are regarded as indigenous on account of their descent from the populations which inhabited the country, or a geographical region to which the country belongs, at the time of conquest or colonisation or the establishment of present state boundaries and who, irrespective of their legal status, retain some or all of their own social, economic, cultural and political institutions.

2. Self-identification as indigenous or tribal shall be re-

garded as a fundamental criterion for determining the groups to which the provisions of this Convention apply.

3. The use of the term "peoples" in this convention shall not be construed as having any implications as regards the rights which may attach to the term under international law.

Article 2. 1. Governments shall have the responsibility for developing, with the participation of the peoples concerned, co-ordinated and systematic action to protect the rights of these peoples and to guarantee respect for their integrity.

2. Such action shall include measures for:

(a) ensuring that members of these peoples benefit on an equal footing from the rights and opportunities which national laws and regulations grant to other members of the population;

(b) promoting the full realisation of the social, economic and cultural rights of these peoples with respect for their social and cultural identity, their customs and traditions and their institutions;

(c) assisting the members of the peoples concerned to eliminate socio-economic gaps that may exist between indigenous and other members of the national community, in a manner compatible with their aspirations and ways of life.

Article 3. 1. Indigenous and tribal peoples shall enjoy the full measure of human rights and fundamental freedoms without hindrance or discrimination. The provisions of the Convention shall be applied without discrimination to male and female members of these peoples.

2. No form of force or coercion shall be used in violation of the human rights and fundamental freedoms of the peoples concerned, including the rights contained in this Convention.

Article 4. 1. Special measures shall be adopted as appropriate for safeguarding the persons, institutions, property, labour, cultures and environment of the peoples concerned.

2. Such special measures shall not be contrary to the freely-expressed wishes of the peoples concerned.

3. Enjoyment of the general rights of citizenship, without discrimination, shall not be prejudiced in any way by such special measures.

Article 5. In applying the provisions of this Convention:

(a) the social, cultural, religious and spiritual values and practices of these peoples shall be recognised and protected, and due account shall be taken of the nature of the problems which face them both as groups and as individuals;

(b) the integrity of the values, practices and institutions of these peoples shall be respected;

(c) policies aimed at mitigating the difficulties experienced by these peoples in facing new conditions of life and work shall be adopted, with the participation and co-operation of the peoples affected.

Article 6. In applying the provisions of this Convention, governments shall:

(a) consult the peoples concerned, through appropriate procedures and in particular through their representative institutions, whenever consideration is being given to legislative or administrative measures which may affect them directly;

(b) establish means by which these peoples can freely participate, to at least the same extent as other sectors of the population, at all levels of decision-making in elective institutions and administrative and other bodies responsible for policies and programmes which concern them;

(c) establish means for the full development of these peoples' own institutions and initiatives, and in appropriate cases provide the resources necessary for this purpose.

2. The consultations carried out in application of this Convention shall be undertaken, in good faith and in a form appropriate to the circumstances, with the objective of achieving agreement or consent to the proposed measures.

Article 7. 1. The peoples concerned shall have the right to decide their own priorities for the process of development as it affects their lives, beliefs, institutions and spiritual well-being and the lands they occupy or otherwise use, and to excercise control, to the extent possible, over their own economic, social and cultural development. In addition, they shall participate in the formulation, implementation and evaluation of plans and programmes for national and regional development which may affect them directly.

2. The improvement of the conditions of life and work and level of health and education of the peoples concerned, with their participation and co-operation, shall be a matter of priority in plans for the overall economic development of areas they inhabit. Special projects for development of the areas in question shall also be so designed as to promote such improvement.

3. Governments shall ensure that, whenever appropriate, studies are carried out, in co-operation with the peoples concerned, to assess the social, spiritual, cultural and environmental impact on them of planned development activities. The results of these studies shall be considered as fundamental criteria for the implementation of these activities.

4. Government shall take measures, in co-operation with the peoples concerned, to protect and preserve the environment of the territories they inhabit.

Article 8. 1. In applying national laws and regulations to the peoples concerned, due regard shall be had to their customs or customary laws.

2. These peoples shall have the right to retain their own customs and institutions, where these are not incompatible with fundamental rights defined by the national legal system and with internationally recognized human rights. Procedures shall be established, whenever necessary, to resolve conflicts which may arise in the application of this principle.

3. The application of paragraphs 1 and 2 of this Article shall not prevent members of these peoples from exercising the rights granted to all citizens and from assuming the corresponding duties.

Article 9. 1. To the extent compatible with the national legal system and internationally recognized human rights, the methods customarily practised by the peoples concerned for dealing with offences committed by their members shall be respected.

2. The customs of these peoples in regard to penal matters shall be taken into consideration by the authorities and courts dealing with such cases.

Article 10. In imposing penalties laid down by general law on members of these peoples account shall be taken of their economic, social and cultural characteristics.

2. Preference shall be given to methods of punishment other than confinement in prison.

Article 11. The exaction from members of the peoples concerned of compulsory personal services in any form, whether paid or unpaid, shall be prohibited and punishable by law, except in cases prescribed by law for all citizens.

Article 12. The peoples concerned shall be safeguarded against the abuse of their rights and shall be able to take legal proceedings, either individually or through their representative bodies, for the effective protection of these rights. Measures shall be taken to ensure that members of these peoples can understand and be understood in legal proceedings, where necessary through the provision of interpretation or by other effective means.

Part II. Land

Article 13. 1. In applying the provisions of this Part of the Convention governments shall respect the special importance for the cultures and spiritual values of the peoples concerned of their relationship with the lands or territories, or both as applicable, which they occupy or otherwise use, and in particular the collective aspects of this relationship.

2. The use of the term "lands" in Articles 15 and 16 shall include the concept of territories, which covers the total environment of the areas which the peoples concerned occupy or otherwise use.

Article 14. 1. The rights of ownership and possession of the peoples concerned over the lands which they traditionally occupy shall be recognised. In addition, measures shall be taken in appropriate cases to safeguard the right of the peoples concerned to use lands not exclusively occupied by them, but to which they have traditionally had access for their subsistence and traditional activities. Particular attention shall be paid to the situation of nomadic peoples and shifting cultivators in this respect.

2. Governments shall take steps as necessary to identify the lands which the peoples concerned traditionally occupy, and to guarantee effective protection of their rights of ownership and possession.

3. Adequate procedures shall be established within the national legal system to resolve land claims by the peoples concerned.

Article 15. 1. The rights of the peoples concerned to the natural resources pertaining to their lands shall be specially safeguarded. These rights include the right of these peoples to participate in the use, management and conservation of these resources.

2. In cases in which the State retains the ownership of mineral or sub-surface resources or rights to other resources pertaining to lands, governments shall establish or maintain procedures through which they shall consult these peoples, with a view to ascertaining whether and to what degree their interests would be prejudiced, before undertaking or permitting any programmes for the exploration or exploitation of such resources pertaining to their lands. The peoples concerned shall wherever possible participate in the benefits of such activities, and shall receive fair compensation for any damages which they may sustain as a result of such activities.

Article 16. 1. Subject to the following paragraphs of this Article, the peoples concerned shall not be removed from the lands which they occupy.

2. Where the relocation of these peoples is considered necessary as an exceptional measure, such relocation shall take place only with their free and informed consent. Where their consent cannot be obtained, such relocation shall take place only following appropriate procedures es-

I

tablished by national laws and regulations, including public inquiries where appropriate, which provide the opportunity for effective representation of the peoples concerned.

3. Whenever possible, these peoples shall have the right to return to their traditional lands, as soon as grounds for relocation cease to exist.

4. When such return is not possible, as determined by agreement or, in the absence of such agreement, through appropriate procedures, these peoples shall be provided in all possible cases with lands of quality and legal status at least equal to that of the lands previously occupied by them, suitable to provide for their present needs and future development. Where the peoples concerned express a preference for compensation in money or in kind, they shall be so compensated under appropriate guarantees.

5. Persons thus relocated shall be fully compensated for any resulting loss or injury.

Article 17. 1. Procedures established by the peoples concerned for the transmission of land rights among members of these peoples shall be respected.

2. The peoples concerned shall be consulted whenever consideration is being given to their capacity to alienate their lands or otherwise transmit their rights outside their own community.

3. Persons not belonging to these peoples shall be prevented from taking advantage of their customs or of lack of understanding of the laws on the part of their members to secure the ownership, possession or use of land belonging to them.

Article 18. Adequate penalties shall be established by law for unauthorised intrusion upon, or use of, the lands of the peoples concerned, and governments shall take measures to prevent such offences.

Article 19. National agrarian programmes shall secure to the peoples concerned treatment equivalent to that accorded to other sectors of the population with regard to:

(a) the provision of more land for these peoples when they have not the area necessary for providing the essentials of a normal existence, or for any possible increase in their numbers;

(b) the provision of the means required to promote the development of the lands which these peoples already possess.

Part III. Recruitment and Conditions of Employment

Article 20. 1. Governments shall, within the framework of national laws and regulations, and in co-operation with the peoples concerned, adopt special measures to ensure the effective protection with regard to recruitment and conditions of employment of workers belonging to these peoples, to the extent that they are not effectively protected by laws applicable to workers in general.

2. Governments shall do everything possible to prevent any discrimination between workers belonging to the peoples concerned and other workers, in particular as regards:

(a) admission to employment, including skilled employment, as well as measures for promotion and advancement;

(b) equal remuneration for work of equal value;

(c) medical and social assistance, occupational safety and health, all social security benefits and any other occupationally related benefits, and housing;

(d) the right of association and freedom for all lawful trade union activities, and the right to conclude collective agreements with employers or employers' organisations.

3. The measures taken shall include measures to ensure:

(a) that workers belonging to the peoples concerned, including seasonal, casual and migrant workers in agricultural and other employment, as well as those employed by labour contractors, enjoy the protection afforded by national law and practice to other such workers in the same sectors, and that they are fully informed of their rights under labour legislation and of the means of redress available to them;

(b) that workers belonging to these peoples are not subjected to working conditions hazardous to their health, in particular through exposure to pesticides or other toxic substances;

(c) that workers belonging to these peoples are not subjected to coercive recruitment systems, including bonded labour and other forms of debt servitude;

(d) that workers belonging to these peoples enjoy equal opportunities and equal treatment in employment for men and women, and protection form sexual harassment.

4. Particular attention shall be paid to the establishment of adequate labour inspection services in areas where workers belonging to the peoples concerned undertake wage employment, in order to ensure compliance with the provisions of this Part of this Convention.

Part IV. Vocational Training, Handicrafts and Rural Industries

Article 21. Members of the peoples concerned shall enjoy opportunities at least equal to those of other citizens in respect of vocational training measures.

Article 22. 1. Measures shall be taken to promote the voluntary participation of members of the peoples concerned in vocational training programmes of general application.

2. Whenever existing programmes of vocational training of general application do not meet the special needs of the peoples concerned, governments shall, with the participation of these peoples, ensure the provision of special training programmes and facilities.

3. Any special training programmes shall be based on the economic environment, social and cultural conditions and practical needs of the peoples concerned. Any studies made in this connection shall be carried out in co-operation with these peoples, who shall be consulted on the organisation and operation of such programmes. Where feasible, these peoples shall progressively assume responsibility for the organisation and operation of such special training programmes, if they so decide.

Article 23. 1. Handicrafts, rural and community based industries, and subsistence economy and traditional activities of the peoples concerned, such as hunting, fishing, trapping and gathering, shall be recognised as important factors in the maintenance of their cultures and in their economic self-reliance and development. Governments shall, with the participation of these people and whenever appropriate, ensure that these activities are strengthened and promoted.

2. Upon the request of the peoples concerned, appropriate technical and financial assistance shall be provided wherever possible, taking into account the traditional technologies and cultural characteristics of these peoples, as well as the importance of sustainable and equitable development.

Part V. Social Security and Health

Article 24. Social security schemes shall be extended progressively to cover the peoples concerned, and applied without discrimination against them.

Article 25. 1. Governments shall ensure that adequate health services are made available to the peoples concerned, or shall provide them with resources to allow them to design and deliver such services under their own responsibility and control, so that they may enjoy the highest attainable standard of physical and mental health.

2. Health services shall, to the extent possible, be community-based. These services shall be planned and administered in co-operation with the peoples concerned and take into account their economic, geographic, social and cultural conditions as well as their traditional preventive care, healing practices and medicines.

3. The health care system shall give preference to the training and employment of local community health workers, and focus on primary health care while maintaining strong links with other levels of health care services.

4. The provision of such health services shall be co-ordinated with other social, economic and cultural measures in the country.

Part VI. Education and Means of Communication

Article 26. Measures shall be taken to ensure that members of the peoples concerned have the opportunity to acquire education at all levels on at least an equal footing with the rest of the national community.

Article 27. 1. Education programmes and services for the peoples concerned shall be developed and implemented in co-operation with them to address their special needs, and shall incorporate their histories, their knowledge and technologies, their value systems and their further social, economic and cultural aspirations.

2. The competent authority shall ensure the training of members of these peoples and their involvement in the formulation and implementation of education programmes, with a view to the progressive transfer of responsibility for the conduct of these programmes to these peoples as appropriate.

3. In addition, governments shall recognize the right of these peoples to establish their own educational institutions and facilities, provided that such institutions meet minimum standards established by the competent authority in consultation with these peoples. Appropriate resources shall be provided for this purpose.

Article 28. 1. Children belonging to the peoples concerned shall, wherever practicable, be taught to read and write in their own indigenous language or in the language most commonly used by the group to which they belong. When this is not practicable, the competent authorities shall undertake consultations with these peoples with a view to the adoption of measures to achieve this objective.

2. Adequate measures shall be taken to ensure that these peoples have the oportunity to attain fluency in the national language or in one of the official languages of the country.

3. Measures shall be taken to preserve and promote the development and practice of the indigenous languages of the peoples concerned.

Article 29. The imparting of general knowledge and skills that will help children belonging to the peoples concerned to participate fully and on an equal footing in their own community and in the national community shall be an aim of education for these peoples.

Article 30. 1. Governments shall adopt measures appropriate to the traditions and cultures of the peoples concerned, to make known to them their rights and duties, especially in regard to labour, economic opportunities, education and health matters, social welfare and their rights deriving from this Convention.

2. If necessary, this shall be done by means of written translations and through the use of mass communications in the languages of these peoples.

Article 31. Educational measures shall be taken among all sections of the national community, and particularly among those that are in most direct contact with the peoples concerned, with the object of eliminating prejudices that they may harbour in respect of these peoples. To this end, efforts shall be made to ensure that history textbooks and other educational materials provide a fair, accurate and informative portrayal of the societies and cultures of these peoples.

Part VII. Contacts and Co-operation across Borders

Article 32. Governments shall take appropriate measures, including by means of international agreements, to facilitate contacts and co-operation between indigenous and tribal peoples across borders, including activities in the economic, social, cultural, spiritual and environmental fields.

Part VIII. Administration

Article 33. 1. The governmental authority responsible for the matters covered in this Convention shall ensure that agencies or other appropriate mechanisms exist to administer the programmes affecting the peoples concerned, and shall ensure that they have the means necessary for proper fulfilment of the functions assigned to them.

2. These programmes shall include:

(a) the planning, co-ordination, execution and evaluation, in co-operation with the peoples concerned, of the measures provided for in this convention;

(b) the proposing of legislative and other measures to the competent authorities and supervision of the application of the measures taken, in co-operation with the peoples concerned.

Part IX. General Provisions

Article 34. The nature and scope of the measures to be taken to give effect to this Convention shall be determined in a flexible manner, having regard to the conditions characteristic of each country.

Article 35. The application of the provisions of this Convention shall not adversely affect rights and benefits of the peoples concerned pursuant to other Conventions and Recommendations, international instruments, treaties, or national laws, awards, custom or agreements.

Part X. Final Provisions

Article 36. This Convention revises the Indigenous and Tribal Populations Convention, 1957.

Article 37. The formal ratifications of this Convention shall be communicated to the Director-General of the International Labour Office for registration.

Article 38. 1. This Convention shall be binding only upon those Members of the International Labour Organisation whose ratifications have been registered with the Director-General.

2. It shall come into force twelve months after the date

813

on which the ratifications of two Members have been registered with the Director-General.

3. Thereafter, this Convention shall come into force for any Member twelve months after the date on which its ratification has been registered.

Article 39. 1. A Member which has ratified this Convention may denounce it after the expiration of ten years from the date on which the Convention first comes into force, by an act communicated to the Direcor-General of the International Labour Office for registration. Such denunciation shall not take effect until one year after the date on which it is registered.

2. Each Member which has ratified this Convention and which does not, within the year following the expiration of the period of ten years mentioned in the preceding paragraph, excercise the right of denunciation provided for in this Article, will be bound for another period of ten years and, thereafter, may denounce this Convention at the expiration of each period of ten years under the terms provided for in this Article.

Article 40. 1. The Director-General of the International Labour Office shall notify all Members of the International Labour Organisation of the registration of all ratifications and denunciations communicated to him by the Members of the Organisation.

2. When notifying the Members of the Organisation of the registration of the second ratification communicated to him, the Director-General shall draw the attention of the Members of the Organisation to the date upon which the Convention will come into force.

Article 41. The Director-General of the International Labour Office shall communicate to the Secretary-General of the United Nations for registration in accordance with Article 102 of the Charter of the United Nations full particulars of all ratifications and acts of denunciation registered by him in accordance with the provisions of the preceding Articles.

Article 42. At such times as it may consider necessary the Governing Body of the International Labour Office shall present to the General Conference a report on the working of this Convention and shall examine the desirability of placing on the agenda of the Conference the question of its revision in whole or in part.

Article 43. 1. Should the Conference adopt a new Convention revising this Convention in whole or in part, then, unless the new Convention otherwise provides—

(a) the ratification by a Member of the new revising Convention shall *ipso jure* involve the immediate dennunciation of this Convention, notwithstanding the provisions of Article 39 above, if and when the new revising Convention shall have come into force;

(b) as from the date when the new revising Convention comes into force this Convention shall cease to be open to ratification by the Members.

2. This Convention shall in any case remain in force in its actual form and content for those Members which have ratified it but have not ratified the revising Convention.

Article 44. The English and French versions of the text of this Convention are equally authoritative.

SEE ALSO *Indigenous Populations Conventions: ILO Action; Indigenous Populations: Study of Problem of Discrimination; Indigenous Rights: Draft Universal Declaration; Indigenous Rights Year; Working Group on Indigenous Populations.*

ILO INVALIDITY, OLD AGE AND SURVIVORS' BENEFITS CONVENTION (1967).

Formally entitled Convention (No. 128) concerning Invalidity, Old-Age and Survivors' Benefits, the convention amends and updates a number of earlier agreements relating to old-age insurance, invalidity insurance, and survivors' benefits, permitting States parties to provide levels of benefits consistent with their economic development. It was adopted by the INTERNATIONAL LABOR CONFERENCE (51st session) on 29 June 1967 and entered into force on 1 November 1969. The text, with the exception of the ILO STANDARD FINAL PROVISIONS (articles 47–54) and an annex setting out an International Standard Industrial Classification of all Economic Activities, is as follows:

The General Conference of the International Labour Organisation,

Having been convened at Geneva by the Governing Body of the International Labour Office, and having met in its Fifty-first Session on 7 June 1967, and

Having decided upon the adoption of certain proposals with regard to the revision of the Old-Age Insurance (Industry, etc.) Convention, 1933, the Old-Age Insurance (Agriculture) Convention, 1933, the Invalidity Insurance (Industry, etc.) Convention, 1933, the Invalidity Insurance (Agriculture) Convention, 1933, the Survivors' Insurance (Industry, etc.) Convention, 1933, and the Survivors' Insurance (Agriculture) Convention, 1933, which is the fourth item on the agenda of the session, and

Having determined that these proposals shall take the form of an international Convention,

adopts this twenty-ninth day of June of the year one thousand nine hundred and sixty-seven the following Convention, which may be cited as the Invalidity, Old-Age and Survivors' Benefits Convention, 1967:

Part I. General Provisions

Article 1. In this Convention—

(a) the term "legislation" includes any social security rules as well as laws and regulations;

(b) the term "prescribed" means determined by or in virtue of national legislation;

(c) the term "industrial undertaking" includes all undertakings in the following branches of economic activity: mining and quarrying; manufacturing; construction; electricity, gas, water and sanitary services; and transport, storage and communication;

(d) the term "residence" means ordinary residence in the territory of the Member, and the term "resident" means a person ordinarily resident in the territory of the Member;

(e) the term "dependent" refers to a state of dependency which is presumed to exist in prescribed cases;

(f) the term "wife" means a wife who is dependent on her husband;

(g) the term "widow" means a woman who was dependent on her husband at the time of his death;

(h) the term "child" covers—

(i) a child under school-leaving age or under 15 years of age, whichever is the higher; and

(ii) a child under a prescribed age higher than that

specified in clause (i) of this subparagraph and who is an apprentice or student or has a chronic illness or infirmity disabling him for any gainful activity, under prescribed conditions: Provided that this requirement shall be deemed to be met where national legislation defines the term so as to cover any child under an age appreciably higher than that specified in clause (i) of this subparagraph;

(i) the term "qualifying period" means a period of contribution, or a period of employment, or a period of residence, or any combination thereof, as may be prescribed;

(j) the terms "contributory benefits" and "non-contributory benefits" mean respectively benefits the grant of which depends or does not depend on direct financial participation by the persons protected or their employer or on a qualifying period of occupational activity.

Article 2. Each Member for which this Convention is in force shall comply with—

(a) Part I;

(b) at least one of Parts II, III and IV;

(c) the relevant provisions of Parts V and VI; and

(d) Part VII.

2. Each Member shall specify in its ratification in respect of which of Parts II to IV it accepts the obligations of the Convention.

Article 3. 1. Each Member which has ratified this Convention may subsequently notify the Director-General of the International Labour Office that it accepts the obligations of the Convention in respect of one or more of Parts II to IV not already specified in its ratification.

2. The undertakings referred to in paragraph 1 of this Article shall be deemed to be an integral part of the ratification and to have the force of ratification as from the date of notification.

Article 4. 1. A Member whose economy is sufficiently developed may avail itself, by a declaration accompanying its ratification, of the temporary exceptions provided for in the following Articles: Article 9, paragraph 2; Article 13, paragraph 2; Article 16, paragraph 2; and Article 22, paragraph 2. Any such declaration shall state the reason for such exceptions.

2. Each Member which has made a declaration under paragraph 1 of this Article shall include in its reports upon the application of this Convention submitted under article 22 of the Constitution of the International Labour Organisation a statement in respect of each exception of which it avails itself—

(a) that its reason for doing so subsists; or

(b) that it renounces its right to avail itself of the exception in question as from a stated date.

3. Each Member which has made a declaration under paragraph 1 of this Article shall increase the number of employees protected as circumstances permit.

Article 5. Where, for the purpose of compliance with any of the Parts II to IV of this Convention which are to be covered by its ratification, a Member is required to protect prescribed classes of persons constituting not less than a specified percentage of employees or of the whole economically active population, the Member shall satisfy itself, before undertaking to comply with any such Part, that the relevant percentage is attained.

Article 6. For the purpose of compliance with Parts II, III or IV of this Convention, a Member may take account of protection effected by means of insurance which, although not made compulsory by its legislation for the persons to be protected—

(a) is supervised by the public authorities or adminis-

tered, in accordance with prescribed standards, by joint operation of employers and workers;

(b) covers a substantial part of the persons whose earnings do not exceed those of the skilled manual male employee; and

(c) complies, in conjunction with other forms of protection, where appropriate, with the relevant provisions of the Convention.

Part II. Invalidity Benefit

Article 7. Each Member for which this Part of this Convention is in force shall secure to the persons protected the provision of invalidity benefit in accordance with the following Articles of this Part.

Article 8. The contingency covered shall include incapacity to engage in any gainful activity, to an extent prescribed, which incapacity is likely to be permanent or persists after the termination of a prescribed period of temporary or initial incapacity.

Article 9. 1. The persons protected shall comprise—

(a) all employees, including apprentices; or

(b) prescribed classes of the economically active population, constituting not less than 75 percent of the whole economically active population; or

(c) all residents, or residents whose means during the contingency do not exceed limits prescribed in such a manner as to comply with the requirements of Article 28.

2. Where a declaration made in virtue of Article 4 is in force, the persons protected shall comprise—

(a) prescribed classes of employees, constituting not less than 25 per cent of all employees;

(b) prescribed classes of employees in industrial undertakings, constituting not less than 50 per cent of all employees in industrial undertakings.

Article 10. The invalidity benefit shall be a periodical payment calculated as follows:

(a) where employees or classes of the economically active population are protected, in such a manner as to comply either with the requirements of Article 26 or with the requirements of Article 27;

(b) where all residents or all residents whose means during the contingency do not exceed prescribed limits are protected, in such a manner as to comply with the requirements of Article 28.

Article 11. 1. The benefit specified in Article 10 shall, in a contingency covered, be secured at least—

(a) to a person protected who has completed, prior to the contingency, in accordance with prescribed rules, a qualifying period which may be 15 years of contribution or employment, or ten years of residence; or

(b) where, in principle, all economically active persons are protected, to a person protected who has completed, prior to the contingency, in accordance with prescribed rules, a qualifying period of three years of contribution and in respect of whom, while he was of working age, the prescribed yearly average number or yearly number of contributions has been paid.

2. Where the invalidity benefit is conditional upon a minimum period of contribution, employment or residence, a reduced benefit shall be secured at least—

(a) to a person protected who has completed, prior to the contingency, in accordance with prescribed rules, a qualifying period of five years of contribution, employment or residence; or

(b) where, in principle, all economically active persons

are protected, to a person protected who has completed, prior to the contingency, in accordance with prescribed rules, a qualifying period of three years of contribution and in respect of whom, while he was of working age, half of the yearly average number or of the yearly number of contributions prescribed in accordance with subparagraph (b) of paragraph 1 of this Article has been paid.

3. The requirements of paragraph 1 of this Article shall be deemed to be satisfied where a benefit calculated in conformity with the requirements of Part V but at a percentage of ten points lower than shown in the Schedule appended to that Part for the standard beneficiary concerned is secured at least to a person protected who has completed, in accordance with prescribed rules, five years of contribution, employment or residence.

4. A proportional reduction of the percentage indicated in the Schedule appended to Part V may be effected where the qualifying period for the benefit corresponding to the reduced percentage exceeds five years of contribution, employment or residence but is less than 15 years of contribution or employment or ten years of residence; a reduced benefit shall be payable in conformity with paragraph 2 of this Article.

5. The requirements of paragraphs 1 and 2 of this Article shall be deemed to be satisfied where a benefit calculated in conformity with the requirements of Part V is secured at least to a person protected who has completed, in accordance with prescribed rules, a qualifying period of contribution or employment which shall not be more than five years at a prescribed minimum age and may rise with advancing age to not more than a prescribed maximum number of years.

Article 12. The benefit specified in Articles 10 and 11 shall be granted throughout the contingency or until an old-age benefit becomes payable.

Article 13. 1. Each Member for which this Part of this Convention is in force shall, under prescribed conditions—

(a) provide rehabilitation services which are designed to prepare a disabled person wherever possible for the resumption of his previous activity, or, if this is not possible, the most suitable alternative gainful activity, having regard to his aptitudes and capacity; and

(b) take measures to further the placement of disabled persons in suitable employment.

2. Where a declaration made in virtue of Article 4 is in force, the Member may derogate from the provisions of paragraph 1 of this Article.

Part III. Old-Age Benefit

Article 14. Each Member for which this Part of this Convention is in force shall secure to the persons protected the provision of old-age benefit in accordance with the following Articles of this Part.

Article 15. 1. The contingency covered shall be survival beyond a prescribed age.

2. The prescribed age shall be not more than 65 years or such higher age as may be fixed by the competent authority with due regard to demographic, economic and social criteria, which shall be demonstrated statistically.

3. If the prescribed age is 65 years or higher, the age shall be lowered, under prescribed conditions, in respect of persons who have been engaged in occupations that are deemed by national legislation, for the purpose of old-age benefit, to be arduous or unhealthy.

Article 16. 1. The persons protected shall comprise—

(a) all employees, including apprentices; or

(b) prescribed classes of the economically active population, constituting not less than 75 per cent of the whole economically active population; or

(c) all residents or residents whose means during the contingency do not exceed limits prescribed in such a manner as to comply with the requirements of Article 28.

2. Where a declaration made in virtue of Article 4 is in force, the persons protected shall comprise—

(a) prescribed classes of employees, constituting not less than 25 percent of all employees; or

(b) prescribed classes of employees in industrial undertakings, constituting not less than 50 per cent of all employees in industrial undertakings.

Article 17. The old-age benefit shall be a periodical payment calculated as follows:

(a) where employees or classes of the economically active population are protected, in such a manner as to comply either with the requirements of Article 26 or with the requirements of Article 27;

(b) where all residents or all residents whose means during the contingency do not exceed prescribed limits are protected, in such a manner as to comply with the requirements of Article 28.

Article 18. 1. The benefit specified in Article 17 shall, in a contingency covered, be secured at least—

(a) to a person protected who has completed, prior to the contingency, in accordance with prescribed rules, a qualifying period which may be 30 years of contribution or employment, or 20 years of residence; or

(b) where, in principle, all economically active persons are protected, to a person protected who has completed, prior to the contingency, a prescribed qualifying period of contribution and in respect of whom, while he was of working age, the prescribed yearly average number of contributions has been paid.

2. Where the old-age benefit is conditional upon a minimum period of contribution or employment, a reduced benefit shall be secured at least—

(a) to a person protected who has completed, prior to the contingency, in accordance with prescribed rules, a qualifying period of 15 years of contribution or employment; or

(b) where, in principle, all economically active persons are protected, to a person protected who has completed, prior to the contingency, a prescribed qualifying period of contribution and in respect of whom, while he was of working age, half of the yearly average number of contributions prescribed in accordance with subparagraph (b) of paragraph 1 of this Article has been paid.

3. The requirements of paragraph 1 of this Article shall be deemed to be satisfied where a benefit calculated in conformity with the requirements of Part V but at a percentage of ten points lower than shown in the Schedule appended to that Part for the standard beneficiary concerned is secured at least to a person protected who has completed, in accordance with prescribed rules, ten years of contribution or employment, or five years of residence.

4. A proportional reduction of the percentage indicated in the Schedule appended to Part V may be effected where the qualifying period for the benefit corresponding to the reduced percentage exceeds ten years of contribution or employment or five years of residence but is less than 30 years of contribution or employment or 20 years of residence; if such qualifying period exceeds 15 years of contri-

bution or employment, a reduced benefit shall be payable in conformity with paragraph 2 of this Article.

Article 19. The benefit specified in Articles 17 and 18 shall be granted throughout the contingency.

Part IV. Survivors' Benefit

Article 20. Each Member for which this Part of this Convention is in force shall secure to the persons protected the provision of survivors' benefit in accordance with the following Articles of this Part.

Article 21. 1. The contingency covered shall include the loss of support suffered by the widow or child as the result of the death of the breadwinner.

2. In the case of a widow the right to a survivors' benefit may be made conditional on the attainment of a prescribed age. Such age shall not be higher than the age prescribed for old-age benefit.

3. No requirement as to age may be made if the widow—

(a) is invalid, as may be prescribed; or

(b) is caring for a dependent child of the deceased.

4. In order that a widow who is without a child may be entitled to a survivors' benefit, a minimum duration of marriage may be required.

Article 22. 1. The persons protected shall comprise—

(a) the wives, children and, as may be prescribed, other dependents of all breadwinners who were employees or apprentices; or

(b) the wives, children and, as may be prescribed, other dependants of breadwinners in prescribed classes of the economically active population, which classes constitute not less than 75 percent of the whole economically active population; or

(c) all widows, all children and all other prescribed dependants who have lost their breadwinner, who are residents and, as appropriate, whose means during the contingency do not exceed limits prescribed in such a manner as to comply with the provisions of Article 28.

2. Where a declaration made in virtue of Article 4 is in force, the persons protected shall comprise—

(a) the wives, children and, as may be prescribed, other dependants of breadwinners, in prescribed classes of employees, which classes constitute not less than 25 per cent of all employees; or

(b) the wives, children and, as may be prescribed, other dependants of breadwinners in prescribed classes of employees in industrial undertakings, which classes constitute not less than 50 per cent of all employees in industrial undertakings.

Article 23. The survivors' benefit shall be a periodical payment calculated as follows:

(a) where employees or classes of the economically active population are protected, in such a manner as to comply either with the requirements of Article 26 or with the requirements of Article 27;

(b) where all residents or all residents whose means during the contingency do not exceed prescribed limits are protected, in such a manner as to comply with the requirements of Article 28.

Article 24. 1. The benefit specified in Article 23 shall, in a contingency covered, be secured at least—

(a) to a person protected whose breadwinner has completed, in accordance with prescribed rules, a qualifying period which may be 15 years of contribution or employment, or ten years of residence: Provided that, for a benefit payable to a widow, the completion of a prescribed quali-

fying period of residence by such widow may be required instead; or

(b) where, in principle, the wives and children of all economically active persons are protected, to a person protected whose breadwinner has completed, in accordance with prescribed rules, a qualifying period of three years of contribution and in respect of whose breadwinner, while he was of working age, the prescribed yearly average number or the yearly number of contributions has been paid.

2. Where the survivors' benefit is conditional upon a minimum period of contribution or employment, a reduced benefit shall be secured at least—

(a) to a person protected whose breadwinner has completed, in accordance with prescribed rules, a qualifying period of five years of contribution or employment; or

(b) where, in principle, the wives and children of all economically active persons are protected, to a person protected whose breadwinner has completed, in accordance with prescribed rules, a qualifying period of three years of contribution and in respect of whose breadwinner, while he was of working age, half of the yearly average number or of the yearly number of contributions prescribed in accordance with subparagraph (b) of paragraph 1 of this Article has been paid.

3. The requirements of paragraph 1 of this Article shall be deemed to be satisfied where a benefit calculated in conformity with the requirements of Part V but at a percentage of ten points lower than shown in the Schedule appended to that Part for the standard beneficiary concerned is secured at least to a person protected whose breadwinner has completed, in accordance with prescribed rules, five years of contribution, employment or residence.

4. A proportional reduction of the percentage indicated in the Schedule appended to Part V may be effected where the qualifying period for the benefit corresponding to the reduced percentage exceeds five years of contribution, employment or residence but is less than 15 years of contribution or employment or ten year of residence; if such qualifying period is one of contribution or employment, a reduced benefit shall be payable in conformity with paragraph 2 of this Article.

5. The requirements of paragraphs 1 and 2 of this Article shall be deemed to be satisfied where a benefit calculated in conformity with the requirements of Part V is secured at least to a person protected whose breadwinner has completed, in accordance with prescribed rules, a qualifying period of contribution or employment which shall not be more than five years at a prescribed minimum age and may rise with advancing age to not more than a prescribed maximum number of years.

Article 25. The benefit specified in Articles 23 and 24 shall be granted throughout the contingency.

Part V. Standards to Be Complied with by Periodical Payments

Article 26. 1. In the case of a periodical payment to which this Article applies, the rate of the benefit, increased by the amount of any family allowances payable during the contingency, shall be such as to attain, in respect of the contingency in question, for the standard beneficiary indicated in the Schedule appended to this Part, at least the percentage indicated therein of the total of the previous earnings of the beneficiary or his breadwinner and of the amount of any family allowances payable to a person protected with the same family responsibilities as the standard beneficiary.

2. The previous earnings of the beneficiary or his breadwinner shall be calculated according to prescribed rules, and, where the persons protected or their breadwinners are arranged in classes according to their earnings, their previous earnings may be calculated from the basic earnings of the classes to which they belonged.

3. A maximum limit may be prescribed for the rate of the benefit or for the earnings taken into account for the calculation of the benefit, provided that the maximum limit is fixed in such a way that the provisions of paragraph 1 of this Article are complied with where the previous earnings of the beneficiary or his breadwinner are equal to or lower than the wage of a skilled manual male employee.

4. The previous earnings of the beneficiary or his breadwinner, the wage of the skilled manual male employee, the benefit and any family allowances shall be calculated on the same time basis.

5. For the other beneficiaries the benefit shall bear a reasonable relation to the benefit for the standard beneficiary.

6. For the purpose of this Article, a skilled manual male employee shall be—

(a) a fitter or turner in the manufacture of machinery other than electrical machinery; or

(b) a person deemed typical of skilled labour selected in accordance with the provisions of the following paragraph; or

(c) a person whose earnings are such as to be equal to or greater than the earnings of 75 per cent of all the persons protected, such earnings to be determined on the basis of annual or shorter periods as may be prescribed; or

(d) a person whose earnings are equal to 125 per cent of the average earnings of all the persons protected.

7. The person deemed typical of skilled labour for the purposes of subparagraph (b) of the preceding paragraph shall be a person employed in the major group of economic activities with the largest number of economically active male persons protected in the contingency in question, or of the breadwinners of the persons protected, as the case may be, in the division comprising the largest number of such persons or breadwinners; for this purpose, the international standard industrial classification of all economic activities, adopted by the Economic and Social Council of the United Nations at its Seventh Session on 27 August 1948, as amended up to 1958 and reproduced in the Annex to this Convention, or such classification as at any time further amended, shall be used.

8. Where the rate of benefit varies by region, the skilled manual male employee may be determined for each region in accordance with paragraphs 6 and 7 of this Article.

9. The wage of the skilled manual male employee shall be determined on the basis of the rates of wages for normal hours of work fixed by collective agreements, by or in pursuance of national legislation, where applicable, or by custom, including cost-of-living allowances if any; where such rates differ by region but paragraph 8 of this Article is not applied, the median rate shall be taken.

Article 27. 1. In the case of a periodical payment to which this Article applies, the rate of the benefit, increased by the amount of any family allowances payable during the contingency, shall be such as to attain, in respect of the contingency in question, for the standard beneficiary indicated in the Schedule appended to this Part, at least the percentage indicated therein of the total of the wage of an ordinary adult male labourer and of the amount of any family allowances payable to a person protected with the same family responsibilities as the standard beneficiary.

2. The wage of the ordinary adult male labourer, the benefit and any family allowances shall be calculated on the same time basis.

3. For the other beneficiaries, the benefit shall bear a reasonable relation to the benefit for the standard beneficiary.

4. For the purpose of this Article, the ordinary adult male labourer shall be—

(a) a person deemed typical of unskilled labour in the manufacture of machinery other than electrical machinery; or

(b) a person deemed typical of unskilled labour selected in accordance with the provisions of the following paragraph.

5. The person deemed typical of unskilled labour for the purpose of subparagraph (b) of the preceding paragraph shall be a person employed in the major group of economic activities with the largest number of economically active male persons protected in the contingency in question, or of the breadwinners of the persons protected, as the case may be, in the division comprising the largest number of such persons or breadwinners; for this purpose the international standard industrial classification of all economic activities, adopted by the Economic and Social Council of the United Nations at its Seventh Session on 2 August 1948, as amended up to 1958 and reproduced in the Annex to this Convention, or such classifications as at any time further amended, shall be used.

6. Where the rate of benefit varies by region, the ordinary adult male labourer may be determined for each region in accordance with paragraphs 4 and 5 of this Article.

7. The wage of the ordinary adult male labourer shall be determined on the basis of the rates of wages for normal hours of work fixed by collective agreements, by or in pursuance of national legislation, where applicable, or by custom, including cost-of-living allowances if any; where such rates differ by region but paragraph 6 of this Article is not applied, the median rate shall be taken.

Article 28. In the case of a periodical payment to which this Article applies—

(a) the rate of the benefit shall be determined according to a prescribed scale or a scale fixed by the competent public authority in conformity with prescribed rules;

(b) such rate may be reduced only to the extent by which the other means of the family of the beneficiary exceed prescribed substantial amounts or substantial amounts fixed by the competent public authority in conformity with prescribed rules;

(c) the total of the benefit and any other means, after deduction of the substantial amounts referred to in subparagraph (b), shall be sufficient to maintain the family of the beneficiary in health and decency, and shall be not less than the corresponding benefit calculated in accordance with the requirements of Article 27;

(d) the provisions of subparagraph (c) shall be deemed to be satisfied if the total amount of benefits paid under the Part concerned exceeds by at least 30 per cent the total amounts of benefits which would be obtained by applying the provisions of Article 27 and the provisions of—

(i) Article 9, paragraph 1, subparagraph (b) for Part II;

(ii) Article 16, paragraph 1, subparagraph (b) for Part III;

(iii) Article 22, paragraph 1, subparagraph (b) for Part IV.

Article 29. 1. The rates of cash benefits currently payable pursuant to Article 10, Article 17 and Article 23 shall be reviewed following substantial changes in the general level of earnings or substantial changes in the cost of living.

2. Each Member shall include the findings of such reviews in its reports upon the application of this Convention submitted under article 22 of the Constitution of the International Labour Organisation, and shall specify any action taken. . . .

Part VI. Common Provisions

Article 30. National legislation shall provide for the maintenance of rights in course of acquisition in respect of contributory invalidity, old-age and survivors' benefits under prescribed conditions.

Article 31. 1. The payment of invalidity, old-age or survivors' benefit may be suspended, under prescribed conditions, where the beneficiary is engaged in gainful activity.

2. A contributory invalidity, old-age or survivors' benefit may be reduced where the earnings of the beneficiary exceed a prescribed amount; the reduction in benefit shall not exceed the earnings.

3. A non-contributory invalidity, old-age or survivors' benefit may be reduced where the earnings of the beneficiary or his other means or the two taken together exceed a prescribed amount.

Article 32. 1. A benefit to which a person protected would otherwise be entitled in compliance with any of Parts II to IV of this Convention may be suspended to such extent as may be prescribed—

(a) as long as the person concerned is absent from the territory of the Member, except, under prescribed conditions, in the case of a contributory benefit;

(b) as long as the person concerned is maintained at public expense or at the expense of a social security institution or service;

(c) where the person concerned has made a fraudulent claim;

(d) where the contingency has been caused by a criminal offence committed by the person concerned;

(e) where the contingency has been wilfully caused by the serious misconduct of the person concerned;

(f) in appropriate cases, where the person concerned, without good reason, neglects to make use of the medical or rehabilitation services placed at his disposal or fails to comply with rules prescribed for verifying the occurrence or continuance of the contingency or for the conduct of beneficiaries; and

(g) in the case of survivors' benefit for a widow, as long as she is living with a man as his wife.

2. In the case and within the limits prescribed, part of the benefit otherwise due shall be paid to the dependants of the person concerned.

Article 33. 1. If a person protected is or would otherwise be eligible simultaneously for more than one of the benefits provided for in this Convention, these benefits may be reduced under prescribed conditions and within prescribed limits; the person protected shall receive in total at least the amount of the most favourable benefit.

2. If a person protected is or would otherwise be eligible for a benefit provided for in this Convention and is in receipt of another social security cash benefit for the same contingency, other than a family benefit, the benefit under this Convention may be reduced or suspended under prescribed conditions and within prescribed limits, subject to the art of the benefit which is reduced or suspended not exceeding the other benefit.

Article 34. 1. Every claimant shall have a right of appeal in the case of refusal of benefit or complaint as to its quality or quantity.

2. Procedures shall be prescribed which permit the claimant to be represented or assisted, where appropriate, by a qualified person of his choice or by a delegate of an organisation representative of persons protected.

Article 35. 1. Each Member shall accept general responsibility for due provision of the benefits provided in compliance with this Convention and shall take all measures required for this purpose.

2. Each Member shall accept general responsibility for the proper administration of the institutions and services concerned in the application of this Convention.

Article 36. Where the administration is not entrusted to an institution regulated by the public authorities or to a government department responsible to a legislature, representatives of the persons protected shall participate in the management under prescribed conditions; national legislation may likewise decide as to the participation of representatives of employers and of the public authorities.

Part VII. Miscellaneous Provisions

Article 37. Any Member whose legislation protects employees may, as necessary, exclude from the application of this Convention—

(a) persons whose employment is of a casual nature;

(b) members of the employer's family living in his house, in respect of their work for him;

(c) other categories of employees, which shall not exceed in number 10 per cent of all employees other than those excluded under subparagraphs (a) and (b) of this Article.

Article 38. 1. Any Member whose legislation protects employees may, by a declaration accompanying its ratification, temporarily exclude from the application of this Convention the employees in the sector comprising agricultural occupations who are not yet protected by its legislation at the time of the ratification.

2. Each Member which has made a declaration under paragraph 1 of this Article shall indicate in its reports upon the application of this Convention submitted under article 22 of the Constitution of the International Labour Organisation to what extent effect is given and what effect is proposed to be given to the provisions of the Convention in respect of the employees in the sector comprising agricultural occupations and any progress which may have been made with a view to the application of the Convention to such employees or, where there is no change to report, furnish all the appropriate explanations.

3. Each Member which has made a declaration under paragraph 1 of this Article shall increase the number of employees protected in the agriculture sector to the extent and with the speed that the circumstances permit.

Article 39. 1. Any Member which ratifies this Convention may, by a declaration accompanying its ratification, exclude from the application of the Convention—

(a) seafarers, including sea fishermen,

(b) public servants,

where these categories are protected by special schemes, which provide in the aggregate benefits at least equivalent to those required by this Convention.

2. Where a declaration under paragraph 1 of this Article is in force, the Member may exclude the persons belonging to the category or categories excluded from the application

of the Convention from the number of persons taken into account when calculating the percentages specified in paragraph 1, subparagraph (b), and paragraph 2, subparagraph (b), of Article 9; paragraph 1, subparagraph (b), and paragraph 2, subparagraph (b), of Article 16; paragraph 1, subparagraph (b), and paragraph 2, subparagraph (b), of Article 22; and subparagraph (c) of Article 37.

3. Any Member which has made a declaration under paragraph 1 of this Article may subsequently notify the Director-General of the International Labour Office that it accepts the obligations of this Convention in respect of a category or categories excluded at the time of its ratification.

Article 40. If a person protected is entitled, under national legislation, in case of death of the breadwinner, to periodical benefits other than a survivors' benefit, such periodical benefits may be assimilated to the survivor's benefit for the application of this Convention.

Article 41. 1. A Member which—

(a) has accepted the obligations of this Convention in respect of Parts II, III and IV, and

(b) covers a percentage of the economically active population which is at least ten points higher than that required by Article 9, paragraph 1, subparagraph (b), Article 16, paragraph 1, subparagraph (b), and Article 22, paragraph 1, subparagraph (b), or complete with Article 9, paragraph 1, subparagraph (c), Article 16, paragraph 1, subparagraph (c), and Article 22, paragraph 1, subparagraph (c), and

(c) secures in respect of at least two of the contingencies covered by Parts II, III and IV benefits of an amount corresponding to a percentage at least five points higher than the percentages specified in the Schedule appended to Part V,

may take advantage of the provisions of the following paragraph.

2. Such Member may—

(a) substitute, for the purpose of Article 11, paragraph 2, subparagraph (b), and Article 24, paragraph 2, subparagraph (b), a period of five years for the period of three years specified therein;

(b) determine the beneficiaries of survivors' benefits in a manner which is different from that required by Article 21, but which ensures that the total number of beneficiaries does not fall short of the number of beneficiaries which would result from the application of Article 21.

3. Each Member which has taken advantage of the provisions of paragraph 2 of this Article shall indicate in its reports upon the application of this Convention submitted under article 22 of the Constitution of the International Labour Organisation the position of its law and practice as regards the matters dealt with in that paragraph and any progress made towards complete application of the terms of the Convention.

Article 42. 1. A Member which—

(a) has accepted the obligations of this Convention in respect of Parts II, III and IV, and

(b) covers a percentage of the economically active population which is at least ten points higher than that required by Article 9, paragraph 1, subparagraph (b), Article 16, paragraph 1, subparagraph (b), and Article 22, paragraph 1, subparagraph (b), or complies with Article 9, paragraph 1, subparagraph (c), Article 16, paragraph 1, subparagraph (c), and Article 22, paragraph 1, subparagraph (c),

may derogate from particular provisions of Parts II, III and IV: on condition that the total amount of benefits paid under the Part concerned shall be at least equal to 110 per cent of the total amount which would be obtained by applying all the provisions of that Part.

2. Each Member which has made such a derogation shall indicate in its reports upon the application of this Convention submitted under article 22 of the Constitution of the International Labour Organisation the position of its law and practice as regards such derogation and any progress made towards complete application of the terms of the Convention.

Article 43. This Convention shall not apply to—

(a) contingencies which occurred before the coming into force of the relevant Part of the Convention for the Member concerned;

(b) benefits in contingencies occurring after the coming into force of the relevant Part of the Convention for the Member concerned in so far as the rights to such benefits are derived from periods preceding that date.

Article 44. 1. This Convention revises, on the terms set forth in this Article, the Old-Age Insurance (Industry, etc.) Convention 1933, the Old-Age Insurance (Agriculture) Convention, 1933, the Invalidity Insurance (Industry, etc.) Convention, 1933, the Invalidity Insurance (Agriculture) Convention, 1933, the Survivors' Insurance (Industry, etc). Convention, 1933, and the Survivors' Insurance (Agriculture) Convention, 1933.

2. The legal effect of the acceptance of the obligations of this Convention by a Member which is a party to one or more of the Conventions which have been revised, when this Convention shall have come into force, shall be as follows for that Member:

(a) acceptance of the obligations of Part II of the Convention shall, *ipso jure,* involve the immediate denunciation of the Invalidity Insurance (Industry, etc.) Convention, 1933, and the Invalidity Insurance (Agriculture) Convention, 1933;

(b) acceptance of the obligations of Part III of the Convention shall, *ipso jure,* involve the immediate denunciation of the Old-Age Insurance (Industry, etc.) Convention, 1933, and the Old-Age Insurance (Agriculture) Convention, 1933;

(c) acceptance of the obligations of Part IV of the Convention shall, *ipso jure,* involve the immediate denunciation of the Survivors' Insurance (Industry, etc.) Convention, 1933, and the Survivors' Insurance (Agriculture) Convention, 1933.

Article 45. 1. In conformity with the provisions of Article 75 of the Social Security (Minimum Standards) Convention, 1952, the following Parts of that Convention and the relevant provisions of other Parts thereof shall cease to apply to any Member having ratified this Convention as from the date at which this Convention is binding on that Member and no declaration under Article 38 is in force:

(a) Part IX where the Member has accepted the obligations of this Convention in respect of Part II;

(b) Part V where the Member has accepted the obligations of this Convention in respect of Part III;

(c) Part X where the Member has accepted the obligations of this Convention in respect of Part IV.

2. Acceptance of the obligations of this Convention shall, on condition that no declaration under Article 38 is in force, be deemed to constitute acceptance of the obliga-

tions of the following parts of the Social Security (Minimum Standards) Convention, 1952, and the relevant provisions of other Parts thereof, for the purpose of Article 2 of the said Convention:

(a) Part IX where the Member has accepted the obligations of this Convention in respect of Part II;

(b) Part V where the Member has accepted the obligations of this Convention in respect of Part III;

(c) Part X where the Member has accepted the obligations of this Convention in respect of Part IV.

Article 46. If any Convention which may be adopted subsequently by the Conference concerning any subject or subjects dealt with in this Convention so provides, such provisions of this Convention as may be specified in the said Convention shall cease to apply to any Member having ratified the said Convention as from the date at which the said Convention comes into force for that Member....

SEE ALSO *ILO Social Security (Basic Aims and Standards) Convention; ILO Social Security (Minimum Standards) Convention; ILO Workers with Family Responsibilities Convention; Social Security.*

ILO LABOR INSPECTION CONVENTION (1947).

Formally entitled Convention (No. 81) concerning Labor Inspection in Industry and Commerce, the convention was adopted on 11 July 1947 by the INTERNATIONAL LABOR CONFERENCE (30th session) and entered into force on 7 April 1950.

The ILO had long considered it to be of great importance that every country should have a labor inspection service worthy of the name, it being obvious that labor legislation that did not provide for inspection represented more of a theoretical exercise than a binding obligation. The convention establishes standards for operational inspection programs.

The text of the convention (*International Labour Conventions and Recommendations, 1919–1981*, p. 170), with the exception of the ILO STANDARD FINAL PROVISIONS (articles 32–39) and provisions relating to declarations of application to non-metropolitan territories (articles 30 and 31), is as follows:

The General Conference of the International Labour Organisation,

Having been convened at Geneva by the Governing Body of the International Labour Office, and having met in its Thirtieth Session on 19 June 1947, and

Having decided upon the adoption of certain proposals with regard to the organisation of labour inspection in industry and commerce, which is the fourth item on the agenda of the Session, and

Having determined that these proposals shall take the form of an international Convention,

adopts this eleventh day of July of the year one thousand nine hundred and forty-seven the following Convention, which may be cited as the Labour Inspection Convention, 1947:

Part I. Labour Inspection in Industry

Article 1. Each Member of the International Labour Organisation for which this Convention is in force shall maintain a system of labour inspection in industrial workplaces.

Article 2. 1. The system of labour inspection in industrial workplaces shall apply to all workplaces in respect of which legal provisions relating to conditions of work and the protection of workers while engaged in their work are enforceable by labour inspectors.

2. National laws or regulations may exempt mining and transport undertakings or parts of such undertakings from the application of this Convention.

Article 3. 1. The functions of the system of labour inspection shall be:

(a) to secure the enforcement of the legal provisions relating to conditions of work and the protection of workers while engaged in their work, such as provisions relating to hours, wages, safety, health and welfare, the employment of children and young persons, and other connected matters, in so far as such provisions are enforceable by labour inspectors;

(b) to supply technical information and advice to employers and workers concerning the most effective means of complying with the legal provisions;

(c) to bring to the notice of the competent authority defects or abuses not specifically covered by existing legal provisions.

2. Any further duties which may be entrusted to labour inspectors shall not be such as to interfere with the effective discharge of their primary duties or to prejudice in any way the authority and impartiality which are necessary to inspectors in their relations with employers and workers.

Article 4. 1. So far as is compatible with the administrative practice of the Member, labour inspection shall be placed under the supervision and control of a central authority.

2. In the case of a federal State, the term "central authority" may mean either a federal authority or a central authority of a federated unit.

Article 5. The competent authority shall make appropriate arrangements to promote:

(a) effective co-operation between the inspection services and other government services and public or private institutions engaged in similar activities; and

(b) collaboration between officials of the labour inspectorate and employers and workers or their organisations.

Article 6. The inspection staff shall be composed of public officials whose status and conditions of service are such that they are assured of stability of employment and are independent of changes of government and of improper external influences.

Article 7. 1. Subject to any conditions for recruitment to the public service which may be prescribed by national laws or regulations, labour inspectors shall be recruited with sole regard to their qualifications for the performance of their duties.

2. The means of ascertaining such qualifications shall be determined by the competent authority.

3. Labour inspectors shall be adequately trained for the performance of their duties.

Article 8. Both men and women shall be eligible for appointment to the inspection staff; where necessary, special duties may be assigned to men and women inspectors.

Article 9. Each Member shall take the necessary measures to ensure that duly qualified technical experts and specialists, including specialists in medicine, engineering, electricity and chemistry, are associated in the work of inspection, in such manner as may be deemed most appropriate under national conditions, for the purpose of securing the enforcement of the legal provisions relating to the protection of the health and safety of workers while engaged in their work and of investigating the effects of processes, materials and methods of work on the health and safety of workers.

Article 10. The number of labour inspectors shall be sufficient to secure the effective discharge of the duties of the inspectorate and shall be determined with due regard for:

(a) the importance of the duties which inspectors have to perform, in particular—

(i) the number, nature, size and situation of the workplaces liable to inspection;

(ii) the number and classes of workers employed in such workplaces; and

(iii) the number and complexity of the legal provisions to be enforced;

(b) the material means placed at the disposal of the inspectors; and

(c) the practical conditions under which visits of inspection must be carried out in order to be effective.

Article 11. 1. The competent authority shall make the necessary arrangements to furnish labour inspectors with—

(a) local offices, suitably equipped in accordance with the requirements of the service, and accessible to all persons concerned;

(b) the transport facilities necessary for the performance of their duties in cases where suitable public facilities do not exist.

2. The competent authority shall make the necessary arrangements to reimburse to labour inspectors any travelling and incidental expenses which may be necessary for the performance of their duties.

Article 12. 1. Labour inspectors provided with proper credentials shall be empowered:

(a) to enter freely and without previous notice at any hour of the day or night any workplace liable to inspection;

(b) to enter by day any premises which they may have reasonable cause to believe to be liable to inspection; and

(c) to carry out any examination, test or enquiry which they may consider necessary in order to satisfy themselves that the legal provisions are being strictly observed, and in particular—

(i) to interrogate, alone or in the presence of witnesses, the employer or the staff of the undertaking on any matters concerning the application of the legal provisions;

(ii) to require the production of any books, registers or other documents the keeping of which is prescribed by national laws or regulations relating to conditions of work, in order to see that they are in conformity with the legal provisions, and to copy such documents or make extracts from them;

(iii) to enforce the posting of notices required by the legal provisions;

(iv) to take or remove for purposes of analysis samples of materials and substances used or handled, subject to the employer or his representative being notified of any samples or substances taken or removed for such purposes.

2. On the occasion of an inspection visit, inspectors shall notify the employer or his representative of their presence, unless they consider that such a notification may be prejudicial to the performance of their duties.

Article 13. 1. Labour inspectors shall be empowered to take steps with a view to remedying defects observed in plant, layout or working methods which they may have reasonable cause to believe constitute a threat to the health or safety of the workers.

2. In order to enable inspectors to take such steps they shall be empowered, subject to any right of appeal to a judicial or administrative authority which may be provided by law, to make or to have made orders requiring—

(a) such alterations to the installation or plant, to be carried out within a specified time limit, as may be necessary to secure compliance with the legal provisions relating to the health or safety of the workers; or

(b) measure with immediate executory force in the event of imminent danger to the health or safety of the workers.

3. Where the procedure prescribed in paragraph 2 is not compatible with the administrative or judicial practice of the Member, inspectors shall have the right to apply to the competent authority for the issue of orders or for the initiation of measures with immediate executory force.

Article 14. The labour inspectorate shall be notified of industrial accidents and cases of occupational disease in such cases and in such manner as may be prescribed by national laws or regulations.

Article 15. Subject to such exceptions as may be made by national laws or regulations, labour inspectors—

(a) shall be prohibited from having any direct or indirect interest in the undertakings under their supervision;

(b) shall be bound on pain of appropriate penalties or disciplinary measures not to reveal, even after leaving the service, any manufacturing or commercial secrets or working processes which may come to their knowledge in the course of their duties; and

(c) shall treat as absolutely confidential the source of any complaint bringing to their notice a defect or breach of legal provisions and shall give no intimation to the employer or his representative that a visit of inspection was made in consequence of the receipt of such a complaint.

Article 16. Workplaces shall be inspected as often and as thoroughly as is necessary to ensure the effective application of the relevant legal provisions.

Article 17. 1. Persons who violate or neglect to observe legal provisions enforceable by labour inspectors shall be liable to prompt legal proceedings without previous warning: Provided that exceptions may be made by national laws or regulations in respect of cases in which previous notice to carry out remedial or preventive measures is to be given.

2. It shall be left to the discretion of labour inspectors to give warning and advice instead of instituting or recommending proceedings.

Article 18. Adequate penalties for violations of the legal provisions enforceable by labour inspectors and for obstructing labour inspectors in the performance of their duties shall be provided for by national laws or regulations and effectively enforced.

Article 19. 1. Labour inspectors or local inspection offices, as the case may be, shall be required to submit to the central inspection authority periodical reports on the results of their inspection activities.

2. These reports shall be drawn up in such manner and deal with such subjects as may from time to time be prescribed by the central authority; they shall be submitted at least as frequently as may be prescribed by that authority and in any case not less frequently than once a year.

Article 20. 1. The central inspection authority shall publish an annual general report on the work of the inspection services under its control.

2. Such annual reports shall be published within a reasonable time after the end of the year to which they relate and in any case within twelve months.

3. Copies of the annual reports shall be transmitted to the Director-General of the International Labour Office within a reasonable period after their publication and in any case within three months.

Article 21. The annual report published by the central inspection authority shall deal with the following and other relevant subjects in so far as they are under the control of the said authority:

(a) laws and regulations relevant to the work of the inspection service;

(b) staff of the labour inspection service;

(c) statistics of workplaces liable to inspection and the number of workers employed therein;

(d) statistics of inspection visits;

(e) statistics of violations and penalties imposed;

(f) statistics of industrial accidents;

(g) statistics of occupational diseases.

Part II. Labour Inspection in Commerce

Article 22. Each Member of the International Labour Organisation for which this Part of this Convention is in force shall maintain a system of labour inspection in commercial workplaces.

Article 23. The system of labour inspection in commercial workplaces shall apply to workplaces in respect of which legal provisions relating to conditions of work and the protection of workers while engaged in their work are enforceable by labour inspectors.

Article 24. The system of labour inspection in commercial workplaces shall comply with the requirements of Articles 3 to 21 of this Convention in so far as they are applicable.

Part III. Miscellaneous Provisions

Article 25. 1. Any Member of the International Labour Organisation which ratifies this Convention may, by a declaration appended to its ratification, exclude Part II from its acceptance of the Convention.

2. Any Member which has made such a declaration may at any time cancel that declaration by a subsequent declaration.

3. Every Member for which a declaration made under paragraph 1 of this Article is in force shall indicate each year in its annual report upon the application of this Convention the position of its law and practice in regard to the provisions of Part II of this Convention and the extent to which effect has been given, or is proposed to be given, to the said provisions.

Article 26. In any case in which it is doubtful whether any undertaking, part or service of an undertaking or workplace is an undertaking, part, service or workplace to which this Convention applies, the question shall be settled by the competent authority.

Article 27. In this Convention the term "legal provisions" includes, in addition to laws and regulations, arbitration awards and collective agreements upon which the force of law is conferred and which are enforceable by labour inspectors.

Article 28. There shall be included in the annual reports to be submitted under Article 22 of the Constitution of the International Labour Organisation full information concerning all laws and regulations by which effect is given to the provisions of this Convention.

Article 29. 1. In the case of a Member the territory of which includes large areas where, by reason of the sparseness of the population or the stage of development of the area, the competent authority considers it impracticable to enforce the provisions of this Convention, the authority may exempt such areas from the application of this Convention either generally or with such exceptions in respect of particular undertakings or occupations as it thinks fit.

2. Each Member shall indicate in its first annual report upon the application of this Convention submitted under article 22 of the Constitution of the International Labour Organisation any areas in respect of which it proposes to have recourse to the provisions of the present Article and shall give the reasons for which it proposes to have recourse thereto; no Member shall, after the date of its first annual report, have recourse to the provisions of the present Article except in respect of areas so indicated.

3. Each Member having recourse to the provisions of the present Article shall indicate in subsequent annual reports any areas in respect of which it renounces the right to have recourse to the provisions of the present Article. . . .

SEE ALSO ILO Working Environment (Air Pollution, Noise and Vibration) Convention.

ILO LABOR RELATIONS (PUBLIC SERVICE) CONVENTION (1978).

Formally entitled Convention (No. 151) concerning Protection of the Right to Organize and Procedures for Determining Conditions of Employment in the Public Service, the convention protects the right of public employees to organize and to be protected against anti-union discrimination. It was adopted by the INTERNATIONAL LABOR CONFERENCE (64th session) on 27 June 1978 and entered into force on 25 February 1981.

The text of the convention (*International Labour Conventions and Recommendations, 1919–1981*, p. 25), with the exception of the ILO STANDARD FINAL PROVISIONS (articles 10–17), is as follows:

Part I. Scope and Definitions

Article 1. 1. This Convention applies to all persons employed by public authorities, to the extent that more favourable provisions in other international labour Conventions are not applicable to them.

2. The extent to which the guarantees provided for in this Convention shall apply to high-level employees whose functions are normally considered as policy-making or managerial, or to employees whose duties are of a highly confidential nature, shall be determined by national laws or regulations.

3. The extent to which the guarantees provided for in this Convention shall apply to the armed forces and the police shall be determined by national laws or regulations.

Article 2. For the purpose of this Convention, the term "public employee" means any person covered by the Convention in accordance with Article 1 thereof.

Article 3. For the purpose of this Convention, the term

"public employees' organisation" means any organisation, however composed, the purpose of which is to further and defend the interests of public employees.

Part II. Protection of the Right to Organise

Article 4. 1. Public employees shall enjoy adequate protection against acts of anti-union discrimination in respect of their employment.

2. Such protection shall apply more particularly in respect of acts calculated to—

(a) make the employment of public employees subject to the condition that they shall not join or shall relinquish membership of a public employees' organisation;

(b) cause the dismissal of or otherwise prejudice a public employee by reason of membership of a public employees' organisation or because of participation in the normal activities of such an organisation.

Article 5. 1. Public employees' organisations shall enjoy complete independence from public authorities.

2. Public employees' organisations shall enjoy adequate protection against any acts of interference by a public authority in their establishment, functioning or administration.

3. In particular, acts which are designed to promote the establishment of public employees' organisations under the domination of a public authority, or to support public employees' organisations by financial or other means, with the object of placing such organisations under the control of a public authority, shall be deemed to constitute acts of interference within the meaning of this Article.

Part III. Facilities to Be Afforded to Public Employees' Organisations

Article 6. 1. Such facilities shall be afforded to the representatives of recognised public employees' organisations as may be appropriate in order to enable them to carry out their functions promptly and efficiently, both during and outside their hours of work.

2. The granting of such facilities shall not impair the efficient operation of the administration or service concerned.

3. The nature and scope of these facilities shall be determined in accordance with the methods referred to in Article 7 of this Convention, or by other appropriate means.

Part IV. Procedures for Determining Terms and Conditions of Employment

Article 7. Measures appropriate to national conditions shall be taken, where necessary, to encourage and promote the full development and utilisation of machinery for negotiation of terms and conditions of employment between the public authorities concerned and public employees' organisations, or of such other methods as will allow representatives of public employees to participate in the determination of these matters.

Part V. Settlement of Disputes

Article 8. The settlement of disputes arising in connection with the determination of terms and conditions of employment shall be sought, as may be appropriate to national conditions, through negotiation between the parties or through independent and impartial machinery, such as mediation, conciliation and arbitration, established in such

a manner as to ensure the confidence of the parties involved.

Part VI. Civil and Political Rights

Article 9. Public employees shall have, as other workers, the civil and political rights which are essential for the normal exercise of freedom of association, subject only to the obligations arising from their status and the nature of their functions. . . .

ILO MATERNITY PROTECTION CONVENTION, REVISED (1952). Formally entitled Convention (No. 103) concerning Maternity Protection (Revised 1952), the convention provides that an employed woman, after producing a medical certificate indicating that she is pregnant and stating the presumed date of her confinement, shall be entitled to a period of maternity leave of at least 12 weeks, including a period of compulsory leave after confinement. It applies to women employed in industrial undertakings and in non-industrial and agricultural occupations, including women wage-earners working at home.

The convention was adopted by the INTERNATIONAL LABOR CONFERENCE (35th session) on 28 June 1952 and entered into force on 7 September 1955. The text of the convention (*International Labour Conventions and Recommendations, 1919–1981*, p. 693), with the exception of the ILO STANDARD FINAL PROVISIONS (articles 8, 9, and 12–17), and provisions relating to declarations of application to non-metropolitan territories (articles 10 and 11), is as follows:

Article 1. 1. This convention applies to women employed in industrial undertakings and in non-industrial and agricultural occupations, including women wage earners working at home.

2. For the purpose of this convention, the term "industrial undertaking" comprises public and private undertakings and any branch thereof and includes particularly:

(a) Mines, quarries, and other works for the extraction of minerals from the earth;

(b) Undertakings in which articles are manufactured, altered, cleaned, repaired, ornamented, finished, adapted for sale, broken up or demolished, or in which materials are transformed, including undertakings engaged in shipbuilding, or in the generation, transformation or transmission of electricity or motive power of any kind;

(c) Undertakings engaged in building and civil engineering work, including constructional, repair, maintenance, alteration and demolition work;

(d) Undertakings engaged in the transport of passengers or goods by road, rail, sea, inland waterway or air, including the handling of goods at docks, quays, wharves, warehouses or airports.

3. For the purpose of this convention, the term "non-industrial occupations" includes all occupations which are carried on in or in connexion with the following undertakings or services, whether public or private:

(a) Commercial establishments;

(b) Postal and telecommunication services;

(c) Establishments and administrative services in which the persons employed are mainly engaged in clerical work;

(d) Newspaper undertakings;

(e) Hotels, boarding houses, restaurants, clubs, cafés and other refreshment houses;

(f) Establishments for the treatment and care of the sick, infirm or destitute and of orphans;

(g) Theatres and places of public entertainment;

(h) Domestic work for wages in private households; and any other non-industrial occupations to which the competent authority may decide to apply the provisions of the convention.

4. For the purpose of this convention, the term "agricultural occupations" includes all occupations carried on in agricultural undertakings, including plantations and large-scale industrialized agricultural undertakings.

5. In any case in which it is doubtful whether this convention applies to an undertaking, branch of an undertaking or occupation, the question shall be determined by the competent authority after consultation with the representative organisations of employers and workers concerned where such exist.

6. National laws or regulations may exempt from the application of this convention undertakings in which only members of the employer's family, as defined by national laws or regulations, are employed.

Article 2. For the purpose of this convention, the term "woman" means any female person, irrespective of age, nationality, race or creed, whether married or unmarried, and the term "child" means any child whether born of marriage or not.

Article 3. 1. A woman to whom this convention applies shall, on the production of a medical certificate stating the presumed date of her confinement, be entitled to a period of maternity leave.

2. The period of maternity leave shall be at least twelve weeks, and shall include a period of compulsory leave after confinement.

3. The period of compulsory leave after confinement shall be prescribed by national laws or regulations, but shall in no case be less than six weeks; the remainder of the total period of maternity leave may be provided before the presumed date of confinement or following expiration of the compulsory leave period or partly before the presumed date of confinement and partly following the expiration of the compulsory leave period as may be prescribed by national laws or regulations.

4. The leave before the presumed date of confinement shall be extended by any period elapsing between the presumed date of confinement and the actual date of confinement and the period of compulsory leave to be taken after confinement shall not be reduced on that account.

5. In case of illness medically certified arising out of pregnancy, national laws or regulations shall provide for additional leave before confinement, the maximum duration of which may be fixed by the competent authority.

6. In case of illness medically certified arising out of confinement, the woman shall be entitled to an extension of the leave after confinement, the maximum duration of which may be fixed by the competent authority.

Article 4. 1. While absent from work on maternity leave in accordance with the provisions of article 3, the woman shall be entitled to receive cash and medical benefits.

2. The rates of cash benefit shall be fixed by national laws or regulations so as to ensure benefits sufficient for the full

and healthy maintenance of herself and her child in accordance with a suitable standard of living.

3. Medical benefits shall include pre-natal, confinement and post-natal care by qualified midwives or medical practitioners as well as hospitalization care where necessary; freedom of choice of doctor and freedom of choice between a public and private hospital shall be respected.

4. The cash and medical benefits shall be provided either by means of compulsory social insurance or by means of public funds; in either case they shall be provided as a matter of right to all women who comply with the prescribed conditions.

5. Women who fail to qualify for benefits provided as a matter of right shall be entitled, subject to the means test required for social assistance, to adequate benefits out of social assistance funds.

6. Where cash benefits provided under compulsory social insurance are based on previous earnings, they shall be at a rate of not less than two-thirds of the woman's previous earnings taken into account for the purpose of computing benefits.

7. Any contribution due under a compulsory social insurance scheme providing maternity benefits and any tax based upon payrolls which is raised for the purpose of providing such benefits shall, whether paid both by the employer and the employees or by the employer, be paid in respect of the total number of men and women employed by the undertakings concerned, without distinction of sex.

8. In no case shall the employer be individually liable for the cost of such benefits due to women employed by him.

Article 5. 1. If a woman is nursing her child she shall be entitled to interrupt her work for this purpose at a time or times to be prescribed by national laws or regulations.

2. Interruption of work for the purpose of nursing are to be counted as working hours and remunerated accordingly in cases in which the matter is governed by or in accordance with laws and regulations; in cases in which the matter is governed by collective agreement, the position shall be as determined by the relevant agreement.

Article 6. While a woman is absent from work on maternity leave in accordance with the provisions of article 3 of this convention, it shall not be lawful for her employer to give her notice of dismissal during such absence, or to give her notice of dismissal at such a time that the notice would expire during such absence.

Article 7. 1. Any Member of the International Labour Organisation which ratifies this convention may, by a declaration accompanying its ratification, provide for exceptions from the application of the convention in respect of:

(a) Certain categories of non-industrial occupations;

(b) Occupations carried on in agricultural undertakings, other than plantations;

(c) Domestic work for wages in private households;

(d) Women wage earners working at home;

(e) Undertakings engaged in the transport of passengers or goods by sea.

2. The categories of occupations or undertakings in respect of which the Member proposes to have recourse to the provisions of paragraph 1 of this article shall be specified in the declaration accompanying its ratification.

3. Any Member which has made such a declaration may at any time cancel that declaration, in whole or in part, by a subsequent declaration.

4. Every Member for which a declaration made under paragraph 1 of this article is in force shall indicate each year in its annual report upon the application of this con-

vention the position of its law and practice in respect of the occupations or undertakings to which paragraph 1 of this article applies in virtue of the said declaration and the extent to which effect has been given or is proposed to be given to the convention in respect of such occupations or undertakings.

5. At the expiration of five years from the first entry into force of this convention, the Governing Body of the International Labour Office shall submit to the conference a special report concerning the application of these exceptions, containing such proposals as it may think appropriate for further action in regard to the matter. . . .

ILO MEDICAL CARE AND SICKNESS BENEFITS CONVENTION (1969).

Entitled Convention (No. 130) concerning Medical Care and Sickness Benefits, 1969, the convention revises two conventions adopted by the ILO in 1927: the Sickness Insurance (Industry) Convention and the Sickness Insurance (Agriculture) Convention. It provides for regulation by the contracting States of the scope and character of State medical care (Part I) and of sickness benefits (Part II), with a view to ensuring that such care and benefits are made available to all eligible persons on a basis of equality and without discrimination.

The convention was adopted by the INTERNATIONAL LABOR CONFERENCE (53d session) on 25 June 1969 and entered into force on 27 May 1972. The text of the convention (*International Labour Conventions and Recommendations, 1919–1981*, p. 579), with the exception of the ILO STANDARD FINAL PROVISIONS (articles 38–45) is as follows:

The General Conference of the International Labour Organisation,

Having been convened at Geneva by the Governing Body of the International Labour Office, and having met in its Fifty-third Session on 4 June 1969, and

Having decided upon the adoption of certain proposals with regard to the revision of the Sickness Insurance (Industry) Convention, 1927, and the Sickness Insurance (Agriculture) Convention, 1927, which is the fifth item on the agenda of the session, and

Having determined that these proposals shall take the form of an international Convention,

adopts this twenty-fifth day of June of the year one thousand nine hundred and sixty-nine the following Convention, which may be cited as the Medical Care and Sickness Benefits Convention, 1969:

Part 1. General Provisions

Article 1. In this Convention—

(a) the term "legislation" includes any social security rules as well as laws and regulations;

(b) the term "prescribed" means determined by or in virtue of national legislation;

(c) the term "industrial undertaking" includes all undertakings in the following branches of economic activity: mining and quarrying; manufacturing; construction; electricity, gas and water; and transport, storage and communication;

(d) the term "residence" means ordinary residence in the territory of the Member and the term "resident" means a person ordinarily resident in the territory of the Member;

(e) the term "dependent" refers to a state of dependency which is presumed to exist in prescribed cases;

(f) the term "wife" means a wife who is dependent on her husband;

(g) the term "child" covers—

(i) a child under school-leaving age or under 15 years of age, whichever is the higher: Provided that a Member which has made a declaration under Article 2 may, while such declaration is in force, apply the Convention as if the term covered a child under school-leaving age or under 15 years of age; and

(ii) a child under a prescribed age higher than that specified in clause (i) of this subparagraph and who is an apprentice or student or has a chronic illness or infirmity disabling him for any gainful activity, under prescribed conditions: Provided that this requirement shall be deemed to be met where national legislation defines the term so as to cover any child under an age appreciably higher than that specified in clause (i) of this subparagraph;

(h) the term "standard beneficiary" means a man with a wife and two children;

(i) the term "qualifying period" means a period of contribution, or a period of employment, or a period of residence, or any combination thereof, as may be prescribed;

(j) the term "sickness" means any morbid condition, whatever its cause;

(k) the term "medical care" includes allied benefits.

Article 2. 1. A Member whose economy and medical facilities are insufficiently developed may avail itself, by a declaration accompanying its ratification, of the temporary exceptions provided for in Article 1, subparagraph (g), clause (i); Article 11; Article 14; Article 20; and Article 26, paragraph 2. Any such declaration shall state the reason for such exceptions.

2. Each Member which has made a declaration under paragraph 1 of this Article shall include in its reports upon the application of this Convention submitted under article 22 of the Constitution of the International Labour Organisation a statement in respect of each exception of which it avails itself—

(a) that its reason for doing so subsists; or

(b) that it renounces its right to avail itself of the exception in question as from a stated date.

3. Each Member which has made a declaration under paragraph 1 of this Article shall, as appropriate to the terms of such declaration and as circumstances permit—

(a) increase the number of persons protected;

(b) extend the range of medical care provided;

(c) extend the duration of sickness benefit.

Article 3. 1. Any Member whose legislation protects employees may, by a declaration accompanying its ratification, temporarily exclude from the application of this Convention the employees in the sector comprising agricultural occupations who, at the time of the ratification, are not yet protected by legislation which is in conformity with the standards of this Convention.

2. Each Member which has made a declaration under paragraph 1 of this Article shall indicate in its reports upon the application of this Convention submitted under article 22 of the Constitution of the International Labour Organisation to what extent effect is given and what effect

is proposed to be given to the provisions of the Convention in respect of the employees in the sector comprising agricultural occupations and any progress which may have been made with a view to the application of the Convention to such employees or, where there is no change to report, shall furnish all the appropriate explanations.

3. Each Member which has made a declaration under paragraph 1 of this Article shall increase the number of employees protected in the sector comprising agricultural occupations to the extent and with the speed that the circumstances permit.

Article 4. 1. Any Member which ratifies this Convention may, by a declaration accompanying its ratification, exclude from the application of the Convention—

(a) seafarers, including sea fishermen,

(b) public servants,

where these categories are protected by special schemes which provide in the aggregate benefits at least equivalent to those required by this Convention.

2. Where a declaration under paragraph 1 of this Article is in force, the Member may—

(a) exclude the persons belonging to the category or categories excluded from the application of the Convention from the number of persons taken into account when calculating the percentages specified in Article 5, subparagraph (c); Article 10, subparagraph (b); Article 11; Article 19, subparagraph (b); and Article 20;

(b) exclude the persons belonging to the category or categories excluded from the application of the Conventions, as well as the wives and children of such persons, from the number of persons taken into account when calculating the percentage specified in Article 10, subparagraph (c).

3. Any Member which has made a declaration under paragraph 1 of this Article may subsequently notify the Director-General of the International Labour Office that it accepts the obligation of this Convention in respect of a category or categories excluded at the time of its ratification.

Article 5. Any Member whose legislation protects employees may, as necessary, exclude from the application of this Convention—

(a) persons whose employment is of a casual nature;

(b) members of the employer's family living in his house, in respect of their work for him;

(c) other categories of employees, which shall not exceed in number 10 per cent of all employees other than those excluded under subparagraphs (a) and (b) of this Article.

Article 6. For the purpose of compliance with this Convention, a Member may take account of protection effected by means of insurance which, although not made compulsory by its legislation at the time of ratification for the persons to be protected—

(a) is supervised by the public authorities or administered, in accordance with prescribed standards, by joint operation of employers and workers;

(b) covers a substantial proportion of the persons whose earnings do not exceed those of the skilled manual male employee defined in Article 22, paragraph 6; and

(c) complies, in conjunction with other forms of protection, where appropriate, with the provisions of the Convention.

Article 7. The contingencies covered shall include—

(a) need for medical care of a curative nature and, under prescribed conditions, need for medical care of a preventive nature;

(b) incapacity for work resulting from sickness and involving suspension of earnings, as defined by national legislation.

Part II. Medical Care

Article 8. Each Member shall secure to the persons protected, subject to prescribed conditions, the provision of medical care of a curative or preventive nature in respect of the contingency referred to in subparagraph (a) of Article 7.

Article 9. The medical care referred to in Article 8 shall be afforded with a view to maintaining, restoring or improving the health of the person protected and his ability to work and to attend to his personal needs.

Article 10. The persons protected in respect of the contingency referred to in subparagraph (a) of Article 7 shall comprise—

(a) all employees, including apprentices, and the wives and children of such employees; or

(b) prescribed classes of the economically active population, constituting not less than 75 per cent of the whole economically active population, and the wives and children of persons in the said classes; or

(c) prescribed classes of residents constituting not less than 75 per cent of all residents.

Article 11. Where a declaration made in virtue of Article 2 is in force, the persons protected in respect of the contingency referred to in subparagraph (a) of Article 7 shall comprise—

(a) prescribed classes of employees, constituting not less than 25 percent of all employees, and the wives and children of employees in the said classes; or

(b) prescribed classes of employees in industrial undertakings, constituting not less than 50 per cent of all employees in industrial undertakings, and the wives and children of employees in the said classes.

Article 12. Persons who are in receipt of a social security benefit for invalidity, old age, death of the breadwinner or unemployment, and, where appropriate, the wives and children of such persons, shall continue to be protected, under prescribed conditions, in respect of the contingency referred to in subparagraph (a) of Article 7.

Article 13. The medical care referred to in Article 8 shall comprise at least—

(a) general practitioner care, including domiciliary visiting;

(b) specialist care at hospitals for in-patients and out-patients, and such specialist care as may be available outside hospitals;

(c) the necessary pharmaceutical supplies on prescription by medical or other qualified practitioners;

(d) hospitalisation where necessary;

(e) dental care, as prescribed; and

(f) medical rehabilitation, including the supply, maintenance and renewal of prosthetic and orthopaedic appliances, as prescribed.

Article 14. Where a declaration made in virtue of Article 2 is in force, the medical care referred to in Article 8 shall comprise at least—

(a) general practitioner care, including, wherever possible, domiciliary visiting;

(b) specialist care at hospitals for in-patients and out-patients, and, wherever possible, such specialist care as may be available outside hospitals;

(c) the necessary pharmaceutical supplies on prescription by medical or other qualified practitioners; and

(d) hospitalisation where necessary.

Article 15. Where the legislation of a Member makes the right to the medical care referred to in Article 8 conditional upon the fulfilment of a qualifying period by the person protected or by his breadwinner, the conditions governing the qualifying period shall be such as not to deprive of the right to benefit persons who normally belong to the categories of persons protected.

Article 16. 1. The medical care referred to in Article 8 shall be provided throughout the contingency.

2. Where a beneficiary ceases to belong to the categories of persons protected, further entitlement to medical care for a case of sickness which started while he belonged to the said categories may be limited to a prescribed period which shall not be less than 26 weeks: Provided that the medical care shall not cease while the beneficiary continues to receive a sickness benefit.

3. Notwithstanding the provisions of paragraph 2 of this Article, the duration of medical care shall be extended for prescribed diseases recognised as entailing prolonged care.

Article 17. Where the legislation of a Member requires the beneficiary or his breadwinner to share in the cost of the medical care referred to in Article 8, the rules concerning such cost sharing shall be so designed as to avoid hardship and not to prejudice the effectiveness of medical and social protection.

Part III. Sickness Benefit

Article 18. Each Member shall secure to the person protected, subject to prescribed conditions, the provision of sickness benefit in respect of the contingency referred to in subparagraph *(b)* of Article 7.

Article 19. The persons protected in respect of the contingency specified in subparagraph (b) of Article 7 shall comprise—

(a) all employees, including apprentices; or

(b) prescribed classes of the economically active population, constituting not less than 75 per cent of the whole economically active population; or

(c) all residents whose means during the contingency do not exceed limits prescribed in such a manner as to comply with the requirements of Article 24.

Article 20. Where a declaration made in virtue of Article 2 is in force, the persons protected in respect of the contingency referred to in subparagraph *(b)* of Article 7 shall comprise—

(a) prescribed classes of employees, constituting not less than 25 per cent of all employees; or

(b) prescribed classes of employees in industrial undertakings, constituting not less than 50 per cent of all employees in industrial undertakings.

Article 21. The sickness benefit referred to in Article 18 shall be a periodical payment and shall—

(a) where employees or classes of the economically active population are protected, be calculated in such a manner as to comply either with the requirements of Article 22 or with the requirements of Article 23;

(b) where all residents whose means during the contingency do not exceed prescribed limits are protected, be calculated in such a manner as to comply with the requirements of Article 24.

Article 22. 1. In the case of a periodical payment to which this Article applies, the rate of the benefit, increased by the amount of any family allowances payable during the contingency, shall be such as to attain for the standard ben-

eficiary, in respect of the contingency referred to in subparagraph (b) of Article 7, at least 60 per cent of the total of the previous earnings of the beneficiary and of the amount of any family allowances payable to a person protected with the same family responsibilities as the standard beneficiary.

2. The previous earnings of the beneficiary shall be calculated according to prescribed rules, and, where the persons protected are arranged in classes according to their earnings, their previous earnings may be calculated from the basic earnings of the classes to which they belonged.

3. A maximum limit may be prescribed for the rate of the benefit or for the earnings taken into account for the calculation of the benefit, provided that the maximum limit is fixed in such a way that the provisions of paragraph 1 of this Article are complied with where the previous earnings of the beneficiary are equal to or lower than the wage of a skilled manual male employee.

4. The previous earnings of the beneficiary, the wage of the skilled manual male employee, the benefit and any family allowances shall be calculated on the same time basis.

5. For the other beneficiaries the benefit shall bear a reasonable relation to the benefit for the standard beneficiary.

6. For the purpose of this Article, a skilled manual male employee shall be—

(a) a fitter or turner in the manufacture of machinery other than electrical machinery; or

(b) a person deemed typical of skilled labour selected in accordance with the provisions of the following paragraph; or

(c) a person whose earnings are such as to be equal to or greater than the earnings of 75 per cent of all the persons protected, such earnings to be determined on the basis of annual or shorter periods as may be prescribed; or

(d) a person whose earnings are equal to 125 per cent of the average earnings of all the persons protected.

7. The person deemed typical of skilled labour for the purposes of sub-paragraph (b) of the preceding paragraph shall be a person employed in the major group of economic activities with the largest number of economically active male persons protected in the contingency referred to in subparagraph (b) of Article 7 in the division comprising the largest number of such persons; for this purpose, the International Standard Industrial Classification of All Economic Activities adopted by the Economic and Social Council of the United Nations at its Seventh Session on 27 August 1948, as amended up to 1968 and reproduced in the Annex to this Convention, or such classification as at any time further amended, shall be used.

8. Where the rate of benefit varies by region, the skilled manual male employee may be determined for each region in accordance with paragraphs 6 and 7 of this Article.

9. The wage of the skilled manual male employee shall be determined on the basis of the rates of wages for normal hours of work fixed by collective agreements, by or in pursuance of national legislation, where applicable, or by custom, including cost-of-living allowances if any: where such rates differ by region but paragraph 8 of this Article is not applied, the median rate shall be taken.

Article 23. 1. In the case of a periodical payment to which this Article applies, the rate of the benefit, increased by the amount of any family allowances payable during the contingency, shall be such as to attain for the standard beneficiary, in respect of the contingency referred to in subparagraph *(b)* of Article 7, at least 60 per cent of the total of the wage of an ordinary adult male labourer and of the amount of any family allowances payable to a person protected with the same family responsibilities as the standard beneficiary.

2. The wage of the ordinary adult male labourer, the benefit and any family allowances shall be calculated on the same time basis.

3. For the other beneficiaries, the benefit shall bear a reasonable relation to the benefit for the standard beneficiary.

4. For the purpose of this Article, the ordinary adult male labourer shall be—

(a) a person deemed typical of unskilled labour in the manufacture of machinery other than electrical machinery; or

(b) a person deemed typical of unskilled labour selected in accordance with the provisions of the following paragraph.

5. The person deemed typical of unskilled labour for the purpose of sub-paragraph *(b)* of the preceding paragraph shall be a person employed in the major group of economic activities with the largest number of economically active male persons protected in the contingency referred to in subparagraph (b) of Article 7 in the division comprising the largest number of such persons; for this purpose, the International Standard Industrial Classification of All Economic Activities adopted by the Economic and Social Council of the United Nations at its Seventh Session on 27 August 1948, as amended up to 1968 and reproduced in the Annex to this Convention, or such classification as at any time further amended, shall be used.

6. Where the rate of benefit varies by region, the ordinary adult male labourer may be determined for each region in accordance with paragraphs 4 and 5 of this Article.

7. The wage of the ordinary adult male labourer shall be determined on the basis of the rates of wages for normal hours of work fixed by collective agreements, by or in pursuance of national legislation, where applicable, or by custom, including cost-of-living allowances, if any; where such rates differ by region but paragraph 6 of this Article is not applied, the median rate shall be taken.

Article 24. In the case of a periodical payment to which this Article applies—

(a) the rate of the benefit shall be determined according to a prescribed scale or a scale fixed by the competent public authority in conformity with prescribed rules;

(b) such rate may be reduced only to the extent by which the other means of the family of the beneficiary exceed prescribed substantial amounts or substantial amounts fixed by the competent public authority in conformity with prescribed rules;

(c) the total of the benefit and any other means, after deduction of the substantial amounts referred to in subparagraph (b), shall be sufficient to maintain the family of the beneficiary in health and decency, and shall be not less than the corresponding benefit calculated in accordance with the requirements of Article 23;

(d) the provisions of subparagraph (c) shall be deemed to be satisfied if the total amount of sickness benefits paid under this Convention exceeds by at least 30 per cent the total amount of benefits which would be obtained by applying the provisions of Article 23 and the provisions of subparagraph (b) of Article 19.

Article 25. Where the legislation of a Member makes the right to the sickness benefit referred to in Article 18 conditional upon the fulfilment of a qualifying period by the person protected, the conditions governing the qualifying period shall be such as not to deprive of the right to benefit persons who normally belong to the categories of persons protected.

Article 26. 1. The sickness benefit referred to in Article 18 shall be granted throughout the contingency: Provided that the grant of benefit may be limited to not less than 52 weeks in each case of incapacity, as prescribed.

2. Where a declaration made in virtue of Article 2 is in force, the grant of the sickness benefit referred to in Article 18 may be limited to not less than 26 weeks in each case of incapacity, as prescribed.

3. Where the legislation of a Member provides that sickness benefit is not payable for an initial period of suspension of earnings, such period shall not exceed three days.

Article 27. 1. In the case of the death of a person who was in receipt of, or qualified for, the sickness benefit referred to in Article 18, a funeral benefit shall, under prescribed conditions, be paid to his survivors, to any other dependants or to the person who has borne the expense of the funeral.

2. A member may derogate from the provision of paragraph 1 of this Article where—

(a) it has accepted the obligations of Part IV of the Invalidity, Old-Age and Survivors' Benefits Convention, 1967;

(b) it provides in its legislation for cash sickness benefit at a rate of not less than 80 per cent of the earnings of the persons protected; and

(c) the majority of persons protected are covered by voluntary insurance which is supervised by the public authorities and which provides a funeral grant.

Part IV. Common Provisions

Article 28. 1. A benefit to which a person protected would otherwise be entitled in compliance with this Convention may be suspended to such extent as may be prescribed—

(a) as long as the person concerned is absent from the territory of the Member;

(b) as long as the person concerned is being indemnified for the contingency by a third party, to the extent of the indemnity;

(c) where the person concerned has made a fraudulent claim;

(d) where the contingency has been caused by a criminal offence committed by the person concerned;

(e) where the contingency has been caused by the serious and wilful misconduct of the person concerned;

(f) where the person concerned, without good cause, neglects to make use of the medical care or the rehabilitation services placed at his disposal, or fails to comply with rules prescribed for verifying the occurrence or continuance of the contingency or for the conduct of beneficiaries;

(g) in the case of the sickness benefit referred to in Article 18, as long as the person concerned is maintained at public expense or at the expense of a social security institution or service; and

(h) in the case of the sickness benefit referred to in Article 18, as long as the person concerned is in receipt of another social security cash benefit, other than a family benefit, subject to the part of the benefit which is suspended not exceeding the other benefit.

2. In the cases and within the limits prescribed, part of the benefit otherwise due shall be paid to the dependents of the person concerned.

Article 29. 1. Every claimant shall have a right of appeal in the case of refusal of the benefit or complaint as to its quality or quantity.

I

2. Where in the application of this Convention a government department responsible to a legislature is entrusted with the administration of medical care, the right of appeal provided for in paragraph 1 of this Article may be replaced by a right to have a complaint concerning the refusal of medical care or the quality of the care received investigated by the appropriate authority.

Article 30. 1. Each Member shall accept general responsibility for the due provision of the benefits provided in compliance with this Convention and shall take all measures required for this purpose.

2. Each Member shall accept general responsibility for the proper administration of the institutions and services concerned in the application of this Convention.

Article 31. Where the administration is not entrusted to an institution regulated by the public authorities or to a government department responsible to a legislature—

(a) representatives of the persons protected shall participate in the management under prescribed conditions;

(b) national legislation shall, where appropriate, provide for the participation of representatives of employers;

(c) national legislation may likewise decide as to the participation of representatives of the public authorities.

Article 32. Each Member shall, within its territory, assure to non-nationals who normally reside or work there equality of treatment with its own nationals as regards the right to the benefits provided for in this Convention.

Article 33. 1. A Member—

(a) which has accepted the obligations of this Convention without availing itself of the exceptions and exclusions provided for in Article 2 and Article 3,

(b) which provides over-all higher benefits than those provided in this Convention and whose total relevant expenditure on medical care and sickness benefits amounts to at least 4 per cent of its national income, and

(c) which satisfies at least two of the three following conditions:

(i) it covers a percentage of the economically active population which is at least ten points higher than the percentage required by Article 10, subparagraph (b), and by Article 19, subparagraph (b), or a percentage of all residents which is at least ten points higher than the percentage required by Article 10, subparagraph (c),

(ii) it provides medical care of a curative and preventive nature of an appreciably higher standard than that prescribed by Article 13,

(iii) it provides sickness benefit corresponding to a percentage at least ten points higher than is required by Articles 22 and 23,

may, after consultation with the most representative organisations of employers and workers, where such exist, make temporary derogations from particular provisions of Parts II and III of this Convention on condition that such derogation shall neither fundamentally reduce nor impair the essential guarantees of this Convention.

2. Each Member which has made such a derogation shall indicate in its reports upon the application of this Convention submitted under article 22 of the Constitution of the International Labour Organisation the position of its law and practice as regards such derogation and any progress made towards complete application of the terms of the Convention.

Article 34. This Convention shall not apply to—

(a) contingencies which occurred before the coming into force of the Convention for the Member concerned;

(b) benefits in contingencies occurring after the coming into force of the Convention for the Member concerned in so far as the rights to such benefits are derived from periods preceding that date.

Part V. Final Provisions

Article 35. This Convention revises the Sickness Insurance (Industry) Convention, 1927, and the Sickness Insurance (Agriculture) Convention, 1927.

Article 36. 1. In conformity with the provisions of Article 75 of the Social Security (Minimum Standards) Convention, 1952, Part III of that Convention and the relevant provisions of other Parts thereof shall cease to apply to any Member having ratified this Convention as from the date at which this Convention is binding on that Member and no declaration under Article 3 is in force.

2. Acceptance of the obligations of this Convention shall, on condition that no declaration under Article 3 is in force, be deemed to constitute acceptance of the obligations of Part III of the Social Security (Minimum Standards) Convention, 1952, and the relevant provisions of other Parts thereof, for the purpose of Article 2 of the said Convention.

Article 37. If any Convention which may be adopted subsequently by the Conference concerning any subject or subjects dealt with in this Convention so provides, such provisions of this Convention as may be specified in the said Convention shall cease to apply to any Member having ratified the said Convention as from the date at which the said Convention comes into force for that Member. . . .

SEE ALSO *ILO Social Security (Minimum Standards) Convention.*

ILO MIGRANT WORKERS (SUPPLEMENTARY PROVISIONS) CONVENTION (1975). Formally entitled Convention (No. 143) concerning Migrations in Abusive Conditions and the Promotion of Equality of Opportunity and Treatment of Migrant Workers, the convention supplements the earlier ILO MIGRATION FOR EMPLOYMENT CONVENTION and provides that the States parties undertake to respect the basic human rights of all MIGRANT WORKERS, take steps to eliminate abusive work conditions, and actively promote equality of opportunity and treatment.

The convention was adopted by the INTERNATIONAL LABOUR CONFERENCE (60th session) on 24 June 1975 and entered into force on 9 December 1978. The text of the convention *(International Labour Conventions and Recommendations, 1919–1981,* p. 821), with the exception of the ILO STANDARD FINAL PROVISIONS (articles 17–24), is as follows:

The General Conference of the International Labour Organisation,

Having been convened at Geneva by the Governing Body of the International Labour Office, and having met in its Sixtieth Session on 4 June 1975, and

Considering that the Preamble of the Constitution of the International Labour Organisation assigns to it the task of

830

protecting "the interests of workers when employed in countries other than their own", and

Considering that the Declaration of Philadelphia reaffirms, among the principles on which the Organisation is based, that "labour is not a commodity", and that "poverty anywhere constitutes a danger to prosperity everywhere", and recognises the solemn obligation of the ILO to further programmes which will achieve in particular full employment through "the transfer of labour, including for employment . . .",

Considering the ILO World Employment Programme and the Employment Policy Convention and Recommendation, 1964, and emphasising the need to avoid the excessive and uncontrolled or unassisted increase of migratory movements because of their negative social and human consequences, and

Considering that in order to overcome underdevelopment and structural and chronic unemployment, the governments of many countries increasingly stress the desirability of encouraging the transfer of capital and technology rather than the transfer of workers in accordance with the needs and requests of these countries in the reciprocal interest of the countries of origin and the countries of employment, and

Considering the right of everyone to leave any country, including his own, and to enter his own country, as set forth in the Universal Declaration of Human Rights and the International Covenant on Civil and Political Rights, and

Recalling the provisions contained in the Migration for Employment Convention and Recommendation (Revised), 1949, in the Protection of Migrant Workers (Underdeveloped Countries) Recommendation, 1955, in the Employment Policy Convention and Recommendation, 1964, in the Employment Service Convention and Recommendation, 1948, and in the Fee-Charging Employment Agencies Convention (Revised), 1949, which deal with such matters as the regulation of the recruitment, introduction and placing of migrant workers, the provision of accurate information relating to migration, the minimum conditions to be enjoyed by migrants in transit and on arrival, the adoption of an active employment policy and international collaboration in these matters, and

Considering that the migration of workers due to conditions in labour markets should take place under the responsibility of official agencies for employment or in accordance with the relevant bilateral or multilateral agreements, in particular those permitting free circulation of workers, and

Considering that evidence of the existence of illicit and clandestine trafficking in labour calls for further standards specifically aimed at eliminating these abuses, and

Recalling the provisions of the Migration for Employment Convention (Revised), 1949, which require ratifying Members to apply to immigrants lawfully within their territory treatment not less favourable than that which they apply to their nationals in respect of a variety of matters which it enumerates, in so far as these are regulated by laws or regulations or subject to the control of administrative authorities, and

Recalling that the definition of the term "discrimination" in the Discrimination (Employment and Occupation) Convention, 1958, does not mandatorily include distinctions on the basis of nationality, and

Considering that further standards, covering also social security, are desirable in order to promote equality of opportunity and treatment of migrant workers and, with regard to matters regulated by laws or regulations or subject to the control of administrative authorities, ensure treatment at least equal to that of nationals, and

Noting that, for the full success of action regarding the very varied problems of migrant workers, it is essential that there be close co-operation with the United Nations and other specialised agencies, and

Noting that, in the framing of the following standards, account has been taken of the work of the United Nations and of other specialised agencies and that, with a view to avoiding duplication and to ensuring appropriate co-ordination, there will be continuing co-operation in promoting and securing the application of the standards, and

Having decided upon the adoption of certain proposals with regard to migrant workers, which is the fifth item on the agenda of the session, and

Having determined that these proposals shall take the form of an international Convention supplementing the Migration for Employment Convention (Revised), 1949, and the Discrimination (Employment and Occupation) Convention, 1958,

adopts this twenty-fourth day of June of the year one thousand nine hundred and seventy-five the following Convention, which may be cited as the Migrant Workers (Supplementary Provisions) Convention, 1975:

Part I. Migrations in Abusive Conditions

Article 1. Each Member for which this Convention is in force undertakes to respect the basic human rights of all migrant workers.

Article 2. 1. Each Member for which this Convention is in force shall systemically seek to determine whether there are illegally employed migrant workers on its territory and whether there depart from, pass through or arrive in its territory any movements of migrants for employment in which the migrants are subjected during their journey, on arrival or during their period of residence and employment to conditions contravening relevant international multilateral or bilateral instruments or agreements, or national laws or regulations.

2. The representative organisations of employers and workers shall be fully consulted and enabled to furnish any information in their possession on this subject.

Article 3. Each Member shall adopt all necessary and appropriate measures, both within its jurisdiction and in collaboration with other Members—

(a) to suppress clandestine movements of migrants for employment and illegal employment of migrants, and

(b) against the organisers of illicit or clandestine movements of migrants for employment departing from, passing through or arriving in its territory, and against those who employ workers who have immigrated in illegal conditions, in order to prevent and to eliminate the abuses referred to in Article 2 of this Convention.

Article 4. In particular, Members shall take such measures as are necessary, at the national and the international level, for systematic contact and exchange of information on the subject with other States, in consultation with representative organisations of employers and workers.

Article 5. One of the purposes of the measures taken under Articles 3 and 4 of this Convention shall be that the authors of manpower trafficking can be prosecuted whatever the country from which they exercise their activities.

Article 6. 1. Provision shall be made under national laws or regulations for the effective detection of the illegal employment of migrant workers and for the definition and the application of administrative, civil and penal sanctions, which include imprisonment in their range, in respect of the illegal employment of migrant workers, in respect of the organisation of movements of migrants for employment defined as involving the abuses referred to in Article 2 of this Convention, and in respect of knowing assistance to such movements, whether for profit or otherwise.

2. Where an employer is prosecuted by virtue of the provision made in pursuance of this Article, he shall have the right to furnish proof of his good faith.

Article 7. The representative organisations of employers and workers shall be consulted in regard to the laws and regulations and other measures provided for in this Convention and designed to prevent and eliminate the abuses referred to above, and the possibility of their taking initiatives for this purpose shall be recognised.

Article 8. 1. On condition that he has resided legally in the territory for the purpose of employment, the migrant workers shall not be regarded as in an illegal or irregular situation by the mere fact of the loss of his employment, which shall not in itself imply the withdrawal of his authorisation of residence or, as the case may be, work permit.

2. Accordingly, he shall enjoy equality of treatment with nationals in respect in particular of guarantees of security of employment, the provision of alternative employment, relief work and retraining.

Article 9. 1. Without prejudice to measures designed to control movements of migrants for employment by ensuring that migrant workers enter national territory and are admitted to employment in conformity with the relevant laws and regulations, the migrant worker shall, in cases in which these laws and regulations have not been respected and in which his position cannot be regularised, enjoy equality of treatment for himself and his family in respect of rights arising out of past employment as regards remuneration, social security and other benefits.

2. In case of dispute about the rights referred to in the preceding paragraph, the worker shall have the possibility of presenting his case to a competent body, either himself or through a representative.

3. In case of expulsion of the worker or his family, the cost shall not be borne by them.

4. Nothing in this Convention shall prevent Members from giving persons who are illegally residing or working within the country the right to stay and to take up legal employment.

Part II. Equality of Opportunity and Treatment

Article 10. Each Member for which the Convention is in force undertakes to declare and pursue a national policy designed to promote and to guarantee, by methods appropriate to national conditions and practice, equality of opportunity and treatment in respect of employment and occupation, of social security, of trade union and cultural rights and of individual and collective freedoms for persons who as migrant workers or as members of their families are lawfully within its territory.

Article 11. 1. For the purpose of this Part of this Convention, the term "migrant worker" means a person who migrates or who has migrated from one country to another with a view to being employed otherwise than on his own account and includes any person regularly admitted as a migrant worker.

2. This Part of this Convention does not apply to—

(a) frontier workers;

(b) artistes and members of the liberal professions who have entered the country on a short-term basis;

(c) seamen;

(d) persons coming specifically for purposes of training or education;

(e) employees of organisations or undertakings operating within the territory of a country who have been admitted temporarily to that country at the request of their employer to undertake specific duties or assignments, for a limited and defined period of time, and who are required to leave that country on the completion of their duties or assignments.

Article 12. Each Member shall, by methods appropriate to national conditions and practice—

(a) seek the co-operation of employers' and workers' organisations and other appropriate bodies in promoting the acceptance and observance of the policy provided for in Article 10 of this Convention;

(b) enact such legislation and promote such educational programmes as may be calculated to secure the acceptance and observance of the policy;

(c) take measures, encourage educational programmes and develop other activities aimed at acquainting migrant workers as fully as possible with the policy, with their rights and obligations and with activities designed to give effective assistance to migrant workers in the exercise of their rights and for their protection;

(d) repeal any statutory provisions and modify any administrative instructions or practices which are inconsistent with the policy;

(e) in consultation with representative organisations of employers and workers, formulate and apply a social policy appropriate to national conditions and practice which enables migrant workers and their families to share in advantages enjoyed by its nationals while taking account, without adversely affecting the principle of equality of opportunity and treatment, of such special needs as they may have until they are adapted to the society of the country of employment;

(f) take all steps to assist and encourage the efforts of migrant workers and their families to preserve their national and ethnic identity and their cultural ties with their country of origin, including the possibility for children to be given some knowledge of their mother tongue;

(g) guarantee equality of treatment, with regard to working conditions, for all migrant workers who perform the same activity whatever might be the particular conditions of their employment.

Article 13. 1. A Member may take all necessary measures which fall within its competence and collaborate with other Members to facilitate the reunification of the families of all migrant workers legally residing in its territory.

2. The members of the family of the migrant worker to which this Article applies are the spouse and dependent children, father and mother.

Article 14. A Member may—

(a) make the free choice of employment, while assuring migrant workers the right to geographical mobility, subject to the conditions that the migrant worker has resided lawfully in its territory for the purpose of employment for a prescribed period not exceeding two years or, if its laws or regulations provide for contracts for a fixed term of less than two years, that the worker has completed his first work contract;

(b) after appropriate consultation with the representative

organisations of employers and workers, make regulations concerning recognition of occupational qualifications acquired outside its territory, including certificates and diplomas;

(c) restrict access to limited categories of employment or functions where this is necessary in the interests of the State.

Part III. Final Provisions

Article 15. This Convention does not prevent Members from concluding multilateral or bilateral agreements with a view to resolving problems arising from its application.

Article 16. 1. Any Member which ratifies this Convention may, by a declaration appended to its ratification, exclude either Part I or Part II from its acceptance of the Convention.

2. Any Member which has made such a declaration may at any time cancel that declaration by a subsequent declaration.

3. Every Member for which a declaration made under paragraph 1 of this Article is in force shall indicate in its reports upon the application of this Convention the position of its law and practice in regard to the provisions of the Part excluded from its acceptance, the extent to which effect has been given, or is proposed to be given, to the said provision and the reasons for which it has not yet included them in its acceptance of the Convention. . . .

ILO MIGRATION FOR EMPLOYMENT CONVENTION, REVISED (1949).

Formally entitled Convention (No. 97) Concerning Migration for Employment (Revised 1949), this is one of several ILO instruments dealing with the problems of MIGRANT WORKERS. It aims at assisting migrants in their search for employment and in achieving equality of treatment in respect of their human rights and fundamental freedoms.

The revised convention was adopted by the INTERNATIONAL LABOR CONFERENCE (32d session) on 1 July 1949 and entered into force on 22 January 1952. The text of the convention (*International Labour Conventions and Recommendations, 1919–1981*, p. 785), with the exception of the article on authoritative texts of the ILO STANDARD FINAL PROVISIONS (article 23), is as follows:

The General Conference of the International Labour Organisation,

Having been convened at Geneva by the Governing Body of the International Labour Office, and having met in its Thirty-second Session on 8 June 1949, and

Having decided upon the adoption of certain proposals with regard to the revision of the Migration for Employment Convention, 1939, adopted by the Conference at its Twenty-fifth Session, which is included in the eleventh item on the agenda of the session, and

Considering that these proposals must take the form of an international Convention,

adopts this first day of July of the year one thousand nine hundred and forty-nine the following Convention, which may be cited as the Migration for Employment Convention (Revised), 1949:

Article 1. Each Member of the International Labour Organisations for which this Convention is in force undertakes to make available on request to the International Labour Office and to other Members—

(a) information on national policies, laws and regulations relating to emigration and immigration;

(b) information on special provisions concerning migration for employment and the conditions of work and livelihood of migrants for employment;

(c) information concerning general agreements and special arrangements on these questions concluded by the Member.

Article 2. Each Member for which this Convention is in force undertakes to maintain, or satisfy itself that there is maintained, an adequate and free service to assist migrants for employment, and in particular to provide them with accurate information.

Article 3. 1. Each Member for which this Convention is in force undertakes that it will, so far as national laws and regulations permit, take all appropriate steps against misleading propaganda relating to emigration and immigration.

2. For this purpose, it will where appropriate act in co-operation with other Members concerned.

Article 4. Measures shall be taken as appropriate by each Member, within its jurisdiction, to facilitate the departure, journey and reception of migrants for employment.

Article 5. Each Member for which this Convention is in force undertakes to maintain, within its jurisdiction, appropriate medical services responsible for—

(a) ascertaining, where necessary, both at the time of departure and on arrival, that migrants for employment and the members of their families authorised to accompany or join them are in reasonable health;

(b) ensuring that migrants for employment and members of their families enjoy adequate medical attention and good hygienic conditions at the time of departure, during the journey and on arrival in the territory of destination.

Article 6. 1. Each Member for which this Convention is in force undertakes to apply, without discrimination in respect of nationality, race, religion or sex, to immigrants lawfully within its territory, treatment no less favourable than that which it applies to its own nationals in respect of the following matters:

(a) in so far as such matters are regulated by law or regulations, or are subject to the control of administrative authorities—

(i) remuneration, including family allowances where these form part of remuneration, hours of work, overtime arrangements, holidays with pay, restrictions on home work, minimum age for employment, apprenticeship and training, women's work and the work of young persons;

(ii) membership of trade unions and enjoyment of the benefits of collective bargaining;

(iii) accommodation;

(b) social security (that is to say, legal provision in respect of employment injury, maternity, sickness, invalidity, old age, death, unemployment and family responsibilities, and any other contingency which, according to national laws or regulations, is covered by a social security scheme), subject to the following limitations:

(i) there may be appropriate arrangements for the maintenance of acquired rights and rights in course of acquisition;

(ii) national laws or regulations of immigration countries may prescribe special arrangements concerning benefits or portions of benefits which are payable wholly out of public funds, and concerning allowances paid to persons who do not fulfil the contribution conditions prescribed for the award of a normal pension;

(c) employment taxes, dues or contributions payable in respect of the person employed; and

(d) legal proceedings relating to the matters referred to in this Convention.

2. In the case of a federal State the provisions of this Article shall apply in so far as the matter dealt with are regulated by federal law or regulations or are subject to the control of federal administrative authorities. The extent to which and manner in which these provisions shall be applied in respect of matters regulated by the law or regulations of the constituent States, provinces or cantons, or subject to the control of the administrative authorities thereof, shall be determined by each Member. The Member shall indicate in its annual report upon the application of the Convention the extent to which the matters dealt with in this Article are regulated by federal law or regulations or are subject to the control of federal administrative authorities. In respect of matters which are regulated by the law or regulations of the constituent States, provinces or cantons, or are subject to the control of the administrative authorities thereof, the Member shall take the steps provided for in paragraph 7 *(b)* of article 19 of the Constitution of the International Labour Organisation.

Article 7. 1. Each Member for which this Convention is in force undertakes that its employment service and other services connected with migration will co-operate in appropriate cases with the corresponding services of other Members.

2. Each Member for which this Convention is in force undertakes to ensure that the services rendered by its public employment service to migrants for employment are rendered free.

Article 8. 1. A migrant for employment who has been admitted on a permanent basis and the members of his family who have been authorised to accompany or join him shall not be returned to their territory of origin or the territory from which they emigrated because the migrant is unable to follow his occupation by reason of illness contracted or injury sustained subsequent to entry, unless the person concerned so desires or an international agreement to which the Member is a party so provides.

2. When migrants for employment are admitted on a permanent basis upon arrival in the country of immigration the competent authority of that country may determine that the provisions of paragraph 1 of this Article shall take effect only after a reasonable period which shall in no case exceed five years from the date of admission of such migrants.

Article 9. Each Member for which this Convention is in force undertakes to permit, taking into account the limits allowed by national laws and regulations concerning export and import of currency, the transfer of such part of the earnings and savings of the migrant for employment as the migrant may desire.

Article 10. In cases where the number of migrants going from the territory of one Member to that of another is sufficiently large, the competent authorities of the territories concerned shall, whenever necessary or desirable, enter into agreements for the purpose of regulating matters of common concern arising in connection with the application of the provisions of this Convention.

Article 11. 1. For the purpose of this Convention the term "migrant for employment" means a person who migrates from one country to another with a view to being employed otherwise than on his own account and includes any person regularly admitted as a migrant for employment.

2. This Convention does not apply to—

(a) frontier workers;

(b) short-term entry of members of the liberal professions and artistes; and

(c) seamen. . . .

Articles 12 and 13. Ratifications and entry into force: standard final provisions.

Article 14. 1. Each Member ratifying this Convention may, by a declaration appended to its ratification, exclude from its ratification any or all of the Annexes to the Convention.

2. Subject to the terms of any such declaration, the provisions of the Annexes shall have the same effect as the provisions of the Convention.

3. Any Member which makes such a declaration may subsequently by a new declaration notify the Director-General that it accepts any or all of the Annexes mentioned in the declaration; as from the date of the registration of such notification by the Director-General the provisions of such Annexes shall be applicable to the Member in question.

4. While a declaration made under paragraph 1 of this Article remains in force in respect of any Annex, the Member may declare its willingness to accept that Annex as having the force of a Recommendation. . . .

Articles 15 and 16. Declarations of application to non-metropolitan territories.

Article 17. Paragraphs 1 and 2: standard final provisions on denunciation.

3. At any time at which this Convention is subject to denunciation in accordance with the provisions of the preceding paragraphs any Member which does not so denounce it may communicate to the Director-General a declaration denouncing separately any Annex to the Convention which is in force for that Member.

4. The denunciation of this Convention or of any or all of the Annexes shall not affect the rights granted thereunder to a migrant or to the members of his family if he immigrated while the Convention or the relevant Annex was in force in respect of the territory where the question of the continued validity of these rights arises. . . .

Articles 18–21. Notification, registration and examination of revision: standard final provisions.

Article 22. 1. The International Labour Conference may, at any session at which the matter is included in its agenda, adopt by a two-thirds majority a revised text of any one or more of the Annexes to this Convention.

2. Each Member for which this Convention is in force shall, within the period of one year, or, in exceptional circumstances, of eighteen months, from the closing of the session of the Conference, submit any such revised text to the authority or authorities within whose competence the matter lies, for the enactment of legislation or other action.

3. Any such revised text shall become effective for each Member for which this Convention is in force on communication by that Member to the Director-General of the International Labour Office of a declaration notifying its acceptance of the revised text.

4. As from the date of the adoption of the revised text of the Annex by the Conference, only the revised text shall be open to acceptance by Members. . . .

Annex I
Recruitment, Placing and Conditions of Labour of Migrants for Employment Recruited Otherwise than Under Government-Sponsored Arrangements for group Transfer

Article 1. This Annex applies to migrants for employment who are recruited otherwise than under Government-sponsored arrangements for group transfer.

Article 2. For the purpose of this Annex—

(a) the term "recruitment" means—

(i) the engagement of a person in one territory on behalf of an employer in another territory, or

(ii) the giving of an undertaking to a person in one territory to provide him with employment in another territory,

together with the making of any arrangements in connection with the operations mentioned in (i) and (ii) including the seeking for and selection of emigrants and the preparation for departure of the emigrants;

(b) the term "introduction" means any operations for ensuring or facilitating the arrival in or admission to a territory of persons who have been recruited within the meaning of paragraph (a) of this Article; and

(c) the term "placing" means any operations for the purpose of ensuring or facilitating the employment of persons who have been introduced within the meaning of paragraph (b) of this Article.

Article 3. 1. Each Member for which this Annex is in force, the laws and regulations of which permit the operations of recruitment, introduction and placing as defined in Article 2, shall regulate such of the said operations as are permitted by its laws and regulations in accordance with the provisions of this Article.

2. Subject to the provisions of the following paragraph, the right to engage in the operations of recruitment, introduction and placing shall be restricted to—

(a) public employment offices or other public bodies of the territory in which the operations take place;

(b) public bodies of a territory other than that in which the operations take place which are authorised to operate in that territory by agreement between the Governments concerned;

(c) any body established in accordance with the terms of an international instrument.

3. In so far as national laws and regulations or a bilateral arrangement permit, the operations of recruitment, introduction and placing may be undertaken by—

(a) the prospective employer or a person in his service acting on his behalf, subject, if necessary in the interest of the migrant, to the approval and supervision of the competent authority;

(b) a private agency, if given prior authorisation so to do by the competent authority of the territory where the said operations are to take place, in such cases and under such conditions as may be prescribed by—

(i) the laws and regulations of that territory, or

(ii) agreement between the competent authority of the territory of emigration or any body established in accordance with the terms of an international instrument and the competent authority of the territory of immigration.

4. The competent authority of the territory where the operations take place shall supervise the activities of bodies and persons to whom authorisations have been issued in pursuance of paragraph 3 (b), other than any body established in accordance with the terms of an international instrument, the position of which shall continue to be governed by the terms of the said instrument or by any agreement made between the body and the competent authority concerned.

5. Nothing in this Article shall be deemed to permit the acceptance of a migrant for employment for admission to the territory of any Member by any person or body other than the competent authority of the territory of immigration.

Article 4. Each Member for which this Annex is in force undertakes to ensure that the services rendered by its public employment service in connection with the recruitment, introduction or placing of migrants for employment are rendered free.

Article 5. 1. Each Member for which this Annex is in force which maintains a system of supervision of contracts of employment between an employer, or a person acting on his behalf, and a migrant for employment undertakes to require—

(a) that a copy of the contract of employment shall be delivered to the migrant before departure or, if the Governments concerned so agree, in a reception centre on arrival in the territory of immigration;

(b) that the contract shall contain provisions indicating the conditions of work and particularly the remuneration offered to the migrant;

(c) that the migrant shall receive in writing before departure, by a document which relates either to him individually or to a group of migrants of which he is a member, information concerning the general conditions of life and work applicable to him in the territory of immigration.

2. Where a copy of the contract is to be delivered to the migrant on arrival in the territory of immigration, he shall be informed in writing before departure, by a document which relates either to him individually or to a group of migrants of which he is a member, of the occupational category for which he is engaged and the other conditions of work, in particular the minimum wage which is guaranteed to him.

3. The competent authority shall ensure that the provisions of the preceding paragraphs are enforced and that appropriate penalties are applied in respect of violations thereof.

Article 6. The measures taken under Article 4 of the Convention shall, as appropriate, include—

(a) the simplification of administrative formalities;

(b) the provision of interpretation services;

(c) any necessary assistance during an initial period in the settlement of the migrants and members of their families authorised to accompany or join them; and

(d) the safeguarding of the welfare, during the journey and in particular on board ship, of migrants and members of their families authorised to accompany or join them.

Article 7. 1. In cases where the number of migrants for employment going from the territory of one Member to that of another is sufficiently large, the competent authorities of the territories concerned shall, whenever necessary or desirable, enter into agreements for the purpose of regulating matters of common concern arising in connection with the application of the provisions of this Annex.

2. Where the members maintain a system of supervision over contracts of employment, such agreements shall indicate the methods by which the contractual obligations of the employers shall be enforced.

Article 8. Any person who promotes clandestine or illegal immigration shall be subject to appropriate penalties.

Annex II
Recruitment, Placing and Conditions of Labour of Migrants for Employment Recruited Under Government-sponsored Arrangements for Group Transfer

Article 1. This Annex applies to migrants for employment who are recruited under Government-sponsored arrangements for group transfer.

Article 2. For the purpose of this Annex—

(a) the term "recruitment" means—

(i) the engagement of a person in one territory on behalf of an employer in another territory under a Government-sponsored arrangement for group transfer, or

(ii) the giving of an undertaking to a person in one territory to provide him with employment in another territory under a Government-sponsored arrangement for group transfer,

together with the making of any arrangements in connection with the operations mentioned in (i) and (ii) including the seeking for and selection of emigrants and the preparation for departure of the emigrants;

(b) the term "introduction" means any operations for ensuring or facilitating the arrival in or admission to a territory of persons who have been recruited under a Government-sponsored arrangement for group transfer within the meaning of subparagraph (a) of this paragraph; and

(c) the term "placing" means any operations for the purpose of ensuring or facilitating the employment of persons who have been introduced under a Government-sponsored arrangement for group transfer within the meaning of subparagraph (b) of this paragraph.

Article 3. 1. Each Member for which this Annex is in force, the laws and regulations of which permit the operations of recruitment, introduction and placing as defined in Article 2, shall regulate such of the said operations as are permitted by its laws and regulations in accordance with the provisions of this Article.

2. Subject to the provisions of the following paragraph, the right to engage in the operations of recruitment, introduction and placing shall be restricted to—

(a) public employment offices or other public bodies of the territory in which the operations take place;

(b) public bodies of a territory other than that in which the operations take place which are authorised to operate in that territory by agreement between the Governments concerned;

(c) any body established in accordance with the terms of an international instrument.

3. In so far as national laws and regulations or a bilateral arrangement permit, and subject, if necessary in the interest of the migrant, to the approval and supervision of the competent authority, the operations of recruitment, introduction and placing may be undertaken by—

(a) the prospective employer or a person in his service acting on his behalf;

(b) private agencies.

4. The right to engage in the operations of recruitment, introduction and placing shall be subject to the prior authorisation of the competent authority of the territory where the said operations are to take place in such cases and under such conditions as may be prescribed by—

(a) the laws and regulations of that territory, or

(b) agreement between the competent authority of the territory of emigration or any body established in accordance with the terms of an international instrument and the competent authority of the territory of immigration.

5. The competent authority of the territory where the operations take place shall, in accordance with any agreements made between the competent authorities concerned, supervise the activities of bodies and persons to whom authorisations have been issued in pursuance of the preceding paragraph, other than any body established in accordance with the terms of an international instrument, the position of which shall continue to be governed by the terms of the said instrument or by any agreement made between the body and the competent authority concerned.

6. Before authorising the introduction of migrants for employment the competent authority of the territory of immigration shall ascertain whether there is not a sufficient number of persons already available capable of doing the work in question.

7. Nothing in this Article shall be deemed to permit the acceptance of a migrant for employment for admission to the territory of any Member by any person or body other than the competent authority of the territory of immigration.

Article 4. 1. Each Member for which this Annex is in force undertakes to ensure that the services rendered by its public employment service in connection with the recruitment, introduction or placing of migrants for employment are rendered free.

2. The administrative costs of recruitment, introduction and placing shall not be borne by the migrants.

Article 5. In the case of collective transport of migrants from one country to another necessitating passage in transit through a third country, the competent authority of the territory of transit shall take measures for expediting the passage, to avoid delays and administrative difficulties.

Article 6. 1. Each Member for which this Annex is in force which maintains a system of supervision of contracts of employment between an employer, or a person acting on his behalf, and a migrant for employment undertakes to require—

(a) that a copy of the contract of employment shall be delivered to the migrant before departure or, if the Governments concerned so agree, in a reception centre on arrival in the territory of immigration;

(b) that the contract shall contain provisions indicating the conditions of work and particularly the remuneration offered to the migrant;

(c) that the migrant shall receive in writing before departure, by a document which relates either to him individually or to a group of migrants of which he is a member, information concerning the general conditions of life and work applicable to him in the territory of immigration.

2. Where a copy of the contract is to be delivered to the migrant on arrival in the territory of immigration, he shall be informed in writing before departure, by a document which relates either to him individually or to a group of migrants of which he is a member, of the occupational category for which he is engaged and the other conditions of work, in particular the minimum wage which is guaranteed to him.

3. The competent authority shall ensure that the provisions of the preceding paragraphs are enforced and that appropriate penalties are applied in respect of violations thereof.

Article 7. 1. The measures taken under Article 4 of this Convention shall, as appropriate, include—

(a) the simplification of administrative formalities;

(b) the provision of interpretation services;

(c) any necessary assistance, during an initial period in the settlement of the migrants and members of their families authorised to accompany or join them;

(d) the safeguarding of the welfare, during the journey and in particular on board ship, of migrants and members of their families authorised to accompany or join them; and

(e) permission for the liquidation and transfer of the property of migrants for employment admitted on a permanent basis.

Article 8. Appropriate measures shall be taken by the competent authority to assist migrants for employment, during an initial period, in regard to matters concerning their conditions of employment; where appropriate, such measures may be taken in co-operation with approved voluntary organisations.

Article 9. If a migrant for employment introduced into the territory of a Member in accordance with the provisions of Article 3 of this Annex fails, for a reason for which he is not responsible, to secure the employment for which he has been recruited or other suitable employment, the cost of his return and that of the members of his family who have been authorised to accompany or join him, including administratives fees, transport and maintenance charges to the final destination, and charges for the transport of household belongings, shall not fall upon the migrant.

Article 10. If the competent authority of the territory of immigration considers that the employment for which a migrant for employment was recruited under Article 3 of this Annex has been found to be unsuitable, it shall take appropriate measures to assist him in finding suitable employment which does not prejudice national workers and shall take such steps as will ensure his maintenance pending placing in such employment, or his return to the area of recruitment if the migrant is willing or agreed to such return at the time of his recruitment, or his resettlement elsewhere.

Article 11. If a migrant for employment who is a refugee or a displaced person and who has entered a territory of immigration in accordance with Article 3 of this Annex becomes redundant in any employment in that territory, the competent authority of that territory shall use its best endeavours to enable him to obtain suitable employment which does not prejudice national workers, and shall take such steps as will ensure his maintenance pending placing in suitable employment or his resettlement elsewhere.

Article 12. 1. The competent authorities of the territories concerned shall enter into agreements for the purpose of regulating matters of common concern arising in connection with the application of the provisions of this Annex.

2. Where the Members maintain a system of supervision over contracts of employment, such agreements shall indicate the methods by which the contractual obligations of the employer shall be enforced.

3. Such agreements shall provide, where appropriate, for co-operation between the competent authority of the territory of emigration or a body established in accordance with the terms of an international instrument and the competent authority of the territory of immigration, in respect of the assistance to be given to migrants concerning their conditions of employment in virtue of the provisions of Article 8.

Article 13. Any person who promotes clandestine or illegal immigration shall be subject to appropriate penalties.

Annex III
Importation of the Personal Effects, Tools and Equipment of Migrants for Employment

Article 1. 1. Personal effects belonging to recruited migrants for employment and members of their families who have been authorised to accompany or join them shall be exempt from customs duties on arrival in the territory of immigration.

2. Portable hand-tools and portable equipment of the kind normally owned by workers for the carrying out of their particular trades belonging to recruited migrants for employment and members of their families who have been authorised to accompany or join them shall be exempt from customs duties on arrival in the territory of immigration if such tools and equipment can be shown at the time of importation to be in their actual ownership or possession, to have been in their possession and use for an appreciable time, and to be intended to be used by them in the course of their occupation.

Article 2. 1. Personal effects belonging to migrants for employment and members of their families who have been authorised to accompany or join them shall be exempt from customs duties on the return of the said persons to their country of origin if such persons have retained the nationality of that country at the time of their return there.

2. Portable hand-tools and portable equipment of the kind normally owned by workers for the carrying out of their particular trades belonging to migrants for employment and members of their families who have been authorised to accompany or join them shall be exempt from customs duties on return of the said persons to their country of origin if such persons have retained the nationality of that country at the time of their return there and if such tools and equipment can be shown at the time of importation to be in their actual ownership or possession, to have been in their possession and use for an appreciable time, and to be intended to be used by them in the course of their occupation.

ILO MINIMUM AGE CONVENTION (1973). Formally entitled Convention (No. 138) concerning Minimum Age for Admission for Employment, the convention aims at the abolition of CHILD LABOR and the establishment of a minimum age for employment high enough to ensure the fullest physical and mental development of young persons. It provides that each State party shall specify a minimum age for admission to employment or work within its territory and not permit anyone under that age to work in any occupation and that the minimum age specified shall not be less than the age of completion of compulsory schooling and, in any case, not less than 15 years. It revises all earlier ILO conventions relating to minimum age of employment to conform to its standard.

The convention was adopted by the INTERNATIONAL LABOR CONFERENCE (58th session) on 26 June 1973 and entered into force on 19 June 1976. The text of the convention (*International Labour Conventions and Recommendations, 1919–1981*, page 730), with the exception of the ILO STANDARD FINAL PROVISIONS (articles 11–18), is as follows:

The General Conference of the International Labour Organisation,

Having been convened at Geneva by the Governing Body of the International Labour Office, and having met in its Fifty-eighth Session on 6 June 1973, and

Having decided upon the adoption of certain proposals with regard to minimum age for admission to employment, which is the fourth item on the agenda of the session, and

Noting the terms of the Minimum Age (Industry) Convention, 1919, the Minimum Age (Sea) Convention, 1920, the Minimum Age (Agriculture) Convention, 1921, the Minimum Age (Trimmers and Stokers) Convention, 1921, the Minimum Age (Non-Industrial Employment) Convention, 1932, the Minimum Age (Sea) Convention (Revised), 1936, the Minimum Age (Industry) Convention (Revised), 1937, the Minimum Age (Non-Industrial Employment) Convention (Revised), 1937, the Minimum Age (Fishermen) Convention, 1959, and the Minimum Age (Underground Work) Convention, 1965, and

Considering that the time has come to establish a general instrument on the subject, which would gradually replace the existing ones applicable to limited economic sectors, with a view to achieving the total abolition of child labour, and

Having determined that these proposals shall take the form of an international Convention,

adopts this twenty-sixth day of June of the year one thousand nine hundred and seventy-three the following Convention, which may be cited as the Minimum Age Convention, 1973:

Article 1. Each Member for which this Convention is in force undertakes to pursue a national policy designed to ensure the effective abolition of child labour and to raise progressively the minimum age for admission to employment or work to a level consistent with the fullest physical and mental development of young persons.

Article 2. 1. Each Member which ratifies this Convention shall specify, in a declaration appended to its ratification, a minimum age for admission to employment or work within its territory and on means of transport registered in its territory; subject to Articles 4 to 8 of this Convention, no one under that age shall be admitted to employment or work in any occupation.

2. Each Member which has ratified this Convention may subsequently notify the Director-General of the International Labour Office, by further declarations, that it specifies a minimum age higher than that previously specified.

3. The minimum age specified in pursuance of paragraph 1 of this Article shall not be less than the age of completion of compulsory schooling and, in any case, shall not be less than 15 years.

4. Notwithstanding the provisions of paragraph 3 of this Article, a Member whose economy and educational facilities are insufficiently developed may, after consultation with the organisations of employers and workers concerned, where such exist, initially specify a minimum age of 14 years.

5. Each Member which has specified a minimum age of 14 years in pursuance of the provisions of the preceding paragraph shall include in its reports on the application of this Convention submitted under article 22 of the Constitution of the International Labour Organisation a statement—

(a) that its reason for doing so subsists; or

(b) that it renounces its right to avail itself of the provisions in question as from a stated date.

Article 3. 1. The minimum age for admission to any type of employment or work which by its nature or the circumstances in which it is carried out is likely to jeopardise the health, safety or morals of young persons shall not be less than 18 years.

2. The types of employment or work to which paragraph 1 of this Article applies shall be determined by national laws or regulations or by the competent authority, after consultation with the organisations of employers and workers concerned, where such exist.

3. Notwithstanding the provisions of paragraph 1 of this Article, national laws or regulations or the competent authority may, after consultation with the organisations of employers and workers concerned, where such exist, authorise employment or work as from the age of 16 years on condition that the health, safety and morals of the young persons concerned are fully protected and that the young persons have received adequate specific instruction or vocational training in the relevant branch of activity.

Article 4. 1. In so far as necessary, the competent authority, after consultation with the organisations of employers and workers concerned, where such exist, may exclude from the application of this Convention limited categories of employment or work in respect of which special and substantial problems of application arise.

2. Each Member which ratifies this Convention shall list in its first report on the application of the Convention submitted under article 22 of the Constitution of the International Labour Organisation any categories which may have been excluded in pursuance of paragraph 1 of this Article, giving the reasons for such exclusion, and shall state in subsequent reports the position of its law and practice in respect of the categories excluded and the extent to which effect has been given or is proposed to be given to the Convention in respect of such categories.

3. Employment or work covered by Article 3 of this Convention shall not be excluded from the application of the Convention in pursuance of this Article.

Article 5. 1. A Member whose economy and administrative facilities are insufficiently developed may, after consultation with the organisations of employers and workers concerned, where such exist, initially limit the scope of application of this Convention.

2. Each Member which avails itself of the provisions of paragraph 1 of this Article shall specify, in a declaration appended to its ratification, the branches of economic activity or types of undertakings to which it will apply the provisions of the Convention.

3. The provisions of the Convention shall be applicable as a minimum to the following: mining and quarrying; manufacturing; construction; electricity, gas and water; sanitary services; transport, storage and communication; and plantations and other agricultural undertakings mainly producing for commercial purposes, but excluding family and small-scale holdings produced for local consumption and not regularly employing hired workers.

4. Any Member which has limited the scope of application of this Convention in pursuance of this Article—

(a) shall indicate in its reports under article 22 of the Constitution of the International Labour Organisation the general position as regards the employment or work of young persons and children in the branches of activity which are excluded from the scope of application of this Convention and any progress which may have been made towards wider application of the provisions of the Convention;

(b) may at any time formally extend the scope of application by a declaration addressed to the Director-General of the International Labour Office.

Article 6. This Convention does not apply to work done by children and young persons in schools for general, vocational or technical education or in other training institutions, or to work done by persons at least 14 years of age in undertakings, where such work is carried out in accordance with conditions prescribed by the competent authority, after consultation with the organisations of employers and workers concerned, where such exist, and is an integral part of—

(a) a course of education or training for which a school or training institution is primarily responsible;

(b) a programme of training mainly or entirely in an undertaking, which programme has been approved by the competent authority; or

(c) a programme of guidance or orientation designed to facilitate the choice of an occupation or of a line of training.

Article 7. 1. National laws or regulations may permit the employment or work of persons 13 to 15 years of age on light work which is—

(a) not likely to be harmful to their health or development; and

(b) not such as to prejudice their attendance at school, their participation in vocational orientation or training programmes approved by the competent authority or their capacity to benefit from the instruction received.

2. National laws or regulations may also permit the employment or work of persons who are at least 15 years of age but have not yet completed their compulsory schooling on work which meets the requirements set forth in subparagraphs (a) and (b) of paragraph 1 of this Article.

3. The competent authority shall determine the activities in which employment or work may be permitted under paragraphs 1 and 2 of this Article and shall prescribe the number of hours during which and the conditions in which such employment or work may be undertaken.

4. Notwithstanding the provisions of paragraphs 1 and 2 of this Article, a Member which has availed itself of the provisions of paragraph 4 of Article 2 may, for as long as it continues to do so, substitute the ages 12 and 14 for the ages 13 and 15 in paragraph 1 and the age 14 for the age 15 in paragraph 2 of this Article.

Article 8. 1. After consultation with the organisations of employers and workers concerned, where such exist, the competent authority may, by permits granted in individual cases, allow exceptions to the prohibition of employment or work provided for in Article 2 of this Convention, for such purposes as participation in artistic performances.

2. Permits so granted shall limit the number of hours during which and prescribe the conditions in which employment or work is allowed.

Article 9. 1. All necessary measures, including the provision of appropriate penalties, shall be taken by the competent authority to ensure the effective enforcement of the provisions of this Convention.

2. National laws or regulations or the competent authority shall define the persons responsible for compliance with the provisions giving effect to the Convention.

3. National laws or regulations or the competent authority shall prescribe the registers or other documents which shall be kept and made available by the employer; such registers or documents shall contain the names and ages or dates of birth, duly certified wherever possible, of persons whom he employs or who work for him and who are less than 18 years of age.

Article 10. 1. This Convention revises, on the terms set forth in this Article, the Minimum Age (Industry) Convention, 1919, the Minimum Age (Sea) Convention, 1920, the Minimum Age (Agriculture) Convention, 1921, the Minimum Age (Trimmers and Stokers) Convention, 1921, the Minimum Age (Non-Industrial Employment) Convention, 1932, the Minimum Age (Sea) Convention (Revised), 1936, the Minimum Age (Industry) Convention (Revised), 1937, the Minimum Age (Non-Industrial Employment) Convention (Revised), 1937, the Minimum Age (Fishermen) Convention, 1959, and the Minimum Age (Underground Work) Convention, 1965.

2. The coming into force of this Convention shall not close the Minimum Age (Sea) Convention (Revised), 1936, the Minimum Age (Industry) Convention (Revised), 1937, the Minimum Age (Non-Industrial Employment) Convention (Revised), 1937, the Minimum Age (Fishermen) Convention, 1959, or the Minimum Age (Underground Work) Convention, 1965, to further ratification.

3. The Minimum Age (Industry) Convention, 1919, the Minimum Age (Sea) Convention, 1920, the Minimum Age (Agriculture) Convention, 1921, and the Minimum Age (Trimmers and Stokers) Convention, 1921, shall be closed to further ratification when all the parties thereto have consented to such closing by ratification of this Convention or by a declaration communicated to the Director-General of the International Labour Office.

4. When the obligations of this Convention are accepted—

(a) by a Member which is a party to the Minimum Age (Industry) Convention (Revised), 1937, and a minimum age of not less than 15 years is specified in pursuance of Article 2 of this Convention, this shall *ipso jure* involve the immediate denunciation of that Convention,

(b) in respect of non-industrial employment as defined in the Minimum Age (Non-Industrial Employment) Convention, 1932, by a Member which is a party to that Convention, this shall *ipso jure* involve the immediate denunciation of that Convention,

(c) in respect of non-industrial employment as defined in the Minimum Age (Non-Industrial Employment) Convention (Revised), 1937, by a Member which is a party to that Convention, and a minimum age of not less than 15 years is specified in pursuance of Article 2 of this Convention, this shall *ipso jure* involve the immediate denunciation of that Convention,

(d) in respect of maritime employment, by a Member which is a party to the Minimum Age (Sea) Convention (Revised), 1936, and a minimum age of not less than 15 years is specified in pursuance of Article 2 of this Convention or the Member specifies that Article 3 of this Convention applies to maritime employment, this shall *ipso jure* involve the immediate denunciation of that Convention,

(e) in respect of employment in maritime fishing, by a Member which is a party to the Minimum Age (Fishermen) Convention, 1959, and a minimum age of not less than 15 years is specified in pursuance of Article 2 of this Convention or the Member specifies that Article 3 of this Convention applies to employment in maritime fishing, this shall *ipso jure* involve the immediate denunciation of that Convention,

(f) by a Member which is a party to the Minimum Age (Underground Work) Convention, 1965, and a minimum age of not less than the age specified in pursuance of that Convention is specified in pursuance of Article 2 of this Convention or the Member specifies that such an age applies to employment underground in mines in virtue of Article 3 of this Convention, this shall *ipso jure* involve the immediate denunciation of that Convention,
if and when this Convention shall have come into force.

5. Acceptance of the obligations of this Convention—

(a) shall involve the denunciation of the Minimum Age (Industry) Convention, 1919, in accordance with Article 12 thereof,

(b) in respect of agriculture shall involve the denunciation of the Minimum Age (Agriculture) Convention, 1921, in accordance with Article 9 thereof,

(c) in respect of maritime employment shall involve the denunciation of the Minimum Age (Sea) Convention, 1920, in accordance with Article 10 thereof, and of the Minimum Age (Trimmers and Stokers) Convention, 1921, in accordance with Article 12 thereof,
if and when this Convention shall have come into force.

SEE ALSO Convention on the Rights of the Child; Declaration of the Rights of the Child.

ILO MINIMUM WAGE FIXING CONVENTION (1970).

Formally entitled Convention (No. 131) concerning Minimum Wage Fixing, with Special Reference to Developing Countries, the convention establishes a system of minimum wages and the machinery by which they may be adjusted periodically, supplementing the ILO EQUAL REMUNERATION CONVENTION of 1951 and devoting special attention to the problems of the developing countries. It was adopted by the INTERNATIONAL LABOR CONFERENCE (54th session) on 22 June 1970 and entered into force on 29 April 1972. The text of the convention *(International Labour Conventions and Recommendations, 1919–1981,* page 230), with the exception of the ILO STANDARD FINAL PROVISIONS (articles 7–14), is as follows:

The General Conference of the International Labour Organisation,

Having been convened at Geneva by the Governing Body of the International Labour Office, and having met in its Fifty-fourth Session on 3 June 1970, and

Noting the terms of the Minimum Wage-Fixing Machinery Convention, 1928, and the Equal Remuneration Convention, 1951, which have been widely ratified, as well as of the Minimum Wage Fixing Machinery (Agriculture) Convention, 1951, and

Considering that these Conventions have played a valuable part in protecting disadvantaged groups of wage earners, and

Considering that the time has come to adopt a further instrument complementing these Conventions and providing protection for wage earners against unduly low wages, which, while of general application, pays special regard to the needs of developing countries, and

Having decided upon the adoption of certain proposals

with regard to minimum wage fixing machinery and related problems, with special reference to developing countries, which is the fifth item on the agenda of the session, and

Having determined that these proposals shall take the form of an international Convention,
adopts this twenty-second day of June of the year one thousand nine hundred and seventy the following Convention, which may be cited as the Minimum Wage Fixing Convention, 1970:

Article 1. 1. Each Member of the International Labour Organisation which ratifies this Convention undertakes to establish a system of minimum wages which covers all groups of wage earners whose terms of employment are such that coverage would be appropriate.

2. The competent authority in each country shall, in agreement or after full consultation with the representative organisations of employers and workers concerned, where such exist, determine the groups of wage earners to be covered.

3. Each Member which ratifies this Convention shall list in the first report on the application of the Convention submitted under article 22 of the Constitution of the International Labour Organisation any groups of wage earners which may not have been covered in pursuance of this Article, giving the reasons for not covering them, and shall state in subsequent reports the position of its law and practice in respect of the groups not covered, and the extent to which effect has been given or is proposed to be given to the Convention in respect of such groups.

Article 2. 1. Minimum wages shall have the force of law and shall not be subject to abatement, and failure to apply them shall make the person or persons concerned liable to appropriate penal or other sanctions.

2. Subject to the provisions of paragraph 1 of this Article, the freedom of collective bargaining shall be fully respected.

Article 3. The elements to be taken into consideration in determining the level of minimum wages shall, so far as possible and appropriate in relation to national practice and conditions, include:

(a) The needs of workers and their families, taking into account the general level of wages in the country, the cost of living, social security benefits, and the relative living standards of other social groups;

(b) Economic factors, including the requirements of economic development, levels of productivity and the desirability of attaining and maintaining a high level of employment.

Article 4. 1. Each Member which ratifies this Convention shall create and/or maintain machinery adapted to national conditions and requirements whereby minimum wages for groups of wage earners covered in pursuance of Article 1 thereof can be fixed and adjusted from time to time.

2. Provision shall be made, in connexion with the establishment, operation and modification of such machinery, for full consultation with representative organisations of employers and workers concerned or, where no such organisations exist, representatives of employers and workers concerned.

3. Wherever it is appropriate to the nature of the minimum wage fixing machinery, provision shall also be made for the direct participation in its operation of:

(a) Representatives of organisations of employers and workers concerned or, where no such organisations exist, representatives of employers and workers concerned, on a basis of equality;

(b) Persons having recognised competence for representing the general interests of the country and appointed after full consultation with representative organisations of employers and workers concerned, where such organisations exist and such consultation is in accordance with national law or practice.

Article 5. Appropriate measures, such as adequate inspection reinforced by other necessary measures, shall be taken to ensure the effective application of all provisions relating to minimum wages.

Article 6. This Convention shall not be regarded as revising any existing Convention. . . .

ILO NIGHT WORK (WOMEN) CONVENTION, REVISED (1948).

Formally entitled Convention (No. 89) concerning Night Work of Women Employed in Industry, the convention was adopted by the INTERNATIONAL LABOR CONFERENCE (31st session) on 9 July 1948 and entered into force on 27 February 1951. It increases the restrictions on industrial night-work employment of women previously established in the ILO Night Work (Women) Convention (1919) and the ILO Night Work (Women) Convention, Revised (1934). The text of the convention (*International Labour Conventions and Recommendations, 1919–1981,* page 706), with the exception of the ILO STANDARD FINAL PROVISIONS (articles 13–20) and provisions for modifications in the application of the convention to India and Pakistan (articles 10–12), is as follows:

The General Conference of the International Labour Organisation,

Having been convened at San Francisco by the Governing Body of the International Labour Office, and having met in its Thirty-first Session on 17 June 1948, and

Having decided upon the adoption of certain proposals with regard to the partial revision of the Night Work (Women) Convention, 1919, adopted by the Conference at its First Session, and the Night Work (Women) Convention (Revised), 1934, adopted by the Conference at its Eighteenth Session, which is the ninth item on the agenda of the session, and

Considering that these proposals must take the form of an international Convention,

adopts this ninth day of July of the year one thousand nine hundred and forty-eight the following Convention, which may be cited as the Night Work (Women) Convention (Revised), 1948:

Part I. General Provisions

Article 1. 1. For the purpose of this Convention, the term "industrial undertakings" includes particularly—

(a) mines, quarries, and other works for the extraction of minerals from the earth;

(b) undertakings in which articles are manufactured, altered, cleaned, repaired, ornamented, finished, adapted for sale, broken up or demolished, or in which materials are transformed, including undertakings engaged in shipbuild-

ing or in the generation, transformation or transmission of electricity or motive power of any kind;

(c) undertakings engaged in building and civil engineering work, including constructional, repair, maintenance, alteration and demolition work.

2. The competent authority shall define the line of division which separates industry from agriculture, commerce and other non-industrial occupations.

Article 2. For the purpose of this Convention the term "night" signifies a period of at least eleven consecutive hours, including an interval prescribed by the competent authority of at least seven consecutive hours falling between ten o'clock in the evening and seven o'clock in the morning; the competent authority may prescribe different intervals for different areas, industries, undertakings or branches of industries or undertakings, but shall consult the employers' and workers' organisations concerned before prescribing an interval beginning after eleven o'clock in the evening.

Article 3. Women without distinction of age shall not be employed during the night in any public or private industrial undertaking, or in any branch thereof, other than an undertaking in which only members of the same family are employed.

Article 4. Article 3 shall not apply—

(a) in case of *force majeure,* when in any undertaking there occurs an interruption of work which it was impossible to foresee, and which is not of a recurring character;

(b) in cases where the work has to do with raw materials or materials in course of treatment which are subject to rapid deterioration when such night work is necessary to preserve the said materials from certain loss.

Article 5. 1. The prohibition of night work for women may be suspended by the government, after consultation with the employers' and workers' organisations concerned, when in case of serious emergency the national interest demands it.

2. Such suspension shall be notified by the government concerned to the Director-General of the International Labour Office in its annual report on the application of the Convention.

Article 6. In industrial undertakings which are influenced by the seasons and in all cases where exceptional circumstances demand it, the night period may be reduced to ten hours on sixty days of the year.

Article 7. In countries where the climate renders work by day particularly trying, the night period may be shorter than that prescribed in the above Articles if compensatory rest is accorded during the day.

Article 8. This Convention does not apply to—

(a) women holding responsible positions of a managerial or technical character; and

(b) women employed in health and welfare services who are not ordinarily engaged in manual work.

Part II. Special Provisions for Certain Countries

Article 9. In those countries where no government regulation as yet applies to the employment of women in industrial undertakings during the night, the term "night" may provisionally, and for a maximum period of three years, be declared by the government to signify a period of only ten hours, including an interval prescribed by the competent authority of at least seven consecutive hours falling between ten o'clock in the evening and seven o'clock in the morning. . . .

I

ILO OCCUPATIONAL SAFETY AND HEALTH CONVENTION (1981). Formally entitled Convention (No. 155) concerning Occupational Safety and Health and the Working Environment, the convention requires States parties to adopt a coherent national policy on occupational safety, occupational health, and the working environment, aimed at preventing accidents and injury to health by minimizing, so far as is reasonably practicable, the causes of hazards inherent in the working environment.

The convention was adopted by the INTERNATIONAL LABOR CONFERENCE (67th session) on 22 June 1981 and entered into force on 11 August 1983. The text (*International Labour Conventions and Recommendations, 1919–1981,* page 350), with the exception of the ILO STANDARD FINAL PROVISIONS (articles 22–30), is as follows:

The General Conference of the International Labour Organisation,

Having been convened at Geneva by the Governing Body of the International Labour Office, and having met in its Sixty-seventh Session on 3 June 1981, and

Having decided upon the adoption of certain proposals with regard to safety and health and the working environment, which is the sixth item on the agenda of the session, and

Having determined that these proposals shall take the form of an international Convention,

adopts this twenty-second day of June of the year one thousand nine hundred and eighty-one the following Convention, which may be cited as the Occupational Safety and Health Convention, 1981:

Part I. Scope and Definitions

Article 1. 1. This Convention applies to all branches of economic activity.

2. A Member ratifying this Convention may, after consultation at the earliest possible stage with the representative organisations of employers and workers concerned, exclude from its application, in part or in whole, particular branches of economic activity, such as maritime shipping or fishing, in respect of which special problems of a substantial nature arise.

3. Each Member which ratifies this Convention shall list, in the first report on the application of the Convention submitted under article 22 of the Constitution of the International Labour Organisation, any branches which may have been excluded in pursuance of paragraph 2 of this Article, giving the reason for such exclusion and describing the measures taken to give adequate protection to workers in excluded branches, and shall indicate in subsequent reports any progress towards wider application.

Article 2. 1. This Convention applies to all workers in the branches of economic activity covered.

2. A Member ratifying this Convention may, after consultation at the earliest possible stage with the representative organisations of employers and workers concerned, exclude from its application, in part or in whole, limited categories of workers in respect of which there are particular difficulties.

3. Each Member which ratifies this Convention shall list, in the first report on the application of the Convention submitted under article 22 of the Constitution of the International Labour Organisation, any limited categories of workers which may have been excluded in pursuance of paragraph 2 of this Article, giving the reasons for such exclusion, and shall indicate in subsequent reports any progress towards wider application.

Article 3. For the purpose of this Convention—

(a) the term "branches of economic activity" covers all branches in which workers are employed, including the public service;

(b) the term "workers" covers all employed persons, including public employees;

(c) the term "workplace" covers all places where workers need to be or to go by reason of their work and which are under the direct or indirect control of the employer;

(d) the term "regulations" covers all provisions given force of law by the competent authority or authorities;

(e) the term "health", in relation to work, indicates not merely the absence of disease or infirmity; it also includes the physical and mental elements affecting health which are directly related to safety and hygiene at work.

Part II. Principles of National Policy

Article 4. 1. Each Member shall, in the light of national conditions and practice, and in consultation with the most representative organisations of employers and workers, formulate, implement and periodically review a coherent national policy on occupational safety, occupational health and the working environment.

2. The aim of the policy shall be to prevent accidents and injury to health arising out of, linked with or occurring in the course of work, by minimising, so far as is reasonably practicable, the causes of hazards inherent in the working environment.

Article 5. The policy referred to in Article 4 of this Convention shall take account of the following main spheres of action in so far as they affect occupational safety and health and the working environment:

(a) design, testing, choice, substitution, installation, arrangement, use and maintenance of the material elements of work (workplaces, working environment, tools, machinery and equipment, chemical, physical and biological substances and agents, work processes);

(b) relationships between the material elements of work and the persons who carry out or supervise the work, and adaptation of machinery, equipment, working time, organisation of work and work processes to the physical and mental capacities of the workers;

(c) training, including necessary further training, qualifications and motivations of persons involved, in one capacity or another, in the achievement of adequate levels of safety and health;

(d) communication and co-operation at the levels of the working group and the undertaking and at all other appropriate levels up to and including the national level;

(e) the protection of workers and their representatives from disciplinary measures as a result of actions properly taken by them in conformity with the policy referred to in Article 4 of this Convention.

Article 6. The formulation of the policy referred to in Article 4 of this Convention shall indicate the respective functions and responsibilities in respect of occupational safety and health and the working environment of public authorities, employers, workers and others, taking account both of the complementary character of such responsibilities and of national conditions and practice.

Article 7. The situation regarding occupational safety and health and the working environment shall be reviewed at appropriate intervals, either over-all or in respect of particular areas, with a view to identifying major problems, evolving effective methods for dealing with them and priorities of action, and evaluating results.

Part III. Action at the National Level

Article 8. Each Member shall, by laws or regulations or any other method consistent with national conditions and practice and in consultation with the representative organisations of employers and workers concerned, take such steps as may be necessary to give effect to Article 4 of this Convention.

Article 9. 1. The enforcement of laws and regulations concerning occupational safety and health and the working environment shall be secured by an adequate and appropriate system of inspection.

2. The enforcement system shall provide for adequate penalties for violations of the laws and regulations.

Article 10. Measures shall be taken to provide guidance to employers and workers so as to help them to comply with legal obligations.

Article 11. To give effect to the policy referred to in Article 4 of this Convention, the competent authority or authorities shall ensure that the following functions are progressively carried out:

(a) the determination, where the nature and degree of hazards so require, of conditions governing the design, construction and layout of undertakings, the commencement of their operations, major alterations affecting them and changes in their purposes, the safety of technical equipment used at work, as well as the application of procedures defined by the competent authorities;

(b) the determination of work processes and of substances and agents the exposure to which is to be prohibited, limited or made subject to authorisation or control by the competent authority or authorities; health hazards due to the simultaneous exposure to several substances or agents shall be taken into consideration;

(c) the establishment and application of procedures for the notification of occupational accidents and diseases, by employers and, when appropriate, insurance institutions and others directly concerned, and the production of annual statistics on occupational accidents and diseases;

(d) the holding of inquiries, where cases of occupational accidents, occupational diseases or any other injuries to health which arise in the course of or in connection with work appear to reflect situations which are serious;

(e) the publication, annually, of information on measures taken in pursuance of the policy referred to in Article 4 of this Convention and on occupational accidents, occupational diseases and other injuries to health which arise in the course of or in connection with work;

(f) the introduction or extension of systems, taking into account national conditions and possibilities, to examine chemical, physical and biological agents in respect of the risk to the health of workers.

Article 12. Measures shall be taken, in accordance with national law and practice, with a view to ensuring that those who design, manufacture, import, provide or transfer machinery, equipment or substances for occupational use—

(a) satisfy themselves that, so far as is reasonably prac-

ticable, the machinery, equipment or substance does not entail dangers for the safety and health of those using it correctly;

(b) make available information concerning the correct installation and use of machinery and equipment and the correct use of substances, and information on hazards of machinery and equipment and dangerous properties of chemical substances and physical and biological agents or products, as well as instructions on how hazards are to be avoided;

(c) undertake studies and research or otherwise keep abreast of the scientific and technical knowledge necessary to comply with subparagraphs (a) and (b) of this Article.

Article 13. A worker who has removed himself from a work situation which he has reasonable justification to believe presents an imminent and serious danger to his life or health shall be protected from undue consequences in accordance with national conditions and practice.

Article 14. Measures shall be taken with a view to promoting in a manner appropriate to national conditions and practice, the inclusion of questions of occupational safety and health and the working environment at all levels of education and training, including higher technical, medical and professional education, in a manner meeting the training needs of all workers.

Article 15. 1. With a view to ensuring the coherence of the policy referred to in Article 4 of this Convention and of measures for its application, each Member shall, after consultation at the earliest possible stage with the most representative organisations of employers and workers, and with other bodies as appropriate, make arrangements appropriate to national conditions and practice to ensure the necessary co-ordination between various authorities and bodies called upon to give effect to Parts II and III of this Convention.

2. Whenever circumstances so require and national conditions and practice permit, these arrangements shall include the establishment of a central body.

Part IV. Action at the Level of the Undertaking

Article 16. 1. Employers shall be required to ensure that, so far as is reasonably practicable, the workplaces, machinery, equipment and processes under their control are safe and without risk to health.

2. Employers shall be required to ensure that, so far as is reasonably practicable, the chemical, physical and biological substances and agents under their control are without risk to health when the appropriate measures of protection are taken.

3. Employers shall be required to provide, where necessary, adequate protective clothing and protective equipment to prevent, so far is reasonably practicable, risk of accidents or of adverse effects on health.

Article 17. Whenever two or more undertakings engage in activities simultaneously at one workplace, they shall collaborate in applying the requirements of this Convention.

Article 18. Employers shall be required to provide, where necessary, for measures to deal with emergencies and accidents, including adequate first-aid arrangements.

Article 19. There shall be arrangements at the level of the undertaking under which—

(a) workers, in the course of performing their work, co-operate in the fulfilment by their employer of the obligations placed upon him;

(b) representatives of workers in the undertaking co-operate with the employer in the field of occupational safety and health;

(c) representatives of workers in an undertaking are given adequate information on measures taken by the employer to secure occupational safety and health and may consult their representative organisations about such information provided they do not disclose commercial secrets;

(d) workers and their representatives in the undertaking are given appropriate training in occupational safety and health;

(e) workers or their representatives and, as the case may be, their representative organisations in an undertaking, in accordance with national law and practice, are enabled to enquire into, and are consulted by the employer on, all aspects of occupational safety and health associated with their work; for this purpose technical advisers may, by mutual agreement, be brought in from outside the undertaking;

(f) a worker reports forthwith to his immediate supervisor any situation which he has reasonable justification to believe presents an imminent and serious danger to his life or health; until the employer has taken remedial action, if necessary, the employer cannot require workers to return to a work situation where there is continuing imminent and serious danger to life or health.

Article 20. Co-operation between management and workers and/or their representatives within the undertaking shall be an essential element of organisational and other measures taken in pursuance of Articles 16 to 19 of this Convention.

Article 21. Occupational safety and health measures shall not involve any expenditure for the workers. . . .

SEE ALSO *ILO Labor Inspection Convention; ILO Working Environment (Air Pollution, Noise and Vibration) Convention.*

ILO PAID EDUCATIONAL LEAVE CONVENTION (1974). Formally entitled Convention (No. 140) concerning Paid Educational Leave, the convention was adopted on 24 June 1974 by the INTERNATIONAL LABOR CONFERENCE (59th session) and entered into force on 23 September 1976. The text of the convention *(International Labour Conventions and Recommendations, 1919–1981,* p. 327), with the exception of the ILO STANDARD FINAL PROVISIONS (articles 12–19), is as follows:

The General Conference of the International Labour Organisation,

Having been convened at Geneva by the Governing Body of the International Labour Office, and having met in its Fifty-ninth Session on 5 June 1974, and

Noting that Article 26 of the Universal Declaration of Human Rights affirms that everyone has the right to education, and

Noting further the provisions contained in existing international labour Recommendations on vocational training and the protection of workers' representatives concerning the temporary release of workers, or the granting to them of time off, for participation in education or training programmes, and

Considering that the need for continuing education and training related to scientific and technological development and the changing pattern of economic and social relations calls for adequate arrangements for leave for education and training to meet new aspirations, needs and objectives of a social, economic, technological and cultural character, and

Considering that paid educational leave should be regarded as one means of meeting the real needs of individual workers in a modern society, and

Considering that paid educational leave should be conceived in terms of a policy of continuing education and training to be implemented progressively and in an effective manner, and

Having decided upon the adoption of certain proposals with regard to paid educational leave, which is the fourth item on the agenda of the session, and

Having determined that these proposals shall take the form of an international Convention,

adopts this twenty-fourth day of June of the year one thousand nine hundred and seventy-four the following Convention, which may be cited as the Paid Educational Leave Convention, 1974:

Article 1. In this Convention, the term "paid educational leave" means leave granted to a worker for educational purposes for a specified period during working hours, with adequate financial entitlements.

Article 2. Each Member shall formulate and apply a policy designed to promote, by methods appropriate to national conditions and practice and by stages as necessary, the granting of paid educational leave for the purpose of—

(a) training at any level;

(b) general, social and civic education;

(c) trade union education.

Article 3. That policy shall be designed to contribute, on differing terms as necessary—

(a) to the acquisition, improvement and adaptation of occupational and functional skills, and the promotion of employment and job security in conditions of scientific and technological development and economic and structural change;

(b) to the competent and active participation of workers and their representatives in the life of the undertaking and of the community;

(c) to the human, social and cultural advancement of workers; and

(d) generally, to the promotion of appropriate continuing education and training, helping workers to adjust to contemporary requirements.

Article 4. The policy shall take account of the stage of development and the particular needs of the country and of different sectors of activity, and shall be co-ordinated with general policies concerning employment, education and training as well as policies concerning hours of work, with due regard as appropriate to seasonal variations of hours of work or of volume of work.

Article 5. The means by which provision is made for the granting of paid educational leave may include national laws and regulations, collective agreements, arbitration awards, and such other means as may be consistent with national practice.

Article 6. The public authorities, employers' and workers' organisations, and institutions or bodies providing education and training shall be associated, in a manner appropriate to national conditions and practice, with the formulation and application of the policy for the promotion of paid educational leave.

Article 7. The financing of arrangements for paid educational leave shall be on a regular and adequate basis and in accordance with national practice.

Article 8. Paid educational leave shall not be denied to workers on the ground of race, colour, sex, religion, political opinion, national extraction or social origin.

Article 9. As necessary, special provisions concerning paid educational leave shall be established—

(a) where particular categories of workers, such as workers in small undertakings, rural or other workers residing in isolated areas, shift workers or workers with family responsibilities, find it difficult to fit into general arrangements;

(b) where particular categories of undertakings, such as small or seasonal undertakings, find it difficult to fit into general arrangements, it being understood that workers in these undertakings would not be excluded from the benefit of paid educational leave.

Article 10. Conditions of eligibility for paid educational leave may vary according to whether such leave is intended for—

(a) training at any level;

(b) general, social or civic education; or

(c) trade union education.

Article 11. A period of paid educational leave shall be assimilated to a period of effective service for the purpose of establishing claims to social benefits and other rights deriving from the employment relation, as provided for by national laws or regulations, collective agreements, arbitration awards or such other means as may be consistent with national practice. . . .

ILO PROTECTION OF WAGES CONVENTION

(1949). Formally entitled Convention (No. 95) concerning the Protection of Wages, the convention was adopted on 1 July 1949 by the INTERNATIONAL LABOR CONFERENCE (32d session) and entered into force on 24 September 1952. The text of the convention (*International Labour Conventions and Recommendations, 1919–1981*, p. 237), with the exception of the ILO STANDARD FINAL PROVISIONS (articles 18, 19, and 22–27) and the provisions relating to declarations of application to non-metropolitan territories (articles 20 and 21) made in accordance with article 35 of the INTERNATIONAL LABOR ORGANIZATION: CONSTITUTION, is as follows:

The General Conference of the International Labour Organisation,

Having been convened at Geneva by the Governing Body of the International Labour Office, and having met in its Thirty-second Session on 8 June 1949, and

Having decided upon the adoption of certain proposals concerning the protection of wages, which is the seventh item on the agenda of the session, and

Having determined that these proposals shall take the form of an international Convention,

adopts this first day of July of the year one thousand nine hundred and forty-nine the following Convention, which may be cited as the Protection of Wages Convention, 1949:

Article 1. In this Convention, the term "wages" means remuneration or earnings, however designated or calculated, capable of being expressed in terms of money and fixed by mutual agreement or by national laws or regulations, which are payable in virtue of a written or unwritten contract of employment by an employer to an employed person for work done or to be done or for services rendered or to be rendered.

Article 2. 1. This Convention applies to all persons to whom wages are paid or payable.

2. The competent authority may, after consultation with the organisations of employers and employed persons directly concerned, if such exist, exclude from the application of all or any of the provisions of the Convention categories of persons whose circumstances and conditions of employment are such that the application to them of all or any of the said provisions would be inappropriate and who are not employed in manual labour or are employed in domestic service or work similar thereto.

3. Each Member shall indicate in its first annual report upon the application of this Convention submitted under article 22 of the Constitution of the International Labour Organisation any categories of persons which it proposes to exclude from the application of all or any of the provisions of the Convention in accordance with the provisions of the preceding paragraph; no Member shall, after the date of its first annual report, make exclusions except in respect of categories of persons so indicated.

4. Each member having indicated in its first annual report categories of persons which it proposes to exclude from the application of all or any of the provisions of the Convention shall indicate in subsequent annual reports any categories of persons in respect of which it renounces the right to have recourse to the provisions of paragraph 2 of this Article and any progress which may have been made with a view to the application of the Convention to such categories of persons.

Article 3. 1. Wages payable in money shall be paid only in legal tender, and payment in the form of promissory notes, vouchers or coupons, or in any other form alleged to represent legal tender, shall be prohibited.

2. The competent authority may permit or prescribe the payment of wages by bank cheque or postal cheque or money order in cases in which payment in this manner is customary or is necessary because of special circumstances, or where a collective agreement or arbitration award so provides, or, where not so provided, with the consent of the worker concerned.

Article 4. 1. National laws or regulations, collective agreements or arbitration awards may authorise the partial payment of wages in the form of allowances in kind in industries or occupations in which payment in the form of such allowances is customary or desirable because of the nature of the industry or occupation concerned; the payment of wages in the form of liquor of high alcoholic content or of noxious drugs shall not be permitted in any circumstances.

2. In cases in which partial payment of wages in the form of allowances in kind is authorised, appropriate measures shall be taken to ensure that—

(a) such allowances are appropriate for the personal use and benefit of the worker and his family; and

(b) the value attributed to such allowances is fair and reasonable.

Article 5. Wages shall be paid directly to the worker concerned except as may be otherwise provided by national laws or regulations, collective agreement or arbitration award or where the worker concerned has agreed to the contrary.

Article 6. Employers shall be prohibited from limiting in any manner the freedom of the worker to dispose of his wages.

Article 7. 1. Where works stores for the sale of commodities to the workers are established or services are operated in connection with an undertaking, the workers concerned shall be free from any coercion to make use of such stores or services.

2. Where access to other stores or services is not possible, the competent authority shall take appropriate measures with the object of ensuring that goods are sold and services provided at fair and reasonable prices, or that stores established and services operated by the employer are not operated for the purpose of securing a profit but for the benefit of the workers concerned.

Article 8. 1. Deductions from wages shall be permitted only under conditions and to the extent prescribed by national laws or regulations or fixed by collective agreement or arbitration award.

2. Workers shall be informed, in the manner deemed most appropriate by the competent authority, of the conditions under which and the extent to which such deductions may be made.

Article 9. Any deduction from wages with a view to ensuring a direct or indirect payment for the purpose of obtaining or retaining employment, made by a worker to an employer or his representative or to any intermediary (such as a labour contractor or recruiter), shall be prohibited.

Article 10. 1. Wages may be attached or assigned only in a manner and within limits prescribed by national laws or regulations.

2. Wages shall be protected against attachment or assignment to the extent deemed necessary for the maintenance of the worker and his family.

Article 11. 1. In any event of the bankruptcy or judicial liquidation of an undertaking, the workers employed therein shall be treated as privileged creditors either as regards wages due to them for service rendered during such a period prior to the bankruptcy or judicial liquidation as may be prescribed by national laws or regulations, or as regards wages up to a prescribed amount as may be determined by national laws or regulations.

2. Wages constituting a privileged debt shall be paid in full before ordinary creditors may establish any claim to a share of the assets.

3. The relative priority of wages constituting a privileged debt and other privileged debts shall be determined by national laws or regulations.

Article 12. 1. Wages shall be paid regularly. Except where other appropriate arrangements exist which ensure the payment of wages at regular intervals, the intervals for the payment of wages shall be prescribed by national laws or regulations or fixed by collective agreement or arbitration award.

2. Upon the termination of a contract of employment, a final settlement of all wages due shall be effected in accordance with national laws or regulations, collective agreement or arbitration award or, in the absence of any applicable law, regulation, agreement or award, within a reasonable period of time having regard to the terms of the contract.

Article 13. 1. The payment of wages where made in cash shall be made on working days only and at or near the workplace, except as may be otherwise provided by national laws

or regulations, collective agreement or arbitration award, or where other arrangements known to the workers concerned are considered more appropriate.

2. Payment of wages in taverns or other similar establishments and, where necessary to prevent abuse, in shops or stores for the retail sale of merchandise and in places of amusement shall be prohibited except in the case of persons employed therein.

Article 14. Where necessary, effective measures shall be taken to ensure that workers are informed, in an appropriate and easily understandable manner—

(a) before they enter employment and when any changes take place, of the conditions in respect of wages under which they are employed; and

(b) at the time of each payment of wages, of the particulars of their wages for the pay period concerned, in so far as such particulars may be subject to change.

Article 15. The laws or regulations giving effect to the provisions of this Convention shall—

(a) be made available for the information of persons concerned;

(b) define the persons responsible for compliance therewith;

(c) prescribe adequate penalties or other appropriate remedies for any violation thereof;

(d) provide for the maintenance, in all appropriate cases, of adequate records in an approved form and manner.

Article 16. There shall be included in the annual reports to be submitted under article 22 of the Constitution of the International Labour Organisation full information concerning the measures by which effect is given to the provisions of this Convention.

Article 17. 1. In the case of a Member the territory of which includes large areas where, by reason of the sparseness of the population or the stage of development of the area, the competent authority considers it impracticable to enforce the provisions of this Convention, the authority may, after consultation with the organisations of employers and workers concerned, where such exist, exempt such areas from the application of this Convention either generally or with such exceptions in respect of particular undertakings or occupations as it thinks fit.

2. Each Member shall indicate in its first annual report upon the application of this Convention submitted under article 22 of the Constitution of the International Labour Organisation any areas in respect of which it proposes to have recourse to the provisions of the present Article and shall give the reasons for which it proposes to have recourse thereto; no Member shall, after the date of its first annual report, have recourse to the provisions of the present Article except in respect of areas so indicated.

3. Each Member having recourse to the provisions of this Article shall, at intervals not exceeding three years, reconsider in consultation with the organisations of employers and workers concerned, where such exist, the practicability of extending the application of the Convention to areas exempted in virtue of paragraph 1.

4. Each Member having recourse to the provisions of this Article shall indicate in subsequent annual reports any areas in respect of which it renounces the right to have recourse to the provisions of this Article and any progress which may have been made with a view to the progressive application of the Convention in such areas. . . .

ILO RIGHT OF ASSOCIATION (AGRICULTURE) CONVENTION (1921). In this first ILO convention on freedom of association, formally entitled Convention (No. 11) concerning the Rights of Association and Combination of Agricultural Workers, contracting States undertake to ensure to agricultural workers the same rights of association and combination as are ensured to industrial workers. Adopted by the INTERNATIONAL LABOR CONFERENCE (third session) on 12 November 1921, the convention entered into force on 11 May 1923. The text of the convention (*International Labour Conventions and Recommendations, 1919–1981,* page 3), with the exception of the ILO STANDARD FINAL PROVISIONS (articles 2, 4, and 7–9) and other final provisions (articles 1, 3 and 5–6), is as follows:

The General Conference of the International Labour Organisation,

Having been convened at Geneva by the Governing Body of the International Labour Office, and having met in its Third Session on 25 October 1921, and

Having decided upon the adoption of certain proposals with regard to the rights of association and combination of agricultural workers, which is included in the fourth item of the agenda of the Session, and

Having determined that these proposals shall take the form of an international Convention,

adopts the following Convention, which may be cited as the Right of Association (Agriculture) Convention, 1921, for ratification by the Members of the International Labour Organisation in accordance with the provisions of the Constitution of the International Labour Organisation:

Article 1. Each Member of the International Labour Organisation which ratifies this Convention undertakes to secure to all those engaged in agriculture the same rights of association and combination as to industrial workers, and to repeal any statutory or other provisions restricting such rights in the case of those engaged in agriculture . . .

SEE ALSO *Assembly and Association; ILO Collective Bargaining Convention; ILO Freedom of Association and Protection of the Right to Organize Convention; ILO Right to Organize and Collective Bargaining Convention; ILO Rural Workers' Organizations Convention.*

ILO RIGHT TO ORGANIZE AND COLLECTIVE BARGAINING CONVENTION (1949). Formally entitled Convention (No. 98) concerning the Application of the Principles of the Right to Organize and to Bargain Collectively, 1949, the convention was adopted on 1 July 1949 by the INTERNATIONAL LABOR CONFERENCE (32d session) and entered into force on 18 July 1951. It aims at providing safeguards against acts of anti-union discrimination. The text of the convention (*International Labour Conventions and Recommendations, 1919–1981,* page 7), with the exception of the ILO STANDARD FINAL PROVISIONS (articles 7–8, 11–16) and articles relating to declarations of application to non-metropolitan territories (articles 9 and 10), is as follows:

The General Conference of the International Labour Organisation,

Having been convened at Geneva by the Governing Body of the International Labour Office, and having met in its thirty-second session on 8 June 1949, and

Having decided upon the adoption of certain proposals concerning the application of the principles of the right to organise and to bargain collectively, which is the fourth item on the agenda of the session, and

Having determined that these proposals shall take the form of an international Convention,

Adopts this first day of July of the year one thousand nine hundred and forty-nine the following Convention, which may be cited as the Right to Organise and Collective Bargaining Convention 1949:

Article 1. 1. Workers shall enjoy adequate protection against acts of anti-union discrimination in respect of their employment.

2. Such protection shall apply more particularly in respect of acts calculated to:

(a) Make the employment of a worker subject to the condition that he shall not join a union or shall relinquish trade union membership;

(b) Cause the dismissal of or otherwise prejudice a worker by reason of union membership or because of participation in union activities outside working hours or, with the consent of the employer, within working hours.

Article 2. 1. Workers' and employers' organisations shall enjoy adequate protection against any acts of interference by each other or each other's agents or members in their establishment, functioning or administration.

2. In particular, acts which are designed to promote the establishment of workers' organisations under the domination of employers or employers' organisations, or to support workers' organisations by financial or other means, with the object of placing such organisations under the control of employers or employers' organisations, shall be deemed to constitute acts of interference within the meaning of this article.

Article 3. Machinery appropriate to national conditions shall be established, where necessary, for the purpose of ensuring respect for the right to organise as defined in the preceding articles.

Article 4. Measures appropriate to national conditions shall be taken, where necessary, to encourage and promote the full development and utilisation of machinery for voluntary negotiation between employers or employers' organisations and workers' organisations, with a view to the regulation of terms and conditions of employment by means of collective agreements.

Article 5. 1. The extent to which the guarantees provided for in this Convention shall apply to the armed forces and the police shall be determined by national laws or regulations.

2. In accordance with the principle set forth in paragraph 8 of article 19 of the Constitution of the International Labour Organisation the ratification of this Convention by any Member shall not be deemed to affect any existing law, award, custom or agreement in virtue of which members of the armed forces or the police enjoy any right guaranteed by this Convention.

I

Article 6. This Convention does not deal with the position of public servants engaged in the administration of the State, nor shall it be construed as prejudicing their rights or status in any way. . . .

SEE ALSO Assembly and Association; ILO Collective Bargaining Convention; ILO Freedom of Association and Protection of Right to Organize Convention.

ILO RURAL WORKERS' ORGANIZATIONS CONVENTION (1975).

Formally entitled Convention (No. 141) concerning Organizations of Rural Workers and their Role in Economic and Social Development, the convention requires States parties to ensure freedom of association to rural workers. It was adopted by the INTERNATIONAL LABOR CONFERENCE (60th session) on 23 June 1975 and entered into force on 24 November 1977. The text of the convention *(International Labour Conventions and Recommendations, 1919–1981,* page 15), with the exception of the ILO STANDARD FINAL PROVISIONS (articles 7–14) is as follows:

The General Conference of the International Labour Organisation,

Having been convened at Geneva by the Governing Body of the International Labour Office, and having met in its Sixtieth Session on 4 June 1975, and

Recognising that the importance of rural workers in the world makes it urgent to associate them with economic and social development action if their conditions of work and life are to be permanently and effectively improved, and

Noting that in many countries of the world and particularly in developing countries there is massive under-utilisation of land and labour and that this makes it imperative for rural workers to be given every encouragement to develop free and viable organisations capable of protecting and furthering the interests of their members and ensuring their effective contribution to economic and social development, and

Considering that such organisations can and should contribute to the alleviation of the persistent scarcity of food products in various regions of the world, and

Recognising that land reform is in many developing countries an essential factor in the improvement of the conditions of work and life of rural workers and that organisation of such workers should accordingly co-operate and participate actively in the implementation of such reform, and

Recalling the terms of existing international labour Conventions and Recommendations—in particular the Right of Association (Agriculture) Convention, 1921, the Freedom of Association and Protection of the Right to Organise Convention, 1948, and the Right to Organise and Collective Bargaining Convention, 1949—which affirm the right of all workers, including rural workers, to establish free and independent organisations, and the provisions of numerous international labour Conventions and Recommendations applicable to rural workers which call for the participation, inter alia, of workers' organisations in their implementation, and

Noting the joint concern of the United Nations and the specialised agencies, in particular the International La-

bour Organisation and the Food and Agriculture Organisation of the United Nations, with land reform and rural development, and

Noting that the following standards have been framed in co-operation with the Food and Agriculture Organisation of the United Nations and that, with a view to avoiding duplication, there will be continuing co-operation with that Organisation and with the United Nations in promoting and securing the application of these standards, and

Having decided upon the adoption of certain proposals with regard to organisations of rural workers and their role in economic and social development, which is the fourth item on the agenda of the session, and

Having determined that these proposals shall take the form of an international Convention,

adopts this twenty-third day of June of the year one thousand nine hundred and seventy-five the following Convention, which may be cited as the Rural Workers' Organisations Convention, 1975:

Article 1. This Convention applies to all types of organisations of rural workers, including organisations not restricted to but representative of rural workers.

Article 2. 1. For the purposes of this Convention, the term "rural workers" means any person engaged in agriculture, handicrafts or a related occupation in a rural area, whether as a wage earner or, subject to the provisions of paragraph 2 of this Article, as a self-employed person such as a tenant, sharecropper or small owner-occupier.

2. This Convention applies only to those tenants, sharecroppers or small owner-occupiers who derive their main income from agriculture, who work the land themselves, with the help only of their family or with the help of occasional outside labour and who do not—

(a) permanently employ workers; or

(b) employ a substantial number of seasonal workers; or

(c) have any land cultivated by sharecroppers or tenants.

Article 3. 1. All categories of rural workers, whether they are wage earners or self-employed, shall have the right to establish and, subject only to the rules of the organisation concerned, to join organisations of their own choosing without previous authorisation.

2. The principles of freedom of association shall be fully respected; rural workers' organisations shall be independent and voluntary in character and shall remain free from all interference, coercion or repression.

3. The acquisition of legal personality by organisations of rural workers shall not be made subject to conditions of such a character as to restrict the application of the provisions of the preceding paragraphs of this Article.

4. In exercising the rights provided for in this Article rural workers and their respective organisations, like other persons or organised collectivities, shall respect the law of the land.

5. The law of the land shall not be such as to impair, nor shall it be so applied as to impair, the guarantees provided for in this Article.

Article 4. It shall be an objective of national policy concerning rural development to facilitate the establishment and growth, on a voluntary basis, of strong and independent organisations of rural workers as an effective means of ensuring the participation of rural workers, without discrimination as defined in the Discrimination (Employment and Occupation) Convention, 1958, in economic and social development and in the benefits resulting therefrom.

Article 5. 1. In order to enable organisations of rural workers to play their role in economic and social development, each Member which ratifies this Convention shall adopt and carry out a policy of active encouragement to these organisations, particularly with a view to eliminating obstacles to their establishment, their growth and the pursuit of their lawful activities, as well as such legislative and administrative discrimination against rural workers' organisations and their members as may exist.

2. Each Member which ratifies this Convention shall ensure that national laws or regulations do not, given the special circumstances of the rural sector, inhibit the establishment and growth of rural workers' organisations.

Article 6. Steps shall be taken to promote the widest possible understanding of the need to further the development of rural workers' organisations and of the contribution they can make to improving employment opportunities and general conditions of work and life in rural areas as well as to increasing the national income and achieving a better distribution thereof. . . .

SEE ALSO ILO Right of Association (Agriculture) Convention.

ILO SOCIAL POLICY (BASIC AIMS AND STANDARDS) CONVENTION (1962).

Formally entitled Convention (No. 117) concerning Basic Aims and Standards of Social Policy, 1962, the convention was adopted by the INTERNATIONAL LABOR CONFERENCE (46th session) on 23 June 1962 and entered into force on 23 April 1964. Its basic aim is to improve STANDARDS OF LIVING and thereby to promote social progress. The text of the convention (*International Labour Conventions and Recommendations, 1919–1981*, page 145), with the exception of the ILO STANDARD FINAL PROVISIONS (articles 17–25), is as follows:

The General Conference of the International Labour Organisation,

Having been convened at Geneva by the Governing Body of the International Labour Office, and having met in its Forty-sixth Session on 6 June 1962, and

Having decided upon the adoption of certain proposals concerning the revision of the Social Policy (Non-Metropolitan Territories) Convention, 1947, which is the tenth item on the agenda of the session, primarily with a view to making its continued application and ratification possible for independent States, and

Considering that these proposals must take the form of an international Convention, and

Considering that economic development must serve as a basis for social progress, and

Considering that every effort should be made, on an international, regional or national basis, to secure financial and technical assistance safeguarding the interests of the population, and

Considering that, in appropriate cases, international, regional or national action should be taken with a view to establishing conditions of trade which would encourage production at a high level of efficiency and make possible the maintenance of a reasonable standard of living, and

Considering that all possible steps should be taken by appropriate international, regional and national measures to promote improvement in such fields as public health, housing, nutrition, education, the welfare of children, the status of women, conditions of employment, the remuneration of wage earners and independent producers, the protection of migrant workers, social security, standards of public services and general production, and

Considering that all possible steps should be taken effectively to interest and associate the population in the framing and execution of measures of social progress, adopts this twenty-second day of June of the year one thousand nine hundred and sixty-two the following Convention, which may be cited as the Social Policy (Basic Aims and Standards) Convention, 1962:

Part I. General Principles

Article 1. 1. All policies shall be primarily directed to the well-being and development of the population and to the promotion of its desire for social progress.

2. All policies of more general application shall be formulated with due regard to their effect upon the well-being of the population.

Part II. Improvement of Standards of Living

Article 2. The improvement of standards of living shall be regarded as the principal objective in the planning of economic development.

Article 3. 1. All practicable measures shall be taken in the planning of economic development to harmonise such development with the healthy evolution of the communities concerned.

2. In particular, efforts shall be made to avoid the disruption of family life and of traditional social units, especially by—

(a) close study of the causes and effect of migratory movements and appropriate action where necessary;

(b) the promotion of town and village planning in areas where economic needs result in the concentration of population;

(c) the prevention and elimination of congestion in urban areas;

(d) the improvement of living conditions in rural areas and the establishment of suitable industries in rural areas where adequate manpower is available.

Article 4. The measures to be considered by the competent authorities for the promotion of productive capacity and the improvement of standards of living of agricultural producers shall include—

(a) the elimination to the fullest practicable extent of the causes of chronic indebtedness;

(b) the control of the alienation of agricultural land to non-agriculturalists so as to ensure that such alienation takes place only when it is in the best interests of the country;

(c) the control, by the enforcement of adequate laws or regulations, of the ownership and use of land and resources to ensure that they are used, with due regard to customary rights, in the best interests of the inhabitants of the country;

(d) the supervision of tenancy arrangements and of working conditions with a view to securing for tenants and labourers the highest practicable standards of living and an equitable share in any advantages which may result from improvements in productivity or in price levels;

(e) the reduction of production and distribution costs by

all practicable means and in particular by forming, encouraging and assisting producers' and consumers co-operatives.

Article 5. 1. Measures shall be taken to secure for independent producers and wage earners conditions which will give them scope to improve living standards by their own efforts and will ensure the maintenance of minimum standards of living as ascertained by means of official inquiries into living conditions, conducted after consultation with the representative organisations of employers and workers.

2. In ascertaining the minimum standards of living, account shall be taken of such essential family needs of the workers as food and its nutritive value, housing, clothing, medical care and education.

Part III. Provisions Concerning Migrant Workers

Article 6. Where the circumstances under which workers are employed involve their living away from their homes, the terms and conditions of their employment shall take account of their normal family needs.

Article 7. Where the labour resources of one area are used on a temporary basis for the benefit of another area, measures shall be taken to encourage the transfer of part of the workers' wages and savings from the area of labour utilisation to the area of labour supply.

Article 8. 1. Where the labour resources of a country are used in an area under a different administration, the competent authorities of the countries concerned shall, whenever necessary or desirable, enter into agreements for the purpose of regulating matters of common concern arising in connection with the application of the provisions of this Convention.

2. Such agreements shall provide that the worker shall enjoy protection and advantages not less than those enjoyed by workers resident in the area of labour utilisation.

3. Such agreements shall provide for facilities for enabling the worker to transfer part of his wages and savings to his home.

Article 9. Where workers and their families move from low-cost to higher-cost areas, account shall be taken of the increased cost of living resulting from the change.

Part IV. Remuneration of Workers and Related Questions

Article 10. 1. The fixing of minimum wages by collective agreements freely negotiated between trade unions which are representative of the workers concerned and employers or employers' organisations shall be encouraged.

2. Where no adequate arrangements exist for the fixing of minimum wages by collective agreement, the necessary arrangements shall be made whereby minimum rates of wages can be fixed in consultation with representatives of the employers and workers, including representatives of their respective organisations, where such exist.

3. The necessary measures shall be taken to ensure that the employers and workers concerned are informed of the minimum wage rates in force and that wages are not paid at less than these rates in cases where they are applicable.

4. A worker to whom minimum rates are applicable and who, since they became applicable, has been paid wages at less than these rates shall be entitled to recover, by judicial or other means authorised by law, the amount by which he has been underpaid, subject to such limitation of time as may be determined by law or regulation.

Article 11. 1. The necessary measures shall be taken to ensure the proper payment of all wages earned and employers shall be required to keep registers of wage payments, to issue to workers statements of wage payments and to take other appropriate steps to facilitate the necessary supervision.

2. Wages shall normally be paid in legal tender only.

3. Wages shall normally be paid direct to the individual worker.

4. The substitution of alcohol or other spirituous beverages for all or any part of wages for services performed by the worker shall be prohibited.

5. Payment of wages shall not be made in taverns or stores, except in the case of workers employed therein.

6. Unless there is an established local custom to the contrary, and the competent authority is satisfied that the continuance of this custom is desired by the workers, wages shall be paid regularly at such intervals as will lessen the likelihood of indebtedness among the wage earners.

7. Where food, housing, clothing and other essential supplies and services form part of remuneration, all practicable steps shall be taken by the competent authority to ensure that they are adequate and their cash value properly assessed.

8. All practicable measures shall be taken—

(a) to inform the workers of their wage rights;

(b) to prevent any unauthorised deductions from wages; and

(c) to restrict the amounts deductible from wages in respect of supplies and services forming part of remuneration to the proper cash value thereof.

Article 12. 1. The maximum amounts and manner of repayment of advances on wages shall be regulated by the competent authority.

2. The competent authority shall limit the amount of advances which may be made to a worker in consideration of his taking up employment; the amount of advances permitted shall be clearly explained to the worker.

3. Any advance in excess of the amount laid down by the competent authority shall be legally irrecoverable and may not be recovered by the withholding of amounts of pay due to the worker at a later date.

Article 13. 1. Voluntary forms of thrift shall be encouraged among wage earners and independent producers.

2. All practicable measures shall be taken for the protection of wage earners and independent producers against usury, in particular by action aiming at the reduction of rates of interest on loans, by the control of the operations of money lenders, and by the encouragement of facilities for borrowing money for appropriate purposes through co-operative credit organisations or through institutions which are under the control of the competent authority.

Part V. Non-Discrimination on Grounds of Race, Colour, Sex, Belief, Tribal Association or Trade Union Affiliation

Article 14. 1. It shall be an aim of policy to abolish all discrimination among workers on grounds of race, colour, sex, belief, tribal association or trade union affiliation in respect of—

(a) labour legislation and agreements which shall afford equitable economic treatment to all those lawfully resident or working in the country;

(b) admission to public or private employment;

(c) conditions of engagement and promotion;

(d) opportunities for vocational training;

(e) conditions of work;

(f) health, safety and welfare measures;

(g) discipline;

(h) participation in the negotiation of collective agreements;

(i) wage rates, which shall be fixed according to the principle of equal pay for work of equal value in the same operation and undertaking.

2. All practicable measures shall be taken to lessen, by raising the rates applicable to the lower-paid workers, any existing differences in wage rates due to discrimination by reason of race, colour, sex, belief, tribal association or trade union affiliation.

3. Workers from one country engaged for employment in another country may be granted in addition to their wages benefits in cash or in kind to meet any reasonable personal or family expenses resulting from employment away from their homes.

4. The foregoing provisions of this Article shall be without prejudice to such measures as the competent authority may think it necessary or desirable to take for the safeguarding of motherhood and for ensuring the health, safety and welfare of women workers.

Part VI. Education and Training

Article 15. 1. Adequate provision shall be made to the maximum extent possible under local conditions, for the progressive development of broad systems of education, vocational training and apprenticeship, with a view to the effective preparation of children and young persons of both sexes for a useful occupation.

2. National laws or regulations shall prescribe the school-leaving age and the minimum age for and conditions of employment.

3. In order that the child population may be able to profit by existing facilities for education and in order that the extension of such facilities may not be hindered by a demand for child labour, the employment of persons below the school-leaving age during the hours when the schools are in session shall be prohibited in areas where educational facilities are provided on a scale adequate for the majority of the children of school age.

Article 16. 1. In order to secure high productivity through the development of skilled labour, training in new techniques of production shall be provided in suitable cases.

2. Such training shall be organised by or under the supervision of the competent authorities, in consultation with the employers' and workers' organisations of the country from which the trainees come and of the country of training. . . .

ILO SOCIAL SECURITY (MINIMUM STANDARDS) CONVENTION (1952). Formally entitled Convention (No. 102) Concerning Minimum Standards of Social Security, the convention was adopted on 28 June 1952 by the INTERNATIONAL LABOR CONFERENCE (35th session) and entered into force on 27 April 1955. The text of the convention (*International Labour Conventions and Recommendations, 1919–1981*, p. 533), with the exception of the ILO STANDARD FINAL PROVISIONS (articles 78, 79, and 82–87), and the provisions relating to declarations of application to non-metropolitan territories (articles 80 and 81) made in accordance

with article 35 of the INTERNATIONAL LABOR ORGANIZATION CONSTITUTION, is as follows:

The General Conference of the International Labour Organisation,

Having been convened at Geneva by the Governing Body of the International Labour Office, and having met in its Thirty-fifth Session on 4 June 1952, and

Having decided upon the adoption of certain proposals with regard to minimum standards of social security, which are included in the fifth item on the agenda of the session, and

Having determined that these proposals shall take the form of an international Convention,

adopts this twenty-eight day of June of the year one thousand nine hundred and fifty-two the following Convention, which may be cited as the Social Security (Minimum Standards) Convention, 1952:

Part I. General Provisions

Article 1. 1. In this Convention—

(a) the term "prescribed" means determined by or in virtue of national laws or regulations;

(b) the term "residence" means ordinary residence in the territory of the Member and the term "resident" means a person ordinarily resident in the territory of the Member;

(c) the term "wife" means a wife who is maintained by her husband;

(d) the term "widow" means a woman who was maintained by her husband at the time of death;

(e) the term "child" means a child under school-leaving age or under 15 years of age, as may be prescribed;

(f) the term "qualifying period" means a period of contribution, or a period of employment, or a period of residence, or any combination thereof, as may be prescribed.

2. In Articles 10, 34 and 49 the term "benefit" means either direct benefit in the form of care or indirect benefit consisting of a reimbursement of the expenses borne by the person concerned.

Article 2. Each member for which this Convention is in force—

(a) shall comply with—

(i) Part I;

(ii) at least three of Parts II, III, IV, V, VI, VII, VIII, IX and X, including at least one of Parts IV, V, VI, IX and X;

(iii) the relevant provisions of Parts XI, XII and XIII; and

(iv) Part XIV; and

(b) shall specify in its ratification in respect of which of Parts II to X it accepts the obligations of the Convention.

Article 3. 1. A Member whose economy and medical facilities are insufficiently developed may, if and for so long as the competent authority considers necessary, avail itself, by a declaration appended to its ratification, of the temporary exceptions provided for in the following Articles: 9 (d); 12 (2); 15 (d); 18 (2); 21 (c); 27 (d); 33 (b); 34 (3); 41 (d); 48 (c); 55 (d); and 61 (d).

2. Each Member which has made a declaration under paragraph 1 of this Article shall include in the annual report upon the application of this Convention submitted under article 22 of the Constitution of the International Labour Organisation a statement, in respect of each exception of which it avails itself—

(a) that its reason for doing so subsists; or

(b) that it renounces its right to avail itself of the exception in question as from a stated date.

Article 4. 1. Each Member which has ratified this Convention may subsequently notify the Director-General of the International Labour Office that it accepts the obligations of the Convention in respect of one or more of Parts II to X not already specified in its ratification.

2. The undertakings referred to in paragraph 1 of this Article shall be deemed to be an integral part of the ratification and to have the force of ratification as from the date of notification.

Article 5. Where, for the purpose of compliance with any of the Parts II to X of this Convention which are to be covered by its ratification, a Member is required to protect prescribed classes of persons constituting not less than a specified percentage of employees or residents, the Member shall satisfy itself, before undertaking to comply with any such Part, that the relevant percentage is attained.

Article 6. For the purpose of compliance with Parts II, III, IV, V, VIII (in so far as it relates to medical care), IX or X of this Convention, a Member may take account of protection effected by means of insurance which, although not made compulsory by national laws or regulations for the persons to be protected—

(a) is supervised by the public authorities or administered, in accordance with prescribed standards, by joint operation of employers and workers;

(b) covers a substantial part of the persons whose earnings do not exceed those of the skilled manual male employee; and

(c) complies, in conjunction with other forms of protection, where appropriate, with the relevant provisions of the Convention.

Part II. Medical Care

Article 7. Each Member for which this Part of this Convention is in force shall secure to the persons protected the provision of benefit in respect of a condition requiring medical care of a preventive or curative nature in accordance with the following Articles of this Part.

Article 8. The contingencies covered shall include any morbid condition, whatever its cause, and pregnancy and confinement and their consequences.

Article 9. The persons protected shall comprise—

(a) prescribed classes of employees, constituting not less than 50 per cent. of all employees, and also their wives and children; or

(b) prescribed classes of economically active population, constituting not less than 20 per cent. of all residents, and also their wives and children; or

(c) prescribed classes of residents, constituting not less than 50 per cent. of all residents; or

(d) where a declaration made in virtue of Article 3 is in force, prescribed classes of employees constituting not less than 50 per cent. of all employees in industrial workplaces employing 20 persons or more, and also their wives and children.

Article 10. 1. The benefit shall include at least—

(a) in case of a morbid condition—

(i) general practitioner care, including domiciliary visiting;

(ii) specialist care at hospitals for in-patients and out-patients, and such specialist care as may be available outside hospitals;

(iii) the essential pharmaceutical supplies as prescribed by medical or other qualified practitioners; and

(iv) hospitalisation where necessary; and

(b) in case of pregnancy and confinement and their consequences—

(i) pre-natal, confinement and post-natal care either by medical practitioners or by qualified midwives; and

(ii) hospitalisation where necessary.

2. The beneficiary or his breadwinner may be required to share in the cost of the medical care the beneficiary receives in respect of a morbid condition; the rules concerning such cost-sharing shall be so designed as to avoid hardship.

3. The benefit provided in accordance with this Article shall be afforded with a view to maintaining, restoring or improving the health of the person protected and his ability to work and to attend to his personal needs.

4. The institutions or Government departments administering the benefit shall, by such means as may be deemed appropriate, encourage the persons protected to avail themselves of the general health services placed at their disposal by the public authorities or by other bodies recognised by the public authorities.

Article 11. The benefit specified in Article 10 shall, in a contingency covered, be secured at least to a person protected who has completed, or whose breadwinner has completed, such qualifying period as may be considered necessary to preclude abuse.

Article 12. 1. The benefit specified in Article 10 shall be granted throughout the contingency covered, except that, in case of a morbid condition, its duration may be limited to 26 weeks in each case, but benefit shall not be suspended while a sickness benefit continues to be paid, and provision shall be made to enable the limit to be extended for prescribed diseases recognised as entailing prolonged care.

2. Where a declaration made in virtue of Article 3 is in force, the duration of the benefit may be limited to 13 weeks in each case.

Part III. Sickness Benefit

Article 13. Each member for which this Part of this Convention is in force shall secure to the persons protected the provision of sickness benefit in accordance with the following Articles of this Part.

Article 14. The contingency covered shall include incapacity for work resulting from a morbid condition and involving suspension of earnings, as defined by national laws or regulations.

Article 15. The persons protected shall comprise—

(a) prescribed classes of employees, constituting not less than 50 per cent. of all employees; or

(b) prescribed classes of the economically active population, constituting not less than 20 per cent. of all residents; or

(c) all residents whose means during the contingency do not exceed limits prescribed in such a manner as to comply with the requirements of Article 67; or

(d) where a declaration made in virtue of Article 3 is in force, prescribed classes of employees constituting not less than 50 per cent. of all employees in industrial workplaces employing 20 persons or more.

Article 16. 1. Where classes of employees or classes of the economically active population are protected, the benefit shall be a periodical payment calculated in such a manner as to comply either with the requirements of Article 65 or with the requirements of Article 66.

2. Where all residents whose means during the contingency do not exceed prescribed limits are protected, the benefit shall be a periodical payment calculated in such a manner as to comply with the requirements of Article 67.

Article 17. The benefit specified in Article 16 shall, in a contingency covered, be secured at least to a person protected who has completed such qualifying period as may be considered necessary to preclude abuse.

Article 18. 1. The benefit specified in Article 16 shall be granted throughout the contingency, except that the benefit may be limited to 26 weeks in each case of sickness, in which event it need not be paid for the first three days of suspension of earnings.

2. Where a declaration made in virtue of Article 3 is in force, the duration of the benefit may be limited—

(a) to such period that the total number of days for which the sickness benefit is granted in any year is not less than ten times the average number of persons protected in that year; or

(b) to 13 weeks in each case of sickness, in which event it need not be paid for the first three days of suspension of earnings.

Part IV. Unemployment Benefit

*Article 19.*Each Member for which this Part of this Convention is in force shall secure to the persons protected the provisions of unemployment benefit in accordance with the following Articles of this Part.

Article 20. The contingency covered shall include suspension of earnings, as defined by national laws or regulations, due to inability to obtain suitable employment in the case of a person protected who is capable of, and available for, work.

Article 21. The persons protected shall comprise—

(a) prescribed classes of employees, constituting not less than 50 per cent. of all employees; or

(b) all residents whose means during the contingency do not exceed limits prescribed in such a manner as to comply with the requirements of Article 67; or

(c) where a declaration made in virtue of Article 3 is in force, prescribed classes of employees, constituting not less than 50 per cent. of all employees in industrial workplaces employing 20 persons or more.

Article 22. 1. Where classes of employees are protected, the benefit shall be a periodical payment calculated in such manner as to comply either with the requirements of Article 65 or with the requirements of Article 66.

2. Where all residents whose means during the contingency do not exceed prescribed limits are protected, the benefit shall be a periodical payment calculated in such a manner as to comply with the requirements of Article 67.

Article 23. The benefit specified in Article 22 shall, in a contingency covered, be secured at least to a person protected who has completed such qualifying period as may be considered necessary to preclude abuse.

Article 24. 1. The benefit specified in Article 22 shall be granted throughout the contingency, except that its duration may be limited—

(a) where classes of employees are protected, to 13 weeks within a period of 12 months, or

(b) where all residents whose means during the contingency do not exceed prescribed limits are protected, to 26 weeks within a period of 12 months.

2. Where national laws or regulations provide that the duration of the benefit shall vary with the length of the contribution period and/or the benefit previously received within a prescribed period, the provisions of subparagraph (a) of paragraph 1 shall be deemed to be fulfilled if the average duration of benefit is at least 13 weeks within a period of 12 months.

3. The benefit need not be paid for a waiting period of the first seven days in each case of suspension of earnings, counting days or unemployment before and after temporary employment lasting not more than a prescribed period as part of the same case of suspension of earnings.

4. In the case of seasonal workers the duration of the benefit and the waiting period may be adapted to their conditions of employment.

Part V. Old-Age Benefit

Article 25. Each Member for which this Part of this Convention is in force shall secure to the persons protected the provision of old-age benefit in accordance with the following Articles of this Part.

Article 26. 1. The contingency covered shall be survival beyond a prescribed age.

2. The prescribed age shall be no more than 65 years or such higher age as may be fixed by the competent authority with due regard to the working ability of elderly persons in the country concerned.

3. National laws or regulations may provide that the benefit of a person otherwise entitled to it may be suspended if such person is engaged in any prescribed gainful activity or that the benefit, if contributory, may be reduced where the earnings of the beneficiary exceed a prescribed amount and, if non-contributory, may be reduced where the earnings of the beneficiary or his other means or the two taken together exceed a prescribed amount.

Article 27. The persons protected shall comprise—

(a) prescribed classes of employees, constituting not less than 50 per cent. of all employees; or

(b) prescribed classes of the economically active population, constituting not less than 20 per cent. of all residents; or

(c) all residents whose means during the contingency do not exceed limits prescribed in such a manner as to comply with the requirements of Article 67; or

(d) where a declaration made in virtue of Article 3 is in force, prescribed classes of employees, constituting not less than 50 per cent. of all employees in industrial workplaces employing 20 persons or more.

Article 28. The benefit shall be a periodical payment calculated as follows:

(a) where classes of employees or classes of the economically active population are protected, in such a manner as to comply either with the requirements of Article 65 or with the requirements of Article 66;

(b) where all residents whose means during the contingency do not exceed prescribed limits are protected, in such a manner as to comply with the requirements of Article 67.

Article 29. 1. The benefit specified in Article 28 shall, in a contingency covered, be secured at least—

(a) to a person protected who has completed, prior to the contingency, in accordance with prescribed rules, a qualifying period which may be 30 years of contribution or employment, or 20 years of residence; or

(b) where, in principle, all economically active persons are protected, to a person protected who has completed a prescribed qualifying period of contribution and in respect of whom, while he was of working age, the prescribed yearly average number of contributions has been paid.

2. Where the benefit referred to in paragraph 1 is conditional upon a minimum period of contribution or employment, a reduced benefit shall be secured at least—

(a) to a person protected who has completed, prior to the contingency, in accordance with prescribed rules, a qualifying period of 15 years of contribution or employment; or

(b) where, in principle, all economically active persons are protected, to a person protected who has completed a prescribed qualifying period of contribution and in respect of whom, while he was of working age, half the yearly average number of contributions prescribed in accordance with subparagraph (b) of paragraph 1 of this Article has been paid.

3. The requirements of paragraph 1 of this Article shall be deemed to be satisfied where a benefit calculated in conformity with the requirements of Part XI but at a percentage of ten points lower than shown in the Schedule appended to that Part for the standard beneficiary concerned is secured at least to a person protected who has completed, in accordance with prescribed rules, ten years of contribution or employment, or five years of residence.

4. A proportional reduction of the percentage indicated in the Schedule appended to Part XI may be effected where the qualifying period for the benefit corresponding to the reduced percentage exceeds ten years of contribution or employment but is less than 30 years of contribution or employment; if such qualifying period exceeds 15 years, a reduced benefit shall be payable in conformity with paragraph 2 of this Article.

5. Where the benefit referred to in paragraphs 1, 3 or 4 of this Article is conditional upon a minimum period of contribution or employment, a reduced benefit shall be payable under prescribed conditions to a person protected who, by reason only of his advanced age when the provisions concerned in the application of this Part come into force, has not satisfied the conditions prescribed in accordance with paragraph 2 of this Article, unless a benefit in conformity with the provisions of paragraphs 1, 3 or 4 of this Article is secured to such person at an age higher than the normal age.

Article 30. The benefits specified in Articles 28 and 29 shall be granted throughout the contingency.

Part VI. Employment Injury Benefit

Article 31. Each Member for which this Part of this Convention is in force shall secure to the persons protected the provision of employment injury benefit in accordance with the following Articles of this Part.

Article 32. The contingencies covered shall include the following where due to accident or a prescribed disease resulting from employment:

(a) a morbid condition;

(b) incapacity for work resulting from such a condition and involving suspension of earnings, as defined by national law or regulations;

(c) total loss of earning capacity or partial loss thereof in excess of a prescribed degree, likely to be permanent, or corresponding loss of faculty; and

(d) the loss of support suffered by the widow or child

as the result of the death of the breadwinner; in the case of a widow, the right to benefit may be made conditional on her being presumed, in accordance with national laws or regulations, to be incapable of self-support.

Article 33. The persons protected shall comprise—

(a) prescribed classes of employees, constituting not less than 50 per cent. of all employees, and, for benefit in respect of death of the breadwinner, also their wives and children; or

(b) where a declaration made in virtue of Article 3 is in force, prescribed classes of employees, constituting not less than 50 per cent. of all employees in industrial workplaces employing 20 persons or more, and, for benefit in respect of death of the breadwinner, also their wives and children.

Article 34. 1. In respect of a morbid condition, the benefit shall be medical care as specified in paragraphs 2 and 3 of this Article.

2. The medical care shall comprise—

(a) general practitioner and specialist in-patient care and out-patient care, including domiciliary visiting;

(b) dental care;

(c) nursing care at home or in hospital or other medical institutions;

(d) maintenance in hospitals, convalescent homes, sanatoria or other medical institutions;

(e) dental, pharmaceutical and other medical or surgical supplies, including prosthetic appliances, kept in repair, and eyeglasses; and

(f) the care furnished by members of such other professions as may at any time be legally recognised as allied to the medical profession, under the supervision of a medical or dental practitioner.

3. Where a declaration made in virtue of Article 3 is in force, the medical care shall include at least—

(a) general practitioner care, including domiciliary visiting;

(b) specialist care at hospitals for in-patients and out-patients, and such specialist care as may be available outside hospitals;

(c) the essential pharmaceutical supplies as prescribed by a medical or other qualified practitioner; and

(d) hospitalisation where necessary.

4. The medical care provided in accordance with the preceding paragraphs shall be afforded with a view to maintaining, restoring or improving the health of the person protected and his ability to work and to attend to his personal needs.

Article 35. 1. The institutions or Government departments administering the medical care shall co-operate, wherever appropriate, with the general vocational rehabilitation services, with a view to the re-establishment of handicapped persons in suitable work.

2. National laws or regulations may authorise such institutions or departments to ensure provision for the vocational rehabilitation of handicapped persons.

Article 36. 1. In respect of incapacity for work, total loss of earning capacity likely to be permanent or corresponding loss of faculty, or the death of the breadwinner, the benefit shall be a periodical payment calculated in such a manner as to comply either with the requirements of Article 65 or with the requirements of Article 66.

2. In the case of partial loss of earning capacity likely to be permanent, or corresponding loss of faculty, the benefit, where payable, shall be a periodical payment representing a suitable proportion of that specified for total loss of earning capacity or corresponding loss of faculty.

3. The periodical payment may be commuted for a lump sum—

(a) where the degree of incapacity is slight; or

(b) where the competent authority is satisfied that the lump sum will be properly utilised.

Article 37. The benefit specified in Articles 34 and 36 shall, in a contingency covered, be secured at least to a person protected who was employed in the territory of the Member at the time of the accident if the injury is due to accident or at the time of contracting the disease if the injury is due to a disease and, for periodical payments in respect of death of the breadwinner, to the widow and children of such person.

Article 38. The benefit specified in Article 34 and 36 shall be granted throughout the contingency, except that, in respect of incapacity for work, the benefit need not be paid for the first three days in each case of suspension of earnings.

Part VII. Family Benefit

Article 39. Each Member for which this Part of this Convention is in force shall secure to the persons protected the provision of family benefit in accordance with the following Articles of this Part.

Article 40. The contingency covered shall be responsibility for the maintenance of children as prescribed.

Article 41. The persons protected shall comprise—

(a) prescribed classes of employees, constituting not less than 50 per cent. of all employees; or

(b) prescribed classes of the economically active population, constituting not less than 20 per cent. of all residents; or

(c) all residents whose means during the contingency do not exceed prescribed limits; or

(d) where a declaration made in virtue of Article 3 is in force, prescribed classes of employees, constituting not less than 50 per cent. of all employees in industrial workplaces employing 20 persons or more.

Article 42. The benefit shall be—

(a) a periodical payment granted to any person protected having completed the prescribed qualifying period; or

(b) the provision to or in respect of children, of food, clothing, housing, holidays or domestic help; or

(c) a combination of (a) and (b).

Article 43. The benefit specified in Article 42 shall be secured at least to a person protected who, within a prescribed period, has completed a qualifying period which may be three months of contribution or employment, or one year of residence, as may be prescribed.

Article 44. The total value of the benefits granted in accordance with Article 42 to the persons protected shall be such as to represent—

(a) 3 per cent. of the wage of an ordinary adult male labourer, as determined in accordance with the rules laid down in Article 66, multiplied by the total number of children of persons protected; or

(b) 1.5 per cent. of the said wage, multiplied by the total number of children of all residents.

Article 45. Where the benefit consists of a periodical payment, it shall be granted throughout the contingency.

Part VIII. Maternity Benefit

Article 46. Each Member for which this Part of this Convention is in force shall secure to the persons protected the provision of maternity benefit in accordance with the following Articles of this Part.

Article 47. The contingencies covered shall include pregnancy and confinement and their consequences, and suspension of earnings, as defined by national laws or regulations, resulting therefrom.

Article 48. The persons protected shall comprise—

(a) all women in prescribed classes of employees, which classes constitute not less than 50 per cent. of all employees and, for maternity medical benefit, also the wives of men in these classes; or

(b) all women in prescribed classes of the economically active population, which classes constitute not less than 20 per cent. of all residents, and, for maternity medical benefit, also the wives of men in these classes; or

(c) where a declaration made in virtue of Article 3 is in force, all women in prescribed classes of employees, which classes constitute not less than 50 per cent. of all employees in industrial workplaces employing 20 persons or more, and, for maternity medical benefit, also the wives of men in these classes.

Article 49. 1. In respect of pregnancy and confinement and their consequences, the maternity medical benefit shall be medical care as specified in paragraphs 2 and 3 of this Article.

2. The medical care shall include at least—

(a) pre-natal, confinement and post-natal care either by medical practitioners or by qualified midwives; and

(b) hospitalisation where necessary.

3. The medical care specified in paragraph 2 of this Article shall be afforded with a view to maintaining, restoring or improving the health of the woman protected and her ability to work and to attend to her personal needs.

4. The institutions or Government departments administering the maternity medical benefit shall, by such means as may be deemed appropriate, encourage the women protected to avail themselves of the general health services placed at their disposal by the public authorities or by other bodies recognised by the public authorities.

Article 50. In respect of suspension of earnings resulting from pregnancy and from confinement and their consequences, the benefit shall be a periodical payment calculated in such a manner as to comply either with the requirements of Article 65 or with the requirements of Article 66. The amount of the periodical payment may vary in the course of the contingency, subject to the average rate thereof complying with these requirements.

Article 51. The benefit specified in Articles 49 and 50 shall, in a contingency covered, be secured at least to a woman in the classes protected who has completed such qualifying period as may be considered necessary to preclude abuse, and the benefit specified in Article 49 shall also be secured to the wife of a man in the classes protected where the latter has completed such qualifying period.

Article 52. The benefit specified in Articles 49 and 50 shall be granted throughout the contingency, except that the periodical payment may be limited to 12 weeks, unless a longer period of abstention from work is required or authorised by national laws or regulations, in which event it may not be limited to a period less than such longer period.

Part IX. Invalidity Benefit

Article 53. Each Member for which this Part of this Convention is in force shall secure to the persons protected the provision of invalidity benefit in accordance with the following Articles of this Part.

Article 54. The contingency covered shall include inability to engage in any gainful activity, to an extent prescribed, which inability is likely to be permanent or persists after the exhaustion of sickness benefit.

Article 55. The persons protected shall comprise—

(a) prescribed classes of employees, constituting not less than 50 per cent. of all employees; or

(b) prescribed classes of the economically active population, constituting not less than 20 per cent. of all residents; or

(c) all residents whose means during the contingency do not exceed limits prescribed in such a manner as to comply with the requirements of Article 67; or

(d) where a declaration made in virtue of Article 3 is in force, prescribed classes of employees, constituting not less than 50 per cent. of all employees in industrial workplaces employing 20 persons or more.

Article 56. The benefit shall be a periodical payment calculated as follows:

(a) where classes of employees or classes of the economically active population are protected, in such a manner as to comply either with the requirements of Article 65 or with the requirements of Article 66;

(b) where all residents whose means during the contingency do not exceed prescribed limits are protected, in such a manner as to comply with the requirements of Article 67.

Article 57. 1. The benefit specified in Article 56 shall, in a contingency covered, be secured at least—

(a) to a person protected who has completed, prior to the contingency, in accordance with prescribed rules, a qualifying period which may be 15 years of contribution or employment, or 10 years of residence; or

(b) where, in principle, all economically active persons are protected, to a person protected who has completed a qualifying period of three years of contribution and in respect of whom, while he was of working age, the prescribed yearly average number of contributions has been paid.

2. Where the benefit referred to in paragraph 1 is conditional upon a minimum period of contribution or employment, a reduced benefit shall be secured at least—

(a) to a person protected who has completed, prior to the contingency, in accordance with prescribed rules, a qualifying period of five years of contribution or employment; or

(b) where, in principle, all economically active persons are protected, to a person protected who has completed a qualifying period of three years of contribution and in respect of whom, while he was of working age, half the yearly average number of contributions prescribed in accordance with subparagraph (b) of paragraph 1 of this Article has been paid.

3. The requirements of paragraph 1 of this Article shall be deemed to be satisfied where a benefit calculated in conformity with the requirements of Part XI but at a percentage of ten points lower than shown in the Schedule appended to that Part for the standard beneficiary concerned is secured at least to a person protected who has completed, in accordance with prescribed rules, five years of contributions, employment or residence.

4. A proportional reduction of the percentage indicated in the Schedule appended to Part XI may be effected where the qualifying period for the pension corresponding to the reduced percentage exceeds five years of contribution or employment but is less than 15 years of contribution or employment; a reduced pension shall be payable in conformity with paragraph 2 of this Article.

Article 58. The benefit specified in Article 56 and 57 shall be granted throughout the contingency or until an old-age benefit becomes payable.

Part X. Survivors' Benefit

Article 59. Each Member for which this Part of this Convention is in force shall secure to the persons protected the provision of survivors' benefit in accordance with the following Articles of this Part.

Article 60. 1. The contingency covered shall include the loss of support suffered by the widow or child as the result of the death of the breadwinner; in the case of a widow, the right to benefit may be made conditional on her being presumed, in accordance with national laws or regulations, to be incapable of self-support.

2. National laws or regulations may provide that the benefit of a person otherwise entitled to it may be suspended if such person is engaged in any prescribed gainful activity or that the benefit, if contributory, may be reduced where the earnings of the beneficiary exceed a prescribed amount, and, if non-contributory, may be reduced where the earnings of the beneficiary or his other means or the two taken together exceed a prescribed amount.

Article 61. The persons protected shall comprise—

(a) the wives and the children of breadwinners in prescribed classes of employees, which classes constitute not less than 50 per cent. of all employees; or

(b) the wives and the children of breadwinners in prescribed classes of the economically active population, which classes constitute not less than 20 per cent. of all residents; or

(c) all resident widows and resident children who have lost their breadwinner and whose means during the contingency do not exceed limits prescribed in such a manner as to comply with the requirements of Article 67; or

(d) where a declaration made in virtue of Article 3 is in force, the wives and the children of breadwinners in prescribed classes of employees, which classes constitute not less than 50 per cent. of all employees in industrial workplaces employing 20 persons or more.

Article 62. The benefit shall be a periodical payment calculated as follows:

(a) where classes of employees or classes of the economically active population are protected, in such a manner as to comply either with the requirements of Article 65 or with the requirements of Article 66;

(b) where all residents whose means during the contingency do not exceed prescribed limits are protected, in such a manner as to comply with the requirements of Article 67.

Article 63. 1. The benefit specified in Article 62 shall, in a contingency covered, be secured at least—

(a) to a person protected whose breadwinner has completed, in accordance with prescribed rules, a qualifying period which may be 15 years of contribution or employment, or 10 years of residence; or

(b) where, in principle, the wives and children of all economically active persons are protected, to a person protected whose breadwinner has completed a qualifying period of three years of contribution and in respect of whose breadwinner, while he was of working age, the prescribed yearly average number of contributions has been paid.

2. Where the benefit referred to in paragraph 1 is conditional upon a minimum period of contribution or employment, a reduced benefit shall be secured at least—

(a) to a person protected whose breadwinner has completed, in accordance with prescribed rules, a qualifying period of five years of contribution or employment; or

(b) where, in principle, the wives and children of all economically active persons are protected, to a person protected whose breadwinner has completed a qualifying period of three years of contribution and in respect of whose breadwinner, while he was of working age, half the yearly average number of contributions prescribed in accordance with subparagraph (b) of paragraph 1 of this Article has been paid.

3. The requirements of paragraph 1 of this Article shall be deemed to be satisfied where a benefit calculated in conformity with the requirements of Part XI but a percentage of ten points lower than shown in the Schedule appended to that Part for the standard beneficiary concerned is secured at least to a person protected whose breadwinner has completed, in accordance with prescribed rules, five years of contribution, employment or residence.

4. A proportional reduction of the percentage indicated in the Schedule appended to Part XI may be effected where the qualifying period for the benefit corresponding to the reduced percentage exceeds five years of contribution or employment but is less than 15 years of contribution or employment; a reduced benefit shall be payable in conformity with paragraph 2 of this Article.

5. In order that a childless widow presumed to be incapable of self-support may be entitled to a survivor's benefit, a minimum duration of the marriage may be required.

Article 64. The benefit specified in Articles 62 and 63 shall be granted throughout the contingency.

Part XI. Standards to Be Complied with by Periodical Payments

Article 65. 1. In the case of a periodical payment to which this Article applies, the rate of the benefit, increased by the amount of any family allowances payable during the contingency, shall be such as to attain, in respect of the contingency in question, for the standard beneficiary indicated in the Schedule appended to this Part, at least the percentage indicated therein of the total of the previous earnings of the beneficiary or his breadwinner and of the amount of any family allowances payable to a person protected with the same family responsibilities as the standard beneficiary.

2. The previous earnings of the beneficiary or his breadwinner shall be calculated according to prescribed rules, and, where the persons protected or their breadwinners are arranged in classes according to their earnings, their previous earnings may be calculated from the basic earnings of the classes to which they belonged.

3. A maximum limit may be prescribed for the rate of the benefit or for the earnings taken into account for the calculation of the benefit, provided that the maximum limit is fixed in such a way that the provisions of paragraph 1 of this Article are complied with where he previous earnings of the beneficiary of his breadwinner are equal to or lower than the wage of a skilled manual male employee.

4. The previous earnings of the beneficiary or his breadwinner, the wage of the skilled manual male employee, the benefit and any family allowances shall be calculated on the same time basis.

5. For the other beneficiaries, the benefit shall bear a reasonable relation to the benefit for the standard beneficiary.

6. For the purpose of this Article, a skilled manual male employee shall be—

(a) a fitter or turner in the manufacture of machinery other than electrical machinery; or

(b) a person deemed typical of skilled labour selected in accordance with the provisions of the following paragraph; or

(c) a person whose earnings are such as to be equal to or greater than the earnings of 75 per cent. of all the persons protected, such earnings to be determined on the basis of annual or shorter periods as may be prescribed; or

(d) a person whose earnings are equal to 125 per cent. of the average earnings of all the persons protected.

7. The person deemed typical of skilled labour for the purposes of subparagraph (b) of the preceding paragraph shall be a person employed in the major group of economic activities with the largest number of economically active male persons protected in the contingency in question, or of the breadwinners of the persons protected, as the case may be, in the division comprising the largest number of such persons or breadwinners; for this purpose, the international standard industrial classification of all economic activities, adopted by the Economic and Social Council of the United Nations at its Seventh Session on 27 August 1948, and reproduced in the Annex to this Convention, or such classification as at any time amended, shall be used.

8. Where the rate of benefit varies by region, the skilled manual male employee may be determined for each region in accordance with paragraphs 6 and 7 of this Article.

9. The wage of the skilled manual male employee shall be determined on the basis of the rates of wages for normal hours of work fixed by collective agreements, by or in pursuance of national laws or regulations, where applicable, or by custom, including cost-of-living allowances if any; where such rates differ by region but paragraph 8 of this Article is not applied, the median rate shall be taken.

10. The rates of current periodical payments in respect of old age, employment injury (except in case of incapacity for work), invalidity and death of breadwinner, shall be reviewed following substantial changes in the general level of earnings where these result from substantial changes in the cost of living.

Article 66. 1. In the case of a periodical payment to which this Article applies, the rate of the benefit, increased by the amount of any family allowances payable during the contingency, shall be such as to attain, in respect of the contingency in question, for the standard beneficiary indicated in the Schedule appended to this Part, at least the percentage indicated therein of the total of the wage of an ordinary adult male labourer and of the amount of any family allowances payable to a person protected with the same family responsibilities as the standard beneficiary.

2. The wage of the ordinary adult male labourer, the benefit and any family allowances shall be calculated on the same time basis.

3. For the other beneficiaries, the benefit shall bear a reasonable relation to the benefit for the standard beneficiary.

4. For the purpose of this Article, the ordinary adult male labourer shall be—

(a) a person deemed typical of unskilled labour in the

manufacture of machinery other than electrical machinery; or

(b) a person deemed typical of unskilled labour selected in accordance with the provisions of the following paragraph.

5. The person deemed typical of unskilled labour for the purpose of subparagraph (b) of the preceding paragraph shall be a person employed in the major group of economic activities with the largest number of economically active male persons protected in the contingency in question, or of the breadwinners of the persons protected, as the case may be, in the division comprising the largest number of such persons or breadwinners; for this purpose, the international standard industrial classification of all economic activities, adopted by the Economic and Social Council of the United Nations at its Seventh Session on 27 August 1948, and reproduced in the Annex to this Convention, or such classification as at any time amended, shall be used.

6. Where the rate of benefit varies by region, the ordinary adult male labourer may be determined for each region in accordance with paragraphs 4 and 5 of this Article.

7. The wage of the ordinary adult male labourer shall be determined on the basis of the rates of wages for normal hours of work fixed by collective agreements, by or in pursuance of national laws or regulations, where applicable, or by custom, including cost-of-living allowances if any; where such rates differ by region but paragraph 6 of this Article is not applied, the median rate shall be taken.

8. The rates of current periodical payments in respect of old age, employment injury (except in case of incapacity for work), invalidity and death of breadwinner, shall be reviewed following substantial changes in the general level of earnings where these result from substantial changes in the cost of living.

Article 67. In the case of a periodical payment to which this Article applies—

(a) the rate of the benefit shall be determined according to a prescribed scale or a scale fixed by the competent public authority in conformity with prescribed rules;

(b) such rate may be reduced only to the extent by which the other means of the family of the beneficiary exceed prescribed substantial amounts or substantial amounts fixed by the competent public authority in conformity with prescribed rules;

(c) the total of the benefit and any other means, after deduction of the substantial amounts referred to in subparagraph (b), shall be sufficient to maintain the family of the beneficiary in health and decency, and shall be not less than the corresponding benefit calculated in accordance with the requirements of Article 66;

(d) the provisions of subparagraph (c) shall be deemed to be satisfied if the total amount of benefits paid under the Part concerned exceeds by at least 30 per cent. the total amount of benefits which would be obtained by applying the provisions of Article 66 and the provisions of:

(i) Article 15 (b) for Part III;

(ii) Article 27 (b) for Part V;

(iii) Article 55 (b) for Part IX;

(iv) Article 61 (b) for Part X. . . .

Part XII. Equality of Treatment of Non-National Residents

Article 68. 1. Non-national residents shall have the same rights as national residents: Provided that special rules concerning non-nationals and nationals born outside the territory of the Member may be prescribed in respect of

benefits or portions of benefits which are payable wholly or mainly out of public funds and in respect of transitional schemes.

2. Under contributory social security schemes which protect employees, the persons protected who are nationals of another Member which has accepted the obligations of the relevant Part of the Convention shall have, under that Part, the same rights as nationals of the Member concerned: Provided that the application of this paragraph may be made subject to the existence of a bilateral or multilateral agreement providing for reciprocity.

Part XIII. Common Provisions

Article 69. A benefit to which a person protected would otherwise be entitled in compliance with any of Parts II to X of this Convention may be suspended to such extent as may be prescribed—

(a) as long as the person concerned is absent from the territory of the Member;

(b) as long as the person concerned is maintained at public expense, or at the expense of a social security institution or service, subject to any portion of the benefit in excess of the value of such maintenance being granted to the dependants of the beneficiary;

(c) as long as the person concerned is in receipt of another social security cash benefit, other than a family benefit, and during any period in respect of which he is indemnified for the contingency by a third party, subject to the part of the benefit which is suspended not exceeding the other benefit or the indemnity by a third party;

(d) where the person concerned has made a fraudulent claim;

(e) where the contingency has been caused by a criminal offence committed by the person concerned;

(f) where the contingency has been caused by the wilful misconduct of the person concerned;

(g) in appropriate cases, where the person concerned neglects to make use of the medical or rehabilitation services placed at his disposal or fails to comply with rules prescribed for verifying the occurrence or continuance of the contingency or for the conduct of beneficiaries;

(h) in the case of unemployment benefit, where the person concerned has failed to make use of the employment services placed at his disposal;

(i) in the case of unemployment benefit, where the person concerned has lost his employment as a direct result of a stoppage of work due to a trade dispute, or has left it voluntarily without just cause; and

(j) in the case of survivors' benefit, as long as the widow is living with a man as his wife.

Article 70. 1. Every claimant shall have a right of appeal in case of refusal of the benefit or complaint as to its quality or quantity.

2. Where in the application of this Convention a Government department responsible to a legislature is entrusted with the administration of medical care, the right of appeal provided for in paragraph 1 of this Article may be replaced by a right to have a complaint concerning the refusal of medical care or the quality of the care received investigated by the appropriate authority.

3. Where a claim is settled by a special tribunal established to deal with social security questions and on which the persons protected are represented, no right of appeal shall be required.

Article 71. 1. The cost of the benefits provided in compliance with this Convention and the cost of the administration of such benefits shall be borne collectively by way of insurance contributions or taxation or both in a manner which avoids hardship to persons of small means and takes into account the economic situation of the Member and of the classes of persons protected.

2. The total of the insurance contributions borne by the employees protected shall not exceed 50 per cent. of the total of the financial resources allocated to the protection of employees and their wives and children. For the purpose of ascertaining whether this condition is fulfilled, all the benefits provided by the Member in compliance with this Convention, except family benefit and, if provided by a special branch, employment injury benefit, may be taken together.

3. The Member shall accept general responsibility for the due provision of the benefits provided in compliance with this Convention, and shall take all measures required for this purpose; it shall ensure, where appropriate, that the necessary actuarial studies and calculations concerning financial equilibrium are made periodically and, in any event, prior to any change in benefits, the rate of insurance contributions, or the taxes allocated to covering the contingencies in question.

Article 72. 1. Where the administration is not entrusted to an institution regulated by the public authorities or to a Government department responsible to a legislature, representatives of the persons protected shall participate in the management, or be associated therewith in a consultative capacity, under prescribed conditions; national laws or regulations may likewise decide as to the participation of representatives of employers and of the public authorities.

2. The Member shall accept general responsibility for the proper administration of the institutions and services concerned in the application of the Convention.

Part XIV. Miscellaneous Provisions

Article 73. This Convention shall not apply to—

(a) contingencies which occurred before the coming into force of the relevant Part of the Convention for the Member concerned;

(b) benefits in contingencies occurring after the coming into force of the relevant Part of the Convention for the Member concerned in so far as the rights to such benefits are derived from periods preceding that date.

Article 74. This Convention shall not be regarded as revising any existing Convention.

Article 75. If any Convention which may be adopted subsequently by the Conference concerning any subject or subjects dealt with in the Convention so provides, such provisions of this Convention as may be specified in the said Convention shall cease to apply to any Member having ratified the said Convention as from the date at which the said Convention comes into force for that Member.

Article 76. 1. Each Member which ratifies this Convention shall include in the annual report upon the application of this Convention submitted under article 22 of the Constitution of the International Labour Organisation—

(a) full information concerning the laws and regulations by which effect is given to the provisions of the Convention; and

(b) evidence, conforming in its presentation as closely as is practicable with any suggestions for greater uniformity of presentation made by the Governing Body of the International Labour Office, of compliance with the statistical conditions specified in—

(i) Articles 9 (a), (b), (c) or (d); 15 (a), (b) or (d); 21 (a) or (c); 27 (a), (b) or (d); 33 (a) or (b); 41 (a), (b) or (d); 48 (a), (b) or (c); 55 (a), (b) or (d); 61 (a), (b) or (d), as regards the number of persons protected;

(ii) Articles 44, 65, 66 or 67, as regards the rates of benefit;

(iii) subparagraph (a) of paragraph 2 of Article 18, as regards duration of sickness benefit;

(iv) paragraph 2 of Article 24, as regards duration of unemployment benefit; and

(v) paragraph 2 of Article 71, as regards the proportion of the financial resources constituted by the insurance contributions of employees protected.

2. Each Member which ratifies this Convention shall report to the Director-General of the International Labour Office at appropriate intervals, as requested by the Governing Body, on the position of its law and practice in regard to any of Parts II to X of the Convention not specified in its ratification or in a notification made subsequently in virtue of Article 4.

Article 77. 1. This Convention does not apply to seamen or seafishermen; provision for the protection of seamen and seafishermen has been made by the International Labour Conference in the Social Security (Seafarers) Convention, 1946, and the Seafarers' Pensions Convention, 1946.

2. A Member may exclude seamen and seafishermen from the number of employees, of the economically active population or of residents, when calculating the percentage of employees or residents protected in compliance with any of Parts II to X covered by its ratification. . . .

SEE ALSO *European Code of Social Security and Protocol; European Convention on Social Security; ILO Equality of Treatment (Social Security) Convention; Social Security.*

ILO STANDARD FINAL PROVISIONS. During the first ten sessions of the INTERNATIONAL LABOR CONFERENCE, the final provisions of the conventions adopted varied widely. Beginning with the 11th session (1928), however, the conference framed the final provisions of all conventions in a form that became standardized under six main headings: ratifications, entry into force, denunciations, notification of ratification to members, examination of revision, and authoritative texts. In 1929, the conference added a seventh standard final provision, relating to the effect of revision of the convention; and, in 1946, an eighth was added, relating to notification of ratification to the Secretary-General of the United Nations.

Brief references to these standard final provisions may be found at the end of many ILO conventions reproduced in the present publication. The texts of the provisions are as follows:

Standard Final Provisions

Ratifications. The formal ratifications of this Convention shall be communicated to the Director-General of the International Labour Office for registration.

Entry into Force. 1. This Convention shall be binding only upon those Members of the International Labour Organisation whose ratifications have been registered with the Director-General.

2. It shall come into force twelve months after the date on which the ratifications of two Members have been registered with the Director-General.

3. Thereafter, this Convention shall come into force for any Member twelve months after the date on which its ratification has been registered.

Denunciation. 1. A Member which has ratified this Convention may denounce it after the expiration of ten years from the date on which the Convention first comes into force, by an act communicated to the Director-General of the International Labour Office for registration. Such denunciation shall not take effect until one year after the date on which it is registered.

2. Each Member which has ratified this Convention and which does not, within the year following the expiration of the period of ten years mentioned in the preceding paragraph, exercise the right of denunciation provided for in this Article, will be bound for another period of ten years and, thereafter, may denounce this Convention at the expiration of each period of ten years under the terms provided for in this Article.

Notification of Ratifications to Members. 1. The Director-General of the International Labour Office shall notify all Members of the International Labour Organisation of the registration of all ratifications and denunciations communicated to him by the Members of the Organisation.

2. When notifying the Members of the Organisation of the registration of the second ratification communicated to him, the Director-General shall draw the attention of the Members of the Organisation to the date upon which the Convention will come into force.

Communication to the United Nations. The Director-General of the International Labour Office shall communicate to the Secretary-General of the United Nations for registration in accordance with article 102 of the Charter of the United Nations full particulars of all ratifications and acts of denunciation registered by him in accordance with the provisions of the preceding Articles.

Note: This provision does not appear in Conventions Nos. 1–67. However, it is made applicable to these Conventions by Article 1, paragraph 3, of the Final Articles Revision Convention, 1946 (No. 80).

Examination of Revision. At such times as it may consider necessary the Governing Body of the International Labour Office shall present to the General Conference a report on the working of this Convention and shall examine the desirability of placing on the agenda of the Conference the question of its revision in whole or in part.

Note: In Conventions Nos. 1–98 this provision originally provided for reports by the Governing Body every ten years after entry into force. It was replaced in these Conventions by the present text, under the terms of the Final Articles Revision Convention. 1961 (No. 116).

Effect of Revising Convention. 1. Should the Conference adopt a new Convention revising this Convention in whole or in part, then, unless the new Convention otherwise provides—

(a) the ratification by a Member of the new revising Convention, shall *ipso jure* involve the immediate denunciation of this Convention, notwithstanding the provisions of Article 3 above, if and when the new revising Convention shall have come into force;

(b) as from the date when the new revising Conven-

tion comes into force this Convention shall cease to be open to ratification by the Members.

2. This Convention shall in any case remain in force in its actual form and content for those Members which have ratified it but have not ratified the revising Convention.
Note: This provision does not appear in Conventions Nos. 1–26. Conventions Nos. 27–33 do not contain the words "then, unless the new Convention otherwise provides".

Authoritative Texts. The English and French versions of the text of this Convention are equally authoritative.
Note: In Conventions Nos. 1–67 this provision reads "The French and English texts of this Convention shall both be authentic."

ILO WORKERS' REPRESENTATIVES CONVENTION (1971).

Formally entitled Convention (No. 135) concerning Protection and Facilities to be Afforded to Workers' Representatives in the Undertaking, the convention reinforces two basic conventions relating to trade union rights: the ILO FREEDOM OF ASSOCIATION AND PROTECTION OF THE RIGHT TO ORGANIZE CONVENTION, 1948, and the ILO RIGHT TO ORGANIZE AND COLLECTIVE BARGAINING CONVENTION, 1949. It aims at ensuring that the representatives of workers are protected against dismissal or other discriminatory acts because of their status or activities and puts responsibility upon employers to provide those representatives with facilities which will enable them to perform their functions promptly and efficiently.

The convention was adopted by the INTERNATIONAL LABOR CONFERENCE (56th session) on 23 June 1971 and entered into force on 30 June 1973. The text of the convention (*International Labour Conventions and Recommendation, 1919–1981*, page 9), with the exception of the ILO STANDARD FINAL PROVISIONS (articles 7–14), is as follows:

The General Conference of the International Labour Organisation,

Having been convened at Geneva by the Governing Body of the International Labour Office, and having met in its fifty-sixth session on 2 June 1971, and

Noting the terms of the Right to Organise and Collective Bargaining Convention, 1949, which provides for protection of workers against acts of anti-union discrimination in respect of their employment, and

Considering that it is desirable to supplement these terms with respect to workers' representatives, and

Having decided upon the adoption of certain proposals with regard to protection and facilities afforded to workers' representatives in the undertaking, which is the fifth item on the agenda of the session, and

Having determined that these proposals shall take the form of an international Convention,

Adopts this twenty-third day of June of the year one thousand nine hundred and seventy-one the following Convention, which may be cited as the Workers' Representatives Convention, 1971:

Article 1. Workers' representatives in the undertaking

shall enjoy effective protection against any act prejudicial to them, including dismissal, based on their status or activities as a workers' representative or on union membership or participation in union activities, in so far as they act in conformity with existing laws or collective agreements or other jointly agreed arrangements.

Article 2. 1. Such facilities in the undertaking shall be afforded to workers' representatives as may be appropriate in order to enable them to carry out their functions promptly and efficiently.

2. In this connection account shall be taken of the characteristics of the industrial relations system of the country and the needs, size and capabilities of the undertaking concerned.

3. The granting of such facilities shall not impair the efficient operation of the undertaking concerned.

Article 3. For the purpose of this Convention the term "workers' representatives" means persons who are recognised as such under national law or practise, whether they are:

(a) trade union representatives, namely, representatives designated or elected by trade unions or by the members of such unions; or

(b) elected representatives, namely, representatives who are freely elected by the workers of the undertaking in accordance with provisions of national laws or regulations or of collective agreements and whose functions do not include activities which are recognised as the exclusive prerogative of trade unions in the country concerned.

Article 4. National laws or regulations, collective agreements, arbitration awards or court decisions may determine the type or types of workers' representatives which shall be entitled to the protection and facilities provided for in this Convention.

Article 5. Where there exist in the same undertaking both trade union representatives and elected representatives, appropriate measures shall be taken, wherever necessary, to ensure that the existence of elected representatives is not used to undermine the position of the trade unions concerned or their representatives and to encourage co-operation on all relevant matters between the elected representatives and the trade unions concerned and their representatives.

Article 6. Effect may be given to this Convention through national laws or regulations or collective agreements, or in any other manner consistent with national practice. . . .

ILO WORKERS WITH FAMILY RESPONSIBILITIES CONVENTION (1981).

Formally entitled Convention (No. 156) concerning Equal Opportunities and Equal Treatment for Men and Women Workers with Family Responsibilities, the convention was adopted by the INTERNATIONAL LABOR CONFERENCE (67th session) on 23 June 1981 and entered into force on 11 June 1983. It updates the ILO DISCRIMINATION (EMPLOYMENT AND OCCUPATION) CONVENTION, 1958, taking into account the perceived need for a change in the traditional role of men, as well as in the role of women in society and in the family, as a prerequisite to the achievement of full equality between men and women.

The text of the convention (*International Labour Conventions and Recommendations, 1919–1981,* page 52), with the exception of the ILO STANDARD FINAL PROVISIONS (articles 12–19) is as follows:

The General Conference of the International Labour Organisation,

Having been convened at Geneva by the Governing Body of the International Labour Office and having met in its Sixty-seventh Session on 3 June 1981, and

Noting the Declaration of Philadelphia concerning the Aims and Purposes of the International Labour Organisation which recognises that "all human beings, irrespective of race, creed or sex, have the right to pursue their material well-being and their spiritual development in conditions of freedom and dignity, of economic security and equal opportunity", and

Noting the terms of the Declaration of Equality of Opportunity and Treatment for Women Workers and of the resolution concerning a plan of actions with a view to promoting equality of opportunity and treatment for women workers, adopted by the International Labour Conference in 1975, and

Noting the provisions of international labour Conventions and Recommendations aimed at ensuring equality of opportunity and treatment for men and women workers, namely the Equal Remuneration Convention and Recommendation, 1951, the Discrimination (Employment and Occupation) Convention and Recommendation, 1958, and Part VIII of the Human Resources Development Recommendation, 1975, and

Recalling that the Discrimination (Employment and Occupation) Convention, 1958, does not expressly cover distinctions made on the basis of family responsibilities, and considering that supplementary standards are necessary in this respect, and

Noting the terms of the Employment (Women with Family Responsibilities) Recommendation, 1965, and considering the changes which have taken place since its adoption, and

Noting that instruments on equality of opportunity and treatment for men and women have also been adopted by the United Nations and other specialised agencies, and recalling, in particular, the fourteenth paragraph of the Preamble of the United Nations Convention on the Elimination of All Forms of Discrimination against Women, 1979, to the effect that States Parties are "aware that a change in the traditional role of men as well as the role of women in society and in the family is needed to achieve full equality between men and women", and

Recognising that the problems of workers with family responsibilities are aspects of wider issues regarding the family and society which should be taken into account in national policies, and

Recognising the need to create effective equality of opportunity and treatment as between men and women workers with family responsibilities and between such workers and other workers, and

Considering that many of the problems facing all workers are aggravated in the case of workers with family responsibilities and recognising the need to improve the conditions of the latter both by measures responding to their special needs and by measures designed to improve the conditions of workers in general, and

Having decided upon the adoption of certain proposals

with regard to equal opportunities and equal treatment for men and women workers: workers with family responsibilities, which is the fifth item on the agenda of the session, and

Having determined that these proposals shall take the form of an international Convention,

adopts this twenty-third day of June of the year one thousand nine hundred and eighty-one the following Convention, which may be cited as the Workers with Family Responsibilities Convention, 1981:

Article 1. 1. This Convention applies to men and women workers with responsibilities in relation to their dependent children, where such responsibilities restrict their possibilities of preparing for, entering, participating in or advancing in economic activity.

2. The provisions of this Convention shall also be applied to men and women workers with responsibilities in relation to other members of their immediate family who clearly need their care or support, where such responsibilities restrict their possibilities of preparing for, entering, participating in or advancing in economic activity.

3. For the purposes of this Convention, the terms "dependent child" and "other members of the immediate family who clearly needs care or support" mean persons defined as such in each country by one of the means referred to in Article 9 of this Convention.

4. The workers covered by virtue of paragraphs 1 and 2 of this Article are hereinafter referred to as "workers with family responsibilities".

Article 2. This Convention applies to all branches of economic activity and all categories of workers.

Article 3. 1. With a view to creating effective equality of opportunity and treatment for men and women workers, each Member shall make it an aim of national policy to enable persons with family responsibilities who are engaged or wish to engage in employment to exercise their right to do so without being subject to discrimination and, to the extent possible, without conflict between their employment and family responsibilities.

2. For the purposes of paragraph 1 of this Article, the term "discrimination" means discrimination in employment and occupation as defined by Articles 1 and 5 of the Discrimination (Employment and Occupation) Convention, 1958.

Article 4. With a view to creating effective equality of opportunity and treatment for men and women workers, all measures compatible with national conditions and possibilities shall be taken—

(a) to enable workers with family responsibilities to exercise their right to free choice of employment; and

(b) to take account of their needs in terms and conditions of employment and in social security.

Article 5. All measures compatible with national conditions and possibilities shall further be taken—

(a) to take account of the needs of workers with family responsibilities in community planning; and

(b) to develop or promote community services, public or private, such as child-care and family services and facilities.

Article 6. The competent authorities and bodies in each country shall take appropriate measures to promote information and education which engender broader public understanding of the principle of equality of opportunity and treatment for men and women workers and of the problems of workers with family responsibilities, as well as a climate of opinion conducive to overcoming these problems.

Article 7. All measures compatible with national conditions and possibilities, including measures in the field of vocational guidance and training, shall be taken to enable workers with family responsibilities to become and remain integrated in the labour force, as well as to re-enter the labour force after an absence due to those responsibilities.

Article 8. Family responsibilities shall not, as such, constitute a valid reason for termination of employment.

Article 9. The provisions of this Convention may be applied by laws or regulations, collective agreements, work rules, arbitration awards, court decisions or a combination of these methods, or in any other manner consistent with national practice which may be appropriate, account being taken of national conditions.

Article 10. 1. The provisions of this Convention may be applied by stages if necessary, account being taken of national conditions: Provided that such measures of implementation as are taken shall apply in any case to all the workers covered by Article 1, paragraph 1.

2. Each Member which ratifies this Convention shall indicate in the first report on the application of the Convention submitted under article 22 of the Constitution of the International Labour Organisation in what respect, if any, it intends to make use of the faculty given by paragraph 1 of this Article, and shall state in subsequent reports the extent to which effect has been given or is proposed to be given to the Convention in that respect.

Article 11. Employers' and workers' organisations shall have the right to participate, in a manner appropriate to national conditions and practice, in devising and applying measures designed to give effect to the provisions of this Convention. . . .

SEE ALSO *Women Workers: ILO Plan of Action on Equality of Opportunity and Treatment of Men and Women in Employment.*

ILO WORKING ENVIRONMENT (AIR POLLUTION, NOISE AND VIBRATION) CONVENTION

(1977). Formally entitled Convention (No. 148) concerning the Protection of Workers against Occupational Hazards in the Working Environment Due to Air Pollution, Noise and Vibration, the convention requires States parties to take measures for the prevention and control of, and protection against, occupational hazards in the working environment due to air pollution, noise, and vibration. They may accept the obligations of the convention separately in respect of each of the three hazards.

The convention was adopted by the INTERNATIONAL LABOR CONFERENCE (63d session) on 20 June 1977 and entered into force on 11 July 1979. The text of the convention (*International Labour Conventions and Recommendations, 1919–1981*, page 408), with the exception of the ILO STANDARD FINAL PROVISIONS (articles 17, 18, and 20–24), and article 19, which provides for denunciation of the Convention "in whole or in respect of one or more of the categories of hazards referred to in article 2 thereof," is as follows:

The General Conference of the International Labour Organisation,

Having been convened at Geneva by the Governing Body of the International Labour Office and having met in its Sixty-third Session on 1 June 1977, and

Noting the terms of existing international labour Conventions and Recommendations which are relevant and, in particular, the Protection of Workers' Health Recommendation, 1953, the Occupational Health Services Recommendation, 1959, the Radiation Protection Convention and Recommendation, 1960, the Guarding of Machinery Convention and Recommendation, 1963, the Employment Injury Benefits Convention, 1964, the Hygiene (Commerce and Offices) Convention and Recommendation, 1964, the Benzene Convention and Recommendation, 1971, and the Occupational Cancer Convention and Recommendation, 1974, and

Having decided upon the adoption of certain proposals with regard to working environment: atmospheric pollution, noise and vibration, which is the fourth item on the agenda of the session, and

Having determined that these proposals shall take the form of an international Convention,

adopts this twentieth day of June of the year one thousand nine hundred and seventy-seven the following Convention, which may be cited as the Working Environment (Air Pollution, Noise and Vibration) Convention, 1977:

Part I. Scope and Definitions

Article 1. 1. This Convention applies to all branches of economic activity.

2. A Member ratifying this Convention may, after consultation with the representative organisations of employers and workers concerned, where such exist, exclude from the application of the Convention particular branches of economic activity in respect of which special problems of a substantial nature arise.

3. Each Member which ratifies this Convention shall list in the first report on the application of the Convention submitted under article 22 of the Constitution of the International Labour Organisation any branches which may have been excluded in pursuance of paragraph 2 of this Article, giving the reasons for such exclusion, and shall state in subsequent reports the position of its law and practice in respect of the branches excluded, and the extent to which effect has been given or is proposed to be given to the Convention in respect of such branches.

Article 2. 1. Each Member, after consultation with the representative organisations of employers and workers, where such exists, may accept the obligations of this Convention separately in respect of—

(a) air pollution;

(b) noise; and

(c) vibration.

2. A Member which does not accept the obligations of the Convention in respect of one or more of the categories of hazards shall specify this in its ratification and shall give reasons in the first report on the application of the Convention submitted under article 22 of the Constitution of the International Labour Organisation; it shall state in subsequent reports the position of its law and practice in respect of the category or categories of hazards excluded and the extent to which effects has been given or is proposed to be given to the Convention in respect of each such category of hazards.

3. Each Member which has not on ratification accepted the obligations of this Convention in respect of all the categories of hazards shall subsequently, when it is satisfied that conditions permit this, notify the Director-General of the International Labour Office that it accepts the obligations of the Convention in respect of a category or categories previously excluded.

Article 3. For the purpose of this Convention—

(a) the term "air pollution" covers all air contaminated by substances, whatever their physical state, which are harmful to health or otherwise dangerous;

(b) the term "noise" covers all sound which can result in hearing impairment or be harmful to health or otherwise dangerous;

(c) the term "vibration" covers any vibration which is transmitted to the human body through solid structures and is harmful to health or otherwise dangerous.

Part II. General Provisions

Article 4. 1. National laws or regulations shall prescribe that measures be taken for the prevention and control of, and protection against, occupational hazards in the working environment due to air pollution, noise and vibration.

2. Provisions concerning the practical implementation of the measures so prescribed may be adopted through technical standards, codes of practice and other appropriate methods.

Article 5. 1. In giving effect to the provisions of this Convention, the competent authority shall act in consultation with the most representative organisations of employers and workers concerned.

2. Representatives of employers and workers shall be associated with the elaboration of provisions concerning the practical implementation of the measures prescribed in pursuance of Article 4.

3. Provision shall be made for as close a collaboration as possible at all levels between employers and workers in the application of the measures prescribed in pursuance of this Convention.

4. Representatives of the employer and representatives of the workers of the undertaking shall have the opportunity to accompany inspectors supervising the application of the measures prescribed in pursuance of this Convention, unless the inspectors consider, in the light of the general instructions of the competent authority, that this may be prejudicial to the performance of their duties.

Article 6. 1. Employers shall be made responsible for compliance with the prescribed measures.

2. Whenever two or more employers undertake activities simultaneously at one workplace, they shall have the duty to collaborate in order to comply with the prescribed measures, without prejudice to the responsibility of each employer for the health and safety of his employees. In appropriate circumstance, the competent authority shall prescribe general procedures for this collaboration.

Article 7. 1. Workers shall be required to comply with safety procedures relating to the prevention and control of, and protection against, occupational hazards due to air pollution, noise and vibration in the working environment.

2. Workers or their representatives shall have the right to present proposals, to obtain information and training and to appeal to appropriate bodies so as to ensure protection against occupational hazards due to air pollution, noise and vibration in the working environment.

Part III. Preventive and Protective Measures

Article 8. 1. The competent authority shall establish criteria for determining the hazards of exposure to air pollution, noise and vibration in the working environment and, where appropriate, shall specify exposure limits on the basis of these criteria.

2. In the elaboration of the criteria and the determination of the exposure limits the competent authority shall take into account the opinion of technically competent persons designated by the most representative organisations of employers and workers concerned.

3. The criteria and exposure limits shall be established, supplemented and revised regularly in the light of current national and international knowledge and data, taking into account as far as possible any increase in occupational hazards resulting from simultaneous exposure to several harmful factors at the workplace.

Article 9. As far as possible, the working environment shall be kept free from any hazard due to air pollution, noise or vibration—

(a) by technical measures applied to new plant or processes in design or installation, or added to existing plant or processes; or, where this is not possible,

(b) by supplementary organisational measures.

Article 10. Where the measures taken in pursuance of Article 9 do not bring air pollution, noise and vibration in the working environment within the limits specified in pursuance of Article 8, the employer shall provide and maintain suitable personal protective equipment. The employer shall not require a worker to work without the personal protective equipment provided in pursuance of this Article.

Article 11. 1. There shall be supervision at suitable intervals, on conditions and in circumstances determined by the competent authority, of the health of workers exposed or liable to be exposed to occupational hazards due to air pollution, noise or vibration in the working environment. Such supervision shall include a preassignment medical examination and periodical examinations, as determined by the competent authority.

2. The supervision provided for in paragraph 1 of this Article shall be free of cost to the worker concerned.

3. Where continued assignment to work involving exposure to air pollution, noise or vibration is found to be medically inadvisable, every effort shall be made, consistent with national practice and conditions, to provide the worker concerned with suitable alternative employment or to maintain his income through social security measures or otherwise.

4. In implementing this Convention, the rights of workers under social security or social insurance legislation shall not be adversely affected.

Article 12. The use of processes, substances, machinery and equipment, to be specified by the competent authority, which involve exposure of workers to occupational hazards in the working environment due to air pollution, noise or vibration, shall be notified to the competent authority and the competent authority, as appropriate, may authorise the use on prescribed conditions or prohibit it.

Article 13. All persons concerned shall be adequately and suitably—

(a) informed of potential occupational hazards in the working environment due to air pollution, noise and vibration; and

(b) instructed in the measures available for the pre-

vention and control of, and protection against, those hazards.

Article 14. Measures taking account of national conditions and resources shall be taken to promote research in the field of prevention and control of hazards in the working environment due to air pollution, noise and vibration.

Part IV. Measures of Application

Article 15. On conditions and in circumstances determined by the competent authority, the employer shall be required to appoint a competent person, or use a competent outside service or service common to several undertakings, to deal with matters pertaining to the prevention and control of air pollution, noise and vibration in the working environment.

Article 16. Each Member shall—

(a) by laws or regulations or any other method consistent with national practice and conditions take such steps, including the provision of appropriate penalties, as may be necessary to give effect to the provisions of this Convention;

(b) provide appropriate inspection services for the purpose of supervising the application of the provisions of this Convention, or satisfy itself that appropriate inspection is carried out. . . .

SEE ALSO ILO *Labor Inspection Convention;* ILO *Occupational Safety and Health Convention.*

IMPRISONMENT: TRANSFER AND TREATMENT OF FOREIGN PRISONERS. The Seventh United Nations Congress on the Prevention of Crime and the Treatment of Offenders, held in Milan from 26 August to 6 September 1985, recognized the difficulties confronting foreigners detained in prison establishments abroad owing to such factors as differences in language, culture, customs, and religion and expressed the view that the social resettlement of offenders could best be achieved by giving foreign prisoners the opportunity to serve their sentence within their country of nationality or residence.

The congress accordingly prepared and adopted (1) the Model Agreement on the Transfer of Foreign Prisoners, and (2) a series of recommendations on the treatment of foreign prisoners (United Nations publication, Sales No. E.86.IV.2, chap. D [1] and [2]), both of which are reproduced below.

The congress invited member States to take the Model Agreement and the recommendations into account in dealing with questions relating to foreign prisoners. The General Assembly endorsed its decisions on 29 November 1985 (resolution 40/32).

Model Agreement on the Transfer of Foreign Prisoners
Preamble

The _____ and the
_____,

Desirous of further developing mutual co-operation in the field of criminal justice,

Believing that such co-operation should further the ends of justice and the social resettlement of sentenced persons,

Considering that those objectives require that foreigners who are deprived of their liberty as the result of a criminal offence should be given the opportunity to serve their sentences within their own society,

Convinced that this aim can best be achieved by transferring foreign prisoners to their own countries,

Bearing in mind that the full respect for human rights, as laid down in universaly recognized principles, should be ensured,

Have agreed on the following:

I. General Principles

1. The social resettlement of offenders should be promoted by facilitating the return of persons convicted of crime abroad to their country of nationality or of residence to serve their sentence at the earliest possible stage. In accordance with the above, States should afford each other the widest measure of co-operation.

2. A transfer of prisoners should be effected on the basis of mutual respect for national sovereignty and jurisdiction.

3. A transfer of prisoners should be effected in cases where the offence giving rise to conviction is punishable by deprivation of liberty by the judicial authorities of both the sending (sentencing) State and the State to which the transfer is to be effected (administering State) according to their national laws.

4. A transfer may be requested by either the sentencing or the administering State. The prisoner, as well as close relatives, may express to either State their interest in the transfer. To that end, the contracting State shall inform the prisoner of their competent authorities.

5. A transfer shall be dependent on the agreement of both the sentencing and the administering State, and should also be based on the consent of the prisoner.

6. The prisoner shall be fully informed of the possibility and of the legal consequences of a transfer, in particular whether or not he might be prosecuted because of other offences committed before his transfer.

7. The administering State should be given the opportunity to verify the free consent of the prisoner.

8. Any regulation concerning the transfer of prisoners shall be applicable to sentences of imprisonment as well as to sentences imposing measures involving deprivation of liberty because of the commission of a criminal act.

9. In cases of the person's incapability of freely determining his will, his legal representative shall be competent to consent to the transfer.

II. Other Requirements

10. A transfer shall be made only on the basis of a final and definitive sentence having executive force.

11. At the time of the request for a transfer, the prisoner shall, as a general rule, still have to serve at least six months of the sentence; a transfer should, however, be granted also in cases of indeterminate sentences.

12. The decision whether to transfer a prisoner shall be taken without any delay.

13. The person transferred for the enforcement of a sentence passed in the sentencing State may not be tried again in the administering State for the same act upon which the sentence to be executed is based.

III. Procedural Regulations

14. The competent authorities of the administering State shall: (a) continue the enforcement of the sentence immediately or through a court or administrative order; or (b) convert the sentence, thereby substituting for the sanction imposed in the sentencing State a sanction prescribed by the law of the administering State for a corresponding offence.

15. In the case of continued enforcement, the administering State shall be bound by the legal nature and duration of the sentence as determined by the sentencing State. If, however, this sentence is by its nature or duration incompatible with the law of the administering State, this State may adapt the sanction to the punishment or measure prescribed by its own law for a corresponding offence.

16. In the case of conversion of sentence, the administering State shall be entitled to adapt the sanction as to its nature or duration according to its national law, taking into due consideration the sentence passed in the sentencing State. A sanction involving deprivation of liberty shall, however, not be converted to a pecuniary sanction.

17. The administering State shall be bound by the findings as to the facts in so far as they appear from the judgement imposed in the sentencing State. Thus the sentencing State has the sole competence for a review of the sentence.

18. The period of deprivation of liberty already served by the sentenced person in either State shall be fully deducted from the final sentence.

19. A transfer shall in no case lead to an aggravation of the situation of the prisoner.

20. Any costs incurred because of a transfer and related to transportation should be borne by the administering State, unless otherwise decided by both the sentencing and administering States.

IV. Enforcement and Pardon

21. The enforcement of the sentence shall be governed by the law of the administering State.

22. Both the sentencing and the administering State shall be competent to grant pardon and amnesty.

V. Final Clauses

23. This agreement shall be applicable to the enforcement of sentences imposed either before or after its entry into force.

24. This agreement is subject to ratification. The instruments of ratification shall be deposited as soon as possible in _____.

25. This agreement shall enter into force on the thirtieth day after the day on which the instruments of ratification are exchanged.

26. Either Contracting Party may denounce this agreement in writing to the _____. Denunciation shall take effect six months following the date on which the notification is received by the _____.

In witness whereof the undersigned, being duly authorized thereto by the respective Governments, have signed this treaty.

Recommendations on the Treatment of Foreign Prisoners

1. The allocation of a foreign prisoner to a prison establishment should not be effected on the grounds of his nationality alone.

2. Foreign prisoners should have the same access as national prisoners to education, work and vocational training.

3. Foreign prisoners should in principle be eligible for measures alternative to imprisonment, as well as for prison leave and other authorized exits from prison according to the same principles as nationals.

4. Foreign prisoners should be informed promptly after reception into a prison, in a language which they understand and generally in writing, of the main features of the prison régime, including relevant rules and regulations.

5. The religious precepts and customs of foreign prisoners should be respected.

6. Foreign prisoners should be informed without delay of their right to request contacts with their consular authorities, as well as of any other relevant information regarding their status. If a foreign prisoner wishes to receive assistance from a diplomatic or consular authority, the latter should be contacted promptly.

7. Foreign prisoners should be given proper assistance, in a language they can understand, when dealing with medical or programme staff and in such matters as complaints, special accommodation, special diets and religious representation and counselling.

8. Contacts of foreign prisoners with families and community agencies should be facilitated, by providing all necessary opportunities for visits and correspondence, with the consent of the prisoner. Humanitarian international organizations, such as the International Committee of the Red Cross, should be given the opportunity to assist foreign prisoners.

9. The conclusion of bilateral and multilateral agreements on supervision of and assistance to offenders given suspended sentences or granted parole could further contribute to the solution of the problems faced by foreign offenders.

IMPUNITY: NGO REACTION. In a communication circulated as an official document to the UN COMMISSION ON HUMAN RIGHTS in February 1988 (UN Doc. E/CN.4/1988/NGO/51), 18 non-governmental organizations in consultative status with the Economic and Social Council expressed their deep concern about indiscriminate amnesty laws which provide what they described as impunity to repressive forces responsible for gross violations of human rights. The communication reads as follows:

We, concerned non-governmental organizations, have noted an alarming trend in many parts of the world: civilian Governments, and in some cases the military themselves, are allowing virtual impunity to repressive forces which have been responsible for crimes of torture, "disappearance", murder—in some cases to the point of genocide—and other human rights violations.

This impunity has been accomplished through various means: amnesty laws granted by Governments, constitutional statutes and decrees, and the simple *de facto* method of failure by Governments to implement existing laws. We call this cluster of methods immunity because it places criminals above the law and leaves crimes unpunished, which in essence reinforces these patterns of behaviour by military, paramilitary and security forces and gives them

the freedom to continue these practices, or to threaten to do so.

At the trial of Klaus Barbie, the Nazi criminal, it was clear that the end of the Second World War and the passage of 40 years did not diminish the horror of the atrocities committed nor the necessity for justice to be done. Yet under national security doctrines and counter-insurgency programmes, crimes of great magnitude have also been carried out more recently in many countries, and in others are still being carried out.

In a number of countries in Latin America, Africa and Asia, civilian Governments have in fact absolved or ignored the crimes of armies and individuals, and are still doing so in some cases. This effort is explained as necessary to consolidate democracy or avoid more bloodshed. In other countries where military rule still exists, although there are loudly proclaimed moves towards democracy, military rulers have taken measures to avoid ever being prosecuted for human rights violations. Sometimes, these provisions for impunity have been taken to the level of the national constitutions or "legalized" in national law. Often, in fact, civilian Governments and new "democracies" are subservient to former military rulers precisely because impunity has been granted to them by these Governments.

We state very firmly that the issue is larger than a single nation's constitution or internal law. It is an issue of international human rights law. Since the Nürnberg trials following the Second World War, international law has been clear on the necessity for the military of each country to respect the principles of human rights. The 1984 United Nations Convention against Torture and Other Cruel, Inhuman or Degrading Treatment or Punishment, in upholding the Nürnberg decision concerning the use of torture, stated: "No exceptional circumstances whatsoever, whether a state of war or a threat of war, internal political instability or any other public emergency, may be invoked as a justification of torture." Other international standards uphold absolute respect for human rights, including the International Convention on Civil and Political Rights and the 1968 Convention on the Non-Applicability of Statutory Limitations to War Crimes and Crimes against Humanity. Yet, the kinds of impunity laws being granted to military and repressive forces place them above international law and thus threaten all of civilization.

It has been argued that granting this sort of impunity is a necessary price for establishing democracy. While we welcome the transition to constitutional rule in countries which have suffered serious violations of human rights by armies in power, we see this as only the first step towards real democracy. We believe that laws granting impunity, rather than consolidating democracy, in fact weaken constitutional rule and may open the way for its reversal by a defiant army. These laws prevent justice from being done and allow powerful military forces to continue their domination behind the scenes through a persistent climate of intimidation and terror. Moreover, they perpetuate the bitter divisions that have plagued society. Democracy is more than formal elections or the turning over of government from military forces to civilians. Democracy must mean, among other things, an effective set of laws and a judiciary that can hold accountable criminals and violators of human rights. There can be no real democracy in a society where there is no justice, where murderers and torturers go free, where victims can achieve no legitimate rights for their loved ones and there is no accounting of what happened.

We believe that this issue, due to its magnitude, deserves

the attention of the Commission on Human Rights. Some background work has been done by non-governmental organizations, human rights organizations, concerned individuals and this coalition, but we consider it necessary for the United Nations to start addressing this problem. In this sense we suggest the following measures:

1. Approval of a resolution expressing concern for indiscriminate amnesty and laws and measures leading to impunity;

2. Appointment of an *ad hoc* group of experts to study the consequences for human rights of granting impunity laws and decrees to repressive forces, expanding the work of document E/CN.4/Sub.2/1987/16 on the administration of justice and the human rights of detainees, particularly the practice of administrative detention without charge or trial;

3. Request to the Sub-Commission on Prevention of Discrimination and Protection of Minorities to analyze the problem in death, as it has affected many peoples;

4. Reaffirmation of existing international law covering crimes against humanity, and work towards a convention to prevent impunity for these crimes.

We know that full implementation of the measures here could take a long time, but we feel it is necessary for the United Nations to send a visible signal to all concerned, especially to the peoples who have suffered widespread and gross violations of human rights. Civilian Governments must see that the world cares and supports their efforts to democratize. Victims of past repression must see others join their demand for justice. Military and repressive forces must see that they cannot act with impunity and trample international and national law as well as respect for human rights.

SEE ALSO *Convention on the Non-Applicability of Statutory Limitations to War Crimes and Crimes against Humanity; Principles of International Law Recognized in the Charter of the Nurmberg Tribunal and in the Judgment of the Tribunal; War Crimes File; War Criminals: Prosecution and Punishment.*

INDIA. The Republic of India is a country in southern Asia occupying most of the Indian sub-continent, located between the Arabian Sea and the Bay of Bengal; it also includes three groups of islands: the Andamans (204 islands) and the Nicobars (19 islands) in the Bay of Bengal and the Laccadives (14 islands) in the Arabian Sea. It has borders with Bangladesh, Bhutan, China, Myanmar, Nepal, and Pakistan. It achieved independence from Great Britain in 1947 and became a member of the United Nations in 1945. Its population is estimated by the UN (1990) to be 827,152,000. Ethnic groups include Indo–Aryan (72%), Dravidian (25%), and Mongoloid (2%). The population also includes members of "scheduled castes" and "scheduled tribes," for which special provisions are included in the 1950 constitution with the aim of helping them to attain equality in real terms; these provisions, and a wide variety of special programs and measures undertaken by the government, are not considered by the government to violate the

principle of equality but rather to benefit all the peoples of India. Over 200 languages are in common use, including Hindi (official) and 14 languages recognized in the constitution: Assamese, Bengali, Gujarati, Kannada, Kannarese, Kashmiri, Malayam, Marathi, Oriya, Punjabi, Sindhi, Tamil, Telegu, and Urdu. Religions practiced include Hinduism (83%), Islam (11%), Christianity (3%), Animism (1%), and others including the Sikh, Jain, Parsi, and Buddhist faiths (2%). Literacy is estimated at 40%.

The government (1990) took the form of a republic and member of the Commonwealth of Nations, of which the British sovereign is the symbolic head. It is described in the constitution as "a Sovereign, Socialist, Secular, Democratic Republic." The president, elected by popular vote for a term of five years, is head of State. He appoints, and is advised by, the prime minister and cabinet, who represent the party or coalition given a majority in a popular election. Parliament is bicameral, consisting of the Council of States *(Rajya Sabha)* and the House of the People *(Lok Sabha)*. Members of the Council of States represent the constituent units of the republic: 22 states and nine union territories. Members of the House of the People are elected by popular vote for terms of five years. Political parties include the Congress Party, the Lok Dal Party, the Congress II Party, the Communist Party and the Communist Party of India.

History has made India the home of people with diverse origin, many of whom came from beyond the country's borders. Hinduism, Buddhism, Jainism and later Sikhism were faiths cradled by India. Christianity, in the coastal regions of Western India, goes back to apostolic times. Islam came to India within the first century of its emergence. India is thus composed of a wonderful mosaic of different religions and cultures. It has a tolerant, eclectic society where people of many different faiths and persuasions have joined together in building the world's largest democracy, a democracy in which universally recognized human rights and fundamental freedoms are guaranteed to all without any discrimination on grounds of creed or community. At the time of the 1981 census the total population of India was 683,997,512. Since 1971 it had shown an increase of 24.78 per cent. The census mentions that over 1,500 languages are spoken in the country. Of these 15 are specified and recognized in the VIIIth schedule of the Constitution; 90 per cent of the Indian population speaks one of these 15 languages.

In spite of the diversity, India is the largest democracy in the world where elections are held periodically on the basis of universal and equal adult franchise; and article 325 of the constitution provides that no person shall be ineligible for inclusion in the general electoral roll on grounds only of religion, race, caste, sex, or any of them. Indian citizens enjoy the right to participate in public affairs, and all Indians have equal access to employment in the public services. While guaranteeing these rights, the constitution provides for reservations in favor of the scheduled castes and tribes and other disadvantaged classes.

India's traditional lack of any sort of unity—physical, political, social, linguistic, or religious—periodically gives rise to serious human rights problems. Controlled by force during the early years of British colonial rule, which began in 1757, these problems multiplied soon after World War I when the All–India Congress Party, led by Mohandas K. Gandhi, spearheaded non-violent but effective revolts against British authority. The party's main demand was for a measure of self-government for india, which had sent more than six million troops into the war. The British responded in 1919 by giving India a federal form of government and a measure of self-rule.

In 1942, as Japanese troops approached India's eastern borders, the Congress Party demanded that the British leave India. In an effort to avoid further confrontations, the Indian government arrested Gandhi and other party leaders and announced its determination to transfer power to "responsible Indian hands" by June 1948 even if a constitution recognizing Indian independence had not been completed by that time.

In June 1947, Lord Mountbatten, as viceroy, reached an agreement on independence which called for the partitioning of British India into two dominions: India, with a Hindu majority, and Pakistan, with a Moslem majority. Two provinces, Bengal and the Punjab, which the Moslems had claimed, were to be split between the two new states. The Indian Independence Act was quickly adopted by the British Parliament and received royal assent on 8 July 1947. On 15 August, the Indian empire passed into history.

The resultant flight of large groups of Hindus and Moslems who suddenly found themselves in hostile territory was accompanied by the outright murder of millions of refugees as communal passions exceeded all bounds. The hostility between India and newly established Pakistan was subsequently aggravated by warfare over the princely states of Hyderabad and Kashmir.

In today's India, the most persistent human rights problem relates to the situation of the "scheduled castes" and "scheduled tribes," designated as such by presidential orders in accordance with articles 341 and 342 of the constitution. According to the 1981 census, the population of scheduled castes was 104,754,623

and that of scheduled tribes was 51,628,638; together they comprise about 24% of the country's population.

In a report submitted to the United Nations on 26 June 1986 (UN Doc. CERD/C/149/Add. 11, para. 14–22), the government of India stated that:

The Constitution prescribes protection and safeguards for the scheduled castes and scheduled tribes and other weaker sections, either specially or by way of insisting on their general rights as citizens, with the object of promoting their educational and economic interests and of removing the social disabilities. The main safeguards are:

(i) Abolition of "untouchability" and forbidding of its practice in any form (art. 17);

(ii) Promotion of their educational and economic interests and their protection from social injustice and all forms of exploitation (art. 46);

(iii) Throwing open by law of Hindu religious institutions of a public character to all classes and sections of Hindus (art. 25b);

(iv) Removal of any disability, liability, restriction or condition with regard to access to shops, public restaurants, hotels and places of public entertainment or the use of wells, tanks, bathing ghats, roads and places of public resort maintained wholly or partially out of State funds or dedicated to the use of the general public (art. 15(2));

(v) Curtailment by law in the interests of any scheduled tribe, of the general rights of all citizens to move freely, reside and settle in any part of India (art. 19(5));

(vi) Permitting the State to make reservation for the backward classes in public services in case of inadequate representations and requiring the State to consider the claims of the scheduled castes and scheduled tribes in the making of appointments to public services (arts. 16 and 335);

(vii) Reservation of seats in the *Lok Sabha* and the State Legislatures *(vidhan sabhas)* to scheduled castes and tribes (arts. 330, 332 and 334);

(viii) The setting up of tribes advisory councils and separate departments in the states and the appointment of a special officer at the centre to promote their welfare and safeguard their interests (arts. 244 and 338 and 5th Schedule);

(ix) Special provision for the administration and control of scheduled and tribal areas (art. 244 and 5th and 6th Schedules); and

(x) Prohibition of traffic in human beings and forced labour (art. 23).

To enlarge the scope and make the penal provision more stringent, the Untouchability (Offences) Act, 1955 was comprehensively amended by the Untouchability (Offences) Amendment and Miscellaneous Provisions Act, 1976, which came into force from 19 November 1976. With this amendment, the name of the principal Act has been changed to the Protection of Civil Rights Act, 1955. The Act provides penalties for preventing a person, on the ground of untouchability, from enjoying the rights accruing out of abolition of untouchability. Enhanced penalties/punishment have also been provided for subsequent offences.

Under section 8 of the Representation of the People Act, 1951, a person who is convicted of an offence under the Act is disqualified from contesting elections to Parliament and State legislatures for a period of six years commencing from the date of such conviction.

The Protection of Civil Rights Act, 1955, is administered by the state governments also from time to time. Under a provision in the Act, the Government also lays before each House of Parliament an annual report on the working of the provisions of section 15A of the Act.

Under articles 330 and 332 of the Constitution, seats are reserved for scheduled castes and scheduled tribes in the *Lok Sabha* or the Lower House of Parliament and State *vidhan sabhas* or legislatures in proportion to their population. This concession was initially for a period of 10 years from the commencement of the Constitution but has been extended, through amendments up to 25 January 1990. Parliamentary Acts provide for such reservations in the Union territories having legislatures. Following the introduction of *panchayati raj,* safeguards have been provided for proper representation of the members of the scheduled castes and tribes by reserving seats for them in the *gram panchayats* and other local bodies.

Article 335 of the Constitution provides that the claims of the members of the scheduled castes and scheduled tribes shall be taken into consideration, consistent with the maintenance of efficiency of administration, in making appointments to posts and services, in connection with the affairs of the Union or of a state. Article 16(4) permits reservation in favour of citizens of backward classes, who may not be adequately represented in services. In pursuance of these provisions, the Government has made reservations for scheduled castes and scheduled tribes in the services under their control.

A Commission for the scheduled castes and scheduled tribes consisting of a chairman and four members, including the special officer appointed under article 338 of the Constitution known as the Commissioner for Scheduled Castes and Scheduled Tribes, was set up in August 1978. The Commission is to investigate all matters relating to Constitutional safeguards, reservation in public services; to study the implementation of the Protection of Civil Rights Act, 1955, with particular reference to the objective of removal of untouchability and invidious discrimination arising therefrom; and to ascertain the socio-economic and other relevant circumstances responsible for the commission of offences against persons belonging to scheduled castes and tribes with a view to recommending appropriate remedial measures.

A number of voluntary organizations also promote the welfare of the scheduled castes and scheduled tribes. Important organizations of all-India character are: Harijan Sevak Sangh, Delhi; Bharatiya Depressed Classes League, New Delhi; Ishwar Saran Ashram, Allahabad; Indian Red Cross Society, New Delhi; Hind Sweepers Sevak Samaj, New Delhi; Ramakrishnan Mission, Narendrapur, West Bengal; Bharatiya Adimjati Sevak Sangh, New Delhi; Andhra Rashtra Adimjati Sevak Sangh, Nellore, Remakrishna Mission, Cheerapunchi, Ranchi, Puri, Silchar and Shillong; Thakkar Bapa Ashram, Numakhandi, Orissa; Servants of India Society, Pune; and Social Work and Research Centre, Tilonia, Rajasthan.

Government provides grants-in-aid to non-official voluntary organizations working among scheduled castes and scheduled tribes.

In addition, the Indian government sponsors a plan for rehabilitation of freed bonded laborers, started in 1978, which provides for matching assistance to the extent of 50% of the total cost subject to a ceiling of 2,000 rupees per bonded laborer. The individual state governments have been asked to treat the program as a national program for the effective and permanent rehabilitation of identified and freed bonded labor. By 30 September 1983, 158,946 bonded laborers had been identified and freed; of these, 116,917 had been rehabilitated.

Nevertheless, despite the government's efforts to end BONDED LABOR schemes, the practice continues to be a major human rights problem. The ANTI-SLAVERY SOCIETY FOR THE PROTECTION OF HUMAN RIGHTS, a nongovernmental organization in consultative status, submitted the following information to the WORKING GROUP ON CONTEMPORARY FORMS OF SLAVERY at the working group's 1988 session (UN Doc. E/CN.4/Sub.2/AC.2/1988/7/Add.1):

In its report to the Working Group on Slavery last year, the Anti-Slavery Society pointed out that it had several times raised the issue of bonded labour in India in the United Nations. On each occasion, the official response, as relayed by the Indian representative on the Sub-Commission on Prevention of Discrimination and Protection of Minorities, was that the problem was being resolved with all the despatch and vigour that Delhi and the State capitals could command. Therefore there was no cause for concern.

The Anti-Slavery Society maintains there is cause for concern. India is not the only country where debt bondage occurs, but it is home to the largest number of bonded labourers in the world. By extrapolation, and using the 1983 judgement of the Supreme Court of India, those trapped in debt bondage could form 10 per cent of the population: 80 million bonded labourers, the greatest number of contemporary slaves on the face of the earth.

The Anti-Slavery Society has recently finished its own investigation into the malleable nature of contemporary bonded labour, particularly as it affects the landless in and migrating from Bihar.

Bihar has been described as being India's most feudal State. Thousands of Biharis migrate to economically more advanced areas every year, and frequently they are forced to do so by the village money-lender. This may sometimes lead to the debtor being able, eventually, to pay off his debt because the money he earns away from his home and family is significantly more than is available in Bihar. Until the loan is repaid in full, the debtor is in bondage and his family form a living surety for his return or repayment.

North Bihar provides seasonal workers for Punjab's agrarian sector. These come from the scheduled castes. South Bihar annually provides some 10,000 migrant workers drawn from the scheduled tribes. These become agricultural workers bonded to creditor-employers or labour contractors in Punjab itself.

Share-cropping continues to be a means of entrapping borrowers into debt bondage. Land ownership in Bihar is unequal—72 per cent of cultivators own fewer than five acres—and the 1961 Bihar Land Reform Act had the unintended consequence of increasing dependence on large landowners. Tenants were evicted and re-engaged as simple share-croppers.

A poor peasant farmer may become a share-cropper

when, during a lean period, he falls further into debt and his land is taken in lieu of unredeemed loans. He then joins the ranks of the landless.

A landless labourer or a poor peasant with insufficient land may be forced through circumstance and the lack of alternative local employment to share-crop for a large landlord or rich peasant. He becomes indebted to his "partner" through taking out loans, in cash or in kind, in order to perform his role as a share-cropper.

The eventual result is an increase in debt bondage.

It is the view of the Anti-Slavery Society that the introduction of new technology in the more economically advanced States, particularly in Punjab and Haryana, has aggravated and not relieved the age-old condition of debt bondage in India. This development, allied with traditional practices and obligations, has resulted in an increase in contemporary slavery.

The Anti-Slavery Society repeats its pleas of previous years made in this Working Group, and urges the Government of India to take all measures not only to free its most vulnerable people from slavery, but to ensure freed bonded labourers receive the full rehabilitation sums due to them under the 1976 Bonded Labour (Abolition) Act.

Of particular concern is the problem of child bonded labor, especially in the carpetmaking industry. Child carpet weavers, usually boys below the age of 15, are reported to suffer from practices similar to slavery. In its 1988 report to the Working Group on Contemporary Forms of Slavery, the Anti-Slavery Society for the Protection of Human Rights furnished the following information:

Professor B.N. Juyal quotes Shridar Mishra, a leading figure in India's carpet-making industry, as saying that the Government is considering proposals "to raise the minimum wages on the pretext of regulating the wages of bonded child workers, which shall prove suicidal to the development of the industry."

This is revealing on two counts: it implies ruthless employment practices and it explicitly admits the existence of bonded child labour.

Carpet-making is an officially designated hazardous industry and, consequently, children are prohibited from working in it by article 24 of the Constitution and by the 1938 Employment of Children Act.

Even under the much-criticized new legislation, the Child Labour (Regulation) Act, 1986, children are prohibited from making carpets except as part of a family labour force and in familial conditions.

The Anti-Slavery Society's latest research into labour conditions in the Mirzapur-Varanasi-Bhadohi carpet belt in the State of Uttar Pradesh reveals that school-age boys are being employed in contravention of the law, and that they are underpaid (if paid at all), ill-treated, badly fed, unhealthy, kept illiterate and innumerate, kidnapped and sold deliberately or naively into bondage.

India today has at least 100,000 juvenile carpet-making slaves. They are slaves as defined by the United Nations 1956 Supplementary Convention on the Abolition of Slavery, the Slave Trade and Institutions and Practices similar to Slavery because:

(a) They suffer gross labour exploitation;
(b) They are below the age of 15;

(c) 15 per cent of them are aged between 6 and 11;
(d) Some of them have been sold into debt bondage.

It is difficult to know the precise number of bonded children. It is certain that in the main they come from the scheduled casts and scheduled tribes of Bihar, and that sometimes they are kidnapped. When this occurs, the parents do not even receive the approximately £25 which is the common advance on the wages their children will supposedly earn.

In addition, the "industry" is composed of some 55,000 looms located in about 15,000 villages scattered over a large area. The loom owners in fact are frequently tied to specific manufacturers who have advanced them the money to buy the loom. Because they are one-man-and-a-couple-of-boys operations, they do not even have to register under either the Factory Act or the Shops and Establishment Act. These unregistered premises account for 95 per cent of the carpet belt's production.

The boys working at the looms are passed off as sons or nephews, and this in spite of about half the child labour force having been brought in from other areas.

What is greatly disturbing is that the Indian authorities not only know about the gross exploitation of the carpet-making boys, are not only aware of the daily and wholesale contravention of legislation, but they may be regarded as being originally responsible for this contemporary form of slavery. In 1975, the Government set up training centres for children who were required to work over six hours a day and so denied schooling. In 1981, the Government claimed to be turning out 30,000 child carpet-makers under the age of 15.

A recital of statistics does not convey the misery of exploited child labour.

The Anti-Slavery Society appreciates the difficulties involved in eradicating exploitative child labour in the carpet industry. It does not advocate emancipation in a void; accordingly, it is proud to announce the founding of Project Mala.

Project Mala aims to raise the standard of life and the future expectations of children working in the carpet industry by offering them benefits which are in fact guaranteed under the Indian Constitution: education, training, health and an adequate diet. Although it is only boys who work at the looms, Project Mala will not discriminate sexually, and girls will be entitled to equal benefit.

It is intended to set up six schools during the next three years. Each school will serve a cluster of villages so that children will be able to walk to and from school each day. One of the schools will, however be a boarding school to cater for those children who have been "imported", by whatever means, from further afield. This boarding school will almost certainly be established in the Palamau region on the Uttar Pradesh-Bihar border, since it is from there that the majority of bonded children come.

The school day will be divided into two: one half will be devoted to basic education along the Gandhian lines and the other half to vocational training of an appropriate kind. For the boys, this vocational training may indeed centre on carpet-weaving but girls will learn other skills which will help them to generate their own incomes and thus relieve them from utter dependency on their menfolk. By education along Gandhian lines is meant a learning process which will be relevant to the children's circumstances and way of life, rather than an externally imposed system to which they would find it difficult to relate.

Great importance will be attached to personal hygiene

and, since tuberculosis is endemic in the region, children will be regularly screened so that the disease can be caught in its earliest stages when it is relatively easy to cure. Care for the children's health will be reinforced by the good, well-balanced midday meal which will be provided in all the schools. In the boarding school all meals as well as decent accommodation will be provided.

The conditions in which the weavers work, and this applies to adults as well as to children, are usually very bad. The weaving huts are badly lit, with poor ventilation, and the looms themselves are usually of rudimentary and inefficient design. The Intermediate Technology Group has been asked to advise on improvements to both the looms and the huts. It is hoped that this will result in much better working conditions, as well as a reduction in the quantity of rejected carpets. This improved efficiency will increase significantly the income from each loom as well as providing a better quality of goods.

Children are driven to difficult work by a simple economic necessity. The weavers are usually poor farmers who turn to carpet-making to eke out a penurious living during slack seasons or when harvests are poor. Now that there is an increased demand for carpets, weaving tends to occupy more of a family's time and it is this increased demand which has given rise to abuses such as the sale or kidnapping of children. Essentially, it is sheer poverty, allied to the lack of educational and other facilities, which drives children to work. Without the children's income most families would be hard put to it to survive.

Project Mala takes account of this economic necessity by paying a stipend to each child in school and this stipend will increase annually so that the family will suffer no loss of income; indeed, with girls as well as boys benefiting in this way, a family's income should be significantly greater. It is hoped that this simple economic fact will help overcome the inherent conservatism of the villagers and that they will accept the opportunity for improving their children's chances in life which Project Mala offers.

The scheme is unique in that it brings together for the first time a group of voluntary organizations, the State Government of Uttar Pradesh and representatives of the carpet industry. The scheme also enjoys the blessing of the Union Ministry of Labour in Delhi and is attracting the interest and support of both the British Overseas Development Administration and the European Community in Brussels. The International Labour Organisation is also following the scheme's progress with interest and with its moral support.

A site for the first school has been found near Mirzapur. The buildings already *in situ* are readily adaptable for the purposes of the school, vocational training centre and other facilities. Project Mala should have its first school in operation by the end of the year, and it is hoped that this collaborative effort may serve as a model for similar schemes in other industries and, perhaps, in other countries.

Although India, unlike many third world countries, has succeeded in preserving its constitutional democracy and has improved its national income, its health standards, and its production of food, the improvements have not kept pace with the rapid increase in its population. Observance of the 40th anniversary of India's independence on 15 August 1987 evoked a flood of soul-searching introspection about its future.

One problem is the declining efficiency of the civil service bureaucracy; once so well trained that it was able to assume the responsibilities of government overnight when the British left the country, it has been wracked by disclosures of systematic bribery, illicit kickback payments, and tax evasion. Another is that the separation of church and State, enshrined in the constitution, has been threatened by resurgencies of domination by the Hindu majority and by clashes between religious extremists and the government. A third is that little, if any, new leadership has emerged to fight for reform and to compel the nation to pay more attention to the plight of its poor and deprived. A fourth is that the Congress Party, which since the days of Mahatma Gandhi held the confidence and respect of the Indian people, seems to have lost some of its mass support.

In recent years, one of India's major human rights problems have involved antagonisms between religious groups. In 1984, Prime Minister Indira Ghandi ordered a military invasion of the Golden Temple in Amritsar to rout out military Sikhs who had occupied it, demanding restoration of their civil rights. Four months later, she was assassinated by her Sikh bodyguards. Her son and successor, Rajiv Ghandi, fought a continuous and sometimes successful battle against Sikh terrorists but never won their trust. Prime Minister V.P. Singh, who took office in December 1989, journeyed to Amritsar to pray at the Golden Temple as his first official trip outside New Delhi and set up a non-partisan conference to deal with the Sikh demands for an independent homeland to be known as Khalistan.

In Kashmir Valley, a predominantly Muslim territory largely occupied by India, there have been frequent attacks on Indian officials and installations by militants demanding the withdrawal of Indian troops and the holding of a United Nations-supervised plebescite. India has persistently refused to permit such a plebescite in its part of the Muslim-majority valley; however Pakistan, which occupies the remainder, strongly favors it, knowing that Kashmir's population feels strongly bound to it by ties of religion.

Islamic militancy has swept through Kashmir Valley on the ground that India has failed to make good its promises of economic development and better links with the outside world. Calling themselves "Allah's Tigers," long-unemployed young men have taken to roaming the streets of Srinagar in groups, halting the sale of alcoholic drinks, and monitoring the dress of women. Their stated aim is restoration of the human rights of the Kashmiri people and ending what they term the Indian "reign of terror."

INDIAN COUNCIL OF SOUTH AMERICA. An international non-governmental organization in consultative status (Roster) with the UN Economic and Social Council, best known by its Spanish title *Consejo Indio de Sudamérica (CISA)*, the council is affiliated with 15 organizations in 10 American countries.

Established in 1980 with the participation of delegations from 10 South American countries, CISA works to promote and secure the human rights of Indians of Latin America, to improve the economies of Indian communities, and to regain territory taken from indigenous peoples. CISA publishes *Pueblo Indio* (in Peruvian and international editions) and *Boletín Informativo CISA* (in Spanish).

Indian Council of South America. Address: Av. J. de Canterac 373, Apdo Postal 2054, Correo Central, Lima 100, Peru. Telephone: 236955. Coordinator General: Asunción Ontiveros Yulquila.

INDIGENOUS POPULATIONS CONVENTION: ILO ACTION. The action taken by the International Labor Organization to revise the ILO Indigenous and Tribal Populations Convention, 1957 (No. 107), shows how work continues on formerly established and accepted documents in order to bring them up-to-date with changing world conditions and attitudes. These deliberations are described in a statement (UN Doc. E/CN.4/Sub.2/AC.4/1988/3/Add.1) submitted to the 1988 session of the WORKING GROUP ON INDIGENOUS POPULATIONS by the International Labor Office, as follows:

At its 75th Session, in June 1988, the International Labour Conference held the first of two discussions leading to the revision of the ILO Indigenous and Tribal Populations Convention, 1957 (No. 107). The Committee appointed by the Conference met from 2 to 18 June, and its report was adopted by the Conference in plenary session on 21 June.

The Committee's report (Conference Provisional Record No. 32) includes a summary of its deliberations. The Committee had before it proposed conclusions prepared by the International Labour Office on the basis of consultations with the ILO's constituents. The Committee's deliberations comprised a general discussion, followed by an examination of the proposed conclusions point by point. The Office is now preparing a draft revised Convention on the basis of the conclusions adopted by the Committee. This draft will be sent to all member States in early August 1988, for their comments and for the comments of workers' and employers' organisations, in accordance with the ILO's tripartite structure. Their replies will be due on 30 November 1988, and on the basis of the replies received a second draft of the Convention will be circulated in March 1989. These two documents will be placed before the Conference at its 76th Session, beginning on 7 June 1989, for the second and final discussion.

At the 76th Session of the Conference, the same procedures will be followed. A special committee will be established to discuss the question, meeting throughout the Conference. Its report and a draft revised Convention will be submitted to the plenary Session of the Conference for adoption, which must be by a two-thirds vote.

In accordance with the ILO Constitution, when the revised Convention is adopted by the Conference in 1989, it must be submitted to the "competent authorities" of each member State within a year (or at most 18 months) after its adoption, "for the enactment of legislation or other action" (article 19, para. 5 of the Constitution). This means that the revised Convention will be put before the legislative authority of each country, along with a recommendation by the Government of what action should be taken on it. Information must then be supplied to the ILO on the measures taken.

It is expected that the Conference will decide in 1989 that Convention No. 107 will be closed to further ratifications, when the revised Convention comes into force (that is, when it is ratified by a specified minimum number of countries, usually two). Convention No. 107 would, however, remain in force for countries which have ratified it but not ratified the revised Convention.

Finally, when the report was put before the plenary of the Conference for adoption, a representative of the Indian Council of South America spoke in the name of several other NGOs in putting on the official record of the Conference the views of these NGOs. Another speaker, a native American who was a member of the employers' delegation from a member State, also spoke very movingly and convincingly to the Conference to support the report and ask for further progress.

Substantive Questions. While it is too early to discuss substantive results of the Conference in detail, some points already appear clear. First, the Conference adopted without question the basic recommendation made by the 1986 Meeting of Experts, and by the United Nations' Special Rapporteur, Mr. Martinez Cobo. This consists of changing the orientation of the Convention away from the integrationist approach adopted in 1957, to respect for the cultures, ways of life and very existence of indigenous and tribal peoples, and of incorporating requirements for consultation and participation. Indeed, in many cases the Conference showed a willingness on the part of governments as well as the other social partners to adopt requirements for the full participation of indigenous and tribal peoples in the planning and administration of programmes and other measures adopted for their benefit. In some cases, it is also foreseen in the Committee's conclusions that actual control of programmes intended for them, especially in regard to health and education, would gradually be transferred to their own administration, and resources made available by governments to run them.

On the other hand, no agreement has yet been reached on two important issues. On the question of whether to use the designation "peoples" or "populations" in the revised Convention, the Committee was unable to reach full agreement this year. The fear was expressed by a number of government delegates that the use of the term "peoples" without qualifying language might lead to claims of the right to self-determination in the sense of separation from the countries in which these people live. The Committee was unable to reach agreement in 1988 on language which would satisfy all the concerns expressed with a view to limiting the impact of the use of this term. It therefore decided to include in the draft Convention the expression "(peoples/populations)" in order to indicate that no decision had yet been taken.

Discussions of another key issue, concerning land rights, also could not be completed in 1988, and final decision was deferred until the second discussion. It emerged from the general discussion which was held, that one point of disagreement was whether to use the term "lands" or "territories". As for other questions of terminology, fears were expressed by some that the term "territories" might carry implications beyond a mere description of the way in which indigenous and tribal peoples see their relationship to the territories they occupy. Another unresolved issue is the extent to which and the way in which these peoples will be protected against involuntary removals from their lands, and from exploration for and exploitation of nonrenewable resources. These questions have been deferred to 1989 for a final resolution.

The Committee was frequently reminded by various speakers that the Conference was engaged in drafting a Convention, which when ratified would create binding legal obligations. It was stated on a number of occasions that it was necessary to ensure that the provisions included in the draft not be such as to make it difficult for countries to ratify the Convention. In this connection, the complementary nature of the standard-setting procedures currently operating in the ILO and in the United Nations, was evoked a number of times.

Participation of NGOs in the Deliberations. NGOs took a very prominent part in the deliberations leading up to and during the Conference discussion in 1988. This participation was unprecedented in its magnitude at a comparable level in a standard-setting exercise, either for the ILO or for other intergovernmental organisations.

To summarise briefly, the ILO Governing Body requested all governments to consult representatives of indigenous and tribal populations in their countries when preparing their replies to the initial questionnaire in 1987, and to do whatever was possible to include representatives of these peoples in their delegations. A number of such representatives did attend the Conference as members of Government, employer and worker delegations. . . .

As for the direct participation of representatives of these organisations, the Governing Body extended invitations to all the international NGOs which expressed their wish to attend the Conference as observers under Article 56 of the Standing Orders. Also under this Article, these organisations were able to request the right to intervene in the discussions, which they did on a number of occasions. They agreed among themselves to coordinate their statements and for one organisation to speak in the name of all of them, for each separate subject.

Other NGOs present, who did not have international status and thus could not participate directly in the formal meetings, were given a possibility to speak in their own names at a specially-convened informal session of the Committee, attended by all its members. They also remained in contact with the international NGOs, and made their opinions known through these NGOs.

All such interventions were co-ordinated by an Indigenous Rights Group of NGOs formed for this purpose at the Conference. . . .

The result of these deliberations is the recently adopted ILO INDIGENOUS AND TRIBAL PEOPLES CONVENTION.

INDIGENOUS POPULATIONS: STUDY OF THE PROBLEM OF DISCRIMINATION.

The *Study of Discrimination against Indigenous Populations,* prepared by Mr. Jose R. Martinez-Cobo (Ecuador), special rapporteur of the SUB-COMMISSION ON PREVENTION OF DISCRIMINATION AND PROTECTION OF MINORITIES, was authorized by the Economic and Social Council on recommendation of the Sub-Commission in 1971 (resolution 1589 [L]) and completed in 1985. At the request of the council (decision 1985 [137]), Parts I and II of the study were issued as a consolidated document (UN Doc. E/CN.4/Sub. 2/1986/7), while Part III, setting out the Special Rapporteur's conclusions, proposals, and recommendations, was printed (UN publication, Sales No. E.86.XIV.3).

Parts I and I contain chapters on the following subjects:

I. Measures adopted by the United Nations
II. Action taken by the specialized agencies
III. Action taken by the Organization of American States
IV. Other international action
V. Definition of indigenous populations
VI. Composition of the population
VII. Basic principles
VIII. General measures for the prohibition, prevention and elimination of discrimination
IX. Fundamental policy
X. Administrative arrangements
XI. Health, medical care and social services
XII. Housing
XIII. Education
XIV. Language
XV. Culture and cultural, social and legal institutions
XVI. Occupation, employment and vocational education
XVII. Land
XVIII. Political rights
XIX. Religious rights and practices
XX. Equality in the administration of justice and legal assistance

One of the questions considered in detail in Part III is that of the definition of "indigenous populations" from the international point of view. In this connection, the special rapporteur points out that "the fundamental assertion must be that indigenous populations must be recognized according to their own perception and conception of themselves in relation to other groups; there must be no attempt to define them according to the perception of others through the values of foreign societies or of the dominant sections in such societies." On this subject, he continues (para. 369–382; 402–403):

The right of indigenous peoples themselves to define what and who is indigenous must be recognized.

The correlative of this faculty is, obviously, the faculty of defining or determining what or who is not indigenous.

No State may take, by legislation, regulations or other

means, measures that interfere with the power of indigenous nations or groups to determine who are their members.

Artificial, arbitrary or manipulatory definitions must, in any event, be rejected.

As regards the circumstance that gave rise to the notion of indigenous populations, it must be said that the special position of indigenous populations within the society of nation-States existing today derives from their historical rights to their lands, as well as from their right to be different and to be considered as different.

Much of their land has been taken away and whatever land is left to them is subject to constant encroachment. Their culture and their social and legal institutions and systems have been constantly under attack at all levels, through the media, the law and the public educational systems. It is only natural, therefore, that there should be resistance to further loss of their land and rejection of the distortion or denial of their history and culture and defensive/offensive reaction to the continual linguistic and cultural aggressions and attacks on their way of life, their social and cultural integrity and their very physical existence. They have a right to continue to exist, to defend their lands, to keep and to transmit their culture, their language, their social and legal institutions and systems and their way of life, which have been illegally and unjustifiably attacked.

It is in the context of these situations and these rights that the question of definition should arise. Social scientists have reached the conclusion that ethnic groups can be characterized only by the distinctions which they themselves perceive between themselves and other groups with which they have to interact. They exist as such ethnic groups as long as they consider themselves different from those other groups. Ethnic groups determine their rules concerning membership, contemplating inclusion or exclusion of individuals whom they may accept or reject as members, or those they will adopt or ostracize, and those who may or may not represent them. On an individual basis, belonging to such groups depends on two main factors: self-identification as members of the group (group consciousness) and recognition by the group that those given individuals belong to it (acceptance by the group). Thus the group may, under its own rules governing membership, and inclusion and exclusion of individuals, accept or reject some persons as its members, while adopting or ostracizing others. It may, further, keep these rules unchanged or modify them as it wishes, without any outside interference.

It is clear that indigenous peoples consider themselves to be different from the other groups that form the society of present-day nation-States in which they now find themselves included. They consider themselves to be the historical successors of the peoples and nations that existed on their territories before the coming of the invaders of these territories, who eventually prevailed over them and imposed on them colonial or other forms of subjugation, and whose historical successors now form the predominant sectors of society. It is also abundantly clear that indigenous peoples consider themselves different from those other peoples and demand the right to be considered different by other sectors of society and by the international community.

Indigenous peoples wish to keep whatever territory has been left to them and to regain land illegally taken from them, so as to have an adequate land base for their existence as different peoples. They also want their culture,

language, social and legal institutions, which they consider essential for their own organization and existence, to be respected and recognized in those nation-States. They wish to keep, develop and transmit to future generations their territories, social and legal institutions and systems, their culture and their language.

Indigenous populations may, therefore, be defined as follows for the purposes of international action that may be taken affecting their future existence:

Indigenous communities, peoples and nations are those which, having a historical continuity with pre-invasion and pre-colonial societies that developed on their territories, consider themselves distinct from other sectors of the societies now prevailing in those territories, or parts of them. They form at present nondominant sectors of society and are determined to preserve, develop and transmit to future generations their ancestral territories, and their ethnic identity, as the basis of their continued existence as peoples, in accordance with their own cultural patterns, social institutions and legal systems.

This historical continuity may consist of the continuation, for an extended period reaching into the present, of one or more of the following factors:

(a) Occupation of ancestral lands, or at least of part of them;

(b) Common ancestry with the original occupants of these lands;

(c) Culture in general, or in specific manifestations (such as religion, living under a tribal system, membership of an indigenous community, dress, means of livelihood, life-style, etc.);

(d) Language (whether used as the only language, as mother-tongue, as the habitual means of communication at home or in the family, or as the main, preferred, habitual, general or normal language);

(e) Residence in certain parts of the country, or in certain regions of the world;

(f) Other relevant factors.

On an individual basis, an indigenous person is one who belongs to these indigenous populations through self-identification as indigenous (group consciousness) and is recognized and accepted by these populations as one of its members (acceptance by the group).

This preserves for these communities the sovereign right and power to decide who belongs to them, without external interference. . . .

Diversity is not, in itself, contrary to unity, any more than uniformity itself necessarily produces the desired unity. Indeed, there can be weakness and hostility within artificially produced uniformity, just as there can be strength in diversity co-ordinated within a harmonious, yet many-faceted whole, based on respect for the special nature of each component part.

Pluralism, self-management, self-government, autonomy and self-determination within a policy of ethnic development, as defined in the San José Declaration, appear to be the formula called for by the times in which we are now living and to do justice to the aspirations and desires of indigenous populations, which have for so long been subjected to interference and imposed conditions of all kinds. The Special Rapporteur is convinced that, following these guidelines would not be promoting artificial distinctions or separatist aspirations where such feelings do not exist, but would simply be recognizing the multiform nature of the societies of States with indigenous populations. It is essential not to prevent such groups from fully regaining a historical awareness of their own existence as such and to enable them to control their future according to their own aspirations and traditions. To do otherwise is to prolong the subjugation and oppression of groups and cultures capable of making a significant contribution to mankind, today as in the past. They should be afforded that opportunity like any other people on our planet, if frictions and conflicts caused by lack of understanding and injustice are to be avoided.

The special rapporteur then suggests a number of steps which, in his view, should be taken by the governments of countries having indigenous populations with a view to eliminating discrimination against such populations and their individual members, as follows (para. 405):

Governments which have not yet done so should consider establishing institutions, machinery and specialized administrative procedures, since entities with specific and clearly defined mandates are in a better position to accord due attention to solving the difficult and complex problems currently facing indigenous populations in the countries in which they live.

A second question considered in detail in Part II of the study relates to the status of the treaties which govern the relationships between various indigenous populations and the states in which they live. Because of the paramount importance of this question, the special rapporteur proposes that a thorough and careful study should be made of the subject in its entirety, including the official force of such treaties; the observance, or lack of observance, of their provisions; and the consequences for the population concerned.

As regards the policy to be adopted in dealing with the problem of discrimination against indigenous populations, the special rapporteur offers the following views (para. 399–401; 406–412):

The Special Rapporteur is fully aware that each country will determine its ethnic, cultural, linguistic and religious policies on the basis of prevailing conditions and other criteria which it deems pertinent. The suggestions put forward in this regard are based on the existing alternatives and the preferences which the needs of indigenous populations and current world thinking appear to demand. While the recommendations do not represent any attempt to dictate policies to any sovereign State, a number of suggestions can nevertheless be made.

States should seek to gear their policies to the wish of indigenous populations to be considered different, as well as to the ethnic identity explicitly defined by such populations. In the view of the Special Rapporteur, this should be done within a context of socio-cultural and political pluralism which affords such populations the necessary degree of autonomy, self-determination and self-management commensurate with the concepts of ethnic development described in *chapter IX* and *XV*.

The unity which is a legitimate concern of many States, particularly those which have most recently acceded to independence, can be achieved most fully and profoundly through a genuine diversity which respects differences between existing groups aspiring to a distinct identity within society as a whole. The desired unity will be achieved more fully if it is based on diversity, rather than on an imposed uniformity inconsistent with the genuine feelings of the population. Within that diversity, each group would participate more fully since it would do so on the basis of its own conceptions, values and patterns, rather than attempting to use modes of expression which are foreign to it. . . .

Governments which have divided responsibility for indigenous population affairs among a number of ministries, departments or institutions should consider the advantages of setting up a special body to co-ordinate such efforts. They should also consider the possibility of authorizing that or some other body to co-ordinate and harmonize private programmes with government policy.

Governments with parliamentary systems should endeavour to set up legislative committees and sub-committees specializing in indigenous affairs, with a view to according more careful study and specialized consideration to legislation in this area.

Governments should consider setting up consultative or advisory bodies, either of a general or a specialized nature, and at the national or local level, to make use of the specialized knowledge of non-governmental experts and, in particular, to encourage the participation of authentic representatives of indigenous populations. This would ensure the greater involvement of those populations in the formulation and implementation of official policy and programmes, the revision and amendment of which should be based on their points of view.

The selection and immovability of the staff of departments concerned with indigenous affairs should be governed by the norms generally applicable to civil service or administrative personnel. Special measures should be adopted, however, to secure the services of specially qualified individuals and, in particular, of members of indigenous communities, to occupy such posts, with a number of key and decision-making posts being reserved for them. Pre-service or in-service training programmes on the problems of indigenous populations and possible solutions should also be regarded as essential for the effective preparation and utilization of available staff and resources.

Special efforts should be made to ensure the adequate funding of institutions and administrative programmes concerned with indigenous affairs at all times. Consideration should be given to the possibility of establishing trust funds to provide the necessary stability for certain budgetary provisions and to supplement regular appropriations in specific critical areas. Entities or undertakings which generate their own income should be subjected to annual reviews by joint consultative or advisory bodies (governmental and non-governmental, indigenous and non-indigenous), in order to ensure that the attainment of the proposed income targets does not conflict with general policy, which should constitute a compact and meaningful body of guiding principles serving the interests of indigenous populations, as they themselves conceive such interests.

Governments should consider ways of encouraging non-governmental organizations and, in particular, those established by indigenous populations, through normative measures and the necessary financial assistance, and of promoting the participation of indigenous communities in consultative and advisory bodies and proceedings.

Governments should recognize the pertinence and special competence of indigenous communities and organizations in this area and should increasingly incorporate them into policy-making and policy-implementing bodies and processes and programmes of fundamental importance to indigenous populations. The need for the participation of such communities and organizations in advisory and consultative procedures should be recognized explicitly, and increasing efforts should be made in daily life with regard to indigenous affairs.

As areas requiring special attention if discrimination against indigenous populations is to be eliminated, the special rapporteur cites health, housing, education, language, culture, employment, land use and development, political rights, and religious rights and practices.

His basic proposal for dealing with the problem of discrimination against indigenous populations is to begin by formulating specific principles for use as guidelines by governments in their relationships with such populations, on a basis of respect for the ethnic identity of such populations and for the rights and freedoms to which they are entitled:

Such principles [he concludes] must necessarily contain any additional and specific provisions which, following careful study, may be deemed necessary for the fuller recognition and protection of the indispensable rights and freedoms of indigenous populations. . . . When the ideas and measures considered fundamental have been organized into a set of principles, the Sub-Commission may deem it advisable to recommend to its subsidiary organs the need to prepare a declaration of the rights and freedoms of indigenous populations as a possible basis for a convention on that question.

In fact, the sub-commission did enlist the assistance of its WORKING GROUP ON INDIGENOUS POPULATIONS in preparing the draft Universal Declaration on Indigenous Rights (see below).

SEE ALSO ILO Indigenous and Tribal Peoples Convention.

INDIGENOUS RIGHTS: DRAFT UNIVERSAL DEC-LARATION.

In 1985, the WORKING GROUP ON INDIGE-NOUS POPULATIONS decided to proceed with the preparation of a draft declaration on indigenous rights for eventual adoption by the General Assembly. Pursuant to this decision, it adopted, in 1985 and 1987, a provisional text consisting of 14 draft principles. In 1987, it recommended that its chairman/ rapporteur, Mrs. Erica-Irene A. Daes (Greece), be entrusted with the preparation of a working paper consisting of a full set of preambular paragraphs and principles for insertion in the draft declaration. Its recommendation was subsequently approved by its parent bodies, the Sub-Commission on Prevention of Discrimination and Protection of Minorities (resolu-

tion 1987/16), the Commission on Human Rights (resolution 1988/49), and the Economic and Social Council (resolution 1988/36).

The chairman/ rapporteur's working paper (UN Doc. E/CN.4/Sub. 2/1988/25) was accepted by the working group at its 1988 session and was forwarded to the sub-commission as an annex to the working group's report (UN. Doc E/CN.4/Sub.2/1988/24, annex II). The sub-commission examined it at its 1988 session, endorsed (resolution 1988/18) the working group's decision to adopt it as the framework for the drafting of a universal declaration on indigenous rights, and requested the Secretary-General to transmit the working group's report to governments, indigenous peoples, and to intergovernmental and non-governmental organizations, for their specific comments and proposals. It recommended that the chairman-rapporteur should later be entrusted with preparing a revised text of the draft declaration on the basis of the comments and proposals received and the discussion in the working group.

The working group, at its 1989 session, examined the first revised text of the draft Universal Declaration on the Rights of Indigenous Peoples (UN Doc. E/ CN.4/Sub.2/1989/33) and recommended that its chairman-rapporteur be entrusted with the task of preparing and presenting in 1990 a further revision based on comments received in writing and those made at sessions of the working group. The first revised text of the draft declaration was as follows:

The General Assembly,
Considering indigenous peoples born free and equal in dignity and rights in accordance with existing international standards while recognizing the right of all individuals and groups to be different, to consider themselves different and to be regarded as such,
Considering that all peoples and human groups have contributed to the progress of civilizations and cultures which constitute the common heritage of humankind,
Recognizing the specific need to promote and protect those rights and characteristics which stem from indigenous history, philosophy of life, traditions, culture and legal, social and economic structures, especially as these are tied to the lands which the groups have traditionally occupied,
Concerned that many indigenous peoples have been unable to enjoy and assert their inalienable human rights and fundamental freedoms, frequently resulting in insufficient land and resources, poverty and deprivation, which in turn may lead them to voice their grievances and to organize themselves in order to bring an end to all forms of discrimination and oppression which they face,
Convinced that all doctrines and practices of racial, ethnic or cultural superiority are legally wrong, morally condemnable and socially unjust,
Reaffirming that indigenous peoples in the exercise of their rights should be free from adverse distinction or discrimination of any kind,

Endorsing calls for the consolidation and strengthening of indigenous societies and their cultures and traditions through development based on their own needs and value systems and comprehensive participation in and consultation about all other relevant development efforts,

Emphasizing the need for special attention to the rights and skills of indigenous women and children,

Believing that indigenous peoples should be free to manage their own affairs to the greatest possible extent, while enjoying equal rights with other citizens in the political, economic and social life of States,

Bearing in mind that nothing in this declaration may be used as a justification for denying to any people, which otherwise satisfies the criteria generally established by human rights instruments and international law, its right to self-determination,

Calling on States to comply with and effectively implement all international human rights instruments as they apply to indigenous peoples,

Acknowledging the need for minimum standards taking account of the diverse realities of indigenous peoples in all parts of the world,

Solemnly proclaims the following declaration on rights of indigenous peoples and calls upon all States to take prompt and effective measures to implement the declaration in conjunction with the indigenous peoples.

Part I

1. The right to the full and effective enjoyment of all fundamental rights and freedoms, as well as the observance of the corresponding responsibilities, which are universally recognized in the Charter of the United Nations and in existing international human rights instruments.

2. The right to be free and equal to all the other human beings in dignity and rights and to be free from adverse distinction or discrimination of any kind.

Part II

3. The [collective] right to exist as distinct peoples and to be protected against genocide, as well as the [individual] rights to life, physical integrity, liberty and security of person.

4. The [collective] right to maintain and develop their ethnic and cultural characteristics and distinct identity, including the right of peoples and individuals to call themselves by their proper names.

5. The individual and collective right to protection against ethnocide. This protection shall include, in particular, prevention of any act which has the aim or effect of depriving them of their ethnic characteristics or cultural identity, of any form of forced assimilation or integration, of imposition of foreign life-styles and of any propaganda derogating their dignity and diversity.

6. The right to preserve their cultural identity and traditions and to pursue their own cultural development. The rights to the manifestations of their cultures, including archaeological sites, artefacts, designs, technology and works of art, lie with the indigenous peoples or their members.

7. The right to require that States grant—within the resources available—the necessary assistance for the maintenance of their identity and their development.

8. The right to manifest, teach, practise and observe their own religious traditions and ceremonies, and to maintain, protect and have access to sacred sites and burial-grounds for these purposes.

9. The right to develop and promote their own languages, including an own literary language, and to use them for administrative, juridical, cultural and other purposes.

10. The right to all forms of education, including in particular the right of children to have access to education in their own languages, and to establish, structure, conduct and control their own educational systems and institutions.

11. The right to promote intercultural information and education, recognizing the dignity and diversity of their cultures, and the duty of States to take the necessary measures, among other sections of the national community, with the object of eliminating prejudices and of fostering understanding and good relations.

Part III

12. The right of collective and individual ownership, possession and use of the lands or resources which they have traditionally occupied or used. The lands may only be taken away from them with their free and informed consent as witnessed by a treaty or agreement.

13. The right to recognition of their own land-tenure systems for the protection and promotion of the use, enjoyment and occupancy of the land.

14. The right to special measures to ensure their ownership and control over surface and substance of resources pertaining to the territories they have traditionally occupied or otherwise used including flora and fauna, waters and ice sea.

15. The right to reclaim land and surface resources or where this is not possible, to seek just and fair compensation for the same, when the property has been taken away from them without consent, in particular, if such deprival has been based on theories such as those related to discovery, *terra nullius*, waste lands or idle lands. Compensation, if the parties agree, may take the form of land or resources of quality and legal status at least equal to that of the property previously owned by them.

16. The right to protection of their environment and in particular against any action or course of conduct which may result in the destruction, deterioration or pollution of their traditional habitat, land, air, water, sea ice, wildlife or other resources without free and informed consent of the indigenous peoples affected. The right to just and fair compensation for any such action or course of conduct.

17. The right to require that States consult with indigenous peoples and with both domestic and transnational corporations prior to the commencement of any large-scale projects, particularly natural resource projects or exploitation of mineral and other subsoil resources in order to enhance the projects' benefits and to mitigate any adverse economic, social, environmental and cultural effect. Just and fair compensation shall be provided for any such activity or adverse consequence undertaken.

Part IV

18. The right to maintain and develop within their areas of lands or territories their traditional economic structures and ways of life, to be secure in the traditional economic structures and ways of life, to be secure in the enjoyment of their own traditional means of subsistence, and to engage freely in their traditional and other economic activities, including hunting, fresh- and salt-water fishing, herding, gathering, lumbering and cultivation, without adverse discrimination. In no case may an indigenous people be de-

prived of its means of subsistence. The right to just and fair compensation if they have been so deprived.

19. The right to special State measures for the immediate, effective and continuing improvement of their social and economic conditions, with their consent, that reflect their own priorities.

20. The right to determine, plan and implement all health, housing and other social and economic programmes affecting them, and as far as possible to develop, plan and implement such programmes through their own institutions.

Part V

21. The right to participate on an equal footing with all the other citizens and without adverse discrimination in the political, economic and social life of the State and to have their specific character duly reflected in the legal system and in political and socio-economic institutions, including in particular proper regard to end recognition of indigenous laws and customs.

22. The right to participate fully at the State level, through representatives chosen by themselves, in decision-making about and implementation of all national and international matters which may affect their life and destiny.

23. The [collective] right to autonomy in matters relating to their own internal and local affairs, including education, information, culture, religion, health, housing, social welfare, traditional and other economic activities, land and resources administration and the environment, as well as internal taxation for financing these autonomous functions.

24. The right to decide upon the structures of their autonomous institutions, to select the membership of such institutions, and to determine the membership of the indigenous people concerned for these purposes.

25. The right to determine the responsibilities of individuals to their own community, consistent with universally recognized human rights and fundamental freedoms.

26. The right to maintain and develop traditional contacts and co-operation, including cultural and social exchanges and trade, with their own kith and kin across State boundaries and the obligation of the State to adopt measures to facilitate such contacts.

27. The right to claim that States honour treaties and other agreements concluded with indigenous peoples.

Part VI

28. The individual and collective right to access to and prompt decision by mutually acceptable and fair procedures for resolving conflicts or disputes and any infringement, public or private, between States and indigenous peoples, groups, or individuals. These procedures should include, as appropriate, negotiations, mediation, arbitration, national courts and international and regional human rights review and complaints mechanisms.

Part VII

29. These rights constitute the minimum standards for the survival and the well-being of the indigenous peoples of the world.

30. Nothing in this Declaration may be interpreted as implying for any State, group or individual any right to engage in any activity or to perform any act aimed at the destruction of any of the rights and freedoms set forth herein.

INDIGENOUS RIGHTS YEAR. In May 1988, the ECONOMIC AND SOCIAL COUNCIL, on recommendation of the COMMISSION ON HUMAN RIGHTS and the SUBCOMMISSION ON PREVENTION OF DISCRIMINATION AND PROTECTION OF MINORITIES, recommended (resolution 1988/37) that the General Assembly should proclaim an international year of the world's indigenous populations. In September of that year, the sub-commission proposed (resolution 1988/19) that an international year for indigenous rights should be proclaimed to coincide with the end of the Second Decade for Action to Combat Racism and Radical Discrimination, i.e., 1993. The General Assembly, however, took no action on the matter at its 1988 session.

INDIGENOUS WORLD ASSOCIATION. An international non-governmental organization in consultative status (Category II) with the UN Economic and Social Council, the IWA is affiliated with six organizations in four countries.

Founded in 1981, the association promotes the values and programs of the United Nations and the rights of indigenous peoples, refugees, migrant workers, and minorities. It promotes the development of international human rights law and supports the work of the WORKING GROUP ON INDIGENOUS POPULATIONS. IWA publishes the *IWA Bulletin*.

Indigenous World Association. Address: 275 Grand View Avenue, San Francisco, CA 94114 (USA). Telephone: (415) 647-1966. Directors: Roxanne Dunbar Ortiz and Chockie Cottier.

INDIVIDUALS AS SUBJECTS OF INTERNATIONAL LAW. On 8 May 1981, the UN Economic and Social Council authorized (decision 1981/142) the Sub-Commission on Prevention of Discrimination and Protection of Minorities to appoint one of its members, Mrs. Erica-Irene A. Daes (Greece) as special rapporteur to undertake a study on the status of the individual and contemporary international law.

The final report on the study was presented to the sub-commission at its 1989 session (UN Doc. E/CN.4/Sub.2/1989/40). Based on the information received, in response to a questionnaire, from 38 States, four specialized agencies, the Office of the United Nations High Commissioner for Refugees, and a number of international agencies and organizations, the special rapporteur reviewed developments relating to the subjectivity of the individual in international law with the aim of demonstrating, both from the theoretical and from the practical point of view, that the individual is indeed a bearer of international rights and responsibilities and that he has a restricted procedural capacity directly under international law and should be considered, at least alongside the State, as a subject of contemporary international law.

Her final conclusions were (1) that the individual is the beneficiary of international law and, in certain cases, bears the liabilities and disabilities which it imposes; (2) that the growing and ever-changing needs and the interdependence of communities and the real interest of modern society require, in most cases, the existence of various subjects of international law; and (3) that the individual, at the present time, should at least be considered on a parallel with the State as a subject of international law.

On the basis of these conclusions, the special rapporteur proposed that the sub-commission consider making the following recommendations to the Commission on Human Rights (chap. X, para. 567–568):

A. *General Recommendations.* (a) Greater popularization of the international standards of human rights and dissemination of information concerning the promotion, protection and restoration of universally-recognized human rights, especially of measures related to teaching and education for the promotion of, respect for, and the implementation of international human rights.

(b) It is considered necessary to use the mass communication media, such as radio, television, newspapers and magazines to the greatest possible extent for constant campaigning on issues related in particular to the international protection of human rights. In this connection, it is important not only to refer to reports of human rights violations but also to the popularization of international rights standards and to every aspect that might contribute to the exaltation of the individual as the worthiest creature in the universe, over and above all racial, national, social, cultural, ideological or political differences.

(c) In some less developed countries, individuals should, when necessary, be enlightened with regard to their rights and in the manner in which they should be protected and safeguarded mainly at the regional and international level.

(d) The petition system in the Human Rights Committee represents a considerable advance over any other system of implementation existing at the universal level within the framework of the United Nations, but it is still inadequate.

(e) The creation of more effective institutions is considered of great importance. These should be accessible to the individual for the protection of their rights. Thus, it is recommended the establishment and development of international rules and procedures for more effective protection of the individual in international law, for example, on the lines of the individual's right to petition under article 25 of the European Convention on Human Rights.

(f) Developing new mechanisms by which individuals might seek international judicial review of alleged violations of their human rights, once domestic remedies have been exhausted.

(g) Adopting proper enforcement mechanisms capable of ensuring the redress of specific human rights violations. The individual must have some form of ultimate international redress.

(h) The individual should have the right to appeal to procedures provided by international law when his fundamental human rights are being violated.

(i) The individual must be given his place at the centre of international courts and international law; he must have easier access to international courts and tribunals, not only for actions falling within the competence of municipal courts but also for all real and major actions directly related to international law.

(j) The revision of the provisions of the Statute of the International Court of Justice should be considered by States and the United Nations so that even the World Court may offer free access to every individual who may be denied justice in the courts of any municipal jurisdiction.

(k) International treaties, other intergovernmental instruments relating in particular to the protection of the human rights and fundamental freedoms of every individual, should be duly ratified by the States in order to become municipal law and to be applied by the competent authorities as substantive law.

(l) States should recognize that true supranational protection and enforcement of human rights norms is essential for the practical enjoyment of human rights by every individual.

(m) Rules of international law, including humanitarian and human rights law, and resolutions of the competent organs and bodies of the United Nations system, related in particular to the international protection of the individual should be fully respected by every State of the international community.

(n) In particular, the disrespect and violation of human rights resolutions by Governments should be strongly condemned by the competent United Nations organs.

(o) The individual should be accorded personality under international law and should have certain rights and responsibilities as a subject of international law.

B. *Specific Recommendations.* (a) A study should be undertaken on the status of the liberation movements and contemporary international law. It should be noted that there are clear signs that recognized liberation movements are in a state of transition, which may well have an important impact on the norms of international law pertaining to them. Taking into account this ongoing evolution, it may be appropriate to delay the implementation of this recommendation until developments provide the United Nations with a clearer and firmer basis for formulating relevant criteria and standards;

(b) A study should be undertaken on the status of the "Indigenous Peoples and Nations" under contemporary international law. The study of the Problem of Discrimination Against Indigenous Populations, prepared by J.R. Martinez Cobo, Special Rapporteur of the Sub-Commission, the reports of the United Nations Working Group on Indigenous Populations, the relevant reports and the work of the ILO, including, in particular, the relevant work on the revision of the Convention No. 107/1957, and the Draft Universal Declaration on the rights of indigenous peoples under elaboration, will, *inter alia,* constitute sources of information and the key-documents for the justification of such a study. In addition to these sources, the report of the United Nations Seminar on the Effects of Racism and Racial Discrimination on the Social and Economic Relations between Indigenous Peoples and States provides a wealth of relevant information, data and reasons, and valuable conclusions and recommendations;

(c) Action should be taken by the competent bodies and organs of the United Nations and efforts should be doubled to revive the appropriate procedures for the consideration of the establishment of an objective international criminal jurisdiction;

(d) The formulation and adoption of certain general principles which could lead to international norms and standards related specifically to the status of the individual in contemporary international law; and,

(e) The present study should be transmitted through the appropriate United Nations channels to the International Law Commission for its information.

The sub-commission, which had examined a draft of the report at its 1988 session, received and considered the final version at its 1989 session. On 1 September 1989, it expressed (resolution 1989/46) its appreciation to the special rapporteur and recommended that her study, entitled "The Status of the Individual and Contemporary International Law," should be published and widely disseminated by the United Nations.

INDONESIA. The Republic of Indonesia is a country in southeastern Asia consisting of the Malay Archipelago, a large island group in the Indian Ocean, including the Sunda Islands (including Java and Sunatra), the Lesser Sundas (including Bali), Borneo, the Celebes, and the Moluccas. It has borders with Malaysia and Papua New Guinea. It achieved independence from the Netherlands in 1945 and became a member of the United Nations in 1950. Its population is estimated by the UN (1990) to be 181,539,000. The complex ethnic structure of the population is the result of several great migrations, many centuries ago, from Asia and the South Pacific. The Chinese are the most numerous of the non-indigenous peoples. The so-called Coast Malays, who inhabit the coastal areas of the major islands, are of mixed stock: Chinese, Arab, East Indian, and Malayan. Languages commonly used include Bahasa Indonesian (official), Javanese, Dutch, and English. Islam is the predominant religion (90%); Christianity, Buddhism, and Hinduism comprise the remaining 10%.

The government (1990) took the form of a republic. The president, elected by the 920-member People's Assembly, serves as head of State and government. The House of Representatives, composed of 464 members of the assembly, is the legislative authority. The house meets at least once a year; the assembly only once every five years. Political parties include the Sekber Golkar Party, the Islamic United Development Party, and the Democratic Party.

Occupied by the Japanese during World War II, the Dutch colony of Indonesia enjoyed virtual self-government until the Japanese surrendered to the Allies on 17 August 1945, at which time President Sukarno proclaimed his country's independence from the Netherlands. British troops fought the Indonesian nationalists until Dutch units arrived; then Dutch and Indonesian forces fought sporadically until leaders of the two countries agreed upon terms of a Dutch–Indonesian union under the Dutch crown. But the union, established in 1949, was abrogated by Indonesia in 1956.

Indonesia was involved in an international dispute concerning the right of self-determination in 1963–1964, relating to the formation of Malaysia. A United Nations mission determined that the people of Sabah and Sarawak had decided to realize their independence through freely chosen association with the people of the Federation of Malaysia and Singapore, with whom they felt ties of ethnic association, heritage, language, religion, culture, ideals, and objectives. When the Federation of Malaysia was proclaimed on 16 September 1963, Indonesia's representative at the United Nations objected. In January 1965, after Malaysia had been seated as a member of the Security Council, Indonesia withdrew from the United Nations. However, it resumed participation in UN activities in September 1966.

During the two decades when President Sukarno was in power in Indonesia, the influence of the Indonesian Communist Party gradually increased, until fear of a takeover led to an attempted *coup d'etat*. The coup, directed against Sukarno, was thwarted by the army under the command of Gen. Suharto and was followed by an intensive campaign against "subversives" in which thousands are said to have "disappeared" or lost their lives.

Gen. Suharto replaced Sukarno as president in 1967, stabilized the country economically, and reorganized its government. However, the "disappearance" continued and, indeed, intensified between 1982 and 1984 under the influence of legislation that made it a crime, subject to the death penalty, to undertake action aimed at undermining or contradicting the ideology of the State.

President Suharto was elected to a fifth term of office on 10 March 1988. He was the only candidate.

INDONESIA: CONSTITUTION. The Constitution of the Republic of Indonesia, adopted in 1945 when the Republic was established, includes the following provisions (articles 26 to 34) specifically relating to human rights and fundamental freedoms:

Chapter X. Citizens

Article 26. (1) Citizens shall be persons who are native-born Indonesians and persons of other nationality who are legalised by statute as being citizens.

(2) Conditions with regard to citizenship shall be prescribed by statute.

Article 27. (1) Without any exception, all citizens shall have equal positions in Law and Government and shall be obliged to uphold that Law and Government.

(2) Every citizen shall have the right to work, and to a living, befitting for human beings.

Article 28. Freedom of association and assembly, of expressing thoughts and of issuing writing and the like, shall be prescribed by statute.

Chapter XI. Religion

Article 29. (1) The State shall be based upon Belief in the One, Supreme God.

(2) The State shall guarantee freedom to every resident to adhere to his respective religion and to perform his religious duties in conformity with that religion and that faith.

Chapter XII. Defence

Article 30. (1) Every citizen shall have the right and the duty to participate in the defence effort of the State.

(2) Conditions concerning defence shall be regulated by statute.

Chapter XIII. Education

Article 31. (1) Every citizen shall have the right to obtain an education.

(2) The Government shall establish and conduct a national educational system which shall be regulated by statute.

Article 32. The Government shall advance the national culture of Indonesia.

Chapter XIV. Social Well-being

Article 33. (1) The economy shall be organised as a common endeavour based upon the principle of the family system.

(2) Branches of production which are important for the State and which affect the life of most people shall be controlled by the State.

(3) Land and water and the natural riches contained therein shall be controlled by the State and shall be made use of for the people.

Article 34. The poor, and destitute children, shall be cared for by the State.

INFORMATION AND COMMUNICATION. On 18 December 1978, the UN General Assembly affirmed (resolution 33/115 B) the need to establish a new, more just, and more effective international information and communication order, intended to strengthen peace and international understanding and based on the free circulation and wider and better-balanced dissemination of information. On the same date one year later, the assembly affirmed (resolution 34/182) its primary role in elaborating, coordinating, and harmonizing policies and activities in this field and requested the director-general of UNESCO to submit to it a progress report on the establishment of a new world information and communication order.

The UNESCO General Conference, convened in Belgrade in Oct.–Nov. 1980, adopted (resolution 21 C/19) the following considerations upon which a new world information and communication order could be based:

(a) elimination of the imbalances and inequalities which characterize the present situation;

(b) elimination of the negative effects of certain monopolies, public or private, excessive concentrations;

(c) removal of the internal and external obstacles to a free flow and wider and better balanced dissemination of information and ideas;

(d) plurality of sources and channels of information;

(e) freedom of the press and information;

(f) freedom of journalists and all professionals in the communication media, a freedom inseparable from responsibility;

(g) the capacity of developing countries to achieve improvement of their own situations, notably by providing their own equipment, by training their personnel, by improving their infrastructures, and by making their information and communication media suitable to their needs and aspirations;

(h) the sincere will of developed countries to help them attain these objectives;

(i) respect for each people's cultural identity and for the right of each nation to inform the world public about its interests, its aspirations, and its social and cultural values;

(j) respect for the right of all peoples to participate in international exchanges of information on the basis of equality, justice, and mutual benefit; and

(k) respect for the right of public, ethnic, and social groups and of individuals to have access to information sources and to participate actively in the communication process.

UNESCO has continued to conduct studies on the notion of a new world information and communication order; the studies have dealt with differents aspects of the right to communicate, such as the democratization of communication, communication and human rights, obstacles to the free flow of information, and the legal implications of an international instrument on the subject.

The General Conference approved (resolution 21 C 4.20) the UNESCO INTERNATIONAL PROGRAM FOR THE DEVELOPMENT OF COMMUNICATION had been formulated by the second session of the program's Intergovernmental Council held in Acapulco from 18 to 25 January 1982. UNESCO's director-general has since submitted annual reports on the implementation of the international program to the UN General Assembly.

At its 1989 session, the assembly, after considering reports of the secretary-general (UN Doc. A/44/653) and of the assembly's Committee on Information (UN Doc. A/44/21) on questions relating to information, adopted a resolution entitled "Information in the Service of Mankind" (resolution 44/50, Part I), in which it urged the full implementation of the following recommendations:

(1) All countries, the United Nations system as a whole and all others concerned should, reaffirming their commitment to the principles of the Charter of the United Nations and adhering to the principles of freedom of the press and freedom of information, as well as to those of the independence, pluralism and diversity of the media, co-operate and interact in responding to the call for the establishment of a new world information and communication order, seen as an evolving and continuous process, aimed at eliminating the existing imbalances between developed and developing countries in the field of information and communication, at reducing existing disparities in information flows at the international as well as the national level and at improving the media infrastructure and communication technology in the developing countries in order to increase their participation in the communication process, based on the free flow and wider and better balanced dissemination of information as well as on the meaningful and equal participation of all countries in the field of information and communication, ensuring the diversity of sources of and free access to information and intended to advance the mutual knowledge and understanding of peoples through all means of mass communication as an important contribution towards strengthening international peace and understanding. The central role of the United Nations Educational, Scientific and Cultural Organization in this regard, in line with that organization's strategies, should be reaffirmed;

(2) Fully aware of the important role that the media world-wide can freely play, the mass media should be encouraged to give wider and objective coverage to the efforts of the international community towards global development and, in particular, the efforts of the developing countries to achieve economic, social and cultural progress;

(3) All countries are urged to assure to journalists the free and effective performance of their professional tasks; all physical attacks against them should be resolutely condemned;

(4) Aware of the existing imbalances in the international distribution of news, particularly that affecting the developing countries, it is recommended that urgent attention should be given to the elimination of existing inequalities and the reduction of existing disparities in information flows at the international as well as the national level, to the encouragement of the free flow and the promotion of wider and better balanced dissemination of information, without any obstacle to freedom of expression, and to the advancement of mutual knowledge and understanding of peoples through the diversification of sources of information, respecting the interests, aspirations and socio-cultural values of all peoples;

(5) The United Nations system as a whole, particularly the United Nations Educational, Scientific and Cultural Organization, and the developed countries should be urged to co-operate in a concerted manner with the developing countries and their media, public, private and other, with a view to strengthening the information and communication infrastructure in the latter countries and promoting their access to advanced communication technology, in accordance with their needs and the priorities attached to such areas by the developing countries, so as to enable them and their media to develop their own information and communication policies freely and independently and in the light of their social and cultural values, adhering to the principle of freedom of information and freedom of the press. In this regard, support should be provided for the continuation and strengthening of practical training programmes for broadcasters and journalists from developing countries;

(6) Regional efforts and co-operation among developing countries, as well as co-operation between developed and developing countries, to strengthen communication capacities and to develop further the media infrastructure in the developing countries, especially in the areas of training and dissemination of information, should be enhanced so as to encourage the free flow and promote wider and better balanced dissemination of information;

(7) The United Nations system, particularly the United Nations Educational, Scientific and Cultural Organization, in addition to bilateral co-operation, should aim at providing all possible support and assistance to the developing countries and their media, public and private or other, with due regard to their interests and needs in the field of information and to action already adopted within the United Nations system, including, in particular:

(a) The development of the human and technical resources that are indispensable for the improvement of information and communication systems in developing countries and support for the continuation and strengthening of practical training programmes, such as those already operating under both public and private auspices throughout the developing world;

(b) The creation of conditions that will enable developing countries and their media, public, private or other, to have, by using their national and regional resources, the communication technology suited to their national needs, as well as the necessary programme material, especially for radio and television broadcasting;

(c) Assistance in establishing and promoting telecommunication links at the subregional, regional and interregional levels, especially among developing countries;

(8) Full support should be provided for the International Programme for the Development of Communication of the United Nations Educational, Scientific and Cultural Organization, which should support both public and private media.

SEE ALSO UNESCO *Declaration on Fundamental Principles concerning the Contribution of the Mass Media to Strengthening Peace and International Understanding, to the Promotion of Human Rights and to Countering Racialism,* Apartheid *and Incitement to War.*

INKATHA. An anti-*apartheid* organization founded in 1976 and led by Chief Mangosuthu Gatsha Buthelezi of KwaZulu, the Zulu nation in South Africa, Inkatha's members, numbering about 1.5 million, are mainly Zulus from Natal Province. In recent years, they have engaged in factional warfare with the United Democratic Front, a coalition of anti-*apartheid* groups that supports the AFRICAN NATIONAL CONGRESS OF SOUTH AFRICA. The frequent clashes have brought death and destruction to a number of black townships in Durban, Pietermaritzburg, and other townships. In the last five years, more than 3,000 lives have been lost due to the warfare.

Inkatha stands firmly against the African National Congress because of the ANC's endorsement of armed struggle against white rule, economic sanctions, and the nationalization of sections of the South African economy, measures which Inkatha supporters feel hurt black South Africans more than help the majority. Chief Buthelezi has called the ANC undemocratic and communist-influenced and has accused the ANC of suppressing other black anti-*apartheid* organizations, including his own, that advocate less radical measures.

In July 1990, Chief Buthelezi took steps to convert his movement into a multi-racial party and to enter into negotiations with the ANC and South African government (*New York Times,* 15 July 1990).

INTER-AMERICAN CHARTER OF SOCIAL GUAR-ANTEES (1948). The charter is a proclamation of principles to protect workers of all kinds, setting out the rights to which they are entitled in the American States. Its purpose is to encourage the raising of STANDARDS OF LIVING throughout the American continent through economic development linked to co-operation between workers and employers. It was adopted as a resolution by the Ninth International Conference of American States, convened at Bogota, on 2 May 1948, and included in the Final Act of the Conference. The text of the charter is as follows:

General Principles

Article 1. It is the aim of the present Charter of Social Guarantees to proclaim the fundamental principles that must protect workers of all kinds, and it sets forth the minimum rights they must enjoy in the American States, without prejudice to the fact that the laws of each State may extend such rights or recognize others that are more favourable.

This Charter of Social Guarantees gives equal protection to men and women.

It is recognized that the supremacy of these rights and the progressive raising of the standard of living of the community in general depend to a large degree upon the development of economic activities, upon increased productivity, and upon co-operation between workers and employers, expressed in harmonious relations and in mutual respect for and fulfilment of their rights and duties.

Article 2. The following principles are considered to be fundamental in the social legislations of the American countries:

(a) Labour is a social function; it enjoys the special protection of the State and must not be considered as a commodity.

(b) Every worker must have the opportunity for a decent existence and the right to fair working conditions.

(c) Intellectual, as well as technical and manual labour,

must enjoy the guarantees established in labour laws, with the distinctions arising from the application of the law under the different circumstances.

(d) There should be equal compensation for equal work, regardless of the sex, race, creed or nationality of the worker.

(e) The rights established in favour of workers may not be renounced, and the laws that recognize such rights are binding on and benefit all the inhabitants of the territory, whether nationals or aliens.

Article 3. Every worker has the right to engage in his occupation and to devote himself to whatever activity suits him. He is likewise free to change employment.

Article 4. Every worker has the right to receive vocational and technical training in order to perfect his skills and knowledge, obtain a greater income from his work, and contribute effectively to the advancement of production. To this end, the State shall organize adult education and the apprenticeship of young people, in such a way as to assure effective training in a given trade or work, at the same time that it provides for their cultural, moral and civic development.

Article 5. Workers have the right to share in the equitable distribution of the national well-being, by obtaining the necessary food, clothing, and housing at reasonable prices. To achieve these purposes, the State must sponsor the establishment and operation of popular farms and restaurants and of consumer and credit co-operatives, and should organize institutions to promote and finance such farms and establishments, as well as to supply low-cost, comfortable, hygienic housing for labourers, salaried employees and rural workers.

Individual Labour Contracts

Article 6. The law shall regulate individual labour contracts, for the purpose of guaranteeing the rights of workers.

Collective Labour Contracts and Agreements

Article 7. The law shall recognize and regulate collective labour contracts and agreements. In the enterprises that are governed by these contracts and agreements, the provisions shall apply not only to the workers affiliated with the trade association that signed them, but also to the other workers who are or shall be employed in those enterprises. The law shall establish the procedure for extending collective contracts and agreements to all the activities in respect to which they were made and for widening the geographical sphere of their application.

Wages

Article 8. Every worker has the right to earn a minimum wage, fixed periodically with the participation of the State and of workers and employers, which shall be sufficient to cover his normal home needs, material, moral and cultural, taking into account the characteristics of each type of work, the special conditions of each region and each job, the cost of living, the worker's relative aptitude, and the wage systems prevalent in the enterprises.

A minimum occupational wage shall also be set up for those activities in which this matter is not regulated by a collective contract or agreement.

Article 9. Workers have the right to an annual bonus; in proportion to the number of days worked during the year.

Article 10. Wages and social benefits, in the amount fixed by law, are not subject to attachment, with the exception of payments for support that the worker has been ordered by a court to pay.

Wages should be paid in cash in legal tender. The value of wages and social benefits constitutes a privileged claim in the case of the bankruptcy of the employer, or a meeting of his creditors.

Article 11. Workers have the right to a fair share in the profits of the enterprises in which they work, in the form and amount and under the conditions that the law provides.

Work Periods, Rest and Vacations

Article 12. The ordinary effective work period should not exceed eight hours a day or forty-eight hours a week. The maximum duration of the work period in agricultural, livestock, or forestry work, shall not exceed nine hours a day or fifty-four hours a week. The daily limits may be extended up to one hour in each case, provided that the work period of one or more days during the week is shorter than the indicated limit, without prejudice to the provisions with respect to a weekly rest period. The period for night work, and that for dangerous or unhealthful work, shall be less than the daytime work period.

The work period limitation shall not apply in cases of *force majeure*.

Overtime work shall not exceed a daily and weekly maximum. In work that is by nature hazardous or unhealthful, the limit of the work period may not be exceeded by means of overtime work.

The laws of each country shall determine both the length of the intervals that are to interrupt the work period when for reasons of health the nature of the task demands it, and the intervals that should come between two work periods.

Workers may not exceed the limit of the work period, whether working for the same or for another employer.

Night and overtime work shall give the right to extra pay.

Article 13. Every worker has a right to a weekly paid rest period in the form established by the law of each country.

Workers who do not enjoy the rest period referred to in the foregoing paragraph shall be entitled to special pay for the services rendered on those days and to a compensatory rest period.

Article 14. Workers shall also have the right to a paid rest period on the civil and religious holidays established by law, with the exceptions that the law itself may determine, for the same reasons that justify work on the weekly days of rest. Those who do not enjoy the rest period on these days have a right to extra pay.

Article 15. Every worker who has to his credit a minimum of service rendered during a given period shall be entitled to paid annual vacations, on work days, the length of such vacations to be in proportion to the number of years of service. Monetary compensation may not be given in lieu of vacations, and the obligation of the worker to take them shall follow from the obligation of the employer to grant them.

Child Labour

Article 16. Persons less than fourteen years of age, and those who, having reached that age, are still subject to the compulsory education laws of the country, may not be employed in any type of work. The authorities responsible for supervising the work of such minors may authorize their employment when it is essential for their own maintenance, or that of their parents or brothers and sisters, provided that the minimum compulsory education requirements are met.

The work period for those under sixteen years of age may not be greater than six hours daily or thirty-six hours weekly in any type of work.

Article 17. Night work and work hazardous or injurious to health is forbidden for persons under eighteen years of age; exceptions concerning weekly rest set forth in the laws of the respective countries may not be applied to such workers.

The Work of Women

Article 18. In general, night work is forbidden for women in industrial establishments, whether public or private, and in work that is hazardous or injurious to health, except in cases where only the members of the same family are employed, in cases of *force majeure* that render it necessary, in cases where women perform administrative or responsible duties not normally requiring manual labour, and in other cases expressly provided for by law.

By industrial establishments and by work that is hazardous or injurious to health are understood those so defined by law or by international labour conventions.

Exceptions concerning weekly rest set forth in the laws of the respective countries may not be applied to women.

Tenure

Article 19. The law shall guarantee stability of employment, due consideration being given to the nature of the respective industries and occupations and justifiable causes for dismissal. In case of unjustified discharge, the worker shall have the right to indemnification.

Apprenticeship Contracts

Article 20. Apprenticeship contracts shall be regulated by a law, to assure to the apprentice instruction in his trade or occupation, just treatment, fair pay and the benefits of social security and welfare.

Work at Home

Article 21. Work at home is subject to social legislation. Home workers have the right to an officially determined minimum wage, to compensation for time lost because of the employer's delay in ordering or receiving the work, or for arbitrary or unjustified suspension of the supply of work. Home workers shall be entitled to a legal status similar to that of other workers, due consideration being given to the special nature of their work.

Domestic Work

Article 22. Domestic workers have a right to the protection of the law with respect to wages, work periods, rest periods, vacations, dismissal pay and social benefits in general; the extent and nature of this protection shall be determined with due regard to the conditions and special nature of their work. Those who render services of a domestic nature in industrial, commercial, social and other similar establishments should be considered as manual workers, and granted the rights to which such workers are entitled.

Work in the Merchant Marine and Aviation

Article 23. The law shall regulate the contracts of those serving in the merchant marine and in aviation, in accordance with the special character of their work.

Public Employees

Article 24. Public employees have the right to be protected in their administrative careers by being guaranteed, so long as they perform their duties satisfactorily, permanent employment, the right to promotion, and the benefits of social security. Such employees also have the right to be protected by a special court of administrative-contentious jurisdiction and, in case penalties are imposed, the right to defend themselves in the respective proceedings.

Intellectual Workers

Article 25. Independent intellectual workers and the product of their activity should be the subject of protective legislation.

The Right of Association

Article 26. Workers and employers, without distinction as to sex, race, creed or political ideas, have the right freely to form associations for the protection of their respective interests, by forming trade associations or unions, which in turn may form federations among themselves. These organizations have the right to enjoy juridical personality and to be duly protected in the exercise of their rights. Their suspension or dissolution may not be ordered save by due process of law.

Conditions of substance and of form that must be met for the constitution and functioning of trade and union organizations should not go so far as to restrict freedom of associations.

The organization, functioning and dissolution of federations and confederations shall be subject to the same formalities as those prescribed for unions.

Members of boards of directors of trade unions, in the number established by the respective law and during their term of office, may not be discharged, transferred or given less satisfactory working conditions, without just cause having been previously determined by competent authority.

The Right to Strike

Article 27. Workers have the right to strike. The law shall regulate the conditions and exercise of that right.

Social Security and Welfare

Article 28. It is the duty of the State to provide measures of social security and welfare for the benefit of workers.

Article 29. States should promote and provide for recreational and welfare centres that can be freely utilized by workers.

Article 30. The State should take adequate measures to ensure healthful, safe and moral conditions at places of work.

Article 31. Workers, including agricultural workers; home workers; domestic workers; public servants; apprentices, even when not receiving wages; and independent workers, when it is possible to include them, have the right to a system of compulsory social security designed to realize the following objectives:

(a) To provide for the elimination of hazards that might deprive workers of their wage-earning ability and means of support;

(b) To re-establish as quickly and as completely as possible the wage-earning ability lost or reduced as a result of illness or accident;

(c) To supply means of support in case of the termination or interruption of occupational activity as a result of illness or accident, maternity, temporary or permanent disability, unemployment, old age, or premature death of the head of the family.

Compulsory social security should provide for protection of the members of the worker's family and should establish additional benefits for those of the insured who have large families.

Article 32. In countries where a social security system does not yet exist, or in those in which one does exist but does not cover all occupational and social hazards, employers shall be responsible for providing adequate welfare and assistance benefits.

Article 33. Every working woman shall be entitled to have leave with pay for a period of not less than six weeks before and six weeks after childbirth, to keep her job, and to receive medical attention for herself and the child and financial assistance during the nursing period.

The law shall make it obligatory for employers to instal and maintain nurseries and playrooms for the children of workers.

Article 34. Independent workers have a right to the co-operation of the State in joining associations of social protection organized to given them benefits equal to those of wage earners. Persons who practise the liberal professions and are not employed by third parties have a similar right.

Supervision of Labour Conditions

Article 35. Workers have a right to have the State maintain a service of trained inspectors to ensure faithful compliance with legal provisions in regard to labour and social security, assistance and welfare, to study the results of such provisions and to suggest the indicated improvements.

Labour Courts

Article 36. Each State shall have a special system of labour courts and an adequate procedure for the prompt settlement of disputes.

Conciliation and Arbitration

Article 37. It is the duty of the State to promote conciliation and arbitration as means of obtaining peaceful solutions for collective labour disputes.

Rural Work

Article 38. Rural or farm workers have the right to be guaranteed an improvement in their present standard of living, to be furnished proper hygienic conditions and to have effective social assistance organized for them and their families.

The State shall carry on planned and systematic activity directed towards putting agricultural development on a rational basis, organizing and distributing credit, improving rural living conditions, and achieving the progressive economic and social emancipation of the rural population.

The law shall establish the technical and other conditions, consistent with the national interest of each State, under which effect shall be given to the exercise of the right which the State recognizes on behalf of associations of rural workers, and individuals suited to agricultural work who lack land or do not possess it in sufficient quantity, to be granted land and the means necessary to make it productive.

Article 39. In countries where the problem of an indigenous population exists, the necessary measures shall be adopted to give protection and assistance to the Indians, safeguarding their life, liberty and property, preventing their extermination, shielding them from oppression and exploitation, protecting them from want and furnishing them an adequate education.

The State shall exercise its guardianship in order to preserve, maintain and develop the patrimony of the Indians or their tribes; and it shall foster the exploitation of the natural, industrial or extractive resources or any other sources of income proceeding from or related to the aforesaid patrimony, in order to ensure in due time the economic emancipation of the indigenous groups.

Institutions or agencies shall be created for the protection of Indians, particularly in order to ensure respect for their lands, to legalize their possession thereof, and to prevent encroachment upon such lands by outsiders.

SEE ALSO American Convention on Human Rights and protocols; American Declaration on the Rights and Duties of Man; European Social Charter and Protocol.

INTER-AMERICAN COMMISSION OF WOMEN.

The Commission is an autonomous specialized agency of the ORGANIZATION OF AMERICAN STATES, established in 1928 by the Sixth International Conference of American States, meeting in Havana, and accorded permanent status in 1938 by the Eighth International Conference, meeting in Lima.

The OAS was the first intergovernmental organization to take action against discrimination on the ground of sex and to create a body expressly for the purpose of insuring recognition and enjoyment of the political rights of women. As a result of the Inter-American Commission's pioneering studies on the nationality of married women, the American republics adopted a convention on this subject at their seventh conference, held in Montevideo in 1933. Two years later, the League of Nations recommended this convention to all countries for signature. At the ninth International Conference of American States, held in Bogota in 1948, two inter-American conventions dealing with women's rights were adopted, one relating to the granting of political rights to women and the other to the granting of civil rights to women. The experience gained in the preparation and implementation of these regional agreements proved useful in the preparation by the United Nations of such international instruments as the CONVENTION ON THE POLITICAL RIGHTS OF WOMEN (1952), the DECLARATION ON THE ELIMINATION OF DISCRIMINATION AGAINST WOMEN (1967) and the CONVENTION ON THE ELIMINATION OF ALL FORMS OF DISCRIMINATION AGAINST WOMEN (1979).

The functions of the Inter-American Commission of Women may be summarized as follows: (1) to formulate strategies to bring about a new concept of the roles of men and women in the new social structure, considering them as two beings of equal worth, equally responsible for the fate of humanity; (2) to analyze the problems of women in the Americas and to identify those areas requiring more intensive action for their development, the realization of their just aspirations, and their participation in the integral development of their countries; (3) to mobilize, train, and organize women for effective, conscious, and continuing participation in the process of planning and executing development programs, providing them with the channels required to bring about such participation; (4) to promote the effective participation of women of all levels and all ages and social conditions in educational opportunities on an integral and continuing basis; and (5) to inform the governments of the American States and the OAS General Assembly about the civil, political, social, economic, and cultural status of women in the Americas and on the progress made in these fields, as well as on problems that, in its opinion, should be considered and to propose to them possible solutions to those problems.

The Commission is composed of one representative of each State member of the Organization of American States. Each member State appoints a principal delegate and such alternates and advisors as it may consider appropriate. All delegates, alternates, and advisors serve at the will of their governments. Regular sessions of the Assembly of Delegates, the supreme organ of the commission, are held every two years; special session are convened as required. Unless otherwise decided, sessions of the commission are held at its headquarters in Washington, D.C.

The commission's subsidiary bodies include (1) the Executive Committee, composed of six member States under the chairmanship of the president of the Assembly of Delegates, which meets as required either at the headquarters of the commission or in any country of the Americas; (2) the National Committees of Cooperation, organized, directed, and presided over by the respective delegates; and (3) the Permanent Secretariat, appointed by the OAS Secretary-General to provide the staff of the commission.

SEE ALSO Commission on the Status of Women (UN).

INTER-AMERICAN COMMISSION ON HUMAN RIGHTS.

The Inter-American Commission on Human Rights of the ORGANIZATION OF AMERICAN STATES was established in 1959 and in 1965 was authorized to examine complaints received from individuals alleging violations of the principles set out in the AMERICAN DECLARATION ON THE RIGHTS AND DUTIES OF MAN. Under the AMERICAN CONVENTION OF HUMAN RIGHTS, which entered into force on 18 July 1978, the commission is authorized °(a) to develop an awareness of human rights among the people of America; (b) to make recommendations to the governments of the member States for the adoption of progessive measures in favor of human rights; (c) to prepare studies and reports; (d) to request the governments of member States to supply it with information on the measures adopted by them in matters of human rights; (e) to respond, through the General Secretariat of the Organization of American States, to inquiries made by the member States on matters related to human rights and, within the limited of its possibilities, to provide those States with the advisory services they request; (f) to take action on petitions and other communications under the provisions of the convention; and (g) to submit an annual report to the General Assembly of the Organization of American States.

Under article 42 of the convention, States parties transmit to the commission copies of the reports that they submit annually to the Executive Committee of the INTER-AMERICAN ECONOMIC AND SOCIAL COUNCIL and the INTER-AMERICAN COUNCIL FOR EDUCATION, SCIENCE AND CULTURE. The task of the commission with regard to such reports is to "watch over the promotion of human rights implicit in the economic, social, educational, scientific and cultural standards set forth in the Charter of the Organization of American States as amended by the Protocol of Buenos Aires."

Under article 45, any State party to the convention may declare that it recognizes the competence of the commission to receive and examine communications in which a State party alleges that another State party has committed a violation of a human right set forth in the convention. The committee may examine such communications only if they are presented by a State that has made such a declaration and are directed against a State that has also made such a declaration. The commission first considers the admissibility of such communications (articles 46 and 47). In the case of those found to be admissible, it requests relevant information from the government of the State indicated as being responsible for the alleged violations. On the basis of such information, it may close the case. If not, it first establishes the facts and then seeks to secure a friendly settlement. If such a settlement is reached, it draws up a report to be transmitted to the petitioner and to the States parties to the convention, as well as to the secretary-general for publication. If unsuccessful, it draws up a report setting out the facts and stating its conclusions, to be transmitted to the States concerned. If the matter has not been settled or submitted to the INTER-AMERICAN COURT OF HUMAN RIGHTS within three months, the commission may set forth its opinions and conclusions, make pertinent recommendations, and prescribe a period within which the State may be expected to take measures to remedy the situation. If the prescribed period expires without action, the commission may decide by majority vote (a) whether the State has taken adequate measures and (b) whether to publish its report on the situation. In addition to such reports, the commission submits an annual report to the General Assembly of the Organization of American States.

The commission consists of seven members, elected by the OAS General Assembly from a list of candidates proposed by the governments of member States; they serve in their personal capacity for a term of four years. The commission usually holds three session per year at its headquarters, the General Secretariat of the Organization of American States, Washington, D.C. Occasionally, it meets elsewhere, or upon invitation conducts on-site observation in a particular country.

Rules relating to the Functions of the Commission. The regulations of the commission (OAS Doc. OEA/Ser. L/V/II.65, Doc. 6) set out rules relating to the handling of the petitions and communications regarding States parties to the American Convention on Human Rights, as follows:

Title II—Procedures

Chapter I
General Provisions

Article 25. Official Languages. 1. The official languages of the Commission shall be Spanish, French, English and Portuguese. The working languages shall be those decided on by the Commission every two years, in accordance with the languages spoken by its members.

2. A member of the Commission may allow omission of the interpretation of debates and the preparation of documents in his language.

Article 26. Presentation of Petitions. 1. Any person or group of persons or nongovernmental entity legally recognized in one or more of the Member States of the Organization may submit petitions to the Commission, in accordance with these Regulations, on one's own behalf or on behalf of third persons, with regard to alleged violations of a human rights recognized, as the case may be, in the American Convention on Human Rights or in the American Declaration of the Rights and Duties of Man.

2. The Commission may also, *motu proprio,* take into consideration any available information that it considers pertinent and which might include the necessary factors to begin processing a case which in its opinion fulfills the requirements for the purpose.

Article 27. Form. 1. The petition shall be lodged in writing.

2. The petitioner may appoint, in the petition itself, or in another written petition, an attorney or other person to represent him before the Commission.

Article 28. Special Missions. The Commission may designate one or more of its members or staff members of the Secretariat to take specific measures, investigate facts or make the necessary arrangements for the Commission to perform its functions.

Article 29. Precautionary Measures. 1. The Commission may, at its own initiative, or at the request of a party, take any action it considers necessary for the discharge of its functions.

2. In urgent cases, when it becomes necessary to avoid irreparable damage to persons, the Commission may request that provisional measures be taken to avoid irreparable damage in cases where the denounced facts are true.

3. If the Commission is not in session, the Chairman, or in his absence, one of the Vice-Chairmen, shall consult with the other members, through the Secretariat, on implementation of the provisions of paragraphs 1 and 2 above. If it is not possible to consult within a reasonable time, the Chairman shall take the decision on behalf of the Commission and shall so inform its members immediately.

4. The request for such measures and their adoption shall not prejudice the final decision.

Article 30. Initial Processing. 1. The Secretariat of the Commission shall be responsible for the study and initial processing of petitions lodged before the Commission and that fulfill all the requirements set forth in the Statute and in these Regulations.

2. If a petition or communication does not meet the requirements called for in these Regulations, the Secretariat of the Commission may request the petitioner or his representative to complete it.

3. If the Secretariat has any doubt as to the admissibility of a petition, it shall submit it for consideration to the Commission or to the Chairman during recesses of the Commission.

Chapter II
Petitions and Communications Regarding States Parties to the American Convention on Human Rights

Article 31. Condition for Considering the Petition. The Commission shall take into account petitions regarding alleged violations by a state party of human rights defined in the American Convention on Human Rights, only when they fulfill the requirements set forth in that Convention, in the Statute and in these Regulations.

Article 32. Requirements for the Petitions. Petitions addressed to the Commission shall include:

a. the name, nationality, profession or occupation, postal address, or domicile and signature of the person or persons making the denunciation; or in cases where the petitioner in a nongovernmental entity, its legal domicile or postal address, and the name and signature of its legal representative or representatives;

b. an account of the act or situation that is denounced, specifying the place and date of the alleged violations and, if possible, the name of the victims of such violations as well as that of any official that might have been apprised of the act or situation that was denounced;

c. an indication of the state in question which the petitioner considers responsible, by commission or omission, for the violation of a human right recognized in the American Convention on Human Rights in the case of States Parties thereto, even if no specific reference is made to the article alleged to have been violated;

d. information on whether the remedies under domestic law have been exhausted or whether it has been impossible to do so.

Article 33. Omission of Requirements. Without prejudice to the provisions of Article 26, if the Commission considers that the petition is inadmissible or incomplete, it shall no-

tify the petitioner, whom it shall ask to complete the requirements omitted in the petition.

Article 34. Initial Processing. 1. The Commission, acting initially through its Secretariat, shall receive and process petitions lodged with it in accordance with the standards set forth below:

a. it shall enter the petition in a register especially prepared for that purpose, and the date on which it was received shall be marked on the petition or communication itself;

b. it shall acknowledge receipt of the petition to the petitioner, indicating that it will be considered in accordance with the Regulations;

c. if it accepts, in principle, the admissibility of the petition, it shall request information from the government of the State in question and include the pertinent parts of the petitions.

2. In serious or urgent cases or when it is believed that the life, personal integrity or health of a person is in imminent danger, the Commission shall request the promptest reply from the government, using for this purpose the means it considers most expeditious.

3. The request for information shall not constitute a prejudgment with regard to the decision the Commission may finally adopt on the admissibility of the petition.

4. In transmitting the pertinent parts of a communication to the government of the State in question, the identity of the petitioner shall be withheld, as shall any other information that could identify him, except when the petitioner expressly authorizes in writing the disclosure of his identity.

5. The Commission shall request the affected government to provide the information requested within 90 days after the date on which the request is sent.

6. The government of the State in question may, with justifiable cause, request a 30 day extension, but in no case shall extensions be granted for more than 180 days after the date on which the first communication is sent to the government of the State concerned.

7. The pertinent parts of the reply and the documents provided by the government shall be made known to the petitioner or to his representative, who shall be asked to submit his observations and any available evidence to the contrary within 30 days.

8. On receipt of the information or documents requested, the pertinent parts shall be transmitted to the government, which shall be allowed to submit its final observations within 30 days.

Article 35. Preliminary Questions. The Commission shall proceed to examine the case and decide on the following matters:

a. whether the remedies under domestic law have been exhausted, and it may determine any measures it considers necessary to clarify any remaining doubts;

b. other questions related to the admissibility of the petition of its manifest inadmissibility based upon the record or submission of the parties;

c. whether grounds for the petition exist or subsist, and if not, to order the file closed.

Article 36. Examination by the Commission. The record shall be submitted by the Secretariat to the Commission for consideration at the first session held after the period referred to in Article 31, paragraph 5, if the government has not provided the information on that occasion, or after the periods indicated in paragraphs 7 and 8 have elapsed if the petitioner has not replied or if the government has not submitted its final observations.

Article 37. Exhaustion of Domestic Remedies. 1. For a petition to be admitted by the Commission, the remedies under domestic jurisdiction must have been invoked and exhausted in accordance with the general principles of international law.

2. The provisions of the preceding paragraph shall not be applicable when:

a. the domestic legislation of the State concerned does not afford due process of law for protection of the right or rights that have allegedly been violated;

b. the party alleging violation of his rights has been denied access to the remedies under domestic law or has been prevented from exhausting them;

c. there has been unwarranted delay in rendering a final judgment under the aforementioned remedies.

3. When the petitioner contends that he is unable to prove exhaustion as indicated in this Article, it shall be up to the government against which this petition has been lodged to demonstrate to the Commission that the remedies under domestic law have not previously been exhausted, unless it is clearly evident from the background information contained in the petition.

Article 38. Deadline for the Presentation of Petitions. 1. The Commission shall refrain from taking up those petitions that are lodged after the six-month period following the date on which the party whose rights have allegedly been violated has been notified of the final ruling in cases where the remedies under domestic law have been exhausted.

2. In the circumstances set forth in Article 34, (2) of these Regulations, the deadline for presentation of a petition to the Commission shall be within a reasonable period of time, in the Commission's judgment, as from the date on which the alleged violation of rights has occurred, considering the circumstances of each specific case.

Article 39. Duplication of Procedures. 1. The Commission shall not consider a petition in cases where the subject of the petition:

a. is pending settlement in another procedure under an international governmental organization of which the State concerned is a member;

b. essentially duplicates a petition pending or already examined and settled by the Commission or by another international governmental organization of which the state concerned is a member.

2. The Commission shall not refrain from taking up and examining a petition in cases provided for in paragraph 1 when:

a. the procedure followed before the other organization or agency is one limited to an examination of the general situation on human rights in the State in question and there has been no decision on the specific facts that are the subject of the petition submitted to the Commission, or is one that will not lead to an effective settlement of the violation denounced;

b. the petitioner before the Commission or a family member is the alleged victim of the violation denounced and the petitioner before the organizations in reference is a third party of a nongovernmental entity having no mandate from the former.

Article 40. Separation and Combination of Cases. 1. Any petition that states different facts that concern more than one person, and that could constitute various violations that are unrelated in time and place shall be separated and processed as separate cases, provided the requirements set forth in Article 32 are met.

2. When two petitions deal with the same facts and persons, they shall be combined and processed in a single file.

Article 41. Declaration of Inadmissibility. The Commission shall declare inadmissible any petition when:

a. any of the requirements set forth in Article 32 of these Regulations has not been met;

b. when the petition does not state facts that constitute a violation of rights referred to in Article 31 of these Regulations in the case of the States Parties to the American Convention on Human Rights;

c. the petition is manifestly groundless or inadmissible on the basis of the statement by the petitioner himself or the government.

Article 42. Presumption. The facts reported in the petition whose pertinent parts have been transmitted to the government of the State in reference shall be presumed to be true if, during the maximum period set by the Commission under the provision of Article 34 paragraph 5, the government has not provided the pertinent information, as long as other evidence does not lead to a different conclusion.

Article 43. Hearing. 1. If the file has not been closed and in order to verify the facts, the Commission may conduct a hearing following a summons to the parties and proceed to examine the matter set forth in the petition.

2. At that hearing, the Commission may request any pertinent information from the representative of the State in question and shall receive, if so requested, oral or written statements presented by the parties concerned.

Article 44. On-site Investigation. 1. If necessary and advisable, the Commission shall carry out an on-site investigation, for the effective conduct of which it shall request, and the States concerned shall furnish to it, all necessary facilities.

2. However, in serious and urgent cases, only the presentation of a petition or communication that fulfills all the formal requirements of admissibility shall be necessary in order for the Commission to conduct an on-site investigation with the prior consent of the State in whose territory a violation has allegedly been committed.

3. Once the investigatory stage has been completed, the case shall be brought for consideration before the Commission, which shall prepare its decision in a period of 180 days.

Article 45. Friendly Settlement. 1. At the request of any of the parties, or on is own initiative, the Commission shall place itself at the disposal of the parties concerned, at any stage of the examination of a petition, with a view to reaching a friendly settlement of the matter on the basis of respect for the human rights recognized in the American Convention on Human Rights.

2. In order for the Commission to offer itself as an organ of conciliation for a friendly settlement to the matter it shall be necessary for the positions and allegations of the parties to be sufficiently precise; and in the judgment of the Commission, the nature of the matter must be susceptible to the use of the friendly settlement procedure.

3. The Commission shall accept the proposal to act as an organ of conciliation for a friendly settlement presented by one of the parties if the circumstances described in the above paragraph exist and if the other party to the dispute expressly accepts the procedure.

4. The Commission, upon accepting the role of an organ of conciliation for a friendly settlement shall designate a Special Commission or an individual from among its members. The Special Commission or the member so desig-

nated shall inform the Commission within the time period set by the Commission.

5. The Commission shall fix a time for the reception and gathering of evidence, it shall set dates for the holding of hearings, if appropriate, it shall plan an on-site observation, which will be carried out following the receipt of consent of the State to be visited and it shall fix a time for the conclusion of the procedure, which the Commission may extend.

6. If a friendly settlement is reached, the Commission shall prepare a report which shall be transmitted to the parties concerned and referred to the Secretary General of the Organization of American States for publication. This report shall contain a brief statement of the facts and of the solution reached. If any party in the case so requests, it shall be provided with the fullest possible information.

7. In a case where the Commission finds, during the course of processing the matter, that the case, by its very nature, is not susceptible to a friendly settlement; or finds that one of the parties does not consent to the application of this procedure; or does not evidence good will in reaching a friendly settlement based on the respect for human rights, the Commission, at any stage of the procedure shall declare its role as organ of conciliation for a friendly settlement to have terminated.

Article 46. Preparation of the Report. 1. If a friendly settlement is not reached, the Commission shall examine the evidence provided by the government in question and the petitioner, evidence taken from witnesses to the facts or that obtained from documents, records, official publications, or through an on-site investigation.

2. After the evidence has been examined, the Commission shall prepare a report stating the facts and conclusions regarding the case submitted to it for its study.

Article 47. Proposals and Recommendations. 1. In transmitting the report, the Commission may make such proposals and recommendations as it sees fit.

2. If, within a period of three months from the date of the transmittal of the report of the Commission to the States concerned, the matter has not been settled or submitted by the Commission, or by the State concerned, to the Court and its jurisdiction accepted, the Commission may, by the vote of an absolute majority of its members, set forth its opinion and conclusions concerning the question submitted for its consideration.

3. The Commission may make the pertinent recommendation and prescribe a period within which the government in question must take the measures that are incumbent upon it to remedy the situation examined.

4. If the report does not represent, in its entirety, or, in part, the unanimous opinion of the members of the Commission, any member may add his opinion separately to that report.

5. Any verbal or written statement made by the parties shall also be included in the report.

6. The report shall be transmitted to the parties concerned, who shall not be authorized to publish it.

Article 48. Publication of the Report. 1. When the prescribed period has expired, the Commission shall decide by the vote of an absolute majority of its members whether the State has taken suitable measures and whether to publish its report.

2. That report may be published by including it in the Annual Report to be presented by the Commission to the General Assembly of the Organization or in any other way the Commission may consider suitable.

Article 49. Communications from a Government. 1. Communications presented by the government of a State Party to the American Convention on Human Rights, which has accepted the competence of the Commission to receive and examine such communications against other States Parties, shall be transmitted to the State Party in question, whether or not it has accepted the competence of the Commission. Even if it has not accepted such competence, the communication shall be transmitted so that the State can exercise its option under the provisions of Article 45, (3) of the Convention to recognize the Commission's competence in the specific case that is the subject of the communication.

2. Once the State in question has accepted the competence of the Commission to take up the communication of the other State Party, the corresponding procedure shall be governed by the provisions of Chapter II insofar as they may be applicable.

Article 50. Referral of the Case to the Court. 1. If a State Party to the Convention has accepted the Court's jurisdiction in accordance with Article 62 of the Convention, the Commission may refer the case to the Court, subsequent to transmittal of the report referred to in Article 46 of these Regulations to the government of the State in question.

2. When it is ruled that the case is to be referred to the Court, the Executive Secretary of the Commission shall immediately notify the Court, the petitioner and the government of the State in question.

3. If the State Party has not accepted the Court's jurisdiction, the Commission may call upon that State to make use of the option referred to in Article 62, paragraph 2 of the Convention to recognize the Court's jurisdiction in the specific case that is the subject of the report.

Chapter III
Petitions Concerning States that Are Not Parties to the American Convention on Human Rights

Article 51. Receipt of the Petitions. The Commission shall receive and examine any petition that contains a denunciation of alleged violations of the human rights set forth in the American Declaration of the Rights and Duties of Man, concerning the Member States of the Organization that are not parties to the American Convention on Human Rights.

Article 52. Applicable Procedure. The procedure applicable to petitions concerning Member States of the Organization that are not parties to the American Convention on Human Rights shall be that provided for in the General Provisions included in Chapter I of Title II, in Articles 32 to 43 of these Regulations, and in the articles indicated below.

Article 53. Final Decision. 1. In addition to the facts and conclusions, the Commission's final decision shall include any recommendations the Commission deems advisable and a deadline for their implementation.

2. That decision shall be transmitted to the State in question.

3. If the State does not adopt the measures recommended by the Commission within the deadline referred to in paragraphs 1 or 3, the Commission may publish its decision.

4. The decision referred to in the preceding paragraph may be published in the Annual Report to be presented by the Commission to the General Assembly of the Organization or in any other manner the Commission may see fit.

Article 54. Request for Reconsideration. 1. When the State in question, prior to the expiration of the 90 day deadline, invokes new facts or legal arguments which have not been previously considered, it may request a reconsideration of the conclusions or recommendations of the Commission's Report. The Commission shall decide to maintain or modify its decision, fixing a new deadline for compliance, where appropriate.

2. The Commission, if it considers it necessary, may request the petitioner to present any observations to the affected State's request for reconsideration.

3. The reconsideration procedure may be utilized only once.

4. The Commission shall consider the request for reconsideration during the first regular session following its presentation.

5. If the State does not adopt the measures recommended by the Commission within the deadline referred to in paragraph 1, the Commission may publish its decision in conformity with Article 48 (2) and 53 (4) of the present Regulations.

Chapter IV
On-Site Observations

Article 55. Designation of the Special Commission. On-site observations shall be carried out in each case by a Special Commission named for that purpose. The number of members of the Special Commission and the designation of its Chairman shall be determined by the Commission. In cases of great urgency, such decision may be made by the Chairman subject to the approval of the Commission.

Article 56. Disqualification. A member of the Commission who is a national of or who resides in the territory of the State in which the on-site observation is to be carried out shall be disqualified from participating therein.

Article 57. Schedule of Activities. The Special Commission shall organize its own activities. To that end, it may appoint its own members and, after hearing the Executive Secretary, any staff members of the Secretariat or personnel necessary to carry out any activities related to its mission.

Article 58. Necessary Facilities. In extending an invitation for an on-site observation or in giving its consent, the government shall furnish to the Special Commission all necessary facilities for carrying out its mission. In particular, it shall bind itself not to take any reprisals of any kind against any persons or entities cooperating with the Special Commission or providing information or testimony.

Article 59. Other Applicable Standards. Without prejudice to the provisions in the preceding article, any on-site observation agreed upon by the Commission shall be carried out in accordance with the following standards:

a. the special Commission or any of its members shall be able to interview freely and in private, any persons, groups, entities or institutions, and the government shall grant the pertinent guarantees to all those who provide the Commission with information, testimony or evidence of any kind;

b. the members of the Special Commission shall be able to travel freely throughout the territory of the country, for which purpose the government shall extend all the corresponding facilities, including the necessary documentation;

c. the government shall ensure the availability of local means of transportation;

d. the members of the Special Commission shall have access to the jails and all other detention and interrogation centers and shall be able to interview in private those persons imprisoned or detained;

e. the government shall provide the Special Commission with any document related to the observance of human rights that it may consider necessary for the presentation of its reports;

f. the Special Commission shall be able to use any method appropriate for collecting, recording or reproducing the information it considers useful;

g. the government shall adopt the security measures necessary to protect the Special Commission;

h. the government shall ensure the availability of appropriate lodging for the members of the Special Commission;

i. the same guarantees and facilities that are set forth here for the members of the Special Commission shall also be extended to the Secretariat staff;

j. any expenses incurred by the Special Committee, any of its members and the Secretariat staff shall be borne by the Organization, subject to the pertinent provisions.

INTER-AMERICAN COMMISSION ON HUMAN RIGHTS: STATUTE. The statute of the Inter-American Commission on Human Rights, approved by the OAS General Assembly (resolution 447) at its ninth regular session, held in La Paz, Bolivia, in October 1979, is as follows:

Chapter I
Nature and Purposes

Article 1. The Inter-American Commission on Human Rights is an organ of the Organization of the American States, created to promote the observance and defense of human rights and to serve as consultative organ of the Organization in this matter.

2. For the purposes of the present Statute, human rights are understood to be:

a. The rights set forth in the American Convention on Human Rights, in relation to the States Parties thereto;

b. The rights set forth in the American Declaration of the Rights and Duties of Man, in relation to the other member states.

Chapter II
Membership and Structure

Article 2. 1. The Inter-American Commission on Human Rights shall be composed of seven members, who shall be persons of high moral character and recognized competence in the field of human rights.

2. The Commission shall represent all the member states of the Organization.

Article 3. 1. The members of the Commission shall be elected in a personal capacity by the General Assembly of the Organization from a list of candidates proposed by the governments of the member states.

2. Each government may propose up to three candidates, who may be nationals of the state proposing them or of any other Member State of the Organization. When a slate of three is proposed, at least one of the candidates shall be a national of a State other then the proposing state.

Article 4. 1. At least six months prior to completion of the term of office for which the members of the Commission were elected, the Secretary General shall request, in writing, each Member State of the Organization to present its candidates within 90 days.

2. The Secretary General shall prepare a list in alphabetical order of the candidates nominated, and shall transmit it to the member states of the Organization at least thirty days prior to the next General Assembly.

Article 5. The members of the Commission shall be elected by secret ballot of the General Assembly from the list of candidates referred to in Article 3 (2). The candidates who obtain the largest number of votes and an absolute majority of the votes of the member states shall be declared elected. Should it become necessary to hold several ballots to elect all the members of the Commission, the candidates who receive the smallest number of votes shall be eliminated successively, in the manner determined by the General Assembly.

Article 6. The members of the Commission shall be elected for a term of four years and may be reelected only once. Their terms of office shall begin on January 1 of the year following the year in which they are elected.

Article 7. No two nationals of the same State may be members of the Commission.

Article 8. 1. Membership on the Inter-American Commission on Human Rights is incompatible with engaging in other functions that might affect the independence or impartiality of the member or the dignity or prestige of his post on the Commission.

2. The Commission shall consider any case that may arise regarding incompatibility in accordance with the provisions of the first paragraph of this Article, and in accordance with the procedures provided by its Regulations.

If the Commission decides, by an affirmative vote of a least five of its members, that a case of incompatibility exists, it will submit the case, with its background, to the General Assembly for decision.

3. A declaration of incompatibility by the General Assembly shall be adopted by a majority of two thirds of the member states of the Organization and shall occasion the immediate removal of the member of the Commission from his post, but it shall not invalidate any action in which he may have participated.

Article 9. The duties of the members of the Commission are:

1. Except when justifiably prevented, to attend the regular and special meetings the Commission holds at its permanent headquarters or in any other place to which it may have decided to move temporarily.

2. To serve, except when justifiably prevented, on the special committees which the Commission may form to conduct on-site observations, or to perform any other duties within their ambit.

3. To maintain absolute secrecy about all matters which the Commission deems confidential.

4. To conduct themselves in their public and private life as befits the high moral authority of the office and the importance of the mission entrusted to the Commission.

Article 10. 1. If a member commits a serious violation of any of the duties referred to in Article 9, the Commission, on the affirmative vote of five of its members, shall submit the case to the General Assembly of the Organization, which shall decide whether he should be removed from office.

2. The Commission shall hear the member in question before taking its decision.

Article 11. 1. When a vacancy occurs for reasons other than the normal completion of a member's term of office,

the Chairman of the Commission shall immediately notify the Secretary General of the Organization, who shall in turn inform the member states of the Organization.

2. In order to fill vacancies, each government may propose a candidate within a period of 30 days from the date of receipt of the Secretary General's communication that a vacancy has occurred.

3. The Secretary General shall prepare an alphabetical list of the candidates and shall transmit it to the Permanent Council of the Organization, which shall fill the vacancy.

4. When the term of office is due to expire within six months following the date on which a vacancy occurs, the vacancy shall not be filled.

Article 12. 1. In those member states of the Organization that are Parties to the American Convention on Human Rights, the members of the Commission shall enjoy, from the time of their election and throughout their term of office, such immunities as are granted to diplomatic agents under international law. While in office, they shall also enjoy the diplomatic privileges required for the performance of their duties.

2. In those member states of the Organization that are not Parties to the American Convention on Human Rights, the members of the Commission shall enjoy the privileges and immunities pertaining to their posts that are required for them to perform their duties with independence.

3. The system of privileges and immunities of the members of the Commission may be regulated or supplemented by multilateral or bilateral agreements between the Organization and the member states.

Article 13. The members of the Commission shall receive travel allowances and per diem and fees, as appropriate, for their participation in the meetings of the Commission or in other functions which the Commission, in accordance with its Regulations, entrusts to them, individually or collectively. Such travel and per diem allowances and fees shall be included in the budget of the Organization, and their amounts and conditions shall be determined by the General Assembly.

Article 14. 1. The Commission shall have a Chairman, a First Vice-Chairman and a Second Vice-Chairman, who shall be elected by an absolute majority of its members for a period of one year; they may be re-elected only once in each four-year period.

2. The Chairman and the two Vice-Chairmen shall be the officers of the Commission, and their function shall be set forth in the Regulations.

Article 15. The Chairman of the Commission may go to the Commission's headquarters and remain there for such time as may be necessary for the performance of his duties.

Chapter III
Headquarters and Meetings

Article 16. 1. The headquarters of the Commission shall be in Washington, D.C.

2. The Commission may move to and meet in the territory of any American State when it so decided by an absolute majority of votes, and with the consent, or at the invitation of the government concerned.

3. The Commission shall meet in regular and special sessions, in conformity with the provisions of the Regulations.

Article 17. 1. An absolute majority of the members of the Commission shall constitute a quorum.

2. In regard to those States that are Parties to the Convention, decisions shall be taken by an absolute majority

vote of the members of the Commission in those cases established by the American Convention on Human Rights and the present Statute. In other cases, an absolute majority of the members present shall be required.

3. In regard to those States that are not Parties to the Convention, decisions shall be taken by an absolute majority vote of the members of the Commission, except in matters of procedure, in which case, the decisions shall be taken by simple majority.

Chapter IV
Functions and Powers

Article 18. The Commission shall have the following powers with respect to the member states of the Organization of American States:

a. to develop an awareness of human rights among the peoples of the Americas;

b. to make recommendations to the governments of the States on the adoption of progressive measures in favor of human rights in the framework of their legislation, constitutional provisions and international commitments, as well as appropriate measures to further observance of those rights;

c. to prepare such studies or reports as it considers advisable for the performance of its duties;

d. to request that the governments of the States provide it with reports on measures they adopt in matters of human rights;

e. to respond to inquiries made by any Member State through the General Secretariat of the Organization on matters related to human rights in the State and, within its possibilities, to provide those States with the advisory services they request;

f. to submit an annual report to the General Assembly of the Organization, in which due account shall be taken of the legal regime applicable to those State Parties to the American Convention on Human Rights and of that system applicable to those that are not Parties;

g. to conduct on-site observations in a state, with the consent or at the invitation of the government in question; and

h. to submit the program-budget of the Commission to the Secretary General, so that he may present it to the General Assembly.

Article 19. With respect to the States Parties to the American Convention on Human Rights, the Commission shall discharge its duties in conformity with the powers granted under the Convention and in the present Statute, and shall have the following powers in addition to those designated in Article 18:

a. to act on petitions and other communications, pursuant to the provisions of Articles 44 to 51 of the Convention;

b. to appear before the Inter-American Court of Human Rights in cases provided for in the Convention;

c. to request the Inter-American Court of Human Rights to take such provisional measures as it considers appropriate in serious and urgent cases which have not yet been submitted to it for consideration, whenever this becomes necessary to prevent irreparable injury to persons;

d. to consult the Court on the interpretation of the American Convention on Human Rights or of other treaties concerning the protection of human rights in the American states;

e. to submit additional draft protocols to the American Convention on Human rights to the General Assembly, in order to progressively include other rights and freedoms under the system of protection of the Convention, and

f. to submit to the General Assembly, through the Secretary General, proposed amendments to the American Convention on Human Rights, for such action as the General Assembly deems appropriate.

Article 20. In relation to those member states of the Organization that are not Parties to the American Convention on Human Rights, the Commission shall have the following powers, in addition to those designated in Article 18:

a. to pay particular attention to the observance of the human rights referred to in Articles I, II, III, IV, XVIII, XXV, and XXVI of the American Declaration of the Rights and Duties of Man;

b. to examine communications submitted to it and any other available information, to address the government of any Member State not a Party to the Convention for information deemed pertinent by this Commission, and to make recommendations to it, when it finds this appropriate, in order to bring about more effective observance of fundamental human rights; and

c. to verify, as a prior condition to the exercise of the powers granted under subparagraph b. above, whether the domestic legal procedures and remedies of each Member State not a Party to the Convention have been duly applied and exhausted.

Chapter V
Secretariat

Article 21. 1. The Secretariat services of the Commission shall be provided by a specialized administrative unit under the direction of an Executive Secretary. This unit shall be provided with the resources and staff required to accomplish the tasks the Commission may assign to it.

2. The Executive Secretary, who shall be a person of high moral character and recognized competence in the field of human rights, shall be responsible for the work of the Secretariat and shall assist the Commission in the performance of its duties in accordance with the Regulations.

3. The Executive Secretary shall be appointed by the Secretary General of the Organization, in consultation with the Commission. Furthermore, for the Secretary General to be able to remove the Executive Secretary, he shall consult with the Commission and inform its members of the reasons for his decision.

Chapter VI
Statute and Regulations

Article 22. 1. The present Statute may be amended by the General Assembly.

2. The Commission shall prepare and adopt its own Regulations, in accordance with the present Statute.

Article 23. 1. In accordance with the provisions of Articles 44 to 51 of the American Convention on Human Rights, the Regulations of the Commission shall determine the procedure to be followed in cases of petitions or communications alleging violation of any of the rights guaranteed by the Convention, and imputing such violation to any State Party to the Convention.

2. If the friendly settlement referred to in Articles 44–51 of the Convention is not reached, the Commission shall draft, within 180 days, the report required by Article 50 of the Convention.

Article 24. 1. The Regulations shall establish the procedure to be followed in cases of communications containing accusations or complaints of violations of human rights imputable to States that are not Parties to the American Convention on Human Rights.

2. The Regulations shall contain, for this purpose, the pertinent rules established in the Statute of the Commission approved by the Council of the Organization in resolutions adopted on May 25 and June 8, 1960, with the modifications and amendments introduced by Resolution XXII of the Second Special Inter-American Conference, and by the Council of the Organization at its meeting held on April 24, 1968, taking into account resolutions CP/RES. 253 (343/78), "Transition from the present Inter-American Commission on Human Rights to the Commission provided for in the American Convention on Human Rights," adopted by the Permanent Council of the Organization on September 20, 1979.

Chapter VII
Transitory Provisions

Article 25. Until the Commission adopts its new Regulations, the current Regulations (OEA/Ser.L/VII. 17, doc. 26) shall apply to all the member states of the Organization.

Article 26. 1. The present Statute shall enter into effect 30 days after its approval by the General Assembly.

2. The Secretary General shall order immediate publication of the Statute, and shall give it the widest possible distribution.

INTER-AMERICAN CONVENTION OF CONFLICT OF LAWS CONCERNING THE ADOPTION OF MINORS (1984).

The aim of the convention is to eliminate, insofar as possible, legal or social discrimination against adopted children in cases where the domicile of the adopting parent or parents is in one State party and the habitual residence of the adoptee is in another State party.

The convention was adopted at La Paz on 24 May 1984 by the Third Inter-American Specialized Conference on Private International Law and entered into force on 26 May 1988. The text (*OAS Treaty Series* 62) is as follows:

The Governments of the Member States of the Organization of American States, desirous of concluding a convention on conflict of laws concerning the adoption of minors, have agreed as follows:

Article 1. This Convention shall apply to the adoption of minors in the form of full adoption, adoptive legitimation and other similar institutions that confer on the adoptee a legally established filiation, when the domicile of the adopter (or of the adoptee) is in one State Party and the habitual residence of the adoptee is in another State Party.

Article 2. When signing, ratifying or acceding to this Convention, any State Party may declare that it applies to any other form of international adoption of minors.

Article 3. The law of the habitual residence of the minor shall govern capacity, consent, and other requirements for adoption, as well as those procedures and formalities that are necessary for creating the relationship.

Article 4. The law of the domicile of the adopter (or adopters) shall govern:

a. The capacity to be an adopter;

b. The age and marital status requirement to be met by an adopter;

c. The consent of an adopter's spouse, if required, and

d. The other requirements for being an adopter.

If, however, the requirements of the law of the adopter (or adopters) are manifestly less strict than those of the law of the adoptee's habitual residence, the law of the adoptee shall govern.

Article 5. Adoptions that are in conformity with this Convention shall produce their effects unconditionally in the States Parties, and the exception of the unknown institution may not be invoked.

Article 6. The requirements of publication and registration of adoption shall be subject to the law of the State in which they are to be satisfied.

The particular features and type of adoption shall be stated in the registration.

Article 7. Where called for, the secrecy of the adoption shall be guaranteed. However, whenever possible, medical background information on the minor and on the birth parents, if it is known, shall be communicated to the legally appropriate person, without mention of their names or of other data whereby they may be identified.

Article 8. In adoptions governed by this Convention, the authorities granting the adoption may require the adopter (or adopters) to provide evidence of his physical, moral, psychological and economic capacity, through public or private institutions; the specific purpose is to protect minors. These institutions must be specifically authorized by some State or by some international organization.

The institutions that certify the capacity referred to above shall undertake to report to the authority granting the adoption on the conditions under which the adoption has developed over a period of one year. To this end, the authority granting the adoption shall inform the certifying institution that the adoption has been granted.

Article 9. In case of full adoption, adoptive legitimation, and similar institutions:

a. The relations between the adopter (or adopters) and the adoptee, including support relations, and the relations between the adoptee and the family of the adopter (or adopters), shall be governed by the same law as would govern the relations between the adopter (or adopters) and his legitimate family;

b. Ties between the adoptee and his family of origin shall be considered dissolved. However, impediments to marriage shall continue.

Article 10. In the case of adoptions other than full adoption, adoptive legitimation, and similar institutions, relations between the adopter (or adopters) and the adoptee shall be governed by the law of the domicile of the adopter (or adopters).

The relations between the adoptee and his family of origin shall be governed by the law of his habitual residence at the time of adoption.

Article 11. The rights of succession of the adoptee or the adopter (or adopters) shall be governed by the rules applicable to the respective successions.

In case of full adoption, adoptive legitimation, and similar institutions, the adoptee, and the adopter (or adopters) and the family thereof, shall have the same rights of succession as those of legitimate family members.

Article 12. Adoptions referred to in Article 1 are irrevocable. Revocation of adoptions referred to in Article 2 shall be governed by the law of the habitual residence of the adoptee at the time of adoption.

Article 13. Where it is permitted, conversion of the simple adoption into full adoption, adoptive legitimation, or similar institutions shall be governed, at the choice of the petitioner, by the law of the habitual residence of the adoptee at the time of the adoption, or by that of the State in which the adopter (or adopters) has his domicile at the time the conversion is requested.

If the adoptee is more than 14 years of age, his consent shall be required.

Article 14. Annulment of the adoption shall be governed by the law under which it was granted. An annulment shall be decreed only by judicial authorities, and the interest of the minor shall be protected in accordance with Article 19 of this Convention.

Article 15. The authorities of the State of the habitual residence of the adoptee shall be competent to grant the adoptions referred to in this Convention.

Article 16. The judges of the State where the adoptee was habitually resident at the time the adoption was granted shall be competent to decide on annulment or revocation of the adoption.

The authorities of the State of habitual residence of the adoptee at the time of the adoption; those of the State of domicile of the adopter (or adopters); or those of the State of domicile of the adoptee, if he has a domicile of his own at the time the conversion is requested, shall be competent, at the option of the petitioner, to decide on the conversion, where it is permitted, of simple adoption into full adoption, adoptive legitimation, or similar institutions.

Article 17. The judges of the State of the domicile of the adopter (or adopters) shall be competent to rule on matters concerning the relations between the adoptee and the adopter (or adopters) and the family thereof until the adoptee has a domicile of his own.

As soon as the adoptee has his own domicile, the judge of the domicile of the adoptee or that of the adopter (or adopters) shall, at the option of the petitioner, have jurisdiction.

Article 18. The authorities of a State Party may refuse to apply the law declared applicable under this Convention when the law is manifestly contrary to its public policy (*ordre public*).

Article 19. The terms of this Convention and the laws applicable under it shall be interpreted consistently and in favor of the validity of the adoption and the best interests of the adoptee.

Article 20. A State Party may at any time declare that this Convention applies to adoptions of minors habitually resident in it by persons also habitually resident in it when, in the opinion of the authority concerned, the circumstances of a given case indicate that the adopter (or adopters) plans to establish his domicile in another State Party after the adoption has been granted.

Article 21. This Convention shall be open for signature by the Member States of the Organization of American States.

Article 22. This Convention is subject to ratification. The instruments of ratification shall be deposited with the General Secretariat of the Organization of American States.

Article 23. This Convention shall remain open for accession by any other State. The instruments of accession shall be deposited with the General Secretariat of the Organization of American States.

Article 24. Each State may, at the time of signature, ratifi-

cation or accession, make reservations to this Convention, provided that each reservation concerns one or more specific provisions.

Article 25. Adoptions granted according to domestic law when the adoptee and the adopter (or adopters) have their domicile or habitual residence in the same State Party shall produce their effects unconditionally in the other States Parties, without prejudice to their being governed by the law of the new domicile of the adopter (or adopters).

Article 26. This Convention shall enter into force on the thirtieth day following the date of deposit of the second instrument of ratification.

For each State ratifying or acceding to the Convention after the deposit of the second instrument of ratification, the Convention shall enter into force on the thirtieth day after deposit by such State of its instrument of ratification or accession.

SEE ALSO *European Convention on the Adoption of Children.*

INTER-AMERICAN CONVENTION ON DIPLOMATIC ASYLUM (1954).

Under the convention, States parties may grant asylum to persons being sought for political reasons or political offenses in its legations, war vessels, or military camps or aircraft located in the territory of another State until that territorial State permits the asylee to depart from the country under government guarantees ensuring his safety. The convention was adopted by the Tenth Inter-American Conference of American States, convened at Caracas, on 28 March 1954 and entered into force on 29 December 1954. The text of the convention (*OAS Treaty Series* 18) is as follows:

The governments of the Member States of the Organization of American States, desirous of concluding a convention on diplomatic asylum, have agreed to the following articles:

Article 1. Asylum granted in legations, war vessels, and military camps or aircraft, to persons being sought for political reasons or for political offences, shall be respected by the territorial State in accordance with the provisions of this convention.

For the purposes of this convention, a legation is any seat of a regular diplomatic mission, the residence of chiefs of mission, and the premises provided by them for the dwelling places of asylees when the number of the latter exceeds the normal capacity of the buildings.

War vessels or military aircraft that may be temporarily in shipyards, arsenals, or shops for repair may not constitute a place of asylum.

Article 2. Every State has the right to grant asylum; but it is not obligated to do so or to state its reasons for refusing it.

Article 3. It is not lawful to grant asylum to persons who, at the time of requesting it, are under indictment or on trial for common offences or have been convicted by competent regular courts and have not served the respective sentence, nor to deserters from land, sea, and air forces, save when the acts giving rise to the request for asylum, whatever the case may be, are clearly of a political nature.

Persons included in the foregoing paragraph who *de facto*

enter a place that is suitable as an asylum shall be invited to leave or, as the case may be, shall be surrendered to the local authorities, who may not try them for political offences committed prior to the time of the surrender.

Article 4. It shall rest with the State granting asylum to determine the nature of the offence or the motives for the persecution.

Article 5. Asylum may not be granted except in urgent cases and for the period of time strictly necessary for the asylee to depart from the country with the guarantees granted by the government of the territorial State, to the end that his life, liberty, or personal integrity may not be endangered, or that the asylee's safety is ensured in some other way.

Article 6. Urgent cases are understood to be those, among others, in which the individual is being sought by persons or mobs over whom the authorities have lost control, or by the authorities themselves, and is in danger of being deprived of his life or liberty because of political persecution and cannot, without risk, ensure his safety in any other way.

Article 7. If a case of urgency is involved, it shall rest with the State granting asylum to determine the degree of urgency of the case.

Article 8. The diplomatic representative, commander of a warship, military camp, or military airship, shall, as soon as possible after asylum has been granted, report the fact to the Minister of Foreign Affairs of the territorial State, or to the local administrative authority if the case arose outside the capital.

Article 9. The official furnishing asylum shall take into account the information furnished to him by the territorial government in forming his judgement as to the nature of the offence or the existence of related common crimes; but his decision to continue the asylum or to demand a safe-conduct for the asylee shall be respected.

Article 10. The fact that the government of the territorial State is not recognized by the State granting asylum shall not prejudice the application of the present convention, and no act carried out by virtue of this convention shall imply recognition.

Article 11. The government of the territorial State may, at any time, demand that the asylee be withdrawn from the country, for which purpose the said State shall grant a safe-conduct and the guarantees stipulated in article 5.

Article 12. Once asylum has been granted, the State granting asylum may request that the asylee be allowed to depart for foreign territory, and the territorial State is under obligation to grant immediately, except in case of *force majeure,* the necessary guarantees, referred to in article 5, as well as the corresponding safe-conduct.

Article 13. In the cases referred to in the preceding articles, the State granting asylum may require that the guarantees be given in writing, and may take into account, in determining the rapidity of the journey, the actual conditions of danger involved in the departure of the asylee.

The State granting asylum has the right to transfer the asylee out of the country. The territorial State may point out the preferable route for the departure of the asylee, but this does not imply determining the country of destination.

If the asylum is granted on board a warship or military airship, departure may be made therein, but complying with the previous requisite of obtaining the appropriate safe-conduct.

Article 14. The State granting asylum cannot be held responsible for the prolongation of asylum caused by the need for obtaining the information required to determine whether or not the said asylum is proper, or whether there are circumstances that might endanger the safety of the asylee during the journey to a foreign country.

Article 15. When, in order to transfer an asylee to another country, it may be necessary to traverse the territory of a State that is a party to this convention, transit shall be authorized by the latter, the only requisite being the presentation, through diplomatic channels, of a safe-conduct, duly countersigned and bearing a notation of his status as asylee by the diplomatic mission that granted asylum.

En route, the asylee shall be considered under the protection of the State granting asylum.

Article 16. Asylees may not be landed at any point in the territorial State or at any place near thereto, except for exigencies of transportation.

Article 17. Once the departure of the asylee has been carried out, the State granting asylum is not bound to settle him in its territory; but it may not return him to his country of origin, unless this is the express wish of the asylee.

If the territorial State informs the official granting asylum of its intention to request the subsequent extradition of the asylee, this shall not prejudice the application of any provision of the present convention. In that event, the asylee shall remain in the territory of the State granting asylum until such time as the formal request for extradition is received, in accordance with the juridical principles governing that institution in the State granting asylum. Preventive surveillance over the asylee may not exceed thirty days.

Payment of the expenses incurred by such transfer and of preventive control shall devolve upon the requesting State.

Article 18. The official furnishing asylum may not allow the asylee to perform acts contrary to the public peace or to interfere in the internal politics of the territorial State.

Article 19. If as a consequence of a rupture of diplomatic relations the diplomatic representative who granted asylum must leave the territorial State, he shall abandon it with the asylees.

If this is not possible for reasons independent of the wish of the asylee or the diplomatic representative, he must surrender them to the diplomatic mission of a third State, which is a party to this convention, under the guarantees established in the convention.

If this is also not possible, he shall surrender them to a state that is not a party to this convention and that agrees to maintain the asylum. The territorial State is to respect the said asylum.

Article 20. Diplomatic asylum shall not be subject to reciprocity. Every person is under its protection, whatever his nationality.

Article 21. The present convention shall be open for signature by the Member States of the Organization of American States and shall be ratified by the signatory States in accordance with their respective constitutional procedures.

Article 22. The original instrument, whose texts in the English, French, Portuguese, and Spanish languages are equally authentic, shall be deposited in the Pan American Union, which shall send certified copies to the governments for the purpose of ratification. The instruments of ratification shall be deposited in the Pan American Union, and the said organization shall notify the signatory governments of the said deposit.

Article 23. The present convention shall enter into force among the States that ratify it in the order in which their respective ramifications are deposited.

Article 24. The present convention shall remain in force indefinitely, but may be denounced by any of the signatory States by giving advance notice of one year, at the end of which period it shall cease to have effect for the denouncing State, remaining in force, however, among the remaining signatory States. The denunciation shall be transmitted to the Pan American Union, which shall inform the other signatory States thereof.

SEE ALSO *Inter-American Convention on Territorial Asylum.*

INTER-AMERICAN CONVENTION OF EXTRADITION (1981).

The convention supplements the Convention on Extradition prepared under the auspices of the ORGANIZATION OF AMERICAN STATES and adopted in Montevideo on 26 December 1933 (*League of Nations Treaty Series* 162, p. 45), which systematized the process of extradition for OAS member States. It supplements, clarifies, and simplifies the extradition procedures set out in the earlier convention and, in particular, defines extraditable offenses as those punishable "by a penalty of not less than two years of deprivation of liberty under the laws of both the requesting State and the requested State."

Drafted by the Inter-American Council of Jurists and approved by the INTER-AMERICAN JURIDICAL COMMITTEE, the convention was adopted by the OAS General Assembly, meeting at Caracas, on 25 February 1981.

The text of the convention (*OAS Treaty Series* 60) is as follows:

Reaffirming their goal of strengthening international cooperation in legal and criminal law matters, which was the inspiration for the agreements reached in Lima on March 27, 1879, in Montevideo on January 23, 1889, in Mexico City on January 28, 1902, in Washington on February 7, 1923, in Havana on February 20, 1928, in Montevideo on December 26, 1933, in Guatemala City on April 12, 1934, and in Montevideo on March 19, 1940;

Taking into consideration resolutions CVII of the Tenth Inter-American Conference (Caracas, 1954), VII of the Third Meeting of the Inter-American Council of Jurists (Mexico, 1956), IV of the Fourth Meeting of that Council (Santiago, Chile, 1959), and AG/RES.91 (II-O/72), 183 (V-O/75) and 310 (VII-O/77) of the General Assembly of the Organization of American States, as well as the draft Conventions proposed by the Inter-American Juridical Committee in 1954, 1957, 1973, and 1977;

Believing that the close ties and the cooperation that exist in the Americas call for the extension of extradition to ensure that crime does not go unpunished, and to simplify procedures and promote mutual assistance in the field of criminal law on a wider scale than provided for by the treaties in force, with due respect to the human rights embodied in the American Declaration of the Rights and Duties of Man and the Universal Declaration of Human Rights; and

Conscious that the fight against crime at the international level will enhance the fundamental value of justice in criminal law matters,

The Member States of the Organization of American States adopt the following Inter-American Convention on Extradition:

Article 1. Obligation to Extradite. The States Parties bind themselves, in accordance with the provisions of this Convention, to surrender to other States Parties that request their extradition persons who are judicially required for prosecution, are being tried, have been convicted or have been sentenced to a penalty involving deprivation of liberty.

Article 2. Jurisdiction. 1. For extradition to be granted, the offense that gave rise to the request for extradition must have been committed in the territory of the requesting State.

2. When the offense for which extradition is requested has been committed outside the territory of the requesting State, extradition shall be granted provided the requesting State has jurisdiction to try the offense that gave rise to the request for extradition and to pronounce judgment thereon.

3. The requested State may deny extradition when it is competent, according to its own legislation, to prosecute the person whose extradition is sought for the offense on which the request is based. If it denies extradition for this reason, the requested State shall submit the case to its competent authorities and inform the requesting State of the result.

Article 3. Extraditable Offenses. 1. For extradition to be granted, the offense for which the person is sought shall be punishable at the time of its commission, by reason of the acts that constitute it, disregarding extenuating circumstances and the denomination of the offense, by a penalty of not less than two years of deprivation of liberty under the laws of both the requesting State and the requested State. Where the principle of retroactivity of penal law exists, it shall be applied only when it is favorable to the offender.

2. If the extradition is to be carried out between States whose laws establish minimum and maximum penalties, the offense for which extradition is requested shall be punishable, under the laws of the requesting and the requested States, by an average penalty of at least two years of deprivation of liberty. Average penalty is understood to be one-half of the sum of the minimum and maximum terms of each penalty of deprivation of liberty.

3. Where the extradition of an offender is requested for the execution of a sentence involving deprivation of liberty, the duration of the sentence still to be served must be at least six months.

4. In determining whether extradition should be granted to a State having a federal form of government and separate federal and state criminal legislation, the requested State shall take into consideration only the essential elements of the offense and shall disregard elements such as interstate transportation or use of the mails or other facilities of interstate commerce, since the sole purpose of such elements is to establish the jurisdiction of the federal courts of the requesting State.

Article 4. Grounds for Denying Extradition. Extradition shall not be granted:

1. When the person sought has completed his punishment or has been granted amnesty, pardon or grace for the offense for which extradition is sought, or when he has been acquitted or the case against him for the same offense has been dismissed with prejudice;

2. When the prosecution or punishment is barred by the statute of limitations according to the laws of the requesting State or the requested State prior to the presentation of the request for extradition;

3. When the person sought has been tried or sentenced or is to be tried before an extraordinary or *ad hoc* tribunal of the requesting State;

4. When, as determined by the requested State, the offense for which the person is sought is a political offense, an offense related thereto, or an ordinary criminal offense prosecuted for political reasons. The requested State may decide that the fact that the victim of the punishable act in question performed political functions does not in itself justify the designation of the offenses as political;

5. When, from the circumstances of the case, it can be inferred that persecution for reasons of race, religion or nationality is involved, or that the position of the person sought may be prejudiced for any of these reasons;

6. With respect to offenses that in the requested State cannot be prosecuted unless a complaint or charge has been made by a party having a legitimate interest.

Article 5. Specific Offenses. No provision of this Convention shall preclude extradition regulated by a treaty or Convention in force between the requesting State and the requested State whose purpose is to prevent or repress a specific category of offenses and which imposes on such States an obligation to either prosecute or extradite the person sought.

Article 6. Right of Asylum. No provision of this Convention may be intercepted as a limitation on the right of asylum when its exercise is appropriate.

Article 7. Nationality. 1. The nationality of the person sought may not be invoked as a ground for denying extradition, except when the law of the requested State otherwise provides.

2. In the case of convicted persons, the States Parties may negotiate the mutual surrender of nationals so that they may serve their sentences in the States of which they are nationals.

Article 8. Prosecution by the Requested State. If, when extradition is applicable, a State does not deliver the person sought, the requested State shall, when its laws or other treaties so permit, be obligated to prosecute him for the offense with which he is charged, just as if it had been committed within its territory, and shall inform the requesting State of the judgment handed down.

Article 9. Penalties Excluded. The States Parties shall not grant extradition when the offense in question is punishable in the requesting State by the death penalty, by life imprisonment, or by degrading punishment, unless the requested State has previously obtained from the requesting State, through the diplomatic channel, sufficient assurances that none of the above-mentioned penalties will be imposed on the person sought or that, if such penalties are imposed, they will not be enforced.

Article 10. Transmission of Request. The request for extradition shall be made by the diplomatic agent of the requesting State, or, if none is present, by its consular officer, or, when appropriate, by the diplomatic agent of a third State to which is entrusted, with the consent of the government of the requested State, the representation and protection of the interests of the requesting State. The request may also be made directly from government to government, in accordance with such procedure as the governments concerned may agree upon.

Article 11. Supporting Documents. 1. The request for extra-

dition shall be accompanied by the documents listed below, duly certified in the manner prescribed by the laws of the requesting State:

a. A certified copy of the warrant for arrest, or other document of like nature, issued by a competent judicial authority, or the *Ministerio Público* as well as a certified copy of evidence that, according to the laws of the requested State, is sufficient for the arrest and commitment for trial of the person sought. The last mentioned requirement shall not apply if the laws of the requesting State and of the requested State do not so provide. If the person has been tried and convicted of the offense by the courts of the requesting State, a certified verbatim copy of the final judgment shall suffice.

b. The text of the legal provisions that define and penalize the alleged crime, as well as those of the statute of limitations governing prosecution and punishment.

2. The request for extradition shall also be accompanied by the translation into the language of the requested State, if appropriate, of the documents enumerated in the previous paragraph, as well as by any personal data that will permit identification of the person sought, indication of his nationality, and, whenever possible, his location within the territory of the requested State, photographs, fingerprints, or any other satisfactory means of identification.

Article 12. Supplementary Information and Legal Assistance. 1. The requested State, when it considers that the documents presented are insufficient, in accordance with the provisions of Article 11 of this Convention, shall so inform the requesting State as soon as possible. The requesting State shall correct any omissions or defects observed within a period of thirty days in the event the person sought is already detained or subject to precautionary measures. If, because of special circumstances, the requesting State is unable to correct the omissions or defects within that term, it may ask the requested State to extend the term by thirty days.

2. The requested State shall provide, at no cost to the requesting State, legal assistance to protect the interests of the requesting State before the competent authorities of the requested State.

Article 13. Rule of Speciality. 1. A person extradited under this Convention shall not be detained, tried or punished in the territory of the requesting State for an offense, committed prior to the date of the request for extradition, other than that for which extradition has been granted unless:

a. That person leaves the territory of the requesting State after extradition and voluntarily returns to it; or

b. That person does not leave the territory of the requesting State within thirty days after being free to do so; or

c. The competent authority of the requested State consents to that person's detention, trial or punishment for another offense. In such case, the requested State may require the requesting State to submit the documents mentioned in Article 11 of this Convention.

2. When extradition has been granted, the requesting State shall inform the requested State of the final resolution of the case against the person extradited.

Article 14. Provisional Detention and Precautionary Measures. 1. In urgent cases, a State Party may request by the means of communication provided for in Article 10 of this Convention, or any other such means, the detention of the person who is judicially required for prosecution, is being tried, has been convicted, or has been sentenced to a penalty involving deprivation of liberty, and may also request the seizure of the objects related to the offense. The request for provisional detention shall contain a statement of intention to present the formal request for the extradition of the person sought, a statement of the existence of a warrant of arrest or of a judgment of conviction against that person issued by a judicial authority, and a description of the offense. The request for provisional detention shall be the sole responsibility of the requesting State.

2. The requested State shall order provisional detention and, when appropriate, the seizure of objects and shall immediately inform the requesting State of the date on which provisional detention commenced.

3. If the request for extradition, accompanied by the documents referred to in Article 11 of this Convention, is not presented within sixty days of the date on which the provisional detention referred to in paragraph 1 of this article commenced, the person sought shall be set free.

4. After the period of time referred to in the preceding paragraph has expired, the detention of the person sought may not be again requested except upon presentation of the documents required under Article 11 of this Convention.

Article 15. Requests by more than One State. When the extradition is requested by more than one State for the same offense, the requested State shall give preference to the request of the State in which the offense was committed. If the requests are for different offenses, preference shall be given to the State seeing the individual for the offense punishable by the most severe penalty, in accordance with the laws of the requested State. If the requests involve different offenses that the requested State considers to be of equal gravity, preference shall be determined by the order in which the requests are received.

Article 16. Legal Rights and Assistance. 1. The person sought shall enjoy in the requested State all the legal rights and guarantees granted by the laws of that State.

2. The person sought shall be assisted by legal counsel, and if the official language of the country is other than his own, he shall also be assisted by an interpreter.

Article 17. Communication of the Extradition Decision. The requested State shall promptly inform the requesting State of its decision on the request for extradition and the reasons for its approval or denial.

Article 18. Non bis in idem. Once the request for extradition of a person has been denied, a request may not be made again for the same offense.

Article 19. Surrender of the Person Sought and Delivery of Property. 1. The surrender of the person sought to the agents of the requesting State shall be carried out at a place determined by the requested State. This place shall, if possible, be an airport from which direct international flights depart for the requesting State.

2. If the request for provisional detention or for extradition is accompanied by a request for the seizure of documents, money or other objects that result from the alleged offense or may serve as evidence, such objects shall be collected and deposited under inventory by the requested State for subsequent delivery to the requesting State when the extradition is granted and even though the extradition is impeded by *force majeure,* unless the law of the requested State forbids such delivery. In any event, the rights of the third parties shall not be affected.

Article 20. Deferral of Surrender. 1. When the person is being tried or is serving a sentence in the requested State for an offense other than that for which the extradition is requested, his surrender may be deferred until he is entitled to be set free by virtue of acquittal, completed service or commutation of sentence, dismissal, pardon, amnesty or grace. No civil suit that the person sought may have pending against him in the requested State may prevent or defer his surrender.

2. When the surrender of the person sought would, for reasons of health, endanger his life, his surrender may be deferred until it would no longer pose such a danger.

Article 21. Simplified Extradition. The requested State may grant extradition without a formal extradition proceeding if:

a. Its laws do not expressly prohibit it;

b. The person sought irrevocably consents in writing to the extradition after being advised by a judge or other competent authority of his right to a formal extradition proceeding and the protection afforded by such a proceeding.

Article 22. Period for Taking Custody of the Person Sought. If the extradition has been granted, the requesting State shall take custody of the person sought within a period of thirty days from the date on which he was placed at its disposal. If it does not take custody within that period, the person sought shall be set free and may not be subjected to a new extradition procedure for the same offense or offenses. This period, however, may be extended for thirty days if the requesting State is unable, owing to circumstances beyond its control, to take custody of the person sought and escort him out of the territory of the requested State.

Article 23. Custody. The agents of the requesting State who are in the territory of another State Party to take custody of a person whose extradition has been granted shall be authorized to have custody of him and escort him to the territory of the requesting State, provided, however, that such agents shall be subject to the jurisdiction of the State in which they are.

Article 24. Transit. 1. If prior notification has been given from government to government through diplomatic or consular channels, the States Parties shall permit and cooperate in the transit through their territories of a person whose extradition has been granted under the custody of agents of the requesting State and/or the requested State, as the case may be, upon presentation of a copy of the order granting the extradition.

2. Such prior notification shall not be necessary when air transport is used and no landing is scheduled in the territory of the State Party that will be flown over.

Article 25. Expenses. Expenses incurred in the detention, custody, maintenance, and transportation of both the person extradited and of the objects referred to in Article 19 of this Convention shall be borne by the requested State up to the moment of surrender and delivery, and thereafter such expenses shall be borne by the requesting State.

Article 26. Waiver of Legalization. When the documents provided for in this Convention are communicated through the diplomatic or consular channel, or direct from government to government, their legalization shall not be required.

Article 27. Signature. This Convention shall be open for signature by the member states of the Organization of American States.

Article 28. Ratification. This Convention is subject to ratification. The instruments of ratification shall be deposited with the General Secretariat of the Organization of American States.

Article 29. Accession. 1. This Convention shall be open to accession by any American State.

2. This Convention shall be open to accession by States

having the status of permanent observer to the Organization of American States, following approval of the pertinent request by the General Assembly of the Organization.

Article 30. Reservations. Each State may, at the time of signature, approval, ratification, or accession, make reservations to this Convention, provided that each reservation concerns one or more specific provisions and is not incompatible with the object and purpose of the Convention.

Article 31. Entry into Force. 1. This Convention shall enter into force on the thirtieth day following the date of deposit of the second instrument of ratification.

2. For each State ratifying or acceding to the Convention after the deposit of the second instrument of ratification, the Convention shall enter into force on the thirtieth day after deposit by such State of its instrument of ratification or accession.

Article 32. Special Cases of Territorial Application. 1. If a State Party has two or more territorial units in which different systems of law apply in relation to the matters dealt with in this Convention, it shall, the time of signature, ratification, or accession, declare that this Convention shall extend to all its territorial units or only to one or more of them.

2. Such declaration may be modified by subsequent declarations, which shall expressly indicate the territorial unit or units to which this Convention applies. Such subsequent declarations shall be transmitted to the General Secretariat of the Organization of American States, and shall become effective thirty days after the date of their receipt.

Article 33. Relations with other Conventions on Extradition. 1. This Convention shall apply to the States Parties that ratify it or accede to it and shall not supersede multilateral or bilateral treaties that are in force or were concluded earlier unless the States Parties concerned otherwise expressly declare or agree, respectively.

2. The State Parties may decide to maintain in force as supplementary instruments treaties entered into earlier.

Article 34. Duration and Denunciation. This Convention shall remain in force indefinitely, but any of the States Parties may denounce it. The instrument of denunciation shall be deposited with the General Secretariat of the Organization of American States. After one year from the date of deposit of the instrument of denunciation, the Convention shall no longer be in effect for the denouncing State, but shall remain in effect for the other States Parties.

SEE ALSO *European Convention on Extradition and protocols.*

INTER-AMERICAN CONVENTION ON TERRITORIAL ASYLUM (1954). Under the convention, States parties undertake to recognize and respect the right of every State to admit into its territory such persons as it deems advisable without, by so doing, giving rise to a complaint by any other State, as well as the right of every State to refuse to expel or extradite from its territory persons persecuted for political reasons or offenses elsewhere. The convention was adopted by the Tenth Inter-American Conference of American States, convened at Caracas, on 28 March 1954 and entered into force on 29 December 1954. The text of the convention (*OAS Treaty Series* 19), is as follows:

The governments of the Member States of the Organization of American States, desirous of concluding a convention regarding territorial asylum, have agreed to the following articles:

Article 1. Every State has the right, in the exercise of its sovereignty, to admit into its territory such persons as it deems advisable, without, through the exercise of this right, giving rise to complaint by any other State.

Article 2. The respect which, according to international law, is due the jurisdictional right of each State over the inhabitants in its territory, is equally due, without any restriction whatsoever, to that which it has over persons who enter it proceeding from a State in which they are persecuted for their beliefs, opinions, or political affiliations, or for acts which may be considered as political offences.

Any violation of sovereignty that consists of acts committed by a government or its agents in another State against the life or security of an individual, carried out on the territory of another State, may not be considered attenuated because the persecution began outside its boundaries or is due to political considerations or reasons of state.

Article 3. No State is under the obligation to surrender to another State, or to expel from its own territory, persons persecuted for political reasons or offences.

Article 4. The right of extradition is not applicable in connexion with persons who, in accordance with the qualification of the solicited State, are sought for political offences, or for common offences committed for political ends, or when extradition is solicited for predominantly political motives.

Article 5. The fact that a person has entered into the territorial jurisdiction of a State surreptitiously or irregularly does not affect the provisions of this convention.

Article 6. Without prejudice to the provisions of the following articles, no State is under the obligation to establish any distinction in its legislation, or in its regulations or administrative acts applicable to aliens, solely because of the fact that they are political asylees or refugees.

Article 7. Freedom of expression of thought, recognized by domestic law for all inhabitants of a State, may not be ground of complaint by a third State on the basis of opinions expressed publicly against it or its government by asylees or refugees, except when these concepts constitute systematic propaganda through which they incite to the use of force or violence against the government of the complaining State.

Article 8. No State has the right to request that another State restrict for the political asylees or refugees the freedom of assembly or association which the latter State's internal legislation grants to all aliens within its territory, unless such assembly or association has as its purpose fomenting the use of force or violence against the government of the soliciting State.

Article 9. At the request of the interested State, the State that has granted refuge or asylum shall take steps to keep watch over, or to intern at a reasonable distance from its border, those political refugees or asylees who are notorious leaders of a subversive movement, as well as those against whom there is evidence that they are disposed to join it.

Determination of the reasonable distance from the border, for the purpose of internment, shall depend upon the judgment of the authorities of the State of refuge.

All expenses incurred as a result of the internment of political asylees and refugees shall be chargeable to the State that makes the request.

Article 10. The political internees referred to in the preceding article shall advise the government of the host State whenever they wish to leave its territory. Departure therefrom will be granted, under the condition that they are not to go to the country from which they came; and the interested government is to be notified.

Article 11. In all cases in which a complaint or request is permissible in accordance with this convention, the admissibility of evidence presented by the demanding State shall depend on the judgement of the solicited State.

Article 12. This convention remains open to the signature of the Member States of the Organization of American States, and shall be ratified by the signatory States in accordance with their respective constitutional procedures.

Article 13. The original instrument, whose texts in the English, French, Portuguese, and Spanish languages are equally authentic, shall be deposited in the Pan American Union, which shall send certified copies to the governments for the purpose of ratification. The instruments of ratification shall be deposited in the Pan American Union; this organization shall notify the signatory governments of said deposit.

Article 14. This convention shall take effect among the States that ratify it in the order in which their respective ratifications are deposited.

Article 15. This convention shall remain effective indefinitely, but may be denounced by any of the signatory States by giving advance notice of one year, at the end of which period it shall cease to have effect for the denouncing State, remaining, however, in force among the remaining signatory States. The denunciation shall be forwarded to the Pan American Union, which shall notify the other signatory States thereof.

SEE ALSO *Inter-American Convention on Diplomatic Asylum.*

INTER-AMERICAN CONVENTION ON THE FORCED DISAPPEARANCE OF PERSONS (DRAFT). In its annual report for 1986/1987, the INTER-AMERICAN COMMISSION ON HUMAN RIGHTS proposed to the OAS General Assembly that it consider the possibility of adopting an Inter-American Convention on the Forced Disappearance of Persons, designed to prevent and punish that abominable practice (OAS Doc. OEA/Ser. L/V/II.71, Doc. 9 rev. 1, chap. V [I]).

At its 1987 session, the OAS General Assembly endorsed the proposal and invited member States to submit their comments and observations on it. The commission prepared a preliminary text at its 72d regular session, in 1987, and requested interested non-governmental human rights organizations, as well as governments, to submit their observations and comments. On the basis of the documentation available to it, the commission completed its elaboration of the draft convention in 1988 and approved the following text which it proposed to the OAS General Assembly for consideration (OAS Doc. OEA/Ser. L/V/II.74, doc. 10/Rev. 1, chap. V [II]):

The American States party to the present Convention,

Reaffirming their intent to consolidate, in this hemisphere, within the framework of democratic institutions, a system of personal freedom and social justice based on respect for the rights of the human person;

Considering that the forced disappearance of persons constitutes an extremely serious form of repression, one that violates basic human rights enshrined in the American Declaration of the Rights and Duties of Man, the Universal Declaration of Human Rights, the International Covenant on Political and Civil Rights and the American Convention on Human Rights;

Bearing in mind that, while the acts which comprise the forced disappearance constitute both a violation of fundamental rights and freedoms guaranteed in the aforementioned international instruments as well as the commission of crimes set forth in the respective national laws, it is nonetheless important to devise an instrument which characterizes the forced disappearance of persons as a specific crime in and of itself, setting forth norms designed to punish and prevent and regulate its international effects;

Observing that, because of its inherent cruelty and contempt for human dignity, the practice of forced disappearances is an affront to the conscience of the hemisphere;

Recalling that the General Assembly of the Organization of American States has declared that the forced disappearance of persons constitutes a crime against humanity;

Convinced that an inter-American Convention to prevent and to punish the perpetrators of forced disappearance of persons will contribute to the elimination of this horrendous crime, and that it will constitute a decisive advance in the protection of the rights to life, integrity and personal freedom,

Have agreed to the following:

Article 1. The States Parties commit themselves to prevent and to punish the perpetrators of forced disappearances of persons, and undertake to act jointly to contribute by all means within their power to eradicating the practice of it.

Article 2. For the purposes of this Convention, forced disappearance is understood to be the abduction or detention of any person by an agent of a State or by a person acting with the consent or acquiescence of a State in circumstances where, after a reasonable period of time there has been made available no information that would permit the determination as of the fate or whereabouts of the person abducted or detained.

Article 3. Without prejudice to the fact that the component elements of the crime of forced disappearance may not be punishable under national laws, the States Parties shall adopt new penal standards sanctioning the forced disappearance of persons. The crime resulting therefrom shall be considered continuous or permanent until the fate or whereabouts of the victim has been ascertained.

Article 4. The forced disappearance of a person is a crime against humanity. Under the terms of this Convention, it engages the personal responsibility of its perpetrators and the responsibility of the State whose authorities executed the disappearance or consented to it.

Article 5. 1. The acts constituting a forced disappearance shall be considered a crime in every State Party to this Convention. Consequently, every State Party shall undertake to establish its jurisdiction over the cause in the following cases:

a. When the forced disappearance has occurred within its jurisdiction;

b. When the alleged perpetrator is a national of that State;

c. When the alleged perpetrator is found in its territory.

2. In the event of a conflict of jurisdiction, the criminal procedure and sentence, as well as possible civil action for compensatory damages against the perpetrators of forced disappearances, shall take place in the order set forth in the preceding paragraph.

Article 6. The crime referred to in Article 2 shall be deemed to be included among the extraditable crimes in every extradition treaty entered into between States Parties. The States Parties undertake to include the crime of forced disappearance as an extraditable offence in every extradition treat to be concluded between them.

Every State Party that makes extradition conditional on the existence of a treaty may, if it receives a request for extradition from another State Party with which it has no extradition treaty, consider this Convention as the legal basis for extradition in respect of the crime of forced disappearance. Extradition shall be subject to the other conditions that may be required by the law of the requested State.

State Parties which do not make extradition conditional on the existence of a treaty shall recognize such crimes as extraditable offences between themselves, subject to the conditions required by the law of the requested State.

Article 7. Penal action arising out of the forced disappearance of persons, and penalties imposed by the judicial system against those responsible shall not be subject to a statute of limitations.

Article 8. The perpetrators of forced disappearances shall not benefit from any legal act adopted by the Executive or Legislative branches of government that might have the effect of exempting such persons from punishment.

Article 9. In penal action for the acts mentioned in Article 2, the defense based on obedience to superior orders shall not be admitted.

Article 10. No privileges, special courts, or exclusive jurisdictions for the trial of the crime of forced disappearance shall be permitted. Such acts shall not be considered crimes committed in the course of military duties for the purpose of determining jurisdiction or the applicability of military penal legislation.

Article 11. The forced disappearance of persons shall be considered common crimes for the purposes of extradition.

Article 12. The States Parties to this Convention undertake not to grant political asylum to the perpetrators of forced disappearances regardless of the motives for their actions.

Article 13. Notwithstanding the provisions of the foregoing articles, the States Parties if necessary, may establish mitigating or exculpatory circumstances for those who, having taken part in a person's disappearance, contribute to bringing that person forward alive or give voluntary information to the authorities making it possible to solve the case, unless they themselves committed acts of torture or committed homicide.

Article 14. The States Parties to the Convention shall adopt any legislative, administrative and jurisdictional measures necessary to prevent the crime of forced disappearances.

Article 15. Even during a state of emergency or during the suspension of individual guarantees, the States Parties shall not suspend any judicial guarantee including *habeas corpus* as a means of determining the whereabouts of a detainee,

his or her state of health or the warrant from the authority leading to the arrest. In such a proceeding, the appropriate officials shall have free and immediate access to all detention centers and to each part thereof, as well as to any place in which an abducted or detained person may be presumed to be, including places subject to military jurisdiction.

Article 16. The States Parties shall establish and maintain public and centralized registries of all persons detained in all parts of their national territory, to be updated on a daily basis, and shall make them available to family members, magistrates, attorneys, and other authorities.

Article 17. The States Parties shall establish standards in their domestic laws indicating those officials authorized to order arrests or detentions, the conditions under which they may be ordered, as well as sanctions for those officials who wilfully refuse to provide information on a person's arrest or detention.

Article 18. By means of ratification or accession to this Convention, the States Parties adopt the United Nations Standard Minimum Rules for the Treatment of Prisoners (Resolution 663 C [XXIV] of the Economic and Social Council, of July 31, 1957) as an integral part of their domestic law.

Article 19. The States Parties shall combine their efforts to prevent and sanction the appropriation of children of disappeared parents or children born during the mother's clandestine captivity and their release to other families for irregular adoption. To that end, they shall punish, in their domestic law, crimes involving the alteration of, or the suppression of proof, of the civil status of any person and the abduction of minors.

Article 20. The States Parties shall cooperate in the search for, identification and ascertainment of the parental relationship of children who have been removed from the territory where they or their parents disappeared and to cooperate in returning them to their legitimate families.

Article 21. The States Parties to this Convention shall allow the International Committee of the Red Cross regular and periodic access to all centers of confinement and detention.

Article 22. For the purposes of this Convention, the processing of complaints regarding forced disappearances is subject to the procedures established in the American Convention on Human Rights and the Statutes and Regulations of the Inter-American Commission and and the Inter-American Court of Human Rights.

Article 23. Without prejudice to the provisions of the preceding article, when the Inter-American Commission on Human Rights receives a complaint or information regarding a forced disappearance, within fourteen days of the act its Executive Secretariat shall urgently transmit the complaint or information received to the respective government and shall request that government to provide any relevant information as soon as possible, especially with regard to measures being taken to determine the whereabouts of the disappeared person.

Article 24. 1. If the government's response to a request in the terms of Article 21, fails to indicate the whereabouts of the alleged victim, the Commission, or if the IACHR is not in session, the President of the Commission or in the event of his unavailability, one of the Vice Presidents, through the Executive Secretary, shall instruct the Executive Secretary to request that the Inter-American Court of Human Rights adopt such provisional measures as it deems pertinent pursuant to the provisions of Article 63.2 of the American Convention on Human Rights, especially measures designed to lead the government to present the abducted person or detainee before the competent judicial authorities and to guarantee the protection of the family of the victim as well as the original complainants.

2. For purposes of this article, the States Parties to this Convention, which have not yet recognized the compulsory jurisdiction of the Inter-American Court of Human Rights, agree to grant the Court competence, in cases of forced disappearance, in order to enable it to adopt the provisional measures referred to in the foregoing paragraph.

Article 25. 1. The practice of forced disappearance in a member State of the OAS, as a deliberate and systematic policy adopted by the government of that State which affects a significant number of people, shall be considered to be an urgent problem and one that is of common interest to the American states.

2. The Inter-American Commission on Human Rights may decide, with the affirmative vote of five of its members, that forced disappearances are practiced in a State as the manifestation of a deliberate and systematic policy of the government of that State.

3. In the event that the Commission adopts the decision set forth in the foregoing paragraph, it shall so inform the Permanent Council of the Organization so that any member state may request, in accordance with the provisions of Article 60 of the Charter of the OAS, convocation of a Meeting of Consultation of Ministers of Foreign Affairs, to take cognizance of the situation in respect of that State, and adopt any pertinent measures.

Article 26. This Convention is open to signature by the member states of the Organization of American States.

Article 27. This Convention is subject to ratification. The instruments of ratification shall be deposited with the General Secretariat of the Organization of American States.

Article 28. This Convention is open to accession by any other State. The instruments of accession shall be deposited with the General Secretariat of the Organization of American States.

Article 29. The State Parties may, at the time of approval, signature, ratification, or accession, make reservations to this Convention, provided that such reservations are not incompatible with the object and purpose of the Convention and concern one or more specific provisions.

Article 30. This Convention shall enter into force on the thirtieth day following the date on which the second instrument of ratification is deposited. For each State ratifying or acceding to the Convention after the second instrument of ratification has been deposited, the Convention shall enter into force on the thirtieth day following the date on which that State deposits its instrument of ratification or accession.

Article 31. This Convention shall remain in force indefinitely, but may be denounced by any State Party. The instrument of denunciation shall be deposited with the Secretariat of the Organization of American States. After one year from the date of deposit of the instrument of denunciation, this Convention shall cease to be in effect for the denouncing State but shall remain in force for the remaining States Parties.

Article 32. The original instrument of this Convention, the English, French, Portuguese, and Spanish texts of which are equally authentic, shall be deposited with the Secretariat of the Organization of American States, which shall send a certified copy to the Secretariat of the United Nations for registration and publication, in accordance with the provisions of Article 102 of the United Nations

Charter. The Secretariat of the Organization of American States shall notify the member states of the Organization and the states that have acceded to the Convention, of signatures and of deposits of instruments of ratification, accession, and denunciation, as well as of reservations, if any.

SEE ALSO *Argentina: Disappearances of Children; Disappearance of Persons; Disappearances: Statistical Summary; Disappearances: UN Draft Declaration; Guatemala: Disappearances; Honduras: Inter-American Court Hearings on Disappearances and Velasques Rodriguez Case entries; Peru: Disappearances.*

INTER-AMERICAN CONVENTION ON THE GRANTING OF CIVIL RIGHTS TO WOMEN (1948).

This convention, and the INTER-AMERICAN CONVENTION ON THE GRANTING OF POLITICAL RIGHTS TO WOMEN (1948), emerged from a single draft, on the granting of civil and political rights to women, prepared by the INTER-AMERICAN COMMISSION OF WOMEN.

The Inter-American Convention on the Granting of Civil Rights to Women sets out in terms of an international legal commitment the agreement of the governments of the American States that women shall enjoy the same civil rights as men. It was adopted by the Ninth International Conference of the American States, convened at Bogota, on 2 May 1948 and entered into force on 22 April 1949. The text (*OAS Treaty Series* 23) is as follows:

The Governments represented at the Ninth International Conference of American States,

Considering:

That the majority of the American Republics, inspired by lofty principles of justice, have granted civil rights to women;

That it has been a constant aspiration of the American Community of nations to equalize the status of men and women in the enjoyment and exercise of civil rights;

That Resolution XX of the Eighth International Conference of American States expressly declares:

"That women have the right to the enjoyment of equality as to civil status";

That long before the women of America demanded their rights they were able to carry out nobly all their responsibilities side by side with men;

That the principle of equality of human rights for men and women is contained in the Charter of the United Nations,

Have resolved:

To authorize their respective representatives, whose full powers have been found to be in good and due form, to sign the following articles:

Article 1. The American States agree to grant to women the same civil rights that men enjoy.

Article 2. The present Convention shall be open for signature by the American States and shall be ratified in accordance with their respective constitutional procedures. The original instrument, the English, French, Portuguese and Spanish texts of which are equally authentic, shall be deposited with the General Secretariat of the Organization of American States, which shall transmit certified copies to the Governments for the purpose of ratification. The instruments of ratification shall be deposited with the General Secretariat of the Organization of American States, which shall notify the signatory Governments of the said deposit. Such notification shall serve as an exchange of ratifications.

INTER-AMERICAN CONVENTION ON THE GRANTING OF POLITICAL RIGHTS TO WOMEN (1948).

This convention, and the INTER-AMERICAN CONVENTION ON THE GRANTING OF CIVIL RIGHTS TO WOMEN (1948), emerged from a single draft, on the granting of civil and political rights to women, prepared by the INTER-AMERICAN COMMISSION OF WOMEN.

The Inter-American Convention on the Granting of Political Rights to Women sets out in terms of an international legal commitment the agreement of the governments of American States that women shall enjoy the same political rights enjoyed by men. It was adopted by the Ninth International Conference of American States, convened at Bogota, on 2 May 1948 and entered into force on 22 April 1949. The text (*OAS Treaty Series* 3) is as follows:

The Governments represented at the Ninth International Conference of American States,
Considering:
That the majority of the American Republics, inspired by lofty principles of justice, have granted political rights to women;
That it has been a constant aspiration of the American community of nations to equalize the status of men and women in the enjoyment and exercise of political rights;
That Resolution XX of the Eighth International Conference of American States expressly declares:
"That women have the right to political treatment on the basis of equality with men";
That long before the women of America demanded their rights they were able to carry out nobly all their responsibilities side by side with men;
That the principle of equality of human rights for men and women is contained in the Charter of the United Nations;
Have resolved:
To authorize their respective representatives, whose full powers have been found to be in good and due form, to sign the following articles:
Article 1. The High Contracting Parties agree that the right to vote and to be elected to national office shall not be denied or abridged by reason of sex.
Article 2. The present Convention shall be open for signature by the American States and shall be ratified in accordance with their respective constitutional procedures. The original instrument, the English, French, Portuguese and Spanish texts of which are equally authentic, shall be deposited with the General Secretariat of the Organization of American States, which shall transmit certified copies to the Governments for the purpose of ratification. The instruments of ratification shall be deposited with the General Secretariat of the Organization of American States, which shall notify the signatory Governments of the said deposit. Such notification shall serve as an exchange of ratifications.

INTER-AMERICAN CONVENTION TO PREVENT AND PUNISH TORTURE (1985).

Under the convention, open for acceptance by States members of the ORGANIZATION OF AMERICAN STATES, the States parties undertake to take effective measures to prevent and punish TORTURE, which is defined in article 2, and other cruel, inhuman, or degrading treatment or punishment within their jurisdiction. They agree to make torture, and attempts to commit it, offenses under their penal law punishable by severe penalties. They also undertake to prohibit public servants or employees from using torture at any stage of interrogation, detention, or arrest; to guarantee that every victim of torture shall have the right to an impartial examination of his case; to provide adequate compensation for the victims of torture; and to extradite anyone accused of having committed the crime of torture or sentenced for the commission of that crime.

States parties also agree to inform the INTER-AMERICAN COMMISSION ON HUMAN RIGHTS of the measures taken to apply the provisions of the convention and of the results achieved. The commission is authorized to monitor and analyze in its annual reports the situation existing in the OAS member States as regards the prevention and elimination of torture.

The convention was drafted at the request of the OAS GENERAL ASSEMBLY by the INTER-AMERICAN JURIDICAL COMMITTEE in coordination with the Inter-American Commission on Human Rights. It was examined and revised by the OAS PERMANENT COUNCIL in the light of observations and comments on the draft submitted by the governments of member States. On the basis of the revised draft, the OAS General Assembly adopted the convention and opened it for signature on 9 December 1985 (AG/RES. 783 [XV–0/85]). The text of the convention, annexed to the assembly's resolution, is as follows:

The American States signatory to the present Convention,
Aware of the provision of the American Convention on Human Rights that no one shall be subjected to torture or to cruel, inhuman, or degrading punishment or treatment;
Reaffirming that all acts of torture or any other cruel, inhuman, or degrading treatment or punishment constitute an offense against human dignity and a denial of the principles set forth in the Charter of the Organization of American States and in the Charter of the United Nations and are violations of the fundamental human rights and freedoms proclaimed in the American Declaration of the Rights and Duties of Man and the Universal Declaration of Human Rights;
Noting that, in order for the pertinent rules contained in the aforementioned global and regional instruments to take effect, it is necessary to draft an Inter-American Convention that prevents and punishes torture;

Reaffirming their purpose of consolidating in this hemisphere the conditions that allow for recognition of and respect for the inherent dignity of man, and ensure the full exercise of his fundamental rights and freedoms,

Have agreed upon the following:

Article 1. The States Parties shall prevent and punish torture in accordance with the terms of this Convention.

Article 2. For the purposes of this Convention, torture shall be understood to be any act intentionally performed whereby physical or mental pain or suffering is inflicted on a person for purposes of criminal investigation, as a means of intimidation, as personal punishment, as a preventive measure, as a penalty, or for any other purpose. Torture shall also be understood to be the use of methods upon a person intended to obliterate the personality of the victim or to diminish his physical or mental capacities, even if they do not cause physical pain or mental anguish.

The concept of torture shall not include physical or mental pain or suffering that is inherent in or solely the consequence of lawful measures, provided that they do not include the performance of the acts or use of the methods referred to in this article.

Article 3. The following shall be held guilty of the crime of torture:

a. A public servant or employee who acting in that capacity orders, instigates or induces the use of torture, or who directly commits it or who, being able to prevent it, fails to do so.

b. A person who at the instigation of a public servant or employee mentioned in subparagraph (a) orders, instigates or induces the use of torture, directly commits it or is an accomplice thereto.

Article 4. The fact of having acted under orders of a superior shall not provide exemption from the corresponding criminal liability.

Article 5. The existence of circumstances such as a state of war, threat of war, state of siege or of emergency, domestic disturbance or strife, suspension of constitutional guarantees, domestic political instability, or other public emergencies or disasters shall not be invoked or admitted as justification for the crime of torture.

Neither the dangerous character of the detainee or prisoner, nor the lack of security of the prison establishment or penitentiary shall justify torture.

Article 6. In accordance with the terms of Article 1, the States Parties shall take effective measures to prevent and punish torture within their jurisdiction.

The States Parties shall ensure that all acts of torture and attempts to commit torture are offenses under their criminal law and shall make such acts punishable by severe penalties that take into account their serious nature.

The States Parties likewise shall take effective measures to prevent and punish other cruel, inhuman, or degrading treatment or punishment within their jurisdiction.

Article 7. The States Parties shall take measures so that, in the training of police officers and other public officials responsible for the custody of persons temporarily or definitively deprived of their freedom, special emphasis shall be put on the prohibition of the use of torture in interrogation, detention, or arrest.

The States Parties likewise shall take similar measures to prevent other cruel, inhuman, or degrading treatment or punishment.

Article 8. The States Parties shall guarantee that any person making an accusation of having been subjected to torture within their jurisdiction shall have the right to an impartial examination of his case.

Likewise, if there is an accusation or well-grounded reason to believe that an act of torture has been committed within their jurisdiction, the States Parties shall guarantee that their respective authorities will proceed ex officio and immediately to conduct an investigation into the case and to initiate, whenever appropriate, the corresponding criminal process.

After all the domestic legal procedures of the respective State and the corresponding appeals have been exhausted, the case may be submitted to the international fora whose competence has been recognized by that State.

Article 9. The State Parties undertake to incorporate into their national laws regulations guaranteeing adequate compensation for victims of torture.

None of the provisions of this article shall affect the right to receive compensation that the victim or other persons may have by virtue of existing national legislation.

Article 10. No statement that is verified as having been obtained through torture shall be admissible as evidence in a legal proceeding, except in a legal action taken against a person or persons accused of having elicited it through acts of torture, and only as evidence that the accused obtained such statement by such means.

Article 11. The States Parties shall take the necessary steps to extradite anyone accused of having committed the crime of torture or sentenced for commission of that crime, in accordance with their respective national laws on extradition and their international commitments on this matter.

Article 12. Every State Party shall take the necessary measures to establish its jurisdiction over the crime described in this Convention in the following cases:

a. When torture has been committed within its jurisdiction;

b. When the alleged criminal is a national of that State; or

c. When the victim is a national of that State and it so deems appropriate.

Every State Party shall also take the necessary measures to establish its jurisdiction over the crime described in this Convention when the alleged criminal is within the area under its jurisdiction and it does not proceed to extradite him in accordance with Article 11.

This Convention does not exclude criminal jurisdiction exercised in accordance with domestic law.

Article 13. The crime referred to in Article 2 shall be deemed to be included among the extraditable crimes in every extradition treaty entered into between States Parties. The States Parties undertake to include the crime of torture as an extraditable offence in every extradition treaty to be concluded between them.

Every State Party that makes extradition conditional on the existence of a treaty may, if it receives a request for extradition from another State Party with which it has no extradition treaty, consider this Convention as the legal basis for extradition in respect of the crime of torture. Extradition shall be subject to the other conditions that may be required by the law of the requested State.

States Parties which do not make extradition conditional on the existence of a treaty shall recognize such crimes as extraditable offences between themselves, subject to the conditions required by the law of the requested State.

Extradition shall not be granted nor shall the person sought be returned when there are grounds to believe that his life is in danger, that he will be subjected to torture or to cruel, inhuman or degrading treatment, or that he will be tried by special or ad hoc courts in the requesting State.

Article 14. When a State Party does not grant the extradition, the case shall be submitted to its competent authorities as if the crime had been committed within its jurisdiction, for the purposes of investigation, and when appropriate, for criminal action, in accordance with its national law. Any decision adopted by these authorities shall be communicated to the State that has requested the extradition.

Article 15. No provision of this Convention may be interpreted as limiting the right of asylum, when appropriate, nor as altering the obligations of the States Parties in the matter of extradition.

Article 16. This Convention shall not affect the provisions of the American Convention on Human Rights, other conventions on the subject, or the Statues of the Inter-American Commission on Human Rights, with respect to the crime of torture.

Article 17. The States Parties shall inform the Inter-American Commission on Human Rights of any legislative, judicial, administrative, or other measures they adopt in application of this Convention.

In keeping with its duties and responsibilities, the Inter-American Commission on Human Rights will endeavor in its annual report to analyze the existing situation in the member states of the Organization of American States in regard to the prevention and elimination of torture.

Article 18. This Convention is open to signature by the member states of the Organization of American States.

Article 19. This Convention is subject to ratification. The instruments of ratification shall be deposited with the General Secretariat of the Organization of American States.

Article 20. This Convention is open to accession by any other American state. The instruments of accession shall be deposited with the General Secretariat of the Organization of American States.

Article 21. The States Parties may, at the time of approval, signature, ratification, or accession, make reservations to this Convention, provided that such reservations are not incompatible with the object and purpose of the Convention and concern one or more specific provisions.

Article 22. This Convention shall enter into force on the thirtieth day following the date on which the second instrument of ratification is deposited. For each State ratifying or acceding to the Convention after the second instrument of ratification has been deposited, the Convention shall enter into force on the thirtieth day following the date on which that State deposits its instrument of ratification or accession.

Article 23. This Convention shall remain in force indefinitely, but may be denounced by any State Party. The instrument of denunciation shall be deposited with the General Secretariat of the Organization of American States. After one year from the date of deposit of the instrument of denunciation, this Convention shall cease to be in effect for the denouncing State but shall remain in force for the remaining States Parties.

Article 24. The original instrument of this Convention, the English, French, Portuguese, and Spanish texts of which are equally authentic, shall be deposited with the General Secretariat of the Organization of American States, which shall send a certified copy to the Secretariat of the United Nations for registration and publication, in accordance with the provisions of Article 102 of the United Nations Charter. The General Secretariat of the Organiza-

tion of American States shall notify the member states of the Organization and the states that have acceded to the Convention of signatures and of deposits of instruments of ratification, accession, and denunciation, as well as reservations, if any.

SEE ALSO *Body of Principles for the Protection of All Persons under Any Form of Detention or Imprisonment; Convention against Torture and Other Cruel. . .Punishment; Declaration on the Protection of All Persons from Being Subjected to Torture. . .; European Convention for the Prevention of Torture and Inhuman. . .Punishment.*

INTER-AMERICAN COUNCIL FOR EDUCATION, SCIENCE AND CULTURE.

The purpose of the council, as set out in article 99 of the ORGANIZATION OF AMERICAN STATES CHARTER, "is to promote friendly relations and mutual understanding between the peoples of the Americas through educational, scientific and cultural cooperation and exchange between Member States, in order to raise the cultural level of the peoples, reaffirm their dignity as individuals, prepare them fully for the tasks of progress, and strengthen the devotion to peace, democracy and social justice that has characterized their evolution."

The council's functions, powers, and organizational arrangements are set out in Chapters XI and XIV of the Organization of American States Charter. It is composed of one principle representative, of the highest rank, of each member State, especially appointed by the respective government.

INTER-AMERICAN COURT OF HUMAN RIGHTS.

The Inter-American Court of Human Rights of the ORGANIZATION OF AMERICAN STATES was established in accordance with article 33 of the AMERICAN CONVENTION ON HUMAN RIGHTS, which entered into force on 18 July 1978. It is an autonomous judicial institution whose purpose is the application and interpretation of the convention. As regards application, the court may adjudicate disputes relating to charges that a State party has violated the convention. As regards interpretation, it may interpret the convention and certain other human rights treaties in proceedings in which it is not called upon to adjudicate a specific dispute. Only the States parties and the INTER-AMERICAN COMMISSION ON HUMAN RIGHTS have the right to submit a case to the court (article 61.1 of the convention); this, however, does not mean that a case arising out of an individual's complaint cannot reach the court but only that it must be referred to the court by the Inter-American Commission or by a State party to the convention. (See, for example, HONDURAS: VELASQUEZ RODRIGUEZ CASE).

A State party does not subject itself to the contentious jurisdiction of the court by ratifying the convention; it must, in addition, recognize the court's jurisdiction either by a special declaration or a special agreement (art. 63). After hearing a case, the court must decide whether there has been a breach of the convention and, if so, what rights the injured party should be accorded. Moreover, the court may also determine the steps that should be taken to remedy the breach and the amount of damages to which the injured party is entitled (art. 63.1). In addition to regular judgments, the court also has the power to grant temporary injunctions "in cases of extreme gravity and urgency, and when necessary to avoid irreparable damage to persons" (art. 63.2). Judgments of the court are final and not subject to appeal, and all States parties to the convention have undertaken to comply with such judgments in any case to which they are parties. Enforcement of judgments of the court is the responsibility of the OAS GENERAL ASSEMBLY.

As regards the court's advisory jurisdiction, it is authorized to interpret the provisions of any OAS treaty concerning the protection of human rights in the American States at the request of any OAS member State or of OAS organs such as the Commission on Human Rights and the Commission of Women on matters within their competence (art. 64).

The court consists of seven judges, "nationals of the member States of the OAS, elected in an individual capacity from among jurists of the highest moral authority and of recognized competence in the field of human rights, who possess the qualifications required for the exercise of the highest judicial functions in conformity with the law of the State of which they are nationals or of the State that proposes them as candidates. . . . No two judges may be nationals of the same State. . . . The judges shall be elected by secret ballot by an absolute majority vote of the States Parties to the Convention in the General Assembly of the Organization, from a panel of candidates proposed by those States. . . ." (arts. 52–53). The term of office is six years.

The court submits a report on its work during the previous year to each regular session of the OAS General Assembly. In the report, the court specifies, in particular, any cases in which a State has not complied with its judgments and makes any pertinent recommendations (art. 65).

The Court has its seat in San Jose, Costa Rica.

Rules Relating to the Functions of the Court. Rules relating to the handling of cases brought before the court were adopted by the court at its third regular session, held from 30 July to 9 August 1980, and are set out in the court's *Rules of Procedure* (OAS Doc. OAE/Ser. 1/V/II.65, Doc. 6, Title II, chaps. 1-V) as follows:

Title II
Chapter I: General Rules

Article 19. Official Languages. 1. The official languages of the Court are those of the Organization of American States.

2. The working languages are those of the nationalities of the judges and, whenever required, those of the parties as long as they are the official languages.

3. The working language shall be determined at the beginning of the proceedings in each case.

4. The Court may authorize any party, agent, advocate, adviser, witness, expert, or other person who appears before it to use his own language if he does not have sufficient knowledge of an official language. The Court shall, in that event, make the necessary arrangements for the interpretation of the statements of such persons into the working language mentioned in the preceding paragraphs.

5. In all cases the authentic text shall be designated accordingly.

Article 20. Representation of the Parties. The parties shall be represented by agents who may have the assistance of advocates, advisers, or any other person of their choice.

Article 21. Representation of the Commission. The Commission shall be represented by the delegates whom it designates. These delegates may, if they so wish, have the assistance of any person of their choice.

Article 22. Communications, Notifications and Summonses Addressed to Persons other than the Agents of the Parties or Delegates of the Commission. 1. If, for any communication, notification or summons addressed to persons other than the agents of the parties or delegates of the Commission, the Court considers it necessary to have the assistance of the government of the State on whose territory such communication, notification or summons is to have effect, the President shall address an appropriate request to that government to obtain the same.

2. The same procedure shall apply when the Court wishes to undertake or arrange for an investigation in the territory of a State for the purpose of establishing the facts or procuring evidence, or when it orders the appearance of a person resident in, or having to cross, that territory.

Article 23. Interim Measures. 1. At any stage of the proceeding involving cases of extreme gravity and urgency and when necessary to avoid irreparable damage to persons, the Court may, in matters it has under consideration, adopt whatever provisional measures, based on the provisions of Article 63 (2) of the Convention, it deems appropriate.

2. With respect to matters not yet submitted to it, the Court may act at the request of the Commission.

3. Such request may be presented to the President or any judge of the Court by any means of communication.

4. If the Court is not sitting, the President shall convoke it immediately. Pending the meeting of the Court, the President, in consultation with the Permanent Commission or with the judges, if possible, shall call upon the parties, whenever necessary, to act so as to permit any decision of the Court regarding the request for provisional measures to have its appropriate effect.

5. The Court may at any time determine, *motu proprio* at the request of one of the parties, whether the circumstances of the case require the adoption of provisional measures.

Article 24. Procedure by Default. 1. When a party fails to appear in or to continue with a case, the Court shall, *motu proprio*, subject to the provisions of Article 42 of these Rules,

...er measures are necessary to complete consid-... the case.

...2. When a party, having the right to enter a case, does so at a later stage, it shall take the proceedings at that stage.

Chapter II
Institution of the Proceedings

Article 25. Filing of the Application. 1. A State Party which intends to bring a case before the Court in accordance with the provisions of Article 61 of the Convention shall file with the Secretary an application, in twenty copies, indicating the object of the application, the human rights involved, and the name and address of its agent, including, if pertinent, its objections to the opinion of the Commission. On receipt of the application, the Secretary shall immediately request the report of the Commission.

2. If the Commission intends to bring a case before the Court in accordance with the provisions of Article 61 of the Convention, it shall file with the Secretary, together with its report, in twenty copies, its duly signed application which shall indicate the object of the application, the human rights involved, and the names of its delegates.

Article 26. Communication of the Application. 1. On receipt of the application provided for in Article 25 of these Rules, the Secretary shall notify the Commission whenever the application is submitted under Article 25 (1) as well as the States concerned in the case, transmitting copies thereof to them.

2. The Secretary shall inform the other States Parties and the Secretary General of the OAS of the receipt of the application.

3. When giving the notice provided for in paragraph 1, the Secretary shall request the State concerned to designate, within a period of two weeks, an agent who shall have an address for service at the seat of the Court to which all communications concerning the case shall be sent. If the State does not do so, a decision shall be deemed to have been notified twenty-four hours after it was rendered.

Article 27. Preliminary Objections. 1. A preliminary objection must be filed, in twenty copies, no later than the expiration of the time fixed for the beginning of the written proceedings with respect to the party making the objection.

2. The preliminary objection shall set out the facts and the law on which the objection is based, the submissions and a list of the documents in support; it shall mention any evidence which the party may wish to produce. Copies of the supporting documents shall be attached.

3. The receipt by the Secretary of a preliminary objection shall not cause the suspension of the proceedings on the merits. The Court, or the President, if the Court is not sitting, shall fix the time-limit within which the other party may present a written statement of its observations and submissions.

4. The Court shall, after having received the replies or comments of every other party and of the delegates of the Commission, give its decision on the objection or join the objection to the merits.

Chapter III
Examination of the Cases

Article 28. Stages of the Proceedings. The proceedings before the Court shall consist of a written and an oral part.

Article 29. Fixing of Time-limits. Before the Court meets, the President shall ascertain the views of the agents of the parties and the delegates of the Commission or, if they have not yet been appointed, the Chairman of the Commission, regarding the procedure to be followed. He shall then direct in what order and within what time-limits memorials, counter-memorials and other documents are to be filed.

Article 30. Written Proceeding. 1. The written part of the proceedings in a case shall consist of a Memorial and a Counter-Memorial.

2. The Court may, in special circumstances, authorize additional written submissions consisting of a Reply and a Rejoinder.

3. A Memorial shall contain a statement of the relevant facts, a statement of law, and the submissions.

4. A Counter-Memorial shall contain an admission or denial of the facts stated in the Memorial; any additional facts, if necessary; observations concerning the statement of law in the Memorial; a statement of law in answer thereto; and the submissions.

5. The Reply and Rejoinder, whenever authorized by the Court, shall not merely repeat the contentions of the parties, but shall be directed to bringing out the issues that still divide them.

6. The Memorials, Counter-Memorials, and accompanying documents shall be deposited with the Secretary in twenty copies. The Secretary shall send copies of this documentation to the agents of the parties and the delegates of the Commission.

Article 31. Joinder of Cases. 1. In the event that two cases are presented which have common elements, the Court shall decide whether to join the cases.

2. The Court may at any time direct that the proceedings in two or more cases be joined.

Article 32. Oral Proceedings. When the case is ready for hearing, the President shall, after consulting the agents of the parties and the delegates of the Commission, fix the date for the opening of the oral proceedings.

Article 33. Conduct of the Hearings. The President shall direct the hearings. He shall prescribe the order in which the agents, the advocates or advisers of the parties, and the delegates of the Commission, as well as any other person appointed by them in accordance with Article 21, shall be called upon to speak.

Article 34. Inquiry, Expert Opinion and other Measures for Obtaining Information. 1. The Court may, at the request of a party or the delegates of the Commission, or *motu proprio*, decide to hear as a witness, expert, or in any other capacity, any person whose testimony or statements seem likely to assist it in carrying out its functions.

2. The Court may, in consultation with the parties, entrust any body, office, commission, or authority of its choice with the task of obtaining information, expressing an opinion, or making a report upon any specific point.

3. Any report prepared in accordance with the preceding paragraph shall be sent to the Secretary and shall not be published until so authorized by the Court.

Article 35. Convocation of Witnesses, Experts and other Persons. 1. Witnesses, experts, or other persons whom the Court decides to hear, shall be summoned by the Secretary. If they are called by a party, the expenses of their appearance shall be fixed by the President and borne by that party. In other cases, such expenses shall be fixed by the President and borne by the Court.

2. The summons shall indicate:

    a. the name of the party or parties;

    b. the object of the inquiry, expert opinion, or any other measure for obtaining information ordered by the Court;

c. any provision for the payment of the sum due to the person summoned.

Article 36. Oath or Solemn Declaration by Witness and Experts. 1. After the establishment of his identity and before giving evidence, every witness shall take the following oath or make the following solemn declaration: "I swear"—or "I solemnly declare upon my honor and conscience"—"that I will speak the truth, the whole truth and nothing but the truth."

2. After the establishment of his identity and before carrying out his task, every expert shall take the following oath or make the following solemn declaration: "I swear"—"I solemnly declare"—"that I will discharge my duty as an expert honorably and conscientiously."

3. This oath shall be taken or this declaration made before the Court or before any of its judges who have been so delegated by the Court.

Article 37. Objection to a Witness or Expert; Hearing of a Person for Purpose of Information. The Court shall decide any dispute arising from an objection to a witness or expert. If the Court considers it necessary, it may nevertheless, hear, for purposes of information, a person who cannot be heard as a witness.

Article 38. Questions Put During the Hearing. 1. Any judge may put questions to the agents, advocates, or advisers of the parties, to the witnesses and experts, to the delegates of the Commission, and to any other person appearing before the Court.

2. Subject to the control of the President, who has the power to decide as to the relevance of the questions put, the witnesses, experts, and other persons referred to in Article 34, may be examined by the agents, advocates or advisers of the parties, by the delegates of the Commission, and by any person appointed by them in accordance with Article 21.

Article 39. Failure to Appear or False Evidence. 1. When without good reason, a witness or any other person who has been duly summoned, fails to appear or refuses to give evidence, the Secretary shall, on being so required by the President, inform the State to whose jurisdiction such witness or other person is subject. The same provision shall apply when a witness or expert has, in the opinion of the Court, violated the oath or solemn declaration mentioned in Article 36.

2. The State may not try any person on account of their testimony before the Court. The Court may, however, request the States to take the measures provided for in their domestic legislation against those who, in the opinion of the Court, have violated the oath or solemn declaration.

Article 40. Minutes of Hearings. 1. Minutes shall be made of each hearing; they shall be signed by the President and the Secretary.

2. These minutes shall include:

a. the names of the judges present;

b. the names of the agents, advocates, advisers, and delegates of the Commission present;

c. the names, description and residence of the witnesses, experts, or other persons heard;

d. the declaration expressly made for insertion in the minutes on behalf of the parties or the Commission;

e. a summary record of the questions put by the judges and the responses thereto;

f. any decision by the Court delivered during the hearing.

3. Copies of the minutes shall be given to the agents of the parties and the delegates of the Commission.

4. The minutes shall be deemed to constitute the certified record.

Article 41. Transcript of the Hearings. 1. The Secretary shall ensure that a transcript of the hearings be made.

2. The agents, advocates, and advisers of the parties, the delegates of the Commission and witnesses, experts, and other persons mentioned in Articles 21 and 34, shall receive the transcript of their arguments, statements or evidence, to enable them, subject to the control of the Secretary, to make corrections within the time-limits fixed by the President.

Article 42. Discontinuance. 1. When the party which has brought the case before the Court notifies the Secretary of its intention not to proceed with the case and when the other parties agree to such discontinuance, the Court shall, after having obtained the opinion of the Commission, decide whether it is appropriate to approve the discontinuance and, accordingly, to strike the case off its list.

2. When, in a case brought before the Court by the Commission, the Court is informed of a friendly settlement, arrangement or other fact of a kind to provide a solution of the matter, it may, after having obtained the opinion, if necessary, of the delegates of the Commission, strike the case off its list.

3. The Court may, having regard to its responsibilities, decide that it should proceed with the consideration of the case, notwithstanding the notice of discontinuance, friendly settlement, arrangement or other fact referred to in the two preceding paragraphs.

Article 43. Question of the Application of Article 63 (1) of the Convention. If proposals or observations on the question of the application of Article 63 (1) of the Convention have not been presented to the Court in the document instituting the proceedings, they may be presented by a party or by the Commission at any stage of the written or oral proceedings.

Article 44. Decisions. 1. The judgments, advisory opinions, and the interlocutory decisions that put an end to a case or proceedings, shall be decided by the Court.

2. The other decisions shall be taken by the Court, if it is sitting, or, if not, by the President, pursuant to the instructions of the Court.

Chapter IV: Judgments

Article 45. Contents of the Judgment. 1. A judgment shall contain:

a. the names of the judges and the Secretary;

b. the date on which it was delivered at a hearing in public;

c. a description of the party or parties;

d. the names of agents, advocates or advisers of the party or parties;

e. the names of the delegates of the Commission;

f. the statement of the proceedings;

g. the submission of the party or parties and, if any, of the delegates of the Commission;

h. the facts of the case;

i. the legal arguments;

j. the operative provisions of the judgment;

k. the allocation, if any, of compensation;

l. the decision, if any, in regard to costs;

m. the number of judges constituting the majority;

n. a statement as to which text is authentic.

2. Where the Court finds that there is a breach of the Convention, it shall give in the same judgment a decision on the application of Article 63 (1) of the Convention if

that question, after being raised under Article 43 of these Rules, is ready for decision; if the question is not ready for decision, the Court shall decide on the procedure to follow. If, on the other hand, the matter has not been raised under Article 43, the Court shall determine the period within which it may be presented by a party or by the Commission.

3. If the Court is informed that an agreement has been reached between the victim of the violation and the State Party concerned, it shall verify the equitable nature of such agreement.

Article 46. Delivery and Communication of the Judgment. 1. When the case is ready for a decision, the Court shall meet in private, take a preliminary vote, name one or more rappporteurs among the judges of the respective majority and minority, and fix the date of the deliberation and final vote.

2. In the final deliberation, the Court shall take a final vote, approve the wording of the judgment, and fix the date of the public hearing at which it shall be communicated to the parties.

3. Until the aforementioned communication, the votes and details thereof, the texts, and the legal arguments shall remain secret.

4. The judgments shall be signed by all of the judges who participated in the voting and the dissents and concurring opinions shall be signed by the judges supporting them. A judgment shall, however, be valid if signed by a majority of the judges.

5. An order of communication and execution, sealed and signed by the President and the Secretary, shall appear at the end of the judgment.

6. The originals of the decisions shall be placed in the archives of the Court. The Secretary shall send certified copies to the party or parties, the Commission, the Chairman of the Permanent Council, the Secretary General, and any other person directly concerned.

7. The Secretary shall transmit the judgment to all the States Parties.

Article 47. Publication of Judgments, Decision and Other Documents. 1. The Secretary shall be responsible for the publication of:

a. judgments and other decisions of the Court;

b. documents relating to the proceedings, including the report of the Commission, but excluding any particulars relating to the attempt to reach a friendly settlement;

c. the transcripts of the public hearings;

d. any other document whose publication the President considers useful.

2. Documents deposited with the Secretary and not published shall be accessible to the public unless otherwise decided by the President, either on his own initiative, at the request of a party, the Commission, or any other person concerned.

Article 48. Request for an Interpretation of a Judgment. 1. Requests for an interpretation allowed under the terms of Article 67 of the Convention shall be presented in twenty copies and shall indicate precisely the points in the operative provision of the judgment on which interpretation is requested. It shall be filed with the Secretary.

2. The Secretary shall communicate the request to any other party and, where appropriate, to the Commission, and shall invite them to submit, in twenty copies, any written comments within a period fixed by the President.

3. The nature of the proceedings shall be determined by the Court.

4. A request for interpretation shall not suspend the effect of the judgment.

Chapter V: Advisory Opinions

Article 49. Interpretation of the Convention. 1. The request for an advisory opinion provided for in Article 64 (1) of the Convention shall be instituted by means of an application that shall state the specific questions on which the opinion of the Court is sought.

2. If an interpretation of the Convention is requested by:

a. A Member State—the application shall indicate the provisions to be interpreted, the considerations giving rise to the consultation, and the name and address of the agent of the applicant;

b. An OAS organ—the application shall indicate the provisions to be interpreted, how the consultation relates to its sphere of competence, the considerations giving rise to the consultation, and the name and address of its delegates.

Article 50. Interpretation of Other Treaties. 1. If an interpretation is requested of other treaties concerning the protection of human rights in the American states, as provided for in Article 64 (1) of the Convention, the application shall indicate the name of, and parties to, the treaty, the specific questions on which the opinion of the Court is sought, and the considerations giving rise to the consultation.

2. In the case of an application submitted by one of the OAS organs referred to in Article 64 (1) of the Convention, the provisions of Article 49 (2) (b) of these rules shall apply, *mutatis mutandis.*

Article 51. Interpretation Relating to Domestic Laws. 1. The request for an advisory opinion, provided for in Article 64 (2) of the Convention, shall be instituted by means of an application that shall identify:

a. the domestic laws, the provisions of the Convention and/or international treaties forming the subject of the consultation;

b. the specific questions on which the opinion of the Court is sought;

c. the name and address of the applicant's agent.

2. Ten copies of the domestic laws referred to in the preceding paragraph shall accompany the application.

Article 52. 1. Upon receipt of the request for an advisory opinion, under Articles 49 and 50 of these Rules, the Secretary shall transmit copies thereof to any State which might be concerned in this matter, as well as to the Secretary General of the OAS for transmission to the organs mentioned in Article 64 (1) of the Convention. He shall likewise inform the aforementioned and the Commission that the Court is prepared to receive within a time-limit fixed by the President their written observations. These observations or other relevant documents shall be filed with the Secretariat in forty copies and shall be transmitted to the Commission, to the States and to the other bodies mentioned in Article 64 (1) of the Convention.

2. At the conclusion of the written proceedings, the Court shall decide upon the format of the oral proceedings, and fix the order of presentation and time-limits for the hearing.

Article 53. When the circumstances require, the Court may apply any of the rules governing contentious proceedings to advisory proceedings.

Article 54. 1. The hearings and advisory opinions shall be public.

2. When the Court has completed its deliberations and

adopted its advisory opinion, it shall be read in public and shall contain:

    a. a statement of the questions submitted to the Court;

    b. the date on which it is delivered;

    c. the names of the judges;

    d. a summary of the proceedings;

    e. a summary of the considerations giving rise to the request;

    f. the conclusions of the Court;

    g. the legal arguments;

    h. a statement indicating which text of the opinion shall be deemed authoritative.

3. A judge may, if he so wishes, attach his individual opinion to the advisory opinion of the Court, whether he dissents from the majority or not, and may record his concurrence or dissent.

Final Title
Chapter VI

Article 55. These Rules may be amended or supplemented by the vote of an absolute majority of the titular judges of the Court.

INTER-AMERICAN COURT OF HUMAN RIGHTS: STATUTE (1979).

The statute of the Inter-American Court of Human Rights, approved by the OAS GENERAL ASSEMBLY (resolution 448) at its ninth regular session, held in La Paz, Bolivia, in October 1979, is as follows:

Chapter I
General Provisions

Article 1. Nature and Legal Organization. The Inter-American Court of Human Rights is an autonomous judicial institution whose purpose is the application and interpretation of the American Convention on Human Rights. The Court exercises its functions in accordance with the provisions of the aforementioned Convention and the present Statute.

Article 2. Jurisdiction. The Court shall exercise adjudicatory and advisory jurisdiction:

1. Its adjudicatory jurisdiction shall be governed by the provisions of Articles 61, 62 and 63 of the Convention, and

2. Its advisory jurisdiction shall be governed by the provisions of Article 64 of the Convention.

Article 3. Seat. 1. The seat of the Court shall be San José, Costa Rica; however, the Court may convene in any Member State of the Organization of American States (OAS) when a majority of the Court considers it desirable, and with the prior consent of the State concerned.

2. The seat of the Court may be changed by a vote of two-thirds of the States Parties to the Convention, in the OAS General Assembly.

Chapter II
Composition of the Court

Article 4. Composition. 1. The Court shall consist of seven judges, nationals of the Member States of the OAS, elected in an individual capacity from among jurists of the highest moral authority and of recognized competence in the field of human rights, who possess the qualifications required for the exercise of the highest judicial functions under the law of the State of which they are nationals or of the State that proposes them as candidates.

2. No two judges may be nationals of the same State.

Article 5. Judicial Terms. 1. The judges of the Court shall be elected for a term of six years and may be re-elected only once. A judge elected to replace a judge whose term has not expired shall complete that term.

2. The terms of office of the judges shall run from January 1 of the year following that of their election to December 31 of the year in which their terms expire.

3. The judges shall serve until the end of their terms. Nevertheless, they shall continue to hear the cases they have begun to hear and that are still pending, and shall not be replaced by the newly elected judges in the handling of those cases.

Article 6. Election of the Judges—Date. 1. Election of judges shall take place, insofar as possible, during the session of the OAS General Assembly immediately prior to the expiration of the term of the outgoing judges.

2. Vacancies on the Court caused by death, permanent disability, resignation or dismissal of the judges shall, insofar as possible, be filled at the next session of the OAS General Assembly. However, an election shall not be necessary when a vacancy occurs within six months of the expiration of a term.

3. If necessary in order to preserve a quorum of the Court, the States Parties to the Convention, at a meeting of the OAS Permanent Council, and at the request of the President of the Court, shall appoint one or more interim judges who shall serve until such time as they are replaced by elected judges.

Article 7. Candidates 1. Judges shall be elected by the States Parties to the Convention, at the OAS General Assembly, from a list of candidates nominated by those States.

2. Each State Party may nominate up to three candidates, nationals of the State that proposes them or of any other Member State of the OAS.

3. When a slate of three is approved, at least one of the candidates must be a national of a state other than the nominating state.

Article 8. Election—Preliminary Procedures. 1. Six months prior to expiration of the terms to which the judges of the Court were elected, the Secretary General of the OAS shall address a written request to each State Party to the Convention that it nominate its candidates within the next ninety days.

2. The Secretary General of the OAS shall draw up an alphabetical list of the candidates nominated, and shall forward it to the States Parties, if possible, at least thirty days before the next session of the OAS General Assembly.

3. In the case of vacancies on the Court, as well as in cases of the death or permanent disability of a candidate, the aforementioned time periods shall be shortened to a period that the Secretary General of the OAS deems reasonable.

Article 9. Voting. 1. The judges shall be elected by secret ballot and by an absolute majority of the States Parties to the Convention, from among the candidates referred to in Article 7 of the present Statute.

2. The candidates who obtain the largest number of votes and an absolute majority shall be declared elected. Should several ballots be necessary, those candidates who receive the smallest number of votes shall be eliminated successively, in the manner determined by the States Parties.

Article 10. Ad Hoc Judges. 1. If a judge is a national of any of the States Parties to a case submitted to the Court, he shall retain his right to hear that case.

2. If one of the judges called upon to hear a case is a national of one of the States Parties to the case, any other

State Party to the case may appoint a person to serve on the Court as an *ad hoc* judge.

3. If among the judges called upon to hear a case, none is a national of the States Parties to the case, each of the latter may appoint an *ad hoc* judge. Should several States have the same interest in the case, they shall be regarded as a single party for purposes of the above provisions. In case of doubt, the Court shall decide.

4. The right of any State to appoint an *ad hoc* judge shall be considered relinquished if the State should fail to do so within thirty days following the written request from the President of the Court.

5. The provisions of Articles 4, 11, 15, 16, 18, 19 and 20 of the present Statue shall apply to *ad hoc* judges.

Article 11. Oath. 1. Upon assuming office, each judge shall take the following oath or make the following solemn declaration: "I swear"—or "I solemnly declare"—"that I shall exercise my functions as a judge honorably, independently and impartially and that I shall keep secret all deliberations."

2. The oath shall be administered by the President of the Court, and, if possible, in the presence of the other judges.

Chapter III
Structure of the Court

Article 12. Presidency. 1. The Court shall elect from among its members a President and Vice-President who shall serve for a period of two years; they may be re-elected.

2. The President shall direct the work of the Court, represent it, regulate the disposition of matters brought before the Court, and preside over its sessions.

3. The Vice-President shall take the place of the President in the latter's temporary absence, or if the office of the President becomes vacant. In the latter case, the Court shall elect a new Vice-President to serve out the term of the previous Vice-President.

4. In the absence of the President and the Vice-President, their duties shall be assumed by other judges, following the order of precedence established in Article 13 of the present Statute.

Article 13. Precedence. 1. Elected judges shall take precedence after the President and Vice-President according to their seniority in office.

2. Judges having the same seniority in office shall take precedence according to age.

3. *Ad hoc* and interim judges shall take precedence after the elected judges, according to age. However, if an *ad hoc* or interim judge has previously served as an elected judge, he shall have precedence over any other *ad hoc* or interim judges.

Article 14. Secretariat. 1. The Secretariat of the Court shall function under the immediate authority of the Secretary, in accordance with the administrative standards of the OAS General Secretariat, in all matters that are not incompatible with the independence of the Court.

2. The Secretary shall be appointed by the Court. He shall be a full-time employee serving in a position of trust to the Court, shall have his office at the seat of the Court and shall attend any meetings that the Court holds away from its seat.

3. There shall be as Assistant Secretary who shall assist the Secretary in his duties and shall replace him in his temporary absence.

4. The Staff of the Secretariat shall be appointed by the Secretary General of the OAS, in consultation with the Secretary of the Court.

Chapter IV
Rights, Duties and Responsibilities

Article 15. Privileges and Immunities. 1. The judges of the Court shall enjoy, from the moment of their election and throughout their term of office, the immunities extended to diplomatic agents under international law. During the exercise of their functions, they shall, in addition, enjoy the diplomatic privileges necessary for the performance of their duties.

2. At no time shall the judges of the Court be held liable for any decisions or opinions issued in the exercise of their functions.

3. The Court itself and its staff shall enjoy the privileges and immunities provided for in the Agreement on Privileges and Immunities of the Organization of American States, of May 15, 1949, *mutatis mutandis,* taking into account the importance and independence of the Court.

4. The provision of paragraph 1, 2 and 3 of this article shall apply to the States Parties to the Convention. They shall also apply to such other Member States of the OAS as expressly accept them, either in general or for specific cases.

5. The system of privileges and immunities of the judges of the Court and of its staff may be regulated or supplemented by multilateral or bilateral agreements between the Court, the OAS and its Member States.

Article 16. Service. 1. The judges shall remain at the disposal of the Court, and shall travel to the seat of the Court or to the place where the Court is holding its sessions as often and for as long a time as may be necessary, as established in the Regulations.

2. The President shall render his service on a permanent basis.

Article 17. Emoluments. 1. The emoluments of the President and the judges of the Court shall be set in accordance with the obligations and incompatibilities imposed on them by Articles 16 and 18, and bearing in mind the importance and independence of their functions.

2. The *ad hoc* judges shall receive the emoluments established by Regulations, within the limits of the Court's budget.

3. The judges shall also receive per diem and travel allowances, when appropriate.

Article 18. Incompatibilities. 1. The position of judge of the Inter-American Court of Human Rights is incompatible with the following positions and activities.

a. Members or high-ranking officials of the executive branch of government, except for those who hold positions that do not place them under the direct control of the executive branch and those of diplomatic agents who are not Chiefs of Missions to the OAS or to any of its member states;

b. Officials of international organizations;

c. Any others that might prevent the judges from discharging their duties, or that might affect their independence or impartiality, or the dignity and prestige of the office.

2. In case of doubt as to incompatibility, the Court shall decide. If the incompatibility is not resolved, the provisions for Article 73 of the Convention and Article 20.2 of the present Statute shall apply.

3. Incompatibilities may lead only to dismissal of the judge and the imposition of applicable liabilities, but shall

not invalidate the acts and decisions in which the judge in question participated.

Article 19. Disqualifications. 1. Judges may not take part in matters in which, in the opinion of the Court, they or members of their family have a direct interest or in which they have previously taken part as agents, counsel or advocates, or as members of a national or international court or an investigatory committee, or in any other capacity.

2. If a judge is disqualified from hearing a case or for some other appropriate reason considers that he should not take part in a specific matter, he shall advise the President of his disqualification. Should the latter disagree, the Court shall decide.

3. If the President considers that a judge has cause for disqualification or for some other pertinent reason should not take part in a given matter, he shall advise him to that effect. Should the judge in question disagree, the Court shall decide.

4. When one or more judges are disqualified pursuant to this article, the President may request the States Parties to the Convention, in a meeting of the OAS Permanent Council, to appoint interim judges to replace them.

Article 20. Disciplinary Regime. 1. In the performance of their duties and at all other times, the judges and staff of the Court shall conduct themselves in a manner that is in keeping with the office of those who perform an international judicial function. They shall be answerable to the Court for their conduct, as well as for any violation, act of negligence or omission committed in the exercise of their functions.

2. The OAS General Assembly shall have disciplinary authority over the judges, but may exercise that authority only at the request of the Court itself, composed for this purpose of the remaining judges. The Court shall inform the General Assembly of the reasons for its request.

3. Disciplinary authority over the Secretary shall lie with the Court, and over the rest of the staff, with the Secretary, who shall exercise that authority with the approval of the President.

4. The Court shall issue disciplinary rules, subject to the administrative regulations of the OAS General Secretariat insofar as they may be applicable in accordance with Article 59 of the Convention.

Article 21. Resignation—Incapacity. 1. Any resignation from the Court shall be submitted in writing to the President of the Court. The resignation shall not become effective until the Court has accepted it.

2. The Court shall decide whether a judge is incapable of performing his functions.

3. The President of the Court shall notify the Secretary General of the OAS of the acceptance of a resignation or a determination of incapacity, for appropriate action.

Chapter V
The Workings of the Court

Article 22. Sessions. 1. The Court shall hold regular and special sessions.

2. Regular sessions shall be held as determined by the Regulations of the Court.

3. Special sessions shall be convoked by the President or at the request of a majority of the judges.

Article 23. Quorum. 1. The quorum for deliberations by the Court shall be five judges.

2. Decisions of the Court shall be taken by a majority voted of the judges present.

3. In the event of a tie, the President shall cast the deciding vote.

Article 24. Hearings, Deliberations, Decisions. 1. The hearings shall be public, unless the Court, in exceptional circumstances, decides otherwise.

2. The Court shall deliberate in private. Its deliberations shall remain secret, unless the Court decides otherwise.

3. The decisions, judgments and opinions of the Court shall be delivered in public session, and the parties shall be given written notification thereof. In addition, the decisions, judgments and opinions shall be published, along with judges' individual votes and opinions and with such other data or background information that the Court may deem appropriate.

Article 25. Rules and Regulations. 1. The Court shall draw up its Rules of Procedure.

2. The Rules of Procedure may delegate to the President or to Committees of the Court authority to carry out certain parts of the legal proceedings, with the exception of issuing final rulings or advisory opinions. Rulings or decisions issued by the President or the Committees of the Court that are not purely procedural in nature may be appealed before the full Court.

3. The Court shall also draw up its own Regulations.

Article 26. Budget, Financial System. 1. The Court shall draw up its own budget and shall submit it for approval to the General Assembly of the OAS, through the General Secretariat. The latter may not introduce any changes in it.

2. The Court shall administer its own budget.

Chapter VI
Relations with Governments and Organizations

Article 27. Relations with the Host Country, Governments and Organizations. 1. The relations of the Court with the host country shall be governed through a headquarters agreement. The seat of the Court shall be international in nature.

2. The relations of the Court with governments, with the OAS and its organs, agencies and entities and with other international governmental organizations involved in promoting and defending human rights shall be governed through special agreements.

Article 28. Relations with the Inter-American Commission on Human Rights. The Inter-American Commission on Human Rights shall appear as a party before the Court in all cases within the adjudicatory jurisdiction of the Court, pursuant to Article 2.1 of the present Statute.

Article 29. Agreements of Cooperation. 1. The Court may enter into agreements of cooperation with such nonprofit institutions and law schools, bar associations, courts, academies and educational or research institutions dealing with related disciplines in order to obtain their cooperation and to strengthen and promote the juridical and institutional principles of the Convention in general and of the Court in particular.

2. The Court shall include an account of such agreements and their results in its Annual Report to the OAS General Assembly.

Article 30. Report to the OAS General Assembly. The Court shall submit a report on its work of the previous year to each regular session of the OAS General Assembly. It shall indicate those cases in which a State has failed to comply with the Court's ruling. It may also submit to the OAS General Assembly proposals or recommendations on ways to improve the inter-American system of human rights, insofar as they concern the work of the Court.

Chapter VII
Final Provisions

Article 31. Amendments to the Statute. The present Statute may be amended by the OAS General Assembly, at the initiative of any Member State or of the Court itself.

Article 32. Entry into Force. The present Statute shall enter into force on January 1, 1980.

INTER-AMERICAN DECLARATION ON RACIAL INTEGRATION IN THE AMERICAS (1965). In the declaration, the Inter-American Conference clearly restates the basic racial policy of all American states: one of complete integration of all elements of the population without regard to race.

The declaration was adopted at Rio de Janiero on 30 November 1965 by the Second Special Inter-American Conference. The text is as follows:

Whereas:
Distinctions based on racial differences are contrary to the legal principles of human equality;
The entire system for the protection of individuals, of social groups, and of states arises from the preservation of this principle;
The unqualified and nondiscriminating protection of the individual is indispensable if democratic institutions themselves are to survive; and
The foregoing principles have been proclaimed in Article 5.j of the Charter of the Organization of American States and in the American Declaration of the Rights and Duties of Man,
The Second Special Inter-American Conference
Declares:
1. That racial discrimination is deeply contrary to the sense of justice of the peoples of the Americas.
2. That it reiterates that the democratic concept of the state, a basic principle on which the conduct of the nations of the hemisphere is based, must guarantee to all individuals, without regard to race, decent living conditions, access to culture and employment, and opportunities for the pursuit of their legitimate activities.
3. That it reaffirms the goal of all the governments to develop a policy tending toward complete integration of all elements of their citizenry, without distinction of any nature based on racial origin.

INTER-AMERICAN ECONOMIC AND SOCIAL COUNCIL. The council promotes cooperation among the American countries in order to attain accelerated economic and social development in accordance with the standards set forth in Chapter VII of the ORGANIZATION OF AMERICAN STATES CHARTER. Its functions, powers, and organizational arrangements are set out in Chapters XI and XIII of that charter. It is composed of one principal representative, of the highest rank, of each member State, especially appointed by the respective government.

INTER-AMERICAN JURIDICAL COMMITTEE. The committee serves the ORGANIZATION OF AMERICAN STATES as an advisory body on legal matters, promotes the progressive development and the codification of international law, and studies other legal problems. It is composed of 11 jurists, elected by the General Assembly for terms of four years. Candidates are nominated by member States and are chosen with a view to equitable geographical representation; no two members of the committee may be nationals of the same State.

The committee has its headquarters in Rio de Janeiro but may meet elsewhere after consultation with the member States concerned. Its functions, powers, and organizational arrangements are set out in Chapter XV of the ORGANIZATION OF AMERICAN STATES CHARTER.

INTER-AMERICAN PRESS ASSOCIATION. An international non-governmental organization in consultative status with the UN Economic and Social Council (Category II), and with UNESCO, IAPA has over 1,300 associate life members (newspapers and magazines published six or more times a year) in 34 countries, mostly in Latin and South America. It is a non-profit organization of western hemisphere publications devoted to the promotion and protection of freedom of the press and the people's right to know in the New World.

The seed of IAPA was sown in 1926, when the first Pan American Congress of Journalists, held in Washington, D.C., adopted a resolution calling for the establishment of a permanent inter-American organization of journalists. The resolution was forgotten, however, for 16 years; and the seed began to germinate only in 1942, in Mexico City, when the next Pan American Congress created a Permanent Commission.

In 1943, in Havana, the following congress established the organization with its present name. During its first years, the association was largely a Latin American body, and few North Americans attended the meetings. But in 1946, a small group of United States editors and publishers with faith in the organization's future decided to establish the Inter-American Press Association of the United States as a national chapter of the hemispheric institution.

At a meeting in New York in 1950, the U.S. chapter and a group of influential Latin American publishers revised the organization's by-laws and became a *bona fide* organization of publications, sustained exclusively by the dues paid by its members and without any outside interference. From then on, delegates represented no one but their newspapers, each with one vote. IAPA thus proclaimed that it would be totally independent and would recognize no boundaries in matters relating to freedom of the press.

IAPA's objectives are to foster and protect the interests of the daily and periodical press of the Americas; to promote and maintain the dignity, rights, and responsibilities of journalism; to encourage uniform standards of professional and business conduct; to exchange ideas and information which contribute to the cultural, material, and technical development of the press; and to foster a wider knowledge and greater interchange among the peoples of the Americas. The Association campaigns via protests, press releases, and missions on behalf of journalists whose rights are violated or endangered. It has protested against the closing of newspapers in Nicaragua, Panama, and Paraguay.

In addition to its primary concerns, IAPA supports the Inter-American Press Association Scholarship Fund, which awards 10 scholarships annually; the IAPA Technical Center, which provides members—especially those in Latin America—with technical and modern management information; the Office of Certified Circulation, which gives members a tool for measuring circulation; and the IAPA awards, which are presented annually to newspersons and publications in South and Central America for outstanding community and journalistic work and to North American newspapers for their work on behalf of Inter-American friendship and understanding.

IAPA's publication include the *IAPA News, Noticiero SIP,* and *El Boletín del Centro Técnico.*

Inter American Press Association. Address: 2911 N.W. 39th Street, Miami, FL 33142 (USA). Telephone: (305) 634-2465. Cable: SIPRENSA, MIAMI. Telex: 522873. Executive Director: Bill Williamson.

INTERGOVERNMENTAL COMMITTEE FOR MIGRATION. A committee consisting of the representatives of 33 governments, established in Brussels in 1951 as an outgrowth of the International Migration Conference, the Intergovernmental Committee for Migration has observer status with a number of intergovernmental organs rendering assistance to refugees and other migrants, including the UNITED NATIONS HIGH COMMISSIONER FOR REFUGEES and the WORLD HEALTH ORGANIZATION, and also with many non-governmental organizations active in this field such as the INTERNATIONAL CATHOLIC MIGRATION COMMISSION and the LEAGUE OF RED CROSS AND RED CRESCENT SOCIETIES.

Since 1952, ICM has arranged the movement of more than 3.5 million migrants—whether refugees, displaced persons, asylum seekers, or nationals in need of international assistance—to countries of resettlement. Its member governments, and 15 additional governments participating in its work as observers, adhere to the principle of free movement of people. At the request of these governments, ICM provides a wide variety of migration services including recruitment, selection, orientation, counselling, medical examination, provision of medical escorts, reception, placement, immigration assistance, and language training. Its largest emergency operations involved refugees from Hungary in 1956, from Czechoslovakia in 1968, from Uganda in 1972, and from Viet Nam from 1975 onwards. It also assisted in the transfer of detainees out of Chile in 1973, out of Bolivia in 1980/1981, and out of El Salvador in 1983.

Among ICM's publications are the quarterly *International Migration* and the *Monthly Dispatch;* it also issues an annual report entitled *Review of Achievements* and numerous pamphlets, booklets, and leaflets.

Intergovernmental Committee for Migration. Address: 17 Route des Morillons, P. O. Box 71, CH-1211, Geneva 19, Switzerland. Telephone: (41-22) 717-9-11. Cable: Promigrant Geneva. Telex: 22-155/22-193. Director-General: James N.Purcell.

INTERNATIONAL ABOLITIONIST FEDERATION. An international non-governmental organization in consultative status with the UN Economic and Social Council (Category II) and with ILO, UNESCO, and the Council of Europe, IAF has national branches in India, France, Belgium, Switzerland, West Germany, and Great Britain; in addition, it has 40 affiliated organizations in 50 countries and individual members in 60 countries.

The Federation was founded in London in 1875. It engages in scientific study of the problems of prostitution and the traffic in persons, seeking the causes thereof and the means of preventing and eliminating such traffic. It also strives to promote the social rehabilitation of persons engaged in prostitution and victims of traffic in persons. Each year IAF delegates participate in the work of the WORKING GROUP ON CONTEMPORARY FORMS OF SLAVERY of the UN Commission on Human Rights.

IAF publishes *Revue Abolitionniste.*

International Abolitionist Federation. Address: 47 rue de Rivoli, 75001 Paris, France. Telephone: (33-1) 45-08-97-52. Secretary-General: Marie-Renée Jamet.

I

INTERNATIONAL ALLIANCE OF WOMEN. An international non-governmental organization in consultative status with the UN Economic and Social Council (Category I), and with ILO, UNESCO, and the Council of Europe, and also known by its full title, "International Alliance of Women: Equal Rights Equal Reponsibilities," the organization brings together national affiliates in 53 countries.

Founded in 1904 in Berlin, under the name "International Women Suffrage Alliance," the Alliance promotes all reforms necessary to establish a real equality of liberties, status, and opportunities between men and women and urges women to use their rights and influence in public life to ensure respect for the rights of all individuals. The group sponsors a triennal congress and annual regional conferences.

IAW publishes *International Women's News* (six times a year) in English and French.

International Alliance of Women. Address: P.O. Box 355, Valletta, Malta. Telephone: (356) 824098. President: Olive H. Bloomer.

Yearbook of International Organizations 1989/90 (K. G. Saur).

INTERNATIONAL ASSOCIATION AGAINST TORTURE. An international non-governmental organization in consultative status (Category II) with the UN Economic and Social Council, the association has national sections in 14 countries.

Founded in Milan in 1977, the International Association Against Torture organizes campaigns to denounce torture and those who practice it, to investigate its causes, and to assist its victims. The association has published numerous monographs and pamphlets, including *Torture, Executions and Disappearances, The Fate of Political Prisoners in Regimes in Latin America* (1983), *Latin America: A Governmental System* (1984), and *Latin America: A Tortured Continent.*

International Association Against Torture. Address: Via Ugo Foscolo 3, 1-20121, Milan, Italy. Telephone: (02) 259-3189 and (02) 837-3411. International Secretary: Avv. Amanda C. Parra.

Yearbook of International Organizations 1989/90 (K. G. Saur).

INTERNATIONAL ASSOCIATION FOR THE DEFENSE OF RELIGIOUS LIBERTY. An international non-governmental organization in consultative status with the UN Economic and Social Council (Category II) and with UNESCO and the Council of Europe, the association has individual members and national affiliates in 10 countries.

Founded in France in 1946, the International Association crusades against all forms of intolerance and fanaticism and conducts the World Congress on Religious Liberty, jointly with the International Religious Liberty Association. It publishes *Conscience et liberté.*

International Association for the Defense of Religious Liberty. Address: Schosshaldenstrasse 17, CH-3006 Berne, Switzerland. Telephone: (4131) 44-62-62. Secretary General: Gianfranco Rossi.

Yearbook of International Organizations 1989/90 (K. G. Saur).

INTERNATIONAL ASSOCIATION OF DEMOCRATIC LAWYERS. An international non-governmental organization in consultative status with the UN Economic and Social Council (Category II) and UNESCO. At its inception, the IADL brought together lawyers from mainly European countries; however, by the end of 1988, the IADL had 165,000 members from 80 countries.

The IADL was founded on 24 October 1946 by lawyers who had fought fascism, nazism, and militarism during World War II. The organization promotes cooperation among lawyers for defense of peace, support for the principles of the United Nations Charter, support for international law, and defense of fundamental human and peoples' rights. To achieve these goals, IADL supports political, economic, social, cultural, and institutional independence and actively promotes a democratic international order. The association also strives for respect for modern international law as a law of peace and coexistence and attempts to safeguard fundamental rights of defense, in particular through guaranteeing the independence of the judiciary and the Bar. In the past 40 years, IADL has sent working groups and special missions to investigate and report on human rights conditions in countries on all continents; has supported liberation movements in Asia, Africa, and Latin America; and has sent legal observers to trials to insure the defense of political prisoners.

Among its special projects is the IADL Study Centre, created in 1975 to reflect on the main legal themes concerning national and international law for reports for the United Nations and its affiliated agencies; to provide education in law for officers of national or international organizations; and to provide legal advice on behalf of countries, especially third world countries, or organizations which seek it.

IADL's primary publication is the *International Review of Contemporary Law,* and it also publishes reports, pamphlets, and brochures on human rights situations in individual countries.

International Association of Democratic Lawyers. Address: 263 Avenue Albert, 1180 Brussels, Belgium. Telephone: 3451471. Cable: Interjurist–Bruxelles. Secretary General: Amar Bentoumi.

INTERNATIONAL ASSOCIATION OF EDUCATORS FOR WORLD PEACE.

An international non-governmental organization in consultative status with the UN Economic and Social Council (Category II), and with UNESCO, the association has more than 18,500 members in 54 countries.

Founded in the United States in 1969, IAWEP fosters international understanding and world peace, using education as a medium, and furthers the realization of the Universal Declaration of Human Rights through the promotion of social progress, broader international communications at the personal level, and the development of peaceful co-existence.

The Association organizes quadrennial world congresses and publishes *Peace Education* and *Peace Progress* annually. It also issues the IAWEP *Newsletter* from time to time, as well as occasional case studies, monographs, and progress reports.

International Association of Educators for World Peace. Address: P.O. Box 3282, Mastin Lake Station, Huntsville, AL 35810 (USA). Telephone: (205) 534-5501. Executive Vice-President: Dr. Charles Mercieca.

Yearbook of International Organizations 1989/90 (K. G. Saur).

INTERNATIONAL ASSOCIATION OF PENAL LAW.

An international non-governmental organization in consultative status with the UN Economic and Social Council (Category II), and with UNESCO and the Council of Europe, the association has members in 74 countries.

IAPL was founded in Paris in 1924 as the successor to the International Union of Penal Law, which had functioned since 1889. The association encourages the exchange of ideas and close collaboration between those who are concerned with the study or application of criminal law or with research on crime and its causes, with a view to promoting theoretical and practical development of international penal law and rules of procedure. The association has conducted studies on the evolution of the methods and means of penal law, on drug traffic and abuse, on indemnification of victims of penal infractions, and on the suppression of hijacking.

The association publishes the *Revue international de droit pénal* (twice a year) in English and French.

International Association of Penal Law. Address: DePaul University, College of Law, 25 E. Jackson Blvd., Chicago, IL 60604 (USA). Secretary-General: Prof. M. Cherif Bassiouni.

Yearbook of International Organizations 1989/90 (K. G. Saur).

INTERNATIONAL BAR ASSOCIATION.

An international non-governmental organization in consultative status with the UN Economic and Social Council (Category II) and with the Council of Europe, the association has over 100 national or local affiliates and over 10,000 individual members in 114 countries and territories.

Founded in New York in 1947 as a federation of national bar associations, IBA works to establish and maintain permanent relations and exchanges between bar associations and law societies throughout the world, to advance the science of jurisprudence by common study of practical legal problems, to promote uniformity and definition in appropriate fields of law, and to promote the administration of justice under law among the peoples of the world.

The IBA publishes several journals and newsletters: *International Business Lawyer* (11 times a year), *International Bar Journal* (six times a year), *International Legal Practitioner* (four times a year), and the *Journal of Natural Resources Law* (four times a year). It also publishes the *International Code of Professional Ethics,* conference reports, books, pamphlets, and papers on various phases of the law.

International Bar Association. Address: 2 Harewood Place, Hanover Square, London W1R 9HB, UK. Telephone: (44-1) 629-1206. Cable: Inbarassoc London SW1. Telex: 8812664 INBAR G. Fax: (44-1) 409-0456. Executive Director: Madelene May.

Yearbook of International Organizations 1989/90 (K. G. Saur).

INTERNATIONAL BILL OF HUMAN RIGHTS.

A collective term applied to four major international instruments in the field of human rights: the UNIVERSAL DECLARATION OF HUMAN RIGHTS, the INTERNATIONAL COVENANT ON ECONOMIC, SOCIAL AND CULTURAL RIGHTS, the INTERNATIONAL COVENANT ON CIVIL AND POLITICAL RIGHTS and the OPTIONAL PROTOCOL TO THE INTERNATIONAL COVENANT ON CIVIL AND POLITICAL RIGHTS. A fifth instrument, the CONVENTION ON THE ELIMINATION OF ALL FORMS OF RACIAL DISCRIMINATION, is sometimes recognized as part of the International Bill of Human Rights.

I

INTERNATIONAL CATHOLIC CHILD BUREAU.
An international non-governmental organization in consultative status (Category II) with the UN's Economic and Social Council, ICCB is affiliated with 122 organizations in 31 countries.

The bureau studies and documents children's issues and works in areas of non-material needs of refugee children—religious information, spiritual growth, family issues—and many other child-related projects. ICCB participated in the preparation of the DECLARATION OF THE RIGHTS OF THE CHILD and the more recent draft Convention on the Rights of the Child. The bureau has reported on the mental health of refugees, health education in West Africa, the problems of street children, handicapped children, and child pornography.

ICCB publishes the international review *Children Worldwide* tri-annually in English and French and the quarterly *Enfants de partout* (in French), as well as brochures, special statements, reports of workshops and symposia, and specialized publications from national members.

International Catholic Child Bureau. Address: 65 rue de Lausanne, CH-1202 Geneva, Switzerland. Telephone: 31-32-48; 31-17-21. Secretary-General: Dr. François Ruegg.

INTERNATIONAL CATHOLIC MIGRATION COMMISSION. An international non-governmental organization in consultative status with the UN Economic and Social Council (Category II), and with the Council of Europe.

Established by the Holy See in 1951 to deal with problems of refugees, migrants, and displaced persons, ICMC works mainly through 60 national Catholic affiliates for the resettlement of refugees and local integration self-help projects. ICMC publishes the quarterly *Migration News* and the *ICMC Newsletter.*

International Catholic Migration Commission. Address: 37-39 Rue Vermont CP 96, CH-1211 Geneva 20 CIC Switzerland. Telephone:(41-22) 33-41-50. Telex: CH 28100 ICMC CH. Fax: (41-22) 34-7929. Secretary-General: Dr. Elizabeth Winkler.

INTERNATIONAL CATHOLIC UNION OF THE PRESS. An international non-governmental organization in consultative status with the UN Economic and Social Council (Category II), and with UNESCO, ICUP consists of four international federations: the International Federation of Associations of Church Press, the International Federation of Catholic Dailies and Periodicals, the International Federation of

Catholic Journalists, and the International Federation of Catholic Press Agencies.

Founded in Brussels in 1927 as the "International Bureau of Catholic Journalists," ICUP serves as a link for Catholics who exercise an influence on public opinion through the press and supports high standards of professional conscience in its members. It conducts research on the problems of the press and religious news and promotes the Catholic press in developing countries. It has been instrumental in establishing the International Catholic Association of Teachers and Research Fellows in the Sciences and Techniques of Information; the *Union catholique africaine de la press;* the Union of Catholic Asian News; and the Catholic Media Council.

ICUP publishes the quarterly *UCIP Informations* in English, French, and German; and the *UCLAP Newsletter* for Latin America.

International Catholic Union of the Press. Address: UCIP, 37-39 rue de Vermont, CP 197, CH-1211. Geneva 20, Switzerland. Telephone: (41-22) 734-00-17. Cable: PRESSUCIP GENEVE. Secretary-General: P. Bruno Holtz.

Yearbook of International Organizations 1989/90 (K. G. Saur).

INTERNATIONAL CENTER OF SOCIOLOGICAL, PENAL AND PENITENTIARY RESEARCH AND STUDIES. An international non-governmental organization in consultative status with the UN Economic and Social Council (Category II), and with the Council of Europe, INTERCENTER brings together associations in 11 countries and individual members in 20 countries.

Founded in Messina, Italy, in 1977 by a number of leading Italian and international personalities, the center studies various forms of criminality considered to be compromising to democratic society or threatening democratic institutions. INTERCENTER also sponsors international study seminars and round-table discussions, finances research, and conducts courses in higher specialization of police forces. In collaboration with UNESCO, the center also organizes annual human rights sessions.

Since 1978, INTERCENTER has published approximately 50 volumes of proceedings of its various courses and seminars.

International Center of Sociological, Penal and Penitentiary Research and Studies. Address: Via Ghibellina, 59, I 98100 Messina, Italy. Telephone: (39-90)/710553-4. Cable: Intercentr. Telex: 980075 UNIME. Secretary-General: Domenico Cucchiara.

INTERNATIONAL COMMISSION OF HEALTH PROFESSIONALS FOR HEALTH AND HUMAN RIGHTS. An international non-governmental organization in consultative status with the UN Economic and Social Council (Category II) and with WHO, ICHP has national affiliates in three countries.

Founded in Geneva in 1985, the commission works to secure the commitment of health professionals to respect human rights and professional ethics. ICHP investigates general situations and individual cases in which human rights relevant to health questions have been violated and takes action to secure their observance. The commission publishes *Up to Date,* a biannual newsletter, *Health and Human Rights,* a collection of speeches, and reports on its activities.

International Commission of Health Professionals for Health and Human Rights. Address: 15 Route des Morillons, Grand Saconnex, CH-1218, Geneva, Switzerland. Telephone: (41-22) 98-89-81. Telex: 27-935 ICA CH. Secretary-General: Dr. Robert Bannerman.

Yearbook of International Organizations 1989/90 (K. G. Saur).

INTERNATIONAL COMMISSION OF JURISTS. An international non-governmental organization in consultative status with the UN Economic and Social Council (Category II), UNESCO, and the Council of Europe. Membership in the commission is limited to 40 eminent jurists representative of different legal systems, but others may join as associates. The commission has a network of national sections and affiliated legal organizations in more than 60 countries.

Founded in 1952, in Geneva, the commission concentrates upon advancing the principles of justice which constitute the basis of the rule of law, and mobilizing jurists throughout the world to support and defend the rule of law and the legal protection of human rights. ICJ has initiated inquiries and published reports on human rights and political and legal situations in British Guiana, South and South West Africa, Brazil, Uruguay, Chile, Iran, Suriname, and Sri Lanka, among others. It has also established, at its Geneva headquarters, the Centre for the Independence of Judges and Lawyers, to promote the independence of these professions and to organize support by legal organizations for victims of harassment and persecution. For its work, ICJ was awarded in 1980 the first European Human Rights Prize by the Council of Europe; and, in 1985, it received the Wateler Peace Prize.

The organization sponsors several publications: The bi-annual *Review* (in English, French, and Spanish), the quarterly *ICJ Newsletter* (in English), and the bi-annual *Bulletin of the Center for Independence of Judges and Lawyers* (in English, French, and Spanish).

International Commission of Jurists. Address: P.O. Box 120, 109 Route de Chêne, CH-1224, Geneva, Switzerland. Telephone: (41-22) 49-35-45. Cable: INTERJURISTS, GENEVE. Fax: (41-22) 49-31-45. Secretary-General: Niall MacDermot.

INTERNATIONAL COMMITTEE OF THE RED CROSS. An international non-governmental organization in consultative status (Category II) with the UN Economic and Social Council, ICRC has 146 national affiliated societies, with over 250 million individual members.

The International Committee of the Red Cross is an independent, private institution, neutral in regard to politics, ideology, and religion. The Committee was established in Geneva in 1863, based on the humanitarian writings of Henry Dunant, and is the founder body of the Red Cross and Red Crescent Societies. ICRC is composed exclusively of Swiss nationals, not exceeding 25 members, selected by choice or election, and making corporate decisions. In time of international or national armed conflict, ICRC endeavours to ensure that the victims of such conflict, whether civilian or soldiers, receive protection and humanitarian assistance. ICRC also works for the development of international humanitarian law and for the understanding and dissemination of the Geneva Convention. For its humanitarian service, ICRC has been awarded the Nobel Peace Prize three times: in 1917, in 1944, and in 1963, when it shared the Prize with the Red Cross Societies League.

Among its numerous activities, ICRC has instituted two humanitarian divisions, the Central Tracing Agency and the International Tracing Service. The Central Tracing Agency, under various names, has been active since 1870 when it was begun by Swiss humanitarians during the Franco-Prussian War to locate prisoners of war and to notify their families of their location. During World War II, as during World War I, ICRC opened an information agency in Geneva to transmit details concerning military personnel in captivity. Currently, the agency's work consists in registering and forwarding any information obtained on prisoners of war, civilian internees, persons released or repatriated, etc., mainly on the basis of lists of names which it receives. It traces civilians and soldiers missing during conflicts and informs their families. It also draws up captivity and death certificates. The agency has a card index of 60 million cards, representing 30 million individual cases.

The second humanitarian agency is the International Tracing Service, whose headquarters is in

Arolsen, FRG, today the most important center of information concerning persons deported or displaced during the Second World War, whether in Germany or in countries occupied by German troops. Responsibility for administering the service was entrusted to the ICRC in 1955. The International Tracing Service has a card index of 25 million cards, representing 2 million inquiries received since 1951.

ICRC has an extensive publication program, sponsoring books and pamphlets on its own work, international humanitarian law, and human rights. Among its periodical publications are the *ICRC Annual Report, ICRC* (annually), *International Review of the Red Cross* (bi-monthly), *Dissemination* (quarterly), and the *ICRC Bulletin* (monthly). The *ICRC Annual Report, ICRC,* and *Dissemination* are published in English, French, Spanish, German, and Arabic. The *International Review of the Red Cross* and *ICRC Bulletin* are published in English, French, Spanish, and German.

International Committee of the Red Cross. Address: 17 avenue de la Paix, CH-1202 Geneva, Switzerland. Telephone: 22-346001. Cable: INTERCROSS. Fax: 332057. Telex: 22269. President: Alexandre Hay.

SEE ALSO *International Red Cross; League of Red Cross and Red Crescent Societies.*

INTERNATIONAL CONFEDERATION OF FREE TRADE UNIONS.

An international non-governmental organization in consultative status with the UN Economic and Social Council (Category I), and with ILO, UNESCO and FAO, ICFTU has 145 affiliated organizations in 97 countries.

Its constitution, adopted in December 1949, declares that the confederation exists to unite workers organized in free and democratic trade unions throughout the world and to afford a means of consultation and collaboration between them to further the right of individuals to achieve social justice and a full and decent life; to work and choose their own employment; to secure their employment and the income deriving from it; to protect their lives and health in the working environment; to protect workers' interests through independent trade unions; and to guarantee democratic means of changing their government. The confederation also works to raise living standards; to promote international cooperation, peace, and disarmament; to defend fundamental human and trade union rights, and to combat discrimination based on race, color, creed, or sex. These aims are summarized in the motto "Bread, Peace and Freedom."

Among its publications, ICFTU publishes fortnightly the *Free Labour World*. It also publishes annually a survey of violations of trade union rights taking place throughout the world.

International Confederation of Free Trade Unions. Address: Rue Montagne-aux-Herbes-Potagères, 37-41, B-1000 Brussels, Belgium. Telephone: (32-2) 2-17-80-85. Cable: INTERCONFED. Fax: (32-2) 2-18-84-15. Telex: 26-785-ICFTU-Bru. General Secretary: John Vanderveken.

INTERNATIONAL CONFERENCE ON HUMAN RIGHTS.

The conference, which met in Teheran from 22 April to 13 May 1968, was the first worldwide meeting of government representatives to deal with the entire range of human rights and fundamental freedoms. It was attended by representatives of 84 States and a large number of United Nations organs, specialized agencies, and governmental and non-governmental organizations.

Convened by the UN General Assembly in a resolution adopted on 20 December 1965 (resolution 2081 [XX]), the conference aimed "to promote further the principles contained in the Universal Declaration of Human Rights, to develop and guarantee political, civil, economic, social and cultural rights and to end all discrimination and denial of human rights and fundamental freedoms on grounds of race, color, sex, language or religion; and, in particular, to permit the elimination of *apartheid.*" Its specific purposes were: (a) to review the progress which had been made in the field of human rights since the adoption of the Universal Declaration of Human Rights; (b) to evaluate the effectiveness of the methods used by the United Nations in the field of human rights, especially with regard to the elimination of all forms of racial discrimination and the practice of the policy of *apartheid*; and (c) to formulate and prepare a program of further measures to be taken subsequent to the celebration of the International Year for Human Rights. The assembly earlier had designated 1968 as the "International Year for Human Rights."

A major product of the conference was the PROCLAMATION OF TEHERAN, which set forth a consensus on the major human rights problems considered by the conference. In its resolutions, the conference addressed many recommendations to various United Nations bodies, specialized agencies, and member States.

Later in 1968, the General Assembly noted the Final Act of the Conference (UN publication, Sales No. E.68.XIV.2) with approval and called upon all States and organizations to act in accordance with the conference's recommendations.

INTERNATIONAL CONVENTION AGAINST *APARTHEID* **IN SPORTS (1985).** The convention defines *"apartheid"* as meaning "a system of institutionalized racial segregation and discrimination for the purpose of establishing and maintaining domination by one racial group of persons over another racial group of persons and systematically oppressing them, such as that pursued by South Africa," and *"apartheid* in sports" as meaning "the application of the policies and practices of such a system in sports activities, whether organized on a professional or an amateur basis." States which ratify or accede to the convention strongly condemn *apartheid* and undertake to pursue the policy of eliminating the practice of *apartheid* in all its forms from sports.

To monitor implementation of the convention, article 11 authorizes the establishment of a COMMISSION AGAINST *APARTHEID* IN SPORTS, consisting of 15 members of high moral character and committed to the struggle against *apartheid*. Members are to be elected by States parties from among their nationals, having regard to the most equitable geographical distribution and the representation of the principle legal systems, with particular attention being paid to the participation of persons having experience in sports administration.

States parties to the convention undertake (article 12) to submit to the UN Secretary-General, for consideration by the commission, reports on the legislative, judicial, administrative, or other measures which they have adopted to give effect to the provisions of the convention. The commission reports annually to the UN General Assembly on its activities and may make suggestions and general recommendations based on its examination of the reports and information received from the States parties, together with comments, if any, from States parties concerned.

Under article 13, a State party may at any time declare that it recognizes the competence of the commission to receive and examine complaints concerning breaches of the convention submitted by States parties which have also made such a declaration. The commission is authorized to decide on the appropriate measures to be taken in respect of such breaches.

The convention, adopted by the UN General Assembly on 10 December 1985 (resolution 40/64) had not entered into force as of 1 January 1989. The text of the convention, annexed to that resolution, is as follows:

The States Parties to the present Convention,

Recalling the provisions of the Charter of the United Nations, in which all Members pledged themselves to take joint and separate action, in co-operation with the Organization, for the achievement of universal respect for, and observance of, human rights and fundamental freedoms for all without distinction as to race, sex, language or religion,

Considering that the Universal Declaration of Human Rights proclaims that all human beings are born free and equal in dignity and rights and that everyone is entitled to all the rights and freedoms set forth in the Declaration without distinction of any kind, particularly in regard to race, colour or national origin,

Observing that, in accordance with the International Convention on the Elimination of All Forms of Racial Discrimination, States Parties to that Convention particularly condemn racial segregation and *apartheid* and undertake to prevent, prohibit and eradicate all practices of this nature in all fields,

Observing that the General Assembly of the United Nations has adopted a number of resolutions condemning the practice of *apartheid* in sports and has affirmed its unqualified support for the Olympic principle that no discrimination be allowed on the grounds of race, religion, or political affiliation and that merit should be the sole criterion for participation in sports activities,

Considering that the International Declaration against *Apartheid* in Sports, which was adopted by the General Assembly on 14 December 1977, solemnly affirms the necessity for the speedy elimination of *apartheid* in sports,

Recalling the provisions of the International Convention on the Suppression and Punishment of the Crime of *Apartheid* and recognizing, in particular, that participation in sports exchanges with teams selected on the basis of *apartheid* directly abets and encourages the commission of the crime of *apartheid,* as defined in that Convention,

Resolved to adopt all necessary measures to eradicate the practice of *apartheid* in sports and to promote international sports contacts based on the Olympic principle,

Recognizing that sports contact with any country practising *apartheid* in sports condones and strengthens *apartheid* in violation of the Olympic principle and thereby becomes the legitimate concern of all Governments,

Desiring to implement the principles embodied in the International Declaration against *Apartheid* in Sports and to secure the earliest adoption of practical measures to that end,

Convinced that the adoption of an International Convention against *Apartheid* in Sports would result in more effective measures at the international and national levels, with a view to eliminating *apartheid* in sports,

Have agreed as follows:

Article 1. For the purposes of the present Convention:

(a) The expression *"apartheid"* shall mean a system of institutionalized racial segregation and discrimination for the purpose of establishing and maintaining domination by one racial group of persons over another racial group of persons and systematically oppressing them, such as that pursued by South Africa, and *"apartheid* in sports" shall mean the application of the policies and practices of such a system in sports activities, whether organized on a professional or an amateur basis;

(b) The expression "national sports facilities" shall mean any sports facility operated within the framework of a sports programme conducted under the auspices of a national government;

(c) The expression "Olympic principle" shall mean the principle that no discrimination be allowed on the grounds of race, religion or political affiliation;

(d) The expression "sports contracts" shall mean any

contract concluded for the organization, promotion, performance or derivative rights, including servicing, of any sports activity;

(e) The expression "sports bodies" shall mean any organization constituted to organize sports activities at the national level, including national Olympic committees, national sports federations or national governing sports committees;

(f) The expression "team" shall mean a group of sportsmen organized for the purpose of participating in sports activities in competition with other such organized groups;

(g) The expression "sportsmen" shall mean men and women who participate in sports activities on an individual or team basis, as well as managers, coaches, trainers and other officials whose functions are essential for the operation of a team.

Article 2. States Parties strongly condemn *apartheid* and undertake to pursue immediately by all appropriate means the policy of eliminating the practice of *apartheid* in all its forms from sports.

Article 3. States Parties shall not permit sports contact with a country practising *apartheid* and shall take appropriate action to ensure that their sports bodies, teams, and individual sportsmen do not have such contact.

Article 4. States Parties shall take all possible measures to prevent sports contact with a country practising *apartheid* and shall ensure that effective means exist for bringing about compliance with such measures.

Article 5. States Parties shall refuse to provide financial or other assistance to enable their sports bodies, teams and individual sportsmen to participate in sports activities in a country practising *apartheid* or with teams or individual sportsmen selected on the basis of *apartheid.*

Article 6. Each State Party shall take appropriate action against its sports bodies, teams and individual sportsmen that participate in sports activities in a country practising *apartheid* or with teams representing a country practising *apartheid,* which in particular shall include:

(a) Refusal to provide financial or other assistance for any purpose to such sports bodies, teams and individual sportsmen;

(b) Restriction of access to national sports facilities by such sports bodies, teams and individual sportsmen;

(c) Non-enforceability of all sports contracts which involve sports activities in a country practising *apartheid* or with teams or individual sportsmen selected on the basis of *apartheid;*

(d) Denial and withdrawal of national honours or awards in sports to such teams and individual sportsmen;

(e) Denial of official receptions in honour of such teams or sportsmen.

Article 7. States Parties shall deny visas and/or entry to representatives of sports bodies, teams and individual sportsmen representing a country practising *apartheid.*

Article 8. States Parties shall take all appropriate action to secure the expulsion of a country practising *apartheid* from international and regional sports bodies.

Article 9. States Parties shall take all appropriate measures to prevent international sports bodies from imposing financial or other penalties on affiliated bodies which, in accordance with United Nations resolutions, the provisions of the present Convention and the spirit of the Olympic principle, refuse to participate in sports with a country practising *apartheid.*

Article 10. 1. States Parties shall use their best endeavours to ensure universal compliance with the Olympic principles of non-discrimination and the provisions of the present Convention.

2. Towards this end, States Parties shall prohibit entry into their countries of members of teams and individual sportsmen participating or who have participated in sports competitions in South Africa and shall prohibit entry into their countries of representatives of sports bodies, members of teams and individual sportsmen who invite on their own initiative sports bodies, teams and sportsmen officially representing a country practising *apartheid* and participating under its flag. States Parties may also prohibit entry of representatives of sports bodies, members of teams or individual sportsmen who maintain sports contacts with sports bodies, teams or sportsmen representing a country practising *apartheid* and participating under its flag. Prohibition of entry should not violate the regulations of the relevant sports federations which support the elimination of *apartheid* in sports and shall apply only to participation in sports activities.

3. States Parties shall advise their national representatives to international sports federations to take all possible and practical steps to prevent the participation of the sports bodies, teams and sportsmen referred to in paragraph 2 above in international sports competitions and shall, through their representatives in international sports organizations, take every possible measure:

(a) To ensure the expulsion of South Africa from all federations in which it still holds membership as well as to deny South Africa reinstatement to membership in any federation from which it has been expelled;

(b) In case of national federations condoning sports exchanges with a country practising *apartheid,* to impose sanctions against such national federations including, if necessary, expulsion from the relevant international sports organization and exclusion of their representatives from participation in international sports competitions.

4. In cases of flagrant violations of the provisions of the present Convention, States Parties shall take appropriate action as they deem fit, including, where necessary, steps aimed at the exclusion of the responsible national sports governing bodies, national sports federations or sportsmen of the countries concerned from international sports competition.

5. The provisions of the present article relating specifically to South Africa shall cease to apply when the system of *apartheid* is abolished in that country.

Article 11. 1. There shall be established a Commission against *Apartheid* in Sports (hereinafter referred to as "the Commission") consisting of fifteen members of high moral character and committed to the struggle against *apartheid,* particular attention being paid to participation of persons having experience in sports administration, elected by the States Parties from among their nationals, having regard to the most equitable geographical distribution and the representation of the principal legal systems.

2. The members of the Commission shall be elected by secret ballot from a list of persons nominated by the States Parties. Each State Party may nominate one person from among its own nationals.

3. The initial election shall be held six months after the date of the entry into force of the present Convention. At least three months before the date of each election, the Secretary-General of the United Nations shall address a letter to the States Parties inviting them to submit their nominations within two months. The Secretary-General shall

prepare a list in alphabetical order of all persons thus nominated, indicating the States Parties which have nominated them, and shall submit it to the States Parties.

4. Elections of the members of the Commission shall be held at a meeting of States Parties convened by the Secretary-General at United Nations Headquarters. At that meeting, for which two thirds of the States Parties shall constitute a quorum, the persons elected to the Commission shall be those nominees who obtain the largest number of votes and an absolute majority of the votes of the representatives of States Parties present and voting.

5. The members of the Commission shall be elected for a term of four years. However, the terms of nine of the members elected at the first election shall expire at the end of two years; immediately after the first election, the names of these nine members shall be chosen by lot by the Chairman of the Commission.

6. For the filling of casual vacancies, the State Party whose national has ceased to function as a member of the Commission shall appoint another person from among its nationals, subject to the approval of the Commission.

7. States Parties shall be responsible for the expenses of the members of the Commission while they are in performance of Commission duties.

Article 12. 1. States Parties undertake to submit to the Secretary-General of the United Nations, for consideration by the Commission, a report on the legislative, judicial, administrative or other measures which they have adopted to give effect to the provisions of the present Convention within one year of its entry into force and thereafter every two years. The Commission may request further information from the States Parties.

2. The Commission shall report annually through the Secretary-General to the General Assembly of the United Nations on its activities and may make suggestions and general recommendations based on the examination of the reports and information received from the States Parties. Such suggestions and recommendations shall be reported to the General Assembly together with comments, if any, from States Parties concerned.

3. The Commission shall examine, in particular, the implementation of the provisions of article 10 of the present Convention and make recommendations on action to be undertaken.

4. A meeting of States Parties shall be convened by the Secretary-General at the request of a majority of the States Parties to consider further action with respect to the implementation of the provisions of article 10 of the present Convention. In cases of flagrant violation of the provisions of the present Convention, a meeting of States Parties shall be convened by the Secretary-General at the request of the Commission.

Article 13. 1. Any State Party may at any time declare that it recognizes the competence of the Commission to receive and examine complaints concerning breaches of the provisions of the present Convention submitted by States Parties which have also made such a declaration. The Commission may decide on the appropriate measures to be taken in respect of breaches.

2. States Parties against which a complaint has been made, in accordance with paragraph 1 of the present article, shall be entitled to be represented and take part in the proceedings of the Commission.

Article 14. 1. The Commission shall meet at least once a year.

2. The Commission shall adopt its own rules of procedure.

3. The secretariat of the Commission shall be provided by the Secretary-General of the United Nations.

4. The meetings of the Commission shall normally be held at United Nations Headquarters.

5. The Secretary-General shall convene the initial meeting of the Commission.

Article 15. The Secretary-General of the United Nations shall be the depositary of the present Convention.

Article 16. 1. The present Convention shall be open for signature at United Nations Headquarters by all States until its entry into force.

2. The present Convention shall be subject to ratification, acceptance or approval by the signatory States.

Article 17. The present Convention shall be open for accession by all States.

Article 18. 1. The present Convention shall enter into force on the thirtieth day after the date of deposit with the Secretary-General of the United Nations of the twenty-seventh instrument of ratification, acceptance, approval or accession.

2. For each State ratifying, accepting, approving or acceding to the present Convention after its entry into force, the Convention shall enter into force on the thirtieth day after the date of deposit of the relevant instrument.

Article 19. Any dispute between States Parties arising out of the interpretation, application or implementation of the present Convention which is not settled by negotiation shall be brought before the International Court of Justice at the request and with the mutual consent of the States Parties to the dispute, save where the Parties to the dispute have agreed on some other form of settlement.

Article 20. 1. Any State Party may propose an amendment or revision to the present Convention and file it with the depositary. The Secretary-General of the United Nations shall thereupon communicate the proposed amendment or revision to the States Parties with a request that they notify him whether they favour a conference of States Parties for the purpose of considering and voting upon the proposal. In the event that at least one third of the States Parties favour such a conference, the Secretary-General shall convene the conference under the auspices of the United Nations. Any amendment or revision adopted by the majority of the States Parties present and voting at the conference shall be submitted to the General Assembly of the United Nations for approval.

2. Amendments or revisions shall come into force when they have been approved by the General Assembly and accepted by a two-thirds majority of the States Parties, in accordance with their respective constitutional processes.

3. When amendments or revisions come into force, they shall be binding on those States Parties which have accepted them, other States Parties still being bound by the provisions of the present Convention and any earlier amendment or revision which they have accepted.

Article 21. A State Party may withdraw from the present Convention by written notification to the depositary. Such withdrawal shall take effect one year after the date of receipt of the notification by the depositary.

Article 22. The present Convention has been concluded in Arabic, Chinese, English, French, Russian and Spanish, all texts being equally authentic.

SEE ALSO *International Declaration against* Apartheid *in Sports.*

I

INTERNATIONAL CONVENTION AGAINST THE RECRUITMENT, USE, FINANCING AND TRAINING OF MERCENARIES (1989). The convention, adopted and opened for signature, ratification, and accession by the UN General Assembly on 4 December 1989, reflects repeated earlier denunciations of the practice of using mercenaries against developing countries and national liberation movements, denunciations which appeared in resolutions of the General Assembly, the Security Council, the Commission on Human Rights, and other bodies. These organs had affirmed, on many occasions, that the practice of using mercenaries in such circumstances constitutes a criminal act and that the mercenaries themselves are criminals and had called upon governments to enact legislation declaring the recruitment, financing, and training of mercenaries in their territory, or even their transit through it, to be punishable offences.

In 1980, the General Assembly, recognizing that the activities of mercenaries are contrary to the fundamental principles of international law and seriously impede the progress of people struggling for self-determination and against foreign domination, established (resolution 35/48) the *Ad Hoc* Committee on the Drafting of an International Convention against the Recruitment, Use, Financing and Training of Mercenaries, composed of 35 member States, and called upon it to elaborate such a convention at the earliest possible date.

Nine years later, during the 1989 session of the General Assembly, a working group that met during that session succeeded in putting into final form the draft convention which the ad hoc committee had substantially completed. The assembly thereupon adopted, without a recorded vote, the International Convention against the Recruitment, Use, Financing and Training of Mercenaries (resolution 44/34), Annex) as follows:

The States Parties to the present Convention,

Reaffirming the purposes and principles enshrined in the Charter of the United Nations and in the Declaration on the Principles of International Law concerning Friendly Relations and Co-operation among States in accordance with the Charter of the United Nations.

Being aware of the recruitment, use, financing and training of mercenaries for activities which violate principles of international law such as those of sovereign equality, political independence, territorial integrity of States and self-determination of peoples,

Affirming that the recruitment, use, financing and training of mercenaries should be considered as offences of grave concern to all States and that any person committing any of these offences should either be prosecuted or extradited,

Convinced of the necessity to develop and enhance international co-operation among States for the prevention, prosecution and punishment of such offences,

Expressing concern at new unlawful international activities linking drug traffickers and mercenaries in the perpetration of violent actions which undermine the constitutional order of States,

Also convinced that the adoption of a convention against the recruitment, use, financing and training of mercenaries would contribute to the eradication of these nefarious activities and thereby to the observance of the purposes and principles enshrined in the Charter of the United Nations,

Cognizant that matters not regulated by such a convention continue to be governed by the rules and principles of international law,

Have agreed as follows:

Article 1. For the purposes of the present Convention,

1. A mercenary is any person who:

(a) Is specially recruited locally or abroad in order to fight in an armed conflict;

(b) Is motivated to take part in the hostilities essentially by the desire for private gain and, in fact, is promised, by or on behalf of a party to the conflict, material compensation substantially in excess of that promised or paid to combatants of similar rank and functions in the armed forces of that party;

(c) Is neither a national of a party to the conflict nor a resident of territory controlled by a party to the conflict;

(d) Is not a member of the armed forces of a party to the conflict; and

(e) Has not been sent by a State which is not a party to the conflict on official duty as a member of its armed forces.

2. A mercenary is also any person who, in any other situation:

(a) Is specially recruited locally or abroad for the purpose of participating in a concerted act of violence aimed at:

(i) Overthrowing a Government or otherwise undermining the constitutional order of a State; or

(ii) Undermining the territorial integrity of a State;

(b) Is motivated to take part therein essentially by the desire for significant private gain and is prompted by the promise or payment of material compensation;

(c) Is neither a national nor a resident of the State against which such an act is directed;

(d) Has not been sent by a State on official duty; and

(e) Is not a member of the armed forces of the State on whose territory the act is undertaken.

Article 2. Any person who recruits, uses, finances or trains mercenaries, as defined in article 1 of the present Convention, commits an offence for the purposes of the Convention.

Article 3. 1. A mercenary, as defined in article 1 of the present Convention, who participates directly in hostilities or in a concerted act of violence, as the case may be, commits an offence for the purposes of the Convention.

2. Nothing in this article limits the scope of application of article 4 of the present Convention.

Article 4. An offence is committed by any person who:

(a) Attempts to commit one of the offences set forth in the present Convention;

(b) Is the accomplice of a person who commits or attempts to commit any of the offences set forth in the present Convention.

Article 5. 1. States Parties shall not recruit, use, finance or train mercenaries and shall prohibit such activities in accordance with the provisions of the present Convention.

2. States Parties shall not recruit, use, finance or train mercenaries for the purpose of opposing the legitimate exercise of the inalienable right of peoples to self-determination, as recognized by international law, and shall take, in conformity with international law, the appropriate measures to prevent the recruitment, use, financing or training of mercenaries for that purpose.

3. They shall make the offences set forth in the present Convention punishable by appropriate penalties which take into account the grave nature of those offences.

Article 6. States Parties shall co-operate in the prevention of the offences set forth in the present Convention, particularly by:

(a) Taking all practicable measure to prevent preparations in their respective territories for the commission of those offences within or outside their territories, including the prohibition of illegal activities of persons, groups and organizations that encourage, instigate, organize or engage in the perpetration of such offences;

(b) Co-ordinating the taking of administrative and other measures as appropriate to prevent the commission of those offences.

Article 7. States Parties shall co-operate in taking the necessary measures for the implementation of the present Convention.

Article 8. Any State Party having reason to believe that one of the offences set forth in the present Convention has been, is being or will be committed shall, in accordance with its national law, communicate the relevant information, as soon as it come to its knowledge, directly or through the Secretary-General of the United Nations, to the States Parties affected.

Article 9. 1. Each State Party shall take such measures as may be necessary to establish its jurisdiction over any of the offences set forth in the present Convention which are committed:

(a) In its territory or on board a ship or aircraft registered in that State;

(b) By any of its nationals or, if that State considers it appropriate, by those stateless persons who have their habitual residence in that territory.

2. Each State Party shall likewise take such measures as may be necessary to establish its jurisdiction over the offences set forth in articles 2, 3 and 4 of the present Convention in cases where the alleged offender is present in its territory and it does not extradite him to any of the States mentioned in paragraph 1 of this article.

3. The present Convention does not exclude any criminal jurisdiction exercised in accordance with national law.

Article 10. 1. Upon being satisfied that the circumstances so warrant, any State Party in whose territory the alleged offender is present shall, in accordance with its laws, take him into custody or take such other measures to ensure his presence for such time as is necessary to enable any criminal or extradition proceedings to be instituted. The State Party shall immediately make a preliminary inquiry into the facts.

2. When a State Party, pursuant to this article, has taken a person into custody or has taken such other measures referred to in paragraph 1 of this article, it shall notify without delay either directly or through the Secretary-General of the United Nations:

(a) The State Party where the offence was committed;

(b) The State Party against which the offence has been directed or attempted;

(c) The State Party of which the natural or juridical person against whom the offence has been directed or attempted is a national;

(d) The State Party of which the alleged offender is a national or, if he is a stateless person, in whose territory he has his habitual residence;

(e) Any other interested State Party which it considers it appropriate to notify.

3. Any person regarding whom the measures referred to in paragraph 1 of this article are being taken shall be entitled:

(a) To communicate without delay with the nearest appropriate representative of the State of which he is a national or which is otherwise entitled to protect his rights or, if he is a stateless person, the State in whose territory he has his habitual residence;

(b) To be visited by a representative of that State.

4. The provisions of paragraph 3 of this article shall be without prejudice to the right of any State Party having a claim to jurisdiction in accordance with article 9, paragraph 1 (*b*), to invite the International Committee of the Red Cross to communicate with and visit the alleged offender.

5. The State which makes the preliminary inquiry contemplated in paragraph 1 of this article shall promptly report its findings to the States referred to in paragraph 2 of this article and indicate whether it intends to exercise jurisdiction.

Article 11. Any person regarding whom proceedings are being carried out in connection with any of the offences set forth in the present Convention shall be guaranteed at all stages of the proceedings fair treatment and all the rights and guarantees provided for in the law of the State in question. Applicable norms of international law should be taken into account.

Article 12. The State Party in whose territory the alleged offender is found shall, if it does not extradite him, be obliged, without exception whatsoever and whether or not the offence was committed in its territory, to submit the case to its competent authorities for the purpose of prosecution, through proceedings in accordance with the laws of that State. Those authorities shall take their decision in the same manner as in the case of any other offence of a grave nature under the law of that State.

Article 13. 1. State Parties shall afford one another the greatest measure of assistance in connection with criminal proceedings brought in respect of the offences set forth in the present Convention, including the supply of all evidence at their disposal necessary for the proceedings. The law of the State whose assistance is requested shall apply in all cases.

2. The provisions of paragraph 1 of this article shall not affect obligations concerning mutual judicial assistance embodied in any other treaty.

Article 14. The State Party where the alleged offender is prosecuted shall in accordance with its laws communicate the final outcome of the proceeding to the Secretary-General of the United Nations, who shall transmit the information to the other States concerned.

Article 15. 1. The offences set forth in articles 2, 3 and 4 of the present Convention shall be deemed to be included as extraditable offences in any extradition treaty existing between States Parties. States Parties undertake to include such offences as extraditable offences in every extradition treaty to be concluded between them.

2. If a State Party which makes extradition conditional on the existence of a treaty receives a request for extradition

from another State Party with which it has no extradition treaty, it may at its option consider the present Convention as the legal basis for extradition in respect of those offences. Extradition shall be subject to the other conditions provided by the law of the requested State.

3. States Parties which do not make extradition conditional on the existence of a treaty shall recognize those offences as extraditable offences between themselves, subject to the conditions provided by the law of the requested State.

4. The offences shall be treated, for the purpose of extradition between States Parties, as if they had been committed not only in the place in which they occurred but also in the territories of the States required to establish their jurisdiction in accordance with article 9 of the present Convention.

Article 16. The present Convention shall be applied without prejudice to:

(a) The rules relating to the international responsibility of States;

(b) The law of armed conflict and international humanitarian law, including the provisions relating to the status of combatant or of prisoner of war.

Article 17. 1. Any dispute between two or more States Parties concerning the interpretation or application of the present Convention which is not settled by negotiation shall, at the request of one of them, be submitted to arbitration. If, within six months from the date of the request for arbitration, the parties are unable to agree on the organization of the arbitration, any one of those parties may refer the dispute to the International Court of Justice by a request in conformity with the Statute of the Court.

2. Each State may, at the time of signature or ratification of the present Convention or accession thereto, declare that it does not consider itself bound by paragraph 1 of this article. The other States Parties shall not be bound by paragraph 1 of this article with respect to any State Party which has made such a reservation.

3. Any State Party which has made a reservation in accordance with paragraph 2 of this article may at any time withdraw that reservation by notification to the Secretary-General of the United Nations.

Article 18. 1. The present Convention shall be open for signature by all States until 31 December 1990 at United Nations Headquarters in New York.

2. The present Convention shall be subject to ratification. The instruments of ratification shall be deposited with the Secretary-General of the United Nations.

3. The present Convention shall remain open for accession by any State. The instruments of accession shall be deposited with the Secretary-General of the United Nations.

Article 19. 1. The present Convention shall enter into force on the thirtieth day following the date of deposit of the twenty-second instrument of ratification or accession with the Secretary-General of the United Nations.

2. For each State ratifying or acceding to the Convention after the deposit of the twenty-second instrument of ratification or accession, the Convention shall enter into force on the thirtieth day after deposit by such State of its instrument of ratification or accession.

Article 20. 1. Any State Party may denounce the present Convention by written notification to the Secretary-General of the United Nations.

2. Denunciation shall take effect one year after the date on which the notification is received by the Secretary-General of the United Nations.

Article 21. The original of the present Convention, of which the Arabic, Chinese, English, French, Russian and Spanish texts are equally authentic, shall be deposited with the Secretary-General of the United Nations, who shall send certified copies thereof to all States.

In witness whereof the undersigned, being duly authorized thereto by their respective Governments, have signed the present Convention, opened for signature at New York on 4 December 1989.

SEE ALSO *Mercenarism: Violation of the Right to Self-Determination.*

INTERNATIONAL CONVENTION AGAINST THE TAKING OF HOSTAGES (1979).

In 1976, the UN General Assembly decided (resolution 31/103) to establish an *ad hoc* committee to draft an international convention against the taking of HOSTAGES, composed of 35 Member States, and to request it to prepare the draft of such a convention bearing in mind suggestions and proposals received from any State.

In doing so, the Assembly bore in mind that both the UNIVERSAL DECLARATION OF HUMAN RIGHTS and the INTERNATIONAL COVENANT ON CIVIL AND POLITICAL RIGHTS provide that everyone has the right to life, liberty, and security. It also recalled the prohibitions of the taking of hostages in articles 3 and 34 of the GENEVA CONVENTION RELATIVE TO THE PROTECTION OF CIVILIAN PERSONS IN TIME OF WAR of 12 August 1949, the CONVENTION FOR THE SUPPRESSION OF UNLAWFUL ACTS AGAINST THE SAFETY OF CIVIL AVIATION, and the CONVENTION ON THE PREVENTION AND PUNISHMENT OF CRIMES AGAINST INTERNATIONALLY PROTECTED PERSONS, INCLUDING DIPLOMATIC AGENTS, as well as the Assembly's own resolution of 25 November 1970 (resolution 2645 [XXV]), condemning aerial hijacking or interference with civil air travel.

The ad hoc committee completed the draft of a convention against the taking of hostages in 1979; and, on 17 December 1979, the Assembly adopted (resolution 34/146) the International Convention against the Taking of Hostages. The text of the convention, annexed to that resolution, is as follows:

The States Parties to this Convention,

Having in mind the purposes and principles of the Charter of the United Nations concerning the maintenance of international peace and security and the promotion of friendly relations and co-operation among States,

Recognizing, in particular, that everyone has the right to life, liberty and security of person, as set out in the Universal Declaration of Human Rights and the International Covenant on Civil and Political Rights,

Reaffirming the principle of equal rights and self-determination of peoples as enshrined in the Charter of the United Nations and the Declaration on Principles of International Law concerning Friendly Relations and Co-operation among States in accordance with the Charter of the United Nations, as well as in other relevant resolutions of the General Assembly,

Considering that the taking of hostages is an offence of grave concern to the international community and that, in accordance with the provisions of this Convention, any person committing an act of hostage taking shall be either prosecuted or extradited,

Being convinced that it is urgently necessary to develop international co-operation between States in devising and adopting effective measures for the prevention, prosecution and punishment of all acts of taking of hostages as manifestations of international terrorism.

Have agreed as follows:

Article 1. 1. Any person who seizes or detains and threatens to kill, to injure or to continue to detain another person (hereinafter referred to as the "hostage") in order to compel a third party, namely, a State, an international intergovernmental organization, a natural or juridical person, or a group of persons, to do or abstain from doing any act as an explicit or implicit condition for the release of the hostage commits the offence of taking of hostages ("hostage-taking") within the meaning of this Convention.

2. Any person who:

(a) Attempts to commit an act of hostage-taking, or

(b) Participates as an accomplice of anyone who commits or attempts to commit an act of hostage-taking

likewise commits an offence for the purposes of this Convention.

Article 2. Each State Party shall make the offences set forth in article 1 punishable by appropriate penalties which take into account the grave nature of those offences.

Article 3. 1. The State Party in the territory of which the hostage is held by the offender shall take all measures it considers appropriate to ease the situation of the hostage, in particular, to secure his release and, after his release, to facilitate, when relevant, his departure.

2. If any object which the offender has obtained as a result of the taking of hostages comes into the custody of a State Party, that State Party shall return it as soon as possible to the hostage or the third party referred to in article 1, as the case may be, or to the appropriate authorities thereof.

Article 4. States Parties shall co-operate in the prevention of the offences set forth in article 1, particularly by:

(a) Taking all practicable measures to prevent preparations in their respective territories for the commission of those offences within or outside their territories, including measures to prohibit in their territories illegal activities of persons, groups and organizations that encourage, instigate, organize or engage in the perpetration of acts of taking of hostages;

(b) Exchanging information and co-ordinating the taking of administrative and other measures as appropriate to prevent the commission of those offences.

Article 5. 1. Each State Party shall take such measures as may be necessary to establish its jurisdiction over any of the offences set forth in article 1 which are committed:

(a) In its territory or on board a ship or aircraft registered in that State;

(b) By any of its nationals or, if that State considers it appropriate, by those stateless persons who have their habitual residence in its territory;

(c) In order to compel that State to do or abstain from doing any act; or

(d) With respect to a hostage who is a national of that State, if that State considers it appropriate.

2. Each State Party shall likewise take such measures as may be necessary to establish its jurisdiction over the offences set forth in article 1 in cases where the alleged offender is present in its territory and it does not extradite him to any of the States mentioned in paragraph 1 of this article.

3. This Convention does not exclude any criminal jurisdiction exercised in accordance with internal law.

Article 6. 1. Upon being satisfied that the circumstances so warrant, any State Party in the territory of which the alleged offender is present shall, in accordance with its laws, take him into custody or take other measures to ensure his presence for such time as is necessary to enable any criminal or extradition proceedings to be instituted. That State Party shall immediately make a preliminary inquiry into the facts.

2. The custody or other measures referred to in paragraph 1 of this article shall be notified without delay directly or through the Secretary-General of the United Nations to:

(a) The State where the offence was committed;

(b) The State against which compulsion has been directed or attempted;

(c) The State of which the natural or juridical person against whom compulsion has been directed or attempted is a national;

(d) The State of which the hostage is a national or in the territory of which he has his habitual residence;

(e) The State of which the alleged offender is a national or, if he is a stateless person, in the territory of which he has his habitual residence;

(f) The international intergovernmental organization against which compulsion has been directed or attempted;

(g) All other States concerned.

3. Any person regarding whom the measures referred to in paragraph 1 of this article are being taken shall be entitled:

(a) To communicate without delay with the nearest appropriate representative of the State of which he is a national or which is otherwise entitled to establish such communication or, if he is a stateless person, the State in the territory of which he has his habitual residence;

(b) To be visited by a representative of that State.

4. The rights referred to in paragraph 3 of this article shall be exercised in conformity with the laws and regulations of the State in the territory of which the alleged offender is present, subject to the proviso, however, that the said laws and regulations must enable full effect to be given to the purposes for which the rights accorded under paragraph 3 of this article are intended.

5. The provisions of paragraphs 3 and 4 of this article shall be without prejudice to the right of any State Party having a claim to jurisdiction in accordance with paragraph 1 (b) of article 5 to invite the International Committee of the Red Cross to communicate with and visit the alleged offender.

6. The State which makes the preliminary inquiry contemplated in paragraph 1 of this article shall promptly report its findings to the States or organization referred to in paragraph 2 of this article and indicate whether it intends to exercise jurisdiction.

Article 7. The State Party where the alleged offender is prosecuted shall, in accordance with its laws, communicate the final outcome of the proceedings to the Secretary-General of the United Nations, who shall transmit the information to the other States concerned and the international intergovernmental organizations concerned.

Article 8. 1. The State Party in the territory of which the alleged offender is found shall, if it does not extradite him, be obliged, without exception whatsoever and whether or not the offence was committed in its territory, to submit the case to its competent authorities for the purpose of prosecution, through proceedings in accordance with the laws of that State. Those authorities shall take their decision in the same manner as in the case of any ordinary offence of a grave nature under the law of that State.

2. Any person regarding whom proceedings are being carried out in connexion with any of the offences set forth in article 1 shall be guaranteed fair treatment at all stages of the proceedings, including enjoyment of all the rights and guarantees provided by the law of the State in the territory of which he is present.

Article 9. 1. A request for the extradition of an alleged offender, pursuant to this Convention, shall not be granted if the requested State Party has substantial grounds for believing:

(a) That the request for extradition for an offence set forth in article 1 has been made for the purpose of prosecuting or punishing a person on account of his race, religion, nationality, ethnic origin or political opinion; or

(b) That the person's position may be prejudiced:

(i) For any of the reasons mentioned in subparagraph (a) of this paragraph, or

(ii) For the reason that communication with him by the appropriate authorities of the State entitled to exercise rights of protection cannot be effected.

2. With respect to the offences as defined in this Convention, the provisions of all extradition treaties and arrangements applicable between States Parties are modified as between States Parties to the extent that they are incompatible with this Convention.

Article 10. 1. The offences set forth in article 1 shall be deemed to be included as extraditable offences in any extradition treaty existing between States Parties. States Parties undertake to include such offences as extraditable offences in every extradition treaty to be concluded between them.

2. If a State Party which makes extradition conditional on the existence of a treaty receives a request for extradition from another State Party with which it has no extradition treaty, the requested State may at its opinion consider this Convention as the legal basis for extradition in respect of the offences set forth in article 1. Extradition shall be subject to the other conditions provided by the law of the requested State.

3. States Parties which do not make extradition conditional on the existence of a treaty shall recognize the offences set forth in article 1 as extraditable offences between themselves, subject to the conditions provided by the law of the requested State.

4. The offences set fort in article 1 shall be treated, for the purpose of extradition between States Parties, as if they had been committed not only in the place in which they occurred but also in the territories of the States required to establish their jurisdiction in accordance with paragraph 1 of article 5.

Article 11. 1. States Parties shall afford one another the greatest measure of assistance in connexion with criminal proceedings brought in respect of the offences set forth in article 1, including the supply of all evidence at their disposal necessary for the proceedings.

2. The provisions of paragraph 1 of this article shall not affect obligations concerning mutual judicial assistance embodied in any other treaty.

Article 12. In so far as the Geneva Conventions of 1949 for the protection of war victims or the Protocols Additional to those Conventions are applicable to a particular act of hostage-taking, and in so far as States Parties to this Convention are bound under those conventions to prosecute or hand over the hostage-taker, the present Convention shall not apply to an act of hostage-taking committed in the course of armed conflicts as defined in the Geneva Conventions of 1949 and the Protocols thereto, including armed conflicts, mentioned in article 1, paragraph 4, of Additional Protocol 1 of 1977 in which peoples are fighting against colonial domination and alien occupation and against racist régimes in the exercise of their right of self-determination, as enshrined in the Charter of the United Nations and the Declaration on Principles of International Law concerning Friendly Relations and Co-operation among States in accordance with the Charter of the United Nations.

Article 13. This Convention shall not apply where the offence is committed within a single State, the hostage and the alleged offender are nationals of that State and the alleged offender is found in the territory of that State.

Article 14. Nothing in this Convention shall be construed as justifying the violation of the territorial integrity or political independence of a State in contravention of the Charter of the United Nations.

Article 15. The provisions of this Convention shall not affect the application of the Treaties on Asylum, in force at the date of the adoption of this Convention, as between the States which are parties to those Treaties; but a State Party to this Convention may not invoke those Treaties with respect to another State Party to this Convention which is not a party to those Treaties.

Article 16. 1. Any dispute between two or more States Parties concerning the interpretation or application of this Convention which is not settled by negotiation shall, at the request of one of them, be submitted to arbitration. If within six months from the date of the request for arbitration the parties are unable to agree on the organization of the arbitration, any one of those parties may refer the dispute to the International Court of Justice by request in conformity with the Statute of the Court.

2. Each State may at the time of signature or ratification of this Convention or accession thereto declare that it does not consider itself bound by paragraph 1 of this article. The other Sates Parties shall not be bound by paragraph 1 of this article with respect to any State Party which has made such a reservation.

3. Any State Party which has made a reservation in accordance with paragraph 2 of this article may at any time withdraw that reservation by notification to the Secretary-General of the United Nations.

Article 17. 1. This Convention is open for signature by all States until 31 December 1980 at United Nations Headquarters in New York.

2. This Convention is subject to ratification. The instruments of ratification shall be deposited with the Secretary-General of the United Nations.

3. This Convention is open for accession by any State. The instruments of accession shall be deposited with the Secretary-General of the United Nations.

Article 18. 1. This Convention shall enter into force on the thirtieth day following the date of deposit of the twenty-second instrument of ratification or accession with the Secretary-General of the United Nations.

2. For each State ratifying or acceding to the Convention after the deposit of the twenty-second instrument of ratification or accession, the Convention shall enter into force on the thirtieth day after deposit by such State of its instrument of ratification or accession.

Article 19. 1. Any State Party may denounce this Convention by written notification to the Secretary-General of the United Nations.

2. Denunciation shall take effect one year following the date on which notification is received by the Secretary-General of the United Nations.

Article 20. The original of this Convention, of which the Arabic, Chinese, English, French, Russian and Spanish texts are equally authentic, shall be deposited with the Secretary-General of the United Nations, who shall send certified copies thereof to all States.

In witness whereof, the undersigned, being duly authorized thereto by their respective Governments, have signed this Convention, opened for signature at New York on 18 December 1979.

INTERNATIONAL CONVENTION ON THE ELIMINATION OF ALL FORMS OF RACIAL DISCRIMINATION (1965).

The convention is the first human rights instrument adopted by the United Nations to embody international measures of implementation: it authorized establishment of the COMMITTEE ON THE ELIMINATION OF RACIAL DISCRIMINATION, composed of experts serving in their personal capacities, to consider reports from States parties on the legislative, judicial, administrative, or other measures adopted by them and which give effect to the provisions of the convention, to make suggestions and general recommendations based on its examination of those reports and information received from States parties, and to assist in settling disputes among States parties concerning the application of the Convention.

It also provides (article 14) for the committee to receive and consider communications from individuals or groups of individuals within the jurisdiction of a State party claiming to be the victims of a violation of any of the rights set forth in the convention, provided that that State has made a declaration recognizing the competence of the committee to do so.

The International Convention on the Elimination of All Forms of Racial Discrimination was adopted by the UN General Assembly on 21 December 1965 (resolution 2106 [XX]), and entered into force on 2 January 1969. The DECLARATION ON THE ELIMINATION OF ALL FORMS OF RACIAL DISCRIMINATION entered into force on 3 December 1982. The text of the convention, annexed to resolution 2106 (XX), is as follows:

The States Parties to this Convention,

Considering that the Charter of the United Nations is based on the principles of the dignity and equality inherent in all human beings, and that all Member States have pledged themselves to take joint and separate action, in cooperation with the Organization, for the achievement of one of the purposes of the United Nations which is to promote and encourage universal respect for and observance of human rights and fundamental freedoms for all, without distinction as to race, sex, language or religion,

Considering that the Universal Declaration of Human Rights proclaims that all human beings are born free and equal in dignity and rights and that everyone is entitled to all the rights and freedoms set out therein, without distinction of any kind, in particular as to race, colour or national origin,

Considering that all human beings are equal before the law and are entitled to equal protection of the law against any discrimination and against any incitement to discrimination,

Considering that the United Nations has condemned colonialism and all practices of segregation and discrimination associated therewith, in whatever form and wherever they exist, and that the Declaration on the Granting of Independence to Colonial Countries and Peoples of 14 December 1960 (General Assembly resolutions 1514 (XV)) has affirmed and solemnly proclaimed the necessity of bringing them to a speedy and unconditional end,

Considering that the United Nations Declaration on the Elimination of All Forms of Racial Discrimination of 20 November 1963 (General Assembly resolution 1904 (XVIII)) solemnly affirms the necessity of speedily eliminating racial discrimination throughout the world in all its forms and manifestations and of securing understanding of and respect for the dignity of the human person,

Convinced that any doctrine of superiority based on racial differentiation is scientifically false, morally condemnable, socially unjust and dangerous, and that there is no justification for racial discrimination, in theory or in practice, anywhere,

Reaffirming that discrimination between human beings on the grounds of race, colour or ethnic origin is an obstacle to friendly and peaceful relations among nations and is capable of disturbing peace and security among peoples and the harmony of persons living side by side even within one and the same State,

Convinced that the existence of racial barriers is repugnant to the ideals of any human society,

Alarmed by manifestations of racial discrimination still in evidence in some areas of the world and by governmental policies based on racial superiority or hatred, such as policies of *apartheid,* segregation or separation,

Resolved to adopt all necessary measures for speedily eliminating racial discrimination in all its forms and manifestations, and to prevent and combat racist doctrines and practices in order to promote understanding between races and to build an international community free from all forms of racial segregation and racial discrimination,

Bearing in mind the Convention concerning Discrimination in respect of Employment and Occupation adopted by the International Labour Organisation in 1958, and the Convention against Discrimination in Education adopted by the United Nations Educational, Scientific and Cultural Organization in 1960,

Desiring to implement the principles embodied in the United Nations Declaration on the Elimination of All Forms of Racial Discrimination and to secure the earliest adoption of practical measures to that end,

Have agreed as follows:

I

Part I

Article 1. 1. In this Convention, the term "racial discrimination" shall mean any distinction, exclusion, restriction or preference based on race, colour, descent, or national or ethnic origin which has the purpose or effect of nullifying or impairing the recognition, enjoyment or exercise, on an equal footing, of human rights and fundamental freedoms in the political, economic, social, cultural or any other field of public life.

2. This Convention shall not apply to distinctions, exclusions, restrictions or preferences made by a State Party to this Convention between citizens and non-citizens.

3. Nothing in this Convention may be interpreted as affecting in any way the legal provisions of States Parties concerning nationality, citizenship or naturalization, provided that such provisions do not discriminate against any particular nationality.

4. Special measures taken for the sole purpose of securing adequate advancement of certain racial or ethnic groups or individuals requiring such protection as may be necessary in order to ensure such groups or individuals equal enjoyment or exercise of human rights and fundamental freedoms shall not be deemed racial discrimination, provided, however, that such measures do not, as a consequence, lead to the maintenance of separate rights for different racial groups and that they shall not be continued after the objectives for which they were taken have been achieved.

Article 2. 1. States Parties condemn racial discrimination and undertake to pursue by all appropriate means and without delay a policy of eliminating racial discrimination in all its forms and promoting understanding among all races, and, to this end:

(a) Each State Party undertakes to engage in no act or practice of racial discrimination against persons, groups of persons or institutions and to ensure that all public authorities and public institutions, national and local, shall act in conformity with this obligation;

(b) Each State Party undertakes not to sponsor, defend or support racial discrimination by any persons or organizations;

(c) Each State Party shall take effective measures to review governmental, national and local policies, and to amend, rescind or nullify any laws and regulations which have the effect of creating or perpetuating racial discrimination wherever it exists;

(d) Each State Party shall prohibit and bring to an end, by all appropriate means, including legislation as required by circumstances, racial discrimination by any persons, group or organization;

(e) Each State Party undertakes to encourage, where appropriate, integrationist multiracial organizations and movements and other means of eliminating barriers between races, and to discourage anything which tends to strengthen racial division.

2. States Parties shall, when the circumstances so warrant, take, in the social, economic, cultural and other fields, special and concrete measures to ensure the adequate development and protection of certain racial groups or individuals belonging to them, for the purpose of guaranteeing them the full and equal enjoyment of human rights and fundamental freedoms. These measures shall in no case entail as a consequence the maintenance of unequal or separate rights for different racial groups after the objectives for which they were taken have been achieved.

Article 3. States Parties particularly condemn racial segregation and *apartheid* and undertake to prevent, prohibit and eradicate all practices of this nature in territories under their jurisdiction.

Article 4. States Parties condemn all propaganda and all organizations which are based on ideas or theories of superiority of one race or group of persons of one colour or ethnic origin, or which attempt to justify or promote racial hatred and discrimination in any form, and undertake to adopt immediate and positive measures designed to eradicate all incitement to, or acts of, such discrimination and, to this end, with due regard to the principles embodied in the Universal Declaration of Human Rights and the rights expressly set forth in article 5 of this Convention, *inter alia:*

(a) Shall declare an offence punishable by law all dissemination of ideas based on racial superiority or hatred, incitement to racial discrimination, as well as all acts of violence or incitement to such acts against any race or group of persons of another colour or ethnic origin, and also the provision of any assistance to racist activities, including the financing thereof;

(b) Shall declare illegal and prohibit organizations, and also organized and all other propaganda activities, which promote and incite racial discrimination, and shall recognize participation in such organizations or activities as an offence punishable by law;

(c) Shall not permit public authorities or public institutions, national or local, to promote or incite racial discrimination.

Article 5. In compliance with the fundamental obligations laid down in article 2 of this Convention, States Parties undertake to prohibit and to eliminate racial discrimination in all its forms and to guarantee the right of everyone, without distinction as to race, colour, or national or ethnic origin, to equality before the law, notably in the enjoyment of the following rights:

(a) The right to equal treatment before the tribunals and all other organs administering justice;

(b) The right to security of person and protection by the State against violence or bodily harm, whether inflicted by government officials or by any individual group or institution;

(c) Political rights, in particular the rights to participate in elections—to vote and to stand for election—on the basis of universal and equal suffrage, to take part in the Government as well as in the conduct of public affairs at any level and to have equal access to public service;

(d) Other civil rights, in particular:

(i) The right to freedom of movement and residence within the border of the State;

(ii) The right to leave any country, including one's own, and to return to one's country;

(iii) The right to nationality;

(iv) The right to marriage and choice of spouse;

(v) The right to own property alone as well as in association with others;

(vi) The right to inherit;

(vii) The right to freedom of thought, conscience and religion;

(viii) The right to freedom of opinion and expression;

(ix) The right to freedom of peaceful assembly and association;

(e) Economic, social and cultural rights, in particular:

(i) The rights to work, to free choice of employment, to just and favourable conditions of work, to protection against unemployment, to equal pay for equal work, to just and favourable remuneration;

  (ii) The right to form and join trade unions;

  (iii) The right to housing;

  (iv) The right to public health, medical care, social security and social services;

  (v) The right to education and training;

  (vi) The right to equal participation in cultural activities;

  (f) The right of access to any place or service intended for use by the general public, such as transport, hotels, restaurants, cafés, theatres and parks.

Article 6. States Parties shall assure to everyone within their jurisdiction effective protection and remedies, through the competent national tribunals and other State institutions, against any acts of racial discrimination which violate his human rights and fundamental freedoms contrary to this Convention, as well as the right to seek from such tribunals just and adequate reparation or satisfaction for any damage suffered as a result of such discrimination.

Article 7. States Parties undertake to adopt immediate and effective measures, particularly in the fields of teaching, education, culture and information, with a view to combating prejudices which lead to racial discrimination and to promoting understanding, tolerance and friendship among nations and racial or ethnical groups, as well as to propagating the purposes and principles of the Charter of the United Nations, the Universal Declaration of Human Rights, the United Nations Declaration on the Elimination of All Forms of Racial Discrimination, and this Convention.

Part II

Article 8. 1. There shall be established a Committee on the Elimination of Racial Discrimination (hereinafter referred to as the Committee) consisting of eighteen experts of high moral standing and acknowledged impartiality elected by States Parties from among their nationals, who shall serve in their personal capacity, consideration being given to equitable geographical distribution and to the representation of the different forms of civilization as well as of the principal legal systems.

2. The members of the Committee shall be elected by secret ballot from a list of persons nominated by the States Parties. Each State Party may nominate one person from among its own nationals.

3. The initial election shall be held six months after the date of the entry into force of this Convention. At least three months before the date of each election the Secretary-General of the United Nations shall address a letter to the States Parties inviting them to submit their nominations within two months. The Secretary-General shall prepare a list in alphabetical order of all persons thus nominated, indicating the States Parties which have nominated them, and shall submit it to the States Parties.

4. Elections of the members of the Committee shall be held at a meeting of States Parties convened by the Secretary-General at United Nations Headquarters. At that meeting, for which two thirds of the States Parties shall constitute a quorum, the persons elected to the Committee shall be those nominees who obtain the largest number of votes and an absolute majority of the votes of the representatives of States Parties present and voting.

5. (a) The members of the Committee shall be elected

for a term of four years. However, the terms of nine of the members elected at the first election shall expire at the end of two years; immediately after the first election the names of these nine members shall be chosen by lot by the Chairman of the Committee.

  (b) For the filling of casual vacancies, the State Party whose expert has ceased to function as a member of the Committee shall appoint another expert from among its nationals, subject to the approval of the Committee.

6. States Parties shall be responsible for the expenses of the members of the Committee while they are in performance of Committee duties.

Article 9. 1. States Parties undertake to submit to the Secretary-General of the United Nations, for consideration by the Committee, a report on the legislative, judicial, administrative or other measures which they have adopted and which give effect to the provisions of this Convention: (a) within one year after the entry into force of the Convention for the State concerned; and (b) thereafter every two years and whenever the Committee so requests. The Committee may request further information from the States Parties.

2. The Committee shall report annually, through the Secretary-General, to the General Assembly of the United Nations on its activities and may make suggestions and general recommendations based on the examination of the reports and information received from the States Parties. Such suggestions and general recommendations shall be reported to the General Assembly together with comments, if any, from States Parties.

Article 10. 1. The Committee shall adopt its own rules of procedure.

2. The Committee shall elect its officers for a term of two years.

3. The secretariat of the Committee shall be provided by the Secretary-General of the United Nations.

4. The meetings of the Committee shall normally be held at United Nations Headquarters.

Article 11. 1. If a State Party considers that another State Party is not giving effect to the provisions of this Convention, it may bring the matter to the attention of the Committee. The Committee shall then transmit the communication to the State Party concerned. Within three months, the receiving State shall submit to the Committee written explanations or statements clarifying the matter and the remedy, if any, that may have been taken by that State.

2. If the matter is not adjusted to the satisfaction of both parties, either by bilateral negotiations or by any other procedure open to them, within six months after the receipt by the receiving State of the initial communication, either State shall have the right to refer the matter again to the Committee by notifying the Committee and also the other State.

3. The Committee shall deal with a matter referred to it in accordance with paragraph 2 of this article after it has ascertained that all available domestic remedies have been invoked and exhausted in the case, in conformity with the generally recognized principles of international law. This shall not be the rule where the application of the remedies is unreasonably prolonged.

4. In any matter referred to it, the Committee may call upon the States Parties concerned to supply any other relevant information.

5. When any matter arising out of this article is being considered by the Committee, the States Parties concerned shall be entitled to send a representative to take part in the proceedings to the Committee, without voting rights, while the matter is under consideration.

Article 12. 1. (a) After the Committee has obtained and collated all the information it deems necessary, the Chairman shall appoint an *ad hoc* Conciliation Commission (hereinafter referred to as the Commission) comprising five persons who may or may not be members of the Committee. The members of the Commission shall be appointed with the unanimous consent of the parties to the dispute, and its good offices shall be made available to the States concerned with a view to an amicable solution of the matter on the basis of respect for this Convention.

(b) If the States parties to the dispute fail to reach agreement within three months on all or part of the composition of the Commission, the members of the Commission not agreed upon by the States parties to the dispute shall be elected by secret ballot by a two-thirds majority vote of the Committee from among its own members.

2. The members of the Commission shall serve in their personal capacity. They shall not be nationals of the States parties to the dispute or of a State not Party to this Convention.

3. The Commission shall elect its own Chairman and adopt its own rules of procedure.

4. The meetings of the Commission shall normally be held at United Nations Headquarters or at any other convenient place as determined by the Commission.

5. The secretariat provided in accordance with article 10, paragraph 3, of this Convention shall also service the Commission whenever a dispute among States Parties brings the Commission into being.

6. The States parties to the dispute shall share equally all the expenses of the members of the Commission in accordance with estimates to be provided by the Secretary-General of the United Nations.

7. The Secretary-General shall be empowered to pay the expenses of the members of the Commission, if necessary, before reimbursement by the States parties to the dispute in accordance with paragraph 6 of this article.

8. The information obtained and collated by the Committee shall be made available to the Commission, and the Commission may call upon the States concerned to supply any other relevant information.

Article 13. 1. When the Commission has fully considered the matter, it shall prepare and submit to the Chairman of the Committee a report embodying its findings on all questions of fact relevant to the issue between the parties and containing such recommendations as it may think proper for the amicable solution of the dispute.

2. The Chairman of the Committee shall communicate the report of the Commission to each of the States parties to the dispute. These States shall, within three months, inform the Chairman of the Committee whether or not they accept the recommendations contained in the report of the Commission.

3. After the period provided for in paragraph 2 of this article, the Chairman of the Committee shall communicate the report of the Commission and the declarations of the States Parties concerned to the other States Parties to this Convention.

Article 14. 1. A State Party may at any time declare that it recognizes the competence of the Committee to receive and consider communications from individuals or groups of individuals within its jurisdiction claiming to be victims of a violation by that State Party of any of the rights set forth in this Convention. No communication shall be received by the Committee if it concerns a State Party which has not made such a declaration.

2. Any State Party which makes a declaration as provided for in paragraph 1 of this article may establish or indicate a body within its national legal order which shall be competent to receive and consider petitions from individuals and groups of individuals within its jurisdiction who claim to be victims of a violation of any of the rights set forth in this Convention and who have exhausted other available local remedies.

3. A declaration made in accordance with paragraph 1 of this article and the name of any body established or indicated in accordance with paragraph 2 of this article shall be deposited by the State Party concerned with the Secretary-General of the United Nations, who shall transmit copies thereof to the other States Parties. A declaration may be withdrawn at any time by notification to the Secretary-General but such a withdrawal shall not affect communications pending before the Committee.

4. A register of petitions shall be kept by the body established or indicated in accordance with paragraph 2 of this article, and certified copies of the register shall be filed annually through appropriate channels with the Secretary-General on the understanding that the contents shall not be publicly disclosed.

5. In the event of failure to obtain satisfaction from the body established or indicated in accordance with paragraph 2 of this article, the petitioner shall have the right to communicate the matter to the Committee within six months.

6. (a) The Committee shall confidentially bring any communication referred to it to the attention of the State Party alleged to be violating any provision of this Convention, but the identity of the individual or groups of individuals concerned shall not be revealed without his or their express consent. The Committee shall not receive anonymous communications.

(b) Within three months, the receiving State shall submit to the Committee written explanations or statements clarifying the matter and the remedy, if any, that may have been taken by that State.

7. (a) The Committee shall consider communications in the light of all information made available to it by the State Party concerned and by the petitioner. The Committee shall not consider any communication from a petitioner unless it has ascertained that the petitioner has exhausted all available domestic remedies. However, this shall not be the rule where the application of the remedies is unreasonably prolonged.

(b) The Committee shall forward its suggestions and recommendations, if any, to the State Party concerned and to the petitioner.

8. The Committee shall include in its annual report a summary of such communications and, where appropriate, a summary of the explanations and statements of the States Parties concerned and of its own suggestions and recommendations.

9. The Committee shall be competent to exercise the functions provided for in this article only when at least ten

States Parties to this Convention are bound by declarations in accordance with paragraph 1 of this article.

Article 15. 1. Pending the achievement of the objectives of the Declaration on the Granting of Independence to Colonial Countries and Peoples, contained in General Assembly resolutions 1514 (XV) of 14 December 1960, the provisions of this Convention shall in no way limit the right of petition granted to these peoples by other international instruments or by the United Nations and its specialized agencies.

2. (a) The Committee established under article 8, paragraph 1, of this Convention shall receive copies of the petitions from, and submit expressions of opinion and recommendations on these petitions to, the bodies of the United Nations which deal with matters directly related to the principles and objectives of this Convention in their consideration of petitions from the inhabitants of Trust and Non-Self-Governing Territories and all other territories to which General Assembly resolution 1514 (XV) applies, relating to matters covered by this Convention which are before these bodies.

(b) The Committee shall receive from the competent bodies of the United Nations copies of the reports concerning the legislative, judicial, administrative or other measures directly related to the principles and objectives of this Convention applied by the administering Powers within the Territories mentioned in subparagraph (a) of this paragraph, and shall express opinions and make recommendations to these bodies.

3. The Committee shall include in its report to the General Assembly a summary of the petitions and reports it has received from United Nations bodies, and the expressions of opinion and recommendation of the Committee relating to the said petitions and reports.

4. The Committee shall request from the Secretary-General of the United Nations all information relevant to the objectives of this Convention and available to him regarding the Territories mentioned in paragraph 2 (a) of this article.

Article 16. The provisions of this Convention concerning the settlement of disputes or complaints shall be applied without prejudice to other procedures for settling disputes or complaints in the field of discrimination laid down in the constituent instruments of, or in conventions adopted by, the United Nations and its specialized agencies, and shall not prevent the States Parties from having recourse to other procedures for settling a dispute in accordance with general or special international agreements in force between them.

Part III

Article 17. 1. This Convention is open for signature by any State Member of the United Nations or member of any of its specialized agencies, by any State Party to the Statute of the International Court of Justice, and by any other State which has been invited by the General Assembly of the United Nations to become a Party to this Convention.

2. This Convention is subject to ratification. Instruments of ratification shall be deposited with the Secretary-General of the United Nations.

Article 18. 1. This Convention shall be open to accession by any State referred to in article 17, paragraph 1, of the Convention.

2. Accession shall be effected by the deposit of an instrument of accession with the Secretary-General of the United Nations.

Article 19. 1. This Convention shall enter into force on the thirtieth day after the date of the deposit with the Secretary-General of the United Nations of the twenty-seventh instrument of ratification or instrument of accession.

2. For each State ratifying this Convention or acceding to it after the deposit of the twenty-seventh instrument of ratification or instrument of accession, the Convention shall enter into force on the thirtieth day after the date of the deposit of its own instrument of ratification or instrument of accession.

Article 20. 1. The Secretary-General of the United Nations shall receive and circulate to all States which are or may become Parties to this Convention reservations made by States at the time of ratification or accession. Any State which objects to the reservation shall, within a period of ninety days from the date of the said communication, notify the Secretary-General that it does not accept it.

2. A reservation incompatible with the object and purpose of this Convention shall not be permitted, nor shall a reservation the effect of which would inhibit the operation of any of the bodies established by this Convention be allowed. A reservation shall be considered incompatible or inhibitive if at least two thirds of the States Parties to this Convention object to it.

3. Reservations may be withdrawn at any time by notification to this effect addressed to the Secretary-General. Such notification shall take effect on the date on which it is received.

Article 21. A State Party may denounce this Convention by written notification to the Secretary-General of the United Nations. Denunciation shall take effect one year after the date of receipt of the notification by the Secretary-General.

Article 22. Any dispute between two or more States Parties with respect to the interpretation or application of this Convention, which is not settled by negotiation or by the procedures expressly provided for in this Convention, shall, at the request of any of the parties to the dispute, be referred to the International Court of Justice for decision, unless the disputants agree to another mode of settlement.

Article 23. 1. A request for the revision of this Convention may be made at any time by any State Party by means of a notification in writing addressed to the Secretary-General of the United Nations.

2. The General Assembly of the United Nations shall decide upon the steps, if any, to be taken in respect of such a request.

Article 24. The Secretary-General of the United Nations shall inform all States referred to in article 17, paragraph 1, of this Convention of the following particulars:

(a) Signatures, ratifications and accessions under articles 17 and 18;

(b) The date of entry into force of this Convention under article 19;

(c) Communications and declarations received under articles 14, 20 and 23;

(d) Denunciations under article 21.

Article 25. 1. This Convention, of which the Chinese, English, French, Russian and Spanish texts are equally authentic, shall be deposited in the archives of the United Nations.

2. The Secretary-General of the United Nations shall transmit certified copies of this Convention to all States belonging to any of the categories mentioned in article 17, paragraph 1, of the Convention.

SEE ALSO Decades to Combat Racism and Racial Discrimination; Declaration of the Second World Conference to Combat Racism and Racial Discrimination; Racial Discrimination; Racial Discrimination: National and Local Recourses; Racial Prejudice: Prevention; Racism and Racial Discrimination: Second Decade Action Program.

INTERNATIONAL CONVENTION ON THE SUPPRESSION AND PUNISHMENT OF THE CRIME OF *APARTHEID* (1973).

For many years, the UN General Assembly and Security Council have periodically drawn attention to the inalienable right of the people of South Africa to SELF-DETERMINATION and freedom and have affirmed that the practice of *apartheid*—the policy of racial segregation and discrimination imposed by the government upon the inhabitants of that country and, before its independence in 1989, on those of Namibia—constitutes a crime against humanity and a total negation of the purposes and principles of the UNITED NATIONS CHARTER.

On 30 November 1973, the General Assembly adopted and opened for signature, ratification, or accession (resolution 3068 [XXVIII]) the International Convention on the Suppression and Punishment of the Crime of *Apartheid*, modelled after the CONVENTION ON THE PREVENTION AND PUNISHMENT OF THE CRIME OF GENOCIDE, and urged that it be accepted and implemented without delay. The convention entered into force on 18 July 1976.

Article 7 of the convention calls for reports to be submitted periodically by the States parties on the legislative, administrative, or other measures that they have adopted and that give effect to the provisions of the Convention. Article 9 authorizes the appointment, by the chairman of the UN COMMISSION ON HUMAN RIGHTS, of the GROUP OF THREE, consisting of three members of the commission who are also representatives of States parties to the convention. The Group of Three is established at each annual session of the commission and examines and reports on the periodic reports of States parties.

The text of the convention (annexed to General Assembly resolution 3068 [XXVIII]), is as follows:

The States Parties to the Present Convention,

Recalling the provisions of the Charter of the United Nations, in which all Members pledged themselves to take joint and separate action in co-operation with the Organization for the achievement of universal respect for, and observance of, human rights and fundamental freedoms for all without distinction as to race, sex, language or religion,

Considering the Universal Declaration of Human Rights, which states that all human beings are born free and equal in dignity and rights and that everyone is entitled to all the rights and freedoms set forth in the Declaration, without distinction of any kind, such as race, colour or national origin,

Considering the Declaration on the Granting of Independence to Colonial Countries and Peoples, in which the General Assembly stated that the process of liberation is irresistible and irreversible and that, in the interests of human dignity, progress and justice, an end must be put to colonialism and all practises of segregation and discrimination associated therewith,

Observing that, in accordance with the International Convention on the Elimination of All Forms of Racial Discrimination, States particularly condemn racial segregation and *apartheid* and undertake to prevent, prohibit and eradicate all practices of this nature in territories under their jurisdiction,

Observing that, in the Convention on the Prevention and Punishment of the Crime of Genocide, certain acts which may also be qualified as acts of *apartheid* constitute a crime under international law,

Observing that, in the Convention on the Non-Applicability of Statutory Limitations to War Crimes and Crimes Against Humanity, "inhuman acts resulting from the policy of *apartheid*" are qualified as crimes against humanity,

Observing that the General Assembly of the United Nations has adopted a number of resolutions in which the policies and practices of *apartheid* are condemned as a crime against humanity,

Observing that the Security Council has emphasized that *apartheid* and its continued intensification and expansion seriously disturb and threaten international peace and security,

Convinced that an International Convention on the Suppression and Punishment of the Crime of *Apartheid* would make it possible to take more effective measures at the international and national levels with a view to the suppression and punishment of the crime of *apartheid*,

Have agreed as follows:

Article 1. 1. The States Parties to the present Convention declare that *apartheid* is a crime against humanity and that inhuman acts resulting from the policies and practices of *apartheid* and similar policies and practices of racial segregation and discrimination, as defined in article 2 of the Convention, are crimes violating the principles of international law, in particular the purposes and principles of the Charter of the United Nations, and constituting a serious threat to international peace and security.

2. The States Parties to the present Convention declare criminal those organizations, institutions and individuals committing the crime of *apartheid*.

Article 2. For the purpose of the present Convention, the term "the crime of *apartheid*", which shall include similar policies and practices of racial segregation and discrimination as practised in southern Africa, shall apply to the following inhuman acts committed for the purpose of establishing and maintaining domination by one racial group of persons over any other racial group of persons and systemically oppressing them:

(a) Denial to a member or members of a racial group or groups of the right to life and liberty of person:

(i) By murder of members of a racial group or groups;

(ii) By the infliction upon the members of a racial

group or groups of serious bodily or mental harm, by the infringement of their freedom or dignity, or by subjecting them to torture or to cruel, inhuman or degrading treatment or punishment;

(iii) By arbitrary arrest and illegal imprisonment of the members of a racial group or groups;

(b) Deliberate imposition on a racial group or groups of living conditions calculated to cause its or their physical destruction in whole or in part;

(c) Any legislative measures and other measures calculated to prevent a racial group or groups from participation in the political, social, economic and cultural life of the country and the deliberate creation of conditions preventing the full development of such a group or groups, in particular by denying to members of a racial group or groups basic human rights and freedoms, including the right to work, the right to form recognized trade unions, the right to education, the right to leave and to return to their country, the right to a nationality, the right to freedom of movement and residence, the right to freedom of opinion and expression, and the right to freedom of peaceful assembly and association;

(d) Any measures, including legislative measures, designed to divide the population along racial lines by the creation of separate reserves and ghettos for the members of a racial group or groups, the prohibition of mixed marriages among members of various racial groups, the expropriation of landed property belonging to a racial group or groups or to members thereof;

(e) Exploitation of the labour of the members of a racial group or groups, in particular by submitting them to forced labour;

(f) Persecution of organizations and persons, by depriving them of fundamental rights and freedoms, because they oppose *apartheid*.

Article 3. International criminal responsibility shall apply, irrespective of the motive involved, to individuals, members of organizations and institutions and representatives of the State, whether residing in the territory of the State in which the acts are perpetrated or in some other State, whenever they:

(a) Commit, participate in, directly incite or conspire in the commission of the acts mentioned in article II of the present Convention;

(b) Directly abet, encourage or co-operate in the commission of the crime of *apartheid*.

Article 4. The States Parties to the present Convention undertake:

(a) To adopt any legislative or other measures necessary to suppress as well as to prevent any encouragement of the crime of *apartheid* and similar segregationist policies or their manifestations and to punish persons guilty of that crime;

(b) To adopt legislative, judicial and administrative measures to prosecute, bring to trial and punish in accordance with their jurisdiction persons responsible for, or accused of, the acts defined in article II of the present Convention, whether or not such persons reside in the territory of the State in which the acts are committed or are nationals of that State or of some other State or are stateless persons.

Article 5. Persons charged with the acts enumerated in article II of the present Convention may be tried by a competent tribunal of any State Party to the Convention which may acquire jurisdiction over the person of the accused or by an international penal tribunal having jurisdiction with

respect to those States Parties which shall have accepted its jurisdiction.

Article 6. The States Parties to the present Convention undertake to accept and carry out in accordance with the Charter of the United Nations the decisions taken by the Security Council aimed at the prevention, suppression and punishment of the crime of *apartheid*, and to co-operate in the implementation of decisions adopted by other competent organs of the United Nations with a view to achieving the purposes of the Convention.

Article 7. 1. The States Parties to the present Convention undertake to submit periodic reports to the group established under article 9 on the legislative, judicial, administrative or other measures that they have adopted and that give effect to the provisions of the Convention.

2. Copies of the reports shall be transmitted through the Secretary-General of the United Nations to the Special Committee on *Apartheid*.

Article 8. Any State Party to the present Convention may call upon any competent organ of the United Nations to take such action under the Charter of the United Nations as it considers appropriate for the prevention and suppression of the crime of *apartheid*.

Article 9. 1. The Chairman of the Commission on Human Rights shall appoint a group consisting of three members of the Commission on Human Rights, who are also representatives of States Parties to the present Convention, to consider reports submitted by States Parties in accordance with article 7.

2. If, among the members of the Commission on Human Rights, there are no representatives of States Parties to the present Convention or if there are fewer than three such representatives, the Secretary-General of the United Nations shall, after consulting all States Parties to the Convention, designate a representative of the State Party or representatives of the States Parties which are not members of the Commission on Human Rights to take part in the work of the group established in accordance with paragraph 1 of this article, until such time as representatives of the States Parties to the Convention are elected to the Commission on Human Rights.

3. The group may meet for a period of not more than five days, either before the opening or after the closing of the session of the Commission on Human Rights, to consider the reports submitted in accordance with article 7.

Article 10. 1. The States Parties to the present Convention empower the Commission on Human Rights:

(a) To request United Nations organs, when transmitting copies of petitions under article 15 of the International Convention on the Elimination of All Forms of Racial Discrimination, to draw its attention to complaints concerning acts which are enumerated in article 2 of the present Convention;

(b) To prepare, on the basis of reports from competent organs of the United Nations and periodic reports from States Parties to the present Convention, a list of individuals, organizations, institutions and representatives of States which are alleged to be responsible for the crimes enumerated in article 2 of the Convention, as well as those against whom legal proceedings have been undertaken by States Parties to the Convention;

(c) To request information from the competent United Nations organs concerning measures taken by the authorities responsible for the administration of Trust and Non-Self-Governing Territories, and all other Territories to which General Assembly resolution 1514 (XV) of 14 December 1960 applies, with regard to such individuals alleged to be responsible for crimes under article 2 of the Convention who are believed to be under their territorial and administrative jurisdiction.

2. Pending the achievement of the objectives of the Declaration on the Granting of Independence to Colonial Countries and Peoples, contained in General Assembly resolution 1514 (XV), the provisions of the present Convention shall in no way limit the right of petition granted to those peoples by other international instruments or by the United Nations and its specialized agencies.

Article 11. 1. Acts enumerated in article 2 of the present Convention shall not be considered political crimes for the purpose of extradition.

2. The States Parties to the present Convention undertake in such cases to grant extradition in accordance with their legislation and with the treaties in force.

Article 12. Disputes between States Parties arising out of the interpretation, application or implementation of the present Convention which have not been settled by negotiation shall, at the request of the States Parties to the dispute, be brought before the International Court of Justice, save where the parties to the dispute have agreed on some other form of settlement.

Article 13. The present Convention is open for signature by all States. Any State which does not sign the Convention before its entry into force may accede to it.

Article 14. 1. The present Convention is subject to ratification. Instruments of ratification shall be deposited with the Secretary-General of the United Nations.

2. Accession shall be effected by the deposit of an instrument of accession with the Secretary-General of the United Nations.

Article 15. 1. The present Convention shall enter into force on the thirtieth day after the date of the deposit with the Secretary-General of the United Nations of the twentieth instrument of ratification or accession.

2. For each State ratifying the present Convention or acceding to it after the deposit of the twentieth instrument of ratification or instrument of accession, the Convention shall enter into force on the thirtieth day after the date of the deposit of its own instrument of ratification or instrument of accession.

Article 16. A State Party may denounce the present Convention by written notification to the Secretary-General of the United Nations. Denunciation shall take effect one year after the date of receipt of the notification by the Secretary-General.

Article 17. 1. A request for the revision of the present Convention may be made at any time by any State Party by means of a notification in writing addressed to the Secretary-General of the United Nations.

2. The General Assembly of the United Nations shall decide upon the steps, if any, to be taken in respect of such request.

Article 18. The Secretary-General of the United Nations shall inform all States of the following particulars:

(a) Signatures, ratifications and accessions under articles 13 and 14;

(b) The date of entry into force of the present Convention under article 15;

(c) Denunciations under article 16;

(d) Notifications under article 17.

Article 19. 1. The present Convention, of which the Chinese, English, French, Russian and Spanish texts are equally authentic, shall be deposited in the archives of the United Nations.

2. The Secretary-General of the United Nations shall transmit certified copies of the present Convention to all States.

SEE ALSO Apartheid: *A Collective Form of Slavery;* Apartheid: *An International Crime;* Apartheid: *Penal Tribunal; Declaration on* Apartheid *and its Destructive Consequences in Southern Africa; Lagos Declaration for Action against* Apartheid*; Slavery-like Practices of* Apartheid *and Colonialism; South Africa: UN Concern about* Apartheid.

INTERNATIONAL COUNCIL FOR ADULT EDUCATION.

An international non-governmental organization in consultative status with the UN Economic and Social Council (Category II), and with UNESCO and FAO.

Founded in 1973 by educators from a number of countries who decided to form a group linking adult education work around the world, the council has grown to include member associations in over 80 countries and to maintain liaison with national and international groups in those countries. Its activities focus on research, training, advocacy, and the exchange of information. Among its primary concerns are health care, problems relating to the equality of men and women, literacy and peace workers' education.

The council publishes *ICAE News* and the newsletter *Convergence,* as well as newsletters from its various programs: *Peace Letter, Voices Rising, Participatory Research International Networking Memo, Health and Popular Education, Education and Criminal Justice,* and *Participatory 'Formation'.*

International Council for Adult Education. Address: 720 Bathurst Street, Suite 500, Toronto, Ontario M5S 2R4, Canada. Telephone: (416) 588-1211. Telex: 06-986766 TOR. Secretary-General: Dr. Budd Hall.

INTERNATIONAL COUNCIL OF ENVIRONMENTAL LAW.

An international non-governmental organization in consultative status (Category II) with the UN Economic and Social Council, ICEL has members in 68 countries.

Founded in 1969 in New Delhi, the council promotes the exchange of information on legal, administrative, and policy aspects of environmental conservation and cooperates with organizations active in those fields. It co-sponsors *Environmental Policy and Law* (issued eight times a year) in English and French and publishes the *ICEL Directory* and *ICEL References.*

International Council of Environmental Law. Address: Adenauerallee 214, D-5300 Bonn 1, FRG. Telephone: (49-228) 2692-240.

Yearbook of International Organizations 1989/90 (K. G. Saur).

INTERNATIONAL COUNCIL OF JEWISH WOMEN.

An international non-governmental organization in consultative status with the UN Economic and Social Council (Category II) and with UNESCO and the Council of Europe, ICJW, established in 1912, links Jewish women from 34 countries in six continents with a total individual membership of approximately 1 million. Among its objectives are cooperation with national and international organizations working for good will and equal rights among all peoples for realization of the principles set out in the Universal Declaration of Human Rights. It participates in the work of inter-governmental human rights bodies including the COMMISSION ON HUMAN RIGHTS, the COMMISSION ON THE STATUS OF WOMEN and the SUBCOMMISSION ON PREVENTION OF DISCRIMINATION AND PROTECTION OF MINORITIES, and encourages its affiliates to take part in the activities of the United Nations.

ICJW published the ICJW *Newsletter,* occasional bulletins, and Action Alerts.

International Council of Jewish Women. Address: 19, rue de Teheran, 75008 Paris, France. Telephone: (331) 45635341. Telex: IC5W12874F. President: Stella Rozan.

INTERNATIONAL COUNCIL OF VOLUNTARY AGENCIES.

An international non-governmental organization in consultative status with the UN Economic and Social Council (Category I), and with ILO and UNICEF, the council brings together 81 organizations worldwide. It is an independent association of non-governmental, non-profit organizations active in the fields of humanitarian assistance and development cooperation. Established in 1962 to promote the development of voluntary agencies, ICVA today provides a permanent international liaison structure for voluntary agency consultation and cooperation. ICVA does not implement relief or development projects itself but provides services and support to its member agencies to enable them to cooperate and perform more effectively.

The council publishes *ICVA News* (ten times a year), *NGO Management* (four times a year), and special reports and publications concerning the activities of voluntary agencies.

International Council of Voluntary Agencies. Address: 13 rue Gautier, CH–1201 Geneva, Switzerland. Telephone: (41-22) 32-66-00. Cable VOLAG (Geneva). Telex: 22891 icva ch. Fax: (41-22) 86-72-37. Executive Director: Anthony J. Kozlowski.

INTERNATIONAL COUNCIL OF WOMEN.

An international non-governmental organization in consultative status with the UN Economic and Social Council (Category I), and with ILO, UNESCO, FAO, and WHO, the international council brings together 75 national councils of women's voluntary organizations.

Founded in Washington, D.C., in 1888, the council seeks to promote the welfare of mankind, the family, and the individual through recognition of and respect for human rights and the removal of all forms of discrimination. It is particularly active in pursuing equal rights and responsibilities for both sexes in all spheres, in stimulating women to participate in public life, and in integrating them in development and decision-making bodies. It is assisted by international standing committees on such subjects as international relations and peace, laws and the status of women, migration, and women and employment.

In addition to issuing its resolutions and reports at regular intervals, ICW publishes the *ICW Newsletter* three times a year, occasional books including *Women and the UN* and *World Anthology of Poetry by Women.*

International Council of Women. Address: 13 rue Caumartin, F-75009 Paris, France. Telephone: (1) 47-42-19-40. General Secretary: Jacqueline Barbet-Massin.

INTERNATIONAL COUNCIL ON SOCIAL WELFARE.

An international non-governmental organization in consultative status with the UN Economic and Social Council (Category I), and with ILO, UNESCO, FAO, WHO, and the Council of Europe, the council has national committees in 59 countries and 21 international members organizations.

Founded in Paris in 1928 at the First International Conference of Social Work as the "Permanent Committee of the International Conference of Social Work," ICSW was reorganized in 1946 and again in 1966, and its constitution was amended in 1982. Its main functions are to foster and promote social development on a global basis, to define social needs and stimulate awareness of these needs, to facilitate the dialogue between different groups of society concerned with the promotion of social justice and human well-being, and in general to act as a catalyst, platform, and resource center for the sharing of knowledge, experience, and information on social development. It organizes international and regional seminars, conferences, and workshops and participates in studies and research regarding the development of effective new social policies.

ICSW publishes *International Social Work* quarterly and issues the proceedings of its Biennial Conferences.

International Council on Social Welfare. Address: Kostlergasse 1/29, A-1060, Vienna, Austria. Telephone: (43 222) 587 81 64. Cable: INCOSOWO WIEN. Secretary-General: Ingrid Gelinek.

Yearbook of International Organizations 1989/90 (K. G. Saur).

INTERNATIONAL COURT OF JUSTICE.

The court, which has its headquarters at the Hague, is the principal judicial organ of the United Nations. The INTERNATIONAL COURT OF JUSTICE STATUTE—based on the Statute of the Permanent Court of International Justice instituted by the League of Nations in 1920 but dissolved in 1946—is an integral part of the UNITED NATIONS CHARTER. All States members of the United Nations are *ipso facto* parties to the statute. A State which is not a UN member may become a party to the statute of the court on conditions to be determined in each case by the UN General Assembly on recommendation of the Security Council.

In accordance with Article 38 of the statute, the court's primary function is "to decide in accordance with international law such disputes as are submitted to it." In so doing, the court applies (1) international conventions, (2) international custom, (3) the general principles of law recognized by civilized nations, and (4) judicial decisions and the teachings of the most highly qualified publicists as subsidiary means for determining the rules of law. The court may also decide a case *ex aequo et bono*—i.e., in accordance with the principles of equity—if the parties concerned agree. The court may also give an advisory opinion on any legal question at the request of the UN General Assembly, the Security Council, or other UN organs or specialized agencies when authorized by the General Assembly. The Security Council can be called upon to determine measures to be taken to effect a judgment of the court if the other party fails to perform its obligations under that judgment. The reports of the International Court of Justice are considered by the General Assembly.

The court is composed of 15 independent judges of different nationalities "from among persons of high moral character who possess the qualifications required in their respective countries for appointment to the highest judicial offices, or are jurisconsults of recognized competence in international law." Candidates are nominated by national groups of legal experts. From the list of candidates, the General Assembly and the Security Council, voting independently, elect the members of the court, an absolute majority being required. If, after three meetings, concurring majorities have not been achieved in the two organs, a special joint conference is applied. Judges are elected for a term of nine years, the terms of five of the 15 judges expiring at the end of every three years.

The court remains permanently in session, except during judicial vacations. It has no subsidiary bodies, but from time to time may establish chambers of three or more judges to deal with particular categories of cases (for example, labor cases). The Registry is the administrative organ of the Court, and the registrar directs the work of the staff, of which he is the head.

Since the court met for the first time in The Hague on 1 April 1946, it has dealt with a number of contentious cases relating to human rights matters, among them: *Haya de la Torre* (Colombia v. Peru), 1950–51; *Nottebohm* (Liechtenstein v. Guatemala), 1951–55; *South West Africa* (Ethiopia v. South Africa; Liberia v. South Africa), 1960–61; *Trial of Pakistani Prisoners of War* (Pakistan v. India), 1973; and *U.S. Diplomatic and Consular Staff in Teheran* (United States of America v. Iran), 1979–81. It has also given advisory opinions on legal questions relating to human rights in a number of cases, among them: *Interpretation of Peace Treaties with Bulgaria, Hungary and Romania* (1949–50), *International Status of South West Africa* (1949–50), *Reservations to the Convention on the Prevention and Punishment of the Crime of Genocide* (1950–51), and *Legal Consequences for States of the Continued Presence of South Africa in Namibia (South West Africa) notwithstanding Security Council resolution 276 (1970)*, (1970–71).

INTERNATIONAL COURT OF JUSTICE: STATUTE (1945).

An integral part of the UNITED NATIONS CHARTER, the Statute of the International Court of Justice was signed on 26 June 1945 at the conclusion of the United Nations Conference on International Organization, in San Francisco, and entered into force on 24 October 1945.

The INTERNATIONAL COURT OF JUSTICE, established as the principal judicial organ of the United Nations by article 7 of the UN Charter, is constituted and functions in accordance with the provisions of the statute, the text of which is as follows:

Article 1. The International Court of Justice established

by the Charter of the United Nations as the principal judicial organ of the United Nations shall be constituted and shall function in accordance with the provisions of the present Statute.

Chapter I
Organization of the Court

Article 2. The Court shall be composed of a body of independent judges, elected regardless of their nationality from among persons of high moral character, who possess the qualifications required in their respective countries for appointment to the highest judicial offices, or are jurisconsults of recognized competence in international law.

Article 3. 1. The Court shall consist of fifteen members, no two of whom may be nationals of the same state.

2. A person who for the purposes of membership in the Court could be regarded as a national of more than one state shall be deemed to be a national of the one in which he ordinarily exercises civil and political rights.

Article 4. 1. The members of the Court shall be elected by the General Assembly and by the Security Council from a list of persons nominated by the national groups in the Permanent Court of Arbitration, in accordance with the following provisions.

2. In the case of Members of the United Nations not represented in the Permanent Court of Arbitration, candidates shall be nominated by national groups appointed for this purpose by their governments under the same conditions as those prescribed for members of the Permanent Court of Arbitration by Article 44 of the Convention of The Hague of 1907 for the pacific settlement of international disputes.

3. The conditions under which a state which is a party to the present Statute but is not a Member of the United Nations may participate in electing the members of the Court shall, in the absence of a special agreement, be laid down by the General Assembly upon recommendation of the Security Council.

Article 5. 1. At least three months before the date of the election, the Secretary-General of the United Nations shall address a written request to the members of the Permanent Court of Arbitration belonging to the states which are parties to the present Statute, and to the members of the national groups, appointed under Article 4, paragraph 2, inviting them to undertake, within a given time, by national groups, the nomination of persons in a position to accept the duties of a member of the Court.

2. No group may nominate more than four persons, not more than two of whom shall be of their own nationality. In no case may the number of candidates nominated by a group be more than double the number of seats to be filled.

Article 6. Before making these nominations, each national group is recommended to consult its highest court of justice, its legal faculties and schools of law, and its national academies and national sections of international academies devoted to the study of law.

Article 7. 1. The Secretary-General shall prepare a list in alphabetical order of all the persons thus nominated. Save as provided in Article 12, paragraph 2, these shall be the only persons eligible.

2. The Secretary-General shall submit this list to the General Assembly and to the Security Council.

Article 8. The General Assembly and the Security Council shall proceed independently of one another to elect the members of the Court.

Article 9. At every election, the electors shall bear in mind not only that the persons to be elected should individually possess the qualifications required, but also that in the body as a whole the representation of the main forms of civilization and of the principal legal systems of the world should be assured.

Article 10. 1. Those candidates who obtain an absolute majority of votes in the General Assembly and in the Security Council shall be considered as elected.

2. Any vote of the Security Council, whether for the election of judges or for the appointment of members of the conference envisaged in Article 12, shall be taken without any distinction between permanent and non-permanent members of the Security Council.

3. In the event of more than one national of the same state obtaining an absolute majority of the votes both of the General Assembly and of the Security Council, the eldest of these only shall be considered as elected.

Article 11. If, after the first meeting held for the purpose of the election, one or more seats remain to be filled, a second and, if necessary, a third meeting shall take place.

Article 12. 1. If, after the third meeting, one or more seats still remain unfilled, a joint conference consisting of six members, three appointed by the General Assembly and three by the Security Council, may be formed at any time at the request of either the General Assembly or the Security Council, for the purpose of choosing by the vote of an absolute majority one name for each seat still vacant, to submit to the General Assembly and the Security Council for their respective acceptance.

2. If the joint conference is unanimously agreed upon any person who fulfills the required conditions, he may be included in its list, even though he was not included in the list of nominations referred to in Article 7.

3. If the joint conference is satisfied that it will not be successful in procuring an election, those members of the Court who have already been elected shall, within a period to be fixed by the Security Council, proceed to fill the vacant seats by selection from among those candidates who have obtained votes either in the General Assembly or in the Security Council.

4. In the event of an equality of votes among the judges, the eldest judge shall have a casting vote.

Article 13. 1. The members of the Court shall be elected for nine years and may be re-elected; provided, however, that of the judges elected at the first election, the terms of five judges shall expire at the end of three years and the terms of five more judges shall expire at the end of six years.

2. The judges whose terms are to expire at the end of the above-mentioned initial periods of three and six years shall be chosen by lot to be drawn up by the Secretary-General immediately after the first election has been completed.

3. The members of the Court shall continue to discharge their duties until their places have been filled. Though replaced, they shall finish any cases which they may have begun.

4. In the case of the resignation of a member of the Court, the resignation shall be addressed to the President of the Court for transmission to the Secretary-General. This last notification makes the place vacant.

Article 14. Vacancies shall be filled by the same method as that laid down for the first election, subject to the following provision: the Secretary-General shall, within one month of the occurrence of the vacancy, proceed to issue the invitations provided for in Article 5, and the date of the election shall be fixed by the Security Council.

Article 15. A member of the Court elected to replace a member whose term of office has not expired shall hold office for the remainder of his predecessor's term.

Article 16. 1. No member of the Court may exercise any political or administrative function, or engage in any other occupation of a professional nature.

2. Any doubt on this point shall be settled by the decision of the Court.

Article 17. 1. No member of the Court may act as agent, counsel, or advocate in any case.

2. No member may participate in the decision of any case in which he has previously taken part as agent, counsel, or advocate for one of the parties, or as a member of a national or international court, or of a commission of enquiry, or in any other capacity.

3. Any doubt on this point shall be settled by the decision of the Court.

Article 18. 1. No member of the Court can be dismissed unless, in the unanimous opinion of the other members, he has ceased to fulfill the required conditions.

2. Formal notification thereof shall be made to the Secretary-General by the Registrar.

3. This notification makes the place vacant.

Article 19. The members of the Court, when engaged on the business of the Court, shall enjoy diplomatic privileges and immunities.

Article 20. Every member of the Court shall, before taking up his duties, make a solemn declaration in open court that he will exercise his powers impartially and conscientiously.

Article 21. 1. The Court shall elect its President and Vice-President for three years; they may be re-elected.

2. The Court shall appoint its Registrar and may provide for the appointment of such other officers as may be necessary.

Article 22. 1. The seat of the Court shall be established at The Hague. This, however, shall not prevent the Court from sitting and exercising its functions elsewhere whenever the Court considers it desirable.

2. The President and the Registrar shall reside at the seat of the Court.

Article 23. 1. The Court shall remain permanently in session, except during the judicial vacations, the dates and duration of which shall be fixed by the Court.

2. Members of the Court are entitled to periodic leave, the dates and duration of which shall be fixed by the Court, having in mind the distance between The Hague and the home of each judge.

3. Members of the Court shall be bound, unless they are on leave or prevented from attending by illness or other serious reasons duly explained to the President, to hold themselves permanently at the disposal of the Court.

Article 24. 1. If, for some special reason, a member of the Court considers that he should not take part in the decision of a particular case, he shall so inform the President.

2. If the President considers that for some special reason one of the members of the Court should not sit in a particular case, he shall give him notice accordingly.

3. If in any such case the member of the Court and President disagree, the matter shall be settled by the decision of the Court.

Article 25. 1. The full Court shall sit except when it is expressly provided otherwise in the present Statute.

2. Subject to the condition that the number of judges available to constitute the Court is not thereby reduced below eleven, the Rules of the Court may provide for allowing one or more judges, according to circumstances and in rotation, to be dispensed from sitting.

3. A quorum of nine judges shall suffice to constitute the Court.

Article 26. 1. The Court may from time to time form one or more chambers, composed of three or more judges as the Court may determine, for dealing with particular categories of cases; for example, labor cases and cases relating to transit and communications.

2. The Court may at any time form a chamber for dealing with a particular case. The number of judges to constitute such a chamber shall be determined by the Court with the approval of the parties.

3. Cases shall be heard and determined by the chambers provided for in this Article if the parties so request.

Article 27. A judgment given by any of the chambers provided for in Articles 26 and 29 shall be considered as rendered by the Court.

Article 28. The chambers provided for in Articles 26 and 29 may, with the consent of the parties, sit and exercise their functions elsewhere than at The Hague.

Article 29. With a view to the speedy dispatch of business, the Court shall form annually a chamber composed of five judges which, at the request of the parties, may hear and determine cases by summary procedure. In addition, two judges shall be selected for the purpose of replacing judges who find it impossible to sit.

Article 30. 1. The Court shall frame rules for carrying out its functions. In particular, it shall lay down rules of procedure.

2. The Rules of the Court may provide for assessors to sit with the Court or with any of its chambers, without the right to vote.

Article 31. 1. Judges of the nationality of each of the parties shall retain their right to sit in the case before the Court.

2. If the Court includes upon the Bench a judge of the nationality of one of the parties, any other party may choose a person to sit as judge. Such person shall be chosen preferably from among those persons who have been nominated as candidates as provided in Articles 4 and 5.

3. If the Court includes upon the Bench no judge of the nationality of the parties, each of these parties may proceed to choose a judge as provided in paragraph 2 of this Article.

4. The provisions of this Article shall apply to the case of Articles 26 and 29. In such cases, the President shall request one or, if necessary, two of the members of the Court forming the chamber to give place to the members of the Court of the nationality of the parties concerned, and, failing such, or if they are unable to be present, to the judges specially chosen by the parties.

5. Should there be several parties in the same interest, they shall, for the purpose of the preceeding provisions, be reckoned as one party only. Any doubt upon this point shall be settled by the decision of the Court.

6. Judges chosen as laid down in paragraphs 2, 3, and 4 of this Article shall fulfill the conditions required by Articles 2, 17 (paragraph 2), 20, and 24 of the present Statute. They shall take part in the decision on terms of complete equality with their colleagues.

Article 32. 1. Each member of the Court shall receive an annual salary.

2. The President shall receive a special annual allowance.

3. The Vice-President shall receive a special allowance for every day on which he acts as President.

4. The judges chosen under Article 31, other than members of the Court, shall receive compensation for each day on which they exercise their functions.

5. These salaries, allowances, and compensation shall be fixed by the General Assembly. They may not be decreased during the term of office.

6. The salary of the Registrar shall be fixed by the General Assembly on the proposal of the Court.

7. Regulations made by the General Assembly shall fix the conditions under which retirement pensions may be given to members of the Court and to the Registrar, and the conditions under which members of the Court and the Registrar shall have their traveling expenses refunded.

8. The above salaries, allowances, and compensation shall be free of all taxation.

Article 33. The expenses of the Court shall be borne by the United Nations in such a manner as shall be decided by the General Assembly.

Chapter II
Competence of the Court

Article 34. 1. Only states may be parties in cases before the Court.

2. The Court, subject to and in conformity with its Rules, may request of public international organizations information relevant to cases before it, and shall receive such information presented by such organizations on their own initiative.

3. Whenever the construction of the constituent instrument of a public international organization or of an international convention adopted thereunder is in question in a case before the Court, the Registrar shall so notify the public international organization concerned and shall communicate to it copies of all the written proceedings.

Article 35. 1. The Court shall be open to the states parties to the present Statute.

2. The conditions under which the Court shall be open to other states shall, subject to the special provisions contained in treaties in force, be laid down by the Security Council, but in no case shall such conditions place the parties in a position of inequality before the Court.

3. When a state which is not a Member of the United Nations is a party to a case, the Court shall fix the amount which that party is to contribute towards the expenses of the Court. This provision shall not apply if such state is bearing a share of the expenses of the Court.

Article 36. 1. The jurisdiction of the Court comprises all cases which the parties refer to it and all matters specially provided for in the Charter of the United Nations or in treaties and conventions in force.

2. The states parties to the present Statute may at any time declare that they recognize as compulsory *ipso facto* and without special agreement, in relation to any other state accepting the same obligation, the jurisdiction of the Court in all legal disputes concerning:

    a. the interpretation of a treaty;

    b. any question of international law;

    c. the existence of any fact which, if established, would constitute a breach of an international obligation;

    d. the nature or extent of the reparation to be made for the breach of an international obligation.

3. The declarations referred to above may be made un-conditionally or on condition of reciprocity on the part of several or certain states, or for a certain time.

4. Such declarations shall be deposited with the Secretary-General of the United Nations, who shall transmit copies thereof to the parties to the Statute and to the Registrar of the Court.

5. Declarations made under Article 36 of the Statute of the Permanent Court of International Justice and which are still in force shall be deemed, as between the parties to the present Statute, to be acceptances of the compulsory jurisdiction of the International Court of Justice for the period which they still have to run and in accordance with their terms.

6. In the event of a dispute as to whether the Court has jurisdiction, the matter shall be settled by the decision of the Court.

Article 37. Whenever a treaty or convention in force provides for reference of a matter to a tribunal to have been instituted by the League of Nations, or to the Permanent Court of International Justice, the matter shall, as between the parties to the present Statute, be referred to the International Court of Justice.

Article 38. 1. The Court, whose function is to decide in accordance with international law such disputes as are submitted to it, shall apply:

    a. international conventions, whether general or particular, establishing rules expressly recognized by the contesting states;

    b. international custom, as evidence of a general practice accepted as law;

    c. the general principles of law recognized by civilized nations;

    d. subject to the provisions of Article 59, judicial decisions and the teachings of the most highly qualified publicists of the various nations, as subsidiary means for the determination of rules of law.

2. This provision shall not prejudice the power of the Court to decide a case *ex aequo et bono,* if the parties agree thereto.

Chapter III
Procedure

Article 39. 1. The official languages of the Court shall be French and English. If the parties agree that the case shall be conducted in French, the judgment shall be delivered in French. If the parties agree that the case shall be conducted in English, the judgment shall be delivered in English.

2. In the absence of an agreement as to which language shall be employed, each party may, in the pleadings, use the language which it prefers: the decision of the Court shall be given in French and English. In this case the Court shall at the same time determine which of the two texts shall be considered as authoritative.

3. The Court shall, at the request of any party, authorize a language other than French or English to be used by that party.

Article 40. 1. Cases are brought before the Court, as the case may be, either by the notification of the special agreement or by a written application addressed to the Registrar. In either case the subject of the dispute and the parties shall be indicated.

2. The Registrar shall forthwith communicate the application to all concerned.

3. He shall also notify the Members of the United Na-

tions through the Secretary-General, and also any other states entitled to appear before the Court.

Article 41. 1. The Court shall have the power to indicate, if it considers that circumstances so require, any provisional measures which ought to be taken to preserve the respective rights of either party.

2. Pending the final decision, notice of the measures suggested shall forthwith be given to the parties and to the Security Council.

Article 42. 1. The parties shall be represented by agents.

2. They may have the assistance of counsel or advocates before the Court.

3. The agents, counsel, and advocates of parties before the Court shall enjoy the privileges and immunities necessary to the independent exercise of their duties.

Article 43. 1. The procedure shall consist of two parts; written and oral.

2. The written proceedings shall consist of the communications to the Court and to the parties of memorials, counter-memorials and, if necessary, replies; also all papers and documents in support.

3. These communications shall be made through the Registrar, in the order and within the time fixed by the Court.

4. A certified copy of every document produced by one party shall be communicated to the other party.

5. The oral proceedings shall consist of the hearing by the Court of witnesses, experts, agents, counsel, and advocates.

Article 44. 1. For the service of all notices upon persons other than the agents, counsel, and advocates, the Court shall apply direct to the government of the state upon whose territory the notice has to be served.

2. The same provision shall apply whenever steps are to be taken to procure evidence on the spot.

Article 45. The hearing shall be under the control of the President or, if he is unable to preside, of the Vice-President; if neither is able to preside, the senior judge present shall preside.

Article 46. The hearing in Court shall be public, unless the Court shall decide otherwise, or unless the parties demand that the public be not admitted.

Article 47. 1. Minutes shall be made at each hearing and signed by the Registrar and the President.

2. These minutes alone shall be authentic.

Article 48. The Court shall make orders for the conduct of the case, shall decide the form and time in which each party must conclude its arguments, and make all arrangements connected with the taking of evidence.

Article 49. The Court may, even before the hearing begins, call upon the agents to produce any document or to supply any explanations. Formal note shall be taken of any refusal.

Article 50. The Court may, at any time, entrust any individual, body, bureau, commission, or other organization that it may select, with the task of carrying out an enquiry or giving an expert opinion.

Article 51. During the hearing any relevant questions are to be put to the witnesses and experts under the conditions laid down by the Court in the rules of procedure referred to in Article 30.

Article 52. After the Court has received the proofs and evidence within the time specified for the purpose, it may refuse to accept any further oral or written evidence that one party may desire to present unless the other side consents.

Article 53. 1. Whenever one of the parties does not appear before the Court, or fails to defend its case, the other party may call upon the Court to decide in favor of its claim.

2. The Court must, before doing so, satisfy itself, not only that it has jurisdiction in accordance with Articles 36 and 37, but also that the claim is well founded in fact and law.

Article 54. 1. When, subject to the control of the Court, the agents, counsel, and advocates have completed their presentation of the case, the President shall declare the hearing closed.

2. The Court shall withdraw to consider the judgment.

3. The deliberations of the Court shall take place in private and remain secret.

Article 55. 1. All questions shall be decided by a majority of the judges present.

2. In the event of an equality of votes, the President or the judge who acts in his place shall have a casting vote.

Article 56. 1. The judgment shall state the reasons on which it is based.

2. It shall contain the names of the judges who have taken part in the decision.

Article 57. If the judgment does not represent in whole or in part the unanimous opinion of the judges, any judge shall be entitled to deliver a separate opinion.

Article 58. The judgment shall be signed by the President and by the Registrar. It shall be read in open court, due notice having been given to the agents.

Article 59. The decision of the Court has no binding force except between the parties and in respect of that particular case.

Article 60. The judgment is final and without appeal. In the event of dispute as to the meaning or scope of the judgment, the Court shall construe it upon the request of any party.

Article 61. 1. An application for revision of a judgment may be made only when it is based upon the discovery of some fact of such a nature as to be a decisive factor, which fact was, when the judgment was given, unknown to the Court and also to the party claiming revision, always provided that such ignorance was not due to negligence.

2. The proceedings for revision shall be opened by a judgment of the Court expressly recording the existence of the new fact, recognizing that it has such a character as to lay the case open to revision, and declaring the application admissible on this ground.

3. The Court may require previous compliance with the terms of the judgment before it admits proceedings in revision.

4. The application for revision must be made at latest within six months of the discovery of the new fact.

5. No application for revision may be made after the lapse of ten years from the date of the judgment.

Article 62. 1. Should a state consider that it has an interest of a legal nature which may be affected by the decision in the case, it may submit a request to the Court to be permitted to intervene.

2. It shall be for the Court to decide upon this request.

Article 63. 1. Whenever the construction of a convention to which states other than those concerned in the case are parties is in question, the Registrar shall notify all such states forthwith.

2. Every state so notified has the right to intervene in the proceedings; but if it uses this right, the construction given by the judgment will be equally binding upon it.

Article 64. Unless otherwise decided by the Court, each party shall bear its own costs.

Chapter IV
Advisory Opinions

Article 65. 1. The Court may give an advisory opinion on any legal question at the request of whatever body may be authorized by or in accordance with the Charter of the United Nations to make such a request.

2. Questions upon which the advisory opinion of the Court is asked shall be laid before the Court by means of a written request containing an exact statement of the question upon which an opinion is required, and accompanied by all documents likely to throw light upon the question.

Article 66. 1. The Registrar shall forthwith give notice of the request for an advisory opinion to all states entitled to appear before the Court.

2. The Registrar shall also, by means of a special and direct communication, notify any state entitled to appear before the Court or international organization considered by the Court, or, should it not be sitting, by the President, as likely to be able to furnish information on the question, that the Court will be prepared to receive, within a time limit to be fixed by the President, written statements, or to hear, at a public sitting to be held for the purpose, oral statements relating to the question.

3. Should any such state entitled to appear before the Court have failed to receive the special communication referred to in paragraph 2 of this Article, such state may express a desire to submit a written statement or to be heard; and the Court will decide.

4. States and organizations having presented written or oral statements or both shall be permitted to comment on the statements made by other states or organizations in the form, to the extent, and within the time limits which the Court, or, should it not be sitting, the President, shall decide in each particular case. Accordingly, the Registrar shall in due time communicate any such written statements to states and organizations having submitted similar statements.

Article 67. The Court shall deliver its advisory opinions in open court, notice having been given to the Secretary-General and to the representatives of Members of the United Nations, of other states and of international organizations immediately concerned.

Article 68. In the exercise of its advisory functions the Court shall further be guided by the provisions of the present Statute which apply in contentious cases to the extent to which it recognizes them to be applicable.

Chapter V
Amendment

Article 69. Amendments to the present Statute shall be effected by the same procedure as is provided by the Charter of the United Nations for amendments to that Charter, subject, however, to any provisions which the General Assembly upon recommendation of the Security Council may adopt concerning the participation of states which are parties to the present Statute but are not Members of the United Nations.

Article 70. The Court shall have power to propose such amendments to the present Statute as it may deem necessary, through written communications to the Secretary-General, for consideration in conformity with the provisions of Article 69.

INTERNATIONAL COVENANT ON CIVIL AND POLITICAL RIGHTS (1966). The covenant is the third instrument—after the UNIVERSAL DECLARATION OF HUMAN RIGHTS and the INTERNATIONAL COVENANT ON ECONOMIC, SOCIAL AND CULTURAL RIGHTS—constituting the INTERNATIONAL BILL OF HUMAN RIGHTS. The fourth is the OPTIONAL PROTOCOL TO THE INTERNATIONAL COVENANT ON CIVIL AND POLITICAL RIGHTS.

The covenant defines the civil and political rights which it aims to protect and the permissible limitations on the enjoyment of those rights, authorizes the establishment of a monitoring organ, the HUMAN RIGHTS COMMITTEE, to supervise the implementation of its provisions, and provides (article 41) for the handling by the committee of complaints by one State party that another State party is not fulfilling its obligations under the covenant, provided that both States have made a declaration recognizing the competence of the committee to receive and consider such communications.

Under the optional protocol, the committee may also deal with complaints from individuals claiming to be victims of violations of any of the rights set out in the covenant provided that the State concerned is a party both to the covenant and to the optional protocol.

The International Covenant on Civil and Political Rights was adopted by the UN General Assembly on 16 December 1966 (resolution 2200 A [XXI]), and entered into force on 23 March 1976. The Declaration Regarding Article 41 of the International Covenant on Civil and Political Rights entered into force on 28 March 1979. The text of the covenant, annexed to resolution 2200 A (XXI), is as follows:

Preamble

The States Parties to the present Covenant,

Considering that, in accordance with the principles proclaimed in the Charter of the United Nations, recognition of the inherent dignity and of the equal and inalienable rights of all members of the human family is the foundation of freedom, justice and peace in the world,

Recognizing that these rights derive from the inherent dignity of the human person,

Recognizing that, in accordance with the Universal Declaration of Human Rights, the ideal of free human beings enjoying civil and political freedom and freedom from fear and want can only be achieved if conditions are created whereby everyone may enjoy his civil and political rights, as well as his economic, social and cultural rights,

Considering the obligation of States under the Charter of the United Nations to promote universal respect for, and observance of, human rights and freedoms,

Realizing that the individual, having duties to other individuals and to the community to which he belongs, is under a responsibility to strive for the promotion and observance of the rights recognized in the present Covenant,

Agree upon the following articles:

I

Part I

Article 1. 1. All peoples have the right of self-determination. By virtue of that right they freely determine their political status and freely pursue their economic, social and cultural development.

2. All peoples may, for their own ends, freely dispose of their natural wealth and resources without prejudice to any obligations arising out of international economic co-operation, based upon the principle of mutual benefit, and international law. In no case may a people be deprived of its own means of subsistence.

3. The States Parties to the present Covenant, including those having responsibility for the administration of Non-Self-Governing and Trust Territories, shall promote the realization of the right of self-determination, and shall respect that right, in conformity with the provisions of the Charter of the United Nations.

Part II

Article 2. 1. Each State Party to the present Covenant undertakes to respect and to ensure to all individuals within its territory and subject to its jurisdiction the rights recognized in the present Covenant, without distinction of any kind, such as race, colour, sex, language, religion, political or other opinion, national or social origin, property, birth or other status.

2. Where not already provided for by existing legislative or other measures, each State Party to the present Covenant undertakes to take the necessary steps, in accordance with its constitutional processes and with the provisions of the present Covenant, to adopt such legislative or other measures as may be necessary to give effect to the rights recognized in the present Covenant.

3. Each State Party to the present Covenant undertakes:

(a) To ensure that any person whose rights or freedoms as herein recognized are violated shall have an effective remedy, notwithstanding that the violation has been committed by persons acting in an official capacity;

(b) To ensure that any person claiming such a remedy shall have his right thereto determined by competent judicial, administrative or legislative authorities, or by any other competent authority provided for by the legal system of the State, and to develop the possibilities of judicial remedy;

(c) To ensure that the competent authorities shall enforce such remedies when granted.

Article 3. The States Parties to the present Covenant undertake to ensure the equal right of men and women to the enjoyment of all civil and political rights set forth in the present Covenant.

Article 4. 1. In time of public emergency which threatens the life of the nation and the existence of which is officially proclaimed, the States Parties to the present Covenant may take measures derogating from their obligations under the present Covenant to the extent strictly required by the exigencies of the situation, provided that such measures are not inconsistent with their other obligations under international law and do not involve discrimination solely on the ground of race, colour, sex, language, religion or social origin.

2. No derogation from articles 6, 7, 8 (paragraphs 1 and 2), 11, 15, 16 and 18 may be made under this provision.

3. Any State Party to the present Covenant availing itself of the right of derogation shall immediately inform the other States Parties to the present Covenant, through the intermediary of the Secretary-General of the United Nations, of the provisions from which it has derogated and of the reasons by which it was actuated. A further communication shall be made, through the same intermediary, on the date on which it terminates such derogation.

Article 5. 1. Nothing in the present Covenant may be interpreted as implying for any State, group or person any right to engage in any activity or perform any act aimed at the destruction of any of the rights and freedoms recognized herein or at their limitation to a greater extent than is provided for in the present Covenant.

2. There shall be no restriction upon or derogation from any of the fundamental human rights recognized or existing in any State Party to the present Covenant pursuant to law, conventions, regulations or custom on the pretext that the present Covenant does not recognize such rights or that it recognizes them to a lesser extent.

Part III

Article 6. 1. Every human being has the inherent right to life. This right shall be protected by law. No one shall be arbitrarily deprived of his life.

2. In countries which have not abolished the death penalty, sentence of death may be imposed only for the most serious crimes in accordance with the law in force at the time of the commission of the crime and not contrary to the provisions of the present Covenant and to the Convention on the Prevention and Punishment of the Crime of Genocide. This penalty can only be carried out pursuant to a final judgment rendered by a competent court.

3. When deprivation of life constitutes the crime of genocide, it is understood that nothing in this article shall authorize any State Party to the present Covenant to derogate in any way from any obligation assumed under the provisions of the Convention on the Prevention and Punishment of the Crime of Genocide.

4. Anyone sentenced to death shall have the right to seek pardon or commutation of the sentence. Amnesty, pardon or commutation of the sentence of death may be granted in all cases.

5. Sentence of death shall not be imposed for crimes committed by persons below eighteen years of age and shall not be carried out on pregnant women.

6. Nothing in this article shall be invoked to delay or to prevent the abolition of capital punishment by any State Party to the present Covenant.

Article 7. No one shall be subjected to torture or to cruel, inhuman or degrading treatment or punishment. In particular, no one shall be subjected without his free consent to medical or scientific experimentation.

Article 8. 1. No one shall be held in slavery; slavery and the slave-trade in all their forms shall be prohibited.

2. No one shall be held in servitude.

3. (a) No one shall be required to perform forced or compulsory labour;

(b) Paragraph 3 (a) shall not be held to preclude, in countries where imprisonment with hard labour may be imposed as a punishment for a crime, the performance of hard labour in pursuance of a sentence to such punishment by a competent court;

(c) For the purpose of this paragraph the term "forced or compulsory labour" shall not include:

(i) Any work or service, not referred to in subparagraph (b), normally required of a person who is under detention in consequence of a lawful order of a court, or of a person during conditional release from such detention;

(ii) Any service of a military character and, in countries where conscientious objection is recognized, any national service required by law of conscientious objectors;

(iii) Any service exacted in cases of emergency or calamity threatening the life or well-being of the community;

(iv) Any work or service which forms part of normal civil obligations.

Article 9. 1. Everyone has the right to liberty and security of person. No one shall be subjected to arbitrary arrest or detention. No one shall be deprived of his liberty except on such grounds and in accordance with such procedure as are established by law.

2. Anyone who is arrested shall be informed, at the time of arrest, of the reasons for his arrest and shall be promptly informed of any charges against him.

3. Anyone arrested or detained on a criminal charge shall be brought promptly before a judge or other officer authorized by law to exercise judicial power and shall be entitled to trial within a reasonable time or to release. It shall not be the general rule that persons awaiting trial shall be detained in custody, but release may be subject to guarantees to appear for trial, at any other stage of the judicial proceedings, and, should occasion arise, for execution of the judgement.

4. Anyone who is deprived of his liberty by arrest or detention shall be entitled to take proceedings before a court, in order that that court may decide without delay on the lawfulness of his detention and order his release if the detention is not lawful.

5. Anyone who has been the victim of unlawful arrest or detention shall have an enforceable right to compensation.

Article 10. 1. All persons deprived of their liberty shall be treated with humanity and with respect for the inherent dignity of the human person.

2. (a) Accused persons shall, save in exceptional circumstances, be segregated from convicted persons and shall be subject to separate treatment appropriate to their status as unconvicted persons;

(b) Accused juvenile persons shall be separated from adults and brought as speedily as possible for adjudication.

3. The penitentiary system shall comprise treatment of prisoners the essential aim of which shall be their reformation and social rehabilitation. Juvenile offenders shall be segregated from adults and be accorded treatment appropriate to their age and legal status.

Article 11. No one shall be imprisoned merely on the ground of inability to fulfil a contractual obligation.

Article 12. 1. Everyone lawfully within the territory of a State shall, within that territory, have the right to liberty of movement and freedom to choose his residence.

2. Everyone shall be free to leave any country, including his own.

3. The above-mentioned rights shall not be subject to any restrictions except those which are provided by law, are necessary to protect national security, public order (*ordre public*), public health or morals or the rights and freedoms of others, and are consistent with the other rights recognized in the present Covenant.

4. No one shall be arbitrarily deprived of the right to enter his own country.

Article 13. An alien lawfully in the territory of a State Party to the present Covenant may be expelled therefrom only in pursuance of a decision reached in accordance with law and shall, except where compelling reasons of national security otherwise require, be allowed to submit the reasons against his expulsion and to have his case reviewed by, and be represented for the purpose before, the competent authority or a person or persons especially designated by the competent authority.

Article 14. 1. All persons shall be equal before the court and tribunals. In the determination of any criminal charge against him, or of his rights and obligations in a suit at law, everyone shall be entitled to a fair and public hearing by a competent, independent and impartial tribunal established by law. The Press and the public may be excluded from all or part of a trial for reasons of morals, public order (*ordre public*) or national security in a democratic society, or when the interest of the private lives of the parties so requires, or to the extent strictly necessary in the opinion of the court in special circumstances where publicity would prejudice the interests of justice; but any judgement rendered in a criminal case or in a suit at law shall be made public except where the interest of juvenile persons otherwise requires or the proceedings concern matrimonial disputes or the guardianship of children.

2. Everyone charged with a criminal offence shall have the right to be presumed innocent until proved guilty according to law.

3. In the determination of any criminal charge against him, everyone shall be entitled to the following minimum guarantees, in full equality:

(a) To be informed promptly and in detail in a language which he understands of the nature and cause of the charge against him;

(b) To have adequate time and facilities for the preparation of his defence and to communicate with counsel of his own choosing;

(c) To be tried without undue delay;

(d) To be tried in his presence, and to defend himself in person or through legal assistance of his own choosing; to be informed, if he does not have legal assistance, of this right; and to have legal assistance assigned to him, in any case where the interests of justice so require, and without payment by him in any such case if he does not have sufficient means to pay for it;

(e) To examine, or have examined, the witnesses against him and to obtain the attendance and examination of witnesses on his behalf under the same conditions as witnesses against him;

(f) To have the free assistance of an interpreter if he cannot understand or speak the language used in court;

(g) Not to be compelled to testify against himself or to confess guilt.

4. In the case of juvenile persons, the procedure shall be such as will take account of their age and the desirability of promoting their rehabilitation.

5. Everyone convicted of a crime shall have the right to his conviction and sentence being reviewed by a higher tribunal according to law.

6. When a person has by a final decision been convicted of a criminal offence and when subsequently his conviction has been reversed or he has been pardoned on the ground that a new or newly discovered fact shows conclusively that there has been a miscarriage of justice, the person who has suffered punishment as a result of such conviction shall be compensated according to law, unless it is proved that the non-disclosure of the unknown fact in time is wholly or partly attributable to him.

7. No one shall be liable to be tried or punished again for

an offence for which he has already been finally convicted or acquitted in accordance with the law and penal procedure of each country.

Article 15. 1. No one shall be held guilty of any criminal offence on account of any act or omission which did not constitute a criminal offence, under national or international law, at the time when it was committed. Nor shall a heavier penalty be imposed than the one that was applicable at the time when the criminal offence was committed. If, subsequent to the commission of the offence, provision is made by law for the imposition of the lighter penalty, the offender shall benefit thereby.

2. Nothing in this article shall prejudice the trial and punishment of any person for any act or omission which, at the time when it was committed, was criminal according to the general principles of law recognized by the community of nations.

Article 16. Everyone shall have the right to recognition everywhere as a person before the law.

Article 17. 1. No one shall be subjected to arbitrary or unlawful interference with his privacy, family, home or correspondence, nor to unlawful attacks on his honour and reputation.

2. Everyone has the right to the protection of the law against such interference or attacks.

Article 18. 1. Everyone shall have the right to freedom of thought, conscience and religion. This right shall include freedom to have or to adopt a religion or belief of his choice, and freedom, either individually or in community with others and in public or private, to manifest his religion or belief in worship, observance, practice and teaching.

2. No one shall be subject to coercion which would impair his freedom to have or to adopt a religion or belief of his choice.

3. Freedom to manifest one's religion or beliefs may be subject only to such limitations as are prescribed by law and are necessary to protect public safety, order, health, or morals or the fundamental rights and freedoms of others.

4. The States Parties to the present Covenant undertake to have respect for the liberty of parents and, when applicable, legal guardians to ensure the religious and moral education of their children in conformity with their own convictions.

Article 19. 1. Everyone shall have the right to hold opinions without interference.

2. Everyone shall have the right to freedom of expression; this right shall include freedom to seek, receive and impart information and ideas of all kinds, regardless of frontiers, either orally, in writing or in print, in the form of art, or through any other media of his choice.

3. The exercise of the rights provided for in paragraph 2 of this article carries with it special duties and responsibilities. It may therefore be subject to certain restrictions, but these shall only be such as are provided by law and are necessary:

(a) For respect of the rights or reputations of others;

(b) For the protection of national security or of public order (*ordre public*), or of public health or morals.

Article 20. 1. Any propaganda for war shall be prohibited by law.

2. Any advocacy of national, racial or religious hatred that constitutes incitement to discrimination, hostility or violence shall be prohibited by law.

Article 21. The right of peaceful assembly shall be recognized. No restrictions may be placed on the exercise of this right other than those imposed in conformity with the law and which are necessary in a democratic society in the interests of national security or public safety, public order (*ordre public*), the protection of public health or morals or the protection of the rights and freedoms of others.

Article 22. 1. Everyone shall have the right to freedom of association with others, including the right to form and join trade unions for the protection of his interests.

2. No restrictions may be placed on the exercise of this right other than those which are prescribed by law and which are necessary in a democratic society in the interests of national security or public safety, public order (*ordre public*), the protection of public health or morals or the protection of the rights and freedoms of others. This article shall not prevent the imposition of lawful restrictions on members of the armed forces and of the police in their exercise to this right.

3. Nothing in this article shall authorize States Parties to the International Labour Organisation Convention of 1948 concerning Freedom of Association and Protection of the Right to Organize to take legislative measures which would prejudice, or to apply the law in such a manner as to prejudice the guarantees provided for in that Convention.

Article 23. 1. The family is the natural and fundamental group unit of society and is entitled to protection by society and the State.

2. The right of men and women of marriageable age to marry and to found a family shall be recognized.

3. No marriage shall be entered into without the free and full consent of the intending spouses.

4. States Parties to the present Covenant shall take appropriate steps to ensure equality of rights and responsibilities of spouses as to marriage, during marriage and at its dissolution. In the case of dissolution, provision shall be made for the necessary protection of any children.

Article 24. 1. Every child shall have, without any discrimination as to race, colour, sex, language, religion, national or social origin, property or birth, the right to such measures of protection as are required by his status as a minor, on the part of his family, society and the State.

2. Every child shall be registered immediately after birth and shall have a name.

3. Every child has the right to acquire a nationality.

Article 25. Every citizen shall have the right and the opportunity, without any of the distinctions mentioned in article 2 and without unreasonable restrictions:

(a) To take part in the conduct of public affairs, directly or through freely chosen representatives;

(b) To vote and to be elected at genuine periodic elections which shall be by universal and equal suffrage and shall be held by secret ballot, guaranteeing the free expression of the will of the electors;

(c) To have access, on general terms of equality, to public service in his country.

Article 26. All persons are equal before the law and are entitled without any discrimination to the equal protection of the law. In this respect, the law shall prohibit any discrimination and guarantee to all persons equal and effective protection against discrimination on any ground such as race, colour, sex, language, religion, political or other opinion, national or social origin, property, birth or other status.

Article 27. In those States in which ethnic, religious or linguistic minorities exist, persons belonging to such minorities shall not be denied the right, in community with the other members of their group, to enjoy their own culture, to profess and practise their own religion, or to use their own language.

Part IV

Article 28. 1. There shall be established a Human Rights Committee (hereafter referred to in the present Covenant as the Committee). It shall consist of eighteen members and shall carry out the functions hereinafter provided.

2. The Committee shall be composed of nationals of the States Parties to the present Covenant who shall be persons of high moral character and recognized competence in the field of human rights, consideration being given to the usefulness of the participation of some persons having legal experience.

3. The members of the Committee shall be elected and shall serve in their personal capacity.

Article 29. 1. The members of the Committee shall be elected by secret ballot from a list of persons possessing the qualifications prescribed in article 28 and nominated for the purpose by the States Parties to the present Covenant.

2. Each State Party to the present Covenant may nominate not more than two persons. These persons shall be nationals of the nominating State.

3. A person shall be eligible for renomination.

Article 30. 1. The initial election shall be held no later than six months after the date of the entry into force of the present Covenant.

2. At least four months before the date of each election to the Committee, other than an election to fill a vacancy declared in accordance with article 34, the Secretary-General of the United Nations shall address a written invitation to the States Parties to the present Covenant to submit their nominations for membership of the Committee within three months.

3. The Secretary-General of the United Nations shall prepare a list in alphabetical order of all the persons thus nominated, with an indication of the States Parties which have nominated them, and shall submit it to the States Parties to the present Covenant no later than one month before the date of election.

4. Elections of the members of the Committee shall be held at a meeting of the States Parties to the present Covenant convened by the Secretary-General of the United Nations at the Headquarters of the United Nations. At that meeting, for which two thirds of the States Parties to the present Covenant shall constitute a quorum, the persons elected to the Committee shall be those nominees who obtain the largest number of votes and an absolute majority of the votes of the representatives of States Parties present and voting.

Article 31. 1. The Committee may not include more than one national of the same State.

2. In the election of the Committee, consideration shall be given to equitable geographical distribution of membership and to the representation of the different forms of civilization and of the principal legal systems.

Article 32. 1. The members of the Committee shall be elected for a term of four years. They shall be eligible for reelection if renominated. However, the terms of nine of the members elected at the first election shall expire at the end of two years; immediately after the first election, the names of these nine members shall be chosen by lot by the Chairman of the meeting referred to in article 30, paragraph 4.

2. Elections at the expiry of office shall be held in accord-

ance with the preceding articles of this part of the present Covenant.

Article 33. 1. If, in the unanimous opinion of the other members, a member of the Committee has ceased to carry out his functions for any cause other than absence of a temporary character, the Chairman of the Committee shall notify the Secretary-General of the United Nations, who shall then declare the seat of that member to be vacant.

2. In the event of the death or the resignation of a member of the Committee, the Chairman shall immediately notify the Secretary-General of the United Nations, who shall declare the seat vacant from the date of death or the date on which the resignation takes effect.

Article 34. 1. When a vacancy is declared in accordance with article 33 and if the term of office of the member to be replaced does not expire within six months of the declaration of the vacancy, the Secretary-General of the United Nations shall notify each of the States Parties to the present Covenant, which may within two months submit nominations in accordance with article 29 for the purpose of filling the vacancy.

2. The Secretary-General of the United Nations shall prepare a list in alphabetical order of the persons thus nominated and shall submit it to the States Parties to the present Covenant. The election to fill the vacancy shall then take place in accordance with the relevant provisions of this part of the present Covenant.

3. A member of the Committee elected to fill a vacancy declared in accordance with article 33 shall hold office for the remainder of the term of the member who vacated the seat on the Committee under the provisions of that article.

Article 35. The members of the Committee shall, with the approval of the General Assembly of the United Nations, receive emoluments from United Nations resources on such terms and conditions as the General Assembly may decide, having regard to the importance of the Committee's responsibilities.

Article 36. The Secretary-General of the United Nations shall provide the necessary staff and facilities for the effective performance of the functions of the Committee under the present Covenant.

Article 37. 1. The Secretary-General of the United Nations shall convene the initial meeting of the Committee at the Headquarters of the United Nations.

2. After its initial meeting, the Committee shall meet at such times as shall be provided in its rules of procedure.

3. The Committee shall normally meet at the Headquarters of the United Nations or at the United Nations Office at Geneva.

Article 38. Every member of the Committee shall, before taking up his duties, make a solemn declaration in open committee that he will perform his functions impartially and conscientiously.

Article 39. 1. The Committee shall elect its officers for a term of two years. They may be re-elected.

2. The Committee shall establish its own rules of procedure, but these rules shall provide, *inter alia,* that:

(a) Twelve members shall constitute a quorum;

(b) Decisions of the Committee shall be made by a majority vote of the members present.

Article 40. 1. The States Parties to the present Covenant undertake to submit reports on the measures they have adopted which give effect to the rights recognized herein and on the progress made in the enjoyment of those rights:

(a) Within one year of the entry into force of the present Covenant for the States Parties concerned;

(b) Thereafter whenever the Committee so requests.

2. All reports shall be submitted to the Secretary-General of the United Nations, who shall transmit them to the Committee for consideration. Reports shall indicate the factors and difficulties, if any, affecting the implementation of the present Covenant.

3. The Secretary-General of the United Nations may, after consultation with the Committee, transmit to the specialized agencies concerned copies of such parts of the reports as may fall within their field of competence.

4. The Committee shall study the reports submitted by the States Parties to the present Covenant. It shall transmit its reports, and such general comments as it may consider appropriate, to the States Parties. The Committee may also transmit to the Economic and Social Council these comments along with the copies of the reports it has received from States Parties to the present Covenant.

5. The States Parties to the present Covenant may submit to the Committee observations on any comments that may be made in accordance with paragraph 4 of this article.

Article 41. 1. A State Party to the present Covenant may at any time declare under this article that it recognizes the competence of the Committee to receive and consider communications to the effect that a State Party claims that another State Party is not fulfilling its obligations under the present Covenant. Communications under this article may be received and considered only if submitted by a State Party which has made a declaration recognizing in regard to itself the competence of the Committee. No communication shall be received by the Committee if it concerns a State Party which has not made such a declaration. Communications received under this article shall be dealt with in accordance with the following procedure:

(a) If a State Party to the present Covenant considers that another State Party is not giving effect to the provisions of the present Covenant, it may, by written communication, bring the matter to the attention of that State Party. Within three months after the receipt of the communication the receiving State shall afford the State which sent the communication an explanation, or any other statement in writing clarifying the matter which should include, to the extent possible and pertinent, reference to domestic procedures and remedies taken, pending, or available in the matter.

(b) If the matter is not adjusted to the satisfaction of both States Parties concerned within six months after the receipt by the receiving State of the initial communication, either State shall have the right to refer the matter to the Committee, by notice given to the Committee and to the other State.

(c) The Committee shall deal with a matter referred to it only after it has ascertained that all available domestic remedies have been invoked and exhausted in the matter, in conformity with the generally recognized principles of international law. This shall not be the rule where the application of the remedies is unreasonably prolonged.

(d) The Committee shall hold closed meetings when examining communications under this article.

(e) Subject to the provisions of sub-paragraph (c), the Committee shall make available its good offices to the States Parties concerned with a view to a friendly solution of the matter on the basis of respect for human rights and fundamental freedoms as recognized in the present Covenant.

(f) In any matter referred to it, the Committee may call upon the States Parties concerned, referred to in sub-paragraph (b), to supply any relevant information.

(g) The States Parties concerned, referred to in sub-paragraph (b), shall have the right to be represented when the matter is being considered in the Committee and to make submissions orally and/or in writing.

(h) The Committee shall, within twelve months after the date of receipt of notice under sub-paragraph (b), submit a report:

(i) If a solution within the terms of sub-paragraph (e) is reached, the Committee shall confine its report to a brief statement of the facts and of the solution reached;

(ii) If a solution within the terms of sub-paragraph (e) is not reached, the Committee shall confine its report to a brief statement of the facts; the written submissions and record of the oral submissions made by the State Parties concerned shall be attached to the report.

In every matter, the report shall be communicated to the States Parties concerned.

2. The provisions of this article shall come into force when ten States Parties to the present Covenant have made declarations under paragraph 1 of this article. Such declarations shall be deposited by the States Parties with the Secretary-General of the United Nations, who shall transmit copies thereof to the other States Parties. A declaration may be withdrawn at any time by notification to the Secretary-General. Such a withdrawal shall not prejudice the consideration of any matter which is the subject of a communication already transmitted under this article; no further communication by any State Party shall be received after the notification of withdrawal of the declaration has been received by the Secretary-General, unless the State Party concerned has made a new declaration.

Article 42. 1. (a) If a matter referred to the Committee in accordance with article 41 is not resolved to the satisfaction of the States Parties concerned, the Committee may, with the prior consent of the States Parties concerned, appoint an *ad hoc* Conciliation Commission (hereinafter referred to as the Commission). The good offices of the Commission shall be made available to the States Parties concerned with a view to an amicable solution of the matter on the basis of respect for the present Covenant;

(b) The Commission shall consist of five persons acceptable to the States Parties concerned. If the States Parties concerned fail to reach agreement within three months on all or part of the composition of the Commission, the members of the Commission concerning whom no agreement has been reached shall be elected by secret ballot by a two-thirds majority vote of the Committee from among its members.

2. The members of the Commission shall serve in their personal capacity. They shall not be nationals of the States Parties concerned, or of a State not party to the present Covenant, or of a State Party which has not made a declaration under article 41.

3. The Commission shall elect its own Chairman and adopt its own rules of procedure.

4. The meetings of the Commission shall normally be held at the Headquarters of the United Nations or at the United Nations Office at Geneva. However, they may be held at such other convenient places as the Commission may determine in consultation with the Secretary-General of the United Nations and the States Parties concerned.

5. The secretariat provided in accordance with article 36 shall also service the commission appointed under this article.

6. The information received and collated by the Committee shall be made available to the Commission and the

Commission may call upon the States Parties concerned to supply any other relevant information.

7. When the Commission has fully considered the matter, but in any event not later than twelve months after having been seized of the matter, it shall submit to the Chairman of the Committee a report for communication to the States Parties concerned:

(a) If the Commission is unable to complete its consideration of the matter within twelve months, it shall confine its report to a brief statement of the status of its consideration of the matter.

(b) If an amicable solution to the matter on the basis of respect for human rights as recognized in the present Covenant is reached, the Commission shall confine its report to a brief statement of the facts and of the solution reached;

(c) If a solution within the terms of sub-paragraph (b) is not reached, the Commission's report shall embody its findings on all questions of fact relevant to the issues between the States Parties concerned, and its views on the possibilities of an amicable solution of the matter. This report shall also contain the written submissions and a record of the oral submissions made by the States Parties concerned;

(d) If the Commission's report is submitted under sub-paragraph (c), the States Parties concerned shall, within three months of the receipt of the report, notify the Chairman of the Committee whether or not they accept the contents of the report of the Commission.

8. The provisions of this article are without prejudice to the responsibilities of the Committee under article 41.

9. The States Parties concerned shall share equally all the expenses of the members of the Commission in accordance with estimates to be provided by the Secretary-General of the United Nations.

10. The Secretary-General of the United Nations shall be empowered to pay the expenses of the members of the Commission, if necessary, before reimbursement by the States Parties concerned, in accordance with paragraph 9 of this article.

Article 43. The members of the Committee, and of the *ad hoc* conciliation commissions which may be appointed under article 42, shall be entitled to the facilities, privileges and immunities of experts on mission for the United Nations as laid down in the relevant sections of the Convention on the Privileges and Immunities of the United Nations.

Article 44. The provisions for the implementation of the present Covenant shall apply without prejudice to the procedures prescribed in the field of human rights by or under the constituent instruments and the conventions of the United Nations and of the specialized agencies and shall not prevent the States Parties to the present Covenant from having recourse to other procedures for settling a dispute in accordance with general or special international agreements in force between them.

Article 45. The Committee shall submit to the General Assembly of the United Nations, through the Economic and Social Council, an annual report on its activities.

Part V

Article 46. Nothing in the present Covenant shall be interpreted as impairing the provisions of the Charter of the United Nations and of the constitutions of the specialized agencies which define the respective responsibilities of the various organs of the United Nations and of the specialized agencies in regard to the matters dealt with in the present Covenant.

Article 47. Nothing in the present Covenant shall be interpreted as impairing the inherent right of all peoples to enjoy and utilize fully and freely their natural wealth and resources.

Part VI

Article 48. 1. The present Covenant is open for signature by any State Member of the United Nations or member of any of its specialized agencies, by any State Party to the Statute of the International Court of Justice, and by any other State which has been invited by the General Assembly of the United Nations to become a party to the present Covenant.

2. The present Covenant is subject to ratification. Instruments of ratification shall be deposited with the Secretary-General of the United Nations.

3. The present Covenant shall be open to accession by any State referred to in paragraph 1 of this article.

4. Accession shall be effected by the deposit of an instrument of accession with the Secretary-General of the United Nations.

5. The Secretary-General of the United Nations shall inform all States which have signed this Covenant or acceded to it of the deposit of each instrument of ratification or accession.

Article 49. 1. The present Covenant shall enter into force three months after the date of the deposit with the Secretary-General of the United Nations of the thirty-fifth instrument of ratification or instrument of accession.

2. For each State ratifying the present Covenant or acceding to it after the deposit of the thirty-fifth instrument of ratification or instrument of accession, the present Covenant shall enter into force three months after the date of the deposit of its own instrument of ratification or instrument of accession.

Article 50. The provisions of the present Covenant shall extend to all parts of federal States without any limitations or exceptions.

Article 51. 1. Any State Party to the present Covenant may propose an amendment and file it with the Secretary-General of the United Nations. The Secretary-General of the United Nations shall thereupon communicate any proposed amendments to the States Parties to the present Covenant with a request that they notify him whether they favour a conference of States Parties for the purpose of considering and voting upon the proposals. In the event that at least one third of the States Parties favours such a conference, the Secretary-General shall convene the conference under the auspices of the United Nations. Any amendment adopted by a majority of the States Parties present and voting at the conference shall be submitted to the General Assembly of the United Nations for approval.

2. Amendments shall come into force when they have been approved by the General Assembly of the United Nations and accepted by a two-thirds majority of the States Parties to the present Covenant in accordance with their respective constitutional processes.

3. When amendments come into force, they shall be binding on those States Parties which have accepted them, other States Parties still being bound by the provisions of the present Covenant and any earlier amendment which they have accepted.

Article 52. Irrespective of the notifications made under

article 48, paragraph 5, the Secretary-General of the United Nations shall inform all States referred to in paragraph 1 of the same article of the following particulars:

(a) Signatures, ratifications and accessions under article 48;

(b) The date of the entry into force of the present Covenant under article 49 and the date of the entry into force of any amendments under article 51.

Article 53. 1. The present Covenant, of which the Chinese, English, French, Russian and Spanish texts are equally authentic, shall be deposited in the archives of the United Nations.

2. The Secretary-General of the United Nations shall transmit certified copies of the present Covenant to all States referred to in article 48.

SEE ALSO *Civil and Political Rights: Human Rights Commission's Views in Particular Cases; Civil and Political Rights: Siracusa Principles; Political Rights; Political Rights: Electoral Processes; Political Rights: Periodic and Genuine Elections.*

INTERNATIONAL COVENANT ON CIVIL AND POLITICAL RIGHTS: OPTIONAL PROTOCOL

(1966). The optional protocol provides for consideration by the HUMAN RIGHTS COMMITTEE of communications from individuals or groups of individuals who claim to be victims of violations of any of the rights set out in the INTERNATIONAL COVENANT ON CIVIL AND POLITICAL RIGHTS. However, States parties to the covenant have the options of accepting, or not accepting, the optional protocol; and such communications can only be considered by the committee if the complaint is directed against a State which has ratified or acceded to the optional protocol.

The optional protocol was adopted by the UN General Assembly on 16 December 1966 (resolution 2200 A [XXI]) and entered into force on 23 March 1976. The text, annexed to that resolution, is as follows:

The States Parties to the Present Protocol,

Considering that in order further to achieve the purposes of the Covenant on Civil and Political Rights (hereinafter referred to as the Covenant) and the implementation of its provisions it would be appropriate to enable the Human Rights Committee set up in part IV of the Covenant (hereinafter referred to as the Committee) to receive and consider, as provided in the present Protocol, communications from individuals claiming to be victims of violations of any of the rights set forth in the Covenant.

Have agreed as follows:

Article 1. A State Party to the Covenant that becomes a party to the present Protocol recognizes the competence of the Committee to receive and consider communications from individuals subject to its jurisdiction who claim to be victims of a violation by that State Party of any of the rights set forth in the Covenant. No communication shall be received by the Committee if it concerns a State Party to the Covenant which is not a party to the present Protocol.

Article 2. Subject to the provisions of article 1, individuals who claim that any of their rights enumerated in the Covenant have been violated and who have exhausted all available domestic remedies may submit a written communication to the Committee for consideration.

Article 3. The Committee shall consider inadmissible any communication under the present Protocol which is anonymous, or which it considers to be an abuse of the right of submission of such communications or to be incompatible with the provisions of the Covenant.

Article 4. 1. Subject to the provisions of article 3, the Committee shall bring any communications submitted to it under the present Protocol to the attention of the State Party to the present Protocol alleged to be violating any provision of the Covenant.

2. Within six months, the receiving State shall submit to the Committee written explanations or statements clarifying the matter and the remedy, if any, that may have been taken by that State.

Article 5. 1. The Committee shall consider communications received under the present Protocol in the light of all written information made available to it by the individual and by the State Party concerned.

2. The Committee shall not consider any communication from an individual unless it has ascertained that:

(a) The same matter is not being examined under another procedure of international investigation or settlement;

(b) The individual has exhausted all available domestic remedies.

This shall not be the rule where the application of the remedies is unreasonably prolonged.

3. The Committee shall hold closed meetings when examining communications under the present Protocol.

4. The Committee shall forward its views to the State Party concerned and to the individual.

Article 6. The Committee shall include in its annual report under article 45 of the Covenant a summary of its activities under the present Protocol.

Article 7. Pending the achievement of the objectives of resolution 1514 (XV) adopted by the General Assembly of the United Nations on 14 December 1960 concerning the Declaration on the Granting of Independence to Colonial Countries and Peoples, the provisions of the present Protocol shall in no way limit the right of petition granted to these peoples by the Charter of the United Nations and other international conventions and instruments under the United Nations and its specialized agencies.

Article 8. 1. The present Protocol is open for signature by any State which has signed the Covenant.

2. The present Protocol is subject to ratification by any State which has ratified or acceded to the Covenant. Instruments of ratification shall be deposited with the Secretary-General of the United Nations.

3. The present Protocol shall be open to accession by any State which has ratified or acceded to the Covenant.

4. Accession shall be effected by the deposit of an instrument of accession with the Secretary-General of the United Nations.

5. The Secretary-General of the United Nations shall inform all States which have signed the present Protocol or acceded to it of the deposit of each instrument of ratification or accession.

Article 9. 1. Subject to the entry into force of the Covenant, the present Protocol shall enter into force three months after the date of the deposit with the Secretary-General of the United Nations of the tenth instrument of ratification or instrument of accession.

2. For each State ratifying the present Protocol or acceding to it after the deposit of the tenth instrument of ratification or instrument of accession, the present Protocol shall enter into force three months after the date of the deposit of its own instrument of ratification or instrument of accession.

Article 10. The provisions of the present Protocol shall extend to all parts of federal States without any limitations or exceptions.

Article 11. 1. Any State Party to the present Protocol may propose an amendment and file it with the Secretary-General of the United Nations. The Secretary-General shall thereupon communicate any proposed amendments to the States Parties to the present Protocol with a request that they notify him whether they favour a conference of States Parties for the purpose of considering and voting upon the proposal. In the event that at least one third of the States Parties favours such a conference, the Secretary-General shall convene the conference under the auspices of the United Nations. Any amendment adopted by a majority of the States Parties present and voting at the conference shall be submitted to the General Assembly of the United Nations for approval.

2. Amendments shall come into force when they have been approved by the General Assembly of the United Nations and accepted by a two-thirds majority of the States Parties to the present Protocol in accordance with their respective constitutional processes.

3. When amendments come into force, they shall be binding on those States Parties which have accepted them, other States Parties still being bound by the provisions of the present Protocol and any earlier amendment which they have accepted.

Article 12. 1. Any State Party may denounce the present Protocol at any time by written notification addressed to the Secretary-General of the United Nations. Denunciation shall take effect three months after the date of receipt of the notification by the Secretary-General.

2. Denunciation shall be without prejudice to the continued application of the provisions of the present Protocol to any communication submitted under article 2 before the effective date of denunciation.

Article 13. Irrespective of the notifications made under article 8, paragraph 5, of the present Protocol, the Secretary-General of the United Nations shall inform all States referred to in article 48, paragraph 1, of the Covenant of the following particulars:

(a) Signatures, ratifications and accessions under article 8;

(b) The date of the entry into force of the present Protocol under article 9 and the date of the entry into force of any amendments under article 11;

(c) Denunciations under article 12.

Article 14. 1. The present Protocol, of which the Chinese, English, French, Russian and Spanish texts are equally authentic, shall be deposited in the archives of the United Nations.

2. The Secretary-General of the United Nations shall transmit certified copies of the present Protocol to all States referred to in article 48 of the Covenant.

INTERNATIONAL COVENANT ON CIVIL AND POLITICAL RIGHTS: SECOND OPTIONAL PROTOCOL, AIMING AT ABOLITION OF THE DEATH PENALTY (1989). The second optional protocol, adopted and opened for signature and ratification or accession by the UN General Assembly on 15 December 1989, provides States that choose to do so the opportunity to join in an international commitment to abolish the death penalty. The purpose of the second optional protocol is to ensure the enjoyment by everyone of the right to life as set out in article 3 of the UNIVERSAL DECLARATION OF HUMAN RIGHTS and in article 6 of the INTERNATIONAL COVENANT ON CIVIL AND POLITICAL RIGHTS. The implementation of its provisions is supervised by the HUMAN RIGHTS COMMITTEE.

The General Assembly requested the UN COMMISSION ON HUMAN RIGHTS to consider the idea of a second optional protocol on 18 December 1982 (resolution 37/192). The commission asked its SUBCOMMISSION ON PREVENTION OF DISCRIMINATION AND PROTECTION OF MINORITIES to prepare a draft text, and the sub-commission entrusted the task to one of its members, Mr. Marc Bossuyt (Belgium) as its special rapporteur.

The special rapporteur submitted his report (UN Doc. E/CN.4/Sub.2/1987/20) to the sub-commission at its 1987 session. On the basis of the special rapporteur's proposals, the sub-commission transmitted a draft of the second optional protocol to the commission in 1988. The commission forwarded the draft, through the Economic and Social Council, to the General Assembly, which considered it in detail in 1989.

The Second Optional Protocol to the International Covenant on Civil and Political Rights, Aiming at the Abolition of the Death Penalty, was adopted and opened for signature, ratification and accession by the General Assembly on 15 December 1989 (resolution 44/128). The text of the second optional protocol, annexed to that resolution, is as follows:

The States parties to the present Protocol,

Believing that abolition of the death penalty contributes to enhancement of human dignity and progressive development of human rights,

Recalling article 3 of the Universal Declaration of Human Rights adopted on 10 December 1948 and article 6 of the International Covenant on Civil and Political Rights adopted on 16 December 1966,

Noting that article 6 of the International Covenant on Civil and Political Rights refers to abolition of the death penalty in terms that strongly suggest that abolition is desirable,

Convinced that all measures of abolition of the death penalty should be considered as progress in the enjoyment of the right to life,

Desirous to undertake hereby an international commitment to abolish the death penalty,

Have agreed as follows:

Article 1. 1. No one within the jurisdiction of a State party to the present Optional Protocol shall be executed.

2. Each State party shall take all necessary measures to abolish the death penalty within its jurisdiction.

Article 2. 1. No reservation is admissible to the present Protocol, except for a reservation made at the time of ratification or accession that provides for the application of the death penalty in time of war pursuant to a conviction for a most serious crime of a military nature committed during wartime.

2. The State party making such a reservation shall at the time of ratification or accession communicate to the Secretary-General of the United Nations the relevant provisions of its national legislation applicable during wartime.

3. The State party having made such a reservation shall notify the Secretary-General of the United Nations of any beginning or ending of a state of war applicable to its territory.

Article 3. The States parties to the present Protocol shall include in the reports they submit to the Human Rights Committee, in accordance with article 40 of the Covenant, information on the measures that they have adopted to give effect to the present Protocol.

Article 4. With respect to the States parties to the Covenant that have made a declaration under article 41, the competence of the Human Rights Committee to receive and consider communications when a State party claims that another State party is not fulfilling its obligations shall extend to the provisions of the present Protocol, unless the State party concerned has made a statement to the contrary at the moment of ratification or accession.

Article 5. With respect to the States parties to the (First) Optional Protocol to the International Covenant on Civil and Political Rights adopted on 16 December 1966, the competence of the Human Rights Committee to receive and consider communications from individuals subject to its jurisdiction shall extend to the provisions of the present Protocol, unless the State party concerned has made a statement to the contrary at the moment of ratification or accession.

Article 6. 1. The provisions of the present Protocol shall apply as additional provisions to the Covenant.

2. Without prejudice to the possibility of a reservation under article 2 of the present Protocol, the right guaranteed in article 1, paragraph 1, of the present Protocol shall not be subject to any derogation under article 4 of the Covenant.

Article 7. 1. The present Protocol is open for signature by any State that has signed the Covenant.

2. The present Protocol is subject to ratification by any State that has ratified the Covenant or acceded to it. Instruments of ratification shall be deposited with the Secretary-General of the United Nations.

3. The present Protocol shall be open to accession by any State that has ratified the Covenant or acceded to it.

4. Accession shall be effected by the deposit of an instrument of accession with the Secretary-General of the United Nations.

5. The Secretary-General of the United Nations shall inform all States that have signed the present Protocol or acceded to it of the deposit of each instrument of ratification or accession.

Article 8. 1. The present Protocol shall enter into force three months after the date of the deposit with the Secretary-General of the United Nations of the tenth instrument of ratification or accession.

2. For each State ratifying the present Protocol or acceding to it after the deposit of the tenth instrument of ratification or accession, the present Protocol shall enter into force three months after the date of the deposit of its own instrument of ratification or accession.

Article 9. The provisions of the present Protocol shall extend to all parts of federal States without any limitations or exceptions.

Article 10. The Secretary-General of the United Nations shall inform all States referred to in article 48, paragraph 1, of the Covenant of the following particulars:

(a) Reservations, communications and notifications under article 2 of the present Protocol;

(b) Statements made under its articles 4 or 5;

(c) Signatures, ratifications and accessions under its article 7;

(d) The date of the entry into force of the present Protocol under its article 8.

Article 11. 1. The present Protocol, of which the Arabic, Chinese, English, French, Russian and Spanish texts are equally authentic, shall be deposited in the archives of the United Nations.

2. The Secretary-General of the United Nations shall transmit certified copies of the present Protocol to all States referred to in article 48 of the Covenant.

SEE ALSO *American Convention on Human Rights: Additional Protocol on the Death Penalty (Draft); Capital Punishment; Capital Punishment: World Survey; European Convention on Human Rights: Protocol VI.*

INTERNATIONAL COVENANT ON ECONOMIC, SOCIAL AND CULTURAL RIGHTS (1966). The covenant is the second instrument—after the UNIVERSAL DECLARATION OF HUMAN RIGHTS—constituting the INTERNATIONAL BILL OF HUMAN RIGHTS, the third and fourth being the INTERNATIONAL COVENANT ON CIVIL AND POLITICAL RIGHTS and the OPTIONAL PROTOCOL TO THE INTERNATIONAL COVENANT ON CIVIL AND POLITICAL RIGHTS, respectively.

The covenant defines the economic, social, and cultural rights which it aims to protect and the permissible limitations on the enjoyment of those rights and authorizes the United Nations ECONOMIC AND SOCIAL COUNCIL to monitor the implementation of its provisions. The council established the COMMITTEE ON ECONOMIC, SOCIAL AND CULTURAL RIGHTS to assist it in this task.

The covenant was adopted by the UN General Assembly on 16 December 1966 (resolution 2200 A [XXI]), and entered into force on 3 January 1976. The text, annexed to that resolution, is as follows:

Preamble

The States Parties to the present Covenant,

Considering that, in accordance with the principles proclaimed in the Charter of the United Nations, recognition of the inherent dignity and of the equal and inalienable rights of all members of the human family is the foundation of freedom, justice and peace in the world,

Recognizing that these rights derive from the inherent dignity of the human person,

Recognizing that, in accordance with the Universal Declaration of Human Rights, the ideal of free human beings enjoying freedom from fear and want can only be achieved if conditions are created whereby everyone may enjoy his economic, social and cultural rights, as well as his civil and political rights,

Considering the obligation of States under the Charter of the United Nations to promote universal respect for, and observance of, human rights and freedoms,

Realizing that the individual, having duties to other individuals and to the community to which he belongs, is under a responsibility to strive for the promotion and observances of the rights recognized in the present Covenant,

Agree upon the following articles:

Part I

Article 1. 1. All peoples have the right of self-determination. By virtue of that right they freely determine their political status and freely pursue their economic, social and cultural development.

2. All peoples may, for their own ends, freely dispose of their natural wealth and resources without prejudice to any obligations arising out of international economic co-operation, based upon the principle of mutual benefit, and international law. In no case may a people be deprived of its own means of subsistence.

3. The States Parties to the present Covenant, including those having responsibility for the administration of Non-Self-Governing and Trust Territories, shall promote the realization of the right of self-determination, and shall respect that right, in conformity with the provisions of the Charter of the United Nations.

Part II

Article 2. 1. Each State Party to the present Covenant undertakes to take steps, individually and through international assistance and co-operation, especially economic and technical, to the maximum of its available resources, with a view to achieving progressively the full realization of the rights recognized in the present Covenant by all appropriate means, including particularly the adoption of legislative measures.

2. The States Parties to the present Covenant undertake to guarantee that the rights enunciated in the present Covenant will be exercised without discrimination of any kind as to race, colour, sex, language, religion, political or other opinion, national or social origin, property, birth or other status.

3. Developing countries, with due regard to human rights and their national economy, may determine to what extent they would guarantee the economic rights recognized in the present Covenant to non-nationals.

Article 3. The States Parties to the present Covenant undertake to ensure the equal right of men and women to the enjoyment of all economic, social and cultural rights set forth in the present Covenant.

Article 4. The States Parties to the present Covenant recognize that, in the enjoyment of those rights provided by the State in conformity with the present Covenant, the State may subject such rights only to such limitations as are determined by law only in so far as this may be compatible with the nature of these rights and solely for the purpose of promoting the general welfare in a democratic society.

Article 5. 1. Nothing in the present Covenant may be interpreted as implying for any State, group or person any right to engage in any activity or to perform any act aimed at the destruction of any of the rights or freedoms recognized herein, or at their limitation to a greater extent than is provided for in the present Covenant.

2. No restriction upon or derogation from any of the fundamental human rights recognized or existing in any country in virtue of law, conventions, regulations or custom shall be admitted on the pretext that the present Covenant does not recognize such rights or that it recognizes them to a lesser extent.

Part III

Article 6. 1. The States Parties to the present Covenant recognize the right to work, which includes the right of everyone to the opportunity to gain his living by work which he freely chooses or accepts, and will take appropriate steps to safeguard this right.

2. The steps to be taken by a State Party to the present Covenant to achieve the full realization of this right shall include technical and vocational guidance and training programmes, policies and techniques to achieve steady economic, social and cultural development and full and productive employment under conditions safeguarding fundamental political and economic freedoms to the individual.

Article 7. The States Parties to the present Covenant recognize the right of everyone to the enjoyment of just and favourable conditions of work which ensure, in particular:

(a) Remuneration which provides all workers, as a minimum, with:

(i) Fair wages and equal remuneration for work of equal value without distinction of any kind, in particular women being guaranteed conditions of work not inferior to those enjoyed by men, with equal pay for equal work;

(ii) A decent living for themselves and their families in accordance with the provisions of the present Covenant;

(b) Safe and healthy working conditions;

(c) Equal opportunity for everyone to be promoted in his employment to an appropriate higher level, subject to no considerations other than those of seniority and competence;

(d) Rest, leisure and reasonable limitation of working hours and periodic holidays with pay, as well as remuneration for public holidays.

Article 8. 1. The States Parties to the present Covenant undertake to ensure:

(a) The right of everyone to form trade unions and join the trade union of his choice, subject only to the rules of the organization concerned, for the promotion and protection of his economic and social interests. No restrictions may be placed on the exercise of this right other than those prescribed by law and which are necessary in a democratic society in the interests of national security or public order or for the protection of the rights and freedoms of others;

(b) The right of trade unions to establish national federations or confederations and the right of the latter to form or join international trade-union organizations;

(c) The right of trade unions to function freely subject to no limitations other than those prescribed by law and which are necessary in a democratic society in the interests of national security or public order or for the protection of the rights and freedoms of others;

(d) The right to strike, provided that it is exercised in conformity with the laws of the particular country.

2. This article shall not prevent the imposition of lawful restrictions on the exercise of these rights by members of the armed forces or of the police or of the administration of the State.

3. Nothing in this article shall authorize States Parties to the International Labour Organisation Convention of 1948 concerning Freedom of Association and Protection of the Right to Organize to take legislative measures which would prejudice, or apply the law in such a manner as would prejudice, the guarantees provided for in that Convention.

Article 9. The States Parties to the present Covenant recognize the right of everyone to social security, including social insurance.

Article 10. The States Parties to the present Covenant recognize that:

1. The widest possible protection and assistance should be accorded to the family, which is the natural and fundamental group unit of society, particularly for its establishment and while it is responsible for the care and education of dependent children. Marriage must be entered into with the free consent of the intending spouses.

2. Special protection should be accorded to mothers during a reasonable period before and after childbirth. During such period working mothers should be accorded paid leave or leave with adequate social security benefits.

3. Special measures of protection and assistance should be taken on behalf of all children and young persons without any discrimination for reasons of parentage or other conditions. Children and young persons should be protected from economic and social exploitation. Their employment in work harmful to their morals or health or dangerous to life or likely to hamper their normal development should be punishable by law. States should also set age limits below which the paid employment of child labour should be prohibited and punishable by law.

Article 11. 1. The States Parties to the present Covenant recognize the rights of everyone to an adequate standard of living for himself and his family, including adequate food, clothing and housing, and to the continuous improvement of living conditions. The States Parties will take appropriate steps to ensure the realization of this right, recognizing to this effect the essential importance of international co-operation based on free consent.

2. The States Parties to the present Covenant, recognizing the fundamental right of everyone to be free from hunger, shall take, individually and through international co-operation, the measures, including specific programmes, which are needed:

(a) To improve methods of production, conservation and distribution of food by making full use of technical and scientific knowledge, by disseminating knowledge of the principles of nutrition and by developing or reforming agrarian systems in such a way as to achieve the most efficient development and utilization of natural resources;

(b) Taking into account the problems of both food-importing and food-exporting countries, to ensure an equitable distribution of world food supplies in relation to need.

Article 12. 1. The States Parties to the present Covenant recognize the right of everyone to the enjoyment of the highest attainable standard of physical and mental health.

2. The steps to be taken by the States Parties to the present Covenant to achieve the full realization of this right shall include those necessary for:

(a) The provision for the reduction of the stillbirthrate and of infant mortality and for the healthy development of the child;

(b) The improvement of all aspects of environmental and industrial hygiene;

(c) The prevention, treatment and control of epidemic, endemic, occupational and other diseases;

(d) The creation of conditions which would assure to all medical service and medical attention in the event of sickness.

Article 13. 1. The States Parties to the present Covenant recognize the right of everyone to education. They agree that education shall be directed to the full development of the human personality and the sense of its dignity, and shall strengthen the respect for human rights and fundamental freedoms. They further agree that education shall enable all persons to participate effectively in a free society, promote understanding, tolerance and friendship among all nations and all racial, ethnic or religious groups, and further the activities of the United Nations for the maintenance of peace.

2. The States Parties to the present Covenant recognize that, with a view to achieving the full realization of this right:

(a) Primary education shall be compulsory and available free to all;

(b) Secondary education in its different forms, including technical and vocational secondary education, shall be made generally available and accessible to all by every appropriate means, and in particular by the progressive introduction of free education;

(c) Higher education shall be made equally accessible to all, on the basis of capacity, by every appropriate means, and in particular by the progressive introduction of free education;

(d) Fundamental education shall be encouraged or intensified as far as possible for those persons who have not received or completed the whole period of their primary education;

(e) The development of a system of schools at all levels shall be actively pursued, an adequate fellowship system shall be established, and the material conditions of teaching staff shall be continuously improved.

3. The States Parties to the present Covenant undertake to have respect for the liberty of parents and, when applicable, legal guardians to choose for their children schools, other than those established by the public authorities, which conform to such minimum educational standards as may be laid down or approved by the State and to ensure the religious and moral education of their children in conformity with their own convictions.

4. No part of this article shall be construed so as to interfere with the liberty of individuals and bodies to establish and direct educational institutions, subject always to the observance of the principles set forth in paragraph 1 of this article and to the requirement that the education given in

such institutions shall conform to such minimum standards as may be laid down by the State.

Article 14. Each State Party to the present Covenant which, at the time of becoming a Party, has not been able to secure in its metropolitan territory or other territories under its jurisdiction compulsory primary education, free of charge, undertakes, within two years, to work out and adopt a detailed plan of action for the progressive implementation, within a reasonable number of years, to be fixed in the plan, of the principle of compulsory education free of charge for all.

Article 15. 1. The States Parties to the present Covenant recognize the right of everyone:

    (a) To take part in cultural life;

    (b) To enjoy the benefits of scientific progress and its applications;

    (c) To benefit from the protection of the moral and material interests resulting from any scientific, literary or artistic production of which he is the author.

2. The steps to be taken by the States Parties to the present Covenant to achieve the full realization of this right shall include those necessary for the conservation, the development and the diffusion of science and culture.

3. The States Parties to the present Covenant undertake to respect the freedom indispensable for scientific research and creative activity.

4. The States Parties to the present Covenant recognize the benefits to be derived from the encouragement and development of international contacts and co-operation in the scientific and cultural fields.

Part IV

Article 16. 1. The States Parties to the present Covenant undertake to submit in conformity with this part of the Covenant reports on the measures which they have adopted and the progress made in achieving the observance of the rights recognized herein.

2. (a) All reports shall be submitted to the Secretary-General of the United Nations, who shall transmit copies to the Economic and Social Council for consideration in accordance with the provisions of the present Covenant;

    (b) The Secretary-General of the United Nations shall also transmit to the specialized agencies copies of the reports, or any relevant parts therefrom, from States Parties to the present Covenant which are also members of these specialized agencies in so far as these reports, or parts therefrom, relate to any matters which fall within the responsibilities of the said agencies in accordance with their constitutional instruments.

Article 17. 1. The States Parties to the present Covenant shall furnish their reports in stages, in accordance with a programme to be established by the Economic and Social Council within one year of the entry into force of the present Covenant after consultation with the States Parties and the specialized agencies concerned.

2. Reports may indicate factors and difficulties affecting the degree of fulfilment of obligations under the present Covenant.

3. Where relevant information has previously been furnished to the United Nations or to any specialized agency by any State Party to the present Covenant, it will not be necessary to reproduce that information, but a precise reference to the information so furnished will suffice.

Article 18. Pursuant to its responsibilities under the Char-

ter of the United Nations in the field of human rights and fundamental freedoms, the Economic and Social Council may make arrangements with the specialized agencies in respect of their reporting to it on the progress made in achieving the observance of the provisions of the present Covenant falling within the scope of their activities. These reports may include particulars of decisions and recommendations on such implementation adopted by their competent organs.

Article 19. The Economic and Social Council may transmit to the Commission on Human Rights for study and general recommendation or, as appropriate, for information the reports concerning human rights submitted by States in accordance with articles 16 and 17, and those concerning human rights submitted by the specialized agencies in accordance with article 18.

Article 20. The States Parties to the present Covenant and the specialized agencies concerned may submit comments to the Economic and Social Council on any general recommendation under article 19 or reference to such general recommendation in any report of the Commission on Human Rights or any documentation referred to therein.

Article 21. The Economic and Social Council may submit from time to time to the General Assembly reports with recommendations of a general nature and a summary of the information received from the States Parties to the present Covenant and the specialized agencies on the measures taken and the progress made in achieving general observance of the rights recognized in the present Covenant.

Article 22. The Economic and Social Council may bring to the attention of other organs of the United Nations, their subsidiary organs and specialized agencies concerned with furnishing technical assistance any matters arising out of the reports referred to in this part of the present Covenant which may assist such bodies in deciding, each within its field of competence, on the advisability of international measures likely to contribute to the effective progressive implementation of the present Covenant.

Article 23. The States Parties to the present Covenant agree that international action for the achievement of the rights recognized in the present Covenant includes such methods as the conclusion of conventions, the adoption of recommendations, the furnishing of technical assistance and the holding of regional meetings and technical meetings for the purpose of consultation and study organized in conjunction with the Governments concerned.

Article 24. Nothing in the present Covenant shall be interpreted as impairing the provisions of the Charter of the United Nations and of the constitutions of the specialized agencies which define the respective responsibilities of the various organs of the United Nations and of the specialized agencies in regard to the matters dealt with in the present Covenant.

Article 25. Nothing in the present Covenant shall be interpreted as impairing the inherent right of all peoples to enjoy and utilize fully and freely their natural wealth and resources.

Part V

Article 26. 1. The present Covenant is open for signature by any State Member of the United Nations or member of any of its specialized agencies, by any State Party to the Statute of the International Court of Justice, and by any other State which has been invited by the General Assembly of the United Nations to become a party to the present Covenant.

2. The present Covenant is subject to ratification. Instruments of ratification shall be deposited with the Secretary-General of the United Nations.

3. The present Covenant shall be open to accession by any State referred to in paragraph 1 of this article.

4. Accession shall be effected by the deposit of an instrument of accession with the Secretary-General of the United Nations.

5. The Secretary-General of the United Nations shall inform all States which have signed the present Covenant or acceded to it of the deposit of each instrument of ratification or accession.

Article 27. 1. The present Covenant shall enter into force three months after the date of the deposit with the Secretary-General of the United Nations of the thirty-fifth instrument of ratification or instrument of accession.

2. For each State ratifying the present Covenant or acceding to it after the deposit of the thirty-fifth instrument of ratification or instrument of accession, the present Covenant shall enter into force three months after the date of the deposit of its own instrument of ratification or instrument of accession.

Article 28. The provisions of the present Covenant shall extend to all parts of federal States without any limitations or exceptions.

Article 29. 1. Any State Party to the present Covenant may propose an amendment and file it with the Secretary-General of the United Nations. The Secretary-General shall thereupon communicate any proposed amendments to the States Parties to the present Covenant with a request that they notify him whether they favour a conference of States Parties for the purpose of considering and voting upon the proposals. In the event that at least one third of the States Parties favours such a conference, the Secretary-General shall convene the conference under the auspices of the United Nations. Any amendment adopted by a majority of the States Parties present and voting at the conference shall be submitted to the General Assembly of the United Nations for approval.

2. Amendments shall come into force when they have been approved by the General Assembly of the United Nations and accepted by a two-thirds majority of the States Parties to the present Covenant in accordance with their respective constitutional processes.

3. When amendments come into force they shall be binding on those States Parties which have accepted them, other States Parties still being bound by the provisions of the present Covenant and any earlier amendment which they have accepted.

Article 30. Irrespective of the notifications made under article 26, paragraph 5, the Secretary-General of the United Nations shall inform all States referred to in paragraph 1 of the same article of the following particulars:

(a) Signatures, ratifications and accessions under article 26;

(b) The date of the entry into force of the present Covenant under article 27 and the date of the entry into force of any amendments under article 29.

Article 31. 1. The present Covenant, of which the Chinese, English, French, Russian and Spanish texts are equally authentic, shall be deposited in the archives of the United Nations.

2. The Secretary-General of the United Nations shall transmit certified copies of the present Covenant to all States referred to in article 26.

SEE ALSO *Economic, Social, and Cultural Rights; Economic, Social and Cultural Rights: ILO Activities; Economic, Social and Cultural Rights: Limburg Principles; Economic, Social and Cultural Rights: Studies; Economic, Social and Cultural Rights: UNESCO Activities; European Social Charter; and individual ILO and UNESCO instruments.*

INTERNATIONAL COVENANT ON ECONOMIC, SOCIAL AND CULTURAL RIGHTS: REPORTING BY STATES.

The COMMITTEE ON ECONOMIC, SOCIAL AND CULTURAL RIGHTS decided to begin, as from its 1989 session, the preparation of general comments based on various articles and provisions of the INTERNATIONAL COVENANT ON ECONOMIC, SOCIAL AND CULTURAL RIGHTS with a view to assisting the States parties to that covenant in fulfilling their reporting obligations.

The committee's first general comment, relating to reporting by States, was adopted at its 19th meeting, on 17 February 1989, as follows (UN Doc. E/1989/22, Annex III, para. 1–9):

The reporting obligations which are contained in part IV of the Covenant are designed principally to assist each State party in fulfilling its obligations under the covenant and, in addition, to provide a basis on which the Council, assisted by the Committee, can discharge its responsibilities for monitoring States parties' compliance with their obligations and for facilitating the realization of economic, social and cultural rights in accordance with the provisions of the Covenant. The Committee considers that it would be incorrect to assume that reporting is essentially only a procedural matter designed solely to satisfy each State party's formal obligation to report to the appropriate international monitoring body. On the contrary, in accordance with the letter and spirit of the Covenant, the processes of preparation and submission of reports by States can, and indeed should, serve to achieve a variety of objectives.

A *first objective,* which is of particular relevance to the initial report required to be submitted within two years of the Covenant's entry into force for the State party concerned, is to ensure that a comprehensive review is undertaken with respect to national legislation, administrative rules and procedures, and practices in an effort to ensure the fullest possible conformity with the Covenant. Such a review might, for example, be undertaken in conjunction with each of the relevant national ministries or other authorities responsible for policy-making and implementation in the different fields covered by the Covenant.

A *second objective* is to ensure that the State party monitors the actual situation with respect to each of the rights on a regular basis and is thus aware of the extent to which the various rights are, or are not, being enjoyed by all individuals within its territory or under its jurisdiction. From the Committee's experience to date, it is clear that the fulfilment of this objective cannot be achieved only by the preparation of aggregate national statistics or estimates, but also requires that special attention be given to any worse-off regions or areas and to any specific groups or subgroups which appear to be particularly vulnerable or disadvantaged. Thus, the essential first step towards promoting the realization of economic, social and cultural rights is diagnosis and knowledge of the existing situation. The Committee is aware that this process of monitoring and gathering information is a potentially time-consuming and costly one and that international assistance and co-operation, as provided for in article 2, paragraph 1 and articles 22 and 23 of the Covenant, may well be required in order to enable some States parties to fulfil the relevant obligations. If that is the case, and the State party concludes that it does not have the capacity to undertake the monitoring process which is an integral part of any process designed to promote accepted goals of public policy and is indispensable to the effective implementation of the Covenant, it may note this fact in its report to the Committee and indicate the nature and extent of any international assistance that it may need.

While monitoring is designed to give a detailed overview of the existing situation, the principal value of such an overview is to provide the basis for the elaboration of clearly stated and carefully targeted policies, including the establishment of priorities which reflect the provisions of the Covenant. Therefore, a *third objective* of the reporting process is to enable the Government to demonstrate that such principled policy-making has in fact been undertaken. While the Covenant makes this obligation explicit only in article 14 in cases where "compulsory primary education, free of charge" has not yet been secured for all, a comparable obligation "to work out and adopt a detailed plan of action for the progressive implementation" of each of the rights contained in the Covenant is clearly implied by the obligation in article 2, paragraph 1 "to take steps . . . by all appropriate means . . ."

A *fourth objective* of the reporting process is to facilitate public scrutiny of government policies with respect to economic, social and cultural rights and to encourage the involvement of the various economic, social and cultural sectors of society in the formulation, implementation and review of the relevant policies. In examining reports submitted to it to date, the Committee has welcomed the fact that a number of States parties, reflecting different political and economic systems, have encouraged inputs by such non-governmental groups into the preparation of their reports under the Covenant. Other States have ensured the widespread dissemination of their reports with a view to enabling comments to be made by the public at large. In these ways, the preparation of the report, and its consideration at the national level can come to be of at least as much value as the constructive dialogue conducted at the international level between the Committee and representatives of the reporting State.

A *fifth objective* is to provide a basis on which the State party itself, as well as the Committee, can effectively evaluate the extent to which progress has been made towards the realization of the obligations contained in the Covenant. For this purpose, it may be useful for States to identify specific bench-marks or goals against which their performance in a given area can be assessed. Thus, for example, it is generally agreed that it is important to set specific goals with respect to the reduction of infant mortality, the extent of vaccination of children, the intake of calories per person, the number of persons per health care provider, etc. In many of these areas, global bench-marks are of limited use,

whereas national or other more specific bench-marks can provide an extremely valuable indication of progress.

In this regard, the Committee wishes to note that the Covenant attaches particular importance to the concept of "progressive realization" of the relevant rights and, for that reason, the Committee urges States parties to include in their periodic reports information which shows the progress over time, with respect to the effective realization of the relevant rights. By the same token, it is clear that qualitative, as well as quantitative, data are required in order for an adequate assessment of the situation to be made.

A *sixth objective* is to enable the State party itself to develop a better understanding of the problems and shortcomings encountered in efforts to realize progressively the full range of economic, social and cultural rights. For this reason, it is essential that States parties report in detail on the "factors and difficulties" inhibiting such realization. This process of identification and recognition of the relevant difficulties then provides the framework within which more appropriate policies can be devised.

A *seventh objective* is to enable the Committee, and the States parties as a whole, to facilitate the exchange of information among States and to develop a better understanding of the common problems faced by States and to develop a better understanding of the common problems faced by States and a fuller appreciation of the type of measure which might be taken to promote effective realization of each of the rights contained in the Covenant. This part of the process also enables the Committee to identify the most appropriate means by which the international community might assist States, in accordance with articles 22 and 23 of the Covenant. In order to underline the importance which the Committee attaches to this objective, a separate general comment on those articles will be discussed by the Committee at its fourth session.

INTERNATIONAL COVENANTS ON HUMAN RIGHTS. Pointing out that the INTERNATIONAL COVENANT ON ECONOMIC, SOCIAL AND CULTURAL RIGHTS and the INTERNATIONAL COVENANT ON CIVIL AND POLITICAL RIGHTS constitute the first all-embracing and legally binding international treaties in the field of human rights and that they, together with the UNIVERSAL DECLARATION OF HUMAN RIGHTS, form the core of the INTERNATIONAL BILL OF HUMAN RIGHTS, the UN General Assembly on 15 December 1989 reaffirmed (resolution 44/129) "that all human rights and fundamental freedoms are indivisible and interrelated and that the promotion and protection of one category of rights should never exempt or excuse States from the promotion and protection of the other."

Reflecting views which had been expressed earlier in 1989 by the Commission on Human Rights (resolution 1989/17) and the Economic and Social Council (resolution 1989/81), the General Assembly recognized the important role played by the HUMAN RIGHTS COMMITTEE in the implementation of the International Covenant on Civil and Political Rights and by the COMMITTEE ON ECONOMIC, SOCIAL AND CULTURAL

RIGHTS in the implementation of the International Covenant on Economic, Social and Cultural Rights. It emphasized the importance of the strictest compliance by States parties to those covenants and, where applicable, to the INTERNATIONAL COVENANT ON CIVIL AND POLITICAL RIGHTS: OPTIONAL PROTOCOL.

The assembly, further, stressed the importance of avoiding the erosion of human rights by DEROGATION and underlined the necessity of strict observance of the agreed conditions and procedures for derogation under article 4 of the International Covenant on Civil and Political Rights, bearing in mind the need for States parties to provide the fullest possible information during states of emergency, so that the justification for and appropriateness of measures taken in these circumstances can be assessed. It also appealed to States parties to the covenants that have exercised their sovereign right to make reservations in accord with the relevant rules of international law to consider whether any such reservation should be reviewed.

INTERNATIONAL CRIMINAL POLICE ORGANIZATION (INTERPOL).

INTERPOL is an intergovernmental organization composed of 138 affiliated countries which provides international coordination for the police authorities in its member States and centralizes documentation pertaining to international crime. Police authorities in each participating country operate a National Central Bureau which is constantly in touch with INTERPOL's headquarters by means of a private radio network of more than 70 stations. Information concerning criminal activities is thus passed rapidly from one country to another to prevent individuals who commit crimes in one country to escape arrest by moving quickly to another, and to expedite extradition proceedings.

INTERPOL endeavors to insure the widest possible mutual assistance between police authorities in the spirit of the UNIVERSAL DECLARATION OF HUMAN RIGHTS and to establish and develop institutions and procedures which will contribute to the prevention and suppression of crime. The organization's constitution strictly forbids it to intervene in any activities of a political, military, religious, or racial character.

Policy questions arising within INTERPOL are dealt with by its General Assembly, which meets annually. On the international level, INTERPOL participates on a continuing basis, under a special arrangement, with the UN ECONOMIC AND SOCIAL COUNCIL and its subsidiary bodies, including the SUB-COMMISSION ON PREVENTION OF DISCRIMINATION AND PROTECTION OF MINORITIES. In particular, it supplies information when available concerning institutions

and practices resembling slavery or the slave trade to the sub-commission's WORKING GROUP ON CONTEMPORARY FORMS OF SLAVERY.

INTERPOL publishes the *International Criminal Police Review* (issued 10 times per year) and the *INTERPOL Information Bulletin*. It also conducts seminars and training courses on various aspects of police work.

International Criminal Police Organization. Address: 26, rue Armengaud BP 205, F-92212, Saint-Cloud CEDEX, France. Telephone: (33) 42 02 55 50. Secretary-General: Raymond E. Kendall.

INTERNATIONAL DECLARATION AGAINST *APARTHEID* IN SPORTS (1977).

In 1968, the UN INTERNATIONAL CONFERENCE ON HUMAN RIGHTS strongly recommended that international sports federations and associations should exclude South Africa from membership until *apartheid* had been brought to an end in that country. In 1971, the UN General Assembly (resolution 2775 [XXVI]) declared its unqualified support of the Olympic principle that no discrimination be allowed on the grounds of race, religion, or political affiliation; affirmed that merit should be the sole criterion for participation in sports activities; and called upon all national and international sports organizations to uphold the Olympic principle of non-discrimination and to discourage and deny support to sporting events organized in violation of this principle. It called upon individual sportsmen to refuse to participate in any sports activity in a country in which there is an official policy of racial discrimination or *apartheid* in the field of sports and urged all States to promote adherence to the Olympic principle of non-discrimination and to encourage their sports organizations to withhold support from sporting events organized in violation of this principle.

Six years later, the Assembly adopted, on 14 December 1977 (resolution 32/105), the International Declaration against *Apartheid* in Sports. The text of the declaration is as follows:

The General Assembly,

Recalling the provisions of the Charter of the United Nations, in which Member States pledge to take joint and separate action in co-operation with the Organization for the achievement of universal respect for, and observance of, human rights and fundamental freedoms for all without distinction as to race, sex, language, or religion,

Considering the Universal Declaration of Human Rights, which states that all human beings are born free and equal in dignity and rights and that everyone is entitled to all the rights and freedoms set forth in the Declaration without distinction of any such kind such as race, colour or national origin,

Recalling that, in accordance with the principles of the

International Convention on the Elimination of All Forms of Racial Discrimination, States undertake not to sponsor, defend or support racial discrimination,

Recalling further that the International Convention on the Suppression and Punishment of the Crime of *Apartheid* declares that *apartheid* is a crime violating the principles of international law, in particular the purposes and principles of the Charter of the United Nations, and constituting a serious threat to international peace and security,

Recalling that the General Assembly has adopted a number of resolutions in which the policies and practices of *apartheid*, including the application of *apartheid* in the field of sport, and collaboration with the racist régime in all areas, are condemned,

Reaffirming the legitimacy of the struggle of the people of South Africa for the total elimination of *apartheid* and racial discrimination,

Recognizing that the eradication of *apartheid* and rendering of assistance to the South African people to establish a non-racial society is one of the primary concerns of the international community,

Convinced that more effective measures must be taken as a matter of priority, during the International Anti-*Apartheid* Year and the Decade to Combat Racism and Racial Discrimination, to eliminate *apartheid* in all its manifestations,

Reaffirming its unqualified support for the Olympic principle that no discrimination be allowed on the grounds of race, religion or political affiliation and its belief that merit should be the sole criterion for participation in sports activities,

Considering that international representative sporting contacts based on the Olympic principle can play a positive role in promoting peace and the development of friendly relations among nations of the world,

Recognizing that there can be neither adherence to the principle of merit selection nor fully integrated non-racial sport in any country practising *apartheid* until the *apartheid* system itself is eradicated,

Condemning the enforcement, by the racist régime of South Africa, of racial discrimination and segregation in sports,

Commending the sportsmen inside South Africa who are struggling against *apartheid* and upholding the principle of non-racialism in sport,

Condemning the repressive measures taken by the racist *apartheid* régime against the non-racial sports bodies and their leaders in South Africa,

Rejecting the policy of so-called "multinational" sport, enunciated by the South African racist régime, as no more than a device for perpetuating *apartheid* in sports and an attempt by the régime to mislead international public opinion in order to gain acceptance for participation in international sport,

Recognizing the importance in the international campaign against *apartheid* of the boycott of South African sports teams selected on the basis of *apartheid*,

Convinced that an effective campaign for the total boycott of South African sports teams can be an important measure in demonstrating the abhorrence of *apartheid* by Governments and peoples,

Commending all Governments, sportsmen, sports bodies and other organizations which have taken action against *apartheid* in sports,

Noting with concern that some national and international sports bodies have continued contacts with racist *apartheid* sports bodies in violation of the Olympic principle and resolutions of the United Nations,

Recognizing that participation in sports exchanges with teams selected on the basis of *apartheid* violates the fundamental human rights of the great majority of the people of South Africa and directly abets and encourages the commission of the crime of *apartheid*, as defined in the International Convention on the Suppression and Punishment of the Crime of *Apartheid*, and encourages the racist régime in its pursuit of *apartheid*,

Condemning sports contacts with any country practising *apartheid* and recognizing that participation in *apartheid* in sports condones and strengthens *apartheid* and thereby becomes the legitimate concern of all Governments,

Convinced that an international declaration against *apartheid* in sports would make it possible to take more effective measures at the international and national levels with a view to completely isolating and eliminating *apartheid*,

Proclaims this International Declaration against *Apartheid* in Sports:

Article 1. States affirm and support this Declaration as an expression of international condemnation of *apartheid* and as a measure to contribute towards the total eradication of the system of *apartheid*, and to this end resolve to take strong action and to exert the greatest possible influence in order to ensure the total elimination of *apartheid* in sports.

Article 2. States shall take all appropriate action to bring about the total cessation of sporting contact with any country practising *apartheid* and shall refrain from official sponsorship, assistance or encouragement of such contacts.

Article 3. States shall take all appropriate action towards the exclusion or expulsion of any county practising *apartheid* from international and regional sports bodies. They shall give full support to national sports bodies attempting to exclude such countries from membership of international and regional sports associations or to prevent such countries from participation in sports activities.

Article 4. 1. States shall publicly declare and express total opposition to *apartheid* in sports as well as full and active support for the total boycott of all teams and sportsmen from the racist *apartheid* sports bodies.

2. States shall pursue a vigorous programme of public education aimed at securing strict adherence to the Olympic principle of non-discrimination in sports and widespread national acceptance for the spirit and letter of United Nations resolutions on *apartheid* in sports.

3. Sports bodies shall be actively encouraged to withhold any support from sporting events organized in violation of the Olympic principle and United Nations resolutions. To this end, States shall convey the United Nations resolutions on *apartheid* in sports to all national sports bodies, urging them:

(a) To disseminate such information to all their affiliates and branches;

(b) To take all necessary action to ensure strict compliance with those resolutions.

Article 5. States shall take appropriate actions against their sporting teams and organizations whose members collectively or individually participate in sports activities in any country practising *apartheid* or with teams from a country practising *apartheid*, which in particular shall include:

(a) Refusal to provide financial or other assistance to enable sports bodies, teams or individuals to participate in sports activities in countries practising *apartheid* or with teams and individual sportsmen selected on the basis of *apartheid;*

(b) Refusal to provide financial or other assistance for any purpose to sports bodies whose team members or affiliates participate in such sporting activities;

(c) Withdrawal of access to national sporting facilities to such teams or individuals;

(d) Non-recognition by States of all professional sporting contracts which involve sporting activities in any country practising *apartheid,* or with teams or individual sportsmen selected on the basis of *apartheid;*

(e) Denial and withdrawal of national honours or awards to such teams or individuals;

(f) Denial of official receptions to teams or sportsmen participating in sports activities with teams or individual sportsmen from any country practising *apartheid.*

Article 6. States shall deny visas and/or entry to representatives of sports bodies, members of teams or individual sportsmen from any country practising *apartheid.*

Article 7. States shall establish national regulations and guidelines against participation with *apartheid* in sports and shall ensure that effective means exist for bringing about compliance with such guidelines.

Article 8. States shall co-operate with anti-*apartheid* movements and other organizations which are engaged in promoting the implementation of the principles of this Declaration.

Article 9. States undertake to encourage actively and publicly all official bodies, private enterprises and other groups engaged in promoting, organizing or servicing sports activities to refrain from undertaking any action which in any way supports, assists or enables the organization of activities involving *apartheid* in sports.

Article 10. States shall urge all their regional, provincial and other authorities to take whatever steps are necessary to ensure the strict compliance with the provisions of this Declaration.

Article 11. States agree to use their best endeavours to terminate the practice of *apartheid* in sports, in accordance with the principles contained in this Declaration and, to this end, States agree to work towards the prompt preparation and adoption of an international convention against *apartheid* in sports based on the principles contained in this Declaration which would include sanctions for violation of its terms.

Article 12. 1. States and international, regional and national sports bodies shall actively support projects, undertaken in collaboration with the Organization of African Unity and the South African liberation movements recognized by it, towards the formation of non-racial teams truly representative of South Africa.

2. To this end, States and all appropriate organizations shall encourage, assist and recognize genuine non-racial sports bodies in South Africa endorsed by the Special Committee against *Apartheid,* the Organization of African Unity and the South African liberation movements recognized by it.

3. States shall also give active support to sportsmen and sports administrators in their opposition to *apartheid* in sports.

Article 13. International, regional and national sports bodies shall uphold the Olympic principle and cease all sports contact with the racist *apartheid* sports bodies.

Article 14. International sports bodies shall not impose financial or other penalties on affiliated bodies which, in accordance with United Nations resolutions and the spirit of the Olympic Charter, refuse to participate in sports contact with any country practising *apartheid.*

Article 15. National sports bodies shall take appropriate action to persuade their international federation to exclude racist *apartheid* sports bodies from membership and from all international activities.

Article 16. All national Olympic committees shall declare their opposition to *apartheid* in sports and to sports contact with South Africa, and shall actively encourage all affiliates and constituent members to end all sports contact with South Africa.

Article 17. The provisions of this Declaration concerning the boycott of South African sports teams shall not apply to non-racial sports bodies endorsed by the Special Committee against *Apartheid,* the Organization of African Unity and the South African liberation movements recognized by it and their members.

Article 18. All international, regional and national sports bodies and Olympic committees shall endorse the principles of this Declaration and support and uphold all provisions contained therein.

SEE ALSO *International Convention against* Apartheid *in Sports.*

INTERNATIONAL FEDERATION OF BUSINESS AND PROFESSIONAL WOMEN. An international non-governmental organization in consultative status with the UN Economic and Social Council (Category I) and with ILO, UNESCO, and the Council of Europe.

Established as an international organization in 1930, the federation has 76 affiliated organizations in 67 countries, with an individual membership of approximately 250,000. Its main function is to encourage women and girls to acquire advanced education land occupational training. It also strives for equal opportunities for all and for improved status for women in all phases of economic, civil, and political life.

To accomplish these goals, the federation employs concerted action to press governments to ratify such instruments as the CONVENTION ON THE ELIMINATION OF ALL FORMS OF DISCRIMINATION AGAINST WOMEN, makes statements on women's rights to organs within the United Nations system, and issue general statements in support of peace and in condemnation of *apartheid.*

IFBPW publishes two journals, the quarterly *Widening Horizons* and the monthly *Circular.* In addition, it gives wide circulation to the proceedings and the resolutions of its conferences.

International Federation of Business and Professional Women. Address: Cloisters House, 8 Battersea Park Rd., SW 8 4 BG, UK. Telephone: (44.1) 738-8323. Cable: PROFED LONDON SW 8. Fax: (44.1) 738-8325. General Secretary: Marianne Haslegrave.

INTERNATIONAL FEDERATION OF HUMAN RIGHTS. An international non-governmental organization in consultative status with the UN Economic and Social Council (Category II) and with UNESCO and the Council of Europe, best known by its French title, *Federation internationale des droits de l'homme* (FIDH), the federation has a membership of national leagues or associations in or from 36 countries.

FIDH is primarily concerned with the application of the UNIVERSAL DECLARATION ON HUMAN RIGHTS and with disseminating in all countries the principles of justice, liberty, and equality laid down in the French declarations of the rights of man of 1789 and 1793. It specializes in sending missions to countries (more than 125 missions to more than 50 countries since 1960) in which human rights violations are reported; these missions of inquiry and observation have in many cases resulted in improvements in the realization of human rights in such countries.

FIDH publishes reports of its investigative missions, the weekly *La lettre de la FIDH,* and the *Revue annuelle de la Fédération internationale des droits de l'homme.*

International Federation of Human Rights. Address: 27 rue Jean-Dolent, 75014 Paris, France. Telephone: (1) 43.31.94.95. President: Etienne Jaudel.

INTERNATIONAL FEDERATION OF NEWSPAPER PUBLISHERS. A non-governmental organization in consultative status with the UN Economic and Social Council (Roster), and with UNESCO, also known by its French title, *Fédération internationale des éditeurs de journaux (FIEJ),* the federation is a union of national organizations of newspaper publishers and directors (full members) and individuals (associate members). It has members in 24 countries.

Founded in Paris in 1948, the federation promotes the free flow of ideas by word and image and defends freedom of information. It also works to safeguard the ethical and economic interests of the press by studying and supporting all means to promote press activities. It holds an annual congress.

The federation publishes the quarterly *FIEJ Bulletin* in French and English.

International Federation of Newspaper Publishers. Address: 6 rue du Faubourg Poissonnière, F-75010 Paris, France. Telephone: (33-1) 45-23-38-88. Director: Timothy Balding.

Yearbook of International Organizations 1989/90 (K. G. Saur).

INTERNATIONAL FEDERATION OF RURAL ADULT CATHOLIC MOVEMENTS. An international non-governmental organization in consultative status with the UN Economic and Social Council (Roster), and with UNESCO, the federation has affiliated and associated movements in 39 countries and territories.

Founded in 1964 at Fatima, Portugal, the International Federation of Rural Adult Catholic Movements promotes a life-long human and Christian education of rural adults, thereby contributing to the development of rural populations. The federation holds a quadrennial general assembly and continental regional sessions between assemblies. It publishes the quarterly *Cahiers du monde rural* in English, French, Portuguese, and Spanish; and *Voix du monde rural* in English, French, Portuguese, and Spanish.

International Federation of Rural Adult Catholic Movements. Secretary-General: Joseph Pirson. Address: Rue Africaine 92, B-1050 Brussels, Belgium. Telephone: (32-2) 538-78-42.

Yearbook of International Organizations 1989/90 (K. G. Saur).

INTERNATIONAL FEDERATION OF SOCIAL WORKERS. An international non-governmental organization in consultative status with the UN Economic and Social Council (Category II) and with UNESCO, WHO, OAS, and the Council of Europe, IFSW has as members national associations of social workers in 49 countries.

A successor to the International Permanent Secretariat of Social Workers which was launched in Paris in 1928, the International Federation of Social Workers was established in 1956 at the Munich International Conference on Social Welfare. Its principal activities are to promote social work as a profession, to represent that profession on the international level, to organize international symposia and regional seminars for discussion of the problems of social workers. In addition, IFSW has assisted in liberating social workers held as prisoners of conscience in Chile, the Philippines, and South Africa. In 1987, it was awarded the designation as "Peace Messenger" by the UN Secretary General in connection with the observance of the International Year of Peace.

Among its publications, IFSW issues the quarterly journal *International Social Work,* the triannual *IFSW Newsletter,* the International Social Workers Code of Ethics, and Policy Paper on Human Rights.

International Federation of Social Workers. Address: 33 rue de l'Athénée, CH-1206 Geneva, Switzerland. Telephone: (22) 47.12.36. Telex: 423118A TXC CH FOR APOSTOL. Secretary General: Andrew Mouravieff-Apostol.

INTERNATIONAL FEDERATION OF THE PERIODICAL PRESS. An international non-governmental organization in consultative status with the UN Economic and Social Council (Roster), and with UNESCO and the Council of Europe, the federation has national sections in 29 countries.

Founded in 1910 in Brussels, the federation develops the interests of the periodical press by supporting freedom in the dissemination of the news, protecting its ethical and material interests, and raising its standards. The federation holds a biennial congress.

International Federation of the Periodical Press. Address: Grosvenor Gardens House, Suite 19, 35-37 Grosvenor Gardens, London SW1W OBS, UK. Telephone: (44-1) 828-13-66. Fax: (44-1) 834-4357. Director: Robin Wharmby.

Yearbook of International Organizations 1989/90 (K. G. Saur).

INTERNATIONAL FEDERATION OF UNIVERSITY WOMEN. An international non-governmental organization in consultative status with the UN Economic and Social Council (Category II), and with UNESCO, the federation was founded in 1919 by women graduates who wanted to do all they could to prevent another catastrophe such as World War I. Since its foundation, IFUW has been concerned and active in education, the advancement of women, and the promotion of international understanding, working primarily for the elimination of all forms of discrimination against women. IFUW undertakes studies and compiles reports dealing with the legal, social, economic, and educational status of women. Individual national affiliates (of which there are 50, representing some 230,000 university women internationally) carry out a variety of activities: vocational guidance for school-aged girls, literacy projects, adult education, self-help training for rural women, hostels for working young women and students, child care, and scholarships—among other endeavors.

IFUW publishes the *IFUW Newsletter* annually in English, French, and Spanish; and publishes irregularly the *IFUW Communiqué* in English and French.

International Federation of University Women. Address: 37 Quai Wilson CH-1201 Geneva, Switzerland. Telephone: (41-22) 31-23-80. Cable: Ifederuw. Secretary General: Dorothy Davies.

INTERNATIONAL FEDERATION OF WOMEN IN LEGAL CAREERS. An international non-governmental organization in consultative status with the UN Economic and Social Council (Category II), and

with ILO, UNESCO, and FAO, the federation's membership includes national associations in 72 countries as well as individual members.

Founded in 1929, the federation works to establish relations between women of all countries and to promote their access to all careers in the legal profession. IFWLC also studies on an international level the various rules of law, particularly those relating to the family and the individual, with a view to putting forward a law of the individual and of the family equally acceptable in all countries. It sets up mutual aid and legal research projects for women who are students of law, economics, or social or political sciences from developing countries, particularly Africa. It also campaigns to publicize questions such as the prostitution of children, the legal rights of women in rural areas, and the problems of migrant workers and their families.

IFWLC publishes the *IFWLC Bulletin* (quarterly) in English and French. Other publications include the *Dictionaire international des professions juridiques, Some Aspects of Family, Children whose Parents are in Prison,* and *Information Tour on the Human Rights Situation in Chile, Argentina, Uruguay, Paraguay and Brazil.*

International Federation of Women in Legal Careers. Address: Ms. Brugiatelli, FIFCJ, Via R Giovagnoli 6, 1-10052 Roma, Italy.

INTERNATIONAL FEDERATION OF WOMEN LAWYERS. An international non-governmental organization in consultative status with the UN Economic and Social Council (Category II), and with ILO and UNESCO, the federation has affiliated organizations and individual members in 66 countries.

Founded in 1944 in Mexico City during the third Conference of the Inter-American Bar Association, IFWL works to establish friendly international relations on a basis of equality and mutual respect of all peoples, to promote the principles and aims of the United Nations in their legal and social aspects, and to enhance and promote the welfare of women and children. To assist in this work, it has established a number of standing committees, including committees on comparative civil and commercial law, on domestic relations, on immigration, on nationality and naturalization, and on the legal status of women.

IFWL publishes *La Abogada Newsletter* six times a year, for distribution to its members; and occasionally issues *La Abogada Internacional.*

International Federation of Women Lawyers. Address: 186 Fifth Avenue, New York, NY 10010 (USA). President: Angela Cuevas de Dolmetsch.

Yearbook of International Organizations 1989/90 (K. G. Saur).

INTERNATIONAL FELLOWSHIP OF RECONCILIATION. An international non-governmental organization in consultative status with the UN Economic and Social Council (Category II), and with UNESCO. As inter-religious movement, the fellowship is committed to non-violence as a principle of life for a world community of peace and liberation. Founded in Holland in 1919, IFOR now has over 100,000 members internationally in 30 affiliated branches. The abolition of war has long been an IFOR goal, and the group advocates total disarmament and works for the creation of nuclear-weapon-free zones as steps toward disarmament. IFOR also strives for solidarity among peoples and non-violent change and works for human rights for all peoples. The fellowship has given special attention to working for the release of "prisoners of peace"—those arrested and imprisoned for their human rights and non-violence. Through coordinated efforts, including petitions, letter-writing campaigns, and visits with government officials, IFOR has helped to free political prisoners in Argentina, Vietnam, and South Africa. Adolfo Perez Esquivel, 1980 Nobel Peace Prize winner, was the focus of such an IFOR campaign that began with his imprisonment in 1977.

Five times annually, IFOR publishes *Reconciliation International.*

International Fellowship of Reconciliation. Address: Spoorstraat 38, 1815 BK, Alkmaar, Holland. Telephone: 072-12-30-14. General Secretary: David Atwood.

INTERNATIONAL HELSINKI FEDERATION FOR HUMAN RIGHTS. A non-governmental organization, with NGO relations with the "Watch" groups (AMERICAS WATCH, ASIA WATCH, HELSINKI WATCH, etc.), the federation promotes compliance with the human rights provisions of the HELSINKI ACCORD: FINAL ACT OF THE CONFERENCE ON SECURITY AND COOPERATION IN EUROPE by the 35 States that signed the accord in 1975. The federation gathers information on human rights situations in the signatory countries, acts as a clearinghouse for this information, and publishes reports on its findings.

International Helsinki Federation for Human Rights. Address: Rummelhardtgasse 2/18, A-1090 Vienna, Austria. Telephone: (43-222) 427-387. Executive Director: Gerald Nagler.

Yearbook of International Organizations 1989/90 (K. G. Saur).

INTERNATIONAL HUMANIST AND ETHICAL UNION. An international non-governmental organization in consultative status with the UN Economic and Social Council (Roster) and with UNESCO and the Council of Europe, the union brings together 20 national organizations and more than 3 million individual members.

IHEU endeavors to bring into active association groups and individuals throughout the world interested in promoting ethical and scientific humanism. It stimulates cooperation and the exchange of information between its members in various fields, including human rights and, in 1983, established its own International Humanist *Ombudsman*—since renamed IHEU Commissioner for Human Rights. In addition to investigating and reporting on allegations concerning violations of human rights, the union also deals with infringements of the principle of Church and State and provides legal services to persons in need.

IHEU issues the quarterly publication *International Humanist.* It also issues the proceedings of its congresses.

International Humanist and Ethical Union. Address: Oudkerkhof 11, 3512 Utrecht, Netherlands. Telephone: 030-312155. Telex: 70104 human nl. Executive Director: Ernst van Brakel.

INTERNATIONAL HUMAN RIGHTS INTERNSHIP PROGRAM. An international non-governmental organization in consultative status with the UN Economic and Social Council (Roster), the program was initiated in 1976 with a grant from the Ford Foundation. Its purpose is to strengthen human rights structures and education by the placement of interns with organizations concerned with the international protection of human rights.

Since its inception, IHRIP has assisted more than 125 individuals in 45 human rights organizations in Asia, Africa, Europe, Latin America, and North America, providing them with practical training in the implementation of human rights and strengthening the network of human rights workers. Fellows participate in programs of the host organizations for a period of one year.

International Human Rights Internship Program. Address: 229-19th Ave. South, Minneapolis, MN 55455 (USA). Telephone: (1-612) 625-5027. Chairman: David Weissbrodt.

INTERNATIONAL INDIAN TREATY COUNCIL. An international non-governmental organization in consultative status (Category II) with the UN Economic and Social Council, the council includes representatives from 98 Indian nations in the Americas.

Founded in 1974 in the United States of America, the council works to inform the international community about treaty rights of Indians of the western hemisphere and about human rights violations and denial of land rights of this indigenous people. IITC publishes the *IITC Newsletter.*

International Indian Treaty Council. Address: 1529 Folsom St., San Francisco, CA 94103 (USA). Telephone: (1-415) 863-7733. Executive Director: William Means.

Yearbook of International Organizations 1989/90 (K. G. Saur).

INTERNATIONAL INSTITUTE OF HUMANITARIAN LAW. An international non-governmental organization in consultative status with the UN Economic and Social Council (Category II) and with UNESCO and the Council of Europe, the institute was founded in San Remo, Italy, in September 1970, to reaffirm, develop, and disseminate the principles of international humanitarian law, which is primarily concerned with the protection of combatants and civilians and the protection of refugees, in time of war. It organizes courses on the law of armed conflicts and on international refugee law. It is also concerned with protection of the rights of victims of disasters and migrations.

IIHL conducts an extensive publications program and disseminates documentation generated by its program of conferences, symposia, round-tables, and meetings of experts. Its publications include *International Protection of Refugees in Armed Conflicts* (1981), *International Humanitarian Law of Coerced Movements of People across State Boundaries* (1983), *The Status of Refugees in Denmark* (1985), and *El Derecho de los Refugiados y el Articulo 2 de la Convencion Americana sobre Derechos Humanos* (1987).

International Institute of Humanitarian Law. Address: Villa Nobel, Corso Cavallotti 112, 18038 San Remo, Italy. Telephone: 184-690848. Cable: HUMANLAW SANREMO. Secretary-General: Dr. Ugo Genesio.

INTERNATIONAL INSTITUTE ON AGING. The institute, authorized by the UN Economic and Social Council in 1987 (resolution 1987/41), was inaugurated by the UN secretary-general on 15 April 1988. With headquarters in Valletta, Malta, the institute is funded from voluntary contributions by govern-

ments, non-governmental organizations, and philanthropic institutions and individuals.

The institute provides training in gerontology to policymakers, planners, program executives, educators, scientists, professionals, and para-professionals. It promotes cooperation on various aspects of AGING and analyzes and disseminates information on aging to the developing countries. It operates under the direction of an international board, which formulates principles and guidelines for its activities, approves its work program and budget, and assists in fundraising activities. The UN secretary-general has appointed the director-general of the United Nations office at Vienna as chairperson of the board.

INTERNATIONAL LABOR CONFERENCE. The popular name of the General Conference of the INTERNATIONAL LABOR ORGANIZATION, established and functioning in accordance with provisions of the INTERNATIONAL LABOR ORGANIZATION CONSTITUTION (articles 2–6).

INTERNATIONAL LABOR OFFICE. The Office, which comprises the staff of the INTERNATIONAL LABOR ORGANIZATION, consists of more than 3,000 international civil servants appointed and directed by the Director-General under regulations approved by the governing body. In accordance with the INTERNATIONAL LABOR ORGANIZATION CONSTITUTION, the responsibilities of the Director-General and of the staff are exclusively international in character (article 9). Their main functions include the collection and distribution of information on all subjects relating to the international adjustment of conditions of industrial life and labor, particularly the examination of subjects which it is proposed to bring before the International Labor Conference with a view to the conclusion of international conventions and the conduct of such investigations as may be ordered by the conference or by the governing body (article 10).

INTERNATIONAL LABOR ORGANIZATION. In accordance with the INTERNATIONAL LABOR ORGANIZATION CONSTITUTION of 1919, the ILO was established as an autonomous permanent intergovernmental organization mandated to promote world wide programs to achieve (1) full employment and the raising of standards of living; (2) the employment of workers in occupations in which they can have the satisfaction of giving the fullest measure of their skill and attainments and can make their contribution to the common well-being; (3) the provision, as a means to attaining this end, and under adequate guarantees for all concerned, of facilities for training and the transfer of labor, including migration for employment and settlement; (4) policies in regard to wages and earnings, hours and other conditions of work, calculated to insure a just share of the fruits of progress to all, and a minimum living wage to all employed and in need of such protection; (5) the effective recognition of the right of collective bargaining, the cooperation of management and labor in the continuous improvement of productive efficiency, and the collaboration of workers and employers in the preparation and application of social and economic measures; (6) the extension of social security measures to provide a basic income to all in need of such protection and comprehensive medical care; (7) adequate protection for the life and health of workers in all occupations; (8) provision for child welfare and maternity protection; (9) the provision of adequate nutrition, housing, and facilities for recreation and culture; and (10) the assurance of equality of educational and vocational opportunity. A complete list of all ILO documents, known as the International Labor Code, adopted to accomplish the ILO's mandate, can be found in **APPENDIX E.**

A total of 151 States are members of the International Labor Organization: they include all States members of the United Nations with the exceptions of Albania, Bhutan, Gambia, Maldives, Oman, St. Christopher and Nevis, St. Vincent, South Africa, and Vanuatu; and San Marino, Switzerland, and Namibia (formerly represented by the UN Council for Namibia). ILO's main organs are the General Conference, composed of representatives of each member State, and the Governing Body composed of 56 members— 28 of them representing governments, 14 representing employees, and 14 representing employers. The conference elects members of the Governing Body, sets international labor standards by preparing and adopting conventions and recommendations, and provides a forum for the discussion of questions relating to the treatment of labor. The Governing Body elects the director-general, establishes administrative policy and work programs, and supervises the activities of the International Labor Office (the ILO secretariat, headed by the director-general).

The General Conference meets annually for a period of about three weeks, usually at the United Nations office in Geneva during the month of June. The Governing Body holds three sessions per year, the first in February/March, the second in May/June, and the third in November, all in Geneva.

The Governing Body has two standing committees which deal with human rights matters: the ILO FREEDOM OF ASSOCIATION COMMITTEE and the ILO COMMIT-

TEE OF EXPERTS ON THE APPLICATION OF CONVENTIONS AND RECOMMENDATIONS. The former considers and investigates complaints alleging infringement of trade union rights; the latter supervises the application of a number of international instruments that deal with human rights matters, prepared under the auspices of the ILO. In addition, the Governing Body from time to time establishes tri-partite committees to examine representations made under article 24 of the ILO constitution relating to discrimination in employment; most of these allege non-observance of the ILO DISCRIMINATION (EMPLOYMENT AND OCCUPATION) CONVENTION.

INTERNATIONAL LABOR ORGANIZATION: CONSTITUTION (1919).

Originally adopted as Part 13 of the Treaty of Versailles, which concluded World War I, the ILO constitution entered into force along with that treaty on 10 January 1920, its membership consisting of all member States of the LEAGUE OF NATIONS. After the league ceased to function, the ILO constitution was amended by the addition of the "Declaration Concerning the Aims and Purposes of the International Labor Organization," popularly known as the "Philadelphia Declaration," adopted by the International Labor Conference (26th session), convened in Philadelphia, on 10 May 1944.

The ILO's main function is to advance the economic and social welfare of working people throughout the world. It accomplishes this by establishing high international labor standards and by supervising the realization of those standards in its member States. Over the years, it has continuously sought to protect the right to work, to put an end to certain forms of forced or compulsory labor, and to ensure enjoyment of the right to form and join trade unions.

The ILO is unique among international organizations because its main organs include delegates representing workers and employers as well as delegates representing States. Thus, the INTERNATIONAL LABOR CONFERENCE consists of four representatives from each member State, of whom two are government delegates and the remaining two represent employers and workers. Similarly, the ILO Governing Body is composed of 48 persons, of whom 24 represent governments, 12 represent employers, and 12 represent workers.

The text of the ILO constitution, as amended (United Nations, *Treaty Series,* vol. 466, p. 323) is as follows:

Preamble

Whereas universal and lasting peace can be established only if it is based upon social justice;

And whereas conditions of labour exist involving such injustice, hardship and privation to large numbers of people as to produce unrest so great that the peace and harmony of the world are imperilled; and an improvement of those conditions is urgently required as, for example, by the regulation of the hours of work, including the establishment of a maximum working day and week, the regulation of the labour supply, the prevention of unemployment, the provision of an adequate living wage, the protection of the worker against sickness, disease and injury arising out of his employment, the protection of children, young persons and women, provision for old age and injury, protection of the interests of workers when employed in countries other than their own, recognition of the priniciple of equal remuneration for work of equal value, recognition of the principle of freedom of association, the organisation of vocational and technical education and other measures;

Whereas also the failure of any nation to adopt humane conditions of labour is an obstacle in the way of other nations which desire to improve the conditions in their own countries;

The High Contracting Parties, moved by sentiments of justice and humanity as well as by the desire to secure the permanent peace of the world, and with a view to attaining the objectives set forth in the Preamble, agree to the following Constitution of the International Labour Organisation:

Chapter I—Organisation

Article 1. 1. A permanent organisation is hereby established for the promotion of the objects set forth in the Preamble to this Constitution and in the Declaration concerning the aims and purposes of the International Labour Organisation adopted at Philadelphia on 10 May 1944 the text of which is annexed to this Constitution.

2. The Members of the International Labour Organisation shall be the States which were Members of the Organisation on 1 November 1945, and such other States as may become Members in pursuance of the provisions of paragraphs 3 and 4 of this article.

3. Any original Member of the United Nations and any State admitted to membership of the United Nations by a decision of the General Assembly in accordance with the provisions of the Charter may become a Member of the International Labour Organisation by communicating to the Director-General of the International Labour Office its formal acceptance of the obligations of the Constitution of the International Labour Organisation.

4. The General Conference of the International Labour Organisation may also admit Members to the Organisation by a vote concurred in by two-thirds of the delegates attending the session, including two-thirds of the Government delegates present and voting. Such admission shall take effect on the communication to the Director-General of the International Labour Office by the government of the new Member of its formal acceptance of the obligations of the Constitution of the Organisation.

5. No Member of the International Labour Organisation may withdraw from the Organisation without giving notice of its intention so to do to the Director-General of the International Labour Office. Such notice shall take effect two years after the date of its reception by the Director-General, subject to the Member having at that time fulfilled all financial obligations arising out of its membership. When a Member has ratified any international labour Convention, such withdrawal shall not affect the continued validity for the period provided for in the Convention of all obligations arising thereunder or relating thereto.

6. In the event of any State having ceased to be a Member of the Organisation, its readmission to membership shall be governed by the provisions of paragraph 3 or paragraph 4 of this article as the case may be.

Article 2. The permanent organisation shall consist of—

(a) a General Conference of representatives of the Members;

(b) a Governing Body composed as described in article 7; and

(c) an International Labour Office controlled by the Governing Body.

Article 3. 1. The meetings of the General Conference of representatives of the Members shall be held from time to time as occasion may require, and at least once in every year. It shall be composed of four representatives of each of the Members, of whom two shall be Government delegates and the two others shall be delegates representing respectively the employers and the workpeople of each of the Members.

2. Each delegate may be accompanied by advisers, who shall not exceed two in number for each item on the agenda of the meeting. When questions specially affecting women are to be considered by the Conference, one at least of the advisers should be a woman.

3. Each Member which is responsible for the international relations of non-metropolitan territories may appoint as additional advisers to each of its delegates—

(a) persons nominated by it as representatives of any such territory in regard to matters within the self-governing powers of that territory; and

(b) persons nominated by it to advise its delegates in regard to matters concerning non-self-governing territories.

4. In the case of a territory under the joint authority of two or more Members, persons may be nominated to advise the delegates of such Members.

5. The Members undertake to nominate non-Government delegates and advisers chosen in agreement with the industrial organisations, if such organisations exist, which are most representative of employers or workpeople, as the case may be, in their respective countries.

6. Advisers shall not speak except on a request made by the delegate whom they accompany and by the special authorisation of the President of the Conference, and may not vote.

7. A delegate may by notice in writing addressed to the President appoint one of his advisers to act as his deputy, and the adviser, while so acting, shall be allowed to speak and vote.

8. The names of the delegates and their advisers will be communicated to the International Labour Office by the government of each of the Members.

9. The credentials of delegates and their advisers shall be subject to scrutiny by the Conference, which may, by two-thirds of the votes cast by the delegates present, refuse to admit any delegate or adviser whom it deems not to have been nominated in accordance with this article.

Article 4. 1. Every delegate shall be entitled to vote individually on all matters which are taken into consideration by the Conference.

2. If one of the Members fails to nominate one of the non-Government delegates whom it is entitled to nominate, the other non-Government delegate shall be allowed to sit and speak at the Conference, but not to vote.

3. If in accordance with article 3 the Conference refuses admission to a delegate of one of the Members, the provisions of the present article shall apply as if that delegate had not been nominated.

Article 5. The meetings of the Conference shall, subject to any decisions which may have been taken by the Conference itself at a previous meeting, be held at such place as may be decided by the Governing Body.

Article 6. Any change in the seat of the International Labour Office shall be decided by the Conference by a two-thirds majority of the votes cast by the delegates present.

Article 7. 1. The Governing Body shall consist of forty-eight persons—Twenty-four representing governments, Twelve representing the employers, and Twelve representing the workers.

2. Of the twenty-four persons representing governments, ten shall be appointed by the Members of chief industrial importance, and fourteen shall be appointed by the Members selected for that purpose by the Government delegates to the Conference, excluding the delegates of the ten Members mentioned above.

3. The Governing Body shall as occasion requires determine which are the Members of the Organisation of chief industrial importance and shall make rules to ensure that all questions relating to the selection of the Members of chief industrial importance are considered by an impartial committee before being decided by the Governing Body. Any appeal made by a Member from the declaration of the Governing Body as to which are the Members of chief industrial importance shall be decided by the Conference, but an appeal to the Conference shall not suspend the application of the declaration until such time as the Conference decides the appeal.

4. The persons representing the employers and the persons representing the workers shall be elected respectively by the Employers' delegates and the Workers' delegates to the Conference.

5. The period of office of the Governing Body shall be three years. If for any reason the Governing Body elections do not take place on the expiry of this period, the Governing Body shall remain in office until such elections are held.

6. The method of filling vacancies and of appointing substitutes and other similar questions may be decided by the Governing Body subject to the approval of the Conference.

7. The Governing Body shall, from time to time, elect from its number a chairman and two vice-chairmen, of whom one shall be a person representing a government, one a person representing the employers, and one a person representing the workers.

8. The Governing Body shall regulate its own procedure and shall fix its own times of meeting. A special meeting shall be held if a written request to that effect is made by at least sixteen of the representatives on the Governing Body.

Article 8. 1. There shall be a Director-General of the International Labour Office, who shall be appointed by the Governing Body, and, subject to the instructions of the Governing Body, shall be responsible for the efficient conduct of the International Labour Office and for such other duties as may be assigned to him.

2. The Director-General or his deputy shall attend all meetings of the Governing Body.

Article 9. 1. The staff of the International Labour Office shall be appointed by the Director-General under regulations approved by the Governing Body.

2. So far as is possible with due regard to the efficiency of the work of the Office, the Director-General shall select persons of different nationalities.

3. A certain number of these persons shall be women.

4. The responsibilities of the Director-General and the staff shall be exclusively international in character. In the performance of their duties, the Director-General and the staff shall not seek or receive instructions from any government or from any other authority external to the Organisation. They shall refrain from any action which might reflect on their position as international officials responsible only to the Organisation.

5. Each Member of the Organisation undertakes to respect the exclusively international character of the responsibilities of the Director-General and the staff and not to seek to influence them in the discharge of their responsibilities.

Article 10. 1. The functions of the International Labour Office shall include the collection and distribution of information on all subjects relating to the international adjustment of conditions of industrial life and labour, and particularly the examination of subjects which it is proposed to bring before the Conference with a view to the conclusion of international Conventions, and the conduct of such special investigations as may be ordered by the Conference or by the Governing Body.

2. Subject to such directions as the Governing Body may give, the Office shall—

(a) prepare the documents on the various items of the agenda for the meetings of the Conference;

(b) accord to governments at their request all appropriate assistance within its power in connection with the framing of laws and regulations on the basis of the decisions of the Conference and the improvement of administrative practices and systems of inspection;

(c) carry out the duties required of it by the provisions of this Constitution in connection with the effective observance of Conventions;

(d) edit and issue, in such languages as the Governing Body may think desirable, publications dealing with problems of industry and employment of international interest.

3. Generally, it shall have such other powers and duties as may be assigned to it by the Conference or by the Governing Body.

Article 11. The government departments of any of the Members which deal with questions of industry and employment may communicate directly with the Director-General through the representative of their government on the Governing Body of the International Labour Office or, failing any such representative, through such other qualified official as the government may nominate for the purpose.

Article 12. 1. The International Labour Organisation shall cooperate within the terms of this Constitution with any general international organisation entrusted with the coordination of the activities of public international organisations having specialised responsibilities and with public international organisations having specialised responsibilities in related fields.

2. The International Labour Organisation may make appropriate arrangements for the representatives of public international organisations to participate without vote in its deliberations.

3. The International Labour Organisation may make suitable arrangements for such consultation as it may think desirable with recognised non-governmental international

organisations, including international organisations of employers, workers, agriculturists and co-operators.

Article 13. 1. The International Labour Organisation may make such financial and budgetary arrangements with the United Nations as may appear appropriate.

2. Pending the conclusion of such arrangements or if at any time no such arrangements are in force—

(a) each of the Members will pay the travelling and subsistence expenses of its delegates and their advisers and of its representatives attending the meetings of the Conference or the Governing Body, as the case may be;

(b) all other expenses of the International Labour Office and of the meetings of the Conference or Governing Body shall be paid by the Director-General of the International Labour Office out of the general funds of the International Labour Organisation;

(c) the arrangements for the approval, allocation and collection of the budget of the International Labour Organisation shall be determined by the Conference by a two-thirds majority of the votes cast by the delegates present, and shall provide for the approval of the budget and of the arrangements for the allocation of expenses among the Members of the Organisation by a committee of Government representatives.

3. The expenses of the International Labour Organisation shall be borne by the Members in accordance with the arrangements in force in virtue of paragraph 1 or paragraph 2 (c) of this article.

4. A Member of the Organisation which is in arrears in the payment of its financial contribution to the Organisation shall have no vote in the Conference, in the Governing Body, in any committee, or in the elections of members of the Governing Body, if the amount of its arrears equals or exceeds the amount of the contributions due from it for the preceding two full years: Provided that the Conference may by a two-thirds majority of the votes cast by the delegates present permit such a Member to vote if it is satisfied that the failure to pay is due to conditions beyond the control of the Member.

5. The Director-General of the International Labour Office shall be responsible to the Governing Body for the proper expenditure of the funds of the International Labour Organisation.

Chapter II—Procedure

Article 14. 1. The agenda for all meetings of the Conference will be settled by the Governing Body, which shall consider any suggestion as to the agenda that may be made by the government of any of the Members or by any representative organisation recognised for the purpose of article 3, or by any public international organisation.

2. The Governing Body shall make rules to ensure thorough technical preparation and adequate consultation of the Members primarily concerned, by means of a preparatory conference or otherwise, prior to the adoption of a Convention or Recommendation by the Conference.

Article 15. 1. The Director-General shall act as the Secretary-General of the Conference, and shall transmit the agenda so as to reach the Members four months before the meeting of the Conference, and through them, the non-Government delegates when appointed.

2. The reports on each item of the agenda shall be dispatched so as to reach the Members in time to permit adequate consideration before the meeting of the Conference.

The Governing Body shall make rules for the application of this provision.

Article 16. 1. Any of the governments of the Members may formally object to the inclusion of any item or items in the agenda. The grounds for such objection shall be set forth in a statement addressed to the Director-General who shall circulate it to all the Members of the Organisation.

2. Items to which such objection has been made shall not, however, be excluded from the agenda, if at the Conference a majority of two-thirds of the votes cast by the delegates present is in favour of considering them.

3. If the Conference decides (otherwise than under the preceding paragraph) by two-thirds of the votes cast by the delegates present that any subject shall be considered by the Conference, that subject shall be included in the agenda for the following meeting.

Article 17. 1. The Conference shall elect a president and three vice-presidents. One of the vice-presidents shall be a Government delegate, one an Employers' delegate and one a Workers' delegate. The Conference shall regulate its own procedure and may appoint committees to consider and report on any matter.

2. Except as otherwise expressly provided in this Constitution or by the terms of any Convention or other instrument conferring powers on the Conference or of the financial and budgetary arrangements adopted in virtue of article 13, all matters shall be decided by a simple majority of the votes cast by the delegates present.

3. The voting is void unless the total number of votes cast is equal to half the number of the delegates attending the Conference.

Article 18. The Conference may add to any committees which it appoints technical experts without power to vote.

Article 19. 1. When the Conference has decided on the adoption of proposals with regard to an item on the agenda, it will rest with the Conference to determine whether these proposals should take the form: (a) of an international Convention, or (b) of a Recommendation to meet circumstances where the subject, or aspect of it, dealt with is not considered suitable or appropriate at that time for a Convention.

2. In either case a majority of two-thirds of the votes cast by the delegates present shall be necessary on the final vote for the adoption of the Convention or Recommendation, as the case may be, by the Conference.

3. In framing any Convention or Recommendation of general application the Conference shall have due regard to those countries in which climatic conditions, the imperfect development of industrial organisation, or other special circumstances make the industrial conditions substantially different and shall suggest the modifications, if any, which it considers may be required to meet the case of such countries.

4. Two copies of the Convention or Recommendation shall be authenticated by the signatures of the President of the Conference and of the Director-General. Of these copies one shall be deposited in the archives of the International Labour Office and the other with the Secretary-General of the United Nations. The Director-General will communicate a certified copy of the Convention or Recommendation to each of the Members.

5. In the case of a Convention—

(a) the Convention will be communicated to all Members for ratification;

(b) each of the Members undertakes that it will, within the period of one year at most from the closing of the session of the Conference, or if it is impossible owing to exceptional circumstances to do so within the period of one year, then at the earliest practicable moment and in no case later than 18 months from the closing of the session of the Conference, bring the Convention before the authority or authorities within whose competence the matter lies, for the enactment of legislation or other action;

(c) Members shall inform the Director-General of the International Labour Office of the measures taken in accordance with this article to bring the Convention before the said competent authority or authorities, with particulars of the authority or authorities regarded as competent, and of the action taken by them;

(d) if the Member obtains the consent of the authority or authorities within whose competence the matter lies, it will communicate the formal ratification of the Convention to the Director-General and will take such action as may be necessary to make effective the provisions of such Convention;

(e) if the Member does not obtain the consent of the authority or authorities within whose competence the matter lies, no further obligation shall rest upon the Member except that it shall report to the Director-General of the International Labour Office, at appropriate intervals as requested by the Governing Body, the position of its law and practice in regard to the matters dealt with in the Convention, showing the extent to which effect has been given, or is proposed to be given, to any of the provisions of the Convention by legislation, administrative action, collective agreement or otherwise and stating the difficulties which prevent or delay the ratification of such Convention.

6. In the case of a Recommendation—

(a) the Recommendation will be communicated to all Members for their consideration with a view to effect being given to it by national legislation or otherwise;

(b) each of the Members undertakes that it will, within a period of one year at most from the closing of the session of the Conference, or if it is impossible owing to exceptional circumstances to do so within the period of one year, then at the earliest practicable moment and in no case later than 18 months after the closing of the Conference, bring the Recommendation before the authority or authorities within whose competence the matter lies for the enactment of legislation or other action;

(c) the Members shall inform the Director-General of the International Labour Office of the measures taken in accordance with this article to bring the Recommendation before the said competent authority or authorities with particulars of the authority or authorities regarded as competent, and of the action taken by them;

(d) apart from bringing the Recommendation before the said competent authority or authorities, no further obligation shall rest upon the Members, except that they shall report to the Director-General of the International Labour Office, at appropriate intervals as requested by the Governing Body, the position of the law and practice in their country in regard to the matters dealt with in the Recommendation, showing the extent to which effect has been given, or is proposed to be given, to the provisions of the Recommendation and such modifications of these provisions as it has been found or may be found necessary to make in adopting or applying them.

7. In the case of a federal State, the following provisions shall apply:

(a) in respect of Conventions and Recommendations which the federal government regards as appropriate under its constitutional system for federal action, the obligations of the federal State shall be the same as those of Members which are not federal States;

(b) in respect of Conventions and Recommendations which the federal government regards as appropriate under its constitutional system, in whole or in part, for action by the constituent states, provinces, or cantons rather than for federal action, the federal government shall—

(i) make, in accordance with its Constitution and the Constitutions of the states, provinces or cantons concerned, effective arrangements for the reference of such Conventions and Recommendations not later than 18 months from the closing of the session of the Conference to the appropriate federal, state, provincial or cantonal authorities for the enactment of legislation or other action;

(ii) arrange, subject to the concurrence of the state, provincial or cantonal governments concerned, for periodical consultations between the federal and the state, provincial or cantonal authorities with a view to promoting within the federal State co-ordinated action to give effect to the provisions of such Conventions and Recommendations;

(iii) inform the Director-General of the International Labour Office of the measures taken in accordance with this article to bring such Conventions and Recommendations before the appropriate federal, state, provincial or cantonal authorities with particulars of the authorities regarded as appropriate and of the action taken by them;

(iv) in respect of each such Convention which it has not ratified, report to the Director-General of the International Labour Office, at appropriate intervals as requested by the Governing Body, the position of the law and practice of the federation and its constituent states, provinces or cantons in regard to the Convention, showing the extent to which effect has been given, or is proposed to be given, to any of the provisions of the Convention by legislation, administrative action, collective agreement, or otherwise;

(v) in respect of each such Recommendation, report to the Director-General of the International Labour Office, at appropriate intervals as requested by the Governing Body, the position of the law and practice of the federation and its constituent states, provinces or cantons in regard to the Recommendation, showing the extent to which effect has been given, or is proposed to be given, to the provisions of the Recommendation and such modifications of these provisions as have been found or may be found necessary in adopting or applying them.

8. In no case shall the adoption of any Convention or Recommendation by the Conference, or the ratification of any Convention by any Member, be deemed to affect any law, award, custom or agreement which ensures more favourable conditions to the workers concerned than those provided for in the Convention or Recommendation.

Article 20. Any Convention so ratified shall be communicated by the Director-General of the International Labour Office to the Secretary-General of the United Nations for registration in accordance with the provisions of article 102 of the Charter of the United Nations but shall only be binding upon the Members which ratify it.

Article 21. 1. If any Convention coming before the Conference for final consideration fails to secure the support of two-thirds of the votes cast by the delegates present, it shall nevertheless be within the right of any of the Members of the Organisation to agree to such Convention among themselves.

2. Any Convention so agreed to shall be communicated by the governments concerned to the Director-General of

the International Labour Office and to the Secretary-General of the United Nations for registration in accordance with the provisions of article 102 of the Charter of the United Nations.

Article 22. Each of the Members agrees to make an annual report to the International Labour Office on the measures which it has taken to give effect to the provisions of Conventions to which it is a party. These reports shall be made in such form and shall contain such particulars as the Governing Body may request.

Article 23. 1. The Director-General shall lay before the next meeting of the Conference a summary of the information and reports communicated to him by Members in pursuance of articles 19 and 22.

2. Each Member shall communicate to the representative organisations recognised for the purpose of article 3 copies of the information and reports communicated to the Director-General in pursuance of articles 19 and 22.

Article 24. In the event of any representation being made to the International Labour Office by an industrial association of employers or of workers that any of the Members has failed to secure in any respect the effective observance within its jurisdiction of any Convention to which it is a party, the Governing Body may communicate this representation to the government against which it is made, and may invite that government to make such statement on the subject as it may think fit.

Article 25. If no statement is received within a reasonable time from the government in question, or if the statement when received is not deemed to be satisfactory by the Governing Body, the latter shall have the right to publish the representation and the statement, if any, made in reply to it.

Article 26. 1. Any of the Members shall have the right to file a complaint with the International Labour Office if it is not satisfied that any other Member is securing the effective observance of any Convention which both have ratified in accordance with the foregoing articles.

2. The Governing Body may, if it thinks fit, before referring such a complaint to a Commission of Inquiry, as hereinafter provided for, communicate with the government in question in the manner described in article 24.

3. If the Governing Body does not think it necessary to communicate the complaint to the government in question, or if, when it has made such communication, no statement in reply has been received within a reasonable time which the Governing Body considers to be satisfactory, the Governing Body may appoint a Commission of Inquiry to consider the complaint and to report thereon.

4. The Governing Body may adopt the same procedure either of its own motion or on receipt of a complaint from a delegate to the Conference.

5. When any matter arising out of article 25 or 26 is being considered by the Governing Body, the government in question shall, if not already represented thereon, be entitled to send a representative to take part in the proceedings of the Governing Body while the matter is under consideration. Adequate notice of the date on which the matter will be considered shall be given to the government in question.

Article 27. The Members agree that, in the event of the reference of a complaint to a Commission of Inquiry under article 26, they will each, whether directly concerned in the complaint or not, place at the disposal of the Commission all the information in their possession which bears upon the subject-matter of the complaint.

Article 28. When the Commission of Inquiry has fully considered the complaint, it shall prepare a report embodying its findings on all questions of fact relevant to determining the issue between the parties and containing such recommendations as it may think proper as to the steps which should be taken to meet the complaint and the time within which they should be taken.

Article 29. 1. The Director-General of the International Labour Office shall communicate the report of the Commission of Inquiry to the Governing Body and to each of the governments concerned in the complaint, and shall cause it to be published.

2. Each of these governments shall within three months inform the Director-General of the International Labour Office whether or not it accepts the recommendations contained in the report of the Commission; and if not, whether it proposes to refer the complaint to the International Court of Justice.

Article 30. In the event of any Member failing to take the action required by paragraphs 5 (b), 6 (b) or 7 (b) (i) of article 19 with regard to a Convention or Recommendation, any other Member shall be entitled to refer the matter to the Governing Body. In the event of the Governing Body finding that there has been such a failure, it shall report the matter to the Conference.

Article 31. The decision of the International Court of Justice in regard to a complaint or matter which has been referred to it in pursuance of article 29 shall be final.

Article 32. The International Court of Justice may affirm, vary or reverse any of the findings or recommendations of the Commission of Inquiry, if any.

Article 33. In the event of any Member failing to carry out within the time specified the recommendations, if any, contained in the report of the Commission of Inquiry, or in the decision of the International Court of Justice, as the case may be, the Governing Body may recommend to the Conference such action as it may deem wise and expedient to secure compliance therewith.

Article 34. The defaulting government may at any time inform the Governing Body that it has taken the steps necessary to comply with the recommendations of the Commission of Inquiry or with those in the decision of the International Court of Justice, as the case may be, and may request it to constitute a Commission of Inquiry to verify its contention. In this case the provisions of articles 27, 28, 29, 31 and 32 shall apply, and if the report of the Commission of Inquiry or the decision of the International Court of Justice is in favour of the defaulting government, the Governing Body shall forthwith recommend the discontinuance of any action taken in pursuance of article 33.

Chapter III—General

Article 35. 1. The Members undertake that Conventions which they have ratified in accordance with the provisions of this Constitution shall be applied to the non-metropolitan territories for whose international relations they are responsible, including any trust territories for which they are the administering authority, except where the subject-matter of the Convention is within the self-governing powers of the territory or the Convention is inapplicable owing to the local conditions or subject to such modifications as may be necessary to adapt the Convention to local conditions.

2. Each Member which ratifies a Convention shall as soon as possible after ratification communicate to the

Director-General of the International Labour Office a declaration stating in respect of the territories other than those referred to in paragraphs 4 and 5 below the extent to which it undertakes that the provisions of the Convention shall be applied and giving such particulars as may be prescribed by the Convention.

3. Each Member which has communicated a declaration in virtue of the preceding paragraph may from time to time, in accordance with the terms of the Convention, communicate a further declaration modifying the terms of any former declaration and stating the present position in respect of such territories.

4. Where the subject-matter of the Convention is within the self-governing powers of any non-metropolitan territory the Member responsible for the international relations of that territory shall bring the Convention to the notice of the government of the territory as soon as possible with a view to the enactment of legislation or other action by such government. Thereafter the Member, in agreement with the government of the territory, may communicate to the Director-General of the International Labour Office a declaration accepting the obligations of the Convention on behalf of such territory.

5. A declaration accepting the obligations of any Convention may be communicated to the Director-General of the International Labour Office—

(a) by two or more Members of the Organisation in respect of any territory which is under their joint authority; or

(b) by any international authority responsible for the administration of any territory, in virtue of the Charter of the United Nations or otherwise, in respect of any such territory.

6. Acceptance of the obligations of a Convention in virtue of paragraph 4 or paragraph 5 shall involve the acceptance on behalf of the territory concerned of the obligations stipulated by the terms of the Convention and the obligations under the Constitution of the Organisation which apply to ratified Conventions. A declaration of acceptance may specify such modification of the provisions of the Conventions as may be necessary to adapt the Convention to local conditions.

7. Each Member or international authority which has communicated a declaration in virtue of paragraph 4 or paragraph 5 of this article may from time to time, in accordance with the terms of the Convention, communicate a further declaration modifying the terms of any former declaration or terminating the acceptance of the obligations of the Convention on behalf of the territory concerned.

8. If the obligations of a Convention are not accepted on behalf of a territory to which paragraph 4 or paragraph 5 of this article relates, the Member or Members or international authority concerned shall report to the Director-General of the International Labour Office the position of the law and practice of that territory in regard to the matters dealt with in the Convention and the report shall show the extent to which effect has been given, or is proposed to be given, to any of the provisions of the Convention by legislation, administrative action, collective agreement or otherwise and shall state the difficulties which prevent or delay the acceptance of such Convention.

Article 36. Amendments to this Constitution which are adopted by the Conference by a majority of two-thirds of the votes cast by the delegates present shall take effect when ratified or accepted by two-thirds of the Members of

the Organisation including five of the ten Members which are represented on the Governing Body as Members of chief industrial importance in accordance with the provisions of paragraph 3 of article 7 of this Constitution.

Article 37. 1. Any question or dispute relating to the interpretation of this Constitution or of any subsequent Convention concluded by the Members in pursuance of the provisions of this Constitution shall be referred for decision to the International Court of Justice.

2. Notwithstanding the provisions of paragraph 1 of this article the Governing Body may make and submit to the Conference for approval rules providing for the appointment of a tribunal for the expeditious determination of any dispute or question relating to the interpretation of a Convention which may be referred thereto by the Governing Body or in accordance with the terms of the Convention. Any applicable judgment or advisory opinion of the International Court of Justice shall be binding upon any tribunal established in virtue of this paragraph. Any award made by such a tribunal shall be circulated to the Members of the Organisation and any observations which they may make thereon shall be brought before the Conference.

Article 38. 1. The International Labour Organisation may convene such regional conferences and establish such regional agencies as may be desirable to promote the aims and purposes of the Organisation.

2. The powers, functions and procedure of regional conferences shall be governed by rules drawn up by the Governing Body and submitted to the General Conference for confirmation.

Chapter IV—Miscellaneous Provisions

Article 39. The International Labour Organisation shall possess full juridical personality and in particular the capacity—

(a) to contract;

(b) to acquire and dispose of immovable and movable property;

(c) to institute legal proceedings.

Article 40. 1. The International Labour Organisation shall enjoy in the territory of each of its Members such privileges and immunities as are necessary for the fulfilment of its purposes.

2. Delegates to the Conference, members of the Governing Body and the Director-General and officials of the Office shall likewise enjoy such privileges and immunities as are necessary for the independent exercise of their functions in connection with the Organisation.

3. Such privileges and immunities shall be defined in a separate agreement to be prepared by the Organisation with a view to its acceptance by the States Members.

Annex
Declaration concerning the Aims and Purposes of the International Labour Organisation

The General Conference of the International Labour Organisation, meeting in its Twenty-sixth Session in Philadelphia, hereby adopts, this tenth day of May in the year nineteen hundred and forty-four, the present Declaration of the aims and purposes of the International Labour Organisation and of the principles which should inspire the policy of its Members.

I. The Conference reaffirms the fundamental principles on which the Organisation is based and, in particular, that—

(a) labour is not a commodity;

(b) freedom of expression and of association are essential to sustained progress;

(c) poverty anywhere constitutes a danger to prosperity everywhere;

(d) the war against want requires to be carried on with unrelenting vigour within each nation, and by continuous and concerted international effort in which the representatives of workers and employers, enjoying equal status with those of governments, join with them in free discussion and democratic decision with a view to the promotion of the common welfare.

II. Believing that experience has fully demonstrated the truth of the statement in the Constitution of the International Labour Organisation that lasting peace can be established only if it is based on social justice, the Conference affirms that—

(a) all human beings, irrespective of race, creed or sex, have the right to pursue both their material well-being and their spiritual development in conditions of freedom and dignity, of economic security and equal opportunity;

(b) the attainment of the conditions in which this shall be possible must constitute the central aim of national and international policy;

(c) all national and international policies and measures, in particular those of an economic and financial character, should be judged in this light and accepted only in so far as they may be held to promote and not to hinder the achievement of this fundamental objective;

(d) it is a responsibility of the International Labour Organisation to examine and consider all international economic and financial policies and measures in the light of this fundamental objective;

(e) in discharging the tasks entrusted to it the International Labour Organisation, having considered all relevant economic and financial factors, may include in its decisions and recommendations any provisions which it considers appropriate.

III. The Conference recognises the solemn obligation of the International Labour Organisation to further among the nations of the world programmes which will achieve:

(a) full employment and the raising of standards of living;

(b) the employment of workers in the occupations in which they can have the satisfaction of giving the fullest measure of their skill and attainments and make their greatest contribution to the common well-being;

(c) the provision, as a means to the attainment of this end and under adequate guarantees for all concerned, of facilities for training and the transfer of labour, including migration for employment and settlement;

(d) policies in regard to wages and earnings, hours and other conditions of work calculated to ensure a just share of the fruits of progress to all, and a minimum living wage to all employed and in need of such protection;

(e) the effective recognition of the right of collective bargaining, the co-operation of management and labour in the continuous improvement of productive efficiency, and the collaboration of workers and employers in the preparation and application of social and economic measures;

(f) the extension of social security measures to provide a basic income to all in need of such protection and comprehensive medical care;

(g) adequate protection for the life and health of workers in all occupations;

(h) provision for child welfare and maternity protection;

(i) the provision of adequate nutrition, housing and facilities for recreation and culture;

(j) the assurance of equality of educational and vocational opportunity.

IV. Confident that the fuller and broader utilisation of the world's productive resources necessary for the achievement of the objectives set forth in this Declaration can be secured by effective international and national action, including measures to expand production and consumption, to avoid severe economic fluctuations, to promote the economic and social advancement of the less developed regions of the world, to assure greater stability in world prices of primary products, and to promote a high and steady volume of international trade, the Conference pledges the full co-operation of the International Labour Organisation with such international bodies as may be entrusted with a share of the responsibility for this great task and for the promotion of the health, education and well-being of all peoples.

V. The Conference affirms that the principles set forth in this Declaration are fully applicable to all peoples everywhere and that, while the matter of their application must be determined with due regard to the stage of social and economic development reached by each people, their progressive application to peoples who are still dependent, as well as to those who have already achieved self-government, is a matter of concern to the whole civilised world.

INTERNATIONAL LAW COMMISSION. Established by the Statute of the International Law Commission, adopted by the UN General Assembly on 21 November 1947 (resolution 174 [II]), the commission endeavors to promote the progressive development of international law and its codification. The term "progressive development of international law" is defined in article 15 of the statute as meaning the preparation of draft conventions on subjects which have not been heretofore regulated by international law, or in regard to which the law has not yet sufficiently developed in the practice of States. The term "codification of international law" is defined as meaning the more precise formulation and systemization of rules of international law in fields where there already has been extensive State practice, precedent, and doctrine.

In accordance with the statute, as amended by the General Assembly (resolutions 1103 [XI], 1647 [XVI], and 36/39), the commission consists of 34 members "who shall be persons of recognized competence in international law." Members are elected by the Assembly from a list of candidates nominated by the governments of member States, prepared by the Secretary-General. Under the terms of the statute, the electors bear in mind that the persons chosen should individually possess the qualifications required and that, in the commission as a whole, representation of the main forms of civilization and of the principal legal systems of the world should be insured. Under resolution 36/39, members are elected according to the following pattern: eight nationals from African States; seven from Asian States, three from Eastern European States; six from Latin American States; eight from Western European and other States; one from African or Eastern European States, in rotation; and one from Asian or Latin American States, in rotation. The term of office is five years.

Normally, the Commission holds one session, of 12 weeks' duration, each year at the United Nations European office in Geneva. It has occasionally held meetings at other places, including New York City (first session), Paris (sixth session), and Monaco (2d part of its 17th session). The commission reports annually to the General Assembly.

The commission frequently appoints one of its members as special rapporteur to prepare a study and report on a topic of its agenda and takes action on the basis of such a study or report. It occasionally makes use of a drafting committee composed so as to achieve a balance between its working languages or sets up small working groups or sub-committees to deal with particular topics.

As regards human rights, the commission was responsible for drafting several important international instruments, including the CONVENTION ON THE NATIONALITY OF MARRIED WOMEN, the CONVENTION ON THE REDUCTION OF STATELESSNESS, and the CONVENTION RELATING TO THE STATUS OF STATELESS PERSONS.

On 21 November 1947, the UN General Assembly directed the commission (resolution 177 [II]) to: (a) formulate the principles of international law recognized in the charter of the Nurnberg Tribunal and in the judgment of the tribunal, and (b) prepare a draft code of offenses against the peace and security of mankind, indicating clearly the place to be accorded to the principle mentioned in (a) above.

At its 1950 session, the commission adopted a formulation of the PRINCIPLES OF INTERNATIONAL LAW RECOGNIZED IN THE CHARTER OF THE NURMBERG TRIBUNAL AND IN THE JUDGMENT OF THE TRIBUNAL, and submitted these principles to the General Assembly. In 1954, it completed and submitted to the General Assembly a draft code of offenses against the peace and security of mankind.

At that time, the General Assembly concluded (resolution 897 [IX]) that the draft code formulated by the commission raised questions closely related to those of the definition of AGGRESSION, which it had entrusted to a special committee. It, therefore, postponed consideration of the draft code until the special committee had completed its work.

On 14 December 1974, the assembly adopted (resolution 3314 [XXIX]) the definition of aggression. Some time later, it invited the International Law Commission to resume its work on elaborating the proposed draft code of offenses against the peace and security of mankind.

The commission appointed one of its members, Mr. Doudou Thiam (Senegal), as its special rapporteur for the topic. On the basis of his reports (UN Doc. A/CN.4/387, 398, 404, and 411), it was able to adopt provisionally, between 1985 and 1989, articles 1–8 and 10–15 of the draft code. The texts thus adopted are reproduced in the entry entitled CRIMES AGAINST THE PEACE AND SECURITY OF MANKIND.

INTERNATIONAL LAW COMMISSION: STATUTE (1947). The statute, adopted by the UN General Assembly on 21 November 1947 (resolution 174 [II]) and subsequently amended by the Assembly on 12 December 1950 (resolution 485 [V]), 3 December 1955 (resolutions 984 and 985 [X]), and 6 November 1961 (resolution 1647 [XVI]), authorizes the establishment of the International Law Commission to promote the progressive development of international law and its codification. The text of the statute (annexed to resolution 174 [II]), as amended, is as follows:

Article 1. 1. The International Law Commission shall have for its object the promotion of the progressive development of international law and its codification.

2. The Commission shall concern itself primarily with public international law, but is not precluded from entering the field of private international law.

Chapter I
Organization of the International Law Commission

Article 2. 1. The Commission shall consist of twenty-five members who shall be persons of recognized competence in international law.

2. No two members of the Commission shall be nationals of the same State.

3. In case of dual nationality a candidate shall be deemed to be a national of the State in which he ordinarily exercises civil and political rights.

Article 3. The members of the Commission shall be elected by the General Assembly from a list of candidates nominated by the Governments of States Members of the United Nations.

Article 4. Each Member may nominate for election not more than four candidates, of whom two may be nationals of the nominating State and two nationals of other States.

Article 5. The names of the candidates shall be submitted in writing by the Governments to the Secretary-General by the first of June of the year in which an election is held, provided that a Government may in exceptional circumstances substitute for a candidate whom it has nominated before the first of June another candidate whom it shall name not later than thirty days before the opening of the General Assembly.

Article 6. The Secretary-General shall as soon as possible communicate to the Governments of States Members the names submitted, as well as any statements of qualifications of candidates that may have been submitted by the nominating Governnments.

Article 7. The Secretary-General shall prepare the list referred to in article 3 above, comprising in alphabetical order the names of all the candidates duly nominated, and shall submit this list to the General Assembly for the purposes of the election.

Article 8. At the election the electors shall bear in mind that the persons to be elected to the Commission should individually possess the qualifications required and that in the Commission as a whole representation of the main forms of civilization and of the principal legal systems of the world should be assured.

Article 9. 1. The twenty-five candidates who obtain the greatest number of votes and not less than a majority of the votes of the Members present and voting shall be elected.

2. In the event of more than one national of the same State obtaining a sufficient number of votes for election the one who obtains the greatest number of votes shall be elected and if the votes are equally divided the elder or eldest candidate shall be elected.

Article 10. The members of the Commission shall be elected for five years. They shall be eligible for re-election.

Article 11. In the case of a casual vacancy, the Commission itself shall fill the vacancy having due regard to the provisions contained in article 2 and 8 of this Statute.

Article 12. The Commission shall sit at the European Office of the United Nations at Geneva. The Commission shall, however, have the right to hold meetings at other places after consultation with the Secretary-General.

Article 13. Members of the Commission shall be paid travel expenses, and shall also receive a special allowance, the amount of which shall be determined by the General Assembly.

Article 14. The Secretary-General shall, so far as he is able, make available staff and facilities required by the Commission to fulfil its task.

Chapter II.
Functions of the International Law Commission

Article 15. In the following articles the expression "progressive development of international law" is used for convenience as meaning the preparation of draft conventions on subjects which have not yet been regulated by international law or in regard to which the law has not yet been sufficiently developed in the practice of States. Similarly, the expression "codification of international law" is used for convenience as meaning the more precise formulation and systematization of rules of international law in fields where there already has been extensive State practice, precedent and doctrine.

A. Progressive Development of International Law

Article 16. When the General Assembly refers to the Commission a proposal for the progressive development of international law, the Commission shall follow in general a procedure on the following lines:

(a) It shall appoint one of its members to be Rapporteur;

(b) It shall formulate a plan of work;

(c) It shall circulate a questionnaire to the Governments, and shall invite them to supply within a fixed period of time data and information relevant to items included in the plan of work;

(d) It may appoint some of its members to work with the Rapporteur on the preparation of drafts pending receipt of replies to this questionnaire;

(e) It may consult with scientific institutions and individual experts; these experts need not necessarily be nationals of Members of the United Nations. The Secretary-General will provide, when necessary and within the limits of the budget, for the expenses of these consultations of experts;

(f) It shall consider the drafts proposed by the Rapporteur;

(g) When the Commission considers a draft to be satisfactory, it shall request the Secretary-General to issue it as a Commission document. The Secretariat shall give all necessary publicity to this document which shall be accompanied by such explanations and supporting material as the Commission considers appropriate. The publication shall include any information supplied to the Commission in reply to the questionnaire referred to in sub-paragraph (c) above;

(h) The Commission shall invite the Governments to submit their comments on this document within a reasonable time;

(i) The Rapporteur and the members appointed for that purpose shall reconsider the draft taking into consideration these comments and shall prepare a final draft and explanatory report which they shall submit for consideration and adoption by the Commission;

(j) The Commission shall submit the draft so adopted with its recommendations through the Secretary-General to the General Assembly.

Article 17. 1. The Commission shall also consider proposals and draft multilateral conventions submitted by Members of the United Nations, the principal organs of the United Nations other than the General-Assembly, specialized agencies, or official bodies established by intergovernmental agreement to encourage the progressive development of international law and its codification, and transmitted to it for that purpose by the Secretary-General.

2. If in such cases the Commission deems it appropriate to proceed with the study of such proposals or drafts, it shall follow in general a procedure on the following lines:

(a) The Commission shall formulate a plan of work, and study such proposals or drafts, and compare them with any other proposals and drafts on the same subjects;

(b) The Commission shall circulate a questionnaire to all Members of the United Nations and to the organs, specialized agencies and official bodies mentioned above which are concerned with the question, and shall invite them to transmit their comments within a reasonable time;

(c) The Commission shall submit a report and its recommendations to the General Assembly. Before doing so, it may also, if it deems it desirable, make an interim report to the organ or agency which has submitted the proposal or draft;

(d) If the General Assembly should invite the Commission to proceed with its work in accordance with a suggested plan, the procedure outlined in article 16 above shall apply. The questionnaire referred to in paragraph (c) of that article may not, however, be necessary.

B. Codification of International Law

Article 18. 1. The Commission shall survey the whole field of international law with a view to selecting topics for codification, having in mind existing drafts whether governmental or not.

2. When the Commission considers that the codification of a particular topic is necessary or desirable, it shall submit its recommendations to the General Assembly.

3. The Commission shall give priority to requests of the General Assembly to deal with any question.

Article 19. 1. The Commission shall adopt a plan of work appropriate to each case.

2. The Commission shall, through the Secretary-General, address to Governments a detailed request to furnish the texts of laws, decrees, judicial decisions, treaties, diplomatic correspondence and other documents relevant to the topic being studied and which the Commission deems necessary.

Article 20. The Commission shall prepare its drafts in the form of articles and shall submit them to the General Assembly together with a commentary containing:

(a) Adequate presentation of precedents and other relevant data, including treaties, judicial decisions and doctrine;

(b) Conclusions relevant to:

(i) The extent of agreement on each point in the practice of States and in doctrine;

(ii) Divergencies and disagreements which exist, as well as arguments invoked in favour of one or another solution.

Article 21. 1. When the Commission considers a draft to be satisfactory, it shall request the Secretary-General to issue it as a Commission document. The Secretariat shall give all necessary publicity to the document including such explanations and supporting material as the Commission may consider appropriate. The publication shall include any information supplied to the Commission by Governments in accordance with article 19. The Commission shall decide whether the opinions of any scientific institution or individual experts consulted by the Commission shall be included in the publication.

2. The Commission shall request Governments to submit comments on this document within a reasonable time.

Article 22. Taking such comments into consideration, the Commission shall prepare a final draft and explanatory report which it shall submit with its recommendations through the Secretary-General to the General Assembly.

Article 23. 1. The Commission may recommend to the General Assembly:

(a) To take no action, the report having already been published;

(b) To take note of or adopt the report by resolution;

(c) To recommend the draft to Members with a view to the conclusion of a convention;

(d) To convoke a conference to conclude a convention.

2. Whenever it deems it desirable, the General Assembly may refer drafts back to the Commission for reconsideration or redrafting.

Article 24. The Commission shall consider ways and means for making the evidence of customary international law more readily available, such as the collection and publication of documents concerning State practice and of the decisions of national and international courts on questions of international law, and shall make a report to the General Assembly on this matter.

Chapter III.
Co-operation With Other Bodies

Article 25. 1. The Commission may consult, if it considers it necessary, with any of the organs of the United Nations on any subject which is within the competence of that organ.

2. All documents of the Commission which are circulated to Governments by the Secretary-General shall also be circulated to such organs of the United Nations as are concerned. Such organs may furnish any information or make any suggestions to the Commission.

Article 26. 1. The Commission may consult with any international or national organizations, official or non-official, on any subject entrusted to it if it believes that such a procedure might aid it in the performance of its functions.

2. For the purpose of distribution of documents of the Commission, the Secretary-General, after consultation with the Commission, shall draw up a list of national and international organizations concerned with questions of international law. The Secretary-General shall endeavour to include on this list at least one national organization of each Member of the United Nations.

3. In the application of the provisions of this article, the Commission and the Secretary-General shall comply with the resolutions of the General Assembly and the other principal organs of the United Nations concerning relations with Franco's Spain and shall exclude both from consultations and from the list, organizations which have collaborated with the nazis and fascists.

4. The advisability of consultation by the Commission with inter-governmental organizations whose task is the codification of international law such as those of the Pan American Union, is recognized.

INTERNATIONAL LEAGUE FOR HUMAN RIGHTS. An international non-governmental organization in consultative status with the UN Economic and Social Council (Category II), and with ILO, UNESCO, OAS, and the Council of Europe, the league has 41 affiliates in 26 countries and individual members in 60 countries.

Founded in 1941 in New York City as the "International League for the Rights of Man," the league now seeks to promote realization of the human rights and fundamental freedoms set out in the Universal Declaration of Human Rights and other international human rights instruments. It monitors the application of those instruments, investigates human rights violations, intervenes directly with governments, makes representations before international bodies, conducts research and educational programs, publishes special reports on human rights conditions, assists victims, sends observers to political trials, dispatches special investigative missions to inquire into specific violations and to effect redress, supports and helps establish human rights national groups, and, in general, works to establish international human rights standards. It awards a Human Rights Prize annually. It publishes the monthly *Human Rights Bulletin* and the *ILHR Annual Review.*

International League for Human Rights. Address: 432 Park Avenue South, New York, N.Y. 10002 (U.S.A.). Telephone: (212) 684-1221. Executive Director: Felice Gaer.

Yearbook of International Organizations 1989/90 (K. G. Saur)

INTERNATIONAL LEAGUE FOR THE RIGHTS AND LIBERATION OF PEOPLES.

An international non-governmental organization in consultative status with the UN Economic and Social Council (Roster), the league has individual members and national branches in 24 countries.

Founded in Rome in 1976, the league works to uphold and promote the principles of the Declaration on the Granting of Independence to Colonial Countries and Peoples. It publishes the quarterly *Peoples* in English, French, Spanish, and Italian; and the *Dossier* in Italian with English summaries.

International League for the Rights and Liberation of Peoples. Address: Via Bagutta 12, 1-20121 Milan, Italy. Telephone: (39-2) 78-08-11. Secretary General: Piero Basso.

Yearbook of International Organizations 1989/90 (K. G. Saur).

INTERNATIONAL MOVEMENT ATD FOURTH WORLD.

An international non-governmental organization in consultative status with the UN Economic and Social Council (Category II) and with UNESCO and the Council of Europe, the movement has 18 national affiliates and individual members in 117 countries.

The Fourth World Movement was founded by Fr. Joseph Wresinski and the poor people of the shantytown Noisy-le-Grand, France, in 1957. The movement defends human rights by fighting against the cultural and economic insecurity into which the poor are born and works to enable the poorest and most excluded to participate in their communities and to change their destiny; it campaigns on both grassroots and international levels for decent housing, health care, job training, education, and an understanding of the problems of the poor. In February 1987, the Economic and Social Council of France adopted the movement's "Report on Economic and Social Poverty and Insecurity," which includes a detailed plan to combat poverty. The plan is now being implemented in 12 of France's 95 *départements* on an experimental basis.

The movement publishes the monthly journals *The Fourth World Journal* and *Tapori* (for children). It has also produced the books *Children of our Time, The Fourth World Speaks, Children Lead the Way in Burkina Faso, Blessed are You the Poor,* and *Passport to Bringing Computers to the Most Disadvantaged.*

International Movement ATD Fourth World. Address: 107 Avenue du General Leclerc, F-95480 Pierrelaye, France. Telephone: (33) 34-64-69-63. Secretariat: J. Wresinki.

INTERNATIONAL MOVEMENT FOR FRATERNAL UNION AMONG RACES AND PEOPLES.

An international non-governmental organization in consultative status with the UN Economic and Social Council (Category II) and with UNESCO, the movement was founded in Paris in 1952 and currently has national branches in 41 countries.

The purpose of the movement is to promote mutual understanding and fraternal collaboration among races and peoples in the spirit of the Universal Declaration of Human Rights. Since the majority of its members are women, it accords high priority to questions relating to the status of women and children, especially in situations of oppression and underdevelopment.

The movement publishes the *Grail Review* in English and the *UFER Bulletin* and *Intercom* in English and French.

International Movement for Fraternal Union among Races and Peoples. Address: UFER, Rue Eugene Smits 74, B-1030 Brussels, Belgium. Secretary-General: Magda Van Malder.

Yearbook of International Organizations 1989/90 (K. G. Saur).

INTERNATIONAL ORGANIZATION FOR THE ELIMINATION OF ALL FORMS OF RACIAL DISCRIMINATION.

An international non-governmental organization in consultative status with the UN Economic and Social Council (Category II) and with UNESCO, EAFORD unites individual members in 20 countries.

Established in 1976 in Tripoli by an international symposium on Zionism, the organization seeks to advance understanding of international law and world consensus on the question of racism; to further the elimination of all forms of racial discrimination; to conduct, support, and publish scholarly research on racism and racial conflict; and to engage in other activities and projects aimed at the protection of human rights and the elimination of racial discrimination. EAFORD investigates racism, in particular, as it relates to the Palestine conflict, the situation in South Africa, and the conditions of indigenous peoples everywhere. Among its publications are *Treatment of Palestinians in Israeli-occupied West Bank and Gaza* (1978) and *Witness of War Crimes in Lebanon* (1983).

International Organization for the Elimination of all Forms of Racial Discrimination. Address: 41, Rue de Zurich, 1201 Geneva, Switzerland. Telephone: 32-55-34. Telex: 289712 IPBCH.

INTERNATIONAL ORGANIZATION OF JOURNALISTS.

An international non-governmental organization in consultative status with the UN Economic and Social Council (Category II) and with UNESCO, the organization has over 250,000 members in 120 countries.

Founded in Copenhagen in 1946, IOJ is the oldest and largest organization of professional journalists. It endeavors, by stimulating the flow of free and true information, to help maintain peace and friendship between nations; to defend freedom of the press and of journalists, in particular; to fight for better material and social conditions for journalists; and to support friendly cooperation among journalists all over the world, especially those engaged in dangerous missions. It organizes conferences, seminars, and training courses to achieve these purposes, conducts mass media research, and establishes data bases.

The organization has published more than 250 textbooks, handbooks, and pamphlets on journalism. It also produces the monthly journal *Democratic Journalists* and the bimonthly *Newsletter.*

International Organization of Journalists. Address: Parizska 9, 110 01 Prague 1, Czechoslovakia. Telephone: 2328015, 232-83-71, or 232-59-89. Cable: INTORGJOUR PRAGUE. Telex: 122631 JOUR C. General Secretary: Dusan Ulcak.

INTERNATIONAL PRESS INSTITUTE.

An international non-governmental organization in consultative status with the UN Economic and Social Council (Roster) and with UNESCO and the Council of Europe, IPI has 1,800 members in 65 countries.

Founded in Paris in 1951, the institute promotes free access to news, free expression of views, and free publication of newspapers. It also promotes understanding among editors, the exchange of accurate and balanced news, and the improvement of journalistic practices. The institute's Press Center provides information on press freedom and editorial research. IPI also conducts Asian conferences and African training programs, as well as seminars in Africa, the Americas, Asia, and Europe.

The institute publishes the monthly *IPI Report* in English.

International Press Institute. Address: Dilke House, Malet Street, London WC1E 7JA, UK. Telephone: 636-0703; 636-0704. Cable: PRESSINT London WC1. Fax: (44-1) 580-8349. Director: Peter Galliner.

Yearbook of International Organizations 1989/90 (K. G. Saur).

INTERNATIONAL PROGRESS ORGANIZATION.

An international non-governmental organization in consultative status with the UN Economic and Social Council (Roster) and with UNESCO, IPO has members in 58 countries.

The organization was founded in 1972 in Innsbruck, Austria, by students from Europe, Asia, and Africa who were concerned about human rights. IPO sponsors international conferences and research seminars on topics such as human rights, international law, and economic development. It encourages cultural exchanges between all nations, attempts to promote tolerance towards all nationalities and cultures, and emphasizes human liberties, social and economic development, and peace.

IPO conducts an extensive publication program, most prominently the series "Studies in International Relations," which includes among its titles *Cultural Self-Comprehension of Nations* (1978), *The Principles of International Law and Human Rights* (1981), *The Principles of Non-Alignment* (1982), and *Democracy in International Relations* (1986). Among its published monographs are *The Concept of Monotheism in Islam and Christianity* (1982), *The Crisis of Representative Democracy* (1986), and *Ethical Relativism Versus Human Rights* (1987).

International Progress Organization. Address: Kohlmarkt 4, A-1010 Vienna, Austria. Telephone: (43-222) 5332877. Cable: Interprogress. Fax: (43-222) 533296221. Telex: 613222950 IPOA. President: Dr. Hans Koechler.

INTERNATIONAL RED CROSS.

This organization comprises the INTERNATIONAL COMMITTEE OF THE RED CROSS, the LEAGUE OF RED CROSS AND RED CRESCENT SOCIETIES, and about 145 national Red Cross and Red Crescent Societies. The International Red Cross oversees the realization, in all parts of the Red Cross/Red Crescent movement, of certain basic principles: humanity, impartiality, neutrality, independence, voluntary service, unity and universality.

The first Red Cross national societies came into being in 1863; in 1864, the emblem of a red cross on a white background—the inverse of the Swiss flag—was created to insure the protection of those wounded in war and those who care for them. The emblem has no religious significance; however, in 1876, during the Russo–Turkish war, the Ottoman Society for Relief to the Wounded replaced the cross with a red crescent. The red crescent has since been adopted by a number of Islamic countries and is recognized and granted equal status with the red cross.

The work of the national societies in time of armed conflict is well known; originally created for service in wartime, to help army medical personnel care for the sick and wounded, the national societies moved off the battlefields to help civilian victims of conflicts. In addition, the societies expanded their efforts to help in peacetime. After World War I, the national societies used their training and experience to attend to the urgent medical and social needs of populations ravaged by that conflict. Since that time, the national societies have played important roles in founding hospitals, training nurses, and conducting education programs in child care and public health; in pioneering ambulances, mountain, and sea rescue services; in providing first-aid training; and in caring for the elderly and the handicapped.

Nearly every society has a youth section and promotes blood transfusion services. Since World War II, the national societies in industrialized countries have further widened their field of activities to address social problems like drug addiction, unemployment, and delinquency. In developing countries, the societies work for improved health and welfare, engaging in projects to combat fatal infantile diseases, give basic health education, and mount intensive vaccination campaigns.

Finally, throughout the 1980s, due to the enormous increase in refugees, especially in third world countries, the national societies have provided relief and social services for this population. In addition to its many other services, the national societies continue one of their oldest peacetime activities: providing relief and emergency services for victims of natural disasters.

International Red Cross. Address: 17 Avenue de la Paix, CH-1202 Geneva, Switzerland. Telephone: 22-346001. Cable: INTERCROIXROUGE. Telex: 22269. Contact: Michel Testuz.

INTERNATIONAL RESEARCH AND TRAINING INSTITUTE FOR THE ADVANCEMENT OF WOMEN.

In 1975, the World Conference of the International Women's Year recommended the establishment of an International Training and Research

Center for the Advancement of Women which would (1) undertake research and the collection and dissemination of information as the basis for the formulation of programs and policies for the effective participation of women; (2) assist in the design of research for the monitoring of changes in the situation of women and the impact on their lives of economic, social, and technological changes; and (3) develop, adapt, and provide training programs for women, in particular those of the developing countries, which would enable them to undertake national research, to assume leadership roles within their own societies, and to increase their earning possibilities.

The UN General Assembly decided in principle on 15 December 1975 (resolution 3520 [XXX]) to establish such an institute, and the Economic and Social Council set it up on 21 May 1976 (resolution 1998 [LX]) as "an autonomous body under the auspices of the United Nations, funded through voluntary contributions." In May 1979, the council decided that the institute should be located in the Dominican Republic; and, by May 1981, an agreement had been concluded between the United Nations and the government of that country concerning the installation of the institute at Santo Domingo and the appointment of a Director.

The institute, in full operation, assists in the advancement of women and in their integration in the development process through research, training programs, and the collection and dissemination of information. It works in close cooperation with the competent organs and agencies of the United Nations system and pays special attention to the needs of women in developing countries. The institute reports on its activities through the Economic and Social Council to the General Assembly; its report is also provided to the COMMISSION ON THE STATUS OF WOMEN.

The institute is governed by a Board of Trustees appointed by the Economic and Social Council; its members serve a three-year term. Members of the board are nominated by States members of the United Nations. They serve in their personal capacity. The board holds a session of about one week each year, usually in January at the headquarters of the institute, Santo Domingo, Dominican Republic.

In 1989, the UN Economic and Social Council considered the report of the Board of Trustees of the institute (UN Doc. E/1989/46); and later that year, the General Assembly examined the report of the institute (UN Doc. A/44/416, annex). Both bodies noted that the institute would observe in 1990 the tenth anniversary of its establishment, and both expressed satisfaction at the significance and scope of its activities on behalf of women and at the special importance which it had attached to research, training, information, documentation, and communication relating to women and development.

The council noted with special interest (resolution 1989/43) that the institute had organized an "International Consultative Meeting on Communications for Women" and authorized wide dissemination of the report of that meeting. The assembly noted, in particular, (resolution 44/60) that the institute, in consultation with other United Nations bodies, had launched its new research program for the elaboration of special methodologies for the monitoring and evaluation of programs and projects for women, as the assembly had requested it to do in 1987.

INTERNATIONAL SOCIAL SERVICE. An international non-governmental organization in consultative status with the UN Economic and Social Council (Category II), ISS has national branches in 14 countries.

Founded in 1921 by the World YWCA and originally called the "International Migration Service," ISS assists individuals who, as a consequence of voluntary or forced migration or other social problems of an international character, have to overcome personal or family difficulty. It also studies, from an international viewpoint, the conditions and consequences of migration regarding the individual and family life. The ISS General Secretariat in Geneva handles annually about 500 cases involving individual or family difficulty arising from migration or from residence in a foreign country. The service also works with groups and communities as required and endeavors to procure legal documents, where needed.

ISS publishes annual activity reports and has published *International Naming and Addressing Directory, ISS History,* and *60 Years of International Service Service.*

International Service Service. Address: 32 Quai du Seujet, CH-1201, Geneva, Switzerland. Telephone: 31-74-54 or 31-74-55. Cable: Migranto Geneva. Telex: 28-92-83. Secretary-General: Marcelle L. Brisson.

Yearbook of International Organizations 1989/90 (K. G. Saur).

INTERNATIONAL SOCIETY FOR HUMAN RIGHTS. An international non-governmental organization in consultative status with the Council of Europe, ISHR brings together 18 national organizations in 17 countries.

Founded in 1972 in Frankfurt–Main—originally as the "Society for Human Rights"—ISHR works to achieve universal respect for and observance of human rights, to provide support and relief to victims of discrimination, and to support the Universal Declaration of Human Rights and other international human rights instruments. It defends non-violent human rights activists and assists "prisoners of conscience" and their families. It also promotes family reunions within the framework of the HELSINKI ACCORD: FINAL ACT.

Among the society's publications are *Menschenrechte, Menschenrechte in Latein Amerika, Menschenrechte in Afrika, DDR Heute, Boletin en America Latina, USSR Aktuell,* and *Human Rights in Brief.*

International Society for Human Rights. Address: Kaiserstrasse 72, Postfach 101132, D-6000 Frankfurt/ Main 1, German FR. Telephone: 69-23-69-71. Telex: 4-185-181-IGFM. Fax: (49-69) 23-41-00. Executive Director: Ivan Agrusow.

INTERNATIONAL STUDIES ASSOCIATION. An international non-governmental organization in consultative status (Roster) with the UN Economic and Social Council, ISA is associated with 16 organizations in 21 countries. It has more than 2,000 individual members, including scientists, students, officials of governments and international organizations, and officials of transnational corporations.

The association focuses primarily on issues of academic freedom and the unimpeded transnational flow of persons and ideas. ISA organizes an annual international convention (with approximately 1,200 attendees) and the biennial World Assembly of International Studies Research.

In addition to individual papers and studies, ISA regularly publishes the *International Studies Newsletter* (10 times per year), *International Studies Quarterly,* and *IS Notes* (four times per year).

International Studies Association. Address: Byrnes International Center, University of South Carolina, Columbia, SC 29208 (USA). Telephone: (803) 777-2933. Telex: 805038. USC INTL CLB. Executive Director: William A. Welsh.

INTERNATIONAL UNION OF LAWYERS. An international non-governmental organization in consultative status with the UN Economic and Social Council (Category II) and with the Council of Europe, best known by its French title, *Union internationale des avocats* (UIA), the organization is affiliated with regional associations and national bar associations (55) in 41 countries.

Founded in 1927 in Belgium, the union works to establish permanent relations and exchanges between national federations or associations of lawyers and supports their action and work. It promotes joint study of questions concerning legal organization and contributes to the establishment of an international legal order. The union publishes *Bulletin de l'UIA*.

International Union of Lawyers. Address: 18 Ave. Charles de Gaulle, F-92200 Neuilly, France. Telephone: (33-1) 47-38-13-11. Telex: UIAPARI 620101F. Fax: (33-1) 47-38-61-38.

Yearbook of International Organizations 1989/90 (K. G. Saur).

INTERNATIONAL UNION OF STUDENTS.

An international non-governmental organization in consultative status with the UN Economic and Social Council (Category I) and with UNESCO, the union brings together over 100 organizations of students in 105 countries.

Founded in 1946 in Prague, the union works for the right of all young people to enjoy primary, secondary, and higher education, regardless of sex, economic circumstances, social standing, political or religious convictions, color, or race. It organizes and sponsors conferences, seminars, and winter and summer sports and work camps. It also supports student campaigns for peace, student relief and welfare activities, and works against colonialism and racial discrimination. The union also arranges student exchanges, travel, and cultural events and operates a documentation center.

Among IUS' publications are the monthly *World Student News,* published in English, French, Spanish and German; and the *Democratization of Education, Sports Bulletin,* and *Young Cinema and Theatre,* in English, French, and Spanish.

International Union of Students. Address: 17th November Street, P.O. Box 58, 110 01 Prague 01, Czechoslovakia. Telephone: 2312812. Cable: UNISTUD PRAGUE. Telex: 122858 IUS Prague. Secretary-General: Michaelides Giorgos.

Yearbook of International Organizations 1989/90 (K. G. Saur).

INTERNATIONAL UNION OF YOUNG CHRISTIAN DEMOCRATS.

An international non-governmental organization in consultative status with the UN Economic and Social Council (Category II) and with UNESCO, IUYCD has national affiliates in 42 countries.

Founded in 1959, the union supports the establishment throughout the world of a social, economic, and political democracy based on Christian democratic ideals. In addition to its quadrennial world congress, it conducts international, regional, and national congresses, seminars, and round-table discussions, focusing on issues related to human rights, social justice, and pluralism in society.

IUYCD publishes the *IUYCD Newsletter* fortnightly in three languages and *Debate* triannually, also in three languages.

International Union of Young Christian Democrats. Address: Rue de La Victoire, B-1060 Brussels, Belgium. Secretary General: Filippo Lombardi.

Yearbook of International Organizations 1989/90 (K. G. Saur)

INTERNATIONAL WOMEN'S TRIBUNE CENTRE.

An international non-governmental organization in consultative status with the UN Economic and Social Council (Roster), IWTC serves as a communication link for 14,000 individual and group members in 160 countries in Latin America, Africa, Asia, the Caribbean, and the South Pacific. It is supported by grants from the development agencies of the Governments of Canada, Sweden, the Netherlands, Norway, and Australia, with additional funds coming from church and foundation groups in the United States.

The centre was established in 1976 following the International Women's Year Tribune (a nongovernmental conference) in Mexico City in 1975. IWTC promotes equal rights and opportunities for women worldwide, in particular supporting the initiatives of third world women who are working to promote the more equitable and active participation of women within the development process. Through a program of technical assistance and training, information and networking services, IWTC's work focuses on four areas: organizing women, coordinating communication services, promoting community economic development, and training individuals and groups in appropriate technology.

Among its resources for women, IWTC has an extensive publication program. Its principal organ is *The Tribune* (in English, French, and Spanish), published quarterly since 1976. The centre also publishes newsletter collections, training manuals, and reports of workshops and meetings on women's issues. It also produces posters and postcards and slide-tape sets.

International Women's Tribune Centre. Address: 777 United Nations Plaza, New York, NY 10017 (USA). Telephone: (212) 687-8633. Cable: TRIBCEN NEWYORK. Director: Dr. Anne S. Walker.

INTERNATIONAL WOMEN'S YEAR (1975). On 18 December 1972, the UN General Assembly proclaimed (resolution 3010 [XXVII]) the year 1975 as International Women's Year. The highlight of the year was the World Conference of the International Women's Year, convened in Mexico City from 19 June to 2 July 1975 by the United Nations at the invitation of the Government of Mexico.

The conference adopted as its principal decisions the DECLARATION OF MEXICO ON THE EQUALITY OF WOMEN AND THEIR CONTRIBUTION TO DEVELOPMENT AND PEACE and the World Plan of Action for the Implementation of the Objectives of the International Women's Year. Acting on recommendations of the conference, the General Assembly on 15 December 1975 proclaimed (resolution 3520 [XXX]) the period from 1976 to 1985 as the "United Nations Decade for Women: Equality, Development and Peace," and decided to convene, in 1980, at the mid-point of the decade, a world conference to review progress made in implementing the objectives specified by the Mexico City conference. The world conference was held at Copenhagen from 14 to 30 July 1980 and was followed by the World Conference to Review and Appraise the Achievements of the United Nations Decade for Women: Equality, Development and Peace, convened in Nairobi from 15 to 26 July 1985. The latter conference prepared and adopted the NAIROBI FORWARD-LOOKING STRATEGIES FOR THE ADVANCEMENT OF WOMEN.

INTERNATIONAL YEAR FOR HUMAN RIGHTS (1968). The year 1968, which marked the 20th anniversary of the UNIVERSAL DECLARATION OF HUMAN RIGHTS, was designated by the UN General Assembly (resolution 2081 [XX]) as the International Year for Human Rights. The highlight of the year was the INTERNATIONAL CONFERENCE ON HUMAN RIGHTS, convened in Teheran from 22 April to 13 May 1968. The conference reviewed the progress achieved in the field of human rights since the adoption of the declaration, evaluated the effectiveness of international human rights activities, prepared a program for future work in this field, and adopted the PROCLAMATION OF TEHERAN.

INTERNATIONAL YEAR OF THE CHILD (1979). In General Assembly resolutions 31/169, 32/109, and 33/83, the United Nations designated the year 1979 as the International Year of the Child. At the conclusions of that year, the General Assembly declared UNICEF as the United Nations' lead agency for the concerns of children worldwide.

INTERNATIONAL YOUNG CATHOLIC STUDENTS. An international non-governmental organization in consultative status with the UN Economic and Social Council (Roster) and with UNESCO and the Council of Europe, YCS has affiliated organizations and individual members in 81 countries.

Founded in 1946, as the *Centre international de documentation et d'information, Brussels,* International Young Catholic Students supports student movements in all countries. Its regional secretariats organize study sessions. The group publishes *Lettre du Conseil* (quarterly) in English, French, and Spanish; *Info-Rapid* (bi-monthly); *SPES: Boletin de Información para los Movimientos de América Latina* (quarterly) in Spanish; and the *YCS Newsletter* in English and French, among others.

International Young Catholic Students (Regional Offices). *Pan African Office:* P.O. Box 44335, Nairobi, Kenya. *Latin American Office:* Secretariado, Latinoamericano JECI–MIEC, Ap. Aereo 14-0330 Lima, Peru. *North American Office:* Sec. Nat. JEC, 5323 rue Brébeuf, Montreal H2J 3L8, Canada. *European Office:* Rue du Marteau 19, B-1040, Brussels, Belgium. *Asian Office:* YCS Asia, Block Q, Rm. 1204-77, Ngau Tau Kok Rd., Kowloon, Hong Kong.

Yearbook of International Organizations 1989/90 (K. G. Saur).

INTERNATIONAL YOUNG CHRISTIAN WORKERS. An international non-governmental organization in consultative status with the UN Economic and Social Council (Category II) and with ILO, UNESCO, FAO, and the Council of Europe, IYCW brings together national organizations in 71 countries.

Founded in 1945 in Brussels as the "European Young Christian Workers," International Young Christian Workers—through surveys, meetings, and congresses—studies aspects of young workers lives: working conditions, displacements, living conditions, etc. The group organizes young working people in groups to discuss their problems and means of solving them. IYCW publishes the quarterly *Info* in English, French, and Spanish.

International Young Christian Workers. Address: Rue Plantin 11, B-1070 Brussels, Belgium. Telephone: (32-2) 521-69-83. Cable: JOCINT Bruxelles. International President: Felix Ollarves Sanchez.

Yearbook of International Organizations 1989/90 (K. G. Saur).

INTERNATIONAL YOUTH AND STUDENT MOVEMENT FOR THE UNITED NATIONS. An international non-governmental organization in consultative status with the UN Economic and Social Council (Category I) and with UNESCO, the movement has corresponding members in 42 countries and territories.

Founded in Rome in 1948 as the "Student Commission of the World Federation of United Nations Associations," the International Youth and Student Movement for the United Nations is now an independent organization. It works with students and young people to promote national liberation; economic, social, and cultural justice; and peace, disarmament, and human rights. It opposes colonialism, neocolonialism, imperialism, and repression in all forms and promotes a wider knowledge of the UN's activities and of its potential.

ISMUN publishes the monthly *ISMUN Newsletter* and *Analysis and Action Reports.* An occasional publication is the *Human Rights Bulletin.*

International Youth and Student Movement for the United Nations. Address: Palais des Nations, CH-1211 Geneva 10, Switzerland. Telephone: (41-22) 98-94-79 or (41-22) 98-58-50, Ext. 249-250. Cable: ISMUNAT Geneva. Secretary General: Juan Carlos Giacosa.

Yearbook of International Organizations 1989/90 (K. G. Saur).

INTER-PARLIAMENTARY UNION. An international non-governmental organization in consultative status with the UN Economic and Social Council (Category II) and with UNESCO and WHO, IPU is composed of Inter-Parliamentary national groups from 108 countries.

The union was the first worldwide political organization to promote the concept of peace and international arbitration. Its origins date back to 1889, when the first Inter-Parliamentary Conference for International Arbitration met in Paris. From its inception, IPU has been active in the peace movement and was instrumental in setting up what is now the Permanent Court of Arbitration in the Hague. Over the years, eight Nobel Peace Prizes—including the first three awards—were shared by leading personalities of the IPU.

IPU addresses all international problems suitable for settlement by parliamentary action and promotes improvements in the working methods of parliamentary institutions. Through organizing specialized world-wide or regional meetings, IPU studies problems in the fields of international security, economic development, and social affairs, including problems in European security and cooperation, disarmament, the environment, population, health, employment, drug control, and women's and children's rights. IPU also safeguards the rights of parliamentarians; in a 1987 report of the Special Committee on Violations of the Human Rights of Parliamentarians, the committee stated that, in its ten years of operation, it has investigated nearly 600 individual situations in 47 countries and has examined cases involving violations of freedom of expression, exile, disappearance, murder and execution, and restriction or suspension of civil and political rights.

IPU publishes the *Inter-Parliamentary Bulletin,* its official organ, issued quarterly in English and French.

Inter-Parliamentary Union. Address: P.O. Box 438, 1211 Geneva 19, Switzerland. Telephone: (022) 344150. Cable: Interparlement. Telex: 289784 IPU CH. Fax: (41-22) 33-31-41. Secretary General: Pierre Cornillon.

INTIFADAH **(UPRISING) OF THE PALESTINIAN PEOPLE.** Beginning on 9 December 1987, the Palestinian people residing in the territories occupied by Israel staged an uprising (*intifadah*) against the occupation, one which received significant attention and sympathy from world public opinion. However, the uprising caused the human rights situation in the territories to deteriorate dramatically. The resulting situation was described by the chairman of the SPECIAL COMMITTEE TO INVESTIGATE ISRAELI PRACTICES AFFECTING THE HUMAN RIGHTS OF THE POPULATION OF THE OCCUPIED TERRITORIES in his letter transmitting the 1988 report of the special committee (UN Doc. A/43/694) to the UN Secretary-General, as follows:

The accumulation of frustrations suffered by the civilian population over the years as a result of the persistent policy of annexation and colonization pursued by the Government of Israel in the territories occupied in June 1967, and the humiliation and suffering brought about by that policy, were bound to provoke a violent reaction on the part of the oppressed civilians. The restrictions imposed in the framework of the "iron fist policy" since 1985 and the increasing determination of the young generation of Palestinians to oppose the arbitrary rules set by the occupants had prepared the ground for such a confrontation. Thus, the explosion of violence sparked off by an incident in the Gaza Strip in December 1987 quickly spread to the entire occupied territories, giving rise to what has since been called the uprising against the occupation.

The uprising has been marked by a heavy toll of casualties among the Palestinian population. Hundreds of civilians have been killed by security forces, settlers, or under various other circumstances. The death toll has included casualties caused by shooting, beating, gas inhalation or electrocution. While several thousands of civilians have been physically injured, the entire Palestinian population has suffered as a result of the implementation by the Israeli authorities of the policy of "force, power and blows".

The day-to-day life in the occupied territories since the start of the uprising has been characterized by constant unrest and violent clashes, sparing almost no single village or locality; the now familiar pattern of disturbances usually includes demonstrations, stone-throwing, commercial strikes on the one hand, and the use of tear gas, clubs, rubber and live bullets, the imposition of curfews and various economic sanctions by the occupation authorities on the other. Acts of aggression committed by Israel settlers against Palestinians have contributed to a further deterioration in the climate of tension and terror prevailing in the occupied territories. Information and evidence collected by the Special Committee reveal other serious infringements of fundamental rights and freedoms, including the arbitrary deportation of Palestinians from the occupied territories; the illegal demolition of houses used as a form of collective punishment; the severe limitations on the freedom of expression, tending in particular to limit or prevent an adequate media coverage of events related to the uprising; the general closure of all educational institutions for several months, resulting in the loss of an academic year for students and serious delays in the schooling of Palestinian children.

The new situation in the occupied territories has endangered a considerable amount of administrative and other forms of detentions. Several thousand Palestinians, including minors, have been or continue to be detained in various prisons and detention centres, sometimes even inside Israel itself. Many of these cases illustrate the fact that legal guarantees such as the right to fair trial are often denied to Palestinians. Furthermore, this unprecedented increase in the prison population has also aggravated the already critical conditions of detention and the plight of the detainees.

The Special Committee has endeavoured, within the constraints and self-restrictions imposed by the financial situation of the United Nations, to provide in its report a faithful and accurate picture of the human rights situation prevailing in the occupied territories. The tragic developments that have cast their shadow over the civilian population clearly illustrate the responsibility of the international community, which so far has unfortunately not been able to adopt effective measures to improve the human rights situation of the Palestinians under occupation. It is the sincere hope of the Special Committee that the present report may serve as a means of assessing the gravity of the plight of the civilian population in the occupied territories and the urgent need to improve its conditions. . . .

With reference to the *intifadah,* the UN General Assembly on 3 November 1988 (resolution 43/21), and again on 6 October 1989 (resolution 44/2), condemned

those policies and practices of Israel, the occupying Power, which violate the human rights of the Palestinian people in the occupied Palestinian territory, including Jerusalem, and, in particular, such acts as the opening of fire by the Israeli army and settlers that result in the killing and wounding of defenceless Palestinian civilians, the beating and breaking of bones, the deportation of Palestinian civilians, the imposition of restrictive economic measures, the demolition of houses, the ransacking of real or personal property belonging individually or collectively to private persons, collective punishment and detentions, etc.

The assembly demanded that Israel abide scrupulously by the GENEVA CONVENTION RELATIVE TO THE PROTECTION OF CIVILIAN PERSONS IN TIME OF WAR, and desist immediately from those policies and practices that are in violation of the provisions of the convention. It reaffirmed that the occupation by Israel of the Palestinian territory since 1967, including Jerusalem, and of other Arab territories, in no way changes the legal status of those territories and requested the Security Council to examine with urgency the situation in the occupied Palestinian territory with a view to considering measures needed to provide international protection to the Palestinian civilians in the Palestinian territory occupied by Israel. It invited member states, the organizations of the United Nations system; governmental, intergovernmental and non-governmental organizations; and the mass communications media to continue and enhance their support for the Palestinian people.

SEE ALSO *Israel entries; Palestinian People's Rights.*

IRAN. The Islamic Republic of Iran is a country in southern Asia, on the Caspian Sea, the Gulf of Oman, and the Persian Gulf. It has borders with Afghanistan, Iraq, Pakistan, Turkey, and the Union of Soviet Socialist Republics. It achieved independence in 1925 from Russia and England, which had divided the country (then known as Persia) into two spheres of influence, when Gen. Reza Pahlavi seized the government and was elected hereditary shah; and became a member of the United Nations in 1945. Its population is estimated by the UN (1990) to be 49,897,000. Ethnic groups include persons of Turkish, Kurdish and Syrian descent. Languages commonly used include Farsi (Persian), various Turkic vernaculars, Kurdish, Luri, and Baluchi. Islam (Shi'ite, 96%; Sunni, 3%) is the predominant religion; non-Muslim denominations account for the remainder.

The government (1990) took the form of a republic. Under the constitution, the president, elected for a term of four years, exercises executive authority. He appoints the prime minister and members of the cabinet, subject to the approval of the unicameral National Consultative Assembly, members of which are elected by popular vote for terms of four years. The judicial system is based on Islamic law. However, from 1982 to the end of 1988 all State policy was determined by a religious leader, the Ayatollah Ruhollah Khomeini, who, together with the National Consultative Assembly, aimed to ensure adherence to Islamic principles in every aspect of Iranian life.

In ancient days, the territory now known as Iran lay at the heart of the Persian Empire, one of the greatest empires the world has ever known. In 626 A.D., Arab invaders brought foreign rule, and the new religion of Islam, to the country. Independence was re-established many centuries later when the Safavid dynasty (1499–1733), under its leader Shah Ismael, drove out the Arabs and converted the population to the Shi'ite branch of Islam. Subsequently, Iran experienced periods of prosperity and expansion mixed with periods of conquest and exploitation of its vast natural resources by various European countries, including England, Portugal, and Russia.

Gen. Reza Pahlavi was deposed as Shah in 1941 in favor of his son, Mohammed Reza Pahlavi. Although conditions of life improved notably in Iran during the regime of the new shah, he was widely criticized for his efforts to modernize the country and to improve the status of its women, as well as for misuse of the secret police force known as *Sadak* to suppress opposition. In 1968, Iran acted as host to the International Conference on Human Rights, held to commemorate the 20th anniversary of the Universal Declaration of Human Rights.

Massive demonstrations demanding the return to Iran of opposition leader Ayatollah Ruhollah Khomeini from France, where he had lived for some years in exile, led to the imposition of martial law in 1978. When riots and strikes continued despite the appointment of another opposition leader, Shahpur Bakhtiar, as premier, Shah Mohammed Reza Pahlavi handed over power to a regency council and left Iran on 16 January 1979. Khomeini returned to Iran on 1 February and established a new government based on fundamentalist Islamic concepts. The shah died on 17 July 1980 after being admitted to the United States of America for treatment of his terminal cancer.

Since militant "students" invaded the U.S. embassy at Teheran on 4 November 1979 and seized a number of staff members as hostages, the United Nations has been deeply concerned about the human rights situation in Iran. A unanimous appeal by the Security Council demanding release of the hostages was rejected by the Iranian government, and it was not until Iran's conditions—including release of $8 billion in frozen Iranian assets, return of assets held by the former imperial family, and cancellation of any damage claims against Iran by the U.S.—were met that 52 American hostages were released after 444 days in captivity.

The Security Council, the General Assembly, the Commission on Human Rights, the Sub-Commission on Prevention of Discrimination and Protection of Minorities, and other United Nations bodies have repeatedly, since then, expressed their concern at reports of continuing serious violations of human rights in the Islamic Republic of Iran, and the commission has appointed a special representative to assist it in monitoring the situation.

The special representative was first appointed by the commission at its 1984 session (resolution 1984/54); the special representative's mandate later was extended, at each annual commission session, for a one-year period. The special representative is Mr. Reynaldo Galindo Pohl (El Salvador). He prepares, each year, an interim report for consideration by the General Assembly and a final report for consideration by the Commission on Human Rights.

Up to December 1989, all reports of the special reresentative were based on information made available to him by the government of the Islamic Republic of Iran and by other sources including governmental and non-governmental organizations. In noting with appreciation the 1989 interim report, however, the General Assembly also took note of the special rapporteur's recommendation that, in order to achieve full cooperation between the Iranian government and the special representative, there was a need to proceed to another stage in the discharge of the special representative's mandate. Accordingly, the Assembly welcomed (resolution 44/163) the invitation by the Islamic Republic of Iran to the special representative to visit that country (UN Doc. A/C.3/44/9) and requested the secretary-general to give the special representative as necessary assistance.

Accordingly, Mr. Pohl visited Iran between 20 and 28 January 1990 and met with many representatives of the executive, judicial and legislative branches of its government. Earlier, between 8 and 19 January 1989, he had heard a number of witnesses in connection with the human rights situation in that country; and, during the period between the announcement of the invitation and the departure of the special representative, some 1,500 Iranian emigres or relatives of Iranians living abroad addressed communications to him. Their allegations related to alleged cases of executions, torture, disappearances, and mistreatment of prisoners. Information was also obtained from the Iranian and the international press and from organizations of many types.

The special representative's visit was described in detail, and the information placed at his disposal was analyzed, in the report which he presented to the Commission on Human Rights at its 1990 session (UN Doc. E/CN.4/1990/24, chaps. I to IV). His conclusions and recommendations (chap. V, para. 232–253) were as follows:

This final report marks a major development in the fulfilment of the Special Representative's mandate and in the resolutions adopted by the General Assembly and the Commission on Human Rights: the visit to the Islamic Republic of Iran and the on-the-spot examination of the human rights situation. For the first time since the mandate was issued in 1984, the Government invited the Special Representative to visit the Islamic Republic of Iran.

The Special Representative wishes to place on record his gratitude to the Government of the Islamic Republic of Iran for its co-operation in the course of the visit, the facilities afforded to him in his task and its readiness to extend the visit, although this was not possible in view of the strict time-limits imposed by the imminent start of the Commission's work.

On his return to Geneva, the Special Representative discovered that the press or the media attributed to him statements made following the visit to the Islamic Republic of Iran. The Commission on Human Rights should know that neither he nor any member of the group that visited the country made any statement whatsoever. Even though he is unaware of the substance of the statements attributed to him, the Special Representative would point out most emphatically that he made no statement whatsoever, either in public or in private, and that he has not even spoken with anybody about the subject, because it was his firm intention that the report should be drawn up without interpretations or speculations that would compromise its objectiveness and that nothing should be said before the Commission received it.

Communication between the Special Representative and the Government of the Islamic Republic of Iran is at a suitably high level and there is no topic, problem or issue that cannot be openly discussed through expeditious channels. As a result of the visit, further possibilities of communication were opened up.

The report sets out information received before and during the visit. It should be noted that allegations similar to those of previous years were still being received and that, during the period under review, there was a considerable increase in assertions, testimony and documents about terrorism. During the visit, terrorism also featured a great deal in the statements by Iranian officials and many witnesses.

The allegations of human rights violations have been arranged under different headings, to deal with them more easily, and the testimony has been split up, where appropriate, and placed under the heading involved. It was physically impossible to accommodate everyone who wished to make a statement, but sufficient testimony was gathered to establish or fill out the headings into which the available information is classed. To hear all of the people who wished to speak about their experiences, it would have been necessary to extend the visit not only by a few days, but probably by a few weeks. Some witnesses were unable to keep the appointment they had been given. This was due, among other things, to the people crowding outside the United Nations Development Programme's office, who literally blocked off the path for anyone who wanted to enter and they were disorderly in their behaviour.

Authorities and officials contacted by the Special Representative spoke about general issues and said the Government of the Islamic Republic of Iran had been friendly to all nations, particularly neighbouring countries, but had not met with a positive response. They went on to speak of kinds of pressure from abroad, help to armed gangs, terrorism, disinformation, the eight-year war and the July

1988 invasion. Generally, their points were: the international community listens to terrorist groups; information abroad has been and still is being manipulated; United Nations bodies apply two different standards as far as human rights are concerned because for political reasons a very close eye is kept on some countries, whereas others which commit serious human rights violations do not come under any international monitoring procedure.

The Special Representative observed that there is a deep split in Iranian society as a result of the hectic revolutionary period and that one ingredient in this split has been the armed struggle, in which terrorism has had a part, sometimes with devastating effects. Complaints are heard on all sides and among all social classes, from some who deplore and condemn the armed struggle, from others who are distressed by the punishment meted out and reject it in the belief that it has been applied improperly and undermined the dignity of prisoners, and a significant number who maintain that their ideals have been crushed and their youthful naivety has been exploited. The meetings of mothers and of wives of the dead are a symbol of the social polarization: outside the office of the United Nations Development Programme, large groups of women were demonstrating against terrorism, to which they attributed their troubles and the loss of their loved ones, whereas, at the other end of Tehran at the Behest Zahra cemetery, mothers and wives of the executed were meeting, as they do every Thursday and Friday afternoon, to weep for their loved ones, the executed and those buried in common graves.

The Special Representative, as in earlier reports, condemns terrorism in all its forms, whatever the motive, pretext or aim. During the visit to the Islamic Republic of Iran, he received ample official and private information about the disastrous effects of this kind of political activity. However, it has to be borne in mind that the parties to international instruments are States and are, of course, represented by Governments, and hence the grievances are chiefly directed against them. By extension and in keeping with recent practice, it has been understood that insurgent groups should also respect human rights, although Governments recognized by the international community and insurgents are not on the same footing.

The testimony gathered reiterated complaints received in Geneva about unlawful executions, torture, substitute prisoners, imprisonment beyond the period specified in the sentence, spontaneous decisions by low-ranking officials and the absence of counsel for the defence. Other witnesses stated the opposite because they had been arrested in the course of clandestine activities against the Government, had been treated leniently and subsequently pardoned. Testimony was also gathered on restrictions on the right of association. A study of the testimony, representing two different kinds of personal experience and views, is in itself illuminating.

The Special Representative was able to verify that four persons shown on lists of executed persons were still alive. With a copy of the list of executed persons, these four people presented their identity cards, which included photographs, and their identity was established so far as was possible without laboratory proof. Another dozen persons also maintained that they had been included on the lists, but they did not have their identity cards on them when the case was examined in the course of a collective interview in the Hotel Azadi.

The allegation that political prisoners had been executed under false charges of drug trafficking was given special attention during the visit. In the light of the testimony received and published in earlier reports about such indications as hearing somebody shout that he was not a drug trafficker, the explanations given by the Special Prosecutor for Drug Trafficking Offences and the testimony from leading figures in the political opposition who are living in the country, the Special Representative considers it his duty to acquaint the Commission with his conviction on this matter. He has always treated this information cautiously and taken it as a point of departure for further inquiry. Three witnesses from the political opposition, who were well informed and spoke on other issues that were not precisely favourable to the Government, said they were not aware of a single case of a political prisoner being executed as if he were a drug trafficker. It would be strange if, living in the place and following events so closely, such persons had not learned of facts of such great significance. In the light of his conviction and in all honesty, the Special Representative considers that, unless specific proof is submitted to him in this regard, this allegation involves elements of speculation and he rules it out.

The number of executions and the guarantees of due process of law were topics that arose in many conversations. The Special Representative repeatedly brought up the subject of the number of executions and adduced reasons for doing so, on the basis of international instruments and on humanitarian grounds. Many drug traffickers can be rehabilitated and reincorporated into society and should in any event enjoy the guarantees of due process of law. Certainly the deterrent character of the executions has disappeared because there have been none in public for five months, but many persons, probably hundreds, are still awaiting execution. As he was leaving the country, the Special Representative presented a request for clemency in this regard. He has gained the impression that this harsh policy could become a good deal less severe.

The guarantees of due process of law now include appeal and review and they are operative with regard to convictions in general and review usually applies in respect of the revolutionary courts. The Supreme Court of Justice has the last word. Criticisms are made, for some lawyers would like an appeal to lie not only against the sentence, but against other rulings in the trial, but this remedy does exist, and it may be broadened.

Admittedly, the Iranian Constitution provides for the assistance of a lawyer and makes no exception in any case whatever. However, many witnesses speak of the absence of counsel and such testimony is still being received. The Special Representative believes he has identified two gaps that might explain why some proceedings are held without a lawyer for the defence: when the accused person refuses to accept such assistance or when the lawyer called upon refuses to take over the defence. The practical effects in these two cases are that some proceedings, particularly trials for drug trafficking and political offences, may be held without counsel for the defence. The Special Representative believes that a way of overcoming these gaps should be examined, for they turn into opportunities to make sure that there is no defence counsel; in this connection, he would suggest that the right to legal assistance should be declared an inalienable right and that a rule should be adopted that no criminal proceedings may be instituted, pursued and completed without continuous assistance from a lawyer, who would be afforded sufficient time to gather evidence and make a plea based on legal reasoning or lenience on humanitarian grounds.

Moreover, the testimony gathered during the visit to the Islamic Republic of Iran repeats a number of allegations communicated to the Government in the past. In the matter of issuing passports, the higher authorities should look into the way in which the lower authorities are keeping to the law and to the regulations established by the higher authorities because there may be some problem of enforcement at the administrative level.

There were repetitions of allegations about prisoners completing their sentence and still being held in custody indefinitely, and persons completing their sentence and then being executed. Testimony collected privately and statements taken at Evin prison in the presence of prison officials again spoke of ill-treatment and torture. The Special Representative has also insisted that detailed replies to these and other allegations are necessary as part of the process of studying the human rights situation.

The Government of the Islamic Republic of Iran has been receptive to some criticisms made in earlier reports by the Special Representative, for example, about public and mass executions of drug traffickers and about incorporating in the penalty the time that has been served before the sentence is handed down. This receptiveness indicates that other suggestions and criticisms could well be taken into account. In the course of the actual visit, the following suggestions were, in principle, favourably received: regular visits by the International Committee of the Red Cross to prisons throughout the country in order to ascertain the conditions of imprisonment and, in particular, to look into the situation of political prisoners; the possibility of the Centre for Human Rights providing technical assistance to the Government of the Islamic Republic of Iran in matters pertaining to human rights; the acceptance of a programme to identify clashes or inconsistencies between Islamic law and international law, particularly internationally recognized human rights, so as to make it easier for the Iranian Government to bring its system into line with international standards; and consideration of requests the Special Representative may transmit on purely humanitarian grounds. The Special Representative handed over a request for a marked reduction in death sentences and about the case of a person in urgent need of medical treatment outside prison walls.

The Special Representative received information on frequent clemency measures. While this report was being completed, he received from the Permanent Mission of the Islamic Republic of Iran to the United Nations Office at Geneva an announcement of a clemency measure for persons sentenced by military courts: persons sentenced to one year will be freed and longer sentences will be reduced by half.

The information gathered by the Special Representative in Geneva on the situation of the Baha'is was confirmed in Tehran by the testimony of two members of this group. They supplied a circular from the Prime Minister, whose duties were later taken up by the President of the Republic, instructing the authorities about the treatment of the Baha'is. The circular was satisfactory to the visitors and to the other members of this faith. In addition, the witnesses said that a ruling by the Supreme Court of Justice had been in their favour and established a marked precedent, although it has not yet been enforced. The Special Representative's impression is that the situation of the Baha'is is moving towards quite broad *de facto* tolerance.

At the round table held at the Ministry of Foreign Affairs to sum up the visit, the Special Representative expressed the opinion that the Government's next step could consist in providing detailed replies to the allegations transmitted to it. In order for these replies to be prepared, the allegations would have to be investigated; it might well prove that some officials had failed in the performance of their duties and that disciplinary measures or punishment would be needed or, on the contrary, that it would be appropriate to demonstrate that the allegations were inaccurate, false or mistaken. Both the Government and the procedure established by the Commission on Human Rights would benefit from such concrete co-operation. The visit needs to be supplemented by these replies so that the consideration of the alleged cases may continue and conclusions may be reached on the situation as a whole.

In view of these facts and considerations, it is the Special Representative's conclusion that, in his view, the Commission should continue to monitor the human rights situation in the Islamic Republic of Iran and that another visit seems desirable, and even necessary, in order to broaden the study with many cases which it was not possible to collect, to go deeper into situations which still call for greater knowledge of the facts and to listen to many persons who felt disappointed because so little time was available.

Having examined the report, which in its view marked a major development in the fulfilment of the mandate of the special representative and opened up further possibilities of communication on a high level, the Commission on Human Rights adopted, on 7 March 1990, a resolution (resolution 1990/79) containing the following operative paragraphs:

The Commission on Human Rights, . . .

1. Takes note with appreciation of the report of the Special Representative (E/CN.4/1990/24), which was prepared after a visit to the country, and the conclusions and recommendations contained therein;

2. Welcomes the decision of the Government of the Islamic Republic of Iran to invite the Special Representative of the Commission on Human Rights to visit that country and the co-operation provided by the Government of the Islamic Republic of Iran in the course of the visit, as well as its commitment to continue the co-operation;

3. Welcomes also the invitation of the Government of the Islamic Republic of Iran extended to the Representative for a further visit to the country;

4. Takes note of the Special Representative's view that the Commission on Human Rights should continue to monitor the human rights situation in the Islamic Republic of Iran in order to broaden his study, to go deeper into certain situations, and to listen to many persons who could not see the Special Representative due to the short duration of his stay in Iran;

5. Endorses the Special Representative's opinion that the Government of the Islamic Republic of Iran continue to provide the Special Representative with replies on all allegations of human rights violations that have been transmitted to it;

6. Notes that the Special Representative, as in earlier reports, condemns terrorism in all its forms, whatever the motive, pretext or aim, and that during his visit to the Islamic Republic of Iran, he received ample official and private information about the disastrous effects of this kind of activity;

7. Expresses its concern that testimony gathered by the Special Representative reiterated complaints about unlawful executions, torture, substitute prisoners, imprisonment beyond the period specified in the sentence, spontaneous decisions by low-ranking officials and the absence of council for defence as well as restrictions on the right to assemble and recognizes that testimony was also gathered representing the opposite and thus two different kinds of personal experience and view were received;

8. Recognizes that the Special Representative rules out allegations that political prisoners had been executed under false charges of drug trafficking, unless specific proof is submitted to him in this regard;

9. Welcomes the clemency measures taken by the Government of the Islamic Republic of Iran;

10. Notes the receptiveness of the Government of the Islamic Republic of Iran to some criticisms in earlier reports by the Special Representative and encourages the Government of the Islamic Republic of Iran to respond to the recommendations contained in the Special Representative's reports;

11. Welcomes the favourable reception by the Government of the Islamic Republic of Iran to the Special Representative's suggestions: that the International Committee of the Red Cross be permitted to make regular visits to prisons throughout the Islamic Republic of Iran in order to ascertain the conditions of imprisonment, and in particular to look into the situation of political prisoners; that there be a programme, or study, to identify clashes or inconsistencies between Islamic law and international law, particularly internationally recognized human rights; that consideration be given to requests transmitted by the Special Representative on purely humanitarian grounds; and that the possibility of technical assistance from the United Nations in the field of human rights be examined;

12. Encourages the Islamic Republic of Iran to comply with international instruments on human rights, including the International Covenant on Civil and Political Rights to which the Islamic Republic of Iran is a party, and to ensure that all individuals within its territory and subject to its jurisdiction enjoy the rights recognized in these instruments;

13. Decides to extend the mandate of the Special Representative, as contained in its resolution 1984/54 of 14 March 1984, for a further year;

14. Requests the Special Representative to present an interim report to the General Assembly at its forty-fifth session on the human rights situation in the Islamic Republic of Iran, including the situation of minority groups, such as the Bahai's, and a final report to the Commission at its forty-seventh session;

15. Requests the Secretary-General to give all necessary assistance to the Special Representative of the Commission;

16. Decides to continue its consideration of the situation of human rights and fundamental freedoms in the Islamic Republic of Iran as a matter of priority at its forty-seventh session.

IRAQ. The Republic of Iraq is an Arab country in western Asia, once known as Mesopotamia. It has borders with Iran, Jordan, Kuwait, Saudi Arabia, Syria, and Turkey. It achieved independence in 1932, after 12 years as a League of Nations mandate under British administration, and became a member of the United Nations in 1945. Its population is estimated by the UN (1990) to be 18,760,000. Arabs and Kurds are the largest ethnic groups; the Kurds are largely concentrated in the northern areas. Numerically, the next largest ethnic group are the Turcomans who, although scattered throughout the country, are concentrated mainly in the area of Kirkuk. Other minorities are the Assyrians, the Chaldeans, and the Armenians, who are concentrated mainly in the governates of Nineva and Dohuk. Languages spoken include Arabic (official), Kurdish, Turcoman, Syrian, and Armenian. Islam is the predominant religion, 96%; Christians, Sabeans, Yazidis, and Jews make up the remaining 4%. Literacy is estimated at 50%.

The government (1990) took the form of a republic. However, since the revolution of 17 July 1968, the Iraqi government has been directed by the Arab Ba'ath Socialist Party through a council of Command of the Revolution and a Council of Ministers, both headed by the president who acts as head of State and of government. Legislation is prepared by the National Assembly. The courts are independent of other branches of government and may award damages to any person found to have suffered moral or material harm as a result of violation of his human rights.

In September 1980, Iraq became involved in a war with neighboring Iran which arose out of a dispute over control of a waterway between the two countries. The war took many thousands of lives on both sides.

One result of the war was the "disappearance" of large numbers of persons in Iraq between 1980 and 1984. Many of the "disappeared" were Iraqi Shi'ites who were arrested at the outbreak of hostilities and later expelled to Iran. More recent cases, reported to the **WORKING GROUP ON ENFORCED OR INVOLUNTARY DIS- APPEARANCES** of the Commission on Human Rights, include 16 women said to have been arrested in reprisal against their husbands. The working group's 1990 report to the Commission on Human Rights indicated that it had transmitted a total of 3,045 cases to the government of Iraq, of which 36 had been clarified by government responses and 17 by non-governmental sources, leaving 2,992 cases outstanding. None of these cases had occurred in the latest year of the survey, 1989.

Iraq has also been engaged in recent years in an undeclared conflict with Kurdish guerrillas and a group of Shi'ite extremists known as *Al Daawa* (The Call), both operating in its northern regions. Both groups claim violation of their human rights as cause for the conflict, but others consider it to be an effort, sponsored covertly by Iran, to harass the Iraqi government and to divert its energies from the southern borders.

Traditionally, however, Iraq has provided a good example in the handling of its Kurdish population to neighboring countries with large numbers of Kurds,

including Iran, Syria, Turkey, and the Union of Soviet Socialist Republics. Article 8(c) of the Iraqi constitution provides that "the region in which the majority of the population are Kurds shall enjoy autonomy in accordance with the provisions of the law." Revolutionary Command Council decision 288 of 11 March 1970, which has the force of law, contains the following guidelines for autonomy (UN Doc. CCPR/C/37/ Add. 3, para. 260):

(a) One of the vice-presidents of the Republic must be a Kurd;
(b) In administrative units where the majority of the population is Kurdish, civil servants must be Kurds or proficient in the Kurdish language;
(c) There must be no discrimination between Kurds and others in regard to access to public office, including key positions in the State such as ministries and army commands, subject to the requirements of competence.

As regards the official language and the language of education in the autonomous region, article 2 of Act. No. 33 of 1974 stipulates that (*Ibid.,* para. 264):

(a) In addition to Arabic, Kurdish shall be an official language in the region;
(b) Arabic and Kurdish shall be the languages of education, at all stages and in all establishments, for Kurds in the region, in accordance with paragraph (e) of this article;
(c) Educational facilities for members of the Arab ethnic group shall be established in the region. In such facilities, instruction shall be in Arabic and the Kurdish language shall be taught as a compulsory subject;
(d) All residents of the region, regardless of their mother tongue, shall have the right to choose the schools in which they wish to be taught;
(e) All stages of education in the region shall be governed by the general education policy of the State.

As regards the rights of Iraqi citizens in the autonomous region, article 3 of the same act provides that (*Ibid.,* para. 266):

(a) The rights and freedoms of Arabs and members of minority groups in the region shall be safeguarded in accordance with the provisions of the Constitution, the law and the decisions promulgated in connection therewith. The autonomous administration shall be under an obligation to guarantee the exercise of the said rights and freedoms;
(b) Arabs and members of minority groups in the region shall be represented in all the autonomous institutions on the basis of their number in proportion to the total population of the region and they shall have access to public office in accordance with the regulations and decisions pertaining thereto.

In Iraq as a whole, legislation protects the rights of persons belonging to ethnic, religious, and linguistic minorities and guarantees the freedom of all communities to engage in religious observance. The following information on the subject was provided to the HUMAN RIGHTS COMMITTEE in a report dated 21 April 1986 (*Ibid.*, para. 203–205).

Article 1, paragraph 5, of Act No. 50 promulgated on 23 May 1981 stipulates that the responsibilities of the Ministry of Awqaf (Mortmain) and Religious Affairs includes looking after the welfare of religious communities and, in particular, regulating matters pertaining to the administration of their religious endowments and places of worship.

Under the terms of Ordinance No. 32 promulgated on 19 September 1981, the Ministry of Awqaf and Religious Affairs assumed responsibility for the welfare and support of religious communities. The following list of the religious communities that are officially recognized in Iraq was attached to that ordinance:

(1) the Chaldean community; (2) the Assyrian community; (3) the Assyrian Catholic community; (4) the Syrian Orthodox community; (5) the Syrian Catholic community; (6) the Armenian Orthodox community; (7) the Armenian Catholic community; (8) the Greek Orthodox community; (9) the Greek Catholic community; (10) the Roman Catholic community; (11) the National Evangelical Protestant community; (12) the Assyrian Evangelical Protestant community; (13) the Seventh Day Adventist community; (14) the Orthodox Coptic community; (15) the Yazidi community; (16) the Sabaean community; and (17) the Jewish community.

The support that the religious communities receive from the State can be summarized as follows:

(a) Exemption of all churches and places of worship from charges for the supply of water and electricity;

(b) Exemption of Christian ministers of religion from compulsory military service and their assignment to their churches after completion of the period of basic training;

(c) Payment of the amounts needed for the renovation and furnishing of the churches, places of worship and residences of the ministers of religion of all communities;

(d) Payment by the Ministry of the amounts needed for the construction of churches and places of worship and their connection to the water and electric power supply;

(e) Granting of land, free of charge, for the establishment of churches, places of worship and cemeteries for the religious communities;

(f) Exemption from customs duty of materials imported from abroad for the purpose of the observance of religious rites;

(g) Provision of financial assistance for religious communities. By the middle of 1984, this assistance had totalled 1,160,000 dinars.

As regards religious instruction in Iraq, the government stated (*Ibid.*, para. 206) that "the teaching syllabuses in all schools include religious educational studies in accordance with the religious beliefs of students. No student belonging to any religious community is compelled to receive instruction in religious beliefs other than his own."

Iraq has been the subject of international attention since 1984 because of allegations concerning its use of CHEMICAL WEAPONS against Iranian forces and against Kurdish rebels. As early as 1982, the UN General Assembly had requested the secretary-general (resolution 37/98) to investigate, with the assistance of qualified experts, information brought to his attention by any member State concerning activities that may constitute a violation of the PROTOCOL FOR THE PROHIBITION OF THE USE OF ASPHYXIATING, POISONOUS OR OTHER GASES, AND OF BACTERIOLOGICAL METHODS OF WARFARE, signed at Geneva on 17 June 1925, or of the relevant rules of customary international law. Accordingly, the secretary-general dispatched missions to investigate allegations by the Islamic Republic of Iran, and of Iraq, concerning the use of chemical weapons in March 1984, April 1985, February–March 1986, April–May 1987, March–April 1988, and twice in July 1988. The results were summarized by the secretary-general as follows (UN Doc. E/CN.4/Sub.2/1989/4, para. 36–38):

In its report of 8 May 1987, the mission stated that, in areas inspected by the mission, chemical weapons had been used against Iranian positions. In addition to military personnel, civilians had also been injured in these attacks. After investigation undertaken in Iran in 1984, 1986 and 1987, in hospitals in Europe in 1985 and in Iraq in 1987, the mission concluded that [UN Doc. S/18852, paras. 18–19]:

"(a) There has been repeated use of chemical weapons against Iranian forces by Iraqi forces, employing aerial bombs and, very probably, rockets. The chemical agents used are mustard gas (yperite) and probably, on some occasions, nerve agents;

"(b) A new dimension is that civilians in Iran also have been injured by chemical weapons;

"(c) Iraqi military personnel have sustained injuries from chemical warfare agents, which are mustard gas (yperite) and a pulmonary irritant, possibly phosgene".

At the request of the Secretary-General, Dr. M. Domingues, a medical specialist, accompanied by Mr. James Holger, a senior official of the United Nations Secretariat, conducted between 8 and 11 April 1988 an investigation into the alleged use of chemical weapons in the Iran-Iraq conflict. He came to the following conclusions [UN Doc. S/19823, para. 16–17]:

"(a) On the basis of the clinical examinations I conducted in the Islamic Republic of Iran, I was able to determine that patients had been affected by chemical weapons. A considerable number of those affected were civilians;

"(b) On the basis of clinical examinations I conducted in Iraq, I was able to determine that the patients—all military personnel—had been affected by chemical weapons".

In its resolutions 612 of 9 May 1988 and 620 of 16 August 1988, the Security Council, having reviewed reports on the investigative missions dispatched to the region by the Secretary-General in April, July and in August, condemned the use of chemical weapons in the conflict between Iran and Iraq. All three missions' reports confirmed the use of chemical weapons in the war [UN Docs. S/19823, S/20060 and Add. 1, S/20063 and Add 1, and S/2 0134].

In September 1988, officials in Turkey charged that Iraq had used chemical weapons in its military campaign against Kurdish rebels within its own borders, causing thousands of Kurds to seek refuge in Turkey. An investigation by United Nations experts was proposed by Belgium, Great Britain, Japan, the Netherlands, the United States of America, and West Germany. Although Iraq denied that chemical weapons had been used, it refused to cooperate with the proposed investigation on the ground that it would constitute an interference in its internal affairs.

On 2 August 1990, Iraq's armed forces invaded neighboring KUWAIT. This action was condemned by the UN Security Council on the following day (resolution 660 [1990]). On 6 August, the council imposed a mandatory trade embargo against Iraq and occupied Kuwait, calling upon all member States to halt their trade and transportation links with those countries (resolution 661 [1990]). Only twice before had the council imposed mandatory economic sanctions, as authorized by chap. VII of the UNITED NATIONS CHARTER—against Southern Rhodesia in 1965 and against South Africa in 1977. The sanctions were adopted by a vote of 13 to 0, with Cuba and Yemen abstaining. In addition to the United Nations, the Arab League voted in a tumultuous meeting to condemn Iraq's aggression against its Arab neighbor, by a vote of 13 to 0, with the remaining eight members either abstaining or boycotting the meeting.

The United States of America promptly imposed a trade embargo on Iraq and sent military forces to defend Saudi Arabia at the request of the Saudi government. Iraq formally annexed Kuwait on 8 August 1990, an act repudiated by the UN Security Council on the following day.

On 18 August 1990, the Security Council demanded the release of foreign hostages—called "guests" by the Iraqi government. These foreign citizens were trapped in Iraq and occupied Kuwait and reportedly to be used as "human shields" against military attack; all "guests" were released by Christmas 1990. On 15 August 1990, the council gave the United States and other countries with warships in the Persian Gulf area the authority to enforce the blockade by halting shipping headed for Iraq or Kuwait.

On 29 November 1990, the Security Council noted that, despite all its efforts, Iraq had refused to implement resolution 660 and subsequent resolutions, and, in resolution 678 (1990), authorized UN member States cooperating with the legitimate government of Kuwait "to use all necessary means" to uphold and implement its resolutions, unless Iraq were to fully implement them by 15 January 1991.

When Iraq ignored the deadline, the allied coalition began a devastating air attack on military targets in Iraq and occupied Kuwait on 16 January 1991. On 25 February, having achieved air supremacy, the allies undertook a massive ground offensive, which decimated the demoralized Iraqi ground forces. By 27 February, Kuwait had been fully liberated and offensive combat operations were suspended, provided that Iraq would immediately comply with the Security Council's resolutions.

On 2 March 1991, the Security Council, having received assurances of Iraq's compliance, reaffirmed the force and effect of its previous decrees and called upon Iraq (a) to rescind immediately its actions purporting to annex Kuwait; (b) to acknowledge in principle its liability for any loss, damage, or injury resulting from the occupation; (c) to release all Kuwaiti and third-country nationals who had been detained; and (d) to return immediately all seized Kuwaiti property.

IRELAND. A country in Western Europe, occupying about 84% of the land area of the second largest of the British Isles, situated in the Atlantic Ocean west of Great Britain, from which it is separated by the Irish Sea, the Republic of Ireland has a border with Nothern Ireland, which occupies the remainder of the island. It achieved self-rule in 1921 when the Irish Free State was recognized after prolonged anti-British agitation and guerrilla warfare; however, six northern counties chose to remain as part of the United Kingdom. Full independence came with the proclamation of the Republic of Ireland on 18 April, 1949, and Ireland became a member of the United Nations in 1955. Its population is estimated by the UN (1990) to be 3,843,000. Ethnic groups include descendents of Celtic tribes who conquered the island before the Christian era, and of the English invaders who eventually replaced them. Languages commonly used include English and Irish (Gaelic). Christianity (Roman Catholic, 95%; Anglican, 5%) is the predominant religion. Literacy is estimated at 99%.

The government (1990) took the form of a republic. The prime minister (*Taoiseach*), representing the party or coalition given the majority in a popular election, is appointed by the president on nomination by the House of Representatives (*Dáil Eireann*), to which he is responsible. The legislature consists of the president, who signs and promulgates all laws, the 166-member House of Representatives, and the 60-member Senate (*Seanad Eireann*). Members of the House are elected by proportional representation. Members of the Senate are nominated in the following manner: 11 by the prime minister, six by the universities, and 43 by vocational panels. Members of both bodies serve for a maximum term of five years.

There is an independent judiciary, to which judges are appointed by the president. Political parties include the *Fianna Fáil, Fine Gael,* Labour, Progressive Democrats, Workers' Party and the Independents.

Efforts to reunite the republic and the six northern provinces—now joined to the United Kingdom—continue sporadically. However, the government in Dublin has outlawed the extremist Irish Republican Army (IRA) and has detained and punished IRA guerrillas operating in territories under its control.

Concerning freedom of religion, members of the Protestant minority have maintained that laws relating to mixed marriages force the children of such unions into the Catholic faith and that Protestant parents are compelled to pay educational costs considerably higher than those paid by Catholics.

ISLAMIC CALL SOCIETY. An international non-governmental organization in consultative status with the UN Economic and Social Council (Roster) and with UNESCO, the society has affiliated organizations and individual members in 36 countries.

Founded in 1972, the group aims to make known the call of Islam in the world by all peaceful means, in particular by diffusing Islamic culture and the Arabic language, promoting peace and international cooperation, classifying Islamic law, compiling and publishing reference works, and creating centers of education.

Islamic Call Society. Address: P.O. Box 2549, Tripoli, Libya. Secretary-General: Mohamed Ahmed Sharif.

ISRAEL. The State of Israel is a country in western Asia, on the Mediterranean Sea. It has borders with Egypt, Jordan, Lebanon, and Syria. Formerly Palestine, a League of Nations mandate under the administration of Great Britain, the foreign minister of the Provincial Government of Israel informed the UN Security Council of the "Proclamation of an Independent State of Israel in Palestine" (UN Doc. S/747) on 15 May 1948, one day after the expiration of the mandate. Israel became a member of the United Nations in 1949. Its population is estimated by the UN (1990) to be 4,617,000. The demographic composition of the population (as of 1983) included Jews (84%), Muslims (13%), Christians (2.3%) and Druze (1.3%). Languages in common use include Hebrew and Arabic (both official), English, and the many national tongues of the immigrant population. Arabic is employed in official publications and as necessary in government offices; it is used by members of the parliament if they so choose, such speeches being simultaneously rendered into Hebrew; and it is used in the the publication of ordinances, official notices, and in the press and other media. The *Sharia* (Muslim religious) courts, which have exclusive jurisdiction over members of the Muslim community in matters of personal status (marriage, divorce, inheritance, etc.), conduct their proceedings in Arabic, while, in other courts, translators are appointed to assist those who do not know Hebrew. Literacy is estimated at 94% among Jews and 84% among those of other beliefs.

Among the Jewish population of Israel, there tend to be four main divisions: the non-observant, 45%; the traditional, mostly immigrants from Muslim countries, 35%; the Orthodox, 15%; and the ultra-orthodox Haredim, 5%. Their points of view sometimes conflict, mainly on the question of whether or not Israel should remain a secular State.

While basically secular, Israel has preserved the system of religious communities, or millets, of earlier Turkish and British administrations. Under that system, members of religious communities are governed by the laws of their own religion in matters of personal status, such as marriage, divorce, maintenance, guardianship, etc. For this purpose, the recognized religious communities may establish and administer their own religious courts under rules supervised by the Ministry of Religious Affairs. In addition, recognized communities are governed by religious and cultural councils or boards, which have the capacity to acquire and administer property, to enter into contracts, to raise funds, and to execute deeds. In some cases, they may also have the power to impose upon members of the community contributions and fees for communal purposes.

The government (1990) took the form of a republic, although it does not have a written constitution. The president, elected by the *Knesset* for a term of five years, is head of State. The cabinet, headed by the prime minister, who represents the party or coalition given the majority in a popular election, exercises executive authority. The *Knesset* is composed of 120 members elected for terms of four years under a system of proportional representation. Citizens of Israel vote for national parties rather than for individuals, and any party getting even 1% of the vote wins a seat in parliament. With 17 parties represented in 1990, none could gain a majority without joining with several others.

A special body, independent of the executive, was established in 1971: the Commissioner for Complaints from the Public (or *Ombudsman*). Its function is to examine complaints submitted by anyone who claims to have been injured by an act of a public authority and to seek redress in appropriate cases.

For more than 20 years, the question of the violation of human rights in Arab territories occupied by Israel has been on the agenda of a number of United Nations organs, including the General Assembly, the Security Council, the UN Commission on Human Rights, and various specialized agencies and intergovernmental organizations. On the basis of reports prepared periodically by the SPECIAL COMMITTEE TO INVESTIGATE ISRAELI PRACTICES AFFECTING THE HUMAN RIGHTS OF THE POPULATION OF THE OCCUPIED TERRITORIES, the question has been considered year after year by the UN General Assembly as a matter of highest priority.

A major change in the composition of Israel's population began in 1988, when restrictions on the emigration of Jews from the Soviet Union were relaxed, while visa requirements for immigration into the United States of America were tightened. The stream of Soviet Jews thus diverted towards Israel was encouraged by that country's economic assistance, which, in some cases, included payment of airfare and of some post-arrival living expenses. As a result, 444 arrivals in April 1989 swelled to more than 10,000 in April 1990, and as many as a million more are expected by 1993.

On the one hand, this influx tended to calm the fears of the Jewish population, fears which had been aroused by the rapid population growth among the 650,000 Arabs resident in Israel and the 1.7 million Palestinians living in the occupied West Bank and the Gaza Strip. On the other hand, it raised serious problems of economic and social integration, such as finding suitable housing and employment for the newcomers.

In June 1990, U.S.S.R. President Mikhail Gorbachev, at a news conference in Washington, D.C. after his meetings with American President George Bush, remarked that the Soviet Union might reconsider granting exit visas to Jews unless Israel assured it that no Jewish immigrants would settle in the occupied Arab territories. The Arab League welcomed the idea, but caretaker Prime Minister Yitzhak Shamir responded that Israel would never tell its citizens where they could live "in the land of Israel." At that time, it was estimated that as many as 10% of Soviet Jewish immigrants had settled either in the occupied territories or in East Jerusalem. For specific information on the Palestinian situation in the State of Israel and the Occupied Territories, see the following entries on Israel, INTIFADAH, and PALESTINIAN PEOPLE'S RIGHTS.

ISRAEL: APPLICATION OF THE FOURTH GENEVA CONVENTION TO THE TERRITORIES OCCUPIED SINCE 1967. The UN General Assembly, after examining the 1989 report of the SPECIAL COMMITTEE TO INVESTIGATE ISRAELI PRACTICES AFFECTING

THE HUMAN RIGHTS OF THE POPULATION OF THE OCCUPIED TERRITORIES (UN Doc. A/44/599) and other relevant documentation, reaffirmed on 8 December 1989 (resolution 44/48 B) that the GENEVA CONVENTION RELATIVE TO THE PROTECTION OF CIVILIAN PERSONS IN TIME OF WAR is applicable to the Palestinian and other Arab territories occupied by Israel since 1967, including Jerusalem, and condemned again—as it had done in 16 earlier resolutions adopted annually since 1973—the failure of Israel, the occupying power, to acknowledge the applicability of the convention to those territories.

The assembly strongly demanded that Israel, a party to the convention, acknowledge and comply with its provisions and urgently called upon all States parties to the convention to exert all efforts in order to ensure respect for and compliance with those provisions.

The assembly, further, expressed grave anxiety and concern (resolution 44/48 C) at the serious situation in the Palestinian and other occupied Arab territories, including Jerusalem, as a result of the continued Israeli occupation and the measures and actions taken by Israel, the occupying power, designed to change the legal status, geographical nature, and demographic composition of those territories. It determined that all such measures and actions are in violation of the relevant provisions of the Fourth Geneva Convention, and constitute a serious obstacle to the efforts to achieve a comprehensive, just, and lasting peace in the Middle East, and, therefore, have no legal validity. It strongly deplored the persistence of Israel in carrying out such measures, and demanded that Israel desist forthwith from taking any action that would result in changing the legal status, geographical nature, or demographic composition of the Palestinian and other Arab territories occupied since 1967, including Jerusalem.

ISRAEL: DETENTION AND DEPORTATION OF PALESTINIANS. The UN General Assembly, after examining the 1989 report of the SPECIAL COMMITTEE TO INVESTIGATE ISRAELI PRACTICES AFFECTING THE HUMAN RIGHTS OF THE POPULATION OF THE OCCUPIED TERRITORIES (UN Doc. A/44/599), and other relevant documentation, deplored (resolution 44/48 D) "the Israeli arbitrary detention or imprisonment of thousands of Palestinians as a result of their resistance against occupation in order to attain self-determination" and called upon Israel to release all Palestinians and other Arabs arbitrarily detained or imprisoned.

At the same time, the assembly demanded (resolution 44/48 E) "that the Government of Israel, the occupying Power, rescind the illegal measures taken by the Israeli authorities in deporting Palestinians and that it facilitate their immediate return."

The assembly called upon the Secretary-General to report to it as soon as possible on the implementation of these resolutions.

ISRAEL: EFFECTIVE ANNEXATION OF THE SYR-IAN ARAB GOLAN. In resolution 44/48 F of 8 December 1989, the UN General Assembly, after examining the 1989 report of the SPECIAL COMMITTEE TO INVESTIGATE ISRAELI PRACTICES AFFECTING THE HUMAN RIGHTS OF THE POPULATION OF THE OCCUPIED TERRITORIES (UN Doc. A/44/599) and other relevant documentation, reaffirmed once more, as it had done in many earlier resolutions, the illegality of Israel's decision of 14 December 1981 to impose its laws, jurisdiction, and administration on the Syrian Arab Golan, which had resulted in the effective annexation of that territory.

Pointing out that the acquisition of territory by force is inadmissible under the UNITED NATIONS CHARTER and that all territories thus occupied by Israel must be returned, the assembly strongly condemned Israel, the occupying power, or its refusal to comply with the relevant resolutions, particularly Security Council resolution 497 (1981) in which the council, *inter alia,* decided that the Israeli decision to impose its laws, jurisdiction, and administration on the Syrian Arab Golan was null and void and without international legal effect and demanded that Israel should rescind its decision forthwith.

The assembly determined that all legislative and administrative measures and actions taken or to be taken by Israel that purport to alter the character and legal status of the Syrian Arab Golan are null and void and constitute a flagrant violation of the Fourth Geneva Convention and have no legal effect, strongly condemned Israel for its attempts to impose forcibly Israeli citizenship and Israeli identity cards on the Syrian citizens in the occupied Syrian Arab Golan, and called upon it to cease and desist from its repressive measures against the population of the Syrian Arab Golan. It also called upon UN member States not to recognize any of the legislative or administrative actions referred to above.

ISRAEL: HARASSMENT OF EDUCATIONAL INSTITUTIONS IN OCCUPIED PALESTINIAN TERRITORY. In resolution 44/48 G of 8 December 1989, the UN General Assembly, after examining the 1989 report of the SPECIAL COMMITTEE TO INVESTIGATE ISRAELI PRACTICES AFFECTING THE HUMAN RIGHTS OF THE POPULATION OF THE OCCUPIED TERRITORIES (UN Doc. A/

44/599) and other relevant documentation, condemned Israeli policies and practices against Palestinian students and faculties in schools, universities, and other educational institutions in the occupied Palestinian territory, especially the opening of fire on defenseless students, causing many casualties.

The assembly also condemned "the systematic Israeli campaign of repression against and closing of universities, schools and other educational and vocational institutions in the occupied Palestinian territory, in large numbers and for prolonged periods, restricting and impeding the academic activities of Palestinian universities by subjecting the selection of courses, textbooks and educational programs, the admission of students and the appointment of faculty members to the control and supervision of the military occupation authorities, in flagrant contravention of the Geneva Convention. The assembly demands that Israel, the occupying Power, comply with the provisions of that Convention, rescind all actions and measures against all educational institutions, ensure the freedom of those institutions, and refrain forthwith from hindering the effective operation of the universities, schools and other educational institutions." It requested the Secretary-General to report to it on the implementation of the resolution.

ITALY. The Italian Republic is a country in southern Europe, occupying a peninsula extending into the Mediterranean Sea and several islands including Lampedusa, Linosa, Pantellaria, Sardinia, and Sicily. It has borders with Austria, France, Switzerland, and Yugoslavia. It achieved independence originally as the Roman Empire, which disintegrated after 1713. Reunited by Giuseppe Garibaldi under Victor Emmanuel II, it was a monarchy until Benito Mussolini seized power as dictator in 1922. After World War II, in which it participated as part of the Rome–Berlin Axis, the resumption of its independence was recognized in the peace treaty of 15 September 1947. Under the peace treaty, Italy renounced all claims in Ethiopia and Greece, ceded the Dodecanese Islands to Greece and five Alpine areas to France, and turned over much of the Istrian Peninsula to Yugoslavia.

Italy became a member of the United Nations in 1955. Its population is estimated by the UN to be (1990) 57,563,000. Ethnic groups include communities of Albanian, Catalan, Croatian, Germanic, Greek, Gypsy, Sardinian, and Slavic origin; linguistic communities whose mother tongue is French, Franco–Provencal, German, Ladin, Occitan, or Slovene; and foreign workers and refugees, mostly of Mediterranean background. Languages commonly used include Italian and the above-mentioned minority languages. Christianity (Roman Catholic) is the predominant religion. Literacy is estimated at 98%.

The government (1990) took the form of a republic. The constitution, promulgated on 1 January 1948, establishes a bicameral parliament consisting of a 315-member Senate and a 630-member Chamber of Deputies; members are elected for five-year terms. The executive branch consists of a Council of Ministers (cabinet), headed by the president of the council (prime minister). The president of the republic is elected for a term of seven years by parliament sitting jointly with a small number of regional delegates. The resident nominates the prime minister, who chooses the other ministers. The judicial system is based on Roman law, as modified by the Napoleonic Code and subsequent statutes, and there is a Constitutional Court which passes on the constitutionality of laws.

There are many political parties. The Christian Democratic Party is the largest, and Italy's stability is largely due to the fact that it has represented the majority, either alone or in coalition with other parties, since 1945, although Italy has had more than 40 prime ministers during that period. The Italian Communist Party, the second largest, has at times received as much as 34% of the popular vote; in 1983, it won 29.9% of that vote. Other parties include the Italian Socialist Party, the Italian Social Movement, the Italian Republican Party, the Italian Social Democratic Party, the Italian Liberal Party, and the Radical Party.

Bettino Craxi, Italy's first socialist premier, was chosen for that post after the election of June 1983. However, his government suffered an internal crisis after the October 1985 hijacking of the cruise ship *Achille Lauro* and the downing of an Egyptian plane carrying the hijackers and Abu Abbas, a PLO leader believed to have organized the hijacking. The release of Abbas and refusal to turn the hijackers over to U.S. authorities brought Craxi's government to an impasse, and Craxi was forced to resign. He was succeeded in June 1987 by a Christian Democrat, Giovanni Goria, who, in turn, was replaced by Ciriaco De Mita in April 1988.

In recent years, Italy has been plagued by frequent outbursts of lawlessness and terrorism, carried out by well-organized bands of kidnappers. In February 1990, the government took steps to reduce the problem by enacting measures lengthening prison terms for cases in which kidnapping victims are ill, very young, or very old, and those in which cruel treatment is involved. At the same time, it called upon parliament to approve a far-reaching policy under which all relatives of a kidnapping victim would immediately have their assets frozen by the State to prevent them from raising money for payment of ransom and would be prohibited from seeking financial help from banks and similar sources. Moreover, an existing ban that makes it illegal for Italian insurance companies to sell anti-kidnapping policies would be extended to foreign companies.

Italy has also experienced an influx of foreigners, attracted by the relative prosperity of the country. The presence among the newcomers of Africans and Gypsies has occasionally been the subject of protests and public demonstrations.

As regards the treatment of Italy's linguistic minorities, the government stated, in a report presented to the United Nations on 9 June 1987 (UN Doc. CERD/C/156/Add. 1., para. 6–8), that:

The various linguistic minorities present on Italian territory are equally protected by the law, both in their existence and their cultural characteristics, and such laws promote their participation in social and economic development. Any difference in treatment among the minorities are the consequence of the application of international conventions concluded by Italy with some neighbouring countries.

The participation of the minorities in the political life of the country is assured by the inclusion of the various ethnic groups in the political parties and by the right to vote and run for office, as far as Italian citizens are concerned. Minority groups, as such, do not have representatives either at the national level or at the municipal, provincial, or regional levels. However, it should be noted that articles 12 and 22 of Law 18 of 24 January 1978 on Elections of Italian Representatives to the European Parliament contain provisions which tend to favour the political representation of the French-speaking minorities of the Valle d'Aosta, the German-speaking minorities of the Province of Bolzano, and the Slovene-speaking minorities of Friuli-Venezia Giulia.

The First Permanent Commission of the Chamber of Deputies is currently examining various bills concerning the protection of linguistic minorities. The text of these provisions confirms the principle that Italy safeguards the language and culture of the populations of Albanian, Catalan, Germanic, Greek, Slavic and Gypsy origin, and of those who speak Latin, Franco-Provençal, and Occitan. It also protects the language and culture of the Friulian and Sardinian populations. The comprehensive texts of the bills contain numerous provisions concerning school programmes in the various languages. The law recognizes that the regions with special Statutes and the Provinces of Bolzano and Trento can adopt, on the basis of their legislative competencies, further measures for the protection of the various linguistic groups.

Concerning particular linguistic minorities, the report stated (para. 10–13):

(a) *German-speaking Minority.* As is known, the German minority is present mainly in Alto Adige. The principle measures taken for the protection of this minority concern situations stemming from the pre-war period as well as the protection of its current relations with the Italian-speaking population. This protection consists mainly in the right to use the mother tongue in communicating with public offices, including tribunals; the right to obtain instruction for one's children in the German language; the right of access to public employment in proportional representation, etc.

French-speaking Minority. The protection of this minority is mainly guaranteed by Law 196 of 16 May 1978 on Implementation of the Special Statute of the Valle d'Aosta, which guarantees the use of the French language, especially in school, educational and cultural programmes. It also establishes, among other things, the obligation of the local administrations to employ, if possible, civil servants who originate from the region or who know French. Other regional provisions protect the French minority of the Valle d'Aosta in the domain of radio and television communications and publishing (Law of 14 April 1975 and Law 416 of 5 August 1981) and the Franco-Provençal, Occitan and Walser minorities in Piedmont (Law 30 of 20 June 1979). It is also to be noted that radio and television broadcasts in French for the autonomous region of Valle d'Aosta began in February 1986.

Slovene-speaking Minorities. Currently the Senate First Commission on Constitutional Affairs is proceeding to examine separately various bills concerning the protection of the Slovene minority, with a view to introducing a comprehensive programme for the Slovenes of the Provinces of Trieste and Gorizia and the Slovenes of the Province of Udine, who are protected by different norms, in relation to the various international instruments which concern them. In particular, Bill 1016 contains provisions for the global protection of the Slovene minority, and is based on the principle that Italy protects the historic settlement territory of the Slovene minority in the Provinces of Gorizia, Trieste and Udine, and ensures the minority as a whole the conditions for its own social, economic, and cultural development, eliminating any territorial diversity in application.

Ladin-Speaking Minority. Parliament is in the process of examining some bills (No. 19 of 19 July 1983 and No. 22 of 19 July 1983) which should grant the Ladin minority the use of its language in schools of all types and grades as well as in the schools in the Province of Bolzano, and a certain administrative autonomy (representation of the Ladin group within the regional and provincial Council of Trento, preferential system for access to employment in the public sector, etc.). It is to be noted that a radio station which broadcasts various programmes in Ladin recently began operating in Bolzano.

As regards nomads, the report stated that (para. 15–16):

The competent authorities, and in particular the Ministry of the Interior, have many times intervened to call attention to the need to facilitate in all ways the incorporation of the nomads into Italian economic and social life. In this way many local bodies and communities have become more sensitive to the need to guarantee, in respect of constitutional principles and international order, the real equality of those who belong to nomadic groups—Italian citizens for the most part—and other citizens. The interventions aim to meet the primary needs of the nomadic populations, maintaining the greatest respect for the extremely diversified cultural traditions of the various ethnic groups which are found among the nomads. It has been pointed out that the interventions in favour of the nomads are often rendered fruitless, as for example in the health

sector, by their mobility and by the absence of their inclusion in the register of the resident population. In consideration of the complex problems which result from this, an interministerial committee was established by a Decree of the President of the Council of Ministers on 4 June 1986, in order to co-ordinate the initiatives of the various State administrative bodies, with the goal of protecting the civil rights of the groups of nomadic origin.

It should be noted that, while a number of initiatives aim to ensure access to schools for nomads, the protection of their cultural heritage and their incorporation into the context of Italian economic and social life, concern over the increase in criminal activity, linked to the presence in Italy of a considerable number of juvenile nomads, especially of Slavic origin, has emerged. These criminal activities are materially committed by nomadic minors, who are however themselves the object of considerable exploitation, to the extent that the condition of nomadic juveniles has been considered in relation to the provisions of the Supplementary Convention on the Abolition of Slavery, the Slave Trade, and Institutions and Practices Similar to Slavery, signed in Geneva on 7 September 1956. The phenomenon, while on the one hand creating serious concern, on the other hand is the object of constant and continuous interventions, especially by the Juvenile Courts, which protect minors. It has been emphasized many times that it is unjust, ethically and legally, that only the juveniles are subjected to restrictive measures on their personal freedom as a consequence of crimes which they commit but which are planned by others or which they are forced to commit.

Finally, as regards foreign workers, the report stated that (para. 17):

It is known that in recent years there has been a significant influx of foreign citizens to Italy, who, although lacking regular residence permits, and therefore work, in fact engage in "clandestine" employment activity, thereby lending themselves to exploitation in relation to both working conditions (number of hours worked, social insurance, hygienic conditions, etc.) and remuneration. In order to remedy this situation and to regulate the entry of foreigners in the future, Parliament is examining two different bills. One contains rules for the entry and the residence of foreigners (No. 3641, tabled on 2 April 1986) and the other concerns the employment and treatment of immigrant workers and discourages clandestine immigration (No. 1820, already approved by the Chamber of Deputies on 7 May 1986 and currently under consideration by the Senate). The new rules, which should be finally approved and enter in force shortly, grant the right for foreign workers who find themselves in Italy without resident and work permits to regularize their position. In this way, the clandestine immigrant worker obtains the recognition of all rights, if already employed, or inclusion in the lists of those available for work in the case of unemployed workers. On the other hand, the new norms concerning immigration to Italy are inspired by the principle of moderating the spirit of liberality governing the conditions of admission to the country, due to the exigencies which derive from terrorist phenomena, and are therefore designed to provide an adequate system to regulate the presence of foreigners on Italian territory.

I

IVORY COAST. The *Republique de la Cote d'Ivoire*, which officially changed its name from Ivory Coast in 1985, is a country in western Africa, on the Gulf of Guinea. It has borders with Burkina Faso, Ghana, Guinea, Liberia, and Mali. It achieved independence from France in 1960 and became a member of the United Nations the same year. Its population is estimated by the UN (1990) to be 11,658,000.

A French trading center and protectorate from 1842, the area was recognized as an autonomous republic in the French Union after World War II. As an independent State, it was once one of the most prosperous and stable tropical African nations. Its population includes more than 60 ethnic groups, among them peoples of many national and racial backgrounds. Languages commonly used are French (official), Diaula, and other African languages. Religions practiced include Animism (45%), Christianity (30%), and Islam (25%). Literacy is estimated at 40%.

The government (1990) took the form of a republic. Its constitution provides for the president, elected by popular vote for a term of five years, to act as head of State and of government. There is a 175-member unicameral National Assembly, also elected by popular vote, and an independent judiciary modelled after the French system of justice. Suffrage is universal for those 21 years of age or over. The Democratic Party of the Ivory Coast is the only political party.

Early in 1990, when world prices for coffee, cocoa, and other products of Africa dipped to their lowest levels in many years, the long-celebrated "economic miracle" of the Ivory Coast slacked off as the country experienced its worst recession since achieving independence.

In mid-February 1990, university students demonstrated in the streets of Abidjan to protest increased school fees, lowered wages, and cuts in scholarships. The government responded by sending police and army units to disperse them with tear gas, stun grenades, and rubber truncheons. But in March a far larger protest march was organized to oppose the government's new austerity program and, incidentally, to complain that money spent by President Felix Houphouët-Boigny—out of his personal funds—to build a Roman Catholic basilica at his birthplace could better have been spent on health care and housing for the poor. This time the police used stun guns and tear gas to turn the marchers back. As the confrontation escalated, groups of college students threw firebombs at the police and were met with concussion grenades. Demonstrating secondary-school students were sprayed with tear gas by paramilitary troops. And most civil servants in Abidjan, including school personnel, went on strike.

The protests were aimed, at least in part, at ending single-party rule in the Ivory Coast, where President Houphouët-Boigy, at 84, is Africa's oldest and longest-serving leader.

In April 1990, under growing pressure, the government announced postponement of some of the austerity measures and the creation of a special government panel to review efforts to counter the severe economic downturn.

J

JAMAICA. Jamaica is a country occupying an island of the West Indies, situated in the Caribbean Sea south of Cuba and west of Haiti. It achieved independence from Great Britain in 1962 and became a member of the United Nations the same year. Its population is estimated by the UN (1990) to be 2,521,000. Ethnic groups include (according to the 1970 census) Negro/Black (90%), White (.7%), Mixed (5.8%), East Indian (1.7%), Chinese (.7%), and others (1.1%). Languages commonly used are English and Creole. Religions practiced include Christianity (Anglican, Baptist, and other Protestant denominations, and Roman Catholic), and Ras Tafarianism (belief in the spiritual leadership of Emperor Haile Selassie I of Ethiopia). Literacy is estimated at 75%.

The government (1990) took the form of a monarchy and member of the Commonwealth of Nations, of which the British monarch is the symbolic head. The governor-general, representing the crown, appoints as prime minister the person who, in his view, is best able to command the confidence of a majority of the members of the House of Representatives. The legislature includes, in addition to the 60-member house, elected by popular vote, a 21-member Senate nominated by the governor-general. The judiciary is independent and modelled after the British system of justice. Political parties include the Jamaica Labour Party and the People's National Party.

Provisions against discrimination are entrenched in Jamaica's constitution; any proposal to amend or delete such provisions would require a two-thirds' majority in both the House of Representatives and the Senate.

JAPAN. A country which occupies an archipelago off the eastern coast of Asia, between the Pacific Ocean and the Sea of Japan. Its main islands are Hokkaido, Honshu (on which Tokyo and other principal cities are located), Shikoku, and Kyushu. In addition, about 1,000 smaller islands lie in an arc between the ocean and the sea.

Japan resumed its independence under the Japanese Peace Treaty of 1951 and became a member of the United Nations in 1956. Its population is estimated by the UN (1990) to be 123,866,000. Ethnic groups include Japanese (99.4%), Korean (0.5%), and Chinese (0.1%). Among the Japanese, there are the remnants of a section of the indigenous population traditionally considered as outcastes because of their occupations (killing animals, handling the dead, etc.), and sometimes segregated in special communities (*Tokushu Buraku*). Discrimination against these "Burakumin" has been illegal for many years, but behavior towards them often resembles that directed against India's outcaste groups. In addition, naturalized Korean and Chinese citizens of Japan have often complained about discrimination in housing and employment, leading some foreign-born citizens to adopt Japanese names to prevent such problems.

Japanese is the predominant language, with English and German in frequent use. Religions practiced include Buddhism, Christianity, Confucianism, and Shintoism. Many Japanese observe both Shinto and Buddhist rituals; and Buddhism has developed special Japanese denominations such as Jodo, Shingon, Nicheren, and Zen. Literacy is estimated at 99%.

The government (1990) took the form of a constitutional monarchy; the institution of emperor exists but no longer is considered to have divine rights. Executive authority is exercised by the Cabinet, nominated by the Diet from among its members, and its chairman, the prime minister. The Diet consists of a 512-member House of Representatives, the members of which are elected for terms of four years; and a 252-member House of Councilors, half of its members being elected every three years for terms of five years. The judicial system is one of civil law, based on Roman Law. Political parties include the Liberal Democratic Party, the Socialist Party, the Clean Government Party, the Communist Party, the Democratic Socialist Party, and the New Liberal Club. The Liberal Democratic Party, which has governed without interruption for 35 years, was returned to power in elections held on 18 February 1990.

After invading Manchuria in 1931 and setting up

the state of Manchukuo, Japan resigned from the League of Nations in 1933. Three years later is signed the "anti-Comintern" pact with Germany.

After invading China in 1937, Japan launched its attack on Pearl Harbor in 1941, bringing the United States of America into World War II. After three years and nine months of warfare, in which 3 million Japanese lost their lives, Japan signed an instrument of surrender shortly after the atomic bombings of Hiroshima and Nagasaki.

As a result, Japan lost all of its overseas possessions and renounced its claims to Formosa. Manchukuo was dissolved and Manchuria returned to China. The southern Sakhalin and Kuriles Islands were occupied by the Soviet Union.

After the war, Japan was placed under international control of the Allied powers through Supreme Commander General Douglas MacArthur, who ruled Japan through Japanese officials and a freely elected legislature. This arrangement provided for a progressive and orderly transition from strict military control to the eventual restoration of full sovereignty.

Japan's constitution, prepared under American sponsorship, includes a pledge of the people of Japan to uphold human rights and the ideas of democracy and to end the emperor's "divine rights." Accordingly, the emperor now has no powers with respect to the government.

The people of Japan join organs of the State in protecting human rights through a system of voluntary civil liberties commissioners, to whom the Ministry of Justice entrusts the task of keeping a close watch in their own communities to ensure that the human rights of residents are not violated and of taking prompt remedial action if indicated. The commissioners, who include people working in agriculture, industry, forestry, and business, give advice and counsel to citizens on matters relating to their rights and freedoms and organize campaigns to promote respect for those rights.

In a report presented to the **HUMAN RIGHTS COMMITTEE** on 24 March 1988 (UN Doc. CCPR/C/42/Add. 4), the Government of Japan provided the following information concerning the human rights provisions of the Japanese constitution and the Japanese system of human rights protection, as follows:

Respect for Fundamental Human Rights in the Constitution. (a) The Constitution of Japan is based on the principle of popular sovereignty. Together with its pacifism, respect for human rights is one of the important pillars of the Constitution. The idea of popular sovereignty is stated in the preamble of the Constitution as follows: "Government is a sacred trust of the people, the authority for which is derived from the people, the powers of which are exercised by the representatives of the people, and the benefits of which

are enjoyed by the people." Pacifism is also expressed in the preamble: "We, the Japanese people, . . . resolved that never again shall we be visited with the horrors of war through the action of Government". No freedom exists without peace and we cannot enjoy freedom as far as there exists a war or a threat of war. In this sense, pacifism and respect for fundamental human rights have a close relation to each other.

(b) The fundamental human rights guaranteed by the Constitution "are conferred upon this and future generations in trust, to be held for all time inviolable" (article 97 of the Constitution), and the idea of respect for these rights is declared in a straightforward manner in the provisions of article 13: "All of the people shall be respected as individuals". These fundamental human rights include civil liberties, such as the right to liberty, the right to freedom of thought, speech and religion, political right as a means of the people's participation in the execution of State power, and social and economic rights, such as the right to work for people to lead a decent life and the right to maintain the minimum standards of wholesome and cultured living. In particular, the Constitution of Japan has 10 articles for guaranteeing the rights of the accused and suspects involved in criminal cases. This attests to the fact that the Constitution attaches great importance to the rights of indivuals.

(c) The Constitution provides that human rights may be restricted on account of "public welfare" (artifcle 12 and 13). But "public welfare" is strictly interpreted as a principle inherent in fundamental human rights which serves to harmonize conflicting fundamental rights so that individuals' rights will be equally respected, and it is not a concept to place unreasonable limits upon human rights.

Guarantee of Human Rights and Governing Structure. (a) In Japan, the three powers, legislature, administration and judicature, are given to the Diet, the Cabinet and the Courts, respectively. Protection of human rights is also ensured through their strict mutual restraint.

(b) The Diet is the "highest organ of State power" and consists of the duly elected representatives of the people. As the "sole law-making organ," it exercises legislative power to defend the rights and freedom of the people. The Cabinet (Government) similarly makes efforts to protect the rights and freedoms by implementing sincerely the laws enacted by the Diet (national institutions for the protection of human rights, which are directly engaged in human rights protection activities as government agencies, is described in Appendix 1). When the rights of the people are violated, there is a judicial remedy at court (article 32 of the Constitution stipulates that "No person shall be denied the right of access to the courts".). To ensure an independent and fair trial, the Constitution provides that "All judges shall be independent in the exercise of their conscience and shall be bound only by this Constitution and the laws" (article 76, paragraph 3).

In an appendix to the report (*Ibid.,* Appendix I), the government of Japan summarized the work of national institutions for the protection and promotion of human rights as follows:

The respect of fundamental human rights of the people is one of the important pillars of the Constitution of Japan. To protect these human rights, special administrative organs were established: The Civil Liberties Bureau of the Ministry of Justice, and its lower organizations, Regional Legal Affairs Bureaux and District Legal Affairs Bureaux. In addition, there is the system of Civil Liberties Commissioners, who are appointed by the Minister of Justice from among civilians.

1. National Institutions for the Protection and Promotion of Human Rights

Civil Liberties Bureau of the Ministry of Justice and Its Lower Organizations. The Civil Liberties Bureau is established in the Ministry of Justice as a central administrative organ for the protection of human rights of the people (including foreigners in Japan; the same hereinafter). And as the lower organizations of the Bureau, the Civil Liberties Department and Civil Liberties Division are established in the Regional Legal Affairs Bureaux and the District Legal Affairs Bureaux, respectively. These organs are performing duties assigned to them.

Civil Liberties Commissioners. Civil Liberties Commissioners are the volunteer civilians who are assigned to perform activities for the protection of human rights.

The system of these Commissioners was created on the basis of the idea that it would be desirable to protect human rights by obtaining co-operation from those selected from among residents in each community who are of fine character and of wisdom and by sharing the daily life of the people of each community.

Civil Liberties Commissioners are selected and assigned by the Minister of Justice from among those residents in each municipality who are considered well-qualified to pursue the task of protecting human rights. For selecting these Commissioners, democratic and deliberate procedures are established as follows:

(a) The chief executive officers of cities, towns and villages listen to the opinions of the assemblies of these municipalities and recommend, as candidates for the Commissioners, those who are of fine character and of wisdom, are familiar with social situations broadly and have deep understanding of protection of human rights.

(b) The Minister of Justice assigns these candidates to Civil Liberties Commissioners after he consults the Bar Association and the Prefectural Federation of Consultative Assemblies of Civil Liberties Commissioners.

In this way, Civil Liberties Commissioners are selected from almost all walks of life. As of 1 January 1987, there are about 11,500 Civil Liberties Commissioners all over Japan.

2. Activities of National Institutions for the Protection and Promotion of Human Rights

Public Information and Educational Programmes for the Promotion of Universal Respect for Human Rights. The officials of the Civil Liberties Bureau and Civil Liberties Commissioners are closely co-operating with each other to achieve the popularization and promotion of human rights ideas.

(a) General activities for enlightenment:

These activities are for the general public. They take diverse forms: lecture meetings, round-table discussions, discussion meetings, film shows; TV and radio programmes; press releases, public relations publications; distribution of pamphlets, leaflets and other printed matters; posters, banners, signboards; tours of public relations cars; and exhibitions of human right-related articles.

"Human right model districts" activity is one of them, too. Every year, about 20 local municipalities are chosen across the country as "human rights model districts." In these districts, activities for protection of human rights are positively organized with the aim of spreading the spirit of respect for human rights which are developed in these municipalities among other areas. Active enlightenment campaigns are carried out by co-operation from those of municipal governments and assemblies and from residents.

(b) Individual Activities for Enlightenment:

These activities are for particular individuals. They include investigation and settlement of cases of infringement of human rights and counselling service on human rights, and aim at solving specific problems of human rights.

As described above, activities for enlightenment on the importance of universal respect for human rights are organized in diverse ways. These activities reach a peak in the "human rights week" ending on 10 December every year, during which large-scale enlightenment campaigns are organized. The National Federation of Consultative Assemblies of Civil Liberties Commissioners designates 1 June as the "Day of Civil Liberties Commissioners" commemorating the day when the Civil Liberties Commissioners Law was enacted (1 June 1949). Since 1982, the Federation has carried out nation-wide activities for human rights enlightenment on this day.

Counselling Service on Human Rights. The Regional Legal Affairs Bureaux and District Legal Affairs Bureaux and their branches have a permanent human rights counselling office. In addition, temporary human rights counselling offices are established at department stores, public halls, etc. At these offices, officials of the Bureaux and Civil Liberties Commissioners offer counselling service on human rights. Civil Liberties Commissioners provide this service at their home, too.

Counselling service is free, and no complex procedures are required. And the secrecy of counselling is strictly observed.

The problems on which counselling service has been requested cover a very broad range; they include family troubles relating to divorce, inheritance and support of family, disputes with neighbours and problems relating to rented land or houses. The number of counselling cases is increasing year after year. In 1986, the figure reached about 392,000, some 158,000 of them were handled by Civil Liberties Commissioners.

Upon request for counselling, the official of the Bureau or Civil Liberties Commissioner gives advice on the procedure needed to protect human rights, refers the person to the competent government or public authorities, or helps him otherwise according to the nature of the problem.

Investigation and Settlement of Cases of Infringement of Human Rights. National institutions for the protection of human rights look into whether there is an actual violation of human rights regarding alleged cases, and take proper steps in accordance with the results of the investigation. They also carry out activities for enlightenment on the importance of universal respect for human rights which would lead to ensure further protection of human rights.

Violation of human rights handled by these institutions is not limited to acts in violation of laws and orders; it includes "any act which is against the idea of respect for human rights, one of the fundamental principles of the Constitution" as well.

If an act of violation of human rights comes under the object of a criminal or civil procedure, these institutions do not deal with such a case in principle, as such an act should be referred to the court, the Public Prosecutor's Office and the police, etc.

In 1986, the number of alleged cases of violation totalled about 15,000.

If investigation reveals that violation of human rights is continued, measures are taken to stop such violations, and relieve the victim. If acts of violation have already been committed, the person who has committed a violation and those who are in a position to supervise the person are advised to take proper steps, in writing or orally. In case some administrative reform is considered necessary, the fact is reported to the authorities concerned.

Legal Aid System. This is a system under which the State provides financial aid to those who are unable to file a civil suit due to poverty (including foreigners in Japan), by making advance payments for all expenses, including lawyer's fees. In actual practice, this legal aid is delegated to the Legal Aid Association; the Civil Liberties Bureau supplies necessary funds to the Association from among subsidies it receives from the national treasury, and supervises the affairs of the Association.

In a second appendix to the report (*Ibid.*, Appendix II), the government outlines the criminal procedure available to victims of violations of their human rights, as follows:

If an act of infringement of human rights constitutes a crime, the victim may lodge a complaint or an accusation in accordance with the Code of Criminal procedure. Article 230 of the Code provides that "A person who has been injured by an offence may file a complaint", while Article 231 stipulates the right of the legal representative and relations of the victim to lodge an independent complaint. And Article 239, paragraph 1 says that "Any person who believes that an offence has been committed may lodge an accusation".

The Code of Criminal Procedure of Japan adopts the principle of State prosecution, and provides that "Prosecution shall be instituted by a public prosecutor" (Article 247). Thus, no prosecution by a private person is recognized. But to reflect the popular will on the execution of the right to public action and to attain proper use of this right, there is the system under which the Prosecution Examination Council examines the appropriateness of dispositions by public prosecutors not to institute a public prosecution. Those who have lodged a complaint or an accusation or injured parties may apply to the Council for such examination (Prosecution Examination Council Law).

The Code of Criminal Procedure establishes a special criminal procedure (quasi-procedure for prosecution) in its Article 262 *et seq.* As to abuse of authority by a public offender, abuse of authority by a special public officer, use of violence and cruelty by special public officials (Articles 193 to 196 of the Penal Code), etc., those who have lodged a complaint or an accusation and who are dissatisfied with the position taken by a public prosecutor not to prosecute may apply to a court for committing the case to a court for trial. If a court accepts this application and renders a ruling to commit the case to a court for trial, prosecution shall be deemed to have been instituted, and the practising attorney designated by the court sustains the prosecution.

JAYCEES INTERNATIONAL An international non-governmental organization in consultative status with the UN Economic and Social Council (Category II) and with UNESCO and the Council of Europe, JAYCEES International has members in 80 countries and territories.

Founded in 1944 in Mexico as the "Junior Chamber International," JAYCEES International coordinates the activities of member organizations to develop the individual abilities of young people for the purpose of improving the economic, social, and spiritual well-being of all peoples. JCI encourages an awareness and acceptance of the responsibilities of citizenship, active participation in planning and executing programs for the development of the individual and the community, and furtherance of understanding, good will, and cooperation among all peoples. It adopts major themes in which all members world-wide participate; recent themes have included "Outlook for Children" and "North/South Dialogue."

JCI publishes the quarterly *JCI World* in Chinese, English, French, Japanese, Korean, and Spanish.

JAYCEES International. Address: 400 University Drive, P.O. Box 140577, Coral Gables, FL 33114 (USA). Telephone: (305) 446-7608. Cable: JAYCEES. Telex: 441084. Fax: (1-305) 442-0041. Secretary-General: W. Daniel Lamey.

Yearbook of International Organizations 1989/90 (K. G. Saur).

JORDAN. The Hashemite Kingdom of Jordan, formerly know as Transjordan, is an Arab country in western Asia. It has borders with Iraq, Israel, Saudi Arabia, and Syria. A part of the Ottoman Empire from the 16th century until the end of World War I, Jordan became a part of the Palestine mandate of the League of Nations. Great Britain, which administered the mandate, agreed in 1923 to recognize Jordan's independence under Abdullah, a son of Husein ibn Ali of the Hashemite family. The loyalty of Jordan in World War II led to the termination of the mandate and the proclamation of the kingdom in 1946. Jordan became a member of the United Nations in 1955. Its population is estimated by the UN (1990) to be 4,291,000. Ethnic groups include Armenians, Circassians, and Kurds. Languages commonly used include Arabic (official), English, and French. Religions practiced include Islam (95%), Christianity (4%), and others (1%). Literacy is estimate at 70%.

The government (1990) took the form of a monarchy, with the king as ruler and head of State. Under the 1952 constitution, executive authority is exercised by the Council of Ministers, of which the prime minister is chairman. The council is responsible to Parliament, which consists of the Chamber of Deputies, the 60 members of which are elected by popular vote for terms of four years, and the Senate, the 30 members of which are appointed by the king. Disputes arising between individuals in matters of personal status, such as divorce, maintenance, and child custody, fall within the jurisdiction of religious courts, which deliver judgments enforceable by the authorities who execute judgment delivered by civil and criminal courts. Political parties have been banned since 1957.

Jordan acquired control of Jerusalem's Old City and the area on the west bank of the Jordan River in the hostilities of 1948 but lost both to Israel in 1967. For many years, Jordan continued to provide financial and other support to West Bank municipalities, but this policy has been discontinued. Jordan broke diplomatic relations with Egypt in 1979 as a protest against the peace treaty between Egypt and Israel; relations were, however, resumed in 1984.

JOURNALISTS: PROTECTION OF THEIR HUMAN RIGHTS. The safety and protection of journalists was considered by the SUB-COMMISSION ON PREVENTION OF DISCRIMINATION AND PROTECTION OF MINORITIES at its 1989 session. The sub-commission recalled (resolution 1989/2) that the press and other forms of mass media have served, and continue to serve, as very valuable and indispensable sources of information on gross violations of human rights and that they perform an honorable and useful role under most difficult circumstances, often when their very lives are being constantly threatened.

It expressed its appreciation to the journalists and other mass media personnel who promote human rights and provide valuable information on human rights violations worldwide and called upon them to carry out their mission to expose such violations and to inform the public with maximum neutrality, fairness, and objectivity. It requested one of its members, Mr. Waleed Sadi (Jordan), to prepare a report on the feasibility of a study on ways and means to extend additional protection and assistance to journalists and mass media personnel while they carry out their duties with objectivity and fairness.

The question of the safety and protection of journalists was later drawn to the attention of the UN Commission on Human Rights, at its 1990 session, by the INTERNATIONAL ORGANIZATION OF JOURNALISTS, which urged the commission to take immediate action to put an end to what it described as a "grave situation." In its statement to the commission (E/CN.4/1990/NGO/72), the organization pointed out that (para. 2–5):

The journalistic profession has become one of the most dangerous professions in the world. Journalists have been exposed in recent years to increasing risks and dangers. In many instances they have been subjected to harassment, arrest, torture, denial of their rights, and even physical liquidation to prevent them from performing their professional duties. This process of silencing journalists and the media is increasing to an alarming level. Dictatorial régimes and those forces opposed to the responsible flow of information are more and more resorting to violence to prevent journalists from performing their professional duties.

Data at the disposal of the IOJ for the last four years (1986–1989) clearly reflects the gravity of the problem:

(a) Killed: in 1986, 19 journalists; in 1987, 25 journalists; in 1988, 38 journalists; in 1989, 60 journalists. (b) Kidnapped: in 1986, 13 journalists; in 1987, 10 journalists; in 1988, 6 journalists; in 1989, 3 journalists. (c) Detained: in 1986, 178 journalists; in 1987, 188 journalists; in 1988, 98 journalists; in 1989, 269 journalists.

At present the lives of two journalists—from Great Britain and the United States—John McCarthy and Terry Andersson, continue to be in jeopardy. They were kidnapped in 1985 in the Lebanon while performing their professional duties and nothing has been heard of their fate.

Drug traffickers, particularly in Colombia, have especially targeted journalists for their wrath. It is reported that they have killed 13 journalists and attacked a number of newspapers, notably *El Espectador* newspaper.

JUDICIARY. Courts—including courts of general jurisdiction, constitutional courts, special courts and tribunals, and administrative courts and tribunals, all having as one of their functions the protection and promotion of human rights—operate within the framework of the judicial system of nearly every country in the world. As described in the UN Secretary-General's report entitled *National Institutions for the Protection and Promotion of Human Rights* (UN Doc. E/CN.4/1987/37, para. 19–43) prepared at the request of the General Assembly (resolution 42/123):

The judiciary plays a central role in enforcing and safeguarding human rights at the national level. Courts, and in particular, courts of general jurisdiction, are endowed with great powers through which they may exercise their ability to enforce human rights, including the very basic function of providing a fair, open and impartial hearing for persons accused of crimes and other illegal acts.

The forum of a court room may provide the accused with the opportunity to hear for the first time all of the specified crimes with which he is charged. Clearly, such information is essential in the preparation of an effective defence for the accused. Moreover, it is the court which provides the accused with the opportunity to speak in his own defence, should he choose to do so, and to confront the witnesses who may testify against him. Such provisions are essential to ensure the protection of the rights of the accused, particularly in penal cases where a great advantage is held by the prosecution, which generally has all organs of the State, including the police, at its disposal while prosecuting a case.

Courts of general jurisdiction also provide forums in which individuals can challenge legislative or executive acts, as well as actions by public authorities which may be illegal. Such a recourse is important in that it helps to hold public officials legally accountable for their actions.

In case of deprivation of liberty, one of the most essential requirements for a fair and equitable administration of justice is the existence of effective remedies. Such remedies are generally provided in all legal systems. Particular mention should be made of the procedures of *habeas corpus* and *amparo* (enforcement of constitutional rights)—a procedure found in Latin American countries.

In many countries, the constitution or other laws provide for the special remedies of *habeas corpus* and *amparo* to redress an unlawful violation of fundamental rights. Both *habeas corpus* and *amparo* are procedures primarily designed to provide speedy relief for the individual who has been the victim of wrongful detention or deprivation of liberty, affected for reasons or in a manner not prescribed by law. Such an action may be the result of a civil or criminal matter.

Although countries may apply different rules as regards access to these procedures, the common factor of *habeas corpus* and *amparo* procedures is the speed and simplicity with which these remedies are effected. Generally, a detained person will submit to the competent judge or authority a "petition alleging unlawful custody". The court will then require the responsible official to appear before the court and explain the reasons for detaining the person in custody. The responsible officer must also, at this time, present the detainee to the court. If the judge decides that the person in custody has indeed been unlawfully detained, then the judge must order that the detained person be released immediately.

For example, according to the Constitution of Venezuela, every person who becomes subject to a deprivation or restriction of his or her liberty in violation of constitutional guarantees, has the right to ask the competent judge to issue a writ of *habeas corpus*. The judge shall immediately order the official in whose custody the aggrieved person is held to report within 24 hours, and shall initiate a summary verification. If the judge decides that the legal formalities for deprivation or restriction of liberty were not met, he or she must order the immediate release of the aggrieved or an end to the restriction imposed within 96 hours after the time that request was originally submitted. Moreover, recent decisions of the Venezuelan Supreme Court of Justice have broadened the application of the remedy of *amparo* to the violation of any fundamental right.

Finally, in many countries, actions of *habeas corpus* or *amparo* may be presented directly to the Supreme Court, High Court or Constitutional Court, and no exhaustion of other legal remedies is necessary. This is the case in El Salvador, India and Spain.

Constitutional Courts

One of the most important ways in which the courts may strengthen the protection of human rights is through judicial examination of the constitutional validity of enacted laws and administrative measures. Courts of this nature have been established in a number of countries. They are solely concerned with determining the constitutionality of enacted laws and are often called constitutional courts. For instance, the Spanish Constitutional Court may declare a law invalid if it contravenes the rights guaranteed under the Constitution. Similarly, in Ecuador, the Constitutional Guarantees Court, created in 1945 and re-established in 1978 after a period of suspension, seeks to ensure respect for the human rights guaranteed by the Constitution. Composed of three judges, the members of the Ecuadorian Constitutional Guarantees Court are elected by the national legislature, the President of the Supreme Court of Justice, the Attorney-General, the President of the Supreme Electoral court, a representative of the President of the Republic, a representative of the workers, a representative of industrial organizations and two citizens' representatives.

While in many countries separate constitutional courts have been created, a large number of other States have empowered their supreme courts or high courts to determine the constitutionality of laws. In Singapore, for instance, in addition to its authority to hear all disputes and claims, the High Court is also empowered to hear and adjudicate all constitutional disputes. In accordance with section 42 (2) of the Nigerian Constitution, the High Court has special jurisdiction to hear and decide cases of alleged violations of the human rights guaranteed in the Constitution. Similarly, the Canadian Supreme Court at the federal level has ultimate jurisdiction to ensure the conformity of both federal and provincial statutes or administrative measures to the Charter of Rights and Freedoms set out in the Constitution. The United States Supreme Court hears appeals from the decisions of the State courts in cases involving questions of constitutional interpretation, in addition to its authority to adjudicate cases on appeal from federal courts. The Court may declare any executive Act, Congressional Act or State law unconstitutional if such a law denies or abridges the guaranteed civil liberties of the people.

Although the functions of most courts which examine the constitutionality of laws are quite similar, countries vary greatly in granting the right of direct access to such courts. Most countries have strictly limited the access of individuals to such courts. For instance, actions filed with the Spanish Constitutional Court must be filed by either the President, the People's Advocate, 50 deputies, 50 senators, the executive collegiate bodies of the Autonomous Communities, or their legislative assemblies. A judge or a court, either *ex officio* or at the request of a party, may, however, refer a question on the constitutional validity of a law applicable to the case at hand to the Constitutional Court.

Some courts, like the Supreme Court of Papua New Guinea, however, determine questions of constitutional law presented by other courts, organizations or governmental bodies, as well as by individuals. Similarly, the Ecuadorian Constitutional Guarantees Court may receive complaints from individuals or any entity concerning alleged violations of human rights. The Federal Constitutional Court of the Federal Republic of Germany may hear an appeal from any individual who considers that his rights guaranteed in the Basic Law have been violated. In Sri Lanka, every individual has the Constitutional right to apply to the Supreme Court with respect to an alleged infringement or imminent infringement, by executive or administrative action, of a fundamental right recognized by the Constitution. Similarly, the Indian Constitution gives each individual the legal right to challenge before the Supreme Court the measures adopted by the State which affect or threaten to affect his civil and political rights. In some Latin America countries, like El Salvador, Panama and Venezuela, the *acción popular de inconstitucionalidad* permits every citizen, even those not directly affected, to appeal to the Supreme Court to declare any specific law unconstitutional if it violates the rights guaranteed by the constitution. For example, article 112 of the Venezuelan Organic Law of the Supreme Court of Justice states that any person whose rights or interests are affected by a law, regulation, ordinance or other act, created by national deliberative bodies at the State or municipal level or by the national executive power, may demand before the Supreme Court that such an act be declared void for reasons of unconstitutionality or illegality. In India complainants may appeal to the Supreme Court, even at first instance, to challenge the constitutionality of measures affecting their civil and political rights.

In Canada and the Federal Republic of Germany, complainants are required to exhaust all available State and local remedies before seeking recourse to the Constitutional or Supreme Court for a determination of the constitutionality of a law or action.

Special Courts and Tribunals

Increasingly, the legal systems in many countries have provided specialized judicial bodies with limited competence, which function apart from courts of general jurisdiction. Such specialized courts are created for a number of reasons. In some instances, they are established to deal with issues of a socially or politically sensitive nature. Moreover, the character of some legal issues and questions may require a certain level of technical knowledge for a fair adjudication of the matter. Clearly, the creation of such courts helps to ease the case-load of the courts of general jurisdiction, which are frequently too overburdened to provide aggrieved parties with a timely decision on their case. Specialized courts are frequently incorporated into the judicial framework in many countries throughout the world to deal with a number of questions. Labour courts and juvenile and children's courts may be mentioned as examples of special courts.

1. Labour Courts. During recent years a large number of countries have begun to establish courts, designed to settle, conciliate or arbitrate disputes arising from labour relations between employers, employees and workers' unions. For instance, the constitution of Yugoslavia calls for the establishment of "self-management courts", empowered to conciliate and arbitrate labour dispute. These self-management courts are composed of permanent judges and workers from organized labour, State organs and other self-managed organizations and communities. In Norway, special courts—the *Arbeidsretten*—have been created to adjudicate labour disputes. The decisions of these courts cannot be appealed to ordinary courts or courts of general jurisdiction. Labour courts have also been established in many other countries, including Barbados, the Federal Republic of Germany, India, Kenya, Papua New Guinea and Thailand.

In some countries the organs dealing with the settlement of disputes in the area of labour relations are not always considered fully-fledged judicial bodies. They settle such disputes in quasi-judicial proceedings. For instance, the main competence of the Canadian Labour Relations Board lies in its statutory and regulatory powers. However the Board may hear appeals against safety rulings in cases where imminent danger has been alleged. The Board also rules on complaints by employees that they have been discriminated against or punished for exercising their rights in relation to safety. An important part of the Board's activities is concerned with granting or reviewing certification on the application of trade unions to act as bargaining agents for groups of employees. The Labour Code of some countries—France and Tunisia for example—provides for the establishment of Conseils de Prud'hommes (Councils of Elders), with competence to rule in disputes between workers and employees.

2. Juvenile and Children's Courts. The establishment of juvenile and children's courts is based on the principle that children and young persons need special care and different treatment from that accorded to adults under the law. Definitions of the terms "infants", "children", "minors", "young persons", and "juveniles" vary from country to country. Distinctions are also made according to cases. For example, a "minor" in penal matters may not be so considered in civil cases. Juvenile and children's courts usually have broad discretion for the settlement of cases, ranging from the imposition of a sentence, often suspended, upon the accused, to ordering his or her placement in a rehabilitative institution or school, or merely warning or reprimanding the accused.

Children's courts in Australia are entitled to hear all complaints against children concerning summary offences as well as charges against children accused of committing indictable offences other than homicide, or offences punishable by penal servitude for life. In El Salvador, the Juvenile Courts have exclusive competence to try infractions regarded as crimes or offences under ordinary law and attributed to minors of 18 years of age or under, to investigate the situation of minors of 18 years of age or under who are in a state of moral or physical abandon or in danger, and to adopt suitable measures for the care, treatment, placement, supervision and education of minors.

In Tunisia, minors between 13 and 18 years of age charged with a transgression regarded as a crime, or offence, are brought before the children's judge or the Minors' Penal court. The judges in such cases are required to order appropriate measures of protection, assistance, supervision and education. Where the circumstances and the personality of the delinquent appear to warrant this, the Court may deliver a penal sentence against a minor of over 13 years old, in which case the sentence is served in a special establishment.

Some States select individuals to sit on the juvenile court from among professionals in the community who are qualified to bring particular sociological or psychological expertise to the panel, in addition to the legally certified judges who usually sit on the judicial panel in such courts. For instance, in Italy, the Special Juvenile Court, which tries minors of 18 years of age, is composed of a judge of the Court of Appeals and two citizens (a man and a woman) over 30 years of age who are professionals in biology, psychiatry, clinical anthropology or psychology.

Many juvenile and children's courts are concerned with maintaining the privacy of minors in court proceedings. In Barbados for example, the Juvenile Offenders Act provides that juvenile courts may convene in different places and at different times from ordinary courts. The Act also prohibits the publication of information likely to lead to the identification of any juvenile offender. Similarly, in France, the Juvenile Court and the Juvenile Assize Court are always held in private, without a public audience apart from close relatives. Decisions are, however, delivered in open court.

Finally, it is important to note that some States do not try juvenile delinquents before an organized court. In Cyprus, for example, cases involving delinquent minors do not appear before the Court except when a very serious crime has been committed. Instead, in most cases, delinquent minors are supervised by social workers in their own environment.

3. *Other Specialized Courts.* In addition to juvenile courts and labour courts, many countries have reported the existence of a wide range of quasi-judicial organs to settle disputes involving diverse categories of rights. For instance, New Zealand reports the existence of the Maori Land Court, established to adjudicate the land claims of its indigenous population. In the same country, a Deportation Review Tribunal was created in 1978 to examine administrative orders for the expulsion and deportation of foreigners. A special Social Insurance Court or *Trygderetten,* whose decisions may be brought before the ordinary courts, has been created in Norway.

Administrative Courts and Tribunals

The protection of human rights may be provided either within a unitary judicial system, or under a dual system of civil courts (competent to hear civil disputes and penal cases) and administrative courts (competent to rule on complaints against administrative acts). Such a dual system is employed in France, where the *Cour de cassation,* at the top of the judicial hierarchy, deals with criminal and civil cases, and the *Conseil d'Etat* is the judicial authority which exercises ultimate control of the administration by giving final rulings on appeal from the Administrative Tribunals *(Tribunaux administratifs).* The *Conseil d'Etat* may declare void administrative acts which are contrary to the law as well as acts by State or local authorities which have exceeded their jurisdiction. Additionally, the *Conseil d'Etat* may declare measures void, if it finds that they have been exercised for purposes other than those intended by the law. The available remedies of the *Conseil d'Etat* are the annulment of challenged acts and the granting of compensation to the victim, which is paid by the administration.

Administrative courts of a similar nature are also found in other countries, notably in Belgium, Greece and Tunisia. For instance, the Tunisian Administrative Tribunal, which was created in 1972, may hear appeals for compensation from the civil courts and appeals for annulment on grounds of misuse of authority lodged against acts of the administration, local public authorities or public administrative bodies.

JUDICIARY: STUDY ON INDEPENDENCE AND IMPARTIALITY.

In 1980, the UN Economic and Social Council authorized the SUB-COMMISSION ON PREVENTION OF DISCRIMINATION AND PROTECTION OF MINORITIES (decision 1980/124) to entrust one of its members, Mr. M. L. Singhvi (India) with the preparation of a report on the independence and impartiality of the judiciary, jurors, and assessors and the independence of lawyers "to the end that there should be no discrimination in the administration of justice and that human rights and fundamental freedoms might be maintained and safeguarded."

The special rapporteur's report on the subject (UN Doc. E/CN.4/Sub.2/1985/18 and Add. 1–6) was presented to the sub-commission at its 1985 session and included the draft of a Universal Declaration on the Independence of Justice (*Ibid.,* Add. 5/Rev. 1). The sub-commission, after reviewing the report, decided (decision 1985/107) (a) to postpone consideration of the report to its 1986 session, (b) to request the Secretary-General to circulate the study to members of the sub-commission and to invite those wishing to do so to submit written comments for transmittal to Mr. Singhvi, (c) to request the Secretary-General to circulate the comments received to all members of the sub-commission, and (d) to request Mr. Singhvi to take those comments into account when presenting his report at the 1986 session of the sub-commission.

At its 1987 session, the sub-commission examined the special rapporteur's report in detail, expressed (resolution 1987/23) its appreciation and thanks to him, and decided to examine the draft declaration annexed to the report at its 1988 session, on a priority basis as a separate agenda item. It further decided that the draft declaration should meanwhile be transmitted by the Secretary-General to member States and to the UN Centre for Social Development and Humanitarian Affairs for their comments, and called upon the special rapporteur to prepare a report on the draft declaration in the light of such comments and the deliberations in the sub-commission.

The COMMISSION ON HUMAN RIGHTS, in January 1988, approved (resolution 1988/40) these arrangements. It called upon the sub-commission to review and finalize the draft declaration with a view to submitting it to the commission for consideration in 1989.

The sub-commission, in August 1988, received, a report by the special rapporteur (UN Doc. E/CN.4/Sub.2/1988/20 and Add. 1) in which he analyzed the comments he had received, accepted or accommodated most of them, and presented a revised text of the draft declaration. The sub-commission amended the title of the draft declaration to read "Draft Declaration on the Independence and Impartiality of the Judiciary, Jurors and Assessors, and the Independence of Lawyers," and decided (resolution 1988/25) to refer the revised draft declaration, and the relevant documentation, to the Commission on Human Rights for further consideration.

The text of the draft Declaration on the Independence and Impartiality of the Judiciary, Jurors and Assessors, and the Independence of Lawyers is as follows (UN Doc. E/CN.4/Sub.2/1988/20/Add. 1, as amended by sub-commission resolution 1988/25):

The General Assembly,
Whereas the peoples of the world have, in the Charter of the United Nations, proclaimed their determination to reaffirm faith in fundamental human rights, in the dignity and worth of the human person and in the equal rights of

men and women, and to promote social progress and better standards of life in larger freedom,

Whereas the Charter sets forth, as one of the purposes of the United Nations, the promotion and encouragement of respect for human rights and fundamental freedoms for all without distinction as to race, sex, language or religion.

Whereas the Universal Declaration of Human Rights proclaims in article 2 that everyone is entitled to all the rights and freedoms set forth in that Declaration without distinction of any kind such as race, colour, sex, language, religion, political or other opinion, national or social origin, property, birth or other status, or the status of the territory to which he belongs,

Whereas the Universal Declaration proclaims in article 10 that everyone is entitled in full equality to a fair and public hearing by an independent and impartial tribunal, in the determination of his rights and obligations and of any criminal charge against him,

Mindful of the Statute of the International Court of Justice, which postulates and provides for the principle of the independence of judges,

Recalling that the International Covenant on Civil and Political Rights embodies provisions to ensure access to effective remedy to any person whose rights or freedoms are violated and to develop the possibilities of judicial remedy,

Considering that a number of international instruments have proclaimed that all human beings are equal before the law and are entitled to equal protection of the law,

Recalling resolution 3144 (XXVIII) of the General Assembly with reference to draft principles relating to equality in the administration of justice,

Proceeding on the basis of the resolution 5 (XXXII) of the Sub-Commission on Prevention of Discrimination and Protection of Minorities and in the light of the discussions in and decisions of the Sub-Commission in its successive sessions,

Recognizing that the principle of the impartiality and independence of the judiciary, jurors and assessors and the independence of lawyers is the foundation of the rule of law, equal protection of the law, prevention of discrimination and protection of minorities,

Bearing in mind the Basic Principles on the Independence of the Judiciary adopted by the Seventh United Nations Congress on the Prevention of Crime and the Treatment of Offenders in 1985 at Milan which the General Assembly welcomed by its resolution 40/146 of 13 December 1985, inviting Governments to respect them and to take them into account within the framework of their national legislation and practice and encouraging the Sub-Commission on Prevention of Discrimination and Protection of Minorities to take them into account in making its final recommendations,

Recalling resolution 42/143 of the General Assembly, resolution 1986/10 of the Economic and Social Council and the importance of progress with regard to the draft Body of Principles for the Protection of All Persons under Any Form of Detention or Imprisonment,

Noting that, notwithstanding the diversities of political systems and legal mechanisms in different countries, there is a basic and substantial consensus on the principles and minimum standards relating to the independence of justice in the constitutions and legal systems of the world,

Concerned that there exists a gap between the vision underlying the universally accepted principles on the independence of justice and the actual situation in many parts of the world,

Believing that the restatement and elaboration of the principles of the independence of justice and the application of standards based on them will contribute to an improvement in the administration of justice and strengthening of the institutional culture of the rule of law,

Desirous of promoting world-wide solidarity on the principles and standards relating to the independence of justice,

Convinced that an International Declaration on the Independence of Justice will help to advance justice, strengthen freedom and promote rule of law and also to develop legal institutions and enlarge the possibilities of judicial remedies as contemplated in article 2 (3) (b) of the International Covenant on Civil and Political Rights,

1. Solemnly proclaims this Universal Declaration on the Independence of Justice;

2. Calls upon Member States to adhere to the principles and standards contained in this Declaration, to foster its widest possible dissemination particularly among judges, lawyers, jurors and assessors, and to develop programmes for strengthening legal institutions and judicial remedies;

3. Invites intergovernmental and non-governmental organizations to secure the widest possible dissemination of the principles and standards contained in this Declaration and to pledge their sustained endeavour to ensure their universal observance.

Judges

Objectives and Functions. 1. The objectives and functions of the judiciary shall include:

(a) Administering the law impartially irrespective of parties;

(b) Promoting, within the proper limits of the judicial function, the observance and the attainment of human rights;

(c) Ensuring that all peoples are able to live securely under the rule of law.

Independence. 2. Judges individually shall be free, and it shall be their duty, to decide matters before them impartially in accordance with their assessment of the facts and their understanding of the law without any restrictions, influences, inducements, pressure, threats or interferences, direct or indirect, from any quarter or for any reason.

3. In the decision-making process, judges shall be independent *vis-à-vis* their judicial colleagues and superiors. Any hierarchical organization of the judiciary and any difference in grade or rank shall, in no way, interfere with the right of the judge to pronounce his judgement freely. Judges, on their part, individually and collectively, shall exercise their functions with full responsibility of the discipline of law in their legal system.

4. The judiciary shall be independent of the Executive and Legislature.

5. (a) The judiciary shall have jurisdiction, directly or by way of review, over all issues of a judicial nature, including issues of its own jurisdiction and competence.

(b) No *ad hoc* tribunals shall be established to displace jurisdiction properly vested in the courts.

(c) Everyone shall have the right to be tried with all due expedition and without undue delay by the ordinary courts or judicial tribunals under law subject to review by the courts.

(d) Some derogations may be permitted in times of grave public emergency which threatens the life of the nation but only under conditions prescribed by law, only to the extent strictly consistent with internationally recognized minimum standards and subject to review by the courts.

(e) In such times of emergency, the State shall endeavour to provide that civilians charged with criminal offences of any kind shall be tried by ordinary civilian courts, and, detention of persons administratively without charge shall be subject to review by courts or other independent authority by way of *habeas corpus* or similar procedures so as to ensure that the detention is lawful and to inquire into any allegations of ill-treatment.

(f) The jurisdiction of military tribunals shall be confined to military offences. There shall always be a right of appeal from such tribunals to a legally qualified appellate court or tribunal or a remedy by way of an application for annulment.

(g) No power shall be so exercised as to interfere with the judicial process.

(h) The Executive shall not have control over the judicial functions of the courts in the administration of justice.

(i) The Executive shall not have the power to close down or suspend the operation of the courts.

(j) The Executive shall refrain from any act or omission which pre-empts the judicial resolution of a dispute or frustrates the proper execution of a court decision.

6. No legislation or executive decree shall attempt retroactively to reverse specific court decisions or to change the composition of the court to affect its decision-making.

7. Judges shall be entitled to take collective action to protect their judicial independence.

8. Judges shall always conduct themselves in such a manner as to preserve the dignity and responsibilities of their office and the impartiality and independence of the judiciary. Subject to this principle, judges shall be entitled to freedom of thought, belief, speech, expression, professional association, assembly and movement.

Qualifications, Selection and Training. 9. Candidates chosen for judicial office shall be individuals of integrity and ability. They shall have equality of access to judicial office; except in case of lay judges, they should be well-trained in the law.

10. In the selection of judges, there shall be no discrimination on the grounds of race, colour, sex, language, religion, political or other opinion, national, linguistic or social origin, property, income, birth or status, but it may however be subject to citizenship requirements and consideration of suitability for judicial office.

11. (a) The process and standards of judicial selection shall give due consideration to ensuring a fair reflection by the judiciary of the society in all its aspects.

(b) Any methods of judicial selection shall scrupulously safeguard against judicial appointments for improper motives.

(c) Participation in judicial appointments by the Executive or the Legislature or the general electorate is consistent with judicial independence so far as such participation is not vitiated by and is scrupulously safeguarded against improper motives and methods. To secure the most suitable appointments from the point of view of professional ability and integrity and to safeguard individual independence, integrity and endeavour shall be made, in so far as possible, to provide for consultation with members of the judiciary and the legal profession in making judicial appointments or to provide appointments or recommendations for appointments to be made by a body in which members of the judiciary and the legal profession participate effectively.

12. Continuing education shall be available to judges.

Posting, Promotion and Transfer. 13. Where the law provides for the discretionary assignment of a judge to a post on his appointment or election to judicial office such assignment shall be carried out by the judiciary or by a superior council of the judiciary where such bodies exist.

14. Promotion of a judge shall be based on an objective assessment of the judge's integrity, independence, professional competence, experience, humanity and commitment to uphold the rule of law. No promotions shall be made from an improper motive.

15. Except pursuant to a system of regular rotation or promotion, judges shall not be transferred from one jurisdiction or function to another without their consent, but when such transfer is in pursuance of a uniform policy formulated after due consideration by the judiciary, such consent shall not be unreasonably withheld by an individual judge.

Tenure. 16. (a) The term of office of the judges, their independence, security, adequate remuneration and conditions of service shall be secured by law and shall not be altered to their disadvantage.

(b) Subject to the provisions relating to discipline and removal set forth herein, judges whether appointed or elected, shall have guaranteed tenure until a mandatory retirement age or expiry of their legal term of office.

17. There may be probationary periods for judges following their initial appointment but in such cases the probationary tenure and the conferment of permanent tenure shall be substantially under the control of the judiciary or a superior council of the judiciary.

18. (a) During their terms of office, judges shall receive salaries and after retirement, they shall receive pensions.

(b) The salaries and pensions of judges shall be adequate, commensurate with the status, dignity and responsibility of their office, and shall be periodically reviewed to overcome or minimize the effect of inflation.

(c) Retirement age shall not be altered for judges in office without their consent.

19. The executive authorities shall at all times ensure the security and physical protection of judges and their families.

Immunities and Privileges. 20. Judges shall be protected from the harassment of personal litigation against them in respect of their judicial functions and shall not be sued or prosecuted except under an authorization of an appropriate judicial authority.

21. Judges shall be bound by professional secrecy in relation to their deliberations and to confidential information acquired in the course of their duties other than in public proceedings. Judges shall not be required to testify on such matters.

Disqualifications. 22. Judges may not serve in a nonjudicial capacity which compromises their judicial independence.

23. Judges and courts shall not render advisory opinions except under an express constitutional or statutory provision.

24. Judges shall refrain from business activities, except as incidental to their personal investments or their ownership of property. Judges shall not engage in law practice.

25. A judge shall not sit in a case where a reasonable apprehension of bias on his part or conflict of interest of incompatibility of functions may arise.

Discipline and Removal. 26. (a) A complaint against a judge shall be processed expeditiously and fairly under an appropriate practice and the judge shall have the opportunity to comment on the complaint at the initial stage. The examination of the complaint at its initial stage shall be kept confidential, unless otherwise requested by the judge.

(b) The proceedings for judicial removal or discipline when such are initiated shall be held before a Court or a Board predominantly composed of members of the judiciary. The power of removal may, however, be vested in the Legislature by impeachment or joint address, preferably upon a recommendation of such a Court or Board.

27. All disciplinary action shall be based upon established standards of judicial conduct.

28. The proceedings for discipline of judges shall ensure fairness to the judge and the opportunity of a full hearing.

29. Judgements in disciplinary proceedings instituted against judges, whether held *in camera* or in public, shall be published.

30. A judge shall not be subject to removal except on proved grounds of incapacity or misbehaviour rendering him unfit to continue in office.

31. In the event a court is abolished, judges serving on that court, except those who are elected for a specified term, shall not be affected, but they may be transferred to another court of the same status.

Court Administration. 32. The main responsibility for court administration including supervision and disciplinary control of administration personnel and support staff shall vest in the judiciary, or in a body in which the judiciary is represented and has an effective role.

33. It shall be a priority of the highest order for the State to provide adequate resources to allow for the due administration of justice, including physical facilities appropriate for the maintenance of judicial independence, dignity and efficiency; judicial and administrative personnel; and operating budgets.

34. The budget of the courts shall be prepared by the competent authority in collaboration with the judiciary having regard to the needs and requirements of judicial administration.

35. The judiciary shall alone be responsible for assigning cases to individual judges or to sections of a court composed of several judges, in accordance with law or rules of court.

36. The head of the court may exercise supervisory powers over judges only in administrative matters.

Miscellaneous. 37. A judge shall ensure the fair conduct of the trial and inquire fully into any allegations made of a violation of the rights of a party or of a witness, including allegations of ill-treatment.

38. Judges shall accord respect to the members of the Bar, as well as to assessors, procurators, public prosecutors and jurors as the case may be.

39. The State shall ensure the due and proper execution of orders and judgements of the Courts; but supervision over the execution of orders and over the service or process shall be vested in the judiciary.

40. Judges shall keep themselves informed about international conventions and other instruments establishing human rights norms, and shall seek to implement them as far as feasible, within the limits set by their national constitutions and laws.

41. These principles and standards shall apply to all persons exercising judicial functions, including assessors, arbitrators, public prosecutors and procurators who perform judicial functions, unless a reference to the context necessarily makes them inapplicable or inappropriate.

42. An assessor may either perform the functions of a judge or an associate or auxiliary judge or a consultant or a legal or technical expert. In performing any of these functions the assessors shall discharge their duties and perform their functions impartially and independently. Principles and standards which apply to judges are applicable to assessors unless a reference to the context necessarily make them inapplicable or inappropriate.

43. Assessors or Peoples' Assessors, or *Nyaya Panchas*, may be elected for specified terms on the basis of such franchise and by such electorates as may be provided by law to participate in the collegiate process of adjudication along with elected or appointed judges. There shall be no discrimination by reason of race, colour, sex, language, religion, political or other opinion, national or social origin property, birth or status among citizens in the matter of their eligibility for election as assessors. On their election, such assessors may be empanelled for short and limited periods to discharge their functions as assessors. Assessors may also be appointed or empanelled for technical advice or assistance on the basis of their specialized knowledge in a case or a class of cases. Lay judges or citizen judges may also be appointed to discharge certain simple adjudicating functions.

44. Assessors shall be duly and adequately compensated with a reasonable allowance for the duration of their service as assessors by the State except when they receive such allowance paid to them in their place of employment.

45. Assessors who are elected to participate in the process of adjudication or are appointed to render technical and other assistance shall be free from any restrictions, influences, inducements, pressure, threats or interferences, direct or indirect, except that elected assessors may give periodic explanations to their electorate as a part of the system of citizen participation in the justice system.

46. Assessors shall be independent of the judges and of the Executive and Legislature and shall be entitled to participate in the process of adjudication to the extent and in the manner provided for in the law and practice of the legal system. Peoples' assessors who are elected to participate in the process of adjudication shall also be entitled to record their minutes of dissent which shall form a part of the record.

47. Any method of empanelment of assessors shall scrupulously safeguard against any improper motive in the matter of empanelment.

48. A provision may be made for the orientation and instruction for Peoples' Assessors or *Nyaya Panchas* elected to participate in the process of adjudication.

49. An assessor may be recalled by the electorate or may be disqualified or removed or his appointment may be terminated, but always strictly in accordance with the procedure established by law.

Jurors and Assessors

Selection of Prospective Jurors. 50. The opportunity for jury service shall be extended without distinction of any kind by reason of race, colour, sex, religion, political or other opinion, national, linguistic or social origin, property, income, birth or status, but it may, however, be subject to citizenship requirements.

51. The names of prospective jurors shall be drawn from a jury source list compiled from one or more regularly maintained lists of persons residing in the court jurisdiction.

52. The jury source list shall be representative and shall be as inclusive of the adult population in the jurisdiction as is feasible.

53. The Court shall periodically review the jury source list for its representativeness and inclusiveness. Should the Court determine that improvement is needed in the representativeness or inclusiveness of the jury source list, appropriate corrective action shall be taken.

54. Random selection procedures shall be used at all stages throughout the jury selection process except as provided herein.

55. The frequency and the length of time that persons are called upon to perform jury service and to be available therefor, shall be the minimum consistent with the needs of justice.

56. Except as may be expressly provided for by law, all automatic excuses or exemptions from jury service shall be avoided.

57. Eligible persons who are summoned may be excused from jury service only for valid reason by the court, or with its authorization.

Selection of a Particular Jury. 58. Examination of prospective jurors shall be limited to matters relevant to determining whether to remove a juror for cause and to exercising peremptory challenges.

59. If the judge determines during the examination of prospective jurors that an individual is unable or unwilling to hear the particular case before the court fairly and impartially, that individual shall be removed from the panel. Such a determination may be made on motion of a party or on the judge's own initiative.

60. In jurisdictions where peremptory challenges are permitted, their number and the procedure for exercising them shall be uniform for the same type of case.

61. Peremptory challenges shall be limited to a number no larger than necessary to provide reasonable assurance of obtaining an unbiased jury.

Administration of the Jury System. 62. The responsibility for the administration of the jury system shall be under the control of the judiciary.

63. The notice summoning a person to jury service shall be in writing, easily understandable, and delivered sufficiently in advance.

64. Courts shall employ the services of prospective jurors so as to achieve the best possible use of them with a minimum of inconvenience.

65. Courts shall provide adequate protection for jurors from threat and intimidation.

66. Courts shall provide an adequate and suitable environment for jurors, and jury facilities shall be arranged to minimize contact between jurors and parties, counsel and the public.

67. Persons called for jury service shall receive a reasonable allowance from the State except when they receive such allowance in their place of employment.

68. Employers shall be prohibited from penalizing employees who are called for jury service.

Jury Consideration and Deliberation. 69. Procedures shall be provided to prevent a trial from being terminated because of unforeseen circumstances which would reduce the number of jurors.

70. Courts shall provide some form of orientation or instruction to persons called for jury service to increase prospective jurors' understanding of the judicial system and prepare them to serve competently as jurors.

71. In simple language the trial judge shall:

(a) Directly following empanelment of the jury, give preliminary explanations of the jury's role and of trial procedures;

(b) Direct the jury on the law.

72. (a) A jury's deliberations shall be held in secrecy. Jurors shall not make public reasons for their decisions.

(b) A jury shall be sequestered only for the purpose of insulating its members from improper information or influence.

(c) Standard procedures shall be promulgated to make certain that the inconvenience and discomfort of the sequestered jurors is minimized.

Lawyers

Definitions. 73. In this chapter:

(a) "Lawyer" means a person qualified and authorized to plead and act on behalf of his clients, to engage in the practice of law and appear before the courts and to advise and represent his clients in legal matters, and shall, for the purposes of this chapter, include agents, assistants, procuradores, paraprofessionals and other persons authorized and permitted to perform one or more of the functions of lawyers, unless a reference to the context makes such inclusion inappropriate or inapplicable;

(b) "Bar Association" means a professional association, guild, faculty, college, bureau, council or any other recognized professional body under any nomenclature within a given jurisdiction, and shall, for the purposes of this chapter, include any association under any nomenclature of gents, assistants, procuradores, paraprofessionals and other persons who are authorized and permitted to perform one or more of the functions of lawyers, unless a reference to the context makes such inclusion inappropriate or inapplicable.

General Principles. 74. The independence of the legal profession constitutes an essential guarantee for the promotion and protection of human rights.

75. There shall be a fair and equitable system of administration of justice which guarantees the independence of lawyers in the discharge of their professional duties without any restrictions, influences, inducements, pressures, threats or interference, direct or indirect, from any quarter or for any reason.

76. All persons shall have effective access to legal services provided by an independent lawyer of their choice, to protect and establish their economic, social and cultural as well as civil and political rights.

Legal Education and Entry into the Legal Profession. 77. Legal education and entry into the legal profession shall be open to all persons with requisite qualifications and no one shall be denied such opportunity by reason of race, colour, sex, religion, political or other opinion, national, linguistic or social origin, property, income, birth or status.

78. Legal education shall be designed to promote in the public interest, in addition to technical competence, awareness of the ideals and ethical duties of the lawyer and of human rights and fundamental freedoms recognized by national and international law.

79. Programmes of legal education shall have regard to the social responsibilities of the lawyer, including cooperation in providing legal services to the poor and the promotion and defence of economic, social and cultural rights in the process of development.

80. Every person having the necessary qualifications, integrity and good character shall be entitled to become a

lawyer and to continue to practise as a lawyer without discrimination on the ground of race, colour, sex, religion or political or other opinion, national, linguistic, or social origin, property, income, birth or status or for having been convicted of an offence for exercising his internationally recognized civil or political rights. The conditions for the disbarment, disqualification or suspension of a lawyer shall, as far as practicably, be specified in the statutes, rules or precedents applicable to lawyers and others performing the functions of lawyers.

Education of the Public Concerning the Law. 81. It shall be the responsibility of the lawyers and Bar Associations to educate the members of the public about the principles of the rule of law, the importance of the independence of the judiciary and of the legal profession and the important role lawyers, judges, jurors, and assessors play in protecting fundamental rights and liberties and to inform the members of the public about their rights and duties and the relevant and available remedies. In particular, the Bar Associations shall prepare and implement appropriate educational programmes for lawyers as well as for the general public, and shall collaborate with the authorities, non-governmental organizations, bodies of citizens and educational institutions in promoting and co-ordinating such programmes.

Duties and Rights of Lawyers. 82. The duties of a lawyer towards his client include:

(a) Advising the client as to his legal rights and obligations, and as to the working of the legal system in so far as it is relevant to the client's legal rights and obligations;

(b) Assisting the client in every appropriate way, and taking legal action to protect him and his interests; and

(c) Representing him before courts, tribunals or administrative authorities.

83. The lawyer in discharging his duties shall at all times act freely, diligently and fearlessly in accordance with the wishes of his client and subject to the established rules, standards and ethics of his profession without any inhibition or pressure from the authorities or the public.

84. Every person and group of persons is entitled to call upon the assistance of a lawyer to defend his or its interests or cause within the law and it is the duty of the lawyer to do so to the best of his ability and with integrity and independence. Consequently, the lawyer is not to be identified by the authorities or the public with his client or his client's cause, however popular or unpopular it may be.

85. No lawyer shall suffer or be threatened with penal, civil, administrative, economic or other sanctions by reason of his having advised or assisted any client or for having represented any client's cause.

86. Save and except when the right of representation by a lawyer before an administrative department or a domestic forum may have been excluded by law, or when a lawyer is suspended, disqualified or disbarred by an appropriate authority, no court or administrative authority shall refuse to recognize the right of a lawyer to appear before it for his client, provided, however, that such exclusion, suspension, disqualification or disbarment shall be subject to independent judicial review.

87. It is the duty of a lawyer to show proper respect towards the judiciary. He shall have the right to raise an objection to the particulation or continued participation of a judge in a particular case, or to the conduct of a trial or hearing.

88. If any proceedings are taken against a lawyer for failing to show proper respect towards a court, no sanction against him shall be imposed by a judge or judges who participated in the proceedings which gave rise to the charge against the lawyer, except that the judge or judges concerned may in such a case suspend the proceedings and decline to continue to hear the lawyer concerned.

89. Save as provided in these principles, a lawyer shall enjoy civil and penal immunity for relevant statements made in good faith in written or oral pleadings or in his professional appearances before a court, tribunal or other legal or administrative authority.

90. The independence of lawyers in advising, assisting and representing persons deprived of their liberty shall be guaranteed so as to ensure that such persons have free and fair legal assistance. Safeguards shall be built to avoid any possible suggestion of collusion, arrangement or dependence between the lawyer who acts for them and the authorities.

91. Lawyers shall have all such other facilities and privileges as are necessary to fulfil their professional responsibilities effectively, including:

(a) Confidentiality of the lawyer-client relationship and the right to refuse to give testimony if it impinges on such confidentiality;

(b) The right to travel and to consult with their clients freely born within their own country and abroad;

(c) The right to visit, to communicate with and to take instructions from their clients;

(d) The right freely to seek, to receive and, subject to the rules of their profession, to impart information and ideas relating to their professional work;

(e) The right to accept or refuse a client or a brief on reasonable personal or professional grounds.

92. Lawyers shall enjoy freedom of belief, expression, association and assembly; and in particular they shall have the right to:

(a) Take part in public discussion of matters concerning the law and the administration of justice;

(b) Join or form freely local, national and international organizations;

(c) Propose and recommend well considered law reforms in the public interest and inform the public about such matters;

(d) Take full and active part in the political, social and cultural life of their country.

93. Rules and regulations governing the fees and remunerations of lawyers shall be designed to ensure that they earn a fair and adequate income, and legal services are made available to the public on reasonable terms.

Legal Service for the Poor. 94. It is a necessary corollary of the concept of an independent bar that its members shall make their services available to all sectors of society and particularly to its weaker sections, so that free legal aid may be given in appropriate cases, no one may be denied justice, and the Bar may promote the cause of justice by protecting economic, social, cultural, civil and political human rights of individuals and groups.

95. Governments shall be responsible for providing sufficient funding for appropriate legal service programmes for those who cannot afford the expenses on their legitimate litigation. Governments shall also be responsible for laying down the criteria and prescribing the procedure for making such legal services available in such cases.

96. Lawyers engaged in legal service programmes and organizations, which are financed wholly or in part from public funds, shall receive adequate remuneration and enjoy full guarantees of their professional independence in particular by:

(a) The direction of such programmes or organizations being entrusted to Bar Associations or independent boards composed mainly or entirely of members of the profession, with effective control over its policies, allocated budget and staff;

(b) Recognition that, in serving the cause of justice, the lawyer's primary duty is towards his client, whom he must advise and represent in conformity with his professional conscience and judgement.

The Bar Association. 97. There may be established in each jurisdiction one or more independent and self-governing associations of lawyers recognized in law, whose council or other executive body shall be freely elected by all the members without interference of any kind by any other body or person. This shall be without prejudice to their right to form or join in addition other professional associations of lawyers and jurists.

98. In order to foster the solidarity and maintain the independence of the legal profession, it shall be the duty of a lawyer to enrol himself as a member of an appropriate Bar Association.

Functions of the Bar Association. 99. The functions of a Bar Association in ensuring the independence of the legal professional shall be *inter alia*:

(a) To promote and uphold the cause of justice, without fear of favour;

(b) To maintain the honour, dignity, integrity, competence, ethics, standards of conduct and discipline of the profession;

(c) To defend the role of lawyers in society and preserve the independence of the profession;

(d) To protect and defend the dignity and independence of the judiciary;

(e) To promote the free and equal access of the public to the system of justice, including the provision of legal aid and advice;

(f) To promote the right of everyone to a fair and public hearing before a competent, independent and impartial tribunal and in accordance with proper procedures in all such proceedings,

(g) To promote and support law reform, and to comment upon and promote public discussion on the substance, interpretation and application of existing and proposed legislation;

(h) To promote a high standard of legal education as a prerequisite for entry into the profession;

(i) To ensure that there is free access to the profession for all persons having the requisite professional competence and good character, without discrimination of any kind, and to give assistance to new entrants into the profession;

(j) To promote the welfare of members of the profession and render assistance to a member of his family in appropriate cases;

(k) To affiliate with and participate in the activities of international organizations of lawyers.

100. Where a person involved in litigation wishes to engage a lawyer from another country to act with a local lawyer, the Bar Association shall, as far as practicable, cooperate in assisting the foreign lawyer to obtain the necessary right of audience.

101. To enable the Bar Association to fulfil its function of preserving the independence of lawyers it shall be informed immediately of the reason and legal basis for the arrest or detention of any of its members or any lawyer practising within its jurisdiction; and for the same purpose the Association shall have notice of:

(a) Any search of his person or property;

(b) Any seizure of documents in his possession;

(c) Any decision to take proceedings affecting or calling into question the integrity of a lawyer.

In such cases, the Bar Association shall be entitled to be represented by its president or nominee to follow the proceedings and in particular to ensure that professional secrecy and independence are safeguarded.

Disciplinary Proceedings. 102. The Bar Association shall establish and enforce in accordance with the law a code of professional conduct of lawyers. Such a code of conduct may also be established by legislation.

103. The Bar Association or an independent statutory authority consisting mainly of lawyers shall ordinarily have the primary competence to conduct disciplinary proceeding against lawyers on its own initiative or at the request of a litigant or a public spirited citizen. A court or a public authority may also report a case to the Bar Association or the statutory authority which may on that basis initiate disciplinary proceedings.

104. Disciplinary proceedings shall be conducted in the first instance by a disciplinary committee established by the Bar Association.

105. An appeal shall lie from a decision of the disciplinary committee to an appropriate appellate body.

106. Disciplinary proceedings shall be conducted with full observance of the requirements of fair and proper procedure, in the light of the principles expressed in this Declaration.

SEE ALSO *Basic Principles of the Independence of the Judiciary; Basic Principles of the Independence of the Judiciary: Procedures for Implementation.*

K

KENYA. The Republic of Kenya is a country in eastern Africa, on the Indian Ocean. It has borders with Ethiopia, Somalia, Sudan, Uganda, and Tanzania. It achieved independence from Great Britain in 1963 and became a member of the United Nations the same year. Its population is estimated by the United Nations (1990) to be 25,414,000. Ethnic groups include the Kikuyu (21%), Luhya (14%), Luo (13%), Kalenjin (11%), Kamba (11%), Kisii (6%), and others (24%). Languages commonly used include Kiswahili (official), Bantu, Kikuyu, Luhya, Luo, and English. Religions practiced include Christianity (Roman Catholic, 28%; Protestant denominations, 28%), Islam (6%), and Animism (38%). Literacy is estimated at 50%.

The government (1990) took the form of a republic and member of the Commonwealth of Nations, of which the British monarch is the symbolic head. Under the 1963 constitution, the president is elected by popular vote in a general election in which suffrage is universal. He is head of State and government and commander-in-chief of the armed forces. Legislative functions are performed by the 171-member unicameral National Assembly, members of which are elected for terms of five years. The judicial system is modeled along British lines; however, Islamic courts exercise limited jurisdiction in matters of personal status where local populations are predominantly of that faith. The Kenyan African National Union is the only political party.

Kenya's most serious human rights problem stems from the fact that its population growth rate—about 4.1% per year, estimated to be among the world's highest—is rapidly outstripping its foodcrop production. Widespread crop failures in 1979 and 1984, and increasing population of the land once available for agriculture, have signalled serious problems in this area and have made large-scale food imports necessary.

In response to a communication circulated to the Commission on Human Rights at its 1990 session, in which a non-governmental organization alleged that hundreds of Kenyan citizens of Somali origin had been deported from Kenya, the government of Kenya arranged for the following statement to be distributed as a document of the commission (UN Doc. E/CN.4/1990/90):

In November 1989, the Kenya Government began a screening process of all Kenyan citizens of Somali origin at the request of political, religious and civil leaders of Kenyan Somali ethnic origin. This request came amid widespread incidences of banditry, thuggery, illegal entry, murder of tourists in game parks and forged Kenyan identity documents. These acts were nearly all committed by aliens from neighbouring countries. Given this situation, there has been suspicion and outrage against Kenyan people of Somali ethnic origin. The neighbouring government are fully briefed and aware of these incidences and these governments have themselves expressed concern at the adverse publicity such acts have generated against the governments and people of the region.

The Task Force to identify and reregister Kenyan Somalis was headed by a very senior Kenyan citizen of Somali ethnic origin and Provincial Commissioner, Rift Valley Province. The exercise of weeding out illegal aliens and criminal elements who use physical similarities to Somali people as cover, has further strengthened Kenya-Somali relations which the Kenya Government has worked hard over the years to strengthen and maintain.

Finally the exercise is not one of screening but one of registration to protect legitimate Kenyan citizens of Somali ethnic origin and has been carried out with no malicious intention.

KHARTOUM DECLARATION. The *Khartoum Declaration: Towards a Human-Focused Approach to Socio-economic Recovery and Development in Africa* was adopted on 8 March 1988 by the International Conference on the Human Dimension of Africa's Economic Recovery and Development, Khartoum, Sudan. On 28 July 1988, the UN General Assembly welcomed (resolution 1988/66) the thrust of the declaration and the commitment of States members of the Economic Commission for Africa to implement its recommendations. The Assembly urged international financial institutions, bilateral and multilateral donors, organizations of the United Nations system, and non-governmental organizations to contribute actively to the implementation of the recommendations contained in the declaration, with a view to ensuring that concern for the human dimension is adequately taken into account in their programs of assistance to African countries, and urged the UN Secretary-General to institute the action necessary to mobilize the UN system and the international community in support of the implementation of those recommendations.

The text of the declaration is as follows (UN Doc. A/43/430):

Preamble

1. Under the auspices of the United Nations, an International Conference on the Human Dimension of Africa's Economic Recovery and Development took place at Khartoum, the Sudan, from 5 to 8 March 1988 as part of the follow-up to the implementation of the United Nations Programme of Action for African Economic Recovery and Development 1986–1990 (UN-PAAERD) and Africa's Priority Programme for Economic Recovery 1986–1990 (APPER) and as a sequel to the International Conference on Africa: The Challenge of Economic Recovery and Accelerated Development, held at Abuja, Nigeria, in June 1987. The Conference brought together a gathering of about 200 policy-and decision-makers, government officials, professional and technical experts in the field of development and other related fields mostly from various African countries, as well as representatives of governmental and non-governmental organizations, agencies of the United Nations system, including the International Monetary Fund and the World Bank, bilateral and multilateral donor organizations and other resource personnel.

2. The Conference was organized with the whole-hearted support of the Government and people of the Sudan and participants enjoyed the warm hospitality of the Sudanese people. His Excellency Mr. El Sadik El Mahdi, Prime Minister of the Republic of Sudan, addressed the opening of the Conference. The proceedings were conducted in seven plenary sessions and six working groups. The Conference made a deep and detailed analysis of the African situation, particularly the current economic crisis and all its ramifications on the people of Africa. The Conference is unanimous in its conviction that the crisis that confronts the African continent is one that affects the total human condition of the continent and its people, men and women alike. It is a crisis that challenges the very survival of the African people. It is a crisis of Africa's environment as the desert rapidly overcomes the fertility of the land and the coastlines also recede. It is a crisis of the continent's natural resources exploited more for the benefit of external interests than to meet Africa's dire needs. It is a crisis of the rich cultures of the African people and the cohesion of families broken up by the desperate circumstances of the African reality. It is a crisis that threatens to overwhelm Africa and her people and, *in extremis,* to reduce them to the helpless gaze depicted in the starving faces of Africa's children in the international media. But it is a crisis that can and must be overcome through the concerted and determined action of the African people and their societies and States, as they develop a clearer understanding of the implications of the current predicament and fashion a decisive and coherent plan of action, with the assistance and understanding of the international community.

3. We are encouraged in this view by the fact that although Africa has been sorely squeezed by the pressures of recent years and millions of Africans have suffered severely, no objective observer can fail to be impressed by the vitality and human creativity which strive and flourish in spite of everything. The large cutbacks and constraints of government and urban production has stimulated communities to devise their own solutions to the problem of meeting their own basic human needs. Self-help groups abound in every country; the extended family, though strained, has often provided the means of survival of many of its members; examples of community action can be found in almost every village. It is important to recognize the enormous potential of the human energy and creativity and find ways to harness it rather than ignore it in the total process of national recovery and development. For these and other reasons we repeat that Africa's crisis, though dire, CAN AND MUST BE OVERCOME.

4. As participants in this event, the overwhelming majority of whom come from the African continent, we are moved to place on record our collective voice on the issues we discussed and we accordingly make this Khartoum Declaration.

I. Overall Assessment of the Human Condition in Africa

5. Since the human being is the centre of all development, the human condition is the only final measure of development. Improving that condition is essential for the poor and vulnerable human beings who comprise the majority of our peoples in Africa. Africa's men and women are the main factors and the ends for whom and by whom any programme and implementation of development must be justified.

6. Regrettably, over the past decade the human condition of most Africans has deteriorated calamitously. Real incomes of almost all households and families have declined sharply. Malnutrition has risen massively, food production has fallen relative to population, the quality and quantity of health and education services have deteriorated. Famine and war have made tens of millions of human beings refugees and displaced persons. In many cases, the slow decline of infant mortality and of death from preventable, epidemic diseases has been reversed. Meanwhile the unemployment and underemployment situation has worsened markedly.

7. Acts of destabilization and aggression, being perpetrated against the countries of southern Africa by the South Africa régime, have also imposed massive human and economic costs, greatly in excess of military budgets or battle casualties. Of the approximately 1 million human beings dead in southern Africa as a result of South African aggression over 1980–1986 about 100,000 were war-dead, narrowly defined. Of the approximately $30,000,000,000 in lost production, most relates to the creation of chaos and the loss of peasants' crops and national production.

8. Production and other economic aspects of development—especially distribution—are of crucial importance. Production by the poor is vital if they are to become more able to meet at least their basic needs. But it is just as important who produces what. Production of food, of basic consumer goods, of agricultural inputs and construction materials, of basic services such as health, education, and pure water, as well as of exports are central to improving the human condition. Unsustainable imbalances do matter.

9. Nutrition imbalances are as crucial as trade imbalances. High infant mortality requires just as immediate and as serious an attention as high rates of inflation or huge

budget deficits. Ultimately the trade, inflation and budget imbalances are serious obstacles to development because they are barriers to enabling the poor to produce more; to the vulnerable to surviving and rehabilitating themselves; and to the state and the society achieving universal access to basic services.

10. Therefore, a basic test for all stabilization, adjustment and development programmes is whether they will improve the human condition from their inception or, on the contrary, worsen it. Social services and human resources development programmes have high short-, medium- and long-term payoffs on economic as well as on broader development criteria.

11. They are relevant to the reversal of unsustainable imbalances since survival and rehabilitation assistance to the most vulnerable groups—international refugees and displaced persons, disabled persons, youth, women and children—is an important element in reversing production losses. Similarly, the engagement of Africa's most basic resource—its approximately 250 million economically active people—in production is essential to restoring growth as well as development.

12. The human-centred strategy to the implementing of the Lagos Plan of Action, APPER and UN-PAAERD is vital for reaching out to the aspirations and needs of Africa's peoples and *especially* their poor and vulnerable majorities. It is deliverable through the appropriate mobilization, allocation and use of resources. To bring this about it will be essential to restore the strained and torn fabrics of our societies, make popular participation in decision-making processes effective, ensure the preservation of basic human rights and fundamental freedoms and eliminate policies that discriminate against minorities and vulnerable groups.

13. Progress in advancing the human condition in Africa depends on the structure, pattern and political context of socio-economic development. The problems and weaknesses in these areas must therefore be recognized and attempts must be made to tackle them in order to achieve the objectives of social and human development. This is also necessary because the economic crisis which Africa faced from the late 1970s found fertile ground in the structural and political weaknesses that bred the germs that hastened the intolerable deterioration in the human condition.

14. A fundamental problem is the fast rate of population growth and the uneven and uneconomic distribution of the population in the different age groups. The youthful population makes high demands on educational, medical and other social services, while the large number of college graduates and school leavers that enter the labour market each year creates an imbalance between labour supply and demand.

15. A further structural factor is the urban bias and socially unequal distribution of critical factors and resources for human development such as employment, income, food and nutrition and health and education. As is well known, this distribution is biased against the majority of the population living mainly in the rural areas and in favour of the politically vocal minority in the urban enclaves. Economic issues have overshadowed social concerns and have prevented African countries from according the needed centrality to the human dimension and the human factor.

16. Finally, the political context for promoting healthy human development has been marred, for more than two decades, by instability, war, intolerance, restrictions on the freedom and human rights of individuals and groups as well as overcentralization of power with attendant restric-

tions on popular participation in decision-making. In such a context, the motivation of many Africans to achieve their best in productivity and the enhancement of their own and society's well-being has been severely constrained. In times of economic crisis, the politically stronger social groups and individuals survive while the weaker ones go under in increasing deprivation, social dislocation, hunger, ill-health or death.

II. The Human Dimension of Structural Adjustment Programmes

17. From the causes mentioned so far flow the consequences of wretched misery, marginalization and—for millions—very literally premature death. The severity of the African crisis is such that country after country has been putting in place structural adjustment programmes in their effort to halt their economic degradation and achieve a turn-around. Unfortunately, far too many of these programmes—whether nationally conceived or in collaboration with the World Bank, the International Monetary Fund and the donor community—are rending the fabric of the African society. Rather than improve the human condition, some Structural Adjustment Programmes have aggravated it because they are incomplete, mechanistic and of too short a time perspective.

18. Structural Adjustment Programmes are *incomplete* because they are often implemented as if fiscal, trade and price balances are ends in themselves and are virtually complete sets of means to production increases. Human condition imbalances as related to employment, incomes, nutrition, health and education do not receive equal priority in attention to macro-economic imbalances. Unless and until they make the elimination of these human condition imbalances central targets, stabilization and adjustment programmes cannot provide Africa's growth and development dynamic.

19. They are too *mechanistic* in being inadequately grounded in or sensitive to specific national economic, human and cultural realities. This is aggravated by an incomplete articulation which allows the gaps between macro models and contextual realities to remain largely unobserved, nor can we evaluate how rapidly production can be expanded, where, by whom and of what. Thus their human condition impact remains inadequately projected instead of being at the centre of target-setting, policy formulation and programme or project choice.

20. They are in *too short* a time perspective. Africa cannot wait for the attainment of external equilibrium and fiscal balance before seeking to improve the human condition, nor can long-term human investment to strengthen the institutional, scientific, technical and productive capacity operating in environmental balance be postponed. That is essential to attaining the more stable and less vulnerable economic position that we aspire to for the African continent.

21. Further, we must place squarely on record that the external context confronting Africa continues to deteriorate. The terms of trade losses of 1986 vastly exceeded net resource transfers to Africa. APPER is not receiving either the new concessional transfer support or the debt burden relief it projects as essential or which UN-PAAERD committed the international community to providing. This is not simply an African view—the World Bank has repeatedly said the same thing as has the Secretary-General's Advisory

Group on Financial Flows for Africa, a majority of whom are practising bankers.

22. We welcome the increased concern for the human dimension in stabilization and adjustment programmes, broadly expressed within the international community, but this is far from being enough. The gap between the expression of concern and actual programme implementation remains wide. Human dimension elements are additions, often long after programme initiation, rather than integral parts of their overall design. Those poor and vulnerable groups to be served are often narrowed down to those who are the victims of the stabilization programme, rather than addressing the human condition of all the absolutely poor and vulnerable people.

23. In the light of all the foregoing, we do not hesitate to reiterate the central position that the human dimension should be accorded in stabilization and structural adjustment programmes, for we are convinced beyond doubt that no nation can be great and prosperous if the majority of its people are poor, malnourished, illiterate, miserable and perpetually vulnerable.

24. Overall, we identify five distinct areas on which greater awareness and action must be focused by the African Governments, the international financial institutions and the international community at large. Firstly, all structural adjustment programmes in Africa must be designed, implemented and monitored as part of the long-term framework of Africa's development. These programmes must, therefore, be incontrovertibly compatible with the objectives and aspirations of the African people as outlined in the Lagos Plan of Action and the Final Act of Lagos. Secondly, the human dimension must be the fulcrum of the adjustment programmes. Thirdly, the structural adjustment policies must incorporate the relevant adjustments of the social sector. Fourthly, considerations must be made of the consequences of macro-policies on the poor and vulnerable not only so as to design temporary and independent compensatory additional programmes but to make the alleviation of absolute and relative poverty and the elimination of gender biases integral parts and factors of the adjustment programmes. Lastly, the entire process of monitoring the stabilization and structural adjustment programmes must incorporate the social aspects and criteria.

25. We regard it as the primary responsibility of African Governments to develop a richer articulation of the total macro-framework within which to reorientate these programmes.

26. Structural adjustment programmes must be made to complement the efforts of African Governments to attain their long-term development objectives. Consequently, they should, through their effects on the economy and the African social fabric, contribute to the preservation of basic human rights and fundamental freedoms and help to eliminate policies that discriminate against minority and vulnerable groups. Above all, the application of structural adjustment measures should restore, not corrode, the dignity of the African as a human being.

27. It is with these concerns in mind that we set forth in the pages that follow our conclusions and detailed recommendations.

III. Recommendations

28. In the light of the foregoing analysis, the following conclusions and recommendations are proposed for the most careful consideration of African countries and the interna-

tional community. It is our earnest hope that these recommendations will be taken into account when the mid-term review of UN-PAAERD is undertaken by the General Assembly of the United Nations at its forty-third session in 1988. Even before that, we hope that individual Governments, international agencies and non-governmental organizations will take them fully into account and implement these recommendations in whatever way they may find appropriate, given their respective mandates.

A. Incorporating the Human Factor in the Recovery and Structural Adjustment Process

29. Since structural adjustment is intended to improve prospects for longer-term development, the design and context of structural adjustment programmes should incorporate the goals and objectives of long-term development. As the improvement of human condition and welfare is the ultimate objective of development, structural adjustment programmes need to incorporate the human factor into their design and implementation. Towards the achievement of this goal, we call for the following actions at the national, subregional, regional and international levels:

Action at the National Level. (i) There is an urgent need to restore the centrality in Africa of long-term development goals and actions.

(ii) To this end, there is a need for African countries to design their structural adjustment programmes as part and parcel of their long-term development goals. These indigenous programmes should serve as the basis for discussion with the donor community, multilateral as well as bilateral.

(iii) In this process, the human dimension needs to be brought out both in the definition of the long-term goals and in the priorities and components of the structural adjustment process.

(iv) Each African Government should translate its pronouncements—regarding the centrality of the social sectors in the process of economic recovery and development, as expressed in APPER and UN-PAAERD—into concrete action. In particular, a special appeal is to be made to the Governments to speedily carry out their pledge to commit 20 to 25 per cent of their annual budgets to the agricultural sector.

(v) In designing adjustment programmes, a careful analysis should be made of what categories of the population are most severely affected during the adjustment period, of the magnitude of their needs and of the ways and means that these needs, especially of the poor, can be met during the process of adjustment and beyond.

(vi) In making the protection of the poor an integral part of adjustment, the primary strategy should be that of enhancing their productive capacity through better access to productive resources and assets.

(vii) In the design of adjustment and development programmes, explicit attention must be paid to gender issues so as to accelerate the integration of women in the whole development process. With the clear awareness of women's major contribution to development, there is a new opportunity for making major progress in this direction.

(viii) Special attention should be paid to the vulnerable groups, particularly children, the aged, the disabled and refugees and displaced persons. The design of adjustment programmes should incorporate aspects of support of the retrenched employees to enable them to become viable entrepreneurs. Such support should include provision of loans and extension and advisory services.

(ix) In making policy decisions on the question of subsidies, a thorough analysis of the impact of such decisions on the most affected groups should be made and, if possible, alternative approaches should be found, especially as regards the poor and vulnerable.

(x) Food security and its indispensable adjunct of food self-sufficiency should be treated with the utmost priority in the design of adjustment, recovery and development policies.

(xi) There should be greater openness in the process of designing the adjustment package, both within government and beyond. In particular, employers, trade unions and other relevant groups should be closely associated with the process both to improve the design of the programmes and to ensure their fuller understanding and support.

Action at the Regional and Subregional Levels. (i) National actions will be greatly helped or hindered to the extent that regional and subregional environments are conducive. To this end, African countries need to take more positive steps towards peace, stability, human rights and African solidarity.

(ii) Subregional and regional data banks, such as the Pan-African Documentation and Information Service (PADIS) should strengthen their programmes in order to generate and disseminate current information and data on the social and human conditions in Africa, in order, *inter alia,* to facilitate the monitoring and implementation of Structural Adjustment Programmes.

(iii) Exchange of experience and in-depth studies should be undertaken by African countries and institutions as well as international organizations about structural adjustment options that would, *inter alia,* take fully into account:

(a) The human dimension;

(b) Compatibility with long-term development;

(c) Full participation of the people in the design and implementing of the alternative.

(iv) Subregional and regional institutions should take appropriate action to strengthen and improve the capabilities and skills of African countries in their negotiations with their development partners, especially on issues related to structural adjustment.

(v) In the long term, greater subregional and regional co-operation is needed to ensure the acceleration and sustainability of long-term African development. In this context, African Governments should also try to harmonize the activities of their various institutions in the field of human resources development.

Action at the International Level. (i) Having due regard to the high social costs of structural adjustment programmes, the IMF and the World Bank should endeavour to ensure that adequate and comprehensive safeguards for the protection of vulnerable groups and the human dimension are built into such programmes from the beginning. In this connection, we welcome the recent undertaking by the Bank and IMF to this effect and we urge its rapid implementation.

(ii) International organizations should intensify their efforts in the development and use of appropriate indicators for closely monitoring the human and social dimensions of the adjustment process.

(iii) The World Bank and the United Nations Development Programme, in their various roles as co-ordinators of consultative groups and round tables, should pay full atten-

tion to the human dimension of adjustment in the preparation and documentation for and the discussion at these meetings.

B. Paying Special Attention to the Social Sector and the Vulnerable Groups

30. Africa's people are her most valuable asset. Their healthy social development is a *sine qua non* for achieving a productive and sustainable transformation in the continent. Yet, for far too long, the vast majority of the African people, especially women and youth, have been locked into poverty and vulnerability, along with the traditionally disadvantaged, the disabled, refugees and displaced persons. Where the most affected groups inhabit the neglected rural and peri-urban areas, their living conditions have often become intolerable in recent years as a result of the economic crisis and structural adjustment measures. The fundamental problem is that of late official policies have paid only scant attention and have given very low priority to the social sector and the vulnerable groups in society.

31. Therefore, we strongly recommend the following urgent actions:

Action at the National Level. (i) Measures should be adopted to promote equitable patterns of development based on the democratization and decentralization of the decision-making process.

(ii) Even in times of severe resource constraints, such as experienced during periods of economic adjustment, attempts should be made to ensure acceptable minimum levels of and access to food and social services, particularly for the vulnerable groups. Furthermore, food aid, being an important portion of ODA to Africa, must be used in direct support of food security, particularly to ensure access to food by the vulnerable groups in times of structural adjustment.

(iii) Investment priorities should be focused on the rural sector so as to raise rural employment, productivity and incomes and to reduce rural poverty.

(iv) Governments that have not already done so should formulate and implement national population policies as stipulated by the 1984 Kilimanjaro Programme of Action.

(v) To arrest the current drought and desertification, resulting from long-continuing misuse of renewable natural resources and endangering mostly the vulnerable persons in the rural areas, sustainable development and long-term considerations, rather than immediate, quick benefits, should be made the overriding principle governing all development plans, programmes and projects. In each and every socio-economic development plan, programme and project, conservation of nature and natural resources and maintenance of ecosystems and environmental balances should be an in-built primary component.

(vi) Opportunities should be given to women for greater participation in the nation's political and decision-making processes at all levels, especially at the national centres of power. Where necessary, appropriate training should be given to them to ensure this.

(vii) Accelerated child development and survival strategies (for example, low-cost immunization and oral rehydration therapy) should be implemented so as to reduce the very high levels of infant and child mortality and morbidity.

(viii) Greater efforts should be made to provide youth

with productive employment opportunities and to integrate them more effectively in the development process.

(ix) Concerted efforts should be made to change prevailing attitudes towards the disabled so as to rehabilitate them and bring them into the mainstream of development.

Action at the Subregional and Regional Levels. (i) Subregional and regional development, research and training and financing institutions should give priority attention in their work programmes to the issues of African women, children, youth and vulnerable groups, particularly the aged, disabled, refugees and displaced persons.

(ii) Governments of each subregion should devise policies and plans for collectively dealing with the root causes of the problems of refugees and displaced persons. Where possible arrangements should be made to facilitate the voluntary return of refugees to their home countries.

Action at the International Level. 32. International organizations should intensify their efforts, in co-operation with African countries, in the development and use of appropriate indicators for closely monitoring and measuring progress in the improvement of conditions of human well-being. Instruments should also be developed to provide early warning on deteriorating human conditions.

C. Manpower Development and Utilization for the Long Term

33. Africa's long-term development prospects depend on its human resources, and for African countries to achieve the goals of APPER, UN-PAAERD and the Lagos Plan of Action a significant strengthening of their capabilities to develop and adequately utilize their human resources is called for. These efforts should be aimed at reinforcing, expanding and making more relevant, the human resources base, avoiding wastage through under-utilization of manpower, or loss through the brain drain, and raising productivity levels, particularly in agriculture, through various support policies and programmes and public sector interventions.

34. In the light of the foregoing observations, the following are recommended:

Action at the National Level. (i) Efforts should be intensified to expand primary and basic education, especially in the urban peripheries and in the rural areas.

(ii) Higher and technical education must, of urgent necessity, be significantly strengthened and reoriented so as to build within them those capabilities that would enable African countries to produce the required middle- and high-level manpower.

(iii) Governments should strive to seek greater relevance in education and training so that the outputs of education and training systems are more readily employable and can function better as job-creators rather than as job-seekers, particularly in the rural areas and the agricultural sector.

(iv) Greater emphasis should be placed on improvements in the teaching of science and technology in African countries, and more effective mechanisms should be evolved for the dissemination of the results of scientific and technological research for purposes of application and development.

(v) Governments should review education expenditure policies with a view to maximizing effectiveness in all areas of education.

35. In view of the seriousness of the unemployment and underemployment problems in African countries and the bleak prognosis for the future in this domain, it is strongly recommended that:

(i) Every development plan should have as major expressed objectives the generation of employment and incomes and the reduction of absolute poverty and income inequality among the people, and to this end effective monitoring and implementation mechanisms should be established to ensure the achievement of these objectives.

(ii) Investment priorities should be focused on the rural sector so as to raise rural employment, productivity and incomes and to reduce rural poverty.

(iii) Opportunities should be increased for women to have a greater access to education and training in order to increase their skill levels and enable them to raise their efficiency as a significant group in the African work-force.

(iv) Greater efforts should be made to provide youth with productive employment opportunities and to integrate them more effectively in the development process.

(v) Governments should provide a more congenial environment for the development of the informal sector which has a high potential for employment creation in African countries and is a rich and fertile ground for the development of indigenous entrepreneurship.

Action at the Subregional and Regional Levels. 36. Governments of the various subregions and of the region as a whole are urged to strengthen their bonds of co-operation in the area of manpower development and utilization. Accordingly, they are urged to:

(i) Intensify their efforts to create, maintain and strengthen regional and subregional institutions with specialization in specific fields of learning and research for the common use of member States.

(ii) Develop joint research programmes among groups of countries at the subregional and regional levels to focus on common problems of development in fields such as science and technology, medicine, engineering, agriculture, management etc.

(iii) Strive to expand employment markets within a subregional context by embarking upon joint employment-generation investment programmes accompanied by an opening up of subregional employment markets and the promotion of the free movement of people in order to reduce the unemployment problems facing African countries.

(iv) Enter into agreement among themselves within a subregional context to promote the exchange of experts and to make it easier for skilled manpower from countries within their subregions to find employment in other countries as a means of reducing the brain drain from Africa.

(v) Participate as fully as possible in ECA's Return of Skills Programme for Africa by exploiting this Programme for the identification and recruitment of high-level manpower to fill vacancies in their public and private sectors, higher learning institutions as well as technical assistance posts within their countries.

D. Role of Regional, International and Non-governmental Organizations

1. *Bilateral Donors.* 37. The Conference calls upon the industrialized countries, particularly OECD and CMEA, to report on the reforms and resource allocations they are making and will undertake in support of their commitments under UN-PAAERD.

2. *Role of Regional and Subregional Organizations.* 38. One cannot overstate the fact that international actions and sup-

port are vital to the success of the whole programme of African recovery and development. In the subregional and regional levels several actions are vital:

(i) African countries should rationalize the structure of their regional organizations and make better use of key organizations vital to the co-ordination of African development.

(ii) Regional organizations should accord the highest priority to the human dimension in the design and implementation of the recovery and development programmes of the continent, including the resolution of regional conflicts so that scarce resources are further saved to protect the human dimension.

(iii) Co-operation at the regional and subregional levels should focus on collective self-reliance to protect the human dimension during the recovery period and beyond.

(iv) African Governments are at a disadvantage in international negotiations with the International Monetary Fund and the World Bank. This disadvantage must be overcome. African Governments should turn, for assistance, to regional organizations, like the ECA, ADB and OAU, which have the capacity to provide technical and political expertise. In particular, the comparative information provided by the ECA on the nature, details and constraints of structure adjustment programmes should be exploited to the maximum in order to improve the negotiating position of the African Governments.

3. *Role of International Organizations.* 39. International organizations can and should play a more positive role in Africa's recovery. The major preoccupation of the Conference is the fact that such organizations should be more sensitive and more responsive to the realities of the African countries and societies since political, social and cultural realities condition the dynamics of adjustment, recovery and development. Accordingly, it is proposed that:

(i) International organizations involved in Africa should undertake high priority actions aimed at supporting and enhancing the human dimension in the recovery and development programmes of Africa.

(ii) The Conference endorses the proposal of UNDP for the establishment of an inter-agency task force for the assessment of Africa's human resources needs and the development of an appropriate United Nations system-wide programme of action in the field of human resources development. This task force could, *inter alia,* establish the modalities and mechanisms for improving co-ordination in the delivery of mutual co-operation in the field of human resources, public sector resources management, use of resources for human resources development and for the creation of information systems and an integrated data base for human resources development and management. Regional monitoring and information exchange will be conducted by ECA. To this end, the task force should, in consultation with national governments, draw up a detailed human resources development plan for submission to and approval by a special ECA meeting of ministers.

(iii) The international financial institutions should make prompt and urgent efforts to catalyse the implementation of the recommendations of the report of the Advisory Group on Financial Flows for Africa and to bring the attention of the international community to the fact that additional resources and debt reductions are urgently required for Africa's adjustment efforts to succeed.

(iv) International agencies should strengthen their regional and national units by decentralizing power, responsibilities and resources to the regional offices. Increasingly,

decision-making on resource allocation should be decentralized to the regional, subregional and field offices.

(v) International organizations ought to ensure that their priorities are in line with the aspirations of African countries. In this context, their priorities should be compatible with the stated objectives, priorities and strategies of APPER and UN-PAAERD and the Lagos Plan of Action.

(vi) United Nations organizations should make every effort to collaborate and to co-ordinate their programmes in order to conserve resources and avoid waste.

4. *Role of Non-governmental Organizations.* 40. There is increasing evidence that non-governmental organizations can make an effective contribution at the grass-roots level to the process of recovery and development. The NGOs present a number of advantages which must be built upon and strengthened, especially in the context of improving the human condition in Africa. The proposals below are made with the conviction that, if they are adopted, there is a lot to be gained by Africa's poor and vulnerable during the recovery period and by the African people at large during the process of development:

(i) NGOs should always respect Africa's own priorities and sectoral choices as this is the most sure way of contributing to overall national efforts.

(ii) NGOs based in donor countries should review their technical assistance with a view to using national expertise as much as possible and, to the extent possible, transferring power to local NGOs.

(iii) African Governments should give due recognition to African NGOs and create the legal and fiscal framework for their activities. NGOs should improve their policy analysis so as to incorporate longer-term perspectives and commitments.

(iv) NGOs should have an important role at the international level in monitoring the implementation of international commitments and improving public awareness among their nationals, of the realities of the African countries and societies. African NGOs should be encouraged, as appropriate, to respond to the human and social needs of the poor, especially in rural areas where structural adjustment programmes have resulted in the reduction of social services.

IV. Conclusion and Follow-up

41. This Declaration, then, affirms and asserts that the human dimension is the *sine qua non* of economic recovery. We, the delegates here assembled, will not abide economic rationale, will not tolerate economic formulas, will not apply economic indices, will not legitimize economic policies which fail to assert the primacy of the human condition. That means, quite simply, that no structural adjustment programme or economic recovery programme should be formulated or can be implemented without having, at its heart, detailed social and human priorities. There can be no real structural adjustment or economic recovery in the absence of the human imperative.

42. And how is that imperative defined?

43. Fundamentally, it means that the vulnerable and the impoverished, the uprooted and the ravaged, women, children, youth, disabled, aged, the rural poor and the urban poor, every group and individual in society who is in some way disadvantaged, must be given paramount consideration in the socio-economic development process. That is a sacrosanct principle. And in the service of that principle, health, education, welfare and all related social sectors be-

come indispensable components of every national policy, every national programme, every national plan, and every regional or subregional collaboration.

44. So should Africa conduct itself. But Africa cannot do it alone. The centre-piece of UN-PAAERD 1986–1990—of which this Declaration is an organic part of the follow-up— enshrines a shared partnership between Africa and the rest of the international community.

45. The understanding is explicit: Africa acts and the international community commensurately responds through its own donor reforms and increased levels of assistance. Fidelity begets fidelity. It is a mutual pact. Both sides have binding obligations.

46. Alas, the international community has not yet fulfilled its part of the bargain. African economic recovery continues to be threatened on every front by catastrophic debt, collapsed commodity prices, stagnating concessional flows, and crippling terms of trade. Because the front-line of recovery is the human dimension, the human dimension is at greatest risk. If structural adjustment with a human face does not succeed, then the failure, in considerable measure, will be laid at the feet of the international community.

47. It is this sense of urgency which has animated this Conference and suffuses this Declaration. We are nearly two years from the thirteenth special session of the General Assembly. We are on the eve of the Secretary-General's mid-term review. The United Nations Programme of Action ends in 1990. We are in a desperate race with time. No one pretends that African economic recovery is a short-term proposition, but the prospects for the human dimension of recovery will be writ in the actions of the next two years.

48. It is therefore our collective recommendation that this Declaration be endorsed by the Third ECA Conference of African Ministers Responsible for Human Resources Planning, Development and Utilization, which follows immediately. It is then our hope that the Ministers will transmit this Declaration to the Thirtieth Anniversary Session of the ECA Conference of Ministers scheduled for Niamey, Niger, in mid-April of 1988. If, then, as we would wish the Declaration is again embraced, it can be transmitted directly to the General Assembly of the United Nations to be considered by the whole international community of sovereign States, in the highest of forums, as an integral part of the follow-up to the United Nations Programme of Action.

49. When the Prime Minister of the Sudan opened this Conference, to which this Declaration stands as an enduring testament, he called for the restoration of the dignity of the African person, for peaceful relations among peoples and States, and for the pursuit of fundamental human rights rooted in the consent of the governed.

50. In so speaking, he mirrors the principles of the Charter of the United Nations. This Declaration, with its total focus on the human dimension, is a challenge to Africa and to the world to turn yearning into reality.

SEE ALSO Declaration of Abijan; Lagos Declaration . . . .

KOREA, NORTH. The Democratic People's Republic of Korea is a country in east Asia occupying the part of a peninsula jutting into the Sea of Japan and the Yellow Sea that lies above the 38th parallel Military Demarcation Line, which is its border with South Korea.

It also has a border with China. It achieved independence in 1948 and has observer status at the United Nations, although it is not a member. Its population is estimated by the UN (1990) to be 22,939,000. Ethnic groups are not in evidence because the Korean people are of a homogeneous nature, sharing one language and one culture. There is, however, a small Chinese minority. Religion has been officially discouraged since 1945, but small groups of Buddhists and Christians continue to practice their faith. Literacy is estimated at 99%.

The government (1990) took the form of a republic. The Korean Workers' (Communist) Party exercises power through its control of the organs of government. The general secretary of the party is president, chairman of the Central People's Committee and head of State. The Supreme People's Assembly, composed of 615 deputies elected by popular vote for four-year terms of office, is the chief organ of government but meets rarely and only for short periods. The judicial system is headed by the Supreme Court. There are also military courts, which are subordinate to the Supreme People's Assembly.

The independence of Korea as a whole was recognized in the treaty that ended the Sino–Japanese War of 1894–1895; but, in 1910, Japan annexed the country. At the conclusion of World War II, the Potsdam Conference designated the 38th parallel as the line dividing occupation by Russian troops in the north and American troops in the south. The Democratic People's Republic was founded in May 1948 in the northern zone, with Pyongyang as its capital.

On 25 June 1950, North Korean military forces attacked the Republic of Korea all along the 38th parallel, and the UN Security Council called for immediate cessation of hostilities. Two days later, the council, noting that North Korea had neither ceased hostilities nor withdrawn its forces, recommended that all UN member States furnish such assistance to the Republic of Korea as might be necessary to restore international peace and security in the area. On the same day, the United States ordered its naval and sea forces to provide cover and support to the South Korean troops; and, three days later, it set up a naval blockade of the Korean coast. By 8 July, General Douglas MacArthur had been designated commanding general of a command which unified troops provided by 16 member States, and the United Nations embarked upon its first armed conflict to halt aggression.

By the first week of August 1950, the combined UN forces had been trapped in a 4,000-square-mile beachhead in southeast Korea. After standing off North Korean attacks until 15 September, they launched a major amphibious attack at Inchon, behind the communist lines and, by 30 September, were again in complete control of South Korea. Moving northward, they were attacked by military units of the People's Republic of China and were eventually forced to retreat below the 38th parallel.

Truce negotiations between the opposing military commanders began in July 1951, but hostilities did not cease until after the signing of an armistice agreement on 27 July 1953, at Panmunjom. The armistice remains in effect after a conference of participants in the hostilities, convened in Geneva in 1954, failed to reach an agreed solution.

In the absence of a peace treaty, North Korea maintains that the two Koreas should become autonomous, equal governments in a Confederal Republic of Koryo (Korea's name for several years in the 10th century). In such a unified republic, North and South Korea would each maintain its own economic and political systems. South Korea, rejecting such an arrangement as unworkable, has for some time sought without success to arrange a summit meeting at which the two sides can discuss and resolve the issues that continue to divide the country.

Because North Korea functions as a closed society dominated since 1948 by the Korean Workers' (Communist) Party and its leader, Kim Il Sung, little information is available concerning the enjoyment of human rights and fundamental freedoms by its citizens. For many years, Kim Il Sung has been the object of a personality cult unequaled in the modern world; and a similar cult is developing around his son, Kim Chong Ill, who is being groomed to succeed him.

As a party to both the INTERNATIONAL COVENANT ON CIVIL AND POLITICAL RIGHTS and the INTERNATIONAL COVENANT ON ECONOMIC, SOCIAL AND CULTURAL RIGHTS, North Korea submits reports on its implementation of those covenants to the HUMAN RIGHTS COMMITTEE and the UN ECONOMIC AND SOCIAL COUNCIL from time to time. The situation in the country, as summarized in its initial report to the council submitted on 8 July 1986, was as follows (UN Doc. E/1986/3/Add. 5, para. 1):

Today the Democratic People's Republic of Korea has been turned into a people's paradise, where all the people are leading a happy life while working and studying to their heart's content without any worries about food, clothing and medical treatment. . . .

In 1983, 17 persons, including four South Korean cabinet ministers, were killed by a bombing in Rangoon; two North Korean army officers who confessed to setting the bomb were later sentenced to death by Burmese authorities. In 1988, a woman who claimed to be a North Korean agent confessed that she had planted the bomb that had destroyed Korean Airlines flight 858 on 29 November 1987 over the Andaman Sea, off the coast of Burma, with 115 persons aboard. The bombing, she said, had been intended to frighten those who planned to participate in the Olympic games in Seoul.

On 20 February 1988, the U.S. State Department placed North Korea on its list of States supporting terrorism after concluding that "the evidence of North Korean culpability is compelling."

KOREA, SOUTH. The Republic of Korea is a country in east Asia occupying the part of a peninsula jutting into the Sea of Japan and the Yellow Sea that lies below the 38th parallel military demarcation line, which is its border with North Korea. It achieved independence in 1948 and has observer status at the United Nations, although is not a member. Its population is estimated by the UN (1990) to be 44,828,000. Ethnic groups are not reported. There is, however, a small Chinese minority. Religions practiced by those who profess a religious belief include Buddhism (37%), Christianity (Protestant denominations, 26%, Roman Catholic, 5%), Animism (2%), and Confucianism (1.8%). Literacy is estimated at 93%.

The government (1990) took the form of a republic. Under the 1980 constitution, the president is elected by an electoral college chosen by popular vote for a term of seven years and serves as head of State. He appoints, and leads, a Council of Ministers. The prime minister, representing the party or coalition given the majority in the parliamentary election, is head of government. The unicameral legislature, the National Assembly, consists of 276 members, of which 184 are elected by popular vote and 92 appointed under a system of proportional representation. Political parties include the Democratic Justice Party, the New Korea Democratic Party, and the Korean National Party.

Throughout much of its history, Korea has been invaded, influenced, and fought over by its neighbors. It became a vassal of China in the early 17th century and was so isolated from foreign contact that it became known as the "Hermit Kingdom." All non-Chinese influences were excluded until Japan annexed Korea in 1910 and initiated a colonial era characterized by almost total control from Tokyo and ruthless efforts to replace the Korean language and culture by that of Japan. This period ended only after Japan's defeat in World War II.

The United States and the Soviet Union agreed at Yalta that the Japanese forces would surrender to the United States south of the 38th parallel and to the Soviet Union north of that line. This temporary arrangement was formalized in 1948 by the establishment of the Korean Republic in the south, with its capital at Seoul, and the People's Republic of Korea in the north, with its capital at Pyongyang. An election held in the south under United Nations supervision resulted in the choice of Syngman Rhee as president of the Republic. An election held in the north under Soviet supervision resulted in the choice of Kim Il Sung, a former Soviet Army major, as president of the People's Republic. On 12 December 1948, the United Nations declared the Republic of Korea to be the only lawful government in Korea.

After the United Nations command withdrew in 1949, North Korean forces invaded South Korea in 1950. The United Nations, thereupon, organized its first collective action to restore the peace by setting up the United Nations Command, to which 16 nations contributed troops and assistance. This international effort was led by the United States, which contributed the largest contingent.

As United Nations forces advanced northward, they were met by Korean forces and "volunteers" from the Chinese Army and forced to withdraw. The battle line finally stabilized north of Seoul, near the 38th parallel. Hostilities continued until 1953, when an armistice agreement was signed at Panmunjom. The armistice called for an international conference to solve the problem of Korea's division, but the conference—held at Geneva in April 1954—ended inconclusively.

Syngman Rhee served as president of the Republic until forced to step down in 1960 by demonstrations of university students against irregularities in the presidential election of that year. There followed a series of shifts between civilian and military rule, the most successful regime being that of Maj. Gen. Park Chung Hee, who was elected president in 1963 and re-elected in 1967, 1971, and 1978—a period marked by rapid industrialization, economic growth, and modernization. However, Park was assassinated in October 1979; and, after a brief power struggle, Maj. Gen. Chun Doo Hwan took over as president.

Chun's opponents demonstrated vigorously through the spring of 1980, and, in mid-May, the government declared martial law, banned all demonstrations, and arrested many political leaders and dissidents. This led to a confrontation in Kwangju City, which left 170 dead according to official estimates.

A new constitution, adopted in October 1980, limited the chief executive to a single seven-year term. A new electoral college in 1981 elected President Chun to such a term, and he vowed to step down in 1988.

In 1986 and 1987, students, intellectuals, and clergy, fearing that a way might be found to re-elect Chun, joined in organizing demonstrations demanding an open, free election in which opposition candidates could participate without fear of reprisal. Some of the demonstrations were marked by considerable violence. They subsided only after fair elections practices were guaranteed.

On 25 February 1988, Chun's hand-picked successor, Rho Tae Woo, assumed the presidency after the first genuine presidential election since 1971. Although given only 36.6% of the popular vote, he had emerged victorious because a badly splintered opposition divided its support.

Mr. Rho began his term by pledging "a great era for ordinary people through democratic reforms and national reconciliation." In his inaugural speech, he stated that "the day when freedom and human rights could be slighted in the name of economic growth and national security has ended. The day when repressive force and torture in secret chambers were tolerated is over. At the same time, the day when confusion was irresponsibly created on the pretext of freedom and participation must also come to an end."

Under the new government, the Olympic Games were held in Seoul without serious disruption. However, demonstrations against government policies preceded the games and resumed after they had ended.

KUWAIT. The State of Kuwait is an Arab country situated in western Asia, on the Persian Gulf. It has borders with Iraq and Saudi Arabia. It achieved independence in 1961 and became a member of the United Nations in 1963. Its population is estimated by the UN (1990) to be 2,230,000. Ethnic groups include Arabs (84%), Iranians and other Southeast Asians (16%). Non-Kuwaitis constitute about 75% of the total workforce and draw comparatively high pay. Languages commonly used include Arabic (official) and English. Religions practiced include Islam, the official State religion, (92%), Christianity (6%), and others (2%). Literacy is estimated at 71%.

On 2 August 1990, Kuwait was invaded by the armed forces of its neighbor IRAQ and was promptly claimed by Iraq as its province. Before the Iraqi occupation, the Kuwaiti government took the form of a monarchy. The amir was ruler and head of State. Upon his death, he was succeeded by the crown prince, who, up to then, had served as prime minister. A new crown prince was then selected, subject to approval by the National Assembly, by members of the Sabah family, which had controlled succession in the State since 1751. The crown prince was chosen from among the direct descendants of Mubarak the Great.

The National Assembly was a 50-member unicameral body elected by vote of the adult males who lived in Kuwait prior to 1920, or their male descendants. Women, police officers, and members of the military were not eligible to vote. The assembly prepared legislative decrees which were promulgated by the amir. The judicial system, which was independent, was strongly influenced by Islamic legal concepts. There was a constitutional court which interpreted constitutional texts, issued rulings in disputes and heard appeals, and the Administrative Division of the General Court which considered disputes arising between individuals and administrative authorities. There were no political parties.

Prior to the Iraqi invasion, many Kuwaitis had begun to call for democratization of their country, denouncing one-party rule and demanding the return of Parliament, which was abolished by the ruling amir in 1986. They also called for the lifting of press censorship and for the recognition and protection by the government of all human rights and fundamental freedoms.

The Iraqui occupation lasted for more than six months and caused enormous human suffering to the Kuwaiti population, to the non-Kuwaiti workforce, and to other foreigners in that country. During the occupation, civilians remaining in Kuwait were compelled to live under perilous conditions while attacks upon the country's infrastructure undermined their enjoyment of economic, social, cultural, civil, and political rights. Noting that the treatment of prisoners of war and detained civilians in occupied Kuwait failed to conform to international principles, the UN General Assembly on 18 December 1990 (resolution 45/170) condemned the Iraqi authorities and forces "for their serious violations of human rights against the Kuwaiti people and third-State nationals, and for acts of torture, arrests, summary executions, disappearances and abductions in violation of all relevant international standards of human rights and international law."

An allied coalition—headed by the United States of America and including armed forces of Great Britain, France, Saudi Arabia, Egypt, Syria, and many others—undertook a war to liberate Kuwait on 16 January 1991, acting on the authority of the UN Security Council to enforce 12 resolutions which the council had adopted following Iraq's act of aggression. The alliance forces prevailed, and the Iraqi occupation collapsed on 27 February 1991. Kuwait's independence was thus restored.

One of the wealthiest countries in the world because of its oil revenues, Kuwait's primary human rights problem has related to the treatment of the thousands of non-Kuwaiti workers attracted to the country each year. The situation was explained in a report presented to the United Nations by the government of Kuwait on 15 February 1984 in the following terms (UN Doc. CERD/C/118/Add. 3, para. 29–32):

The following statistics on non-national manpower in Kuwait are taken from the general population censuses: in 1965, the percentage of non-Kuwaitis amounted to 71 per cent of the total labour force of 184,297; in 1970, the latter figure increased to 242,197, of which non-Kuwaitis constituted 73 percent; in 1975, out of a total labour force of 304,582, 69.8 per cent were non-Kuwaiti, while in 1980 non-Kuwaitis constituted 77.6 per cent of the total workforce of 487,880. In the period from 1 April 1978 to 7 December 1983, a total of 439,908 work permits were issued to persons of 132 different nationalities.

Since migrant workers rarely stay in Kuwait for long periods, this non-national labour force is constantly changing in composition as its members return to their home countries. Consequently, non-nationals have not participated to a great extent in trade union activities, although those who have settled in the country for longer periods are strongly represented in professional organizations. . . .

With regard to the question as to whether a distinction is made between temporary and long-term workers from the standpoint of health, social security and other benefits, there are no temporary workers since employment is regulated in accordance with the needs of the country and the periods required for the completion of development projects in order to avoid the problem of unemployment among members of the national or non-national labour force. It is well known that the Government is providing numerous benefits in the fields of health, education and social security and is ensuring the availability of foodstuffs at appropriate prices for all residents. All persons enjoy free medical treatment and numerous hospitals and health centres provide free services for all residents in the territory of Kuwait, in keeping with the principle set forth in article 15 of the Constitution. . . .

Since embarking on its economic and social development programme, Kuwait has pursued an open-door policy with regard to migrant workers and this policy has enabled the Kuwait labour market to attract large numbers of skilled and unskilled workers of various nationalities, races and religions. Over the years, this demographic mixture has enjoyed a secure and dignified life free from racial discrimination and forced labour since Kuwaiti society is a hard-working community which is attempting to achieve the planned degree of social prosperity of which Kuwait is the standard-bearer. . . .

L

LAGOS DECLARATION FOR ACTION AGAINST APARTHEID (1977).

LAGOS DECLARATION FOR ACTION AGAINST APARTHEID (1977). In this declaration, the World Conference for Action against *Apartheid*, convened in Lagos from 22 to 26 August 1977 by the United Nations, reflected the unequivocal opposition of the African people to the policies of *apartheid* imposed by the Government of South Africa upon the peoples of that country and of Namibia. The declaration was adopted by the Conference on 26 August 1977 and endorsed by the UN General Assembly on 14 December 1977 (resolution 32/105 B).

The text of the declaration, as set out in the report of the world conference (UN Doc. A/CONF.91/9, chap. X), is as follows:

I

The Conference reiterates the universal abhorrence of *apartheid* and racism in all its forms and manifestations and the determination of the international community to secure its speedy elimination.

The Conference reaffirms support and solidarity for the oppressed peoples of southern Africa and their national liberation movements, and the commitment of Governments and peoples of the world to take actions to contribute towards the eradication of *apartheid*.

Apartheid, the policy of institutionalized racist domination and exploitation, imposed by a minority régime in South Africa, is a flagrant violation of the Charter of the United Nations and the Universal Declaration of Human Rights. It rests on the dispossession, plunder, exploitation and social deprivation of the African people since 1652 by colonial settlers and their descendents. It is a crime against the conscience and dignity of mankind. It has resulted in immense suffering and involved the forcible moving of millions of Africans under special laws restricting their freedom of movement; and the denial of elementary human rights to the great majority of the population, as well as the violation of the inalienable right to self-determination of all of the people of South Africa. This inhuman policy has been enforced by ruthless measures of repression and has led to escalating tension and conflict.

The *apartheid* régime in South Africa is the bastion of racism and colonialism in southern Africa and is one of the main opponents of the efforts of the United Nations and the international community to promote self-determination and independence in the area.

It has continued illegally to occupy the Territory of Namibia, for which the United Nations has a special responsibility and extended *apartheid* to that international Territory.

It has sustained and supported the illegal racist minority régime in Southern Rhodesia, and has constantly resorted to threats against neighbouring independent African States and violations of their sovereignty. Since the end of colonial rule in Angola and Mozambique it has engaged in a series of acts of aggression against neighbouring States and has connived at acts of aggression by the illegal régime in Southern Rhodesia. Its massive invasion of Angola and constant violations of the territorial integrity of Zambia have been condemned by the United Nations Security Council. It continues to violate the territorial integrity of neighbouring independent African States.

The policies and actions of the South African régime have already created an explosive situation in the whole of southern Africa and events have moved into a phase of acute crisis. The *apartheid* régime has intensified its military activities along the borders of independent African States and in constructing and expanding new military bases. It is reinforcing its enormous military arsenal and the production of nuclear weapons is within its reach. The possession of this arsenal and the acquisition of nuclear weapons by this racist and aggressive régime constitutes a menace to all independent African States and the whole world.

II

The World Conference recalls with admiration the valiant efforts of the South African people for many decades for an end to racial discrimination and for the establishment of a non-racial society. By their courageous struggle at heavy sacrifice, the South African people, under the leadership of their national liberation movement, have made a significant contribution to the purposes of the United Nations.

The United Nations has solemnly recognized the legitimacy of the struggle of the South African people for freedom and human equality, and for enabling all the people of the country irrespective of race, colour or creed, to participate as equals in the determination of the destiny of the nation. It has proclaimed that the United Nations and the international community have a special responsibility towards the oppressed people of South Africa and their national liberation movement, and towards those imprisoned, restricted or exiled for their struggle against *apartheid*.

The World Conference pledges its full support to the legitimate aspirations of the South African people and urges Governments, organizations and individuals to provide all appropriate assistance to the oppressed people of South Africa and their national liberation movement in their just struggle for freedom and human equality.

The Conference rejects all aspects of the *apartheid* system, including the imposition of "bantustans" which divide the population, deprive the African people of their citizenship and inalienable right to self-determination, and deny them a just share of the wealth of the country. There can be no international co-operation with bantustans and other entities based on racism.

The Conference condemns all manoeuvres by the South African régime aimed at preserving racist domination and the system of exploitation and oppression in South Africa, and in southern Africa as a whole.

It calls upon all Governments to enact legislation declaring the recruitment, assembly, financing and training of mercenaries in their territories to be punishable as a criminal act and to do their utmost to discourage and prohibit their nationals from serving as mercenaries.

It declares that South Africa belongs to all its people irrespective of race, colour or creed and that all have the right to live and work there in conditions of full equality. The system of racist domination must be replaced by majority rule and the participation of all the people on the basis of equality in all phases of national life, in freely determining the political, economic and social character of their society and in freely disposing their natural resources.

III

The Conference calls upon Governments, intergovernmental and non-governmental organizations to intensify the campaign for the further isolation of the *apartheid* régime with a view to complementing the efforts of the South African people and their national liberation movement and to ensure:

(a) The immediate and total elimination of the policy and practice of *apartheid* and granting equal rights to all its inhabitants, including equal political rights;

(b) The termination of all measures, under whatever name, which forcibly separate elements of the population on the basis of race;

(c) The dismantling of the system of *apartheid* and the policy of bantustanization, and abrogation of all racially discriminatory laws and measures;

(d) The ending of repression against the opponents of *apartheid,* and the immediate and unconditional release of all persons, imprisoned, detained, restricted or exiled for their opposition to *apartheid*;

(e) The exercise, freely and on the basis of equality, of the inalienable right to self-determination of the people of South Africa as a whole;

(f) The removal of the illegal South African forces of occupation in Namibia and compliance by the *apartheid* régime with the relevant Security Council resolutions, particularly resolution 385 (1976);

(g) Compliance by the South African régime with Security Council resolutions on the question of Southern Rhodesia, and full implementation of sanctions against the illegal racist minority régime, including the oil embargo;

(h) The immediate cessation by the *apartheid* régime of all aggressive acts and threats against the independence, sovereignty and territorial integrity of African States;

(i) The immediate cessation by the *apartheid* régime of military and nuclear build-up which constitutes a serious danger to international peace and security.

The World Conference recognizes that the continuation of the prevailing situation in South Africa, and in southern Africa as a whole, will inevitably lead to greater conflict in Africa with enormous repercussions to international peace and security.

The World Conference condemns the South African régime for its ruthless repressive measures which are designed to perpetuate white racist domination. It recognizes and respects the inalienable right of the oppressed South African people and their national liberation movement to resort to all available and appropriate means of their choice to secure their freedom, and the need to assist them to achieve freedom. It declares that the international community has an inescapable duty to take all necessary measures to ensure the triumph of freedom and human equality in South Africa.

It further calls upon the international community to assist States which have been subjected to pressure, threats and acts of aggression by the South African régime because of their opposition to *apartheid* and implementations of United Nations resolutions for action against *apartheid.*

Governments and organizations participating in the World Conference pledge to use their separate and collective efforts forthwith, and on a continuing basis, to bring about the elimination of *apartheid,* to provide assistance to the victims of oppression, and to lend appropriate support to their national liberation movements in consultation with the United Nations and the Organization of African Unity, in their legitimate struggle to eliminate *apartheid,* and to attain the inalienable right to self-determination of the South African people as a whole.

The Conference commends those States and organizations which have provided assistance to the oppressed people and their national liberation movement, and appeals to all States and organizations to increase such assistance.

It draws attention to the International Convention on the Suppression and Punishment of the Crime of *Apartheid.*

The Conference calls upon all States for the cessation of any assistance or co-operation enabling South Africa to obtain nuclear capability. It further calls upon all States to prevent companies or institutions within their jurisdiction, from any nuclear co-operation with South Africa.

The Conference solemnly calls upon all States to cease forthwith all sales and supplies of arms and military equipment, spare parts and components thereof; to withdraw all licenses for the manufacture of arms and military equipment in South Africa and to refrain from any assistance to the South African régime in its military build-up or any military co-operation with that régime. It further recommends the setting up of a watchdog committee to follow up the observance of the arms embargo.

It calls on the United Nations Security Council to take all necessary measures, under Chapter VII of the Charter, to ensure the full implementation of the arms embargo against South Africa.

The Conference recognizes the urgent need for economic, and other measures, universally applied, to secure the elimination of *apartheid*. It commends all Governments which have taken such measures in accordance with United Nations resolutions. It calls upon the United Nations and all Governments, as well as economic interests, including transnational corporations, urgently to consider such measures, including the cessation of loans to, and investments in, South Africa. It requests the Special Committee against *Apartheid,* in co-operation with the Organization of African Unity and all other appropriate organizations, to promote the implementation of the above recommendations.

The Conference urges States, and international and national sporting bodies to take all appropriate steps within their jurisdiction to bring about the termination of all sporting contacts with South Africa.

It commends all public organizations which have taken actions in accordance with United Nations resolutions and in support of the legitimate struggle of the oppressed people of South Africa.

IV

The World Conference calls on all the Governments and peoples of the world to lend their full support to international efforts, under the auspices of the United Nations and in co-operation with the Organizations of African Unity and the liberation movements recognized by it, to eliminate *apartheid* and enable the South African people as a whole to attain their inalienable right to self-determination.

The Conference expresses its solidarity with the oppressed people of South Africa and with all political prisoners and detainees in South Africa, and pledges the total support of all participants to continue and intensify their campaign for the immediate and unconditional release of all political prisoners and detainees. It further pledges its unswerving support to all efforts to end arbitrary arrests, detentions and political trials in South Africa.

It endorses the proposal to proclaim 1978 as the International Anti-*apartheid* Year and appeals to all Governments and organizations to observe it in the spirit of this Declaration.

The liberation of southern Africa as a whole from colonial and racist rule will be the final step in the emancipation of the continent of Africa from centuries of domination and humiliation. It will be a major contribution to the elimination of racism and racial discrimination in the world, and to the strengthening of international peace and security.

The World Conference calls on all Governments and peoples to make their fullest contribution in this historic and crucial effort for freedom, peace and international co-operation.

SEE ALSO Apartheid; Apartheid: *Adverse Effects of Assistance to South Africa;* Apartheid: *UN Program of Action; Declaration on* Apartheid *and its Destructive Consequences in Southern Africa; International Convention on the Suppression and Punishment of the Crime of* Apartheid; *South Africa: UN Concern about* Apartheid.

LAOS. The Lao People's Democratic Republic is a country in southeastern Asia, located on the Indochinese Peninsula. It has borders with Cambodia, China, Myanmar, Thailand, and Viet Nam. It achieved independence within the French Union in 1950, and full sovereignty under the Paris Agreements of 29 December 1954; and became a member of the United Nations in 1955. Its population is estimated by the UN (1990) to be 4,648,000.

The census of 1982 indicated the presence of 68 ethnic groups falling into three major groupings: the Lao Loum, who are plain dwellers and make up approximately 50% of the population; the Lao Sung, who are mountain dwellers and make up approximately 33%; and the Lao Theung, who live on the high plateaus and account for the remainder. Languages commonly used include Lao (official), Lao Sung, French, and English. Each ethnic group is free to preserve its own culture, language, and traditions; however, the only official language is Lao, which must be learned by all national ethnic groups. Religions practiced include Buddhism (Therevada), Animism, and various tribal beliefs. Literacy is estimated at 45%.

The government (1990) took the form of a republic. The president, sometimes advised by the former king (who abdicated in 1975), is head of State. Executive authority is exercised by the premier, who leads the only political party, the Lao People's Revolutionary Party *(Pathet Lao)*.

A small number of American servicemen, missing since the war in Indochina, are alleged to be held by Pathet Lao elements. In 1985, the government cooperated in an effort to locate them, but the search produced few results.

The 50,000 Vietnamese troops once stationed in Laos have been withdrawn, and the country has developed good relations with its neighbors: Cambodia, China, Myanmar, and Viet Nam. For many years dependent upon support from the Soviet Union and other eastern European countries for development assistance, Laos has recently sought improved relations with Great Britain, Japan, and the United States. However, it has made no move towards discarding its rigid one-party system.

LATIN AMERICAN FEDERATION OF ASSOCIATIONS OF FAMILIES OF THE DISAPPEARED AND DETAINED. An international non-governmental organization—best known by its Spanish title, *Federación Latinoamericana de Asociaciones Familiares de Detenidos-Desaprecidos* (FEDEFAM)—in consultative status (Category II) with the Un Economic and Social Council, FEDEFAM was founded in 1981 in San José, Costa Rica. The federation works to secure the release of all people who have forcibly disappeared in Latin America, seeks to locate children who were kidnapped or born in jails, and strives for their reunification with their legitimate families. FEDEFAM also provides social and medical assistance to families and victims after their release. In 1982, FEDEFAM proposed to the United Nations the adoption of a Convention Against the Enforced Disappearance of Persons.

The federation publishes the bi-monthly bulletin *Hasta Encontrarlos* and the annual magazine *FEDEFAM*.

Latin American Federation of Associations of Families of the Disappeared and Detained. Address: P.O. 2444, Carmelitas 1010-A, Caracas, Venezuela. Telephone: (02) 5611174. Telex: 21381–26274 CABIC VCF–4144. Executive Secretary: Loyola Guzman.

LEAGUE OF ARAB STATES. An intergovernmental organization composed of the governments of 21 countries of the Arab world, established in Cairo in 1945 and transferred temporarily to Tunis in 1979.

The functions of the Arab League—as it is popularly known—are to strengthen ties between its member States, to coordinate their political planning, and to safeguard their independence and sovereignty. The league is concerned with a wide variety of matters, including questions of economics and finance, transportation, communications, cultural and social affairs; questions of health; and questions related to nationality, passports, visas, and inter-state travel. It supports African development and anti-colonial movements and occasionally plays a role in the settlement of regional disputes and in the reinforcement of collective security.

A large number of specialized bodies have been established under the auspices of the Arab League, including the Arab Human Rights Committee and the Organization of Arab Petroleum Exporting Countries (OAPEC). It has also sponsored occasional Arab summit conferences.

League of Arab States. Address: Jamiat Adduwal Al Arabia, 37 Ave. Khereddine Pacha, Tunis, Tunisia. Telephone: 89-01-00. Telex: 13241 TN. Secretary-General: Chedli Klibi.

LEAGUE OF NATIONS. Founded at the close of World War I as "a society of nations" for the purpose of maintaining the peace, the League of Nations was the predecessor of the United Nations. The covenant of the league—incorporated in the peace treaty signed at Versailles on 28 June 1919, makes no reference to the rights of freedoms of individuals; indeed, a mild proposal by Japan to include a call for racial equality was hastily set aside on the insistence of Australia.

However, the covenant broke new ground in establishing the first international "mandates" system to protect those residents of former German colonies who were considered not yet capable of self-government. Provisions in peace treaties with Austria, Hungary, Bulgaria, and Turkey and in special treaties with Poland, Czechoslovakia, Romania, Yugoslavia, and Greece placed the protection of racial, religious, and linguistic minorities in those States—particularly the minorities created by changes in national boundary lines—under the protection of the league. Moreover, the league was directly involved in activities connected with the abolition of slavery and suppression of the slave trade, and with a wide variety of questions relating to the plight of refugees and of stateless persons.

Under the mandates system, former German colonies were assigned to more economically and industrially advanced States, who were expected to administer them not on their own behalf but as trustees of the League of Nations. Togoland and the Cameroons were divided between France and Great Britain, German East Africa was split between Great Britain and Belgium, and South West Africa was assigned to South Africa. The thinking behind the system was that, in the case of peoples "not yet able to stand by themselves under the strenuous conditions of the modern world," the mandatory States should apply the principle that the well-being and development of such peoples is a sacred trust of civilization.

In accordance with the peace treaties and the special treaties concerning minorities, the governments concerned agreed to ensure full and complete protection of life and liberty to all the inhabitants of the mandated territories, without distinction as to birth, nationality, language, race, or religion. All were guaranteed the free exercise, in public and in private, of any creed, religion, or belief the practice of which would not be inconsistent with public order or public morals. All were further guaranteed the free use of any language in private business and in private schools and the right to instruction in public primary schools in their own language, if they constituted a sizeable proportion of the population. In a few cases, particular privileges, such as the right of Jews to observe their sabbath as a holiday, were ensured. The protection of the rights set out in the treaties was placed in the hands of the League of Nations, and the specific guarantees could not be modified except with consent of a majority of the council of the league.

The States thus charged with guaranteeing the rights of members of minorities vigorously opposed the treaty provisions and maintained that they had been unfairly compelled to do something which no other State had done, or would do, voluntarily. They looked upon the league's "minorities system" as an infringement upon their sovereignty and feared that it would inflame the separatist tendencies of the minorities concerned and otherwise stir up trouble. But the victorious "Great Powers" insisted that their demands were in the interest of peace in Europe and compelled acceptance of the guarantees.

Thus, while, to a certain extent, the League of Nations was concerned with the rights of individuals as well as the rights of States, this concern was never very broad or well-developed. Its efforts to protect the rights of individuals applied mainly to persons who formed part of an underprivileged group—a people, a class, or a minority—and it was only rarely concerned with the situation of other human beings.

There were, however, two notable exceptions. The first was that the league established, in 1921, the Office of the High Commissioner for Refugees. This office—which arranged repatriation or asylum where possible for persons who had left their native land either because they had been expelled or had fled to escape persecution, and which issued international ("Nansen") passports to enable them to move about and find new homes—considerably eased the plight of many such persons. The second was that, under the auspices of the league, the International Slavery Convention was signed at Geneva on September 25, 1926. This important treaty placed responsibility upon the league for the progressive abolition of slavery and suppression of the slave trade and established international machinery for this purpose within the framework of the League. (For an updated version of this instrument, see SLAVERY CONVENTION SIGNED AT GENEVA ON 25 SEPTEMBER 1926, AS AMENDED)

As a power for peace, the League of Nations collapsed soon after World War II began, in 1939. The league was formally dissolved in 1946.

LEAGUE OF RED CROSS AND RED CRESCENT SOCIETIES.

A non-governmental organization in consultative status with the UN Economic and Social Council (Category I), and with UNESCO, WHO, and FAO, the league, together with the INTERNATIONAL COMMITTEE OF THE RED CROSS, form the International Red Cross and Red Crescent Movement, which includes 145 national Red Cross and Red Crescent societies with a total membership of more than 230 individuals.

The league, acting as a permanent coordination and liaison body, encourages and assists all forms of humanitarian action on the part of its national affiliates designed to prevent or to alleviate human suffering. In recognition of its efforts, it received the Nobel Peace Prize in 1963, sharing that honor with the International Committee of the Red Cross.

Although the INTERNATIONAL RED CROSS was founded in 1863, the league itself, as a coordinating body, was not instituted until 1919, after the end of World War I, when national societies turned their attention to helping famine victims and the homeless, especially in eastern Europe. Few countries had health min-

istries at the time, and there were no international bodies capable of organizing large-scale relief operations. Henry P. Davison, of the American Red Cross, convened an international medical conference in 1919 at which he proposed "to federate the Red Cross Societies of the different countries into an organization comparable to that of the League of Nations, in view of a permanent worldwide crusade to improve health, prevent sickness and alleviate suffering." Davison's proposal gained immediate support, and LORCS was established in Paris. Since 1939, its headquarters have been in Geneva.

The league performs a number of duties for the national societies. It contributes to the development of new national societies by providing advisers, equipment, and subsidies. It also acts as an international-level coordinator for emergency operations being carried out by a national society during a natural disaster. Based on information and requests it receives from the afflicted area, it appeals to other member societies for assistance; forwards donations, foods, or other supplies not available in the stricken area; and, if needed, sends experts—in particular, medical teams—to help in relief operations. In countries often at risk from natural disasters, the league helps the national societies to minimize the toll on human life by developing disaster-preparedness plans, for example, the construction of shelters and the institution of warning systems. The league has also established an international network of warehouses to enable relief supplies to be sent to disaster zones with a minimum of delay.

In addition to its work with national societies, the league also assists refugees outside of conflict areas, a responsibility it often undertakes at the request of the Office of the UNITED NATIONS HIGH COMMISSIONER FOR REFUGEES. In the area of health protection, the league has developed a variety of national society activities in the fields of community health care, health education, blood transfusion services, and large-scale vaccination campaigns. The "Child Alive" program, launched in 1984, aims to support national societies and local authorities in their fights against infantile diseases. Finally, to support the many national societies that have responsibility for blood services, the league actively encourages the dissemination of the "Code of Ethics for Blood Donation and Transfusion," established in 1980 by the International Blood Transfusion Society.

The League of the Red Cross and Red Crescent Societies. Address: Chemin des Crêts 17, Petit-Saconnex, CP 372, CH–1211 Geneva 19, Switzerland. Telephone: (41-22) 34-55-80. Cable: LICROSS–GENEVE. Telex: 22555 LRCS CH.

LEBANON. The Republic of Lebanon is an Arab country in western Asia, on the Mediterranean Sea. It has borders with Israel and Syria. It achieved independence from France in 1943 and became a member of the United Nations in 1945. Its population is estimated by the UN (1990) to be 2,967,000. Ethnic groups include Arabs (93%) and Armenians (7%). Languages commonly used include Arabic (official), French, and English. Religions practiced include Christianity (Greek Orthodox, Catholic, Maronite, and various Protestant denominations), Islam (Sunni and Shi'ia), and Druze. Literacy is estimated at 75%.

The government (1990) took the form of a republic. Under the constitution, the president is elected by Parliament for a six-year term and serves as head of State. He appoints the Council of Ministers, headed by the premier; the council is responsible to Parliament. Members of Parliament are elected by universal suffrage by numbers proportionate to the division of religious groups within the population. The judicial system includes religious as well as secular courts. Political parties organized along religious and ethnic considerations are numerous but ineffective because of the absence of parliamentary elections after 1972.

Religion has been a key factor in Lebanese history for many centuries. Together with Syria, Lebanon came under Roman domination and was included in the Byzantine Empire until part of it fell to the Arabs in the 7th century. Long before that, the Maronites, affiliated with the Roman Catholic Church, had established themselves, with the result that Lebanon became predominantly Christian, while Syria became predominantly Muslim. Adherents of the Druze sect, a group deriving from Islam but differing greatly from it, also settled in Lebanon and adjacent portions of Syria, and dissention between the Maronites and Druze led to frequent disturbances. The crusaders were active in Lebanon, and the Christians assisted them. After that time, until World War I, Lebanon was part of the Ottoman Empire.

Massacres of Maronites by Druzes took place in 1841 and 1860, and gave rise to pressure for the protection of Lebanese Christians by European governments. As a result, some local autonomy was granted to Lebanon. When the empire was broken up after the war, Lebanon and Syria were combined in the Levant States Mandate of the League of Nations and placed under French administration. Lebanon remained in French hands until, after being seized from the Vichy regime by the Free French in 1941, it achieved full independence in 1943.

Lebanon was able to achieve political unity at that time under an agreement between its religious factions known as the National Covenant of 1943, which provided that the president would be a Maronite Christian; the prime minister, a Sunni Muslim; and the president of the National Assembly, a Shi'a Muslim. Article 95 of its constitution provides that religious communities are to be equitably represented in public employment and in the composition of the cabinet.

However, as years passed, it became increasingly clear that Muslims had begun to outnumber Christians. The government did not take an official census, but Muslim leaders in 1977 put the ratio at 55% Muslim and 45% Christian and demanded greater representation in the government.

Full-scale internal conflict broke out in 1975 over difficulties stemming from the large number of Palestinian refugees in the country and the presence of Palestinian commandos. Late in 1976, the Arab Deterrent Force, composed largely of Syrian troops, moved in and separated the combatants.

Invasion of Lebanon by Israel in 1979 provoked the UN Security Council to create the UN International Force in Lebanon. A second invasion by Israel, in 1982, resulted in dispersal of Palestinian Liberation Organization units to other Arab countries. However, the assassination of Lebanon's president-elect on 14 September 1982 and the massacre of hundreds of Palestinian refugees in the Sabra and Shatila camps in Beirut a few days later stepped up the conflict. A multi-national peacekeeping force composed of American, British, French, and Italian elements was established in 1983 but withdrew in 1984 after 260 American marines and 60 French soldiers died as a result of suicide bombings.

After Israeli forces withdrew in 1985, conflict intensified between divergent Muslim elements, and Shi'ite extremists hijacked a TWA jet plane to Beirut where they held 39 Americans hostage for 17 days. Syrian troops were sent in, in increasing strength, to monitor a bewildering series of ceasefire and peacekeeping agreements, none of which proved effective, except for an accord reached in July 1986 under which all militia offices were closed.

The situation which prevailed in Lebanon in recent years made realization of human rights almost impossible for anyone in the country and provoked massive violations of those rights which have been of deep concern to the international community.

On 10 March 1988, the UN COMMISSION ON HUMAN RIGHTS expressed its concern (resolution 1988/66) about "the continuation of the acts of aggression and the arbitrary practices of the Israeli occupation forces in southern Lebanon which constitute a flagrant violation of the provisions of the Charter of the United Nations, the principles of international law, the Universal Declaration of Human Rights, the Geneva Convention relative to the Protection of Civilian Persons in Time of War and the Hague Convention IV of 1907." The commission strongly condemned Israel's persistence in violating human rights manifested in acts of aggression, bombardments of civilian populations, detentions, and other arbitrary practices, and called upon that country to put an immediate end to such repressive practices and to implement Security Council resolutions 425 (1978) and 509 (1982), which require its immediate, total, and unconditional withdrawal from all Lebanese territory and respect for the sovereignty, independence, and territorial integrity of Lebanon. Further, the commission called upon those governments assisting Israel politically, economically, and militarily to exert pressure on the government of Israel to put an end to its aggressive and expansionist policy in southern Lebanon.

The SUB-COMMISSION ON PREVENTION OF DISCRIMINATION AND PROTECTION OF MINORITIES, on 1 September 1988, expressed (resolution 1988/23) its deep concern at the continuing detention of foreign and Lebanese HOSTAGES in Lebanon in violation of the basic principles of human rights. Taking note of the repetitive deplorations and condemnations expressed by the government of Lebanon of all the acts of abduction which took place on its territory and its intention to cooperate within its power with all the international parties concerned to release those hostages as soon as possible, the sub-commission called upon all parties, local and regional, involved in the war in Lebanon, to release immediately and unconditionally all their detainees and hostages held for political, religious, or ethnical reasons, or any other reason inconsistent with the norms of human rights, and to use whatever influence they have on those in direct control of detainees and hostages.

In October 1988, the UN secretary-general reported to the General Assembly (UN Doc. A/43/727) that, in view of the critical economic situation in Lebanon, the organizations of the United Nations system had substantially increased their emergency relief activities and upgraded their presence there and that the relief assistance provided by the international community had helped to alleviate the suffering of the Lebanese people. He indicated that the United Nations would continue its efforts to mobilize all possible support in terms of emergency relief aid, as well as assistance for the reconstruction and development of Lebanon, and appealed to the parties concerned to do everything possible to promote the restoration of peace and stability in Lebanon.

In response, the General Assembly (resolution 43/207) called upon the organs, organizations, and bodies of the United Nations system to intensify their programs of assistance and to expand them in response to the pressing needs of Lebanon.

The Sub-Commission on Prevention of Discrimination and Protection of Minorities, at its 1989 session, adopted two resolutions relating to Lebanon.

In the first, on the situation in that country (resolution 1989/8), the sub-commission expressed grave concern about the escalating violence in Lebanon, which had caused extensive loss of life, and called upon all parties in the country to initiate measures towards the restoration of peaceful democratic processes. It expressed the view that restoration of confidence among Lebanese groups was possible only through restoration of Lebanon's sovereignty and territorial integrity, and called for full compliance with the relevant resolutions of the Security Council. Further, it pointed out that humanitarian aid should reach all parts of the civilian population without discrimination and must not be used for achieving political purposes, selectively depriving parts of the population of their access to basic needs.

In the second resolution, the sub-commission dealt with the problem of detainees and hostages in Lebanon. It expressed concern (resolution 1989/29) at the continuing detention of such hostages in violation of the basic principles of human rights and expressed the view that a lasting solution to the tragedy of the hostages in Lebanon should be sought primarily by helping that country to recover its sovereignty and legal authority and to re-establish the rule of law in its territory. It called upon all parties involved in the war in Lebanon to release immediately and unconditionally all their detainees and hostages detained for political, religious, or ethnic reasons or any other reason inconsistent with the norms of human rights, and to use whatever influence they have on those in direct control of detainees and hostages.

The General Assembly, on 19 December 1989, noted (resolution 44/180) the deterioration of the economic situation in Lebanon, which had been compounded by extensive damage to the basic infrastructure of the country and to its utilities, and reaffirmed the urgent need for further international action to assist the government in its continuing efforts for reconstruction and development. It called upon all organs, organizations and bodies of the United Nations system to intensify their programs of assistance and to expand them in response to the pressing needs of Lebanon.

Because of the civil war, Lebanon has had no general elections for 18 years. Syria controls two-thirds of the country, having maintained about 40,000 troops there since 1976, and supports the government headed by President Elias Hrawi. Christian units of the Lebanese army number about 20,000, and are commanded by General Michel Aoun; they control less than one-third of the country, the remainder—a strip six miles deep and 50 miles long in southern Lebanon—being occupied by Israel as a "security zone."

In addition to the Syrians, Muslim forces in Lebanon include units of the Lebanese army, which include some 17,000 Druze, Shi'ite, and Sunni soldiers; Amal, a Shi'ite Muslim militia which includes about 6,500 fighters armed by Syria; the Druze militia of the Progressive Socialist Party, with about 5,000 armed men; and the Party of God (*Hezbollah*), with about 3,500 Shi'ite militia.

Christian forces, in addition to the Lebanese army units, include the Maronite militia of about 6,000 and the South Lebanon Army of about 2,500. Both, backed by Israel, patrol the area of Lebanon north of the "security zone."

LEGAL AID. A national institution established within the framework of the judicial system of most countries, having as one of its functions the protection and promotion of human rights. As described in the UN Secretary-General's report entitled *National Institutions for the Protection and Promotion of Human Rights* (UN Doc. E/CN.4/1987/37, para. 53–57) prepared at the request of the General Assembly (resolution 40/123):

One of the most important institutions for safeguarding the rights of the individual within the judicial framework is the system of legal assistance services provided in most countries to persons who are financially or otherwise unable to defend themselves competently in a legal action. Generally such assistance may be granted when: (a) the accused is financially unable to retain counsel; (b) the accused is mentally or physically incapable of presenting his or her own defence to the court; or (c) when the statutes or laws relevant to the case are of such a complex nature that legal expertise is required to present an effective defence. Many countries have included provisions in their constitutions or laws making legal assistance mandatory in some types of criminal case. For instance, legal assistance is viewed as indispensable in the interest of justice in cases in which: (a) the defendant is charged with a capital offence; (b) the accused is a minor, deaf or mute, or is mentally unsound; (c) the accused does not have a command of the language used in court. In some countries, such provisions may be waived by the accused.

To illustrate, the following examples may be mentioned. In Barbados the Community Legal Services provide free legal assistance only to persons charged with such indictable offences as murder, manslaughter and rape, who have insufficient means to retain their own defence counsel. Similarly, the Nigerian Legal Aid Council restricts its grant of free legal aid to defendants with inadequate resources in criminal proceedings. In Norway, legal aid is granted to all who apply for it in criminal cases. In civil cases, applicants must demonstrate that they are without sufficient means. This stipulation applies to all requests for free legal advice, even in cases where judicial proceedings have not been in-

stituted. When an accused person does not have counsel, courts in the Federal Republic of Germany will appoint a lawyer, especially in cases where the accused is charged with a crime which carries a minimum prison sentence of one year. Counsel is also appointed for the accused when such assistance appears to be necessary because of the gravity of the act or because of difficulties of fact or law, or when it is obvious that the accused cannot defend himself. In these cases, an accused person without sufficient means may be assisted at no cost by an attorney appointed by the Court. No proof of lack of financial means is required. However, if convicted, the accused must bear the cost of both the proceedings and court-appointed counsel. In Morocco, every accused person may, at any stage of the proceedings, have recourse to the assistance of defence counsel. Appointment of such counsel is mandatory when accused persons are under 16 years of age, or when they are blind or disabled. The Finnish Act on Public Legal Aid, makes free legal assistance available to foreigners and stateless persons, as well as citizens. In the United States Public Defender Offices are located throughout the country, to provide legal assistance to the accused. The Public Defender is appointed by State or local authorities if a defendant in a criminal prosecution cannot afford to retain a lawyer. The staff of the Public Defender offices may be selected through civil service procedures, appointed by the judiciary or elected. The public defender systems are financed by public funds. The right to defence counsel in the United States has been expanded to include any case in which the defendant might be imprisoned and cannot provide his or her own attorney. In the USSR and the Ukrainian SSR, colleges of advocates are available to give legal assistance to citizens and organizations. In cases provided for by law, citizens shall be given legal aid free of charge.

Finally, various countries have made provisions to extend special legal aid services to persons who do not understand the language in which the court proceedings are conducted or to persons belonging to specific population groups. For instance, in Canada, legal services are provided to the indigenous population through the Native Court-workers' Association and the *Makiganik Tukisiiniakvik* Legal Services Centre.

Free legal aid services, in general, are provided by bar associations, legal aid societies or other similar bodies which may or may not receive financial assistance from the Government, by court appointed lawyers, who are not in government service or by lawyers employed by the Government, known as public defenders, who are usually appointed by State or local authorities and are full-time, salaried lawyers.

Some States require that the accused request legal assistance before the court will appoint a lawyer to the case. In others, the court appoints a lawyer to defend the accused, whether or not the defendant has so requested. In still other States, like Costa Rica, the court will only appoint a lawyer for the defence, if the accused has not chosen a lawyer within a certain time.

LEGISLATIVE ORGANS. Institutions, established within the framework of the government of nearly every country, which enact the laws and regulations which promote and protect human rights and fundamental freedoms. Their role and functions in this respect are described in a report by the UN Secretary-General entitled *National Institutions for the Protection and Promotion of Human Rights* (UN Doc. E/CN.4/1987/37, para. 7–15) submitted to the UN Commission on Human Rights at the request of the General Assembly (resolution 40/123):

In most countries the basic foundation for the protection of the human rights of individuals at the national level is established in the Constitution and developed by legislative organs. It is indeed the role of these organs to enact laws and regulations with a view to implementing the principles formulated in the Constitution. Countries which do not function under a written constitution, generally rely on the parliament or on the equivalent legislative organ to ensure the protection of human rights.

The essential function of parliament is, of course, its power to abrogate old laws and make new ones. Because of the importance of careful drafting of legislation, many parliaments have created select committees, whose primary function is to scrutinize and draft all proposed legislation.

To strengthen further the role of parliament in the protection of human and civil rights, many countries have instituted organs functioning within the parliament, to heighten parliament's awareness of corruption in the government, and increase the parliament's ability to respond to allegations brought by constituents whose rights may have been violated by illegal or unconstitutional acts, or by public authorities. These legislative organs fall into four basic categories: committees which seek to protect citizens from infringement of rights by the Executive; committees designed to draft and scrutinize legislation; committees which may receive petitions from citizens asking for a parliamentary investigation into a matter of public or private interest; and inquiry or investigatory committees.

Committees which are created to protect the rights of citizens from infringement by the Executive, may be either standing committees or *ad hoc* committees. Standing committees are permanent parliamentary committees which conduct ongoing investigations throughout the year on a particular agenda of issues. *Ad hoc* committees are created to respond to a particular situation or allegation requiring an investigation, which involves the public interest. Both standing and *ad hoc* committees may investigate allegations and report their findings to the entire parliament, urging that appropriate action be taken. The purpose of these committees is to exercise control over the Executive, with a view to restraining it from acting in an arbitrary or oppressive manner, to influence the policies of the government and to act as a liaison between the government and the general public.

The power of parliament to check the powers and activities of the executive branch can also be exercised through its authority to initiate investigations of executive offices. In Poland, for example, in accordance with the Constitution, the parliament can authorize the Supreme Chamber to investigate State officers or authorities which it suspects may be guilty of a breach of law.

Increasingly, legislative bodies in many countries have created standing and *ad hoc* commissions of inquiry or investigation. These commission are designed primarily to inquire into matters of public interest which may involve arbitrary action or violations of law. Both Houses of Congress in the United States frequently set up standing or *ad hoc* committees to investigate a wide range of matters of public interest. In 1974, one such committee, the United States Senate Select Committee, conducted hearings which led to the resignation of the President of the United States. Committees of this nature are generally comprised only of members of the legislative organ concerned, who have lawyers and independent investigators at their disposal. While such committees do not have punitive powers or judicial authority, they may examine witnesses under oath and take testimony.

Many countries throughout the world recognize the right of individual citizens to petition the parliament or other legislative bodies for the redress of grievances. In the United Kingdom, for example, the Committee of Petitions, appointed by the House of Commons, may receive petitions from citizens with the aim of redressing grievances. Similarly, in India, in 1952, the Lower House created a Committee on Petitions to inquire into general grievances against the Government.

To redress the grievances of citizens who believe that incorrect information, omissions or unauthorized data about themselves has been recorded in the State computer system, New Zealand passed the Wanganui Computer Act in 1976, which provides for the appointment of a Wanganui Computer Centre Privacy Commissioner as an officer of Parliament. Not a civil servant, and answerable only to Parliament, the Privacy Commissioner may, if he/she deems it justified after the completion of an investigation, direct the department concerned to make such deletions or alterations as may be deemed necessary by the commission. The departments in question are required to comply with the Commissioner's directions.

The Spanish Standing Commission on Petitions, which functions within the Congress of Deputies (the lower house of the Cortes), is required to consider each individual or collective petition received by Congress. The Commission may refer any of these petitions to the President of the Chamber, the Commission of Congress most suited to respond to the matter in question, the Senate, the Government, the Courts, or the Office of the Government Attorney. Finally, the Presidiums of the Supreme Soviets in the USSR have the power to receive and consider petitions from citizens.

LESOTHO. The Kingdom of Lesotho is a country in southern Africa, surrounded by the territory of South Africa except for a border with the Republic of Transkei, a South African bantustan. Formerly known as the Basutoland Protectorate, Lesotho achieved independence from Great Britain in 1966 and became a member of the United Nations the same year. Its population is estimated by the UN (1990) to be 1,731,000. Ethnic groups include Sothos (99%), Europeans (0.6%), and Asians (0.4%). Languages commonly used include English and Sesotho (both official). Christianity (Roman Catholic, 44%; Lesotho Evangelical, 30%; Anglican, 12%; and other Protestant denominations, 14%) is the predominant religion. Literacy is estimated at 65%.

The government (1990) took the form of a monarchy and member of the Commonwealth of Nations, of which the British Sovereign is the symbolic head. The king, recognized as head of State and ruler, does not participate in political activities. Executive functions are performed by the prime minister, appointed by the king, and his cabinet.

On 1 January 1986, South Africa blockaded Lesotho which it claimed had given sanctuary to military units organizing an attempt to overthrow the South African government. A severe economic crisis resulted; and, on 20 January, the government headed by Chief Jonathan was outed by a military coup. Five days later, the blockade was lifted after the military government agreed to expel the rebel units.

Political parties in Lesotho include the Basotho National Party, the Basutoland Congress, the Marematlou Freedom Party, and the United Democratic Party; they are, however, inactive.

LIBERATION. An international non-governmental organization in consultative status (Roster) with the UN Economic and Social Council. Founded in London in 1954 as the Movement of Colonial Freedom, Liberation promotes the rights of peoples to full independence, including self-determination and freedom from external political, economic, and military domination. Liberation also supports economic aid and technical assistance, free of external regulations, to underdeveloped nations and territories. The group publishes the magazine *Liberation* six times a year.

Liberation. Address: 490 Kingsland Road, London E8 4AE, UK. Telephone: (44-1) 254–6223. Secretary-General: Tony Gilbert.

Yearbook of International Organizations 1989/90 (K. G. Saur).

LIBERIA. The Republic of Liberia is a country in western Africa, on the Atlantic Ocean. It has borders with Guinea, the Ivory Coast, and Sierra Leone. Founded in 1822 by the American Colonization Society as a place where freed American slaves could resettle, it achieved independence as the Free and Independent Republic of Liberia in 1847 and became a member of the United Nations in 1945.

Liberia's population is estimated by the UN (1990) to be 2,577,000. Ethnic groups include indigenous tribes (among them the Kpelle, Bassa, Gio, Kru, Grebo, Mano, Krahn, Gola, Gbandi, Loma, Kissi, Vai, Mandingo, and Belle communities) (95%), and descendants of freed American slaves (5%). Languages commonly used include English (official) and a number of African vernaculars. Religions practiced include Islam (20%), Christianity (15%), and Animism and other traditional beliefs (65%). Literacy is estimated at 24%.

The government (1990) took the form of a republic. However, on 12 April 1980, Liberia was placed under military rule, directed by the 17-member People's Redemption Council. In 1984, the Council was replaced by an appointed National Assembly. There is a civilian court system and a military tribunal; the latter was established to deal with persons charged with crimes against the security of the State.

Government, employment, and social activity remain in the hands of the descendants of American slaves, although they constitute only about 5% of the total population. Only rarely are members of the indigenous populations permitted to exercise their civil rights. Efforts to raise the educational level of those populations have not been notably successful.

Once a progressive, well-ordered country, Liberia in recent years has been the scene of serious outbreaks of violence which have caused many citizens to move to Guinea or to the Ivory Coast. These outbreaks have been centered mainly in Nimba County, in the northeast, and have involved guerillas opposed to Liberia's president, General Samuel K. Doe, who himself seized power in a 1980 coup.

Government troops sent to Nimba County attacked civilian as well as military targets and Liberian civilians as well as invaders. An estimated 500 civilians lost their lives, and at least 70,000 fled to the Ivory Coast. The government's failure to control its troops gave rise to fear of prolonged civil strife.

In the summer of 1990, fighting between the government and insurgent forces graduated to a full-scale civil war, with the rebels gaining ground and approaching the capital city of Monrovia. Civilians fled to neighboring countries, and atrocities were reported against both sides. On 9 September 1990, Pres. Doe was captured by rebel forces—and reportedly 60 other persons were killed—when he left the headquarters of the five-nation West African peacekeeping forces, which had been sent into Liberia. Prince Johnson, leader of one of the rebel factions, said that he was declaring himself president of the country until elections could be held. After his capture, Doe was tortured and killed.

In 1987, Liberia became the only country in Africa ever suspended from International Monetary Fund and World Bank borrowing.

LIBERTY. The right of everyone to liberty is proclaimed in the UNIVERSAL DECLARATION OF HUMAN RIGHTS in the following terms:

Article 3. Everyone has the right to life, liberty and security of person.

The right to liberty is elaborated in two articles of the **INTERNATIONAL COVENANT ON CIVIL AND POLITICAL RIGHTS** as follows:

Article 9. 1. Everyone has the right to liberty and security of person. No one shall be subjected to arbitrary arrest or detention. No one shall be deprived of his liberty except on such grounds and in accordance with such procedure as are established by law.

2. Anyone who is arrested shall be informed, at the time of arrest, of the reasons for his arrest and shall be promptly informed of any charges against him.

3. Anyone arrested or detained on a criminal charge shall be brought promptly before a judge or other officer authorized by law to exercise judicial power and shall be entitled to trial within a reasonable time or to release. It shall not be the general rule that persons awaiting trial shall be detained in custody, but release may be subject to guarantees to appear for trial, at any other stage of the judicial proceedings, and, should occasion arise, for execution of the judgment.

4. Anyone who is deprived of his liberty by arrest or detention shall be entitled to take proceedings before a court, in order that that court may decide without delay on the lawfulness of his detention and order his release if the detention is not lawful.

5. Anyone who has been the victim of unlawful arrest or detention shall have an enforceable right to compensation.

Article 10. 1. All persons deprived of their liberty shall be treated with humanity and with respect for the inherent dignity of the human person.

2. (a) Accused persons shall, save in exceptional circumstances, be segregated from convicted persons and shall be subject to separate treatment appropriate to their status as unconvicted persons;

(b) Accused juvenile persons shall be separated from adults and brought as speedily as possible for adjudication.

3. The penitentiary system shall comprise treatment of prisoners the essential aim of which shall be their reformation and social rehabilitation. Juvenile offenders shall be segregated from adults and be accorded treatment appropriate to their age and legal status.

The **AMERICAN CONVENTION ON HUMAN RIGHTS,** open for acceptance by member States of the **ORGANIZATION OF AMERICAN STATES,** deals with the right to personal liberty in the following article:

Article 7. 1. 1. Every person has the right to personal liberty and security.

2. No one shall be deprived of his physical liberty except for the reasons and under the conditions established beforehand by the constitution of the State Party concerned or by a law established pursuant thereto.

3. No one shall be subject to arbitrary arrest or imprisonment.

4. Anyone who is detained shall be informed of the reasons for his detention and shall be promptly notified of the charge or charges against him.

5. Any person detained shall be brought promptly before a judge or other officer authorized by law to exercise judicial power and shall be entitled to trial within a reasonable time or to be released without prejudice to the continuation of the proceedings. His release may be subject to guarantees to assure his appearance for trial.

6. Anyone who is deprived of his liberty shall be entitled to recourse to a competent court, in order that the court may decide without delay on the lawfulness of his arrest or detention and order his release if the arrest or detention is unlawful. In State Parties whose laws provide that anyone who believes himself to be threatened with deprivation of his liberty is entitled to recourse to a competent court in order that it may decide on the lawfulness of such threat, this remedy may not be restricted or abolished. The interested party or another person in his behalf is entitled to seek these remedies.

7. No one shall be detained for debt. This principle shall not limit the orders of a competent judicial authority issued for nonfulfillment of duties of support.

The **AFRICAN CHARTER ON HUMAN AND PEOPLE'S RIGHTS,** open for acceptance by member States of the **ORGANIZATION OF AFRICAN UNITY,** contains the following provision:

Article 6. Every individual shall have the right to liberty and to the security of his person. No one may be deprived of his freedom except for reasons and conditions previously laid down by law. In particular, no one may be arbitrarily arrested or detained.

The **EUROPEAN CONVENTION ON HUMAN RIGHTS,** open for acceptance by member States of the **COUNCIL OF EUROPE,** provides that:

Article 5. 1. 1. Everyone has the right to liberty and security of person. No one shall be deprived of his liberty save in the following cases and in accordance with a procedure prescribed by law;

a. the lawful detention of a person after conviction by a competent court;

b. the lawful arrest or detention of a person for noncompliance with the lawful order of a court or in order to secure the fulfillment of any obligation prescribed by law;

c. the lawful arrest or detention of a person effected for the purpose of bringing him before the competent legal authority on reasonable suspicion of having committed an offence or when it is reasonably considered necessary to prevent his committing an offence or fleeing after having done so;

d. the detention of a minor by lawful order for the purpose of educational supervision or his lawful detention for the purpose of bringing him before the competent legal authority;

e. the lawful detention of persons for the prevention of the spreading of infectious diseases, of persons of unsound mind, alcoholics or drug addicts or vagrants;

f. the unlawful arrest or detention of a person to prevent his effecting an unauthorised entry into the country or of a person against whom action is being taken with a view to deportation or extradition.

2. Everyone who is arrested shall be informed promptly,

in a language which he understands, of the reasons for his arrest and of any charge against him.

3. Everyone arrested or detained in accordance with the provisions of paragraph 1(*c*) of this Article shall be brought promptly before a judge or other officer authorised by law to exercise judicial power and shall be entitled to trial within a reasonable time or to release pending trial. Release may be conditioned by guarantees to appear for trial.

4. Everyone who is deprived of his liberty by arrest or detention shall be entitled to take proceedings by which the lawfulness of his detention shall be decided speedily by a court and his release ordered if the detention is not lawful.

5. Everyone who has been the victim of arrest or detention in contravention of the provisions of this Article shall have an enforceable right to compensation.

The EUROPEAN CONVENTION ON HUMAN RIGHTS, PROTOCOL IV, adds the following provision:

Article 1. No one shall be deprived of his liberty merely on the ground of inability to fulfil a contractual obligation.

After examining reports submitted by States parties to the International Covenant on Civil and Political Rights in accordance with article 40 of that instrument, the HUMAN RIGHTS COMMITTEE adopted, in 1982, general comments on articles 9 and 10 of that instrument, as follows (UN Doc. A/37/40, Annex V):

Article 9, which deals with the right to liberty and security of persons, has often been somewhat narrowly understood in reports by States parties, and they have therefore given incomplete information. The Committee points out that paragraph 1 is applicable to all deprivations of liberty, whether in criminal cases or in other cases such as, for example, mental illness, vagrancy, drug addiction, educational purposes, immigration control, etc. It is true that some of the provisions of article 9 (part of paragraph 2 and the whole of paragraph 3) are only applicable to persons against whom criminal charges are brought. But the rest, and in particular the important guarantees laid down in paragraph 4, i.e. the right to control by a court of the legality of the detention, applies to all persons deprived of their liberty by arrest or detention. Furthermore, States parties have in accordance with article 2 (3) also to ensure that an effective remedy is provided in other cases in which an individual claims to be deprived of his liberty in violation of the Covenant.

Paragraph 3 of article 9 requires that in criminal cases any person arrested or detained has to be brought "promptly" before a judge or other officer authorized by law to exercise judicial power. More precise time limits are fixed by law in most States parties and, in the view of the Committee, delays must not exceed a few days. Many States have given insufficient information about the actual practices in this respect.

Another matter is the total length of detention pending trial. In certain categories of criminal cases in some countries this matter has caused some concern within the Committee, and members have questioned whether their practices have been in conformity with the entitlement "to trial within a reasonable time or to release" under paragraph 3. Pre-trial detention should be an exception and as short as possible. The Committee would welcome information concerning mechanisms existing and measures taken with a view to reducing the duration of such detention.

Also if so-called preventive detention is used, for reasons of public security, it must be controlled by these same provisions, i.e., it must not be arbitrary, and must be based on grounds and procedures established by law (paragraph 1), information available (paragraph 4) as well as compensation in the case of a breach (paragraph 5). And if, in addition, criminal charges are brought in such cases, the full protection of article 9 (2) and (3), as well as article 14, must also be granted.

Article 10, paragraph 1, of the Covenant provides that all persons deprived of their liberty shall be treated with humanity and with respect for the inherent dignity of the human person. However, by no means all the reports submitted by State parties have contained information on the way in which this paragraph of the article is being implemented. The Committee is of the opinion that it would be desirable for the reports of States parties to contain specific information on the legal measures designed to protect that right. The Committee also considers that reports should indicate the concrete measures being taken by the competent State organs to monitor the mandatory implementation of national legislation concerning the humane treatment and respect for the human dignity of all persons deprived of their liberty that paragraph 1 requires.

The Committee notes in particular that paragraph 1 of this article is generally applicable to persons deprived of their liberty, whereas paragraph 2 deals with accused as distinct from convicted persons, and paragraph 3 with convicted persons only. This structure quite often is not reflected in the reports, which mainly have related to accused and convicted persons. The wording of paragraph 1, its context—especially its proximity to article 9, paragraph 1, which also deals with all deprivations of liberty—and its purpose support a broad application of the principle expressed in that provision. Moreover, the Committee recalls that this article supplements article 7 as regards the treatment of all persons deprived of their liberty.

The humane treatment and the respect for the dignity of all persons deprived of their liberty is a basic standard of universal application which cannot depend entirely on material resources. While the Committee is aware that in other respects the modalities and conditions of detention may vary with the available resources, they must always be applied without discrimination, as required by article 2 (1).

Ultimate responsibility for the observance of this principle rests with the State as regards all institutions where persons are lawfully held against their will, not only in prisons but also, for example, hospitals, detention camps or correctional institutions.

Subparagraph 2 (a) of the article provides that, save in exceptional circumstances, accused persons shall be segregated from convicted persons and shall receive separate treatment appropriate to their status as unconvicted persons. Some reports have failed to pay proper attention to this direct requirement of the Covenant and, as a result, to provide adequate information on the way in which the treatment of accused persons differs from that of convicted persons. Such information should be included in future reports.

Subparagraph 2 (b) of the article calls, *inter alia,* for accused juvenile persons to be separated from adults. The information in reports shows that a number of States are not taking sufficient account of the fact that this is an unconditional requirement of the Covenant. It is the Committee's opinion that, as is clear from the text of the Covenant, deviation from States parties' obligations under subparagraph 2 (b) cannot be justified by any consideration whatsoever.

In a number of cases, the information appearing in reports with respect to paragraph 3 of the article has contained no concrete mention either of legislative or of administrative measures or of practical steps to promote the reformation and social rehabilitation of prisoners, by, for example, education, vocational training and useful work. Allowing visits, in particular by family members, is normally also such a measure which is required for reasons of humanity. There are also similar lacunae in the reports of certain States with respect to information concerning juvenile offenders, who must be segregated from adults and given treatment appropriate to their age and legal status.

The Committee further notes that the principles of humane treatment and respect for human dignity set out in paragraph 1 are the basis for the more specific and limited obligations of States in the field of criminal justice set out in paragraphs 2 and 3 of article 10. The segregation of accused persons from convicted ones is required in order to emphasize their status as unconvicted persons who are at the same time protected by the presumption of innocence stated in article 14, paragraph 2. The aim of these provisions is to protect the groups mentioned, and the requirements contained therein should be seen in that light. Thus, for example, the segregation and treatment of juvenile offenders should be provided for in such a way that it promotes their reformation and social rehabilitation.

SEE ALSO *Arbitrary Arrest, Detention or Exile.*

LIBYA. The Socialist People's Libyan Arab Jamahiriya is a country in northern Africa, on the Mediterranean Sea. It has borders with Algeria, Chad, Egypt, Niger, Sudan, and Tunisia. It achieved independence from Italy in 1951 and became a member of the United Nations in 1955. Its population is estimated by the UN (1990) to be 4,331,000. Ethnic groups include Arabs, Berbers, Arab–Berbers, Touaregs, and Tebous. Languages commonly used include Arabic and Italian. Religions practiced include Islam (Sunni), 97%; others, 3%. Literacy is estimated at 55%.

The Government (1990) took the form of a *jamahiriya,* or "mass State," composed of multi-layered popular assemblies (People's Congresses) and executive institutions (People's Committees), guided by the General People's Congress. Under military rule since 1969, the Revolutionary Council that establishes all State policy has been re-named the General Secretariat of the General People's Congress. The sole political party is the Arab Socialist Union Organization.

Ruled successively in antiquity by the Phoenicians, the Greeks, the Romans, the Vandals, and the Byzantines, Libya was conquered by the Arabs in the 7th century and by the Ottoman Turks in the 16th century. Italy invaded and seized it in 1911 and held it as a colony until forced to relinquish all claims under the terms of the 1947 peace treaty with the Allies. The treaty provided that Libya's final disposition was to be determined by France, the United Kingdom, the United States of America, and the Soviet Union by 15 September 1948. When those powers failed to reach agreement, they referred the problem to the General Assembly of the United Nations, which decided that Libya should become independent not later than 1 January 1952. A UN commissioner was appointed to assist the Libyans in drawing up a constitution and establishing an independent government.

On 2 December 1950, the Libyan National Assembly declared that Libya should be a federal State with King Idris I, the Emir of Cyrenaica—who had led Libyan resistance to Italian occupation between the two world wars—as head of State. When Libya declared its independence on 24 December 1951, it was the first country to achieve independence through the United Nations. In 1955, 1958, and 1960, the General Assembly adopted resolutions recognizing the special responsibility of the United Nations for the future of the country and providing it with technical and economic assistance. However, the discovery of significant oil reserves in 1959 changed Libya overnight from a poor country to a wealthy one measured in terms of per capita resources and made further outside assistance unnecessary.

The Kingdom of Libya was ruled by King Idris until 1 September 1969, when the government was overthrown in a *coup d'etat* led by the military. The Revolutionary Command Council, which seized power, abolished the monarchy, pledged itself to improve and to encourage domestic policies, and promised an equitable distribution of wealth. By 1970, it had succeeded in closing down British military installations at Tobruk and El Adem and American facilities at Wheelus Air Force Base near Tripoli.

Under Col. Mu'ammar al-Qadhafi, the revolutionary leader who emerged as chairman of the Revolutionary Command Council and *de facto* head of State, the Libyan government in 1977 convened a General People's Congress which proclaimed the establishment of "people's power," changed the name of the country to Socialist People's Libyan Arab Jamahiriya, and assumed authority as a legislative body and as an intermediary between the masses and the leadership. Libyan embassies abroad were re-named "People's Bureaus" and their extended staffs sought to win new recruits to revolutionary philosophy and to take direct action to control Libyan nationals abroad. The United States government closed the Libyan Embassy in Washington in 1981 and accused Libya of supporting international terrorism.

In the same year, American and Libyan warplanes fought in the airspace above the Gulf of Sidra, which

Libya claimed to be within its territory but which the United States held to be an international waterway. Two Libyan Soviet-built SU-22s were shot down by missiles launched by American F-14s. The U.S. Air Force claimed that its planes had merely returned fire in self-defense, but Libya charged that the incident had been carefully planned and provoked.

In December 1985, Libya's Press Bureau praised as "heroic" terrorist attacks by Arab gunmen—said to be linked to the Abu Nidal terrorist group then believed to be based in Libya—who hurled grenades at check-in counters of El Al, Israel's national airline, in airports at Rome and Vienna, killing 18 persons and wounding 111.

In March 1986, U.S. and Libyan naval units skirmished in the Gulf of Sidra and two Libyan patrol boats were sunk. In April of that year—after an American serviceman had been killed in a terrorist attack on a West German discotheque—the United States launched an air raid aimed at Tripoli, Benghazi, and nearby "terrorist-related" targets. President Ronald Reagan announced that he had ordered the air strikes in retaliation for the bombing of the discotheque and to deter future Libyan-directed terrorist attacks and warned of further military action unless Libya ended its alleged support of anti-American terrorism.

The bombing attack, which threatened the lives of Col. Mu'ammar al-Qadhafi and his family (an 18-month old daughter was killed), was later condemned by the Organization of African Unity and the Organization of the Islamic Conference. The United Nations General Assembly, in resolution 41/38 of 20 November 1986, also condemned the action, which in its view constituted a serious threat to peace and security in the Mediterranean region. The assembly called upon the government of the United States to refrain from the threat or use of force in the settlement of disputes with Libya and to resort to peaceful means in accordance with the Charter of the United Nations. It further called upon all States to refrain from extending any assistance or facilities for perpetrating acts of aggression against Libya, and affirmed Libya's right to receive appropriate compensation for the material and human losses which had been inflicted upon it.

In a matter some consider a coincidence and others consider a result of the American retaliatory bombings, American State Department reports showed a distinct drop in the number of international acts of terrorism in 1987. In the same year, Libyan armed forces suffered a humiliating defeat when Chadian forces captured a strategic airstrip at Wadi Doum, bringing the Libyan offensive against Chad to

a halt. In September 1989, Libya and Chad signed a peace treaty to end 16 years of hostility.

In January 1989, intelligence experts in the United States of America reached the conclusion that West German companies had assisted Libya in designing and constructing a plant for the production of chemical weapons and in helping it to develop a capacity for refueling its French-made fighter planes. These reports surfaced again early in March 1990, when Libya was reported to have produced 30 tons of mustard gas and an unknown quantity of Sarin, a nerve gas, in the Rabta plant. Libyan officials maintain that the plant produces only pharmaceuticals. In a related matter, late in March, President Vaclev Havel of Czechoslovakia, at a news conference in London, revealed that the ousted Communist government in Prague had shipped 1,000 tons of Semtex—a pliable, odorless explosive plastic substance undetectable by conventional methods—to Libya, which had passed it on to terrorist organizations in various parts of the world. He added that his country no longer exported Semtex.

LIECHTENSTEIN. The Principality of Liechtenstein is a country in the Alps of western Europe. It has borders with Austria and Switzerland. An independent State since it withdrew from the German Confederation in 1866, it maintains a customs and monetary union with Switzerland, which also administers its postal services. Its population is estimated by the UN (1990) to be 30,000, and includes persons of Alemannic (south German) descent (95%) and of Italian descent (5%). Languages in common use are German (official) and various Alemannic dialects. Christianity (Roman Catholic, 85%; Protestant, 8%) is the predominant religion. Literacy is estimated at 100%.

Liechtenstein is not a member of the United Nations. Its government (1990) took the form of a monarchy, headed since 1938 by Prince Franz Josef II but ruled in fact since 1984 by his son, Prince Hans Adam, after his father had given up the responsibilities but not his title to the throne.

Under its 1921 constitution, the premier acts as head of government. There is a 15-member legislature, the *Landtag*, elected by direct male suffrage. Women were granted the right to vote only in a referendum held on 1 July 1984. The main political parties are the Homeland Union and the Progressive Citizens Party.

The principality abolished its army in 1868 and has since remained neutral. Because of its low tax rates, it has attracted many international corporations and about one-third of its population consists of workers from other countries.

L

LUTHERAN WORLD FEDERATION. An international non-governmental organization in consultative status (Category II) with the UN Economic and Social Council, LWF has 104 member Churches and 15 recognized congregations in 88 countries.

Founded in 1947 in Lund, Sweden, as the successor to the Lutheran World Convention, the federation acts as a free association of Lutheran churches and serves as their agent in such matters as they may assign to it. LWF cultivates unity of the Lutheran faith and fosters Lutheran interest, concern for, and participation in ecumenical movements. LWF also assists mission and church programs globally, aids in welfare work, develops communications, and sponsors scholarships and exchange programs for leadership training.

Among LWF's publications are *Lutheran World Information* and the *Lutheran Directory*.

Lutheran World Federation. Address: 150 route de Ferney, P.O. Box 66, CH-1211, Geneva 20, Switzerland. Telephone: (41-22) 916111. Cable: LUTHWORLD. Telex: 23423 OIK CH. Secretary-General: Rev. Gunnar Johan Stalsett.

Yearbook of International Organizations 1989/90 (K. G. Saur).

LUXEMBOURG. The Grand Duchy of Luxembourg is a country in western Europe. It has borders with Belgium, the Federal Republic of Germany, and France. It achieved independence from the Netherlands in 1839 and became a member of the United Nations in 1945. Its population is estimated by the UN (1990) to be 362,000. Ethnic groups include Germans and Celts. Aliens constitute over 25% of the population, including Portuguese, Italians, French, Germans, and Belgians. Languages commonly used include Luxembourgish, French, German, and English. Christianity (Roman Catholic) is the predominant religion. Literacy is estimated at 100%.

The government (1990) took the form of a monarchy. The Grand Duke is ruler and head of State. The prime minister, representing the party or coalition given a majority in the Chamber of Deputies, exercises executive authority as head of government. Parliament consists of a 59-member Chamber of Deputies, members of which are elected by popular vote for terms of five years. There is also a Council of State. Political parties include the Christian Social Party, the Socialist Labor Party, the Democratic Party, the Communist Party, and the Green Alternative Party.

Originally one of the largest fiefs of the Holy Roman Empire, Luxembourg passed from Spanish to Austrian to French rule before the Congress of Vienna in 1815 made it a Grand Duchy loosely united to the Netherlands. It joined Belgium in revolting against the Netherlands; and, although Belgium on gaining independence in 1839 took over most of the territory of the Grand Duchy, the remainder declared its independence and joined the German Confederation. At the London Conference of 1857, the Grand Duchy was declared a neutral territory. That neutrality was violated twice by Germany, once in 1914 and again in 1940; the country finally was liberated by Allied troops in 1944. In 1948, its permanent neutrality was abolished by revision of the constitution.

As of 31 December 1984, the total population of Luxembourg was 365,900, of which 96,700 (slightly more than 26%) were aliens. The largest groups of aliens was the Portuguese (29,300), followed by Italians (22,300), French (11,900), Germans (8,900), and Belgians (7,900). There were also 813 stateless persons and 98 persons of undetermined nationality. The government, feeling that these alien residents have made a substantial contribution to the development of the country and that their presence will also in the future constitute an essential element in the efficient functioning of its economy, undertakes to combat any form of xenophobia and considers that the solution of problems requires a voluntarist integration policy which respects cultural identities.

As regards measures to promote understanding between the people of Luxembourg and its immigrants and alien residents, the government has established consultative services and has reorganized its system of education. In a report presented to the United Nations on 18 March 1986, the government stated that (UN Doc. CERD./C/128/Add. 2, para. 47):

The whole organization of education in Luxembourg promotes understanding, tolerance and friendship between countries and racial or ethnic groups. As to the various levels, within Luxembourg itself distinctions are made between pre-school, primary, secondary and non-university higher education. Schools at all these levels are open without distinction to the school-age children of any person residing in the Grand Duchy. Generally speaking, pupils of all ethnic groups mix with Luxembourg pupils in all school activities. The Luxembourg authorities are anxious to avoid the development of school "ghettos". Reception classes are, however, organized for the children of recent immigrants in order to familiarize them with the languages of instruction (French and German) and the Luxembourg language. In addition to these regular programmes, foreign language courses are organized in co-operation with the various embassies. They are held in school premises which are made available free of charge to the persons concerned.

M

MADAGASCAR. The Democratic Republic of Madagascar is a country in eastern Asia occupying one of the largest islands in the world, situated in the Indian Ocean off the Mozambique Channel. It achieved independence from France in 1960 and became a member of the United Nations the same year. Its population is estimated by the UN to be 11,575,000. Ethnic groups include Malagasy tribes, Comorans, and persons of Chinese, French, Indian, Malaysian, and Polynesian origin. Languages commonly spoken include Malagasy (official) and French. Religions practiced include Christianity (40%), Islam (5%), and Animism (55%). Article 39 of the constitution provides that "freedom of conscience and religion shall be guaranteed by the neutrality of the State with respect of all beliefs." Literacy is estimated at 53%.

The government (1990) took the form of a republic. Under the 1975 constitution, executive authority is exercised by the president, elected by popular vote for a term of seven years. Policy is determined by the Supreme Council of the Revolution and carried out by the prime minister. Legislation is prepared by the unicameral 137-member National Popular Assembly, members of which are elected by popular vote for terms of five years. The judiciary includes a Supreme Court, a High Court of Justice, and a Constitutional High Court. The only political party is the National Front for the Defense of the Revolution, which consists of seven revolutionary organizations. Its leader, Adm. Didier Ratsiraka, president for 15 years, was the subject of an attempted *coup d'etat* on 13 May 1990 by rebels who claimed he had impoverished the country. Thirteen persons who seized the Tananarive radio station were subdued by a commando team armed with tear gas.

Since 1979, the United Nations General Assembly has considered at each annual session the question of the Malagasy islands of the Glorieuses, Juan de Nova, and Bassas da India, separated by France from Madagascar at the time of independence, and has urged France to initiate negotiations with Madagascar with a view to reintegrating those islands as part of Madagascar's territory.

In a report presented to the **COMMITTEE ON THE ELIMINATION OF RACIAL DISCRIMINATION** in June 1984 (UN Doc. CERD/C/118/Add. 10, para. 4–8), the government of Madagascar provided the following information:

The long history of the Malagasy people's struggle for emancipation, first against the colonialists and later against the neo-colonial regime, led to formal independence in 1960 and to the choice of the Socialist Revolution on 16 June 1975. The popular movements throughout this history were the expression of one and the same struggle, the class struggle between exploiters and exploited, oppressors and oppressed, rich and poor. During the colonial period, this struggle was transformed in order to further the interests of the colonialists into a racial struggle (tribalism) and into a struggle for position amongst the national bourgeoisie. Tribalism was a political instrument for division, exploitation and domination. In order to take up the challenge and eradicate the racial prejudice created and maintained among the Malagasy people, the political leaders who have succeeded one another in Madagascar since independence have been determined to encourage and achieve national unity.

The aims and scope of the socialist choice made by the Malagasy people in their massive vote on 21 December 1975 for the new Constitution and the Charter of the Malagasy Socialist Revolution, are clearly stated:

The eradication of the exploitation of man by man;

The elimination of social injustice and inequality as a source of division, by means of a fair distribution of wealth and factors of production;

Equal access to culture;

The appropriation by the State and the people of the principal means of production;

An end to all discrimination based on race or religion; and

Freedom of religion and the holding of private property where this does not conflict with the programme and the objectives of the revolution.

In the same report (para. 21–25), the government summarized the goals of the Democratic Republic as follows:

The Malagasy people having decided to construct a new type of State expressing the interests of the toiling masses, and to build up a society in conformity with the socialist principles set forth in the Charter of the Malagasy Socialist Revolution, the Constitution stipulates that fundamental freedoms and individual rights are guaranteed under this Charter. Moreover, no right or freedom may be invoked by a citizen who has not fulfilled his obligations to the community and no right may be invoked to thwart the State in its task of setting up the socialist order. Further, under the terms of article 16 of the Constitution:

"Anyone abusing constitutional or legal freedoms to combat the revolution, delay the advent of the socialist State, violate the Constitution, damage the interests of the community or endanger national unity shall be deprived of his rights and freedoms."

It follows that all dynamic elements in the nation are called upon to join together to build the new type of socialist society whose principles and aims are described in the Charter and the Constitution. The Charter defines national unity, in relation to its aim, in the following terms:

"As long as crying injustices persist, as long as Malagasys are not considered as equally Malagasys, as long as flagrant inequalities exist between regions, between town and country, between social classes and individuals, there cannot be true national unity, which is an absolute condition for our national liberation and independence."

The phrase "endanger national unity" may be interpreted as meaning concretely to aggravate tribalism and to foment ethnic division. Anyone guilty of such acts is deprived of his rights and freedoms, the maximum possible penalty.

MALAWI. The Republic of Malawi is a country in eastern Africa, totally surrounded by Mozambique, Tanzania, and Zambia, and bordered on the east by Lake Malawi. Formerly known as Nyasaland, it achieved independence from Great Britain in 1964 and became a member of the United Nations the same year. Its population is estimated by the UN (1990) to be 8,190,000. Ethnic groups include the Chewa, Nyanja, Tumbuka, Yao, Lomwe, Sena, Tonga, and Ngoni communities and persons of European and Asian descent. Languages commonly used are English and Chichewa (both official). Religions practiced include Christianity (Protestant and Roman Catholic denominations) (60%), Islam (20%), and Animism (20%). Literacy is estimated at 25%.

The government (1990) took the form of a republic and member of the Commonwealth of Nations, of which the British sovereign is the symbolic head. Under the 1966 constitution, the president is head of State and government; President Hastings Kamuzu Banda, who came into office in 1966, has since been designated "Life President." There is a 107-member unicameral National Assembly and a judiciary including both magisterial and traditional courts. The Malawi Congress Party is the only political party.

Between 1977 and 1980, the UN COMMISSION ON HUMAN RIGHTS received and examined a number of complaints to the effect that thousands of Jehovah's Witnesses had been deprived of their basic human rights and fundamental freedoms in Malawi between 1972 and 1975 because of religious intolerance. The government of Malawi did not cooperate with the commission in its investigation of the matter, which substantiated the allegations. On recommendation of the commission, the Economic and Social Council publicized the situation and expressed the hope that the human rights of all citizens of Malawi had been fully restored and that adequate measures had been taken to provide a remedy to those who might have suffered injustice.

In a report presented to the commission in 1987 (UN Doc. E/CN.4/1987/34, para. 11–12), the government of Malawi indicated that

the problem [of religious intolerance] does not exist in Malawi at present although it did, on occasion, in the past. This related to cases concerning such groups as the Jehova's Witnesses and Watch Tower, known variously as Acitawala, Ampatuko, Mboni and Achoonadi, which, because of their activities, were declared unlawful under section 64 (2) (ii) of the Malawi Penal Code.

Although the Malawi Government guarantees freedom of religion, thought and conscience, it may not tolerate the extent of freedom that will interfere with the smooth running of the legitimate government.

More recently, refugees from neighboring Mozambique have swarmed into Malawi—more than 600,000 in 1988 alone—and continue to do so at a rate of about 1,200 a month. They have fled the civil war between the government of Mozambique and the Mozambique National Resistance and have totally disrupted normal life in the host country. Malawi has been hospitable to them, despite food shortages and infestations of insects, and has endeavored to follow the dictum of President Banda: "We are all brothers." By April 1990, one out of every ten persons in Malawi came from Mozambique; in many locations, refugees vastly outnumber citizens. Food production and water resources in the affected areas are insufficient to satisfy the needs of the Malawi population and the displaced persons; the ecological environment has been severely damaged by woodcutting on, and expanding cultivation to, fragile hillsides; and health, education, and community services have been severely strained. A United Nations interagency mission sent to Malawi to determine the type and magnitude of the assistance required concluded that the Malawi economy would not be able to cope with the expanding emergency conditions without major support from the international community and substantial development investment.

In a report to the 1988 session of the UN General Assembly, the secretary-general described the situation as follows (UN Doc. A/43/536, para. 5 and 31–32):

While refugees began arriving in Malawi in substantial numbers as of late 1980, Mozambicans have been registered during the 1970s and early 1980s. In some cases, ethnic background, family ties, language and intermarriage facilitated the entry and spontaneous settlement of these refugees into the rural areas of Malawi. These persons regularly crossed the border to tend to their own fields in Mozambique and, as such, were self-sufficient. Those who arrived from the southern areas of Mozambique, however, concentrated in camp-like locations as there were no integration possibilities owing to a lack of land and linguistic and kinship groups. In the early 1980s, only a few hundred Mozambicans, mostly of urban background, were considered of direct concern to the Office of the United Nations High Commissioner for Refugees (UNHCR) and subsequently individual assistance was provided to those persons through the office of the United Nations Development Programme (UNDP) in Malawi. However, in June 1986, the number of Mozambicans entering Malawi began to rise substantially and, by the end of September, it was estimated that a total of 70,000 persons had sought refuge, the majority being settled in border regions, primarily in the central and southern regions. . . .

While voluntary repatriation remains the most desirable solution for the refugees in Malawi, it appears that large-scale return is unlikely in the immediate future. While every effort will be made to avoid undue dependency, it is clear that the Government of Malawi and the international community are facing a care and maintenance operation for the foreseeable future.

The response of the international community to the Secretary-General's appeal, calling for generous contributions to assist refugees and displaced persons in Malawi, has yet to meet with an adequate response, particularly in respect of projects which are development related. This has meant that progress has been slow in formulating some of the projects needed to strengthen overburdened essential services and facilities in localities where refugees are concentrated.

The UN General Assembly, on 8 December 1988, noted (resolution 43/138) the secretary-general's report, commended the measures that the government of Malawi had taken to provide material and humanitarian assistance of refugees and displaced persons in spite of the serious economic situation it faced, and stressed the need for additional resources to lessen the impact of the presence of refugees and displaced persons on the country's long-term development process, appealing to member States and international organizations and institutions to continue providing Malawi with the necessary resources to implement development assistance projects.

The secretary-general's report on the subject to the 1989 session of the General Assembly (UN Doc. A/44/403) indicated that the situation continued to be serious.

MALAYSIA. A country in southeastern Asia, occupying the southern portion of the Malay Peninsula and including the territories of Sabah and Sarawak, located on the island of Borneo. West Malaysia, in the mainland, has borders with Singapore and Thailand. East Malaysia, on Borneo, has borders with Borneo and Brunei. The Federation of Malaysia achieved independence from Great Britain in 1957 and became a member of the United Nations the same year, Malaysia's population is estimated by the UN (1990) to be 17,298,000. Ethnic groups include persons of Malay and indigenous origins (59%), Chinese (32%), and Indian (9%). Languages commonly used include Malay (official), Chinese and Chinese dialects, Tamil, and English. Religions practiced include Islam (official), Buddhism, Christianity, Confucianism, Hinduism, and Taoism. Literacy is estimated at 80% in peninsular Malaysia, 60% in Sabah and Sarawak.

The government (1990) took the form of a monarchy and member of the Commonwealth of Nations, of which the British sovereign is the symbolic head. The "Paramount Ruler," elected by the hereditary rulers of the States from among themselves, is head of State. He is advised by the prime minister and cabinet. The prime minister, representing the party or coalition given a majority of seats in the House of Representatives, exercises executive authority as head of government. There is a bicameral parliament including the 68-member Senate—partly elected by the legislative assemblies of the various states and partly appointed by the paramount ruler to represent minority and special interests—and the 180-member House of Representatives, members of which are elected by popular vote for terms of five years. The judiciary is organized along British lines. Political parties include the National Front, which is a broad coalition of 11 parties; the Democratic Action Party; the Islamic Party; and the Independents.

Tensions occur frequently in Malaysia as a result of feelings within the Malay community that the Chinese and Indian minorities, which together outnumber the Malays and control a large share of the nation's wealth, will assume control of the country in spite of a constitutional provision that the head of State must always be a Malay of the Islamic faith—a provision that, in fact, means that the prime minister is selected by about 1,500 members of the United Malays National Organization.

The Communist Party of Malaysia ended one of the world's longest insurgencies on 2 December 1989 by signing separate agreements with the government of Malaysia and the Internal Security Operations Command of Thailand, pledging to lay down their arms and return to civilian life. The communist "war of liberation" had started in 1948, when Malaya was a British colony. About 1,200 guerillas were involved. The Malaysian government undertook to allow the disbanded units to participate in political activities within the framework of the country's constitution and laws, while the communists agreed to respect the laws of Malaysia and Thailand and to take part in social and economic development.

In April 1990, the UN HIGH COMMISSIONER FOR REFUGEES drew attention to the fact that Malaysia was again refusing permission to land, to ethnic Chinese refugees from Viet Nam—"boat people"—in violation of an agreement which it had made in June 1989 at a conference in Geneva convened at Malaysia's request. Under the agreement, Malaysia and other "first asylum countries" were to provide temporary shelter for all new arrivals until they could be screened to determine who among them were real refugees with a "well-founded fear of persecution" and who were "economical migrants." Resettlement countries would then take those judged to be refugees, while the economic migrants would be repatriated.

MALDIVES. The Republic of Maldives is a country in southern Asia, occupying about 1,250 atolls in the Pacific Ocean, southwest of Sri Lanka. Formerly a protectorate known as the Maldive Islands, Maldives achieved independence from Great Britain in 1965 and became a member of the United Nations the same year. Its population is estimated by the UN (1990) to be 215,000. Ethnic groups include Sinhalese, South Indians, and Arabs. The language in common use is Divehi. Islam (Sunni) is the predominant religion.

The government (1990) took the form of a republic and member of the Commonwealth of Nations, of which the British sovereign is the symbolic head. There are no political parties. President Maumoon Abdul Gayoom is head of State.

The situation as regards human rights was summarized by the government in a report presented to the GROUP OF THREE of the UN Commission on Human Rights on 24 October 1986, under article 7 of the INTERNATIONAL CONVENTION ON THE SUPPRESSION AND PUNISHMENT OF THE CRIME OF APARTHEID, as follows (UN Doc. E/CN.4/1987/26/Add. 11, para. 1–13):

The Republic of Maldives has a democratic Government where supreme power is vested in the people and their elected representatives. The unicameral legislature of Maldives, called the Citizen's *Majlis* (parliament), is elected by universal adult franchise.

All Maldivians above the age of 21 possess all the political rights including the right of suffrage. Any qualified citizen may stand for election to the *Majlis* which consists of 48 members; two members elected from each atoll—rural administrative units—and two members from the Capital Malé, which has 25.5 per cent of the total population—181, 453 (1985 census), and eight members elected by the President.

Any eligible Maldivian can seek election for the supreme post of the President of the Republic. The *Majlis* nominates a President by secret ballot and this nomination is confirmed or rejected in a nationwide public referendum also by secret ballot. The term of office for the *Majlis* as well as for the Presidency is five years.

The *Majlis* has the power to question government Ministers and to call for their removal. The President is also answerable to the *Majlis* and liable to impeachment and punishment if the case so warrants.

The Constitution of Maldives and all its laws must be approved by the *Majlis* or by a Citizen's Special *Majlis*.

The Constitution guarantees all basic human rights and the Government upholds them. Individuals are free to pursue private interests as long as they do not violate the civil law or the shariah (the Islamic Legal Code).

The Constitution guarantees equality before the law and equal protection by the law. It specifically provides that unlawful practices, such as arbitrary arrest, detention, exilement or torture, should never be perpetrated either by the Government or individuals. A person accused of a crime is given a fair trial and appropriate opportunity to defend himself. Freedom of speech and expression or oral and written thought exists "so long as the specific provisions of shariah and the law are not contravened" and academic freedoms are guaranteed in the Constitution.

Immunities against interception of private property, premises and dwellings, letters, telephone conversations, telegrams, etc., are provided for in the Constitution.

Basic rights concerning freedom of movement, assembly and association, the forming of trade unions, marriage, public health, medical care, social services, choice of employment, just and favourable conditions of work, just and favourable remuneration, changing of jobs, foreign travel and emigration are guaranteed to everyone in accordance with the existing rules and regulations without any discrimination.

Women enjoy free, equal status with men and a conscious effort is being made to broaden opportunities for them.

All Maldivians are Sunni (Orthodox) Muslims of the Shafiite sect and there is no religious disharmony among them. As the belief in equality of all mankind is a tenet of Islam, Maldivians condemn all kinds of racial discrimination. There is no discrimination against followers of other creeds and religions who visit Maldives or are employed in the country in any way.

Maldives has always condemned and incriminated all forms of racial discrimination and resolutely supported measures for their elimination. In particular, Maldives resolutely condemns the policy of racial discrimination and *apartheid* practised by the South African régime in South Africa and Namibia and considers it a crime against humanity.

Maldives does not have diplomatic, economic, cultural or any other relations with the South African régime. Maldives denounces the aggressive terrorist activities of South Africa against her neighbouring front-line States and believes that if these actions are unchecked it will disrupt international peace and security.

In his report to the 1989 session of the Commission on Human Rights, the special rapporteur on the question of the use of mercenaries recalled that (UN Doc. E/CN.4/1989/14, para. 13):

When introducing his second report to the Third Committee of the General Assembly, the Special Rapporteur referred to press reports to the effect that a force of mercenaries coming from Sri Lanka had tried to overthrow the Government of Maldives on 3 November 1988. In the light of that situation, the Special Rapporteur had sent letters on 28 November 1988 to the permanent representatives to the United Nations in New York of the Governments of Maldives, Sri Lanka and India, expressing his concern at those events and adding that he believed the Government of Maldives had requested the support of the Government of India to repel the mercenary aggression, which had failed, an indeterminate number of mercenaries being held prisoner, pending the necessary investigations, in Maldives. For those reasons, the Special Rapporteur had asked the Governments concerned to co-operate by furnishing him with any information which they regarded as relevant to the fulfillment of his mandate. By the date of the completion of this report, the Special Rapporteur had received replies from the Governments of India and Sri Lanka. The latter State had replied by means of a letter dated 16 December 1988 from Mr. Daya Perera, Permanent Representative to the United Nations in New York, who confirmed the accuracy of the account given above. Mr. Perera added that the Sri Lankan nationals recruited as mercenaries were, according to the information received, "members of Tamil secessionist terrorist groups" and that the recruited agents were alleged to have been "Maldivian nationals". Lastly, he added that his Government had offered its full co-operation to the Government of Maldives for any investigation that it might consider necessary to carry out in Sri Lanka. For its part, India had informed the Special Rapporteur on 3 January 1989 that the Government of Maldives could supply information on the subject.

In this connection, the government of the Maldives presented to the special rapporteur, and circulated to the commission, the following statement (UN Doc. E/CN.4/1989/80, para. 1–14):

The Government of Maldives would like to convey the following facts in respect of paragraphs 13 and 195 of the report contained in document E/CN.4/1989/14 dealing with an attempted *coup* in the Maldives. The Government of Maldives was unable either to brief the Commission or to make a prior statement as it felt that it would be premature to do so until an exact factual assessment was made and a clear picture of the episode had emerged.

A heavily armed foreign mercenary/terrorist force landed at Malé, the capital of Maldives, in two small Sri Lankan fishing trawlers at 4 a.m. on 3 November 1988 and proceeded to attack the National Security Headquarters, situated a few hundred yards from the water front, the President's residence and some key government installations. Two Maldivians, Abdulla Luthfy, a businessman living in Sri Lanka, and Sager Nasir, a former seaman, also took part in the hostile operations.

The attackers who, as subsequent investigations have revealed, belonged to a militant Tamil group from Sri Lanka, the People's Liberation Organization of Tamil Elam (PLOT), were armed with assault rifles, machine-guns, mortars, RPG-7 rockets, grenades and explosives. Their main objective was to seize the National Security Service (NSS) Headquarters, and to capture the President and a number of Cabinet Ministers in a bid to overthrow the legitimate Government of President Maumoon Abdul Gayoom, undermine the constitutional order of the State and turn it into a Tamil terrorist base from which they could launch subversive operations in Sri Lanka.

The attackers failed to achieve their objectives owing to the stiff resistance put up by the NSS and the Presidential guards with the result that they were not able to enter the NSS Headquarters or the residence of the President. However, the fighting lasted 18 hours and left eight National Security Servicemen and four civilians dead and 36 wounded. At least three of the attackers were killed, and many more injured.

The armed aggressors also surrounded the main power house and the central telecommunications building in Malé. Although they forced the engineers to cut off the power supply to the entire city, the terrorists were not skilled enough to sever the international telephone links. They also violated the sanctity of the Islamic Centre and Grand Mosque while the early morning prayers were being conducted and took a number of worshippers hostage, including the elderly imam of the Mosque.

Considering the fact that the safety of a large number of civilians as well as the sovereignty and territorial integrity of the nation were at stake, President Gayoom appealed to the Indian Government for military assistance to stop the aggression. This crucial step was taken by the President in the light of his concern over the possibility of reinforcements reaching the invading force, which would inevitably have led to more fierce fighting, resulting in heavy loss of life and destruction of key government buildings, private homes and other infrastructure.

Their failure to capture the President and the courage with which the NSS fought the terrorists, together with the impending arrival of the Indian troops, caused panic among the mercenaries. In their hurry to escape, they captured a Maldivian cargo ship *Progress Light* and resorted to hostage-taking. A total of 28 persons, including the Minister of Transport and Shipping, his wife, and a Member of Parliament who is a senior official at the Ministry of Trade and Industries, were taken as hostages on board the *Progress Light*. One of the fishing craft in which the mercenary group had arrived left Malé before noon, while the other had escaped at about 9 p.m.

On 4 November 1988, at the request of the Maldives Government, Indian navy and air-force planes tracked down the *Progress Light* which was travelling towards Colombo. Two warships of the Indian navy were also directed to intercept the hijacked vessel in an effort to rescue the hostages and apprehend the terrorists. On being ordered to stop and hand over the hostages, the terrorists refused and continued their course towards Colombo.

Negotiations between the Maldivian officials on board the Indian frigates and the mercenaries/terrorists at sea, which continued for two days, were of no avail. Finally, and with the explicit approval of the Maldives Government, the Indian frigates on 6 November 1988 used forced to stop the commandeered vessel, rescue the hostages and capture the fleeing terrorists. The terrorists had killed two of the hostages in cold blood, including the imam of the Islamic Centre. After the rescue operation was over, five more hostages were found dead.

A total of 68 mercenaries, along with the two Maldivian collaborators, Abdulla Luthfy and Sagar Nasir, were apprehended and placed in custody in the Maldives. The investigation of the incident and examination of the evidence is currently being carried out in accordance with the laws of the Republic of Maldives and thereafter the trial of the terrorists will begin.

The Government of Maldives is convinced that the 3 November episode was not merely an attempted *coup d'état* but that it was a foreign mercenary/terrorist aggression aimed at subverting the sovereignty, territorial integrity and political independence of the Republic of Maldives and converting it into a terrorist base which would endanger the security and stability of the South Asian region as a whole. The Government of Maldives has already conveyed the facts of the 3 November aggression to the Secretary-General of the United Nations and has also addressed the issue in other international forums.

The Republic of Maldives condemns in the strongest terms any mercenary or terrorist activities which threaten the sovereignty, political independence and territorial integrity of any State, or create instability in any region. Terrorism and mercenarism have been growing in recent times in different parts of the world. The Republic of Maldives had repeatedly emphasized the urgent need to tackle this menace in the global context and take strong, effective and concerted action, in various international forums.

The Government of Maldives has also addressed the question of mercenaries before the Commonwealth forum and more particularly, has discussed the subject in the regional forum of the South Asian Association for Regional Co-operation (SAARC). The SAARC Regional Convention on Suppression of Terrorism which came into force in August 1988, provides a framework for the countries of the region to co-operate in combatting the menace of terrorism.

The Government of Maldives would appreciate the inclusion of the above statement in the report of the Special Rapporteur on the question of the use of mercenaries to the Commission on Human Rights at its forty-fifth session currently being held in Geneva.

MALI. The Republic of Mali is a landlocked country in western Africa. It has borders with Algeria, Burkina Faso, Guinea, the Ivory Coast, Mauritania, Niger, and Senegal. Formerly known as French Sudan and from June until August 1960 as the Sudanese Republic, Mali achieved independence from France in 1960 and became a member of the United Nations the same year. Its population is estimated by the UN (1990) to be 9,362,000. Ethnic groups include two main racial branches (which and black, each living in a particular area of the national territory); however, the people are cosmopolitan, and racially mixed in the urban centers. Languages commonly used include French (official), Bambara, and numerous languages of the various ethnic groups. Religions practiced include Islam (90%), Animism (9%), and Christianity (1%). The members of the white racial group are almost 99% Muslim. Literacy is estimated at 10%.

The government (1990) took the form of a republic. Under the 1974 constitution, President Gen. Moussa Iraore is head of State and of government.

There is a unicameral legislature and a Supreme Court vested with administrative as well as judicial powers. The only political party is the Democratic Union of the Malian People; the secretary-general of the party is president of the country.

A report presented to the COMMITTEE ON THE ELIMINATION OF RACIAL DISCRIMINATION in April 1985 by the government of Mali (UN Doc. CERD/C/105/Add. 7, para. 5–7) provides the following details about the ethnic situation in that country:

Mali occupies a culturally advantageous position, in that it is at the crossroads of the Arab–Berber and black–African worlds. This fact explains the existence of two major racial groups:
—the white racial group which comprises the Tuaregs, the Peul, the Arabs and the Moors, and
—the black racial group which comprises a large number of ethnic groups including Bambara, Malinke, Solinke, Dogon, Sonrghai, Senufo, Minianka, Bozo, Somono, and Kakoro.

The black racial group is by far the largest; apart from some 600,000 Peul, 200,000 Tuareg, and 60,000 Moors, the rest of the population of 7 million is made up of black ethnic groups. But it cannot be said that there is cultural homogeneity; each of these ethnic groups claims its own culture. Of all the ethnic groups, however, the Bambara group is the largest in number, with more than 2 million people, and the Bambara language is by far the most widely spoken, especially when the neighboring languages (Malinke, Dioula, and Kassomke), which are closely related to Bambara, are taken into account.

The Malian population, therefore, is quite diversified; this diversity occurs over a territory whose frontiers are not very favorable to any kind of homogeneity, since they are the result of successive divisions by the former colonizers designed to form simple administrative units with no regard whatsoever for historical, ethnic or cultural factors; in most cases, frontiers were, quite literally, drawn with a ruler. Mali has virtually no natural frontiers with the seven countries surrounding it. . . . .

MALTA. The Republic of Malta is a country in southern Europe, occupying the islands of Malta, Gozo, and Comingo in the Mediterranean Sea, 60 miles south of Sicily. It achieved independence from Great Britain in 1964 and became a member of the United Nations the same year. Its total population is estimated by the UN (1990) to be 396,000. Ethnic groups include Arabs, Italians, and British. Languages commonly used include Maltese and English, both official, and Italian, French, German, and Arabic. Christianity (Roman Catholic) is the predominant religion. Literacy is estimated at 90%.

The government (1990) took the form of a republic and member of the Commonwealth of Nations, of which the British monarch is the symbolic head. The 1964 constitution is based on the Universal Declaration of Human Rights. Under that constitution, the president is head of State and the prime minister head of government. The prime minister, representing the party or coalition given the majority in a popular election, exercises executive authority with the assistance of his cabinet; he is directly responsible to the 65-member House of Representatives, members of which are elected by popular vote. Legislation is prepared by the House of Representatives. The judiciary, modelled after the British system, includes the Constitutional Court. Political parties include the Malta Labor Party and the Nationalist Party.

Students of many countries, races, beliefs, and backgrounds are welcome to study in Malta. During 1987–1988, 710 foreign students attended various primary, secondary, and trade schools, the university, the Libyan–Arab School, and medical and nursing school; they came from the United States, Canada, the United Kingdom, South Africa (refugees), Namibia, Ghana, Nigeria, Tanzania, Swaziland, Libya, Pakistan, India, Egypt, Jordan, and several eastern European countries. Malta has special arrangements with the Palestine Liberation Organization for the free education of Palestinian students. Under the "Commonwealth Scheme," it provided education to 14 Namibians and 8 South African refugee students in 1989.

Since Malta ratified the European Convention on Human Rights in 1987, individuals may take complaints concerning violations of human rights to the European Commission on Human Rights after exhausting domestic remedies, in accordance with article 25 of that convention.

MAPUTO DECLARATION ON THE LIBERATION OF NAMIBIA (1977). The declaration adopted by the International Conference in Support of the Peoples of Zimbabwe and Namibia, held at Maputo, Mozambique, from 16 to 21 May 1977, provides an indication of the firmness of the resolve of the peoples of Africa to liquidate once and for all the last bastions of colonialism and racism in that continent. (The Declaration on the Liberation of Zimbabwe, adopted by the Conference at the same time, is not reproduced here in view of the fact that Zimbabwe achieved independence and self-government in 1980).

The text of the Declaration on the Liberation of Namibia (*Report of the International Conference in Support of the Peoples of Zimbabwe and Namibia,* UN Doc. A/ 32/109/Rev. 1, annex V, part B, para. 22–33) is as follows:

The Conference solemnly proclaims its full support for the struggle of the people of Namibia under the leadership of their sole and authentic liberation movement, the South West Africa People's Organization, to achieve self-determination, freedom and independence in a united Namibia. It recognizes that the Namibian people have been forced to resort to armed struggle after many years of arduous attempts to achieve those objectives by peaceful means. It reaffirms the right of the people of Namibia to decide on the means of their struggle, in the light of the conditions in the Territory. The development of the armed struggle and continued efforts of the international community have created positive conditions for a negotiated settlement. It is encouraging and inspiring to see the unity and solidarity of the Namibian people in their efforts to fulfil their true aspirations and legitimate interests under the leadership of their liberation movement. Despite a ferocious oppressor, the determination, competence and heroism of Namibian patriots have gained for them the respect and admiration of the international community. It is imperative that all freedom-loving forces in the international community give maximum support to the South West Africa People's Organization to ensure the victory of the people of Namibia in their struggle against the forces of colonialism and racism.

The Conference strongly condemns the colonial and illegal occupation of Namibia by South Africa, which constitutes an act of aggression against the Namibian people and against the United Nations, in defiance of repeated demands for its withdrawal by the Security Council and the General Assembly. The policies of the illegal South African administration are a systematic violation of its obligations under the Charter of the United Nations, the Universal Declaration of Human Rights and the Declaration on the Granting of Independence to Colonial Countries and Peoples. The United Nations Council for Namibia as the legal authority to administer that Territory until independence has the responsibility to assist the Namibian people in their struggle against South African aggression and occupation. It is therefore imperative that appropriate measures be formulated and implemented to counter decisively South Africa's continued defiance of the authority of the United Nations.

The Conference strongly condemns the policies of *apartheid* and homelands which the Pretoria régime has extended to Namibia. In order to perpetuate its exploitation of the people and natural resources of the Territory, the illegal South African administration in Namibia follows a policy of brutal institutionalized terrorism against the Namibian people. Many Namibian patriots have perished under this régime. The illegal administration in Namibia imprisons and tortures men and women under its violently repressive racist system. It carries out massive transfers of population, thus causing untold suffering to thousands of innocent men, women and children. In this respect, the Conference invites all States to implement the Declaration and Programme of Action adopted at the Dakar Conference on Namibia and Human Rights. The Conference considers furthermore that all possible pressure should be brought to bear upon the Pretoria régime to cease its barbaric repression of the Namibian people in their efforts to achieve self-determination, freedom and independence in a united Namibia.

The Conference recognizes Walvis Bay as an integral part of Namibia and rejects the attempts of South Africa to separate it from the rest of Namibia with which it is inextricably linked by geographical, historical, economic, cultural and ethnic bonds. All States should endeavour to dissuade South Africa from pursuing its efforts to separate Walvis Bay from Namibia.

The Conference strongly condemns the increasing militarization of Namibia by the racist Pretoria régime. In its increasingly aggressive posture, South Africa has expanded its military apparatus in Namibia in order to give itself the capability to attack neighbouring African countries, in a policy of continuous intimidation. It enacted the Defence Amendment Act in 1976 in order to carry out aggression far beyond its borders. Therefore, the sale or supply of any arms or military material, the transfer of technology and the provision of the means to produce weapons, as well as any nuclear collaboration with South Africa, ultimately support the acts of aggression by South Africa against the Namibian people and the United Nations. It is therefore imperative that all States cease and desist from any form of direct or indirect military consultation, co-operation or collaboration with South Africa. In order to meet the continuous threat of the minority régime to international peace and security in southern Africa, the Security Council should be called upon to impose a mandatory arms embargo against South Africa.

The Conference strongly denounces the Turnhalle tribal talks as a South African stratagem to perpetuate its ruthless colonial and racist policies and practices under false pretenses. South Africa has brought together in the Turnhalle tribal talks the fanatical racist promoters of *apartheid* and tribal puppets to prepare a so-called charter for the purpose of misleading the international community on its true intentions in Namibia. The so-called charter is to be the basis for a provisional government fabricated by South Africa, which would pretend to be an advance towards a pseudo-independent Namibia. The international community, especially all States Members of the United Nations, should act to frustrate South Africa's tactics of political deception. No recognition should be accorded to any group which the illegal South African administration may install as a consequence of the current fraudulent constitutional talks or any other manoeuvres in Namibia. Any independence talks regarding Namibia must be between the representatives of the South West Africa People's Organization and South Africa under the auspices of the United Nations for the sole purpose of discussing the modalities for the transfer of power to the Namibian people.

The Conference reaffirms that, in order that the people of Namibia shall be enabled freely to determine their own future, free elections should be held urgently under the supervision and control of the United Nations in the whole of Namibia as one political entity. However, prior to such elections, conditions for a negotiated settlement should be created in Namibia in accordance with all relevant decisions and resolutions of the United Nations and, in particular, Security Council resolution 385 (1976) of 30 January 1976.

The Conference solemnly reaffirms the responsibility of the United Nations for Namibia until the Territory attains full independence. The General Assembly has declared that Namibia is a direct responsibility of the United Nations and has entrusted the United Nations Council for Namibia with the exercise of *de jure* internal and external sovereignty over Namibia. Therefore, the Council is empowered to protect the rights and to represent the interests of the Namibian people, with the full participation of the South West African People's Organization. The Conference recognizes the United Nations Council for Namibia as the legal Administering Authority of Namibia until independence, an indispensable role which it is fulfilling. It is imperative that the international community strengthen its support for the Council in its efforts to promote the le-

gitimate aspirations of the Namibian people for self-determination, freedom and independence in a united Namibia. The Conference calls upon all Member States to implement the provisions contained in the United Nations resolution granting full participation of the United Nations Council for Namibia in all conferences, specialized agencies and other organizations of the United Nations system.

The Conference solemnly proclaims its support for the Nationhood Programme for Namibia contained in General Assembly resolution 31/153 of 20 December 1976. The Council received from the General Assembly at its thirty-first session the mandate to elaborate, in consultation with the South West Africa People's Organization, the guidelines and policies for such a programme and to direct and co-ordinate the implementation of the Programme. The Nationhood Programme shall cover the present period of struggle for independence and the initial years of the independence of Namibia. It is imperative that the international community ensure the success of the Nationhood Programme by taking measures to increase the programmes of concrete assistance to the people of Namibia through their liberation movement, the South West Africa People's Organization.

The Conference solemnly declares that the natural resources of Namibia are the birth-right of the Namibian people. The exploitation of those resources by foreign economic interests, under the protection of the repressive racist colonial administration and in violation of all principals of the Charter of the United Nations and of the pertinent resolutions of the Security Council and the General Assembly, is illegal and contributes to the maintenance of the illegal occupation régime. The rapid depletion of the natural resources of the Territory due to the reckless plunder in which foreign economic interests engage in collusion with the illegal South African administration is a grave threat to the integrity and prosperity of an independent Namibia. It is imperative that the activities of foreign economic interests engaged in Namibia should be the object of systematic denunciation so that their actions, which are detrimental to the Namibian people, will be exposed to the full scrutiny and condemnation of the international community.

The Conference welcomes the report and recommendations of the mission of the United Nations Council for Namibia to the specialized agencies and other United Nations organizations with headquarters in Europe. In this regard, it urges all specialized agencies and other United Nations organizations to give all possible concrete assistance within their spheres of competence to the Council in the discharge of the mandate entrusted to it, so as to expedite the implementation of the relevant United Nations resolutions on Namibia, in particular resolution 31/153 on the Nationhood Programme for Namibia. The Conference calls upon those specialized agencies and other United Nations organizations in which South Africa still illegally purports to represent Namibia to terminate such relationships forthwith and to grant full membership to the United Nations Council for Namibia as the Administering Authority of Namibia until independence.

The Conference commends the international community for the invaluable moral, political and material assistance it is giving to the South West Africa People's Organization. It further commends all non-governmental organizations which are giving their solidarity and support to the cause of the liberation of Namibia from illegal South African occupation. The Conference solemnly appeals to all States

Members of the United Nations and intergovernmental and non-governmental organizations to intensify their assistance to the South West Africa People's Organization in this crucial and final stage in the emancipation of Africa.

SEE ALSO Namibia; Namibia: Constitution; South West Africa Peoples Organization.

MARRIAGE AND THE FAMILY. The right to marry and to found a family is proclaimed in the UNIVERSAL DECLARATION OF HUMAN RIGHTS in the following terms:

Article 16. 1. Men and women of full age, without any limitation due to race, nationality or religion, have the right to marry and to found a family. They are entitled to equal rights as to marriage, during marriage and at its dissolution.

2. Marriage shall be entered into only with the free and full consent of the intending spouses.

3. The family is the natural and fundamental group unit of society and is entitled to protection by society and the State.

The INTERNATIONAL COVENANT ON ECONOMIC, SOCIAL AND CULTURAL RIGHTS provides for special measures to be taken to protect the family, mothers, and children, as follows:

Article 10. The States Parties to the present Covenant recognize that:

1. The widest possible protection and assistance should be accorded to the family, which is the natural and fundamental group unit of society, particularly for its establishment and while it is responsible for the care and education of dependent children. Marriage must be entered into with the free consent of the intending spouses.

2. Special protection should be accorded to mothers during a reasonable period before and after childbirth. During such period working mothers should be accorded paid leave or leave with adequate social security benefits.

3. Special measures of protection and assistance should be taken on behalf of all children and young persons without any discrimination for reasons of parentage or other conditions. Children and young persons should be protected from economic and social exploitation. Their employment in work harmful to their morals or health or dangerous to life or likely to hamper their normal development should be punishable by law. States should also set age limits below which the paid employment of child labour should be prohibited and punishable by law.

The INTERNATIONAL COVENANT ON CIVIL AND POLITICAL RIGHTS also calls for special measures to be taken to protect the family, mothers, and children, as follows:

Article 23. 1. The family is the natural and fundamental group unit of society and is entitled to protection by society and the State.

2. The right of men and women of marriageable age to marry and to found a family shall be recognized.

3. No marriage shall be entered into without the free and full consent of the intending spouses.

4. State Parties to the present Covenant shall take appropriate steps to ensure equality of rights and responsibilities of spouse as to marriage, during marriage and at its dissolution. In the case of dissolution, provision shall be made for the necessary protection of any children.

Article 24. 1. Every child shall have, without any discrimination as to race, colour, sex, language, religion, national or social origin, property or birth, the right to such measures of protection as are required by his status as a minor, on the part of his family, society and the State.

2. Every child shall be registered immediately after birth and shall have a name.

3. Every child has the right to acquire a nationality.

The INTERNATIONAL CONVENTION ON THE ELIMINATION OF ALL FORMS OF RACIAL DISCRIMINATION contains the following provision:

Article 5. In compliance with the fundamental obligations laid down in article 2 of this Convention, States parties undertake to prohibit and to eliminate racial discrimination in all its forms and to guarantee the right of everyone, without distinction as to race, colour, or national or ethnic origin, to equality before the law, notably in the enjoyment of the following rights. . . .

(d) Other civil rights, in particular: . . . .

(iv) The right to marriage and choice of spouse.

The CONVENTION ON THE ELIMINATION OF ALL FORMS OF DISCRIMINATION AGAINST WOMEN contains extensive provisions concerning marriage and the family, as follows:

Article 4. 2. Adoption by States parties of special measures, including those measures contained in the present Convention, aimed at protecting maternity, shall not be considered discriminatory. . . .

Article 12. 1. States parties shall take all appropriate measures to eliminate discrimination against women in the field of health care in order to ensure, on a basis of equality of men and women, access to health care services, including those related to family planning.

2. Notwithstanding the provisions of paragraph 1 of this article, States parties shall assure to women appropriate services in connection with pregnancy, confinement and the post-natal period, granting free services where necessary, as well as adequate nutrition during pregnancy and lactation. . . .

Article 16. 1. States Parties shall take all appropriate measures to eliminate discrimination against women in all matters relating to marriage and family relations and in particular shall ensure, on a basis of equality of men and women:

(a) The same right to enter into marriage;

(b) The same right freely to choose a spouse and to enter into marriage only with their free and full consent;

(c) The same rights and responsibilities during marriage and at its dissolution;

(d) The same rights and responsibilities as parents, irrespective of their marital status, in matters relating to their children; in all cases the interests of the children shall be paramount;

(e) The same rights to decide freely and responsibly on the number and spacing of their children and to have access to the information, education and means to enable them to exercise these rights;

(f) The same rights and responsibilities with regard to guardianship, wardship, trusteeship and adoption of children, or similar institutions where these concepts exist in national legislation; in all cases the interests of the children shall be paramount;

(g) The same personal rights as husband and wife, including the right to choose a family name, a profession and an occupation;

(h) The same rights for both spouses in respect of ownership, acquisition, management, administration, enjoyment and disposition of property, whether free of charge or for a valuable consideration.

2. The betrothal and the marriage of a child shall have no legal effect, and all necessary action, including legislation, shall be taken to specify a minimum age for marriage and to make the registration of marriages in an official registry compulsory.

The EUROPEAN CONVENTION ON HUMAN RIGHTS, PROTOCOL VII, adds the following provision to the text of the convention:

Article 5. Spouses shall enjoy equality of rights and responsibilities of a private law character between them, and in their relations with their children, as to marriage, during marriage and in the event of its dissolution. This Article shall not prevent States from taking such measures as are necessary in the interests of the children.

Consent to Marriage, Minimum Age for Marriage, and Registration of Marriages. At the suggestion of the conference of plenipotentiaries convened in 1956 to prepare the Supplementary Convention on the Abolition of Slavery, the Slave Trade and Institutions and Practices Similar to Slavery, the UN COMMISSION ON THE STATUS OF WOMEN initiated a study of the question of marriage with the objective of drawing attention to the desirability of free consent of both parties to a marriage and of the establishment of a minimum age for marriage.

The commission decided that it would prepare both an international convention and a recommendation on this subject and was able to complete preliminary drafts of both at its 1960 and 1961 sessions.

The CONVENTION ON CONSENT TO MARRIAGE, MINIMUM AGE FOR MARRIAGE AND REGISTRATION OF MARRIAGES was completed, adopted, and opened for signature and ratification by the General Assembly in 1962 (resolution 1763 [XVII]). The recommendation on the same subject was adopted and proclaimed by the assembly three years later (resolution 2018 [XX]).

The convention sets out three measures aimed at ensuring that no marriage shall be legally entered into without the full and free consent of both parties. The first (article 1) is that consent must be expressed by the two intending spouses in person after due publicity and in the presence of an authority competent to solemnize the marriage. The second (article 2) is that each State party must specify by law a minimum age for marriage. The third (article 3) is that all marriages must be registered in an appropriate official register by the competent authority.

The convention provides for a limited exception from the general rule requiring the presence of both parties at the solemnization of the marriage. One of the parties may be absent if the competent authority is satisfied that the circumstances are exceptional and that the party has, before a competent authority and in such a manner as may be prescribed by law, expressed and not withdrawn consent.

The convention also permits an exception from the general rule that no marriage shall be legally entered into by a person under the age specified by the law of the State. This exception applies when the competent authority has, in the interests of the intending spouses and for serious reasons, granted a dispensation as to age.

The recommendation, intended to apply generally to all States not parties to the convention, deals with the same problems. However, whereas the convention does not specify a minimum age for marriage, the recommendation expressly provides that the minimum age to be specified in State legislation shall not be less than 15 years.

International Year of the Family. At its 1987 session, the UN General Assembly invited all States (resolution 42/134) to make known their views concerning possible proclamation of an international year of the family and to offer their comments and proposals thereon to the Secretary-General before 30 April 1988. In doing so, it was guided by the relevant provisions of the Universal Declaration of Human Rights; the International Covenant on Economic, Social and Cultural Rights; and the Declaration on Social Progress and Development, as well as the Guiding Principles for Developmental Social Welfare Policies and Programmes in the Near Future, which it had endorsed (resolution 42/125) and which calls for social welfare policies to give greater attention to the family.

Taking note of the positive responses reflected in the report submitted by the Secretary-General in 1988 (UN Doc. A/43/570), the General Assembly on 8 December 1988 requested him (resolution 43/135) to submit to its 1989 session a report containing a proposed date and a comprehensive outline of a possible program for an International Year of the Family. Member States, specialized agencies, and interested intergovernmental and non-governmental organizations were, at the same time, invited to submit proposals on their participation in such an international year.

MAURITANIA. The Islamic Republic of Mauritania is a country in western Africa, on the Atlantic Ocean. It has borders with Algeria, Senegal, and Western Sahara. It achieved independence from France in 1960 and became a member of the United Nations in 1961. Its population is estimated by the UN (1990) to be 2,220,000. Ethnic groups include Moors, Arabs, Berbers, and a black minority (Poulars, Soninkes, and Wolofs). Languages commonly used include Hassaniya Arabic (national) and French (official), Toucouleur, Fula, Sarakole, and Wolof. Islam is the predominant religion. Literacy is estimated at 17%.

The government (1990) took the form of a republic; however, the constitution of 1961 was abolished by decree in 1978 after a military *coup d'etat,* and the army chief of staff assumed the presidency after a *coup d'etat* of 12 December 1984. The president is also head of the Military Committee for National Salvation, which has assumed all legislative functions. The courts, under the Ministry of Justice and Islamic Affairs, follow the *Sharia* (Islamic law).

In 1984, a mission to study the situation prevailing in Mauritania as regards slavery and the slave trade visited the country at the request of the UN Sub-Commission on Prevention of Discrimination and Protection of Minorities, Commission on Human Rights, and Economic and Social Council and on invitation of the government of the country. The mission reported to the sub-commission at its 1984 session, at which time the observer for Mauritania indicated that his government was determined to eradicate slavery but faced major economic and social problems in implementing this policy. In 1985, the Commission on Human Rights received further information and called upon international and regional organizations to consider what assistance they could give to Mauritania as a contribution towards the eradication of slavery, and authorized the sub-commission to continue to monitor the situation.

In a final report on the mission, prepared by an expert of the sub-commission, the government of Mauritania is quoted as follows (UN Doc. E/CN.4/Sub.2/1987/27, para. 18):

The Ministry first wishes to recall that "the abolition of slavery," provided for in Ordinance No. 81-234 of 9 November 1981 reflected in practice the desire of the Mauritanian authorities to eradicate "consequences" which persisted essentially in attitudes and mentalities.

This desire has resulted in the establishment of a body of legal texts and accompanying measures in various areas (rural development, land tenure, justice, education, information, etc.) whose objective, rather than to abolish practices which by then no longer existed, was to promote a general policy designated to correct social inequalities and to raise the living standard of all citizens.

This desire has also been given effect through the sincere and comprehensive exploration of all possible ways to attain the stated objective.

Thus the government of Mauritania took the initiative, in August 1981, of inviting the Sub-Commission to send a mission to carry out an on-the-spot inquiry into the reality of what has been termed "the question of slavery" in Mauritania, whereas in fact, as the expert's report testifies, what are involved are only "consequences", neither more nor less. . . .

The Sub-Commission, in resolution 1987/30 of 4 September 1987, encouraged that government to implement those measures and policies fully in order to eliminate the consequences of slavery and to intensify further its efforts in adopting measures guaranteeing effective emancipation for former slaves.

The New York Times, on 20 July 1989, reported that "nearly 40,000 blacks have been forced out of Mauritania since early May in what relief workers and Senegalese officials say are racially motivated expulsions. The flow of refugees began after a minor border dispute between Senegalese farmers and Mauritanian herders erupted into riots. About 100,000 Mauritanian nationals in Senegal and 85,000 Senegalese in Mauritania were repatriated at that time, most of them in an international airlift. Since then, a growing stream of black Mauritanians, many with Mauritanian passports and other national identity papers, have been forced by Government officials across the Senegal River from Mauritania into Senegal." According to the dispatch, the expulsions were directed against black Mauritanians suspected of being Senegalese nationals. About one-third of Mauritania's people are black, while others are of Arab and Berber origin; most Senegalese are black.

MAURITANIA: QUESTION OF SLAVERY. In 1982, the **SUB-COMMISSION ON PREVENTION OF DISCRIMINATION AND PROTECTION OF MINORITIES** authorized its chairman (resolution 1982/15) to appoint two of its members, Mr. Marc Bossuyt (Belgium) and Mr. Mohamed Yousif Mudawi (Sudan) to visit Mauritania, pursuant to the invitation of the government of that country, in order to study the situation prevailing there with respect to slavery and the slave trade and the country's needs in its struggle to end those practices.

The sub-commission's mission, consisting of Mr. Bossuyt alone, accompanied by three members of the UN Secretariat, visited Mauritania from 14 to 22 January

1984. Mr. Peter Davies, director of the ANTI-SLAVERY SOCIETY FOR THE PROTECTION OF HUMAN RIGHTS, also accompanied the mission, having been personally invited by the government of Mauritania.

In his report (UN Doc. E/CN.4/Sub.2/1984/23), Mr. Bossuyt expressed the conviction that he had gathered enough information and had heard a sufficient range of views to be able to assert that slavery as an institution protected by law had been genuinely abolished in Mauritania, although it could not be ruled out that, in remote corners of the country over which the administration had little control, certain situations of *de facto* slavery might still persist.

In 1985, THE ECONOMIC AND SOCIAL COUNCIL called upon Mr. Bossuyt to prepare a follow-up report after obtaining information on further developments. That report, submitted to the sub-commission in 1987 (UN Doc. E/CN.4/Sub.2/1987/27), included the texts of two communications received from Mauritanian authorities. The first, dated 8 February 1986, included the following paragraphs:

The Ministry first wishes to recall that "the abolition of slavery" provided for in Ordinance No. 81-234 of 9 November 1981 reflected in practice the desire of the Mauritanian authorities to eradicate "consequences" which persisted essentially in attitudes and mentalities.

This desire has resulted in the establishment of a body of legal texts and accompanying measures in various areas (rural development, land tenure, justice, education, information, etc.) whose objective, rather than to abolish practices which by then no longer existed, was to promote a general policy designed to correct social inequalities and to raise the living standard of all citizens.

This desire has also been given effect through the sincere and comprehensive exploration of all possible ways to achieve the stated objective.

Thus the Government of Mauritania took the initiative, in August 1981, of inviting the Sub-Commission to send a mission to carry out an on-the-spot inquiry into the reality of what had been termed "the question of slavery" in Mauritania, whereas in fact, as the expert's report testifies, what are involved are only "consequences", neither more nor less.

The second communication, dated 17 June 1987, stated that:

The Ministry wishes to reaffirm the determination of the government of Mauritania to eliminate for good all "consequences" of slavery in Mauritania.

This desire has already been reflected in the adoption of Ordinance No. 81-234 of 9 November 1981 and is supported by continuous political, social and economic action.

The mass education media play a leading role in this matter thanks to their ideals of equality and justice and their public information and awareness campaigns to modify backward attitudes and mentalities.

The Government of Mauritania is convinced that the legal abolition of slavery, together with political action, will be insufficient unless they are accompanied by measures guaranteeing effective emancipation for former slaves.

This conviction has been given practical effect—despite Mauritania's current difficult economic situation—with the establishment of several organs designed to complete the incorporation of former slaves into the various sectors of socio-economic activity.

Having taken, within the framework of the exercise of its national sovereignty and with the valued co-operation of the United Nations mission, all appropriate measures gradually to eradicate the last vestiges of slavery in its country, the Government of Mauritania considers that the time for consideration of this question in the various international forums is now past.

In concluding the follow-up report, Mr. Bossuyt thanked the Mauritanian government for its cooperation and for taking a number of measures covered by recommendations set out in his report. He regretted, however, that that government had not seen fit to set up a specific body which would be entrusted with coordinating the struggle against slavery and to which any person experiencing difficulties in that field could apply, to involve former slaves in the struggle against the consequences of slavery, or to develop sociological research on Mauritanian society.

At the same time, he welcomed the initiative taken by the UN Secretary-General to send an inter-agency mission to Mauritania in July 1986, in connection with the third country program for Mauritania prepared by the administrator of the United Nations Development Program (UNDP), and noted that several UNDP donor countries had committed themselves to an assistance effort for Mauritania.

In conclusion, he wrote (para. 55–56):

The expert is pleased to have had the opportunity to contribute to assisting Mauritania in its efforts to rid itself of the consequences of slavery. The first step was to gain a better understanding of the actual extent of the problem in its historical and socio-economic context. Next, the Mauritanian Government had to be encouraged to step up its efforts in this area, and all States and international bodies and agencies in a position to do so had to be invited to provide development assistance to Mauritania.

Efforts have been made to respond to the concerns expressed. Admittedly, the expert would have hoped for even more energetic action on both sides and more generous assistance. In any event, he remains convinced that the attention the international community has focused on this question, on the initiative of the Anti-Slavery Society and through the Sub-Commission, has, thanks mainly to the positive attitude of the Mauritanian Government, had a beneficial influence in the interest of all those concerned by this question.

The sub-commission considered the follow-up report at its 1987 session and (resolution 1987/30) expressed its appreciation to Mr. Bossuyt and to the government of the Islamic Republic of Mauritania and invited governments, United Nations organs, and specialized agencies to undertake additional and specific efforts in order to assist Mauritania in accelerating its development and in eliminating the consequences of slavery.

MAURITIUS. Mauritius is a country in eastern Africa, occupying an island in the Indian Ocean, east of Madagascar. It achieved independence from Great Britain in 1968 and became a member of the United Nations the same year. Its population is estimated by the UN (1990) to be 1,140,000. Ethnic groups include Indo–Mauritians (68%), Creoles (27%), Sino–Mauritians (3%), and Franco–Mauritians (2%). The Indo–Mauritian majority includes descendents of laborers brought from India to work in the sugar plantations after the abolition of slavery in 1934. Languages commonly used include English (official), French, Creole, Hindi, Urdu, Hakka, and Bojpoori. More than 140 religious denominations have followers in the country; the predominant religions are Hinduism and Islam. Under its constitution, Mauritius is a secular State and maintains a system whereby major religious organizations are subsidized by the government. Literacy is estimated at 79%.

The government (1990) took the form of a monarchy and member of the Commonwealth of Nations, of which the British sovereign is the symbolic head. The governor-general, representing the crown, selects as prime minister the member of the Legislative Assembly representing the party or coalition holding the majority there. The 70-member Legislative Assembly is composed of 62 members elected by voters and eight chosen from among the unsuccessful candidates. The judicial system is organized along British lines. Political parties include the Mauritian Socialist Movement, the Mauritian Labour Party, the Mauritian Social Democratic Party, and the *Organisation du Peuple Rodriguais,* and the *Mouvement Militant Mauricien.*

In a report submitted to the COMMITTEE ON THE ELIMINATION OF RACIAL DISCRIMINATION, the government stated that (UN Doc. CERD/C/131/Add. 8, para. 30):

A multiracial, multireligious, multilingual and multicultural State, Mauritius maintains that the only valid, realistic and progressive form of nationalism is pluricultural Mauritianism, which is defined as (i) the preservation of all positive cultural traits specific to all the cultural sections of the population; (ii) knowing one's ancestral culture but learning, understanding and appreciating the cultural values of others; (iii) avoiding intolerance, arrogance, chauvinism, dogmatism, sexism, racism and sectarianism so as to encourage cultural sharing and exchange; and (iv) fostering new cultural expressions based on local reality so as to promote cross-culture integration.

MEDICAL WOMEN'S INTERNATIONAL ASSOCIATION. An international non-governmental organization in consultative status with the UN Economic and Social Council (Category II) and with WHO and UNICEF, MWIA is affiliated with national associations and has members in 55 countries.

Founded in 1919 in New York, the association brings together women in medical fields to study health problems, in particular as these relate to women. MWIA promotes international communication among women in medical areas. It also publishes scientific proceedings and reports of its biennial congresses.

Medical Women's International Association. Address: Herbert–Lewin–Strasse 5, Lindenthal, D-5000 Köln 41, FRG. Telephone (49-221) 400-42-35. Hon. Secretary-General: Dr. Carolyn Motzel.

Yearbook of International Organizations 1989/90 (K. G. Saur).

MENTALLY ILL PERSONS. The question of protecting the human rights of persons considered to be mentally ill has been a matter of concern to international organs and agencies for many years, with the WORLD HEALTH ORGANIZATION assuming the leading role. The nature and extent of the problem is outlined by WHO in a memorandum presented to the 1970 session of the UN General Assembly (UN Doc. A/8055/ Add. 1, para. 91–97), as follows:

Mental health is no less a human right than physical health and reasonable social comfort and security. Treatment methods in psychiatry are classified as psychological, biological and social. Biological methods of treatment differ little from those in other branches of medicine, and include the use of drugs, biological products, electricity and surgery. Psychiatric illness may affect the patient's intelligence, judgement, insight and responsibility and if a patient is lacking in one or more of these faculties, his behaviour may be impaired to the extent that he is not aware of what he is doing or that he is a danger to himself or others or is behaving in a way that is an affront to others. Therefore, it may, on occasion, be reasonable to apply treatment for his own good without his consent, since he may be unable to understand the situation and give his consent. Provided that reasonable and acceptable medical care is applied with good judgement and that established ethical practice is followed, there is no question of infringement of human rights. Human rights would be infringed only if treatment were applied to someone who did not require that particular type of treatment or who is not mentally ill and to whom treatment is applied without his understanding and consent.

As a result of the major progress in the treatment of mentally disordered and mentally retarded persons which has occurred during the past three decades, it is now possible for many individuals with mental illness to be treated while living in the community and/or be transferred from institutional care, to the open life of the community and to be usefully employed, to the benefit both of themselves and of the community. If they are refused the right to work because of mental illness their resocialization is slow and their human rights are infringed. In general it is now possible to envisage the necessary after care as one of the functions of the basic health services.

Traditionally mental institutions have always attracted a sometimes undeserved reputation for the infringement of human rights. In consequence systems for external supervision of the work of these institutions, and for appeals against unwarranted detention, have been established and should continue to work satisfactorily and prevent infringement of human rights in this context. Doubts however have been expressed about the human rights aspects of psychotherapy, chemotherapy and psychosurgery.

The misuse of these most helpful methods of treatment is a breach of medical ethics and might constitute a violation of human rights. But such misuse would be no different from delicts in other branches of medicine and surgery.

Mentally retarded individuals constitute a special group which governments must always be concerned to protect whether they are in institutions or living with their families or guardians.

Mentally retarded children and adults accommodated in institutions were undoubtedly used in the past for therapeutic trials and the like, and in some cases, e.g. vaccine trials, were exposed to physical risk.

The tendency to use these groups for such purposes has happily diminished and where they are so used, the appropriate authorities usually ensure that the investigators follow strict codes of conduct and practice, in order to prevent any infringement of human rights.

In 1980, the SUB-COMMISSION ON PREVENTION OF DISCRIMINATION AND PROTECTION OF MINORITIES entrusted one of its members, Mrs. Erica-Irene A. Daes (Greece) with the task of elaborating guidelines and principles for the protection of mentally ill persons (resolution 11 [XXXIII]). It received and considered her report on the subject (UN Doc. E/CN.4/Sub.2/1983/17 and Add. 1) at its 1983 session.

On 16 December 1983, the General Assembly, having noted with satisfaction the progress made by the sub-commission, called upon it to expedite its consideration of the problems of the mentally ill and to prepare a draft body of principles and guidelines for their protection for its consideration. The sub-commission set up a sessional Working Group on the Question of Persons Detained on the Ground of Mental Ill-health or Suffering from Mental Disorder.

At its 1988 session, the sub-commission, after considering the report of the working group at that session containing a draft body of principles and guarantees, adopted (resolution 1988/28) the working group's text and submitted it to the COMMISSION ON HUMAN RIGHTS for consideration.

The commission, however, found that because the working group had made only limited progress, the sub-commission was still far from concluding its con-

sideration of the draft body of principles and guarantees. It reiterated (resolution 1988/62) the urgent need for such principles and guarantees to prevent the misuse of psychiatry and to safeguard the rights of all individuals, and requested the sub-commission (a) to attach much greater emphasis at its 1989 session to the working group and its drafting assignments, (b) to complete the work on the draft body of guidelines, principles, and guarantees as a matter of urgency at that session, and (c) to take into account the memorandum presented to the commission by the World Health Organization (UN Doc. E/CN.4/1988/66; see below) and to submit it to the working group for consideration. For more information, see WORKING GROUP ON THE DRAFT BODY OF PRINCIPLES AND GUARANTEES FOR THE PROTECTION OF MENTALLY ILL PERSONS AND THE IMPROVEMENT OF MENTAL HEALTH CARE.

Later in 1988, the General Assembly took note (resolution 43/109) of the sub-commission's action in adopting the draft body of principles and guarantees prepared by its working group and invited the Commission on Human Rights to consider the subject further at its 1989 session. In doing so, the Assembly expressed deep concern at the repeated evidence of the misuse of psychiatry to detain persons on nonmedical grounds and reaffirmed its conviction that detention of persons in mental institutions on account of their political views or on other non-medical grounds is a violation of their human rights.

Views of the World Health Organization. In February 1988, the World Health Organization submitted to the UN Commission on Human Rights a written statement on the question of persons detained on the grounds of mental ill-health or suffering from mental disorders (UN Doc. E/CN.4/1988/66), in which it expressed its continued interest in this matter and offered to cooperate in its further development. The statement, in part, was as follows:

. . . . WHO has considerable experience in this field, having worked on a number of projects designed to enhance the care of the mentally ill. It has also carried out studies on legislation related to the care of the mentally ill, most recently in 1976 carrying out an empirical study across 35 jurisdictions, examining the legal statutes relating to mental health. The results of this research, as well as an analysis of the handling of the mentally ill across a number of cultures and economic conditions is reported on in the WHO publication *The Law and Mental Health: Harmonizing Objectives* (W.J. Curran and T. Harding, [Geneva: WHO, 1978]). This document still provides a most valuable source of information and guidance on this topic. Over the last two years WHO has obtained advice on the protection of the rights of the mentally ill from members of its expert advisory panel in a number of developed and developing countries, and from a range of non-governmental organizations representing a variety of professional and academic concerns. WHO has convened a number of informal consultations with non-governmental organizations in order to try and obtain a consensus of opinion from a number of perspectives on this subject (March 1987, May 1987, August 1987 and February 1988 in WHO headquarters, Geneva). WHO has also convened a consultation of lawyers and psychiatrists (June 1987, The Hague) in order to formulate a plan of action whereby the organization could assist the United Nations in further developing these principles, guidelines and guarantees.

As a result of these consultations, several points have come to the fore.

1. *Protection Against Neglect as well as Protection Against Abuse.* Although the report of the Special Rapporteur and the guidelines provided in annex 2 of the report cover many aspects concerning the protection of the civil rights of the mentally ill, it would be desirable to expand the treatment of economic and social rights so as to cover, in particular, the protection of the mentally ill against neglect. WHO recognizes the need for the protection of the mentally ill from potential abuse, and for ensuring that a label of mental illness is not used as an excuse for limiting the rights of people inappropriately. Equally important, however, are the needs of the mentally ill for care and treatment aimed at integrating them within the community. Experiences in some countries have demonstrated that blocking the access of people with mental illness to treatment can result in more deplorable conditions for the mentally ill person and for his or her family and community than if he or she were confined in a mental health facility. The disturbed mental processes of some of those with mental illness make them especially liable to neglect and unable to take advantage of health and social services even when they are provided for their care. It is to be hoped that any international declaration concerning the mentally ill would provide guidance for the treatment, care and protection of the mentally ill against neglect, in addition to the protection that should be provided against abuse and loss of civil rights.

2. *The Desirability of Treating Mental Illness in the Same Way as Other Illnesses.* Most patients with mental illness do not have to be hospitalized and, of those hospitalized, most are admitted at their own request. Only a minority are kept at health care facilities. The laws and regulations governing the treatment of mental patients at their own request and with their own consent should be no different from those governing the treatment of a person with any other illness. To do otherwise is a form of unjustified discrimination against those with mental illness. Similarly the laws and regulations governing the administration of hospitals or parts of hospitals for the mentally ill in voluntary treatment, should be no different from the laws and regulations governing any other hospital.

Nevertheless, a minority of mental patients do have to be kept at health care facilities. This may be because their mental processes are so disturbed that they are incompetent, from a medical point of view, to make their own decisions and run their own lives or it may be because they pose a threat to themselves or others. Under these circumstances it is necessary to have laws and regulations which regulate the conditions under which they may be kept in health care facilities for treatment. Because such patients cannot leave such facilities, the standard of care may need greater regulation than where patients have the option of leaving or refusing treatment. In addition, in situations where patients can be compelled to receive treatment, means have

to be available to ensure that such compulsion is in conformity with the relevant laws and regulations.

Recent trends have shown the intention to promote the incorporation of laws and regulations governing the compulsory treatment of the mentally ill into other legislation and regulations governing the compulsory treatment and retention in health care facilities of patients with any illness requiring such a course of action (e.g. quarantine laws governing those with infectious illnesses, treatment for any illness of minors or others not considered competent to make their own decisions). In this case, it is argued, discrimination against those with mental illness, as opposed to those with physical illness, will be diminished. Nevertheless, the particular problems related to mental illness will need to be dealt with, separately, in special legislations and regulations. Guiding principles for this would therefore be of considerable value.

3. *The Problem of Encompassing the Needs of Very Divergent Groups Around the World.* In the context of a declaration of the kind envisaged, there is a particular problem related to the divergent legal, cultural and economic situations of the States Members of the United Nations. The report states outright in its introductory comments that not all of the guidelines are appropriate for all Member States at their present level of development. It is hoped that solutions can be found with a view to developing a set of ideals that are attainable by the maximum number of Member States. This might require some sacrifice of specificity in the guidelines so that the cost of fulfilling their requirements and the administrative infrastructure needed might be within the means of both developed and developing nations.

4. *The Need for Prior Agreement on a Set of Principles for Protecting the Mentally Ill.* Experience dictates that the greater the detail and specificity that any body of recommendations provides, the greater the difficulty in implementing the measures on an international basis. Consideration could therefore be given to dividing annex 2 of the report into two parts. The first part would be an extract from the draft declaration of universal principles for the treatment, care and protection of the mentally ill, and the second part would provide more specific guidelines for implementing the principles. The set of principles, which would be clearly separated from the guidelines, would provide the conceptual framework necessary for a universal set of goals. The subsequent guidelines would be more dependent on the means and cultural traditions of the Member States. Guidelines would thus be more like a set of suggestions (for example, as is provided by the WHO *List of Essential Drugs* which provides suggestions to Member States) that could be followed in order to adhere to the principles. This would be one way of enabling an international instrument to provide both the breadth and depth that the repot envisages. It is appreciated that the task is difficult. A first step could be to ensure that there is complete agreement on the part of all concerned on a set of principles for the care, treatment and protection of the mentally ill. A list of issues which would have to be addressed in the formulation of such principles is as follows:

4.1 The promotion of humanitarian values in the treatment of the mentally ill;

4.2 The protection of the legal rights of the mentally ill including protection against:

(a) Confinement for political, racial or other reasons not directly related to mental illness;

(b) Confinement for reasons of family conflict;

(c) Confinement based on economic interests or gain;

(d) Confinement on the ostensible grounds of mental illness, when the individual does not meet acceptable diagnostic criteria;

(e) Abuses;

4.3 The need to be able to provide treatment and care to the mentally ill under circumstances in which the patient's own judgement is impaired;

4.4 The need for a provision by which those detained or being treated compulsorily can appeal against this decision;

4.5 The protection of the mentally ill against neglect and inadequate treatment. The provision of treatment, care, support and other resources where necessary for patients to be able to live within the community;

4.6 The need for specific guidelines that will be adapted to different cultural contexts with due attention to basic values and the limitations in financial and health resources of the societies in which they will be used;

4.7 The need to take into account differences in legal traditions around the world;

4.8 Facilitation of help for those voluntarily seeking treatment, in order that they can do so in a dignified manner, with easy access, which allows them to maintain their autonomy and self-determination;

4.9 Encouragement of the development of treatment options which may be less intrusive on the individual and the provision of appropriate resources for this;

4.10 Clear conceptualization of the important distinctions which may influence an individual's legal rights between: (a) voluntary and involuntary admission; (b) competency and incompetency to make decisions; and (c) informed consent to treatment and the right to refuse treatment;

4.11 Protection of the patient's rights to privacy and confidentiality with regard to information about his or her treatment;

4.12 Provision for a patient's access to his or her own treatment information or, where this is not possible, access to such information by an advocate on behalf of the patient;

4.13 Provision of appropriate and universal guidelines for situations where it is unclear whether a person should be handled by the mental health or criminal system;

4.14 Precise and consistent definition of fundamental terms, such as (a) mental illness, (b) patient, (c) mental health care facility, (d) dangerousness to self and others, (e) mental health care provider;

4.15 Provision of special procedures concerning treatments which may be hazardous, irreversible or especially intrusive;

4.16 Protection of mental patients if they are to be involved in medical and psychosocial research.

WHO is at present considering issues of this kind within the framework of its own activities, and would be prepared to contribute further to the debate in the working group of the Subcommission on Prevention of Discrimination and Protection of Minorities or as the case may be in the Commission on Human Rights itself, in accordance with the procedural decisions that the Commission may wish to take in this respect.

MENTALLY ILL PERSONS: DRAFT PRINCIPLES FOR THEIR PROTECTION.

MENTALLY ILL PERSONS: DRAFT PRINCIPLES FOR THEIR PROTECTION. Individuals in all parts of the world diagnosed as "mentally ill" require special measures of protection because they lack the ca-

pacity to provide for their own needs, to request aid, to testify, or to educate public opinion about their situation.

In 1977, the UN Commission on Human Rights requested its **SUB-COMMISSION ON PREVENTION OF DISCRIMINATION AND PROTECTION OF MINORITIES** (resolution 10 A [XXXIII] to study, with a view to formulating guidelines, if possible, the question of the protection of those detained on the ground of mental ill-health against treatment that may adversely affect the human personality and its physical and intellectual integrity. In 1979, the General Assembly urged (resolution 33/53) that the study be given priority. In 1980, the sub-commission entrusted preparation of the study to one of its members, Mrs. Erica-Irene A. Daes (Greece), as special rapporteur. The study (UN Doc. E/CN.4/Sub.2/1983/17) was completed and submitted to the sub-commission at its 1983 session. It contained (annex II) a series of draft principles formulated by the special rapporteur.

With the approval of its parent bodies, the sub-commission in 1985 established a sessional working group to consider the special rapporteur's draft principles. The working group completed its task during the sub-commission's 1988 session, and the sub-commission adopted them (resolution 1988/28) and forwarded them to the Commission on Human Rights for further consideration.

At its 1988 session, the General Assembly welcomed (resolution 43/109) the progress made by the sub-commission and its working group and invited the commission on Human Rights to consider the question in the light of the sub-commission's recommendations. The commission responded (resolution 1989/40) by establishing its own working group, open to all its members, to examine, revise, and simplify as necessary the draft body of principles.

Taking note of this development, the assembly called upon the commission to consider the subject at its 1990 session with a view to submitting the draft principles and guarantees to the assembly the same year (resolution 44/134). In doing so, it expressed the belief that all mentally ill persons should be treated with humanity and respect for the inherent dignity of the human person and reaffirmed its conviction that the misuse of psychiatry to detain persons in mental institutions on account of their political views or on other non-medical grounds, as reflected in the special rapporteur's report, is a violation of their human rights.

The Commission on Human Rights decided, on 6 March 1989, to establish an open-ended working group of the commission to examine, revise, and simplify as necessary the draft body of principles prepared by the sub-commission and requested the working group to meet for a period of two weeks prior to the commission's 1990 session. This development was endorsed by the Economic and Social Council (resolution 1989/76) and by the General Assembly (resolution 44/134).

The WORKING GROUP ON THE DRAFT BODY OF PRINCI-PLES AND GUARANTEES FOR THE PROTECTION OF MENTALLY-ILL PERSONS AND FOR THE IMPROVEMENT OF MENTAL HEALTH CARE accordingly met at the United Nations of-fice in Geneva from 8 to 19 January 1990. After put-ting aside for later consideration the question of the title of the draft as a whole, and also the definitions of terms contained in article 2 of the sub-commission's draft, the working group proceeded to revise and sim-ply that text, taking into account comments and sug-gestions from governments and intergovernmental and non-governmental organizations.

The articles thus adopted by the working group at its 1990 session are as follows:

Title [To be discussed]

Article 1. These Principles and Guarantees shall be applied without discrimination of any kind such as disability, race, colour, sex, language, religion, political or other opinion, national or social origin, social status, age, property or birth.

Article 2. [To be discussed].

Article 3. 1. All persons have the right to the best available mental health care, which shall be part of the health and so-cial care system.

2. All persons with a mental illness or who are being treated as such persons shall be treated with humanity and respect for the inherent dignity of the human person.

3. All persons with a mental illness or who are being treated as such persons have the right to protection from exploitation, physical or other abuse and degrading treat-ment.

4. There shall be no discrimination on the grounds of mental illness. Special measures taken for the sole purpose of protecting the rights, or securing the advancement, of persons with mental illness shall not be deemed to be dis-crimination. Discrimination does not include any distinc-tion, exclusion or preference undertaken in accordance with the procedures in these Principles and necessary to protect the human rights of a person with a mental illness or of other individuals. ["Discrimination" means any dis-tinction, exclusion or preference that has the effect of nul-lifying or impairing equal enjoyment of rights.]

5. Every person with a mental illness shall have the right to exercise all civil, political, economic, social and cultural rights as recognized in the Universal Declaration of Human Rights, International Covenant on Economic, Social and Cultural Rights, International Covenant on Civil and Politi-cal Rights and the Declaration on the Rights of Disabled Persons, subject within the limits prescribed by those in-struments to the provisions of domestic law relating to inca-pacity which include those providing for the judicial review of any relevant decision.

6. Where a court or other competent tribunal finds that a person with mental illness is unable to manage his or her own affairs, measures shall be taken, so far as is necessary and appropriate to that person's condition, to ensure the protection of his or her interests.

Article 4. 1. A patient in a mental health facility shall be informed as soon as possible after admission in a form and a language which the patient understands of all his or her rights in accordance with these Principles and Guarantees and under domestic law, which information shall include an explanation of these rights and how to exercise them.

2. If and for so long as a patient is unable to understand such information, the rights of the patient shall be commu-nicated to the person or persons best able to represent the patient's interests and willing to do so.

3. A patient who has the necessary capacity has the right to nominate a person who should be informed on his or her behalf.

Article 5. 1. Every patient in a mental health facility shall, in particular, have the right to full respect for his or her:

(a) privacy;

(b) freedom of communication which includes free-dom to communicate with other persons in the facility; freedom to send and receive uncensored private communi-cations; freedom to receive, in private, visits from a legal or other representative and, at all reasonable times, from other visitors; and freedom of access to postal and tele-phone services and to newspapers, radio and television;

(c) freedom of religion or belief.

2. The environment and living conditions in mental health facilities shall be as close as possible to those of the normal life of persons of similar age and in particular shall include:

(a) facilities for recreational and leisure activities;

(b) facilities for education;

(c) facilities to purchase or receive items for daily liv-ing, recreation and communication;

(d) facilities, and encouragement to use such facili-ties, for his or her engagement in active occupation suited to his or her social and cultural background and for train-ing designed to promote rehabilitation and reintegration in the community.

3. In no circumstances shall a patient be subject to forced labour.

4. The labour of a patient in a mental health facility shall not be exploited. Every such patient shall have the right to receive the same remuneration for any work which he or she does as would, according to domestic law or custom, be paid for such work to a non-patient. Every such patient shall in any event have the right to receive a fair share of any remuneration which is paid to the mental health facility for his or her work.

Article 5 (bis). The right of a [patient] to confidentiality of information concerning him or her shall be respected.

Article 6. 1. A determination that a person has a mental illness shall be in accordance with internationally accepted medical standards.

2. A determination of mental illness shall never be made on the basis of political, economic or social status, or mem-bership in a cultural, racial or religious group, or any other reason not directly relevant to mental health status.

3. Family or professional conflict, or non-conformity with moral, social, cultural or political values or religious beliefs prevailing in a person's community, shall never be a determining factor in diagnosing mental illness.

4. A background of past treatment or hospitalization as a patient shall not of itself justify any present or future deter-mination of mental illness.

5. No person or authority should classify a person as hav-

ing, or otherwise indicate that a person has, a mental illness except for purposes directly relating to mental illness or the consequences of mental illness.

Article 6(a). No person shall be compelled to undergo mental examination with a view to determining whether or not he or she has a mental illness except in accordance with a procedure authorized by domestic law.

Article 7. 1. Every patient shall have the right to be treated and cared for, as far as possible, in the community in which he or she lives.

2. Where treatment takes place in a mental health facility, a patient shall have the right, whenever possible, to be treated near his or her home or the home of his or her relatives or friends and shall have the right to return to the community as soon as possible.

3. Every patient shall have the right to treatment suited to his or her cultural background.

Article 8. 1. Every patient shall have the right to receive such health and social care as is appropriate to his or her health needs, and is entitled to care and treatment in accordance with:

(a) the same standards as other ill persons; and

(b) the internationally accepted standards of the mental health professions, including the Principles of Medical Ethics adopted by the United Nations General Assembly.

2. Every patient shall be protected from harm, including unjustified medication, abuse by other patients or staff or other acts causing mental distress or physical discomfort.

Article 9. 1. A mental health facility shall have access to the same resources as any other health establishment, and in particular:

(a) qualified medical and other appropriate professional staff in sufficient numbers and adequate space to provide the patient with a programme of appropriate and active therapy and privacy;

(b) diagnostic and therapeutic equipment for the patient;

(c) appropriate professional care; and

(d) adequate, regular and comprehensive treatment, including supplies of medication.

2. Every mental health facility shall be inspected by the competent authorities with sufficient frequency to ensure that the conditions, treatment, and care of patients comply with these [Principles].

Article 10. 1. Every patient shall have the right to be treated in the least restrictive environment and with the least restrictive or intrusive treatment appropriate to the patient's health needs and the need to protect the physical safety of others.

2. The treatment and care of every patient shall be based on an individually prescribed plan, discussed with the patient, reviewed regularly, revised as necessary and provided by qualified professional staff.

3. Psychiatric knowledge and skills shall never be abused.

4. The treatment of every patient shall be directed towards preserving and enhancing personal autonomy.

Article 11. 1. Medication shall meet the best health needs of the patient and shall be given to a patient only for therapeutic or diagnostic purposes and shall never be administered as a punishment, or for the convenience of others. Subject to the provisions of Article 12 of these Principles, mental health practitioners shall only administer medication of known or demonstrated efficacy.

2. All medication shall be prescribed by a medical practitioner or by another trained person authorized by law and shall be recorded in the patient's records.

Article 12. 1. No treatment shall be given to a patient without his or her informed consent, except as provided for in paragraphs 6, 7 and 8.

2. Informed consent is consent obtained freely without threats or improper inducements after appropriate disclosure to the patient of adequate and understandable information in a form and language understood by the patient of:

(a) the diagnostic assessment;

(b) the purpose, method, likely duration and expected benefit of the proposed treatment;

(c) alternative modes of treatment, including those less intrusive; and

(d) possible pain or discomfort, risks and side effects of the proposed treatment.

3. A patient may request the presence of a person or persons of the patient's choosing during the procedure for granting consent.

4. Patients have the right to refuse or stop treatment except as provided for in paragraphs, 6, 7 and 8. The consequences of refusing or stopping treatment must be explained to the patient.

5. A patient shall never be invited or induced to waive the right to informed consent. If the patient should seek to do so, it shall be explained to the patient that the treatment cannot be given without informed consent.

6. Except as provided in paragraph 7 or in paragraphs 12, 13, and 14, a proposed plan of treatment may be given to a patient without a patient's informed consent if the following conditions are satisfied:

(a) the patient is, at the relevant time, held as an involuntary patient; and

(b) a competent and independent authority, established or prescribed by domestic law and having in its possession all relevant information, including the information specified in paragraph 2, is satisfied that, at the relevant time, the patient lacks the capacity to give or withhold informed consent to the proposed plan of treatment; and

(c) the competent authority is satisfied that the proposed plan of treatment is in the best interests of the patient's health needs.

7. Paragraph 6 does not apply to a patient who is a minor or to any other patient with a legal representative empowered by law to consent to treatment for the patient; but except as provided in paragraphs 12, 13 and 14, treatment may be given to such a patient without his or her informed consent if the legal representative, having been given the information described in paragraph 2, consents on the patient's behalf.

8. Except as provided in paragraphs 12, 13 and 14, treatment may also be given to any patient without the patient's informed consent if a qualified medical practitioner or another trained person authorized by law determines that it is urgently necessary in order to prevent immediate or imminent harm to the patient or to other persons. Such treatment shall not be prolonged beyond the period which is strictly necessary for this purpose.

9. Where any treatment is authorized without the patient's informed consent, every effort shall nevertheless be made to inform the patient about the nature of the treatment and any possible alternatives, and to involve the patient as far as practicable in the development of the treatment plan.

10. [All treatment shall be immediately recorded in the patient's medical records, with an indication of whether involuntary or voluntary].

11. Physical restraint or involuntary seclusion of a patient shall not be employed except in accordance with the officially approved procedures of the mental health facility and only when it is the only means available to prevent immediate or imminent harm to the patient or others. It shall not be prolonged beyond the period which is strictly necessary for this purpose. All instances of physical restraint or involuntary seclusion, the reasons for them, and their nature and extent shall be recorded in the patient's medical record. A patient who is restrained or secluded shall be kept under humane conditions and be under the care and close and regular supervision of qualified members of the staff. The parents of minors or any legal representative shall be given prompt notice of any physical restraint or involuntary seclusion of the patient.

12. Sterilization shall never be carried out as a treatment for mental illness. Notwithstanding the provisions of paragraphs 6, 7 and 8, sterilization can be carried out on a person with a mental illness only where it is considered that it would best serve the health needs of the patient and where the patient gives informed consent, except that where the patient is unable to give informed consent, sterilization should be authorized only after independent external review.

13. Notwithstanding the provisions of paragraphs 6, 7 and 8, psychosurgery and castration can never be carried out on a patient who is an involuntary patient in a mental health facility and can be carried out on any other patient only where the patient has given informed consent and an independent external body has satisfied itself that there is genuine informed consent and that the treatment best serves the health needs of the patient.

14. Clinical trials and experimental treatment shall never be carried out on any patient without informed consent, except that a patient who is unable to give informed consent may be admitted to a clinical trial or given experimental treatment only with the approval of a competent, independent review body specifically constituted for this purpose.

Article 13. 1. Where a patient needs treatment in a mental health facility, every effort shall be made to avoid involuntary admission.

2. Access to a mental health facility shall be administered in the same way as access to any other facility for any other illness.

3. Every patient not admitted involuntarily shall have the right to leave the mental health facility at any time unless the criteria for his or her retention as an involuntary patient, as set forth in Article 15, apply, and he or she shall be informed of that right.

Article 14. [Deleted, as it becomes paragraph 3 of Article 13].

Article 15. 1. A person shall—

(a) be admitted involuntarily to a mental health facility as a patient; or

(b) having already been admitted voluntarily as a patient, be retained as an involuntary patient in the mental health facility,

if and only if a qualified clinician authorized by law for that purpose determines [in accordance with Article 6] that that person has a mental illness and considers:

(i) that, because of that mental illness, there is a serious likelihood of immediate or imminent harm to that person or to other persons; or

(ii) that, in the case of a person whose mental illness is severe and whose judgment is impaired, failure to admit or retain that person is likely to lead to a serious deterioration in his or her condition or will prevent the giving of treatment which can only be given by admission to a mental health facility in accordance with the principle of the least restrictive alternative.

In the case referred to in sub-paragraph (ii), a second such clinician should be consulted if possible and, if such consultation takes place, the involuntary admission or retention may not take place unless the second clinician concurs.

2. Involuntary admission or retention shall initially be for a short period specified by domestic law for observation and preliminary treatment pending review of the patient's admission or retention by a judicial or other independent and impartial review body established by domestic law (hereinafter referred to as "the review body") and in accordance with procedures laid down in domestic law. The fact of the admission or retention and the grounds for it shall be communicated without delay to the review body, to the patient's representative (if any), and, unless the patient objects, to the patient's family.

Draft General Limitation Clause. The exercise of the rights set forth in these Principles and Guarantees may be subject only to such limitations as are prescribed by law and are necessary to protect the health or safety of the person concerned or of others or otherwise to protect public safety, order, health or morals or the fundamental rights and freedoms of others.

MERCENARISM: VIOLATION OF RIGHT TO SELF-DETERMINATION. In 1986, the Economic and Social Council (resolution 1986/43) expressed its deep concern at the loss of life, substantial damage to property and the long-term negative effects on the economy of southern Africa countries resulting from mercenary aggression, and condemned the increased recruitment, financing, training, assembly, transit and use of mercenaries, as well as other forms of support to mercenaries, including so-called humanitarian aid, for the purpose of destabilizing and overthrowing the governments of southern African States and fighting against the national liberation movements of people struggling for the exercise of their right to self-determination. The Council denounced any State that persists in the recruitment, or permits or tolerates the recruitment, of mercenaries and provides facilities to them; and called upon States to exercise the utmost vigilance against the menace posed by the activities of mercenaries and to ensure, by both administrative and legislative measures, that their territory and other territories under their control, as well as their nationals, are not used for the recruitment, assembly, financing, training, and transit of mercenaries, or the planning of such activities designed to destabilize or overthrow the government of any State and to fight the national liberation movements struggling against racism, apartheid, colonial domination, and foreign intervention or occupation for their independence, territorial integrity, and national unity.

The council urged the COMMISSION ON HUMAN RIGHTS to appoint a special rapporteur on the subject, and its action was later endorsed by the General Assembly (resolution 41/102). The commission decided on 9 January 1987 (resolution 1987/16) to appoint such a rapporteur "to examine the question of the use of mercenaries as a means of violating human rights and of impeding the exercise of the right of peoples to self-determination." Mr. Enrique Bernales Ballesteros (Peru) was subsequently designated as special rapporteur.

In his first report to the Commission (UN Doc. E/CN./1988/14), the special rapporteur outlined the current state of international law on the subject of mercenarism as reflected in the GENEVA CONVENTION RELATIVE TO THE PROTECTION OF CIVILIAN PERSONS IN THE TIME OF WAR: PROTOCOL I, the OAU Convention for the Elimination of Mercenarism in Africa, and the INTERNATIONAL CONVENTION AGAINST THE RECRUITMENT, USE, FINANCING, AND TRAINING OF MERCENARIES, then under preparation in the UN General Assembly and since adopted.

The commission, at its 1988 session, took note (resolution 1988/7) of the report with appreciation and continued the special rapporteur's mandate for one year, requesting him (a) to develop further the position that mercenary acts and mercenarism in general are a means of violating human rights and thwarting the self-determination of peoples, (b) to strengthen his cooperation and coordination with the various bodies concerned with mercenarism within the United Nations system, and (c) to study credible and reliable reports of mercenary activity in African and other developing countries in order to determine the scope and implications of such activities and the possible responsibility of third parties by means, *inter alia,* of on-site visits where appropriate.

The commission also called upon the special rapporteur to submit to it, in 1989, a report on the question of the use of mercenaries as a means of impeding the exercise of the right of peoples to self-determination, together with his conclusions and recommendations; and to submit a preliminary report on the subject to the General Assembly at its 1988 session.

In its resolution, the commission expressed its concern at the loss of life, the substantial damage to property, and the long-term negative effects of the economy of African, Central American, and other developing countries resulting from mercenary aggressions, and strongly condemned the racist regime of South Africa for its increasing use of groups of armed mercenaries against national liberation movements and for the destabilization of the governments of southern African States. It condemned the increased recruitment, financing, training, assembly, transit, and use of mercenaries, as well as other forms of support to mercenaries for the purpose of destabilizing and overthrowing the governments of Africa and Central America and of other developing States and fighting against the national liberation movements of peoples struggling for the exercise of their right to self-determination. It branded as inadmissible the use of channels of humanitarian and other assistance to finance, train and arm mercenaries, and denounced any State that persists in the recruitment, or permits or tolerates the recruitment, of mercenaries and provides facilities to them for launching armed aggression against other States. Finally, the commission called upon all States to exercise the utmost vigilance against the menace posed by the activities of mercenaries and to ensure, by both administrative and legislative measures, that the territory of those States and other territories under their control, as well as their nationals, are not used in any manner in the use or encouragement of mercenarism.

On December 1988, the General Assembly (resolution 43/107) welcomed the provisions of Commission on Human Rights resolution 1988/7 and expressed its appreciation to the special rapporteur for his report and especially for his preliminary conclusions and recommendations.

The special rapporteur has since submitted reports annually to the Commission on Human Rights and the General Assembly, providing up-to-date information on the situation of mercenarism in various parts of the world and offering his recommendations for putting an end to this scourge.

In his report to the 1990 session of the Commission on Human Rights, he presented the following conclusions (UN Doc. E/CN.4/1990/11, chap. X, para. 157–170):

It is to be concluded from the information, reports and observations received by the Special Rapporteur during 1989 from Member States, recognized national liberation movements, international organizations and non-governmental organizations that mercenary activities have been clearly condemned and repudiated. Such activities have tended to decrease in the armed conflicts in which they were mentioned and which have been or are being settled, thereby highlighting the tendency to make use of mercenaries in low-intensity conflicts. Thus it may be noted that, as the use of mercenaries declines or ceases, there may also be a fall in the number of reports of mercenary activities connected with such conflicts.

Notwithstanding the above conclusion, it can be observed from the reports received that, regrettably, the world offers a supply of individuals who, because of their military experience, for ideological reasons, or for reasons of adventurism, lifestyle or financial motivation, are prepared to hire out their services for unlawful mercenary activities. Such individuals, in turn, are usually involved with organizations which recruit, train and employ them, at the request of third parties, in activities which violate international law, State sovereignty, the exercise of the right of peoples to self-determination, the stability of constitutional governments and human rights. In this way, it may be concluded that the notion of a mercenary has changed as far as the traditional characteristics are concerned and has become a kind of independent criminal occupation. This is so because of the readiness to participate in unlawful acts and acts which may objectively be characterized as mercenary or terrorist acts, by virtue of both the individual perpetrating them and the damage caused in the territory and among the population affected, causing serious prejudice to territorial sovereignty and human life, even when the context in which they occur is not necessarily that of an international armed conflict.

The use of mercenaries is something that particularly affects small States, notably archipelagic States, especially when their geographical position places them close to areas of acute conflict, or when they are of strategic importance to third parties involved in activities relating to the political, military or economic control of the entire area which has been or is intended to be placed under their influence. These small States, many of them recently established, are extremely vulnerable to expansionist policies, invasion from outside, or to internal conspiracies to destabilize the government that make[s] use of mercenaries. Proven mercenary activity in the cases of Benin, Seychelles, Maldives and the Comoros in recent years demonstrates that there are small States exposed to dangerous situations in which mercenaries are used to jeopardize their sovereignty, their right to self-determination, their constitutional stability and the human rights of their peoples.

As regards mercenary activities in southern Africa, the Special Rapporteur would point out that the process of détente and peace embarked upon by Angola and South Africa, and the current process leading to independence in Namibia, have led to a marked reduction in mercenary activity in that part of southern Africa. In fact the Special Rapporteur has received no new reports of operations of that kind. However, he cannot but mention that, until the internal military conflict in Angola is settled and effective national reconciliation achieved, Angola will remain exposed to the risk of mercenary activities on the part of such groups or individuals employed by UNITA. It is well known that the UNITA rebel guerrilla group receives military assistance and funds from outside which, as indicated in the third report (E/CN.4/1989/14, paras. 179–180), are used in part to hire mercenaries. The Special Rapporteur has also received information from Botswana about mercenary attacks; consequently, the mercenary presence cannot be said to have totally disappeared from southern Africa.

The invasion of Maldives by mercenary groups on 3 November 1988 was thwarted, and the mercenaries of Tamil origin were tried under Maldivian law. The Special Rapporteur has kept in touch with the Maldivian authorities, which have pointed to the vulnerability of Maldivian territory and the risk of invasion, terrorist attacks and other forms of violence while an atmosphere of tension reigns in the Indian Ocean region and could spread to threaten Maldives too. The Maldivian authorities have not ruled out the possibility that mercenaries might be used again in an attack on the sovereignty of the State, and have invited the Special Rapporteur to examine the situation in Maldives on the spot.

On December 4, 1989 the General Assembly adopted the International Convention aginst the Recruitment, Use, Financing and Training of Mercenaries. The text of the Convention was prepared by an *ad hoc* committee set up under resolution 35/48 of 4 December 1980. The complex work of discussion and preparation culminated in a convergence of views which broadens, deepens and refines the scope of the definition of a mercenary, the elements and situations which combine to characterize mercenary activity and the qualifications of both the mercenary acts, and any actions which deliberately advance them, as indictable offences. In this sense, the Convention fills a gap, constitutes an important instrument to enable member States to adapt their national legislation on this subject, and also confirms the legal scope of the many United Nations declarations and resolutions condemning mercenary activities.

It is to be concluded from the text, the preamble and the body of the Convention that the extent and the variety of forms of mercenary practices are recognized. Noteworthy in this regard is the preamble to the Convention, which acknowledges the links between the drug traffic and mercenary activities in its reference to "new unlawful international activities linking drug traffickers and mercenaries in the perpetration of violent actions which undermine the constitutional order of the States" (preamble, fifth paragraph). In this regard, as well as through the broad definition in article 1, the Convention brings matters up to date in a way which should contribute to proper observance of the purposes and principles set out in the Charter of the United Nations, without prejudice to the fact that matters which are not regulated will continue to be governed by the rules and principles of international law. After the Convention has been in force for a reasonable period of time, it would be desirable to analyse and review a number of objections raised to the text, for example the requirement that mercenaries must be foreigners, or the amount of payment made.

Lastly, it can be seen from the text that the Convention contains no provision establishing machinery to minitor implementation. However, such monitoring will be a task for the domestic courts of the States parties. Bearing in mind that the Convention refers to the basic rights of peoples, such as political freedoms, human rights, State sovereignty and self-determination, which may be affected by mercenary activities, the Special Rapporteur concludes that part of the international machinery for monitoring this instrument may fall within the competence of the Commission on Human Rights. If this is the case, reports of mercenary activities of various kinds, such as those wich have been reaching the Special Rapporteur, might better be studied within flexible Commission machinery under the mandate of the Special Rapporteur, without prejudice to actions falling within the scope of the competent domestic forums. In this way the Commission could contribute to effective implementation of this Convention.

In reply to letters sent by the Special Rapporteur, nongovernmental organizations and the Government of Colombia itself referred to the serious cases of violence which are systematicallly disrupting public order and affecting individuals and public and private property in that country. Preliminary information indicates that such acts of violence involve groups with a political motivation and also paramilitary gangs in the pay of organized drug traffickers. According to this preliminary information, evidence and facts of public record highlight a criminal association between Colombian drug traffickers and mercenaries recruited for them, who have participated in the formation and training of paramilitary gangs. These mercenaries, reported to be of Israeli and British nationality, are said to have prepared and taken part in large-scale attacks and criminal acts designed to subject the Colombian government to pressure on the part of these illegal groups and secure advantages for the drug traffickers. It may thus be concluded that this unlawful association between drug traffickers and mercenaries affects the sovereignty and constitutional stability of the Government of Colombia and the people, creating a situation presenting serious risks for Colombia and the international community itself.

Various press reports have taken up the generally accepted fact of the mercenary invasion of Comoros on 26 November 1989 in a *coup d'etat* which led to the overthrow and assassination of President Ahmed Abdallah Abderemane. The invasion was carried out by Bob Denard and a group of about 30 French and Belgian mercenaries. The mercenaries stayed in the Comoros until 15 December 1989, and then left for Johannesburg on a South African cargo plane. The departure of the mercenaries was essentially due to French action in support of the sovereignty and legitimate authorities of the Comoros. This event highlighted the vulnerability of the Comoros and, once again, the active presence of mercenaries in Africa. The Special Rapporteur considered it pertinent to draw the attention of the Commission on Human Rights to this serious occurrence, as well as the withdrawal of the mercenaries to South African territory, and would point out the need for a thorough investigation, for which reason he has made appropriate requests for full and detailed information on this regrettable event.

As to the Central American conflict and the role played in it by the United States of America, the Special Rapporteur has continued to examine the extensive information and documentation obtained when he visited the United States. Although open to further analysis, all the material examined so far indicates that, under the Administration of President Reagan and in the context of policy decisions designed to provide assistance to the Nicaraguan resistance and—as the administration saw it—prevent the Sandinista Government from helping the FMLN guerrillas in El Salvador, covert actions and operations did indeed take place and they went beyond the legal authority granted by Congress for aid and funds for the Nicaraguan resistance (or contras). Some of these covert operations, carried out to raise funds for the contras or to perform acts of sabotage against Nicaragua, involved the creation of all-purpose networks and the recruitment and active participation of some foreign mercenaries. This participation by foreigners, on terms corresponding to mercenarism, has been noted in the Iran-*Contra* Affair report prepared by the Committees of the United States Congress, as well as in reports drawn up by experts and investigators working in United States non-governmental organizations dealing with human rights matters. However, it may also be concluded from the information which has been gathered that these illegal acts were carried out by officials acting without authorization from the highest government authorities or from Congress. The United States Government neither recognizes nor acknowledges any connection with mercenary activities, and has stated that any such activities as may have taken place are the sole responsibility of the private organizations which made use of them.

On the basis of the documentation studied, it may also be concluded that the United States public is greatly aware of the Central American issue, opposes anything that might involve the United States in a military conflict and is against anything that might affect the principles and values of United States democracy. It is also important to note that the Bush administration has stated its readiness to contribute to peace in the region, on the understanding that the most appropriate tool for such purpose is the implementation of the Esquipulas II Agreement as a comprehensive and indivisible set of obligations for all the parties. This stance underlies the bipartisan agreement and the Congress's policy of not granting the Nicaraguan resistance funds for military purposes.

The effort made by Central American leaders to promote political negotiation, détente and peace, despite differences of view between some of them, is a matter of record. In this context, the Esquipulas II, Alajuela, Costa del Sol and Tela agreements, and recently those adopted in San Isidro de Coronado, demonstrate a determination on the part of the Governments of Central America to seek and implement effective solutions to achieve peace in Central America. There is no doubt that demobilization of the Nicaraguan resistance, voluntary repatriation of its members to Nicaragua or third countries, resumption of dialogue and holding democratic elections, which are now under way, can constitute genuine measures to accelerate the process of restoring peace and democracy throughout the Central American region.

As a contribution to international co-operation in the relaxation of tension, the United Nations has set up observer machinery and an International Support and Verification Commission (CIAV) to study issues relating to demobilization, such as the acceptance of returned weapons and ammunition and repatriation as well as assistance to persons deciding to return to Nicaragua or resettle in third countries. On the basis of the Tela and San Isidro de Coronado agreements, and the positions in this regard taken up by the Governments of Honduras and Nicaragua, it may be concluded that such United Nations machinery is the most appropriate means of guaranteeing the implementation of the various arrangements for bringing about reconciliation and peace. Consequently, the stronger this machinery and the guarantees for its operation and the greater resources and funds for its activities, the more rapidly and effectively will it be possible to achieve the desired result of peace in Central America.

On the basis of the information he had received and analyzed, and on the conclusions he had drawn, the special rapporteur submitted the following recommendations for consideration by the commission (chap. XI, para. 172–186):

Bearing in mind that, despite the rejection and condemnation of mercenary activities by the United Nations, they are still being carried out; it is desirable for such a stand to be maintained and strengthened by provisions on concrete measures and actions to help eliminate mercenary activities of all kinds. To this end it will be necessary to take into account the methods used in recent conflict situations in which one of the parties has made use of mercenaries to subject the other to military action and inflict material damage, or to destabilize a sovereign State internally.

Condemnation and punishment of mercenary activities should apply both to the mercenary agents directly involved in such activities and to those who make use of them, as well as to the bodies or individuals recruiting and training them at the request of third parties for participation in actions in violation of international rules, State sovereignty, the excercise of the right of peoples to self-determination, the stability of constitutional Governments and human rights. In addition, to ensure that this recommendation is effectively applied, it should be borne in mind that there are a variety of ways of making use of mercenaries and that mercenaries now form a kind of independent criminal occupation by virtue of their readiness to take part, on agreed terms, in unlawful acts, as well as acts which may objectively be characterized as mercenary acts, by virtue of both the individual perpetrating them and the damage caused to the population and the territory affected.

The use of mercenaries has been particularly intense against small States, especially archipelagic States, when their geographical position places them close to areas of acute conflict, or when they are of strategic importance to the interests of third parties involved in activities relating to the political, military or economic control of the area which has been or is intended to be placed under their influence. In this context, and bearing in mind attacks by mercenary gangs against Benin, Seychelles, Maldives and the Comoros, it is desirable for the Commission to look into the vunerability of small States and strenghten the principles of self-determination and the unrestricted realization of the human rights of their peoples, by warning against attempts at expansionist policies, invasions from outside or destabilizing internal conspiracies involving the use of mercenaries, thereby violating the sovereignty, self-determination, domestic constitutional order and human rights of nations.

In view of the variety and scope of the uses to which mercenaries may be put, all States should be urged to exercise maximum vigilance and apply legislative and administrative measures to prevent and punish the use of their territory and other territories under their control, as well as their nationals, for the recruitment, concentration, funding, training and transit of mercenaries, as well as their use in activities designed to destabilize or overthrow the Government of any State or combat national liberation movements fighting against racism, *apartheid*, colonial domination and foreign intervention and occupation and for their independence, territorial integrity and national unity.

As to the principles underlying United Nations action, it would be desirable to point out the incompatibility with international rules of any external assistance which can be objectively demonstrated as for use in intervening in the internal affairs of other States and for attacks against the exercise of the rights of peoples to self-determination. The recommendation on incompatibility should include any diversion of programmes of humanitarian or other assistance to cover up actual situations in which mercenaries are financed, trained or used.

In view of the fact that on 4 December 1989 the General Assembly adopted the International Convention against the Recruitment, Use, Financing and Training of Mercenaries, it is desirable for the Commission to express its satisfaction at the successful finalization of the work of the *Ad hoc* Committee and the adoption of the Convention and declare at the same time that this constitutes a meaningful step forward and an important instrument for Member States to adapt their national legislation in this area, and also express the hope that the Convention will be signed by the greatest possible number of States in the shortest possible time, so as to ensure prompt entry into force.

In view of the text of the Convention itself and the fact that there are few States in which domestic legislation specifically classes mercenary activities as unlawful and provides for the prohibition of such activities and the prosecution and punishment of those responsible, States should once again be urged to establish in their domestic legislation that mercenary activities are an offence and stipulate the appropriate penalties.

It is of relevance to point out that the Convention contains no provisions establishing machinery to monitor implementation. Given the legal precedents and the subject-matter of the Convention, it is desirable for the Commission to bear in mind that it can itself form part of the monitoring machinery, in all matters relating to the unrestricted applicability and the protection of human rights. In this context, reports of mercenary activities in violation of the right to self-determination and the human rights of peoples received by the Special Rapporteur might better be studied under the mandate of the Special Rapporteur—without prejudice to any legal action initiated in competent national courts.

In connection with the peace process in the southern African region, and in the light of the peace agreements signed by Angola and South Africa, as well as the current independence process in Namibia, it is recommended that these initiatives should be supported, together with the relaxation of tension discernible in the region, for their successful culmination may consolidate independence in Namibia and lasting peace in Angola. Mercenary practices arose in the context of the existing violence and conflicts in the region, and hence it is to be hoped that halting them will contribute to the disappearance of mercenary activities once and for all. For this same reason, this recommendation should include a reference to internal military conflict in Angola, expressing support for a national reconciliation process which will lead to the disappearance of the UNITA guerrilla movement, together with its use of mercenaries, and seeking peace among Angolans, and their contribution to, and political participation in, the development of their country.

Bearing in mind the fact that, according to a number of reports, mercenary activities have not ceased in Africa, and indeed the recent occupation of the Comoros by a mercenary force highlights the existence of groups intended to effect the sovereignty, self-determination and stability of the Governments of certain States, it is recommended that the Commission should clearly comdemn this situation, express full support for the sovereign rights of States and peoples in the region and demand an explanation from the Government of South Africa about its alleged connection with mercenary activities, or in any event, the protection of persons taking part in them.

With regard to the invasion of Maldives by mercenary groups on 3 November 1988, the prosecution and punishment of the mercenaries found guilty of the invasion, and the concern expressed by the Government of Maldives in drawing attention to the vunerability of its territory and the risk of exposure to invasion, attacks, and other forms of violence affecting its sovereignty, self-determination and political stability and the human rights of its people, it is desirable for the Commission to condemn the mercenary agression to which Maldives was subjected and express support for the country's sovereign rights. At the same time, the Commission might reiterate its call on the Governments concerned to continue co-operating with the Special Rapporteur in this regard.

In the light of the reports and evidence which highlight criminal links between organized groups of Colombian drug traffickers and foreign mercenaries recruited to work for them and participate in the formation and training of paramilitary groups and in acts of extreme violence that have disrupted public order and affected individuals and public and private property in Colombia, it is desirable for the Commission to condemn this serious unlawful association, and at the same time assure the Government of Colombia of its readiness to co-operate within the Commission's field of competence in eliminating this association that affects the sovereignty and constitutional stability of Colombia.

The Commission should vigorously condemn the occupation of the Comoros by a mercenary force on 26 November 1989, express support for the sovereign rights of the people of the Comoros, and welcome the French initiative which helped to bring the mercenary occupation of the country to an end and re-establish the sovereignty and constitutional authority of the Comorian Government. At the same time, this recommendation should include the need for an exhaustive investigation of the causes of, and responsibility for, this mercenary act, as well as the legal situation of the mercenaries who have been publicly accused of perpetrating it.

As regards the Central American conflict, particularly the armed actions in Nicaragua which have caused objective harm to its sovereignty, population, territory and economy, and bearing in mind that, in this context, there has been external interference to help one of the parties to the conflict, and mercenaries have been recruited and used through the use of outside funds raised by covert operations that ignored and exceeded the legal authorizations by the United States Congress and the authorities for aid to the Nicaraguan resistance, it is desirable to reaffirm the right of Nicaragua and the other countries in the Central American region to non-interference in their internal affairs, self-determination and full sovereignty, while condemning the mercenary activities of foreigners recruited as mercenaries and the practices and operations that made those activities possible.

Finally, noting the process of détente which has begun in the Central American region by express and agreed decision of the five presidents; that the Esquipulas II, Alajuela, Costa del Sol, Tela and San Isidro de Coronado agreements set out solutions, machinery and procedures for the settlement of all aspects of the conflict in a manner that is satisfactory to all parties; that, in addition to the United States of America, through the bipartisan agreement, has indicated its readiness to co-operate in seeking a peaceful political solution for Central America on the basis of the comprehensive application to the Esquipulas II agreements as an indivisible whole; and that machinery for observation (ONUCA) and verification (the International Support and Verification Commission) has been established under the United Nations to contribute to democratization, détente and demobilization in the region—the Special Rapporteur considers it desirable for the Commission to express explicit support for this comprehensive peaceful political negotiation process, support the initiatives set out in the San Isidro de Coronado agreement designed to speed up the process of comprehensive application of the peace agreements, and invite all Member States to express their support for and co-operation in the negotiations and political settlement under way and in the demobilization of the Nicaraguan resistance forces and

their voluntary repatriation to their own or a third country, as well as undertaking to respect the sovereignty and self-determination of the peoples of Central America and their contribution to all actions that strengthen democracy and development in the region as a whole.

After examining the report of the special rapporteur at its 1990 session, the Commission on Human Rights on 19 February 1990 took note of it with appreciation (resolution 1990/7) and extended the special rapporteur's mandate for two years. It requested him, in carrying out his mandate, to continue to study credible and reliable reports of mercenary activity in developing countries, in particular smaller states, to determine the scope and implications of such activities and the possible responsibility of third parties by means, *inter alia,* of on-site visits where appropriate; and requested him to seek the point of view of those governments in whose territories mercenaries may have been recruited or trained or may have been provided with facilities for launching armed agression against other States.

The commission condemned the increased recruitment, financing, training, assembly, transit and use of mercenaries, as well as other forms of support to them for the purpose of destabilizing or overthrowing the governments of southern Africa, the Comoros, Maldives, and Nicaragua and of other developing countries and fighting against the national liberation movements of peoples struggling for the exercise of their right to self-determination; and considered it inadmissible to use channels of humanitarian and other assistance to finance, train, and arm mercenaries, and denounced any State that persists in the recruitment, or permits or tolerates the recruitment, of mercenaries and provides facilities for them for launching armed agression against other States.

The commmission also expressed the hope that the International Convention against the Recruitment, Use, Financing and Training of Mercenaries will be signed and ratified by the largest possible number of States in order to ensure its entry into force in the shortest possible time. It requested the special rappoteur to follow closely the process of ratification and the mode of application of the convention, and to use his good offices to encourage States to become parties to it.

MEXICO. The United Mexican States constitute a country in the southern part of North America, between the Pacific Ocean and the Gulf of Mexico. Mexico has borders with Belize, Guatemala, and the United States of America. It achieved independence from Spain in 1821 and became a member of the United Nations in 1945. Its population is estimated by the UN (1990) to be 89,012,000. There are 56 ethnic groups living in 23 states of the republic, including the following: Huasteco, Huichol, Maya, Mazahva, Mazateco, Mixteco, Nahuatl, Otomi, Tarahumara, Tarasco, Totonaco, Tzeltal, Tzotzil, and Zapoteco; members of these groups together constitute about 8.5% of the country's total population. Languages commonly used include Spanish and a wide variety of indigenous vernaculars. Christianity (Roman Catholic, 97%; Protestant denominations, 3%) is predominant among those who profess a religious belief. Literacy is estimated at 74%.

The government (1990) took the form of a republic, composed of 31 federated states and a federal district. Each state has its own governor, legislature, and judiciary; the mayor of the federal district is appointed by the president. National executive power is exercised by the president, elected by popular vote for a term of six years and ineligible to succeed himself; he appoints a cabinet to assist him in this function. National legislative matters are dealt with by a bicameral Congress consisting of a 64-member Senate, members of which are elected for terms of six years, and a 400-member Chamber of Deputies, members of which are elected for three-year terms. The national judiciary includes federal and local systems and a Supreme Court. Major political parties include the Institutional Revolutionary Party, the *Partido Acción Nacional,* and the Unified Socialist Party.

Hernan Cortés undertook the conquest of Mexico for Spain in 1519; and, from that time until 1810, Spanish colonists exploited the country's natural resources while endeavoring to convert to Christianity descendents of the ancient Maya, Axtec, and Zapotec civilizations. By the time Mexico took advantage of Napoleon's subjugation of Spain to revolt and achieve independence in 1821, the country's population had developed into three main groups: the white Spaniards, the Amerindians, and the Mestizos (mixed). Although loosely bound together by adherence to the Roman Catholic faith, there was antagonism between these groups: the Spanish-born and Mexican-born white elements vied for economic and political power, while the Amerindians and Mestizos fought a losing battle against sinking into poverty and even peonage.

Liberal reforms instituted by the constitution of 1857, including secularization of Church property, restrictions on the military, and some land distribution improved the lot of the most severely disadvantaged groups but outraged conservatives who, with the help of Napoleon III, established Maximilian as Emperor in 1864. However, the empire lasted only three years; and the regime of Porfirio Diaz, which followed, was one of outstanding national development, unfortunately sometimes at the expense of the underprivileged classes who lost lands, homes, and jobs in the process.

In the 20th century, after a series of revolts and revolutions, Lazaro Cardenas was installed as president in 1934 and initiated a series of measures to improve the lot of the underprivileged, including the indigenous populations. However, Mexico's financial crises of 1983 and 1984, which had worldwide repercussions when the government was unable to make payments on its foreign debt, produced high unemployment and continues to upset the economic balance of the country and its people.

Every presidential election since 1929 has been won by a candidate nominated by the Institutional Revolutionary Party, although voters have frequently expressed displeasure over 60 years of one-party rule. In 1988, Carlos Salinas de Gortari, son of a former president, was elected for a six-year term with the support of that party and of a coalition of smaller organizations known as the National Democratic Front. He took office on 1 December 1988 as Mexico struggled to end its worst economic decline in 50 years, committing himself to reform and modernization of the troubled economy and the somewhat discredited political system.

As regards human rights problems, the most vulnerable groups in Mexico are the indigenous and peasant populations in the states of Oaxaca and Chiapas. Members of these groups are frequently subjected to ill-treatment by the police and security forces; and many cases of abduction, disappearance, and torture have not been resolved by those forces. The government body responsible for the welfare of the indigenous peoples is the National Indigenous Institute. Its objectives include strengthening the capacity of those peoples to defend their individual and social status; and its programs for the promotion of cultural heritage help them to exercise their right to enjoy their own cultural life, to profess and practice their own religions or beliefs, and to use their own language. The Department of Public Information, through its Indigenous Education Office, offers a bilingual-bicultural primary education program in which nearly 500,000 students take part.

In a report to the **HUMAN RIGHTS COMMITTEE,** submitted in 1988, the Mexican government stated that (UN Doc. CCPR/C/46/Add. 3, para. 460–462):

The Government of Mexico respects the country's indigenous cultures and the rights of the Indian peoples. It is, however, aware that there are economic conditions and age-old problems, some of which date from as far back as the colonial era and which result in the social inequality and marginalization of ethnic groups.

M

These problems include the geographical isolation and dispersion of indigenous population centres, the unfavourable system of trade through intermediaries, uncertainty with regard to land ownership and the growing erosion of the indigenous and traditional values that shape ethnic identity.

In view of the foregoing, the Government of Mexico is actively promoting the preservation of the Indian peoples' cultures and traditions by framing a policy with the indigenous peoples and not only for them. Efforts are being made to check the process of the reduction of their territory, preserve and use for their benefit the natural resources which belong to them, carry out improvements in the communities, extend basic services and eliminate the system of intermediaries in order to make the individual guarantees and social rights enshrined in the Constitution of the Republic for all Mexicans a reality for indigenous groups.

MIGRANT WORKERS. In 1972, the UN Economic and Social Council noted with alarm and indignation (resolution 1706 [LIII]) newspaper reports of incidents which involved the illegal transportation of African workers to European countries by criminal elements, and the exploitation of those workers in conditions akin to slavery or forced labor. The council condemned all such clandestine trafficking and exploitation, appealed to the governments concerned to put an end to such practices, and called upon the UN COMMISSION ON HUMAN RIGHTS to study the problem and to prepare recommendations for further action.

Later the same year, the General Assembly also expressed concern (resolution 2920 [XXVII] about the *de facto* discrimination against foreign workers in Europe and elsewhere and urged governments to step up their efforts to eliminate such discrimination. In particular, it recommended that governments which had not done so should ratify the ILO MIGRATION FOR EMPLOYMENT CONVENTION (revised, 1949).

In 1973, the Economic and Social Council (resolution 1789 [LIV] requested the COMMISSION ON THE STATUS OF WOMEN and the SUB-COMMISSION ON PREVENTION OF DISCRIMINATION AND PROTECTION OF MINORITIES to study the question in depth and to recommend further measures to protect the human rights of foreign workers. The sub-commission responded by appointing one of its members, Ms. Halima Warzazi (Morocco) as special rapporteur to prepare a comprehensive study of the subject.

Ms. Warzazi's study, entitled *Exploitation of Labor Through Illicit and Clandestine Trafficking* (UN publication, Sales No. E.86.XIV.1), was considered by the sub-commission at its 1986 session. The sub-commission noted it with appreciation and forwarded it to the Commission on Human Rights.

Meanwhile, the General Assembly had examined the question further under the agenda item "Measures to Improve the Situation and Ensure the Human Rights and Dignity of All Migrant Workers." On 16 December 1977, it adopted a resolution (resolution 32/120) calling upon all States, "taking into account the provisions of the relevant instruments adopted by the International Labor Organization and of the International Convention on the Elimination of all Forms of Racial Discrimination, to take measures to prevent and put to an end all discrimination against migrant workers and to ensure the implementation of such measures."

In particular, the assembly invited all States:

(a) to extend to migrant workers having regular status in their territories treatment equal to that enjoyed by their own nationals with regard to the enjoyment of fundamental human rights, with particular reference to equality of opportunity and of treatment in respect of employment and occupation, social security, trade union and cultural rights and individual and collective freedoms;

(b) to promote and facilitate by all the means in their power the implementation of the relevant international instruments and the adoption of bilateral agreements designed, *inter alia,* to eliminate the illicit traffic in alien workers; and

(c) to take all necessary and appropriate measures to ensure that the fundamental human rights and acquired social rights of all migrant workers, irrespective if their immigration status, are fully respected under their national legislation.

In 1980, the General Assembly established (resolution 34/172) the Working Group on the Drafting of an International Convention on the Protection of the Rights of All Migrant Workers and their Families, open to all States, to elaborate such an international convention. The working group held sessions during and between annual sessions of the General Assembly but, as at 15 December 1989, had not been able to complete its task. On that date, the assembly, having examined the progress made by the working group, took note of that progress with satisfaction (resolution 44/155) and called upon the Secretary-General to entrust to the CENTER FOR HUMAN RIGHTS the technical revision of the text of the articles of the draft convention approved up to that time by the working group with a view to ensuring uniformity of terminology and gender and to harmonizing the versions in the official languages of the United Nations. The Secretary-General was to transmit the results of the technical revision to governments as soon as possible, at least one month before the 1990 meeting of the working group. The working group would then hold a meeting of two week's duration with a view to completing the remaining articles and considering the results of the technical revision.

SEE ALSO *Charter of Rights for Migrant Workers in Southern Africa; European Convention on the Legal Status of Migrant Workers; European Convention on Establishment and Protocol; ILO Migrant Workers (Supplementary Provisions) Convention.*

MILAN PLAN OF ACTION. The Seventh United Nations Congress on the Prevention of Crime and the Treatment of Offenders, convened at Milan from 26 August to 6 September 1985, adopted a number of instruments, among them the Milan Plan of Action, with a view to strengthening international cooperation in the field of crime prevention and criminal justice. The plan, representing the collective endeavor of the international community to deal with a major human-rights-related problem whose disruptive and destabilizing impact upon society is certain to increase unless concrete and constructive action is taken on a priority basis, is reproduced below.

Annexed to the plan is a series of "Guiding Principles for Crime Prevention and Criminal Justice in the Context of Development and a New International Order," section C of which is entitled "The Responsiveness of the Criminal Justice System to Development and Human Rights." The section is also reproduced below.

The General Assembly, on 29 November 1985, approved (resolution 40/32) the Milan Plan of Action as a useful and effective means of strengthening international cooperation in dealing with criminal activity. It recommended the guiding principles for national, regional, and international action, as appropriate, taking into account the political, economic, social, and cultural circumstances and traditions of each country on the basis of the principles of the sovereign equality of States and of non-interference in their internal affairs. It invited governments to be guided by the Milan Plan of Action in the formulation of appropriate legislation and policy directives.

On 24 May 1989, the Economic and Social Council received a report prepared by the Secretary-General, which it had requested in 1986 (resolution 86/10), developing a number of proposals for concerted international action against the forms of crime identified in the Milan Plan of Action (UN Doc. E/AC.57/1988/16). Taking note of the report, the council expressed (resolution 1989/62) its alarm at the marked increase in the transnational dimensions of grave forms of crime and by the comparative im-

munity enjoyed by the perpetrators of such criminality and its dismay at the shortcomings of existing international cooperation arrangements and instruments for the prevention of transnational criminality. In particular, it was concerned at the growing tendency of some governments and transnational corporations to facilitate the dumping of toxic nuclear and industrial waste in developing countries and at the devastating damage to the environment which is the direct outcome of harmful and illicit practices, such as the dumping of toxic waste, the thoughtless depletion of non-renewable resources, the extermination of animal species, the massive use of herbicides and defoliants, and the release into the atmosphere of harmful gases and radioactive substances. It was also concerned about the sustained pillage of archeological sites and the illicit trade in objects belonging to the cultural heritage of nations and the ensuing damage to the national identity of peoples.

Accordingly, the council invited governments, intergovernmental and non-governmental organizations, and other decisionmaking bodies to examine the Secretary-General's recommendations, with a view to implementing them. In particular, it urged governments to examine existing domestic legislation, with a view to enacting provisions that protect the natural environment and that establish adequate compensation for the victims of such practices, and invited them to exercise stricter and more effective control over the industrial and other sectors that could be involved in the dumping of toxic nuclear or industrial waste in developing countries. Finally, it called upon the Eighth United Nations Congress on the Prevention of Crime and the Treatment of Offenders to consider the topics of transnational crimes against the environment and against the cultural patrimony of countries, with a view to formulating comprehensive policies of international cooperation for the prevention of such offenses; and called upon the Secretary-General to submit an expanded report on proposals for concerted international action against the forms of crime identified in the Milan Plan of Action to the Eighth Congress.

The Milan Plan of Action, adopted by consensus by the Seventh United Nations Congress on the Prevention of Crime and the Treatment of Offenders, is set out in the report of the congress (UN publication, sales no. E.86.IV.1, chap. 1 [A]) as follows:

1. Crime is a major problem of national and, in some cases, international dimensions. Certain forms of crime can hamper the political, economic, social and cultural development of peoples and threaten human rights, fundamental freedoms, and peace, stability and security. In certain cases it demands a concerted response from the community of nations in reducing the opportunities to

commit crime and address the relevant socio-economic factors, such as poverty, inequality and unemployment. The universal forum of the United Nations has a significant role to play and its contribution to multilateral co-operation in this field should be made more effective.

2. The past years have witnessed rapid and far-reaching social and economic transformations in many countries. Development is not criminogenic *per se*, especially where its fruits are equitably distributed among all the peoples, thus contributing to the improvement of overall social conditions; however, unbalanced or inadequately planned development contributes to an increase in criminality.

3. The success of criminal justice systems and strategies for crime prevention depend on the progress achieved in preserving peace, improving social conditions, making progress towards a new international economic order and enhancing the quality of life. The multisectoral and interdisciplinary nature of crime prevention and criminal justice, including their linkages to peace, demands the co-ordinated attention of various agencies and disciplines.

4. Crime prevention and criminal justice should be considered in the context of economic development, political systems, social and cultural values and social change, as well as in the context of the new international economic order. The criminal justice system should be fully responsive to the diversity of political, economic and social systems and to the constantly evolving conditions of society.

5. In the light of those general considerations, the following recommendations are made as essential elements of an effective plan of action for consideration by the United Nations General Assembly:

(a) Governments should accord high priority to crime prevention and criminal justice through, *inter alia,* the strengthening of national crime prevention mechanisms and the allocation of adequate resources;

(b) Interested Governments should co-operate bilaterally and multilaterally, to the fullest extent possible, with a view to strengthening crime prevention measures and the criminal justice process by undertaking action-oriented programmes and projects;

(c) Since criminality is a dynamic concept, the United Nations and Member States should continue to strengthen their research capacity and to take action to develop the required data bases on crime and criminal justice. In particular, attention should be given to possible interrelationships between criminality and specific aspects of development, such as population structure and growth, urbanization, industrialization, housing, migration and employment opportunities;

(d) There is also need for further study of crime and criminality in relation to human rights and fundamental freedoms and for investigation of traditional and new forms of crime;

(e) Member States should adopt concrete and urgent measures to eradicate racial discrimination, particularly *apartheid,* and other forms of oppression and discrimination against peoples, and should refrain from committing any acts which would undermine the sovereignty and independence of countries;

(f) Priority must be given to combating terrorism in all its forms including, when appropriate, by co-ordinated and concerted action by the international community;

(g) It is imperative to launch a major effort to control and eventually eradicate the destructive phenomena of illicit drug traffic and abuse and of organized crime, both of which disrupt and destabilize societies;

(h) Continued attention should be given to the improvement of criminal justice systems so as to enhance their responsiveness to changing conditions and requirements in society and to the new dimension of crime and criminality. The United Nations should facilitate the exchange of information and experiences between Member States and should undertake study and policy research, drawing on available expertise;

(i) Non-governmental organizations should continue to be effectively involved in the work of the United Nations in the field of crime prevention and criminal justice;

(j) The Secretary-General of the United Nations is requested to review, in consultation with the Committee on Crime Prevention and Control, the functioning and programme of work of the United Nations in the field of crime prevention and criminal justice, including the United Nations regional and interregional institutes, in order to establish priorities and to ensure the continuing relevance and responsiveness of the United Nations to emerging needs. In such a review, special attention should be given to improving the co-ordination of relevant activities within the United Nations in all related areas. Given the diversity of economic, social and cultural situations, it is also imperative to initiate and strengthen the subregional, regional and interregional programmes of the United Nations in the field of crime prevention and criminal justice with the concurrence of concerned Member States;

(k) The regional and interregional institutes of the United Nations should be strengthened and their programmes reinforced to meet the requirements of their respective constituencies. Action should be taken for the immediate establishment in Africa of the long-delayed regional institute for the prevention of crime and the treatment of offenders;

(l) The capacity of the United Nations to extend technical co-operation to developing countries, upon their request, should be urgently reinforced, particularly in the areas of training, planning, exchange of information and experiences, reappraisal of legal systems in relation to changing socio-economic conditions and appropriate measures to combat criminality in all forms. Necessary action should be taken to promote regional advisory services in this field. All of those efforts require adequate resources;

(m) Member States should intensify their efforts in developing the widest possible public participation in preventing and combating crime and to this end efforts should be made to engender the widest public education.

6. Member States are urged to implement the Plan of Action as the collective endeavour of the international community to deal with a major problem whose disruptive and destabilizing impact on society is bound to increase unless concrete and constructive action is taken on an urgent and priority basis.

Annex
Guiding Principles for Crime Prevention and Criminal Justice in the Context of Development and a New International Economic Order

. . . C. The Responsiveness of the Criminal Justice System to Development and Human Rights

Development and Fundamental Human Rights. Socio-economic programmes and national planning should be conducive to the promotion, protection and efficacy of social justice, fundamental freedoms and human rights. Existing socio-economic policies and programmes should be examined in the light of their implications for the achievement of those objectives.

Legal Systems, Criminal Justice and Development. Legal systems, including criminal justice, should be instrumental in promoting beneficial and equitable development and due regard to human rights and social justice considerations, in ensuring that those performing judicial or quasi-judicial functions exercise them in a manner that is independent of personal or group interest and in maintaining impartiality in the staffing of the courts, in the conduct of criminal court proceedings and in the provision of public access to them.

Periodic Reappraisal of Criminal Justice Policies and Practices. There should be in every country, regardless of its stage of development, a periodic reappraisal of the existing criminal justice policies and practices in relation to both formal and informal means of social control, so as to foster their concordance and responsiveness to emerging requirements deriving from socio-economic, cultural and other changes.

Written Laws and Societal Structures and Values. The conflicts existing in many countries between indigenous institutions and traditions for the solution of socio-legal problems and the frequently imported or superimposed foreign legislation and codes should be reviewed with a view to assuring that official norms appropriately reflect current societal values and structures.

Unrestricted Access to the Legal System. Legal systems should endeavour, through appropriate policies aimed at overcoming socio-economic, ethnic, cultural and political inequalities or disparities whenever they exist, to optimize access to justice for all segments of society, especially the most vulnerable ones. Appropriate mechanisms for legal aid and the protection of basic human rights, in accordance with the demands of justice, should be established wherever they do not exist. Legal systems should also provide readily available, less costly and non-cumbersome procedures for the peaceful settlement of disputes and litigation or arbitration, so as to ensure prompt and just parajudicial and judicial action for everybody while offering the means for widespread legal assistance for the effective defence of all those in need.

Community Participation. Various forms of community participation should be explored and encouraged in order to create suitable alternatives to purely judicial interventions, which would provide more readily accessible methods of administering justice, such as mediation, arbitration and conciliation courts. Community participation in all phases of crime prevention and criminal justice processes should, therefore, be further promoted and strengthened, paying full attention to the protection of human rights.

Mass Media and Education. The role of the mass media and its impact on aspects of crime prevention and criminal justice should be examined and evaluated, since public perceptions of criminal policies and public attitudes are central to the effectiveness and fairness of the legal system. In this connection, the mass media should be encouraged to contribute positively to the education of the public on issues of crime prevention and criminal justice, as an important tool of socialization, together with programmes of civic and legal education.

Human Rights, Social Justice and Effective Crime Prevention. While protecting human rights and promoting social justice, improvements in the effectiveness of crime prevention and criminal justice policies should be encouraged

through the use of community and other alternatives to incarceration, by avoiding unnecessary delay in the administration of justice, by fostering staff training evaluation and by scientific and technological innovations and action-oriented research, especially when there is need to maximize limited financial and human resources.

Traditional Forms of Social Control. When new crime prevention measures are introduced, necessary precautions should be taken not to disrupt the smooth and effective functioning of traditional systems, full attention being paid to the preservation of cultural identities and the protection of human rights.

New Forms of Crime and Criminal Sanctions. Criminal sanctions, generally applied to counteract conventional criminality, should also be oriented towards new forms and dimensions of crime through the adoption of new legislative instruments and measures adequate to meet the challenges and by means of innovative techniques for detection, investigation, prosecution and sentencing. Appropriate instruments and mechanisms for international co-operation should likewise be devised and applied in order to cope effectively with such new and dangerous manifestations of crime.

Overall Re-examination of Criminal Justice Measures. The limited resources of the criminal justice system should be allocated on the basis of careful consideration of the benefits and costs associated with alternative strategies, taking into account not only the direct and indirect costs of crime, but also the social consequences associated with its control. In this connection, constant efforts should be made to consider the use of alternatives to judicial intervention and institutionalization procedures, including community-oriented alternatives, thus decreasing the level of undue criminalization and penalization and reducing its social and human costs.

Modern Technology and Potential for Abuses. New developments in science and technology should be used everywhere in the interest of the people and thus also for effective crime prevention. However, since modern technology may produce new forms of crime, appropriate measures should be taken against potential abuses. In particular, as computer systems may result in the accumulation of personal data that could be used to violate human rights, including the right to privacy, or to engage in other abuses, appropriate safeguards should be adopted, confidentiality ensured and a system of individual access to such data and of correction of errors should be established, together with appropriate procedures for expurgating such data in order to alleviate these and other discriminatory aspects deriving from their possible abuse.

Social Marginality and Inequality. In view of the staggering dimensions of social, political, cultural and economic marginality of many segments of the population in certain countries, criminal policies should avoid transforming such deprivation into likely conditions for the application of criminal sanctions. Effective social policies should, on the contrary, be adopted to alleviate the plight of the disadvantaged, and equality, fairness and equity in the processes of law enforcement, prosecution, sentencing and treatment should be ensured so as to avoid discriminatory practices based on socio-economic, cultural, ethnic, national or political backgrounds, on sex or on material means. It is necessary to proceed from the principle that the establishment of genuine social justice in the distribution of material and spiritual good among all members of society, the elimination of all forms of exploitation and of social and economic inequality and oppression, and the real assurance of all basic human rights and freedoms represent a principal hope for the successful combating of crime and its eradication from the life of society in general.

SEE ALSO Code of Conduct for Law Enforcement Officials; Code of Conduct for Law Enforcement Officials: Guidelines for Implementation; Crime Prevention, Development, and Human Rights; Declaration on Permanent Sovereignty over Natural Resources; Environment: Toxic and Dangerous Wastes; Equality: Administration of Justice; Racism: Administration of Criminal Justice; Right to Life: Disposal of Dangerous Products and Wastes; Toxic and Dangerous Products and Wastes; UNESCO Convention on the Means of Prohibiting and Preventing the Illicit Import, Export and Transfer of Ownership of Cultural Property; UNESCO Recommendation concerning the Preservation of Cultural Property Endangered by Public or Private Works.

MINISTERIO PÚBLICO. A national organ established within the framework of the judicial system in several Latin American countries, having as one of its functions the protection and promotion of human rights. As described in the UN Secretary-General's report entitled *National Institutions for the Protection and Promotion of Human Rights* (UN Doc. E/CN.4/1987/37, para. 45–46), prepared at the request of the General Assembly (resolution 40/123):

The *Ministerio Público* has a broad range of responsibilities consisting in an overall supervision of the administration of justice. Each category of existing court or tribunal in the country is generally provided with a corresponding agent of the *Ministerio Público*. Agents of the *Ministerio Público* may act on their own initiative, or upon complaints addressed to them by individuals or groups requesting the office's intervention. In some countries, the *Ministerio Público* is elected by the legislature. In others, the *Ministerio Público* is appointed by the President from a list of suggested candidates submitted by the State Council. This is the procedure followed in Guatemala.

The competence of the *Ministerio Público* extends to the activities of all judicial courts and administrative tribunals. Although the *Ministerio Público* does not have power to change laws or quash any administrative or judicial decision, agents of its offices are empowered to prosecute, sue, request that disciplinary action be taken, impeach public officials before the competent courts and act as a party in proceedings. In Colombia, for example, the *Ministerio Público* has a broad range of responsibilities and duties. Generally, it may receive complaints of violations of human rights from individuals, investigate such complaints and take appropriate action on them, supervise the official conduct of public officials and employees (particularly those in the judicial branch), ensure that the competent authorities investigate acts by public officials or employees that might constitute a criminal offence, and represent the interests of the nation in the judicial forum, either in person or through its agents. In Venezuela, the *Ministerio Público* is an independent institution which primarily supervises the actions of public officials. In accordance with Venezuelan Organic Law, the *Ministerio Público* is, *inter alia*, responsible for ensuring that tribunals of the Republic apply the law correctly and uniformly in penal cases, investigating cases of alleged arbitrary detention, and promoting action to bring about the end of such unlawful detention, defending the independence and autonomy of judges in the exercise of their duties, ensuring that police officials in prisons and other prison personnel maintain respect for the human rights of prisoners.

MINORITIES: SEXUAL. In a resolution adopted on 26 May 1983, entitled "Suppression of the traffic in persons and of the exploitation of the prostitution of others," The UN ECONOMIC AND SOCIAL COUNCIL requested the CENTER FOR HUMAN RIGHTS to prepare, in liaison with the United Nations agencies and organs concerned and with the competent non-governmental organizations, two complementary studies: one on the sale of children and the other on the legal and social problems of sexual minorities, including male prostitution, and to submit those studies as soon as possible to the SUB-COMMISSION ON PREVENTION OF DISCRIMINATION AND PROTECTION OF MINORITIES.

The study entitled "The Legal and Social Problems of Sexual Minorities," (UN Doc. E/CN.4Sub.2/1988/31), prepared by Mr. Jean Fernand-Laurent at the invitation of the Secretary-General, was transmitted to the sub-commission at its 1988 session. It endeavored to answer two questions in particular: (a) Are sexual minorities subjected to *de facto* or *de jure* discrimination and (b) if so, is such discrimination justified on any valid grounds?

The study deals, in the words of the author, "not with occasional and individual breaches of collective moral standards, but, rather, only with groups of persons who are, implicitly or explicitly, protesting against the established order, who refuse to play the role assigned to them as men or women and who, when possible, set up groups to demand the satisfaction of their particular needs and to help one another. This definition covers male and female homosexuals (lesbians), who set themselves apart by having a relationship with a partner of the same sex, and transsexuals, who refuse the legal sex assigned to them. They will henceforth be referred to as sexual minorities." It attempts to answer the question whether the UNIVERSAL DECLARATION OF HUMAN RIGHTS is compatible with legislation, regulations, and practices relating to sexual minorities, and to show whether discrimination which might have occurred is justified by valid reasons, such as the protection of the minorities themselves against economic exploitation, concern for public health, and the protection of children.

The study recalls that, in 1982, the HUMAN RIGHTS COMMITTEE adopted views under article 5 (4) of the INTERNATIONAL COVENANT ON CIVIL AND POLITICAL RIGHTS:

OPTIONAL PROTOCOL, with reference to a communication submitted by five Finnish journalists represented by the Organization for Sexual Equality of Finland. The authors of the communication contended that Finnish authorities, including organs of the State-controlled Finnish Broascasting Company, had interfered with their right of freedom of expression and information, as laid down in article 19 of the Covenant, by imposing sanctions against participants in, or censuring, radio and television programs dealing with homosexuality. At the heart of the dispute was paragraph 9 of chapter 20 of the Finnish Penal Code, which reads:

If someone publicly engages in an act violating sexual morality, thereby giving offense, he shall be sentenced for publicly violating sexual morality to imprisonment for at most six months or to a fine.

Anyone who publicly encourages indecent behavior between persons of the same sex shall be sentenced for encouragement to indecent behavior between members of the same sex as decreed in sub-section 1.

The Finnish Government, while admitting that paragraph 9 of chapter 20 of the Penal Code constitutes a certain restriction on freedom of expression, referred to article 19 (3) of the covenant, which states that the exercise of the rights provided for in article 19 (2) may be subject to certain restrictions, in so far as these are provided by law and are necessary for the protection of public order, or of public health or morals.

The committee, after considering the merits of the communication, found (UN Doc. A/37/40, Annex XIV)

that it cannot question the decision of the responsible organs of the Finnish Broadcasting Corporation that radio and TV are not the appropriate forums to discuss issues related to homosexuality, as far as a program could be judged as encouraging homosexual behavior. According to article 19 (3), the exercise of the rights provided for in article 19 (2) carries with it special duties and responsibilities for these organs. As far as radio and TV programs are concerned, the audience cannot be controlled. In particular, harmful effects on minors cannot be excluded. Accordingly, the Human Rights Committee is of the view that there has been no violation of the rights of the authors of the communication under article 19 (2) of the Covenant.

The study also recalls that between 1976 and 1981 the EUROPEAN COMMISSION ON HUMAN RIGHTS and the EUROPEAN COURT OF HUMAN RIGHTS considered a petition brought by a British subject against his Government, complaining of the existence in Northern Ireland of laws which had the effect of establishing as offenses certain homosexual acts between consenting adults. The Court's judgment, dated 22 October 1981, led to an order by the British Government decriminalizing homosexual acts committed in private by two consenting adults aged 21 or more in Northern Ireland, thus bringing Northern Irish law on this issue into line with the law in force for the rest of the United Kingdom.

After examining in some detail the numerous problems, including those of prejudice and discrimination, encountered by male and female homosexuals, transsexuals, and male prostitutes, the study concludes with the following comments and proposals (para. 95–106):

In considering three sexual minorities (homosexuals, lesbians and transsexuals), we have approached the depths of human nature and have come upon the most disturbing mysteries on which scholars have been unable to shed any light. These facts are very humbling and keep us from making any hard and fast judgements.

Our research brought us up against one of the basic structures of every society—the distinction between the sexes. It took us into the area of sexual activity which, together with power and money, forms one of the focal points of all private and social morality, and of all ethical thinking. However, the governing rules of morality, which have been widely challenged over the last 30 years in Western societies, no longer apply for young people, or even for some members of their parents' generation. They are no longer an insurmountable obstacle to the realization of any desires. Admittedly, this questioning attitude and trend towards permissiveness have thus far affected only the industrialized market-economy countries, but neither the socialist countries nor the third world can consider themselves safe from such changes. Moreover, in so far as the law is determined to a large extent by social mores, some impact has begun to be seen in the Western countries, in both legislation and court decisions. Moral permissiveness, encouraged by the media, advertising and cultural industries and only tenuously reined in by the courts, may thus be approaching the point where a continuing deterioration would provoke a backlash in the form of a sudden return to traditional moral values and traditional sanctions, and thus the remarginalization of sexual minorities. The Commission for Social Development, in an effort to ensure the physical and mental equilibrium of the child, is already considering proposing to the Economic and Social Council a major United Nations effort on behalf of the family. It is perhaps for the Commission on Human Rights, without questioning the usefulness of such an initiative, to consider which rights of the human person are at stake in the situation experienced by individuals who, because of sexual proclivity, find themselves excluded from a society in which the family constitutes the basic unit.

In individual cases, we have seen a great deal of suffering engendered more often than not by the feeling of being confined in a ghetto. The members of sexual minorities, who are the victims rather than the instigators of this confinement, are asking not that we should pity them, but that we should respect their difference and that our behaviour should be based on fellowship. We must make every effort to eliminate the causes of their suffering and afford them the possibility of escaping from the ghetto and fitting into society.

It would be worthwhile drawing up a general strategy taking account, in particular, of the fact that many of the situations studied are encouraged, if not determined, by the attitude of society. It is likely that societies have emphasized the distinction between the sexes more than necessary to ensure a happy and fruitful family life, and has established excessively hard and fast male and female prototypes. It is more than likely that the assertion of a purported male supremacy has had a deeply disturbing effect on many women and that there would be fewer lesbians if men were able to be more affectionate, more attentive and more tactful. Also, the virility model presented to men, seeming unattainable to many of them, has caused them to drift towards alternative forms of sexual activity. There would be less impotence and homosexuality if men did not feel called on by the social model to achieve with their female partners an exceptionally high level of sexual performance. In short, a considerable effort would have to be made for the long term, through improved education and a thorough review of the conduct of the media, to eliminate the artificiality of the contrast between the sexes and promote more equality and reciprocity between them. This would bring closer that future time hoped for by Ranier Maria Rilke, when "love would no longer be a relationship between man and woman but a relationship between one human being with another. Being more human, it will be infinitely sensitive and considerate, good and clear in all things which it initiates and resolves. It will be that love for which we work so hard—two solitudes protecting one another, complementing one another, limiting one another and yielding to one another."

In view of the foregoing observations, the Sub-Committee on Prevention of Discrimination and Protection of Minorities may wish to propose that the Commission on Human Rights should recommend to Member States the adoption of a set of coherent measures, first and foremost in the areas of education and communication, the preventive strategy suggested in the following two paragraphs. (Italics found in study.)

The first preventive action will consist of a policy in support of the family unit and the educational capacity of the parents. At the same time, in formal education, and particularly as part of the moral education and civics training which should begin at nursery school, it would be as well to institute, instead of or in conjunction with simple sex education, education in respect for life, respect for feelings and for the body and mutual respect between the sexes, which would also provide an early preparation for parental responsibilities. These goals are already provided for in a number of ongoing UNESCO programmes (studies of the image presented of men and women in textbooks, research into the influence of the media on the image of women) encouraged by the Economic and Social Council (resolution 1983/30, para. 11).

With regard to the media (cinema, radio and television, the press, cartoon strips, video cassettes, telephone, telematics, etc.) and advertising in the press, on the screen and on hoardings, it would be worth establishing multidisciplinary advisory commissions on which both parents and teachers were represented, as is already the case with regard to the cinema in a number of countries. These commissions would encourage the media to adopt a deontology of respect for women and children and would formulate guidelines which could be approved by Governments, with a view to protecting children against the spread of pornography which could upset the psychological equilibrium of the most insecure individuals and turn them into sex maniacs.

In addition, in the area of positive law, we have noted that changes in moral values have resulted in the non-application of a number of existing laws, so that the public is no longer quite sure what is permitted and what is not; we have also noted that existing laws vary considerably from one country to another and even within countries with federal systems. There should therefore be greater coherence between the law and judicial practice and greater harmony between the laws of various countries. As for the guiding principles, these should of course be, first and foremost, freedom, equality and non-discrimination as embodied in the Universal Declaration of Human Rights (articles 2 and 7) and in the Covenants, together with the principle of respect for privacy (article 12 of the Universal Declaration) and of the "special safeguards" needed by the child (International Declaration of the Rights of the Child, adopted by the United Nations General Assembly on 20 November 1959).

In the interests of non-discrimination and respect for privacy, the Sub-Commission on Prevention of Discrimination and Protection of Minorities may wish to propose to the Commission on Human Rights that it should recommend that Member States which have not already done so should take the legislative or regulatory measures described below as the second phase of an overall policy. (Italics found in study.)

(a) As in the case of racism, any violence or discrimination practised against an individual because of sexual proclivity to be made punishable by law. Norwegian law already provides for this.

(b) All sexual practices to be tolerated between consenting adults, provided that they are practised in private and do not offend public decency.

(c) A genuine transsexual who has obtained a change of sex by medical means to be entitled to a change of civil status to conform to the new identity. This is already provided for by law in the Federal Republic of Germany and Sweden, among others.

(d) Sexual minorities to be authorized to form associations provided their activities do not contravene the law on associations or other laws.

However, as the guardian of the welfare of the community, the State has the right, and perhaps also the duty, to take, in respect of sexual minorities, precautions similar to those which it takes, without being reproached for it, with regard to any activity likely to present a danger to the natural environment, the human environment or the person engaging in the activity himself (as in the case of fishing, hunting, operation of powered equipment, possession and carrying of weapons, selling of alcoholic beverages and drugs, gambling, etc). In this respect, common sense coincides with the underlying ethics of the Universal Declaration of Human Rights in that, in order to make freedom and equality as accessible as possible to all, individuals and the State itself are called on, in a spirit of brotherhood, to protect the weakest and most vulnerable. This leads to the conclusion that, in addition to protecting sexual minorities . . . against any kind of persecution, the State can and must protect society against the potential dangers which such practices represent for "morality, public order and the general welfare" (article 29, 2, of the Universal Declaration). Furthermore, in the event of a conflict between the respective rights of men, women and children, the guiding principle should be to provide greater protection for the most vulnerable person—in many cases women, and in all cases the child.

As part of their social defence responsibility, Governments and parliaments which feel unable to remain neutral with regard to such burning ethical and social issues could contemplate adopting (as the third element of an overall policy) the following legislation or regulations. (Italics found in study.)

(a) *With regard to transsexuality,* protect:

The transsexual himself by imposing a period of reflection, requiring him to attend consultations before deciding to undergo an irreversible operation, and even establishing a minimum age for such operations;

The medical profession against the temptation of deriving profit from requests for unnecessary treatment, by making the administering of hormones and sex change operations subject to certain rules;

The spouse against the distortion, by a transsexual spouse, of the meaning and purpose of marriage by according the right to present any objections before an irreversible operation and affording him the possibility of a divorce on the basis of the decision taken.

(b) *With regard to homosexuality,* protect the health of the population and of homosexuals themselves by taking the precautions recommended by the World Health Organization, in so far as the male homosexual community is known . . . to be one of the groups exposed to a number of contagious diseases.

With regard to homosexuals in positions of authority over children (teachers, etc.), a frequently raised question . . . a choice must be made between the wish to avoid exposing children to the influence of a deviant model and the wish to eliminate any possible discrimination against a minority. Although no specific answer will be suggested here, attention is again drawn to the principle, recognized in the International Declaration of the Rights of the Child, of the special safeguards to be afforded to children by virtue of their vulnerability.

(c) *With regard to propaganda for any abnormal sexual practice,* to protect the mental and moral well-being of the population, and in particular of young people, by regulating freedom of expression to the extent authorized by article 19, paragraph 3, of the International Covenant on Civil and Political Rights, by imposing on propaganda for such practices "certain restrictions, but these shall only be such as are provided by law and are necessary: (a) for respect of the rights or reputations of others; (b) for the protection of national security or of public order (ordre publique) or of public health or morals". This power of the State was recognized by the Human Rights Committee when considering a complaint against Finland.

(d) *With regard to paedophilia,* since minors are unable to protect themselves against adults, prohibit and severely punish any sexual relations between minors and adults (active paedophilia), even if the minor declares himself to be consenting. In view of the opportunities afforded to paedophiles by international tourism, standardize the age of sexual majority (age of consent) in all countries and for both girls and boys. This recommendation has already been made by the Council of Europe Parliamentary Assembly.

(e) *Concerning male prostitution,* proceed as recommended for female prostitution in Economic and Social Council resolution 1983/30, and, in particular, protect:

Young people by prohibiting, among other things, active soliciting in public places and the access of minors to certain establishments;

Prostitutes themselves against exploitation, by punishing procuring and collectively or bilaterally combating international traffic by *inter alia,* prohibiting the residence of foreign prostitutes.

The foregoing three groups of suggestions . . . obviously call for numerous consultations and lengthy consideration in order to weigh the advantages and disadvantages of legislating on moral values which are in a state of transition, in the knowledge that the criminalization of an act generally forces it underground, whereas its decriminalization (as in the case of abortion) leads to its proliferation. Another question is whether the measures . . . designed to protect young people do not run the risk—which it is hoped to avoid—of placing the individuals concerned under surveillance, making their marginalization official and even, as those concerned fear, encouraging a witch hunt. Consequently, the question of the advisability of a measure which would clearly be legitimate under the Universal Declaration of Human Rights and the Covenants, must be considered in the cultural and political context of each State.

The sub-commission was not able to consider the study at its 1987 session because, although completed, it had not been issued as a sub-commission document. The sub-commission requested (resolution 1987/31) that it be made available in document form and made available to it at the 1988 session. At that session, the study (UN Doc. E/CN.4/Sub.2/1988/31) was examined in connection with item 14 A of the agenda, "Question of slavery and the slave trade in all their practices and manifestations, including the slavery-like practices of *apartheid* and colonialism."

SEE ALSO Homosexuality: Discrimination; Transsexualism.

MINORITY RIGHTS. Protection of the rights of "minorities" has been a highly controversial question for the international community for many decades. The League of Nations devoted much time and attention to this question between the two world wars and served as a protective agency for a number of ethnic, linguistic, and national groups living in various countries, particularly in central Europe. But this machinery ceased to exist when the circumstances which had led to its creation ended with the close of the World War II, and the emphasis of the United Nations has since been upon protecting the enjoyment of all human rights by every individual rather than upon protecting special rights of any particular groups.

When the UN General Assembly adopted and proclaimed the **UNIVERSAL DECLARATION OF HUMAN RIGHTS** in 1948, it decided that it would not include a specific provision on the question of minorities. At the same time, it stated (resolution 217 C [III]) "that the United Nations cannot remain indifferent to the fate of minorities" and added that "it is difficult to adopt a uniform solution of this complex and delicate question, which has special aspects in each State in which it arises."

In 1953, the Economic and Social Council recommended (resolution 502 F [XVI] that "in the preparation of any international treaties, decisions of international organs, or other acts which establish new States, or new boundary lines between States, special attention should be paid to the protection of any minority which may be created thereby."

Several general international instruments, and at least one of regional application, touch upon the question of special protective measures for ethnic, religious, or linguistic groups. The CONVENTION ON THE PREVENTION AND PUNISHMENT OF THE CRIME OF GENOCIDE, for example, defines genocide as any of a number of acts "committed with intent to destroy, in whole or in part, a national, ethnical, racial or religious group, as such," and the contracting parties "confirm that genocide, whether committed in time of peace or in time of war, is a crime under international law which they undertake to prevent and punish." The ILO INDIGENOUS AND TRIBAL PEOPLES CONVENTION places upon governments (article 2) "the primary responsibility for developing co-ordinated and systematic action for the protection of the populations concerned and their progressive integration into the life of their respective countries," and provides (article 3) that "so long as the social, economic and cultural conditions of the populations concerned prevent them from enjoying the benefits of the general laws of the country to which they belong, special measures should be adopted for the protection of the institutions, persons property and labor of these populations." In the UNESCO CONVENTION AGAINST DISCRIMINATION IN EDUCATION, the States parties agree (article 5 [c]) that "it is essential to recognize the right of members of national minorities to carry on their own educational activities, including the maintenance of schools and, depending on the educational policy of each State, the use or the teaching of their own language," and set out the circumstances in which this right may be exercised. The EUROPEAN CONVENTION ON HUMAN RIGHTS contains a provision (article 14) in which "association with a national minority" is listed among a series of grounds upon which discrimination is prohibited. And the INTERNATIONAL COVENANT ON CIVIL AND POLITICAL RIGHTS, adopted by the UN General Assembly in 1966, includes an article on the rights of persons belonging to minorities which reads:

Article 27. In those States in which ethnic, religious or linguistic minorities exist, persons belonging to such minorities shall not be denied the right, in community with other members of their group, to enjoy their own culture, to profess and practice their own religion, or to use their own language.

Among the decisions of principal organs of the United Nations which have dealt with the question of special protective measures for ethnic, religious, or linguistic groups are three resolutions of the General Assembly: (1) on the future government of Palestine (resolution 181 [II]), (2) on the question of the disposal of the former Italian colonies (resolution 289 [IV]), and (3) on the question of Eritrea (resolution 390 [V]). In addition, the Statute of the City of Jerusalem, approved by the TRUSTEESHIP COUNCIL on 4 April 1950, provides special protective measures for ethnic, religious, or linguistic groups in articles dealing with human rights and fundamental freedoms (article 9), the legislative council (article 21), the judicial system (article 28), official and working languages (article 31), the educational system and cultural and benevolent institutions (article 32), and broadcasting and television (article 33).

From the texts of the instruments and decisions mentioned above, it may be inferred that the term "minority" is applied internationally to two distinct categories of persons: (a) minorities whose members desire equality with dominant groups in the sole sense of non-discrimination, and (b) those whose members desire equality with dominant groups in the sense of non-discrimination and the recognition of certain special rights and the rendering of certain positive services. The kind of "minority rights" that they feel they are entitled to claim if their equality within the State is to be real includes one or more of the following:

(a) provision of adequate primary and secondary education for the minority in its own language and its cultural traditions;

(b) provision for maintenance of the culture of the minority through the establishment and operation of schools, libraries, museums, media of information, and other cultural and educational institutions;

(c) provision of adequate facilities to the minority for the use of its language, either orally or in writing, in the legislature, before the courts, and in administration, and the granting of the right to use that language in private intercourse;

(d) provision for respect of the family law and personal status of the minority and their religious practices and interests; and

(e) provision of a certain degree of autonomy.

The rendering of such services may be effected either out of public funds or at the expense of the minority.

Study of the Rights of Minorities. At its 1967 session,

the UN SUB-COMMISSION ON PREVENTION OF DISCRIMINA-TION AND PROTECTION OF MINORITIES decided (resolution 9 [XX]) to initiate a study of the implementation of the principles set out in article 27 of the International Covenant on Civil and Political Rights, "with special reference to analyzing the concept of the minority taking into account the ethnic, religious and linguistic factors and considering the position of ethnic, religious and linguistic factors and considering the position of ethnic, religious or linguistic groups in multinational societies." The study was entrusted by the sub-commission to one of its members, Mr. Francesco Capotorti (Italy).

Completed in 1977, the study (UN Doc. E/CN.4/Sub.2/384 and Add. 1–7) was examined by the sub-commission at its session held in August of that year. The sub-commission expressed its appreciation (resolution 5 [XXX]) to the special rapporteur, endorsed his conclusions and recommendations, and requested him to present the report to the COMMISSION ON HUMAN RIGHTS at its 1978 session. It recommended that the commission consider the possibility of drafting a declaration on the rights of minorities within the framework of the principles set out in article 27 of the International Covenant on Civil and Political Rights.

In the study, the special rapporteur presented a tentative definition of the term "minority," drawn up with the application of article 27 in mind, suggesting that the term may be taken to mean

a group numerically inferior to the rest of the population of a State, in a non-dominant position, whose members—being nationals of the State—possess ethnic, religious or linguistic characteristics differing from those of the rest of the population and show, if only implicitly, a sense of solidarity, directed towards preserving their culture, traditions, religion or language.

The special rapporteur also made a number of recommendations for dealing with the problems of minorities, including (a) full use of the procedures of implementation contained in the International Covenant on Civil and Political Rights with regard to article 27 thereof; (b) provision of adequate procedures at the national level to deal effectively with violations of the rights granted to members of minority groups under article 27, and (c) preparation of a draft declaration on the rights of members of minority groups within the framework of the principles set forth in article 27. The special rapporteur also expressed his belief that bilateral agreements dealing with minority rights concluded between States where minorities lived and States from which such minorities originated (especially between neighboring countries) would be extremely useful, provided that coopera-

tion with regard to the rights of members of minority groups was based on mutual respect for the principles of the sovereignty and territorial integrity of the States concerned and non-interference in their internal affairs.

The sub-commission, (resolution 5 [XXX]) recommended that the commission consider the drafting of a declaration on the rights of members of minorities, as had been suggested by the special rapporteur. The commission established an open-ended working group for this purpose at its 1978 session and referred to it the draft of a declaration proposed by Yugoslavia (UN Doc. E/CN.4/L. 1367/Rev.1).

The working group was unable to complete its task during the commission's 1978 session. Similar working groups were set up each year to examine and revise the draft declaration. However, the text was not in form to be considered by the commission as late as 1988. The commission decided (resolution 1988/64) to establish another such working group for this purpose at its 1989 session.

The sub-commission, which had been following the slow progress of the commission in this endeavor, took up the question of the protection of minorities again at its 1988 session and expressed the view that there was a need to explore more practical approaches to the subject in line, *inter alia,* with the conclusions of its special rapporteur on the subject, Mr. Capotori. Accordingly, it invited (resolution 1988/36) one of its members, Ms. Claire Palley (United Kingdom) to prepare a working paper on possible ways and means to facilitate the peaceful and constructive resolution of situations involving racial, national, religious, and linguistic minorities.

In the working paper which she presented to the sub-commission at its 1989 session (E/CN.4/Sub.2/1989/43), Ms. Palley made the following proposal (sect. 5, para. 23–25):

In its resolution on the "fate of minorities", the General Assembly observed 40 years ago that it is "difficult to adopt a uniform solution to this complex and delicate question, which has special aspects in each State in which it arises". This remains valid, and cautions against any attempt to construct solutions from general theories or a small sample of national experiences. At the same time, it would appear preferable to adopt a thematic approach to the study of situations involving minorities, because this affords a more global perspective and balance than methods which respond to particular cases.

It is also clear that a study of minorities must initially focus on the analysis of examples of successful national action, so that it is possible to determine what kinds of United Nations action, if any, can strengthen the minorities is still an ongoing concern. Since national situations are so varied and complex, the ultimate goal of the exercise must be to contribute to the formation of effective national institutions, based on comparative experience and some useful models, rather than to develop a catalogue of specific prescriptive measures.

To begin this work, the Sub-Commission may wish to consider the appointment of a special rapporteur to prepare a survey of relevant national experience based on information available from all sources with a view to:

(a) identifying positive examples of achieving or surpassing the requirements of article 27, which can serve as models;

(b) identifying situations in which the programme of advisory services could be used effectively to strengthen or restore unity by supporting relevant national institutions for minorities.

Ms. Palley further suggested that in carrying out the mandate, the special rapporteur might be guided by the following principles (sect. 6, para. 26):

(a) the paramount importance of non-discrimination, as well as the full participation of all individuals and groups, as contained in the two International Covenants of Human Rights and in the Declaration on the Right to Development;

(b) the necessity of promoting the rights and development of minorities in a manner that is consistent with the unity and stability of States, in light of the Declaration of Principles on Friendly Relations and Co-operation Among States;

(c) the dangers posed by ethnic conflict for regional as well as national security;

(d) the importance of both negative (non-discrimination) and positive (special assistance or status) measures for the effective protection of minorities;

(e) the role of the development process in removing economic and social obstacles to co-operation and mutual respect among all groups in national society;

(f) the necessity of ensuring that measures adopted to protect minorities also respect the human rights of majorities.

Finally, Ms. Palley suggested that, as a first step in developing a useful analysis, the special rapporteur circulate a questionnaire to governments and to interested non-governmental organizations, soliciting information of a specific and practical nature. He would then be in a position to present an analytical report for discussion at the sub-commission's 1991 session. She included in the working paper, as an annex, the following proposed questionnaire on national experience in the protection of minorities:

The extent to which minorities:

(1) are recognized in States' legal/political institutions;

(2) enjoy educational or cultural institutions specifically designed to meet their needs, or different forms of autonomy;

(3) have continued to use and to be educated in their own languages, and how practical difficulties in this, if any, have been overcome;

(4) have been able to achieve improvements in their social and economic conditions, relative to national society as a whole;

(5) benefit from positive measures or affirmative action, and the experience gained from the use of such measures;

(6) maintain contacts with other members of their group across State borders, and any difficulties experienced with this;

(7) enjoy direct representation in national legislative bodies and participated in elections, holding public office, and public service generally;

(8) participate in the planning, implementation and benefits of development activities, and by what institutional means;

(9) have benefited from agrarian reform or resettlement programmes, and any difficulties encountered.

The sub-commission, having examined Ms. Palley's working paper, concluded (resolution 1989/44) that it could best contribute to preventing situations involving minorities by studying and promoting positive measures for the development of minorities and for the peaceful and constructive solution of problems concerning them within the States in which they live. Convinced of the need for the study and dissemination of positive and practical approaches to questions of the assimilation, integration, or autonomy of minorities, it expressed its appreciation to Ms. Palley for her proposals and decided to entrust another of its members, Mr. Asbjorn Eide (Norway) with the preparation of a further report on national experience in this field, in accordance with the guidelines and principles contained in the working paper. Mr. Eide was invited to present a progress report to the sub-commission at its 1990 session.

SEE ALSO *Ethnic Minorities: World Guide; Minorities: Sexual; Working Group on the Rights of Persons Belonging to National, Ethnic, Religious and Linguistic Minorities.*

MINORITY RIGHTS GROUP. An international non-governmental organization in consultative status (Roster) with the UN Economic and Social Council, MRG is affiliated with 17 organizations in 16 countries.

The Minority Rights Group was established in the late 1960s following the Biafra conflict in Nigeria. MRG is a global, impartial, and independent specialized research and information unit that has three principal aims: (1) to secure justice for groups suffering discrimination, by investigating their situation and publicizing the facts to educate and alert public opinion throughout the world; (2) to help prevent, through publicity about violations of human rights, such problems from developing into destructive conflicts; and (3) to foster, by its research findings, international understanding of factors which create prejudiced treatment and group tensions. To implement its goals, MRG monitors developments worldwide in minority situations, prepares impartial reports on these subjects, and disseminates the reports to several hundred newspapers and television and radio stations throughout the world, as well as making them available to universities, libraries, schools, and interested individuals. The group also organizes meeting and lectures and commissions multi-disciplinary research into the causes of human rights problems and their possible solution. In 1982, in recognition of its work, MRG was awarded the United Nations Association Media Peace Prize.

MRG has an extensive publication program. Its primary publication is the newsletter *Outsider.* Since its inception, MRG has published 77 reports and updates on minority situations, including *Japan's Minorities, Roma: Europe's Gypsies, The Amerindians of South America, Western Europe's Migrant Workers, The Social Psychology of Minorities,* and *The Falashas: the Jews of Ethiopia.* On average, MRG produces five new reports and ten up-dated reports annually.

Minority Rights Group. Address: 29 Craven Street, London WC2N 5NT, UK. Telephone: 930-6659. Director: Alan Phillips.

MONACO. The Principality of Monaco is a country in western Europe, on the Mediterranean Sea, almost totally surrounded by France. After 800 years of independence, Monaco was annexed to France in 1793. It was under the protection of Sardinia from 1815 to 1861, when it returned to French guardianship as an independent nation. Although not a member of the United Nations, it has observer status there.

Monaco's population is estimated by the UN (1990) to be 28,000. Ethnic and national groups include Monegasque (16%), French (47%), and Italian (16%). Languages in common use include French (official), Italian, and Monegasque. Christianity (Roman Catholic, 95%) is the predominant religion. Literacy is estimated at 99%.

The government (1990) took the form of a monarchy. Under the constitution of 1962, the ruler, Prince Rainier III, is head of State. He is assisted by an 18-member National Council, members of which are elected by popular vote for terms of five years. Executive authority is vested in the Minister of State, who is the head of government. The judicial system includes the Court of First Instance, the Court of Appeal, the Court of High Appeal, the Criminal Court, and the Supreme Court. The only political party is the National and Democratic Union.

MONGOLIA. Formerly known as Outer Mongolia, the Mongolian People's Republic is a country in east Asia that once was the home of the Mongols under the leadership of Kublai Khan. It has borders with China and the Union of Soviet Socialist Republics. From 1689 to 1912, it was under Manchu rule; but, after the fall of the Manchus, it declared its independence and expelled the Chinese officials. Soviet troops entered the country in 1921 and assisted in the establishment of a Socialist Republic, which was recognized as an independent country in the Chinese–Russian Treaty of 1945. It became a member of the United Nations in 1961. Its total population is estimated by the UN (1990) to be 2,188,000. Ethnic groups include the Kazakh minority, the Kahlka-speaking Mongols, and other Mongolian-language groups: Durbets, Bayts, Buryats, Zalehchins, Olets, and Torguts. Languages commonly used include Mongolian, Kahlka, and a number of native languages. Buddhism (Lamaistic) is the religion practiced by those who profess a religion or belief, but the number of adherents has declined since the establishment of the People's Republic in 1924. There is a Buddhist temple in Ulan Bator, in which lamas hold prayer services and to which citizens who are believers have free access; attached to it there is a religious school which trains priests. Under article 86 of the constitution, religion is separate from the State and from schools. Literacy is estimated at 80%.

The government (1990) took the form of a republic. The Great People's Khural (parliament) is the organ of State power; its members are elected by popular vote for terms of four years, and it is convened annually. The presidium of the Khural consists of a chairman, two vice chairmen, a secretary, and six members. The chairman of the presidium is head of State. Executive powers are exercised by the Council of Ministers, also set up by the Khural, and by its chairman, who serves as premier. The courts and the procurator's offices of the Mongolian People's Republic are obliged, under the constitution, the Act on the Judicial System, and the Acts on Procuratorial Supervision, directly to safeguard all the rights and interests of citizens.

As regards the situation of nationalities and ethnic groups in Mongolia, the government stated in a report presented to the **COMMITTEE ON THE ELIMINATION OF RACIAL DISCRIMINATION** on 12 February 1987 (UN Doc. CERD/149/Add. 23):

Twenty-five nationalities and ethnic groups live in Mongolia. Of these the most numerous are the Kazakhs, who form 5.4 per cent of the population. The Bayan-Uul *aimak* (region), where most of the Kazakhs live, has rapidly developing industry, agriculture, transport, communications and culture.

Its regional construction industry undertakes building work not only within the region itself, but also in the neighbouring five *aimaks.* Apart from food industry enterprises, there are also fuel and power enterprises, and these supply all the needs of the region. As a result of the rapid introduction of modern methods in stock-raising and the reinforcement of its material foundation, the sector, which consists of 11 agricultural combines (co-operatives), two State farms and one inter-combine enterprise, has developed intensively.

The level of social and cultural development of Kazakh workers may be indicated simply by recalling that in all *somons* (main administrative districts) there is an eight-year school, an inter-*somon* united hospital or medical station, a mobile cinema, a library, a kindergarten, a creche, an hotel, shops, a cafeteria, a domestic services department, and other social amenities. There are 74 hospital beds per 1,000 *aimak* residents and a doctor for every 900 people.

Much attention is being focused on the development of the culture of national minorities. The material foundation of art and culture existing in the country today consists of more than 20 professional art institutions, 23 palaces of culture, more than 300 clubs, 470 libraries with 9 million books, 640 reading rooms and 36 museums; this serves the equal development of the culture of nationalities, national groups and the whole population of the country.

In the areas inhabited by national minorities, theatres and musical and drama groups have been set up. The Bayan-Uul *aimak* has its own Kazakh theatre of music and drama, which puts on plays in the Kazakh language. The theatre has drama, orchestral and dance sections, and also a musical group which plays the national musical instrument, the dombre.

There is an ethnographic museum in the *aimak* which shows the development of Kazakh culture and art, as well as a printing house which publishes books in the Kazakh language, and national libraries. The cinemas show films in both Kazakh and Mongolian.

The national arts festival which takes place throughout the country every five years is another effective way of developing the culture of nationalities and national groups. More than 100,000 of the 450,000 participants at the 1986 festival worked in livestock-raising and farming. All the nationalities and national groupings were represented here. . . .

With regard to the employment of human rights, the government stated in the same report that:

Citizens of the Mongolian People's Republic are guaranteed a wide range of civil, political, economic, social and cultural rights.

The country's Constitution and legislation on the one hand proclaim and guarantee equal rights for all citizens without distinction, exception, limitation or privilege, and on the other hand prohibit and punish discrimination, including racial, national or ethnic discrimination.

In particular, article 83 of the Mongolian Constitution provides: "Citizens of the Mongolian People's Republic, irrespective of their nationality, have equal rights in all spheres of the economic, cultural, social and political life of the country. Any direct or indirect restriction of the rights of citizens on account of their nationality or race and the advocacy of the ideas of chauvinism or nationalism are forbidden by law".

This constitutional principle is reflected in a series of other pieces of legislation which contains norms that develop this principle and make it more specific, proclaim

and guarantee the equality of citizens and the preclusion of discrimination in the areas of public life to which they apply, provide for sanctions for violations of the principle of equality and measures to verify its observance, and set up a procedure for appeal against acts of discrimination and for the restoration of the violated rights and compensation for damage caused in the event of discrimination.

The system of State and administrative bodies in the Mongolian People's Republic, the way they are established, and all the institutions of constitutional law ensure that it is impossible to found an organization which has aims contradictory to our country's Constitution, or to establish associations of people, including organizations, which propagate theories and ideas of racial superiority.

The provisions of the Constitution and of other legislative acts which prohibit racial and national discrimination have equal force for all bodies of State power and for all officials.

An important role in ensuring that all the activities of State bodies comply with this requirement is played by the Procurator's Offices and people's control bodies, which supervise and monitor the observation of the law by all institutions, organizations, officials and citizens.

An important guarantee affirmed in the Constitution (article 85) is the right of citizens to lodge an appeal against illegal and discriminatory actions by State bodies which violate the principle of equality. . . .

MONGOLIA: CONSTITUTION.

The Constitution of the Mongolian People's Republic contains the following provisions (articles 76–89) specifically relating to human rights and fundamental freedoms:

Chapter 7
The Basic Rights and Freedoms of Citizens and Their Guarantees

Article 76. Citizens of the Mongolian People's Republic have equal rights irrespective of sex, race, and nationality, religious persuasion, social origin and status.

Article 77. Citizens of the MPR have the right to work and to payment for their work in accordance with its quantity and quality.

This right is ensured by all the advantages of the socialist economic system established in the MPR, which gives every citizen of MPR full opportunity to apply his or her knowledge and labour without let or hindrance in any branch of the economy and culture and to receive a guaranteed remuneration in accordance with the labour expended.

Article 78. Citizens of the MPR have the right to rest and leisure.

This right is ensured by the establishment of an eight-hour working day, reduction of the working day for a number of special trades and professions, the fixing of a weekly day of rest, and the establishment of annual vacations for workers and other employees with retention of pay, and the provision for working people of sanatoria and holiday homes, theatres, clubs, and other institutions serving the working people.

The policy of the MPR shall be directed to increasing the working people's free time in the future, as the country's productive forces are developed, by reducing working time and improving various services and bringing them closer to the working people so that they can use their free time more and more not only for leisure but also for their physical and intellectual development and to improve their knowledge.

Article 79. Citizens of the MPR have the right to financial aid in old age, in case of loss of working capacity, illness and loss of the breadwinner.

This right is ensured by providing working people with assistance through a system of social insurance, state retirement pensions, special funds of co-operative organisations, by broad development of a system of therapeutic institutions and health resorts, by free medical aid for working people, and by the development of a system of labour protection.

Article 80. Citizens of the MPR have the right to education. This right is ensured by free education, broad development of a system of general schools, secondary specialist institutions, higher educational establishments, development of a system for improving skills and raising qualifications, and a system of state grants for students of secondary specialist institutions and higher schools.

Article 81. Citizens of the MPR have the right to participate freely in governing the state and society and in directing the country's economic affairs both through their representative bodies and directly. This right is ensured by providing all citizens with a real opportunity for broad participation in all spheres of the country's national, political, economic, and cultural development, and in particular in elections, referendums, in providing the state control, the organisation of various democratic societies, and so on.

All citizens of the MPR, who have reached 18 years of age, with the exception of persons certified as insane, shall be granted the right to vote and to be elected to all organs of state authority.

Article 82. Citizens of the MPR have the right to associate in public and social organisations: trade unions, co-operative associations, youth, sport, and other organisations; cultural and scientific societies, and societies for furthering peace and friendship among nations, etc.

The most active and conscientious citizens from the ranks of the workers, co-operative arats, and working intelligentsia, are united in the Mongolian People's Revolutionary Party, which is the vanguard and leader of all state and other mass organisations of the working people.

Article 83. Citizens of the MPR, irrespective of their nationality, have equal rights in all spheres of the country's state, economic, cultural, social and political affairs.

Any direct or indirect limitations of the rights of citizens for reasons of race or nationality, and any preaching of ideas of chauvinism and nationalism are forbidden by law. The MPR ensures members of all nationalities living on its territory the opportunity to develop their national culture, and to study and carry on business in their native language.

The MPR accords the right of asylum to foreign citizens persecuted for defending the interests of the working people, for involvement in the national liberation struggle, for activity to further peace, or for scientific activity.

Article 84. Women are accorded equal rights with men in the MPR in all spheres of economic, state, cultural, and socio-political affairs. Exercise of these rights is ensured by granting women equal conditions with men for work, leisure, social insurance, and education, and by state protection of the interests of mother and child, state assistance for mothers of many children, the granting of paid leave to women during pregnancy and after childbirth, and extension of the system of maternity homes, creches, and kindergartens.

It is prohibited by law to impair women's equality in any form whatsoever.

Article 85. Every citizen of the Mongolian People's Republic has the right freely to apply to any body of state authority and administration and to submit written or verbal complaints and statements concerning the unlawful actions of state bodies or individual officials, and concerning cases of a display of bureaucracy and red tape. State bodies and officials are obliged to consider statements and complaints received without delay, take steps to eliminate breaches of law and order, and give the complainant an answer to the substance of his or her application or complaint.

Article 86. Religions is separated from the state and school in the Mongolian People's Republic. Citizens of the MPR are accorded freedom of conscience and of anti-religious propaganda.

Article 87. In accordance with the interests of the working people and in order to develop and consolidate the state system of the MPR, citizens of the MPR are guaranteed by law:

1. freedom of speech;
2. freedom of the press;
3. freedom of assembly and meeting;
4. freedom of demonstration and procession.

These rights and freedoms shall be ensured by granting working people and their organisations the material conditions needed to exercise them.

Article 88. Citizens of the Mongolian People's Republic are ensured inviolability of the person and of their dwellings and the secrecy of their correspondence. No one may be arrested other than by a court order or the warrant of a procurator.

Chapter 8
The Basic Duties of Citizens

Article 89. All citizens of the Mongolian People's Republic are obliged:

(1) to devote all their strength and knowledge to the building of socialism, remembering that honest, conscientious labour for the good of society is the source of the socialist state's growth in wealth and might and of improving the well-being of the working people;

(2) to observe strictly the Constitution of the MPR, to carry out its laws exactly and abide by labour discipline, to observe the rules of the socialist way of life and to fight actively against all anti-social phenomena;

(3) to ensure unity of personal and social interests, and to put the interests of society and the state first;

(4) to guard the sacred and inviolable basis of the socialist system—public socialist property—as the apple of their eye, and to strengthen and multiply it in every way;

(5) to consider the furthering of international friendship of nations in every way an objective necessity, and by deed in their own sector through their practical activities to promote the strengthening of friendship and solidarity of the working people and unity and solidarity of the peoples of the socialist camp headed by the Soviet Union, to fight resolutely against phenomena of any kind liable to damage that sacred friendship and unity;

(6) to bring up the rising generation in a spirit of industry, discipline and good organisation, collectivism, and respect for society's interests, in the spirit of a communist attitude to work and socialist property, of boundless devotion to the socialist Motherland, the ideas of communism,

and the principles of proletarian internationalism, and in a spirit of respect for all working people without distinction of nationality;

(7) to co-operate actively in strengthening the people's democratic system, to guard state secrets strictly, and to be vigilant as regards enemies;

(8) to defend the socialist Motherland scrupulously against the enemies of socialism, military service in the People's Army of the MPR being an honourable duty of citizens of the MPR;

(9) to fulfil all their civil duties exactly and require the same of other citizens.

MOROCCO. The Kingdom of Morocco is a country in northern Africa, on the Atlantic Ocean. It has borders with Algeria and Mauritania. It achieved independence from France in 1956 and became a member of the United Nations the same year. Its population is estimated by the UN (1990) to be 24,616,000. Moroccans are largely of Arab–Berber descent, but the national census provides no breakdown as to race, language, or ethnic group. Languages commonly used include Arabic (official), French, Spanish, and several Berber vernaculars. Islam is the religion of the State; Jewish and Christian communities practice their religion in accordance with Moroccan law, which vests them with legal personality and enables them to own immovable property. Literacy is estimated at 28%.

The government (1990) took the form of a monarchy, with the king as ruler and head of State. Executive authority as head of government is exercised by the prime minister, who represents the party of coalition given the majority of elected seats in the 306-member Chamber of Deputies (of the 306 members, 204 are elected by popular vote, while the remainder is chosen by local councils and groups). Political parties include the Constitutional Union Party, the National Democratic Party, the Popular Movement, and *Isviglol.*

Throughout most of its history, Morocco has been invaded and occupied by colonial forces. Once an outpost of the Roman Empire, it was seized by the Vandals after the Roman collapse. Later the Arabs invaded and brought Islam to the country, all but wiping out Christianity. Jewish colonies in Morocco, however, retained their religion, prospered, and increased in size.

Morocco first became an independent State in 788. But, after a period of unrest, its coastline was seized by Spain and Portugal soon after they had dispelled the Moors (people from Morocco) from the Iberian Peninsula. The Spanish remained in the country through the 20th century.

In the 20th century, France seized some of its territory, and the Germans threatened to take it away by force. They agreed, instead, to recognize Morocco as a French protectorate in exchange for the cession of French territory in Equatorial Africa. French Morocco remained loyal to the Vichy government even after the fall of France in 1940, at which time both France and Germany rushed to reorganize its economy in order to feed their people. Spanish Morocco, however, was partly occupied by Mauritania and eventually the Spanish, who had promised the territory self-determination, withdrew.

The question of Moroccan independence was raised in the UN General Assembly in 1951, when six Arab States complained of violations by France of the principles of the UNITED NATIONS CHARTER and of the UNIVERSAL DECLARATION OF HUMAN RIGHTS and asked the assembly to look into the matter. When the assembly postponed consideration of the matter, the question of Morocco was raised again at the next session of the assembly by 13 States which charged that stringent French rule had compromised the sovereignty of the country and that the national movement in Morocco was being oppressed. In a resolution adopted on 19 December 1952, the assembly expressed its confidence that France would "endeavor to further fundamental liberties of the people of Morocco" and that the parties would "continue negotiations toward developing the free political institutions of the people of Morocco."

In 1953, 15 Asian and African countries requested an urgent meeting of the UN Security Council to investigate the danger to international peace and security arising out of the intervention of France in Morocco and the overthrow of its legitimate sovereign, Sultan Mohammed V. The issue was not included in the council's agenda, France maintaining that the United Nations had no right to intervene since the question was one of domestic jurisdiction. The issue was later discussed at three sessions of the General Assembly.

On 2 March 1956, a joint declaration on the status of Morocco was signed by France and Morocco by which France recognized the independence of Morocco.

Western Sahara. In 1975, many thousands of Moroccans marched into Spanish Sahara in support of their government's claim that the northern part of the area was legally a part of Morocco. The Moroccan government subsequently annexed the northern two-thirds of Spanish Morocco, and Mauritania annexed the southern one-third. Spain withdrew, giving up its earlier demand for self-determination for the peoples of the sparsely populated area which is rich in phosphates.

The Polisario Front, a guerrilla movement, declared Spanish Sahara to be independent and launched attacks against the two annexing States. Morocco, with military and economic assistance from the United

States of America, retained its hold on the northern portion of the territory, but Mauritania withdrew from the southern portion in 1979 after signing a treaty with the Polisario Front. Morocco then completed its annexation of the entire Spanish Sahara. In the face of protests by the leaders of neighboring African countries, Morocco in 1981 agreed to an internationally supervised referendum to determine the fate of the area.

Since 1986, the chairman of the Organization of African Unity and the UN secretary-general have joined in offering their good offices with a view to promoting a just and lasting solution of the question of Western Sahara. On 30 August 1988, their proposals concerning the referendum were agreed in principle by the Kingdom of Morocco and the *Frente Popular.* However, the conditions necessary for holding the referendum—without any administrative or military constraints, and organized and supervised by the United Nations in cooperation with the OAU—had not been met up to 11 December 1989, when the General Assembly appealed (resolution 44/88) to both parties to display the cooperation and the political goodwill necessary to achieve an acceptable solution.

MOVEMENT AND RESIDENCE. The right to freedom of movement and residence is proclaimed in article 13 of the UNIVERSAL DECLARATION OF HUMAN RIGHTS, which reads:

Article 13. 1. Everyone has the right to freedom of movement and residence within the borders of each State.

2. Everyone has the right to leave any country, including his own, and to return to his country.

Freedom of movement and residence is also the subject of articles 12 and 13 of the INTERNATIONAL COVENANT ON CIVIL AND POLITICAL RIGHTS, which read as follows:

Article 12. 1. Everyone lawfully within the territory of a State shall, within that territory, have the right to liberty of movement and freedom to choose his residence.

2. Everyone shall be free to leave any country, including his own.

3. The above-mentioned rights shall not be subject to any restrictions except those which are provided by law, are necessary to protect national security, public order (*ordre public*), public health or morals or the rights and freedoms of others, and are consistent with the other rights recognized in the present Covenant.

4. No one shall be arbitrarily deprived of the right to enter his own country.

Article 13. An alien lawfully in the territory of a State Party to the present Covenant may be expelled therefrom only in pursuance of a decision reached in accordance with law and shall, except where compelling reasons of national security otherwise require, be allowed to submit the reasons against his expulsion and to have his case reviewed by, and be represented for the purpose before, the competent authority or a person or persons especially designated by the competent authority.

Discrimination denying freedom of movement and residence on the grounds of race, color, or national or ethnic origin is prohibited by article 5 of the INTERNATIONAL CONVENTION ON THE ELIMINATION OF ALL FORMS OF RACIAL DISCRIMINATION, which reads in part as follows:

Article 5. In compliance with the fundamental obligations laid down in article 2, States Parties undertake to prohibit and to eliminate racial discrimination in all its forms and to guarantee the right of everyone, without distinction as to race, colour, or national or ethnic origin, to equality before the law, notably in the enjoyment of the following rights:. . . .

(d) other civil rights, in particular:

(i) The right to freedom of movement and residence within the border of the State;

(ii) The right to leave any country, including his own, and to return to one's country. . . .

(f) The right of access to any place or service intended for use by the general public, such as transport, hotels, restaurants, cafes, theatres, and parks.

Discrimination denying freedom of movement and residence on the ground of sex is prohibited by article 15 of the CONVENTION ON THE ELIMINATION OF ALL FORMS OF DISCRIMINATION AGAINST WOMEN, which reads in part as follows:

Article 15. 4. States parties shall accord to men and women the same rights with regard to the law relating to the movement of persons and the freedom to choose their residence and domicile.

The AMERICAN CONVENTION ON HUMAN RIGHTS, open for acceptance by member States of the ORGANIZATION OF AMERICAN STATES, provides that:

Article 22. 1. Every person lawfully in the territory of a State Party has the right to move about in it, and to reside in it subject to the provisions of the law.

2. Every person has the right to leave any country freely, including his own.

3. The exercise of the foregoing rights may be restricted only pursuant to a law to the extent necessary in a democratic society to prevent crime or to protect national security, public safety, public order, public morals, public health, or the rights or freedoms of others.

4. The exercise of the rights recognized in paragraph 1 may also be restricted by law in designated zones for reasons of public interest.

The AFRICAN CHARTER OF HUMAN AND PEOPLE'S RIGHTS, open for acceptance by member States of the ORGANIZATION OF AFRICAN UNITY, contains the following provision:

Article 12. 1. Every individual shall have the right to freedom of movement and residence within the borders of a State provided he abides by the law.

2. Every individual shall have the right to leave any country including his own, and to return to his country. This right may only be subject to restrictions, provided for by law for the protection of national security, law and order, public health or morality.

3. Every individual shall have the right, when persecuted, to seek and obtain asylum in other countries in accordance with the laws of those countries and international conventions.

4. A non-national legally admitted in a territory of a State Party to the present Charter, may only be expelled from it by virtue of a decision taken in accordance with the law.

5. The mass expulsion of non-nationals shall be prohibited. Mass expulsion shall be that which is aimed at national, racial, ethnic or religious groups.

The EUROPEAN CONVENTION ON HUMAN RIGHTS: PROTOCOL IV adds the following provisions to the text of the convention:

Article 2. 1. Everyone lawfully within the territory of a State shall, within that territory, have the right to liberty of movement and freedom to choose his residence.

2. Everyone shall be free to leave any country, including his own.

3. No restrictions shall be placed on the exercise of these rights other than such as are in accordance with law and are necessary in a democratic society in the interests of national security or public safety, for the maintenance of *ordre public,* for the prevention of crime, for the protection of health or morals, or for the protection of the rights and freedoms of others.

4. The rights set forth in paragraph 1 may also be subject, in particular areas, to restrictions imposed in accordance with law and justified by the public interest in a democratic society.

Article 3. 1. No one shall be expelled, by means either of an individual or of a collective measure, from the territory of the State of which he is a national.

2. No one shall be deprived of the right to enter the territory of the State of which he is a national.

Article 4. Collective expulsion of aliens is prohibited.

The EUROPEAN CONVENTION ON HUMAN RIGHTS, PROTOCOL VI, adds the following provision:

Article 1. 1. An alien lawfully resident in the territory of a State shall not be expelled therefrom except in pursuance of a decision reached in accordance with law and shall be allowed:

    a. to submit reasons against his expulsion,

    b. to have his case reviewed, and

    c. to be represented for these purposes before the competent authority or a person or persons designated by that authority.

2. An alien may be expelled before the exercise of his rights under paragraph 1(a), (b) and (c) of this Article, when such expulsion is necessary in the interests of public order or is grounded on reasons of national security.

Expulsion. After examining reports submitted by States parties on the International Covenant on Civil and Political Rights in accordance with article 40 of that instrument, the HUMAN RIGHTS COMMITTEE adopted, in 1986, general comments on article 13 of that instrument, as follows (UN Doc.A/41/40, Annex VI, para. 9–10):

Many reports have given insufficient information on matters relevant to article 13. That article is applicable to all procedures aimed at the obligatory departure of an alien, whether described in national law as expulsion or otherwise. If such procedures entail arrest, the safeguards of the Covenant relating to deprivation of liberty (arts. 9 and 10) may also be applicable. If the arrest is for the particular purpose of extradition, other provisions of national and international law may apply. Normally an alien who is expelled must be allowed to leave for any country that agrees to take him. The particular rights of article 13 only protect those aliens who are lawfully in the territory of a State party. This means that national law concerning the requirements for entry and stay must be taken into account in determining the scope of that protection, and that illegal entrants and aliens who have stayed longer than the law or their permits allow, in particular, are not covered by its provisions. However, if the legality of an alien's entry or stay is in dispute, any decision on this point leading to his expulsion or deportation ought to be taken in accordance with article 13. It is for the competent authorities of the State party, in good faith and in the exercise of their powers, to apply and interpret the domestic law, observing, however, such requirements under the Covenant as equality before the law (art. 26).

Article 13 directly regulates only the procedure and not the substantive grounds for expulsion. However, by allowing only those carried out "in pursuance of a decision reached in accordance with law", its purpose is clearly to prevent arbitrary expulsions. On the other hand, it entitles each alien to a decision in his own case and, hence, article 13 would not be satisfied with laws or decisions providing for collective or mass expulsions. This understanding, in the opinion of the Committee, is confirmed by further provisions concerning the right to submit reasons against expulsion and to have the decision reviewed by and to be represented before the competent authority or someone designated by it. An alien must be given full facilities for pursuing his remedy against expulsion so that this right will in all the circumstances of his case be an effective one. The principles of article 13 relating to appeal against expulsion and the entitlement to review by a competent authority may only be departed from when "compelling reasons of national security" so require. Discrimination may not be made between different categories of aliens in the application of article 13.

SEE ALSO European Agreement on Regulations concerning the Movement of Persons between Member States of the Council of Europe; European Convention on Human Rights: Protocol IV; Helsinki Accord: Cooperation in Humanitarian and Other Fields; Helsinki Accord: Final Act of the Conference on Security and Cooperation in Europe; Helsinki Accord: Human Dimension of the Conference on Security and Cooperation in Europe; Right to Leave Any Country, including One's Own, and to Return to One's Own Country.

MOZAMBIQUE. The People's Republic of Mozambique is a country in eastern Africa, on the Indian Ocean. It has borders with Malawi, South Africa, Swaziland, Tanzania, Zambia, and Zimbabwe. It achieved independence from Portugal in 1975 and became a member of the United Nations the same year. Its population is estimated by the UN (1990) to be 16,416,000. Ethnic groups include many indigenous tribal groups and persons of European, Euro–African, and Indian descent. Languages commonly used are Portuguese (official) and a number of Bantu vernaculars. Religions practiced include Animism (48%), Christianity (17%), and Islam (17%). Literacy is estimated at 15%.

The government (1990) took the form of a republic. President Joaquim Alberto Chissano, as head of State and Government, exercises executive authority with the assistance of a cabinet which he appoints. Legislation is prepared by the People's Assembly. The judiciary is modelled on the Portuguese system of civil law. The only political party is the National Front for the Liberation of Mozambique (FRELIMO), which was led through the 10-year war for independence by Mr. Chissano.

A Portuguese colony for 470 years, Mozambique won its guerrilla war for independence after its national liberation movement, FRELIMO, overwhelmed 40,000 troops sent from Portugal and forced a ceasefire in 1974, an event which promised independence. However, the new Marxist government spent the following 14 years in fighting anti-government guerrillas backed by South Africa and in trying to feed its people suffering from a prolonged drought.

Mozambique's economic problems were intensified by the immigration of nearly all the country's white farmers, civil servants, and professionals, many of whom had been subjected to brutality by the insurgents, by increasing indebtedness, by the continuing war against guerrilla forces, and by widespread and persistent shortages of food.

MUSLIM WORLD LEAGUE. An international non-governmental organization in consultative status with the UN Economical and Social Council (Category II), and with UNESCO. Founded in 1962, the league explains and publicizes Islamic culture, its teachings, and ideology. It seeks to further Islamic unity and coordinate Muslim policies and to strengthen the struggle of the Muslim people for the restoration of their religious rights.

MWL's publications include *Akhbar Al-Alam Al-Islami* (weekly) in Arabic; *Majalla Rabitah Al-Alam Al-Islami* (monthly) in Arabic; and *The Journal* (monthly) in English.

Muslim World League. Address: Rabita, P.O. Box 538, Makkah, Saudi Arabia.

Yearbook of International Organizations 1989/90 (K. G. Saur).

MYANMAR. The Union of Myanmar, formerly known as Burma, is a country in southeastern Asia, on the Bay of Bengal, occupying the northwest portion of the Indochinese Peninsula. It has borders with Bangladesh, China, India, Laos, and Thailand. It achieved independence from Great Britain in 1948 and became a member of the United Nations the same year. Its population is estimated by the UN (1990) to be 40,848,000. Ethnic groups include the Burmese (70%), Shan (9%), Karen (7%), Rakhine (4%), Chinese (5%), and Indian (2%). Languages commonly used include Burmese and English. Hinayana Buddhism is the religion of 85% of the population; the remaining 15% practice Christianity, Islam or Animism. Literacy is estimated at 78%.

The government (1990) took the form of a republic. Up to 1988, the Burma Socialist Program Party held a monopoly on power which lasted for 26 years and was dedicated to the creation of a socialist welfare State. However, on 10 September 1988, that party was forced by widespread anti-government rioting to end that monopoly and to call for multi-party elections. Later that month, the demonstrations for democracy were crushed by military gunfire, said to have killed more than 3,000 persons and to have forced thousands of student to flee the country.

On 8 March 1989, the UN COMMISSION ON HUMAN RIGHTS adopted a decision entitled "Situation in Burma" (decision 1989/112) in which it expressed concern at the reports and allegations of violations of human rights in Myanmar in 1988 and also at the obstacles to be overcome in the way of the implementation of the democratic aspirations of the people. The commission decided (a) to encourage the government authorities to take all measures necessary to assure fundamental freedoms, including freedom of expression, freedom of assembly, and freedom of association, with a view to enhancing the prospects for democracy; (b) to note that the Myanmar authorities have been responding to the requests by rapporteurs on specific subjects; (c) to welcome the undertaking by the government authorities to organize free and fair multi-party democratic elections; (d) to urge the Myanmar authorities to implement their undertaking as early as possible with a view to assuring the human rights and fundamental freedoms of the people of Myanmar; and (e) to invite the Myanmar delegation to continue to provide the commission with the necessary information on this question.

The name of Burma was changed to Myanmar on 18 June 1989, and the secretary-general requested the permanent representative of Myanmar to the United Nations office at Geneva to submit any information the government might wish to provide in accordance with commission decision 1989/112. In a *note verbale* dated 29 January 1990, the permanent representative made the following statement, which was circulated to the Commission on Human Rights at its 1990 session (UN Doc. E/CN.4/1990/69, para. 3):

(a) It is certainly the intention of the Government of the Union of Myanmar to continue to co-operate with the Commission on Human Rights by providing it with the information requested in paragraph (e) of the Commission's aforementioned decision.

(b) The independent five-member Multi-party Democracy General Elections Commission has, as of the date of this note, completed about 70% of the works preparatory to the holding of the general elections which are scheduled to be held on 27 May 1990.

(c) According to the 14-month timetable drawn up by the Multi-party Democracy General Elections Commission, January and February 1990 will be the most fateful months when political parties contesting elections are required to nominate candidates and subsequently start off a fully-fledged public political campaign for canvassing of votes with full democratic rights subject only to the maintenance of public order and morality.

(d) The Elections Commission has also announced dates for the nomination, scrutinization and withdrawal of nominations of candidates. The period for the nomination of Pyithu Hluttaw (Parliament) candidates for various constituencies was from 28 December 1989 to 3 January 1990. The period for the scrutinization of the nominations of candidates was from 5 to 9 January 1990. The last date for withdrawal of the nominations of candidates was 22 January 1990.

(e) It is encouraging to note that the initial announcements made by the political parties indicate the following position:
— 117 political parties will be contesting the elections
— 6 of them (namely National League for Democracy (NLD), National Unity Party (NUP), Democracy Party, Union Nationals Democracy Party (UNDP), Coalition League for Democratic Multi-party Unity and League for Democracy and Peace (LDP), will contest in more than 300 constituencies (there are altogether 492 constituencies))
— 4 will contest between 101 and 200 constituencies
— 4 will contest between 51 and 100 constituencies
— 31 will contest between 11 and 50 constituencies
— 72 will contest between 3 and 10 constituencies.

(f) As of 9 January 1990, a total of 2,392 Pyithu Hluttaw candidates (83 independents and 2,309 from 100 political parties) have put up nomination papers, indicating broad participation in the forthcoming general elections by the whole spectrum of political parties and organizations. It is worth noting that none of the candidates had withdrawn his or her candidatures on or before the closing date for such withdrawal—22 January 1990.

(g) The Government of the Union of Myanmar will arrange to have a delegation to participate in the work of the Commission in the capacity of an observer as in previous years and report to the Commission at an appropriate time and in an appropriate manner during its forth-sixth session in keeping with the provisions of decision 1989/112.

(h) In the meanwhile, as part of the process to keep the Commission informed of the matter, the Permanent Mission of the Union of Myanmar in Geneva will be keeping in close touch with all State members of the Commission on Human Rights.

In the country's first multi-party general elections in 30 years, held as scheduled on 27 May 1990, the opposition National League for Democracy won a stunning upset victory, winning two-thirds of the popular vote and a majority of the 485 National Assembly seats. The National Unity Party, backed by the military regime, received one-third of the popular vote but won only a few assembly seats. In all, 93 political parties took part in the election.

The first demand of the National League for Democracy was that the military regime release 400 of its members held under house arrest or other forms of detention, including its leader, Daw Aung San Suu Kyi, the 44-year-old daughter of the country's founder, U Aung San. It then faced the problem of establishing the modalities and a timetable for transition to civilian rule.

N

NAIROBI FORWARD-LOOKING STRATEGIES FOR THE ADVANCEMENT OF WOMEN.

NAIROBI FORWARD-LOOKING STRATEGIES FOR THE ADVANCEMENT OF WOMEN. Adopted by consensus by the World Conference to Review and Appraise the Achievements of the United Nations Decade for Women: Equality, Development and Peace, which met in Nairobi, Kenya, from 15 to 26 July 1985, the Nairobi Forward-looking Strategies for the Advancement of Women was endorsed by the UN General Assembly on 13 December 1985 (resolution 40/108). In the resolution, the General Assembly pointed out that implementation of the forward-looking strategies should result in the elimination of all forms of inequality between men and women and in the complete integration of women into the development process, achievements which should guarantee broad participation by women in efforts to strengthen peace and security in the world.

The Assembly called upon governments to allocate adequate resources and to take effective appropriate measures to implement the forward-looking strategies as a matter of high priority, including the establishment or reinforcement, as appropriate, of national machineries to promote the advancement of women and to monitor the implementation of these strategies with a view to ensuring the full integration of women in the political, economic, social, and cultural life of their countries. In particular, it called upon all governments of member States to appoint women to decision-making positions, bearing in mind their contribution to national development.

The Assembly emphasized the central role of the COMMISSION ON THE STATUS OF WOMEN in matters related to the advancement of women and called upon it to promote the implementation of the forward-looking strategies to the year 2000 based on the goals of the United Nations Decade for Women: Equality, Development and Peace, and the sub-themes of employment, health, and education. It urged all organizations of the United Nations system to cooperate with the commission in this task.

The text of the forward-looking strategies is as follows:

Introduction
A. Historical Background

1. The founding of the United Nations after the victory in the Second World War and the emergence of independent States following decolonization were some of the important events in the political, economic and social liberation of women. The International Women's Year, the World Conference held at Mexico City in 1975 and Copenhagen in 1980, and the United Nations Decade for Women: Equality, Development and Peace contributed greatly to the process of eliminating obstacles to the improvement of the status of women at the national, regional and international levels. In the early 1970s, efforts to end discrimination against women and to ensure their equal participation in society provided the impetus for most initiatives taken at all of those levels. Those efforts were also inspired by the awareness that women's reproductive and productive roles were closely linked to the political, economic, social, cultural, legal, educational and religious conditions that constrained the advancement of women and that factors intensifying the economic exploitation, marginalization and oppression of women stemmed from chronic inequalities, injustices and exploitative conditions at the family, community, national, subregional, regional and international levels.

2. In 1972, the General Assembly, in its resolution 3010 (XXVII), proclaimed 1975 International Women's Year, to be devoted to intensified action to promote equality between men and women, to ensure the full integration of women in the total development effort and to increase women's contribution to the strengthening of world peace. The World Plan of Action for the Implementation of the Objectives of the International Women's Year, adopted by the World Conference of the International Women's Year at Mexico City in 1975, was endorsed by the General Assembly in its resolution 3520 (XXX). The General Assembly, in that resolution, proclaimed 1976–1985 the United Nations Decade for Women: Equality, Development and Peace. In its resolution 33/185, the General Assembly decided upon the sub-theme "Employment, Health and Education" for the World Conference of the United Nations Decade for Women: Equality, Development and Peace, to be held at Copenhagen to review and evaluate the progress made in the first half of the Decade.

3. In 1980, at the mid-point of the Decade, the Copenhagen World Conference adopted the Programme of Action for the Second Half of the United Nations Decade for Women: Equality, Development and Peace, which further elaborated on the existing obstacles and on the existing international consensus on measures to be taken for the advancement of women. The Programme of Action was endorsed by the General Assembly that year in its resolution 35/136.

4. Also in 1980, the General Assembly, in its resolution 35/56, adopted the International Development Strategy for the Third United Nations Development Decade and re-affirmed the recommendations of the Copenhagen World Conference (General Assembly resolution 35/56, annex, para. 51). In the Strategy, the importance of the participation of women in the development process, as both agents and beneficiaries, was stressed. Also, the Strategy called for appropriate measures to be taken in order to bring about profound social and economic changes and to eliminate the structural imbalances that compounded and perpetu-ated women's disadvantages in society.

5. The strategies contained in the World Plan of Action and in the Programme of Action were important contribu-tions towards enlarging the perspective for the future of women. In most areas, however, further action is required. In this connection the General Assembly confirmed the goals and objectives of the Decade—equality, development and peace—stressed their validity for the future and indica-ted the need for concrete measures to overcome the obsta-cles to their achievement during the period 1986–2000.

6. The Forward-looking Strategies for the Advancement of Women during the Period from 1986 to the Year 2000 set forth in the present document present concrete measures to overcome the obstacles to the Decade's goals and objec-tives for the advancement of women. Building on princi-ples of equality also espoused in the Charter of the United Nations, the Universal Declaration of Human Rights, the International Covenant on Civil and Political Rights, the International Covenant on Economic, Social and Cul-tural Rights, the Convention on the Elimination of All Forms of Discrimination against Women, and the Declara-tion on the Participation of Women in Promoting Interna-tional Peace and Co-operation, the Forward-looking Strategies reaffirm the international concern regarding the status of women and provide a framework for renewed commitment by the international community to the ad-vancement of women and the elimination of gender-based discrimination. The efforts for the integration of women in the development process should be strengthened and should take into account the objectives of a new interna-tional economic order and the International Development Strategy for the Third United Nations Development Dec-ade.

7. The Nairobi World Conference is taking place at a critical moment for the developing countries. Ten years ago, when the Decade was launched, there was hope that accelerated economic growth, sustained by growing inter-national trade, financial flows and technological develop-ments, would allow the increased participation of women in the economic and social development of those coun-tries. These hopes have been belied owing to the persist-ence and, in some cases, the aggravation of an economic crisis in the developing countries, which has been an im-portant obstacle that endangers not only the pursuance of new programmes in support of women but also the mainte-nance of those that were already under way.

8. The critical international economic situation since the end of the 1970s has particularly adversely affected devel-oping countries and, most acutely, the women of those countries. The overall picture for the developing countries, particularly the least developed countries, the drought-stricken and famine-stricken areas of Africa, the debt-ridden countries and the low-income countries, has reached a critical point as a result of structural imbalances and the continuing critical international economic situa-

tion. The situation calls for an increased commitment to improving and promoting national policies and multilat-eral co-operation for development in support of national programmes, bearing in mind that each country is respon-sible for its own development policy. The gap between the developed and developing countries, particularly the least developed among them, instead of narrowing, is widening further. In order to stem such negative trends and mitigate the current difficulties of the developing countries, which affect women the most, one of the primary tasks of the in-ternational community is to pursue with all vigour the ef-forts directed towards the establishment of a New International Economic Order founded on equity, sover-eign equality, interdependence and common interest.

B. Substantive Background of the Forward-looking Strategies

9. The three objectives of the Decade—equality, develop-ment and peace—are broad, interrelated and mutually re-inforcing, so that the achievement of one contributes to the achievement of another.

10. The Copenhagen World Conference interpreted equality as meaning not only legal equality, the elimination of *de jure* discrimination, but also equality of rights, respon-sibilities and opportunities for the participation of women in development, both as Beneficiaries and as active agents.

11. Equality is both a goal and a means whereby individu-als are accorded equal treatment under the law and equal opportunities to enjoy their rights and to develop their po-tential talents and skills so that they can participate in na-tional political, economic, social and cultural development and can benefit from its results. For women in particular, equality means the realization of rights that have been de-nied as a result of cultural, institutional, behavioural and at-titudinal discrimination. Equality is important for development and peace because national and global ineq-uities perpetuate themselves and increase tensions of all types.

12. The role of women in development is directly related to the goal of comprehensive social and economic develop-ment and is fundamental to the development of all socie-ties. Development means total development, including development in the political, economic, social, cultural and other dimensions of human life, as well as the develop-ment of the economic and other material resources and the physical, moral, intellectual and cultural growth of human beings. It should be conducive to providing women, partic-ularly those who are poor or destitute, with the necessary means for increasingly claiming, achieving, enjoying and utilizing equality of opportunity. More directly, the increas-ingly successful participation of each woman in societal ac-tivities as a legally independent agent will contribute to further recognition in practice of her right to equality. De-velopment also requires a moral dimension to ensure that it is just and responsive to the needs and rights of the individ-ual and that science and technology are applied within a so-cial and economic framework that ensures environmental safety for all life forms on our planet.

13. The full and effective promotion of women's rights can best occur in conditions of international peace and se-curity where relations among States are based on the re-spect for the legitimate rights of all nations, great and small, and peoples to self-determination, independence, sovereignty, territorial integrity and the right to live in peace within their national borders.

Peace depends on the prevention of the use or threat of the use of force, aggression, military occupation, interference in the internal affairs of others, the elimination of domination, discrimination, oppression and exploitation, as well as of gross and mass violation of human rights and fundamental freedoms.

Peace includes not only the absence of war, violence and hostilities at the national and international levels but also the enjoyment of economic and social justice, equality and the entire range of human rights and fundamental freedoms within society. It depends upon respect for the Charter of the United Nations and the Universal Declaration of Human Rights, as well as international covenants and the other relevant international instruments on human rights, upon mutual co-operation and understanding among all States irrespective of their social political and economic systems and upon the effective implementation by States of the fundamental human rights standards to which their citizens are entitled.

It also embraces the whole range of actions reflected in concerns for security and implicit assumptions of trust between nations, social groups and individuals. It represents goodwill toward others and promotes respect for life while protecting freedom, human rights and the dignity of peoples and of individuals. Peace cannot be realized under conditions of economic and sexual inequality, denial of basic human rights and fundamental freedoms, deliberate exploitation of large sectors of the population, unequal development of countries, and exploitative economic relations. Without peace and stability there can be no development. Peace and development are interrelated and mutually reinforcing.

In this respect special attention is drawn to the final document of the tenth special session of the General Assembly, the first special session devoted to disarmament encompassing all measures thought to be advisable in order to ensure that the goal of general and complete disarmament under effective international control is realized. This document describes a comprehensive programme of disarmament, including nuclear disarmament, which is important not only for peace but also for the promotion of the economic and social development of all, particularly in the developing countries, through the constructive use of the enormous amount of material and human resources otherwise expended on the arms race.

Peace is promoted by equality of the sexes, economic equality and the universal enjoyment of basic human rights and fundamental freedoms. Its enjoyment by all requires that women be enabled to exercise their right to participate on an equal footing with men in all spheres of the political, economic and social life of their respective countries, particularly in the decision-making process, while exercising their right to freedom of opinion, expression, information and association in the promotion of international peace and co-operation.

14. The effective participation of women in development and in the strengthening of peace, as well as the promotion of the equality of women and men, require concerted multi-dimensional strategies and measures that should be people-oriented. Such strategies and measures will require continual upgrading and the productive utilization of human resources with a view to promoting equality and producing sustained, endogenous development of societies and groups of individuals.

15. The three goals of the Decade—equality, development and peace—are inextricably linked to the three sub-themes—employment, health and education. They constitute the concrete basis on which equality, development and peace rest. The enhancement of women's equal participation in development and peace requires the development of human resources, recognition by society of the need to improve women's status, and the participation of all in the restructuring of society. It involves, in particular, building a participatory human infrastructure to permit the mobilization of women at all levels, within different spheres and sectors. To achieve optimum development of human and material resources, women's strengths and capabilities, including their great contribution to the welfare of families and to the development of society, must be fully acknowledged and valued. The attainment of the goals and objectives of the Decade requires a sharing of this responsibility by men and women and by society as a whole and requires that women play a central role as intellectuals, policy-makers, decision-makers, planners, and contributors and beneficiaries of development.

16. The need for women's perspective on human development is critical since it is in the interest of human enrichment and progress to introduce and weave into the social fabric women's concept of equality, their choices between alternative development strategies and their approach to peace, in accordance with their aspirations, interests and talents. These things are not only desirable in themselves but are also essential for the attainment of the goals and objectives of the Decade.

17. The review and appraisal of progress achieved and obstacles encountered at the national level in the realization of the goals and objectives of the United Nations Decade for Women: Equality, Development and Peace (see A/CONF.116/5 and Add.1–14) identifies various levels of experience. Despite the considerable progress achieved and the increasing participation of women in society, the Decade has only partially attained its goals and objectives. Although the earlier years of the Decade were characterized by relatively favourable economic conditions in both the developed and developing countries, deteriorating economic conditions have slowed efforts directed towards promoting the equal participation of women in society and have given rise to new problems. With regard to development, there are indications that in some cases, although the participation of women is increasing, their benefits are not increasing proportionately.

18. Many of the obstacles discussed in the Forward-looking Strategies were identified in the review and appraisal (see A/CONF.116/5 and Add.1–14). The overwhelming obstacles to the advancement of women are in practice caused by varying combinations of political and economic as well as social and cultural factors. Furthermore, the social and cultural obstacles are sometimes aggravated by political and economic factors such as the critical international economic situation and the consequent adjustment programmes, which in general entail a high social cost. In this context, the economic constraints due in part to the prevailing macro-economic factors have contributed to the aggravation of economic conditions at the national level. Moreover, the devaluation of women's productive and reproductive roles, as a result of which the status of women continued to be regarded as secondary to that of men, and the low priority assigned to promoting the participation of women in development are historical factors that limit women's access to employment, health and education, as well as to other sectoral resources, and to the effective integration of women in the decision-making process.

Regardless of gains, the structural constraints imposed by a socio-economic framework in which women are second-class persons still limit progress. Despite changes in some countries to promote equity in all spheres of life, the "double burden" for women of having the major responsibility for domestic tasks and of participating in the labour force remains. For example, several countries in both the developed and developing world identify as a major obstacle the lack of adequate supportive services for working women.

19. According to responses from the developing countries, particularly the least developed, to the United Nations questionnaire to Governments (see A/CONF.116/5 and Add. 1–14), poverty is on the increase in some countries and constitutes another major obstacle to the advancement of women. The exigencies created by problems of mass poverty, compounded by scarce national resources, have compelled Governments to concentrate on alleviating the poverty of both women and men rather than on equality issues for women. At the same time, because women's secondary position increases their vulnerability to marginalization, those belonging to the lowest socio-economic strata are likely to be the poorest of the poor and should be given priority. Women are an essential productive force in all economies; therefore it is particularly important in times of economic recession that programmes and measures designed to raise the status of women should not be relaxed but rather intensified.

20. To economic problems, with their attendant social and cultural implications, must be added the threat to international peace and security resulting from violations of the principles of the United Nations Charter. This situation, affecting *inter alia* the lives of women, constitutes a most serious obstacle to development and thus hinders the fulfilment of the Forward-looking Strategies.

21. What is now needed is the political will to promote development in such a way that the strategy for the advancement of women seeks first and foremost to alter the current unequal conditions and structures that continue to define women as secondary persons and give women's issues a low priority. Development should now move to another plane in which women's pivotal role in society is recognized and given its true value. That will allow women to assume their legitimate and core positions in the strategies for effecting the changes necessary to promote and sustain development.

C. Current Trends and Perspectives to the Year 2000

22. In the absence of major structural changes or technological breakthroughs, it can be predicted that up to the year 2000 recent trends will, for the most part, be extended and adjusted. The situation of women, as it evolves during the period 1986–2000, will also cause other changes, establishing a process of cause and effect of great complexity. Changes in women's material conditions, consciousness and aspirations, as well as societal attitudes towards women, are themselves social and cultural processes having major implications and a profound influence on institutions such as the family. Women's advancement has achieved a certain momentum that will be affected by the social and economic changes of the next 15 years, but it will also continue to exist as a force to be reckoned with. Internal processes will exercise a major influence in the economic sphere, but the state of the global economic system and of the political, social, cultural, demographic and communication processes

directly affected by it will invariably have a more profound impact on the advancement of women.

23. At the beginning of the Decade there was an optimistic outlook for development, but during the early 1980s the world economy experienced a widespread recession due, *inter alia*, to sharp inflationary pressures that affected regions and some groups of countries, irrespective of their level of development or economic structure. During the same period, however, the countries with centrally planned economies as a group experienced stable economic growth. The developed market economy countries also experienced growth after the recession.

Despite the recovery in the developed market economy countries which is being felt in the world economy, the immediate outlook for recovery in developing countries, especially in the low-income and the least developed countries, remains bleak, particularly in view of their enormous public and private external debts and the cost of servicing that debt, which are an evident manifestation of this critical situation. This heavy burden has serious political, economic and social consequences for them. No lasting recovery can be achieved without rectifying the structural imbalances in the context of the critical international economic situation and without continued efforts towards the establishment of a new international economic order. The present situation clearly has serious repercussions for the status of women, particularly underprivileged women, and for human resource development.

Women, subject to compound discrimination on the basis of race, colour, ethnicity and national origin, in addition to sex, could be even more adversely affected by deteriorating economic conditions.

24. If current trends continue, the prospects for the developing world, particularly the low-income and least developed countries, will be sombre. The overall growth in the developing countries as currently projected will be lower in the period 1980–2000 than that experienced in the period 1960–1980. In order to redress this outlook and thereby promote the advancement of women, policies should be reoriented and reinforced to promote world trade, in particular so as to promote market access for the exports of developing countries. Similarly, policies should be pursued in other areas which would also promote growth and development in developing countries, for example, in respect of further lowering interest rates and pursuit of non-inflationary growth policies.

25. It is feared that, if there is slow growth in the world economy, there will inevitably be negative implications for women since, as a result of diminished resources, action to combat women's low position, in particular, their high rates of illiteracy, low levels of education, discrimination in employment, their unrecognized contribution to the economy and their special health needs, may be postponed. A pattern of development promoting just and equitable growth on the basis of justice and equality in international economic relations could make possible the attainment of the goals and objectives of the International Development Strategy, which could make a significant improvement in the status of women while enhancing women's effective contribution to development and peace. Such a pattern of development has its own internal dynamics that would facilitate an equitable distribution of resources and is conducive to promoting sustained, endogenous development, which will reduce dependence.

26. It is very important that the efforts to promote the economic and social status of women should rely in particular

on the development strategies that stem from the goals and objectives of the International Development Strategy and the principles of a new international economic order. These principles include, *inter alia*, self-reliance, collective self-reliance, the activation of indigenous human and material resources. The restructuring of the world economy, viewed on a long-term basis, is to the benefit of all people— women and men of all countries.

27. According to estimates and projections of the International Labour Office, women constitute 35 per cent of the world's labour force, and this figure is likely to increase steadily to the year 2000. Unless profound and extensive changes are made, the type of work available to the majority of women, as well as the rewards, will continue to be low. Women's employment is likely to be concentrated in areas requiring lower skills and lower wages and minimum job security. While women's total input of labour in the formal and informal sector will surpass that of men by the year 2000, they will receive an unequal share of the world's assets and income. According to recent estimates, it seems that women have sole responsibility for the economic support of a large number of the world's children, approximately one third and higher in some countries, and the numbers seem to be rising. Forward-looking strategies must be progressive, equitable and designed to support effectively women's roles and responsibilities as they evolve up to the year 2000. It will continue to be necessary to take specific measures to prevent discrimination and exploitation of their economic contribution at national and international levels.

28. During the period from 1986 to the year 2000, changes in the natural environment will be critical for women. One area of change is that of the role of women as intermediaries between the natural environment and society with respect to agro-ecosystems, as well as the provision of safe water and fuel supplies and the closely associated question of sanitation. The problem will continue to be greatest where water resources are limited—in arid and semi-arid areas—and in areas experiencing increasing demographic pressure. In a general manner, an improvement in the situation of women could bring about a reduction in mortality and morbidity as well as better regulation of fertility and hence of population growth, which would be beneficial for the environment and, ultimately, for women, children and men.

29. The issues of fertility rates and population growth should be treated in a context that permits women to exercise effectively their rights in matters pertaining to population concerns, including the basic right to control their own fertility which forms an important basis for the enjoyment of other rights, as stated in the report of the International Population Conference held at Mexico City in 1984. (The Holy See delegation reserved its position with respect to paragraph 29 because it had not joined in the consensus at the International Conference on Population [Mexico City, 1984] and did not agree with the substance of paragraph 29.)

30. It is expected that the ever-expanding communications network will be better attuned than before to the concerns of women and that planners in this field will provide increasing information on the objectives of the Decade—equality, development and peace—on the Forward-looking Strategies, and on the issues included in the subtheme—employment, health and education. All channels, including computers, formal and non-formal education and the media, as well as traditional mechanisms of communication involving the cultural media of ritual, drama, dialogue, oral literature and music, should be used.

31. Political and governmental factors that are likely to affect prospects for the achievement of progress by women during the period 1986–2000 will depend in large measure upon the existence or absence of peace. If widespread international tensions continue, with threats not only of nuclear catastrophe but also of localized conventional warfare, then the attention of policy-makers will be diverted from tasks directly and indirectly relevant to the advancement of women and men, and vast resources will be further applied to military and related activities. This should be avoided and these resources should be directed to the improvement of humanity.

32. To promote their interests effectively, women must be able to enjoy their right to take part in national and international decision-making processes, including the right to dissent publicly and peacefully from their Government's policies, and to mobilize to increase their participation in the promotion of peace within and between nations.

33. There is no doubt that, unless major measures are taken, numerous obstacles will continue to exist which retard the participation of women in political life, in the formulation of policies that affect them and in the formulation of national women's policies. Success will depend in large measure upon whether or not women can unite to help each other to change their poor material circumstances and secondary status and to obtain the time, energy and experience required to participate in political life. At the same time, improvements in health and educational status, legal and constitutional provisions and networking will increase the effectiveness of the political action taken by women so that they can obtain a much greater share in political decision-making than before.

34. In some countries and in some areas, women have made significant advances, but overall progress has been modest during the Decade, as is evident from the review and appraisal. During this period, women's consciousness and expectations have been raised, and it is important that this momentum should not be lost, regardless of the poor performance of the world economy. The changes occurring in the family, in women's roles and in relationships between women and men may present new challenges requiring new perspectives, strategies and measures. At the same time, it will be necessary to build alliances and solidarity groups across sexual lines in an attempt to overcome structural obstacles to the advancement of women.

35. The World Plan of Action for the Implementation of the objectives of the International Women's Year, the Declaration of Mexico on the Equality of Women and their Contribution to Development and Peace, 1975, regional plans of action, the Programme of Action for the Second Half of the United Nations Decade for Women: Equality, Development and Peace, and the sub-theme—employment, health and education—the Declaration on the Participation of Women in Promoting International Peace and Co-operation and the Convention on the Elimination of All Forms of Discrimination against Women remain valid and therefore constitute the basis for the strategies and concrete measures to be pursued up to the year 2000. The continuing relevance of the goals of the United Nations Decade for Women: Equality, Development and Peace— and of its sub-theme—health, education and employment—should be stressed, as should the implementation of the relevant recommendations of the 1975 Plan of Action and the 1980 Programme of Action, so as to ensure the

complete integration of women in the development process and the effective realization of the objectives of the Decade. The challenge now is for the international community to ensure that the achievements of the Decade become strong building blocks for development and to promote equality and peace, especially for the sake of future generations of women. The obstacles of the next 15 years must be met through concerted global, regional and national efforts. By the year 2000 illiteracy should have been eliminated, life expectancy for all women increased to at least 65 years of good quality life and opportunities for self-supporting employment made available. Above all, laws guaranteeing equality for women in all spheres of life must by then be fully and comprehensively implemented to ensure a truly equitable socio-economic framework within which real development can take place. Forward-looking Strategies for the advancement of women at the regional level should be based on a clear assessment of demographic trends and development forecasts that provide a realistic context for their implementation. (Reservations to paragraph 35 were formulated by Australia, Belgium, Canada, Denmark, Finland, Germany, Federal Republic of, Iceland, Ireland, Israel, Italy, Luxembourg, Netherlands, New Zealand, Norway, Sweden, Switzerland and United States of America. The United States reserved its position on the reference in paragraph 35 to the Declaration of Mexico on the Equality of Women and their Contribution to Development and Peace, 1975.)

36. The Forward-looking Strategies and multidimensional measures must be pursued within the framework of a just international society in which equitable economic relations will allow the closing of the gap that separates the industrialized countries from the developing countries. In this regard, all countries are called upon to show their commitment as was decided in General Assembly resolution 34/138 and, therefore, to continue informal consultations on the launching of global negotiations, as decided by the General Assembly in decision 39/454.

D. Basic Approach to the Formulation of the Forward-looking Strategies

37. It is necessary to reiterate the unity, inseparability and interdependence of the objectives of the Decade—equality, development and peace—as regards the advancement of women and their full integration in economic, political, social and cultural development, for which purpose the objectives should remain in effect in the operational strategies for the advancement of women to the year 2000.

38. The Forward-looking Strategies are intended to provide a practical and effective guide for global action on a long-term basis and within the context of the broader goals and objectives of a new international economic order. Measures are designed for immediate action, with monitoring and evaluation occurring every five years, depending on the decision of the General Assembly. Since countries are at various stages of development, they should have the option to set their own priorities based on their own development policies and resource capabilities. What may be possible for immediate action in one country may require more long-range planning in another, and even more so in respect of countries which are still under colonialism, domination and foreign occupation. The exact methods and procedures of implementing measures will depend upon the nature of the political process and the administrative capabilities of each country.

39. Some measures are intended to affect women and others directly and are designed to make the societal context less obstructive and more supportive of their progress. These measures would include the elimination of sex-based stereotyping, which is at the root of continuing discrimination. Measures to improve the situation of women are bound to have a ripple effect in society, since the advancement of women is without doubt a pre-condition for the establishment of a humane and progressive society.

40. The feasibility of policies, programmes and projects concerning women will be affected not only by their numbers and socio-economic heterogeneity but also by the different life-styles of women and by the constant changes in their life cycle.

41. The Forward-looking Strategies not only suggest measures for overcoming obstacles that are fundamental and operational, but also identify those that are emerging. Thus, the strategies and measures presented are intended to serve as guidelines for a process of continuous adaptation to diverse and changing national situations at speeds and modes determined by overall national priorities, within which the integration of women in development should rank high. The Forward-looking Strategies, acknowledging existing and potential obstacles, include separate basic strategies for the achievement of equality, development and peace. In line with the recommendations of the Commission on the Status of Women, acting as the Preparatory Body for the Conference at its second session, particular attention is given to "especially vulnerable and underprivileged groups of women, such as rural and urban poor women; women in areas affected by armed conflicts, foreign intervention and international threats to peace; elderly women; young women; abused women; destitute women; women victims of trafficking and women in involuntary prostitution; women deprived of their traditional means of livelihood; women who are sole supporters of families; physically and mentally disabled women; women in detention; refugee and displaced women; migrant women; minority women; and indigenous women."

42. Although addressed primarily to Governments, international and regional organizations, and non-governmental organizations, an appeal is made to all women and men in a spirit of solidarity. In particular, it is addressed to those women and men who now enjoy certain improvements in their material circumstances and who have achieved positions where they may influence policy-making, development priorities and public opinion to change the current inferior and exploited condition of the majority of women in order to serve the goals of equality for all women, their full participation in development, and the achievement and strengthening of peace.

I. Equality
A. Obstacles

43. One of the objectives of the Decade entails the full observance of the equal rights of women and the elimination of *de jure* and *de facto* discrimination. This is a critical first step towards human resource development. In developing countries inequality is, to a great extent, the result of underdevelopment and its various manifestations, which in turn are aggravated by the unjust distribution of the benefits of the international economy. The United Nations system, particularly the Commission on the Status of Women, has worked for four decades to establish international standards and to identify and propose measures to prevent

discrimination on the basis of sex. Although much progress has been made in legislation, measures are necessary for effective implementation and enforcement. Legislative enactment is only one element in the struggle for equality, but an essential one as it provides the legitimate basis for action and acts as a catalyst for societal change.

44. The inequality of women in most countries stems to a very large extent from mass poverty and the general backwardness of the majority of the world's population caused by underdevelopment, which is a product of imperialism, colonialism, neo-colonialism, *apartheid,* racism, racial discrimination and of unjust international economic relations. The unfavourable status of women is aggravated in many countries, developed and underdeveloped, by *de facto* discrimination on the grounds of sex. (The United States reserved its position on paragraph 44 because it did not agree that the obstacles listed should be considered the main reasons for the inequality of women in most countries.)

45. One of the fundamental obstacles to women's equality is that *de facto* discrimination and inequality in the status of women and men derive from larger social, economic, political and cultural factors that have been justified on the basis of physiological differences. Although there is no physiological basis for regarding the household and family as essentially the domain of women, for the devaluation of domestic work and for regarding the capacities of women as inferior to those of men, the belief that such a basis exists perpetuates inequality and inhibits the structural and attitudinal changes necessary to eliminate such inequality.

46. Women, by virtue of their gender, experience discrimination in terms of denial of equal access to the power structure that controls society and determines development issues and peace initiatives. Additional differences, such as race, colour and ethnicity, may have even more serious implications in some countries, since such factors can be used as justification for compound discrimination.

47. Fundamental resistance creates obstacles, which have wide-ranging implications for the objectives of the Decade. Discrimination promotes an uneconomic use of women's talents and wastes the valuable human resources necessary for development and for the strengthening of peace. Ultimately, society is the loser if the talents of women are under-utilized as a result of discrimination.

48. The sharp contrasts between legislative changes and effective implementation of these changes are a major obstacle to the full participation of women in society. *De facto* and indirect discrimination, particularly by reference to marital or family status, often persists despite legislative action. The law as a recourse does not automatically benefit all women equally, owing to the socio-economic inequalities determining women's knowledge of and access to the law, as well as their ability to exercise their full legal rights without fear of recrimination or intimidation. The lack or inadequacy of the dissemination of information on women's rights and the available recourse to justice has hampered, in many instances, the achievement of expected results.

49. Some legislative changes are made without a thorough understanding of the relationship between existing legal systems. In practice, however, certain aspects of the law—for instance, customary provisions—may be in operation in societies with multiple and conflicting legal systems. Emerging and potential obstacles resulting from possible contradictions should be anticipated so that preventive measures can be taken. When passing new legislation, whatever its subject-matter, all possible care should be taken to ensure that it implies no direct or indirect discrimination so that women's right to equality is fully respected in law.

50. In some countries, discriminatory legislative provisions in the social, economic and political spheres still exist, including civil, penal and commercial codes and certain administrative rules and regulations. Civil codes in some instances have not yet been adequately studied to determine action for repealing those laws that still discriminate against women and for determining, on the basis of equality, the legal capacity and status of women, married women in particular, in terms of nationality, inheritance, ownership and control of property, freedom of movement and the custody and nationality of children. Above all, there is still a deeply rooted resistance on the part of conservative elements in society to the change in attitude necessary for a total ban on discriminatory practices against women at the family, local, national and international levels.

B. Basic Strategies

51. The political commitment to establish, modify, expand or enforce a comprehensive legal base for the equality of women and men and on the basis of human dignity must be strengthened. Legislative changes are most effective when made within a supportive framework promoting simultaneous changes in the economic, social, political and cultural spheres, which can help bring about a social transformation. For true equality to become a reality for women, the sharing of power on equal terms with men must be a major strategy.

52. Governments should take the relevant steps to ensure that both men and women enjoy equal rights, opportunities and responsibilities so as to guarantee the development of their individual aptitudes and capacities and enable women to participate as beneficiaries and active agents in development.

53. Changes in social and economic structures should be promoted which would make possible the full equality of women and their free access to all types of development as active agents and beneficiaries, without discrimination of any kind, and to all types of education, training and employment. Special attention should be paid to implementing this right to the maximum extent possible for young women.

54. In order to promote equality of women and men, Governments should ensure, for both women and men, equality before the law, the provision of facilities for equality of educational opportunities and training, health services, equality in conditions and opportunities of employment, including remuneration, and adequate social security. Governments should recognize and undertake measures to implement the right of men and women to employment on equal conditions, regardless of marital status, and their equal access to the whole range of economic activities.

55. Effective institutions and procedures must be established or strengthened to monitor the situation of women comprehensively and identify the causes, both traditional and new, of discrimination and to help formulate new policies and effectively carry out strategies and measures to end discrimination. These arrangements and procedures must be integrated within a coherent policy for development but cannot wait indefinitely for such a policy to be formulated and implemented.

56. The obstacles to the equality of women created by stereotypes, perceptions of and attitudes towards women

should be totally removed. Elimination of these obstacles will require, in addition to legislation, education of the population at large through formal and informal channels, including the media, non-governmental organizations, political party platforms and executive action.

57. Appropriate governmental machinery for monitoring and improving the status of women should be established where it is lacking. To be effective, this machinery should be established at a high level of government and should be ensured adequate resources, commitment and authority to advise on the impact on women of all government policies. Such machinery can play a vital role in enhancing the status of women, *inter alia,* through the dissemination of information to women on their rights and entitlements, through collaborative action with various ministries and other government agencies and with non-governmental organizations and indigenous women's societies and groups.

58. Timely and reliable statistics on the situation of women have an important role to play in the elimination of stereotypes and the movement towards full equality. Governments should help collect statistics and make periodic assessment in identifying stereotypes and inequalities, in providing concrete evidence concerning many of the harmful consequences of unequal laws and practices and in measuring progress in the elimination of inequities.

59. The sharing of domestic responsibilities by all members of the family and equal recognition of women's informal and invisible economic contributions in the mainstream of society should be developed as complementary strategies for the elimination of women's secondary status, which has fostered discrimination.

C. Measures for the Implementation of the Basic Strategies at the National Level

1. *Constitutional and Legal.* Governments that have not yet done so are urged to sign the Convention on the Elimination of All Forms of Discrimination against Women and to take all the necessary steps to ensure its ratification, or their accession to it. They should consider the possibility of establishing appropriate bodies charged with reviewing the national legislation concerned and with drawing up recommendations thereon to ensure that the provisions of the Convention and of the other international instruments to which they are parties that are relevant to the role, status and material circumstances of women are complied with.

61. Governments that have not yet done so should establish appropriate institutional procedures whereby the application of a revised set of laws and administrative measures may be effectively enforced from the village level up and may be adequately monitored so that individual women may, without obstruction or cost to themselves, seek to have discriminatory treatment redressed. Legislation that concerns women as a group should also be effectively enforced and monitored so that areas of systemic or *de facto* discrimination against women can be redressed. To this end, positive action policy should be developed.

62. Agrarian reform measures have not always ensured women's rights even in countries where women predominate in the agricultural labour force. Such reforms should guarantee women's constitutional and legal rights in terms of access to land and other means of production and should ensure that women will control the products of their labour and their income, as well as benefits from agricul-

tural inputs, research, training, credits and other infrastructural facilities.

63. National research institutions, both governmental and private, are urged to undertake investigations of the problems associated with the relationship between the law and the role, status and material circumstances of women. These should be integrated into the curricula of relevant educational institutions in an attempt to promote general knowledge and awareness of the law.

64. In the past decade there have been significant advances in the development of statistical concepts and methods for measuring inequality between women and men. The capabilities of national institutions concerned with statistics and women's issues should be improved to implement these concepts and methods in the regular statistical programmes of countries and to make effective use of these statistics in the policy-planning process. Training for producers and users of statistics on women should play a key role in this process.

65. In-depth research should be undertaken to determine instances when customary law may be discriminatory or protective of women's rights and the extent to which the interfaces between customary and statutory law may retard progress in the implementation of new legislative measures. Particular attention should be paid to double standards in every aspect of life, with a view to abolishing them.

66. Law-reform committees with equal representation of women and men from Governments and from non-governmental organizations should be set up to review all laws, not only as a monitoring device but also with a view to determining research-related activities, amendments and new legislative measures.

67. Employment legislation should ensure equity and provide benefits for women not only in the conventional and formal labour force but also in the informal sector, particularly with regard to migrant and service workers, by providing minimum wage standards, insurance benefits, safe working conditions and the right to organize. Opportunities for similar guarantees and benefits should also be extended to women making vital economic contributions in activities involving food production and processing, fisheries and food distribution through trade. These benefits should also pertain to women working in family enterprises and, if possible, to other self-employed women in an effort to give due recognition to the vital contribution of all these informal and invisible economic activities to the development of human resources.

68. Civil codes, particularly those pertaining to family law, should be revised to eliminate discriminatory practices where these exist and wherever women are considered minors. The legal capacity of married women should be reviewed in order to grant them equal rights and duties.

69. Such social and economic development should be encouraged as would secure the participation of women as equal partners with men in all fields of work, equal access to all positions of employment, equal pay for work of equal value and equal opportunities for education and vocational training, and would co-ordinate the legislation on the protection of women at work with the need for women to work and be highly productive producers and managers of all political, economic and social affairs and would develop branches of the social services to make domestic duties easier for women and men. (The United States reserved its position on paragraphs 69, 72 and 137 specifically because it did not agree with the concept of "equal pay for work of

equal value" and maintained the principle of "equal pay for equal work".)

70. Measures for the implementation of legislation relating to working conditions for women must be taken.

71. Legislative and/or other measures should be adopted and implemented to secure for men and women the same right to work and to unemployment benefits, as well as to prohibit, through, *inter alia,* the imposition of sanctions, dismissal on the grounds of pregnancy or of maternity leave and discrimination in dismissals on the grounds of marital status. Legislative and other measures should be adopted and implemented to facilitate the return to the labour market of women who have left it for family reasons and to guarantee the right of women to return to work after maternity leave.

72. Governments should continue to take special action to institute programmes that would inform women workers of their rights under legislation and other remedial measures. The importance of freedom of association and the protection of the right to organize should be emphasized, this being particularly relevant to the position of women in employment. Special measures should be taken to ratify and implement in national legislation the relevant conventions and recommendations of the International Labour Organisation concerning the rights of women as regards access to equal employment opportunities, equal pay for work of equal value, equal working conditions, job security and maternity protection.

73. Marriage agreements should be based on mutual understanding, respect and freedom of choice. Careful attention should be paid to the equal participation and valuation of both partners so that the value of housework is considered equivalent of financial contributions.

74. The right of all women, in particular married women, to own, administer, sell or buy property independently should be guaranteed as an aspect of their equality and freedom under the law. The right to divorce should be granted equally to both partners under the same conditions, and custody of children decided in a non-discriminatory manner with full awareness of the importance of the input from both parents in the maintenance, rearing and socialization of children. Women should not forfeit their right to custody of their children or to any other benefits and freedoms simply because they have initiated a divorce. Without prejudice to the religious and cultural traditions of countries, and taking into account the *de facto* situations, legal or other appropriate provisions should be made to eliminate discrimination against single mothers and their children.

75. Appropriate action is necessary to ensure that the judiciary and all paralegal personnel are fully aware of the importance of the achievement by women of rights set out in internationally agreed instruments, constitutions and the law. Appropriate forms of in-service training and re-training should be designed and carried out for this purpose, with special attention given to the recruitment and training of women.

76. Special attention should be given in criminology training to the particular situation of women as victims of violent crimes, including crimes that violate women's bodies and result in serious physical and psychological damage. Legislation should be passed and laws enforced in every country to end the degradation of women through sex-related crimes. Guidance should be given to law enforcement and other authorities on the need to deal sensibly and sensitively with the victims of such crimes.

2. *Equality in Social Participation.* A comprehensive and sustained public campaign should be launched by all Governments, in close collaboration with non-governmental organizations, women's pressure groups, where they exist, and research institutions, as well as the media, educational institutions and traditional institutions of communication, to challenge and abolish all discriminatory perceptions, attitudes and practices by the year 2000. Target groups should include policy-makers and decision-makers, legal technical, advisers, bureaucrats, labour and business leaders, business persons, professionals and the general public.

78. By the year 2000, all Governments should have adequate comprehensive and coherent national women's policies to abolish all obstacles to the full and equal participation of women in all spheres of society.

79. Governments should take all appropriate measures to ensure to women, on equal terms with men and without discrimination, the opportunity to represent their Government at all levels on delegations to subregional, regional and international meetings. More women should be appointed as diplomats and to decision-making posts within the United Nations system, including posts in fields relating to peace and development activities. Support services, such as educational facilities and day care, for families of diplomats and other civil servants stationed abroad, of United Nations officials, as well as employment of spouses at the duty station, wherever possible, should be strongly encouraged.

80. As future parents, young people and children should be educated and mobilized to act as stimulators for and monitors of changes in attitudes towards women at all levels of society, particularly with regard to the need for greater flexibility in the assignment of roles between women and men.

81. Research activities should be promoted to identify discriminatory practices in education and training and to ensure quality at those two levels. One priority area for research should be the impact of sexual discrimination on the development of human resources.

82. Governments and private institutions are urged to include in the curricula of all schools, colleges and universities courses and seminars on women's history and roles in society and to incorporate women's issues in the general curriculum and to strengthen research institutions in the area of women's studies by promoting indigenous research activities and collaboration.

83. New teaching methods should be encouraged, especially audio-visual techniques, to demonstrate clearly the equality of the sexes. Programmes, curricula and standards of education and training should be the same for females and males. Textbooks and other teaching materials should be continuously evaluated, updated and, where necessary, redesigned, rewritten to ensure that they reflect positive, dynamic and participatory images of women and to present men actively involved in all aspects of family responsibilities.

84. Governments are urged to encourage the full participation of women in the whole range of occupations, especially in fields previously regarded as male preserves, in order to break down occupational barriers and taboos. Employment equity programmes should be developed to integrate women into all economic activities on an equal basis with men. Special measures designed to redress the imbalance imposed by centuries of discrimination against women should be promoted to accelerate *de facto* equality between men and women. Those measures should not be considered discriminatory or entail

the maintenance of unequal or separate standards. They are to be discontinued when the objectives of equality of opportunity and treatment have been achieved. Governments should ensure that their public service is an exemplary equal opportunity employer.

85. High priority should be given to substantial and continuing improvement in the portrayal of women in the mass media. Every effort should be made to develop attitudes and to produce materials that portray positive aspects of women's roles and status in intellectual and other activities as well as egalitarian relations of sexes. Steps also should be taken to control pornography, other obscene portrayals of women and the portrayal of women as sex objects. In this regard all measures should be taken to ensure that women participate effectively in relevant councils and review bodies regarding mass media, including advertisement, and in the implementation of decisions of these bodies.

3. *Equality in Political Participation and Decision-making.* Governments and political parties should intensify efforts to stimulate and ensure equality of participation by women in all national and local legislative bodies and to achieve equity in the appointment, election and promotion of women to high posts in executive, legislative and judiciary branches in these bodies. At the local level, strategies to ensure equality of women in political participation should be pragmatic, should bear a close relationship to issues of concern to women in the locality and should take into account the suitability of the proposed measures to local needs and values.

87. Governments and other employers should devote special attention to the broader and more equitable access and inclusion of women in management in various forms of popular participation, which is a significant factor in the development and realization of all human rights.

88. Governments should effectively secure participation of women in the decision-making processes at a national, state and local level through legislative and administrative measures. It is desirable that governmental departments establish a special office in each of them, headed preferably by a woman, to monitor periodically and accelerate the process of equitable representation of women. Special activities should be undertaken to increase the recruitment, nomination and promotion of women, especially to decision-making and policy-making positions, by publicizing posts more widely, increasing upward mobility and so on, until equitable representation of women is achieved. Reports should be compiled periodically on the numbers of women in public service and on their levels of responsibility in their areas of work.

89. With respect to the increase in the number of couples in which both partners are employed in the public service, especially the foreign service, Governments are urged to consider their special needs, in particular the couple's desire to be assigned to the same duty station, with a view to reconciling family and professional duties.

90. Awareness of women's political rights should be promoted through many channels, including formal and informal education, political education, non-governmental organizations, trade unions, the media and business organizations. Women should be encouraged and motivated and should help each other to exercise their right to vote and to be elected and to participate in the political process at all levels on equal terms with men.

91. Political parties and other organizations such as trade unions should make a deliberate effort to increase and improve women's participation within their ranks.

They should institute measures to activate women's constitutional and legal guarantees of the right to be elected and appointed by selecting candidates. Equal access to the political machinery of the organizations and to resources and tools for developing skills in the art and tactics of practical politics, as well as effective leadership capabilities, should be given to women. Women in leadership positions also have a special responsibility to assist in this field.

92. Governments that have not already done so should establish institutional arrangements and procedures whereby individual women, as well as representatives of all types of women's interest groups, including those from the most vulnerable, least privileged and most oppressed groups, may participate actively in all aspects of the formulation, monitoring, review and appraisal of national and local policies, issues and activities.

II. Development
A. Obstacles

93. The United Nations Decade for Women has facilitated the identification and overcoming of obstacles encountered by Member States in integrating women into society effectively and in formulating and implementing solutions to current problems. The continuation of women's stereotyped reproductive and productive roles, justified primarily on physiological, social and cultural grounds, has subordinated them in the general as well as sectoral spheres of development, even where some progress has been achieved.

94. There are coercive measures of an economic, political and other nature that are promoted and adopted by certain developed States and are directed towards exerting pressure on developing countries, with the aim of preventing them from exercising their sovereign rights and of obtaining from them advantages of all kinds, and furthermore affect possibilities for dialogue and negotiation. Such measures, which include trade restrictions, blockades, embargoes and other economic sanctions incompatible with the principles of the United Nations Charter and in violation of multilateral or bilateral commitments, have adverse effects on the economic, political and social development of developing countries and therefore directly affect the integration of women in development, since that is directly related to the objective of general social, economic and political development. (The United States abstained in the vote on paragraph 94 because of unacceptable language relating to economic measures by developed countries against developing States.)

95. One of the main obstacles to the effective integration of women in the process of development is the aggravation of the international situation, resulting in a continuing arms race, which now may spread also to outer space. As a result, immense material and human resources needed for development are wasted. Other major obstacles to the implementation of goals and objectives set by the United Nations in the field of the advancement of women include imperialism, colonialism neo-colonialism, expansionism, *apartheid* and all other forms of racism and racial discrimination, exploitation, policies of force and all forms of manifestations of foreign occupation, domination and hegemony, and the growing gap between the levels of economic development of developed and developing countries. (The United States reserved its position on paragraph 95 because it did not agree with the listing of those obstacles categorized as being major impediments to the advancement of women.)

96. The efforts of many countries to implement the objectives of the United Nations Decade for Women were undermined by a series of grave economic crises that have had severe repercussions, especially for many developing countries because of their generally greater vulnerability to external economic factors as well as because the main burden of adjustment to the economic crises has been borne by the developing countries, pushing the majority of them towards economic collapse.

97. The worsening of the social situation in many parts of the world, and particularly in Africa, as a result of the disruptive consequences of the economic crisis had a great negative impact on the process of effective and equal integration of women in development. This adverse social situation reflects the lack of implementation of relevant United Nations conventions, declarations and resolutions in the social and economic fields, and of the objectives and overall development goals adopted and reaffirmed in the International Development Strategy for the Third United Nations Development Decade.

98. The lack of political will of certain developed countries to eliminate obstacles to the practical realization of such fundamental documents adopted by the United Nations as the Declaration of Social Progress and Development (General Assembly resolution 2542 (XXIV)), the Charter of Economic Rights and Duties of States (General Assembly resolution 3281 (XXIX)), the Declaration and the Programme of Action on the Establishment of a New International Economic Order (General Assembly resolutions 3201 (S-VI) and 3202 (S-VI), respectively), the International Development Strategy for the Third United Nations Development Decade (General Assembly resolution 35/56, annex), aimed at the restructuring of international economic relations on a just and democratic basis, should be counted among the main reasons for the conservation of the unfavourable and unequal position of women from the point of view of development, especially in the developing countries. (The United States requested a vote on paragraph 98 and voted against the paragraph.)

99. The last years of the Decade have witnessed a deterioration of the general economic situation in the developing countries. The financial, economic and social crisis of the developing world has worsened the situation of large sectors of the population, especially women. In particular, the decline in economic activity is having a negative impact on an already unbalanced distribution of income, as well as on the high levels of unemployment, which affect women more than men.

100. Protectionism against developing countries' exports in all its forms, the deterioration in the terms of trade, monetary instability, including high interest rates and the inadequate flow of official development assistance have aggravated the development problems of the developing countries, and consequently have complicated the difficulties hampering the integration of women in the development process. (The United States reserved its position on paragraph 100 because it did not accept the underlying philosophy of the paragraph as it concerned the economic situation in debtor and developing countries.)

One of the principal obstacles now confronting the developing countries is their gigantic public and private external debt, which constitutes a palpable expression of the economic crisis and has serious political, economic and social consequences for these countries. The amount of the external debt obliges the developing countries to devote enormous sums of their already scarce export income to the servicing of the debt, which affects their peoples' lives and possibilities of development, with particular effects on women. In many developing countries there is a growing conviction that the conditions for the payment and servicing of the external debt cause those countries enormous difficulties and that the adjustment policies traditionally imposed are inadequate and lead to a disproportionate social cost.

The negative effects of the present international economic situation on the least developed countries have been particularly grave and have caused serious difficulties in the process of integrating women in development.

The growth prospects of the low-income countries have seriously deteriorated owing to the reduction in international economic co-operation, particularly the inadequate flow of official development assistance and the growing trade protectionism in the developed countries, which restricts the capacity of the low-income countries to attain the objectives of the United Nations Decade for Women.

This situation is even more grave in the developing countries that are afflicted by drought, famine and desertification.

101. Despite significant efforts in many countries to transfer tasks traditionally performed by women to men or to public services, traditional attitudes still continue to persist and in fact have contributed to the increased burden of work placed on women. The complexity and multidimensional aspects of changing sex roles and norms and the difficulty of determining the specific structural and organizational requirements of such a change have hindered the formulation of measures to alter sex roles and to develop appropriate perspectives on the image of women in society. Thus, despite gains made by a few women, for the majority subordination in the labour force and in society has continued, though the exploitative conditions under which women often work have become more visible.

102. The effective participation of women in development has also been impeded by the difficult international economic situation, the debt crisis, poverty, continued population growth, rising divorce rates, increasing migration, and the growing incidence of female-headed households. Yet, neither the actual expansion of employment for women nor the recognition that women constitute a significant proportion of producers has been accompanied by social adjustments to ease women's burden of child and household care. The economic recession led to a reduction in investments, particularly in those services that allow greater societal sharing of the social and economic costs of child care and housework.

103. Insufficient awareness and understanding of the complex and multifaceted relationships between development and the advancement of women have continued to make policy, programme and project formulation difficult. While during the earlier part of the Decade the belief that economic growth would automatically benefit women was more widely shared, an evaluation of the experience of the Decade has shed considerable doubt on this over-simplified premise. Consequently, the need to understand better the relationship between development and the advancement of women and to gather, analyse and disseminate information for the more effective formulation of policies, programmes and projects has become greater.

104. Although throughout history and in many societies women have been sharing similar experiences, in the developing countries the problems of women, particularly those pertaining to their integration in the development process,

are different from the problems women face in the industrialized countries and are often a matter of survival. Failure to recognize these differences leads, *inter alia*, to neglect the adverse effect of the insufficient progress made towards improvement in national policies or programmes and the present international economic situation as well as the interrelationships that exist between the goals and objectives of the International Development Strategy for the Third United Nations Development Decade and the objectives of equality, development and peace.

105. The lack of political will and commitment continued to retard action to promote effective participation by women in development. Exclusion of women from policy-making and decision-making made it difficult for women and women's organizations to include in their preferences and interests the largely male-dominated choices of progress and development. Furthermore, because the issue of women in development has often been perceived as a welfare problem, it has received low priority, viewed simply as a cost to society rather than as a contribution. Thus, the specific formulation of targets, programmes and projects concerning women and development has often received little attention, awaiting the attainment of development rather than being instrumental to it. This, in turn, caused a parallel weakness in the institutional, technical and material resources devoted to the promotion of activities for effective participation by women in development.

106. Appropriate national machinery for the effective integration of women in the development process has been either insufficient or lacking. Where the machinery exists, it often lacks the resources, focus, responsibility and authority to be effective.

B. Basic Strategies

107. The commitment to remove obstacles to the effective participation of all women in development as intellectuals, policy-makers and decision-makers, planners, contributors and beneficiaries should be strengthened according to the specific problems of women in different regions and countries and the needs of different categories of women in them. That commitment should guide the formulation and implementation of policies, plans, programmes and projects, with the awareness that development prospects will be improved and society advanced through the full and effective participation of women.

108. Different socio-economic and cultural conditions are to be taken into account when identifying the foremost obstacles to the advancement of women. The current economic situation and the imbalances within the world monetary and financial system need adjustment programmes to overcome the difficulties. These programmes should not adversely affect the most vulnerable segments of society among whom women are disproportionately represented.

109. Development, being conceived as a comprehensive process, must be characterized by the search for economic and social objectives and goals that guarantee the effective participation of the entire population, especially women, in the process of development. It is also necessary to work in favour of the structural changes needed for the fulfilment of these aspirations. In line with these concerns, one should endeavour to speed up social and economic development in developing countries; accelerate the development of the scientific and technological capabilities of those countries; promote an equitable distribution of national income; and eradicate absolute poverty, experienced

disproportionately by women and children, with the shortest possible delay by applying an overall strategy that, on the one hand, eliminates hunger and malnutrition and, on the other, works towards the construction of more just societies, in which women may reach their full development.

110. As the primary objective of development is to bring about sustained improvement in the well-being of the individual and of society and to bestow benefits on all, development should be seen not only as a desirable goal in itself but also as an important means of furthering equality of the sexes and the maintenance of peace.

111. Women should be an integral part of the process of defining the objectives and modes of development, as well as of developing strategies and measures for their implementation. The need for women to participate fully in political processes and to have an equal share of power in guiding development efforts and in benefiting from them should be recognized. Organizational and other means of enabling women to bring their interests and preferences into the evaluation and choice of alternative development objectives and strategies should be identified and supported. This would include special measures designed to enhance women's autonomy, bringing women into the mainstream of the development process on an equal basis with men, or other measures designed to integrate women fully in the total development effort.

112. The actual and potential impact on women of macro-economic processes operating at the international and national levels, as well as of financial spatial and physical development policies, should be assessed and appropriate modifications made to ensure that women are not adversely affected. Initial emphasis should be placed on employment, health and education. Priority should be given to the development of human resources, bearing in mind the need to avoid further increases in the work-load of women, particularly when alternative policies are formulated to deal with the economic and debt crisis.

113. With due recognition of the difficulties involved, Governments, international and regional organizations, and non-governmental organizations should intensify their efforts to enhance the self-reliance of women in a viable and sustained fashion. Because economic independence is a necessary pre-condition for self-reliance, such efforts should above all be focused on increasing women's access to gainful activities. Grass-roots participatory processes and planning approaches using local talent, expertise and resources are vital and should be supported and encouraged.

114. The incorporation of women's issues in all areas and sectors and at the local, national, regional and international levels should be institutionalized. To this end, appropriate machinery should be established or strengthened, and further legislative action taken. Sectoral policies and plans should be developed, and the effective participation of women in development should be integrated both in those plans and in the formulation and implementation of mainstream programmes and projects and should not be confined solely to statements of intent within plans or to small-scale, transitory projects relating to women.

115. The gender bias evident in most development programmes should be eliminated and the prejudices hindering the solution of women's problems removed. Particular attention should be given to the restructuring of employment, health and education systems and to ensuring equal access to land, capital and other productive resources. Emphasis should be placed on strategies to assist women in generating and keeping income, including measures de-

signed to improve women's access to credit. Such strategies must focus on the removal of legal, customary and other barriers and on strengthening women's capacity to use existing credit systems.

116. Governments should seek means to increase substantially the number of women who are decision-makers, policy-makers, managers, professionals and technicians in both traditional and non-traditional areas and sectors. Women should be provided with equal opportunities for access to resources, especially education and training, in order to facilitate their equal representation at higher managerial and professional levels.

117. The role of women as a factor of development is in many ways linked to their involvement in various forms and levels of decision-making and management in economic and social structures, such as worker participation in management, industrial democracy, worker self-management, trade unions and co-operatives. The development of these forms of participation, which have an impact on the development and promotion of working and living conditions, and the inclusion of women in these forms of participation on an equal footing with men is of crucial importance.

118. The relationships between development and the advancement of women under specific socio-cultural conditions should be studied locally to permit the effective formulation of policies, programmes and projects designed for stable and equitable growth. The findings should be used to develop social awareness of the need for effective participation of women in development and to create realistic images of women in society.

119. It is vital that the link between the advancement of women and socio-economic and political development be emphasized for the effective mobilization of resources for women.

120. The remunerated and, in particular, the unremunerated contributions of women to all aspects and sectors of development should be recognized, and appropriate efforts should be made to measure and reflect these contributions in national accounts and economic statistics and in the gross national product. Concrete steps should be taken to quantify the unremunerated contribution of women to agriculture, food production, reproduction and household activities.

121. Concerted action should be directed towards the establishment of a system of sharing parental responsibilities by women and men in the family and by society. To this end, priority should be given to the provision of a social infrastructure that will enable society to share these responsibilities with families and, simultaneously, to bring about changes in social attitudes so that new or modified gender roles will be accepted, promoted and become exercisable. Household tasks and parental responsibilities, including decision-making regarding family size and child spacing, should be re-examined with a view to a better sharing of responsibilities between men and women and therefore, be conducive to the attainment of women's and men's self-reliance and to the development of future human resources.

122. Monitoring and evaluation efforts should be strengthened and directed specifically towards women's issues and should be based on a thorough review and extensive development of improved statistics and indicators on the situation of women as compared with men, over time and in all fields.

123. Appropriate national machinery should be established and should be utilized to integrate women effectively in the development process. To be effective, this machinery should be provided with adequate resources, commitment and authority to encourage and enhance development efforts.

124. Regional and international co-operation, within the framework of technical co-operation among developing countries, should be strengthened and extended to promote the effective participation of women in development.

C. Measures for the Implementation of the Basic Strategies at the National Level

1. *Overall.* Appropriate machinery with sufficient resources and authority should be established at the highest level of government as a focal point to ensure that the full range of development policies and programmes in all sectors recognizes women's contribution to development and incorporates strategies to include women and to ensure that they receive an equitable share of the benefits of development.

126. To achieve the goal of development, which is inseparably linked to the goals of equality and peace, Governments should institutionalize women's issues by establishing or strengthening appropriate machinery in all areas and sectors of development. In addition, they should direct specific attention to effecting a positive change in the attitudes of male decision-makers. Governments should ensure the establishment and implementation of legislation and administrative policies and mobilize communications and information systems to create social awareness of the legal rights of women to participate in all aspects of development at all levels and at all stages—that is, planning, implementation and evaluation. Governments should stimulate the formation and growth of women's organizations and women's groups and give financial and organizational support to their activities when appropriate.

127. National resources should be directed so as to promote the participation of women at all levels and in all areas and sectors. Governments should establish national and sectoral plans and specific targets for women in development; equip the machinery in charge of women's issues with political, financial and technical resources; strengthen intersectoral co-ordination in promoting women's participation; and establish institutional mechanisms to address the needs of especially vulnerable groups of women.

128. Governments should recognize the importance of and the need for the full utilization of women's potential for self-reliance and for the attainment of national development goals and should enact legislation to ensure this. Programmes should be formulated and implemented to provide women's organizations, co-operatives, trade unions and professional associations with access to credit and other financial assistance and to training and extension services. Consultative mechanisms through which the views of women may be incorporated in governmental activities should be set up, and supportive ties with women's grassroots organizations, such as self-help community development and mutual aid societies and non-governmental organizations committed to the cause of women should be created and maintained to facilitate the integration of women in mainstream development.

129. There should be close co-ordination between Governments, agencies and other bodies at the national and local level. The effectiveness of national machinery, including the relationship between Governments and non-governmental organizations, should be evaluated and strengthened with a view to improving co-operation. Posi-

tive experiences and good models should be widely publicized.

130. Governments should compile gender-specific statistics and information and should develop or reorganize an information system to take decisions and action on the advancement of women. They should also support local research activities and local experts to help identify mechanisms for the advancement of women, focusing on the self-reliant, self-sustaining and self-generating social, economic and political development of women.

131. Governmental mechanisms should be established for monitoring and evaluating the effectiveness of institutional and administrative arrangements and of delivery systems, plans, programmes and projects to promote an equitable participation of women in development.

2. *Areas for Specific Action.* (a) *Employment.* Special measures aimed at the advancement of women in all types of employment should be consistent with the economic and social policies promoting full productive and freely chosen employment.

133. Policies should provide the means to mobilize public awareness, political support, and institutional and financial resources to enable women to obtain jobs involving more skills and responsibility, including those at the managerial level, in all sectors of the economy. These measures should include the promotion of women's occupational mobility, especially in the middle and lower levels of the work-force, where the majority of women work.

134. Governments that have not yet done so should ratify and implement the Convention on the Elimination of All Forms of Discrimination against Women and other international instruments relating to the improvement of the condition of women workers.

135. Measures based on legislation and trade union action should be taken to ensure equity in all jobs and avoid exploitative trends in part-time work, as well as the tendency towards the feminization of part-time, temporary and seasonal work.

136. Flexible working hours for all are strongly recommended as a measure for encouraging the sharing of parental and domestic responsibilities by women and men, provided that such measures are not used against the interests of employees. Re-entry programmes, complete with training and stipends, should be provided for women who have been out of the labour force for some time. Tax structures should be revised so that the tax liability on the combined earnings of married couples does not constitute a disincentive to women's employment.

137. Eliminating all forms of employment discrimination, *inter alia* through legislative measures, especially wage differentials between women and men carrying out work of equal value, is strongly recommended to all parties concerned. Additional programmes should help to overcome still existing disparities in wages between women and men. Differences in the legal conditions of work of women and men should also be eliminated, where there are disadvantages to women, and privileges should be accorded to male and female parents. Occupational desegregation of women and men should be promoted.

138. The public and private sectors should make concerted efforts to diversify and create new employment opportunities for women in the traditional, non-traditional and high productivity areas and sectors in both rural and urban areas through the design and implementation of incentive schemes for both employers and women employees and through widespread dissemination of information.

Gender stereotyping in all areas should be avoided and the occupational prospects of women should be enhanced.

139. The working conditions of women should be improved in all formal and informal areas by the public and private sectors. Occupational health and safety and job security should be enhanced and protective measures against work-related health hazards effectively implemented for women and men. Appropriate measures should be taken to prevent sexual harassment on the job or sexual exploitation in specific jobs, such as domestic service. Appropriate measures for redress should be provided by Governments and legislative measures guaranteeing these rights should be enforced. In addition, Governments and the private sector should put in place mechanisms to identify and correct harmful working conditions.

140. National planning should give urgent consideration to the development and strengthening of social security and health schemes and maternity protection schemes in keeping with the principles laid down in the ILO maternity protection convention and maternity protection recommendation and other relevant ILO conventions and recommendations as a prerequisite to the hastening of women's effective participation in production, and all business and trade unions should seek to promote the rights and compensations of working women and to ensure that appropriate infrastructures are provided. Parental leave following the birth of a child should be available to both women and men and preferably shared between them. Provision should be made for accessible child-care facilities for working parents.

141. Governments and non-governmental organizations should recognize the contribution of older women and the importance of their input in those areas that directly affect their well-being. Urgent attention should be paid to the education and training of young women in all fields. Special retraining programmes including technical training should also be developed for young women in both urban and rural sectors, who lack qualifications and are ill-equipped to enter productive employment. Steps should be taken to eliminate exploitative treatment of young women at work, in line with ILO Convention No. 111 concerning discrimination in respect of employment and occupation, 1958 and ILO Convention No. 122 concerning employment policy, 1964.

142. National planning, programmes and projects should launch a twofold attack on poverty and unemployment. To enable women to gain access to equal economic opportunities, Governments should seek to involve and integrate women in all phases of the planning, delivery and evaluation of multisectoral programmes that eliminate discrimination against women, provide required supportive services and emphasize income generation. An increased number of women should be hired in national planning mechanisms. Particular attention should be devoted to the informal sector since it will be the major employment outlet of a considerable number of underprivileged urban and rural women. The co-operative movement could play an indispensable role in this area.

143. Recognition and application should be given to the fact that women and men have equal rights to work and, on the same footing, to acquire a personal income on equal terms and conditions, regardless of the economic situation. They should be given opportunities in accordance with the protective legislation of each country and especially in the labour market, in the context of measures to stimulate economic development and to promote employment growth.

144. In view of the persistence of high unemployment levels in many countries, Governments should endeavour to strengthen the efforts to cope with this issue and provide more job opportunities for women. Given that in many cases women account for a disproportionate share of total unemployment, that their unemployment rates are higher than those of men and that, owing to lower qualifications, geographical mobility and other barriers, women's prospects for alternative jobs are mostly limited, more attention should be given to unemployment as it affects women. Measures should be taken to alleviate the consequences of unemployment for women in declining sectors and occupations. In particular, training measures must be instituted to facilitate the transition.

145. Although general policies designed to reduce unemployment or to create jobs may benefit both men and women, by their nature they are often of greater assistance to men than to women. For this reason, specific measures should be taken to permit women to benefit equally with men from national policies to create jobs.

146. As high unemployment among youth, wherever it exists, is a matter of serious concern, policies designed to deal with this problem should take into account that unemployment rates for young women are often much higher than those for young men. Moreover, measures aimed at mitigating unemployment among youth should not negatively affect the employment of women in other age groups—for example, by lowering minimum wages. Women should not face any impediment to employment opportunities and benefits in cases where their husbands are employed.

147. Governments should also give special attention to women in the peripheral or marginal labour market, such as those in unstable temporary work or unregulated part-time work, as well as to the increasing number of women working in the informal economy.

(b) *Health.* The vital role of women as providers of health care both inside and outside the home should be recognized, taking into account the following: the creation and strengthening of basic services for the delivery of health care, with due regard to levels of fertility and infant and maternal mortality and the needs of the most vulnerable groups and the need to control locally prevalent endemic and epidemic diseases. Governments that have not already done so should undertake, in co-operation with the World Health Organization, the United Nations Children's Fund and the United Nations Fund for Population Activities, plans of action relating to women in health and development in order to identify and reduce risks to women's health and to promote the positive health of women at all stages of life, bearing in mind the productive role of women in society and their responsibilities for bearing and rearing children. Women's participation in the achievement of Health for All by the Year 2000 should be recognized, since their health knowledge is crucial in their multiple roles as health providers and health brokers for the family and community, and as informed consumers of adequate and appropriate health care.

149. The participation of women in higher professional and managerial positions in health institutions should be increased through appropriate legislation; training and supportive action should be taken to increase women's enrolment at higher levels of medical training and training in health-related fields. For effective community involvement to ensure the attainment of the World Health Organization's goal of Health for All by the Year 2000 and respon-

siveness to women's health needs, women should be represented in national and local health councils and committees. The employment and working conditions of women health personnel and health workers should be expanded and improved at all levels. Female traditional healers and birth attendants should be more fully and constructively integrated in national health planning.

150. Health education should be geared towards changing those attitudes and values and actions that are discriminatory and detrimental to women's and girls' health. Steps should be taken to change the attitudes and health knowledge and composition of health personnel so that there can be an appropriate understanding of women's health needs. A greater sharing by men and women of family and health-care responsibilities should be encouraged. Women must be involved in the formulation and planning of their health education needs. Health education should be available to the entire family not only through the health care system, but also through all appropriate channels and in particular the educational system. To this end, Governments should ensure that information meant to be received by women is relevant to women's health priorities and is suitably presented.

151. Promotive, preventive and curative health measures should be strengthened through combined measures and a supportive health infrastructure which, in accordance with the International Code of Marketing of Breast Milk Substitutes, should be free of commercial pressure. To provide immediate access to water and sanitary facilities for women, Governments should ensure that women are consulted and involved in the planning and implementation of water and sanitation projects, trained in the maintenance of water-supply systems, and consulted with regard to technologies used in water and sanitation projects. In this regard, recommendations arising from the activities generated by the International Drinking Water Supply and Sanitation Decade and other public health programmes should be taken into account.

152. Governments should take measures to vaccinate children and pregnant women against certain endemic local diseases as well as other diseases as recommended by the vaccination schedule of the World Health Organization and to eliminate any differences in coverage between boys and girls (cf. WHO report EB 75/22). In regions where rubella is prevalent, vaccinations should preferably be given to girls before puberty. Governments should ensure that adequate arrangements are made to preserve the quality of vaccines. Governments should ensure the quality of vaccines. Governments should also ensure the full and informed participation of women in programmes to control chronic and communicable diseases.

153. The international community should intensify efforts to eradicate the trafficking, marketing and distribution of unsafe and ineffective drugs and to disseminate information on their ill effects. Those efforts should include educational programmes to promote the proper prescription and informed use of drugs. Efforts should also be strengthened to eliminate all practices detrimental to the health of women and children. Efforts should be made to ensure that all women have access to essential drugs appropriate to their specific needs and as recommended in the WHO List of Essential Drugs as applied in 1978. It is imperative that information on the appropriate use of such drugs is made widely available to all women. When drugs are imported or exported Governments should use the WHO Cer-

tification Scheme on the Quality of Pharmaceutical Products Moving in International Commerce.

154. Women should have access to and control over income to provide adequate nutrition for themselves and their children. Also, Governments should foster activities that will increase awareness of the special nutritional needs of women; provide support to ensure sufficient rest in the last trimester of pregnancy and while breast-feeding; and promote interventions to reduce the prevalence of nutritional diseases such as anaemia in women of all ages, particularly young women, and promote the development and use of locally produced weaning food.

155. Appropriate health facilities should be planned, designed, constructed and equipped to be readily accessible and acceptable. Services should be in harmony with the timing and patterns of women's work, as well as with women's needs and perspectives. Maternal and child-care facilities, including family planning services, should be within easy reach of all women. Governments should also ensure that women have the same access as men to affordable curative, preventive and rehabilitative treatment. Wherever possible, measures should be taken to conduct general screening and treatment of women's common diseases and cancer. In view of the unacceptably high levels of maternal mortality in many developing countries, the reduction of maternal mortality from now to the year 2000 to a minimum level should be a key target for Governments and non-governmental organizations, including professional organizations.

156. The ability of women to control their own fertility forms an important basis for the enjoyment of other rights. As recognized in the World Population Plan of Action and reaffirmed at the International Conference on Population, 1984, all couples and individuals have the basic human right to decide freely and informedly the number and spacing of their children; maternal and child health and family-planning components of primary health care should be strengthened; and family-planning information should be produced and services created. Access to such services should be encouraged by Governments irrespective of their population policies and should be carried out with the participation of women's organizations to ensure their success. (The Holy See delegation reserved its position with respect to paragraphs 156 to 159 because it did not agree with the substance of those paragraphs.)

157. Governments should make available, as a matter of urgency, information, education and the means to assist women and men to take decisions about their desired number of children. To ensure a voluntary and free choice, family-planning information, education and means should include all medically approved and appropriate methods of family planning. Education for responsible parenthood and family-life education should be widely available and should be directed towards both men and women. Non-governmental organizations, particularly women's organizations, should be involved in such programmes because they can be the most effective media for motivating people at that level. (The Holy See delegation reserved its position with respect to paragraphs 156 to 159 because it did not agree with the substance of those paragraphs.)

158. Recognizing that pregnancy occurring in adolescent girls, whether married or unmarried, has adverse effects on the morbidity and mortality of both mother and child, Governments are urged to develop policies to encourage delay in the commencement of childbearing. Governments should make efforts to raise the age of entry into marriage in countries in which this age is still quite low. Attention should also be given to ensuring that adolescents, both girls and boys, receive adequate information and education. (The Holy See delegation reserved its position with respect to paragraphs 156 to 159 because it did not agree with the substance of those paragraphs.)

159. All Governments should ensure that fertility-control methods and drugs conform to adequate standards of quality, efficiency and safety. This should also apply to organizations responsible for distributing and administering these methods. Information on contraceptives should be made available to women. Programmes of incentives and disincentives should be neither coercive nor discriminatory and should be consistent with internationally recognized human rights, as well as with changing individual and cultural values. (The Holy See delegation reserved its position with respect to paragraphs 156 to 159 because it did not agree with the substance of those paragraphs.)

160. Governments should encourage local women's organizations to participate in primary health-care activities including traditional medicine, and should devise ways to support women, especially underprivileged women, in taking responsibility for self-care and in promoting community care, particularly in rural areas. More emphasis should be placed on preventive rather than curative measures.

161. The appropriate gender-specific indicators for monitoring women's health that have been or are being developed by the World Health Organization should be widely applied and utilized by Governments and other interested organizations in order to develop and sustain measures for treating low-grade ill health and for reducing high morbidity rates among women, particularly when illnesses are psychosomatic or social and cultural in nature. Governments that have not yet done so should establish focal points to carry out such monitoring.

162. Occupational health and safety should be enhanced by the public and private sectors. Concern with the occupational health risks should cover female as well as male workers and focus among other things on risks endangering their reproductive capabilities and unborn children. Efforts should equally be directed at the health of pregnant and lactating women, the health impact of new technologies and the harmonization of work and family responsibilities.

(c) *Education.* Education is the basis for the full promotion and improvement of the status of women. It is the basic tool that should be given to women in order to fulfil their role as full members of society. Governments should strengthen the participation of women at all levels of national educational policy and in formulating and implementing plans, programmes and projects. Special measures should be adopted to revise and adapt women's education to the realities of the developing world. Existing and new services should be directed to women as intellectuals, policy-makers, decision-makers, planners, contributors and beneficiaries, with particular attention to the UNESCO Convention against Discrimination in Education (1960). Special measures should also be adopted to increase equal access to scientific, technical and vocational education, particularly for young women, and evaluate progress made by the poorest women in urban and rural areas.

164. Special measures should be taken by Governments and the international organizations, especially UNESCO, to eliminate the high rate of illiteracy by the year 2000, with the support of the international community. Governments should establish targets and adopt appropriate measures

for this purpose. While the elimination of illiteracy is important to all, priority programmes are still required to overcome the special obstacles that have generally led to higher illiteracy rates among women than among men. Efforts should be made to promote functional literacy, with special emphasis on health, nutrition and viable economic skills and opportunities, in order to eradicate illiteracy among women and to produce additional material for the eradication of illiteracy. Programmes for legal literacy in low-income urban and rural areas should be initiated and intensified. Raising the level of education among women is important for the general welfare of society and because of its close link to child survival and child spacing.

165. The causes of high absenteeism and drop-out rates of girls in the educational system must be addressed. Measures must be developed, strengthened and implemented that will, *inter alia,* create the appropriate incentives to ensure that women have an equal opportunity to acquire education at all levels, as well as to apply their education in a work or career context. Such measures should include the strengthening of communication and information systems, and implementation of appropriate legislation and the reorientation of educational personnel. Moreover, Governments should encourage and finance adult education programmes for those women who have never completed their studies or were forced to interrupt their studies, owing to family responsibilities, lack of financial resources or early pregnancies.

166. Efforts should be made to ensure that available scholarships and other forms of support from governmental, non-governmental and private sources are expanded and equitably distributed to girls and boys and that boarding and lodging facilities are equally accessible to them.

167. The curricula of public and private schools should be examined, textbooks and other educational materials reviewed and educational personnel retrained in order to eliminate all discriminatory gender stereotyping in education. Educational institutions should be encouraged to expand their curricula to include studies on women's contribution to all aspects of development.

168. The Decade has witnessed the rise of centres and programmes of women's studies in response to social forces and to the need for developing a new scholarship and a body of knowledge on women's studies from the perspective of women. Women's studies should be developed to reformulate the current models influencing the constitution of knowledge and sustaining a value system that reinforces inequality. The promotion and application of women's studies inside and outside and conventional institutions of learning will help to create a just and equitable society in which men and women enjoy equal partnership.

169. Encouragement and incentives, as well as counselling services, should be provided for girls to study scientific, technical and managerial subjects at all levels, in order to develop and enhance the aptitudes of women for decision-making, management and leadership in these fields.

170. All educational and occupational training should be flexible and accessible to both women and men. It should aim to improve employment possibilities and promotion prospects for women including those areas where technologies are improving rapidly, and vocational training programmes, as well as workers' educational schemes dealing with co-operatives, trade unions and work associations, should stress the importance of equal opportunity for women at all levels of work and work-related activities.

171. Extensive measures should be taken to diversify women's vocational education and training in order to extend their opportunities for employment in occupations that are non-traditional or are new to women and that are important to development. The present educational system, which in many countries is sharply divided by sex, with girls receiving instruction in home economics and boys in technical subjects, should be altered. Existing vocational training centres should be opened to girls and women instead of continuing a segregated training system.

172. A fully integrated system of training, having direct linkages with employment needs, pertinent to future employment and development trends should be created and implemented in order to avoid wastage of human resources.

173. Educational programmes to enable men to assume as much responsibility as women in the upbringing of children and the maintenance of the household should be introduced at all levels of the educational system.

(d) *Food, Water and Agriculture.* Women, as key food producers in many regions of the world, play a central role in the development and production of food and agriculture, participating actively in all phases of the production cycle, including the conservation, storage, processing and marketing of food and agricultural products. Women therefore make a vital contribution to economic development, particularly in agriculturally based economies, which must be better recognized and rewarded. Development strategies and programmes, as well as incentive programmes and projects in the field of food and agriculture, need to be designed in a manner that fully integrates women at all levels of planning, implementation, monitoring evaluation in all stages of the development process of a project cycle, so as to facilitate and enhance this key role of women and to ensure that women receive proper benefits and remuneration commensurate with their important contribution in this field. Moreover, women should be fully integrated and involved in the technological research and energy aspects of food and agricultural development.

175. During the Decade, the significant contribution of women to agricultural development has been more widely recognized, particularly their contribution in working hours to agricultural, fishery and forestry production and conservation, and to various parts of the food system. There are indications, however, that poverty and landlessness among rural women will increase significantly by the year 2000. In order to stem this trend, Governments should implement, as a matter of priority, equitable and stable investment and growth policies for rural development to ensure that there is a reallocation of the country's resources which, in many cases, are largely derived from the rural areas but allocated to urban development.

176. Governments should establish multisectoral programmes to promote the productive capacity of rural poor women in food and animal production, create off-farm employment opportunities, reduce their work-load, *inter alia,* by supporting the establishment of adequate child-care facilities and that of their children, reverse their pauperization, improve their access to all sources of energy, and provide them with adequate water, health, education, effective extension services and transportation within their region. In this connection it should be noted that the World Conference on Agrarian Reform and Rural Development, held at Rome in 1979, recognized women's vital role in the socio-economic life in both agricultural and non-agricultural activities as a prerequisite for successful rural development policies, planning and programmes, and pro-

posed specific measures for improving their condition, which are still valid. The Programme of Action for the Second Half of the United Nations Decade for Women also included specific measures to improve the situation of women in food and agriculture, which remain a valid guide for action.

177. The General Assembly, in resolution 39/165 on the critical situation of food production and agriculture in Africa, confirmed the growing concern of the international community at the dramatic deterioration in African food and agricultural production and the resulting alarming increase in the number of people, especially women and children, exposed to hunger, malnutrition and even starvation. Concrete measures and adequate resources for the benefit of African women should be a priority. The international community, particularly donor countries, should be urged to assist African women by continuing and, where possible, by increasing financial assistance to enhance the role of women as food producers, with an emphasis on providing training in food technologies, thereby alleviating the problems of the continent resulting from extended drought and a severe shortage of food. Donor countries should also contribute to the special funds that have been launched by various organizations—for example, the United Nations Development Fund for Women. Emergency assistance should be increased and accelerated to alleviate the suffering of starving and dying women and children under famine conditions in Africa. Furthermore, given the critical food situation in Africa, aggravated *inter alia* by demographic pressures, the international community is urged to give priority to and provide support for the efforts of the African countries to overcome this serious situation. These efforts include the Lagos Plan of Action and the Nairobi Programme of Action, as well as the consultation by African Governments on the role of women in food production and food security.

178. Governments should give priority to supporting effective participation by women in food production and in food security programmes and should develop specific plans of action for this purpose. This would ensure that resources are directed towards women's programmes, that women are integrated in all mainstream rural development projects and that projects are located within technical ministries as well as ministries of social affairs. Governments should promote integrated solutions, such as national food policies, which are diversified according to specific natural regions for the improvement of self-reliance in food production, instead of resorting to palliatives or fragmented remedies.

179. Mechanisms should also include monitoring and evaluation and, where necessary should modify the allocation of resources between women and men in mixed projects; should restructure rural development schemes to respond to women's needs; should assess women's projects in terms of technical and economic viability, as well as on social grounds; and should develop gender-specific statistics and information that reflect accurately women's contribution to food staples. Women's participation in programmes and projects to promote food security should be enhanced by providing them with opportunities to hold official positions, to receive training in leadership, administration and financial management and to organize on a co-operative basis. Research and experimentation should be conducted on food production and storage techniques to improve traditional knowledge and introduce modern technology.

180. Animal husbandry, fishery and forestry program-

mes should give greater attention to the effective participation of women as contributors and beneficiaries. Similarly, all other off-farm rural production programmes, as well as rural settlement, health, educational and social service programmes, should secure the participation of women as planners, contributors and beneficiaries.

181. Also important are the dissemination of information to rural women through national information campaigns, using all available media and established women's groups; the exposure of local populations to innovation and creativity through open-air films, talks, visits to areas where needs are similar, and demonstrations of scientific and technological innovations; the participation of women farmers in research and information campaigns; and the involvement of women in technical co-operation among developing countries and the exchange of information.

182. Rural women's access to land, capital, technology, know-how and other productive resources should be secured. Women should be given full and effective rights to land ownership, registration of land titles and allocation of tenancies on irrigation or settlement schemes and should also benefit from land reform. Women's customary land and inheritance rights under conditions of land shortage, land improvement or shifts into cash-cropping should be protected. Implementation of inheritance laws should be modified so that women can inherit a fair share of livestock, agricultural machinery and other property. Women's access to investment finance to increase their productivity and income should be supported by removing legal and institutional restrictions and by promoting women's savings groups and co-operatives and intermediary institutions, as well as training in and assistance with financial management, savings and investments and reallocation of land resources, with priority placed on production, especially of staple foods.

183. Women should be integrated into modern technology programmes that introduce new crops and improved varieties, rotation of crops, mixed farming, mixed and intercropping systems, low-cost soil fertility techniques, soil and water conservation methods and other modern improvements. In this connection, women's involvement in the construction, management and maintenance of irrigation schemes should be promoted.

184. Appropriate food-processing technologies can free women from time- and energy-consuming tasks and thus effect improvements in their health. Appropriate technologies can also increase the productivity and income of women, either directly or by freeing them to engage in other activities. Such technologies should be designed and introduced, however, in a manner that ensures women's access to the new technology and to its benefits and does not displace women from means of livelihood when alternative opportunities are not available. Appropriate labour-saving technologies should utilize local human and material resources and inexpensive sources of energy. The design, testing and dissemination of the technology should be appropriate also to the women who will be the users. Nongovernmental organizations can play a valuable role in this process. Appropriate and affordable food-processing technologies should be made widely available to rural women, along with appropriate and affordable storage, marketing and transportation facilities to reduce post-harvest and income losses. Information on improved methods which have been ecologically confirmed of reducing post-harvest food loss and of preserving and conserving food products should be widely disseminated.

185. Financial, technical, advisory and institutional support should be provided to women's organizations and groups to enhance the self-reliance of rural women. Women's co-operatives should be promoted to operate on a larger scale by improving farm input provisions, primary processing and the wholesale marketing of women's production. Comprehensive support should be given to women's organizations to facilitate the acquisition of farm inputs and information and to facilitate the marketing of produce.

186. Governments should set targets for increased extension contracts with rural women, reorient the training of male extension workers and train adequate numbers of female extension workers. Women should be given access to training programmes at different levels that develop various types of skills to widen the range of methods and technologies used for agricultural production.

187. Governments should involve women in the mobilization and distribution of food aid in countries affected by the drought, as well as in the fight against desertification, through large-scale afforestation campaigns (planting of woodlots, collective farms and seedlings).

188. Governments should pay greater attention to the preservation and the maintenance free from pollution of any kind of sources of water supply for irrigation and domestic consumption, applying special remedial measures to relieve the burden placed on women by the task of fetching water. To this end, they should construct wells, boreholes, dams and locally made water-catchment devices sufficient for all irrigation and domestic needs, including those of livestock. Women should be included by Governments and agencies in all policy planning, implementation and administration of water supply projects and trained to take responsibility for the management of hydraulic infrastructures and equipment and for its maintenance.

(e) *Industry*. The problems related to the industrial development of the developing countries reflect the dependent nature of their economies and the need to promote transformation industries based on domestic agricultural production as a fundamental issue of development. Women are an important part of the agricultural workforce; therefore, there should be special interest in the promotion of the technical training of women in this particular field. In this respect, Governments should take into account the following recommendations:

(a) There should be a link between agriculture and industry;

(b) Steps should be taken to eliminate the particular obstacles to industrialization and to the participation of women in industry, such as energy, the limited markets of some developing countries, the rural exodus, poor infrastructure, a lack of technical know-how, the dependence of the industries of some countries and a lack of financial resources;

(c) Steps should also be taken to promote women's equitable and increased participation in industry by enabling them to have equal access to and to participate in adult education and in-service programmes that teach not only literacy but also saleable income-generating skills, and by encouraging women to participate in collective organizations, including trade unions;

(d) Industrial co-operation among developing countries should be promoted by creating subregional industries;

(e) International organizations and developed countries should assist developing countries in their industrialization effort and the integration of women in that process.

190. Governments should ensure that, at all levels of the planning process, women participate both directly in decision-making and indirectly through effective consultation with the potential beneficiaries of programmes and projects. To this end, resources should be allocated to prepare women, through training, vocational guidance and career counselling and through increased incentives and other support measures, for increased participation in policy-making and decision-making roles and to integrate them by means of special measures at all levels.

191. Women should be viewed as users and agents of change in science and technology, and their technological and managerial skills should be enhanced in order to increase national self-reliance in industrial production and to promote innovations in productive design, product adaptation and production techniques. At the same time, industrial technologies should be applied appropriately to the needs and situations of women so as to free them from time- and energy-consuming tasks.

192. The introduction of advanced technologies in industry in particular, must allow women to enter into sectors from which they have been so far excluded.

193. Governments should direct their efforts to expanding women's employment opportunities in the modern, traditional and self-employed sectors of both the rural and urban economy and to avoiding the exploitation of female labour. Efforts to improve the absolute and relative levels of women's earnings and working conditions should be directed simultaneously to all three sectors.

194. In accordance with accepted international labour standards, particularly, though not exclusively, in the field of female employment, appropriate legislation should be adopted and fully implemented at the national level. Specific consideration should be given to the removal of discriminatory practices concerning employment conditions, health and safety, and to guaranteeing provisions for pregnant women and maternity benefits and child care. Social security benefits, including unemployment benefits, should be guaranteed to women on an equal footing with men. Recruitment of female workers in existing or new capital-intensive, high-productivity sectors should be encouraged.

195. Governments should recognize the importance of improving the conditions and structure of the informal sector for national industrial development and the role of women within it. Traditional craft and cottage industries, as well as the small industrial efforts of women, should be supported with credits, training facilities marketing opportunities and technological guidance. To this end, producers' co-operatives should be supported and women should be encouraged to establish, manage and own small enterprises.

196. Governments should design and promote as well as encourage the design and promotion of programmes and should allocate resources to prepare women to take up traditional and non-traditional industrial activities in organized and small enterprises, as well as in the informal sector, through innovative approaches to training, and should prepare and disseminate training materials and provide training to the trainers. They should support self-employment initiatives and offer guidance and career counselling.

(f) *Trade and Commercial Services*. Governments should recognize the potential impact of short-term economic adjustment policies on women in the areas of trade and commerce. Government policies should promote the full participation and integration of women in these areas. Alternative sources of finance and new markets should be sought to maintain and increase women's participation in these activities. Not only should appropriate measures be taken to ensure that legal and administrative impediments that prevent women from enjoying effective and equal access to finance and credit are removed but in addition positive measures such as loan guarantees, technical advice and marketing development services should be introduced.

198. Governments should also recognize the positive contribution of women traders to local and national economies and should adopt policies to assist and organize these women. The infrastructure and management of markets, transportation and social services should be improved to increase the efficiency, security and income of women traders and to reduce their work-load and the hazards to their health, as well as to avoid wastage of marketable produce. Training opportunities in bookkeeping, finance, packaging, standardization and processing technology should be provided to women traders. Such training should also aim at opening up employment opportunities to these women in other marketing and credit institutions. Governments should design innovative mechanisms to provide women traders with access to credit and to encourage the establishment and reinforcement of women's trade associations.

199. Efforts should be made to encourage enterprises to train women in economic sectors that traditionally have been closed to them, to promote diversification of women's employment and to eliminate gender bias from labour markets.

(g) *Science and Technology.* The full and effective participation of women in the decision-making and implementation process related to science and technology, including planning and setting priorities for research and development, and the choice, acquisition, adaptation, innovation and application of science and technology for development should be enhanced. Governments should reassess their technological capabilities and monitor current processes of change so as to anticipate and ameliorate any adverse impact on women, particularly adverse effects upon the quality of job.

201. The involvement of women in all of the peaceful uses of outer space should be enhanced, and effective measures should be undertaken to integrate women into all levels of decision-making and the implementation of such activities. In all countries special efforts should be made by Governments and non-governmental organizations to provide women and women's organizations with information on the peaceful uses of outer space. Special incentives should be provided to enable women to obtain advanced education and training in areas related to outer space in order to expand their participation in the application of outer space technology for peaceful uses, especially in the high-priority development areas of water, health, energy, food production and nutrition. To achieve these goals, increased opportunities and encouragement should be given to women to study science, mathematics and engineering at the university level and to girls to study mathematics and science at the pre-university level.

202. Women with appropriate skills should be employed at managerial and professional levels and not restricted to service-level jobs. Special measures should be taken to improve working conditions for women in the science and technology fields, to eliminate discriminatory classification of jobs and to protect the right of women to promotion. Ef-

forts should be made to ensure that women obtain their fair share of jobs at all levels in new technology industries.

203. Major effects should be undertaken and effective incentives created to increase the access of women to both scientific and technological education and training. To achieve these goals, efforts should be made by Governments and women themselves to enhance, where necessary, the change of attitudes towards women's performance in scientific fields.

204. The potential and actual impact of science and technology on the developments that affect women's integration into the various sectors of the economy, as well as on their health, income and status, should be assessed. Relevant findings should be integrated in policy formulation to ensure that women benefit fully from available technologies and that any adverse effects are minimized.

205. Efforts in the design and delivery of appropriate technology to women should be intensified, and attention should be given to the achievement of the best possible standard in such technologies. In particular, the implications of advances in medical technology for women should be carefully examined.

(h) *Communications.* In view of the critical role of this sector in eliminating stereotyped images of women and providing women with easier access to information, the participation of women at all levels of communications policy and decision-making and in programme design, implementation and monitoring should be given high priority. The media's portrayal of stereotyped images of women and also that of the advertising industry can have a profoundly adverse effect on attitudes towards and among women. Women should be made an integral part of the decision-making concerning the choice and development of alternative forms of communication and should have an equal say in the determination of the content of all public information efforts. The cultural media, involving ritual, drama, dialogue, oral literature and music, should be integrated in all development efforts to enhance communication. Women's own cultural projects aimed at changing the traditional images of women and men should be promoted and women should have equal access to financial support. In the field of communication, there is ample scope for international co-operation regarding information related to the sharing of experience by women and to projecting activities concerning the role of women in development and peace in order to enhance the awareness of both accomplishments and the tasks that remain to be fulfilled.

207. The enrolment of women in publicly operated mass communication networks and in education and training should be increased. The employment of women within the sector should be promoted and directed towards professional, advisory and decision-making positions.

208. Organizations aimed at promoting the role of women in development as contributors and beneficiaries should be assisted in their efforts to establish effective communications and information networks.

(i) *Housing, Settlement, Community Development and Transport.* Governments should integrate women in the formulation of policies, programmes and projects for the provision of basic shelter and infrastructure. To this end, enrolment of women in architectural, engineering and related fields should be encouraged, and qualified women graduates in these fields should be assigned to professional and policy-making and decision-making positions. The shelter and infrastructural needs of women should be assessed and specifically incorporated in housing, community development, and slum and squatter projects.

210. Women and women's groups should be participants in and equal beneficiaries of housing and infrastructure construction projects. They should be consulted in the choice of design and technology of construction and should be involved in the management and maintenance of the facilities. To this end, women should be provided with construction, maintenance and management skills and should be participants in related training and educational programmes. Special attention must be given to the provision of adequate water to all communities, in consultation with women.

211. Housing credit schemes should be reviewed and women's direct access to housing construction and improvement credits secured. In this connection, programmes aimed at increasing the possibilities of sources of income for women should be promoted and existing legislation or administrative practices endangering women's ownership and tenancy rights should be revoked.

212. Government efforts for the International Year of Shelter for the Homeless should incorporate assessments of the shelter needs of women and encourage the design and implementation of innovative projects that will increase women's access to services and finance. In these efforts special attention should be paid to women who are the sole supporters of their families. Low-cost housing and facilities should be designed for such women.

213. All measures to increase the efficiency of land, water and air transportation should be formulated with due regard to women as producers and consumers. All national and local decisions concerning transportation policies, including subsidies, pricing, choice of technology for construction and maintenance, and means of transport, should consider women's needs and should be based on consideration of the possible impact on the employment, income and health of women.

214. Women's roles as operators and owners of means of transport should be promoted through greater access to credit for women and other appropriate means and equal consideration with regard to the allocation of contracts. This is particularly important for women's groups and collectives, especially in rural areas, that are usually well organized but are cut off from serviceable means of transport and communication.

215. Rural transportation planning in developing countries should aim at reducing the heavy burden on women who carry agricultural produce, water and fuelwood as head-loads. In exploring modes of transportation, efforts should be made to avoid loss of income and employment for women by introducing costs that may be too high for them.

216. In the choice of modes of transportation and the design of transport routes, the increasing ratio of women whose income is essential for family survival should be taken into account.

217. In the design and choice of both commercial and appropriate vehicular technology, the needs of women, especially those with young children, should be taken into consideration. Institutional support to give women access to appropriate vehicles should be provided.

(j) *Energy.* Measures developed to rationalize energy consumption and to improve energy systems, especially of hydrocarbons, and to increase technical training should be formulated with a view to women as producers, users and managers of energy sources.

219. In conventional and non-conventional national energy programmes, women should be integrated as contributors and beneficiaries with a view to their needs, as determined by specific socio-cultural factors at local and national levels and in both rural and urban contexts. Assessment of new energy sources, energy technologies and energy-delivery systems should specifically consider the reduction of the drudgery that constitutes a large part of the work of poor urban and rural women.

220. The grass-roots participation of women in energy-needs assessment, technology and energy conservation, management and maintenance efforts should be supported.

221. Priority should be given to substituting energy for muscle in the performance of the industrial and domestic work of women without loss of their jobs and tasks to men. In view of the high percentage of domestic use in total energy consumption in low-income countries, the implications of increasing energy costs, and the current threats posed by inflation, immediate attention should be directed towards action concerning adapted technologies, fuel conservation and improved or new sources of energy, such as biomass, solar and wind energy, geothermal and nuclear energy, as well as mini-hydroelectric power plants. Improved stoves should be designed and disseminated to reduce the drudgery involved in the collection of fuel by women.

222. In order to prevent depletion of the forest areas on which most rural women rely for much of their energy needs and income, innovative programmes, such as farm woodlot development, should be initiated with the involvement of both women and men. In the commercialization of fuelwood energy, measures should be taken to avoid the loss of women's income to middlemen and urban industries. Development of fuelwood plantations, diffusion of fast-growing varieties of trees and technologies for more efficient production of charcoal should be accelerated with a view to poor rural and urban women being the major beneficiaries. The use of solar energy and biogas should be promoted with due regard to affordability, as well as to use and management by women who are the principal consumers.

223. The involvement of women at all levels of decision-making and implementation of energy-related decisions including peaceful use of nuclear energy should be enhanced. Special efforts should be made by Governments and non-governmental organizations to provide women and women's organizations with information on all sources and uses of energy, including nuclear energy. Special incentives should be provided to enable women to obtain advanced levels of education and training in all energy-related areas in order to expand their participation in decision-making relating to the application of nuclear technology for peaceful uses especially in high priority development areas of water, health, energy, food production and nutrition. To achieve these goals, increased opportunities and encouragement should be given to women to study science, mathematics and engineering at the university level and for girls to study mathematics and science at the pre-university level.

(k) *Environment.* Deprivation of traditional means of livelihood is most often a result of environmental degradation resulting from such natural and man-made disasters as droughts, floods, hurricanes, erosion, desertification, deforestation and inappropriate land use. Such conditions have already pushed great numbers of poor women into marginal environments where critically low levels of water supplies, shortages of fuel, over-utilization of grazing and arable lands and population density have deprived them of their livelihood. Most seriously affected are women in drought-afflicted arid and semi-arid areas and in urban slums and squatter settlements. These women need options for alternative means of livelihood. Women must have the same opportunity as men to participate in the wage-earning labour force in such programmes as irrigation and tree planting and in other programmes needed to upgrade urban and rural environments. Urgent steps need to be taken to strengthen the machinery for international economic co-operation in the exploration of water resources and the control of desertification and other environmental disasters.

225. Efforts to improve sanitary conditions, including drinking water supplies, in all communities should be strengthened, especially in urban slums and squatter settlements and in rural areas, with due regard to relevant environmental factors. These efforts should be extended to include improvements of the home and the work environment and should be effected with the participation of women at all levels in the planning and implementation process.

226. Awareness by individual women and all types of women's organizations of environmental issues and the capacity of women and men to manage their environment and sustain productive resources should be enhanced. All sources of information dissemination should be mobilized to increase the self-help potential of women in conserving and improving their environment. National and international emphasis on ecosystem management and the control of environmental degradation should be strengthened and women should be recognized as active and equal participants in this process.

227. The environmental impact of policies, programmes and projects on women's health and activities, including their sources of employment and income, should be assessed and the negative effects eliminated.

(l) *Social Services*. Governments are urged to give priority to the development of social infrastructure, such as adequate care and education for the children of working parents, whether such work is carried out at home, in the fields or in factories, to reduce the "double burden" of working women in both urban and rural areas. Likewise they are urged to offer incentives to employers to provide adequate child-care services which meet the requirements of parents regarding opening hours. Employers should allow either parent to work flexible hours in order to share the responsibilities of child care. Simultaneously, Governments and non-governmental organizations should mobilize the mass media and other means of communication to ensure public consensus on the need for men and society as a whole to share with women the responsibilities of producing and rearing children, who represent the human resource capabilities of the future.

229. Governments should further establish ways and means of assisting women consumers through the provision of information and the creation of legislation that will increase consumer consciousness and protect consumers from unsafe goods, dangerous drugs, unhealthy foods and unethical and exploitative marketing practices. (The General Assembly adopted guidelines for consumer protection in resolution 39/248 of 9 April 1985.) Non-governmental organizations should work towards establishing strong and active organization for consumer protection.

230. Public expenditure directed towards health, educa-

tion and training and towards providing health-care and child-care services for women should be increased.

231. Governments should undertake effective measures, including mobilizing community resources, to identify, prevent and eliminate all violence, including family violence, against women and children and to provide shelter, support and reorientation services for abused women and children. These measures should notably be aimed at making women conscious that maltreatment is not an incurable phenomenon, but a blow to their physical and moral integrity, against which they have the right (and the duty) to fight, whether they are themselves the victims or the witnesses. Beyond these urgent protective measures for maltreated women and children, as well as repressive measures for the authors of this maltreatment, it would be proper to set in motion long-term supportive machineries of aid and guidance for maltreated women and children, as well as the people, often men, who maltreat them.

III. Peace
A. Obstacles

232. The threat to peace resulting from continuing international tension and violations of the United Nations Charter, resulting in the unabated arms race, in particular in the nuclear field, as well as wars, armed conflicts, external domination, foreign occupation, acquisition of land by force, aggression, imperialism, colonialism, neo-colonialism, racism, *apartheid,* gross violation of human rights, terrorism, repression, the disappearance of persons and discrimination on the basis of sex are major obstacles to human progress, specifically to the advancement of women.

233. Such obstacles, some of which occur with increasing frequency, continually reinforce and are reinforced by historically established hostile attitudes, ignorance and bigotry between countries, ethnic groups, races, sexes, socio-economy groups and by lack of tolerance and respect for different cultures and traditions. Their negative effects are increased by poverty, tensions in international economic and political relations which are often aggravated, as well as by the arms race, both nuclear and conventional. The arms race in particular diverts resources which could be used for developmental and humanitarian purposes, hinders national and international development efforts and further handicaps the well-being of the poorest nations and the most disadvantaged segments of the population.

234. Despite the achievements of the Decade, women's involvement in governmental and non-governmental activities, decision-making processes related to peace, mobilization efforts for peace, education for peace and peace research remains limited. Their participation in the struggle to eradicate colonialism, neo-colonialism, imperialism, totalitarianism including fascism and similar ideologies, alien occupation, foreign domination, aggression, racism, racial discrimination, *apartheid* and other violations of human rights has often gone unnoticed.

235. Universal and durable peace cannot be attained without the full and equal participation of women in international relations, particularly in decision-making concerning peace, including the processes envisaged for the peaceful settlement of disputes under the Charter of the United Nations nor without overcoming the obstacles mentioned in paragraph 232.

236. Full equality between women and men is severely hampered by the threats to international peace and security, lack of satisfying progress in the field of disarmament,

including the spread of the arms race to outer space, violation of the principle of the right of peoples under alien and colonial domination and foreign occupation to self-determination and independence and respect for the national sovereignty and territorial integrity of States as well as justice, equality and mutual benefit in international relations.

237. It is evident that women all over the world have manifested their love for peace and their wish to play a greater role in international co-operation, amity and peace among different nations. All obstacles at national and international levels in the way of women's participation in promoting international peace and co-operation should be removed as soon as possible.

238. It is equally important to increase women's understanding and awareness of constructive negotiations aimed at reaching positive results for international peace and security. Governments should take measures to encourage the full and effective participation of women in negotiations on international peace and security. The rejection of the use of force or of the threat of the use of force and foreign interference and intervention should become widespread.

B. Basic Strategies

239. The main principles and directions for women's activities aimed at strengthening peace and formulated in the Declaration on the Participation of Women in Promoting International Peace and Co-operation should be put into practice. The Declaration calls for Governments, the United Nations system, non-governmental organizations, relevant institutions and individuals to strengthen women's participation in this sphere and it provides the overall framework for such activities.

240. Women and men have an equal right and the same vital interest in contributing to international peace and co-operation. Women should participate fully in all efforts to strengthen and maintain international peace and security and to promote international co-operation, diplomacy, the process of détente, disarmament in the nuclear field in particular, and respect the for the principles of the Charter of the United Nations, including respect for the sovereign rights of States, guarantees of fundamental freedoms and human rights, such as recognition of the dignity of the individual and self-determination, and freedom of thought, conscience, expression, association, assembly, communication and movement without distinction as to race, sex, political and religious beliefs, language or ethnic origin. The commitment to remove the obstacles to women's participation in the promotion of peace should be strengthened.

241. In view of the fact that women are still very inadequately represented in national and international political processes dealing with peace and conflict settlement, it is essential that women support and encourage each other in their initiatives and action relating either to universal issues, such as disarmament and the development of confidence-building measures between nations and people, or to specific conflict situations between or within States.

242. There exist situations in several regions of the world where the violation of principles of non-use of force, non-intervention, non-interference, non-aggression and the right to self-determination endangers international peace and security and creates massive humanitarian problems which constitute an impediment to the advancement of women and hence to the full implementation of the

Forward-looking Strategies. In regard to these situations strict adherence to and respect for the cardinal principles enshrined in the Charter of the United Nations and implementation of relevant resolutions consistent with the principles of the Charter are an imperative requirement with a view to seeking solutions to such problems, thereby ensuring a secure and better future for the people affected, most of whom are invariably women and children.

243. Since women are one of the most vulnerable groups in the regions affected by armed conflicts, special attention has to be drawn to the need to eliminate obstacles to the fulfilment of the objectives of equality, development and peace and the principles of the Charter of the United Nations.

244. One of the important obstacles to achieving international peace is the persistent violation of the principles and objectives of the Charter of the United Nations and the lack of political will of Governments of some countries to promote constructive negotiations aimed at decreasing international tension on the issues that seriously threaten the maintenance of international peace and security. For this reason, the strategies in this field should include the mobilization of women in favour of all acts and actions that tend to promote peace, in particular, the elimination of wars and danger of nuclear war.

245. Immediate and special priority should be given to the promotion and the effective enjoyment of human rights and fundamental freedoms for all without distinction as to sex, the full application of the rights of peoples to self-determination and the elimination of colonialism, neo-colonialism, *apartheid*, of all forms of racism and racial discrimination, oppression and aggression, foreign occupation, as well as domestic violence and violence against women.

246. In South-West Asia women and children have endured serious suffering owing to the violation of the Charter of the United Nations, leading, among other things, to the vast problem of refugees in neighbouring countries.

247. The situation of violence and destabilization that exists in Central America constitutes the most serious obstacle to the achievement of peace in the region and thus hinders the fulfilment of the Forward-looking Strategies vital to the advancement of women. In this regard and to promote conditions favourable to the objectives of the Strategies, it is important to reiterate the principles of non-intervention and self-determination, as well as the non-use of force or rejection of the threat of use of force in the solution of conflicts in the region. Therefore, the validity of the United Nations resolutions that establish the right of all sovereign States in the area to live in peace, free from all interference in their internal affairs, should be reaffirmed. It is necessary to support the negotiated political solutions and the peace proposals that the Central American States adopt under the auspices of the Contadora Group, as the most viable alternative for the solution of the crisis in Central America for the benefit of their people. In this sense it is important that the five Central American Governments speed up their consultations with the Contadora Group with the aim of bringing to a conclusion the negotiation process with the early signing of the Contadora Act on Peace and Co-operation in Central America (see A/39/562-S/16775, annex).

248. Women have played and continue to play an important role in the self-determination of peoples, including through national liberation, in accordance with the United Nations Charter. Their efforts should be recognized and

commended and used as one basis for their full participation in the construction of their countries, and in the creation of humane and just social and political systems. Women's contribution in this area should be ensured by their equal access to political power and their full participation in the decision-making process.

249. Strategies at the national, regional and the global levels should be based on a clear recognition that peace and security, self-determination and national independence are fundamental for the attainment of the three objectives of the Decade: equality, development and peace.

250. Safeguarding world peace and averting a nuclear catastrophe is one of the most important tasks today in which women have an essential role to play, especially by supporting actively the halting of the arms race followed by arms reduction and the attainment of a general and complete disarmament under effective international control, and thus contributing to the improvement of their economic position. Irrespective of their socio-economic system, the States should strive to avoid confrontation and to build friendly relations instead, which should be also supported by women.

251. Peace requires the participation of all members of society, women and men alike, in rejecting any type of intervention in the domestic affairs of States, whether it is openly or covertly carried out by other States or by transnational corporations. Peace also requires that women and men alike should promote respect for the sovereign right of a State to establish its own economic, social and political system without undergoing political and economic pressures or coercion of any type.

252. There exists a relationship between the world economic situation, development and the strengthening of international peace and security, disarmament and the relaxation of international tension. All efforts should be made to reduce global expenditures on armaments and to reach an agreement on the internationally agreed disarmament goals in order to prevent the waste of immense material and human resources, some part of which might otherwise be used for development, especially of the developing countries, as well as for the improvement of standards of living and well-being of people in each country. In this context, particular attention should be given to the advancement of women, including to the participation of women in the promotion of international peace and co-operation and the protection of mothers and children who represent a disproportionate share of the most vulnerable group, the poorest of the poor.

253. Women's equal role in decision-making with respect to peace and related issues should be seen as one of their basic human rights and as such should be enhanced and encouraged at the national, regional and international levels. In accordance with the Convention on the Elimination of All Forms of Discrimination against Women, all existing impediments to the achievement by women of equality with men should be removed. To this end, efforts should be intensified at all levels to overcome prejudices, stereotyped thinking, denial to women of career prospects and appropriate educational possibilities, and resistance by decision-makers to the changes that are necessary to enable equal participation of women with men in the international and diplomatic service.

254. Mankind is confronted with a choice: to halt the arms race and proceed to disarmament or face annihilation. The growing opposition of women to the danger of war, especially a nuclear war, which will lead to a nuclear holocaust, and their support for disarmament must be respected. States should be encouraged to ensure unhindered flow and access to information, including to women, with regard to various aspects of disarmament to avoid dissemination of false and tendentious information concerning armaments and to concentrate on the danger of the escalation of the arms race and on the need for general and complete disarmament under effective international control. The resources released as a result of disarmament measures should be used to help promote the well-being of all peoples and improve the economic and social conditions of the developing countries. Under such conditions, States should pay increased attention to the urgent need to improve the situation of women.

255. Peace education should be established for all members of society, particularly children and young people. Values, such as tolerance, racial and sexual equality, respect for and understanding of others, and good-neighbourliness should be developed, promoted and strengthened.

256. Women of the world, together with men, should as informal educators and socialization agents, play a special role in the process of bringing up younger generations in an atmosphere of compassion, tolerance, mutual concern and trust, with an awareness that all people belong to the same world community. Such education should be part of all formal and informal educational processes as well as of communications, information and mass-media systems.

257. Further action should be taken at family and neighbourhood levels, as well as at national and international levels, to achieve a peaceful social environment compatible with human dignity. The questions of women and peace and the meaning of peace for women cannot be separated from the broader question of relationships between women and men in all spheres of life and in the family. Discriminatory practices and negative attitudes towards women should be eliminated and traditional gender norms changed to enhance women's participation in peace.

258. Violence against women exists in various forms in everyday life in all societies. Women are beaten, mutilated, burned, sexually abused and raped. Such violence is a major obstacle to the achievement of peace and the other objectives of the Decade and should be given special attention. Women victims of violence should be given particular attention and comprehensive assistance. To this end, legal measures should be formulated to prevent violence and to assist women victims. National machinery should be established in order to deal with the question of violence against women within the family and society. Preventive policies should be elaborated, and institutionalized forms of assistance to women victims provided.

C. Women and Children Under Apartheid

259. Women and children under *apartheid* and other racist minority régimes suffer from direct inhumane practices such as massacres and detention, mass population removal, separation from families and immobilization in reservations. They are subjected to the detrimental implications of the labour migrant system pass laws and of relegation to the homelands where they suffer disproportionately from poverty, poor health and illiteracy. The Programme of Action of the World Conference to Combat Racism and Racial Discrimination (1978) provides an overall framework for action. Its objective is to eradicate *apartheid* and to enable black African people in South Africa to enjoy their full sovereign rights in their country. Governments that have not

already done so are urged to sign and ratify the International Convention on the Suppression and Punishment of the Crime of *Apartheid* of 30 November 1973. (The United States voted against paragraph 259 because of its opposition to the references in the eighth and ninth subparagraphs to the imposition of sanctions and aid to liberation movements.)

Full international assistance should be given to the most oppressed group under *apartheid*—women and children. The United Nations system, Governments and non-governmental organizations should identify the basic needs of women and children under *apartheid* and other racist minority régimes, including women in refugee camps in southern Africa, and provide them with adequate, legal, humanitarian, medical and material assistance as well as education, training and employment.

Assistance should be given to women's sections in national liberation movements in order to strengthen their work for women's equal opportunities, education and training so as to prepare them to play an important political role in the present struggle and in nation-building after liberation.

The Forward-looking Strategies should take into account the destabilizing effects of *apartheid* on the economic infrastructure of neighbouring independent African States, which impede the development of the subregion.

Institutionalized *apartheid* in South Africa and Namibia as realized in the day-to-day political, legal, social and cultural life remains an enormous obstacle and hindrance to advancement, equality and peace in the African region.

The Forward-looking Strategies should aim at the speedy and effective implementation of Security Council resolution 435 (1978) concerning the independence of Namibia. The total and unconditional liberation of Namibia should be a major objective of the Forward-looking Strategies, which should also aim at the improvement of the condition of women and children.

The United Nations and the international community must strengthen their resolve to see the abhorrent *apartheid* system eradicated and Namibia freed from the forces of occupation. Owing to South Africa's position in the international political and economic structure, the international community has the greatest responsibility to ensure that peace and human dignity are restored to southern Africa.

In addition to measures already taken, further effective measures, including sanctions, should be taken to terminate all collaboration with the racist régime of South Africa in the political, military, diplomatic and economic fields with a view to eliminating untold misery and loss of the oppressed people, the majority of whom are black women and children.

The international community must insist upon the effective implementation of Security Council resolution 435 (1978) concerning the independence of Namibia and all the United Nations resolutions calling for sanctions against South Africa, its isolation and abandonment of its racist policies. All efforts should be made for the immediate and unconditional withdrawal of South African forces from Angola.

The international community must condemn the direct aggression committed by the armed forces of the racist régime of South Africa against the front-line countries as well as the recruitment, training and financing of mercenaries and of armed bandits who massacre women and children and who are used to overthrow the legitimate

Governments of these countries by reason of their support for the people of South Africa and Namibia.

The international community should provide greater moral and material assistance to all the bodies struggling to remove *apartheid*, especially the national liberation movements—the African National Congress of South Africa, the Pan Africanist Congress of Azania and the South West Africa People's Organization—the African front-line States, the Organization of African Unity, the Movement of Non-Aligned Countries and non-governmental organizations.

Women, together with their Governments, should strengthen their commitment to the eradication of *apartheid* and support to their struggling sisters in all possible ways. To this end, women and women's organizations should keep themselves constantly informed about the situation of women and children under *apartheid*, disseminate information widely and build up awareness in their countries about the situation by organizing national solidarity and support committees where these do not yet exist as a means to educate the public about the evils of *apartheid* and its brutal oppression of women and children in South Africa and Namibia.

D. Palestinian Women and Children

260. For more than three decades, Palestinian women have faced difficult living conditions in camps and outside, struggling for the survival of their families and the survival of the Palestinian people who were deprived of their ancestral lands and denied the inalienable rights to return to their homes and their property, their right to self-determination, national independence and sovereignty (see A/CONF.116/6). Palestinian women are vulnerable to imprisonment, torture, reprisals and other oppressive practices by Israel in the occupied Arab territories. The confiscation of land and the creation of further settlements has affected the lives of Palestinian women and children. Such Israeli measures and practices are a violation of the Geneva Convention. The Palestinian woman as part of her nation suffers from discrimination in employment, health care and education. (The United States voted against this paragraph because of its strong objection to the introduction of tendentious and unnecessary elements into the Forward-looking Strategies document which have only a nominal connection with the unique concerns of women.)

The situation of violence and destabilization which exists in southern Lebanon and the Golan Heights put Arab women and children who are living under Israeli occupation in severe situations. Lebanese women are also suffering from discrimination and detention. Therefore, all relevant United Nations resolutions, in particular Security Council resolutions 497 (1981), 508 (1982) and 509 (1982), should be implemented.

The implementation of the Programme of Action for the Achievement of Palestinian Rights should be kept under review and co-ordinated between the United Nations units and agencies concerned, with emphasis on the role of Palestinian women in preserving their national identity, traditions and heritage and in the struggle for sovereignty. Palestinian people must recover their rights to self-determination and the right to establish an independent State in accordance with all relevant United Nations resolutions. The special and immediate needs of Palestinian women and children should be identified and appropriate provision made. United Nations projects should be initiated to help Palestinian women in the fields of health, education, and vocational training. Their living conditions inside and outside the occupied territories should be studied by the appropriate United Nations units and agencies assisted, as appropriate, by specialized research institutes from various regions. The results of these studies should be given broad publicity to promote actions at all levels. The international community should exert all efforts to stop the establishment of new Israeli settlements in the West Bank and the Gaza Strip. Palestinian women should be allowed to enjoy security in a liberated homeland also in accordance with United Nations resolutions.

E. Women in Areas Affected by Armed Conflicts, Foreign Intervention and Threats to Peace

261. Armed conflicts and emergency situations impose a serious threat to the lives of women and children, causing constant fear, danger of displacement, destruction, devastation, physical abuse, social and family disruption, and abandonment. Sometimes these result in complete denial of access to adequate health and educational services, loss of job opportunities and overall worsening of material conditions.

262. International instruments, ongoing negotiations and international discussions aimed at the limitation of armed conflicts, such as the Fourth Geneva Convention of 1949 and the First Additional Protocol to the Geneva Conventions of 1949, adopted in 1977, provide a general framework for the protection of civilians in times of hostilities and the basis of provisions of humanitarian assistance and protection to women and children. Measures proposed in the 1974 Declaration on the Protection of Women and Children in Emergency and Armed Conflict (General Assembly resolution 3318 (XXIX) should be taken into account by Governments.

F. Measures for the Implementation of the Basic Strategies at the National Level

1. *Women's Participation in Efforts for Peace.* Governments should follow the overall framework of action for disarmament as provided by the Final Document of the tenth special session of the General Assembly, which was devoted to disarmament (resolution S-10/2). Women's participation in the World Disarmament Campaign and their contribution to education for disarmament should be supported.

264. Publicity should be given by Governments and non-governmental organizations to the main treaties concluded in the field of arms control and disarmament, and to other relevant documents. More should be done to mobilize women to overcome social apathy and helplessness in relation to disarmament and to generate wide support for the implementation of these agreements. Publicity should also be given to the declaration by the General Assembly of 1986 as the International Year of Peace, and the participation of women in the programme for the Year should be encouraged.

265. Non-governmental organizations should be encouraged to play an active role in promoting the restoration of peace in areas of conflict, in accordance with United Nations resolutions.

266. Women should be able to participate actively in the decision-making process related to the promotion of international peace and co-operation. Governments should take the necessary measures to facilitate this participation by institutional, educational and organizational means. Empha-

sis should be given to the grass-roots participation and co-operation of women's organizations with other non-governmental organizations in this process.

267. Governments which have not done so should undertake all appropriate measures to eliminate existing discriminatory practices towards women and to provide them with equal opportunities to join, at all levels, the civil service, to enter the diplomatic service and to represent their countries as members of delegations to national, regional and international meetings, including conferences on peace, conflict resolution, disarmament, and meetings of the Security Council and other United Nations bodies.

268. Women should be encouraged and given financial support to take university courses in government, international relations and diplomacy in order to obtain the necessary professional qualifications for careers in fields relating to peace and international security.

269. Governments should encourage women's participation in the promotion of peace at decision-making levels by providing information on opportunities for such participation in public service and by promoting equitable representation of women in governmental and non-governmental bodies and activities.

270. Non-governmental organizations should provide opportunities for women to learn how to develop self-reliance and leadership capabilities in order to promote peace, disarmament, human rights and international co-operation more effectively. They should emphasize the participation of women from trade unions and organizations in rural areas that have not as yet received sufficient attention and should make periodic assessments of strategies for women's participation in the promotion of peace at all levels, including the highest decision-making levels.

271. National machinery should be established to deal with the question of domestic violence. Preventive policies should be elaborated and institutionalized economic and other forms of assistance and protection for women and child victims should be provided. Legislative measures should be strengthened and legal aid provided.

2. *Education for Peace.* Governments, non-governmental organizations, women's groups and the mass media should encourage women to engage in efforts to promote education for peace in the family, neighbourhood and community. Special attention should be given to the contribution of women's grass-roots organizations. The multiple skills and talents of women artists, journalists, writers, educators and civic leaders can contribute to promoting ideas of peace if encouraged, facilitated and supported.

273. Special attention should be given to the education of children for life in peace within an atmosphere of understanding, dialogue and respect for others. In this respect, suitable concrete action should be taken to discourage the provision of children and young persons with games and publications and other media promoting the notion of favouring war, aggression, cruelty, excessive desire for power and other forms of violence, within the broad processes of the reparation of society for life in peace.

274. Governments, educational institutions, professional associations and non-governmental organizations should co-operate to develop a high-quality content for and to achieve widespread dissemination of books and programmes on education for peace. Women should take an active part in the preparation of those materials, which should include case studies of peaceful settlements of disputes, non-violent movements and passive resistance and the recognition of peace-seeking individuals.

275. Governments should create the conditions that would enable women to increase their knowledge of the main problems in contemporary international relations. Information should be widely and freely disseminated among women, thereby contributing to their full understanding of those problems. All existing obstacles and discriminatory practices regarding women's civil and political education should be removed. Opportunities should be provided for women to organize and choose studies, training programmes and seminars related to peace, disarmament, education for peace and the peaceful settlement of disputes.

276. The participation of women in peace research, including research on women and peace, should be encouraged. Existing barriers to women researchers should be removed and appropriate resources provided for peace researchers. Co-operation amongst peace researchers, government officials, non-governmental organizations and activists should be encouraged and fostered.

IV. Areas of Special Concern

277. There is an increasing number of categories of women who, because of their special characteristics, are experiencing not only the common problems indicated under the separate themes but also specific difficulties due to their socio-economic and health condition, age, minority status or a combination of these factors. Moreover, in many countries increasing demographic pressure, deteriorating political conditions have been exacerbated by the current economic recession, leading to the dislocation of large sections of populations. In this process women experience particular difficulties and are often the more vulnerable because of their traditional lack of access to development opportunities.

278. The special groups of women identified below are extremely diverse, and their problems vary tremendously from one country to another. No single strategy or set of measures can apply adequately to all cases, and the present document is therefore limited to highlighting their special circumstances and the need for each country, as well as the international community, to give these issues the necessary attention. The basic strategy must remain one of fundamentally changing the economic conditions that produce such deprivation and of upgrading women's low status in society, which accounts for their extreme vulnerability to such conditions, especially to poverty. This is aggravated by the increase in drug-dependence, which adversely affects all sectors of society, including women. Building an organizational base for such change is a crucial strategy that can provide a rallying point for solidarity among women. Measures needed to provide immediate emergency assistance should be supplemented by longer-term efforts to enable women to break out of these situations. In many cases, permanent solutions to these issues can only be found through the broader efforts directed towards the reallocation of resources and decision-making power and towards the elimination of inequality and injustice.

279. There is a need to recognize the survival mechanisms already developed by these women as basic strategies in their own right and to build on them. A first priority would be to strengthen their organization capabilities by providing physical, financial and human resources, as well as education and training. Also of extreme importance is the need to revitalize these women's aspirations in order to eliminate the chronic despair that characterizes their daily lives.

280. The economic, social, cultural and political conditions of those groups of women should be improved basically by the implementation of the measures proposed for the attainment of equality, development and peace for women in general. Additional efforts should be directed towards ensuring the gainful and productive inclusion of these women in mainstream development and in political activities. Priority emphasis should be placed upon income-generating opportunities and for the independent and sustained improvement of their condition and by the full integration and active participation of women as agents and beneficiaries of development.

281. Policies, programmes and projects aimed at or incorporating especially vulnerable and underprivileged groups of women should recognize the particular difficulties of removing the multiple obstacles facing such groups and should place equal emphasis on addressing the social, economic and human dimensions of their vulnerability and their underprivileged positions. Measures needed to provide them with immediate assistance should be supplemented by comprehensive long-term plans to achieve lasting solutions to their problems. These will usually necessitate global efforts in resolving the special problems of vulnerable groups, of which women are a significant part.

282. Basic to all efforts to improve the condition of these women should be the identification of their needs and hence the gathering of gender-specific data and economic indicators sensitive to conditions of extreme poverty and oppression. Such data should contain spatial, socio-economic and longitudinal characteristics and should be designed specifically for use in policy, programme and project formulation and implementation. Monitoring efforts at national, subregional, regional and international levels should be intensified.

A. Women in Areas Affected by Drought

283. During the Decade, the phenomenon of drought and desertification grew and developed incessantly, no longer affecting merely some localities in a single country but several entire countries. The scale and persistence of drought constitutes a grave threat, particularly for the countries of the Sahel, in which famine and a far-reaching deterioration of the environment set in as a result of the desertification process. Hence, despite the considerable efforts of the international community, the living conditions of the peoples, particularly those of women and children, which were already precarious, have become particularly miserable.

In view of that situation steps should be taken to promote concerted programmes between the countries concerned for combating drought and desertification. Efforts should be intensified for the formulation and implementation of programmes aimed at food security and self-sufficiency, in particular by the optimum control and exploitation of hydro-geological resources.

A distinction should be made between emergency aid and productive activities. Emergency aid should be intensified when necessary and as far as ever possible directed towards development aid.

Measures should be adopted to take into account women's contribution to production, involve them more closely in the design, implementation and evaluation of the programmes envisaged and ensure ample access for them to the means of production and processing and preservation techniques.

B. Urban Poor Women

284. Urbanization has been one of the major socio-economic trends over the past few decades and is expected to continue at an accelerating rate. Although the situation varies considerably from one region to another, it can generally be expected that by the year 2000 close to half the number of women in the world will be living in urban areas. In developing countries, the number of urban women could nearly double by the year 2000, and it is envisaged that there could be a considerable increase in the number of poor women among them.

285. To deal effectively with the issue, Governments should organize multi-sectoral programmes with emphasis on economic activities, elimination of discrimination and the provision of supportive services and, *inter alia*, adequate child-care facilities and, where necessary, workplace canteens to enable women to gain access to economic, social and educational opportunities on an equal basis with men. Particular attention should be devoted to the informal sector, which constitutes a major outlet for employment of a considerable number of urban poor women.

C. Elderly Women

286. The International Plan of Action on Aging adopted by the World Assembly on Aging in 1982 emphasized both the humanitarian and developmental aspects of aging. The recommendations of the Plan of Action are applicable to women and men with a view to providing them with protection and care, and ensuring their involvement and participation in social life and development. However, the Plan of Action recognizes a number of specific areas of concern for elderly women since their longer life expectancy frequently means an old age aggravated by economic need for isolation for both unmarried women and widows, possibly with little or no prospect of paid employment. This applies particularly to those women whose lifetimes were spent in unpaid and unrecognized work in the home with little or no access to a pension. If women have an income, it is generally lower than men's, partly because their former employment status has in the majority of cases been broken by maternity and family responsibilities. For this reason, the Plan of Action also noted the need for long-term policies directed towards providing social insurance for women in their own right. Governments and non-governmental organizations should, in addition to the measures recommended, explore the possibilities of employing elderly women in productive and creative ways and encouraging their participation in social and recreational activities.

It is also recommended that the care of elderly persons, including women, should go beyond disease orientation and should include their total well-being. Further efforts, in particular primary health care, health services and suitable accommodation and housing as strategies should be directed at enabling elderly women to lead a meaningful life as long as possible, in their own home and family and in the community.

Women should be prepared early in life, both psychologically and socially, to face the consequences of longer life expectancy. Although, while getting older, professional and family roles of women are undergoing fundamental changes, aging, as a stage of development, is a challenge for women. In this period of life, women should be enabled to cope in a creative way with new opportunities. The social consequences arising from the stereotyping of elderly women should be recognized and eliminated. The media should assist by presenting positive images of women, particularly emphasizing the need for respect because of their past and continuing contributions to society.

Attention should be given to studying and treating the health problems of aging, particularly in women. Research should also be directed towards the investigation and slowing down of the process of premature aging due to a lifetime of stress, excessive work-load, malnutrition and repeated pregnancy.

D. Young Women

287. Initiatives begun for the 1985 International Youth Year should be extended and expanded so that young women are protected from abuse and exploitation and assisted to develop their full potential. Girls and boys must be provided with equal access to health, education and employment to equip them for adult life. Both girls and boys should be educated to accept equal responsibilities for parenthood.

Urgent attention should be paid to the educational and vocational training of young women in all fields of occupation, giving particular emphasis to those who are socially and economically disadvantaged. Self-employed young women and girls should be assisted to organize co-operatives and ongoing training programmes to improve their skills in production, marketing and management techniques. Special retraining programmes should also be developed for teenage mothers and girls who have dropped out of school and are ill equipped to enter productive employment.

Steps should be taken to eliminate exploitative treatment of young women at work in line with ILO Convention No. 111 concerning discrimination in respect of employment and occupation, 1958 and ILO Convention No. 122 concerning employment policy, 1964. Legislative measures guaranteeing young women their rights should be enforced.

Governments should recognize and enforce the rights of young women to be free from sexual violence, sexual harassment and sexual exploitation. In particular, Governments should recognize that many young women are victims of incest and sexual abuse in the family, and should take steps to assist the victims and to prevent such abuse by education, by improving the status of women and by appropriate action against offenders. Young women should be educated to assert their rights. Particular attention should also be given to sexual harassment and exploitation in employment, especially those areas of employment such as domestic service, where sexual harassment and exploitation are more prevalent.

Governments must also recognize their obligation to provide housing for young women who because of unemployment and low incomes suffer special problems in obtaining housing. Homeless young women are particularly vulnerable to sexual exploitation.

In the year 2000 women aged 15–24 will constitute over 8 per cent of both rural and urban populations in developing countries. The great majority of these women will be out of school and in search of jobs. For those employed, frequent exploitation, long working hours and stress have serious implications for their health. Low nutritional levels and unplanned and repeated pregnancies are also aggravating factors.

E. Abused Women

288. Gender-specific violence is increasing and Governments must affirm the dignity of women, as a priority action.

Governments should therefore intensify efforts to establish or strengthen forms of assistance to victims of such violence through the provision of shelter, support, legal and other services.

In addition to immediate assistance to victims of violence against women in the family and in society, Governments should undertake to increase public awareness of violence against women as a societal problem, establish policies and legislative measures to ascertain its causes and prevent and eliminate such violence, in particular by suppressing degrading images and representations of women in society, and finally encourage the development of educational and re-educational measures for offenders.

F. Destitute Women

289. Destitution is an extreme form of poverty. It is estimated that its effects on large segments of the population in developing and developed countries are on the increase. Forward-looking Strategies to promote the objectives of the United Nations Decade for Women: Equality, Development and Peace at the national and international levels are the basis for dealing with this problem. In addition strategies already specified for the implementation of the International Development Strategy for the Third United Nations Development Decade and the new international economic order are suggested in these recommendations. Governments should therefore ensure that the special needs and concerns of destitute women are given priority in the above-mentioned strategies. Moreover, efforts being undertaken for the International Year of Shelter for the Homeless (1987) should focus attention on the particular situation of women commensurate with their relative needs.

G. Women Victims of Trafficking and Involuntary Prostitution

290. Forced prostitution is a form of slavery imposed on women by procurers. It is, *inter alia,* a result of economic degradation that alienates women's labour through processes of rapid urbanization and migration resulting in underemployment and unemployment. It also stems from women's dependence on men. Social and political pressures produce refugees and missing persons. Often these include vulnerable groups of women who are victimized by procurers. Sex tourism, forced prostitution and pornography reduce women to mere sex objects and marketable commodities.

291. States Parties to the United Nations Convention for the Suppression of the Traffic in Persons and of the Exploitation of the Prostitution of Others should implement the provisions dealing with the exploitation of women as prostitutes. Urgent consideration should also be given to the improvement of international measures to combat trafficking in women for the purposes of prostitution. Resources for the prevention of prostitution and assistance in the professional, personal and social reintegration of prostitutes should be directed towards providing economic opportunities, including training, employment, self-employment and

health facilities for women and children. Governments should also endeavour to co-operate with non-governmental organizations to create wider employment possibilities for women. Strict enforcement provisions must also be taken at all levels to stem the rising tide of violence, drug abuse and crime related to prostitution. The complex and serious problems of the exploitation of and violence against women associated with prostitution call for increased and co-ordinated efforts by police agencies internationally.

H. Women Deprived of Their Traditional Means of Livelihood

292. The excessive and inappropriate exploitation of land by any party for any purpose, *inter alia,* by transnational corporations, as well as natural and man-made disasters are among the predominant causes of deprivation of traditional means of livelihood. Droughts, floods, hurricanes and other forms of environmental hazards, such as erosion, desertification and deforestation, have already pushed poor women into marginal environments. At present the pressures are greatest in drought-afflicted arid and semi-arid areas. Urban slums and squatter settlements are also seriously affected. Critically low levels of water supplies, shortage of fuel, over-utilization of grazing and arable lands, and population density are all factors that deprive women of their livelihood.

293. National and international emphasis on ecosystem management should be strengthened, environmental degradation should be controlled and options provided for alternative means of livelihood. Measures should be established to draw up national conservation strategies aimed at incorporating women's development programmes, among which are irrigation and tree planting and also orientation in the area of agriculture, with women constituting a substantial part of the wage-earning labour force for those programmes.

I. Women who are the Sole Supporters of Families

294. Recent studies have shown that the number of families in which women are the sole supporters is on the increase. Owing to the particular difficulties (social, economic and legal) which they face, many such women are among the poorest people concentrated in urban informal labour markets and they constitute large numbers of the rural unemployed and marginally employed. Those with very little economic, social and moral support face serious difficulties in supporting themselves as well as in bringing up their children alone. This has serious repercussions for society in terms of the quality, character, productivity and human resource capabilities of its present and future citizenry.

295. The assumptions that underlie a large part of the relevant legislation, regulations and household surveys that confine the role of supporter and head of household to men hinder women's access to credit, loans and material and non-material resources. Changes are needed in these areas to secure for women equal access to resources. There is a need to eliminate terms such as "head of household" and introduce others that are comprehensive enough to reflect women's role appropriately in legal documents and household surveys to guarantee the rights of these women. In the provision of social services, special attention has to be given to the needs of these women. Governments are urged to ensure that women with sole responsibility for their families receive a level of income and social support

sufficient to enable them to attain or maintain economic independence and to participate effectively in society. To this end, the assumptions that underlie policies, including research used in policy development, and legislation that confines the role of supporter or head of household to men should be identified and eliminated. Special attention, such as accessible, quality child care, should be given to assisting those women in discharging their domestic responsibilities and to enabling them to participate in and benefit from education, training programmes and employment. The putative father should be made to assist in the maintenance and education of those children born out of wedlock.

J. Women with Physical and Mental Disabilities

296. It is generally accepted that women constitute a significant number of the estimated 500 million people who are disabled as a consequence of mental, physical or sensory impairment. Many factors contribute to the rising numbers of disabled persons, including war and other forms of violence, poverty, hunger, nutritional deficiencies, epidemics and work-related accidents. The recognition of their human dignity and human rights and the full participation by disabled persons in society is still limited, and this presents additional problems for women who may have domestic and other responsibilities. It is recommended that Governments should adopt the Declaration on the Rights of Disabled Persons (1975) and the World Programme of Action concerning Disabled Persons (1982) which provide an overall framework for action and also refer to problems specific to women that have not been fully appreciated by society because they are still not well known or understood. Community-based occupational and social rehabilitation measures, support services to help them with their domestic responsibilities, as well as opportunities for the participation of such women in all aspects of life should be provided. The rights of intellectually disabled women to obtain health information and advice and to consent to or refuse medical treatment should be respected; similarly, the rights of intellectually disabled minors should be respected.

K. Women in Detention and Subject to Penal Law

297. One of the major areas of current concern in the field of crime prevention and criminal justice is the need for equal treatment of women by the criminal justice system. In the context of changing socio-economic and cultural conditions some improvements have taken place but more need to be made. The number of women in detention has increased over the Decade and this trend is expected to continue. Women deprived of freedom are exposed to various forms of physical violence, sexual and moral harassment. The conditions of their detention are often below acceptable hygienic standards and their children are deprived of maternal care. The recommendations of the Sixth United Nations Congress on the Prevention of Crime and the Treatment of Offenders, held at Caracas, in 1980, and the principles of the Caracas Declaration with special reference to the "fair and equal treatment of women", should be taken into account in designing and implementing concrete measures at the national and international levels. The proportions of indigenous women imprisoned in some countries is a matter of concern.

L. Refugee and Displaced Women and Children

298. The international community recognizes a humanitarian responsibility to protect and assist refugees and displaced persons. In many cases refugee and displaced women are exposed to a variety of difficult situations affecting their physical and legal protection as well as their psychological and material well-being. Problems of physical debility, physical safety, emotional stress and socio-psychological effects of separation or death in the family, as well as changes in women's roles, together with limitations often found in the new environment including lack of adequate food, shelter, health care and social services call for specialized and enlarged assistance. Special attention has to be offered to women with special needs. Furthermore, the potential and capacities of refugee and displaced women should be recognized and enhanced.

299. It is recognized that a lasting solution to the problems of refugees and displaced women and children should be sought in the elimination of the root causes of the flow of refugees and durable solutions should be found leading to their voluntary return to their homes in conditions of safety and honour and their full integration in the economic, social and cultural life of their country of origin in the immediate future. Until such solutions are achieved, the international community, in an expression of international solidarity and burden-sharing, should continue providing relief assistance and also launching special relief programmes taking into account the specific needs of refugee women and children in countries of first asylum. Similarly, relief assistance and special relief programmes should also continue to be provided to returnees and displaced women and children. Legal, educational, social, humanitarian and moral assistance should be offered as well as opportunities for their voluntary repatriation, return or resettlement. Steps should also be taken to promote accession by Governments to the 1951 Convention relating to the Status of Refugees and to implement, on a basis of equity for all refugees, provisions contained in this Convention and its 1967 Protocol.

M. Migrant Women

300. The Decade has witnessed the increasing involvement of women in all forms of migration, including rural-rural, rural-urban and international movements of a temporary, seasonal or permanent nature. In addition to their lack of adequate education, skills and resources, migrant women may also face severe adjustment problems due to differences in religion, language, nationality, and socialization as well as separation from their original families. Such problems are often accentuated for international migrants as a result of the openly-expressed prejudices and hostilities, including violation of human rights in host countries. Thus recommendations of the World Population Plan of Action and the Programme of Action for the Second Half of the United Nations Decade for Women pertaining to migrant women should be implemented and expanded in view of the anticipated increase in the scope of the problem. It is also urgent to conclude the elaboration of the draft International Convention on the Protection of the Rights of All Migrant Workers and their Families, as agreed by the General Assembly in the relevant resolutions.

301. The situation of migrant women, who are subject to double discrimination as women and as migrants, should be given special attention by the Governments of host countries, particularly with respect to protection and main-

tenance of family unity, employment opportunities and equal pay, equal conditions of work, health care, benefits to be provided in accordance with the existing social security rights in the host country, and racial and other forms of discrimination. Particular attention should also be given to the second generation of migrant women, especially with regard to education and professional training, to allow them to integrate themselves in their countries of adoption and to work according to their education and skills. In this process, loss of cultural values of their countries of origin should be avoided.

N. Minority and "Indigenous" Women

302. Some women are oppressed as a result of belonging to minority groups or populations which have historically been subjected to domination and suffered dispossession and dispersal. These women suffer the full burden of discrimination based on race, colour, descent, ethnic and national origin and the majority experienced serious economic deprivation. As women, they are therefore doubly disadvantaged. Measures should be taken by Governments in countries in which there are minority and indigenous populations to respect, preserve and promote all of their human rights, their dignity, ethnic, religious, cultural and linguistic identity and their full participation in societal change.

303. Governments should ensure that the fundamental human rights and freedoms as enshrined in relevant international instruments are fully guaranteed also to women belonging to minority groups and indigenous populations. Governments in countries in which there are indigenous and minority populations should ensure respect for the economic, social and cultural rights of these women and assist them in the fulfilment of their family and parental responsibilities. Specific measures should address dietary deficiencies, high levels of infant and maternal mortality and other health problems, lack of education, housing and child care. Vocational, technical, professional and other training should be provided to enable these women to secure employment or to participate in income-generating activities and projects, and to secure adequate wages, occupational health and safety and their other rights as workers. As far as possible, Governments should ensure that these women have access to all services in their own languages.

304. Women belonging to minority groups or indigenous populations should be fully consulted and should participate in the development and implementation of programmes affecting them. The Governments of countries where minorities and indigenous populations exist should take proper account of the work of bodies such as the Committee on the Elimination of Racial Discrimination and the Sub-Commission on Prevention of Discrimination and Protection of Minorities, in particular its Working Group which is developing a set of international standards to protect the rights of indigenous populations. The General Assembly should consider the advisability of designating an international year of indigenous and traditional cultures in order to promote international understanding and to emphasize the distinctive role of women in sustaining the identity of their people.

V. International and Regional Co-operation
A. Obstacles

305. Insufficient attention has been devoted during the Decade at the international level and in some regions to the need to advance the status of women in relation to the goals and objectives of the Decade—equality, development and peace. International tensions, arms race, threat of nuclear war, failure to respect human rights and fundamental freedoms and failure to observe the principles of the United Nations Charter as well as global economic recession and other critical situations combined with dissatisfaction due to inadequate progress in multilateral and international co-operation since the Copenhagen World Conference has substantially affected the scope and ability for international and regional co-operation including the role of the United Nations. The progress in the developing world has slackened or in some cases turned negative under conditions of serious indebtedness, economic and monetary instability, resource constraints and unemployment. This has also affected prospects for economic and technical co-operation among developing countries, particularly with regard to women. Nevertheless some progress has been made in terms of achieving equality between women and men, and a greater appreciation of the role of women in development and peace which should also contribute toward effective international co-operation.

306. International and regional organizations have been called upon during the Decade to advance the position of their women staff and to extend hiring practices to include qualified women. The results have been highly uneven and in some cases the situation has actually worsened during the Decade in the face of resource constraints and other limiting criteria, such as geographical distribution and attitudinal barriers. In particular, women are absent from the senior management levels, which seriously limits their influence on decision-making.

307. In order to institutionalize interorganizational exchanges of information and co-operation in relation to women's advancement, several United Nations agencies, non-governmental organizations and regional bodies have designated, in response to pressures applied during the Decade, focal points for women's activities. However, in many cases, insufficient tenure and resources accompanied those actions, thus limiting their long-term effectiveness. Moreover, activities that promote the integration of women in development have often been confined to these focal points and have not been integrated into all organizational planning and programme activities. Progress has also been limited in this area by the inadequate training of many of the staff members of international agencies and organizations with respect to the centrality of women's role in development.

308. International and regional co-operation strategies must be formulated on the premise that effective development requires the full integration of women in the development process as both agents and beneficiaries. Development agencies should take full cognizance of women as a development resource. This requires that all international and regional development institutions adopt explicit policies in this regard and put in place the management systems necessary to ensure the effective implementation and evaluation of these policies in the full range of their programmes and activities. Such policies should incorporate the principles endorsed in the Forward-looking Strategies of Implementation for the Advancement of Women. Strong and visible commitment to and interest in integrating women in the development process should be demonstrated by the senior-level management of development agencies.

B. Basic Strategies

309. Effective consultative and reporting arrangements are required to collect information on action taken to implement the Forward-looking Strategies and on successful ways and means used to overcome obstacles. Monitoring and evaluation should, therefore, be carried out at international, regional and subregional levels based on national-level monitoring, including input from non-governmental organizations.

310. Technical co-operation, training and advisory services should promote endogenous development and self-reliance with greater emphasis on economic and technical co-operation among developing countries. The special needs of women should be periodically assessed and methods developed to integrate women's concerns into the planning and evaluation of development activities. The participation of women in the formulation of technical co-operation policies and programmes should be ensured.

311. International, regional and subregional institutional co-ordination should be strengthened, particularly in relation to the exchange of information on the advancement of women and the establishment of collaborative arrangements to undertake activities with interrelated components.

312. Research and policy analysis should focus greater attention on the economic role of women in society, including access to economic resources such as land and capital. Research and policy analysis related to women should be action-oriented without losing sight of key analytical considerations. Further investment in evolving adequate gender-specific data is also required.

313. Steps should be taken to increase the participation of women in international, regional and subregional level activities and decision-making, including those directly or indirectly concerned with the maintenance of peace and security, the role of women in development and the achievement of equality between women and men.

314. Information on progress in achieving the goals of the Decade and on implementing the Forward-looking Strategies should be widely disseminated in the period from 1985 to the year 2000 at international, regional, subregional and national levels, based on experience gained during the Decade. Greater reliance is needed on audiovisual communications and expansion of networks for disseminating information on programmes and activities for women. Discriminatory, stereotyped and degrading images of women must be eliminated in the media.

315. On the basis of the results of the review and appraisal in the United Nations system that indicated the need for continued efforts to ensure the recruitment, promotion and retention of women, all United Nations bodies, the regional commissions and the specialized agencies should take all measures necessary to achieve an equitable balance between women and men staff members at managerial and professional levels in all substantive areas, as well as in field posts, with particular attention to promoting equitable regional representation of women. Women should be appointed to decision-making and management posts within the United Nations system in order to increase their participation in activities at the international and regional levels, including such areas as equality, development and peace.

316. In view of the difficulties of spouses of United Nations officials in securing employment at the various duty stations, the United Nations is urged to make every possible effort to provide the establishment of educational facilities and day care centres for families of officials in order to facilitate the employment of spouses at these duty stations.

C. Measures for the Implementation of the Basic Strategies

1. *Monitoring.* The implementation of the goals and objectives of the Decade—equality, development and peace—and of the Forward-looking Strategies should be monitored during the period 1986 to the year 2000. Monitoring at the international level should be based on reviews, at the regional, subregional and national levels, of action taken, resources allocated and progress achieved. The national reviews should take the form of a response to a regular statistical reporting request from the United Nations Secretariat, which should include indicators of the situation of women. The statistical reporting basis should be developed by the Statistical Commission, in consultation with the Commission on the Status of Women. The United Nations Secretariat should compile the results of such monitoring in consultation with the appropriate bodies of Governments, including national machinery established to monitor and improve the status of women. The action taken and progress achieved at the national level should reflect consultation with non-governmental organizations and integration of their concerns at all levels of government planning, implementation and evaluation, as appropriate.

318. The specialized agencies and other United Nations organizations, including the regional commissions, should establish monitoring capabilities and procedures to analyse the situation of women in their sectoral or geographical areas, and submit their reports regularly to their respective governing bodies and to the Commission on the Status of Women, which is the main intergovernmental body within the United Nations system concerned with women.

319. The Commission on the Status of Women should consider on a regular basis reports on the progress made and concrete measures implemented at national, regional and international levels to advance the status of women in relation to the goals of the Decade—equality, development and peace—and the sub-theme—employment, health and education—and the strategies and measures to the year 2000. The United Nations system should continue to carry out a comprehensive and critical review of progress achieved in implementing the provisions of the World Plan of Action and of the Programme for the Second Half of the Decade. The central role in carrying out this review and appraisal should be played by the Commission on the Status of Women. The Commission should also monitor progress in the implementation of international standards, codes of conduct, strategies, conventions and covenants as they pertain to women. In view of this important function, high-level expertise and representation on the Commission should be given priority, including officials with substantive policy responsibilities for the advancement of women.

320. The preparation of new instruments and strategies such as the overall strategies for international development, should pay specific, appropriate attention to the advancement of women. Intergovernmental bodies of the United Nations system, particularly those concerned with the monitoring, review and appraisal of the existing instruments, strategies, plans and programmes that may be of direct or indirect relevance to women, are urged as a matter of priority to develop explicit policies and reviewable plans

of action for the integration of women in their regular work programmes.

321. The methods and procedures employed for collecting information from Governments, regional commissions, non-governmental organizations and other international organizations and bodies should be streamlined and based on guidelines to be discussed by the Commission on the Status of Women.

2. *Technical Co-operation, Training and Advisory Services.* Measures of technical co-operation, training and advisory services directed towards improving women's status at the international, interregional and regional levels, including co-operation among developing countries, need some impetus. This would require the re-ordering of principles for the allocation of resources as well as targeted financial, material and human resource assistance. Notwithstanding resource constraints, the United Nations should continue the important role of reinforcing these increased benefits for women.

323. Technical co-operation should be approached with a new concept that will break the cycle of dependency, emphasize local needs, and use local materials and resources as well as local creativity and expertise and be based on the full integration of women as agents and beneficiaries in all technical co-operation activities. Local associations and mechanisms should be oriented to play a more active role in planning and policy-making. Emphasis should be given to broader access by women to capital for self-help projects, income-generating activities, enterprise development and projects designed to reduce the drudgery in work performed by women. Innovative demonstration projects, particularly with respect to the integration of women in non-traditional sector activities, should be an essential element in technical co-operation activities.

324. Agencies which do not have specific guidelines or project procedures relating to women in development interlinked with the other aims of the period up to the year 2000 should ensure that they are developed. Such guidelines and procedures should apply to all aspects of the project cycle. Existing guidelines and procedures have to be applied more vigorously and consistently; in particular, each project document should contain a strategy to ensure that the project has a positive impact on the situation of women.

325. Substantive staff training is needed to enhance the ability of staff to recognize and deal with the centrality of women's role in development, and adequate resources must be made available for this purpose. Implementation of policies concerning women is the responsibility of the particular organization as a whole. Responsibility is not merely a matter of personal persuasion. Systems should be developed which allocate responsibility and accountability.

326. Governments should strengthen and improve their institutional arrangements for technical co-operation so that policy is effectively linked to local-level implementing mechanisms, and should promote sustained, endogenous development. In these efforts Governments may wish to make use of the accumulated experience, activities and resources of the whole United Nations system.

327. While technical co-operation should be focused equally on women and men, the incorporation of women's needs and aspirations in the formulation and review of technical co-operation policies and programmes should be ensured and the potential negative effects on women of technical assistance should be minimized. Technical co-operation and women must be linked to overall national development objectives and priorities, and technical assistance plans and programmes should be managed so as to ensure the full integration of activities specific to women. As a standard component of technical co-operation policies, women should be full and equal participants in technical co-operation projects and activities. The needs of especially vulnerable and underprivileged groups of women should be addressed in the technical co-operation programmes.

328. Participation of non-governmental organizations as a means to enhance the relevance and impact of technical co-operation activities of benefit to women should be encouraged.

329. In allocating multilateral and bilateral assistance, agencies, in consultation with recipient Governments, should establish measurable and reviewable plans of action, with goals and time frames. They should also give adequate impetus to sustained and real increases in the flow of resources for technical co-operation activities of benefit to women, including greater mobilization of resources from non-governmental sources and the private sector. Bilateral and multilateral aid agencies should give special consideration to assisting the least developed countries in their efforts to integrate women in development. In this regard, particular attention should be given to projects in the fields of health, education and training, and the creation of employment opportunities for women, especially in rural areas.

330. Bilateral and multilateral aid agencies should take a corporate-wide response to the integration of women in development. Bilateral aid agencies' policies for women in development should involve all parts of donors' organizations and programmes, including participation of multilateral and bilateral programmes, training, technical assistance and financial aid. Policies for women in development should be incorporated into all applicable aid and agency procedures relating to sectoral and project levels.

331. In order to enable women to define and defend their own interests and needs, the United Nations system and aid agencies should provide assistance for programmes and projects which strengthen women's autonomy, in particular in the integration process.

332. International non-governmental organizations, including such organizations as trade unions, should be encouraged to involve women in their day-to-day work and to increase their attention to women's issues. The capacity of non-governmental organizations at all levels to reach women and women's groups should receive greater recognition and support. The potential role of those non-governmental organizations could be fully utilized by international and governmental agencies involved in development co-operation.

333. Technical and advisory assistance should be provided by the United Nations system at the national level to improve systematically statistical and other forms of gender-specific indicators and information that can help redirect policy and programmes for the more effective integration of women in development as contributors and beneficiaries.

334. Technical co-operation among developing countries should be strengthened in the service of women at all levels and in all sectors of activity, focusing particularly on promoting the exchange of experience, expertise, technology and know-how, as well as on diffusing innovative organizational models suitable for strengthening the self-reliance of women. The urgent need for information flows to facilitate the process of integrating women in development, and

the need for relevant, transferable and appropriate information should be a priority of regional co-operation within the framework of technical co-operation among developing countries. Regional co-operation to assist disadvantaged groups of women should also be promoted in this context.

335. Technical assistance should be given by the United Nations system and other international and non-governmental organizations to women involved in the promotion of international peace and co-operation.

336. The United Nations system should continue to strengthen training programmes for women, in particular in the least developed countries, through fellowships and other means of assistance, particularly in the fields of economic planning, public affairs and public administration, business management and accounting, and farming and labour relations, and in scientific, engineering and technical fields. It is necessary to support and expand technical and economic activities for women by means of collaboration with international development assistance agencies. In this respect, the United Nations Development Fund for Women is particularly recognized for its innovative contribution in the area of development and technical assistance for disadvantaged women, and its continuation and expansion beyond the Decade is considered of vital importance to the development needs of women.

337. The participation of women in technical assistance monitoring, planning, programming, evaluation and follow-up missions should be promoted, and guidelines should be developed and applied to assess the relevance and impact of development assistance projects on women. The United Nations funding agencies, such as the United Nations Development Programme, the United Nations Fund for Population Activities, the United Nations Children's Fund and the World Food Programme, as well as the World Bank, should ensure that women benefit from and participate in all projects and programmes funded by them.

3. *Institutional Co-ordination.* System-wide co-ordination of work on issues relating to women needs to be strengthened. The Economic and Social Council should be encouraged to play a more forceful and dynamic role in reviewing and co-ordinating all relevant United Nations activities in the field of women's issues. Regular consultations between United Nations agencies and organizations should be institutionalized in conjunction with meetings of the Commission on the Status of Women in order to exchange information on programme activities and co-ordinate future planning and programming with a view to ensuring adequate resource-allocation that would facilitate action and limit the unnecessary duplication of activities.

339. Future medium-term plans of the United Nations and the specialized agencies should contain intersectoral presentations of the various programmes dealing with issues of concern to women. In order to achieve greater coherence and efficiency of the policies and programmes of the United Nations system related to women and development, the Secretary-General, in his capacity as Chairman of the Administrative Committee on Co-ordination and in conformity with Economic and Social Council resolution 1985/46 of 31 May 1985, should take the initiative in formulating a system-wide medium-term plan for women and development.

340. The Centre for Social Development and Humanitarian Affairs of the Department of International Economic and Social Affairs, in particular the Branch of the Advance-

ment of Women, should continue to serve as the focal point for co-ordination of, consultation on, promotion of and advice on matters relevant to women in the United Nations system and to co-ordinate information on system-wide activities related to the future implementation on the goals and objectives of the Decade and the Forward-looking Strategies. In this context, the United Nations system should explore ways and means of developing further collaboration between its organizations, including the regional commissions, the International Research and Training Institute for the Advancement of Women and the United Nations Development Fund for Women, in particular in connection with the holding of United Nations world conferences on women on a regular basis, if necessary, for example every five years. It is recommended that at least one world conference be held during the period between 1985 and the year 2000, taking into account that the General Assembly will take the decision on the holding of the conference in each case within existing financial resources.

341. Existing sectoral inter-agency task forces in the United Nations system should always include issues related to the advancement of women in their agenda.

342. Inter-agency co-ordination should be complemented where possible by networking, particularly in the fields of information, research, training and programme development, in order to facilitate the availability of data and information in these fields and the exchange of experience with national machinery.

343. Resolutions of the United Nations General Assembly, of governing bodies of the specialized agencies and of other organizations which promote the improvement of the status of women should be implemented. All institutions within the United Nations system that have not yet established special internal arrangements and procedures with respect to women's policies are urged to take the necessary measures to do so.

344. International machineries that promote and support education for peace should co-ordinate their efforts and include the role of women in promoting peace in their curricula. Particular attention should be paid to the Declaration on the Participation of Women in Promoting International Peace and Co-operation adopted by the General Assembly in 1982. The University for Peace should play a leading role in this regard.

4. *Research and Policy Analysis.* Institutes of women's affairs at the regional level should be strengthened or, where they do not exist, their establishment should be considered for the promotion of regional collaboration in undertaking research and analyses on emerging women's issues in order to facilitate and promote regional and international co-operation and understanding in this field.

346. Measures should be taken by the United Nations system to strengthen the capabilities of the United Nations Secretariat to provide assistance to Governments and other international organizations and bodies concerned with integrating women in policy formulation and in assessing the impact of development policies on women. The Branch for the Advancement of Women should act as the focal point for co-ordinating the exchange of information, providing advice on matters related to the advancement of women and monitoring and evaluating the progress of other bodies in that connection. The United Nations should develop guidelines for this purpose based on comparative analyses of experience world wide.

347. Guidelines should also be developed by the United Nations for action to remove gender-specific discrimina-

tory perceptions, attitudes and behaviour based on models of successful initiatives.

348. The United Nations system should undertake research and prepare guidelines, case studies and practical approaches on integrating women on an equal basis with men into political life. Training programmes for and consultations between women already engaged in political life should be organized.

349. Research should be carried out and a report prepared by the United Nations, in consultation with other organizations and specialized agencies and in co-operation with Governments, on establishing effective institutional arrangements at the national level for the formulation of policies on women, including guidelines and summaries of national case studies.

350. United Nations agencies and, in particular, the Centre for Social Development and Humanitarian Affairs of the United Nations Secretariat, as part of its regular programme of work, should undertake in-depth research on the positive and negative effects of legislative change, the persistence of *de facto* discrimination and conflicts between customary and statutory laws. In carrying out this research, full use should be made of the work of the Committee on the Elimination of All Forms of Discrimination against Women.

351. In the context of the Third United Nations Development Decade and any subsequent decade, the implications for women of international decisions especially pertaining to international trade and finance, agriculture and technology transfer should be assessed by the United Nations system in consultation with the appropriate international organizations, bodies and research institutes, including the United Nations Research Institute for Social Development, the International Research and Training Institute for the Advancement of Women and any others established by the United Nations University. The lack of reliable data prevents the assessment of relative improvements in women's status in the various sectors. It is therefore essential that the Statistical Commission, the Commission on the Status of Woman and the International Research and Training Institute for the Advancement of Women should co-operate at the institutional level in the collection, analysis, utilization and dissemination of statistical data on the question of women. The data base on women's role in national, regional and international economic activities should be further developed by the United Nations in co-operation with Governments, specialized agencies and the regional commissions of the United Nations system.

352. The United Nations regional commissions, with a view to integrating women's concerns at all levels in each commission's overall programme of work, should undertake further research on the status of women in their regions to the year 2000 by developing the necessary data base and indicators and by drawing upon inputs from the national and local levels, including perspectives on and by women at the grass-roots level. To this end, the regional commissions should include in their annual reports an analysis of changes in the situation of women in their regions.

353. It is also necessary to strengthen the activities of the International Research and Training Institute for the Advancement of Women which performs an important role in the field of research, training, information and communication, and to request States and appropriate organizations, in particular, the organizations of the United Nations system, to continue to collaborate with the Institute in its work for the improvement of the status of women. The In-

stitute should continue its work in appraising and evaluating what has been done by Governments and the United Nations system in promoting the status of women and it should be given increased voluntary financial support.

354. The United Nations should incorporate within its activities related to the World Disarmament Campaign the preparation of a study on the specific consequences of the arms race and modern warfare for women in general, especially aged or pregnant women and young children. Such a study should be given wide publicity in order to mobilize researchers, politicians and non-governmental organizations, as well as women themselves, for the promotion of disarmament.

355. The United Nations system and other intergovernmental, governmental and non-governmental organizations should encourage women, women's organizations and all the appropriate governmental bodies from different countries to discuss and study various aspects of promoting peace and other related issues in order to increase knowledge, facilitate understanding and develop friendly relations between countries and people. Exchange visits among women from different countries, and meetings and seminars in which women participate fully should be organized at regional and international levels.

5. *Participation of Women in Activities at the International and Regional Levels and in Decision-making.* The United Nations system should take all necessary measures to achieve an equitable balance between women and men staff members at managerial and professional levels in all substantive areas, as well as in field posts. Regular reporting to the General Assembly, the governing bodies of the specialized agencies, the regional commissions and the Commission on the Status of Women on the establishment and implementation of targets for the equal representation of women in professional posts should be continued.

357. Women and women's organizations from different countries should be encouraged to discuss and study various aspects of promoting peace and development issues in order to increase knowledge, facilitate understanding and develop friendly relations between countries and peoples. Exchange visits of women from different countries and meetings with full participation by women should be encouraged.

358. In order to ensure that programmes and activities of concern to women are given the necessary attention and priority, it is essential that women should participate actively in the planning and formulation of policies and programmes and in decision-making and appraisal processes in the United Nations. To this end, international, regional and national organizations have been called upon during the Decade to advance the status of their female staff and to increase the number of women recruited. In the absence of overall targets and effective mechanisms for their achievement, however, greater efforts are needed to ensure the recruitment, promotion and career development of women. All bodies and organizations of the United Nations system should therefore take all possible measures to achieve the participation of women on equal terms with men at all levels by the year 2000. To achieve this goal, the secretariats of the United Nations and all the organizations and bodies within the system should take special measures, such as the preparation of a comprehensive affirmative action plan including provisions for setting intermediate targets and for establishing and supporting special mechanisms—for example, co-ordinators—to improve the status of women staff. Progress made to implement those measures should

be reported to the General Assembly, the Economic and Social Council and the Commission on the Status of Women on a regular basis.

359. Women should be assured of the opportunity to participate in international, regional and subregional meetings and seminars, including those organized by the United Nations system, particularly those related to equality, development and peace, including peace education, and those directed to promoting the role of women in development through research activities, seminars and conferences to exchange experience and expertise. Similarly, women Parliamentarians should always be included in delegations to inter-parliamentary meetings organized by the Inter-Parliamentary Union and regional inter-parliamentary organizations.

360. The participation of women in promoting peace and in the struggle against the obstacles to peace at the international level should be encouraged. Networking of women at high decision-making levels related to peace and disarmament, including women leaders, peace researchers and educators, should also be encouraged in connection with United Nations system activities such as the International Year of Peace (1986). "Women and peace" should be a separate item in the programme for that Year.

361. In order to provide a firm basis for the integration of issues of concern to women in the overall development process, a greater effort is needed to define such issues and to develop useful models for action in socio-cultural, economic and political contexts. Work in this area can be undertaken in the national and regional research institutions, as well as in the United Nations and other international agencies. In this context, attention should also be given to increasing the planning capabilities of women.

362. Special efforts should be made at both the national and regional levels to ensure that women have equal access to all aspects of modern science and technology, particularly in educational systems. The use of science and technology can be a powerful instrument for the advancement of women. Special research to evolve appropriate technology for rural women should be carried out, and existing and new technology should be disseminated as widely as possible. The co-ordination of such activities in the regions should be the responsibility of the regional commissions, in co-operation with other intergovernmental bodies and agencies that deal with the status of women and technology.

363. Governments and non-governmental organizations should organize regular training programmes that are aimed at improving the status of women workers and widening women's access to and improving their performance in managerial positions in the sectors of employment or self-employment. In this connection, the United Nations is urged to support programmes on network and exchange of expertise in vocational training being carried out by regional and subregional organizations.

364. Regional and subregional groups have an important role to play in strengthening the roles of women in development. Existing regional and subregional information systems on women should be reinforced. A stronger data and research base on women should be developed in the developing countries and in the regional commissions, in collaboration with the appropriate specialized agencies, and the sharing of information and research data should be encouraged. Information systems at the national level should be strengthened or, where they do not exist, should be established.

365. International, regional, and subregional and national organizations should be strengthened through the injection of additional human and financial resources and through the placement of more women at policy- and decision-making levels.

6. *Information Dissemination.* International programmes should be designed and resources allocated to support national campaigns to improve public consciousness of the need for equality between women and men and for eliminating discriminatory practices. Special attention should be given to information about the Convention on the Elimination of All Forms of Discrimination against Women.

367. Studies must be carried out by the United Nations system on sex stereotyping in advertising and in the mass media, especially degrading images of women in articles and programmes disseminated world wide. Steps should be taken to promote the elimination or reduction of sex stereotyping in the media.

368. In order to promote peace, social justice and the advancement of women, wide publicity should be given by the United Nations to legal instruments and the United Nations resolutions and reports relating to women and the objectives of the Decade, that is, equality, development and peace. The mass media, including United Nations radio and television, should disseminate information on the role of women in achieving these objectives, particularly in promoting co-operation and understanding among peoples and the maintenance of international peace and security. Cultural mechanisms of communication should also be used to disseminate the importance of the concepts of peace and international understanding for the advancement of women.

369. It is essential that women be trained in the use of audio-visual forms of information dissemination, including visual display units and computers, and participate more actively in developing programmes on the advancement of women and for women at the international, regional, subregional and national levels.

370. The present United Nations weekly radio programme and co-production of films on women should be continued with adequate provision for distributing them in different languages.

371. The Joint United Nations Information Committee should continue to include women's issues in its programmes of social and economic information. Adequate resources should be made available for these activities.

372. Governments and the organizations of the United Nations system, including the regional commissions and the specialized agencies, are urged to give the Forward-looking Strategies the widest publicity possible and to ensure that their content is translated and disseminated in order to make authorities and the public in general, especially women's grass-root organizations, aware of the objectives of that document and of the recommendations contained therein.

On 26 May 1988, the Economic and Social Council, at the request of the General Assembly, approved (resolution 1988/22) a comprehensive reporting system to monitor, review, and appraise the implementation of the Nairobi Forward-looking Strategies (the resolution is reproduced below) and decided that its intergovernmental subsidiary bodies, including the regional commissions, should perform the monitoring function under the leadership of the Commission on the Status of Women. Under the five-year cycle of reporting, quinquennial reviews and appraisals are scheduled for 1990, 1995, and 2000. The reporting system was endorsed by the General Assembly on 8 December 1988 (resolution 43/101).

I. Biennial Monitoring of Progress Made by the Organizations of the United Nations System

1. The Secretary-General should prepare a biennial report on monitoring of the implementation of the Forward-looking Strategies by the organizations of the United Nations system, including monitoring at the regional level. The report should address the three interrelated and mutually reinforcing objectives of the Forward-looking Strategies: equality, development and peace. Each objective should be reported on separately, as appropriate.

2. An introductory commentary covering the basic strategies, relevant institutions, mandates and programmes of action employed to advance each objective should be included.

3. An account of measures taken for the implementation of the basic strategies for international and regional co-operation set out in chapter V of the Forward-looking Strategies should be included under each objective.

4. The report should contain specific information on:

(a) Measures to ensure the integration of the Forward-looking Strategies in the programmes of the organizations of the United Nations system, including measures to strengthen institutional co-ordination and focal points on the status of women;

(b) Progress made by each organization in establishing and meeting five-year targets at each level for the percentage of women in professional and decision-making positions, as called for by the General Assembly.

5. Reports should be prepared according to a standardized format.

6. In order to minimize duplication of effort, the biennial monitoring report should make use of reports prepared to meet other reporting requirements, *inter alia,* any other reports required under subprogramme 5A of the proposed revisions to the medium-term plan for 1984–1989 to cover the period 1990–1991, the biennial reports requested by the General Assembly in resolution 42/178 of 11 December 1987 and reports on the improvement of the status of women in the United Nations Secretariat as requested by the General Assembly.

II. Quinquennial Review and Appraisal

7. The review and appraisal will be based on responses from Member States to a questionnaire on the progress achieved in the implementation of the Forward-looking Strategies, including an assessment of the effectiveness of methods and programmes introduced and an account of new programmes planned as a result of the national review and appraisal.

8. The national reports should address the three interrelated and mutually reinforcing objectives of the Forward-looking Strategies: equality, development and peace. Each objective should be monitored and reported on separately.

9. Each national report should include an introductory commentary covering the basic strategies and programmes of action employed to advance each objective and a review and appraisal of their effectiveness.

10. The national reports should include, under each of the three objectives, an account of measures for the implementation of the basic strategies for international and regional co-operation set out in paragraphs 356 to 365 of the Forward-looking Strategies.

11. The questionnaires should be simple and direct and structured according to the Forward-looking Strategies.

12. The national reports should include an account of the measures taken to meet relevant international standards, such as the Convention on the Elimination of All Forms of Discrimination against Women, the International Convention on the Elimination of All Forms of Racial Discrimination and the conventions of the International Labour Organisation.

13. Non-governmental bodies should be invited to submit reports for the review and appraisal.

14. The biennial statistical reports provided by the Secretary-General to the Commission on the Status of Women for monitoring progress at the national level should be consolidated and made available to the Commission for the review and appraisal.

15. Every five years, the Commission on the Status of Women should review its conclusions on priority themes on the basis of a compilation of relevant resolutions and select priority themes for the following five-year period.

16. Reports of Member States to relevant international supervisory bodies, such as the Committee on the Elimination of Discrimination against Women, the Committee on the Elimination of Racial Discrimination, the International Labour Organisation and the United Nations Educational, Scientific and Cultural Organization, and the *World Survey on the Role of Women in Development* should be made available in a consolidated form to the Commission on the Status of Women for consideration in the review and appraisal.

17. Reports prepared by the regional commissions on change in the situation of women within their region, as requested by the General Assembly in resolution 42/178 of 11 December 1987, should be made available to the Commission on the Status of Women every five years, for the review and appraisal.

SEE ALSO *Convention on the Elimination of All Forms of Discrimination against Women; Convention on the Political Rights of Women; Declaration of Mexico on the Equality of Women and Their Contribution to Development and Peace; Declaration on the Elimination of Discrmination against Women; Inter-American Convention on the Granting of Civil Rights to Women; Inter-American Convention on the Granting of Political Rights to Women; International Women's Year.*

NAMIBIA. Once a German colony and later the Territory of South West Africa mandated by the League of Nations to South Africa, Namibia has been the subject of intense international contention since 1946. When it achieved independence on 21 March 1990—the last African colony to do so—it became the 160th State member of the United Nations, the 52nd State member of the Organization of African States, and the 50th State member of the Commonwealth of Nations.

The country, which is rich in natural resources, has borders with Angola, Botswana, South Africa, and

Zambia. Its total population is estimated (1990) to be 1,288,000, of which 82,000 are white; 52,000, colored (mixed), and the remainder, a wide variety of ethnic groups, including 641,000 Ovambo, 120,000 Kavango, 97,000 Damara, 97,000 Herero, 62,000 Nama, 48,000 Caprivian, 37,000 Bushmen, 32,000 Baster, and 8,000 Tswana. Languages in common use include Africaans, English, German, and numerous regional vernaculars. Christianity is the predominant religion, although animism and other indigenous beliefs are widely practiced. Literacy is estimated at 90% for white Africans, 30% for non-whites.

Recent international developments with reference to Namibia were summarized by the AD HOC WORKING GROUP OF EXPERTS ON SOUTHERN AFRICA in its report to the 1990 session of the UN Commission on Human Rights as follows (UN Doc. E/CN.4/1990/7, para. 230–249):

After World War I, the League of Nations assigned Namibia, which was known as German South West Africa, to South Africa as a mandated territory. However, because of grave abuses and violations of contractual obligations by South Africa, the United Nations General Assembly revoked the mandate in 1966. The International Court of Justice adjudicated several times that South Africa has been in illegal occupation of Namibia ever since.

In 1976, the Security Council unanimously adopted resolution 385, which required withdrawal of South Africa and transfer of power to the United Nations. It was proposed that elections would then be held under the aegis of the United Nations, to select delegates to draft a constitution for an independent Namibia.

On 10 April 1978, the United States, United Kingdom, France, West Germany and Canada submitted the main "proposals for a settlement of the Namibian situation" (see S/12636). The aforementioned countries became known as the Contact Group. On 29 August and 28 September 1978, the Secretary-General issued two subsidiary documents (S/12827 and S/12869, respectively) for the purpose of implementing the proposals of the Contact Group and by way of an explanation of the proposals. On the basis of the foregoing the Security Council adopted resolution 435 on 29 September 1978 which, *inter alia,* provides for the establishment of the United Nations Transition Assistance Group (UNTAG), which includes both a civilian and a military component, functioning under the authority of the Security Council resolution 435 (1978) and assisting the Special Representative of the Secretary-General for Namibia in his task of monitoring and supervising the free and fair election of a Constituent Assembly. It may be mentioned that not only the elections but also all aspects of the preceding and subsequent political process must be free and fair.

It may be noted that many units now operating under the effective control of, or in co-operation with, the South African Defence Force (SADF) did not exist when Security Council resolution 435 (1978) was adopted. The South West African Territorial Force (SWATF) and the Counterinsurgency Unit (COIN), popularly known as "Koevoet" ("crowbar"), are examples of such units.

In December 1988, as a result of negotiations held by the parties concerned, the independence agreement for Namibia was concluded (see Annex). It included the following provisions:

    (1) Release of political prisoners
    (2) Return of political exiles
    (3) Repatriation of refugees
    (4) Abolition of all discriminatory laws.

On 16 February 1989, the Security Council adopted resolution 632 (1989) by which it decided to implement its resolution 435 (1978) of 29 September 1978 in its original and definitive form to ensure conditions in Namibia which would allow the Namibian people to participate freely and without intimidation in the electoral process under the supervision and control of the United Nations leading to early independence of the territory.

The implementation of the settlement plan began in April 1989, entrusting UNTAG with the task of monitoring the territory's transition to independence.

As in previous years, the Working Group analysed the situation of human rights in Namibia on the basis of the testimonies and other relevant material received from various sources. In addition, taking into account the specificity of the current situation prevailing in Namibia, the Working Group relied extensively on the information contained in the report of the Secretary-General of the United Nations submitted to the Security Council in accordance with paragraph 9 of Council resolution 640 (1989) of 29 August 1989 (see S/20883 and S/20883/Add.1).

As stated in the report of the Secretary-General, under paragraphs 7 (b) and 7 (c) of the United Nations settlement plan, all Namibian political prisoners were required to be set free. It was stated in the report of the United Nations Mission on Detainees that, on 24 May 1989, UNTAG military observers stationed in Angola had been enabled to interview about 201 former detainees who had been released by SWAPO. On 4 July 1989, 153 ex-detainees, including 18 children, were repatriated to Namibia from Angola, followed by two further groups of 63 and 16 on 29 July 1989 and 8 August 1989, respectively.

On 20 July 1989, 25 Namibian political prisoners were released from the central prison in Windhoek by the South African authorities. It was alleged that both SWAPO and the South African authorities were still holding detainees. In reply to these allegations, the Administrator-General for Namibia, on behalf of the South African Government, replied that the persons on the lists submitted to him had either been released or were unknown to the South African authorities.

SWAPO stated that it no longer held any detainees, and invited the international community to conduct an investigation.

The Mission on Detainees, established by the Special Representative of the Secretary-General in pursuance of paragraphs 7 (c) and 7 (d) of the settlement proposal for Namibia visited Angola and Zambia from 2 to 21 September 1989. Its main purpose was to ascertain whether any Namibians were still being detained by SWAPO, at locations already identified or elsewhere in Angola and Zambia, and if so, to ensure that appropriate arrangements for their release and voluntary repatriation were promptly made in order to enable them to participate in the electoral process. Prior to the departure of the Mission, a consolidated list was prepared of the names of persons allegedly detained. It included about 1,100 names of persons reported to have died or to have been released and/or repatriated, and was intended to form a comprehensive reference source.

From 2 to 12 September 1989, the Mission visited a total of 22 locations in Angola, after which, from 14 to 20 September 1989 it visited a total of 8 locations in Zambia. The Mission visited virtually all of the sites where persons had been reported to be held in the two countries. On the basis of its findings, the Mission unanimously concluded that there were no detainees, in any of the alleged detention centres and other places which it visited, and the majority of persons allegedly detained or missing had been repatriated or otherwise accounted for.

The report of the Secretary-General stated that, on 6 June 1989, an amnesty was granted to all Namibian exiles. This permitted the beginning of the repatriation operation which had been entrusted to the United Nations High Commissioner for Refugees (UNHCR).

UNHCR established three air and three land entry points as well as five reception centres in central and northern Namibia, to receive, register and materially assist the returnees. By 29 September 1989, it was reported that 41,748 Namibians from 46 countries had returned home, and all but 579 had resettled in their former communities.

The planned return of Namibian refugees scheduled for mid-May was threatened with delay because of a dispute over abolishing all discriminatory laws, as required by Security Council resolution 435 (1978). The key obstacle reportedly was Proclamation AG.8, a law that makes provision for racially segregated administrations under the territory's two-tier governmental system. South Africa's Administrator-General, Mr. Louis Pienaar, insisted that by merely dissolving the political compound, the administrations themselves can continue to function within the terms of resolution 435 (1978). In the opinion of the Working Group, the delay in the return of refugees could have affected their participation in the electoral process.

The registration of voters began on 3 September 1989 and ended on 23 September 1989. Almost 700,000 voters were registered, with only 593 applications being rejected, in each case with the concurrence of the UNTAG supervisor.

According to information received by the Working Group, the Administrator-General for Namibia issued instructions that schools in Namibia were to remain closed from 30 October to 10 November 1989, to accommodate preparations for the elections.

The following political parties presented electoral candidates:

    (1) Action Christian National
    (2) Democratic Turnhalle Alliance
    (3) Federal Convention of Namibia
    (4) Namibian Christian Democratic Party
    (5) Namibian National Front
    (6) National Patriotic Front of Namibia
    (7) South West Africa People's Organization
    (8) SWAPO - Democrats
    (9) United Democratic Front
    (10) Namibia National Democratic Party.

The elections, which took place from 7 to 11 November 1989, enabled the elected delegates to form a constituent assembly that will enact a constitution for Namibia. The results of the elections which took place under the supervision of UNTAG were announced on 13 November 1989, with 7 of the 10 parties contesting the elections gaining representation. SWAPO won 41 seats, the Democratic Turnhalle Alliance won 21 seats, the United Democratic Front won 4 seats, the Action Christian National won 3 seats, and 3 smaller parties secured 1 seat each. The electoral process was described as "an exemplary lesson in democracy". As SWAPO had been unable to obtain a clear two-thirds majority, it was necessary for them to form an alliance with other parties.

After completing the above-mentioned report, the ad hoc working group visited Namibia from 12 to 17 February 1990. In a further report to the commission, prepared at Windhoek, it presented its analysis of the human rights provisions of the "Constitution for an Independent Namibia," which had been adopted unanimously by the Namibian Constituent Assembly and which later became operative as the **NAMIBIA: CONSTITUTION** on 21 March 1990, the day of independence. The analysis was as follows (UN Doc. E/CN.4/1990/7/Add. 1, para. 39–44):

. . . . . The *Ad Hoc* Working Group has studied the main elements of the Constitution, which proclaims the Republic of Namibia as a sovereign, secular, democratic and unitary State based on the principles of democracy, the rule of law and justice for all. The multi-party democratic State has the characteristics of a presidential system. Chapter 3 (articles 5 to 25) incorporates most of the fundamental rights and freedoms laid down in the Universal Declaration of Human Rights, subject only to the declaration of a state of emergency (article 26), which must first be approved by a resolution of the National Assembly. In article 4, the Constitution deals with the acquisition and loss of citizenship. Article 26 elaborates circumstances in which a state of emergency may be declared.

Articles 79, 80 and 81 refer to the administration of justice. The Constitution provides for an independent judicial machinery capable of protecting basic human rights. It contains provisions for legal safeguards through the judicial power vested in the courts, and through the establishment of an ombudsman who is competent to provide individuals with legal assistance or advice as required. Under article 91(a) of the Constitution, the ombudsman has "the duty to investigate complaints concerning alleged or apparent instances of violations of fundamental rights and freedoms, abuse of power, unfair, harsh, insensitive or discourteous treatment of an inhabitant of Namibia by an official in the employ of any organ of government (whether national or local), manifest injustice, or corruption or conduct by such official which would properly be regarded as unlawful, oppressive or unfair in a democratic society".

These fundamental rights and freedoms cannot be set aside easily and laws cannot be amended by a simple majority of the members of the Parliament. Mention should also be made of the provisions contained in chapter 11 relating to the principles of State policy, in particular articles 95, 97, and 98. Article 131 in chapter 19 of the Constitution contains provisions which entrench fundamental rights and freedoms, as provided for in chapter 3 of the said Constitution.

All rights provided for in the International Covenant on Civil and Political Rights are taken into account. The Constitution further contains provisions on the rights of the child under article 15, the right to private property in article 16 and the right to education in article 20. The Constitution provides for primary education that is compulsory and free of charge and the right of individuals to create their own educational establishments.

Human rights and fundamental freedoms may be derogated from to a certain extent. Article 22 contains a clause on the "limitation upon fundamental rights and freedoms", and article 24 has a clause on "derogation". This clause is linked to the powers of the President to derogate from human rights during a state of emergency under article 26, and particular reference is made to rules applicable to persons under detention. Derogations are not permitted in respect of a series of fundamental rights which correspond to article 4 of the International Covenant on Civil and Political Rights. The provisions in regard to public emergency, state of national defence and martial law are regulated by way of parliamentary and judicial control.

Whilst the Constitution contains provisions on human rights which, in the opinion of the Working Group, are quite satisfactory and follow the principles developed within the United Nations, the real value of such a Constitution will depend on its implementation in the future.

In the further report, the ad hoc working group also presented to the Commission on Human Rights the following observations and recommendations (UN Doc. E/CN.4/1990/7/Add. 1. para. 45–46):

A. Observations

(a) The *Ad Hoc* Group of Experts wishes to take this opportunity to express to the Government of the Republic of South Africa its thanks for the co-operation extended to it, which allowed the Group to undertake this visit to Namibia. It therefore expresses the hope that such continued co-operation will enable the Group to visit South Africa in the near future, in accordance with Commission on Human Rights resolution 1989/5, paragraph 29.

(b) The Group welcomes the implementation of Security Council resolution 435 (1978), which culminated in the participation of the Namibian people in free and democratic elections in a general climate of peace and political pluralism provided for in the Constitution adopted on 9 February 1990.

(c) A preliminary examination of the Constitution reveals that due account has been taken of the provisions of the international covenants on civil and political rights, and economic, social and cultural rights. The Constitution also provides guarantees in the event of restrictions on the exercise of human rights during a state of emergency. In the opinion of the Group, these guarantees are in general consistent with the relevant international standards. The Constitution prohibits discrimination based on race, colour, ethnic origin, sex or religion, creed or social or economic status.

Exercise of Civil and Political Rights. (d) While, on one hand, the discriminatory laws and measures which might curtail the objectives of free and fair elections have been repealed, in accordance with Security Council resolution 435 (1978), the Working Group notes that most of the measures based on *apartheid* or other discriminatory concepts remain in force.

(e) The Working Group took note of the proclamation by the Administrator-General (AG 13 of 1989) granting amnesty to certain persons. Nevertheless, the Group questions whether such an amnesty should also automatically benefit all former members of the anti-riot units known as "Koevoet", in view of the atrocities committed for years against peaceful citizens. The Group is of the opinion that the amnesty law should not benefit this category of persons.

(f) Furthermore, the Group notes with concern that, under the terms of article 1, paragraph 3, of the above-mentioned Proclamation, the Administrator-General is given discretionary power to determine the category of persons eligible to be granted amnesty.

(g) Information and testimony received by the Group shows that not all Namibians who have lived abroad in order to take part in the liberation struggle of their people have returned to the country. Their absence is profoundly upsetting to their families who, given the situation, are likely to regard those who have not returned as disappeared persons. However, apart from the figures submitted to the Group, the exact number of persons who fall into this category is not known. All the political sources that have provided the Group with information on this question agree that the matter should be clarified and that the co-operation and assistance of all concerned, as well as of the international community, remains indispensable given the impact of this problem on the prospects for the essential task of building understanding and reconciliation in Namibia.

(h) The Group also received information to the effect that, contrary to what the international community had believed, the South African Government has not released all political prisoners. There is also controversy regarding the interpretation to be given to the term "political prisoner". This applies in particular to the case of Leonard Sheehama, as mention above (paras. 27 to 32). The case has not yet been settled and Mr. Sheehama remains in prison in South Africa. The Group believe that the concept of a political prisoner should be considered in accordance with the Geneva Conventions of 1949 and the first Additional Protocol of 1977. In this regard, the Group considers that the motive of the perpetrator and the circumstances of the act committed should also be taken into consideration.

(i) Regarding the administration of justice, the information received reveals that independent and impartial justice cannot be expected in a general legal context in which the national legislation continues to be based on the policy and philosophy of *apartheid*. However, some isolated cases have shown a certain measure of independence of the judiciary vis-à-vis the Executive.

(j) The Group notes that the investigations into the assassination of white SWAPO member Anton Lubowski are reported to be continuing and some suspects have been arrested.

Economic, Social and Cultural Rights. (k) The Group would point out that enjoyment of these rights depends on the general standard of living of a population and on the general political context in which it lives. In the case of Namibia, subjected for years to the policy of *apartheid* and its associated practices, the Group noted that no significant progress had been achieved because all the factors are so interrelated as to produce negative effects.

(l) In a society where unemployment prevails and access to a good education has long been the privilege of whites alone, and where menial work has always been done by the black population, there can be no expectation of any rapid change or immediate major transformation. The wages paid to black workers in Namibia are too low to provide them with decent and proper accommodation or appropriate health care.

(m) The same may be said of the right to education. Discrimination in access to schools solely on the basis of colour or rase has theoretically been abolished. However, the Group notes that, for the majority of the black population, little has changed due to a number of elements inherited from the former regime. It is clear that pupils who have received a so-called Bantu education, with all that that implies in terms of lack of qualified teachers, shortage of equipment and educational facilities, combined with the fact that they have been brought up in a different environment, cannot suddenly become competitive, even if they are admitted to good schools.

B. Recommendations

In view of the aforementioned observations, the *Ad Hoc* Working Group of Experts on southern Africa recommends the following:

(a) The future Government of independent Namibia should repeal all laws and measures based on *apartheid* and discrimination.

(b) All political prisoners should be unconditionally released.

(c) The amnesty declared by the Administrator-General in Proclamation AG 13 of 1989 should not be extended to those members of the "Koevoet" who have committed or have been convicted of atrocities against innocent civilians.

(d) The international community should grant the Namibian people all necessary assistance to enable them effectively to enjoy their economic and social rights and, notably, the right to health, to well remunerated work in proper conditions of safety and health, and to decent housing.

(e) The Commission on Human Rights should invite the Working Group on Enforced or Involuntary Disappearances, in close co-operation with the Government of independent Namibia, to shed light on the situation of persons who are alleged to have disappeared.

(f) The Government should take all necessary steps to ensure that the human rights provisions of the Constitution are effectively implemented in practice.

In addition, the ad hoc working group reiterated the following recommendations made in its earlier report (UN Doc. E/CN.4/1990/7, para. 281 (c), (d), (e), and (f):

(c) Since the people of Namibia, during the illegal occupation of their country, have suffered in many forms; since many innocent persons have been tortured and wrongfully convicted and imprisoned, and since private property has been destroyed during the illegal occupation of Namibia, the Group recommends the Commission to adopt a resolution:

(i) requesting an in-depth study of all damage caused during the illegal occupation of Namibia; and

(ii) recommending the setting up of a mechanism for settlement by which the damage occasioned could be compensated in an equitable manner.

(d) In the light of the development of the situation prevailing in Namibia and its accession to independence, and considering that the United Nations should be able to assist any country in accordance with Articles 55 and 56 of the Charter of the United Nations with a view to promoting universal respect for and observance of human rights and fundamental freedoms, the *Ad Hoc* Group of Experts recommends that the Commission on Human Rights should request the Secretary-General to provide any advisory services and any other appropriate forms of assistance in human rights that may be requested by the future Namibian Government in order to promote democratic development and to strengthen the institutions responsible for ensuring respect for and promotion of human rights. Such assistance, both technical as well as legal, could be provided by designating a body that would contribute to the proper functioning of the above-mentioned institutions and report to the Commission on Human Rights in close co-operation with the Namibian authorities.

(e) The Commission on Human Rights should . . . organize a seminar on human rights in post-colonial Namibia and the situation of children in consultation with the future Namibian Government.

(f) The Commission on Human Rights should recommend that the Government of independent Namibia should accede to all international human rights instruments."

SEE ALSO *South West Africa People's Organization.*

NAMIBIA: CONSTITUTION. On 9 February 1990, the Constituent Assembly of Namibia, meeting in Windhoek, approved by consensus the "Constitution for an Independent Namibia." The constitution, which entered into force on the day Namibia achieved its independence, 21 March 1990, contains the following provisions (articles 1–29, 32–46, 49–50, 63–70, 74–75, 78–84, 89–102, and 131–132) specifically relating to human rights and fundamental freedoms (UN Doc. S/20967/Add. 2, pp. 10–63):

Preamble

Whereas recognition of the inherent dignity and of the equal and inalienable rights of all members of the human family is indispensable for freedom, justice and peace;

Whereas the said rights include the right of the individual to life, liberty and the pursuit of happiness, regardless of race, colour, ethnic origin, sex, religion, creed or social or economic status;

Whereas the said rights are most effectively maintained and protected in a democratic society, where the government is responsible to freely elected representatives of the people, operating under a sovereign constitution and a free and independent judiciary;

Whereas these rights have for so long been denied to the people of Namibia by colonialism, racism and apartheid;

Whereas we the people of Namibia—

have finally emerged victorious in our struggle against colonialism, racism and apartheid;

are determined to adopt a Constitution which expresses for ourselves and our children our resolve to cherish and to protect the gains of our long struggle;

desire to promote amongst all of us the dignity of the individual and the unity and integrity of the Namibian nation among and in association with the nations of the world;

will strive to achieve national reconciliation and to foster peace, unity and a common loyalty to a single state;

committed to these principles, have resolved to constitute the Republic of Namibia as a sovereign, secular, democratic and unitary State securing to all our citizens justice, liberty, equality and fraternity,

Now therefore, we the people of Namibia accept and adopt this Constitution as the fundamental law of our Sovereign and Independent Republic.

Chapter 1
The Republic

Article 1. Establishment of the Republic of Namibia and Identification of its Territory. (1) The Republic of Namibia is hereby established as a sovereign, secular, democratic and unitary State founded upon the principles of democracy, the rule of law and justice for all.

(2) All power shall vest in the people of Namibia who shall exercise their sovereignty through the democratic institutions of the State.

(3) The main organs of the State shall be the Executive, the Legislature and the Judiciary.

(4) The national territory of Namibia shall consist of the whole of the territory recognised by the international community through the organs of the United Nations as Namibia, including the enclave, harbour and port of Walvis Bay, as well as the off-shore islands of Namibia, and its southern boundary shall extend to the middle of the Orange River.

(5) Windhoek shall be the seat of central Government.

(6) This Constitution shall be the Supreme Law of Namibia.

Article 2. National Symbols. (1) Namibia shall have a National Flag, the description of which is set out in Schedule 6 hereof.

(2) Namibia shall have a National Coat of Arms, a National Anthem and a National Seal to be determined by Act of Parliament, which shall require a two-thirds majority of all the members of the National Assembly for adoption and amendment.

(3) (a) The National Seal of the Republic of Namibia shall show the Coat of Arms, circumscribed with the word 'NAMIBIA' and the motto of the country, which shall be determined by Act of Parliament as aforesaid.

(b) The National Seal shall be in the custody of the President or such person whom the President may designate for such purpose and shall be used on such official documents as the President may determine.

Article 3. Language. (1) The official language of Namibia shall be English.

(2) Nothing contained in this Constitution shall prohibit the use of any other language as a medium of instruction in private schools or in schools financed or subsidised by the State, subject to compliance with such requirements as may be imposed by law, to ensure proficiency in the official language, or for pedagogic reasons.

(3) Nothing contained in Sub-Article (1) hereof shall preclude legislation by Parliament which permits the use of a language other than English for legislative, administrative and judicial purposes in regions or areas where such other language or languages are spoken by a substantial component of the population.

Chapter 2
Citizenship

Article 4. Acquisition and Loss of Citizenship. (1) The following persons shall be citizens of Namibia by birth:

(a) those born in Namibia before the date of Independence whose fathers or mothers would have been Namibian citizens at the time of the birth of such persons, if this Constitution had been in force at that time; and

(b) those born in Namibia before the date of Independence, who are not Namibian citizens under Sub-Article (a) hereof, and whose fathers or mothers were ordinarily resident in Namibia at the time of the birth of such persons: provided that their fathers or mothers were not then persons:

(aa) who were enjoying diplomatic immunity in Namibia under any law relating to diplomatic privileges; or

(bb) who were career representatives of another country; or

(cc) who were members of any police, military or security unit seconded for service within Namibia by the Government of another country: provided further that this Sub-Article shall not apply to persons claiming citizenship of Namibia by birth if such persons were ordinarily resident in Namibia at the date of Independence and had been so resident for a continuous period of not less than five (5) years prior to such date, or if the fathers or mothers of such persons claiming citizenship were ordinarily resident in Namibia at the date of the birth of such persons and had been so resident for a continuous period of not less than five (5) years prior to such date;

(c) those born in Namibia after the date of Independence whose fathers or mothers are Namibian citizens at the time of the birth of such persons;

(d) those born in Namibia after the date of Independence who do not qualify for citizenship under Sub-Article (c) hereof, and whose fathers or mothers are ordinarily resident in Namibia at the time of the birth of such persons: provided that their fathers or mothers are not then persons:

(aa) enjoying diplomatic immunity in Namibia under any law relating to diplomatic privileges; or

(bb) who are career representatives of another country; or

(cc) who are members of any police, military or security unit seconded for service within Namibia by the Government of another country; or

(dd) who are illegal immigrants:
provided further that Sub-Articles (aa), (bb), (cc), and (dd) hereof will not apply to children who would otherwise be stateless.

(2) The following persons shall be citizens of Namibia by descent:

(a) those who are not Namibian citizens under Sub-Article (1) hereof and whose fathers or mothers at the time of the birth of such persons are citizens of Namibia or whose fathers or mothers would have qualified for Namibian citizenship by birth under Sub-Article (1) hereof, if this Constitution had been in force at that time; and

(b) who comply with such requirements as to registration of citizenship as may be required by Act of Parliament: provided that nothing in this Constitution shall preclude Parliament from enacting legislation which requires the birth of such persons born after the date of Independence to be registered within a specific time either in Namibia or at an embassy, consulate or office of a trade representative of the Government of Namibia.

(3) The following persons shall be citizens of Namibia by marriage:

(a) those who are not Namibian citizens under Sub-Article (1) or (2) hereof and who:

(aa) in good faith marry a Namibian citizen or, prior to the coming into force of this Constitution, in good faith married a person who would have qualified for Namibian citizenship if this Constitution had been in force, and

(bb) subsequent to such marriage have ordinarily resided in Namibia as the spouse of such person for a period of not less than two (2) years, and

(cc) apply to become citizens of Namibia.

(b) For the purposes of this Sub-Article (and without derogating from any effect that it may have for any other purposes) a marriage by customary law shall be deemed to be a marriage: provided that nothing in this Constitution shall preclude Parliament from enacting legislation which defines the requirements which need to be satisfied for a marriage by customary law to be recognised as such for the purposes of this Sub-Article.

(4) Citizenship by registration may be claimed by persons who are not Namibian citizens under Sub-Articles (1), (2), or (3) hereof and who were ordinarily resident in Namibia at the date of Independence, and had been so resident for a continuous period of not less than five (5) years prior to such date: provided that application for Namibian citizenship under this Sub-Article is made within a period of twelve (12) months from the date of Independence, and prior to making such application, such persons renounce the citizenship of any other country of which they are citizens.

(5) Citizenship by naturalisation may be applied for by persons who are not Namibian citizens under Sub-Articles (1), (2), (3) or (4) hereof and who:

(a) are ordinarily resident in Namibia at the time when the application for naturalisation is made; and

(b) have been so resident in Namibia for a continuous period of not less than five (5) years (whether before or after the date of Independence); and

(c) satisfy any other criteria pertaining to health, morality, security or legality of residence as may be prescribed by law.

(6) Nothing contained herein shall preclude Parliament from authorizing by law the conferment of Namibia citizenship upon any fit and proper person by virtue of any special skill or experience or commitment to or services rendered to the Namibian nation either before or at any time after the date of Independence.

(7) Namibian citizenship shall be lost by persons who renounce their Namibian citizenship by voluntarily signing a formal declaration to that effect.

(8) Nothing in this Constitution shall preclude Parliament from enacting legislation providing for the loss of Namibian citizenship by persons who, after the date of Independence:

(a) have acquired the citizenship of any other country by any voluntary act; or

(b) have served or volunteered to serve in the armed or security forces of any other country without the written permission of the Namibian Government; or

(c) have taken up permanent residence in any other country and have absented themselves thereafter from Namibia for a period in excess of two (2) years without the written permission of the Namibian Government:

provided that no person who is a citizen of Namibia by birth or descent may be deprived of Namibian citizenship by such legislation.

(9) Parliament shall be entitled to make further laws not inconsistent with this Constitution regulating the acquisition or loss of Namibian citizenship.

Chapter 3
Fundamental Human Rights and Freedoms

Article 5. Protection of Fundamental Rights and Freedoms. The fundamental rights and freedoms enshrined in this Chapter shall be respected and upheld by the Executive, Legislature and Judiciary and all organs of the Government and its agencies and, where applicable to them, by all natural and legal persons in Namibia, and shall be enforceable by the Courts in the manner hereinafter prescribed.

Article 6. Protection of Life. The right to life shall be respected and protected. No law may prescribe death as a competent sentence. No Court or Tribunal shall have the power to impose a sentence of death upon any person. No executions shall take place in Namibia.

Article 7. Protection of Liberty. No persons shall be deprived of personal liberty except according to procedures established by law.

Article 8. Respect for Human Dignity. (1) The dignity of all persons shall be inviolable.

(2) (a) In any judicial proceedings or in other proceedings before any organ of the State, and during the enforcement of a penalty, respect for human dignity shall be guaranteed.

(b) No persons shall be subject to torture or to cruel, inhuman or degrading treatment or punishment.

Article 9. Slavery and Forced Labour. (1) No persons shall be held in slavery or servitude.

(2) No persons shall be required to perform forced labour.

(3) For the purposes of this Article, the expression "forced labour" shall not include:

(a) any labour required in consequence of a sentence or order of a Court;

(b) any labour required of persons while lawfully detained which, though not required in consequence of a sentence or order of a Court, is reasonably necessary in the interests of hygiene;

(c) any labour required of members of the defence force, the police force and the prison service in pursuance of their duties as such or, in the case of persons who have conscientious objections to serving as members of the defence force, any labour which they are required by law to perform in place of such service;

(d) any labour required during any period of public emergency or in the event of any other emergency or calamity, which threatens the life and well-being of the community, to the extent that requiring such labour is reasonably justifiable in the circumstances of any situation arising or existing during that period or as a result of that other emergency or calamity, for the purpose of dealing with that situation;

(e) any labour reasonably required as part of reasonable and normal communal or other civic obligations.

Article 10. Equality and Freedom from Discrimination. (1) All persons shall be equal before the law.

(2) No persons may be discriminated against on the grounds of sex, race, colour, ethnic origin, religion, creed or social or economic status.

Article 11. Arrest and Detention. (1) No persons shall be subject to arbitrary arrest or detention.

(2) No persons who are arrested shall be detained in custody without being informed promptly in a language they understand of the grounds for such arrest.

(3) All persons who are arrested and detained in custody shall be brought before the nearest Magistrate or other judicial officer within a period of forty-eight (48) hours of their arrest or, if this is not reasonably possible, as soon as possible thereafter, and no such persons shall be detained in custody beyond such period without the authority of a Magistrate or other judicial officer.

(4) Nothing contained in Sub-Article (3) hereof shall apply to illegal immigrants held in custody under any law dealing with illegal immigration: provided that such persons shall not be deported from Namibia unless deportation is authorised by a Tribunal empowered by law to give such authority.

(5) No persons who have been arrested and held in custody as illegal immigrants shall be denied the right to consult confidentially legal practitioners of their choice, and there shall be no interference with this right except such as is in accordance with the law and is necessary in a democratic society in the interest of national security or for public safety.

Article 12. Fair Trial. (1) (a) In the determination of their civil rights and obligations or any criminal charges against them, all persons shall be entitled to a fair and public hearing by an independent, impartial and competent Court or Tribunal established by law, provided that such Court or Tribunal may exclude the press and/or the public from all or any part of the trial for reasons of morals, the public order or national security, as is necessary in a democratic society.

(b) A trial referred to in Sub-Article (a) hereof shall take place within a reasonable time, failing which the accused shall be released.

(c) Judgments in criminal cases shall be given in public, except where the interests of juvenile persons or morals otherwise require.

(d) All persons charged with an offence shall be presumed innocent until proven guilty according to law, after having had the opportunity of calling witnesses and cross-examining those called against them.

(e) All persons shall be afforded adequate time and facilities for the preparation and presentation of their defence, before the commencement of and during their trial, and shall be entitled to be defended by a legal practitioner of their choice.

(f) No persons shall be compelled to give testimony against themselves or their spouses, who shall include partners in a marriage by customary law, and no Court shall admit in evidence against such persons testimony which has been obtained from such persons in violation of Article 8(2)(b) hereof.

(2) No persons shall be liable to be tried, convicted or punished again for any criminal offence for which they have already been convicted or acquitted according to law: provided that nothing in this Sub-Article shall be construed as changing the provisions of the common law defences of "previous acquittal" and "previous conviction".

(3) No persons shall be tried or convicted for any criminal offence or on account of any act or omission which did not constitute a criminal offence at the time when it was committed, nor shall a penalty be imposed exceeding that which was applicable at the time when the offence was committed.

Article 13. Privacy. (1) No persons shall be subject to interference with the privacy of their homes, correspondence or communications save as in accordance with law and as is necessary in a democratic society in the interests of national security, public safety or the economic well-being of the country, for the protection of health or morals, for the prevention of disorder or crime or for the protection of the rights or freedoms of others.

(2) Searches of the person or the homes of individuals shall only be justified:

(a) where these are authorised by a competent judicial officer;

(b) in cases where delay in obtaining such judicial authority carries with it the danger of prejudicing the objects of the search or the public interest, and such procedures as are prescribed by Act of Parliament to preclude abuse are properly satisfied.

Article 14. Family. (1) Men and women of full age, without any limitation due to race, colour, ethnic origin, nationality, religion, creed or social or economic status shall have the right to marry and to found a family. They shall be entitled to equal rights as to marriage, during marriage and at its dissolution.

(2) Marriage shall be entered into only with the free and full consent of the intending spouses.

(3) The family is the natural and fundamental group unit of society and is entitled to protection by society and the State.

Article 15. Children's Rights. (1) Children shall have the right from birth to a name, the right to acquire a nationality and, subject to legislation enacted in the best interests of children, as far as possible the right to know and be cared for by their parents.

(2) Children are entitled to be protected from economic exploitation and shall not be employed in or required to perform work that is likely to he hazardous or to interfere with their education, or to be harmful to their health or physical, mental, spiritual, moral or social development. For the purposes of this Sub-Article children shall be persons under the age of sixteen (16) years.

(3) No children under the age of fourteen (14) years shall be employed to work in any factory or mine, save under conditions and circumstances regulated by Act of Parliament. Nothing in this Sub-Article shall be construed as derogating in any way from Sub-Article (2) hereof.

(4) Any arrangement or scheme employed on any farm or other undertaking, the object or effect of which is to compel the minor children of an employee to work for or in the interest of the employer of such employee, shall for the purposes of Article 9 hereof be deemed to constitute an arrangement or scheme to compel the performance of forced labour.

(5) No law authorising preventive detention shall permit children under the age of sixteen (16) years to be detained.

Article 16. Property. (1) All persons shall have the right in any part of Namibia to acquire, own and dispose of all forms of immovable and movable property individually or in association with others and to bequeath their property to their heirs or legatees: provided that Parliament may by legislation prohibit or regulate as it deems expedient the right to acquire property by persons who are not Namibian citizens.

(2) The State or a competent body or organ authorised by law may expropriate property in the public interest sub-

ject to the payment of just compensation, in accordance with requirements and procedures to be determined by Act of Parliament.

Article 17. Political Activity. (1) All citizens shall have the right to participate in peaceful political activity intended to influence the composition and policies of the Government. All citizens shall have the right to form and join political parties and, subject to such qualifications prescribed by law as are necessary in a democratic society, to participate in the conduct of public affairs, whether directly or through freely chosen representatives.

(2) Every citizen who has reached the age of eighteen (18) years shall have the right to vote and who has reached the age of twenty-one (21) years to be elected to public office, unless otherwise provided herein.

(3) The rights guaranteed by Sub-Article (2) hereof may only be abrogated, suspended or be impinged upon by Parliament in respect of specified categories of persons on such grounds of infirmity or on such grounds of public interest or morality as are necessary in a democratic society.

Article 18. Administrative Justice. Administrative bodies and administrative officials shall act fairly and reasonably and comply with the requirements imposed upon such bodies and officials by common law and any relevant legislation, and persons aggrieved by the exercise of such acts and decisions shall have the right to seek redress before a competent Court or Tribunal.

Article 19. Culture. Every person shall be entitled to enjoy, practise, profess, maintain and promote any culture, language, tradition or religion subject to the terms of this Constitution and further subject to the conditions that the rights protected by this Article do not impinge upon the rights of others or the national interest.

Article 20. Education. (1) All persons shall have the right to education.

(2) Primary education shall be compulsory and the State shall provide reasonable facilities to render effective this right for every resident within Namibia, by establishing and maintaining State schools at which primary education will be provided free of charge.

(3) Children shall not be allowed to leave school until they have completed their primary education or have attained the age of sixteen (16) years, whichever is the sooner, save in so far as this may be authorised by Act of Parliament on grounds of health or other considerations pertaining to the public interest.

(4) All persons shall have the right, at their own expense, to establish and to maintain private schools, or colleges or other institutions of tertiary education, provided that:

(a) such schools, colleges or institutions of tertiary education are registered with a Government department in accordance with any law authorising and regulating such registration;

(b) the standards maintained by such schools, colleges or institutions of tertiary education are not inferior to the standards maintained in comparable schools, colleges or institutions of tertiary education funded by the State;

(c) no restrictions of whatever nature are imposed with respect to the admission of pupils based on race, colour or creed;

(d) no restrictions of whatever nature are imposed with respect to the recruitment of staff based on race or colour.

Article 21. Fundamental Freedoms. (1) All persons shall have the right to:

(a) freedom of speech and expression, which shall include freedom of the press and other media;

(b) freedom of thought, conscience and belief, which shall include academic freedom in institutions of higher learning;

(c) freedom to practise any religion and to manifest such practise;

(d) assemble peaceably and without arms;

(e) freedom of association, which shall include freedom to form and join associations or unions, including trade unions and political parties;

(f) withhold their labour without being exposed to criminal penalties;

(g) move freely throughout Namibia;

(h) reside and settle in any part of Namibia;

(i) leave and return to Namibia;

(j) practise any profession, or carry on any occupation, trade or business.

(2) The fundamental freedoms referred to in Sub-Article (1) hereof shall be exercised subject to the law of Namibia, in so far as such law imposes reasonable restrictions on the exercise of the rights and freedoms conferred by the said Sub-Article, which are necessary in a democratic society and are required in the interests of the sovereignty and integrity of Namibia, national security, public order, decency or morality, or in relation to contempt of court, defamation or incitement to an offence.

Article 22. Limitation upon Fundamental Rights and Freedoms. Whenever or wherever in terms of this Constitution the limitation of any fundamental rights or freedoms contemplated by this Chapter is authorised, any law providing for such limitation shall:

(a) be of general application, shall not negate the essential content thereof, and shall not be aimed at a particular individual;

(b) specify the ascertainable extent of such limitation and identify the Article or Articles hereof on which authority to enact such limitation is claimed to rest.

Article 23. Apartheid and Affirmative Action. (1) The practice of racial discrimination and the practice and ideology of apartheid from which the majority of the people of Namibia have suffered for so long shall be prohibited and by Act of Parliament such practices, and the propagation of such practices, may be rendered criminally punishable by the ordinary Courts by means of such punishment as Parliament deems necessary for the purposes of expressing the revulsion of the Namibian people at such practices.

(2) Nothing contained in Article 10 hereof shall prevent Parliament from enacting legislation providing directly or indirectly for the advancement of persons within Namibia who have been socially, economically or educationally disadvantaged by past discriminatory laws or practices, or for the implementation of policies and programmes aimed at redressing social, economic or educational imbalances in Namibian society arising out of past discriminatory laws or practices, or for achieving a balanced structuring of the public service, the police force, the defence force and the prison service.

(3) In the enactment of legislation and the application of any policies and practices contemplated by Sub-Article (2) hereof, it shall be permissible to have regard to the fact that women in Namibia have traditionally suffered special discrimination and that they need to be encouraged and enabled to play a full, equal and effective role in the political, social, economic and cultural life of the nation.

Article 24. Derogation. (1) Nothing contained in or done

under the authority of Article 26 hereof shall be held to be inconsistent with or in contravention of this Constitution to the extent that it authorises the taking of measures during any period when Namibia is in a state of national defence or any period when a declaration of emergency under this Constitution is in force.

(2) Where any persons are detained by virtue of such authorisation as is referred to in Sub-Article (1) hereof, the following provisions shall apply:

(a) they shall, as soon as reasonably practicable and in any case not more than five (5) days after the commencement of their detention, be furnished with a statement in writing in a language that they understand specifying in detail the grounds upon which they are detained and, at their request, this statement shall be read to them;

(b) not more than fourteen (14) days after the commencement of their detention, a notification shall be published in the Gazette stating that they have been detained and giving particulars of the provision of law under which their detention is authorised;

(c) not more than one (1) month after the commencement of their detention and thereafter during their detention at intervals of not more than three (3) months, their cases shall be reviewed by the Advisory Board referred to in Article 26(5)(c) hereof, which shall order their release from detention if it is satisfied that it is not reasonably necessary for the purposes of the emergency to continue the detention of such persons;

(d) they shall be afforded such opportunity for the making of representations as may be desirable or expedient in the circumstances, having regard to the public interest and the interests of the detained persons.

(3) Nothing contained in this Article shall permit a derogation from or suspension of the fundamental rights or freedoms referred to in Article 5, 6, 8, 9, 10, 12, 14, 15, 18, 19 and 21(1)(a), (b), (c) and (e) hereof, or the denial of access by any persons to legal practitioners or a Court of law.

Article 25. Enforcement of Fundamental Rights and Freedoms. (1) Save in so far as it may be authorised to do so by this Constitution, Parliament or any subordinate legislative authority shall not make any law, and the Executive and the agencies of Government shall not take any action which abolishes or abridges the fundamental rights and freedoms conferred by this Chapter, and any law or action in contravention thereof shall to the extent of the contravention be invalid: provided that:

(a) a competent Court, instead of declaring such law or action to be invalid, shall have the power and the discretion in an appropriate case to allow Parliament, any subordinate legislative authority, or the Executive and the agencies of Government, as the case may be, to correct any defect in the impugned law or action within a specified period, subject to such conditions as may be specified by it. In such event and until such correction, or until the expiry of the time limit set by the Court, whichever be the shorter, such impugned law or action shall be deemed to be valid;

(b) any law which was in force immediately before the date of Independence shall remain in force until amended, repealed or declared unconstitutional. If a competent Court is of the opinion that such law is unconstitutional, it may either set aside the law, or allow Parliament to correct any defect in such law, in which event the provisions of Sub-Article (a) hereof shall apply.

(2) Aggrieved persons who claim that a fundamental right or freedom guaranteed by this Constitution has been infringed or threatened shall be entitled to approach a competent Court to enforce or protect such a right or freedom, and may approach the Ombudsman to provide them with such legal assistance or advice as they require, and the Ombudsman shall have the discretion in response thereto to provide such legal or other assistance as he or she may consider expedient.

(3) Subject to the provisions of this Constitution, the Court referred to in Sub-Article (2) hereof shall have the power to make all such orders as shall be necessary and appropriate to secure such applicants the enjoyment of the rights and freedoms conferred on them under the provisions of this Constitution, should the Court come to the conclusion that such rights or freedoms have been unlawfully denied or violated, or that grounds exist for the protection of such rights or freedoms by interdict.

(4) The power of the Court shall include the power to award monetary compensation in respect of any damage suffered by the aggrieved persons in consequence of such unlawful denial or violation of their fundamental rights and freedoms, where it considers such an award to be appropriate in the circumstances of particular cases.

Chapter 4
Public Emergency, State of National Defence and Martial Law

Article 26. State of Emergency, State of National Defence and Martial Law. (1) At a time of national disaster or during a state of national defence or public emergency threatening the life of the nation or the constitutional order, the President may by Proclamation in the Gazette declare that a state of emergency exists in Namibia or any part thereof.

(2) A declaration under Sub-Article (1) thereof, if not sooner revoked, shall cease to have effect:

(a) in the case of a declaration made when the National Assembly is sitting or has been summoned to meet, at the expiration of a period of seven (7) days after publication of the declaration; or

(b) in any other case, at the expiration of a period of thirty (30) days after publication of the declaration; unless before the expiration of that period, it is approved by a resolution passed by the National Assembly by a two-thirds majority of all its members.

(3) Subject to the provisions of Sub-Article (4) hereof, a declaration approved by a resolution of the National Assembly under Sub-Article (2) hereof shall continue to be in force until the expiration of a period of six (6) months after being so approved or until such earlier date as may be specified in the resolution: provided that the National Assembly may, by resolution by a two-thirds majority of all its members, extend its approval of the declaration for periods of not more than six (6) months at a time.

(4) The National Assembly may by resolution at any time revoke a declaration approved by it in terms of this Article.

(5) (a) During a state of emergency in terms of this Article or when a state of national defence prevails, the President shall have the power by Proclamation to make such regulations as in his or her opinion are necessary for the protection of national security, public safety and the maintenance of law and order.

(b) The powers of the President to make such regulations shall include the power to suspend the operation of any rule of the common law or statute or any fundamental right or freedom protected by this Constitution, for such period and subject to such conditions as are reasonably justifiable for the purpose of dealing with the situation which has given rise to the emergency: provided that nothing in this Sub-Article shall enable the President to act contrary to the provisions of Article 24 hereof.

(c) Where any regulation made under Sub-Article (b) hereof provides for detention without trial, provision shall also be made for an Advisory Board, to be appointed by the President on the recommendation of the Judicial Service Commission, and consisting of no more than five (5) persons, of whom no fewer than three (3) persons shall be Judges of the Supreme Court or the High Court or qualified to be such. The Advisory Board shall perform the function set out in Article 24(2)(c) hereof.

(6) Any regulations made by the President pursuant to the provisions of Sub-Article (5) hereof shall cease to have legal force if they have not been approved by a resolution of the National Assembly within fourteen (14) days from the date when the National Assembly first sits in session after the date of the commencement of any such regulations.

(7) The President shall have the power to proclaim or terminate martial law. Martial law may be proclaimed only when a state of national defence involving another country exists or when civil war prevails in Namibia: provided that any proclamation of martial law shall cease to be valid if it is not approved within a reasonable time by a resolution passed by a two-thirds majority of all the members of the National Assembly.

Chapter 5
The President

Article 27. Head of State and Government. (1) The President shall be the Head of State and of the Government and the Commander-in-Chief of the Defence Force.

(2) The executive power of the Republic of Namibia shall vest in the President and the Cabinet.

(3) Except as may be otherwise provided in this Constitution or by law, the President shall in the exercise of his or her functions be obliged to act in consultation with the Cabinet.

Article 28. Election. (1) The President shall be elected in accordance with the provisions of this Constitution and subject thereto.

(2) Election of the President shall be:

(a) by direct, universal and equal suffrage; and

(b) conducted in accordance with principles and procedures to be determined by Act of Parliament: provided that no person shall be elected as President unless he or she has received more than fifty (50) per cent of the votes cast and the necessary number of ballots shall be conducted until such result is reached.

(3) Every citizen of Namibia by birth or descent, over the age of thirty-five (35) years, and who is eligible to be elected to office as a member of the National Assembly shall be eligible for election as President.

(4) The procedures to be followed for the nomination of candidates for election as President, and for all matters necessary and incidental to ensure the free, fair and effective election of a President, shall be determined by Act of Parliament: provided that any registered political party shall be entitled to nominate a candidate, and any person supported by a minimum number of registered voters to be determined by Act of Parliament shall also be entitled to be nominated as a candidate.

Article 29. Term of Office. (1) (a) The President's term of office shall be five (5) years unless he or she dies or resigns before the expiry of the said term or is removed from office.

(b) In the event of the dissolution of the National Assembly in the circumstances provided for under Article 57(1) hereof, the President's term of office shall also expire.

(2) A President shall be removed from office if a two-thirds majority of all the members of the National Assembly, confirmed by a two-thirds majority of all the members of the National Council, adopts a resolution impeaching the President on the ground that he or she has been guilty of a violation of the Constitution or guilty of a serious violation of the laws of the land or otherwise guilty of such gross misconduct or ineptitude as to render him or her unfit to hold with dignity and honour the office of President.

(3) A person shall hold office as President for not more than two terms.

(4) If a President dies, resigns or is removed from office in terms of this Constitution, the vacant office of President shall be filled for the unexpired period thereof as follows:

(a) if the vacancy occurs nor more than one (1) year before the date on which Presidential elections are required to be held, the vacancy shall be filled in accordance with the provisions of Article 34 hereof;

(b) if the vacancy occurs more than one (1) year before the date on which Presidential elections are required to be held, an election for the President shall be held in accordance with the provisions of Article 28 hereof within a period of ninety (90) days from the date on which the vacancy occurred, and pending such election the vacant office shall be filled in accordance with the provisions of Article 34 hereof.

(5) If the President dissolves the National Assembly under Articles 32(3)(a) and 57(1) hereof, a new election for President shall be held in accordance with the provisions of Article 28 hereof within ninety (90) days, and pending such election the President shall remain in office, and the provisions of Article 58 hereof shall be applicable.

(6) If a person becomes President under Sub-Article (4) hereof, the period of time during which he or she holds office consequent upon such election or succession shall not be regarded as a term for the purposes of Sub-Article (3) hereof. . . .

Article 32. Functions, Powers and Duties. (1) As the Head of State, the President shall uphold, protect and defend the Constitution as the Supreme Law, and shall perform with dignity and leadership all acts necessary, expedient, reasonable and incidental to the discharge of the executive functions of the Government, subject to the overriding terms of this Constitution and the laws of Namibia, which he or she is constitutionally obliged to protect, to administer and to execute.

(2) In accordance with the responsibility of the executive branch of Government to the legislative branch, the President and the Cabinet shall each year during the consideration of the official budget attend Parliament. During such session the President shall address Parliament on the state of the nation and on the future policies of the Government, shall report on the policies of the previous year and shall be available to respond to questions.

(3) Without derogating from the generality of the functions and powers contemplated by Sub-Article (1) hereof, the President shall preside over meetings of the Cabinet and shall have the power, subject to this Constitution to:

(a) dissolve the National Assembly by Proclamation in the circumstances provided for in Article 57(1) hereof;

(b) determine the times for the holding of special sessions of the National Assembly, and to prorogue such sessions;

(c) accredit, receive and recognize ambassadors, and to appoint ambassadors, plenipotentiaries, diplomatic representatives and other diplomatic officers, consuls and consular officers;

(d) pardon or reprieve offenders, either unconditionally or subject to such conditions as the President may deem fit;

(e) negotiate and sign international agreements, and to delegate such power;

(f) declare martial law or, if it is necessary for the defence of the nation, declare that a state of national defence exists: provided that this power shall be exercised subject to the terms of Article 26(7) hereof;

(g) establish and dissolve such Government departments and ministries as the President may at any time consider to be necessary or expedient for the good government of Namibia;

(h) confer such honours as the President considers appropriate on citizens, residents and friends of Namibia in consultation with interested and relevant persons and institutions;

(i) appoint the following persons:
(aa) the Prime Minister;
(bb) Ministers and Deputy-Ministers;
(cc) the Attorney-General;
(dd) the Director-General of Planning;
(ee) any other person or persons who are required by any other provision of this Constitution or any other law to be appointed by the President.

(4) The President shall also have the power, subject to this Constitution, to appoint:

(a) on the recommendation of the Judicial Service Commission:
(aa) the Chief Justice, the Judge-President of the High Court and other Judges of the Supreme Court and the High Court;
(bb) the Ombudsman;
(cc) the Prosecutor-General;

(b) on the recommendation of the Public Service Commission:
(aa) the Auditor-General;
(bb) the Governor and the Deputy-Governor of the Central Bank;

(c) on the recommendation of the Security Commission:
(aa) the Chief of the Defence Force;
(bb) the Inspector-General of Police;
(cc) the Commissioner of Prisons.

(5) Subject to the provisions of this Constitution dealing with the signing of any laws passed by Parliament and the promulgation and publication of such laws in the Gazette, the President shall have the power to:

(a) sign and promulgate any Proclamation which by law he or she is entitled to proclaim as President;

(b) initiate, in so far as he or she considers it necessary and expedient, laws for submission to and consideration by the National Assembly;

(c) appoint as members of the National Assembly but without any vote therein, not more than six (6) persons by virtue of their special expertise, status, skill or experience.

(6) Subject to the provisions of this Constitution or any other law, any person appointed by the President pursuant to the powers vested in him or her by this Constitution or any other law may be removed by the President by the same process through which such person was appointed.

(7) Subject to the provisions of this Constitution and of any other law of application in this matter, the President may, in consultation with the Cabinet and on the recommendation of the Public Service Commission:

(a) constitute any office in the public service of Namibia not otherwise provided for by any other law;

(b) appoint any person to such office;

(c) determine the tenure of any person so appointed as well as the terms and conditions of his or her service.

(8) All appointments made and actions taken under Sub-Articles (3), (4), (5), (6) and (7) hereof shall be announced by the President by Proclamation in the Gazette.

(9) Subject to the provisions of this Constitution and save where this Constitution otherwise provides, any action taken by the President pursuant to any power vested in the President by the terms of this Article shall be capable of being reviewed, reversed or corrected on such terms as are deemed expedient and proper should there be a resolution proposed by at least one-third of all the members of the National Assembly and passed by a two-thirds majority of all the members of the National Assembly disapproving any such action and resolving to review, reverse or correct it.

(10) Notwithstanding the review, reversal or correction of any action in terms of Sub-Article (9) hereof, all actions performed pursuant to any such action during the period preceding such review, reversal or correction shall be deemed to be valid and effective in law, until and unless Parliament otherwise enacts.

Article 33. Remuneration. Provision shall be made by Act of Parliament for the payment out of the State Revenue Fund of remuneration and allowances for the President, as well as for the payment of pensions to former Presidents and, in the case of their deaths, to their surviving spouses.

Article 34. Succession. (1) If the office of President becomes vacant or if the President is otherwise unable to fulfill the duties of the office, the following persons shall in the order provided for in this Sub-Article act as President for the unexpired portion of the President's term of office or until the President is able to resume office, whichever is the earlier:

(a) the Prime Minister.
(b) the Deputy-Prime Minister;
(c) a person appointed by the Cabinet.

(2) Where it is regarded as necessary or expedient that a person deputize for the President because of a temporary absence from the country or because of pressure of work, the President shall be entitled to nominate any person enumerated in Sub-Article (1) hereof to deputize for him or her in respect of such specific occasions or such specific matters and for such specific periods as in his or her discretion may be considered wise and expedient, subject to consultation with the Cabinet.

Chapter 6
The Cabinet

Article 35. Composition. (1) The Cabinet shall consist of the President, the Prime Minister and such other Ministers as the President may appoint from the members of the National Assembly, including members nominated under Article 46(1)(b) hereof, for the purposes of administering and executing the functions of the Government.

(2) The President may also appoint a Deputy-Prime Min-

ister to perform such functions as may be assigned to him or her by the President or the Prime Minister.

(3) The President or, in his or her absence, the Prime Minister or other Minister designated for this purpose by the President, shall preside at meetings of the Cabinet.

Article 36. Functions of the Prime Minister. The Prime Minister shall be the leader of Government business in Parliament, shall co-ordinate the work of the Cabinet and shall advise and assist the President in the execution of the functions of Government.

Article 37. Deputy-Ministers. The President may appoint from the members of the National Assembly, including members nominated under Article 46(1)(b) hereof, and the National Council such Deputy-Ministers as he or she may consider expedient, to exercise or perform on behalf of Ministers any of the powers, functions and duties which may have been assigned to such Ministers.

Article 38. Oath or Affirmation. Before assuming office, a Minister or Deputy-Minister shall make and subscribe to an oath or solemn affirmation before the President or a person designated by the President for this purpose, in the terms set out in Schedule 2 hereof.

Article 39. Vote of No Confidence. The President shall be obliged to terminate the appointment of any member of the Cabinet, if the National Assembly by a majority of all its members resolves that it has no confidence in that member.

Article 40. Duties and Functions. The members of the Cabinet shall have the following functions:

(a) to direct, co-ordinate and supervise the activities of Ministries and Government departments including para-statal enterprises, and to review and advise the President and the National Assembly on the desirability and wisdom of any prevailing subordinate legislation, regulations or orders pertaining to such para-statal enterprises, regard being had to the public interest;

(b) to initiate bills for submission to the National Assembly;

(c) to formulate, explain and assess for the National Assembly the budget of the State and its economic development plans, and to report to the National Assembly thereon;

(d) to carry out such other functions as are assigned to them by law or are incidental to such assignment;

(e) to attend meetings of the National Assembly and to be available for the purposes of any queries and debates pertaining to the legitimacy, wisdom, effectiveness and direction of Government policies;

(f) to take such steps as are authorised by law to establish such economic organisations, institutions and para-statal enterprises on behalf of the State as are directed or authorised by law;

(g) to formulate, explain and analyse for the members of the National Assembly the goals of Namibian foreign policy and its relations with other States and to report to the National Assembly thereon;

(h) to formulate, explain and analyse for the members of the National Assembly the directions and content of foreign trade policy and to report to the National Assembly thereon;

(i) to assist the President in determining what international agreements are to be concluded, acceded to or succeeded to and to report to the National Assembly thereon;

(j) to advise the President on the state of national defence and the maintenance of law and order and to inform the National Assembly thereon;

(k) to issue notices, instructions and directives to facilitate the implementation and administration of laws administered by the Executive, subject to the terms of this Constitution or any other law;

(l) to remain vigilant and vigorous for the purposes of ensuring that the scourges of apartheid, tribalism and colonialism do not again manifest themselves in any form in a free and independent Namibia and to protect and assist disadvantaged citizens of Namibia who have historically been the victims of these pathologies.

Article 41. Ministerial Accountability. All Ministers shall be accountable individually for the administration of their own Ministries and collectively for the administration of the work of the Cabinet, both to the President and to Parliament.

Article 42. Outside Employment. (1) During their tenure of office as members of the Cabinet, Ministers may not take up any other paid employment, engage in activities inconsistent with their positions as Ministers, or expose themselves to any situation which carried with it the risk of a conflict developing between their interests as Ministers and their private interests.

(2) No members of the Cabinet shall use their positions as such or use information entrusted to them confidentially as such members of the Cabinet, directly or indirectly to enrich themselves.

Article 43. Secretary to the Cabinet. (1) There shall be a Secretary to the Cabinet who shall be appointed by the President and who shall perform such functions as may be determined by law and such functions as are from time to time assigned to the Secretary by the President or the Prime Minister. Upon appointment by the President, the Secretary shall be deemed to have been appointed to such office on the recommendation of the Public Service Commission.

(2) The Secretary to the Cabinet shall also serve as a depository of the records, minutes and related documents of the Cabinet.

Chapter 7
The National Assembly

Article 44. Legislative Power. The legislative power of Namibia shall be vested in the National Assembly with the power to pass laws with the assent of the President as provided in this Constitution subject, where applicable, to the powers and functions of the National Council as set out in this Constitution.

Article 45. Representative Nature. The members of the National Assembly shall be representative of all the people and shall in the performance of their duties be guided by the objectives of this Constitution, by the public interest and by their conscience.

Article 46. Composition. (1) The composition of the National Assembly shall be as follows:

(a) seventy-two (72) members to be elected by the registered voters by general, direct and secret ballot. Every Namibian citizen who has the qualifications described in Article 17 hereof shall be entitled to vote in the elections for members of the National Assembly and, subject to Article 47 hereof, shall be eligible for candidature as a member of the National Assembly;

(b) not more than six (6) persons appointed by the President under Article 32(5)(c) hereof, by virtue of their special expertise, status, skill or experience: provided that such members shall have no vote in the National Assembly, and shall not be taken into account for the purpose of determining any specific majorities that are required under this Constitution or any other law.

(2) Subject to the principles referred to in Article 49 hereof, the members of the National Assembly referred to in Sub-Article (1) (a) hereof shall be elected in accordance with procedures to be determined by Act of Parliament. . . .

Article 49. Elections. The election of members in terms of Article 46(1) (a) hereof shall be on party lists and in accordance with the principles of proportional representation as set out in Schedule 4 hereof.

Article 50. Duration. Every National Assembly shall continue for a maximum period of five (5) years, but it may before the expiry of its term be dissolved by the President by Proclamation as provided for in Article 32(3) (a) and 57 (1) hereof. . . .

Article 63. Functions and Powers. (1) The National Assembly, as the principal legislative authority in and over Namibia, shall have the power, subject to this Constitution, to make and repeal laws for the peace, order and good government of the country in the best interest of the people of Namibia.

(2) The National Assembly shall further have the power and function, subject to this Constitution:

(a) to approve budgets for the effective government and administration of the country;

(b) to provide for revenue and taxation;

(c) to take such steps as it considers expedient to uphold and defend this Constitution and the laws of Namibia and to advance the objectives of Namibian independence;

(d) to consider and decide whether or not to succeed to such international agreements as may have been entered into prior to Independence by administrations within Namibia in which the majority of the Namibian people have historically not enjoyed democratic representation and participation;

(e) to agree to the ratification of or accession to international agreements which have been negotiated and signed in terms of Article 32(3) (e) hereof;

(f) to receive reports on the activities of the Executive, including para-statal enterprises, and from time to time to require any senior official thereof to appear before any of the committees of the National Assembly to account for and explain his or her acts and programmes;

(g) to initiate, approve or decide to hold a referendum on matters of national concern;

(h) to debate and to advise the President in regard to any matters which by this Constitution the President is authorised to deal with;

(i) to remain vigilant and vigorous for the purposes of ensuring that the scourges of apartheid, tribalism and colonialism do not again manifest themselves in any form in a free and independent Namibia and to protect and assist disadvantaged citizens of Namibia who have historically been the victims of these pathologies;

(j) generally to exercise any other functions and powers assigned to it by this Constitution or any other law and any other functions incidental thereto.

Article 64. Withholding of Presidential Assent. (1) Subject to the provisions of this Constitution, the President shall be entitled to withhold his or her assent to a bill approved by the National Assembly if in the President's opinion such bill would upon adoption conflict with the provisions of this Constitution.

(2) Should the President withhold assent on the grounds of such opinion, he or she shall so inform the Speaker who shall inform the National Assembly thereof, and the

Attorney-General, who may then take appropriate steps to have the matter decided by a competent Court.

(3) Should such Court thereafter conclude that such bill is not in conflict with the provisions of this Constitution, the President shall assent to the said bill if it was passed by the National Assembly by a two-thirds majority of all its members. If the bill was not passed with such majority, the President may withhold his or her assent to the bill, in which event the provisions of Article 56(3) and (4) hereof shall apply.

(4) Should such Court conclude that the disputed bill would be in conflict with any provisions of this Constitution, the said bill shall be deemed to have lapsed and the President shall not be entitled to assent thereto.

Article 65. Signature and Enrolment of Acts. (1) When any bill has become an Act of Parliament as a result of its having been passed by Parliament, signed by the President and published in the Gazette, the Secretary of the National Assembly shall promptly cause two (2) fair copies of such Act in the English language to be enrolled in the office of the Registrar of the Supreme Court and such copies shall be conclusive evidence of the provisions of the Act.

(2) The public shall have the right of access to such copies subject to such regulations as may be prescribed by Parliament to protect the durability of the said copies and the convenience of the Registrar's staff.

Article 66. Customary and Common Law. (1) Both the customary law and the common law of Namibia in force on the date of Independence shall remain valid to the extent to which such customary or common law does not conflict with this Constitution or any other statutory law.

(2) Subject to the terms of this Constitution, any part of such common law or customary law may be repealed or modified by Act of Parliament, and the application thereof may be confined to particular parts of Namibia or to particular periods.

Article 67. Requisite Majorities. Save as provided in this Constitution, a simple majority of votes cast in the National Assembly shall be sufficient for the passage of any bill or resolution of the National Assembly.

Chapter 8
The National Council

Article 68. Establishment. There shall be a National Council which shall have the powers and functions set out in this Constitution.

Article 69. Composition. (1) The National Council shall consist of two (2) members from each region referred to in Article 102 hereof, to be elected from amongst their members by the Regional Council for such region.

(2) The elections of members of the National Council shall be conducted according to procedures to be prescribed by Act of Parliament.

Article 70. Term of Office of Members. (1) Members of the National Council shall hold their seats for six (6) years from the date of their election and shall be eligible for re-election.

(2) When a seat of a member of the National Council becomes vacant through death, resignation or disqualification, an election for a successor to occupy the vacant seat until the expiry of the predecessor's term of office shall be held, except in the instance where such vacancy arises less than six (6) months before the expiry of the term of the National Council, in which instance such vacancy need not be filled. Such election shall be held in accordance with the

procedures prescribed by the Act of Parliament referred to in Article 69(2) hereof. . . .

Article 74. Powers and Functions. (1) The National Council shall have the power to:

(a) consider in terms of Article 75 hereof all bills passed by the National Assembly;

(b) investigate and report to the National Assembly on any subordinate legislation, reports and documents which under law must be tabled in the National Assembly and which are referred to it by the National Assembly for advice;

(c) recommend legislation on matters of regional concern for submission to and consideration by the National Assembly;

(d) perform any other functions assigned to it by the National Assembly or by an Act of Parliament.

(2) The National Council shall have the power to establish committees and to adopt its own rules and procedures for the exercise of its powers and the performance of its functions. A committee of the National Council shall be entitled to conduct all such hearings and collect such evidence as it considers necessary for the exercise of the National Council's powers of review and investigations, and for such purposes shall have the powers referred to in Article 59(3) hereof.

(3) The National Council shall in its rules of procedure make provision for such disclosure as may be considered to be appropriate in regard to the financial or business affairs of its members.

(4) The duties of the members of the National Council shall include the following:

(a) all members of the National Council shall maintain the dignity and image of the National Council both during the sittings of the National Council as well as in their acts and activities outside the National Council;

(b) all members of the National Council shall regard themselves as servants of the people of Namibia and desist from any conduct by which they seek improperly to enrich themselves or alienate themselves from the people.

(5) Rules providing for the privileges and immunities of members of the National Council shall be made by Act of Parliament and all members shall be entitled to the protection of such privileges and immunities.

Article 75. Review of Legislation. (1) All bills passed by the National Assembly shall be referred by the Speaker to the National Council.

(2) The National Council shall consider bills referred to it under Sub-Article (1) hereof and shall submit reports thereon with its recommendations to the Speaker.

(3) If in its report to the Speaker the National Council confirms a bill, the Speaker shall refer it to the President to enable the President to deal with it under Article 56 and 64 hereof.

(4) (a) If the National Council in its report to the Speaker recommends that the bill be passed subject to the amendments proposed by it, such bill shall be referred by the Speaker back to the National Assembly.

(b) If a bill is referred back to the National Assembly under Sub-Article (a) hereof, the National Assembly may reconsider the bill and may make any amendments thereto, whether proposed by the National Council or not. If the bill is again passed by the National Assembly, whether in the form in which it was originally passed, or in an amended form, the bill shall not again be referred to the National Council, but shall be referred by the Speaker to the President to enable it to be dealt with under Articles 56 and 64 hereof.

(5) (a) If a majority of two-thirds of all the members of the National Council objects to the principle of a bill, this shall be mentioned in its report to the Speaker. In that event, the report shall also indicate whether or not the National Council proposes that amendments be made to the bill, if the principle of the bill is confirmed by the National Assembly under Sub-Article (b) hereof, and if amendments are proposed, details thereof shall be set out in the report.

(b) If the National Council in its report objects to the principle of the bill, the National Assembly shall be required to reconsider the principle. If upon such reconsideration the National Assembly reaffirms the principle of the bill by a majority of two-thirds of all its members, the principle of the bill shall no longer be an issue. If such two-thirds majority is not obtained in the National Assembly, the bill shall lapse.

(6) (a) If the National Assembly reaffirms the principle of the bill under Sub-Article 5(b) hereof by a majority of two-thirds of all its members, and the report of the National Council proposed that in such event amendments be made to the bill, the National Assembly shall then deal with the amendments proposed by the National Council, and in that event the provisions of Sub-Article 4(b) shall apply *mutatis mutandis.*

(b) If the National Assembly reaffirms the principle of the bill under Sub-Article 5(b) hereof by a majority of two-thirds of all its members, and the report of the National Council did not propose that in such event amendments be made to the bill, the National Council shall be deemed to have confirmed the bill, and the Speaker shall refer the bill to the President to be dealt with under Articles 56 and 64 hereof.

(7) Sub-Articles (5) and (6) hereof shall not apply to bills dealing with the levying of taxes or the appropriation of public monies.

(8) The National Council shall report to the Speaker on all bills dealing with the levying of taxes or appropriations of public monies within thirty (30) days of the date on which such bills were referred to it by the Speaker, and on all other bills within three (3) months of the date of referral by the Speaker, failing which the National Council will be deemed to have confirmed such bills and the Speaker shall then refer them promptly to the President to enable the President to deal with the bills under Articles 56 and 64 hereof.

(9) If the President withholds his or her assent to any bill under Article 56 hereof and the bill is then dealt with in terms of that Article, and is again passed by the National Assembly in the form in which it was originally passed or in an amended form, such bill shall not again be referred to the National Council, but shall be referred by the Speaker directly to the President to enable the bill to be dealt with in terms of Articles 56 and 64 hereof. . . .

Chapter 9
The Administration of Justice

Article 78. The Judiciary. (1) The judicial power shall be vested in the Courts of Namibia, which shall consist of:

(a) a Supreme Court of Namibia;

(b) a High Court of Namibia;

(c) Lower Courts of Namibia.

(2) The Courts shall be independent and subject only to this Constitution and the law.

(3) No member of the Cabinet or the Legislature or any other person shall interfere with Judges or judicial officers

in the exercise of their judicial functions, and all organs of the State shall accord such assistance as the Courts may require to protect their independence, dignity and effectiveness, subject to the terms of this Constitution or any other law.

(4) The Supreme Court and the High Court shall have the inherent jurisdiction which vested in the Supreme Court of South-West Africa immediately prior to the date of Independence, including the power to regulate their own procedures and to make court rules for that purpose.

Article 79. The Supreme Court. (1) The Supreme Court shall consist of a Chief Justice and such additional Judges as the President, acting on the recommendation of the Judicial Service Commission, may determine.

(2) The Supreme Court shall be presided over by the Chief Justice and shall hear and adjudicate upon appeals emanating from the High Court, including appeals which involve the interpretation, implementation and upholding of this Constitution and the fundamental rights and freedoms guaranteed thereunder. The Supreme Court shall also deal with matters referred to it for decision by the Attorney-General under this Constitution, and with such other matters as may be authorised by Act of Parliament.

(3) Three (3) Judges shall constitute a quorum of the Supreme Court when it hears appeals or deals with matters referred to it by the Attorney-General under this Constitution: provided that provision may be made by Act of Parliament for a lesser quorum in circumstances in which a Judge seized of an appeal dies or becomes unable to act at any time prior to judgment.

(4) The jurisdiction of the Supreme Court with regard to appeals shall be determined by Act of Parliament.

Article 80. The High Court. (1) The High Court shall consist of a Judge-President and such additional Judges as the President, acting on the recommendation of the Judicial Service Commission, may determine.

(2) The High Court shall have original jurisdiction to hear and adjudicate upon all civil disputes and criminal prosecutions, including cases which involve the interpretation, implementation and upholding of this Constitution and the fundamental rights and freedoms guaranteed thereunder. The High Court shall also have jurisdiction to hear and adjudicate upon appeals from Lower Courts.

(3) The jurisdiction of the High Court with regard to appeals shall be determined by Act of Parliament.

Article 81. Binding Nature of Decisions of the Supreme Court. A decision of the Supreme Court shall be binding on all other Courts of Namibia and all persons in Namibia unless it is reversed by the Supreme Court itself, or is contradicted by an Act of Parliament lawfully enacted.

Article 82. Appointment of Judges. (1) All appointments of Judges to the Supreme Court and the High Court shall be made by the President on the recommendation of the Judicial Service Commission and upon appointment Judges shall make an oath or affirmation of office in the terms set out in Schedule 1 hereof.

(2) At the request of the Chief Justice the President may appoint Acting Judges of the Supreme Court to fill casual vacancies in the Court from time to time, or as *ad hoc* appointments to sit in cases involving constitutional issues or the guarantee of fundamental rights and freedoms, if in the opinion of the Chief Justice it is desirable that such persons should be appointed to hear such cases by reason of their special knowledge of or expertise in such matters.

(3) At the request of the Judge-President, the President may appoint Acting Judges of the High Court from time to

time to fill casual vacancies in the Court, or to enable the Court to deal expeditiously with its work.

(4) All Judges, except Acting Judges, appointed under this Constitution shall hold office until the age of sixty-five (65) but the President shall be entitled to extend the retiring age of any Judge to seventy (70). It shall also be possible by Act of Parliament to make provision for retirement at ages higher than those specified in this Article.

Article 83. Lower Courts. (1) Lower Courts shall be established by Act of Parliament and shall have the jurisdiction and adopt the procedures prescribed by such Act and regulations made thereunder.

(2) Lower Courts shall be presided over by Magistrates or other judicial officers appointed in accordance with procedures prescribed by Act of Parliament.

Article 84. Removal of Judges from Office. (1) A Judge may be removed from office before the expiry of his or her tenure only by the President acting on the recommendation of the Judicial Service Commission.

(2) Judges may only be removed from office on the ground of mental incapacity or for gross misconduct, and in accordance with the provisions of Sub-Article (3) hereof.

(3) The Judicial Service Commission shall investigate whether or not a Judge should be removed from office on such grounds, and if it decides that the Judge should be removed, it shall inform the President of its recommendation.

(4) If the deliberations of the Judicial Service Commission pursuant to this Article involve the conduct of a member of the Judicial Service Commission, such Judge shall not participate in the deliberations and the President shall appoint another Judge to fill such vacancy.

(5) While investigations are being carried out into the necessity of the removal of a Judge in terms of this Article, the President may, on the recommendation of the Judicial Service Commission and, pending the outcome of such investigations and recommendations, suspend the Judge from office.

Chapter 10
The Ombudsman

Article 89. Establishment and Independence. (1) There shall be an Ombudsman, who shall have the powers and functions set out in this Constitution.

(2) The Ombudsman shall be independent and subject only to this Constitution and the law.

(3) No member of the Cabinet or the Legislature or any other person shall interfere with the Ombudsman in the exercise of his or her functions and all other organs of the State shall accord such assistance as may be needed for the protection of the independence, dignity and effectiveness of the Ombudsman.

(4) The Ombudsman shall either be a Judge of Namibia, or a person possessing the legal qualifications which would entitle him or her to practise in all the Courts of Namibia.

Article 90. Appointment and Term of Office. (1) The Ombudsman shall be appointed by Proclamation by the President on the recommendation of the Judicial Service Commission.

(2) The Ombudsman shall hold office until the age of sixty-five (65) but the President may extend the retiring age of any Ombudsman to seventy (70).

Article 91. Functions. The functions of the Ombudsman shall be defined and prescribed by an Act of Parliament and shall include the following:

(a) the duty to investigate complaints concerning alleged or apparent instances of violations of fundamental rights and freedoms, abuse of power, unfair, harsh, insensitive or discourteous treatment of an inhabitant of Namibia by an official in the employ of any organ of Government (whether central or local), manifest injustice, or corruption or conduct by such official which would properly be regarded as unlawful, oppressive or unfair in a democratic society;

(b) the duty to investigate complaints concerning the functioning of the Public Service Commission, administrative organs of the State, the defence force, the police force and the prison service in so far as such complaints relate to the failure to achieve a balanced structuring of such services or equal access by all to the recruitment of such services or fair administration in relation to such services;

(c) the duty to investigate complaints concerning the over-utilization of living natural resources, the irrational exploitation of non-renewable resources, the degradation and destruction of ecosystems and failure to protect the beauty and character of Namibia;

(d) the duty to investigate complaints concerning practices and actions by persons, enterprises and other private institutions where such complaints allege that violations of fundamental rights and freedoms under this Constitution have taken place;

(e) the duty and power to take appropriate action to call for the remedying, correction and reversal of instances specified in the preceding Sub-Articles through such means as are fair, proper and effective, including:

(aa) negotiation and compromise between the parties concerned;

(bb) causing the complaint and his or her finding thereon to be reported to the superior of an offending person;

(cc) referring the matter to the Prosecutor-General;

(dd) bringing proceedings in a competent Court for an interdict or some other suitable remedy to secure the termination of the offending action or conduct, or the abandonment or alteration of the offending procedures;

(ee) bringing proceedings to interdict the enforcement of such legislation or regulation by challenging its validity if the offending action or conduct is sought to be justified by subordinate legislation or regulation which is grossly unreasonable or otherwise *ultra vires;*

(ff) reviewing such laws as were in operation before the date of Independence in order to ascertain whether they violate the letter or the spirit of this Constitution and to make consequential recommendations to the President, the Cabinet or the Attorney-General for appropriate action following thereupon;

(f) the duty to investigate vigorously all instances of alleged or suspected corruption and the misappropriation of public monies by officials and to take appropriate steps, including reports to the Prosecutor-General and the Auditor-General, pursuant thereto;

(g) the duty to report annually to the National Assembly on the exercise of his or her powers and functions.

Article 92. Powers of Investigation. The powers of the Ombudsman shall be defined by Act of Parliament and shall include the power:

(a) to issue subpoenas requiring the attendance of any person before the Ombudsman and the production of any document or record relevant to any investigation by the Ombudsman;

(b) to cause any person contemptuous of any such subpoena to be prosecuted before a competent Court;

(c) to question any person;

(d) to require any person to co-operate with the Ombudsman and to disclose truthfully and frankly any information within his or her knowledge relevant to any investigation of the Ombudsman.

Article 93. Meaning of "Official." For the purposes of this Chapter the word "official" shall, unless the context otherwise indicates, include any elected or appointed official or employee of any organ of the central or local government, any official of a para-statal enterprise owned or managed or controlled by the State, or in which the State or the Government has substantial interest, or any officer of the defence force, the police force or the prison service, but shall not include a Judge of the Supreme Court or the High Court or, in so far as a complaint concerns the performance of a judicial function, any other judicial officer.

Article 94. Removal from Office. (1) The Ombudsman may be removed from office before the expiry of his or her term of office by the President acting on the recommendation of the Judicial Service Commission.

(2) The Ombudsman may only be removed from office on the ground of mental incapacity or for gross misconduct, and in accordance with the provisions of Sub-Article (3) hereof.

(3) The Judicial Service Committee shall investigate whether or not the Ombudsman shall be removed from office on the grounds referred to in Sub-Article (2) hereof and, if it decides that the Ombudsman shall be removed, it shall inform the President of its recommendation.

(4) While investigations are being carried out into the necessity of the removal of the Ombudsman in terms of this Article, the President may, on the recommendation of the Judicial Service Commission and, pending the outcome of such investigations and recommendation, suspend the Ombudsman from office.

Chapter 11
Principles of State Policy

Article 95. Promotion of the Welfare of the People. The State shall actively promote and maintain the welfare of the people by adopting, *inter alia,* policies aimed at the following:

(a) enactment of legislation to ensure equality of opportunity for women, to enable them to participate fully in all spheres of Namibian society; in particular, the Government shall ensure the implementation of the principle of non-discrimination in remuneration of men and women; further, the Government shall seek, through appropriate legislation, to provide maternity and related benefits for women;

(b) enactment of legislation to ensure that the health and strength of the workers, men and women, and the tender age of children are not abused and that citizens are not forced by economic necessity to enter vocations unsuited to their age and strength;

(c) active encouragement of the formation of independent trade unions to protect workers' rights and interests, and to promote sound labour relations and fair employment practices;

(d) membership of the International Labour Organisation (ILO) and, where possible, adherence to and action in accordance with the international Conventions and Recommendations of the ILO;

(e) ensurance that every citizen has a right to fair and

reasonable access to public facilities and services in accordance with the law;

(f) ensurance that senior citizens are entitled to and do receive a regular pension adequate for the maintenance of a decent standard of living and the enjoyment of social and cultural opportunities;

(g) enactment of legislation to ensure that the unemployed, the incapacitated, the indigent and the disadvantaged are accorded such social benefits and amenities as are determined by Parliament to be just and affordable with due regard to the resources of the State;

(h) a legal system seeking to promote justice on the basis of equal opportunity by providing free legal aid in defined cases with due regard to the resources of the State;

(i) ensurance that workers are paid a living wage adequate for the maintenance of a decent standard of living and the enjoyment of social and cultural opportunities;

(j) consistent planning to raise and maintain an acceptable level of nutrition and standard of living of the Namibian people and to improve public health;

(k) encouragement of the mass of the population through education and other activities and through their organisations to influence Government policy by debating its decisions;

(l) maintenance of ecosystems, essential ecological processes and biological diversity of Namibia and utilization of living natural resources on a sustainable basis for the benefit of all Namibians, both present and future; in particular, the Government shall provide measures against the dumping or recycling of foreign nuclear and toxic waste on Namibia territory.

Article 96. Foreign Relations. The State shall endeavour to ensure that in its international relations it:

(a) adopts and maintains a policy of non-alignment;

(b) promotes international co-operation, peace and security;

(c) creates and maintains just and mutually beneficial relations among nations;

(d) fosters respect for international law and treaty obligations;

(e) encourages the settlement of international disputes by peaceful means.

Article 97. Asylum. The State shall, where it is reasonable to do so, grant asylum to persons who reasonably fear persecution on the ground of their political beliefs, race, religion or membership of a particular social group.

Article 98. Principles of Economic Order. (1) The economic order of Namibia shall be based on the principles of a mixed economy with the objective of securing economic growth, prosperity and a life of human dignity for all Namibians.

(2) The Namibian economy shall be based, *inter alia,* on the following forms of ownership:

(a) public;

(b) private;

(c) joint public-private;

(d) co-operative;

(e) co-ownership;

(f) small-scale family.

Article 99. Foreign Investments. Foreign investments shall be encouraged within Namibia subject to the provisions of an Investment Code to be adopted by Parliament.

Article 100. Sovereign Ownership of Natural Resources. Land, water and natural resources below and above the surface of the land and in the continental shelf and within the territorial waters and the exclusive economic zone of Namibia shall belong to the State if they are not otherwise lawfully owned.

Article 101. Application of the Principles contained in this Chapter. The principles of state policy contained in this Chapter shall not of and by themselves be legally enforceable by any Court, but shall nevertheless guide the Government in making and applying laws to give effect to the fundamental objectives of the said principles. The Courts are entitled to have regard to the said principles in interpreting any laws based on them.

Chapter 12
Regional and Local Government

Article 102. Structures of Regional and Local Government. (1) For purposes of regional and local government, Namibia shall be divided into regional and local units, which shall consist of such regions and Local Authorities as may be determined and defined by Act of Parliament.

(2) The delineation of the boundaries of the regions and Local Authorities referred to in Sub-Article (1) hereof shall be geographical only, without any reference to the race, colour or ethnic origin of the inhabitants of such areas.

(3) Every organ of regional and local government shall have a Council as the principal governing body, freely elected in accordance with this Constitution and the Act of Parliament referred to in Sub-Article (1) hereof, with an executive and administration which shall carry out all lawful resolutions and policies of such Council, subject to this Constitution and any other relevant laws.

(4) For the purposes of this Chapter a Local Authority shall include all municipalities, communities, village councils and other organs of local government defined and constituted by Act of Parliament.

(5) There shall be a Council of Traditional Leaders to be established in terms of an Act of Parliament in order to advise the President on the control and utilization of communal land and on all such other matters as may be referred to it by the President for advice. . . .

Chapter 19
Amendment of the Constitution

Article 131. Entrenchment of Fundamental Rights and Freedoms. No repeal or amendment of any of the provisions of chapter 3 hereof, in so far as such repeal or amendment diminishes or detracts from the fundamental rights and freedoms contained and defined in that chapter, shall be permissible under this Constitution, and no such purported repeal or amendment shall be valid or have any force or effect.

Article 132. Repeal and Amendment of the Constitution. (1) Any bill seeking to repeal or amend any provision of this Constitution shall indicate the proposed repeals and/or amendments with reference to the specific articles sought to be repealed and/or amended and shall not deal with any matter other than the proposed repeals or amendments.

(2) The majorities required in Parliament to the repeal and/or amendment of any of the provisions of this Constitution shall be:

(a) two-thirds of all the members of the National Assembly; and

(b) two-thirds of all the members of the National Council.

(3) (a) Notwithstanding the provisions of Sub-Article (2) hereof, if a bill proposing a repeal and/or amendment of

any of the provisions of this Constitution secures a majority of two-thirds of all the members of the National Assembly, but fails to secure a majority of two-thirds of all the members of the National Council, the President may by Proclamation make the bill containing the proposed repeals and/or amendments the subject of a national referendum.

(b) The national referendum referred to in Sub-Article (a) hereof shall be conducted in accordance with procedures prescribed for the holding of referenda by Act of Parliament.

(c) If upon the holding of such a referendum the bill containing the proposed repeals and/or amendments is approved by a two-thirds majority of all the votes cast in the referendum, the bill shall be deemed to have been passed in accordance with the provisions of this Constitution, and the President shall deal with it in terms of Article 56 hereof.

(4) No repeal or amendment of this Sub-Article or Sub-Articles (2) or (3) hereof in so far as it seeks to diminish or detract from the majorities required in Parliament or in a referendum shall be permissible under this Constitution, and no such purported repeal or amendment shall be valid or have any force or effect.

(5) Nothing contained in this Article:

(a) shall detract in any way from the entrenchment provided for in Article 131 hereof of the fundamental rights and freedoms contained and defined in Chapter 3 hereof;

(b) shall prevent Parliament from changing its own composition or structures by amending or repealing any of the provisions of this Constitution: provided always that such repeals or amendments are effected in accordance with the provisions of this Constitution.

NATIONALITY. The right to a nationality is proclaimed in the UNIVERSAL DECLARATION OF HUMAN RIGHTS in the following terms:

Article 15.1. Everyone has the right to a nationality.
2. No one shall be arbitrarily deprived of his nationality nor denied the right to change his nationality.

The INTERNATIONAL COVENANT ON CIVIL AND POLITICAL RIGHTS contains the following provision:

Article 24.3. Every child has the right to acquire a nationality.

The INTERNATIONAL CONVENTION ON THE ELIMINATION OF ALL FORMS OF RACIAL DISCRIMINATION provides that:

Article 5. In compliance with the fundamental obligation laid down in article 2 of this Convention, States parties undertake to prohibit and to eliminate racial discrimination in all its forms and to guarantee the right of everyone, without distinction as to race, colour, or national or ethnic origin, to equality before the law, notably in the enjoyment of the following rights:. . . .
(d). Other civil rights, in particular:. . . .
(iii). The right to nationality.

The CONVENTION ON THE ELIMINATION OF ALL FORMS OF DISCRIMINATION AGAINST WOMEN provides that:

Article 9.1. States parties shall grant women equal rights with men to acquire, change or retain their nationality. They shall ensure in particular that neither marriage to an alien nor change of nationality by the husband during marriage shall automatically change the nationality of the wife, render her stateless or force upon her the nationality of her husband.
2. States parties shall grant women equal rights with men with respect to the nationality of their children.

The AMERICAN CONVENTION ON HUMAN RIGHTS, open for acceptance by member States of the ORGANIZATION OF AMERICAN STATES, provides that:

Article 20.1. Every person has the right to a nationality.
2. Every person has a right to the nationality of the State in whose territory he was born if he does not have the right to any other nationality.
3. No one shall be arbitrarily deprived of his nationality or of the right to change it.

Conflicts of Nationality Laws. Nationality is a term which refers to a legal bond reflecting a genuine connection between an individual and a particular State by which the individual gives his allegiance to that State and it, in turn, protects and assists him when he is outside the territory under its jurisdiction.

Normally, nationality coincides with citizenship, but some States restrict their citizenship to those who enjoy full political rights. Each State determines who are its nationals by operation of its laws, and the question of whether a particular individual is a national of a particular State can only be determined by that State itself by reference to those laws.

Most individuals acquire nationality automatically by the fact of birth in a particular State. Later, they may acquire another nationality by marriage, naturalization, or otherwise, sometimes retaining and sometimes losing their original nationality in the process. Or they may lose their original nationality (by expulsion, persecution, or failure to comply with legal requirements) without acquiring a new one, and thus become stateless.

International nationality problems arise most frequently out of conflicts between the nationality laws of various States which give rise either to multiple nationality or to statelessness. From the international point of view, it is essential that everyone should have a nationality—preferably not more than one at a time.

One of the most persistent problems in this field is that relating to the nationality of married women. The Hague Convention on Certain Questions Relating to the Conflict of Nationality Laws, of 12 April

1930, was the earliest multilateral instrument prepared to deal with this problem; it endeavored primarily to reconcile various national legislations so as to eliminate cases of conflicts of nationality laws leading to statelessness. Later, the two Montevideo conventions of 26 December 1933, on the nationality of married women, proclaimed for the first time the principle of equality of the sexes as regards nationality. Article 1 of the first of these conventions provided that "there shall be no distinction based on sex as regards nationality" in the legislation or practice of states parties. Articles 5 and 6 of the second convention provided that "neither matrimony nor its dissolution will affect the nationality of the husband or wife," and that "naturalization or loss of nationality by the husband will not affect any members of his family."

On the basis of a survey of existing national legislation prepared by the Secretary-General, the COMMISSION ON THE STATUS OF WOMEN identified the urgent need for a new multilateral convention on the nationality of married women which would ensure such women equality with men in the exercise of the right to a nationality and prevent them from becoming stateless, or otherwise suffering hardships, as a consequence of conflicts in nationality laws. The commission prepared the draft of such an instrument, and, on 29 January 1957, the CONVENTION ON THE NATIONALITY OF MARRIED WOMEN was completed and adopted by the General Assembly (resolution 1040 [XI]). It was opened for signature and ratification on 20 February of the same year.

Statelessness. There are two categories of stateless persons: *de jure* and *de facto.* Stateless persons *de jure* are persons who are not nationals of any State, either because at birth or subsequently they were not given any nationality or because during their lifetime they lost their own nationality and did not acquire a new one. Stateless persons *de facto* are persons who, having left the country of which they were nationals, no longer enjoy the protection and assistance of their national authorities, either because these authorities refuse to grant them protection and assistance or because they themselves renounce the protection and assistance of the countries of which they were nationals. A stateless person, in short, is one who is unable or unwilling to avail himself of the protection of the government of his country of nationality or former nationality.

Statelessness is a recurrent source of difficulty for the country of reception, the country of origin, and the stateless person himself. These difficulties were described in the booklet entitled *A Study of Statelessness* (United Nations publication, Sales No. 1949.

XIV.2), issued by the United Nations in 1949, as follows:

For the country of reception:

1. The stateless person does not fit smoothly into the legal administrative or social life of his country of sojourn. The provisions of international law which determine the status of foreigners are designed to apply to foreigners having a nationality. The stateless person is an anomaly and for reasons of principle or method it is often impossible to deal with him in accordance with the legal provisions designed to apply to foreigners who receive the assistance of their national authorities, and who must, in certain cases, be repatriated by the countries of which they are nationals.

2. Administrative authorities which have to deal with stateless persons, having no definite legal status and without protection, encounter very great and often insurmountable difficulties. Officials must possess rare professional and human qualities if they are to deal adequately with these defenceless beings, who have no clearly defined rights and live by virtue of good-will and tolerance.

3. The fact that large numbers of persons are obliged to live outside the law, as it were, that they are at the mercy of the administrative authorities and are led to adopt various extra-legal procedures to win the favour of those authorities, creates a state of affairs incompatible with a healthy conception of the law.

4. The uncertain status of stateless persons exposes the nationals of the reception countries to various risks. Because of this uncertainty, some abstain from dealing with stateless persons, others protect themselves from risk by imposing onerous conditions. As a consequence, relations between nationals and stateless persons are strained.

For the country of origin:

When the *de jure* or *de facto* stateless person is a political refugee, he often retains a very strong resentment against the regime of the country from which he has fled.

His hope is that sooner or later, thanks to a change of regime, he will be able to return to his own country. He looks forward to that day and in certain cases may seek by his activities and hostile propaganda to hasten its coming.

Once settled in a country where he can re-establish himself, and often set up a home by marrying a national whose nationality he will acquire, his attitude changes. He will become more or less assimilated in the reception country, and it is there that he will tend to focus his interests and affections; his children will feel fully at home there and will have no thought of returning. The process of peaceful resettlement is complete.

For the stateless person:

Normally every individual belongs to a national community and feels himself a part of it. He enjoys the protection and assistance of the national authorities. When he is abroad, his own national authorities look after him and provide him with certain advantages. The organization of the entire legal and economic life of the individual residing in a foreign country depends upon his possession of a nationality.

The fact that the stateless person has no nationality

places him in an abnormal and inferior position which reduces his social value and destroys his own self-confidence.

During the long period of peace and social stability at the end of the nineteenth and the beginning of the twentieth centuries, stateless persons were few and their situation was tolerable. Life was not highly organized as it is today and foreigners, whatever their status, enjoyed considerable freedom. The stateless person succeeded in making a place for himself in a country and finding a *milieu* to his liking. He was free to find employment as a wage-earner, to practice a craft or engage in trade. If his conduct was unobjectionable he was not troubled by the police, which exercised no special supervision over foreigners, and he could lead a more or less normal existence, without his legal disability causing him any serious difficulties.

Since the First World War, in Europe at any rate, the situation has completely changed. The re-establishment of the passport and visa system, the increased control over foreigners, the regulations governing all aspects of social life (work, exercise of professions, food, housing, movement within the country, and so on) bring the stateless person in constant contact with the authorities and make him conscious of his handicapped status.

A number of international problems resulting from statelessness were examined by the INTERNATIONAL LAW COMMISSION in 1953 and 1954, when it prepared a draft Convention on the Elimination of Future Statelessness and a draft Convention on the Reduction of Future Statelessness (UN Docs. A/2456 and A/2693). In April 1954, the Economic and Social Council convened (resolution 526 A [XVII]) an International Conference of Plenipotentiaries to consider the two draft conventions. On 28 September of that year, the conference was able to adopt, and open for signature and ratification, one of the proposed instruments, the CONVENTION RELATING TO THE STATUS OF STATELESS PERSONS.

A second instrument on the subject, the CONVENTION ON THE REDUCTION OF STATELESSNESS, was adopted and opened for signature and ratification by another conference of plenipotentiaries, this one convened by the General Assembly (resolution 896 [IX]).

The Convention relating to the Status of Stateless Persons applies to "a person who is not considered as a national by any State under the operation of its law." The convention calls for stateless persons to be given the same treatment as that accorded to refugees under the CONVENTION RELATING TO THE STATUS OF REFUGEES. However, the convention places stateless persons in a position less favorable than that provided for refugees, in that they are not to be accorded the "most favored nation" treatment given refugees but only "treatment not less favorable than that accorded to aliens."

Under the Convention on the Reduction of Statelessness, a contracting State shall grant its nationality to a person born in its territory who would otherwise be stateless and shall not deprive a person of his nationality if such deprivation would render him stateless. Further, a contracting State may not deprive any person or group of persons of nationality on racial, ethnic, religious, or political grounds.

SEE ALSO *Convention on the Nationality of Married Women; Convention on the Rights of the Child; Declaration on the Human Rights of Individuals who are not Nationals of the Country in which They Live; European Convention on Establishment and Protocol; Declaration on the Rights of the Child; Universal Declaration on Human Rights.*

NAURU. The Republic of Nauru is a country in Micronesia occupying an island in the Pacific Ocean about 2,500 miles southwest of Honolulu. It achieved independence in 1968 and, although a UN trust territory from 1947 to 1948, is not a member of the United Nations. Its population is estimated by the UN (1990) to be 8,000. Ethnic groups include Nauruan (58%), other Pacific Island peoples (26%), Chinese (8%), and European (8%). Languages commonly used include Nauruan (official) and English. Christianity (Christian-Nauruan Congregational Church, Nauru Independence Church, and Roman Catholic Church) is the predominant religion. Literacy is estimated at 99%.

The government (1990) took the form of a republic. Under the 1968 constitution, the unicameral 18-member Parliament, members of which are elected by popular vote for terms of three years, elects the president from its membership. The president is head of State and government and exercises executive power with the assistance of a five-member cabinet. The judicial system includes the Family Court, the District Court, and the Supreme Court. There is no political party.

Annexed by Germany in 1888, Nauru was a League of Nations mandate under joint Australian, New Zealand, and British administration after World War I and a United Nations trust territory under the same administration after World War II.

NEPAL. The Kingdom of Nepal is a landlocked country in southern Asia. It has borders with India and the Tibetan autonomous region of China. It achieved independence from Great Britain in 1923 and became a member of the United Nations in 1955. Its population is estimated by the UN (1990) to be 18,470,000. Ethnic groups include Bhotias, Brahmans, Chetris, Gurungs, Limbus, Magars, Newars, Rais, Sherpas, and Tamangs. Languages commonly used include Nepali (official), Newari, Bhotia, and a variety of local languages. Religions practiced include Hinduism

(90%), Buddhism (5%), and Islam (5%). Literacy is estimated at 20%.

The government (1990) took the form of a monarchy. The king, as ruler, is head of State; his continued rule was approved by voters in an election held in 1980. He appoints the prime minister, who exercises executive authority as head of government. A unicameral National *Panchayat* (parliament) is provided under the 1962 constitution, and there is a judiciary headed by the Supreme Court. Political parties were banned in 1960.

Occasional conflicts arise because the population is divided into many tribes, speaking a wide variety of Tibeto–Burman languages, and because of the presence of numerous refugees from the Tibet. The refugees enjoy all the rights of Nepalese citizens except political rights.

In the 1950s, Nepal was a multiparty democracy, ruled first by the Rana family and, from 1955 onwards, by King Mahendra Bir Bikram Shah. In 1960, the king ousted the elected government of Prime Minister Bisweshwar Prasad Koirala, put its leaders into prison, and banned all political parties. In 1962, he promulgated a new constitution which provided for a political system without political parties and a unicameral legislature. This so-called "Panchayat system," consisting of a heirarchy of village, district, town, and national councils, was opposed by the Nepali Congress Party, the only organized political opposition; but its attacks against the government, although supported strongly by India, were not successful.

In 1972, Prince Birendra Bir Bikram Shah Dev succeeded Mahendra as king of Nepal. In 1979, his reign was shaken by a revolt of students in Katmandu. On 2 May 1980, in the first election held in 22 years, voters were called upon to choose between the Panchayat system and a multiparty system; the non-party system won with 55% of the vote. Claiming that the vote had been rigged, the Congress Party boycotted nationwide elections held in 1981 and 1986.

On 18 February 1990, thousands of students and political militants turned out in Katmandu, on a day which the government had designated as "Democracy Day," to demonstrate for democracy. They were supported by a general strike and a ban on vehicles arranged by the Movement to Restore Democracy and Human Rights. They were met, however, with clubs, tear gas, and showers of bricks and stones. More than ten were killed, scores were injured, and hundreds were arrested by the police and troops. King Birendra called for calm in a radio address in which he maintained that the Panchayat system was better suited to Nepal than a multiparty democracy.

By April 1990, however, the continuing protests against human rights abuses and the street demonstrations in many cities of Nepal for free multiparty elections caused the king to give the matter further thought. Unexpectedly, on 8 April, he announced that he was lifting the ban on political activity and called for the establishment of an interim government that would organize the supervise free elections in the country within a year.

On 19 April, Krishna Prasad Bhattarai was sworn in as prime minister—the first time in 30 years that a politician opposed to the monarchy had been asked to head a government. Besides Mr. Bhattarai, the cabinet included three other members of the Nepalese Congress Party, three communists, two independent human rights advocates, and two persons nominated by the king. The new government's primary function is to write a new democratic constitution.

Despite the speedy transition, angry crowds rioted briefly in Katmandu on 23 April to protest what they perceived as "the slow pace of change." The four-day-old government ordered a curfew after being informed that ten had been killed and 50 injured in a series of clashes with the police.

NEPAL: CONSTITUTION. The Constitution of Nepal, as amended by the First, Second, and Third Amendments, includes the following provisions (articles 9–17) specifically relating to human rights and fundamental freedoms:

Part 3
Fundamental Duties and Rights

9. Fundamental Duties of Citizen. The fundamental duties of every citizen shall be to act as follows—

(a) To render devotion and loyalty towards the Kingdom of Nepal;

(b) To exercise one's rights with due regard to the law and without infringing upon the rights of others;

(c) To follow the system established under the Constitution;

(d) To maintain harmony in the society by refraining from taking any action, on grounds of caste, tribe, region, race, sect, class, religion or on similar grounds, resulting to hatred, enmity, contempt, or destruction of or damage to public or private property, which may undermine the sovereignty, integrity and unity of Nepal.

10. Right to Equality. (1) All citizens shall have the right to equal protection of the laws.

(2) No discrimination shall be made against any citizen in the application of general laws on grounds of religion, race, sex, caste, tribe or any of them.

(3) There shall be no discrimination against any citizen in respect of appointment to the government service or any other public service only on grounds of religion, race, sex, caste, tribe or any of them.

11. Right to Freedom. (1) No person shall be deprived of his life or personal liberty save in accordance with the law.

(2) Subject to the other provisions of this Part all citizens shall have the right to the following freedoms—

(a) freedom of speech and expression;

(b) freedom to assemble peaceably and without arms;

(c) freedom to form unions and associations;

(d) freedom to move to or reside in any part of Nepal; and

(e) freedom to acquire and enjoy property or to dispose it of by sale or otherwise.

(2a) Notwithstanding anything contained in clause (2), no political party or any other organisation, union or association motivated by party politics shall be formed or caused to be formed or run.

(3) No person shall be punished for an act which was not punishable by law when the act was done, nor shall any person be subjected to a punishment greater than that prescribed by law for an offence when the offence was committed.

(4) No person shall be prosecuted and punished more than once for the same offence in any court.

(5) No person accused of any offence shall be compelled to be a witness against himself.

(6) No person who is arrested shall be detained in custody without being informed, as is practicable, of the grounds of such arrest, nor shall he be denied the right to consult and be defended by a legal practitioner of his choice. *Explanation.* For the purpose of this clause, "legal practitioner" includes any person who, under the law for the time being in force, is authorised to represent any other person in any court.

(7) Every person who is arrested and detained in custody shall be produced before a judicial authority within a period of twenty-four hours of such arrest, excluding the period of journey from the place of arrest to such authority, and no such person shall be detained in custody beyond the said period except on the order of such authority.

(8) Nothing in clauses (6) and (7) shall apply to a person who—

(a) is a citizen of an enemy state; or

(b) is arrested or detained under a law providing for preventive detention.

12. Right against Exile. No citizen shall be exiled.

13. Right against Exploitation. Traffic in human beings, slavery and forced labour are prohibited. Provided that the prohibition on forced labour shall not be a bar to provide for compulsory service by law for public purposes.

14. Right to Religion. Every person may profess his own religion as handed down from ancient times and may practise it having regard to the traditions. Provided that no person shall be entitled to convert another person from one religion to another.

15. Right to Property. No person shall be deprived of his property save in accordance with the law.

16. Right to Constitutional Remedies. Right to proceed in accordance with Article 71, for the enforcement of the rights conferred by this Part, is guaranteed.

17. Restrictions on the Exercise of Fundamental Rights for Public Goods. (1) Laws may be made for the sake of public good to regulate or control the exercise of fundamental rights specified in this Part.

(2) If it is stated in the preamble of any Act that it has been made for any or all of the following purposes, such Act, as well as any rule, order or byelaws made under such Act and having the force of law, shall be deemed to be a law made for the public good—

(a) For the preservation of the security of Nepal;

(b) For the maintenance of law and order;

(c) For the maintenance of friendly relations with foreign states;

(d) For the maintenance of good relations among the people of different classes or professions or between the people of different areas;

(e) For the maintenance of good conduct, health, comfort, economic interest, decency or morality of the people in general;

(f) For the protection of the interest of minors or women;

(g) For the prevention of internal disturbance or external invasion;

(h) For the prevention of contempt of court or contempt of the National Panchayat;

(i) For the prevention of any attempt to subvert this Constitution or any other law for the time being in force or for the prevention of any other attempt of like nature; and

(j) For the compliance of the fundamental duties.

NETHERLANDS. The Kingdom of the Netherlands consists of three countries: the Netherlands, the Netherlands Antilles, and the Island of Aruba—all linked under a legal framework laid down in the charter of the Kingdom of the Netherlands proclaimed on 15 December 1954. The Netherlands is a country in western Europe, on the North Sea, and has borders with Belgium and the Federal Republic of Germany. Its independence was first achieved in 1581 under the Union of Utrecht and was most recently restored after its second period of occupation by Germans in 1945. It became a member of the United Nations the same year. Its population is estimated by the UN (1990) to be 14,748,000.

The Netherlands Antilles consist of five islands: Curacao, Bonaire, St. Maarten, St. Eustatius, and Saba, with a total population of 176,500. Aruba, formerly a part of the Antilles, has a population of 61,900; it is the process of exercising its rights to self-determination, to be realized in 1996. Ethnic groups in the Netherlands include migrants from Suriname, the Moluccan Islands, the Netherland Antilles, and various Mediterranean countries; and non-nationals from Africa, Asia, Europe, the Americas, Oceania, and Hong Kong. Religions practiced include Christianity (Roman Catholic, Dutch Reformed, and other denominations), 55%; Islam, 5%; Judaism, 2%; and other or unaffiliated, 38%. The language commonly used is Dutch (official). Literacy is estimated at 99%. The Antillian community consists of a number of different races and cultural groups; they live together in harmony and without racial discrimination. The normal language of instruction is Dutch. On Curacao, Aruba, and Bonaire, the mother tongue Papiamente is used in some classes in addition to Dutch. On Saba, St. Eustatius, and St. Meerten, the mother tongue English is used as well as Dutch.

The government described the structure of the Kingdom of the Netherlands in a report presented to the **HUMAN RIGHTS COMMITTEE** on 1 August 1988 in the following terms (UN Doc. CCPR/C/42/Add. 6, para. 3–5):

The present constitutional structure of the Kingdom of the Netherlands dates back to 1954, when, after several years of study, discussion and negotiation, it was decided by the Netherlands, Suriname and the Netherlands Antilles (then including Aruba) to establish a new constitutional order under which they (according to the Charter for the Kingdom, the constitutional document which was promulgated) "will conduct their internal affairs autonomously and in their common interests on a basis of equality and will accord each other reciprocal assistance". Thus the Kingdom, while remaining one sovereign entity under international law, came to consist of three co-equal partners which have distinct identities and are fully autonomous in their internal affairs.

Since then, two important changes have taken place. In 1975 Suriname decided—with the full assent of the partners—to leave the Kingdom and become a sovereign State in its own right. In 1986 Aruba became a separate country within the Kingdom, under the Charter, and therefore now has the same constitutional status as the two other countries, the Netherlands and the Netherlands Antilles.

The Charter, the highest constitutional instrument of the Kingdom, is a legal document *sui generis,* which is based upon its voluntary acceptance by the three countries. It falls into three essential parts. The first part defines the association between the three countries, which is federal in nature. The fact that together the three countries form one sovereign entity implies that a number of matters need to be administered by the countries together, through the institutions of the Kingdom (wherever possible, the organs of the countries shall participate in the conduct of these affairs). These matters are called Kingdom affairs. They are enumerated in the Charter, and include the maintenance of independence, defence, foreign relations, and the safeguarding of fundamental human rights and freedoms, legal stability and proper administration. The second part deals with the relationship between the countries as autonomous entities. Their partnership implies that the countries respect each other and render one another aid and assistance, materially and otherwise and that they shall consult and co-ordinate in matters which are not Kingdom affairs but in which a reasonable degree of co-ordination is in the interest of the Kingdom as a whole. The third part of the Charter defines the autonomy of the countries, which is the principle underlying the Charter; the countries govern themselves according to their own wishes, subject only to certain conditions imposed by their being part of the Kingdom. Elementary principles of democratic government, observance of the Charter and Kingdom legislation, and the adequate functioning of the organs of the country are matters of concern to the whole of the realm. Conversely, although Kingdom affairs are matters for the Kingdom as a whole, the countries play active roles in the way they are conducted. In foreign relations, for example, the countries themselves, under the aegis of the Kingdom, deal with matters the substance of which is in their autonomous sphere.

Within the framework provided by the chapter, the government of the Netherlands (1990) took the form of a monarchy. The queen, acting as head of State, appoints the premier, who represents the party or coalition given the majority in popular elections. There is a bi-cameral parliament composed of a 75-member Upper Chamber elected by representative bodies of the provinces for terms of six years, so arranged that one-half of the members retire every three years; and a 150-member Lower Chamber elected by popular vote for terms of four years. The Lower Chamber initiates legislation and amends bills. The judiciary is headed by the Supreme Court of Justice. Justices are appointed by the crown. Political parties include Christian Democrats, Liberals, Democrats, and the Labor Party.

The island territories enjoy autonomy in their domestic affairs. Each has its own governor, appointed by the crown, its own unicameral *Staten* (parliament), its own judicial system, and its own political parties.

In a report presented to the **COMMITTEE ON THE ELIMINATION OF DISCRIMINATION** on 29 November 1988, the Netherlands government provided the following breakdown of the country's demographic composition (UN Doc. CERD/C/158/Add. 9, para. 6–8):

On 1 January 1987 568,000 foreign nationals were resident in the Netherlands. This represents nearly 4 per cent of the total population of the country. About one half of these foreign nationals were either Turks (162,000) or Moroccans (123,000). West Germans (41,000), Britons (38,000), Belgians (23,000), Spaniards (18,000) and Italians (17,000) between them accounted for about one quarter of the foreign population of the Netherlands.

The number of foreign national in the Netherlands increased by about 15,000 in 1986. This increase was mainly the result of net immigration: the number of foreign nationals entering the country exceeded the number of those leaving by some 29,000.

In 1986 about ± 23,000 foreign nationals acquired Dutch citizenship. This figure is considerably down on 1985, when there was a bunching effect caused by the entry into force of the Netherlands Nationality Act.

As regards ethnic minorities, the government indicated in the above-mentioned report to the Human Rights Committee that measures are being taken to improve the situation of members of such groups in fields such as housing, employment, education, and welfare services. The report states that (UN Doc. CCPR/C/42/Add. 6, para. 202–210):

The main features of this policy were set out in the policy document on minorities which appeared in September 1983 following extensive consultation with the organizations involved. The document was presented to the Lower House of parliament where it was debated and approved. It indicates the direction to be taken by minorities policy in the coming years, the objective of which is to create a society in which members of minority groups living in the Netherlands will, both individually and collectively, have the same rights and opportunities as the rest of the population. The three principal aspects of this overall goal are:

(a) To create the conditions needed for the emancipation of members of minority groups and for their participation in society. Mutual adjustment and acceptance must be encouraged among all sections of the population. Emancipation is interpreted in a broad sense, encompassing the dual process of strengthening the self-esteem and self-awareness of minority groups and their individual members and of influencing the surrounding society in such a way as to ensure that it provides lasting scope for their development;

(b) To eliminate the social and economic disadvantages of members of minority groups;

(c) To prevent discrimination, eliminate it where it does occur and, where necessary, improve the legal status of minority groups.

The principal ethnic minorities in the Netherlands are Moluccans, persons of Surinamese and Netherlands antillean origin, migrant workers recruited from Turkey, Morocco and elsewhere, and their families, Netherlands Gypsies and non-Netherlands Gypsies who are legally resident in the Netherlands and refugees. The Netherlands Government regards these sections of the population as forming an integral part of Netherlands society. Caravan dwellers are also classified on pragmatic grounds as a minority group to allow them to benefit from the effects of minorities policy.

The policy document sets out the measures to be taken to afford minorities the same opportunities for development as other residents of the Netherlands. Emphasis is placed first and foremost on ensuring that minorities benefit from general policies to the same extent as all Netherlands citizens. This requires not only measures geared specifically to the needs of minorities, but additional measures in the framework of general policy to ensure that all available facilities are accessible to these sections of the population.

In June 1985 a national advisory and consultative body on minorities policy was instituted. Its members are drawn from minority groups and from organizations seeking to promote the interests of minorities. The following groups are represented:

(a) Persons of Moluccan origin (approx. 42,000);

(b) Migrant workers of Turkish origin (approx. 154,000);

(c) Migrant workers of Moroccan and Tunisian origin (approx. 100,000);

(d) Migrant workers of northern Mediterranean origin (Greeks, Italians and Spaniards) (approx. 73,000);

(e) Persons of Surinamese origin (approx. 181,000);

(f) Persons of Netherlands Antillean origin (approx. 40,000);

(g) Refugees and persons granted asylum (approx. 30,000);

(h) Caravan dwellers and Gypsies (approx. 23,000).

It should also be noted that a Bill submitted to parliament (Lower House 1984–1985, 19076) is designed to permit the appointment of non-Netherlands nationals to public service posts other than those for which Netherlands nationality is deemed by the Government to be indispensable (for example the police, the armed forces and the judiciary). A considerable number of jobs will thus be made accessible within the foreseeable future to residents from minority groups who do not possess Netherlands nationality.

Finally, the Government has studied the report "Fewer rights for minorities?" which catalogues over 1,300 statutory provisions which distinguish between persons on the grounds of nationality, residence, ethnic background, beliefs and language, and has concluded that the vast majority of these distinctions are insignificant, warranted or non-discriminatory. Every year the progress in changing provisions in Netherlands legislation which distinguish between persons in an unjustified way is reported to parliament by the Government.

In recent years, through financial and other forms of assistance, the Government has encouraged and supported the formation of new ethnic minority organizations and the strengthening of existing ones. Priority has been given to women's and young people's organizations. To make it possible for non-Dutch-speaking members of ethnic minorities to make themselves understood in their own languages when dealing with public bodies and services, a national network of interpreters' centres has been in existence for some years, providing interpretation services by telephone free of charge. This was the case during the period when the present report was drawn up.

Increasing attention has been given to the cultural development and cultural awareness of members of ethnic minorities in drama, the visual arts and literature.

Separate Status of Aruba. In the same report, the Netherlands government provided the following information (*Ibid.,* para. 211; 213–214):

Aruba's separate status, its emergence on 1 January 1986 as a separate constituent part of the Kingdom of the Netherlands, signified an important constitutional reorganization of the Kingdom and brought with it a number of political, economic, financial and monetary changes. . . .

The country of Aruba is a parliamentary democracy, as defined in its Constitution. Her Majesty the Queen—who reigns over the Kingdom and over each of the countries—is represented in Aruba by the Governor, who also represents the Kingdom Government. The Aruban Council of Ministers consists of the Prime Minister and six Ministers (General Welfare, Economic Affairs and Tourism, Justice and Public Health, Transport and Communications, Finance, Utilities and Public Works). The *Staten* (parliament) are elected by proportional representation; elections are held at least every four years. Aruba is represented in the Netherlands by a Minister Plenipotentiary who is a member of the Council of Ministers of the Realm.

Common observance of the rule of law in the Kingdom is ensured, *inter alia,* by the existence of a Common Court of Justice of the Netherlands Antilles and Aruba, whose judges are appointed by the Queen; in addition, the Supreme Court of the Netherlands is the court of cassation for the whole of the Kingdom.

NEW INTERNATIONAL ECONOMIC ORDER. In 1980, the UN Economic and Social Council (decision 1980/126) authorized the SUB-COMMISSION ON PREVENTION OF DISCRIMINATION AND PROTECTION OF MINORI-

TIES to appoint one of its members, Mr. Raul Ferrero (Peru), as its special rapporteur to prepare a study on the new international economic order and the promotion of human rights, taking into account the conclusions of the seminar scheduled to be held later in 1980 within the framework of the program of UN AD-VISORY SERVICES IN THE FIELD OF HUMAN RIGHTS on "The Effects of the Existing Unjust International Economic Order on the Economies of the Developing Countries and the Obstacle that This Represents for the Implementation of Human Rights and Fundamental Freedoms, particularly the Right to Enjoy Adequate Standards of Living as Proclaimed in Article 25 of the Universal Declaration of Human Rights."

One conclusion of the seminar, which was widely supported although no consensus was reached, was that the present unjust international order placed obstacles in the way of exercise of the RIGHT TO DEVELOPMENT by developing countries. These obstacles were identified as (UN Doc. ST/HR/SER A/8, chap. V):

(i) ideological obstacles, reflected in the priority given to the arms race rather than to development;
(ii) institutional obstacles, reflected in the observance of comprehensive negotiating frameworks and the glaring inadequacy of existing institutions;
(iii) legal obstacles in the form of obsolete concepts and principles of international law based on colonial approaches to international trade and contractual undertakings, the lack of control on transnational enterprises, unfavourable structure of the patent system and the refusal to accept the concept of "permanent sovereignty";
(iv) international trade and related obstacles, characterized by unequal exchange of goods and services, inadequate institutional arrangement for commodity trade, tariff and non-tariff barriers and emphasis on unfair concepts such as reciprocity among developed and developing countries;
(v) obstacles to access to finance due to anachronistic objectives and spirit prevailing in international financial institutions, and an unjust approach to the external debt problems of developing countries;
(vi) inadequate mechanisms to promote transfer of technology for a balance growth in scientific and technological development in both developing and developed countries.

The seminar also drew a comparison between the present international economic order and the economic orders of the European countries at the end of the 19th century, as follows:

At that time, national economies in their liberal setting had come to the point where the system-promoted interests of the haves, the entrepreneurs, became incompatible with the system-neglected interests of the have-nots, the working masses. On the brink of violent revolution the ruling classes were forced to allow restriction of liberal enterprise by the enactment of special legislation, which provided for a gradually expanding minimum of social security and economic welfare for the hitherto exploited. In other words, to meet the demands of the less privileged the three basic principles of liberalism underwent the following changes: the principle of freedom was restricted by the introduction of the principle of protection; the principle of legal equality was in part replaced by that of material equality; and the principle of reciprocity was conditioned by the fact that the working class was endowed with rights which restricted the operational freedom of the entrepreneurs. Today, one can observe the tendency towards a similar development on the international scene.

The sub-commission received the special rapporteur's study, entitled *The New International Economic Order and the Promotion of Human Rights,* in 1983 (issued in 1985 as United Nations publication, Sales No. E.85.XIV.6). In the study, after examining the relevant documentation, the special rapporteur presented the following conclusions (Chap. XIII A, para. 250–294):

In discussing the present situation regarding world economic relations, it is not entirely appropriate to speak of an international economic order, for it is not so much an "order" as a world-wide interaction of economic forces and powers resulting from historical causes that need to be understood.

The present economic order began to be imposed at a time when the vast majority of developing countries were still dependent territories and consequently unable to take part in its establishment; it was therefore inevitably inequitable and contrary to their interests. It is well known that international economic and monetary relations are based on three liberal principles, namely, freedom, equality and reciprocity. These principles could well suffice to bring prosperity for all, but in a world of equals, not in a world of unequals. In a world of "potentates" on one side and the "poor" on the other, it is not right to expect the poor to accept principles which profit the powerful alone and harm the weak; in such conditions, the relationship tends to give rise to exploitation, legal equality to produce material inequality, and reciprocal concessions to widen still further the already immense gap between the rich and the poor countries.

The present order is a serious obstacle to the realization of the human rights and fundamental freedoms proclaimed in the Universal Declaration of Human Rights, more particularly in article 25, which declares that everyone has the right to a standard of living adequate for the health and well-being of himself and of his family. However, the fact that an unjust international economic order exists cannot be used to justify failure to secure the realization or observance of human rights. In any event, there are two needs that have to be met side by side. One is the need to change the present international economic order into a more equitable order, and the other is the need to promote and protect human rights and fundamental freedoms in each and every country; they are interrelated needs, but neither of them is a prerequisite for the realization of the other.

A process of decolonization has given birth to innumerable independent States since the Second World War. Unfortunately, such political independence has not generally been followed by economic, social or cultural independence, which are equally important.

As Janez Stanovnik has pointed out, the demand for the new international economic order is of a political nature. The underprivileged peoples who are championing the new order have neither the military nor the economic power to match the dominant forces in the present world. Their strength lies rather in inevitable historical evolution and is therefore essentially on the political plane.

It must be recognized that it was at the Fourth Conference of Heads of State or Government of Non-Aligned Countries, held at Algiers from 5 to 9 September 1973, that the first ideas concerning a new international economic order were formulated. Conceptually, this new order represents the economic aspect of the policy of non-alignment, that is to say, the application of its general principles to the economic sphere. The above-mentioned Conference adopted an Economic Declaration and an Action Programme for Economic Co-operation, confirming that the new objective of the movement would be to seek to establish "a new type of international economic relations" and a new and just international division of labour. Both instruments benefited from the fact that all the non-aligned countries are also members of the Group of 77 and participate in the work of UNCTAD so that they have vast experience in such matters. Another important source of valuable ideas and concepts was the International Development Strategy for the Second United Nations Development Decade, adopted in 1970.

The existing system not only nullifies all efforts to narrow the gap between developing and developed countries, but, still worse, magnifies that difference by depriving the former of their rightful say in decisions on international economic and commercial questions of vital interest to them. The gap between the levels of living of developed and developing countries continues to widen—from roughly 10:1 in the 1950s to 14:1 at the end of the 1970s.

The industrialized countries are trying to solve their unemployment and inflation problems at the expense of the poor countries. To attain the price stability that suits them, they are holding down the prices of primary commodities from the developing world. As a result of this drop in commodity prices compared with those of industrial products, developing countries, which are mainly exporters of primary products, are forced to export a growing volume of raw materials each year in order to acquire the industrial products needed for their development. This phenomenon has been dubbed the "external strangulation of development."

The Brandt Commission has made the dramatic point that in some low-income countries studies have shown as many as 40 per cent of pre-school children exhibiting clinical signs of malnutrition. No one can state the exact numbers in the world who suffer from hunger and malnutrition, but all estimates indicate that they amount to hundreds of millions: millions of persons who will die from lack of food or have their physical development impaired. It is an intolerable situation. The food problem is extremely serious, but what is even worse is that it is continuing to grow more acute, to the extent that one third of mankind is now suffering from hunger.

To resolve the urgent food problem, the developing countries must put an end to the neglect into which agriculture has fallen; in the late 1950s and during the whole of the 1960s, their concern for industrial development led them to disregard the extremely important complementary role which rural development should play. This led to an abandonment of the countryside, the consequences of which we are suffering today.

World Bank projections indicate only modest growth for the developing countries' exports in the next 10 years. But it will be simply impossible to maintain this growth if the protectionist barriers erected by the developed nations are maintained or continue to grow as they have done recently. The fact is that this trend towards protectionism and restrictive trade practices is gathering momentum in all the industrialized nations.

It is essential to establish an international trade organization—as was proposed when the World Bank and IMF were set up—which would carry out the functions both of GATT and of UNCTAD, assuming responsibility for sponsoring agreements, *inter alia,* on such vital issues as the commercial practices of transnational corporations, international investment, problems of double taxation, the transfer of technology and so on, and in its turn act as a forum (as does UNCTAD) for dialogue, debate and negotiations in trade matters.

Insufficient attention is paid to developing countries' interests when establishing monetary and financial policies at the world level. The World Bank and IMF, which came into being as a result of the agreements adopted at the United Nations Monetary and Financial Conference held at Bretton Woods, New Hampshire, in 1944, were two corner-stones of the monetary system established after the Second World War, but they began to display serious limitations in the 1970s, and today these have developed into grave defects and failure to adapt to the needs of developing countries.

At present, the developing countries hold 38.5 per cent of the votes in the World Bank, in comparison with 42.5 per cent for the main industrialized countries and 19 per cent for the other industrialized countries. The fact that the participation of the developing countries is so limited has led to a proposal that votes should be divided equally between developed countries and developing countries. Similar pressure is being exerted in IMF, where the developing countries hold only 28 percent of the votes.

It is essential to change the prevailing view that IMF is a "lender of last resort" and place greater emphasis on the advisability, as indicated by IMF itself, of encouraging countries to seek its assistance when a need first arises and not when the situation has already become critical.

The conditions imposed today by certain international organizations, such as IMF, when granting balance-of-payments assistance, oblige developing countries to impose specified domestic policies which have extremely dangerous consequences, such as growing rates of inflation and unemployment.

One way to iron out the blatant inequalities between developing and developed countries would be to implement the International Development Strategy for the Third United Nations Development Decade, which reiterates the objective proclaimed by the General Assembly, in paragraph 43 of its resolution 2626 (XXV) of 24 October 1970, that the developed countries should provide developing countries with a minimum net amount of 0.7 per cent of their GNP each year in the form of official development assistance.

At the Seventh Conference of Heads of State or Government of Non-Aligned Countries, held in New Delhi in 1983, was pointed out that, despite the growing need on the part of developing countries for assistance on favourable terms, such assistance was in fact decreasing. The net expenditure of all members of DAC on official development assistance in fact amounted to only 0.35 per cent of their GNP in 1981, as compared with 0.51 per cent in 1960. After two decades, the figure attained is barely half the target figure set by the Untied Nations, namely, 0.7 per cent of the GNP of the developed countries.

Efforts in the field of science and technology are directed mainly at improving living standards in the developed countries, and when science and technology can be applied to the problems of the poor countries, the cost is sometimes virtually prohibitive. In addition, technology is rarely developed with the aim of meeting the needs of the developing countries, so that any technology transfer to those countries is mostly inadequate or, what is worse, obsolete.

The gap between the developed and the developing countries in the area of technology is much greater than the corresponding economic gap. While the developing countries have on average a per capita income 15 times lower than that of the developed countries, the application of modern scientific and technological knowledge in the developing countries is some 50 times less than in the developed countries. This explains the frequent references to the "technological gap".

As pointed out in the report of the Director-General for Development and International Economic Co-operation, transnational corporations have acquired considerable market power *vis-à-vis* the Governments and enterprises of developing countries. This has been due in part to their command over resources of various kinds—finance, management, marketing networks and skills, technology and "know-how" generally, in part to their ability to combine and deploy such resources across the world, and in part to the fact that transnational corporations, particularly those enjoying monopolistic positions, have generally integrated their subsidiaries and affiliates into the company as a whole, rather than into the economy of the host countries. Transnational corporations have been able to take advantage of their strong bargaining positions in a variety of ways—on occasion by interfering in the political affairs of the host country—and the relationships between transnational corporations and host countries have often involved patterns of growth and industrialization which have led to the inequitable distribution of the earnings from investment and associated activities and have limited the ability of developing countries to achieve self-reliant development.

The role of disarmament should also be emphasized. Let us imagine for a moment what it would mean if the huge resources devoted to military ends were used for civilian purposes. How much could be achieved and how many development programmes could be launched? It is moreover essential to bear in mind how difficult it is for the developing countries, in view of the world's armaments-oriented structure, to pursue their own paths towards progress if at the same time they are confronted with threats of intervention and intimidation from outside. As the report of the Secretary-General on the international dimensions of the right to development concluded, disarmament is crucial to realization of the right to development, as it is to realization of the right to peace, the achievement of a new international economic order and the promotion of respect for all human rights.

It is highly alarming that world expenditures on arms in a single year are, on the one hand, equal to the income of half the world's population in the same year and, on the other hand, of a similar order to the total external debt of the developing countries.

The most serious world recession since 1930 is the worst moment for the international financial institutions to impose more stringent conditions on borrowers and cut back their operations with them. It is counter-productive for IMF and the World Bank to have taken such an attitude at precisely the time when the developing countries have to face high oil prices, low prices for their primary goods and high interest rates on existing debts, all this within the context of a general recession on world markets. Countries that are heavily in debt to the developed countries are precisely their best customers, and any serious reduction in lending will have repercussions in the developed countries in the form of reduced demand and fewer imports in the developing countries.

Although the external debt of some countries may be so great as to appear unmanageable, it must not be forgotten that if the international banking system suddenly stops lending, the developing countries will not be able to pay their existing debts either.

No analysis of the crisis centring round the growing indebtedness of the developing countries can disregard the profound consequences which this crisis may have, above all for the most indebted countries. These countries cannot be expected to confine themselves simply to paying their debts conscientiously, neglecting their internal problems or leaving aside their most important concern, namely, their own development. If these countries are subjected to constraint and pressure, the resulting social problems can come as no surprise.

The current situation with regard to the external debt of the developing countries is extremely serious, and it has now reached the point where whole countries are on the verge of collapse. Unless realistic and urgent measures are taken, the entire international financial system may also collapse. However, the problem has not yet been tackled, except through short-term measures which do not provide any genuine medium-term or long-term solution, and the danger of a widespread cessation of payments therefore remains.

The extremely high level of indebtedness of the developing countries makes it necessary to think in terms of global and realistic solutions. It might be useful to consider the advantages of a system whereby the developed countries would buy from private banks the loans granted to countries with payment difficulties. The loans would of course be brought at a rate lower than the nominal value, which would mean that the private banks would lose a certain amount but would recover a considerable part of the total loan. The acquiring Governments would then negotiate a long-term refinancing scheme with the debtor countries, reducing the annual payments to appropriate or bearable levels based on capacity to pay. The debt might perhaps be converted into negotiable instruments guaranteed in some way by the national treasuries or equivalent institutions in the developed countries.

The effect of this colossal indebtedness on human rights is now being seen. Third world countries are making considerable cuts in their development programmes, Governments have had virtually to halt all public works projects, and unemployment and underemployment are increasing uncontrollably.

All this is giving rise to a bad social atmosphere which affects the poorest classes and helps generate a dangerous climate of political insecurity. In the last two years, the construction of schools, hospitals and houses and the improvement of social security services, for example, have become almost a luxury for the developing countries.

It is extremely important to stress the indivisible and interdependent nature of all human rights, without giving priority to any category in particular. The main difficulty is not to settle on the priority but to establish a flexible relationship between civil and political rights and economic, social and cultural rights and take each country's level of socio-economic development fully into account; to do so, it must be appreciated that the implementation of economic, social and cultural rights depends largely on each State's level of development, while the implementation of civil and political rights depends exclusively on the political will of Governments.

The concept of human rights has evolved gradually. After the traditional classification into civil and political rights, or what could be termed "first generation" rights, came economic, social and cultural rights, which may be place in the second generation, and only in recent times has the need been maintained to recognize the existence of the "rights of solidarity"—which include the right to development, to a healthy environment, to peace and to the common heritage of mankind, and other rights that make up what could be called the third generation in this evolution. These rights, however, have scarcely taken shape and to implement them will require a major effort along a difficult road ahead.

These three categories, or generations, of human rights are to some extent equivalent to the three fundamental principles of the French Revolution of 1789: liberty, equality and fraternity. The human rights which were first recognized, namely civil and political rights, are those based on the "freedom" of the person. Economic, social and cultural rights, which arise in the second stage, may be said to be based on the "equality" of human beings. The rights of solidarity, which represent a third stage, still in process of maturing, are those based on "fraternity" between men and between peoples.

Those who live in absolute poverty cannot even satisfy the minimum needs of a decent life: enough food, a minimum of clothing, living space, drinking water, satisfactory sanitary installations, elementary hygiene, basic schooling for children, etc. The hundreds of millions of people who live in these conditions are permanently denied most of the fundamental and inalienable human rights proclaimed in the Universal Declaration of Human Rights.

Justice and the search for greater equality should be the guiding principles for international action aimed at eliminating the growing disparities between some countries and others. It must be remembered that the very objective of a new international economic order does not relate solely to economic issues as such. Its aim is not only the reassessment of things and their more equitable distribution, but also the development of all men and of all aspects of man, in a global cultural process which embodies values and encompasses the national context, social relations, education and well-being, with the idea of also providing a basis for the development of the international community itself.

The existing unjust international economic order is a genuine obstacle to realization of the human rights and fundamental freedoms proclaimed in the Universal Declaration of Human Rights, in particular in article 25, which states that everyone has the right to a standard of living adequate for the health and well-being of himself and of his family. More than 30 years after the adoption of the Universal Declaration of Human Rights, 850 million people, that is, approximately 40 per cent of the inhabitants of the developing countries, are still living in dire poverty.

It must therefore be emphasized that the central or basic element in its establishment must be man, whose essential dignity must be defined and protected; it must accordingly be understood that the ultimate goal of the new order is respect for human rights and fundamental freedoms.

Interdependence does not mean uniformity. Genuine development does not consist in grafting life-styles from developed countries onto developing countries. It must be understood that interdependence presupposes relations between countries that are different. International co-operation should be aimed at remedying the lack or scarcity of economic resources, and the recipient States are under an obligation to participate in such co-operation. It is implicit in the right to development that States should agree to assist one another when external factors obstruct the effective implementation of human rights.

One method whereby human rights can be truly and effectively safeguarded internally is through fair participation in which the people can express their own will in a free and responsible manner, thus enabling all the members of the community to fulfil themselves and exercise conscious freedom of choice. Workers and their organizations should participate not only in the management of public, economic, social and cultural affairs as part of the democratization of the State, but also in the decision-making processes of economic, labour and social planning, in the determination of social development goals and in the creation of conditions for achieving those goals.

The principle of participation in developing countries with indigenous populations implies the equal recognition of those peoples' right to participate fully in the economic, political and social life of the States of which they form a part, as well as their right to maintain their traditions, customs, languages and other special characteristics, which are expressed in the right to be different. Alienation as an instrument of national and international policy leads to loss of identity for those against whom it is applied.

Any form of economic aggression, as committed by some developed States against developing States, is similarly unacceptable and must therefore be categorically rejected; such forms of aggression include the use of threats, commercial sanctions or any other form of blockade and measures of coercion or blackmail to the extent that they involve means of political pressure aimed at influencing sovereign decisions.

The new order must take into consideration two important sets of principles contained in the Charter of Economic Rights and Duties of States: (i) the sovereignty, territorial integrity and political independence of States, the sovereign equality of all States, the principles of non-aggression, non-intervention and peaceful coexistence, equal rights and self-determination of peoples and the peaceful settlement of disputes; (ii) the right of the developing countries and of the people of territories under colonial and racial domination or foreign occupation to achieve their liberation and to regain effective control over their natural resources and economic activities.

The concept of "development" should not be interpreted solely in terms of economic and material well-being but in much broader terms covering the physical, moral, intellectual and cultural growth of human beings.

Development is a concept which ought to focus on the human element, on people, who must be both its agents and its beneficiaries, and it should be based on the individual definition which each society forms of it, founded on its own values and objectives.

It is essential today to incorporate the standards applicable to human rights and the corresponding goals into development plans. This is what is known as the "integrated approach to development". If the new international economic order is to produce a substantial improvement in the extent to which the impoverished and oppressed peoples of the world enjoy human rights, it is important for that goal to be fully incorporated in development strategies, national as well as international.

On the basis of these conclusions and the supporting documentation, the special rapporteur formulated the following recommendations (Chap. XIII B para. 295–310):

It must be recognized that not much has been achieved through the existing international systems and machinery, and it is therefore essential for the international organizations to adopt a realistic approach to the requirements of the world today, starting with the United Nations, which must be given greater drive by its Member States. In other words, instead of the international organizations being bypassed in the establishment of a new order, as some prefer or seem to prefer, they must be used as tools for correcting the current unjust international relations which allow a few countries to become steadily richer while the vast majority of countries grow poorer and poorer. Today, a stronger and more vigorous United Nations system is needed, and one that is used more effectively.

The new international economic order must be established through action by States in the context of their relations with other States, so as to change existing links, which favour only a small minority of States. This must be the main and immediate task of global negotiations in the framework of the United Nations, which is the organization called upon to direct this task—the more so today, now that a representative of the third world has been elected to the highest office in the Organization.

The global nature of the structural crisis in international economic relations calls for global solutions also. The trend towards bilateralism may have harmful consequences. A new multilateralism is therefore needed, founded on co-ordinated policies in which all groups of countries would take part on an international basis.

Since the establishment of a new international economic order will require a concerted effort on the part of all States, it is essential that the States of Eastern Europe should play a more active and constructive role than has been the case to date. As Leon Zurawicki recently stated ("The NIEO: an Eastern European point of view," *Development and Socio-Economic Progress* (Cairo), 21, (1983/1): 94.), the Eastern European countries should not only specify their own revised doctrine concerning the new international economic order and the related problems but should also indicate a forum where these ideas could be discussed.

It is certainly somewhat discouraging that at the summit meetings of the major developed countries held at Versailles in June 1982 and at Williamsburg in May 1983, those countries failed to grasp fully the immense significance of the demands of the developing countries; the same thing happened at the sixth session of the United Nations Conference on Trade and Development, held in Belgrade in June 1983. This attitude must change, for otherwise the former countries will themselves be largely responsible for the extremely serious consequences which this lack of understanding may have on a world careering towards an unprecedented crisis. Are we not perhaps already on the threshold of a world catastrophe which will have a profound impact on the basic human rights?

On the basis of a survey of the major United Nation instruments relating to the establishment of the new international economic order, it is apparent that the importance of the link between respect for human rights and the establishment of an equitable international order has long been recognized—most notably perhaps in the Charter of the United Nations and in article 28 of the Universal Declaration of Human Rights. In many respects these instruments demonstrate that the programme for the new international economic order is conceptually founded upon the human rights notion of self-determination. It should also be acknowledged, however, that while these instruments contain many references to human rights-related objectives, they tend only very occasionally to use the exact term "human rights". Moreover, references to the relationship between human rights and the new international economic order have tended to go only in one direction—that is to say, while frequent reference is made to the contribution which the new international economic order could make to the realization of human rights, mention is rarely made of the converse position.

Another important issue which has frequently arisen in international forums, although usually not discussed explicitly, is whether the reaffirmation of the objectives of the new international economic order in essentially human rights-related contexts, and vice versa, serves primarily to assure integration of the two objectives, or rather to distract attention from whichever may be treated as the issue of major immediate concern. While such concern may sometimes be justified, it is nevertheless important to ensure that human rights concerns are related to the overall structural framework in which they arise and that they are acknowledged within the mainstream of international negotiations.

The establishment of a linkage or *quid pro quo* between respect for human rights and promotion of the new international economic order has on occasion been proposed by some scholars. The relevant United Nations instruments on the new international economic order, however, have not endorsed such an approach, although there would appear to be general support for the proposition that progress on both fronts should be sought simultaneously.

The major objective of the present study has been to demonstrate the fundamental links that exist between the achievement of full respect for human rights and the establishment of an equitable international economic order. These links are manifold and complex and it has not been possible either to examine every relevant issue or to go into great detail with respect to some of the more important issues.

The present study has been designed to lay the basic groundwork for the future examination of other specific issues. In this regard it has already borne fruit in the form of the study on the right to adequate food as a human right which the Sub-Commission on Prevention of Discrimination and Protection of Minorities proposed at its thirty-fifth session. Moreover in the course of the stimulating debates

1146

that have taken place in the Sub-Commission in recent years, a number of other topics have been proposed for more detailed consideration. Some of them certainly merit separate studies, which could be undertaken in the future by the Sub-Commission.

One of the broad conclusions that emerges very clearly from the present study is that recent progress towards the adoption of specific elements of the package of demands formulated within the framework of the new international economic order has been painfully slow and in some respects non-existent. The very meagre results achieved at the sixth session of the United Nations Conference on Trade and Development have only served to highlight the critical impasse that has been reached. It is therefore imperative that the global negotiations on international economic co-operation for development, the launching of which continues to be stalled, should not be approached by all States concerned with a renewed sense both of commitment and of overriding urgency. The continued deferral of the global negotiations can only have an adverse impact on the prospects for the full realization of human rights, particularly in developing countries.

With respect to more specific issues, one of the most prominent recommendations that emerges from the present study concerns the impact on human rights of the policies and practices of the major international financial institutions, most notably the World Bank and IMF. The study has made clear the seriousness of the current world debt crisis and has emphasized the need to ensure the continuing, and indeed increased, availability of financial resources to facilitate the development efforts of all developing countries and particularly the least developed.

By the same token, it is clear that the assistance provided by the international financial institutions must be of such a nature that its impact on the enjoyment of human rights is positive. The precise implications of this requirement need, however, to be examined in greater detail. Thus, for example, the question of "conditionality" of assistance has been raised in the present study but its deeper ramifications have not been examined. Similarly, the relevance of political concerns in the decision-making of the international financial institutions needs to be examined frankly, as does the issue of equitable global participation in the management of the relevant institutions. If a new Bretton Woods-type conference is to be convened, as has been proposed, an examination of these and other human rights-related issues should be undertaken in advance.

Another issue which would appear to warrant future consideration by the Sub-Commission is the status of the goal, established and accepted well over a decade ago, that developed countries should provide developing countries with a minimum net amount of 0.7 per cent of the GNP each year in the form of official development assistance. At present the amount provided is less than half of that target, and it is clear that the ability of developing countries to ensure the full enjoyment of human rights of their entire populations has suffered accordingly. Many proposals have been made for the creation of mechanisms designed to ensure a regular, guaranteed transfer of resources to developing countries to support their development efforts. Very little progress has been made, however, with respect to an examination of the obligations and entitlements of States to official development assistance under present international law.

The importance of regional endeavours to promote economic co-operation, including, in particular, economic co-operation among developing countries, has also been noted in the present study. One potential means by which human rights concerns might perhaps be more fully taken into account in regional economic decision-making would be the appointment, perhaps within the framework of the United Nations regional commissions, of regional advisers on human rights, as proposed by the Assistant Secretary-General, Centre for Human Rights, Mr. Herndl, in his opening statement to the thirty-ninth session of the Commission on Human Rights, on 31 January 1983.

In concluding the present study, it must be emphasized that the basic challenge, which is to ensure that the establishment of the new international economic order and the promotion of respect for human rights go hand in hand, is never going to be resolved simply by focusing on one particular issue, such as development assistance, commodity prices or the role of transnational corporations. The challenge is in fact a far more pervasive one and requires constant vigilance to see that economic relations, at the international as much as at the national level, are approached in such a way as to ensure that the concepts of the dignity of every individual and of human solidarity are the guiding principles. In the establishment of a new international economic order, full respect for human rights must be seen both as an end in itself and as an essential means.

After examining the study, the sub-commission (resolution 1983/35) transmitted it to the COMMISSION ON HUMAN RIGHTS, drawing attention to the conclusions and recommendations reproduced above. On recommendation of the sub-commission, endorsed by the Commission on Human Rights, the Economic and Social Council (decision 1984/133) decided that the study should be published and given the widest possible distribution in all the official languages of the United Nations.

Two years later, the sub-commission decided (resolution 1985/34) that it would consider certain items on its agenda—among them the item entitled "The New International Economic Order and the Promotion of Human Rights"—on a biennial basis starting at its 1986 session. However, the sub-commission did not meet in 1986 due to the financial situation of the United Nations. The subject was considered again only at the 1989 session, when the sub-commission decided (resolution 1989/1) that thenceforth it would consider the item on an annual basis.

SEE ALSO Foreign Debt.

NEW ZEALAND. A country in Oceania, southeast of Australia, the dominion of New Zealand occupies two principal islands—North Island and South Island—as well as Stewart Island and the Chatham Islands. In addition, it administers Niue and the Cook Islands, which have achieved self-governing status; Tokelau; and the Antarctic region known as the Ross Dependency. It achieved independence from Great Britain as a self-governing dominion in 1907 and became a member of the United Nations in 1945. Its population is estimated by the UN (1990) to be 3,464,000. Ethnic groups include Europeans (86.8%), Maoris (8.9%), and communities such as the Cook Island Maori, Niuean, Tokellauan, Samoan, Tongan, Chinese, and Indian. Languages commonly used include English and Maori (both official). Christianity is the predominant religion (Roman Catholic, 15%; Anglican, 29%, Presbyterian, 18% and others 38%. Literacy is estimated at 99%.

The government (1990) took the form of a monarchy and member of the Commonwealth of Nations, of which the British sovereign is the symbolic head. The governor-general, representing the crown, appoints the prime minister, representing the party of coalition given the majority in popular elections. The prime minister exercises executive authority as head of government with the assistance of his appointed cabinet. The cabinet is responsible to a unicameral House of Representatives composed of 95 members elected by popular vote for a three-year term of office. The judicial system includes magistrate's courts, the Supreme Court, and the Court of Appeals. Political parties include the Labour Party, the National Party, and the Social Party.

As regards the situation of its indigenous Maori people, the government has in recent years placed a new emphasis on encouraging Maori economic development, educational advancement, and the greater use of the Maori language. There has also been a positive policy of appointing Maoris to positions where they can make the Maori point of view heard. In addition, a significant debate was engendered in the country on human rights questions as a result of the government's preparation and publication of a white paper which includes a draft bill of rights for the country. The draft bill would guarantee those fundamental rights and freedoms embodied in the INTERNATIONAL COVENANT ON CIVIL AND POLITICAL RIGHTS. In the light of the significant constitutional change that the adoption of a bill of rights would mean for New Zealand, the government has been concerned that there should be the widest possible debate on the measure before it is taken further. Accordingly, the white paper and draft bill have been referred to a parliamentary select committee and public submissions have been called for. The submissions received were examined by the Justice and Law Reform Select Committee, which concluded that further public education on the issues is necessary.

The government is also considering the desirability of altering the structure and functions of the New Zealand Human Rights Commission and the Race Relations Office, and there is a possibility that the two bodies may be merged. The commission has recommended the appointment of an extra commissioner with special responsibility for Maori affairs, thereby enabling the commission to take a more active educational role in assisting all New Zealanders to understand the issues stemming from the New Zealand–Maori Treaty of Waitangi.

On the subject of the treaty and its implications, the government of New Zealand supplied the following information in a report presented to the HUMAN RIGHTS COMMITTEE on 2 August 1988 (UN Doc. CCPR/C/37/Add. 8, para. 143–152):

The Treaty of Waitangi was signed in 1840 between representative Maori chiefs of different tribes and the British Crown. In recent years, a positive and dynamic view of the Treaty has emerged whereby it is seen as a living social contract and the corner-stone of a positive bicultural relationship between Maori people and other New Zealanders. Accordingly, the Treaty has been given an enhanced status which has in turn led, amongst other things, to a greater awareness of Maori cultural values.

Government policy introduced in 1986 states that "all future legislation referred to Cabinet at the policy approval stage should draw attention to any implications for recognition of the principles of the Treaty of Waitangi".

The Treaty of Waitangi Tribunal (referred to in New Zealand's reply of 10 November 1983) was established in 1975 to hear grievances and make recommendations about alleged breaches of the Treaty by the Crown. In 1985, its jurisdiction was extended and now Maoris may submit claims arising from the prejudicial consequences of any legislation, policy or action of the Crown since 1840.

In 1987, the Treaty of Waitangi was the subject of one of the most important cases heard before the New Zealand Courts (*New Zealand Maori Council v. Attorney-General* [1987] 1 NZLR 641: a copy of the Court of Appeal's decision is attached as annex Y). The Maori Council had sought to restrain the Crown from transferring certain assets to State-owned enterprises alleging that that would be in breach of a legislative provision which required the Crown not to act inconsistently with the principles of the Treaty. The Court upheld the Maori Council's case declaring that the Crown assets could not be transferred before there was a system in place to ensure that the transfer was consistent with the Treaty's principles. The Court of Appeal Judges placed emphasis on the Treaty as a partnership requiring "the upmost good faith" and calling for the partners to act reasonably towards each other. The interests at issue in the case have since been settled by agreement between the parties and given legislative form in the Treaty of Waitangi (State Enterprises) Act 1988.

These developments all reflect a new awareness of the importance of the Treaty. At the heart of these changes lies a cultural and political resurgence in the Maori community. The governmental machinery for administering Maoridom's needs is undergoing dramatic change. The Department of Maori Affairs leads this change and has itself been the subject of a thorough review. The "Devolution" Programme (*Tukua Te Rangatiratanga*) has as its objective the giving back of *Rangatiratanga* (autonomy) to Maori people. The first step in this process is the transfer of many of the current functions of the Department of Maori Affairs to *Iwi* (or tribal) Authorities.

Other government departments are taking up Maori suggestions in order to introduce a greater cultural awareness and Maori perspective into their fields of responsibility. The *Maatu Whanqai* (and see para. 53 above) programme, jointly funded by the Departments of Justice, Social Welfare and Maori Affairs, has as its aim to prevent the flow of Maori people into penal institutions and to take them out of those institutions and into the care of *Whanau-iwi* (family and tribe). The Department of Justice has recently published a paper entitled "The Maori and the Criminal Justice System: A New Perspective—*He Whaipaanga Hou*". The paper is the first stage of a project to develop a Maori conceptual framework for research into Maori crime. This will be followed by consultation within the Maori community to ascertain further Maori views on the justice system.

Of great importance in the cultural field is the passage of the Maori Language Act 1987, referred to in paragraph 75 above. The Act declares *Te Reo Maori* (the Maori language) to be an official language of New Zealand and establishes the Maori Language Commission. The functions of the Commission include the initiation, development, co-ordination and implementation of policies and procedures to promote the Maori language as an official language of New Zealand. The Commission is to consider and report on any matter relating to the Maori language referred to it by the Minister of Maori Affairs and to promote the Maori language as an ordinary means of communication. The Commission is also vested with the authority to issue certificates of competency in the Maori language. The certificates of competency will be in either interpretation, translation or interpretation and translation of the Maori language. An endorsement may be made on the certificate of competency that the holder is competent to translate and/or interpret in legal proceedings if the Commission is satisfied that the person meets certain criteria. As already noted, the Act gives to persons involved in legal proceedings the right to speak Maori in such proceedings.

Maori as a spoken language is also being given a new boost through the *Kohanga Reo* (language nests) programme. These are family groups where Maori language, values and customs are naturally acquired by pre-school children from their *Kaumatua* (elders). Its purpose is to create a Maori language and cultural environment where Maori pre-schoolers can became fluent in Maori and be culturally competent.

A Maori Radio Board has recently been established with responsibility for setting up an Auckland based national Maori radio network; the network is being funded through the Department of Maori Affairs. Some Maori communities, who feel that a national organization is inappropriate, have proceeded independently to establish local Maori radio stations.

An interdepartmental committee is co-ordinating a review of Maori involvement in the news media, including broadcasting. Its objectives are to report on the current situation and suggest strategies to increase Maori influences in this sphere.

Territories. The government of New Zealand administers the Cook Islands and Niue, both of which have achieved self-governing status, the Ross Dependency, an Antarctic region placed under its administration in 1923; and Tokelau, an island of the Gilbert–Ellice group, placed under its administration in 1925.

As regards Tokelau, the UN General Assembly on 22 November 1988 reaffirmed (resolution 43/35) the inalienable right of its people to self-determination and independence and urged the New Zealand government to continue to respect the wishes of those people in carrying out the territory's political and economic development, in order to preserve their social, cultural, and traditional heritage. At the same time, it urged the administering power, other member States, and organizations of the United Nations system to continue to extend to Tokelau the maximum assistance possible for the rehabilitation and reconstruction of the islands in order to overcome the losses incurred in natural disasters in 1987.

NICARAGUA. The Republic of Nicaragua is a country in Central America, located between the Pacific Ocean and the Caribbean Sea. It achieved independence from Spain in 1838 and became a member of the United Nations in 1945. Its population is estimated by the UN (1990) to be 3,871,000. Ethnic groups include descendents of settlers from Spain (19%), and from Jamaica and other Caribbean islands (9%), as well as Amerindians (5%) and Mestizos (mixed Spanish and Amerindian) (67%). Christianity (Roman Catholic, 98%; Protestant denominations, 2%) is the predominant religion. Spanish is the language in common use. Literacy is estimated at 87%.

The government (1990) took the form of a republic. Under a new constitution, which came into effect on 9 January 1987, guarantees are made of freedom of religion, freedom of expression and access to uncensored news, the rights to work and to health, to hold private property, to strike, and to hold meetings and lawful demonstrations. However, most of these liberties may be suspended by the president "in case of war or when national security, economic conditions or national catastrophe require it." The state of emergency, which had been in effect since 1982, was reimposed for the period through 1987 by the president immediately after signing the new constitution into law. Under normal conditions, the president, elected by popular vote for a term of six years, is head of State and government. Legislation is prepared by the Council of State and the 96-member elected National Assembly. The judiciary includes the Supreme Court, members of which are appointed by the president; and there is a Supreme Electoral Commission to monitor elections. Political parties include the Sandinista National Liberation Front, the Democratic Conservative Party, the Independent Liberal

Party, the Popular Social Christian Party, the Socialist Party, the Nicaragua Communist Party, and the Popular Marxist Alliance.

A Spanish colony from 1522 to 1838, Nicaragua was occupied by small contingents of American armed forced between 1912 and 1933 partly because of sporadic outbreaks of civil disorder and party because the United States held an option to build a canal through the country and to establish naval bases there.

Guerrillas under Gen. Cesar Augusto Sandino fought the U.S. troops from 1927 until the Americans withdrew in 1933. In 1934, Sandino was assassinated and Gen. Anastasio Somaza Garcia established a military dictatorship in the country. When Somoza was himself assassinated in 1956, he was succeeded by his son Luis. Another son, Maj. General Anastasio Somoza Debayle, became president in 1967.

On 25 August 1978, a coalition of political parties and trade unions launched a national work stoppage, seeking the resignation of President Anastasio Somoza. The government responded with massive arrests. On 8 September, the Sandinista Liberation Front—named after Gen. Sandino—called for a general uprising; and, on 12 September, the government imposed martial law. Major confrontations between the national guard and the Sandinistas took place in the larger cities, and the government again responded with widespread and often indiscriminate waves of arrests and killings. By the beginning of October, the uprising was largely crushed, and the Sandinistas and their followers fled from the cities.

Between 3 and 12 October 1978, the INTER-AMERICAN COMMISSION ON HUMAN RIGHTS carried out an on-site observation in Nicaragua. In its report, the commission concluded that "the Government of Nicaragua is responsible for serious attempts against the right to life, in violation of international humanitarian norms, in repressing, in an excessive and disproportionate manner, the insurrections that occurred last September in the major cities of the country." The report also stated that "many persons were executed in a summary and collective fashion for the mere reason of living in neighborhoods or districts where there had been activity by the *Frente Sandinista de Liberacion Nacional;* and young people and defenceless children were killed."

By November 1978, 27,000 Nicaraguans had fled to Honduras, while about 30,000 had taken refuge in Costa Rica. An AMNESTY INTERNATIONAL research mission collected data on about 600 individual cases of political imprisonment in Nicaragua and documentation indicating that many of the prisoners detained by the national guard had been summarily executed, often after torture, rape, or mutilation. The mission

also confirmed reports of widespread summary executions of entire families, wounded persons, health workers, and refugees. On 20 November, Amnesty International released a list of 519 Nicaraguan citizens known to be detained by the government.

On 7 December 1978, martial law was lifted. A few days later the United Nations General Assembly, in resolution 33/76 of 15 December 1978, censured the repression of the civilian population of Nicaragua and urged the Nicaraguan authorities to ensure respect for the human rights of the citizens of Nicaragua in accordance with their international commitments and the Charter of the United Nations.

However, the pattern of arbitrary arrests, torture, and summary executions continued unabated in 1979. The UN Commission on Human Rights, in resolution 14 (XXXV) of 13 March 1979, condemned these violations, expressed concern that the government of Nicaragua had taken no steps to respect the human rights of the population, and demanded that the government put an end to the grave situation which existed and restore respect for human rights and fundamental freedoms.

On 23 June 1979, a meeting of foreign ministers of the ORGANIZATION OF AMERICAN STATES adopted a resolution demanding the immediate and definite replacement of President Somoza. On 17 July, Somoza resigned and left the country.

When the Sandinistas assumed political power two days later, they promised to maintain a non-aligned foreign policy and a multi-party political system. In 1981, however, the United States charged that Nicaragua had aligned itself with Cuba and the Soviet Union in supplying aid to rebels in El Salvador—a charge the Sandinistas denied. Later that year, Nicaraguan counter-revolutionaries, known as "contras," began a guerrilla war to overthrow the Sandinistas.

Daniel Ortega Saavedra, a Sandinista coordinator, won 63% of the vote in elections held on 4 November 1984 and was inaugurated as president on 10 January 1985. Nevertheless, the contras, with the backing of the United States, continued their attacks, sometimes from bases in neighboring Honduras. In October 1985, civil liberties were suspended in Nicaragua; and, in 1986, the sole opposition newspaper, *La Prensa,* was forced to cease publication.

On 6 April 1984, Nicaragua accused the United States of America of mining its ports and called upon the INTERNATIONAL COURT OF JUSTICE to halt these activities. The court, on 10 May, ruled that all actions designed to blockade or to mine Nicaragua's ports should halt immediately.

In 1985, the U.S. Congress rejected a request by President Ronald Reagan for military aid to the contras; however, it authorized funds to be used for humanitarian assistance to members of that guerrilla group. In June 1986, the U.S. Congress for the first time approved overt assistance—military as well as non-military—to the contras.

The revelation that the procceds of a secret arms sale to Iran by the U.S. government had been diverted to assist the contras—an act specifically prohibited by law—provoked a major scandal in the United States, popularly known as the "Iran-Contra Affair." A congressional committee studied the affair; its findings have been published as *Report of the Congressional Committee Investigating the Iran-Contra Affair, With Supplemental, Minority, and Additional Views* (Washington: 1987). Criminal indictments against some of the perpetrators of the plot have been brought by a special prosecutor.

In 1987, leaders of neutral Central American countries signed the Contadora Peace Plan, sponsored by the president of Costa Rica, Oscar Arias Sanchez, that called for an end to outside support of the parties to the conflict and for negotiations between them. The U.S. Congress later prohibited further military aid to the contras. A ceasefire, arranged after the first direct meetings between the Sandinistas and the contras, went into effect on 1 April 1988. But further talks between the two sides broke down; and, in September, thousands of contra guerrillas moved out of Nicaragua and settled in base camps in the neighboring Honduras. In February 1989, the five Central American presidents who had signed the Contadora Peace Plan agreed that the contras should be demobilized; and President Ortega, concurring, undertook to hold free elections in Nicaragua in 1990.

The national election, held on 25 February 1990, resulted in a landslide victory for Mrs. Violeta Barrios de Chamorro, widow of the newspaper editor, Pedro Joaquin Chamorro Cardenal, whose assassination in 1978 had touched off the uprising that became the Sandinista revolution. Mrs. Chamorro, not a member of any political party, was the candidate of the National Opposition Union, an alliance of 14 political parties and groups ranging from conservatives to radicals and supported by Nicaragua's indigenous Miskito Indian population. Her election was monitored by nearly 2,000 official observers, including 239 from the United Nations, 435 from the Organization of American States, and 39 from the Carter Center and Council of Free-Elected Heads of State, led by former American President Jimmy Carter. She was inaugurated as president on 25 April 1990.

Nicaragua's Miskito Indians, an indigenous population living on the country's isolated east coast, were also engaged in guerrilla warfare against the govern-

ment of Nicaragua over a period of about six years. For a time, the Miskitos received financial assistance from the U.S. government but were cut off after refusing to unite with the contras.

The Indians charged multiple violations of their rights by the Sandinista regime. The government acknowledged, in 1987, that it had mistreated them and invited them to return to their homelands from Honduras, where many had taken refuge.

In October 1987, the commander of 400 of the Indian guerrillas, Uriel Vanagas, signed an agreement with the government under which his men would retain their weapons and serve as police or militia units to defend Indian villages.

NIGER. The Republic of Niger is a country in western Africa. It has borders with Algeria, Benin, Burkina Faso, Chad, Libya, Mali, and Nigeria. It achieved independence from France in 1960 and became a member of the United Nations the same year. Its population is estimated by the UN (1990) to be 7,109,000. Ethnic groups include the Hausa (54%), Jerma (23%), Fulani (10%), Beriberi–Manga (9%), and Tuareg (3%). Languages in common use include French (official), Hausa, Jerma, Peul, Tamashek, Kanuri, Arabic, Toubou, and Gourmanche. Religions practiced include Islam (90%), Animism (9%), and Christianity (1%). Literacy is estimated at 6%.

The government (1990) took the form of a republic. Its constitution was, however, suspended and civilian government displaced by a military regime which assumed power in April 1974. It is administered by the Supreme Military Council of 12 officers led by the president, who is head of State. The president is assisted by the Council of Ministers appointed by himself, and by the prime minister, who exercises executive authority as head of government. There is a 150-member National Development Council, which has limited legislative powers, and a system of elected local development councils. There have been no active political parties or elections since the suspension of the constitution.

In a report presented to the **COMMITTEE ON THE ELIMINATION OF RACIAL DISCRIMINATION** on 19 January 1988, the government provided the following information (UN Doc. CERD/C/172/Add. 1, para. 2–11):

. . . . On 4 August 1983, by Ordinance No. 83-27, a National Development Council was established, with the task of "proposing to the Government the fundamental options for an accelerated, coherent and harmonious development policy, based on the effective participation of all the social levels of the Nation."

With 150 members, representing the basic development

councils and the various components of society organized in social and vocational associations, this institution, a forum for the discussion of economic and social development issues, charged with preparing, between 1984 and 1987, a draft National Charter, which was submitted to the people of the Niger in the referendum on 14 June 1987.

The draft National Charter, which was approved by 99.5 per cent of the people of the Niger, determines the institutional framework for the activities of representatives of the Nation and the State. It defines the rights and duties of citizens, as well as the purview of the relations of the State of the Niger with the rest of the world. The Charter is the foundation for the Constitution. In the provisions relating to the elimination of all forms of racial discrimination, the Charter affirms the following principles.

The Niger is a State subject to the rule of law, a democratic and secular republic, which consistently guarantees the primacy of the law against all violations, whether perpetrated by the State, a community, a group or an individual.

Thus, upon its accession to independence, the Niger proclaimed its commitment to the universal principles of human rights. In doing so, it declared its support for the principle of fundamental freedoms. (The National Charter accordingly enumerates all the rights and freedoms contained in the Universal Declaration of Human Rights.) The laws and regulations concerning relations between the State and the citizen are promulgated in the light of these principles.

A participatory democracy, which is one of the objectives of the Development Society, will be achieved by the establishment of an egalitarian dialogue among all levels of society.

The Charter proclaims the need for the people to struggle with determination against any trace of regionalism or racism, religious intolerance, clan manifestation or partition ideology.

In its options, the National Charter affirmed the following principles in the area of cultural activities:

(i) The recognition of cultural pluralism, diversity and equality;

(ii) The democratization of culture, by means of its direct and widespread dissemination to the various population groups.

The National Charter also identifies the main trends of the foreign policy of the Niger and states that:

(i) The objective of the defense of national interests leads the Niger to give priority to a policy of good neighbourliness and dialogue with all peace-loving countries;

(ii) Its commitment to African unity calls for the total condemnation of *apartheid,* and of all systems based on racism and oppression;

(iii) Niger resolutely opposes any form of colonialism, neo-colonialism and imperialism in the world and demands freedom for all oppressed peoples.

All the policies and principles contained in the National Charter will be developed and reaffirmed in the Constitution, which is in the process of being drafted.

As stated in the previous report, international conventions duly ratified by the Niger may be invoked at any time in the courts, following their publication in the *Journal Officiel* of the Republic of the Niger. Thus, the implementation of the various international conventions does not require the promulgation of legislation or special regulations.

NIGERIA. The Federal Republic of Nigeria is a country in western Africa, on the Gulf of Guinea. It has borders with Benin, Cameroon, Chad, and Niger. It achieved independence from Great Britain in 1960 and became a member of the United Nations the same year. Its population is estimated by the UN (1990) to be 113,343,000. Ethnic groups include the Hausa, the Fulani, and the Kanuri, who are most numerous in the north; and the Yoruba and Ibo, who predominate in the south. Languages commonly used include English (official), Igbo, Efik, Hausa, and Yoruba. Religions practiced include Islam (48%), Christianity (Roman Catholic, 17%, and Protestant denominations, 17%), Animism and other faiths (18%). Literacy is estimated at 42%.

Since 1970, Nigeria has struggled to recover from its disastrous civil war which began in 1966 and which involved intensive conflict between the predominantly Muslim Hausas and the predominantly Christian Ibos. The war led to the secession of the Republic of Biafra in 1967 but ended with its surrender to federal authorities the following year. Nigeria is now believed to have a Muslim majority, but no census has been taken for more than 20 years, partly out of fear of inflaming religious passions by indicating the current population ratios.

The Government (1990) took the form of a republic and a member of the Commonwealth of Nations, of which the British sovereign is the symbolic head. However, it has been under military rule since 31 December 1983, when a democratically elected civilian government, which had been established in 1979, was overthrown by a *coup d'etat* led by Major-General Muhammadu Buhari. That military ruler was, in turn, ousted on 27 August 1985 by a junta led by Major-General Ibrahim Babangida, who was installed as president.

The military governments suspended a number of provisions of the 1979 constitution of the Federal Republic of Nigeria, most significantly those dealing with features of the national and State assemblies and elections. The 28-member Armed Forces Ruling Council was set up as the main decisionmaking organ of the government, while the 22-member Federal Cabinet presides over the government executive departments. Military governors were appointed to head Nigeria's 19 states.

In a report submitted to the COMMITTEE ON THE ELIMINATION OF RACIAL DISCRIMINATION on 6 August 1987, the new government stated that (UN Doc. CERD/C/149/Add. 25, para. 3–6):

. . . . Nigeria continued in its efforts for national unity and especially its bid to defuse ethnic, religious and linguistic tensions. The new administration moved quickly to demonstrate its commitment to human rights. The controversial Decree No. 4 of 1984 which inhibited press freedom and under which two journalists were sent to gaol by the previous administration was repealed and the two journalists were granted State pardon. As a demonstration of the further commitment of the present military administration to the cause of human rights, the following panels have been set up:

(a) Tribunal of Inquiry for the review of cases of persons convicted under the Recovery of Public Property (Special Military Tribunals) Decree, No. 3 of 1984, headed by a Justice of the Supreme Court;

(b) Tribunal of Inquiry to review the cases of persons convicted under the Exchange Control (Anti-Sabotage) Decree No. 7 of 1984; and

(c) The Special Tribunal to review cases of persons convicted under the (Miscellaneous Offences) Decree, No. 20 of 1984.

The new administration also set up a special panel for the investigation of cases of persons conditionally released from detention and persons still in detention under the State Security (Detention of Persons) Decree, No. 2 of 1984, and the Recovery of Public Property (Special Military Tribunal) Decree, No. 3 of 1984.

All these Tribunals headed by judges have since submitted their recommendations which have been implemented by the Government.

In pursuance of the objective of the present administration, the administration has released approximately 150 persons detained without charges and remanded to the Criminal Court System common criminals detained by security agencies. This fact is confirmed by the report published by the United States Committee on Foreign Relations on Human Rights in Nigeria.

NIGERIA: CONSTITUTION. The Nigerian constitution contains the following provisions (articles 30–31, 33–37, 39, and 42) specifically relating to human rights and fundamental freedoms:

Article 30. (1) Every person has a right to life, and no one shall be deprived intentionally of his life, save in execution of the sentence of a court in respect of a criminal offence of which he has been found guilty in Nigeria.

Article 31. (1) Every individual is entitled to respect for the dignity of his person, and accordingly—

(a) no person shall be subjected to torture or to inhuman and degrading treatment;

(b) no person shall be held in slavery or servitude; and

(c) no person shall be required to perform forced or compulsory labour. . . .

Article 33. (1) In the determination of his civil rights and obligations, including any question or determination by or against any government or authority, a person shall be entitled to a fair hearing within a reasonable time by a court or other tribunal established by law and constituted in such manner as to secure its independence and impartiality.

Article 34. The privacy of citizens, their homes, correspondence, telephone conversations and telegraphic communications is hereby guaranteed and protected.

Article 35. (1) Every person shall be entitled to freedom of thought, conscience and religion, including freedom to change his religion or belief, and freedom (either alone or in community with others, and in public or in private) to manifest and propagate his religion or belief in worship, teaching, practice and observance.

(2) No person attending any place of education shall be required to receive religious instruction or to take part in or attend any religious ceremony or observance if such instruction, ceremony or observance related to a religion other than his own, or a religion not approved by his parent or guardian.

(3) No religious community or denomination shall be prevented from providing religious instruction for pupils of that community or denomination in any place of education maintained wholly by that community or denomination.

Article 36. (1) Every person shall be entitled to freedom of expression, including freedom to hold opinions and to receive and impart ideas and information without interference.

Article 37. Every person shall be entitled to assemble freely and associate with other persons, and in particular he may form or belong to any political party, trade union or any other association for the protection of his interests:

Provided that—

(a) the provisions of this section shall not derogate from the powers conferred by this Constitution on the Federal Electoral Commission with respect to political parties to which that Commission does not accord recognition; and

(b) a person elected to a legislative house as a candidate who was not sponsored by any political party shall not be entitled to join or declare himself to be a member of a political party until the general election next following his election as such candidate. . . .

Article 39. (1) A citizen of Nigeria of a particular community, ethnic group, place of origin, sex, religion or political opinion shall not, by reason only that he is such a person—

(a) be subjected either expressly by, or in the practical application of, any law in force in Nigeria or any executive or administrative action of the government to disabilities or restrictions to which citizens of Nigeria of other communities, ethnic groups, places of origin, sex, religions, or political opinions are not made subject; or

(b) be accorded either expressly by, or in the practical application of, any law in force in Nigeria or any such executive or administrative action, any privilege or advantage that is not accorded to citizens of Nigeria of other communities, ethnic groups, places of origin, sex, religions or political opinions.

(2) No citizen of Nigeria shall be subjected to any disability or deprivation merely by reason of the circumstances of his birth.

(3) Nothing in subsection (1) of this section shall invalidate any law by reason only that the law imposes restrictions with respect to the appointment of any person to any office under the State or as a member of the armed forces of the Federation or a member of the Nigeria Police Force or to an office in the service of a body corporate established by any law in force in Nigeria. . . .

Article 42. (1) Any person who alleges that any of the provisions of this Chapter has been, is being or likely to be contravened in any State in relation to him may apply to a High Court in that State for redress.

(2) Subject to the provisions of this Constitution, a High Court shall have original jurisdiction to hear and determine any application made to it in pursuance of the provisions of this section and may make such orders, issue such

writs and give such directions as it may consider appropriate for the purpose of enforcing or securing the enforcement within that State of any rights to which the person who makes the application may be entitled under this Chapter.

NORWAY. The Kingdom of Norway is a country in northern Europe, on the Norwegian Sea. It has borders with Finland and Sweden. It achieved independence as a kingdom, in personal union with Sweden, in 1814 and became a member of the United Nations in 1945. Its population is estimated by the UN (1990) to be 4,177,000. Ethnic groups include descendents of Germanic peoples (Alpine, Baltic, and Nordic), Gypsies, and Sami (Lapplanders) who are concentrated in Arctic areas where they fish and tend herds of reindeer. Languages commonly used are Norwegian (official) and Lappish. The predominant religion is Christianity, and the Evangelical Lutheran denomination is recognized as the State Church. Literacy is estimated at 100%.

The government (1990) took the form of a monarchy. Under the 1814 constitution, the king is sovereign and head of State. The prime minister, representing the party or coalition given the majority in the *Storting* (parliament), exercises executive authority as head of government. The *Storting* comprises 157 members elected by popular vote under a system of proportional representation; its member vote as a single body on political and financial questions but divide themselves into two bodies (*Lagting* and *Odelsting*) when considering legislation. The judiciary includes the Supreme Court. Political parties include the Labor Party, the Conservative Party, the Christian Democratic Party, the Center Party, the Socialist Left Party, and the Party of Progress.

Norway has about 100,000 foreign nationals among its population, including 62,080 from Europe, 3,357 from Africa, 20,042 from Asia, 13,479 from America, 573 from Oceania, and several hundred stateless; and questions have been raised about the difference between nationals of Nordic countries and other nationals with regard to the period of residence required in order to obtain Norweigian citizenship. The government replied to such questions in a report presented to the COMMITTEE ON THE ELIMINATION OF RACIAL DISCRIMINATION on 15 February 1984 as follows (UN Doc. CERD/C/107/Add. 4, para. 10–11):

The previous Norwegian report mentioned the difference between nationals of Nordic countries and other nationals with regard to the period of residence required in order to obtain Norwegian citizenship. With reference to the question on this point we would answer as follows:
According to paragraph 6 of Act no. 3 of 8 December 1950 relating to Norwegian Nationality one of the general conditions for being granted Norwegian citizenship is that the foreign national has been permanently resident in the realm for the last seven years. Exceptions to this requirement can be made in respect of Nordic nations, among others. In practice, the period of residence required of them is now two years. This is in accordance with a request from the Nordic Council.

Underlying this special rule is the consideration that conditions in the Nordic countries are very similar. The reasons for stipulating a period of residence do not therefore apply to their nationals to the same extent as to others. Nordic nationals integrate easily into Norwegian society because of their closeness geographically, linguistically and culturally. The shorter period of residence required does not, therefore, imply any discrimination in relation to other nationals. Reference can moreover be made to paragraph 3 of article 1 of the Convention, since this is not a question of discrimination "against any particular nationality", either.

With reference to the treatment of its Sami population, which is scattered over the country but concentrated in inner Finnmark and which is large engaged in the breeding and care of reindeer, the government stated in the same report (para. 23–24) that:

According to the Act relating to the Primary School, children in Sami regions are to be taught Sami as their mother tongue if their parents so demand. During the last two years of the primary school, Sami-speaking pupils can choose Sami as one of their two language forms. Attempts are also being made to promote recruitment of Sami-speaking teachers to Sami regions, for instance by offering courses at the college of education in Alta specially designed for Sami students.

The Council for Sami Education, and at the Nordic level the Nordic Sami Institute, which is a permanent institution financed out of the Nordic cultural budget, have each contributed significantly to increasing Sami awareness of their own cultural identity.

With regard to its effort to improve the lot of its Gypsy population, the government furnished the following information in the same report (para. 41–43):

Since 1981, there have been no significant changes in the work for Gypsies. It should nevertheless be mentioned that the Government appointed an independent researcher in 1981 to evaluate the work done on behalf of Norwegian Gypsies since such work first took organized shape about 10 years ago. The expert presented his report in July 1982.

Among favourable developments, the report especially points out that most Gypsy families now have homes; most have homes of their own, but some are in rented apartments. Their municipality of residence (Oslo) has plans ready for providing the remainder with homes.

Work among Gypsies is difficult to organize in such a way that they are able to exercise a real influence themselves. One reason seems to be that public aid is built up and organized in ways which prevents measures from being sufficiently flexible, and makes them difficult for the Gypsies to relate to actively.

NORWAY: CONSTITUTION. The Constitution of the Kingdom of Norway, as laid down on 17 May 1814 by the Constituent Assembly at Eidsvoll, with subsequent amendments, contains the following provisions specifically relating to human rights:

Article 2. All inhabitants of the Realm shall have the right to free exercise of their religion. The Evangelical-Lutheran religion shall remain the official religion of the State. The inhabitants professing it are bound to bring up their children in the same. . . .

Article 16. The King ordains all public church services and public worship, all meetings and assemblies dealing with religious matters, and ensures that public teachers of religion follow the norms prescribed for them. . . .

Article 49. The people exercises Legislative Power through the *Storting*, which consists of two departments, the *Lagting* and the *Odelsting*.

Article 50. Those entitled to vote are Norwegian citizens, men and women, who, at the latest in the year when the election is held, have completed their 18th year. . . .

Article 96. No one may be convicted except according to law, or be punished except after a court judgement. Interrogation by torture must not take place. . . .

Article 99. No one may be taken into custody except in the cases determined by law and in the manner prescribed by law. For unwarranted arrest, or illegal detention, the officer concerned is accountable to the person imprisoned.

Article 100. There shall be liberty of the Press. No person may be punished for any writing, whatever its contents, which he has caused to be printed or published, unless he wilfully and manifestly has either himself shown or incited others to disobedience to the laws, contempt of religion, morality or the constitutional powers, or resistance to their orders, or has made false and defamatory accusations against anyone. Everyone shall be free to speak his mind frankly on the administration of the State and on any other subject whatsoever. . . .

Article 102. Search of private homes shall not be made except in criminal cases. . . .

Article 110. It is the responsibility of the authorities of the State to create conditions enabling every person capable of work to earn a living by his work.

NUCLEAR DISARMAMENT. For many years, the UN General Assembly, alarmed by the threat to the survival of mankind and to the life-sustaining system posed by nuclear weapons and by their use and conscious of an increased danger of nuclear war as a result of the intensification of the nuclear-arms race and the serious deterioration of the international situation, has called upon all States to participate actively in efforts to bring about conditions in international relations among States in which a code of peaceful conduct of nations in international affairs could be agreed upon and that would preclude the use or threat of use of nuclear weapons. In this connection, it has repeatedly affirmed that the use of nuclear weapons would be a violation of the Charter of the United Nations and a crime against humanity.

On 15 December 1989, the assembly noted with regret (resolution 44/117 C) that the Conference on Disarmament had not been able during that year to undertake negotiations with a view to achieving agreement on an international convention prohibiting the use or threat of use of nuclear weapons under any circumstances and repeated the request it had made on several earlier occasions, calling upon the conference to commence negotiations as a matter of priority, taking as a basis the draft Convention on the Prohibition of the Use of Nuclear Weapons annexed to the resolution and reproduced below:

The States Parties to this Convention,

Alarmed by the threat to the very survival of mankind posed by the existence of nuclear weapons,

Convinced that any use of nuclear weapons constitutes a violation of the Charter of the United Nations and a crime against humanity,

Convinced that this Convention would be a step towards the complete elimination of nuclear weapons leading to general and complete disarmament under strict and effective international control,

Determined to continue negotiations for the achievement of this goal,

Have agreed as follows:

Article 1. The States Parties to this Convention solemnly undertake not to use or threaten to use nuclear weapons under any circumstances.

Article 2. This Convention shall be of unlimited duration.

Article 3. 1. This Convention shall be open to all States for signature. Any State that does not sign the Convention before its entry into force in accordance with paragraph 3 of this article may accede to it at any time.

2. This Convention shall be subject to ratification by signatory States. Instruments of ratification or accession shall be deposited with the Secretary-General of the United Nations.

3. This Convention shall enter into force on the deposit of instruments of ratification by twenty-five Governments, including the Governments of the five nuclear-weapon States, in accordance with paragraph 2 of this article.

4. For States whose instruments of ratification or accession are deposited after the entry into force of this Convention, it shall enter into force on the date of the deposit of their instruments of ratification or accession.

5. The depository shall promptly inform all signatory and acceding States of the date of each signature, the date of deposit of each instrument of ratification or accession and the date of the entry into force of this Convention, as well as of the receipt of other notices.

6. This Convention shall be registered by the depository in accordance with Article 102 of the Charter of the United Nations.

Article 4. This Convention, of which the Arabic, Chinese,

English, French, Russian and Spanish texts are equally authentic, shall be deposited with the Secretary-General of the United Nations, who shall send duly certified copies thereof to the Government of the signatory and acceding States.

In witness whereof, the undersigned, being duly author ized thereto by their respective Governments, have signed this Convention, opened for signature at ____ on the ____ day of ____ one thousand nine hundred and ____.

SEE ALSO *Declaration on the Prevention of Nuclear Castrophe.*

O

OAS. *SEE Organization of American States.*

OAS GENERAL ASSEMBLY. The General Assembly is the supreme organ of the Organization of American States. Its functions, powers, and organizational arrangements are set out in Chapter XI of the ORGANIZATION OF AMERICAN STATES CHARTER.

The General Assembly's basic task is to determine and monitor the general action and policy of the organization, exercising its powers in accordance with the charter and other Inter-American treaties. All member States of the OAS are entitled to be represented in the assembly, which normally convenes once a year.

OAS MEETING OF CONSULTATION OF MINISTERS OF FOREIGN AFFAIRS. Composed of ministers of foreign affairs of all member States of the OAS, it meets at the request of any member State to consider problems of an urgent nature and of common interest. It considers any threat to the peace and security of the American hemisphere in accordance with the Inter-American Treaty of Reciprocal Assistance, signed in Rio de Janeiro in 1947. Its organization and terms of reference are set out in the ORGANIZATION OF AMERICAN STATES CHARTER, Chapter XII.

OAS PERMANENT COUNCIL. The Permanent Council is the organ of the Organization of American States which assists member States in the peaceful settlement of their disputes. Its functions, powers, and organizational arrangements are set out in Chapters XI and XII of the ORGANIZATION OF AMERICAN STATES CHARTER. It is composed of one representative of each member State, especially appointed by the respective government, with the rank of ambassador.

OAS SPECIALIZED CONFERENCES. Arrangements for the convening of intergovernmental meetings to deal with technical matters or to develop specific aspects of inter-American cooperation are set out in Chapter XX of the ORGANIZATION OF AMERICAN STATES CHARTER.

OAS SPECIALIZED ORGANIZATIONS. Six organizations which have specific functions with respect to technical matters of common interest to the American States are recognized by the Organization of American States as specialized organizations. They are: The Inter-American Children's Institute, the INTER-AMERICAN COMMISSION OF WOMEN, the Inter-American Indian Institute, the Inter-American Institute for Cooperation on Agriculture, the Pan American Health Organization, and the Pan American Institute of Geography and History. Rules governing relations between the OAS and these specialized organizations are set out in Chapter XXI of the ORGANIZATION OF AMERICAN STATES CHARTER.

OAU. *SEE Organization of African Unity.*

OMAN. The Sultanate of Oman is an Arab country in western Africa, located on the southeastern tip of the Arabian peninsula, fronting on the Arabian Sea and the Gulf of Oman. It attained independence from Turkey in 1741 and became a member of the United Nations in 1971. Its population is estimated by the UN (1990) to be 1,457,000. Ethnic groups include small communities of Arab, Baluchi, Indian, and Zanzibari origins. Languages commonly used include Arabic (official), English, Baluchi, and several Indian dialects. Islam (Ibadhi, 75%, Sunni and Shi'ite, 10%) is the predominant religion; Hinduism is the religion of immigrants from India and their descendants. Literacy is estimated at 20%.

The government (1990) took the form of a monarchy. The sultan is head of State and of government. He is assisted by the Council of Ministers, the Consultative Council, six specialized councils, and a number of personal advisors. There is no legislature. The courts, for the most part, apply traditional Islamic law. There are no political parties.

O

OMBUDSMAN. An ombudsman is a unique institution established in various forms in a number of countries to protect individuals against unjust acts on the part of government officials or agencies. The role and functions of ombudsmen are described in the Secretary-General's report entitled *National Institutions for the Protection and Promotion of Human Rights* (UN Doc. E/CN.4/1987/37), prepared at the request of the General Assembly (resolution 40/123, para. 99–111), as follows:

It would be difficult to classify the ombudsman as a legislative, judicial or administrative organ. It is indeed an institution of a *sui generis* nature, having a multi-faceted character. The ombudsman is an independent mediator—and in some instances, a collegiate body—whose primary role is to protect the rights of the individual who believes he is the victim of unjust acts on the part of the public administration. Generally appointed to office by the legislative body, the ombudsman in many instances functions in a supervisory capacity on behalf of parliament, acting on complaints received from aggrieved persons against government officials or agencies. The ombudsman is often perceived as a Scandinavian institution, since it had its beginnings in early nineteenth century Sweden, and is firmly established in Denmark, Norway and Finland. In the past several decades, however, the ombudsman or the office of the mediator has been established in a number of countries outside Scandinavia. Australia, Austria, Barbados, Canada, France, Ghana, Guyana India, Jamaica, Japan, Mauritius, New Zealand, Portugal, Spain, Trinidad and Tobago, the United Kingdom and certain areas in the United States have all utilized the ombudsman system in one form or another. Moreover, several African countries (Nigeria, the Sudan, Tanzania and Zambia) have established collegiate bodies or commissions, which function with the authority and jurisdiction of the ombudsman.

Essentially, the ombudsman in all countries follows similar procedures in the performance of his duties. He receives complaints from aggrieved parties, and subsequently initiates an investigation if the claim has merit and falls within his jurisdiction. The ombudsman is generally granted access to documents of all authorities within his jurisdiction, which are pertinent to the investigation. He then usually issues a statement of recommendation based on his investigation, which is given to both the complainant and the office or authority against whom the complaint has been lodged. If the recommendation is not acted upon, the ombudsman may then submit his recommendation to parliament. In the Scandinavian countries, the ombudsman may also call both parties to the case to a hearing if necessary, and he is empowered to examine witnesses under oath. In Sweden, the Ombudsman's investigation generally results in a letter to both parties, stating his opinion on the conduct of the official, and stating his interpretation of the law in question. He may recommend that damages be paid to the injured party by the official, or out of public funds. In rare cases involving major faults, the Swedish Ombudsman may order prosecution before the courts. In minor cases, when the investigation reveals faults, delay or neglect, the Ombudsman may issue a reminder to the official concerned that his handling of the case was faulty or improper. Additionally, in almost all countries, the ombudsman submits an annual report to parliament or the corresponding legislative body. Each country may require its ombudsman to include specific information or recommendations in his report. For instance, the Swedish Ombudsman's annual report may include an opinion on inadequacies in legislation, as well as his views on the meaning of existing laws and statutes and how they should be interpreted and applied. He may also suggest new legislation. Similarly, the French Ombudsman, *le Médiateur,* may suggest in his reports amendments to the laws and regulations. The Austrian *Volksanwaltschaft* may make recommendations to the highest executive authorities in addition to his annual activity report, which is submitted to the *Nationalrat.*

Although he submits annual reports to parliament, the ombudsman is essentially an independent office. The office of ombudsman is frequently provided for in a constitution or by an act of the legislature. As such, the ombudsman is accountable to the legislature, and in most cases, the legislative body will conduct an annual review of the ombudsman's office. Despite annual review by parliament or the Executive, the ombudsman nevertheless enjoys relative independence. For example, the Swedish Ombudsman cannot be removed from office unless a Parliamentary Committee issues a petition for his removal. In the United Kingdom, the Parliamentary Commissioner (Ombudsman) is subject to review by a Select Committee of the House of Commons, but he can only be removed by an address from both Houses of Parliament.

Ombudsmen may sometimes be accountable to the Executive. For example, while the Nigerian Public Complaints Commission and the Sudanese People's Assembly for Administrative Control are accountable to Parliament, the Tanzanian Permanent Commission of Inquiry and the Zambian Commission for Investigations are directly responsible to the head of State.

In most cases, the ombudsman initiates an investigation based on a complaint received at his offices. He may, however, initiate an investigation without such a complaint. For instance, in Sweden, the Ombudsman frequently may begin an investigation on the basis of a newspaper report about illegalities and maladministration. France also provides for investigations by the *Médiateur* without receipt of a complaint, by giving members of parliament the right to request that the *Médiateur* investigate a matter of concern to parliament. Some countries limit recourse to the ombudsman to those complainants who have actually been injured by the challenged act or authority. This is a requirement in Guyana and in Trinidad and Tobago. Recourse to the Austrian *Volksanwaltschaft,* however, is granted to non-citizens and citizens who are "concerned by alleged abuses in the administration of the *Bund*". Spain merely requires that the complainant assert a legitimate interest in the complaint.

Several countries (Austria, Jamaica, New Zealand and the United Kingdom) require that the complainant first exhaust all alternative legal remedies before approaching the ombudsman. While there is generally no statute of limitations on the time within which the complainant must lodge his or her grievance with the ombudsman, there is often a requirement that the complaint to an ombudsman be made within one year of notification of the decision complained of. None the less, some ombudsmen have discretion to consider older grievances.

Access to the ombudsman by an individual complainant varies from country to country. In many countries (Denmark, Finland, New Zealand, Norway, Sweden, the United Republic of Tanzania and Zambia for example) individuals may lodge their complaints directly with the ombudsman's office. Israel additionally provides that the ombudsman may receive sealed complaints in writing from prisoners. However, in France, the Sudan and the United Kingdom, complaints must be submitted to a member of parliament, who forwards to the ombudsman those complaints which fall within his jurisdiction. For example, the French *Médiateur* receives individual complaints first addressed to Deputies or Senators who transfer them to the *Médiateur*. In practice, members of parliament generally forward all complaints received to the ombudsman. Complainants whose cases fall outside the ombudsman's jurisdiction may then receive a communication from the ombudsman's office, explaining why he is unable to act on the complaint.

Complaints made to the ombudsman are generally confidential, and the identity of the complainant will not be disclosed without his consent. In most countries, the identity of the complainant and that of the official against whom the complaint has been lodged are not revealed in the ombudsman's annual report. In Sweden however, upon the completion of a case, the Ombudsman's file is, in most cases, open to inspection by the press.

The jurisdiction of the ombudsman's authority generally reaches all offices of public administration. Nevertheless, the scope of the ombudsman's jurisdiction varies from country to country. For example, Finland and Denmark vest power over Ministers in the Ombudsman. Austria, Australia, New Zealand and Sweden do not permit their ombudsmen to investigate complaints against Ministers. The Tanzanian Permanent Commission has jurisdiction over central and local government, and practically all statutory bodies, as well as over the party and party affiliates. The Commission does not, however, have jurisdiction over residential decisions, or matters of government or public policy. In Nigeria, complaints to the Public Complaints Commission may be made against government departments, functionaries, employers and employees, individuals in the public and private sectors, State governments and local authorities. The Sudan People's Assembly Committee may investigate any complaint charging that an administration decision is the result of: (a) nepotism, corruption or bias, (b) failure to observe sound administrative bases, (c) negligence in carrying out duty, (d) misuse of discretion, (e) incompetence, (f) loss of documents and papers, (g) tardiness and delay, (h) unjust segregation or (i) any similar matter. The Parliamentary Commissioner of the United Kingdom is empowered to investigate maladministration in most departments and authorities dealing with the public. Maladministration is defined as including: incompetence, delay, neglect and bias, but *not* policy. Policy questions fall within the jurisdiction of Parliament. The Commissioner does not have the power to investigate the merits of discretionary decisions. Nor does his jurisdiction extend to the national health service, local government or the police, since other organs exist which are empowered to investigate complaints against these institutions. The Ombudsman of New Zealand has jurisdiction over acts or omissions of the departments of State, a small number of statutory administrative tribunals and local organizations. He has no control over any matter in which there is a right of appeal or review on the merits of the case to any court, no direct control over a Minister, and may not alter a decision he believes is wrong. In Finland, Sweden and the United Republic of Tanzania, the ombudsman is allowed to investigate complaints against the judiciary. Other countries, such as Austria, Denmark and Norway, have left judges entirely outside the ombudsman's jurisdiction

because of a strong concern for maintaining the independence of the courts.

In the countries in which the ombudsman has supervisory power over Ministers, the authorities in question are required to support the ombudsman in the exercise of his investigation, including providing all requested documents and testimony. Despite this requirement however, in some instances, Ministers may refuse to give information to the ombudsman if, in the Minister's judgement, the exposure of such information would be prejudicial to national security or defence. In order to prevent abuse of this exception by Ministers, the United Kingdom introduced a provision in its Parliamentary Commissioner Act which grants the Ombudsman access to all information relevant to his investigation, but which gives the Minister the power to prohibit him from disclosing in his report, any information which, in the Minister's judgement, would be "prejudicial to the safety of the State or otherwise contrary to the public interest."

Responsibility for heightening public awareness of the duties and functions of the office seems to rest with the ombudsman's office itself. Radio messages, pamphlets and television documentaries on the history and role of the ombudsman are all methods which may be used to inform the public about the ombudsman's office as an important resource. For example, the Tanzanian and Zambian ombudsman commissions hold public meetings in villages in rural areas to explain the work done by their commission, and to increase their accessibility to individuals residing in outlying areas, who may have grievances against public officials. After these public meetings, the commissions' representatives hold private sessions in which aggrieved parties may report their complaints. These complaints are subsequently investigated and, if necessary, additional visits are made to the villages for follow-up contacts. In its first year, members of the Tanzanian commission visited 14 regions, 53 districts and addressed over 64,000 persons.

The ombudsman is a potentially effective human rights organ, which can be adapted to various political and social systems. A large number of countries have successfully incorporated the ombudsman into their administrative systems. Naturally, the ombudsman's office may only be as effective as its authority and jurisdiction permits. While countries may differ on the breadth of jurisdiction to be bestowed upon that office, it is clear, for instance, that the right to view documents and to question authorities under the parameters of that jurisdiction, appears to be essential for a thorough and accurate investigation. In addition, the effectiveness of the ombudsman's office is largely dependent on the ability of a potential complainant to utilize the services provided by the ombudsman. Therefore, it is important that individuals are not encumbered by confusing petition processes, when attempting to present their grievances to the ombudsman's office. While it is true that most ombudsmen may initiate investigations on their own, independent of a private complaint, the primary function of the office is to provide a recourse to the individual who has been the victim of injustice resulting from governmental or administrative action. As such, all efforts must be made to ensure that the ombudsman's office is easily accessible to all members of the public.

The Danish Ombudsman. The Danish Ombudsman Act No. 203 of 11 June 1954, as amended, is a typical national statute setting out the functions and powers of an ombudsman and establishing the procedures to be followed by such an official in supervising government administration. The text of the act is as follows:

1. (1) After every general election and when a vacancy occurs the Folketing shall elect an Ombudsman to supervise, on its behalf, civil and military central government administration and local government administration. The jurisdiction of the Ombudsman shall not extend to the functions of judge, chief administrative officers of the courts of justice, the head of the Probate Division of the Copenhagen City Court, clerks of the Supreme Court, and assistant judges.

(2) Upon a general election, the Ombudsman shall continue in office until the new Folketing has elected an Ombudsman as provided in subsection (1) above, and, if he is not re-elected, until the new Ombudsman has taken office. The term of office of the outgoing Ombudsman shall not, except with the consent of the Folketing, exceed six months from the date of the general election.

(3) In the event of the death of the Ombudsman, the Ombudsman Committee of the Folketing shall determine who shall carry out the functions of Ombudsman until the Folketing has elected a new Ombudsman.

(4) Should the Ombudsman cease to enjoy the confidence of the Folketing, it may dismiss him.

2. The Ombudsman, who may not be a member of the Folketing shall be a law graduate.

3. The Folketing shall lay down general rules governing the activities of the Ombudsman. Subject to these rules, the Ombudsman shall be independent of the Folketing in the discharge of his functions.

4. (1) The jurisdiction of the Ombudsman shall extend to ministers, civil servants and all other persons in government service except as provided in section 1, subsection (1).

(2) Persons in local government service shall likewise fall within the jurisdiction of the Ombudsman in so far as regards matters in which recourse to a central government authority is provided for. The activities of local government councils acting as a body shall not fall within the jurisdiction of the Ombudsman except as provided in section 6, subsection (5).

(3) In the exercise of his powers the Ombudsman shall take account of the special conditions under which local governments function.

5. The Ombudsman shall keep himself informed as to whether the persons referred to in section 4 make themselves guilty of errors or neglect in the performance of their duties.

6. (1) Any person may lodge a complaint with the Ombudsman against any of the persons referred to in section 4. Any person deprived of his personal liberty shall be entitled to address written communications to the Ombudsman in sealed envelopes.

(2) A complainant shall state his name and lodge his complaint within twelve months after the commission of the act complained of.

(3) Complaints against decisions which may be set aside by a superior administrative authority cannot be lodged with the Ombudsman until the superior authority has taken a decision in the matter. In that event the time-limit referred to in subsection (2) of this section shall be reckoned from the date of that authority's decision.

(4) The Ombudsman shall determine whether a complaint offers sufficient grounds for investigation.

(5) The Ombudsman may take up a matter for investigation on his own initiative. In that event the restrictions referred to in section 4, subsection (2) shall not apply where violation of essential legal interests is postulated.

7. (1) The persons referred to in section 4 shall be under obligation to furnish the Ombudsman with such information and to produce such documents and records as he may demand *ex officio*.

(2) Demands for information made by the Ombudsman in pursuance of subsection (1) of this section shall be subject to restrictions corresponding to those laid down in section 169, subsections (1) and (3), section 170, subsection (1), the principal rule of section 170, subsection (4), and section 749 of the Administration of Justice Act.

(3) If the Ombudsman wants to take action on a complaint against any of the persons referred to in section 4, the complaint shall, except where absolutely incompatible with the investigation of the matter, be notified to the person complained of at the earliest opportunity. If the person complained of is a civil servant he may always demand that the matter be dealt with under the provisions of section 17, cf. section 18, of the Civil Servants (Salaries and Pensions) Act. If he is a local government official he may, if the by-laws of the local government concerned provide for disciplinary action, demand that the matter be dealt with under the provisions of such by-laws.

(4) The Ombudsman may subpoena persons to give evidence in court on any matter of importance to his investigations. Such procedure shall be subject to the rules governing examination of witnesses for purposes of investigation, cf. Part 74 of the Administration of Justice Act. The hearings shall not be held in open court. The person complained of shall be entitled to attend such examinations of witnesses and to bring a counsel. The rules in force at any given time with respect to payment of the costs of counsel, etc. in cases of disciplinary prosecution of civil servants shall apply by analogy.

8. The Ombudsman shall observe secrecy in any matter coming to his knowledge in the performance of his duty, provided that secrecy is necessary *ipso facto*. The obligation of the Ombudsman to observe secrecy shall not lapse on his retirement.

9. (1) The Ombudsman may direct the Public Prosecutor to institute a preliminary investigation or bring a charge before a court of justice for misconduct in public service or office, subject to the provisions of sections 16 and 60 of the Constitution of 5 June 1953 (The Court of the Realm).

(2) The Ombudsman may direct the appropriate central government administrative authority to institute disciplinary proceedings. Where the by-laws of a local government provide for disciplinary proceedings, he may direct the appropriate local government authority to institute such proceedings.

(3) The Ombudsman may always state his own views of a case to the person complained of.

10. (1) Should the Ombudsman learn of major mistakes or derelictions on the part of any of the persons referred to in section 4, he shall report the matter to the folketing and the responsible minister. In the case of mistakes or derelictions on the part of any of the persons referred to in section 4, subsection (2), he shall report the matter also to the local government concerned.

International Ombudsman Institute. The first international conference of ombudsmen, held in Edmonton, Canada in 1976, resulted in the establishment of the International Ombudsman Institute, with headquarters at the Law Center for the University of Alberta, Edmonton, in 1978.

IOI promotes the concept of ombudsmanship by conducting research into problems confronting ombudsmen and organizing conferences and seminars on the subject. It publishes the IOI *Newsletter* every two months and also issues the *IOI Directory of Ombudsmen and Other Complaint-handlers* and the *IOI Bibliography*. In addition, it issues annually the *Ombudsman Journal, Ombudsman and other Complaint-handling Systems Survey, Ombudsman Office Profiles,* and *Court Cases of Interest to the Institution of Ombudsman.*

Membership of the institute consists of ombudsman offices having a legislative status in 40 countries and academies in 20 countries and territories.

OPINION AND EXPRESSION. Freedom of opinion and expression is proclaimed in the UNIVERSAL DECLARATION OF HUMAN RIGHTS in the following terms:

Article 19. Everyone has the right to freedom of opinion and expression; this right includes freedom to hold opinions without interference and to seek, receive, and impart information and ideas through any media and regardless of frontiers.

This freedom is dealt with in two articles of the INTERNATIONAL COVENANT ON CIVIL AND POLITICAL RIGHTS, as follows:

Article 19. 1. Everyone shall have the right to hold opinions without interference.

2. Everyone shall have the right to freedom of expression; this right shall include freedom to seek, receive and impart information and ideas of all kinds, regardless of frontiers, either orally, in writing or in print, in the form of art, or through any other media of his choice.

3. The exercise of the rights provided for in paragraph 2 of this article carries with it special duties and responsibilities. It may therefore be subject to certain restrictions, but these shall only be such as are provided by law and are necessary:

(a) For respect of the rights or reputations of others;

(b) For the protection of national security or of public order (*ordre public*), or of public health or morals.

Article 20. 1. Any propaganda for war shall be prohibited by law.

2. Any advocacy of national, racial or religious hatred that constitutes incitement to discrimination, hostility or violence shall be prohibited by law.

The INTERNATIONAL CONVENTION ON THE ELIMINATION OF ALL FORMS OF RACIAL DISCRIMINATION refers to freedom of opinion and expression in two of its articles, as follows:

Article 4. States Parties condemn all propaganda and all organizations which are based on ideas or theories of superiority of one race or group of persons of one colour or ethnic origin, or which attempt to justify or promote racial hatred and discrimination in any form, and undertake to adopt immediate and positive measures designed to eradicate all incitement to, or acts of, such discrimination, and to this end, with due regard to the principles embodied in the Universal Declaration of Human Rights and the rights expressly set forth in article 5 of this Convention, *inter alia:*

(a) Shall declare an offence punishable by law all dissemination of ideas based on racial superiority or hatred, incitement to racial discrimination, as well as acts of violence or incitement to such acts against any race or group of persons of another colour or ethnic origin, and also the provision of any assistance to racist activities, including the financing thereof;

(b) Shall declare illegal and prohibit organizations, and also organized and all other propaganda activities, which promote and incite racial discrimination, and shall recognize participation in such organizations or activities as an offence punishable by law;

(c) Shall not permit public authorities or public institutions, national or local, to promote or incite racial discrimination.

Article 5. In compliance with the fundamental obligations laid down in article 2, States Parties undertake to prohibit and to eliminate racial discrimination in all its forms and to guarantee the right of everyone, without distinction as to race, colour, or national or ethnic origin, to equality before the law, notably in the enjoyment of the following rights: . . .

(d) Other civil rights, in particular: . . .

(viii) The right to freedom of opinion and expression.

The AMERICAN CONVENTION ON HUMAN RIGHTS, open for acceptance by member States of the ORGANIZATION OF AMERICAN STATES, provides that:

Article 13. 1. Everyone has the right to freedom of thought and expression. This right includes freedom to seek, receive, and impart information and ideas of all kinds, regardless of frontiers, either orally, in writing, in print, in the form of art, or through any other medium of one's choice.

2. The exercise of the right provided for in the foregoing paragraph shall not be subject to prior censorship but shall be subject to subsequent imposition of liability, which shall be expressly established by law to the extent necessary to ensure:

a. respect for the rights or reputations of others; or

b. the protection of national security, public order, or public health or morals.

3. The right of expression may not be restricted by indirect methods or means, such as the abuse of government or private controls over newsprint, radio broadcasting frequencies, or equipment used in the dissemination of information, or by any other means tending to impede the communication and circulation of ideas and opinions.

4. Notwithstanding the provisions of paragraph 2 above, public entertainments may be subject by law to prior censorship for the sole purpose of regulating access to them for the moral protection of childhood and adolescence.

5. Any propaganda for war and any advocacy of national,

racial, or religious hatred that constitute incitements to lawless violence or to any other similar illegal action against any person or group of persons on any grounds including those of race, color, religion, language, or national origin shall be considered as offenses punishable by law.

The AFRICAN CHARTER OF HUMAN AND PEOPLES' RIGHTS, open for acceptance by member States of the ORGANIZATION OF AFRICAN UNITY, provides that:

Article 9. (1) Every individual shall have the right to receive information.
(2) Every individual shall have the right to express and disseminate his opinions within the law.

The EUROPEAN CONVENTION ON HUMAN RIGHTS, open for acceptance by members of the COUNCIL OF EUROPE, provides that:

Article 10. (1) Everyone has the right to freedom of expression. This right shall include freedom to hold opinions and to receive and impart information and ideas without interference by public authority and regardless of frontiers. This Article shall not prevent States from requiring the licensing of broadcasting, television or cinema enterprises.
(2) The exercise of these freedoms, since it carries with it duties and responsibilities, may be subject to such formalities, conditions, restrictions or penalties as are prescribed by law and are necessary in a democratic society, in the interests of national security, territorial integrity or public safety, for the prevention of disorder or crime, for the protection of health or morals, for the protection of the reputation or rights of others, for preventing the disclosure of information received in confidence, or for maintaining the authority and impartiality of the judiciary.

After examining reports submitted by States parties to the INTERNATIONAL CONVENTION ON THE ELIMINATION OF ALL FORCES OF RACIAL DISCRIMINATION in accordance with article 9 of that instrument, the COMMITTEE ON THE ELIMINATION OF RACIAL DISCRIMINATION adopted, in 1972, the following general comments concerning the implementation of article 4:

On the basis of the consideration at its fifth session of reports submitted by States Parties under article 9 of the International Convention on the Elimination of all Forms of Racial Discrimination, the Committee found that the legislation of a number of countries did not include the provisions envisaged under article 4 (a) and (b) of the Convention, the implementation of which (with due regard to the principles embodied in the Universal Declaration of Human Rights and the rights expressly set forth in article 5 of the Convention) is obligatory under the Convention for all States parties.
The Committee accordingly recommends that the States parties whose legislation is deficient in this request should consider, in accordance with their national legislative procedures, the question of supplementing their legislation with provisions conforming to the requirements of article 4 (a) and (b) of the Convention.

After examining reports submitted by States parties to the International Covenant on Civil and Political Rights in accordance with article 40 of that instrument, the HUMAN RIGHTS COMMITTEE adopted, in 1983, the following general comments relating to the implementation of articles 19 and 20:

Comments on article 19. 1. Paragraph 1 requires protection of "the right to hold opinions without interference". This is a right to which the Covenant permits no exception or restriction. The Committee would welcome information from States parties concerning paragraph 1.
2. Paragraph 2 requires protection of the right of freedom of expression, which includes not only freedom to "impart information and ideas of all kinds", but also freedom to "seek" and "receive" them "regardless of frontiers" and in whatever medium, "either orally, in writing or in print, in the form of art, or through any other media" of one's choice. Not all States parties have provided information concerning all aspects of the freedom of expression. For instance, little attention has so far been given to the fact that, because of the development of modern mass media, effective measures are necessary to prevent such control of the media as would interfere with the right of everyone to freedom of expression in a way that is not provided for in paragraph 3.
3. Many reports of States parties confine themselves to mentioning that freedom of expression is guaranteed under the Constitution or the law. However, in order to know the precise régime of freedom of expression, in law and in practice, the Committee needs in addition pertinent information about the rules which either define the scope of freedom of expression or which set forth certain restrictions, as well as any other conditions which in practice affect the exercise of this right. It is the interplay between the principle of freedom of expression and such limitations and restrictions which determines the actual scope of the individual's right.
4. Paragraph 3 expressly stresses that the exercise of the right to freedom of expression carries with it special duties and responsibilities and, for this reason, certain restrictions on that right are permitted which may relate either to the interests of other persons or to those of the community as a whole. However, when a State party imposes certain restrictions on the exercise of freedom of expression, these may not put in jeopardy the right itself. Paragraph 3 lays down conditions and it is only subject to these conditions that restrictions may be imposed: the restrictions must be "provided by law"; they may only be imposed for one of the purposes set out in subparagraphs (a) and (b) of paragraph 3; and they must be justified as being "necessary" for that State party for one of those purposes.
Comments on article 20. 1. Not all reports submitted by States parties have provided sufficient information as to the implementation of article 20 of the Covenant. In view of the nature of article 20, States parties are obliged to adopt the necessary legislative measures prohibiting the actions referred to therein. However, the reports have shown that in some States such actions are neither prohibited by law nor are appropriate efforts intended or made to prohibit them. Furthermore, many reports failed to give sufficient information concerning the relevant national legislation and practice.
2. Article 20 of the Covenant states that any propaganda

for war and any advocacy of national, racial or religious hatred that constitutes incitement to discrimination, hostility or violence shall be prohibited by law. In the opinion of the Committee, these required prohibitions are fully compatible with the right of freedom of expression as contained in article 19, the exercise of which carries with it special duties and responsibilities. The prohibition under paragraph 1 extends to all forms of propaganda threatening or resulting in an act of aggression or breach of the peace contrary to the Charter of the United Nations, while paragraph 2 is directed against any advocacy of national, racial or religious hatred that constitutes incitement to discrimination, hostility or violence, whether such propaganda or advocacy has aims which are internal or external to the State concerned. The provisions of article 20, paragraph 1, do not prohibit advocacy of the sovereign right of self-defence or the right of peoples to self-determination and independence in accordance with the Charter. For article 20 to become fully effective there ought to be a law making it clear that propaganda and advocacy as described therein are contrary to public policy and providing for an appropriate sanction in case of violation. The Committee, therefore, believes that States parties which have not yet done so should take the measures necessary to fulfil the obligations contained in article 20, and should themselves refrain from any such propaganda or advocacy.

Detention of Persons who Exercise the Right to Freedom of Opinion and Expression. At annual sessions held between 1984 and 1988, the UN COMMISSION ON HUMAN RIGHTS repeatedly expressed its concern (resolutions 1984/26, 1985/17, 1986/46, 1987/32, and 1988/37) at the extensive occurrence in many parts of the world of detention of persons who exercise their right to freedom of opinion and expression as affirmed in the Universal Declaration of Human Rights and the International Covenant on Civil and Political Rights. The commission appealed to all States to ensure respect and support for the rights of all persons who exercise the right to freedom of opinion and expression and, where any persons have been detained solely for exercising that right, to release them immediately.

In resolution 1988/37, the commission welcomed releases of persons who had been detained for exercising the right to freedom of opinion and expression, encouraged further progress in this regard in all parts of the world, and expressed the view that the effective promotion of the human rights of persons who exercise that right is of fundamental importance to the safeguarding of human dignity. The commission requested its SUB-COMMISSION ON PREVENTION OF DISCRIMINATION AND PROTECTION OF MINORITIES to continue its consideration of the right to freedom of opinion and expression as laid down in the covenant and to make recommendations to the commission on further measures which may be required at the national and international levels to safeguard the right.

The sub-commission, at its 1988 session, requested one of its members (decision 1988/110), Mr. Danilo Türk (Yugoslavia), to prepare a working paper containing a proposal for carrying out the study aimed at clarifying the conceptual and methodological questions involved.

The Commission on Human Rights at its 1989 session took note (resolution 1989/31) of the sub-commission's request to Mr. Türk and decided to review the question of freedom of opinion and expression when Mr. Türk's study had been completed.

In the working paper that Mr. Türk later prepared for the sub-commission (UN Doc. E/CN.4/Sub.2/26), he made the following recommendations (para.63–65):

Given the nature of the *problematique* dealt with in this paper, I suggest that the Sub-Commission appoint two of its members to work jointly on the study entitled "The right to freedom of opinion and expression: current problems of its realization and measures necessary for its strengthening and promotion".
The priority area within the scope of the study should be the political dimension of the right to freedom of opinion and expression. Within this priority area special attention should be paid to the following problems:
(a) the legal regulation of limitations and restrictions constituting the actual régimes of the right to freedom of expression;
(b) the questions of negative sanctions affecting individuals who express their opinion (particular attention should be paid to the problems relating to detention);
(c) the question of measures (legislative, administrative and others) which are to be taken to promote, safeguard and strengthen the right to freedom of opinion and expression.
At the initial phase of the preparation of the study particular attention should be paid to the methods of collection of information and to other methodological questions.

Approving these recommendations, the sub-commission decided (resolution 1989/14) that, subject to approval of its parent bodies, it would entrust preparation of the study to two of its members, Mr. Türk and Mr. Louis Joinet (France).

The Commission on Human Rights examined Mr. Türk's working paper in some detail at its 1990 session. It noted, in particular, (resolution 1990/32) the views expressed therein including those on the intrinsic link between the right to freedom of opinion and expression and the rights to freedom of thought, conscience, and religion; of peaceful assembly; of freedom of association; and of the right to take part in the conduct of public affairs as set out in articles 18, 21, 22, and 25 of the International Covenant on Civil and Political Rights. It also noted the relevance to the protection of the right to freedom of opinion and expression of work under way on the drafting of a declaration on the right and responsibility of individuals, groups, and organs of society to promote and protect human rights (see **WORKING GROUP ON A DRAFT DECLARATION ON THE RIGHT AND RESPONSIBILITY TO PROMOTE AND PROTECT HUMAN RIGHTS**). It expressed the view that the effective promotion of the human rights of persons who exercise the right to freedom of opinion and expression is of fundamental importance to the safeguarding of human dignity.

The commission expressed its concern at the extensive occurrence in many parts of the world of detention of, or discrimination against, persons who exercise the right to freedom of opinion and expression; and at the extensive occurrence in many parts of the world of detention of, or discrimination against, persons who exercise the intrinsically linked rights to freedom of thought, conscience, and religion; of peaceful assembly and association; and of freedom to take part in the conduct of public affairs. It appealed to all States to ensure respect and support for the rights of all persons who exercise, or who seek to promote and defend these rights and freedoms, and to ensure that such persons are not discriminated against—particularly in such areas as employment, housing, and social services—or harassed.

The commission, and later the Economic and Social Council, approved the sub-commission's request to Mr. Joinet and Mr. Türk to prepare a study on the right to freedom of opinion and expression.

ORGANIZATION OF AFRICAN UNITY.

An intergovernmental organization within the United Nations system composed of the governments of 50 African States, including the island States of Comoros and Madagascar but excluding South Africa.

The organization endeavors to promote the unity and solidarity of African States: to coordinate and intensify their cooperation and their efforts to achieve a better life for the peoples of Africa; to defend their sovereignty, territorial integrity, and independence; to eradicate all forms of colonialism from Africa; to promote international cooperation, having due regard for the **UNITED NATIONS CHARTER** and the **UNIVERSAL DECLARATION OF HUMAN RIGHTS**; and to coordinate and harmonize members' political, diplomatic, economic, educational, cultural, health, welfare, scientific, technical, and defense policies.

OAU's organizational structure includes the Assembly of Heads of State and Government, the supreme organ, which meets once a year to perform the functions set out in articles 8 to 11 of the **ORGANIZATION OF AFRICAN UNITY CHARTER;** the Council of Ministers, which meets two times during the year to perform the functions set out in articles 7 and 8 of the

charter, and the OAU General Secretariat, headed by a Secretary-General and assistant secretaries-general for West, Central, North, East, and Southern Africa.

The OAU Coordinating Committee for the Liberation of Africa organizes, support, and channels financial, military, and logistic support to recognized African liberation movements including the **AFRICAN NATIONAL CONGRESS** and the **SOUTH WEST AFRICAN PEOPLE'S ORGANIZATION.** Through the efforts of the committee, the United Nations was persuaded to recognize the legitimacy of those movements and to grant them status as observers.

Organization of African Unity. Address: P.O. Box 3243, Addis Ababa, Ethiopia. Telephone: 47480. Cable: OAU ADDIS ABABA. Secretary-General: Peter Onu.

ORGANIZATION OF AFRICAN UNITY: CHARTER (1963).

The Charter of the OAU, open to acceptance by any independent sovereign African State, including Madagascar and the islands surrounding Africa but excluding South Africa, was adopted by the heads of African States and Governments, convened at Addis Ababa, on 25 May 1963. It entered into force on 13 September 1963.

The charter is supplemented by the **OAU PROTOCOL OF THE COMMISSION OF MEDIATION, CONCILIATION AND ARBITRATION**, signed at Cairo on 21 July 1964 by the heads of African States and Governments.

The text of the charter (United Nations, *Treaty Series,* vol. 479, p. 39) is as follows:

We, the Heads of African States and Governments assembled in the City of Addis Ababa, Ethiopia;

Convinced that it is the inalienable right of all people to control their own destiny;

Conscious of the fact that freedom, equality, justice and dignity are essential objectives for the achievement of the legitimate aspirations of the African peoples;

Conscious of our responsibility to harness the natural and human resources of our continent for the total advancement of our peoples in spheres of human endeavour;

Inspired by a common determination to promote understanding among our peoples and co-operation among our States in response to the aspirations of our peoples for brotherhood and solidarity, in a larger unity transcending ethnic and national differences;

Convinced that, in order to translate this determination into a dynamic force in the cause of human progress, conditions for peace and security must be established and maintained;

Determined to safeguard and consolidate the hard-won independence as well as the sovereignty and territorial integrity of our States, and to fight against neo-colonialism in all its forms;

Dedicated to the general progress of Africa;

Persuaded that the Charter of the United Nations and the Universal Declaration of Human Rights, to the principles of which we reaffirm our adherence, provide a solid foundation for peaceful and positive co-operation among states;

Desirous that all African States should henceforth unite so that the welfare and well-being of their peoples can be assured;

Resolved to reinforce the links between our states by establishing and strengthening common institutions;

Have agreed to the present Charter.

Establishment

Article 1. 1. The High Contracting Parties do by the present Charter establish an Organization to be known as the *Organization of African Unity.*

2. The Organization shall include the Continental African States, Madagascar and other Islands surrounding Africa.

Purposes

Article 2. 1. The Organization shall have the following purposes:

a. to promote the unity and solidarity of the African States;

b. to coordinate and intensify their co-operation and efforts to achieve a better life for the peoples of Africa;

c. to defend their sovereignty, their territorial integrity and independence;

d. to eradicate all forms of colonialism from Africa; and

e. to promote international co-operation, having due regard to the Charter of the United Nations and the Universal Declaration of Human Rights.

2. To these ends, the Member States shall coordinate and harmonise their general policies, especially in the following fields:

a. political and diplomatic co-operation;

b. economic co-operation, including transport and communications;

c. educational and cultural co-operation;

d. health, sanitation, and nutritional co-operation;

e. scientific and technical co-operations; and

f. co-operation for defence and security.

Principles

Article 3. The Member States, in pursuit of the purposes stated in Article 2, solemnly affirm and declare their adherence to the following principles

1. the sovereign equality of all Member States;

2. non-interference in the internal affairs of States;

3. respect for the sovereignty and territorial integrity of each State and for its inalienable right to independent existence;

4. peaceful settlement of disputes by negotiation, mediation, conciliation or arbitration;

5. unreserved condemnation, in all its forms, of political assassination as well as of subversive activities on the part of neighbouring States or any other State;

6. absolute dedication to the total emancipation of the African territories which are still dependent;

7. affirmation of a policy of non-alignment with regard to all blocs.

Membership

Article 4. Each independent sovereign African State shall be entitled to become a Member of the Organization.

Rights and Duties of Member States

Article 5. All Member States shall enjoy equal rights and have equal duties.

Article 6. The Member States pledge themselves to observe scrupulously the principles enumerated in Article 3 of the present Charter.

Institutions

Article 7. The Organization shall accomplish its purposes through the following principal institutions:

1. the Assembly of Heads of State and Government;

2. the Council of Ministers;

3. the General Secretariat;

4. the Commission of Mediation, Conciliation and Arbitration.

The Assembly of Heads of State and Government

Article 8. The Assembly of Heads of State and Government shall be the supreme organ of the Organization. It shall, subject to the provisions of this Charter, discuss matters of common concern to Africa with a view to co-ordinating and harmonizing the general policy of the Organization. It may in addition review the structure, functions and acts of all the organs and any specialized agencies which may be created in accordance with the present Charter.

Article 9. The Assembly shall be composed of the Heads of State and Government or their duly accredited representatives and it shall meet at least once a year. At the request of any Member State and on approval by a two-thirds majority of the Member States, the Assembly shall meet in extraordinary session.

Article 10. 1. Each Member State shall have one vote.

2. All resolutions shall be determined by a two-thirds majority of the Members of the Organization.

3. Questions of procedure shall require a simple majority. Whether or not a question is one of procedure shall be determined by a simple majority of all Member States of the Organization.

4. Two-thirds of the total membership of the Organization shall form a quorum at any meeting of the Assembly.

Article 11. The Assembly shall have the power to determine its own rules of procedure.

The Council of Ministers

Article 12. The Council of Ministers shall consist of Foreign Ministers or such other Ministers as are designated by the Governments of Member States.

2. The Council of Ministers shall meet at least twice a year. When requested by any Member State and approved by two-thirds of all Member States, it shall meet in extraordinary session.

Article 13. 1. The Council of Ministers shall be responsible to the Assembly of Heads of State and Government. It shall be entrusted with the responsibility of preparing conferences of the Assembly.

2. It shall take cognisance of any matter referred to it by the Assembly. It shall be entrusted with the implementation of the decision of the Assembly, of Heads of State and Government. It shall coordinate inter-African cooperation in accordance with the instructions of the Assembly and in conformity with Article 2 (2) of the present Charter.

Article 14. 1. Each Member State shall have one vote.

2. All resolutions shall be determined by a simple majority of the members of the Council of Ministers.

3. Two thirds of the total membership of the Council of Ministers shall form a quorum for any meeting of the Council.

Article 15. The Council shall have the power to determine its own rules of procedure.

General Secretariat

Article 16. There shall be an Administrative Secretary-General of the Organization, who shall be appointed by the Assembly of Heads of State and Government. The Administrative Secretary-General shall direct the affairs of the Secretariat.

Article 17. There shall be one or more Assistant Secretaries-General of the Organization who shall be appointed by the Assembly of Heads of State and Government.

Article 18. The functions and conditions of services of the Secretary-General, of the Assistant Secretaries-General and other employees of the Secretariat shall be governed by the provisions of this Charter and the regulations approved by the Assembly of Heads of State and Government.

1. In the performance of their duties the Administrative Secretary-General and the staff shall not seek or receive instructions from any government or from any other authority external to the Organization. They shall refrain from any action which might reflect on their position as international officials responsible only to the Organization.

2. Each member of the Organization undertakes to respect the exclusive character of the responsibility of the Administrative Secretary-General and the Staff and not to seek to influence them in the discharge of their responsibilities.

Commission of Mediation, Conciliation and Arbitration

Article 19. Member States pledge to settle all disputes among themselves by peaceful means and, to this end decide to establish a Commission of Mediation, Conciliation and Arbitration, the composition of which and conditions of service shall be defined by a separate Protocol to be approved by the Assembly of Heads of State and Government. Said Protocol shall be regarded as forming an integral part of the present Charter.

Specialized Commissions

Article 20. The Assembly shall establish such Specialized Commissions as it may deem necessary, including the following:

    1. Economic and Social Commission;
    2. Educational and Cultural Commission;
    3. Health, Sanitation and Nutrition Commission;
    4. Defence Commission;
    5. Scientific, Technical and Research Commission.

Article 21. Each Specialized Commission referred to in Article 20 shall be composed of the Ministers concerned or other Ministers or Plenipotentiaries designated by the Governments of the Member States.

Article 22. The functions of the Specialized Commissions shall be carried out in accordance with the provisions of the present Charter and of the regulations approved by the Council of Ministers.

The Budget

Article 23. The budget of the Organization prepared by the Administrative Secretary-General shall be approved by the Council of Ministers. The budget shall be provided by contributions from Member States in accordance with the scale of assessment of the United Nations; provided, however, that no Member State shall be assessed an amount exceeding twenty percent of the yearly regular budget of the Organization. The Member States agree to pay their respective contributions regularly.

Signature and Ratification of Charter

Article 24. 1. This Charter shall be open for signature to all independent sovereign African States and shall be ratified by the signatory States in accordance with their respective constitutional processes.

2. The original instrument, done, if possible in African languages, in English and French, all texts being equally authentic, shall be deposited with the Government of Ethiopia which shall transmit certified copies thereof to all independent sovereign African States.

3. Instruments of ratification shall be deposited with the Government of Ethiopia, which shall notify all signatories of each such deposit.

Entry into Force

Article 25. This Charter shall enter into force immediately upon receipt by the Government of Ethiopia of the instruments of ratification from two thirds of the signatory States.

Registration of the Charter

Article 26. This Charter shall, after due ratification, be registered with the Secretariat of the United Nations through the Government of Ethiopia in conformity with Article 102 of the Charter of the United Nations.

Interpretation of the Charter

Article 27. Any question which may arise concerning the interpretation of this Charter shall be decided by a vote of two thirds of the Assembly of Heads of State and Government of the Organization.

Adhesion and Accession

Article 28. 1. Any independent sovereign African State may at any time notify the Administrative Secretary-General of its intention to adhere or accede to this Charter.

2. The Administrative Secretary-General shall, on receipt of such notification, communicate a copy of it to all the Member States. Admission shall be decided by a simple majority of the Member States. The decision of each Member State shall be transmitted to the Administrative Secretary-General, who shall, upon receipt of the required number of votes, communicate the decision to the State concerned.

Miscellaneous

Article 29. The working languages of the Organization and all its institutions shall be, if possible African languages, English and French.

Article 30. The Administrative Secretary-General may accept on behalf of the Organization gifts, bequests and other donations made to the Organization, provided that this is approved by the Council of Ministers.

Article 31. The Council of Ministers shall decide on the privileges and immunities to be accorded to the personnel of the Secretariat in the respective territories of the Member States.

Cessation of Membership

Article 32. Any State which desires to renounce its membership shall forward a written notification to the Administrative Secretary-General. At the end of one year from the date of such notification, if not withdrawn, the Charter shall cease to apply with respect to the renouncing State, which shall thereby cease to belong to the Organization.

Amendment of the Charter

Article 33. This Charter may be amended or revised if any Member State makes a written request to the Administrative Secretary-General to that effect; provided, however, that the proposed amendment is not submitted to the Assembly for consideration until all the Member States have been duly notified of it and a period of one year has elapsed. Such an amendment shall not be effective unless approved by at least two thirds of all the Member States.

ORGANIZATION OF AFRICAN UNITY: PROTOCOL OF THE COMMISSION OF MEDIATION, CONCILIATION AND ARBITRATION (1964).

The protocol, approved by the Assembly of the Heads of State of African States and Governments, convened at Cairo, on 21 July 1964, is considered to be an integral part of the ORGANIZATION OF AFRICAN UNITY CHARTER (1963). The text of the protocol (*International Legal Materials* 3, p. 1116) is as follows:

Article 1. The Commission of Mediation, Conciliation and Arbitration established by Article XIX of the Charter of the Organization of African Unity shall be governed by the provisions of the present Protocol.

Article 2. 1. The Commission shall consist of twenty-one members elected by the Assembly of Heads of State and Government.

2. No two Members shall be nationals of the same State.

3. The Members of the Commission shall be persons with recognized professional qualifications.

4. Each Member State of the Organization of African Unity shall be entitled to nominate two candidates.

5. The Administrative Secretary-General shall prepare a list of the candidates nominated by Member States and shall submit it to the Assembly of Heads of State and Government.

Article 3. 1. Members of the Commission shall be elected for a term of five years and shall be eligible for re-election.

2. Members of the Commission whose terms of office have expired shall remain in office until the election of a new Commission.

3. Notwithstanding the expiry of their terms of office, Members shall complete any proceedings in which they are already engaged.

Article 4. Members of the Commission shall not be removed from office except by decision of the Assembly of Heads of State and Government, by a two-thirds majority of the total membership, on the grounds of inability to perform the functions of their office or of proved misconduct.

Article 5. 1. Whenever a vacancy occurs in the Commission, it shall be filled in conformity with the provisions of Article II.

2. A Member of the Commission elected to fill a vacancy shall hold office for the unexpired term of the Member he has replaced.

Article 6. 1. A President and two Vice-Presidents shall be elected by the Assembly of Heads of State and Government from among the Members of the Commission who shall each hold office for five years. The President and the two Vice-Presidents shall not be eligible for re-election as such officers.

2. The President and the two Vice-Presidents shall be full-time members of the Commission, while the remaining eighteen shall be part-time Members.

Article 7. The President and the two Vice-Presidents shall constitute the Bureau of the Commission and shall have the responsibility of consulting with the parties as regards the appropriate mode of settling the dispute in accordance with this Protocol.

Article 8. The salaries and allowances of the Members of the Bureau and the remuneration of the other Members of the Commission shall be determined in accordance with the provisions of the Charter of the Organization of African Unity.

Article 9. 1. The Commission shall appoint a Registrar and may provide for such other officers as may be deemed necessary.

2. The terms and conditions of service of the Registrar and other administrative officers of the Commission shall be governed by the Commission's Staff Regulations.

Article 10. The Administrative expenses of the Commission shall be borne by the Organization of African Unity. All other expenses incurred in connection with the proceedings before the Commission shall be met in accordance with the Rules of Procedure of the Commission.

Article 11. The Seat of the Commission shall be at Addis Ababa, Ethiopia.

Part II
General Provisions

Article 12. The Commission shall have jurisdiction over disputes between States only.

Article 13. 1. A dispute may be referred to the Commission jointly by the parties concerned, by a party to the dispute, by the Council of Ministers or by the Assembly of Heads of State and Government.

2. Where a dispute has been referred to the Commission as provided in paragraph 1, and one or more of the parties have refused to submit to the jurisdiction of the Commission, the Bureau shall refer the matter to the Council of Ministers for consideration.

Article 14. The consent of any party to a dispute to submit to the jurisdiction of the Commission may be evidenced by:

(a) a prior written undertaking by such party that there shall be recourse to Mediation, Conciliation or Arbitration;

(b) reference of a dispute by such party to the Commission; or

(c) submission by such party to the jurisdiction in respect of a dispute referred to the Commission by another State, by the Council of Ministers, or by the Assembly of Heads of State and Government.

Article 15. Member States shall refrain from any act or omission that is likely to aggravate a situation which has been referred to the Commission.

Article 16. Subject to the provisions of this Protocol and any special agreement between the parties, the Commission shall be entitled to adopt such working methods as it deems to be necessary and expedient and shall establish appropriate rules of procedure.

Article 17. The Members of the Commission, when engaged in the business of the Commission, shall enjoy diplomatic privileges and immunities as provided for in the Convention on Privileges and Immunities of the Organization of African Unity.

Article 18. Where, in the course of Mediation, Conciliation or Arbitration, it is deemed necessary to conduct an investigation or inquiry for the purpose of elucidating facts or circumstances relating to a matter in dispute, the parties concerned and all other Member States shall extend to those engaged in any such proceedings the fullest cooperation in the conduct of such investigation or inquiry.

Article 19. In case of a dispute between Member States, the parties may agree to resort to any one of these modes of settlement: Mediation, Conciliation and Arbitration.

Part III
Mediation

Article 20. When a dispute between Member States is referred to the Commission for Mediation, the President shall, with the consent of the parties, appoint one or more members of the Commission to mediate the dispute.

Article 21. 1. The role of the mediator shall be confined to reconciling the views and claims of the parties.

2. The mediator shall make written proposals to the parties as expeditiously as possible.

3. If the means of reconciliation proposed by the mediator are accepted, they shall become the basis of a protocol of arrangement between the parties.

Part IV
Conciliation

Article 22. 1. A request for the settlement of a dispute by conciliation may be submitted to the Commission by means of a petition addressed to the President by one or more of the parties to the dispute.

2. If the request is made by only one of the parties, that party shall indicate that prior written notice has been given to the other party.

3. The petition shall include a summary explanation of the grounds of the dispute.

Article 23. 1. Upon receipt of the petition, the President shall, in agreement with the parties, establish a Board of Conciliators, of whom three shall be appointed by the President from among the Members of the Commission, and one each by the parties.

2. The Chairman of the Board shall be a person designated by the President from among the three Members of the Commission.

3. In nominating persons to serve as Members of the Board, the parties to the dispute shall designate persons in such a way that no two Members of it shall be nationals of the same State.

Article 24. 1. It shall be the duty of the Board of Conciliators to clarify the issues in dispute and to endeavour to bring about an agreement between the parties upon mutually acceptable terms.

2. The Board shall consider all questions submitted to it and may undertake any inquiry or hear any person capable of giving relevant information concerning the dispute.

3. In the absence of disagreement between the parties, the Board shall determine its own procedure.

Article 25. The parties shall be represented by agents, whose duty shall be to act as intermediaries between them and the Board. They may moreover be assisted by counsel and experts and may request that all persons whose evidence appears to the Board to be relevant shall be heard.

Article 26. 1. At the close of the proceedings, the Board shall draw up a report stating either:

(a) that the parties have come to an agreement and, if the need arises, the terms of the agreement and any recommendations for settlement made by the Board; or

(b) that it has been impossible to effect a settlement.

2. The Report of the Board of Conciliators shall be communicated to the parties and to the President of the Commission without delay and may be published only with the consent of the parties.

Part V
Arbitration

Article 27. 1. Where it is agreed that arbitration should be resorted to, the Arbitral Tribunal shall be established in the following manner:

(a) each party shall designate one arbitrator from among the Members of the Commission having legal qualifications;

(b) the two arbitrators thus designated shall, by common agreement, designate from among the Members of the Commission a third person who shall act as Chairman of the Tribunal;

(c) where the two arbitrators fail to agree, within one month of their appointment, in the choice of the person to be Chairman of the Tribunal, the Bureau shall designate the Chairman.

2. The President may, with the agreement of the parties, appoint to the Arbitral Tribunal two additional Members who need not be Members of the Commission but who shall have the same powers as the other Members of the Tribunal.

3. The arbitrators shall not be nationals of the parties, or have their domicile in the territories of the parties, or be employed in their service, or have served as mediators or conciliators in the same dispute. They shall all be of different nationalities.

Article 28. Recourse to arbitration shall be regarded as submission in good faith to the award of the Arbitral Tribunal.

Article 29. 1. The parties shall, in each case, conclude a *compromis* which shall specify:

(a) the undertaking of the parties to go to arbitration, and to accept as legally binding, the decision of the Tribunal;

(b) the subject matter of the controversy; and

(c) the seat of the Tribunal.

2. The *compromis* may specify the law to be applied by the Tribunal and the power, if the parties so agree, to adjudicate *ex aequo et bono*, the time-limit within which the award of the arbitrators shall be given, and the appointment of agents and counsel to take part in the proceedings before the Tribunal.

Article 30. In the absence of any provision in the *compromis* regarding the applicable law, the Arbitral Tribunal shall decide the dispute according to treaties concluded between the parties, International Law, the Charter of the Organization of African Unity, the Charter of the United Nations and, if the parties agree, *ex aequo et bono*.

Article 31. 1. Hearings shall be held in *camera* unless the arbitrators decide otherwise.

2. The record of the proceedings signed by the arbitrators and the Registrar shall alone be authoritative.

3. The arbitral award shall be in writing and shall, in respect of every point decided, state the reasons on which it is based.

Part VI
Final Provisions

Article 32. The present Protocol shall, after approval by the Assembly of Heads of State and Government, be an integral part of the Charter of the Organization of African Unity.

Article 33. This Protocol may be amended or revised in accordance with the provisions of Article 33 of the Charter of the Organization of African Unity.

In faith whereof, We the Heads of African State and Government, have signed this Protocol.

SEE ALSO *Good Offices, Mediation, or Conciliation Commissions.*

ORGANIZATION OF AMERICAN STATES. A regional intergovernmental organization composed of 32 countries of North, South, and Central America: Antigua and Barbuda, Argentina, Bahamas, Barbados, Bolivia, Brazil, Chile, Colombia, Costa Rica, Cuba, Dominica, Dominican Republic, Ecuador, El Salvador, Grenada, Guatemala, Haiti, Honduras, Jamaica, Mexico, Nicaragua, Panama, Paraguay, Peru, St. Christopher–Nevis, St. Lucia, St. Vincent–Grenadines, Suriname, Trinidad–Tobago, the United States of America, Uruguay, and Venezuela. However, the government of Cuba has been excluded from participation in the Inter-American System since 1962.

The OAS developed out of the International Union of American Republics, established on 14 April 1890 by the First International Conference of American States, convened in Washington. The name of the organization was first changed, in 1910, to Union of American Republics, then changed again to Organization of American States on 30 April 1948 when the Ninth International Conference of American States adopted the ORGANIZATION OF AMERICAN STATES CHARTER. The 1948 conference also adopted the AMERICAN DECLARATION ON THE RIGHTS AND DUTIES OF MAN.

In 1959, the INTER-AMERICAN COMMISSION ON HUMAN RIGHTS was authorized by the Fifth Meeting of Consultation of Ministers of Foreign Affairs, convened in Santiago, Chile. The INTER-AMERICAN COMMISSION ON HUMAN RIGHTS STATUTE, approved by the council, provided that the commission would function as an autonomous entity of OAS and that the human rights referred to in the statute were those set forth in the American Declaration of the Rights and Duties of Man.

The 1981 Inter-American Conference of American States adopted and opened for signature and ratification or accession the AMERICAN CONVENTION ON HUMAN RIGHTS, also known as the Pact of San Jose. When this convention entered into force in 1978, authority was provided for the establishment of the INTER-AMERICAN COURT OF HUMAN RIGHTS.

In 1985, the OAS General Assembly, at a special session in Cartagena, Colombia, approved the Protocol of Amendment to the Charter of the Organization of American States, also known as the Protocol of Cartagena de Indias. The protocol entered into force in November 1988 upon ratification by two-thirds of the present OAS membership.

In its annual report for 1985–1986 (OAS Doc. OEA/ Ser. L/V/II.68, Doc. 8 rev. 1), the Inter-American Commission on Human Rights submitted to the OAS General Assembly, as the Assembly had requested in resolution 778 (XV-O/85), a draft AMERICAN CONVENTION ON HUMAN RIGHTS: ADDITIONAL PROTOCOL, incorporating economic, social, and cultural rights into the convention. The additional protocol was approved unanimously by the OAS General Assembly on 17 November 1988.

Under the OAS charter, as amended by the Protocol of Cartagena de Indias, the essential purposes of the organization are (article 2):

(a) To strengthen the peace and security of the continent;

(b) To promote and consolidate representative democracy, with due respect for the principle of nonintervention;

(c) To prevent possible causes of difficulties and to ensure the pacific settlement of disputes that may arise among the Member States;

(d) To provide for common action on the part of those States in the event of aggression;

(e) To seek the solution of political, juridical, and economic problems that may arise among them;

(f) To promote, by cooperative action, their economic, social and cultural development, and

(g) To achieve an effective limitation of conventional weapons that will make it possible to devote the largest amount of resources to the economic and social development of the Member States.

Under the charter, as amended, the following principles are reaffirmed (article 3):

(a) International law is the standard of conduct of States in their reciprocal relations;

(b) International order consists essentially of respect for the personality, sovereignty, and independence of States, and the faithful fulfillment of obligations derived from treaties and other sources of international law;

(c) Good faith shall govern the relations between States;

(d) The solidarity of the American States and the high aims which are sought through it require the political organization of those States on the basis of the effective exercise of representative democracy;

(e) Every State has the right to choose, without external interference, its political, economic, and social system and to organize itself in the way best suited to it, and has the duty to abstain from intervening in the affairs of another State. Subject to the foregoing, the American States shall cooperate fully among themselves, independently of the nature of their political, economic, and social systems;

(f) The American States condemn war of aggression: victory does not give rights;

(g) An act of aggression against one American State is an act of aggression against all the other American States;

(h) Controversies of an international character arising between two or more American States shall be settled by peaceful procedures;

(i) Social justice and social security are bases of lasting peace;

(j) Economic cooperation is essential to the common welfare and prosperity of the peoples of the continent;

(k) The American States proclaim the fundamental rights of the individual without distinction as to race, nationality, creed, or sex;

(l) The spiritual unity of the continent is based on respect for the cultural values of the American countries and requires their close cooperation for the high purposes of civilization;

(m) The education of peoples should be directed toward justice, freedom and peace.

The functions and procedures of the major organs of the Organization of American States are set out in the charter, as amended, as follows:

OAS General Assembly (Chapter XI);

OAS Meeting of Consultation of Ministers of Foreign Affairs (Chapter XII);

OAS Permanent Council (Chapters XIII and XIV):

Inter-American Economic and Social Council (Chapters XIII and XV),

Inter-American Council for Education, Science and Culture (Chapters XIII and XVI);

Inter-American Juridical Committee (Chapter XVII);

Inter-American Commission on Human Rights (Chapter XVIII);

OAS General Secretariat (Chapter XX); and

Inter-American Specialized Organizations (Chapter XXI).

Organization of American States. Address: 17th and Constitution Avenue, Northwest, Washington. D.C., 20006, USA. Telephone: (202) 789-3000. Cable: OAS-WSHDC. Telex: 64128-24838. Secretary-General: Joao Clemente Baena Soares.

ORGANIZATION OF AMERICAN STATES: CHARTER (1948).

The charter was opened for signature on 30 April 1948 at the Ninth International Conference of American States and entered into force on 13 December 1951. It was amended first by the protocol known as the "Protocol of Buenos Aires," signed on 27 February 1967 at the Third Special Inter-American Conference, which entered into force on 27 February 1970, and later by the protocol known as the "Protocol of Cartagena de Indias," which entered into force on 16 November 1988.

The integrated text of the charter, as amended by the protocols, is as follows (*OAS Treaty Series* 1-D):

In the name of their peoples, the States represented at the Ninth International Conference of American States,

Convinced that the historic mission of America is to offer to man a land of liberty and a favorable environment for the development of his personality and the realization of his just aspirations;

Conscious that that mission has already inspired numerous agreements, whose essential value lies in the desire of the American peoples to live together in peace and, through their mutual understanding and respect for the sovereignty of each one, to provide for the betterment of all, in independence, in equality and under law;

Convinced that representative democracy is an indispensable condition for the stability, peace and development of the region;

Confident that the true significance of American solidarity and good neighborliness can only mean the consolidation on this continent, within the framework of democratic institutions, of a system of individual liberty and social justice based on respect for the essential rights of man;

Persuaded that their welfare and their contribution to the progress and the civilization of the world will increasingly require intensive continental cooperation;

Resolved to persevere in the noble undertaking that humanity has conferred upon the United Nations, whose principles and purposes they solemnly reaffirm;

Convinced that juridical organization is a necessary condition for security and peace founded on moral order and on justice; and

In accordance with Resolution IX of the Inter-American Conference on Problems of War and Peace, held in Mexico City,

Have agreed upon the following

Part One

Chapter I
Nature and Purposes

Article 1. The American States establish by this Charter the international organization that they have developed to achieve an order of peace and justice, to promote their solidarity, to strengthen their collaboration, and to defend their sovereignty, their territorial integrity, and their independence. Within the United Nations, the Organization of American States is a regional agency.

The Organization of American States has no powers other than those expressly conferred upon it by this Charter, none of whose provisions authorizes it to intervene in matters that are within the internal jurisdiction of the Member States.

Article 2. The Organization of American States, in order to put into practice the principles on which it is founded and to fulfill its regional obligations under the Charter of the United Nations, proclaims the following essential purposes:

(a) To strengthen the peace and security of the continent;

(b) To promote and consolidate representative democracy, with due respect for the principle of nonintervention;

(c) To prevent possible causes of difficulties and to ensure the pacific settlement of disputes that may arise among the Member States;

(d) To provide for common action on the part of those States in the event of aggression;

(e) To seek the solution of political, juridical, and economic problems that may arise among them;

(f) To promote, by cooperative action, their economic, social, and cultural development; and

(g) To achieve an effective limitation of conventional weapons that will make it possible to devote the largest amount of resources to the economic and social development of the Member States.

Chapter II
Principles

Article 3. The American states reaffirm the following principles:

(a) International law is the standard of conduct of States in their reciprocal relations;

(b) International order consists essentially of respect for the personality, sovereignty, and independence of States, and the faithful fulfillment of obligations derived from treaties and other sources of international law;

(c) Good faith shall govern the relations between States;

(d) The solidarity of the American States and the high aims which are sought through it require the political organization of those States on the basis of the effective exercise of representative democracy;

(e) Every State has the right to choose, without external interference, its political, economic, and social system and to organize itself in the way best suited to it, and has the duty to abstain from intervening in the affairs of another State. Subject to the foregoing, the American States shall cooperate fully among themselves, independently of the nature of their political, economic, and social systems;

(f) The American States condemn war of aggression: victory does not give rights;

(g) An act of aggression against one American State is an act of aggression against all the other American States;

(h) Controversies of an international character arising between two or more American States shall be settled by peaceful procedures;

(i) Social justice and social security are bases of lasting peace;

(j) Economic cooperation is essential to the common welfare and prosperity of the peoples of the continent;

(k) The American States proclaim the fundamental rights of the individual without distinction as to race, nationality, creed, or sex;

(l) The spiritual unity of the continent is based on respect for the cultural values of the American countries and requires their close cooperation for the high purposes of civilization;

(m) The education of peoples should be directed toward justice, freedom, and peace.

Chapter III
Members

Article 4. All American States that ratify the present Charter are Members of the Organization.

Article 5. Any new political entity that arises from the union of several Member States and that, as such, ratifies the present Charter, shall become a Member of the Organization. The entry of the new political entity into the Organization shall result in the loss of membership of each one of the States which constitute it.

Article 6. Any other independent American State that desires to become a Member of the Organization should so indicate by means of a note addressed to the Secretary General, in which it declares that it is willing to sign and ratify the Charter of the Organization and to accept all the obligations inherent in membership, especially those relating to collective security expressly set forth in Articles 27 and 28 of the Charter.

Article 7. The General Assembly, upon the recommendation of the Permanent Council of the Organization, shall determine whether it is appropriate that the Secretary General be authorized to permit the applicant State to sign the Charter and to accept the deposit of the corresponding instrument of ratification. Both the recommendation of the Permanent Council and the decision of the General Assembly shall require the affirmative vote of two thirds of the Member States.

Article 8. Membership in the Organization shall be confined to independent States of the Hemisphere that were members of the United Nations as of December 10, 1985, and the nonautonomous territories mentioned in document OEA/Ser. P, AG/doc.1939/85, of November 5, 1985, when they become independent.

Chapter IV
Fundamental Rights and Duties of States

Article 9. States are juridically equal, enjoy equal rights and equal capacity to exercise these rights, and have equal duties. The rights of each State depend not upon its power to ensure the exercise thereof, but upon the mere fact of its existence as a person under international law.

Article 10. Every American State has the duty to respect the rights enjoyed by every other State in accordance with international law.

Article 11. The fundamental rights of States may not be impaired in any manner whatsoever.

Article 12. The political existence of the State is independent of recognition by other States. Even before being recognized, the State has the right to defend its integrity and independence, to provide for its preservation and prosperity, and consequently to organize itself as it sees fit, to legislate concerning its interests, to administer its services, and to determine the jurisdiction and competence of its courts. The exercise of these rights is limited only by the exercise of the rights of other States in accordance with international law.

Article 13. Recognition implies that the State granting it accepts the personality of the new State, with all the rights and duties that international law prescribes for the two States.

Article 14. The right of each State to protect itself and to live its own life does not authorize it to commit unjust acts against another State.

Article 15. The jurisdiction of States within the limits of their national territory is exercised equally over all the inhabitants, whether nationals or aliens.

Article 16. Each State has the right to develop its cultural, political, and economic life freely and naturally. In this free development, the State shall respect the rights of the individual and the principles of universal morality.

Article 17. Respect for and the faithful observance of treaties constitute standards for the development of peaceful relations among States. International treaties and agreements should be public.

Article 18. No State or group of States has the right to intervene, directly or indirectly, for any reason whatever, in the internal or external affairs of any other State. The foregoing principle prohibits not only armed force but also any other form of interference or attempted threat against the personality of the State or against its political, economic, and cultural elements.

Article 19. No State may use or encourage the use of coercive measures of an economic or political character in order to force the sovereign will of another State and obtain from it advantages of any kind.

Article 20. The territory of a State is inviolable; it may not be the object, even temporarily, of military occupation or of other measures of force taken by another State, directly or indirectly, on any grounds whatever. No territorial acquisitions or special advantages obtained either by force or by other means of coercion shall be recognized.

Article 21. The American States bind themselves in their international relations not to have recourse to the use of force, except in the case of self-defense in accordance with existing treaties or in fulfillment thereof.

Article 22. Measures adopted for the maintenance of peace and security in accordance with existing treaties do not constitute a violation of the principles set forth in Articles 18 and 20.

Chapter V
Pacific Settlement of Disputes

Article 23. International disputes between Member States shall be submitted to the peaceful procedures set forth in this Charter.

This provision shall not be interpreted as an impairment of the rights and obligations of the Member States under Articles 34 and 35 of the Charter of the United Nations.

Article 24. The following are peaceful procedures: direct negotiation, good offices, mediation, investigation and conciliation, judicial settlement, arbitration, and those which the parties to the dispute may especially agree upon at any time.

Article 25. In the event that a dispute arises between two or more American States which, in the opinion of one of them, cannot be settled through the usual diplomatic channels, the parties shall agree on some other peaceful procedure that will enable them to reach a solution.

Article 26. A special treaty will establish adequate means for the settlement of disputes and will determine pertinent procedures for each peaceful means such that no dispute between American States may remain without definitive settlement within a reasonable period of time.

Chapter VI
Collective Security

Article 27. Every act of aggression by a State against the territorial integrity or the inviolability of the territory or against the sovereignty or political independence of an American State shall be considered an act of aggression against the other American States.

Article 28. If the inviolability or the integrity of the territory or the sovereignty or political independence of any American State should be affected by an armed attack or by an act of aggression that is not an armed attack, or by an extracontinental conflict, or by a conflict between two or more American States, or by any other fact or situation that might endanger the peace of America, the American States, in furtherance of the principles of continental solidarity or collective self-defense, shall apply the measures and procedures established in the special treaties on the subject.

Chapter VII
Integral Development

Article 29. The Member States, inspired by the principles of inter-American solidarity and cooperation, pledge themselves to a united effort to ensure international social justice in their relations and integral development for their peoples, as conditions essential to peace and security. Integral development, encompasses the economic, social, educational, cultural, scientific, and technological fields through which the goals that each country sets for accomplishing it should be achieved.

Article 30. Inter-American cooperation for integral development is the common and joint responsibility of the Member States, within the framework of the democratic principles and the institutions of the inter-American system. It should include the economic, social, educational, cultural, scientific, and technological fields, support the achievement of national objectives of the Member States, and respect the priorities established by each country in its development plans, without political ties or conditions.

Article 31. Inter-American cooperation for integral development should be continuous and preferably channeled through multilateral organizations, without prejudice to bilateral cooperation between Member States.

The Member States shall contribute to inter-American cooperation for integral development in accordance with their resources and capabilities and in conformity with their laws.

Article 32. Development is a primary responsibility of each country and should constitute an integral and continuous process for the establishment of a more just economic and social order that will make possible and contribute to the fulfillment of the individual.

Article 33. The Member States agree that equality of opportunity, equitable distribution of wealth and income, and the full participation of their peoples in decisions relating to their own development are, among others, basic objectives of integral development. To achieve them, they likewise agree to devote their utmost efforts to accomplishing the following basic goals:

(a) Substantial and self-sustained increase of per capita national product;

(b) Equitable distribution of national income;

(c) Adequate and equitable systems of taxation;

(d) Modernization of rural life and reforms leading to equitable and efficient land-tenure systems, increased agricultural productivity, expanded use of land, diversification of production and improved processing and marketing systems for agricultural products; and the strengthening and expansion of the means to attain these ends;

(e) Accelerated and diversified industrialization, especially of capital and intermediate goods;

(f) Stability of domestic price levels, compatible with sustained economic development and the attainment of social justice;

(g) Fair wages, employment opportunities, and acceptable working conditions for all;

(h) Rapid eradication of illiteracy and expansion of educational opportunities for all;

(i) Protection of man's potential through the extension and application of modern medical science;

(j) Proper nutrition, especially through the acceleration of national efforts to increase the production and availability of food;

(k) Adequate housing for all sectors of the population;

(l) Urban conditions that offer the opportunity for a healthful, productive, and full life;

(m) Promotion of private initiative and investment in harmony with action in the public sector; and

(n) Expansion and diversification of exports.

Article 34. The Member States should refrain from practicing policies and adopting actions or measures that have serious adverse effects on the development of other Member States.

Article 35. Transnational enterprises and foreign private investment shall be subject to the legislation of the host countries and to the jurisdiction of their competent courts and to the international treaties and agreements to which said counties are parties, and should conform to the development policies of the recipient countries.

Article 36. The Member States agree to join together in seeking a solution to urgent or critical problems that may arise whenever the economic development or stability of any Member State is seriously affected by conditions that cannot be remedied through the efforts of that State.

Article 37. The Member States shall extend among themselves the benefits of science and technology by encouraging the exchange and utilization of scientific and technical knowledge in accordance with existing treaties and national laws.

Article 38. The Member States, recognizing the close interdependence between foreign trade and economic and social development, should make individual and united efforts to bring about the following:

(a) Favorable conditions of access to world markets for the products of the developing countries of the region, particularly through the reduction or elimination, by importing countries, of tariff and nontariff barriers that affect the exports of the Member States of the Organization, except when such barriers are applied in order to diversify the economic structure, to speed up the development of the less-developed Member States, and intensify their process of economic integration, or when they are related to national security or to the needs of economic balance;

(b) Continuity in their economic and social development by means of:

i. Improved conditions for trade in basic commodities through international agreements, where appropriate; orderly marketing procedures that avoid the disruption of markets, and other measures designed to promote the expansion of markets and to obtain dependable incomes for producers, adequate and dependable supplies for consumers, and stable prices that are both remunerative to producers and fair to consumers;

ii. Improved international financial cooperation and the adoption of other means for lessening the adverse impact of sharp fluctuations in export earnings experienced by the countries exporting basic commodities;

iii. Diversification of exports and expansion of export opportunities for manufactured and semimanufactured products from the developing countries; and

iv. Conditions conducive to increasing the real export earnings of the Member States, particularly the developing countries of the region, and to increasing their participation in international trade.

Article 39. The Member States reaffirm the principle that when the more developed countries grant concessions in international trade-agreements that lower or eliminate tariffs or other barriers to foreign trade so that they benefit the less-developed countries, they should not expect reciprocal concessions from those countries that are incompatible with their economic development, financial, and trade needs.

Article 40. The Member States, in order to accelerate their economic development, regional integration, and the expansion and improvement of the conditions of their commerce, shall promote improvement and coordination of transportation and communication in the developing countries and among the Member States.

Article 41. The Member States recognize that integration of the developing countries of the Hemisphere is one of the objectives of the inter-American system and, therefore, shall orient their efforts and take the necessary measures to accelerate the integration process, with a view to establishing a Latin American common market in the shortest possible time.

Article 42. In order to strengthen and accelerate integration in all its aspects, the Member States agree to give adequate priority to the preparation and carrying out of multinational projects and to their financing, as well as to encourage economic and financial institutions of the inter-American system to continue giving their broadest support to regional integration institutions and programs.

Article 43. The Member States agree that technical and financial cooperation that seeks to promote regional economic integration should be based on the principle of harmonious, balanced, and efficient development, with particular attention to the relatively less-developed countries, so that it may be a decisive factor that will enable them to promote, with their own efforts, the improved development of their infrastructure programs, new lines of production, and export diversification.

Article 44. The Member States, convinced that man can only achieve the full realization of his aspirations within a just social order, along with economic development and true peace, agree to dedicate every effort to the application of the following principles and mechanisms:

(a) All human beings, without distinction as to race, sex, nationality, creed, or social condition, have a right to material well-being and to their spiritual development, under circumstances of liberty, dignity, equality of opportunity, and economic security;

(b) Work is a right and a social duty, it gives dignity to the one who performs it, and it should be performed under conditions, including a system of fair wages, that ensure life, health, and a decent standard of living for the worker and his family, both during his working years and in his old age, or when any circumstance deprives him of the possibility of working;

(c) Employers and workers, both rural and urban, have the right to associate themselves freely for the defense and promotion of their interests, including the right to collective bargaining and the workers' right to strike, and recognition of the juridical personality of associations and the protection of their freedom and independence, all in accordance with applicable laws;

(d) Fair and efficient systems and procedures for consultation and collaboration among the sectors of production, with due regard for safeguarding the interests of the entire society;

(e) The operation of systems of public administration, banking and credit, enterprise, and distribution and sales, in such a way, in harmony with the private sector, as to meet the requirements and interests of the community;

(f) The incorporation and increasing participation of the marginal sectors of the population, in both rural and urban areas, in the economic, social, civic, cultural, and political life of the nation, in order to achieve the full integration of the national community, acceleration of the process of social mobility, and the consolidation of the democratic system. The encouragement of all efforts of popular promotion and cooperation that have as their purpose the development and progress of the community;

(g) Recognition of the importance of the contribution of organizations such as labor unions, cooperatives, and cultural, professional, business, neighborhood, and community associations to the life of the society and to the development process;

(h) Development of an efficient social security policy; and

(i) Adequate provision for all persons to have due legal aid in order to secure their rights.

Article 45. The Member States recognize that, in order to facilitate the process of Latin American regional integration, it is necessary to harmonize the social legislation of the developing countries, especially in the labor and social security fields, so that the rights of the workers shall be equally protected, and they agree to make the greatest efforts possible to achieve this goal.

Article 46. The Member States will give primary importance within their development plans to the encouragement of education, science, technology, and culture, oriented toward the overall improvement of the individual, and as a foundation for democracy, social justice, and progress.

Article 47. The Member States will cooperate with one another to meet their educational needs, to promote scientific research, and to encourage technological progress for their integral development. They will consider themselves individually and jointly bound to preserve and enrich the cultural heritage of the American peoples.

Article 48. The Member States will exert the greatest efforts, in accordance with their constitutional processes, to ensure the effective exercise of the right to education, on the following bases:

(a) Elementary education, compulsory for children of school age, shall also be offered to all others who can benefit from it. When provided by the State it shall be without charge;

(b) Middle-level education shall be extended progressively to as much of the population as possible, with a view to social improvement. It shall be diversified in such a way that it meets the development needs of each country without prejudice to providing a general education; and

(c) Higher education shall be available to all, provided that, in order to maintain its high level, the corresponding regulatory or academic standards are met.

Article 49. The Member States will give special attention to the eradication of illiteracy, will strengthen adult and vocational education systems, and will ensure that the benefits of culture will be available to the entire population. They will promote the use of all information media to fulfill these aims.

Article 50. The Member States will develop science and technology through educational, research, and technological development activities and information and dissemination programs. They will stimulate activities in the field of technology for the purpose of adapting it to the needs of their integral development. They will organize their cooperation in these fields efficiently and will substantially increase exchange of knowledge, in accordance with national objectives and laws and with treaties in force.

Article 51. The Member States, with due respect for the individuality of each of them, agree to promote cultural exchange as an effective means of consolidating inter-American understanding; and they recognize that regional integration programs should be strengthened by close ties in the fields of education, science, and culture.

Part Two

Chapter VIII
The Organs

Article 52. The Organization of American States accomplishes its purposes by means of:

(a) The General Assembly;

(b) The Meeting of Consultation of Ministers of Foreign Affairs;

(c) The Councils;

(d) The Inter-American Juridical Committee;

(e) The Inter-American Commission on Human Rights;

(f) The General Secretariat;

(g) The Specialized Conferences; and

(h) The Specialized Organizations.

There may be established, in addition to those provided for in the Charter and in accordance with the provisions thereof, such subsidiary organs, agencies, and other entities as are considered necessary.

Chapter IX
The General Assembly

Article 53. The General Assembly is the supreme organ of the Organization of American States. It has as its principal powers, in addition to such others as are assigned to it by the Charter, the following:

(a) To decide the general action and policy of the Organization, determine the structure and functions of its organs, and consider any matter relating to friendly relations among the American States;

(b) To establish measures for coordinating the activities of the organs, agencies, and entities of the Organization among themselves, and such activities with those of the other institutions of the inter-American system;

(c) To strengthen and coordinate cooperation with the United Nations and its specialized agencies;

(d) To promote collaboration, especially in the economic, social, and cultural fields, with other international organizations whose purposes are similar to those of the Organization of American States;

(e) To approve the program-budget of the Organization and determine the quotas of the Member States;

(f) To consider the reports of the Meeting of Consultation of Ministers of Foreign Affairs and the observations and recommendations presented by the Permanent Council with regard to the reports that should be presented by the other organs and entities, in accordance with the provisions of paragraph f of Article 90, as well as the reports of any organ which may be required by the General Assembly itself;

(g) To adopt general standards to govern the operations of the General Secretariat; and

(h) To adopt its own rules of procedure and, by a two-thirds vote, its agenda.

The General Assembly shall exercise its powers in accordance with the provisions of the Charter and of other inter-American treaties.

Article 54. The General Assembly shall establish the bases for fixing the quota that each Government is to contribute to the maintenance of the Organization, taking into account the ability to pay of the respective countries and their determination to contribute in an equitable manner. Decisions on budgetary matters require the approval of two thirds of the Member States.

Article 55. All member States have the right to be represented in the General Assembly. Each State has the right to one vote.

Article 56. The General Assembly shall convene annually during the period determined by the rules of procedure and at a place selected in accordance with the principle of rotation. At each regular session the date and place of the next regular session shall be determined, in accordance with the rules of procedure.

If for any reason the General Assembly cannot be held at the place chosen, it shall meet at the General Secretariat, unless one of the Member States should make a timely offer of a site in its territory, in which case the Permanent Council of the Organization may agree that the General Assembly will meet in that place.

Article 57. In special circumstances and with the approval of two thirds of the Member States, the Permanent Council shall convoke a special session of the General Assembly.

Article 58. Decisions of the General Assembly shall be adopted by the affirmative vote of an absolute majority of the Member States, except in those cases that require a two-thirds vote as provided in the Charter or as may be provided by the General Assembly in its rules of procedure.

Article 59. There shall be a Preparatory Committee of the General Assembly, composed of representatives of all the Member States, which shall:

(a) Prepare the draft agenda of each session of the General Assembly;

(b) Review the proposed program-budget and the draft resolution on quotas, and present to the General Assembly a report thereon containing the recommendations it considers appropriate; and

(c) Carry out such other functions as the General Assembly may assign to it.

The draft agenda and the report shall, in due course, be transmitted to the Governments of the Member States.

Chapter X
The Meeting of Consultation of Ministers
of Foreign Affairs

Article 60. The Meeting of Consultation of Ministers of Foreign Affairs shall be held in order to consider problems of an urgent nature and of common interest to the American States, and to serve as the Organ of Consultation.

Article 61. Any Member State may request that a Meeting of Consultation be called. The request shall be addressed to the Permanent Council of the Organization, which shall decide by an absolute majority whether a meeting should be held.

Article 62. The agenda and regulations of the Meeting of Consultation shall be prepared by the Permanent Council of the Organization and submitted to the Member States for consideration.

Article 63. If, for exceptional reasons, a Minister of Foreign Affairs is unable to attend the meeting, he shall be represented by a special delegate.

Article 64. In case of an armed attack on the territory of an American State or within the region of security delimited by the treaty in force, the Chairman of the Permanent Council shall without delay call a meeting of the Council to decide on the convocation of the Meeting of Consultation, without prejudice to the provisions of the Inter-American Treaty of Reciprocal Assistance with regard to the States Parties to that instrument.

Article 65. An Advisory Defense Committee shall be established to advise the Organ of Consultation on problems of military cooperation that may arise in connection with the application of existing special treaties on collective security.

Article 66. The Advisory Defense Committee shall be composed of the highest military authorities of the American States participating in the Meeting of Consultation. Under exceptional circumstances the Governments may appoint substitutes. Each State shall be entitled to one vote.

Article 67. The Advisory Defense Committee shall be convoked under the same conditions as the Organ of Consultation, when the latter deals with matters relating to defense against aggression.

Article 68. The Committee shall also meet when the General Assembly or the Meeting of Consultation or the Governments, by a two-thirds majority of the Member States, assign to it technical studies or reports on specific subjects.

Chapter XI
The Councils of the Organization

Common Provisions

Article 69. The Permanent Council of the Organization, the Inter-American Economic and Social Council, and the Inter-American Council for Education, Science, and Culture are directly responsible to the General Assembly and each has the authority granted to it in the Charter and other inter-American instruments, as well as the functions assigned to it by the General Assembly and the Meeting of Consultation of Ministers of Foreign Affairs.

Article 70. All Member States have the right to be represented on each of the Councils. Each State has the right to one vote.

Article 71. The Councils may, within the limits of the Charter and other inter-American instruments, make recommendations on matters within their authority.

Article 72. The Councils, on matters within their respective competence, may present to the General Assembly studies and proposals, drafts of international instruments, and proposals on the holding of specialized conferences, on the creation, modification, or elimination of specialized organizations and other inter-American agencies, as well as on the coordination of their activities. The Councils may also present studies, proposals, and drafts of international instruments to the Specialized Conferences.

Article 73. Each Council may, in urgent cases, convoke

Specialized Conferences on matters within its competence, after consulting with the Member States and without having to resort to the procedure provided for in Article 127.

Article 74. The Councils, to the extent of their ability, and with the cooperation of the General Secretariat, shall render to the Governments such specialized services as the latter may request.

Article 75. Each Council has the authority to require the other Councils, as well as the subsidiary organs and agencies responsible to them, to provide it with information and advisory services on matters within their respective spheres of competence. The Councils may also request the same services from the other agencies of the inter-American system.

Article 76. With the prior approval of the General Assembly, the Councils may establish the subsidiary organs and the agencies that they consider advisable for the better performance of their duties. When the General Assembly is not in session, the aforesaid organs or agencies may be established provisionally by the corresponding Council. In constituting the membership of these bodies, the Councils, insofar as possible, shall follow the criteria of rotation and equitable geographic representation.

Article 77. The Councils may hold meetings in any Member State, when they find it advisable and with the prior consent of the Government concerned.

Article 78. Each Council shall prepare its own statutes and submit them to the General Assembly for approval. It shall approve its own rules of procedure and those of its subsidiary organs, agencies, and committees.

Chapter XII
The Permanent Council of the Organization

Article 79. The Permanent Council of the Organization is composed of one representative of each Member State, especially appointed by the respective Government, with the rank of ambassador. Each Government may accredit an acting representative, as well as such alternates and advisers as it considers necessary.

Article 80. The office of Chairman of the Permanent Council shall be held by each of the representatives, in turn, following the alphabetic order in Spanish of the names of their respective countries. The office of Vice Chairman shall be filled in the same way, following reverse alphabetic order.

The Chairman and the Vice Chairman shall hold office for a term of not more than six months, which shall be determined by the statutes.

Article 81. Within the limits of the Charter and of inter-American treaties and agreements, the Permanent Council takes cognizance of any matter referred to it by the General Assembly or the Meeting of Consultation of Ministers of Foreign Affairs.

Article 82. The Permanent Council shall serve provisionally as the Organ of Consultation in conformity with the provisions of the special treaty on the subject.

Article 83. The Permanent Council shall keep vigilance over the maintenance of friendly relations among the Member States, and for that purpose shall effectively assist them in the peaceful settlement of their disputes, in accordance with the following provisions.

Article 84. In accordance with the provisions of this Charter, any party to a dispute in which none of the peaceful procedures provided for in the Charter is under way may resort to the Permanent Council to obtain its good offices.

The Council, following the provisions of the preceding article, shall assist the parties and recommend the procedures it considers suitable for peaceful settlement of the dispute.

Article 85. In the exercise of its functions and with the consent of the parties to the dispute, the Permanent Council may establish ad hoc committees.

The ad hoc committees shall have the membership and the mandate that the Permanent Council agrees upon in each individual case, with the consent of the parties to the dispute.

Article 86. The Permanent Council may also, by such means as it deems advisable, investigate the facts in the dispute, and may do so in the territory of any of the parties, with the consent of the Government concerned.

Article 87. If the procedure for peaceful settlement of disputes recommended by the Permanent Council or suggested by the pertinent ad hoc committee under the terms of its mandate is not accepted by one of the parties, or one of the parties declares that the procedure has not settled the dispute, the Permanent Council shall so inform the General Assembly, without prejudice to its taking steps to secure agreement between the parties or to restore relations between them.

Article 88. The Permanent Council, in the exercise of these functions, shall take its decisions by an affirmative vote of two thirds of its members, excluding the parties to the dispute, except for such decisions as the rules of procedure provide shall be adopted by a simple majority.

Article 89. In performing their functions with respect to the peaceful settlement of disputes, the Permanent Council and the respective ad hoc committee shall observe the provisions of the Charter and the principles and standards of international law, as well as take into account the existence of treaties in force between the parties.

Article 90. The Permanent Council shall also:

(a) Carry out those decisions of the General Assembly or of the Meeting of Consultation of Ministers of Foreign Affairs the implementation of which has not been assigned to any other body;

(b) Watch over the observance of the standards governing the operation of the General Secretariat and, when the General Assembly is not in session, adopt provisions of a regulatory nature that enable the General Secretariat to carry out its administrative functions;

(c) Act as the Preparatory Committee of the General Assembly, in accordance with the terms of Article 59 of the Charter, unless the General Assembly should decide otherwise;

(d) Prepare, at the request of the Member States and with the cooperation of the appropriate organs of the Organization, draft agreements to promote and facilitate cooperation between the Organization of American States and the United Nations or between the Organization and other American agencies of recognized international standing. These draft agreements shall be submitted to the General Assembly for approval;

(e) Submit recommendations to the General Assembly with regard to the functioning of the Organization and the coordination of its subsidiary organs, agencies, and committees;

(f) Consider the reports of the other Councils, of the Inter-American Juridical Committee, of the Inter-American Commission on Human Rights, of the General Secretariat, of specialized agencies and conferences, and of other bodies and agencies, and present to the General Assembly any observations and recommendations it deems necessary; and

(g) Perform the other functions assigned to it in the Charter.

Article 91. The Permanent Council and the General Secretariat shall have the same seat.

Chapter XIII
The Inter-American Economic and Social Council

Article 92. The Inter-American Economic and Social Council is composed of one principal representative, of the highest rank, of each Member State, especially appointed by the respective Government.

Article 93. The purpose of the Inter-American Economic and Social Council is to promote cooperation among the American countries in order to attain accelerated economic and social development, in accordance with the standards set forth in Chapter VII.

Article 94. To achieve its purpose the Inter-American Economic and Social Council shall:

(a) Recommend programs and courses of action and periodically study and evaluate the efforts undertaken by the Member States;

(b) Promote and coordinate all economic and social activities of the Organization;

(c) Coordinate its activities with those of the other Councils of the Organization;

(d) Establish cooperative relations with the corresponding organs of the United Nations and with other national and international agencies, especially with regard to coordination of inter-American technical assistance programs; and

(e) Promote the solution of the cases contemplated in Article 36 of the Charter, establishing the appropriate procedure.

Article 95. The Inter-American Economic and Social Council shall hold at least one meeting each year at the ministerial level. It shall also meet when convoked by the General Assembly, the Meeting of Consultation of Ministers of Foreign Affairs, at its own initiative, or for the cases contemplated in Article 36 of the Charter.

Article 96. The Inter-American Economic and Social Council shall have a Permanent Executive Committee, composed of a Chairman and no less than seven other members, elected by the Council for terms to be established in the statutes of the Council. Each member shall have the right to one vote. The principles of equitable geographic representation and of rotation shall be taken into account, insofar as possible, in the election of members. The Permanent Executive Committee represents all of the Member States of the Organization.

Article 97. The Permanent Executive Committee shall perform the tasks assigned to it by the Inter-American Economic and Social Council, in accordance with the general standards established by the Council.

Chapter XIV
The Inter-American Council for Education, Science, and Culture

Article 98. The Inter-American Council for Education, Science, and Culture is composed of one principal representative, of the highest rank, of each Member State, especially appointed by the respective Government.

Article 99. The purpose of the Inter-American Council for Education, Science, and Culture is to promote friendly relations and mutual understanding between the peoples of the Americas through educational, scientific, and cultural cooperation and exchange between Member States, in order to raise the cultural level of the peoples, reaffirm their dignity as individuals, prepare them fully for the tasks of progress, and strengthen the devotion to peace, democracy, and social justice that has characterized their evolution.

Article 100. To accomplish its purpose the Inter-American Council for Education, Science, and Culture shall:

(a) Promote and coordinate the educational, scientific, and cultural activities of the Organization;

(b) Adopt or recommend pertinent measures to give effect to the standards contained in Chapter VII of the Charter;

(c) Support individual or collective efforts of the Member States to improve and extend education at all levels, giving special attention to efforts directed toward community development;

(d) Recommend and encourage the adoption of special educational programs directed toward integrating all sectors of the population into their respective national cultures;

(e) Stimulate and support scientific and technological education and research, especially when these relate to national development plans;

(f) Foster the exchange of professors, research workers, technicians, and students, as well as of study materials; and encourage the conclusion of bilateral or multilateral agreements on the progressive coordination of curricula at all educational levels and on the validity and equivalence of certificates and degrees;

(g) Promote the education of the American peoples with a view to harmonious international relations and a better understanding of the historical and cultural origins of the Americas, in order to stress and preserve their common values and destiny;

(h) Systematically encourage intellectual and artistic creativity, the exchange of cultural works and folklore, as well as the interrelationships of the different cultural regions of the Americas;

(i) Foster cooperation and technical assistance for protecting, preserving, and increasing the cultural heritage of the Hemisphere;

(j) Coordinate its activities with those of the other Councils. In harmony with the Inter-American Economic and Social Council, encourage the interrelationship of programs for promoting education, science, and culture with national development and regional integration programs;

(k) Establish cooperative relations with the corresponding organs of the United Nations and with other national and international bodies;

(l) Strengthen the civic conscience of the American peoples, as one of the bases for the effective exercise of democracy and for the observance of the rights and duties of man;

(m) Recommend appropriate procedures for intensifying integration of the developing countries of the Hemisphere by means of efforts and programs in the fields of education, science, and culture; and

(n) Study and evaluate periodically the efforts made by the Member States in the fields of education, science, and culture.

Article 101. The Inter-American Council for Education, Science, and Culture shall hold at least one meeting each year at the ministerial level. It shall also meet when convoked by the General Assembly, by the Meeting of Consultation of Ministers of Foreign Affairs, or at its own initiative.

Article 102. The Inter-American Council for Education, Science, and Culture shall have a Permanent Executive Committee, composed of a Chairman and no less than seven other members, elected by the Council for terms to be established in the statutes of the Council. Each member shall have the right to one vote. The principles of equitable geographic representation and of rotation shall be taken into account, insofar as possible, in the election of members. The Permanent Executive Committee represents all of the Member States of the Organization.

Article 103. The Permanent Executive Committee shall perform the tasks assigned to it by the Inter-American Council for Education, Science, and Culture, in accordance with the general standards established by the Council.

Chapter XV
The Inter-American Juridical Committee

Article 104. The purpose of the Inter-American Juridical Committee is to serve the Organization as an advisory body on juridical matters; to promote the progressive development and the codification of international law; and to study juridical problems related to the integration of the developing countries of the Hemisphere and, insofar as may appear desirable, the possibility of attaining uniformity in their legislation.

Article 105. The Inter-American Juridical Committee shall undertake the studies and preparatory work assigned to it by the General Assembly, the Meeting of Consultation of Ministers of Foreign Affairs, or the Councils of the Organization. It may also, on its own initiative, undertake such studies and preparatory work as it considers advisable, and suggest the holding of specialized juridical conferences.

Article 106. The Inter-American Juridical Committee shall be composed of eleven jurists, nationals of Member States, elected by the General Assembly for a period of four years from panels of three candidates presented by Member States. In the election, a system shall be used that takes into account partial replacement of membership and, insofar as possible, equitable geographic representation. No two members of the Committee may be nationals of the same State.

Vacancies that occur for reasons other than normal expiration of the terms of office of the members of the Committee shall be filled by the Permanent Council of the Organization in accordance with the criteria set forth in the preceding paragraph.

Article 107. The Inter-American Juridical Committee represents all of the Member States of the Organization, and has the broadest possible technical autonomy.

Article 108. The Inter-American Juridical Committee shall establish cooperative relations with universities, institutes, and other teaching centers, as well as with national and international committees and entities devoted to study, research, teaching, or dissemination of information on juridical matters of international interest.

Article 109. The Inter-American Juridical Committee shall draft its statutes, which shall be submitted to the General Assembly for approval.

The Committee shall adopt its own rules of procedure.

Article 110. The seat of the Inter-American Juridical Committee shall be the city of Rio de Janeiro, but in special cases the Committee may meet at any other place that may be designated, after consultation with the Member State concerned.

Chapter XVI
The Inter-American Commission on Human Rights

Article 111. There shall be an Inter-American Commission on Human Rights, whose principal function shall be to promote the observance and protection of human rights and to serve as a consultative organ of the Organization in these matters.

An inter-American convention on human rights shall determine the structure, competence, and procedure of this Commission, as well as those of other organs responsible for these matters.

Chapter XVII
The General Secretariat

Article 112. The General Secretariat is the central and permanent organ of the Organization of American States. It shall perform the functions assigned to it in the Charter, in other inter-American treaties and agreements, and by the General Assembly, and shall carry out the duties entrusted to it by the General Assembly, the Meeting of Consultation of Ministers of Foreign Affairs, or the Councils.

Article 113. The Secretary General of the Organization shall be elected by the General Assembly for a five-year term and may not be reelected more than once or succeeded by a person of the same nationality. In the event that the office of Secretary General becomes vacant, the Assistant Secretary General shall assume his duties until the General Assembly shall elect a new Secretary General for a full term.

Article 114. The Secretary General shall direct the General Secretariat, be the legal representative thereof, and, notwithstanding the provisions of Article 90.b, be responsible to the General Assembly for the proper fulfillment of the obligations and functions of the General Secretariat.

Article 115. The Secretary General, or his representative, may participate with voice but without vote in all meetings of the Organization.

The Secretary General may bring to the attention of the General Assembly or the Permanent Council any matter which in his opinion might threaten the peace and security of the Hemisphere or the development of the Member States.

The authority to which the preceding paragraph refers shall be exercised in accordance with the present Charter.

Article 116. The General Secretariat shall promote economic, social, juridical, educational, scientific, and cultural relations among all the Member States of the Organization, in keeping with the actions and policies decided upon by the General Assembly and with the pertinent decisions of the Councils.

Article 117. The General Secretariat shall also perform the following functions:

(a) Transmit *ex officio* to the Member States notice of the convocation of the General Assembly, the Meeting of Consultation of Ministers of Foreign Affairs, the Inter-American Economic and Social Council, the Inter-American Council for Education, Science, and Culture, and the Specialized Conferences;

(b) Advise the other organs, when appropriate, in the preparation of agenda and rules of procedure;

(c) Prepare the proposed program-budget of the Organization on the basis of programs adopted by the Councils, agencies, and entities whose expenses should be included in the program-budget and, after consultation with the Councils or their permanent committees, submit it to the Preparatory Committee of the General Assembly and then to the Assembly itself;

(d) Provide, on a permanent basis, adequate secretariat services for the General Assembly and the other organs, and carry out their directives and assignments. To the extent of its ability, provide services for the other meetings of the Organization;

(e) Serve as custodian of the documents and archives of the Inter-American Conferences, the General Assembly, the Meetings of Consultation of Ministers of Foreign Affairs, the Councils, and the Specialized Conferences;

(f) Serve as depository of inter-American treaties and agreements, as well as of the instruments of ratification thereof;

(g) Submit to the General Assembly at each regular session an annual report on the activities of the Organization and its financial condition; and

(h) Establish relations of cooperation, in accordance with decisions reached by the General Assembly or the Councils, with the Specialized Organizations as well as other national and international organizations.

Article 118. The Secretary General shall:

(a) Establish such offices of the General Secretariat as are necessary to accomplish its purposes; and

(b) Determine the number of officers and employees of the General Secretariat, appoint them, regulate their powers and duties, and fix their remuneration.

The Secretary General shall exercise this authority in accordance with such general standards and budgetary provisions as may be established by the General Assembly.

Article 119. The Assistant Secretary General shall be elected by the General Assembly for a five-year term and may not be reelected more than once or succeeded by a person of the same nationality. In the event that the office of Assistant Secretary General becomes vacant, the Permanent Council shall elect a substitute to hold that office until the General Assembly shall elect a new Assistant Secretary General for a full term.

Article 120. The Assistant Secretary General shall be the Secretary of the Permanent Council. He shall serve as advisory officer to the Secretary General and shall act as his delegate in all matters that the Secretary General may entrust to him. During the temporary absence or disability of the Secretary General, the Assistant Secretary General shall perform his functions.

The Secretary General and the Assistant Secretary General shall be of different nationalities.

Article 121. The General Assembly, by a two-thirds vote of the Member States, may remove the Secretary General or the Assistant Secretary General, or both, whenever the proper functioning of the Organization so demands.

Article 122. The Secretary General shall appoint, with the approval of the respective Council, the Executive Secretary for Economic and Social Affairs and the Executive Secretary for Education, Science, and Culture, who shall also be the secretaries of the respective Councils.

Article 123. In the performance of their duties, the Secretary General and the personnel of the Secretariat shall not seek or receive instructions from any Government or from any authority outside the Organization, and shall refrain from any action that may be incompatible with their position as international officers responsible only to the Organization.

Article 124. The Member States pledge themselves to respect the exclusively international character of the responsibilities of the Secretary General and the personnel of the General Secretariat, and not to seek to influence them in the discharge of their duties.

Article 125. In selecting the personnel of the General Secretariat, first consideration shall be given to efficiency, competence, and integrity; but at the same time, in the recruitment of personnel of all ranks, importance shall be given to the necessity of obtaining as wide a geographic representation as possible.

Article 126. The seat of the General Secretariat is the city of Washington, D.C.

Chapter XVIII
The Specialized Conferences

Article 127. The Specialized Conferences are intergovernmental meetings to deal with special technical matters or to develop specific aspects of inter-American cooperation. They shall be held when either the General Assembly or the Meeting of Consultation of Ministers of Foreign Affairs so decides, on its own initiative or at the request of one of the Councils or Specialized Organizations.

Article 128. The agenda and rules of procedure of the Specialized Conferences shall be prepared by the Councils or Specialized Organizations concerned and shall be submitted to the Governments of the Member States for consideration.

Chapter XIX
The Specialized Organizations

Article 129. For the purposes of the present Charter, Inter-American Specialized Organizations are the intergovernmental organizations established by multilateral agreements and having specific functions with respect to technical matters of common interest to the American States.

Article 130. The General Secretariat shall maintain a register of the organizations that fulfill the conditions set forth in the foregoing Article, as determined by the General Assembly after a report from the Council concerned.

Article 131. The Specialized Organizations shall enjoy the fullest technical autonomy, but they shall take into account the recommendations of the General Assembly and of the Councils, in accordance with the provisions of the Charter.

Article 132. The Specialized Organizations shall transmit to the General Assembly annual reports on the progress of their work and on their annual budgets and expenses.

Article 133. Relations that should exist between the Specialized Organizations and the Organization shall be defined by means of agreements concluded between each organization and the Secretary General, with the authorization of the General Assembly.

Article 134. The Specialized Organizations shall establish cooperative relations with world agencies of the same character in order to coordinate their activities. In concluding agreements with international agencies of a worldwide character, the Inter-American Specialized Organizations shall preserve their identity and their status as integral parts of the Organization of American States, even when they perform regional functions of international agencies.

Article 135. In determining the location of the Specialized Organizations consideration shall be given to the interest of all of the Member States and to the desirability of selecting the seats of these organizations on the basis of a geographic representation as equitable as possible.

O

Part Three

Chapter XX
The United Nations

Article 136. None of the provisions of this Charter shall be construed as impairing the rights and obligations of the Member States under the Charter of the United Nations.

Chapter XXI
Miscellaneous Provisions

Article 137. Attendance at meetings of the permanent organs of the Organization of American States or at the conferences and meetings provided for in the Charter, or held under the auspices of the Organization, shall be in accordance with the multilateral character of the aforesaid organs, conferences, and meetings and shall not depend on the bilateral relations between the Government of any Member State and the Government of the host country.

Article 138. The Organization of American States shall enjoy in the territory of each Member such legal capacity, privileges, and immunities as are necessary for the exercise of its functions and the accomplishment of its purposes.

Article 139. The representatives of the Member States on the organs of the Organization, the personnel of their delegations, as well as the Secretary General and the Assistant Secretary General shall enjoy the privileges and immunities corresponding to their positions and necessary for the independent performance of their duties.

Article 140. The juridical status of the Specialized Organizations and the privileges and immunities that should be granted to them and to their personnel, as well as to the officials of the General Secretariat, shall be determined in a multilateral agreement. The foregoing shall not preclude, when it is considered necessary, the concluding of bilateral agreements.

Article 141. Correspondence of the Organization of American States, including printed matter and parcels, bearing the frank thereof, shall be carried free of charge in the mails of the Member States.

Article 142. The Organization of American States does not allow any restriction based on race, creed, or sex, with respect to eligibility to participate in the activities of the Organization and to hold positions therein.

Article 143. Within the provisions of this Charter, the competent organs shall endeavor to obtain greater collaboration from countries not members of the Organization in the area of cooperation for development.

Chapter XXII
Ratification and Entry Into Force

Article 144. The present Charter shall remain open for signature by the American States and shall be ratified in accordance with their respective constitutional procedures. The original instrument, the Spanish, English, Portuguese, and French texts of which are equally authentic, shall be deposited with the General Secretariat, which shall transmit certified copies thereof to the Governments for purposes of ratification. The instruments of ratification shall be deposited with the General Secretariat, which shall notify the signatory States of such deposit.

Article 145. The present Charter shall enter into force among the ratifying States when two thirds of the signatory States have deposited their ratifications. It shall enter into force with respect to the remaining States in the order in which they deposit their ratifications.

Article 146. The present Charter shall be registered with the Secretariat of the United Nations through the General Secretariat.

Article 147. Amendments to the present Charter may be adopted only at a General Assembly convened for that purpose. Amendments shall enter into force in accordance with the terms and the procedure set forth in Article 145.

Article 148. The present Charter shall remain in force indefinitely, but may be denounced by any Member State upon written notification to the General Secretariat, which shall communicate to all the others each notice of denunciation received. After two years from the date on which the General Secretariat receives a notice of denunciation, the present Charter shall cease to be in force with respect to the denouncing State, which shall cease to belong to the Organization after it has fulfilled the obligations arising from the present Charter.

Chapter XXIII
Transitory Provisions

Article 149. The Inter-American Committee on the Alliance for Progress shall act as the permanent executive committee of the Inter-American Economic and Social Council as long as the Alliance is in operation.

Article 150. Until the inter-American convention on human rights, referred to in Chapter XVI, enters into force, the present Inter-American Commission on Human Rights shall keep vigilance over the observance of human rights.

Article 151. The Permanent Council shall not make any recommendation nor shall the General Assembly take any decision with respect to a request for admission on the part of a political entity whose territory became subject, in whole or in part, prior to December 18, 1964, the date set by the First Special Inter-American Conference, to litigation or claim between an extracontinental country and one or more Member States of the Organization, until the dispute has been ended by some peaceful procedure. This article shall remain in effect until December 10, 1990.

P

PAKISTAN. The Islamic Republic of Pakistan is a country in southern Asia occupying the northwestern portion of the Indian sub-continent, on the Arabian Sea. It has borders with Afghanistan, India, and Iran. It achieved independence from Great Britain in 1947 and became a member of the United Nations the same year. Its population is estimated by the UN (1990) to be 112,226,000. Ethnic groups include Baluchi, Pathan, Punjabi, Sindhi, and Urdu-speaking Indian elements; precise data on ethnic origin are not collected by the government. Languages commonly used include Urdu (official), Baluchi, English, Punjabi, Pushto, and Sindhi. Islam is the predominant religion, accounting for about 97% of those who profess a religious belief; Christianity and Hinduism account for the remaining 3%. Literacy is estimated at 26%.

The government (1990) took the form of a republic. The military dictatorship of President Mohammed Zia ul-Haq, who came to power in a military coup in 1977 when he deposed Prime Minister Zulfikar Ali Bhutto, ended on 17 August 1988 when the dictator died in an unexplained airplane crash. In free national elections held in November 1988, the Pakistan People's Party won 92 of 215 contested seats in the lower house of Parliament and its leader, Benazir Bhutto—daughter of the former prime minister—was given a chance to form a government by Acting President Ghulam Ishaq Khan. She succeeded in doing so over the opposition of the Islamic Democratic Alliance led by former supporters of General Zia. Other political parties include the Awami National Party, composed largely of ethnic Pathans, and the Mohajir Qaumi Movement, composed largely of descendents of Indians who migrated to Pakistan when British India was divided in 1947.

Created in 1947 out of areas of British India that were predominantly Muslim in population, Pakistan has endeavored to ensure that the rights of its minorities are protected and that minority members do not face any problems which are peculiar to their belonging to a minority community. A Ministry of Minorities' Affairs has been established to deal with (a) safeguarding the rights of minorities, (b) promo-

tion of the welfare of minorities, (c) protection of minorities against discrimination, (d) international agreements and commitments in respect of minorities and their implementation, and (e) all other matters relating to minorities.

The government of Pakistan stated, in a report presented to the **COMMITTEE ON THE ELIMINATION OF RACIAL DISCRIMINATION** in 1986 (UN Doc. CERD/C/149/Add. 12) that it is "committed to protecting and promoting the cultural identity of minorities" in accordance with the constitution which provides that "any section of citizens having a distinct language, script or culture shall have the right to preserve and promote the same and subject to law established institutions for that purpose."

As regards people living in the tribal areas (federally administered tribal areas consisting of seven agencies and four frontier regions and having a population of 2,175,000), their participation in the national decisionmaking process is ensured through constitutional provisions and administrative instructions; their representation is eight seats in the National Assembly and an equal number of seats in the Senate. In addition, a special quota is reserved in central superior and other services for tribal people to facilitate their entry into the service of Pakistan and provincial services.

With reference to one religious community in Pakistan, the **SUB-COMMISSION ON PREVENTION OF DISCRIMINATION AND PROTECTION OF MINORITIES,** in resolution 1985/21 of 29 August 1985, expressed grave concern over Government Ordinance No. XX of 1984 which appeared to single out the Ahmadis for differential treatment. The ordinance, promulgated "to amend the law to prohibit the Quadiani group and Ahmadis from indulging in anti-Islamic activities," was said by the sub-commission to violate "the right to liberty and security of persons, the right to freedom from arbitrary arrest or detention, the right to freedom of thought, expression, conscience and religion, the right of religious minorities to profess and practice their own religion, and the right to an effective legal remedy." The sub-commission further expressed concern that persons charged with and arrested for violations of the ordinance had reportedly been subjected to various punishments and confiscation of personal property and that the affected groups as a whole had been subjected to discrimination in employment and education and to the defacement of their religious property. The sub-commission requested the COMMISSION ON HUMAN RIGHTS to call on the government of Pakistan to repeal Ordinance XX and to restore the human rights and fundamental freedoms of all persons within its jurisdiction and alerted the commission to the situation in Pakistan which, in its view, was one with great potential to cause a mass exodus, especially of members of the Ahmadi community.

The commission took no action on the sub-commission's request at any open meeting of its 1986 session, and the sub-commission did not meet in August of that year, as scheduled, because of financial constraints. Towards the close of the commission's 1987 session, on 6 March 1987, the ANTI-SLAVERY SOCIETY FOR THE PROTECTION OF HUMAN RIGHTS, a non-governmental organization in consultative status, circulated a communication to the commission entitled "Violations of Basic Human Rights of Ahmadi Muslims in Pakistan" (UN Doc. E/CN.4/1987/NGO/67) which read as follows:

Since the promulgation of Ordinance XX of 26 April 1984 by the then military Government of Pakistan, fundamental human rights of members of the Ahmadiyya Muslim Community in Pakistan have been violated persistently. The following few facts may be noted by all whose concern is the protection of human rights all over the world:

(1) Ordinance XX forbids in clear, unequivocal terms members of the Ahmadiyya Muslim Community in Pakistan to profess, practise and propagate their beliefs, a fact which cannot be denied by any "interpretation" of the said Ordinance;

(2) President Zia of Pakistan declared in a message to an anti-Ahmadiyya conference held in London on 5 August 1985, his measures to "exterminate the cancer of Ahmadiyyat". This, too, is a documented fact;

(3) The Sub-Commission on Prevention of Discrimination and Protection of Minorities in its findings came to the conclusion that the Government of Pakistan was guilty of grossly violating human rights of Ahmadi Muslims. (See resolution 1985/21 of 29 August 1985);

(4) Both the Universal Declaration of Human Rights and the Constitution of Pakistan (art. 20) guarantee the right of religious freedom, whereas Ordinance XX contravenes these provisions;

(5) The issue of a passport is refused to a Muslim in Pakistan if he does not declare in writing that the Founder of the Ahmadiyya Movement in Islam was a liar and an impostor.

Martial law was in force until 30 December 1985. Our organization was told that the lifting of martial law would allow things to improve and normal conditions would return. Yet, in the case of Ahmadi Muslims things have even worsened and their persecution continues unabated, with greater backing by the authorities. Some more facts in this connection may also be noted:

(i) The provisions of Ordinance XX, which was challenged by the Sub-Commission as a grave violation of basic human rights, have been incorporated in the Constitution of the country, thus perpetuating the "legalized" persecution of Ahmadi Muslims;

(ii) Although martial law was lifted on 30 December 1985, sentences of death against two Ahmadi Muslims were announced in February 1986 as having been passed by a special military court (Sahiwal case);

(iii) Two weeks after the above sentences, two more death sentences by a military court were announced in the Sukkur case against Ahmadi Muslims;

(iv) On 11 May 1986, two Ahmadis were brutally murdered in Sukkur;

(v) On 9 May 1986, the Ahmadiyya mosque in Quetta was attacked by a mob under the very eyes of local authorities; 85 Ahmadis were taken into custody, and the mosque was sealed by police;

(vi) On 9 June 1986, an Ahmadi lady was shot dead in Mardan for having visited the Ahmadiyya mosque to offer her prayers;

(vii) That mosque was later (on 17 August 1986) razed to the ground with police and other government officials as onlookers;

(viii) On 9 July 1986, an ex-Amir of Hyderabad was stabbed to death;

(ix) On 9 September 1986, an Ahmadi Muslim of Peshawar was sentenced to seven years gaol and a fine of PRs 10,000 for wearing the insignia bearing his article of faith;

(x) For the same "crime", two more Ahmadi Muslims were sentenced on 17 September 1986 in Mardan to five years gaol and a fine of PRs 25,000 each;

(xi) On 9 September 1986, an Ahmadi of Rabwah was shot dead in Darra Adam Khel;

(xii) In early February 1987, two Ahmadi Muslims of Lyallpur (Faisalabad) were taken to gaol in handcuffs for having displayed the words "Is God not sufficient for His servant?" and "O Living One, the Sustainer". The logic behind these arrests being that such professions of faith by Ahmadi Muslims "injured the religious feelings" of others;

(xiii) The latest news which reached our organization in March 1987 is that yet another Ahmadi Muslim has been murdered in cold blood in the District of Jhelum.

It becomes quite obvious from these incidents that the persecution of Ahmadis in Pakistan has been stepped up since martial law was lifted. The Government is getting itself involved more and more in the campaign of "exterminating" the "cancer" of Ahmadiyyat. These incidents show beyond doubt that the findings of the Sub-Commission were right and its fears well-based.

The Anti-Slavery Society for the Protection of Human Rights urges the Commission on Human Rights to pay greater attention to the simple enough request made by the Sub-Commission in its resolution 1985/21 of 29 August 1985.

The government of Prime Minister Benazir Bhutto has strong support from the voters of Pakistan, who are proud to have elected a woman as head of an Islamic State and also proud to have returned their country to democracy without demonstrations, violence, or bloodshed. However opposition leaders, joined in the Islamic Democratic Alliance, have sought to remove her from power either by charging her with corruption or favoritism or by presenting motions of "no-confidence" in the National Assembly. Such a motion, put to the vote on 1 November 1989, was supported by 107 of the 236 members—only 12 short of the 119 votes required for passage.

Pakistan's most serious problem of recent years—providing refuge for three million refugees from neighboring Afghanistan—has eased considerably as Soviet troops withdrew; however, the continued political uncertainty in Afghanistan has not permitted a final settlement to be achieved.

PALESTINE LIBERATION ORGANIZATION (PLO).

An organization representing the Palestinian people which participates in the work of the UN General Assembly and other United Nations organs as an observer.

The assembly granted observer status to the PLO on 22 November 1974 (resolution 3237 [XXIX]), and to the SOUTH WEST AFRICA PEOPLE'S ORGANIZATION (SWAPO) on 20 December 1976 (resolution 31/152). Later, on 9 December 1988, it decided (resolution 43/160) that both organizations were entitled to have their communications relating to the sessions and the work of the assembly issued and circulated directly, and without intermediary, as official assembly documents; and that both were also entitled to have their communications relating to the sessions and work of all international conferences issued and circulated directly, and without intermediary, as official documents of such conferences. These steps were taken with a view to facilitating the work of the two organizations.

At the 1989 General Assembly session a number of States submitted and supported the adoption of a draft resolution aimed at recognition of the Palestine Liberation Organization as the government of an independent Palestinian State. The proposal was vigorously opposed by the United States of America, the Union of Soviet Socialist Republics, and by a number of developing countries. The sponsors of the draft resolution, however, did not press it to a vote.

PALESTINIAN PEOPLE'S RIGHTS. In its first re-
port, submitted to the UN General Assembly in 1976 (UN Doc. A/31/35), the COMMITTEE ON THE EXERCISE OF THE INALIENABLE RIGHTS OF THE PALESTINIAN PEOPLE made a number of recommendations designed to enable the Palestinian people to attain and exercise its human rights in Palestine. These recommendations were first endorsed by the General Assembly on 24 No-

vember 1976 (resolution 31/20) as a basis for the solution of the question of Palestine. The recommendations are reproduced below (Annex).

In each of its subsequent annual reports to the Assembly, the committee reaffirmed the original recommendations and called for their implementation. On each occasion, they were endorsed overwhelmingly by the Assembly, which has repeatedly renewed and, as necessary, expanded the committee's mandate. However, despite the increasing urgency of the appeals by the committee, the recommendations have not been acted on by the Security Council.

In its report to the 1988 session of the General Assembly (UN Doc. A/43/35), the committee pointed out that, during that year, its efforts to promote a comprehensive, just, and lasting solution to the Arab–Israeli conflict—the core of which is the question of Palestine—had acquired particular urgency in light of the grave deterioration of the situation in the occupied Palestinian territories as a consequence of the repressive policies and practices of Israel, the occupying power, in its efforts to quell the Palestinian uprising (INTIFADAH) against the occupation, which began in December 1987. The committee expressed the greatest concern at the mounting casualties and suffering inflicted on the Palestinian people and warned that the intransigience of Israel would further exacerbate the situation, jeopardize international efforts towards a just and lasting settlement, and further endanger international peace and security. The committee reasserted its view that no solution could be achieved as long as Palestinians are denied their inlienable rights in Palestine, including those to SELF-DETERMINATION without external interference, to national independence and sovereignty, to return to their homes and property, and to establish their own sovereign State, and as long as the Palestinian and other Arab territories remained occupied.

In the report, the committee summarized its recommendations in the following terms (UN Doc. A/43/35, para. 141–148):

The year under review was marked by the courageous uprising (the *intifadah*) of the Palestinian people in the occupied Palestinian territories against 20 years of Israeli occupation and for the achievement of its inalienable rights. The uprising brought to a new level the understanding of the question of Palestine and support for a comprehensive, just and lasting solution of this long-standing conflict among public opinion internationally and within Israel itself. The intensification of repressive measures by Israel, the occupying Power, in an effort to crush the uprising and its armed attacks against States in the region have been universally condemned and have aroused the most serious concern for the safety of the Palestinian people under occupation. The situation has given a new impetus to efforts to reach a peaceful settlement in accordance with

United Nations resolutions and particularly through the convening of the International Peace Conference on the Middle East as called for in General Assembly resolutions 38/58 C and 41/43 D.

The Committee reaffirms that, in view of the critical situation, urgent positive action by the Security Council is required on the recommendations formulated by the Committee in its first report and those adopted by the International Conference on the Question of Palestine held at Geneva in 1983, which have been repeatedly endorsed by the General Assembly, and annexes them to the present report (annex I, reproduced below). The Committee reaffirms that these recommendations are solidly founded on fundamental and internationally accepted principles and that the recognition, attainment and exercise of the inalienable rights of the Palestinian people are indispensable conditions in the solution of the question of Palestine, the core of the Arab-Israeli conflict in the Middle East. The Committee further reasserts that the Israeli evacuation of the territories occupied by force and in violation of the principles of the Charter and relevant resolutions of the United Nations is a *conditio sine qua non* for the exercise by the Palestinian people of its inalienable rights in Palestine.

The Committee noted the action taken by the Central Council of the Palestine Liberation Organization in the light of the decision of Jordan relative to the West Bank, and the response of the Executive Committee of the Palestine Liberation Organization to assume full responsibility to maintain as well the functioning of the administrative structure in the occupied Palestinian territories of the West Bank and the Gaza Strip. The Committee asserts that the question of representation of the Palestinian people is definitively settled and the Palestine Liberation Organization is the sole and legitimate representative of the Palestinian people. The Committee noted the universal demand for the withdrawal of Israeli forces from the occupied Palestinian people to establish its own independent sovereign State on Palestinian territory, voiced by participants in seminars and NGO symposia and meetings organized under the Committee's auspices, as well as by many intergovernmental organizations and Governments.

The Committee is convinced that these important developments open the way for the Palestinian people to establish an independent Arab State in Palestine as envisaged in General Assembly resolution 181 (II) of 29 November 1947, which has only been implemented in part. The Committee is further convinced that the United Nations and the international community as a whole must now urgently intensify their efforts to bring this about.

The Committee considers that it has now become imperative for the Security Council to take positive action towards the convening of the International Peace Conference on the Middle East in accordance with the guidelines and other provisions contained in General Assembly resolutions 38/58 C and 41/43 D. That Conference remains the most comprehensive and widely accepted proposal for the attainment of a peaceful settlement. The Committee appeals to the Secretary-General to do everything in his power to ensure that active consultations are undertaken within the framework of the Security Council for this purpose. In the past year, the international consensus in favour of the convening of the Conference has clearly been consolidated. The Committee therefore intends to further intensify its efforts towards this objective, and to make it once again the focal point of its work programme in the coming year.

Noting that the Secretary-General has reported that sufficient agreement does not exist, either among the parties directly concerned or within the Security Council, to permit the convening of the Conference, the Committee recommends that the General Assembly should call once again for additional concrete and constructive efforts by all Governments, in particular the permanent members of the Security Council, for the convening of the Conference and for setting up the preparatory committee for the Conference in accordance with General Assembly resolution 41/43 D; and renew the mandate of the Secretary-General, in consultation with the Security Council, to continue his efforts with a view to convening the Conference.

Pending the attainment by the Palestinian people of its inalienable rights, the Committee wishes to reaffirm in the strongest terms the urgent need for effective measures to ensure the safety and protection of the Palestinian population in the occupied Palestinian territories. The Committee calls on the international community, and in particular on the High Contracting Parties to the Geneva Convention relative to the Protection of Civilian Persons in Time of War, to do all in their power to ensure respect for the Convention by Israel, the occupying Power. The Committee calls on the Security Council to take the necessary measures to ensure compliance by Israel with Security Council resolutions 605 (1987), 607 (1988) and 608 (1988). The Committee also calls upon the Security Council to act positively on the recommendations of the Secretary-General contained in his report submitted under resolution 605 (1987) (S/19443), and in particular to make a solemn appeal to the High Contracting Parties to the Fourth Geneva Convention that have diplomatic relations with Israel, drawing their attention to their obligation to ensure respect for the Convention in all circumstances and urging them to use all the means at their disposal to urge Israel to abide by and to give effect to the provisions of the Convention. The Committee also calls upon the Security Council to give positive consideration to the Secretary-General's recommendations and observations concerning other ways and means available to the international community, including physical protection, legal protection, general assistance, and protection by publicity. The Committee further calls on the international organizations to sustain and increase their assistance to the Palestinian people, in close co-operation with the PLO.

The Committee noted with satisfaction the increased awareness and mobilization of international public opinion in support of the inalienable rights of the Palestinian people and of United Nations recommendations for a comprehensive, just and lasting solution of the Palestinian question. The Committee believes that its programme of regional seminars and NGO meetings and symposia, as well as the journalists' encounters and other informational activities sponsored by the Committee, have played a valuable role in this process, and will continue to strive to achieve maximum effectiveness in carrying out this programme and to intensify its efforts in the implementation of its mandate.

In its report to the 1989 session of the assembly (UN Doc. A/44/35), the committee reviewed the situation relating to the question of Palestine and efforts to implement its recommendations as follows (chap. IV, para. 20-31):

The Committee was alarmed at the further aggravation of the situation in the occupied Palestinian territory as a result of the intensification of efforts by Israel to suppress the Palestinian *intifadah*, including the increasing resort to armed force and settler vigilantism, and other Draconian measures.

The Committee monitored the situation in the occupied Palestinian territory on an ongoing basis through the media, the reports of United Nations organs and agencies, as well as information collected by non-governmental organizations, individual experts and persons from the occupied territory who participated in meetings held under the auspices of the Committee, Governments and other sources .

The Committee noted that the *intifadah*, the uprising of the Palestinian people against military occupation and gradual annexation by Israel of the Palestinian territory occupied since 1967, had continued despite overwhelming odds since 9 December 1987. Palestinians, often children and youths, have continued to challenge the Israeli occupying forces with stones, barricades, burning tyres *[sic]* and other means. In order to suppress the *intifadah*, the Israeli troops have resorted to excessive and indiscriminate use of force, which was reported to have been condoned and even encouraged at the highest level of government, with the apparent intent to punish and intimidate the population, resulting in an extensive and unprecedented range of human rights violations. Live ammunition, including rubber and plastic bullets fired at close range, was used liberally and increasingly, even in non-life-threatening situations. There was an apparently deliberate misuse of tear gas, fired, for example, into hospitals or homes. Thousands of Palestinians were the victims of beatings, deliberately aimed at breaking bones, while in the hands of the army or security personnel. As at 15 September 1989, according to the Data-Base Project on Palestinian Human Rights, a respected human rights organization, the number of Palestinians shot to death by the Israeli forces or armed settlers had reached a total of 537 identified cases. Another 212 Palestinians had died from beatings, suffocation from tear gas, and other causes related to actions by the occupying forces. The Committee was particularly alarmed at what appeared to be the deliberate targeting of children in such attacks, as at least 20 per cent of the fatalities were children under 16. That percentage had increased to 28 per cent since March 1989 and 46 per cent during the month of August 1989.

In addition to protest demonstrations, mass strikes and tax boycotts have been organized by Palestinians in the occupied territory, and hundreds of popular committees have been set up with the objective of creating alternative structures to the Israeli Civil Administration. Initially organized to provide food and medical supplies to refugee camps under curfew, those committees were then reported to have grown and to have expanded their goals. They became responsible for the co-ordination of strike activities, alternative education, health needs, guard duties and the organization of a survival economy centred on a return to family agriculture. A number of Palestinian employees of the Israeli Civil Administration, particularly police officials, have resigned from their posts.

The Israeli authorities have resorted to increasingly harsh measures in their attempt to suppress such activities. A number of Palestinian newspapers and institutions were closed down and the popular committees proscribed. Currency restrictions were introduced to control money going to families and institutions in the occupied territory. New identity cards were issued in the Gaza Strip to monitor the population more closely. Sixty Palestinians were deported in violation of the fourth Geneva Convention relative to the Protection of Civilian Persons in Time of War, of 12 August 1949, and numerous Security Council resolutions. Villages, towns and refugee camps have been put under prolonged curfew, sometimes for a month or more, during which time electricity, water and telephones have often been disconnected and food and medical supplies interrupted. At least 100,000 productive trees have been uprooted and crops ruined. There was a dramatic increase in the number of house demolitions in the past year, as a form of punishment of entire villages for supporting the *intifadah*. At least 236 Palestinian homes were destroyed for "security" reasons between December 1987 and August 1989, while another 675 buildings were destroyed on the pretext that they had been built illegally.

The Committee noted that, in their efforts to suppress the Palestinian leadership of the *intifadah*, the Israeli authorities had waged campaigns of mass arrests. It was estimated that, as at September 1989, more than 40,000 Palestinians had been in prison at one time or another, of whom only 18,000 had actually been sentenced. The Israeli authorities had also increasingly relied on the use of administrative detention without detention orders was extended to all officers with the rank of colonel and above. At the same time, previously existing judicial safeguards, which gave the detainees a measure of protection, were removed. Lawyers representing Palestinian detainees have maintained that the withholding of evidence for "security reasons" and administrative and other practical obstacles imposed by the Israeli authorities have made it nearly impossible to represent their clients properly. In August, the standard period of administrative detention was doubled from six months to a year. It was reported that administrative detention was increasingly used to detain prisoners of conscience. All sectors of Palestinian society were included, such as trade unionists, students, journalists, doctors, lawyers, academics, teachers, members of voluntary organizations and human rights workers, as well as labourers and the unemployed. About 13,600 Palestinians, including children, were reported to be in detention as at September 1989, 4,400 of whom were held under harsh conditions at the Ansar III camp in the Negev desert in Israel, where they had been taken in violation of the provisions of the fourth Geneva Convention.

The Committee was gravely concerned at the intensification of violations of the Palestinians' right to education during the second year of the *intifadah*. Measures taken by the occupying Power included the complete closure of universities and the long-term and repeated closure of schools, the prohibition of home study and compensation classes in alternative locations, the use of schools as military outposts, the destruction of school property, and military raids on schools and alternative classes. Arrests, deportations and administrative detention were used against faculty, administrators and students. It was estimated that primary and secondary school children, numbering about 400,000, had been taught school for only about five months altogether during the period from autumn of 1987 to June 1989. About 100,000 children between 6 to 8 years of age had been unable to begin first grade. About 20,000 university students had their education completely interrupted. The Committee noted with great concern the assessment by educators that the imposition of those restrictions penalizes present and future generations of Palestinians and will create serious dysfunctions in the educational system that will be extremely difficult to compensate at a later stage.

The Committee further noted that the health situation in the occupied Palestinian territory had continued to deteriorate and was a matter of the most serious concern. It was reported that, since the beginning of the occupation, Israeli policies had resulted in a lack of basic sanitary infrastructure and health services. The number of health personnel and hospital beds, the quantity and quality of services, the medical equipment and supplies, were increasingly insufficient to meet the needs of the Palestinian population. There was no structured health system and no long-term health planning specific to the occupied territory and independent of the Israeli system, which drained the resources of the occupied territory without providing corresponding services. The estimated 40,00, Palestinians injured during the *intifadah*, who were in need of physiotherapeutical rehabilitation, had created enourmous strains on the already inadequate facilities. The Committee also noted with great concern continuing reports that access to medical care, even in emergency cases, was often rendered difficult by travel restrictions and curfews imposed by the ocupying Power, and that hospitals had been attacked and patients arrested.

The committee also noted with concern that, in his report on the situation of workers of the occupied Arab territories, based on the results of a fact-finding mission to the occupied Palestinian territory, the Director-General of the International Labour Organization (ILO), had stated that economic and other measures taken by the Israeli authorities to supress the *intifadah* had led to a substantial deterioration in the standard of living of the Palestinian people—by as much as 50 per cent, according to some observers. Palestinian employees and workers were of the opinion that any development for their benefit had been reduced to a minimum in recent years, and that any efforts that they themselves had undertaken for genuine development had been slowed or wrecked in order to keep the Palestinian economy as dependent as possible on that of Israel. Palestinian workers continued to suffer from fundamental inequities in training and employment opportunities and in the level and conditions of employment and social insurance system, contributing to their vulnerability and dependence. The Israeli authorities had also continued to engage in grave infringements of the Palestinians' right to freedom of association, including raids on and closure of trade union premises, arrest, house arrest, expulsion or threat of expulsion, administrative detention and physical harassment and interrogation of trade unionists.

Taking into account the continuing serious aggravation of the situation in the occupied territory, which affected every aspect of Palestinian life and society, the Committee deplored that Israel, the occupying Power, had denied entry to the territory to a number of United Nations bodies and agencies seeking to investigate the situation, in particular, the Special Committee to Investigate Israeli Practices Affecting the Human Rights of the Population of the Occupied Territories, the Commission on the Status of Women and the Special Committee of Experts of the World Health Organization (WHO). The Rapporteur and expert missions of the United Nations Educational, Scientific and Cultural Organization (UNESCO) to investigate the needs of Palestinian educational institutions had also been unable to visit the occupied Palestinian territory. The Committee associated itself with the call made in General Assembly resolution 43/233 of 20 April 1989 for the Secretary-General to submit periodic reports on developments in the occupied Palestinian territory.

The Committee wishes to draw once again the most urgent attention of the General Assembly and the Security Council to the policies and practices of Israel, the occupying Power, which are in flagrant violation of the Geneva Convention relative to the Protection of Civilian Persons in Time of War, of 12 August 1949, and which prevent the Palestinian people from attaining its inalienable rights, and thwart international efforts to bring about a peaceful settlement of the question of Palestine, the core of the Arab-Israeli conflict in the Middle East. The Committee reiterates its most urgent appeal to the Security Council and the international community as a whole to take all necessary measures to ensure the safety and protection of the Palestinians in the occupied territory, pending the withdrawl of Israeli forces and the achievement of a settlement.

The Committee further considered that, above and beyond protective and emergency relief measures, the international community must take all possible measures to halt the current economic crisis and to develop socio-economic structures that will lead to the genuine and autonomous development of the occupied Palestinian territory. The Palestinian struggle for independent nationhood requires, and is entitled to, the full support and concrete assistance of the United Nations system, in accordance with the relevent provisions of the Charter of the United Nations and United Nations resolutions. In that connection, the Committee noted that, in resolution 43/178 of 20 December 1988, entitled "Assistance to the Palestinian People", the General Assembly affirmed that the Palestinian people cannot develop their national economy as long as the Israeli occupation persists and it expressed awareness of the increasing need to provide economic and social assistance to the Palestinian people. The resolution contained a number of requests for action by the United Nations system and by Governments and intergovernmental and non-governmental organizations. The Committee also noted with appreciation the efforts of the Economic and Social Council and the relevant United Nations agencies and bodies, as well as the recommendations emanating from meetings of non-governmental organizations organized under its auspices. The Committee called on all concerned to sustain and increase their assistance to the Palestinian people, in close co-operation with the Palestinian Liberation Organization, as a necessary accompaniment of renewed efforts to achieve a political solution to the Palestinian question.

On the basis of the information available to it, the committee presented the following recomendations to the General Assembly (chap. VI, para. 110–117):

The year under review brought about events of momentous signifcance in the long history of the struggle of the Palestinian people to regain and exercise its inalienable rights. The continuing uprising of the Palestinian people against over 20 years of Israeli occupation and oppression, the proclamation of the State of Palestine, and the Palestinian peace initiative announced by President Yasser Arafat at the meetings of the forty-third session of the General Assembly, held at Geneva in December 1988, have created new conditions and opportunities for concerted international action aimed at achieving a comprehensive, just and lasting settlement of the problem. The growing deterioration of the situation in the occupied Palestinian territory, where hundreds of Palestinians have been killed and tens of thousands wounded, maimed and detained since the beginning of the *intifadah*, is a matter of utmost concern that imposes a moral duty on the United Nations and the international community as a whole to bring about expeditiously such a settlement, as well as to ensure the safety and protection of the Palestinian people under occupation.

The Committee considers that it is incumbent upon the Security Council to take concrete and effective action to secure those goals. The Committee believes that the recomendations contained in its first report, which have been repeatedly endorsed by the General Assembly by overwhelming majorities, provide a constructive programme for the implementation of the exercise of the inalienable rights of the Palestinian people. The Committee has accordingly annexed those recommendations to the present report (see annex I) and calls for urgent positive action thereon by the Security Council. The committee further reaffirms the validity of the Declaration and Programme of Action adopted by the International Conference on the Question of Palestine, held at Geneva in 1983, which made a valuable contribution towards the achievement of Palestinian rights. The Committee reaffirms that those recommendations are solidly founded on fundamental and internationally accepted principles and that the recognition, attainment and exercise of the inalienable rights of the Palestinian people are indispensable conditions in the solution of the question of Palestine, the core of the Arab-Israeli conflict in Middle East. The Committee further reasserts that the Israeli evacuation of the territories occupied by force and in violation of the principles of the Charter of the United Nations and relevant resolutions of the United Nations is a *condito sine qua non* for the exercise by the Palestinian people of its inalienable rights in Palestine.

The committee reaffirms the international consensus that the Palestine Liberation Organization is the sole and legitimate representative of the Palestinian people, whose participation on an equal footing is indispensable in any efforts and deliberations aimed at the achievement of a comprehensive, just and lasting peace in the Middle East. The Committee welcomes the Declaration of Independence adopted by the Palestine National Council at its meeting held at Algiers on 15 November 1988, and reiterates that the proclamation of the independent Arab State of Palestine is in fulfilment of General Assembly resolution 181 (II) of 29 November 1947. Accordingly, the Committee considers that the State of Palestine should be accorded its rightful place within the international community and the United Nations Organization. The Committee notes the widespread international support for the Palestinian peace initiative and it deeply regrets that Israel has so far failed to respond positively to it and has continued to refuse to acknowledge the inalienable national rights of the Palestinian people. The Committee accordingly urges Israel to reverse its position and to join the international consensus.

The Committee considers that it has now become imperative for the Security Council to take positive action towards the convening of the international Peace Conference on the Middle East on the basis of the framework and elements set out in General Assembly resolution 43/176 of 15 December 1988, which has the overwhelming support of the international community. The Committee reaffirms the principles for the achievement of a comprehensive peace contained in Assembly resolution 43/176, namely:

the withdrawal of Israel from the Palestinian territory occupied since 1967, including Jerusalem, and from the other occupied Arab territories; guaranteeing arrangements for security of all States in the region, including those named in Assembly resolution 181 (II), within secure and internationally recognized boundaries; resolving the problem of the Palestine refugees in conformity with Assembly resolution 194 (III) of 11 December 1948, and subsequent relevant resolutions; dismantling the Israeli settlements in the territories occupied since 1967; and guaranteeing freedom of access to Holy Places, religious buildings and sites.

In the past year, the international consensus in favour of the convening of the International Peace Conference has clearly been further consolidated. The Committee accordingly urges the Secretary-General to do everything in his power to ensure that active consultations are undertaken within the framework of the Security Council for that purpose. The Committee intends to continue to intensify its efforts towards that objective and to make it once again the focal point of its work programme in the coming year.

Noting that the Secretary-General has reported that his attempts to pave the way to an effective negotiating process have until now proved inconclusive, the Committee recommends that the General Assembly should call once again upon the Security Council, and in particular the permanent members, to consider measures needed to convene the International Peace Conference on the Middle East, including the establishment of a preparatory committee, and to consider guarantees for security measures in accordance with Assembly resolution 43/176, to renew the mandate of the Secretary-General to continue his efforts with the parties concerned and, in consultation with the Security Council, to facilitate the convening of the Conference.

The Committee protests in the strongest terms the intensification of repression by Israel, the occupying Power, against Palestinians in the occupied Palestinian territory, including children, particularly the liberal use of live ammunition, random beatings, raids and mass arrests, the increased use of administrative detention, deportations and collective punishment. The Committee condemns the unchecked violence by Israeli settlers. It also condemns the measures taken by the occupying Power to deprive the Palestinian population of their right to education, as well as administrative, economic and other measures taken to control all aspects of Palestinian life and to prevent the development of autonomous socio-economic structures. The Committee welcomes the action taken by Governments, non-governmental organizations and other bodies to denounce those measures, and welcomes the partial opening of schools as a result of that international pressure. The Committee recalls Security Council resolutions 636 (1989) of 6 July 1989 and 641 (1989) of 30 August 1989 and calls upon all concerned to redouble their efforts to expose, protest and put an end to those Israeli policies and practices, which are in violation of the Geneva Convention relative to the Protection of Civilian Persons in Time of War, of 12 August 1949. Given the grave situation created by such policies and practices, the Committee calls once again upon the Security Council to consider urgently measures needed to provide international protection to the Palestinian civilians in the Palestinian territory occupied by Israel since 1967, including Jerusalem. The Committee also calls for appropriate international action to alleviate the sufferings of the Palestinians living under occupation, especially women and children.

The Committee further reasserts that the United Nations has a historical duty and responsibility to render all assistance necessary to promote the autonomous economic development of the occupied Palestinian territory in preparation for the attainment of independence in accordance with the relevant United Nations resolutions. The Committee accordingly reiterates its call upon the organizations of the United Nations system, as well as on Governments and on intergovernmental and non-governmental organizations, to sustain and increase their economic and social assistance to the Palestinian people, in close co-operation with the Palestine Liberation Organization.

The Committee noted with satisfaction the increased awareness and mobilization of international public opinion in support of the attainment of the inalienable rights of the Palestinian people and of United Nations recommendations for a comprehensive, just and lasting solution of the question of Palestine. The Committee believes that its programme of regional seminars and meetings and symposia of non-governmental organizations, as well as the journalists' encounters and other informational activities sponsored by the Committee, have played a valuable role in this process, and will continue to strive to achieve maximum effectiveness in carrying out this programme and to intensify its efforts in the implementation of its mandates.

After examining the committee's report at its 1989 session, the General Assembly on 6 December 1989 endorsed (resolution 44/41 A) the committee's recommendations contained in para. 110 to 118 of the report and drew the attention of the Security Council to the fact that action on those recomendations, which had been repeatedly endorsed by the assembly, was still awaited.

In resolution 44/41 B, the assembly invited all governments and organizations to cooperate with the committee; and, in resolution 44/41 C, it requested the Department of Public Information of the UN Secretariat to continue its special information program on the question of Palestine, with particular emphasis on public opinion in Europe and North America.

Resolution 44/42, adopted on the same day, contained the following paragraphs, stating that the General Assembly

1. Reaffirms the urgent need to achieve a just and comprehensive settlement of the Arab-Israeli conflict, the core of which is the question of Palestine;
2. Calls once again for the convening of the International Peace Conference on the Middle East, under the auspices of the United Nations, with the participation of all parties to the conflict, including the Palestine Liberation Organization, on an equal footing, and the five permanent members of the Security Council, based on Security Council resolutions 242 (1967) of 22 November 1967 and 338 (1973) of 22 October 1973 and the legitimate national rights of the Palestinian people, primarily the right to self-determination;
3. Reaffirms the following principles for the achievement of comprehensive peace:
(a) The withdrawal of Israel from the Palestinian territory occupied since 1967, including Jerusalem, and from the other occupied Arab territories;

(b) Guaranteeing arrangements for security of all States in the region, including those named in resolution 181 (II) of 29 November 1947, within secure and internationally recognized boundaries;
(c) Resolving the problem of the Palestine refugees in conformity with General Assembly resolution 194 (III) of 11 December 1948, and subsequent relevant resolutions;
(d) Dismantling the Israeli settlements in the territories occupied since 1967;
(e) Guaranteeing freedom of access to Holy Places, religious buildings and sites;
4. Notes the expressed desire and endeavours to place the Palestinian territory occupied since 1967, including Jerusalem, under the supervision of the United Nations for a limited period, as a part of the peace process;
5. Once again invites the Security Council to consider measures needed to convene the International Peace Conference on the Middle East, including the establishment of a preparatory committee, and to consider guarantees for security measures agreed upon by the Conference for all States in the region;
6. Requests the Secretary-General to continue his efforts with the parties concerned, and in consultation with the Security Council, to facilitate the convening of the Conference, and to submit progress reports on developments in this matter.

ANNEX

Recommendations of the Committee. The recommendations of the committee, endorsed by the UN General Assembly at its 1976 session, are as follows (UN Doc. A/31/35, para. 59–72):

I. Basic Considerations and Guidelines

The question of Palestine is at the heart of the Middle East problem, and consequently, the Committee stresses its belief that no solution in the Middle East can be envisaged which does not fully take into account the legitimate aspirations of the Palestinian people.

The legitimate and inalienable rights of the Palestinian people to return to their homes and property and to achieve self-determination, national independence and sovereignty are endorsed by the Committee in the conviction that the full implementation of these rights will contribute decisively to a comprehensive and final settlement of the Middle East crisis.

The participation of the Palestine Liberation Organization, the representative of the Palestinian people, on an equal footing with other parties, on the basis of General Assembly resolutions 3236 (XXIX) and 3375 (XXX) is indispensable in all efforts, deliberations and conferences on the Middle East which are held under the auspices of the United Nations.

The Committee recalls the fundamental principle of the inadmissibility of the acquisition of territory by force and stresses the consequent obligation for complete and speedy evacuation of any territory so occupied.

The Committee considers that it is the duty and responsibility of all concerned to enable the Palestinians to exercise their inalienable rights.

The Committee recommends an expanded and more influential role by the United Nations and its organs in promoting a just solution to the question of Palestine and in the implementation of such a solution. The Security Council, in particular, should take appropriate action to facilitate the exercise by the Palestinians of their right to return to their homes, lands and property. The Committee, furthermore, urges the Security Council to promote action towards a just solution, taking into account all the powers conferred on it by the Charter of the United Nations.

It is with this perspective in view and on the basis of the numerous resolutions of the United Nations, after due consideration of all the facts, proposals and suggestions advanced in the course of its deliberations, that the Committee submits its recommendations on the modalities for the implementation of the exercise of the inalienable rights of the Palestinian people.

II. The Right of Return

The natural and inalienable right of Palestinians to return to their homes is recognized by resolution 194 (III), which the General Assembly has reaffirmed almost every year since its adoption. This right was also unanimously recognized by the Security Council in its resolution 237 (1967); the time for the urgent implementation of these resolutions is long overdue.

Without prejudice to the right of all Palestinians to return to their homes, lands and property, the Committee considers that the programme of implementation of the exercise of this right may be carried out in two phases:

Phase One. The first phase involves the return to their homes of the Palestinians displaced as a result of the war of June 1967. The Committee recommends that:

(i) The Security Council should request the immediate implementation of its resolution 237 (1967) and that such implementation should not be related to any other condition;

(ii) The resources of the International Committee of the Red Cross (ICRC) and/or of the United Nations Relief and Works Agency for Palestine Refugees in the Near East, suitably financed and mandated, may be employed to assist in the solution of any logistical problems involved in the resettlement of those returning to their homes. These agencies could also assist, in co-operation with the host countries and the Palestine Liberation Organization, in the identification of the displaced Palestinians.

Phase Two. The second phase deals with the return to their homes of the Palestinians displaced between 1948 and 1967. The Committee recommends that:

(i) While the first phase is being implemented, the United Nations in co-operation with the States directly involved, and the Palestine Liberation Organization as the interim representative of the Palestinian entity, should proceed to make the necessary arrangements to enable Palestinians displaced between 1948 and 1967 to exercise their right to return to their homes and property, in accordance with the relevant United Nations resolutions, particularly General Assembly resolution 194 (III);

(ii) Palestinians not choosing to return to their homes should be paid just and equitable compensation as provided for in resolution 194 (III).

III. The Right to Self-determination, National Independence and Sovereignty

The Palestinian people has the inherent right to self-determination, national independence and sovereignty in Palestine. The Committee considers that the evacuation of the territories occupied by force and in violation of the principles of the Charter and relevant resolutions of the United Nations is a *conditio sine qua non* for the exercise by the Palestinian people of its inalienable rights in Palestine. The Committee considers furthermore, that upon the return of the Palestinians to their homes and property and with the establishment of an independent Palestinian entity, the Palestinian people will be able to exercise its rights to self-determination and to decide its form of government without external interference.

The Committee also feels that the United Nations has an historical duty and responsibility to render all assistance necessary to promote the economic development and prosperity of the Palestinian entity.

To these ends, the Committee recommends that:

(a) A timetable should be established by the Security Council for the complete withdrawal by Israeli occupation forces from those areas occupied in 1967; such withdrawal should be completed no later than 1 June 1977;

(b) The Security Council may need to provide temporary peace-keeping forces in order to facilitate the process of withdrawal;

(c) Israel should be requested by the Security Council to desist from the establishment of new settlements and to withdraw during this period from settlements established since 1967 in the occupied territories. Arab property and all essential services in these areas should be maintained intact;

(d) Israel should also be requested to abide scrupulously by the provisions of the Geneva Convention relative to the Protection of Civilian Persons in Time of War, of 12 August 1949 and to declare, pending its speedy withdrawal from these territories, its recognition of the applicability of that Convention;

(e) The evacuated territories, with all property and services intact, should be taken over by the United Nations, which with the co-operation of the League of Arab States, will subsequently hand over these evacuated areas to the Palestine Liberation Organization as the representative of the Palestinian people;

(f) The United Nations should, if necessary, assist in establishing communications between Gaza and the West Bank;

(g) As soon as the independent Palestinian entity has been established, the United Nations, in co-operation with the States directly involved and the Palestinian entity, should, taking into account General Assembly resolution 3375 (XXX), make further arrangements for the full implementation of the inalienable rights of the Palestinian people, the resolution of outstanding problems and the establishment of a just and lasting peace in the region, in accordance with all relevant United Nations resolutions;

(h) The United Nations should provide the economic and technical assistance necessary for the consolidation of the Palestinian entity.

SEE ALSO *Geneva Declaration on Palestine; Israel; Israel: Application of the Fourth Geneva Convention to the Territories Occupied since 1967; Israel: Detention and Deportation of Palestinians; Israel: Effective Annexation of the Syrian Arab Golan; Israel: Harassment of Educational Institutions in Occupied Palestinian Territory.*

P

PAN AFRICANIST CONGRESS OF AZANIA. A liberation movement of the South African people, recognized as such by the ORGANIZATION OF AFRICAN UNITY and by the UN General Assembly, the congress participates in the work of the General Assembly and of other United Nations bodies as an observer and thus enjoys a status similar to that accorded to non-member States.

Founded in 1959 by elements of the AFRICAN NATIONAL CONGRESS who broke away under the leadership of Robert Sobukwe, the Pan-Africanist Congress was outlawed in 1960 and went into exile in Dar es Salaam, Tanzania. It invited into its ranks "everybody who owes his only loyalty to Africa and who is prepared to accept the democratic rule of the African majority."

Unlike the ANC, the PAC espouses a philosophy of black consciousness and has only a few white members. It maintains that the country's white minority would not be entitled to any special form of protection in a post-apartheid society and has not been willing to enter into any form of political dialogue with the government. While it criticizes the ANC for accepting assistance from communist elements, it has itself accepted assistance from China.

The announcement by PAC's President Zephania Mothopeng that the organization will not participate in negotiations between blacks and whites on South Africa's future left the ANC unchallenged in its talks with South African government officials, which began in 1990. Standing aside, PAC maintains that only a victorious guerrilla struggle can force the white minority government to end *apartheid*.

PANAMA. The Republic of Panama is a country in Central America, between the Pacific Ocean and the Caribbean Sea. It has borders with Colombia and Costa Rica. It achieved independence from Colombia in 1903 and became a member of the United Nations in 1945. Its population is estimated by the UN (1990) to be 2,418,000. Ethnic groups include descendents of white and black workers employed in the building of the Panama Canal (15%), American Indians (6%), and Mestizos (mixed) (79%). Languages in common use include Spanish (official) and English. Christianity (Roman Catholic, 93%, Protestant denominations, 6%) is the predominant religion. Literacy is estimated at 90%.

The government (1990) took the form of a republic. Under the 1972 constitution, as revised, the president and vice president are elected by popular vote for six-year terms. The president is head of State and of government. Legislation is dealt with by a 57-member Legislative Council, also elected by popular vote. Overall policy matters are considered by the 505-member National Assembly of Community Representatives, composed of representatives of municipal districts chosen on a community rather than a party basis. Political parties include the Democratic Revolutionary Party, the Authentic Panamenista Party, the Liberal Party, the Christian Democratic Party, the Popular Action Party, the Nationalist Republican Liberal Movement, the Popular Nationalist Party, the Labor Party, the People's Party, and the Republican Party.

As regards Panama's indigenous populations, the government stated, in a report presented to the COMMITTEE ON THE ELIMINATION OF RACIAL DISCRIMINATION on 17 April 1986 (UN Doc. CERD/C/149, Add. 4, para. 58–62) that:

Article 120 of the Constitution provides that the State shall give special attention to rural and indigenous communities with a view to promoting their economic, social and political participation in national life. This provision is supplemented by article 123 containing protective measures with respect to land tenure, as follows:

"The State shall guarantee to indigenous communities the reservation of the necessary lands and the collective ownership thereof, to ensure their economic and social welfare. The law shall regulate the procedures to be followed for this purpose and the boundaries within which private appropriation of land is prohibited".

There are three well-known indigenous groups in Panama: the Cunas, Guaymíes and the Emberás; however there are smaller, less well-known groups such as the Teribes and the Bocotás. The Cuna group inhabits the Atlantic coast of the isthmus and occupies the territory of the San Blas *Comarca;* the Guaymíes live in areas of Veraguas, Chiriquí and Bocas del Toro Provinces; the Emberá group, formerly known as the Chocoes, occupies what is now the Emberá *Comarca* in Darién Province; and the other two groups live in small areas of Bocas del Toro Province.

With the participation of these indigenous groups, the National Government has in recent years prepared various draft legislative texts, one of which became Act No. 22, of 8 November 1983, establishing the Emberá *Comarca*. Some of the other drafts are not yet entirely completed and are therefore subject to technical amendment as appropriate. These drafts include one intended to update the special arrangements for the San Blass *Comarca* established by Act No. 16 of 19 February 1953.

Broadly speaking, the above-mentioned drafts and the Embará *Comarca* Act deal with the following aspects: delimitation of the *Comarca* and political division, private property rights, government and administration, administration of justice, economy, natural resources, archeological sites and objects, and education.

A draft legislative text establishing the Cuna reservation of Madugundí de Alto Bayano was also drawn up and was approved by the Cuna leaders on 8 October 1985. The boundaries of the reservation were approved on 11 September 1985. To ensure that these agreements are effective and to control the entry of strangers into the area, the boundaries of the reservation are being marked by boundary stones and wire fences.

In the same report, the government of Panama describes "discrimination on the ground of nationality" allegedly practiced against citizens of Panama who are employees of the Panama Canal Commission and who reside in the Canal Zone. The government states that *(Ibid.,* para. 4–9):

Article XIII, paragraph 3, of the Agreed Minute on the Implementation of article III of the Panama Canal Treaty of 1977 stipulates that, five years after the entry into force of the Treaty, the employees of the Canal Commission who are citizens of the United States and their dependants shall not be authorized to use the military postal services or commissaries, i.e., these privileges end on 30 September 1983. Despite the foregoing, the United States Congress, through Public Law 96–70, adopted on 27 September 1979, section 1206, unilaterally and in contradiction with the Panama Canal Treaty, established a cost-of-living allowance (COLA) not only for United States citizens, but also for personnel recruited from outside the Republic of Panama, whatever their nationality, who were to lose the above-mentioned privileges on 30 September 1984.

By means of this legislation, the United States laid the legal foundation for granting economic benefits to those persons, discriminating on the ground of nationality by failing to establish similar provisions for the Panamanians residing in the Canal Zone Area who, on 1 October 1979, lost their right of eligibility and access to benefits such as housing, fuel, commissary, electricity, water, telephone, and so on. This is an overt downgrading of the terms and conditions of employment of the Panamanian personnel, and constitutes a violation of the provisions of article X, paragraph 2 (b) of the Treaty, which categorically prohibits this type of downgrading.

At the meeting of the Board of Directors of the Panama Canal Commission on 11 and 12 July 1984, the Administrator of the Canal Commission, basing himself on section 1206 of the aforementioned Public Law 96/70 submitted a recommendation, for which he obtained the approval of the United States members of the Board, for granting the following privileges, to be paid out of the Commission budget, to United States employees who lost the use of certain military facilities on 1 October 1984:

(a) Free housing and electricity;

(b) Full use of the diplomatic bag, including the dispatch and receipt of parcels;

(c) Annual travel to the United States of America;

(d) Payment of a transport differential for employees assigned to the Atlantic sector of the Canal Zone Area; and

(e) Two yearly return journeys for dependent students studying outside the Republic of Panama.

The Republic of Panama has opposed this decision, since the Panama Canal Treaty of 1977 does not contain any provision stipulating that the income of the Canal should be used to pay subsidies to United States citizens and their dependents in the employ of the Panama Canal Commission who, on 30 September 1984, lost the above-mentioned privileges, much less to the category of employees referred to in section 1206 of Public Law 96/70.

This is nothing other than an indirect subsidy, the effect of which is to perpetuate the privileges of the United States employees of the Commission, and is a flagrant act of discrimination against the employees of Panamanian nationality.

The Republic of Panama, through its members on the Board of Directors of the Canal Commission, opposed the allocation of the allowances and privileges by the Board since these are not provided for by article X, paragraph 6, of the Treaty, and represent open discrimination against Panamanian employees performing identical work. In addition, these benefits entail substantial additional costs which decrease the profits from the operation of the canal and thus directly reduce the proportion of economic benefits accruing to Panama. In this way, Panama is unjustly and illegally obliged, through a cut in its legitimate revenues, to subsidize the costs of a measure adopted against its judgement and constituting discrimination in remuneration against its own citizens.

A ten-day suspension of certain constitutional guarantees of human rights in June 1987 was explained by the government, in a report presented to the HUMAN RIGHTS COMMITTEE on 8 November 1988 (UN document CCPR/C/42/Add. 7, para. 30–37), as follows:

The constitutional guarantees were suspended on account of continuous disturbances of public order on Tuesday, 9 and Wednesday, 10 June 1987 in the cities of Panamá and Colón. On 10 June, since these disturbances were the outcome of constant incitement to violence by individuals and political groups of neo-fascist orientation, obviously bent on overthrowing the Government and assuming power through violence, the Government acting under article 51 of the Constitution, proclaimed a state of emergency and the temporary suspension of the individual guarantees contained in articles 21, 22, 23, 26, 27, 29, 37, 38 and 44 of the Constitution.

In view of the disorder caused by certain opposition groups for patently subversive purposes, the President of the Republic called a meeting of his Cabinet, at which it was decided to exercise the constitutional power provided for in article 51, authorizing the suspension of guarantees "in the event of an internal disturbance threatening peace and public order". The Cabinet Council accordingly enacted Decree No. 56 of 10 June 1987, the preamble to which stated that "the political forces of the opposition, which have made incessant efforts to prolong the disturbances that occurred during the last electoral contest, have embarked on activities designed to extend the subversion to the rest of the country".

In fact, the opposition groups organizing the disturbances had decided to call a general strike to overthrow the constituted authorities and set up a Provisional Government Junta. There were outbreaks of violence in some parts of the capital which affected normal living, involving serious disruption of traffic and clashes with anti-riot squads of the Defence Forces, deployed to protect the life and personal integrity of members of society and private property. There were several instances of looting of commercial establishments in Colón. The disturbances resulted in casualties and damage to property which compelled the authorities to call out the forces of law and order.

The basic guarantees suspended were:

(a) The guarantee of not being deprived of liberty except by virtue of a written order of the competent authorities, issued in accordance with the legal formalities and for a reason previously defined by law (article 21);

(b) The guarantee of not being detained without being informed of the grounds for detention (article 22);

(c) The presumption of innocence (article 22);

(d) The remedy of *habeas corpus* (article 23);

(e) Freedom of movement (article 27);

(f) The inviolability of correspondence and of private telephone communications (article 29);

(g) Freedom to express ideas in the form of the written word or by any other means, without prior censorship (article 37);

(h) The right of assembly (article 38);

(i) The guarantee of private property acquired in accordance with the law (article 44);

The other guarantees remained in force, including those relating to inviolability of the home, equality before the law, the absence of extradition for political offences, religious liberty and the absence of the death penalty and the penalty of confiscation of property. It should also be noted that, although the right of freedom of movement was suspended, the authorities did not order curfews within the national territory or the use of military check-points on public highways.

Ten days later, since the cause for the state of emergency persisted, the Executive, again acting under article 51 of the Constitution, decided to maintain the state of emergency throughout the national territory by Decree No. 57 of 19 June 1987. The Cabinet Council further requested the President of the Republic to call on the Legislative Assembly to take cognizance of the measures adopted.

The Legislative Assembly, also exercising its constitutional and legal powers and having regard to the action taken by the Cabinet Council and the circumstances necessitating the proclamation of a state of emergency and the suspension of the above-mentioned constitutional provisions, decided, through Decree No. 57 of 19 June 1987, fully to endorse the decisions taken by the Cabinet Council.

When the causes responsible for the above-mentioned measures had ceased to exist, the Legislative Assembly, through resolution No. 22 of 29 June 1987, decided to lift the state of emergency and restore the validity of the articles of the Constitution of the Republic of Panama that had been suspended.

In February 1988, General Antonio Noriega, commander of Panama's armed forces, was indicted by grand juries in Miami and Tampa, Florida, U.S.A., on drug-trafficking charges. Panamanian President Eric Arturo Delvalle dismissed Noriega, but Delvalle himself was dismissed by the Panamanian National Assembly.

An election to replace the president was held in May 1989, but international observers, led by former U.S. President Jimmy Carter, found much of the voting to be fraudulent. The government nullified the election before its results had been announced.

On 15 December 1989, the legislature declared Panama in a "state of war" with the United States of America, and appointed General Noriega to prepare a response. On the following day, a U.S. marine lieutenant was killed by Panamanian soldiers who claimed that he had fired shots at Noriega's military headquarters.

On 20 December, American troops were sent to Panama with a view to seizing Noriega, protecting American lives, preserving the integrity of the Panama Canal, and restoring democracy. After seeking refuge at the Vatican embassy, Noriega turned himself over to American authorities and was transferred to Miami, where he was arraigned. In a letter to US President George Bush, he asserted that he was a prisoner of war. His defense lawyers maintained, without success, that he should be tried only in a neutral country by an international court.

On 29 December, the UN General Assembly (resolution 44/240) reaffirmed the sovereign and inalienable right of Panama to determine freely its social, economic, and political system and to develop its international relations without any form of foreign intervention, interference, subversion, coercion, or threat; and recalled that, in accordance with article 2, paragraph 4, of the charter of the United Nations, all member States shall refrain in their international relations from the threat or use of force against the territorial integrity or political independence of any State, or in any other manner inconsistent with the purposes of the United Nations. It also reaffirmed the need to restore conditions which will guarantee the full exercise of the human rights and fundamental freedoms of the Panamanian people, and expressed its concern at the serious consequences the armed intervention by the United States of America in Panama might have for peace and security in the Central American region.

The assembly deplored the intervention in Panama by the armed forces of the United States of America, "which constitutes a flagrant violation of international law and of the independence, sovereignty and territorial integrity of States;" demanded the immediate cessation of the intervention and the withdrawal from Panama of the armed invasion forces of the United States; and demanded also full respect for and strict observance of the letter and spirit of the Torrijos–Carter Treaties.

The UN Commission on Human Rights adopted a similar resolution on the situation in Panama (resolution 1990/10) on 20 February 1990.

PAN PACIFIC AND SOUTH-EAST ASIA WOMEN'S ASSOCIATION. An international non-governmental organization in consultative status with the UN Economic and Social Council (Category II), and UNESCO, the association has members in 14 countries.

The Pan Pacific and South-East Asia Women's Association was founded in 1928 in Honolulu, Hawaii, at the second Conference of Pan Pacific Women, and was originally called the Pan Pacific Women's Association. It works to promote peace by fostering understanding and friendship among women of the Pacific and Southeast Asian areas and to encourage study and improvement of social conditions. One of the PPSEAWA's principal activities is to provide finances and volunteers for projects in a number of countries to aid women in participating in rural and small business development.

The association publishes *PPSEAWA Bulletin.*

Pan Pacific and South-East Asia Women's Association. Address: 2234 New Petchburi Road, Bangkok 10310, Thailand. President: Khunying Sumalee Chartikavanij.

Yearbook of International Organizations 1989/90 (K. G. Saur).

PAPUA NEW GUINEA. Papua New Guinea is a country in Melanesia, occupying the eastern half of the island of New Guinea, in the Pacific Ocean north of Australia. It has a border with the Indonesian province of Irian Jaya, which occupies the western half of the island. It achieved independence from Australia in 1975 and became a member of the United Nations the same year. Its population is estimated by the UN (1990) to be 3,955,000. Ethnic groups include Melanesians, Europeans, Asians, Chinese, Indians, and Africans. Languages commonly used include English, Melanesian Pidgin, Moto, and more than 700 local dialects. Christianity is the predominant religion (Protestant denominations, 65%; Roman Catholic, 33%); Animism is the faith of the remaining 2%. Literacy is estimated at 32%.

The government (1990) took the form of a monarchy and member of the Commonwealth of Nations, of which the British sovereign is the symbolic head. The governor-general represents the crown and appoints as prime minister the head of the party or coalition given the majority in a popular election. The prime minister exercises executive authority as head of government and is assisted by an appointed cabinet. Legislative matters are dealt with by the unicameral 109-member Parliament, elected by popular vote. The judiciary includes the Supreme Court and the National Court. Political parties include the Pangu Party, the People's Progress Party, the United Party, the People's Democratic Movement, the National Party, the Melanesian Alliance, and the League for National Advancement.

In a report presented to the **COMMITTEE ON THE ELIMINATION OF RACIAL DISCRIMINATION** on 16 August 1983, the government of Papua New Guinea stated (UN Doc. CERD/C/101/Add. 4, para. 3–5 and 7–13) that:

Prior to Independence and self-government, during the early years of the then administration of Papua New Guinea, a degree of racial discrimination existed within Papua New Guinea. With the advent of self-government, and later independence, discrimination on the ground of race virtually disappeared.

There now exists a non-discriminatory multiracial society in Papua New Guinea. The Government is fully conscious of the need to maintain a high degree of harmony amongst the various ethnic groups represented in Papua New Guinea. The Government believes that such harmony can best be maintained by:

(a) the process of education, both formal and nonformal;

(b) the daily interaction of the various ethnic groups in the fields of employment and social and cultural affairs; and

(c) the provision of legal sanctions which punish conduct contrary to that advocated by the International Convention.

The Government is vigilant in ensuring the racial discrimination does not arise. However, it believes that all persons living in Papua New Guinea, whether nationals or non-nationals, are fundamentally opposed to racial discrimination and that this attitude is demonstrated in their daily interaction. . . .

The Constitution provides that citizens of Papua New Guinea have the same rights, privileges, obligations and duties irrespective of race, tribe, place of origin, political opinion, colour, creed, religion or sex (section 55). Section 55 is enforceable under S.57 on application by the person affected or any other person with an interest in the maintenance of the rule of law. In addition, the Supreme and National Courts of Papua New Guinea (which are the two superior Courts) may take enforcement action on their own initiative.

The Constitution also establishes a body called the "Ombudsman Commission" which, *inter alia,* has jurisdiction to investigate complaints of discrimination by governmental bodies.

The Constitution also recognizes and provides for the enjoyment or exercise of basic human rights and fundamental freedoms in the political, social, cultural and economic life of the people. It guarantees the following for all persons: (a) right to life; (b) freedom from inhuman treatment; (c) protection of the law; (d) liberty of the person; (e) freedom from forced labour; (f) freedom from arbitrary search and entry; (g) freedom from conscience, thought, and religion; (h) freedom of expression; (i) freedom of assembly and association; (j) freedom of employment; and (k) right to privacy.

Citizens have special additional rights granted by the Constitution which are: (a) the right to vote and stand for public office; (b) the right to freedom of information; (c) the right to freedom of movement; (d) protection from unjust deprivation of property; and (e) the right to acquire freehold land.

[In addition,] the Discriminatory Practices Act prohibits discriminatory practices by any person based on reasons of colour, race, ethnic, tribal or national origin. It provides for offences relating to the performance of discriminatory practices and incitement to racial hatred punishable by fines and terms of imprisonment.

P

PAPUA NEW GUINEA: CONSTITUTION. The Constitution of Papua New Guinea contains the following provisions (articles 35 to 57) specifically relating to human rights and fundamental freedoms:

Subdivision B.—Fundamental Rights.

35. Right to Life. (1) No person shall be deprived of his life intentionally except—

(a) in execution of a sentence of a court following his conviction of an offence for which the penalty of death is prescribed by law; or

(b) as the result of the use of force to such an extent as is reasonable in the circumstances of the case and is permitted by any other law—

(i) for the defence of any person from violence; or

(ii) in order to effect a lawful arrest or to prevent the escape of a person lawfully detained; or

(iii) for the purpose of suppressing a riot, an insurrection or a mutiny; or

(iv) in order to prevent him from committing an offence; or

(v) for the purpose of suppressing piracy or terrorism or similar acts; or

(c) as the result of a lawful act of war.

(2) Nothing in Subsection (1)(b) relieves any person from any liability at law in respect of the killing of another.

36. Freedom from Inhuman Treatment. (1) No person shall be submitted to torture (whether physical or mental), or to treatment or punishment that is cruel or otherwise inhuman, or is inconsistent with respect for the inherent dignity of the human person.

(2) The killing of a person in circumstances in which Section 35(1)(a) (right to life) applies does not, of itself, contravene Subsection (1), although the manner or the circumstances of the killing may contravene it.

37. Protection of the Law. (1) Every person has the right to the full protection of the law, and the succeeding provisions of this section are intended to ensure that that right is fully available, especially to persons in custody or charged with offences.

(2) Except, subject to any Act of the Parliament to the contrary, in the case of the offence commonly known as contempt of court, nobody may be convicted of an offence that is not defined by, and the penalty for which is not prescribed by, a written law.

(3) A person charged with an offence shall, unless the charge is withdrawn, be afforded a fair hearing within a reasonable time, by an independent and impartial court.

(4) A person charged with an offence—

(a) shall be presumed innocent until proved guilty according to law, but a law may place upon a person charged with an offence the burden of proving particular facts which are, or would with the exercise of reasonable care be, peculiarly within his knowledge; and

(b) shall be informed promptly in a language which he understands, and in detail, of the nature of the offence with which he is charged, and

(c) shall be given adequate time and facilities for the preparation of his defence; and

(d) shall be permitted to have without payment the assistance of an interpreter if he cannot understand or speak the language used at the trial of the charge; and

(e) shall be permitted to defend himself before the court in person or, at his own expense, by a legal representative of his own choice, or if he is a person entitled to legal aid, by the Public Solicitor or another legal representative assigned to him in accordance with law; and

(f) shall be afforded facilities to examine in person or by his legal representative the witnesses called before the court by the prosecution, and to obtain the attendance and carry out the examination of witnesses and to testify before the court on his own behalf, on the same conditions as those applying to witnesses called by the prosecution.

(5) Except with his own consent, the trial shall not take place in his absence unless he so conducts himself as to render the continuance of the proceedings in his presence impracticable and the court orders him to be removed and the trial to proceed in his absence, but provision may be made by law for a charge that a person has committed an offence the maximum penalty for which does not include imprisonment, (except in default of payment of a fine), to be heard summarily in his absence if it is established that he has been duly served with a summons in respect of the alleged offence.

(6) Nothing in Subsection (4)(f) invalidates a law which imposes reasonable conditions that must be satisfied if witnesses called to testify on behalf of a person charged with an offence are to be paid their expenses out of public funds.

(7) No person shall be convicted of an offence on account of any act that did not, at the time when it took place, constitute an offence, and no penalty shall be imposed for an offence that is more severe in degree or description than the maximum penalty that might have been imposed for the offence at the time when it was committed.

(8) No person who shows that he has been tried by a competent court for an offence and has been convicted or acquitted shall again be tried for that offence or for any other offence of which he could have been convicted at the trial for that offence, except upon the order of a superior court made in the course of appeal or review proceedings relating to the conviction or acquittal.

(9) No person shall be tried for an offence for which he has been pardoned.

(10) No person shall be compelled in the trial of an offence to be a witness against himself.

(11) A determination of the existence or extent of a civil right or obligation shall not be made except by an independent and impartial court or other authority prescribed by law or agreed upon by the parties, and proceedings for such a determination shall be fairly heard within a reasonable time.

(12) Except with the agreement of the parties, or by order of the court in the interests of national security, proceedings in any jurisdiction of a court and proceedings for the determination of the existence or extent of any civil right or obligation before any other authority, including the announcement of the decision of the court or other authority, shall be held in public.

(13) Nothing in Subsection (12) prevents a court or other authority from excluding from the hearing of the proceedings before it persons, other than the parties and their legal representatives, to such an extent as the court or other authority—

(a) is by law empowered to do and considers necessary or expedient in the interests of public welfare or in circumstances where publicity would prejudice the interests of justice, the welfare of persons under voting age or the protection of the private lives of persons concerned in the proceedings; or

(b) is by law empowered or required to do in the interests of defence, public safety or public order.

(14) In the event that the trial of a person is not commenced within four months of the date on which he was committed for trial, a detailed report concerning the case shall be made by the Chief Justice to the Minister responsible for the National Justice Administration.

(15) Every person convicted of an offence is entitled to have his conviction and sentence reviewed by a higher court or tribunal according to law.

(16) No person shall be deprived by law of a right of appeal against his conviction or sentence by any court that existed at that time of the conviction or sentence, as the case may be.

(17) All persons deprived of their liberty shall be treated with humanity and with respect for the inherent dignity of the human person.

(18) Accused persons shall be segregated from convicted persons and shall be subject to separate treatment appropriate to their status as unconvicted persons.

(19) Persons under voting age who are in custody in connexion with an offence or alleged offence shall be separated from other persons in custody and be accorded treatment appropriate to their age.

(20) An offender shall not be transferred to an area away from that in which his relatives reside except for reasons of security or other good cause and, if such a transfer is made, the reason for so doing shall be endorsed on the file of the offender.

(21) Nothing in this section—

(a) derogates Division III.4 (principles of natural justice); or

(b) affects the powers and procedures of village courts.

(22) Notwithstanding Subsection 21(b) the powers and procedures of village courts shall be exercised in accordance with the principles of natural justice.

Subdivision C.—Qualified Rights.
General.

38. General Qualifications on Qualified Rights. (1) For the purposes of this Subdivision, a law that complies with the requirements of this section is a law that is made and certified in accordance with Subsection (2), and that—

(a) regulates or restricts the exercise of a right or freedom referred to in this Subdivision to the extent that the regulation or restriction is necessary—

(i) taking account of the National Goals and Directive Principles and the Basic Social Obligations, for the purpose of giving effect to the public interest in (A) defence; or (B) public safety; or (C) public order; or (D) public welfare; or (E) public health (including animal and plant health); or (F) the protection of children and persons under disability (whether legal or practical); or (G) the development of under-privileged or less advanced groups or areas; or

(ii) in order to protect the exercise of the rights and freedoms of others; or

(b) makes reasonable provision for cases where the exercise of one such right may conflict with the exercise of another,

to the extent that the law is reasonably justifiable in a democratic society having a proper regard for the rights and dignity of mankind.

(2) For the purposes of Subsection (1), a law must—

(a) be expressed to be a law that is made for that purpose; and

(b) specify the right or freedom that it regulates or restricts; and

(c) be made, and certified by the Speaker in his certificate under Section 110 (certification as to making of laws) to have been made, by an absolute majority.

(3) The burden of showing that a law is a law that complies with the requirements of Subsection (1) is on the party relying on its validity.

39. "Reasonably Justifiable in a Democratic Society," Etc. (1) The question, whether a law or act is reasonably justifiable in a democratic society having a proper regard for the rights and dignity of mankind, is to be determined in the light of the circumstances obtaining at the time when the decision on the question is made.

(2) A law shall not be declared not to be reasonably justifiable in a democratic society having a proper regard for the rights and dignity of mankind except by the Supreme Court or the National Court, or any other court prescribed for the purpose by or under an Act of the Parliament, and unless the court is satisfied that the law was never so justifiable such a declaration operates as a repeal of the law as at the date of the declaration.

(3) For the purposes of determining whether or not any law, matter or thing is reasonably justifiable in a democratic society that has a proper regard for the rights and dignity of mankind, a court may have regard to—

(a) the provisions of this Constitution generally, and especially the National Goals and Directive Principles and the Basic Social Obligations; and

(b) the Charter of the United Nations; and

(c) the Universal Declaration of Human Rights and any other declaration, recommendation or decision of the General Assembly of the United Nations concerning human rights and fundamental freedoms; and

(d) the European Convention for the Protection of Human Rights and Fundamental Freedoms and the Protocols thereto, and any other international conventions, agreements or declarations concerning human rights and fundamental freedoms; and

(e) judgements, reports and opinions of the International Court of Justice, the European Commission of Human Rights, the European Court of Human Rights and other international courts and tribunals dealing with human rights and fundamental freedoms; and

(f) previous laws, practices and judicial decisions and opinions in the country; and

(g) laws, practices and judicial decisions and opinions in other countries; and

(h) the Final Report of the pre-Independence Constitutional Planning Committee dated 13 August 1974 and presented to the pre-Independence House of Assembly on 16 August 1974, as affected by decisions of that House on the report and by decisions of the Constituent Assembly on the draft of this Constitution; and

(i) declarations by the International Commission of Jurists and other similar organizations; and

(j) any other material that the court considers relevant.

40. Validity of Emergency Laws. Nothing in this Part invalidates an emergency law as defined in Part X (emergency powers), but nevertheless so far as is consistent with their purposes and terms all such laws shall be interpreted and applied so as not to affect or derogate a right or freedom referred to in this Division to an extent that is more than is reasonably necessary to deal with the emergency concerned and matters arising out of it, but only so far as is reasonably justifiable in a democratic society having a proper regard for the rights and dignity of mankind.

41. Proscribed acts. (1) Notwithstanding anything to the contrary in any other provision of any law, any act that is done under a valid law but in the particular case—

(a) is harsh or oppressive; or

(b) is not warranted by, or is disproportionate to, the requirements of the particular circumstances or of the particular case; or

(c) is otherwise not, in the particular circumstances, reasonably justifiable in a democratic society having a proper regard for the rights and dignity of mankind,

is an unlawful act.

(2) The burden of showing that Subsection (1)(a), (b) or (c) applies in respect of an act is on the party alleging it, and may be discharged on the balance of probabilities.

(3) Nothing in this section affects the operation of any other law under which an act may be held to be unlawful or invalid.

Rights of All Persons.

42. Liberty of the Person. (1) No person shall be deprived of his personal liberty except—

(a) in consequence of his unfitness to plead a criminal charge; or

(b) in the execution of the sentence or order of a court in respect of an offence of which he has been found guilty, or in the execution of the order of a court of record punishing him for contempt of itself or another court or tribunal; or

(c) by reason of his failure to comply with the order of a court made to secure the fulfilment of an obligation (other than a contractual obligation) imposed upon him by law; or

(d) upon reasonable suspicion of his having committed, or being about to commit, an offence; or

(e) for the purpose of bringing him before a court in execution of the order of a court; or

(f) for the purpose of preventing the introduction or spread of a disease or suspected disease, whether of humans, animals or plants, or for normal purposes of quarantine; or

(g) for the purpose of preventing the unlawful entry of a person into Papua New Guinea, or for the purpose of effecting the expulsion, extradition or other lawful removal of a person from Papua New Guinea, or the taking of proceedings for any of those purposes; or

(h) in the case of a person who is, or is reasonably suspected of being of unsound mind or addicted to drugs or alcohol—

(i) for the purpose of his care or treatment or the protection of the community, under an order of a court; or

(ii) for the purpose of taking prompt legal proceedings to obtain an order of a court of a type referred to in Subparagraph (i).

(2) A person who is arrested or detained—

(a) shall be informed promptly, in a language that he understands, of the reasons for his arrest or detention and of any charge against him; and

(b) shall be permitted whenever practicable to communicate without delay and in private with a member of his family or a personal friend, and with a lawyer of his choice (including the Public Solicitor if he is entitled to legal aid); and

(c) shall be given adequate opportunity to give instructions to a lawyer of his choice in the place in which he is detained,

and shall be informed immediately on his arrest of his rights under this subsection.

(3) A person who is arrested or detained—

(a) for the purpose of being brought before a court in the execution of an order of a court; or

(b) upon reasonable suspicion of his having committed, or being about to commit, an offence,

shall, unless he is released, be brought without delay before a court or a judicial officer and, in a case referred to in paragraph (b), shall not be further held in custody in connexion with the offence except by order of a court or judicial officer.

(4) The necessity or desirability of interrogating the person concerned or other persons, or any administrative requirement or convenience, is not a good ground for failing to comply with Subsection (3), but exigencies of travel which in the circumstances are reasonable may, without derogating any other protection available to the person concerned, be such a ground.

(5) Where complaint is made to the National Court or a Judge that a person is unlawfully or unreasonably detained—

(a) the National Court or a Judge shall inquire into the complaint and order the person concerned to be brought before it or him; and

(b) unless the Court or Judge is satisfied that the detention is lawful, and in the case of a person being detained on remand pending his trial does not constitute an unreasonable detention having regard, in particular, to its length, the Court or a Judge shall order his release either unconditionally or subject to such conditions as the Court or Judge thinks fit.

(6) A person arrested or detained for an offence (other than treason or wilful murder as defined by an Act of the Parliament) is entitled to bail at all times from arrest or detention until acquittal or conviction unless the interests of justice otherwise require.

(7) Where a person to whom Subsection (6) applies is refused bail—

(a) the court or person refusing bail shall, on request by the person concerned or his representative, state in writing the reason for the refusal; and

(b) the person or his representative may apply to the Supreme Court or the National Court in a summary manner for his release.

(8) Subject to any other law, nothing in this section applies in respect of any reasonable act of the parent or guardian of a child, or a person into whose care a child has been committed, in the course of the education, discipline or upbringing of the child.

(9) Subject to any Constitutional Law or Act of the Parliament, nothing in this section applies in respect of a person who is in custody under the law of another country—

(a) while in transit through the country; or

(b) as permitted by or under an Act of the Parliament made for the purposes of Section 206 (visiting forces).

43. Freedom from Forced Labour. (1) No person shall be required to perform forced labour.

(2) In Subsection (1), "forced labour" does not include—

(a) labour required by the sentence or order of a court; or

(b) labour required of a person while in lawful custody, being labour that, although not required by the sentence or order of a court, is necessary for the hygiene of, or for the maintenance of, the place in which he is in custody; or

(c) in the case of a person in custody for the purpose of his care, treatment, rehabilitation or welfare, labour reasonably required for that purpose; or

(d) labour required of a member of a disciplined force in pursuance of his duties as such a member; or

(e) subject to the approval of any local government body for the area in which he is required to work, labour reasonably required as part of reasonable and normal communal or other civic duties; or

(f) labour of a reasonable amount and kind (including in the case of compulsory military service, labour required as an alternative to such service in the case of a person who has conscientious objections to military service) that is required in the national interest by an Organic Law that complies with Section 38 (general qualifications on qualified rights).

44. Freedom from Arbitrary Search and Entry. No person shall be subjected to the search of his person or property or to entry of his premises, except to the extent that the exercise of that right is regulated or restricted by a law—

(a) that makes reasonable provision for a search or entry—

(i) under an order made by a court; or

(ii) under a warrant for a search issued by a court or judicial officer on reasonable grounds, supported by oath or affirmation, particularly describing the purpose of the search; or

(iii) that authorizes a public officer or government agent of Papua New Guinea or an officer of a body corporate established by law for a public purpose to enter, where necessary, on the premises of a person in order to inspect those premises or anything in or on them in relation to any rate or tax or in order to carry out work connected with any property that is lawfully in or on those premises and belongs to the Government or any such body corporate; or

(iv) that authorizes the inspection of goods, premises, vehicles, ships or aircraft to ensure compliance with lawful requirements as to the entry of persons or importation of goods into Papua New Guinea or departure of persons or exportation of goods from Papua New Guinea or as to standards of safe construction, public safety, public health, permitted use or similar matters, or to secure compliance with the terms of a licence to engage in manufacture or trade; or

(v) for the purpose of inspecting or taking copies of documents relating to (A) the conduct of a business, trade, profession or industry in accordance with a law regulating the conduct of that business, trade, profession or industry; or (B) the affairs of a company in accordance with a law relating to companies; or

(vi) for the purpose of inspecting goods or inspecting or taking copies of documents, in connexion with the collection, or the enforcement of payment of taxes or under a law prohibiting or restricting the importation of goods into Papua New Guinea or the exportation of goods from Papua New Guinea; or

(b) that complies with Section 38 (general qualifications on qualified rights).

45. Freedom of Conscience, Thought and Religion. (1) Every person has the right to freedom of conscience, thought and religion and the practice of his religion and beliefs, including freedom to manifest and propagate his religion and beliefs in such a way as not to interfere with the freedom of others, except to the extent that the exercise of that right is regulated or restricted by a law that complies with Section 38 (general qualification on qualified rights).

(2) No person shall be compelled to receive religious instruction to take part in a religious ceremony or observance, but this does not apply to the giving of religious instruction to a child with the consent of his parent or guardian or to the inclusion in a course of study of secular instruction concerning any religion or belief.

(3) No person is entitled to intervene unsolicited into the religious affairs of a person of a different belief, or to attempt to force his or any religion (or irreligion) on another, by harassment or otherwise.

(4) No person may be compelled to take an oath that is contrary to his religion or belief, or to take an oath in a manner or form that is contrary to his religion or belief.

(5) A reference in this section to religion includes a reference to the traditional religious beliefs and customs of the peoples of Papua New Guinea.

46. Freedom of Expression. (1) Every person has the right to freedom of expression and publication, except to the extent that the exercise of that right is regulated or restricted by a law—

(a) that imposes reasonable restrictions on public office-holders; or

(b) that imposes restrictions on non-citizens; or

(c) that complies with Section 38 (general qualifications on qualified rights).

(2) In Subsection (1), "freedom of expression and publication" includes—

(a) freedom to hold opinions, to receive ideas and information and to communicate ideas and information, whether to the public generally or to a person or class of persons; and

(b) freedom of the press and other mass-communication media.

(3) Notwithstanding anything in this section, an Act of the Parliament may make reasonable provision for securing reasonable access to mass-communication media for interested persons and associations—

(a) for the communication of ideas and information; and

(b) to allow rebuttal of false or misleading statements concerning their acts, ideas or beliefs,

and generally for enabling and encouraging freedom of expression.

47. Freedom of Assembly and Association. Every person has the right peacefully to assemble and associate and to form or belong to, or not to belong to, political parties, industrial organizations or other associations, except to the extent that the exercise of that right is regulated or restricted by a law—

(a) that makes reasonable provision in respect of the registration of all or any associations; or

(b) that imposes reasonable restrictions on public office-holders; or

(c) that imposes restrictions on non-citizens; or

(d) that complies with Section 38 (general qualifications on qualified rights).

48. Freedom of Employment. (1) Every person has the right to freedom of choice of employment in any calling for which he has the qualifications (if any) lawfully required, except to the extent that that freedom is regulated or restricted voluntarily or by a law that complies with Section 38 (general qualifications on qualified rights), or a law that imposes restrictions on non-citizens.

(2) Subsection (1) does not prohibit reasonable action or provision for the encouragement of persons to join industrial organizations or for requiring membership of an industrial organization for any purpose.

49. Right to Privacy. Every person has the right to reasonable privacy in respect of his private and family life, his communications with other persons and his personal papers and effects, except to the extent that the exercise of that right is regulated or restricted by a law that complies with Section 38 (general qualifications on qualified rights).

Special Rights of Citizens.

50. Right to Vote and Stand for Public Office. (1) Subject to the express limitations imposed by this Constitution, every citizen who is of full capacity and has reached voting age, other than a person who—

(a) is under sentence of death or imprisonment for a period of more than nine months; or

(b) has been convicted, within the period of three years next preceding the first day of the polling period for the election concerned, of an offence relating to elections that is prescribed by an Organic Law or an Act of the Parliament for the purposes of this paragraph,

has the right, and shall be given a reasonable opportunity—

(c) to take part in the conduct of public affairs, either directly or through freely chosen representatives; and

(d) to vote for, and to be elected to, elective public office at genuine, periodic, free elections; and

(e) to hold public office and to exercise public functions.

(2) The exercise of those rights may be regulated by a law that is reasonably justifiable for the purpose in a democratic society having a proper regard for the rights and dignity of mankind.

51. Right to Freedom of Information. (1) Every citizen has the right of reasonable access to official documents, subject only to the need for such secrecy as is reasonably justifiable in a democratic society having a proper regard for the rights and dignity of mankind in respect of—

(a) matters relating to national security, defence or international relations of Papua New Guinea (including Papua New Guinea's relations with the Government of any other country or with any international organization); or

(b) records of meetings and decisions of the National Executive Council and of such executive bodies and elected governmental authorities as are prescribed by Organic Law or Act of the Parliament; or

(c) trade secrets, and privileged or confidential commercial or financial information obtained from a person or body; or

(d) parliamentary papers that are the subject of parliamentary privilege; or

(e) reports, official registers and memoranda prepared by governmental authorities or authorities established by government, prior to completion; or

(f) papers relating to lawful official activities for investigation and prosecution of crime; or

(g) the prevention, investigation and prosecution of crime; or

(h) the maintenance of personal privacy and security of the person; or

(i) matters contained in or related to reports prepared by, on behalf of or for the use of a governmental authority responsible for the regulation or supervision of financial institutions; or

(j) geological or geophysical information and data concerning wells and ore bodies.

(2) A law that complies with Section 38 (general qualifications on qualified rights) may regulate or restrict the right guaranteed by this section.

(3) Provision shall be made by law to establish procedures by which citizens may obtain ready access to official information.

(4) This section does not authorize—

(a) withholding information or limiting the availability of records to the public except in accordance with its provisions, or

(b) withholding information from the Parliament.

52. Right to Freedom of Movement. (1) Subject to Subsection (3), no citizen may be deprived of the right to move freely throughout the country, to reside in any part of the country and to enter and leave the country, except in consequence of a law that provides for deprivation of personal liberty in accordance with Section 42 (liberty of the person).

(2) No citizen shall be expelled or deported from the country except by virtue of an order of a court made under a law in respect of the extradition of offenders, or alleged offenders, against the law of some other place.

(3) A law that complies with Section 38 (general qualifications on qualified rights) may regulate or restrict the exercise of the right referred to in Subsection (1), and in particular may regulate or restrict the freedom of movement of persons convicted of offences and of members of a disciplined force.

53. Protection from Unjust Deprivation of Property. (1) Subject to Section 54 (special provision in relation to certain lands) and except as permitted by this section, possession may not be compulsorily taken of any property, and no interest in or right over property may be compulsorily acquired, except in accordance with an Organic Law or an Act of the Parliament, and unless—

(a) the property is required for—

(i) a public purpose; or

(ii) a reason that is reasonably justifiable in a democratic society having a proper regard for the rights and dignity of mankind,

that is so declared and so described, for the purposes of this section, in an Organic Law or an Act of the Parliament; and

(b) the necessity for the taking of possession or acquisition for the attainment of that purpose or for that reason is such as to afford reasonably justification for the causing of any resultant hardship to any person affected.

(2) Subject to this section, just compensation must be made on just terms by the expropriating authority, giving full weight to the National Goals and Directive Principles and having due regard to the national interest and to the expression of that interest by the Parliament, as well as to the person affected.

(3) For the purposes of Subsection (2), compensation shall not be deemed not to be just and on just terms solely by reason of a fair provision for deferred payment, payment by instalments or compensation otherwise than in cash.

(4) In this section, a reference to the taking of possession of property, or the acquisition of an interest in or right over property, includes a reference to—

(a) the forfeiture; or

(b) the extinction or determination (otherwise than by way of a reasonable provision for the limitation of actions or a reasonable law in the nature of prescription or adverse possession),

of any right or interest in property.

(5) Nothing in the preceding provisions of this section prevents—

(a) the taking of possession of property, or the acquisition of an interest in or right over property, that is authorized by any other provision of this Constitution; or

(b) any taking of possession or acquisition—

(i) in consequence of an offence or attempted offence against, or a breach or attempted breach of, or other failure to comply with a law; or

(ii) in satisfaction of a debt or civil obligation; or

(iii) subject to Subsection (6), where the property is or may be required as evidence in proceedings or possible proceedings before a court or tribunal,

in accordance with a law that is reasonably justifiable in a democratic society having a proper regard for the rights and dignity of mankind; or

(c) any taking of possession or acquisition that was an incident of the grant or acceptance of, or of any interest in or right over, that property or any other property by the holder of any of his predecessors in title; or

(d) any taking of possession or acquisition that is in accordance with custom; or

(e) any taking of possession or acquisition of ownerless or abandoned property (other than customary land); or

(f) any restriction on the use of or on dealing with property or any interest in or right over any property that is reasonably necessary for the preservation of the environment or of the national cultural inheritance.

(6) Subsection (5)(b)(iii) does not authorize the retention of any property after the end of the period for which its retention is reasonably required for the purpose referred to in that paragraph.

(7) Nothing in the preceding provisions of this section applies to or in relation to the property of any person who is not a citizen and the power to compulsorily take possession of, or to acquire an interest in, or right over, the property of any such person shall be as provided for by an Act of the Parliament.

54. Special provision in relation to certain lands. Nothing in Section 37 (protection of the law) or 53 (protection from unjust deprivation of property) invalidates a law that is reasonably justifiable in a democratic society having a proper regard for the rights and dignity of mankind and that provides—

(a) for the recognition of the claimed title of Papua New Guinea to land where—

(i) there is a genuine dispute as to whether the land was acquired validly or at all from the customary owners before Independence Day; and

(ii) if the land were acquired compulsorily the acquisition would comply with Section 53(1) (protection from unjust deprivation of property); or

(b) for the settlement by extra-judicial means of disputes as to the ownership of customary land that appear not to be capable of being reasonably settled in practice by judicial means; or

(c) for the prohibition or regulation of the holding of certain interests in, or in relation to, some or all land by non-citizens.

55. Equality of Citizens. (1) Subject to this Constitution, all citizens have the same rights, privileges, obligations and duties irrespective of race, tribe, place of origin, political opinion, colour, creed, religion or sex.

(2) Subsection (1) does not prevent the making of laws for the special benefit, welfare, protection or advancement of females, children and young persons, members of underprivileged or less advanced groups or residents of less advanced areas.

(3) Subsection (1) does not affect the operation of a pre-Independence law.

56. Other Rights and Privileges of Citizens. (1) Only citizens may—

(a) vote in elections for, or hold, elective public offices; or

(b) acquire freehold land.

(2) An Act of the Parliament may—

(a) define the offices that are to be regarded as elective public offices; and

(b) define the forms of ownership that are to be regarded as freehold; and

(c) define the corporations that are to be regarded as citizens,

for the purposes of Subsection (1).

(3) An Act of the Parliament may make further provision for rights and privileges to be reserved for citizens.

Subdivision D.—Enforcement.

57. Enforcement of Guaranteed Rights and Freedoms. (1) A right or freedom referred to in this Division shall be protected by, and is enforceable in, the Supreme Court or the National Court or any other court prescribed for the purpose by an Act of the Parliament, either on its own initiative or on application by any person who has an interest in its protection and enforcement, or in the case of a person who is, in the opinion of the court, unable fully and freely to exercise his rights under this section by a person acting on his behalf, whether or not by his authority.

(2) For the purposes of this section—

(a) the Law Officers of Papua New Guinea; and

(b) any other persons prescribed for the purpose by an Act of the Parliament; and

(c) any other persons with an interest (whether personal or not) in the maintenance of the principles commonly known as the Rule of Law such that, in the opinion of the court concerned, they ought to be allowed to appear and be heard on the matter in question,

have an interest in the protection and enforcement of the rights and freedoms referred to in this Division, but this subsection does not limit the persons or classes of persons who have such an interest.

(3) A court that has jurisdiction under Subsection (1) may make all such orders and declarations as are necessary or appropriate for the purposes of this section, and may make an order or declaration in relation to a statute at any time after it is made (whether or not it is in force).

(4) Any court, tribunal or authority may, on its own initiative or at the request of a person referred to in Subsection (1), adjourn, or otherwise delay a decision in, any proceedings before it in order to allow a question concerning the effect or application of this Division to be determined in accordance with Subsection (1).

(5) Relief under this section is not limited to cases of actual or imminent infringement of the guaranteed rights and freedoms, but may, if the court thinks it proper to do

so, be given in cases in which there is a reasonable probability of infringement, or in which an action that a person reasonably desires to take is inhibited by the likelihood of, or a reasonable fear of, an infringement.

(6) The jurisdiction and powers of the courts under this section are in addition to, and not in derogation of, their jurisdiction and powers under any other provision of this Constitution.

58. Compensation. (1) This section is in addition to, and not in derogation of, Section 57 (enforcement of guaranteed rights and freedoms).

(2) A person whose rights or freedoms declared or protected by this Division are infringed (including any infringement caused by a derogation of the restrictions specified in Part X.5 (internment) on the use of emergency powers in relation to internment is entitled to reasonable damages and, if the court thinks its proper, exemplary damages in respect of the infringement.

(3) Subject to Subsections (4) and (5), damages may be awarded against any person who committed, or was responsible for, the infringement.

(4) Where the infringement was committed by a government body, damages may be awarded either—

(a) subject to Subsection (5), against a person referred to in Subsection (3); or

(b) against the governmental body to which any such person was responsible, or against both, in which last case the court may apportion the damages between them.

(5) Damages shall not be awarded against a person who was responsible to a governmental body in respect of the action giving rise to the infringements if—

(a) the action was an action made unlawful only by Section 41(1) (proscribed acts); and

(b) the action taken was genuinely believed by that person to be required by law,

but the burden of proof of the belief referred to in paragraph (b) is on the party alleging it.

Division 4.—Principles of Natural Justice.

59. Principles of Natural Justice. (1) Subject to this Constitution and to any statute, the principles of natural justice are the rules of the underlying law known by that name developed for control of judicial and administrative proceedings.

(2) The minimum requirement of natural justice is the duty to act fairly and, in principle, to be seen to act fairly.

PARAGUAY. The Republic of Paraguay is a landlocked country in tropical South America. It has borders with Argentina, Bolivia, and Brazil. It achieved independence from Spain in 1811 and became a member of the United Nations in 1945. Its population is estimated by the UN (1990) to be 4,118,000. Ethnic groups include whites (3%), Amerindians (2%), and Mestizos (95%). Languages commonly used include Spanish and Guarani. Christianity is the predominant religion; the Roman Catholic Church is the established church and numbers among its adherents 95% of those who profess a religious belief, while Protestant denominations account for the remaining 5%. Literacy is estimated at 81%.

The government (1990) took the form of a republic. The president is elected by popular vote for a term of five years; he is head of State and of government and appoints his own cabinet. The legislature consists of a 30-member Senate and a 60-member Chamber of Deputies, all members being elected by popular vote for terms of five years. Two-thirds of the seats in each chamber is allocated to the majority party, and the remaining one-third is shared among the minority parties in proportion to the votes cast. There is also a Council of State, composed of representatives of the government, the armed forces, and other bodies; when Parliament is in recess, the president can govern by decree through that council.

Paraguay had a single president, Gen. Alfredo Stroessner, from 1954, when he seized power in a military coup, to 1989, when he lost it in the same way. He ruled as a dictator under a state of siege until 1965, but then was elected to eight successive terms as president; in the eighth, on 14 February 1988, he received 88.6% of the popular vote.

Under Stroessner's rule, Paraguay prospered but became notorious for its suppression of dissent, its mistreatment of its indigenous peoples, and the role it played as a hideout for international criminals, refusing to extradite them to countries where they were wanted for trial for serious offences, including war crimes and crimes against humanity. Stroessner's regime ended suddenly on 3 February 1989 when a military coup led by Gen. Andres Rodriguez forced him to resign as president and commander-in-chief of the armed forces. Gen. Rodriguez took over those functions immediately, and, on 5 February, Stroessner was flown into exile in Brazil.

Under Stroessner, the government's policies towards the Ache Indians of Paraguay's east coast—said to have reduced many of them to involuntary servitude—and its persistent detention of political prisoners were the subjects of much regional and international criticism.

The **INTER-AMERICAN COMMISSION ON HUMAN RIGHTS,** in its annual report issued on 26 September 1986 (OAS Doc. OEA/Ser.L/...), reviewed the status of human rights in Paraguay and reported the following conclusions:

As regards the massive and most serious violations of the right to life and humane treatment, which were frequent in Paraguay in earlier decades, it is to be pointed out that during the period covered by this report there were no cases of disappearances; the incidence of torture committed by the police authorities has diminished, as well as assassinations for political reasons, although at least one major exception occurred during this period that must be mentioned here....

Constant violations still occur in Paraguay of important

rights recognized by the American Declaration of the Rights and Duties of Man. These violations affect, in particular, the right to a fair trial and due process; personal liberty and safety; recognition of legal capacity and other political rights and civil liberties, such as freedom to organize, freedom of association, residence and movement, and freedom of thought and expression.

The Commission once again regrets the continuous and indiscriminate application of the emergency laws contained in Laws Nos. 294 of 1955 and 209 of 1970 on "Defense of Democracy" and "Defence of Public Order and Individual Liberty", as well as the permanent state of siege established in Article 79 of the Constitution, which without fail has been extended, without interruption, every three months.

The absence of a truly autonomous judiciary has been evidenced by a paralysis of the investigations and the failure to bring to trial senior officials and authorities who may be involved in crimes. This happened, for example, with important government authorities who were presumed to have participated in the theft of several hundred million dollars in foreign exchange from the Central Bank, which was reported at the end of 1985. Initially, the courts had sentenced more than a dozen individuals supposedly implicated in the fraud to jail, but all are currently free.

Habeas corpus, a right that is guaranteed under Article 78 of the National Constitution does not function in practice and is not an available remedy: the Supreme Court has continued to abdicate its functions by disqualifying itself from hearing writs of *habeas corpus* filed during the state of siege.

In the area of political and civil rights, the Government continues to regard the opposition parties that make up the "National Accord" as being "illegal" or "irregular". They are not allowed to participate in elections, nor were they permitted to organize ever since the time they were founded in 1970. The Government has also flatly rejected the planned National Dialogue that the Episcopal Conference of the Paraguayan Catholic Church encouraged in early 1986 in an attempt to gain the participation of all political and social sectors in a common, unified effort to facilitate a political transition by peaceful change towards full democracy.

In that context of lack of conditions for the exercise of democracy, the ruling Colorado Party again won municipal elections in October 1985 by an 88% majority of all votes cast in the country. At the same time, notable members of the militant wing of the Colorado Party floated President Stroessner's candidacy for an eighth presidential term in 1988–1993.

. . . . There has been a new wave of mass arrests and attacks on opposition leaders, and a move by the Government and para-police forces to contain and repress demonstrations by the political opposition and the popular demands and protests of the various segments of the population seeking greater democracy in the country. . . .

It should be noted that in most of the cases described here, the detentions lasted for a few hours or days, after which the persons arrested were freed or brought before the appropriate court authorities.

The persons filing the complaints stated that the police and para-police authorities acted with unjustified violence when they broke up the group of the demonstrators, firing their weapons practically over the heads of the marchers and beating them with knuckle-dusters and the butts of their rifles. They also used water cannons and extraordinarily potent, asphyxiating tear-gas.

Freedom of thought, freedom of expression and freedom to publish have continued under severe restrictions, in an atmosphere of an increased number of arrests, threats and intimidation of journalists, newspaper publishers and editors, and managers of radio stations and news agencies.

PARLIAMENTARY ASSOCIATION FOR EURO-ARAB COOPERATION.

An international non-governmental organization in consultative status (Roster) with the UN Economic and Social Council, PAEAC has members in 15 countries; individual members come from the European community national parliaments and the European Parliament of the Council of Europe.

Founded in 1974 in Paris, the association supports a European-Arab dialogue for cooperation between the European and Arab worlds; particular emphasis is laid on the Palestinian question. PAEAC expresses the Arab point of view through the Parliamentary Assembly of the Council of Europe and supports recognition of the PLO and the establishment of a Palestinian State in Palestine.

Parliamentary Association for Euro-Arab Cooperation. Address: Avenue d' Auderghem 33-35, B–1040, Brussels, Belgium. Telephone: (32-2) 231-1300. Fax: (32-2) 231-0646. Secretary-General: Hans Peter Kotthaus.

Yearbook of International Organizations 1989/90 (K. G. Saur).

PAX CHRISTI, INTERNATIONAL CATHOLIC PEACE MOVEMENT.

An international non-governmental organization in consultative status with the UN Economic and Social Council (Category II) and with UNESCO, and the Council of Europe, Pax Christi has national sections in 15 countries.

Founded in 1945, Pax Christi aims to work with all men for universal peace, to help build a world which is genuinely more humane for all people everywhere—a world founded on respect for the life, conscience, and rights of each human being—and to promote the freedom and political and social responsibilities of individuals and communities.

Pax Christi has created international meeting centers, open to all but particularly to young people; it organizes an annual peace march, *"Route international de la paix,"* always in a different country, where participants walk and pray together; and works with other interested organizations on matter of disarmament, development, and human rights.

Pax Christi publishes the quarterly *International Pax Christi Bulletin* in English and French.

Pax Christi. Address: Plantin en Moretuslei 174,

B-2018 Antwerp, Belgium. Telephone: (32-3) 235-36-40. Telex: 32675 Bavel b. International Secretary: Etienne de Jonghe.

Yearbook of International Organizations 1989/90 (K. G. Saur).

PAX ROMANA, INTERNATIONAL CATHOLIC MOVEMENT FOR INTELLECTUAL AND CULTURAL AFFAIRS.

An international non-governmental organization in consultative status with the UN Economic and Social Council (Category II), and with UNESCO and the Council of Europe, ICMICA has members in 66 countries.

Founded in 1947, when "Pax Romana" was split into two autonomous divisions—ICMICA and PAX ROMANA, INTERNATIONAL MOVEMENT OF CATHOLIC STUDENTS (IMCS)—the International Catholic Movement for Intellectual and Cultural Affairs works to unite Catholic university graduates to search for solutions to problems posed by modern life and to place their intellectual and moral resources at the service of peace. ICMICA has four professional secretariats: lawyers, engineers, agronomists, and industry officials.

ICMICA publishes *Convergence* (in conjunction with the IMCS) in English and French and the *ICMICA Newsletter* in English, French, and Spanish.

Pax Romana, International Catholic Movement for Intellectual and Cultural Affairs. Address: 37–39 rue de Vermont, P.O. Box 85, CH-1211 Geneva 20-CIC, Switzerland. Telephone: (41-22) 33-67-40. Secretary General: Victor P. Karunan.

Yearbook of International Organizations 1989/90 (K.G. Saur).

PERMANENT COURT OF ARBITRATION.

The court, also known as the Hague Tribunal, was established in 1899 in accordance with the International Convention for the Pacific Settlement of International Disputes, concluded at the Hague on 29 July 1899. Under the convention, several means for the peaceful settlement of disputes between States are recognized, including the use of mediation, of good offices, and of international commissions of inquiry and arbitration. The Permanent Court of Arbitration formally came into being with the adoption of a revised version of the convention on 18 October 1907 in the course of the Second International Peace Conference at the Hague.

Each State party to the convention appoints up to four jurists versed in international law to the court. A case is initiated when two or more States agree to submit their dispute to arbitration. The disputants may either select arbitrators from the panel of jurists to hear their case or have two arbitrators choose an umpire before whom the hearing will be held. Tribunals normally sit at the Hague.

After World War I, the Permanent Court of Arbitration lost much of its influence first to the World Court and, after 1945, to the INTERNATIONAL COURT OF JUSTICE.

PERSONS BORN OUT OF WEDLOCK.

Discrimination against people born out of wedlock is the subject of a study completed in 1967 by Judge Vieno Voitto Saario (Finland), a special rapporteur appointed by the UN SUB-COMMISSION ON PREVENTION OF DISCRIMINATION AND PROTECTION OF MINORITIES.

Based on data assembled from 71 countries, the study concludes that persons born out of wedlock are frequently the victims of discrimination because they cannot establish a legal relationship with their mother, their father, or both, and thus are left without any family status or even without a birth record or a name. It reveals a general trend towards greater flexibility in the methods used for establishing filiation, despite serious restrictions applied in a number of countries.

Regarding maternal filiation, the study concludes (Chapter V) that:

In a large number of countries, the very fact that a woman has given birth to a child results in *de jure* recognition of the maternal relationship. This rule appears to be most beneficial to persons born out of wedlock who can thus, as a consequence of birth, automatically enjoy status as regards their mother.

A variety of methods of acknowledgement, including tacit acknowledgement resulting from the fact that the mother has openly and constantly treated her child as her own, can be discerned in those systems of law requiring express acknowledgement by the mother. The same purpose is fulfilled where the acknowledgement is effected by the mere mention of the mother's name in the birth record if she does not oppose it, or, as is the case in at least one country, where the director of the public institution where the birth took place has the authority to record officially the declaration of acknowledgement made by the mother. Where the mother is incapacitated or dead, and therefore cannot herself acknowledge the child, the maternal grandparents are, in some instances, permitted to acknowledge him.

In a number of countries where the law requires express acknowledgement by the mother, such acknowledgement may occur at any time during the life of the person born out of wedlock, sometimes before the birth, once conception has taken place, or even after his death. However, some special conditions are to be met when acknowledgement occurs after the birth has been registered. In any case, where a system of express acknowledgement is maintained, the procedure should be made as simple and informal as possible.

Analysis of the available data reveals that while the laws of most countries provide for the judicial establishment of the maternal filiation of a person born out of wedlock, in some countries the law does not provide for its establishment as such, the question being solved for each particular case if and when filiation is challenged. In a few instances, the judicial establishment of maternal filiation is not provided for at all. It goes without saying that the right to establish maternal filiation judicially should be embodied in the law of all countries.

As regards the evidence admissible in the proof of maternal filiation, there may sometimes be differences in the admissibility of evidence in cases of births in wedlock and births out of wedlock. It seems of primary importance that every type of evidence to the effect of establishing the respective identities of the mother and the child, as well as the fact of birth, should be admitted in both situations. As is the case in various countries, any party having a legitimate interest should have the right to establish maternal filiation judicially.

Regarding paternal filiation when the parents are married to each other, the study concludes that:

Analysis of the available data reveals that the rule *"pater is est quem nuptiae demonstrant"* is incorporated in the legislation of all countries surveyed. This principle is interpreted, in one group of countries, to mean that the husband is presumed to be the father of the children conceived by his wife during the subsistence of the marriage, while in some other countries the presumption is extended to children either conceived or born during the existence of the marriage. According to this wider interpretation, children conceived before the marriage but born during it, children conceived and born during the marriage, and children conceived during the marriage but born after its dissolution are all presumed to be the offspring of the husband and wife. It is evident that this wider interpretation of the rule is preferable, because it establishes paternal filiation within marriage with all its consequences, in all situations mentioned above.

The legislation of most countries provides for a predetermined period of gestation which usually varies from a minimum of 180 days to a maximum of 302 days. A certain flexibility in this regard would certainly seem to be in accordance with present-day medical knowledge. When no specific period of gestation is provided for, reliance on expert medical evidence should be the rule.

In nearly all countries the law recognizes the right of the husband to disavow paternity, mostly through court proceedings, whether as a principal cause of action or in connexion with other proceedings whereby the enforcement of the legal right depends on the legitimacy of the person concerned. Sometimes, however, children conceived before the celebration of the marriage may be disavowed by a mere declaration of non-paternity made in the appropriate manner. Except for the latter case the presumption of paternity is usually destroyed only upon evidence of circumstances establishing that sexual relations did not take place during the period of conception and that paternity of the husband is impossible. Such a trend should be encouraged and the grounds admitted should be always very serious and strictly limited.

The right to disavow or to challenge paternity is usually granted to the husband, sometimes also to the person concerned as well as to their respective heirs. In a few instances, such right is enjoyed by the wife and by any person having a legitimate interest. In some countries the competent public authority may *ex efficio* initiate proceedings and this is usually the case when the interest of the child or of his descendants so requires. Generally, the action has to be exercised within short time-limits. It is evident that the opportunities of initiating proceedings to disavow or challenge paternity should be as limited as possible, in order not to upset the prevailing family situation.

It should be recalled here that the disavowal or challenge of paternity, when it is admitted in connexion with other proceedings where the issue is relevant, can be made usually at any time and by any person whose interest is affected.

As regards paternal filiation when the parents are not married to each other, the study concludes that:

The legislation of most countries provides for the establishment of the paternal filiation of a person born out of wedlock whether it entails a status that is a set of rights and duties, equal or inferior to that of a person born in wedlock or hardly any status at all, but only very limited rights. In some countries the law does not recognize any relationship between a person born out of wedlock and his father. No doubt the child has a fundamental right to have a father and to enjoy status in relation to him. It is, therefor, essential that the paternal filiation of a person born out of wedlock be recognized in law and that provisions to this effect be accordingly made.

The legislation of a great number of countries requires that the acknowledgement of the father be made according to strictly determined forms. The law of various other countries provides for a wide range of forms including, among others, tacit acknowledgement, operation of the presumption of paternity under specific circumstances, the recording of the acknowledgement by the director of the institution where the birth took place. Undoubtedly, this last approach secures paternal filiation in the largest number of cases of birth out of wedlock.

The information gathered for this study reveals that sometimes the approval of the mother is necessary in order for the acknowledgement made by the father to be effective. This requirement constitutes an infringement upon the right of the child to have his paternal filiation established. Because this right should not be denied, the approval of the mother should never constitute a prerequisite to the acknowledgement by the father.

The legislation of a few countries allows the paternal grandfather to acknowledge the child when the natural father is incapacitated or dead. This right should be extended to either paternal grandparent.

In many countries, the judicial establishment of paternal filiation is possible only in a limited number of cases, and in a few instances it is not provided for by law. This is a serious obstacle to securing paternal filiation and status. In order to improve the situation in this regard, the judicial establishment of paternity should be allowed whenever the court is satisfied that sexual relations took place during the time of conception which resulted in the birth. The possibility of establishing paternal relationship should not be denied in case of misconduct of the mother or relations with another man during the legal period of conception, as seems to be the situation in a few countries. If the court is satisfied that the man alleged to be the father is the natural father of the child, paternal filiation should be established.

Paternal filiation is established through court proceedings. However, mention has been made of a simpler form of establishment consisting in a summons to a man to declare before a judge that he believes he is the natural father. In case of default, acknowledgement is considered made. Such procedure permits establishment of paternal filiation in a quick, easy and inexpensive way.

The right to initiate proceedings for the establishment of paternal filiation should be granted to all persons who have a legal interest in doing so, including the competent guardianship or other authorities. As is sometimes the case, these authorities should play an active role in determining paternity by making the necessary investigations and encouraging voluntary acknowledgements of paternity whenever the father of a child born out of wedlock has been identified. In this connexion, the duty to disclose the identity of the father to the competent authorities should be imposed upon all persons having such knowledge as well as direct knowledge of the pregnancy or birth. Such disclosure should be subject to the rules of professional secrecy.

In various countries prohibitions and restrictions exist either as to the acknowledgement or as to the judicial establishment, or both, of the paternal filiation of persons born as a result of adulterous, incestuous or sacrilegious relations. In others, all persons born out of wedlock whether their parents were free or not to marry each other at the time of conception or birth, are entitled to have their paternal filiation established. This last trend should be followed and in so far as possible all existing prohibitions and restrictions should be eliminated so that these categories of persons born out of wedlock may not be denied the right to have a legally recognized paternal filiation.

On the basis of his analysis of the information available to him, the special rapporteur concluded that:

. . . it appears that the institution of adoption might indeed by considered an effective means to upgrade the status of a person born out of wedlock. It has gained wide acceptance in the major juridical systems of the world and has become an integral part of the family law of almost all of the jurisdictions studied. Also, the fundamental principles under which it is developing are generally agreed upon. These two points indicate that further progress could be achieved which would serve to make the institution still more useful, and transform it into an instrument which would help alleviate the discriminatory practices which persist against persons born out of wedlock.

Additional legislative measures appear to be required because of the numerous provisions which limit the effects of adoption or which may prevent the person born out of wedlock from being adopted, or when he is adopted, from being fully integrated into the adopter's family. Measures of this type are already in force in a few countries, but their general extension could be proposed as they would not conflict with the basic objectives of the laws of any of the countries studies. Such measures, moreover, would not affect the nature of the laws in force; they would only enlarge their scope and the extent of rights already granted.

Some adoption laws restrict the right to adopt in the case of persons who are not of the same religion as that of the child to be adopted. The primary consideration of the competent authorities should be the interest of the child; consequently, they should take the most liberal view, one that would make it possible for the child to be adopted whether or not he belongs to the same race or ethnic or religious group as the adoptive parents.

In the analysis of legal requirements for a valid adoption, it was observed that a number of countries prohibit adoption if the adopter already has children of his own. While the existence of previous children is indeed worthy of factual consideration before an adoption takes place, it does not seem necessary that it should lead to a legal prohibition of adoption. Some latitude could be given to the judge or the competent public authority to at least decide on the merits of each individual case. Better still, this decision should be left to the individual persons concerned.

A similar remark could be made regarding the prohibition of adoption when the prospective adopter is the father or mother of the person to be adopted. Such adoption should not, in principle, be prohibited in any case where the law permits the establishment of filiation. Furthermore, it could even be envisaged that adoption should be authorized in cases where the law prohibits the establishment of filiation.

As has been observed, only the type of adoption called "adoption with full effects" of blood relationship leads to an equalization of rights between the person adopted and the person born to the adopter in lawful wedlock. But the analysis above reveals also that this type of adoption is practised mainly in countries where the law disregards the fact of birth out of wedlock. In countries which differentiate between the two categories of persons, and where therefore the status of persons born out of wedlock is generally inferior to that of persons born in wedlock, the most common type of adoption found is "regular adoption" which grants rights subject to limitations and usually restricts the effects of adoption to a relationship between the adopted and the adoptee. Efforts leading to a more liberal attitude should be encouraged, as the possibility for integration of the person adopted into the adopter's family is absent where it is most needed. In particular, the question of recognition of family relationship should be re-examined in order that "regular adoption" may place the adopted person, with all the consequences that such a step implies, on an equal footing with the person born to the adopter in lawful wedlock.

Finally, when the adoptee is a minor, he should be allowed to acquire, *ipso facto,* the nationality of the adopter in order to facilitate the process of integration.

After examining the conclusions and recommendations set out in the study, the Sub-Commission on Prevention of Discrimination and Protection of Minorities adopted (in 1967) a series of draft principles on equality and non-discrimination in respect of persons born out of wedlock. These draft principles were as follows:

Part I

1. Every person born out of wedlock shall be entitled to legal recognition of his maternal and paternal filiation in so far as compatible with the principle of the protection of the family.

2. The fact of birth of a child shall by itself establish maternal filiation to the woman who gives birth to the child.

3. The establishment of paternal filiation shall be provided for by law through a variety of means, including acknowledgement, recognition of legal presumptions and judicial decision. Judicial proceedings to establish paternal filiation shall not be subject to any time-limits.

4. The husband shall be presumed to be the father of any child born to his wife whether he is conceived or born during the marriage. This presumption may be overcome only by a judicial decision based upon evidence that the husband is not the father. Proceedings to that end shall be initiated within a limited period of time.

5. Any child born of parents who intermarry after the birth of that child shall be considered to be born of that marriage.

6. Every person born in wedlock, or considered to be born in wedlock as a result of the subsequent marriage of his parents, shall retain his status notwithstanding the invalidity or annulment of the marriage.

Part II

7. Every person, once his filiation has been established, shall have the same legal status as a person born in wedlock.

8. Every person born out of wedlock whose filiation is established in relation to both parents shall have the right to bear a surname determined as in the case of a person born in wedlock. If his filiation is established in relation only to his mother, he shall be entitled to bear her surname, modified, if necessary, in such a manner as not to reveal the fact of birth out of wedlock.

9. The rights and obligations pertaining to parental authority shall be the same, whether the child is born in wedlock or out of wedlock. Unless otherwise decided by the court in the best interest of the child born out of wedlock, parental authority shall be exercised according to the same rules as for a child born in wedlock if his filiation is established in relation to both parents, or by his mother alone if his paternal filiation is not established.

10. The domicile of any child born out of wedlock whose filiation is established in relation to both parents shall be determined according to the same rules as for children born in wedlock.

If the filiation is established in relation to the mother alone, appropriate rules shall ensure in any case that the child has a domicile.

11. Every person born out of wedlock shall, once his filiation has been established, have the same maintenance rights as persons born in wedlock. Birth out of wedlock shall not affect the order of priority of claimants.

12. Every person born out of wedlock shall, once his filiation has been established, have the same inheritance rights as persons born in wedlock. Legal limitations or restrictions on the freedom of a testator to dispose of his property shall afford equal protection to persons entitled to inheritance, whether they are born in wedlock or out of wedlock.

13. The nationality or citizenship of a person born out of wedlock shall be determined by the same rules as those applicable to persons born in wedlock.

Special protection against statelessness shall be provided for persons born out of wedlock. In particular, when only the maternal filiation of a person born out of wedlock is established, its effects shall be the same as in the case of paternal filiation.

14. Political, social, economic and cultural rights shall be enjoyed equally by all persons, whether they are born in wedlock or out of wedlock, without prejudice as regards social welfare services, to the special care which shall be provided to children born out of wedlock and their mothers, by the State or society, when necessary.

Part III

15. Information in birth and other registers containing personal data which might disclose the fact of birth out of wedlock shall be available only to persons or authorities having a legitimate interest with respect to filiation.

In referring to persons born out of wedlock, any designation which might carry a derogatory connotation shall be avoided.

16. The adoption of a child born out of wedlock shall be subject to the same rules and provisions and shall have the same consequences as the adoption of children born in wedlock.

Restrictions on the right to adopt shall be limited to such requirements as are necessary to establish a parent-child relationship and to assure the best interest of the adoptee. In particular, no restrictions based solely on a difference of race, colour or national origin shall be permitted.

Adoption procedure should be carried out under the supervision of the State and/or a competent social welfare agency to ensure full protection of the child and his wellbeing.

The study and the draft general principles were reviewed by the COMMISSION ON THE STATUS OF WOMEN at its 1967 session in connection with that commission's consideration of questions relating to the status of the unmarried mother. On the initiative of the commission, the Economic and Social Council adopted resolution 1514 (XLVIII) of 28 May 1970, in which it urged States to take adequate measures of social assistance in favor of the unmarried mother and the child born out of wedlock and invited them to study the problems posed by the integration of the unmarried mother and her child in all spheres of society.

Later, again on the initiative of the Commission on the Status of Women, the Economic and Social Council adopted resolution 1679 (LII) of 2 June 1972, in which it recommended that governments take all possible measures to eliminate any prevailing legal and social discrimination against the family consisting of an unmarried mother and her child and to offer such families all necessary advice and assistance, seeking to obtain a greater comprehension by society of their situation and with a view to eliminating the harm caused by lack of understanding and to securing them an acceptance on an equal footing with other members of society. The council recommends the following general principles for achieving that end:

(a) Maternal filiation shall be recognized in law, in all cases, automatically as a consequence of the fact of birth;

(b) Whatever the legal system applying in the case of married parents, the unmarried mother, whether paternal filiation is established or not, shall enjoy in all cases, as a parent, the fullest set of rights and duties provided for by law, in particular:

(i) If maternal filiation only is established, the surname of the mother should be transmitted to her child, if possible, in such a manner as not to reveal the fact of birth out of wedlock;

(ii) If maternal filiation only is established, the nationality of the unmarried mother shall be transmitted to her child as a consequence of the fact of birth; if both maternal and paternal filiations are established, the nationality of the child shall be governed by the same rules as those which apply in the case of birth in wedlock;

(iii) The unmarried mother should be vested in law with full parental authority over her child, in all cases, as an automatic consequence of the fact of birth; a family consisting of an unmarried mother and her child should not be subjected to any special control or supervision by the authorities different from that given to other families;

(iv) Maintenance rights and obligations as between the unmarried mother and her child should be the same as between a sole parent and a child born in wedlock; when both paternal and maternal filiations are established, the maintenance obligations of the parents to the child should be the same as if the child was born in wedlock; all appropriate assistance should be offered by the competent authority to the mother to help her (a) to establish paternal filiation and (b) to obtain an agreement by the father or a decision by the competent authority or court for the support of the child by his father; if the father does not fulfil his maintenance obligations, or if it is not possible to establish paternity, benefit should be available from appropriate public sources for the support of the mother and her child according to their needs;

(v) There should be no discrimination against the offspring of unmarried mothers in all matters of inheritance;

(vi) The unmarried mother should enjoy all the measures of social assistance and social security devised for mothers in general and for single parents in particular;

(vii) There should be no discrimination against the the unmarried mother in matters of employment, education and training as well as in access to child care facilities;

The council also recommended, in the same resolution, that member States should consider the development of programs designed to increase awareness of the existing double standard in allocating social responsibility for births out of wedlock, so as to bring about a balance in these social attitudes towards members of both sexes in the responsibility for such births.

PERU. The Republic of Peru is a country in tropical South America, on the Pacific Ocean. It has borders with Bolivia, Brazil, Chile, Colombia, and Ecuador. It achieved independence from Spain in 1821 and became a member of the United Nations in 1945. Its population is estimated by the UN (1990) to be 22,332,000. There is no up-to-date statistical information on the ethnic composition of the population because it is unlawful to indicate such information on any official document. However, it is estimated that 45% of the people are of Indian origin, 37% of Mestizo (mixed) origin, 15% of European origin, and the remainder of African or Asian origin. Languages commonly used include Spanish (official), Quechua, and Aymara. Christianity (Roman Catholic) is the predominant religion; the Roman Catholic faith is protected by the State, and only Roman Catholic religious instruction is permitted in the schools. Literacy is estimated at 72%.

The government (1990) took the form of a republic. Under the 1980 constitution, the president and members of the legislature are elected, by separate ballots, for terms of five years, voting being compulsory for all citizens over the age of 18. The president, as head of State, exercises executive power with the assistance of a premier and the Council of Ministers. The legislature consists of the 60-member Senate and the 180-member Chamber of Deputies. Political parties include the American Popular Revolutionary Alliance, the Democratic Convergence Party, the Popular Action Party, and the United Left (comprising six Marxist parties).

In a report presented to the **GROUP OF THREE** of the UN Commission on Human Rights on 20 December 1985, the government of Peru provided the following information concerning human rights in that country (UN Doc.E/CN.4/1986/29/Add. 1, para. 1–3):

Article 80 of the Constitution establishes, among other duties of the State, that of guaranteeing the full exercise of human rights. A special role in fulfilling this mandate is played by the judiciary; by the Office of the Government Attorney, which ensures the independence of judicial bodies and acts as the defender of the people before the administration; and by the National Elections Board, the Court of Constitutional Guarantees and the Commission on Human Rights of the Chamber of Deputies.

In order better to guarantee the full exercise of human rights, the legislative bodies have enacted a set of laws relating, for example, to suffrage for illiterate persons, measures to speed up the judicial process, the establishment of the Reprieve Assessment Commission, the Organizational Law on the Office of the Government Attorney the law reestablishing the Ministry of Justice and the Organizational Law on the Court of Constitutional Guarantees. In addition to these provisions, there is a new *amparo* and *habeas corpus* act; these laws are all designed to guarantee the full exercise of human rights. Parliament is also studying a number of bills and draft codes which must be brought into line with the new mandates of the Constitution currently in force in Peru.

Peru is a zealous defender of human rights and the legislative bodies are currently faced with the challenge either of giving the country new provisions to improve the implementation of the relevant provisions of the Constitution or of adapting already existing ones.

In 1985, although the country was engulfed in an acute economic, social, and financial crisis, an elected president was able to transfer power to a constitutionally elected successor for the first time since 1945.

However, Peruvians protest regularly to the government about sub-standard living conditions; and, in 1988, one member of a group of 300 slum dwellers—demanding tap water and electricity in their homes—was killed when an armored car charged into the crowd.

The government has also been preoccupied, for some time, with efforts to control the *Sendero Luminoso* guerrillas, a Maoist group which persistently engages in terrorist activities.

PERU: DISAPPEARANCES. The WORKING GROUP ON ENFORCED OR INVOLUNTARY DISAPPEARANCES has twice sent missions to Peru to study the situation as regards enforced or involuntary disappearances there, first in 1985 in response to an invitation extended by the government of then-President Fernando Belaunde Terry and again in 1986 in response to a further invitation extended by the government by his replacement, President Alan Garcia Perez. The working group was presented on both visits by two of its members, Mr. Toine van Dongen (Netherlands) and Mr. Luis Varela Quiros (Costa Rica).

The reports of the two visits (UN Docs. E/CN.4/ 1986/18/Add. 1 and E/CN.4/1987/15/Add. 1) together provide a picture of the evolving situation regarding enforced and involuntary disappearances which plagued Peru at that time and of the measures taken by the two governments to deal with the problem. The working group's concluding observations, prepared after the second visit, were as follows (UN Doc. E/CN.4/1987/15/Add. 1, para, 42–52):

The Working Group is grateful to the Peruvian Government for providing an opportunity to review the progress made in combating the phenomenon of disappearances in Peru, following its first visit in June of 1985.

As already stated in last year's report, in assessing the situation of missing persons in Peru, the Working Group has to pay due regard to the overall context of violence in which disappearances have been reported to it. For, in both intellectual and practical terms, it is not feasible to divorce the issue of disappearances completely from related violations of human rights or from the socio-political processes that have engendered them. If it did so, the Group would not be exercising its mandate properly in the manner consistently supported over the years by the Commission on Human Rights.

Being faced with a terrorist movement such as Sendero Luminoso amidst a variety of urgent economic and social problems is not an enviable position for any government to be in. Terrorist violence rages unabated, without the least respect for life, limb or property. Worse still, although for a long time it was confined to some provinces of Ayacucho and neighbouring departments, insurgence has now spread to the Departments of Cerro de Pasco(north of Ayacucho) and of Cuzco and Puno(to the south) and the capital itself has become affected. In consequence, the area covered by the state of emergency has been extended.

Clearly, in its contacts with the Working Group, the previous Government was loath to admit that disappearances had indeed occurred in significant numbers and avoided apportioning responsibility for any excesses to the armed forces or the police. It was heartening, therefore, to note that the new President declared upon taking office that his administration would not fight "barbarism with barbarism". Indeed, that promise as well as concrete action bear witness to a firm resolve to call a halt to disappearances and other violations of human rights by government forces. Civil participation has been sought in finding long-term solutions for internal strife and in promoting the cause of human rights. Establishing the National Council for Human Rights is but one example. The present Government has also resolutely opened its doors to international scrutiny of Peru's human rights record. It has taken a much more cooperative attitude towards the Group, swiftly responding to cases transmitted to it and making immediate efforts to clarify them.

In parliament, interest for human rights seems to have increased markedly and this has led to the introduction of legislation designed to remedy lacunae in Peruvian human rights law.

One of the major concerns expressed in the previous report concerned the wide latitude granted by the central Government to the armed forces and the police to fight Sendero Luminoso and restore public order in the manner they saw fit. At the time it was argued that such latitude would almost inevitably lead sooner or later to disappearances and concomitant violations of human rights. It would seem that the present administration has made great strides towards regaining control over the counter-insurgence strategy followed by the armed forces. Consequently, the incidence of disappearances has decreased considerably, particularly since the end of 1985. This is clear from the graph in the annex.

However, disappearances still continue to occur in Peru on an appreciable scale, and other forms of violence at the hands of government forces appear to have increased, particularly since the middle of 1986. The Working Group has transmitted to the Government some 160 cases that occurred in the emergency zone between August 1985 and November 1986. About half of these cases have subsequently been clarified: detention was acknowledged or subjects were turned over to the police by the armed forces or released. While this shows a welcome increase in the measure of responsiveness of the armed forces, it is also indicative of the practice of short-term disappearances as a method of counter-insurgency in breach of Peruvian law.

In last year's report attention was drawn to what was described as some sort of institutional paralysis pertaining to the protection of human rights in the emergency zone. Little progress can be reported in that regard. In the majority of cases prosecutors are still obstructed in their efforts to follow up on denunciations of disappearances. The Judiciary seems ill at ease with *habeas corpus* proceedings, which in any case meet with lack of co-operation from the respondents. Almost without exception civilian courts refer cases involving military and police personnel to military courts, despite the fact that the Code of Military Justice does not cover homicide, maltreatment and the like. The broad powers concentrated in the hands of the military in the

P

emergency zone further diminish the role which civil institutions might otherwise play in applying the rule of law.

Establishing a Human Rights Office under the auspices of the Attorney-General has admirably expedited the processing of cases of missing persons. Yet that fact in itself has not substantially enhanced the measure of protection extended to citizens at large. Undoubtedly, adequate access to registers of arrests maintained by the armed forces would have not only a curative but also a preventive effect. At any rate, the armed forces must be prevailed upon to cooperate more closely in the emergency zone with prosecutors and judicial authorities. Moreover, the latter are in dire need of material and human resources, as was pointed out in last year's report.

The situation of the victims among the indigenous population in the affected areas remains dismal. Humanitarian aid from national and international sources is an increasingly vital necessity. A long-term development strategy, designed to eliminate the poverty and neglect which are among the root causes of the Ayacuchan drama, is slowly getting under way, even though efforts have been set back by terrorist onslaughts.

Violence cannot be countered with violence alone. Only when the structural factors that contributed to the spiral of terror and counter-terror are properly dealt with, can there be any hope of preventing a recurrence of the excesses of the past. The Peruvian Government seems keenly aware of that fact. Its task remains a formidable one.

SEE ALSO *Disappearances: UN Draft Declaration; Inter-American Convention on the Forced Disappearance of Persons (Draft).*

PHILIPPINES. The Republic of the Philippines is a country occupying an archipelago of more than 7,000 islands in the Pacific Ocean, off the southeastern coast of Asia, of which the largest are Luzon, Mindanao, Samar, Negros, Palawan, Panay, and Mindoro. It achieved independence from the United States of America in 1946 and became a member of the United Nations in 1945. Its population is estimated by the UN (1990) to be 60,974,000. Ethnic groups include Malaysians, Chinese, and persons of mixed blood. Languages commonly used include Filipino (the national language, based on Tagalog, a Malaysian dialect), English (the language of the government and of higher education), and more than 75 languages of the Malayo–Polynesian family. Christianity (Roman Catholic, 85%; Aglipayan, 4%; and Protestant denominations, 3%) is the predominant religion; Islam is the religion of about 4%, and Animism and related beliefs the faith of the remaining 4%. Members of the Islamic religion are concentrated on Mindanao and other southern islands of the Sulu Archipelago. Literacy is estimated at 88%.

The government (1990) took the form of a republic. President Corazon Aquino, who took office on 25 February 1986, suspended parliament and set up a provisional government pending preparation of a new constitution. Political parties include the Philippine Democratic Party, the United Nationalist Democratic Organization, the New Society Movement, and the *Partido Nacionalista Philipina.*

Although a Spanish expedition led by Portuguese explorer Ferdinand Magellan first visited the Philippines in 1521, Spanish conquest of the islands—named Las Felipinas after King Philip II—began in earnest only 40 years later, when an expedition arrived and quickly established dominance over thousands of small independent communities which had never had central rule. The Filipino population at that time consisted of local chiefs, freemen who did not pay tribute to the chiefs, freedmen or liberated slaves who were heavily in debt to the chiefs, and slaves who were the chiefs' personal property. Spanish missionaries—Augustinians, Franciscans, Jesuits, and Dominicans—soon won most of that population either to the Roman Catholic Church or to the Philippine Independent (Aglipayan) Church, an offshoot of Catholicism, with the exception of the Moros who were concentrated on Mindanao and the Sulu Peninsula and who retained their Islamic faith.

After British defeat of the Spanish Armada in 1588, Spanish influence declined in the Philippines, but the religious orders took over some government functions and amassed great wealth and property. Opposition to these activities of the clergy led to the formation of a liberation movement which accepted American aid during the Spanish–American war. After the victory of Adm. Dewey in Manila Bay in 1898, an insurrection broke out. Although it was successful, the treaty that ended the war transferred the Philippines to the United States instead of grating it independence. This led to a revolt against the United States; and, after the islands were subdued, the question of independence for the Philippines remained a political issue for many years. Finally, under the Tydings–McDuffie Independence Act of 1934, the islands began a ten-year transition period of controlled autonomy as the Commonwealth of the Philippines, with complete independence scheduled for 4 July 1946.

However, on 7 December 1941, the Japanese attacked the Philippines without warning and destroyed most of the U.S. aircraft stationed there after wrecking the Cavite Naval Base. After Manila was bombed and occupied on 2 January 1942 after being declared an open city, American and Filipino forces, commanded by Gen. Douglas MacArthur, were compelled to withdraw to the Bataan Peninsula. MacArthur was ordered to go to Australia, but the 36,000-man garrison he left on Bataan was forced to surrender and its survivors were subjected by the Japanese to a brutal "death march" in which thousands perished and those who survived were eventually crowded into concentration camps where they were subjected to cruel and inhuman treatment.

American troops liberated the Philippines and freed thousands of prisoners in mid-1945, and by September of that year all military rule ended. On 4 July 1946, President Truman proclaimed the independence of the Philippines.

The United States played a major role in rebuilding the government and the economy of the islands, and, until 1972, the country enjoyed democratic rule under its 1935 constitution. In 1972, however, President Ferdinand Marcos declared martial law, blaming his action on increasing lawlessness, urban terrorism, and threats of open rebellion by the New People's Army, alleged to be a military wing of the Philippine Communist Party. During the eight-year period of martial law, Marcos ruled largely by decree and progressively restricted democratic institutions and civil liberties. Although a new constitution came into effect in 1973, the Marcos government acted until 1981 under its transitory provisions.

Mounting popular dissatisfaction with the regime and with the deteriorating national economy was further aroused by the assassination, in 1983, of the leader of the opposition, Benigno Aquino, upon his return from exile in the United States. In December 1985, Marcos called for an unscheduled presidential election to be held in February 1986. Although his party won the official election tally, impartial observers, including a delegation of U.S. congressmen, supported the claim of the opposition that it had actually received a large majority of the votes cast. A civilian-military uprising forced Marcos to flee the country and Corazon Aquino, widow of Benigno Aquino and leader of the opposition party, was declared winner of the election. As president, Mrs. Aquino was given extensive powers under a provisional constitution.

A new **PHILIPPINES: CONSTITUTION,** containing a Bill of Rights (article 3), was ratified by the people of the Philippines on 2 February 1987. Its policies and provisions are implemented mainly through the Revised Penal Code, the Civil Code, the Administrative Code, and various executive orders, proclamations, and directives, as well as by laws adopted by the congress.

Under article 13 of the constitution, a national Commission on Human Rights was created with a mandate to investigate, on its own or on a complaint from any party, all forms of human rights violations involving civil and political rights. These rights can be protected and enforced through the regular judicial system or through administrative bodies such as the Civil Service Commission and the National Police Commission.

On 6 May 1988, the Commission on Human Rights of the Philippines issued a "Statement on Human Rights" and "Guidelines on Visitation and the Conduct of Arrest, Detention and Related Operations" (both reproduced below) to which the secretary of National Defense, the chief of staff of the armed forces, and the director-general of the Integrated National Police have conformed.

In a report submitted to the HUMAN RIGHTS COMMITTEE on 26 August 1988, the government of the Philippines provided the following information (UN Doc. CCPR/C/50/Add. 1, para. 10–11):

The Philippines is currently facing a serious insurgency problem and certain extraordinary measures have been taken by the government authorities to cope with the problem. One of these is Executive Order No. 272 issued on 25 July 1987 increasing the period within which, under article 125 of the Revised Penal Code of the Philippines, a person who is detained on legal grounds is to be delivered to the proper judicial authorities: within 12 hours for crimes or offences punishable by light penalties, 18 hours for crimes or offences punishable by correctional penalties, and 36 hours for crimes or offences punishable by afflictive or capital penalties. The previous period of detention allowed was 6, 9 and 18 hours, respectively. Also, the amount of the bail bond for persons accused of bailable offences has been increased by 10 times in certain cases, such as subversion, sedition, rebellion, illegal possession of firearms, car stealing, drug trafficking and other serious offences.

As already stated in paragraph 10, the current serious insurgency problem has given rise to reported violations of human rights allegedly committed by elements of the military and paramilitary civilian groups as well as by elements of rebel and secessionist groups. Reports of such violations are being investigated by the Commission on Human Rights and, where investigations show that violations have indeed occurred, the perpetrators are recommended for immediate prosecution under existing Philippine laws.

Statement on Human Rights. The "Statement on Human Rights" issued by the Commission on Human Rights of the Philippines, reads as follows (UN Doc. CCPR/C/50/Add. 1, annex III):

The Commission on Human Rights reiterates its position that the human rights of every person must be observed and respected at all times. This statement encompasses the human rights most affected in the current insurgency situation.

Human Rights are the supreme and inherent rights to life, to dignity and to self-development. It is the essence of these rights that makes man human.

The policy of our constitutional government on Human Rights is embodied in Section 11, Article II of the Constitution, which states:

"The State values the dignity of every human person and guarantees full respect for human rights."

The Constitution guarantees these rights to every human person and has mandated the Commission on Human Rights as an independent constitutional body to investigate, on its own or on complaint by any party, all forms of human rights violations involving civil and political rights (Par. 1, Sec. 18, Article XIII).

The Bill of Rights enshrined in our Constitution (Article III) specifies the rights guaranteed to every person, without distinction as to race, sex, color, religion, or political persuasion. Among these are the right to life, to equal protection under our laws, to freedom from unreasonable searches and seizures, the right to assemble peacefully for redress of grievances and the right to due process, to be heard and to be assisted by legal counsel.

A person may not be detained unlawfully. During his detention, the following are prohibited:

1. The use of torture, force, violence, threat or any means that vitiate his free will;

2. The use of secret detention places, solitary, incommunicado and other similar forms of detention;

3. The employment of physical, psychological, or degrading punishment, or the use of inhuman facilities.

Every Filipino, regardless of whether he is a member of the military force or the police organization, a civilian, or an insurgent, and even a foreigner residing in or visiting the country, is guaranteed these rights.

Corollary to these rights, however, is the primary obligation of every Filipino citizen to protect and defend the Constitution, to respect the rights of others, to uphold the authority of the State, and to observe its laws.

Our government's commitment to human rights is founded in the Filipino's inherent respect for the dignity of man and his human rights enunciated not only in its state policies but also in its commitment to the principles embodied in, among others, the Universal Declaration of Human Rights adopted by the General Assembly of the United Nations on 10 December 1948, the Declaration of the Rights of the Child, the International Covenant on Civil and Political Rights, the International Covenant of Economic, Social and Cultural Rights, and to Protocol II relating to Protection of Victims of Non-International Armed Conflicts adopted on 12 August 1949 by the Geneva Convention.

We enjoin every Filipino citizen, most especially those in the government service whose functions directly involve the protection of the security of the state and its people, to observe and protect these human rights, and enforce laws, substantive and procedural, that uphold them.

Guidelines on Visitation and the Conduct of Investigation, Arrest, Detention and Related Operations. These guidelines, adopted by the Commission on Human Rights of the Philippines, are as follows (UN Doc. CCPR/C/50/Add. 1, annex IV):

1. Section 18, Article XIII of the 1987 Constitution specifically grants the Commission on Human Rights certain powers and functions, among which are the following:

(i) Investigate, on its own or on complaint by any party, all forms of human rights violations involving civil and political rights;

(ii) Protect the rights of Filipinos in the Philippines and overseas;

(iii) Exercise visitorial powers over jails, prisons, detention facilities; and

(iv) Request the assistance of any department, bureau, office or agency in the performance of its functions.

2. The armed Forces of the Philippines, the National Police and other law enforcement agencies have the obligation to protect the human rights of citizens and ensure the security of the state and its people. In the performance of these duties, utmost observance and respect for human rights is required.

3. Accordingly, the following guidelines on visitation and the conduct of investigation, arrest, detention and related operations are hereby promulgated for the strict and immediate implementation of all law enforcement agencies:

3.1 The Heads of the various law enforcement agencies shall be responsible for promulgating the rules and regulations to be disseminated to all members of their units or agencies to ensure observance of the rights guaranteed in the Constitution, especially those enumerated in the Commission on Human Rights statement promulgated May 6, 1988, which are incorporated herein by reference.

3.2 Commanders and elements of all units under their command shall extend maximum cooperation and courtesy to members of the Commission on Human Rights and/or their authorized representatives in the exercise of their constitutional authority and functions.

3.3 Recognizing the crucial role of complainants and witnesses in human rights cases, commanders and elements of all units under their command are responsible for their safety and security from potentially adverse or hostile actions.

3.4 Immediate members of the family, extended members of the family, legal counsel and spiritual advisers shall have free access to detained persons, subject to the provisions of applicable laws, rules and regulations.

3.5 An official report on any arrest, detention, investigation or similar operations shall be submitted to the Commission on Human Rights at the Integrated Bar of the Philippines Building, Dona Julia Vargas Avenue, Pasig, Metro Manila or to any of its twelve (12) regional offices, on a quarterly basis concerning the conduct of the foregoing operations and the names and status of all persons arrested or detained by virtue thereof unless a special report is required by the Commission or any of its regional offices.

3.6 In effecting arrests, conducting investigations and during detention, the use of unnecessary force must always be avoided. The resolution of the National Police Commission prescribing policies on arrests and investigations and enjoining strict adherence to Rule 113 of the Rules of Court must be followed, not only by the National Police, but also by other law enforcement agencies.

PHILIPPINES: CONSTITUTION. The Constitution of the Republic of the Philippines, ratified by the Filipino people on 2 February 1987, contains the following provisions (articles III and XIII) relating specifically to human rights and fundamental freedoms (UN Doc. CCPR/C/50/Add. 1, pp. 4–6):

Article III
Bill of Rights

Section 1. No person shall be deprived of life, liberty, or property without due process of law, nor shall any person be denied the equal protection of the laws.

Sec. 2. The right of the people to be secure in their persons, houses, papers, and effects against unreasonable searches and seizures of whatever nature and for any purpose shall be inviolable, and no search warrant or warrant of arrest shall issue except upon probable cause to be determined personally by the judge after examination under oath or affirmation of the complainant and the witnesses he may produce, and particularly describing the place to be searched and the persons or things to be seized.

Sec. 3. (1) The privacy of communication and correspondence shall be inviolable except upon lawful order of the court, or when public safety or order requires otherwise as prescribed by law.

(2) Any evidence obtained in violation of this or the preceding section shall be inadmissible for any purpose in any proceeding.

Sec. 4. No law shall be passed abridging the freedom of speech, of expression, or of the press, or the right of the people peaceably to assemble and petition the government for redress of grievances.

Sec. 5. No law shall be made respecting an establishment of religion, or prohibiting the free exercise thereof. The free exercise and enjoyment of religious profession and worship, without discrimination or preference, shall forever be allowed. No religious test shall be required for the exercise of civil or political rights.

Sec. 6. The liberty of abode and of changing the same within the limits prescribed by law shall not be impaired except upon lawful order of the court. Neither shall the right to travel be impaired except in the interest of national security, public safety, or public health, as may be provided by law.

Sec. 7. The right of the people to information on matters of public concern shall be recognized. Access to official records, and to documents, and papers pertaining to official acts, transactions, or decisions, as well as to government research data used as basis for policy development, shall be afforded the citizen, subject to such limitations as may be provided by law.

Sec. 8. The right of the people, including those employed in the public and private sectors, to form unions, associations, or societies for purposes not contrary to law shall not be abridged.

Sec. 9. Private property shall not be taken for public use without just compensation.

Sec. 10. No law impairing the obligation of contracts shall be passed.

Sec. 11. Free access to the courts and quasi-judicial bodies and adequate legal assistance shall not be denied to any person by reason of poverty.

Sec. 12. (1) Any person under investigation for the commission of an offense shall have the right to be informed of his right to remain silent and to have competent and independent counsel preferably of his own choice. If the person cannot afford the services of counsel, he must be provided with one. These rights cannot be waived except in writing and in the presence of counsel.

(2) No torture, force, violence, threat, intimidation, or any other means which vitiate the free will shall be used against him. Secret detention places, solitary, *incommunicado,* or other similar forms of detention are prohibited.

(3) Any confession of admission obtained in violation of this or Section 17 hereof shall be inadmissible in evidence against him.

(4) The law shall provide for penal and civil sanctions for violations of this section as well as compensation to and rehabilitation of victims of torture or similar practices, and their families.

Sec. 13. All persons, except those charged with offenses punishable by *reclusion perpetua* when evidence of guilt is strong, shall, before conviction, be bailable by sufficient sureties, or be released on recognizance as may be provided by law. The right to bail shall not be impaired even when the privilege of the writ of *habeas corpus* is suspended. Excessive bail shall not be required.

Sec. 14. (1) No person shall be held to answer for a criminal offense without due process of law.

(2) In all criminal prosecutions, the accused shall be presumed innocent until the contrary is proved, and shall enjoy the right to be heard by himself and counsel, to be informed of the nature and cause of the accusation against him, to have a speedy, impartial, and public trial, to meet the witnesses face to face, and to have compulsory process to secure the attendance of witnesses and the production of evidence in his behalf. However, after arraignment, trial may proceed notwithstanding the absence of the accused provided that he has been duly notified and his failure to appear is unjustifiable.

Sec. 15. The privilege of the writ of *habeas corpus* shall not be suspended except in cases of invasion or rebellion when the public safety requires it.

Sec. 16. All persons shall have the right to a speedy disposition of their cases before all judicial, quasi-judicial, or administrative bodies.

Sec. 17. No person shall be compelled to be a witness against himself.

Sec. 18. (1) No person shall be detained solely by reason of his political beliefs and aspirations.

(2) No involuntary servitude in any form shall exist except as a punishment for a crime whereof the party shall have been duly convicted.

Sec. 19. (1) Excessive fines shall not be imposed, nor cruel, degrading or inhuman punishment inflicted. Neither shall death penalty be imposed, unless, for compelling reasons involving heinous crimes, the Congress hereafter provides for it. Any death penalty already imposed shall be reduced to *reclusion perpetua.*

(2) The employment of physical, psychological, or degrading punishment against any prisoner or detainee or the use of substandard or inadequate penal facilities under subhuman conditions shall be dealt with by law.

Sec. 20. No person shall be imprisoned for debt or nonpayment of a poll tax.

Sec. 21. No person shall be twice put in jeopardy of punishment for the same offense. If an act is punished by a law and an ordinance, conviction or acquittal under either shall constitute a bar to another prosecution for the same act.

Sec. 22. No *ex post facto* law or bill of attainder shall be enacted.

Article XIII
Human Rights

Sec. 17. (1) There is hereby created an independent office called the Commission on Human Rights.

(2) The Commission shall be composed of a Chairman and four members who must be natural-born citizens of the Philippines and a majority of whom shall be members of the Bar. The term of office and other qualifications and disabilities of the Members of the Commission shall be approved by law.

(3) Until this Commission is constituted, the existing Presidential Committee on Human Rights shall continue to exercise its present functions and powers.

(4) The approved annual appropriations of the Commission shall be automatically and regularly released.

Sec. 18. The Commission on Human Rights shall have the following powers and functions:

(1) Investigate, on its own or on complaint by any party, all forms of human rights violations involving civil and political rights;

(2) Adopt its operational guidelines and rules of procedure, and cite for contempt for violations thereof in accordance with the Rules of Court;

(3) Provide appropriate legal measures for the protection of human rights of all persons within the Philippines, as well as Filipinos residing abroad, and provide for preventive measures and legal aid services to the underprivileged whose human rights have been violated or need protection;

(4) Exercise visitatorial powers over jails, prisons, or detention facilities;

(5) Establish a continuing program of research, education, and information to enhance respect for the primacy of human rights;

(6) Recommend to the Congress effective measures to promote human rights and to provide for compensation to victims of violations of human rights, or their families;

(7) Monitor the Philippine Government's compliance with international treaty obligations on human rights;

(8) Grant immunity from prosecution to any person whose testimony or whose possession of documents or other evidence is necessary or convenient to determine the truth in any investigations conducted by it or under its authority;

(9) Request the assistance of any department, bureau, office, or agency in the performance of its functions;

(10) Appoint its officers and employees in accordance with law; and

(11) Perform such other duties and functions as may be provided by law.

Sec. 19. The Congress may provide for other cases of violations of human rights that should fall within the authority of the Commission, taking into account its recommendations.

POLAND. The Polish People's Republic is a country in eastern Europe, on the Baltic Sea. It has borders with Czechoslovakia, the former German Democratic Republic, and the Union of Soviet Socialist Republics. Occupied by Germany during World War II, Poland's boundaries were redefined in 1945 by the establishment of a *de facto* western frontier along the Oder and Neisse Rivers under an agreement reached in Berlin by American President Harry S. Truman, British Prime Minister Clement Attlee and U.S.S.R. Premier Joseph Stalin, and by a treaty with the Union of Soviet Socialist Republics delimiting the Polish-U.S.S.R. frontier. Poland became a member of the United Nations the same year. Its population is estimated by the UN (1990) to be 38,513,000. It includes small national minorities of Byelorussians and Ukrainians. Although religious activity is not officially encouraged, 90% of the Polish people are said to maintain religious beliefs; among them, Christian-

ity is predominant (Roman Catholic, 93%; Eastern Orthodox, 5%; Protestant denominations, 1%), while Islam is professed by .5% of the population and Judaism by .5%. State–Church relationships are regulated by laws, including those adopted by Parliament on 17 May 1989 giving the Roman Catholic Church legal status, the right to buy and sell property, and to operate businesses, and authorizing the government to return Church property it had seized in the 1950s. Literacy is estimated at 98%.

The government (1990) took the form of a republic. Under the 1989 "round table" agreements between the State authorities, the union Solidarity *(Solidarnošč)*, and other groups concerned, open elections were held on 4 June 1989 for the first time in 40 years to fill 161 open seats in the 460-member *Sejm*, or lower house of parliament, and 100 seats in the newly created Senate. Candidates sponsored by Solidarity won 160 *Sejm* seats and 92 Senate seats. Thus reconstructed, the National Assembly, on 19 July 1989, elected Gen. Wojciech Jaruzelski, who had been general secretary of the United Workers' (Communist) Party and head of State since 1981, as Poland's president. Tadeusz Mazowiecki, a Solidarity official, was elected as Poland's first postwar non-Communist prime minister and took office on 29 July 1989. In elections held in December 1990, Solidarity leader Lech Walesa replaced Gen. Jaruzelski as president.

Poland's fate was controlled for many centuries by its neighbors—Austria, Germany, and Russia—and, for more than a century beginning in 1795, it totally disappeared from the map after those powers had partitioned it among themselves.

World War I gave Poland an opportunity to recover its independence, and the armistice of 11 November 1918 led to its reconstitution as an independent State. The Treaty of Versailles gave it access to the Baltic Sea and made Danzig a free city but left it with the problem of reconciling the conflicting interests of numerous linguistic and ethnic minorities, including Germans, Ukrainians, Byelorussians, Lithuanians, and Jews. The Polish Jews, protected in the Middle Ages by the kings, had later suffered intolerance and discrimination in their own country.

In 1939, Adolph Hitler, brushing aside a ten-year non-aggression pact he had signed in 1934, abruptly demanded the return of Danzig to Germany. Poland refused; and, on 1 September 1939, Nazi troops invaded Poland from the west, precipitating World War II. Soviet troops moved in from the east on 17 September, and a German–Russian agreement partitioned Poland between the two countries. However, after the German attack on Russia in June 1941, all of Poland was occupied by Germany.

During the war years, Nazi occupation authorities

proceeded methodically to exterminate large segments of the Polish population by massacres, starvation, and mass incineration in concentration camps. Of more than 3 million Polish Jews, all but 100,000 were put to death; nevertheless, Jewish men and women participated in an effective underground resistance movement that culminated in the Warsaw uprising of 1944.

The last German troops were expelled from Poland in 1945 by Russian forces that had entered the country and set up a provisional government at Lublin. When elections were held in 1947, the Polish Committee for National Liberation, with Russian recognition and support, proclaimed itself the Provisional Government of Poland. A new constitution was adopted in 1952, under which Poland became the Polish People's Republic. Poland joined the Warsaw Pact the same year.

In 1980, persistent economic decline led to strikes and rioting in Poland. Largest of the strikes was one organized by a joint committee of workers in the Gdansk (formerly Danzig), Gydnia, and Sopot shipyards, led by Lech Walesa, demanding the right to strike and to form independent unions, abolition of censorship, access to the media of information and release of political prisoners. It ended with the signing of the "Gdansk Agreements" by Walesa and government officials, recognizing the right of workers to form independent unions and to go on strike.

Shortly thereafter, the leadership of Poland changed, with Edward Heirek stepping down as first secretary of the Communist Party and being replaced by Stanislaw Kania.

On 17 September 1980, a number of trade unions joined in a national confederation, Solidarity, and applied for legal status, which was granted after some hesitation on 29 October. Early in 1981, Solidarity launched a drive for a five-day week for workers in many enterprises. A crisis was narrowly averted when Defense Minister General Wojciech Jaruzelski assumed the added responsibility of prime minister and arranged a moratorium. Jaruzelski became first secretary of the Communist Party after Kania resigned that post on 18 October.

On 13 December 1981, the Council of State imposed martial law throughout Poland, suspended most political and civil liberties, and established a 20-member Military Council of National Salvation to maintain law and order. The union Solidarity was banned, and its leaders were detained along with many political prisoners.

On 8 October 1982, the *Sejm* adopted a law dissolving all registered trade unions, including Solidarity, and establishing a new union system permitting the establishment of trade unions in workplaces but re-quiring that they pledge support for the Communist Party and the constitution before being accorded recognition. Martial law was suspended in December 1982 and lifted completely in July 1983, and all internees were released. Although Lech Walesa and other Solidarity leaders were freed as internees, 11 of them—not including Walesa—were immediately arrested and charged with political offenses. This "Group of Eleven" was freed only in July 1984.

In November 1983, Lech Walesa was awarded the Nobel Peace Prize. His wife travelled to Oslo to accept it on his behalf. In October 1984 the kidnapping and murder of Father Jerzy Popieluszko, a supporter of Solidarity, shocked and angered the Polish people; the subsequent trial and conviction of four officers of the Polish Security Police was an unprecedented event in the nation.

Earlier, on 10 March, 1982, the Commission on Human Rights of the United Nations had expressed deep concern about reports of widespread violations of human rights in Poland and had requested the secretary-general, or a person designated by him, to make a thorough study of the human rights situation in that country. The secretary-general followed the situation closely and, on 21 December 1982, designated Under-Secretary-General Hugo Gobbi to continue the task on his behalf.

In 1983, the commission received Mr. Gobbi's report, indicating that the Polish authorities had not cooperated either with him or with the secretary-general. The commission deplored their attitude in the matter and reaffirmed the right of the Polish people to pursue its political, social, and cultural development free from outside interference. It called upon the Polish authorities to terminate the restrictive measures they had imposed on the exercise of human rights and to review the severe prison sentences which had been imposed in the context of the state of martial law.

In September 1983, Mr. Gobbi forwarded a detailed request for information to the government of Poland. That government did not reply. Under-Secretary-General Patricio Ruedas, who succeeded Mr. Gobbi as the secretary-general's representative, reported to the commission at its February 1984 session, presenting information which had reached the secretary-general and Mr. Gobbi from a wide variety of sources, including personal contacts between the secretary-general and Polish authorities during a visit to Poland.

In the report, Under-Secretary-General Patricio Ruedas presented the following conclusions (UN Doc. E/CN.4/1984/26, para. 38–41):

A difficult economic and social situation has existed, and

continues to exist, since 1981 in Poland, taxing to the utmost the resources and the stamina of the Polish people and of the Polish Government. Poland is in the process of change. Martial law, imposed in December 1981, lasted formally for 19 months. During that period, numerous arrests were made, including those for political reasons. Furthermore, some Polish citizens died as a result of clashes between demonstrators and the police: at least two, in 1981; at least one in 1982 and at least two in 1983. That the figures are under dispute is not so important as that deaths actually occurred, for one single case is one too much. This is also the view of the Polish authorities, as reported to the Secretary-General.

The suspension and, thereafter, the lifting of martial law, as well as the enactment and implementation of the clemency measures and, subsequently, the amnesty law, have produced conditions favourable to a reconciliation between different sectors of Polish society. The figures. . . are significant in this regard—particularly if comparison is made between the figure of about 1,500 persons detained for political reasons as of 4 January 1983 (E/CN.4/ 1983/18, para. 35) and that of 281 detainees— most of them on a temporary basis—as of 18 February 1984. These are certainly encouraging developments, to be seen as such by any independent observer.

Some questions can nevertheless be entertained regarding some of the recent (1983) legislation, be it ever temporary. Thus, for example, the amendment to the Polish penal code. . . seems to perpetuate a similar provision which existed in Article 46 (1) of the now defunct martial law. Also the "Special Legal Regulations in the Period of Overcoming the Socio-Economic Crisis", . . ., while temporary in nature, provide for extensive powers to the authorities in several domains, including education. As regards the possible exercise of these powers, the writer of this report is impressed by the spirit of moderation evidenced by all members of the Polish Government who met with him, and is authorized by the Secretary-General to say that he, too, noted favourably that spirit. This has permitted the Secretary-General to state that what he heard in Poland was "very encouraging on all fronts".

In the operative paragraph 4 of its resolution 1983/30, the Commission on Human Rights called upon the Polish authorities "to realize fully and without further delay their stated intention to terminate the restrictive measures imposed on the exercise of human rights and fundamental freedoms, particularly in relation to a review of the severe prison sentences imposed in the context of the state of martial law, the lifting of restrictions on the free flow of information, and the repeal of the new restrictions imposed on the Polish people". In the light of the information contained in this report, it seems clear that in at least one very important aspect—the review of prison sentences—effect has been given to the resolution through enactment and implementation of the clemency measures and the amnesty law.

The reports of Under-Secretaries-General Gobbi and Ruedas made it clear that the government of Poland had seemingly solved one of its major problems by adopting a new law on trade unions which provided for a complete new trade union structure in the country and abolished all existing trade unions without exception. However, this raised the question whether such action was permissible under the terms of relevant international instruments such as the ILO FREEDOM OF ASSOCIATION AND PROTECTION OF THE RIGHT TO ORGANIZE CONVENTION, 1948, and the ILO RIGHT TO ORGANIZE AND COLLECTIVE BARGAINING CONVENTION, 1949, especially when taken in a period of emeregency affecting trade union affairs. Analysis of the new law by the INTERNATIONAL LABOR OFFICE raised doubts as to its compatibility with those conventions, and there was a general consensus that the matter could be settled satisfactorily only by utilizing the complaints procedure established in accordance with the 1948 convention. Thereafter, the Commission on Human Rights took no further action relating to the situation in Poland.

After a long period of ever-increasing labor unrest over wages and living conditions, government authorities organized a series of "round table negotiations" for discussion of issues relating to the trade union movement and the broadening of civil liberties. On 9 March 1989, these talks between the regime and the opposition, which included Solidarity, resulted in the adoption of a program of major political reform.

The program called for the creation of an upper house of parliament which would be democratically elected and which would supplement the work of the 460-member *Sejm*; the two houses together would constitute the National Assembly. All the senators would be chosen by the people in free elections. The 161 open seats in the *Sejm* would likewise be filled by free elections, open to opposition candidates and independents. The president would then be elected by the National Assembly as a whole and would have strong executive powers, including the ability to dissolve the National Assembly. In addition, three dissident organizations were to be legalized: Solidarity, Rural Solidarity, and the Independent Students Association.

Although the round table agreements were not totally satisfactory to either side, they were signed on 5 April 1989 as—in the words of Solidarity's chief negotiator—"one step in a process through which democracy may be rebuilt in an evolutionary manner, not upsetting the political balance or stability."

When General Jaruzelski was inaugurated as president, Solidarity turned down offers to participate in a coalition government and did not permit its members to serve in the cabinet either in their official or individual capacities. It, however, organized a "shadow cabinet" in the National Assembly to prepare for the time when it would be called upon to assume power, as occurred in 1989.

Aside from its political and economic problems, Poland has been plagued from time to time by manifestations of intolerance and discrimination directed against Jews. Once numbering more than 3 million, the bulk of the Jewish population of the country died of starvation or perished in the Nazi death camps on Polish soil during World War II. Only about 250,000 remained in 1967 and 1968 when an official anti-Semitic campaign reflecting a power struggle in the Communist Party caused 9,000 Jewish workers to lose their jobs and drove more than 20,000 to leave the country after being stripped of their citizenship and provided with one-way travel documents. The campaign, supported by Wladyslaw Gomulka, then head of the Polish Community Party, took the form of party and factory meetings all over Poland denouncing "Zionists" and proclaiming war against liberals and intellectuals, many of whom were Jews. These actions were condemned as "infamous and an embarrassment to Poland" by the Polish Communist Party weekly *Polityka* some 20 years later, on 18 February 1988.

As of 1990, between 6,000 and 10,000 Jews remain in Poland, and public expressions of anti-Semitism have increased within the framework of newly realized freedom of expression.

However, Poland's new government has resumed full relations with Israel—broken in 1967 as a result of the Arab–Israeli war—and has arranged for the passage through Warsaw of charter flights carrying 500 Soviet Jews per week to Israel. Besides easing the movement of Jews from the Soviet Union, Poland has chances for investment and markets for their products to successful Israeli business men, many of whom are of Polish origin.

POLITICAL RIGHTS. The right of everyone to take part in the government of his country is proclaimed in the UNIVERSAL DECLARATION OF HUMAN RIGHTS in the following terms:

Article 2. (1). Everyone has the right to take part in the government of his country, directly or through freely chosen representatives.

(2). Everyone has the right of equal access to public service in his country.

(3). The will of the people shall be the basis of the authority of government; this will shall be expressed in periodic and genuine elections which shall be by universal and equal suffrage and shall be held by secret vote or by equivalent free voting procedures.

The INTERNATIONAL COVENANT ON CIVIL AND POLITICAL RIGHTS deals with the subject in article 25, which reads:

Article 25. (1). Every citizen shall have the right and the opportunity, without any of the distinctions mentioned in article 2 and without unreasonable restrictions:

(a) To take part in the conduct of public affairs, directly or through freely chosen representatives;

(b) To vote and to be elected at genuine periodic elections which shall be by universal and equal suffrage and shall be held by secret ballot, guaranteeing the free expression of the will of the electors;

(c) To have access, on general terms of equality, to public service in his country.

Article 5 of the INTERNATIONAL CONVENTION ON THE ELIMINATION OF ALL FORMS OF RACIAL DISCRIMINATION provides that:

Article 5. In compliance with the fundamental obligations laid down in article 2 of this Convention, States parties undertake to prohibit and to eliminate racial discrimination in all its forms and to guarantee the right of everyone, without distinction as to race, colour, or national or ethnic origin, to equality before the law, notably in the enjoyment of the following rights:. . . .

(c) Political rights, in particular the rights to participate in elections, to vote and to stand for election—on the basis of universal and equal suffrage, to take part in the Government as well as in the conduct of public affairs at any level and to have equal access to public service;. . . .

Discrimination against women in respect of the right of everyone to take part in the government of his country is dealt with in the CONVENTION ON THE ELIMINATION OF ALL FORMS OF DISCRIMINATION AGAINST WOMEN as follows:

Article 7. States Parties take all appropriate measures to eliminate discrimination against women in the political and public life of the country and, in particular, shall ensure to women, on equal terms with men, the right:

(a) To vote in all elections and public referenda and to be eligible for election to all publicly elected bodies;

(b) To participate in the formulation of government policy and the implementation thereof and to hold public office and perform all public functions at all levels of government;

(c) To participate in non-governmental organizations and associations concerned with the public and political life of the country.

Article 8. States Parties shall take all appropriate measures to ensure to women, on equal terms with men and without any discrimination, the opportunity to represent their Governments at the international level and to participate in the work of international organizations.

The AMERICAN CONVENTION ON HUMAN RIGHTS, open for acceptance by members of the ORGANIZATION OF AMERICAN STATES, contains the following provision:

Article 23. (1). Every citizen shall enjoy the following rights and opportunities:

a. to take part in the conduct of public affairs, directly or through freely chosen representatives;

b. to vote and to be elected in genuine periodic elections, which shall be by universal and equal suffrage and by secret ballot that guarantees the free expression of the will of the voters; and

   c. to have access, under general conditions of equality, to the public service of his country.

   2. The law may regulate the exercise of the rights and opportunities referred to in the preceding paragraph only on the basis of age, nationality, residence, language, education, civil and mental capacity, or sentencing by a competent court in criminal proceedings.

The **AFRICAN CHARTER OF HUMAN AND PEOPLE'S RIGHTS,** open for acceptance by member States of the **ORGANIZATION OF AFRICAN UNITY,** states that:

Article 13. 1. Every citizen shall have the right to participate freely in the government of his country, either directly or through freely chosen representatives in accordance with the provisions of the law.

   2. Every citizen shall have the right of equal access to the public service of his country.

   3. Every individual shall have the right of access to public property and services in strict equality of all persons before the law.

Studies on Discrimination in the Political Sphere. The UN **SUB-COMMISSION ON PREVENTION OF DISCRIMINATION AND PROTECTION OF MINORITIES** first considered the preparation of a study of discrimination in the matter of political rights in 1952. It decided to proceed with such a study at its 1956 session and appointed Mr. Hernan Santa Cruz (Chile) as its special rapporteur for the study.

The sub-commission considered the special rapporteur's final report at its 1962 session. On the basis of drafts presented in that report, it formulated a series of "General Principles on Freedom and Non-Discrimination in the Matter of Political Rights," reproduced below. The report, to which the general principles were annexed, was published by the United Nations in 1963 (UN Publication, Sales No. 63.XIV.2).

The sub-commission transmitted the report and general principles to the **COMMISSION ON HUMAN RIGHTS** for further consideration. The commission did not elaborate them into a separate international instrument, as had been proposed, but took them into account when it prepared drafts which later were adopted by the General Assembly as the **DECLARATION ON THE ELIMINATION OF ALL FORMS OF RACIAL DISCRIMINATION** and the **INTERNATIONAL CONVENTION ON THE ELIMINATION OF ALL FORMS OF RACIAL DISCRIMINATION.**

The General Assembly, at its 1988 session, recalled the provisions of those instruments relating to political rights and stressed (resolution 43/157) its conviction that periodic and genuine elections are a necessary and indispensable element of sustained efforts to protect the rights and interests of the governed, and that, as a matter of practical experience,

the right of everyone to take part in the government of his or her country is a crucial factor in the effective enjoyment by all of a wide range of other human rights and fundamental freedoms, including political, economic, social, and cultural rights. The assembly declared, further, "that determining the will of the people requires an electoral process which accommodates distinct alternatives, and that this process should provide an equal opportunity for all citizens to become candidates and put forward their political views, individually and in co-operation with others."

The assembly also reaffirmed its oft-stated view that *apartheid* should be abolished, that the systematic denial or abridgement of the right to vote on grounds of race or color is a gross violation of human rights and an affront to the conscience and dignity of mankind, and that the right to participate in a political system based on common and equal citizenship and universal franchise is essential for the exercise of the principle of periodic and genuine elections.

The assembly called upon the Commission on Human Rights to consider appropriate ways and means of enhancing the effectiveness of the principle of periodic and genuine elections, in the context of full respect for the sovereignty of member States, and to report to it on this question in 1989.

General Principles on Freedom and Non-discrimination in the Matter of Political Rights Preamble

Whereas the peoples of the world in the Charter of the United Nations have proclaimed their determination to reaffirm faith in fundamental human rights, in the dignity and worth of the human person, in the equal rights of men and women and of nations large and small, and to promote social progress and better standards of life in larger freedom,

Whereas the Charter sets forth, as one of the purposes of the United Nations, the promotion and encouragement of respect for human rights and fundamental freedoms for all without distinction as to race, sex, language or religion,

Whereas the Universal Declaration of Human Rights, further elaborating the principle of non-discrimination, proclaims that everyone is entitled to all the rights and freedoms set forth therein without distinction of any kind, including political opinion, and provides that no distinction shall be made on the basis of the political, jurisdictional or international status of the country or territory to which a person belongs,

Whereas, since the interests of the many are often disregarded when political power is in the hands of the few, the right of everyone to take part in the government of his country is the condition indispensable for the effective enjoyment by all of other human rights, including economic, social and cultural rights,

Whereas the exercise of political rights is directly linked to the existence of freedom of opinion and expression and freedom of peaceful assembly and association,

Whereas these rights can only be effectively guaranteed in a world in which the principles of the Charter, especially the principle of self-determination, and the principles enshrined in the declaration on the granting of independence to colonial territories and peoples, contained in General Assembly resolution 1514 (XV) of 14 December 1960, shall have full application.

Now therefore the following general principles are proclaimed to ensure recognition of the right of everyone to take part in the government of his country and of other related political rights, and to prevent discrimination in the enjoyment of these rights:

1. *The Right of All Peoples to Self-determination.* All peoples have the right to self-determination; by virtue of that right they freely determine their political status and freely pursue their economic, social and cultural development.

2. *Political Rights of Nationals.* (a) Every national of a country is entitled within that country to full and equal political rights without distinction of any kind, such as race, colour, sex, language, religion, political or other opinion, national or social origin, property, birth or other status.

(b) No one shall be denied nationality, or deprived of nationality, as a means of denying him or depriving him of political rights.

(c) The age, length of residence and other conditions prescribed by law for the exercise of any particular political right shall be the same for all nationals of a country or inhabitants of a political unit, as the case may be.

3. *Freedom of Opinion and Association.* Freedom of opinion and expression and freedom of peaceful assembly and association are essential to the enjoyment of political rights. These freedoms, and the access to the facilities and means for their exercise, shall be ensured to all persons at all times.

4. *Universality of Suffrage.* Every national is entitled to vote in any national election, referendum or plebiscite held in his country, and in any such public consultation held in the political or administrative unit thereof in which he resides. The right to vote shall not be dependent upon literacy or any other educational qualifications.

5. *Equality of Suffrage.* (a) Every national is entitled to vote in any election, or other public consultation for which he is eligible, on equal terms, and each vote shall have the same weight.

(b) When voting is conducted on the basis of electoral districts, the said districts shall be established on an equitable basis such as would make the results most accurately and completely reflect the will of all the voters.

(c) For any election or public consultation held by direct vote there shall be one general election roll, and every eligible national shall be included in that roll.

6. *Secrecy of the Vote.* (a) Every voter shall be able to vote in such a manner as not to involve disclosure of how he has voted or intends to vote.

(b) No voter shall be compelled to state, in any legal proceeding or otherwise, how he voted, or intends to vote, and no one shall attempt to obtain from any voter, directly or otherwise, information as to how he has voted or intends to vote.

7. *Periodicity of Elections.* Elections to all elective public offices shall be held at reasonable intervals, in order to ensure that the will of the people shall at all times be the basis of the authority of government.

8. *Genuine Character of Elections and Other Public Consultations.* (a) Every voter shall be free to vote for the candidate or list of candidates he prefers in any election to public of-

fice, and shall not be compelled to vote for any specified candidate or list of candidates.

(b) Every voter shall be free to vote for or against any proposal submitted to a plebiscite, referendum, or other public consultation.

(c) The conduct of elections and other public consultations, including the preparation and periodic revision of the electoral roll, shall be supervised by authorities whose independence and impartiality are ensured and whose decisions are subject to appeal to the judicial authorities or other independent and impartial bodies.

(d) Full freedom shall be ensured for the peaceful expression of political opposition, and also for the organization and free functioning of political parties and the right to present candidates for election.

9. *Access to Elective Public Office.* (a) Every national shall be eligible on equal terms for election to any elective public office in his country or in any political or administrative unit thereof in which he resides.

(b) The extent to which this principle shall be applied to those whose election might result in a conflict between their duties or personal interests and the interests of the community as a whole, shall be determined by law.

10. *Access to Non-elective Public Office.* (a) Every national shall be eligible on equal terms to hold any non-elective public office in his country or in any political or administrative unit thereof in which he resides.

(b) The extent to which this principle shall be applied to those whose appointment or assignment to a non-elective public office might result in a conflict between their duties or personal interests and the interests of the community as a whole, shall be determined by law.

(c) All appointments to the career civil service of a country shall be made on an objective and impartial basis.

11. *Measures Which Shall not Be Considered Discriminatory.* The following measures prescribed by law or regulation shall not be considered discriminatory:

(a) Reasonable requirements for the exercise of the right to vote or the right of access to elective public office;

(b) Reasonable qualifications for appointment to public office which stem from the nature of the duties of the office;

(c) Measures establishing a reasonable period which must elapse before naturalized persons may exercise their political rights, provided that they are combined with a liberal naturalization policy.

(d) Special measures taken to ensure:

(i) The adequate representation of an element of the population of a country whose members are in fact prevented by political, economic, religious, social, historical, or cultural conditions from enjoying equality with the rest of the population in the matter of political rights;

(ii) The balanced representation of the different elements of the population of a country;
provided that such measures are continued only so long as there is need for them, and only to the extent that they are necessary.

12. *Limitations.* The rights and freedoms proclaimed above shall in no case be exercised contrary to the purposes and principles of the United Nations. They shall be subject only to such limitations as are determined by law solely for the purpose of securing due recognition and respect for the rights and freedoms of others and of meeting the just requirements of public order (*ordre public*), morality and the general welfare in a democratic society. Any limitation

which may be imposed shall be consistent with the purposes and principles of the United Nations.

13. *Constitutional Guarantee.* The rights and freedoms proclaimed above shall in no case be subject to repeal or alteration by ordinary legislative procedure.

14. *Recourse to Independent Tribunals.* Any denial or violation of these rights and freedoms shall entitle the aggrieved person or persons to recourse to independent and impartial tribunals.

15. *Application of Principles.* These principles shall apply to all independent countries and to countries which are under alien domination.

SEE ALSO *Civil and Political Rights entries; State of Emergency entries.*

POLITICAL RIGHTS: ELECTORAL PROCESSES.
On 15 December 1989, the UN General Assembly adopted a resolution (resolution 44/147) entitled "Respect for the Principles of National Sovereignty and Non-interference in the Internal Affairs of States in their Electoral Processes" in which it reconfirmed the principle set out in the UNITED NATIONS CHARTER (article 2, para. 7) that nothing contained in the charter shall authorize the United Nations to intervene in matters which are essentially within the domestic jurisdiction of any State or shall require the members to submit such matters to settlement under the charter. The assembly recognized that the principles of national sovereignty and non-interference in the internal affairs of any State, as set out in the charter and in other international instruments, including the DECLARATION ON THE GRANTING OF INDEPENDENCE TO COLONIAL COUNTRIES AND PEOPLES and THE DECLARATION OF PRINCIPLES OF INTERNATIONAL LAW CONCERNING FRIENDLY RELATIONS AND CO-OPERATION AMONG STATES IN ACCORDANCE WITH THE CHARTER OF THE UNITED NATIONS, should be respected in the holding of elections. It also recognized that there is no single political system or single model for electoral processes equally suited to all nations and their peoples and that political systems and electoral processes are subject to historical, political, cultural, and religious factors.

The assembly accordingly reiterated that, by virtue of the principle of equal rights and SELF-DETERMINATION of people enshrined in the UN Charter, all peoples have the right freely to determine, without external interference, their political status and to pursue their economic, social, and cultural development and that every State has the duty to respect that right in accordance with the provisions of the charter. It affirmed that it is the sole concern of peoples to determine methods and to establish institutions regarding the electoral process, as well as the ways for its implementation according to constitutional and national legislation. And it also affirmed that any extra-neous activities that attempt, directly or indirectly, to interfere in the free development of national electoral processes, in particular in the developing countries, or that tend to sway the results of such processes, violate the spirit and the letter of the principles established in the charter and in the Declaration of Principles of International Law.

The assembly urged all States to respect the principle of non-interference in the internal affairs of States and the sovereign rights of peoples to determine their political, economic, and social system; and strongly appealed to all States to abstain from financing or providing, directly or indirectly, any other form of overt or covert support for political parties or groups and from taking actions to undermine the electoral processes in any country. It condemned any act of armed AGGRESSION or threat or use of force against peoples, elected governments, or their legitimate leaders.

Finally, the assembly called upon the Commission on Human Rights, at its 1990 session, to give priority to the review of the fundamental factors that negatively affect the observance of the principle of national sovereignty and non-interference in the internal affairs of States in their electoral processes and to report on that review to the assembly's 1990 session.

POLITICAL RIGHTS: PERIODIC AND GENUINE ELECTIONS. The UN General Assembly has twice dealt in almost identical terms (resolutions 43/157 of 8 December 1988 and 44/146 of 15 December 1989) with the question of enhancing the effectiveness of the principle of periodic and genuine elections, reaffirming the relevant provisions of the UNIVERSAL DECLARATION OF HUMAN RIGHTS (article 21) and of the INTERNATIONAL COVENANT ON CIVIL AND POLITICAL RIGHTS (article 25). Similar views were expressed by the Commission on Human Rights at its 1989 session (resolution 1989/51).

In resolution 44/146, as in the earlier resolution 43/157, the assembly recalls that all States enjoy sovereign equality and that each State has the right freely to choose and develop its political, social, economic, and cultural systems; and recognizes that there is no single political system or electoral method equally suited to all nations and their people. It further states (para. 1–7) that it:

Underscores the significance of the Universal Declaration of Human Rights and the International Covenant on Civil and Political Rights, which establish that the authority to govern shall be based on the will of the people, as expressed in periodic and genuine elections;

Stresses its conviction that periodic and genuine elections are a necessary and indispensable element of sustained efforts to protect the rights and interests of the governed and that, as a matter of practical experience, the right of everyone to take part in the government of his or her country is a crucial factor in the effective enjoyment by all of a wide range of other human rights and fundamental freedoms, embracing political, economic, social and cultural rights;

Declares that determining the will of the people requires an electoral process that provides an equal opportunity for all citizens to become candidates and put forward their political views, individually and in co-operation with others within constitutional and national legislation;

Recognizes that the efforts of the international community to enhance the effectiveness of the principle of periodic and genuine elections should not call into question each State's sovereign right freely to choose and develop its political, social, economic and cultural systems, whether or not they conform to the preference of other States;

Underscores the duty of each member of the international community to respect the decisions taken by other States in freely choosing and developing their electoral institutions;

Reaffirms that *apartheid* must be abolished, that the systematic denial or abridgement of the right to vote on the grounds of race or color is a gross violation of human rights and an affront to the conscience and dignity of mankind, and that the right to participate in a political system based on common and equal citizenship and universal franchise is essential for the exercise of the principle of periodic and genuine elections;

Rejects the tricameral parliament established under the system of *apartheid* as an abhorrent expression of a fundamentally oppressive and flagrantly inhuman political system. . . .

The assembly called upon the Commission on Human Rights, at its 1990 session, to continue its consideration of appropriate ways and means of enhancing the effectiveness of the principle of periodic and genuine elections, in the context of full respect for the sovereignty of member States, and to submit a report on that subject for consideration by the assembly in 1990.

The commission, in resolution 1989/51 of 7 March 1989, recommended to the assembly the adoption of the "Framework for Future Efforts" in this field, reproduced below. The Economic and Social Council forwarded the recommendation to the assembly on 24 May 1989 (decision 1989/145):

I. The Will of the People Expressed Through Periodic and Genuine Elections as the Basis for the Authority of Government

A. Universal and equal suffrage.

B. The right to take part in the government of one's country, directly or through freely chosen representatives.

C. The right to equal access to public service in one's country.

D. The need for a secret vote or equivalent free voting procedures, guaranteeing the free expression of the will of the electors.

E. The importance of the right to freedom of peaceful assembly.

F. The importance of the right to freedom of association.

G. The importance of the right to freedom of opinion and expression, including the freedom to seek, receive and impart information and ideas of all kinds, either orally, in writing or in print, in the form of art, or through any other media.

H. The right of citizens of a State to change their governmental system through appropriate constitutional means.

II. The Activities of Candidates for Public Office

A. Equal opportunity for all citizens to become candidates.

B. The right of candidates to put forward their political views, individually and in co-operation with others.

III. Operational Aspects: National Institutions

National institutions should ensure universal and equal suffrage, as well as impartial administration. There is particular need for independent supervision, appropriate voter registration, reliable balloting procedures and methods for preventing electoral fraud and resolving disputes.

IV. Co-operative Activities of the International Community

The host country may wish to invite observers or seek advisory services. Either or both may be available from regional organizations or from the United Nations system.

POPULAR PARTICIPATION. The UN GENERAL ASSEMBLY, the ECONOMIC AND SOCIAL COUNCIL, and the COMMISSION ON HUMAN RIGHTS have repeatedly, since 1979, reaffirmed that popular participation in all sectors of public life, including the participation of workers in management and workers' self-management where they exist, constitutes an important factor in socio-economic development and in the full realization of all human rights and the dignity of the human person.

In 1975 the council defined (resolution 1929 [LVIII]) popular participation as connoting the voluntary and democratic involvement of people in:

(a) contributing to the development effort;

(b) sharing equitably in the benefits derived therefrom; and

(c) decisionmaking in respect of setting goals, formulating policies, and planning and implementing economic and social development programs.

The council noted in particular that, to be effective, popular participation should be consciously promoted by governments, with full recognition of civil, political, economic, and cultural rights and through innovative measures, including structural changes and institutional reform and development, as well as through the encouragement of all forms of education, particularly compulsory primary education, designed to involve actively all segments of society. It recommended that governments:

(a) Adopt popular participation as a basic policy measure in national development strategy;

(b) Encourage the widest possible active participation of all individuals and national non-governmental organizations, such as trade unions and youth and women's organizations, in the development process in setting goals, formulating policies and implementing plans;

(c) Include popular participation as an integral element in local, regional and national development plans and programmes in ways that will ensure maximum citizen participation consistent with the requirements of economic growth, social equity and administrative efficiency;

(d) Adopt measures, including structural changes and institutional arrangements, that will facilitate the contribution of the people to the development effort, their equitable sharing in the benefits derived therefrom and their involvement in making decisions on those matters which directly affect their economic advancement and social progress;

(e) Encourage the study, documentation and dissemination, for the information and benefit of other Member States, of innovative measures adopted by them for promoting popular participation in development and for monitoring and assessing their effectiveness; and

(f) Encourage organized training programmes to impart to government officials and local leaders knowledge and skills in promoting and sustaining effective participation by the people in national, regional and local development plans and programmes.

In 1983, the council (resolution 1983/21) requested the Secretary-General "to undertake a comprehensive analytical study on the right to popular participation in its various forms as an important factor in the full realization of all human rights." The resulting study (UN Doc. E/CN.4/1985/10 and Add. 1 and 2) was received and noted by the Commission on Human Rights (resolution 1985/44) and later by the General Assembly (resolution 40/99). Both the commission and the assembly invited the Secretary-General to obtain the comments of governments, the concerned specialized agencies and organs of the United Nations system, and the relevant non-governmental organizations of the study; and the assembly requested the commission to continue to consider the question and to inform the assembly, at its regular 1989 session, of the results of that consideration.

At that session, the commission received the secretary-general's study of the laws and practices regarding popular participation (UN Doc. E/CN.4/1989/12) and his report reproducing the comments received on the earlier study of popular participation in its various forms as an important factor in development and in the full realization of all human rights

(UN Doc. E/CN.4/1989/11). While taking note of these reports, the commission again invited comments on the earlier one (resolution 1989/14), and requested the secretary-general to submit a further report on the subject for consideration at its 1990 session. The General Assembly, confirming the commission's decision, invited the commission to consider the question further at its 1991, 1992, and 1993 sessions, and to inform the assembly in 1993 of the results.

At its 1990 session, the commission received the secretary-general's report on the substantive replies received up to that time (UN Doc. E/CN.4/1990/8).

PORTUGAL. The Portuguese Republic is a country occupying the western part of the Iberian Peninsula, on the Atlantic Ocean; it includes also the Atlantic archipelagos of the Azores and Madeira. It has a border with Spain. Portugal achieved independence from Spain during the 12th century and became a Member of the United Nations in 1955. Its population is estimated by the UN (1990) to be 1,543,000. Ethnic groups include persons of Mediterranean origin and a small African minority. The language in common use is Portuguese. Christianity (Roman Catholic, 97%; Protestant denominations, 3%) is the predominant religion. Literacy is estimated at 80%.

The government (1990) took the form of a republic. Under the 1982 constitution, the president is directly elected for a term of five years; he may serve for a maximum of two consecutive terms. As head of State, he appoints the premier, representing the party or coalition given the majority in a popular election. On advice of the prime minister, he also appoints other members of the Council of Ministers and the secretaries and under-secretaries of State, who are outside the council. Legislation is handled by the 250-member Assembly of the Republic, elected for four-year terms by universal adult suffrage under a system of proportional representation. Political parties include the Social Democratic Party, the Democratic Renewal Party, the United People Alliance, and the Centre Social Democrats. As autonomous regions, the Azores and Madeira have their own governments and legislatures.

Portuguese explorers such as Vasco da Gama, Bartholomeu Dias, and Pedro Alvares Cabral helped to found the widespread Portuguese empire which included territories in Africa, South America, and the Far East. Today Portugal's only overseas territory is Macao, consisting of a peninsula and two small islands on the South China coast, not far from Hong Kong.

In 1926, a prominent university professor and

economist, Dr. Antonio Salazar, was brought into the government of Portugal as an expert to solve serious fiscal problems. In 1928, he was appointed finance minister; and, by 1932, he had become prime minister. He ruled Portugal as an authoritarian "corporate" State for 36 years, keeping it neutral during World War II but leasing air and naval bases to the Allies after 1943. His successor, Marcello Caetano, continued the tradition after Salazar died in 1970.

On 25 April 1974, leftist army officers launched a revolution and established the Junta of National Salvation, which called for negotiation with the independence movements in Angola, Portuguese Guinea, and Mozambique; the end of the "corporate" police state; and the introduction of social and economic reforms which would benefit the lower classes.

Once in power, the junta granted independence to Portuguese Guinea, which became the Republic of Guinea-Bissau on 10 September 1974. Following an attempted rightist coup on 11 March 1975, the junta was dissolved, and the Portuguese Communist Party assumed control of the government. The Supreme Revolutionary Council was formed and remained in control until 25 April 1976, when a new constitution was promulgated providing for a government committed to socialist principles. Meanwhile, Mozambique achieved independence on 25 June 1975 and Angola on 11 November 1975.

General Antonio Ramhalo Eanes was elected to a four-year term as president in 1976 with the support of three major parties and chose Mario Alberto Soares to serve as prime minister. Soares' minority socialist government fell in December 1977, but he was elected to the presidency in 1986.

A new constitution, replacing the one promulgated in 1976, was adopted on 12 August 1982. Under it, Portugal is a sovereign, unitary republic and all citizens possess fundamental rights and duties before the law. In a report presented to the COMMITTEE ON THE ELIMINATION OF RACIAL DISCRIMINATION on 14 November 1986, the government presented the following information relating to that constitution (UN Doc. CERD/C/126/Add. 3, para. 11–16):

The Portuguese Constitution repeatedly reflects the concern to ensure that human rights are protected and it consistently upholds the principle of full equality before the law and of non-discrimination.

Not unexpectedly, therefore, the fundamental principles of the Constitution include the following:

"The Portuguese Republic is a democratic State subject to the rule of law, founded on the sovereignty of the people, respect for and the safeguard of fundamental rights and freedoms . . ." (art. 2);

"In its international relations Portugal shall abide by the principles . . . of respect for human rights . . ." (art. 7, para. 1);

"The fundamental tasks of the State shall be . . .

"(b) To guarantee fundamental rights and freedoms and respect for the principles of a democratic State subject to the rule of law . . ." (art. 9).

13. Also, the section on fundamental rights and duties stipulates that:

"All citizens shall enjoy the rights and shall be subject to the duties laid down in the Constitution . . ." (art. 12, para. 1).

Article 13, for its part, provides:

"1. All citizens shall have the same dignity at the social level and shall be equal before the law.

"2. No one may be privileged, favoured, disadvantaged, deprived of any right or exempt of any duty by virtue of ancestry, sex, race, language, place of origin, religion, political or ideological convictions, education, financial situation or social status."

This principle of equality likewise applies to foreigners and stateless persons, since article 15 of the Constitution stipulates:

"1. Aliens and stateless persons temporarily or permanently resident in Portugal shall enjoy the same rights and be subject to the same duties as Portuguese citizens.

"2. The preceding paragraph shall not apply to political rights, the performance of public duties that are not primarily technical, and rights and duties confined to Portuguese citizens under the Constitution and by law."

The terms of the Constitution and the law are interpreted and applied in accordance with the Universal Declaration of Human Rights (art. 16) and therefore prohibit any provisions to the contrary, particularly as regards racial discrimination. The validity of the laws and acts of the State is dependent on whether they are in conformity with the Constitution (art. 3, para. 3) and any person who violates these fundamental principles will be subject to the legal régime prescribed for the protection of fundamental rights, which provides for appeal to the courts, responsibility of offenders, etc. . . .

POVERTY. The UN Economic and Social Council, at its first regular 1988 session, expressed its concern that a significant percentage of the world's population lives in conditions of extreme poverty and is forced to live increasingly at the margins of society and noted that insufficient attention had been paid to this phenomenon, which tends to elude international and intergovernmental action and current statistical methods.

Taking into account the provision of the DECLARATION ON SOCIAL PROGRESS AND DEVELOPMENT to the effect that social progress and development are the common concerns of the international community, which shall supplement, by concerted international action, national efforts to raise the living standards of peoples, the council urged the COMMISSION FOR SOCIAL DEVELOPMENT to suggest, on the basis of an assessment of its studies, strategies that will help put an end to the marginalization of people living in extreme poverty, irrespective of the economic and social system to which they belong, and to submit its views to the council in 1991.

The General Assembly, on 20 December 1988, joined the council (resolution 43/195) in expressing its concern about the situation and emphasized the need for new and imaginative approaches to eradicating poverty in developing countries as an integral part of the promotion of growth and development. It urged the international community to achieve, as a priority, a supportive international economic environment for growth and development that will reinforce the efforts of developing countries to revitalize their development process and eradicate poverty; and requested the UN regional commissions to study options, including new approaches oriented towards the revitalization of developing countries, in order to enable them to address effectively the eradication of poverty.

In the resolution, the General Assembly requested the secretary-general to prepare a report analyzing the impact of the economic crisis in developing countries on the intensity of poverty and recommending effective international policy measures for dealing with this problem.

The secretary-general's report on International Co-operation for the Eradication of Poverty (UN Doc. A/44/467) was presented to the General Assembly at its 1989 session. Its analysis of the extent and intensity of poverty in the developing countries was as follows (para. 2–4):

Constituting close to half of the population of the developing countries as a whole (not including China), the poor during past decades did not share equally in economic progress. During the 1980s, they absorbed much of the brunt of the economic and other crises that beset most developing countries.

Although a heterogeneous group in terms of their economic interests, the poor have one thing in common: their extremely low incomes. Taking as a comparative cut-off line a level of annual income based on detailed studies of extreme poverty in Kenya, which amounts to $US 300 per capita in constant 1980 dollars, two broad trends are revealed. . . On the one hand, estimates of the share of the total population living in poverty during the 1970s and 1980s show that a significant improvement has occurred. On the other hand, the number of people living in poverty increased substantially during this period because the population itself grew rapidly. The same overall trends are discernible. . . with respect to absolute poverty levels, that is to say, the income levels established by regions below which a minimum nutritionally adequate diet plus essential non-food requirements is not deemed affordable. Poverty being a normative concept, the absolute levels below which the conditions of life are viewed as intolerable vary by region in broad accordance with the general level of development of each region. For instance, the absolute poverty threshold in Latin America is at a higher cut-off income level than in Africa.

A closer look at the data. . . shows a worsening incidence of poverty, both numerically and as a share of the total population, in both Africa and Latin America during the 1980s. In Latin America, moreover, the magnitude of poverty shifted from the rural to the urban areas, reflecting the effects of continued high rates of rural emigration and the impact of the fall in urban incomes in most countries of the region. In Africa, the relatively rapid growth of rural poverty has been due primarily to high population growth rates, continuing low levels of agricultural productivity, and the destitution created in the early 1980s by the worst drought in 15 years. As for the Asian region, what most stands out is that, while the share of the population in poverty improved steadily during the past two decades, the extent and depth of poverty remained staggering. In general, moreover, it can be seen that the share of the population in the 1980s earning less than $US 300 per annum has been considerably higher in Asia and Africa than in Latin America.

As regards the capacity of the poor to cope with the situation in which they found themselves in the decade of the 1980s, the secretary-general reported that (para. 25–30)

Income and consumption findings are necessary for gauging and analysing the incidence and changes in poverty, but are not sufficient in explaining the full scope of the changes in circumstances experienced by the extremely poor during the present decade. Bearing in mind the risks of generalizing when faced with a wide diversity of conditions and needs, it appears that in various ways the most salient dimension of poverty during the present decade has been the increased vulnerability of the poor.

The coping mechanisms of the poor were put to a severe test during much of the decade. Those mechanisms consisted as ever of continued attempts at diversifying risks and opportunities, with an eye to the future as well as the present; in particular, this has usually meant making use of the ability and willingness of different household members to do different things in different places. Household strategies have typically consisted of keeping some family members on the farm or in nearby off-farm activities, having others migrate to cities or even abroad for work and educating the brightest children as an investment for the future. Such strategies have resulted in a high degree of intersectoral labour mobility, with the dry season usually the main time of the year available for such diversification.

As already noted, such anti-destitution strategies were severely tested in the 1980s. In much of Africa, in particular, rural-based livelihoods were reduced or wiped out by drought, environmental degradation and civil conflicts. Many of the rural poor lost, mortgaged or sold in distress most or all of their assets in order to survive until famine relief arrived. Others ended up in refugee camps or withdrew into subsistence farming.

The viability of the migration option also declined. With opportunities for work in cities and abroad substantially reduced, rural school leavers were deployed on family farms and many displaced urban workers returned to live with their families in the rural areas. In some cases, returned migrants who used to work abroad, had to be accommodated, as when Ghana's nationals returned from Nigeria.

What has most stood out has been the tenacity and long

view adopted by the poor in attempting to preserve their assets and self-respect in the face of extreme adversity. They, for example, typically went hungry rather than lose the basis of their livelihood. Sacrificing the future to salvage the present was resorted to only as a last resort. Despite their attempts to avoid destitution, however, millions of poor people were subjected to the horrors of famine and malnutrition, war-related violence, the loss or forced sale of all productive assets and holdings and refugee uprooting.

Traditional values of wider family obligation and support systems have played a crucial role, especially in African societies, in enabling the poor and vulnerable to survive the wrenching adjustments of the present decade. Mutual support arrangements and networks, however, came under stress as family and kinship groups became less able to help one another, and especially to help their poorest members. Modernizing trends also weakened traditional support and mutual obligation systems. The privatization of natural resources, such as grazing lands and water resources, and the increasing commercialization of economic activities further marginalized weaker social groups and members who more than ever have had to buy things which they formerly were accustomed to receiving in the form of traditional claims. Such trends, while historically inevitable, have had the effect of further augmenting the vulnerability of the poorest of the poor.

On the basis of his study, the secretary-general drew the following conclusions (para. 80–82):

The economic crisis of the 1980s has had a generally adverse impact on poverty in Africa and brought to a halt the amelioration in the conditions of the poor achieved in Latin America during previous years. As a result, poverty has once again become a major issue of concern for many developing countries and the international community.

International co-operation is essential if progress is to be made towards achieving the goal of eradicating poverty on an urgent, lasting and comprehensive basis. Co-operation on international trade and debt matters would help restore the conditions necessary for renewed economic growth in countries undergoing adjustment. Such growth would expand investment and employment opportunities, support increased social expenditures, and thus raise the incomes and living standards of a majority of the poor. Equally, international co-operation in the form of increased official development assistance could play an important role as seed capital in launching poverty-oriented programmes before the effects of economic growth are felt, and as a contribution to special programmes targeted on those pockets of hard-core poverty that lie beyond the spread effects of growth. For their part, it would help if developing country Governments would restructure the composition of their social expenditure to improve the scope and depth of poverty programmes, as well as reform or remove those laws and regulations that make it hard for the poor to start or expand a small shop or enterprise, put a roof over their heads, or help themselves through organized participation.

A variety of approaches—ranging from short-run welfare measures to long-term human capital formation, and from small-scale, targeted activities to macroeconomic policies—may contribute to poverty eradication in important ways. As examined in the present report, the formulation and implementation of policies that have the aim of increasing the earnings capacity of the poor and making them less vulnerable to future crises remain a major and urgent challenge to policy makers and multilateral agencies.

After examining the report at its 1989 session, the General Assembly on 22 December 1989 (resolution 44/212) expressed its deep concern that more than one billion people throughout the world, mostly in developing countries, are still living in abject poverty and misery, with hunger, malnutrition, disease, illiteracy, and premature death as a integral part of their lives, and called upon the international community to strengthen its work, on a priority basis, towards action-oriented programs for the eradication of poverty in support of developing countries' own efforts.

The assembly requested the secretary-general to coordinate such activities and to submit to its 1990 session a progress report and to its 1991 session a comprehensive report containing, *inter alia*: (a) an analysis of the diversified impact of adverse international economic conditions on the intensification of poverty in developing countries, (b) a summary of the experience of developing countries in their efforts to combat poverty, (c) specific recommendations for effective policy measures for urgently and permanently eradicating poverty, and (d) an account of the implementation of resolution 44/212.

The COMMISSION ON HUMAN RIGHTS also examined the question, "Human Rights and Extreme Poverty" at its 1990 session and expressed (resolution 1990/15) concern that, despite the progress achieved by the international community in ensuring the effective enjoyment of the rights of the person, poverty continues to spread throughout the world, seriously affecting the most vulnerable and disadvantaged individuals, families, and groups in all countries, thus hindering them in the exercise of their human rights and fundamental freedoms.

The commission drew the attention of all United Nations bodies to the contradiction between the existence of situations of extreme poverty and exclusion from society, and the ability to enjoy human rights fully. It urged the COMMITTEE ON ECONOMIC, SOCIAL AND CULTURAL RIGHTS to give the necessary attention, in its work, to the question of extreme poverty and exclusion from society, and called upon the SUB-COMMISSION ON PREVENTION OF DISCRIMINATION AND PROTECTION OF MINORITIES to examine that question in greater depth and to carry out a specific study of the question.

SEE ALSO Food; Health; Homelessness; Housing; Hunger and Malnutrition; Shelter; Standard of Living.

PRINCIPLES GOVERNING THE USE BY STATES OF ARTIFICIAL EARTH SATELLITES FOR INTERNATIONAL DIRECT TELEVISION BROADCASTING (1982).

In 1972, the Union of Soviet Socialist Republics called upon the UN General Assembly (UN Doc. A/8771) to adopt an international convention on principles governing the use by States of artificial earth satellites for direct television broadcasting and submitted the draft of such a convention to the Assembly. In referring the request to its Committee on the Peaceful Uses of Outer Space, the Assembly noted (resolution 2917 [XXVII]) that the work which had been done earlier on the draft convention on FREEDOM OF INFORMATION might be useful in the discussion and elaboration of international instruments or other United Nations arrangements relative to direct television broadcasting.

Between 1972 and 1982, the question was considered by the Committee on the Peaceful Uses of Outer Space, by its Working Group on Direct Broadcast Satellites, and by its legal sub-committee. On the basis of the committee's recommendation, the Assembly adopted on 10 December 1982 the following declaration of principles (resolution 37/92, annex):

A. Purposes and Objectives

1. Activities in the field of international direct television broadcasting by satellite should be carried out in a manner compatible with the sovereign rights of States, including the principle of non-intervention as well as with the right of everyone to seek, receive and impart information and ideas as enshrined in the relevant United Nations instruments.

2. Such activities should promote the free dissemination and mutual exchange of information and knowledge in cultural and scientific fields, assist in educational, social and economic development, particularly in the developing countries, enhance the qualities of life of all peoples and provide recreation with due respect to the political and cultural integrity of States.

3. These activities should accordingly be carried out in a manner compatible with the development of mutual understanding and the strengthening of friendly relations and co-operation among all States and peoples in the interest of maintaining international peace and security.

B. Applicability of International Law

4. Activities in the field of international direct television broadcasting by satellite should be conducted in accordance with international law, including the Charter of the United Nations, the Treaty on Principles Governing the Activities of States in the Exploration and Use of Outer Space, including the Moon and Other Celestial Bodies, of 27 January 1967, the relevant provisions of the International Telecommunication Convention and its Radio Regulations and of international instruments relating to friendly relations and co-operation among States and to human rights.

C. Rights and Benefits

5. Every State has an equal right to conduct activities in the field of international direct television broadcasting by satellite and to authorize such activities by persons and entities under its jurisdiction. All States and peoples are entitled to and should enjoy the benefits from such activities. Access to the technology in this field should be available to all States without discrimination on terms mutually agreed by all concerned.

D. International Co-operation

6. Activities in the field of international direct television broadcasting by satellite should be based upon and encourage international co-operation. Such co-operation should be the subject of appropriate arrangements. Special consideration should be given to the needs of the developing countries in the use of international direct television broadcasting by satellite for the purpose of accelerating their national development.

E. Peaceful Settlement of Disputes

7. Any international dispute that may arise from activities covered by these principles should be settled through established procedures for the peaceful settlement of disputes agreed upon by the parties to the dispute in accordance with the provisions of the Charter of the United Nations.

F. State Responsibility

8. States should bear international responsibility for activities in the field of international direct television broadcasting by satellite carried out by them or under their jurisdiction and for the conformity of any such activities with the principles set forth in this document.

9. When international direct television broadcasting by satellite is carried out by an international intergovernmental organization, the responsibility referred to in paragraph 8 above should be borne both by that organization and by the States participating in it.

G. Duty and Right to Consult

10. Any broadcasting or receiving State within an international direct television broadcasting satellite service established between them requested to do so by any other broadcasting or receiving State within the same service should promptly enter into consultations with the requesting State regarding its activities in the field of international direct television broadcasting by satellite, without prejudice to other consultations which these States may undertake with any other State on that subject.

H. Copyright and Neighbouring Rights

11. Without prejudice to the relevant provisions of international law, States should co-operate on a bilateral and multilateral basis for protection of copyright and neighbouring rights by means of appropriate agreements between the interested States of the competent legal entities acting under their jurisdiction. In such co-operation they should give special consideration to the interests of developing countries in the use of direct television broadcasting for the purpose of accelerating their national development.

I. Notification to the United Nations

12. In order to promote international co-operation in the peaceful exploration and use of outer space, States conducting or authorizing activities in the field of international direct television broadcasting by satellite should inform the Secretary-General of the United Nations, to the greatest extent possible, of the nature of such activities. On receiving this information, the Secretary-General should disseminate it immediately and effectively to the relevant specialized agencies, as well as to the public and the international scientific community.

J. Consultations and Agreements Between States

13. A State which intends to establish or authorize the establishment of an international direct television broadcasting satellite service shall without delay notify the proposed receiving State or States of such intention and shall promptly enter into consultation with any of those States which so requests.

14. An international direct television broadcasting satellite service shall only be established after the conditions set forth in paragraph 13 above have been met and on the basis of agreements and/or arrangements in conformity with the relevant instruments of the International Telecommunication Union and in accordance with these principles.

15. With respect to the unavoidable overspill of the radiation of the satellite signal, the relevant instruments of the International Telecommunication Union shall be exclusively applicable.

SEE ALSO *European Convention on Transfrontier Television; UNESCO Declaration of Guiding Principles on the Use of Satellite Broadcasting for the Free Flow of Information, the Spread of Education and Greater Cultural Exchange.*

PRINCIPLES OF INTERNATIONAL CO-OPERATION IN THE DETECTION, ARREST, EXTRADITION AND PUNISHMENT OF PERSONS GUILTY OF WAR CRIMES AND CRIMES AGAINST HUMANITY (1973).

Finding it appropriate to stimulate the prosecution and punishment of persons guilty of war crimes and crimes against humanity, the UN General Assembly formulated nine principles to be observed universally and adopted and proclaimed them on 3 December 1973 (resolution 3074 [XXVIII]). The text of the principles, annexed to that resolution, is as follows:

The General Assembly

Declares that the United Nations, in pursuance of the principles and purposes set forth in the Charter concerning the promotion of co-operation between peoples and the maintenance of international peace and security, proclaims the following principles of international co-operation in the detection, arrest, extradition and punishment of persons guilty of war crimes and crimes against humanity:

1. War crimes and crimes against humanity, wherever they are committed, shall be subject to investigation and the persons against whom there is evidence that they have committed such crimes shall be subject to tracing, arrest, trial and, if found guilty, to punishment.

2. Every State has the right to try its own nationals for war crimes or crimes against humanity.

3. States shall co-operate with each other on a bilateral and multilateral basis with a view to halting and preventing war crimes and crimes against humanity, and shall take the domestic and international measures necessary for that purpose.

4. States shall assist each other in detecting, arresting and bringing to trial persons suspected of having committed such crimes and, if they are found guilty, in punishing them.

5. Persons against whom there is evidence that they have committed war crimes and crimes against humanity shall be subject to trial and, if found guilty, to punishment, as a general rule in the countries in which they committed those crimes. In that connexion, States shall co-operate on questions of extraditing such persons.

6. States shall co-operate with each other in the collection of information and evidence which would help bring to trial the persons indicated in paragraph 5 above and shall exchange such information.

7. In accordance with article 1 of the Declaration on Territorial Asylum of 14 December 1967, States shall not grant asylum to any person with respect to whom there are serious reasons for considering that he has committed a crime against peace, a war crime or a crime against humanity.

8. States shall not take any legislative or other measures which may be prejudicial to the international obligations they have assumed in regard to the detection, arrest, extradition and punishment of persons guilty of war crimes and crimes against humanity.

9. In co-operating with a view to the detection, arrest and extradition of persons against whom there is evidence that they have committed war crimes and crimes against humanity and, if found guilty, their punishment, States shall act in conformity with the provisions of the Charter of the United Nations and of the Declaration of Principles of International Law concerning Friendly Relations and Co-operation among States in accordance with the Charter of the United Nations.

SEE ALSO *Convention on the Non-Applicability of Statutory Limitations to War Crimes and Crimes against Humanity; Convention on the Prevention and Punishment of Genocide; Crimes against the Peace and Security of Mankind; European Convention on the Non-Applicability of Statutory Limitations to Crimes against Humanity and War Crimes; Genocide; Principles of International Law Recognized in the Charter of the Nurmberg Tribunal and in the Judgment of the Tribunal; War Crimes File; War Criminals: Prosecution and Punishment.*

PRINCIPLES OF INTERNATIONAL LAW RECOGNIZED IN THE CHARTER OF THE NURMBERG TRIBUNAL AND IN THE JUDGMENT OF THE TRIBUNAL (1950).

The principles, formulated by the **INTERNATIONAL LAW COMMISSION** as requested by the General Assembly on 21 November 1947 (resolution 177 [II]), and completed by the commission at its 1950 session, are as follows:

Principle 1. Any person who commits an act which constitutes a crime under international law is responsible therefor and liable to punishment.

Principle 2. The fact that internal law does not impose a penalty for an act which constitutes a crime under international law does not relieve the person who committed the act from responsibility under international law.

Principle 3. The fact that a person who committed an act which constitutes a crime under international law acted as Head of state or responsible Government official does not relieve him from responsibility under international law.

Principle 4. The fact that a person acted pursuant to order of his Government or of a superior does not relieve him from responsibility under international law, provided a moral choice was in fact possible to him.

Principle 5. Any person charged with a crime under international law has the right to a fair trial on the facts and law.

Principle 6. The crimes hereinafter set out are punishable as crimes under international law:

(a) Crimes against peace:

(i) Planning, preparation, initiation or waging of war of aggression or a war in violation of international treaties, agreements or assurances;

(ii) Participation in a common plan or conspiracy for the accomplishment of any of the acts mentioned under (i).

(b) War crimes: Violations of the laws or customs of war which include, but are not limited to, murder, ill-treatment or deportation to slave-labour or for any other purpose of civilian population of or in occupied territory; murder or ill-treatment of prisoners of war, of persons on the seas, killing of hostages, plunder of public or private property, wanton destruction of cities, towns, or villages, or devastation not justified by military necessity.

(c) Crimes against humanity: Murder, extermination, enslavement, deportation and other inhuman acts done against any civilian population, or persecutions on political, racial or religious grounds, when such acts are done or such persecutions are carried on in execution of or in connexion with any crime against peace or any war crime.

Principle 7. Complicity in the commission of a crime against peace, a war crime, or a crime against humanity as set forth in Principle VI is a crime under international law.

SEE ALSO *Convention on the Non-Applicability of Statutory Limitations to War Crimes and Crimes against Humanity; War Crimes Files; War Criminals: Prosecution and Punishment.*

PRINCIPLES OF MEDICAL ETHICS RELEVANT TO THE ROLE OF HEALTH PERSONNEL, PARTICULARLY PHYSICIANS, IN THE PROTECTION OF PRISONERS AND DETAINEES AGAINST TORTURE AND OTHER CRUEL, INHUMAN OR DEGRADING TREATMENT OR PUNISHMENT

(1982). In 1976, the UN General Assembly invited the WORLD HEALTH ORGANIZATION to prepare "a draft code of medical ethics relevant to the protection of persons subjected to any form of detention or imprisonment against torture and other cruel, inhuman or degrading treatment or punishment." The Executive Board of WHO decided, in 1979, to endorse the general principles on this subject which had been prepared by the Council for International Organisations of the Medical Sciences, entitled "Principles of Medical Ethics Relevant to the Role of Health Personnel in the Protection of Persons Against Torture and other Cruel, Inhuman or Degrading Treatment or Punishment." On the basis of these principles, the General Assembly adopted a more restricted set of principles directed in particular at the protection of prisoners and detainees.

The Principles of Medical Ethics was adopted by the General Assembly on 18 December 1982 (resolution 37/194). Their text, annexed to that resolution, is as follows:

Principle 1. Health personnel, particularly physicians, charged with the medical care of prisoners and detainees have a duty to provide them with protection of their physical and mental health and treatment of disease of the same quality and standard as is afforded to those who are not imprisoned or detained.

Principle 2. It is a gross contravention of medical ethics, as well as an offence under applicable international instruments, for health personnel, particularly physicians, to engage, actively or passively, in acts which constitute participation in, complicity in, incitement to or attempts to commit torture or other cruel, inhuman or degrading treatment or punishment.

Principle 3. It is a contravention of medical ethics for health personnel, particularly physicians, to be involved in any professional relationship with prisoners or detainees the purpose of which is not solely to evaluate, protect or improve their physical and mental health.

Principle 4. It is a contravention of medical ethics for health personnel, particularly physicians:

(a) To apply their knowledge and skills in order to assist in the interrogation of prisoners and detainees in a manner that may adversely affect the physical or mental health or condition of such prisoners or detainees and which is not in accordance with the relevant international instruments;

(b) To certify, or to participate in the certification of, the fitness of prisoners or detainees for any form of treatment or punishment that may adversely affect their physical or mental health and which is not in accordance with the relevant international instruments, or to participate in any way in the infliction of any such treatment or punishment which is not in accordance with the relevant international instruments.

Principle 5. It is a contravention of medical ethics for health personnel, particularly physicians, to participate in any procedure for restraining a prisoner or detainee unless such a procedure is determined in accordance with purely medical criteria as being necessary for the protection of the physical or mental health or the safety of the prisoner or detainee himself, of his fellow prisoners or detainees, or of his guardians, and presents no hazard to his physical or mental health.

Principle 6. There may be no derogation from the foregoing principles on any ground whatsoever, including public emergency.

PRINCIPLES ON THE EFFECTIVE PREVENTION AND INVESTIGATION OF EXTRA-LEGAL, ARBITRARY AND SUMMARY EXECUTIONS (1989).

In 1978, and frequently thereafter, the UN General Assembly expressed deep concern at reports from various parts of the world relating to enforced or involuntary disappearances and called upon governments to search for the "disappeared" persons and to investigate disappearances with speed and impartiality. More recently, the General Assembly has on a number of occasions strongly condemned the large number of summary or arbitrary executions, including extra-legal executions, occurring in some areas.

In 1986, the Economic and Social Council requested the COMMITTEE ON CRIME PREVENTION AND CONTROL to examine the question of extra-legal, arbitrary, and summary executions with a view to elaborating principles for the effective prevention and investigation of such practices. On recommendation of the committee, the council approved, on 24 May 1989, a series of Principles on the Effective Prevention and Investigation of Extra-legal, Arbitrary or Summary Executions and recommended that they should be taken into account and respected by governments within the framework of their national legislation and practices, and should be brought to the attention of law enforcement and criminal justice officials, military personnel, lawyers, members of the executive and legislative bodies of the government, and the public in general. The council requested the Committee on Crime Prevention and Control to keep the recommendations under constant review, including the implementation of the principles, taking into account the various socio-economic, political, and cultural circumstances in which extra-legal, arbitrary, and summary executions occur.

The Principles on the Effective Prevention and Investigation of Extra-legal, Arbitrary and Summary Executions adopted by the council (resolution 1989/65, Annex) are as follows:

Prevention. 1. Governments shall prohibit by law all extra-legal, arbitrary and summary executions and shall ensure that any such executions are recognized as offences under their criminal laws, and are punishable by appropriate penalties which take into account the seriousness of such offences. Exceptional circumstances including a state of war or threat of war, internal political instability or any other public emergency may not be invoked as a justification of such executions. Such executions shall not be carried out under any circumstances including, but not limited to, situations of internal armed conflict, excessive or illegal use of force by a public official or other person acting in an official capacity or a person acting at the instigation, or with the consent or acquiescence of such person, and situations in which deaths occur in custody. This prohibition shall prevail over decrees issued by governmental authority.

2. In order to prevent extra-legal, arbitrary and summary executions, Governments shall ensure strict control, including a clear chain of command over all officials responsible for the apprehension, arrest, detention, custody and imprisonment as well as those officials authorized by law to use force and firearms.

3. Governments shall prohibit orders from superior officers or public authorities authorizing or inciting other persons to carry out any such extra-legal, arbitrary or summary executions. All persons shall have the right and duty to defy such orders. Training of law enforcement officials shall emphasize the above provisions.

4. Effective protection through judicial or other means shall be guaranteed to individuals and groups who are in danger of extra-legal, arbitrary or summary executions, including those who receive death threats.

5. No one shall be involuntarily returned or extradited to a country where there are substantial grounds for believing that he or she may become a victim of extra-legal, arbitrary or summary execution in that country.

6. Governments shall ensure that persons deprived of their liberty are held in officially recognized places of custody, and that accurate information on their custody and whereabouts, including transfers, is made promptly available to their relatives and lawyer or other persons of confidence.

7. Qualified inspectors, including medical personnel, or an equivalent independent authority, shall conduct inspections in places of custody on a regular basis, and be empowered to undertake unannounced inspections on their own initiative, with full guarantees of independence in the exercise of this function. The inspectors shall have unrestricted access to all persons in such places of custody, as well as to all their records.

8. Governments shall make every effort to prevent extra-legal, arbitrary and summary executions through measures such as diplomatic intercession, improved access of complainants to intergovernmental and judicial bodies, and public denunciation. Intergovernmental mechanisms shall be used to investigate reports of any such executions and to take effective action against such practices. Governments, including those of countries where extra-legal, arbitrary and summary executions are reasonably suspected to occur, shall co-operate fully in international investigations on the subject.

Investigation. 9. There shall be a thorough, prompt and impartial investigation of all suspected cases of extra-legal, arbitrary and summary executions, including cases where complaints by relatives or other reliable reports suggest unnatural death in the above circumstances. Governments shall maintain investigative offices and procedures to undertake such inquiries. The purpose of the investigation shall be to determine the cause, manner and time of death, the person responsible, and any pattern or practice which may have brought about that death. It shall include an adequate autopsy, collection and analysis of all physical and documentary evidence, and statements from witnesses. The investigation shall distinguish between natural death, accidental death, suicide and homicide.

10. The investigative authority shall have the power to obtain all the information necessary to the inquiry. Those persons conducting the investigation shall have at their disposal all the necessary budgetary and technical resources for effective investigation. They shall also have the authority to oblige officials allegedly involved in any such executions to appear and testify. The same shall apply to any

witness. To this end, they shall be entitled to issue summons to witnesses, including the officials allegedly involved, and to demand the production of evidence.

11. In cases in which the established investigative procedures are inadequate because of lack of expertise or impartiality, because of the importance of the matter or because of the apparent existence of a pattern of abuse, and in cases where there are complaints from the family of the victim about these inadequacies or other substantial reasons, Governments shall pursue investigations through an independent commission of inquiry or similar procedure. Members of such a commission shall be chosen for their recognized impartiality, competence and independence as individuals. In particular, they shall be independent of any institution, agency or person that may be the subject of the inquiry. The commission shall have the authority to obtain all information necessary to the inquiry and shall conduct the inquiry as provided for under these Principles.

12. The body of the deceased person shall not be disposed of until an adequate autopsy is conducted by a physician, who shall, if possible, be an expert in forensic pathology. Those conducting the autopsy shall have the right of access to all investigative data, to the place where the body was discovered, and to the place where the death is thought to have occurred. If the body has been buried and it later appears that an investigation is required, the body shall be promptly and competently exhumed for an autopsy. If skeletal remains are discovered, they should be carefully exhumed and studied according to systematic anthropological techniques.

13. The body of the deceased shall be available to those conducting the autopsy for a sufficient amount of time to enable a thorough investigation to be carried out. The autopsy shall, at a minimum, attempt to establish the identity of the deceased and the cause and manner of death. The time and place of death shall also be determined to the extent possible. Detailed colour photographs of the deceased shall be included in the autopsy report in order to document and support the findings of the investigation. The autopsy report must describe any and all injuries to the deceased including any evidence of torture.

14. In order to ensure objective results, those conducting the autopsy must be able to function impartially and independently of any potentially implicated persons or organizations or entities.

15. Complainants, witnesses, those conducting the investigation and their families shall be protected from violence, threats of violence or any other form of intimidation. Those potentially implicated in extra-legal, arbitrary or summary executions shall be removed from any position of control or power, whether direct or indirect, over complainants, witnesses and their families, as well as over those conducting investigations.

16. Families of the deceased and their legal representatives shall be informed of, and have access to, any hearing as well as to all information relevant to the investigation, and shall be entitled to present other evidence. The family of the deceased shall have the right to insist that a medical or other qualified representative be present at the autopsy. When the identity of a deceased person has been determined, a notification of death shall be posted, and the family or relatives of the deceased immediately informed. The body of the deceased shall be returned to them upon completion of the investigation.

17. A written report shall be made within a reasonable period of time on the methods and findings of such investigations. The report shall be made public immediately and shall include the scope of the inquiry, procedures and methods used to evaluate evidence as well as conclusions and recommendations based on findings of fact and on applicable law. The report shall also describe in detail specific events that were found to have occurred, and the evidence upon which such findings were based, and list the names of witnesses who testified, with the exception of those whose identities have been withheld for their own protection. The Government shall, within a reasonable period of time, either reply to the report of the investigation, or indicate the steps to be taken in response to it.

Legal Proceedings. 18. Governments shall ensure that persons identified by the investigation as having participated in extra-legal, arbitrary or summary executions in any territory under their jurisdiction are brought to justice. Governments shall either bring such persons to justice or co-operate to extradite any such persons to other countries wishing to exercise jurisdiction. This principle shall apply irrespective of who and where the perpetrators or the victims are, their nationalities or where the offence was committed.

19. Without prejudice to Principle 3 above, an order from a superior officer or a public authority may not be invoked as a justification for extra-legal, arbitrary or summary executions. Superiors, officers or other public officials may be held responsible for acts committed by officials under their hierarchical authority if they had a reasonable opportunity to prevent such acts. In no circumstances, including a state of war, siege or other public emergency, shall blanket immunity from prosecution be granted to any person allegedly involved in extra-legal, arbitrary or summary executions.

20. The families and dependents of victims of extra-legal, arbitrary or summary executions shall be entitled to fair and adequate compensation within a reasonable period of time.

SEE ALSO *Executions: Report of Special Rapporteur.*

PRISONS: PRIVATIZATION. At its 1989 session, the UN SUB-COMMISSION ON PREVENTION OF DISCRIMINATION AND PROTECTION OF MINORITIES, on recommendation of its WORKING GROUP ON DETENTION, decided to request the chairman of the working group at that session, Mr. Miguel Alfonso Martinez (Cuba), to prepare a working paper containing proposals as to the best way for the sub-commission to study further the issue of privatization of prisons. The working paper was to be submitted to the sub-commission at its 1990 session for consideration under the item "The Administration of Justice and the Human Rights of Detainees."

PRIVACY. The right of everyone to privacy is set out in the UNIVERSAL DECLARATION OF HUMAN RIGHTS in the following terms:

Article 12. No one shall be subjected to arbitrary interference with his privacy, family, home or correspondence, nor to attacks upon his honour and reputation. Everyone has the right to the protection of the law against such interference or attacks.

The INTERNATIONAL COVENANT ON CIVIL AND POLITICAL RIGHTS contains the following provision on the subject:

Article 17. (1). No one shall be subjected to arbitrary or unlawful interference with his privacy, family, home or correspondence.
(2). Everyone has the right to the protection of the law against such interference or attacks.

The AMERICAN CONVENTION ON HUMAN RIGHTS, open for acceptance by member States of the ORGANIZATION OF AMERICAN STATES, deals with the right to privacy in the following provision:

Article 11. 1. Everyone has the right to have his honor respected and his dignity recognized.
2. No one may be the object of arbitrary or abusive interference with his private life, his family, his home, or his correspondence, or of unlawful attacks on his honor or reputation.
3. Everyone has the right to the protection of the law against such interference or attacks.

The EUROPEAN CONVENTION ON HUMAN RIGHTS, open for acceptance by member States of the COUNCIL OF EUROPE, contains the following provision:

Article 8. 1. Everyone has the right to respect for his private and family life, his home and his correspondence.
2. There shall be no interference by a public authority with the exercise of this right except such as in accordance with the law and is necessary in a democratic society in the interests of national security, public safety or the economic well-being of the country, for the prevention of disorder or crime, for the protection of health or morals, or for the protection of the rights and freedoms of others.

After examining reports submitted by States parties to the International Covenant on Civil and Political Rights in accordance with article 40 of that instrument, the HUMAN RIGHTS COMMITTEE adopted, in 1988, a general comment setting out its views on the meaning of the right to privacy as formulated in article 17 of the covenant, as follows (UN Doc.A/43/40, Annex VI):

1. Article 17 provides for the right of every person to be protected against arbitrary or unlawful interference with his privacy, family, home or correspondence, as well as against unlawful attacks on his honour and reputation. In the view of the Committee, this right is required to be guaranteed against all such interferences and attacks whether they emanate from State authorities or from natural or legal persons. The obligations imposed by this article require

the State to adopt legislative and other measures to give effect to the prohibition against such interferences and attacks as well as to the protection of this right.
2. In this connection, the Committee wishes to point out that, in the reports of States parties to the Covenant, the necessary attention is not being given to information concerning the manner in which respect for this right is guaranteed by legislative, administrative or judicial authorities and in general by the competent organs established in the State. In particular, insufficient attention is paid to the fact that article 17 of the Covenant deals with protection against both unlawful and arbitrary interference. That means that it is precisely in State legislation above all that provision must be made for the protection of the right set forth in that article. At present, the reports either say nothing about such legislation or provide insufficient information on the subject.
3. The term "unlawful" means that no interference can take place except in cases envisaged by the law. Interference authorized by States can only take place on the basis of law, which itself must comply with the provisions, aims and objectives of the Covenant.
4. The expression "arbitrary interference" is also relevant to the protection of the right provided for in article 17. In the Committee's view, the expression "arbitrary interference" can also extend to interference provided for under the law. The introduction of the concept of arbitrariness is intended to guarantee that even interference provided for by law should be in accordance with the provisions, aims and objectives of the Covenant and should be, in any event, reasonable in the particular circumstances.
5. Regarding the term "family", the objectives of the Covenant require that, for the purposes of article 17, this term be given a broad interpretation to include all those comprising the family as understood in the society of the State party concerned. The term "home" in English, *"manzel"* in Arabic, *"zhùzhái"* in Chinese, *"domicile"* in French, *"zhilishche"* in Russian and *"domicilio"* in Spanish, as used in article 17 of the Covenant, is to be understood to indicate the place where a person resides or carries out his usual occupation. In this connection, the Committee invites States to indicate in their reports the meaning given in their society to the term "family" and "home".
6. The Committee considers that the reports should include information on the authorities and organs set up within the legal system of the State which are competent to authorize interference allowed by the law. It is also indispensable to have information on the authorities which are entitled to exercise control over such interference with strict regard for the law, and to know in what manner and through which organs persons concerned may complain of a violation of the right provided for in article 17 of the Covenant. In their reports, States should make clear the extent to which actual practice conforms to the law. State party reports should also contain information on complaints lodged in respect of arbitrary or unlawful interference, and the number of any findings in that regard, as well as the remedies provided in such cases.
7. As all persons live in society, the protection of privacy is necessarily relative. However, the competent public authorities should only be able to call for such information relating to an individual's private life, the knowledge of which is essential in the interests of society as understood under the Covenant. Accordingly, the Committee recommends that States should indicate in their reports the laws and reg-

ulations that govern authorized interferences with private life.

8. Even with regard to interferences that conform to the Covenant, relevant legislation must specify in detail the precise circumstances in which such interferences may be permitted. A decision to make use of such authorized interference must be made only by the authority designated under the law, and on a case-by-case basis. Compliance with article 17 requires that the integrity and confidentiality of correspondence should be guaranteed *de jure* and *de facto*. Correspondence should be delivered to the addressee without interception and without being opened or otherwise read. Surveillance, whether electronic or otherwise, interceptions of telephonic, telegraphic and other forms of communication, wire-tapping and recording of conversations should be prohibited. Searches of a person's home should be restricted to a search for necessary evidence and should not be allowed to amount to harassment. So far as personal and body searches are concerned, effective measures should ensure that such searches are carried out in a manner consistent with the dignity of the person who is being searched. Persons being subjected to a body search by State officials, or medical personnel acting at the request of the State, should only be examined by persons of the same sex.

9. States parties are under a duty themselves not to engage in interferences inconsistent with article 17 of the Covenant and to provide the legislative framework prohibiting such acts by natural or legal persons.

10. The gathering and holding of personal information on computers, data banks and other devices, whether by public authorities or private individuals or bodies, must be regulated by law. Effective measures have to be taken by States to ensure that information concerning a person's private life does not reach the hands of persons who are not authorized by law to receive, process and use it, and is never used for purposes incompatible with the Covenant. In order to have the most effective protection of his private life, every individual should have the right to ascertain, in an intelligible form, whether, and if so, what personal data is stored in automatic data files and for what purposes. Every individual should also be able to ascertain which public authorities or private individuals or bodies control or may control their files. If such files contain incorrect personal data or have been collected or processed contrary to the provisions of the law, every individual should have the right to request rectification or elimination.

11. Article 17 affords protection to personal honour and reputation and States are under an obligation to provide adequate legislation to that end. Provision must also be made for everyone effectively to be able to protect himself against any unlawful attacks that do occur and to have an effective remedy against those responsible. States parties should indicate in their reports to what extent the honour or reputation of individuals is protected by law and how this protection is achieved according to their legal system.

PRIVACY: COMPUTERIZED PERSONAL DATA FILES. The PROCLAMATION OF TEHERAN, adopted by the International Conference on Human Rights on 13 May 1968, contains the following paragraph 18:

While recent scientific discoveries and technological ad-

vances have opened vast prospects for economic, social and cultural progress, such developments may nevertheless endanger the rights and freedoms of individuals and will require continuing attention.

On 19 December 1968, the General Assembly invited the Secretary-General to undertake (resolution 2450 [XXIII]) a study of the problems in connection with human rights arising from developments in science and technology, including one on the uses of electronics which might affect the rights of the person and the limits which should be placed on such uses in a democratic society.

That study, the first part of which is concerned with "computerized personal data systems," was presented to the UN COMMISSION ON HUMAN RIGHTS at its 1974 session (UN Doc. E/CN.4/1142 and Corr. 1, and Add. 1 and 2).

The General Assembly, at its 1975 session, adopted the DECLARATION ON THE USE OF SCIENTIFIC AND TECHNO-LOGICAL PROGRESS IN THE INTERESTS OF PEACE AND FOR THE BENEFIT OF MANKIND, in which it proclaimed that:

. . . All States shall take appropriate measures to prevent the use of scientific and technological developments, particularly by the State organs, to limit or interfere with the enjoyment of the human rights and fundamental freedoms of the individual as enshrined in the Universal Declaration of Human Rights, the International Covenants on Human Rights and other relevant international instruments . . .

In 1977, when the Commission on Human Rights was able to consider the sub-commission's study, it called upon the sub-commission (resolution 10 B [XXXIII]) to examine this and other studies in the light of the provisions of the declaration and to submit its recommendations for further action.

The sub-commission, at its 1980 session, noted (resolution 12 [XXXIII]) that one of the consequences of the use of computers was the increasingly frequent recourse to computerized personal files; that the concentration of personal particulars in such files entailed grave risks of interference with the privacy of individuals and the exercise of their freedoms; and that, apart from States, international, intergovernmental, and regional organizations were keeping an increasing number of computerized personal files. It requested its chairman to designate one of its members to undertake a study of guidelines to be adopted in this area.

Mrs. Nicole Questiaux (France) was designated for this task on the understanding that it would be carried out by her alternate, Mr. Louis Joinet. Mr. Joinet, who in the meantime replaced Mrs. Questiaux as a member of the sub-commission, submitted an interim report in 1981 and the final report (UN Doc. E/CN.4/Sub.2/1983/18) in 1983.

In the report, Mr. Joinet noted that, as early as 1966, the Nordic Council, a regional organization comprising the Scandinavian countries, had set up a special committee to promote the harmonization of legislation on data processing and freedoms in member States, and that, with time, this committee had become an effective organ for cooperation among the national bodies responsible for the supervision of data files. Further, he noted that the COUNCIL OF EUROPE and the Organization for Economic Co-operation and Development (OECD) had proposed for adoption by their member States—in the form of resolutions, recommendations, and even a convention—minimum rules, commonly known as the "hard core," which governments should take into account in the rules they were drafting. In particular, the Council of Europe's Council of Ministers adopted, on 28 January 1981, the EUROPEAN CONVENTION FOR THE PROTECTION OF INDIVIDUALS WITH REGARD TO AUTOMATIC PROCESSING OF PERSONAL DATA, and the OECD Council of Ministers adopted, on 23 September 1980, a recommendation concerning guidelines on the protection of privacy and transborder flows of personal data.

On the basis of these precedents and other materials available to him, Mr. Joinet concluded his study with two main proposals, the first relating to the promotion of human rights in domestic law (para. 136–148) and the second relating to the files of international organizations and agencies (para. 149–152) as follows:

A. The Promotion of Human Rights in Domestic Law. In order, firstly, to encourage States to promote protective regulations in their domestic legislation, and secondly, to avoid excessive discrepancies between one legislation and another, guidelines should be proposed for adoption by the competent United Nations bodies, possibly in the form of a recommendation, which might be along the following lines:

States should take steps to give effect to the following basic principles in their domestic legislation:

Principle of Fairness: information about persons should not be collected or processed in unfair or unlawful ways.

Principle of Accuracy: persons responsible for data files should be obliged to check the accuracy of the data recorded and to ensure that they are kept up to date.

Principle of Purpose Specification: the main purpose which a file is to serve should be known before it is established in order to make it possible subsequently to check whether: (a) the personal data collected and recorded are relevant to the purpose to be served; (b) the personal data are not used for purposes other than those for which the file was intended; and (c) the period for which the personal data are kept does not exceed that which would enable the objective for which they were recorded to be achieved.

Principle of Openness: measures should be taken to ensure that any person may be in a position to know of the existence of a personal data file.

Principle of Individual Access: any person, irrespective of nationality or place of residence, should have the right: (1) to know whether information concerning him is being processed; (2) if the need arises, to have such information communicated to him in an intelligible form, without excessive delay or expense; (3) to have appropriate rectification or erasures made in the case of erroneous, unlawful or inaccurate entries.

Principle of Security: appropriate measures should be taken to ensure the essential security of data files and of access to restricted information.

Departures from the application of one or other of these principles might be admitted in regulations concerning security files (police, defence, courts, intelligence), medical records, scientific and statistical data, and press files, provided that the limits of the exceptions were specified and they were embodied in laws or special regulations promulgated in accordance with the juridical system of each State.

Information on racial origin, sexual proclivities, political opinions, religious or philosophical convictions, or trade-union membership should not be recorded. Departures from these prohibitions should not be authorized except by law and should be subject to more rigorous safeguards.

A supervisory body should be established with adequate guarantees of impartiality both for the purpose of advising the persons affected by these new legislative measures and in order to ensure that the above principles are complied with.

The above principles and rules should, at the very least, be applied to public or private computerized files containing data relating to natural persons.

Particular provision might be made to extend the application of these provisions to manual data systems.

B. The Files of International Organizations and Agencies. The international organizations and agencies using computerized personnel files should be recommended to take appropriate protective measures unless they accept local jurisdiction where such exists.

The internal statutes and rules of international organizations and agencies should make provision, as concerns their own files, for the application of the aforementioned principles of fairness, accuracy, purpose specification, openness, individual access and security.

A supervisory authority, either of a collegiate or "ombudsman" type, set up under a procedure offering adequate guarantees of impartiality, should be appointed within each organization or agency.

Its task would be to advise those responsible for the operation of data files and to ensure effective enforcement of internal regulations.

Mr. Joinet recommended that the sub-commission prepare a resolution embodying in some appropriate way the twofold proposal above, for submission to the Commission on Human Rights. At the same time, he suggested that, as an immediate step, as far as United Nations computerized files are concerned, one member of the sub-commission should be appointed to study draft internal regulations with the assistance of the Secretariat.

Guidelines concerning Computerized Personal Data Files. In the *Study of the Relevant Guidelines in the Field of Computerized Personnel Files* (UN Doc. E/CN.4/Sub. 2/

P

1983/18) prepared for the SUB-COMMISSION ON PREVENTION OF DISCRIMINATION AND PROTECTION OF MINORITIES by its special rapporteur, Mr. Louis Joinet (France), the author elaborated a series of provisional draft guidelines on the use of such files with a view to encouraging States to adopt the regulations necessary to ensure the right to privacy.

At the request of the sub-commission, the Secretary-General transmitted the provisional draft guidelines to member States and interested international organizations with a request that they submit their comments. The guidelines were revised in the light of the comments received and presented to the sub-commission at its 1988 session (UN Doc. E/CN.4/Sub.2/1988/22).

On 1 September 1988, the sub-commission, expressing its satisfaction with the revised draft guidelines, forwarded them through the Commission on Human Rights and the Economic and Social Council to the General Assembly with a recommendation for their adoption (resolution 1988/29). The assembly, after examining them, invited the special rapporteur (resolution 44/132) to submit to the commission, at its 1990 session, a revised version taking into account the comments and suggestions submitted by eight governments. The special rapporteur accordingly submitted a revised text of the "Guidelines concerning Computerized Personal Data Files", reproduced below, to the commission at its 1990 session (UN Doc. E/CN.4/1990/72):

The procedures for implementing regulations concerning computerized personal data files are left to the initiative of each State subject to the following orientations:

A. Principles concerning the Minimum Guarantees that Should Be Provided in National Legislations

1. *Principle of Lawfulness and Fairness.* Information about persons should not be collected or processed in unfair or unlawful ways, nor should it be used for ends contrary to the purposes and principles of the Charter of the United Nations.

2. *Principle of Accuracy.* Persons responsible for the compilation of files or those responsible for keeping them have an obligation to conduct regular checks on the accuracy and relevance of the data recorded and to ensure that they are kept as complete as possible in order to avoid errors of omission and that they are kept up to date regularly or when the information contained in a file is used, as long as they are being processed.

3. *Principle of the Purpose-Specification.* The purpose which a file is to serve and its utilization in terms of that purpose should be specified, legitimate and, when it is established, receive a certain amount of publicity or be brought to the attention of the person concerned, in order to make it possible subsequently to ensure that:

(a) All the personal data collected and recorded remain relevant and adequate to the purposes so specified;

(b) None of the said personal data is used or disclosed, except with the consent of the person concerned, for purposes incompatible with those specified;

(c) The period for which the personal data are kept does not exceed that which would enable the achievement of the purpose so specified.

4. *Principle of Interested-Person Access.* Everyone who offers proof of identity has the right to know whether information concerning him is being processed and to obtain it in an intelligible form, without undue delay or expense, and to have appropriate rectifications or erasures made in the case of unlawful, unnecessary or inaccurate entries and, when it is being communicated, to be informed of the addresses. Provision should be made for a remedy, if need be with the supervisory authority specified in principle 8 below. The cost of any rectification shall be borne by the person responsible for the file. It is desirable that the provisions of this principle should apply to everyone, irrespective of nationality or place of residence.

5. *Principal of Non-Discrimination.* Subject to cases of exceptions restrictively envisaged under principle 6, data likely to give rise to unlawful or arbitrary discrimination, including information on racial or ethnic origin, colour, sex life, political opinions, religious, philosophical or other beliefs as well as membership of an association or trade union, should not be compiled.

6. *Power to Make Exceptions.* Departures from principles 1 to 4 may be authorized only if they are necessary to protect national security, public order, public health or morality, as well as, *inter alia,* the rights and freedoms of others, especially persons being persecuted (humanitarian clause) provided that such departures are expressly specified in a law or equivalent regulation promulgated in accordance with the internal legal system which expressly states their limits and sets forth appropriate safeguards.

Exceptions to principle 5 relating to the prohibition of discrimination, in addition to being subject to the same safeguards as those prescribed for exceptions to principles 1 and 4, may be authorized only within the limits prescribed by the International Bill of Human Rights and the other relevant instruments in the field of protection of human rights and the prevention of discrimination.

7. *Principle of Security.* Appropriate measures should be taken to protect the files against both natural dangers, such as accidental loss or destruction and human dangers, such an unauthorized access, fraudulent misuse of data or contamination by computer viruses.

8. *Supervision and Sanctions.* The law of every country shall designate the authority which, in accordance with its domestic legal system, is to be responsible for supervising observance of the principles set forth above. This authority shall offer guarantees of impartiality, independence vis-à-vis persons or agencies responsible for processing and establishing data, and technical competence. In the event of violation of the provisions of the national law implementing the aforementioned principles, criminal or other penalties should be envisaged together with the appropriate individual remedies.

9. *Transborder Data Flows.* When the legislation of two or more countries concerned by a transborder data flow offers comparable safeguards for the protection of privacy, information should be able to circulate as freely as inside each of the territories concerned. If there are no reciprocal safeguards, limitations on such circulation may not be imposed unduly and only in so far as the protection of privacy demands.

10. *Field of Application.* The present principles should be

1232

made applicable, in the first instance, to all public and private computerized files as well as, by means of optional extension and subject to appropriate adjustments, to manual files. Special provision, also optional, might be made to extend all or part of the principles to files on legal persons particularly when they contain some information on individuals.

Application of the Guidelines to Personal Data Files Kept by Governmental International Organizations

The present guidelines should apply to personal data files kept by governmental international organizations, subject to any adjustments required to take account of any differences that might exist between files for internal purposes such as those that concern personnel management and files for external purposes concerning third parties having relations with the organization.

Each organization should designate the authority statutorily competent to supervise the observance of these guidelines.

Humanitarian clause: a derogation from these principles may be specifically provided for when the purpose of the file is the protection of human rights and fundamental freedoms of the individual concerned or humanitarian assistance.

A similar derogation should be provided in national legislation for governmental international organizations whose headquarters agreement does not preclude the implementation of the said national legislation as well as for non-governmental international organizations to which this law is applicable.

PROCEDURAL ASPECTS OF INTERNATIONAL LAW INSTITUTE.

An international organization in consultative status (Roster) with the UN Economic and Social Council, PAIL was founded in 1965, initially to study international procedures for the protection of human rights. It conducts research on various procedural aspects of international law and disseminates its findings through publications, seminars and, conferences. In 1978, PAIL established the International Human Rights Law Group, which has functioned as a separate organization since 1983.

Among the publications in the PAIL series are the following: John Carey, *UN Protection of Civil and Political Rights* (1970); Frank G. Dawson and Ivan L. Head, *International Law, National Tribunals, and the Rights of Aliens* (1970); Richard B. Lillich, *Humanitarian Intervention and the United Nations* (1973); David Harris, *The European Social Charter* (1984); Hurst Hannum, ed., *Guide to International Human Rights Practice* (1984); Hurst Hannum and Richard B. Lillich, *Materials on International Human Rights and U.S. Constitutional Law* (1985); and Hurst Hannum, *The Right to Leave and Return in International Law and Practice* (1987).

Procedural Aspects of International Law Institute. Address: 910 17th Street, N.W., Washington, D.C. (USA) 20006. Telephone: (202) 659-3228. Executive Director: L Hurst Hannum.

PROCEDURAL GUARANTEES.

Provisions which prescribe the manner in which rights may be exercised or enforced, and which provide safeguards to ensure justly administered remedies in the case of violation of those rights. Certain principles relating to procedural guarantees are set out in articles 6, 10, and 11 of the UNIVERSAL DECLARATION OF HUMAN RIGHTS, as follows:

Article 6. Everyone has the right to recognition everywhere as a person before the law. . . .

Article 10. Everyone is entitled in full equality to a fair and public hearing by an independent and impartial tribunal, in the determination of his rights and obligations and of any criminal charge against him.

Article 11. (1). Everyone charged with a penal offense has the right to be presumed innocent until proved guilty according to law in a public trial at which he has had all the guarantees necessary for his defence.

(2). No one shall be held guilty of any penal offence on account of any act or omission which did not constitute a penal offence, under national or international law, at the time when it was committed. Nor shall a heavier penalty be imposed than the one that was applicable at the time the penal offence was committed.

The subject of procedural guarantees is dealt with extensively in the INTERNATIONAL COVENANT ON CIVIL AND POLITICAL RIGHTS, in articles 14 to 16, as follows:

Article 14. 1. All persons shall be equal before the courts and tribunals. In the determination of any criminal charge against him, or of his rights and obligations in a suit at law, everyone shall be entitled to a fair and public hearing by a competent, independent and impartial tribunal established by law. The Press and the public may be excluded from all or part of a trial for reasons of morals, public order (*ordre public*) or national security in a democratic society, or when the interest of the private lives of the parties so requires, or to the extent strictly necessary in the opinion of the court in special circumstances where publicity would prejudice the interests of justice; but any judgement rendered in a criminal case or in a suit at law shall be made public except where the interest of juvenile persons otherwise requires or the proceedings concern matrimonial disputes of the guardianship of children.

2. Everyone charged with a criminal offence shall have the right to be presumed innocent until proved guilty according to law.

3. In the determination of any criminal charge against him, everyone shall be entitled to the following minimum guarantees, in full equality:

(a) To be informed promptly and in detail in a language which he understands of the nature and cause of the charge against him;

(b) To have adequate time and facilities for the preparation of his defence and to communicate with counsel of his own choosing;

(c) To be tried without undue delay;

(d) To be tried in his presence, and to defend himself in person or through legal assistance of his own choosing; to be informed, if he does not have legal assistance, of this right; and to have legal assistance assigned to him, in any case where the interests of justice so require, and without payment by him in any such case if he does not have sufficient means to pay for it;

(e) To examine, or have examined, the witnesses against him and to obtain the attendance and examination of witnesses on his behalf under the same condition as witnesses against him;

(f) To have the free assistance of an interpreter if he cannot understand or speak the language used in court;

(g) Not to be compelled to testify against himself or to confess guilt.

4. In the case of juvenile persons, the procedure shall be such as will take account of their age and the desirability of promoting their rehabilitation.

5. Everyone convicted of a crime shall have the right to his conviction and sentence being reviewed by a higher tribunal according to law.

6. When a person has by a final decision been convicted of a criminal offence and when subsequently his conviction has been reversed or he has been pardoned on the ground that a new or newly discovered fact shows conclusively that there has been a miscarriage of justice, the person who has suffered punishment as a result of such conviction shall be compensated according to law, unless it is proved that the non-disclosure of the unknown fact in time is wholly or partly attributable to him.

7. No one shall be liable to be tried or punished again for an offence for which he has already been finally convicted or acquitted in accordance with the law and penal procedure of each country.

Article 15. 1. No one shall be held guilty of any criminal offence on account of any act or omission which did not constitute a criminal offence, under national or international law, at the time when it was committed. Nor shall a heavier penalty be imposed than the one that was applicable at the time when the criminal offence was committed. If, subsequent to the commission of the offence, provision is made by law for the imposition of the lighter penalty, the offender shall benefit thereby.

2. Nothing in this article shall prejudice the trial and punishment of any person for any act or omission which, at the time when it was committed, was criminal according to the general principles of law recognized by the community of nations.

Article 16. Everyone shall have the right to recognition everywhere as a person before the law.

The **INTERNATIONAL CONVENTION ON THE ELIMINATION OF ALL FORMS OF RACIAL DISCRIMINATION** deals with procedural guarantees briefly, as follows:

Article 5. In compliance with the fundamental obligations laid down in article 2 of this Convention, States parties undertake to prohibit and to eliminate racial discrimination in all its forms and to guarantee the right of everyone, without distinction as to race, colour, or national or ethnic origin, to equality before the law, notably in the enjoyment of the following rights: (a) the right to equal

treatment before the tribunals and all other organs administering justice. . . .

The **CONVENTION ON THE ELIMINATION OF ALL FORMS OF DISCRIMINATION AGAINST WOMEN** contains the following provisions:

Article 15. (2). States Parties shall accord to women, in civil matters, a legal capacity identical to that of men and the same opportunities to exercise that capacity. In particular, they shall give women equal rights to conclude contracts and to administer property and shall treat them equally in all stages of procedure in courts and tribunals.

(3) States parties agree that all contracts and all other private instruments of any kind with a legal effect which is directed at restricting the legal capacity of women shall be deemed null and void.

The subject of procedural guarantees is dealt with in the **CONVENTION AGAINST TORTURE AND OTHER CRUEL, INHUMAN OR DEGRADING TREATMENT OR PUNISHMENT,** as follows:

Article 12. Each State party shall ensure that its competent authorities proceed to a prompt and impartial investigation, wherever there is reasonable ground to believe that an act of torture has been committed in any territory under its jurisdiction.

Article 13. Each State party shall ensure that any individual who alleges he has been subjected to torture in any territory under its jurisdiction has the right to complain to, and to have his case promptly and impartially examined by, its competent authorities. Steps shall be taken to ensure that the complainant and witnesses are protected against all ill-treatment or intimidation as a consequence of his complaint or any evidence given.

Article 14. (1). Each State party shall ensure in its legal system that the victim of an act of violence obtains redress and has an enforceable right to fair and adequate compensation, including the means for as full rehabilitation as possible. In the event of the death of the victim as a result of an act of torture, his dependents shall be entitled to compensation.

(2). Nothing in this article shall affect any right of the victim or other persons to compensation which may exist under national law.

Article 15. Each State party shall ensure that any statement which is established to have been made as a result of torture shall not be invoked as evidence in any proceedings, except against a person accused of torture as evidence that the statement was made.

The **AMERICAN CONVENTION ON HUMAN RIGHTS,** open for acceptance by member States of the **ORGANIZATION OF AMERICAN STATES,** provides that:

Article 3. Every person has the right to recognition as a person before the law. . . .

Article 8. 1. Every person has the right to a hearing, with due guarantees and within a reasonable time, by a competent, independent, and impartial tribunal, previously established by law, in the substantiation of any accusation of a criminal nature made against him or for the determination of his rights and obligations of a civil, labor, fiscal, or any other nature.

2. Every person accused of a criminal offense has the right to be presumed innocent so long as his guilt has not been proven according to law. During the proceedings, every person is entitled, with full equality, to the following minimum guarantees:

a. the right of the accused to be assisted without charge by a translator or interpreter, if he does not understand or does not speak the language of the tribunal or court;

b. prior notification in detail to the accused of the charges against him;

c. adequate time and means for the preparation of his defense;

d. the right of the accused to defend himself personally or to be assisted by legal counsel of his own choosing, and to communicate freely and privately with his counsel;

e. the inalienable right to be assisted by counsel provided by the state, paid or not as the domestic law provides, if the accused does not defend himself personally or engage his own counsel within the time period established by law;

f. the right of the defense to examine witnesses present in the court and to obtain the appearance, as witnesses, of experts or other persons who may throw light on the facts;

g. the right not to be compelled to be a witness himself or to plead guilty; and

h. the right to appeal the judgment to a higher court.

3. A confession of guilt by the accused shall be valid only if it is made without coercion of any kind.

4. An accused person acquitted by a nonappealable judgment shall not be subjected to a new trial for the same cause.

5. Criminal proceedings shall be public, except insofar as may be necessary to protect the interests of justice.

The **AFRICAN CHARTER ON HUMAN AND PEOPLE'S RIGHTS,** open for acceptance by member States of the **ORGANIZATION OF AFRICAN UNITY,** contains the following provisions:

Article 5. Every individual shall have the right to the respect of the dignity inherent in a human being and to the recognition of his legal status. . . .

Article 7. 1. Every individual shall have the right to have his cause heard. This comprises:

a. The right to an appeal to competent national organs against acts violating his fundamental rights as recognized and guaranteed by conventions, laws, regulations and customs in force;

b. the right to be presumed innocent until proved guilty by a competent court or tribunal;

c. the right to defence, including the right to be defended by counsel of his choice;

d. the right to be tried within a reasonable time by an impartial court or tribunal.

2. No one may be condemned for an act or omission which did not constitute a legally punishable offence at the time it was committed. No penalty may be inflicted for an offence for which no provision was made at the time it was committed. Punishment is personal and can be imposed only on the offender.

The **EUROPEAN CONVENTION ON HUMAN RIGHTS,** open for acceptance by member States of the **COUNCIL OF EUROPE,** provides that:

Article 6. 1. In the determination of his civil rights and obligations or of any criminal charge against him, everyone is entitled to a fair and public hearing within a reasonable time by an independent and impartial tribunal established by law. Judgment shall be pronounced publicly but the press and public may be excluded from all or part of the trial in the interest of morals, public order or national security in a democratic society, where the interests of juveniles or the protection of the private life of the parties so require, or to the extent strictly necessary in the opinion of the court in special circumstances where publicity would prejudice the interests of justice.

2. Everyone charged with a criminal offence shall be presumed innocent until proved guilty according to law.

3. Everyone charged with a criminal offence has the following minimum rights:

a. to be informed promptly, in a language which he understands and in detail, of the nature and cause of the accusation against him;

b. to have adequate time and facilities for the preparation of his defence;

c. to defend himself in person or through legal assistance of his own choosing or, if he has not sufficient means to pay for legal assistance, to be given it free when the interests of justice so require;

d. to examine or have examined witnesses against him and to obtain the attendance and examination of witnesses on his behalf under the same conditions as witnesses against him;

e. to have the free assistance of an interpreter if he cannot understand or speak the language used in court.

Article 7. 1. No one shall be held guilty of any criminal offence on account of any act or omission which did not constitute a criminal offence under national or international law at the time when it was committed. Nor shall a heavier penalty be imposed than the one that was applicable at the time the criminal offence was committed.

2. This Article shall not prejudice the trial and punishment of any person for any act or omission which, at the time when it was committed, was criminal according to the general principles of law recognized by civilised nations.

The **EUROPEAN CONVENTION ON HUMAN RIGHTS: PROTOCOL VII,** adds the following provisions to the text of the convention:

Article 2. 1. Everyone convicted of a criminal offence by a tribunal shall have the right to have conviction or sentence reviewed by a higher tribunal. The exercise of this right, including the grounds on which it may be exercised, shall be governed by law.

2. This right may be subject to exceptions in regard to offences of a minor character, as prescribed by law, or in cases in which the person concerned was tried in the first instance by the highest tribunal or was convicted following an appeal against acquittal.

Article 3. When a person has by a final decision been convicted of a criminal offence and when subsequently his conviction has been reversed, or he has been pardoned, on the ground that a new or newly discovered fact shows conclusively that there has been a miscarriage of justice, the persons who has suffered punishment as a result of such conviction shall be compensated according to the law or the practice of the State concerned, unless it is proved that the non-disclosure of the unknown fact in time is wholly or partly attributable to him.

Article 4. 1. No one shall be liable to be tried or punished again in criminal proceedings under the jurisdiction of the same State for an offence for which he has already been finally acquitted or convicted in accordance with the law and penal procedure of that State.

2. The provisions of the preceding paragraph shall not prevent the reopening of the case in accordance with the law and penal procedure of the State concerned, if there is evidence of new or newly discovered facts, or if there has been a fundamental defect in the previous proceedings, which could affect the outcome of the case.

3. No derogation from this Article shall be made under Article 15 of the Convention.

After examining reports submitted by States parties to the International Covenant on Civil and Political Rights in accordance with its article 40, the HUMAN RIGHTS COMMITTEE adopted in 1984 a general comment on article 14 of that covenant in which it set out the committee's views on the use of procedural guarantees to ensure the proper administration of justice in the following terms (UN Doc. A/39/40, Annex VI):

1. The Committee notes that article 14 of the Covenant is of a complex nature and that different aspects of its provisions will need specific comments. All of these provisions are aimed at ensuring the proper administration of justice, and to this end uphold a series of individual rights such as equality before the courts and tribunals and the right to a fair and public hearing by a competent, independent and impartial tribunal established by law. Not all reports provided details on the legislative or other measures adopted specifically to implement each of the provisions of article 14.

2. In general, the reports of States parties fail to recognize that article 14 applies not only to procedures for the determination of criminal charges against individuals but also to procedures to determine their rights and obligations in a suit at law. Laws and practices dealing with these matters vary widely from State to State. This diversity makes it all the more necessary for States parties to provide all relevant information and to explain in greater detail how the concepts of "criminal charge" and "rights and obligations in a suit at law" are intercepted in relation to their respective legal systems.

3. The Committee would find it useful if, in their future reports, States parties could provide more detailed information on the steps taken to ensure that equality before the courts, including equal access to courts, fair and public hearings and competence, impartiality and independence of the judiciary are established by law and guaranteed in practice. In particular, States parties should specify the relevant constitutional and legislative texts which provide for the establishment of the courts and ensure that they are independent, impartial and competent, in particular with regard to the manner in which judges are appointed, the qualifications for appointment, and the duration of their terms of office; the conditions governing promotion, transfer and cessation of their functions and the actual independence of the judiciary from the executive branch and the legislature.

4. The provisions of article 14 apply to all courts and tribunals within the scope of that article whether ordinary or specialized. The Committee notes the existence, in many countries, of military or special courts which try civilians. This could present serious problems as far as the equitable, impartial and independent administration of justice is concerned. Quite often the reason for the establishment of such courts is to enable exceptional procedures to be applied which do not comply with normal standards of justice. While the Covenant does not prohibit such categories of courts, nevertheless the conditions which it lays down clearly indicate that the trying of civilians by such courts should be very exceptional and take place under conditions which genuinely afford the full guarantees stipulated in article 14. The Committee has noted a serious lack of information in this regard in the reports of some States parties whose judicial institutions include such courts for the trying of civilians. In some countries such military and special courts do not afford the strict guarantees of the proper administration of justice in accordance with the requirements of article 14 which are essential for the effective protection of human rights. If States parties decide in circumstances of a public emergency as contemplated by article 4 to derogate from normal procedures required under article 14, they should ensure that such derogations do not exceed those strictly required by the exigencies of the actual situation, and respect the other conditions in paragraph 1 of article 14.

5. The second sentence of article 14, paragraph 1, provides that "everyone shall be entitled to a fair and public hearing". Paragraph 3 of the article elaborates on the requirements of a "fair hearing" in regard to the determination of criminal charges. However, the requirements of paragraph 3 are minimum guarantees, the observance of which is not always sufficient to ensure the fairness of a hearing as required by paragraph 1.

6. The publicity of hearings is an important safeguard in the interest of the individual and of society at large. At the same time article 14, paragraph 1, acknowledges that courts have the power to exclude all or part of the public for reasons spelt out in that paragraph. It should be noted that, apart from such exceptional circumstances, the Committee considers that a hearing must be open to the public in general, including members of the press, and must not, for instance, be limited only to a particular category of persons. It should be noted that, even in cases in which the public is excluded from the trial, the judgement must, with certain strictly defined exceptions, be made public.

7. The Committee has noted a lack of information regarding article 14, paragraph 2, and, in some cases, has even observed that the presumption of innocence, which is fundamental to the protection of human rights, is expressed in very ambiguous terms or entails conditions which render it ineffective. By reason of the presumption of innocence, the burden of proof of the charge is on the prosecution and the accused has the benefit of doubt. No guilt can be presumed until the charge has been proved beyond reasonable doubt. Further, the presumption of innocence implies a right to be treated in accordance with this principle. It is therefore a duty for all public authorities to refrain from prejudging the outcome of a trial.

8. Among the minimum guarantees in criminal proceedings prescribed by paragraph 3, the first concerns the right of everyone to be informed in a language which he understands of the charge against him (subparagraph (a)). The Committee notes that State reports often do not explain how this right is respected and ensured. Article 14, subparagraph 3 (a) applies to all cases of criminal charges, including those of persons not in detention. The Committee notes further that the right to be informed of the charge "promptly" requires that information is given in the manner described as soon as the charge is first made by a competent authority. In the opinion of the Committee this right must arise when in the course of an investigation a court or an authority of the prosecution decides to take procedural steps against a person suspected of a crime or publicly names him as such. The specific requirements of subparagraph 3 (a) may be met by stating the charge either orally or in writing, provided that the information indicates both the law and the alleged facts on which it is based.

9. Subparagraph 3 (b) provides that the accused must have adequate time and facilities for the preparation of his defence and to communicate with counsel of his own choosing. What is "adequate time" depends on the circumstances of each case, but the facilities must include access to documents and other evidence which the accused requires to prepare his case, as well as the opportunity to engage and communicate with counsel. When the accused does not want to defend himself in person or request a person or an association of his choice, he should be able to have recourse to a lawyer. Furthermore, this subparagraph requires counsel to communicate with the accused in conditions giving full respect for the confidentiality of their communications. Lawyers should be able to counsel and to represent their clients in accordance with their established professional standards and judgement without any restrictions, influences, pressures or undue interference from any quarter.

10. Subparagraph 3 (c) provides that the accused shall be tried without undue delay. This guarantee relates not only to the time by which a trial should commence, but also the time by which it should end and judgement be rendered; all stages must take place "without undue delay". To make this right effective, a procedure must be available in order to ensure that the trial will proceed "without undue delay", both in first instance and on appeal.

11. Not all reports have dealt with all aspects of the right of defence as defined in subparagraph 3 (d). The Committee has not always received sufficient information concerning the protection of the right of the accused to be present during the determination of any charge against him nor how the legal system assures his right either to defend himself in person or to be assisted by counsel of his own choosing, or what arrangements are made if a person does not have sufficient means to pay for legal assistance. The accused or his lawyer must have the right to act diligently and fearlessly in pursuing all available defences and the right to challenge the conduct of the case if they believe it to be unfair. When exceptionally for justified reasons trials *in absentia* are held, strict observance of the rights of the defence is all the more necessary.

12. Subparagraph 3 (e) states that the accused shall be entitled to examine or have examined the witnesses against him and to obtain the attendance and examination of witnesses on his behalf under the same conditions as witnesses against him. This provision is designed to guarantee to the accused the same legal powers of compelling the attendance of witnesses and of examining or cross-examining any witnesses as are available to the prosecution.

13. Subparagraph 3 (f) provides that if the accused cannot understand or speak the language used in court he is entitled to the assistance of an interpreter free of any charge. This right is independent of the outcome of the proceedings and applies to aliens as well as to nationals. It is of basic importance in cases in which ignorance of the language used by a court or difficulty in understanding may constitute a major obstacle to the right of defence.

14. Subparagraph 3 (g) provides that the accused may not be compelled to testify against himself or to confess guilt. In considering this safeguard the provisions of article 7 and article 10, paragraph 1, should be borne in mind. In order to compel the accused to confess or to testify against himself frequently methods which violate these provisions are used. The law should require that evidence provided by means of such methods or any other form of compulsion is wholly unacceptable.

15. In order to safeguard the rights of the accused under paragraphs 1 and 3 of article 14, judges should have authority to consider any allegations made of violations of the rights of the accused during any stage of the prosecution.

16. Article 14, paragraph 4, provides that in the case of juvenile persons, the procedure shall be such as will take account of their age and the desirability of promoting their rehabilitation. Not many reports have furnished sufficient information concerning such relevant matters as the minimum age at which a juvenile may be charged with a criminal offence, the maximum age at which a person is still considered to be a juvenile, the existence of special courts and procedures, the laws governing procedures against juveniles and how all these special arrangements for juveniles take account of "the desirability of promoting their rehabilitation". Juveniles are to enjoy at least the same guarantees and protection as are accorded to adults under article 14.

17. Article 14, paragraph 5, provides that everyone convicted of a crime shall have the right to his conviction and sentence being reviewed by a higher tribunal according to law. Particular attention is drawn to the other language versions of the word "crime" *("infraction", "delito", "prestuplenie")* which show that the guarantee is not confined only to the most serious offences. In this connection, not enough information has been provided concerning the procedures of appeal, in particular the access to and the powers of reviewing tribunals, what requirements must be satisfied to appeal against a judgement and the way in which the procedures before review tribunals take account of the fair and public hearing requirements of paragraph 1 of article 14.

18. Article 14, paragraph 6, provides for compensation according to law in certain cases of a miscarriage of justice as described therein. It seems from many State reports that this right is often not observed or insufficiently guaranteed by domestic legislation. States should, where necessary, supplement their legislation in this area in order to bring it into line with the provisions of the Covenant.

19. In considering State reports differing views have often been expressed as to the scope of paragraph 7 of article 14. Some States parties have even felt the need to make reservations in relation to procedures for the resumption of criminal cases. It seems to the Committee that most States parties make a clear distinction between a resumption of a trial justified by exceptional circumstances and a

retrial prohibited pursuant to the principle of *ne bis in idem* as contained in paragraph 7. This understanding of the meaning of *ne bis in idem* may encourage States parties to reconsider their reservations to article 14, paragraph 7.

SEE ALSO Arbitrary Arrest, Detention or Exile; Arrested Person's Right to Communicate; Body of Principles for the Protection of All Persons under any Form of Detention or Imprisonment; Convention against Torture and Other Cruel, Inhuman or Degrading Treatment or Punishment; Declaration on the Protection of all Persons from being Subjected to Torture and Other Cruel, Inhuman or Degrading Treatment or Punishment; Fair Trial; Imprisonment; Liberty; Principles on the Effective Prevention and Investigation of Extra-Legal, Arbitrary and Summary Executions; Standard Minimum Rules for the Treatment of Prisoners.

PROCLAMATION OF TEHERAN (1968). In the proclamation, prepared and adopted by the INTERNATIONAL CONFERENCE ON HUMAN RIGHTS which convened in Teheran from 22 April to 13 May 1968, the conference affirmed "its faith in the principles of the Universal Declaration of Human Rights and other international instruments in this field" and urged all peoples and nations to dedicate themselves to these principles and "to reduce their efforts to provide for all human beings a life consonant with freedom and dignity and conducive to physical, mental, social and spiritual welfare."

In paragraph 2 of the proclamation, the conference recognized that "the Universal Declaration of Human Rights states a common understanding of the peoples of the world concerning the inalienable and inviolable rights of all members of the human family and constitutes an obligation for the members of the international community." This evaluation of the significance of the universal declaration went beyond any that had been made previously by a world-wide international organ.

The proclamation was adopted by the conference on 13 May 1968. The text (*Final Act of the International Conference on Human Rights,* United Nations publication, Sales No. E.68.XIV.2, chap. II) is as follows:

The International Conference on Human Rights,

Having met at Teheran from April 22 to May 13, 1968 to review the progress made in the twenty years since the adoption of the Universal Declaration of Human Rights and to formulate a programme for the future,

Having considered the problems relating to the activities of the United Nations for the promotion and encouragement of respect for human rights and fundamental freedoms,

Bearing in mind the resolutions adopted by the Conference,

Noting that the observance of the International Year for Human Rights takes place at a time when the world is undergoing a process of unprecedented change,

Having regard to the new opportunities made available by the rapid progress of science and technology,

Believing that, in an age when conflict and violence prevail in many parts of the world, the fact of human interdependence and the need for human solidarity are more evident than ever before,

Recognizing that peace is the universal aspiration of mankind and that peace and justice are indispensable to the full realization of human rights and fundamental freedoms,

Solemnly proclaims that:

1. It is imperative that the members of the international community fulfil their solemn obligations to promote and encourage respect for human rights and fundamental freedoms for all without distinctions of any kind such as race, colour, sex, language, religion, political or other opinions;

2. The Universal Declaration of Human Rights states a common understanding of the peoples of the world concerning the inalienable and inviolable rights of all members of the human family and constitutes an obligation for the members of the international community;

3. The International Covenant on Civil and Political Rights, the International Covenant on Economic, Social and Cultural Rights, the Declaration on the Granting of Independence to Colonial Countries and Peoples, the International Convention on the Elimination of All Forms of Racial Discrimination as well as other conventions and declarations in the field of human rights adopted under the auspices of the United Nations, the specialized agencies and the regional intergovernmental organizations, have created new standards and obligations to which States should conform;

4. Since the adoption of the Universal Declaration of Human Rights the United Nations has made substantial progress in defining standards for the enjoyment and protection of human rights and fundamental freedoms. During this period many important international instruments were adopted but much remains to be done in regard to the implementation of those rights and freedoms;

5. The primary aim of the United Nations in the sphere of human rights is the achievement by each individual of the maximum freedom and dignity. For the realization of this objective, the laws of every country should grant each individual, irrespective of race, language, religion or political belief, freedom of expression, of information, of conscience and of religion, as well as the right to participate in the political, economic, cultural and social life of his country;

6. States should reaffirm their determination effectively to enforce the principles enshrined in the Charter of the United Nations and in other international instruments that concern human rights and fundamental freedoms;

7. Gross denials of human rights under the repugnant policy of *apartheid* is a matter of the gravest concern to the international community. This policy of *apartheid,* condemned as a crime against humanity, continues seriously to disturb international peace and security. It is therefore imperative for the international community to use every possible means to eradicate this evil. The struggle against *apartheid* is recognized as legitimate;

8. The peoples of the world must be made fully aware of the evils of racial discrimination and must join in combating them. The implementation of this principle of nondiscrimination, embodied in the Charter of the United Nations, the Universal Declaration of Human Rights, and other international instruments in the field of human rights, constitutes a most urgent task of mankind at the international as well as at the national level. All ideologies

based on racial superiority and intolerance must be condemned and resisted;

9. Eight years after the General Assembly's Declaration on the Granting of Independence to Colonial Countries and Peoples the problems of colonialism continue to preoccupy the international community. It is a matter of urgency that all Member States should co-operate with the appropriate organs of the United Nations so that effective measures can be taken to ensure that the Declaration is fully implemented;

10. Massive denials of human rights, arising out of aggression or any armed conflict with their tragic consequences, and resulting in untold human misery, engender reactions which could engulf the world in ever growing hostilities. It is the obligation of the international community to co-operate in eradicating such scourges;

11. Gross denials of human rights arising from discrimination on grounds of race, religion, belief or expressions of opinion outrage the conscience of mankind and endanger the foundations of freedom, justice and peace in the world;

12. The widening gap between the economically developed and developing countries impedes the realization of human rights in the international community. The failure of the Development Decade to reach its modest objectives makes it all the more imperative for every nation, according to its capacities, to make the maximum possible effort to close this gap;

13. Since human rights and fundamental freedoms are indivisible, the full realization of civil and political rights without the enjoyment of economic, social and cultural rights is impossible. The achievement of lasting progress in the implementation of human rights is dependent upon the sound and effective national and international policies of economic and social development;

14. The existence of over seven hundred million illiterates throughout the world is an enormous obstacle to all efforts at realizing the aims and purposes of the Charter of the United Nations and the provisions of the Universal Declaration of Human Rights. International action aimed at eradicating illiteracy from the face of the earth and promoting education at all levels requires urgent attention;

15. The discrimination of which women are still victims in various regions of the world must be eliminated. An inferior status for women is contrary to the Charter of the United Nations as well as the provisions of the Universal Declaration of Human Rights. The full implementation of the Declaration on the Elimination of Discrimination against Women is a necessity for the progress of mankind;

16. The protection of the family and of the child remains the concern of the international community. Parents have a basic human right to determine freely and responsibly the number and the spacing of their children;

17. The aspirations of the younger generation for a better world, in which human rights and fundamental freedoms are fully implemented, must be given the highest encouragement. It is imperative that youth participate in shaping the future of mankind;

18. While recent scientific discoveries and technological advances have opened vast prospects for economic, social and cultural progress, such developments may nevertheless endanger the rights and freedoms of individuals and will require continuing attention;

19. Disarmament would release immense human and material resources now devoted to military purposes. These resources should be used for the promotion of human rights and fundamental freedoms. General and complete disarmament is one of the highest aspirations of all peoples;

Therefore,

The International Conference on Human Rights,

1. Affirming its faith in the principles of the Universal Declaration of Human Rights and other international instruments in this field,

2. Urges all peoples and governments to dedicate themselves to the principles enshrined in the Universal Declaration of Human Rights and to redouble their efforts to provide for all human beings a life consonant with freedom and dignity and conducive to physical, mental, social and spiritual welfare.

PROCLAMATION OF THE INTERNATIONAL YEAR OF PEACE (1985).

In 1982, the UN General Assembly declared (resolution 37/16) the year 1986 to be the International Year of Peace as a commemoration of the 40th anniversary of the United Nations. The Proclamation of the International Year of Peace approved by the General Assembly on 24 October 1985 (resolution 40/3) links the promotion and achievement of the ideals of peace to the promotion and protection of human right—both being fundamental purposes of the UNITED NATIONS CHARTER. The text of the proclamation, annexed to resolution 40/3, is as follows:

Whereas, the General Assembly has decided unanimously to proclaim solemnly the International Year of Peace on 24 October 1985, the fortieth anniversary of the United Nations,

Whereas the fortieth anniversary of the United Nations provides a unique opportunity to reaffirm the support for and commitment to the purposes and principles of the Charter of the United Nations,

Whereas peace constitutes a universal ideal and the promotion of peace is the primary purpose of the United Nations,

Whereas the promotion of international peace and security requires continuing and positive action by States and peoples aimed at the prevention of war, removal of various threats to peace—including the nuclear threat—respect for the principle of non-use of force, the resolution of conflicts and peaceful settlement of disputes, confidence-building measures, disarmament, maintenance of outer space for peaceful uses, development, the promotion and exercise of human rights and fundamental freedoms, decolonization in accordance with the principle of self-determination, elimination of racial discrimination and *apartheid,* the enhancement of the quality of life, satisfaction of human needs and protection of the environment,

Whereas peoples must live together in peace and practise tolerance, and it has been recognized that education, information, science and culture can contribute to that end,

Whereas the International Year of Peace provides a timely impetus for initiating renewed thought and action for the promotion of peace,

Whereas the International Year of Peace offers an opportunity to Governments, intergovernmental, non-governmental organizations and others to express in practical terms the common aspiration of all peoples for peace,

Whereas the International Year of Peace is not only a celebration or commemoration, but an opportunity to reflect and act creatively and systematically in fulfilling the purposes of the United Nations,

Now, therefore,

The General Assembly

Solemnly proclaims 1986 to be the International Year of Peace and calls upon all peoples to join with the United Nations in resolute efforts to safeguard peace and the future of humanity.

PROCURATOR'S OFFICE. A national institution established within the framework of the judicial system of the Union of Soviet Socialist Republics and other eastern European countries including Bulgaria, Hungary, Romania, Czechoslovakia, Poland, and Yugoslavia, and in the Democratic People's Republic of Korea, having as one of its functions the protection and promotion of human rights. As described in the UN Secretary-General's report entitled *National Institutions for the Protection and Promotion of Human Rights* (UN Doc. E/CN.4/1987/37, para. 48–52), prepared at the request of the General Assembly (resolution 40/123):

The Procurator's Office was designed to protect the constitutionally guaranteed rights and legally protected interests of citizens of the USSR, as well as to protect the rights and legally protected interests of State institutions. In order to provide the Procurator's Office with the means to fulfil this broad responsibility, the State grants the Procurator far-reaching authority and jurisdiction. For instance the Procurator's powers include the right to demand documents and information, and all State bodies and officials must submit the necessary information to the Procurator's Office upon request.

Unlike the Scandinavian ombudsman, with which the Procurator's Office is frequently compared, the Procurator-General is empowered to monitor the legality and validity of verdicts, decisions, judgements and orders of judicial organs in criminal and civil cases. In accordance with this authority, the Procurator may appeal to a higher court if, in his view, a court sentence in a criminal case or a ruling in a civil case is unlawful and unjustified. He may not however, challenge a sentence of acquittal, which is irreversible after one year from the date on which the sentence was passed.

The Procurator is further charged with the supervision of administrative bodies. To that end, the Procurator's Office may act on its own initiative or on the basis of complaints received from aggrieved citizens. Considerable importance is attached to these complaints. Ensuring respect for the law in the examinations of such complaints is one of the Procurator's most important duties. The law governing this matter imposes upon all administrative organs seized of a complaint, the obligation to make a careful investigation, to communicate to the plaintiffs in writing and orally, the decision taken, and to state the grounds for negative decisions. Furthermore, the Administration must attempt to draw general conclusions on the complaints

received with a view to eliminating the causes of the violations. Penalties are imposed in the case of a breach of the complaints procedure, bureaucratic unco-operativeness or victimization of the plaintiff.

Generally, the Procurator's Office is also charged with the prevention of crime and the prosecution of criminals. Included in this prosecutory power is the obligation to ensure that the organs of inquiry and preliminary investigation strictly observe the criminal investigation procedures established by the law. The Procurator is also empowered to investigate the lawfulness of administrative detention of a citizen. Moreover, the Procurator must ensure that no arrest is made unless it has been ordered by a court or approved by the Procurator's Office. In addition, the Procurator has a duty immediately to release any person illegally deprived of liberty or detained in custody for longer than the term provided for by the law or by a court sentence.

The Procurator of the USSR is elected by the Supreme Soviet for a term of seven years' service. Only the Supreme Soviet may remove the Procurator-General from Office. He is responsible for appointing the Procurators of the Union Republics, the autonomous republics, the territories, the regions and the autonomous regions. The various agencies of the Procurator's Office are then established, according to the division of the Republic, into administrative units. Although the Procurator's Office is virtually an independent organ, the Procurator-General must submit an annual activity report to the Supreme Soviet.

SEE ALSO Ministerio Publico, Ombudsman.

PROPERTY. The right of everyone to own property is proclaimed in the UNIVERSAL DECLARATION OF HUMAN RIGHTS in the following terms:

Article 17. (1). Everyone has the right to own property alone as well as in association with others.

(2). No one shall be arbitrarily deprived of his property.

The prohibition of discrimination in respect of the right is set out in article 5 of the INTERNATIONAL CONVENTION ON THE ELIMINATION OF ALL FORMS OF DISCRIMINATION, which provides that:

Article 5. In compliance with the fundamental obligations laid down in article 2 of this Convention, States Parties undertake to prohibit and to eliminate racial discrimination in all its forms and to guarantee the right of everyone, without distinction as to race, colour, or national or ethnic origin, to equality before the law, notably in the enjoyment of the following rights:. . . .

(d) Other civil rights, in particular:. . . .

(v) The right to own property alone as well as in association with others;

(vi) The right to inherit. . . .

The CONVENTION ON THE ELIMINATION OF DISCRIMINATION AGAINST WOMEN contains the following provisions:

Article 13. States Parties shall take all appropriate measures to eliminate discrimination against women in other areas of economic and social life in order to ensure, on a basis of equality of men and women, the same rights, in particular:

(a) The right to family benefits;

(b) The right to bank loans, mortgages and other forms of financial credit;

(c) The right to participate in recreational activities, sports and all aspects of cultural life. . . .

Article 15. (2). States parties shall accord to women, in civil matters, a legal capacity identical to that of men and the same opportunities to exercise that capacity. In particular, they shall give women equal rights to conclude contracts and to administer property and shall treat them equally in all stages of procedure in courts and tribunals.

The AMERICAN CONVENTION ON HUMAN RIGHTS, open for acceptance by member States of the ORGANIZATION OF AMERICAN STATES, provides that:

Article 21. 1. Everyone has the right to the use and enjoyment of his property. The law may subordinate such use and enjoyment to the interest of society.

2. No one shall be deprived of his property except upon payment of just compensation, for reasons of public utility or social interest, and in the cases and according to the forms established by law.

3. Usury and any form of exploitation of man by man shall be prohibited by law.

The AFRICAN CHARTER OF HUMAN AND PEOPLE'S RIGHTS, open for acceptance by member States of the ORGANIZATION OF AFRICAN UNITY, provides that:

Article 14. The right to property shall be guaranteed. It may only be encroached upon in the interest of public need or in the general interest of the community and in accordance with the provisions of appropriate laws.

The right of property, set out in general terms in article 17 of the Universal Declaration of Human Rights, is not mentioned in either of the International Covenants on Human Rights, the drafters of the covenants having been unable to reach agreement of the appropriate formulation of the right, its legitimate limitations, or the restrictions which should properly be placed upon action by the state. However, this right is dealt with, as shown above, in several other international conventions; and both the DECLARATION ON SOCIAL PROGRESS AND DEVELOPMENT and the DECLARATION ON THE RIGHT TO DEVELOPMENT assign a role to property in the implementation of human rights and fundamental freedoms.

In recent years, the right of property has been examined mainly in the General Assembly and the COMMISSION ON HUMAN RIGHTS.

In 1986, the UN General Assembly expressed (resolution 41/132) the conviction that the full enjoyment by everyone of the right to own property, alone as well as in association with others, is of particular significance in fostering widespread enjoyment of other basic human rights and contributes to securing the goals of economic and social development enshrined in the UNITED NATIONS CHARTER. The resolution called upon the Secretary-General to prepare a report, taking into account the views of member States, specialized agencies, and other competent bodies of the United Nations system, on (a) the relationship between the full enjoyment by individuals of human rights and fundamental freedoms, in particular the right of everyone to own property alone as well as in association with others, as set forth in article 17 of the Universal Declaration of Human Rights, and the economic and social development of member States; and (b) the role of the same right in ensuring the full and free participation of individuals in the economic and social systems of states. The assembly requested the Secretary-General to report his findings to it through the Economic and Social Council.

In 1987, the General Assembly recognized (resolution 42/115) that there exist in member States many forms of legal property ownership, including private, communal, and state forms, each of which should contribute to ensuring the effective development and utilization of human resources through the establishment of sound bases for political, economic, and social justice; and called upon States to ensure that their national legislation with regard to all forms of property shall preclude any impairment of the enjoyment of human rights and fundamental freedoms, without prejudice to their right freely to choose and develop their political, social, economic, and cultural system.

Also in 1987, the Commission on Human Rights dealt with the right to own property in two resolutions. In the first (resolution 1987/17), it urged States to provide, where they have not done so, adequate constitutional and legal provisions to protect the right of everyone to own property alone as well as in association with others and the right not to be deprived arbitrarily of one's property. In the second (resolution 1987/18), it reaffirmed the statement in article 6 of the Declaration on Social Progress and Development, that social progress and development require the establishment, in conformity with human rights and fundamental freedoms, and with the principles of justice and the social function of property, of forms of ownership of land and of the means of production which preclude any kind of exploitation of man, ensure equal rights to property for all, and create conditions leading to genuine equality among people.

The Commission on Human Rights, at its 1988 session, appealed (resolution 1988/18) to member

States, specialized agencies, and other competent bodies of the United Nations systems to respond as constructively and factually as possible to the invitation of the General Assembly to communicate their views on the subject to the Secretary-General. In a resolution on the impact of property upon the enjoyment of human rights and fundamental freedoms (resolution 1988/19), it called upon states to ensure that their national legislation with regard to all forms of property precludes any impairment and reiterated the views which had been expressed by the assembly on this subject in assembly resolution 42/115. And in another resolution, on the recovery of nations' assets illegally removed by violators of human rights (resolution 1988/20), it joined with the SUB-COMMISSION ON PREVENTION OF DISCRIMINATION AND PROTECTION OF MINORITIES in requesting all States concerned to cooperate in the speedy recovery of the assets belonging to the peoples of the Philippines and Haiti illegally removed by the Marcos and Duvalier families, respectively.

In a note presented to the Economic and Social Council and to the General Assembly in 1988 (UN Doc. E/1988/24), the Secretary-General informed those bodies of the progress made in preparing his report and pointed out that each of the above-mentioned resolutions had brought forward important issues to be considered, among them the following (para. 9–11):

The principal focus of Assembly resolution 41/132 and 42/115 and Commission resolutions 1987/17 and 1988/18 [is]on the legal protection of the right to property as a human right and its relationship to the economic and social development of the individual, within his socio-economic system. In those resolutions, the Assembly and the Commission on Human Rights emphasized the right not to be deprived of one's property arbitrarily (art. 17 of the Universal Declaration of Human Rights), that the right to property should be subject only to such limitations as are determined by law solely for the purpose of securing due recognition and respect for the rights and freedoms of others and of meeting the just requirements of morality, public order and the global welfare in a democratic society (art. 29 of the Universal Declaration of Human Rights), that no State, group or person should be engaged in any activity or perform any act aimed at the destruction of, *inter alia,* the right to property (art. 30 of the Universal Declaration of Human Rights) and that States should establish national legislation to protect the rights of everyone to own property alone as well as in association with others. They also stressed the role of individual initiative as a valuable resource in promoting economic and social development.

In Assembly resolution 42/115 and Commission resolutions 1987/18 and 1988/19, other elements were brought forward relating to the links between the right to own property and the right to self-determination, the right to sovereignty over all natural wealth and resources and the establishment of a new international economic order. Referring to article 6 of the Declaration on Social Progress

and Development, the Assembly and the Commission reaffirmed that social progress and development require the establishment, in conformity with human rights and fundamental freedoms and with the principles of justice and the social function of property, of forms of ownership of land and of the means of production which preclude any kind of human exploitation, ensure equal rights to property for all and create conditions leading to genuine equality among people.

The Assembly and the Commission in those resolutions also emphasized the role of the public sector in promoting the economic development of developing countries, expressed their conviction that social justice is a prerequisite for lasting peace and that man can achieve complete fulfilment of his aspirations only within a just social order and called upon States to ensure that their national legislation with regard to all forms of property precludes any impairment of the enjoyment of human rights and fundamental freedoms, without prejudice to their right freely to choose and develop their political, social, economic and cultural systems. Finally, those resolutions dealt with the specific issues of transnational corporations and urged them to ensure that their activities do not adversely affect the process of implementing the human rights in developing countries.

As regards the materials made available for use in the preparation of his report, the Secretary-General stated that (para. 12–16)

The communications which have so far been received reflect the broad approach to the issue taken by the Assembly and the Commission by describing the different forms of property which exist in countries and their role in promoting economic and social progress.

Governments in their replies generally refer to constitutional provisions or national legislation regulating the protection of the right to property. Some governmental replies describe the role that the different forms of property play in their countries in promoting the socio-economic development process and in creating conditions in which the individuality of every member of the society can flourish.

Other communications received from competent bodies of the United Nations system and non-governmental organizations, emphasize the need to utilize all human resources for the social and economic development and to guarantee equal opportunity for all to participate in these processes. Referring to the various forms of property, it is stated that property rights may be conceived as one of the means for enlarging people's participation in, and the acceleration of, their social and economic development, particularly in developing countries. It is said that the right of everyone to own property has to be seen in the context of general social conditions of the individual. If such a concept is to be established, it should particularly refer to the needs of under-developed regions and of special and disadvantaged social groups.

Various replies refer to the relationship between the right of everybody to own property and other political, economic and social rights. Mention is made in this context to the right to freedom of association, freedom from discrimination, freedom of labour, the right to equivalent pay for the work done or service rendered and other rights. Certain replies stressed that holding of property should not increase social discrimination or injustice, prevent or impeded social integration or full participation in the economic or social policy-making processes, increase unemployment and neglect social responsibility. In this regard, attention is drawn to discriminatory factors which may exist to restrict the social integration and advancement of women, the poor, the aged or the young in many parts of the world.

A number of replies argue that the principal issue was to find and guarantee effective ways and means of enabling socially and economically disadvantaged people to have access to different forms of legal property ownership, including private, communal or State forms. It is said that in the development of these ways and means, national distribution and redistribution policies, as well as land and other social and economic reforms had to be taken into account. It is also emphasized that respect for the right of everybody to own property includes the elimination of all forms of discrimination against specific social groups.

Late in 1988, the General Assembly considered (resolution 43/123) two aspects of the right of property. First, it repeated the earlier call of the Commission on Human Rights requesting States to provide adequate constitutional and legal provisions to protect the right to own property alone as well as in association with others and the right not to be deprived arbitrarily of one's property. Secondly, it requested the Secretary-General to seek the views of member States, specialized agencies, and other competent bodies of the United Nations system on the means whereby and the degree to which the right to own property, contributes to the development of individual liberty and initiative which serve to foster, strengthen, and enhance the exercise of other human rights and fundamental freedoms. It suggested that member States, specialized agencies, and other competent bodies of the United Nations system may wish to address, in particular, the right to own the following types of property: (a) personal property, including the residence of one's self and family; and (b) economically productive property, including property associated with agriculture, commerce, and industry.

PROTOCOL AMENDING THE SLAVERY CONVENTION (1953).

The protocol, which amends the Slavery Convention opened for signature under the auspices of the League of Nations on 25 September 1926 to place it under the auspices of the United Nations, was adopted by the UN General Assembly on 23 October 1953 and entered into force on 7 July 1955. As authorized in article 4 of the protocol, the Secretary-General subsequently published the protocol and the SLAVERY CONVENTION SIGNED AT GENEVA ON 25 SEPTEMBER 1926, AS AMENDED.

The text of the protocol (General Assembly resolution 794 [VIII], Annex), is as follows:

The States Parties to the present Protocol,

Considering that under the Slavery Convention signed at Geneva on 25 September 1926 (hereinafter called "the Convention") the League of Nations was invested with certain duties and functions, and

Considering that it is expedient that these duties and functions should be continued by the United Nations,

Have agreed as follows:

Article 1. The State Parties to the present Protocol undertake that as between themselves they will, in accordance with the provisions of the Protocol, attribute full legal force and effect to and duly apply the amendments to the Convention set forth in the annex to the Protocol.

Article 2. 1. The present Protocol shall be open for signature or acceptance by any of the States Parties to the Convention to which the Secretary-General has communicated for this purpose a copy of the Protocol.

2. States may become Parties to the present Protocol by:

    (a) Signature without reservation as to acceptance;

    (b) Signature with reservation as to acceptance, followed by acceptance;

    (c) Acceptance.

3. Acceptance shall be effected by the deposit of a formal instrument with the Secretary-General of the United Nations.

Article 3. 1. The present Protocol shall come into force on the date on which two States shall have become Parties thereto, and shall therefore come into force in respect of each State upon the date on which it becomes a Party to the Protocol.

2. The amendments set forth in the annex to the present Protocol shall come into force when twenty-three States shall have become Parties to the Protocol, and consequently any State becoming a Party to the Convention, after the amendments thereto have come into force, shall become a Party to the Convention as so amended.

Article 4. In accordance with paragraph I of Article 102 of the Charter of the United Nations and the regulations pursuant thereto adopted by the General Assembly, the Secretary-General of the United Nations is authorized to effect registration of the present Protocol and of the amendments made in the Convention by the Protocol on the respective dates of their entry into force and to publish the Protocol and the amended text of the Convention as soon as possible after registration.

Article 5. The present Protocol, of which the Chinese, English, French, Russian and Spanish texts are equally authentic, shall be deposited in the archives of the United Nations Secretariat. The texts of the Convention to be amended in accordance with the annex being authentic in the English and French languages only, the English and French texts of the annex shall be equally authentic, and the Chinese, Russian and Spanish texts shall be translations. The Secretary-General shall prepare certified copies of the Protocol, including the annex, for communication to State Parties to the Convention, as well as to all other States Members of the United Nations. He shall likewise prepare for communication to States including States not Members of the United Nations, upon the entry into force of the amendments as provided in article III, certified copies of the Convention as so amended.

In witness whereof the undersigned, being duly authorized thereto by their respective Governments, signed the present Protocol on the date appearing opposite their respective signatures.

Done at the Headquarters of the United Nations, New

York, this seventh day of December one thousand nine hundred and fifty-three.

Annex to the Protocol Amending the Slavery Convention Signed at Geneva on 25 September 1926

In article 7 "the Secretary-General of the United Nations" shall be substituted for "the Secretary-General of the League of Nations".

In article 8 "the International Court of Justice" shall be substituted for the "Permanent Court of International Justice", and "the Statute of the International Court of Justice" shall be substituted for "the Protocol of December 16th, 1920, relating to the Permanent Court of International Justice".

In the first and second paragraphs of article 10 "the United Nations" shall be substituted for "the League of Nations".

The last three paragraphs of article 11 shall be deleted and the following substituted:

"The present Convention shall be open to accession by all States, including States which are not Members of the United Nations, to which the Secretary-General of the United Nations shall have communicated a certified copy of the Convention.

"Accession shall be effected by the deposit of a formal instrument with the Secretary-General of the United Nations, who shall give notice thereof to all States Parties to the Convention and to all other States contemplated in the present article, informing them of the date on which each such instrument of accession was received in deposit."

In article 12 "the United Nations" shall be substituted for "the League of Nations".

PROTOCOL FOR THE PROHIBITION OF THE USE IN WAR OF ASPHYXIATING, POISONOUS OR OTHER GASES, AND OF BACTERIOLOGICAL METHODS OF WARFARE (1925).
The protocol, concluded and signed in Geneva on 17 June 1925, was the first international instrument of universal scope to prohibit the use in war of poisonous and other gases, and of bacteriological methods of warfare. The subject, however, had been mentioned earlier in several peace treaties concluded at the close of the first world war, including the Treaty of Versailles.

The protocol entered into force for each signatory power as from the date of deposit of its instrument of ratification. The text (94 LNTS 65) is as follows:

The Undersigned Plenipotentiaries, in the name of their respective Governments:

Whereas the use in war of asphyxiating, poisonous or other gases, and of all analogous liquids, materials or devices, has been justly condemned by the general opinion of the civilized world; and

Whereas the prohibition of such use has been declared in Treaties to which the majority of Powers of the world are Parties; and

To the end that this prohibition shall be universally accepted as a part of International Law, binding alike the conscience and the practice of nations;

Declare:

That the High Contracting Parties, so far as they are not already Parties to Treaties prohibiting such use, accept this prohibition, agree to extend this prohibition to the use of bacteriological methods of warfare and agree to be bound as between themselves according to the terms of this declaration.

The High Contracting Parties will exert every effort to induce other States to accede to the present Protocol. Such accession will be notified to the Government of the French Republic, and by the latter to all signatory and acceding Powers, and will take effect on the date of the notification by the Government of the French Republic.

The present Protocol, of which the French and English texts are both authentic, shall be ratified as soon as possible. It shall bear to-day's date.

The ratifications of the present Protocol shall be addressed to the Government of the French Republic, which will at once notify the deposit of such ratification to each of the signatory and acceding Powers.

The instruments of ratification of and accession to the present Protocol will remain deposited in the archives of the Government of the French Republic.

The present Protocol will come into force for each signatory Power as from the date of deposit of its ratification, and, from that moment, each Power will be bound as regards other Powers which have already deposited their ratifications.

In witness whereof the Plenipotentiaries have signed the present Protocol.

Done at Geneva in a single copy, the seventeenth day of June, One Thousand Nine Hundred and Twenty-Five.

SEE ALSO Chemical Weapons; Chemical Weapons: Declaration on their Prohibition; Convention on the Prohibition of the Development, Production and Stockpiling of Bacteriological (Biological) and Toxin Weapons and on their Destruction.

PUBLIC EMERGENCY.
Article 4 of the INTERNATIONAL COVENANT ON CIVIL AND POLITICAL RIGHTS reads as follows:

1. In time of public emergency which threatens the life of the nation and the existence of which is officially proclaimed, the States Parties to the present Covenant may take measures derogating from their obligations under the present Covenant to the extent strictly required by the exigencies of the situation, provided that such measures are not inconsistent with their other obligations under international law and do not involve discrimination solely on the ground of race, colour, sex, language, religion or social origin.
2. No derogation from articles 6, 7, 8 (paragraphs 1 and 2), 11, 15, 16 and 18 may be made under this provision.
3. Any State party to the present Covenant availing itself of the right of derogation shall immediately inform the other States Parties to the present Covenant, through the intermediary of the Secretary-General of the United Nations, of the provisions from which it has derogated and of the reasons by which it was actuated. A further communication shall be made, through the same intermediary, on the date on which it terminates the derogation.

A study of the protection of human rights in time of public emergency appears as Part Three of the more comprehensive study entitle *The Individual's Duties to the Community and the Limitations on Human Rights and Freedoms Under Article 29 of the Universal Declaration of Human Rights,* prepared by Mrs. Erica-Irene A. Daes (Greece), special rapporteur for the SUB-COMMISSION ON PREVENTION OF DISCRIMINATION AND PROTECTION OF MINORITIES, published in 1983 (United Nations publication, Sales No. E.82.XIV.1). In the study, the special rapporteur reviews the legislative history of the preparation of article 4 of the International Covenant on Civil and Political Rights and sets out the requirements for the existence of a public emergency. Her conclusions and recommendations on this subject are as follows (para. 171–195):

A. Conclusions

From the foregoing analysis of article 4 of the International Covenant of Civil and Political Rights, the examination of relevant provisions of other international instruments on human rights, the study of the replies of Governments and certain national constitutions and the review of certain cases dealt with by international organs of implementation, the following conclusions may be drawn.

The only kind of emergency envisaged in article 4 is a "public emergency" and according to paragraph 1, such an emergency can occur only when "the life of the nation" is threatened and only when its existence has been "officially proclaimed" by the State party concerned. The concept "public emergency" is of recent date. It was introduced to eliminate, where possible, from legal instruments the "state of war" which has not existed in international law since the Second World War. It also replaces the traditional term "state of siege".

This formulation was chosen in order to provide for a qualification of the kind of public emergency in which a State would be entitled to make derogations from the rights protected by the Covenant which would not be open to abuse.

The present wording requires that the public emergency should be of such a magnitude as to threaten the life of a nation as a whole.

Article 4 rightly does not include war as a form of public emergency, because the United Nations was established with the object of preventing war.

"Public emergency" is a restrictive term which does not cover, for example, natural disasters, which very often, justify a State party in derogating from some, at least, of the rights recognized in the Covenant.

The provision of article 4, paragraph 1, of the Covenant to the effect that the existence of a public emergency should be "officially proclaimed" by the State party concerned is essential in order to prevent States from derogating arbitrarily from their obligations where such action is not warranted by events.

In most countries a public emergency can be declared only under conditions defined by law, and that guarantee would be lost if a requirement of public proclamation were not provided for.

The provisions of article 4 should in no way imply that constitutional and legal limits imposed upon the powers of Governments during a public emergency can be derogated from or that the executive power is not responsible for taking measures which might conflict with national guarantees.

The measures which a State party may take in derogation of its obligations under the Covenant after a public emergency has been proclaimed are subject to three conditions which are specified in paragraph 1 of the article: (*a*) they must be "to the extent strictly required by the exigencies of the situation"; (*b*) they must not be "inconsistent with [the State party's] other obligations under international law"; and (*c*) they must "not involve discrimination solely on the ground of race, colour, sex, language, religion or social origin".

In particular, the measures which may be taken in derogation of the obligations of a State party under the Covenant should not be inconsistent with the purposes and principles of the Charter of the United Nations, the Universal Declaration of Human Rights and other international instruments on human rights.

Paragraph 2 of article 4 of the Covenant enumerates the provisions of the Covenant from which no derogations may be made.

No derogation may be made, even in time of public emergency, from the provisions of the following articles: article 6 (right to life); article 7 (freedom from torture and cruel, inhuman or degrading treatment or punishment and from medical or scientific experimentation); article 8 (freedom from slavery, servitude and forced labour); article 11 (right not to be imprisoned for inability to fulfil a contractual obligation); article 15 (prohibition of retroactive application of criminal law); article 16 (recognition as a person before the law); and article 18 (freedom of thought, conscience and religion).

When a State party avails itself of the right of derogation in time of public emergency, it is required, by paragraph 3 of article 4 of the Covenant, to comply with three steps concerning notifications of its actions. It must in each case "immediately inform" the other States parties, through the intermediary of the Secretary-General: (*a*) of the provisions of the Covenant from which it has derogated; (*b*) of the reasons by which it was actuated; and (*c*) of the date on which it terminates such derogation.

The proclamation of a public emergency and consequential derogation from the provisions of the Covenant is a matter of the gravest concern and the States parties have the right to be notified of such action.

The derogating State should also furnish the reasons by which it was actuated, although this might not include every detail of each particular measure taken. Notification should also be furnished of the date on which the derogation was terminated.

Certain of the international instruments on human rights contain express provisions spelling out that States may interfere with nationally and internationally guaranteed human rights in time of public emergency.

It is often precisely through action of this kind that the rights and freedoms of the individual are violated.

States of public emergency and their effects need to be scrutinized by the organs charged with the implementation of the relevant international bill of human rights.

The implementation provisions of the Covenant should apply to article 4 of the Covenant.

The onus of proof as to the existence of a public emergency and to the necessity of the measure should rest on the respondent Government.

Immeasurable criteria such as the margin of appreciation, the onus and standard of proof and the elements of good faith and reasonableness merely constitute useful tools at the disposal of those exercising functions of a judicial or quasi-judicial nature.

States of exception should not always be equated with violations of human rights.

Even in a state of public emergency the fundamental principle of the rule of law should prevail.

B. Recommendations

In connection with the protection of human rights in a state of public emergency, and in the light and spirit of the conclusions set forth in section A above, the Special Rapporteur proposes that the Sub-Commission on Prevention of Discrimination and Protection of Minorities should consider making the following recommendations to the Commission on Human Rights:

(1) The Commission should recommend to the Economic and Social Council that it authorize the Sub-Commission to elaborate a declaratory resolution containing common principles, guidelines and standards relating to the protection of human rights in time of public emergency.

(2) The Commission should recommend to the Economic and Social Council that it authorize the Sub-Commission to study all other aspects related to the question of the protection of human rights in time of public emergency, including such aspects as whether public emergency is an issue falling within the domestic jurisdiction of a State and the interrelationship of economic and social development and the state of emergency.

SEE ALSO *Assembly and Association; Civil and Political Rights: Siracusa Principles; Derogation; State of Emergency; State of Emergency: Essential Judicial Guarantees; State of Emergency: Freedom of Association.*

Q

QATAR. The State of Qatar is an Arab country in western Asia, occupying the Qatar Peninsula that extends into the Persian Gulf from the Arabian Peninsula. It has boundaries with Saudi Arabia and the United Arab Emirates. It achieved independence from Great Britain in 1971 and became a member of the United Nations the same year. Its population is estimated by the UN (1990) to be 413,000 and includes members of foreign communities needed for the country's socio-economic development plans. These foreign communities consist of Asians from Iraq, India, Pakistan, Afghanistan, Iran, Thailand, Korea, the Philippines, Japan, and China; Arab and non-Arab nationals from African countries, and Europeans from Great Britain, France, Germany, Italy, Greece, and other countries. The language commonly used is Arabic. Islam is the predominant religion, and all nationals of Qatar are Muslims. Literacy is estimated at 40%.

The government (1990) took the form of a monarchy. The amir, as ruler, is assisted by the 30-member Advisory Council. There is no legislative body as such; all decrees are issued by the amir. There are five courts of justice which proclaim judgements in the name of the amir; only Arab lawyers are permitted to practice before them. There are no political parties.

In regard to the restrictions placed upon the practice of law, the government provided the following information to the **COMMITTEE ON THE ELIMINATION OF RACIAL DISCRIMINATION** in a report presented to that body on 11 October 1983 (UN Doc. CERD/C/104/ Add. 1, para. 39–44):

The practice of law and legal consultancy in Qatar are regulated by Act No. 20 of 1980, article 1 of which restricts the exercise of this profession to jurists listed in the permanent or provisional rolls of lawyers. Under articles 2 and 3, inclusion in the permanent and provisional rolls is restricted to Qataris and non-Qatari Arabs, respectively. However, under article 15, lawyers who are not registered in Qatar may be appointed by litigants to plead before the Qatari courts in particular cases, subject to the following conditions:

The lawyer thus appointed must be an Arab national licensed to practise law in his country. He must work in co-operation with a lawyer entered either in the permanent or in the provisional roll in Qatar. Special permission must be obtained from the Minister of Justice. Such treatment must be granted on a reciprocal basis.

This does not constitute discrimination in favour of Arab lawyers. The purpose of this regulation is to further the interests of litigants, since, in addition to familiarity with Arabic, which is the official language of the country, such lawyers are also acquainted with Arab practices, customs and traditions. Moreover, there is considerable similarity between the laws in force in the various Arab countries and it is therefore fairly easy for this category of lawyers to obtain a sound grasp of the laws applicable in the State of Qatar. This type of regulation is applied in a large number of other countries, particularly those whose circumstances are similar to our own.

QATAR: CONSTITUTION. The amended Provisional Constitution of the State of Qatar contains the following provisions (articles 6 to 16) specifically relating to human rights and fundamental freedoms:

Article 6. Economic Principles. (a) Property, capital and labour shall be basic elements in the social structure of the State, and they are individual rights serving social ends as prescribed by law.

(b) The State shall guarantee free enterprise within the limits of public interests.

The State shall have the right to supervise the national economy in a manner that will ensure its safety for the good of the country. Such supervision shall be regulated, and its limits shall be defined by law, as may be required in the public interest.

(c) The State shall direct economic advancement through scientific planning and technical co-operation with specialised international organisations, in a manner that will realise such prosperity in the country as will ensure honourable life for its citizens.

Article 7. Social Principles. (a) The basis of society is the family, based on religion, morality and patriotism. The law shall prescribe the means for the protection of the family against such elements as may weaken its ties, and for supporting its structure, and strengthening its bonds and fostering motherhood and child care within the family.

(b) The State shall endeavour to instill proper Islamic religious principles in society, and to purify it from all manifestations of moral disintergration.

(c) The State shall provide care and guidance for the rising generations, and shall protect them from immorality and corruption, exploitation and the evils of physical and spiritual neglect.

(d) The State shall endeavour to provide equal opportunities for all citizens, and to make it possible for them to exercise the right to work under laws that will ensure social justice.

(e) The State shall do everything in its power to protect its citizens against the causes of ignorance and poverty.

(f) The State shall provide means for the care of the health of its citizens.

(g) The State shall adopt a social security plan that will ensure assistance to citizens in case of old age, sickness, disasters and other causes of disability.

Article 8. (a) Education is a basic factor in the progress and well-being of society, and is the right of every citizen. The State shall endeavour to realize the implementation of compulsory general education, free of charge at all levels.

(b) Education is the means to culture. It shall be guaranteed and fostered by the State.

(c) The goal of education is the creation of citizens who are strong in body, mind and character, believing in God, possessing good morals, proud of their Arab-Islamic heritage, enlightened with knowledge, aware of their responsibilities and mindful of their rights.

(d) The State shall foster, preserve and assist in the spreading of the cultural heritage of the nation, and shall promote science, arts, literature and scientific research.

Part Three
Public Rights and Duties

Article 9. All persons shall enjoy equal public rights and shall be subject to equal public duties without distinction on grounds of race, sex or religion.

Article 10. (a) The provisions of the laws shall only apply to acts or events which take place on or after the date on which such laws come into effect, and they shall not affect any acts or events which take place prior to that date. However, subject to the provisions of the next following paragraph, a law may contain a provision to the contrary.

(b) No act may be considered a criminal offence, and no criminal penalty may be imposed except under a law that has been previously enacted.

Article 11. A person who is accused of a criminal offence shall be considered innocent until he is proven guilty. He shall have the right to be fairly tried before a court, and to defend himself either personally or through an attorney.

Article 12. The sanctity of homes shall be guaranteed and entry thereto without the permission of the persons residing therein shall be prohibited except in the cases determined by law, and in the manner prescribed therein.

Article 13. The freedom of publication and the press shall be guaranteed in accordance with the law.

Article 14. The holding of public office is a national service to be rendered by the office holder. The goal of a civil servant in the discharge of the duties of his office shall be the promotion of the public interest exclusively.

Article 15. Maintenance of public order and respect of public morals is the duty of every person living in the State.

Article 16. Individual and collective ownership of property shall be respected, and this right of ownership may not be taken away except in the public interest and in accordance with the law.

R

RACE: UNESCO STATEMENT ON SCIENTIFIC FACTS. Four statements on the concept of race were prepared by groups of experts on the subject, brought together by the UNITED NATIONS EDUCATIONAL, SCIENTIFIC AND CULTURAL ORGANIZATION in 1950, 1951, 1964, and 1967, as part of its program to make known the scientific facts about race and to combat racial prejudice. The findings of the four statements were taken into account in the preparation of the UNESCO DECLARATION ON RACE AND RACIAL PREJUDICE, adopted by the UNESCO General Conference in 1978.

The texts of the four statements are reproduced below. The names and qualifications of the experts responsible for the preparation of each of the statements appear at the end of each. Statement II, entitled "Statement on the Nature of Race and Race Differences," is preceded by an explanation of the reasons for convening the second meeting of experts.

I. Statement on Race, Prepared at Paris, July 1950.

1. Scientists have reached general agreement in recognizing that mankind is one: that all men belong to the same species, *homo sapiens*. It is further generally agreed among scientists that all men are probably derived from the same common stock; and that such differences as exist between different groups of mankind are due to the operation of evolutionary factors of differentiation such as isolation, the drift and random fixation of the material particles which control heredity (the genes), changes in the structure of these particles, hybridization, and natural selection. In these ways groups have arisen of varying stability and degree of differentiation which have been classified in different ways for different purposes.

2. From the biological standpoint, the species *homo sapiens* is made up of a number of populations, each one of which differs from the others in the frequency of one or more genes. Such genes, responsible for the hereditary differences between men, are always few when compared to the whole genetic constitution of man and to the vast number of genes common to all human beings regardless of the population to which they belong. This means that the likenesses among men are far greater than their differences.

3. A race, from the biological standpoint, may therefore be defined as one of the group of populations constituting the species *homo sapiens*. These populations are capable of interbreeding with one another but, by virtue of the isolating barriers which in the past kept them more or less separated, exhibit certain physical differences as a result of their somewhat different biological histories. These represent variations, as it were, on a common theme.

4. In short, the term "race" designates a group or population characterized by some concentrations, relative as to frequency and distribution, of hereditary particles (genes) or physical characters, which appear, fluctuate, and often disappear in the course of time by reason of geographic and/or cultural isolation. The varying manifestations of these traits in different populations are perceived in different ways by each group. What is perceived is largely preconceived, so that each group arbitrarily tends to misinterpret the variability which occurs as a fundamental difference which separates that group from all others.

5. These are the scientific facts. Unfortunately, however, when most people use the term 'race' they do not do so in the sense above defined. To most people, a race is any group of people whom they choose to describe as a race. Thus, many national, religious, geographic, linguistic or cultural groups have, in such loose usage, been called 'race', when obviously Americans are not a race, nor are Englishmen, nor Frenchmen, nor any other national group. Catholics, Protestants, Moslems, and Jews are not races, nor are groups who speak English or any other language thereby definable as a race; people who live in Iceland or England or India are not races; nor are people who are culturally Turkish or Chinese or the like thereby describable as races.

6. National, religious, geographic, linguistic and cultural groups do not necessarily coincide with racial groups: and the cultural traits of such groups have no demonstrated genetic connexion with racial traits. Because serious errors of this kind are habitually committed when the term 'race' is used in popular parlance, it would be better when speaking of human races to drop the term 'race' altogether and speak of ethnic groups.

7. Now what has the scientist to say about the groups of mankind which may be recognized at the present time? Human races can be and have been differently classified by different anthropologists, but at the present time most anthropologists agree on classifying the greater part of the present-day mankind into three major divisions as follows: (a) the Mongoloid division; (b) the Negroid division; and (c) the Caucasoid division. The biological processes which the classifier has here embalmed, as it were, are dynamic, not static. These divisions were not the same in the past as they are at present, and there is every reason to believe that they will change in the future.

8. Many sub-groups or ethnic groups within these divisions have been described. There is no general agreement upon their number, and in any event most ethnic groups

have not yet been either studied or described by the physical anthropologists.

9. Whatever classification the anthropologist makes of man, he never includes mental characteristics as part of those classifications. It is now generally recognized that intelligence tests do not in themselves enable us to differentiate safely between what is due to innate capacity and what is the result of environmental influences, training and education. Wherever it has been possible to make allowances for differences in environmental opportunities, the tests have shown essential similarity in mental characters among all human groups. In short, given similar degrees of cultural opportunity to realize their potentialities, the average achievement of the members of each ethnic group is about the same. The scientific investigations of recent years fully support the dictum of Confucius (551–478 B.C.): "Men's natures are alike; it is their habits that carry them far apart."

10. The scientific material available to us at present does not justify the conclusion that inherited genetic differences are a major factor in producing the differences between the cultures and cultural achievements of different peoples or groups. It does indicate, however, that the history of the cultural experience which each group has undergone is the major factor in explaining such differences. The one trait which above all others has been at a premium in the evolution of men's mental characters has been educability, plasticity. This is a trait which all human beings possess. It is indeed, a species character of *homo sapiens*.

11. So far as temperament is concerned, there is no definite evidence that there exist inborn differences between human groups. There is evidence that whatever group differences of the kind there might be are greatly overridden by the individual differences, and by the differences springing from environmental factors.

12. As for personality and character, these may be considered raceless. In every human group a rich variety of personality and character types will be found, and there is no reason for believing that any human group is richer than any other in these respects.

13. With respect to race mixture, the evidence points unequivocally to the fact that this has been going on from the earliest times. Indeed, one of the chief processes of race formation and race extinction or absorption is by means of hybridization between races or ethnic groups. Furthermore, no convincing evidence has been adduced that race mixture of itself produces biologically bad effects. Statements that human hybrids frequently show undesirable traits, both physically and mentally, physical disharmonies and mental degeneracies, are not supported by the facts. There is, therefore, no biological justification for prohibiting intermarriage between persons of different ethnic groups.

14. The biological fact of race and the myth of 'race' should be distinguished. For all practical social purposes 'race' is not so much a biological phenomenon as a social myth. The myth of 'race' has created an enormous amount of human and social damage. In recent years it has taken a heavy toll in human lives and caused untold suffering. It still prevents the normal development of millions of human beings and deprives civilization of the effective co-operation of productive minds. The biological differences between ethnic groups should be disregarded from the standpoint of social acceptance and social action. The unity of mankind from both the biological and social viewpoints is the main thing. To recognize this and to act accordingly is the first requirement of modern man. It is but to recognize what a great biologist wrote in 1875: 'As man advances in civilization, and small tribes are united into larger communities, the simplest reason would tell each individual that he ought to extend his social instincts and sympathies to all the members of the same nation, though personally unknown to him. This point being once reached, there is only an artificial barrier to prevent his sympathies extending to the men of all nations and races.' These are the words of Charles Darwin in *The Descent of Man* (2nd ed., 1875, p. 187–8). And, indeed, the whole of human history shows that a co-operative spirit is not only natural to men, but more deeply rooted than any self-seeking tendencies. If this were not so we should not see the growth of integration and organization of his communities which the centuries and the millenniums plainly exhibit.

15. We now have to consider the bearing of these statements on the problem of human equality. It must be asserted with the utmost emphasis that equality as an ethical principle in no way depends upon the assertion that human beings are in fact equal in endowment. Obviously individuals in all ethnic groups vary greatly among themselves in endowment. Nevertheless, the characteristics in which human groups differ from one another are often exaggerated and used as a basis for questioning the validity of equality in the ethical sense. For this purpose we have thought it worth while to set out in a formal manner what is at present scientifically established concerning individual and group differences.

(a) In matters of race, the only characteristics which anthropologists can effectively use as a basis for classifications are physical and physiological.

(b) According to present knowledge there is no proof that the groups of mankind differ in their innate mental characteristics, whether in respect of intelligence or temperament. The scientific evidence indicates that the range of mental capacities in all ethnic groups is much the same.

(c) Historical and sociological studies support the view that genetic differences are not of importance in determining the social and cultural differences between different groups of *homo sapiens*, and that the social and cultural changes in different groups have, in the main, been independent of changes in inborn constitution. Vast social changes have occurred which were not in any way connected with changes in racial type.

(d) There is no evidence that race mixture as such produces bad results from the biological point of view. The social results of race mixture whether for good or ill are to be traced to social factors.

(e) All normal human beings are capable of learning to share in a common life, to understand the nature of mutual service and reciprocity, and to respect social obligations and contracts. Such biological differences as exist between members of different ethnic groups have no relevance to problems of social and political organization, moral life and communication between human beings.

Lastly, biological studies lend support to the ethic of universal brotherhood; for man is born with drives toward co-operation, and unless these drives are satisfied, men and nations alike fall ill. Man is born a social being who can reach his fullest development only through interaction with his fellows. The denial at any point of this social bond between men and man brings with it disintegration. In this sense, every man is his brother's keeper. For every man is a piece of the continent, a part of the main, because he is involved in mankind.

Original statement drafted at Unesco House, Paris, by the following experts: Professor Ernest Beaglehole (New Zealand); Professor Juan Comas (Mexico); Professor L. A. Costa Pinto (Brazil); Professor Franklin Frazier (United States of America); Professor Morris Ginsberg (United Kingdom); Dr. Humayun Kabir (India); Professor Claude Levi-Strauss (France); Professor Ashley Montagu (United States of America) (rapporteur). Text revised by Professor Ashley Montagu, after criticism submitted by Professors Hadley Cantril, E. G. Conklin, Gunnar Dahlberg, Theodosius Dobzhansky, L. C. Dunn, Donald Hager, Julian S. Huxley, Otto Klineberg, Wilbert Moore, H. J. Muller, Gunnar Myrdal, Joseph Needham, Curt Stern.

II. Statement on the Nature of Race and Race Differences, Prepared at Paris, June 1951.

[Explanation:] Race is a question of interest to many different kinds of people, not only to the public at large, but to sociologists, anthropologists and biologists, especially those dealing with problems of genetics. At the first discussion on the problem of race, it was chiefly sociologists who gave their opinions and framed the "Statement on Race". That statement had a good effect, but it did not carry the authority of just those groups within whose special province fall the biological problems of race, namely the physical anthropologists and geneticists. Secondly, the first statement did not, in all its details, carry conviction of these groups and, because of this, it was not supported by many authorities in these two fields.

In general, the chief conclusions of the first statement were sustained, but with differences in emphasis and with some important deletions.

There was no delay or hesitation or lack of unanimity in reaching the primary conclusion that there were no scientific grounds whatever for the racialist position regarding purity of race and the hierarchy of inferior and superior races to which this leads.

We agreed that all races were mixed and that intraracial variability in most biological characters was as great as, if not greater than, interracial variability.

We agreed that races had reached their present states by the operation of evolutionary factors by which different proportions of similar hereditary elements (genes) had become characteristic of different, partially separated groups. The source of these elements seemed to all of us to be the variability which arises by random mutation, and the isolating factors bringing about racial differentiation by preventing intermingling of groups with different mutations, chiefly geographical for the main groups such as African, European and Asiatic.

Man, we recognized, is distinguished as much by his culture as by his biology, and it was clear to all of us that many of the factors leading to the formation of minor races of men have been cultural. Anything that tends to prevent free exchange of genes amongst groups is a potential race-making factor and these partial barriers may be religious, social and linguistic, as well as geographical.

We were careful to avoid dogmatic definitions of race, since, as a product of evolutionary factors, it is a dynamic rather than a static concept. We were equally careful to avoid saying that, because races were all variable and many of them graded into each other, therefore races did not exist. The physical anthropologists and the man in the street both know that races exist; the former, from the scientifically recognizable and measurable congeries of traits which he uses in classifying the varieties of man; the latter from the immediate evidence of his senses when he sees an African, a European, an Asiatic and an American Indian together.

We had no difficulty in agreeing that no evidence of differences in innate mental ability between different racial groups has been adduced, but that here too intraracial variability is at least as great as interracial variability. We agreed that psychological traits could not be used in classifying races, nor could they serve as parts of racial descriptions.

We were fortunate in having as members of our conference several scientists who had made special studies of the results of intermarriage between members of different races. This meant that our conclusion that race mixture in general did not lead to disadvantageous results was based on actual experience as well as upon study of the literature. Many of our members thought it quite likely that hydridization of different races could lead to biologically advantageous results, although there was insufficient evidence to support any conclusion.

Since race, as a word, has become coloured by its misuse in connexion with national, linguistic and religious differences, and by its deliberate abuse by racialists, we tried to find a new word to express the same meaning of a biologically differentiated group. On this we did not succeed, but agreed to reserve race as the word to be used for anthropological classification of groups showing definite combinations of physical (including physiological) traits in characteristic proportions.

We also tried hard, but again we failed, to reach some general statement about the inborn nature of man with respect to his behaviour toward his fellows. It is obvious that members of a group show co-operative or associative behaviour towards each other, while members of different groups may show aggressive behaviour towards each other and both of these attitudes may occur within the same individual. We recognized that the understanding of the psychological origin of race prejudice was an important problem which called for further study.

Nevertheless, having regard to the limitations of our present knowledge, all of us believed that the biological differences found amongst human racial groups can in no case justify the views of racial inequality which have been based on ignorance and prejudice, and that all of the differences which we know can well be disregarded for all ethical human purposes.

L. C. Dunn (rapporteur), June 1951

Text of Statement

1. Scientists are generally agreed that all men living today belong to a single species, *homo sapiens,* and are derived from a common stock, even though there is some dispute as to when and how different human groups diverged from this common stock.

The concept of race is unanimously regarded by anthropologists as a classificatory device providing a zoological frame within which the various groups of mankind may be arranged and by means of which studies of evolutionary processes can be facilitated. In its anthropological sense, the word "race" should be reserved for groups of mankind possessing well-developed and primarily heritable physical differences from other groups. Many populations can be so classified but, because of the complexity of human history, there are also many populations which cannot easily be fitted into a racial classification.

2. Some of the physical differences between human groups are due to differences in hereditary constitution and some to differences in the environments in which they have been brought up. In most cases, both influences have been at work. The science of genetics suggests that the hereditary differences among populations of a single species are the results of the action of two sets of processes. On the one hand, the genetic composition of isolated populations is constantly but gradually being altered by natural selection and by occasional changes (mutations) in the material particles (genes) which control heredity. Populations are also affected by fortuitous changes in gene frequency and by marriage customs. On the other hand, crossing is constantly breaking down the differentiations so set up. The new mixed populations, in so far as they, in turn, become isolated, are subject to the same processes, and these may lead to further changes. Existing races are merely the result, considered at a particular moment in time, of the total effect of such processes on the human species. The hereditary characters to be used in the classification of human groups, the limits of their variation within these groups, and thus the extent of the classificatory sub-divisions adopted may legitimately differ according to the scientific purpose in view.

3. National, religious, geographical, linguistic and cultural groups do not necessarily coincide with racial groups; and the cultural traits of such groups have no demonstrated connexion with racial traits. Americans are not a race, nor are Frenchmen, nor Germans; nor *ipso facto* is any other national group. Moslems and Jews are no more races than are Roman Catholics and Protestants; nor are people who live in Iceland or Britain or India, or who speak English or any other language, or who are culturally Turkish or Chinese and the like, thereby describable as races. The use of the term 'race' in speaking of such groups may be a serious error, but it is one which is habitually committed.

4. Human races can be, and have been, classified in different ways by different anthropologists. Most of them agree in classifying the greater part of existing mankind into at least three large units, which may be called major groups (in French *grand-races*, in German *Hauptrassen*). Such a classification does not depend on any single physical character, nor does for example, skin colour by itself necessarily distinguish one major group from another. Furthermore, so far as it has been possible to analyse them, the differences in physical structure which distinguish one major group from another give no support to popular notions of any general "superiority" or "inferiority" which are sometimes implied in referring to these groups.

Broadly speaking, individuals belonging to different major groups of mankind are distinguishable by virtue of their physical character, but individual members, or small groups belonging to different races within the same major group are usually not so distinguishable. Even the major groups grade into each other, and the physical traits by which they and the races within them are characterized overlap considerably. With respect to most, if not all, measurable characters, the differences among individuals belonging to the same race are greater than the differences that occur between the observed averages for two or more races within the same major group.

5. Most anthropologists do not include mental characteristics in their classification of human races. Studies within a single race have shown that both innate capacity and environmental opportunity determine the results of tests of intelligence and temperament, though their relative importance is disputed.

When intelligence tests, even non-verbal, are made on a group of non-literate people, their scores are usually lower than those of more civilized people. It has been recorded that different groups of the same race occupying similarly high levels of civilization may yield considerable differences in intelligence tests. When, however, the two groups have been brought up from childhood in similar environments, the differences are usually very slight. Moreover, there is good evidence that, given similar opportunities, the average performance (that is to say, the performance of the individual who is representative because he is surpassed by as many as he surpasses), and the variation round it, do not differ appreciably from one race to another.

Even those psychologists who claim to have found the greatest differences in intelligence between groups of different racial origin and have contended that they are hereditary, always report that some members of the group of inferior performance surpass not merely the lowest ranking member of the superior group but also the average of its members. In any case, it has never been possible to separate members of two groups on the basis of mental capacity, as they can often be separated on a basis of religion, skin colour, hair form or language. It is possible, though not proved, that some types of innate capacity for intellectual and emotional responses are commoner in one human group than in another, but it is certain that, within a single group, innate capacities vary as much as, if not more than, they do between different groups.

The study of the heredity of psychological characteristics is beset with difficulties. We know that certain mental diseases and defects are transmitted from one generation to the next, but we are less familiar with the part played by heredity in the mental life of normal individuals. The normal individual, irrespective of race, is essentially educable. It follows that his intellectual and moral life is largely conditioned by his training and by his physical and social environment.

It often happens that a national group may appear to be characterized by particular psychological attributes. The superficial view would be that this is due to race. Scientifically, however, we realize that any common psychological attribute is more likely to be due to a common historical and social background, and that such attributes may obscure the fact that, within different populations consisting of many human types, one will find approximately the same range of temperament and intelligence.

6. The scientific material available to us at present does not justify the conclusion that inherited genetic differences are a major factor in producing the differences between the cultures and cultural achievements of different peoples or groups. It does indicate, on the contrary, that a major factor in explaining such differences is the cultural experience which each group has undergone.

7. There is no evidence for the existence of so-called 'pure' races. Skeletal remains provide the basis of our limited knowledge about earlier races. In regard to race mixture, the evidence points to the fact that human hybridization has been going on for an indefinite but considerable time. Indeed, one of the processes of race formation and race extinction or absorption is by means of hybridization between races. As there is no reliable evidence that disadvantageous effects are produced thereby, no biological justification exists for prohibiting intermarriage between persons of different races.

8. We now have to consider the bearing of these statements on the problem of human equality. We wish to emphasize that equality of opportunity and equality in law in no way depend, as ethical principles, upon the assertion that human beings are in fact equal in endowment.

9. We have thought it worth while to set out in a formal manner what is at present scientifically established concerning individual and group differences:

(a) In matters of race, the only characteristics which anthropologists have so far been able to use effectively as a basis for classification are physical (anatomical and physiological).

(b) Available scientific knowledge provides no basis for believing that the groups of mankind differ in their innate capacity for intellectual and emotional development.

(c) Some biological differences between human beings within a single race may be as great as, or greater than, the same biological differences between races.

(d) Vast social changes have occurred that have not been connected in any way with changes in racial type. Historical and sociological studies thus support the view that genetic differences are of little significance in determining the social and cultural differences between different groups of men.

(e) There is no evidence that race mixture produces disadvantageous results from a biological point of view. The social results of race mixture, whether for good or ill, can generally be traced to social factors.

Text drafted at Unesco House, Paris, on 8 June 1951, by: Professor R. A. M. Borgman, Royal Tropical Institute, Amsterdam; Professor Gunnar Dahlberg, Director, State Institute for Human Genetics and Race Biology, University of Uppsala; Professor L. C. Dunn, Department of Zoology, Columbia University, New York; Professor J. B. S. Haldane, Head, Department of Biometry, University College, London; Professor M. F. Ashley Montagu, Chairman, Department of Anthropology, Rutgers University, New Brunswick, N.J.; Dr. A. E. Mourant, Director, Blood Group Reference Laboratory, Lister Institute, London; Professor Hans Nachtsheim, Director, Institut für Genetik, Freie Universität, Berlin; Dr. Eugène Schreider, Directeur adjoint du Laboratoire d'Anthropologie Physique de l'Ecole des Hautes Etudes, Paris; Professor Harry L. Shapiro, Chairman, Department of Anthropology, American Museum of Natural History, New York; Dr. J. C. Trevor, Faculty of Archaeology and Anthropology, University of Cambridge; Dr. Henri V. Vallois, Professeur au Museum d'Histoire Naturelle, Directeur du Musée de l'Homme, Paris; Professor S. Zuckerman, Head, Department of Anatomy, Medical School, University of Birmingham; Professor Th. Dobzhansky, Department of Zoology, Columbia University, New York; Dr. Julian Huxley contributed to the final wording.

III. Proposals on the Biological Aspects of Race, Prepared at Moscow, 18 August 1964.

The undersigned, assembled by Unesco in order to give their views on the biological aspects of the race question and in particular to formulate the biological part for a statement foreseen for 1966 and intended to bring up to date and to complete the declaration on the nature of race and racial differences signed in 1951, have unanimously agreed on the following:

1. All men living today belong to a single species, *homo sapiens,* and are derived from a common stock. There are differences of opinion regarding how and when different human groups diverged from this common stock.

2. Biological differences between human beings are due to differences in hereditary constitution and to the influence of the environment on this genetic potential. In most cases, those differences are due to the interaction of these two sets of factors.

3. There is great genetic diversity within all human populations. Pure races—in the sense of genetically homogeneous populations—do not exist in the human species.

4. There are obvious physical differences between populations living in different geographical areas of the world, in their average appearance. Many of these differences have a genetic component.

Most often the latter consist in differences in the frequency of the same hereditary characters.

5. Different classifications of mankind into major stocks, and of those into more restricted categories (races, which are groups of populations, or single populations) have been proposed on the basis of hereditary physical traits. Nearly all classifications recognize at least three major stocks.

Since the pattern of geographic variation of the characteristics used in racial classification is a complex one, and since this pattern does not present any major discontinuity, these classifications, whatever they are, cannot claim to classify mankind into clearcut categories; moreover, on account of the complexities of human history, it is difficult to determine the place of certain groups within these racial classifications, in particular that of certain intermediate populations.

Many anthropologists, while stressing the importance of human variation, believe that the scientific interest of these classifications is limited, and even that they carry the risk of inviting abusive generalizations.

Differences between individuals within a race or within a population are often greater than the average differences between races or populations.

Some of the variable distinctive traits which are generally chosen as criteria to characterize a race are either independently inherited or show only varying degrees of association between them within each population. Therefore, the combination of these traits in most individuals does not correspond to the typological racial characterization.

6. In man as well as in animals, the genetic composition of each population is subject to the modifying influence of diverse factors: natural selection, tending towards adaptation to the environment, fortuitous mutations which lead to modifications of the molecules of deoxyribonucleic acid which determine heredity, or random modifications in the frequency of qualitative hereditary characters, to an extent dependent on the patterns of mating and the size of populations.

Certain physical characters have a universal biological value for the survival of the human species, irrespective of the environment. The differences on which racial classifications are based do not affect these characters, and therefore, it is not possible from the biological point of view to speak in any way whatsoever of a general inferiority or superiority of this or that race.

7. Human evolution presents attributes of capital importance which are specific to the species.

The human species which is now spread over the whole world, has a past rich in migrations, in territorial expansions and contractions.

As a consequence, general adaptability to the most diverse environments is in man more pronounced than his adaptation to specific environments.

For long millenniums progress made by man, in any field, seems to have been increasingly, if not exclusively, based on culture and the transmission of cultural achievements and not on the transmission of genetic endowment. This implies a modification in the role of natural selection in man today.

On account of the mobility of human populations and of social factors, mating between members of different human groups which tend to mitigate the differentiations acquired, has played a much more important role in human history than in that of animals. The history of any human population or of any human race, is rich in instances of hybridization and those tend to become more and more numerous.

For man, the obstacles to interbreeding are geographical as well as social and cultural.

8. At all times, the hereditary characteristics of the human populations are in dynamic equilibrium as a result of this interbreeding and of the differentiation mechanisms which were mentioned before. As entities defined by sets of distinctive traits, human races are at any time in a process of emergence and dissolution.

Human races in general present a far less clearcut characterization than many animal races and they cannot be compared at all to races of domestic animals, these being the result of heightened selection for special purposes.

9. It has never been proved that interbreeding has biological disadvantages for mankind as a whole.

On the contrary, it contributes to the maintenance of biological ties between human groups and thus to the unity of the species in its diversity.

The biological consequences of a marriage depend only on the individual genetic make-up of the couple and not on their race.

Therefore, no biological justification exists for prohibiting intermarriage between persons of different races, or for advising against it on racial grounds.

10. Man since his origin has at his disposal ever more efficient cultural means of nongenetic adaptation.

11. Those cultural factors which break social and geographic barriers, enlarge the size of the breeding populations and so act upon their genetic structure by diminishing the random fluctuations (genetic drift).

12. As a rule, the major stocks extend over vast territories encompassing many diverse populations which differ in language, economy, culture, etc.

There is no national, religious, geographic, linguistic or cultural group which constitutes a race *ipso facto;* the concept of race is purely biological.

However, human beings who speak the same language and share the same culture have a tendency to intermarry, and often there is as a result a certain degree of coincidence between physical traits on the one hand, and linguistic and cultural traits on the other. But there is no known causal nexus between these and therefore it is not justifiable to attribute cultural characteristics to the influence of the genetic inheritance.

13. Most racial classifications of mankind do not include mental traits or attributes as a taxonomic criterion.

Heredity may have an influence in the variability shown by individuals within a given population in their responses to the psychological tests currently applied.

However, no difference has ever been detected convincingly in the hereditary endowments of human groups in regard to what is measured by these tests. On the other hand, ample evidence attests to the influence of physical, cultural and social environment on differences in response to these tests.

The study of this question is hampered by the very great difficulty of determining what part heredity plays in the average differences observed in so-called tests of over-all intelligence between populations of different cultures.

The genetic capacity for intellectual development, like certain major anatomical traits peculiar to the species, is one of the biological traits essential for its survival in any natural or social environment.

The peoples of the world today appear to possess equal biological potentialities for attaining any civilizational level. Differences in the achievements of different peoples must be attributed solely to their cultural history.

Certain psychological traits are at times attributed to particular peoples. Whether or not such assertions are valid, we do not find any basis for ascribing such traits to hereditary factors, until proof to the contrary is given.

Neither in the field of hereditary potentialities concerning the over all intelligence and the capacity for cultural development, nor in that of physical traits, is there any justification for the concept of "inferior" and "superior" races.

The biological data given above stand in open contradiction to the tenets of racism. Racist theories can in no way pretend to have any scientific foundation and the anthropologists should endeavour to prevent the results of their researches from being used in such a biased way that they would serve non-scientific ends.

Professor Nigel Barnicot, Department of Anthropology, University College, London; Professor Jean Benoist, Director, Department of Anthropology, University of Montreal, Montreal; Professor Tadeusz Bielicki, Institute of Anthropology, Polish Academy of Sciences, Wroclaw; Dr. A. E. Boyo, Head, Federal Malaria Research Institute, Department of Pathology and Haematology, Lagos University Medical School, Lagos; Professor V. V. Bunak, Institute of Ethnography, Moscow; Professor Carleton S. Coon, Curator, The University Museum, University of Pennsylvania, Philadelphia, Pa. (United States); Professor G. F. Debetz, Institute of Ethnography, Moscow; Mrs. Adelaide G. de Diaz Ungria, Curator, Museum of Natural Sciences, Caracas; Professor Santiago Genoves, Institute of Historical Research, Faculty of Sciences, University of Mexico, Mexico; Professor Robert Gessain, Director, Centre of Anthropological Research, Musée de l'Homme, Paris; Professor Jean Hiernaux, (Scientific Director of the meeting), Laboratory of Anthropology, Faculty of Sciences, University of Paris, Institute of Sociology, Free University of Brussels; Dr. Yaya Kane, Director, Senegal National Centre of Blood Transfusion, Dakar; Professor Ramakhrishna Mukherjee, Head, Sociological Research Unit, Indian Statistical Institute, Calcutta; Professor Bernard Rensch, Zoological Institute, Westfälische Wilhelms-Universität, Münster (Federal Republic of Germany); Professor Y. Y. Roguinski, Institute of Ethnography, Moscow; Professor Francisco M. Salzano, Institute of Natural Sciences, Pôrto Alegre, Rio Grande do Sul (Brazil); Professor Alf Sommerfelt, Rector, Oslo University, Oslo; Professor James N. Spuhler, Department of Anthropology, University of Michigan, Ann Arbor, Mich. (United States); Professor Hisashi Suzuki, Department of Anthropology, Faculty of Science, University of Tokyo, Tokyo; Professor J. A. Valsik, Department of Anthropology and Genetics, J. A. Komensky University, Bratislava (Czechoslovakia); Dr. Joseph S. Weiner, London School of Hygiene and Tropical Medicine, University of London, London; Professor V. P. Yakimov, Moscow State University, Institute of Anthropology, Moscow.

IV. Statement on Race and Racial Prejudice, Prepared at Paris, September 1967.

1. "All men are born free and equal both in dignity and in rights." This universally proclaimed democratic principle stands in jeopardy wherever political, economic, social and cultural inequalities affect human group relations. A particularly striking obstacle to the recognition of equal dignity for all is racism. Racism continues to haunt the world. As a major social phenomenon it requires the attention of all students of the sciences of man.

2. Racism stultifies the development of those who suffer from it, perverts those who apply it, divides nations within themselves, aggravates international conflict and threatens world peace.

3. Conference of experts meeting in Paris in September 1967, agreed that racist doctrines lack any scientific basis whatsoever. It reaffirmed the propositions adopted by the international meeting held in Moscow in 1964 which was called to re-examine the biological aspects of the statements on race and racial differences issued in 1950 and 1951. In particular, it draws attention to the following points:

(a) All men living today belong to the same species and descend from the same stock.

(b) The division of the human species into 'races' is partly conventional and partly arbitrary and does not imply any hierarchy whatsoever. Many anthropologists stress the importance of human variation, but believe that 'racial' divisions have limited scientific interest and may even carry the risk of inviting abusive generalization.

(c) Current biological knowledge does not permit us to impute cultural achievements to differences in genetic potential. Differences in the achievements of different peoples should be attributed solely to their cultural history. The peoples of the world today appear to possess equal biological potentialities for attaining any level of civilization. Racism grossly falsifies the knowledge of human biology.

4. The human problems arising from so-called 'race' relations are social in origin rather than biological. A basic problem is racism, namely, antisocial beliefs and acts which are based on the fallacy that discriminatory intergroup relations are justifiable on biological grounds.

5. Groups commonly evaluate their characteristics in comparison with others. Racism falsely claims that there is a scientific basis for arranging groups hierarchically in terms of psychological and cultural characteristics that are immutable and innate. In this way it seeks to make existing differences appear inviolable as a means of permanently maintaining current relations between groups.

6. Faced with the exposure of the falsity of its biological doctrines, racism finds ever new stratagems for justifying the inequality of groups. It points to the fact that groups do not intermarry, a fact which follows, in part, from the divisions created by racism. It uses this fact to argue the thesis that this absence of intermarriage derives from differences of a biological order. Whenever it fails in its attempts to prove that the source of group differences lies in the biological field, it falls back upon justifications in terms of divine purpose, cultural differences, disparity of educational standards or some other doctrine which would serve to mask its continued racist beliefs. Thus, many of the problems which racism presents in the world today do not arise merely from its open manifestations, but from the activities of those who discriminate on racial grounds but are unwilling to acknowledge it.

7. Racism has historical roots. It has not been a universal phenomenon. Many contemporary societies and cultures show little trace of it. It was not evident for long periods in world history. Many forms of racism have arisen out of the conditions of conquest, out of the justification of Negro slavery and its aftermath of racial inequality in the West, and out of the colonial relationship. Among other examples is that of anti-semitism, which has played a particular role in history, with Jews being the chosen scapegoat to take the blame for problems and crises met by many societies.

8. The anti-colonial revolution of the twentieth century has opened up new possibilities for eliminating the scourge of racism. In some formerly dependent countries, people formerly classified as inferior have for the first time obtained full political rights. Moreover, the participation of formerly dependent nations in international organizations in terms of equality has done much to undermine racism.

9. There are, however, some instances in certain societies in which groups, victims of racialistic practices, have themselves applied doctrines with racist implications in their struggle for freedom. Such an attitude is a secondary phenomenon, a reaction stemming from men's search for an identity which prior racist theory and racialistic practices denied them. None the less, the new forms of racist ideology, resulting from this prior exploitation, have no justification in biology. They are a product of a political struggle and have no scientific foundation.

10. In order to undermine racism it is not sufficient that biologists should expose its fallacies. It is also necessary that psychologists and sociologists should demonstrate its causes. The social structure is always an important factor. However, within the same social structure, there may be great individual variation in racialistic behaviour, associated with the personality of the individuals and their personal circumstances.

11. The committee of experts agreed on the following conclusions about the social causes of race prejudice:

(a) Social and economic causes of racial prejudice are particularly observed in settler societies wherein are found conditions of great disparity of power and property, in certain urban areas where there have emerged ghettoes in which individuals are deprived of equal access to employment, housing, political participation, education, and the administration of justice, and in many societies where social and economic tasks which are deemed to be contrary to the ethics or beneath the dignity of its members are assigned to a group of different origins who are derided, blamed, and punished for taking on these tasks.

(b) Individuals with certain personality troubles may be particularly inclined to adopt and manifest racial prejudices. Small groups, associations, and social movements of a certain kind sometimes preserve and transmit racial prejudices. The foundations of the prejudices lie, however, in the economic and social system of a society.

(c) Racism tends to be cumulative. Discrimination deprives a group of equal treatment and presents that group as a problem. The group then tends to be blamed for its own condition, leading to further elaboration of racist theory.

12. The major techniques for coping with racism involve changing those social situations which give rise to prejudice, preventing the prejudiced from acting in accordance

with their beliefs, and combating the false beliefs themselves.

13. It is recognized that the basically important changes in the social structure that may lead to the elimination of racial prejudice may require decisions of a political nature. It is also recognized, however, that certain agencies of enlightenment, such as education and other means of social and economic advancement, mass media, and law can be immediately and effectively mobilized for the elimination of racial prejudice.

14. The school and other instruments for social and economic progress can be one of the most effective agents for the achievement of broadened understanding and the fulfilment of the potentialities of man. They can equally much be used for the perpetuation of discrimination and inequality. It is therefore essential that the resources for education and for social and economic action of all nations be employed in two ways:

(a) The schools should ensure that their curricula contain scientific understandings about race and human unity, and that invidious distinctions about peoples are not made in texts and classrooms.

(b) (i) Because the skills to be gained in formal and vocational education become increasingly important with the processes of technological development, the resources of the schools and other resources should be fully available to all parts of the population with neither restriction nor discrimination;

(ii) Furthermore, in cases where, for historical reasons, certain groups have a lower average education and economic standing, it is the responsibility of the society to take corrective measures. These measures should ensure, so far as possible, that the limitations of poor environments are not passed on to the children.

In view of the importance of teachers in any educational programme, special attention should be given to their training. Teachers should be made conscious of the degree to which they reflect the prejudices which may be current in their society. They should be encouraged to avoid these prejudices.

15. Governmental units and other organizations concerned should give special attention to improving the housing situations and work opportunities available to victims of racism. This will not only counteract the effects of racism, but in itself can be a positive way of modifying racist attitudes and behaviour.

16. The media of mass communication are increasingly important in promoting knowledge and understanding, but their exact potentiality is not fully known. Continuing research into the social utilization of the media is needed in order to assess their influence in relation to formation of attitudes and behavioural patterns in the field of race prejudice and race discrimination. Because the mass media reach vast numbers of people at different educational and social levels, their role in encouraging or combating race prejudice can be crucial. Those who work in these media should maintain a positive approach to the promotion of understanding between groups and populations. Representation of peoples in stereotypes and holding them up to ridicule should be avoided. Attachment to news reports of racial designations which are not germane to the accounts should also be avoided.

17. Law is among the most important means of ensuring equality between individuals and one of the most effective means of fighting racism.

The Universal Declaration of Human Rights of 10 December 1948 and the related international agreements and conventions which have taken effect subsequently can contribute effectively, on both the national and international level, to the fight against any injustice of racist origin.

National legislation is a means of effectively outlawing racist propaganda and acts based upon racial discrimination. Moreover, the policy expressed in such legislation must bind not only the courts and judges charged with its enforcement, but also all agencies of government of whatever level or whatever character.

It is not claimed that legislation can immediately eliminate prejudice. Nevertheless, by being a means of protecting the victims of acts based upon prejudice, and by setting a moral example backed by the dignity of the courts, it can, in the long run, even change attitudes.

18. Ethnic groups which represent the object of some form of discrimination are sometimes accepted and tolerated by dominating groups at the cost of their having to abandon completely their cultural identity. It should be stressed that the effort of these ethnic groups to preserve their cultural values should be encouraged. They will thus be better able to contribute to the enrichment of the total culture of humanity.

19. Racial prejudice and discrimination in the world today arise from historical and social phenomena and falsely claim the sanction of science. It is, therefore, the responsibility of all biological and social scientists, philosophers, and others working in related disciplines, to ensure that the results of their research are not misused by those who wish to propagate racial prejudice and encourage discrimination.

This statement was prepared by a committee of experts on race and racial prejudice which met at Unesco House, Paris, from 18 to 26 September 1967. The following experts took part in the committee's work: Professor Muddathir Abdel Rahim, University of Khartoum (Sudan); Professor Georges Balandier, Université de Paris (France); Professor Celio de Oliveira Borja, University of Guanabara (Brazil); Professor Lloyd Braithwaite, University of the West Indies (Jamaica); Professor Leonard Broom, University of Texas (United States); Professor G. F. Debetz, Institute of Ethnography, Moscow (U.S.S.R.); Professor J. Djordjevic, University of Belgrade (Yugoslavia); Dean Clarence Clyde Ferguson, Howard University (United States); Dr. Dharam P. Ghai, University College (Kenya); Professor Louis Guttman, Hebrew University (Israel); Professor Jean Hiernaux, Université Libre de Bruxelles (Belgium); Professor A. Kloskowska, University of Lodz (Poland); Judge Kéba M'Baye, President of the Supreme Court (Senegal); Professor John Rex, University of Durham (United Kingdom); Professor Mariano R. Solveira, University of Havana (Cuba); Professor Hisashi Suzuki, University of Tokyo (Japan); Dr. Romila Thapar, University of Delhi (India); Professor C. H. Waddington, University of Edinburgh (United Kingdom).

RACE AND RACIAL PREJUDICE: IMPACT OF THE UNESCO DECLARATION. Action taken by the UNITED NATIONS EDUCATIONAL, SCIENTIFIC AND CULTURAL ORGANIZATION in 1987 and 1988 to implement the UNESCO DECLARATION ON RACE AND RACIAL PREJUDICE is described in a memorandum submitted to the 1988 session of the Sub-Commission on Prevention of Discrimination and Protection of Minorities by the Director-General of

UNESCO (UN Doc. E/CN.4/Sub.2/1988/4), as follows:

The first report on the UNESCO Declaration on Race and Racial Prejudice, which was adopted by the UNESCO General Conference in 1978, was prepared for the UNESCO General Conference in October/November 1983. A second report was submitted to the General Conference in October/November 1987. The report (UNESCO Doc. 24 C/14, para. 93), concludes that racial prejudice and discrimination are still widely prevalent in the world today and sometimes are increasing: In spite of the fact that constitutional and legal guarantees of equality now exist in most countries, with the exception of *apartheid* South Africa, the situation with regard to racial prejudice and discrimination remains a serious one. Indeed in some areas where a great deal of progress has, over the past decades, been achieved, the present economic crisis and in some cases the crisis in values has led to the slowing down of measures aimed at equality or to the recurrence of overt racism.

During 1989 UNESCO will prepare an evaluation of the impact of the Declaration on Race and Racial Prejudice since its adoption, and of the procedures for submission of reports.

RACIAL DISCRIMINATION. A practice characterized as "the very negation of the principle of EQUALITY, and therefore an affront to human dignity," in the *Study of Racial Discrimination* prepared in 1976 (United Nations publication, Sales No. E.76.XIV.2) by Mr. Hernan Santa Cruz (Chile), special rapporteur of the SUB-COMMISSION ON PREVENTION OF DISCRIMINATION AND PROTECTION OF MINORITIES.

As Mr. Santa Cruz explains (para. 68–69):

The principle of equality does not, as one might assume, exclude all possible differentiations between individuals. In particular, it is not concerned with differentiations based upon such individual qualities as mental or physical capacity, talent or innate ability; nor is it concerned with differentiations based upon the individual's capacities, merits, or behaviour in so far as these are within his control. It is rather concerned with differentiations based on factors over which he has no control, such as his race, his colour, his descent, and his national or ethnic origin.

The principle of equality, in short, recognizes that those elements of body and spirit in which all human beings are essentially alike far outweigh and transcend those purely accidental differentiations over which the individual has no control. The principle flows from a basic ethical concept, that of human dignity, which implies, in its simplest terms, that every human being is an end in himself, not a mere means to an end.

It is for these reasons that Mr. Santa Cruz considers racial discrimination "the very negation of the principle of equality" and adds that "it is a negation, also, of the social nature of man, who can reach his fullest development only through interaction with his fellows."

The special rapporteur selects, as the most care-fully prepared and widely accepted definition of the term "racial discrimination," the one which appears in article 1 of the INTERNATIONAL CONVENTION ON THE ELIMINATION OF ALL FORMS OF RACIAL DISCRIMINATION and which reads as follows:

In this Convention, the term "racial discrimination" shall mean any distinction, exclusion, restriction of preference based on race, colour, descent, or national or ethnic origin which has the purpose or effect of nullifying or impairing the recognition, enjoyment or exercise, on an equal footing, of human rights and fundamental freedoms in the political, economic, social, cultural or any other field of public life. . . .

Special measures taken for the sole purpose of securing adequate advancement of certain racial or ethnic groups or individuals requiring such protection as may be necessary in order to ensure to such groups or individuals equal enjoyment or exercise of human rights and fundamental freedoms shall not be deemed racial discrimination, provided, however, that such measures do not, as a consequence, lead to the maintenance of separate rights for different racial groups and that they shall not be continued after the objectives for which they were taken have been achieved.

This definition, he explains, while intended to serve only for the purpose of the convention, serves to clarify the meaning of "racial discrimination" in a number of ways:

It specifies the grounds upon which such discrimination may be based: race, colour, descent, and national or ethnic origin. It indicates the kind of acts which lead to discrimination; distinctions, exclusions, restrictions and preferences. It stipulates that discriminatory acts include not only those having the effect of discriminating, but also those having this intent or purpose. It brands as discriminatory those acts which wholly nullify, as well as those which only partially impair, the recognition, enjoyment or exercise of human rights and fundamental freedoms. It spells out not only what discrimination is, but also what it is not, and provides for the measures necessary to secure the advancement of backward racial or ethnic groups or individuals in order to ensure to them the equal enjoyment or exercise of human rights and fundamental freedoms.

One strong cause of racial prejudice and discrimination, according to the special rapporteur, is racism, or "the superiority complex," consisting of a set of popular beliefs which includes the following elements: (1) that the differences between groups are due to hereditary biology and nothing can change them; (2) that habits, attitudes, beliefs, behavior, and all the things we learn are determined for us before we are born; (3) that all differences between the non-dominant group and the dominant group are thought to be examples of inferiority on the part of members of the non-dominant group; and (4) that, if there should be biological crossing of the groups, the children will be more degenerate than either of the parent groups. These racist beliefs, he adds, have been so widespread that, although authoritatively and consistently proved erroneous, they still continue to be an important cause of prejudice.

SEE ALSO Committee on the Elimination of Racial Discrimination; Decades to Combat Racism and Racial Discrimination; Declaration of the Second World Conference to Combat Racism and Racial Discrimination; Declaration on the Elimination of all Forms of Racial Discrimination; Racism and Racial Discrimination: Second Decade Action Program.

RACIAL DISCRIMINATION: NATIONAL AND LOCAL RECOURSES.

At its 1980 session, the UN SUB-COMMISSION ON PREVENTION OF DISCRIMINATION AND PROTECTION OF MINORITIES requested the Secretary-General (resolution 4 C [XXXIII]) to prepare a report setting out measures which the sub-commission might recommend to governments with a view to enhancing and strengthening national and local recourse procedures available to victims of racial discrimination.

In the report, the Secretary-General enumerated (UN Doc. E/CN.4/Sub.2/1982/9) the forms of national and local recourse procedures available, evaluated their impact and effectiveness, and indicated which had been found to be most effective. Excerpts from the report (para. 3–39) are reproduced below.

Forms of Recourse Procedures Available

Although the principle of equality of all in the enjoyment of rights and freedoms is now generally accepted by the international community, the proclaimed human rights and fundamental freedoms, in order to be meaningful, must be sanctioned by effective recourse procedures easily available to victims of racial discrimination.

The establishment of such procedures implies the determination and precise definition of the acts which constitute punishable offences. It is essential to examine carefully the various and subtle forms that racial discrimination can take, in order to determine the most opportune forms of procedure to deal with it.

Bearing in mind the multifaceted aspects of the problem of racial discrimination, a wide range of measures have been envisaged by Governments with a view to providing relevant safeguards against the various forms of discrimination.

A. Legislative Procedures. The constitutional and other legislative provisions of many countries include recognition of the principle of non-discrimination and legal means to combat all forms of racial discrimination. These provisions bear upon various fields such as labour, family, economic, social and cultural life. Many countries have adopted legislation which declares illegal racist propaganda and racist organizations. Moreover, international instruments adopted in the field of racial discrimination have usually had an important impact on national legislations, either by having an immediate effect at the national level or by leading to the adoption of special laws in order to comply with the relevant provisions of such instruments.

B. Judicial Procedures. Protection against discrimination can be provided through penal codes and procedures. Victims of racial discrimination can also find a remedy in procedures before the civil courts. In some cases, public prosecutors can play an important role in acting against discrimination by making an investigation *ex officio* if reasonable grounds exist for believing that an offence has been committed, even if no complaint has been lodged by a victim of racial discrimination. The public prosecutor is also, as a rule, under the obligation to institute criminal proceedings *ex officio* if he feels that an offence has been committed. Should the public prosecutor decide not to institute such proceedings, the victims are, according to the law, entitled to institute criminal proceedings on their own.

C. Administrative Procedures. Special procedures have been introduced by some countries for implementation by the administrative authorities with a view to ensuring equality or treatment and access to public places and services.

Among such procedures, mention may be made of the role of institutions such as the ombudsman or similar officials.

The ombudsman is a public official whose function is to represent the individual in cases where the rights of the individual under the law may have been infringed upon or abused by the State or another public authority.

In some countries, the ombudsman has authority to check and investigate inappropriate performance by public officials, including discriminatory acts. He also devotes special attention to the problems of immigrants and helps them to become familiar with the legal system and legal remedies available to them.

Similar institutions exist in other countries: for instance, in some cases the "Chancellor of Justice" of the Government performs functions concerning the investigation of claims of racial discrimination similar to those of an ombudsman, while in other cases the Procurator is entrusted with safeguarding legality. In some developing countries, similar institutions have been established, with some modifications to take account of their respective needs and experience. The Office Lokpal (Protector of the Law) of India, set up to inquire into allegations of misconduct against public men, can be cited as an example of this type of institution.

D. Other Forms of Procedure. Among various other forms of recourse procedure reference may be made to the roles played by the following institutions:

(i) National and local commissions on human rights, it has been said, have an important role in the fight against discriminatory action. They can bring about rapid action, particularly in urgent cases such as those relating to housing, employment and similar situations. They can also play a conciliatory role or make necessary arrangements for legal aid;

(ii) Trade unions can initiate action to curtail discriminatory practices, such as discriminatory contracts or conditions of work. Union management grievance procedures sometimes deal with complaints of racial discrimination;

(iii) In addition to legalistic procedures, some countries have encouraged conciliation and informal procedures for the settlement of cases involving violations of human rights; these procedures have usually proved to be useful;

(iv) In some countries political parties can serve as a means of focusing attention on violations of human rights, and provide an effective means of attacking racial practices;

(v) In other countries, the church has played a valuable role as a powerful means of providing assistance to victims of racial discrimination;

(vi) Finally, an important role can be played in supplementing national recourse procedures, by means provided under the pertinent international legal instruments dealing with racial discrimination. In this regard, great importance is attached to the recognition of the individual right to petition as an effective means of recourse.

Impact and Effectiveness of Existing Recourse Procedures

Reference has been made above to various forms of recourse procedures available to victims of racial discrimination. However, the mere establishment of such procedures cannot suffice to ensure their effectiveness. A number of criteria have to be taken into account in order to determine the real impact of the recourse procedures in practice.

A. Accessibility of Recourse Procedures. The first problem which arises in connection with existing recourse procedures is to ensure that they are universally available to all persons and groups, without any distinction between citizens and non-citizens.

However, access to recourse procedures, even when universally available, might prove quite difficult in practice to those portions of the population which, owing to ignorance or insufficient information on existing rights and ways to exercise them usually are the most vulnerable to acts of racial discrimination. Psychological obstacles also sometimes prevent victims of racial discrimination from using recourse procedures. In order to ensure better access to these procedures, in some countries specific information about available recourse procedures is channelled through regional bureaux for legal assistance established by trade unions, or through "law shops", which offer free legal advice and facilitate access to the courts for disadvantaged groups through reducing psychological and financial barriers.

B. Flexible Rules for Initiation of Complaints. In many cases the complexity of the rules relating to the initiation of complaints constitutes an obstacle. In a number of countries it has been noted that very few complaints dealing with racial discrimination are submitted to the courts or other competent institutions. This often stems from lack of information and knowledge about how to initiate a complaint, or from frustration with the complexity of rules relating to the initiation of complaints.

C. Flexible Evidentiary Criteria and Standards of Proof. Evidence to prove discrimination can be very difficult to obtain, as some of the discriminatory acts can take a subtle form and be unamenable to physical proof.

Questions of possible discrimination cannot be investigated like ordinary legal problems for which the question is basically one of deciding whether an illegal act has been committed or not. Thus, investigating bodies have to be flexible regarding the sort of evidence they can regard as admissible evidence, and both direct and/or indirect or circumstantial evidence have to be taken into account.

The same principle applies to standard of proof, for which flexibility is also required. In cases where the objective of the investigation is to obtain redress for an individual the standard of proof should be much less than that required by many investigating bodies. On the other hand,

stricter standards of proof should be observed if the investigation extends to the trial of someone on criminal charges.

D. Effectiveness and Speed of Action. There is a need for prompt and speedy resolution of the cases brought before the competent organs or bodies in order to avoid any kind of denial of justice. In some countries, internal legislation provide for time limits, not only for the action of the administration in response to a complaint but also in matters of control of the constitutionality of laws.

Flexible recourse procedures can play an important role in eliminating undue delay and problems of backlog.

E. Ability to Grant Legal and Other Assistance. The granting of legal aid to victims of racial discrimination to bring actions before the courts can contribute in improving the effectiveness of recourse procedures.

In many countries free legal aid is fully or partially available to persons requiring it. In some cases, the State has complete carriage of a case from beginning to end. Other forms of assistance include the provision, at State expense, of the services of an interpreter. In some countries private attorneys are mandated by the State, at its expense, to provide legal assistance to those requiring it. The wide dissemination of legal literature and information constitutes another form of legal assistance improving the effectiveness of recourse procedures.

Recommended Procedures and Activities

The importance attached, within the United Nations system, to the struggle against racism and racial discrimination, has led, among other things to the organization under the Programme of the Decade for the Action to Combat Racism and Racial Discrimination, of a number of seminars. Some of these seminars dealt more specifically with recourse procedures available to victims of racial discrimination.

Among the conclusions of these various seminars, many can be retained as concrete and extremely useful suggestions regarding measures that Governments might wish to adopt with a view to enhance and strengthen recourse procedures available to victims of racial discrimination at national and local levels.

Establishment of Recourse Procedures

Effective recourse procedures, it has been argued, should be instituted as a means of guaranteeing victims of racial discrimination the application of legal provisions relating to the substance of the law. Therefore, common standards should be established in combating racial discrimination and securing the principle of equality. Thus, all States should ratify international instruments adopted under the auspices of the United Nations and dealing with racial discrimination, such as the International Convention on the Elimination of All Forms of Racial Discrimination, the International Covenant on Civil and Political Rights, and the International Covenant on Economic, Social and Cultural Rights.

Variety of Approaches

Different approaches, it has been emphasized, should be envisaged in the form and content of recourse procedures, bearing in mind the various root causes and manifestations of racial discrimination, and the differing realities in each country. The forms and efficiency of recourse procedures depend, among other things, on the type of violation dealt with and the socio-economic conditions prevailing in each given society. Particular attention should be given to the specific problems and realities of each situation. Therefore, in order to identify the most effective means of dealing with problems raised by racial discrimination, efforts should be made to detect and study the various causes and manifestations of racial discrimination.

Conditions of Effectiveness of Recourse Procedures

A number of conditions, it has been stressed, should be filled by recourse procedures in order to render them effective. These procedures should be adequate, efficient and easy to initiate, and cover areas of civil as well as general law and administrative disputes. To this end, it has been said that all countries should ensure that the conditions of access to recourse procedures are as broad as possible, and that these procedures are made available to all persons without any distinction between citizens and non-citizens or exclusion of any specific group. Furthermore, the rules for initiation of complaints should be simple and flexible. Complaints of racial discrimination should be dealt with expeditiously. It has been further argued that different standards of proofs should be promoted, such as the balance of probability or preponderance of the evidence. Another proposal strongly recommended is that victims of racial discrimination should be afforded appropriate financial and legal assistance necessary for the investigation and execution of their complaints.

Compensation of Victims

With regard to the question of compensation of victims it has been recommended that, in addition to repressive action, States should ensure that measures are taken with a view to providing fair and tangible compensation to victims of acts of racial discrimination, as provided for in article 6 of the International Convention on the Elimination of All Forms of Racial Discrimination. Compensation should be provided for material and moral damages, and cover general as well as special damages. Even in cases where the awarding of moral damages is already provided for in the legislation, specific national legislation on the matter of compensation of victims of acts of racial discrimination would reduce ambiguities.

Appeal Procedures

With respect to appeal procedures, it has been said that the streamlining of appeals procedures would help strengthen the recourse procedures available to victims of racial discrimination, who frequently depend on fair and effective appeals system in their pursuit of redress.

Information Activities

In the field of information, it has been suggested that all countries should by all appropriate means publicize effective recourse procedures. Without an appropriate dissemination of information on their availability, such procedures would be meaningless. Among the various measures which could be taken as regards information activities in this field, the following can be cited:

(i) Publishing popular literature about efforts undertaken to combat racial discrimination and for the realization of civil, political, economic, social and cultural rights;

(ii) Dissemination of information through offices of ombudsmen and similar institutions;

(iii) Giving publicity to the operation of the recourse procedures available;

(iv) Dissemination of information for victims or potential victims of racial discrimination;

(v) Radio and television programmes designed to combat racism;

(vi) Articles and publications on recourse procedures available against racial discrimination;

(vii) Dissemination of legal information through special activities to be carried out by central and local administrative bodies and lawyers associations.

Educational Measures

Educational measures have been mentioned as an important factor in strengthening the recourse procedures. Governments should introduce, or where it already exists, strengthen and promote teaching relating to human rights in general and to problems connected with racial discrimination in particular. Among particular educational measures which could be used, are suitable training of teachers; grants to schools towards the cost of employing extra teachers where needed; extra staff employed at schools with concentration of children of foreign workers; subsidies granted for bicultural education. Pupils from the primary level upwards should be made aware of racial problems and the dangers of racism. Students should be in a position to know that domestic as well as international remedies are available to them if their rights are infringed. Another educational measure which could help strengthen recourse procedures would be the dissemination of human rights documents, including those concerned with racial discrimination, among minority groups, in their respective languages.

Institutions of Independent Mediators

It has been emphasized that States should be encouraged to adopt the system of ombudsman or independent mediators. The role of such mediators could differ from country to country, depending on differences of economic and social systems and the varying problems with which countries are faced at different stages of development. The ombudsman system assumes an independent supervisory role over courts as well as administrative bodies in order to leave no gap in protective mechanisms for individual rights. This system represents an additional guarantee for the protection of human rights. The independent mediator should be entitled to make inspections of governmental and administrative bodies in order to suggest improvements in their administrative procedures. This jurisdiction should be as wide as possible, and should operate at all levels of government.

National and Local Human Rights Institutions

As regards institutions in the field of human rights, it has been recommended that human rights committees and similar national and local institutions for the protection and promotion of human rights be established and enabled to function adequately. Such institutions should be empowered to investigate infringements of human rights and act in a conciliatory capacity. To this end, they should be protected from government persecution or repression.

Among the various tasks national and local institutions for human rights should be entitled to perform in connection with the protection of victims of racial discrimination, reference may be made to the following:

(i) National and local institutions should assist in the provision of free legal aid to the needy;

(ii) They should be authorized within the framework

of their constitution and competence, to investigate complaints alleging that citizens are being deprived of their basic rights;

(iii) They should be authorized, within the framework of their constitution and competence, to apply concrete remedies to individual cases of human rights violations;

(iv) They should, while discharging their functions of fact finding, conciliation or redress, be empowered, in the conduct of their inquiry, with due process of law, into any matter affecting human rights at the national level, to summon witnesses and have access to relevant evidence.

Protection of Minority Groups

It has also been agreed that States should adopt specific measures to enhance and strengthen recourse procedures available to minority groups particularly vulnerable to acts of racial discrimination, such as indigenous populations or migrant workers.

With regard to indigenous populations, the distinctiveness of the problems of discrimination in each region require innovative approaches in devising recourse procedures. Alongside national and local human rights bodies, such as human rights commissions or race relations commissions, every Government whose population includes indigenous peoples might establish a national ombudsman on the human rights of indigenous peoples, whose task would be to promote and protect the human rights of indigenous peoples. Members of indigenous peoples who are victims of racial discrimination should be afforded appropriate financial and other assistance necessary for the investigation of their complaints.

The ombudsman institution could also play a constructive role in dealing with problems of racial discrimination against migrant workers, who generally are not familiar with the legal system and legal remedies available to them. States should also eliminate, through legislative, judicial and administrative measures, discriminatory practices against migrant workers.

SEE ALSO Equality: National Constitutional and Legislative Provisions on Non-Discrimination; Ministerio Público, *Ombudsman.*

RACIAL PREJUDICE: PREVENTION. The COMMITTEE ON THE ELIMINATION OF RACIAL DISCRIMINATION has from time to time considered ways and means of preventing, or combatting, attitudes and prejudices based on race, color, or national or ethnic origin, which often give rise to overt acts of racial discrimination. In 1977, the committee decided to draw to the attention of States parties to the INTERNATIONAL CONVENTION ON THE ELIMINATION OF ALL FORMS OF RACIAL DISCRIMINATION the importance of the provisions of article 7 thereof and to invite them to furnish detailed information on the measures which they had adopted in order to give effect to those provisions. It also considered the need to provide the states parties with some guidance on the manner in which the provisions could most effectively be applied and on the

role that UNESCO might be willing to play in assisting the committee and the States parties.

In the course of formulating an appropriate recommendation, the committee heard the representative of UNESCO, who stated that the development of the teaching of human rights could constitute an excellent means of implementing article 7. He analyzed a number of UNESCO activities in human rights teaching, e.g., the preparation of instructional material, teacher training, and the teaching of human rights in the framework of disciplines other than law; and added that UNESCO was organizing an international conference on the teaching of human rights at the university level which would take place in Vienna in September 1978. He also drew the attention of the committee to UNESCO's preparation of a UNESCO DECLARATION ON RACE AND RACIAL PREJUDICE, which aimed at illuminating the biological, sociological, cultural, economic, and political aspects, as well as the juridical, of the race question, thereby going well beyond the legal effects of condemning racism and racial discrimination. The declaration would, therefore, constitute an extension and a deepening of the convention and might, because of its multidisciplinary approach, also become a useful element in the committee's interpretation of the convention and a synthetic document for the implementation of article 7.

On 13 April 1977, the committee adopted a recommendation on the subject and authorized its chairman to transmit it to UNESCO with a request for that body's cooperation. The recommendation was also transmitted by the UN Secretary-General to States parties to the convention for any comments they might wish to make. The recommendations was as follows (UN Doc. A/32/18, Chap. VIII, decision 3 [XV], General Recommendation V):

The Committee on the Elimination of Racial Discrimination,

Bearing in mind the provisions of articles 7 and 9 of the International Convention on the Elimination of All Forms of Racial Discrimination,

Convinced that combating prejudices which lead to racial discrimination, promoting understanding, tolerance and friendship among racial and ethnic groups, and propagating the principles and purposes of the Charter of the United Nations and of the human rights declarations and other relevant instruments adopted by the General Assembly of the United Nations, are important and effective means of eliminating racial discrimination,

Considering that the obligations under article 7 of the Convention, which are binding on all States parties, must be fulfilled by them, including States which declare that racial discrimination is not practised on the territories under their jurisdiction, and that therefore all States parties are required to include information on their implementation of the provisions of that article in the reports they submit in accordance with article 9, paragraph 1, of the Convention,

Noting with regret that few States parties have included, in the reports they have submitted in accordance with article 9 of the Convention, information on the measures which they have adopted and which give effect to the provisions of article 7 of the Convention, and that that information has often been general and perfunctory,

Recalling that, in accordance with article 9, paragraph 1, of the Convention, the Committee may request further information from the States parties,

1. Requests every State party which has not already done so to include—in the next report it will submit in accordance with article 9 of the Convention, or in a special report before its next periodic report becomes due—adequate information on the measures which it has adopted and which give effect to the provisions of article 7 of the Convention;

2. Invites the attention of States parties to the fact that, in accordance with article 7 of the Convention, the information to which the preceding paragraph refers should include information on the "immediate and effective measures" which they have adopted, "in the fields of teaching, education, culture and information", with a view to:

(a) "Combating prejudices which lead to racial discrimination";

(b) "Promoting understanding, tolerance and friendship among nations and racial or ethnical groups";

(c) "Propagating the purposes and principles of the Charter of the United Nations, the Universal Declaration of Human Rights, the United Nations Declaration on the Elimination of All Forms of Racial Discrimination" as well as the International Convention on the Elimination of All Forms of Racial Discrimination.

The Committee on the Elimination of Racial Discrimination has since given special attention to the implementation of article 7 by the national bodies concerned; has included in each annual report to the General Assembly a section indicating to what extent the States parties appear to be conforming to the rules laid out in that article; and has highlighted each positive achievement reported to it. However, in 1982, the committee found it necessary to prepare additional guidelines for the implementation of article 7 (UN Doc. A/37/18, chap. IX, decision 2 [XXV]), as follows:

1. The reports should provide as much information as possible on each of the main subjects mentioned in article 7 under the following separate headings: (1) Education and teaching, (2) Culture, (3) Information.

2. Within these broad parameters, the information provided should reflect the measures taken by the States parties;

(a) To combat prejudices which lead to racial discrimination,

(b) To promote understanding, tolerance and friendship among nations and racial and ethnic groups.

I. Education and Teaching

3. This part should describe legislative and administrative measures, including some general information on the educational system, taken in the field of education and teaching to combat racial prejudices which lead to racial discrimination.

4. It should indicate whether any steps have been taken to include in school curricula and in the training of teachers and other professionals, programmes and subjects to help promote human rights issues which would lead to better understanding, tolerance and friendship among nations and racial or ethnic groups.

5. It should also provide information on whether the purposes and principles of the instruments mentioned in the Committee's general guidelines (CERD/C/70, art. 7, letter C) are included in education and teaching.

II. Culture

6. Information should be provided in this part of the report on the role of institutions or associations working to develop national culture and traditions, to combat racial prejudices and to promote intra-national and intra-cultural understanding, tolerance and friendship among nations and racial or ethnic groups.

7. Information should also be included on the work of solidarity committees or United Nations Associations to combat racism and racial discrimination and the observance by States parties of Human Rights Days or campaigns against racism and *apartheid*.

III. Information

8. This part should provide information:

(a) On the role of State media in the dissemination of information to combat racial prejudices which lead to racial discrimination and to inculcate better understanding of the purposes and principles of the above-mentioned instruments;

(b) On the role of the mass information media, i.e. the press, radio and television, in the publicizing of human rights and disseminating information on the purposes and principles of the above-mentioned human rights instruments.

In 1983, the *Study on the Implementation of Article 7 of the International Convention on the Elimination of all Forms of Racial Discrimination* (UN Doc. A/CONF. 119/11) was prepared by a special rapporteur, Mr. Georges Tenekides, a former member of the committee. The committee endorsed the study as its contribution to the Second World Conference to Combat Racism and Racial Discrimination.

The study indicated clearly that a number of States parties to the convention had not adequately fulfilled their obligations under article 7. The most frequently advanced explanation was the absence of racial discrimination in territories under their control. Another was that the existence of anti-discriminatory provisions in the national constitution made it unnecessary to adopt additional legislative, administrative, or other measures. Still another was that certain matters, particularly in the field of information, were outside the authority of the national authorities. The committee did not consider such explanations to be valid or acceptable, maintaining, for example, that the simple assertion that racism does not exist in a particular country in no way absolves the State from its obligation to take appropriate measures under article 7, since it is never known what the future might hold in terms, for example, of a re-emergence of racism as a result of new social conditions such as a sudden influx of foreign migrant workers.

After considering the committee's report, the General Assembly on 3 December 1982 (resolution 37/44) appealed to all States parties to the International Convention on the Elimination of all Forms of Racial Discrimination to fulfil their obligations under the Convention and to submit their reports within the appropriate time.

The significance of the provisions of article 7, and their important human, social, and international implications, are aptly summarized in the conclusions set out by the special rapporteur in the above-mentioned study, which are as follows (UN Doc. A/CONF. 119/11, para. 105–109):

The guidelines contained in article 7 of the Convention are universal in scope since good relations between individuals, States or various ethnic groups will, in the final analysis, depend on the implementation of these and other measures. In any event, article 7 is unique in that, generally speaking, no provision exists, either in the various internal codes regulating social relations or in international treaties, which contains measures designed to prevent the infringement of the provisions of such instruments. To mention only two basic examples, the Charter of the United Nations and the Covenants on human rights do not provide for any measure in the fields of teaching, education, culture or information to encourage governments or individuals to devote greater attention to the fundamental objectives of those instruments, such as the ideals of peaceful co-operation, respect for the sovereign equality of States and respect for the dignity of the human person. The reason for this is that, in the area of racial prejudice, more than for any other social affliction subject to legal, political or economic sanctions, preventive action is called for to shape mental attitudes through teaching, education, culture and the information media.

It is essential that the concrete measures described above should become a reality. States are trusted to implement them. However, since the State is an abstract entity, the responsibility for ensuring the implementation of the relevant measures devolves upon its organs. The insistent and effective implementation of the principles of non-discrimination, understanding, tolerance and friendship among nations or racial or ethnic groups depends on the cultural background and the sense of the universal within an egalitarian perspective, primarily of teachers, but also, to a certain extent, of legislators, members of the administrative and the executive in general and judges, and on the initiatives of the potential victims.

But it is, for CERD, too, to exercise vigilance and to remind States at every opportunity—particularly during consideration of their periodic reports—of their duties under article 7. A similar responsibility devolves upon the United Nations General Assembly, which, when considering CERD's annual report, has the duty—making use of its moral prestige and vast dissemination facilities—to call upon States who have failed to do so to fulfil their obligations. Similar responsibilities are also incumbent on men of culture and writers. In South Africa, Afrikaner writers such as André Brink and Nadine Gordimer have, through their writings, worked effectively for racial equality and against *apartheid*.

Article 7 carries the seeds of part of the philosophy underlying the fundamental provisions of the Charter of the United Nations. For, today, humanity must be seen as oscillating between interdependence dictated by economic and political circumstances and the reality of cultural pluralism, where more and more is heard of multicultural societies. Never before has man gone so far to promote the one-world ideology, and, at the same time, to ensure the acceptance of the individual by the international community on his own terms.

Thus, the right to be different is being claimed on all sides. Positive law in the sphere of human rights proclaims equality with a view to eliminating discrimination, but not to impose a standardization which could prove oppressive, or even, in some cases, repressive. The system for the safeguarding of human rights combines or pairs unity with diversity and interdependence with freedom, and sees the equal dignity of all within the context of the individuality of each.

Every ethnic group and every State, regardless of the politico-social system to which it belongs, has the right to culture in general and to its own culture. If the duty to promote understanding, tolerance and friendship among nations or racial or ethnic groups is added to this, it will be seen that the result prescribed by article 7, namely fruitful dialogue between men of goodwill, accompanied by the unparalleled fertility of a dialogue of cultures, can be achieved only at the expense of an authentic dialogue encompassing all mankind. Healthy dialogue, with the conditions which it presupposes (good faith of the parties involved, dedication to the values advocated by the United Nations), is a means, a mechanism for piercing the veil which separates individuals and peoples. It provides access to understanding and rapprochement with others and saves us from isolation, which is the cause of many forms of anguish or disillusionment at the individual or social level. To withdraw selfishly into oneself, to seek only gain, or to be indifferent or contemptuous towards individuals in general is to render the civic spirit unattainable and the sense of international solidarity inconceivable. By promoting intolerance and enmity this egotistical attitude threatens individuals and society alike. If man wishes to achieve a full understanding of the time in which he lives and to overcome the crises which beset him on all sides, he will reject the unilateral in favour of the universal. The adoption of the universal perspective and the acceptance of flows from other continents which can fertilize any civilization, indisputably contribute to man's vital potential, to his ability to invent and create. At which point, man, in achieving fulfilment, will find infinite joy, and that euphoria will improve him. The achievement of understanding, tolerance and friendship among nations and racial and ethnic groups, is a process which takes place at both the logical and temporal levels. The resulting rapprochement between human beings will contribute effectively to the development of the spirit of international solidarity, to the safeguarding of the security of States and to the strengthening of *peace within justice*, which is the ultimate aim of the United Nations.

R

RACIAL, RELIGIOUS, AND NATIONAL HATRED.

In 1960, both the SUB-COMMISSION ON PREVENTION OF DISCRIMINATION AND PROTECTION OF MINORITIES (resolution 3 B [XII]) and the UN COMMISSION ON HUMAN RIGHTS (resolution 1510 [XV]) took note of "the manifestations of anti-Semitism and other forms of racial and national hatred and religious and racial prejudices of a similar character which have occurred in various countries, reminiscent of the crimes and outrages committed by the Nazis prior to and during the Second World War" and expressed their gratification that governments, peoples, and private organizations had spontaneously reacted in opposition to those manifestations.

On recommendation of the commission and subcommission, the UN General Assembly on 12 December 1960 expressed the principle (resolution 1510 [XV]) "that the United Nations is duty bound to combat these manifestations, to establish the facts and the causes of their origin, and to recommend resolute and effective measures which can be taken against them." The Assembly, further, resolutely condemned all manifestations and practices of racial, religious, and national hatred in the political, economic, social, educational, and cultural spheres of the life of society as violations of the the UNITED NATIONS CHARTER and the UNIVERSAL DECLARATION OF HUMAN RIGHTS; and called upon the governments of all States to take all necessary measures to prevent all manifestations of such hatred.

RACISM: ADMINISTRATION OF CRIMINAL JUSTICE.

At its 1979 session, the SUB-COMMISSION ON PREVENTION OF DISCRIMINATION AND PROTECTION OF MINORITIES examined a preliminary study on the independence and impartiality of the judiciary, jurors, and assessors, prepared by the Secretary-General (UN Doc. E/CN.4/Sub.2/428), and decided (resolution 4 A [XXXIII]) to appoint one of its members, Mr. Justice Abu Sayeed Chowdhury (Bangladesh) as its special rapporteur to study the subject further.

The special rapporteur's final report (UN Doc. E/CN.4/Sub.2/1982/7) was considered by the sub-commission at its 1982 session. Entitled "Study on discriminatory treatment of members of racial, ethnic, religious or linguistic groups at the various levels in the administration of criminal justice, such as police, military, administrative and judicial investigations, arrest, detention, trial and execution of sentences, including the ideologies or beliefs which contribute or lead to racism in the administration of criminal justice," it set out the following conclusions and recommendations:

Conclusions. Discriminatory treatment against members of racial, ethnic, religious or linguistic groups at the various levels in the administration of justice is, in a number of juridictions, a fact of current life. It would seem that as politically and economically subordinate minority groups seek to achieve self-determination and rise in the social structure, they are continually confronted by the legal structure. Many minority group members feel that the criminal legal system is heavily weighted against them and that the police represent a foreign, alien power.

If legal systems are to deal effectively with mounting attacks from minority group members, the issues and allegations at hand will have to be frankly discussed. The Special Rapporteur has attempted to address the relationship between the structure of the criminal justice system and minority groups. Rather than looking at one phase of this relationship, he has included the issues of police conduct, police and the community, factors of arrest and detention, the question of violence by the police, the factor of judicial proceedings, and finally, military justice.

The use of force by the police, causing great bodily harm and even death, figures prominently in complaints of minority groups against the police. That some policemen are killed is sufficiently impressive to underscore what might be termed the "dangerous" nature of the job, although the public image and the image of the police themselves have been known to exaggerate the real danger considerably. At any rate, society equips the policeman with instruments of violence for his own protection, because it is in society's interest that he be able to protect himself.

On the basis of certain statistics, it would appear that many more people are killed by the police than there are police killed in the line of duty. Homicides committed by police officers are of particular concern to certain minority groups since they continue to be the victims of these killings at a very disproportionate rate.

There is little indication, if any, that the norms which define the permissible use of violence by the police have, as a general rule, been internalized. Given the wide discretion and the absence of effective sanctions the police are apt to conform not to the requirements of due process of law, but rather to the pressures of the politically powerful.

Much of the friction between law officers and minority communities might be said to stem from the under-representation of members of minority groups in the police force of many communities.

The quality of the relationship between the police and the community is of utmost importance. How a policeman handles day-to-day contacts with citizens and minority groups in particular will, to a large extent, shape the relationship between the police and community.

The criminal court is one of the most crucial institutions in the criminal justice system. It is expected to meet society's demands to convict and punish serious offenders while at the same time ensuring that the innocent and unfortunate are not oppressed. The administration of criminal justice is an issue of great public concern; particularly as it relates to members of minority groups. The pervasive mistrust of such groups of the criminal justice system is said to be an important contributing factor to social discontent and upheaval; the police and the courts have been identified as sources of conflict between the dominant and non-dominant groups.

During periods when we are witnessing what might be termed a proliferation of military hostilities, one can see the need for adopting, subscribing to and adhering to rules and regulations pertaining to the conduct of such hostilities among civilized nations. During these periods, certain rights of combatants and non-combatants must be observed. Perhaps, in the light of today's advanced war technology, new rules and regulations of an international character might be called for.

Recommendations. (1) Legislative provisions generally provide important safeguards to supplement the ordinary law, where ordinary law guarantees do not exist or do not operate satisfactorily. It is suggested that national legislation should recognize the need for special protection to ensure that the basic rights of minorities are observed.

(2) Provision should be made for effective and enforceable remedies, reporting procedures, complaint and investigative procedures and conciliation machinery and processes. In this connection, complementary action should be taken by administrative and executive authorities concurrent with action taken by legislative and judicial authorities.

(3) It is recognized that the *Principles on Equality in the Administration of Justice* formulated by Mr. Mohammed A. Abu Rannat in his *Study* on that subject [UN Doc. E/CN.4/Sub.2/296] apply to all groups of society in general. It is suggested that in the administration of criminal justice the special needs and circumstances of minority groups should be given consideration in the interest of equity and justice. Courts should be relatively free and should have discretionary powers to interpret the law to fit situations not foreseen by the legal draughtsman.

(4) Efforts should be made to bring minority groups into the various processes of government and administration so that their views can be adequately represented and also to enable them to identify with these processes.

(5) Criminal justice services should have officers recruited among minorities.

(6) Affirmative action where deemed necessary would induce confidence and provide the services with personnel capable of understanding problems of minority groups.

SEE ALSO Equality: Administration of Justice.

RACISM AND RACIAL DISCRIMINATION: SECOND DECADE ACTION PROGRAM.

The Second World Conference to Combat Racism and Racial Discrimination, convened by the General Assembly (resolution 37/41) at the European office of the United Nations in Geneva from 14 to 25 August 1983, adopted and included in its report to the Assembly (UN publication, Sales No. E.83.XIV.4) a comprehensive "Program of Action for the Second Decade to Combat Racism and Racial Discrimination," reproduced below. On 22 November 1983, the General Assembly (resolution 38/14) proclaimed the ten-year period beginning on 10 December 1983 as the Second Decade to Combat Racism and Racial Discrimination, approved the program of action, and invited governments, United Nations bodies, the specialized agencies, and other intergovernmental organizations, as well as interested non-governmental organizations in consultative status with the Economic and Social Council, to participate in the celebration of the second decade by intensifying and extending their efforts to ensure the rapid elimination of racism and racial discrimination.

A. Action to Combat Apartheid

1. The Conference calls upon all States, United Nations organs and intergovernmental and non-governmental organizations to ensure the full and universal implementation of mandatory Security Council resolutions and to make efforts to implement other United Nations resolutions. Particular attention should be paid to specific measures, including those contained in the present Program of Action, designed to ensure the implementation of the provisions relating to *apartheid.*

2. The Conference reaffirms that the system of *apartheid* in South Africa is the most extreme form of institutionalized racism, a crime against humanity and an affront to the conscience and dignity of mankind, and that South Africa's policies and practices constitute serious breaches of and threats to regional stability and to international peace and security. The Conference calls upon all States, international organizations, private institutions and non-governmental organizations to render increased political and material assistance to the oppressed peoples of South Africa and Namibia, and to accelerate greatly campaigns for obtaining the release of all political prisoners imprisoned for their activities against *apartheid.*

3. The Conference further reaffirms the legitimacy of the struggle of the oppressed peoples of South Africa and Namibia and their national liberation movements for the elimination of *apartheid* by all available means, including armed struggle, and the special responsibility of the United Nations and the international community to provide them with moral, political and material assistance in the realization of their quest to exercise their right to self-determination.

4. The Conference reiterates the commitment of the United Nations to the total eradication of *apartheid* and to the establishment of a democratic society in which all the people of South Africa as a whole, irrespective of race, colour, sex or creed, will enjoy equal and full human rights and fundamental freedoms and participate freely in the determination of their destiny.

5. The Conference reaffirms the international community's rejection of the "bantustanization" policy and similar measures which are an integral part of the discriminatory *apartheid* system and which deny the black majority their legitimate rights to their land and to their citizenship of South Africa.

6. The Conference further confirms the international community's rejection of the régime's so-called reforms, especially the limited parliamentary representation for the Coloureds and Asians designed to split the black alliance and buttress the *apartheid* system.

7. The Conference calls upon all States to implement strictly the embargo on the sale and transfer of arms and related military materials imposed against South Africa under Security Council resolution 418 (1977) of 4 November 1977. The Conference further urges the Security Council to adopt urgent measures to strengthen the arms embargo, in accordance with the recommendations of the Council's committee established under its resolution 421 (1977) of 9 December 1977.

8. The Conference calls upon the Security Council to

consider urgently the imposition of mandatory sanctions, under Chapter VII of the Charter of the United Nations, against the *apartheid* régime of South Africa, and in particular:

(a) The cessation of all collaboration with South Africa in the nuclear field, as such collaboration would enhance South Africa's capacity to develop nuclear weapons;

(b) The prohibition of all technological assistance or collaboration in the manufacture of arms in South Africa and the provision of military supplies to South Africa;

(c) The cessation of foreign investments in, and financial loans to, South Africa;

(d) An embargo on the supply of petroleum, petroleum products, and other strategic commodities that would enable South Africa to continue implementing its *apartheid* policy;

(e) The interruption of trade relations with South Africa.

9. The Conference strongly condemns the racist régime of South Africa for its systematic oppression of and discrimination against the overwhelming majority of the population of South Africa and for its continuing illegal occupation of Namibia. The Conference also condemns acts of military aggression and acts of political and economic destabilization perpetrated by South Africa against the independent neighbouring States of Angola, Botswana, Lesotho, Mozambique, Seychelles, Swaziland, Zambia and Zimbabwe, as well as South Africa's activities to recruit, train, finance and arm mercenaries for aggression against and destabilization of the neighbouring States, creating instability in this part of the world.

10. The Conference calls for increased international assistance and support to the front-line States and other independent States in the subregion that are subjected to threats and acts of aggression and destabilization by the *apartheid* régime of South Africa, in order to enable them to strengthen their defence capacity, defend their sovereignty and territorial integrity, fight the adverse South African and other propaganda that undermines racial harmony and peace in the subregion, and peacefully rebuild and develop their countries.

11. The Conference calls upon States to sever all sporting, cultural and scientific links with the racist régime and with organizations or institutions in South Africa which practise *apartheid*, and to discourage their nationals from having any such contacts.

12. The Conference calls upon all States that have not yet done so:

(a) To refrain from any relations with the *apartheid* régime which could contribute to the continuance of the *apartheid* policy;

(b) To discourage or prevent all business enterprises, including transnational corporations, in so far as they are under their jurisdiction or control, from collaborating in any way with the racist régime of South Africa, as such collaboration may contribute towards the continuance of its *apartheid* policy.

13. The Conference, reaffirming the direct responsibility of the United Nations for Namibia pending its achievement of genuine self-determination, national independence and territorial integrity, demands the immediate and unconditional implementation of Security Council resolution 435 (1978) of 29 September 1978 and calls upon all States, intergovernmental organizations, private institutions and non-governmental organizations to make an active contribution to this aim. The Conference further calls upon all Govern-

ments and transnational corporations to implement Decree No. 1 for the Protection of the Natural Resources of Namibia, enacted by the United Nations Council for Namibia on 27 September 1974, and also calls for the implementation of the measures referred to in General Assembly resolution 37/233 C of 20 December 1982 on Namibia.

14. The Conference calls upon all States, intergovernmental organizations, private institutions and non-governmental organizations to continue to take all necessary measures to ensure the termination of all economic and financial collaboration with the racist régime of South Africa, as such assistance will contribute to the continuance of the policies of *apartheid*, and to refrain from taking any action that might imply recognition of or support for the illegal occupation of the Namibian territory by that régime. In this connection, the Conference cautions against unilateral attempts to relax the application of the sanctions already imposed by the Security Council.

15. The Conference urges the World Bank and the International Monetary Fund, as well as similar institutions, to refrain from extending any credits to the racist régime of South Africa.

B. Education, Teaching and Training

16. The Conference calls upon all States to use effectively education, teaching and training to create a favourable atmosphere for the eradication of racism and racial discrimination. These media should serve as channels for exposing the myths and fallacies of theories, philosophies, ideas and attitudes that are inherent in discriminatory actions based on differences of race, colour, descent and national or ethnic origin. It is imperative for all States to apply strictly the principle of non-discrimination and equality in the matter of education as set forth in the Convention against Discrimination in Education, adopted by the United Nations Educational, Scientific and Cultural Organization. The Conference invites States:

(a) To examine history, geography and social studies textbooks with a view to correcting any erroneous assessment of historical and social data, or their unbalanced presentation, which could give rise to racial prejudice;

(b) To ensure that teachers are made conscious of the degree to which they may reflect the prejudices of their society and are instructed to avoid such prejudices;

(c) To provide adequate opportunities in schools and institutions of higher learning for the study of the activities of the United Nations in combating racism, racial discrimination and *apartheid;*

(d) To provide pupils and students at all levels with access to literature and documentation on racism, racial discrimination and *apartheid;*

(e) To ensure that the composition of the teaching staff of institutions reflects, as far as possible, the racial and ethnic composition of the community; affirmative action programmes should be instituted to facilitate the hiring of teachers who represent the racial, ethnic and linguistic composition of the community;

(f) To make available the resources of schools and of teaching and training facilities to persons belonging to all population groups;

(g) To take remedial measures in instances where particular racial, ethnic, linguistic or other groups have had a history of being placed at a disadvantage because of their origin and where such a situation has contributed to a lower level of education and a lower standard of living for persons belonging to various population groups; this is the responsibility of society. It might necessitate special educational programmes at all levels of the society;

(h) To make law enforcement agents aware in their training of the possibility that they may reflect the prejudices of their society;

(i) To ensure that school curricula promote a dialogue between persons belonging to the various groups of the society; the curricula should be responsive to the needs and backgrounds of all these persons and foster, where possible, an interchange of cultural experience; in this regard, persons belonging to minority ethnic and racial groups should be allowed to introduce students to the practices and values of the respective cultures; efforts should also be made to allow the topic of human rights to permeate the curricula.

17. National institutions should inform the general public of the nature of their human rights as provided for in the existing international instruments directed towards combating racism, racial discrimination and *apartheid,* as well as in other instruments based on the principles contained in the Universal Declaration of Human Rights or as otherwise covered in national legislation. The general public should be advised by the national institutions on the means of enforcing their rights in accordance with national law. National institutions should ensure that persons are made aware of their own rights and those of others and should assist them in the matter of protecting and enforcing their rights. These institutions should mobilize public opinion in their countries against violations of human rights, especially gross and massive violations, in particular against the practice of *apartheid,* racism and genocide.

18. One of the fundamental objectives of programmes of education and scientific research undertaken in national institutions should be the elimination of racial discrimination and prejudice.

19. It is imperative that all States apply strictly the principle of non-discrimination and equality in the matter of education and adhere to the principles set forth in the Convention against Discrimination in Education. It is important that the right to enter any school should be guaranteed to every child. The availability of special or supplementary education for children belonging to disadvantaged racial and ethnic groups may be appropriate in some cases for their development.

20. International agencies such as the United Nations Educational, Scientific and Cultural Organization should continue their work in the field of human rights education and promote such programmes on a continuing basis as guidelines for textbook analysis, teacher training, curriculum development and other undertakings and, in particular, should develop materials explaining how discrimination inherent in the system and institutionalized can be addressed through remedial programmes such as affirmative action plans.

21. As was recommended by the International Conference on *Apartheid* and Health, held at Brazzaville from 16 to 20 November 1981, the World Health Organization should continue to implement the Plan of Action in favour of the victims of *apartheid,* in particular in the fields of health, education and training.

C. Dissemination of Information and the Role of the Mass Media in Combating Racism and Racial Discrimination

22. The mass media should play a vital role in disseminating information on methods and techniques used in combating racism, racial discrimination and *apartheid.* Taking into account the Declaration on fundamental principles concerning the contribution of the mass media to strengthening peace and international understanding, to the promotion of human rights and countering racialism, *apartheid* and incitement to war, adopted by the United Nations Educational, Scientific and Cultural Organization on 28 November 1978, the mass media should regard it as their task, by disseminating information on the aims, aspirations, cultures and needs of all peoples, to contribute to eliminating ignorance and misunderstanding between peoples, to making nationals of a country sensitive to the needs and desires of others, to ensuring respect for the rights and dignity of all nations, all peoples and all individuals without distinction as to race, sex, language, religion or nationality and in that way to contribute to protecting them against the influence of any propaganda supporting racism and racist régimes.

23. The mass media should contribute to making the peoples more aware of the close link between the struggle against *apartheid* and all forms of racism and racial discrimination and the struggle for international peace and security, in conformity with the provisions of the above-mentioned Declaration.

24. Lack of self-expression through the mass media for persons belonging to racial and ethnic minorities in society can often cause the mass media to become one-sided or distorted. Media of all kinds—radio, television, films, the press, advertising, booklets and public meetings—as well as traditional forms such as drama and story-telling could play a vital role.

25. Events and activities aimed at combating racism and racial discrimination should be given broad coverage by the media. Mention may be made of such activities as the coverage of conferences, seminars, workshops and round-tables, as well as of meetings of United Nations organs dealing with a particular question, and the publication and wide distribution of pertinent resolutions and decisions of such bodies. Success stories in combating racial discrimination through legislation, executive action or community action programmes should be given publicity, and the negative and evil side of racism and racial discrimination highlighted. Comic strips, films and magazines for children and adults should be screened with a view to eliminating any form of racial stereotyping, whether favourable or unfavourable. Events having a racial aspect should be presented in their economic and social, cultural and political context; they should not be treated as mere news items.

26. The negative and positive influences exercised by the media in their role as information-conveyors, entertainers, educators and advertisers should be studied. In addition, the media should seek to raise public consciousness about the positive roles and achievements of racial and ethnic groups from all walks of life throughout history. Efforts should be made to produce radio and television programmes depicting the evils of racial discrimination in a vivid way—for example, by illustrating the plight of individual victims of racial discrimination. Such audio and visual presentations are likely to have great impact, particularly in areas where literacy is not widespread.

27. There should be adequate opportunity within the mass media for persons belonging to groups which are victims of discrimination to express their own points of view, particularly by producing programmes or reports themselves. In addition, persons belonging to such groups should have equal access to the professions within the mass media, especially journalism.

28. National institutions should publicize widely basic texts on the elimination of racism, racial discrimination and *apartheid,* as well as other human rights texts.

D. Measures for the Promotion and Protection of the Human Rights of Persons Belonging to Minority Groups, Indigenous Populations and Peoples and Migrant Workers who are Subjected to Racial Discrimination

Throughout the various regions of the world there is a diversity of peoples, cultures, traditions and religions that encompasses, in many instances, various minority groups. There is a need for constant effort and continued vigilance on the part of all Governments to obviate any form of discrimination based on race, colour, descent or national or ethnic origin, in accordance with article 1 of the International Convention on the Elimination of All Forms of Racial Discrimination.

National and local institutions, as adapted to the needs and conditions of each country, can play an important role in the promotion and protection of human rights, in the prevention of discrimination and the protection of the rights of persons belonging to national and ethnic minorities, of indigenous populations and of refugees. Such national and local institutions could be of varying types, including judicial, administrative, conciliatory, social and educational. Any or all of these types of institutions could be utilized by individual countries according to their own circumstances and needs.

In the area of legislation, Governments should abolish and prohibit any discrimination within their jurisdiction. Such legislation should seek to promote and protect the human rights of persons belonging to minority groups, in accordance with the Universal Declaration of Human Rights, the International Covenant on Civil and Political Rights, the International Convention on the Elimination of All Forms of Racial Discrimination and other relevant international instruments. Persons belonging to minorities should enjoy all human rights and fundamental freedoms without any discrimination as to national or ethnic origin, language, religion or sex.

Governments should create favourable conditions and take measures that will enable persons belonging to national or ethnic minorities within their jurisdiction to express their characteristics freely and to develop their education, culture, language, traditions and customs and to participate on a non-discriminatory and equitable basis in the cultural, social, economic and political life of the country in which they live. In maintaining their culture and traditions such persons should be in a position to develop the necessary contacts inside and outside their country, with due respect for the sovereignty, territorial integrity and political independence of the States concerned and for the principle of non-interference by one State in the internal affairs of another State.

States should undertake to combat the causes of intergroup antagonism by adopting concrete measures designed to promote understanding, co-operation and harmonious relations among members of population groups. Where tension and friction exist, their elimination cannot be achieved if the realities of political, economic, cultural, religious and linguistic differences between the various components of the society concerned are not taken into account.

With respect to indigenous populations, Governments should recognize and respect the basic rights of such populations:

(a) To call themselves by their proper name and to express freely their own identity;

(b) To have official status and to form their own representative organizations;

(c) To maintain within the areas where they live their traditional economic structure and way of life; this should in no way affect their right to participate freely on an equal basis in the economic, social and political development of the country;

(d) To maintain and use their own language, wherever possible, for administration and education;

(e) To enjoy freedom of religion or belief;

(f) To have access to land and natural resources, particularly in the light of the fundamental importance of rights to land and natural resources to their traditions and aspirations;

(g) To structure, conduct and control their own educational systems.

Indigenous populations should be free to manage their own affairs to the fullest practicable extent, and should be consulted in all matters concerning their interests and welfare, wherever possible through formal consultative arrangements. Special measures should be taken to remedy past dispossession, dispersal and systematic discrimination.

Funds should be made available by the national authorities for investments, the uses of which are to be determined with the participation of the indigenous populations themselves, in the economic life of the areas concerned, as well as in all spheres of cultural activity.

Governments should allow indigenous populations within their territories to develop cultural and social links with related or similar populations, taking into account the important role of international organizations or associations of indigenous populations, and with due respect for the sovereignty, territorial integrity and political independence of those countries in which indigenous populations live.

The Conference further urges States to facilitate and support the establishment of representative non-governmental international organizations for indigenous populations, through which they can share experiences and promote common interests. The Sub-Commission on Prevention of Discrimination and Protection of Minorities should ensure that the urgent work being carried out by its Working Group on Indigenous Populations is continued so that the complex issues involved can be analysed and appropriate measures taken at the international and national levels.

In view of the vulnerability of indigenous populations to discrimination and violations of their human rights, and of the gravity of the threat faced by indigenous populations in some parts of the world, Governments should pay close attention to situations in which the rights of indigenous populations may be violated or denied, in order to prevent such violations, which should be widely publicized as soon as they are detected.

States receiving migrant workers should eliminate all discriminatory practices against such workers and their families by giving them treatment no less favourable than that accorded to their own nationals. Host countries should eliminate from their legislation any type of legal or other provisions which may discriminate against migrant workers on the basis of their nationality. This should pertain, *inter alia,* to vocational training, the type of posts that migrants may occupy, the type of contracts accorded to migrant workers, their right to seek employment in any part of the country, regulations governing working conditions, trade-union activity and access to judicial and administrative tribunals to air grievances concerning discrimination. With a view to combating xenophobia, host countries should develop information campaigns in order to disseminate the idea of equality between nationals and migrant workers.

The following measures could also be undertaken by Governments to protect the rights of migrant workers:

(a) The General Assembly should complete, as soon as possible, the elaboration of an international convention on the protection of the rights of all migrant workers and their families; the Conference considers that the conclusion of this convention by the United Nations would constitute an important contribution to its endeavours to protect fundamental human rights, because the convention would be added to the other instruments protecting these rights; the Conference recommends, pending the conclusions of the above-mentioned convention, that a joint consultative mechanism should be established in host countries with a view to contributing to good relations and mutual understanding;

(b) States should ratify, accede to and implement the international instruments aimed at protecting migrant workers from discrimination, including the relevant conventions of the International Labour Organisation;

(c) Migrant workers and members of their families should have the same rights as nationals of the State concerned as regards access to and treatment by the courts and tribunals;

(d) All migrant workers should enjoy treatment no less favourable than that accorded to nationals of the host State in respect of remuneration;

(e) Migrant workers should be ensured equal treatment with national workers in the field of social security, including the right to a retirement pension and similar social rights, while they have lawful residence in the host country;

(f) Host countries should be invited to co-operate with countries of origin to provide migrant workers and their families with the necessary facilities in the fields of education and information to safeguard their cultural identity;

(g) The children of migrant workers should be enabled to receive education in their mother tongue and on different aspects of their cultural heritage with a view to preserving their national identity;

(h) The State of origin and the State of employment should co-operate, as far as possible, with a view to helping to create new job opportunities for migrant workers returning to the State of origin.

E. Recourse Procedures for Victims of Racial Discrimination

42. The Conference invites States to take into account, within their domestic recourse procedures, the following considerations:

(a) Access to such procedures should be as broad as possible;

(b) Existing recourse procedures should be publicized within their respective jurisdictions, and victims of racial discrimination should be assisted in utilizing the procedures where appropriate;

(c) In each jurisdiction the rules relating to the initiation of complaints should be made simple and flexible and capable of being entertained in the language of the complainant;

(d) Complaints of racial discrimination should be

dealt with as expeditiously as possible and there should be a reasonable time-limit with regard to the length of investigations;

(e) Indigent victims of racial discrimination should receive legal aid and assistance in prosecuting their complaint in civil or criminal proceedings, with the help of an interpreter when necessary.

43. Victims of racial discrimination should have the right to seek from tribunals just and adequate reparation or satisfaction for any damage suffered as a result of such discrimination.

F. Implementation of the International Convention on the Elimination of All Forms of Racial Discrimination and Other Related International Instruments

44. The Conference urges States which have not yet become parties to the International Convention on the Elimination of All Forms of Racial Discrimination to do so as part of their contribution to the objectives of the Decade for Action to Combat Racism and Racial Discrimination and until such States ratify the Convention they should utilize its provisions as guidelines in combating racial discrimination and in securing the realization of the principles of equality at both the national and international levels. The Conference calls upon States parties to the Convention to consider the possibility of making the Declaration provided for in article 14 of the Convention.

45. Those States should enact, as a matter of the highest priority, appropriate legislation and other suitable measures to prohibit and bring to an end racial discrimination, to abrogate, amend, rescind or nullify any policies or regulations that have the effect of creating or perpetuating racial hatred and to declare the dissemination of ideas based on racial superiority and hatred to be an offence punishable by law, taking duly into account the provisions of the International Convention on the Elimination of All Forms of Racial Discrimination.

46. The Conference also appeals to States which have not yet done so to consider ratifying or acceding to as soon as possible other relevant international instruments adopted under the aegis of the United Nations and of the specialized agencies, such as the Convention on the Prevention and Punishment of the Crime of Genocide, the International Covenant on Economic, Social and Cultural Rights, the International Covenant on Civil and Political Rights, the Convention on the Non-Applicability of Statutory Limitations to War Crimes and Crimes against Humanity, the International Convention on the Suppression and Punishment of the Crime of *Apartheid,* the Convention concerning Discrimination in Respect of Employment and Occupation adopted by the International Labour Organisation on 25 June 1958, the Convention against Discrimination in Education adopted by the United Nations Educational, Scientific and Cultural Organization and the Convention on the Elimination of All Forms of Discrimination against Women; States are urged to comply with the reporting requirements called for by the relevant conventions.

G. National Legislation and Institutions

47. The Conference suggests that States that have not already done so should consider the urgent enactment, as a matter of the highest priority, of appropriate legislation and other suitable measures to prohibit and bring to an end racial discrimination, to abrogate, amend, rescind or nullify any policies or regulations that have the effect of

R

creating or perpetuating racial hatred and, with due regard to the principles embodied in the Universal Declaration of Human Rights, the United Nations Declaration on the Elimination of All Forms of Racial Discrimination, the Declaration on Fundamental Principles concerning the Contribution of the Mass Media to Strengthening Peace and International Understanding, to the Promotion of Human Rights and to Countering Racialism, *Apartheid* and Incitement to War, the Declaration on Race and Racial Prejudice adopted by the United Nations Educational, Scientific and Cultural Organization on 27 November 1978, and the rights set forth in the International Convention on the Elimination of All Forms of Racial Discrimination, to declare the dissemination of ideas based on racial superiority and hatred to be an offence punishable by law.

48. The Conference calls upon all States that have not yet done so to take effective legislative and other measures, including in the field of penal law, to prevent the recruitment, use, financing and training, transit and transport of mercenaries, in particular when they are aimed at assisting racist régimes, and to punish such mercenaries as common criminals. The Conference urges the *Ad Hoc* Committee on the Drafting of an International Convention against the Recruitment, Use, Financing and Training of Mercenaries, established by the General Assembly at its thirty-fifth session, to complete, as soon as possible, the draft international convention.

49. The Conference urges all States to adopt strict legislation to declare any dissemination of ideas based on racial superiority or hatred to be an offence punishable by law and to prohibit organizations based on racial prejudice and hatred, including neo-Nazi and Fascist organizations, and private clubs and institutions established on the basis of racial criteria or propagating ideas of racial discrimination and *apartheid*.

50. With regard to national legislation, the Conference recommends that:

(a) Governments, where necessary, should guarantee non-discrimination on grounds of race and equal rights for all individuals in their constitutions and legislation;

(b) Governments, where necessary, should undertake to review and update all national legislation and remove from it any discriminatory provisions;

(c) Legislation should be consistent with international standards embodied in relevant international instruments;

(d) Victims of discrimination should be informed and advised of their rights, by all possible means, and given assistance in securing those rights;

(e) Governments should, where necessary, establish appropriate and effective mechanisms, including conciliation and mediation procedures and national commissions, to ensure that such legislation is enforced effectively, and thereby to promote equality of opportunity and good race relations.

51. A system of regular review and appraisal should be continued to enable Member States, all organizations of the United Nations system, including relevant regional bodies and non-governmental organizations, to assess the measures taken towards achieving the aims and objectives of the Decade.

52. Within the framework of their national legislation and policy, and according to their means, States should set up national institutions for the promotion and protection of human rights. Those institutions should study legal developments and review the laws and policies of the Government with a view to ensuring the elimination of all discriminatory laws, prejudices and practices based on race, sex, colour, descent and national and ethnic origin.

H. Seminars and Studies

53. The Conference recommends that, in the context of future activities to combat racism and racial discrimination, consideration should be given to the organization of international and regional seminars on such subjects as:

(a) Political, historical, economic, social and cultural factors leading to racism, racial discrimination and *apartheid;*

(b) International assistance and support to peoples and movements struggling against colonialism, racism, racial discrimination and *apartheid;*

(c) Ways and means of denying support to racist régimes with a view to making them change their policies;

(d) The historical and current dimensions of tribalism;

(e) Main obstacles to the full eradication of racism, racial discrimination and *apartheid;*

(f) The human rights of persons belonging to ethnic groups in countries of immigration;

(g) Equality of treatment for persons belonging to ethnic and racial minorities and disadvantaged groups, such as indigenous populations;

(h) Community relations commissions and their functions.

54. The Conference also recommends that studies should be continued regarding ways and means of ensuring implementation of United Nations resolutions on *apartheid*, racism and racial discrimination. In particular, the Conference strongly encourages the United Nations Institute for Training and Research to continue to research, study and conduct seminars on racism and racial discrimination.

I. Action by Non-Governmental Organizations

55. By virtue of their independent status, non-governmental organizations, individually and collectively, have an important contribution to make to the achievement of the objectives of the Decade for Action to Combat Racism and Racial Discrimination. Through various activities sponsored by them, non-governmental organizations can be effective in identifying and publicizing areas of racial discrimination which otherwise might not come to light, and in helping to create greater practical understanding among young people of the importance of actively combating all forms of discrimination, in their own countries as well as in the international community.

56. Non-governmental organizations have the opportunity to create and sustain awareness among their members and in society at large of the evils of racism and racial discrimination. Such awareness can be transmitted from a national to an international organization with all the added benefits of the concrete experience of a particular country. Governments should therefore ensure that non-governmental organizations shall be enabled to function freely and openly within their societies and thus make an effective contribution to the elimination of racism and racial discrimination throughout the world.

J. International Co-operation

57. In order to obtain the full promotion and protection of the human rights of individuals and peoples, it is necessary to intensify national, regional and international action

aimed at combating and eliminating the causes of the policies and practices of racism, racial discrimination and *apartheid*.

58. The Conference underlines that the maintenance and strengthening of international co-operation and peace, the implementation of human rights and the combating of *apartheid* and racial discrimination are clearly linked. In order to improve mutual understanding among peoples, exchange visits should be increased and educational, cultural and scientific exchange programmes should be expanded. The free flow of information and ideas with respect to combating racism and racial discrimination should be ensured. The Conference calls on States to exchange information and ideas with respect to combating racism and racial discrimination.

59. The Conference calls upon the World Conference to Review and Appraise the Achievements of the United Nations Decade for Women, to be held in 1985, to contribute to the struggle against racism, racial discrimination and *apartheid* by recommending the adoption of measures aimed at ensuring the active participation of women in the struggle against those evils.

60. The Conference recommends that, in the context of International Youth Year, in 1985, the United Nations and the specialized agencies should undertake activities to encourage the effective contribution of youth to the struggle against racism, racial discrimination and *apartheid*.

61. The Conference calls upon all Governments and international organizations to make every effort to change the economic, political and social conditions on which policies and practices of racism, racial discrimination and *apartheid* are based and to give all their support to the victims of racism, racial discrimination and *apartheid*, and declares that the struggle against the remnants of colonialism and support of the liberation movements recognized by the regional organizations are worthy of particular attention.

62. Article 28 of the Universal Declaration of Human Rights establishes that everyone is entitled to a social and international order in which the rights and freedoms set forth in the Declaration can be fully realized. For this purpose, it is necessary to work for the establishment of a just and fair international order. The establishment of a new international economic order would be an important means of combating the causes which generate racism and racial discrimination.

63. The national, regional and international action to combat and eliminate the causes of the policies and practices of racism, racial discrimination and *apartheid* should include measures aimed at improving the conditions of life of peoples and individuals in the economic, political, social and cultural spheres in order that the great inequalities now existing in the fields of employment, nutrition, health, housing and education, among others, may disappear. International development co-operation has an important role to play in securing the resources required by the developing countries to realize these objectives.

At its regular 1987 session, the General Assembly noted with concern (resolution 42/47) that, despite the efforts of the international community, the principal objectives of the First Decade for Action to Combat Racism and Racial Discrimination had not been attained and that millions of human beings continued to be the victims of varied forms of racism, racial

discrimination, and *apartheid;* and decided that the international community, in general, and the United Nations in particular, should continue to give the highest priority to programs for combatting racism, racial discrimination, and *apartheid,* and to intensify their efforts, during the Second Decade to Combat Racism and Racial Discrimination, to provide assistance and relief to the victims of racism and all forms of racial discrimination and *apartheid,* especially in South Africa and Namibia and in occupied territories and territories under alien domination.

The Assembly took note of a report by the Secretary-General on activities proposed to give effect to the program of action for the second decade (UN Doc. A/42/493) and requested him to ensure the effective and immediate implementation of those activities. It also requested him to prepare and issue as soon as possible a collection of model legislation for the guidance of governments in the enactment of further legislation against racial discrimination.

In addition, the Assembly invited the UNITED NATIONS EDUCATIONAL, SCIENTIFIC AND CULTURAL ORGANIZATION to expedite the preparation of teaching materials and teaching aids to promote teaching, training, and educational activities on human rights and against racism and racial discrimination, with particular emphasis on activities at the primary and secondary levels of education, and called upon the SUB-COMMISSION ON PREVENTION OF DISCRIMINATION AND PROTECTION OF MINORITIES to complete as soon as possible its study of the results achieved and the obstacles encountered during the first Decade and the first half of the Second Decade for Action to Combat Racism and Racial Discrimination.

Finally, the Assembly approved the plan of activities for the period 1990–1993, reproduced below, and invited the Secretary-General to proceed with the implementation of those activities, according the highest priority to measures for combating *apartheid.*

At its 1988 session, the Assembly again affirmed (resolution 43/91) the need for the implementation of the plan of activities and requested the Secretary-General (1) to accord the highest priority, in executing the plan, to measures for combatting *apartheid,* and (2) to continue to give special attention to the situation of migrant workers and their families. In addition, it reiterated its request to the Economic and Social Council to submit to it each year, throughout the second decade, a report containing *inter alia* (a) an enumeration of the activities undertaken or contemplated to achieve the objectives of the second decade, including the activities of governments, United Nations bodies, the specialized agencies, and other international and regional organizations, as well as non-governmental organizations; (b) a review and appraisal of those activities; and (c) its suggestions and recommendations.

Plan of Activities to be Implemented During the Second Half of the Second Decade to Combat Racism and Racial Discrimination, 1990–1993

1. The following activities should take place during the biennium 1990–1991 and be reflected in the proposed programme budget for that biennium:

(a) Global survey of the extent to which the children of migrant workers are able to receive education in their mother tongue;

(b) Meeting of experts to review national experience in the operation of schemes of local, internal self-government for indigenous populations;

(c) Expert study on the impact of article 27 of the International Covenant on Civil and Political Rights in providing guarantees of equality to persons belonging to minorities;

(d) Regional workshops on the adoption of legislation to combat racism and racial discrimination;

(e) Seminar on community relations commissions and their functions;

(f) Seminar to assess experience gained in the implementation of the International Convention on the Elimination of All Forms of Racial Discrimination;

(g) International campaign to contribute to the early independence of Namibia, in conformity with Security Council resolution 435 (1978) of 29 September 1978.

2. The following activities should take place during the biennium 1992–1993 and be reflected in the proposed programme budget for that biennium:

(a) Round table of experts to discuss the preparation of teaching materials to combat racism and racial discrimination;

(b) Issuance in three additional languages of the handbook of recourse procedures available to victims of racism and racial discrimination;

(c) Two regional workshops on the adoption of legislation to combat racism and racial discrimination;

(d) International campaign on the main obstacles to the full eradication of racism, racial discrimination and *apartheid,* and on ways and means of bringing about the early disappearance of these scourges;

(e) Study on the treatment of political prisoners and detainees in South Africa and Namibia, particularly women and children;

(f) Global survey on the extent of dissemination of the International Convention on the Elimination of All Forms of Racial Discrimination.

SEE ALSO Apartheid: *ILO Declaration and Program of Action;* Apartheid: *UN Program of Action; Decades to Combat Racism and Racial Discrimination; Declaration of the Second World Conference to Combat Racism and Racial Discrimination; Declaration on the Elimination of all Forms of Racial Discrimination; Human Rights: Teaching; Indigenous Populations: Study of Problem of Discrimination; Inter-American Declaration on Racial Integration in the Americas; International Convention against Recruitment, Use, Financing and Training of Mercenaries; International Convention on the Elimination of all Forms of Racial Discrimination; International Convention on the Suppression and Punishment of the Crime of* Apartheid; *International Covenant on Civil and Political Rights and Protocols; International Covenant on Economic, Social, and Cultural Rights and Protocols; Migrant Workers; Minority Rights.*

RACIST PROPAGANDA AND ORGANIZATIONS.
Article 4 of the INTERNATIONAL CONVENTION ON THE ELIMINATION OF ALL FORMS OF RACIAL DISCRIMINATION reads as follows:

States parties condemn all propaganda and all organizations which are based on ideas or theories of superiority of one race or group of persons of one colour or ethnic origin, or which attempt to justify or promote racial hatred and discrimination in any form, and undertake to adopt immediate and positive measures designed to eradicate all incitement to, or acts of, such discrimination and, to this end, with due regard to the principles embodied in the Universal Declaration of Human Rights and expressly set forth in article 5 of this Convention, *inter alia:*

(a) Shall declare an offence punishable by law all dissemination of ideas based on racial superiority or hatred, incitement to racial discrimination, as well as all acts of violence or incitement to such acts against any race or group of persons of another coulour or ethnic origin, and also the provision of any assistance to racist activities, including the financing thereof;

(b) Shall declare illegal and prohibit organizations, and also organized and all other propaganda activities, which promote and incite racial discrimination, and shall recognize participation in such organization or activities as an offence punishable by law;

(c) Shall not permit public authorities or public institutions, national or local, to promote or incite racial discrimination.

In examining the reports submitted by States parties to the convention, the COMMITTEE ON THE ELIMINATION OF RACIAL DISCRIMINATION has consistently maintained that article 4 requires them to enact legislation imposing specific penalties for all acts of a discriminatory nature, as provided in sub-paragraphs (a) and (b), and that no State could be said to have effectively implemented the convention until it had done so. It has not accepted the position of some States parties that article 4 should be interpreted as requiring such States to adopt further legislative measures only insofar as racist propaganda and organizations actually exist in their countries and territories and has maintained that the adoption of specific and appropriate legislation is required for deterrent purposes even in countries free of racism, since no one can foresee what the future holds in store.

Nor has the committee accepted the view of some States parties that article 4 cannot be read in isolation from the rest of the convention and should be interpreted as requiring States to adopt further legislative measures only insofar as such measures were consistent with the fundamental right of freedom of opinion and expression, to which reference is made in article 5 of the convention.

The Study on the Implementation of Article 4 of the International Convention on the Elimination of all Forms of Racial Discrimination, prepared by a member of the Committee on the Elimination of Racial Discrimination, Mr. Jose D. Ingles (Philippines), and approved by the committee (UN Doc. A/CONF.119/10, later issued as UN publication, Sales No. E.85.XIV.2), was presented to the Second World Conference to Combat Racism and Racial Discrimination, convened at the European office of the United Nations, Geneva, from 1 to 12 August 1983. In the study, Mr. Ingles included the following background information (para. 2–11):

Article 4 has been aptly described as the "key article" of the Convention. It was the consensus in the General Assembly that the article, as finally adopted, afforded a compromise between those who wished the enactment of positive legislation to penalize not only "incitement to discrimination" but also the "dissemination of ideas based on racial superiority or hatred", and those who did not wish to see freedom of speech or assembly impaired. For example, the representative of the United Kingdom would not accept punishment for the bare expression of an idea or mere incitement to racial discrimination, unless there was incitement to violence. Indeed, the original draft of article 4 *(a)* submitted by the Sub-Commission on Prevention of Discrimination and Protection of Minorities, as subsequently adopted by the Commission on Human Rights, provided for the punishment by law of "all incitement to racial discrimination resulting in or likely to cause acts of violence".

The compromise text proposed by Nigeria (A/ C.3/ L.1250) broadened the scope of article 4 *(a)* by providing for the punishment by law of "all dissemination of ideas based on superiority or hatred, incitement to racial discrimination, as well as acts of violence or incitement to such acts against any race or group of persons . . .".

That text also included in the introductory paragraph of article 4 the clause "with due regard to the principles embodied in the Universal Declaration of Human Rights and the rights expressly set forth in article 5 of the Convention". This was interpreted by the advocates of free speech and assembly as "not imposing on a State party the obligation to take any action impairing the right to freedom of speech and freedom of association". However, article 29, paragraph 2, of the Universal Declaration of Human Rights allows the limitation of everyone's rights and freedoms "as are determined by law solely for the purpose of securing due recognition and respect for the rights and freedoms of others and of meeting the just requirements of morality, public order and the general welfare in a democratic society". It is clear that a balance must be struck between article 4 *(a)* of the Convention and the right of free speech, and between article 4 *(b)* and the right of free association.

When the Convention entered into force on 4 January 1969, many of the States parties had not yet enacted legislation to implement that particular article. The situation did not change substantially when the number of States parties increased to 118, from the original 28 in 1969. There were a few States parties that had enacted the necessary legislation prior to ratification or accession to the Convention, and still fewer States whose existing legislation may be said to comply substantially with the provisions of article 4.

A few were of the erroneous opinion that, having become parties to the Convention, they had done all that was required of them as States parties. It was contended that, the Convention having become part of domestic law by incorporation with or without transformation, no further measures were necessary to give effect to the Convention.

Others cited the provisions of their respective constitutions prohibiting racial discrimination or racial propaganda, but did not provide legislative texts to carry out the constitutional injunction. In the absence of legislative provisions, a few stated that racial discrimination or incitement thereto, as well as racist organizations and propaganda, would be unconstitutional.

Some stated in their reports that, since racial discrimination did not exist or was unknown in their respective countries, it was not necessary or might even be counterproductive to prohibit it, much less to take measures to eradicate incitement to, or acts of, such discrimination.

The problem of implementation arose in view of the guidelines adopted by the Committee at its first session, on 28 January 1970 (CERD/C/R.12), to assist the States parties in preparing the reports they were required to submit under article 9, paragraph 1, of the Convention. It was asked, *inter alia,* what administrative, legislative, judicial or other measures they had taken to comply with the provisions of article 4 of the Convention.

On 24 February 1972, the Committee adopted general recommendation I, as follows:

"On the basis of the consideration at its fifth session of reports submitted by States parties under article 9 of the International Convention on the Elimination of All Forms of Racial Discrimination, the Committee found that the legislation of a number of States parties did not include the provisions envisaged in article 4 *(a)* and *(b)* of the Convention, the implementation of which (with due regard to the principles embodied in the Universal Declaration of Human Rights and the rights expressly set forth in article 5 of the Convention) is obligatory under the Convention for all States parties.

"The Committee accordingly recommends that the States parties whose legislation was deficient in this respect should consider, in accordance with their national legislative procedures, the question of supplementing their legislation with provisions conforming to the requirements of article 4 *(a)* and *(b)* of the Convention."

The revised general guidelines concerning the form and contents of reports by States parties under article 9, paragraph 1, of the Convention, adopted by the Committee on 9 April 1980 (CERD/C/70), required *inter alia:*

A. Information on the legislative, judicial, administrative or other measures which give effect to the provisions of article 4 of the Convention, in particular measures taken to give effect to the undertaking to adopt immediate and positive measures designed to eradicate all incitement to, or acts of, racial discrimination [with due regard to the principles embodied in the Universal Declaration of Human Rights and the rights expressly set forth in article 5 of the Convention]; in particular:

(1) To declare an offence punishable by law all dissemination of ideas based on racial superiority and hatred, incitement to racial discrimination, as well as all acts of violence or incitement to such acts against any race or group of persons of another colour or ethnic origin, and

also the provision of any assistance to racist activities, including the financing thereof;

(2) To declare illegal and prohibit organizations, and also organized and all other propaganda activities, which promote and incite racial discrimination, and to recognize participation in such organizations or activities as an offence punishable by law;

(3) Not to permit public authorities or public institutions, national or local, to promote or incite racial discrimination.

B. Information on appropriate measures taken to give effect to general recommendation I, of 24 February 1972, by which the Committee recommended that the States parties whose legislation was deficient in respect of the implementation of article 4 should consider, in accordance with their national legislative procedures, the question of supplementing their legislation with provisions conforming to the requirements of article 4 *(a)* and *(b)* of the Convention;

C. Information in response to decision 3 (VII) adopted by the Committee on 4 May 1973, by which the Committee requested the States parties:

(1) To indicate what specific penal internal legislation designed to implement the provisions of article 4 *(a)* and *(b)* has been enacted in their respective countries and to transmit to the Secretary-General in one of the official languages the texts concerned, as well as such provisions of general penal law as must be taken into account when applying such specific legislation;

(2) Where no such specific legislation has been enacted, to inform the Committee of the manner and the extent to which the provisions of the existing penal laws, as applied by the courts, effectively implement their obligations under article 4 *(a)* and *(b),* and to transmit to the Secretary-General in one of the official languages the texts of those provisions.

Mr. Ingles' conclusions and recommendations, set out in Chapter IV of the study (para. 210–246), are as follows:

The practice of States parties in the implementation of the Convention, particularly of article 4, has not been uniform.

Some States point out that their existing legislation prior to the entry into force of the Convention already satisfies the requirements of article 4. In rare instances the claim seems to be justified.

Others have enacted legislation to conform to the Convention before ratification or accession to the Convention. In some cases such legislation is adequate to meet the requirements of article 4.

Many have amended their existing legislation after accession to, or ratification of, the Convention. Some amendments comply fully with article 4.

A few have adopted entirely new legislation to fulfil the conditions laid down in article 4.

Some are still considering the enactment of the necessary legislation, sometimes through special commissions set up for the purpose.

Unlike other articles of the Convention, article 4 is not self-executing. Despite the incorporation or transformation of the Convention as part of domestic law, article 4 can be implemented only if legislation is enacted to do what the article ordains.

The other articles of the Convention vest States parties with ample discretion to adopt such measures as they may deem appropriate to achieve the objectives of the Convention. The introductory paragraph of article 4 follows this general trend in the undertaking of States parties "to adopt immediate and positive measures designed to eradicate all incitement to, or acts of, such discrimination".

However, paragraphs *(a)* and *(b)* of article 4 are not discretionary, but mandatory. These paragraphs are clear-cut and unambiguous. They provide that States parties "shall declare an offence punishable by law" certain acts enumerated in paragraph *(a)* and "shall declare illegal and prohibit organizations, and also organized and all other propaganda activities which promote and incite racial discrimination" as well as "recognize participation in such organization or activities as an offence punishable by law", as required by paragraph *(b).*

While article 4 (see the introductory paragraph) is generally directed at the eradication of racial discrimination or incitement to such discrimination, paragraphs *(a)* and *(b)* are directed mainly against incitement, or promotion and incitement, to racial discrimination.

It is evident that many States parties have not yet fulfilled all the requirements of article 4 *(a)* and *(b)* of the Convention. This is due in the first instance to the claims of some States parties that there is no racial discrimination in their respective jurisdictions.

However, States parties are bound to enact implementing legislation in accordance with article 4 *(a)* and *(b)* even if they allege that racial discrimination is unknown or that there are no racist organizations in their respective jurisdictions. Article 4 aims at prevention rather than cure; the penalty of the law is supported to deter racism or racial discrimination as well as activities aimed at their promotion or incitement. Of course other measures are recommended by the Convention, particularly in article 7, through teaching, information, education and acculturation, to combat prejudices which lead to racial discrimination and to promote understanding, tolerance and friendship among nations and racial or ethnic groups. But it is also recognized that penal legislation is educative as well as punitive.

Certain States parties have sought to retain the discretion to determine whether and when it is necessary to enact legislation in accordance with the mandatory provisions of article 4. It has been said that this kind of reservation is incompatible with the object and purpose of the Convention and cannot be permitted under article 20, paragraph 2, of the Convention.

It is true that the second sentence of article 20, paragraph 2, provides that "a reservation shall be considered incompatible or inhibitive if at least two thirds of the States parties to this Convention object to it". But this is certainly only one of the modes of determining whether or not a reservation is incompatible with the Convention, withal an extraordinary one. Article 22 of the Convention gives the International Court of Justice the ultimate function of resolving disputes with respect to the interpretation or application of the Convention.

In the absence of a definitive judicial ruling on the admissibility of the reservation in question, the State party concerned might be asked to withdraw its reservation. Indeed, the Committee has made such a recommendation to one State party.

Another factor hindering the full application of article 4 of the Convention is the interpretation that implementation of that article might impair or jeopardize freedom of opinion and expression and of peaceful assembly and association. This is the extreme position. Midway lies the proposition that a "balance" has to be struck between article 4 *(a)* and freedom of speech, and between article 4 *(b)* and freedom of association. The weight of opinion inclines to the view that the rights of free speech and of free association are not absolute, but subject to limitations.

Liberty is not licence. As the former Secretary-General of the United Nations, Dag Hammarskjöld, aptly said: "There is not now and never has been any such thing as unlimited liberty . . . Each man's freedom is limited by that of his neighbours . . . The very existence of a society . . . imposes certain limitations of the freedom of action of all its members, no matter how loose or disorderly the society or communities may be. Limitations . . . on the liberty of individuals are thus inevitable."

Article 29, paragraph 2, of the Universal Declaration of Human Rights is explicit that the exercise of the rights and freedoms guaranteed therein shall be subject only to such limitations as may be determined by law solely for the purpose of securing due recognition and respect for the rights and freedoms of others, and of meeting the just requirements of morality, public order and the general welfare of a democratic society.

While article 30 of the Universal Declaration provides that nothing in the Declaration may be interpreted as implying for any State, group or person any right to engage in any activity or to perform any act aimed at the destruction of any of the rights and freedoms set forth therein, this does not preclude or prohibit reasonable limitations as are expressly set forth in article 29, paragraph 2, which do not have the purpose or effect of destroying those rights and freedoms. Moreover, article 29, paragraph 3, of the Universal Declaration provides that those rights and freedoms many in no case be exercised contrary to the purposes and principles of the United Nations, as set forth in Articles 1 and 2 of the Charter of the United Nations.

Article 19, paragraph 3, of the International Covenant on Civil and Political Rights expressly authorizes restrictions on the exercise of the right to freedom of expression such as are provided by law and are necessary, *(a)* for respect of the rights or reputation of others, or *(b)* for the protection of national security or of public order or of public health or morals.

Article 21 of the International Covenant on Civil and Political Rights also authorizes such restrictions on the right of peaceful assembly as are in conformity with law and are necessary in a democratic society in the interests of national security or public safety, public order, the protection of public health or morals or the protection of the rights and freedoms of others.

Even in societies most zealous of safeguarding the right of free speech, there are laws against defamation and sedition. Laws against incitement to racial discrimination or hatred are certainly no less necessary to protect public order or the rights of others. The majority of the Committee is convinced that the same applies without distinction to the dissemination of ideas based on racial superiority.

Moreover, racial discrimination is a crime under international law and its eradication is a treaty obligation of the States parties to the Convention. More than that, the eradication of racial discrimination has become a peremptory norm of international law *(jus cogens)*.

Many States parties have incorporated in their Constitutions the principle of equality in the enjoyment of human rights guaranteed therein. Others have provided in their Constitutions the principle of nondiscrimination, particularly on grounds of race or colour. Some of these countries contend as a consequence that any act of discrimination or violation of the principle of equality would be unconstitutional. The victim of an unconstitutional act may apply to the competent court for redress. Some countries, however, also provide for the extraordinary remedy of *amparo* as a constitutional right.

The remedy of *amparo* is generally available in case a public official or authority commits the unconstitutional act of discrimination or of violation of the principle of equality. In the event of an affirmative finding by the appropriate tribunal, the public official or authority concerned is ordered to desist from continuing the commission of the offence. If the public official or authority persists, then the official or officials concerned are summarily dismissed from office. It is possible that the remedy of *amparo* is also available to the victim of incitement to racial discrimination in case the offender is a public official. But it is clear that, in the absence of legislation, no remedy is available to the victim of racial discrimination, or incitement thereto, if the offender is a private person.

The legislation of some State parties subject the "dissemination of ideas based on racial superiority or hatred" or "incitement to racial discrimination" to certain conditions, for example that the dissemination or incitement must be intentional, or must have certain objectives such as "to stir up hatred", or that they be "threatening, abusive or insulting", or accompanied by "mocking, slander, insult, threat or other means". Obviously, these conditions are restrictive and ignore the fact that article 4 *(a)* of the Convention declares punishable the mere act of dissemination or incitement, without any conditions.

Most penal codes penalize acts of violence or incitement to such acts directed against any individual or group of individuals. These should satisfy one of the requirements of article 4 *(a)*, although it would be within the spirit, if not the letter, of that article to enact legislation specifically referring to violence or incitement thereto directed against "any race or group of persons of another colour or ethnic origin", perhaps making it an aggravating circumstance.

General penal legislation making accomplices or accessories to crime also punishable would cover "the provision of any assistance to racist activities, including the financing thereof", if such racist activities are made a crime in the first place.

Some States parties have Constitutions which guarantee the right of peaceful assembly and association and also provide that associations may be established only for a lawful purpose. The establishment of an organization or association with promotes or incites to racial discrimination would thus be unconstitutional because it was not established for a lawful purpose. The remedy in such a case varies from denial of permit or registration to dissolution, in the event that the organization or association has already been registered or granted a permit. In any case, legislation would still be necessary to penalize those who form or create such an organization or association, or those who participate in its illegal activities, that is, in the promotion of and incitement to racial discrimination.

There is also legislation in most countries against the establishment of associations or organizations with an illegal purpose. In the absence of such legislation, some countries contend that existing legislation penalizing the promotion of or incitement to discimination, has the effect of discouraging the establishment of organizations dedicated to such purposes. The Committee takes the view that further legislation is necessary to declare illegal and prohibit such organizations.

Some States prohibit organizations vested with an unlawful purpose. Legislation is directed either to the prohibition of their registration or their dissolution thereafter, or both. In common law countries, the term "unlawful" is distinguished from "illegal" in the sense that an unlawful act may not always give rise to penal sanctions. Unlawful acts usually result in civil liability, as in the case of torts. It follows that the imposition of civil liability falls short of the requirement in article 4 to declare certain acts or activities "as an offence punishable by law".

Article 4 *(b)* requires States parties not only to "declare illegal and prohibit organizations, and also organized and all other propaganda activities, which promote and incite racial discrimination", but also to "recognize participation in such organizations or activities as an offence punishable by law".

It is obvious that this provision of the Convention or any similar provision in the Constitution of a State party requires implementing legislation. *A fortiori*, this applies also to article 4 *(a)*. The Constitution of a State, like the Convention, can only decree that certain acts should be punishable by law. Rarely does a Constitution itself provide the penalty, as in the case of high treason, for example.

It is clear that constitutional provisions alone, without implementing legislation, would not satisfy the mandatory requirements of article 4 of the Convention for States parties to declare an offence punishable by law the acts enumerated in paragraphs *(a)* and *(b)*.

It will be seen that many States parties require time in order to be able to comply with their obligations under the Convention. It is realized that adoption of legislation is a slow process. Nowhere is this observation more apt than with reference to article 4.

It is not enough that the executive should recommend to the legislature or to parliament the enactment of legislation to implement article 4. The experience of at least four States parties shows that the executive should follow up its recommendation. The legislature, no less than the executive, is bound to take action.

However, it should be stated that States parties should complete the process of adjusting their legislation in accordance with article 4 within a reasonable time. A certain amount of political will is necessary to give impetus to the legislative process. It is an accepted principle that treaties should be observed in good faith by contracting parties. *Pacta sunt servanda.*

SEE ALSO *Totalitarian Ideologies.*

RECOMMENDATION ON CONSENT TO MARRIAGE, MINIMUM AGE FOR MARRIAGE AND REGISTRATION OF MARRIAGES (1965). The recommendation deals with the same problems as the CONVENTION ON CONSENT TO MARRIAGE, MINIMUM AGE FOR MARRIAGE AND REGISTRATION OF MARRIAGES (1962) and is intended to apply to States which have not become parties to the convention. Whereas the convention does not specify a minimum age for marriage, the recommendation provides that the minimum age to be specified by States should be not less than 15 years of age.

The recommendation was adopted by the General Assembly on 1 November 1965 (resolution 2018 [XX]); the text, annexed to the resolution, is as follows:

The General Assembly,

Recognizing that the family group should be strengthened because it is the basic unit of every society, and that men and women of full age have the right to marry and to found a family, that they are entitled to equal rights as to marriage and that marriage shall be entered into only with the free and full consent of the intending spouses, in accordance with the provisions of article 16 of the Universal Declaration of Human Rights,

Recalling its resolution 843 (IX) of 17 December 1954,

Recalling further article 2 of the Supplementary Convention on the Abolition of Slavery, the Slave Trade, and Institutions and Practices Similar to Slavery of 1956, which makes certain provisions concerning the age of marriage, consent to marriage and registration of marriages,

Recalling also that Article 13, paragraph 1 b, of the Charter of the United Nations provides that the General Assembly shall make recommendations for the purpose of assisting in the realization of human rights and fundamental freedoms for all without distinction as to race, sex, language or religion,

Recalling likewise that, under Article 64 of the Charter, the Economic and Social Council may make arrangements with the Members of the United Nations to obtain reports on the steps taken to give effect to its own recommendations and to recommendations on matters falling within its competence made by the General Assembly,

1. Recommends that, where not already provided by existing legislative or other measures, each Member State should take the necessary steps, in accordance with its constitutional processes and its traditional and religious practices, to adopt such legislative or other measures as may be appropriate to give effect to the following principles:

Principle I. (a) No marriage shall be legally entered into without the full and free consent of both parties, such consent to be expressed by them in person, after due publicity and in the presence of the authority competent to solemnize the marriage and of witnesses, as prescribed by law.

(b) Marriage by proxy shall be permitted only when the competent authorities are satisfied that each party has, before a competent authority and in such manner as may be prescribed by law, fully and freely expressed consent before witnesses and not withdrawn such consent.

Principle II. Member States shall take legislative action to specify a minimum age for marriage, which in any case shall not be less than fifteen years of age; no marriage shall be legally entered into by any person under this age, except where a competent authority has granted a dispensation as to age, for serious reasons, in the interest of the intending spouses.

Principle III. All marriages shall be registered in an appropriate official register by the competent authority.

2. Recommends that each Member State should bring the Recommendation on Consent to Marriage, Minimum Age for Marriage and Registration of Marriages contained in the present resolution before the authorities competent to enact legislation or to take other action at the earliest

practicable moment and, if possible, no later than eighteen months after the adoption of the Recommendation;

3. Recommends that Member States should inform the Secretary-General, as soon as possible after the action referred to in paragraph 2 above, of the measures taken under the present Recommendation to bring it before the competent authority or authorities, with particulars regarding the authority or authorities considered as competent:

4. Recommends further that Member States should report to the Secretary-General at the end of three years, and thereafter at intervals of five years, on their law and practice with regard to the matters dealt with in the present Recommendation, showing the extent to which effect has been given or is proposed to be given to the provisions of the Recommendation and such modifications as have been found or may be found necessary in adapting or applying it;

5. Requests the Secretary-General to prepare for the Commission on the Status of Women a document containing the reports received from Governments concerning methods of implementing the three basic principles of the present Recommendation;

6. Invites the Commission on the Status of Women to examine the reports received from Member States pursuant to the present Recommendation and to report thereon to the Economic and Social Council with such recommendations as it may deem fitting.

REFUGEES. An international term defined in the Statute of the Office of the UNITED NATIONS HIGH COMMISSIONER FOR REFUGEES (Section 6 B) as "any . . . person who is outside the country of his nationality or, if he has no nationality, the country of his former habitual residence, because he has or had well-founded fear of persecution by reason of his race, religion, nationality or political opinion and is unable or, because of such fear, is unwilling to avail himself of the protection of the government of the country of his nationality, or, if he has no nationality, to return to the country of his former habitual residence."

The UNIVERSAL DECLARATION OF HUMAN RIGHTS proclaims that:

Article 13. 2. Everyone has the right to leave any country, including his own, and to return to his country.

Article 14. 1. Everyone has the right to seek and enjoy in other countries asylum from persecution.

2. This right may not be invoked in the case of prosecutions genuinely arising from non-political crimes or from acts contrary to the purposes and principles of the United Nations.

The DECLARATION ON TERRITORIAL ASYLUM recognizes "that the grant of asylum by a State to persons entitled to invoke article 14 of the Universal Declaration of Human Rights is a peaceful and humanitarian act and that, as such, it cannot be regarded as unfriendly by any other State." It recommends that States should base themselves, in their practices relating to territorial asylum, on the following principles:

Article 1. 1. Asylum granted by a State, in the exercise of its sovereignty, to persons entitled to invoke article 14 of the Universal Declaration of Human Rights, including persons struggling against colonialism, shall be respected by all other States.

2. The right to seek and to enjoy asylum may not be invoked by any person with respect to whom there are serious reasons for considering that he has committed a crime against peace, a war crime or a crime against humanity, as defined in the international instruments drawn up to make provision in respect of such crimes.

3. It shall rest with the State granting asylum to evaluate the grounds for the grant of asylum.

Article 2. 1. The situation of persons referred to in article 1, paragraph 1, is, without prejudice to the sovereignty of States and the purposes and principles of the United Nations, of concern to the international community.

2. Where a State finds difficulty in granting or continuing to grant asylum, States individually or jointly or through the United Nations shall consider, in a spirit of international solidarity, appropriate measures to lighten the burden on that State.

Article 3. 1. No person referred to in article 1, paragraph 1, shall be subjected to measures such as rejection at the frontier or, if he has already entered the territory in which he seeks asylum, expulsion or compulsory return to any State where he may be subjected to persecution.

2. Exception may be made to the foregoing principle only for overriding reasons of national security or in order to safeguard the population, as in the case of a mass influx of persons.

3. Should a State decide in any case that exception to the principle stated in paragraph 1 of this article would be justified, it shall consider the possibility of granting to the person concerned, under such conditions as it may deem appropriate, an opportunity, whether by way of provisional asylum or otherwise, of going to another State.

Article 4. States granting asylum shall not permit persons who have received asylum to engage in activities contrary to the purposes and principles of the United Nations.

At the regional level, the main instrument defining standards for the treatment of refugees is the AFRICAN CONVENTION GOVERNING THE SPECIFIC ASPECTS OF REFUGEE PROBLEMS IN AFRICA.

Various aspects of the situation of refugees are dealt with in the CONVENTION RELATING TO THE STATUS OF REFUGEES and its PROTOCOL, which define the term "refugee" and define the juridical status and the rights of persons falling within this category.

Under the Statute of the Office of the United Nations High Commissioner for Refugees, such an office is established, and the high commissioner is authorized to provide international protection to refugees and to seek permanent solutions for their problems. The high commissioner follows policy directives given him by the UN General Assembly and is assisted in his work by the Executive Committee of the High Commissioner's Program.

In his report to the 1988 session of the General Assembly, the high commissioner summed up the work of his office during the latter half of 1987 and the early months of 1988 as follows (UN Doc. A/43/12, chap. I, para. 9–15):

Developments in the field of international protection of refugees, during the reporting period, have once again demonstrated the magnitude and complexity of the refugee problem. Concentrations and flows of refugees can be found in all parts of the world. While the circumstances leading to these refugee flows are varied and intricate, their common feature is that the persons concerned have been compelled to leave their respective countries of origin in order to find security and protection elsewhere and they are all in need of, and entitled to, international protection.

It is the responsibility of UNHCR to provide this protection to refugees to compensate for their lack or the denial of national protection. This task can, however, only be achieved through effective co-operation of States and relevant intergovernmental and non-governmental organizations.

The largest concentrations of refugees are currently located in the Asian and Middle Eastern regions. Some of the refugee situations in those regions are also among the most protracted; more than one has now lasted for well over a decade. This is the case, for example, in South-East Asia where several refugee flows have lasted for over 13 years. The period under review saw the onset of further restrictive tendencies in the region with States seeking, at times with appalling results, to stem the flow of asylum-seekers. If further deaths and suffering of refugees are to be avoided, a concerted effort must be undertaken involving the international community at large in support of the first asylum countries in the region. Elsewhere in the Asian region, positive developments occurred that may lead to the cessation of the hostilities that had originally provoked one of the largest refugee flows in recent times. It is hoped that, with the co-operation of all the parties involved, circumstances may now be created that may allow for the voluntary return of the refugees.

To the already substantial portion of the refugee population that is found on the African continent, the period under review witnessed an increase of well over half a million refugees. Even though, in many instances, the reception of the refugees entailed great sacrifices for the receiving countries, they continued, in the main, their policy of hospitality. At the same time, close to 150,000 refugees returned voluntarily to their respective countries of origin. By and large the voluntary repatriats were able to return in conditions of safety and dignity. Experience shows, however, that if larger numbers are to be afforded an opportunity to avail themselves of voluntary repatriation, countries concerned must redress the causes that originally led to the refugee flow. A particular concern in the region was the vulnerable situation in which many of the refugees find themselves because of the fact that they are located within, or in the vicinity of, conflict areas. In several instances, refugees were subjected to military and armed attacks.

In the American hemisphere, the situation of refugees from Central American countries continued to be the main source of concern to the Office. As in other parts of the world, the refugee phenomenon is but part of a larger political, social and economic situation that rendered the task of providing international protection extremely difficult. Even so, encouraging developments took place during the reporting period as the countries in the region sought to find peaceful and humanitarian solutions to the refugee problem. More than 10,000 refugees returned to their countries of origin voluntarily. Nevertheless, considerable problems remain, in particular with regard to the physical safety of the refugees and the need to gain respect by all parties concerned for the strictly humanitarian and civilian character of the refugees' status.

As far as Europe is concerned, the High Commissioner continued a series of consultations with countries in the region with a view to reaching humane solutions to the problems of refugees and asylum-seekers. The primary preoccupation of the Governments concerned continued to be the arrival of non-European asylum-seekers into Western Europe. This situation was compounded by xenophobic attitudes adopted by segments of the population, and the countries concerned responded with a variety of legal and administrative measures aimed at containing the situation. Such measures ranged from continuing to apply an unduly restrictive interpretation of the refugee definition contained in the United Nations Convention of 1951 relating to the Status of Refugees to the rejection of asylum-seekers at the border on the sole ground that they had been present in another country where they could have sought asylum. In seeking humane solutions to the problems of those who, as a result of persecution or out of fear for their safety, seek asylum in European countries, UNHCR also reinforced its co-operation with the European Community as well as with the network of non-governmental organizations established by the European Consultation on Refugees and Exiles.

Although States have generally continued their efforts to ensure that refugees and asylum-seekers are protected, serious problems emerged, sometimes with extremely serious consequences for the refugees and asylum-seekers concerned. Thus, grave problems remain in the areas of admission and asylum, expulsion and detention and the physical protection of refugees. Increased efforts by the international community and UNHCR in these and related areas of the international protection of refugees are needed to ensure that all refugees, irrespective of their race, country or region of origin, ethnic origin, membership of a particular social group or political opinion are treated in accordance with accepted international standards.

In his report, the high commissioner further sums up the existing situation as regards recognition and enjoyment of the principles of international protection and refugee rights as follows (*Ibid.*, chap. I, B, para. 16–35):

1. Admission and Asylum

For refugees to enjoy basic protection, it is essential that they be admitted into the territory of a State and granted at least temporary asylum. The main international refugee instruments, however, contain no provisions dealing directly with admission and asylum. The closest they come to addressing the issue is in their *non-refoulement* provisions that protect a refugee from forceful return to a country where he or she may face persecution, as well as in articles that hold that refugees should not be penalized for having entered the territory of a State in an illegal manner if they come directly from their country of origin.

The Universal Declaration of Human Rights embodies

the principle that everyone has the right to seek and enjoy in other countries asylum from persecution. A similar provision is contained in the 1967 United Nations Declaration on Territorial Asylum, contained in General Assembly resolution 2312 (XXII) of 14 December 1967. Asylum remains, however, an attribute of State sovereignty and the right to be granted, as opposed to seeking asylum, has not been translated into a binding international legal norm.

Given the absence of firm legal obligations to grant asylum, it is encouraging to note that many States continue liberal asylum policies. Whether persons flee their countries for fear of persecution in the sense of article 1 of the United Nations Convention of 1951 relating to the Status of Refugees, or as a result of armed conflict, foreign aggression or occupation, gross violations of human rights or internal upheavals, there is widespread recognition that they should be admitted and granted at least temporary asylum. Thus, the majority of today's asylum-seekers continue to be admitted into the territory of States and granted, *de jure* or *de facto*, some form of asylum. It should be noted that the majority of these countries—particularly those accommodating large-scale influxes—are among the world's poorest.

If the overall situation with respect to admission and asylum remains on the whole positive, some worrying trends need to be highlighted. One of these involves asylum-seekers who sought asylum in countries far away from their own. Sometimes they travelled uninterruptedly from their country, travelling through some other States to a third country. In other instances, they travelled from a country where they might appear already to have found protection, in order to seek asylum or a durable solution in another State, without first obtaining the consent of the authorities of that State. In many instances, the concerned asylum-seekers, in addition, travelled on forged documents and/or destroyed their documents en route with a view to misleading the authorities and frustrating their efforts to return the asylum-seekers to an intermediate country.

Partly as a result of these movements, a growing number of States introduced, or further reinforced, measures aimed at restricting the entry of asylum-seekers. These included: visa restrictions for growing numbers of nationalities, penalties on airlines carrying insufficiently documented asylum-seekers, penalties on persons assisting in organizing the illegal entry of asylum-seekers into the territories of States, screening procedures at national borders, restrictions in assistance and the right to work, and systematic and prolonged detention of asylum-seekers.

At the same time, some States also continued to resort to much stricter interpretations of the notion of a refugee, as defined in the United Nations Convention of 1951 relating to the Status of Refugees and its 1967 Protocol. Some of these States, furthermore, required that asylum-seekers meet unduly high or unrealistic standards of proof. The combined effect of such measures was that large numbers of persons were frustrated in their efforts to seek asylum from persecution and, even when fulfilling refugee criteria in the sense of the United Nations Convention of 1951 relating to the Status of Refugees, were denied the protection stipulated in that Convention.

An equally worrying trend consisted in the practice of some States to refuse admission to asylum-seekers on the grounds that they could, or should, have sought it elsewhere. In some instances, this led to the creation of "orbit" situations, some of which eventually resulted in *refoulement*. In one particular case involving asylum-seekers travelling by small boats, a comparable practice adopted by one country was reported to have resulted in the deaths of more than 100 persons.

A fundamental tenet of the international system for providing protection to refugees is that the granting of asylum is a peaceful and non-hostile act. Nevertheless, in one instance, as a result of the pressure exerted on neighbouring countries by one particular State, refugees from that country could not, for reasons of national security, be granted asylum in those former countries. Other States in the region offered asylum, however, and several hundred asylum-seekers were relocated to these States during the reporting period.

2. Non-refoulement and Other Rights

The most fundamental of protection principles and the first of refugee rights is that of *non-refoulement*, which provides that no person shall be subjected to measures such as rejection at the border, or, if already in the territory of a country of refuge, expulsion or compulsory return to any country where he or she may have reason to fear persecution or danger to life, liberty or freedom because of reasons pertinent to refugee status. Apart from being embodied in a large number of international treaties and declarations, this principle is today considered as part of general international law.

As in previous years, most States continued to adhere to the principle of *non-refoulement*. Nevertheless, the reporting period also saw several noteworthy exceptions. Thus, some countries continued their practice of pushing back asylum-seekers. Other States occasionally resorted to the *refoulement* of larger groups of asylum-seekers and even some recognized refugees. The total number of refugees and asylum-seekers who were subject to *refoulement* during the reporting period exceeded several thousand. This constitutes an extremely worrisome and noteworthy deterioration in recent years.

Another basic principle of refugee protection embodied in article 32 of the 1951 United Nations Convention prohibits States from expelling refugees who are lawfully in their territory except on grounds of national security or public order. During the reporting period, expulsions in disregard of article 32 were limited in number but nevertheless affected several groups of refugees. In one instance, many of the expelled refugees were allowed to return to the asylum country concerned after seeking judicial remedy.

Unjustified detention of refugees and asylum-seekers is contrary to basic principles of refugee protection. It will be recalled that, in 1986, the Executive Committee of the Programme of the High Commissioner at its thirty-seventh session, adopted a conclusion on this matter. Through this conclusion, the members of the Executive Committee confirmed that detention of refugees and asylum-seekers should only be resorted to if necessary and only on grounds prescribed by law for certain purposes. Those purposes were defined as being to verify identity; to determine the elements on which the claim to refugee status was based; to deal with cases where refugees and asylum-seekers have destroyed their travel and/or identity documents or have used false documents; and to protect national security or public order.

Even so, many hundreds of refugees and asylum-seekers were detained during the reporting period for no other reason than illegal entry or for having overstayed the validity of their entry visa. Such detentions were in violation of article 31 of the United Nations Convention of 1951 relating to the

Status of Refugees and disregarded the fact that their illegal entry or presence was due entirely to the need to find asylum. In several instances, detention measures were enforced as a means of discouraging further arrivals and/or were part of a deliberate government policy to deny asylum to persons coming from certain countries or regions. In some instances, the conditions of detention gave rise to particular concern as they did not meet internationally-recognized minimum standards of detention. Also worrisome were the facts that many refugees and asylum-seekers had to spend considerable periods in detention, sometimes exceeding one year, with no possibility of judicial or administrative review of the detention measure, and that detention measures were applied equally to refugee children.

Economic and social rights of refugees are important, not only so as to facilitate their integration, but also to preserve their dignity and self-respect; these latter reasons applying equally to asylum-seekers and those who have only received temporary asylum. The most fundamental of these rights—the right to gainful occupation—is reflected in both the United Nations Convention of 1951 relating to the Status of Refugees and in other international instruments, such as the Universal Declaration of Human Rights and the International Covenant on Economic, Social and Cultural Rights (General Assembly resolution 2200 A [XXI], annex).

The enjoyment by refugees of economic and social rights are, however, fraught with limitations. In some situations, this is due to the absence of specific programmes aimed at assisting refugees to find work, obtain training and other facilities, all of which may be required in countries with high rates of unemployment. In some countries, the sheer number of refugees makes the enjoyment of these rights meaningless as no employment is to be found. The difficulty of finding work may be further increased by the absence of appropriate mechanisms whereby refugee status can be recognized, thereby putting the refugees on a par with ordinary aliens or illegal immigrants. As regards asylum-seekers whose status had not been determined, their situation was even more difficult, particularly in countries which introduced or strengthened already existing restrictions on their right to work.

Limitations also existed on the refugees' right to education. Many countries do not have enough educational institutions to meet the needs of their own citizens let alone those of refugees and asylum-seekers. Special assistance programmes went a long way to meet the basic education needs of refugees living in settlements and camps, whereas the needs of refugees living in urban centres were largely unmet.

At its thirty-eighth session, the Executive Committee of the Programme of the High Commissioner considered the issue of Convention travel documents. Although the great majority of States parties to the United Nations Convention of 1951 relating to the Status of Refugees follow the provisions of article 28 of that Convention on the issuance of such documents, certain problems remained. These related in particular to the issuance and renewal of Convention travel documents, their geographic or temporal validity, their recognition for visa and admission purposes and the transfer of responsibility for their issue. In its conclusion on travel documents for refugees, the Executive Committee, *inter alia*, urged States parties to the United Nations Convention of 1951 relating to the Status of Refugees and/or its 1967 Protocol to take appropriate legislative or administrative measures to implement effectively the provisions of these instruments concerning the issue of Convention travel documents.

Many States continued to issue identity documents to refugees during the reporting period, sometimes with UNHCR assistance. In most instances, these documents attested not only to the holders' identity but also to their refugee status, thereby enabling them to benefit from the various rights of refugees.

3. Family Reunification

During the period under review, UNHCR noted that certain Governments introduced measures to facilitate family reunification, such as the lifting of restrictions which limited the rights to family reunification to those refugees who had sufficient means to support their family members; or in accepting family members belonging to the extended family, namely, siblings, parents, grandparents, etc. Progress was further achieved in connection with documentation requirements, whereby some States have been more flexible in cases where refugees were unable to provide documentary evidence in support of claimed family relationships. Positive results were also achieved with respect to reuniting refugees with family members who had remained in their country of origin.

Despite the progress made in some areas, obstacles still remained in many countries. These included the length of the administrative procedures prevailing mainly in countries with heavy backlogs in the processing of asylum requests; the lack of resources to support dependent family members; difficulties in securing employment and adequate housing; the inability of some refugees to prove family relationships; and the requirement to obtain exit permits from countries of origin for the purpose of family reunification abroad. As regards the lack of documentation, the Office was particularly concerned that some countries did not hesitate to contact the authorities of the refugee's country of origin to seek verification of documentation.

After considering the report, the General Assembly on 8 December 1988 (resolution 43/117), recognizing that the enhancement of basic economic and social rights is essential to the achievement of self-sufficiency and family security for refugees, as well as to the process of re-establishing the dignity of the human person and realizing durable solutions to refugee problems, commended those states that, despite severe economic and development problems of their own, continue to admit large numbers of refugees and displaced persons and emphasized the need to share the burden of those states to the maximum extent possible through international assistance.

Stressing the need for the international community to continue to provide adequate resettlement opportunities for those refugees for whom no other durable solution may be in sight, in particular for refugees who have already spent an inordinately long time in camps, the Assembly urged all States to support the high commissioner in his efforts to achieve durable solutions to the problem of refugees and displaced persons, primarily through voluntary rapatriation or return, including assistance as appropriate to returnees or, wherever appropriate, through integration into countries of asylum or through resettlement in third countries. It also expressed deep appreciation for the valuable material and humanitarian response of receiving countries and urged the international community, in accordance with the principle of international solidarity and burden-sharing, to assist those countries to enable them to cope with the additional burden that the care for refugees and asylum-seekers represents.

REFUGEES: CHILDREN. The particular problems experienced by children who are refugees, which often expose them to practices having effects similar to those of slavery, have for some time been a matter of special concern to the Office of the UNITED NATIONS HIGH COMMISSIONER FOR REFUGEES. A standing Working Group on Refugee Children At Risk was established in that office early in 1987 to monitor those problems and to suggest ways of ameliorating or remedying them.

In October 1987, the high commissioner presented a paper to his executive committee (UN Doc. EC/SCP/46) enumerating the problems and the possible solutions. After examining the subject, the executive committee adopted a series of conclusions on refugee children, in which it:

(a) Expressed appreciation to the High Commissioner for his Report on Refugee Children (EC/SCP/46) and noted with serious concern the violations of their human rights in different areas of the world and their special needs and vulnerability within the broader refugee population;

(b) Recognized that refugee children constitute approximately one half of the world's refugee population and that the situation in which they live often gives rise to special protection and assistance problems as well as to problems in the area of durable solutions;

(c) Reiterated the widely-recognized principle that children must be among the first to receive protection and assistance;

(d) Stressed that all action taken on behalf of refugee children must be guided by the principle of the best interests of the child as well as by the principle of family unity;

(e) Condemned the exposure of refugee children to physical violence and other violations of their basic rights, including through sexual abuse, trade in children, acts or piracy, military or armed attacks, forced recruitment, political exploitation or arbitrary detention, and called for national and international action to prevent such violations and assist the victims;

(f) Urged States to take appropriate measures to register the births of refugee children born in countries of asylum;

(g) Expressed its concern over the increasing number of cases of statelessness among refugee children;

(h) Recommended that children who are accompanied by their parents should be treated as refugees if either of the parents is determined to be a refugee;

(i) Underlined the special situation of unaccompanied children and children separated from their parents, who are in the care of other families, including their needs as regards determination of their status, provision for their physical and emotional support and efforts to trace parents or relatives; and in this connection, recalled the relevant paragraphs of Conclusion No. 24 (XXXII) on Family Reunification;

(j) Called upon the High Commissioner to ensure that individual assessments are conducted and adequate social histories prepared for unaccompanied children and children separated from their parents, who are in the care of other families, to facilitate provision for their immediate needs, the analysis of the long-term as well as immediate viability of existing foster arrangements, and the planning and implementation of appropriate durable solutions;

(k) Noted that while the best durable solution for an unaccompanied refugee child will depend on the particular circumstances of the case, the possibility of voluntary repatriation should at all times be kept under review, keeping in mind the best interests of the child and the possible difficulties of determining the voluntary character of repatriation;

(l) Stressed the need for internationally and nationally supported programmes geared to preventive action, special assistance and rehabilitation for disabled refugee children and encouraged States to participate in the "Twenty or More" Plan providing for the resettlement of disabled refugee children;

(m) Noted with serious concern the detrimental effects that extended stays in camps have on the development of refugee children and called for international action to mitigate such effects and provide durable sessions as soon as possible;

(n) Recognized the importance of meeting the special psychological, religious, cultural and recreational needs of refugee children in order to ensure their emotional stability and development;

(o) Reaffirmed the fundamental right of refugee children to education and called upon all States, individually and collectively, to intensify their efforts, in co-operation with the High Commissioner, to ensure that all refugee children benefit from primary education of a satisfactory quality, that respects their cultural identity and is oriented towards an understanding of the country of asylum;

(p) Recognized the need of refugee children to pursue further levels of education and recommended that the High Commissioner consider the provision of post-primary education within the general programme of assistance;

(q) Called upon all States, in co-operation with UNHCR and concerned agencies, to develop and/or support programmes to address nutritional and health risks faced by refugee children, including programmes to ensure an adequate, well-balanced and safe diet, general immunization and primary health care;

(r) Recommended regular and timely assessment and review of the needs of refugee children, either on an individual basis or through sample surveys, prepared in co-operation with the country of asylum, taking into account all relevant factors such as age, sex, personality, family, religion, social and cultural background and the situation of the local population, and benefiting from the active involvement of the refugee community itself;

(s) Reaffirmed the need to promote continuing and expanded co-operation between UNHCR and other concerned agencies and bodies active in the fields of assistance to refugee children and protection, including through the development of legal and social standards;

(t) Noted the importance of further study of the needs of refugee children by UNHCR, other intergovernmental and non-governmental agencies and national authorities, with a view to identification of additional support programmes and reorientation as necessary of existing ones;

(u) Called upon the High Commissioner to develop further, in consultation with concerned organizations, guidelines to promote co-operation between UNHCR and these organizations to improve the international protection, physical security, well-being and normal psycho-social development of refugee children;

(v) Called upon the High Commissioner to maintain the UNHCR Working Group on Refugee Children at Risk as his focal point on refugee children, to strengthen the Working Group and to inform the members of the Executive Committee, on a regular basis, of its work.

REFUGEES: MASSIVE EXODUSES. At its 1980 session, the attention of the UN COMMISSION ON HUMAN RIGHTS was drawn to movements of large masses of refugees and displaced persons, in various parts of the world, and the immense burden which such massive movements of population—which were frequently the results of violations of human rights—placed on the first host countries. The commission requested the Secretary-General (resolution 30/XXXVI), in cases where any large-scale exoduses became a matter of international concern, to make concrete recommendations for ameliorating them. Later that year, the General Assembly also expressed deep concern (resolution 35/196) at the large-scale exoduses and displacements and called upon the commission to recommend solutions for the problems they caused.

In 1981, the commission invited its chairman (resolution 29 [XXXVII]) to appoint an individual of recognized international standing as special rapporteur to study the question of human rights and mass exoduses. Sadruddin Aga Khan, former UN High Commissioner for Refugees, was entrusted with this task.

In his *Study on Human Rights and Massive Exoduses* (UN Doc. E/CN.4/1503), presented to the commission at its 1982 session, the special rapporteur pointed out (para. 1–5) that:

The phenomenon of mass movements of people is not new. From earliest times men have been fleeing one another's intolerance or migrating in search of land and livelihood. For the last several years, however, the number and magnitude of flows of refugees and displaced persons have been such as to cause increasing concern within the international community. By the beginning of the 1980s, numbers exceeded ten million, with the exodus from certain countries reaching haemorrhage proportions. At the same time, increasingly large migratory movements within coun-

tries and regions have begun to pose economic and social problems not hitherto experienced on quite the same scale.

In the last 35 years, with the emergence from colonialism of about a hundred new States, often after a considerable struggle and with an inheritance of artificial national boundaries, fragile national unity, underdeveloped economies, too few cadres and boundless logistical problems, the world has seen an unprecedented proliferation of tensions and conflicts. New ideologies misunderstood by and unacceptable to portions of the population, blatant racial discrimination, civil wars, the terror tactics of more than one dictator, foreign invasion or acute economic hardship have caused millions to decide that any life outside their own country must be more bearable than the present one.

The recent mass flights of people to neighbouring countries not only represent wholescale human deprivation and misery, but have come to place upon their hosts and upon the international community as a whole burdens which it is proving increasingly difficult to bear. The three solutions which until recently enabled most refugee situations to be resolved, namely voluntary repatriation, local settlement and resettlement in third countries, can no longer suggest an answer in every case. While circumstances in the home country remain substantially the same and as long as there is no dialogue between the governments most directly concerned, there is no hope of paving the way to a voluntary return. Where the refugees are numbered in hundreds of thousands—or even millions—and land and other resources are scarce, programmes of local integration are practically unthinkable. As for resettlement in third countries, the Indo-Chinese diaspora brought home to over twenty countries which had offered special quotas at the height of the crisis in South East Asia in mid-1979 the difficulty of integrating refugees from an entirely different ethnic and cultural background. Few have found it possible to renew their generous offers of places at anything like the same level—if at all.

Meanwhile, in some underdeveloped areas the presence of millions of uprooted people, sometimes accompanied by as many head of livestock, is playing havoc with the struggling economies of the host countries and posing a dire ecological threat which should not go unchecked. As for economic migrants, world-wide economic recession has meant that they are no longer in demand on the same scale as before. Yet millions still strive to reach more affluent countries in the hope of finding work and a better life.

As a result of all these factors, many governments have reached the conclusion that serious attention must be paid to analysing the forces which get people on the move, with a view particularly to considering whether means can be found to avert new large-scale refugee situations. At the same time, the need has been felt to study the phenomenon of mass exodus in the context of human rights. Hence the initiative of the United Nations Commission on Human Rights contained in its Resolution 29 (XXXVII) to appoint a Special Rapporteur.

Data presented in the study indicate, in the words of the special rapporteur, that "all mass exodus which took place during the decade under review (1971–1981) poured forth from regions where the prevailing situation prevented individual citizens from exercising their political rights. It should be noted, however, that this constraint is not, in itself, the essential cause for large movements of population. Indeed, some countries seem to have succeeded in compensating the absence of democracy by ensuring that their peoples have access to material well being. This, coupled with restrictions on freedom of movement, appears to have stemmed the flow of what is still limited one-way traffic from some countries."

A second major cause of mass exodus is described as "conflict between the desire of certain nationalities absorbed within nation-states to retain at least part of their cultural heritage (including their own language), and the policy of the central authorities to phase out (or stamp out) the distinct linguistic and cultural patterns of a homogenous national population. Such conflict between centralization and regionalism has sometimes been violent enough to lead to an exodus of quite considerable proportions."

The special rapporteur's conclusions, based on his analysis of mass exodus situations which had developed during the decade under review in 22 countries, in many of which he had personally played a role in his former capacity as United Nations High Commissioner for Refugees, were as follows (para. 114–129):

To summarize very briefly the foregoing, the overview of the past decade amply demonstrates that the consequences of mass exodus situations may be measured in terms not only of human suffering but also of threats to national or regional peace and stability.

People leave for a variety of reasons, and usually as a combination of factors rather than a single one. The social contract has failed temporarily or permanently. Modernization and progress have made casualties of people who held certain customs and traditions too dear. In the chaos of war and post-war reconstruction, populations may have been repeatedly uprooted, and thereby conditioned for a further uprooting—from their country—when the going is hard. Colonialism left a heritage of artificial boundaries and structurally imbalanced economies. The repressive tactics of white minority régimes have made many victims. Most provisions of the Declaration of Human Rights have been violated.

These "push factors" must be viewed against a series of economic realities in developing countries, such as high population growth, global food insecurity and a hunger-induced rise in death rates, inflation, unemployment, the flight of skilled manpower and ecological deterioration—which taken in combination may bring large sectors of the population of the world's poorest countries to the threshold of economic distress. Deficiencies in infrastructure, the high cost of equipping modern armed forces, loss or reduction in both trade and aid and the calamitous impact of oil price rises have in the last ten years further handicapped young nations lacking any tradition of statehood. One result has frequently been the attempt to create national cohesion along somewhat authoritarian single-party lines, a fact which helps explain what may be termed the "integrative revolution" facing many developing nations following their accession to independence. Hence the difficulty in creating conditions in which normal human rights could

be enjoyed, and hence a high incidence of mass exodus in the countries classified as some of the poorest in the world.

The other side of the coin is a series of "pull factors" which include an increasingly free flow of information from North to South on economic opportunity, and a belief widely shared by beleaguered potential refugees/migrants that their problems will be better understood by the authorities of countries which uphold human rights. The existence of liberalized immigration regulations or refugee quotas must exert some degree of magnetism, particularly in the case of skilled manpower seeking upward mobility, as may the institutionalization of aid close to a troubled country's border.

As a consequence of all these factors, mass movements have become more commonplace, and the principle of the law of asylum has been eroded. It would seem to be time to update refugee, nationality and labour law, and to re-examine asylum practice. Furthermore, to ensure greater clarity in mass influx situations as to numbers of people to be assisted, a mechanism seems to be called for to carry out refugee population census in an impartial manner.

Since mass exodus frequently takes place from economically-disadvantaged countries, and since those governments which generally provide the means to mount humanitarian assistance programmes are very often those which are giving development aid, there appears to be a strong case for a more integrated approach to the planning of aid. Various ways in which this might be tackled are suggested in the preceding chapter. At the same time, when mass exodus does occur, it is important to see the problem in the broad perspective of the position of both "refugee-producing" and "refugee-receiving" countries. A simultaneity of approach should help in identifying the long-term solution, and with regard to the administration of humanitarian assistance, will ensure that this in itself does not constitute a "pull factor" by there being any imbalance in the overall picture. Moreover, standardization of multilateral aid criteria will help to iron out other "wrinkles" in the international community's approach to these most important questions.

It is suggested that the basic concept of an appropriate United Nations presence can be extended to humanitarian emergencies, as distinct from peace-keeping operations in the accepted sense.

It has been found in studying mass exodus that all these situations conform to a certain pattern common to which is the involvement, at an earlier or later stage, of a miscellany of concerned parties, particularly in relation to the provision of essential relief and the production of a considerable volume of informed comment after the event. Yet all the characteristics of this pattern of upheaval and exodus taken together point to certain lacunae which it will be well to attempt to fill if there is to be a lessening of human suffering and of related frictions between States. Three observations are called for here.

Firstly, there is an obvious lack of contact in man-made exodus situations between the authorities of the country of origin and those of the country (or countries) of asylum. It would appear that those who leave are "written off" by their government, more often than not being labelled as traitors, criminals, undesirables, subversives or, at best, misguided elements, while the receiving government is left to handle matters. To be sure, when political circumstances change and negotiated settlements can be initiated, bilateral talks are a prelude to any mass repatriation. Governments seldom get together whilst the exodus is underway, however, and indeed they may not even be enjoying normal diplomatic relations at the time which would permit them to do so.

As a result, the receiving countries with the help of international agencies mount relief and resettlement operations which may develop and grow in a vacuum without any relation to, or detailed knowledge of, the origins or causes of the problem or its likely resolution. Relief agencies, whether they be intergovernmental or non-governmental, continue to refrain from going far into the background to mass movements on the grounds that they have a humanitarian mandate to fulfil and cannot concern themselves with controversial matters, usually of a political nature.

Thus the need for meaningful dialogue with those principally responsible on how to contain the problem remains unmet. Even if the countries or origin should offer a version of the causes which trigger movement which some might qualify as slanted, their responsibility towards their own nationals needs to be upheld—particularly if there is a danger of economic and social disruption in the receiving country and the undermining of peaceful relations between States which share a common border.

Secondly, because funds for humanitarian emergencies are finite, one has to think in both "lateral" and "vertical" terms about the co-ordination of humanitarian assistance. By "lateral" is meant the range of emergencies for which assistance is supplied, extending through man-made disasters to economic difficulties in individual countries. By "vertical" we refer to the co-ordination of humanitarian assistance through the successive phases of relief, rehabilitation, reconstruction and longer-term development. Just as the international community had reached a perception of the need for approaches to development co-operation to be integrated, so, increasingly, it is recognized that contributions must be used in the most cost-effective way possible.

Already it has been seen that in the not infrequent cases where the origins of an exodus are compounded by famine, the apportioning of aid and timely distribution within the country of origin may contribute to circumscribing the flow. At the same time, the presence of international relief officials may help to create a measure of hope and confidence. An improvement in the psychological climate is indeed a key factor in stemming the departure of groups who tend to influence each other until the movement snowballs beyond control. Conversely, in some situations the availability of international assistance very close to the border but exclusively within the receiving country may help precipitate the flow. It seems to be time to take a broader view and fill the existing lacunae.

Thirdly, appropriate organs of the United Nations called upon to deal with causes and, by inference, with prevention tend to be compartmentalized and ponderous, or may be hamstrung by political constraints. At the same time, agencies, subsidiary organs, intergovernmental and non-governmental bodies assisting displaced populations which are victims of man-made or natural disasters have little or no contact with those bodies whose responsibility it is to address the causes. In this, as in other domains, effective co-ordination remains a chronic problem despite the existence of studies and committees dealing with streamlining and restructuring.

As we have recalled in four case studies and an overview of exodus situations of the past decade, large-scale humanitarian emergencies have consistently been met by *ad hoc* measures and the designation of "focal points" or "lead agencies", as well as the appointment of a co-ordinator or special represent-

ative of the Secretary-General whose responsibility did not specifically extend to a liaison function, in the case of mass exodus, between the "refugee-producing" country ("cause") and the "refugee-receiving" countries and/or corresponding humanitarian operations ("effect").

The international community is increasingly concerned with causes behind mass exodus and measures to avert new flows of refugees. The General Assembly, at its last session, dealt *inter alia* with this question in Resolution 36/148. This resolution calls for the Group of Experts to take into account the Study submitted by the Special Rapporteur. It is hoped that the two undertakings will be complementary, bearing in mind the distinct history and terms of reference of each initiative. In a wider context, attention should be drawn also to the General Assembly Resolution 36/136 on the proposal for the promotion of a New International Humanitarian Order.

On the basis of these conclusions, the special rapporteur discusses ''what might be feasible in terms of prognosis and prescription, prevention and cure,'' in the following terms (para. 131–140):

In order to give birth to an "early-warning system", it would be necessary to gather, on an ongoing basis, impartial information from proven sources such as governments, the United Nations presence in the countries concerned (whether the UNDP Resident Representative, Specialized Agencies, UNIC or other) and further informed parties in order to gain an understanding of the background and all the facets of a situation, including the ethnic, economic, political and social aspects. Of necessity, there would be visits to the field. After assessing all available data, an appreciation to include a number of possible scenarios for the future development of the situation would be given to the Secretary-General of the United Nations and to the competent intergovernmental organs.

A "trigger mechanism" would be provided by the Secretary-General deciding, after due study of the material and using his executive authority, what action would be required on the part of the United Nations. The Secretary-General might call for further study of the situation, including discussion with the government or governments most closely concerned and/or with the appropriate regional body (Arab League, Council of Europe, Organization of African Unity, Organization of American States) to try to determine how regional containment of the problem cold be achieved, to save it becoming internationalized (that is to say requiring involvement of large-scale United Nations operations).

In the next stage, the executive entrusted with the task would bring the situation to the attention of those who deal with causes (as distinct from effects) to try to encourage, as appropriate, preventive action before the start of a mass movement. In the case of a political question, he would propose to the Secretary-General that the latter take the initiative appearing most indicated, whether it be consulting interested States or drawing the attention of the Security Council, in a suitable manner, to the problem. In the case of human rights issues, the responsible officer would relay the situation to the Commission on Human Rights which could make an investigation and ensure follow up.

It is suggested that after this, there should be liaison on an informal basis with the humanitarian agencies for purposes of consultation. They would thus be alerted and enabled to act swiftly if an exodus did indeed occur, which could be the case even if action were being taken at the source to remove or dissipate the cause(s) of such exodus.

The executive encrusted with responsibility in the situation would keep abreast of the relevant work of the General Assembly, the Security Council, the Commission on Human Rights or other competent body tackling "causes", as the case might be, while at the same time ensuring that humanitarian needs were being covered. He would be responsible for seeing that the question were kept under review by the relevant bodies. Simultaneously, he would be in a position to advise on the best way to apportion aid as between areas affected by the crisis in order to reduce to the maximum extent possible the stress/distress involved. Where necessary, an agency or agencies not so far working on the problem whose expertise were seen to be needed would be invited to participate.

Follow-up work could include monitoring of developments in order to report them to the Secretary-General and informal reporting to governments on the progress of the international effort. In the longer term, work could be carried out on seeking to promote regional reflexes to crisis situations, for example through encouraging the creation and/or development of regional human rights mechanisms, in co-operation with the Commission on Human Rights, and through promoting an active interest in the New International Humanitarian Order.

Measures to be undertaken should be speedy. Their success would be largely dependent on an informed appreciation of each complex situation and its respective origins, based on ongoing research and analysis. Only an impartial monitoring of situations could lead to a more balanced assessment of circumstances lying at the root of potential exodus and contribute thereby to a more adapted response from humanitarian agencies.

Few events go unnoticed in the world today, and the media has been remarkably effective in bringing violations of human rights to the attention of the public. Yet these and other "push factors" are rarely cause for sufficiently active concern until refugees are on the move. Those who could not leave may pay an even higher price for the apparent indifference of their fellow men.

Such an approach as has been outlined is no panacea. It may not always circumscribe exodus but could lead in certain cases to containing or diminishing movement.

The fact that an undertaking is difficult does not mean that it should not be attempted, Governments will inevitably expect that something should be done on this account if there is to be any confidence that the necessary level of humanitarian response to need and distress will be attained.

The special rapporteur's recommendations, at the conclusion of the study, are as follows:

It is recommended that consideration be given to the following:
(1) An updating of refugee, nationality and labour law and fresh consideration of asylum practice in the context of the promotion of a New International Humanitarian Order;
(2) A reappraisal of developing countries' economic needs in relation to possible causes of exodus;
(3) Standardization of international aid criteria;
(4) Simultaneity in approach to the country of origin and country of asylum to gain a comprehensive view of the overall situation and thus be able to plan better;
(5) A "bi-multi" aid approach: multilateral aid should take into account bilateral aid, to prevent duplication and ensure an integrated approach;
(6) The introduction of an effective census mechanism to work independently of relief agencies in order to determine in an impartial and professional way the numbers of border-crossers requiring assistance in mass influx situations;
(7) The introduction of an early-warning system based on impartial information gathering and data collection concerning potential mass exodus situations, leading to expeditious reporting to the Secretary-General of the United Nations and competent intergovernmental organs for the purpose of timely action, if required;
(8) The appointment of a Special Representative for Humanitarian Questions whose task, defined briefly in the preceding section, would basically be (a) to forewarn; (b) to monitor; (c) to de-politicize humanitarian situations; (d) to carry out those functions which humanitarian agencies cannot assume because of institutional/mandatory constraints; (e) to serve as an intermediary of goodwill betweeen the concerned parties;
(9) The identification from among groups experienced in humanitarian questions of men and women willing and able to be called upon to form a corps of "humanitarian observers" which, in case of need, could monitor situations and contribute through their presence to a deescalation of tensions. A prerequisite for this role would be the concurrence of the governments concerned. The crops would facilitate the work of the Special Representative for Humanitarian Questions.

The report of the special rapporteur was examined in detail by the Group of Governmental Experts on International Co-operation to Avert New Flows of Refugees, which, in turn, presented a comprehensive report on the subject (UN Doc. A/41/324) to the General Assembly in 1986. After endorsing the conclusions and recommendations contained in the report of the group of experts and calling upon member States to respect them, the Assembly—as had been recommended by the group—urged the main organs of the United Nations to make fuller use of their respective competences under the UN Charter as a means of preventing new massive flows of refugees.

At its 1988 session, the Commission on Human Rights welcomed (resolution 1988/70) the steps taken up to that time by the Secretary-General to establish an early warning system, as well as steps taken by other United Nations bodies to examine the problem of massive outflows of refugees and displaced persons in all its aspects, including its root causes; and invited all governments and concerned international organizations to intensify their cooperation and assistance in world-wide efforts to address these serious problems.

The General Assembly, on 8 December 1988, recognized (resolution 43/154) the fact that human rights violations are one of the multiple and complex factors causing mass exoduses of refugees and displaced persons, as indicated in the study of the special rapporteur and in the report of the Group of Governmental Experts on International Cooperation to Avert New Flows of Refugees. Concerned about the increasingly heavy burden being imposed by these sudden mass exoduses and displacements of population upon developing countries with limited resources of their own and upon the international community as a whole, the Assembly requested all governments to ensure the effective implementation of the relevant international instruments, in particular in the field of human rights, as this would contribute to averting new massive flows of refugees and displaced persons.

REFUGEES: SECURITY. As pointed out in the report of the UN HIGH COMMISSIONER FOR REFUGEES to the 1988 session of the UN General Assembly, covering the period from mid-1987 to mid-1988 (UN Doc. A/43/12, chap. I, C para. 36–40):

The minimum content of the international protection of refugees consists in the enjoyment of fundamental human rights necessary for survival in safety and dignity. This implies, as the *non-refoulement* principle recognizes, protection from loss of life, injury and other bodily harm as well as from any other action that might endanger, or threaten to endanger, the safety and dignity of refugees. As a fundamental element of this protection, the right of refugees to security is fully recognized in international law.

During the reporting period, the security of refugees continued to be at issue, including during flight, in countries of refuge or in connection with their voluntary return to their country of origin. The most flagrant example of the violation of the right to security remained, as in previous years, military and armed attacks on refugee camps and settlements as well as on refugees living in urban centres. Many of these attacks occurred in Africa, the Middle East and in Asia, with resulting loss of life. In one country alone, some 33 attacks were launched on 21 out of 26 settlements that were located in an area suffering from civil strife and armed uprisings. As a result, some 25 refugees lost their lives, 100 were injured, over 150 were raped and between 300 and 400 were abducted.

At its thirty-eighth session, the Executive Committee, for the sixth consecutive year, considered the problem of military and armed attacks on refugee camps and settlements. The Executive Committee adopted a conclusion on this subject which, *inter alia,* condemned all violations of the rights and safety of refugees and asylum-seekers and, in particular, military and armed attacks on refugee camps and settlements; urged States to abstain from these violations, which are against the principles of international law and cannot, therefore, be justified; called upon States and competent international organizations to provide all necessary assistance to relieve the plight of the victims of such attacks; and urged States to take every possible measure to prevent the occurrence of attacks, including measures to ensure that the civilian and humanitarian character of refugee camps and settlements is maintained.

In some refugee situations, the security of refugees is jeopardized through their forced recruitment into armed groups, guerilla bands or regular armies. Such practices continued during the reporting period and affected considerable numbers of young male refugees. Coercing refugees to take part, as active combatants in an armed struggle, amounts to a clear threat to their survival and integrity, is incompatible with their status as refugees and undermines their access to international protection. Furthermore, these violations are contrary to the concept that refugees are civilians, as well as the tenet, reconfirmed by the Executive Committee in its conclusions on military and armed attacks on refugee camps and settlements, that such camps and settlements have a strictly civilian and humanitarian character and that it is essential that States of refuge do all within their capacity to ensure that this character is maintained.

Further examples of violations of the security of refugees were found in the waters of South-East Asia where pirates continued, during the reporting period, to attack asylum-seekers travelling in boats. Efforts to curb such attacks were maintained under the Anti-Piracy Programme previously established by the Royal Thai Government, in co-operation with UNHCR and funded by several donor countries. Similarly, the Rescue at Sea Resettlement Offers (RASRO) scheme and the Disembarkation Resettlement Offers (DISERO) scheme benefited large numbers of asylum-seekers in distress at sea. Elsewhere, national authorities and UNHCR increased their vigilance along flight routes to ensure that refugees in search of protection were not killed, injured, raped or abducted. Even so, during the period under review, several reports reached the Office of violations of refugees' right to security.

After examining the report, the General Assembly on 8 December 1988 (resolution 43/117) noted with particular concern the continued violation, in certain situations, of the principle of *non-refoulement,* stressed the need to strengthen measures to protect refugees against such action and appealed to all states to abide by their international obligations, taking fully into account their legitimate security concerns.

The Assembly condemned all violations of the rights and safety of refugees and asylum-seekers, in particular those perpetrated by military or armed attacks against refugees camps and settlements and other forms of violence; endorsed again the conclusions on military and armed attacks adopted by the Executive Committee of the Programme of the High Commissioner; and renewed its call to all states to observe these principles.

REFUGEES: STUDENTS IN SOUTHERN AFRICA. In 1976, the UN General Assembly expressed concern about the continued influx of large numbers of South African student refugees to Botswana, Lesotho, and Swaziland, which imposed a heavy burden on the limited resources of those countries, and requested the secretary-general (resolution 31/126) to consult with the governments of those countries and the liberation movements concerned with a view to organizing and providing emergency financial and other forms of assistance for the care, subsistence, and education of these student refugees. The program was later enlarged to include student refugees from Namibia and to add Zambia to the list of receiving countries.

The UNITED NATIONS HIGH COMMISSIONER FOR REFUGEES, in cooperation with the secretary-general, continues to organize and implement the program of assistance and to report thereon to the Economic and Social Council and the General Assembly. Several other organizations, intergovernmental as well as non-governmental, provide assistance in the field of education; and, in Zambia, the national liberation movements recognized by the Organization of African Unity play a crucial implementing role for UNHCR-assisted humanitarian programs in the field of education.

The secretary-general's report to the 1988 session of the General Assembly, covering the period from 1 July 1987 to 30 June 1988 (UN Doc. A/43/594) provided the following information (para. 6–17):

Botswana. The number of South African and Namibian refugees did not change appreciably during the reporting period: 1,000 South Africans and some 200 Namibians, the majority of whom live in urban areas.

Refugee students living in Dukwe Settlement (180 South Africans and 120 Namibians) continued to benefit from the educational facilities (academic and vocational) which are offered at primary, secondary and tertiary levels. A junior secondary school, open both to refugees and nationals, was being constructed with European Economic Community (EEC) and UNHCR funding, while the Educational Resource Centre provided informal adult education.

For the urban case-load, UNHCR and other organizations were involved in the provision of educational assistance at various levels—academic as well as vocational—as needed to improve refugees' chances of obtaining gainful employment.

Swaziland. There were 14,550 officially registered refugees in Swaziland, with an estimated similar number having spontaneously settled in the border areas. This official case-load represented an increase of some 30 percent since 1984, and was comprised of 6,500 South Africans, 5,500 Mozambicans, and others of various nationalities. The South African refugees, mainly of Swazi ethnic origin and of rural background, left South Africa in the late 1970s.

UNHCR assistance activities on behalf of South Africa refugees were centred at Ndzevane Rural Settlement, where the majority of the refugees were located.

At the request of the Government, UNHCR was also providing assistance aimed at facilitating the transfer of individual South Africans to second countries of asylum. Meanwhile, UNHCR continued to provide basic care and maintenance.

The number of South Africans receiving educational assistance from UNHCR during the period under review increased to over 220; of these, more than 50 percent were in the academic levels. There were no Namibian refugee students sponsored in Swaziland during this period.

Zambia. The majority of the 3,200 refugees were affiliated to the African National Congress (ANC). The Namibian refugees in the country, mainly affiliates of the South West Africa People's Organization (SWAPO), numbered 7,300. The majority of the urban case-load consisted of South Africans (400), Namibians (200) and Malawians (450). Non-affiliated refugees number approximately 400.

Other refugees from South Africa and Namibia benefited from educational assistance provided by UNHCR and other agencies, both intergovernmental and non-governmental.

Lesotho. The Government estimate of the total number of persons in a refugee-like situation remained stable at 11,500 since the end of 1986 through March 1987; of these, 269 were registered as refugees and some 114 received assistance from UNHCR. Nearly all of these refugees originated from South Africa and were predominantly of urban background, with males constituting a large proportion (70 percent). In 1986, 317 new arrivals were recorded while 375 persons departed for resettlement to third countries.

Since 1967, Lesotho increasingly became a temporary asylum country for South African refugees, particularly for those affiliated to national liberation movements. This trend is likely to continue in the foreseeable future, with possible negative implications for refugees who have been in the country for an extended period and who are already well integrated.

UNHCR's assistance activities in Lesotho continued to focus on individual refugees. Refugees continued to receive various forms of assistance, mainly in education (at the primary and secondary levels) and local integration, through the establishment of small-scale income-generating projects, counselling, supplementary aid and resettlement to another country.

Noting with concern that the discriminatory and repressive policies that continued to be applied in South Africa and Namibia caused a continued and increasing influx of student refugees into Botswana, Lesotho, Swaziland, and Zambia, the General Assembly (resolution 43/149) took note of the report with satisfaction, expressed its appreciation to the governments of the receiving countries for making educational and other facilities available to the student refugees in spite of the pressure that the continuing influx of those refugees exerted on facilities in their countries, and noted with appreciation the financial and material support provided for the student refugees by member States, the Office of the United Nations High Commissioner for Refugees, other bodies of the United Nations system, and intergovernmental and non-governmental organizations. It urged continued assistance to the countries of asylum, materially and otherwise, to enable them to continue to discharge their humanitarian obligations towards refugees.

R

REFUGEES: VOLUNTARY REPATRIATION. As indicated in the report of the UNITED NATIONS HIGH COMMISSIONER FOR REFUGEES to the 1988 session of the UN General Assembly, covering the period from mid-1987 to mid-1988 (UN Doc. A/43/12, chap. 1, E), at least 150,000 refugees returned voluntarily to their countries of origin during that period, the vast majority on the African continent. Significant numbers of refugees, however, also returned to several Central American countries. Voluntary repatriation movements elsewhere were almost negligible. According to the report (para. 46–48):

A considerable proportion of the refugees concerned returned spontaneously. In one situation, their decision to return was no doubt influenced by the seriously deteriorating security situation in the part of the country of asylum where they had previously found refuge. Elsewhere, the return took place in an organized fashion in which transportation and immediate assistance needs were met both during the return and during the initial period back in the country of origin.

Although by and large the voluntary returns took place in safety and dignity, there were some exceptions. At least one refugee lost his life as a result of violence and many others were subjected to harassment upon return. Yet other refugees faced considerable problems in the reintegration process and several returning refugees were subjected to detention measures. Part of these problems resulted from the fact that returning refugees were denied proper documentation by their countries of origin, thereby denying them effective national protection.

Voluntary repatriation, whenever feasible, is the preferred solution to any refugee situation. It achieves the basic goal of international protection, namely, the re-establishment of refugees in a community, in this case, their own. It is, however, also one of the most delicate solutions to implement. It is, therefore, of the utmost importance that the Office be able to count on the full support and cooperation of the countries concerned, including receiving the requisite material and human resources. If voluntary repatriation is to become a viable solution for more significant numbers of refugees, it is essential that States attend to the root causes of refugee movements. Only by removing the conditions that led to the original flight can larger numbers of refugees return voluntarily to their respective countries of origin in safety and dignity. This task, which is largely political, must be pursued more vigorously by States.

After considering the report, the General Assembly on 8 December 1988 (resolution 43/117) recognized that voluntary repatriation or return remains the most desirable solution to the problems facing refugees and displaced persons, welcomed the fact that in various parts of the world it had been possible for significant numbers of them to return voluntarily to their countries of origin, and urged all States to support the high commissioner's efforts to solve the basic problems of refugees and displaced persons primarily through voluntary repatriation or return.

REFUGEES: WOMEN AND CHILDREN. As indicated in the report of the UNITED NATIONS HIGH COMMISSIONER FOR REFUGEES to the 1988 session of the UN General Assembly, covering the period from mid-1987 to mid-1988 (UN Doc. A/43/12, chap. 1, D, para. 41–44):

In recent years, UNHCR has paid particular attention to the protection needs of refugee women and children. It will be recalled that, in 1985, the Executive Committee of the Programme of the High Commissioner adopted a conclusion on the protection of refugee women in recognition of the fact that refugee women and girls in certain situations are more vulnerable than the refugee population at large. Since then, the Office has worked with States and non-governmental organizations to sensitize them to the particular protection needs of refugee women and girls. Specific measures have also been adopted in a number of refugee situations, as for example, within the framework of the Anti-Piracy Programme referred to above.

Nevertheless, refugee women and girls continue to suffer physical violence, sexual abuse and discrimination. During the reporting period, refugee women were beaten, raped and subjected to other forms of sexual abuse, such as exploitation for the purpose of prostitution. In some instances, such abuse was inflicted on women under the threat of being denied recognition of their refugee status. In other instances, it seemed, at least in part, to be linked to the absence of adequate assistance programmes geared to the specific needs of the female refugee population. The tensions resulting from living in closed camps during protracted periods of time also increased the level of violence of which women were primarily the victims.

The situation of refugee children was subjected to special scrutiny by the Office during the period under review, and was discussed by the Executive Committee of the Programme of the High Commissioner at its thirty-eighth session. In many instances, refugee children are exposed to physical violence, exploitation, forced recruitment and detention. At times they also face particular problems with respect to their registration, determination of their refugee status and their nationality.

In its conclusion on the subject, the Executive Committee recognized that refugee children have special needs within the broader refugee population, and stressed that all action taken on their behalf must be guided by the principle of the best interests of the child, as well as the principle of family unity. It called for national and international action to prevent violations of the basic rights of children and to assist victims. States were also urged to ensure that the births of refugee children born in countries of asylum were registered. Finally, the Executive Committee addressed the situation of particularly vulnerable groups of refugee children, including unaccompanied minors.

After examining the report, the General Assembly on 8 December 1988 (resolution 43/117) commended the high commissioner for the work undertaken by his office to identify and meet the special needs of refugee children and invited him to pursue his efforts on their behalf, drawing on the valuable contributions of non-governmental organizations in this area.

The Assembly also urged States to extend their full cooperation to the high commissioner in his efforts to ensure that the special needs of refugee women in the fields of protection, assistance, and durable solutions are met.

REGIONAL COUNCIL ON HUMAN RIGHTS IN ASIA.

An international non-governmental organization in consultative status (Roster) with the UN Economic and Social Council, the council's members are civil rights leaders in five Asian and Pacific countries.

Founded in Manila in 1982, the the first General Assembly of the Council adopted, in 1983, the Declaration of the Basic Duties of ASEAN Peoples and Governments, a "regional Declaration of Human Rights" that reflects the culture, values, and aspirations of the people of the ASEAN region. The council—which consists of civil rights leaders from Indonesia, Malaysia, the Philippines, Singapore, and Thailand—promotes respect for individual and collective civil, political, social, economic, and cultural human rights; receives complaints and petitions; assists in redressing violations of these rights; and encourages governments of the region to ratify or concur in the International Covenants on Human Rights. Since 1984, the council has campaigned for the release of political prisoners in the region.

Regional Council on Human Rights in Asia. Secretary-General: Socorro Diokno. Address: Station Mesa, P.O. Box 417, Manila, 2806, Philippines.

Yearbook of International Organizations 1989/90 (K. G. Saur).

RELIGIOUS INTOLERANCE AND DISCRIMINATION: SPECIAL RAPPORTEUR.

At its 1986 session, the UN COMMISSION ON HUMAN RIGHTS decided (resolution 1986/20) to appoint a special rapporteur to examine incidents and governmental actions which are inconsistent with the provisions of the DECLARATION ON THE ELIMINATION OF ALL FORMS OF INTOLERANCE AND OF DISCRIMINATION BASED ON RELIGION and designated Mr. Angelo Vidal d'Almeida Ribero as its special rapporteur.

The special rapporteur's reports to the 1987 and 1988 sessions of the commission (UN Docs.E/CN.4/1987/35 and E/CN.4/1988/45 and Add. 1, respectively) presented an analysis, based on the information available to him, of the principal factors which hamper the implementation of the declaration. After examining them, the commission (resolutions 1987/15 and 1988/55) urged States to provide, where they have not already done so, adequate constitutional and legal guarantees of freedom of thought, conscience, religion and belief, including the provision of effective remedies where there is intolerance or discrimination based on religion or belief; and urged them also to take all appropriate measures to combat intolerance and to encourage understanding, tolerance, and respect in matters relating to freedom of religion or belief; and, in this context, to examine, where necessary, the supervision and training of their civil servants, educators, and other public officials to ensure that, in the course of their official duties, they respect different religions and beliefs and do not discriminate against persons professing other religions or beliefs.

In his report to the 1990 session of the commission, the special rapporteur presented the following analysis of the information which he had collected (UN Doc. E/CN.4/1990/46, paras. 102–108):

Since his appointment, the Special Rapporteur has been able to gather a considerable amount of information regarding the factors hampering the implementation of the Declaration, the infringements of the rights defined in the Declaration and the various situations in which religious intolerance and discrimination can lead to the violation of other human rights. The Special Rapporteur has pointed out that the most important factors hampering the implementation of the Declaration are: the existence of legal provisions that run counter to the spirit and letter of the Declaration; practices by governmental authorities contradicting not only the principles embodied in international instruments but even provisions enshrined in domestic law which prohibit discrimination on religious grounds; the persistence of political, economic and cultural factors which result from complex historical processes and which are at the basis of current expressions of religious intolerance.

A large number of incidents brought to the attention of the Special Rapporteur, which involved clashes between members of various religious communities, appear to have resulted from the sectarian and intransigent attitude of the followers of a particular religion or belief. In addition to conflicts between entire religious communities, there are situations in which the activities of extremist or fanatical factions are the main cause of discriminatory practices or of violent outbursts of a religious nature. In fact, the intransigence of extremist elements and their demand for a literal interpretation, without consideration of the context of certain religious precepts, is at the root of many of the current manifestations of religious conflicts in the world.

The last few years have seen the emergence of such sectarian and intransigent attitudes regarding religious matters. This regrettable phenomenon has not only affected the freedoms and rights of minority communities in the countries where they have occurred, but has also become a destabilizing factor in the international system and a source of tension and conflict between States. As is usually the case with the different expressions of religious intolerance, these attitudes have led to attempts at curtailing a wide variety of human rights. For example, the condemnation to death of an author of a book which expresses views considered to be offensive by followers of a world religion and the death threats addressed to his publishers have been a matter of serious concern for the Special Rapporteur, not least because such attitudes violate basic principles of international law. The Special Rapporteur implores those responsible for the above-mentioned death threats not to carry them out, as this would constitute a flagrant violation of universally accepted human rights standards.

As in previous years, this year's alleged infringement of the rights defined in the Declaration affect a whole range of rights and freedoms, such as the right to have, to manifest and to practise the religion or belief of one's choice (Declaration, arts. 1 and 6); the freedom from discriminatory treatment on the grounds of religion or belief (Declaration, arts. 2–4); and the right to bring up children in accordance with the religion or belief chosen by their parents (Declaration, art. 5). As regards, for example, the right to have, to manifest and to practise the religion or belief of one's choice, allegations have been received in relation to restrictions on the right to manifest one's religion in public; sanctions for belonging to a specific denomination; the destruction, enforced closure, evacuation or arbitrary occupation of places of worship or assembly for a religion or belief; prohibition of the opening of new places of worship or assembly, or repair of existing premises; restriction of certain activities of a cultural nature relating to a religion or belief; seizure or confiscation of religious property or articles of worship; prohibition on importing, possessing, exhibiting or distributing certain articles of worship; prohibition on publishing, importing or distributing publications relating to a religion or belief; restriction or prohibition of religious publications, sermons or addresses; use for secular purposes of places considered to be sacred for certain religions or beliefs; profanation of burial places; restrictions on the right to set up seminaries to train clergy and on the possibilities for seminarists to receive adequate instruction; and restrictions on the right to appoint sufficient numbers of clergy. Regarding discrimination on the grounds of religion and belief, the allegations received refer to discriminatory measures in relation to access to education, employment, health services, and food rations, as well as to the permanent exclusion of certain groups or movements from public service, the refusal to give injured parties their legal compensation and the denial of the right to obtain a passport on the grounds of religion or belief. Where the education of children in accordance with the religion or belief of their parents is concerned, the allegations received by the Special Rapporteur indicate the continued existence of restrictions on the enjoyment of this freedom.

As has already been noted, and as it becomes clear from careful analysis of the allegations transmitted to Governments by the Special Rapporteur in the present and previous reports, the infringements of the rights and freedoms embodied in the Declaration usually result in the infringement of other human rights, such as the right to life, physical integrity, liberty and security of the person; freedom of movement; and freedom of opinion and expression. Indeed, many persons are still detained, either in prisons, labour camps or psychiatric hospitals, for reasons of religion or belief, while many more are silenced, persecuted or expelled from their countries on the same grounds. Persons held for religious reasons have in some cases allegedly been subjected to ill-treatment and to corporal punishment. Believers and members of the clergy of many denomination or persons holding certain beliefs continue, in a number of regions of the world, to be subjected to death threats, in-

timidation, physical assault, enforced re-education or enforced indoctrination. Most important, this year there has been an increase in alleged violations of the right to life in connection with the enjoyment of the rights and freedoms of religion and belief. In some cases, these violations affect individuals or groups and result from clashes with governmental forces; in others, they affect individuals or groups and result from communal clashes. In some cases, law enforcement authorities appear to have intervened in time to reduce the damage; in others it seems that they have not taken any measures; in yet others, they appear to have actively encouraged clashes.

The Special Rapporteur wishes to acknowledge the progress made by certain countries in introducing changes in their constitutional and legal systems in order to bring them into line with prevailing international standards in the field of religious rights and freedoms. He also wishes to express his satisfaction with improvements in the policies of certain Governments regarding matters of religion and conscience. The growing co-operation of Governments in the fulfilment of his mandate is also an encouraging development. However, infringements of the rights defined in the Declaration on the Elimination of All Forms of Intolerance and of Discrimination Based on Religion or Belief seem to persist in most regions of the world, as illustrated in the allegations transmitted to Governments by the Special Rapporteur in the course of this year. They concern all the provisions of the Declaration.

Despite the above-mentioned negative trends, the Special Rapporteur wishes once more to express his satisfaction with the positive impact of the policy of openness and transparency in the sphere of religious freedom and manifestations of worship in Eastern Europe. The Special Rapporteur has particularly noted significant improvement in the relations between the Orthodox Church and the Government of the Union of Soviet Socialist Republics. Among the encouraging signs worth mentioning is the election of His Holiness the Patriarch of Moscow and all Russia and two church dignitaries as deputies to the Supreme Soviet, as well as the opening of more than 1,700 new Orthodox parishes; the opening of a new seminary at Zhiovitzy in the Minsk region which adds to the four existing ones in Smolensk, Minsk, Kishinev and Stavropol; the opening of the competition for the design of a Memorial Cathedral to commemorate the 1,000th anniversary of Christianity in Russia; and the publication by the Moscow Patriarchate of a weekly paper entitled "The Church Messenger". Furthermore, the dialogue initiated at the highest level with the Roman Catholic Church during the recent official visit by the President of the Soviet Union, Mr. Gorbatchev, to the Holy See is yet another positive manifestation of this new policy.

On the basis of the above analysis, the special rapporteur submitted to the commission the following conclusions and recommendations (*Ibid.*, paras. 109–123):

During the past year, the Special Rapporteur has continued to receive allegations of infringements of the rights and freedoms set out in the Declaration occurring in most regions of the world, especially the right to have the religion or belief of one's choice and freedom from discrimination on grounds of religion or belief. The Special Rapporteur is concerned with the persistence of alarming infringements of other human rights arising out of attacks on freedom of thought, conscience, religion or belief. Noteworthy among them is the growing number of extra-judicial killings that have allegedly taken place in the context of clashes between religious groups or between such groups and security forces. Resorting to violence or the threat of its use in dealing with problems or antagonisms of a religious nature is also a disturbing development which, if unchecked, might endanger international peace. Despite the growing number of allegations concerning infringements of the principles embodied in the Declaration, the Special Rapporteur also wishes to note that the information collected also attests to a definite interest in overcoming the existing restrictions on the enjoyment of the rights and freedoms of thought, conscience, religion or belief. Significant progress achieved in Eastern Europe is particularly encouraging, and the increasing co-operation of almost all States in connection with the mandate of the Special Rapporteur is also praiseworthy.

The Special Rapporteur would like to emphasize that he is aware of the difficulties involved in distinguishing between religions, sects and religious associations. In his view, aspects having to do with the antiquity of a religion, its revealed character and the existence of a scripture, while important, are not sufficient to make a distinction. Even belief in the existence of a Supreme Being, a particular ritual or a set of ethical and social rules are not exclusive to religions but can also be found in political ideologies. So far, a satisfactory and acceptable distinction has not been arrived at. Given the rapid proliferation of religious associations, the lack of a genuine distinction between religions, sects and religious associations sometimes poses serious problems. Experience has shown that many newer sects and religious associations seem to engage in activities which are not always of a legal nature. The Special Rapporteur believes that, in the absence of an international convention which would be more explicit in this regard, the Declaration is the best instrument at the disposal of the international community allowing a distinction to be made between the legal and illegal practices of sects and religious associations. Indeed, the Declaration protects not only religious but also theistic, non-theistic and atheistic beliefs and stipulates in article 1, paragraph 3, that freedom to manifest one's religion or belief is subject only to such limitations as are prescribed by law and are necessary to protect public safety, order, health or morals, or the fundamental rights and freedoms of others.

Regarding communications informing of legal action taken against certain members of sects or religious associations, the Special Rapporteur believes it would be appropriate to await the final decisions of the courts, although he wishes to add that such legal proceedings should be concluded within a reasonable time. Long procedural delays can be harmful to the parties to a dispute and detrimental to the image of a State. Moreover, to allow a trial to drag on for years is a denial of justice sometimes more serious than the allegations that led to the legal action. In any event, the Special Rapporteur is of the opinion that the possible sentencing of one or more individuals in a criminal trial does not mean a condemnation of the religion or belief that they consider themselves to serve. All religions have already experienced similar situations without being themselves affected.

The Special Rapporteur also wishes to express his concern about the difficulties created by certain States in regard to the religious practices of foreigners who hold religious beliefs different from those held by the majority of the nationals of those States. In many cases, such difficulties consist not only in the prohibition of the building of either churches or chapels, but even in the prohibition of private worship. In some cases, such restrictions are imposed by Governments which have been authorized to build places of worship in the countries of origin of those whom they prevent from practising their faith in public. Not long ago, Pope John Paul II said in reference to this situation: "Allow me to confide in you. It is not difficult to understand the astonishment and frustration felt by Christians, say in Europe, who readily welcome believers of other religions and allow them to practise their faith, when they are refused similar rights in countries where such believers are a majority and their religion is the State religion." The Special Rapporteur believes that what is lacking here is the respect for the principle of reciprocity, widely accepted in international law and the day-to-day practice of international relations. Respect for this principle in the context described above, would certainly contribute to enhancing religious tolerance on a world-wide scale.

The Special Rapporteur would like to draw attention to another limitation in the existing international instruments with regard to freedom of thought, conscience, religion or belief. A broadly based school of legal thought maintains that the individual should be free not only to choose among different theistic creeds and to practise the one of his choice freely, but also to have the right to view life from a non-theistic perspective without facing disadvantages *vis-à-vis* believers. The Special Rapporteur thinks that, in the same way as believers must enjoy their right to practise their religion unhindered, non-believers (freethinkers, agnostics and atheists) should not be discriminated against. The rights of non-believers should be properly guaranteed in a new international instrument.

In the analysis of the information received, the Special Rapporteur has established that the most important obstacles to the implementation of the Declaration are, *inter alia*: the existence of provisions in national laws which run counter to the spirit and letter of the Declaration; governmental practices which often conflict with both national laws and international instruments on the matter; persistent economic, political and cultural factors; the influence of complex historical processes on current manifestations of religious intolerance, such as distrust and clashes between members of various religious communities which generate sectarian and intransigent attitudes; extremist and fanatical opinions originating from a literal interpretation of certain religious precepts which result in violent outbursts; extra-judicial killings, death threats, intimidation, enforced re-education, confinement to psychiatric or labour camps; profanation of places of worship and burial grounds, destruction, closing, evacuation or occupation of such places of worship; seizure or confiscation of articles of worship and property; hindering or prohibition of religious publications and their dissemination, their censorship as well as that of sermons, etc. These regrettable phenomena adversely affect not only the rights and freedoms of religious communities but also those of minorities and represent a destabilizing factor in international relations and a source of tensions and conflict between States. The violation or non-respect of religious rights often results in the infringement of other human rights, such as the right to life, physical integrity, liberty and security of the person, freedom of movement and freedom of opinion and expression.

The Special Rapporteur also wishes to underline that

progress has been made in this area as well. An example is the introduction of appropriate changes in constitutions and legal systems made by certain countries to bring them into greater accord with international instruments; improved policies of certain Governments regarding matters of religion and conscience; the positive impact of the policy of openness and transparency in Eastern Europe, especially the new dialogue between the Government of the Soviet Union and the Orthodox and Roman Catholic Churches.

Since his appointment, the Special Rapporteur has been collecting information transmitted to him by the Governments, non-governmental organizations and other religious and lay sources, regarding constitutional and legal guarantees of freedom of thought, conscience, religion and belief, measures taken by States to combat intolerance, and incidents and governmental actions which might be inconsistent with the provisions of the Declaration. The information thus gathered has constantly been examined by the Special Rapporteur, since it contains important elements to be taken into account by any future drafters of a new international instrument. The Special Rapporteur, should the Commission decide to renew his mandate, intends to include in his next report a brief analysis of the material collected over the years since his first appointment.

Although the international system already has a number of mandatory norms in the area of freedom of religion or belief, the persistence of the problem of intolerance and discrimination in this field calls for the preparation of an international instrument dealing specifically with the elimination of this phenomenon. The Special Rapporteur is of the opinion that the adoption of such an instrument could give a broader and more profound dimension to international protection against manifestations of intolerance based on religion or belief. Furthermore, the mandatory nature of the provisions of such an instrument could impose on States parties a number of requirements, such as the submission of reports on the application of its provisions, which might encourage greater respect for religious rights and freedoms by such States.

For the purpose of elaborating such an international instrument, the international community might usefully draw upon the principles laid down in the 1981 Declaration, as well as on the practical experience acquired in recent years by the Commission on Human Rights in this regard. The Special Rapporteur would like to insist on the advantage of establishing, within the Commission on Human Rights or its Sub-commission on Prevention of Discrimination and Protection of Minorities, an open-ended working group to consider the possibility of preparing a new binding international instrument. In his view, such a group should be able to count on the broad participation of States, non-governmental organizations and religious denominations. While such an international instrument is being prepared, the Commission on Human Rights should endeavour to maintain its vigilance and continue to apply the procedure it has introduced with a view to monitoring and, if possible, reducing incidents and measures inconsistent with the provisions of the 1981 Declaration.

In this connection, the Special Rapporteur has noted with interest the report (E/CN.4/Sub.2/1989/32) prepared by Mr. Theo van Boven, expert of the Sub-Commission on Prevention of Discrimination and Protection of Minorities, pursuant to Commission to resolution 1988/55. In relation to the new binding international instrument itself, Mr. van Boven stresses that it should build on the standard already elaborated by the international community;

take into account the complexity of the issues involved and, in particular, the need for broad international acceptance on the part of States which would have to undertake legal obligations.

The Special Rapporteur wishes once more to urge States which have not already ratified the relevant international instruments to do so, making provision, in accordance with the norms laid down by those instruments, for the necessary constitutional and legal guarantees for freedom of thought, conscience, religion and belief, including effective remedies in the event of intolerance or discrimination based on religion or belief.

Advantage should be taken of the advisory services made available by the United Nations in the field of human rights, as follows:

(a) Provision of expert advisory services to countries which express the desire to have them for the drafting of new legislative provisions or the adaptation of existing legislation in conformity with the principles set out in the 1981 Declaration; for the establishment of a machinery for the promotion and protection of human rights, particularly in respect of freedom of religion and belief, such as national commissions, the institution of an ombudsman or of reconciliation commissions; or for the inclusion in school curricula of teaching of the ideals of tolerance, understanding and mutual respect among all religious groups;

(b) Organization of regional, subregional and national training courses aimed at greater familiarization with existing principles, norms and remedies in the sphere of freedom of religion and belief. These training courses would be particularly intended for persons occupying key posts in their respective countries, such as legislators, judges, lawyers, law-enforcement officials, members of the administration and educators;

(c) Organization of international, regional and national workshops for representatives of non-governmental organizations in the sphere of human rights, and for representatives of specific religions and ideologies, on the theme of promotion of tolerance and understanding as regards religion and belief and encouragement of inter-denominational dialogue;

(d) Organization, with the collaboration of UNESCO, of media briefings aimed at a broader dissemination of the principles contained in the Declaration so as to prevent the spreading of stereotypes which might lead to lack of comprehension and tolerance.

The Special Rapporteur wishes to insist that non-governmental organizations in general, and groups representing specific religions or ideologies in particular, can and should play an active role in assuring respect for and promoting tolerance and freedom of religion and belief by initiating an inter-denominational dialogue at the national and international levels, in the form of meetings, conferences and seminars whose topics would be aimed at emphasizing the similarities among various religions and beliefs rather than their differences.

Finally, victims of intolerance and discrimination based on religion or belief should have effective remedies available to them. In this connection, the Special Rapporteur is of the opinion that it would be desirable for information on the norms laid down by the 1981 Declaration to be given widespread dissemination among persons responsible for protecting the right to freedom of religion or belief, particularly lawmakers, judges, lawyers and civil servants.

SEE ALSO Thought, Conscience, and Religion.

REMEDY. The means by which an individual may enforce his right, prevent it from being violated, or seek redress or compensation in case of its violation. The right to an effective remedy is proclaimed in article 8 of the UNIVERSAL DECLARATION OF HUMAN RIGHTS, which reads:

Article 8. Everyone has the right to an effective remedy by the competent national tribunals for acts violating the fundamental rights granted him by the constitution or by law.

A corresponding provision is to be found in article 2 (3) of the INTERNATIONAL COVENANT ON CIVIL AND POLITICAL RIGHTS, which reads:

Article 2. (3). Each State Party to the present Covenant undertakes:

(a) To ensure that any person whose rights or freedoms as herein recognized are violated shall have an effective remedy, notwithstanding that the violation has been committed by persons acting in an official capacity;

(b) To ensure that any person claiming such a remedy shall have his right thereto determined by competent judicial, administrative or legislative authorities, or by any other competent authority provided for by the legal system of the State, and to develop the possibilities of judicial remedy;

(c) To ensure that the competent authorities shall enforce such remedies when granted.

A provision on the subject also appears in article 6 of the INTERNATIONAL CONVENTION ON THE ELIMINATION OF ALL FORMS OF RACIAL DISCRIMINATION, as follows:

Article 6. States Parties shall assure to everyone within their jurisdiction effective protection and remedies, through the competent national tribunals and other State institutions, against any acts of racial discrimination which violate his human rights and fundamental freedoms contrary to this Convention, as well as the right to seek from such tribunals just and adequate reparation or satisfaction for any damage suffered as a result of such discrimination.

Articles 13 and 14 of the CONVENTION AGAINST TORTURE AND OTHER CRUEL, INHUMAN OR DEGRADING TREATMENT OR PUNISHMENT provides for the right to an adequate remedy in the case of victims of torture in the following articles:

Article 13. Each State Party shall ensure that any individual who alleges he has been subjected to torture in any territory under its jurisdiction has the right to complain to, and to have his case promptly and impartially examined by, its competent authorities. Steps shall be taken to ensure that the complainant and witnesses are protected against all ill-treatment or intimidation as a consequence of his complaint or any evidence given.

Article 14. 1. Each State Party shall ensure in its legal system that the victim of an act of torture obtains redress and has an enforceable right to fair and adequate compensation, including the means for as full rehabilitation as possible. In the event of the death of the victim as a result of an act of torture, his dependants shall be entitled to compensation.

2. Nothing in this article shall affect any right of the victim or other persons to compensation which may exist under national law.

The AMERICAN CONVENTION ON HUMAN RIGHTS, open for acceptance by member States of the ORGANIZATION OF AMERICAN STATES, provides that:

Article 10. Every person has the right to be compensated in accordance with the law in the event he has been sentenced by a final judgement through a miscarriage of justice.

The EUROPEAN CONVENTION ON HUMAN RIGHTS, open for acceptance by members of the COUNCIL OF EUROPE, provides that:

Article 13. Everyone whose rights and freedoms as set forth in this Convention are violated shall have an effective remedy before a national authority notwithstanding that the violation has been committed by persons acting in an official capacity.

After examining reports submitted by states parties to the International Covenant on Civil and Political Rights in accordance with article 40 of that instrument, the HUMAN RIGHTS COMMITTEE adopted, in 1981, a general comment relating to article 2 of the covenant in the following terms (UN Doc. A/36/40, Annex VII para. 1–2):

The Committee notes that article 2 of the Covenant generally leaves it to the States parties concerned to choose their method of implementation in their territories within the framework set out in that article. It recognizes, in particular, that the implementation does not depend solely on constitutional or legislative enactments, which in themselves are often not *per se* sufficient. The Committee considers it necessary to draw the attention of States parties to the fact that the obligation under the Covenant is not confined to the respect of human rights, but that States parties have also undertaken to ensure the enjoyment of these rights to all individuals under their jurisdiction. This aspect calls for specific activities by the States parties to enable individuals to enjoy their rights. This is obvious in a number of articles (e.g. article 3 which is dealt with in general comment 4/13 below), but in principle this undertaking relates to all rights set forth in the Covenant.

In this connexion, it is very important that individuals should know what their rights under the Covenant (and the Optional Protocol, as the case may be) are and also that all administrative and judicial authorities should be aware of the obligations which the State party has assumed under

R

the Covenant. To this end, the Covenant should be publicized in all official languages of the State and steps should be taken to familiarize the authorities concerned with its contents as part of their training. It is desirable also to give publicity to the State party's co-operation with the Committee.

SEE ALSO *African Commission on Human and People's Rights; Commission on Human Rights; Compensation for Victims of Human Rights Violations; Complaints and Other Communications concerning Human Rights; Constitutional Councils; Courts of Human Rights; Equality: National Constitutional and Legislative Provisions on Non-Discrimination; European Commission on Human Rights; European Court of Human Rights; Honduras: Velasquez Rodriguez Case—Compensatory Damages; Human Rights Agencies: Aid to Particular Groups; Human Rights Commissions: National and Local; Human Rights Commissions: Universal and Regional; Individuals as Subjects of International Law; Inter-American Commission of Human Rights; Inter-American Court of Human Rights; Legal Aid; Legislative Organs;* Ministerio Público; *Ombudsman; State of Emergency: Essential Judicial Guarantees; and individual constitutions of nations.*

RIGHT TO DEVELOPMENT. In 1981, the Commission on Human Rights established (resolution 36 [XXXVII]) the WORKING GROUP OF GOVERNMENTAL EXPERTS ON THE RIGHT TO DEVELOPMENT, composed of 15 governmental experts appointed by its chairman, and instructed it to study "the scope and contents of the right to development and the most effective means to ensure the realization, in all countries, of the economic, social, and cultural rights enshrined in various international instruments, paying particular attention to the obstacles encountered by developing countries in their efforts to secure the enjoyment of human rights."

The final report of the working group (UN Doc. E/CN.4/1985/11), containing the draft of a declaration on the right to development, was submitted to the commission at its 1985 session. The commission forwarded it to the General Assembly, which on 4 December 1986 was able to adopt and proclaim (resolution 41/128) the DECLARATION ON THE RIGHT TO DEVELOPMENT. At the same time, the assembly welcomed (resolution 41/131) the commission's decision to entrust further tasks to the working group relating to the realization of the provisions of the declaration.

In adopting the declaration, the assembly confirmed that "the right to development is an inalienable human right and that equality of opportunity for development is a prerogative both of nations and of individuals who make up nations."

The declaration itself defines the right to development as "an inalienable human right by virtue of which every human person and all peoples are entitled to participate in, contribute to and enjoy eco-

nomic, social, cultural and political development, in which all human rights and fundamental freedoms can be fully realized." It adds that "the human right to development also implies the full realization of the right of peoples to self-determination, which includes, subject to the relevant provisions of both International Covenants on Human Rights, the exercise of their inalienable right to full sovereignty over all their natural wealth and resources."

After examining the working group's 1988 report (UN Doc. E/CN.4/1988/10), which contained a set of recommendations in tentative form, the Commission on Human Rights took note of it with approval (resolution 1988/26), requested the Secretary-General to transmit it to the General Assembly, and agreed that future work on the question of the right to development should proceed step-by-step and in stages. It invited the Secretary-General to obtain further comments and views on the subject and to include them in an expanded analytical compilation which would also include relevant statements made during the discussions in the commission and the Economic and Social Council; and called upon the working group to prepare final recommendations on how an evaluation system for the implementation and further enhancement of the declaration could be set up.

The General Assembly on 8 December 1988 endorsed (resolution 43/127) the views expressed, and the requests made, by the Commission. It called upon the Commission to decide at its 1989 session, on the basis of the working group's report and the views expressed by its own members, on the future course of action on the question, in particular on practical measures for the implementation and enhancement of the declaration.

In a separate resolution on the subject adopted the same day (resolution 43/126), the General Assembly reiterated the importance of the right to development for all countries, particularly developing countries. It stressed that the achievement of that right requires a concerted international and national effort to eliminate economic deprivation, hunger, and disease in all parts of the world without discrimination; and emphasized that, to this end, international cooperation should aim at the maintenance of stable and sustained economic growth with simultaneous action to increase concessional assistance to developing countries, build world food security, resolve the debt burden, eliminate trade barriers, promote stability, and enhance scientific cooperation.

After examining the report of the working group on its 1989 session (UN Doc. E/CN.4/1989/10), which reflected the views expressed during that session on the implementation and further enhancement of the declaration, the commission requested the Secretary-General (resolution 1989/45) to circulate it to all governments, United Nations organs and specialized agencies, and other governmental and non-governmental organizations, drawing their attention to the analytical compilation of replies (UN Doc. E/CN.4/AC.39/1989/1). It also called upon the Secretary-General to transmit a questionnaire to governments, United Nations organs and specialized agencies, as well as to other governmental and non-governmental organizations, including those active in development and human rights, in order to elicit from them additional updated and more specific views on the subject of the implementation and further enhancement of the declaration.

In the same resolution, the commission invited the Secretary-General to organize, in 1989, a global consultation on the realization of the right to development involving experts with relevant experience gained at the national level and representatives of organizations and agencies within the United Nations system, including those active in development and human rights, to focus on the fundamental problems posed by the implementation of the declaration, the criteria which might be used to identify progress, and the mechanisms for stimulating and evaluating such progress.

The Global Consultation on the Realization of the Right to Development as a Human Right took place at the United Nations office in Geneva from 8 to 12 January 1990. Leading experts in the various fields were invited to prepare short background papers and to participate in the consultation by introducing their topics and taking part in the ensuing discussions.

In addition to the speakers under each item of the agenda, representatives of specialized agencies; concerned units of the United Nations Secretariat; international trade, development, and financial institutions; and non-governmental organizations participated in the discussions. A special effort was made to ensure the participation of representatives of development-related non-governmental organizations and, in particular, those with direct experience in development projects. The consultation began with a round-table exchange of views on "Development and Human Rights: Global Perspectives and New Policy Directions," which provided a framework for the ensuing debates of the consultation.

In addition to the expert participants, ten United Nations bodies, two intergovernmental organizations, 36 non-governmental organizations, and 53 States were represented at the consultation, with more than 170 persons attending in one capacity or another.

RIGHT TO LEAVE ANY COUNTRY, INCLUDING ONE'S OWN, AND TO RETURN TO ONE'S OWN COUNTRY. In 1960, the UN Sub-Commission on Discrimination and Protection of Minorities decided (resolution 5 [XII]) to initiate a study of discrimination in respect of the right of everyone to leave any country, including his own, and to return to his country, as provided in article 13, para. 2, of the UNIVERSAL DECLARATION OF HUMAN RIGHTS. Mr. Jose D. Ingles (Philippines), a member of the sub-commission, was appointed as special rapporteur to carry out the study.

The special rapporteur completed his study in 1963, and it was published the following year (UN publication, Sales No. 64.XIV.2). It concluded with proposals for action by States and by the international community which included the adoption of a series of principles. Draft principles, formulated by the special rapporteur, were set out in annex VI of the study. After examination by the sub-commission, they were forwarded to the Commission on Human Rights for further consideration and adoption.

However, it was only in 1973 that the study received the attention of the Commission on Human Rights and the Economic and Social Council. At that time, the council took no action other than to request the commission to deal with the subject further at three-year intervals.

In 1982, the sub-commission called upon one of its members, Mr. C.L.C. Mubanga-Chipoya (Zambia), to prepare an analysis of current trends and developments in respect of the right of everyone to leave any country, including his own, and to return to his country. The analysis (UN Doc. E/CN.4/Sub.2/1988/35 and Add. 1 and Corr. 1), submitted to the sub-commission in 1988, included the special rapporteur's proposal for a revised set of draft principles, reproduced below.

At the request of the sub-commission (resolution 1988/39), the secretary-general transmitted the revised draft principles to UN member States and to the intergovernmental and non-governmental organizations concerned, for their comments. The comments received were presented to the sub-commission at its 1989 session (UN Doc. E/CN.4/Sub.2/1989/44).

After considering the draft declaration and comments thereon, the sub-commission requested the secretary-general (resolution 1989/25) to prepare an analytical summary of them. It decided that it would establish, at its 1990 session, an open-ended working group with a view to preparing a revised version of the draft declaration for submission to its parent bodies.

The *Draft Declaration on Freedom and Non-Discrimination in respect of the Right of Everyone to Leave any Country, including his Own, and to Return to his*

Country prepared by special rapporteur Mr. C.L.C. Mubanga-Chipoya is as follows:

Preamble

Whereas the peoples of the United Nations in the Charter solemnly reaffirmed their faith in fundamental human rights, in the dignity and worth of the human person, in the equal rights of men and women and of nations large and small, and expressed their determination to promote social progress and better standards of life in larger freedom,

Whereas the Charter declares that it is one of the purposes of the United Nations to promote and encourage universal respect and observance of human rights and fundamental freedoms for all without distinction as to race, sex, language or religion,

Recognizing that respect for human rights and fundamental freedoms is essential for peace, justice and well-being and is necessary to ensure the development of friendly relations and co-operation among all States,

Recalling that the Universal Declaration of Human Rights, the International Covenant on Civil and Political Rights, and the International Convention on the Elimination of All Forms of Racial Discrimination, as well as regional conventions, recognize the fundamental principle, based on general international law, that everyone has the right to leave any country, including one's own, and to return to one's own country,

Emphasizing that the right of everyone to leave any country and to enter one's own country is indispensable for the full enjoyment of all civil, political, economic, social and culture rights and the free and untrammelled exercise of this right is a sure means of fostering mutual understanding, co-operation and beneficial exchanges among the peoples of the world so that they may practise tolerance and live together in peace as good neighbors,

Recognizing that an individual has duties to himself and to his family as well as to the community in which he lives and in which alone the full and free development of his personality is possible,

Concerned that the denial of this right is the cause of widespread human suffering, a source of international tensions, and an object of international concern,

Whereas this right can only be effectively guaranteed when formally acknowledged in national law consistent with the principles of the Charter of the United Nations, the Universal Declaration of Human Rights and the International Covenant on Civil and Political Rights,

Now therefore the following principles are hereby proclaimed as of universal application to ensure recognition and enjoyment of the right of everyone to leave any country, including his own, and to return to his country, and other related rights, and to prevent discrimination in respect of these rights and urges upon all nations the elaboration, implementation and enforcement of the following principles through effective international machinery and international laws and processes.

Part I
General Provisions

Article 1. Everyone has the right to leave any country, including one's own, and to enter one's own country, without distinction as to race, colour, sex, language, religion, political or other opinion, national or social origin, property, birth, marriage, age (except for minors not *sui juris* independently of their parents) or other status.

Article 2. (a) Every State shall adopt such legislative or other measures as may be necessary to ensure the full and effective enjoyment of the rights set forth in this Declaration.

(b) All laws, administrative regulations or other provisions affecting the enjoyment of these rights shall be published and made easily accessible.

(c) The conditions prescribed by law of administrative regulations for the exercise of this right shall be the same for all nationals of a country.

Part II
Right to Leave

Article 3. Every State shall recognize, implement and enforce, the right of any person to leave its territory, temporarily or permanently.

Article 4. In the implementation of the right to leave every State shall prevent adverse economic consequences through the "brain drain" and shall make bilateral and multilateral arrangements for the benefit of the developing countries concerned.

Article 5. No person nor members of his family shall be subjected to any sanction, penalty, official or unofficial reprisals or harassments for seeking to exercise or for exercising the right to leave a country, such as acts which adversely affect, *inter alia*, employment, housing, residence status of social, economic or educational benefits.

(a) No person shall be required to renounce his or her nationality in order to leave a country, nor shall a person be deprived of his nationality for seeking to exercise or for exercising his right to leave a country.

(b) No person shall be denied the right to leave a country on the grounds that that person wished to renounce or has renounced his or her nationality.

Article 7. (a) No restriction may be imposed on the right to leave any country including one's own or to enter any country except those which are

  (i)   Provided by law;

  (ii) Necessary to protect national security, "public order" (*ordre public*), public health or morals or the rights and freedoms of others;

  (iii) Consistent with internationally recognized human rights and other international legal obligations.

Any such restriction shall be narrowly construed.

(b) Any restriction on the right to leave or enter shall be clear, specific and not subject to arbitrary application.

(c) A restriction shall be considered "necessary" only if it responds to a pressing public and social need, pursues a legitimate aim and is proportionate to that aim.

(d) A restriction based on "national security" may be invoked only in situations where the exercise of the right poses a clear, imminent and serious danger to the State. When this restriction is invoked on the grounds that an individual acquired military secrets, the restriction shall be applicable only for a limited time, appropriate to the specific circumstances, which should not be more than five years after the individual acquired such secrets.

(e) A restriction based on "public order" (*ordre public*) shall be directly related to the specific interest which is sought to be protected. "Public order" (*ordre public*) means the universally accepted fundamental principles, consistent with respect for human rights, on which democratic society is based.

(f) "Public health" may be invoked when there is a serious threat to the health of the population or individual members of the population.

(g) "Public morals" may be invoked when it is essential to the maintenance of respect for fundamental moral values of the community.

(h) A restriction based on "the rights and freedoms of others" shall not imply that relatives (except for parents with respect to minors not *sui juris),* employers or other persons may prevent, by withholding their consent, the departure (entry) of any person seeking to leave (to enter) a country.

Article 8. (a) No fees, taxes or other exactions shall be imposed for seeking to exercise or exercising the right to leave a country, with the exception of nominal fees related to travel documents.

(b) No deposit or other security shall be required to ensure the repatriation or return of any national.

(c) Currency or other economic controls shall not be used as a means of preventing any national from leaving his country.

(d) Any national prevented from leaving his country because of non-compliance with obligations towards the State, or towards another person, shall be allowed to make reasonable arrangements for satisfying these obligations.

Article 9. (a) Any person leaving a country shall be entitled to take out of that country

    (i) His or her personal property, including household effects and property connected with the exercise of that person's profession or skills;

    (ii) All other property or the proceeds thereof, subject only to the satisfaction of legal monetary obligations, such as maintenance obligations to family members, and to general controls imposed by law to safeguard the national economy, provided that such controls do not have the effect of denying the exercise of the right.

(b) Property or the proceeds thereof which cannot be taken out of the country shall remain in the possession of the departing owner, who shall be free to dispose of such property or proceeds within the country.

Part III
The Right to Return

Article 10. (a) No one shall be deprived of the right to enter [to return to] his own country.

(b) The right of everyone to return to his country shall not be subject to any arbitrary restrictions.

(c) No person shall be deprived of nationality or citizenship in order to enforce exile or to prevent that person from exercising the right to enter his or her country.

(d) No entry visa or fees or taxes may be required to enter one's own country.

Article 11. Permament legal residents who leave their country of residence shall not be denied the right to return to that country except for reasonable cause identical to those applicable under article 7 of this Declaration.

Part IV
The Right of a Foreigner to Leave the Country

Article 12. (a) Every foreigner has the right to leave the country of his sojourn.

(b) Every foreigner, legally within the territory of a country shall not be accorded lesser rights than a national in the exercise of his right to leave that country.

(c) The right of every foreigner to leave the country of his sojourn shall not be subject to any arbitrary restrictions.

(d) No foreigner shall be prevented from seeking the diplomatic assistance of his own country in order to ensure the enjoyment of his right to leave the country of his sojourn.

Part V
Travel Documents and Procedural Safeguards

Article 13. (a) Everyone has the right to obtain such travel or other documents as may be necessary to leave any country or to enter one's own country. No one shall be denied such documents and permits.

(b) Such documents shall be issued free of charge or subject only to nominal fees.

Article 14. (a) Any national procedures or requirements affecting the exercise of the rights set forth in this Declaration shall be established by law or administrative regulations adopted pursuant to law.

(b) No State shall refuse to issue the documents referred to in article 13 (a) or shall otherwise impede the exercise of the right to leave, on the grounds of the applicant's inability to present authorization to enter another country.

(c) Procedures for the issuance of the documents referred to in article 13 (a) shall be expeditious and shall not be unreasonably lengthy or burdensome.

(d) Everyone filing an application for any document referred to in article 13 (a) shall be entitled to obtain promptly a duly certified receipt for the application filed. Decisions regarding issuance of such documents shall be taken within a reasonable period of time specified by law. The applicant shall be promptly informed in writing of any decision denying, withdrawing, cancelling or postponing issuance of any such document; the specific reasons therefor; the facts upon which the decision is based; and the administrative or other remedies available to appeal the decision.

Article 15. The right to appeal to higher administrative or judicial authority shall be provided in all instances in which the right to leave or enter is denied. The appellant shall have a full opportunity to present the grounds for the appeal, to be represented by counsel of his or her choice, and to challenge the validity of any fact upon which a denial or restriction has been founded. The results of any appeal, specifying the reasons for the decision, shall be communicated promptly in writing to the appellant.

Article 16. Any person claiming violation of his rights set forth in this Declaration shall have effective recourse to a judicial or other independent tribunal to seek enforcement of those rights.

Article 17. (a) No State may impede communication by any person with an international organization outside the State with regard to the rights set forth in this Declaration. No sanction, penalty, reprisal or harassment may be imposed on anyone exercising this right of communication.

(b) No one shall be hindered in or penalized for communicating with or petitioning the United Nations or other intergovernmental or non-governmental organizations complaining of the denial of the rights set forth in this Declaration or seeking their assistance in the exercise of these rights.

(c) No one shall be penalized for or prevented from communicating with foreign consular or diplomatic officials with a view to obtaining travel documents or permits.

(d) A person who claims to be a national of another State shall not be prevented from seeking the assistance of that State in order to ensure his right to leave or return.

Part VI
Final Provisions

Article 18. The enjoyment of the rights set forth in this Declaration shall not be limited because of activities protected under internationally recognized human rights or other international legal obligations.

Article 19. Nothing in this Declaration shall be interpreted as implying for any State, group or person any right to engage in any activity or perform any act aimed at destroying any of the rights set forth herein or at limiting them to a greater extent than is provided for in this Declaration.

Article 20. The present Declaration shall not be interpreted to limit the enjoyment of any human right protected by international law.

SEE ALSO *Helsinki Accord entries; Movement and Residence.*

RIGHT TO LIFE. A human right proclaimed in the UNIVERSAL DECLARATION OF HUMAN RIGHTS as follows:

Article 3. Everyone has the right to life, liberty and the security of person.

The meaning and scope of the right to life is clarified in the INTERNATIONAL COVENANT ON CIVIL AND POLITICAL RIGHTS in the following provision:

Article 6.(1). Every human being has the inherent right to life. This right shall be protected by law. No one shall be arbitrarily deprived of his life.

(2). In countries which have not abolished the death penalty, sentence of death may be imposed only for the most serious crimes in accordance with the law in force at the time of the commission of the crime and not contrary to the provisions of the present Covenant and to the Convention on the Prevention and Punishment of the Crime of Genocide. This penalty can only be carried out pursuant to a final judgement rendered by a competent court.

(3). When deprivation of life constitutes the crime of genocide, it is understood that nothing in this article shall authorize any State Party to the present Covenant to derogate in any way from any obligation assumed under the provisions of the Convention on the Prevention and Punishment of the Crime of Genocide.

(4). Anyone sentenced to death shall have the right to seek pardon or commutation of the sentence. Amnesty, pardon or commutation of the sentence of death may be granted in all cases.

(5). Sentence of death shall not be imposed for crimes committed by persons below eighteen years of age and shall not be carried out on pregnant women.

(6). Nothing in this article shall be invoked to delay or to prevent the abolition of capital punishment by any State Party to the present Covenant.

The AMERICAN CONVENTION ON HUMAN RIGHTS, open for acceptance by member States of the ORGANIZATION OF AMERICAN STATES, provides that:

Article 4. (1). Every person has the right to have his life respected. This right shall be protected by law and, in general, from the moment of conception. No one shall be arbitrarily deprived of his life.

(2). In countries that have not abolished the death penalty, it may be imposed only for the most serious crimes and pursuant to a final judgment rendered by a competent court and in accordance with a law establishing such punishment, enacted prior to the commission of the crime. The application of such punishment shall not be extended to crimes to which it does not presently apply.

(3). The death penalty shall not be reestablished in states that have abolished it.

(4). In no case shall capital punishment be inflicted for political offenses or related common crimes.

(5). Capital punishment shall not be imposed upon persons who, at the time the crime was committed, were under 18 years of age or over 70 years of age; nor shall it be applied to pregnant women.

(6). Every person condemned to death shall have the right to apply for amnesty, pardon, or commutation of sentence, which may be granted in all cases. Capital punishment shall not be imposed while such a petition is pending decision by the competent authority.

The AFRICAN CHARTER OF HUMAN AND PEOPLES' RIGHTS, open for acceptance by member States of the ORGANIZATION OF AFRICAN UNITY, provides that:

Article 4. Human beings are inviolable. Every human being shall be entitled to respect for his life and the integrity of his person. No one may be arbitrarily deprived of this right.

The EUROPEAN CONVENTION ON HUMAN RIGHTS, open for acceptance by members of the COUNCIL OF EUROPE, provides that:

Article 2. (1). Everyone's right to life shall be protected by law. No one shall be deprived of his life intentionally save in the execution of a sentence of a court following his conviction of a crime for which this penalty is provided by law.

(2). Deprivation of life shall not be regarded as inflicted in contravention of this Article when it results from the use of force which is no more than absolutely necessary:

(a) in defense of any person from unlawful violence;

(b) in order to effect a lawful arrest or to prevent the escape of a person lawfully detained;

(c) in action lawfully taken for the purpose of quelling a riot or insurrection.

The EUROPEAN CONVENTION ON HUMAN RIGHTS, PROTOCOL VI, contains the following provisions:

Article 1. The death penalty shall be abolished. No one shall be condemned to such penalty or executed.

Article 2. A State may make provision in its law for the death penalty in respect of acts committed in time of war or of imminent threat of war; such penalty shall be applied only in the instances laid down in the law and in accordance with its provisions. The State shall communicate to the Secretary-General of the Council of Europe the relevant provisions of the law.

In addition, the COVENTION ON THE PREVENTION AND PUNISHMENT OF THE CRIME OF GENOCIDE and the INTERNATIONAL CONVENTION ON THE SUPPRESSION AND PUNISHMENT OF THE CRIME OF *APARTHEID* both define as crimes the killing of members of certain racial or other groups with a view to bringing about the physical destruction of such a group in whole or in part.

After examining reports submitted by States parties to the International Covenant of Civil and Political Rights in accordance with article 40 of that instrument, the HUMAN RIGHTS COMMITTEE adopted two general comments on article 6 which, although formulated primarily to guide States in the preparation of future reports, incidentally serve to throw light on the meaning and scope which the committee attributes to certain provisions of the covenant. The first such comment, adopted in 1982, reads:

The right to life enunciated in article 6 of the Covenant has been dealt with in all State reports. It is the supreme right from which no derogations is permitted even in time of public emergency which threatens the life of the nation (article 4). However, the Committee has noted that quite often the information given concerning article 6 has been limited to only one or other aspect of this right. It is a right which should not be interpreted narrowly.

The Committee observes that war and other acts of mass violence continue to be a scourge of humanity and take the lives of thousands of innocent human beings every year. Under the Charter of the United Nations the threat or use of force by any State against another State, except in exercise of the inherent right of self-defence, is already prohibited. The Committee considers that States have the supreme duty to prevent wars, acts of genocide and other acts of mass violence causing arbitrary loss of life. Every effort they make to avert the danger of war, especially thermo-nuclear war, and to strengthen international peace and security would constitute the most important condition and guarantee for the safeguarding of the right to life. In this respect, the Committee notes, in particular, a connexion between article 6 and article 20, which states that the law shall prohibit any propaganda for war (paragraph 1) or incitement to violence (paragraph 2) as therein described.

The protection against arbitrary deprivation of life which is explicitly required by the third sentence of article 6 (1) is of paramount importance. The Committee considers that States parties should take measures not only to prevent and punish deprivation of life by criminal acts, but also to prevent arbitrary killing by their own security forces. The deprivation of life by the authorities of the State is a matter of the utmost gravity. Therefore, the law must strictly control and limit the circumstances in which a person may be deprived of his life by such authorities.

States parties should also take specific and effective measures to prevent the disappearance of individuals, something which unfortunately has become all too frequent and leads too often to arbitrary deprivation of life. Further-

more, States should establish effective facilities and procedures to investigate thoroughly cases of missing and disappeared persons in circumstances which may involve a violation of the right to life.

Moreover, the Committee has noted that the right to life has been too often narrowly interpreted. The expression "inherent right to life" cannot properly be understood in a restrictive manner, and the protection of this right requires that States adopt positive measures. In this connexion, the Committee considers that it would be desirable for States parties to take all possible measures to reduce infant mortality and to increase life expectancy, especially in adoping measures to eliminate malnutrition and epidemics.

While it follows from article 6 (2) to (6) that States parties are not obliged to abolish the death penalty totally, they are obliged to limit its use and, in particular, to abolish it for other than the "most serious crimes". Accordingly, they ought to consider reviewing their criminal laws in this light and, in any event, are obliged to restrict the application of the death penalty to the "most serious crimes". The article also refers generally to abolition in terms which strongly suggest (paras. 2 (2) and (6)) that abolition is desirable. The Committee concludes that all measures of abolition should be considered as progress in the enjoyment of the right to life within the meaning of article 40, and should as such be reported to the Committee. The Committee notes that a number of States have already abolished the death penalty or suspended its application. Nevertheless, States' reports show that progress made towards abolishing or limiting the application of the death penalty is quite inadequate.

The Committee is of the opinion that the expression "most serious crimes" must be read restrictively to mean that the death penalty should be a quite exceptional measure. It also follows from the express terms of article 6 that it can only be imposed in accordance with the law in force at the time of the commission of the crime and not contrary to the Covenant. The procedural guarantees therein prescribed must be observed, including the right to a fair hearing by an independent tribunal, the presumption of innocence, the minimum guarantees for the defence, and the right to review by a higher tribunal. These rights are applicable in addition to the particular right to seek pardon or commutation of the sentence.

The second comment, adopted in 1985, reads:

In its general comment 6 (16), adopted at its 378th meeting on 27 July 1982, the Human Rights Committee observes that the right to life enunciated in the first paragraph of article 6 of the International Covenant on Civil and Political Rights is the supreme right from which no derogation is permitted even in time of public emergency. The same right to life is enshrined in article 3 of the Universal Declaration of Human Rights adopted by the General Assembly of the United Nations on 10 December 1948. It is basic to all human rights.

In its previous general comment, the Committee also observes that it is the supreme duty of States to prevent wars. War and other acts of mass violence continue to be a scourge of humanity and take the lives of thousands of innocent human beings every year.

While remaining deeply concerned by the toll of human life taken by conventional weapons in armed conflicts, the Committee has noted that, during successive sessions of the

General Assembly, representatives from all geographical regions have expressed their growing concern at the development and proliferation of increasingly awesome weapons of mass destruction, which not only threaten human life but also absorb resources that could otherwise be used for vital economic and social purposes, particularly for the benefit of developing countries, and thereby for promoting and securing the enjoyment of human rights for all.

The Committee associates itself with this concern. It is evident that the designing, testing, manufacture, possession and deployment of nuclear weapons are among the greatest threats to the right to life which confront mankind today. This threat is compounded by the danger that the actual use of such weapons may be brought about, not only in the event of war, but even through human or mechanical error or failure.

Furthermore, the very existence and gravity of this threat generate a climate of suspicion and fear between States, which is in itself antagonistic to the promotion of universal respect for and observance of human rights and fundamental freedoms in accordance with the Charter of the United Nations and the International Covenants on Human Rights.

The production, testing, possession, deployment and use of nuclear weapons should be prohibited and recognized as crimes against humanity.

The Committee accordingly, in the interest of mankind, calls upon all States, whether parties to the Covenant or not, to take urgent steps, unilaterally and by agreement, to rid the world of this menace.

At its 1987 session, the UN General Assembly adopted a comprehensive resolution (resolution 42/99) on the right to life, based on its conviction that all rights and freedoms, as well as all the material goods and spiritual wealth that both man and nations possess, have a common foundation—the right to life, freedom, peace, and aspiration for happiness.

In the resolution, the assembly reaffirmed that all peoples and all individuals have an inherent right to life and that the safeguarding of this cardinal right is an essential condition for the enjoyment of the entire range of economic, social, and cultural, as well as civil and political, rights. It stressed the urgent need for the international community to make every effort to strengthen peace, remove the growing threat of war, particularly nuclear war, halt the arms race, and achieve general and complete disarmament under effective international control and prevent violations of the principles of the of the United Nations Charter regarding the sovereignty and territorial integrity of States and the self-determination of peoples, thus contributing to ensuring the right to life. It stressed further the foremost importance of the implementation of practical measures of disarmament to bring to an end the waste of valuable resources and to streamline them to fight economic backwardness and poverty and to accelerate social and economic progress, particularly for the benefit of developing countries.

The assembly called upon all States, appropriate United Nations organs, specialized agencies, and intergovernmental and non-governmental organizations concerned to take the necessary measures to ensure that the results of scientific and technological progress, the material and intellectual potential of mankind, are used to solve global problems exclusively in the interests of international peace, for the benefit of mankind, and for promoting and encouraging universal respect for human rights and fundamental freedoms.

It also called upon all States that had not done so to take effective measures with a view to prohibiting, in accordance with the International Covenant on Civil and Political Rights, any propaganda for war, in particular the formulation, propounding, and dissemination of and propaganda for doctrines and concepts aimed at unleashing nuclear war.

The Commission on Human Rights echoed these views at its 1988 session (resolution 1988/60), and expressed profound concern that international peace and security continue to be threatened by the arms race in all its aspects, particularly the nuclear arms race, as well as by violations of the principles of the UNITED NATIONS CHARTER regarding the sovereignty and territorial integrity of States and the SELF-DETERMINATION of peoples. It recognized that peoples want to live in a better and more equitable world based on recognition of the priority of the values common to all mankind; that the widening availability of technology and scientific and technical advances, bringing new possibilities for peaceful and productive enterprise, open new perspectives for the progress of civilization and provide increasing opportunities to better the conditions of life of peoples and nations, but at the same time present new dangers if used for the creation of new types of deadly weapons, which are already able to transform an armed conflict from human tragedy to human annihilation; and that it is only the creative genius of man that makes progress and the development of civilization possible in a peaceful environment and that human life must be recognized as supreme.

Convinced of the need to intensify efforts to foster the spirit of mutual respect, understanding, and confidence and to combat attempts to incite enmity, hatred, and intolerance and to impose "enemy-image" stereotypes, it emphasized the importance of overcoming prejudices based on intolerance, hatred, and stereotypes of this kind.

The commission, finally, requested the Secretary-General, in the light of the comments and views of member States, to submit a report on the implementation of its resolution to the commission at its 1990 session.

On 8 December 1988, the General Assembly (resolution 43/111) again reaffirmed that all people have an inherent right to life, recalled the historic responsibility of the governments of all countries of the world to preserve civilization and to insure that everyone enjoys that right, and called upon all States to do their utmost to assist in implementing the right through the adoption of appropriate measures at both the national and the international levels.

Similarly, on 15 December 1989, the assembly, realizing that it is only the creative genius of man that makes progress and the development of civilization possible in a peaceful environment and that human life must be recognized as supreme and recalling the historic responsibility of the governments of all countries of the world to preserve civilization and to ensure that everyone enjoys his inherent right to life, called upon those Governments (resolution 44/133) to do their utmost to assist in implementing the right to life through the adoption of appropriate measures, at the national and international levels, to ensure that the results of scientific and technological progress and the material and intellectual potential of mankind are used for the benefit of mankind and for promoting and encouraging respect for human rights and fundamental freedoms.

SEE ALSO *Abortion; Amnesty Laws; Capital Punishment entries; Chemical Weapons entries; Convention on the Prohibition of the Development, Production and Stockpiling of Bacteriological . . . and Toxin Weapons. . .; Crimes against the Peace and Security of Mankind; Death Penalty entries; Declaration on the Prevention of Nuclear Catastrophe; Environment entries; Executions: Report of Special Rapporteur; Genocide; Nuclear Disarmament; Standard of Living; Toxic and Dangerous Products and Wastes.*

RIGHT TO LIFE: DISPOSAL OF DANGEROUS PRODUCTS AND WASTES.

On 11 December 1987, the General Assembly expressed concern (resolution 42/183) that part of the international disposal of toxic and dangerous products and wastes is being carried out in contravention of existing national legislation and relevant international legal instruments, as well as internationally accepted guidelines and principles, to the detriment of the environment and public health of all countries, particularly of developing countries. The Assembly requested the Secretary-General to prepare a comprehensive report on the question of illegal traffic in toxic and dangerous products and wastes and its impact on all countries.

Taking into account a preliminary report on the subject submitted by the Secretary-General to the Economic and Social Council (UN Doc. E/1988/72), which drew attention to this problem, the SUB-COMMISSION ON PREVENTION OF DISCRIMINATION AND PROTECTION OF MINORITIES at its 1988 session prepared a draft resolution on the subject which it recommended for adoption by the COMMISSION ON HUMAN RIGHTS.

The draft proposed that the commission, bearing in mind the right of all peoples to life and of the future generation to enjoy its heritage, should note that the movement and dumping of toxic and dangerous products endanger basic human rights such as the right to life, the right to live in a sound and healthy environment, and, consequently, the right to health; and should request the governments of those countries producing toxic and dangerous wastes to ban their exportation to States which do not have the technical capability for their environmentally sound disposal and to take proper measures to ensure that they do not imperil human health and the ecosystem in their countries, as well as in other countries of the world.

SEE ALSO *Environment: Toxic and Dangerous Wastes.*

ROMANIA. The Socialist Republic of Romania is a country in eastern Europe, on the Black Sea. It has borders with Bulgaria, Hungary, the Union of Soviet Socialist Republics, and Yugoslavia. It proclaimed its independence from Turkey in 1877, and its status as an independent State was confirmed by the Treaty of Berlin in 1878. It became a kingdom in 1881 and a constitutional monarchy in 1886.

After the election of a communist-dominated government in 1946, King Michael abdicated, and the country became the People's Republic of Romania. As such, it joined the Warsaw Treaty Organization and the United Nations in 1955. Under a new constitution, its name was changed to the Socialist Republic of Romania in 1965.

Nicolae Ceausescu, who succeeded Gheorghe Gheorghiu-Dej as communist party chief in 1965, presided over a government which harshly suppressed dissidents, mistreated the large Hungarian ethnic minority, and totally disregarded consumer needs. Drastic cuts in the use of energy and in the production of the necessities of life, initiated in 1981 with a view to eliminating a foreign debt of more than $11 billion by the end of the decade, reduced living standards to an unbearable level. By 1987, factory workers marched in protest through the streets of several Romanian cities.

The human rights situation in Romania was first examined by the UN COMMISSION ON HUMAN RIGHTS at its 1989 session on the basis of alarming information received from a number of reliable sources. On 9 March 1989, the commission expressed its concern (resolution 1989/75) about serious violations of human rights having occurred in the country and authorized its chairman to appoint a special rapporteur to look into the situation and prepare a report.

Appointed as the special rapporteur, Mr. Joseph Voyame (Switzerland) completed a report (UN Doc. E/-CN.4/1990/28) on 18 December 1989 for presentation to the 1990 session of the commission, scheduled to be convened on 29 January 1990. However, he later found it necessary to prepare an addendum to the report (UN Doc. E/CN.4/1990/28/Rev. 1) in order to take into account the revolutionary events which occurred in Romania between 19 December and 18 February 1989. He submitted the addendum to the commission on 22 February 1990.

In the basic report, the special rapporteur presented the following general information about Romania (para. 27–36):

Romania has a surface area of 237,500 square kilometres and a population of about 23 million. Nearly half the population (11.8 million persons) live in urban areas. Until the latest administrative reform of 17 April 1989, the country was divided into 40 departments, plus the municipality of Bucharest, 237 towns and 2,705 communes comprising 13,123 villages (which do not have their own administrative structure).

In historical terms, the union, in January 1859, of Moldavia and Walachia laid the foundations for the modern Romanian State. Romania's independence was proclaimed in 1877 and recognized by the Congress of Berlin in 1878. Following the First World War and the dismantling of the Austro-Hungarian Empire, under the 1920 Treaty of Trianon, Romania acquired Transylvania, Bessarabia and Bukovina. During the Second World War, northern Transylvania was attached to Hungary. Northern Bukovina and Bessarabia were ceded to the Soviet Union and southern Dobruja to Bulgaria. The Peace Treaty signed in Paris on 10 February 1947 re-established the 1920 border between Hungary and Romania and Romanian sovereignty over all of Transylvania.

A pro-Soviet Government headed by Petru Groza was installed in March 1945. After the 1946 elections, most government posts were given to the communists. In December 1947, following the abdication of the King, Parliament announced the establishment of a People's Republic (renamed the Socialist Republic of Romania in 1965). The first Constitution of the Republic was adopted in 1948.

According to the 1965 Constitution (republished in 1987), Romania is a unitary State and a socialist republic, where "the Romanian Communist Party is the leading political force of all of society" (art. 3).

The supreme organ of State power is the Grand National Assembly, the sole legislative organ, which usually meets twice a year. Under the electoral law, the Democracy and Socialist Unity Front, (which is composed of all the country's political and social forces and all grass-roots and civic organizations) organizes elections under the leadership of the Communist Party and "nominates deputies to the Grand National Assembly and the people's councils" (art. 3).

The Council of State, the supreme organ of State power which functions on a permanent basis, is subordinate to, and elected by, the Grand National Assembly. The Council is presided over by the President of the Republic. The current President of the Republic, Nicolae Ceausescu, was elected in March 1974 and re-elected in 1975, 1980 and 1985 and has been President of the Council of State since December 1967. He has also been General Secretary of the Romanian Communist Party since March 1965 and President of the Democracy and Socialist Unity Front. In addition, he is President of the National Workers' Council, the National Agricultural Council, the Supreme Economic and Social Development Council, to which the State Planning Committee was recently added, and the Defence Council.

The functions of the Council of State are, *inter alia:* to draft legislation (although it is unable to amend the Constitution); to appoint and dismiss the Prime Minister and the Council of Ministers if the Grand National Assembly is not in session; and to interpret the laws in force. The people's councils, which are local organs of State power, are responsible for local government. They ensure "the economic, social, cultural and civic development of the administrative-territorial units where they have been elected, the defence of socialist property, the protection of the rights of citizens, socialist legality and the maintenance of public order" (Constitution, art. 86). The Council of Ministers is an administrative organ which monitors implementation of the decisions of the Grand National Assembly.

Under the Constitution, justice is administered by the Supreme Court, the district courts, the magistrates' courts and the military courts (art. 101). The Supreme Court is elected by the Grand National Assembly. The Procurator-General, who is responsible for the work of the Procurator's Office, is also elected by the Grand National Assembly. The Procurator's Office "monitors the work of the criminal prosecution and sentencing bodies" and ensures respect for legality and the defence of the socialist régime (art. 112). The people's judges and assessors and the chief prosecutors of the departments and the municipality of Bucharest are elected by the people's councils. The Grand National Assembly and, between sessions, the Council of State are empowered to grant amnesty. In the past few years, amnesties have regularly been granted by decree (17 since 1965), notably in 1981, 1984, 1986, 1987 and 1988. Under the amnesty decree published on 27 January 1988, all persons sentenced to 10 years' imprisonment or less were amnestied. Sentences of more than 10 years were reduced by half, and death sentences were commuted to 20 years' imprisonment.

Until the Second World War, there were some 60 religious sects in Romania. Under Decree No. 177/1948 of 1948, sects wishing to organize their activities have to be recognized by decree of the Council of State on the recommendation of the Department of Worship. At present, 14 religious sects carry out their activities on the basis of statutes adopted by agreement with the State. The Orthodox Church has between 16 and 18 million members. The second largest Church is the Roman Catholic Church, with some 1.3 million members, of whom most (about 700,000) are of Hungarian ethnic origin and about 100,000 of German origin. Of the Protestant churches, the largest is the Reformed Church, which is composed primarily of Hungarians. Mention may also be made of the Lutheran Church, composed mainly of Germans, and the Baptist Church. The Jewish community had about 400,000 members after the Second World War, but most of them have emigrated and only about 20,000 are now left. The Churches which are not legally recognized include the

Greek (Uniate) Catholic Church, which was officially disbanded by governmental decree on 1 December 1948 and is reported to have more than 1.5 million members, the Army of the Lord, with about 400,000 members, the Jehovah's Witnesses, and the Nazarene Church.

In addition to ethnic Romanians (89.1 per cent of the total population, according to the 1977 census), Romania comprises minorities which are officially known as "co-inhabiting nationalities" and include ethnic Hungarians, who are estimated at between 1.7 and 2.5 million (7.7 per cent of the population) gypsies, estimated at between several hundred thousand and over 1 million (0.4 per cent of the population), ethnic Germans, estimated at some 250,000 (1.5 per cent of the population), ethnic Ukrainians, Serbo-Croatians and Jews (0.3 per cent, 0.2 per cent and 0.1 per cent of the population, respectively), and ethnic Russians, Tartars, Slovaks and Turks (each group less than 0.1 per cent of the population). All the above figures are based on the 1977 census. There is also a Catholic Hungarian-speaking community, the Csangos, who have lived in Moldavia for several centuries and number about 250,000 persons. The Csangos are not officially regarded as one of the "co-inhabiting nationalities"....

The special rapporteur's conclusions and recommendations, as set out in the basic report, were as follows (chap. V, para. 211–235):

The Special Rapporteur has endeavoured to carry out his mandate as fully and objectively as possible. To this end, he has tried to secure the co-operation of the Romanian authorities and to conduct investigations in Romania itself. To his great regret, he met with a refusal; the Romanian Government deems null and void Commission on Human Rights resolution 1989/75, in which the Commission decided to appoint a special rapporteur to examine the human rights situation in Romania. None the less, the Special Rapporteur has studied the Romanian constitutional, legislative and regulatory provisions as fully as possible, to the extent that they relate to his mandate. In addition, he has made every effort to take the position of the Romanian authorities into account on the basis of the reports which they have sent to various United Nations bodies or specialized agencies.

In order to compile the information necessary for the fulfilment of his mandate, he interviewed a large number of persons who had come to Geneva to provide him with information. In addition, he went to Hungary, specifically in the vicinity of the Romanian-Hungarian frontier. There he was able to interview some 60 recent emigrants from Romania who belonged to various ethnic groups and came from all sectors of Romanian society.

Lastly, he consulted a very large number of documents relating to the human rights situation in Romania.

The information thus gathered does not, of course, enable the Special Rapporteur to draw absolutely certain conclusions, such as might derive from a thorough inquiry in Romania itself. Nevertheless, this information is sufficiently precise and consistent for reasonably reliable observations to be made. In this regard, the Special Rapporteur emphasizes that he has not taken account of isolated allegations; each of the points noted is based on several sources of mutually corroborative information. As to the numerous cases listed in annex 1, they are essentially intended to illustrate observations based on more general information.

Lastly, the Special Rapporteur has taken into consideration only relatively recent information and has not in principle, dealt with the period before 1980, even though many violations prior to that date were brought to his attention.

In these circumstances, the Special Rapporteur finds that the Commission on Human Rights has justifiably concerned itself with the situation in Romania. This country is indeed a party to most of the international conventions formulated within the United Nations system which universally protect human rights; it submits the reports called for under these instruments and takes part in discussions on them. It is also a party to the Final Act of the Helsinki Conference on Security and Co-operation in Europe, and to the Concluding Document of the Vienna Meeting relating to the Follow-up to the Helsinki Agreements. It should nevertheless be noted that, in practice, these international instruments are frequently ignored or are only partially implemented in Romania. In these conclusions, the Special Rapporteur will not recapitulate everything stated in the earlier parts of this report. He will simply point out what, in his view, constitute the major violations of the various instruments which protect human rights and by which Romania is bound.

With regard to the right to life, the Special Rapporteur was informed of various cases of deaths or disappearances, either following ill-treatment during interrogations or detention periods, or in the course of attempts to leave the country without authorization. He was unable to elucidate these cases.

As to the right to physical and moral integrity, the reports received are numerous and consistent enough to prompt the conclusion that this right is frequently violated: brutal treatment of persons arrested during attempts to cross the frontier illegally; intimidation, psychological humiliation and maltreatment, including torture, of detainees in order to obtain confessions; poor conditions of detention.

Respect for privacy is frequently violated through arbitrary interference, such as searches and seizures, wiretapping, confiscation or monitoring of correspondence, restriction of personal or telephone contacts, and gynaecological examinations to prevent interruptions of pregnancy.

With regard to the administration of justice, the Romanian Constitution and laws provide guarantees which are in conformity with international standards. But these guarantees are restricted by decrees, ministerial orders and directives, some of which are not published. Thus, searches and arrests are often carried out without a judicial warrant, detainees are sometimes held incommunicado for several months, and prisoners are frequently deprived of their right to know the charges against them, to communicate with their relatives and to be assisted by a lawyer of their choosing. Furthermore, trials are often held *in camera*, and restricted residence is imposed, even though this measure is not provided for under Romanian law.

Freedom of movement is subject to many restrictions. For instance, young people who have completed their education are required to accept the job assigned to them for several years, often far from their families. The right to leave the country is restricted and is frequently applied in an arbitrary fashion; would-be emigrants are often subjected to harassment, sometimes lose their jobs, or are demoted or even imprisoned; persons who attempt to cross the frontier illegally risk prosecution, and it is not unusual for the families of those who have emigrated without authorization to suffer reprisals. It is interesting to note that, despite these dangers, more than 20,000 persons emigrated clandestinely between mid-1987 and October 1989. Lastly, many families are split because their members who have stayed in Romania are not allowed to leave the country.

Freedom of thought, conscience, religion and belief is restricted. Fourteen Churches are recognized; others, such as the Romanian Greek (Uniate) Catholic Church are illegal. The recognized Churches are subject to supervision by the Department of Worship. Faculties of theology can accept students only according to very limited quotas, and even these are being reduced. Religious literature is insufficient; the importation of Bibles, in particular, is subject to severe restrictions. Church members are not allowed to take up certain professions, such as teaching. Some of them have even been subjected to harassment or other penalties.

The broad and sometimes arbitrary interpretation of certain constitutional and legislative provisions leads to serious restrictions on freedom of opinion and expression. Criticism of governmental policy is not permitted. Many persons have for this reason been subjected to various repressive measures, such as police surveillance and summonses, searches, restricted residence, a ban on receiving visitors, disconnection of telephone service, monitoring of correspondence, and even ill-treatment, loss of employment and imprisonment. In addition, writers, journalists and poets have been deprived of the right to publish their works. Contacts with foreign visitors are strictly monitored, as is the possession of typewriters and photocopying machines. Persons who lose their jobs for political reasons are sometimes later prosecuted and convicted of "parasitism".

Freedom of assembly and association is similarly restricted. The general and vague wording of certain constitutional and legislative provisions has made it possible to prohibit any exercise of this freedom which is not in line with governmental policy. In particular, various penalties, including imprisonment, may be imposed on persons who attempt to exercise their right to take part in public affairs by joining a disbanded party, attempting to form a new party or organizing groups of students and young workers who are critical of governmental policy.

The right to work is subject to many infringements. The linking of remuneration to the total output of an enterprise often entails major wage cuts for workers in enterprises which are unable to achieve norms owing to shortages of electricity, raw materials or adequate tools. Working extra hours is common. It should also be noted that workers are assigned to jobs in areas far from their homes and, for various reasons, some are subject to discrimination in the choice of occupation or job and in opportunities for promotion. Trade union rights are also severely restricted. In particular, workers cannot form trade union organizations of their choice and strikes have been harshly suppressed.

The right to an adequate standard of living is relative and depends, of course, on the country's economic situation. It must be admitted, however, that it is not sufficiently guaranteed in Romania. A large segment of the population has great difficulty in obtaining adequate food, especially for young children. In winter, inadequate heating makes life difficult in homes and work places. The rural systematization policy and the abandonment or demolition of individual houses which it entails seem to have aggravated housing conditions, despite the efforts of the authorities to build new homes. Lastly, medical care is often inadequate. Postnatal mortality is high, and elderly persons generally receive only limited medical care.

Cultural rights are under attack in various ways. The cultural heritage is threatened by demolitions in the cities, which have already resulted in the disappearance of many monuments of artistic or historic interest. Similarly, the rural systemization plan is endangering the rich Romanian popular culture, which has been preserved and developed in the villages in particular. Literary and artistic freedom can be exercised only within narrow limits. As stated earlier, authors who criticize the Government's policy are frequently barred from publication or penalized in other ways. The theatres are subject to control by the authorities and very few foreign publications are imported.

The rights of members of minorities are particularly hard hit. In this regard, the Special Rapporteur would point out that, in order to ensure the survival and development of minorities, it is not sufficient to make them subject to the same rules as those applicable to the population as a whole. They must be given special treatment, appropriate to their identity and needs. Nothing of the sort can be seen in Romania. In the first place, it is obvious that minorities, more than the majority, suffer most of the human rights violations referred to above. Thus, the posting of young people to work places far from their families in the long run results in a dispersal of the ethnic minorities and a mixing of populations which places their survival in jeopardy. Likewise, being cut off from home affects them more than the majority, because they need contacts with the outside populations with whom they share language and culture.

In addition, there is a definite trend towards the Romanization of ethnic minorities. Thus, the use of Hungarian and German is disappearing from the civil administration, the courts and enterprises, and from the names of towns and villages and road signs.

This trend is also apparent in education. With a few exceptions, higher education courses are now in Romanian only. In primary, secondary and vocational education, the number of schools and classes in which Hungarian is the language of instruction has declined markedly in favour of Romanian. Restrictions on access to higher education and arbitrary postings, have even led to a shortage of teachers of Hungarian in Transylvania. Moreover, it is not uncommon for ethnic Hungarian or German parents to opt for their children to be educated in Romanian from the beginning, in the expectation that they will thus have better prospects.

At the cultural level, there has been a decrease in creativity and activities in the minority languages. This phenomenon is particularly apparent in the theatre, and on television and radio. While publications in Hungarian are still relatively numerous, they are concentrated in a single publishing house, and the importation of publications from Hungary has been stopped.

The situation of the churches in which a majority of members are ethnic Hungarians or Germans is particularly precarious. The number of theology students, for example, is specially limited and available religious literature is inadequate. Moreover, severe restrictions limit relations with sister Churches in Hungary and other countries. And it seems that, in some Churches, senior members who have been placed in office with official backing themselves help to persecute members of the clergy and congregations who express views critical of governmental policy.

In general, the minorities complain of living in a hostile climate, which is aggravated by the media and schoolbooks.

These are the main points which the Special Rapporteur

wishes to highlight. However, it is apparent from a review of the documents forwarded by the Romanian authorities that they deny that human rights are violated in their country or maintain that they limit such violations to isolated cases.

The Special Rapporteur wishes to state that he fully appreciates what has been achieved in Romania during the past few years or decades: the repayment of the external debt, major industrialization, 10 years of compulsory education for all, a figure which is expected to be raised to 12 in 1990. However, he is of the view that these achievements do not justify the infringements of human rights to which he has drawn attention.

In conclusion, the Special Rapporteur proposes to the Commission on Human Rights that it should make the following recommendations to the Romanian authorities:

(a) They should bring all laws, decrees, regulations and directives into line with the international instruments for the protection of human rights to which Romania is a party, and should make them public if they have not already done so;

(b) They should ensure that these international instruments are strictly implemented in practice;

(c) In so doing, they should pay special attention to the situations noted in this report.

In the addendum to the report, the special rapporteur first presented a chronology of events which had occurred since the completion of the basic report and which had materially altered the situation in Romania. The chronology, based primarily on news items in the international press, was as follows (UN Doc. E/CN.4/1990/28/Add. 1, para. 9–28):

16/17 December 1989. Riots against the Ceausescu Government broke out in Timisoara and were violently put down by the forces of law and order, more particularly the Securitate (State police). The forces of law and order fired into the crowd, killing and wounding many people; the exact number still has not been accurately determined.

21 December 1989. A large demonstration was arranged by the Government in Bucharest to support President Ceausescu. However, the demonstration turned against the régime and so triggered the revolution. As a result of attempts to put down the movement, a large number of people were killed and wounded in the capital.

22 December 1989. A group of former dissidents and members of the military, proclaiming that they formed the National Salvation Front, announced on television that they had taken control; violent fighting still continued between the army, which had joined the revolution, and members of the Securitate. The Presidential Palace was taken over by the crowd and the President and his wife fled from the capital.

23 December 1989. The National Salvation Front announced the release of all political prisoners and the arrest of President Ceausescu and his wife, Elena. Fighting was still going on between the army and the Securitate.

24 December 1989. The fighting continued and Mr. Ion Iliescu, the Front's spokesman, proclaimed that the revolution was victorious. He also announced that the presidential couple would be tried by a military court.

25 December 1989. The National Salvation Front announced that Nicolae and Elena Ceausescu had been sentenced to death and executed for the following reasons: the genocide of more than 60,000 people in the course of their reign; infiltration by the State by organizing armed action against the people and the authorities; theft and destruction of public property (by demolishing certain buildings and razing towns and villages); misappropriation of the national economy; attempted escape to recover more than 1,000 million dollars in foreign banks.

26 December 1989. Mr. Ion Iliescu was appointed Chairman of the Council of the National Salvation Front.

27 December 1989. At its first plenary meeting, the Council of the National Salvation Front adopted a number of urgent measures to establish emergency courts to try "terrorists", repeal certain laws of the previous régime, and make arrangements for the distribution of food products.

28 December 1989. Mr. Ion Iliescu, Chairman of the Council of the National Salvation Front, described the new organization of power in Romania. The Council, consisting of 36 members, was intended to head the country until elections were held in April 1990. The Council proceeded to appoint members of the government and adopt measures to do away with some earlier legislation and to reorganize the system of government. The Council had an 11-member Executive Bureau headed by Mr. Ion Iliescu.

29 December 1989. The Government announced that the new name for the Romanian State was "Romania".

31 December 1989. The Chairman of the Council of the National Salvation Front announced the abolition of the death penalty, the introduction of a five-day working week from March onwards and the start of a programme to redistribute collectivized land to the peasants. It was also announced that the Securitate had been dissolved and that its former chief, Iulian Vlad, had been arrested.

12 January 1990. At a demonstration by several thousand people in Bucharest, the Chairman of the Front announced that a referendum would be held on 20 January 1990 on restoring the death penalty for "terrorists" and on outlawing the Romanian Communist Party.

17 January 1990. The Council of the National Salvation Front repealed the two decrees of 12 January 1990 mentioned above.

23 January 1990. The Council of the National Salvation Front announced that free elections were to be held on 20 May 1990 and that the Front, as such, would be a candidate.

27 January 1990. The trial began in the Bucharest Military Court of four leaders of the previous régime: Emil Bobu, former number three; Ion Dinca, former Deputy Prime Minister; Manea Manescu, former Deputy Chairman of the Council of State; and Tudor Postelnicu, former Minister of the Interior. On 2 February 1990 they were given life sentences.

28/29 January 1990. A demonstration was called in Bucharest by the traditional political parties to protest against the Front's decision to take part in the elections, and a counter-demonstration also took place.

3 February 1990. A Provisional Council of National Unity was established to replace the Council of the National Salvation Front. It consists of 241 members, half of the seats being reserved for the political parties (three members each) and the other half for various leading non-governmental figures who played a role in the revolution, as well as for representatives of national minorities.

9 February 1990. The Provisional Council of National Unity held its first meeting.

13 February 1990. The Provisional Council of National

Unity elected Mr. Ion Iliescu Chairman by consensus. The Council decided on a 21-member Executive Bureau. Sixteen standing commissions were set up: Commission on Reconstruction, Economic Development and Foreign Trade; Commission on Agriculture; Commission on Youth; Commission on Foreign Policy; Commission on Science and Technology; Commission on Education; Commission on Culture; Commission on the Environment and Ecological Balance; Commission on National Minorities; Commission on Local Administration; Commission on Organization; National Commission to Consider and Settle Claims and Complaints by Victims of the Dictatorship; Commission on Health; Commission on the Constitution and Human Rights; Commission on Labour and Social Protection; and Commission on Abuses under the Previous Régime.

18 February 1990. In a demonstration the government headquarters were stormed and Mr. Gelu Voican-Voiculescu, Deputy Prime Minister of the Provisional Government, was manhandled by demonstrators. In the evening the army took back the government headquarters, after clashes leaving 3 soldiers dead and 20 injured.

While these extraordinary events were taking place, the special rapporteur requested the new Romanian authorities to cooperate with him in discharging the mandate given him by the Commission on Human Rights, including the possibility of a one-week visit to Romania to examine the situation on the spot. The request was granted, and the visit took place from 12 to 16 February 1990.

While in Romania, the special rapporteur was also able to talk to the leaders of a number of political parties and factions, to representatives of non-governmental organizations concerned with human rights issues, with former dissidents and political prisoners, and with members of the Hungarian and other minorities.

In the addendum to his report to the Commission on Human Rights, the special rapporteur summarized and analyzed the information he had received or compiled (chap. II) and presented his conclusions and recommendations (chap. III). The conclusions and recommendations are as follows (UN Doc. E/CN.4/1990/28/Add. 1, para. 65–69):

The Special Rapporteur is pleased to note that respect for human rights has improved considerably in Romania since the revolution of December 1989. The authorities with whom he met were, moreover, unanimous in expressing their firm determination to guarantee both a return to genuine democracy and the full restoration of human rights in all their aspects. They have already taken a number of legislative and regulatory measures for this purpose, together with restructuring measures.

However, although the texts are generally satisfactory, human rights have not actually been re-established; quite frequently, their exercise encounters *de facto* obstacles.

The Special Rapporteur was unable to shed light on the specific cases brought to his attention. He was, however, able to see that there is still an atmosphere of suspicion, if not fear, in Romania and that it will definitely take time to rebuild confidence. Moreover, the idea of the existence of human rights is still not very widespread among the population and measures will have to be taken to make them better known.

The Special Rapporteur particularly wishes to stress that a number of persons who are prominent in political life are still being subjected to threats, including death threats; many are still wary of the Securitate; real freedom to establish and disseminate newspapers and magazines is not yet fully guaranteed; and the problem of ethnic minorities will still require careful consideration and appropriate measures. The Special Rapporteur is obviously not unaware that, in the space of two months, it is impossible to reform institutions, amend legislation and, above all, change ways of thinking in order to re-establish respect for human rights, which have been disregarded for decades. That is a long-term process. For that reason, however, the process calls for constant vigilance on the part of the authorities and citizens.

The Special Rapporteur therefore recommends that the Commission on Human Rights should:

(a) Take note of the considerable improvement in respect for human rights that has taken place in Romania;

(b) Recommend that the Romanian authorities should:

(i) Continue their action to ensure that human rights in all their aspects are respected in their country, both *de jure* and *de facto;*

(ii) Pay particular attention to the points raised in this report by the Special Rapporteur;

(iii) Consider the possibility of using the Voluntary Fund for Advisory Services set up by the Centre for Human Rights in order to establish national institutions for the promotion and protection of human rights and to strengthen existing institutions.

After examining the reports of the special rapporteur, the Commission on Human Rights on 6 March 1990 (resolution 1990/50) took note of the considerable improvement in respect for human rights that has taken place in Romania.

The commission recommended that the Romanian authorities continue their action to ensure that human rights in all their aspects are respected in their country, both *de jure* and *de facto,* and pay particular attention to the points raised in the special rapporteur's latter report (UN doc. E/CN.4/1990/28/add. 1). It also recommended that the Romanian authorities consider the possibility of using the UNITED NATIONS VOLUNTARY FUND FOR ADVISORY SERVICES as suggested by the special rapporteur. Taking note with appreciation of the readiness of the government of Romania to cooperate with the commission and its special rapporteur, the commission decided to continue its consideration of the human rights situation in Romania at its 1991 session.

On 20 May 1990, Romanian voters went to the polls to participate in the first free national elections in half a century and chose Ion Iliescu as their president. The Iliescu candidacy was opposed, on the one hand, by two long-established political groups, the Peasants Party and the National Liberal Party, and, on the other hand, by a number of new groups, including the Hungarian Democratic Union and the Ecologists Party. Only the Democratic Union, representing the Hungarian minority of more than two million living mostly in Transylvania, made a better-than-expected showing, polling more than 6% of the vote for seats in Parliament.

ROMANIA: "A SPECIAL VIEW ON THE ROMANIAN CASE." At its 1989 session, the UN SUB-COMMISSION ON PREVENTION OF DISCRIMINATION AND PROTECTION OF MINORITIES examined and took note of the report entitled *Human Rights and Youth* (UN Doc. E/CN.4/Sub.2/1989/41 and Add. 1), prepared at its request by its special rapporteur, Mr. Dumitru Mazilu (Romania).

In the addendum to the report, Mr. Mazilu presents "A Special View on the Romanian Case," in which he describes with revulsion the situation confronting young people in Romania and other countries like it where dictatorial regimes have destroyed traditional values, negated human rights and fundamental freedoms, and courted economic disaster while maintaining that they are democratic.

Once a member of the Romanian State Security Council, a representative of his country at many international conferences, and a propagandist for the Ceausescu regime, Mr. Mazilu wrote from first-hand experience and obvious conviction. However, he was not authorized by the competent Romanian authorities to travel to Geneva in 1987 or 1988 to present his report to the sub-commission, and the report itself was issued by the United Nations only after the International Court of Justice had been requested by the UN Economic and Social Council for an advisory opinion. The Court's opinion, delivered on 15 December 1989, is reproduced in the entry entitled SPECIAL RAPPORTEURS: PRIVILEGES AND IMMUNITIES.

On 22 December 1989, a group calling itself the Council of National Salvation announced that it had overthrown the Ceausescu regime and would form a provisional government. Mr. Dumitru Mazilu was first deputy chairman of the council and chairman of its Constitutional, Legal and Human Rights Working Committee. The chairman of the council, Ion Iliescu, later was elected president of Romania.

Unwilling to examine Mr. Mazilu's report in detail in his absence, the sub-commission on 1 September 1989 called upon him (resolution 1989/45) to update it and decided to consider it at its August 1990 session. The text is as follows:

I. Unprecedented Aggression against the Rights and Freedoms of the Younger Generation. Grave Dangers to the Moral Health of Young People

Niccolò Machiavelli came to the conclusion that politics was immoral, that rules behaved cynically and that "the end justified the means"—he was referring to the need to establish a unitary national State in Italy under the aegis of absolute monarchy. Many theorists since his day have exposed the use of political methods and means that conflict with ethical requirements. Jean-Jacques Rousseau disapproves the use of such methods and means, while Montesquieu argues that Government needs to be based on certain laws which, "in the broadest sense, are the necessary relationships that derive from the nature of affairs".

The passage of time has brought to the fore, with ever-increasing insistence, the moral prerequisites for any Government, making it plain that falsehood, hypocrisy and imposture deeply undermine the foundations of any society, endangering the moral health of the younger generations. While anyone is shocked by the falsification of the truth, by the onslaught of falsehood, shuddering when he finds that hypocrisy has become the habitual formula of Government in some countries such as Romania, and that attempts to unmask imposters are put down with a violence and brutality hard to describe, the young generations are simply traumatized by the injustices and wrongs they find proliferating around them. More than once the desperate cries of the youngest among us have profoundly shaken us and brought us back to the earth of some of the crudest realities, reminding us of the nightmare world we have been thrown into by odious tyrants to whom the most elementary human feelings are unknown and whose "morality" consists in crushing the individual, destroying his personality and keeping him in slavery.

How can it be, the young Romanians ask us, that in our century, in which civilization has attained unimagined heights, whole peoples should be terrorized in the world's plain sight, while criminal tyrants, instead of being removed and punished as they should be, are glorified by a cult of disgusting vulgarity?

How can it be, they wonder, that the greatest imposters should install themselves at the head of nations and become their absolute spokesmen?

How is it possible to endure such humiliation, such violence and such feudal despotism?

What contempt for man, what effrontery and what barbarity have been shown by tyrants who, labelling millions of people as enemies of the people, traitors to the country or foreign agents, have sent them to their deaths with a mere signature, ordering them to be basely executed in death camps!

How has civil society been able for so many decades to allow a few tyrants to expropriate all the property of its members, to reduce their homes to rubble, to destroy their way of life, to crush their personality?

What kind of civil society is this, in which a person's life no longer counts, the individual being transformed into a beast of burden useful only to put into practice the tyrants' plans of aggrandisement, so as to assure their immortality?

How has it been possible to reach the point at which a person is denied the right to food and to heating for his home in severe winters, while children and old people are robbed even of the right to survive?

Not even in a nightmare world does it seem possible to hear that—as is happening in Romania—newly born babies are denied registration for the first three to four weeks, while old people are refused aid in case of need if they have reached the age of 60, and while medicine is out of the question altogether. "Irresponsibility, indifference, recklessness; what is it all about?" civilized society asks itself, and wonders.

There is no doubt that torturing millions of people means bringing together in one place all the filth and all the vileness of the most aberrant and odious dictators known to history.

Only in our own day, after several decades of infinite sufferings, have the younger generations' questions, their desperate cries, begun to receive frank answers. Obviously it is very late but, anyway, better late than never.

The young people's reprobation and bitterness pour out in waves: "How has it been, and how is it still, possible in some countries that evil should reach unimaginable dimensions and the reaction of civil society be paralysed or quasi-paralysed?"

The younger generations vehemently condemn these odious deeds, but at the same time demand guarantees that they will never be repeated.

Gradually madness is giving way to reason. The peoples have begun to expose and condemn the crimes of Stalin and the other tyrants, unmasking the brutal violation of the elementary rights of hundreds of millions of people.

But if the truth comes to light only after the tyrants' death, it means that the societies which have had the misfortune to fall into the hands of despots are condemned to bear unimagined torments until they pass from the scene.

However, the younger generations and contemporary civil society will not accept this any more. Millions upon millions of young people in Romania demand that an end should be put to the repressive barbarity, oppression, humiliation and slavery and that respect for the human being should be guaranteed in a truly civilized society.

The veil of falsehood and hypocrisy has fallen. Anyone who tries to hide behind it nowadays is building vain hopes that he will not be unmasked.

A. The Attempt to Mislead Millions of People by Empty Promises and to Conceal from Them the Truth Concerning the Economic Disaster into which They Have Been Plunged by a Despotic Government is not Merely a Profoundly Immoral Act but an Unspeakable Crime

1. *The High-handedness of Dictators Means the Failure of a Whole National Economy.* For modern society, in which science and technology have reached such high levels, it is unimaginable that one individual, having reached the summit of the social hierarchy—as is happening in Romania—should dictate the installation of large economic units, fix their parameters of operation and draw up their programmes of activity without a single specialized study or a single economic calculation. Any rational person understands that this is an act of madness.

Then how are we to explain the incredible fact that the best specialists in the field concerned have not given their opinion, while ministers, heads of economic departments, their deputies and other managerial staff comply with insane directives, setting economic objectives and building on them, even ahead of time, while aware that they will be a failure, that they will go bankrupt, before they have managed to carry out their production programmes?

If it were a matter of an isolated case, we would doubtless try to find some attenuating circumstances. But when it is a matter of dozens, of hundreds of similar cases, one shudders!

Only by economic diktat has it been possible in Romania to spend billions of dollars buying obsolete factories abroad and to install them in the national territory without a single prospect of marketing their products. The only objective attained has been to save foreign firms from bankruptcy and to increase the foreign debt of the countries concerned by several billion dollars.

Only by economic diktat has it been possible to establish giant petrochemical plants in Romania without having assured raw materials and without any of the necessary commodity markets. In this way, millions of people have been deprived of the strictly necessary fuel for public and private transport.

Only by economic diktat has it been possible to establish mammoth iron and steel plants in this country at a time when the civilized countries have been closing down their large works owing to the inefficiency of this sector. The only "objective" attained has been to increase the dependence of the people in question on sources of raw materials and energy in other countries, even on other continents, and to maintain bankrupt sectors that have no chance of recovery. The population concerned have been deprived of the necessary light and heat for their homes.

The economic diktat in Romania has led to the establishment of industrial sectors at random, in the absence of assured sources of raw materials and energy and of outlets for their products, not to speak of skilled manpower for the peak areas of modern technology.

Folly enthroned, with just enough "gumption" to order, to demand the doing of what is objectively impossible, has cost and is costing the peoples concerned billions of dollars to maintain bankrupt economies. Every month ministers of finance are forced to squeeze money out of dry stone in order to prolong the agony of economic colossi maintained with the means of subsistence snatched from the mouths of millions of people, merely in order that the "genius" of the tyrants who dictated their installation should not be alled into question.

But the price is too high. The truth has come to light. The economic disaster is experienced by everybody.

An economy built on the high-handedness of dictators, on incompetence and defiance of the most elementary requirements of modern science and technology, is turning into an unbearable burden for the peoples concerned.

Neither concealment of the real figures nor their systematic falsification can cover up the disaster in Romania any longer.

Then why do not the economic summits demand that the race to catastrophe should be brought to an end immediately?

Romanian youth is horrified by the indolence and lack of dignity of the ruling hierarchy.

The ruling hierarchy, however, is terrorized by the repressive measures of the dictatorial clan. Everyone is afraid to act, especially when that means not only losing one's job but also losing one's freedom and life. Everyone is waiting for the natural dénouement—the disappearance of the tyrants—and hoping for a new order of affairs thereafter. A sad and barbarous option!

Why should we accept falsehood and hypocrisy? Who gains from them? Not even the dictators. No one believes any longer in the claim that they are ignorant of the sad reality.

At first people were surprised that those around the tyrants paved their way with invented achievements, but when they found that even they required them to embellish the reality and conceal the disaster, they grasped the unbelievable dimensions of the enthroned falsehood.

Cowards lie to you and you lie in your turn to others. What vileness! What human squalor!

2. *Two Worlds: the Palaces of the Despots, and Concentration Camps for Millions of People.* While heaping the most savage curses on the leaders who preceded them, accusing them of having ground down and exploited their own peoples, the new masters install themselves in their castles after having invested billions to rebuild them in an incredible profusion of luxury and wealth.

To the existing palaces, ultramodern new ones are added, as is happening in Romania: palaces at a level of luxury unknown even to the most extravagant monarchs. Sumptuous villas and pleasure grounds scattered all over the national territory; fabulous sums in accounts at the biggest international banks; all the countries' forests as hunting grounds, with the game prepared and lured within range of the tyrants' guns; special aircraft that bring in gowns and luxurious furs from famous fashion houses in exchange for exorbitant sums; culinary preparations of the most sophisticated kind, flown in in special containers . . . And when you think that the dictators do not even have a salary that can be increased or reduced according to need!

This is the world in which the dictatorial cliques take their ease, while millions of people live in some sort of "matchboxes", grouped together in a kind of concentration camp, with wages that do not afford them even the most wretched level of subsistence. In Romania they chase about desperately in search of a morsel of bread with which to feed their children. Unhappily, however, they often return home empty-handed.

No one claims that those invested with certain responsibilities should not benefit from living conditions that allow them to devote their full time to the proper conduct of public affairs, but the concentration of so much display and luxury at one extreme and of squalor and indigence at the other builds up the hatred and indignation of the oppressed against the flagrant injustices sanctioned with the most shameless effrontery by the dictators.

And when you think that the new rulers in Romania sneaked into power with slogans of condemnation directed at the wrongs and injustices committed by previous societies!

Today, with the most alluring promises concerning right, truth and justice, the Romanian people have seen themselves reduced to the cruellest poverty by rulers whose only "merit" consists in lying with even greater shamelessness and subjecting human beings to tortures that even the most ferocious tyrants never imagined.

3. *The Megalomania of Dictators Means the Proliferation of People's Sufferings.* After having assumed discretionary powers for life, the dictators want to remain in history, enduring even after death. The Pharaohs organized the building of the pyramids. The *Roi Soleil* sponsored the erection of Versailles.

The reigning princes of smaller countries have raised churches, cathedrals and other places of worship. Whenever they emerged victorious in the struggle against foreign invaders, they built a holy place in which to raise a hymn of thanksgiving to Almighty God.

The despots of today wish to distinguish themselves, not by erecting holy places, but by destroying them, as is happening in Romania today.

Gigantic structures, of a quality and taste that are dubious to say the least, take the place of old and durable civilizations. They set tens of thousands of men to changing watercourses and building all kinds of canals for which there is not a single practical use, save only to secure their immortality.

And as the despots' desire to endure for centuries grows stronger, their megalomania takes on insane dimensions. And while the tyrants, for the sake of history, raise megalomaniac edifices in immortal memory of themselves, the national economies of their countries are destroyed and the sufferings of millions upon millions of people attain paroxysmal levels.

Even the most faithful disciples of the dictators sense the disaster, glimpse the catastrophe. Natural questions are put with ever-increasing insistence: "Until when?" "How far is it possible to go?"

Until the youngest scion of Romania wants to know why the truth, the bare and unvarnished truth, is not told about the economic depression. Why people lack the necessary shred of dignity to throw their guilt, all their guilt, in the dictators' faces.

"Through your folly and diktat you have overturned the peoples' traditional values!"

"Through your folly and diktat you have destroyed the national economy!"

"Through a megalomaniac and despotic vision you have brought us to the brink of bankruptcy!"

"Through your Government, you have shown the greatest contempt and the deepest disdain for the human being!"

"You must answer to the peoples for your criminal deeds!"

But for falsehood and hypocrisy to be eliminated once and for all from the activity of any Government, that Government must be built on consistently democratic foundations, so that dictatorship and dictators will no longer find a place.

II. The Younger Generation Has Been Swept Clean of Any Faith in a Political Régime Which, While Practising the Most Odious Dictatorship, Has the Audacity to Maintain That It Is Profoundly Democratic

Since the most ancient times, the world's great thinkers have spoken out in favour of stable social orders based on democracy. Heracleitus holds that the progress of society can be assured if men will learn to promote, to heed and to respect the best among them. Marcus Tullius Cicero points out that democracy ensures freedom and equality, the State being conceived as *res populi* or *res publica*. Thomas Jefferson has demonstrated that the foundation of democracy and progress is liberty, while Nicolae Bălcescu has shown that a true democracy is "the rule of the people by the people". In his view a democratic republic is one in which "the people will be sovereign, that is to say their own master", and will obey only "officials of their own choosing". These officials—says the great thinker—must act and work only in the name and interest of the people, being always prepared "to give back the office that has been entrusted to them, when the time for which they received it has come to an end". The same thinker points out that "the first condition for the moral development of a State, for its political existence, is freedom of the people and equal rights".

In our own day Raymond Aron, Sartre, André Malraux, Allain Touraine, Marian Irish, James Prothro, René Cassin and virtually all the great thinkers of the world regard freedom and equality as the indispensable foundations of democracy.

A. Discretionary Dissociation

Democracy has always aimed to participate both in the preparation of decisions and guidelines for economic and social development and in their execution, their practical application. Even the very supporters of forms of Government based on dictatorship recognize, at least theoretically, that participation must be assured, in certain forms, for both components of the leadership. The dissociation of these fundamental components, through the right of decision being monopolized by a few individuals or even by a single individual—as is happening in Romania—is a discretionary act that demonstrates the abandonment of any appearance of democracy and the installation of despotic forms of Government.

1. *The Dictation of Decisions. Unlimited Power Takes Maniacal Forms.* There can be no doubt that the process of decision-making constitutes the most sensitive aspect of Government. For this very reason, precise rules have been framed and laid down concerning the drafting, definition and adoption of decisions with a view to satisfying the requirements of objectivity and timeliness and, more particularly, the requirements of economic and social progress within one or other country. The broader, freer and more genuine the participation in the drafting and preparation of political, economic, social or cultural decisions, the steadier, more useful and more efficient those decisions will be. At the opposite extreme, the more closely restricted and more incompetent the participation in such preparation, the more arbitrary it will prove, regularly conflicting with the most elementary requirements of progress and development.

Notwithstanding these major desiderata, the decision-making process has nevertheless attained in some countries—in Romania for example—such a degree of concentration that nearly all the problems of development are in practice decided by one person or at most two. From economic development plans for the longer or shorter term to the way wheat, barley or maize is to be sown or harvested or some strictly necessary accessories are to be imported, to the approval of a few dollars with which to send a specialist abroad, everything is decided by a single person, who has accumulated powers that are unimaginable save in the most absolute of feudal monarchies. One or two persons lead the sole party that exists, hold all executive power, and subordinate the legislative and judicial powers.

The effects are disastrous, especially in the long term, since in particular, as we have seen, arbitrary decisions on economic problems of major concern have set veritable catastrophes in train and many years of toil and efforts will be needed to set matters right.

2. *The Slavery of Execution.* In the few despotic régimes that still survive, to the great shame of our century, execution of the tyrants' decisions is a field in which no right is reserved any longer, but instead a binding obligation to participate that rests on all members of the society concerned, from elementary schoolchildren to the old and the sick.

When it comes to putting their discretionary decisions into practice, the dictators fix the time, schedule and apply penalties, suspend the payment of wages, dismiss and appoint, send for trial and convict thousands, tens of thousands of people. In the field of execution they are generous, desiring and inviting a very wide, a unanimous participation.

And in order to mark, once again, the "rightness" of the despots' decisions, people are further required to enthuse when they carry out those decisions, to raise hymns of praise and devotion to the "enlightened chiefs, titans among the titans of the world", as the Romanians are required to do. And if they do not do so, they risk their job, with the scrap of remuneration that comes with it; the persecution of whole families; labelling as enemies of the people; conviction, and even death.

Participation only in the execution of the decisions, through discretionary dissociation from participation in their adoption, has become a form of slavery that dishonours the societies which have fallen into the hands of the despots, dishonours the continents on which tyrannical régimes still exist that stand out like so many dark blots on the whole of contemporary civilization.

People, and especially young ones who have greater working capacity, are transformed into a species of robots, being forced to put into effect decisions which have been proved to be not only useless but manifestly harmful.

And when the régimes that practise such forms of dictatorship still have the audacity to maintain that they are profoundly democratic, they show how deep the gulf has become between the rulers and the ruled.

More and more young Romanians are demanding that an end should be put to the barbarity and that there should be a return to civilized ways of governing. They cite more and more frequently the example of the countries where democracy and freedom have triumphed and where officials who do not work in the people's interest are immediately dismissed, while political, economic and social decisions are subject to the direct approval of the people, not through formal and mendacious referenda but through real ones. In these popular consultations, the will of every person counts. He feels that the decisions adopted take this point of view into account.

The younger generations are demanding more and more insistently that their life should no longer be darkened by odious dictatorships and that Government based on democracy and freedom should prevail in all the countries of the world.

B. Unprecedented Aggression against Man, Pulverization of Freedom and Annihilation of the Personality

Freedom endures, more than ever, not only in philosophical studies but in political, legal and sociological studies also. Famous poets and writers have dedicated masterpieces to it, while the most talented painters and sculptors have immortalized it in symbolic form.

Freedom, however, is not an abstract idea or merely a subject of theoretical speculation but a major component of people's everyday life. In many countries it has become a shining reality, in others it is recognized but not respected, and in a few countries it continues to be brutally violated.

Developments in several countries over the past few years have led to the release of the adult generations from many sufferings and have filled the hearts of the younger generations with new hopes. The torch of freedom has begun to flicker again even where the chances were thought to be least. Its overwhelming importance in the life of people and of society has started to be rediscovered. Opinions of value concerning it have been taken off the forbidden list, and dogmas are more and more being abandoned and even repudiated.

Many have remembered that Aristotle regards freedom as a major premise of human progress, while Plato regards it as an expression of culture and civilization. Adam Smith appreciates that free initiative lies at the foundation of the modern development of society, while David Ricardo shows that, without freedom, society would mark time, being exposed to phenomena of stagnation with all the adverse consequences that flow from it.

Marx and Engels have shown that freedom is a rational necessity, and on this basis Stalin decreed that anyone who did not understand the requirements of the revolution was not free.

Stalin placed his own interpretations upon the revolution and advanced the thesis that "he who is not with the revolution is against it!" Gradually the diktat made its way in all political, economic, social and military affairs.

In a number of countries, including Romania, the components and manifestations of freedom, one by one, have been negated, stripped of all content, pulverized.

Free initiative has been outlawed and condemned, and its advocates exiled or executed.

The small peasant farm has been wiped out, and those who tried to resist have vanished without trace.

Great personalities have been reduced to silence. The only voice that can be heard is that of the leader. He thinks for everybody. He thinks best and most boldly. All must listen and submit, and those who did not do so have disappeared into the death camps. Millions of crimes, millions of deaths, more millions of sufferings for which there is no cure. . . .

In order to survive, you have only one course: to renounce freedom, dignity and personality and to live in falsehood and hypocrisy.

Pol Pot in Kampuchea went further. In three years he murdered more than a million people. All those who had in some way succeeded in life, all individuals who had accumulated a certain baggage of knowledge, all intellectuals, were executed without mercy and thrown into common graves.

1. *Violence and Barbarous Aggression by Bulldozers against Human Beings.* In our own day, we have met with even more enterprising despots, who have decided to continue the "revolution" with the aid of bulldozers. Thus in Romania small villas, pretty cottages, traditional rural dwellings—the expression of an entire civilization—have been condemned to disappear because they are regarded as "a breeding-ground of bourgeois liberalism" that still perpetuates "forms of private property". The bulldozers have gone into action! Hundreds of thousands, millions of people have begun to be expropriated overnight. The home erected with such pains and labour or handed down from generation to generation is razed from the face of the earth at the rulers' behest.

Those who have the strength to survive this barbarous vandalism are thrown into some sort of prefabricated concrete boxes in which the last individual liberties are pulverized in a collectivism characteristic of concentration camps. People are obliged to prepare their food in common kitchens, to wash in common bathrooms, to use common lavatories.

Many Romanians have put an end to their lives, unable to bear any longer the barbarous aggression of the bulldozers, the inhuman way of life provided by tyrants. The survivors remain marked for ever.

The young people shudder to find that such horrors can be perpetrated in our century. Everyone's personality is destroyed.

The sufferings are infinite. The tears of mothers are shed in torrents, and old people's hearts are broken.

The civilized world refuses to understand how such violent aggression against man can be borne.

An X-ray, however succinct, of the societies concerned enables us to reveal the concerted and offensive character of the oppression practised by tyrants who have made contempt for man and his needs into their preferred instrument of government.

2. *Hunger, Cold and Fear in the Service of the Subjugation of Man.* The starving of human beings was one method used even in ancient times by the more powerful armies against cities which did not surrender.

In Romania today the acute shortage of strictly necessary foodstuffs, such as milk for children and daily bread, is of such concern to many large human communities that all other problems, however complex and serious they may be, are relegated to the background.

It is even worse when people are deprived of the heating that is so necessary in the cold seasons. Even if the tyrants advise their subjects to put another coat on, there is no way of tricking the cold. Thousands upon thousands of children and old people are carried off without mercy by the bitter cold. And the struggle for survivial keeps more and more individuals away from political and social disturbances.

Many Romanians are saying straight out: "First let my kids escape from this pitiless winter!" or "Help my mother and father to survive!", and then: "I'm not going to bother about other problems any more."

A person who is struggling all-out to feed his children, or to save them from dying of the cold to which they have been exposed by the insane measures of the dictators, no longer has the strength to concentrate on ways of improving the Government, much less on the far more complex and far more risky enterprise of changing it.

If we add to hunger and cold the fear generated by merciless systems of repression such as that of Romania, we shall have a fairly complete picture of the inhuman means of government used by tyrants who are increasingly distinguished by their violent offensive against inherent human rights and freedoms.

As the dictators' failures grow more resounding and the discontent of the population spreads, the machinery of oppression comes into more intensive use. No means is too costly for the dictatorial cliques when it comes to hunting down and annihilating those who dare to oppose the insane course of events. Their correspondence is violated, their telephone conversations are intercepted, contacts with foreigners are forbidden them or strictly monitored, and individual trips abroad are virtually impossible.

A dense fabric of collaborationists is being woven around the inhabitants of the country. Distrust of friends, colleagues and even relatives grows day by day. The oppressors maintain that he who does not love the leader does not love the country, and anyone who dare fail to show his devotion to him or who makes any observation about him is put on the blacklist, hunted down, arrested, tortured and condemned. His life is in jeopardy.

Many young Romanians, learning from the terrible experience of their elders in the matter of barbarous repression, prefer to survive, without renouncing the struggle. They engage is a stealthy battle which they wage with resolution and perseverance, sabotaging the despots' plans of grandeur and splendour, exposing the horrors committed and defusing whenever possible the acts of aggression directed against man, human rights and human freedoms.

The struggle is hard and is waged with unequal forces

and resources. The pressure against the human being in Romania grow steadily greater, and the dangers that combine to weaken civil society grow ever more numerous.

3. *The Destruction of Human Values Is Sweeping Away Some Shining Ideals of the Younger Generation.* As the imposture becomes more harmful and the tyrants lose more and more of the ground from under their feet, the repression of potential rivals assumes increasingly offensive and violent forms. In Romania, for example, any leader who comes to public notice, any chief with a fair amount of personality who enjoys the respec⸜ of those around him and, especially, those who have gained greater popularity through their personal qualities, capacity for work and civilized behaviour in dealings with people, are immediately discredited, removed from the important public offices they hold, and thrown into the remotest recesses of the economic and social machinery, so that nothing more is heard of them.

Even to mention the name of one of those who have been removed is considered a grave affront to the dictatorial cliques and is reprimanded with the greatest severity. And if there is still anyone in the ruling hierarchy bold enough to pay them a last tribute on the occasion of their death, the gesture is classified even more seriously as entering into compacts with "the class enemy", and the courageous one incurs risks that are difficult to imagine.

In Romania one single leader, one single name is cultivated continuously, insistently, exasperatingly—that of the dictator. Around him are kept or drawn only biddable men, passionate admirers of the "bold thinking" and "innovating activity" of the "titan among titans", of the "hero among heroes", of the "great chief".

If any one of them ventures to open his mouth and say something that is not to the liking of the dictator and his clan, he risks never having his voice heard again, and if someone is inspired to raise his head, he loses it before he begins to be noticed.

Understanding the tragedy of the situation, many of the dictator's collaborators develop a split personality: in public they say what pleases the tyrants and sometimes, in private, with many precautions and great prudence, what they truly think. What a chasm, what a horrifying abyss!

Not only the political field, however, but all other fields fall under the pitiless axe of tyranny. Gradually, but with diabolical persistence and perseverance, all persons of value in science and culture and from all sectors of human creativity are compromised, dishonoured, removed and destroyed.

Some of them, humiliated and discouraged, take the road of exile, trying to do, and sometimes succeeding in doing, there what has been denied them in their homeland. Others give up, no longer having the strength to withstand the onslaught of imposture and of a pitiless oppression.

There nevertheless remain a fair number of valiant people whom only unwavering belief in the rightness of their cause and determination to serve their own nation to the end have impelled to continue creative work and scientific activity, enduring with boundless stoicism the pressures devised by tyrants against them. Devotion to science and creativity and sincere love of country give them the strength to endure anonymity. They do not speak of their research even if it is of national or universal value; they do not mention their creations even if they are exceptional.

A deep silence settles over everything that is bright, bold, advanced.

From time to time there is talk of collectives of creative workers, in a barbarous endeavour to dissolve individual merit in a formula of amorphous, standardizing collectivism.

And when you think that all this is only in order to accredit tyrants and members of their clan as the greatest "creators", the most valuable persons of science and culture", who should enjoy "the widest possible international recognition"! Scientific diplomas and certificates are collected from everywhere, by dint of the most persistent intervention and at vast expense.

In this way, as the years of oppression and violence pass, the dictators acquire, alongside the "status" of "political titans", that of "men of science", of "culture". They are the greatest, the most powerful and, at the same time, "the most learned"!

Young Romanians are horrified by so much human baseness, especially when they observe with stupefaction that, even after they have cornered countless certificates and diplomas, the tyrants have not even learned their own language properly. A feeling of fury and indignation takes hold of the young people of Romania when they break through into the basement of the sham dictatorial edifice.

The most intimate and most cherished ideals of the younger generation are swept away when they are deprived of the opportunity to glimpse on the horizon the great lights of science, culture and human creativity; when the examples of their predecessors are denied them; when in literature, in art, in the most widely different branches of science and technology, the leading figures disappear.

The example of prominent personalities has always exerted a powerful force of attraction upon the younger generations. Many young people have become the disciples of scholars, great creative artists, research workers who have devoted their lives to the knowledge and progress of the world. Prominent personalities have always represented shining ideals for the youngest members of the human community. Respect for values stimulates values.

In Romania, contempt for prominent personalities levels, standardizes, blocks material and spiritual progress in all segments of society.

All nations have secured their place in history, not through despotic acts of coercion and oppression by tyrants, but through the contribution made to the advancement of science, culture and human civilization by the great personalities to whom they have given birth. The denial and destruction of real values, the discrediting and ruin of prominent personalities, have grave repercussions on the evolution of human civilization.

Millions upon millions of young people understanding the profound sense of these perennial truths, are boldly raising the banners of struggle and hope, reminding the human community that, the more aggressive, barbarous and reckless the offensive against freedom grows, the closer will come the moment of its rebirth.

C. Discriminatory Policies and Practices Continue to Do Violence to the Human Being, to Trample His Fundamental Rights and Freedoms

The old saw "Divide and rule" has not disappeared from the theory and practice of the dictators of our times. We observe with sorrow that there are still rulers who have made *apartheid*, segregation and racial discrimination into a State policy, continuing to spread racial "superiority" and hatred and to pursue a policy of discrimination in all spheres of political, economic, social and cultural life. Measures of force assimilation are applied to national minorities by the denial of traditions and customs, by attempts to destroy an entire past of history and civilization. Neither the cries of millions of the oppressed nor the strenuous protests of the international community cause dictators to cease their oppression. Acts of persecution and discrimination take ever harsher forms; intolerence makes life impossible.

To the young scions of contemporary society, discriminatory policies and practices, restrictions or preferences based on race, colour or national or ethnic origin are the anachronisms of feudal despots which have been perpetuated by brutal interference with the progressive course of history in this century of human civilization.

The United Nations has given priority attention to the elimination of acts of discrimination and of discriminatory policies and practices, describing them as instruments for the degradation and humiliation of the human being. The General Assembly of the world body has demanded the immediate elimination of discrimination inviting the Administering Powers to repeal discriminatory provisions and to lift discriminatory measures. The United Nations has issued normative instruments condemning discriminatory measures; it has established specialized organs for the elimination of racial discrimination; it has organized long-term programmes of action; it has prepared studies and surveys; it has drawn up very useful recommendations to Member States. The approach to these problems has drawn the attention of the international community to the importance and urgency of solving them.

But despite these measures *apartheid* is maintained, segregation and racial discrimination continue stubbornly to be practised.

Tens of thousands of young people who rise against these anachronistic practices, long condemned by history, fall victim to savage oppression, but they do not give up the struggle.

The disastrous national economic policy of certain dictators has led to the mass exodus of ethnic minorities, for the rulers have made a source of revenue out of the sums collected for each emigrant, as is happening in Romania. A shameful trade, a tragic trade!

Many ethnic groups remind us that "there is nothing more precious than freedom!" "If we cannot attain it any other way, we are ready to give everything we have gained in life in order to see our sons and daughters free!" Trading in people's freedom nevertheless remains a deeply immoral act, precisely because it is so inhuman.

The past years have refocused attention on the complex problem of inter-ethnic relations. Hopes of freedom have been reborn for many ethnic communities in different parts of the world. Millions of people are demanding safeguards for their cultural and religious traditions and recognition of their natural, elementary right to use their language officially and to keep up their customs.

It has been confirmed once again that ethnic problems cannot be solved by discriminatory measures, by oppression, by cultural and social genocide, by displacing millions upon millions of people, by deporting them or by sending them to concentration camps.

A lasting solution to all ethnic questions can be found only through consistent application of the principles of freedom and non-discrimination, principles proven by life and confirmed by social practice.

Young people are deeply attached to these noble principles and express the conviction that only on the basis of those principles will the ethnic communities to which they belong develop and thrive steadily, securing and guaranteeing respect for man and the dignity of the human being.

III. Manipulation of Relations with Other Countries

The younger generation has begun to decode many of the mechanisms of operation of the monolithic societies ruled over by tyrannical, despotic régimes. One of the most critical has proved to be the manipulation of relations with other countries. This mechanism comprises a co-ordinated system in which every link is tested and retested, conversations are controlled, the places to be visited are carefully chosen, the goods offered to foreigners are selected, and so on.

The concern to embellish reality, and hence to falsify truth, which is present in all other fields of action of tyrannical political régimes, becomes positively obsessive in relations with foreigners, as is happening in Romania for example.

The dictators, knowing themselves to blame for political repression, for their economic failures and for cultural stagnation in their respective countries, take quite exceptional measures to block the circulation of real information, trying to sell foreigners "truths" made up of whole cloth.

In Romania, for example, this is done by establishing a special body of people for contact with foreigners. They escort them continuously, are present at foreigners' conversations with authorized persons, provide them with facts prepared in advance and take them to visit specially laid-out sectors or areas. Foreigners are accorded a hospitality that is out of the common. They are put up in special guesthouses or luxury hotels. They are treated to sumptuous meals washed down with choice wines of which the citizens of the countries concerned do not partake even in their wildest dreams. And in the case of important visiting figures, in view of the difficulty of winning their good opinion, special recreation facilities are made available.

The cynicism of certain tyrants has reached the point where they personally place articles of advertisement, and large sums from the budgets of the countries concerned are squandered on their publication.

Romanian youth is revolted by this profoundly immoral form of manipulation of foreigners. The "truths" which are served up to them represent gross falsehoods, a deliberate attempt to mislead. Any means is good enough when it comes to preventing discovery of the discontent and sufferings of the people oppressed by tyrants. But as a rule the lie is exposed and the truth comes to light.

Instead of being wasted on falsifying the truth, such efforts should have been concentrated on giving people the pleasures they deserve, the freedoms that belong to them, a dignified and happy life. There is not a single young person who thinks otherwise.

But then there would be nothing hidden, nothing falsified.

IV. Non-interference in Domestic Affairs Is not a Tool for Covering Up the Crimes of Tyrants against Man

The principle of non-interference in domestic affairs (non-intervention) was conceived as an instrument for protecting and guaranteeing the sovereign equality of States and the right of peoples to self-determination and to international peace and security. It is unanimously acknowledged that interference or intervention in domestic affairs means an attempt to stifle the aspirations of peoples to free development. Several cases are known in which a great Power, finding that the constitutional Government of a country which is under its influence has attempted to give greater freedom to the people in question, has intervened brutally, stifling in blood the aspirations of millions of people to free development. And to keep up appearances, they have set up puppet Governments which have labelled the constitutional representatives of the countries concerned as "enemies of the people" and have asked foreign Powers to intervene. As a result, it has been only a matter of time before the strivings for freedom of the peoples in question were crushed under the tracks of the foreign tanks invited to intervene.

But whereas in this case we are concerned with intervention of a violent brutality in the domestic affairs of other countries, how can the expression "interference in domestic affairs" be applied to a notification concerning the violation by certain rulers of international undertakings to respect human rights?

To plead non-interference in domestic affairs, as the Romanian rulers are doing, in cases of brutal and systematic violation of the Universal Declaration of Human Rights, the International Covenants on human rights and other commitments assumed concerning respect for the inherent rights and freedoms of the human being, including countries' own constitutions, is not only an illegal act but also a profoundly immoral one.

An attempt to cover up acts of violent oppression of the fundamental rights and freedoms of millions upon millions of people by torturing them individually and destroying their personalities, while maintaining that this should be a matter within the domestic competence of the rulers, forms part of the arsenal that the tyrants bring into play in order to give themselves a free hand in committing crimes of varying degrees of gravity in the countries in which they have cornered power. Disregarding any standard of justice or morality, they behave like the most odious of feudal despots, regarding the country in which they exercise their dictatorship as their own estate and the people as their own slaves.

They ostentatiously reject any critical observation concerning the abuses and crimes they commit, admonishing everybody that they are interfering in their domestic affairs and reminding everyone that "at home they do as they see fit!"

They are not interested in what is right and what is wrong, what is legal and what is illegal, much less in what is moral and what is immoral. Their cynicism reaches the point of declaring that "they do everything for the people's good", whereas those who venture to make critical observations "are unacquainted with reality".

It is plain for anyone to see that concern for the respect of the fundamental rights and freedoms of the human being constitutes a national and international duty of the first order, since man represents the supreme value and since all activities within the frontiers of nations, as well as those within the framework of international co-operation, should be subordinated to his well-being and happiness. The Charter of the United Nations specifies among its purposes and principles priority for international co-operation in promoting and encouraging respect for human rights and for fundamental freedoms for all. At the same time the Charter lays on Member States the obligation to fulfil in good faith the obligations assumed by them.

In the light of these fundamental principles, who can be allowed any longer to maintain that an action to put an end to crimes directed against man would be an interference in domestic affairs?

Who nowadays can have the impudence to assert that, by reminding certain rulers that they are disregarding their own international undertakings in keeping hundreds of thousands of people in terror and slavery we are violating their "right" to apply the world regulations as they choose?

If we add to this the assessments of some great theorists of international law, we shall understand even better the inconsistency of pleading non-interference in domestic affairs when it is a matter of violence being done to such generally recognized values as the freedom and dignity of man. Great thinkers like Oppenheim, Lauterpacht, J. Fawcett, I. Brownlie and others have convincingly demonstrated that concern to assure and guarantee human rights cannot be described as interference in domestic affairs, considering that these values enjoy universal protection. This legal and doctrinal point of view is considered natural in all the civilized countries of the world.

The only people who dispute it are the despots, the tyrants, who are still to be found here and there, evoking periods of the saddest memory from human history.

They, the tyrants who still exist to the shame of the blue planet, reject any critical observation. They, the despots who remind us of barbarism, want to manipulate their subjects without international rules, without criticism, without comments from outside. They, the tyrants, despots and dictators, have no need of outside arbitration. They are the arbiters of their own deeds. And they always note with satisfaction and nonchalance that it works out fine.

RWANDA. The Republic of Rwanda is a landlocked country in eastern Africa. It has borders with Burundi, Uganda, Tanzania, and Zaire. Formerly part of the UN trust territory of Rwanda–Urundi under Belgian administration, it became independent in 1962 and became a member of the United Nations the same year. Its population is estimated by the UN (1990) to be 7,179,000. Ethnic groups include the Batwa, the Bahutu, and the Batutsi; the first belongs to the pygmoid group; the second, to the Bantu group; and the third, to the Nilo–Hamitic group. The Batwa, Bahuti, and Batutsi intermarry, speak the same language, and share the same culture. Kinyarwanda is the only language spoken by all Rwandese; French is sometimes used in commerce and education. Religions practiced include Christianity (Roman Catholic, 56%; Protestant denominations, 12%), Islam (10%), and Animism and other beliefs (22%).

The government (1990) took the form of a republic. However, it was placed under military rule by a *coup d'etat* of 5 July 1973, at which time its elected president was replaced by an army officer Maj.-Gen. Juvenal Habyarimana. A new constitution, adopted in December 1978, provides for an elected Assembly and a single political party, the National Revolutionary Development Movement.

In 1960 Belgium, the administering authority for Rwanda–Urundi, a former German colony which was a League of Nations mandate before becoming a

United Nations trust territory, set up a provisional government there and announced its intention of holding elections for the purpose of constituting a national assembly. Belgium invited the United Nations to send a mission to observe the election, but the General Assembly decided that it should be held under UN supervision.

The election, held on 25 September 1960, produced a legislative body which proceded to establish a constitutional democracy in the territory. The General Assembly set up a five-member commission in February 1962 to ensure the achievement of essential objectives before independence. After considering the report of the commission, it decided to terminate the trusteeship agreement; and, on 1 July 1962, two independent and sovereign States emerged—Rwanda and Burundi.

Maintaining the peaceful co-existence of the Batwa, Bahutu, and Batutsi groups has been a primary concern of the government of Rwanda, which does all it can to ensure that the members of those groups enjoy equality in law and in practice. Recently, special measures were taken on behalf of the Batwa, who had lived in cramped and rudimentary huts; the government granted subsidies for housing improvements and, in particular, made corrugated iron available to the Batwa for building purposes.

In a report presented to the COMMITTEE ON THE ELIMINATION OF RACIAL DISCRIMINATION on 22 April 1985, the government described its efforts to eliminate discrimination against, and between, minority groups as follows (UN Doc. CERD/C/115/Add. 2, para. 11–15):

With a view to avoiding a preponderance of certain ethnic groups or of certain strata of the population, the Rwandese Government has for several years been pursuing a policy of equilibrium, consisting in the equitable allocation of jobs in the public and private sector and also in teaching, based on a representation of each ethnic group *pro rata* to the population as a whole. The three ethnic groups of which the Rwandese population is composed presumably each spoke their own language before becoming fully integrated; but it is difficult to determine at what point Kinyarwanda—the national language—became the one and only language in the country. The three ethnic groups can be recognized by their physical type. The Batutsi belong to the Nilo-Hamitic group, the Bahutu to the Bantu group and the Batwa to the pygmoid group. Interethnic marriages tend, however, to blur this distinction.

Special measures have been taken in the social, economic and cultural fields with a view to guaranteeing the proper development and protection of minority groups, particularly on behalf of the Batwa group who were very backward by comparison with the other groups. Special measures have been taken to assist the Batwa in the field of education, ... and a major effort has been undertaken to alert them to the need to become more fully integrated in the national community. In addition, since Rwandans share the same culture, an endeavour has also been made to make this group play a more active part in the expression of this culture.

The feudal régime has been formally abolished by the Constitution, article 2 of which provides that "the monarchy is hereby abolished and cannot be reinstated". Furthermore, the Code of Civil and Commercial Procedure prohibits certain procedures in evidence, the use of which is a relic of feudal-colonialist bondage. For instance, the oath invoking the name of Mwami (the King, when there was a monarchy) and of the Kalinga (the sacred drum of the ancient royalty) is forbidden. It can be said that there are no longer any vestiges of feudalism in our country, particularly since the National Revolutionary Movement for Development (MRND) has adopted, among other aims, the elimination from the Rwandese mentality of the survival of such feudal attitudes as caste, the currying of favour, and intrigue, which act as an impediment to national development.

S

SAFEGUARDS GUARANTEEING THE PROTECTION OF THE RIGHTS OF THOSE FACING THE DEATH PENALTY (1984).

The UN Economic and Social Council, at its first regular session for 1984, acknowledged the work done by the UN COMMISSION ON HUMAN RIGHTS and its SUB-COMMISSION ON PREVENTION OF DISCRIMINATION AND PROTECTION OF MINORITIES in the areas of CAPITAL PUNISHMENT concerning summary or arbitrary executions, as well as the relevent views and comments of the HUMAN RIGHTS COMMITTEE, and strongly condemned and deplored (resolution 1984/50) the practice of arbitrary or summary executions in various parts of the world. It approved the "Safeguards Guaranteeing Protection of the Rights of those Facing the Death Penalty," which had been formulated and recommended by the COMMITTEE ON CRIME PREVENTION AND CONTROL, on the understanding that these safeguards would never be invoked to delay or to prevent the abolition of capital punishment.

The text of the safeguards, annexed to resolution 1984/50, is as follows:

1. In countries which have not abolished the death penalty, capital punishment may be imposed only for the most serious crimes, it being understood that their scope should not go beyond intentional crimes with lethal or other extremely grave consequences.

2. Capital punishment may be imposed only for a crime for which the death penalty is prescribed by law at the time of its commission, it being understood that if, subsequent to the commission of the crime, provision is made by law for the imposition of a lighter penalty, the offender shall benefit thereby.

3. Persons below 18 years of age at the time of the commission of the crime shall not be sentenced to death, nor shall the death sentence be carried out on pregnant women, or on new mothers, or on persons who have become insane.

4. Capital punishment may be imposed only when the guilt of the person charged is based upon clear and convincing evidence leaving no room for an alternative explanation of the facts.

5. Capital punishment may only be carried out pursuant to a final judgement rendered by a competent court after legal process which gives all possible safeguards to ensure a fair trial, at least equal to those contained in article 14 of the International Covenant on Civil and Political Rights, including the right of anyone suspected of or charged with a crime for which capital punishment may be imposed to adequate legal assistance at all stages of the proceedings.

6. Anyone sentenced to death shall have the right to appeal to a court of higher jurisdiction, and steps should be taken to ensure that such appeals shall become mandatory.

7. Anyone sentenced to death shall have the right to seek pardon, or commutation of sentence; pardon or commutation of sentence may be granted in all cases of capital punishment.

8. Capital punishment shall not be carried out pending any appeal or other recourse procedure or other proceeding relating to pardon or commutation of the sentence.

9. Where capital punishment occurs, it shall be carried out so as to inflict the minimum possible suffering.

SEE ALSO Death Penalty: Safeguards; Executions: Report of Special Rapporteur; Principles on the Effective Prevention and Investigation of Extra-Legal, Arbitrary and Summary Executions.

ST. KITTS AND NEVIS.

The Federation of St. Kitts and Nevis is a country occupying two of the Leeward Islands, in the eastern Caribbean Sea, separated by a narrow strait. St. Kitts and Nevis became a dependency of Great Britain under the 1713 Peace of Utrecht. The islands achieved independence from Great Britain in 1983 and became a member of the United Nations the same year. Their combined population is estimated by the UN (1990) to be 50,000. Ethnic groups include descendents of British and French settlers, African slaves, and Carib Indians. The language commonly used is English. Christianity (Anglican, 36%; Methodist, 32%; other Protestant denominations, 8%; and Roman Catholic, 10%) is the predominant religion.

The government (1990) took the form of a monarchy and member of the Commonwealth of Nations, of which the British sovereign is the symbolic head. The governor-general, representing the crown, appoints the prime minister, who represents the party or coalition given the majority in a popular election. There is a unicameral legislature consisting of 11 elected members (eight from St. Kitts and three from Nevis), and three senators appointed by the governor-general. Nevis, in addition, has its own Island Assembly. Nevis also has the right of secession.

The judiciary is independent and modelled after the British court system. Political parties include the People's Action Movement, the Labor Party, and the Nevis Reformation Party.

On 12 October 1989, the UN General Assembly expressed distress (resolution 44/3) at the large number of afflicted persons and the destruction wrought by Hurricane Hugo, which, on 16 September 1989, devastated St. Kitts and Nevis, and urged all States to contribute generously to its relief, rehabilitation, and reconstruction efforts.

ST. KITTS AND NEVIS: CONSTITUTION. The Constitution of St. Kitts and Nevis contains the following provisions (Chapter II, articles 3–15) specifically relating to human rights and fundamental freedoms:

Chapter II—Protection of Fundamental Rights and Freedoms

3. Whereas every person in Saint Christopher and Nevis is entitled to the fundamental rights and freedoms, that is to say, the right, whatever his race, place of origin, birth, political opinions, colour, creed or sex, but subject to respect for the rights and freedoms of others and for the public interest, to each and all of the following, namely—

(a) life, liberty, security of the person, equality before the law and the protection of the law;

(b) freedom of conscience, of expression and of assembly and association; and

(c) protection for his personal privacy, the privacy of his home and other property and from deprivation of property without compensation,

the provisions of this Chapter shall have effect for the purpose of affording protection to those rights and freedoms subject to such limitations of that protection as are contained in those provisions, being limitations designed to ensure that the enjoyment of those rights and freedoms by any person does not impair the rights and freedoms of others or the public interest.

4. Protection of right to life. (1) A person shall not be deprived of his life intentionally save in execution of the sentence of a court in respect of a criminal offence of treason or murder under any law of which he has been convicted.

(2) A person shall not be regarded as having been deprived of his life in contravention of subsection (1) if he dies as the result of the use, to such extent and in such circumstances as are permitted by law, of such force as is reasonably justifiable—

(a) for the defence of any person from violence or for the defence of property;

(b) in order to effect a lawful arrest, or to prevent the escape, of a person lawfully detained;

(c) for the purpose of suppressing a riot, insurrection or mutiny; or

(d) in order to prevent the commission by that person of a criminal offence,

or if he dies as the result of a lawful act of war.

5. Protection of right to personal liberty. (1) A person shall not be deprived of his personal liberty save as may be authorised by law in any of the following cases, that is to say—

(a) in consequence of his unfitness to plead to a criminal charge;

(b) in execution of the sentence or order of a court, whether established for Saint Christopher and Nevis or some other country, in respect of a criminal offence of which he has been convicted;

(c) in execution of the order of the High Court or the Court of Appeal punishing him for contempt of that court or of another court or tribunal;

(d) in execution of the order of a court made to secure the fulfilment of any obligation imposed on him by law;

(e) for the purpose of bringing him before a court in execution of the order of a court;

(f) upon reasonable suspicion of his having committed, or being about to commit, a criminal offence under any law;

(g) under the order of a court or with the consent of his parent or guardian, for his education or welfare during any period ending not later than the date when he attains the age of eighteen years;

(h) for the purpose of preventing the spread of an infectious or contagious disease;

(i) in the case of a person who is, or is reasonably suspected to be, of unsound mind, addicted to drugs or alcohol, or a vagrant, for the purpose of his care or treatment or the protection of the community;

(j) for the purpose of preventing the unlawful entry of that person into Saint Christopher and Nevis or for the purpose of effecting the expulsion, extradition or other lawful removal of that person from Saint Christopher and Nevis or for the purpose of restricting that person while he is being conveyed through Saint Christopher and Nevis in the course of his extradition or removal as a convicted prisoner from one country to another, or

(k) to such extent as may be necessary in the execution of a lawful order requiring that person to remain within a specified area within Saint Christopher and Nevis, or prohibiting him from being within such an area, or to such extent as may be reasonably justifiable for the taking of proceedings against that person with a view to the making of any such order or relating to such an order after it has been made, or to such extent as may be reasonably justifiable for restraining that person during any visit that he is permitted to make to any part of Saint Christopher and Nevis in which, in consequence of any such order, his presence would otherwise be unlawful.

(2) Any person who is arrested or detained shall with reasonable promptitude and in any case not later than forty-eight hours after such arrest or detention be informed in a language that he understands of the reasons for his arrest or detention and be afforded reasonable facilities for private communication and consultation with a legal practitioner of his own choice and, in the case of a person under the age of eighteen years, with his parents or guardian.

(3) Any person who is arrested or detained—

(a) for the purpose of bringing him before a court in execution of the order of a court; or

(b) upon reasonable suspicion of his having committed, or being about to commit, a criminal offence under any law

and who is not released, shall be brought before a court without undue delay and in any case not later than seventy-two hours after his arrest or detention.

(4) Where any person is brought before a court in execution of the order of a court in any proceedings or upon suspicion of his having committed or being about to com-

mit a criminal offence, he shall not be thereafter further held in custody in connection with those proceedings or that offence save upon the order of a court.

(5) If any person arrested or detained as mentioned in subsection (3)(b) is not tried within a reasonable time, then, without prejudice to any further proceedings that may be brought against him, he shall be released either unconditionally or upon reasonable conditions, including in particular such conditions as are reasonably necessary to ensure that he appears at a later date for trial or for proceedings preliminary to trial, and such conditions may include bail so long as it is not excessive.

(6) Any person who is unlawfully arrested or detained by any other person shall be entitled to compensation therefor from that other person or from any other person or authority on whose behalf that other person was acting:

Provided that a judge, a magistrate or a justice of the peace or an officer of a court or a police officer acting in pursuance of the order of a judge, a magistrate or a justice of the peace shall not be under any personal liability to pay compensation under this subsection in consequence of any act performed by him in good faith in the discharge of the functions of his office and any liability to pay any such compensation in consequence of any such act shall be a liability of the Crown.

(7) For the purpose of subsection (1)(b) a person charged before a court with a criminal offence in respect of whom a special verdict has been returned that he was guilty of the act or omission charged but was insane when he did the act or made the omission or that he is not guilty by reason of insanity shall be regarded as a person who has been convicted of a criminal offence and the detention of that person in consequence of such a verdict shall be regarded as detention in execution of the order of a court.

6. Protection from Slavery or Forced Labour. (1) A person shall not be held in slavery or servitude.

(2) No person shall be required to perform forced labour.

(3) For the purposes of this section, the expression "forced labour" does not include—

(a) any labour required in consequence of the sentence or order of a court;

(b) labour required of any person while he is lawfully detained that though not required in consequence of the sentence or order of a court, is reasonably necessary in the interests of hygiene or for the maintenance of the place at which he is detained;

(c) any labour required of a member of a disciplined force in pursuance of his duties as such or, in the case of a person who has conscientious objections to service as a member of a defence force, any labour that that person is required by law to perform in place of such service; or

(d) any labour required during any period of public emergency or in the event of any accident or natural calamity that threatens the life and well-being of the community, to the extent that the requiring of such labour is reasonably justifiable in the circumstances of any situation arising or existing during that period or as a result of that accident or natural calamity, for the purpose of dealing with that situation.

7. Protection from Inhuman Treatment. A person shall not be subjected to torture or to inhuman or degrading punishment or other like treatment.

8. Protection from Deprivation of Property. No property of any description shall be compulsorily taken possession of, and no interest in or right over property of any description shall be compulsorily acquired, except for a public purpose and by or under the provisions of a law that prescribes the principles on which and the manner in which compensation therefore is to be determined and given.

(2) Every person having an interest in or right over property that is compulsorily taken possession of or whose interest in or right over any property is compulsorily acquired shall have a right of direct access to the High Court for—

(a) the determination of his interest or right, the legality of the taking of possession or acquisition of the property, interest or right and the amount of any compensation to which he is entitled; and

(b) the purpose of enforcing his right to prompt payment of that compensation:

Provided that, if the legislature so provides in relation to any matter referred to in paragraph (a) the right of access shall be by way of appeal (exercisable as of right at the instance of the person having the interest in or right over the property) from a tribunal or authority, other than the High Court, having jurisdiction under any law to determine that matter.

(3) The Chief Justice may make rules with respect to the practice and procedure of the High Court or, subject to such provision as may have been made in that behalf by the legislature, with respect to the practice and procedure of any other tribunal or authority in relation to the jurisdiction conferred on the High Court by subsection (2) or exercisable by the other tribunal or authority for the purpose of that subsection (including rules with respect to the time within which applications or appeals to the High Court or applications to the other tribunal or authority may be brought).

(4) A person who is entitled to compensation by virtue of subsection (1) shall not be prevented from remitting, within a reasonable time after he has received any amount of that compensation in the form of a sum of money or, as the case may be, has received any such amount in some other form and has converted any of that amount into a sum of money, the whole of that sum of money (subject to any tax that applies generally to persons remitting moneys but free from any other deduction, charge or tax made or levied in respect of its remission) to any country of his choice outside Saint Christopher and Nevis.

(5) Nothing contained in or done under the authority of any law shall be held to be inconsistent with or in contravention of subsection (4) to the extent that the law in question authorises—

(a) the attachment, by order of a court, of any amount of compensation to which a person is entitled in satisfaction of the judgment of a court or pending the determination of civil proceedings to which he is a party;

(b) the imposition of reasonable restrictions on the manner in which any sum of money is to be remitted; or

(c) the imposition of reasonable restrictions upon the remission of any sum of money in order to prevent or regulate the transfer to a country outside Saint Christopher and Nevis of capital raised in Saint Christopher and Nevis or in some other country or derived from the natural resources of Saint Christopher and Nevis.

(6) Nothing contained in or done under the authority of any law shall be held to be inconsistent with or in contravention of subsection (1)—

(a) to the extent that the law in question makes provision for the taking of possession of or acquisition of any property, interest or right—

(i) in satisfaction of any tax, rate or due;

(ii) by way of penalty for breach of any law or forfeiture in consequence of breach of any law;

(iii) as an incident of a lease, tenancy, mortgage charge, bill of sale, pledge or contract;

(iv) in the execution of judgments or orders of a court in proceedings for the determination of civil rights or obligations;

(v) in circumstances where it is reasonably necessary so to do because the property is in a dangerous state or likely to be injurious to the health of human beings, animals or plants;

(vi) in consequence of any law with respect to the limitation of actions; or

(vii) for so long only as may be necessary for those purposes, for the purposes of any examination, investigation, trial or inquiry or, in the case of land, for the purposes of the carrying out thereon of work of soil conservation or the conservation of other natural resources or work relating to agricultural development or improvement (being work relating to such development or improvement that the owner or occupier of the land has been required and has without reasonable excuse refused or failed, to carry out),

and except so far as that provision or, as the case may be, the thing done under the authority thereof is shown not to be reasonably justifiable in a democratic society; or

(b) to the extent that the law in question makes provision for the taking of possession of or acquisition of any of the following property (including an interest in or right over property), that is to say—

(i) enemy property;

(ii) property of a deceased person, a person of unsound mind or a person who has not attained the age of eighteen years, for the purpose of its administration for the benefit of the persons entitled to the beneficial interest therein;

(iii) property of a person adjudged bankrupt or a body corporate in liquidation, for the purpose of its administration for the benefit of the creditors of the bankrupt or body corporate and, subject thereto, for the benefit of other persons entitled to the beneficial interest in the property; or

(iv) property subject to a trust, for the purpose of vesting the property in persons appointed as trustees under the instrument creating the trust or by a court or, by order of a court, for the purpose of giving effect to the trust.

(7) Nothing contained in or done under the authority of any law enacted by Parliament shall be held to be inconsistent with or in contravention of this section to the extent that the law in question makes provision for the compulsory acquisition of any interest in or right over property, where that property, interest or right is held by a body corporate established by law for public purposes in which no moneys have been invested other than moneys provided by Parliament.

(8) Nothing contained in or done under the authority of any law enacted by the Nevis Island Legislature shall be held to be inconsistent with or in contravention of this section to the extent that the law in question makes provision for the compulsory taking of possession of any property, or the compulsory acquisition of any interest in or right over property, where that property, interest or right is held by a body corporate established by law for public purposes in which no moneys have been invested other than moneys provided by that Legislature.

9. Protection from Arbitrary Search or Entry. (1) Except with his own consent, a person shall not be subject to the search of his person or his property or the entry by others on his premises.

(2) Nothing contained in or done under the authority of any law shall be held to be inconsistent with or in contravention of this section to the extent that the law in question makes provision—

(a) that is reasonably required in the interests of defence, public safety, public order, public morality, public health, town and country planning, the development and utilisation of mineral resources or the development or utilisation of any property for a purpose beneficial to the community;

(b) that is reasonably required for the purpose of protecting the rights or freedoms of other persons;

(c) that authorises an officer or agent of the Government, the Nevis Island Administration, a local government authority or a body corporate established by law for public purpose to enter on the premises of any person in order to inspect those premises or anything thereon for the purpose of any tax, rate or due or in order to carry out work connected with any property that is lawfully on those premises and that belongs to that Government, Administration, authority or body corporate, as the case may be; or

(d) that authorises, for the purpose of enforcing the judgment or order of a court in any civil proceedings, the search of any person or property by order of a court or entry upon any premises by such an order,

and except so far as that provision or, as the case may be, anything done under the authority thereof is shown not to be reasonably justifiable in a democratic society.

10. Provisions to Secure Protection of Law. (1) If any person is charged with a criminal offence, then, unless the charge is withdrawn, the case shall be afforded a fair hearing within a reasonable time by an independent and impartial court established by law.

(2) Every person who is charged with a criminal offence—

(a) shall be presumed to be innocent until he is proved or has pleaded guilty;

(b) shall be informed as soon as reasonably practicable, in a language that he understands and in detail, of the nature of the offence charged;

(c) shall be given adequate time and facilities for the preparation of his defence;

(d) shall be permitted to defend himself before the court in person or, at his own expense, by a legal practitioner of his own choice;

(e) shall be afforded facilities to examine in person or by his legal representative the witnesses called by the prosecution before the court, and to obtain the attendance and carry out the examination of witnesses to testify on his behalf before the court on the same conditions as those applying to witnesses called by the prosecution; and

(f) shall be permitted to have without payment the assistance of an interpreter if he cannot understand the language used at the trial,

and except with his own consent the trial shall not take place in his absence unless he so conducts himself as to render the continuance of the proceedings in his presence impracticable and the court has ordered him to be removed and the trial to proceed in his absence:

Provided that the trial may take place in his absence in any case in which it is so provided by a law under which he is entitled to adequate notice of the charge and the date, time and place of the trial and to a reasonable opportunity of appearing before the court.

(3) When a person is tried for any criminal offence, the accused person or any person authorised by him in that behalf shall, if he so requires and subject to payment of such reasonable fee as may be prescribed by law, be given within a reasonable time after judgment a copy for the use of the accused person of any record of the proceedings made by or on behalf of the court.

(4) A person shall not be held to be guilty of a criminal offence on account of any act or omission that did not, at the time it took place, constitute such an offence, and no penalty shall be imposed for any criminal offence that is severer in degree or description than the maximum penalty that might have been imposed for that offence at the time when it was committed.

(5) A person who shows that he has been tried by a competent court for a criminal offence and either convicted or acquitted shall not again be tried for that offence or for any other criminal offence of which he could have been convicted at the trial for that offence, save upon the order of a superior court in the course of appeal or review proceedings relating to the conviction or acquittal.

(6) A person shall not be tried for a criminal offence if he shows that he has been pardoned for that offense.

(7) A person who is tried for a criminal offence shall not be compelled to give evidence at the trial.

(8) Any court or other authority prescribed by law for the determination of the existence or extent of any civil right or obligation shall be established by law and shall be independent and impartial; and where proceedings for such a determination are instituted by any person before such a court or other authority the case shall be given a fair hearing within a reasonable time.

(9) Where the existence or extent of any civil right or obligation has been determined in proceedings in any court or before any other authority any party to those proceedings shall, if he so requires and subject to payment of such reasonable fee as may be prescribed by law, be entitled to obtain within a reasonable time after the judgment or other determination a copy of any record of the proceedings made by or on behalf of the court or other authority.

(10) Except with the agreement of all the parties thereto, all proceedings of every court and all proceedings for the determination of the existence or extent of any civil right or obligation before any other authority, including the announcement of the decision of the court or other authority, shall be held in public.

(11) Nothing in subsection (10) shall prevent the court or other adjudicating authority from excluding from the proceedings persons other than the parties thereto and the legal practitioners representing them to such extent as the court or other authority—

(a) may by law be empowered to do and may consider necessary or expedient in circumstances where publicity would impair the interests of justice or in interlocutory proceedings or in the interests of public morality, the welfare of persons under the age of eighteen years or the protection of the private lives of persons concerned in the proceedings; or

(b) may by law be empowered or required to do in the interests of defence, public safety or public order.

(12) Nothing contained in or done under the authority of any law shall be held to be inconsistent with or in contravention of—

(a) subsection (2)(a) to the extent that the law in

question imposes upon any person charged with a criminal offence the burden of proving particular facts;

(b) subsection (2)(e) to the extent that the law in question imposes reasonable conditions that must be satisfied if witnesses called to testify on behalf of an accused person are to be paid their expenses out of public funds; or

(c) subsection (5) to the extent that the law in question authorises a court to try a member of a disciplined force for a criminal offence notwithstanding any trial and conviction or acquittal of that member under the disciplinary law of that force, so, however, that any court so trying such a member and convicting him shall in sentencing him to any punishment take into account any punishment awarded him under that disciplinary law.

(13) In the case of any person who is held in lawful detention subsection (1), paragraphs (d) and (e) of subsection (2) and subsection (3) shall not apply in relation to his trial for a criminal offence under the law regulating the discipline of persons held in such detention.

(14) In this section "criminal offence" means a criminal offence under a law.

11. Protection of Freedom of Conscience. (1) Except with his own consent, a person shall not be hindered in the enjoyment of his freedom of conscience including freedom of thought and of religion, freedom to change his religion or belief and freedom, either alone or in community with others, and both in public and in private, to manifest and propagate his religion or belief in worship, teaching, practice and observance.

(2) Except with his own consent (or, if he is a person under the age of eighteen years, the consent of a person who is his parent or guardian) a person attending any place of education, detained in any prison or corrective institution or serving in a defence force shall not be required to receive religious instruction or to take part in or attend any religious ceremony or observance if that instruction, ceremony or observance relates to a religion that is not his own.

(3) Every religious community shall be entitled, at its own expense, to establish and maintain places of education and to manage any place of education that it wholly maintains and such a community shall not be prevented from providing religious instruction for persons of that community in the course of any education that it wholly maintains or in the course of any education that it otherwise provides.

(4) A person shall not be compelled to take any oath that is contrary to his religion or belief or to take any oath in a manner that is contrary to his religion or belief.

(5) Nothing contained in or done under the authority of any law shall be held to be inconsistent with or in contravention of this section to the extent that the law in question makes provision that is reasonably required—

(a) in the interests of defence, public safety, public order, public morality or public health;

(b) for the purpose of protecting the rights and freedoms of other persons, including the right to observe and practise any religion without the unsolicited intervention of members of any other religion; or

(c) for the purpose of regulating educational institutions in the interests of the persons who receive or may receive instruction in them,

and except so far as that provision or, as the case may be, the thing done under the authority thereof is shown not to be reasonably justifiable in a democratic society.

(6) References in this section to a religion shall be construed as including references to a religious denomination, and cognate expressions shall be construed accordingly.

12. Protection of Freedom of Expression. (1) Except with his own consent, a person shall not be hindered in the enjoyment of his freedom of expression, including freedom to hold opinions without interference, freedom to receive ideas and information without interference, freedom to communicate ideas and information without interference (whether the communication is to the public generally or to any person or class of persons) and freedom from interference with his correspondence.

(2) Nothing contained in or done under the authority of any law shall be held to be inconsistent with or in contravention of this section to the extent that the law in question makes provision—

(a) that is reasonably required in the interests of defence, public safety, public order, public morality or public health;

(b) that is reasonably required for the purpose of protecting the reputations, rights and freedoms of other persons or the private lives of persons concerned in legal proceedings, preventing the disclosure of information received in confidence, maintaining the authority and independence of the courts or regulating telephony, telegraphy, posts, wireless broadcasting or television; or

(c) that imposes restrictions upon public officers that are reasonably required for the proper performance of their functions,
and except so far as that provision or, as the case may be, the thing done under the authority thereof is shown not to be reasonably justifiable in a democratic society.

13. Protection of Freedom of Assembly and Association. (1) Except with his own consent, a person shall not be hindered in the enjoyment of his freedom of assembly and association, that is to say, his right to assemble freely and associate with other persons and in particular to form or belong to trade unions or other associations for the protection of his interests or to form or belong to political parties or other political associations.

(2) Nothing contained in or done under the authority of any law shall be held to be inconsistent with or in contravention of this section to the extent that the law in question makes provision—

(a) that is reasonably required in the interests of defence, public safety, public order, public morality or public health;

(b) that is reasonably required for the purpose of protecting the rights or freedoms or other persons; or

(c) that imposes restrictions upon public officers that are reasonably required for the proper performance of their functions,
and except so far as that provision or, as the case may be, the thing done under the authority thereof is shown not to be reasonably justifiable in a democratic society.

14. Protection of Freedom of Movement. (a) A person shall not be deprived of his freedom of movement, that is to say, the right to move freely throughout Saint Christopher and Nevis, the right to reside in any part of Saint Christopher and Nevis, the right to enter Saint Christopher and Nevis, the right to leave Saint Christopher and Nevis and immunity from expulsion from Saint Christopher and Nevis.

(2) Any restriction on a person's freedom of movement that is involved in his lawful detention shall not be held to be inconsistent with or in contravention of subsection (1).

(3) Nothing contained in or done under the authority of any law shall be held to be inconsistent with or in contravention of subsection (1) to the extent that the law in question makes provision—

(a) for the imposition of restrictions on the movement or residence within Saint Christopher and Nevis of any person or on any person's right to leave Saint Christopher and Nevis that are reasonably required in the interests of defence, public safety or public order;

(b) for the imposition of restrictions on the movement or residence within Saint Christopher and Nevis or on the right to leave Saint Christopher and Nevis of persons generally or any class of persons in the interests of defence, public safety, public order, public morality or public health and except so far as that provision or, as the case may be, the thing done under the authority thereof is shown not to be reasonably justifiable in a democratic society;

(c) for the imposition of restrictions, by order of a court, on the movement or residence within Saint Christopher and Nevis of any person or on any person's right to leave Saint Christopher and Nevis either in consequence of his having been found guilty of a criminal offence under any law or for the purpose of ensuring that he appears before a court at a late date for trial of such a criminal offence or for proceedings preliminary to trial or for proceedings relating to his extradition or lawful removal from Saint Christopher and Nevis;

(d) for the imposition of restrictions on the freedom of movement of any person who is not a citizen;

(e) for the imposition of restrictions on the acquisition or use by any person of land or other property in Saint Christopher and Nevis;

(f) for the imposition of restrictions upon the movement or residence within Saint Christopher or on the right to leave Saint Christopher and Nevis of any public officer that are reasonably required for the proper performance of his functions;

(g) for the removal of a person from Saint Christopher and Nevis to be tried or punished in some other country for a criminal offence under the law of that other country or to undergo imprisonment in some other country in execution of the sentence of a court in respect of a criminal offence under a law of which he has been convicted; or

(h) for the imposition of restrictions on the right of any person to leave Saint Christopher and Nevis that are reasonably required in order to secure the fulfilment of any obligations imposed on that person by law,
and except so far as that provision or, as the case may be, the thing done under the authority thereof is shown not to be reasonably justifiable in a democratic society.

(4) If any person whose freedom of movement has been restricted by virtue of such a provision as is referred to in subsection (3)(a) so requests at any time during the period of that restriction not earlier than twenty-one days after the order imposing the restriction was made or, as the case may be, three months after he last made such a request, his case shall be reviewed by an independent and impartial tribunal presided over by a person appointed by the Chief Justice from among persons who hold the office of magistrate or who are legal practitioners.

(5) On any review by a tribunal in pursuance of subsection (4) of the case of any person whose freedom of movement has been restricted, the tribunal may make recommendations concerning the necessity or expediency of the continuation of that restriction to the authority by whom it was ordered but, unless it is otherwise provided by law, that authority shall not be obliged to act in accordance with any such recommendations.

15. Protection from Discrimination on Grounds of Race etc. (1) Subject to subsections (4), (5) and (7), no law shall make any provision that is discriminatory either of itself or in its effect.

(2) Subject to subsections (6), (7), (8) and (9), a person shall not be treated in a discriminatory manner by any persons acting by virtue of any written law or in the performance of the functions of any public office or any public authority.

(3) In this section the expression "discriminatory" means affording different treatment to different persons attributable wholly or mainly to their respective descriptions by race, place of origin, birth out of wedlock, political opinions or affiliations, colour, sex or creed whereby persons of one such description are subjected to disabilities or restrictions to which persons of another such description are not made subject or are accorded privileges or advantages that are not accorded to persons of another such description.

(4) Subsection (1) shall not apply to any law so far as that law makes provision—

(a) for the appropriation of public revenues or other public funds;

(b) with respect to persons who are not citizens;

(c) for the application, in the case of persons of any such description as is mentioned in subsection (3) (or of persons connected with such persons) of the law with respect to adoption, marriage, divorce, burial, devolution of property on death or other like matters that is the personal law of persons of that description; or

(d) whereby persons of any such description as is mentioned in subsection (3) may be subjected to any disability or restriction or may be accorded any privilege or advantage that, having regard to its nature and to special circumstances pertaining to those persons or to persons of any other such description, is reasonably justifiable in a democratic society.

(5) Nothing contained in any law shall be held to be inconsistent with or in contravention of subsection (1) to the extent that it makes provision with respect to standards or qualifications (not being standards or qualifications specifically relating to race, place of origin, birth out of wedlock, political opinions or affiliations, colour, creed or sex) to be required of any person who is appointed to or to act in any office under the Crown, any office in the service of a local government authority or any office in a body corporate established by law for public purposes.

(6) Subsection (2) shall not apply to anything that is expressly or by necessary implication authorised to be done by any such provision of law as is referred to in subsection (4) or (5).

(7) Nothing contained in or done under the authority of any law shall be held to be inconsistent with or in contravention of subsection (1) or (2) to the extent that the law in question makes provision whereby persons of any such description as is mentioned in subsection (3) may be subjected to any restriction on the rights and freedoms guaranteed by sections 9, 11, 12, 13 and 14, being such a restriction as is authorised by section 9(2), 11(5), 12(2) or 13(2) or, as the case may be, paragraph (a), (b), or (c) of section 14(3).

(8) Nothing in subsection (2) shall affect any discretion relating to the institution, conduct or discontinuance of civil or criminal proceedings in any court that is vested in any person by or under any law.

(9) Nothing in subsection (2) shall apply in relation to the exercise of any function vested in any person or authority by any of the provisions of this Constitution except sections 78(1), 79(2), 80(1), 81(1), 82(1), 83 and 85 (which relate to the appointment etc. of public officers).

16. Emergency Measures Derogating from s.5 or 15. Nothing contained in or done under the authority of a law enacted by Parliament shall be held to be inconsistent with or in contravention of section 5 or 15 to the extent that the law authorises the taking during any period of public emergency of measures that are reasonably justifiable for dealing with the situation that exists in Saint Christopher and Nevis or part of Saint Christopher and Nevis during that period.

ST. LUCIA. A country which occupies one of the Windward Islands of the West Indies, located off the northern coast of South America, south of Martinique and between the Atlantic Ocean and the Caribbean Sea, St. Lucia achieved independence from Great Britain in 1979 and became of member of the United Nations the same year. Its population is estimated by the UN (1990) to be 139,000. Ethnic groups include Carib Indians, East Indians, and descendents of British and French settlers and their slaves. Languages commonly used include English and a local *patois*. Christianity (Roman Catholic, 92%; Church of England, 3%; and other Protestant denominations, 5%) is the predominant religion. Literacy is estimated at 78%.

The government (1990) took the form of a monarchy and a member of the Commonwealth of Nations, of which the British sovereign is the symbolic head. The governor-general, representing the crown, appoints the prime minister, representing the party or coalition given the majority in a popular election. Members of the 17-member House of Assembly are elected for a term of five years; members of the 11-member Senate are appointed by the governor-general, six on advice of the prime minister, three on advice of the leader of the opposition party, and two on nomination by appropriate non-governmental bodies. The judiciary is independent and modelled after the British system of justice. Political parties include the United Workers' Party, the St. Lucia Labour Party, and the Progressive Labour Party.

ST. VINCENT AND THE GRENADINES. A country which occupies one of the Windward Islands of the West Indies and a chain of nearly 600 small islets extending for 60 miles, all located 100 miles west of Barbados in the Caribbean Sea, St. Vincent and the Grenadines achieved independence from Great Britain in 1979 and became a member of the United Nations in 1980. Its population is estimated by the UN (1990) to be 111,000. Ethnic groups include Carib Indians and descendents of British and French settlers and their slaves, as well as a few Portuguese and East Indians. The language commonly used is English. Christianity (Anglican, 47%; Methodist, 28%; and Roman Catholic, 13%) is the predominant religion. Literacy is estimated at 78%.

The government (1990) took the form of a monarchy and member of the Commonwealth of Nations, of which the British sovereign is the symbolic head. The governor-general, representing the crown, appoints the prime minister, who represents the party or coalition given the majority in a popular election, and who exercises executive authority. The legislature includes 13 members elected by voters for five-year terms and six senators appointed by the governor-general, four on the advice of the prime minister, and two on the advice of the leader of the opposition. The judiciary is modelled after the British system. Political parties include the New Democrats and the St. Vincent Labor Party.

SALVATION ARMY. An international non-governmental organization in consultative status with the UN Economic and Social Council (Category II) and with UNESCO, the Salvation Army has about 25,000 full-time ministers and "commissioned offices" and about 1.5 million "soldiers" (members subscribing to its doctrines and providing voluntary support in religious service) in 89 countries and territories.

Founded in 1865 in London by Gen. William Booth and his wife Catherine as the Christian Mission, the Salvation Army works to relieve poverty and to carry out charitable activities throughout the world. The Salvation Army promotes a Christian evangelical ministry and provides social services for the needy of all ages and groups, irrespective of race or religion, through educational, medical, agricultural, and rehabilitation programs, especially in developing countries.

The Salvation Army has an extensive publication program, including the weeklies *The War Cry, The Salvationist,* and *The Young Soldier;* the bi-monthlies *All the World* and *The Deliverer;* and *The Salvation Army Year Book.*

Salvation Army. Address: 101 Queen Victoria Street, P.O. Box 249, London EC4P 4EP, UK. Telephone: (44-1) 236-5222. Cable: Salvation London EC4. Telex: 8954847. Secretary General: Eva Burrows.

Yearbook of International Organizations 1989/90 (K. G. Saur).

SAMOA. The Independent State of Western Samoa is a Polynesian country occupying an island in the South Pacific Ocean 800 miles northeast of Fiji. Administered by New Zealand from 1914 to 1947 as a League of Nations mandate, and subsequently as a United Nations trust territory, it achieved independence on 1 January 1962. As Samoa, it became a member of the United Nations in 1976. Its population is estimated by the UN (1990) to be 169,000. Ethnic groups include Europeans, New Zealanders, Polynesians, and Euronesians (mixed). Languages commonly used include Samoan, Polynesian, and English. Christianity (Congregational, 50%; Roman Catholic, 22%; and Methodist, 16%) is the predominant religion; many adhere to local religions or beliefs or to none at all. Literacy is estimated at 95%.

The government (1990) took the form of a republic. Under the constitution approved in a plebescite held under United Nations supervision on 9 May 1961, the incumbent Head of State for Life will be succeeded by heads of State elected by the Legislative Assembly for terms of five years. The head of State appoints the prime minister and, on advice of the prime minister, eight ministers to form the cabinet; all executive authority is vested in these officials. Of the 47 members in the Legislative Assembly, 45 are elected by the titleholders (chiefs) of the largest family groups, and two are elected by universal adult suffrage to represent those not belonging to one of those groups. The judiciary includes the Supreme Court.

SAN MARINO. The Most Serene Republic of San Marino is a landlocked country in southern Europe, totally surrounded by Italy. It achieved independence, according to legend, in 301 A.D. and, although not a member of the United Nations, is a party to the statute of the International Court of Justice. Its population is estimated by the UN (1990) to be 23,000. Ethnic groups include persons of Sammarinese and Italian origin. The language in common use is Italian. Christianity (Roman Catholic) is the predominant religion. Literacy is estimated at 97%.

The government (1990) took the form of a republic. Two coregents acts as heads of State. Executive authority is exercised by an 11-member Congress of State. Legislative functions are performed by the 60-member unicameral Grand and General Council. The judiciary is headed by the Council of Twelve, which is the court of final appeal. Political parties include the Christian Democratic Party, the Communist Party, the United Socialist Party, the Democratic Socialist Party, and the Republican Party.

San Marino is said to be the oldest republic in the world. Its citizens retain the right to vote regardless of residence abroad.

SAO TOME AND PRINCIPE. The Democratic Republic of Sao Tome and Principe is a country in middle Africa, occupying four islands in the Gulf of Guinea, about 150 miles off the coast of Africa. It achieved independence from Portugal in 1975 and became a member of the United Nations the same year. Its population is estimated by the UN (1990) to be 112,000. Ethnic groups include descendents of Portuguese settlers and their slaves. Portuguese is the only language commonly used. Christianity (Roman Catholic, 80%; Evangelical Protestant, Seventh Day Adventist, and other Protestant denominations, 20%) is the predominant religion. Literacy is estimated at 50%.

The government (1990) took the form of a republic. The president is elected by members of the People's Assembly from candidates nominated by the Movement for the Liberation of Sao Tome and Principe, the only legal political party. The People's Assembly, composed of members elected for terms of four years, is granted supreme power under the 1975 constitution.

The Portuguese used slave labor to develop extensive sugar and cacao plantations on the islands of Sao Tome and Principe during the 17th century. It was the scene of labor riots in 1953, which ended with the killing of several hundred African laborers and the development of a liberation movement.

When the Portuguese departed from Sao Tome and Principe in 1975, they abandoned one of Africa's poorest countries. Because they had not trained the African population to maintain the roads and bridges or to manage the coffee and cocoa plantations, the economic situation deteriorated rapidly. In 1981, food riots erupted when the government could no longer afford to import dried fish. Since that time, however, governments and international organizations have provided massive assistance and the country has achieved food-sufficiency in coffee, sugar, and cooking oil. Much of the international aid was provided by the World Food Program.

SAUDI ARABIA. The Kingdom of Saudi Arabia is an Arab country occupying most of the Arabian Peninsula, on the Red Sea, the Gulf of Aqaba, and the Arabian Gulf. It has borders with Iraq, Jordan, Kuwait, Oman, Qatar, the United Arab Emirates, and Yemen. It achieved independence in 1932 when King Ibn Saud united Hejaz and Nejd into a single kingdom and became a member of the United Nations in 1945. Its population is estimated by the UN (1990) to be 13,988,000. Ethnic groups include Arabs (90% of the population), and a variety of Afro–Asian mixtures. The language in common use is Arabic. Islam (Sunni, 85%; Shi'ite, 15%) is the predominant religion. Literacy is estimated at 80%.

The government (1990) took the form of a monarchy based on the *Sharia* (Islamic law). There is no formal constitution. King Fahd ibn Abdul Aziz Al Saud is prime minister and head of State and government. There is a 21-member Council of Ministers to advise the king and to prepare legislation; all laws and regulations are promulgated in the form of royal or ministerial decrees. The religious law of Islam is the law of the land, and it is administered by religious courts headed by a chief judge who is also responsible for the Department of *Sharia* Affairs. There are no political parties.

In recent years, Saudi Arabia has periodically experienced difficultues with Iranian pilgrims to Mecca, who have numbered over 150,000 in some years and have caused severe damage to Muslim holy places. In 1988, Saudi Arabia limited the number of Iranians permitted to enter Mecca, and severed diplomatic relations with Teheran. It has since supported Kuwait in what they consider to be Iranian-supported terrorism in the Arab Gulf.

SAVE THE CHILDREN ALLIANCE. An international non-governmental organization in consultative status (Category II) with the UN Economic and Social Council, Save the Children has affiliated organizations in 21 countries and territories.

The alliance was founded in 1979, as an international consortium of independent voluntary organizations and agencies. The group acts as a consultative and coordinating body to help underprivileged children anywhere in the world regardless of race, nationality, creed, or political background. Save the Children organizes and cooperates in programs in child health, education, and nutrition. It operates a data bank that holds information on all humanitarian and development assistance programs of its members.

Save the Children Alliance. Address: 4 Brogaardsvaenget, DK-2820 Gentofte, Denmark. Telephone: (45-01) 68-05-45. Cable: SCALLIANCE-COPENHAGEN. Telex: 16088 ALIANS DK. Secretary: Ellis Wagner Johansen.

Yearbook of International Organizations 1989/90 (K. G. Saur).

SCIENCE AND TECHNOLOGY. The impact of scientific and technological developments on the realization of human rights and fundamental freedoms was considered informally, but in some detail, at a seminar organized by the UN Division of Human Rights in cooperation with the government of Austria and held in Vienna from 19 June to 1 July 1972. Expert participants and alternates, designated by 25 countries but serving in their capacity as individuals, took part in the seminar, together with observers from four additional countries and the representatives of a large number of intergovernmental and non-governmental organizations.

Those who attended the seminar realized that, whereas scientific and technological developments could improve the life of human beings in many spheres, they could at the same time, if applied without planning or built-in safeguards, lead to the violation of human rights in other spheres. They put forward a number of proposals and policies to ensure that all scientific discoveries and their technological applications are utilized in the interest of society as a whole but ultimately came to the conclusion that it was inappropriate for such an informal gathering to adopt common conclusions or recommendations.

The report of the seminar (UN Doc. ST/TAO/HR/45) reflects the extreme complexity of the problem and the wide diversity of views of the participants. The following extracts indicate the main trends of thinking, particularly as regards the impact of science and technology upon the right to privacy, the right to enjoy democratic government, the right to work, the right to rest and leisure, the right to health, the right to food, and the right to education and culture (*Ibid.*, para. 21–61):

There was diversity of opinion as to what were the really important problems in relation to human rights and scientific and technological developments. Some speakers felt that the vital issues were not so much possible invasions of the right of privacy or questions arising from heart transplants as the use of modern science and technology to promote economic, social and cultural rights, including the rights to health, food and housing and threats to the rights to work posed by automation. It was noted that in the developing societies the concern to preserve respect for privacy was felt as strongly as in the industrialized societies; however, the need for specific local laws dealing with scientific and technological developments had not yet been felt with such urgency; all the more so in Islamic countries for instance where private life as well as public life was impregnated with religion, which was a balancing factor. It was remarked that one of the greatest dangers to the right to life itself were the advanced technologies of warfare. Attention was drawn also to the danger that science might be used to interfere with the integrity and sovereignty of nations, for instance through the use of observation satellites or devices used for espionage. Further, it was pointed out that until the basic rights of food, work and shelter had been realized, there ought to be a more careful use of resources by developing countries for the sophisticated technology. It was asserted by other speakers that the socialist form of government had led to very great developments in science and technology. Science and technology were also well developed in other countries which had other socio-economic bases.

Many participants wished to emphasize that science in general was a positive force in society for increasing production and improving the conditions of life of the citizens. Several participants felt that often scientific techniques had evolved for the benefit of an *élite* and that great sums of money were directed towards projects such as space research or sophisticated weaponry that did not necessarily benefit the pressing needs of humanity at large. It was said that the new phenomenon of the large multinational corporations which often pollute the air and water and disrupt the economic and social fabric of developing countries should be studied. Other speakers pointed to the need for technology assessment, since scientific and technological advances which appear to be an unmitigated good on a small or laboratory or pilot plant scale, might have unforeseen consequences when applied on a massive international scale. These were unexpected effects which occurred in the environment or in man, irrespective of the social system.

Participants in the seminar pointed out that contemporary scientific and technological progress had a very great influence on all aspects of social life in all societies. Advances in science and technology created vast opportunities for the development of the economy and culture of various countries, the improvement of the material welfare of peoples and the consolidation of peace, friendship and co-operation between peoples and States. Yet it would be a great mistake to view scientific and technological progress in the abstract or collectively, without taking account of the existence in the modern world of different social and political systems, or to disregard the major qualitative differences in the social consequences of the scientific and technological revolution in socialist, capitalist and developing countries. Scientific and technological progress could, of course, have negative effects too, but science itself and peoples were able to cope with them. There were therefore no grounds for pessimism, panic or fear.

Other participants doubted whether there was any fundamental difference between the disadvantages and possible dangers arising out of science and technology as between one system and another. The problems now arising from technological advance were the same in kind whenever they occurred, though they no doubt differed in degree. They could understand that solutions adopted might well differ according to the political, economic and social system, and that in some systems a given solution might be more readily accepted than in others.

Several speakers advocated the adoption of international instruments dealing with human rights and scientific and technological developments, as was envisaged by the preamble to General Assembly resolution 2450 (XXIII) and paragraph 10 of Commission on Human Rights resolution 10 (XXVII). Reference was made in this connexion to the possibility of adopting one or more conventions, declarations, model laws or regulations or minimum standards.

(a). Right to Privacy (article 12 of the Universal Declaration of Human Rights). The threats posed to the right of privacy due to surreptitious surveillance devices were pointed out by various participants. Whereas previously one could often detect intrusions, now the methods were more clandestine.

Computers might be used for storing vast quantities of information on individuals and questions arose concerning invasion of privacy and the right to access to such information. Several participants described national computer systems used for health and social purposes and the measures being taken to prohibit or prevent the use of an individual's records for other than intended purposes. The use of drugs to obtain confessions was deplored. The importance of protecting a private sphere was emphasized by several speakers, but it was recognized that a specific right to privacy had not been explicitly defined in many countries. Moreover it was pointed out that the prevention of an assault on privacy by other individuals or private institutions was often more difficult to control than State intervention. Large data banks were being kept by commercial firms and personal information was published by newspapers and the electronic media to wide segments of the population. Some participants emphasized that the simple proclamation of a right was not enough; technological safeguards should also be sought, penal consequences for violations would be appropriate, but the real guarantees lay in a sensitive social and political system. Religious and legal attitudes of respect for inviolability of the person, family and home were also important bulwarks against invasion of privacy.

Attention was drawn to the invasion of privacy due to such features as new construction techniques, which result in the use of inferior materials such as thin walls in housing. An element of discrimination was pointed out; this type of housing was the only one that some could afford. Hence, an implied consent is given by the inhabitants to the violation of their right to privacy. The assault on this right caused by the noise, pollution and advertising present in advanced, industrialized countries was also recognized. The adverse effects of noise, pollution and advertising especially in the industrially advanced countries, were also recognized. In particular, the conditioning of the consumer by television, radio and abusive advertising might sometimes constitute a veritable rape of the mind.

(b). Right to Enjoy Democratic Government (article 21). Several participants drew attention to the importance of radio and television and the other media of information for informing the electorate of political events and making better informed choices of their representatives. The advent of copying machines, an improved communication network, computers and other modern machines had resulted in better and more efficient public administrators. Many countries had voting machines which permitted a prompt and accurate calculation of the results of elections.

Other participants emphasized the danger of technocracy and the fear that computers would greatly influence many important decision-making functions. It was pointed out that if a computer made a determination and only one group had complete information, it would be very difficult to dispute the resulting decision. The inhibiting psychological impact of challenging the machine may often be a great danger to democratic participation in government. However, it had to be realized that many governmental decisions had in fact become highly technical and complex and beyond the ken of the average layman.

It was stated that the influencing of the electorate through the electronic media and use of sophisticated social science surveys and opinion polls can have a significant impact on the results of elections. It was pointed out that there were tendencies towards monopoly in the control of mass media. The cost of campaigning for office had risen in many countries due to the need for costly technology.

The use of surveillance devices and data banks, which violated the right to privacy, was also seen to threaten the rights to peaceful assembly, freedom of speech, thought and the press. The important question of access to computerized information kept by governments as well as private organizations was discussed. It was remarked that the use of tranquilizing drugs might render a whole population more docile.

Several participants told the seminar of positive social used to which computers and other technological tools were being put in their respective countries, emphasizing that a stable economic and social environment was the best guarantee for democratic government. Towards this end participants from the developing world stresses the necessity of an increased transfer of technology.

(c). Right to Work (article 23). The increasing specialization necessary because of new technological requirements could, if remedial measures were not taken, exacerbate the employment situation for unskilled workers. Several speakers stated that the development of automation often displaced workers. Several participants spoke of the need for relatively frequent retraining. Because of the rapid advancement of technology, even technical, professional and managerial staff might be unemployed. Computer services intended to match vacancies with those looking for jobs had been adopted by one Government. Attention was drawn to the question of the scientific workers' right to refuse to continue certain socially dangerous research; they should be protected against the possibility of losing their jobs or of any sort of persecution. The attention of participants in the seminar was directed to the need to guarantee for all people employment, democratic education and an improvement in its quality, and retraining for workers without reduction in salary; to establish public control of the introduction and use of new technology in the interests of the people; to prevent industrial accidents and to ensure real and effective participation by the workers in the management of the affairs of State and of society at all levels.

Attention was drawn to the use and abuse of psychological tests and personal data banks to assess a prospective employee's suitability for work and the use of secret surveillance methods and computer records to observe employees' performance and conduct.

Many participants described the care that their countries were taking to ensure safe and healthy working conditions when installing new technological processes. Female workers were given special protection in particular when working with potentially dangerous chemical substances.

Several participants mentioned the importance that computers and other scientific and technological developments had in the industries of their respective countries and in the stimulation of economic growth and therefore the creation of more jobs.

The need to provide everyone with a fair opportunity for decent employment was recognized by all participants. Attention was drawn to the dehumanizing tendency of automated industry, which often severely lowered the job satisfaction of the workers. However, the assumption that work itself was essential to the quality of life was challenged. Reference was made to shorter working weeks and earlier retirement, with the consequent need to stimulate education for the creative use of leisure.

Stress was laid upon the importance of continuing consultation and planning by government, employers and employees in anticipation of change so as to minimize disruption and redundancy when it came.

One participant suggested that article 23 of the Universal Declaration of Human Rights was itself offensive to human dignity in that it implied a subordination of the worker to his employer and reflected traditional conflicts which were now out of date. The emphasis now should be upon participation in productive processes on the basis of co-operation, not conflict.

(d). *Right to Rest and Leisure (article 24)*. Many of the participants described the new facilities, being made available in their countries, for their citizens to enjoy the outdoors, take up sports, rest and pursue cultural activities. As the need for long hours of work declined, this sphere of human activity was becoming more important. Labour-saving devices abounded in the house to reduce the time necessary for household chores. Furthermore improved transportation made access to places of rest and recreation increasingly possible. Recreational equipment was mass-produced and increasingly available.

The destruction of the environment and the stresses caused by industrialization and urbanization were threats to the rights to rest and leisure. Better city planning was suggested to reverse adverse trends.

The social alienation characterized by the new technological age was mentioned. Better planning of man's social needs was suggested so that man might be able to fulfil himself creatively during his non-working hours.

(e). *Right to Health (article 25)*. The term "technogenic" diseases was introduced to the seminar to characterize those diseases which were a direct result of technological advances. Occupational diseases and mental disorders caused by the urban environment were examples of such threats to the right to health posed by new technological developments. Science was continuously discovering the harmful effect which certain activities have on the health of man. Recent tests, for instance, had shown that cigarette smoke inhaled by non-smokers in the proximity of smokers in unventilated or poorly ventilated areas could be harmful to the non-smoker.

Several participants addressed themselves to the questions raised by organ transplantation, including the definition of death, attitudes to which were changing in the light of the possibility of maintaining heart and lung functioning after cessation of brain activity. Experimentation on human subjects also received considerable attention and participants discussed what constitutes "informed consent" for the purpose of such experiments. Several speakers drew attention to the psychological inferiority felt by patients entering modern hospitals. In some areas, patients had been abused for research or demonstration purposes and some feared that they might become involved in organ transplantation against their will.

The subjects of artificial fertilization, abortion, production of children in test tubes, compulsory sterilization and mutation of germinal cells were also touched upon. It was pointed out that it was possible to determine prior to birth that a foetus had Down's syndrome and it was asked whether the parents or society had a right to abort such a child.

Since the right to health and the application of science in these fields was involved, several participants stated that deontological codes should be more precise and should be constantly adjusted to discoveries and rapid changes.

It was pointed out that the effects of certain technological developments could have effects on later generations through production of mutations.

The dangers of air pollution were again referred to in the context of the right to health. The question of legal responsibility for the car exhaust which caused smog, and ultimately contributed to disability and death were referred to.

Several participants drew attention to the difficulties which inevitably arose in present conditions of scarcity in selecting beneficiaries of "iron lungs", the dialysis machines used by patients with kidney disease and other types of costly and scarce machinery, or costly surgical procedures, including organ transplantation and the "artificial" prolongation of life. It was also pointed out that sophisticated life-prolonging procedures were being used while many suffered a lack of basic medical attention. On the other hand, attention was drawn to certain dramatic recent events such as the development of a successful and inexpensive anti-polio vaccine.

It was observed that in numerous ways, technology was reducing the extent to which the individual must indulge in beneficial exercise.

(f). *Right to Food (article 25)*. Several participants and observers referred to the importance of "the green revolution" in meeting food shortages in various countries. It was explained that this progress had come about through improved agricultural practices including improved seeds, synthetic fertilizers, pesticides and fungicides and better water and soil management. Certain pesticides and fungicides were recognized as being ecologically disruptive. Prudence was advocated in their use as well as in that of artificial growth stimulants for animals and chemical additives in food, for which purpose adequate protective legislation might be necessary. It was also recognized that in order to improve methods of production, conservation and distribution of food, it was necessary in many countries to develop or reform the agrarian structure. The improvement of international trade practices in agricultural products was also deemed important.

DDT was recognized to have some long-range undesirable effects in the environment, but for many regions it was deemed necessary until a inexpensive substitute could be found. Since malnutrition was widespread in large areas of the world, the negative aspects of modern chemistry in the production of food should be kept in proper perspective.

The population growth rate stimulated by improved health services was recognized as having placed large demands on agriculturalists to ensure an adequate supply of food. The interdependence of fertility control and the right to food was noted.

(g). *Right to Education and Culture (article 26 and 27)*. The need for continuous education and even frequent retraining in the present era of rapid technological advances was stressed by several participants. The content of the educational curriculum must be regularly brought up to date and the demands placed on teachers were particularly great. Some participants in the seminar noted in their statements the democratic and advanced nature of education and the flowering of culture in socialist countries.

Others pointed out that in any case the freedom of research and of artistic creation should be safeguarded.

Modern audio-visual aids could make important contributions to education. Several participants referred to the importance of radio and television in educating their people, perhaps especially in rural areas. It was noted, however, that pictures and sound had to be augmented by high quality commentary in order to produce desirable results. Computers were playing an important part in the social sciences.

Reference was made to the phenomenon of cultural misrepresentation and interference being perpetuated against developing countries through certain types of advertising and commercial films and television shows.

It was said that violence portrayed on television had been shown to lead to anti-social behaviour in some children, who were unable fully to distinguish fact from fantasy, or who were otherwise susceptible to having their behaviour influenced through viewing television.

It was maintained that it should be possible to keep museums and libraries open free of charge in the evening and on weekends for the benefit of all.

Special emphasis was placed on the fact that the great technological advances should be used for progress in education and culture in developing countries.

One participant in the seminar stressed that the steps taken in some socialist countries to complete the transition to universal secondary education in condition of scientific and technological progress were of great social import.

SEE ALSO Declaration on the Use of Scientific and Technological Progress in the Interests of Peace and for the Benefit of Mankind.

SCIENTIFIC AND TECHNOLOGICAL DEVELOPMENTS: EFFECT ON HUMAN RIGHTS.

On 13 May 1968, the International Conference on Human Rights, convened in Teheran, adopted the PROCLAMATION OF TEHERAN, in which it pointed out (para. 18) that "while recent scientific discoveries and technological advances have opened vast prospects for economic, social and cultural progress, such developments may nevertheless endanger the rights and freedoms of individuals and will require continuing attention."

On proposal of the conference, the General Assembly invited the Secretary-General (resolution 2450 [XXIII]) to study the problems in connection with human rights arising from developments in science and technology, in particular from the following standpoints: (a) respect for the privacy of individuals and the integrity and sovereignty of nations in the light of advances in recording and other techniques; (b) protection of the human personality and its physical and intellectual integrity in the light of advances in biology, medicine, and biochemistry; (c) uses of electronics which might affect the rights of the person and the limits which should be placed on such uses in a democratic society; and (d) more generally, the balance which should be established between scientific and technological progress and the intellectual, spiritual, cultural, and moral advancement of humanity.

In the following years, the Secretary-General prepared a number of studies on various aspects of the subject, including studies entitled "The impact of scientific and technological developments on economic, social and cultural rights" (UN Doc. E/CN.4/1084), "The impact of science and technology on the right to work and certain related rights" (UN Doc. E/CN.4/1115), "Respect for the privacy of individuals and the integrity and sovereignty of nations in the light of advances in recording and other techniques" (UN Doc. E/CN.4/1116 and Add. 1-4), "The impact of science and technology on the right to rest and leisure and the right to social security" (UN Doc. E/CN.4/1141), and "Uses of electronics which might affect the rights of the person and the limits which should be placed on such uses in a democratic society" (UN Doc. E/CN.4/1142 and Add. 1). These studies—and a UNESCO report on the impact of scientific developments on the right to education, the right to culture, and authors' rights—were considered by the COMMISSION ON HUMAN RIGHTS at its 1974 session.

The commission (resolution 2 [XXX]) called upon all States "to develop further international cooperation to ensure that the results of scientific and technological developments are used in the interests of strengthening international peace and security, realization of the peoples' right to self-determination and respect for national sovereignty, freedom and independence and for the purpose of economic and social development and improving the quality of life for the entire population." The Secretary-General was requested to bring the studies to the attention of governments and to seek their observations on the use to which science and technology can be put: (a) to strengthen international peace and security and the fundamental rights of peoples; (b) to promote and insure general respect for the human rights proclaimed in the UNIVERSAL DECLARATION OF HUMAN RIGHTS and the International Covenants on Human Rights; and (c) through raising their standard of living, to facilitate and protect the enjoyment by all peoples of their right to employment, education, food, health, and economic, social, and cultural well-being. He was further requested to prepare an analysis of the observations received in order to enable the Commission to consider possible guidelines or standards which could be included in appropriate international instruments.

The General Assembly, in 1975, examined a draft declaration on the use of scientific and technological progress in the interests of peace and for the benefit of mankind which had been submitted to it in 1974 by Bangladesh, Czechoslovakia, the German Democratic Republic, Mauritius, Poland, and the Union of Soviet Socialist Republics (UN Doc. A/C.3/L.2144). On 10 November 1975, it proclaimed the DECLARATION ON THE USE OF SCIENTIFIC AND TECHNOLOGICAL PROGRESS IN THE INTERESTS OF PEACE AND FOR THE BENEFIT OF MANKIND. The declaration emphasizes the incalculable potential of scientific and technological developments but, at the same time, identifies the harmful consequences that might result from the improper use of technological advances; and it appeals to states to coordinate their actions by means of scientific and technological cooperation with a view to solving some of the problems that confront mankind.

The Commission on Human Rights has since devoted its efforts primarily to exploring ways and means of implementing the provisions of the declaration. In 1977, it considered a number of relevant reports, including reports by the Secretary-General on the protection of the human personality and its physical and intellectual integrity in the light of biology, medicine, and biochemistry (UN Docs. E/CN.4/1172 and Adds. 1–3, and E/CN.4/1173); on the balance which should be established between scientific and technological progress and the intellectual, spiritual, cultural, and moral advancement of humanity (UN Doc. E/CN.4/1199 and Add. 1); on developments relating to science and technology elsewhere in the United Nations system (UN Doc. E/CN.4/1234); on national technological assessment machinery (UN Doc. E/ CN.4/1235); and on human rights and international machinery for technological assessment (UN Doc. E/CN.4/1237). In addition, UNESCO submitted to it a report on the impact of scientific and technological developments on the right to education, the right to culture, and author's rights (UN Doc. E/CN.4/ 1196); and WHO submitted a report on the human rights implications of the genetic manipulation of microbes (UN Doc. E/CN.4/1236). The commission noted (resolution 10 A [XXXIII]) these reports and requested the SUB-COMMISSION ON PREVENTION OF DISCRIMINATION AND PROTECTION OF MINORITIES to study, with a view to formulating guidelines if possible, the question of the protection of those detained on the ground of mental ill-health against treatment that may adversely affect the human personality and its physical and intellectual capacity.

The sub-commission has since studied the problems of MENTALLY ILL PERSONS but has not completed that work as at the end of 1989. Meanwhile, the commission has repeatedly called upon the sub-commission to initiate a study on the use of the achievements of scientific and technological progress to insure the right to work and development (resolutions 38 [XXXVII], 1982/4, 1984/29, 1986/11, and 1988/61), a task which the sub-commission itself had not undertaken up to the end of 1989.

The General Assembly, at its 1988 session, invited the commission (resolution 43/110) to take appropriate measures and to assist the sub-commission in preparing the study. Realizing that the science and technology of our times create possibilities for providing an abundance of material wealth on earth and establishing conditions for the prosperity of society as well as the all-around development of every person, the Assembly expressed serious concern that the results of scientific and technological progress could be used for the arms race and the development of new types of weapons to the detriment of international peace, security, and social progress; human rights and fundamental freedoms; and the dignity of the human person. It called upon all States to make every effort to use the achievements of science and technology in order to promote peaceful social, economic, and cultural development and progress and to put an end to the use of these achievements for military purposes; and to take all necessary measure to place the achievements of science and technology at the service of mankind and to ensure that they do not lead to the degradation of the natural environment.

SEE ALSO *Mentally Ill: Draft Principles for Their Protection; UNESCO Rocommendation on the Status of Scientific Researchers.*

SCIENTIFIC AND TECHNOLOGICAL DEVELOPMENTS: UN UNIVERSITY STUDY.

Recognizing that the effects of scientific and technological developments on human rights and fundamental freedoms have both beneficial and harmful aspects, and therefore must be examined in their totality, the UN COMMISSION ON HUMAN RIGHTS, on 10 March 1986 (resolution 1986/9), invited the UNITED NATIONS UNIVERSITY, in cooperation with other interested academic and research institutions, to study both the positive and the negative impacts of scientific and technological developments on human rights and fundamental freedoms.

The university submitted a preliminary report on its "Project on Human Rights and Scientific Development" (UN Doc. E/CN.4/1988/48) to the commission at its 1988 session, informing the commission that it had established a steering committee to coordinate the project. The steering committee held two sessions in 1987, at which it had considered means for carrying out its task of developing a conceptual framework which will discern both positive and negative impacts of scientific and technological developments on human rights and fundamental freedoms. In the course of its deliberations, the following ideas for future research, as summarized in the report, emerged:

(a) The Committee considered the necessity for international technology impact assessment in relation to technology related projects, especially in the context of the developing world. The Committee recognized that some developing countries experience special difficulty at the present time in marshalling technical expertise requisite for analysing the impact of proposed technology transfers on human rights within their respective societies. Many suggestions have been made to assist in resolving these problems. The Committee is of the view that it is urgently necessary to commission research examining these various proposals and their ideological and practical implications. It, therefore, proposes to initiate a study to consider these implications and to identify mechanisms for resolving these problems.

(b) The Committee also considered the massive damage to human rights resulting from such incidents as the Bhopal disaster, and the need for normative and institutional safeguards in relation to technology already in operation. The Committee perceived that the answers should be both national and international and was of the view that a study should be commissioned to investigate the ways, including early-warning systems, in which existing monitoring standards could be raised and more effectively enforced.

(c) While being conscious of the studies in the field of intellectual property made by the World Intellectual Property Organization and other institutions, the Committee was of the view that the human rights aspect of intellectual property, with particular reference to developing countries, has not yet been adequately explored. The Committee felt that a study is required of how the rights and interests of intellectual property owners should be balanced against those of society without damaging the necessary incentives for stimulating technology innovations.

(d) The Committee considered the fact that a very small proportion of scientific talent (estimated at barely 1 per cent in the Brandt report) is devoted to problems of development. The Committee considered it an urgent need to study the reasons for this imbalance and seek ways in which the scientific community could be stimulated to devote a greater proportion of its time and attention to the problems of poverty, development and the environment.

(e) The Committee considered it important to promote research in "Science Studies", devoted to an examination of the ways in which scientific knowledge and technological information are produced, processed, distributed, and utilized, and the implications of this for human rights.

The commission at its 1988 session welcomed (resolutions 1988/59) and preliminary report, in particular the future research ideas described therein, and invited the university to continue the study with a view to making its results available to the commission at its 1990 session.

SECURITY COUNCIL. The Security Council of the United Nations was established in accordance with article 7 of the UNITED NATIONS CHARTER. Its principal functions and powers are (1) to investigate any disputes or situation which might give rise to a dispute in order to determine whether the continuance of the dispute or situation is likely to endanger the maintenance of international peace and security; (2) to decide on such procedures or recommend such terms of settlement as it may consider appropriate; (3) to make recommendations or decide to take enforcement measures in order to maintain or restore international peace and security; and (4) if it decides that these measures are, or have proved to be, inadequate, to take such action by air, sea, or land forces as may be necessary to restore international peace and security. The council's enforcement action may take the form of measures not involving the use of armed force, such as complete or partial interruption of economic relations and of rail, sea, air, postal, telegraphic, radio, and other means of communication, and the severance of diplomatic relations; or "action by land, sea or land forces, including demonstrations, blockades, and other operations conducted by the armed forces of UN Member States."

The council is so organized as to be able to function continuously; a representative of each of its members must be present at UN headquarters at all times. The council meets in its own chamber at UN headquarters in New York; it has met elsewhere only occasionally, e.g., in Addis Ababa in 1972 and in Panama in 1973. It prepares annual and special reports for consideration by the General Assembly.

In accordance with article 23 of the UN Charter, as amended by resolution 1991 A (XVIII) of 17 December 1963, which entered into force on 31 August 1965, the council consists of five permanent members (China, France, Union of Soviet Socialist Republics, United Kingdom of Great Britain and Northern Ireland, and the United States of America) and ten non-permanent members elected by the General Assembly. In 1963, the General Assembly decided that the non-permanent members of the Security Council should be elected according to the following pattern: five from African and Asian States, one from eastern European States, two from Latin American States, and two from western European and other States. The election is held by secret ballot, and there are no nominations. Non-permanent members are elected by a two-thirds' majority, and a retiring non-permanent member is not eligible for immediate re-election. For non-permanent members, the term of office is two years.

On 18 October 1989, the UN General Assembly, in accordance with article 23 of the United Nations Charter and rule 142 of its rules of procedure, elected, on the first secret ballot, *Cote d'Ivoire,* Cuba, Democratic Yemen, Romania, and Zaire as non-permanent members of the Security Council for a two-year term of office beginning on 1 January 1990. As a result, the Council is composed of the following 15 member States: Canada (term expires 31 December 1990), China (permanent member), Colombia (term expires 31 December 1990), *Cote d'Ivoire* (term expires 31 December 1991), Cuba (term expires 31 December 1991), Democratic Yemen (term expires 31 December 1991), Ethiopia (term expires 31 December 1990), Finland (term expires 31 December 1990), France (permanent member), Malaysia (term expires 31 December 1990), Romania (term expires 31 December 1991), U.S.S.R. (permanent member), United Kingdom (permanent member), United States of America (permanent member), and Zaire (term expires 31 December 1991).

The council has two standing committees: the Committee of Experts, which studies and advises on rules of procedure and other technical matters, and the Committee on the Admission of New Members. Each committee is composed of all members of the council. In addition, the Military Staff Committee, composed of the chiefs of staff of the five permanent members or their representatives, was established under article 47 of the UN Charter to advise and assist the Council on such matters as its military requirements for maintaining peace, the strategic direction of armed forces placed at its disposal, the regulation of armaments, and possible disarmament.

SELF-DETERMINATION. The inalienable right of all peoples to self-determination was first proclaimed by the international community in the DECLARATION ON THE GRANTING OF INDEPENDENCE TO COLONIAL COUNTRIES AND PEOPLES, adopted by the UN General Assembly on 14 December 1960 (resolution 1514 [XV]), in the following terms:

1. The subjection of peoples to alien subjugation, domination and exploitation constitutes a denial of fundamental human rights, is contrary to the Charter of the United Nations and is an impediment to the promotion of world peace and co-operation.
2. All peoples have the right to self-determination; by virtue of that right they freely determine their political status and freely pursue their economic, social and cultural development.
3. Inadequacy of political, economic, social or educational preparedness should never serve as a pretext for delaying independence. . . .

Both International Covenants on Human Rights contain an identical article 1 on the subject, which reads as follows:

Article 1. 1. All peoples have the right of self-determination. By virtue of that right they freely determine their political status and freely pursue their economic, social and cultural development.
2. All peoples may, for their own ends, freely dispose of their natural wealth and resources without prejudice to any obligations arising out of international economic co-operation, based upon the principle of mutual benefit, and international law. In no case may a people be deprived of its own means of subsistence.

3. The States Parties to the present Covenant, including those having responsibility for the administration of Non-Self-Governing and Trust Territories, shall promote the realization of the right of self-determination, and shall respect that right, in conformity with the provisions of the Charter of the United Nations.

In the DECLARATION ON PRINCIPLES OF INTERNATIONAL LAW CONCERNING FRIENDLY RELATIONS AND CO-OPERATION AMONG SATES IN ACCORDANCE WITH THE CHARTER OF THE UNITED NATIONS, adopted by the General Assembly in 1970 (resolution 2625 [XXV]), the Assembly proclaimed the following "principle of equal rights and self-determination of peoples:"

By virtue of the principle of equal rights and self-determination of peoples enshrined in the Charter of the United Nations, all peoples have the right freely to determine, without external interference, their political status and to pursue their economic, social and cultural development, and every State has the duty to respect this right in accordance with the provisions of the Charter.

Every State has the duty to promote, through joint and separate action, realization of the principle of equal rights and self-determination of peoples, in accordance with the provisions of the Charter, and to render assistance to the United Nations in carrying out the responsibilities entrusted to it by the Charter regarding the implementation of the principle, in order:
(a) To promote friendly relations and co-operation among States; and
(b) To bring a speedy end to colonialism, having due regard to the freely expressed will of the peoples concerned;
and bearing in mind that subjection of peoples to alien subjugation, domination and exploitation constitutes a violation of the principle, as well as a denial of fundamental human rights, and is contrary to the Charter.

Every State has the duty to promote through joint and separate action universal respect for and observance of human rights and fundamental freedoms in accordance with the Charter.

The establishment of a sovereign and independent State, the free association or integration with an independent State or the emergence into any other political status freely determined by a people constitute modes of implementing the right of self-determination by that people.

Every State has the duty to refrain from any forcible action which deprives peoples referred to above in the elaboration of the present principle of their right to self-determination and freedom and independence. In their actions against, and resistance to, such forcible action in pursuit of the exercise of their right to self-determination, such peoples are entitled to seek and to receive support in accordance with the purposes and principles of the Charter.

The territory of a colony or other Non-Self-Governing Territory has, under the Charter, a status separate and distinct from the territory of the State administering it; and such separate and distinct status under the Charter shall exist until the people of the colony or Non-Self-Governing Territory have exercised their right of self-determination in accordance with the Charter, and particularly its purposes and principles.

Nothing in the foregoing paragraphs shall be construed as authorizing or encouraging any action which would dismember or impair, totally or in part, the territorial integrity or political unity of sovereign and independent States conducting themselves in compliance with the principle of equal rights and self-determination of peoples as described above and thus possessed of a government representing the whole people belonging to the territory without distinction as to race, creed or colour.

Every State shall refrain from any action aimed at the partial or total disruption of the national unity and territorial integrity of any other State or country.

The **AFRICAN CHARTER OF HUMAN AND PEOPLE'S RIGHTS** open for acceptance by member States of the **ORGANIZATION OF AFRICAN UNITY,** contains the following provisions:

Article 19. All peoples shall be equal; they shall enjoy the same respect and shall have the same rights. Nothing shall justify the domination of a people by another.

Article 20. 1. All peoples shall have right to existence. They shall have the unquestionable and inalienable right to self-determination. They shall freely determine their political status and shall pursue their economic and social development according to the policy they have freely chosen.

2. Colonized or oppressed peoples shall have the right to free themselves from the bonds of domination by resorting to any means recognized by the international community.

3. All peoples shall have the right to the assistance of the States Parties to the present Charter in their liberation struggle against foreign domination, be it political, economic or cultural.

Article 21. 1. All peoples shall freely dispose of their wealth and natural resources. This right shall be exercise (sic) in the exclusive interest of the people. In no case shall a people be deprived of it.

2. In case of spoliation the dispossessed people shall have the right to the lawful recovery of its property as well as to an adequate compensation.

3. The free disposal of wealth and natural resources shall be exercised without prejudice to the obligation of promoting international economic cooperation based on mutual respect, equitable exchange and the principles of international law.

4. States parties to the present Charter shall individually and collectively exercise the right to free disposal of their wealth and natural resources with a view to strengthening African unity and solidarity.

5. States Parties to the present Charter shall undertake to eliminate all forms of foreign economic exploitation particularly that practised by international monopolies so as to enable their peoples to fully benefit from the advantages derived from their national resources.

After examining reports submitted by states parties to the **INTERNATIONAL COVENANT ON CIVIL AND POLITICAL RIGHTS** in accordance with article 40 of that covenant, the **HUMAN RIGHTS COMMITTEE** adopted in 1984 a general comment on article 1 of that instrument. Although formulated by the committee primarily to guide states in preparing the reports called for by the covenant, such comments incidentally serve to throw light on the committee's interpretation of certain provisions. The comments on article 1 are as follows (UN Doc. A/39/40, Annex VI, para. 1–8):

In accordance with the purposes and principles of the Charter of the United Nations, article 1 of the International Covenant on Civil and Political Rights recognizes that all peoples have the right of self-determination. The right of self-determination is of particular importance because its realization is an essential condition for the effective guarantee and observance of individual human rights and for the promotion and strengthening of those rights. It is for that reason that States set forth the right of self-determination in a provision of positive law in both Covenants and placed this provision as article 1 apart from and before all of the other rights in the two Covenants.

Article 1 enshrines an inalienable right of all peoples as described in its paragraphs 1 and 2. By virtue of that right they freely "determine their political status and freely pursue their economic, social and cultural development". The article imposes on all States parties corresponding obligations. This right and the corresponding obligations concerning its implementation are interrelated with other provisions of the Covenant and rules of international law.

Although the reporting obligations of all States parties include article 1, only some reports give detailed explanations regarding each of its paragraphs. The Committee has noted that many of them completely ignore article 1, provide inadequate information in regard to it or confine themselves to a reference to election laws. The Committee considers it highly desirable that States parties' reports should contain information on each paragraph of article 1.

With regard to paragraph 1 of article 1, States parties should describe the constitutional and political processes which in practice allow the exercise of this right.

Paragraph 2 affirms a particular aspect of the economic content of the right of self-determination; namely the right of peoples, for their own ends, freely to "dispose of their natural wealth and resources without prejudice to any obligations arising out of international economic co-operation, based upon the principle of mutual benefit, and international law. In no case may a people be deprived of its own means of subsistence". This right entails corresponding duties for all States and the international community. States should indicate any factors or difficulties which prevent the free disposal of their natural wealth and resources contrary to the provisions of this paragraph and to what extent that affects the enjoyment of other rights set forth in the Covenant.

Paragraph 3, in the Committee's opinion, is particularly important in that it imposes specific obligations on States parties, not only in relation to their own peoples but *vis-à-vis* all peoples which have not been able to exercise or have been deprived of the possibility of exercising their right to self-determination. The general nature of this paragraph is confirmed by its drafting history. It stipulates that "The States Parties to the present Covenant, including those having responsibility for the administration of Non-Self-Governing and Trust Territories, shall promote the realization of the right of self-determination, and shall respect that right, in conformity with the provisions of the Charter of the United Nations". The obligations exist irrespective of whether a people entitled to self-determination depends on a State party to the Covenant or not. It follows that all States parties to the Covenant should take positive action to facilitate realization of and respect for the right of peoples to self-determination. Such positive action must be consistent with the States' obligations under the Charter of the United Nations and under international law: in particular, States must refrain from interfering in the internal affairs of other States and thereby adversely affecting the exercise of the right to self-determination. The reports should contain information on the performance of these obligations and the measures taken to that end.

In connection with article 1 of the Covenant the Committee refers to other international instruments concerning the right of all peoples to self-determination, in particular the Declaration on Principles of International Law concerning Friendly Relations and Co-operation among States in accordance with the Charter of the United Nations, adopted by the General Assembly on 24 October 1970 (General Assembly resolution 2625 (XXV)).

The Committee considers that history has proved that the realization of and respect for the right of self-determination of peoples contributes to the establishment of friendly relations and co-operation between States and to strengthening international peace and understanding.

SELF-DETERMINATION: DEFINITION AND IMPLEMENTATION. The definition, scope, and legal nature of the right of peoples under colonial and alien domination to self-determination, and the means by which the implementation of that right has been promoted and monitored by the international community, are set out in the study entitled *The Right to Self-Determination: Implementation of United Nations Resolutions*, prepared by Mr. Hector Gros Espiell (Uruguay), special rapporteur of the UN Sub-Commission on Prevention of Discrimination and Protection of Minorities. The study was issued in 1979 (UN publication, Sales No. E/79.XIV.5).

As the special rapporteur points out, the right of peoples to self-determination is enshrined in the UNITED NATIONS CHARTER, both International Covenants on Human Rights, the DECLARATION ON THE INADMISSIBILITY OF INTERVENTION AND INTERFERENCE IN THE INTERNAL AFFAIRS OF STATES, the Declaration on the Strengthening of International Security, the DECLARATION ON PRINCIPLES OF INTERNATIONAL LAW CONCERNING FRIENDLY RELATIONS AND CO-OPERATION AMONG STATES, the definition of AGGRESSION, the Charter of Economic Rights and Duties of States, the DECLARATION ON SOCIAL PROGRESS AND DEVELOPMENT, and in numerous and repeated resolutions of the General Assembly, including the momentous and historic DECLARATION ON THE GRANTING OF INDEPENDENCE TO COLONIAL COUNTRIES AND PEOPLES, which has been termed the Magna Carta of decolonization and which marks the beginning of the modern attitude to the subject and of the irreversible trend towards full decolonization.

As the special rapporteur points out (para. 50):

This is one of the spheres in which the Organization's achievements are unanimously acknowledged to be of outstanding value and of historic significance. The affirmation and implementation by the United Nations of the right of peoples to self-determination brought about the crisis of colonialism and set in motion the process of its universal elimination. What in the Covenant of the League of Nations and in the international law of that era was a principle, as is the case with nationalities, applicable preferentially or, rather, almost exclusively in Europe, which did not imply the rejection of colonialism in Africa, Asia and Latin America, what in the Charter of the United Nations was only the mention of a principle in Articles 1 (paragraph 2) and 73, was transformed, as a result of the work done by the Organization from 1952 onwards, but more particularly since 1960, into a basic principle, of universal applicability, into a right of all peoples and into a peremptory norm of international law which, with the end of the traditional colonialism—save for a few surviving remants—led to a complete change in international society.

In the study, the special rapporteur deals with questions relating to the definition, scope and legal nature of the right to self-determination (Chapter I), reviews the state of realization of United Nations decisions relating to that right (Chapter II), refers to specific situations involving that right which have been dealt with by United Nations organs (Chapter III), and puts forward his recommendations for further action to be taken by the international community (Chapters IV and V).

As regards the question of definition, the special rapporteur presents the following views (para. 56–63):

Self-determination is essentially a right of peoples. The divergence of opinion among legal theorists which existed on this point until a few years ago has been overcome; the Declaration adopted in resolution 1514 (XV) and the International Covenants on Human Rights have provided the basis for unquestioned acceptance in international law of the fact that self-determination is a right of peoples under colonial and alien domination. To characterize self-determination as a collective right possessed by peoples raises awkward theoretical problems, because of the difficulty of defining the concept of a people and drawing a clear distinction between that and other similar concepts. Self-determination of peoples is a right of peoples, in other words of a specific type of human community sharing a common desire to establish an entity capable of functioning to ensure a common future. It is Peoples as such which are entitled to the right to self-determination. Under contemporary international law minorities do not have this right. People and Nation are two closely related concepts; they may be one and the same, but they are not synonymous. Modern international law has deliberately attributed the right to Peoples, and not to Nations and States. However, when the People and the Nation are one and the same, and when a People has established itself as a State, clearly that Nation and that State are, as forms or manifestations of the same People, implicitly entitled to the right to self-determination. There is no doubt that the theoretical and practical difficulties involved in these concepts are very great and the Special Rapporteur cannot possibly make a thorough and conclusive analysis of these concepts. All he can do is to make clear his ideas on the subject, even if they are only his first thoughts and presented in summarized form. Apart from such difficulties, however, it is evident that, both politically and practically, the right of peoples to self-determination is one of the major realities of the present day and that the invocation and recognition of this right have radically changed international society as it existed until a few years ago. In their replies, the Government of the Philippines stated that a minority or a foreign State cannot invoke the right of self-determination, and the Government of Iraq stressed the need to distinguish between peoples and minorities, since only peoples possess the right of self-determination. The reply of the Government of the German Democratic Republic gave a full analysis of the reasons why all peoples should be recognized as possessing it.

To assert that self-determination constitutes a collective right of peoples does not mean that an individual right, to which all human beings are entitled, cannot exist at the same time. A right can be simultaneously an individual right and a collective right. The presumed incompatibility between the two types of rights is inadmissible. This conclusion, already recognized, for instance, with respect to the right to development, the right to form trade unions and the right to freedom of information, is perfectly applicable to the case of the right to self-determination.

In the Special Rapporteur's judgement, it is important likewise to try to conceptualize the right to self-determination as a right of the individual. The Commission on Human Rights has repeatedly invoked it as such, without giving a precise reason for that conception and without distinguishing self-determination as a right of the individual from self-determination as a condition or prerequisite for the effective exercise of the other rights and freedoms. In the Special Rapporteur's view, self-determination may be regarded also, as a consequence or its initial recognition, as a right of peoples, as a right of the individual, in that it is every person's right that the people of which he is a member—if it is under colonial and alien domination—should be recognized as having the right to determine freely its own political, economic, social and cultural condition. The Special Rapporteur considers, moreover, that self-determination as a right of the human being is a consequence of the necessary recognition of the political rights of citizens and of the civil, economic, social and cultural rights of all individuals without any discrimination. The self-determination of citizens, individually, on the basis of the recognition of their political rights, is a prerequisite of the effective realization of self-determination as the people's collective right. This view is referred to in paragraph 284 of this study.

In addition, however, the effective exercise of a people's right to self-determination is an essential condition or prerequisite, although not necessarily excluding other conditions, for the genuine existence of the other human rights and freedoms. Only when self-determination has been achieved can a people take the measures necessary to ensure human dignity, the full enjoyment of all rights, and the political, economic, social and cultural progress of all human beings, without any form of discrimination. Consequently, human rights and fundamental freedoms can only exist truly and fully when self-determination also exists. Such is the fundamental importance of self-determination as a human right and a prerequisite for the enjoyment of all the other rights and freedoms. It is with awareness and appreciation of these characteristics of self-determination

that the Special Rapporteur has approached the present study.

The United Nations has established the right of self-determination as a right of peoples under colonial and alien domination. The right does not apply to peoples already organized in the form of a State which are not under colonial and alien domination, since resolution 1514 (XV) and other United Nations instruments condemn any attempt aimed at the partial or total disruption of the national unity and the territorial integrity of a country. If, however, beneath the guise of ostensible national unity, colonial and alien domination does in fact exist, whatever legal formula may be used in an attempt to conceal it, the right of the subject people concerned cannot be disregarded without international law being violated. The Declaration on Principles of International Law concerning Friendly Relations and Co-operation among States in accordance with the Charter of the United Nations (General Assembly resolution 2625 (XXV)) uses particularly apt language in spelling out this idea: it reaffirms the need to reserve the territorial integrity of sovereign and independent States, but ties this concept to the requirement that the States must be "possessed of a government representing the whole people belonging to the territory without distinction as to race, creed or colour".

This right of peoples gives rise to the corresponding duty of all States to recognize it and to promote it. The international community and all States not only have a legal duty to refrain from opposing and impeding the exercise of the right to self-determination, but also are under a positive obligation to help in securing its realization, by promoting its exercise and by co-operating in every possible way to ensure that peoples under colonial and alien domination achieve their independence and that those peoples which have already become independent as a result of exercising their right to self-determination achieve their complete sovereignty and full development. These considerations have a particular bearing on the question of the legitimacy of the use of force to achieve self-determination, and the corresponding duty to display solidarity. The Special Rapporteur will pay special attention to this in paragraph 93.

The right of peoples under colonial and alien domination to self-determination is not contingent on any kind of condition or requirement. In particular, resolution 1514 (XV) precludes any opposition to the exercise of the right to self-determination on the pretext that a people has not reached a sufficiently high level of development to lead an independent existence.

Peoples under colonial and alien domination accordingly have rights and obligations conferred by contemporary international law. They therefore possess an international personality and as regards the exercise of their rights and the performance of their duties can be regarded as subjects of international law. Clearly, not all subjects of law have the same status, nor are their rights and duties identical. That is why the view that peoples are now, within the limits indicated above, subjects of law is tenable.

In examining the political, economic, social, and cultural aspects of the right of peoples to self-determination, the special rapporteur emphasizes that each of these specific and necessary aspects of the general concept is closely and indissolubly linked to all the others, since they are interdependent and each can only be fully realized through the complete recognition and implementation of the others. His view on these aspects are as follows:

Political Aspects (para. 114). From the political point of view, the right of peoples under colonial and alien domination to self-determination has as its corollary their right to achieve independence, free association or integration with another independent State or the acquisition of any other freely determined status. The achievement of any of these objectives "in the effective exercise of national sovereignty against any hegemony and independence" must be the result of a free decision by the people concerned. Where the exercise of self-determination results in the establishment of a new, sovereign and independent State, the right to self-determination itself provides the basis for the right of the people of the new State freely to chose its political system. Thus the right to self-determination does not cease when independence or another possible status is achieved and recognized; it extends into the permanent defence and maintenance of the independence or other status achieved as a result of the initial exercise of the right to self-determination.

Economic Aspects (para. 135–137). The economic aspects of the right of peoples to self-determination are manifested, first, in the right of all peoples to determine in freedom and sovereignty, the economic system or régime under which they are to live. Where a people is still subject to colonial or alien domination this right already exists, even though the colonial Power may ignore it and violate it. Where the people has formed a free and sovereign State or has established some other political formula through the exercise of the right to self-determination, the people of that State naturally retains its right freely to determine the economic régime which is to exist in that State. This right will be of lasting efficacy and will continue to take effect in the future, which is of particular significance, in view of all the neo-colonialistic and neo-imperialistic schemes, whatever form they make take, to dominate the new States which have come into being as a result of the exercise of the right to political self-determination, through their power or unlawful intervention in the economic field.

Without prejudice to this general meaning of self-determination from the economic standpoint, it is necessary to specify that the economic content of the right of peoples to self-determination finds its expression in particular—without prejudice to many other different manifestations—in their right to permanent sovereignty over natural resources, a question which covers the problems raised by nationalizations and the harmful activities that may be undertaken in this area by transnational or multinational enterprises.

This right of peoples to self-determination exists, in its economic aspects, in all the above-mentioned manifestations, both in cases where the people concerned has not yet attained its political self-determination and is still struggling against colonial and alien domination, and where the people has formed a political entity or sovereign State as a result of the prior exercise of its right to self-determination.

Social Aspects (para. 152–154). Every people has the right to choose and determine the social system under which it is to live, in accordance with its free and sovereign will and with due respect for its traditions and special characteristics.

More specifically, it may be said that the social aspects of the right of peoples to self-determination are related, in particular, to the promotion of social justice, to which every people is entitled and which, in its broadest sense, implies the right to the effective enjoyment by all the individual members of a particular people of their economic and social rights without any discrimination whatsoever.

This aspect of self-determination is covered by various General Assembly resolutions, especially the Declaration on Social Progress and Development, which proclaims "national independence based on the right of peoples to self-determination" to be a primary condition of social progress and development. Other provisions of the Declaration are directly concerned with various aspects of the right of peoples to self-determination. The Declaration of Mexico on the Equality of Women and their Contribution to Development and Peace also refers to the question.

Cultural Aspects (para. 158–160). Every people, in the exercise of its right to self-determination, has the right to determine and establish the cultural régime or system under which it is to live; this implies recognition of its right to regain, enjoy and enrich its cultural heritage, and the affirmation of the right of all its members to education and culture.

A people subject to colonial and alien domination has the right to struggle to prevent its heritage, values and cultural identity from being destroyed or affected by the colonial or alien Power. Where that people, through the exercise of its right to self-determination, has formed a political entity or established a sovereign State, the cultural content of its right to self-determination remains in effect, even though it is now governed by the legal and political situation which this people has freely accepted.

The efficacy of the right of peoples to self-determination in its cultural aspects is essential in order that a people may be aware of its rights and consequently be fully capable of fighting for their recognition and implementation.

Conclusions regarding the Work Done by the United Nations in This Field. after reviewing in some detail the relevant activities of all organizations and organs within the United Nations system, including the specialized agencies concerned, the special rapporteur records his conclusions as follows (para. 243–245).

This action taken by the entire United Nations system to secure recognition of the right of peoples under colonial and alien domination to self-determination has without doubt led to highly positive results as regards the final objective sought.

What has been achieved in this respect affords one of the most outstanding examples of the effectiveness and importance of the work done by the United Nations. The end of the great colonial empires and traditional colonialism and the creation of an international society based on effective recognition of the right of peoples to self-determination, with the result that 151 sovereign independent States are now Members of the United Nations, have to a large extent been achieved through United Nations efforts. These achievements and the problems raised by the right of peoples to self-determination, as well as future prospects, are summed up in paragraph 6 of the Declaration on the Occasion of the Twenty-Fifth Anniversary of the United Nations, adopted by the General Assembly in 1970 (resolution 2627

(XXV)). The terms of this paragraph deserve to be reproduced:

"We acclaim the role of the United Nations in the past twenty-five years in the process of the liberation of peoples of colonial, Trust and other Non-Self-Governing Territories. As a result of this welcome development, the number of sovereign States in the Organization has been greatly increased and colonial empires have virtually disappeared. Despite these achievements, many Territories and peoples continue to be denied their right to self-determination and independence, particularly in Namibia, Southern Rhodesia, Angola, Mozambique and Guinea (Bissau), in deliberate and deplorable defiance of the United Nations and world opinion by certain recalcitrant States and by the illegal régime of Southern Rhodesia. We reaffirm the inalienable right of all colonial peoples to self-determination, freedom and independence and condemn all actions which deprive any people of these rights. In recognizing the legitimacy of the struggle of colonial peoples for their freedom by all appropriate means at their disposal, we call upon all Governments to comply in this respect with the provisions of the Charter, taking into account the Declaration on the Granting of Independence to Colonial Countries and Peoples adopted by the United Nations in 1960. We re-emphasize that these countries and peoples are entitled, in their just struggle, to seek and to receive all necessary moral and material help in accordance with the purposes and principles of the Charter."

However, despite the exceptional importance of what has been done, the problem has not yet been solved entirely, even from the political standpoint alone, nor has the right to self-determination become a reality everywhere. Many colonial situations still exist and there are still many United Nations resolutions on specific cases which have not yet been fully implemented. Hence the need to persevere, to maintain and, if possible, speed up the process of decolonization, and to consider, systematically and globally, the work done and the procedures employed, in order to determine what new measures are required and what approach should be taken with regard to the implementation of the resolutions already adopted.

Recommendations. In presenting his recommendations for further action to implement the right to self-determination, the special rapporteur points out that (para. 247–250):

There can be no overlooking the difficulties which even today are seriously hampering the full achievement of the objectives of the Charter and General Assembly resolution 1514 (XV) with regard to the recognition of the right of peoples under colonial and alien domination to self-determination.

In addition to the negative influence exerted by undeniable political and military interests, there are the effects of other interests, particularly economic ones.

United Nations action to eliminate colonialism should take realistic account of the existence and impact of these adverse interests and should adopt a global, systematic and unified approach to the struggle for the recognition of the right to self-determination in every field, in all the competent organs and all the organizations of the United Nations system.

But while there is reason to think that this systematic and constant effort by the international community will shortly put an end to traditional colonialism, although there still remain some particularly serious problems inherent in that form of colonialism to be solved, inasmuch as the violation of the right to self-determination of peoples occurs openly, repeatedly, flagrantly and deliberately, it should not be forgotten that other problems continue to exist in this connexion and that new forms of violation of this right of peoples have appeared. Indeed, economic neo-imperialism and the new forms of colonialism, particularly serious for developing countries and especially for small States which have achieved independence in the last stage of the process of decolonization, constitute manifestations of the violation of the right to self-determination of peoples which may have the effect of cancelling out, to a large extent, the results achieved by the process of political decolonization. This is why it is essential for the United Nations to pay particular attention in the future to this question, which is directly related to the economic, social and cultural aspects of the right to self-determination.

The first of two general recommendations put forward by the special rapporteur is (para. 287):

. . . . that all United Nations organizations and all organizations within the United Nations system should continue to take systematic and coordinated action to promote decolonization, in order that peoples under colonial and alien domination may enjoy the right to self-determination in all its political, economic, social and cultural aspects. The right of peoples to self-determination has been affirmed, recognized and accepted by the international community; its characteristics have been defined, and direct and indirect methods and procedures have been devised, to ensure that subject peoples may exercise it with the assistance and co-operation of the United Nations and of all States; the consequences of all this must be weighed with honesty and clarity for the time when recognition of principles must give way to effective action. Colonialism is doomed. The right of peoples to self-determination must now become fully realized, as the basis for a new international society in which international peace and security and human rights must be more effectively assured. The Special Rapporteur can only conceive of this new international society as being based on respect for all human rights and freedoms, including the right to self-determination, and on the international guarantee of their effective protection on the basis of non-discrimination.

The second recommendation is of a formal and juridical nature and is stated in the following terms:

Starting with the historic resolution 1514 (XV) of 14 December 1960, the General Assembly and other United Nations organs have put forth large numbers of resolutions covering political, military, legal, economic, social and cultural aspects of the right to self-determination. The novel and varied problems which have had to be confronted during this period have entailed the formulation of a long and complicated series of instruments which have now become a veritable maze of law. Nineteen years after the adoption of resolution 1514 (XV), which marked the beginning of a new stage in international law, the Special Rapporteur believes that a declaratory resolution should be drafted for adoption by the General Assembly to systematize, codify and up-date, in view of their progressive development, all the various matters relating to the right of peoples under colonial and alien domination to self-determination which have been the subject of the general resolutions adopted hitherto, and to deal with some new problems which contemporary international law must take up and resolve in this context, as stated in chapter IV of the resent study. This instrument, the drafting of which the Special Rapporteur believes should be started forthwith and which would be both an up-to-date representation of and a tribute to the principles set forth in resolution 1514(XV), would preside over the final stages in the implementation of the right of peoples to self-determination and over the end of colonialism, while being a further contribution to full and effective respect for human rights.

The SUB-COMMISSION ON PREVENTION OF DISCRIMINATION AND PROTECTION OF MINORITIES considered the special rapporteur's final report (UN Doc. E/C.4/Sub.2/405) at its 1978 session and recommended (resolution 4 A [XXXI]) that it should be printed and given the widest possible distribution. It requested the Commission on Human Rights to entrust the special rapporteur, Mr. Hector Gros Espiell, with the preliminary draft of the international instrument proposed in his report. Further, in resolution 4 B (XXXI), it affirmed that the right to self-determination is a well-established principle of international law; recognized that the self-rule, home rule, or self-government formulae are entirely different from the principle of self-determination of peoples; and called upon all UN member states to observe faithfully their obligations under the Charter and relevant United Nations resolutions and to extend their support to the countries and peoples under colonial or alien domination or foreign occupation.

The General Assembly, later in 1978, noted (resolution 33/24) the study. The Commission on Human Rights, at its 1979 session, recommended (decision 3[XXXV]) that the study should be published but took no decision on the sub-commission's request that Mr. Hector Gros Espiell be entrusted to prepare the preliminary draft of an international instrument dealing with the right to self-determination.

SELF-DETERMINATION: DEVELOPMENT OF THE RIGHT. The *Study of the Historical and Current Development of the Right to Self-Determination*, prepared by Mr. Aureliu Cristescu (Romania), special rapporteur of the UN Sub-Commission on Prevention of Discrimination and Protection of Minorities, was authorized by the Economic and Social Council in 1974 (resolution 1865 [LVI]) and completed in 1978. It was issued in printed form in 1980 (United Nations publication, Sales No. E.80.XIV.3).

The opening chapters of the study trace the gradual development of the concept of the right of peoples and nations to self-determination through a number of major international instruments, including the UNITED NATIONS CHARTER, the International Covenants on human rights, and the DECLARATION ON PRINCIPLES OF INTERNATIONAL LAW CONCERNING FRIENDLY RELATIONS AND CO-OPERATION AMONG STATES IN ACCORDANCE WITH THE CHARTER OF THE UNITED NATIONS. Chapters III to VIII deal with a number of legal and political aspects of the concept, including the related right of peoples freely to determine their political status and to pursue their economic, social, and cultural development.

The special rapporteur presents the conclusions of his study in Chapter VIII, para. 679–713, as follows:

The historical and current development of the right to self-determination shows that it has become one of the most important and dynamic concepts in contemporary international life and that it exercises a profound influence on the political, legal, economic, social and cultural planes, in the matter of fundamental human rights and on the life and fate of peoples and of individuals.

The proclamation in the Charter of the United Nations of the principle of equal rights and self-determination of peoples as one of the bases for friendly relations and co-operation among States constitutes a development of historic importance, in terms both of the recognition of that principle as a binding principle of international law and of its further elaboration and impact on various aspects of the life of peoples. The principle of equal rights and self-determination of peoples is a vital feature of the Charter; it is regarded as the basis for the development, on the one hand, of friendly relations among nations and the link between friendly relations and international co-operation and, on the other, of respect for the principle laid down by the provisions of Article 1, paragraph 2, and Article 55 of the Charter. The embodiment of that principle in the Charter of the United Nations is the culmination of a fairly long development. It marks not only the recognition of the concept as a legal principle and a principle of contemporary international law, but also the point of departure of a new process—the increasingly dynamic development of the principle and its legal content, its implementation, and its application to the most varied situation of international life. The importance of this principle is generally recognized, and the far-reaching changes which have occurred since the adoption of the Charter have brought out with ever-increasing force the importance which the principle has gained, on the one hand, from its role in achieving the purposes of the United Nations and, on the other, from its significant position in contemporary international law and in the legal system derived from the Charter of the United Nations.

The principle of equal rights and self-determination of peoples is the most important of the principles of international law concerning friendly relations and co-operation among States, and constitutes the basis for the other principles. Thus, the international co-operation which is the fundamental theme of United Nations activities is incompatible with any form of subjection or pressure exerted by the strong against the weak and must be based on the sovereign equality of States and the equal rights and self-determination of peoples has as its corollary sovereign equality, a fundamental principle of the United Nations which is closely bound up with the struggle to achieve equal rights, self-determination and independence and with the strengthening of national sovereignty. Non-intervention, another principle of international law concerning friendly relations and co-operation among States, should not be used as a cover for violations of self-determination: it should protect States and peoples struggling for their independence, since acts of intervention are violations of the principle of equal rights and self-determination of peoples. Though the principle of non-intervention of peoples is linked to the principle of non-resort to the threat or use of force, which protects the political independence and territorial integrity of States, aggression—the use or threat of force—is a violation not only of the principle of the non-use of force but also and more particularly, of the principle of equal rights and self-determination of peoples. Colonial domination and oppression, the practice of racism and foreign occupation, are clear cases of aggression against the peoples subjected to them.

The reaffirmation of the right of peoples to self-determination in the Declaration on the Granting of Independence to Colonial Countries and Peoples (General Assembly resolution 1514 (XV) of 14 December 1960) is of great importance, since, from the practical point of view, the principle was to constitute the driving force in the decolonization activities undertaken by the United Nations. The United Nations recognized the passionate yearning for freedom of all dependent peoples and the decisive role of those peoples in the attainment of their independence, expressed its conviction that all peoples had an inalienable right to complete freedom, the exercise of their sovereignty and the integrity of their national territory, and declared that all peoples had the right to self-determination and that, by virtue of that right, they freely determined their political status and freely pursued their economic, social and cultural development. By other special resolutions, the General Assembly has affirmed, *in concreto,* the right of particular peoples to self-determination. Thus the abolition of colonialism and the granting of independence to colonial countries and peoples have played a decisive role in the far-reaching development of the right of subject peoples to national independence and sovereignty. The various rules proclaimed by the United Nations, which define not only the content of the right of those peoples to political self-determination but also the measure to be adopted to that end, amount to a general law of decolonization. The decolonization activities of the United Nations, based on that law, have been of enormous scope and have led to profound changes on the international scene. Those activities must be resolutely pursued, and a determined effort must be made to ensure the full implementation of United Nations resolutions. The affront to human civilization constituted by colonial domination is now approaching its end, and the time when all peoples of the world will enjoy the benefits of independence and freedom is near.

Linked with colonial domination are racial discrimination and *apartheid,* which represent an affront to human conscience and dignity, a total negation of the purposes and principles of the Charter of the United Nations and a crime against humanity, based as they are on doctrines or exclusions on grounds of racial difference or ethnic or religious superiority, all of which are scientifically false, mor-

ally reprehensible and socially unjust. The United Nations must ensure the full implementation of the instruments which it has adopted with a view to eliminating these evils, which afflict peoples in a considerable part of the world. Firm support for such implementation from States and the discontinuance of all assistance to the racist régimes are essential to the success of this effort.

Universal respect for fundamental human rights and lasting world peace cannot be achieved so long as the unjust conditions recognized in resolutions of the United Nations General Assembly continue to exist and peoples under foreign occupation continue to be prevented from exercising their fundamental right to freedom, independence and self-determination. Accordingly, the United Nations must, as a matter of urgency, make fresh efforts to implement its resolutions concerning the cessation of foreign occupation and the right of peoples still under such occupation to self-determination.

The international community must persevere in its endeavours to eliminate all vestiges of colonialism, racism and foreign occupation and make a concerted effort to provide the peoples struggling against those evils with all the moral, political and material support they need. The national movements of peoples fighting for their liberation must be recognized as the authentic representatives of the peoples concerned.

The elimination of imperialism, colonialism, aggression, foreign occupation, all forms of discrimination and *apartheid* and threats against national sovereignty and territorial integrity is a prerequisite for the realization of the right of peoples to self-determination and for the social and economic advancement of peoples. The combined force of the movements for national and social liberation, which have shaken the old structures of our rapidly changing world to their very foundations, on the one hand, and the sustained impetus of the scientific and technological revolution, on the other, are paving the way for the full liberation of all mankind.

While colonialism, in the traditional sense, is nearing its end, imperialism and the policy of force and diktat continue to exist and may persist in the future, under the guise of neo-colonialism and power relationships. The exploitation by colonialist forces of the difficulties and problems confronting developing or recently liberated countries, interference in the internal affairs of those States and attempts to maintain, especially in the economic sector, a relationship based on inequality are serious threats to the new States. Colonialism, neo-colonialism and imperialism resort to various devices to impose their will on independent nations. Economic pressure and domination, interference, racial discrimination, subversion, intervention and the threat of force are neo-colonialist devices against which the newly independent nations must guard.

The countries which have acquired their national independence after years of struggle are reaffirming their determination, based in particular on the right of their peoples to self-determination, to resist, by any means available to them, any attempt to impair their sovereignty or to violate their territorial integrity. International relations are currently entering a phase characterized by increased interdependence and by the desire of States to pursue an independent policy. The democratization of international relations is therefore an imperative need at the present time. Some major Powers exhibit an unfortunate tendency to monopolize decision-making in regard to global problems which are of vital concern to all countries of the world.

The true independence of States, as distinct from formal sovereignty, is incompatible with any form of interference in the internal affairs of States. Policies of interference are largely conducted through a wide variety of highly subtle and refined indirect techniques—economic aggression, subversion and the defamation of Governments—designed to break up States and their institutions.

For small and medium-sized States, interference in their internal affairs gives cause for deep concern. Although the decolonization process has made remarkable progress, there are some cases in which the independence of States has not been ensured. The policy of pressure and domination continues to pose a serious threat to the independence of States. Measures designed to sow division and disorder threaten internal security and create political confusion and economic chaos. Interference takes many forms—political, economic and military—and is also practised through the information media. One manifestation of such interference is the use of mercenaries to undermine the independence of sovereign States and the national liberation struggle against colonial domination.

International life has brought out the importance of ensuring that States enjoy full and genuine independence, as opposed to mere formal sovereignty. Unequal relations between States, accompanied as they often are by domination and even the extinction of States' hard-won freedoms, remain a matter for concern. The major issue of the present day is the fight against the unequal relations and domination deriving from colonialism and related forms of domination.

The right to self-determination is a collective right, a fundamental human right forming part of the legal system established by the Charter of the United Nations, the beneficiaries of which are peoples—whether or not constituted as independent States—nations and States. Individuals participate, both directly and through the realization of other human rights, in the exercise of this right. Similarly, national minorities exercise this right through the enjoyment of the rights granted to them by article 27 of the International Covenant on Civil and Political Rights and of other individual human rights, whether civil, political, economic, social or cultural. Since the principles of international law concerning friendly relations and co-operation among States are interrelated, the exercise of the right to self-determination must contribute to safeguarding the political independence and territorial integrity of States, ensuring non-interference in their internal affairs and promoting international co-operation. To respect the independence of peoples and their existence and personality is also to respect the sovereignty and integrity of their States, which are essential elements in the exercise of the right of peoples to independence, namely their right to determine their own future and to organize their national life as they please. Respect for the sovereign rights of nations and peoples makes it possible to establish international relations based on friendship and co-operation. The violation of the principle of equal rights and self-determination of peoples, on the other hand, constitutes a danger to the very existence of those peoples; it is an offence against international legality and a threat to world peace. The principle of equal rights and self-determination of peoples is therefore a fundamental element of the international order.

Although the principle of equal rights and self-determination of peoples constitutes a collective right, it nevertheless concerns each individual, since deprivation of that right would entail the loss of individual rights. The right to self-determination is a fundamental right without which other rights cannot be fully enjoyed. Consequently, the enjoyment of that right is essential to the exercise of all individual rights and freedoms. That is why it is accorded pride of place in the International Covenants on Human Rights. States therefore have an obligation to respect the right of peoples freely to determine their political status and to pursue their economic, social and cultural development. The right also implies that Governments owe their existence and powers to the assent of their people; the will of the people is the necessary basis of the Government's authority. It was with this in mind that the right to self-determination was incorporated in international instruments, and not with a view to encouraging secessionist or irredentist movements or foreign interference and aggression. By virtue of this principle, it is necessary to safeguard the political independence and territorial integrity of States which respect the equal rights of peoples and their right to self-determination and possess a Government representative of the population as a whole. Accordingly, the universal realization of the right to self-determination is of great importance for the effective guarantee and observance of fundamental human rights. At the same time, the promotion and protection of human rights and fundamental freedoms contributes to the implementation of the right to self-determination; the guarantee and observance of the various individual human rights and freedoms contribute, in the area of their exercise, to the realization of the different aspects—political, economic, social or cultural—of the right to self-determination.

The right to self-determination, which is a fundamental human right, plays an important part in the realization of the other human rights and freedoms, by creating the general framework and foundation for the implementation and promotion of human rights. At the same time, respect for each individual human right contributes to the exercise of the right to self-determination.

The political aspect of the right to self-determination continues to play a preponderant role, ensuring respect for the existence, sovereignty, independence and territorial integrity of nation States. However, the economic, social and cultural aspects of the right to self-determination are currently assuming increasing importance and are exercising a growing influence on the life of peoples, on the effort to establish a new international economic order, on balanced and integrated development and on the implementation and promotion of economic, social and cultural and civil and political human rights.

The recognition by the International Covenants on Human Rights and other important United Nations instruments of the economic, social and cultural aspects of the right to self-determination represented a milestone in the development of the content of that right. The interdependence of the various aspects of development, based on the right to self-determination, is now commonly recognized throughout the world and has led to the formulation of the concept of balanced and integrated development, which is playing an increasingly important part in the efforts to establish a new international economic order. At the same time, the elaboration of the various economic, social and cultural aspects of the right to self-determination has resulted in the adoption of new rule forming a veritable international law of development.

The right of peoples to self-determination has acquired importance as an essential pillar in the construction of the new international economic and political order, since the political, economic, social and cultural problems of mankind are intimately linked and call for concerted action and because economic emancipation is an essential factor for the elimination of political domination. It is undeniable that there is a close link between political and economic questions and it would be illogical to deal with economic problems separately from political problems. A complete change of political attitude and proof of political will are a first essential step in achieving the new international economic order. A feature of the present international situation is the intensification of the struggle of the peoples of the world for political and economic independence, for peace and progress and for an international political and economic order based on the principles of self-determination, justice, equality and peaceful coexistence among the peoples and nations of the world.

A new international economic order must put an end to the exploitation of the weak and the poor by the strong and the rich. The efforts of the developing countries to secure co-operation in the establishment of a new international economic order have not been successful and have not obtained a satisfactory response from the developed countries. The economic gap between developed and developing countries is still widening, the rich becoming richer and the poor becoming even poorer. The developing countries are being denied their right to equality and to effective participation in international progress. The technological revolution, which is currently the monopoly of the wealthy countries, should constitute one of the main opportunities for the advancement of the developing countries. World solidarity is not only just a cause, it is a clear necessity. It is intolerable that some should today be enjoying a peaceful and comfortable existence at the expense of others condemned to poverty and misery.

A prerequisite for, and a vital component of, the new international economic order is a new political order for the system of inter-State relations, in other words, the construction of those relations on the basis of the fundamental principles and norms of international law in such a manner as to guarantee and ensure, in practice, full equality of rights for peoples, respect for their independence and national sovereignty, non-interference in their internal affairs and mutual advantage. Such a universal application of these principles and norms should, in practice, ensure the right of every people to be the master of its own affairs and a political order in which all States participate effectively in the preparation and adoption of decisions concerning the international community.

The permanent sovereignty of peoples over their wealth and natural resources, which is a component element of their right to self-determination and a new concept of international law deriving from the decolonization process and the formulation of human rights and freedoms, is giving rise to a review of the rules of traditional international law and, at the economic and social level, has become the corner-stone of development. Responsibility for development lies primarily with the developing countries themselves, which must mobilize to this end all their wealth and resources, but their permanent sovereignty over their wealth and resources must be respected and strengthened, permanent sovereignty being also a basic factor for their economic and social development and their political independence. Wealth and natural resources constitute the material basis which ensures for peoples the exercise of their right to self-determination and the exercise of the other fundamental human rights. Consequently, any action aimed at destroying the permanent sovereignty of peoples over their wealth and natural resources is a violation of international law and an attack on the international order.

The economic development of peoples poses many problems for the international community, which is seeking a new order that will be more just and more equitable. Industrialization is a prerequisite for economic development and for development in the areas of food and agriculture. The development and establishment of a new international economic order call for measures to stimulate an equitable expansion of international trade and economic co-operation among States that excludes all forms of pressure and interference in the internal affairs of States and makes international trade an effective instrument for economic development. Science and technology, which are genuine sources of civilization, power, well-being and progress, must be used for the general advancement of peoples, including that of the developing countries. New resources must be mobilized for financing the economic and social development of the developing countries. Economic development must be accompanied by social development and a just social order, which are prerequisites for the full satisfaction of the aspirations of mankind and for contributing to guaranteed international peace and solidarity.

The promotion of human, economic, social and cultural rights helps to strengthen the general development of peoples. A prerequisite for the observance, assurance and promotion of human, economic, social and cultural rights and the development of the human personality to the present level achieved by civilization is the achievement of the right of peoples to self-determination and to the exercise of permanent sovereignty over their wealth and natural resources, and their right to choose their own economic system and to ensure their economic, social and cultural development. In order to secure such a guarantee and the genuine promotion of fundamental human rights and such economic, social and cultural development, it is imperative to establish a new international economic order based on the sovereign equality of States and respect for the equal rights of all peoples, an order that also guarantees the integrated economic, social and cultural development of every people and every State, in accordance with its aspirations to progress and well-being. The members of the international community have a responsibility and a duty to create the necessary conditions for the full achievement of economic, social and cultural rights as an essential means of ensuring the effective enjoyment of civil and political rights and fundamental freedoms.

The right to development possessed by all peoples, whether they constitute sovereign States or not, is becoming vitally important for the progress of humanity as a whole. The affirmation, the observance and the promotion of this right must be a matter of major concern for the whole international community. The urgency of the question of this right is dictated by the imperative development needs felt throughout the world and particularly in the most backward areas, which constitute an affront to human dignity and to civilization. The international community cannot tolerate such an injustice, such an inequality and such an imbalance between levels of development and in the degree of participation of its various constituent parts in the progress and advances of modern civilization and culture, at a time when scientific progress has brought a hitherto unknown abundance within reach of a part of mankind.

The right to development is a means of attaining the noble purposes of the Charter of the United Nations, including the promotion of "social progress and better standards of life in larger freedom", the ending of the division of the world into zones of poverty and zones of abundance and the ensuring of prosperity for all.

The right to development is an instrument of peace, since it can help the peoples of the developing countries to achieve a higher standard of living and thus avoid the danger to international peace and security constituted by the widening gap between the levels of living of peoples, stemming from privileges, extremes of wealth and poverty and social injustice.

The right of peoples to ensure their economic, social and cultural development is becoming an essential factor in the context of the establishment of a new international economic order.

The realization of the right to development, which is a primary task of States and international organizations, calls for the elimination from society of all the evils and barriers to social progress, particularly inequality, exploitation, war, colonialism and racism.

The right to development is a means of ensuring social justice at the national and international levels, a better distribution of income, wealth and social services, the elimination of poverty and the improvement of living conditions for the whole population. In order to achieve a greater social justice, there must be an expansion of the national product, and specific social and economic policies that are oriented towards a distribution of income and wealth must be adopted. In this connexion, the redistribution of income through transfers and the provision of social services without charge or at low cost are merely corrective measures; the initial organization of the distribution of income is a determining factor in its structure and the principal instrument for the achievement of greater equality, having a direct impact on the level of income and wealth of individuals and groups. It is an economic and social measure that has repercussions in all fields, particularly on employment and wages, investment, the democratization of wealth, fiscal policy and social welfare. However, public ownership of the means of production, which is practised by a steadily increasing number of countries, is still the determining factor for an equitable distribution of the national income, for economic and social democratization and for social justice. Thus, economic growth, social and cultural development and social justice are integrated and complementary objectives of the International Development Strategy, but social justice at the national level is clearly linked with international social justice, particularly in regard to trade, credits and financial assistance, prices and the marketing of products. The achievement of international social justice requires a new international economic order, since the existing order is in direct conflict with the contemporary international trends in political and economic relations, and there is a close correlation between the prosperity of the developed countries and the growth and development of the developing countries. The prosperity of the international community as a whole is linked with the prosperity of its constituent elements. Consequently, international co-operations for development is the goal and the common duty of all countries. In other words, the political, economic and social well-being of present and future generations depends, more than ever, on the existence among all the members of the international community of a spirit of co-operation based on sovereign equality and the elimination of the imbalance between them, on the realization of

their aspirations and on the right of all peoples to ensure their political, economic, social and cultural development.

The real purpose of the new international economic order is not the material growth of nations, but the development of all men and women in every way, in a comprehensive cultural process involving profound values and embracing the national environment, social relations, education and welfare; in other words, the achievement of man's economic, social and cultural rights, or human development, for the benefit of man, must be the central factor in the development process. He is the key factor in economic and social development, which must be directed towards fulfiling the needs of an evolving and constantly diversifying human existence, and the unhampered affirmation, at all levels, of the human personality. The general goal of development must be to create equal social conditions for all individuals, in order that they may achieve their potential, as distinct personalities, in accordance with their capacities and aptitudes.

The fundamental element of the right to development and of the right of peoples to self-determination is permanent sovereignty over natural resources. Today, the right of peoples to self-determination can no longer be viewed from a purely political standpoint, but must also be seen increasingly from an economic social and cultural point of view, for development in all is forms creates a sound basis for political independence, and the first step in such development is achievement of the permanent sovereignty of peoples and States over their natural resources and wealth. Any action, whether direct or indirect, designed to prevent a people or a State from exercising permanent sovereignty over its wealth and natural resources undermines the development of the peoples concerned and violates their right to self-determination. Respect for and promotion of the right of peoples to permanent sovereignty over their wealth and natural resources are prerequisite for the achievement of the right to development and the right to self-determination of peoples, and are essential for the strengthening of co-operation and universal peace. The promotion of the right of peoples to permanent sovereignty over their wealth and natural resources must be reflected in concrete fashion by legal measures that will ensure respect for this right and by the development of principles and measures designed to prevent and combat speculative fluctuations in and imbalances between the prices of raw materials and those of industrial products, so as to ensure the normal development of international economic relations and thus to eliminate world economic insecurity, which is detrimental to the national planning of all countries and particularly of the developing countries, and to ensure the realization and promotion of the right of peoples to integrated and balanced economies and to social and cultural development.

The creation of suitable conditions at the international level is of vital importance for securing and promoting the right of peoples and individuals to development. Peaceful coexistence, friendly relations and active co-operation among States encourage the development of peoples. The success of international and national development activities will depend largely on improvement of that overall international situation and particularly on the concrete progress which must be made towards general disarmament, the elimination of colonialism, racial discrimination, *apartheid* and the foreign occupation of territories, and on promotion of equality of political, economic, social and cultural rights for all members of society. At the same time, the promotion of the right to development and the balanced economic and social development of peoples are prerequisite for ensuring the maintenance of peace and international security.

Development can be neither exported nor imported. On the contrary, it implies the taking into account of many economic, technical and social parameters and a choice of priorities and growth rates on the basis of a knowledge of specific needs, conditions and possibilities, and the participation of the whole community, animated by a common ideal and by individual and collective creativity, in the search for the solutions which are best adapted to the local conditions, needs and aspirations. The irreplaceable framework for such development, therefore, is State organization and the driving forces are the peoples and nations themselves, which have a direct interest in their own development. Peoples and States will be able to organize their development effectively only by ensuring the full exercise of their sovereignty, particularly in such matters as the choice of the form of social and political organization, control over natural resources, the choice of the development approach, the directions and pace of their economic and social development and the form of their participation in international trade. Rapid and economic social progress also requires structures and institutions that will ensure the creative participation of the people, fairness in the distribution of the fruits of development and the focusing of all efforts on the main directions of development. Bearing in mind that the national efforts of each people constitute the primary factor for development substantial and effective international assistance must be given to those efforts, for the elimination of under-development is not only a moral imperative and an essential requirement for equity, it is also the expression of the general interest of peoples at all levels. At a time when the economic interdependence of States is increasing and when no country can remain insulated from world economic processes, all States, whatever their social system, their territorial extent or their economic potential, must contribute actively to the solution of the world's present major economic problems and to the development of peoples.

The right to economic, social and cultural development and to political progress is based on respect for the dignity and value of the human person, on the immediate and complete elimination of all forms of inequality, exploitation of peoples and individuals, colonialism and racism, including Nazism, *apartheid* and all other principles of the United Nations concerning the recognition and effective observance of civil and political rights and economic, social and cultural rights, without any discrimination. At the same time, development also ensures the promotion of human rights and social justice.

Realization of the Right to Development. Development provides a vital contribution to the observance and promotion of human rights and fundamental freedoms. This most important idea has often been emphasized by the General Assembly, which stressed, in its resolution 2027 (XX) of 18 November 1965, the need, during the first United Nations Development Decade, to devote special attention at both the national and the international level to progress in the field of human rights, and to encourage the adoption of measures designed to accelerate the promotion of respect for and observance of human rights and fundamental freedoms. In its resolution 2586 (XXIV) of 15 December 1969, the General Assembly considered that, in the preparation of the strategy for the Second United Nations Devel-

opment Decade, the final aim must be the attainment of a rapid and sustained rate of economic and social development, especially in developing countries, and also the well-being, freedom and dignity of all human beings, and the enjoyment of all the civil, political, economic, social and cultural rights recognized by the Universal Declaration of Human Rights and guaranteed by the two International Covenants on Human Rights. Since the right of peoples to self-determination forms the basis for the enjoyment and development of individual human rights and also has major implications for the political, economic, social and cultural advancement of every nation, it remains a corner-stone of the new international order. Promotion by the United Nations of the right of peoples to self-determination and the progressive development of this right will be an essential means of achieving a new international order and a better, more just and more equitable world.

The special rapporteur's recommendation for international action to ensure enjoyment of the right to self-determination are presented in Chapter IX (para. 714–729) of the study, as follows:

Respect for the right to self-determination—a right proclaimed by the United Nations as a fundamental principle of the Charter—must be the basis of any action taken by the United Nations itself or by the Member States. If this fundamental right of peoples is to be attained, it is essential that the action already initiated by the United Nations and its Members should be continued and that measures calculated to ensure, in particular, the execution and full realization of this right in the areas of greatest contemporary concern should be adopted. In this connexion, the elimination of colonialism, neo-colonialism, racism, *apartheid* and other forms of the violation of the right to self-determination, and the adoption of strong measures to establish truly democratic relations between States and peoples are an urgent necessity at the present time. The United Nations must continue to take vigorous and firm action to bring about the prompt eradication of the vestiges of colonialism, a shameful anachronism which is blatantly at variance with the international ethics and principles unanimously proclaimed by the peoples of the world. The United Nations and the Member States must take effective measures to ensure the immediate and complete liberation of all peoples from any form of foreign subjugation, to eliminate all manifestations of exploitation and discrimination, racism and *apartheid*, and to repress any action intended to revive such practices. With the same object, the United Nations must devise specific measures to end all support to the colonial and racist régimes that disregard the right to self-determination, and take practical action to support the movements for the liberation of peoples from colonialism, neo-colonialism, racism, *apartheid* and foreign occupation, and to ensure the adequate representation of such movements within the United Nations by establishing favourable conditions for the work of their observers and preparing, under United Nations auspices, detailed programmes of effective multilateral assistance for these movements.

The provisions of the Charter which are based on the concept of the recognition of the rights of some countries to administer and dominate other countries and peoples are totally inconsistent with the realities of the modern world. The Charter should proclaim with complete clarity the total and permanent abolition of colonialism, neo-colonialism and racism, and the determination of the States Members of the United Nations to eliminate all practices engendered thereby; it should prohibit any form of interference by one State in the internal affairs of other States, pressure by one State on another, the dependence of one State on another, and the subordination of one State to another. The Charter should clearly affirm the right to self-determination as a fundamental principle of contemporary international law, and the right of peoples to exercise permanent sovereignty over their natural wealth and resources and to develop their material and human potential, in accordance with their interests and aspirations. It should reflect the principles of law and justice which necessarily derive from the development of the right to self-determination and provide for the equalization of the levels of economic development of all countries, as a genuine basis for the democratization of international life. At the same time, it should affirm with the greatest possible clarity the need for the establishment of a new international economic order calculated to ensure the economic and social progress of all peoples and the unrestricted access of all peoples, in particular the least developed peoples, to the achievements of modern civilization and to open up the prospect of a better and more just world. The Charter of the United Nations should thus be the charter for the eradication of colonialism, neo-colonialism and racism, and of all forms of domination, oppression, inequity and inequality in international relations. It should be a charter of the rights of peoples, nations and States, and of fundamental human rights, and an international instrument such as to ensure full, multifaceted and unrestricted approval by every people and thereby open up the prospect of progress and peace for the whole world.

The political aspect of the right to self-determination, in other words the right of peoples to choose their political status, continues to be of particular importance, because this right will always ensure respect for the existence, sovereignty and territorial integrity of States. Consequently, the United Nations must always be capable of guaranteeing this right by combating any form of aggression, intervention or pressure against States and peoples, and of protecting their sovereignty and territorial integrity. The United Nations can no longer today permit the re-emergence, in any form whatsoever, of the domination of one State by another State or those forms of neo-colonialism which perpetuate the spoliation of peoples; it must combat any form of domination or subjugation which engenders international tension and conflict, wars with harmful and unforeseeable consequences, the arms race, the maintenance and accentuation of economic and social disparities between peoples and the phenomenon of economic crisis and instability.

Apartheid, all forms of racial discrimination, colonialism, foreign occupation, aggression and threats against national sovereignty, national unity or territorial integrity, and the refusal to recognize the fundamental rights of peoples to self-determination and of any nation to exercise its full sovereignty over its natural wealth and resources constitute factors which, by their very nature, are and engender, massive and flagrant violations of all the human rights and fundamental freedoms of peoples and individuals.

Consequently, the United Nations must continue forcefully to emphasize the harmful effect on the attainment of human rights, of the persistence of colonialism, aggression and threats against national sovereignty, national unity or territorial integrity, foreign occupation, discrimination in all its forms, *apartheid* and all forms of domination of one State by another.

At the same time, in connexion with the need to develop the right to self-determination, the United Nations must increase its contribution to the promotion, in international life, of new relations between peoples, nations and States. To this end, the preparation and adoption, within the context of the United Nations, of a universal code of conduct proclaiming the fundamental rights and duties of States will be of particular importance. Such a code will have to define standards to ensure rigorous respect for the right to self-determination, the incompatibiity of that right with all forms of domination or pressure, genuine equality of rights for peoples, full political independence, respect for the territorial integrity of peoples, the illegality of military occupation and of the acquisition of territory through the use of force, and the elimination from international life of the possibility of misusing self-determination for purposes of interference or to undermine the national unity of States.

The international economic situation, characterized as it is by major disparities in development, is having an unfavourable effect on the achievement of the right to self-determination and on the social situation within the various countries, especially the developing countries; social distress and poverty can be eliminated only if the preconditions are established for economic growth and balanced and generalized social development. It is therefore incumbent upon the United Nations to tackle those economic and social problems that are of vital importance for the peace, progress and prosperity of the peoples of mankind as a whole, to analyse them in depth and systematically, and to devise and adopt, for the purpose of establishing the new international economic order, precise standards calculated to commit all Member States and special action programmes aimed at the attainment of this new order.

If the right to self-determination is to be achieved, the efforts made at the national level must be continued, so as to promote progress and development in the economic, social, cultural and political sectors, in order to meet the fundamental needs of the peoples concerned. Particularly important measures include the promotion of a more equitable distribution of income and wealth at the national level, the elimination of hunger and malnutrition, the reduction of unemployment and under-employment, the improvement of the distribution of social services and the broad democratic participation of people in the management of the political, economic and social life of their country. The United Nations can contribute to such efforts as a centre for the harmonization of the activities of Member States and for the exchange of experience among them, and by furnishing advisory services and providing the necessary financial assistance to enable measures to be taken in these areas.

In the exercise of the right to self-determination, particular importance must be attached to the urgent need to ensure, at the international level, respect for the principles, and the implementation of the decisions, relating to the establishment of the new international economic order, and respect for the objectives and the implementation of the measures provided for in the International Development Strategy for the Second United Nations Development Decade—an essential condition for the success of the measures aimed at eliminating poverty and ensuring genuine social progress in the developing countries. To this same end, the developed countries which have so far failed to do so must act in a spirit of co-operation and interdependence, so as to ensure the social and economic development of the developing countries.

The ideal of the dignity and value of the individual, free and liberated from fear and poverty, can be achieved only if conditions are established to enable everyone to enjoy his economic, social and cultural rights, and his civil and political rights, and if all States fulfil the obligation to respect the purposes and principles of the Charter of the United Nations and to bring about international co-operation by resolving international problems of an economic, social, cultural or humanitarian nature, and by developing and encouraging respect for the human rights and fundamental freedoms of all, at the same time taking account of the varied nature of the problems which exist in the different societies and of the economic, social and cultural realities of each society. It is in this spirit that the United Nations must take due account, in its work concerning the execution and implementation of human rights, of the experience and over-all situation of the developing countries, and of the efforts made by these countries to give effect to human rights and fundamental freedoms. The United Nations must support these efforts through practical, far-reaching and long-term measures calculated to promote the economic, social and cultural progress of peoples and to create the international atmosphere of peace which is essential if progress is to be achieved in this area. In this context, too, more intensive efforts must be made within the United Nations to contribute to the execution and implementation of the economic, social and cultural rights of the individual, and to the affirmation, elaboration and implementation of the right to development as a fundamental human right.

To the same end, the United Nations must systematically and continuously support those efforts by States which are specifically reflected in structural measures aimed at ensuring the achievement of fundamental human rights, the elimination of social inequalities and all forms of discrimination, and the establishment of equal, genuine and effective rights to work, instruction, education, culture and the benefits of civilization.

The United Nations must take increasing account of the effect of mass information activities on international life and relations, and support national and international efforts to disseminate to the masses information which will promote the *rapprochement* of, and friendship among, peoples, the strengthening of respect for the traditions and culture of each people, and the dissemination of all of mankind's best achievements in all spheres of human activity and knowledge.

The United Nations must examine from an overall standpoint the progress achieved, firstly, in the establishment of a new international economic order, and secondly, in the implementation of the right to self-determination in all its aspects—political, economic, social and cultural—and in the execution and application of economic, social and cultural rights, and of civil and political rights. It would seem necessary to ensure co-ordination, within the international development strategy, between economic, social and cultural development, on the one hand, and human rights on the other, and to undertake a thorough examination of the progress achieved in this sphere. An over-all view of the achievement of the economic, social and cultural aspects of the right to self-determination and of its political aspect is necessary, because at present these different aspects come within the province of a variety of bodies within the United Nations and the specialized agencies. It is the responsibility of the Commission on Human Rights and the Sub-Commission on Prevention of Discrimination and Protection of Minorities to adopt this over-all approach to the achievement of the various aspects of the right to self-determination and the other fundamental human rights.

The progress achieved in social development must therefore be analysed in conjunction with the progress achieved in the sphere of human rights. This requires more effective co-ordination between the work of the United Nations bodies which deal with social questions and those which deal with fundamental human rights.

The United Nations must continue to study the relationship between the progress achieved in the implementation of economic, social and cultural rights, on the one hand, and civil and political rights, on the other, within the context of the realization of the right to self-determination. The attainment of the right to self-determination in all its aspects must constitute a continuing concern of the United Nations. In this connexion, on the basis of information received from Governments, the United Nations is able to publish reports on the attainment of this right. The violation of the right to self-determination and the right of peoples to free themselves from colonial domination, racism and *apartheid* constitutes an international crime. In specific cases of the violation of this right, the provisions of the international conventions relating to the prevention of genocide, racism and *apartheid* must be implemented.

The study of the most salient aspects of the achievement of the right to self-determination, as mentioned above, is the responsibility of the United Nations bodies and the specialized agencies, which must pay continuing attention to, and take an increasing interest in, that matter, acting both individually and jointly. At the same time, in order to assist the United Nations in carrying out its tasks in these areas, with all their complexity and contemporary relevance, conferences, debates, seminars, round tables, etc. might be organized, with the broad participation of States and international non-governmental organizations. Such discussions would make possible a broad and deep analysis serving as a basis for the new measures which might be recommended and for the realization by international public opinion of the urgent need for a solution to the major problems on which the full enjoyment by all peoples of their right to self-determination depends.

SELF-DETERMINATION: UNIVERSAL RECOGNITION OF THE RIGHT. The list of territories which have become self-governing since the United Nations Charter entered into force in 1945 is an impressive one and provides a clear indication of the success of international efforts to promote the universal realization of the right of peoples to self-determination.

The list includes (1) Algeria, (2) Angola, (3) Antigua and Barbuda, (4) Bahamas, (5) Bahrain, (6) Bangladesh, (7) Barbados, (8) Belize, (9) Benin, (10) Bhutan, (11) Botswana, (12) Brunei Darussalam, (13) Burkina Faso, (14) Burundi, (15) Cameroon, (16) Cape Verde, (17) Central African Republic, (18) Chad, (19) Comoros, (20) Congo, (21) Cote d'Ivoire, (22) Cyprus,

(23) Democratic Kampuchea, (24) Democratic Yemen, (25) Djibouti, (26) Dominica, (27) Equatorial Guinea, (28) Fiji, (29) Gabon, (30) Gambia, (31) Ghana, (32) Grenada, (33) Guinea, (34) Guinea-Bissau, (35) Guyana, (36) Indonesia, (37) Jamaica, (38) Kenya, (39) Kuwait, (40) Lao People's Democratic Republic, (41) Lesotho, (42) Libyan Arab Jamahiriya, (43) Madagascar, (44) Malawi, (45) Malaysia, (46) Maldives, (47) Mali, (48) Malta, (49) Mauritania, (50) Morocco, (51) Namibia, (52) Niger, (53) Nigeria, (54) Oman, (55) Qatar, (56) Rwanda, (57) Saint Lucia, (58) Saint Vincent and the Grenadines, (59) Samoa, (60) Sao Tome and Principe, (61) Senegal, (62) Sierra Leone, (63) Singapore, (64) Solomon Islands, (65) Somalia, (66) Sudan, (67) Suriname, (68) Togo, (69) Trinidad and Tobago, (70) Tunisia, (71) Uganda, (72) United Arab Emirates, (73) United Republic of Tanzania, (74) Vanuatu, (75) Zaire, (76) Zambia, and (77) Zimbabwe.

Despite this progress towards universal recognition of the right of peoples to self-determination, both the UN Commission on Human Rights and the General Assembly have repeatedly, since 1980, expressed concern at the continuation of acts or threats of foreign military intervention and occupation that are threatening to suppress, or have already suppressed, the right to self-determination of a number of sovereign peoples and nations.

On 8 December 1988, the General Assembly reaffirmed (resolution 44/80) that the universal realization of the right of all peoples, including those under colonial, foreign, and alien domination, to self-determination is a fundamental condition for the effective guarantee and observance of human rights and for the preservation and promotion of such rights and declared its firm opposition to acts of foreign military intervention, aggression, and occupation, since these have resulted in the suppression of the right to self-determination and other human rights in certain parts of the world.

The assembly called upon those States responsible to cease immediately their military intervention and occupation of foreign countries and territories and all acts of repression, discrimination, exploitation, and maltreatment, particularly the brutal and inhuman methods reportedly employed for the execution of these acts against the peoples concerned. It deplored the plight of the millions of refugees and displaced persons who have been uprooted as a result of such acts and reaffirmed their right to return to their homes voluntarily in safety and honor.

The assembly, finally, called upon the Commission on Human Rights to continue to give special attention to the violation of human rights, especially the right to self-determination, resulting from foreign military intervention, aggression, or occupation.

SENEGAL. The Republic of Senegal is a country in western Africa, fronting on the Atlantic Ocean. It has borders with Gambia (with which it is joined in the Confederation of Senegambia), Guinea, Guinea-Bissau, Mali, and Mauritania. It achieved independence from France in 1960 and became a member of the United Nations the same year. Its population is estimated by the UN (1990) to be 7,377,000. Its ethnic groups are classified by the government as follows:

(a) the Sahel–Sudanese group, which is 40% Wolof and 18% Serer, and lives mainly in the capital Dakar and the central regions;

(b) the Al–Poular group, which is 15% Peul and 10% Tukulor, and lives in the Senegal River valley and in the Ferlo;

(c) the Sub-Guinean group, which represents 13% of the population, and which is composed of Diolas, Balantes, Bassaris, and Sarakoles; and

(d) the Mande group, which is numerically the smallest and lives in the southern part of the country.

With regard to religion, the population is divided as follows: Islam, 90%; Christians, 5%, and others, 5%.

Senegal has provided refuge for more than 5,000 refugees from other parts of Africa, who receive assistance administered by the UNITED NATIONS HIGH COMMISSIONER FOR REFUGEES. There are, in addition, nearly one million foreigners in Senegal, who are subject to the laws of the country and are granted equal protection with nationals in the enjoyment of human rights.

Literacy, estimated to be between 10 and 25%, has been below expectations for many years, and the government set up a National Literacy Department in the late 1970s to promote all types of activities and initiatives relating to the subject. The resulting literacy campaigns endeavor not only to teach people to read and write but also to encourage them to apply what they have learned to every aspect of their daily lives. These efforts are beginning to bear fruit and many of the country's workers are moving gradually away from the dependent situation to which they were confined by their lack of education.

The government (1990) took the form of a republic. Under the 1963 constitution, as amended, the president is head of State and of government; he is assisted by the Council of Ministers, which he himself appoints. Legislation is enacted by a 120-member National Assembly, members of which are elected for five-year terms: 60 by single-member constituencies and 60 by a form of proportional representation. Judges of the Supreme Court are appointed by the president. There are more than 15 political parties, including the Socialist Party, the Senegalese Democratic Party, and the *Rassemblement National Democratique*.

In 1980, the country's leader since independence, President Leopold Senghor, retired, turning over power to Abdou Diouf. President Diouf was elected with 83% of the votes in 1983 and re-elected to a second five-year term in 1988. As president of Senegal, Mr. Diouf also serves as president of the Confederation of Senegambia.

SERVICE FOR JUSTICE AND PEACE IN LATIN AMERICA. An international non-governmental organization in consultative status with the UN Economic and Social Council (category II) and with UNESCO, the organization endeavors to develop ways of freeing the poor from oppression and of creating a free, just, and humane society. It promotes education, based on Christian and humanitarian principles, for peace and human rights. It also supports and practices the principle of non-violence.

Also known by its Spanish title, *Servicio Paz y Justicia en América Latina,* the service, founded in 1974, has 11 affiliated national groups in 10 Latin American countries.

Service for Justice and Peace in Latin America. Address: Rua da Lapa 180, Suite 1107, 20021 Rio de Janiero, Brazil. Telephone: 232-8535. Co-ordinator General: Creuza Rosa Maciel.

SEYCHELLES. The Republic of Seychelles is a country in eastern Africa occupying an archipelago consisting of 112 islands in the Indian Ocean north of Madagascar, the largest of which are Mahe, Praslin, and La Digue. It achieved independence from Great Britain in 1976 and became a member of the United Nations the same year. Its population is estimated by the UN (1990) to be 90,000. Ethnic groups include Asian, African, European, and Creole elements. Languages commonly used include Creole, spoken by 95% of the population; and English and French, both of which are official. Christianity (Roman Catholic, 90%; Anglican and other Protestant denominations, 10%) is the predominant religion. Literacy is estimated at 80%.

The government (1990) took the form of a republic and member of the Commonwealth of Nations, of which the British sovereign is the symbolic head. The president, elected for a term of five years, is head of State and government; he nominates and leads the Council of Ministers. There is a 25-member unicameral People's Assembly, of which 23 are elected for four-year terms and two are nominated by the president. However, both the constitution and the assembly have been suspended since 1977; and the sole political party is the Seychelles People's Progressive Front, which nominates all candidates for election.

SHELTER. At its 1980 session, the UN General Assembly concluded (resolution 35/76) that a special year devoted to the problems of homeless people in urban and rural areas of the developing countries could be an appropriate occasion to focus the attention of the international community on their problems and proclaimed the Year 1987 International Year of Shelter for the Homeless. It decided that the objective of activities before and during the year would be to improve the shelter and neighborhoods of some of the poor and disadvantaged by 1987 and to demonstrate by the year 2000 ways and means of improving the shelter and neighborhoods of such people all over the world.

During the Year of Shelter for the Homeless, activities organized by the United Nations Centre for Human Settlements were undertaken in all parts of the world. In these activities, special attention was given to: (a) securing renewed political commitment by the international community to the improvement of the shelter and neighborhoods of the poor and disadvantaged and to the provision of shelter for the homeless; (b) consolidating and sharing relevant knowledge and experience in the field; (c) developing and demonstrating new approaches to the problem; and (d) exchanging experience and providing support among countries to meet the objectives of the Year.

At the close of the international year, the General Assembly received and noted (resolution 42/191) the reports of the executive director of the United Nations Centre for Human Settlements entitled *Shelter and services for the poor—a call to action* (UN Doc. HS/C/10/3) and *A new agenda for human settlements* (UN Doc. HS/C/10/2 and Corr. 1 and 4), and a summary of the comments made by governments at the tenth (commemorative) session of the Commission on Human Settlements (UN Doc. A/42/8).

Recognizing that adequate and secure shelter is a basic human right and is vital for the fulfilment of human aspirations and that a squalid residential environment is a constant threat to health and to life itself, thereby constituting a drain on human resources, a nation's most valuable asset, the Assembly expressed deep concern about the existing situation in which, despite the efforts of governments at the national and local levels and of international organizations, more than one billion people find themselves either completely without shelter or living in homes unfit for human habitation; and that, owing to prevailing demographic trends, the already formidable problems will escalate in the coming years unless concerted, determined efforts are taken immediately.

Encouraged by action which had been taken in many countries in order to prepare national shelter strategics and launch other measures to promote achievement of the goal of shelter for all, the Assembly decided that there shall be a Global Strategy for Shelter to the Year 2000, including a plan of action for its implementation, monitoring and evaluation, and that its objective would be to stimulate measures to facilitate adequate shelter for all by the year 2000. It requested the executive director of the centre for Human Settlements to prepare a proposal for such a global strategy and called upon the Commission on Human Settlements to formulate the strategy for consideration by the Assembly in 1988.

On 20 December 1988, the General Assembly, bearing in mind the VANCOUVER DECLARATION ON HUMAN SETTLEMENTS and noting that the Commission on Human Settlements had prepared a Global Strategy for Shelter to the Year 2000 as requested (UN Doc. A/43/8/Add.1), adopted a series of guidelines for steps to be taken at the national and international levels, reproduced below, in support of the Global Strategy. The assembly requested the Commission on Human Settlements, as the body designated to coordinate implementation of the strategy, to report biennially on the progress made.

I. Guidelines for Steps to be Taken at the National Level

A. *Considerations for Governments When Formulating a National Shelter Strategy.* 1. A national shelter strategy must spell out clear operational objectives for the development of shelter conditions both in terms of the construction of new housing and the upgrading and maintenance of existing housing stock and infrastructure and services.

2. In the definition of those objectives, development of shelter should be seen as a process whereby conditions are gradually improved for both men and women. The objectives need to address the scale of the problem, while the "adequate" standard aimed at should be identified on the basis of an analysis of the standards and options affordable to the target population and society at large. The objectives should be based on a comprehensive view of the magnitude and nature of the problem and of the available resource base, including the potential contribution of men and women. In addition to finance, land, manpower and institutions, building materials and technology also have to be considered irrespective of whether they are held by the public or private, formal or informal sector.

3. The objectives of the shelter sector need to be linked to the goals of overall economic policy, social policy, settlement policy and environmental policy.

4. The strategy needs to outline the action through which the objectives can be met. In an enabling strategy actions such as the provision of infrastructure may mean the direct involvement of the public sector in shelter construction. The objective of "facilitating adequate shelter for all"

also implies that direct government support should mainly be allocated to the most needy population groups.

5. The public sector is responsible for developing and implementing measures for national shelter policies and for the adoption of measures to stimulate the desired action by other sectors. This can happen through measures in areas such as the locally based small-scale building-materials industry, appropriate financial schemes or training programmes.

6. Another important component is the development of administrative, institutional and legislative tasks that are the direct responsibility of the Government, for example, land registration and regulation of construction.

7. An analysis of affordability will provide the criteria for defining the right priorities and appropriate approaches and standards for public sector involvement. Likewise, such an analysis gives the criteria for planning the indirect involvement of the public sector, that is, the type of activities to be promoted and the appropriate way of going about it.

8. The appropriate institutional framework for the implementation of a strategy must be identified, which may require much institutional reorganization. Each agency involved must have a clear understanding of its role within the overall organization framework and of the tasks expected of it. Mechanisms for the co-ordination of inter- and intra-agency activities need to be developed. Mechanism such as shelter coalitions are recommended and may be developed in partnership with the private and non-governmental sectors. Finally, arrangements for the continuous monitoring, review and revision of the strategy must be developed.

B. *Steps to be Taken by Governments When Implementing a National Strategy.* 9. Organize work for the preparation of the strategy. For instance, a task force may be appointed for the actual work and a steering committee ensuring high-level political commitment set up to guide its work. Alternately it may be possible to use existing mechanisms. Equal participation of women should be ensured at all levels.

10. Assess needs and resources. Estimates are required of the needs in housing construction and in upgrading and maintenance (including housing-related infrastructure), as well as of the resources that can be mobilized over the period to the year 2000 to cover those needs.

11. Analyse shelter options and standards that are affordable by the target groups and society at large, taking into account both the scale of need and all the resources available—finance, land, manpower and institutions, building materials and technology.

12. Set objectives for the construction of new housing and for the upgrading and maintenance of the existing housing stock in terms both of the scale of the activities and of the housing standards to be met.

13. Identify action through which those objectives can be realistically met. The estimated required resources for this action must not exceed those that can be made available by society. The action includes both direct government involvement and measures needed to encourage, facilitate and integrate active participation of other sectors in shelter delivery.

14. Prepare a plan of action in consultation and partnership with non-governmental organizations, people and their representatives, which:

    (a) Lists the activities that are the direct responsibility of the public sector;

    (b) Lists the activities to be taken to facilitate and encourage the other actors to carry out their part of the task;

(c) Outlines resource allocation to the aforementioned activities;

(d) Outlines the institutional arrangements for the implementation, co-ordination, monitoring and review of the strategy;

(e) Outlines a schedule for the activities of the various agencies.

II. Guidelines for Steps to be Taken at the International Level

15. International action will be necessary to support the activities of countries in their endeavour to improve the housing situation of their poor and disadvantaged inhabitants. Such assistance should support national programmes and use know-how available locally and within the international community.

16. The goal of external assistance should be to enhance and support national capabilities to develop and implement national action components of the Global Strategy for Shelter to the Year 2000.

17. Mutual co-operation and exchange of information and expertise between developing countries in human settlement work stimulate and enrich national human settlement work.

18. The United Nations Centre for Human Settlements (Habitat) will act as the co-ordinating agency in the implementation of the global Strategy for Shelter to the Year 2000, on the basis of biennial plans to be drawn up with the involvement of experts working with Governments and the Centre on a regional and subregional basis.

19. As the co-ordinating agency for the Strategy, the United Nations Centre for Human Settlements (Habitat) will stimulate international and national action by incorporating the Strategy in its future medium-term plans and biennial work programmes.

20. An inter-agency-level working arrangement will be made within the existing budget to provide continuous co-ordination of the Strategy.

21. The United Nations Centre for Human Settlements (Habitat) will prepare a reporting format to facilitate monitoring by the Commission on Human Settlements of progress achieved in the implementation of the Global Strategy.

SEE ALSO *Homelessness; Housing.*

SIERRA LEONE. The Republic of Sierra Leone is a country in western Africa, on the Atlantic Ocean. It has borders with Guinea and Liberia. It achieved independence from Great Britain in 1961 and became a member of the United Nations the same year. Its total population is estimated by the UN (1990) to be 3,968,000. Ethnic groups include Temnes (30%), Mendis (29%), and Creoles (2%). Languages commonly used include English (official), Krio (the *lingua franca),* Tenne, Menda, and other African languages. Religions practiced include Islam (39%), Animism and traditional tribal faiths (53%), and Christianity (Protestant, 6%; Roman Catholic, 2%). Literacy is estimated at 15%.

The government (1990) took the form of a republic and member of the Commonwealth of Nations, of which the British sovereign is the symbolic head. Under the 1978 constitution, the All Peoples' Congress Party is the only legal political party. The president, elected unopposed in 1985, is head of State and government. Legislation is prepared by the 104-member parliament which includes 85 members nominated by the All Peoples' Congress Party, 12 paramount chiefs, and seven members appointed by the president. Judges of the Supreme Court are appointed by the president.

Founded in 1788 by British settlers as a home for runaway slaves who had sought refuge in London and for blacks discharged from the British armed forces, Sierra Leone was a British protectorate from 1896 to 1961. It declared itself a republic in 1971 after two coup attempts by army officers had failed; however, since April 1978, the only political party has been the All People's Congress.

SINGAPORE. The Republic of Singapore is a country in southeastern Asia; it occupies Singapore Island, which lies off the southern tip of the Malay Peninsula between the South China Sea and the Indian Ocean, and 54 nearby islets. It achieved independence in 1965 upon withdrawing from the Federation of Malaysia and became a member of the United Nations the same year. Its population is estimated by the UN (1990) to be 2,707,000. Ethnic groups include Chinese (77%), Malays (15%), Indians (6%), and others (2%). Languages commonly used include English (the language of government and of higher education), Malay, Chinese, and Tamil; all are considered to be official languages. Religions practiced include Buddhism, Christianity, Confucianism, Hinduism, Islam, and Taoism. Literacy is estimated at 85%.

The government (1990) took the form of a republic and member of the Commonwealth of Nations, of which the British sovereign is the symbolic head. The president is head of State, and is assisted by a presidential council. The prime minister is head of government and represents the party or coalition given a majority in popular elections. There is a unicameral 79-member Parliament, members of which are elected for terms ranging up to five years from single-member constituencies. The judiciary is organized along British lines and includes the Supreme Court, the High Court, the Court of Appeal, and the Court of Criminal Appeal. The predominant political party is the People's Action Party; there are a number of opposition parties.

SLAVERY: IMPLEMENTATION OF INTERNATIONAL CONVENTIONS. At its second session, in 1976, the WORKING GROUP ON CONTEMPORARY FORMS OF SLAVERY (then known as the Working Group on Slavery and Slavery-like Practices) noted that, although article 8 of the SUPPLEMENTARY CONVENTION ON THE ABOLITION OF SLAVERY, THE SLAVE TRADE AND INSTITUTIONS AND PRACTICES SIMILAR TO SLAVERY requires States parties to forward to the Secretary-General copies of new laws, regulations, and administrative measures enacted or put into effect to implement its provisions, no such reports had been received. At the same session, the working group noted that reports under article 21 of the CONVENTION FOR THE SUPPRESSION OF THE TRAFFIC IN PERSONS AND OF THE EXPLOITATION OF THE PROSTITUTION OF OTHERS were no longer transmitted regularly by States parties, that the number of reporting governments had declined, and that information accumulated since 1958 had not been published. The working group accordingly recommended that the reporting procedures envisaged in the two conventions should be set again in motion.

On recommendation of the working group and the SUB-COMMISSION ON PREVENTION OF DISCRIMINATION AND PROTECTION OF MINORITIES, the COMMISSION ON HUMAN RIGHTS on 12 March 1984 requested the Secretary-General (resolution 1984/40) to call upon States parties to the SLAVERY CONVENTION SIGNED AT GENEVA ON 25 SEPTEMBER 1926, the Supplementary Convention of 1956, and the Convention for the Suppression of the Traffic in Persons and of the Exploitation of the Prostitution of Others to submit regular reports on the situation in their countries, as provided for under the convention; and to call upon other States, intergovernmental organizations, relevant agencies of the United Nations, and concerned non-governmental organizations, and the INTERNATIONAL CRIMINAL POLICE ORGANIZATION (INTERPOL) to supply relevant information to the working group.

SLAVERY AND THE SLAVE TRADE. The UNIVERSAL DECLARATION OF HUMAN RIGHTS calls for the prohibition of these and similar violations of human rights in the following terms:

Article 4. No one shall be held in slavery or servitude; slavery and the slave trade shall be prohibited in all their forms.

International cooperation in endeavors to put an end to slavery, the slave trade, and similar practices, existed for many years prior to the proclamation of the Declaration. In 1890, signatories to the General Act of the Brussels Conference declared their intention to secure the complete suppression of slavery in all its forms, and of the slave trade by land and by sea, and established an elaborate international machinery which proved highly effective in diminishing the trade in slaves. Later, states parties to the SLAVERY CONVENTION SIGNED AT GENEVA ON 25 SEPTEMBER 1926 undertook (a) to prevent and suppress the slave trade and (b) to bring about, progressively and as soon as possible, the complete abolition of slavery in all its forms. To this end, they agreed to adopt all appropriate measures with a view to preventing and suppressing the embarkation, disembarkation, and transport of slaves in their territorial waters and upon all vessels flying their respective flags, to give one another every assistance with the objective of securing the abolition of slavery and the slave trade, and to take all necessary measures to prevent compulsory or forced labor from developing into conditions analogous to slavery. The convention defined slavery as "the status or condition of a person over who any or all of the owners attaching to the right of ownership are exercised," and the slave trade as including "all acts involved in the capture, acquisition or disposal of a person with intent to reduce him to slavery; all acts involved in the acquisition of a slave with a view to selling or exchanging him; all acts of disposal by sale or exchange of a slave acquired with a view to being sold or exchanged, and, in general, every act of trade or transport of slaves."

The convention of 1926 became a United Nations instrument when the PROTOCOL AMENDING THE SLAVERY CONVENTION, adopted by the UN General Assembly in 1953, entered into force on 7 July 1955. However, studies undertaken by expert bodies of the United Nations and the International Labor Organization indicated that it had not effectively eliminated slavery or the slave trade in all parts of the world and that it needed to be augmented (a) to intensify national as well as international efforts to abolish these evils and (b) to make it clear that its definition of "slavery" includes not only literal slavery but also certain institutions and practices having the same effects as slavery, such as debt bondage, serfdom, and the exploitation of the labor of women and children.

Accordingly, the Economic and Social Council convened (resolution 608 [XXI]) a Conference of Plenipotentiaries which met in Geneva and adopted, on 7 September 1956, the SUPPLEMENTARY CONVENTION ON THE ABOLITION OF SLAVERY, THE SLAVE TRADE, AND INSTITUTIONS AND PRACTICES SIMILAR TO SLAVERY. The Convention entered into force on 30 April 1957.

With regard to institutions and practices similar to slavery, the supplementary convention provides that:

Article 1. Each of the States Parties to this Convention

shall take all practicable and necessary legislative and other measures to bring about progressively and as soon as possible the complete abolition or abandonment of the following institutions or practices, where they still exist and whether or not they are covered by the definition of slavery contained in article 1 of the Slavery Convention signed at Geneva on 25 September 1926:

(a) Debt bondage, that is to say, the status or condition arising from a pledge by a debtor of his personal services or of those of a person under his control as security for a debt, if the value of those services as reasonably assessed is not applied towards the liquidation of the debt or the length and nature of those services are not respectively limited and defined;

(b) Serfdom, that is to say, the condition or status of a tenant who is by law, custom or agreement bound to live and labour on land belonging to another person and to render some determinate service to such other person, whether for reward or not, and is not free to change his status;

(c) Any institution or practice whereby:

(i) A woman, without the right to refuse, is promised or given in marriage on payment of a consideration in money or in kind to her parents, guardian, family or any other person or group; or

(ii) The husband of a woman, his family, or his clan, has the right to transfer her to another person for value received or otherwise; or

(iii) A woman on the death of her husband is liable to be inherited by another person;

(d) Any institution or practice whereby a child or young person under the age of 18 years is delivered by either or both of his natural parents or by his guardian to another person, whether for reward or not, with a view to the exploitation of the child or young person or of his labour.

Article 2. With a view to bringing to an end the institutions and practices mentioned in article 1 (c) of this Convention, the States Parties undertake to prescribe, where appropriate, suitable minimum ages of marriage, to encourage the use of facilities whereby the consent of both parties to a marriage may be freely expressed in the presence of a competent civil or religious authority, and to encourage the registration of marriages.

With regard to the slave trade, the supplementary convention provides that:

Article 3. (1) The act of conveying or attempting to convey slaves from one country to another by whatever means of transport, or of being accessory thereto, shall be a criminal offence under the laws of the States Parties to this Convention and persons convicted thereof shall be liable to very severe penalties.

2. (a) The States Parties shall take all effective measures to prevent ships and aircraft authorized to fly their flags from conveying slaves and to punish persons guilty of such acts or of using national flags for that purpose.

(b) The States Parties shall take all effective measures to ensure that their ports, airfields and coasts are not used for the conveyance of slaves.

3. The States Parties to this Convention shall exchange information in order to ensure the practical co-ordination of the measures taken by them in combating the slave trade and shall inform each other of every case of the slave trade, and of every attempt to commit this criminal offence, which comes to their notice.

Article 4. Any slave who takes refuge on board any vessel of a State Party to this Convention shall *ipso facto* be free.

With regard to slavery and institutions and practices similar to slavery, the supplementary convention further provides that:

Article 5. In a country where the abolition or abandonment of slavery, or of the institutions or practices mentioned in article 1 of this Convention, is not yet complete, the act of mutilating, branding or otherwise marking a slave or a person of servile status in order to indicate his status, or as a punishment, or for any other reason, or of being accessory thereto, shall be a criminal offence under the laws of the States Parties to this Convention and persons convicted thereof shall be liable to punishment.

Article 6. 1. The act of enslaving another person or of inducing another person to give himself or a person dependent upon him into slavery, or of attempting these acts, or being accessory thereto, or being a part to a conspiracy to accomplish any such acts, shall be a criminal offence under the laws of the States Parties to this Convention and persons convicted thereof shall be liable to punishment.

2. Subject to the provisions of the introductory paragraph of article 1 of this Convention, the provisions of paragraph 1 of the present article shall also apply to the act of inducing another person to place himself or a person dependent upon him into the servile status resulting from any of the institutions or practices mentioned in article 1, to any attempt to perform such acts, to being accessory thereto, and to being a party to a conspiracy to accomplish any such acts.

The supplementary convention does not establish a special body to monitor the implementation of its provisions but calls for cooperation between the States parties to give effect to those provisions, as follows:

Article 8 (2). The Parties undertake to communicate to the Secretary-General of the United Nations copies of any laws, regulations and administrative measures enacted or put into effect to implement the provisions of this Convention.

3. The Secretary-General shall communicate the information received under paragraph 2 of this article to the other Parties and to the Economic and Social Council as part of the documentation for any discussion which the Council might undertake with a view to making further recommendations for the abolition of slavery, the slave trade or the institutions and practices which are the subject of this Convention.

Long before the promulgation of the Slavery Convention of 1926 and the Supplementary Convention of 1956, the international community had evidenced its concern with a particular practice resembling slavery in its effects—the traffic in women and children—and had prepared a series of instruments aimed at the suppression of such traffic, among them:

(a) The International Agreement of 18 May 1904 for the Suppression of the White Slave Traffic, as amended by the Protocol approved by the UN General Assembly on 3 December 1948;

(b) the International Convention of 4 May 1910 for the Suppression of the White Slave Traffic, as amended by the above-mentioned Protocol;

(c) the International Convention of 30 September 1921 for the Suppression of the Traffic in Women and Children, as amended by the Protocol as approved by the UN General Assembly on 20 October 1947; and

(d) The International Convention of 11 October 1933 for the Suppression of the Traffic in Women of Full Age, as amended by the above-mentioned Protocol.

In attention, the LEAGUE OF NATIONS had prepared, in 1937, a draft convention extending the scope of these instruments but had not been able to finalize or to adopt the text.

In 1949, the concerned United Nations bodies consolidated the proposed draft convention and the four instruments. The resulting CONVENTION FOR THE SUPPRESSION OF THE TRAFFIC IN PERSONS AND OF THE EXPLOITATION OF THE PROSTITUTION OF OTHERS was adopted by the General Assembly (resolution 317 [IV]) on 2 December 1949 and entered into force on 25 July 1951.

The convention provides that:

Article 1. The Parties to the present Convention agree to punish any person who, to gratify the passions of another:

(1) Procures, entices or leads away, for purposes of prostitution, another person, even with the consent of that person;

(2) Exploits the prostitution of another person, even with the consent of that person.

Article 2. The Parties to the present Convention further agree to punish any person who:

(1) Keeps or manages, or knowingly finances or takes part in the financing of a brothel;

(2) Knowingly lets or rents a building or other place or any part thereof for the purpose of the prostitution of others.

Article 3. To the extent permitted by domestic law, attempts to commit any of the offences referred to in articles 1 and 2, and acts preparatory to the commission thereof, shall also be punished.

Article 4. To the extent permitted by domestic law, intentional participation in the acts referred to in articles 1 and 2 above shall also be punishable.

To the extent permitted by domestic law, acts of participation shall be treated as separate offences whenever this is necessary to prevent impunity.

The convention does not provide for the establishment of special international machinery to monitor the implementation of its provisions. However, under article 21, the States parties undertake to communicate to the UN Secretary-General such laws and regulations as have already been promulgated in their countries and, thereafter, such laws and regulations as may be promulgated, relating to the subjects of the Convention, as well as measures taken by them concerning the application of the Convention. The information received is published by the Secretary-General, sent to member and non-member States of the United Nations, and examined by the WORKING GROUP ON CONTEMPORARY FORMS OF SLAVERY.

In 1957, the General Conference of the International Labor Organization reviewed the provisions of ILO FORCED LABOR CONVENTION, 1930, and of the ILO PROTECTION OF WAGES CONVENTION, 1949, and decided that further measures were required in order to put an end of certain forms of compulsory or FORCED LABOR. The General Conference accordingly adopted, on 25 June 1957, the ILO ABOLITION OF FORCED LABOR CONVENTION, which provides that:

Article 1. Each Member of the International Labour Organisation which ratifies this Convention undertakes to suppress and not to make use of any form of forced or compulsory labour:

(a) As means of political coercion or education or as a punishment for holding or expressing political views or views ideologically opposed to the established political, social or economic system;

(b) As a method of mobilising and using labour for purposes of economic development;

(c) As a means of labour discipline;

(d) As a punishment for having participated in strikes;

(e) As a means of racial, social, national or religious discrimination.

Article 2. Each member of the International Labour Organisation which ratifies this Convention undertakes to take effective measures to secure the immediate and complete abolition of forced or compulsory labour as specified in article 1 of this Convention.

The INTERNATIONAL COVENANT ON CIVIL AND POLITICAL RIGHTS, adopted by the UN General Assembly on 16 December 1966, includes the following provision relating to slavery and the slave trade:

Article 8. 1. No one shall be held in slavery; slavery and the slave-trade in all their forms shall be prohibited.

2. No one shall be held in servitude.

3. (a) No one shall be required to perform forced or compulsory labour;

(b) Paragraph 3 (a) shall not be held to preclude in countries where imprisonment with hard labour may be imposed as a punishment for a crime, the performance of hard labour in pursuance of a sentence to such punishment by a competent court;

(c) For the purpose of this paragraph the term "forced or compulsory labour" shall not include:

(i) Any work or service, not referred to in subparagraph (b), normally required of a person who is under detention in consequence of a lawful order of a court, or of a person during conditional release from such detention;

(ii) Any service of a military character and, in countries where conscientious objection is recognized, any national service required by law of conscientious objectors;

(iii) Any service exacted in cases of emergency or calamity threatening the life or well-being of the community;

(iv) Any work or service which forms part of normal civil obligations.

The United Nations Convention on the Law of the Sea, signed at Montego Bay, Jamaica, on 10 December 1982, contains the following provision:

Article 9. Every State shall take effective measure to prevent and punish the transport of slaves in ships authorized to fly its flag and to prevent the unlawful use of its flag for that purpose. Any slave taking refuge on board any ship, whatever its flag, shall *ipso facto* be free.

The AMERICAN CONVENTION ON HUMAN RIGHTS, open for acceptance by member States of the ORGANIZATION OF AMERICAN STATES, provides that:

Article 6. 1. No one shall be subject to slavery or to involuntary servitude, which are prohibited in all their forms, as are the slave trade and traffic in women.

2. No one shall be required to perform forced or compulsory labor. This provision shall not be interpreted to mean that, in those countries in which the penalty established for certain crimes is deprivation of liberty at forced labor, the carrying out of such a sentence imposed by a competent court is prohibited. Forced labor shall not adversely affect the dignity or the physical or intellectual capacity of the prisoner.

3. For the purposes of this article, the following do not constitute forced or compulsory labor:

a. work or service normally required of a person imprisoned in executive [sic] of a sentence or formal decision passed by the competent judicial authority. Such work or service shall be carried out under the supervision and control of public authorities, and any persons performing such work or service shall not be placed at the disposal of any private party, company, or juridical person;

b. military service and, in countries in which conscientious objectors are recognized, national service that the law may provide for in lieu of military service;

c. service exacted in time of danger or calamity that threatens the existence or the well-being of the community; or

d. work or service that forms part of normal civic obligations.

The AFRICAN CHARTER OF HUMAN AND PEOPLES' RIGHTS, open for acceptance by member States of the ORGANIZATION OF AFRICAN UNITY, provides that:

Article 5. Every individual shall have the right to the respect of the dignity inherent in a human being and to the recognition of his legal status. All forms of exploitation and degradation of man particularly slavery, slave trade, torture, cruel, inhuman or degrading punishment and treatment shall be prohibited.

The EUROPEAN CONVENTION ON HUMAN RIGHTS, open for acceptance by members of the COUNCIL OF EUROPE, provides that:

Article 4. 1. No one shall be held in slavery or servitude.

2. No one shall be required to perform forced or compulsory labour.

3. For the purpose of this Article the term 'forced or compulsory labour' shall not include:

a. any work required to be done in the ordinary course of detention imposed according to the provisions of Article 5 of this Convention or during conditional release from such detention;

b. any service of a military character or, in case of conscientious objectors in countries where they are recognised, service exacted instead of compulsory military service;

c. any service exacted in case of an emergency or calamity threatening the life or well-being of the community;

d. any work or service which forms part of normal civic obligations.

International Action to Abolish Slavery in all its Forms and Manifestations. In 1949, shortly after the proclamation of the Universal Declaration of Human Rights, the UN Economic and Social Council authorized the Secretary-General (resolution 238 [IX]) to select a committee of experts to survey the field of slavery and other institutions and customs resembling slavery, to assess the nature and extent of these problems, and to suggest ways of attacking them. The four-member committee reported in 1951 that, apart from slavery in its crudest form, a number of practices analogous to slavery, or resembling slavery in their effects, still existed in various parts of the world. It was on recommendation of the committee that the functions previously exercised by the League of Nations under the Slavery Convention of 1926 were transferred to the United Nations in 1953, and that the Supplementary Convention on the Abolition of Slavery, the Slave Trade, and Institutions and Practices Similar to Slavery was adopted by the General Assembly in 1956.

In 1963, the council requested the Secretary-General (resolution 960 [XXXVI]) to appoint a special rapporteur to compile comprehensive and up-to-date information on the extent to which slavery persisted. The special rapporteur, Mr. Mohamed Awad, in his *Report on Slavery* (UN Publication, Sales No. 67.XIV.2) clearly demonstrated that slavery, the slave trade, and similar institutions and practices continued to exist in some parts of the world and that women and children were among their victims.

After examining and noting the report, the council referred the question of slavery and the slave trade in all their practices and manifestations, including the slavery-like practices of *apartheid* and colonialism, to the COMMISSION ON HUMAN RIGHTS (resolution 1126

[XLI]). The Commission, in turn, called upon its SUB-COMMISSION ON PREVENTION OF DISCRIMINATION AND PROTECTION OF MINORITIES (resolution 13 [XXIII]) to undertake regular consideration of the question, taking into account the *Report on Slavery* and other relevant materials, and to consider information submitted by States parties to the Supplementary Convention of 1956 in accordance with article 8 of that instrument.

In May 1968, the council broadened the sub-commission's mandate in this field, authorizing it (resolution 1330 [XLIV]) "to undertake a study of the measures which might be taken to implement the International Slavery Convention of 1926 and the Supplementary Convention of 1956 on the Abolition of Slavery, the Slave Trade and Institutions and Practices Similar to Slavery and the various recommendations included in the resolutions of the General Assembly, the Economic and Social Council and the Commission on Human Rights relating to the slavery-like practices of *apartheid* and colonialism," and further authorizing it "to initiate a study of the possibilities of international police co-operation to interrupt and punish the transportation of persons in danger of being enslaved, taking into account, as appropriate, the view of the competent international organizations." These studies, completed in 1971 by the sub-commission's special rapporteur (UN Doc. E/CN.4/Sub.2/322), resulted in the adoption of a comprehensive resolution on slavery by the Council in 1972.

In the resolution (resolution 1695 [LII]), the council called upon all eligible States which were not parties to the International Slavery Convention of 1926 and the Supplementary Convention of 1956 to become parties as soon as possible, drew attention to the close relationship between the effects of slavery, *apartheid,* and colonialism and to the need to take concrete measures to ensure the effective implementation of the relevant international conventions and decisions of the United Nations with a view to bringing about the complete elimination of these shameful phenomena, and called upon all States to enact any legislation necessary to prohibit slavery and the slave trade in all their practices and manifestations and to provide effective penal sanctions for persons committing, or ordering to be committed, any of the following acts: abduction, planning the abduction, or giving instructions for the abduction of any person by force, treachery, gifts, abuse of authority or power, or intimidation, which results in that person being placed in a status of slavery or servitude as defined in the International Slavery Convention of 1926 and the Supplementary Convention of 1956. The council also called upon all States to search for persons alleged to have committed, or to have ordered to be committed,

any such acts, and to bring such persons, regardless of their nationality, before its own courts, or to hand such persons over for trial to another state concerned.

The Secretary-General was requested to present a summary of the available information on slavery and the slave trade to the sub-commission at each session, to undertake a survey of national legislation for the purpose of eliminating practices similar to slavery and to prepare a plan of technical cooperation to contribute to the eradication of slavery and the slave trade.

The sub-commission was requested, by the same resolution, to examine the possibility of establishing some form of permanent machinery to give advice on the elimination of slavery and on the suppression of the traffic in persons and exploitation of the prostitution of others. Accordingly, the sub-commission initiated the practice of appointing a working group composed of five of its members to meet for not more than three working days before each sub-commission session "to review developments in the field of slavery and the slave trade in all their practices and manifestations, including the slavery-like practices of *apartheid* and colonialism, the traffic in persons and the exploitation of the prostitution of others as they are defined in the Slavery Convention of 1926, the Supplementary Convention of 1956, and the Convention for the Suppression of the Traffic in Persons and of the Exploitation of the Prostitution of Others of 1949." The mandate of the working group on slavery, the name of which in 1988 was changed to Working Group on Contemporary Forms of Slavery by the Commission on Human Rights (resolution 1988/42), has been progressively interpreted in such a way as to cover a growing number of additional relevant issues such as the sale of children, the exploitation of child labor, the sexual mutilation of female children, abuses against workers and indigenous populations, debt bondage, and the exploitation of the prostitution of others.

In 1980, the sub-commission appointed one of its members, Mr. Benjamin Whitaker (United Kingdom) as special rapporteur to update the *Report on Slavery.* The resulting report, entitled *Slavery,* was presented to the sub-commission in 1982 and published in 1984 (UN publication, Sales No. E.84/XIV.1). In it, the author described the contemporary manifestations of slavery and slavery-like practices and the action which had been taken to combat them by governments, the United Nations and other intergovernmental bodies, and non-governmental organizations, and resented his conclusions and recommendations. Among his conclusions were the following (para. 187–188):

The phenomenon of slavery manifests several of the gravest forms of the violation of human rights: often it combines coercion, severe discrimination and the most extreme form of economic exploitation. As Mr. Masud, a member of the Sub-Commission, pointed out, slavery-like practices have frequently been exploited by elites (initially, often by colonial invaders), and the long-term remedy lies in widening participation democracy and educating people about, and providing them with the means to safeguard, their human rights. Slavery is the ultimate structural abuse of human power; that any vestiges of it should remain in the 1980s is a disgrace to professed international standards.

The cumulative evidence contained in this report substantiates *prima facie* that, although chattelslavery in the former traditional sense no longer persists in any significant degree, the prevalence of several forms of slavery-like practice continues unabated. Indeed, instances of new forms of servitude and gross exploitation have come to light only in recent years, as violators seek to circumvent laws or to take advantage of changing economic and social conditions. Some of the individual cases, although they may appear isolated, highlight wider and deeper problems that deserve attention. Hence the necessity to re-examine continuously both the nature of the problem and the manner in which the international community should deal with it.

The Sub-Commission on Prevention of Discrimination and Protection of Minorities and its working group have since, at each annual session, reviewed in some detail recent developments concerning slavery in its classical and contemporary forms. The 1989 review, prepared by the working group and set out in its report (UN Doc. E/CN.4 Sub.2/1989/39) deals (chap. IV) with prevention of the sale of children, of child prostitution and of child pornography and (chap. V) with other contemporary forms of slavery such as CHILD LABOR, DEBT BONDAGE, TRAFFIC IN PERSONS AND EXPLOITATION OF THE PROSTITUTION OF OTHERS, and the SLAVERY-LIKE PRACTICES OF *APARTHEID* AND COLONIALISM.

After examining the report of the working group, the sub-commission proposed (resolution 1989/42) that the Commission on Human Rights should appoint a special rapporteur to consider matters relating to the sale of children, child prostitution and child pornography, including the problem of adoption of children for commercial purposes; and (resolution 1989/43) that the commission transmit to governments and to intergovernmental and nongovernmental organizations, for their comments, the draft "Program of Action For Prevention of the Sale of Children, Child Prostitution and Child Pornography" prepared by the working group. The program is reproduced below.

The Commission on Human Rights, at its 1990 session, took note (resolution 1990/63) of the report of the working group but did not consider the measures proposed by the sub-commission in resolutions 1989/

42 and 43. Expressing grave concern that slavery, the slave trade, slavery practices, and even modern manifestations of this phenomenon still exist, representing some of the gravest violations of human rights, the commission requested the secretary-general to invite States parties to the Slavery Convention Signed at Geneva on 25 September 1926, as amended, the Supplementary Convention on the Abolition of Slavery, the Slave Trade, and Institutions and Practices similar to Slavery, and the Convention for the Suppression of the Traffic in Persons and of the Exploitation of the Prostitution of Others to submit to the sub-commission regular reports on the situation in their countries as provided under the conventions. It also called upon those eligible States which have not ratified the above-mentioned conventions to consider doing so as soon as possible, and invited them to consider providing information regarding their national legislation and practices in this field. The commission, further, invited intergovernmental organizations, the relevant United Nations agencies, and non-governmental organizations, including those interested in children's and women's rights, to attend sessions of the working group.

Finally, the commission invited all member States to consider the possibility of taking appropriate action for the protection of children and migrant women against exploitation by prostitution and other slavery-like practices, including the possibility of establishing national bodies to achieve these objectives; and requested governments to pursue a policy of information, prevention, and rehabilitation of women victims of the exploitation of prostitution, and to take the appropriate economic and social measures deemed necessary to that effect.

Program of Action for Prevention of Sale of Children, Child Prostitution and Child Pornography
A. General

1. To prevent the sale of children, child prostitution and child pornography, concerted measures are called for at the national and international level, including information, education, assistance and rehabilitation, legislative measures and a strenghtening of law enforcement in this field. Co-ordinating agencies should be appointed or established at the national, regional and global level.

2. At the global level, co-ordination of the Programme of Action should be carried out by the Centre for Human Rights in co-operation with other sections of the United Nations Secretariat including the Centre for the Advancement of Women, and with concerned intergovernmental agencies, in particular UNICEF and UNESCO. Co-operation should also be established with INTERPOL.

Information and Education. 3. An international information campaign to raise public awareness of these abuses should form part of the Programme. Religious and lay organizations should be encouraged to participate. The media should also be called upon in order to help break the practice of silence surounding these issues, while avoiding sensationalism. Law enforcement agencies should be given a significant role in this campaign.

4. To improve the sources of information, studies and investigations of these abuses should be undertaken by public and private institutions. The outcomes should, wherever possible, be made public and exchanged between governmental and non-governmental organizations at the national and international level.

5. To provide a focus for the campaign, a World Day for the Abolition of Contemporary Forms of Slavery might be proclaimed. One possibility is to use the date of 2 December, the anniversary of the adoption of the Convention for the Suppression of the Traffic in Persons and of the Exploitation of the Prostitution of Others.

6. Special educational measures should be adopted, to be directed both at the general public and to specific groups. The education should be based on universally agreed ethical principles including the recognition of every child's fundamental right to the integrity of its own body. Emphasis should be placed on the damaging effects which these abuses have on children, ways in which the abuses can be prevented, discovered and exposed, and ways to assist children who have suffered from such abuse.

7. Preventive educational programmes at the primary and secondary level should make the children understand the dangers of these abuses, including the health dangers such as AIDS, and make them aware of their own right to the integrity of their body and thereby strengthen their defence against abuses.

8. Such education must avoid underplaying the issues but should also avoid sensationalizing it. Great care must be taken in developing educational programmes on these subjects. The age of the children concerned and the culture in which the children are living must be taken into account.

9. For street children, who are particularly affected by these practices, alternative educational programmes should be developed.

10. Social workers, health workers, members of law enforcement agencies and of the judiciary should also receive education on the occurrence of such abuses and the ways in which they can be counteracted.

Social Measures, Development Assistance. 11. It is recognized that these practices are often linked to poverty, and that long-range structural reforms in the social and economic fields will be required for their prevention. In the shorter run, development activities of the United Nations and other international as well as national agencies should have a substantive and positive impact on children. Priority should be given to policies aimed at improving the social, economic and working conditions of women in general and of the poorest women in particular. Local community projects, including collective self-help projects by vulnerable mothers, should also be encouraged.

12. The needs of children exposed to sexual exploitation should be taken into account in development plans and assistance. Special attention should be given to certain groups of street children and children whose mothers are engaged in prostitution. Governments and non-governmental organizations should be encouraged to initiate projects designed to protect street children from sexual abuse (e.g. small-scale enterprise projects for children, "safe houses", emergency centres, etc.). Efforts should also be made to reunite street children in cities with their families in rural areas.

Legal Measures and Law Enforcement. 13. Preventive legislation aimed at protecting children should be strengthened and better enforced. Police, courts and treatment and support systems should focus more on children. Legal aid should be easily available to those who claim to have been sexually violated and to parents or legal guardians in cases of sale of children. Methods should be developed to obtain evidence from the child without further traumatization, and witnesses should be afforded protection.

14. Sexual abuse and traffic in children are serious crimes and must be treated as such. More severe penalties should be imposed on consumers and procurers.

15. Effective legislative and enforcement measures must also be directed against the middlemen and others who encourage and make a profit from the sale and sexual exploitation of children: agents, dealers, brothel-owners, and others involved. The proceeds from such activities should be confiscated.

16. The draft Convention on the Rights of the Child, when adopted, provides protection against sale of children and sexual exploitation. States are encouraged to become parties to the Convention at the earliest possible moment. For its implementation within States, national institutions, with representatives of public agencies and private organizations, might be established to co-ordinate action and to protect children and their rights.

Rehabilitation and Re-Integration. 17. Programmes for rehabilitation and re-integration with an inter-disciplinary approach should be established to assist children who have been victims of sexual exploitation, and their families. Agencies implementing such programmes, whether public or non-governmental, should be given the necessary support and funding.

International Coordination. 18. Bilateral and multilateral co-operation among law enforcement agencies is essential. States should establish their own data base, improve their reporting at all levels, and report to INTERPOL to allow for a special data bank on suspects involved in such abuses across borders. The experience gained in international police co-operation in combating drug traffic should be made use of to prevent international traffic involving the sale and sexual exploitation of children.

B. Sale of Children

19. States should be encouraged to take effective legal and administrative measures to prevent the abduction and sale of children. Laws should be adopted or strengthened which impose penalties on parents and on all others knowingly involved in the traffic of children.

20. Measures should be taken to ensure that international adoptions do not involve the illicit removal of children from parents. Procedures for this purpose should be based on the 1986 United Nations Declaration on Social and Legal Principles relating to the Protection and Welfare of Children with Special Reference to Foster Placement and Adoption Nationally and Internationally, and the Convention on the Rights of the Child when adopted. Under no circumstances must adoption be allowed to involve financial gain for any of the parties involved.

21. States should adopt effective and urgent procedures at the national level and through international co-operation to find abducted, unlawfully removed or disappeared children and to reunite such children with their families.

C. Child Prostitution

22. Legislative and other measures should be taken to prevent sex tourism. Such measures should be adopted both in the countries from which the customer comes (most often the industrialized countries) and the countries to which they go (often to developing countries). Marketing tourism through the enticement of sex with women and children should be penalized on the same level as procurement.

23. The World Tourist Organization should be encouraged to convene a world conference on ways in which to prevent such practices.

24. States having military bases or troops on foreign territories, as well as host States, should take all the necessary measures to prevent such military personnel from being involved in child prostitution. The same applies to other categories of persons who for professional reasons are posted abroad.

25. Legislation should be adopted to prevent new forms of technology from being used for soliciting prostitution.

D. Child Pornography

26. Taking into account, as stated at the INTERPOL symposium in September 1988, that child pornography is the permanent visual depiction of the sexual molestation and exploitation of a child, and that there is an international market for this material, law enforcement agencies should place a higher priority on the investigation of child pornography with particular emphasis placed on the welfare of the child.

27. States are urged to enact legislation, where they have not yet done so, making it a crime to produce, distribute or possess pornographic material involving children.

28. Postal and custom services should be required to detect and prevent the transmission of material containing child pornography. Special attention has to be paid to new technology for producing pornography, including video films.

29. States should be encouraged to protect children from exposure to adult pornography through suitable legislation and appropriate measures of control.

SLAVERY CONVENTION SIGNED AT GENEVA ON 25 SEPTEMBER 1926, AS AMENDED. In the Slavery Convention prepared under the auspices of the League of Nations, opened for signature in Geneva on 25 September 1926, and entering into force on 9 March 1927 (League of Nations, *Treaty Series,* vol. 60, p. 253), States parties agreed upon a definition of slavery and undertook to prevent and suppress the slave trade and to bring about, progressively and as soon as possible, the complete abolition of slavery in all its forms. They further agreed that forced or compulsory labor should be exacted only for public purposes.

The PROTOCOL AMENDING THE SLAVERY CONVENTION adopted by the UN General Assembly on 7 December 1953 (United Nations, *Treaty Series,* vol. 182, p. 51), replaced each reference to the League of Nations by a reference to the United Nations and each reference to the Permanent Court of International Justice by a

reference to the International Court of Justice. The amended text of the convention thus reads as follows:

Whereas the signatories of the General Act of the Brussels Conference of 1889–90 declared that they were equally animated by the firm intention of putting an end to the traffic in African slaves,

Whereas the signatories of the Convention of Saint-Germain-en-Laye of 1919, to revise the General Act of Berlin of 1885, and the General Act and Declaration of Brussels of 1890, affirmed their intention of securing the complete suppression of slavery in all its forms and of the slave trade by land and sea,

Taking into consideration the report of the Temporary Slavery Commission appointed by the Council of the League of Nations on June 12th, 1924,

Desiring to complete and extend the work accomplished under the Brussels Act and to find a means of giving practical effect throughout the world to such intentions as were expressed in regard to slave trade and slavery by the signatories of the Convention of Saint-Germain-en-Laye, and recognising that it is necessary to conclude to that end more detailed arrangements than are contained in that Convention,

Considering, moreover, that it is necessary to prevent forced labour from developing into conditions analogous to slavery,

Have decided to conclude a Convention and have accordingly appointed as their Plenipotentiaries [*names omitted*]

. . . have agreed as follows:

Article 1. For the purpose of the present Convention, the following definitions are agreed upon:

(1) Slavery is the status or condition of a person over whom any or all of the powers attaching to the right of ownership are exercised.

(2) The slave trade includes all acts involved in the capture, acquisition or disposal of a person with intent to reduce him to slavery; all acts involved in the acquisition of a slave with a view to selling or exchanging him; all acts of disposal by sale or exchange of a slave acquired with a view to being sold or exchanged, and, in general, every act of trade or transport in slaves.

Article 2. The High Contracting Parties undertake, each in respect of the territories placed under its sovereignty, jurisdiction, protection, suzerainty or tutelage, so far as they have not already taken the necessary steps:

(a) To prevent and suppress the slave trade;

(b) To bring about, progressively and as soon as possible, the complete abolition of slavery in all its forms.

Article 3. The High Contracting Parties undertake to adopt all appropriate measures with a view to preventing and suppressing the embarkation, disembarkation and transport of slaves in their territorial waters and upon all vessels flying their respective flags.

The High Contracting Parties undertake to negotiate as soon as possible a general Convention with regard to the slave trade which will give them rights and impose upon them duties of the same nature as those provided for in the Convention of June 17th, 1925, relative to the International Trade in Arms (Articles 12, 20, 21, 22, 23, 24, and paragraphs 3, 4 and 5 of Section II of Annex II), with the necessary adaptations, it being understood that this general Convention will not place the ships (even of small tonnage) of any High Contracting Parties in a position different from that of the other High Contracting Parties.

It is also understood that, before or after the coming into force of this general Convention, the High Contracting Parties are entirely free to conclude between themselves, without, however, derogating from the principles laid down in the preceding paragraph, such special agreements as, by reason of their peculiar situation, might appear to be suitable in order to bring about as soon as possible the complete disappearance of the slave trade.

Article 4. The High Contracting Parties shall give to one another every assistance with the object of securing the abolition of slavery and the slave trade.

Article 5. The High Contracting Parties recognize that recourse to compulsory or forced labour may have grave consequences and undertake, each in respect of the territories placed under its sovereignty, jurisdiction, protection, suzerainty or tutelage, to take all necessary measure to prevent compulsory or forced labour from developing into conditions analogous to slavery.

It is agreed that:

(1) Subject to the transitional provisions laid down in paragraph (2) below, compulsory or forced labour may only be exacted for public purposes.

(2) In territories in which compulsory or forced labour for other than public purposes still survives, the High Contracting Parties shall endeavour progressively and as soon as possible to put an end to the practice. So long as such forced or compulsory labour exists, this labour shall invariably be of an exceptional character, shall always receive adequate remuneration, and shall not involve the removal of the labourers from their usual place of residence.

(3) In all cases, the responsibility for any recourse to compulsory or forced labour shall rest with the competent central authorities of the territory concerned.

Article 6. Those of the High Contracting Parties whose laws do not at present make adequate provision for the punishment of infractions of laws and regulations enacted with a view to giving effect to the purposes of the present Convention undertake to adopt the necessary measures in order that severe penalties may be imposed in respect of such infractions.

Article 7. The High Contracting Parties undertake to communicate to each other and to the Secretary-General of the United Nations any laws and regulations which they may enact with a view to the application of the provisions of the present Convention.

Article 8. The High Contracting Parties agree that disputes arising between them relating to the interpretation or application of this Convention shall, if they cannot be settled by direct negotiation, be referred for decision to the International Court of Justice. In case either or both of the States Parties to such a dispute should not be parties to the Statute of the International Court of Justice, the dispute shall be referred, at the choice of the Parties and in accordance with the constitutional procedure of each State, either to the International Court of Justice or to a court of arbitration constituted in accordance with the Convention of October 18th, 1907, for the Pacific Settlement of International Disputes, or to some other court of arbitration.

Article 9. At the time of signature or of ratification or of accession, any High Contracting Party may declare that its acceptance of the present Convention does not bind some or all of the territories placed under its sovereignty, jurisdiction, protection, suzerainty or tutelage in respect of all or any provisions of the Convention; it may subsequently accede separately on behalf of any one of them or in respect of any provision to which any one of them is not a party.

Article 10. In the event of a High Contracting Party wishing to denounce the present Convention, the denunciation shall be notified in writing to the Secretary-General of the United Nations, who will at once communicate a certified true copy of the notification to all the other High Contracting Parties, informing them of the date on which it was received.

The denunciation shall only have effect in regard to the notifying State, and one year after the notification has reached the Secretary-General of the United Nations.

Denunciation may also be made separately in respect of any territory placed under its sovereignty, jurisdiction, protection, suzerainty or tutelage.

Article 11. The present Convention, which will bear this day's date and of which the French and English texts are both authentic, will remain open for signature by the States Members of the United Nations.

The present Convention shall be open to accession by all States, including States which are not members of the United Nations, to which the Secretary-General of the United Nations shall have communicated a certified copy of the Convention.

Accession shall be effected by the deposit of a formal instrument with the Secretary-General of the United Nations, who shall give notice thereof to all States parties to the Convention and to all other States contemplated in the present article, informing them of the date on which each such instrument of accession was received in deposit.

The Secretary-General of the United Nations will subsequently bring the present Convention to the notice of States which have not signed it, including States which are not Members of the United Nations, and invite them to accede thereto.

A State desiring to accede to the Convention shall notify its intention in writing to the Secretary-General of the United Nations and transmit to him the instrument of accession, which shall be deposited in the archives of the organization.

The Secretary-General shall immediately transmit to all the other High Contracting Parties a certified true copy of the notification and of the instrument of accession, informing them of the date on which he received them.

Article 12. The present Convention will be ratified and the instruments of ratification shall be deposited in the office of the Secretary-General of the United Nations. The Secretary-General will inform all the High Contracting Parties of such deposit.

The Convention will come into operation for each State on the date of the deposit of its ratification or of its accession.

In faith whereof the Plenipotentiaries signed the present Convention.

Done at Geneva the twenty-fifth day of September, one thousand nine hundred and twenty-six, in one copy, which will be deposited in the archives of the United Nations. A certified copy shall be forwarded to each signatory State.

SEE ALSO *Supplementary Convention on the Abolition of Slavery, the Slave Trade and Institutions and Practices similar to Slavery.*

S

SLAVERY-LIKE PRACTICES OF *APARTHEID* AND COLONIALISM. Practices under *apartheid*, especially labor practices, which give rise to effects similar to those of slavery or the slave trade and which have caused *apartheid* to be characterized as a "collective form of slavery."

At its 1988 session, the **WORKING GROUP ON CONTEMPORARY FORMS OF SLAVERY** of the **SUB-COMMISSION ON PREVENTION OF DISCRIMINATION AND PROTECTION OF MINORITIES** reviewed recent developments relating to slavery and the slave trade. Its examination of the question of the slavery-like practices *apartheid* and colonialism was summarized in its report to the sub-commission (UN Doc. E/CN.4/Sub.2/1988/32, chap. III, F, para. 74–79) as follows:

The representative of the African National Congress (ANC) brought to the attention of the Working Group the sufferings of the people of South Africa caused by the *apartheid* régime in that country. She informed the Group that arrests of anti-*apartheid* activists continued, that their torture in *apartheid* gaols also continued unabated, and that, despite an international outcry, children continued to be detained for anti-*apartheid* activities under South Africa's security laws and still suffered torture at the hands of the authorities.

The ANC representative stated that various bills before Parliament would, if adopted, entrench *apartheid*. In 1986, the Abolition of Influx Control Act had been passed, setting out *inter alia* to amend Act 38 of 1927, section 5 of which empowered the State President to move any group of Africans at will; it was under that provision that the people of Mogopa had been removed. But section 5 of the law had been replaced by a bill on squatting, which gave the same powers to magistrates, so that the burden of removal was transferred to the judiciary without the benefit of any parliamentary check on those powers. Section 6 of the bill on squatting, on the other hand, empowered committees of local government to decide to evict so-called illegal squatters. The ANC believed that the persons most likely to be affected by that legislation were farm tenant workers, who were likely to be removed when they lost their jobs as well as when they engaged in trade union activities. She also mentioned the new Group Areas Bill, which stipulated heavy fines for people living in areas designated for other racial groups. The ANC anticipated an increase in repression during the period leading up to the coming local authority elections and also during the elections.

The Congress was also concerned at the collusion between the State and the judiciary, and its representative reminded the Working Group that there were currently persons on death row awaiting execution for political activities. She demanded the removal and abolition of *apartheid* and called for comprehensive sanctions against South Africa in an effort to eradicate *apartheid* from that country.

Mr. Diaconu stated that *apartheid* constituted the most serious form of violation of human rights, and pointed out that *apartheid* was practised not only in South Africa but also in other countries. Part of the South African population had been denied land, and people had been sentenced to death and executed during 1988 as a direct result of *apartheid* policies. He advocated sustained action against *apartheid* that should cover economic, social and cultural domains as well as civil and political ones.

Ms. Ksentini stated that, when dealing with the item under consideration, the Working Group should address the problem of *apartheid* and all forms of racial discrimination and self-determination. Referring to the problem of *apartheid*, she emphasized that the practice was a crime against humanity and destabilized the countries of southern Africa. She called for the exercise of moral, political and economic pressure as well as efforts to alleviate the sufferings of the people that were victims of *apartheid*, a practice that had to be abolished. She also spoke about the denial to the Palestinian people of its right to self-determination.

The representatives of the International Movement for Fraternal Union among Races and Peoples, and of the International Organization for the Elimination of All Forms of Racial Discrimination, addressed the Working Group. The representatives of the former equated *apartheid* with slavery, and spoke at length of its pernicious influence on the labour market. The representative of the latter organization said that *apartheid* was a form of slavery practised in South Africa. He stated that when South Africa employed black people to work in its enterprises, the workers often received very low wages and were deprived of their civil rights, being generally treated as an inferior people and race. He said that black persons under the system of *apartheid* lived under worse conditions than serfs in Europe in the Middle Ages. He believed that the exploitation of black people in South Africa was a form of slavery that should be denounced and condemned by the Sub-Commission on Prevention of Discrimination and Protection of Minorities.

On the basis of the discussion summarized above, the working group made three recommendations, as follows: (a) that *apartheid*, including the labor practices under *apartheid*, should continue to be viewed as a collective form of slavery; (b) that the chairman of the Human Rights Commission should be authorized to continue his efforts to bring pressure to bear on the South African Government for the unconditional release of Nelson Mandela, the unconditional pardon and release of persons sentenced to death and awaiting execution for opposition to *apartheid*, and to request the South African Government to engage in meaningful dialogue with the leaders of the black majority for an early establishment of a democratic society in which the slavery-like practices of *apartheid* can be finally brought to an end; and (c) that in future sessions, particular emphasis should be given to the situation of women and children under *apartheid*.

Recommendations along these lines were adopted by the sub-commission (resolution 1988/30) and forwarded to the Commission on Human Rights.

SEE ALSO *African National Congress; Apartheid: A Collective Form of Slavery.*

SOCIAL LIFE. The fact that the realization of human rights is a necessary element for the improvement of social life was recognized by the UN General Assembly in 1988 when it called upon member States (resolution 43/156).

> to make all efforts to promote the accelerated and complete elimination of such fundamental elements hindering economic and social progress and development as colonialism, neo-colonialism, racism and all forms of racial discrimination, *apartheid*, aggression, foreign occupation, alien domination and all forms of inequality and exploitation of peoples, and also to undertake effective measures to lessen international tensions.

In the resolution, the assembly pointed out that it is the right of everyone to enjoy the greatest possible degree of physical and mental health and emphasized that participation in cultural, sports, and recreational activities and the use of leisure without discrimination of any kind promote the improvement of social life. It requested the Secretary-General to include, in his report on the implementation of the DECLARATION ON SOCIAL PROGRESS AND DEVELOPMENT, the results attained in the improvement of social life in the world.

SOCIAL SECURITY. The right of everyone to social security is proclaimed in the UNIVERSAL DECLARATION OF HUMAN RIGHTS in the following terms:

> *Article 25.* (1) Everyone has the right to a standard of living adequate for the health and well-being of himself and of his family, including. . . . the right to social security in the event of unemployment, sickness, disability, widowhood, old age or other lack of livelihood in circumstances beyond his control.

The INTERNATIONAL COVENANT ON ECONOMIC, SOCIAL AND CULTURAL RIGHTS contains the following provision:

> *Article 9.* The States parties to the present Convenant recognize the right of everyone to social security, including social insurance.

Non-discrimination on racial grounds is ensured by the INTERNATIONAL CONVENTION ON THE ELIMINATION OF RACIAL DISCRIMINATION in the following provision:

> *Article 5.* In compliance with the fundamental obligations laid down in article 2 of this Convention, States parties undertake to prohibit and to eliminate racial discrimination in all its forms and to guarantee the right of everyone, without distinction as to race, colour, or national or ethnic origin, to equality before the law, notably in the enjoyment of the following rights:. . . .

> (e) Economic, social and cultural rights, in particular:. . . .
> (iv) The right to public health, medical care, social security and social services. . . .

Non-discrimination on the ground of sex is ensured by the CONVENTION ON THE ELIMINATION OF ALL FORMS OF DISCRIMINATION AGAINST WOMEN in the following provisions:

> *Article 11.* (1) States parties shall take all appropriate measures to eliminate discrimination against women in the field of employment in order to ensure, on a basis of equality of men and women, the same rights, in particular. . . .
> (e) The right to social security, particularly in cases of retirement, unemployment, sickness, invalidity and old age and other incapacity to work, as well as the right to paid leave;. . . .
> *Article 13.* States parties shall take all appropriate measures to eliminate discrimination against women in other areas of economic and social life in order to ensure, on a basis of equality of men and women, the same rights, in particular:. . .
> (e) The right to family benefits. . . .

Within the United Nations system, primary responsibility for the preparation and supervision of international measures relating to the right to social security lies with the INTERNATIONAL LABOR ORGANIZATION. Its basic instruments in this endeavor are the ILO SOCIAL SECURITY (MINIMUM STANDARDS) CONVENTION, adopted by the International Labor Conference in 1952, and the ILO EQUALITY OF TREATMENT (SOCIAL SECURITY) CONVENTION, adopted by the Conference in 1962.

The Social Security (Minimum Standards) Convention, 1952, (ILO Convention No. 102), provides (article 7) that "each State party shall secure to the persons protected the provision of benefit in respect of a condition requiring medical care of a preventive or curative nature in accordance with the following articles of this Part. . . ." The "persons protected" include (article 9) prescribed classes of employees, of the economically active population and of residents and also their wives and children. Benefits are to be paid in the form of periodical payments in case of sickness, unemployment, old age, employment injury, maternity, or invalidity. Standards to be complied with, and methods of calculating the payments, are set out in detail.

The Equality of Treatment (Social Security) Convention, 1962 (ILO Convention No. 118) provides (article 3) that each State party shall grant within its territory to the nationals of any other State party equality of treatment under its legislation with its own nationals, both as regards coverage and as regards the right to benefits, in respect of every branch of social security for which it has accepted the obligations of the Convention.

Both conventions are supervised by the international machinery established by the International Labor Conference in 1926, consisting of two components: on the one hand, a committee of independent experts responsible for examining the reports received from governments on measures they have taken to give effect to the provisions of such instruments; and, on the other hand, the establishment, at each session of the conference, of a committee responsible for reviewing the application of conventions. Government reports are required, annually, under article 22 of the ILO constitution.

In addition to the conventions mentioned above, two recommendations—the ILO Recommendation concerning Income Security (Recommendation No. 67), adopted by the International Labor Conference on 12 May 1944, and its Recommendation Concerning Agreements Relating to Social Security (Recommendation No. 75), adopted by the conference on 6 June 1946, provide guiding principles for action by all States in these particular fields.

SEE ALSO European Code of Social Security and Protocol; European Convention on Social Security.

SOLOMON ISLANDS. The Solomon Islands comprise a country occupying an archipelago in the Coral Sea east of Papua New Guinea, including Guadalcanal, Malaita, San Cristobal, and New Georgia. Once a British protectorate, the islands achieved independence from Great Britain in 1978 and became a member of the United Nations the same year. The population is estimated by the UN (1990) to be 329,000. Ethnic groups include Malanesian (93%); Polynesian (4%); Micronesian (1.5%); Chinese (0.3%); Gilbertese, Europeans, and others (1.2%). Languages in common use include English (official), Melanesian Pidgin, and a large number of vernaculars. Christianity is the predominant religion (Anglican, 34%; South Seas Evangelical, 17%; Roman Catholic, 19%; United Church, 10%; and Seventh Day Adventist, 10%). Literacy is estimated at 15%.

The government (1990) took the form of a monarchy and member of the Commonwealth of Nations, of which the British sovereign is the symbolic head. The governor-general, a citizen of the Solomon Islands, represents the crown as head of State and serves for a term of five years. The prime minister is elected by and from members of Parliament, who themselves are elected by popular vote for four-year terms of office. The judiciary is modelled after the British system and includes a number of native and local courts which specialize in matters relating to customary land titles. Political parties include the United Party, the People's Alliance Party, and the National Democratic Party.

SOMALIA. The Somali Democratic Republic is a country in eastern Africa, on the Indian Ocean and the Gulf of Aden. It has boundaries with Djibouti, Ethiopia, and Kenya. British Somaliland and Italian Somalia joined in 1960 to achieve independence as Somalia, which became a member of the United Nations the same year. Its total population is estimated by the UN (1990) to be 5,169,000; in addition, it has one of the largest refugee populations in the world. Ethnic groups include Somalis (98%), Arabs and Asians (2%). Languages in common use include Arabic and Somali (both official), English, and Italian. Islam (Sunni) is the predominant religion. Literacy is estimated at 40%.

The government (1990) took the form of a republic. Under the 1979 constitution, the president is nominated by the Central Committee of the Somali Revolutionary Socialist Party and elected by the People's Assembly for a term of six years. The assembly consists of 121 members nominated by the party and elected by popular vote for terms of five years, and six members appointed by the President. The judiciary includes district courts, regional courts, courts of appeal, and the Supreme Court.

For many years, Somalia has claimed the Ogaden Desert, the easternmost territory of Ethiopia; and, in 1977, it backed rebels in that area, in which a large proportion of the people are Somalis. In eight months of fighting, Somalia lost most of its army and equipment. In 1978, the remaining Somali troops and rebels were decimated by Cuban units armed by the Soviet Union. Emergency food relief was provided by the United States of America at that time, but weapons sales were withheld because Somalia refused to give up its claims to the Ogaden area. However, in 1980, Somalia agreed to permit U.S. use of military bases in the country in return for $25 million in military aid in 1981 and more in later years.

Since 1980, the United Nations has provided assistance to Somalia in dealing with its refugee problem. At the beginning of 1982, the Somali government and the United Nations agreed on a planning figure of 700,000 refugees; however, by 1986, 140,000 new refugees from the Ogaden region had entered the country. A large proportion of the refugees, all of whom are from Ethiopia, are women and children. They are accommodated in 44 centers located in four regions: 15 in the northeast, 12 in Gedo, 12 in Hiran, and five in Lower Shabelle.

A United Nations interagency mission visited Somalia in September 1987 and reported that 840,000 refugees continue to have a severe impact on Somalia's fragile economy. The report of the mission identified a number of priority areas requiring international assistance, such as water resources development, food and livestock production, health services, educational and vocational training, and the building of roads and ports. Concrete steps have since been taken to implement the mission's recommendations.

The UN General Assembly considered a report by the secretary-general on the situation (UN Doc. A/44/462) at its 1989 session, and noted (resolution 44/152) that circumstances had made it necessary for the UN HIGH COMMISSIONER FOR REFUGEES and the World Food Program to suspend their food and other humanitarian assistance programs for refugees in the northwest districts of Somalia temporarily. It commended the measures taken by the government of Somalia to provide assistance to refugees, in spite of its own limited resources and fragile economy, and called upon the high commissioner and the World Food Program to resume their assistance programs for the refugees in the northwest districts as soon as possible.

The circumstances referred to by the General Assembly included widespread fighting in a civil war that engulfed northern Somalia in mid-1989, in which government forces attacked members of the rebel Somali National Movement in a violent confrontation that caused more than 400,000 of Somali's refugees to flee to neighboring Ethiopia and displaced a like number of people in central and southern Somalia.

SOROPTIMIST INTERNATIONAL. An international non-governmental organization in consultative status with the UN Economic and Social Council (Category I) and with UNESCO, SI is divided into four federations (the Americas; Europe; Great Britain and Ireland; and South West Pacific), consisting of approximately 2,700 "clubs" with approximately 91,000 members, in 85 countries and territories.

Founded in 1928 in Washington, D.C., as the "Soroptimist International Association," SI aims to maintain high ethical standards in business, the professions, and other aspects of life; to strive for human rights for all people and, in particular, to advance the status of women; to develop a spirit of friendship and unity among Soroptimists of all countries; to quicken the spirit of service and human understanding; and to contribute to international understanding and universal friendship. It sponsors a quadrennial convention.

Soroptimist International publishes *The Interna-*

tional Soroptimist quarterly. In addition, periodicals are issued by the regional federations.

Soroptimist International (Federation Secretariats). *SI of the Americas:* 1616 Walnut Street, Philadelphia, PA 19103 (USA); *SI of Europe:* Route de Florissant 72, CH-1206 Geneva, Switzerland; *SI of Great Britain and Ireland:* 63 Bayswater Road, London W2 3PJ, UK; *SI of SW Pacific:* GPO Box 1439, Sydney 2001, Australia.

Yearbook of International Organizations 1989/90 (K. G. Saur).

SOUTH AFRICA. The Republic of South Africa is a country in southern Africa, fronting on the Atlantic Ocean and the Indian Ocean. It has borders with Botswana, Mozambique, Swaziland, and Zimbabwe. The kingdom of Lesotho forms an enclave within its southeastern territory. Also lying within its southeastern territory are the "independent states" of Bophuthatswana, Transkei, Ciskei, and Venda, commonly known as "homelands" or "bantustans."

The union was formed by Great Britain over a period of years by joining territory that it had acquired after the Napoleonic Wars with Natal, Transvaal, and the Orange Free State, which it had acquired after the Boer War. It gained sovereignty as a member of the British Commonwealth of Nations in 1934 and became a member of the United Nations in 1945. On 31 May 1961, it became the independent Republic of South Africa.

The population of South Africa is estimated by the UN (1990) to be 36,754,000. It includes persons of black (70%), white (17%), colored or mixed (10%), and Asian (3%) descent. Languages in common use include English and Afrikaans (both official), Zulu, Xhosa, Sotho, Tswana, and other vernaculars. Christianity is the predominant religion (73%); Animism (13%), Hinduism (2%), and Islam (1%) are also widely practiced. Literacy is estimated at 99% among the white population, 50% among the non-white elements.

The government (1990) took the form of a republic. Under the 1984 constitution, the president—elected for a term of five years—is head of State and of government. Parliament is composed (since 1984) of three chambers: the House of Assembly (white) with 178 members, the House of Representatives for Coloureds (mixed races) with 85 members, and the House of Delegates for Indians, with 45 members. Although less than one person out of five in the country is white, black South Africans are not represented in the parliament.

The president is elected by an electoral college made up of the three houses of parliament; in that college, the House of Assembly has an automatic majority. The independent judiciary is headed by the Supreme Court. Each of the bantustans or homelands has its own unicameral legislature, to which members are elected by resident voters. National political parties, which are racially oriented, include the following: *White:* National Party, Progressive Federal Party, New Republic Party, Conservative Party, and Reconstituted National Party; *Mixed races:* Labor Party, Freedom Party, People's Congress Party, and New Convention People's Party; *Indian:* National People's Party.

The first permanent white settlement in which is now the Republic of South Africa occurred at Capetown in 1652 and was organized by the Dutch East India Company. The indigenous black inhabitants were expelled from their own lands, while the settlers, known as Boers or Afrikaners, established an economy based upon slavery and a government which sought to become an independent republic. But by 1814, at the end of the Napoleonic Wars, Great Britain took possession of the colony and brought in 5,000 settlers. Its action in 1833 to free the slaves so enraged the Africaners that most of them moved northward and founded the republics of Transvaal, the Orange Free State, and Natal. In doing so, they had to fight and defeat the indigenous inhabitants, including the fierce Zulu tribesmen, who were forced into small reservations and forbidden to hold land elsewhere.

Great Britain annexed Natal in 1843. After diamonds had been discovered in the Orange Free State and Transvaal, the influx of prospectors was so great that the Dutch authorities took steps to discourage them. By the end of 1899, the two sides were engaged in the South African War. The Boers were defeated in 1902; and, in 1910, the Union of South Africa was established with Louis Botha, a Boer, as its first prime minister. The union included the British colonies of the Cape and Natal, the Transvaal and the Orange Free State. Two main political parties developed: the Nationalists, who stood for Dutch superiority and restrictions on the non-white population, and the United South African Party which stood for cooperation between the national and racial groups.

Jan Christian Smuts, a stateman and soldier of Dutch stock and British nationality, headed the Unionists and served as prime minister from 1919 to 1924. He became prime minister again in 1939, when J.B.M. Hertzog, then prime minister, opposed South Africa's entry into World War II and was removed by parliament. Made a field marshal, he spent most of that war in England where he held a place in the British war councils and was active in organizing the United Nations. However, he was defeated in the 1948 elections, which were won by the Nationalist Party, and, under the new Prime Minister Daniel Malan, APARTHEID became South Africa's official policy.

To establish and enforce that policy, the South African Parliament adopted an incredible series of laws providing for the complete separation of racial groups in every walk of life, systematically depriving all non-whites of their human rights and fundamental freedoms and protecting the security forces from legal restraints. Millions of non-whites, including Indians, Pakistanis, and blacks, were forced to move out of "white" areas into segregated sections of South African cities. Many of the blacks were compelled to resettle in so-called "homelands"—undesirable enclaves within South Africa bearing such names as Bophuthatswana, Ciskei, Gazankulu, KwaZulu, Lebowa, Transkei, Venda, and QwaQwa. Four of these areas were declared "independent"—Bophuthatswana, Ciskei, Transkei, and Venda—but their sovereignty is recognized only by South Africa. Blacks residing in "independent" areas were compelled to give up their South African citizenship, thus reducing the number and proportion of black South Africans.

The National Party's policies of *apartheid* were continued and intensified under Malan's successor, Prime Minister Henrdick F. Verwoerd. In 1961, the government broke with the British Commonwealth and declared the country to be the Republic of South Africa. In 1963, as racial tensions mounted, Verwoerd was assassinated.

Balthazar J. Vorster, also a Nationalist, succeeded Verwoerd but was forced by a scandal to resign in 1978. Pieter W. Botha replaced him, and was inaugurated as president on 14 September 1984 after a new constitution had replaced parliamentary government by a strong presidency.

During his term of office, Botha took at least one important step towards ameliorating the effects of *apartheid*. In response to ever-increasing domestic and international appeals for change in a policy that had become notorious throughout the world, he offered Nelson Mandela, leader of the AFRICAN NATIONAL CONGRESS who had served 18 years in jail on charges of sabotage and conspiracy to overthrow the government, his freedom if he would renounce violence. Mandela's reply was that he would not do so until the government assumes the initiative in dismantling *apartheid* and in ensuring full political rights to non-white South Africans.

F.W. DeKlerk, a descendent of Africaner politicians who realized that the white minority could not hold the reins in South Africa indefinitely, replaced Botha as president in August 1989. He also interviewed Nelson Mandela and, by the end of 1989, had legalized the African National Congress and 60 other organizations and ended restrictions on the movement of 374 persons. On 11 Feb. 1990, Mandela was released from prison.

On 2 March 1990, the National Executive Committee of the African National Congress elected Mr. Mandela deputy president of the organization, enabling him to control the movement headed by Oliver N. Tambo, who had been hospitalized after suffering a stroke in August 1989. Mr. Mandela later led the ANC delegation which met with Mr. DeKlerk and other officials of the South African government early in May 1990 to discuss such questions as the ending of the state of emergency, the repeal of repressive legislation, the halting of political trials, the removal of troops from black townships and the release of all political prisoners.

The text of the statement issued at the conclusion of the meeting, on 4 May 1990, is as follows *(New York Times,* 4 May 1990):

The Government and the ANC agree on a common commitment toward the resolution of the existing climate of violence and intimidation from whatever quarter as well as a commitment to stability and to a peaceful process of negotiations. Flowing from this commitment, the following was agreed upon:

1. The establishment of a working group to make recommendations on a definition of political offenses in the South African situation; to discuss, in this regard, time scales; and to advise on norms and mechanisms for dealing with the release of political prisoners and the granting of immunity in respect of political offenses to those inside and outside South Africa. All persons who may be affected will be considered.

The working group will bear in mind experiences in Namibia and elsewhere. The working group will aim to complete its work before 21 May 1990. It is understood that the South African Government, in its discretion, may consult other political parties and movements and other relevant bodies. The proceedings of the working group will be confidential.

In the meantime the following offenses will receive attention immediately: a) The leaving of the country without a valid travel document. b) Any offenses related merely to organizations which were previously prohibited.

2. In addition to the arrangements mentioned in Paragraph 1, temporary immunity from prosecution for political offenses committed before today will be considered on an urgent basis for members of the National Executive Committee and selected other members of the ANC from outside the country, to enable them to return and help with the establishment and management of political activities, to assist in bringing violence to an end and to take part in peaceful political negotiations.

3. The Government undertakes to review existing security legislation to bring it into line with the new dynamic situation developing in South Africa in order to insure normal and free political activities.

4. The Government reiterates its commitment to work toward the lifting of the state of emergency. In this context the ANC will exert itself to fulfill the objectives contained in the preamble.

5. Efficient channels of communication between the Government and the ANC will be established in order to curb violence and intimidation from whatever quarter effectively.

The Government and the ANC agree that the objectives contained in this minute should be achieved as early as possible.

SEE ALSO Apartheid *entries.*

SOUTH AFRICA: UN CONCERN ABOUT *APARTHEID.*

The racial policies of South Africa have been under discussion in the United Nations since 1946, when India complained that South Africa had enacted legislation against South Africans of Indian origin. In 1952, the wider question of *apartheid* was placed on the agenda of the General Assembly. The two related questions continued to be discussed separately until 1953; in 1954, they were combined under the title "Policies of *Apartheid* of the Government of South Africa."

At its 1962 session, the General Assembly established a Special Committee on the Policies of *Apartheid* to keep those policies under review when the assembly was not in session and to report, as appropriate, to the assembly or to the council, or to both. In 1970, the assembly renamed the committee "Special Committee on *apartheid.*" In 1974, it again renamed the committee (resolution 3324 D [XXIX]) SPECIAL COMMITTEE AGAINST *APARTHEID.* In accordance with its terms of reference, the committee has since submitted annual and special reports to the assembly and to the Security Council.

In 1965, the assembly established (resolution 2054 B [XX]) the UNITED NATIONS TRUST FUND FOR SOUTH AFRICA. The secretary-general has submitted reports on the operation of the fund to the assembly each year.

On 30 November 1973, the assembly adopted and opened for signature and ratification (resolution 3068 [XXVIII]) the INTERNATIONAL CONVENTION ON THE SUPPRESSION AND PUNISHMENT OF THE CRIME OF *APARTHEID.* The convention entered into force on 18 July 1976.

In 1974, the assembly invited representatives of the South African liberation movements recognized by the ORGANIZATION OF AFRICAN UNITY—the AFRICAN NATIONAL CONGRESS OF SOUTH AFRICA and the PAN AFRICANIST CONGRESS of Azania—to participate as observers in its debates on the question. At that session, also, the assembly rejected the credentials of the South African delegation.

In 1977, the assembly adopted and proclaimed (resolution 32/105 M) the INTERNATIONAL DECLARATION AGAINST *APARTHEID* IN SPORTS and authorized the preparation of an international convention on the subject. In 1965, it adopted (resolution 40/64) the INTERNA-

TIONAL CONVENTION AGAINST *APARTHEID* IN SPORTS. The convention entered into force on 3 April 1988.

In recent years, the assembly has adopted, at each session, a series of resolutions dealing with various aspects of *apartheid*. Its 1989 resolutions are summarized briefly below. The Security Council and the Commission on Human Rights have also considered annually for many years the question of race conflict in South Africa.

The Security Council recognized in 1960 (resolution 134 [1960]) that the situation in South Africa was one that had led to international friction and one that, if continued, might endanger international peace and security. In 1963, it called upon all States (resolution 181 [1963]) to end the sale and shipment of arms, ammunition of all types and military vehicles to that country. This ban, later extended to include the sale of equipment and material for the maintenance and manufacture of arms and ammunition, was reiterated and strengthened in 1964, 1970, and 1972. In 1976, following the shooting of demonstrators in Soweto, the council strongly condemned the government of South Africa (resolution 392 [1976]) for its resort to massive violence against and killings of the African people and called upon it urgently to end such violence and to take urgent steps to eliminate *apartheid* and racial discrimination.

In 1977, the council unanimously imposed a mandatory embargo on military and nuclear cooperation with South Africa, deciding (resolution 418 [1977]) that all States should cease any provision to that country of arms or related materiel of all types, including the sale or transfer of weapons and ammunition, military vehicles and equipment, paramilitary police equipment, and spare parts for them, and further decided that all States should refrain from any cooperation with South Africa in the manufacture and development of nuclear weapons.

Subsequently, the General Assembly recommended on several occasions that the Security Council should impose comprehensive and mandatory sanctions against South Africa under chapter 7 of the UNITED NATIONS CHARTER, but the council was unable to do so because of the "veto" cast by one or more of its permanent members (France, the United Kingdom, and the United States of America).

In August 1984, the council declared (resolution 554 [1984]) that the so-called "new constitution" of South Africa was contrary to the principles of the charter, that the results of the referendum of 2 November 1983 were of no validity whatsoever, and that the enforcement of the so-called "new constitution" and the "elections" that were to be organized in August 1984 for the non-white population would further aggravate the already explosive situation prevailing in South Africa.

In March 1985, the council called upon the Pretoria regime (resolution 560 [1985]) to release unconditionally and immediately all political prisoners and detainees, including Nelson Mandela and all other black leaders with whom it must deal in any meaningful discussion of the future of the country. In July of that year, it strongly condemned (resolution 569 [1985]) the *apartheid* system, the mass arrests and detentions carried out by the Pretroia government, and the murders that had been committed, as well as the establishment of the STATE OF EMERGENCY in 36 districts. It demanded the immediate lifting of the state of emergency and reaffirmed that only the total elimination of *apartheid* and the establishment in South Africa of a free, united, and democratic society on the basis of universal suffrage could lead to a solution of the country's problems.

In November 1986, the council urged all States (resolution 591 [1986]) to prohibit the export to South Africa of items that they have reason to believe are destined for the military and/or police forces of South Africa, have a military capacity, and are intended for military purpose; and to ensure that their national legislation includes provisions for the investigation of violations and circumventions of the arms embargo set out in resolution 418 (1977).

In this connection, the General Assembly on 22 November 1989 again urged the Security Council (resolution 44/27 C) "to consider immediate action under Chapter VII of the Charter of the United Nations with a view to applying comprehensive and mandatory sanctions against the racist regime of South Africa as long as it continues to disregard the demands of the majority of the people of South Africa and of the international community to eradicate *apartheid*."

Shortly thereafter, on 14 December 1989, the assembly, meeting in special session at the headquarters of the United Nations, New York, unanimously adopted the DECLARATION ON *APARTHEID* AND ITS DESTRUCTIVE CONSEQUENCES IN SOUTHERN AFRICA, in which it urged that serious efforts should be made to bring to an end the unacceptable situation prevailing in southern Africa, which is a result of the policies and practices of *apartheid*, through negotiations based on the principle of justice and peace for all.

In addition to the General Assembly and the Security Council, a number of international organizations participate actively in the campaign against *apartheid*. The UN Commission on Human Rights receives and examines, at each annual session, reports and recommendations prepared by its AD HOC WORKING GROUP OF EXPERTS ON SOUTHERN AFRICA as well as by its GROUP OF THREE, established to monitor the implementation of the INTERNATIONAL CONVENTION ON THE SUPPRESSION AND PUNISHMENT OF THE CRIME OF GENOCIDE. The SUB-COMMISSION ON PREVENTION OF DISCRIMINATION AND PROTECTION OF MINORITIES also prepares reports and recommendations on the subject for consideration by the commission.

Among the UN specialized agencies, the INTERNATIONAL LABOR ORGANIZATION and the UNITED NATIONS EDUCATIONAL, SCIENTIFIC AND CULTURAL ORGANIZATION are particularly active in this field; and, among regional intergovernmental bodies, leadership is provided by the ORGANIZATION OF AFRICAN UNITY.

SOUTH WEST AFRICA. *SEE Namibia.*

SOUTH WEST AFRICA PEOPLE'S ORGANIZATION. A liberation movement of the people of NAMIBIA, recognized as such by the ORGANIZATION OF AFRICAN UNITY and by the UN General Assembly, SWAPO participated in the work of the General Assembly and of other United Nations bodies as an observer until Namibia achieved independence on 21 March 1990. Sam Nujoma, SWAPO's leader, was sworn in as Namibia's first president.

SPAIN. The Spanish State is a country in southern Europe occupying 85% of the Iberian Peninsula, on the Atlantic Ocean, the Mediterranean Sea, and the Bay of Biscay; it also includes the Balearic Islands in the Mediterranean and the Canary Islands off the western coast of Africa. It has borders with France and Portugal. It achieved independence in 1492 and became a member of the United Nations in 1955. Its population is estimated by the UN (1990) to be 39,748,000. Ethnic groups include Gypsies, Basques, and Catalonians. Languages in common use include Castilian (official), Basque, Catalan, and Galician; Romany is the language of the Gypsy communities. Christianity (Roman Catholic, 82%) is the predominant religion. Literacy is estimated at 97%.

The government (1990) took the form of a monarchy, headed by the king as head of State. The prime minister, representing the party or coalition given the majority in a popular election, is elected by the Congress of Deputies; he exercises executive power as president of the government. The *Cortes* (parliament) consists of the Congress of Deputies and the Senate; members of both bodies are elected in popular vote. A proportional representation system is used in elections of members of the Congress of Deputies, which has not less than 300 members nor more than 400. In elections of members of the Senate, four senators are selected in each peninsular province, two each are selected by voters in the cities of Ceuta and Melilla, and each autonomous region chooses one or more depending upon the size of its population. The Senate thus has about 200 members. The judiciary includes territorial, provincial, regional and municipal courts, and is headed by the Supreme Tribunal. Judicial authorities are independent of the legislative and executive branches of the government. Political parties include the Spanish Workers' Socialist Party, the Popular Alliance, the Centre Democratic Union, the Social and Democratic Center, the Spanish Communist Party, the Catalonian Party, and the Nationalist Basque Independents.

In elections held in October 1989, Prime Minister Felipe Gonzalez Marquez of the Socialist Workers' Party won a renewed mandate to continue Spain's new democratic tradition and to modernize its economy.

Conquered by Rome in 206 B.C., Spain was a part of the Roman Empire until invaded by Muslims from Africa in 711. Muslim rule continued until the Kingdom of Grenada, its last stronghold, fell to the French in 1492. At that time, Roman Catholicism was established as the official religion and Jews were expelled from the country. By 1500, nearly all Muslims had departed.

With the discovery of America by Columbus in 1492, followed by the conquest of Mexico and Peru, Spain became one of the world's great colonial powers. However, its expansion was abruptly halted in 1588 when its "invincible" Armada was destroyed by British naval vessels, and many of its American outposts were lost during the following centuries.

Neutral during World War I, Spain became a workers' republic in 1931 after King Alphonso XIII had been forced by anti-monarchists to leave the country. Its new constitution disestablished the Catholic Church and secularized the schools. However, in 1936 the army, led by Francisco Franco Bahamonde, mutinied, and its revolt soon developed into a civil war which was fiercely fought for three years and cost the lives of nearly a million people. With the aid of fascist Italy and nazi Germany, Franco's forces finally seized Madrid in March 1939, and Franco was installed as head of State.

Nominally neutral during World War II, Spain maintained close ties with Italy and Germany and remained a totalitarian State after the war concluded. For this and other reasons, its admission to the United Nations was delayed until 1955.

Before he died of a heart attack in November 1975, Franco designated Prince Juan Carlos Alfonso Victor Maria de Bourbon as his successor. Sworn in as king, Juan Carlos quickly ended Spain's fascist institutions and presided over free elections in June 1977. Autonomy was granted to Catalonia and the Basque country in 1980, but the Basque campaign for independence has not ended. Nor has Spain's claim to Gibraltar, held by the British since 1704, been settled.

However, the government in 1990 overturned the decree issued in 1492 by King Ferdinand and Queen Isabella ordering expulsion or conversion of Spain's Jewish population by signing an agreement granting the Jewish and Protestant faiths privileges comparable to those exercised by Roman Catholics. Under the agreement, Jews and Protestants may (a) negotiate with their employers on the observance of religious holidays, (b) receive religious instruction in their own faith in public schools and in the armed forces, (c) observe dietary laws, (d) receive tax and social security benefits, and (e) have their civil marriages recognized as such.

Because there are relatively few non-whites in Spain, racial discrimination is not considered a serious problem. However Arabs from North Africa, illegal immigrants from Argentina and Chile, farm workers from West Africa, and Gypsies often complain of bias due to racist attitudes. The Arabs, numbering about 400,000, and the West Africans, numbering about 150,000, enter the country as migrant workers without visas or work permits, and are shamefully exploited by the farmers who employ them. The Gypsies, traditionally nomadic, suffer as a result of their instability and often need assistance in resolving social and legal problems and in improving their health and in replacing shanty towns by adequate housing units.

Basque separatist movements have operated in Spain for 20 years and are said to have killed about 500 people in their fight for a Basque nation in northern Spain and southern France. For the most part, terrorist attacks have been aimed at government and military targets.

Article 3 of the Spanish constitution states that the wealth of language variations in Spain is a cultural heritage which should be the object of special attention. To meet this goal, teaching in vernacular languages has been introduced in the public schools: Euskera is taught in the Basque country; Catalan, in Catalonia and the Balearic Islands; Galician, in Galicia; and Valencian, in Valencia. The Romany language of the Gypsy community is, however, not taught in the public educational system.

In a report presented to the **COMMITTEE ON THE ELIMINATION OF RACIAL DISCRIMINATION** on 17 July 1985 (UN Doc. CERD/C/118/Add. 29, para. 13–40) the government of Spain presented the following information concerning its Gypsies and the problems encountered with Romany and other vernacular languages:

Gypsies. Royal Decree 250/79 of 11 January established the Interministerial Commission to consider problems affecting the gypsy community, which is still in operation. Its Chairman is the Under-Secretary of the Ministry of Culture.

With regard to the gypsies, many activities have been carried out by special panels covering different fields. Thus, in the area of education, there have been many campaigns for the enrolment of children in school and for adult literacy programmes. Educational action has also been stepped up at the levels of pre-school education, general basic education and vocational training.

In the area of health, there are many provinces in which courses have been given on personal and family hygiene, vaccination campaigns have been conducted or welfare cards have been provided for those gypsies who lack social security.

In the area of housing, most of the activities are designed to eradicate shanty towns. To this end, many housing units have been built under State sponsorship, and used to accommodate members of this group. Campaigns have also been conducted to instruct them in how to use and care for a house so as to obtain maximum benefit from it and foster coexistence with neighbouring non-gypsy communities.

In the social and civic area, the census of the gypsy population in many provinces is significant. In some provinces, free centres for social and legal assistance were provided, and these made it possible to resolve an entire series of irregularities regarding documentation of the gypsies.

To conclude this section, it may be observed that in general, these panels try to undertake any activities which may result in improvements for this minority group.

Regarding the problems of the gypsies, the Spanish Government was asked questions on three points:

(a) Plans for improving the gypsies' situation;

(b) Contents of the report sent to the Council of Ministers by the Chairman of the Interministerial Commission set up to consider the problems of the gypsy community; and

(c) Special measures for increasing the representation of the gypsy population in the civil service.

Regarding the first question, it should be mentioned that the Interministerial Commission set up to consider problems affecting the gypsy community has established, within the Provincial Commissions in each Civil Governor's Office, a special panel for dealing with issues concerning the gypsy community.

The specific purpose of these panels is to carry out a series of actions designed to improve the situation of the gypsy community in the province in question.

Thus measures have been adopted concerning the most urgent problems of this group, such as the elimination of shanty towns through the construction of pre-fabricated housing and State-sponsored housing units where necessary, education through a school enrolment campaign, as a result of which many gypsy children have registered in national educational institutions. Large-scale literacy campaigns have also been carried out for adults and vocational training courses for young people.

In the area of health, there are now a larger number of welfare centres, at which gypsies receive proper medical assistance. Hygiene and sanitary campaigns have also been proposed for the purpose of attempting to improve the health of this group.

Finally, a study has been carried out on the sorts of conflicts gypsies get into for the purpose of discovering and possibly eliminating their causes.

Regarding the second question raised, the report sent to the Council of Ministers by the Chairman of the Interministerial Commission set up to consider problems affecting the gypsy community mentioned a series of actions which the Government is undertaking for the purpose of encouraging the development and promotion of the gypsy people. Among these actions, and by way of conclusion, we may mention the following:

The allocation of funds to the Ministry of Culture in the General State Budget Act of 1981 in order to promote the interests of ethnic minorities;

The public health and sanitary assistance programmes carried out by the Ministry of Labour, Health and Social Security, and the increase of subsidies from the National Social Welfare Fund to gypsy bodies and associations;

In the area of education, a significant agreement was reached between the Ministry of Education and Science and the Episcopal Commission on Emigrations, for the purpose of putting into operation "bridging schools" for gypsy children: the objective of these schools is to prepare gypsy children, through specialized teaching, for integration into ordinary national schools;

A study carried out by the Ministry of Public Works and Town Planning on the housing needs of this group;

Finally, and as part of the general policy for dealing with specific situations, each Ministry has adopted appropriate measures for gradually improving the situation of this group.

With reference to the last question raised, we should like to point out the Government's interest in increasing gypsy representation; to this end article 4 of Royal Decree 250/79, which set up the Interministerial Commission, established within the Commission one or more working groups whose members would include, where appropriate and with the prior agreement of the Commission, representatives of gypsy bodies or associations. The plenary Commission decided that the gypsies should participate in each of the working groups.

Gypsy associations are also being rigorously promoted. An increasing number of such associations are being formed to promote and undertake measures designed to achieve better integration of this ethnic minority into Spanish society.

Romany. The Romany language is not officially included in the educational system. However, the Directorate General of Secondary Education of the Ministry of Education and Science is working on the elimination of all forms of discrimination and paying particular attention to the gypsy race in order to avoid the discrimination situations, which still occur in our schools.

With regard to the Spanish gypsy community's own language, the Directorate General of Secondary Education reports that it has not been introduced at any secondary educational institution in any Self-Governing Community.

Among the reasons which have hindered and are still hindering the adoption of teaching in Romany, mention may be made of the following:

(a) There has not so far been enough demand to make society at large or the national and local authorities feel the need for it;

(b) The gypsy community is scattered in many small groups, which are perhaps not very highly motivated towards regular schooling in their language;

(c) In many cases, schools are far away from the places where members of the gypsy community live;

(d) Members of this community, at least in the past have tended to lead a wandering life;

(e) Properly trained teachers are not available to give instruction in the Romany language.

However, despite what has been said above about the Romany language of the gypsy community in Spain, it should be pointed out that regional languages are all included in the basic educational curriculum. The State lays down a minimum of basic instruction and each Self-Governing Community with its own language includes it in its programmes.

Vernacular Languages. Article 3 of the 1978 Spanish Constitution, after establishing that Castilian is the official language of the State and that the other languages of Spain are also official in the respective Self-Governing Communities, states that the wealth of the different language variations of Spain is a cultural heritage which shall be the object of special attention, respect and protection.

In order to meet this constitutional mandate, in the course of 1979 the nation's education administration, in collaboration with the not-yet self-governing authorities (constituted before approval of the Statutes of Self-Government) introduced teaching in their own languages for those communities which have them, through appropriate legal provisions. To this end, mixed commissions were appointed to supervise the introduction and conduct of such teaching.

Under these legal provisions, which rank as decrees, teaching in the vernacular language was introduced at non-university levels (as far as secondary education is concerned, in the baccalaureate first- and second-degree vocational training and the university preparation course), in the following Self-Governing Communities: Basque Country: Euskera; Catalonia: Catalan, with special attention to Aranés; Galicia: Galician; Valencia: Valencian; Balearic Islands: Catalan, with special attention to all the island variations.

These languages were included in the educational system under similar conditions to Castilian, with regard to their compulsory nature and place in the time-table. However, exemptions were permitted as an exception for those whose circumstances so warranted in the opinion of the local academic authorities.

The necessary material and staff were also supplied, university chairs and lectureships being established to promote better teaching of vernacular languages.

Once the above-mentioned Statutes of Self-Government were approved for these communities through Organizational Laws 3/1979 of 18 December, 4/1979 of 18 December, 1/1981 of 5 April, 5/1982 of 1 July and 2/1983 of 25 February, and the Communities received the services and budgetary allocations they needed in order to perform the functions laid down in their statutes, not just with respect to the teaching of their languages but with respect to all teaching, compliance with article 3 of the Constitution in relation to the teaching and use of vernacular languages has been the responsibility of the respective self-governing authorities.

With regard to the current situation of vernacular teaching, it may generally be stated that:

(a) In all the Self-Governing communities with a vernacular language teaching has been introduced in that language, under conditions similar to those for the Spanish language;

(b) This type of teaching is being expanded in the communities gradually, depending on the extent to which it existed at the outset, the degree of linguistic heterogeneity of the school population, the availability of appropriately trained teachers, etc;

(c) In all of these Self-Governing communities, the programmes have been drawn up in collaboration with the competent linguistic authorities;

(d) University chairs and lectureships have been created in the vernacular language;

(e) In all cases the possibility of exemptions has been provided for in order not to impose vernacular teaching indiscriminately and against their will on pupils whose stay in the Communities may be temporary;

(f) The teaching of historical variations of the same language, when they exist, is respected and encouraged by the local academic authorities;

(g) The Self-Governing Community of Aragon, entirely Castilian-speaking, has authorized teaching in Catalan in the north-eastern area since it is a zone with some remaining bilingualism.

Similarly, many educational institutions in Communities with a strong bilingual component provide secondary teaching in the vernacular language.

Finally, it should be pointed out that although racial discrimination as such is non-existent in our country, an attempt has been made to avoid any type of social discrimination, especially in the area of education, with the enactment of an important piece of legislation. The Royal Decree of 27 April 1983 on compensatory education is a regulation aimed at combating "the inequality of certain people with respect to the educational system owing to their economic capacity, social level or place of residence".

SPAIN: CONSTITUTION. The Spanish Constitution of 1978, passed by the *Cortes Generales* in plenary meetings of the Congress of Deputies and Senate held on 31 October 1978, ratified by the Spanish people in the referendum of 7 December 1978, and sanctioned by the King before the *Cortes* on 27 December 1979, includes the following provisions (articles 9–55) specifically relating to human rights and fundamental freedoms:

Article 9. 1. Citizen and public authorities are bound by the Constitution and all other legal provisions.

2. It is incumbent upon the public authorities to promote conditions which ensure that the freedom and equality of individuals and of the groups to which they belong may be real and effective, to remove the obstacles which prevent or hinder their full enjoyment, and to facilitate the participation of all citizens in political, economic, cultural and social life.

3. The Constitution guarantees the principle of legality, the ranking of legal provisions, the publicity to be given to legal enactments, the non-retroactivity of punitive measures that are unfavourable to or restrict individual rights, the certainty that the rule of law will prevail, the accountability of the public authorities, and the prohibition against arbitrary action on the part of the latter.

Title I
Concerning Fundamental Rights and Duties

Article 10. 1. Human dignity, man's inviolable and inherent rights, the free development of his personality, respect for the law and for the rights of others are fundamental to political order and social peace.

2. The principles relating to the fundamental rights and liberties recognized by the Constitution shall be interpreted in conformity with the Universal Declaration of Human Rights and the international treaties and agreements thereon ratified by Spain.

Chapter One
Concerning Spaniards and Aliens

Article 11. 1. Spanish nationality is acquired, retained and lost in accordance with the provisions of the law.

2. No person of Spanish origin may be deprived of his nationality.

3. The State may negotiate dual-nationality treaties with Latin-American countries or with those which have had or which have special links with Spain. In these countries, Spaniards may become naturalized without losing their nationality of origin, even if said countries do not recognize a reciprocal right in their own citizens.

Article 12. Spaniards legally come of age at eighteen.

Article 13. 1. Aliens shall enjoy the public freedoms guaranteed by the present Title, under the terms to be laid down by treaties and the law.

2. Only Spaniards shall be entitled to the rights recognized in Article 23, except in cases which may be established by treaty or by law concerning the right of active suffrage in municipal elections, in accordance with the principle of reciprocity.

3. Extradition shall be granted only in compliance with a treaty or with the law, on the basis of the principle of reciprocity. Extradition shall be excluded for political offences; but acts of terrorism shall not be regarded as such.

4. The law shall establish the terms under which citizens from other countries and stateless persons may enjoy the right of asylum in Spain.

Chapter Two
Concerning Rights and Liberties

Article 14. Spaniards are equal before the law and may not in any way be discriminated against on account of birth, race, sex, religion, opinion or any other condition or personal or social circumstance.

Section 1—Concerning Fundamental Rights and Public Liberties

Article 15. All have the right to life and to physical and moral integrity, and may under no circumstances be subjected to torture or to inhuman or degrading punishment or treatment. The death penalty shall be abolished, except as provided for by military criminal law in time of war.

Article 16. 1. Freedom of ideology, religion and worship of individuals and communities is guaranteed, with no other restriction on their expression as may be necessary to maintain public order as protected by law.

2. Nobody may be compelled to make statements regarding his religion, beliefs or ideologies.

3. There shall be no State religion. The public authorities shall take the religious beliefs of Spanish society into account and shall in consequence maintain appropriate

co-operation with the Catholic Church and the other confessions.

Article 17. 1. Every person has a right to freedom and security. Nobody may be deprived of his freedom except in accordance with the provisions of this article and in the cases and in the manner provided by the law.

2. Preventive detention may last no longer than the time strictly required in order to carry out the necessary investigations aimed at establishing the facts; in any case the person arrested must be set free or handed over to the judicial authorities within a maximum period of seventy-two hours.

3. Any person arrested must be informed immediately, and in a manner understandable to him, of his rights and of the grounds for his arrest, and may not be compelled to make a statement. The arrested person shall be guaranteed the assistance of a lawyer during the police enquiries or judicial investigation, under the terms to be laid down by the law.

4. A *habeas corpus* procedure shall be regulated by law in order to ensure the immediate handing over to the judicial authorities of any person arrested illegally. Likewise, the maximum period of provisional imprisonment shall be stipulated by law.

Article 18. 1. The right to honour, to personal and family privacy and to personal reputation is guaranteed.

2. The home is inviolable. No entry or search may be made without the consent of the occupant or under a legal warrant, except in cases of *flagrante delicto.*

3. Secrecy of communications is guaranteed, particularly of postal, telegraphic and telephonic communications, except in the event of a court order to the contrary.

4. The law shall limit the use of data processing in order to guarantee the honour and personal and family privacy of citizens and the full exercise of their rights.

Article 19. Spaniards have the right to choose their place of residence freely, and to move about freely within the national territory.

Likewise, they have the right to freely enter and leave Spain subject to the terms to be laid down by the law. This right may not be restricted for political or ideological reasons.

Article 20. 1. The following rights are recognized and protected:

(a) the right to freely express and disseminate thoughts, ideas and opinions by word, in writing or by any other means of communication;

(b) the right to literary, artistic, scientific and technical production and creation;

(c) the right to academic freedom;

(d) the right to freely communicate or receive accurate information by any means of dissemination whatsoever. The law shall regulate the right to invoke personal conscience and professional secrecy in the exercise of these freedoms.

2. The exercise of these rights may not be restricted by any form of prior censorship.

3. The law shall regulate the organization and parliamentary control of the social communications media under the control of the State or any public agency and shall guarantee access to such media to the main social and political groups, respecting the pluralism of society and of the various languages of Spain.

4. These freedoms are limited by respect for the rights recognized in this Title, by the legal provisions implementing it, and especially by the right to honour, to privacy, to personal reputation and to the protection of youth and childhood.

5. The confiscation of publications and recordings and other information media may only be carried out by means of a court order.

Article 21. 1. The right to peaceful assembly without arms is recognized. The exercise of this right shall not require prior authorization.

2. In the case of meetings in public places and of demonstrations, prior notification shall be given to the authorities, who may ban them only when there are well-founded grounds to expect a breach of public order, involving danger to persons or property.

Article 22. 1. The right of association is recognized.

2. Associations which pursue ends or use means classified as criminal offences are illegal.

3. Associations set up on the basis of this article must be recorded in a register for the sole purpose of public knowledge.

4. The associations may only be dissolved or have their activities suspended by virtue of a considered court order.

5. Secret and para-military associations are prohibited.

Article 23. 1. Citizens have the right to participate in public affairs, directly or through their representatives freely elected in periodic elections by universal suffrage.

2. They likewise have the right to access on equal terms to public office, in accordance with the requirements to be provided by law.

Article 24. 1. Every person has the right to obtain the effective protection of the Judges and the Courts in the exercise of his legitimate rights and interests, and in no case may he go undefended.

2. Likewise, all persons have the right of access to the Ordinary Judge predetermined by law; to the defence and assistance of a lawyer; to be informed of the charges brought against them; to a public trial without undue delays and with full guarantees; to the use of the evidence pertinent to their defence; to not make self-incriminating statements; to not declare themselves guilty; and to the presumption of innocence.

The law shall determine the cases in which, for reasons of family relationship or professional secrecy, it shall not be compulsory to make statements regarding alleged criminal offences.

Article 25. 1. No-one may be convicted or sentenced for any act or omission which at the time it was committed did not constitute a felony, misdemeanour or administrative offence according to the law in force at that time.

2. Punishments entailing imprisonment and security measures shall be aimed at rehabilitation and social reintegration and may not consist of forced labour. The person sentenced to a term of imprisonment shall, while serving it, enjoy the fundamental rights contained in this Chapter except those expressly limited by the terms of the sentence, the purpose of the punishment and the penal law. In any case, he shall be entitled to paid employment and to the appropriate Social Security benefits, as well as to access to cultural opportunities and the over-all development of his personality.

3. The Civil Administration may not impose penalties which directly or indirectly imply deprivation of freedom.

Article 26. Courts of Honour are prohibited in the sphere of the Civil Administration and of professional associations.

Article 27. 1. Everyone is entitled to education. Freedom of instruction is recognized.

2. Education shall have as its objective the full development of the human character compatible with respect for

the democratic principles of co-existence and for the basic rights and freedoms.

3. The public authorities guarantee the right of parents to ensure that their children receive religious and moral instruction that is in accordance with their own convictions.

4. Elementary education is compulsory and free.

5. The public authorities guarantee the right of everyone to education, through general planning of education, with the effective participation of all parties concerned and the setting up of teaching establishments.

6. The right of individuals and legal entities to set up teaching establishments is recognized, provided they respect Constitutional principles.

7. Teachers, parents and, when appropriate, pupils, shall share in the control and management of all the centres maintained by the Administration out of public funds, under the terms to be laid down by the law.

8. The public authorities shall inspect and standardize the educational system in order to guarantee compliance with the law.

9. The public authorities shall give aid to teaching establishments which meet the requirements to be laid down by the law.

10. The autonomy of the Universities is recognized, under the terms to be laid down by the law.

Article 28. 1. Everyone has the right to freely join a trade union. The law may limit the exercise of this right or make an exception to it in the case of the Armed Forces or Institutes or other bodies subject to military discipline, and shall regulate the special features of its exercise by civil servants. Trade union freedom includes the right to found trade unions and to join the union of one's choice, as well as the right of the trade unions to form confederations and to found international trade union organizations, or to become members thereof. Nobody may be compelled to join a trade union.

2. The right of workers to strike in defence of their interests is recognized. The law regulating the exercise of this right shall establish the guarantees necessary to ensure the maintenance of essential community services.

Article 29. 1. All Spaniards shall have the right to individual and collective petition, in writing, in the manner and subject to the consequences to be prescribed by law.

2. Members of the Armed Forces or Institutes or bodies subject to military discipline may only exercise this right individually and in accordance with the provisions of the legislation pertaining to them.

Section 2—Concerning the Rights and Duties of Citizens

Article 30 1. Citizens have the right and the duty to defend Spain.

2. The law shall determine the military obligations of Spaniards and shall regulate, with the proper safeguards, conscientious objection as well as other grounds for exemption from compulsory military service; it may also, when appropriate, impose a form of social service in lieu thereof.

3. A civilian service may be established with a view to accomplishing objectives of general concern.

4. The duties of citizens in the event of grave risk, catastrophe or public calamity may be regulated by law.

Article 31. 1. Everyone shall contribute to the public expenditure in proportion to his financial means, through a just and progressive system of taxation based on principles of equality, which shall in no case be confiscatory in character.

2. Public expenditure shall be incurred in such a way that an equitable allocation of public resources may be achieved, and its planning and execution shall comply with criteria of efficiency and economy.

3. Personal or property contributions for public purposes may only be imposed in accordance with the law.

Article 32. 1. Men and women are entitled to marry on a basis of full legal equality.

2. The law shall regulate the forms of marriage, the age at which it may be entered into and the required capacity therefor, the rights and duties of the spouses, the grounds for separation and dissolution, and the consequences thereof.

Article 33. 1. Private property and inheritance rights are recognized.

2. The content of these rights shall be determined by the social function which they fulfil, in accordance with the law.

3. No-one may be deprived of his property and rights, except on justified grounds of public utility or social interest against proper compensation in accordance with the provisions of the law.

Article 34. 1. The right to set up foundations for purposes of general interest is recognized, in conformity with the law.

2. The provisions of clauses 2 and 4 of Article 22 shall also be applicable to foundations.

Article 35. 1. All Spaniards have the duty to work and the right to employment, to free choice of profession or trade, to advancement through their work, and to sufficient remuneration for the satisfaction of their needs and those of their families; moreover, under no circumstances may they be discriminated against on account of their sex.

2. The law shall establish a Worker's Statute.

Article 36. The law shall regulate the special features of the legal status of the Professional Colleges and the exercise of the degree professions. The internal structure and operation of the Colleges must be democratic.

Article 37. 1. The law shall guarantee the right to collective labour bargaining between workers' and employers' representatives, as well as the binding force of the agreements.

2. The law recognizes the right of workers and employers to adopt collective labour dispute measures. The law regulating the exercise of this right shall, without prejudice to the restrictions which it may establish, include the safeguards necessary to ensure the operation of essential community services.

Article 38. Free enterprise is recognized within the framework of a market economy. The public authorities shall guarantee and protect its exercise and the safeguarding of productivity in accordance with the demands of the economy in general and, as the case may be, of its planning.

Chapter Three
Concerning the Governing Principles
of Economic and Social Policy

Article 39. 1. The public authorities shall ensure the social, economic and legal protection of the family.

2. The public authorities likewise shall ensure full protection of children, who shall be equal before the law, irrespective of their parentage, and of mothers, whatever their marital status. The law shall provide for the investigation of paternity.

3. Parents must provide their children, whether born within or outside wedlock, with assistance of every kind while they are still under age and in other circumstances in which the law is applicable.

4. Children shall enjoy the protection provided for in the international agreements which safeguard their rights.

Article 40. 1. The public authorities shall promote favourable conditions for social and economic progress and for a more equitable distribution of personal and regional income within the framework of a policy of economic stability. They shall devote special attention to carrying out a policy directed towards full employment.

2. Likewise, the public authorities shall foster a policy guaranteeing vocational training and retraining; they shall ensure labour safety and hygiene and shall guarantee adequate rest by means of a limited working day, periodic paid holidays, and the promotion of appropriate centres.

Article 41. The public authorities shall maintain a public Social Security system for all citizens which will guarantee adequate social assistance and benefits in needy situations, especially in cases of unemployment. Supplementary assistance and benefits shall be optional.

Article 42. The State shall be especially concerned with safeguarding the economic and social rights of Spanish workers abroad, and shall direct its policy towards securing their return.

Article 43. 1. The right to protection of health is recognized.

2. It is incumbent upon the public authorities to organize and safeguard public health by means of preventive measures and the necessary benefits and services. The law shall establish the rights and duties of all concerned in this respect.

3. The public authorities shall foster health education, physical education and sports. Likewise, they shall encourage the proper use of leisure.

Article 44. 1. The public authorities shall promote and protect access to cultural opportunities, to which all are entitled.

2. The public authorities shall promote science and scientific and technical research in the general interest.

Article 45. 1. Everyone has the right to enjoy an environment suitable for personal development, as well as the duty to preserve it.

2. The public authorities shall safeguard a rational use of all the natural resources with a view to protecting and improving the quality of life and preserving and restoring the environment, by relying on essential public co-operation.

3. Criminal or, where applicable, administrative sanctions, as well as the obligation to make good the damage, shall be imposed, under the terms to be laid down by the law, against those who violate the provisions contained in the foregoing clause.

Article 46. The public authorities shall guarantee the reservation and promote the enrichment of the historic, cultural and artistic heritage of the peoples of Spain and of the property of which it consists, whatsoever its legal status and to whomsoever it may belong. Offences committed against this heritage shall be punished under criminal law.

Article 47. All Spaniards are entitled to enjoy decent and adequate housing. The public authorities shall promote the necessary conditions and shall establish appropriate standards in order to make this right effective, regulating land use in accordance with the general interest in order to prevent speculation.

The community shall participate in the benefits accruing from the town planning policies of the public bodies.

Article 48. The public authorities shall promote conditions directed towards the free and effective participation of young people in political, social, economic and cultural development.

Article 49. The public authorities shall carry out a policy of preventive care, treatment, rehabilitation and integration of the physically and mentally handicapped and those with sensory disabilities—who shall be given the specialized care that they require, and shall afford them special protection in order that they may enjoy the rights conferred by this Title upon all citizens.

Article 50. The public authorities shall guarantee, through adequate and periodically updated pensions, sufficient financial means for citizens during old age. Likewise, and independently of the obligations of their families towards them, they shall promote their welfare through a system of social services which shall provide for their specific problems of health, housing, culture and leisure.

Article 51. 1. The public authorities shall guarantee the protection of consumers and users and shall, by means of effective measures, safeguard their safety, health and legitimate economic interests.

2. The public authorities shall make means available to inform and educate consumer and users, shall encourage their organizations, and shall provide hearings for such organizations on all matters affecting their members, under the terms to be established by law.

3. Within the framework of the provisions of the foregoing clauses, the law shall regulate domestic trade and the system of permits for commercial products.

Article 52. The law shall regulate the professional organizations which contribute to the defence of the economic interests pertaining to them. Their internal structure and operation must be democratic.

Chapter Four
Concerning the Guaranteeing of Fundamental Rights and Liberties

Article 53. 1. The rights and liberties recognized in Chapter Two of the present Title are binding on all public authorities. The exercise of such rights and liberties, which shall be protected in accordance with the provisions of Article 161, 1a), may be regulated only by law which shall, in any case, respect their essential content.

2. Any citizen may assert his claim to the protection of the liberties and rights recognized in Article 14 and in Section 1 of Chapter Two, by means of a referential and summary procedure in the Ordinary Courts and, when appropriate, by submitting an individual appeal for protection ("recurso de amparo") to the Constitutional Court. This latter procedure shall be applicable to conscientious objections as recognized in Article 30.

3. The substantive legislation, judicial practice and actions of the public authorities shall be based on the acknowledgment, respect and protection of the principles recognized in Chapter Three. The latter may only be invoked in the Ordinary Courts in the context of the legal provisions by which they are developed.

Article 54. An organic law shall regulate the institution of Defender of the People, who shall be a high commissioner of the Cortes Generales, appointed by them to defend the rights contained in this Title; for this purpose he may supervise Administration activities and report thereon to the Cortes Generales.

Chapter Five
Concerning the Suspension of Rights and Liberties

Article 55. 1. The rights recognized in Articles 17 and 18, clauses 2 and 3, Articles 19 and 20, clause 1, sub-clauses a) and d) and clause 5, Articles 21 and 28, clause 2, and Article 37, clause 2, may be suspended when the proclamation of a state of emergency or siege (martial law) is decided upon under the terms provided in the Constitution. Clause 3 of Article 17 is excepted from the foregoing provisions in the event of the proclamation of a state of emergency.

2. An organic law may determine the manner and the circumstances in which, on an individual basis and with the necessary participation of the Courts and proper Parliamentary control, the rights recognized in Articles 17, clause 2, and 18, clauses 2 and 3, may be suspended as regards specific persons in connection with investigations of the activities of armed bands or terrorist groups.

Unjustified or abusive use of the powers recognized in the foregoing organic law shall give rise to criminal liability inasmuch as it is a violation of the rights and liberties recognized by the law.

SPECIAL COMMITTEE AGAINST *APARTHEID*. On 6 November 1962, the UN General Assembly established the Special Committee on the Policies of *Apartheid* of the Government of the Republic of South Africa (resolution 1761 [XVII]), which it re-named the Special Committee on *Apartheid* in 1970 and Special Committee against *Apartheid* in 1975.

The special committee has a broad mandate to keep the racial policies of South Africa under constant review. The committee hears petitioners, studies relevant communications and documents, and occasionally sends delegations composed of its members to States bordering South Africa and Namibia to obtain first-hand information on acts of aggression, terrorism, or destabilization directed against those "frontline" States, to consult with the governments concerned on possible action, and to publicize the situation and promote political and material assistance to those States.

The special committee is composed of 19 States: Algeria, the former German Democratic Republic, Ghana, Guinea, Haiti, Hungary, India, Indonesia, Malaysia, Nepal, Nigeria, Peru, Philippines, Somalia, Sudan, Syria, Trinidad and Tobago, the Ukrainian Soviet Socialist Republic, and Zimbabwe. The members' term of office is indeterminate. The committee holds meetings throughout the year, as required. Normally it does not meet, except in cases of emergency, when the General Assembly is in session. The committee submits regular and special reports to the General Assembly and the Security Council.

The special committee is assisted in its work by two

sub-committees and three task forces. As at 1 January 1989, the composition and membership of these subsidiary bodies was as follows: (a) Sub-Committee on the Implementation of United Nations Resolutions and Collaboration with South Africa: Ghana (Chairman), Hungary, India, Indonesia, Peru, and Sudan; (b) Sub-Committee on Petitions and Information: Algeria (Chairman), German Democratic Republic, Nepal, Somalia, and Trinidad and Tobago; (c) Task Force on Women and Children under *Apartheid*: India, Philippines, Sudan (Chairman), and Trinidad and Tobago; (d) Task Force on Political Prisoners: German Democratic Republic, Guinea, India, Malaysia, Peru (Chairman), Somalia, and Syria; and (e) Task Force on the Legal Aspects of *Apartheid*: Hungary, Nigeria (Chairman), Peru, and Syria.

In addition, the special committee works closely with the Intergovernmental Group to Monitor the Supply and Shipping of Oil and Petroleum Products to South Africa, composed of Algeria, Cuba, the former German Democratic Republic, Indonesia, Kuwait (vice chairman), New Zealand, Nicaragua, Nigeria, Norway (chairman), the Ukrainian S.S.R., and the United Republic of Tanzania; with the COMMISSION AGAINST *APARTHEID* IN SPORTS; and with the Support Group of Eminent Women.

In its report to the UN General Assembly and Security Council covering the period from August 1988 to August 1989 (UN Doc. A/44/22), the special committee summarized developments in South Africa in that period (chap. II), analyzed the situation of the South African economy and the effect of sanctions on it (chap. III), reviewed the international, national, and local action taken with a view to putting an end to *apartheid* (chap. IV), and evaluated the effects of its own activities in the field (chap. V). On the basis of this information, it presented to its parent bodies the following conclusions and recommendations (chap. VI, para. 255–275):

Despite a number of developments, the situation in South Africa remains, in essence, as grim as ever and the state of emergency has been renewed for the fourth consecutive year. After a year of continued resistance to repression, culminating in the recent Defiance Campaign, it has become clear that the new leadership of Pretoria is facing a formidable domestic and international challenge. The black majority, through the national liberation movements and the Mass Democratic Movement, and supported by an increasing portion of the white population, have shown that neither the permanent state of emergency nor the efforts of co-option will suppress their quest for freedom and equality. The international community after a brief "wait-and-see" period is expecting initiatives for real change in South Africa.

The régime cannot any longer repackage with immunity the tenets of *apartheid* by promising the future end of white domination, while at the same time denying equality to all

South African citizens. It would have to take substantive steps towards a fundamental change which, through negotiations, will lead to the eradication of *apartheid* in all its forms and the establishment of a democratic and non-racial society. In this regard, the recent declaration of the OAU *Ad Hoc* Committee on Southern Africa on the Question of South Africa provides a blueprint that appears to be amassing increasing international support.

It is not, however, clear that this imperative has been fully understood by Pretoria. Despite recent developments in Namibia regarding the implementation of the Security Council resolution 435 (1978) and despite pronouncements and diplomatic activities, even under the new leadership of Mr. de Klerk, Pretoria has continued to suppress with savagery any peaceful opposition to its policies.

While Mr. de Klerk made pronouncements about the advent of peace and prosperity for all South Africans, the security forces and the arsenal of security laws were used to suppress the anti-*apartheid* opposition. The growing Defiance Campaign organized by the Mass Democratic Movement against not only *apartheid* laws but also the racially segregated elections of 6 September suffered the brunt of the repression. The death of more than 20 protestors, among them children and elderly women, the increasing number of injuries and the more than 1,500 arrests all constitute evidence of the régime's lack of intention to engage in a genuine process of political negotiations with the anti-*apartheid* opposition.

The exclusion of the black majority from the elections to the racially segregated tricameral Parliament intrinsically denies the demands of the black majority for full political rights. It indicates that the régime intends to implement its political "reform" programme for blacks through repression and regardless of the oposition to it.

The widespread boycott of the elections within the Coloured and Indian communities shows once more that most of the Coloureds and Indians, as part of the black majority, reject the Parliament as it is presently constituted. Furthermore, the reduced majority of the National Party and gains made by the liberal Democratic Party suggest that the National Party monolith is gradually eroding, an important development for any future negotiations. The results of the elections, according to Mr. de Klerk, are a mandate for "reforms". But the "reforms" he has espoused in the past in the Five-Year Plan of Action have been not only vague but, more important, a refurbished version of white domination concealed in the rhetoric of "group rights" and "power sharing". In effect, Pretoria is purporting under the group concept to ensure the veto power of whites. Such a programme is no answer to the country's severe political, economic and social conflict.

As recent protests suggest, the opposition to *apartheid* is undiminished and has re-emerged with a new strength. Despite the state of emergency and the bans and restrictions placed on many black leaders and organizations, the Mass Democratic Movement's Defiance Campaign has had a remarkable impact. It was significant that on election day more than 3 million workers and students stayed at home. This growing resistance shows that any effort by the régime to co-opt "moderate" blacks into its constitutional programme will be rejected by the black majority, thereby increasing the possibility of further violent conflict in the country. Only when Mr. de Klerk makes tangible his plans for a democratic society will he be able to convince his oponents both within and outside South Africa that he is serious about a process of fundamental change in the country.

Under the circumstances, the international community has two options: it can take no further action and adopt no new sanctions, thus maintaining a lifeline to *apartheid* and allowing Mr. de Klerk to proceed with his paced "reforms"; or it can step up the pressure, either by adopting comprehensive and mandatory sanctions or by imposing concerted and strictly monitored sanctions on the vulnerable areas of the South African economy, until Pretoria resists no further the need for genuine negotiations. The first option will undoubtedly lead to a deepening of the conflict and further bloodshed and suffering for South Africans and ominous consequences for southern Africa and the world. The second option would lead to a peaceful and prompt end of *apartheid*.

Despite claims made by Pretoria, present sanctions, even if their implementation, monitoring and enforcement has been uncoordinated and lax, have had a serious impact on the economy and have increased the isolation of the white minority. Experts' studies show that sanctions have contributed to slow rates of growth, adding to the chronic structural difficulties of the South African economy. The combined effects of disinvestment, the dearth of new capital investment and the denial of long-term credit have all contributed to undermining South Africa's ability to impose its designs both within and outside its borders. In view of the fact that South Africa remains extremely dependent on the rest of the world for its economic viability, the denial of external trade, transport facilities, foreign financing, foreign technology and expertice remain crucial fro the demise of *apartheid*.

Sanctions do indeed work, as is evident in the mandatory arms embargo, which, in spite of violations, has prevented South Africa from obtaining modern weapons systems, particularly aircraft, a fact that contributed to Pretoria's retreat from Namibia, and in the oil embargo, which has cost Pretoria $25 billion over the past 10 years. Furthermore, the sports and cultural boycotts have increased the sense of isolation of South Africa.

While the vunerability of the economy is clear, measures adopted by those countries imposing sanctions have been inadequate to the objective. South Africa continues to be able to purchase oil and petroleum products, at a premium price, and has managed to expand parts of its armaments production and has even attempted to secure markets for them, as manifested in its participation in armaments fairs in Chile and Turkey. Likewise, South Africa's external trade continues to thrive as a result of uncoordinated sanctions, the loopholes within sanctions and the eagerness of some smaller countries to expand their trade with South Africa and to take advantage of restrictions imposed by other States. While the Nordic States are in the forefront of those that have curtailed trade with South Africa, the Federal Republic of Germany surpassed Japan and has become the first trading partner of South Africa. At the same time, a disturbing shift in regional trade is taking place. Some Far Eastern and Western European States are increasing trade with Pretoria, thus undermining the positive action undertaken by other States. To note, Taiwan, province of China, Hong Kong, the United Kingdom, Turkey, Switzerland, Spain, Portugal, Belgium/Luxembourg and France showed significant increases in trade.

A grave concern to the international community should be in the many reported violations of the mandatory arms embargo which allow Pretoria to pursue its armaments production and to increase its export of armaments through third-party States. In this respect, the most serious violations were reported in Chile, Turkey and the Federal Republic of Germany. In the same vein, the continued collaboration of the government of Israel with South Africa is providing missile technology that is assisting the régime in developing a missile delivery capability.

While the disinvestment campaign has succeeded from the point of view of cutting off new investment capital to South Africa, the mode of disinvestment used by the majority of transnational corporations continues to provide the domestic South African companies with invaluable access to technology, managerial know-how and foreign markets. It is disquieting that the rate of disinvestment from South Africa fell in 1988 compared to the previous year. The retention of non-equity links by more than half of the disinvesting companies allows a flow of licensing and franchise fees to the transnational corporations as well as technology and other skills to South African companies. Non-racial trade unions in South africa have developed guidelines for a fair disinvestment procedure which provide for advance notice, disclosure-of-sale agreement and negotiations between transnational corporations and the relevant trade union on the terms of disinvestment.

As the Commonwealth Committee of Foreign Ministers on Southern Africa concluded, financial sanctions are one of the most effective forms of presure on Pretoria. With an estimated $8.5 billion due for repayment in June 1990, the most important economic constraint facing Pretoria is the need to reschedule payment of its foreign debt, given its reduced access to international capital markets and its more than $1.2 billion losses on foreign exchange. Since short term trade credits, which are still provided by several States, serve to ease the foreign exchange constraints of South Africa, the terms of repayment of the debt next year assume critical importance. The transnational banks should require the normal full payment of the outstanding debt in June 1990. Rescheduling will be construed as a sign of confidence of the banks in the financial and political stability of South Africa and could be interpreted as an endorsement of the *apartheid* régime.

The Special Committee considers that in order to achieve maximum effectiveness sanctions should be mandatory and comprehensive. Pending appropriate action by the Security Council, further sanctions must target explicitly the main areas of dependence and vunerability of the South African economy. Sanctions must be adopted in unison and must be strictly monitored and enforced. The Committee believes that targeted measures could have a significant impact on South Africa by increasing the economic hardship on the white constituency and structures that support *apartheid*. This growing hardship could help persuade the régime to create a climate conducive to negotiations.

Accordingly, the targeted measures should include: non-rescheduling of debt payment, a prohibition by all States of new loans and investments of any sort to South Africa; a ban on the importation of all South African agricultural products; a ban on the importation of all non-strategic South African minerals, including coal, gold, base metals, iron ore, uranium and non-metallic minerals; a restriction on trade credits for sales to South Africa, including both buyers' and suppliers' credits; a ban on the transfer of technology that allows South Africa to circumvent current sanctions, in particular in the areas of arms, oil and computers; a prohibition of the sale of all computers, software and electronic and communication equipment; the imposition of tighter restrictions on the re-export to South Africa of strategic goods and technology, either directly or included in other products; and the extension of the ban on air links to all States other than those in the SADCC region.

A powerful weapon against the régime would be the imposition of a mandatory oil embargo and, short of that, a widening and tightening of the current voluntary oil embargo. As recent events in southern Africa have shown, the mandatory arms embargo, despite its weaknesses, is of extreme significance and should be monitored and enforced more strictly. In addition, all sanctions should apply to South African-controlled firms to prevent them from assisting Pretoria in evading sanctions.

The effectiveness of the above-mentioned measures lies in the willingness of all States to co-ordinae the imposition, monitoring and enforcement of these measures. In addition, such measures must be adopted with speed to prevent South Africa from adapting to new and changing trading partners and conditions. In that context, the Special Committee welcomes existing proposals aimed at the monitoring and enforcement of sanctions of all types. Measures should also be adopted to prevent States from benefiting from the vacuum created by other States that have imposed sanctions. Information on violations of sanctions and economic links with South Africa should be widely publicized, particularly concerning the arms and oil embargoes.

While there are initiatives concerning the region, the impasse continues in South Africa. As long as Pretoria clings to *apartheid* in any form and is unwilling to create a climate conducive to negotiations, a peaceful resolution of the political conflict in South Africa shall remain elusive. Already in 1986 the Commonwealth Group of Eminent Persons concluded that "the South African Government is concerned about the adoption of effective economic measures against it. If it comes to the conclusion that it would always remain protected from such measures, the process of change in South Africa is unlikely to increase in momentum and the descent into violence would be accelerated". The urgent task confronting the international community is now to make sanctions effective by targeting the key areas of the highly vunerable South African ecconomy.

The liberation struggle and international pressure, which is facilitated by recent positive developments in the world political scene, have opened new possibilities for a prompt and peaceful end to *apartheid*. Intensified and co-ordinated pressure by the international community can induce Pretoria to take the steps conducive to a climate for negotiations as spelled out by the General Assembly, OAU and the Movement of Non-Aligned Countries. It would finally bring about a system that has been a cause of profound embarassment to our civilization and of much suffering to the people of southern Africa.

In view of the above, the Special Committee recommends to the General Assembly that it:

(a) Reaffirm its condemnation of the *apartheid* system and the régime's acts of repression, aggression, destabilization and terrorism;

(b) Reiterate that concerned measures should be intensified now to bring a speedy end to the *apartheid* system in the interest of all the people of South Africa and the region;

(c) Reaffirm the legitimacy of the struggle of the black majority of South Africa and its white allies for the total eradication of *apartheid* and for the establishment of a united, non-racial, democratic society in which all the people, irrespective of race, colour or creed, enjoy the same fundamental freedoms and human rights;

(d) Reaffirm its full support to the national liberation movements, the African National Congress of South Africa and the Pan Africanist Congress of Azania, which pursue their noble objectives of eliminating *apartheid* through political, armed and other forms of struggle;

(e) Demand that Pretoria annul the capital punishment imposed on opponents of *apartheid,* including the "Upington 14" and abide by the Geneva Convention of 12 August 1949 and Additional Protocol I of 1977, which accord prisoner-of-war status to captured fighters;

(f) Support the efforts of the majority of the people of South Africa to arrive at a political settlement through genuine negotiations;

(g) Call upon the present régime of South Africa to create the necessary climate for negotiations by:

(i) Lifting the state of emergency;

(ii) Unconditionally releasing Nelson Mandela and all other political prisoners and detainees;

(iii) Lifting the ban on individual and political organizations opposing *apartheid* and repealing press restrictions;

(iv) Withdrawing the troops from black townships;

(v) Ceasing all political trials and executions;

(h) Urge the Security Council to take immediate action under Chapter VII of the Charter of the United Nations with a view to applying comprehensive and mandatory sanctions against the régime as long as it continues to disregard the above demands of the international community;

(i) Urge the Security Council to take concrete steps for the strict implementation of the mandatory arms embargo imposed by its resolutions 418 (1977) and 588 (1984) in order to bring an end to the continued violations of the arms embargo, and strongly urge those States which directly or indirectly infringe the arms embargo and continue to collaborate with South Africa in the military intelligence and technology fields to eliminate forthwith such acts;

(j) Call upon all States, pending the adoption of comprehensive and mandatory sanctions:

(i) To impose embargoes on the supply of oil; petroleum products and oil technology; investments, loans and credits; computer and communication equipment and other high-technology products which may have military application;

(ii) To prohibit the import of coal, gold, other minerals and agricultural products from South Africa;

(iii) To introduce transnational corporations, banks and financial institutions to withdraw effectively from South Africa by ceasing equity investment and cutting off non-equity links, particularly those involving transfer of high technology and know-how

(iv) To deny landing and port rights to South African air and sea carriers and to sever direct transport links with South Africa;

(v) To monitor strictly the implementation of the above measures and adopt, when necessary, legislation providing for penalties on individuals and enterprises violating those merasures;

(k) Urge governmental and private financial institutions to refrain from rescheduling South Africa's foreign debt and terminate any financial support or favourable treatment of South Africa as long as *apartheid* prevails in that country;

(l) Urge Governments and non-governmental organizations to take appropriate measures to ensure the effectiveness of the cultural and sports boycott in accordance with the policies of the United Nations on the cultural and sports isolation of *apartheid* South Africa;

(m) Call upon Governments, intergovernmental and non-governmental organizations and individuals to extend all possible assistance to the struggling people of South Africa, their national liberation movements, South African refugees, particularly women and children, as well as to the front-line States, that are subject to South Africa's destabilization;

(n) Authorize the Special Committee against *Apartheid,* in accordance with its mandate and acting as a focal point, with the support services of the Centre against *Apartheid,* (i) to continue monitoring closely the situation in South Africa and the actions of the international community, particularly regarding the imposition and implementation of sanctions and their impact on *apartheid* South Africa; (ii) to continue mobilizing international action against *apartheid, inter alia,* through collation, analysis and dissemination of information, liaison with non-governmental organizations and relevant individuals and groups able to influence public opinion and decision-making, as well as through hearings, conferences, consultations, missions, publicity and other relevant activities;

(o) Request the Secretary-General to ensure the co-ordination of activities of the United Nations system regarding the struggle against *apartheid* and the support of the oppressed people of South Africa and to undertake appropriate initiatives to facilitate all efforts leading to the peaceful eradication of *apartheid;*

(p) Appeal to all Governments, intergovernmental and non-governmental organizations, information media and individuals to co-operate with the Centre against *Apartheid* and the Department of Public Information of the Secretariat in their respective activities against *Apartheid,* and in particular in monitoring developments concerning international action against *Apartheid* and in disseminating information on the situation in South Africa.

After examining the special committee's report, the General Assembly on 22 November 1989 took note of it and endorsed the recommendations (resolution 44/27 G). The assembly commended the special committee for its work and authorized it (a) to monitor closely the situation in South Africa and the international community regarding the imposition and implementation of sanctions and other restrictive measures and their impact on *apartheid* in South Africa, and (b) to mobilize international action against *apartheid, inter alia* through the collection, analysis, and dissemination of information; through liaison with non-governmental organizations and relevant individuals and groups able to influence public opinion and decisionmaking; and through hearings, conferences, consultations, missions, publicity and other relevant activities. The assembly, further, appealed to all governments and intergovernmental and non-governmental organizations to increase their cooperation with the special committee, and requested all United Nations bodies to assist it and the Center against *Apatheid* in their activities.

SEE ALSO Apartheid *entries; South Africa: UN Concern about* Apartheid

SPECIAL COMMITTEE ON THE SITUATION WITH REGARD TO THE IMPLEMENTATION OF THE DECLARATION ON THE GRANTING OF INDEPENDENCE TO COLONIAL COUNTRIES AND PEOPLES.

Known informally as the Special Committee on Decolonization, the special committee was established by the UN General Assembly on 27 November 1961 (resolution 1654 [XVI]) to promote realization of the DECLARATION ON THE GRANTING OF INDEPENDENCE TO COLONIAL COUNTRIES AND PEOPLES, which the assembly had adopted and proclaimed on 14 December 1960 (resolution 1514 [XV]).

Originally, the special committee was authorized only to follow developments concerning the declaration and to make suggestions and recommendations on the progress and extent of its implementation. Later, however, after the General Assembly dissolved other bodies which it had created to deal with decolonization questions—including the Special Committee on Territories under Portuguese Administration, the Committee on Information from Non-Self-Governing Territories, and the Special Committee on South West Africa—it called upon the new special committee to take over their tasks. A number of new functions was added to its mandate; these, as summarized in GA resolution 41/41 of 2 December 1986, include the request that the special committee continue to seek suitable means for the immediate and full granting of independence to all remaining colonies and territories and, in particular:

(a) to formulate specific proposals for the elimination of the remaining manifestations of colonialism and to report thereon to the General Assembly at its 42d session;

(b) to make concrete suggestions which could assist the Security Council in considering appropriate measures under the Charter with regard to developments in colonial Territories that are likely to pose a threat to international peace and security;

(c) to continue to examine the compliance of member states with resolution 1514 (XV) and other relevant resolutions on decolonization, particularly those relating to Namibia;

(d) to continue to pay special attention to the small territories, in particular through the dispatch of visiting missions to those territories whenever the Special Committee deems it appropriate, and to recommend to the General Assembly the most suitable steps to be taken to enable the populations of those territories to exercise their right to self-determination and independence; and

(e) to take all necessary steps to enlist world-wide support among governments, as well as national and international organizations having a special interest in decolonization, for the achievement of the objectives of the Declaration and the implementation of the relevant resolutions of the UN, particularly as concerns the people of Namibia.

The special committee originally was composed of 17 member states, nominated by the president of the General Assembly. It was enlarged to 24 in 1962 and to 25 in 1980. In 1985, one member state withdrew from the committee. Thus, the committee—popularly known as the "Committee of Twenty-Four" from 1962 to 1980—once again has 24 members. They are Afghanistan, Bulgaria, Chile, China, Congo, Cote d'Ivoire, Cuba, Czechoslovakia, Ethiopia, Fiji, India, Indonesia, Islamic Republic of Iran, Iraq, Mali, Norway, Sierra Leone, Syria, Trinidad and Tobago, Tunisia, Union of Soviet Socialist Republics, United Republic of Tanzania, Venezuela, and Yugoslavia. The term of office of members is indeterminate.

Meetings of the special committee are held as required throughout the year. Its reports are considered by the General Assembly.

The special committee is assisted in its work by a working group and steering committee, consisting of its officers and three additional members; the Sub-Committee on Petitions, Information and Assistance, consisting of 13 of its members; and the Sub-Committee on Small Territories, consisting of 19 of its members.

SPECIAL COMMITTEE TO INVESTIGATE ISRAELI PRACTICES AFFECTING THE HUMAN RIGHTS OF THE PALESTINIAN PEOPLE AND OTHER ARABS OF THE OCCUPIED TERRITORIES.

The UN General Assembly decided, on 19 December 1968 (resolution 2433 [XXIII]) to establish the Special Committee to Investigate Israeli Practices affecting the Population of the Occupied Territories. Twenty-one years later, on 8 December 1989, the assembly changed the name of the committee (resolution 44/48 A) to the Special Committee to Investigate Israeli Practices affecting the Human Rights of the Palestinian People and Other Arabs of the Occupied Territories.

The special committee is composed of the following members, serving in office for indeterminate terms: Mr. Daya Perera, permanent representative of Sri Lanka to the United Nations, chairman; Mr. Alioune Sene, ambassador of Senegal in Bern and permanent representative of Senegal to the United Nations office at Geneva; and Mr. Dragan Jovanic, Yugoslavia.

In its 1989 report to the General Assembly (UN

Doc. A/44/599), the special committee indicated (chap. III, para. 25) that in interpreting its mandate it had determined that

(a) The territories to be considered as occupied territories referred to the areas under Israeli occupation, namely, the occupied Syrian Arab Golan, the West Bank (including East Jerusalem), the Gaza Strip and the Sinai Peninsula. Following the implementation of the Egyptian-Israeli Agreement on Disengagement Forces of 18 January 1974 and the Agreement on Disengagement between Israeli and Syrian Forces of 31 May 1974, the demarcation of the areas under occupation was altered as indicated in the maps attached to those agreements. The areas of Egyptian territory under Israeli military occupation were further modified in accordance with the Treaty of Peace between the Arab Republic of Egypt and the State of Israel, which was signed on 26 March 1979 and which came into force on 25 April 1979. On 25 April 1982, the Egyptian territory remaining under Israeli military occupation was restituted to the Government of Egypt in accordance with the provisions of the aforementioned agreement. Thus, for the purposes of the present report, the territories to be considered as occupied territories are those remaining under Israeli occupation, namely, the occupied Syrian Arab Golan, the West Bank, including East Jerusalem, and the Gaza Strip;

(b) The persons covered by General Assembly resolution 2443 (XXIII) and therefore the subject of the investigation of the Special Committee were the civilian population residing in the areas occupied as a result of the hostilities of June 1967 and those persons normally resident in the areas that were under occupation but who had left those areas because of the hostilities. However, the Committee noted that resolution 2443 (XXIII) referred to the "population" without any qualification as to any segment of the inhabitants of the occupied territories;

(c) The "human rights" of the population of the occupied territories consisted of two elements, namely, those rights which the Security Council referred to as "essential and inalienable human rights" in its resolution 237 (1967) of 14 June 1967 and, secondly, those rights which found their basis in the protection afforded by international law in particular circumstances such as military occupation and, in the case of prisoners of war, capture. In accordance with General Assembly resolution 3005 (XXVII), the Special Committee was also required to investigate allegations concerning the exploitation and the looting of the resources of the occupied territories, the pillaging of the archaeological and cultural heritage of the occupied territories, and interference in the freedom of worship in the Holy Places of the occupied territories;

(d) The "policies" and "practices" affecting human rights that came within the scope of investigation by the Special Committee referred, in the case of "policies", to any course of action consciously adopted and pursued by the Government of Israel as part of its declared or undeclared intent; while "practices" referred to those actions which, irrespective of whether or not they were in implementation of a policy, reflected a pattern of behaviour on the part of the Israeli authorities towards the civilian population in the occupied areas.

In preparing its report, the special committee relied on the following sources: (a) the testimony of persons with first-hand knowledge of the situation of the population of the occupied territories; (b) reports in the Israeli press of pronouncements by responsible persons in the government of Israel; and (c) reports appearing in other news media, including the Arab language press published in the occupied territories in Israel and the international press. The committee also received written statements from the governments of Jordan and the Syrian Arab Republic and from the observer for Palestine. It undertook a series of hearings in Damascus, Amman, and Cairo during its meetings from 22 May to 7 June 1989, at which it heard the testimony of persons having a first-hand knowledge of the human rights situation existing in the occupied territories. It also took note of information reaching it through a variety of sources, such as individuals, organizations, and governments.

In its report, the committee summarized the information which it had examined under the following main headings: (a) general situation; (b) administration of justice, including the right to a fair trial; (c) treatment of civilians; (d) treatment of detainees; (e) annexation and settlements, and (f) information concerning the occupied Syrian Arab Golan. The committee then summarized its conclusions as follows (UN Doc. A/44/599, chap. V, para. 327–338):

During the period relevant to this report, the Government of Israel continued to withhold its co-operation from the Special Committee. However, the Special Committee benefited from the co-operation of the Governments of Egypt, Jordan and the Syrian Arab Republic, and of various Palestinian representatives. The Special Committee, having been precluded from visiting the occupied territories, conducted a series of meetings at Geneva, Damascus, Amman and Cairo in May and June of this year. At Damascus, Amman and Cairo, it heard the evidence of persons who had first-hand knowledge and personal experience of the human rights situation in the occupied territories. In addition, the Special Committee followed the situation in the occupied territories on a day-to-day basis through reports appearing in the Israeli and Palestinian press. The Special Committee examined a number of valuable communications and reports from Governments, organizations and individuals concerning the occupied territories that reached it during the period under review.

The conclusions contained in the present report are formulated on the basis of the information reflected in the periodic report (A/44/352, sect. II) and in section IV of the present report. It must be borne in mind, however, in this connection, that the volume of information received and examined by the Special Committee did not permit its total reflection in these reports; the Special Committee has endeavoured within the constraints imposed by the financial situation of the United Nations to include in the reports, as faithfully as possible, samples of the information it has received in order to illustrate the total reality of the situation of human rights in the occupied territories during the period covered by both reports.

On the basis of information and evidence put before it,

the Special Committee reaches the general conclusion that the situation in the occupied territories has been marked by a dangerous level of violence and repression, which has constantly escalated since the start of the uprising of the Palestinian population against occupation in December 1987.

Information and evidence put before the Special Committee illustrate the fact that Israel has continued, during the period under consideration, to pursue its policy of annexation towards the occupied territories. This policy has led to various measures such as establishing settlements, expropriating property, transferring Israeli citizens to the occupied territories and encouraging or compelling, by various means, Palestinians to leave their homeland. The Special Committee emphasizes once again that such an attitude is in violation of the obligations of Israel as a State party to the fourth Geneva Convention relative to the Protection of Civilian Persons in Time of War. It may be recalled that this Convention stipulates that military occupation is to be considered as a temporary, *de facto* situation, giving no right whatsoever to the occupying Power over the territorial integrity of the occupied territories. Illustrative of the policy and measures of the Government of Israel in that regard is the publication, on 22 December 1988, of a list of eight new settlements whose construction was agreed upon between the Likud and Labour parties, as reported in *Ha'aretz* on 22 December 1988 (see A/44/352, para. 267), or the approval, reported in *Jerusalem Post* on 31 May 1989, by the Knesset Finance Committee of the allocation of IS 30 million (approximately $20 million) for settlements and roads in the territories (para. 313 above). Another illustration would be the ruling, reported by *Ha'aretz* on 4 July 1989, of the President of the Supreme Court about a military seizure order on a piece of land owned by a Palestinian. The President of the Supreme Court ruled that a provisional seizure of land for military purposes was permitted under the "laws of the war" and under international public law.

The reaction of the Israeli authorities to the wave of disturbances and protest waged by the civilians against occupation has been increasingly severe. In this connection, reference can be made to various measures implemented by the Israeli authorities with a view to quell the demonstrations, such as the issuing in January 1989 of new instructions under which all soldiers, i.e. not only officers, were authorized to shoot plastic bullets at demonstrators, as reported in *Ha'aretz* on 5 January 1989 (see A/44/352, para. 35). Another illustration of the Israeli policy in this regard is the statement on 10 June 1989 by Defence Minister Rabin that in order to further calm down the violence in the territories, more means were needed for "selective punishment of activists", as reported in *Ha'aretz* on 11 June 1989 (see para. 42 above). Mention can also be made of the report by *Jerusalem Post* on 21 June 1989 according to which Defence Minister Rabin had asked the Justice Minister and the Attorney-General to devise the legal means to implement several new punitive measures to help deal more effectively with continued violence in the territories.

Such measures have clearly failed to calm the situation in the occupied territories. On the contrary, they have led to yet more violence and suffering and resulted in great losses among the civilian population. Practically every day and in several localities, serious incidents have been reported, such as violent clashes between the civilian population and Israeli defence forces, border policemen, paratroopers or settlers. The clashes often have resulted in deaths and se-

vere injuries, affecting all categories of civilians, including very young children. Several hundreds of Palestinians have been killed, as appears in the tables reproduced in paragraph 48 of document A/44/352 and paragraph 77 of the present document, which provide details concerning the Palestinians killed during the period under consideration. Information appearing in these tables, in particular in paragraph 77 of the present report, also reveals an alarming trend with respect to the killing of dozens of Palestinians suspected of collaboration with Israel. Other incidents have involved tax collection raids, or raids waged by Israeli soldiers to carry out scores of arrests or demolish houses. Numerous cases of severe beatings and the breaking of bones, casualties provoked by tear-gas and rock throwing into houses or other confined areas such as mosques or schools and various other kinds of harassment and ill-treatment have been reported to the Special Committee. Illustrative of this climate of daily confrontation with violence and humiliation was the testimony of an anonymous witness who stated in this regard ". . . life has been steadily deteriorating, it goes from bad to worse. People live in terror, in fear, all the time. Many times we are beaten by the Jews, by the Israeli army. At the beginning we just used to see them in the street, beating people they met in the street; but later they began to attack the houses. They break into houses and drag people out and beat them. You see your children's bones being broken. I have a son, a daughter and my wife, and all three of them have had bones broken . . ."

One of the most severe incidents occurred on 13 April 1989 in Nahalin near Bethlehem, when a border police unit, which raided the village to carry out arrests, was attacked by local youths who threw stones and other objects at them. The border police unit reacted by opening fire. Four youths were killed and at least 13 others were injured, including four seriously. Arab sources put the number of injured at 35. Many others were injured from tear-gas. The incident was reported in *Ha'aretz* and *Jerusalem Post* on 14 and 16 April 1989. The weekend of 5 and 6 May 1989 was also marked by violent clashes in the Gaza Strip which were reported to have been the fiercest and bloodiest since the beginning of the uprising, and by violent incidents in several West Bank localities. According to data on people killed in the territories since the beginning of the uprising up to mid-June 1989, released by the Israeli Information Centre for Human Rights in the Occupied Territories, as reported in *Ha'aretz* on 15 June 1989 and reflected in paragraph 43 above, 20 per cent of those killed were under 16 years of age. Killings were reported to have been caused by gunfire (including plastic bullets), beatings, electrocution, burning and other causes, and over 70 persons, including 30 babies, were reported to have died shortly after being exposed to tear-gas. In addition to physical harm, the situation prevailing in the territories has also borne dramatic psychological effects on the civilian population, in particular among young children, on whom the impact of violence is very difficult to erase and leaves long-term effects, as mentioned in one of the testimonies collected by the Special Committee.

The harassment of citizens has also been characterized by an increasing recourse to various forms of collective reprisal, imposed on the Palestinian population in contravention of the relevant provisions of the fourth Geneva Convention. One such form of reprisal has been the demolition of houses on a very large scale. Reference can be made in this regard to statistics published on 20 March

1989 by the Palestinian human rights monitoring group Al Haq, reported in *Al-Fajr* on 20 March 1989 and showing that at least 672 houses had been demolished in the occupied territories since the outbreak of the uprising, allegedly for having been built without a permit; another illustration of the recourse to house demolition as a means of reprisal was the information, reported in *Jerusalem Post* on 12 May 1989 and reflected in paragraph 159 of the present report, that on 11 May 1989 the Supreme Court upheld the IDF's right to demolish houses in the territories in reaction to petrol bombing, even in cases when the bombs caused no damage. Similarly, the practice of imposing prolonged curfews, with drastic economic consequences on the civilian population, has continued; reference can be made in this regard to the indefinite curfew imposed on 16 May 1989 to the Gaza Strip, and to the declaration by Defence Minister Rabin that the measure was meant to show Palestinians that they could not take their jobs in Israel for granted (as reported in *Ha'aretz* and *Jerusalem Post* on 16, 17 and 18 May 1989 and reflected in paragraph 168 of the present report). Economic sanctions including heavy taxes, the uprooting of trees or the banning of exports have also been imposed on the civilians, as well as various other measures of collective punishment such as the cutting of water, electricity supplies and the severing of telephone lines. Such measures have further aggravated the already critical economic and social situation. Mention can be made in this connection to the information, reported by *Ha'aretz* and *Jerusalem Post* on 18 May 1989, that all Gaza Strip residents would henceforward be required to have an individual permit to cross into Israel for work and business purposes, and that similar restrictions would also be extended to West Bank residents in time.

The period under consideration has also witnessed a considerable increase in the number of deportations from the occupied territories carried out in spite of a wave of protests by the international community including unanimous resolutions by the Security Council against such illegal practice which is in violation of article 49 of the fourth Geneva Convention. This alarming trend towards increased deportations was well illustrated by the information reported in *Jerusalem Post* on 22 May 1989 and reflected in paragraph 186 of the present report, that the Chief of Staff of the IDF had asked the Government to consider tabling legislation to facilitate deporting "convicted terrorists" who were caught a second time. Another preoccupying development was the increasing recent trend to expel Palestinians without a valid "staying visa", as reported in *Ha'aretz* on 31 May 1989 and reflected in paragraphs 187 and 188 of the present report.

The administration of justice is another field which has witnessed a considerable deterioration of the protection of basic human rights. The "quick justice" referred to in last year's report of the Special Committee has continued to characterize court procedures, provoking many protests from lawyers and human rights activists. According to information reported in *Ha'aretz*, *Jerusalem Post* and *Al Fajr* on 3 and 13 February 1989, complaints about military justice were listed by a group of Arab lawyers who waged protest strikes in January, February and July 1989, and included the frequent postponement of trials while suspects remained in gaol, failure to notify families as to where detainees were held, bureaucratic obstacles in order to prevent lawyers from meeting with their clients, the severity of penalties and the use of the Ketziot camp in the Negev desert to hold detainees from the territories. Another problem fre-

quently referred to by witnesses appearing before the Special Committee was that of the confidential files containing charges levelled against Palestinians, which neither the defendant nor his lawyer have access to.

Such complaints do not seem to have deterred the security establishment which decided, as reported on 12 June 1989 by *Ha'aretz*, to impose harsher penalties on persons suspected of subversive activity in the uprising. One of the penalties would be the extension of administrative detention from the present six months to one year, with a possible further extension (see para. 96). The period under consideration has therefore witnessed a large increase in the number of detentions. *Ha'aretz* reported on 14 June 1989 that since the beginning of the uprising, over 49,000 Palestinians from the territories had been detained for various periods in Israeli detention facilities. They included administrative detainees, detainees pending trial, detainees already tried and persons detained for participation in disturbances. The sentences imposed have also usually been particularly severe. On 20 June 1989, for instance, *Ha'aretz* reported that, on the previous day, three Palestinians had been sentenced each to eight and one half years in prison and four and one half years suspended, for harassing shopkeepers who had opened their shops on strike days. In contrast, Israelis charged with murder or ill-treatment of Arab civilians, seem to have benefited from relative leniency from the authorities. In this connection, it was reported in *Jerusalem Post* on 16 December 1988 that a military court in Jaffa had sentenced private Eli Yedid to 18 months imprisonment for manslaughter, for killing Yusuf Abu-Eid from Bidu during a riot in March 1988. Yedid was found guilty of shooting Abu-Eid after seeing him throwing stones.

The general climate of tension and repression in the territories during the period under consideration was also noticeable in the treatment of detainees, whose situation, as a consequence of the arrests of tens of thousands of Palestinians since the outbreak of the uprising, has further deteriorated. In addition to the existing prisons, army detention centres are being increasingly used. Various governmental buildings and even school buildings have been converted to temporary detention centres. Detainees have continued to be held in prisons and detention centres inside Israel itself, such as Ansar 3 or Megiddo, in violation of relevant provision of article 76 of the fourth Geneva Convention. Detainees, including minors and women have been submitted to various forms of ill-treatment, both physical and psychological; they have suffered from a lack of adequate sanitary and medical facilities, nutrition and clothing, and the overcrowding of cells leading to protests by prisoners in the form of widespread hunger strikes. Some detention centres have been reported to be notorious for particularly cruel conditions, such as the Ansar 3 and Megiddo camps where serious riots have taken place leading to injuries from tear-gas and rubber bullets, as reported by *Ha'aretz* and *Jerusalem Post* on 28 April 1989.

The Special Committee also received information on various measures affecting the enjoyment of certain basic freedoms. For example, a number of civilians, both individually and collectively, were the subject of arbitrary orders restricting their freedom of movement, in particular due to the systematic recourse to curfews or the sealing off of entire areas. Another restrictive measure was the issuing by military authorities of identity cards to Gaza Strip residents wishing to enter Israel, as reported in *Jerusalem Post* on 6 June 1989. This measure was described as a further effort to tighten control over the residents. It was reported that some 2,000 residents with security or criminal records would not be entitled to a card. On 18 August, *Ha'aretz* reported that these new regulations went into effect. On 22 August, it was reported that security authorities were considering introducing similar cards to West Bank residents, in order to ban entry to persons who were convicted in the past of a security or a serious criminal offence, or had been served with an administrative detention term. Freedom of association and freedom of the press were also affected by various measures such as closures of newspapers and press agencies, censorship, interference in the work and detention of journalists or trade unionists. Freedom of worship was also affected by arbitrary measures such as the setting on fire of a mosque under construction or the burning of holy books, or the restrictions imposed on worshippers. Freedom of education was seriously hampered by the prolonged closure of educational institutions, including all universities, schools and even kindergartens. The efforts by the Palestinians to provide children with some kind of "popular teaching" in order to compensate for the lack of public education were also jeopardized by obstacles by the Israeli authorities as illustrated in the evidence of Mr. Usama Sayeh and various press reports.

Another grave development in the occupied territories during the period under consideration has been the increase, both in scope and gravity, of acts of violence and aggression by Israeli settlers against the Palestinian population. On 20 March, it was reported in *Al-Fajr* that Jewish settlers killed 16 Palestinians and wounded 107 in the year between December 1987 and December 1988. An illustration of the violent behaviour of settlers is the raid, on 29 May, by 30 settlers on the village of Kifl Harith, where they reportedly carried out a "methodical and prolonged rampage, involving arson and vandalism . . . which climaxed with the shooting of a 13-year-old girl inside her home in a burst of automatic fire", as reported in *Ha'aretz* and *Jerusalem Post* on 31 May 1989. . . . Another example is the creation of vigilante intervention forces by settlers, as reported in *Ha'aretz* and *Jerusalem Post* on 18 April 1989. Reference can also be made in this connection to the Kiryat Arba settlers who, as reported in *Jerusalem Post* on 18 and 19 July 1989, burst on 17 July 1989 into one of the halls of the Patriach's Cave in Hebron, threw Moslem prayer rugs aside and danced until soldiers forced them out.

Finally, the report of the Special Committee also contains information on the tension prevailing in the occupied Syrian Arab Golan, illustrated by widespread demonstrations, violently dispersed by the police and border police forces.

In the opinion of the Special Committee, the overall picture drawn from the evidence and information examined by it during the period under consideration, i.e. 26 August 1988 to 25 August 1989, reveals a very alarming situation and a further deterioration in the level of enjoyment of basic human rights and fundamental freedoms by the civilian population. The provisions of the fourth Geneva Convention, which remains the main international instrument in humanitarian law that applies to the occupied territories, continue to be disregarded and violated. In view of the gravity of such developments, the Special Committee once again stresses that urgent measures must be taken in order to ensure an effective protection of the basic rights and freedoms of the civilians in the occupied territories. Such protection can only be ensured, in the long run, through the negotiation of a comprehensive, just and lasting settlement of the Arab-Israeli conflict acceptable to all concerned. In the mean time, the Special Committee wishes to reiterate the following measures which it already suggested in its twentieth report last year and which could, in the view of the Special Committee, contribute to the restoration of the basic human rights of the civilians in the occupied territories:

(a) The full application, by Israel, of the relevant provisions of the fourth Geneva Convention, which remains the main international instrument in humanitarian law that applies to the occupied territories, and whose applicability to those territories has repeatedly been reaffirmed by the Security Council, the General Assembly and other relevant organs of the United Nations;

(b) The full co-operation of the Israeli authorities with the International Committee of the Red Cross (ICRC) in order to facilitate efforts to protect detained persons, in particular by ensuring full access of ICRC representatives to such persons;

(c) The full support, by Member States, of the activities of the ICRC in the occupied territories, and positive response by Member States to eventual appeals for additional assistance including funds to finance the extra activities required by the unprecedented increase in the number of detained persons;

(d) The full support, by Member States, of UNRWA activities in the occupied territories in order to enable UNRWA to improve the general assistance provided to the refugee population.

Having considered the report of the special committee and other relevant documentation, the General Assembly commended (resolution 44/48A) the special committee for its efforts in performing the tasks which had been assigned to it and for its impartiality. It deplored the continued refusal by Israel to allow the special committee access to the occupied Palestine territory, including Jerusalem, and other Arab territories occupied by Israel since 1967, and demanded that Israel allow the committee access to those territories. It reaffirmed the fact that occupation itself constitutes a grave violation of the human rights of the Palestinian people in all occupied Palestinian territory.

The assembly strongly condemned the following Israeli policies and practices:

(a) annexation of parts of the occupied Palestinian territory, including Jerusalem;

(b) imposition of Israeli laws, jurisdiction and administration on the Syrian Arab Golan, which has resulted in the effective annexation of that territory;

(c) illegal imposition and levy of taxes and dues;

(d) establishment of new Israeli settlements and expansion of the existing settlements on private and public Palestinian and other Arab lands, and transfer of an alien population thereto;

(e) eviction, deportation, expulsion, displacement and transfer of Palestinians and other Arabs of those occupied territories and denial of their right to return;

(f) confiscation and expropriation of private and public Palestinian and other Arab property in those occupied territories and all other transactions for the acquisition of land by the Israeli authorities, institutions or nationals;

(g) excavation and transformation of the landscape and the historical, cultural and religious sites, especially at Jerusalem;

(h) pillaging of archaeological and cultural property;

(i) destruction and demolition of Palestinian and other Arab houses;

(j) collective punishment, mass arrests, administrative detention and ill-treatment of Palestinians and other Arabs;

(k) torture of Palestinians and other Arabs;

(l) interference with religious freedoms and practices, as well as family rights and customs;

(m) interference with the system of education and with the social and economic and health development of the Palestinians and other Arabs in those occupied territories;

(n) interference with the freedom of movement of individuals within the occupied Palestinian territory, including Jerusalem, and other Arab territories occupied by Israel since 1967;

(o) illegal exploitation of the natural wealth, resources and labour of those occupied territories;

The assembly also condemned, in particular, the following Israeli policies and practices:

(a) implementation of an "iron-fist" policy against the Palestinian people in the occupied Palestinian territory;

(b) escalation of Israeli brutality since the beginning of the uprising *(intifadah)* on 9 December 1987;

(c) ill-treatment and torture of children and minors under detention and/or imprisonment;

(d) closure of headquarters and offices of trade unions and social organizations and harassment, including expulsion of their leaders, as well as attacks on hospitals and their personnel;

(e) interference with the freedom of the press, including ownership, detention or expulsion of journalists, closure and suspension of newspapers and magazines, as well as denial of access to international media;

(f) killing and wounding of defenceless demonstrators;

(g) breaking of bones and limbs of thousands of civilians;

(h) house and/or town arrests;

(i) use of toxic gas, which has resulted, *inter alia,* in the killing of many Palestinians;

The assembly demanded that Israel desist forthwith from the above-listed policies and practices. Further, it condemned Israel's refusal to permit persons from the occupied Palestinian territory to appear as witnesses before the special committee or to participate in conferences and meetings held outside that territory.

The assembly called upon the special committee to continue to investigate and report on Israeli practices affecting the human rights of the population of the occupied territories and, in particular, to investigate the treatment of prisoners in those territories.

SEE ALSO Intifadah . . . *of the Palestinian People; Israel: Application of the Fourth Geneva Convention . . . ; Israel: Detention and Deportation of Palestinians; Israel: Effective Annexation of the Syrian Arab Golan; Israel: Harassment of Educational Institutions in Occupied Palestinian Territory; Palestinian People's Rights.*

SPECIAL RAPPORTEURS: PRIVILEGES AND IMMUNITIES.

On 24 May 1989, the UN ECONOMIC AND SOCIAL COUNCIL, responding to urgent calls for action issued by the UN Commission on Human Rights and its Sub-Commission on Prevention of Discrimination and Protection of Minorities, concluded (resolution 1989/75) that a difference had arisen between the United Nations and the government of Romania as to the applicability of the Convention on Privileges and Immunities of the United Nations to Mr. Dumitru Mazilu as special rapporteur of the sub-commission.

The council requested, on a priority basis, an advisory opinion from the INTERNATIONAL COURT OF JUSTICE on the legal question of the applicability of article VI, section 22, of the convention in the case of Mr. Mazilu as special rapporteur of the sub-commission.

The court delivered the following advisory opinion on 15 December 1989:

Applicability of Article VI, Section 22, of the Convention on the Privileges and Immunities of the United Nations

Competence of the Court to give opinion requested—Article 96, paragraph 2, of United Nations Charter—Relevance of lack of consent of State concerned—Opinion requested on applicability of multilateral convention—Dispute settlement clause providing for decisive advisory opinion—Reservation to clause—No reference to clause in request for opinion and no intention to invoke it—Request based exclusively on Article 96 of Charter—Jurisdiction to entertain the request not affected by reservation.

Propriety of giving the opinion—Whether there is any compelling reason to decline—Whether reply would have effect of circumventing principle of consent.

Convention on the Privileges and Immunities of the United Nations—Article VI, Section 22—Meaning of "experts on missions"—Applicability of Section to all missions including those not requiring travel—Applicability to experts in States of which they are nationals or on territory of which they reside.

Status of special rapporteurs of United Nations Sub-Commission on Prevention of Discrimination and Protection of Minorities—Competence of United Nations to decide on retention of particular rapporteur.

Advisory Opinion

Present: President Ruda; *Judges* Lachs, Elias, Oda, Ago, Schwebel, Sir Robert Jennings, Bedjaoui, Ni, Evensen, Tarassov, Guillaume, Shahabuddeen, Pathak; *Registrar* Valencia-Ospina.

Concerning the applicability of Article VI, Section 22, of the Convention on the Privileges and Immunities of the United Nations,

The Court,

composed as above.

gives the following Advisory Opinion:

1. The question upon which the advisory opinion of the Court has been requested is contained in resolution 1989/75 of the United Nations Economic and Social Council (hereinafter called "the Council"), adopted on 24 May 1989. By a letter dated 1 June 1989, addressed by the Secretary-General of the United Nations to the President of the Court, filed in the Registry on 13 June 1989, the Secretary-General formally communicated to the Court the decision by which the Council submitted to the Court for an advisory opinion the question set out in that resolution. The resolution, certified true copies of the English and French texts of which were enclosed with the letter, was in the following terms:

"The Economic and Social Council,

"Having considered resolution 1988/37 of 1 September 1988 of the Sub-Commission on Prevention of Discrimination and Protection of Minorities and Commission on Human Rights resolution 1989/37 of 6 March 1989,

"1. Concludes that a difference has arisen between the United Nations and the Government of Romania as to the applicability of the Convention on the Privileges and Immunities of the United Nations to Mr. Dumitru Mazilu as Special Rapporteur of the Sub-Commission on Prevention of Discrimination and Protection of Minorities;

"2. Requests, on a priority basis, pursuant to Article 96, paragraph 2, of the Charter of the United Nations and in accordance with General Assembly resolution 89 (1) of 11 December 1946, an advisory opinion from the International Court of Justice on the legal question of the applicability of Article VI, Section 22, of the Convention on the Privileges and Immunities of the United Nations in the case of Mr. Dumitru Mazilu as Special Rapporteur of the Sub-Commission."

Also enclosed with the letter were details of the voting on the resolution and on an amendment to the draft thereof whereby the words "on a priority basis" were added in paragraph 2.

2. On 14 June 1989 the Registrar gave the notice of the request for an advisory opinion prescribed by Article 66, paragraph 1, of the Statute of the Court to all States entitled to appear before the Court.

3. By an Order dated 14 June 1989 the President of the Court decided that the United Nations and the States which are parties to the Convention on the Privileges and Immunities of the United Nations adopted by the United Nations General Assembly on 13 February 1946 (hereinafter called "the General Convention") were likely to be able to furnish information on the question, in accordance with Article 66, paragraph 2, of the Statute of the Court. The President, having regard to that paragraph, and considering that in fixing time-limits for the proceedings, it was "necessary to bear in mind that the request for opinion was expressed to be made 'on a priority basis' ", fixed 31 July 1989 as the time-limit within which the Court would be pre-

pared to receive written statements on the question and 31 August 1989 as the time-limit for written comments on written statements. On 14 June 1989 the Registrar addressed the special and direct communication provided for in Article 66, paragraph 2, of the Statute to the United Nations and to these States.

4. Written statements were submitted, within the time-limit so fixed, by the Secretary-General of the United Nations, and by Canada, the Federal Republic of Germany, the Socialist Republic of Romania and the United States of America. Written comments were submitted, within the relevant time-limit, by the United States of America. These statements and comments were communicated by the Registrar to the States to which he had sent the special and direct communication and to the United Nations.

5. The Secretary-General transmitted to the Court, pursuant to Article 65, paragraph 2, of the Statute, a dossier of documents likely to throw light upon the question; these documents were received in the Registry in instalments from 2 August 1989 onwards.

6. The Court decided to hold hearings, opening on 4 October 1989, at which oral statements might be submitted to the Court by any State or organization which had been considered likely to be able to furnish information on the question before the Court.

7. Pursuant to Article 106 of the Rules of Court, the Court decided to make the written statements and comments submitted to the Court accessible to the public, with effect from the opening of the oral proceedings.

8. At public sittings held on 4 and 5 October 1989, oral statements were made before the Court by Mr. Carl-August Fleischhauer, the United Nations Legal Counsel, on behalf of the Secretary-General, and by Mr. Abraham Sofaer, Legal Adviser, Department of State, on behalf of the United States of America. None of the other States which had presented written statements expressed a desire to be heard. Questions were put by Members of the Court to the representative of the Secretary-General, and answered before the close of the oral proceedings.

9. Pursuant to Articles 55 (*c*) and 68 of the Charter of the United Nations, the Council, by resolution 5 (I) of 16 February 1946, supplemented on 18 February 1946, created a Commission on Human Rights (hereinafter called "the Commission"). In 1947 the Commission in its turn set up a Sub-Commission on Prevention of Discrimination and Protection of Minorities (hereinafter called "the Sub-Commission"), and in 1949 the Sub-Commission was given the following mandate:

"(*a*) to undertake studies, particularly in the light of the Universal Declaration of Human Rights and to make recommendations to the Commission on Human Rights concerning the prevention of discrimination of any kind relating to human rights and fundamental freedoms and the protection of racial, national, religious and linguistic minorities; and

"(*b*) to perform any other functions which may be entrusted to it by the Economic and Social Council or the Commission on Human Rights".

10. On 13 March 1984 the Commission, upon nomination by Romania, elected Mr. Dumitru Mazilu, a Romanian national, to serve as a member of the Sub-Commission for a three-year term, due to expire on 31 December 1986. Pursuant to the Commission's resolution 1985/13 calling upon the Sub-Commission to pay due attention to the role of youth in the field of human rights, the Sub-Commission at its thirty-eighth session adopted on 29 August 1985 resolu-

tion 1985/12 whereby it requested Mr. Mazilu to "prepare a report on human rights and youth analysing the efforts and measures for securing the implementation and enjoyment by youth of human rights, particularly, the right to life, education and work" and requested the Secretary-General to provide him with all necessary assistance for the completion of his task. This report was to be submitted under an agenda item entitled "Promotion, protection and restoration of human rights at national, regional and international levels", at the thirty-ninth session of the Sub-Commission scheduled for 1986.

11. The thirty-ninth session of the Sub-Commission, at which Mr. Mazilu's report was to be presented, was not convened in 1986 but was rescheduled for 1987. The three-year mandate of its members—originally due to expire on 31 December 1986—was extended by Council decision 1987/102 for an additional year. When the thirty-ninth session of the Sub-Commission opened in Geneva on 10 August 1987 no report had been received from Mr. Mazilu, nor was he present. By a letter received by the United Nations Office at Geneva on 12 August 1987, the Permanent Mission of Romania to that Office informed it that Mr. Mazilu had suffered a heart attack and was still in hospital. In its written statement to the Court, Romania stated that Mr. Mazilu had fallen seriously ill in May 1987, and that at that time he had not yet begun to draw up the report entrusted to him. According to the written statement of the Secretary-General, a telegram was received in Geneva on 18 August 1987 signed "D. Mazilu" informing the Sub-Commission of his inability, due to heart illness, to attend the current session.

12. In these circumstances, the Sub-Commission adopted decision 1987/112 on 4 September 1987, whereby it deferred consideration of item 14 of its agenda—under which the report on human rights and youth was due to be discussed—to its fourth session scheduled for 1988. Notwithstanding the scheduled expiration on 31 December 1987 of Mr. Mazilu's term as a member of the Sub-Commission, the latter included reference to a report to be submitted by him, identified by name, under the agenda item "Prevention of discrimination and protection of children", on the provisional agenda of its fortieth session, and entered the report under the title "Human rights and youth" in the "List of studies and reports under preparation by members of the Sub-Commission in accordance with the existing legislative authority".

13. After the thirty-ninth session of the Sub-Commission, the Centre for Human Rights of the United Nations Secretariat in Geneva made various attempts to contact Mr. Mazilu and to provide him with assistance in the preparation of his report, including arranging a visit to Geneva. Relevant information submitted by Governments, intergovernmental organizations and non-governmental organizations was sent to him on a regular basis. Having received from Mr. Mazilu two letters postmarked 25 and 29 December 1987, whereby he stated that he had not received the previous communications of the Centre, the Under-Secretary-General for Human Rights, in a telegram dated 19 January 1988 and addressed to the Acting Director of the United Nations Information Centre in Bucharest, requested the latter's assistance in facilitating Mr. Mazilu's work on his report by serving as a channel through which a ticket to Geneva would be provided to Mr. Mazilu; the Under-Secretary-General also asked that a formal invitation be communicated to Mr. Mazilu to come to the Centre for Human Rights for consultations.

14. In its written statement submitted to the Court, Romania stated that at Mr. Mazilu's request he had, from 1 December 1987, been put on the retired list as being unfit for service, and that in 1988 a medical commission, acting in accordance with current Romanian legislation, had re-examined Mr. Mazilu's state of health and decided to extend for a further one-year period his retirement on the grounds of continued unfitness for service. In a letter addressed to the Under-Secretary-General for Human Rights, handed on 15 January 1988 to the Acting Director of the United Nations Information Centre in Bucharest, Mr. Mazilu said that he had been twice in hospital, and that he had been forced to retire, as of 1 December 1987, from his various governmental posts. He stated that despite his willingness to come to Geneva for consultations, the Romanian authorities were refusing him a travel permit. In a series of letters dated 5 April, 19 April, 8 May and 17 May 1988, Mr. Mazilu further described his personal situation; in the first of these letters he alleged that he had refused to comply with a request addressed to him on 22 February 1988 by a special commission from the Romanian Ministry of Foreign Affairs voluntarily to decline to submit his report to the Sub-Commission. He consistently complained that strong pressure had been exerted on him and on his family.

15. On 31 December 1987 the terms of all members of the Sub-Commission, including Mr. Mazilu, expired (see paragraph 11 above). On 29 February 1988 the Commission, upon nomination by their respective Governments, elected new members of the Sub-Commission, among whom was Mr. Ion Diaconu, a Romanian national. In response to a letter from the Permanent Representative of Romania to the United Nations Office at Geneva, dated 27 June 1988, referring to an offer by Mr. Diaconu to prepare a report on human rights and youth, the Under-Secretary-General for Human Rights recalled on 1 July 1988 that Mr. Mazilu had been mandated by the Sub-Commission resolution 1985/12 to prepare the report on that subject, and stated that only the Sub-Commission or a superior body was competent to change the designation; the Secretary-General had therefore to act pursuant to the instructions given by the Sub-Commission in the said resolution "to provide all necessary assistance to Mr. Dumitru Mazilu for the completion of this task".

16. Meanwhile, by a letter dated 6 May 1988 the Under-Secretary-General for Human Rights requested the assistance of the Permanent Representative of Romania to the United Nations Office at Geneva in transmitting to Mr. Mazilu all relevant information which had been submitted by Governments, specialized agencies and non-governmental organizations, and which was necessary for the completion of his report. By a letter of 15 June 1988, the Under-Secretary-General informed the Permanent Representative of Romania that, as an exceptional measure, he had decided to authorize a staff member of the Centre for Human Rights to travel to Bucharest for the purpose of working with Mr. Mazilu on his report, but only on the understanding that Mr. Mazilu would be enabled to present his report to the Sub-Commission in Geneva and to participate in the ensuing debate.

17. All the rapporteurs and special rapporteurs of the Sub-Commission were invited to attend its fortieth session (8 August to 2 September 1988) and the meetings of its working groups; however Mr. Mazilu again did not appear. Following a discussion at the 2nd meeting, held on 9 August 1988, a special invitation was cabled to Mr. Mazilu to go to Geneva to present his report, but the relevant telegrams

were not delivered, and the United Nations Information Centre in Bucharest was unable to locate Mr. Mazilu. During the debate at the 9th meeting, held on 15 August 1988, on the organization of work of the session, various members expressed their views about Mr. Mazilu's situation, and the Chairman stressed the two-fold aim of the Sub-Commission, namely, to ensure that the study entrusted to Mr. Mazilu be brought to a satisfactory conclusion, and to try to ensure its presentation by Mr. Mazilu in person.

18. At its 10th meeting, held on 15 August 1988, the Sub-Commission adopted decision 1988/102, whereby it requested the Secretary-General "to establish contact with the Government of Romania and to bring to the Government's attention the Sub-Commission's urgent need to establish personal contact with its Special Rapporteur Mr. Dumitru Mazilu and to convey the request that the Government assist in locating Mr. Mazilu and facilitate a visit to him by a member of the Sub-Commission and the secretariat to help him in the completion of his study on human rights and youth if he so wished". The Under-Secretary-General for Human Rights informed the Sub-Commission at its 14th meeting, held on 17 August 1988, that in contacts between the Secretary-General's Office and the Chargé d'affaires of the Romanian Permanent Mission to the United Nations in New York, the possibility of establishing contact with Mr. Mazilu was raised.

19. The Under-Secretary-General reported that in these contacts the Chargé d'affaires had stated that any intervention by the United Nations Secretariat and any form of investigation in Bucharest would be considered interference in Romania's internal affairs; the case of Mr. Mazilu was an internal matter between a citizen and his own Government and for that reason no visit to Mr. Mazilu would be allowed.

20. At its 32nd meeting, held on 30 August 1988, the Sub-Commission considered a draft resolution contemplating that an advisory opinion on the applicability of the General Convention to the case of Mr. Mazilu be sought from the Court; it had before it an opinion by the Office of Legal Affairs of the United Nations Secretariat on that question, and a further opinion was obtained from that Office on the legal implications of the reservation made by Romania to Section 30 (the disputes-settlement provision) of the General Convention.

21. The Sub-Commission on 1 September 1988 adopted by 16 votes to 4, with 3 abstentions, resolution 1988/37. Taking into account that "if Mr. Mazilu should be unable for whatever personal reasons to complete and present himself the said report to the Sub-Commission, he should be given any possible assistance by the United Nations enabling him to complete his report, with such assistance, in Romania", the Sub-Commission, according to the terms of the operative part,

"1. Requests the Secretary-General to approach once more the Government of Romania and invoke the applicability of the Convention on the Privileges and Immunities of the United Nations, and request the Government to co-operate fully in the implementation of the present resolution by ensuring that Mr. Mazilu's report be completed and presented to the Sub-Commission at the earliest possible date, either by himself or in the manner indicated above;

"2. Further requests the Secretary-General, in the event the Government of Romania does not concur in the applicability of the provisions of the said Convention in the present case, and thus with the terms of the present resolution, to bring the difference between the United Nations and Romania immediately to the attention of the Commission

on Human Rights at its forthcoming forty-fifth session in 1989;

"3. Requests the Commission on Human Rights, in the latter event, to urge the Economic and Social Council to request, in accordance with General Assembly resolution 89 (I) of 11 December 1946, from the International Court of Justice an advisory opinion on the applicability of the relevant provisions of the Convention on the Privileges and Immunities of the United Nations to the present case and within the scope of the present resolution."

22. Pursuant to the foregoing resolution the Secretary-General on 26 October 1988 addressed a Note Verbale to the Permanent Representative of Romania to the United Nations in New York, in which he invoked the General Convention in respect of Mr. Mazilu and requested the Romanian Government to accord Mr. Mazilu the necessary facilities in order to enable him to complete his assigned task. As no reply had been received to that Note Verbale, the Under-Secretary-General for Human Rights on 19 December 1988 wrote a letter of reminder to the Permanent Representative of Romania to the United Nations Office at Geneva, in which he asked that the Romanian Government assist in arranging for Mr. Mazilu to visit Geneva so that he could discuss with the Centre for Human Rights the assistance it might give him in preparing his report.

23. On 6 January 1989 the Permanent Representative of Romania handed to the Legal Counsel of the United Nations an Aide-Mémoire in which was set forth the Romanian Government's position concerning Mr. Mazilu. On the facts of the case, Romania stated that Mr. Mazilu, who had not prepared or produced anything on the subject entrusted to him, had in 1987 become gravely ill with a serious heart condition and had had repeatedly to go into hospital over a period of several months. In November 1987, according to that Aide-Mémoire, he had "applied personally for disability retirement because of this condition, submitting appropriate medical certificates"; "in accordance with Romanian law, he was examined by a panel of doctors which decided to place him on the retired list on grounds of ill-health for an initial period of one year"; "at the end of the first year of his disability retirement, he was examined by a similar panel of doctors which decided to extend his retirement on grounds of ill-health".

24. On the law, Romania expressed the view in that Aide-Mémoire that "the problem of the application of the General Convention does not arise in this case": the Convention "does not equate rapporteurs, whose activities are only occasional, with experts on missions for the United Nations"; and "even if rapporteurs are given some of the status of experts, . . . they can enjoy only functional immunities and privileges, that is, privileges connected with their activities for the United Nations, during the period of their mission, and then only in the countries in which they perform the mission and in countries of transit". For Romania, it was obvious that "an expert does not enjoy privileges and immunities in the country in which he has his permanent residence but only in the country in which he is on mission and during the period of his mission. Likewise, the privileges and immunities provided by the Convention begin to apply only at the moment when the expert leaves on a journey connected with the performance of his mission." Moreover, "in the country of which he is a national and in countries other than the country to which he is sent on mission, an expert enjoys privileges and immunities only in respect of actual activities spoken or written which he performs in connection with his mission". Romania stated

expressly that it was opposed to a request for advisory opinion from the Court of any kind in this case. Similar contentions were also put forward in the written statement presented by Romania to the Court in the present proceedings.

25. At the forty-fifth session of the Commission in 1989, the Secretary-General presented a Note "pursuant to paragraph 2 of resolution 1988/37 of the Sub-Commission" (see paragraph 21 above), to which was attached his Note Verbale to the Romanian Government of 26 October 1988, and the Romanian Aide-Mémoire of 6 January 1989. The Commission adopted on 6 March 1989, by 26 votes to 5, with 12 abstentions, its resolution 1989/37 recommending that the Council request an advisory opinion from the Court. The Council on 24 May 1989 adopted by 24 votes to 8, with 19 abstentions, its resolution 1989/75 requesting an advisory opinion of the Court, as recommended in Commission resolution 1989/37, on the legal question of the applicability of Article VI, Section 22, of the General Convention in the case of Mr. Mazilu as Special Rapporteur of the Sub-Commission.

26. The Court has also been informed by the Secretary-General of the following events which have occurred since the request for advisory opinion was made. A report on human rights and youth prepared by Mr. Mazilu was circulated as a document of the Sub-Commission bearing the date 10 July 1989; the text of this report had been transmitted by Mr. Mazilu to the Centre for Human Rights in several installments through various channels. At a meeting held on 8 August 1989, the Sub-Commission decided, in accordance with its practice, to invite Mr. Mazilu to participate in the meetings at which his report was to be considered: no reply was received to the invitation extended. By a Note Verbale dated 15 August 1989 from the Permanent Mission of Romania to the United Nations Office at Geneva addressed to that Office, the Permanent Mission referred to "the so-called report" by Mr. Mazilu, expressed surprise "that the medical opinions made available to the Centre for Human Rights . . . have been ignored", and continued: "The fact that the Centre's administration has agreed, in these circumstances, to sponsor the publication of some of Mr. Mazilu's ideas and judgements under the auspices of the United Nations can only harm the standing and credibility of the Organization." In the view of Romania, "Obviously since becoming ill in 1987, Mr. Dumitru Mazilu does not possess the intellectual capacity necessary for making an objective, responsible and unbiased analysis that could serve as the substance of a report consistent with the requirements of the United Nations." At its 40th meeting held on 1 September 1989, the Sub-Commission adopted, by 12 votes to 4 with 2 abstentions, resolution 1989/45 entitled "The report on human rights and youth prepared by Mr. Dumitru Mazilu". The Sub-Commission noted that Mr. Mazilu's report had been prepared in difficult circumstances and that the relevant information collected by the Secretary-General appeared not to have been delivered to Mr. Mazilu. The Sub-Commission *inter alia* requested Mr. Mazilu to update his report and invited him to present it in person to the Sub-Commission at its next session; it also requested the Secretary-General to continue to gather and furnish to Mr. Mazilu information relating to his study, and to provide Mr. Mazilu with all the assistance he might need in updating his report, including consultations with the Centre for Human Rights.

27. The question laid before the Court by the Council is, in the terms of the resolution requesting the advisory opin-

ion (resolution 1989/75, entitled "Status of Special Rapporteurs"), "the legal question of the applicability of Article VI, Section 22, of the Convention on the Privileges and Immunities of the United Nations in the case of Mr. Dumitru Mazilu as Special Rapporteur of the Sub-Commission [on the Prevention of Discrimination and the Protection of Minorities]". According to the written statement submitted to the Court by the Secretary-General, "It should . . . be noted that while the Court has been asked about the applicability of Section 22 of the Convention in the case of Mr. Mazilu, it has not been asked about the consequences of that applicability, that is about what privileges and immunities Mr. Mazilu might enjoy as a result of his status and whether or not these had been violated." During the oral proceedings, the representative of the Secretary-General, when replying to a question put by a Member of the Court, observed that "it is suggestive of the Council's intention in adopting the resolution to note that, having referred to a 'difference', it then did not attempt to have that difference as a whole resolved by the question it addressed to the Court. Rather . . . the Council merely addressed a preliminary legal question to the Court, which appears designed to clarify at most the general status of Mr. Mazilu in respect of the Convention, without resolving the entire issue that evidently separates the United Nations and the Government."

28. The present request for advisory opinion is the first request made by the Council, pursuant to paragraph 2 of Article 96 of the Charter. That paragraph provides that organs of the United Nations, other than the General Assembly and the Security Council, "which may at any time be so authorized by the General Assembly, may also request advisory opinions of the Court on legal questions arising within the scope of their activities". Such authorization in respect of the Council was given by General Assembly resolution 89 (I) of 11 December 1946. The question which is the subject of the request, involving as it does the interpretation of an international convention in order to determine its applicability, is a legal question. Furthermore it is one arising within the scope of the activities of the Council. As indicated in paragraph 10 above, Mr. Mazilu's assignment was pertinent to a function and programme of the Council. The Commission is a subsidiary organ of the Council, and the Sub-Commission, of which he was appointed special rapporteur, is in turn a subsidiary organ of the Commission. Accordingly, the request before the Court fulfils the conditions of Article 96, paragraph 2, of the Charter of the United Nations.

29. The Court has next to consider the contention of Romania, on the basis of the reservation made by it to Section 30 of the General Convention, that the Court "cannot find that it has jurisdiction to give an advisory opinion" in the present case. Section 30 of the General Convention provides:

"All difference arising out of the interpretation or application of the present convention shall be referred to the International Court of Justice, unless in any case it is agreed by the parties to have recourse to another mode of settlement. If a difference arises between the United Nations on the one hand and a Member on the other hand, a request shall be made for an advisory opinion on any legal question involved in accordance with Article 96 of the Charter and Article 65 of the Statute of the Court. The opinion given by the Court shall be accepted as decisive by the parties."

Romania acceded to the General Convention, and its instrument of accession was deposited with the Secretary-

General on 5 July 1956. The instrument of accession contained the following reservation:

"The Romanian People's Republic does not consider itself bound by the terms of section 30 of the Convention which provide for the compulsory jurisdiction of the International Court in differences arising out of the interpretation or application of the Convention; with respect to the competence of the International Court in such differences, the Romanian People's Republic takes the view that, for the purpose of the submission of any dispute whatsoever to the Court for a ruling, the consent of all the parties to the dispute is required in every individual case. This reservation is equally applicable to the provisions contained in the said section which stipulate that the advisory opinion of the International Court is to be accepted as decisive."

30. It is claimed by Romania that, because of the reservation made by it to Section 30, the United Nations cannot, without Romania's consent, submit a request for advisory opinion in respect of its difference with Romania. The reservation, it is said, subordinates the competence of the Court to "deal with any dispute that may have arisen between the United Nations and Romania, including a dispute within the framework of the advisory procedure," to the consent of the parties to the dispute. Romania points out that it did not agree that an opinion should be requested of the Court in the present case and concludes that the Court is without jurisdiction.

31. The jurisdiction of the Court under Article 96 of the Charter and Article 65 of the Statute, to give advisory opinions on legal questions, enables United Nations entities to seek guidance from the Court in order to conduct their activities in accordance with law. These opinions are advisory, not binding. As the opinions are intended for the guidance of the United Nations, the consent of States is not a condition precedent to the competence of the Court to give them. As the Court observed in 1950,

"The consent of States, parties to a dispute, is the basis of the Court's jurisdiction in contentious cases. The situation is different in regard to advisory proceedings even where the Request for an Opinion relates to a legal question actually pending between States. The Court's reply is only of an advisory character: as such, it has no binding force. It follows that no State, whether a Member of the United Nations or not, can prevent the giving of an Advisory Opinion which the United Nations considers to be desirable in order to obtain enlightenment as to the course of action it should take. The Court's Opinion is given not to the States, but to the organ which is entitled to request it; the reply of the Court, itself an 'organ of the United Nations', represents its participation in the activities of the Organization, and, in principle, should not be refused." (*Interpretation of Peace Treaties with Bulgaria, Hungary and Romania, First Phase, Advisory Opinion, I.C.J. Reports 1950*, p. 71.)

This reasoning is equally valid where it is suggested that a legal question is pending, not between two States, but between the United Nations and a member State.

32. Romania however relies on its reservation to Section 30 of the General Convention; but that Section operates on a different plane and in a different context from that of Article 96 of the Charter. When the provisions of the Sections are read in their totality, it is clear that their object is to provide a dispute settlement mechanisms. The first sentence of the Section provides for the case where a difference arises out of the interpretation or application of the General Convention between States parties to it, and contains two elements. The first is the treaty obligation to refer the difference to the Court, unless another mode of settlement is decided upon by the parties; the second is the object of the reference to the Court, namely to settle the difference.

33. The United Nations is itself intimately, and for the most part directly, concerned with the operation of the General Convention. Section 30 was therefore so framed as to take in also the settlement of differences between the United Nations and a State party to the General Convention. If such a difference arises, "a request shall be made for an advisory opinion on any legal question involved in accordance with Article 96 of the Charter and Article 65 of the Statute of the Court. The opinion given by the Court shall be accepted as decisive by the parties." This provision pursues the same intent as expressed in the first sentence of Section 30; the particular nature of the proceeding contemplated is attributable to the status as an international organization of one of the parties to the difference.

34. In case of a request for an advisory opinion made under Section 30, the Court would of course have to consider any reservation which a party to the dispute had made to that Section. In the particular case of Romania, the Court would have to consider whether the effect of its reservation could be to act as a bar to the operation of the procedure of request for advisory opinion, or merely to deprive any opinion given of the decisive effect attributed to such opinions by Section 30. But in the present case, the resolution requesting the advisory opinion made no reference to Section 30, and it is evident from the dossier that, in view of the existence of the Romanian reservation, it was not the intention of the Council to invoke Section 30. The request is not made under that Section, and the Court does not therefore need to determine the effect of the Romanian reservation to that provision.

35. Romania however contends that although the Council resolution 1989/75 dated 24 May 1989 does not allude to Section 30 of the General Convention as the basis of its request for advisory opinion, the question which it raises nevertheless relates to the applicability of a substantive provision of the General Convention "to a concrete case considered to be a dispute between a State party to the Convention and the United Nations". It argues that

"If it were accepted that a State party to the Convention, or the United Nations, might ask for disputes concerning the application or interpretation of the Convention to be brought before the Court on a basis other than the provisions of Section 30 of the Convention, that would disrupt the unity of the Convention, by separating the substantive provisions from those relating to dispute settlement, which would be tantamount to a modification of the content and extent of the obligations entered into by States when they consented to be bound by the Convention."

However, the nature and purpose of the present proceedings are, as explained above, that of a request for advice on the applicability of a part of the General Convention, and not the bringing of a dispute before the Court for determination. Furthermore, the "content and extent of the obligations entered into by States"—and, in particular, by Romania—"when they consented to be bound by the Convention" are not modified by the request and by the present advisory opinion.

36. The Court thus finds that the reservation made by Romania to Section 30 of the General Convention does not affect the Court's jurisdiction to entertain the present request.

37. While, however, the absence of the consent of Roma-

nia to the present proceedings can have no effect on the jurisdiction of the Court, it is a matter to be considered when examining the propriety of the Court giving an opinion. It is well settled in the Court's jurisprudence that when a request is made under Article 96 of the Charter by an organ of the United Nations or a specialized agency for an advisory opinion by way of guidance or enlightenment on a question of law, the Court should entertain the request and give its opinion unless there are "compelling reasons" to the contrary. In the *Western Sahara* case the Court adverted to a possible situation in which such a "compelling reason" might be present. In that case, commenting on its observations in the *Interpretation of Peace Treaties* case, to the effect that its competence to give an opinion does not depend on the consent of the interested States, the Court observed:

"the Court recognized that lack of consent might constitute a ground for declining to give the opinion requested if, in the circumstances of a given case, considerations of judicial propriety should oblige the Court to refuse an opinion. In short, the consent of an interested State continues to be relevant, not for the Court's competence, but for the appreciation of the propriety of giving an opinion.

"In certain circumstances, therefore, the lack of consent of an interested State may render the giving of an advisory opinion incompatible with the Court's judicial character. An instance of this would be when the circumstances disclose that to give a reply would have the effect of circumventing the principle that a State is not obliged to allow its disputes to be submitted to judicial settlement without its consent. If such a situation should arise, the powers of the Court under the discretion given to it by Article 65, paragraph 1, of the Statute, would afford sufficient legal means to ensure respect for the fundamental principle of consent to jurisdiction." *(Western Sahara, Advisory Opinion, I.C.J. Reports 1975,* p. 25, paras. 32–33.)

38. In view of the emphasis placed by Romania on its reservation to Article 30 of the General Convention and the absence of its consent to the present request for advisory opinion, the Court must consider whether in this case "to give a reply would have the effect of circumventing the principle that a State is not obliged to allow its disputes to be submitted to judicial settlement without its consent". The Court considers that in the present case to give a reply would have no such effect. Certainly the Council, in its resolution requesting the opinion, did conclude that a difference had arisen between the United Nations and the Government of Romania as to the *applicability* of the Convention to Mr. Dumitru Mazilu. But this difference, and the question put to the Court in the light of it, are not to be confused with the dispute between the United Nations and Romania with respect to the *application of* the General Convention in the case of Mr. Mazilu.

39. In the present case, the Court thus does not find any compelling reason to refuse an advisory opinion. The Court will therefore proceed now to reply to the legal question on which such an opinion has been requested.

40. In order to determine the applicability of Article VI, Section 22, of the General Convention, to special rapporteurs of the Sub-Commission, and its applicability in the case of Mr. Dumitru Mazilu, the Court must first ascertain the meaning of that text.

41. According to Article 105, paragraph 1, of the Charter of the United Nations "The Organization shall enjoy in the territory of each of its Members such privileges and immunities as are necessary for the fulfilment of its purposes." Furthermore, according to Article 105, paragraph 2, "Rep-

resentatives of the Members of the United Nations and officials of the Organization shall similarly enjoy such privileges and immunities as are necessary for the independent exercise of their functions in connection with the Organization." Lastly, Article 105, paragraph 3, states that the General Assembly "may propose conventions to the Members of the United Nations" with a view to determining the details of the application of paragraphs 1 and 2.

42. Acting in conformity with Article 105 of the Charter, the General Assembly approved the General Convention on 13 February 1946 and proposed it for accession by each Member of the United Nations. One hundred and twenty-four States, including Romania, are parties to the Convention.

43. As contemplated by Article 105 of the Charter, the General Convention determines the privileges and immunities enjoyed by the United Nations as such (Arts. II and III), lays down the privileges and immunities of the representatives of Members of the United Nations (Art. IV), and defines those of the officials of the Organization (Art. V). It contains in addition an Article VI entitled "Experts on Missions for the United Nations", divided into two Sections. Section 22 provides as follows:

"Experts (other than officials coming within the scope of Article V) performing missions for the United Nations shall be accorded such privileges and immunities as are necessary for the independent exercise of their functions during the period of their missions, including the time spent on journeys in connection with their missions. In particular they shall be accorded:

"*(a)* immunity from personal arrest or detention and from seizure of their personal baggage;

"*(b)* in respect of words spoken or written and acts done by them in the course of the performance of their mission, immunity from legal process of every kind. This immunity from legal process shall continue to be accorded notwithstanding that the persons concerned are no longer employed on missions for the United Nations;

"*(c)* inviolability for all papers and documents;

"*(d)* for the purpose of their communications with the United Nations, the right to use codes and to receive papers or correspondence by courier or in sealed bags;

"*(e)* the same facilities in respect of currency or exchange restrictions as are accorded to representatives of foreign governments on temporary official missions;

"*(f)* the same immunities and facilities in respect of their personal baggage as are accorded to diplomatic envoys."

Section 23 adds:

"Privileges and immunities are granted to experts in the interests of the United Nations and not for the personal benefit of the individuals themselves. The Secretary-General shall have the right and the duty to waive the immunity of any expert in any case where, in his opinion, the immunity would impede the course of justice and it can be waived without prejudice to the interests of the United Nations."

Finally, Article VII, Section 26, of the General Convention grants certain facilities to experts when travelling on the business of the Organization.

44. The Court will examine the applicability of Section 22 *ratione personae, ratione temporis* and *ratione loci,* that is to say it will consider first what is meant by "experts on missions" for the purposes of Section 22, and then the meaning to be attached to the expression "period of [the] missions", before considering the position of experts in

their relations with the States of which they are nationals or on the territory of which they reside.

45. The General Convention gives no definition of "experts on missions". All it does is to clarify two points, one negative and the other positive. From Section 22 it is clear, first that the officials of the Organization, even if chosen in consideration of their technical expertise in a particular field, are not included in the category of experts within the meaning of that provision; and secondly that only experts performing missions for the United Nations are covered by Section 22. The Section does not, however, furnish any indication of the nature, duration or place of these missions.

46. Nor is there really any guidance in this respect to be found in the *travaux préparatoires* of the General Convention. The Convention was initially drafted and submitted to the General Assembly by the Preparatory Commission set up at San Francisco in June 1945; that initial draft did not contain anything corresponding to the present Article VI. That article was added by the Sub-Commission on Privileges and Immunities established by the Sixth Committee to examine the draft, but the contemporary official records do not make it possible to ascertain the reasons for the addition.

47. The purpose of Section 22 is nevertheless evident, namely, to enable the United Nations to entrust missions to persons who do not have the status of an official of the Organization, and to guarantee them "such privileges and immunities as are necessary for the independent exercise of their functions". The experts thus appointed or elected may or may not be remunerated, may or may not have a contract, may be given a task requiring work over a lengthy period or a short time. The essence of the matter lies not in their administrative position but in the nature of their mission.

48. In practice, according to the information supplied by the Secretary-General, the United Nations has had occasion to entrust missions—increasingly varied in nature—to persons not having the status of United Nations officials. Such persons have been entrusted with mediation, with preparing reports, preparing studies, conducting investigations or finding and establishing facts. They have participated in certain peace-keeping forces, technical assistance work, and a multitude of other activities. In addition, many committees, commissions or similar bodies whose members serve, not as representatives of States, but in a personal capacity, have been set up within the Organization; for example the International Law Commission, the Advisory Committee on Administrative and Budgetary Questions, the International Civil Service Commission, the Human Rights Committee established for the implementation of the International Covenant on Civil and Political Rights, and various other committees of the same nature, such as the Committee on the Elimination of Racial Discrimination or the Committee on the Elimination of All Forms of Discrimination Against Women. In all these cases, the practice of the United Nations shows that the persons so appointed, and in particular the members of these committees and commissions, have been regarded as experts on missions within the meaning of Section 22.

49. According to that Section, experts enjoy the privileges and immunities therein provided for "during the period of their missions, including the time spent on journeys". The question thus arises whether experts are covered by Section 22 only during missions requiring travel or whether they are also covered when there is no such travel or apart from such travel. To answer this question, it is nec-essary to determine the meaning of the word *"mission"* in French and "mission" in English, the two languages in which the General Convention was adopted. Initially, in keeping with its Latin derivation, the word referred to a task entrusted to a person only if that person was sent somewhere to perform it. It implied a journey. The same connotation is apparent in the words, of the same derivation, "emissary", "missionary" and "missive". The French word *"mission"*, and the English word "mission", have however long since acquired a broader meaning and nowadays embrace in general the tasks entrusted to a person, whether or not those tasks involve travel.

50. The Court considers that Section 22, in its reference to experts performing missions for the United Nations, uses the word "mission" in a general sense. While some experts have necessarily to travel in order to perform their tasks, others can perform them without having to travel. In either case, the intent of Section 22 is to ensure the independence of such experts in the interests of the Organization by according them the privileges and immunities necessary for the purpose. In some cases these privileges and immunities are designed to facilitate the travel of experts and their stay abroad, for instance those concerning seizure or searching of personal baggage. In other cases, however, they are of a far more general nature, particularly with respect to communications with the United Nations or the inviolability of papers and documents. Accordingly, Section 22 is applicable to every expert on mission, whether or not he travels.

51. The question whether experts on missions can invoke these privileges and immunities against the States of which they are nationals or on the territory of which they reside has also been raised. In this connection, the Court notes that Section 15 of the General Convention provides that the terms of Article IV, Sections 11, 12 and 13, relating to the representatives of Members "are not applicable as between a representative and the authorities of the State of which he is a national or of which he is or has been the representative". Article V, concerning officials of the Organization, and Article VI, concerning experts on missions for the United Nations, do not, however, contain any comparable rule. This difference of approach can readily be explained. The privileges and immunities of Articles V and VI are conferred with a view to ensuring the independence of international officials and experts in the interests of the Organization. This independence must be respected by all States including the State of nationality and the State of residence. Some States parties to the General Convention (Canada, the Lao People's Democratic Republic, Nepal, Thailand, Turkey and the United States of America) have indeed entered reservations to certain provisions of Article V, or of Article VI itself (Mexico and the United States of America), as regards their nationals or persons habitually resident on their territory. The very fact that it was felt necessary to make such reservations confirms the conclusion that, in the absence of such reservations, experts on missions enjoy the privileges and immunities provided for under the Convention in their relations with the States of which they are nationals or on the territory of which they reside.

52. To sum up, the Court takes the view that Section 22 of the General Convention is applicable to persons (other than United Nations officials) to whom a mission has been entrusted by the Organization and who are therefore entitled to enjoy the privileges and immunities provided for in this Section with a view to the independent exercise of their

functions. During the whole period of such missions, experts enjoy these functional privileges and immunities whether or not they travel. They may be invoked as against the State of nationality or of residence unless a reservation to Section 22 of the General Convention has been validly made by that State.

53. In the light of the foregoing, the Court will now consider the situation of special rapporteurs of the Sub-Commission. This is a question which touches on the legal position of rapporteurs in general, a category of persons whom the United Nations and the specialized agencies find it necessary to engage for the implementation of increasingly varied functions, and is thus one of importance for the whole of the United Nations system.

54. The establishment in 1946 of the Commission, and the establishment in 1947 of the Sub-Commission and the definition in 1949 of its mandate, have been described in paragraph 9 above. On 28 March 1947, the Council decided that the Sub-Commission would be composed of 12 eminent persons, designated by name, subject to the consent of their respective national Governments. Subsequently the members of the Sub-Commission, at present 25 in number, were chosen by the Human Rights Commission under similar conditions, and the Council in resolution 1983/32 of 27 May 1983, expressly "recall[ed] . . . that members of the Sub-Commission are elected by the Commission on Human Rights as experts in their individual capacity", and concluded that their alternates should therefore be elected and should serve on the same basis. The members of the Sub-Commission, since their status is neither that of a representative of a member State nor that of a United Nations official, and since they perform independently for the United Nations functions contemplated in the remit of the Sub-Commission, must be regarded as experts on missions within the meaning of Section 22.

55. In accordance with the practice followed by many United Nations bodies, the Sub-Commission has from time to time appointed rapporteurs or special rapporteurs with the task of studying specified subjects. These rapporteurs or special rapporteurs are normally selected from among members of the Sub-Commission. However, over the past ten years, special rapporteurs have, on at least three occasions, been appointed from outside the Sub-Commission. Furthermore, in numerous cases, special rapporteurs appointed from among members of the Sub-Commission have completed their reports only after their membership of the Sub-Commission had expired. In any event, rapporteurs or special rapporteurs are entrusted by the Sub-Commission with a research mission. Their functions are diverse, since they have to compile, analyse and check the existing documentation on the problem to be studied, prepare a report making appropriate recommendations, and present the report to the Sub-Commission. Since their status is neither that of a representative of a member State nor that of a United Nations official, and since they carry out such research independently for the United Nations, they must be regarded as experts on missions within the meaning of Section 22, even in the event that they are not, or are no longer, members of the Sub-Commission. Consequently they enjoy, in accordance with Section 22, the privileges and immunities necessary for the exercise of their functions, and in particular for the establishment of any contacts which may be useful for the preparation, the drafting and the presentation of their reports to the Sub-Commission.

56. Having thus pronounced on the applicability of Section 22 to special rapporteurs of the Sub-Commission, the Court must now give its opinion on the question of the applicability of this provision in the case of Mr. Dumitru Mazilu.

57. As has been noted earlier (paragraph 10 above), Mr. Dumitru Mazilu was elected a member of the Sub-Commission on 13 March 1984. On 29 August 1985 the Sub-Commission requested him to prepare a report on human rights and youth. The mandate of Mr. Mazilu as a member of the Sub-Commission expired on 31 December 1987. On that date, the report requested on human rights and youth had not been submitted and Mr. Mazilu was retained as special rapporteur by decisions or resolutions of the Sub-Commission adopted on 4 September 1987, 15 August 1988 and 1 September 1988 (paragraphs 12, 18 and 21 above). The Sub-Commission subsequently received a report by Mr. Mazilu, which was published on 10 July 1989; and by its resolution 1989/45 of 1 September 1989 (paragraph 26 above), the Sub-Commission once again retained Mr. Mazilu as special rapporteur, and requested him to update his report in the light of, *inter alia,* the information collected for him by the Secretary-General. Thus from 13 March 1984 to 29 August 1985 Mr. Mazilu had the status of member of the Sub-Commission. From 29 August 1985 to 31 December 1987, he was both a member and a rapporteur of the Sub-Commission. Finally, although since the last-mentioned date he has no longer been a member of the Sub-Commission, he has remained one of its special rapporteurs. At no time during this period, therefore, has he ceased to have the status of an expert on mission within the meaning of Section 22, or ceased to be entitled to enjoy for the exercise of his functions the privileges and immunities provided for therein.

58. Doubt was nevertheless expressed by Romania whether Mr. Mazilu was capable of performing his task as special rapporteur. Romania emphasized that he had been taken seriously ill in May 1987, and had therefore been placed on the retired list pursuant to decisions taken by the competent medical practitioners, in accordance with the applicable Romanian legislation; according to the Romanian written statement, he was at that time still unable to carry out his mandate as special rapporteur. Mr. Mazilu himself informed the United Nations that the state of his health did not prevent him from preparing the report entrusted to him or from going for this purpose to the Centre for Human Rights in Geneva. When a report by Mr. Mazilu was circulated as a document of the Sub-Commission, Romania expressed the view that it was obvious that "since becoming ill in 1987, Mr. Dumitru Mazilu does not possess the intellectual capacity necessary" for the preparation of "a report consistent with the requirements of the United Nations" (paragraph 26 above).

59. It is not for the Court to pronounce on the state of Mr. Mazilu's health, or on its consequences on the work he has done or is to do for the Sub-Commission. It is sufficient for it to note, first that it was for the United Nations to decide whether in the circumstances it wished to retain Mr. Mazilu as special rapporteur, and secondly to take note that decisions to that effect have been taken by the Sub-Commission.

60. In these circumstances Mr. Mazilu continues to have the status of special rapporteur, and as a consequence must be regarded as an expert on mission within the meaning of Section 22 of the General Convention. That Section is accordingly applicable in the case of Mr. Mazilu.

61. For these reasons,

The Court,

Unanimously,

Is of the opinion that Article VI, Section 22, of the Convention on the Privileges and Immunities of the United Nations is applicable in the case of Mr. Dumitru Mazilu as a special rapporteur of the Sub-Commission on Prevention of Discrimination and Protection of Minorities.

Done in French and in English, the French text being authoritative, at the Peace Palace, The Hague, this fifteenth day of December, one thousand nine hundred and eighty-nine, in two copies, one of which will be placed in the archives of the Court and the other transmitted to the Secretary-General of the United Nations.

Separate Opinion of Judge Shigeru Oda

1. I agree with the Court's Opinion that "Article VI, Section 22, of the Convention on the Privileges and Immunities of the United Nations is applicable in the case of Mr. Dumitru Mazilu as a special rapporteur of the Sub-Commission on Prevention of Discrimination and Protection of Minorities." (Para. 61.) I wonder, however, whether the Court, by simply giving this answer, has adequately responded to what the Economic and Social Council had in mind when formulating resolution 1989/75, in which it requested the Court, "on a priority basis", to give an opinion "on the legal question of the applicability of Article VI, Section 22, of the Convention . . . *in the case* of Mr. Dumitru Mazilu as Special Rapporteur of the Sub-Commission." (Emphasis added.) To my mind, this question would have been framed more restrictively if all that was desired was an unelaborated "yes" or "no" answer. The way it was actually framed gave scope, I believe, to certain pronouncements on the modalities of the *application* of Section 22 of the Convention to the *case* of Mr. Mazilu.

2. As is stated in the Preamble to its resolution, the Economic and Social Council made that request after "[h]*aving considered* resolution 1988/37 of 1 September 1988 of the Sub-Commission on Prevention of Discrimination and Protection of Minorities and Commission on Human Rights resolution 1989/37 of 6 March 1989". The background to the request for an advisory opinion made to the Court by the Council may be reconstructed in a slightly different manner from that adopted by the Court, as I consider that greater emphasis could have been laid upon some facts which are more directly relevant to the motives of the Council in submitting the request.

3. Mr. Mazilu, then a member of the Sub-Commission whose term was to expire on 31 December 1987, had been requested by the Sub-Commission to prepare a report on human rights and youth (resolution 1985/12 of 29 August 1985). Relevant information had been regularly despatched to him from the United Nations Centre for Human Rights in Geneva. However, when the 1987 session of the Sub-Commission opened in Geneva on 10 August 1987, Mr. Mazilu had not presented a report and was absent from the meeting. On 12 August 1987, the Sub-Commission was informed that the Secretariat had just received a letter from the Permanent Mission of Romania in Geneva, by which it had been informed that Mr. Mazilu had suffered a heart attack in June and had been told that, as he was still in hospital, he would not be able to travel to Geneva. A telegram bearing the name "D. Mazilu", received on 18 August 1987 by the Secretariat, likewise conveyed a message that he was unable to attend the current session due to heart illness. On 4 September 1987, the Sub-Commission decided to de-

fer until the 1988 session its consideration of the agenda item under which the report to be submitted by Mr. Mazilu was to have been discussed.

4. Subsequently, the Under-Secretary-General for Human Rights in Geneva attempted, by means of a letter of 3 November and a cable of 17 December 1987, to contact Mr. Mazilu and provide him with assistance in the preparation of his report, including arrangements for him to travel to Geneva. The Centre received from Mr. Mazilu two letters postmarked 25 and 29 December 1987 in which he said that he had not received its previous communications, including the invitation to the 1987 session, and that he could not obtain permission from his Government to come to the session in Geneva. In neither of those letters did Mr. Mazilu make any reference to having suffered from an illness. The Under-Secretary-General for Human Rights tried, on 19 January 1988, to make contact with Mr. Mazilu through the United Nations Information Centre in Bucharest and sent a formal invitation asking Mr. Mazilu to come to the Centre in Geneva for consultations during the two-week period from 15 February 1988.

5. In an undated letter addressed to the Under-Secretary-General, that was handed to the Acting Director of the Information Centre in Bucharest on 15 January 1988 and received in Geneva on 1 February 1988, Mr. Mazilu stated that he had been isolated from contacts with the Centre for Human Rights in Geneva and "because of this impossible situation, [he had] suffered very much". He had twice been in hospital and had been forced to retire, as of 1 December 1987, from his post in the Ministry of Foreign Affairs. He went on to say that, despite his willingness to come to Geneva for consultations, the Romanian authorities had refused him a travel permit. He further stated that he was "ready to go to the Centre at 14 February this year". In a series of six letters dated 5 April, 19 April (two of this date), 8 May (two of this date) and 17 May 1988, Mr. Mazilu further described his personal situation: in the first he declared that he had refused to comply with a request addressed to him on 22 February 1988 by a special commission from the Ministry of Foreign Affairs and asking him to cable the Under-Secretary-General to say that he would not be able to prepare his report and to suggest that the task be handed over to another expert. He consistently complained that various kinds of strong pressure had been exerted on him and his family.

6. By a letter of 6 May 1988, the Under-Secretary-General for Human Rights requested the assistance of the Permanent Representative of Romania in Geneva in transmitting to Mr. Mazilu all the relevant information that he needed for the completion of his report. On the same day, the Under-Secretary-General suggested to Mr. Mazilu that he should travel to Geneva for the period extending from 30 May to 10 June 1988. By a letter dated 15 June 1988, the Under-Secretary-General informed the Permanent Representative of Romania that he had decided, as an exceptional measure, to authorize a staff member of the Centre for Human Rights to travel to Bucharest for the purpose of working with Mr. Mazilu on the draft of his report, on the understanding that Mr. Mazilu would be enabled to travel to Geneva to present his report to the Sub-Commission and participate in the ensuing debate. In a letter of 27 June 1988 the Permanent Representative of Romania, without directly responding on that point, simply referred to an offer to prepare a report on human rights and youth which had been made on 29 March 1988 to the Chairman of the Sub-Commission by a new Romanian member of the Sub-

Commission for the term starting 1988, and which his Mission had transmitted to the Centre on 8 April 1988. On 1 July 1988, the Under-Secretary-General re-stated to the Permanent Representative of Romania his previous decision, which would have entailed Mr. Mazilu's paying a short visit to Geneva.

7. Mr. Mazilu, who was no longer a member of the Sub-Commission but remained entrusted with the completion of a report on human rights and youth, was once again absent when the 1988 session of the Sub-Commission opened in Geneva on 8 August 1988. Further to a decision taken at its meeting on 9 August 1988 to discuss the organization of work, a special invitation was cabled to Mr. Mazilu to come to Geneva to present his report. The telegram was not delivered, and the United Nations Information Centre in Bucharest was unable to locate Mr. Mazilu. On 15 August 1988, the Sub-Commission adopted decision 1988/102, whereby it requested the United Nations Secretary-General to establish contact with the Government of Romania. On 17 August 1988, the Under-Secretary-General informed the Sub-Commission that in those contacts the Chargé d'affaires of the Permanent Mission of Romania in New York had stated that Mr. Mazilu had been ill and had retired from the Foreign Office, so that he had been unable to proceed with his study for the report. He also made it clear that any intervention by the United Nations Secretariat and any form of investigation in Bucharest would be seen by his Government as an intervention in Romania's internal affairs. Romania held the view that the case of Mr. Mazilu was an internal matter between a citizen and his own Government, and for that reason no visit to Mr. Mazilu would be allowed.

8. It was in these circumstances that, on 1 September 1988, the Sub-Commission adopted resolution 1988/37, in which it asked the Secretary-General to "invoke [to the Government of Romania] the applicability of the Convention" and requested that Government "to co-operate fully in the implementation of the . . . resolution by ensuring that Mr. Mazilu's report be completed and presented to the Sub-Commission at the earliest possible date". The Sub-Commission further requested the Secretary-General—"in the event the Government of Romania does not concur in the applicability of the provisions of the said Convention in the present case"—"to bring the difference between the United Nations and Romania immediately to the attention of the Commission on Human Rights at its [1989] session". The Sub-Commission also requested the Commission on Human Rights, "in the latter event", "to urge the Economic and Social Council to request . . . from the International Court of Justice an advisory opinion on the applicability of the relevant provisions of the Convention . . . to [that] case".

9. Pursuant to this resolution of the Sub-Commission, the Secretary-General, on 26 October 1988, addressed a Note Verbale to the Permanent Representative of Romania in New York in which, referring to the legal opinion given by the United Nations Legal Counsel on 23 August 1988, he invoked the Convention on the Privileges and Immunities of the United Nations in respect of Mr. Mazilu and requested the Romanian Government to accord the necessary facilities to Mr. Mazilu in order to enable him to complete his assigned task. As no reply was received, the Under-Secretary-General for Human Rights then sent a letter of reminder on 19 December 1988 to the Permanent Representative of Romania in Geneva.

10. On 6 January 1989, the Permanent Representative of Romania in New York handed to the United Nations Legal Counsel an Aide-Mémoire in which the Romanian Government set forth its position. Romania stated that, because of his illness and retirement, Mr. Mazilu was unable to prepare the report and that the question of the application of the Convention would not arise in his case.

11. On 6 March 1989, the Commission on Human Rights adopted resolution 1989/37 by which the Commission, "[n]oting that the Government of Romania does not concur in the applicability of the provisions of the Convention . . . in the case of Mr. Mazilu", recommended a draft resolution to the Economic and Social Council for adoption. On 24 May 1989 that text became the Council's resolution 1989/75 (which is partly quoted in paragraph 1 above), without any substantive change other than the inclusion of the words "on a priority basis".

12. It is clear from these three resolutions (of the Sub-Commission, the Commission and the Council) that the Sub-Commission on Prevention of Discrimination and Protection of Minorities considered that the Convention on the Privileges and Immunities of the United Nations was applicable in the case of Mr. Mazilu, that the Commission on Human Rights considered that Romania "[did] not concur in the applicability of the provisions of the Convention", and that the Economic and Social Council concluded that "a difference [had] arisen between the United Nations and the Government of Romania as to the applicability of the Convention . . . to Mr. Dumitru Mazilu as Special Rapporteur of the Sub-Commission". What, then, was the "difference [that had] arisen between the United Nations and . . . Romania as to the applicability of the Convention . . . to Mr. Dumitru Mazilu as Special Rapporteur"?

13. Firstly, it should be asked whether or not a special rapporteur of the Sub-Commission on the Prevention of Discrimination and Protection of Minorities falls within the category of "Experts on Missions for the United Nations", within the meaning of Article VI, Section 22, of the Convention. The United Nations affirmed the positive view but Romania was of the view, as expressed in its Aide-Mémoire of 6 January 1989, that "the Convention does not provide for rapporteurs, whose activities are only occasional, to be treated as experts on mission for the United Nations". The Court has concluded that a person exercising that function does fall within the category of "experts on missions" (para. 55).

14. Secondly, in order to reply to the question on the applicability of Section 22 of the Convention in the case of Mr. Mazilu as a special rapporteur of the Sub-Commission, the Court must determine whether or not Mr. Mazilu was a special rapporteur at the time of adoption of the Council's resolution asking the Court to give an opinion (i.e., 24 May 1989), and whether he still continues to have that status. In this connection, it would also have been relevant to ask whether his mission was considered to have been completed by the organ which had entrusted it to him. Apart from the description of the background to the request for an advisory opinion and of the ensuing events (paras. 9–26), the Court's Opinion makes scarcely any reference to Romania's position on this aspect of the question, except by recording its allegation that Mr. Mazilu was incapable of "carry[ing] out his mandate as special rapporteur" (para. 58).

15. In its Aide-Mémoire of 6 January 1989, Romania stated that
"In 1987, Mr. Mazilu became gravely ill with a serious heart ailment and was repeatedly hospitalized over a period

of several months. In November 1987, as a result of this illness, he personally applied for disability pension and furnished the necessary medical certificates. In accordance with Romanian law, he was examined by a medical commission which decided that he should be pensioned off on grounds of ill health for an initial period of one year. . . .

"[Q]uite recently, at the end of his first year on a disability pension, he was subjected to a further examination by a similar medical commission, which decided to extend his retirement on grounds of ill health."

While it did not exactly say as much, the Government of Romania undoubtedly considered that Mr. Mazilu was no longer a special rapporteur towards the end of 1987. One may take it that its holding this position was confirmed by the transmission by the Permanent Mission of Romania, on 8 April 1988, of an offer by a newly elected member from Romania to undertake the preparation of the report (see para. 5, above). Romania's position was reiterated in its written statement presented to the Court on 24 July 1989, in which the Court was told that

"During the month of May 1987 [Mr. Mazilu] fell seriously ill and, for that reason and at his request he was, from 1 December 1987, withdrawn from office as being unfit for service. In 1988, a medical commission, acting in accordance with current Romanian legislation, proceeded to re-examine Mr. Dumitru Mazilu's state of health and decided to extend his retirement for a further one-year period on the grounds of continued unfitness for service. . . .

"At the time of his retirement he had not even begun to draw up the report in question." (Written statement of Romania, p. 7.)

16. The United Nations adopted a different position. On 1 July 1988, the Under-Secretary-General for Human Rights stated in a letter to the Permanent Representative of Romania (which referred to the offer of assistance made by the new Romanian member) that "Professor Mazilu's mandate comes from a decision by the Sub-Commission in its resolution 1985/12 [to prepare the report on the subject] and it would be within the competence only of the Sub-Commission, or a higher policy-making body, to change that designation".

17. Here, the essential question examined by the Court was whether Mr. Mazilu, in spite of his desire to maintain his status as a special rapporteur of the Sub-Commission, had lost that status owing to a decision made by the Romanian Government—or, in other words, whether the Romanian Government could have deprived him of the status of a special rapporteur of the Sub-Commission for whatever reasons. I share the view of the Court that "Mr. Mazilu continues to have the status of special rapporteur"—a conclusion that it reaches at the very end of its Opinion, that is, in paragraph 60.

18. Thirdly, while the Court has not been asked to give a general opinion on the range of privileges and immunities enjoyed by a special rapporteur of the Sub-Commission or an expert on a mission for the United Nations (or, in other words, to say what kind of privileges he is entitled to receive, and to specify when, where and whether he is entitled to judicial immunities before the courts or other immunities elsewhere, at home or abroad), the question put by the Economic and Social Council does imply some requirement of attention to the material consequences of Mr. Mazilu's entitlement to the benefit of Article VI, Section 22, of the Convention.

19. The Government of Romania adverted to these matters in its Aide-Mémoire of 6 January 1989, and its position

therein may best be expressed by quoting from its written statement:

"Even if rapporteurs are to some extent seen as having the status of experts of the United Nations, . . . Section 22, of the Convention . . . make[s] it clearly apparent that an expert is not accorded such privileges and immunities anywhere and everywhere, but only in the country to which he is sent on mission and during the time spent on the mission, and also in the countries through which he must transit when travelling to meet the requirements of the mission. In the same way, the privileges and immunities only come into existence from the expert's time of departure, when he travels to accomplish the mission. In so far as the expert's journey to carry out the mission for the United Nations has not begun, for reasons entirely unconnected with his activity as an expert, there is no legal basis upon which to lay claim to privileges and immunities under the Convention, regardless of whether he is in his country of residence or in another country in a capacity other than that of an expert.

"In the country of which he is a citizen, in the country where he has his permanent residence, or in other countries where he may be for reasons unconnected with the mission in question, the expert is only accorded privileges and immunities in relation to the content of the activity in which he engages during his mission (including his spoken and written communications)." (Written statement of Romania, p. 6.)

20. The United Nations clearly took another view, as can be seen from the Note Verbale of 26 October 1988 from the Secretary-General to the Permanent Representative of Romania, in which the Secretary-General maintained that under Section 22 of the Convention Mr. Mazilu should have been "enabled to establish personal contact with the Under-Secretary-General for Human Rights in order that the Centre for Human Rights might accord to Mr. Mazilu the assistance he require[d]". In his written statement presented to the Court on 31 July 1989, the Secretary-General referred to his Note Verbale of 26 October 1988, "in which he invoked the General Convention in respect of Mr. Mazilu and requested the Romanian Government to accord Mr. Mazilu the necessary facilities, including travel to Geneva, in order to enable him to complete his assigned task" (written statement of the United Nations Secretary-General, para. 24).

21. The Advisory Opinion states, in general terms, that "the intent of Section 22 is to ensure the independence of such experts in the interests of the Organization by according them the privileges and immunities necessary for the purpose. In some cases these privileges and immunities are designed to facilitate the travel of experts and their stay abroad, for instance those concerning seizure or searching of personal baggage. In other cases, however, they are of a far more general nature, particularly with respect to communications with the United Nations or the inviolability of papers and documents. Accordingly, Section 22 is applicable to every expert on mission, whether or not he travels." (Para. 50.)

"The privileges and immunities of Article . . . VI are conferred with a view to ensuring the independence of international officials and experts in the interests of the Organization. This independence must be respected by all States including the State of nationality and the State of residence." (Para. 51.)

Though correct, these pronouncements nevertheless do not seem to focus sufficiently upon the essential aspects of the concrete *case* of Mr. Mazilu, including the fact that he was unable to receive documentation from, enter into contact with, or be approached by the United Nations Centre for Human Rights in Geneva and was prevented by his Government from travelling to Geneva for consultations with the Centre or for the purpose of presenting a report to the Sub-Commission. Confirmation of Mr. Mazilu's possession of a general status conferring privileges and immunities does not, in my view, exhaust the Court's remit.

22. It may be contended that the Court has merely been asked to give its opinion "on the legal question of the *applicability* of Article VI, Section 22, of the Convention" (emphasis added), not to consider the matter of its *application*. I am conscious of the Secretary-General's written statement, referred to in the opinion of the Court, to the effect that "the Court . . . has not been asked about the consequences of [the] applicability [of Section 22 of the Convention], that is about what privileges and immunities Mr. Mazilu might enjoy as a result of his status and whether or not these had been violated" (written statement of the United Nations Secretary-General, para. 2), and appreciate that the Legal Counsel, as the representative of the Secretary-General, stated during the oral proceedings that "the [Economic and Social] Council merely addressed a preliminary legal question to the Court, which appears designed to clarify at most the general status of Mr. Mazilu in respect of the Convention without resolving the entire issue that evidently separates the United Nations and the Government". While this may theoretically justify contenting oneself with a mere statement that Article VI, Section 22, is applicable to Mr. Mazilu as a special rapporteur falling within the category of "experts on missions for the United Nations", it is not, in my view, possible to determine the *applicability* of a provision to a concrete case without adequate reference to the way in which it may apply. In this respect, the Court simply states, in very general terms, that "[rapporteurs and special rapporteurs] enjoy, in accordance with Section 22, the privileges and immunities necessary for the exercise of their functions, and in particular for the establishment of any contacts which may be useful for the preparation, the drafting and the presentation of their reports to the Sub-Commission" (para. 55).

23. In my view the Court should not have neglected to recount and deal explicitly with the way in which Mr. Mazilu, in Romania, was isolated from contacts with the United Nations Centre for Human Rights in Geneva and prevented from travelling to Geneva for the completion of the task entrusted to him by the United Nations, because these aspects are fundamental to the case of Mr. Mazilu which the Court has been requested to examine.

24. In conclusion, I believe that, bearing in mind the necessity that the Court's "participation in the activities of the Organization" (*I.C.J. Reports 1950*, p. 71) should be as useful as possible, the final paragraph of the Opinion could have been slightly expanded, without trenching upon contentious matters of fact. Instead of giving a bald affirmative answer, it should have stated more explicitly: firstly, that a special rapporteur of the Sub-Commission on Prevention of Discrimination and Protection of Minorities falls within the category of "Experts on Missions for the United Nations", secondly, that Mr. Mazilu was, at the time of the request for the opinion by the Economic and Social Council, a special rapporteur of the Sub-Commission and that he still exercises that function; and, finally, that Mr. Mazilu was, in the interest of the United Nations, entitled to receive from all parties to the Convention on the Privileges and Immunities of the United Nations, including his national State, all facilities within their power for the fulfilment of his mission. If the Court had made such a pronouncement, it would usefully have drawn attention to the necessity of allowing Mr. Mazilu unimpeded communication with and access to the United Nations Centre for Human Rights.

Separate Opinion of Judge Jens Evensen

I fully agree with the Advisory Opinion of the Court but have some additional views on one special aspect thereof. The Opinion states in paragraph 14 that "strong pressure had been exerted on him [Mr. Mazilu] and on his family".

Thus in his letter of 5 April 1988 to Mr. Martenson, United Nations Under-Secretary-General for Human Rights, Mr. Mazilu maintains that "unfortunately, a strong pressure on me and on my family continues in order to sign such a paper". The paper here referred to is a letter of resignation as rapporteur on the topic assigned to him on "Human rights and youth". In a letter of 19 April 1988 to the Chairman of the relevant United Nations Sub-Commission he also complains that his own Government "did everything possible to discourage me to prepare it [the report]".

As special incidents of such pressures Mr. Mazilu mentions in his letter of 8 May 1988 that: "Since 15 February 1988 more than twenty policemen are following me, my wife and my son day and night."

In his letters he mentions as additional concrete examples of such harassments that his "access to the UN Information centre in Bucharest was blocked" and his "telephone has been disconnected".

However, the sole question put to the Court in the request of ECOSOC is "the legal question of the applicability of Article VI, Section 22, of the Convention on the Privileges and Immunities". Thus the Court has not been requested to express itself on concrete violations of these provisions. But it seems evident that the pressures exerted have caused concern and hardship not only to Mr. Mazilu but also to his family. It seems obvious that the protection provided for in Article VI, Section 22, of the 1946 Convention cannot be confined only to the "expert Mazilu" but must apply to a reasonable extent to his family. This seems self-evident and has been touched upon in one special relation in Article V, Section 18 (*d*), of the Convention. It states that officials of the United Nations shall "be immune, together with their spouses and relatives dependent on them, from immigration restrictions and alien registration".

However, this provision is one concrete expression of a basic general principle. The integrity of a person's family and family life is a basic human right protected by prevailing principles of international law which derive not only from conventional international law or customary international law but from "general principles of law recognized by civilized nations".

Thus in the Universal Declaration of Human Rights adopted by the United Nations General Assembly on 10 December 1948 the integrity of family and family life was laid down as a basic human right in Article 16, paragraph 3, as follows: "The family is the natural and fundamental group unit of society and is entitled to protection by society and the State." This principle, which is a concrete expression of an established principle of human rights in the modern law of nations, has been similarly expressed in other international law instruments. Thus the European Convention on Human Rights (the Rome Convention) of 4 November

1950 provides in Article 8, paragraph 1: "Everyone has the right to respect for his private and family life, his home and his correspondence."

The respect for a person's family and family life must be considered as integral parts of the "privileges and immunities" that are necessary for "the independent exercise of their functions" under Article VI, Section 22, of the 1946 Convention on the Privileges and Immunities of the United Nations.

Separate Opinion of Judge Mohamed Shahabuddeen

I have voted in favour of the Advisory Opinion but consider it necessary to explain my position on four aspects. These relate to: (i) the priority basis of the request; (ii) Romania's reservation to the Convention on the Privileges and Immunities of the United Nations, 1946; (iii) Romania's case relating to Mr. Mazilu's state of health; and (iv) the applicability of the Convention to enable an expert to leave his State of nationality or residence in connection with his mission.

I. The Priority Basis of the Request

The first aspect concerns the Order of Court of 14 June 1989, as referred to in paragraph 3 of the Advisory Opinion. As appears from the Order, "in fixing time-limits for the proceedings" it was found "necessary to bear in mind that the request for opinion was expressed to be made 'on a priority basis' " (*I.C.J. Reports 1989*, p. 10). The dossier shows that the introduction of those last four quoted words in the formulation of the request was the subject of specific challenge in the proceedings of ECOSOC on the ground "that the Council was not empowered to give the Court guidelines with regard to priorities when it did not know what other questions the Court had before it . . ." (Dossier, doc. No. 98, p. 2, *per* Mr. Mikulka, Czechoslovakia, May 1989). I do not think that the challenge was well founded, but it does raise a point of sufficient importance to require me to say that, in my opinion, it is always for the Court, while giving due and proper weight to any representations by a requesting body, to decide in its own discretion whether the circumstances of any particular case justify a priority hearing. The question has been helpfully noticed by the commentators, but I would like to state an approach limited to the level of certain general principles.

As is suggested by the case of the *Trial of Pakistani Prisoners of War, Interim Protection (I.C.J. Reports 1973*, p. 330, paras. 10–14), the eligibility of a new case to be heard in priority to other pending cases presupposes urgency, and the Court remains competent to adjudicate on urgency even where a case formally falls within a category of priority prescribed by the Rules of Court. This, I apprehend, is because of the overriding judicial character of the Court as established by the Charter and the Statute, with both of which the Rules of Court must of course conform in their provisions, as well as in their interpretation and operation.

As I read the *travaux préparatoires* relating to the establishment of the Permanent Court of International Justice, they show that, in contradistinction to the Permanent Court of Arbitration accommodated under the same roof, the former was intended to be a court of justice as normally understood. That key concept, though derived from municipal law, was intended to be generally controlling and, indeed, its primacy has been repeatedly affirmed both by that Court and by this. The chief characteristic of a court of justice is that it is invested with judicial power. In the nor-

mal case, some external agency possessed of appropriate legislative competence over the jurisdiction of a court, or, failing that (as in this case), the machinery competent to amend the constitution of the court, may well have authority to modify the extent of the court's original endowment of judicial power; but, however that may be, the court itself is powerless to alienate any part of its grant. Even when account is taken of the usual caution relating to the transposition of municipal law concepts to the plane of international law, it seems unpersuasive to appeal to the international status of an international court of justice to suggest that on so fundamental a matter such a court is exempt from the restraints applicable to courts of justice as generally understood.

A decision to hear a new case in priority to other pending cases has consequences both for the hearing of the new case and for that of the others, and hence for the good administration of justice. Such a decision pertains to, and forms part of, the Court's judicial power. Accordingly, the Court's rule-making competence would not embrace the transfer to a party or to an entity in an analogous position, of any part of the power of the Court to determine questions relating to priority (the right to submit any views being another matter). This would be so even in an advisory case, given the essential judicial character of the Court. True, in such cases "the reply of the Court, itself an 'organ of the United Nations', represents its participation in the activities of the Organization" (*Interpretation of Peace Treaties with Bulgaria, Hungary and Romania, I.C.J. Reports 1950*, p. 71); but, of course, it is as a court of justice that the Court participates. The Court no doubt has autonomy in the exercise of its rule-making competence; but, however extensive its autonomy, its competence is not unbounded. A clear and definite limit is discovered by the reflection that, however generously it may be construed, the Court's rule-making competence was intended to be used for the purpose of regulating the exercise of the Court's judicial power, not for the purpose of disposing of it. The Rules of Court are made, and are intended to be read, on the basis of this understanding. The Court remains free, therefore, to determine the need for priority in all cases.

II. The Romanian Reservation to the General Convention

Paragraphs 29 to 36 of the Advisory Opinion deal with Romania's contention that the absence of its consent bars recourse to the advisory jurisdiction of the Court under Article 96 of the Charter. As the Advisory Opinion suggests, Romania logically can only be taking that position if it is also taking the position that its reservation to Section 30 of the General Convention is applicable to the Charter so as to impose a requirement for consent as a pre-condition to recourse to that jurisdiction. I agree with the Court in not accepting this contention but would like to give my reasons.

Aside from the question whether the Charter admits of reservations and apart from the difficulty presented by the notion of a reservation being made to a treaty (in this case, the Charter) by a State after it has become a party to the treaty, it seems to me that the idea of a reservation to one treaty operating also as a reservation to another treaty is essentially not right. In the *Nuclear Tests (Australia v. France)* case (*I.C.J. Reports 1974*, p. 253) the Court had before it a contention that certain reservations contained in a declaration by France accepting the compulsory jurisdiction of the Court under Article 36, paragraph 2, of the Statute applied also to its obligations under the General Act for the Pacific Settlement of International Disputes, 1928. Referring to this contention and to Article 2, paragraph 1 *(d)*, of the Vienna Convention on the Law of Treaties, 1969, the joint minority opinion (Judges Onyeama, Dillard, Jiménez de Aréchaga and Sir Humphrey Waldock) observed:

"in principle, a reservation relates exclusively to a State's expression of consent to be bound by a particular treaty or instrument and to the obligations assumed by that expression of consent. Consequently, the notion that a reservation attached to one international agreement, by some unspecified process, is to be superimposed upon or transferred to another international instrument is alien to the very concept of a reservation in international law; and also cuts across the rules governing the notification, acceptance and rejection of reservations." *(Ibid.,* p. 350.)

The correctness of this statement of principle is scarcely open to challenge.

The effect of the Romanian reservation is on Section 30 of the Convention alone. By contrast, competence to request an advisory opinion is regulated exclusively by Article 96 of the Charter. Section 30 of the Convention does not and cannot confer a competence on anyone to request an advisory opinion; the Section is hinged on any such competence conferred by or under Article 96 of the Charter. All that Section 30 of the Convention does is to make it compulsory for the body vested with appropriate competence by or under Article 96 of the Charter to exercise that competence in relation to certain differences, and incumbent on the parties to such differences to accept the resulting advisory opinion as "decisive". The action of the reservation is exerted on these two additional features and not on the Court's jurisdiction under Article 96 of the Charter. If, because of the reservation, these two features fall away in the case of Romania, the jurisdiction under Article 96 of the Charter remains, as before, unaffected by the reservation. And this, it should be added, is putting at its highest Romania's view of the extent to which the reservation affects Section 30 of the Convention—a view that is open to dispute but which I agree with the Court it is not necessary to examine (see paragraph 34 of the Advisory Opinion).

In sum then, while agreeing with paragraph 36 of the Advisory Opinion that "the reservation made by Romania to Section 30 of the General Convention does not affect the Court's jurisdiction to entertain the present request", I would like to add that the reservation does not affect that jurisdiction because it simply cannot.

III. Romania's Case Relating to Mr. Mazilu's State of Health

On the question of Mr. Mazilu's state of health, I agree with the finding made in paragraph 59 of the Advisory Opinion to the effect "that it was for the United Nations to decide whether in the circumstances it wished to retain Mr. Mazilu as special rapporteur . . ."; but, apart from the circumstance that that proposition is so self-evident that I hesitate to interpret the material as credibly evidencing an intention by Romania to dispute it, it appears to me that the Romanian argument on this branch of the case does not necessarily depend on who has the right to retain Mr. Mazilu as special rapporteur or to terminate his appointment on grounds of illness (governmental appointments being another

matter). What Romania seems to be saying in its written statement to the Court, as I understand it, is something different which may be expressed this way:

(i) even assuming that Mr. Mazilu was and continues to be an expert on mission (as is found by the Court, with which I agree), illness so wholly incapacitated him from carrying out his functions as to preclude him from having any need for, and therefore any entitlement to, the privileges and immunities provided for by the Convention, these being functionally based; and

(ii) Romania has exclusive domestic jurisdiction over the health of its nationals, with the consequence that, Romania having made its own determination of Mr. Mazilu's state of health, that determination is final for all purposes, and any attempt by the United Nations to verify it within Romania or to act contrary to it would be an interference in Romania's internal affairs (paras. 19 and 26 of the Advisory Opinion; Dossier, doc. No. 61, para. 53, and doc. No. 64, para. 42; Romania's written statement to the Court, pp. 7–8; United States written statement to the Court, p. 10; and the Secretary-General's written statement to the Court, paras. 17, 19 and 67).

If indeed this is the Romanian argument, it would not appear to be free from difficulty. Mr. Mazilu's status as a special rapporteur is based on a relationship subsisting exclusively as between himself and the Sub-Commission on Prevention of Discrimination and Protection of Minorities. A decision as to whether a special rapporteur is in such a state of health as to be incapable of functioning is one to be made by the Sub-Commission as the employer. As a stranger in law to the relationship between the Sub-Commission and Mr. Mazilu, Romania had no juridical basis for intervening to impose its own opinion on the point. No doubt States ordinarily have exclusive domestic jurisdiction over questions concerning the health of their nationals and can and do intervene on such questions as between employer and employee. But the settled jurisprudence of the Court makes it clear that a matter which would normally be within a State's domestic jurisdiction ceases to be exclusively so to the extent to which it has come to be also governed by any international obligations undertaken by the State (see the *Nationality Decrees Issued in Tunis and Morocco* case, *P.C.I.J., Series B, No. 4,* pp. 21–24; the *Acquisition of Polish Nationality* case, *P.C.I.J., Series B, No. 7,* p. 16; the *Certain Norwegian Loans* case, *I.C.J. Reports 1957,* pp. 37–38, *per* Judge Lauterpacht; and the *Aegean Sea Continental Shelf* case, *I.C.J. Reports 1978,* pp. 24–25).

In my view, in agreeing to accord privileges and immunities to their nationals for the purpose of enabling them to carry out their functions when appointed as experts on missions, alternatively, by reason of their being parties to the Charter and committed to promoting its objectives, Member States by necessary implication conceded to the United Nations a right in good faith (not questioned in this case) to determine the capacity of such nationals, on grounds of ill health or otherwise, to continue to carry out their functions. If the Romanian position is correct, the United Nations would be wholly excluded from exercising that right once the view was expressed by the State of nationality that an expert was too ill to perform. It is not necessary, in my view, to consider what settlement procedures might be available if a dispute were to arise as to whether the United Nations was acting in good faith.

IV. Applicability of the General Convention to Enable an Expert to Leave His State of Nationality or Residence in Connection with His Mission

The circumstance that the Court's Advisory Opinion specifies some of the more important privileges and immunities available to experts on missions, and therefore to Mr. Mazilu as such an expert, does not perhaps mesh entirely with the view presented by the Secretary-General to the effect that "the Court . . . has not been asked . . . about what privileges and immunities Mr. Mazilu might enjoy as a result of his status . . ." (Advisory Opinion, para. 27). If the Court has in fact acted on a less sparing conception of the scope of the request, this is because, as it appears to me, the view referred to is admissible not by way of modification of the scope of the request, but only by way of interpretation, as it was of course intended; and possible interpretations advanced before the Court do not restrict the range of choice open to it as to the meaning of the governing text of the resolution presenting the request (see the analogous approach taken in the *Factory at Chorzów* case, *P.C.I.J., Series A, No. 13*, pp. 15–16; the *Free Zones of Upper Savoy and the District of Gex* case, *P.C.I.J., Series A, No. 22*, p. 15, and *P.C.I.J., Series A/B, No. 46*, p. 138; the *South West Africa* case, *I.C.J. Reports 1966*, p. 354, *per* Judge Jessup, dissenting; and *Application for Revision and Interpretation of the Judgment of 24 February 1982 in the Case concerning the Continental Shelf* (Tunisia/Libyan Arab Jamahiriya) (*Tunisia v. Libyan Arab Jamahiriya*), *Judgment, I.C.J. Reports 1985*, p. 223).

In settling what interpretation is to be placed on the question before the Court, it would seem best to approach the question "in the light of the actual framework of fact and law in which it falls for consideration" (*Interpretation of the Agreement of 25 March 1951 between the WHO and Egypt, I.C.J. Reports 1980*, p. 76). That framework may be gathered from the terms of the request viewed against the background material submitted by the Secretary-General in relation to the Sub-Commission's own resolution to which the request expressly refers (see the approach taken by Judge Lauterpacht in the *South West Africa* case, *I.C.J. Reports 1956*, p. 36). Interpreted this way, it is reasonably clear that the request is intended to invite an answer not only as to whether Article VI, Section 22, of the General Convention is applicable in principle "in the case of Mr. Dumitru Mazilu as Special Rapporteur of the Sub-Commission", but also, if it is applicable, as to the way in which it is applicable in the particular circumstances of that particular case. When the context and structure of the request are considered, technical distinctions between the concepts of "applicability" and "application" do not have the effect of excluding these aspects, provided that the answer does not trench on any question as to whether any particular privilege or immunity was violated.

In my view, therefore, the Advisory Opinion has correctly gone on to identify particular privileges and immunities available to experts on missions, and hence to Mr. Mazilu as such an expert. But there is one particular right, namely, that relating to travel, which, I believe, merits closer attention. This aspect is linked to paragraph 55 of the Advisory Opinion which states that rapporteurs or special rapporteurs "enjoy, in accordance with Section 22, the privileges and immunities necessary for the exercise of their functions, and in particular for the establishment of any contacts which may be useful for the preparation, the drafting and the presentation of their reports. . . ." I understand this as conveying, among other things, that experts on missions, whether or not assigned to any particular place, are entitled to invoke the privileges and immunities conferred by the Convention to enable them to leave their State of nationality or residence in connection with the performance of their missions. With this view I agree, but I should like to give my reasons for supporting it with a degree of specificity commensurate with the special, if not primary, interest which it manifestly has for the requesting organ, as may be gathered from the several references to it, on one aspect or another, in the Advisory Opinion itself (see paras. 11, 13, 14, 16, 17, 18, 21, 22, 24, 26, 49 and 52).

My reasons may be conveniently set out in relation to the Romanian contention by which the issue was presented. Treating Mr. Mazilu as an expert present in his own State but assigned to function elsewhere (a position which I will assume for the sake of analysis), Romania submitted that—

"Section 22 of the Convention provides that 'experts . . . performing missions for the United Nations shall be accorded such privileges and immunities as are necessary for the independent exercise of their functions'. Those provisions make it clearly apparent that an expert is not accorded such privileges and immunities anywhere and everywhere, but only in the country to which he is sent on mission and during the time spent on the mission, and also in the countries to which he must transit when travelling to meet the requirements of the mission. In the same way, the privileges and immunities only come into existence from the expert's time of departure, when he travels to accomplish the mission. In so far as the expert's journey to carry out the mission for the United Nations has not begun, for reasons entirely unconnected with his activity as an expert, there is no legal basis upon which to lay claim to privileges and immunities under the Convention, regardless of whether he is in his country of residence or in another country, in a capacity other than that of an expert.

"In the country of which he is a citizen, in the country where he has his permanent residence, or in other countries where he may be for reasons unconnected with the mission in question, the expert is only accorded privileges and immunities in relation to the content of the activity in which he engages during his mission (including his spoken and written communications)." (Romania's written statement to the Court, p. 6. And see Advisory Opinion, para. 24.)

I accept as accurate Romania's statement "that an expert is not accorded such privileges and immunities anywhere and everywhere": their functional character clearly excludes so wholesale and undiscriminating an application. Where I have difficulty is in so far as it would seem to follow from Romania's position that an expert present in a Member State who, for reasons entirely unconnected with his activity as an expert, has not in fact begun his outward journey to carry out a mission falling to be discharged elsewhere but who wishes to embark on such a journey, cannot, as a matter of law, invoke those privileges and immunities to enable him to commence the journey. This is because, on Romania's argument, so long as he has not begun his journey, he is not entitled to any privileges and immunities apart from the limited and not relevant exception mentioned in its statement. So, the limited exception apart, not having begun the journey, the expert has no privileges and immunities, and, not having any privileges and immunities, he cannot enforce a right to begin the journey. Locked in within this system, the expert may well be unable to perform the mission which the privileges and immunities were intended to enable him to perform. Possibly, so strange a result could collide with the position taken by the Court as to the "duty [of a party to a treaty] not to deprive [it] of its object and purpose" *(Military and Paramilitary Activities in and against Nicaragua, I.C.J. Reports 1986,* p. 140, para. 280; cf. *ibid.,* p. 249, para. 79, *per* Judge Oda, dissenting). I propose, however, to approach the matter in the following way.

In conferring privileges and immunities on experts "during ... the time spent on journeys in connection with their missions", Article VI, Section 22, of the Convention obviously regards the making of such a journey as an essential step in the discharge of an expert's mission, as, indeed, it plainly is. Equally obviously, an expert may need to commence such a journey from any Member State in which he happens to be, even if he is there for a purpose wholly unconnected with his mission. Accordingly, his entitlement under that provision to "such privileges and immunities as are necessary for the independent exercise of [his] functions during the period of" his mission would extend to enable him to embark on such a journey undertaken in connection with the discharge of those functions. The express reference to "privileges and immunities ... during ... the time spent on journeys in connection with" his mission cannot be read as meaning that privileges and immunities are available only if and when such a journey is in fact in progress but not also for the purpose of enforcing a right to commence the journey in the first place.

Under Article VII, Section 26, of the General Convention (referred to in paragraph 43 of the Advisory Opinion) an expert is entitled to travelling facilities (including the issue of any necessary visas) from a Member State to which or through which he intends to go in connection with his mission. In exercise of this entitlement, the expert may have applied to such a State for visas and other facilities and secured them only to discover that he cannot use them if he cannot rely on the privileges and immunities conferred by Article VI, Section 22, of the Convention to enable him to leave a Member State in which he happens to be present for a purpose unconnected with his mission.

However strict may be the construction to be placed on provisions providing for privileges and immunities (see Alain Plantey, *Droit et pratique de la Fonction publique internationale,* Paris, 1977, p. 409, para. 1298), results as surprising as those indicated above suggest that the privileges and immunities conferred on an expert by Article VI, Section 22, of the Convention must, subject to the limitations prescribed in that Article, be construed as extending to afford protection against all acts which could frustrate their operation or empty them of real content, with the consequence of effectively preventing the expert from embarking on or resuming his mission. The dangers which proverbially lurk in the use of maxims do not seem to forbid recourse in this case to the well-known words *quando lex aliquid alicui concedit concedere videtur et id sine quo res ipsa esse non potest—* when the law gives a man anything, it gives him that also without which the thing itself cannot exist.

Explaining the rarity of references in the judgements of the Court to arbitral decisions, Judge Charles De Visscher wrote, "The rarity of such references is a matter of prudence; the Court is careful not to introduce into its decisions elements whose heterogeneous character might escape its vigilance" (Charles De Visscher, *Theory and Reality in Public International Law,* rev. ed., 1968, p. 391). Judge Jessup's interesting explanation was "The Court, *qua* Court, naturally hesitates to cite individuals or national courts lest it appear to have some bias or predilection" (Judge Philip C. Jessup, letter dated 16 August 1979,

Annuaire de l'Institut de droit international, 1985, Vol. 61, I, p. 253). No doubt these words of caution extend to other decisions as well. But, apart from the fact that there is some flexibility in the case of individual judges, I do believe that the judicial policy concerning such citations, wise as it is, is not of such rigidity as in practice to disable the Court from benefiting from other experience, particularly where specific guidance in its own jurisprudence is lacking, as seems to be the case here.

Without suggesting that it is wholly applicable, I turn accordingly to the general approach taken in the majority opinion of the European Court of Human Rights in the *Golder* case (Judgment of 21 February 1975, Series A, Vol. 18) in which that Court had to construe Article 6, paragraph 1, of the European Convention on Human Rights, reading "In the determination of his civil rights and obligations or of any criminal charge against him, everyone is entitled to a fair and public hearing within a reasonable time by an independent and impartial tribunal established by law ..." Recognizing that this provision did not in terms confer a right of access to the courts, the European Court of Human Rights nevertheless affirmed the existence of such a right in these words: "While the right to a fair, public and expeditious judicial procedure can assuredly apply only to proceedings in being, it does not, however, necessarily follow that a right to the very institution of such proceedings is thereby excluded ..." (*Ibid.,* p. 15, para. 32.) In effect, if it was correct to say that Article 6, paragraph 1, of the European Convention excluded an antecedent right to institute proceedings in a court, it would follow that the right conferred by that provision to a fair, public and expeditious judicial procedure could prove to be largely devoid of substance. Likewise in this case, if it is correct to say that Article VI, Section 22, of the General Convention excludes an antecedent right to commence a journey from a Member State in connection with the performance of the expert's mission where the expert's presence in that State was for a purpose unconnected with the mission, it would follow that the right conferred on him by that provisions to privileges and immunities "during ... the time spent on journeys in connection with" such a mission (not to speak of other privileges and immunities) could turn out to be illusory, with the further result that the mission itself could remain undischarged.

While the situation in the *Golder* case differs in several respects from that here, at the level of principle it would seem to me that the reasoning in that case supports the conclusion that Article VI, Section 22, of the General Convention is applicable to enable an expert to leave any Member State for the purpose of carrying out his mission even if his presence in that State was for a purpose entirely unconnected with the mission.

SEE ALSO *Arrest, Detention, and Abduction of International Civil Servants; Detention: UN Staff Members; Romania: "A Special View on the Romanian Case."*

SRI LANKA. The Democratic Socialist Republic of Sri Lanka is a country in southern Asia occupying a large island in the Indian Ocean off the southeastern tip of the Indian sub-continent. It achieved independence in 1948 as the British Dominion then known as Ceylon and became an independent republic on 22 May 1972.

It became a member of the United Nations in 1955. Its population is estimated by the UN (1990) to be 17,451,000. Ethnic groups include Sinhala (74%), Sri Lanka Tamils (12.7%), Sri Lanka Moors (7%), Indian Tamils (5.5%), Malays (0.29%), Burghers (0.26%), and others (0.2%). The Sinhalese use Sinhala (official), a language of Indo–Aryan origin. The Tamils use Tamil (also official), the national language which is also the language of the Dravidians of southern India. Some Moors use Tamil, others Sinhala. Descendents of European peoples generally use English. Religions practiced include Buddhism, Christianity (Roman Catholic and a number of Protestant denominations), Hinduism, and Islam. Literacy is estimated at 87%.

The government (1990) took the form of a republic and member of the Commonwealth of Nations, of which the British sovereign is the symbolic head. Under the 1978 constitution, the president is elected by popular vote for a six-year term and must receive at least 50% of all votes cast. He serves as head of State, head of the executive and of the government, and commander-in-chief of the armed forces. The prime minister and other ministers, who must be members of parliament, are appointed by the president. Legislation is prepared by the 168-member unicameral Parliament, the members of which normally serve for a period of six years; however, in 1982, the electorate voted to extend the term of the existing parliament for a further six years. The president has no veto over decisions made by the parliament. Political parties include the United National Party, the Tamil United Liberation Front, the Sri Lanka Freedom Party, and the Sri Lanka Mahajaua Party.

The long tradition of amity, cordiality, and mutual cooperation that had characterized relationships between ethnic and religious groups in multiracial and multireligious Sri Lanka over many generations was broken in 1983 by open conflict between the Tamil minority and the Sinhalese majority. The aim of the Tamils was to establish a separate homeland in northern Sri Lanka which would have close ties with the Tamil-speaking peoples of nearby southern India.

The guerrilla insurgency waged by the Tamils in the northern and eastern provinces of Sri Lanka, and the efforts of the government to crush that insurgency by attacks on the city of Jaffna and other portions of the Jaffna Peninsula, resulted in more than 6,000 casualties up to July 1987. At that time, Indian forces entered the country as a peacekeeping force in accordance with an agreement signed by Ceylonese President J.R. Jayewardene and Indian Prime Minister Rajiv Gandhi and began to disarm the Tamil fighters. However, some separatist groups who opposed the peace accord, including the Liberation Tigers of Tamil Eelam, went underground and continued to attack rival Tamil groups and to wreck their offices and the villages in which they lived.

The Indian peacekeeping force, which at one time numbered as many as 50,000 men, spent nearly three years in Sri Lanka but was not able to disarm the Tamil Liberation Tigers, a group of fighters whose goal is a separate Tamil homeland. The force was withdrawn in March 1990 by India's new Prime Minister V. P. Singh at the request of Sri Lanka's new President Ranasinghe Premadasa. Both had won elections in 1989, the latter with a pledge to get the Indians out of the country and with the confidence and cooperation of the People's Front of Liberation Tigers, who hope to become the elected government of a Tamil homeland.

After the withdrawal of the peacekeeping force, thousands of Tamils who had cooperated with it fled to India in ships, hoping to settle in Tamil Nadu, the Indian state of which Madras is capital. India, however, refused to allow them to disembark on the ground that many did not fit the international definition of the term "refugee."

STANDARD MINIMUM RULES FOR THE TREATMENT OF PRISONERS (1957).

The purpose of the Standard Minimum Rules is not to describe in detail how a model system of penal institutions functions but rather to set out what are generally accepted as good principles and practices to be followed in the treatment of prisoners and the management of penal institutions.

The Standard Minimum Rules were adopted by the First United Nations Congress on the Prevention of Crime and the Treatment of Offenders in 1955, and were annexed to the report of that Congress (United Nations publication, Sales No. 1956.IV.4, annex I.A.) They were approved and recommended to States by the UN Economic and Social Council on 31 July 1957. In 1977, the council decided that a new Section E (rule 95) should be added to the rules (resolution 2076 [LXII]). The text, thus amended, is as follows:

Preliminary Observations

1. The following rules are not intended to describe in detail a model system of penal institutions. They seek only, on the basis of the general consensus of contemporary thought and the essential elements of the most adequate systems of today, to set out what is generally accepted as being good principle and practice in the treatment of prisoners and the management of institutions.

2. In view of the great variety of legal, social, economic and geographical conditions of the world, it is evident that not all of the rules are capable of application in all places

and at all times. They should, however, serve to stimulate a constant endeavour to overcome practical difficulties in the way of their application, in the knowledge that they represent, as a whole, the minimum conditions which are accepted as suitable by the United Nations.

3. On the other hand, the rules cover a field in which thought is constantly developing. They are not intended to preclude experiment and practices, provided these are in harmony with the principles and seek to further the purposes which derive from the text of the rules as a whole. It will always be justifiable for the central prison administration to authorize departures from the rules in this spirit.

4. (1) Part I of the rules covers the general management of institutions, and is applicable to all categories of prisoners, criminal or civil, untried or convicted, including prisoners subject to "security measures" or corrective measures ordered by the judge.

(2) Part II contains rules applicable only to the special categories dealt with in each section. Nevertheless, the rules under section A, applicable to prisoners under sentence, shall be equally applicable to categories of prisoners dealt with in sections B, C and D, provided they do not conflict with the rules governing those categories and are for their benefit.

5. (1) The rules do not seek to regulate the management of institutions set aside for young persons such as Borstal institutions or correctional schools, but in general part I would be equally applicable in such institutions.

(2) The category of young prisoners should include at least all young persons who come within the jurisdiction of juvenile courts. As a rule, such young persons should not be sentenced to imprisonment.

Part I—Rules of General Application

Basic Principle. 6. (1) The following rules shall be applied impartially. There shall be no discrimination on grounds of race, colour, sex, language, religion, political or other opinion, national or social origin, property, birth or other status.

(2) On the other hand, it is necessary to respect the religious beliefs and moral precepts of the group to which a prisoner belongs.

Register. 7. (1) In every place where persons are imprisoned there shall be kept a bound registration book with numbered pages in which shall be entered in respect of each prisoner received:

(a) Information concerning his identity;

(b) The reasons for his commitment and the authority therefor;

(c) The day and hour of his admission and release.

(2) No person shall be received in an institution without a valid commitment order of which the details shall have been previously entered in the register.

Separation of Categories. 8. The different categories of prisoners shall be kept in separate institutions or parts of institutions taking account of their sex, age, criminal record, the legal reason for their detention and the necessities of their treatment. Thus,

(a) Men and women shall so far as possible be detained in separate institutions; in an institution which receives both men and women the whole of the premises allocated to women shall be entirely separate;

(b) Untried prisoners shall be kept separate from convicted prisoners;

(c) Persons imprisoned for debt and other civil prisoners shall be kept separate from persons imprisoned by reason of a criminal offence;

(d) Young prisoners shall be kept separate from adults.

Accommodation. 9. (1) Where sleeping accommodation is in individual cells or rooms, each prisoner shall occupy by night a cell or room by himself. If for special reasons, such as temporary overcrowding, it becomes necessary for the central prison administration to make an exception to this rule, it is not desirable to have two prisoners in a cell or room.

(2) Where dormitories are used, they shall be occupied by prisoners carefully selected as being suitable to associate with one another in those conditions. There shall be regular supervision by night, in keeping with the nature of the institution.

10. All accommodation provided for the use of prisoners and in particular all sleeping accommodation shall meet all requirements of health, due regard being paid to climatic conditions and particularly to cubic content of air, minimum floor space, lighting, heating and ventilation.

11. In all places where prisoners are required to live or work,

(a) The windows shall be large enough to enable the prisoners to read or work by natural light, and shall be so constructed that they can allow the entrance of fresh air whether or not there is artificial ventilation;

(b) Artificial light shall be provided sufficient for the prisoners to read or work without injury to eyesight.

12. The sanitary installations shall be adequate to enable every prisoner to comply with the needs of nature when necessary and in a clean and decent manner.

13. Adequate bathing and shower installations shall be provided so that every prisoner may be enabled and required to have a bath or shower, at a temperature suitable to the climate, as frequently as necessary for general hygiene according to season and geographical region, but at least once a week in a temperate climate.

14. All parts of an institution regularly used by prisoners shall be properly maintained and kept scrupulously clean at all times.

Personal Hygiene. 15. Prisoners shall be required to keep their persons clean, and to this end they shall be provided with water and with such toilet articles as are necessary for health and cleanliness.

16. In order that prisoners may maintain a good appearance compatible with their self-respect, facilities shall be provided for the proper care of the hair and beard, and men shall be enabled to shave regularly.

Clothing and Bedding. 17. (1) Every prisoner who is not allowed to wear his own clothing shall be provided with an outfit of clothing suitable for the climate and adequate to keep him in good health. Such clothing shall in no manner be degrading or humiliating.

(2) All clothing shall be clean and kept in proper condition. Underclothing shall be changed and washed as often as necessary for the maintenance of hygiene.

(3) In exceptional circumstances, whenever a prisoner is removed outside the institution for an authorized purpose, he shall be allowed to wear his own clothing or other inconspicuous clothing.

18. If prisoners are allowed to wear their own clothing, arrangements shall be made on their admission to the institution to ensure that it shall be clean and fit for use.

19. Every prisoner shall, in accordance with local or national standards, be provided with a separate bed, and with

separate and sufficient bedding which shall be clean when issued, kept in good order and changed often enough to ensure its cleanliness.

Food. 20. (1) Every prisoner shall be provided by the administration at the usual hours with food of nutritional value adequate for health and strength, of wholesome quality and well prepared and served.

(2) Drinking water shall be available to every prisoner whenever he needs it.

Exercise and Sport. 21. (1) Every prisoner who is not employed in outdoor work shall have at least one hour of suitable exercise in the open air daily if the weather permits.

(2) Young prisoners, and others of suitable age and physique, shall receive physical and recreational training during the period of exercise. To this end space, installations and equipment should be provided.

Medical Services. 22. (1) At every institution there shall be available the services of at least one qualified medical officer who should have some knowledge of psychiatry. The medical services should be organized in close relationship to the general health administration of the community or nation. They shall include a psychiatric service for the diagnosis and, in proper cases, the treatment of states of mental abnormality.

(2) Sick prisoners who require specialist treatment shall be transferred to specialized institutions or to civil hospitals. Where hospital facilities are provided in an institution, their equipment, furnishing and pharmaceutical supplies shall be proper for the medical care and treatment of sick prisoners, and there shall be a staff of suitably trained officers.

(3) The services of a qualified dental officer shall be available to every prisoner.

23. (1) In women's institutions there shall be special accommodation for all necessary pre-natal and post-natal care and treatment. Arrangements shall be made wherever practicable for children to be born in a hospital outside the institution. If a child is born in prison, this fact shall not be mentioned in the birth certificate.

(2) Where nursing infants are allowed to remain in the institution with their mothers, provision shall be made for a nursery staffed by qualified persons, where the infants shall be placed when they are not in the care of their mothers.

24. The medical officer shall see and examine every prisoner as soon as possible after his admission and thereafter as necessary, with a view particularly to the discovery of physical or mental illness and the taking of all necessary measures; the segregation of prisoners suspected of infectious or contagious conditions; the noting of physical or mental defects which might hamper rehabilitation, and the determination of the physical capacity of every prisoner for work.

25. (1) The medical officer shall have the care of the physical and mental health of the prisoners and should daily see all sick prisoners, all who complain of illness, and any prisoner to whom his attention is specially directed.

(2) The medical officer shall report to the director whenever he considers that a prisoner's physical or mental health has been or will be injuriously affected by continued imprisonment or by any condition of imprisonment.

26. (1) The medical officer shall regularly inspect and advise the director upon:

(a) The quantity, quality, preparation and service of food;

(b) The hygiene and cleanliness of the institution and the prisoners;

(c) The sanitation, heating, lighting and ventilation of the institution;

(d) The suitability and cleanliness of the prisoner's clothing and bedding;

(e) The observance of the rules concerning physical education and sports, in cases where there is no technical personnel in charge of these activities.

(2) The director shall take into consideration the reports and advice that the medical officer submits according to rules 25 (2) and 26 and, in case he concurs with the recommendations made, shall take immediate steps to give effect to those recommendations; if they are not within his competence or if he does not concur with them, he shall immediately submit his own report and the advice of the medical officer to higher authority.

Discipline and Punishment. 27. Discipline and order shall be maintained with firmness, but with no more restriction than is necessary for safe custody and well-ordered community life.

28. (1) No prisoner shall be employed, in the service of the institution, in any disciplinary capacity.

(2) This rule shall not, however, impede the proper functioning of systems based on self-government, under which specified social, educational or sports activities or responsibilities are entrusted, under supervision, to prisoners who are formed into groups for the purposes of treatment.

29. The following shall always be determined by the law or by the regulation of the competent administrative authority:

(a) Conduct constituting a disciplinary offence;

(b) The types and duration of punishment which may be inflicted;

(c) The authority competent to impose such punishment.

30. (1) No prisoner shall be punished except in accordance with the terms of such law or regulation, and never twice for the same offence.

(2) No prisoner shall be punished unless he has been informed of the offence alleged against him and given a proper opportunity of presenting his defence. The competent authority shall conduct a thorough examination of the case.

(3) Where necessary and practicable the prisoner shall be allowed to make his defence through an interpreter.

31. Corporal punishment, punishment by placing in a dark cell, and all cruel, inhuman or degrading punishments shall be completely prohibited as punishments for disciplinary offences.

32. (1) Punishment by close confinement or reduction of diet shall never be inflicted unless the medical officer has examined the prisoner and certified in writing that he is fit to sustain it.

(2) The same shall apply to any other punishment that may be prejudicial to the physical or mental health of a prisoner. In no case may such punishment be contrary to or depart from the principle stated in rule 31.

(3) The medical officer shall visit daily prisoners undergoing such punishments and shall advise the director if he considers the termination or alteration of the punishment necessary on grounds of physical or mental health.

Instruments of Restraint. 33. Instruments of restraint, such as handcuffs, chains, irons and strait-jackets, shall never be applied as a punishment. Furthermore, chains or irons shall not be used as restraints. Other instruments of restraint shall not be used except in the following circumstances:

(a) As a precaution against escape during a transfer, provided that they shall be removed when the prisoner appears before a judicial or administrative authority;

(b) On medical grounds by direction of the medical officer;

(c) By order of the director, if other methods of control fail, in order to prevent a prisoner from injuring himself or others or from damaging property; in such instances the director shall at once consult the medical officer and report to the higher administrative authority.

34. The patterns and manner of use of instruments of restraint shall be decided by the central prison administration. Such instruments must not be applied for any longer time than is strictly necessary.

Information to and Complaints by Prisoners. 35. (1) Every prisoner on admission shall be provided with written information about the regulations governing the treatment of prisoners of his category, the disciplinary requirements of the institution, the authorized methods of seeking information and making complaints, and all such other matters as are necessary to enable him to understand both his rights and his obligations and to adapt himself to the life of the institution.

(2) If a prisoner is illiterate, the aforesaid information shall be conveyed to him orally.

36. (1) Every prisoner shall have the opportunity each week day of making requests or complaints to the director of the institution or the officer authorized to represent him.

(2) It shall be possible to make requests or complaints to the inspector of prisons during his inspection. The prisoner shall have the opportunity to talk to the inspector or to any other inspecting officer without the director or other members of the staff being present.

(3) Every prisoner shall be allowed to make a request or complaint, without censorship as to substance but in proper form, to the central prison administration, the judicial authority or other proper authorities through approved channels.

(4) Unless it is evidently frivolous or groundless, every request or complaint shall be promptly dealt with and replied to without undue delay.

Contact with the Outside World. 37. Prisoners shall be allowed under necessary supervision to communicate with their family and reputable friends at regular intervals, both by correspondence and by receiving visits.

38. (1) Prisoners who are foreign nationals shall be allowed reasonable facilities to communicate with the diplomatic and consular representatives of the State to which they belong.

(2) Prisoners who are nationals of States without diplomatic or consular representation in the country and refugees or stateless persons shall be allowed similar facilities to communicate with the diplomatic representative of the State which takes charge of their interests or any national or international authority whose task it is to protect such persons.

39. Prisoners shall be kept informed regularly of the more important items of news by the reading of newspapers, periodicals or special institutional publications, by hearing wireless transmissions, by lectures or by any similar means as authorized or controlled by the administration.

Books. 40. Every institution shall have a library for the use of all categories of prisoners, adequately stocked with both recreational and instructional books, and prisoners shall be encouraged to make full use of it.

Religion. 41. (1) If the institution contains a sufficient number of prisoners of the same religion, a qualified representative of that religion shall be appointed or approved. If the number of prisoners justifies it and conditions permit, the arrangement should be on a full-time basis.

(2) A qualified representative appointed or approved under paragraph (1) shall be allowed to hold regular services and to pay pastoral visits in private to prisoners of his religion at proper times.

(3) Access to a qualified representative of any religion shall not be refused to any prisoner. On the other hand, if any prisoner should object to a visit of any religious representative, his attitude shall be fully respected.

42. So far as practicable, every prisoner shall be allowed to satisfy the needs of his religious life by attending the services provided in the institution and having in his possession the books of religious observance and instruction of his denomination.

Retention of Prisoners' Property. 43. (1) All money, valuables, clothing and other effects belonging to a prisoner which under the regulations of the institution he is not allowed to retain shall on his admission to the institution be placed in safe custody. An inventory thereof shall be signed by the prisoner. Steps shall be taken to keep them in good condition.

(2) On the release of the prisoner all such articles and money shall be returned to him except in so far as he has been authorized to spend money or send any such property out of the institution, or it has been found necessary on hygienic grounds to destroy any article of clothing. The prisoner shall sign a receipt for the articles and money returned to him.

(3) Any money or effects received for a prisoner from outside shall be treated in the same way.

(4) If a prisoner brings in any drugs or medicine, the medical officer shall decide what use shall be made of them.

Notification of Death, Illness, Transfer, etc. 44. (1) Upon the death or serious illness of, or serious injury to a prisoner, or his removal to an institution for the treatment of mental affections, the director shall at once inform the spouse, if the prisoner is married, or the nearest relative and shall in any event inform any other person previously designated by the prisoner.

(2) A prisoner shall be informed at once of the death or serious illness of any near relative. In case of the critical illness of a near relative, the prisoner should be authorized, whenever circumstances allow, to go to his beside either under escort or alone.

(3) Every prisoner shall have the right to inform at once his family of his imprisonment or his transfer to another institution.

Removal of Prisoners. 45. (1) When prisoners are being removed to or from an institution, they shall be exposed to public view as little as possible, and proper safeguards shall be adopted to protect them from insult, curiosity and publicity in any form.

(2) The transport of prisoners in conveyances with inadequate ventilation or light, or in any way which would subject them to unnecessary physical hardship, shall be prohibited.

(3) The transport of prisoners shall be carried out at the expense of the administration and equal conditions shall obtain for all of them.

46. (1) The prison administration, shall provide for the careful selection of every grade of the personnel, since it is

on their integrity, humanity, professional capacity and personal suitability for the work that the proper administration of the institutions depends.

(2) The prison administration shall constantly seek to awaken and maintain in the minds both of the personnel and of the public the conviction that this work is a social service of great importance, and to this end all appropriate means of informing the public should be used.

(3) To secure the foregoing ends, personnel shall be appointed on a full-time basis as professional prison officers and have civil service status with security of tenure subject only to good conduct, efficiency and physical fitness. Salaries shall be adequate to attract and retain suitable men and women; employment benefits and conditions of service shall be favourable in view of the exacting nature of the work.

47. (1) The personnel shall possess an adequate standard of education and intelligence.

(2) Before entering on duty, the personnel shall be given a course of training in their general and specific duties and be required to pass theoretical and practical tests.

(3) After entering on duty and during their career, the personnel shall maintain and improve their knowledge and professional capacity by attending courses of in-service training to be organized at suitable intervals.

48. All members of the personnel shall at all times so conduct themselves and perform their duties as to influence the prisoners for good by their example and to command their respect.

49. (1) So far as possible, the personnel shall include a sufficient number of specialists such as psychiatrists, psychologists, social workers, teachers and trade instructors.

(2) The services of social workers, teachers and trade instructors shall be secured on a permanent basis, without thereby excluding part-time or voluntary workers.

50. (1) The director of an institution should be adequately qualified for his task by character, administrative ability, suitable training and experience.

(2) He shall devote his entire time to his official duties and shall not be appointed on a part-time basis.

(3) He shall reside on the premises of the institution or in its immediate vicinity.

(4) When two or more institutions are under the authority of one director, he shall visit each of them at frequent intervals. A responsible resident official shall be in charge of each of these institutions.

51. (1) The director, his deputy, and the majority of the other personnel of the institution shall be able to speak the language of the greatest number of prisoners, or a language understood by the greatest number of them.

(2) Whenever necessary, the services of an interpreter shall be used.

52. (1) In institutions which are large enough to require the services of one or more full-time medical officers, at least one them shall reside on the premises of the institution or in its immediate vicinity.

(2) In other institutions the medical officer shall visit daily and shall reside near enough to be able to attend without delay in cases of urgency.

53. (1) In an institution for both men and women, the part of the institution set aside for women shall be under the authority of a responsible woman officer who shall have the custody of the keys of all that part of the institution.

(2) No male member of the staff shall enter the part of the institution set aside for women unless accompanied by a woman officer.

(3) Women prisoners shall be attended and supervised only by women officers. This does not, however, preclude male members of the staff, particularly doctors and teachers, from carrying out their professional duties in institutions or parts of institutions set aside for women.

54. (1) Officers of the institutions shall not, in their relations with the prisoners, use force except in self-defence or in cases of attempted escape, or active or passive physical resistance to an order based on law or regulations. Officers who have recourse to force must use no more than is strictly necessary and must report the incident immediately to the director of the institution.

(2) Prison officers shall be given special physical training to enable them to restrain aggressive prisoners.

(3) Except in special circumstances, staff performing duties which bring them into direct contact with prisoners should not be armed. Furthermore, staff should in no circumstances be provided with arms unless they have been trained in their use.

Inspection. 55. There shall be a regular inspection of penal institutions and services by qualified and experienced inspectors appointed by a competent authority. Their task shall be in particular to ensure that these institutions are administered in accordance with existing laws and regulations and with a view to bringing about the objectives of penal and correctional services.

Part II—Rules Applicable to Special Categories
A. Prisoners Under Sentence

Guiding Principles. 56. The guiding principles hereafter are intended to show the spirit in which penal institutions should be administered and the purposes at which they should aim, in accordance with the declaration made under Preliminary Observation 1 of the present text.

57. Imprisonment and other measures which result in cutting off an offender from the outside world are afflictive by the very fact of taking from the person the right of self-determination by depriving him of his liberty. Therefore the prison system shall not, except as incidental to justifiable segregation or the maintenance of discipline, aggravate the suffering inherent in such a situation.

58. The purpose and justification of a sentence of imprisonment or a similar measure deprivative of liberty is ultimately to protect society against crime. This end can only be achieved if the period of imprisonment is used to ensure, so far as possible, that upon his return to society the offender is not only willing but able to lead a law-abiding and self-supporting life.

59. To this end, the institution should utilize all the remedial, educational, moral, spiritual and other forces and forms of assistance which are appropriate and available, and should seek to apply them according to the individual treatment needs of the prisoners.

60. (1) The régime of the institution should seek to minimize any differences between prison life and life at liberty which tend to lessen the responsibility of the prisoners or the respect due to their dignity as human beings.

(2) Before the completion of the sentence, it is desirable that the necessary steps be taken to ensure for the prisoner a gradual return to life in society. This aim may be achieved, depending on the case, by a pre-release régime organized in the same institution or in another appropriate institution, or by release on trial under some kind of supervision

which must not be entrusted to the police but should be combined with effective social aid.

61. The treatment of prisoners should emphasize not their exclusion from the community, but their continuing part in it. Community agencies should, therefore, be enlisted wherever possible to assist the staff of the institution in the task of social rehabilitation of the prisoners. There should be in connexion with every institution social workers charged with the duty of maintaining and improving all desirable relations of a prisoner with his family and with valuable social agencies. Steps should be taken to safeguard, to the maximum extent compatible with the law and the sentence, the rights relating to civil interest, social security rights and other social benefits of prisoners.

62. The medical services of the institution shall seek to detect and shall treat any physical or mental illnesses or defects which may hamper a prisoner's rehabilitation. All necessary medical, surgical and psychiatric services shall be provided to that end.

63. (1) The fulfillment of these principles requires individualization of treatment and for this purpose a flexible system of classifying prisoners in groups; it is therefore desirable that such groups should be distributed in separate institutions suitable for the treatment of each group.

(2) These institutions need not provide the same degree of security for every group. It is desirable to provide varying degrees of security according to the needs of different groups. Open institutions, by the very fact that they provide no physical security against escape but rely on the self-discipline of the inmates, provide the conditions most favourable to rehabilitation for carefully selected prisoners.

(3) It is desirable that the number of prisoners in closed institutions should not be so large that the individualization of treatment is hindered. In some countries it is considered that the population of such institutions should not exceed five hundred. In open institutions the population should be as small as possible.

(4) On the other hand, it is undesirable to maintain prisons which are so small that proper facilities cannot be provided.

64. The duty of society does not end with a prisoner's release. There should, therefore, be governmental or private agencies capable of lending the released prisoner efficient after-care directed towards the lessening of prejudice against him and towards his social rehabilitation.

Treatment. 65. The treatment of persons sentenced to imprisonment or a similar measure shall have as its purpose, so far as the length of the sentence permits, to establish in them the will to lead law-abiding and self-supporting lives after their release and to fit them to do so. The treatment shall be such as will encourage their self-respect and develop their sense of responsibility.

66. (1) To these ends, all appropriate means shall be used, including religious care in the countries where this is possible, education, vocational guidance and training, social casework, employment counselling, physical development and strengthening of moral character, in accordance with the individual needs of each prisoner, taking account of his social and criminal history, his physical and mental capacities and aptitudes, his personal temperament, the length of his sentence and his prospects after release.

(2) For every prisoner with a sentence of suitable length, the director shall receive, as soon as possible after his admission, full reports on all the matters referred to in the foregoing paragraph. Such reports shall always include a report by a medical officer, wherever possible qualified in psychiatry, on the physical and mental condition of the prisoner.

(3) The reports and other relevant documents shall be placed in an individual file. This file shall be kept up to date and classified in such a way that it can be consulted by the responsible personnel whenever the need arises.

Classification and Individualization. 67. The purposes of classification shall be:

(a) To separate from others those prisoners who, by reason of their criminal records or bad characters, are likely to exercise a bad influence;

(b) To divide the prisoners into classes in order to facilitate their treatment with a view to their social rehabilitation.

68. So far as possible separate institutions or separate sections of an institution shall be used for the treatment of the different classes of prisoners.

69. As soon as possible after admission and after a study of the personality of each prisoner with a sentence of suitable length, a programme of treatment shall be prepared for him in the light of the knowledge obtained about his individual needs, his capacities and dispositions.

Privileges. 70. Systems of privileges appropriate for the different classes of prisoners and the different methods of treatment shall be established at every institution, in order to encourage good conduct, develop a sense of responsibility and secure the interest and co-operation of the prisoners in their treatment.

Work. 71. (1) Prison labour must not be of an afflictive nature.

(2) All prisoners under sentence shall be required to work, subject to their physical and mental fitness as determined by the medical officer.

(3) Sufficient work of a useful nature shall be provided to keep prisoners actively employed for a normal working day.

(4) So far as possible the work provided shall be such as will maintain or increase the prisoners' ability to earn an honest living after release.

(5) Vocational training in useful trades shall be provided for prisoners able to profit thereby and especially for young prisoners.

(6) Within the limits compatible with proper vocational selection and with the requirements of institutional administration and discipline, the prisoners shall be able to choose the type of work they wish to perform.

72. (1) The organization and methods of work in the institutions shall resemble as closely as possible those of similar work outside institutions, so as to prepare prisoners for the conditions of normal occupational life.

(2) The interests of the prisoners and of their vocational training, however, must not be subordinated to the purpose of making a financial profit from an industry in the institution.

73. (1) Preferably institutional industries and farms should be operated directly by the administration and not by private contractors.

(2) Where prisoners are employed in work not controlled by the administration, they shall always be under the supervision of the institution's personnel. Unless the work is for other departments of the government the full normal wages for such work shall be paid to the administration by the persons to whom the labour is supplied, account being taken of the output of the prisoners.

74. (1) The precautions laid down to protect the safety

and health of free workmen shall be equally observed in institutions.

(2) Provision shall be made to indemnify prisoners against industrial injury, including occupational disease, on terms not less favourable than those extended by law to free workmen.

75. (1) The maximum daily and weekly working hours of the prisoners shall be fixed by law or by administrative regulation, taking into account local rules of custom in regard to the employment of free workmen.

(2) The hours so fixed shall leave one rest day a week and sufficient time for education and other activities required as part of the treatment and rehabilitation of the prisoners.

76. (1) There shall be a system of equitable remuneration of the work of prisoners.

(2) Under the system prisoners shall be allowed to spend at least a part of their earnings on approved articles for their own use and to send a part of their earnings to their family.

(3) The system should also provide that a part of the earnings should be set aside by the administration so as to constitute a savings fund to be handed over to the prisoner on his release.

Education and Recreation. 77. (1) Provision shall be made for the further education of all prisoners capable of profiting thereby, including religious instruction in the countries where this is possible. The education of illiterates and young prisoners shall be compulsory and special attention shall be paid to it by the administration.

(2) So far as practicable, the education of prisoners shall be integrated with the educational system of the country so that after their release they may continue their education without difficulty.

78. Recreational and cultural activities shall be provided in all institutions for the benefit of the mental and physical health of prisoners.

Social Relations and After-care. 79. Special attention shall be paid to the maintenance and improvement of such relations between a prisoner and his family as are desirable in the best interests of both.

80. From the beginning of a prisoner's sentence consideration shall be given to his future after release and he shall be encouraged and assisted to maintain or establish such relations with persons or agencies outside the institution as may promote the best interests of his family and his own social rehabilitation.

81. (1) Services and agencies, governmental or otherwise, which assist released prisoners to re-establish themselves in society shall ensure, so far as is possible and necessary, that released prisoners be provided with appropriate documents and identification papers, have suitable homes and work to go to, are suitably and adequately clothed having regard to the climate and season, and have sufficient means to reach their destination and maintain themselves in the period immediately following their release.

(2) The approved representatives of such agencies shall have all necessary access to the institution and to prisoners and shall be taken into consultation as to the future of a prisoner from the beginning of his sentence.

(3) It is desirable that the activities of such agencies shall be centralized or co-ordinated as far as possible in order to secure the best use of their efforts.

B. Insane and Mentally Abnormal Prisoners

82. (1) Persons who are found to be insane shall not be detained in prisons and arrangements shall be made to remove them to mental institutions as soon as possible.

(2) Prisoners who suffer from other mental diseases or abnormalities shall be observed and treated in specialized institutions under medical management.

(3) During their stay in a prison, such prisoners shall be placed under the special supervision of a medical officer.

(4) The medical or psychiatric service of the penal institutions shall provide for the psychiatric treatment of all other prisoners who are in need of such treatment.

83. It is desirable that steps should be taken, by arrangement with the appropriate agencies, to ensure if necessary the continuation of psychiatric treatment after release and the provision of social-psychiatric after-care.

C. Prisoners Under Arrest or Awaiting Trial

84. (1) Persons arrested or imprisoned by reason of a criminal charge against them, who are detained either in police custody or in prison custody (jail) but have not yet been tried and sentenced, will be referred to as "untried prisoners" hereinafter in these rules.

(2) Unconvicted prisoners are presumed to be innocent and shall be treated as such.

(3) Without prejudice to legal rules for the protection of individual liberty or prescribing the procedure to be observed in respect of untried prisoners, these prisoners shall benefit by a special régime which is described in the following rules in its essential requirements only.

85. (1) Untried prisoners shall be kept separate from convicted prisoners.

(2) Young untried prisoners shall be kept separate from adults and shall in principle be detained in separate institutions.

86. Untried prisoners shall sleep singly in separate rooms, with the reservation of different local custom in respect of the climate.

87. Within the limits compatible with the good order of the institution, untried prisoners may, if they so desire, have their food procured at their own expence from the outside, either through the administration or through their family or friends. Otherwise, the administration shall provide their food.

88. (1) An untried prisoner shall be allowed to wear his own clothing if it is clean and suitable.

(2) If he wears prison dress, it shall be different from that supplied to convicted prisoners.

89. An untried prisoner shall always be offered opportunity to work, but shall not be required to work. If he chooses to work, he shall be paid for it.

90. An untried prisoner shall be allowed to procure at his own expense or at the expense of a third party such books, newspapers, writing materials and other means of occupation as are compatible with the interests of the administration of justice and the security and good order of the institution.

91. An untried prisoner shall be allowed to be visited and treated by his own doctor or dentist if there is reasonable ground for his application and he is able to pay any expenses incurred.

92. An untried prisoner shall be allowed to inform immediately his family of his detention and shall be given all reasonable facilities for communicating with his family and friends, and for receiving visits from them, subject only to

such restrictions and supervision as are necessary in the interests of the administration of justice and of the security and good order of the institution.

93. For the purposes of his defence, an untried prisoner shall be allowed to apply for free legal aid where such aid is available, and to receive visits from his legal adviser with a view to his defence and to prepare and hand to him confidential instructions. For these purposes, he shall if he so desires be supplied with writing material. Interviews between the prisoner and his legal adviser may be within sight but not within the hearing of a police or institution official.

Civil Prisoners

94. In countries where the law permits imprisonment for debt, or by order of a court under any other non-criminal process, persons so imprisoned shall not be subjected to any greater restriction or severity than is necessary to ensure safe custody and good order. Their treatment shall be not less favourable than that of untried prisoners, with the reservation, however, that they may possibly be required to work.

E. Persons Arrested or Detained Without Charge

95. Without prejudice to the provisions of article 9 of the International Covenant on Civil and Political Rights, persons arrested or imprisoned without charge shall be accorded the same protection as that accorded under part I and part II, section C. Relevant provisions of part II, section A, shall likewise be applicable where their application may be conducive to the benefit of this special group of persons in custody, provided that no measures shall be taken implying that re-education or rehabilitation is in any way appropriate to persons not convicted of any criminal offence.

SEE ALSO Arbitrary Arrest, Detention or Exile; Arrested Person's Right to Communicate; Body of Principles for the Protection of all Persons under any Form of Detention or Imprisonment; Children: Detention; Fair Trial; Imprisonment; Liberty; Prisons; Privatization; United Nations Standard Minimum Rules for the Administration of Juvenile Justice.

STANDARD OF LIVING. The right of everyone to a standard of living adequate for the health and well-being of himself and of his family is proclaimed in the UNIVERSAL DECLARATION OF HUMAN RIGHTS in the following terms:

Article 25. 1. Everyone has the right to a standard of living adequate for the health and well-being of himself and of his family, including food, clothing, housing and medical care and necessary social services, and the right to security in the event of unemployment, sickness, disability, widowhood, old age or other lack of livelihood in circumstances beyond his control.

2. Motherhood and childhood are entitled to special care and assistance. All children, whether born in or out of wedlock, shall enjoy the same social protection.

The INTERNATIONAL COVENANT ON ECONOMIC, SOCIAL AND CULTURAL RIGHTS contain the following provision:

Article 11. 1. The States Parties to the present Covenant recognize the right of everyone to an adequate standard of living for himself and his family, including adequate food, clothing and housing, and to the continuous improvement of living conditions. The States Parties will take appropriate steps to ensure the realization of this right, recognizing to this effect the essential importance of international co-operation based on free consent.

2. The States Parties to the present Covenant, recognizing the fundamental right of everyone to be free from hunger, shall take, individually and through international co-operation, the measures, including specific programmes, which are needed:

(a) To improve methods of production, conservation and distribution of food by making full use of technical and scientific knowledge, by disseminating knowledge of the principles of nutrition and by developing or reforming agrarian systems in such a way as to achieve the most efficient development and utilization of natural resources;

(b) Taking into account the problems of both food-importing and food-exporting countries, to ensure an equitable distribution of world food supplies in relation to need.

Neither document contains a definition of an "adequate standard of living." However, principles to be applied in particular areas which have a bearing upon the provision of an adequate standard of living are set out in articles 22, 23, 24, 26, and 27 of the declaration and articles 6, 7, 8, 10, 11, 12, 13, and 15 of the covenant. These principles are dealt with both in terms of separate rights and freedoms (right to work, right to education, etc.), and collectively in terms of the RIGHT TO DEVELOPMENT.

SEE ALSO Education; Food; Health; Housing; Shelter; Social Life.

STANDARD-SETTING IN THE FIELD OF HUMAN RIGHTS. On 4 December 1986, the UN General Assembly took note (resolution 41/120) of the extensive network of international standards in the field of human rights which it and other bodies, including the specialized agencies, had established. Emphasizing the primacy of the UNIVERSAL DECLARATION OF HUMAN RIGHTS, the INTERNATIONAL COVENANT ON CIVIL AND POLITICAL RIGHTS, and the INTERNATIONAL COVENANT ON ECONOMIC, SOCIAL AND CULTURAL RIGHTS in this network, the assembly reaffirmed that the effective implementation of these international instruments is of fundamental importance.

The assembly called upon member States and United Nations bodies to accord priority to the implementation of existing international standards in the field of human rights and urged broad ratification of, or accession to, existing treaties in this field. It urged those States and bodies engaged in developing new international human rights standards to pay due regard in this work to the established international legal framework and reaffirmed the important role of the UN COMMISSION ON HUMAN RIGHTS, among other appropriate United Nations bodies, in the development of international instruments in the field of human rights.

The assembly, further, invited member States and United Nations bodies to bear in mind the following guidelines in developing international instruments in the field of human rights; such instruments should, *inter alia,*

(a) be consistent with the existing body of international human rights law;

(b) be of fundamental character and derive from the inherent dignity and worth of the human person;

(c) be sufficiently precise to give rise to identifiable and practicable rights and obligations;

(d) provide, where appropriate, realistic and effective implementation machinery, including reporting systems; and

(e) attract broad international support.

STATE OF EMERGENCY. Article 4 of the INTERNATIONAL COVENANT ON CIVIL AND POLITICAL RIGHTS sets out the circumstances in which an emergency may arise which would entitle a state to derogate from its obligations under the covenant, the condition under which measures derogating from those obligations may be taken, and the kind of notifications that are to be submitted thereon. It reads as follows:

Article 4. 1. In time of public emergency which threatens the life of the nation and the existence of which is officially proclaimed, the States Parties to the present Covenant may take measures derogating from their obligations under the present Covenant to the extent strictly required by the exigencies of the situation, provided that such measures are not inconsistent with their other obligations under international law and do not involve discrimination solely on the ground of race, colour, sex, language, religion or social origin.

2. No derogation from articles 6, 7, 8 (paragraphs 1 and 2) 11, 15, 16 and 18 may be made under this provision.

3. Any State Party to the present Covenant availing itself of the right of derogation shall immediately inform the other States Parties to the present Covenant, through the intermediary of the Secretary-General of the United Nations, of the provisions from which it has derogated and of the reasons by which it was actuated. A further communication shall be made, through the same intermediary, on the date on which it terminates such derogation.

The INTERNATIONAL COVENANT ON ECONOMIC, SOCIAL AND CULTURAL RIGHTS contains the following provisions relating to DEROGATION from the rights set out therein:

Article 4. The States Parties to the present Covenant recognize that, in the enjoyment of those rights provided by the State in conformity with the present Covenant, the State may subject such rights only to such limitations as are determined by law only in so far as this may be compatible with the nature of these rights and solely for the purpose of promoting the general welfare in a democratic society.

Article 5. 1. Nothing in the present Covenant may be interpreted as implying for any State, group or person any right to engage in any activity or to perform any act aimed at the destruction of any of the rights or freedoms recognized herein, or at their limitation to a greater extent than is provided for in the present Covenant.

2. No restriction upon or derogation from any of the fundamental human rights recognized or existing in any country in virtue of law, conventions, regulations or custom shall be admitted on the pretext that the present Covenant does not recognize such rights or that it recognizes them to a lesser extent.

The CONVENTION AGAINST TORTURE AND OTHER CRUEL, INHUMAN OR DEGRADING TREATMENT OR PUNISHMENT provides that:

Article 2.(1). No exceptional circumstances whatsoever, whether a state of war or a threat of war, internal political instability or any other public emergency, may be invoked as a justification of torture.

(2) An order from a superior officer or a public authority may not be invoked as a justification for torture.

The INTER-AMERICAN CONVENTION TO PREVENT AND PUNISH TORTURE provides that:

Article 5. The existence of circumstances such as a state of war, threat of war, state of seige or of emergency, domestic disturbance or strife, suspension of constitutional guarantees, domestic political instability, or other public emergencies or disasters shall not be invoked or admitted as justification for the crime of torture.

The EUROPEAN CONVENTION FOR THE PREVENTION OF TORTURE AND INHUMAN OR DEGRADING TREATMENT OR PUNISHMENT contains the following provision:

Article 9.(1). In exceptional circumstances, the competent authorities of the Party concerned may make representations to the Committee [European Committee for the Prevention of Torture and Inhuman or Degrading Treatment or Punishment] against a visit at the time or to the particular place proposed by the Committee. Such representations may only be made on grounds of national defense, public safety, serious disorder in places where persons are deprived of their liberty, the medical condition of a person or that an urgent interrogation relating to a serious crime is in progress.

(2). Following such representations, the Committee and the Party shall immediately enter into consultations in order to clarify the situation and seek agreement on arrangements to enable the Committee to exercise its functions expeditiously. Such arrangements may include the transfer to another place of any person whom the Committee proposed to visit. Until the visit takes place, the Party shall provide information to the Committee about any person concerned.

After examining the reports submitted by States parties to the International Covenant on Civil and Political Rights in accordance with article 40 of that instrument, the HUMAN RIGHTS COMMITTEE adopted, in 1981, general comments on article 4, as follows (UN Doc. A/36/40, Annex VII, para.1–5):

Article 4 of the Covenant has posed a number of problems for the Committee when considering reports from some States parties. When a public emergency which threatens the life of nation arises and it is officially proclaimed, a State party may derogate from a number of rights to the extent strictly required by the situation. The State party, however, may not derogate from certain specific rights and may not take discriminatory measures on a number of grounds. The State party is also under an obligation to inform the other State parties immediately, through the Secretary-General, of the derogations it has made including the reasons therefor and the date on which the derogations are terminated.

States parties have generally indicated the mechanism provided in their legal systems for the declaration of a state of emergency and the applicable provisions of the law governing derogations. However, in the case of a few States which had apparently derogated from Covenant rights, it was unclear not only whether a state of emergency had been officially declared but also whether rights from which the Covenant allows no derogation had in fact not been derogated from and further whether the other States parties had been informed of the derogations and of the reasons for the derogations.

The Committee holds the view that measures taken under article 4 are of an exceptional and temporary nature and may only last as long as the life of the nation concerned is threatened and that in times of emergency, the protection of human rights becomes all the more important, particularly those rights from which no derogations can be made. The Committee also considers that it is equally important for States parties, in times of public emergency, to inform the other States parties of the nature and extent of the derogations they have made and of the reasons therefor and, further, to fulfil their reporting obligations under article 40 of the Covenant by indicating the nature and extent of each right derogated from together with the relevant documentation.

The Committee, therefore, considers that it might assist States parties if special attention were given to a review by specially appointed bodies or institutions of laws or measures which inherently draw a distinction between men and women in so far as those laws or measures adversely affect the rights provided for in the Covenant and, secondly, that States parties should give specific information in their reports about all measures, legislative or otherwise, designed to implement their undertaking under this article.

The Committee considers that it might help the States parties in implementing this obligation, if more use could be made of existing means of international co-operation with a view to exchanging experience and organizing assistance in solving the practical problems connected with the ensurance of equal rights for men and women.

In 1977, the UN SUB-COMMISSION ON PREVENTION OF DISCRIMINATION AND PROTECTION OF MINORITIES expressed concern (resolution 10 [XXX]) at the manner in which certain countries applied the provisions of article 4 of the International Covenant on Civil and Political Rights to situations known as state of seige or emergency, and proposed that a comprehensive study of the implications for human rights of developments in this sphere was justified. It appointed one of its members, Mrs. Nicole Questiaux (France) as special rapporteur for the study.

Mrs. Questiaux presented her final report (UN Doc. E/CN.4/Sub.2/1982/15) to the sub-commission at its 1982 session. In it, she recalled the basic rules of international law and domestic legislation which set out limitation of state power relating to emergency situations with a view to protecting human rights and analyzed the *de facto* impact of states of emergency upon the rule of law and respect for human rights. She observed that, too often, evidence showed that the model of guarantees provided by law was deviated from, and noted that States of emergency tended to become clandestine, permanent, or even institutionalized. The effects were particularly damaging for persons detained on political grounds. She, therefore, strongly recommended a series of measures to strengthen international monitoring of respect for human rights in such circumstances.

The sub-commission endorsed (resolution 1982/32) the special rapporteur's conclusions and recommendations and asked for the final report to be published and widely disseminated. At the same time, it requested the COMMISSION ON HUMAN RIGHTS to authorize it to undertake a closer study of the advisability of strengthening or extending the provisions of article 4, para. 2, of the International Covenant on Civil and Political Rights.

The commission (resolution 1983/18) called upon the sub-commission to give further attention to Mrs. Questiaux's study and to propose concrete measures designed to ensure respect for human rights under states of seige or emergency. The sub-commission accordingly (resolution 1983/30) decided to include in its agenda an item entitled "Implementation of the right of derogation provided for under article 4 of the International Covenant on Civil and Political Rights and violations of human rights" for the purpose of (a) requesting it WORKING GROUP ON DETENTION to draw up and update a list of countries which proclaim or terminate a state of emergency each year and submit a special annual report to the commission on the subject. One year later, it requested (resolution 1984/27) one of its members, Mr. Leandro Despouy (Argentina), to prepare an explanatory paper indicating how the task which it had envisaged could be carried out.

After examining Mr. Despouy's explanatory paper (UN Doc. E/CN.4/Sub.2/19), the sub-commission appointed him (resolution 1985/32) as its special rapporteur to prepare an annual report containing a list of States which, during the year, had proclaimed, extended or terminated a state of emergency.

Because the 1986 session of the sub-commission was postponed, the first annual report, in a revised version (UN Doc. E/CN.4/1987/19/Rev. 1), was considered only in 1987. It set out (Annex I) information concerning the proclamation, extension, or termination of states of emergency by South Africa, Argentina, Bangladesh, Bolivia, Brunei Darussalem, Cameroon, Chile, Colombia, Egypt, El Salvador, Ecuador, Fiji, France, Malaysia, Nicaragua, Pakistan, Panama, Papua New Guinea, Paraguay, Peru, Syria, Sudan, Sri Lanka, Suriname, Turkey, and Zimbabwe. The sub-commission, after examining it, expressed (resolution 1987/25) its appreciation to the special rapporteur and to the governments and organizations which had provided him with information, and called upon him to continue to carry on the work.

The General Assembly, at its 1987, stressed on two separate occasions (resolutions 42/103 and 42/147) the importance of avoiding the erosion of human rights by derogation and observed that the maintenance of states of emergency constitutes the source of frequent violations of human rights and gives rise to the arbitrary intervention of the authorities in the free exercise of democratic activities.

The special rapporteur's 1988 report (UN Doc. E/CN.4/Sub.2/1988/18 and Add. 1) set out (Annex I) information concerning the proclamation, extension, or termination of states of emergency, and the resulting impact on human rights, in Ecuador, Nicaragua, Peru, and Zimbabwe, and indicated that the special rapporteur was in the process of attempting to verify information relating to other countries received from non-governmental sources. The sub-commission (resolution 1988/24) expressed its satisfaction with that report, authorized him to update it so that the Commission on Human Rights would have before it the most recent and accurate information available at its session in January 1989, and invited him to continue to carry out his mandate. In addition, it requested him, in conjunction with the special rapporteur on detention without charge or trial, to submit to the sub-commission draft standard provisions on emergency situations, including situations of internal unrest or tensions.

The Commission on Human Rights examined, at its 1989 session, a revised and updated version of the special rapporteur's report, and approved (decision 1989/105) the sub-commission's request that he continue to prepare such reports for consideration by the commission and the sub-commission.

The special rapporteur's third annual report (UN Doc. E/CN.4/Sub.2/1989/30 and Add. 1 and Add. 2/Rev. 1) indicated that, since November 1988, at least 25 States had proclaimed or extended a state of emergency, or had continued to take emergency measures, in respect of all or part of the territories under their jurisdiction or control. In addition, he indicated that he had received from non-governmental sources information, which he was endeavoring to verify, concerning such action in 11 other States.

On 1 September 1989, the sub-commission expressed (resolution 1989/28) its satisfaction with the report and with the accompanying list of States which have proclaimed, extended or terminated a state of emergency since 1 January 1985. It invited governments to limit the introduction of states of emergency exclusively to situations which are sufficiently serious and exceptional to justify them, particularly in the case of internal unrest, in order to avoid making the use of states of emergency commonplace and thus possibly perpetuating them. Further, it invited governments which have not yet done so to consider the adoption of internal legislation consistent with the requirements of international instruments concerning states of emergency.

In an addendum to his third report, the special rapporteur presented his views on model legal provisions applicable in emergency situations as follows (UN Doc. E/CN.4/Sub.2/1989/30/Rev. 1, para. 28–34):

In his next report, the Special Rapporteur intends to present some model legal provisions that can serve as a reference for States so that their internal legislation on the state of emergency and its implementation will not have a negative impact on human rights and will meet the criteria of lawfulness deriving from relevant norms of public international law.

To this end, the Special Rapporteur would appreciate receiving the preliminary views of the Sub-Commission and the Commission on those of the criteria set out below which they consider to be the most important.

With respect to states of emergency, there clearly exists an international legal framework deriving from prevailing international norms, the practice of international organizations and the internal law of States, which provides a frame of reference for the lawfulness of states of emergency. However, on the basis of the information submitted to him, the Special Rapporteur believes that this legal framework is rarely respected.

The Special Rapporteur is of the opinion that, if, when it proclaims a state of emergency, a State satisfies the criteria of lawfulness derived from that legal framework, then the adverse consequences that the existence of that state of emergency entail for the enjoyment of human rights as a whole are necessarily limited.

Accordingly the Special Rapporteur proposes the establishment of standard criteria and legal provisions based on the following points, which were widely developed in his previous reports:

(a) The emergency situation capable of giving rise to the proclamation of a state of emergency should be clearly defined and delimited by the Constitution, the law or jurisprudence and, regardless of the phraseology employed, the existence of a real and imminent public danger should be clearly specified;

(b) It is essential that the *de facto* situation exhibiting these characteristics should be publicly announced and also reflected in the legal form of the state of emergency, in order to ensure that the population is informed of the restrictions imposed on its rights and freedoms;

(c) The emergency measures taken should be commensurate with the emergency situation for which they are intended;

(d) The part of the territory in which the emergency measures are to be applied should also be commensurate with the geographical extent of the emergency situation and should be officially specified;

(e) Domestic legislation should clearly specify which rights permit of derogation and which rights do not permit of derogation and must be respected in all circumstances; the Special Rapporteur proposes to draw up a list of those inviolable rights on the basis of the various international and regional instruments and international customary law concerning human rights, in order to provide States with a form of guideline to which they can refer;

(f) In all cases, there should be a monitoring mechanism, which could be either parliamentary, upon the proclamation or extension of a state of emergency, or judicial, for the assessment of measures taken against individuals;

(g) By providing for the legal liability of the State, it would be possible to compensate persons who have suffered under emergency measures. This would serve to prevent the misuse of the measures.

The Special Rapporteur believes that, in order to minimize the adverse effects of the existence of a state of emergency on the enjoyment of human rights, it is particularly important that States should endeavour:

(a) to avoid both a legal vacuum and conflicting legislation;

(b) to maintain the powers of the non-military courts and limit the competence of military courts to military crimes and offences;

(c) to maintain the procedural guarantees: in particular, *habeas corpus, amparo* and other remedies having the same purpose should in no circumstances be suspended;

(d) To avoid any *de facto* state of emergency (i.e., a situation in which emergency measures are taken without an official proclamation or in which, after a state of emergency has been offically repealed, exceptional measures are nevertheless maintained). *De facto* states of emergency, like the adoption of excessive measures during an emergency situation, have an extremely adverse effect, not only on the country's internal legal order but also in respect of the most fundamental human rights. Note should also be taken of another serious problem, which the Special Rapporteur proposes to analyse in depth, that exists in some countries, where persons can be arrested and detained, sometimes for very long periods, without a state of emergency having been proclaimed.

The establishment of standard legal provisions as a guideline is thus one way of encouraging States to respect human rights and fulfilling the mandate entrusted to the Special Rapporteur by the Commission on Human Rights, under which he is to propose to the Sub-Commission, for transmittal to the Commission, measures designed to ensure respect throughout the world of human rights and fundamental freedoms in situations where states of siege or emergency exist, especially of those rights referred to in article 4 (2) of the International Covenant on Civil and Political Rights, namely the inviolable rights not permitting of derogation in any circumstances whatsoever.

SEE ALSO *Public Emergency.*

STATE OF EMERGENCY: ESSENTIAL JUDICIAL GUARANTEES.

At the request of the Government of Uruguay, the INTER-AMERICAN COURT OF HUMAN RIGHTS, on 6 October 1987, gave its advisory opinion (Opinion OG -9/7) on respect for judicial guarantees during states of emergency.

The court met to deal with this question on 17 September 1986 and concerned itself mainly with the meaning and scope of the final sentence of article 27, para. 2, of the AMERICAN CONVENTION ON HUMAN RIGHTS. It considered, in particular, the following questions (E/CN.4/Sub.2/1988/18/Rev.1):

(a) What judicial guarantees must remain in force during states of emergency?

(b) Do the guarantees mentioned in the last sentence of article 27, paragraph 2, relate only to the procedures for protecting the rights involved?

(c) Since states of emergency very often involve suspension of certain procedural guarantees, what is the situation regarding the principle of exhaustion of domestic remedies?

In its advisory opinion, the Court states that the issue raised by the request of the Uruguayan Government must be considered within a specific legal, historical and political framework, since states of exception or emergency and respect for human rights and for the essential judicial guarantees constitute a grave problem for human rights in America. The Court therefore considers that its opinion may be of practical value in a context where the basic principles involved have often been questioned.

The unanimous opinion of the members of the Court is as follows:

1. The following should be regarded as essential judicial guarantees which, according to article 27, paragraph 2, of the Convention, are not subject to suspension: the remedy of *habeas corpus* (art. 7, para. 6), the remedy of *amparo* and any other recourse to a judge or competent tribunal (art. 25, para.1) designed to guarantee respect for the rights and freedoms whose suspension is not authorized by the Convention.

2. Also to be considered as essential judicial guarantees which are not subject to suspension are those judicial procedures inherent in the representative, democratic form of government (art 29. para. (c)), provided by the States parties in their domestic law in order to guarantee the full exercise of the rights referred to in article 27, paragraph 2, of the Convention, suppression or restriction of which would result in the rights being left unprotected.

3. The above mentioned judicial guarantees must be exercised in the context and according to the principles of due process of law, enunciated in article 8 of the Convention.

STATE OF EMERGENCY: FREEDOM OF ASSOCIATION.

With regard to possible effects of a state of emergency upon the full exercise of trade union rights, the ILO FREEDOM OF ASSOCIATION COMMITTEE OF THE GOVERNING BODY has adopted the following principles (*ILO Digest of Decisions and Principles of the Freedom of Association Committee, third edition, Geneva: 1985*):

Detentions During a State of Emergency. The Committee, while refraining from expressing an opinion on the political aspects of a state of emergency, has always emphasized that measures involving detention must be accompanied by adequate judicial safeguards applied within a reasonable period and that all detained persons must receive a fair trial at the earliest possible moment.

Where circumstances approximate to a situation of civil war importance is attached to all detained persons receiving a fair trial at the earliest possible moment.

Due process would not appear to be ensured if, under the national law, the effect of a state of siege is that a court cannot examine, and does not examine the merits of the case....

State of Emergency. Emergency legislation aimed at antisocial disruptive elements should not be applied against workers for exercising their legitimate trade union rights.

As regards countries which are in a state of political crisis or have just undergone grave disturbances (civil war, revolution, etc.), the Committee has considered it necessary, when examining the various measures taken by the governments, including some against trade union organizations, to take account of such exceptional circumstances when examining the merits of the allegations.

Where a state of siege exists, it is desirable that the government, in its relations with occupational organisations and their representatives, should rely, as far as possible, on the ordinary law rather than on emergency measure which are liable, by their very nature, to involve certain restrictions on fundamental rights.

Measures taken by the authorities in a state of emergency may constitute serious interference in trade union affairs, contrary to Article 3 of Convention No. 87, except where such measures are necessary because the organisations concerned have diverged from their trade union objectives and have defied the law. In any case, such measures should be subject to appropriate procedures for judicial review that may be invoked without delay.

The Committee has stressed that martial law is incompatible with the full exercise of trade union rights.

SUB-COMMISSION ON PREVENTION OF DISCRIMINATION AND PROTECTION OF MINORITIES.

Established by the UN Commission on Human Rights in 1947 under the authority of Economic and Social Council resolution 9 (II), the sub-commission is a body of 26 experts in the field of human rights, and their alternates, which meets annually for a period of approximately four weeks during the month of August at the United Nations office in Geneva. It reports to the commission and, through the commission, to the council and the General Assembly.

Originally established at 12, the membership of the sub-commission was increased to 13 in 1949, returned to 12 in 1950, and increased to 14 in 1959, to 18 in 1965, and to 26 in 1968. Each member may be assisted by an alternate who is also an expert in the field of human rights. Members and their alternates are elected by the Commission on Human Rights on nomination by their respective governments; the letters of nomination stress candidates' qualifications as experts.

In accordance with council resolution 1334 (XLIV) and decision 1978/21, the geographical membership of the sub-commission is as follows: seven from African States, five from Asian States, six from western European and other States, five from Latin American States, and three from eastern European States. After the 26 members have been elected, the chairman of the commission draws lots to select the 13 members, and their alternates, whose term will expire in two years in accordance with the following pattern: three from African States, three from Asian States, three from western European and other States, three from Latin American States, and one from an eastern European State. The remaining members, and their alternates, serve for terms of four years.

In May 1970, the council authorized (resolution 1503 [XLVIII]) the sub-commission to establish the WORKING GROUP ON COMMUNICATIONS to consider all communications drawn to its attention "which appear to reveal a consistent pattern of gross and reliably-attested violations of human rights and fundamental freedoms within the Sub-Commission's terms of reference." The sub-commission examines the communications thus identified by the working group, together with relevant information supplied by the governments concerned, and decides whether or not to refer the cases to the Commission on Human Rights. The commission may then decide what further consideration it should give to situations thus brought to its attention. The entire procedure is handled on a confidential basis. The working group consists of two members of the sub-commission from African States, two from Asian States, two from Latin American States, one from an eastern European State, and two from western European and other States. Members are designated by the chairman of the sub-commission after consultation with the regional groups and approved by the sub-commission.

The sub-commission has also established, on a continuing basis, the WORKING GROUP ON INDIGENOUS POPULATIONS and the WORKING GROUP ON CONTEMPORARY

FORMS OF SLAVERY, each having a composition similar to that of the Working Group on Communications. These working groups meet annually, either before or during the annual session of the sub-commission.

In addition, the sub-commission has set up, on a sessional basis, the WORKING GROUP ON DETENTION and the WORKING GROUP ON THE QUESTION OF PERSONS DETAINED ON THE GROUNDS OF MENTAL ILL-HEALTH OR SUFFERING FROM MENTAL DISORDER. These working groups are open to all members of the sub-commission; they meet as required during its annual session.

The functions of the sub-commission and its subsidiary bodies, as formulated by the Commission on Human Rights at its first regular session, in 1947, are

(a) in the first instance, to examine what provisions should be adopted in defining the principles to be applied in the field of prevention of discrimination on grounds of race, sex, language or religion, and in the field of the protection of minorities, and to make recommendations to the Commission on urgent problems in these fields; and

(b) to perform any other functions which may be entrusted to it by the Economic and Social Council or the Commission on Human Rights.

These functions were clarified and extended in scope by the commission at its fifth session, in 1949, by revision of the first paragraph to read

(a) to undertake studies, particularly in the light of the Universal Declaration of Human Rights, and to make recommendations to the Commission on Human Rights concerning the prevention of discrimination of any kind relating to human rights and fundamental freedoms and the protection of racial, national, religious and linguistic minorities.

At its 1988 session, the Commission on Human Rights expressed its appreciation (resolution 1988/43) for the positive contribution of the sub-commission to the promotion and protection of human rights, and in particular for its impartiality and objectivity which results from the independent status of its members and alternates. At the same time, however, it drew attention to some critical comments, as well as to some constructive suggestions, which had been made in the commission, and requested the sub-commission to take them into account. It also set out, in the resolution, a series of guidelines designed to ensure the complementarity of the sub-commission's activities with those of the commission and to maximize the effectiveness of its expert contributions to the commission's work; and requested the chairman of the sub-commission to report to it on the implementation of those guidelines.

In the report which he presented to the 1989 session of the commission (UN Doc. E/CN.4/1989/37), the chairman of the sub-commission's 1988 session stated that that body was endeavoring to apply the guidelines in the fulfillment of its functions and duties and that its members had agreed to review its program and methods of work, in future, on a biennial basis.

SUDAN. The Democratic Republic of Sudan is a country in northern Africa, on the Red Sea. It has borders with the Central African Republic, Chad, Egypt, Ethiopia, Kenya, Libya, Uganda, and Zaire. An Anglo–Egyptian condominium from 1899, Sudan achieved independence from Great Britain and Egypt in 1956 and became a member of the United Nations the same year. Its total population is estimated by the UN (1990) to be 24,895,000. Ethnic groups include Arabs, Africans, and Arab–Africans. Languages in common use include Arabic (official), English, and a number of tribal vernaculars. Religions practiced include Islam (73%), Animism (18%), and Christianity (9%). Literacy is estimated at 20%.

The government (1990) took the form of a republic. However, from October 1969 to April 1985, a military regime was in control, headed by Maj. Gen. Gafaar Mohamed Nimeiri, who served first as president of the Council for the Revolution, then as prime minister, and finally, from 1971 onwards, as the nation's first elected president.

At least three attempts to overthrow Nimeiri were unsuccessful but the fourth, staged while he was visiting the United States in 1985, stripped him of the presidency and replaced him by a military caretaker regime headed by his own defense minister, Gen. Abdel Rahman Siwar el-Dahab. This regime was immediately confronted with violent protests and strikes by public workers and supporters of President Nimeiri and, at the same time, challenged by rebels of the Sudan People's Liberation Movement, supported by neighboring Ethiopia. The rebel attacks, at first sporadic, soon developed into full-scale civil war.

A civilian government, headed by Prime Minister Sadiq al-Mahdi, took power in Khartoum in May 1986. But talks with rebel leaders were unsuccessful; the United Nations and the Red Cross were forced to end emergency foodlifts due to the mounting conflict, and the chaos in the south was worsened by an influx of ravaging former government soldiers from Uganda and a consequent rise in banditry.

On 25 July 1987, the chairman of the Supreme Council, Ahmed Ali al-Mirghani, announced the declaration of a year-long nationwide state of emergency "in view of the anarchy prevailing in the markets. . . . the spread of smuggling in all its forms and the lack of security." Prime Minister Mahdi described the emergency decree as an evil meant to prevent a greater evil and said that the state of emergency would be lifted as soon as possible.

Since the Sudan achieved independence in 1956, it has been ruled by the military for more than 24 years. Its most recent civilian government, headed by Sadiq al-Mahdi, was overthrown in June 1989 by a military junta consisting of Lieut. General Omar Hassan al-Bashir and a 15-member council. In April 1988, that government announced that it had foiled an attempted coup and had executed 28 officers involved after summary court martials.

Since seizing power, General Bashir has declared a state of emergency, suspended the constitution, and dissolved parliament, political parties, and trade unions. The government has detained politicians, trade unionists, and human rights workers; and the press has been placed under strict State control.

Before being deposed in 1989, in June 1988, with a view to securing international assistance in dealing with these difficulties, Prime Minister Mahdi requested the UN secretary-general to alert the international community to the grave situation prevailing in the Sudan and to appeal for the emergency assistance needed to respond to the urgent requirements of the affected people. The government also requested the United Nations to support it in undertaking a comprehensive review of the situation; to update data on the number, condition, and background of the affected people; and to develop a comprehensive strategy leading to the early implementation of a program of immediate emergency assistance.

In response to the government's request, the secretary-general, in July 1988, sent a high-level mission to the Sudan to set up a timetable and an operational framework to reach the above objectives. However, the advent of torrential rains and devastating floods in early August 1988 effectively paralyzed Khartoum until mid-September and wrought additional destruction in several parts of the country. The implementation of the program was thus delayed by two months.

A follow-up mission arrived in Khartoum in late September, travelled to all accessible parts of the country where large numbers of displaced persons had been reported. The findings of the mission were drawn to the attention of the General Assembly, which on 18 October 1988 requested the secretary-general (resolution 43/8), in close cooperation with the government of the Sudan, to coordinate efforts of the United Nations system to help the Sudan in its emergency, rehabilitation, and reconstruction efforts; to mobilize resources for the implementation of these programs; and to keep the international community informed of the situation.

On 27 October 1988, the secretary-general, in a report to the General Assembly, described the crisis in the Sudan in the following terms (UN Doc. A/43/755, para. 11–12 and 22–24):

The immediate causes of the current deep-seated social and economic crisis affecting the Sudan include:
(a) Civil strife in the south;
(b) Heavy rains and flooding in the central and northern areas of the Nile basin that have devastated large parts of metropolitan Khartoum and the communities along the northern reaches of the Nile;
(c) Large numbers of refugees seeking extended asylum within its national territory;
(d) Pockets of drought and famine;
(e) Locust depredations.
As a result of the above, a significant portion of the national population is considered severely affected in terms of nutrition, health, water and shelter requirements. It is also clear that the most affected are those who are least able to fend for themselves, i.e. those who have been displaced by war and low-income rural people who have been forced by drought to migrate to the Khartoum metropolitan area. Both groups have come to urban areas or to districts free from civil strife because they can no longer provide adequate food and shelter for their families in their areas of origin. Those who have only recently arrived in Khartoum, and are not yet integrated into the urban economy, have been doubly affected by the impact of the floods that struck the capital in August of this year. . . .
The current emergency is believed to affect over 2 million people who are in urgent need of assistance, although not all are accessible. The population affected is estimated as follows:
In addition, a considerable number of people are reported to have lost their homes to flooding in small settlements along the Blue Nile and Atbara rivers. The extent of damage from locust depredation is not yet known, but this is likely to cause additional hardship for a significant portion of the rural people. Altogether, there may be as many as 2.5 million people in urgent need of food, shelter and/or medical attention.
Defining who must be served is often complicated by the unavailability of accurate statistical data about the various populations. In no case has this been more difficult than in enumerating the displaced. As part of the preparation for the present appeal, a review of data concerning the location and number of the displaced who are accessible to relief assistance was carried out by the government services concerned, in co-operation with the United Nations technical team and non-governmental organizations.

The General Assembly took note of the secretary-general's report and, on 8 December 1988, expressed its concern (resolution 43/52) about the serious plight of over two million Sudanese nationals displaced or seriously affected by civil strife, famine, and drought. It noted that these problems were in addition to those created in the country by the presence of over one million refugees and recognized the urgent need to take emergency action to alleviate the suffering of these victims and to improve the conditions of life of the displaced population.

The assembly expressed its solidarity with the government and the people of the Sudan in facing a grave and complex humanitarian and economic situation, and its gratitude and appreciation to governments and international and non-governmental organizations that had provided support and assistance to the government of the Sudan in its relief and rehabilitation efforts. It took note of the interim assistance program outlined by the secretary-general in his report and welcomed the secretary-general's decision to organize a meeting of bilateral donors and pertinent international institutions and organizations in order to mobilize resources needed to implement a follow-up emergency assistance program covering the rehabilitation and resettlement needs of the displaced persons.

The situation was no better when the secretary-general again reported to the General Assembly at its 1989 session (UN Doc. A/44/426); on the contrary, it had been exacerbated by floods and infestations of insects and by the arrival of thousands of new refugees. Besides dealing with extremely difficult economic and social problems, the Sudan had the additional task, towards the end of 1989, of taking care of more than 1.5 million persons displaced by successive calamities and civil strife in countries to the south.

On 15 December 1989, the General Assembly recognized (resolution 44/151) the heavy burden shouldered by the people and the government of the Sudan and the sacrifices they were making to host more than one million refugees, constituting approximately 7.5% of the total population of the country, and expressed deep concern that the great majority of the refugees had spontaneously settled in various urban and rural communities where they shared with the indigenous population the already meagre resources and services. It appealed to member States and intergovernmental and non-governmental organizations, and to the international financial institutions, to provide the government of the Sudan with the necessary resources for the implementation of development assistance projects, and called upon the secretary-general to mobilize the necessary financial and material assistance for the full implementation of ongoing projects in the areas affected by the presence of refugees.

In another resolution adopted at the same session, the General Assembly noted with appreciation (resolution 44/12) that the Khartoum Plan of Action on Operation Lifeline Sudan, endorsed by a high-level meeting organized jointly by Sudan and the United Nations and held at Khartoum on 8 and 9 March 1989, had been successfully and fully implemented, and that a plan was under preparation for the second phase of Operation Lifeline Sudan in order to meet the relief and rehabilitation requirements of the Sudan's displaced population.

SUDAN: QUESTION OF SLAVERY. In 1988, certain practices resembling slavery in their effects, which had been noted in the context of the armed conflict in Sudan, were drawn to the attention of the WORKING GROUP ON CONTEMPORARY FORMS OF SLAVERY by the ANTI-SLAVERY SOCIETY FOR THE PROTECTION OF HUMAN RIGHTS, a non-governmental organization in consultative status, as follows (UN Doc. E/CN.4/Sub.2/AC.2/1988/7/Add. 1):

Sudan is today experiencing a resurgence of chattel slavery.

The Anti-Slavery Society recently conducted an investigation into slavery in, mainly, the western provinces of Darfur and Kordofan, and in the capital, Khartoum.

The western region, populated largely by Baggara Arabs, borders on the province of Bahr el Ghazal, the home of the African people, the Dinka. The former are Sunni Muslims; the latter animists and Christian.

The present problem has a historical perspective, but it is more than a localized affair. It is a direct consequence of the five-year-old war between Khartoum and the Dinka-dominated Sudan People's Liberation Army (SPLA).

Armed tribal militias, used by Khartoum to counter the advance of the SPLA, are accused of raiding Dinka villages in northern Bahr el Ghazal, southern Darfur and Kordofan. The militia system is used as an offensive strategy to destabilize the Dinka in the countryside and to preclude Dinka support for the SPLA by depopulating the region. In practice this entails terrorism, and the reward for the militia is the booty that they seize—from goods and livestock to slaves.

In general, there is a link between Khartoum and the militia, which are organized along clan lines. Deputy Defence Minister Burma Nasir, who is credited with the military strategy, comes from Kordofan, where the link is particularly firm. There is strong support in the western area for Prime Minister Sadiq el Mahdi's Umma Party which according to its general-secretary, Dr Omar Nur el Daim, has 22,000 men under arms. There is also a connection between the militia and the army, which supplies them with ammunition. Automatic weapons are easily bought for £70 or £80 sterling. Several militia leaders are ex-soldiers who have personal ties with regional military commands.

The serious problem of insecurity in the west is attributable to an abundance of guns and to groups engaging in armed robbery. The make-up and role of the militia are imprecise, and where their actions merge into banditry is unclear. Young men, acting independently of local chiefs and the army, may also raid the Dinka, and it is common for these various armed bands to clash. The economic gain is the main priority, and the Dinka are easy targets. Despite the mixed ancestry of the Rezeigat, in particular Arab-Dinka, there is an ingrained psychology of racism or Arabism which deems the Dinka inferior.

The Society was informed that between 19 December

1986 until March 1988, over 600 Dinka had been killed in the Abyei area and 400 taken as slaves. This figure has been confirmed by Transport Minister Aldo Ajor, himself a Dinka. The captives are being held in Satep, Meram, Datelia, Kolek, Muglad and Tibum in southern Kordofan. They are sold for between about £18 and £36 or are kept by their militia kidnappers. They work as agricultural labourers or house servants. Males between the ages of 15 and 20 cultivate the fields in the rainy season and in the summer tend cattle. Children aged from 7 to 12 look after goats and other livestock or dig wells. Younger children are employed in the house along with the women that the militia captors "marry". Other women are also used as agricultural labour or water carriers.

The Society has been supplied with the names of 15 Dinkas taken from the Abyei area by Baggara militia at the end of February 1988. The militia are generally accused of murdering adult men out of fear that they may join the SPLA, or supply it with cattle. There have also been reports that slaves are killed after the harvest when their labour is no longer required.

The Society is also in possession of the names of 28 people captured by Baggara militia on 2 December 1987 from around Aweil in northern Bahr el Ghazal. The militia had attacked on horseback, firing indiscriminately, houses and crops were burnt, and cattle and livestock seized. Those that failed to escape were roped together and marched into southern Darfur. In the same vicinity in March, a group of displaced Dinka travelling to Safaha on the Bahr el Ghazal-Darfur border were attacked by Baggara who abducted four members of the same family.

The Anti-Slavery Society is in possession of documents relating to the sale and ransom of Dinka captives. Children have been sold for the equivalent of between £30 and £50. The Baggara are also willing to release slaves on payment of a ransom (regarded as "compensation"). The detailed accounts appearing during 1987 in the Sudanese English language press suggest that this is common practice when relatives are able to raise the necessary amount.

Apart from direct capture by the militia, the war has created another avenue for slavery, which is the sale of children by their destitute parents. Since the beginning of the five-year-old conflict, an estimated two million southerners, predominantly Dinka, have been displaced. Militia attacks and the army's scorched earth policy have forced them off their land and deprived them of their cattle, the basis of the local economy and society. They head north, where they hope to find kinsmen and employment. But those who do arrive in Khartoum sink into one of a number of crowded, illegal and insanitary camps on the outskirts of the capital.

Since the beginning of April 20,000 Dinka, who walked from Aweil, have been camped in Safaha, a trading post on the banks of the Bahr el Arab, the riverine border between Darfur and Bahr el Ghazal. The refugees, mostly women and children and the old, are severely undernourished. The young men prefer the refugee camps in Ethiopia to the north of their own country.

Children are also sold to the Rezeigat. The euphemism commonly used is "pawning" or "renting". While in Safaha, the Anti-Slavery Society attempted to buy a seven-year-old boy, making it clear that he would be taken abroad, and was quoted a price of £40 by a merchant from Ed Daein who arranges the transactions. Apparently the system is that a prospective buyer pays the parents a fixed amount through the merchant who takes a £4 commission. During March the child-price was usually £30. To avoid the accusation of slav-ery, the merchant records the names of those involved, and the parents are theoretically able to buy back the child, but at double the original price.

But parents who had sold their children admitted during interviews conducted in Nyala that they did not know the names of the Arab owners, and had no expectation of seeing the children again. Certainly, Rezeigat at Safaha described the children for sale, who were mostly boys between the ages of 6 and 12, as "abid" (slave).

In February, the Society was informed, a child fetched £60; in April the price had fallen to £10.

Despite the testimonies of escaped slaves now living in Khartoum, and who have provided the locations and names of their abductors, the Government continues to deny the existence of slavery and refuses to set up an independent inquiry.

The Anti-Slavery Society notes: that the ruling Umma Party draws its support from the Baggara Arabs, whose militias are responsible for human rights violations, including slavery; that Khartoum, if not advocating racism, is effectively pursuing a racist policy in regard to its African population, in particular the Dinka; that the Dinka people as a whole are being treated as an internal enemy and are considered synonymous with the SPLA.

The Anti-Slavery Society urges the Government of Prime Minister Sadiq el Mahdi: to take all measures to stop the resurgence of chattel slavery; to seek out and punish military and other personnel involved in the practice; and to order regional authorities to end the "renting" of children, and it draws the attention of the Sudanese authorities to the fact that Sudan has ratified the 1956 Supplementary Convention on the Abolition of Slavery, the Slave Trade, and Institutions and Practices Similar to Slavery.

The Society urges the Sudanese authorities to be cognizant of their responsibilities under the Declaration of Human Rights, and the Supplementary Convention on the Abolition of Slavery.

The above information was not considered by the working group at its 1988 session because an understanding had been reached between the society and the government of Sudan for a fact-finding visit to be made to that country in order to obtain more precise information on the subject.

SUPPLEMENTARY CONVENTION ON THE ABOLITION OF SLAVERY, THE SLAVE TRADE, AND INSTITUTIONS AND PRACTICES SIMILAR TO SLAVERY (1956). The supplementary convention adds to, but does not amend or supersede, the SLAVERY CONVENTION SIGNED AT GENEVA ON 25 SEPTEMBER 1926, AS AMENDED. It provides for States parties to take all practicable and necessary legislative and other measures to bring about progressively and as soon as possible the complete abolition or abandonment of a number of institutions and practices—such as DEBT BONDAGE, serfdom, and the sale or involuntary transfer of a woman or child from one person to another—whether or not they are covered by the definition of slavery contained in article 1 of the 1926 Convention as amended.

The supplementary convention was adopted at the European office of the United Nations, Geneva, on 7 September 1956 by a Conference of Plenipotentiaries which had been convened by the UN Economic and Social Council on 30 April 1956 (resolution 608 [XXI]), and entered into force on 30 April 1957. The text of the supplementary convention (United Nations, *Treaty Series,* vol. 266, p. 3) is as follows:

Preamble

The States Parties to the present Convention,

Considering that freedom is the birthright of every human being,

Mindful that the peoples of the United Nations reaffirmed in the Charter their faith in the dignity and worth of the human person,

Considering that the Universal Declaration of Human Rights, proclaimed by the General Assembly of the United Nations as a common standard of achievement for all peoples and all nations, states that no one shall be held in slavery or servitude and that slavery and the slave trade shall be prohibited in all their forms,

Recognizing that, since the conclusion of the Slavery Convention signed at Geneva on 25 September 1926, which was designed to secure the abolition of slavery and of the slave trade, further progress has been made towards this end,

Having regard to the Forced Labour Convention of 1930 and to subsequent action by the International Labour Organisation in regard to forced or compulsory labour,

Being aware, however, that slavery, the slave trade and institutions and practices similar to slavery have not yet been eliminated in all parts of the world,

Having decided, therefore, that the Convention of 1926, which remains operative, should now be augmented by the conclusion of a supplementary convention designed to intensify national as well as international efforts towards the abolition of slavery, the slave trade and institutions and practices similar to slavery,

Have agreed as follows:

Section I
Institutions and Practices Similar to Slavery

Article 1. Each of the States Parties to this Convention shall take all practicable and necessary legislative and other measures to bring about progressively and as soon as possible the complete abolition or abandonment of the following institutions and practices, where they still exist and whether or not they are covered by the definition of slavery contained in article 1 of the Slavery Convention signed at Geneva on 25 September 1926:

(a) Debt bondage, that is to say, the status or condition arising from a pledge by a debtor of his personal services or of those of a person under his control as security for a debt, if the value of those services as reasonably assessed is not applied towards the liquidation of the debt or the length and nature of those services are not respectively limited and defined;

(b) Serfdom, that is to say, the condition or status of a tenant who is by law, custom or agreement bound to live and labour on land belonging to another person and to render some determinate service to such other person, whether for reward or not, and is not free to change his status;

(c) Any institution or practice whereby:

(i) A woman, without the right to refuse, is promised or given in marriage on payment of a consideration in money or in kind to her parents, guardian, family or any other person or group; or

(ii) The husband of a woman, his family, or his clan, has the right to transfer her to another person for value received or otherwise; or

(iii) A woman on the death of her husband is liable to be inherited by another person;

(d) Any institution or practice whereby a child or young person under the age of 18 years, is delivered by either or both of his natural parents or by his guardian to another person, whether for reward or not, with a view to the exploitation of the child or young person or of his labour.

Article 2. With a view to bringing to an end the institutions and practices mentioned in article 1 (c) of this Convention, the States Parties undertake to prescribe, where appropriate, suitable minimum ages of marriage, to encourage the use of facilities whereby the consent of both parties to a marriage may be freely expressed in the presence of a competent civil or religious authority, and to encourage the registration of marriages.

Section II
The Slave Trade

Article 3. 1. The act of conveying or attempting to convey slaves from one country to another by whatever means of transport, or of being accessory thereto, shall be a criminal offence under the laws of the States Parties to this Convention and persons convicted thereof shall be liable to very severe penalties.

2. (a) The States Parties shall take all effective measures to prevent ships and aircraft authorized to fly their flags from conveying slaves and to punish persons guilty of such acts or of using national flags for that purpose.

(b) The States Parties shall take all effective measures to ensure that their ports, airfields and coasts are not used for the conveyance of slaves.

3. The States Parties to this Convention shall exchange information in order to ensure the practical co-ordination of the measures taken by them in combating the slave trade and shall inform each other of every case of the slave trade, and of every attempt to commit this criminal offence, which comes to their notice.

Article 4. Any slave who takes refuge on board any vessel of a State Party to this Convention shall *ipso facto* be free.

Section III
Slavery and Institutions and Practices Similar to Slavery

Article 5. In a country where the abolition or abandonment of slavery, or of the institutions or practices mentioned in article 1 of this Convention, is not yet complete, the act of mutilating, branding or otherwise marking a slave or a person of servile status in order to indicate his status, or as a punishment, or for any other reason, or of being accessory thereto, shall be a criminal offence under the laws of the States Parties to this Convention and persons convicted thereof shall be liable to punishment.

Article 6. 1. The act of enslaving another person or of inducing another person to give himself or a person dependent upon him into slavery, or of attempting these acts, or being accessory thereto, or being a party to a conspiracy to accomplish any such acts, shall be a criminal offence under the laws of the States Parties to this Convention and persons convicted thereof shall be liable to punishment.

2. Subject to the provisions of the introductory paragraph of article 1 of this Convention, the provisions of paragraph 1 of the present article shall also apply to the act of inducing another person to place himself or a person dependent upon him into the servile status resulting from any of the institutions or practices mentioned in article 1, to any attempt to perform such acts, to bring accessory thereto, and to being a party to a conspiracy to accomplish any such acts.

Section IV
Definitions

Article 7. For the purposes of the present Convention:

(a) "Slavery" means, as defined in the Slavery Convention of 1926, the status or condition of a person over whom any or all of the powers attaching to the right of ownership are exercised, and "slave" means a person in such condition or status;

(b) "A person of servile status" means a person in the condition or status resulting from any of the institutions or practices mentioned in article 1 of this Convention;

(c) "Slave trade" means and includes all acts involved in the capture, acquisition or disposal of a person with intent to reduce him to slavery; all acts involved in the acquisition of a slave with a view to selling or exchanging him; all acts of disposal by sale or exchange of a person acquired with a view to being sold or exchanged; and, in general, every act of trade or transport in slaves by whatever means of conveyance.

Section V
Co-operation Between States Parties and Communication of Information

Article 8. 1. The States Parties to this Convention undertake to co-operate with each other and with the United Nations to give effect to the foregoing provisions.

2. The Parties undertake to communicate to the Secretary-General of the United Nations copies of any laws, regulations and administrative measures enacted or put into effect to implement the provisions of this Convention.

3. The Secretary-General shall communicate the information received under paragraph 2 of this article to the other Parties and to the Economic and Social Council as part of the documentation for any discussion which the Council might undertake with a view to making further recommendations for the abolition of slavery, the slave trade or the institutions and practices which are the subject of this Convention.

Section VI
Final Clauses

Article 9. No reservations may be made to this Convention.

Article 10. Any dispute between States Parties to this Convention relating to its interpretation or application, which is not settled by negotiation, shall be referred to the International Court of Justice at the request of any one of the parties to the dispute, unless the parties concerned agree on another mode of settlement.

Article 11. 1. This Convention shall be open until 1 July 1957 for signature by any State Member of the United Nations or of a specialized agency. It shall be subject to ratifica-

tion by the signatory States, and the instruments of ratification shall be deposited with the Secretary-General of the United Nations, who shall inform each signatory and acceding State.

2. After 1 July 1957 this Convention shall be open for accession by any State Member of the United Nations or of a specialized agency, or by any other State to which an invitation to accede has been addressed by the General Assembly of the United Nations. Accession shall be effected by the deposit of a formal instrument with the Secretary-General of the United Nations, who shall inform each signatory and acceding State.

Article 12. 1. This Convention shall apply to all non-self-governing trust, colonial and other non-metropolitan territories for the international relations of which any State Party is responsible; the Party concerned shall, subject to the provisions of paragraph 2 of this article, at the time of signature, ratification or accession declare the non-metropolitan territory or territories to which the Convention shall apply *ipso facto* as a result of such signature, ratification or accession.

2. In any case in which the previous consent of a non-metropolitan territory is required by the constitutional laws or practices of the Party or of the non-metropolitan territory, the Party concerned shall endeavour to secure the needed consent of the non-metropolitan territory within the period of twelve months from the date of signature of the Convention by the metropolitan State, and when such consent has been obtained the Party shall notify the Secretary-General. This Convention shall apply to the territory or territories named in such notification from the date of its receipt by the Secretary-General.

3. After the expiry of the twelve-month period mentioned in the preceding paragraph, the States Parties concerned shall inform the Secretary-General of the results of the consultations with those non-metropolitan territories for whose international relations they are responsible and whose consent to the application of this Convention may have been withheld.

Article 13. 1. This Convention shall enter into force on the date on which two States have become Parties thereto.

2. It shall thereafter enter into force with respect to each State and territory on the date of deposit of the instrument of ratification or accession of that State or notification of application to that territory.

Article 14. 1. The application of this Convention shall be divided into successive periods of three years, of which the first shall begin on the date of entry into force of the Convention in accordance with paragraph 1 of article 13.

2. Any State Party may denounce this Convention by a notice addressed by that State to the Secretary-General not less than six months before the expiration of the current three-year period. The Secretary-General shall notify all other Parties of each such notice and the date of the receipt thereof.

3. Denunciations shall take effect at the expiration of the current three-year period.

4. In cases where, in accordance with the provisions of article 12, this Convention has become applicable to a non-metropolitan territory of a Party, that Party may at any time thereafter with the consent of the territory concerned, give notice to the Secretary-General of the United Nations denouncing this Convention separately in respect of that territory. The denunciation shall take effect one year after the date of the receipt of such notice by the Secretary-General,

who shall notify all other Parties of such notice and the date of the receipt thereof.

Article 15. This Convention, of which the Chinese, English, French, Russian and Spanish texts are equally authentic, shall be deposited in the archives of the United Nations Secretariat. The Secretary-General shall prepare a certified copy thereof for communication to States Parties to this Convention, as well as to all other States Members of the United Nations and of the specialized agencies.

In witness whereof the undersigned, being duly authorized thereto by their respective Governments, have signed this Convention on the date appearing opposite their respective signatures.

Done at the European Office of the United Nations at Geneva, this seventh day of September one thousand nine hundred and fifty-six.

SURINAME. The Republic of Suriname is a country in tropical South America, located on the northeastern coast of the continent, fronting on the Atlantic Ocean. It has borders with Brazil, French Guinea, and Guyana. Formerly known as Dutch Guiana, it achieved independence from the Netherlands in 1975 and became a member of the United Nations the same year. Its population is estimated by the UN (1990) to be 403,000. Ethnic groups include Hindi (37%), Creole (31%), Dutch and Indonesian (22%), and Bush Negro (10%). Languages commonly used include Dutch and English (both official), Surinamese (a *lingua franca),* Creole, and Hindi. Religions practiced include Christianity (Roman Catholic, Lutheran, Jehovah's Witnesses, and Seventh Day Adventists), Hinduism, and Islam. Literacy is estimated at 20%.

The government (1990) took the form of a republic. However, both the 1975 constitution and the elected assembly were suspended in 1980 when a 16-man military junta took over and installed a civilian premier. When the premier resigned in February 1987 because he no longer had the support of the junta, he was replaced by a deputy premier, also a civilian.

A prosperous British settlement on the banks of the Suriname River of northeast South America, Suriname was transferred to the Dutch in 1667 by the Treaty of Breda—the British receiving New York, New Jersey, and Delaware in return. Slaves imported from Africa furnished labor for the vast plantations; and, after slavery was abolished in 1863, indentured laborers were brought in from British India and the Dutch East Indies for this purpose. As a result, Suriname's population represents a mixture of indigenous Amerindians and Bush Negroes, descendents of slaves and migrant workers from Africa, India, and southeast Asia, and descendents of British, Dutch Indonesian, and Brazilian settlers. Surinamese of African descent,

commonly known as Creoles, vie constantly with those of Asian descent for power within the State.

Self-governing since 1948 as a Dutch overseas territory, Suriname was given full independence in 1975 following a period of acute economic recession that triggered unemployment, inflation, and shortages which triggered riots between the completing ethnic groups. After a brief period of constitutional government, a coup d'etat in 1980 placed Lieut. Col. Desi Bouterse, leader of the so-called February 25 Movement, in control.

When, in 1982, 15 Surinamese civic leaders were arrested on suspicion of plotting a coup, then tortured, and summarily executed, charges of widespread human rights violations were made by several governments, including the United States, and by a number of non-governmental organizations, including **AMNESTY INTERNATIONAL**; and aid to Suriname was suspended by Netherlands and the United States.

Similar charges were made between 1985 and 1987 as guerrilla warfare forced some 20,000 Bush Negroes to flee from their homes into the forests in order to avoid harassment and attacks by Surinamese armed forces.

The Commission on Human Rights of the Organization of American States prepared two special reports on the human rights situation in Suriname after investigating the death of the 15 Surinamese citizens in 1982, and a third as a follow-up on the further development of events relating to human rights.

In the first of these reports, issued on 5 October 1983, the OAS commission concluded that high government officials were responsible for the deaths of the 15 persons. In the second, issued on 2 October 1985, the commission "again reiterated to the Government of Suriname the fact that despite the recommendation stated in the first Report, to investigate the tragic events of 8 December 1982, the investigation had not been done and the high government officials responsible for those acts had not been sanctioned."

In the third report, issued on 25 September 1986, the commission noted that the government of Suriname had taken several political measures which might represent steps toward the country's democratization. Among the developments noted were the following (*Annual Report of the Inter-American Commission on Human Rights,* 1985-1986, (OAS publication OEA/Ser. L/II,68, Doc. 8 rev. 1, pp. 186–188):

In the first place, on November 23, 1985, representatives of the Government and of the three principal political parties of the country—NPS (National Party of Suriname), VHP (Progressive Reform Party) and Kaum Tani Persuatan Indonesia (KTPI)—, reached an agreement by which those parties would integrate the country's highest political organ, that is, the Supreme Council (Topberaad).

Subsequently, on February 25, 1986, the Government of Suriname, by decree A-21, put an end to the state of emergency in force throughout the country since September 1980. The Commission, which had recommended such a measure in its 1985 Report, notes this change because it represents a positive step towards reestablishing the rule of law and the civil rights of the Surinamese people.

In May 1986 the three principal political parties the NPS, the KTPI and the VHP accepted the invitation of Colonel Bouterse to participate in the top deliberating council as agreed to in the November 1985 accord. Their participation was limited to political and administrative affairs. The political parties continued to demand general and secret elections before the transitional phase is completed.

On July 16, 1986, Colonel Bouterse named a new government led by Prime Minister Pretapnaarian Radhakishun, a businessman and member of the Progressive Reform Party (VHP). The new government under Radhakishun will remain in office until March 31, 1987, when the transitional phase which began with the appointment of Udenhout's cabinet in 1985 will end. The Government program presented by the new Prime Minister on July 24 made no specific mention of elections and gave few details on the planned April 1987 return to civilian rule. According to the program, further discussions will take place concerning the substance of the political and administrative order. It does not indicate if the military will continue to play a preponderant role in the executive branch of the government. . . .

In compliance with a United Nations recommendation that the member countries establish institutions which warrant the protection of human rights, the Government of Suriname also created the National Institute for Human Rights by Decree A-18 of March 24, 1986. This official institution, staffed with personnel with direct links both to the Government and the military, has among its functions those of investigating and determining responsibility for violations of human rights; submitting the results of its investigations to the pertinent juridical authorities; promoting the teaching of human rights and adapting national legislation so as to conform it to international human rights instruments. . . .

Furthermore, and in compliance with a program for full transition to a civilian government expected to take place in April 1987, the Government of Suriname has pledged that the transition will bring about a democratic and just society; that the rule of law will be guaranteed; that the National Assembly will meet its goal of concluding the transition phase towards a full democracy no later than next April; and a Constitution and the composition of the organ representative of the people be established in accordance with the principles of a true democracy.

However, in spite of this progress, the Commission considers that the right to freedom of opinion, expression and thought dissemination is still severely limited in Suriname. Decree No. 310 of May 7, 1984, mentioned in the Commission's 1983 and 1985 reports, is still in force; it prohibits importation, transportation, distribution, sale, possession, production or reproductions of certain written material.

Although the Commission has no knowledge of arrests being made for political reasons during the period in which this Report has been written, it does know of a case in which a person was arrested for possession of reports on human rights of the United Nations and the Inter-American Commission on Human Rights. Indeed, Dr. Linus Rensch was arrested with his family on February 3, 1986, at the Zanderij airport in Suriname after having found in his baggage a copy of the OAS 1985 Report on Suriname and a UN report on summary executions. Dr. Rensch was taken to Fort Zeelandia, military police central command, where he was interrogated. After having remained in detention for one day without being given anything to eat he was permitted to leave but instructed to report daily to Major Aalspeer of the Military Intelligence Service. Although Mr. Rensch was not permitted to leave the country he now lives abroad.

After several delays, elections were held in Suriname in January 1988, and Ramshewak Shankar, an agricultural expert, was chosen by a 48-to-0 vote of the National Assembly to serve as the first civilian president of the country since the military takeover of 25 February 1980. The military leader, Col. Desi Bouterse, attended the voting procedure, and the army retained a mild oversight role in the government, as had been provided in the constitution approved in September 1987. Shankar's election marked a crucial step in the return to civilian rule in Suriname.

SWAZILAND. The Kingdom of Swaziland is a landlocked country in southern Africa. It has borders with Mozambique and South Africa. Constituted a British protectorate in 1963, it achieved independence in 1968 and became a member of the United Nations the same year. Its population is estimated by the UN (1990) to be 403,000. Ethnic groups include Swazis, Zulus, and persons of non-African descent. Languages commonly used include Siswati and English (both official). Religions practiced include Christianity (77%) and Animism and other indigenous faiths (27%). Literacy is estimated to be 65%.

The government (1990) took the form of a monarchy and member of the Commonwealth of Nations, of which the British monarch is the symbolic head. Swaziland's King Mswati III is ruler and head of State. The prime Minister, appointed by the king, is head of government.

The former king, in 1973, suspended the constitution and political parties and assumed total power for himself. After his death in 1982, a general election was held in 1983 at which 40 members of the National Assembly were elected. The new king, installed in 1986, abolished the Supreme Council that had exercised State power since 1982. The judiciary includes national courts, traditional courts, the High Court, and the Court of Appeal.

SWEDEN. The Kingdom of Sweden is a country occupying the eastern part of the Scandinavian Peninsula in northern Europe, on the Baltic Sea and the Gulf of Bothnia. It has borders with Denmark, Finland, and Norway. It was never other than independent and became a member of the United Nations in 1946. Its total population is estimated by the UN (1990) to be 8,305,000. The Finnish people living in Sweden, in areas close to Finland, comprise a national minority of about 30,000 persons. Ethnic groups include the Sami, about 17,000; Jews, about 16,000; and three distinct Gypsy groups: (1) descendents of immigrants during the 19th century, about 1,400; postwar immigrants from Finland, about 3,000; and other postwar immigrants, about 1,700. Languages commonly used include Swedish (official), Finnish, English, Catalan, Lithuanian, Punjabi, Tamil, and Telegu; in 1982–1983, instruction was given in 55 languages to 55,000 students by 4,300 teachers. Christianity (Swedish Lutheran, the established national Church, 95%; Pentecost Movement, Mission Covenant Church of Sweden, Swedish Baptist Church, and other Protestant denominations, 2%; Roman Catholic and Orthodox Catholic, 2%) is the predominant religion; Judaism is the faith of about 1%. Literacy is estimated at 99%.

The government (1990) took the form of a monarchy. King Carl XVI Gustaf is sovereign and head of State but does not participate in the government. The prime minister, Ingvar Carlsson, elected by the *Riksdag,* exercises executive authority as head of government. Under the 1975 constitution, the unicameral *Riksdag,* composed of 349 members chosen in general elections for terms of three years, is the central organ or government. In the elections, 310 members are picked by voters in the 28 constituencies; the remaining 29 seats constitute a nationwide pool intended to provide proportionality to political parties that receive at least 4% of the vote. The administration of justice is entirely independent of the remainder of the government. The judiciary includes an "Equal Opportunities Ombudsman" to assist in the resolution of disputes or claims of discrimination. Political parties include the Social Democratic Party, the Conservative Party, the Center Party, the Liberal Party, and the Communist Party.

Partly because it averted involvement in both world wars, making neutrality the basis of its foreign policy, Sweden was able to achieve great prosperity and social progress during the 20th century. This enabled it to pioneer actions to ensure all its citizens the right to health, the right to housing, the right to job security, and the elimination of discrimination, particularly on the ground of sex. Supervision of the application of such measures is in the hands of the Equal Opportunities Ombudsman.

Like Norway and Finland, Sweden has a sizable indigenous Sami population living in its northern areas, engaged largely in the breeding of reindeer. Tourism, forestry, and the construction of hydroelectric power plants have intruded on the activities of the Samis; and a government commission to deal with their problems was established in 1982. The main functions of the commission are (a) to give a clear indication of the special needs of the Samis as an indigenous population, (b) to examine the need to strengthen the legal position of the Samis in matters related to reindeer breeding, (c) to consider the need for a new popularly elected Sami body to represent the Samis on various occasions, and (d) to investigate the legislation and practice of the courts as regards the balancing of the interests of the Sami reindeer breeders and those of companies engaged in forestry, municipal development, and mining.

Under the Sami School Ordinance, Sami children have the right to fulfil their compulsory school attendance at a Sami school instead of an ordinary primary school. They are taught in the Sami language as well as in Swedish; they may also be taught the Sami language if they have not learned it at home.

Since 1751, Sweden and Norway have entered into agreements periodically to regulate the right of Swedish and Norwegian Samis to cross the frontier with their reindeer on their way to traditional summer pastures in Norway and winter pastures in Sweden. The latest convention was concluded in 1972.

As regards aliens, immigrants, and other nonnationals, guidelines issued by the Swedish parliament in 1975 provide that all such persons should be treated with the aim of achieving equality. In accordance with this principle, all immigrants are entitled to virtually the same social benefits as native Swedes, non-Swedish persons have the right to vote and to stand for office in local and regional elections if they have been residents of the country for the three preceding years, and all children with a mother tongue other than Swedish are entitled to training and instruction in their "home language," as well as in Swedish, subject to decision by their parents. The aim of this arrangement is to develop bilingualism.

SWEDEN: CONSTITUTION. The Swedish Instrument of Government contains the following provisions (Chapter II, articles 1–20) specifically relating to human rights and fundamental freedoms:

Chapter 2. Fundamental Freedoms and Rights

Article 1. Every citizen shall in relation to the community be guaranteed

1. the freedom of expression: the freedom to communicate information and express ideas, opinions and feelings either orally, in writing, in pictorial representations, or in any other way.

2. the freedom of information: the freedom to obtain and receive information and otherwise to acquaint oneself with the statements of others.

3. the freedom of assembly: the freedom to arrange and to attend any meeting for the purpose of information or expression of opinions or for any other similar purpose or for the purpose of presenting artistic work.

4. the freedom of demonstration: the freedom to arrange and to participate in any demonstration on public grounds.

5. the freedom of association: the freedom to unite with others for public or private purposes.

6. the freedom of religion: the freedom to practice one's religion either alone or together with others.

With regard to the freedom of the press the provisions of the Freedom of the Press Act shall apply. In the said Act there have also been laid down provisions governing the right to have access to public documents.

Article 2. Every citizen shall in relation to the community be protected against any compulsion to make known his opinion in any political, religious, cultural or other such matter. In relation to the community he shall furthermore be protected against any compulsion to participate in any meeting for the purpose of the formation of opinions or in any demonstration or other expression of opinions or to belong to a political association, a religious community or any other association for such opinions as referred to in the first sentence.

Article 3. No recording regarding a citizen in a public register may without his consent be founded exclusively on his political opinion.

Article 4. Capital punishment may not occur.

Article 5. Every citizen shall be protected against corporal punishment. Furthermore, he shall be protected against torture and against any medical influence or encroachment for the purpose of extorting or preventing statements.

Article 6. Every citizen shall in relation to the community be protected against any forced encroachment on his body even in cases other than those referred to in Articles 4 and 5. Furthermore, he shall be protected against any bodily search, search of his home or similar encroachment as well as against any examination of letters or other confidential correspondence and against eaves-dropping or recording of telephone conversation or other confidential communication.

Article 7. No citizen may be expatriated or prevented from entering the Realm.

No citizen who is or has been resident in the Realm may be deprived of his citizenship except if at the same time he becomes a national of another state with his express consent or by his entering into public service. Notwithstanding the foregoing provision it may, however, be prescribed that children under the age of eighteen shall have the same citizenship as their parents or one of them. It may furthermore be prescribed that, in accordance with an agreement with a foreign state, a person who is a national also of the other state since his birth and who is permanently resident there shall forfeit his Swedish nationality at the age of eighteen or later.

Article 8. In relation to the community every citizen shall be protected against being deprived of his liberty. He snall also in other respects be guaranteed the freedom to move within the Realm and to leave the Realm.

Article 9. Where a public authority other than a court has deprived a citizen of his liberty on account of a criminal act or suspicion of such act, such person shall have the right to have the matter tried by a court without undue delay. This shall not, however, apply where the issue is one of transferring to the Realm the execution of a penal sanction involving deprivation of liberty which has been imposed in another State.

If a citizen, for reasons other than those referred to in the first paragraph, has been coercely taken into custody, he shall likewise be entitled to have the matter tried by a court without undue delay. In such a case an examination by a board shall be deemed to rank equally with the trial of a court, provided that the composition of the board is governed by rules of law and the chairman of the board shall be or shall have been a permanent judge.

If such examination as referred to in the first or second paragraph has not been committed to an authority, competent according to the provisions laid down therein, the examination shall be carried out by a court of general jurisdiction.

Article 10. No penalty or other penal sanction may be imposed on account of an act which was not subject to any penal sanction at the time it was committed. Neither may a more severe penal sanction be imposed on account of the act than that which was prescribed at that time. What has thus been provided with respect to penal sanctions shall likewise apply with respect to confiscation or any other special legal effects attached to criminal acts.

No taxes, charges, or fees due the State may be levied to any further extent than what is prescribed in provisions which were in force when the circumstance occurred which gave rise to the liability to pay the taxes, charges or fees. However, if the Riksdag considers that specific reasons so warrant, it may be provided under an Act of law that taxes, charges, or fees due the State shall be levied although such an act had not entered into force when the aforementioned circumstance occurred, provided that the Government or a Committee of the Riksdag had at that time submitted a proposition to this effect to the Riksdag. For the purpose of the foregoing provision any written communication from the Government to the Riksdag announcing that such proposition is to be expected shall be equalled with a proposition. The Riksdag may furthermore prescribe that exceptions shall be made from the provisions of the first sentence if the Riksdag considers that this is warranted by specific reasons connected with war, danger of war, or a severe economic crisis.

Article 11. No court may be instituted for an act already committed, nor for a particular dispute or otherwise for a particular case.

Proceedings in the courts shall be open to the public.

Article 12. The freedoms and rights referred to in Article 1 sub-paragraphs 1–5 in Articles 6 and 8 and in the second paragraph of Article 11 may, to the extent provided for in Articles 13–16, be restricted by law, or by a decree issued upon an authorization given by law in pursuance of sub-paragraph 7 of the first paragraph of Article 7 of Chapter 8 or in pursuance of Article 10 of Chapter 8.

Such restriction as referred to in the preceding paragraph may be made only for the achievement of a purpose which is acceptable in a democratic society. The restriction may never go beyond what is necessary with regard to the purpose which has given rise to it neither may it be extended so far that it constitutes a threat against the free formation of opinions as one of the foundations of democracy. No restriction may be made solely on grounds of political, religious, cultural or other such ideas.

A proposition for any such Act of law as referred to in the first paragraph, or for an Act of law concerning amendment to or repeal of such Act shall, unless it is rejected by the Riksdag, on a motion by not less than ten of its members be pending for a period of not less than twelve months as from the date at which the first report of a Riksdag Committee on the proposition was submitted to the Chamber of the Riksdag. Notwithstanding the foregoing provision the Riksdag may adopt the proposition if not less than five sixths of those voting are in agreement with the decision.

The third paragraph of the present Article shall not apply to any proposition which is to the effect that an Act of law shall continue to be in force for a period of not more than two years. Nor shall the said paragraph apply to any propositions for an Act of law which concerns exclusively

1. prohibitions against revealing such matters as a person has acquired knowledge of in public service, or while performing an official duty, and the secrecy of which is called for in regard to such interests as referred to in Article 2 of Chapter 2 of the Freedom of the Press Act.

2. search of a person's home or similar encroachment, or

3. deprivation of liberty imposed as a penal sanction on account of a specified act or omission.

The committee on the Constitution shall decide on behalf of the Riksdag whether the third paragraph of the present Article is applicable in respect of a specified proposition for an Act of law.

Article 13. The freedom of expression and the freedom of information may be restricted on account of the safety of the Realm, the national economy, public order and security, the integrity of the individual, the sanctity of privacy, or the prevention and prosecution of crime. Furthermore, the freedom to make statements in economic activities may be restricted. The freedom of expression or the freedom of information may otherwise be restricted only where particularly important reasons so warrant.

In judging what restrictions may be made by virtue of the preceding paragraph particular regard shall be paid to the importance of the widest possible freedom of expression and freedom of information in political, religious, professional, scientific and cultural matters.

The issuing of rules and regulations which govern in detail a particular manner of disseminating or receiving statements without regard to the contents of the statements shall not be considered to restrict the freedom of expression or the freedom of information.

Article 14. The freedom of assembly and the freedom of demonstration may be restricted only on account of the safety of the Realm, of public order and security at the meeting or the demonstration, or of the traffic, or for the purpose of counteracting an epidemic.

The freedom of association may be restricted only as regards such associations the activities of which are of a military or similar nature or which involve the persecution of a national group of a particular race, of a particular skin colour, or of a particular ethnic origin.

Article 15. No law or other decree may imply the discrimi-

nation of any citizen on the grounds of his belonging to a minority on account of his race, skin colour, or ethnical origin.

Article 16. No law or other decree may imply the discrimination of any citizen on account of his sex, unless the relevant provision forms part of efforts to bring about equality between men and women or concerns compulsory military service or any corresponding compulsory national service.

Article 17. Any trade union and any employer or any association of employers shall have the right to take strike or lock-out actions or any similar measures, except as otherwise provided by law or ensuing from an agreement.

Article 18. Every citizen whose property is requisitioned by expropriation or by any other such disposition shall be guaranteed compensation for his loss in accordance with principles governed by law.

Article 19. Authors, artists and photographers shall have the right to their work in accordance with provisions laid down by law.

Article 20. Any foreigner within the Realm shall be on equality with a Swedish citizen with regard to

1. protection against any compulsion to participate in meetings or the purpose of the formation of opinions or in a demonstration or other expression of opinions, or to belong to a religious community or other association (Article 2, second sentence),

2. protection against capital punishment, corporal punishment and torture as well as against medical influence or encroachment for the purpose of extorting or preventing statements (Articles 4 and 5),

3. the right to the trial by a court of any deprivation of liberty on account of a criminal act or a suspicion of such act (Article 9 first and third paragraphs),

4. protection against retroactive penal sanctions and other retroactive effects of criminal acts as well as retroactive taxes, charges or fees (Article 10),

5. the protection against the institution of a court for a particular case (Article 11, first paragraph),

6. protection against discrimination on account of race, skin colour, or ethnical origin, or on account of sex (Articles 15 and 16),

7. the right to take strike or lock-out actions (Article 17),

8. the right to compensation in cases of expropriation or other such disposition (Article 18).

Unless otherwise provided by special rules of law, any foreigner within the Realm shall be on equality with a Swedish citizen also with regard to

1. the freedom of expression, the freedom of information, the freedom of assembly, the freedom of demonstration, the freedom of association, and the freedom of religion (Article 1).

SWITZERLAND. The Swiss Confederation is a country in western Europe consisting of 23 sovereign cantons. It has borders with Austria, France, Italy, Liechtenstein, and Germany. It achieved independence from the Holy Roman Empire in 1648, and its independence and neutrality were recognized and guaranteed by the Congress of Vienna in 1815. Although not a member of the United Nations, Switzerland has observer status there.

Switzerland's population is estimated by the UN

(1990) to be 6,387,000. Ethnic groups include persons of Gypsy descent and temporary migrant workers from southern European countries; national groups include German, French, and Italian. Languages in common use include German (65%), French (19%), Italian (8%), and Romansch and others (8%). Christianity (Roman Catholic, 47%; Protestant denominations, 45%; others, 8%) is the predominant religion. Literacy is estimated at 99%.

The government (1990) took the form of a republic. The main organ of government is the bicameral legislature, consisting of the 46-member *Standerat,* or State Council, and the 200-member *Nationalrat,* or National Council. All members are elected for terms of four years. Members of the *Standerat* are elected by the cantons by whatever methods they themselves adopt and are paid by the cantons which they represent. Because two of the 23 cantons are politically divided, each half-canton elects one member. Members of the *Nationalrat* are elected directly by a system of proportional representation; the number of members elected in each canton corresponds to the population of that canton. They are paid out of federal funds. Executive authority is exercised by the *Bundesrat,* or Federal Council, which consists of seven members elected by joint sessions of the two parliamentary bodies. The president of the federal council is called president of the confederation; he serves in this post for one year and is not immediately eligible for re-election. The vice president, elected by the same procedure, also serves for one year. He is not eligible for re-election to this post but may, and usually is, elected to succeed the outgoing president. The judiciary is headed by the *Bundesgericht,* or Federal Tribunal, members of which are appointed by the federal assembly for terms of six years. This court deals primarily with suits between the federation and the cantons and between one canton and another. It is also a court of appeal against decisions of other federal authorities.

In national elections held on 18 October 1987, the four-party coalition government—composed of the Social Democratic Party, the Radical Democratic Party, the Christian-Democratic Party, and the People's Party—retained its overwhelming parliamentary majority. Other political parties include the Liberals, the Independents, the National Campaign/Vigilance, the Evangelical Party, the Progressive Organizations Party, and two environmentalist groups—the Green Party and the Auto Party.

Switzerland has prospered because of its strategic location in central Europe and because of its strict neutrality, maintained through World Wars I and II. Geneva was the seat of the League of Nations and now houses the European office of the United Nations and the headquarters of many intergovernmental organizations, including the INTERNATIONAL LABOR ORGANIZATION and the WORLD HEALTH ORGANIZATION.

In November 1989, the people of Switzerland voted to keep the Swiss army of 625,000 men, although it has not fought in a foreign war since 1915, as the best way of maintaining Swiss neutrality. The vote was taken as a result of an initiative, signed by 111,300 Swiss citizens, to adopt a constitutional amendment which stated that "Switzerland has no army." More than 35% of those who voted—over a million people—favored the amendment, while about 65%—nearly two million—opposed it.

SYRIA. The Syrian Arab Republic is a country in western Asia, on the Mediterranean Sea. It has borders with Iraq, Israel, Jordan, Lebanon, and Turkey. Once part of the Ottoman Empire, Syria was made part of the Levant States mandate by the League of Nations after World War I; Lebanon was also included in that mandate. The French government proclaimed Syria an independent republic in 1941 after Free French forces had invaded it and routed Vichy forces stationed there during World War II. Complete independence was achieved on 1 January 1944, and Syria became a member of the United Nations in 1945. However, in 1958, Syria joined Egypt to form the United Arab Republic. This arrangement ended, and Syria resumed its independence in 1961. Its population is estimated by the UN (1990) to be 12,634,000. Ethnic groups include Arabs (90%), Kurds, Armenians, Circassians, and Turks. Languages commonly used include Arabic (official) (89%), Kurdish (6%), Armenian (3%), and English and French (2%). Religions practiced include Islam (Sunni, Shi'ite, and Ismaili), 90%; Christianity (Greek Orthodox, Greek Catholic, Armenian Orthodox, Syrian Orthodox, Armenian Catholic, and some Protestant denominations), 10%. Literacy is estimated at 78%.

The government (1990) took the form of a republic. Under the 1973 constitution, the Arab Socialist Renaissance (Ba'ath) Party is the leading party in the State and in society. That party, running on a unified ticket with the Syrian Communist and Socialist Parties, won 70% of the seats in the People's Assembly in 1973, 1977, and 1981; its chairman is president of the republic and head of State. The premier, appointed by the president, exercises executive authority as head of government. Legislation is prepared by the 195-member People's Council, members of which are elected by universal suffrage for terms of four years. The judicial system, headed by the Supreme Court, is based on French and Islamic jurisprudence. Political parties, in addition to the Arab Socialist Renaissance

(Ba'ath) Party, include the Syrian Arab Socialist Union, the Union Socialist Party, and the Communist Party of Syria.

As regards the Syrian Arab Golan, occupied by Israel since 1967, the UN Security Council, in resolution 487 (1981) of 17 December 1981, unanimously reaffirmed the principle that the acquisition of territory by force is inadmissible and decided that Israel's decision to impose its laws, jurisdiction, and administration in the occupied area was null and void and without international effect. The council demanded that Israel rescind its decision forthwith and decided unanimously that, if Israel did not comply, the council would meet urgently to consider taking appropriate measures in accordance with the UN Charter.

The UN General Assembly later considered the situation in the occupied Syrian Arab Golan at each regular session and at a special session in 1982. It determined, in resolution 44/40 B of 4 December 1989—as it had done on several earlier occasions—that the continued occupation of that territory since 1967 and its annexation by Israel on 14 December 1981 constitute a continuing threat to international peace and security. In particular, it strongly deplored the negative vote by a permanent member of the Security Council (the United States of America) which had prevented the council from adopting against Israel, under chapter 7 of the UN CHARTER, the "appropriate measures" to which the council had referred in its resolution; and it called upon all member States (a) to refrain from supplying Israel with any weapons and related equipment and to suspend any military assistance that Israel receives from them; (b) to refrain from acquiring any weapons or military equipment from Israel; (c) to suspend economic, financial and technological assistance to and cooperation with Israel; and (d) to sever diplomatic, trade and cultural relations with Israel.

The UN COMMISSION ON HUMAN RIGHTS also considered the situation in the occupied Syrian Arab Golan at its annual sessions and was disturbed in particular by its human rights implications. On 17 February 1989, for example, the commission deplored (resolution 1989/1)

the inhuman treatment, terror and practices contrary to human rights which the Israeli occupation authorities continue to apply against Syrian citizens in the occupied Syrian Arab Golan by reason of their refusal of Israeli citizenship and in order to force them to carry Israeli identity cards, which practices constitute a flagrant violation of the Universal Declaration of Human Rights, the Geneva Convention Relative to the Protection of Civilian Persons in Time of War of 12 August 1949, and the relevant resolutions adopted by the Security Council, the General Assembly and other international bodies and also constitute a threat to international peace and security.

The commission condemned Israel for persisting in its policies and practices of annexation in the occupied Syrian Arab Golan, *inter alia,* appropriating land, establishing settlements thereon and moving Israeli settlers into them, diverting water to those settlements, thus depriving the Golan population of its sources of livelihood, and in particular imposing a boycott on agricultural products, depriving that population of the right to export them. It called upon all States to urge Israel to cease such practices, including boycott measures, and to facilitate the marketing of the agricultural produce of the Golan population.

Finally, the commission emphasized that Israel must allow the evacuees from among the Golan population to return to their homes and to recover their property and places of residence occupied by Israel since 1967, and firmly emphasized the overriding necessity of the total and unconditional withdrawal by Israel from all Syrian and other Arab territories occupied since 1967, including Jerusalem, which is an essential prerequisite for the establishment of peace in the Middle East.

A number of non-governmental organizations, including the Co-ordinating Board of Jewish Organizations, the World Jewish Congress and the World Union for Progressive Judaism, drew the attention of the UN Commission on Human Rights to the plight of Syria's small Jewish population (estimated to total about 4,500) at the commission's 1987 session (UN Doc. E/CN.4/1987/NGO 73). While recognizing that Syrian Jews are allowed to maintain their religious customs and Jewish education, that their economic situation has improved in recent years, and that they enjoy the possibility of travelling abroad for tourism, business, or medical purposes, the organizations maintain that, nevertheless, they live in continuous fear of the future and as virtual hostages. Among the difficulties reported by them to face Syrian Jews are the following:

1. Emigration from the Syrian Arab Republic is prohibited;
2. Whole families are not allowed to leave the Syrian Arab Republic for visits abroad. An individual who wishes to travel must leave a monetary deposit and his family must remain behind as a guarantee of his return;
3. The sale of property and the purchase of other property in exchange must be approved by Syrian authorities;
4. Jews cannot be employed in public posts;
5. The Jewish community is kept under close surveillance by security officials who are fully informed of any movement or disappearance of Jews from the Syrian Arab Republic. The authorities know of any Jew who does not return from an approved visit abroad and maintain close surveillance of any foreigner who visits the Jewish quarter;

6. Unlike other citizens, Syrian Jews alone are identified in their identity documents and passports by a stamp stating that they are "of the Mosaic faith";

7. Jewish girls of marriageable age, of whom there are approximately 300, who are unable to marry in the absence of Jewish single men, are denied exit visas to contract marriages abroad, despite the awareness of the authorities of this acute social problem;

8. Under government orders, the Jewish schools in Damascus and Haleb are run by Moslem principals.

T

TAIWAN. The Republic of China is a country consisting of the island of Taiwan, formerly known as Formosa, which lies in the Pacific about 100 miles off mainland Asia; two islands closer to the Chinese coast known as Quemoy and Matsu; and a string of smaller islands between Taiwan and the mainland known as Pescadores. Over the years, Taiwan was administered successively by the Dutch, the Spanish, the Chinese, the Japanese and again—after World War II—the Chinese.

Taiwan's population is estimated (1990) to be 20,125,000. Ethnic groups include, in addition to Formosans, a small number of aborigines of Malaysian and Indonesian descent and a large population of Han Chinese from the mainland.

The Chinese arrived for the most part in 1949 when the Nationalist government headed by Generalissimo Chiang Kai-shek was overthrown on mainland China. For many years, the general maintained a government-in-exile and a powerful army in Taiwan in the hope of returning to the mainland. Although the United States of America supported his efforts, his one serious attempt to return to China was blocked, in 1953, by the stationing of the American Pacific fleet in the Strait of Formosa.

The government of Taiwan (1990) took the form of a republic. There is a National Assembly and five major governing *Yuans:* the executive, legislative, judicial, control, and examination governing bodies. The president and vice president are elected by the assembly for terms of five years. The Nationalist Party *(Kuomintang)* and the Democratic Progressive Party are the leading political groups.

For more than twenty years, Taiwan, with the assistance of the United States of America and other powers, occupied the seat designated for "China" in various organs of the United Nations. This ended when the United Nations recognized the People's Republic of China as the legitimate representative of the Chinese people in 1971. Taiwan was never admitted separately to UN membership.

Both the Taipei and the Beijing governments consider Taiwan as constituting an integral part of China, but Taiwan has rejected all efforts at reunification.

However, travel and trade between the two countries increased gradually after the death of Chiang Kai-shek in 1975. Chiang Ching-kuo, who succeeded him as president, died in January 1988 and was, in turn, succeeded by Lee Teng-hui, the first native of Taiwan to serve simultaneously as president and chairman of the Nationalist Party.

In July 1988, 1,209 delegates to the party congress elected a new central committee of 180 members, and in the process many elderly party officials were replaced by young, liberal Taiwanese. At the same time, the congress took steps to liberalize relations with mainland China, authorizing increases in trade, the resumption of mail service, visits by Taiwanese to family members on the mainland, and exchanges of certain categories of students.

A large influx of tourists from Taiwan was welcomed by Chinese authorities in the latter half of 1989, compensating in part for the losses suffered by the Chinese tourist industry after the military crackdown in June of that year. More than 500,000 Taiwan citizens visited China during the six-month period, ending a forced separation that had lasted nearly 40 years.

In mid-March 1990, more than 10,000 protesters, organized by the opposition Democratic Progressive Party, gathered in a park in Taipei to demand democratic changes and to call for replacement of 668 deputies in the 752-seat parliament who were elected on the Chinese mainland before 1949. However, in an election held a few days later, the Nationalists prevailed and President Lee Teng-hui—the only candidate—was again selected to serve as president and party chairman. He continues to be under pressure to dissolve the electoral college and to allow general presidential elections; and he is not fully supported by some elderly assemblymen because, as a native of Taiwan, he does not share their dream of a victorious return to China. In May 1990, President Lee Teng-hui selected Defense Minister Hau Pei-tsun, the country's only four-star general, to be prime minister—a move denounced as a "backward step" by the Democratic Progressive Party.

T

TALLINN GUIDELINES FOR ACTION ON HUMAN RESOURCES DEVELOPMENT IN THE FIELD OF DISABILITY. The guidelines, which set out a guiding philosophy and a series of strategies to be undertaken to promote the further development and continued progress of disabled persons, were adopted by the International Meeting on Human Resources in the Field of Disability, convened at Tallinn, Estonian Soviet Socialist Republic, U.S.S.R., from 14 to 22 August 1989. On 8 December 1989, the UN General Assembly requested the secretary-general (resolution 44/70) to bring the guidelines to the attention of member States, national coordinating bodies, and concerned intergovernmental and non-governmental organizations. The guidelines, annexed to resolution 44/70, are as follows:

Introduction

1. The International Meeting on Human Resources in the Field of Disability, convened at Tallinn, Estonian Soviet Socialist Republic, Union of the Soviet Socialist Republics, from 14 to 22 August 1989, having considered the situation of human resources development in the field of disability, particularly in developing countries, firmly believes that the reinforcement of existing as well as new and innovative action is required to promote the further development and continued progress of disabled persons.

2. Following the adoption of the World Programme of Action concerning Disabled Persons by the General Assembly, in its resolution 37/52 of 3 December 1982, there has been a growing need for higher priority to be given to the development of the human resources of disabled persons, with specific reference to education and training, employment, and science and technology. In this connection, the General Assembly also, in its resolution 37/53 of 3 December 1982, proclaimed the United Nations Decade of Disabled Persons, 1983–1992, encouraging Member States to utilize that period as one of the means to implement the World Programme of Action.

3. The main objectives of the World Programme of Action are to promote effective measures for the prevention of disability, for rehabilitation and for the realization of the goals of full participation and equality for persons with disabilities. To accomplish these goals, due regard must be paid to education, training and work opportunities.

4. While it is acknowledged that the living conditions of the general population in developing countries urgently need to be improved, the objectives of the World Programme of Action call for the situation of disabled persons to be given special attention during the remainder of the Decade and beyond. Effective implementation of the World Programme of Action will make an important contribution to the development process of societies through the mobilization of more human resources.

5. While it is also acknowledged that a number of countries have already initiated or carried out activities within the framework of the World Programme of Action, further concerted efforts should be made to integrate the human resources development of disabled persons into intersectoral planning at the national level.

Guiding Philosophy

6. Human resources development is a human-centred process that seeks to realize the full potential and capabilities of human beings. This process is fundamental to the concept of equalization of opportunities, in keeping with the goals of the World Programme of Action.

7. Through human resources development, disabled persons are able effectively to exercise their rights of full citizenship. As full citizens, they have the same rights and responsibilities as other members of society, including the right to life, as declared in international human rights instruments. They also have the same choices as other citizens in the social, cultural, economic and political life of their communities.

8. Because persons with disabilities are agents of their own destiny rather than objects of care, Governments and organizations need to reflect this perception in their policies and programmes. This means that disabled persons, as individuals and as members of organizations, should be involved in the decision-making process as equal partners.

9. The abilities of disabled persons and their families should be strengthened through community-based supplementary services provided by Governments and non-governmental organizations. These services should promote self-determination and enable disabled persons to participate in the development of society. Governments should recognize and support the role of disabled persons' organizations in enabling persons with disabilities to take charge of their own lives.

Strategies

A. Participation of Persons with Disabilities. 10. A statutory basis is required to enable disabled persons to participate as full citizens in decision-making at all levels of the planning, implementation, and monitoring and evaluation of policies and programmes.

11. To facilitate the full participation of disabled persons and enable them to exercise their rights as citizens, access to information is essential. To this end, all information has to be adapted to appropriate formats. These information formats may include Braille script, large print, audio-visual media and sign-language interpretation. Information channels should include television, radio, newspapers and postal services. Governments should work with organizations of disabled persons to identify appropriate information formats and channels to reach disabled citizens.

12. Governments should adopt, enforce and fund legally binding standards and regulations to improve access for persons with disabilities, ensuring that buildings, streets, and road, sea and air transport are barrier-free, architecturally and in all other ways. Communication systems and security and safety measures should be developed and adapted to meet the needs of disabled persons.

13. To facilitate the recruitment of disabled persons and to assist private-sector industries in hiring them, organizations at the national, regional and international levels, including the United Nations, should identify and maintain listings of qualified disabled candidates.

B. Strengthening of Grassroots Initiatives. 14. Local community initiatives should be especially promoted. Disabled persons and their families should be encouraged to form grass-roots organizations, with governmental recognition of their importance and governmental support in the form of financing and training.

15. Governmental and non-governmental organizations

concerned with disability issues should allow disabled persons to participate as equal partners.

16. The efficient functioning of governmental and non-governmental organizations concerned with disability calls for training in organizational and management skills.

C. Promotion of an Integrated Approach. 17. Overall national policy frameworks with supporting legislation should be developed.

18. The essence of an integrated approach is the inclusion of disability issues in all ministries and at every level of government policy and planning. National co-ordination bodies, with linkages at the local, regional and interregional levels, should be established or strengthened. The membership of those bodies should include all government ministries, legislative committees and non-governmental organizations, particularly organizations of disabled persons. The co-ordination body should review existing policies, plans and programmes, identify existing and projected resources and monitor and evaluate the implementation of national policies.

19. National development programmes should include disability components.

20. Disabled women should be included in the existing national and regional programmes aimed at women.

21. At the level of service delivery, an integrated approach entails co-operation and referral among professionals working in organizational settings that provide educational, vocational, health and social services.

D. Promotion of Education and Training. 22. The early years are critical in the overall development of a disabled child and in fostering positive attitudes towards the child. Specific programmes and training materials should be developed to address these needs during the formative infant and pre-school years.

23. Education at the primary, secondary and higher levels should be available to disabled persons within the regular educational system in regular school settings, as well as in vocational training programmes. When such education is provided to deaf students, teachers and/or interpreters who are proficient in the indigenous sign language must be provided.

24. Special education programmes and schools that promote the indigenous sign language and the indigenous deaf culture must be available to deaf people. Deaf people should be employed in such programmes and schools.

25. Cost-effective alternatives to segregated school facilities should be developed and implemented by Governments at the national and local levels. These alternatives include special education teachers as consultants to regular education teachers, resource rooms with specialized personnel and materials, special classrooms in regular schools and interpreters for deaf students.

26. The education of disabled children should involve the co-operation and concerted efforts of health and social services, as well as teachers and parents. It should provide support measures, such as technical aids, especially adapted pedagogical approaches, and incentives for teachers.

27. The content and quality of education and training should ensure the acquisition of skills that are economically viable and that provide opportunities for work. Career education and vocational training programmes should be available to ensure the transition of disabled students into the economic mainstream.

28. In addition to being offered formal skills training and education, disabled persons should be offered training in social and self-help skills to prepare them for independent living. Special efforts should be made to promote education and skills training for disabled girls and women, in both urban and rural areas.

29. General teacher-training curricula should include a course of study in skills for teaching disabled children and young persons in regular schools.

30. Each Government should have a national plan for training and employing an adequate number of health, education and vocational professionals in rehabilitation. Persons with disabilities should be recruited for such training and employment.

31. In fields such as education, labour, health and social services, law, architecture and technical development, which are often involved in the different aspects of rehabilitation, the professional training should include training on the rights and needs of disabled people. Professionals in these fields should also be made aware of the resources available for disabled persons so that appropriate referrals can be made or services provided.

32. Appropriate technology should be considered essential for the utilization of available resources. This may include simple, universally available equipment, as well as computer technology.

E. Promotion of Employment. 33. Disabled persons have the right to be trained for and to work on equal terms in the regular labour force. Community-based rehabilitation programmes should be encouraged to provide better job opportunities in developing countries. Use should be made of the vocational services, guidance and training, placement, employment and related services that already exist for workers in general. On-the-job training may be more effective than conventional training.

34. General development programmes that provide loans, training and equipment for income-generating activities should include disabled persons.

35. Employment opportunities can be promoted primarily by measures relating to employment and salary standards that apply to all workers and secondarily by measures offering special support and incentives. In addition to formal employment, opportunities should be broadened to include self-employment, co-operatives and other group income-generating schemes. Where special national employment drives have been launched for youth and unemployed persons, disabled persons should be included. Disabled persons should be actively recruited, and when a disabled candidate and a non-disabled candidate are equally qualified, the disabled candidate should be chosen.

36. Employers' and workers' organizations should adopt, in co-operation with organizations of disabled persons, policies that promote the training and employment of disabled and non-disabled persons on an equal basis, including disabled women.

37. Policies for affirmative action should be formulated and implemented to increase the employment of disabled women. Governments and non-governmental organizations should support the creation of income-generating projects involving disabled women.

F. Provisions for Funding. 38. In general, funding should be allocated through regular sectoral budgeting systems. A national rehabilitation fund may be established to facilitate the employment or self-employment of disabled persons. This fund could be used to cover the costs of training, equipment, and initial capital outlay.

39. Similarly, funds should be established for loans to small-scale pilot projects at the grass-roots level; such funds could be administered locally using simple procedures.

T

G. Promotion of Community Awareness. 40. To increase community understanding of the rights, needs and potentials of disabled persons, collaborative efforts with disabled persons and their organizations are required to develop and promote a flow of information using mass media, especially film, television, radio and print media. In particular, information for disabled persons and their families on all aspects of living with a disability should be as clear and uncomplicated as possible.

41. Community awareness programmes should include specific strategies for the prevention of disability. Government efforts aimed at early identification, intervention and prevention should be strengthened through community awareness and community involvement in programmes on disability.

42. Persons with mental disability (mental retardation or mental illness) or multiple disabilities are among the most stigmatized groups of citizens. They have the right to make choices, take risks, control their own lives and live in the community. Their adult status, abilities and aspirations must be respected and reinforced by their inclusion in decision-making, although many may need individual advocacy to be clearly understood.

43. It should be acknowledged that people with mental and multiple disabilities benefit from education, skills training and work opportunities. For many of these people, opportunities need to be individualized. Support is required to help them and their families to establish and maintain a positive life-style.

44. The World Programme of Action should be translated into all national languages, through governmental action. Braille, large print and simplified versions should also be made available by the appropriate media to ensure as wide a distribution as possible to all citizens, including disabled persons, their families, and non-governmental and governmental organizations.

H. Improving the Methodology for Human Resources Development. 45. Policies and programmes for human resources development concerning disabled persons should be based on an assessment of their needs and resources as well as on the potential of existing development programmes and services to meet those needs. The implementation of such policies and programmes should be periodically monitored, with adjustments made to ensure effective implementation.

46. Evaluation should be built into programmes at the planning stage so that their overall efficacy in fulfilling policy objectives can be assessed. Persons with disabilities should play an active role in developing the criteria for monitoring and evaluation.

47. Increased attention should be given to services for people with hearing, speech, mental, intellectual or multiple disabilities.

48. The requirements of particular groups, such as disabled children, disabled women, the disabled elderly, disabled migrants and refugees, should also be recognized and met.

49. Governmental and non-governmental organizations should utilize recent developments in education through communications media, also known as distance education, which has been found to be an appropriate methodology in human resources development in the field of disability.

50. The local use of appropriate technologies for producing such items as wheel chairs, prosthetic devices and mobility aids, as well as aids for hearing and seeing, should take into account the technical, socio-economic and cultural conditions in the particular society. Each country should have a national system for the delivery of rehabilitation aids.

I. Regional and International Cooperation. 51. Training programmes in human resources development in the field of disability should be strengthened by collaborative efforts at the regional and/or subregional levels. Such programmes should be co-ordinated through existing intergovernmental and regional organizations, including those of disabled persons.

52. International development aid projects should include a component specifically aimed at supporting organizations of disabled persons and training their members. In addition, employment opportunities should be made available to disabled individuals within these projects.

53. All international development assistance programmes directed at macro-level planning and development, such as those in agriculture or education, should include a specific component ensuring the participation of disabled persons in such schemes.

54. At both the national and interregional levels, Governments should strongly support collaboration with non-governmental agencies in specific areas of disability, to ensure co-ordination and to prevent duplication of services.

55. Linkages between organizations of disabled persons in developed and developing countries should be strengthened. This can be done through the exchange of information, training and meetings to provide forums for disabled persons to share experiences on strategic approaches. Workshops and field studies should be organized to train trainers and the management personnel of organizations of disabled persons.

56. Implementation of these Guidelines relies on effective action at the national level. This action should be supplemented by concerted efforts at the international level, particularly on the part of the United Nations and its focal point for the implementation of the World Programme of Action concerning Disabled Persons, as well as its relevant organizations and specialized agencies. National and international non-governmental organizations, in particular organizations of disabled persons, should be fully involved.

SEE ALSO *Disability.*

TANZANIA. The United Republic of Tanzania, a country in eastern Africa, fronting on the Indian ocean, and including the offshore islands of Zanzibar and Pemba. Mainland Tanzania has borders with Burundi, Kenya, Malawi, Mozambique, Rwanda, Uganda, Zaire, and Zambia. The Protectorate of Tanganyika achieved independence from Great Britain in 1961 as Tanzania and Zanzibar achieved independence in 1963; and they were united in 1964. Tanzania became a member of the United Nations in 1961. The population of the United Republic of Tanzania is estimated by the UN (1990) to be 26,998,000, including about 700,000 residents of Zanzibar. More than 130 ethnic groups are said to exist in the United Republic, but statistics concerning them are not available because of the government's policy of treating the entire population as a single community. Languages commonly used include Kiswahili (official) and English. Religions practiced in mainland Tanzania include Islam (35%), Animism (35%), and Christianity (30%); in Zanzibar, Islam (96%) and Hunduism (4%). Literacy is estimated at 80%.

The government (1990) took the form of a republic and member of the Commonwealth of Nations, of which the British monarch is the symbolic head. Under the constitution, the Tanganyikan African National Union and the Afro-Shirazi Party of Zanzibar were merged into the *Chama Cha Mapinduzi* (Revolutionary Party), which became an organ of State policy. On its nomination, the president, prime minister, first vice president, second vice president (also president of Zanzibar), and deputy prime minister are elected by universal suffrage. Legislation for the United Republic is prepared by the unicameral National Assembly and for Zanzibar alone by the House of Representatives, all members of which are nominated by the single political party. The judiciary is independent. In some Zanzibar courts, the rules of Islamic law prevail.

The single political party, Chama Cha Mapinduzi, functioned in Tanzania for 25 years after being installed by the country's first president, Julius K. Nyerere. Since his voluntary retirement in 1986, there has been some interest shown in the possibility of replacing it by a multi-party system, and even Mr. Nyerere has not ruled out such a possibility. However, this would require a change in the constitution, which would take some time. Meanwhile, Mr. Nyerere retains his position as chairman of the Revolutionary Party, while the new president, Ali Hassan Mwinyi, functions as head of State.

The constitution of Tanzania, adopted in 1977, states (art. 1 [5]) that "the principal aims and objects of the Party shall be: . . . .2. to build socialism on the basis of self-reliance; . . . .11. to safeguard the inherent dignity of human beings in accordance with the Universal Declaration of Human Rights."

An amendment which entered into force in 1984 added a Bill of Rights to the constitution, under which any person who suffers a violation of his rights may invoke its provisions in seeking redress from the courts of law.

TERRORIST ACTS. The Seventh United Nations Congress on the Prevention of Crime and the Treatment of Offenders, which met in Milan from 26 August to 6 September 1985, was deeply disturbed by the prevalence of actual or threatened violent attacks and other concerted acts of violence against innocent persons and agreed that terrorist activities— including kidnapping, murder, hijacking, the taking of HOSTAGES, and the destruction of property—seriously impair freedom and the political stability of communities.

The congress noted that these acts had occurred in spite of being addressed in a number of accepted international instruments, including the CONVENTION ON OFFENCES AND CERTAIN OTHER ACTS COMMITTED ON BOARD AIRCRAFT; the CONVENTION FOR THE SUPPRESSION OF UNLAWFUL SEIZURE OF AIRCRAFT; the CONVENTION FOR THE SUPPRESSION OF UNLAWFUL ACTS AGAINST THE SAFETY OF CIVIL AVIATION; the CONVENTION ON THE PREVENTION AND PUNISHMENT OF CRIMES AGAINST INTERNATIONALLY PROTECTED PERSONS, INCLUDING DIPLOMATIC AGENTS; and the INTERNATIONAL CONVENTION AGAINST THE TAKING OF HOSTAGES.

Gravely concerned at the human, social, and economic cost of such attacks, and the threat they posed to normal international intercourse—particularly in the areas of travel, commerce, and diplomatic relations—and bearing in mind the importance of safeguards and maintenance of basic rights under ordinary legal procedures and in conformity with international human rights standards, the congress called upon all States to take the necessary measures to ensure the full observance of the obligations contained in the relevant conventions to which they are parties, in particular the application of appropriate law enforcement measures under ordinary legal procedures, in conformity with international human rights standards.

The congress, further, invited all States that had not become parties to the above-mentioned conventions to consider taking the necessary steps to do so in an expeditious fashion; urged all States to adopt legislation that, whenever necessary, will strengthen legal measures against those who commit violent acts of terrorism and to facilitate the exchange of information between States in order to improve the abilities of governments to prevent violence, to safeguard their citizens and to respond more effectively in cases of offenses contemplated in the conventions; and also urged them to facilitate, to the fullest extent possible, the effective application of law enforcement measures with respect to those who commit violent acts of terrorism, to rationalize their extradition procedures and practices and other cooperative arrangements with their respective legal processes and to avoid inappropriate exceptions.

SEE ALSO European Convention on the Suppression of Terrorism; European Recommendation concerning International Cooperation in the Presecution and Punishment of Terrorism.

THAILAND. The Kingdom of Thailand is a country in southeastern Asia occupying the western half of the Indochinese Peninsula and the northern two-thirds of the Malayan Peninsula. It has borders with Cambodia, Laos, Malaysia, and Myanmar. It was never other than independent, although occupied by Japanese troops during World War II, and became a member of the United Nations in 1946. Its population is estimated by the UN (1990) to be 55,712,000. Ethnic groups include Thai (75%), Chinese (14%), and others (11%). Languages commonly used include Thai (Siamese), English, French, and several regional vernaculars. Religions practiced include Buddhism (85%), Islam (4%), Christianity (5%), Hinduism (2%), and others (3%). Literacy is estimated at 86%.

The government (1990) took the form of a monarchy. Under the 1978 constitution, King Bhumibol Adulyadej is head of State. The premier, Chatichai Choonhavan, representing the majority party or coalition was appointed by the king and acts as head of government. The National Assembly, which exercises legislative authority, includes the House of Representatives, whose members are elected by universal suffrage, and the Senate, whose members are appointed by the king. The judiciary includes three levels of courts. Judges, appointed by the king, are independent in conducting trials and pronouncing judgments according to the law. Political parties include the Democrat Party, the Thai Nation Party, the Social Action Party, and the United Democratic Party. The Communist Party is prohibited.

Once known officially in English-speaking countries as Siam, Thailand was dominated by Portuguese traders and missionaries after 1511 and was closed to all foreigners in the 17th century after the British, Dutch, and French broke the Portuguese monopoly.

Because trade is chiefly in the hands of the large Chinese minority, tension between Thais and Chinese has existed for many years. In recent years, Thai fishermen were accused of beating and robbing Vietnamese refugees attempting to reach Malaysia by sea, after Thailand had blocked a safer land route through Cambodia. The Thai government considers most Vietnamese reaching its territory to be economic migrants rather than genuine refugees.

THIRD WORLD MOVEMENT AGAINST THE EXPLOITATION OF WOMEN. An international non-governmental organization in consultative status (roster) with the economic and social council, TW–MAE–W initiates or supports protests and other activities directed against the exploitation of women, giving special attention to those activities or attitudes which oppress, or constitute assaults upon, women and girls. It focuses on unethical activities of employment and marriage bureaus, international beauty contests, nudist resorts, etc.; and operates a crisis center for sexual assault. It publishes the TW–MAE–W *Action Bulletin* every two months.

Founded in Manila in 1980, originally to oppose organized "sex tours" from Japan, the organization now functions in more than 40 countries, mainly through the efforts of its individual members.

Third World Movement against the Exploitation of Women. Address: Arbega's Building, 769 Aurora Boulevard, Quezon City, Philippines. Telephone: 706827. Cable: GODSHEPCON Manila. Telex: 40793 OHD PM.

THOUGHT, CONSCIENCE, AND RELIGION. The right to freedom of thought, conscience, and religion is proclaimed in the UNIVERSAL DECLARATION OF HUMAN RIGHTS in the following terms:

Article 18. Everyone has the right to freedom of thought, conscience and religion; this right includes freedom to change his religion or belief, and freedom, either alone or in community with others and in public or in private, to manifest his religion or belief in teaching, practice, worship and observance.

The INTERNATIONAL COVENANT ON ECONOMIC, SOCIAL AND CULTURAL RIGHTS contains the following provisions:

Article 3. 1. The States Parties to the present Covenant recognize the right of everyone to education. They agree that education shall be directed to the full development of the human personality and the sense of its dignity, and shall strengthen the respect for human rights and fundamental freedoms. They further agree that education shall enable all persons to participate effectively in a free society, promote understanding, tolerance and friendship among all nations and all racial, ethnic or religious groups, and further the activities of the United Nations for the maintenance of peace. . . .
3. The States Parties to the present Covenant undertake to have respect for the liberty of parents and, when applicable, legal guardians to choose for their children schools, other than those established by the public authorities, which conform to such minimum educational standards as may be laid down or approved by the State and to ensure the religious and moral education of their children in conformity with their own convictions.

The INTERNATIONAL COVENANT ON CIVIL AND POLITICAL RIGHTS deals with this right in the following provisions:

Article 18. 1. Everyone shall have the right to freedom of thought, conscience and religion. This right shall include freedom to have or to adopt a religion or belief of his choice, and freedom, either individually or in community with others and in public or private, to manifest his religion or belief in worship, observance, practice and teaching.

2. No one shall be subject to coercion which would impair his freedom to have or to adopt a religion or belief of his choice.

3. Freedom to manifest one's religion or beliefs may be subject only to such limitations as are prescribed by law and are necessary to protect public safety, order, health, or morals or the fundamental rights and freedoms of others.

4. The States Parties to the present Covenant undertake to have respect for the liberty of parents and, when applicable, legal guardians to ensure the religious and moral education of their children in conformity with their own convictions.

Article 4 (2) of the covenant specifies that no DERO-GATION may be made from article 18.

The INTERNATIONAL CONVENTION ON THE ELIMINA-TION OF ALL FORMS OF RACIAL DISCRIMINATION contains the following provision:

Article 5. In compliance with the fundamental obligations laid down in article 2 of this Convention, States parties undertake to prohibit and to eliminate racial discrimination in all its forms and to guarantee the right of everyone, without distinction as to race, colour, or national or ethnic origin, to equality before the law, notably in the enjoyment of the following rights:. . . .

(d) other civil rights, in particular. . . .

(vii) The right to freedom of thought, conscience and religion.

The AMERICAN CONVENTION ON HUMAN RIGHTS, open for acceptance by member States of the ORGANIZATION OF AMERICAN STATES, provides that:

Article 12. 1. Everyone has the right to freedom of conscience and of religion. This right includes freedom to maintain or to change one's religion or beliefs, and freedom to profess or disseminate one's religion or beliefs, either individually or together with others, in public or in private.

2. No one shall be subject to restrictions that might impair his freedom to maintain or to change his religion or beliefs.

3. Freedom to manifest one's religion and beliefs may be subject only to the limitations prescribed by law that are necessary to protect public safety, order, health, or morals, or the rights or freedoms of others.

4. Parents or guardians, as the case may be, have the right to provide for the religious and moral education of their children or wards that is in accord with their own convictions.

The AFRICAN CHARTER ON HUMAN AND PEOPLE'S RIGHTS, open for acceptance by member States of the ORGANIZATION OF AFRICAN UNITY, provides that:

Article 8. Freedom of conscience, the profession and free practice of religion shall be guaranteed. No one may, subject to law and order, be submitted to measures restricting the exercise of these freedoms.

The EUROPEAN CONVENTION ON HUMAN RIGHTS, open for acceptance by member States of the COUNCIL OF EUROPE, provides that:

Article 9. 1. Everyone has the right to freedom of thought, conscience and religion; this right includes freedom to change his religion or belief and freedom, either alone or in community with others and in public or private, to manifest his religion or belief, in worship, teaching, practice and observance.

2. Freedom to manifest one's religion or beliefs shall be subject only to such limitations as are prescribed by law and are necessary in a democratic society in the interests of public safety, for the protection of public order, health or morals, or for the protection of the rights and freedoms of others.

The UN SUB-COMMISSION ON PREVENTION OF DISCRIM-INATION AND PROTECTION OF MINORITIES, at its 1956 session, decided to examine the problem of religious discrimination and intolerance, and appointed one of its members, Mr. Arcot Krishnaswami (India), as its special rapporteur. Mr. Krishnaswami's *Study of Discrimination in the Matter of Religious Rights and Practices* was completed in 1959 and published in 1960 (UN publication, Sales No. 60/XIV.2). On the basis of the conclusions and recommendations set out therein, the sub-commission prepared and adopted a series of draft principles on freedom and non-discrimination in the matter of religious rights and practices (subsequently annexed to the published study), which the sub-commission proposed should serve as the basis for an international instrument on the subject.

It was not until 1981, however, that the General Assembly was able to adopt and proclaim (resolution 36/55) the DECLARATION ON THE ELIMINATION OF ALL FORMS OF INTOLERANCE AND OF DISCRIMINATION BASED ON RELIGION OR BELIEF.

At its 1982 session, the General Assembly requested (resolution 37/187) the Commission on Human Rights to consider what measures may be necessary to implement the declaration and to encourage understanding, tolerance, and respect in matters relating to freedom of religion or belief. The commission called upon the sub-commission (resolution 1983/40) to undertake "a comprehensive and thorough study of the current dimensions of the problems of intolerance and of discrimination on grounds of religion or belief," using the declaration as its terms of reference. The sub-commission subsequently appointed (resolution 1983/31) one of its members, Mrs. Elizabeth Odio Benito (Costa Rica) as its special rapporteur for the study.

The special rapporteur's *Study of the Current Dimensions of the Problems of Intolerance and of Discrimination on Grounds of Religion or Belief* (UN Doc. E/CN.4/Sub.2/1987/26) was considered by the sub-commission at its

1987 session. In it, the special rapporteur concludes that intolerance and discrimination based on religion or belief subsist in the contemporary world and indeed that, in some areas, prejudice and bigotry have given rise to outright hatred, persecution, and repression. She describes, as the root causes of such intolerance and discrimination, such factors as ignorance and lack of understanding of the most basic elements of various religions or beliefs, each of which is unique in certain respects; the constant changes in public religiosity which have occurred and still occur in many parts of the world as a result of the struggle for predominance between the phenomenon of secularization or anti-clericalism and the phenomenon of sacralization or clericalism; developments of history, such as the use of religious intolerance and discrimination by colonial powers in their struggle to subdue and conquer the peoples of developing countries; and social tensions which deny their victims—such as foreign immigrants or migrant workers—the right to live in dignity and to enjoy the fruits of social progress.

The sub-commission (resolution 1987/33) welcomed the study's many recommendations, in particular those relating to the need for further study of major aspects of the issue, the need for the elaboration of a binding international instrument, and the need for educational measures to promote tolerance, understanding, and respect in matters relating to religion or belief. It requested its chairman to entrust one of its members with the following tasks: (a) to consider which aspects of this issue should be studied in greater depth by the sub-commission; (b) to examine information, recommendations, and other materials which may be submitted by governments, specialized agencies, non-governmental organizations, academic institutions, and religious bodies; (c) to examine the issues and factors which should be considered before any definitive drafting of a binding international instrument takes place; and (d) to report to the sub-commission at its 1989 session. Mr. Theo van Boven (Netherlands) was assigned to this task.

The sub-commission further recommended that the special rapporteur's study should be published in all official languages of the United Nations and widely disseminated.

On 10 March 1986, the UN Commission on Human Rights recalled (resolution 1986/20) that the General Assembly had requested it to consider measures to implement the Declaration on the Elimination of all Forms of Intolerance and of Discrimination Based on Religion or Belief and expressed deep concern about reports of incidents and governmental actions in all parts of the world which were inconsistent with the provisions of that declaration. Accordingly, it decided to appoint its own special rapporteur to examine such incidents and actions and to recommend remedial measures, including the promotion of a dialogue between communities of religion or belief and their governments. Mr. Angelo Vidal d'Almeida Ribero (Portugal) was later designated as special rapporteur for the study. His activities are summarized under the heading RELIGIOUS INTOLERANCE AND DISCRIMINATION: SPECIAL RAPPORTEUR.

The General Assembly, on 15 December 1989, reaffirmed (resolution 44/131) that freedom of thought, conscience, religion and belief is a right guaranteed to all without discrimination, and urged States therefore to provide, where they have not already done so, adequate constitutional and legal guarantees of that freedom, including the provision of effective remedies where there is intolerance or discrimination based on religion or belief.

The assembly also urged all States to take appropriate measures to combat intolerance and to encourage understanding, tolerance, and respect in matters relating to freedom of religion or belief and, in this context, to examine where necessary the supervision and training of their civil servants, educators, and other public officials to ensure that, in the course of their official duties, they respect different religions and beliefs and do not discriminate against persons professing other religions or beliefs. In addition, it invited the UNITED NATIONS UNIVERSITY and other academic and research institutions to undertake programs and studies on the encouragement of understanding, tolerance, and respect in matters relating to freedom of religion or belief.

TOGO. The Republic of Togo is a country in western Africa, on the Gulf of Guinea. It has borders with Benin, Burkina Faso, and Ghana. A United Nations trust territory under French administration, it achieved independence in 1960 and became a member of the United Nations the same year. Its population is estimated by the UN (1990) to be 3,449,000. There are some 40 ethnic groups, including (1) a southern group, formed by the Ewe, Ouatchi, and Mina communities; (2) the central group, composed of the Akposo; and (3) the norther group, consisting of the Kabye, Cotocoli, and Lamba. Scattered about the country are members of the Fons, Adja and Yoruba communities. The Ewe constitute 22% of the total population; the Kabye, 13%; the Ouatchi, 11%; the Cotocoli, 6%; and the Mina, 6%. In addition, persons of German, American, French, Lebanese, and Syrian descent live in the country. Languages commonly used include French (official), Ewe, Mina, Kabye, Akposa, Adja, Moba, and many regional vernaculars. Religions practiced include Animism

(56%), Christianity (Catholic, 21%; Protestant, 6%), and Islam (17%). Togo is a secular State and gives all religions equal recognition. Literacy is estimated at 18%.

The government (1990) took the form of a republic. Under the constitution of 1980, the executive president is directly elected for a term of seven years. Legislative authority is exercised by a National Assembly of 77 delegates, elected for five-year terms. All candidates are approved by the *Rassemblement du Peuple Togolais*, the only legal political party. The head of the party is president of the country and head of State.

Togoland became a German colony in 1884, and, for many years, it served as a major source of slaves. After World War II, Togoland was divided into two trust territories: Togoland under British administration and Togoland under French administration. Plebiscites were held in both territories under United Nations supervision to determine whether the people desired union with the neighboring Gold Coast, which was on the point of attaining independence, or wished to remain in the trusteeship system. A majority of residents of Togoland under British administration voted in favor of union with an independent Gold Coast, while a majority of residents of Togoland under French administration voted in favor of independence. The governments of France and Togoland agreed that the latter should attain independence on 27 April 1960, and the UN General Assembly terminated the trusteeship agreement as of that date.

TONGA. The Kingdom of Tonga is a country situated on a group of 169 islands in the South Pacific Ocean, the largest of which are Tongatabu, Vavau, and Haabi. Formerly known as the Friendly Islands, they were a British-protected State from 1900 to 1959, when they were granted self-rule within the British Commonwealth. They achieved complete independence on 4 June 1970. The population of the islands is estimated by the UN (1990) to be 120,000. Ethnic groups include Tongan (98%), European (.5%), part European (.7%), and others (.8%). Languages commonly used include Tongan and English. Christianity (Free Wesleyan, Roman Catholic, Free Church of Tonga, Church of Tonga, Latter Day Saints, Seventh Day Adventists, Anglicans, and members of the Assemblies of God) is the predominant religion. Literacy is estimated at 35% in Tongan only, .04% in English only, and 41% in Tongan and English.

The government (1990) took the form of a monarchy and member of the Commonwealth of Nations, of which the British sovereign is the symbolic head. Executive authority is exercised by the king with the as-

sistance of a prime minister and cabinet appointed by himself. Legislation is prepared by a unicameral Legislative Assembly. The judicial system includes magistrates courts, the Land Court, the Supreme Court, and the Court of Appeals. There is no political party.

The vast majority of the population of Tonga is indigenous; the remainder includes foreign workers in the country on a temporary basis. A person from another country who marries a Tongan is required to show that he has a return ticket for the Tongan husband or wife to the non-Tongan's homeland; this provision is intended to protect the rights of Tongan women who, in the past, often were subjected to desertion by their non-Tongan husbands after a marriage of very short duration.

TORTURE. Freedom from torture and other cruel, inhuman or degrading treatment or punishment is proclaimed as a fundamental right of all human beings in the UNIVERSAL DECLARATION OF HUMAN RIGHTS, in the following provision:

Article 5. No one shall be subjected to torture or to cruel, inhuman or degrading treatment or punishment.

The INTERNATIONAL COVENANT ON CIVIL AND POLITICAL RIGHTS contains the following provisions:

Article 7. No one shall be subjected to torture or to cruel, inhuman or degrading treatment or punishment. In particular, no one shall be subjected without his free consent to medical or scientific experimentation. . . .

Article 10. (1). All persons deprived of their liberty shall be treated with humanity and with respect for the inherent dignity of the human person.

(2). (a). Accused persons shall, save in exceptional circumstances, be segregated from convicted persons and shall be subject to separate treatment appropriate to their status as unconvicted persons;

(b). Accused juvenile persons shall be separated from adults and brought as speedily as possible for adjudication.

(3). The penitentiary system shall comprise treatment of prisoners, the essential aim of which shall be their reformation and social rehabilitation. Juvenile offenders shall be segregated from adults and be accorded treatment appropriate to their age and legal status.

Article 4, para. 2, of the covenant provides against any DEROGATION from article 7.

The CONVENTION ON THE PREVENTION AND PUNISHMENT OF THE CRIME OF GENOCIDE defines "genocide" as meaning "any of the following acts committed with intent to destroy, in whole or in part, a national, ethnical, racial, or religious group, as such: . . . (b) causing serious bodily or mental harm to members of the group; (c) deliberately inflicting on the group conditions of life calculated to bring about its physical destruction in whole or in part. . . ."

Similarly, the INTERNATIONAL CONVENTION ON THE SUPPRESSION AND PUNISHMENT OF THE CRIME OF *APARTHEID* defines "the crime of *apartheid*" as applying

to the following inhuman acts committed for the purpose of establishing and maintaining domination by one racial group of persons over any other racial group of persons and systematically oppressing them: (a) Denial to a member of a racial group or groups of the right to life and liberty of person: (i) by murder of members of a racial group or groups; (ii) by the infliction upon the members of a racial group or groups of serious bodily or mental harm, by the infringement of their freedom or dignity, or by subjecting them to torture or to cruel, inhuman or degrading treatment or punishment; (b) Deliberate imposition on a racial group or groups of living conditions calculated to cause its or their physical destruction in whole or in part.

The SUPPLEMENTARY CONVENTION ON THE ABOLITION OF SLAVERY, THE SLAVE TRADE, AND INSTITUTIONS AND PRACTICES SIMILAR TO SLAVERY provides that:

Article 5. In a country where the abolition or abandonment of slavery, or of the institutions or practices mentioned in article 1 of this Convention, is not yet complete, the act of mutilating, branding or otherwise marking a slave or a person of servile status in order to indicate his status, or as a punishment, or for any other reason, or of being accessory thereto, shall be a criminal offence under the laws of the States Parties to this Convention and persons convicted thereof shall be liable to punishment.

The definition and prohibition of torture is further elaborated in the CONVENTION AGAINST TORTURE AND OTHER CRUEL, INHUMAN OR DEGRADING TREATMENT OR PUNISHMENT, as follows:

Article 1. 1. For the purposes of this Convention, the term "torture" means any act by which severe pain or suffering, whether physical or mental, is intentionally inflicted on a person for such purposes as obtaining from him or a third person information or a confession, punishing him for an act he or a third person has committed or is suspected of having committed, or intimidating or coercing him or a third person, or for any reason based on discrimination of any kind, when such pain or suffering is inflicted by or at the instigation of or with the consent or acquiescence of a public official or other person acting in an official capacity. It does not include pain or suffering arising only from, inherent in or incidental to lawful sanctions.

2. This article is without prejudice to any international instrument or national legislation which does or may contain provisions of wider application. . . .

Article 16. 1. Each State Party shall undertake to prevent in any territory under its jurisdiction other acts of cruel, inhuman or degrading treatment or punishment which do not amount to torture as defined in article 1, when such acts are committed by or at the instigation of or with the consent or acquiescence of a public official or other person acting in an official capacity. In particular, the obligations contained in articles 10, 11, 12 and 13 shall apply with the substitution for references to torture of references to other forms of cruel, inhuman or degrading treatment or punishment.

2. The provisions of this Convention are without prejudice to the provisions of any other international instrument or national law which prohibits cruel, inhuman or degrading treatment or punishment or which relates to extradition or expulsion.

The AMERICAN CONVENTION ON HUMAN RIGHTS, open for acceptance by member States of the ORGANIZATION OF AMERICAN STATES, provides that:

Article 5. 1. Every person has the right to have his physical, mental, and moral integrity respected.

2. No one shall be subjected to torture or to cruel, inhuman, or degrading punishment or treatment. All persons deprived of their liberty shall be treated with respect for the inherent dignity of the human person.

3. Punishment shall not be extended to any person other than the criminal.

4. Accused persons shall, save in exceptional circumstances, be segregated from convicted persons, and shall be subject to separate treatment appropriate to their status as unconvicted persons.

5. Minors while subject to criminal proceedings shall be separated from adults and brought before specialized tribunals, as speedily as possible, so that they may be treated in accordance with their status as minors.

6. Punishments consisting of deprivation of liberty shall have as an essential aim the reform and social readaptation of the prisoners.

The INTER-AMERICAN CONVENTION TO PREVENT AND PUNISH TORTURE, also open for acceptance by OAS member States, provides (articles 6–14) that each State party shall take effective measures to prevent and punish torture and other cruel, inhuman, or degrading treatment or punishment within their jurisdiction.

The EUROPEAN CONVENTION ON HUMAN RIGHTS, open for acceptance by COUNCIL OF EUROPE member States, provides that:

Article 3. No one shall be subjected to torture or to inhuman or degrading treatment or punishment.

The EUROPEAN CONVENTION FOR THE PREVENTION OF TORTURE AND INHUMAN OR DEGRADING TREATMENT OR PUNISHMENT, also open for acceptance by Council of Europe member States, provides (para. 7–14) for implementation by States parties within their jurisdiction.

After examining reports submitted by States parties to the International Covenant on Civil and Political Rights in accordance with article 40 of that instrument, the HUMAN RIGHTS COMMITTEE adopted, in 1982, the following general comments on article 7 of the covenant (UN Doc. A/37/40, Annex V, para. 1–3):

In examining the reports of States parties, members of the Committee have often asked for further information under article 7 which prohibits, in the first place, torture or cruel, inhuman or degrading treatment or punishment. The Committee recalls that even in situations of public emergency such as are envisaged by article 4 (1) this provision is non-derogable under article 4 (2). Its purpose is to protect the integrity and dignity of the individual. The Committee notes that it is not sufficient for the implementation of this article to prohibit such treatment or punishment or to make it a crime. Most States have penal provisions which are applicable to cases of torture or similar practices. Because such cases nevertheless occur, it follows from article 7, read together with article 2 of the Covenant, that States must ensure an effective protection through some machinery of control. Complaints about ill-treatment must be investigated effectively by competent authorities. Those found guilty must be held responsible, and the alleged victims must themselves have effective remedies at their disposal, including the right to obtain compensation. Among the safeguards which may make control effective are provisions against detention incommunicado, granting, without prejudice to the investigation, persons such as doctors, lawyers and family members access to the detainees; provisions requiring that detainees should be held in places that are publicly recognized and that their names and places of detention should be entered in a central register available to persons concerned, such as relatives; provisions making confessions or other evidence obtained through torture or other treatment contrary to article 7 inadmissible in court; and measures of training and instruction of law enforcement officials not to apply such treatment.

As appears from the terms of this article, the scope of protection required goes far beyond torture as normally understood. It may not be necessary to draw sharp distinctions between the various prohibited forms of treatment or punishment. These distinctions depend on the kind, purpose and severity of the particular treatment. In the view of the Committee the prohibition must extend to corporal punishment, including excessive chastisement as an educational or disciplinary measure. Even such a measure as solitary confinement may, according to the circumstances, and especially when the person is kept incommunicado, be contrary to this article. Moreover, the article clearly protects not only persons arrested or imprisoned, but also pupils and patients in educational and medical institutions. Finally, it is also the duty of public authorities to ensure protection by the law against such treatment even when committed by persons acting outside or without any official authority. For all persons deprived of their liberty, the prohibition of treatment contrary to article 7 is supplemented by the positive requirement of article 10 (1) of the Covenant that they shall be treated with humanity and with respect for the inherent dignity of the human person.

In particular, the prohibition extends to medical or scientific experimentation without the free consent of the person concerned (article 7, second sentence). The Committee notes that the reports of States parties have generally given little or no information on this point. It takes the view that at least in countries where science and medicine are highly developed, and even for peoples and areas outside their borders if affected by their experiments, more attention should be give to the possible need and means to ensure the observance of this provision. Special protection in regard to such experiments is necessary in the case of persons not capable of giving their consent.

Implementation of the Convention against Torture. The Convention against Torture and other Cruel, Inhuman or Degrading Treatment or Punishment, adopted by the UN General Assembly on 10 December 1984 (resolution 39/46), entered into force on 26 June 1987. In addition to defining "torture," as mentioned above, the convention requires States parties to take effective measures to prevent acts of torture in any territory under their jurisdiction. No exceptional circumstances, such as war or public emergency, can be invoked to justify torture; nor can obedience to an order from a superior officer or a public authority be invoked as justification.

States parties undertake not to expel, return, or extradite a person to another State where there are substantial grounds for believing that he would be in danger of being subjected to torture and to ensure that all acts of torture, attempts to commit torture, complicity, or participation in torture, are offenses punishable under their criminal law.

The convention also provides for prosecution or extradition of persons alleged to have committed acts of torture, and States parties are called upon to afford one another judicial assistance in connection with criminal proceedings concerning acts of torture. It calls for education on the prohibition of torture to be part of the training of law enforcement personnel and other persons involved in the custody, interrogation, or treatment of prisoners or detainees; and it provides that States parties shall ensure legal measures for protection and compensation for victims of torture. Other forms of cruel, inhuman or degrading treatment or punishment, as defined in the convention, which may be committed by persons acting in an official capacity, are also prohibited.

The implementation of the convention is monitored by the COMMITTEE AGAINST TORTURE, consisting of 10 experts, elected by States parties to the convention and serving in their personal capacity. The committee held its first session at the United Nations office in Geneva from 18 to 22 April 1988. States parties to the convention are required to report regularly to the committee on the measures they have taken to give effect to the provisions of the convention. The committee considers such reports, makes general comments on them, and informs the other States parties and the General Assembly of its activity.

Under Article 20 of the convention, if the committee receives reliable information which appears to it to contain well-founded indications that torture is being systematically practised in the territory of a State party, the committee invites that State party to co-operate in the examination of the information and to this end to submit observations with regard to the information concerned. The committee may decide to make an inquiry, including a visit to the territory of the State party concerned, with its agreement. The proceedings of the committee when it undertakes such an inquiry are confidential, but the committee may decide to include a summary account of the results of the proceedings in its annual report to the State parties and to the General Assembly. In ratifying the convention, States may express a reservation with regard to the competence of the committee under Article 20. Of the initial 20 States which have ratified or acceded to the convention, the Governments of Afghanistan, Bulgaria, Byelorussian SSR, Hungary, Ukrainian SSR, and the Soviet Union have declared that they do not recognize the competence of the committee as defined by Article 20 of the convention.

Under Article 21, a State party to the convention may at any time declare that it recognizes the competence of the Committee against Torture to receive and consider communications to the effect that a State party claims that another State party is not fulfilling its obligations under the convention. Under Article 22, a State party to the convention may at any time declare that it recognizes the competence of the committee to receive and consider communications from or on behalf of individuals subject to its jurisdiction who claim to be victims of a violation by a State party of the provisions of the convention.

SEE ALSO *Body of Principles for the Protection of All Persons under Any Form of Detention or Imprisonment; United Nations Voluntary Fund for Victims of Torture.*

TORTURE: SPECIAL RAPPORTEUR.

At its 1985 session, the UN Commission on Human Rights welcomed (resolution 1985/33) the adoption by the General Assembly on 9 December 1984 of the CONVENTION AGAINST TORTURE AND OTHER CRUEL, INHUMAN OR DEGRADING TREATMENT OR PUNISHMENT and decided to appoint a special rapporteur to examine various aspects of the question of torture. Mr. Peter H. Kooijmans (Netherlands) was designated as special rapporteur and instructed to seek and receive credible and reliable information concerning torture from governments, specialized agencies, and intergovernmental and non-governmental organizations and to "respond effectively" to such information.

In his first report (UN Doc. E/CN.4/1986/15), the special rapporteur drew attention to the "grey area" between torture proper and other harsh treatment or punishment and pointed out that he had to take certain practices into account—such as corporal punishment, prolonged stays on death row, detention of minors along with adults, etc.—since they could, in a further analysis, constitute acts of torture. He also presented a preliminary analysis of the information he had received on the practice of torture and put forward some suggestions for preventative measures.

In his second report, the special rapporteur presented a full analysis of the information he had received on the practice of torture, as follows (UN Doc. E/CN.4/1987/13, chap. VI, para. 72–79):

Torture is still a widespread phenomenon in today's world. From the information he has received the Special Rapporteur has been confirmed in his conviction that no society, whatever its political system or ideological colour, is totally immune to torture. Of particular concern to the international community, however, are situations where torture has become a more or less normal element of daily life. In such situations the authorities have either lost control over the security or law-enforcement personnel and condone the practice of torture, seemingly for the sake of more important goals, such as "national unity" or "national security", or cast a benevolent eye on such practices, as they help to create an atmosphere of fear or terror where opposition may be fairly easily stamped out.

The first is usually the case in situations of civil strife, where there is a confrontation of hostile groups. Violence, fed by mutual hatred, becomes the predominant feature of everyday life. Especially where civil strife has taken the form of guerrilla tactics, military and security personnel feel threatened and may gradually fall into the practice of physical abuse and torture to extract information about their opponents. Every person living within the guerrilla area may be seen as a potential enemy who withholds information and may, therefore, be forced to disclose it by all available means. Although in many cases the victims of such abuse are completely innocent, the inevitable effect of such practices is that mutual hatred increases and life becomes ever more violent. Torture breeds hatred and the increased hatred leads to more atrocities which in themselves seem to justify the practice of more severe torture. The Government may genuinely condemn the practice of torture, but feels that, in view of the need to maintain and uphold national integrity and security, it cannot do anything against it. It, therefore, usually closes its eyes to reality and either flatly denies that torture takes place or contends that it is a reaction to the commission of terrorists acts. Governments should realize, however, that the vicious circle in which they seemingly find themselves may well have started with the abuses and the arrogant practices of the representatives of the official authorities. The prohibition and suppression of such practices are not only an obligation under international law but may also be a matter of sound policy.

The Special Rapporteur has received many allegations about the practice of torture in countries where the whole or parts of the country are the scene of civil strife or civil war. In some of these countries the climate of violence has indeed led to a disheartening loss of respect for the physical and mental integrity of the human person and for his dignity. In this respect the Special Rapporteur wishes to mention the situation in Afghanistan. The situation in Sri Lanka, which finds itself caught in a spiral of violence and where civilians are allegedly tortured in order to extract information from them about planned acts of violence by the insurgents is also of great concern. Serious allegations continue to come in about torture practices in El Salvador. In spite of the fact that the Government has once again committed itself to respect and guarantee fundamental human rights, certain parts of the State apparatus have obviously been successful in evading those commitments.

In other countries torture is practised to deter civil strike and to stifle opposition. It is used as a means not only to extract information but also to enforce behaviour in conformity with the prevalent rules. In this respect mention may be made of the situation in Chile and in South Africa. The Special Rapporteur has also received alarming reports about the practice of torture in the Islamic Republic of Iran where behaviour or even opinions that deviate from the norm are not tolerated.

It is significant that in many of the situations referred to above, either a state of emergency is declared for the whole or parts of the country, under which enjoyment of certain basic human rights has been curtailed or suspended, or special security legislation is in force, under which persons may be arrested without warrant and kept incommunicado for a considerable period. It is well known that such situations easily lend themselves to the practice of torture, as torturers may find it quite simple to avoid criminal responsibility for their acts. It is particularly disquieting that torture becomes so endemic in such a society that even a return to normality does not bring an end to the practice. In various cases the Special Rapporteur has continued to receive allegations from countries where either the previous régime has been replaced or a transfer to a civilian (elected) government has taken place. A firm and unrelenting attitude by the new incumbent is, therefore, required, as well as strict rules and retraining programmes for law enforcement personnel.

With regard to some countries the Special Rapporteur has received allegations of torture with regard to certain ethnic or religious groups in particular. In these cases torture usually took the form of gross physical abuses, such as beatings, rape, etc., often combined with robbery, testifying to a serious lack of respect for the dignity of these citizens. In such cases it should come as no surprise if eventually such a situation leads to insurgency of the group concerned, which in its turn will lead to the civil strife described above. Here again, the Government must adopt a firm position.

The Special Rapporteur has also received information concerning maltreatment in places of detention (irrespective of whether these were penal institutions) which amounted to torture as the effect was severe mental or physical pain. Such maltreatment can take the form of acts but also of omissions. In these cases the Special Rapporteur intends to start consultations with the Governments concerned and in one particular case has already done so. In such cases, the detained person, because he feels that his detention is the result of his divergent political views and that he is therefore unjustly detained frequently considers himself justified in resisting detention. This in turn leads to abusive treatment by security personnel which, however, is unacceptable if the detainee's physical or mental integrity is injured.

There are also cases where a specific type of punishment irreparably damages the integrity of the human person. Here also the Special Rapporteur feels that it is most appropriate to enter into consultation with the Governments involved and, in fact, he has tried to do so.

In his conclusions and recommendations, the special rapporteur advised the commission that (*Ibid.*, chap. VII, para. 80–87):

Torture is an extremely complex phenomenon. It takes many forms and occurs in widely divergent situations. Its occurrence is often determined by specific political conditions; and at the same time in spite of the varying circumstances it occurs in a strikingly monotonous pattern.

Therefore, torture may be the derivative of certain political conditions, its source is invariably the same: contempt for the personality of the other individual which has to be destroyed and annihilated. It is for that reason that torture is one of the most heinous violations of human rights as it is the very denial of the essence of human rights, namely the recognition that each living being has a personality of his own which has to be respected.

Therefore, a society that tolerates torture can never claim to respect other human rights; the duty to eradicate torture is thus a primordial obligation. Efforts to realize that goal should first and foremost be concentrated on the prevention of torture. It goes without saying that repressive measures are called for whenever torture has been practised. Those who have committed this offence should be brought to justice; but it is more important to go to the roots of the evil itself and to take away the causes which make torture possible. The Special Rapporteur can, therefore, only repeat the recommendations he made in his first report. In particular he wishes to stress the importance of limiting the period of incommunicado detention under national law, since many of the allegations he has received refer to torture in countries where a detainee may be kept incommunicado for a prolonged period. He also wishes to emphasize the importance of training programmes for law enforcement and security personnel, especially in countries where torture was regularly practised under a previous régime. The United Nations programme of advisory services should be particularly geared to respond favourably to requests made by Governments in this field. In view of the multitude of norms for the conduct of medical personnel, enumerated in chapter III, and the crucial role medical personnel allegedly often play in the practice of torture, the Special Rapporteur recommends that Governments and medical associations take strict measures against all persons belonging to the medical profession who have in that capacity had a function in the practice of torture. He also recommends that the role that the medical profession may play in the practice of torture should be highlighted in all courses on medical ethics.

A measure which may have an important preventive effect is the introduction of a system of periodic visits by a committee of experts to places of detention or imprisonment. On 6 March 1980, the Government of Costa Rica submitted to the Commission on Human Rights a draft optional protocol to the draft convention against torture and other cruel, inhuman or degrading treatment or punishment which provided for such a system of periodic visits. In resolution 1986/56 the Commission noting that the draft European convention against torture was based on similar ideas, recommended that other interested regions where a consensus existed should consider the possibility of preparing draft conventions based on the concept of a system of visits. In this context, it may be mentioned that the Inter-American Convention to Prevent and Punish Torture (concluded on 9 December 1985) does not establish such a system of periodic visits nor any other comparable machinery.

The introduction of systems of periodic visits should be seen as a preventive rather than a repressive measure. Although the determination of actual acts of torture as a result of such visits could lead to repressive action against the offenders, the main emphasis should be on the advice which experts may give after such a visit with regard to steps to be taken to correct and improve the existing régime in places of detention and imprisonment in the country visited. The element of periodicity is designed to ensure that a system of visits is seen as a means of co-operating with Governments rather than as an instrument for denouncing them. The fact that the idea of periodic visits would eventually form part of regional systems for protection of human rights (of which there are currently three, established in the context of the Organization of African Unity, the Organization of American States and the Council of Europe) would not necessarily stand in the way of the conclusion of a world-wide convention to which States which were subject to such a system of visits under a regional instrument could become party. However, the implementation of the world-wide system could be suspended for States subject to a regional system.

Such a system of visits is no more an intrusion in the internal jurisdiction of a State than the visits of staff members of the International Atomic Energy Agency to nuclear plants which may also lead to recommendations for the improvement of existing standards. In both cases such visits would serve a purpose which is recognized by the international community as being of vital importance for the well-being of mankind as they would ensure respect for human dignity and the maintenance of international peace and security, respectively.

Until such systems of periodic visits have been established, the granting of admission to ICRC teams to places of detention and imprisonment must be recommended, as such visits by ICRC may contribute to the prevention of torture and—in fact—in some cases have ostensibly done so.

In this context, the Special Rapporteur may recall his readiness to visit countries with the consent or at the invitation of the Government, not only on account of allegations of torture he has received, but also on any other occasion for which such a visit may be deemed useful by the Government concerned, for instance, when a power has been transferred to a new Government which wishes to take effective measures to eradicate torture practices which occurred under the previous régime.

In 1987, the special rapporteur held consultations in Geneva with the governments of Argentina, Colombia, Peru, and Uruguay with a view to exploring the possibility of carrying out on-the-site consultations on measures to prevent the phenomenon of torture. Having received a favorable reaction, he proposed to visit those countries from 9 to 18 December 1987. All agreed to the proposed dates, except Peru which preferred to postpone the visit to a later stage.

The special rapporteur visited Colombia from 9 to 13 December 1987, Argentina from 13 to 16 December 1987, and Uruguay from 16 to 18 December, and reported on these visits to the Commission on Human Rights at its 1988 session (UN Doc. E/CN.4/1988/17/Add. 1). In the concluding paragraphs of that report, he wrote (para. 21–23):

The visits paid to Colombia, Argentina and Uruguay have greatly expanded the Special Rapporteur's insight into the roots and causes of torture. Both in Uruguay and in Argentina, he was told that the widespread practice of tor-

ture during the military régime was facilitated by the already existing tradition of brutal treatment of detainees by the police; the important role of confession in criminal procedure had been instrumental in this tradition. In both countries it was stressed that the use of torture as a means of extortion and terror was passed from the police to the military not the other way round as is sometimes believed.

Common criminal procedures and the means by which evidence is collected therefore deserve much more attention than they usually get. Torture is very often seen mainly in the context of political controversies as a means of suppressing political opponents—and correctly so. But this focus on situations of political strife may lead us to close our eyes to the fact that the seeds of the use of torture for this particular end are often sown elsewhere and that, therefore, practical measures to prevent torture should also be taken elsewhere.

Another element which seems to be extremely relevant is that, although mentality training is undoubtedly very important, it is clearly not sufficient. The existence of technical expertise and technical equipment is also of vital significance. It is noteworthy that in two of the three countries visited members of the Government made an explicit appeal for assistance by the international community. In the whole concept of international co-operation economic and social development until now have played a preponderant role. This is logical and to the point since in large areas of the world economic and social human rights cannot be guaranteed without the combined efforts of the international community as a whole. The international community has been much less aware that the realization of political and civil rights may also be dependent upon international co-operation. This may be partly due to the fact that political and civil rights are usually seen as obligations for the State to abstain from interfering in the private sphere of the individual. However, for the full enjoyment of those rights, a certain infrastructure is essential. Up till now, hardly any funds have been set aside to comply with requests for assistance in this field. The programme of advisory services of the Centre for Human Rights—useful as it may be, in particular for the near future—will clearly be insufficient if awareness of the possibilities of international co-operation and assistance for the realization of civil and political human rights increases. The Special Rapporteur is of the opinion that the implications of requests for assistance from individual governments better to guarantee civil and political rights should be a matter for reflection in the Commission on Human Rights. Condemnation of systematic violations of human rights are certainly called for in quite a few cases. However, the commission, whose task it is to promote respect for human rights, would only be doing half its work if it turned a deaf ear to a government which asked the international community to help it better to fulfil its commitment to guarantee respect for human rights.

The Commission on Human Rights reviewed the special rapporteur's report at its 1988 session and, in resolution 1988/33, commended him for it and endorsed its conclusions and recommendations. It extended his mandate for two years in order to enable him to submit further conclusions and recommendations for its consideration.

In the course of 1988, the special rapporteur corresponded with the governments of a number of countries, transmitting to them reports of torture having occurred in territories under their jurisdiction without taking a position as to whether or not those reports were well-founded. Countries to which such communications were addressed included Afghanistan, Bahrain, Benin, Brazil, Burma, China, Colombia, Czechoslovakia, El Salvador, France, Greece, Grenada, Guatemala, Haiti, Honduras, India, Indonesia, Islamic Republic of Iran, Israel, Kenya, Mexico, Morocco, Panama, Paraguay, Peru, Philippines, Republic of Korea, Sao Tome and Principe, Saudi Arabia, Singapore, Somalia, Spain, Sri Lanka, Sudan, Syrian Arab Republic, Turkey, the United Kingdom of Great Britain and Northern Ireland, and Viet Nam.

In addition, he brought 42 appeals for urgent action, received during 1988, to the immediate attention of the respective governments on a purely humanitarian basis, to ensure that the right to physical and mental integrity of the individual was protected and requested information on the remedial measures taken in case the allegations were proved correct. Most of the allegations concerned persons subjected to torture during interrogation while being held incommunicado by security police. Countries to which such urgent appeals were addressed included Benin, Burkina Faso, Myanmar, China, Colombia, El Salvador, Guatemala, Haiti, Honduras, Islamic Republic of Iran, Israel, Liberia, Mauritania, Panama, Peru, Philippines, Somalia, South Africa, Syrian Arab Republic, Turkey, United Arab Emirates, and Zaire.

Further, the special rapporteur, on invitation of the governments concerned, visited Peru, the Republic of Korea, and Turkey in the course of 1988. Such investigations were consultative in nature, rather than for the purpose of investigating specific allegations.

In his report to the UN Commission on Human Rights on his 1988 activities, the special rapporteur included the following general recommendations (UN Doc. E/CN.4/1989/15, Chap. V, paras. 239–247):

The great majority of allegations received by the Special Rapporteur refer to torture practised during incommunicado detention. It seems, therefore, that a formal prohibition of incommunicado detention would greatly reduce the number of reported cases of torture.

In this context, the following recommendations are made, which are in conformity with the Declaration of Basic Principles of Justice for Victims of Crime and Abuse of Power, adopted by the General Assembly in resolution 40/34.

Legal provisions prescribing that a person shall be given access to a lawyer not later than 24 hours after he has been arrested usually function as an effective remedy against torture, provided compliance with such provisions is strictly monitored. Security personnel who violate such provisions should, therefore, be severely disciplined. A useful supplementary provision would be the obligation to inform the relatives of an arrested person within 24 hours of both the arrest and the place where the detainee is being held.

At the time of his arrest, a person should undergo a medical inspection; such an inspection should be repeated regularly, but in any case should be compulsory whenever a detainee is transferred from one place of detention to another.

Since many allegations refer to situations in which the victim of torture was blindfolded or the interrogators were made unrecognizable, each interrogation should be initiated with identification of all the persons present.

Interrogation of detainees should only take place at official interrogation centres. Evidence obtained from the detainee in other places and not confirmed by him during interrogation at official locations should not be admitted as evidence in court.

Independent bodies should be established which may regularly inspect places of detention and may speak confidentially with the detainees. Such bodies should report publicly on their findings.

Each detainee should be able to initiate proceedings before a court on the lawfulness of his detention, in conformity with article 9, paragraph 4, of the International Covenant on Civil and Political Rights. It is recommended that this right should also be recognized under a state of siege or emergency. The right of *habeas corpus* should be strictly respected in all circumstances and should never be suspended.

The Code of Conduct for Law Enforcement Officials and the Standard Minimum Rules for the Treatment of Prisoners should be translated into the national language and used as teaching material during training courses for law enforcement personnel. In particular, such personnel should be instructed on their duty to disobey orders received from a superior to practice torture.

In the same report, the special rapporteur presented to the commission his views on the handling of appeals from governments for direct assistance or for advisory services to assist them in the promotion and protection of human rights, as follows (UN Doc. E/CN.4/1989/15, paras. 235–238):

In the course of all his visits, without exception the Special Rapporteur received repeated appeals for assistance and advisory services.

Taking into account different situations, the Special Rapporteur is of the view that the Centre for Human Rights could assist Governments either to correct a given situation or to prevent the recurrence of past errors.

In countries where civil strife prevails, every effort should be made by the international community to spare the physical and mental integrity of the individual and to help newly elected Governments to correct a situation which may lead to a state of lawlessness. Therefore the following programmes are recommended:

(a) Courses in international humanitarian law on situations related to internal conflicts;

(b) Prototype regulations to safeguard human rights under states of emergency;

(c) Courses for medical associations on norms for the conduct of medical personnel, having regard to the role that the medical profession may play in the practice of torture;

(d) Courses for magistrates and law enforcement officials on *amparo* and *habeas corpus* procedures.

In countries where the military authorities have taken power in the recent past, courses on preventive measures may be envisaged. In fact, instruction programmes for security personnel, with emphasis on training for the correct approach to respect for the human rights of the individual, have already been requested by some countries. The Special Rapporteur considers that courses related to provisions contained in international intruments, specifically those contained in the new Convention against Torture, are indispensable.

In the course of 1988, the special rapporteur received invitations to visit Peru, the Republic of Korea, and Turkey from the governments of those countries. He accepted them, feeling that consultations with the authorities *in situ* are an extremely effective instrument for carrying out his mandate. In his report to the commission, he wrote (para. 7):

It should be pointed out that such visits have a consultative character and that the Special Rapporteur does not carry out investigations into specific allegations during such visits. It has been suggested from time to time to the Special Rapporteur that a Government, by extending an invitation to him, would admit that torture is actually practised in that country. The Special Rapporteur wishes to emphasize in this respect that, irrespective of the question whether torture did occur or still occurs in countries visited by him, such a visit should be seen mainly in the light of prevention of torture.

In his report to the Commission on Human Rights, the special rapporteur described his visits to Peru, the Republic of Korea, and Turkey and presented in the case of each country his evaluation and recommendations.

In the course of 1989, the special rapporteur continued his correspondence with the governments concerned and visited Guatemala and Honduras, describing these activities in his report to the 1990 session of the Commission on Human Rights (UN Doc. E/CN.4/1990/17). The conclusions and recommendations set out in that report were as follows (chap. V, paras. 259–272):

Though the fight against torture has considerably intensified during the last decade, torture still remains a common phenomenon in today's world. Over the past few years there have been hopeful developments in a considerable number of countries; in other countries, however, there has been a clear deterioration. The number of countries where torture is systematically applied may have decreased during that period, but at the same time it has become apparent that torture is far from exceptional in situations where it does not form part of a system. The sad conclusion must be drawn that respect for the inherent dignity of all human beings, irrespective of their race, creed and, most of all, their political conviction is still painfully underdeveloped. This should inspire the international community with renewed energy to continue the fight for the eradication of the horrendous crime of torture. All hopes for a stable, just and peaceful world—hopes which have been greatly nourished over the past year—will turn out to be idle if we do not succeed in instilling in mankind the basic requirement for a stable, just and peaceful world: the respect for the inherent dignity of the fellow human being.

The Special Rapporteur was in particular alarmed by the fact that he received a number of allegations referring to torture of children and juveniles. Torture is horrifying in all its forms and emanations, but the idea of children, who are still in their formative stage, being tortured is mind-boggling indeed. The fact that these alleged events took place at about the same time as the adoption by the international community of the Convention on the Rights of the Child glaringly illustrates how far this world is still removed from practising the standards it sets itself.

Education in the field of human rights, therefore, seems one of the most urgent tasks the international community has to tackle. The fact that the United Nations has launched a World Public Information Campaign for Human Rights is an important step in that direction. The primary responsibility for human rights education lies with Governments, who may be assisted in this vast task by private organizations. The world, however, cannot wait until this educational process takes effect; those in particular who are in a position that makes it possible for them to violate their fellow human beings' right to human dignity and physical and mental integrity must receive training how to deal with persons who have been brought under their control. In this respect the adoption by the General Assembly, by its resolution 43/173 of 9 December 1988, of the Body of Principles for the Protection of All Persons under Any Form of Detention or Imprisonment must be highlighted.

This document contains principles which, in part, had already been recognized in human rights conventions and resolutions of the organs of the United Nations—sometimes in even stronger form—such as, for example, the Standard Minimum Rules for the Treatment of Prisoners. The importance of this new Body of Principles lies in the fact that they are now contained in a document which can function as a check-list for Governments to see whether their legal provisions and administrative practices are in conformity with these principles, and to take corrective measures if this is not the case. In the covering resolution the General Assembly "urges that every effort be made so that the Body of Principles becomes generally known and respected", a recommendation which is addressed to all States. Another important aspect is that the Body of Principles applies to all forms of detention or imprisonment, whatever the form of deprivation of liberty may be. Everybody who is deprived of his liberty is entitled to the protection provided by the document. A third element which has to be noted is that no exception is made for times of emergency. Since an earlier draft contained a reference to such situations, it has to be assumed that the principles must be applied under all circumstances. The Body of Principles contains many elements which are of direct relevance to the prevention of torture and actually echo a number of recommendations the Special Rapporteur has made in previous reports; some of these may be referred to here.

Principle 11 states that a person shall not be kept in detention without being given an effective opportunity to be heard *promptly* by a judicial or other authority. Since torture is often practised immediately after arrest, this prompt hearing by a judge may be a guarantee for the arrested person's physical integrity. The legality of his detention can be considered and his right of access to legal counsel can be secured.

Of no less importance are principles 12 and 23, which prescribe the duty to record the circumstances at the time of arrest and of interrogation. Especially relevant is the duty to record the identity of the officials who are responsible for the arrest and the interrogation. Torture usually takes place under conditions which make it impossible for the victim to recognize his interrogators and torturers. Complaints filed afterwards are therefore often unsubstantiated as regards the alleged perpetrators.

Other elements which have relevance to the prevention of torture are the duty to give the detainee access to legal counsel (principles 17 and 18), the duty to inform his relatives promptly about the arrest (principle 19) and to provide him with medical care and have him medically examined (principles 24 and 25). With regard to the latter issue the Special Rapporteur would have preferred a stronger wording in line with the recommendation made by him in last year's report and repeated in paragraph 272 (d) of the present report.

Of similar importance is principle 27, which states that non-compliance with the provisions contained in the Body of Principles in obtaining evidence shall be taken into account in determining the admissibility of such evidence against a detained or imprisoned person. Next to the rule that evidence which itself is obtained by torture is not admissible in court, this provision contributes to reducing the incidence of torture.

Another principle which deserves mention is principle 29, which prescribes regular inspection of all places of detention by an independent inspection team. The significance of such a system of visits, preferably by international teams, as a preventive measure can hardly be overestimated.

Principle 34 states that each death occurring during detention or imprisonment or shortly afterwards must be investigated by a judicial or other impartial authority. This principle is similar to a recommendation the Special Rapporteur made in one of his previous reports.

Finally, principles 7 and 33 are of great importance for the prevention and repression of torture. Principle 33 lays down the right of a detained or imprisoned person to file a complaint about torture or other maltreatment to which he has been subjected. Principle 7 states that any act contrary to the rights and duties contained in the Body of Principles should be prohibited by law and that such acts should be made subject to appropriate sanctions. Highly relevant for the prevention of torture is paragraph 3, which gives any person who has grounds to believe that a violation of the principles has occurred, the right to report the matter to the authorities in order to have it investigated.

Compliance with the Body of Principles, as urged by the General Assembly, would make torture during detention or imprisonment virtually impossible. This will only be the case, however, if the international community responds to requests by Governments for assistance in the field of training and provision of modern equipment which offers better guarantees for the physical and mental integrity of detained persons. Respect for human rights does not come by itself; nor is it merely dependent upon the political will of the authorities, indispensable though this political will may be. Respect for human rights often also calls for costly investments. The Voluntary Fund for Advisory Services and Technical Assistance in the Field of Human Rights is of vital importance in this respect and States should enable it to carry out its task by providing it with the necessary financial means.

In many allegations the practising of torture is ascribed to members of the security forces. In most countries it is a long-established rule that people belonging to the military who are suspected of having committted an offence have to stand trial before a military tribunal. This rule may be explained by the fact that from time immemorial the military have had their own *esprit de corps,* which is still appropriate in the case of offences that have a typically military character, such as desertion or mutiny. The rule, however, makes no sense at all in cases where members of the security forces have seriously violated a civilian's basic human rights. Such an act is an offence against the public civil order and, consequently, should be tried by a civilian court. Torture is forbidden under all circumstances and this prohibition applies to all officials, whether military or civilian. It therefore cannot be seen as having any relationship to the specific functions of the military. As the civilian courts are responsible for the administration of justice in general with a view to protecting the civil public order, the civilian courts should be competent to try all offences against the civil public order, whoever may have committed them.

In the light of the foregoing, the Special Rapporteur wishes to make the following recommendations, most of which will follow the general pattern of the Body of Principles for the Protection of All Persons under Any Form of Detention or Imprisonment:

(a) Since a great number of the allegations received by the Special Rapporteur referred to torture practised during incommunicado detention, incommunicado detention should be prohibited;

(b) Other allegations referred to torture practised during illegal detention before a detainee was presented to a judge. Those who act contrary to the rules prescribed for a lawful arrest should be subjected to appropriate sanctions;

(c) Any person who is arrested should be given access to legal counsel no later than 24 hours after his arrest; his relatives should be informed promptly of his arrest and the place where he is detained;

(d) Any person who is arrested should be medically examined immediately after his arrest. Such examination should take place regularly, and in any case should be compulsory whenever the detainee is transferred to another place of detention;

(e) All interrogation sessions should be recorded; the identity of all persons present should be included in the records. Evidence obtained from the detainee during non-recorded interrogations should not be admitted in court;

(f) All places of detention should be regularly inspected by independent inspection teams. Such teams should be allowed to speak with detainees in private;

(g) In every case of death of a person during his detention or shortly after his release, an inquiry into the cause of death and the circumstances surrounding it should be held by a judicial or other impartial authority;

(h) Everyone should be entitled to file a complaint about torture or severe maltreatment with an indepedent authority; the official in charge of the investigation of the detainee's case cannot be considered to be an independent authority;

(i) Whenever a person is found to be responsible for acts of torture or severe maltreatment he should be brought to trial; if found guilty, be should be severely punished;

(j) The Body of Principles for the Protection of All Persons under Any Form of Detention or Imprisonment, the Code of Conduct for Law Enforcement Officials and the Standard Minimum Rules for the Treatment of Prisoners should be translated into national languages and used as teaching material during training courses for law enforcement personnel and members of the security forces entrusted with the task of protecting internal law and order. In particular, such personnel should be instructed on their duty to disobey orders received from a superior to practise torture.

The Commission on Human Rights examined the 1987 and 1988 reports of the special rapporteur at its 1988 session and, on 8 March 1988 (resolution 1988/32), expressed its serious concern about the alarming number of cases of torture and other cruel, inhuman, or degrading treatment or punishment reported to be taking place in various parts of the world. It recognized that torture constitutes a criminal obliteration of the human personality which can never be justified under any circumstances, by any ideology, or overriding interest and indicated its determination to promote the full implementation of the prohibition under international and national law of the practice of torture.

The commission endorsed most of the special rapporteur's conclusions and recommendations, in particular the conclusion stressing the importance of limiting, and eventually declaring illegal, incommunicado detention under national law, since many alleged cases of torture had been reported to have taken place during incommunicado detention; and the recommendation that governments and medical associations should take strict measures against all persons belonging to the medical profession who have in that capacity had a function in the practice of torture.

The commission extended the mandate of the special rapporteur for two years and called upon him, in carrying out that mandate, to seek and receive credible and reliable information from governments as well as specialized agencies, intergovernmental organizations, and non-governmental organizations.

The special rapporteur's 1990 report was placed on the agenda of the 1990 session of the commission.

TOTALITARIAN IDEOLOGIES. An item concerning "Measures to be taken against Nazi, Fascist and neo-Fascist activities and all other forms of totalitarian ideologies and practices based on apartheid, ra-

cial discrimination and racism, and the systematic denial of human rights and fundamental freedoms" has appeared under this or similar titles on the agenda of the UN General Assembly since 1967, and on that of the UN Commission on Human Rights since 1972.

Both organs have periodically noted with regret, as did the General Assembly at its 1988 session (resolution 43/150) that

in the contemporary world there continue to exist various forms of totalitarian ideologies and practices which entail contempt for the individual or a denial of the intrinsic dignity and equality of all human beings and of equality of opportunity in the civil, political, economic, social and cultural spheres, including the practices of *apartheid,* racial discrimination and racism; [and both have emphasized] that the doctrines of political, racial or ethnic superiority on which the totalitarian entities and régimes are based contradict the spirit and principles of the United Nations and that the application of such doctrines in practice leads to wars, mass and flagrant violations of human rights and crimes against humanity, such as genocide, and creates serious obstacles to friendly relations among nations and the development of all countries.

Both the commission, in resolution 1988/63, and the General Assembly, in resolution 43/150 of 8 December 1988, repeated their earlier condemnations of all totalitarian or other ideologies and practices, including the Nazi, Fascist and neo-Fascist, that are based on *apartheid,* racial discrimination, and racism, or which have such consequences; and both expressed their determination to resist all totalitarian ideologies, and especially their practices, which deprive people of basic human rights and fundamental freedoms and of equality of opportunity. Both called upon all governments to pay constant attention to educating the young in the spirit of respect for international law and fundamental human rights and freedoms and against Fascist, neo-Fascist and other totalitarian ideologies and practices based on terror, hatred, and violence.

Both bodies also called upon all States to take the necessary measures to ensure the thorough investigation, detection, arrest, extradition, and punishment of all war criminals and persons guilty of crimes against humanity who have not yet been brought before a court and appropriately punished.

The commission expressed the view that the pursuit of totalitarian ideologies and practices represents a serious threat to the exercise of the fundamental human rights, including the right to life, liberty, and security of person; and that the free and widespread participation by all levels of the population in democratic institutions based on respect for human rights is one of the most effective forms of defense against all totalitarian ideologies. Accordingly, it called upon all governments and the appropriate intergovernmental and non-governmental organizations to intensify measures against such ideologies and practices.

The General Assembly called upon all States, in accordance with the basic principles of international law, to refrain from practices aimed at the violation of basic human rights, particularly the right to SELF-DETERMINATION; and appealed to States that had not done so to consider becoming parties to the International Covenants on Human Rights, the CONVENTION ON THE PREVENTION AND PUNISHMENT OF THE CRIME OF GENOCIDE, the INTERNATIONAL CONVENTION ON THE ELIMINATION OF ALL FORMS OF RACIAL DISCRIMINATION, the CONVENTION ON THE NON-APPLICABILITY OF STATUTORY LIMITATIONS TO WAR CRIMES AND CRIMES AGAINST HUMANITY, and the INTERNATIONAL CONVENTION ON THE SUPPRESSION AND PUNISHMENT OF THE CRIME OF APARTHEID.

SEE ALSO Racist Propaganda and Organizations.

TOXIC AND DANGEROUS PRODUCTS AND WASTES.

The UN General Assembly, at its 1987 session, expressed concern (resolution 42/183) that part of the international movement of toxic and dangerous products and wastes is being carried out in contravention of existing national legislation and relevant international legal instruments, as well as internationally accepted guidelines and principles, to the detriment of the environment and public health of all countries, particularly of the developing countries. The assembly called upon all governments to cooperate in the prevention and control of illegal traffic in toxic and dangerous products and wastes—that is, traffic in contravention of national legislation and relevant international legal instruments—as well as traffic not carried out in compliance with internationally accepted guidelines and principles.

Taking the assembly resolution into consideration, the Commission on Human Rights at its 1989 session noted (resolution 1989/42) that the movement and dumping of toxic and dangerous products and wastes endangers basic human rights such as the RIGHT TO LIFE and the right to live in a sound and healthy ENVIRONMENT and expressed concern about the growing threat to human health and the ecosystem posed by the increased rate of transboundary movement and dumping of toxic and dangerous products and wastes and also about the clandestine nature of the movement and dumping of those wastes.

The commission called upon the governments of countries that produce toxic and dangerous wastes to ban their export to States that do not have the technical capacity for their environmentally sound disposal and to take proper measures to ensure that those wastes do not imperil human health and the ecosystem in their countries or in other countries.

The commission called upon the UNITED NATIONS ENVIRONMENT PROGRAM to expedite action on the elaboration of a global convention on the control of transboundary movements of hazardous wastes and to maintain its leading role within the United Nations system for dealing with this serious problem. It requested the Secretary-General to report on progress made in the preparation of the above-mentioned convention to the Sub-Commission on Prevention of Discrimination and Protection at its 1990 session.

SEE ALSO Environment: Toxic and Dangerous Wastes

TRAFFIC IN PERSONS AND EXPLOITATION OF THE PROSTITUTION OF OTHERS.

This practice, which gives rise to effects similar to those of slavery and the slave trade, is characterized in the 1949 CONVENTION FOR THE SUPPRESSION OF THE TRAFFIC IN PERSONS AND OF THE EXPLOITATION OF THE PROSTITUTION OF OTHERS as "incompatible with the dignity and worth of the human person."

A subject of international concern at the start of the 20th century, when governments cooperated to provide international protection against what was then known as the "white slave traffic," this practice retained in the late 1980s its high priority on the agenda of the WORKING GROUP ON CONTEMPORARY FORMS OF SLAVERY of the UN SUB-COMMISSION ON PREVENTION OF DISCRIMINATION AND PROTECTION OF MINORITIES.

In 1904, the parties to the International Agreement for the Suppression of the White Slave Traffic pledged themselves to establish in their respective countries "some authority charged with the co-ordination of all information relative to the procuring of women and girls for immoral purposes abroad" and to take concerted measures for securing to women of full age, who have suffered abuse or compulsion, as well as to girls under age, effective protection against that criminal traffic.

In 1910, the contracting parties to the International Convention for the Suppression of the White Slave Traffic undertook to punish any person who, to gratify the passions of others, hired, abducted, or enticed for immoral purposes, even with her consent, a woman or girl under 20 years of age, or over that age in case of violence, threats, fraud, or any compulsion, notwithstanding that the various acts which together constituted the offense were committed in different countries. The case of retention, against her will, of a woman or girl in a house of prostitution was excluded from the framework of this convention because it was considered a question within the exclusive competence of national legislation.

In 1921, the International Convention for the Suppression of the Traffic in Women and Children, concluded under the auspices of the League of Nations, extended the protective measures provided for in the two earlier instruments to minors of either sex and raised the age limit for protection from 20 to 21 years of age.

In 1933, the International Convention for the Suppression of the Traffic in Women of Full Age declared as punishable offenses the acts of procuring, enticing, or leading away, even with her consent, a woman of full age, for immoral purposes to be carried out in another country. Attempts to commit, and acts preparatory to the commission of, these offenses were also made punishable.

None of the above-mentioned instruments dealt directly with the question of prostitution, which continued to be considered a domestic affair. However, special bodies of experts appointed by the League of Nations in 1927 and 1932, respectively, found that it was difficult, if not impossible, to isolate the international question entirely from various forms of commercialized vice where there was no transportation to a foreign country; and noted that a principal factor in the promotion of international traffic in women was the licensed house of prostitution.

For the purpose of securing international cooperation for the abolition of licensed houses and the prosecution and punishment of any person managing such a house or exploiting the prostitution of others, the League of Nations prepared, in 1937, a draft convention on the subject. Owing to the outbreak of the World War II, the draft convention was not adopted under the auspices of the League. It was, however, completed and adopted by the UN General Assembly in December 1949 as the Convention for the Suppression of the Traffic in Persons and of the Exploitation of the Prostitution of Others.

The 1949 convention consolidates the earlier instruments and embodies the policy favored by the League of Nations' expert bodies: abolition of any form of regulation of prostitution. It binds the States parties "to take all necessary measures to repeal or abolish any law, regulation or administrative provision by virtue of which persons who engage in or are suspected of engaging in prostitution are subject either to special registration or to the possession of a special document or to any exceptional requirements for supervision or notification."

Advocates of this "abolitionist" system place empha-

sis upon effective legislation against illicit traffic and the exploitation of the traffic of others, drafted in such a way as to preclude traffickers and profiteers from circumventing them and escaping punishment; and point out that it is more effective than either the "regulationist" system, which legalizes prostitution and the existence of licensed brothels, or the "prohibitionist" system, which transforms prostitution into a criminal offense, giving rise to clandestine prostitution and often to a ruthless underworld organization conducting the illicit traffic in, and exploitation of, women and girls.

Report on Traffic in Persons and Exploitation of the Prostitution of Others. In 1982, the Economic and Social Council requested the Secretary-General (resolution 1982/20) to appoint a special rapporteur to prepare "a synthesis of the surveys and studies on the traffic in persons and the exploitation of the prostitution of others" and to propose "appropriate measures to prevent and suppress these practices that are contrary to the fundamental human rights of human beings."

The special rapporteur, Mr. Jean Fernand-Laurant (France), submitted his report in 1983. It was published in 1985 under the title *Activities for the Advancement of Women: Equality, Development and Peace* (United Nations publication, Sales No. E.85.IV.11). In it, he analyzed the problem of prostitution and its exploitation from the human rights point of view, considering it as a form of slavery, as follows (para. 16–40):

I. A Universal and Interdisciplinary Question

Although prostitution was and still is unknown in many so-called primitive societies, it is also true that it is found today to varying degrees in all States, in all cultures and in all parts of the world, especially where the population is dense and where money changes hands frequently.

The problem can be analysed from several angles, which is why it interests organizations with very different aims. It can be approached from the angle of ethnology, sociology or cultural history, for example; or from the angle of political economy, from which the world of prostitution can be seen as a closed economic system; or from the angle of criminology, as a branch of the criminal world because of the procuring involved. Prostitution can also be judged by the standards of public health, religion or mortality. Without overlooking any of these approaches, this report will take the human rights approach, as does the Economic and Social Council, in which prostitution is considered to be a form of slavery.

A. A Three-way Trade. Like slavery in the usual sense, prostitution has an economic aspect. While being a cultural phenomenon rooted in the image of man and woman given currency by society, it is a market and indeed a lucrative one. The merchandise offered is for men's pleasure, or the pleasure they enjoy in their imagination. This merchandise is unfortunately supplied by physical intimacy with women or children. Thus, the alienation of the person is here more far-reaching than in slavery in its usual sense, where what is alienated is working strength, not intimacy.

The market is created by demand, which is met by supply. The demand comes from the client, who could also be called the "prostitutor". The supply is provided by the prostitute. This is the simplest but also the rarest example. In most cases (8 or 9 times out of 10, according to observers, at least in Europe), a third person comes into the picture, perhaps the most important; this is the organizer and exploiter of the market, in other words, the procurer in his various guises: go-between or recruiter, pimp, owner of a house of prostitution, "massage parlour" or bar, or provider of a hotel room or studio. The procurer is usually a professional, involved to some extent in the world of crime. When it comes to children, it can be an older child who runs a "racket".

In the industrialized market-economy States, a concern not to hamper trade allows an overt market for eroticism and pornography to develop alongside the discreet prostitution market. The two complement and reinforce each other. The streets on which the sex shops are located are those where prostitution is heaviest.

Of the three partners in the three-way relationship: client, prostitute and procurer, least is known about the first mentioned. Since there are no laws or regulations that either punish or restrict the client, he can remain anonymous. There is so far no literature, to the Rapporteur's knowledge, in which the client has himself divulged his motivations. The reasons that prompt a bachelor or a married man to become a client have not as yet been analysed. Meanwhile, one can only suppose that his desires and his behaviour stem from the image that society gives him of his virility and from the conception that he has of women's duty being to serve his pleasure. Military service and the media no doubt play a decisive role here. Insufficient preparation for marriage among women, and also among men, might explain certain unsuccessful marriages that lead the husband to seek sexual satisfaction outside the home.

More is known about the prostitute because she is monitored by social workers and has often been described in literature. Moreover, in recent times, several former prostitutes have given autobiographical accounts of their prostitution experiences. Today, therefore, we know what brings a woman to the point of becoming a prostitute. Economic hardship is the main reason, but it is not enough; not all poor women become prostitutes. In addition to poverty, there must be a loss of respect for moral strictures, frustration or lack of affection (rejection of parents or by parents, desertion by a husband or lover), and a lack of outside assistance or a refusal to use it when it is available. Statistically, most prostitutes have been raised in broken families; a large number of them have been the victims of rape or incest. They therefore do not count on their families if they want to raise children they have had with men who have deserted them (many of them are unmarried mothers: 70 per cent according to the English Collective of Prostitutes, and they are very attached to their children). In the rare cases where the prostitute comes from an affluent family, she is motivated by a desire to challenge conventional morality combined with an excessive interest in money and the satisfaction it can provide. Does not, however, this need for money reflect the deeper need to use the external trappings of wealth to overcome the frustration of one whose personality fails to make a mark on those around her? More basically, a woman of any social level can fall into prostitution as she would fall into alcoholism or drug abuse, or as she would commit suicide: through grief, loneliness, boredom or despair. Then again it can happen in the case of addicts that prostitution seems to be the only means of obtaining drugs. In short, it could be said of most women prostitutes that they have moved from a marginal situation into another one even more marginal.

At any rate, even when prostitution seems to have been chosen freely, it is actually the result of coercion. That was the gist of the testimony given to the Congress of Nice on 8 September 1981 by three "collectives" of women prostitutes from two developed countries: "As prostitutes, we are well aware that *all* prostitution is forced prostitution. Whether we are forced to become prostitutes by lack of money or by housing or unemployment problems, or to escape from a family situation of rape or violence (which is often the case with very young prostitutes), or by a procurer, we would not lead the 'life' if we were in a position to leave it."

The rural exodus in the developing countries figures as a determining cause of prostitution. A survey published in 1978 by the Dakar magazine *Famille et Développement,* shows that employment in the cities is essentially male-oriented. Thus, the first victims in the cities are women. In the country, they have a role as producers; in the city their only role will be that of mothers and wives. Often illiterate and without professional qualifications, they have few alternatives: to be unskilled workers in the few factories where the work force is largely female, to work in domestic service, to ply a small trade or to become prostitutes. In recent years, this last option has been forced on many women as a condition of survival for themselves and their children. In addition, the supply of prostitutes has grown to meet the demand of large-scale tourism.

Emigration, which is often an extension of the rural exodus, produces comparable effects. Women immigrants are, as pointed out in the paper presented at Nice by three collectives, the most vulnerable to exploitation: "Women who have been raped, beaten, forced to work for a pimp (as a prostitute who works for a procurer or a domestic worker in a family), or for illegal wages on the black market, are too afraid of being deported and dare not complain to the police." Further comments will be made on the effects of workers migrations on prostitution.

Wherever foreign troops are present in large numbers, in both the country concerned and neighbouring countries where the soldiers spend their leave the appearance of a prostitution market or expansion of the existing market can be observed. Habits are established among the female population that, after that troops or bases are withdrawn, will be exploited by the tourist networks that take over. One organization of Asian women considers this yet another reason for opposing military alliances and use of the smallest countries in preparation for a new world war.

Occasional prostitution, the so-called "end-of-the-month" type, becomes permanent prostitution once the woman falls into the clutches of a procurer. The procurer is a character more often depicted in literature or in films than met with by the social workers. However, he is well known to the police who, sometimes, too often, use him as an informer. Contempt for women, congenital sloth and a total lack of morals are the characteristics that predispose a man to become a procurer. As a recruiter, he "sells" women to a house of prostitution or to a pimp. The pimps keep virtually all of women's daily earnings. All are involved in the world of crime. The considerable sums earned from procuring actually constitute, according to the police, the "working capital" of organized crime. These funds are sufficient to corrupt, when they are corruptible, those in political circles, the police and other State officials.

The naiveté of young people facilitates the task of the recruiters and pimps, who have several tricks for subjugating their victims without always having to resort to force. The procurer, who has hardly anything else to do, is adept at detecting the weaknesses of his future victims. Among the most frequently used tricks are seduction and a fraudulent promise of marriage or of lucrative employment, followed by a demand for "temporary" prostitution to repay a fictitious debt; sometimes the lure is a contract to join an artistic tour abroad, a tour that ends in a house of prostitution, or a restaurant or place of entertainment that is also used for prostitution; other times it is the offer of travel abroad as an *au pair* or a student in a language-training centre. When force is used, it involves drugs that facilitate kidnapping and sequestration, beating, torture, blackmail involving children and threats of mutilation or murder. Such threats are all the more to be feared since it is known that they are sometimes carried out.

Other tricks and constraints are practised on children. There is no doubt that in the slum belts of certain large cities, children sometimes have no other choice in order to survive but to pick through garbage, beg, steal or become prostitutes. But adults, paedophiles or procurers, often take the initiative by offering money or gifts. In depressed rural areas, where helpless peasant families are heavily in debt to a usurer, the children are sometimes bought or rented by a procurer from their parents, who may or may not be aware of their ultimate fate. If the child is an orphan, an abandoned child, a runaway or temporarily separated from his parents by some natural or man-made disaster, he or she is especially vulnerable and can simply be kidnapped. Paedophile tourists may be involved.

In some industrialized countries, child prostitution has recently been organized to benefit the pornography industry, which produces photograph albums, films and video cassettes. Children are photographed or filmed in indecent positions, and these pictures are sold for high prices through a clandestine network of persons interested in such things. This trade may be national or international.

Procuring does not stop at the activities of recruiter, go-between or pimp. Many laws consider as a procurer and prosecute as such any person who knowingly derives profit from the prostitution of others. This applies to a landlord or tenant who makes premises available, at rates above the average rent, to a prostitute for the pursuit of her activities: these are the offences of procuring through the provision of hotel or other premises. The owner or manager of a bar where waitresses are encouraged to act as prostitutes is also a procurer, although he is rarely prosecuted. An organizer of package tours ("sex tours") where the services of a prostitute are included in the package is also a procurer, although so far there have been no prosecutions. In this same category of procurers should be included the social clubs, or the so-called marriage bureaux, when such enterprises derive a profit from meetings where payment is made for sexual favours (some international marriages of convenience are concluded simply for the sake of prostitution). Should the publisher of a book or newspaper that encourages such practices also be considered a procurer? The human imagination is limitless where there is a profit to be made.

Certain intelligence services and capitalist firms act as procurers when, in order to corrupt or compromise a statesman or businessman, they arrange for him to meet women, styled as hostesses or secretaries, who are trained in this particular form of "high-class" prostitution.

Procurers usually conduct their activities with impunity. Perhaps because the police or the investigating officials are not sufficiently zealous (through negligence, fear or corruption), or because it is sometimes difficult to obtain proof of such offences (in court the victim, fearing reprisals, may withdraw charges made to the police and the investigating officials), or because the procurer is protected as an informer, or because the offender escapes prosecution by crossing the border, the fact remains that repression is ineffectual. In the Western European State that considers itself to be the strictest, repression affects about 1 procurer out of 10: the deterrent effect is very inadequate.

B. A Form of Slavery. A review of the various collective (remote) and individual (immediate) causes of prostitution: poverty, frustration or lack of affection, trickery and coercion on the part of procurers, makes it unnecessary to invoke any kind of mental weakness or supposed vicious inclination to explain why women fall into prostitution.

Once embarked on that course, they enter a state of servitude. Denied any independence, forced, in order to engage in their new activity, to abide by the rules imposed by the "old hands", exposed to the pressures, untempered by any competing influences, of the morality and law of the "underworld", which are neither the morality nor the law of lawful society, subjected by the procurer to a very effective discipline that metes out punishment with an infrequent admixture of reward, they immediately find themselves in a marginal situation and undergo a psychological conditioning such as may be experienced by someone living in a community within a sect. When able to judge objectively, those women who have been able to escape from this environment realize that they were deprived not only of their name, but of their very identity. A woman may also be sold by one procurer to another, as were slaves in the past and as is merchandise today. The relationship between prostitute and procurer, described by prostitutes in the West as "my husband" or "my man", is ambivalent: it is possible that the woman may find in the man, in spite of his brutality, both a husband and the father she never had in childhood. This does not alter the fact that the relationship is one of dominator and dominated, exploiter and exploited, master and slave. The restricted life of a house of prostitution, even when christened "Turkish bath", "sauna", "massage parlour" or "Eros Centre", is even harsher than that of the street corner. The Director-General of the United Nations Educational, Scientific and Cultural Organization (UNESCO), through his spokesperson at the Mexico City World Conference in 1975, drew attention to the tortures sometimes inflicted on inmates. While it is true that not all are tortured, all are nevertheless subjected to the most degrading and destructive form of slavery.

It is easy to slide into prostitution; it is very difficult to escape from it. To free oneself from a procurer, it is usually necessary to pay him a substantial "fine", sometimes equivalent to a whole year's earnings from prostitution. If one has the courage to inform on him to the police, something which is forbidden by the law of the underworld, there is a risk of terrible reprisals: mutilation or even death. Those few prostitutes who are not controlled by a procurer do not find it much easier to break free of their environment, so profoundly have they been marked by it and so strongly do they feel themselves rejected, as in fact they often are, by the "normal" society to which they wish to return. It would not be an exaggeration to say that, if she is to be successfully reintegrated into that society, a prostitute requires heroic courage.

C. International Networks. The International Criminal Police Organization (ICPO or INTERPOL), an intergovernmental organization linked, through a special arrangement, with the Economic and Social Council and composed of the central criminal police bureaux of 134 States, prepared for its General Assembly of October 1975 in Buenos Aires a third report on the traffic in women. That report was published by Kathleen Barry as an annex to her book entitled *Female Sexual Slavery.* Parts of it were quoted by Whitaker in his report. Based on information received from the police in 69 States, the report identifies a number of international networks involved in this traffic: one flowing from Latin America to Puerto Rico and beyond, to southern Europe and the Middle East; one flowing from South-East Asia to the Middle East and central and northern Europe; a regional European market, in part supplied by Latin America and exporting French women to Luxembourg and the Federal Republic of Germany; one supplying some of the richer countries of West Africa from Europe; and a regional market in the Arab countries. The author of the report did not have access to information from East Africa and does not mention the existence, noted by travellers through that region, of slave markets supplying the Middle East. More recently, the migration of African refugees to Europe has involved women who have been found working as prostitutes only a few months later. Family group among migrant workers have also on occasion served as a cover for traffic networks. According to this incomplete information, few regions and few countries, with the possible exception of the centrally planned economy countries, are free of the international traffic in women, and that traffic is far from being confined to a flow from the less developed South to the more developed North: it would be more accurate to say that the movement involves the traffic of poor women towards rich men in all directions. Through these well-disguised networks, not only adult women but even under-age girls are moved from one country to another.

The replies to the annual questionnaire prepared by the Centre for Human Rights, although supplied by only a small minority of States, provide useful specific supplementary information concerning certain types of international traffic. For example, replies to question 10 were given, for the period 1979–1981, by three countries only: France, Singapore and Spain. These replies have been summarized in a report on slavery, provided by the Centre for Human Rights to the Working Group on Slavery for its eighth session in August 1982. They show that the traffic is often carried on under cover of what purport to be marriage bureaux or advertisements for jobs in touring stage shows. They give evidence of procuring networks supplying Geneva from Paris; Switzerland and the Federal Republic of Germany from Bangkok; Singapore from Malaysia and the Philippines; and Spain from France, Cape Verde, South America and the Philippines (109 young Philippine women aged between 16 and 28). Undoubtedly, if equally detailed replies were available from the other States, a clear picture would be established of the methods and routes used in the traffic in persons. In particular, it would be possible to verify and research in more detail the press reports cited by Whitaker (E/CN.4/Sub.2/1982/20, para. 17), indicating that South American prostitutes are shipped from Argentina to Melbourne, young Hawaiian and Californian women to Japan, and Swedish women from Singapore to the Far East.

More conspicuous, and therefore easier to trace, is the other type of traffic that, instead of transporting the prostitute, temporarily transplants the client. This is the channel of the sex tours, in which the services of a prostitute are included in the price the tourist pays for his ticket. This specialized kind of tourism is grafted onto an existing prostitution market and develops it. Several women's associations and the Churches have denounced this traffic, which is a flourishing movement from the developed countries of America, Europe and Asia towards the countries popular with tourists in Africa, Asia and the Caribbean. In September 1980, in Manila, an international workshop on tourism, meeting under the dual sponsorship of the Christian Conference of Asia and the Confederation of Asian Episcopal Conferences, adopted eight recommendations relating to prostitution. In July 1981, an international congress of theologians on "The Community of Men and Women in the Church", meeting in Sheffield, the United Kingdom of Great Britain and Northern Ireland, under the auspices of the World Council of Churches, denounced the phenomenon of sex tours in an "open letter to Christians". In Stockholm, in November 1981, the World Council of Churches organized an international conference on the theme "the Church and tourism", which heard evidence from all regions of the world and put forward a moral code for tourists. Together with this activity by the churches, joint action is being taken by the Asian Women's Association in Japan, the Philippines and the Republic of Korea: with the assistance of trade union organizations, demonstrations have been mounted in airports to coincide with the departure or arrival of sex tours; and a Third World Movement against the Exploitation of Women has been created among the countries of the Association of South-East Asian Nations. In addition, the Asian Confederation of Women's Organisations discussed prostitution at its July 1982 meeting and took cognizance of a document submitted by the Philippines containing recommendations that were studied at the government level at the meeting of the Programme for Women of ASEAN held at Bangkok in January 1983. All these activities have led to a perceptible reduction in organized sex tourism in that region; but will that reduction be lasting? And what of the situation in other regions of the world, such as the Caribbean, where local resistance has not yet become organized? In any event, it is advisable to view this issue in the general context of the cultural impact of tourism. That is the approach taken by the Holy See in its recommendations, virtually a code of ethics, on tourism drafted over several years, while it continues to encourage the religious orders that are dedicated to the rescue of persons engaged in prostitution. It was also in the context of the cultural effects of tourism that prostitution was discussed by a group of experts that met at Vienna in September 1982 to discuss the issue "Women and the International Development Strategy". That group denounced the destructive effects on the local community and on the identity of women produced by the exploitation of prostitution for tourist purposes. In the view of the Special Rapporteur, such tourism is quite plainly the worst possible image of development that the industrialized countries could project. Together with erotic films, publications and advertising, it may, in the developing countries where it is prevalent, provoke hostile reactions to development itself and prompt a return to discriminatory moral strictures that could be an obstacle to the much-needed liberation of women.

The encouragement that the prostitution of young children receives from Western tourism has been highlighted

T

by Tim Bond, a researcher with the "Terre des Hommes" association of Lausanne. In 1980 he carried out three surveys in two countries of South-East Asia, extending their scope to Europe, where he found publications on sale to the public providing information to paedophiles on the opportunities available to them among young boys from poor families in the big cities of South-East Asia and Africa. Bouhdiba referred to these facts in his report, mentioned above, to the Sub-Commission on Prevention of Discrimination and Protection of Minorities (see annex VI). UNICEF gave them wide publicity in *Ideas Forum*.

After examining the special rapporteur's report in 1983, the Economic and Social Council, recalling that the enslavement of women and children subjected to prostitution is incompatible with the dignity and rights of the human person, invited UN Member States (resolution 1983/30) to sign, ratify, and implement the Convention for the Suppression of the Traffic in Persons and of the Exploitation of the Prostitution of Others and the International Convention for the Suppression of the Circulation of and Traffic in Obscene Publications; and recommended that they should draw up policies aimed, to the extent possible, at (a) preventing prostitution by moral education and civics training, in and out of school; (b) increasing the number of women among the State's personnel having direct contact with the populations concerned; (c) eliminating discrimination that ostracizes prostitutes and makes their reabsorption into society more difficult; (d) curbing the pornography industry and the trade in pornography and penalizing them very severely when minors are involved; (e) punishing all forms of procuring in such a way as to deter it, particularly when it exploits minors; and (f) facilitating occupational training for and the reabsorption into society of persons rescued from prostitution.

The council, at the same time, invited member States to cooperate closely with one another in the research for missing persons and in the identification of international networks of procurers and, if they are members of the INTERNATIONAL CRIMINAL POLICE ORGANIZATION, to cooperate with that organization, requesting it to make the suppression of the traffic in persons one of its priorities. Later, the General Assembly invited the council (resolution 40/103) to give further consideration to the whole question of the suppression of the traffic in persons and of the exploitation of the prostitution of others.

Recent Developments relating to the Traffic in Persons and the Exploitation of the Prostitution of Others. At its 1988 session, the WORKING GROUP ON CONTEMPORARY FORMS OF SLAVERY reviewed recent developments relating to the traffic in persons and the exploitation of the prostitution of others. The discussion, as summarized in the working group's report to the 1988

session of the Sub-Commission on Prevention of Discrimination and Protection of Minorities, (UN Doc. E/CN.4/Sub.2/1988/32, chap. III, E para. 65–73), was as follows:

The International Abolitionist Federation referred the Working Group to its Congress of 1984 held at Vienna which highlighted several factors which led, *inter alia*, to the traffic in persons and prostitution. An indifferent public opinion, irresponsible press, the inertia of Governments, fundamental inequality of men and women in many societies and economic crises were viewed as leading factors. The representative of the Federation also criticized the 1949 Convention for the Suppression of the Traffic in Persons and of the Exploitation of the Prostitution of Others on the grounds that its vague terminology and ineffective implementation machinery allowed States to ignore its application. The attention of the Working Group was drawn to resolution 1988/42 adopted by the Commission on Human Rights at its forty-fourth session calling on States and the Sub-Commission to draw up plans for the taking of concrete measures in the field of slavery. It was announced that an Asian regional conference in collaboration with the Federation would be held in November 1988 at New Delhi in India and that the Federation would hold a European Congress at Bern at 1989.

Another report presented by the International Abolitionist Federation concerned France. It pointed out that there were disparities between principles and declarations contained in the laws of France and what actually obtained in practice. It was pointed out, for instance, that although women and children were regarded as elements of society to be promoted and protected, their positions were constantly being undermined by the way in which they were projected in advertisements and pornography, as well as by their exploitation by prostitution. It was also pointed out that, although international and national standards in France opposed the exploitation of the prostitution of others, the Government profited from prostitution by taxing the earnings of prostitutes, as well as from the revenues it received from the operation of *Minitel Rose,* a communications system run by the Ministry of Posts and Communications and often used by those involved in prostitution. The report also indicated and analysed some inconsistencies within the texts of government policies themselves. The report criticized the ambiguities it had illustrated and emphasized the importance of good laws, conforming with established human rights standards, especially with the advent of greater harmonization in Europe. The report referred to the Congress of the International Abolitionist Federation held in Stuttgart in 1987 which called for a study by the United Nations Educational, Scientific and Cultural Organization on the motivations of prostitutes, pimps and clients and indicated that the Federation itself would commence a publication concerning prostitution internationally. The report further indicated that the Federation called on the Secretary-General of the United Nations to press more States to sign the Convention of 1949 and to hold a diplomatic conference consisting of States parties to the Convention to establish means to ensure better implementation of its terms.

With reference to the report made by the International Abolitionist Federation concerning France, the Observer for France indicated that the Government of France was aware of the abuses of such new technology as *Minitel Rose* and was working on ways to prevent this. The Observer also stated that, although the earnings of prostitutes in France were taxed, this was simply because all income in France was taxable and that this in no way meant that the Government acknowledged prostitution as a legitimate profession. As an incentive for prostitutes to become rehabilitated, it was pointed out that they were sometimes exempted from tax whilst they were making such efforts. The Observer for France paid tribute to the role played by non-governmental organizations in the field of prevention and rehabilitation; he stressed the eagerness of his authorities to continue and to increase the co-operation with non-governmental organizations that was already taking place.

Regarding the statement by the Observer for France, the representative of the International Abolitionist Federation raised two issues concerning the taxation of the earnings of prostitutes. The representative questioned whether there was any difference between pimps and the State who both profited from the prostitution of others. The representative also questioned whether prostitutes would not simply have to work harder so that they could meet their payments to their ponces as well as pay their taxes.

The representative of the United Nations Educational, Scientific and Cultural Organization drew the attention of the Working Group to document E/CN.4/Sub.2/AC.2/1988/5, in which many of the organization's efforts in this field were detailed. Mention was made of the International Meeting of Experts held at Madrid in March 1987 during which the causes of prostitution were discussed. It was reported that the Meeting of Experts viewed prostitution as an economic phenomenon, involving the trade of a woman's body as an item of merchandise, as well as a phenomenon partly reflective of social structures and stereotypes. The document also highlighted the discovery of the United Nations Educational, Scientific and Cultural Organization of the contribution that international marriage markets made to the international traffic in persons and prostitution world-wide. The document further emphasized UNESCO's dissatisfaction with the terms of the 1949 Convention for the Suppression of the Traffic in Persons and of the Exploitation of the Prostitution of Others in that they raise a distinction between voluntary and enforced prostitution. UNESCO took the view that there were grounds in contemporary society for believing that such a distinction was unrealistic and that all prostitution violated international human rights standards.

The International Abolitionist Federation drew the attention of the Working Group to reports it had given to previous sessions of the Working Group concerning prostitution in Belgium. The representative of the Federation stated that the Belgian authorities had not only failed to take measures in support of prostitutes in the past but had increasingly commenced to act in a manner contrary to the spirit of the 1949 Convention. It was pointed out that a Belgian law of 1948 permitted the authorities to enact regulations concerning prostitution and that this power was being exercised contrary to the interests of prostitutes and the spirit of the 1949 Convention. It was reported that, in an effort to satisfy public opinion, the establishment of locations used for prostitution was being made more difficult. It was also reported that a regulation forcing prostitutes to work out of the view of passers-by had also been enacted. The representative of the Federation called for the abrogation of all such measures as they had the effect of further marginalizing people who were already the victims of prostitution.

With reference to the report by the International Abolitionist Federation concerning Belgium, the Observer for Belgium denied that the authorities in Belgium were neglecting the problem of prostitution. The Observer supported this by pointing out that Belgium was actively participating in the work of the Working Group and by reporting that the Minister of Justice of Belgium had spoken about prostitution at the Lisbon meeting of Ministers of Justice of the members of the Council of Europe. The Observer stated that the 1949 Convention was a problem in that its term were vague and that they lent themselves to a variety of interpretations.

A report by the International Abolitionist Federation concerning Japan stated that there were laws for the prosecution of those involved in prostitution but that they were largely ineffective as regards the prostitution of foreigners. This was illustrated by pointing out that although only 10 procurers of foreign prostitutes were indicted from 1986 to 1987 over 2,500 procurers in 1987 alone were indicted for employing Japanese prostitutes. The ineffectiveness of the laws regarding the prostitution of foreigners was explained on the basis that the foreigners had language difficulties, little money and that they were simply often deported as illegal immigrants. The report requested the Japanese Government to grant an amnesty to the foreign prostitutes so that they could seek relief from established shelters, find alternative employment and exercise their rights to bring law suits against those that had exploited them. It was requested that the Official Development Assistance from Japan to the rest of South-East Asia be reviewed to ensure that it created jobs in South-East Asian countries in an effort to combat the problem of prostitution. The report pointed out that a survey had been carried out in Japan which revealed that prostitution was viewed there as a problem of society rather than an issue in terms of the human rights of victimized people.

The representative of the Branch for the Advancement of Women from the United Nations Office in Vienna made a statement in which issues were raised concerning relevant international conventions. Mention was also made of possible links which might be established between that office and the Working Group regarding the reports of States parties particularly in the field of human trafficking.

On the basis of the discussion summarized above, the working group made a number of recommendations, as follows:

(a) That urgent consideration be given to the problems of the implementation of the 1949 Convention for the Suppression of the Traffic in Persons and of the Exploitation of the Prostitution of Others, with particular attention to the meaning and scope of its provisions in the light of new forms of prostitution and pornography imposed on children;

(b) That a study be undertaken of ways and means by which an effective implementation mechanism, including reporting systems, may be established for the 1949 Convention for the Suppression of the Traffic in Persons and of the Exploitation of the Prostitution of Others;

(c) That Governments be urged to pursue a policy of information, prevention and rehabilitation of women victims of the exploitation of prostitution and to take all economic and social measures deemed necessary to that effect;

(d) That United Nations institutions, in particular the United Nations Educational, Scientific and Cultural Organization, be encouraged to examine the possibility of organizing expert meetings on the international standards regarding the prevention of traffic in persons and exploitation of the prostitution of others;

(e) That at its future sessions the Working Group should give attention to the dissemination and proliferation of obscene publications and communications, particularly in the light of new technology;

(f) That resolution 1985/23 of the Sub-Commission, endorsed by resolution 1986/34 of the Commission on Human Rights, be submitted for approval to the Economic and Social Council and the General Assembly so that a world day for the abolition of slavery in all its forms can be proclaimed;

(g) That the receiving countries provide protection to migrant women against exploitation in the form of prostitution and other slavery-like practices;

(h) That the receiving and mother countries of migrant women should co-operate closely in protecting migrant women and preventing their exploitation by prostitution and other slavery-like practices;

(i) That all Member States be urged to consider the possibility of establishing national agencies or institutions for the protection of migrant women against exploitation by prostitution and other slavery-like practices.

Recommendations along these lines were adopted by the sub-commission (resolution 1988/30) and forwarded to the Commission on Human Rights.

SEE ALSO Children: Sale and Trafficking.

TRANSSEXUALISM. On 29 September 1989, the Parliamentary Assembly of the COUNCIL OF EUROPE adopted a recommendation (1117 [1989]) that the Committee of Ministers of the Council should draw up a recommendation inviting member States to introduce legislation whereby, in the case of irreversible transsexualism: (a) the reference to the sex of the person concerned is to be rectified in the register of births and in the identity papers, (b) a change of forename is to be authorized, (c) the person's private life is to be protected, and (d) all discrimination in the enjoyment of fundamental rights and freedoms is prohibited in accordance with article 14 of the EUROPEAN CONVENTION ON HUMAN RIGHTS.

In the resolution, the assembly pointed out that transsexualism is a syndrome characterized by a dual personality—one physical, the other psychological—together with such a profound conviction of belonging to the other sex that the transsexual person is prompted to ask for the corresponding bodily "correction" to be made. It noted that transsexualism raises relatively new and complex questions to which States are called upon to find answers compatible with respect for human rights and observed that, in the absence of specific rules, transexuals are often the victims of discrimination and violation of their private life.

SEE ALSO Homosexuality: Discrimination; Minorities: Sexual.

TRINIDAD AND TOBAGO. The Republic of Trinidad and Tobago is a country in tropical South America, occupying two islands off the northeast coast of Venezuela. It achieved independence from Great Britain in 1962 and became a member of the United Nations the same year. Its population is estimated by the UN (1990) to be 1,283,000. Ethnic groups include persons of African (40.8%), East Indian (40.7%), and mixed (18.5%) descent. Languages commonly used include English (official), Hindi, French, and Spanish. Religions practiced include Christianity (Roman Catholic, 33.6%; Anglican, 15%), Hinduism (25%), Islam (6%), and others (20.4%). Literacy is estimated at 95%.

The government (1990) took the form of a republic and member of the Commonwealth of Nations, of which the British monarch is the symbolic head. Under the 1976 constitution, the president is elected by universal suffrage and acts as head of State. The prime minister, representing the party or coalition given the majority in an election, exercises executive authority as head of government. There is a bicameral parliament consisting of a 36-member House of Representatives and a 24-member Senate. The island of Tobago also has its own 15-member House of Assembly. The judiciary includes a Supreme Court, consisting of the High Court and the Court of Appeal. Political parities include the National Alliance for Reconstruction and the People's National Movement.

Section 91 of the constitution of Trinidad and Tobago creates the office of ombudsman. It is the function of the ombudsman to investigate complaints by persons of injustice arising from the exercise of administrative functions of government and quasi-governmental agencies. He may investigate any such matter, under section 93 (2), in any of the following circumstances:

(a) Where a complaint is duly made to the *Ombudsman* by any person alleging that the complainant has sustained an injustice as a result of a fault in the administration;

(b) Where a member of the House of Representatives requests the *Ombudsman* to investigate the matter on the ground that a person or body of persons specified in the request has or may have sustained such injustice;

(c) In any other circumstances in which the *Ombudsman* considers that he ought to investigate the matter on the ground that some body of persons has or may have sustained such injustice.

TRUSTEESHIP COUNCIL. Established in accordance with the UNITED NATIONS CHARTER (article 7) as a principal organ of the United Nations, the council supervises the administration of trust territories by considering reports of the administering authorities, accepting and examining petitions, arranging for periodic visits to the territories, and taking any other action called for by trusteeship agreements. With regard to "strategic" areas, the Trusteeship Council assists the Security Council in exercising the functions assigned to the United Nations. Since 1977, only one of the original 11 trust territories remains within the trusteeship system, the Trust Territory of the Pacific Islands under United States' Territory administration. The Trusteeship Council receives and considers reports on political, economic, social, and other developments in the territory submitted by the administering authority. Because the territory has been designated as a "strategic area," the Trusteeship Council's report on it is directed to the Security Council. Conditions in the territory are also considered by the SPECIAL COMMITTEE ON THE SITUATION WITH REGARD TO THE IMPLEMENTATION OF THE DECLARATION ON THE GRANTING OF INDEPENDENCE TO COLONIAL COUNTRIES AND PEOPLES.

In accordance with article 86 of the UN Charter, the council is composed of UN members administering trust territories and permanent members of the Security Council not administering trust territories. The United States is a Trusteeship Council member because it administers the Pacific Islands; and China France, the USSR, and the United Kingdom are also council members because they are permanent members of the Security Council and do not administer trust territories. Except for permanent members of the Security Council, members of the Trusteeship Council cease to be members when the territories administered by them become independent.

The Trusteeship Council meets as required to perform its functions, normally the headquarters of the United Nations in New York, and has no subsidiary bodies.

TUNISIA. The Republic of Tunisia is a country in northern Africa. It has borders with Algeria and Libya. It achieved independence from France in 1956 and became a member of the United Nations in 1957. Its population is estimated by the UN (1990) to be 7,894,000. Ethnically, the population is homogeneous, consisting mainly of Arab Malekite Moslems. The Berbers, who were the first inhabitants of the country, are scattered, few in number, and integrated into the Arab/Moslem civilization; they do not form a special, geographically located, autonomous community demanding special status. Languages commonly used include Arabic (official) and French. Islam is the predominant religion (98%); Christianity (1.5%) and Judaism (.5%) are also practiced. Literacy is estimated at 64%.

The government (1990) took the form of a republic. Under the constitution of 1959, the president is elected by universal suffrage for a term of five years and is eligible for re-election for two additional terms; however, President Habib Bourguiba was made "President for Life" in 1975 after re-election to a fourth five-year term, the National Assembly amending the constitution for this purpose. The prime minister, representing the party or coalition winning an election, is head of government. The legislature consists of a unicameral 136-member National Assembly, elected by universal suffrage. The judiciary is independent of other branches of government. Political parties include the Socialist Destourian, the Social Democratic Movement, the Popular Unity Party, and the Community Party.

On 27 September 1987 seven members of the Movement for Islamic Tendencies, Tunisia's largest fundamentalist group, were sentenced to death after having been found guilty by the Tunisian Court for State Security of involvement in four hotel bombing incidents that killed 13 persons. Sixty-nine of the defendents, found guilty of lesser crimes, were sentenced to prison terms, while 14 were found not guilty. The government maintained that the trial was aimed at discouraging Iran-backed terrorists whose aim was to turn Tunisia into an Islamic revolutionary State.

After two of the death penalties had been carried out, President Bourguiba ordered a further crackdown on Islamic fundamentalists—a proposal that most government officials feared would plunge the country into turmoil and religious strife. At this point, Prime Minister and former Minister of Security Zine el-Albidene Ben Ali, with the concurrence of government and opposition leaders, deposed the aging "president for life" on the ground of mental deterioration, appointed himself president, and promised to abolish the post of president for life.

Bourguiba, at 84, was confined to a presidential residence south of Tunis, where he continued to receive the respect due the first President of Tunisia. Under his leadership Tunisia had developed into a modern secular State held together and controlled by

T

the ruling Destourian Socialist Party, of which he was the head.

That party was re-named the Democratic Constitutional Rally in 1988, and President Zine el-Albidene Ben Ali, its candidate, ran unopposed in national popular elections held in 1989, winning over 99% of the vote.

TURKEY. The Republic of Turkey is a country in western Asia, on the Black Sea and the Aegean Sea. It has borders with Bulgaria, Greece, Iraq, Iran, Syria, and the Union of Soviet Socialist Republics. It achieved independence in 1923, when the Ottoman Empire was broken up, and became a member of the United Nations in 1945. Its population is estimated by the UN (1990) to be 54,647,000. Ethnic groups include Turks and about 10 million Kurds, who live in the mountaneous eastern part of the country. Turkish is in common use throughout the country; Kurdish is not recognized as a distinct language and its public use is banned. Islam (Sunni) is the predominant religion, with 98.2% of all believers; Christianity and Judaism (Sephardim) account for the remainder. The State is secular; there is no official religion. Literacy is estimated at 80%.

The government (1990) took the form of a republic. Under the 1982 constitution, the main legislative body is the 399-member Grand National Assembly, members of which are elected by universal suffrage. The Grand National Assembly elects the president, who serves for a term of seven years, acting as head of State. The prime minister, representing the party or coalition which was given the majority in the election, is head of government. The judiciary includes the Council of State, which is the highest administration tribunal. There is also the Constitutional Court, empowered to review and annul legislation and, if necessary, to try the president of the republic. There are no religious courts, and religious law is not applied. There is, however, a Department of Religious Affairs, which, under article 136 of the constitution, "shall carry out its duties defined by law, in accordance with the principles of secularism, detached from political views and ideas and making national solidarity and integrity its objective." Political parties include the Motherland Party, the Populist Party, and the National Democracy Party.

Turkey's Kurdish minority has suffered discrimination on the ground of language since the founding of the modern Turkish State in 1923; and its continuous fight for recognition of its language, for autonomy, and eventually for independence, has been checked systematically and continuously by Turkish armed forces garrisoned in Kurdistan. Besides outlawing the use of Kurdish, Turkey has refused any recognition whatsoever to Kurds as a distinct people having a history and culture of their own. Kurds are sometimes disdainfully referred to as "mountain Turks" and characterized as "bandits."

For many years Turkish Kurds based their insurgent activities in neighboring Iran, Iraq, and Syria, all of which have Kurdish minorities of their own. However, in recent years, they have begun to operate openly within Turkey with some aid and support from the Kurdish Workers' Party, based in Syria and aligned with the Soviet Union, which also has a Kurdish minority. The goal of that party is the establishment of an independent Marxist Kurdish State in what is now eastern Turkey.

In 1988, more than 60,000 Kurdish guerillas and their families, fleeing from northern Iraq to escape what was described, over Iraqi denials, as chemical warfare directed against them, were received and sheltered by Turkey on humanitarian grounds. Although the Turkish government announced that it was prepared to offer them sanctuary indefinitely, most of them later returned to Iraq.

TURKEY: CONSTITUTION. The Constitution of the Republic of Turkey, adopted, approved, and directly enacted by the Turkish nation in the refendum of 7 November 1982, includes the following provisions (articles 5, 10, and 12–74) specifically relating to human rights and fundamental freedoms:

Part One—General Principles
Fundamental Aims and Duties of the State

Article 5. The fundamental aims and duties of the State are: to safeguard the independence and integrity of the Turkish Nation, the indivisibility of the country, the Republic and democracy; to ensure the welfare, peace, and happiness of the individual and society; to strive for the removal of political, social and economic obstacles which restrict the fundamental rights and freedoms of the individual in a manner incompatible with the principles of justice and of the social State governed by the rule of law; and to provide the conditions required for the development of the individual's material and spiritual existence. . . .

Equality Before Law

Article 10. All individuals are equal without any discrimination before the law, irrespective of language, race, colour, sex, political opinion, philisophical belief, religion and sect, or any such considerations.

No privilege shall be granted to any individual, family, group or class.

State organs and administrative authorities shall act in compliance with the principle of equality before the law in all their proceedings. . . .

Part Two—Fundamental Rights and Duties
Chapter One—General Provisions
I. Nature of Fundamental Rights and Freedoms

Article 12. Everyone possesses inherent fundamental rights and freedoms which are inviolable and inalienable.

The fundamental rights and freedoms also include the duties and responsibilities of the individual towards society, his family, and other individuals.

II. Restriction of Fundamental Rights and Freedoms

Article 13. Fundamental rights and freedoms may be restricted by law, in conformity with the letter and spirit of the Constitution, with the aim of safeguarding the indivisible integrity of the State with its territory and nation, national sovereignty, the Republic, national security, public order, general peace, the public interest public morals and public health, and also for specific reasons set forth in the relevant articles of the Constitution.

General and specific grounds for restrictions of fundamental rights and freedoms shall not conflict with the requirements of the democratic order of society and shall not be imposed for any purpose other than those for which they are prescribed.

The general grounds for restriction set forth in this article shall apply for all fundamental rights and freedoms.

III. Prohibition of Abuse of Fundamental Rights and Freedoms

Article 14. None of the rights and freedoms embodied in the Constitution shall be exercised with the aim of violating the indivisible integrity of the State with its territory and nation, of endangering the existence of the Turkish State and Republic, of destroying fundamental rights and freedoms, of placing the government of the State under the control of an individual or a group of people, or establishing the hegemony of one social class over others, or creating discrimination on the basis of language, race, religion or sect, or of establishing by any other means of system of government based on these concepts and ideas.

The sanctions to be applied against those who violate these prohibitions, and those who incite and provoke others to the same end shall be determined by law.

No provision of this Constitution shall be interpreted in a manner that would grant the right of destroying the rights and freedoms embodied in the Constitution.

IV. Suspension of the Exercise of Fundamental Rights and Freedoms

Article 15. In times of war, mobilisation, martial law, or state of emergency the exercise of fundamental rights and freedoms can be partially or entirely suspended, or measures may be taken, to the extent required by the exigencies of the situation, which derogate the guarantees embodied in the Constitution, provided that obligations under international law are not violated.

Even under the circumstances indicated in the first paragraph, the individual's right to life, and the integrity of his material and spiritual entity shall be inviolable except where death occurs through lawful acts of warfare and execution of death sentences; no one may be compelled to reveal his religion, conscience, thought or opinion, nor be accused on account of them; offences and penalties may not be made retroactive, nor may anyone be held guilty until so proven by a court judgement.

V. Status of Aliens

Article 16. The fundamental rights and freedoms of aliens may be restricted by law in a manner consistent with international law.

Chapter Two—The Rights and Duties of the Individual
I. Personal Inviolability, Material and Spiritual Entity of the Individual

Article 17. Everyone has the right to life and the right to protect and develop his material and spiritual entity.

The physical integrity of the individual shall not be violated except under medical necessity and in cases prescribed by law; he shall not be subject to scientific or medical experiments without his consent.

No one shall be subjected to torture or ill-treatment; no one shall be subjected to penalty or treatment incompatible with human dignity.

The cases of carrying out of death penalties under court sentences, the act of killing in self-defense, the occurences of death as a result of the use of a weapon permitted by law as a necessary measure in cases of: apprehension, or the execution of warrants of arrest, the prevention of escape of lawfully arrested or convicted persons, the quelling of a riot or insurrection, the execution of the orders of authorized bodies during martial law or state of emergency are outside of the provision of paragraph 1.

II. Prohibition of Forced Labour

Article 18. No one shall be required to perform forced labour. Unpaid compulsory work is prohibited.

The term forced labour does not include work required of an individual while serving a court sentence or under detention, services required from citizens during a state of emergency, and physical or intellectual work necessitated by the requirements of the country as a civic obligation, provided that the form and conditions of such labour are prescribed by law.

III. Personal Liberty and Security

Article 19. Everyone has the right to liberty and security of person.

No one shall be deprived of his liberty except in the following cases where procedure and conditions are prescribed by law: Execution of sentences restricting liberty and the implementation of security measures decided by courts, apprehension or detention of a person as a result of a court order or as a result of an obligation upon him designated by law; execution of an order for the purpose of the educational supervision of a minor or for bringing him before the competent authority; execution of measures taken in conformity with the relevant legal provision for the treatment, education or correction in institutions of a person of unsound mind, an alcholic in institutions of a person of unsound mind, an alcholic or drug addict or vagrant or a person spreading contagious diseases, when such persons constitute a danger to the public; apprehension or detention of a person who enters or attempts to enter illegaly into the country or concerning whom a deportation or exradition order has been issued.

Individuals against whom there are strong indications of having committed an offence can be arrested by decision of judge solely for the purposes of preventing escape, or preventing the destruction or alteration of evidence as well as in similar other circumstances which necessitate detention and are prescibed by law. Apprehension of a person without a decision by a judge shall be resorted to only in cases when a person is caught in the act of committing an offence or in cases where delay is likely to thwart justice; the conditions for such apprehension shall be defined by law.

Individuals arrested or detained shall be promptly notified, and in all cases in writing, or orally, when the former is not possible, of the grounds for their arrest or detention and the charges against them; in cases of offences committed collectively this notification shall be made, at the latest, before the individual is brought before the judge.

The person arrested or detained shall be brought before a judge within 48 hours and within fifteen days in the case of offences committed collectively, excluding the time taken to send him to the court nearest to the place of seizure. No one can be deprived of his liberty without the decision of a judge after the expiry of the above-specified periods. These periods may be extending during a state of emergency, under martial law or in time of war.

Notification of the situation of the person arrested or detained shall be made to the next of kin, except in cases of definite necessities pertaining to the risks of revealing the scope and subject of the investigation compelling otherwise.

Persons under detention shall have the right to request to be tried within a reasonable time or to be released during investigation or prosecution. Release may be made conditional on the presentation of an appropriate guarantee with a view to securing the presence of the person at the trial proceedings and the execution of the court sentence.

Persons deprived of their liberty under any circumstances are entitled to apply to the appropriate judicial authority for speedy conclusion of proceedings regarding their situation and for their release if the restriction placed upon them is not lawful.

Damages suffered by persons subjected to treatment contrary to the above provisions shall be compensated for according to law, by the State.

IV. Privacy and Protection of Private Life
A. Privacy of the Individual's Life

Article 20. Everyone has the right to demand respect for his private and family life. Privacy of individual and family life cannot be violated. Exceptions necessitated by judiciary investigation and prosecution are reserved.

Unless there exists a decision duly passed by a judge in cases explicitly defined by law, and unless there exists an order of an agency authorised by law in cases where delay is deemed prejudicial, neither the person nor the private papers, nor belongings of an individual shall be searched nor shall they be seized.

B. Inviolability of Domicile

Article 21. The domicile of an individual shall not be violated. Unless there exists a decision duly passed by a judge in cases explicitly defined by law, and unless there exists an order of an agency authorised by law in cases where delay is deemed prejudical, no domicile may be entered or searched, or the property therein seized.

C. Freedom of Communication

Article 22. Everyone has the right to freedom of communication.

Secrecy of communication is fundamental.

Communications shall not be impeded nor its secrecy be violated, unless there exists a decision duly passed by a judge in cases explicitly defined by law, and unless there exists an order of an agency authorised by law in cases where delay is deemed prejudicial.

Public establishments or institutions where exceptions to the above may be applied will be defined by law.

V. Freedom of Residence and Movement

Article 23. Everyone has the right to freedom of residence and movement.

Freedom of residence may be restricted by law for the purpose of preventing offences, promoting social and economic development, ensuring sound and orderly urban growth, and protecting public property; freedom of movement may be restricted by law for the purpose of investigation and prosecution of an offence, and prevention of offences. A citizen's freedom to leave the country may be restricted on account of the national economic situation, civic obligations, or criminal investigation or prosecution.

Citizens may not be deported, or deprived of their right of entry into their homeland.

VI. Freedom of Religion and Conscience

Article 24. Everyone has the right to freedom of conscience, religious belief and conviction.

Acts of worship, religious services, and ceremonies shall be conducted freely, provided that they do not violate the provisions of Article 14.

No one shall be compelled to worship, or to participate in religious ceremonies and rites, to reveal religious beliefs and convictions, or be blamed or accused because of his religious beliefs and convictions.

Education and instruction in religion and ethics shall be conducted under State supervision and control. Instruction in religious culture and moral education shall be compulsory in the curricula of primary and secondary schools. Other religious education and instruction shall be subject to the individual's own desire, and in the case of minors, to the request of their legal representatives.

No one shall be allowed to exploit or abuse religion or religious feelings, or things held sacred by religion, in any manner whatsoever, for the purpose of personal or political influence, or for even partially basing the fundamental, social, economic, political, and legal order of the State on religious tenets.

VII. Freedom of Thought and Opinion

Article 25. Everyone has the right to freedom of thought and opinion.

No one shall be compelled to reveal his thoughts and opinions for any reason or purpose; nor shall anyone be blamed or accused on account of his thoughts and opinions.

VIII. Freedom of Expression and Dissemination of Thought

Article 26. Everyone has the right to express and disseminate his thought and opinion by speech, in writing or in pictures, or through other media, individually or collectively. This right includes the freedom to receive and impart information and ideas without interference from official authorities. This provision shall not preclude subjecting transmission by radio, television, cinema, and similar means to a system of licencing.

The exercise of these freedoms may be restricted for the

purposes of preventing crime, punishing offenders, withholding information duly classified as a State secret, protecting the reputation and rights and the private and family life of others, or protecting professional secrets as prescribed by law, or ensuring the proper functioning of the judiciary.

No language prohibited by law shall be used in the exression and dissemination of thought. Any written or printed documents, phonograph records, magnetic or video tapes, and other means of expression used in contravention of this provision shall be seized by a duly issued decision of judge or, in cases where delay is deemed prejudicial, by the competent authority designated by law. The authority issuing the seizure order shall notify the competent judge of its decision within twenty-four hours. The judge shall decide on the matter within three days.

Provisions regulating the use of means of disseminating information and ideas shall not be interpreted as a restriction of the freedom of expression and dissemination unless they prevent the dissemination of information and thoughts.

IX. Freedom of Science and Arts

Article 27. Everyone has the right to study and teach freely, explain, and disseminate science and arts and to carry out research in these fields.

The right to disseminate shall not be exercised for the purpose of changing the provision of Article 1, 2 and 3 of this Constitution.

The provisions of this Article shall not preclude regulation by law of the entry and distribution of foreign publications in the country.

X. Provisions relating to the Press and Publication
A. Freedom of the Press

Article 28. The Press is free, and shall not be censored. The establishment of a printing house shall not be subject to prior permission and to the deposit of a financial guarantee.

Publication shall not be made in any language prohibited by law.

The State shall take the necessary measures to ensure the freedom of the Press and freedom of information.

In the limitation of freedom of the press, Articles 26 and 27 of the Constitution are applicable.

Anyone who writes or prints any news or articles which threaten the internal or external security of the State or the indivisible integrity of the State with its territory and nation, which tend to incite offence, riot or insurrection, or which refer to classified State secrets and anyone who prints or transmits such news or articles to others for the above purposes, shall be held responsible under the law relevant to these offences. Distribution may be suspended as a preventive measure by a decision of judge, or in the event delay is deemed prejudicial by the competent authority designated by law. The authority suspending distribution shall notify the competent judge of its decision within twenty-four hours at the latest. The order suspending distribution shall become null and void unless upheld by the competent judge within forty-eight hours at the latest.

No ban shall be placed on the reporting of events, except by a decision of judge issued to ensure proper functioning of the judiciary, within the limits to be specified by law.

Periodical and non-periodical publications may be seized by a decision of judge in cases of ongoing investigation or prosecution of offences prescribed by law; and, in situations where delay could endanger the indivisible integrity of the State with its territory and nation, national security, public order or public morals, and for the prevention of offence, by order of the competent authority designated by law. The authority issuing the seizure order shall notify the competent judge of its decision within twenty-four hours at the latest. The seizure order shall become null and void unless upheld by the competent court within forty-eight hours at the latest.

The general common provisions shall apply when seizure and confiscation of periodicals and non-periodicals for reasons of criminal investigation and prosecution take place.

Periodicals published in Turkey may be temporarily suspended by court sentence if found guilty of publishing material which contravenes the indivisible integrity of the State with its territory and nation, the fundamental principles of the Republic, national security and public morals. Any publication which clearly bears the characteristics of being the continuation of the suspended periodical is prohibited; and shall be seized by a decision of judge.

B. Right to Publish Periodicals and Non-periodicals

Article 29. Publication of periodicals or non-periodicals shall not be subject to prior authorisation or to the deposit of a financial guarantee.

To publish a periodical it shall suffice to submit the information and documents prescribed by law to the competent authority designated by law. If the information and documents submitted are found to be in contravention of law, the competent authority shall apply to the appropriate court for suspension of publication.

The publication of periodicals, the conditions of publication, the financial resources and rules relevant to the profession of journalism shall be regulated by law. The law shall not impose any political, economic, financial, and technical conditions obstructing or making difficult the free dissemination of news, thought, or beliefs.

Periodicals shall have equal access to the means and facilities of the State, other public corporate bodies, and their agencies.

C. Protection of Printing Facilities

Article 30. A printing press or its annexes duly established as a publishing house under law shall not be seized, confiscated, or barred from operation on the grounds of being an instrument of crime, except in cases where it is convicted of offences against the indivisible integrity of the State with its territory and nation, against the fundamental principles of the Republic or against national security.

D. Right to Use Mass Media Other Than the Press Which are Owned by Public Corporations

Article 31. Individuals and political parties have the right to use mass media and means of communication other than the Press owned by public corporations. The conditions and procedures for such use shall be regulated by law.

The law shall not impose restrictions preventing the public from receiving information or forming ideas and opinions through these media, or preventing public opinion from being freely formed, on grounds other then the general restrictions set forth in Article 13.

E. Right of Rectification and Reply

Article 32. The right of rectification and reply shall be accorded only in cases where personal reputation and honour is attacked or in cases of unfounded allegation and shall be regulated by law.

If a rectification or reply is not published, the judge will decide, within seven days of appeal by the individual involved, whether this publication is required.

XI. Rights and Freedoms of Assembly
A. Freedom of Association

Article 33. Everyone has the right to form associations without prior permission.

Submitting the information and documents stipulated by law to the competent authority designated by law shall suffice to enable an association to be formed. If the information and documents submitted are found to contravene the law, the competent authority shall apply to the appropriate court for the suspension of activities or dissolution of the association involved.

No one shall be compelled to become or remain a member of an association. The formalities, conditions, and procedures governing the exercise of freedom of association shall be prescribed by law.

Associations shall not contravene the general grounds of restriction in Article 13, nor shall they pursue political aims, engage in political activities, receive support from or give support to political parties, or take joint action with labour unions, with public professional organisations or with foundations.

Associations deviating from their original aims or conditions of establishment, or failing to fulfill the obligations stipulated by law shall be considered dissolved.

Associations may be dissolved by decision of a judge in cases prescribed by law. They may be suspended from activity by the competent authority designated by law pending a court decision in cases where delay endangers the indivisible integrity of the State with its territory and nation, national security or sovereignty, public order, the protection of the rights and freedoms of others, or the prevention of crime.

Provisions of the first paragraph of this Article shall not prevent imposition of restrictions on the rights of Armed Forces and Security Forces officials and civil servants to form associations, or the prohibition of the exercise of this right.

This article shall apply equally to foundations and other organisations of the same nature.

B. Right to Hold Meetings and Demonstration Marches

Article 34. Everyone has the right to hold unarmed and peaceful meetings and demonstration marches without prior permission.

The competent administrative authority may determine a site and route for the demonstration march in order to prevent disruption of order in urban life.

The formalities, conditions, and procedures governing the exercise of the right to hold meetings and demonstration marches, shall be prescribed by law.

The competent authority designated by law may prohibit a particular meeting and demonstration march, or postpone it for not more than two months in situations where there is a strong possibility that disturbances may arise which would seriously upset public order, where the requirement of national security may be violated, or where

acts aimed at destroying the fundamental characteristics of the Republic may be committed. In cases where the law forbids all meetings or demonstration marches in districts of a province for the same reasons, the postponement may not exceed three months.

Associations, foundations, labour unions, and public professional organisations shall not hold meetings or demonstration marches exceeding their own scope and aims.

XII. Right of Property

Article 35. Everyone has the right to own and inherit property.

These rights may be limited by law only in view of public interest.

The exercise of the right to own property shall not be in contravention of the public interest.

XIII. Provisions Relating to the Protection of Rights
A. Freedom to Claim Rights

Article 36. Everyone has the right of litigation either as plaintiff or defendant before the courts through lawful means and procedure.

No court shall refuse to hear a case within its jurisdiction.

B. Guarantee of Lawful Judge

Article 37. No one may be tried by any judicial authority other than the legally designated court.

Extraordinary tribunals with jurisdiction that would in effect remove a person from the jurisdiction of his legally designated court shall not be established.

C. Principles Relating to Offences and Penalties

Article 38. No one shall be punished for any act which did not constitute a criminal offence under the law in force at the time it was committed; no one shall be given a heavier penalty for an offence than the penalty applicable at the time when the offence was committed.

The provision of the above paragraph shall also apply to the statute of limitations as offences and penalties and on the results of conviction.

Penalties, and security measures in lieu of penalties, shall be prescribed only by law.

No one shall be held guilty until proven guilty in a court of law.

No one shall be compelled to make a statement that would incriminate himself or his legal next of kin, or to present such incriminating evidence.

Criminal responsibility shall be personal.

General confiscation shall not be imposed as penalty.

The Administration shall not impose any sanction resulting in restriction of personal liberty. Exceptions to this provision may be introduced by law regarding internal order of the Armed Forces.

No citizen shall be extradited to a foreign country on account of an offence.

XIV. Right to Prove an Allegation

Article 39. In libel and defamation suits involving allegations against persons in the public service in connection with their functions or services, the defendant has the right to prove the allegations. A plea for presenting proof shall not be granted in any other case unless proof would serve the public interest or unless the plaintiff consents.

XV. Protection of Fundamental Rights and Freedoms

Article 40. Everyone whose constitutional rights and freedoms are violated has the right to request prompt access to the competent authorities.

Damages incurred by any person through unlawful treatment by holders of public office shall be compensated by the State. The State reserves the right of recourse to the official responsible.

Chapter Three—Social and Economic Rights and Duties
I. Protection of the Family

Article 41. The family is the foundation of Turkish society.

The State shall take the necessary measures and establish the necessary organisation to ensure the peace and welfare of the family, especially the protection of the mother and children, and for family planning education and application.

II. Right and Duty of Training and Education

Article 42. No one shall be deprived of the right of learning and education.

The scope of the right to education shall be defined and regulated by law.

Training and education shall be conducted along the lines of the principles and reforms of Atatürk, on the basis of contemporary science and education methods, under the supervision and control of the State. Institutions of training and education contravening these provisions shall not be established.

The freedom of training and education does not relieve the individual from loyalty to the Constitution.

Primary Education is compulsory for all citizens of both sexes and is free of charge in State schools.

The principles governing the functioning of private primary and secondary schools shall be regulated by law in keeping with the standards set for State schools.

The State shall provide scholarships and other means of assistance to enable students of merit lacking financial means to continue their education. The State shall take necessary measures to rehabilitate those in need of special training so as to render such people useful to society.

Training, education, research, and study are the only activities that shall be pursued at institutions of training and education. These activities shall not be obstructed in any way.

No language other than Turkish shall be taught as mother tongue to Turkish citizens at any institutions of training or education. Foreign languages to be taught in institutions of training and education and the rules to be followed by schools conducting training and education in a foreign language shall be determined by law. The provisions of international treaties are reserved.

III. Public Interest
A. Utilisation of the Coasts

Article 43. The coasts are under the sovereignty and at the disposal of the State.

In the utilisation of the sea coast, lake shores or river banks, and of the coastal strip along the sea and lakes, public interest shall be taken into consideration with priority.

The width of coasts, and coastal strips to be determined according to the purpose of utilization, and the conditions and possibilities of such utilization by individuals shall be determined by law.

B. Land Ownership

Article 44. The State shall take the necessary measures to maintain and develop efficient land cultivation, to prevent its loss through erosion, and to provide land to farmers with insufficient land of their own, or no land. For this purpose, the law may define the size of appropriate land units, according to different agricultural regions and types of farming. Providing of land to farmers with no or insufficient land shall not lead to a fall in production, or to the depletion of forests and other land and underground resources.

Lands distributed for this purpose shall neither be divided nor be transferred to others, except through inheritance, and shall be cultivated only by farmers, to whom they have been distributed, and their heirs. The principles relating to the recovery by the State of the land thus distributed in the event of loss of these conditions shall be prescribed by law.

C. Protection of Agriculture, Animal Husbandry, and Persons Engaged in these Activities

Article 45. The State shall assist farmers and livestock breeders in acquiring machinery, equipment and other inputs in order to prevent improper use and destruction of agricultural land, meadows and pastures and to increase crop and livestock production in accordance with the principles of agricultural planning.

The State shall take necessary measures to promote the values of crop and livestock products, and to enable producers to be paid their real value.

D. Expropriation

Article 46. The State and public corporations shall be entitled, where the public interest requires it, to expropriate privately owned real estate wholly or in part or impose administrative servitude on it in accordance with the principles and procedures prescribed by law, provided that compensation is paid in advance.

The method and procedure for calculating compensation for expropriation shall be prescribed by law. In determining the compensation, the law shall take into account tax Declarations, current value established by official assessment at the time of expropriation, unit prices and construction costs for real estate, and other objective criteria. The procedure for taxing and difference between the sum due in compensation and the value declared in the tax declaration shall be prescribed by law.

Compensation shall be paid in cash and in advance. However, the procedure to be applied in paying compensation for land expropriated in order to carry out land reform, major energy and irrigation projects, and housing and resettlement schemes and afforestation, and to protect the coasts and to build tourist facilites shall be regulated by law. In the previous cases where the law may allow payment in instalments, the payment period shall not exceed five years; whence payment shall be made in equal instalments, and an interest rate equivalent to the highest interest paid on the public debt shall be paid for the remainder of instalments.

Compensation for land expropriated from the small farmer who cultivates his own land shall in all cases be paid in advance.

E. Nationalisation

Article 47. Private enterprises performing public service may be nationalised when this is required by the exigencies of public interest.

Nationalisation shall be carried out on the basis of real value. The methods and procedures for calculating real value shall be prescribed by law.

IV. Freedom to Work and Conclude Contracts

Article 48. Everyone has the freedom to work and conclude contracts in the field of his choice. The establishment of private enterprises is free.

The State shall take measures to ensure that private enterprises operate in accordance with national economic requirements and social objectives and in conditions of security and stability.

V. Provisions Relating to Labour
A. Right and Duty to Work

Article 49. Everyone has the right and duty to work.

The State shall take the necessary measures to raise the standard of living of workers, to protect them in order to improve the general conditions of labour, to promote labour, and to create suitable economic conditions for prevention of unemployment.

The State shall take facilitating and protecting measures in order to secure labour peace in worker-employer relations.

B. Working Conditions and Right to Rest and Leisure

Article 50. No one shall be required to perform work unsuited to his age, sex, and capacity.

Minors, women and persons with physical or mental disabilities, shall enjoy special protection with regard to working conditions.

All workers have the right to rest and leisure.

Rights and conditions relating to paid weekends and holidays, together with paid annual leave, shall be regulated by law.

C. Right to Organise Labour Unions

Article 51. Workers and employers have the right to form labour unions and employers' associations and higher organisations, without prior permission, in order to safeguard and develop their economic and social rights and the interests of their members in their labour relations.

In order to form unions and their higher bodies, it shall suffice to submit the information and documents prescribed by law to the competent authority designated by law. If this information and documentation is not in conformity with law, the competent authority shall apply to the appropriate court for the suspension of activities or the dissolution of the union or the higher body.

Everyone shall be free to become a member of or withdraw from membership in a union.

No one shall be compelled to become a member, remain a member, or withdraw from membership of a union.

Workers and employers cannot hold concurrent memberships in more than one labour union or employers' association.

Employment in a given work-place shall not be made conditional on being, or not being a member of a labour union.

To become an executive in a labour union or in higher

organisations of them it is a prerequisite condition that the worker should have held the status of a labourer for at least ten years.

The status, the administration, and the functioning of the labour unions and their higher bodies should not be inconsistent with the characteristics of the Republic as defined in the Constitution, or with democratic principles.

D. Activities of Labour Unions

Article 52. Labour Unions, in addition to being under the general restrictions set forth in Article 13, also shall not pursue a political cause, engage in political activity, receive support from political parties or give support to them, and shall not act jointly for these purposes with associations public professional organisations, and foundations.

The fact of engaging in labour union activities in a work-place shall not justify failure to perform one's work.

The administrative and financial supervision of labour unions by the State, and their revenues and expenditures, and the method of payment of membership dues to the labour union, shall be regulated by law.

Labour Unions shall not use their revenues beyond the scope of their professional aims, and shall keep all their funds in State banks.

VI. Collective Bargaining, Right to Strike, and Lockout
A. Right of Collective Bargaining

Article 53. Workers and employers have the right to conclude collective bargaining agreements in order to regulate reciprocally their economic and social position and conditions of work.

The procedure to be followed in concluding collective bargaining agreements shall be regulated by law.

More than one collective bargaining agreement at the same place of work for the same period shall not be concluded or put into effect.

B. Right to Strike, and Lockout

Article 54. Workers have the right to strike if a dispute arises during the collective bargaining process. The procedures and conditions governing the exercise of this right and the employer's recourse to a lockout, the scope of both actions, and the exceptions to which they are subject shall be regulated by law.

The right to strike, and lockout shall not be exercised in a manner contrary to the principle of goodwill to the detriment of society, and in a manner damaging national weath.

During a strike, the labour union is liable for any material damage caused in a work-place where the strike is being held, as a result of deliberate negligent behaviour by the workers and the labour union.

The circumstances and places in which strikes and lockouts may be prohibited or postponed shall be regulated by law.

In cases where a strike or a lockout is prohibited or postponed, the dispute shall be settled by the Supreme Arbitration Board at the end of the period of postponement. The disputing parties may apply to the Supreme Arbitration Board by mutual agreement at any stage of the dispute.

The decisions of the Supreme Arbitration Board shall be final and have the force of a collective bargaining agreement.

The organisation and functions of the Supreme Arbitration Board shall be regulated by law.

Politically motivated strikes and lockouts, solidarity

strikes and lockouts, occupation of work premises, labour go-slows, production decreasing, and other forms of obstruction are prohibited.

Those who refuse to go on strike, shall in no way be barred from working at their work-place by strikers.

VII. Guarantee of Fair Wage

Article 55. Wages shall be paid in return for work.

The State shall take the necessary measures to ensure that workers earn a fair wage suitable for the work they perform and that they enjoy other social benefits.

In determining the minimum wage, the economic and social conditions of the country shall be taken into account.

VIII. Health, the Environment and Housing
A. Health Services and Conservation of the Environment

Article 56. Everyone has the right to live in a healthy, balanced environment.

It is the duty of the State and the citizens to improve the natural environment, and to prevent environmental pollution.

To ensure that everyone lead their lives in conditions of physical and mental health and to secure cooperation in terms of human and material resources through economy and increased productivity, the State shall regulate central planning and functioning of the health services.

The State shall fulfill this task by utilizing and supervising the health and social assistance institutions, in both the public and private sectors.

In order to establish widespread health services general health insurance may be introduced by law.

B. Right to Housing

Article 57. The State shall take measures to meet the needs for housing, within the framework of a plan which takes into account the characteristics of cities and environmental conditions and supports community housing projects.

IX. Youth and Sport
A. Protection of Youth

Article 58. The State shall take measures to ensure the training and development of youth into whose keeping our State, independence, and our Republic are entrusted, in the light of contemporary science, in line with the principles and reforms of Atatürk, and in opposition to ideas aiming at the destruction of the indivisible integrity of the State with its territory and nation.

The State shall take necessary measures to protect youth from addiction to alcohol, drug addiction, crime, gambling, and similar vices, and ignorance.

B. Development of Sports.

Article 59. The State shall take measures to develop the physical and mental health of Turkish citizens of all ages, and encourage the spread of sports among the masses.

The State shall protect successful athletes.

X. Social Security Rights
A. Right to Social Security

Article 60. Everyone has the right to social security.

The State shall take the necessary measures and establish the organisation for the provision of social security.

B. Persons Requiring Special Protection in the Field of Social Security

Article 61. The State shall protect the widows and orphans of those killed in war and in the line of duty, together with the disabled and war veterans, and ensure that they enjoy a decent standard of living.

The State shall take measures to protect the disabled and secure their integration into community life.

The aged shall be protected by the State. State assistance to the aged, and other rights and benefits shall be regulated by law.

The State shall take all kinds of measures for social resettlement of children in need of protection.

To achieve these aims the State shall establish the necessary organisations or facilities, or arrange for their establishment by other bodies.

C. Turkish Nationals Working Abroad

Article 62. The State shall take the necessary measures to ensure the family unity, the education of the children, the cultural needs, and the social security of Turkish nationals working abroad, and shall take the necessary measures to safeguard their ties with the country, and to help them on their return home.

XI. Conservation of Historical, Cultural and Natural Wealth

Article 63. The State shall ensure the conservation of the historical, cultural and natural assets and wealth, and shall take supporting and promoting measures towards this end.

Any limitations to be imposed on such assets and wealth which are privately owned, and the compensation and exemptions to be accorded to the owners of such, as a result of these limitations, shall be regulated by law.

XII. Protection of Arts and Artists

Article 64. The State shall protect artistic activities and artists. The State shall take the necessary measures to protect, promote and support works of art and artists, and encourage the spread of art appreciation.

XIII. The Extent of Social and Economic Rights

Article 65. The State shall fulfill its duties as laid down in the Constitution in the social and economic fields, within the limits of its financial resources, taking into consideration the maintenance of economic stability.

Chapter Four—Political Rights and Duties
I. Turkish Citizenship

Article 66. Everyone bound to the Turkish State through the bond of citizenship is a Turk.

The child of a Turkish father or a Turkish mother is a Turk. The citizenship of a child of a foreign father and a Turkish mother shall be defined by law.

Citizenship can be acquired under the conditions stipulated by law, and shall be forfeited only in cases determined by law.

No Turk shall be deprived of citizenship, unless he commits an act incompatible with loyalty to the motherland.

Recourse to the courts, against the decisions and proceedings related to the deprivation of citizenship, shall not be denied.

II. Right to Vote, to be Elected and to Engage in Political Activity

Article 67. In conformity with the conditions set forth in the law, citizens have the right to vote, to be elected, and to engage in political activities independently or in a political party, and to take part in a referendum.

Elections and referendums shall be held under the direction and supervision of the judiciary, according to the principles of free, equal, secret, direct, universal suffrage, and public counting of the votes.

All Turkish citizens over 21 years of age shall have the right to vote in elections and to take part in a referendum.

The exercise of these rights shall be regulated by law.

Privates and corporals serving in the Armed Services, students in military schools, and detainees and convicts in prisons cannot vote.

III. Provisions Relating to Political Parties
A. Forming Parties, Membership, and Withdrawal From Membership in a Party

Article 68. Citizens have the right to form political parties, and to join and withdraw from them in accordance with the established procedure. To become a member of a party one must be over 21 years of age.

Political parties are indispensable elements of the democratic political system.

Political parties shall be founded without prior permission and shall pursue their activities in accordance with the provisions set forth in the Constitution and law.

The statutes and programmes of political parties shall not be in conflict with the indivisible integrity of the State with its territory and nation, human rights, national sovereignty, and the principles of the democratic and secular Republic.

Political parties whose aim is to support and to set up the domination of a class or group, or any kind of dictatorship cannot be formed.

Political parties shall not organise and function abroad, shall not form discriminative auxiliary bodies such as women's or youth branches, nor shall they establish foundations.

Judges and prosecutors, members of higher judicial organs, members of the teaching staff at institutions of higher education, members of the Higher Education Council, civil servants in public organisations and corporations, and other public servants who are not considered to be labourers by virtue of the services they perform, students, and members of the Armed Forces, shall not become members of political parties.

B. Principles to be Observed by Political Parties

Article 69. Political parties shall not engage in activities outside the lines of their statutes and programmes, and shall not contravene the restrictions set forth in Article 14 of the Constitution; those that contravene them shall be dissolved permanently.

Political parties shall not have political ties and engage in political cooperation with associations, unions foundations, cooperatives, and public professional organisations and their higher bodies in order to implement and strengthen their party policies, nor shall they receive material assistance from these bodies.

The internal functioning and the decisions of political parties shall not be contrary to the principles of democracy.

The auditing of political parties shall be carried out by the Constitutional Court.

The Office of the Chief Public Prosecutor shall examine, with priority, the conformity of the statues and programmes of new parties and of the status of their founders in view of the Constitution and the law; and shall also follow their activities.

The dissolution of political parties shall be decided the Constitutional Court after the filing of a suit by the Office of the Chief Public Prosecutor of the Republic.

The founding members and administrators at every level of a political party which has been permanently dissolved shall not become founding members administrators, or comptrollers of a new political party; nor shall any new political party be founded, the majority of whose members are former members of a political party previously dissolved.

Political parties shall not receive assistance in kind or cash from foreign States, international organisations, associations and groups in foreign contries, nor shall they take orders from these bodies, or participate in their decisions and activities which are prejudicial to the independence and territorial integrity of Turkey. Political parties contravening the provisions of this paragraph shall also be dissolved permanently.

The formulation and activities, supervision, and dissolution of political parties shall be regulated by law within the above-mentioned provisions.

IV. Right to Enter the Public Service
A. Entry into the Public Service

Article 70. Every Turk has the right to enter the public service.

No criteria other than the qualifications for the office concerned shall be taken into consideration for recruitment into the public service.

B. Declaration of Assets

Article 71. Declaration of assets by persons entering public service, and the frequently of such declaration, shall be determined by law. Those serving in the legislative and executive organs shall not be exempted from this requirement.

V. National Service

Article 72. National service is the right and duty of every Turk. The manner in which this service shall be performed, or considered as performed, either in the Armed Forces or in the public service shall be regulated by law.

VI. Obligation to pay Taxes

Article 73. Everyone is under the obligation to pay taxes according to his financial resources, in order to meet public expenditures.

An equitable and balanced distribution of the tax burden is the social objective of fiscal policy.

Taxes, fees, duties, and other such financial impositions shall be imposed, amended, or revoked by law.

The Council of Ministers may be empowered to amend the percentages of exemption, exceptions and reductions in taxes, fees, duties and other such financial impositions, within the minimum and maximum limits prescribed by law.

VII. Right of Petition

Article 74. Citizens have the right to apply in writing to the competent authorities and to the Grand National Assembly of Turkey with regard to requests and complaints concerning themselves or the public.

The result of the application concerning himself shall be made known to the petitioner in writing.

The way of exercising this right shall be determined by law.

U

UGANDA. The Republic of Uganda is a country in eastern Africa, on the equator. It has borders with Kenya, Rwanda, Sudan, Tanzania, and Zaire. It achieved independence from Great Britain in 1962 and became a member of the United Nations in 1963. Its population is estimated by the UN (1990) to be 18,426,000. Ethnic groups include the Baganda, from which the country derived its name; Africans of the Hamitic, Milotic, and Sudanese groups; and Congo Pygmies. Languages commonly used include English (official), Swahili, Lugando, Ateso, Luo, and many regional vernaculars. Religions practiced include Christianity (63%), Islam (6%), Animism and other indigenous beliefs (31%). Literacy is estimated at 52%.

The government (1990) took the form of a republic and member of the Commonwealth of Nations, of which the British monarch is the symbolic head. Under the constitution, embodied in the Uganda (Independence) Order in Council, 1962, the crown-appointed governor-general was replaced by a popularly elected president as head of State. Sir Edward Mutesa, the first president, appointed Milton Obote as prime minister; but, four years later, in 1966, Obote seized control of the government with the help of an army officer, Col. Idi Amin. Col. Amin, in turn, deposed President Obote on 25 January 1971.

The period between January 1971 and April 1979, during which Uganda was under military rule, witnessed a dramatic deterioration in race and ethnic relations. The most notable manifestation of discrimination during that period was the expulsion of the people of Asian origin, many of whom were citizens of Uganda, and the expropriation of their properties without due compensation. A drastic reduction of the American/European population occurred during the same period. Furthermore, the military regime, by its policy of divide and rule, engendered deep ethnic divisions within the country. Apart from the effects of general destruction of the economy, ethnicity became a major factor in determining economic benefits and the provision of social services.

Idi Amin, a ruthless dictator who in 1976 had himself proclaimed "President for Life," conducted a systematic reign of terror and torture against his opponents in Uganda, resulting in an estimated 300,000 deaths. He was forced into exile in 1979 by troops from neighboring Tanzania, aided by Ugandans loyal to former President Obote, who successfully invaded the country.

Obote, who had sought refuge in Tanzania, returned to Uganda and led his People's Congress Party to victory in elections held in December 1980. His government announced its commitment to the restoration of constitutionality, the rule and due process of law, and the observance and guarantee of human rights and fundamental freedoms.

However, as time passed, the Obote regime gradually resumed, and even intensified, the massive abuses which had occurred under Amin, including massacres reported by the U.S. government in 1984 to be "among the most grave in the world." The massacres, denied by Obote, were not widely reported in the information media and did not arouse international outrage at the time.

Obote was deposed by army troops on 27 July 1985, at which time Lieut.-Gen. Tito Okello assumed the presidency. However, the Okello regime proved unable to exercise control over its own troops, including elements of Idi Amin's armed forces, who continued to terrorize Ugandan citizens in an orgy of killing, arson, rape, and looting.

The National Resistance Army, composed of some 10,000 teenaged guerrillas, had taken control of the southwestern third of Uganda over the previous six months of fighting; and its 41-year-old leader, Yoweri Museveni, refused to accept a post in the Okello regime unless the behavior of the government troops was curbed. A ceasefire agreement was arranged between the Resistance Army and the government troops but never came into effect. Late in January 1986, the Resistance guerrillas moved northward and seized control of Kampala after heavy street fighting, winning praise and respect for its disciplined and humane behavior, particularly as contrasted with the brutality which had resulted in the death of more than half a million Ugandan citizens in the preceding two decades.

Museveni, installed as president after the collapse of the Okello regime, characterized the seizure of power not as "a mere change of guards" but rather as "a fundamental change in the politics of our Government." He vowed to strive for a unified government, free of tribal rivalries, stressed that "no regime has the right to kill any citizen of Uganda," and referred to the military officers he had overthrown as "criminals." Claiming to have modelled his guerrilla campaign after that of Cuba's Fidel Castro, he insisted that he was a nationalist and not a communist. Admitting that he had been "compelled by circumstances" to accept arms aid from Libya," he denied that he was a "tool" of Libyan leader Col. Muammar el-Qaddafi.

UKRAINIAN S.S.R. The Ukrainian Soviet Socialist Republic is a constituent unit of the UNION OF SOVIET SOCIALIST REPUBLICS. It has borders with the Byelorussian S.S.R., Czechoslovakia, Hungary, the Moldavian S.S.R., Poland, and Romania. In accordance with an agreement reached before the preparation of the United Nations Charter, the Ukrainian S.S.R. became a member of the United Nations in its own right in 1945. Ethnic and national groups include Ukrainians (73%); Russians (21%); Jews (2%); Byelorussians (1%); and Moldavians, Poles, Bulgarians, and others totalling (3%). Languages in common use include Ukrainian and Russian; members of national minorities tend to use their own language in private. Atheism predominates, and anti-religious propaganda and activity occurs. Among those who maintain a religious belief, Christianity (Russian Orthodox, Greek Orthodox, Roman Catholic, Western Ukrainian Uniate, and several Protestant denominations), and Judaism have the most adherents. The Church is separated from the State and the school from the Church.

The government (1990) took the form of a republic within the Union of Soviet Socialist Republics. Under article 12 of its constitution, the Supreme Soviet of the Ukrainian S.S.R. is the highest body of State authority; it is empowered to deal with all matters within the jurisdiction of the republic, to amend its constitution, to approve plans for its economic and social development, and to approve the State budget. It consists of 650 deputies elected by constituencies with equal populations and is convened twice a year. Its presidium, a standing body of 25 members, has many procedural and substantive functions, such as setting dates for elections, interpreting the laws of the republic, granting Ukrainian citizenship, and ratifying or denouncing international treaties.

For provisions of the constitution which relate to human rights, see UKRAINIAN S.S.R.: CONSTITUTION. For detailed information on changes in the law and practice of the Soviet Union as a whole affecting the realization of civil, political, and other human rights and fundamental freedoms, see UNION OF SOVIET SOCIALIST REPUBLICS: IMPLEMENTATION OF THE INTERNATIONAL COVENANT ON CIVIL AND POLITICAL RIGHTS.

Within the Ukrainian S.S.R., one important change was reflected in the forced resignation in February 1990 of several Communist Party and government officials charged with having enjoyed special medical care, housing, and distribution of food and consumer goods not available to the general public; the founding and registration of a rival political party, the Rukh Popular Front; and the participation of Rukh candidates in election contests for 130 of the 150 seats in the Ukrainian Supreme Soviet.

UKRAINIAN S.S.R.: CONSTITUTION. The constitution (fundamental law) of the Ukrainian Soviet Socialist Republic includes the following provisions (articles 31–67) specifically relating to human rights and fundamental freedoms:

Chapter 5
Citizenship of the Ukrainian SSR.
Equality of Citizens' Rights

Article 31. In accordance with uniform federal citizenship established in the USSR, every citizen of the Ukrainian SSR is a citizen of the USSR.

The grounds and procedure for acquiring or forfeiting Soviet citizenship are defined by the Law on Citizenship of the USSR.

Citizens of other Union republics enjoy equal rights with citizens of the Ukrainian SSR throughout the Ukrainian SSR.

When abroad, citizens of the Ukrainian SSR enjoy the protection and assistance of the Soviet state.

Article 32. Citizens of the Ukrainian SSR are equal before the law, without distinction of origin, social or property status, race or nationality, sex, education, language, attitude to religion, type and nature of occupation, domicile, or other status.

The equal rights of the citizens of the Ukrainian SSR are guaranteed in all fields of economic, political, social, and cultural life.

Article 33. Women and men have equal rights in the Ukrainian SSR.

Exercise of these rights is ensured by according women equal access with men to education and vocational and professional training, equal opportunities in employment, remuneration, and promotion, and in social and political, and cultural activity, and by special labour and health protection measures for women; by providing conditions enabling mothers to work; by legal protection, and material and moral support for mothers and children, including paid leaves and other benefits for expectant mothers and mothers, and gradual reduction of working time for mothers with small children.

Article 34. Citizens of the Ukrainian SSR of different races and nationalities have equal rights.

Exercise of these rights is ensured by a policy of all-round development and drawing together of all the nations and nationalities of the USSR, by educating citizens in the spirit of Soviet patriotism and socialist internationalism, and by the possibility to use their native language and the languages of other peoples of the USSR.

Any direct or indirect limitation of the rights of citizens or establishment of direct or indirect privileges on grounds of race or nationality, and any advocacy of racial or national exclusiveness, hostility or contempt, are punishable by law.

Article 35. Citizens of other countries and stateless persons in the Ukrainian SSR are guaranteed the rights and freedoms provided by law, including the right to apply to a court and other state bodies for the protection of their personal, property, family, and other rights.

Citizens of other countries and stateless persons, when in the Ukrainian SSR, are obliged to respect the Constitution of the USSR, the Constitution of the Ukrainian SSR and observe Soviet laws.

Article 36. The Ukrainian SSR grants the right of asylum to foreigners persecuted for defending the interests of the working people and the cause of peace, or for participation in the revolutionary and national-liberation movement, or for progressive social and political, scientific or other creative activity.

Chapter 6
The Basic Rights, Freedoms, and Duties
of Citizens of the Ukrainian SSR

Article 37. Citizens of the Ukrainian SSR enjoy in full the social, economic, political and personal rights and freedoms proclaimed and guaranteed by the Constitution of the USSR, the Constitution of the Ukrainian SSR and by Soviet laws. The socialist system ensures enlargement of the rights and freedoms of citizens and continuous improvement of their living standards as social, economic, and cultural development programmes are fulfilled.

Enjoyment by citizens of their rights and freedoms must not be to the detriment of the interests of society or the state, or infringe the rights of other citizens.

Article 38. Citizens of the Ukrainian SSR have the right to work (that is, to guaranteed employment and pay in accordance with the quantity and quality of their work, and not below the state-established minimum), including the right to choose their trade or profession, type of job and work in accordance with their inclinations, abilities, training and education, with due account of the needs of society.

This right is ensured by the socialist economic system, steady growth of the productive forces, free vocational and professional training, improvement of skills, training in new trades or professions, and development of the systems of vocational guidance and job placement.

Article 39. Citizens of the Ukrainian SSR have the right to rest and leisure.

This right is ensured by the establishment of a working week not exceeding 41 hours, for workers and other employees, a shorter working day in a number of trades and industries, and shorter hours for night work; by the provision of paid annual holidays, weekly days of rest, extension of the network of cultural, educational and health-building institutions, and the development on a mass scale of sport, physical culture, and camping and tourism; by the provision of neighbourhood recreational facilities, and of other opportunities for rational use of free time.

The length of collective farmers' working and leisure time is established by their collective farms.

Article 40. Citizens of the Ukrainian SSR have the right to health protection.

This right is ensured by free, qualified medical care provided by state health institutions; by extension of the network of therapeutic and health-building institutions; by the development and improvement of safety and hygiene in industry; by carrying out broad prophylactic measures; by measures to improve the environment; by special care for the health of the rising generation, including prohibition of child labour, except for the work done by children as a part of the school curriculum; and by developing research to prevent and reduce the incidence of disease and ensure citizens a long and active life.

Article 41. Citizens of the Ukrainian SSR have the right to maintenance in old age, in sickness, and in the event of complete or partial disability or loss of the breadwinner.

This right is guaranteed by social insurance of workers and other employees and collective farmers, by allowances for temporary disability; by the provision by the state or by collective farms of retirement pensions, disability pensions, and pensions for loss of the breadwinner; by providing employment for the partially disabled; by care for the elderly and the disabled; and by other forms of social security.

Article 42. Citizens of the Ukrainian SSR have the right to housing.

This right is ensured by the development and upkeep of state and socially-owned housing; by assistance for cooperative and individual house building; by fair distribution, under public control, of the housing that becomes available through fulfilment of the programme of building well-appointed dwellings, and by low rents and low charges for utility services. Citizens of the Ukrainian SSR shall take good care of the housing allocated to them.

Article 43. Citizens of the Ukrainian SSR have the right to education.

This right is ensured by free provision of all forms of education, by the institution of universal, compulsory secondary education, and broad development of vocational, specialized secondary, and higher education, in which instruction is oriented toward practical activity and production; by the development of correspondence and evening courses; by the provision of state scholarships and grants and privileges for students; by the free issue of school textbooks; by the opportunity to attend a school where teaching is in the native language; and by the provision of facilities for self-education.

Article 44. Citizens of the Ukrainian SSR have the right to enjoy cultural benefits.

This right is ensured by broad access to the cultural treasures of their own land and of the world that are preserved in state and other public collections; by the development and fair distribution of cultural and educational institutions; by developing television and radio broadcasting and the publishing of books, newspapers and periodicals, and by extending the free library service; and by expanding cultural exchanges with other countries.

Article 45. Citizens of the Ukrainian SSR, in accordance with the aims of building communism, are guaranteed freedom of scientific, technical, and artistic work. This freedom is ensured by broadening scientific research, encouraging invention and innovation, and developing literature and the arts. The state provides the necessary material conditions for this and support for voluntary societies and unions of workers in the arts, organizes introduction of inventions and innovations in production and other spheres of activity.

The rights of authors, inventors and innovators are protected by the state.

Article 46. Citizens of the Ukrainian SSR have the right to take part in the management and administration of state and public affairs and in the discussion and adoption of laws and decisions of all-Union and local significance.

This right is ensured by the opportunity to vote and to be elected to Soviets of People's Deputies and other elective state bodies, to take part in nationwide discussions and referendums, in people's control, in the work of state bodies, public organizations, and local community groups, and in meetings at places of work or residence.

Article 47. Every citizen of the Ukrainian SSR has the right to submit proposals to state bodies and public organizations for improving their activity, and to criticize shortcomings in their work.

Officials are obliged, within established time-limits, to examine citizens' proposals and requests, to reply to them, and to take appropriate action.

Persecution for criticism is prohibited. Persons guilty of such persecution shall be called to account.

Article 48. In accordance with the interests of the people and in order to strengthen and develop the socialist system, citizens of the Ukrainian SSR are guaranteed freedom of speech, of the press, and of assembly, meetings, street processions and demonstrations.

Exercise of these political freedoms is ensured by putting public buildings, streets and squares at the disposal of the working people and their organizations, by broad dissemination of information, and by the opportunity to use the press, television, and radio.

Article 49. In accordance with the aims of building communism, citizens of the Ukrainian SSR have the right to associate in public organizations that promote their political activity and initiative and satisfaction of their various interests.

Public organizations are guaranteed conditions for successfully performing the functions defined in their rules.

Article 50. Citizens of the Ukrainian SSR are guaranteed freedom of conscience, that is, the right to profess or not to profess any religion, and to conduct religious worship or atheistic propaganda. Incitement of hostility or hatred on religious grounds is prohibited.

In the Ukrainian SSR, the church is separated from the state, and the school from the church.

Article 51. The family enjoys the protection of the state.

Marriage is based on the free consent of the woman and the man; the spouses are completely equal in their family relations.

The state helps the family by providing and developing a broad system of child-care institutions, by organizing and improving communal services and public catering, by paying grants on the birth of a child, by providing children's allowances and benefits for large families, and other forms of family allowances and assistance.

Article 52. Citizens of the Ukrainian SSR are guaranteed inviolability of the person. No one may be arrested except by a court decision or on the warrant of a procurator.

Article 53. Citizens of the Ukrainian SSR are guaranteed inviolability of the home. No one may, without lawful grounds, enter a home against the will of those residing in it.

Article 54. The privacy of citizens, and of their correspondence, telephone conversations, and telegraphic communications is protected by law.

Article 55. Respect for the individual and protection of the rights and freedoms of citizens are the duty of all state bodies, public organizations, and officials.

Citizens of the Ukrainian SSR have the right to protection by the courts against encroachments on their honour and reputation, life and health, and personal freedom and property.

Article 56. Citizens of the Ukrainian SSR have the right to lodge a complaint against the actions of officials, state bodies and public bodies. Complaints shall be examined according to the procedure and within the time-limit established by law.

Actions by officials that contravene the law or exceed their powers, and infringe the rights of citizens, may be appealed against in a court in the manner prescribed by law.

Citizens of the Ukrainian SSR have the right to compensation for damage resulting from unlawful actions by state organizations and public organizations, or by officials in the performance of their duties.

Article 57. Citizens' exercise of their rights and freedoms is inseparable from the performance of their duties and obligations.

Citizens of the Ukrainian SSR are obliged to observe the Constitution of the USSR, the Constitution of the Ukrainian SSR and Soviet laws, comply with the standards of socialist conduct, and uphold the honour and dignity of Soviet citizens.

Article 58. It is the duty of, and a matter of honour for, every able-bodied citizen of the Ukrainian SSR to work conscientiously in his chosen, socially useful occupation, and strictly to observe labour discipline. Evasion of socially useful work is incompatible with the principles of socialist society.

Article 59. Citizens of the Ukrainian SSR are obliged to preserve and protect socialist property. It is the duty of a citizen of the Ukrainian SSR to combat misappropriation and squandering of state and socially-owned property and to make thrifty use of the people's wealth.

Persons encroaching in any way on socialist property shall be punished according to the law.

Article 60. Citizens of the Ukrainian SSR are obliged to safeguard the interests of the Soviet state, and to enhance its power and prestige.

Defence of the Socialist Motherland is the sacred duty of every citizen of the Ukrainian SSR.

Betrayal of the Motherland is the gravest of crimes against the people.

Article 61. Military service in the ranks of the Armed Forces of the USSR is an honourable duty of citizens of the Ukrainian SSR.

Article 62. It is the duty of every citizen of the Ukrainian SSR to respect the national dignity of other citizens, and to strengthen friendship of the nations and nationalities of the multinational Soviet state.

Article 63. A citizen of the Ukrainian SSR is obliged to respect the rights and lawful interests of other persons, to be uncompromising toward anti-social behaviour, and to help maintain public order.

Article 64. Citizens of the Ukrainian SSR are obliged to concern themselves with the upbringing of children, to train them for socially useful work, and to raise them as worthy members of socialist society. Children are obliged to care for their parents and help them.

Article 65. Citizens of the Ukrainian SSR are obliged to protect nature and conserve its riches.

Article 66. Concern for the preservation of historical

monuments and other cultural values is a duty and obligation of citizens of the Ukrainian SSR.

Article 67. It is the internationalist duty of citizens of the Ukrainian SSR to promote friendship and cooperation with the peoples of other lands and help maintain and strengthen world peace.

UNEMPLOYMENT. In a report to the 1986 session of the UN General Assembly (UN Doc. A/41/472), transmitting the views of governments regarding the proposal to promote a new international humanitarian order, the Secretary-General included a "Survey on Specific Humanitarian Issues in the Contemporary World" based on information solicited or collected from specialized agencies and other bodies within the United Nations system. The survey was prepared at the request of the assembly (resolution 40/126) within the United Nations Secretariat and, in appropriate instances, in consultation with the organizations directly concerned.

Section D of the survey (para. 23–27), entitled "Massive Unemployment," reads as follows:

Unemployment across the world has grown enormously in recent years. In many low-income countries much of what had been underemployment of one kind or another has turned into open unemployment, in some countries rising to well over 20 per cent of the economically active population. In many industrialized countries the era of "full employment" of the 1950s and 1960s has passed, with seemingly chronically high levels being reached in large parts of Western Europe. Only in South-East Asia has unemployment remained low and in a very few countries it has fallen steadily in recent years.

As for the unemployed themselves, youths have attracted most attention; in some countries the unemployment rates for teenagers have exceeded 40 per cent. Even harder hit have been minority groups, such as coloured ethnic groups and immigrants. In southern Africa the majority group has borne the brunt of unemployment, but that is a special case.

Evidence on the incidence of unemployment among men and women is mixed, for in some countries employment of women has been growing, while employment of men has been shrinking. Nevertheless, taking due account of "discouraged workers", unemployment of women in many economies has been chronically high, and many unemployed women have had no other regular source of income to meet their own needs, or those of their children or other relatives.

Finally, there has been the growing phenomenon of older-worker unemployment. Already a majority of the world's population aged over 55 are in low-income countries; there and in many industrialized countries unemployment among older workers has grown massively in recent years, and in many cases workers in their 50s, once unemployed, become permanent rejects from the labour force, demoralized, increasingly prone to acute poverty, ill health and early death.

Co-ordinated international action is required to tackle global unemployment. Most countries that have tried to stimulate their economies in order to boost employment have found it impossible to sustain such efforts in the face of worsening import penetration and balance-of-payments crises. Co-ordinated actions by groups of trading partners are needed, coupled with measures to control inflation that do not place the burden of price changes on the unemployed. A more humanitarian method must be found of checking inflation and maintaining economic growth than the costly and tragic recipe of mass unemployment. It is a matter of human will and a matter of recognizing that the social malaise represented by unemployment deserves to be given very high priority in policy formulation. It is precisely because the unemployed have no effective lobby group working to protect their interest that national politicians and the international community have a special responsibility to work on their behalf.

SEE ALSO *Work.*

UNESCO. *SEE United Nations Educational, Scientific and Cultural Organization.*

UNESCO AGREEMENT ON THE IMPORTATION OF EDUCATIONAL, SCIENTIFIC AND CULTURAL MATERIALS, AND ANNEXED PROTOCOL (1950). The so-called "Florence Agreement" and its annexed protocol were adopted by the UNESCO GENERAL CONFERENCE (fifth session), held in Florence, Italy, on 1 June 1950, and were opened for signature at Lake Success, NY, on 22 November 1950. They were supplemented in 1976 by the UNESCO protocol to the Agreement on the Importation of Educational, Scientific and Cultural Materials.

Under the Florence Agreement, contracting States undertake to abolish customs duties and to remove any trade barriers which impede international exchanges of a number of items, including books, publications, and documents, and other educational, scientific, or cultural materials listed in Annexes A to E. They further undertake to grant licenses and foreign exchange to facilitate the importation of books and publications from other countries and from the United Nations or any of its specialized agencies, and articles designed for the educational, scientific, or cultural advancement of the blind.

The text of the agreement and of the annexed protocol (*UNESCO's Standard-Setting Instruments*, No. IV.A.2) are as follows:

Preamble

The contracting States,

Considering that the free exchange of ideas and knowledge and, in general, the widest possible dissemination of the diverse forms of self-expression used by civilizations are vitally important both for intellectual progress and international understanding, and consequently for the maintenance of world peace;

Considering that this interchange is accomplished primarily by means of books, publications and educational, scientific and cultural materials;

Considering that the Constitution of the United Nations Educational, Scientific and Cultural Organization urges cooperation between nations in all branches of intellectual activity, including 'the exchange of publications, objects of artistic and scientific interest and other materials of information' and provides further that the Organization shall 'collaborate in the work of advancing the mutual knowledge and understanding of peoples, through all means of mass communication and to that end recommend such international agreements as may be necessary to promote the free flow of ideas by word and image';

Recognize that these aims will be effectively furthered by an international agreement facilitating the free flow of books, publications and educational, scientific and cultural materials; and

Have, therefore, agreed to the following provisions:

Article 1. 1. The contracting States undertake not to apply customs duties or other charges on, or in connexion with, the importation of:

(a) Books, publications and documents, listed in Annex A to this Agreement;

(b) Educational, scientific and cultural materials, listed in Annexes B, C, D and E to this Agreement;

which are the products of another contracting State, subject to the conditions laid down in those annexes.

2. The provisions of paragraph 1 of this article shall not prevent any contracting State from levying on imported materials:

(a) Internal taxes or any other internal charges of any kind, imposed at the time of importation or subsequently, not exceeding those applied directly or indirectly to like domestic products;

(b) Fees and charges, other than customs duties, imposed by governmental authorities on, or in connexion with, importation, limited in amount to the approximate cost of the services rendered, and representing neither an indirect protection to domestic products nor a taxation of imports for revenue purposes.

Article 2. 1. The contracting States undertake to grant the necessary licences and/or foreign exchange for the importation of the following articles:

(a) Books and publications consigned to public libraries and collections and to the libraries and collections of public, educational, research or cultural institutions;

(b) Official government publications, that is, official, parliamentary and administrative documents published in their country of origin;

(c) Books and publications of the United Nations or any of its Specialized Agencies;

(d) Books and publications received by the United Nations Educational, Scientific and Cultural Organization and distributed free of charge by it or under its supervision;

(e) Publications intended to promote tourist travel outside the country of importation, sent and distributed free of charge;

(f) Articles for the blind:

(i) Books, publications and documents of all kinds in raised characters for the blind;

(ii) Other articles specially designed for the educational, scientific or cultural advancement of the blind, which are imported directly by institutions or organizations

concerned with the welfare of the blind, approved by the competent authorities of the importing country for the purpose of duty-free entry of these types of articles.

2. The contracting States which at any time apply quantitative restrictions and exchange control measures undertake to grant, as far as possible, foreign exchange and licences necessary for the importation of other educational, scientific or cultural materials, and particularly the materials referred to in the annexes to this Agreement.

Article 3. 1. The contracting States undertake to give every possible facility to the importation of educational, scientific or cultural materials, which are imported exclusively for showing at a public exhibition approved by the competent authorities of the importing country and for subsequent re-exportation. These facilities shall include the granting of the necessary licences and exemption from customs duties and internal taxes and charges of all kinds payable on importation, other than fees and charges corresponding to the approximate cost of services rendered.

2. Nothing in this article shall prevent the authorities of an importing country from taking such steps as may be necessary to ensure that the materials in question shall be re-exported at the close of their exhibition.

Article 4. The contracting States undertake that they will as far as possible:

(a) Continue their common efforts to promote by every means the free circulation of educational, scientific or cultural materials, and abolish or reduce any restrictions to that free circulation which are not referred to in this Agreement;

(b) Simplify the administrative procedure governing the importation of educational, scientific or cultural materials;

(c) Facilitate the expeditious and safe customs clearance of educational, scientific or cultural materials.

Article 5. Nothing in this Agreement shall affect the right of contracting States to take measures, in conformity with their legislation, to prohibit or limit the importation, or the circulation after importation, of articles on grounds relating directly to national security, public order or public morals.

Article 6. This Agreement shall not modify or affect the laws and regulations of any contracting State or any of its international treaties, conventions, agreements or proclamations, with respect to copyright, trade marks or patents.

Article 7. Subject to the provisions of any previous conventions to which the contracting States may have subscribed for the settlement of disputes, the contracting States undertake to have recourse to negotiation or conciliation, with a view to settlement of any disputes regarding the interpretation or the application of this Agreement.

Article 8. In case of a dispute between contracting States relating to the educational, scientific or cultural character of imported materials, the interested Parties may, by common agreement, refer it to the Director-General of the United Nations Educational, Scientific and Cultural Organization for an advisory opinion.

Article 9. 1. This Agreement, of which the English and French texts are equally authentic, shall bear today's date and remain open for signature by all Member States of the United Nations Educational, Scientific and Cultural Organization, all Member States of the United Nations and any non-member State to which an invitation may have been addressed by the Executive Board of the United Nations Educational, Scientific and Cultural Organization.

2. The Agreement shall be ratified on behalf of the signa-

tory States in accordance with their respective constitutional procedure.

3. The instruments of ratification shall be deposited with the Secretary-General of the United Nations.

Article 10. The States referred to in paragraph 1 of Article 9 may accept this Agreement from 22 November 1950. Acceptance shall become effective on the deposit of a formal instrument with the Secretary-General of the United Nations.

Article 11. This Agreement shall come into force on the date on which the Secretary-General of the United Nations receives instruments of ratification or acceptance from 10 States.

Article 12. 1. The States Parties to this Agreement on the date of its coming into force shall each take all the necessary measures for its fully effective operation within a period of six months after that date.

2. For States which may deposit their instruments of ratification or acceptance after the date of the Agreement coming into force, these measures shall be taken within a period of three months from the date of deposit.

3. Within one month of the expiration of the periods mentioned in paragraphs 1 and 2 of this article, the contracting States to this Agreement shall submit a report to the United Nations Educational, Scientific and Cultural Organization of the measures which they have taken for such fully effective operation.

4. The United Nations Educational, Scientific and Cultural Organization shall transmit this report to all signatory States to this Agreement and to the International Trade Organization (provisionally, to its Interim Commission).

Article 13. Any contracting State may, at the time of signature or the deposit of its instrument of ratification or acceptance, or at any time thereafter, declare by notification addressed to the Secretary-General of the United Nations that this Agreement shall extend to all or any of the territories for the conduct of whose foreign relations that contracting State is responsible.

Article 14. 1. Two years after the date of the coming into force of this Agreement, any contracting State may, on its own behalf or on behalf of any of the territories for the conduct of whose foreign relations that contracting State is responsible, denounce this Agreement by an instrument in writing deposited with the Secretary-General of the United Nations.

2. The denunciation shall take effect one year after the receipt of the instrument of denunciation.

Article 15. The Secretary-General of the United Nations shall inform the States referred to in paragraph 1 of Article 9, as well as the United Nations Educational, Scientific and Cultural Organization, and the International Trade Organization (provisionally, its Interim Commission), of the deposit of all the instruments of ratification and acceptance provided for in Articles 9 and 10, as well as of the notifications and denunciations provided for respectively in Articles 13 and 14.

Article 16. At the request of one-third of the contracting States to this Agreement, the Director-General of the United Nations Educational, Scientific and Cultural Organization shall place on the agenda of the next session of the General Conference of that Organization, the question of convoking a meeting for the revision of this Agreement.

Article 17. Annexes A, B, C, D and E, as well as the Protocol annexed to this Agreement are hereby made an integral part of this Agreement.

Article 18. 1. In accordance with Article 102 of the Charter of the United Nations, this Agreement shall be registered by the Secretary-General of the United Nations on the date of its coming into force.

2. In faith whereof the undersigned, duly authorized, have signed this Agreement on behalf of their respective governments.

Done at Lake Success, New York, this twenty-second day of November one thousand nine hundred and fifty in a single copy, which shall remain deposited in the archives of the United Nations, and certified true copies of which shall be delivered to all the States referred to in paragraph 1 of Article 9, as well as to the United Nations Educational, Scientific and Cultural Organization and to the International Trade Organization (provisionally, to its Interim Commission).

Annex A
Books, Publications and Documents

(i) Printed books.

(ii) Newspapers and periodicals.

(iii) Books and documents produced by duplicating processes other than printing.

(iv) Official government publications, that is, official, parliamentary and administrative documents published in their country of origin.

(v) Travel posters and travel literature (pamphlets, guides, time-tables, leaflets and similar publications), whether illustrated or not, including those published by private commercial enterprises, whose purpose is to stimulate travel outside the country of importation.

(vi) Publications whose purpose is to stimulate study outside the country of importation.

(vii) Manuscripts, including typescripts.

(viii) Catalogues of books and publications, being books and publications offered for sale by publishers or booksellers established outside the country of importation.

(ix) Catalogues of films, recordings or other visual and auditory material of an educational, scientific or cultural character, being catalogues issued by or on behalf of the United Nations or any of its Specialized Agencies.

(x) Music in manuscript or printed form, or reproduced by duplicating processes other than printing.

(xi) Geographical, hydrographical or astronomical maps and charts.

(xii) Architectural, industrial or engineering plans and designs, and reproductions thereof, intended for study in scientific establishments or educational institutions approved by the competent authorities of the importing country for the purpose of duty-free admission of these types of articles.

(The exemptions provided by Annex A shall not apply to:

(a) Stationery;

(b) Books, publications and documents (except catalogues, travel posters and travel literature referred to above) published by or for a private commercial enterprise, essentially for advertising purposes;

(c) Newspapers and periodicals in which the advertising matter is in excess of 70 per cent by space;

(d) All other items (except catalogues referred to above) in which the advertising matter is in excess of 25 per cent by space. In the case of travel posters and literature, this percentage shall apply only to private commercial advertising matter.)

Annex B
Works of Art and Collectors' Pieces of an Educational, Scientific or Cultural Character

(i) Paintings and drawings, including copies, executed entirely by hand, but excluding manufactured decorated wares.

(ii) Hand-printed impressions, produced from hand-engraved or hand-etched blocks, plates or other material, and signed and numbered by the artist.

(iii) Original works of art of statuary or sculpture, whether in the round, in relief, or in intaglio, exluding mass-produced reproductions and works of conventional craftsmanship of a commercial character.

(iv) Collectors' pieces and objects of art consigned to public galleries, museums and other public institutions, approved by the competent authorities of the importing country for the purpose of duty-free entry of these types of articles, not intended for resale.

(v) Collections and collectors' pieces in such scientific fields as anatomy, zoology, botany, mineralogy, palaeontology, archaeology and ethnography, not intended for resale.

(vi) Antiques, being articles in excess of 100 years of age.

Annex C
Visual and Auditory Materials of an Educational, Scientific or Cultural Character

(i) Films, filmstrips, microfilms and slides, of an educational, scientific or cultural character, when imported by organizations (including, at the discretion of the importing country, broadcasting organizations), approved by the competent authorities of the importing country for the purpose of duty-free admission of these types of articles, exclusively for exhibition by these organizations or by other public or private educational, scientific or cultural institutions or societies approved by the aforesaid authorities.

(ii) Newsreels (with or without sound track), depicting events of current news value at the time of importation, and imported in either negative form, exposed and developed, or positive form, printed and developed, when imported by organizations (including, at the discretion of the importing country, broadcasting organizations) approved by the competent authorities of the importing country for the purpose of duty-free admission of such films, provided that free entry may be limited to two copies of each subject for copying purposes.

(iii) Sound recordings of an educational, scientific or cultural character for use exclusively in public or private educational, scientific or cultural institutions or societies (including, at the discretion of the importing country, broadcasting organizations) approved by the competent authorities of the importing country for the purpose of duty-free admission of these types of articles.

(iv) Films, filmstrips, microfilms and sound recordings of an educational, scientific or cultural character produced by the United Nations or any of its Specialized Agencies.

(v) Patterns, models and wall charts for use exclusively for demonstrating and teaching purposes in public or private educational, scientific or cultural institutions approved by the competent authorities of the importing country for the purpose of duty-free admission of these types of articles.

Annex D
Scientific Instruments or Apparatus

Scientific instruments or apparatus, intended exclusively for educational purposes or pure scientific research, provided:

(a) That such scientific instruments or apparatus are consigned to public or private scientific or educational institutions approved by the competent authorities of the importing country for the purpose of duty-free entry of these types of articles, and used under the control and responsibility of these institutions;

(b) That instruments or apparatus of equivalent scientific value are not being manufactured in the country of importation.

Annex E
Articles for the Blind

(i) Books, publications and documents of all kinds in raised characters for the blind.

(ii) Other articles specially designed for the educational, scientific or cultural advancement of the blind, which are imported directly by institutions or organizations concerned with the welfare of the blind, approved by the competent authorities of the importing country for the purpose of duty-free entry of these types of articles.

Protocol annexed to the Agreement on the Importation of Educational, Scientific and Cultural Materials

The contracting States,

In the interest of facilitating the participation of the United States of America in the Agreement on the Importation of Educational, Scientific and Cultural Materials, have agreed to the following:

1. The United States of America shall have the option of ratifying this Agreement, under Article IX, or of accepting it, under Article X, with the inclusion of the reservation hereunder.

2. In the event of the United States of America becoming Party to this Agreement with the reservation provided for in the preceding paragraph 1, the provisions of that reservation may be invoked by the Government of the United States of America with regard to any of the contracting States to this Agreement, or by any contracting State with regard to the United States of America, provided that any measure imposed pursuant to such reservation shall be applied on a non-discriminatory basis.

Text of the Reservation

(a) If, as a result of the obligations incurred by a contracting State under this Agreement, any product covered by this Agreement is being imported into the territory of a contracting State in such relatively increased quantities and under such conditions as to cause or threaten serious injury to the domestic industry in that territory producing like or directly competitive products, the contracting State, under the conditions provided for by paragraph 2 above, shall be free, in respect of such product and to the extent and for such time as may be necessary to prevent or remedy such injury, to suspend, in whole or in part, any obligation under this Agreement with respect to such product.

(b) Before any contracting State shall take action pursuant to the provisions of paragraph (a) above, it shall give notice in writing to the United Nations Educational, Scientific and Cultural Organization as far in advance as may be practicable and shall afford the Organization and the contracting States which are Parties to this Agreement an opportunity to consult with it in respect of the proposed action.

(c) In critical circumstances where delay would cause damage which it would be difficult to repair, action under paragraph (a) above may be taken provisionally without prior consultation, on the condition that consultation be effected immediately after taking such action.

UNESCO AGREEMENT ON THE IMPORTATION OF EDUCATIONAL, SCIENTIFIC AND CULTURAL MATERIALS: PROTOCOL (1976).

The protocol, adopted by the UNESCO GENERAL CONFERENCE (19th session), held at Nairobi, Kenya, on 26 November 1976, entered into force on 2 January 1982. Only States parties to the agreement may avail themselves of the provisions of the protocol, which allows such States to exercise a choice concerning the provisions which they undertake to apply. In addition, the protocol provides measures additional to those set out in the agreement designed to stimulate the international movement of educational, scientific, and cultural materials, such as exemption from customs duties and other taxes.

The text of the protocol (UNESCO's Standard-Setting Instruments, No. IV.A.2) is as follows:

The contracting States parties to the Agreement on the Importation of Educational, Scientific and Cultural Materials, adopted by the General Conference of the United Nations Educational, Scientific and Cultural Organization at its fifth session held in Florence in 1950,

Reaffirming the principles on which the Agreement, hereinafter called "the Agreement", is based,

Considering that this Agreement has proved to be an effective instrument in lowering customs barriers and reducing other economic restrictions that impede the exchange of ideas and knowledge,

Considering, nevertheless, that in the quarter of a century following the adoption of the Agreement, technical progress has changed the ways and means of transmitting information and knowledge, which is the fundamental objective of that Agreement,

Considering, further, that the developments that have taken place in the field of international trade during this period have, in general, been reflected in greater freedom of exchanges,

Considering that since the adoption of the Agreement, the international situation has changed radically owing to the development of the international community, in particular through the accession of many States to independence,

Considering that the needs and concerns of the developing countries should be taken into consideration, with a view to giving them easier and less costly access to education, science, technology and culture,

Recalling the provisions of the Convention on the means of prohibiting and preventing the illicit import, export and transfer of ownership of cultural property, adopted by the General Conference of Unesco in 1970, and those of the Convention concerning the protection of the world cultural and natural heritage, adopted by the General Conference in 1972,

Recalling, moreover, the customs conventions concluded under the auspices of the Customs Co-operation Council, in consultation with the United Nations Educational, Scientific and Cultural Organization, concerning the temporary importation of educational, scientific and cultural materials,

Convinced that new arrangements should be made and that such arrangements will contribute even more effectively to the development of education, science and culture which constitute the essential bases of economic and social progress,

Recalling resolution 4.112 adopted by the General Conference of Unesco at its eighteenth session,

Have agreed as follows:

I

1. The contracting States undertake to extend to the materials listed in Annexes A, B, D and E and also, where the annexes in question have not been the subject of a declaration under paragraph 16 (a) below, Annexes C.1, F, G and H, to the present protocol exemption from customs duties and other charges on, or in connexion with, their importation, as set out in Article I, paragraph 1, of the Agreement, provided such materials fulfil the conditions laid down in these annexes and are the products of another contracting State.

2. The provisions of paragraph 1 of this protocol shall not prevent any contracting State from levying on imported materials;

(a) internal taxes or any other internal charges of any kind, imposed at the time of importation or subsequently, not exceeding those applied directly or indirectly to like domestic products;

(b) fees and charges, other than customs duties, imposed by governmental or administrative authorities on, or in connexion with, importation, limited in amount to the approximate cost of the services rendered, and representing neither an indirect protection to domestic products nor a taxation of imports for revenue purposes.

II

3. Notwithstanding paragraph 2 (a) of this protocol, the contracting States undertake not to levy on the materials listed below any internal taxes or other internal charges of any kind, imposed at the time of importation or subsequently:

(a) books and publications consigned to the libraries referred to in paragraph 5 of this protocol;

(b) official, parliamentary and administrative documents published in their country of origin;

(c) books and publications of the United Nations or any of its Specialized Agencies;

(d) books and publications received by the United Nations Educational, Scientific and Cultural Organization and distributed free of charge by it or under its supervision;

(e) publications intended to promote tourist travel outside the country of importation, sent and distributed free of charge;

(f) articles for the blind and other physically and mentally handicapped persons:

(i) books, publications and documents of all kinds in raised characters for the blind;

(ii) other articles specially designed for the educational, scientific or cultural advancement of the blind and other physically or mentally handicapped persons which are imported directly by institutions or organizations concerned with the education of, or assistance to the blind and other physically or mentally handicapped persons approved by the competent authorities of the importing country for the purpose of duty-free entry of these types of articles.

III

4. The contracting States undertake not to levy on the articles and materials referred to in the annexes to this protocol any customs duties, export duties or duties levied on goods leaving the country, or other internal taxes of any kind, levied on such articles and materials when they are intended for export to other contracting States.

IV

5. The contracting States undertake to extend the granting of the necessary licences and/or foreign exchange provided for in Article II, paragraph 1, of the Agreement, to the importation of the following materials:

(a) books and publications consigned to libraries serving the public interest, including the following:

(i) national libraries and other major research libraries;

(ii) general and specialized academic libraries, including university libraries, college libraries, institute libraries and university extra-mural libraries;

(iii) public libraries;

(iv) school libraries;

(v) special libraries serving a group of readers who form an entity, having particular and identifiable subjects of interest, such as government libraries, public authority libraries, industrial libraries and libraries of professional bodies;

(vi) libraries for the handicapped and for readers who are unable to move around, such as libraries for the blind, hospital libraries and prison libraries;

(vii) music libraries, including record libraries;

(b) books adopted or recommended as textbooks in higher educational establishments and imported by such establishments;

(c) books in foreign languages, with the exception of books in the principal native language or languages of the importing country;

(d) films, slides, video-tapes and sound recordings of an educational, scientific or cultural nature, imported by organizations approved by the competent authorities of the importing country for the purpose of duty-free entry of these types of articles.

V

6. The contracting States undertake to extend the granting of the facilities provided for in Article III of the Agreement to materials and furniture imported exclusively for showing at a public exhibition of objects of an educational, scientific or cultural nature approved by the competent authorities of the importing country and for subsequent re-exportation.

7. Nothing in the foregoing paragraph shall prevent the authorities of an importing country from taking such steps as may be necessary to ensure that the materials and furni-

ture in question will in fact be re-exported at the close of the exhibition.

VI

8. The contracting States undertake:

(a) to extend to the importation of the articles covered by the present protocol the provisions of Article IV of the Agreement;

(b) to encourage through appropriate measures the free flow and distribution of educational, scientific and cultural objects and materials produced in the developing countries.

VII

9. Nothing in this protocol shall affect the right of contracting States to take measures, in conformity with their legislation, to prohibit or limit the importation of articles, or their circulation after importation, on grounds relating directly to national security, public order or public morals.

10. Notwithstanding other provisions of this protocol, a developing country, which is defined as such by the practice established by the General Assembly of the United Nations and which is a party to the protocol, may suspend or limit the obligations under this protocol relating to importation of any object or material if such importation causes or threatens to cause serious injury to the nascent indigenous industry in that developing country. The country concerned shall implement such action in a nondiscriminatory manner. It shall notify the Director-General of the United Nations Educational, Scientific and Cultural Organization of any such action, as far as practicable in advance of implementation, and the Director-General of the United Nations Educational, Scientific and Cultural Organnization shall notify all Parties to the protocol.

11. This protocol shall not modify or affect the laws and regulations of any contracting State or any of its international treaties, conventions, agreements or proclamations, with respect to copyright, trade marks or patents.

12. Subject to the provisions of any previous conventions to which they may have subscribed for the settlement of disputes, the contracting States undertake to have recourse to negotiation or conciliation with a view to settlement of any disputes regarding the interpretation or the application of this protocol.

13. In case of a dispute between contracting States relating to the educational, scientific or cultural character of imported materials, the interested parties may, by common agreement refer it to the Director-General of the United Nations Educational, Scientific and Cultural Organization for an advisory opinion.

VIII

14. (a) This protocol, of which the English and French texts are equally authentic, shall bear today's date and shall be open to signature by all States Parties to the Agreement, as the Member States constituting them are also Parties to the protocol.

The term "State" or "Country" as used in this protocol, or in the protocol referred to in paragraph 18, shall be taken to refer also, as the context may require, to the customs or economic unions and, in all matters which fall within their competence with regard to the scope of this protocol, to the whole of the territories of the Member

States which constitute them, and not to the territory of each of these States.

It is understood that, in [becoming] a Contracting Party to his protocol, such customs or economic unions will also apply the provisions of the Agreement on the same basis as is provided in the preceding paragraph with respect to the protocol.

(b) This protocol shall be subject to ratification or acceptance by the signatory States in accordance with their respective constitutional procedures.

(c) The instruments of ratification or acceptance shall be deposited with the Secretary-General of the United Nations.

15. (a) The States referred to in paragraph 14 (a) which are not signatories of this protocol may accede to this protocol.

(b) Accession shall be effected by the deposit of a formal instrument with the Secretary-General of the United Nations.

16. (a) The States referred to in paragraph 14 (a) of this protocol may, at the time of signature, ratification, acceptance or accession, declare that they will not be bound by Part II, Part IV, Annex C.1, Annex F, Annex G and Annex H, or by any of these Parts or Annexes. They may also declare that they will be bound by Annex C.1 only in respect of contracting States which have themselves accepted that Annex.

(b) Any contracting State which has made such a declaration may withdraw it, in whole or in part, at any time by notification to the Secretary-General of the United Nations, specifying the date on which such withdrawal takes effect.

(c) States which have declared, in accordance with sub-paragraph (a) of this paragraph, that they will not be bound by Annex C.1 shall necessarily be bound by Annex C.2. Those which have declared that they will be bound by Annex C.1 only in respect of contracting States which have themselves accepted that Annex shall necessarily be bound by Annex C.2 in respect of contracting States which have not accepted Annex C.1.

17. (a) This protocol shall come into force six months after the date of deposit of the fifth instrument of ratification, acceptance or accession with the Secretary-General of the United Nations.

(b) It shall come into force for every other State six months after the date of the deposit of its instrument of ratification, acceptance or accession.

(c) Within one month following the expiration of the periods mentioned in sub-paragraphs (a) and (b) of this paragraph, the contracting States to this protocol shall submit a report to the United Nations Educational, Scientific and Cultural Organization on the measures which they have taken to give full effect to the protocol.

(d) The United Nations Educational, Scientific and Cultural Organization shall transmit these reports to all States parties to this protocol.

18. The protocol annexed to the Agreement, and made an integral part thereof, as provided for in Article XVII of the Agreement, is hereby made an integral part of this protocol and shall apply to obligations incurred under this protocol and to products covered by this protocol.

19. (a) Two years after the date of the coming into force of this protocol, any contracting State may denounce this protocol by an instrument in writing deposited with the Secretary-General of the United Nations.

(b) The denunciation shall take effect one year after the receipt of the instrument of denunciation.

(c) Denunciation of the Agreement pursuant to Article XIV thereof shall automatically imply denunciation of this protocol.

20. The Secretary-General of the United Nations shall inform the States referred to in paragraph 14 (a), as well as the United Nations Educational, Scientific and Cultural Organization, of the deposit of all the instruments of ratification, acceptance or accession referred to in paragraphs 14 and 15; of declarations made and withdrawn under paragraph 16 of the dates of entry into force of this protocol in accordance with paragraph 17 (a) and (b); and of the denunciations provided for in paragraph 19.

21. (a) This protocol may be revised by the General Conference of the United Nations Educational, Scientific and Cultural Organization. Any such revision, however, shall be binding only upon States that become parties to the revising protocol.

(b) Should the General Conference adopt a new protocol revising this protocol either totally or in part, and unless the new protocol provides otherwise, the present protocol shall cease to be open to signature, ratification, acceptance or accession as from the date of the coming into force of the new revising protocol.

22. This protocol shall not change or modify the Agreement.

23. Annexes A, B, C.1, C.2, D, E, F, G and H are hereby made an integral part of this protocol.

24. In accordance with Article 102 of the Charter of the United Nations, this protocol shall be registered by the Secretary-General of the United Nations on the date of its coming into force.

In faith whereof the undersigned, duly authorized, have signed this protocol on behalf of their respective governments.

Annex A
Books, Publications and Documents

(i) Printed books, irrespective of the language in which they are printed and whatever the amount of space given over to illustrations, including the following:

(a) luxury editions;

(b) books printed abroad from the manuscript of an author resident in the importing country;

(c) children's drawing and painting books;

(d) school exercise books (workbooks) with printed texts and blank spaces to be filled in by the pupils;

(e) crossword puzzle books containing printed texts;

(f) loose illustrations and printed pages in the form of loose or bound sheets and reproduction proofs or reproduction films to be used for the production of books.

(ii) Printed documents or reports of a non-commercial character.

(iii) Microforms of the articles listed under items (i) and (ii) of this Annex, as well as of those listed under items (i) to (vi) of Annex A to the Agreement.

(iv) Catalogues of films, recordings or other visual and auditory material of an educational, scientific or cultural character.

(v) Maps and charts of interest in scientific fields such as geology, zoology, botany, mineralogy, palaeontology, archaeology, ethnology, meteorology, climatology and geophysics, and also meteorological and geophysical diagrams.

(vi) Architectural, industrial or engineering plans and designs and reproductions thereof.

(vii) Bibliographical information material for distribution free of charge.

Annex B
Works of Art and Collectors' Pieces of an Educational, Scientific or Cultural Character

(i) Paintings and drawings, whatever the nature of the materials on which they have been executed entirely by hand, including copies executed by hand, but excluding manufactured decorated wares.

(ii) Ceramics and mosaics on wood, being original works of art.

(iii) Collectors' pieces and objects of art consigned to galleries, museums and other institutions approved by the competent authorities of the importing country for the purpose of duty-free entry of those types of materials, on condition they are not resold.

Annex C.1
Visual and Auditory Materials

(i) Films, filmstrips, microforms and slides.

(ii) Sound recordings.

(iii) Patterns, models and wall charts of an educational, scientific or cultural character, except toy models.

(iv) Other visual and auditory materials, such as:

    (a) video-tapes, kinescopes, video-discs, videograms and other forms of visual and sound recordings;

    (b) microcards, microfiches and magnetic or other information storage media required in computerized information and documentation services;

    (c) materials for programmed instruction, which may be presented in kit form, with the corresponding printed materials, including video-cassettes and audio-cassettes;

    (d) transparencies, including those intended for direct projection or for viewing through optical devices;

    (e) holograms for laser projection;

    (f) mock-ups or visualizations of abstract concepts such as molecular structures or mathematical formulae;

    (g) multi-media kits;

    (h) materials for the promotion of tourism, including those produced by private concerns, designed to encourage the public to travel outside the country of importation.

(The exemptions provided for in the present Annex C.1 shall not apply to:

    (a) unused microform stock and unused visual and auditory recording media and their specific packaging such as cassettes, cartridges, reels;

    (b) visual and auditory recordings with the exception of materials for the promotion of tourism covered by paragraph (iv) (h), produced by or for a private commercial enterprise, essentially for advertising purposes;

    (c) visual and auditory recordings in which the advertising matter is in excess of 25 per cent by time. In the case of the materials for the promotion of tourism covered by paragraph (iv) (h), this percentage applies only to private commercial publicity.)

Annex C.2
Visual and Auditory Materials of an Educational, Scientific or Cultural Character

Visual and auditory materials of an educational, scientific or cultural character, when imported by organizations (including, at the discretion of the importing country, broadcasting and television organizations) or by any other public or private institution or association, approved by the competent authorities of the importing country for the purpose of duty-free admission of these types of materials or when produced by the United Nations or any of its Specialized Agencies and including the following:

(i) films, filmstrips, microfilms and slides;

(ii) newsreels (with or without sound track) depicting events of current news value at the time of importation, and imported in either negative form, exposed and developed, or positive form, printed and developed, it being understood that duty-free entry may be limited to two copies of each subject for copying purposes;

(iii) archival film material (with or without sound track) intended for use in connexion with newsreel films;

(iv) recreational films particularly suited for children and youth;

(v) sound recordings;

(vi) video-tapes, kinescopes, video-discs, videograms and other forms of visual and sound recordings;

(vii) microcards, microfiches and magnetic or other information storage media required in computerized information and documentation services;

(viii) materials for programmed instruction, which may be presented in kit form, with the corresponding printed materials, including video-cassettes and audio-cassettes;

(ix) transparencies, including those intended for direct projection or for viewing through optical devices;

(x) holograms for laser projection;

(xi) mock-ups or visualizations of abstract concepts such as molecular structures or mathematical formulae;

(xii) multi-media kits.

Annex D
Scientific Instruments or Apparatus

(i) Scientific instruments or apparatus, provided:

    (a) that they are consigned to public or private scientific or educational institutions approved by the competent authorities of the importing country for the purpose of duty-free entry of these types of articles, and used for non-commercial purposes under the control and responsibility of these institutions;

    (b) that instruments or apparatus of equivalent scientific value are not being manufactured in the country of importation.

(ii) Spare parts, components or accessories specifically matching scientific instruments or apparatus, provided these spare parts, components or accessories are imported at the same time as such instruments and apparatus, or if imported subsequently, that they are identifiable as intended for instruments or apparatus previously admitted duty-free or entitled to duty-free entry.

(iii) Tools to be used for the maintenance, checking, gauging or repair of scientific instruments, provided these tools are imported at the same time as such instruments and apparatus or, if imported subsequently, that they are identifiable as intended for the specific instruments or apparatus previously admitted duty-free or entitled to duty-free entry, and further provided that tools of equivalent scientific value are not being manufactured in the country of importation.

Annex E
Articles for the Blind and Other Handicapped Persons

(i) All articles specially designed for the educational, scientific or cultural advancement of the blind which are imported directly by institutions or organizations concerned with the education of, or assistance to, the blind, approved by the competent authorities of the importing country for the purpose of duty-free entry of these types of articles, including:

(a) talking books (discs, cassettes or other sound reproductions) and large-print books;

(b) phonographs and cassette players, specially designed or adapted for the blind and other handicapped persons and required to play the talking books;

(c) equipment for the reading of normal print by the blind and partially sighted, such as electronic reading machines, television-enlargers and optical aids;

(d) equipment for the mechanical or computerized production of braille and recorded material, such as stereotyping machines, electronic braille, transfer and pressing machines; braille computer terminals and displays;

(e) braille paper, magnetic tapes and cassettes for the production of braille and talking books;

(f) aids for improving the mobility of the blind, such as electronic orientation and obstacle detection appliances and white canes;

(g) technical aids for the education, rehabilitation, vocational training and employment of the blind, such as braille watches, braille typewriters, teaching and learning aids, games and other instruments specifically adapted for the use of the blind.

(ii) All materials specially designed for the education, employment and social advancement of other physically or mentally handicapped persons, directly imported by institutions or organizations concerned with the education of, or assistance to, such persons, approved by the competent authorities of the importing country for the purpose of duty-free entry of these types of articles, provided that equivalent objects are not being manufactured in the importing country.

Annex F
Sports Equipment

Sports equipment intended exclusively for amateur sports associations or groups approved by the competent authorities of the importing country for the purpose of duty-free entry of these types of articles, provided that equivalent materials are not being manufactured in the importing country.

Annex G
Musical Instruments and Other Musical Equipment

Musical instruments and other musical equipment intended solely for cultural institutions or music schools approved by the competent authorities of the importing country for the purpose of duty-free entry of these types of articles, provided that equivalent instruments and other equipment are not being manufactured in the importing country.

Annex H
Material and Machines Used for the Production of Books, Publications and Documents

(i) Material used for the production of books, publications and documents (paper pulp, recycled paper, newsprint and other types of paper used for printing, printing inks, glue, etc.).

(ii) Machines for the processing of paper pulp and paper and also printing and binding machines, provided that machines of equivalent technical quality are not being manufactured in the importing country.

SEE ALSO *Economic, Social and Cultural Rights: UNESCO Activities.*

UNESCO CONVENTION AGAINST DISCRIMINATION IN EDUCATION (1960).

The convention was adopted on 14 December 1960 at UNESCO headquarters in Paris by the UNESCO GENERAL CONFERENCE (11th session) and entered into force on 22 May 1962. The preparation of such an instrument had been recommended by Mr. Charles D. Ammoun (Lebanon), special rapporteur of the SUB-COMMISSION ON PREVENTION OF DISCRIMINATION AND PROTECTION OF MINORITIES, in the *Study of Discrimination in Education* (United Nations publication, Sales No. 1957.XIV.3), and endorsed by the Sub-Commission, the UN Commission on Human Rights, and the UN Economic and Social Council. The convention aims at eradicating discrimination based on race, color, sex, language, religion, political or other opinion, national or social origin, nationality or birth, in the field of education, and at ensuring to everyone equality of treatment in this field.

When it adopted the convention, the UNESCO General Conference also adopted the Recommendation against Discrimination in Education. With the exception of differences in formulation and statutory scope inherent in the nature of these two categories of instrument, the content of the recommendation is identical to that of the convention.

Two years later, on 10 December 1962, the UNESCO General Conference (12th session) adopted the protocol instituting a conciliation and good offices commission, which entered into force on 24 October 1968.

The text of the convention *(UNESCO's Standard-Setting Instruments,* No. 1.A.1, p. 3) is as follows:

The General Conference of the United Nations Educational, Scientific and Cultural Organization, meeting in Paris from 14 November to 15 December 1960, at its eleventh session,

Recalling that the Universal Declaration of Human Rights asserts the principle of non-discrimination and proclaims that every person has the right to education,

Considering that discrimination in education is a violation of rights enunciated in that Declaration,

Considering that, under the terms of its Constitution, the United Nations Educational, Scientific and Cultural Organization has the purpose of instituting collaboration among the nations with a view to furthering for all universal respect for human rights and equality of educational oportunity,

Recognizing that, consequently, the United Nations Educational, Scientific and Cultural Organization, while respecting the diversity of national educational systems, has the duty not only to proscribe any form of discrimination in education but also to promote equality of opportunity and treatment for all in education,

Having before it proposals concerning the different aspects of discrimination in education, constituting item 17.1.4 of the agenda of the session,

Having decided at its tenth session that this question should be made the subject of an international convention as well as of recommendations to Member States.

Adopts this Convention on the fourteenth day of December 1960.

Article 1. 1. For the purpose of this Convention, the term "discrimination" includes any distinction, exclusion, limitation or preference which, being based on race, colour, sex, language, religion, political or other opinion, national or social origin, economic condition or birth, has the purpose or effect of nullifying or impairing equality of treatment in education and in particular:

(*a*) Of depriving any person or group of persons of access to education of any type or at any level;

(*b*) Of limiting any person or group of persons to education of an inferior standard;

(*c*) Subject to the provisions of article 2 of this Convention, of establishing or maintaining separate educational systems or institutions for persons or groups of persons; or

(*d*) Of inflicting on any person or group of persons conditions which are incompatible with the dignity of man.

2. For the purposes of this Convention, the term "education" refers to all types and levels of education, and includes access to education, the standard and quality of education, and the conditions under which it is given.

Article 2. When permitted in a State, the following situations shall not be deemed to constitute discrimination, within the meaning of article 1 of this Convention:

(*a*) The establishment or maintenance of separate educational systems or institutions for pupils of the two sexes, if these systems or institutions offer equivalent access to education, provide a teaching staff with qualifications of the same standard as well as school premises and equipment of the same quality, and afford the opportunity to take the same or equivalent courses of study;

(*b*) The establishment or maintenance, for religious or linguistic reasons, of separate educational systems or institutions offering an education which is in keeping with the wishes of the pupil's parents or legal guardians, if participation in such systems or attendance at such institutions is optional and if the education provided conforms to such standards as may be laid down or approved by the competent authorities, in particular for education of the same level;

(*c*) The establishment or maintenance of private educational institutions, if the object of the institutions is not to secure the exclusion of any group but to provide educational facilities in addition to those provided by the public authorities, if the institutions are conducted in accordance with that object, and if the education provided conforms with such standards as may be laid down or approved by the competent authorities, in particular for education of the same level.

Article 3. In order to eliminate and prevent discrimina-

tion within the meaning of this Convention, the States Parties thereto undertake:

(*a*) To abrogate any statutory provisions and any administrative instructions and to discontinue any administrative practices which involve discrimination in education;

(*b*) To ensure, by legislation where necessary, that there is no discrimination in the admission of pupils to educational institutions;

(*c*) Not to allow any differences of treatment by the public authorities between nationals, except on the basis of merit or need, in the matter of school fees and the grant of scholarships or other forms of assistance to pupils and necessary permits and facilities for the pursuit of studies in foreign countries;

(*d*) Not to allow, in any form of assistance granted by the public authorities to educational institutions, any restrictions or preference based solely on the ground that pupils belong to a particular group;

(*e*) To give foreign nationals resident within their territory the same access to education as that given to their own nationals.

Article 4. The States Parties to this Convention undertake furthermore to formulate, develop and apply a national policy which, by methods appropriate to the circumstances and to national usage, will tend to promote equality of opportunity and of treatment in the matter of education and in particular:

(*a*) To make primary education free and compulsory; make secondary education in its different forms generally available and accessible to all; make higher education equally accessible to all on the basis of individual capacity; assure compliance by all with the obligation to attend school prescribed by law;

(*b*) To ensure that the standards of education are equivalent in all public education institutions of the same level, and that the conditions relating to the quality of the education provided are also equivalent;

(*c*) To encourage and intensify by appropriate methods the education of persons who have not received any primary education or who have not completed the entire primary education course and the continuation of their education on the basis of individual capacity;

(*d*) To provide training for the teaching profession without discrimination.

Article 5. 1. The States Parties to this Convention agree that:

(*a*) Education shall be directed to the full development of the human personality and to the strengthening of respect for human rights and fundamental freedoms; it shall promote understanding, tolerance and friendship among all nations, racial or religious groups, and shall further the activities of the United Nations for the maintenance of peace;

(*b*) It is essential to respect the liberty of parents and, where applicable, of legal guardians, firstly to choose for their children institutions other than those maintained by the public authorities but conforming to such minimum educational standards as may be laid down or approved by the competent authorities and, secondly, to ensure in a manner consistent with the procedures followed in the State for the application of its legislation, the religious and moral education of the children in conformity with their own convictions; and no person or group of persons should be compelled to receive religious instruction inconsistent with his or their conviction;

(*c*) It is essential to recognize the right of members of

national minorities to carry on their own educational activities, including the maintenance of schools and, depending on the educational policy of each State, the use or the teaching of their own language, provided however:

(i) That this right is not exercised in a manner which prevents the members of these minorities from understanding the culture and language of the community as a whole and from participating in its activities, or which prejudices national sovereignty;

(ii) That the standard of education is not lower than the general standard laid down or approved by the competent authorities; and

(iii) That attendance at such schools is optional.

2. The States Parties to this Convention undertake to take all necessary measures to ensure the application of the principles enunciated in paragraph 1 of this article.

Article 6. In the application of this Convention, the States Parties to it undertake to pay the greatest attention to any recommendations hereafter adopted by the General Conference of the United Nations Educational, Scientific and Cultural Organization defining the measures to be taken against the different forms of discrimination in education and for the purpose of ensuring equality of opportunity and treatment in education.

Article 7. The States Parties to this Convention shall in their periodic reports submitted to the General Conference of the United Nations Educational, Scientific and Cultural Organization on dates and in a manner to be determined by it, give information on the legislative and administrative provisions which they have adopted and other action which they have taken for the application of this Convention, including that taken for the formulation and the development of the national policy defined in article 4 as well as the results achieved and the obstacles encountered in the application of that policy.

Article 8. Any dispute which may arise between any two or more States Parties to this Convention concerning the interpretation or application of this Convention which is not settled by negotiations shall at the request of the parties to the dispute be referred, failing other means of settling the dispute, to the International Court of Justice for decision.

Article 9. Reservations to this Convention shall not be permitted.

Article 10. This Convention shall not have the effect of diminishing the rights which individuals or groups may enjoy by virtue of agreements concluded between two or more States, where such rights are not contrary to the letter or spirit of this Convention.

Article 11. This Convention is drawn up in English, French, Russian and Spanish, the four texts being equally authoritative.

Article 12. 1. This Convention shall be subject to ratification or acceptance by States Members of the United Nations Educational, Scientific and Cultural Organization in accordance with their respective constitutional procedures.

2. The instruments of ratification or acceptance shall be deposited with the Director-General of the United Nations Educational, Scientific and Cultural Organization.

Article 13. 1. This Convention shall be open to accession by all States not Members of the United Nations Educational, Scientific and Cultural Organization which are invited to do so by the Executive Board of the Organization.

2. Accession shall be effected by the deposit of an instrument of accession with the Director-General of the United Nations Educational, Scientific and Cultural Organization.

Article 14. This Convention shall enter into force three months after the date of the deposit of the third instrument of ratification, acceptance or accession, but only with respect to those States which have deposited their respective instruments on or before that date. It shall enter into force with respect to any other State three months after the deposit of its instrument of ratification, acceptance or accession.

Article 15. The States Parties to this Convention recognize that the Convention is applicable not only to their metropolitan territory but also to all non-self-governing, trust, colonial and other territories for the international relations of which they are responsible; they undertake to consult, if necessary, the governments or other competent authorities of these territories on or before ratification, acceptance or accession with a view to securing the application of the Convention to those territories, and to notify the Director-General of the United Nations Educational, Scientific and Cultural Organization of the territories to which it is accordingly applied, the notification to take effect three months after the date of its receipt.

Article 16. 1. Each State Party to this Convention may denounce the Convention on its own behalf or on behalf of any territory for whose international relations it is responsible.

2. The denunciation shall be notified by an instrument in writing, deposited with the Director-General of the United Nations Educational, Scientific and Cultural Organization.

3. The denunciation shall take effect twelve months after the receipt of the instrument of denunciation.

Article 17. The Director-General of the United Nations Educational, Scientific and Cultural Organization shall inform the States Members of the Organization, the States not members of the Organization which are referred to in article 13, as well as the United Nations, of the deposit of all the instruments of ratification, acceptance and accession provided for in articles 12 and 13, and of notifications and denunciations provided for in articles 15 and 16 respectively.

Article 18. 1. This Convention may be revised by the General Conference of the United Nations Educational, Scientific and Cultural Organization. Any such revision shall, however, bind only the States which shall become Parties to the revising convention.

2. If the General Conference should adopt a new convention revising this Convention in whole or in part, then, unless the new convention otherwise provides, this Convention shall cease to be open to ratification, acceptance or accession as from the date on which the new revising convention enters into force.

Article 19. In conformity with Article 102 of the Charter of the United Nations, this Convention shall be registered with the Secretariat of the United Nations at the request of the Director-General of the United Nations Educational, Scientific and Cultural Organization.

Done in Paris, this fifteenth day of December 1960, in two authentic copies bearing the signatures of the President of the eleventh session of the General Conference and of the Director-General of the United Nations Educational, Scientific and Cultural Organization, which shall be deposited in the archives of the United Nations Educational, Scientific and Cultural Organization, and certified true copies of which shall be delivered to all the States referred to in articles 12 and 13 as well as to the United Nations.

The foregoing is the authentic text of the Convention

duly adopted by the General Conference of the United Nations Educational, Scientific and Cultural Organization during its eleventh session, which was held in Paris and declared closed the fifteenth day of December 1960.

In faith whereof we have appended our signatures this fifteenth day of December 1960.

UNESCO CONVENTION AGAINST DISCRIMINATION IN EDUCATION: PROTOCOL INSTITUTING A CONCILIATION AND GOOD OFFICES COMMISSION TO BE RESPONSIBLE FOR SEEKING A SETTLEMENT OF ANY DISPUTES WHICH MAY ARISE BETWEEN STATES PARTIES TO THE CONVENTION AGAINST DISCRIMINATION IN EDUCATION (1962). The protocol was adopted on 10 December 1962 by the UNESCO GENERAL CONFERENCE at its 12th session, held in Paris. It entered into force on 24 October 1968.

The UNESCO Conciliation and Good Offices Commission, established in accordance with the protocol, normally holds at least one session each year at the headquarters of UNESCO, in Paris. Its reports are transmitted to the UNESCO General Conference through its executive board.

The text of the protocol (*UNESCO's Standard-Setting Instruments,* No. 1.A.1, p. 11) is as follows:

The General Conference of the United Nations Educational, Scientific and Cultural Organization, meeting in Paris from 9 November to 12 December 1962, at its twelfth session,

Having adopted, at its eleventh session, the Convention against Discrimination in Education,

Desirous of facilitating the implementation of that Convention, and

Considering that it is important, for this purpose, to institute a Conciliation and Good Offices Commission to be responsible for seeking the amicable settlement of any disputes which may arise between States Parties to the Convention, concerning its application or interpretation,

Adopts this Protocol on the tenth day of December 1962.

Article 1. There shall be established under the auspices of the United Nations Educational, Scientific and Cultural Organization a Conciliation and Good Offices Commission, hereinafter referred to as the Commission, to be responsible for seeking the amicable settlement of disputes between States Parties to the Convention against Discrimination in Education, hereinafter referred to as the Convention, concerning the application or interpretation of the Convention.

Article 2. 1. The Commission shall consist of eleven members who shall be persons of high moral standing and acknowledged impartiality and shall be elected by the General Conference of the United Nations Educational, Scientific and Cultural Organization, hereinafter referred to as the General Conference.

2. The members of the Commission shall serve in their personal capacity.

Article 3. 1. The members of the Commission shall be elected from a list of persons nominated for the purpose by the States Parties to this Protocol. Each State shall, after consulting its National Commission for UNESCO, nominate not more than four persons. These persons must be nationals of States Parties to this Protocol.

2. At least four months before the date of each election to the Commission, the Director-General of the United Nations Educational, Scientific and Cultural Organization, hereinafter referred to as the Director-General, shall invite the States Parties to the present Protocol to send within two months, their nominations of the persons referred to in paragraph 1 of this article. He shall prepare a list in alphabetical order of the persons thus nominated and shall submit it, at least one month before the election, to the Executive Board of the United Nations Educational, Scientific and Cultural Organization, hereinafter referred to as the Executive Board, and to the States Parties to the Convention. The Executive Board shall transmit the aforementioned list, with such suggestions as it may consider useful, to the General Conference, which shall carry out the election of members of the Commission in conformity with the procedure it normally follows in elections of two or more persons.

Article 4. 1. The Commission may not include more than one national of the same State.

2. In the election of members of the Commission, the General Conference shall endeavour to include persons of recognized competence in the field of education and persons having judicial experience or legal experience particularly of an international character. It shall also give consideration to equitable geographical distribution of membership and to the representation of the different forms of civilization as well as of the principal legal systems.

Article 5. The members of the Commission shall be elected for a term of six years. They shall be eligible for reelection if renominated. The terms of four of the members elected at the first election shall, however, expire at the end of two years, and the terms of three other members at the end of four years. Immediately after the first election, the names of these members shall be chosen by lot by the President of the General Conference.

Article 6. 1. In the event of the death or resignation of a member of the Commission, the Chairman shall immediately notify the Director-General, who shall declare the seat vacant from the date of death or the date on which the resignation takes effect.

2. If, in the unanimous opinion of the other members, a member of the Commission has ceased to carry out his functions for any cause other than absence of a temporary character or is unable to continue the discharge of his duties, the Chairman of the Commission shall notify the Director-General and shall thereupon declare the seat of such member to be vacant.

3. The Director-General shall inform the Member States of the United Nations Educational, Scientific and Cultural Organization, and any States not members of the Organization which have become Parties to this Protocol under the provisions of article 23, of any vacancies which have occurred in accordance with paragraphs 1 and 2 of this article.

4. In each of the cases provided for by paragraphs 1 and 2 of this article, the General Conference shall arrange for the replacement of the member whose seat has fallen vacant, for the unexpired portion of his term of office.

Article 7. Subject to the provisions of article 6, a member of the Commission shall remain in office until his successor takes up his duties.

Article 8. 1. If the Commission does not include a member of the nationality of a State which is party to a dispute referred to it under the provisions of article 12 or article 13, that State, or if there is more than one, each of those States, may choose a person to sit on the Commission as a member *ad hoc.*

2. The States thus choosing a member *ad hoc* shall have regard to the qualities required of members of the Commission by virtue of article 2, paragraph 1, and article 4, paragraphs 1 and 2. Any member *ad hoc* thus chosen shall be of the nationality of the State which chooses him or of a State Party to the Protocol, and shall serve in a personal capacity.

3. Should there be several States Parties to the dispute having the same interest they shall, for the purpose of choosing members *ad hoc,* be reckoned as one party only. The manner in which this provision shall be applied shall be determined by the Rules of Procedure of the Commission referred to in article 11.

Article 9. Members of the Commission and members *ad hoc* chosen under the provisions of article 8 shall receive travel and *per diem* allowances in respect of the periods during which they are engaged on the work of the Commission from the resources of the United Nations Educational, Scientific and Cultural Organization on terms laid down by the Executive Board.

Article 10. The Secretariat of the Commission shall be provided by the Director-General.

Article 11. 1. The Commission shall elect its Chairman and Vice-Chairman for a period of two years. They may be re-elected.

2. The Commission shall establish its own Rules of Procedure, but these rules shall provide, *inter alia,* that:

(a) Two-thirds of the members, including the members *ad hoc,* if any, shall constitute a quorum.

(b) Decisions of the Commission shall be made by a majority vote of the members and members *ad hoc* present; if the votes are equally divided, the Chairman shall have a casting vote.

(c) If a State refers a matter to the Commission under article 12 or article 13:

(i) Such State, the State complained against, and any State Party to this Protocol whose national is concerned in such matter may make submissions in writing to the Commission;

(ii) Such State and the State complained against shall have the right to be represented at the hearings of the matter and to make submissions orally.

3. The Commission, on the occasion when it first proposes to establish its Rules of Procedure, shall send them in draft form to the States then Parties to the Protocol who may communicate any observation and suggestion they may wish to make within three months. The Commission shall re-examine its Rules of Procedure if at any time so requested by any State Party to the Protocol.

Article 12. 1. If a State Party to this Protocol considers that another State Party is not giving effect to a provision of the Convention, it may, by written communication, bring the matter to the attention of that State. Within three months after the receipt of the communication, the receiving State shall afford the complaining State an explanation or statement in writing concerning the matter, which should include, to the extent possible and pertinent, references to procedures and remedies taken, or pending, or available in the matter.

2. If the matter is not adjusted to the satisfaction of both parties, either by bilateral negotiations or by any other procedure open to them, within six months after the receipt by the receiving State of the initial communication, either State shall have the right to refer the matter to the Commission, by notice given to the Director-General and to the other State.

3. The provisions of the preceding paragraphs shall not affect the rights of States Parties to have recourse, in accordance with general or special international agreements in force between them, to other procedures for settling disputes including that of referring disputes by mutual consent to the Permanent Court of Arbitration at The Hague.

Article 13. From the beginning of the sixth year after the entry into force of this Protocol, the Commission may also be made responsible for seeking the settlement of any dispute concerning the application or interpretation of the Convention arising between States which are Parties to the Convention but are not, or are not all, Parties to this Protocol, if the said States agree to submit such dispute to the Commission. The conditions to be fulfilled by the said States in reaching agreement shall be laid down by the Commission's Rules of Procedure.

Article 14. The Commission shall deal with a matter referred to it under article 12 or article 13 of this Protocol only after it has ascertained that all available domestic remedies have been invoked and exhausted in the case, in conformity with the generally recognized principles of international law.

Article 15. Except in cases where new elements have been submitted to it, the Commission shall not consider matters it has already dealt with.

Article 16. In any matter referred to it, the Commission may call upon the States concerned to supply any relevant information.

Article 17. 1. Subject to the provisions of article 14, the Commission, after obtaining all the information it thinks necessary, shall ascertain the facts, and make available its good offices to the States concerned with a view to an amicable solution of the matter on the basis of respect for the Convention.

2. The Commission shall in every case, and in no event later than eighteen months after the date of receipt by the Director-General of the notice under article 12, paragraph 2, draw up a report in accordance with the provisions of paragraph 3 below which will be sent to the States concerned and then communicated to the Director-General for publication. When an advisory opinion is requested of the International Court of Justice, in accordance with article 18, the time-limit shall be extended appropriately.

3. If a solution within the terms of paragraph 1 of this article is reached, the Commission shall confine its report to a brief statement of the facts and of the solution reached. If such a solution is not reached, the Commission shall draw up a report on the facts and indicate the recommendations which it made with a view to conciliation. If the report does not represent in whole or in part the unanimous opinion of the members of the Commission, any member of the Commission shall be entitled to attach to it a separate opinion. The written and oral submissions made by the parties to the case in accordance with article 11, paragraph 2 (c), shall be attached to the report.

Article 18. The Commission may recommend to the Executive Board, or to the General Conference if the recommendation is made within two months before the opening of one of its sessions, that the International Court of Justice be requested to give an advisory opinion on any legal question connected with a matter laid before the Commission.

Article 19. The Commission shall submit to the General Conference at each of its regular sessions a report on its activities, which shall be transmitted to the General Conference by the Executive Board.

Article 20. 1. The Director-General shall convene the first meeting of the Commission at the Headquarters of the United Nations Educational, Scientific and Cultural Organization within three months after its nomination by the General Conference.

2. Subsequent meetings of the Commissions shall be convened when necessary by the Chairman of the Commission to whom, as well as to all other members of the Commission, the Director-General shall transmit all matters referred to the Commission in accordance with the provisions of this Protocol.

3. Notwithstanding paragraph 2 of this article, when at least one-third of the members of the Commission consider that the Commission should examine a matter in accordance with the provisions of this Protocol, the Chairman shall on their so requiring convene a meeting of the Commission for that purpose.

Article 21. The present Protocol is drawn up in English, French, Russian and Spanish, all four texts being equally authentic.

Article 22. 1. This Protocol shall be subject to ratification or acceptance by States Members of the United Nations Educational, Scientific and Cultural Organization which are Parties to the Convention.

2. The instruments of ratification or acceptance shall be deposited with the Director-General.

Article 23. 1. This Protocol shall be open to accession by all States not Members of the United Nations Educational, Scientific and Cultural Organization which are Parties to the Convention.

2. Accession shall be effected by the deposit of an instrument of accession with the Director-General.

Article 24. This Protocol shall enter into force three months after the date of the deposit of the fifteenth instrument of ratification, acceptance or accession, but only with respect of those States which have deposited their respective instruments on or before that date. It shall enter into force with respect to any other State three months after the deposit of its instrument of ratification, acceptance or accession.

Article 25. Any State may, at the time of ratification, acceptance or accession or at any subsequent date, declare, by notification to the Director-General, that it agrees, with respect to any other State assuming the same obligation, to refer to the International Court of Justice, after the drafting of the report provided for in article 17, paragraph 3, any dispute covered by this Protocol on which no amicable solution has been reached in accordance with article 17, paragraph 1.

Article 26. 1. Each State Party to this Protocol may denounce it.

2. The denunciation shall be notified by an instrument in writing, deposited with the Director-General.

3. Denunciation of the Convention shall automatically entail denunciation of this Protocol.

4. The denunciation shall take effect twelve months after the receipt of the instrument of denunciation. The State denouncing the Protocol shall, however, remain bound by its provisions in respect of any cases concerning it which have been referred to the Commission before the end of the time-limit stipulated in this paragraph.

Article 27. The Director-General shall inform the States Members of the United Nations Educational, Scientific and Cultural Organization, the States not Members of the Organization which are referred to in article 23, as well as the United Nations, of the deposit of all the instruments of ratification, acceptance and accession provided for in articles 22 and 23, and of the notifications and denunciations provided for in articles 25 and 26 respectively.

Article 28. In conformity with article 102 of the Charter of the United Nations, this Protocol shall be registered with the Secretariat of the United Nations at the request of the Director-General.

Done in Paris, this eighteenth day of December 1962, in two authentic copies bearing the signatures of the President of the twelfth session of the General Conference and of the Director-General of the United Nations Educational, Scientific and Cultural Organization, which shall be deposited in the archives of the United Nations Educational, Scientific and Cultural Organization, and certified true copies of which shall be delivered to all the States referred to in articles 12 and 13 of the Convention against Discrimination in Education as well as to the United Nations.

The foregoing is the authentic text of the Protocol duly adopted by the General Conference of the United Nations Educational, Scientific and Cultural Organization during its twelfth session, which was held in Paris and declared closed the twelfth day of December 1962.

In faith whereof we have appended our signatures this eighteenth day of December 1962.

SEE ALSO *Good Offices, Mediation, or Conciliation Commissions.*

UNESCO CONVENTION CONCERNING THE PROTECTION OF THE WORLD CULTURAL HERITAGE (1972).

The convention, adopted on 16 November 1972 by the UNESCO GENERAL CONFERENCE at its 17th session, held in Paris, entered into force on 17 December 1975. Each State party to the convention undertakes to ensure conservation of elements of the world cultural heritage situated in its territory, to make an inventory of such elements, and to recognize that it is the duty of the international community as a whole to cooperate in conserving that heritage.

The convention provides for the establishment of an intergovernmental committee, known as the World Heritage Committee, to supervise protection of items recognized as forming part of the world's cultural and natural heritage which are of universal value from the point of view of history, art, science, or esthetics, and a fund, known as the World Heritage Fund, to finance such activities.

The text of the convention (*UNESCO's Standard-Setting Instruments,* No. IV.A.5) is as follows:

The General Conference of the United Nations Educational, Scientific and Cultural Organization, meeting in Paris from 17 October to 21 November 1972, at its seventeenth session,

Noting that the cultural heritage and the natural heritage are increasingly threatened with destruction not only by the traditional causes of decay, but also by changing social and economic conditions which aggravate the situation with even more formidable phenomena of damage or destruction,

Considering that deterioration or disappearance of any item of the cultural or natural heritage constitutes a harmful impoverishment of the heritage of all the nations of the world,

Considering that protection of this heritage at the national level often remains incomplete because of the scale of the resources which it requires and of the insufficient economic, scientific and technical resources of the country where the property to be protected is situated,

Recalling that the Constitution of the Organization provides that it will maintain, increase and diffuse knowledge, by assuring the conservation and protection of the world's heritage, and recommending to the nations concerned the necessary international conventions,

Considering that the existing international conventions, recommendations and resolutions concerning cultural and natural property demonstrate the importance, for all the peoples of the world, of safeguarding this unique and irreplaceable property, to whatever people it may belong,

Considering that parts of the cultural or natural heritage are of outstanding interest and therefore need to be preserved as part of the world heritage of mankind as a whole,

Considering that, in view of the magnitude and gravity of the new dangers threatening them, it is incumbent on the international community as a whole to participate in the protection of the cultural and natural heritage of outstanding universal value, by the granting of collective assistance which, although not taking the place of action by the State concerned, will serve as an effective complement thereto,

Considering that it is essential for this purpose to adopt new provisions in the form of a convention establishing an effective system of collective protection of the cultural and natural heritage of outstanding universal value, organized on a permanent basis and in accordance with modern scientific methods,

Having decided, at its sixteenth session, that this question should be made the subject of an international convention,

Adopts this sixteenth day of November 1972 this Convention.

I. Definitions of the Cultural and the Natural Heritage

Article 1. For the purposes of this Convention, the following shall be considered as "cultural heritage",

Monuments: architectural works, works of monumental sculpture and painting, elements or structures of an archaeological nature, inscriptions, cave dwellings and combinations of features, which are of outstanding universal value from the point of view of history, art or science;

Groups of buildings: groups of separate or connected buildings which, because of their architecture, their homogeneity or their place in the landscape, are of outstanding universal value from the point of view of history, art or science;

Sites: works of man or the combined works of nature and of man, and areas including archaeological sites which are of outstanding universal value from the historical, aesthetic, ethnological or anthropological points of view.

Article 2. For the purposes of this Convention, the following shall be considered as "natural heritage":

Nature features consisting of physical and biological formations or groups of such formations, which are of outstanding universal value from the aesthetic or scientific point of view;

Geological and physiographical formations and precisely delineated areas which constitute the habitat of threatened species of animals and plants of outstanding universal value from the point of view of science or conservation;

Natural sites or precisely delineated natural areas of outstanding universal value from the point of view of science, conservation or natural beauty.

Article 3. It is for each State Party to this Convention to identify and delineate the different properties situated on its territory mentioned in Articles 1 and 2 above.

II. National Protection and International Protection of the Cultural and Natural Heritage

Article 4. Each State Party to this Convention recognizes that the duty of ensuring the identification, protection, conservation, presentation and transmission to future generations of the cultural and natural heritage referred to in Articles 1 and 2 and situated on its territory, belongs primarily to that State. It will do all it can to his end, to the utmost of its own resources and, where appropriate, with any international assistance and cooperation, in particular, financial, artistic, scientific and technical, which it may be able to obtain.

Article 5. To ensure that effective and active measures are taken for the protection, conservation and presentation of the cultural and natural heritage situated on its territory, each State Party to this Convention shall endeavour, in so far as possible, and as appropriate for each country:

(a) To adopt a general policy which aims to give the cultural and natural heritage a function in the life of the community and to integrate the protection of that heritage into comprehensive planning programmes;

(b) To set up within its territories, where such services do not exist, one or more services for the protection, conservation and presentation of the cultural and natural heritage with an appropriate staff and possessing the means to discharge their functions;

(c) To develop scientific and technical studies and research and to work out such operating methods as will make the State capable of counteracting the dangers that threaten its cultural or natural heritage;

(d) To take the appropriate legal, scientific, technical, administrative and financial measures necessary for the identification, protection, conservation, presentation and rehabilitation of this heritage; and

(e) To foster the establishment or development of national or regional centres for training in the protection, conservation and presentation of the cultural and natural heritage and to encourage scientific research in this field.

Article 6. 1. Whilst fully respecting the sovereignty of the States on whose territory the cultural and natural heritage mentioned in Articles 1 and 2 is situated, and without prejudice to property rights provided by national legislation, the States Parties to this Convention recognize that such heritage constitutes a world heritage for whose protection it is the duty of the international community as a whole to co-operate.

2. The States Parties undertake, in accordance with the provisions of this Convention, to give their help in the identification, protection, conservation and preservation of the cultural and natural heritage referred to in paragraphs 2

and 4 of Article 11 if the States on whose territory it is situated so request.

3. Each State Party to this Convention undertakes not to take any deliberate measures which might damage directly or indirectly the cultural and natural heritage referred to in Articles 1 and 2 situated on the territory of other States Parties to this Convention.

Article 7. For the purpose of this Convention, international protection of the world cultural and natural heritage shall be understood to mean the establishment of a system of international co-operation and assistance designed to support States Parties to the Convention in their efforts to conserve and identify that heritage.

III. Intergovernmental Committee for the Protection of the World Cultural and Natural Heritage

Article 8. 1. An Intergovernmental Committee for the Protection of the Cultural and Natural Heritage of Outstanding Universal Value, called "the World Heritage Committee", is hereby established within the United Nations Educational, Scientific and Cultural Organization. It shall be composed of 15 States Parties to the Convention, elected by States Parties to the Convention meeting in general assembly during the ordinary session of the General Conference of the United Nations Educational, Scientific and Cultural Organization. The number of States members of the Committee shall be increased to 21 as from the date of the ordinary session of the General Conference following the entry into force of this Convention for at least 40 States.

2. Election of members of the Committee shall ensure an equitable representation of the different regions and cultures of the world.

3. A representative of the International Centre for the Study of the Preservation and Restoration of Cultural Property (Rome Centre), a representative of the International Council of Monuments and Sites (ICOMOS) and a representative of the International Union for Conservation of Nature and Natural Resources (IUCN), to whom may be added, at the request of States Parties to the Convention meeting in general assembly during the ordinary sessions of the General Conference of the United Nations Educational, Scientific and Cultural Organization, representatives of other intergovernmental or non-governmental organizations, with similar objectives, may attend the meetings of the Committee in an advisory capacity.

Article 9. 1. The term of office of States members of the World Heritage Committee shall extend from the end of the ordinary session of the General Conference during which they are elected until the end of its third subsequent ordinary session.

2. The term of office of one-third of the members designated at the time of the first election shall, however, cease at the end of the first ordinary session of the General Conference following that at which they were elected; and the term of office, of a further third of the members designated at the same time shall cease at the end of the second ordinary session of the General Conference following that at which they were elected. The names of these members shall be chosen by lot by the President of the General Conference of the United Nations Educational, Scientific and Cultural Organization after the first election.

3. States members of the Committee shall choose as their representatives persons qualified in the field of the cultural or natural heritage.

Article 10. 1. The World Heritage Committee shall adopt its Rules of Procedure.

2. The Committee may at any time invite public or private organizations or individuals to participate in its meetings for consultation on particular problems.

3. The Committee may create such consultative bodies as it deems necessary for the performance of its functions.

Article 11. 1. Every State Party to this Convention shall, in so far as possible, submit to the World Heritage Committee an inventory of property forming part of the cultural and natural heritage, situated in its territory and suitable for inclusion in the list provided for in paragraph 2 of this Article. This inventory, which shall not be considered exhaustive, shall include documentation about the location of the property in question and its significance.

2. On the basis of the inventories submitted by States in accordance with paragraph 1, the Committee shall establish, keep up to date and publish, under the title of "World Heritage List", a list of properties forming part of the cultural heritage and natural heritage, as defined in Articles 1 and 2 of this Convention, which it considers as having outstanding universal value in terms of such criteria as it shall have established. An updated list shall be distributed at least every two years.

3. The inclusion of a property in the World Heritage List requires the consent of the State concerned. The inclusion of a property situated in a territory, sovereignty or jurisdiction over which is claimed by more than one State shall in no way prejudice the rights of the parties to the dispute.

4. The Committee shall establish, keep up to date and publish, whenever circumstances shall so require, under the title of "List of World Heritage in Danger", a list of the property appearing in the World Heritage List for the conservation of which major operations are necessary and for which assistance has been requested under this Convention. This list shall contain an estimate of the cost of such operations. The list may include only such property forming part of the cultural and natural heritage as is threatened by serious and specific dangers, such as the threat of disappearance caused by accelerated deterioration, large-scale public or private projects or rapid urban or tourist development projects; destruction caused by changes in the use or ownership of the land; major alterations due to unknown causes; abandonment for any reason whatsoever; the outbreak or the threat of an armed conflict; calamities and cataclysms; serious fires, earthquakes, landslides; volcanic eruptions; changes in water level, floods, and tidal waves. The Committee may at any time, in case of urgent need, make a new entry in the List of World Heritage in Danger and publicize such entry immediately.

5. The Committee shall define the criteria on the basis of which a property belonging to the cultural or natural heritage may be included in either of the lists mentioned in paragraphs 2 and 4 of this article.

6. Before refusing a request for inclusion in one of the two lists mentioned in paragraphs 2 and 4 of this article, the Committee shall consult the State Party in whose territory the cultural or natural property in question is situated.

7. The Committee shall, with the agreement of the States concerned, co-ordinate and encourage the studies and research needed for the drawing up of the lists referred to in paragraphs 2 and 4 of this article.

Article 12. The fact that a property belonging to the cultural or natural heritage has not been included in either of the two lists mentioned in paragraphs 2 and 4 of Article 11 shall in no way be construed to mean that it does not have an outstanding universal value for purposes other than those resulting from inclusion in these lists.

Article 13. 1. The World Heritage Committee shall receive and study requests for international assistance formulated by States Parties to this Convention with respect to property forming part of the cultural or natural heritage, situated in their territories, and included or potentially suitable for inclusion in the lists referred to in paragraphs 2 and 4 of Article 11. The purpose of such requests may be to secure the protection, conservation, presentation or rehabilitation of such property.

2. Requests for international assistance under paragraph 1 of this article may also be concerned with identification of cultural or natural property defined in Articles 1 and 2, when preliminary investigations have shown that further inquiries would be justified.

3. The Committee shall decide on the action to be taken with regard to these requests, determine where appropriate, the nature and extent of its assistance, and authorize the conclusion, on its behalf, of the necessary arrangements with the government concerned.

4. The Committee shall determine an order of priorities for its operations. It shall in so doing bear in mind the respective importance for the world cultural and natural heritage of the property requiring protection, the need to give international assistance to the property most representative of a natural environment or of the genius and the history of the peoples of the world, the urgency of the work to be done, the resources available to the States on whose territory the threatened property is situated and in particular the extent to which they are able to safeguard such property by their own means.

5. The Committee shall draw up, keep up to date and publicize a list of property for which international assistance has been granted.

6. The Committee shall decide on the use of the resources of the Fund established under Article 15 of this Convention. It shall seek ways of increasing these resources and shall take all useful steps to this end.

7. The Committee shall co-operate with international and national governmental and nongovernmental organizations having objectives similar to those of this Convention. For the implementation of its programmes and projects, the Committee may call on such organizations, particularly the International Centre for the Study of the Preservation and Restoration of Cultural Property (the Rome Centre), the International Council of Monuments and Sites (ICOMOS) and the International Union for Conservation of Nature and Natural Resources (IUCN), as well as on public and private bodies and individuals.

8. Decisions of the Committee shall be taken by a majority of two-thirds of its members present and voting. A majority of the members of the Committee shall constitute a quorum.

Article 14. 1. The World Heritage Committee shall be assisted by a Secretariat appointed by the Director-General of the United Nations Educational, Scientific and Cultural Organization.

2. The Director-General of the United Nations Educational, Scientific and Cultural Organization, utilizing to the fullest extent possible the services of the International Centre for the Study of the Preservation and the Restoration of Cultural Property (the Rome Centre), the International Council of Monuments and Sites (ICOMOS) and the International Union for Conservation of Nature and Natural Resources (IUCN) in their respective areas of competence

and capability, shall prepare the Committee's documentation and the agenda of its meetings and shall have the responsibility for the implementation of its decisions.

IV. Fund for the Protection of the World Cultural and Natural Heritage

Article 15. 1. A Fund for the Protection of the World Cultural and Natural Heritage of Outstanding Universal Value, called "the World Heritage Fund", is hereby established.

2. The Fund shall constitute a trust fund, in conformity with the provisions of the Financial Regulations of the United Nations Educational, Scientific and Cultural Organization.

3. The resources of the Fund shall consist of:

(a) Compulsory and voluntary contributions made by the States Parties to this Convention,

(b) Contributions, gifts or bequests which may be made by:

(i) other States;

(ii) the United Nations Educational, Scientific and Cultural Organization, other organizations of the United Nations system, particularly the United Nations Development Programme or other intergovernmental organization;

(iii) public or private bodies or individuals;

(c) Any interest due on the resources of the Fund;

(d) Funds raised by collections and receipts from events organized for the benefit of the Fund; and

(e) All other resources authorized by the Fund's regulations, as drawn up by the World Heritage Committee.

4. Contributions to the Fund and other forms of assistance made available to the Committee may be used only for such purposes as the Committee shall define. The Committee may accept contributions to be used only for a certain programme or project, provided that the Committee shall have decided on the implementation of such programme or project. No political conditions may be attached to contributions made to the Fund.

Article 16. 1. Without prejudice to any supplementary voluntary contribution, the States Parties to this Convention undertake to pay regularly, every two years, to the World Heritage Fund, contributions, the amount of which, in the form of a uniform percentage applicable to all States, shall be determined by the General Assembly of States Parties to the Convention, meeting during the sessions of the General Conference of the United Nations Educational, Scientific and Cultural Organization. This decision of the General Assembly requires the majority of the States Parties present and voting, which have not made the declaration referred to in paragraph 2 of this Article. In no case shall the compulsory contribution of States Parties to the Convention exceed 1 per cent of the contribution to the Regular Budget of the United Nations Educational, Scientific and Cultural Organization.

2. However, each State referred to in Article 31 or in Article 32 of this Convention may declare, at the time of the deposit of its instruments of ratification, acceptance or accession, that it shall not be bound by the provisions of paragraph 1 of this Article.

3. A State Party to the Convention which has made the declaration referred to in paragraph 2 of this Article may at any time withdraw the said declaration by notifying the Director-General of the United Nations Educational, Scientific and Cultural Organization. However, the withdrawal of the declaration shall not take effect in regard to the com-

pulsory contribution due by the State until the date of the subsequent General Assembly of States Parties to the Convention.

4. In order that the Committee may be able to plan its operations effectively, the contributions of States Parties to this Convention which have made the declaration referred to in paragraph 2 of this Article, shall be paid on a regular basis, at least every two years, and should not be less than the contributions which they should have paid if they had been bound by the provisions of paragraph 1 of this Article.

5. Any State Party to the Convention which is in arrears with the payment of its compulsory or voluntary contribution for the current year and the calendar year immediately preceding it shall not be eligible as a Member of the World Heritage Committee, although this provision shall not apply to the first election.

The terms of office of any such State which is already a member of the Committee shall terminate at the time of the elections provided for in Article 8, paragraph 1 of this Convention.

Article 17. The States Parties to this Convention shall consider or encourage the establishment of national, public and private foundations or associations whose purpose is to invite donations for the protection of the cultural and natural heritage as defined in Articles 1 and 2 of this Convention.

Article 18. The States Parties to this Convention shall give their assistance to international fund-raising campaigns organized for the World Heritage Fund under the auspices of the United Nations Educational, Scientific and Cultural Organization. They shall facilitate collections made by the bodies mentioned in paragraph 3 of Article 15 for this purpose.

V. Conditions and Arrangements for International Assistance

Article 19. Any State Party to this Convention may request international assistance for property forming part of the cultural or natural heritage of outstanding universal value situated within its territory. It shall submit with its request such information and documentation provided for in Article 21 as it has in its possession and as will enable the Committee to come to a decision.

Article 20. Subject to the provisions of paragraph 2 of Article 13, sub-paragraph (c) of Article 22 and Article 23, international assistance provided for by this Convention may be granted only to property forming part of the cultural and natural heritage which the World Heritage Committee has decided, or may decide, to enter in one of the lists mentioned in paragraphs 2 and 4 of Article 11.

Article 21. 1. The World Heritage Committee shall define the procedure by which requests to it for international assistance shall be considered and shall specify the content of the request, which should define the operation contemplated, the work that is necessary, the expected cost thereof, the degree of urgency and the reasons why the resources of the State requesting assistance do not allow it to meet all the expenses. Such requests must be supported by experts' reports whenever possible.

2. Requests based upon disasters or natural calamities should, by reasons of the urgent work which they may involve, be given immediate, priority consideration by the Committee, which should have a reserve fund at its disposal against such contingencies.

3. Before coming to a decision, the Committee shall carry out such studies and consultations as it deems necessary.

Article 22. Assistance granted by the World Heritage Committee may take the following forms:

(a) Studies concerning the artistic, scientific and technical problems raised by the protection, conservation, presentation and rehabilitation of the cultural and natural heritage, as defined in paragraphs 2 and 4 of Article 11 of this Convention;

(b) Provision of experts, technicians and skilled labour to ensure that the approved work is correctly carried out;

(c) Training of staff and specialists at all levels in the field of identification, protection, conservation, presentation and rehabilitation of the cultural and natural heritage;

(d) Supply of equipment which the State concerned does not possess or is not in a position to acquire;

(e) Low-interest or interest-free loans which might be repayable on a long-term basis;

(f) The granting, in exceptional cases and for special reasons, of non-repayable subsidies.

Article 23. The World Heritage Committee may also provide international assistance to national or regional centres for the training of staff and specialists at all levels in the field of identification, protection, conservation, presentation and rehabilitation of the cultural and natural heritage.

Article 24. International assistance on a large scale shall be preceded by detailed scientific, economic and technical studies. These studies shall draw upon the most advanced techniques for the protection, conservation, presentation and rehabilitation of the natural and cultural heritage and shall be consistent with the objectives of this Convention. The studies shall also seek means of making rational use of the resources available in the State concerned.

Article 25. As a general rule, only part of the cost of work necessary shall be borne by the international community. The contribution of the State benefiting from international assistance shall constitute a substantial share of the resources devoted to each programme or project, unless its resources do not permit this.

Article 26. The World Heritage Committee and the recipient State shall define in the agreement they conclude the conditions in which a programme or project for which international assistance under the terms of this Convention is provided, shall be carried out. It shall be the responsibility of the State receiving such international assistance to continue to protect, conserve and present the property so safeguarded, in observance of the conditions laid down by the agreement.

VI. Educational Programmes

Article 27. 1. The States Parties to this Convention shall endeavour by all appropriate means, and in particular by educational and information programmes, to strengthen appreciation and respect by their peoples of the cultural and natural heritage defined in Articles 1 and 2 of the Convention.

2. They shall undertake to keep the public broadly informed of the dangers threatening this heritage and of activities carried on in pursuance of this Convention.

Article 28. States Parties to this Convention which receive international assistance under the Convention shall take appropriate measures to make known the importance of the property for which assistance has been received and the role played by such assistance.

VII. Reports

Article 29. 1. The States Parties to this Convention shall, in the reports which they submit to the General Conference of the United Nations Educational, Scientific and Cultural Organization on dates and in a manner to be determined by it, give information on the legislative and administrative provisions which they have adopted and other action which they have taken for the application of this Convention, together with details of the experience acquired in this field.

2. These reports shall be brought to the attention of the World Heritage Committee.

3. The Committee shall submit a report on its activities at each of the ordinary sessions of the General Conference of the United Nations Educational, Scientific and Cultural Organization.

VIII. Final Clauses

Article 30. This Convention is drawn up in Arabic, English, French, Russian and Spanish, the five texts being equally authoritative.

Article 31. 1. This Convention shall be subject to ratification or acceptance by States members of the United Nations Educational, Scientific and Cultural Organization in accordance with their respective constitutional procedures.

2. The instruments of ratification or acceptance shall be deposited with the Director-General of the United Nations Educational, Scientific and Cultural Organization.

Article 32. 1. This Convention shall be open to accession by all States not members of the United Nations Educational, Scientific and Cultural Organization which are invited by the General Conference of the Organization to accede to it.

2. Accession shall be effected by the deposit of an instrument of accession with the Director-General of the United Nations Educational, Scientific and Cultural Organization.

Article 33. This Convention shall enter into force three months after the date of the deposit of the twentieth instrument of ratification, acceptance or accession, but only with respect to those States which have deposited their respective instruments of ratification, acceptance or accession on or before that date. It shall enter into force with respect to any other State three months after the deposit of its instrument of ratification, acceptance or accession.

Article 34. The following provisions shall apply to those States Parties to this Convention which have a federal or non-unitary constitutional system:

(a) With regard to the provisions of this Convention, the implementation of which comes under the legal jurisdiction of the federal or central legislative power, the obligations of the federal or central government shall be the same as for those States Parties which are not federal States;

(b) With regard to the provisions of this Convention, the implementation of which comes under the legal jurisdiction of individual constituent States, countries, provinces or cantons that are not obliged by the constitutional system of the federation to take legislative measures, the federal government shall inform the competent authorities of such States, countries, provinces or cantons of the said provisions, with its recommendation for their adoption.

Article 35. 1. Each State Party to this Convention may denounce the Convention.

2. The denunciation shall be notified by an instrument in writing, deposited with the Director-General of the United Nations Educational, Scientific and Cultural Organization.

3. The denunciation shall take effect twelve months after the receipt of the instrument of denunciation. It shall not affect the financial obligations of the denouncing State until the date on which the withdrawal takes effect.

Article 36. The Director-General of the United Nations Educational, Scientific and Cultural Organization shall inform the States members of the Organization, the States not members of the Organization which are referred to in Article 32, as well as the United Nations, of the deposit of all the instruments of ratification, acceptance, or accession provided for in Articles 31 and 32, and of the denunciations provided for in Article 35.

Article 37. 1. This Convention may be revised by the General Conference of the United Nations Educational, Scientific and Cultural Organization. Any such revision shall, however, bind only the States which shall become Parties to the revising convention.

2. If the General Conference should adopt a new convention revising this Convention in whole or in part, then, unless the new convention otherwise provides, this Convention shall cease to be open to ratification, acceptance or accession, as from the date on which the new revising convention enters into force.

Article 38. In conformity with Article 102 of the Charter of the United Nations, this Convention shall be registered with the Secretariat of the United Nations at the request of the Director-General of the United Nations Educational, Scientific and Cultural Organization.

Done in Paris, this twenty-third day of November 1972, in two authentic copies bearing the signature of the President of the seventeenth session of the General Conference and of the Director-General of the United Nations Educational, Scientific and Cultural Organization, which shall be deposited in the archives of the United Nations Educational, Scientific and Cultural Organization, and certified true copies of which shall be delivered to all the States referred to in Articles 31 and 32 as well as to the United Nations.

UNESCO CONVENTION FOR THE PROTECTION OF CULTURAL PROPERTY IN THE EVENT OF ARMED CONFLICT (1954). The Convention, also known as the Hague Convention, together with the UNESCO Protocol to the Convention for the Protection of Cultural Property in the Event of Armed Conflict, was adopted at the Hague on 14 May 1954 by an international conference of States convened by UNESCO. It entered into force on 7 August 1956.

Under the convention, the contracting parties undertake to safeguard cultural property of great importance to the cultural heritage of peoples, irrespective of its origin or ownership, in the event of ARMED CONFLICT; and also to provide special protection for the refuges intended to shelter such property. The procedures for application of the convention are set out in a series of regulations for its execution.

The text of the convention, and of the regulations for its execution, (*UNESCO's Standard-Setting Instru-*

ments, No. IV.A.3, pp. 3–17 and 18–33, respectively), are as follows:

The High Contracting Parties,

Recognizing that cultural property has suffered grave damage during recent armed conflicts and that, by reason of the developments in the technique of warfare, it is in increasing danger of destruction;

Being convinced that damage to cultural property belonging to any people whatsoever means damage to the cultural heritage of all mankind, since each people makes its contribution to the culture of the world;

Considering that the preservation of the cultural heritage is of great importance for all peoples of the world and that it is important that this heritage should receive international protection;

Guided by the principles concerning the protection of cultural property during armed conflict, as established in the Conventions of The Hague of 1899 and of 1907 and in the Washington Pact of 15 April, 1935;

Being of the opinion that such protection cannot be effective unless both national and international measures have been taken to organize it in time of peace;

Being determined to take all possible steps to protect cultural property;

Have agreed upon the following provisions:

Chapter I. General Provisions Regarding Protection

Article 1. Definition of Cultural Property. For the purposes of the present Convention, the term 'cultural property' shall cover, irrespective of origin or ownership:

(a) movable or immovable property of great importance to the cultural heritage of every people, such as monuments of architecture, art or history, whether religious or secular; archaeological sites; groups of buildings which, as a whole, are of historical or artistic interest; works of art; manuscripts, books and other objects of artistic, historical or archaeological interest; as well as scientific collections and important collections of books or archives or of reproductions of the property defined above;

(b) buildings whose main and effective purpose is to preserve or exhibit the movable cultural property defined in sub-paragraph (a) such as museums, large libraries and depositories of archives, and refuges intended to shelter, in the event of armed conflict, the movable cultural property defined in sub-paragraph (a);

(c) centres containing a large amount of cultural property as defined in sub-paragraphs (a) and (b), to be known as 'centres containing monuments'.

Article 2. Protection of Cultural Property. For the purposes of the present Convention, the protection of cultural property shall comprise the safeguarding of and respect for such property.

Article 3. Safeguarding of Cultural Property. The High Contracting Parties undertake to prepare in time of peace for the safeguarding of cultural property situated within their own territory against the foreseeable effects of an armed conflict, by taking such measures as they consider appropriate.

Article 4. Respect for Cultural Property. 1. The High Contracting Parties undertake to respect cultural property situated within their own territory as well as within the territory of other High Contracting Parties by refraining from any use of the property and its immediate surroundings or of the appliances in use for its protection for purposes which are likely to expose it to destruction or damage in the event of armed conflict; and by refraining from any act of hostility directed against such property.

2. The obligations mentioned in paragraph 1 of the present Article may be waived only in cases where military necessity imperatively requires such a waiver.

3. The High Contracting Parties further undertake to prohibit, prevent and, if necessary, put a stop to any form of theft, pillage, or misappropriation of, and any acts of vandalism directed against, cultural property. They shall refrain from requisitioning movable cultural property situated in the territory of another High Contracting Party.

4. They shall refrain from any act directed by way of reprisals against cultural property.

5. No High Contracting Party may evade the obligations incumbent upon it under the present Article, in respect of another High Contracting Party, by reason of the fact that the latter has not applied the measures of safeguard referred to in Article 3.

Article 5. Occupation. 1. Any High Contracting Party in occupation of the whole or part of the territory of another High Contracting Party shall as far as possible support the competent national authorities of the occupied country in safeguarding and preserving its cultural property.

2. Should it prove necessary to take measures to preserve cultural property situated in occupied territory and damaged by military operations, and should the competent national authorities be unable to take such measures, the Occupying Power shall, as far as possible, and in close co-operation with such authorities, take the most necessary measures of preservation.

3. Any High Contracting Party whose government is considered their legitimate government by members of a resistance movement, shall, if possible, draw their attention to the obligation to comply with those provisions of the Convention dealing with respect for cultural property.

Article 6. Distinctive Marking of Cultural Property. In accordance with the provisions of Article 16, cultural property may bear a distinctive emblem so as to facilitate its recognition.

Article 7. Military Measures. 1. The High Contracting Parties undertake to introduce in time of peace into their military regulations or instructions such provisions as may ensure observance of the present Convention, and to foster in the members of their armed forces a spirit of respect for the culture and cultural property of all peoples.

2. The High Contracting Parties undertake to plan or establish in peace-time, within their armed forces, services or specialist personnel whose purpose will be to secure respect for cultural property and to co-operate with the civilian authorities responsible for safeguarding it.

Chapter II. Special Protection

Article 8. Granting of Special Protection. 1. There may be placed under special protection a limited number of refuges intended to shelter movable cultural property in the event of armed conflict, of centres containing monuments and other immovable cultural property of very great importance, provided that they:

(a) are situated at an adequate distance from any large industrial centre or from any important military objective constituting a vulnerable point, such as, for example, an aerodrome, broadcasting station, establishment engaged upon work of national defence, a port or railway station of relative importance or a main line of communication;

(b) are not used for military purposes.

2. A refuge for movable cultural property may also be placed under special protection, whatever its location, if it is so constructed that, in all probability, it will not be damaged by bombs.

3. A centre containing monuments shall be deemed to be used for military purposes whenever it is used for the movement of military personnel or material, even in transit. The same shall apply whenever activities directly connected with military operations, the stationing of military personnel, or the production of war material are carried on within the centre.

4. The guarding of cultural property mentioned in paragraph 1 above by armed custodians specially empowered to do so, or the presence, in the vicinity of such cultural property, of police forces normally responsible for the maintenance of public order shall not be deemed to be used for military purposes.

5. If any cultural property mentioned in paragraph 1 of the present Article is situated near an important military objective as defined in the said paragraph, it may nevertheless by placed under special protection if the High Contracting Party asking for that protection undertakes, in the event of armed conflict, to make no use of the objective and particularly, in the case of a port, railway station or aerodrome, to divert all traffic therefrom. In that event, such diversion shall be prepared in time of peace.

6. Special protection is granted to cultural property by its entry in the 'International Register of Cultural Property under Special Protection'. This entry shall only be made, in accordance with the provisions of the present Convention and under the conditions provided for in the Regulations for the execution of the Convention.

Article 9. Immunity of Cultural Property under Special Protection. The High Contracting Parties undertake to ensure the immunity of cultural property under special protection by refraining, from the time of entry in the International Register, from any act of hostility directed against such property and, except for the cases provided for in paragraph 5 of Article 8, from any use of such property or its surroundings for military purposes.

Article 10. Identification and Control. During an armed conflict, cultural property under special protection shall be marked with the distinctive emblem described in Article 16, and shall be open to international control as provided for in the Regulations for the execution of the Convention.

Article 11. Withdrawal of Immunity. 1. If one of the High Contracting Parties commits, in respect of any item of cultural property under special protection, a violation of the obligations under Article 9, the opposing Party shall, so long as this violation persists, be released from the obligation to ensure the immunity of the property concerned. Nevertheless, whenever possible, the latter Party shall first request the cessation of such violation within a reasonable time.

2. Apart from the case provided for in paragraph 1 of the present Article, immunity shall be withdrawn from cultural property under special protection only in exceptional cases of unavoidable military necessity, and only for such time as that necessity continues. Such necessity can be established only by the officer commanding a force the equivalent of a division in size or larger. Whenever circumstances permit, the opposing Party shall be notified, a reasonable time in advance, of the decision to withdraw immunity.

3. The Party withdrawing immunity shall, as soon as possible, so inform the Commissioner-General for cultural property provided for in the Regulations for the execution of the Convention, in writing, stating the reasons.

Chapter III. Transport of Cultural Property

Article 12. Transport under Special Protection. 1. Transport exclusively engaged in the transfer of cultural property, whether within a territory or to another territory, may, at the request of the High Contracting Party concerned, take place under special protection in accordance with the conditions specified in the Regulations for the execution of the Convention.

2. Transport under special protection shall take place under the international supervision provided for in the aforesaid Regulations and shall display the distinctive emblem described in Article 16.

3. The High Contracting Parties shall refrain from any act of hostility directed against transport under special protection.

Article 13. Transport in Urgent Cases. 1. If a High Contracting Party considers that the safety of certain cultural property requires its transfer and that the matter is of such urgency that the procedure laid down in Article 12 cannot be followed, especially at the beginning of an armed conflict, the transport may display the distinctive emblem described in Article 16, provided that an application for immunity referred to in Article 12 has not already been made and refused. As far as possible, notification of transfer should be made to the opposing Parties. Nevertheless, transport conveying cultural property to the territory of another country may not display the distinctive emblem unless immunity has been expressly granted to it.

2. The High Contracting Parties shall take, so far as possible, the necessary precautions to avoid acts of hostility directed against the transport described in paragraph 1 of the present Article and displaying the distinctive emblem.

Article 14. Immunity from Seizure, Capture and Prize. 1. Immunity from seizure, placing in prize, or capture shall be granted to:

(a) cultural property enjoying the protection provided for in Article 12 or that provided for in Article 13;

(b) the means of transport exclusively engaged in the transfer of such cultural property.

2. Nothing in the present Article shall limit the right of visit and search.

Chapter IV. Personnel

Article 15. Personnel. As far as is consistent with the interests of security, personnel engaged in the protection of cultural property shall, in the interests of such property, be respected and, if they fall into the hands of the opposing Party, shall be allowed to continue to carry out their duties whenever the cultural property for which they are responsible has also fallen into the hands of the opposing Party.

Chapter V. The Distinctive Emblem

Article 16. Emblem of the Convention. 1. The distinctive emblem of the Convention shall take the form of a shield, pointed below, per saltire blue and white (a shield consisting of a royal-blue square, one of the angles of which forms the point of the shield, and of a royal-blue triangle above the square, the space on either side being taken up by a white triangle).

2. The emblem shall be used alone, or repeated three

times in a triangular formation (one shield below), under the conditions provided for in Article 17.

Article 17. Use of the Emblem. 1. The distinctive emblem repeated three times may be used only as a means of identification of:

(a) immovable cultural property under special protection;

(b) the transport of cultural property under the conditions provided for in Articles 12 and 13;

(c) improvised refuges, under the conditions provided for in the Regulations for the execution of the Convention.

2. The distinctive emblem may be used alone only as a means of identification of:

(a) cultural property not under special protection;

(b) the persons responsible for the duties of control in accordance with the Regulations for the execution of the Convention;

(c) the personnel engaged in the protection of cultural property;

(d) the identity cards mentioned in the Regulations for the execution of the Convention.

3. During an armed conflict, the use of the distinctive emblem in any other cases than those mentions in the preceding paragraphs of the present Article, and the use for any purpose whatever of a sign resembling the distinctive emblem, shall be forbidden.

4. The distinctive emblem may not be placed on any immovable cultural property unless at the same time there is displayed an authorization duly dated and signed by the competent authority of the High Contracting Party.

Chapter VI. Scope of Application of the Convention

Article 18. Application of the Convention. 1. Apart from the provisions which shall take effect in time of peace, the present Convention shall apply in the event of declared war or of any other armed conflict which may arise between two or more of the High Contracting Parties, even if the state of war is not recognized by one or more of them.

2. The Convention shall also apply to all cases of partial or total occupation of the territory of a High Contracting Party, even if the said occupation meets with no armed resistance.

3. If one of the Powers in conflict is not a Party to the present Convention, the Powers which are Parties thereto shall nevertheless remain bound by it in their mutual relations. They shall furthermore be bound by the Convention, in relation to the said Power, if the latter has declared that it accepts the provisions thereof and so long as it applies them.

Article 19. Conflicts not of an International Character. 1. In the event of an armed conflict not of an international character occurring within the territory of one of the High Contracting Parties, each party to the conflict shall be bound to apply, as a minimum, the provisions of the present Convention which relate to respect for cultural property.

2. The parties to the conflict shall endeavour to bring into force, by means of special agreements, all or part of the other provisions of the present Convention.

3. The United Nations Educational, Scientific and Cultural Organization may offer its services to the parties to the conflict.

4. The application of the preceding provisions shall not affect the legal status of the parties to the conflict.

Chapter VII. Execution of the Convention

Article 20. Regulations for the Execution of the Convention. The procedure by which the present Convention is to be applied is defined in the Regulations for its execution, which constitute an integral part thereof.

Article 21. Protecting Powers. The present Convention and the Regulations for its execution shall be applied with the co-operation of the Protecting Powers responsible for safeguarding the interests of the Parties to the conflict.

Article 22. Conciliation Procedure. 1. The Protecting Powers shall lend their good offices in all cases where they may deem it useful in the interests of cultural property, particularly if there is disagreement between the Parties to the conflict as to the application or interpretation of the provisions of the present Convention or the Regulations for its execution.

2. For this purpose, each of the Protecting Powers may, either at the invitation of one Party, of the Director-General of the United Nations Educational, Scientific and Cultural Organization, or on its own initiative, propose to the Parties to the conflict a meeting of their representatives, and in particular of the authorities responsible for the protection of cultural property, if considered appropriate on suitably chosen neutral territory. The Parties to the conflict shall be bound to give effect to the proposals for meeting made to them. The Protecting Powers shall propose for approval by the Parties to the conflict a person belonging to a neutral Power or a person presented by the Director-General of the United Nations Educational, Scientific and Cultural Organization, which person shall be invited to take part in such a meeting in the capacity of Chairman.

Article 23. Assistance of Unesco. 1. The High Contracting Parties may call upon the United Nations Educational, Scientific and Cultural Organization for technical assistance in organizing the protection of their cultural property, or in connexion with any other problem arising out of the application of the present Convention or the Regulations for its execution. The Organization shall accord such assistance within the limits fixed by its programme and by its resources.

2. The Organization is authorized to make, on its own initiative, proposals on this matter to the High Contracting Parties.

Article 24. Special Agreements. 1. The High Contracting Parties may conclude special agreements for all matters concerning which they deem it suitable to make separate provision.

2. No special agreement may be concluded which would diminish the protection afforded by the present Convention to cultural property and to the personnel engaged in its protection.

Article 25. Dissemination of the Convention. The High Contracting Parties undertake, in time of peace as in time of armed conflict, to disseminate the text of the present Convention and the Regulations for its execution as widely as possible in their respective countries. They undertake, in particular, to include the study thereof in their programmes of military and, if possible, civilian training, so that its principles are made known to the whole population, especially the armed forces and personnel engaged in the protection of cultural property.

Article 26. Translations Reports. 1. The High Contracting Parties shall communicate to one another, through the Director-General of the United Nations Educational, Scientific and Cultural Organization, the official translations of the present Convention and of the Regulations for its execution.

2. Furthermore, at least once every four years, they shall forward to the Director-General a report giving whatever information they think suitable concerning any measures being taken, prepared or contemplated by their respective administrations in fulfilment of the present Convention and of the Regulations for its execution.

Article 27. Meetings. 1. The Director-General of the United Nations Educational, Scientific and Cultural Organization may, with the approval of the Executive Board, convene meetings of representatives of the High Contracting Parties. He must convene such a meeting if at least one-fifth of the High Contracting Parties so request.

2. Without prejudice to any other functions which have been conferred on it by the present Convention or the Regulations for its execution, the purpose of the meeting will be to study problems concerning the application of the Convention and of the Regulations for its execution, and to formulate recommendations in respect thereof.

3. The meeting may further undertake a revision of the Convention or the Regulations for its execution if the majority of the High Contracting Parties are represented, and in accordance with the provisions of Article 39.

Article 28. Sanctions. The High Contracting Parties undertake to take, within the framework of their ordinary criminal jurisdiction, all necessary steps to prosecute and impose penal or disciplinary sanctions upon those persons, of whatever nationality, who commit or order to be committed a breach of the present Convention.

Final Provisions

Article 29. Languages. 1. The present Convention is drawn up in English, French, Russian and Spanish, the four texts being equally authoritative.

2. The United Nations Educational, Scientific and Cultural Organization shall arrange for translations of the Convention into the other official languages of its General Conference.

Article 30. Signature. The present Convention shall bear the date of 14 May, 1954 and, until the date of 31 December, 1954, shall remain open for signature by all States invited to the Conference which met at The Hague from 21 April, 1954 to 14 May, 1954.

Article 31. Ratification. 1. The present Convention shall be subject to ratification by signatory States in accordance with their respective constitutional procedures.

2. The instruments of ratification shall be deposited with the Director-General of the United Nations Education, Scientific and Cultural Organization.

Article 32. Accession. From the date of its entry into force, the present Convention shall be open for accession by all States mentioned in Article 30 which have not signed it, as well as any other State invited to accede by the Executive Board of the United Nations Educational, Scientific and Cultural Organization. Accession shall be effected by the deposit of an instrument of accession with the Director-General of the United Nations Educational, Scientific and Cultural Organization.

Article 33. Entry into Force. 1. The present Convention shall enter into force three months after five instruments of ratification have been deposited.

2. Thereafter, it shall enter into force, for each High Contracting Party, three months after the deposit of its instrument of ratification or accession.

3. The situations referred to in Articles 18 and 19 shall give immediate effect to ratifications or accessions deposited by the Parties to the conflict either before or after the beginning of hostilities or occupation. In such cases the Director-General of the United Nations Educational, Scientific and Cultural Organization shall transmit the communications referred to in Article 38 by the speediest method.

Article 34. Effective Application. 1. Each State Party to the Convention on the date of its entry into force shall take all necessary measures to ensure its effective application within a period of six months after such entry into force.

2. This period shall be six months from the date of deposit of the instruments or ratification or accession for any State which deposits its instrument of ratification or accession after the date of the entry into force of the Convention.

Article 35. Territorial Extension of the Convention. Any High Contracting Party may, at the time of ratification or accession, or at any time thereafter, declare by notification addressed to the Director-General of the United Nations Educational, Scientific and Cultural Organization, that the present Convention shall extend to all or any of the territories for whose international relations it is responsible. The said notification shall take effect three months after the date of its receipt.

Article 36. Relation to Previous Conventions. 1. In the relations between Powers which are bound by the Conventions of The Hague concerning the Laws and Customs of War on Land (IV) and concerning Naval Bombardment in Time of War (IX), whether those of 29 July, 1899 or those of 18 October, 1907, and which are Parties to the present Convention, this last Convention shall be supplementary to the aforementioned Convention (IX) and to the Regulations annexed to the aforementioned Convention (IV) and shall substitute for the emblem described in Article 5 of the aforementioned Convention (IX) the emblem described in Article 16 of the present Convention, in cases in which the present Convention and the Regulations for its execution provide for the use of this distinctive emblem.

2. In the relations between Powers which are bound by the Washington Pact of 15 April, 1935 for the Protection of Artistic and Scientific Institutions and of Historic Monuments (Roerich Pact) and which are Parties to the present Convention, the latter Convention shall be supplementary to the Roerich Pact and shall substitute for the distinguishing flag described in Article III of the Pact the emblem defined in Article 16 of the present Convention, in cases in which the present Convention and the Regulations for its execution provide for the use of this distinctive emblem.

Article 37. Denunciation. 1. Each High Contracting Party may denounce the present Convention, on its own behalf, or on behalf of any territory for whose international relations it is responsible.

2. The denunciation shall be notified by an instrument in writing, deposited with the Director-General of the United Nations Educational, Scientific and Cultural Organization.

3. The denunciation shall take effect one year after the receipt of the instrument of denunciation. However, if, on the expiry of this period, the denouncing Party is involved in an armed conflict, the denunciation shall not take effect until the end of hostilities, or until the operations of repatriating cultural property are completed, whichever is the later.

Article 38. Notifications. The Director-General of the United Nations Educational, Scientific and Cultural Organization shall inform the States referred to in Articles 30 and 32, as well as the United Nations, of the deposit of all the instruments of ratification, accession or acceptance provided for in Articles 31, 32 and 39 and of the notifications and denunciations provided for respectively in Articles 35, 37 and 39.

Article 39. Revision of the Convention and of the Regulations for its Execution. 1. Any High Contracting Party may propose amendments to the present Convention or the Regulations for its execution. The text of any proposed amendment shall be communicated to the Director-General of the United Nations Educational, Scientific and Cultural Organization who shall transmit it to each High Contracting Party with the request that such Party reply within four months stating whether it:

(a) desires that a Conference be convened to consider the proposed amendment;

(b) favours the acceptance of the proposed amendment without a Conference; or

(c) favours the rejection of the proposed amendment without a Conference.

2. The Director-General shall transmit the replies, received under paragraph 1 of the present Article, to all High Contracting Parties.

3. If all the High Contracting Parties which have, within the prescribed time-limit, stated their views to the Director-General of the United Nations Educational, Scientific and Cultural Organization, pursuant to paragraph 1(b) of this Article, inform him that they favour acceptance of the amendment without a Conference, notification of their decision shall be made by the Director-General in accordance with Article 38. The amendment shall become effective for all the High Contracting Parties on the expiry of ninety days from the date of such notification.

4. The Director-General shall convene a Conference of the High Contracting Parties to consider the proposed amendment if requested to do so by more than one-third of the High Contracting Parties.

5. Amendments to the Convention or to the Regulations for its execution, dealt with under the provisions of the preceding paragraph, shall enter into force only after they have been unanimously adopted by the High Contracting Parties represented at the Conference and accepted by each of the High Contracting Parties.

6. Acceptance by the High Contracting Parties of amendments to the Convention or to the Regulations for its execution, which have been adopted by the Conference mentioned in paragraphs 4 and 5, shall be effected by the deposit of a formal instrument with the Director-General of the United Nations Educational, Scientific and Cultural Organization.

7. After the entry into force of amendments to the present Convention or to the Regulations for its execution, only the text of the Convention or of the Regulations for its execution thus amended shall remain open for ratification or accession.

Article 40. Registration. In accordance with Article 102 of the Charter of the United Nations, the present Convention shall be registered with the Secretariat of the United Nations at the request of the Director-General of the United Nations Educational, Scientific and Cultural Organization.

In faith whereof the undersigned, duly authorized, have signed the present Convention.

Done at The Hague, this fourteenth day of May, 1954, in a single copy which shall be deposited in the archives of the United Nations Educational, Scientific and Cultural Orga-

nization, and certified ered to all the States refer as to the United Nations.

Regulations for the Execution of
Protection of Cultural Pro
Event of Armed Confl

h shall be delivered to all the States refer
and 32 as well
for the

Chapter I. Control

Article 1. International List of Persons. On the entry into of the Convention, the Director-General of the United Nations Educational, Scientific and Cultural Organization shall compile an international list consisting of all persons nominated by the High Contracting Parties as qualified to carry out the functions of the Commissioner-General for Cultural Property. On the initiative of the Director-General of the United Nations Educational, Scientific and Cultural Organization, this list shall be periodically revised on the basis of requests formulated by the High Contracting Parties.

Article 2. Organization of Control. As soon as any High Contracting Party is engaged in an armed conflict to which Article 18 of the Convention applies:

(a) It shall appoint a representative for cultural property situated in its territory; if it is in occupation of another territory, it shall appoint a special representative for cultural property situated in that territory;

(b) The Protecting Power acting for each of the Parties in conflict with such High Contracting Party shall appoint delegates accredited to the latter in conformity with Article 3 below;

(c) A Commissioner-General for Cultural Property shall be appointed to such High Contracting Party in accordance with Article 4.

Article 3. Appointment of Delegates of Protecting Powers. The Protecting Power shall appoint its delegates from among the members of its diplomatic or consular staff or, with the approval of the Party to which they will be accredited, from among other persons.

Article 4. Appointment of Commissioner-General. 1. The Commissioner-General for Cultural Property shall be chosen from the international list of persons by joint agreement between the Party to which he will be accredited and the Protecting Powers acting on behalf of the opposing Parties.

2. Should the Parties fail to reach agreement within three weeks from the beginning of their discussions on this point, they shall request the President of the International Court of Justice to appoint the Commissioner-General, who shall not take up his duties until the Party to which he is accredited has approved his appointment.

Article 5. Functions of Delegates. The delegates of the Protecting Powers shall take note of violations of the Convention, investigate, with the approval of the Party to which they are accredited, the circumstances in which they have occurred, make representations locally to secure their cessation and, if necessary, notify the Commission-General of such violations. They shall keep him informed of their activities.

Article 6. Functions of the Commissioner-General. 1. The Commissioner-General for Cultural Property shall deal with all matters referred to him in connexion with the application of the Convention, in conjunction with the representative of the Party to which he is accredited and with the delegates concerned.

... of decision and appointment in ... present Regulations.

2. He ... ent of the Party to which he is accredited, the case... he right to order an investigation or to ...

3. W... ited, ... ake any representations to the Parties to the cond...their Protecting Powers which he deems useful ... application of the Convention.

con... shall draw up such reports as may be necessary on ful ... plication of the Convention and communicate them ... the Parties concerned and to their Protecting Powers. He shall send copies to the Director-General of the United Nations Educational, Scientific and Cultural Organization, who may make use only of their technical contents.

6. If there is no Protecting Power, the Commissioner-General shall exercise the functions of the Protecting Power as laid down in Articles 21 and 22 of the Convention.

Article 7. Inspectors and Experts. 1. Whenever the Commissioner-General for Cultural Property considers it necessary, either at the request of the delegates concerned or after consultation with them, he shall propose, for the approval of the Party to which he is accredited, an inspector of cultural property to be charged with a specific mission. An inspector shall be responsible only to the Commissioner-General.

2. The Commissioner-General, delegates and inspectors may have recourse to the services of experts, who will also be proposed for the approval of the Party mentioned in the preceding paragraph.

Article 8. Discharge of the Mission of Control. The Commissioners-General for Cultural Property, delegates of the Protecting Powers, inspectors and experts shall in no case exceed their mandates. In particular, they shall take account of the security needs of the High Contracting Party to which they are accredited and shall in all circumstances act in accordance with the requirements of the military situations as communicated to them by that High Contracting Party.

Article 9. Substitutes for Protecting Powers. If a Party to the conflict does not benefit or ceases to benefit from the activities of a Protecting Power, a neutral State may be asked to undertake those functions of a Protecting Power which concern the appointment of a Commissioner-General for Cultural Property in accordance with the procedure laid down in Article 4 above. The Commissioner-General thus appointed shall, if need be, entrust to inspectors the functions of delegates of Protecting Powers as specified in the present Regulations.

Article 10. Expenses. The remuneration and expenses of the Commissioner-General for Cultural Property, inspectors and experts shall be met by the Party to which they are accredited. Remuneration and expenses of delegates of the Protecting Powers shall be subject to agreement between those Powers and the States whose interests they are safeguarding.

Chapter II. Special Protection

Article 11. Improvised Refuges. 1. If, during an armed conflict, any High Contracting Party is induced by unforeseen circumstances to set up an improvised refuge and desires that it should be placed under special protection, it shall communicate this fact forthwith to the Commissioner-General accredited to that Party.

2. If the Commissioner-General considers that such a measure is justified by the circumstances and by the impor-

tance of the cultural property sheltered in this improvised refuge, he may authorize the High Contracting Party to display on such refuge the distinctive emblem defined in Article 16 of the Convention. He shall communicate his decision without delay to the delegates of the Protecting Powers who are concerned, each of whom may, within a time-limit of 30 days, order the immediate withdrawal of the emblem.

3. As soon as such delegates have signified their agreement or if the time-limit of 30 days has passed without any of the delegates concerned having made an objection, and if, in the view of the Commissioner-General, the refuge fulfils the conditions laid down in Article 8 of the Convention, the Commissioner-General shall request the Director-General of the United Nations Educational, Scientific and Cultural Organization to enter the refuge in the Register of Cultural Property under Special Protection.

Article 12. International Register of Cultural Property under Special Protection. 1. An "International Register of Cultural Property under Special Protection" shall be prepared.

2. The Director-General of the United Nations Educational, Scientific and Cultural Organization shall maintain this Register. He shall furnish copies to the Secretary-General of the United Nations and to the High Contracting Parties.

3. The Register shall be divided into sections, each in the name of a High Contracting Party. Each section shall be subdivided into three paragraphs, headed: Refuges, Centres containing Monuments, Other Immovable Cultural Property. The Director-General shall determine what details each section shall contain.

Article 13. Requests for Registration. 1. Any High Contracting Party may submit to the Director-General of the United Nations Educational, Scientific and Cultural Organization an application for the entry in the Register of certain refuges, centres containing monuments or other immovable cultural property situated within its territory. Such application shall contain a description of the location of such property and shall certify that the property complies with the provisions of Article 8 of the Convention.

2. In the event of occupation, the Occupying Power shall be competent to make such application.

3. The Director-General of the United Nations Educational, Scientific and Cultural Organization shall, without delay, send copies of applications for registration to each of the High Contracting Parties.

Article 14. Objections. 1. Any High Contracting Party may, by letter addressed to the Director-General of the United Nations Educational, Scientific and Cultural Organization, lodge an objection to the registration of cultural property. This letter must be received by him within four months of the day on which he sent a copy of the application for registration.

2. Such objection shall state the reasons giving rise to it, the only valid grounds being that:

(a) the property is not cultural property;

(b) the property does not comply with the conditions mentioned in Article 8 of the Convention.

3. The Director-General shall send a copy of the letter of objection to the High Contracting Parties without delay. He shall, if necessary, seek the advice of the International Committee on Monuments, Artistic and Historical Sites and Archaeological Excavations and also, if he thinks fit, of any other competent organization or person.

4. The Director-General, or the High Contracting Party requesting registration, may make whatever representa-

tions they deem necessary to the High Contracting Parties which lodged the objection, with a view to causing the objection to be withdrawn.

5. If a High Contracting Party which has made an application for registration in time of peace becomes involved in an armed conflict before the entry has been made, the cultural property concerned shall at once be provisionally entered in the Register, by the Director-General, pending the confirmation, withdrawal or cancellation of any objection that may be, or may have been, made.

6. If, within a period of six months from the date of receipt of the letter of objection, the Director-General has not received from the High Contracting Party lodging the objection a communication stating that it has been withdrawn, the High Contracting Party applying for registration may request arbitration in accordance with the procedure in the following paragraph.

7. The request for arbitration shall not be made more than one year after the date of receipt by the Director-General of the letter of objection. Each of the two Parties to the dispute shall appoint an arbitrator. When more than one objection has been lodged against an application for registration, the High Contracting Parties which have lodged the objections shall, by common consent, appoint a single arbitrator. These two arbitrators shall select a chief arbitrator from the international list mentioned in Article 1 of the present Regulations. If such arbitrators cannot agree upon their choice, they shall ask the President of the International Court of Justice to appoint a chief arbitrator who need not necessarily be chosen from the international list. The arbitral tribunal thus constituted shall fix its own procedure. There shall be no appeal from its decisions.

8. Each of the High Contracting Parties may declare, whenever a dispute to which it is a Party arises, that it does not wish to apply the arbitration procedure provided for in the preceding paragraph. In such cases, the objection to an application for registration shall be submitted by the Director-General to the High Contracting Parties. The objection will be confirmed only if the High Contracting Parties so decide by a two-third majority of the High Contracting Parties voting. The vote shall be taken by correspondence, unless the Director-General of the United Nations Educational, Scientific and Cultural Organization deems it essential to convene a meeting under the powers conferred upon him by Article 27 of the Convention. If the Director-General decides to proceed with the vote by correspondence, he shall invite the High Contracting Parties to transmit their votes by sealed letter within six months from the day on which they were invited to do so.

Article 15. Registration. 1. The Director-General of the United Nations Educational, Scientific and Cultural Organization shall cause to be entered in the Register, under a serial number, each item of property for which application for registration is made, provided that he has not received an objection within the time-limit prescribed in paragraph 1 of Article 14.

2. If an objection has been lodged, and without prejudice to the provision of paragraph 5 of Article 14, the Director-General shall enter property in the Register only if the objection has been withdrawn or has failed to be confirmed following the procedures laid down in either paragraph 7 or paragraph 8 of Article 14.

3. Whenever paragraph 3 of Article 11 applies, the Director-General shall enter property in the Register if so requested by the Commissioner-General for Cultural Property.

4. The Director-General shall send without delay to the Secretary-General of the United Nations, to the High Contracting Parties, and, at the request of the Party applying for registration, to all other States referred to in Articles 30 and 32 of the Convention, a certified copy of each entry in the Register. Entries shall become effective thirty days after despatch of such copies.

Article 16. Cancellation. 1. The Director-General of the United Nations Educational, Scientific and Cultural Organization shall cause the registration of any property to be cancelled:

(a) at the request of the High Contracting Party within whose territory the cultural property is situated;

(b) if the High Contracting Party with requested registration has denounced the Convention, and when that denunciation has taken effect;

(c) in the special case provided for in Article 14, paragraph 5, when an objection has been confirmed following the procedures mentioned either in paragraph 7 or in paragraph 8 or Article 14.

2. The Director-General shall send without delay, to the Secretary-General of the United Nations and to all States which received a copy of the entry in the Register, a certified copy of its cancellation. Cancellation shall take effect thirty days after the despatch of such copies.

Chapter III. Transport of Cultural Property

Article 17. Procedure to Obtain Immunity. 1. The request mentioned in paragraph 1 of Article 12 of the Convention shall be addressed to the Commissioner-General for Cultural Property. It shall mention the reasons on which it is based and specify the approximate number and the importance of the objects to be transferred, their present location, the location now envisaged, the means of transport to be used, the route to be followed, the date proposed for the transfer and any other relevant information.

2. If the Commissioner-General, after taking such opinions as he deems fit, considers that such transfer is justified, he shall consult those delegates of the Protecting Powers who are concerned, on the measures proposed for carrying it out. Following such consultation, he shall notify the Parties to the conflict concerned of the transfer, including in such notification all useful information.

3. The Commissioner-General shall appoint one or more inspectors, who shall satisfy themselves that only the property stated in the request is to be transferred and that the transport is to be by the approved methods and bears the distinctive emblem. The inspector or inspectors shall accompany the property to its destination.

Article 18. Transport Abroad. Where the transfer under special protection is to the territory of another country, it shall be governed not only by Article 12 of the Convention and by Article 17 of the present Regulations, but by the following further provisions:

(a) while the cultural property remains on the territory of another State, that State shall be its depositary and shall extend to it as great a measure of care as that which it bestows upon its own cultural property of comparable importance;

(b) the depositary State shall return the property only on the cessation of the conflict; such return shall be effected within six months from the date on which it was requested;

(c) during the various transfer operations, and while it remains on the territory of another State, the cultural property shall be exempt from confiscation and may not be disposed of either by the depositor or by the depositary. Nevertheless, when the safety of the property requires it, the depositary may, with the assent of the depositor, have the property transported to the territory of a third country, under the conditions laid down in the present article;

(d) the request for special protection shall indicate that the State to whose territory the property is to be transferred accepts the provisions of the present Article.

Article 19. Occupied Territory. Whenever a High Contracting Party occupying territory of another High Contracting Party transfers cultural property to a refuge situated elsewhere in that territory, without being able to follow the procedure provided for in Article 17 of the Regulations, the transfer in question shall not be regarded as misappropriation within the meaning of Article 4 of the Convention, provided that the Commissioner-General for Cultural Property certifies in writing, after having consulted the usual custodians, that such transfer was rendered necessary by circumstances.

Chapter IV. The Distinctive Emblem.

Article 20. Affixing of the Emblem. 1. The placing of the distinctive emblem and its degree of visibility shall be left to the discretion of the competent authorities of each High Contracting Party. It may be displayed on flags or armlets; it may be painted on an object or represented in any other appropriate form.

2. However, without prejudice to any possible fuller markings, the emblem shall, in the event of armed conflict and in the cases mentioned in Articles 12 and 13 of the Convention, be placed on the vehicles of transport so as to be clearly visible in daylight from the air as well as from the ground. The emblem shall be visible from the ground:

(a) at regular intervals sufficient to indicate clearly the perimeter of a centre containing monuments under special protection;

(b) at the entrance to other immovable cultural property under special protection.

Article 21. Identification of Persons. 1. The persons mentioned in Article 17, paragraph 2(b) and (c) of the Convention may wear an armlet bearing the distinctive emblem, issued and stamped by the competent authorities.

2. Such persons shall carry a special identity card bearing the distinctive emblem. This card shall mention at least the surname and first names, the date of birth, the title or rank, and the function of the holder. The card shall bear the photograph of the holder as well as his signature or his fingerprints, or both. It shall bear the embossed stamp of the competent authorities.

3. Each High Contracting Party shall make out its own type of identity card, guided by the model annexed, by way of example, to the present Regulations. The High Contracting Parties shall transmit to each other a specimen of the model they are using. Identity cards shall be made out, if possible, at least in duplicate, one copy being kept by the issuing Power.

4. The said persons may not, without legitimate reason, be deprived of their identity card or of the right to wear the armlet.

UNESCO CONVENTION FOR THE PROTECTION OF CULTURAL PROPERTY IN THE EVENT OF ARMED CONFLICT: PROTOCOL (1954). The protocol, like the parent convention, was adopted on 14 May 1954 by an intergovernmental conference convened at the Hague under the auspices of the United Nations Educational, Scientific and Cultural Organization on the invitation of the Government of the Netherlands. Under the protocol, contracting states undertake not to export or—failing that—to return, cultural property displaced in the event of an armed conflict. The text of the protocol is as follows:

The High Contracting Parties are agreed as follows:

I

1. Each High Contracting Party undertakes to prevent the exportation, from a territory occupies by it during an armed conflict, of cultural property as defined in article 1 of the Convention for the Protection of Cultural Property in the Event of Armed Conflict signed at The Hague on 14 May 1954.

2. Each High Contracting Party undertakes to take into its custody cultural property imported into its territory either directly or indirectly from any occupied territory. This shall either be effected automatically upon the importation of the property or, failing this, at the request of the authorities of that territory.

3. Each High Contracting Party undertakes to return, at the close of hostilities, to the competent authorities of the territory previously occupied, cultural property which is in its territory, if such property has been exported in contravention of the principle laid down in the first paragraph. Such property shall never be retained as war reparations.

4. The High Contracting Party whose obligation it was to prevent the exportation of cultural property from the territory occupied by it, shall pay an indemnity to the holders in good faith of any cultural property which has to be returned in accordance with the preceding paragraph.

II

5. Cultural property coming from the territory of a High Contracting Party and deposited by it in the territory of another High Contracting Party for the purpose of protecting such property against the dangers of an armed conflict, shall be returned by the latter, at the end of hostilities, to the competent authorities of the territory from which it came.

III

6. The present Protocol shall bear the date of 14 May 1954 and, until the date of 31 December 1954, shall remain open for signature by all States invited to the Conference which met at The Hague from 21 April 1954 to 14 May 1954.

7. (a) The present Protocol shall be subject to ratification by signatory States in accordance with their respective constitutional procedures.

(b) The instruments of ratification shall be deposited with the Director-General of the United Nations Educational, Scientific and Cultural Organization.

8. From the date of its entry into force, the present Protocol shall be open for accession by all States mentioned in

paragraph 6 which have not signed it as well as any other State invited to accede by the Executive Board of the United Nations Educational, Scientific and Cultural Organization. Accession shall be effected by the deposit of an instrument of accession with the Director-General of the United Nations Educational, Scientific and Cultural Organization.

9. The States referred to in paragraphs 6 and 8 may declare, at the time of signature, ratification or accession, that they will not be bound by the provision of section I or by those of section II of the present Protocol.

10. (a) The present Protocol shall enter into force three months after five instruments of ratification have been deposited.

(b) Thereafter, it shall enter into force, for each High Contracting Party, three months after the deposit of its instrument of ratification or accession.

(c) The situations referred to in articles 18 and 19 of the Convention for the Protection of Cultural Property in the Event of Armed Conflict, signed at The Hague on 14 May 1954, shall give immediate effect to ratifications and accession deposited by the parties to the conflict either before or after the beginning of hostilities or occupation. In such cases, the Director-General of the United Nations Educational, Scientific and Cultural Organization shall transmit the communications referred to in paragraph 14 by the speediest method.

11. (a) Each State party to the protocol on the date of its entry into force shall take all necessary measures to ensure its effective application within a period of six months after such entry into force.

(b) This period shall be six months from the date of deposit of the instruments of ratification or accession for any State which deposits its instrument of ratification or accession after the date of the entry into force of the protocol.

12. Any High Contracting Party may, at the time of ratification or accession, or at any time thereafter, declare by notification addressed to the Director-General of the United Nations Educational, Scientific and Cultural Organization, that the present Protocol shall extend to all or any of the territories for whose international relations it is responsible. The said notification shall take effect three months after the date of its receipt.

13. (a) Each High Contracting Party may denounce the present protocol, on its own behalf, or on behalf of any territory for whose international relations it is responsible.

(b) The denunciation shall be notified by an instrument in writing, deposited with the Director-General of the United Nations Educational, Scientific and Cultural Organization.

(c) The denunciation shall take effect one year after receipt of the instrument of denunciation. However, if, on the expiry of this period, the denouncing Party is involved in an armed conflict, the denunciation shall not take effect until the end of hostilities, or until the operations of repatriating cultural property are completed, whichever is the later.

14. The Director-General of the United Nations Educational, Scientific and Cultural Organization shall inform the States referred to in paragraphs 6 and 8, as well as the United Nations, of the deposit of all the instruments of ratification, accession or acceptance provided for in paragraph 7, 8 and 15 and the notifications and denunciations provided for respectively in paragraphs 12 and 13.

15. (a) The present protocol may be revised if revision is requested by more than one-third of the High Contracting Parties.

(b) The Director-General of the United Nations Educational, Scientific and Cultural Organization shall convene a Conference for this purpose.

(c) Amendments to the present protocol shall enter into force only after they have been unanimously adopted by the High Contracting Parties represented at the Conference and accepted by each of the High Contracting Parties.

(d) Acceptance by the High Contracting Parties of amendments to the present Protocol, which have been adopted by the Conference mentioned in sub-paragraphs (b) and (c), shall be effected by the deposit of a formal instrument with the Director-General of the United Nations Educational, Scientific and Cultural Organization.

(e) After the entry into force of amendments to the present protocol, only the text of the said protocol thus amended shall remain open for ratification or accession.

In accordance with Article 102 of the Charter of the United Nations, the present protocol shall be registered with the Secretariat of the United Nations at the request of the Director-General of the United Nations Educational, Scientific and Cultural Organization.

In faith whereof the undersigned, duly authorized, have signed the present protocol.

Done at the The Hague, this fourteenth day of May 1954, in English, French, Russian and Spanish, the four texts being equally authoritative, in a single copy which shall be deposited in the archives of the United Nations Educational, Scientific and Cultural Organization, and certified true copies of which shall be delivered to all the States referred to in paragraphs 6 and 8 as well as to the United Nations.

UNESCO CONVENTION ON TECHNICAL AND VOCATIONAL EDUCATION (1989).

The convention was adopted, and opened for ratification, acceptance, accession, or approval, by the UNESCO GENERAL CONFERENCE (25th session), held in Paris, on 10 November 1989.

Under the convention, contracting States agree to enable young people and adults, by appropriate legislation and other measures, to acquire the knowledge and know-how that are essential to economic and social development as well as to the personal and cultural fulfilment of the individual in society.

The text of the convention is as follows:

Preamble

The General Conference of the United Nations Educational, Scientific and Cultural Organization, meeting at Paris from 17 October 1989 to 16 November 1989 at its twenty-fifth session,

Recalling that it is the Organization's constitutional duty to promote and develop education,

Recalling also the principles set forth in Articles 23 and 26 of the Universal Declaration of Human Rights which relate to the right to work and to education, the principles contained in the Convention against Discrimination in Education, adopted in Paris on 14 December 1960, the International Covenant on Economic, Social and Cultural Rights and the International Covenant on Civil and Political Rights, adopted in New York on 16 December 1966, as well as the Convention on the Elimination of All Forms of Discrimination against Women, adopted by the United Nations General Assembly on 18 December 1979,

Recognizing that the development of technical and vocational education should contribute to the safeguarding of peace and friendly understanding among nations,

Having noted the provisions of the Revised Recommendation concerning Technical and Vocational Education, and the Recommendation concerning Education for International Understanding, Co-operation and Peace and Education relating to Human Rights and Fundamental Freedoms, both adopted by the General Conference at its eighteenth session in 1974,

Having noted further the provisions of the Recommendation on the Development of Adult Education, adopted by the General Conference in 1976, and the Recommendation concerning the Status of Teachers, adopted by the Special Intergovernmental Conference in 1966,

Taking into account the relevant recommendations of the International Conference on Education,

Bearing in mind the provisions of the Convention (No. 142) and Recommendation (No. 150) concerning Vocational Guidance and Vocational Training in the Development of Human Resources, adopted by the International Labour Conference at its sixtieth session in 1975,

Noting further the close collaboration between Unesco and the International Labour Organisation in drawing up their respective instruments so that they pursue harmonious objectives and with a view to continuing fruitful collaboration,

Considering the need to make a special effort to promote the technical and vocational education of women and girls,

Paying special attention to the diversity of education systems and socio-economic and cultural conditions, in particular those in developing countries which need special considerations and provisions,

Considering that, in spite of this diversity, generally similar objectives are pursued and that similar problems arise in many countries, making it desirable to develop common guidelines in technical and vocational education,

Recognizing that the pace of technological, social and economic development has considerably increased the need to expand and improve the technical and vocational education provided for both young people and adults,

Recognizing that technical and vocational education meets the global aim of developing both individuals and societies,

Convinced of the need for the exchange of information and experiences in the development of technical and vocational education and of the desirability of strengthening international co-operation in this field,

Convinced of the utility of an international legal instrument to reinforce international collaboration in the development of technical and vocational education,

Adopts the present Convention this tenth day of November 1989:

Article 1. The Contracting States agree that:

(a) for the purpose of this Convention, "technical and vocational education" refers to all forms and levels of the educational process involving, in addition to general knowledge, the study of technologies and related sciences and the acquisition of practical skills, know-how, attitudes and understanding relating to occupations in the various sectors of economic and social life;

(b) this Convention applies to all forms and levels of technical and vocational education provided in educational institutions or through co-operative programmes organized jointly by educational institutions, on the one hand, and industrial, agricultural, commercial or any other undertaking related to the world of work, on the other;

(c) this Convention shall be applied in accordance with the constitutional provisions and legislation of each Contracting State.

Article 2. 1. The Contracting States agree to frame policies, to define strategies and to implement, in accordance with their needs and resources, programmes and curricula for technical and vocational education designed for young people and adults, within the framework of their respective education systems, in order to enable them to acquire the knowledge and know-how that are essential to economic and social development as well as to the personal and cultural fulfilment of the individual in society.

2. The general framework for the development of technical and vocational education shall be determined in each Contracting State by appropriate legislation or other measures indicating:

(a) the objectives to be attained in technical and vocational fields, taking into consideration economic, social and cultural development needs and the personal fulfilment of the individual;

(b) the relationship between technical and vocational education, on the one hand, and other types of education, on the other, with particular reference to horizontal and vertical articulation of programmes;

(c) the structures for administrative organization of technical and vocational education defined by the responsible authorities;

(d) the roles of the public authorities responsible for economic, social and development planning in the various sectors of the economy and, where applicable, of professional associations, workers, employers and other interested parties.

3. The Contracting States shall guarantee that no individual who has attained the educational level for admission into technical and vocational education shall be discriminated against on grounds of race, colour, sex, language, religion, national or social origin, political or other opinions, economic status, birth, or on any other grounds.

The Contracting States shall work towards the right to equal access to technical and vocational education and towards equality of opportunity to study throughout the educational process.

4. The Contracting States shall pay attention to the special needs of the handicapped and other disadvantaged groups and take appropriate measures to enable these groups to benefit from technical and vocational education.

Article 3. 1. The Contracting States agree to provide and develop technical and vocational education programmes that take account of:

(a) the educational, cultural and social background of the population concerned and its vocational aspirations;

(b) the technical and professional skills, knowledge and levels of qualification needed in the various sectors of the economy, and the technological and structural changes to be expected;

(c) employment opportunities and development prospects at the national, regional and local levels;

(d) protection of the environment and the common heritage of mankind;

(e) occupational health, safety and welfare.

2. Technical and vocational education should be designed to operate within a framework of open-ended and flexible structures in the context of lifelong education and provide:

(a) an introduction to technology and to the world of work for all young people within the context of general education;

(b) educational and vocational guidance and information, and aptitude counselling;

(c) development of an education designed for the acquisition and development of the knowledge and know-how needed for a skilled occupation;

(d) a basis for education and training that may be essential for occupational mobility, improvement of professional qualifications and updating of knowledge, skills and understanding;

(e) complementary general education for those receiving initial technical and vocational training in the form of on-the-job or other training both inside and outside technical and vocational education institutions;

(f) continuing education and training courses for adults with a view, in particular, to retraining as well as to supplementing and upgrading the qualifications of those whose current knowledge has become obsolete because of scientific and technological progress or changes in the employment structure or in the social and economic situation, and also for those in special circumstances.

3. Technical and vocational education programmes should meet the technical requirements of the occupational sectors concerned and also provide the general education necessary for the personal and cultural development of the individual and include, *inter alia,* social, economic, and environmental concepts relevant to the occupation concerned.

4. The Contracting States agree to tender support and advice to undertakings outside educational institutions which take part in co-operative programmes in technical and vocational education.

5. At each occupational level, the competence required must be defined as clearly as possible and curricula must be continuously updated to incorporate new knowledge and technical processes.

6. In assessing the ability to carry out occupational activities and determining appropriate awards in technical and vocational education, account should be taken of both the theoretical and practical aspects of the technical field in question, and this should apply both to persons who have received training and to persons who have acquired occupational experience in employment.

Article 4. The Contracting States agree to review periodically the structure of technical and vocational education, study programmes, plans, training methods and materials, as well as forms of co-operation between the school system and the world of work, so as to ensure that they are constantly adapted to scientific and technological progress, to cultural progress and to changing employment needs in the various sectors of the economy, and that advances in educational research and innovation are taken into account with a view to application of the most effective teaching methods.

Article 5. 1. The Contracting States agree that all persons teaching in the field of technical and vocational education, whether working full time or part time, should have adequate knowledge, theoretical and practical, of their professional field of competence as well as appropriate teaching skills consistent with the type and level of the courses they are required to teach.

2. Persons teaching in technical and vocational education should be given the opportunity to update their technical information, knowledge and skills through special courses, practical training periods in enterprises and any other organized form of activity involving contact with the world of work; in addition, they should be provided with information on and training in educational innovations that may have applications in their particular discipline and be given the opportunity to participate in relevant research and development.

3. Equal employment opportunities should be offered, without discrimination, to teachers and other specialized staff in technical and vocational education, and their employment conditions should be such that it is possible to attract, recruit and retain staff qualified in their areas of competence.

Article 6. To facilitate international co-operation, the Contracting States agree:

(a) to encourage the collection and dissemination of information concerning innovations, ideas and experience in technical and vocational education and to participate actively in international exchanges dealing with study and teacher-training programmes, methods, equipment standards and textbooks in the field of technical and vocational education;

(b) to encourage the use in technical and vocational education of international technical standards applied in industry, commerce and other sectors of the economy;

(c) to promote approaches to achieving the recognition of equivalencies of qualifications acquired through technical and vocational education;

(d) to encourage international exchanges of teachers, administrators and other specialists in technical and vocational education;

(e) to give students from other countries, particularly from developing countries, the opportunity to receive technical and vocational education in their institutions, with a view, in particular, to facilitating the study, acquisition, adaptation, transfer and application of technology;

(f) to promote co-operation in technical and vocational education between all countries, but in particular between industrialized and developing countries, in order to encourage the development of the technologies of the countries;

(g) to mobilize resources for strengthening international co-operation in the field of technical and vocational education.

Article 7. The Contracting States shall specify, in periodic reports submitted to the General Conference of the United Nations Educational, Scientific and Cultural Organization at the dates and in the form determined by it, the legislative provisions, regulations and other measures adopted by them to give effect to this Convention.

Article 8. The following provisions shall apply to those States Parties to this Convention which have a non-unitary constitutional system:

(a) with regard to the provisions of this Convention, the implementation of which comes under the legal jurisdiction of the federal or central legislative power, the obligations of the federal or central government shall be the same as for those States Parties with a centralized system;

(b) with regard to the provisions of this Convention,

the implementation of which comes under the legal jurisdiction of federated States and constituent countries, provinces, autonomous communities or cantons that are not obliged by the general or basic constitutional system of the federation to take legislative measures, the central government shall inform the competent authorities of such States, countries, provinces, autonomous communities or cantons of the said provisions, with its recommendation for their adoption.

Article 9. Member States of Unesco may become Parties to this Convention, as well as non-Member States of Unesco which have been invited by Unesco's Executive Board to become Parties, by depositing with the Director-General of Unesco an instrument of ratification, acceptance, accession, or approval.

Article 10. This Convention shall enter into force three months after the third instrument referred to in Article 9 has been deposited, but solely with respect to the States that have deposited their respective instruments by that date. It shall enter into force for each other State three months after that State has deposited its instrument.

Article 11. 1. Each Contracting State shall have the right to denounce this Convention by formal notification in writing to the Director-General of the United Nations Educational, Scientific and Cultural Organization.

2. The denunciation shall take effect 12 months after the notification has been received.

Article 12. The Director-General of the United Nations Educational, Scientific and Cultural Organization shall inform the Member States of the Organization, the non-Member States covered by Article 9 and also the United Nations of the deposit of all the instruments referred to in Article 9 and the denunciations provided for in Article 11.

Article 13. 1. This Convention may be revised by the General Conference of the United Nations Educational, Scientific and Cultural Organization. Such revision shall, however, be binding only on States Parties to the revised Convention.

2. Should the General Conference adopt a new Convention entailing a total or partial revision of this Convention, and unless the new Convention otherwise provides, this present Convention shall cease to be open to new States Parties from the date of entry into force of the new revised Convention.

Article 14. This Convention has been drawn up in Arabic, Chinese, English, French, Russian and Spanish, the six texts being equally authoritative.

Article 15. In conformity with Article 102 of the Charter of the United Nations, this Convention shall be registered with the Secretariat of the United Nations at the request of the Director-General of the United Nations Educational, Scientific and Cultural Organization.

Done in Paris, this sixteenth day of November 1989, in two authentic copies bearing the signature of the President of the twenty-fifth session of the General Conference and of the Director-General of the United Nations Educational, Scientific and Cultural Organization, which shall be deposited in the archives of the United Nations Educational, Scientific and Cultural Organization, and certified true copies of which shall be delivered to all the States referred to in Article 9 as well as to the United Nations.

SEE ALSO *UNESCO Recommendation concerning Technical and Vocational Education (Revised).*

UNESCO CONVENTION ON THE MEANS OF PROHIBITING AND PREVENTING THE ILLICIT IMPORT, EXPORT AND TRANSFER OF OWNERSHIP OF CULTURAL PROPERTY (1970). The convention was adopted by the UNESCO GENERAL CONFERENCE (16th session), held in Paris, on 14 November 1970. It entered into force on 14 November 1972.

Under the convention, States parties undertake to prevent museums within their territories from acquiring cultural property which has been illegally exported, to prohibit the import of cultural property stolen from a museum or other public institution, and to recover and return stolen and imported cultural property at the request of the State of origin.

The text of the convention (*UNESCO's Standard-Setting Instruments,* No. IV.A.4) is as follows:

The General Conference of the United Nations Educational, Scientific and Cultural Organization, meeting in Paris from 12 October to 14 November 1970, at its sixteenth session,

Recalling the importance of the provisions contained in the Declaration of the Principles of International Cultural Co-operation, adopted by the General Conference at its fourteenth session,

Considering that the interchange of cultural property among nations for scientific, cultural and educational purposes increases the knowledge of the civilization of Man, enriches the cultural life of all peoples and inspires mutual respect and appreciation among nations,

Considering that cultural property constitutes one of the basis elements of civilization and national culture, and that its true value can be appreciated only in relation to the fullest possible information regarding is origin, history and traditional setting,

Considering that it is incumbent upon every State to protect the cultural property existing within its territory against the dangers of theft, clandestine excavation, and illicit export,

Considering that, to avert these dangers, it is essential for every State to become increasingly alive to the moral obligations to respect its own cultural heritage and that of all nations,

Considering that, as cultural institutions, museums, libraries and archives should ensure that their collections are built up in accordance with universally recognized moral principles,

Considering that the illicit import, export and transfer of ownership of cultural property is an obstacle to that understanding between nations which it is part of Unesco's mission to promote by recommending to interested States, international conventions to this end,

Considering that the protection of cultural heritage can be effective only if organized both nationally and internationally among States working in close co-operation,

Considering that the Unesco General Conference adopted a Recommendation to this effect in 1964,

Having before it further proposals on the means of prohibiting and preventing the illicit import, export and transfer of ownership of cultural property, a question which is on the agenda for the session as item 19,

Having decided, at its fifteenth session, that this question should be made the subject of an international convention,

Adopts this Convention on the fourteenth day of November 1970.

Article 1. For the purposes of this Convention, the term "cultural property" means property which, on religious or secular grounds, is specifically designated by each State as being of importance for archaeology, prehistory, history, literature, art or science and which belongs to the following categories:

(a) Rare collections and specimens of fauna, flora, minerals and anatomy, and objects of palaeontological interest;

(b) Property relating to history, including the history of science and technology and military and social history, to the life of national leaders, thinkers, scientists and artists and to events of national importance;

(c) Products of archaeological excavations (including regular and clandestine) or of archaeological discoveries;

(d) Elements of artistic or historical monuments or archaeological sites which have been dismembered;

(e) Antiquities more than one hundred years old, such as inscriptions, coins and engraved seals;

(f) Objects of ethnological interest;

(g) Property of artistic interest, such as:

(i) Pictures, paintings and drawings produced entirely by hand on any support and in any material (excluding industrial designs and manufactured articles decorated by hand);

(ii) Original works of statuary art and sculpture in any material;

(iii) Original engravings, prints and lithographs;

(iv) Original artistic assemblages and montages in any material;

(h) Rare manuscripts and incunabula, old books, documents and publications of special interest (historical, artistic, scientific, literary, etc.) singly or in collections;

(i) Postage, revenue and similar stamps, singly or in collections;

(j) Archives, including sound, photographic and cinematographic archives;

(k) Articles of furniture more than one hundred years old and old musical instruments.

Article 2. 1. The States Parties to this Convention recognize that the illicit import, export and transfer of ownership of cultural property is one of the main causes of the impoverishment of the cultural heritage of the countries of origin of such property and that international co-operation constitutes one of the most efficient means of protecting each country's cultural property against all the dangers resulting therefrom.

2. To this end, the States Parties undertake to oppose such practices with the means at their disposal, and particularly by removing their causes, putting a stop to current practices, and by helping to make the necessary reparations.

Article 3. The import, export or transfer of ownership of cultural property effected contrary to the provisions adopted under this Convention by the States Parties thereto, shall be illicit.

Article 4. The States Parties to this Convention recognize that for the purpose of the Convention property which belongs to the following categories forms part of the cultural heritage of each State:

(a) Cultural property created by the individual or collective genius of nationals of the State concerned, and cultural property of importance to the State concerned created within the territory of that State by foreign nationals or stateless persons resident within such territory;

(b) Cultural property found within the national territory;

(c) Cultural property acquired by archaeological, ethnological or natural science missions, with the consent of the competent authorities of the country of origin of such property;

(d) Cultural property which has been the subject of a freely agreed exchange;

(e) Cultural property received as a gift or purchased legally with the consent of the competent authorities of the country of origin of such property.

Article 5. To ensure the protection of their cultural property against illicit import, export and transfer of ownership, the States Parties to this Convention undertake, as appropriate for each country, to set up within their territories one or more national services, where such services do not already exist, for the protection of the cultural heritage, with a qualified staff sufficient in number for the effective carrying out of the following functions:

(a) Contributing to the formation of draft laws and regulations designed to secure the protection of the cultural heritage and particularly prevention of the illicit import, export and transfer of ownership of important cultural property;

(b) Establishing and keeping up to date, on the basis of a national inventory of protected property, a list of important public and private cultural property whose export would constitute an appreciable impoverishment of the national cultural heritage;

(c) Promoting the development or the establishment of scientific and technical institutions (museums, libraries, archives, laboratories, workshops . . .) required to ensure the preservation and presentation of cultural property;

(d) Organizing the supervision of archaeological excavations, ensuring the preservation *in situ* of certain cultural property, and protecting certain areas reserved for future archaeological research;

(e) Establishing, for the benefit of those concerned (curators, collectors, antique dealers, etc.) rules in conformity with the ethical principles set forth in this Convention; and taking steps to ensure the observance of those rules;

(f) Taking educational measures to stimulate and develop respect for the cultural heritage of all States, and spreading knowledge of the provisions of this Convention;

(g) Seeing that appropriate publicity is given to the disappearance of any items of cultural property.

Article 6. The States Parties to this Convention undertake:

(a) To introduce an appropriate certificate in which the exporting State would specify that the export of the cultural property in question is authorized. The certificate should accompany all items of cultural property exported in accordance with the regulations;

(b) To prohibit the exportation of cultural property from their territory unless accompanied by the above-mentioned export certificate;

(c) To publicize this prohibition by appropriate means, particularly among persons likely to export or import cultural property.

Article 7. The States Parties to this Convention undertake:

(a) To take the necessary measures, consistent with

national legislation, to prevent museums and similar institutions within their territories from acquiring cultural property originating in another State Party which has been illegally exported after entry into force of this Convention, in the States concerned. Whenever possible, to inform a State of origin Party to this Convention of an offer of such cultural property illegally removed from that State after the entry into force of this Convention in both States;

(b) (i) to prohibit the import of cultural property stolen from a museum or a religious or secular public monument or similar institution in another State Party to this Convention after the entry into force of this Convention for the States concerned, provided that such property is documented as appertaining to the inventory of that institution;

(ii) at the request of the State Party of origin, to take appropriate steps to recover and return any such cultural property imported after the entry into force of this Convention in both States concerned, provided, however, that the requesting State shall pay just compensation to an innocent purchaser or to a person who has valid title to that property. Requests for recovery and return shall be made through diplomatic offices. The requesting Party shall furnish, at its expense, the documentation and other evidence necessary to establish its claim for recovery and return. The Parties shall impose no customs duties or other charges upon cultural property returned pursuant to this Article. All expenses incident to the return and delivery of the cultural property shall be borne by the requesting Party.

Article 8. The States Parties to this Convention undertake to impose penalties or administrative sanctions on any person responsible for infringing the prohibitions referred to under Articles 6 (b) and 7 (b) above.

Article 9. Any State Party to this Convention whose cultural patrimony is in jeopardy from pillage of archaeological or ethnological materials may call upon other States Parties who are affected. The States Parties to this Convention undertake, in these circumstances, to participate in a concerted international effort to determine and to carry out the necessary concrete measures, including the control of exports and imports and international commerce in the specific materials concerned. Pending agreement each State concerned shall take provisional measures to the extent feasible to prevent irremediable injury to the cultural heritage of the requesting State.

Article 10. The States Parties to this Convention undertake:

(a) To restrict by education, information and vigilance, movement of cultural property illegally removed from any State Party to this Convention and, as appropriate for each country, oblige antique dealers, subject to penal or administrative sanctions, to maintain a register recording the origin of each item of cultural property, names and addresses of the supplier, description and price of each item sold and to inform the purchaser of the cultural property of the export prohibition to which such property may be subject;

(b) To endeavour by educational means to create and develop in the public mind a realization of the value of cultural property and the threat to the cultural heritage created by theft, clandestine excavations and illicit exports.

Article 11. The export and transfer of ownership of cultural property under compulsion arising directly or indirectly from the occupation of a country by a foreign power shall be regarded as illicit.

Article 12. The States Parties to this Convention shall respect the cultural heritage within the territories for the international relations of which they are responsible, and shall take all appropriate measures to prohibit and prevent the illicit import, export and transfer of ownership of cultural property in such territories.

Article 13. The States Parties to this Convention also undertake, consistent with the laws of each State:

(a) To prevent by all appropriate means transfers of ownership of cultural property likely to promote the illicit import or export of such property;

(b) To ensure that their competent services co-operate in facilitating the earliest possible restitution of illicitly exported cultural property to its rightful owner;

(c) To admit actions for recovery of lost or stolen items of cultural property brought by or on behalf of the rightful owners;

(d) To recognize the indefeasible right of each State Party to this Convention to classify and declare certain cultural property as inalienable which should therefore *ipso facto* not be exported, and to facilitate recovery of such property by the State concerned in cases where it has been exported.

Article 14. In order to prevent illicit export and to meet the obligations arising from the implementation of this Convention, each State Party to the Convention should, as far as it is able, provide the national services responsible for the protection of its cultural heritage with an adequate budget and, if necessary, should set up a fund for this purpose.

Article 15. Nothing in this Convention shall prevent States Parties thereto from concluding special agreements among themselves or from continuing to implement agreements already concluded regarding the restitution of cultural property removed, whatever the reason, from its territory of origin, before the entry into force of this Convention for the States concerned.

Article 16. The States Parties to this Convention shall in their periodic reports submitted to the General Conference of the United Nations Educational, Scientific and Cultural Organization on dates and in a manner to be determined by it, give information on the legislative and administrative provisions which they have adopted and other action which they have taken for the application of this Convention, together with details of the experience acquired in this field.

Article 17. 1. The States Parties to this Convention may call on the technical assistance of the United Nations Educational, Scientific and Cultural Organization, particularly as regards:

(a) Information and education;

(b) Consultation and expert advice;

(c) Co-ordination and good offices.

2. The United Nations Educational, Scientific and Cultural Organization may, on its own initiative conduct research and publish studies on matters relevant to the illicit movement of cultural property.

3. To this end, the United National Educational, Scientific and Cultural Organization may also call on the co-operation of any competent non-governmental organization.

4. The United Nations Educational, Scientific and Cultural Organization may, on its own initiative, make proposals to States Parties to this Convention for its implementation.

5. At the request of at least two States Parties to this Convention which are engaged in a dispute over its implementation, UNESCO may extend its good offices to reach a settlement between them.

Article 18. This Convention is drawn up in English, French, Russian and Spanish, the four texts being equally authoritative.

Article 19. 1. This Convention shall be subject to ratification or acceptance by States members of the United Nations Educational, Scientific and Cultural Organization in accordance with their respective constitutional procedures.

2. The instruments of ratification or acceptance shall be deposited with the Director-General of the United Nations Educational, Scientific and Cultural Organization.

Article 20. 1. This Convention shall be open to accession by all States not members of the United Nations Educational, Scientific and Cultural Organization which are invited to accede to it by the Executive Board of the Organization.

2. Accession shall be effected by the deposit of an instrument of accession with the Director-General of the United Nations Educational, Scientific and Cultural Organization.

Article 21. This Convention shall enter into force three months after the date of the deposit of the third instrument of ratification, acceptance or accession, but only with respect to those States which have deposited their respective instruments on or before that date. It shall enter into force with respect to any other State three months after the deposit of its instrument of ratification, acceptance or accession.

Article 22. The States Parties to this Convention recognize that the Convention is applicable not only to their metropolitan territories but also to all territories for the international relations of which they are responsible; they undertake to consult, if necessary, the governments or other competent authorities of these territories on or before ratification, acceptance or accession with a view to securing the application of the Convention to those territories, and to notify the Director-General of the United Nations Educational, Scientific and Cultural Organization of the territories to which it is applied, the notification to take effect three months after the date of its receipt.

Article 23. 1. Each State Party to this Convention may denounce the Convention on its own behalf or on behalf of any territory for whose international relations it is responsible.

2. The denunciation shall be notified by an instrument in writing, deposited with the Director-General of the United Nations Educational, Scientific and Cultural Organization.

3. The denunciation shall take effect twelve months after the receipt of the instrument of denunciation.

Article 24. The Director-General of the United Nations Educational, Scientific and Cultural Organization shall inform the States members of the Organization, the States not members of the Organization which are referred to in Article 20, as well as the United Nations, of the deposit of all the instruments of ratification, acceptance and accession provided for in Articles 19 and 20, and of the notifications and denunciations provided for in Articles 22 and 23 respectively.

Article 25. 1. This Convention may be revised by the General Conference of the United Nations Educational, Scientific and Cultural Organization. Any such revision shall, however, bind only the States which shall become Parties to the revising convention.

2. If the General Conference should adopt a new convention revising this Convention in whole or in part, then, unless the new convention otherwise provides, this Con-

vention shall cease to be open to ratification, acceptance or accession, as from the date on which the new revising convention enters into force.

Article 26. In conformity with Article 102 of the Charter of the United Nations, this Convention shall be registered with the Secretariat of the United Nations at the request of the Director-General of the United Nations Educational, Scientific and Cultural Organization.

Done in Paris this seventeenth day of November 1970, in two authentic copies bearing the signature of the President of the sixteenth session of the General Conference and of the Director-General of the United Nations Educational, Scientific and Cultural Organization, which shall be deposited in the archives of the United Nations Educational, Scientific and Cultural Organization, and certified true copies of which shall be delivered to all the States referred to in Articles 19 and 20 as well as to the United Nations.

The foregoing is the authentic text of the Convention duly adopted by the General Conference of the United Nations Educational, Scientific and Cultural Organization during its sixteenth session, which was held in Paris and declared closed the fourteenth day of November 1970.

In faith whereof we have appended our signatures this seventeenth day of November 1970.

UNESCO DECLARATION OF GUIDING PRINCIPLES ON THE USE OF SATELLITE BROADCASTING FOR THE FREE FLOW OF INFORMATION, THE SPREAD OF EDUCATION AND GREATER CULTURAL EXCHANGE (1972).

The UN General Assembly noted on 16 December 1970 (resolution 2733 [XXV]) that the potential benefits of satellite broadcasting have particular significance with regard to better understanding among peoples, the expansion of the flow of information, the wider dissemination of knowledge in the world, and the promotion of cultural exchanges; and invited UNESCO to continue to promote the use of satellite broadcasting for these purposes.

This declaration was one of UNESCO's first efforts in this field. Adopted by the UNESCO GENERAL CONFERENCE (17th session), held in Paris, on 15 November 1972, the declaration deals mainly with the questions raised by the development of communications satellites capable of broadcasting to the population of countries other than that of the country of the transmission's origin. Taking into account the principle of FREEDOM OF INFORMATION, it emphasizes the necessity for States to reach or promote prior agreements regulating such direct satellite broadcasting.

The text of the declaration (*UNESCO's Standard-Setting Instruments,* No. IV.C.2) is as follows:

The General Conference of the United Nations Educational, Scientific and Cultural Organization meeting in Paris at its seventeenth session, in 1972,
Recognizing that the development of communication satellites capable of broadcasting programmes for commu-

nity or individual reception establishes a new dimension in international communication,

Recalling that under its Constitution the purpose of Unesco is to contribute to peace and security by promoting collaboration among the nations through education, science and culture, and that, to realize this purpose, the Organization will collaborate in the work of advancing the mutual knowledge and understanding of peoples through all means of mass communication and to that end recommend such international agreements as may be necessary to promote the free flow of ideas by word and image,

Recalling that the Charter of the United Nations specifies, among the purposes and principles of the United Nations, the development of friendly relations among nations based on respect for the principle of equal rights, the non-interference in matters within the domestic jurisdiction of any State, the achievement of international co-operation and the respect for human rights and fundamental freedoms,

Bearing in mind that the Universal Declaration of Human Rights proclaims that everyone has the right to seek, receive and impart information and ideas through any media and regardless of frontiers, that everyone has the right to education and that everyone has the right freely to participate in the cultural life of the community, as well as the right to the protection of the moral and material interests resulting from any scientific, literary or artistic production of which he is the author,

Recalling the Declaration of Legal Principles Governing the Activities of States in the Exploration of Use of Outer Space (resolution 1962 [XVIII] of 13 December 1963), and the Treaty on Principles Governing the Activities of States in the Exploration and Use of Outer Space, including the Moon and Other Celestial Bodies, of 1967, (hereinafter referred to as the Outer Space Treaty),

Taking account of United National General Assembly resolution 110(II) of 3 November 1947, condemning propaganda designed or likely to provoke or encourage any threat to the peace, breach of the peace or act of aggression, which resolution as stated in the preamble to the Outer Space Treaty is applicable to outer space; and the United Nations General Assembly resolution 1721 D (XVI) of 20 December 1961 declaring that communication by means of satellites should be available as soon as practicable on a global and non-discriminatory basis,

Bearing in mind the Declaration of the Principles of International Cultural Co-operation adopted by the General Conference of Unesco, at its fourteenth session,

Considering that radio frequencies are a limited natural resource belonging to all nations, that their use is regulated by the International Telecommunications Convention and its Radio Regulations and that the assignment of adequate frequencies is essential to the use of satellite broadcasting for education, science, culture and information,

Noting the United Nations General Assembly resolution 2733 (XXV) of 16 December 1970 recommending that Member States, regional and international organizations, including broadcasting associations, should promote and encourage international co-operation at regional and other levels in order to allow all participating parties to share in the establishment and operation of regional satellite broadcasting services,

Noting further that the same resolution invites Unesco to continue to promote the use of satellite broadcasting for the advancement of education and training, science and culture, and in consultation with appropriate intergovern-

mental and non-governmental organizations and broadcasting associations, to direct its efforts towards the solution of problems falling within its mandate,

Proclaims on the 15th day of November 1972, this Declaration of Guiding Principles on the Use of Satellite Broadcasting for the Free Flow of Information, the Spread of Education and Greater Cultural Exchange:

Article 1. The use of Outer Space being governed by international law, the development of satellite broadcasting shall be guided by the principles and rules of international law, in particular the Charter of the United Nations and the Outer Space Treaty.

Article 2. 1. Satellite broadcasting shall respect the sovereignty and equality of all States.

2. Satellite broadcasting shall be essentially apolitical and shall be conducted with due regard for the rights of individual persons and non-governmental entities as recognized by States and international law.

Article 3. 1. The benefits of satellite broadcasting should be available to all countries without discrimination and regardless of their degree of development.

2. The use of satellites for broadcasting should be based on international co-operation, world-wide and regional, intergovernmental and professional.

Article 4. 1. Satellite broadcasting provides a new means of disseminating knowledge and promoting better understanding among peoples.

2. The fulfilment of these potentialities requires that account be taken of the needs and rights of audiences, as well as the objectives of peace, friendship and co-operation between peoples, and of economic, social and cultural progress.

Article 5. 1. The objective of satellite broadcasting for the free flow of information is to ensure the widest possible dissemination, among the peoples of the world, of news of all countries, developed and developing alike.

2. Satellite broadcasting, making possible instantaneous world-wide dissemination of news, requires that every effort be made to ensure the factual accuracy of the information reaching the public. News broadcasts shall identify the body which assumes responsibility for the news programme as a whole, attributing where appropriate particular news items to their source.

Article 6. 1. The objectives of satellite broadcasting for the spread of education are to accelerate the expansion of education, extend educational opportunities, improve the content of school curricula, further the training of educators, assist in the struggle against illiteracy, and help ensure life-long education.

2. Each country has the right to decide on the content of the educational programmes broadcast by satellite to its people and, in cases where such programmes are produced in co-operation with other countries, to take part in their planning and production, on a free and equal footing.

Article 7. 1. The objective of satellite broadcasting for the promotion of cultural exchange is to foster greater contact and mutual understanding between peoples by permitting audiences to enjoy, on an unprecedented scale, programmes on each other's social and cultural life including artistic performances and sporting and other events.

2. Cultural programmes, while promoting the enrichment of all cultures, should respect the distinctive character, the value and the dignity of each, and the right of all countries and peoples to preserve their cultures as part of the common heritage of mankind.

Article 8. Broadcasters and their national, regional and

international associations should be encouraged to co-operate in the production and exchange of programmes and in all other aspects of satellite broadcasting including the training of technical and programme personnel.

Article 9. 1. In order to further the objectives set out in the preceding articles, it is necessary that States, taking into account the principle of freedom of information, reach or promote prior agreements concerning direct satellite broadcasting to the population of countries other than the country of origin of the transmission.

2. With respect to commercial advertising, its transmission shall be subject to specific agreement between the originating and receiving countries.

Article 10. In the preparation of programmes for direct broadcasting to other countries, account shall be taken of differences in the national laws of the countries of reception.

Article 11. The principles of this Declaration shall be applied with due regard for human rights and fundamental freedom.

SEE ALSO *European Convention on Transfrontier Television; Principles Governing the Use by States of Artificial Earth Satellites for International Direct Television Broadcasting.*

UNESCO DECLARATION OF THE PRINCIPLES OF INTERNATIONAL CULTURAL CO-OPERATION (1966).

The declaration, adopted by the UNESCO GENERAL CONFERENCE (14th session) held in Paris, on 4 November 1966, the 20th anniversary of the founding of UNESCO, sets out principles for the guidance of governments, authorities, organizations, associations, and institutions responsible for cultural activities. Based on a study authorized by the UN Economic and Social Council in 1960 (resolution 803 [XXX]), the principles are designed to serve as guidelines for bilateral, regional, and international action regarding the relations and exchanges in the fields of education, science, and culture.

The text of the declaration (*UNESCO's Standard-Setting Instruments,* No. IV.C.1) is as follows:

The General Conference of the United Nations Educational, Scientific and Cultural Organization, met in Paris for its fourteenth session, this fourth day of November 1966, being the twentieth anniversary of the foundation of the Organization.

Recalling that the Constitution of the Organization declares that "since wars begin in the minds of men, it is in the minds of men that the defences of peace must be constructed" and that the peace must be founded, if it is not to fail, upon the intellectual and moral solidarity of mankind,

Recalling that the Constitution also states that the wide diffusion of culture and the education of humanity for justice and liberty and peace are indispensable to the dignity of man and constitute a sacred duty which all the nations must fulfill in a spirit of mutual assistance and concern,

Considering that the Organization's Member States, believing in the pursuit of truth and the free exchange of ideas and knowledge, have agreed and determined to develop and to increase the means of communication between their peoples,

Considering that, despite the technical advances which facilitate the development and dissemination of knowledge and ideas, ignorance of the way of life and customs of peoples still presents an obstacle to friendship among the nations, to peaceful co-operation and to the progress of mankind,

Taking account of the Universal Declaration of Human Rights, the Declaration of the Rights of the Child, the Declaration on the Granting of Independence to Colonial Countries and Peoples, the United Nations Declaration on the Elimination of all Forms of Racial Discrimination, the Declaration on the Promotion among Youth of the Ideals of Peace, Mutual Respect and Understanding between Peoples, and the Declaration on the Inadmissibility of Intervention in the Domestic Affairs of States and the Protection of their Independence and Sovereignty, proclaimed successively by the General Assembly of the United Nations,

Convinced by the experience of the Organization's first twenty years that, if international cultural co-operation is to be strengthened, its principles require to be affirmed,

Proclaims this Declaration of the principles of international cultural co-operation, to the end that governments, authorities, organizations, associations and institutions responsible for cultural activities may constantly be guided by these principles; and for the purpose, as set out in the Constitution of the Organization, of advancing, through the educational, scientific and cultural relations of the peoples of the world, the objectives of peace and welfare that are defined in the Charter of the United Nations:

Article 1. 1. Each culture has a dignity and value which must be respected and preserved.

2. Every people has the right and the duty to develop its culture.

3. In their rich variety and diversity, and in the reciprocal influences they exert on one another, all cultures form part of the common heritage belonging to all mankind.

Article 2. Nations shall endeavour to develop the various branches of culture side by side and, as far as possible, simultaneously, so as to establish a harmonious balance between technical progress and the intellectual and moral advancement of mankind.

Article 3. International cultural co-operation shall cover all aspects of intellectual and creative activities relating to education, science and culture.

Article 4. The aims of international cultural co-operation in its various forms, bilateral or multilateral, regional or universal, shall be:

1. To spread knowledge, to stimulate talent and to enrich cultures;

2. To develop peaceful relations and friendship among the peoples and bring about a better understanding of each other's way of life;

3. To contribute to the application of the principles set out in the United Nations Declarations that are recalled in the Preamble to this Declaration;

4. To enable everyone to have access to knowledge, to enjoy the arts and literature of all peoples, to share in advances made in science in all parts of the world and in the resulting benefits, and to contribute to the enrichment of cultural life;

5. To raise the level of the spiritual and material life of man in all parts of the world.

Article 5. Cultural co-operation is a right and a duty for all peoples and all nations, which should share with one another their knowledge and skills.

Article 6. International co-operation, while promoting the enrichment of all cultures through its beneficent action, shall respect the distinctive character of each.

Article 7. 1. Broad dissemination of ideas and knowledge, based on the freest exchange and discussion, is essential to creative activity, the pursuit of truth and the development of the personality.

2. In cultural co-operation, stress shall be laid on ideas and values conducive to the creations of a climate of friendship and peace. Any mark of hostility in attitudes and in expression of opinion shall be avoided. Every effort shall be made, in presenting and disseminating information, to ensure its authenticity.

Article 8. Cultural co-operation shall be carried on for the mutual benefit of all the nations practising it. Exchanges to which it gives rise shall be arranged in a spirit of broad reciprocity.

Article 9. Cultural co-operation shall contribute to the establishment of stable, long-term relations between peoples, which should be subjected as little as possible to the strains which may arise in international life.

Article 10. Cultural co-operation shall be specially concerned with the moral and intellectual education of young people in a spirit of friendship, international understanding and peace and shall foster awareness among States of the need to stimulate talent and promote the training of the rising generations in the most varied sectors.

Article 11. 1. In their cultural relations, States shall bear in mind the principles of the United Nations. In seeking to achieve international co-operation, they shall respect the sovereign equality of States and shall refrain from intervention in matters which are essentially within the domestic jurisdiction of any State.

2. The principles of this Declaration shall be applied with due regard for human rights and fundamental freedoms.

UNESCO DECLARATION ON FUNDAMENTAL PRINCIPLES CONCERNING THE CONTRIBUTION OF THE MASS MEDIA TO STRENGTHENING PEACE AND INTERNATIONAL UNDERSTANDING, TO THE PROMOTION OF HUMAN RIGHTS AND TO COUNTERING RACIALISM, *APARTHEID* AND INCITEMENT TO WAR (1978).

The declaration was adopted and proclaimed by the UNESCO GENERAL CONFERENCE (20th session), meeting in Paris, on 22 November 1978.

The importance of efforts to implement the principles set out in the declaration was emphasized by the UN General Assembly on 10 December 1982 (resolution 37/94)), which called upon all member States and organizations within the United Nations system to make those principles better known through every means at their disposal.

The text of the declaration (*UNESCO's Standard-Setting Instruments*, No. IV.C.3) is as follows:

The General Conference,

Recalling that by virtue of its Constitution the purpose of Unesco is to "contribute to peace and security by promoting collaboration among the nations through education, science and culture in order to further universal respect for justice, for the rule of law and for the human rights and fundamental freedoms" (Art. I, 1), and that to realize this purpose the Organization will strive "to promote the free flow of ideas by work and image" (Art. I, 2),

Further recalling that under the Constitution the Member States of Unesco, "believing in full and equal opportunities for education for all, in the unrestricted pursuit of objective truth, and in the free exchange of ideas and knowledge, are agreed and determined to develop and to increase the means of communication between their peoples and to employ these means for the purposes of mutual understanding and a truer and more perfect knowledge of each other's lives" (sixth preambular paragraph),

Recalling the purposes and principles of the United Nations, as specified in its Charter,

Recalling the Universal Declaration of Human Rights, adopted by the General Assembly of the United Nations in 1948 and particularly Article 19 thereof, which provides that "everyone has the right to freedom of opinion and expression; this right includes freedom to hold opinions without interference and to seek, receive and impart information and ideas through any media and regardless of frontiers"; and the International Covenant on Civil and Political Rights, adopted by the General Assembly of the United Nations in 1966, Article 19 of which proclaims the same principles and Article 20 of which condemns incitement to war, the advocacy of national, racial or religious hatred and any form of discrimination, hostility or violence.

Recalling Article 4 of the International Convention on the Elimination of all Forms of Racial Discrimination, adopted by the General Assembly of the United Nations in 1965, and the International Convention on the Suppression and Punishment of the Crime of Apartheid, adopted by the General Assembly of the United Nations in 1973, whereby the States acceding to these Conventions undertook to adopt immediate and positive measures designed to eradicate all incitement to, or acts of, racial discrimination, and agreed to prevent any encouragement of the crime of apartheid and similar segregationist policies or their manifestations,

Recalling the Declaration on the Promotion among Youth of the Ideals of Peace, Mutual Respect and Understanding between Peoples, adopted by the General Assembly of the United Nations in 1965,

Recalling the declarations and resolutions adopted by the various organs of the United Nations concerning the establishment of a new international economic order and the role Unesco is called upon to play in this respect,

Recalling the Declaration of the Principles of International Cultural Co-operation, adopted by the General Conference of Unesco in 1966,

Recalling Resolution 59(I) of the General Assembly of the United Nations, adopted in 1946 and declaring:

"Freedom of information is a fundamental human right and is the touchstone of all the freedoms to which the United Nations is consecrated;. . .

"Freedom of information requires as an indispensable element the willingness and capacity to employ its privileges without abuse. It requires as a basic discipline the moral obligation to seek the facts without prejudice and to spread knowledge without malicious intent;"

Recalling Resolution 110(II) of the General Assembly of the United Nations, adopted in 1947, condemning all forms of propaganda which are designed or likely to provoke or encourage any threat to the peace, breach of the peace, or act of aggression,

Recalling Resolution 127(II), also adopted by the General Assembly in 1947, which invites Member States to take measures, within the limits of constitutional procedures, to combat the diffusion of false or distorted reports likely to injure friendly relations between States, as well as the other resolutions of the General Assembly concerning the mass media and their contribution to strengthening peace, trust and friendly relations among States,

Recalling Resolution 9.12 adopted by the General Conference of Unesco in 1968, reiterating Unesco's objective to help to eradicate colonialism and racialism, and Resolution 12.1 adopted by the General Conference in 1976, which proclaims that colonialism, neo-colonialism and racialism in all its forms and manifestations are incompatible with the fundamental aims of Unesco,

Recalling Resolution 4.301 adopted in 1970 by the General Conference of Unesco on the contribution of the information media to furthering international understanding and co-operation in the interests of peace and human welfare, and to countering propaganda on behalf of war, racialism, apartheid and hatred among nations, and *aware* of the fundamental contribution that mass media can make to the realizations of these objectives,

Recalling the Declaration on Race and Racial Prejudice adopted by the General Conference of Unesco at its twentieth session,

Conscious of the complexity of the problems of information in modern society, of the diversity of solutions which have been offered to them, as evidenced in particular by the consideration given to them within Unesco, and of the legitimate desire of all parties concerned that their aspirations, points of view and cultural identity be taken into due consideration,

Conscious of the aspirations of the developing countries for the establishment of a new, more just and more effective world information and communication order,

Proclaims on this twenty-eighth day of November 1978 this Declaration on Fundamental Principles concerning the Contribution of the Mass Media to Strengthening Peace and International Understanding, to the Promotion of Human Rights and to Countering Racialism, Apartheid, and Incitement to War.

Article 1. The strengthening of peace and international understanding, the promotion of human rights and the countering of racialism, apartheid and incitement to war demand a free flow and a wider and better balanced dissemination of information. To this end, the mass media have a leading contribution to make. This contribution will be more effective to the extent that the information reflects the difference aspects of the subject dealt with.

Article 2. 1. The exercise of freedom of opinion, expression and information, recognized as an integral part of human rights and fundamental freedoms, is a vital factor in the strengthening of peace and international understanding.

2. Access by the public to information should be guaranteed by the diversity of the sources and means of information available to it, thus enabling each individual to check the accuracy of facts and to appraise events objectively. To this end, journalists must have freedom to report and the fullest possible facilities of access to information. Similarly, it is important that the mass media be responsive to concerns of peoples and individuals, thus promoting the participation of the public in the elaboration of information.

3. With a view to the strengthening of peace and international understanding, to promoting human rights and to countering racialism, apartheid and incitement to war, the mass media throughout the world, by reason of their role, contribute to promoting human rights, in particular by giving expression to oppressed peoples who struggle against colonialism, neo-colonialism, foreign occupation and all forms of racial discrimination and oppression and who are unable to make their voices heard within their own territories.

4. If the mass media are to be in a position to promote the principles of the Declaration in their activities, it is essential that the journalists and other agents of the mass media, in their own country or abroad, be assured of protection guaranteeing them the best conditions for the exercise of their profession.

Article 3. 1. The mass media have an important contribution to make to the strengthening of peace and international understanding and in countering racialism, apartheid and incitement to war.

2. In countering aggressive war, racialism, apartheid and other violations of human rights which are *inter alia* spawned by prejudice and ignorance, the mass media, by disseminating information on the aims, aspirations, cultures and needs of all peoples, contribute to eliminate ignorance and misunderstanding between peoples, to make nationals of a country sensitive to the needs and desires of others, to ensure the respect of the rights and dignity of all nations, all peoples and all individuals without distinction of race, sex, language, religion or nationality and to draw attention to the great evils which afflict humanity, such as poverty, malnutrition and diseases, thereby promoting the formulation by States of the policies best able to promote the reduction of international tension and the peaceful and equitable settlement of international disputes.

Article 4. The mass media have an essential part to play in the education of young peoples in a spirit of peace, justice, freedom, mutual respect and understanding, in order to promote human rights, equality of rights as between all human beings and all nations, and economic and social progress. Equally, they have an important role to play in making known the views and aspirations of the younger generation.

Article 5. In order to respect freedom of opinion, expression and information and in order that information may reflect all points of view, it is important that the points of view presented by those who consider that the information published or disseminated about them has seriously prejudiced their effort to strengthen peace and international understanding, to promote human rights or to counter racialism, apartheid and incitement to war be disseminated.

Article 6. For the establishment of a new equilibrium and greater reciprocity in the flow of information, which will be conducive to the institution of a just and lasting peace and to the economic and political independence of the developing countries, it is necessary to correct the inequalities in the flow of information to and from the developing countries, and between those countries. To this end, it is essential that their mass media should have conditions and resources enabling them to gain strength and expand, and to co-operate both among themselves and with the mass media in developed countries.

Article 7. By disseminating more widely all of the information concerning the universally accepted objectives and principles which are the bases of the resolutions adopted by the different organs of the United Nations, the mass media contribute effectively to the strengthening of peace and international understanding, to the promotion of human rights, and to the establishment of a more just and equitable international economic order.

Article 8. Professional organizations, and people who participate in the professional training of journalists and other agents of the mass media and who assist them in performing their functions in a responsible manner should attach special importance to the principles of this Declaration when drawing up and ensuring application of their codes of ethics.

Article 9. In the spirit of this Declaration, it is for the international community to contribute to the creation of the conditions for a free flow and wider and more balanced dissemination of information, and of the conditions for the protection, in the exercise of their functions, of journalists and other agents of the mass media. Unesco is well placed to make a valuable contribution in this respect.

Article 10. 1. With due respect for constitutional provisions designed to guarantee freedom of information and for the applicable international instruments and agreements, it is indispensable to create and maintain throughout the world the conditions which make it possible for the organizations and persons professionally involved in the dissemination of information to achieve the objectives of this Declaration.

2. It is important that a free flow and wider and better balanced dissemination of information be encouraged.

3. To this end, it is necessary that States facilitate the procurement by the mass media in the developing countries of adequate conditions and resources enabling them to gain strength and expand, and that they support co-operation by the latter both among themselves and with the mass media in developed countries.

4. Similarly, on a basis of equality of rights, mutual advantage and respect for the diversity of the cultures which go to make up the common heritage of mankind, it is essential that bilateral and multilateral exchanges of information among all States, and in particular between those which have different economic and social systems, be encouraged and developed.

Article 11. For this declaration to be fully effective it is necessary, with due respect for the legislative and administrative provisions and the other obligations of Member States, to guarantee the existence of favourable conditions for the operation of the mass media, in conformity with the provisions of the Universal Declaration of Human Rights and with the corresponding principles proclaimed in the International Covenant on Civil and Political Rights adopted by the General Assembly of the United Nations in 1966.

SEE ALSO *Convention on International Right of Correction; European Declaration on Mass Communication Media and Human Rights.*

UNESCO DECLARATION ON RACE AND RACIAL PREJUDICE (1978).

In 1948, the UN Economic and Social Council advised UNESCO (resolution 116 B [VI]) of the interest of the United Nations in effective educational programs to prevent racial discrimina-

tion and suggested collaboration between the UN and UNESCO in the formulation of such programs. In response, the Director-General of UNESCO was authorized by its General Conference to sponsor research on the scientific facts of race.

Four statements on race were prepared by groups of experts convened by UNESCO in 1950, 1951, 1964, and 1967. Each group concluded that doctrines of racism lack any scientific basis whatsoever. (see RACE: UNESCO STATEMENT ON SCIENTIFIC FACTS).

In 1972, the UNESCO General Conference called for the preparation of a Declaration on Race and Racial Prejudice which would take into account the findings of the four groups of experts and would present a set of universal principles. The draft of such a declaration was prepared by a group of eminent specialists convened by the Director-General in 1977, and the declaration was adopted by the General Conference (20th session) on 27 November 1978. The text of the declaration (*UNESCO's Standard-Setting Instruments,* No. III.C.1) is as follows:

The General Conference of the United Nations Educational, Scientific and Cultural Organization, meeting in Paris at its twentieth session, on 27 November 1978 adopted unanimously and by acclamation the following Declaration:

Preamble

The General Conference of the United Nations Educational, Scientific and Cultural Organization, meeting at Paris at its twentieth session, from 24 October to 28 November 1978,

Whereas it is stated in the Preamble to the Constitution of Unesco, adopted on 16 November 1945, that 'the great and terrible war which has now ended was a war made possible by the denial of the democratic principles of the dignity, equality and mutual respect of men, and by the propagation, in their place, through ignorance and prejudice, of the doctrine of the inequality of men and races', and whereas, according to Article I of the said Constitution, the purpose of Unesco 'is to contribute to peace and security by promoting collaboration among the nations through education, science and culture in order to further universal respect for justice, for the rule of law and for the human rights and fundamental freedoms ... which are affirmed for the peoples of the world, without distinction of race, sex, language or religion, by the Charter of the United Nations',

Recognizing that, more than three decades after the founding of Unesco, these principles are just as significant as they were when they were embodied in its Constitution,

Mindful of the process of decolonization and other historical changes which have led most of the peoples formerly under foreign rule to recover their sovereignty, making the international community a universal and diversified whole and creating new opportunities of eradicating the scourge of racism and of putting an end to its odious manifestations in all aspects of social and political life, both nationally and internationally,

Convinced that the essential unity of the human race

and consequently the fundamental equality of all human beings and all peoples, recognized in the loftiest expressions of philosophy, morality and religion, reflect an ideal towards which ethics and science are converging today,

Convinced that all peoples and all human groups, whatever their composition or ethnic origin, contribute according to their own genius to the progress of the civilizations and cultures which, in their plurality and as a result of their interpenetration, constitute the common heritage of mankind,

Confirming its attachment to the principles proclaimed in the United Nations Charter and the Universal Declaration of Human Rights and its determination to promote the implementation of the International Covenants on Human Rights as well as the Declaration on the Establishment of a New International Economic Order,

Determined also to promote the implementation of the United Nations Declaration and the International Convention on the Elimination of all Forms of Racial Discrimination,

Noting the International Convention on the Prevention and Punishment of the Crime of Genocide, the International Convention on the Suppression and Punishment of the Crime of Apartheid and the Convention on the Non-Applicability of Statutory Limitations to War Crimes and Crimes against Humanity,

Recalling also the international instruments already adopted by Unesco, including in particular the Convention and Recommendation against Discrimination in Education, the Recommendation concerning the Status of Teachers, the Declaration of the Principles of International Cultural Co-operation, the Recommendation concerning Education for International Understanding, Co-operation and Peace and Education relating to Human Rights and Fundamental Freedoms, the Recommendation on the Status of Scientific Researchers, and the Recommendation on participation by the people at large in cultural life and their contribution to it,

Bearing in mind the four statements on the race question adopted by experts convened by Unesco,

Reaffirming its desire to play a vigorous and constructive part in the implementation of the programme of the Decade for Action to Combat Racism and Racial Discrimination, as defined by the General Assembly of the United Nations at its twenty-eighth session,

Noting with the gravest concern that racism, racial discrimination, colonialism and apartheid continue to afflict the world in ever-changing forms, as a result both of the continuation of legislative provisions and government and administrative practices contrary to the principles of human rights and also of the continued existence of political and social structures, and of relationships and attitudes, characterized by injustice and contempt for human beings and leading to the exclusion, humiliation and exploitation, or to be forced assimilation, of the members of disadvantaged groups,

Expressing its indignation at these offences against human dignity, *deploring* the obstacles they place in the way of mutual understanding between peoples and *alarmed* at the danger of their seriously disturbing international peace and security,

Adopts and solemnly proclaims this Declaration on Race and Racial Prejudice:

Article 1. 1. All human beings belong to a single species and are descended from a common stock. They are born equal in dignity and rights and all form an integral part of humanity.

2. All individuals and groups have the right to be different, to consider themselves as different and to be regarded as such. However, the diversity of life styles and the right to be different may not, in any circumstances, serve as a pretext for racial prejudice; they may not justify either in law or in fact any discriminatory practice whatsoever, nor provide a ground for the policy of apartheid, which is the extreme form of racism.

3. Identity of origin in no way affects the fact that human beings can and may live differently, nor does it preclude the existence of differences based on cultural, environmental and historical diversity nor the right to maintain cultural identity.

4. All peoples of the world possess equal faculties for attaining the highest level in intellectual, technical, social, economic, cultural and political development.

5. The differences between the achievements of the different peoples are entirely attributable to geographical, historical, political, economic, social and cultural factors. Such differences can in no case serve as a pretext for any rank-ordered classification of nations or peoples.

Article 2. 1. Any theory which involves the claim that racial or ethnic groups are inherently superior or inferior, thus implying that some would be entitled to dominate or eliminate others, presumed to be inferior, or which bases value judgements on racial differentiation, has no scientific foundation and is contrary to the moral and ethical principles of humanity.

2. Racism includes racist ideologies, prejudiced attitudes, discriminatory behaviour, structural arrangements and institutionalized practices resulting in racial inequality as well as the fallacious notion that discriminatory relations between groups are morally and scientifically justifiable; it is reflected in discriminatory provisions in legislation or regulations and discriminatory practices as well as in anti-social beliefs and acts; it hinders the development of its victims, perverts those who practise it, divides nations internally, impedes international co-operation and gives rise to political tensions between peoples; it is contrary to the fundamental principles of international law and, consequently, seriously disturbs international peace and security.

3. Racial prejudice, historically linked with inequalities in power, reinforced by economic and social differences between individuals and groups, and still seeking today to justify such inequalities, is totally without justification.

Article 3. Any distinction, exclusion, restriction or preference based on race, colour, ethnic or national origin or religious intolerance motivated by racist considerations, which destroys or compromises the sovereign equality of States and the right of peoples to self-determination, or which limits in an arbitrary or discriminatory manner the right of every human being and group to full development is incompatible with the requirements of an international order which is just and guarantees respect for human rights; the right to full development implies equal access to the means of personal and collective advancement and fulfilment in a climate of respect for the values of civilizations and cultures, both national and world-wide.

Article 4. 1. Any restriction on the complete self-fulfillment of human beings and free communication between them which is based on racial or ethnic considerations is contrary to the principle of equality in dignity and rights; it cannot be admitted.

2. One of the most serious violations of this principle is

represented by apartheid, which, like genocide, is a crime against humanity, and gravely disturbs international peace and security.

3. Other policies and practices of racial segregation and discrimination constitute crimes against the conscience and dignity of mankind and may lead to political tensions and gravely endanger international peace and security.

Article 5. 1. Culture, as a product of all human beings and a common heritage of mankind, and education in its broadest sense, offer men and women increasingly effective means of adaptation, enabling them not only to affirm that they are born equal in dignity and rights, but also to recognize that they should respect the right of all groups to their own cultural identity and the development of their distinctive cultural life within the national and international context, it being understood that it rests with each group to decide in complete freedom on the maintenance and, if appropriate, the adaptation or enrichment of the values which it regards as essential to its identity.

2. States, in accordance with their constitutional principles and procedures, as well as all other competent authorities and the entire teaching profession, have a responsibility to see that the educational resources of all countries are used to combat racism, more especially by ensuring that curricula and textbooks include scientific and ethical considerations concerning human unity and diversity and that no invidious distinctions are made with regard to any people; by training teachers to achieve these ends; by making the resources of the educational system available to all groups of the population without racial restriction or discrimination; and by taking appropriate steps to remedy the handicaps from which certain racial or ethnic groups suffer with regard to their level of education and standard of living and in particular to prevent such handicaps from being passed on to children.

3. The mass media and those who control or serve them, as well as all organized groups within national communities, are urged—with due regard to the principles embodied in the Universal Declaration of Human Rights, particularly the principle of freedom of expression—to promote understanding, tolerance and friendship among individuals and groups and to contribute to the eradication of racism, racial discrimination and racial prejudice, in particular by refraining from presenting a stereotyped, partial, unilateral or tendentious picture of individuals and of various human groups. Communication between racial and ethnic groups must be a reciprocal process, enabling them to express themselves and to be fully heard without let or hindrance. The mass media should therefore be freely receptive to ideas of individuals and groups which facilitate such communication.

Article 6. 1. The State has prime responsibility for ensuring human rights and fundamental freedoms on an entirely equal footing in dignity and rights for all individuals and all groups.

2. So far as its competence extends and in accordance with its constitutional principles and procedures, the State should take all appropriate steps, *inter alia* by legislation, particularly in the spheres of education, culture and communication, to prevent, prohibit and eradicate racism, racist propaganda, racial segregation and apartheid and to encourage the dissemination of knowledge and the findings of appropriate research in natural and social sciences on the causes and prevention of racial prejudice and racist attitudes, with due regard to the principles embodied in the Universal Declaration of Human Rights and in the International Covenant on Civil and Political Rights.

3. Since laws proscribing racial discrimination are not in themselves sufficient, it is also incumbent on States to supplement them by administrative machinery for the systematic investigation of instances of racial discrimination, by a comprehensive framework of legal remedies against acts of racial discrimination, by broadly based education and research programmes designed to combat racial prejudice and racial discrimination and by programmes of positive political, social, educational and cultural measures calculated to promote genuine mutual respect among groups. Where circumstances warrant, special programmes should be undertaken to promote the advancement of disadvantaged groups and, in the case of nationals, to ensure their effective participation in the decision-making processes of the community.

Article 7. In addition to political, economic and social measures, law is one of the principal means of ensuring equality in dignity and rights among individuals, and of curbing any propaganda, any form of organization or any practice which is based on ideas or theories referring to the alleged superiority of racial or ethnic groups or which seeks to justify or encourage racial hatred and discrimination in any form. States should adopt such legislation as is appropriate to this end and see that it is given effect and applied by all their services, with due regard to the principles embodied in the Universal Declaration of Human Rights. Such legislation should form part of a political, economic and social framework conducive to its implementation. Individuals and other legal entities, both public and private, must conform with such legislation and use all appropriate means to help the population as a whole to understand and apply it.

Article 8. 1. Individuals, being entitled to an economic, social, cultural and legal order, on the national and international planes, such as to allow them to exercise all their capabilities on a basis of entire equality of rights and opportunities, have corresponding duties towards their fellows, towards the society in which they live and towards the international community. They are accordingly under an obligation to promote harmony among the peoples, to combat racism and racial prejudice and to assist by every means available to them in eradicating racial discrimination in all its forms.

2. In the field of racial prejudice and racist attitudes and practices, specialists in natural and social sciences and cultural studies, as well as scientific organizations and associations, are called upon to undertake objective research on a wide interdisciplinary basis; all States should encourage them to this end.

3. It is, in particular, incumbent upon such specialists to ensure, by all means available to them, that their research findings are not misinterpreted, and also that they assist the public in understanding such findings.

Article 9. 1. The principle of the equality in dignity and rights of all human beings and all peoples, irrespective of race, colour and origin, is a generally accepted and recognized principle of international law. Consequently any form of racial discrimination practised by a State constitutes a violation of international law giving rise to its international responsibility.

2. Special measures must be taken to ensure equality in dignity and rights for individuals and groups wherever necessary, while ensuring that they are not such as to appear racially discriminatory. In this respect, particular attention

should be paid to racial or ethnic groups which are socially or economically disadvantaged, so as to afford them, on a completely equal footing and without discrimination or restriction, the protection of the laws and regulations and the advantages of the social measures in force, in particular in regard to housing, employment and health; to respect the authenticity of their culture and values; and to facilitate their social and occupational advancement, especially through education.

3. Population groups of foreign origin, particularly migrant workers and their families who contribute to the development of the host country, should benefit from appropriate measures designed to afford them security and respect for their dignity and cultural values and to facilitate their adaptation to the host environment and their professional advancement with a view to their subsequent reintegration in their country of origin and their contribution to its development; steps should be taken to make it possible for their children to be taught their mother tongue.

4. Existing disequilibria in international economic relations contribute to the exacerbation of racism and racial prejudice; all States should consequently endeavour to contribute to the restructuring of the international economy on a more equitable basis.

Article 10. International organizations, whether universal or regional, governmental or non-governmental, are called upon to co-operate and assist, so far as their respective fields of competence and means allow, in the full and complete implementation of the principles set out in this Declaration, thus contributing to the legitimate struggle of all men, born equal in dignity and rights, against the tyranny and oppression of racism, racial segregation, apartheid and genocide, so that all the peoples of the world may be forever delivered from these scourges.

Resolution for Implementation of the Declaration

The General Conference, at its twentieth session,

Considering that Unesco, by reason of the responsibilities devolving upon it under its Constitution in the fields of education, science, culture and communication, is required to call the attention of States and peoples to the problems related to all aspects of the question of race and racial prejudice,

Having regard to the Unesco Declaration of Race and Racial Prejudice adopted this twenty-seventh day of November 1978,

1. Urges Member States

(a) to consider the possibility of ratifying, if they have not yet done so, the international instruments designed to aid in countering and eliminating racial discrimination, and in particular the International Convention on the elimination of all Forms of Racial Discrimination, the International Convention on the Suppression and Punishment of the Crime of Apartheid and the Unesco Convention against Discrimination in Education;

(b) to take appropriate measures, including the passing of laws, guided by the provisions of Articles 4 and 6 of the International Convention on the Elimination of All Forms of Racial Discrimination, with a view to preventing and punishing acts of racial discrimination and ensuring that fair and adequate reparation is made to the victims of racial discrimination;

(c) to communicate to the Director-General all necessary information concerning the steps they have taken to give effect to the principles set forth in the Declaration;

2. Invites the Director-General:

(a) to prepare a comprehensive report on the world situation in the fields covered by the Declaration, on the basis of the information supplied by Member States and of any other information supported by trustworthy evidence which he may have gathered by such methods as he may think fit, and to enlist for this purpose, if he deems it advisable, the help of one or more independent experts of recognized competence in these fields;

(b) to take due account, when preparing his report, which should be accompanied by any observations he may deem appropriate, of the work of the various international bodies set up to give effect to the legal instruments concerning the struggle against racialism and racial discrimination, or contributing to that struggle through their activities in the general field of human rights;

(c) to present his report to the General Conference and to submit to it for decision, on the basis of the said report and of the discussion it will then have held, with due priority, on the problems of race and racial prejudice, any general comments and any recommendations deemed necessary to promote the implementation of the Declaration;

(d) to ensure the widest possible dissemination of the text of the Declaration and, to that end, to publish and arrange for the distribution of the text not only in the official languages but also in as many languages as is possible with the resources available to him;

(e) to communicate the Declaration to the Secretary-General of the United Nations with a request that he place before the United Nations General Assembly appropriate proposals for strengthening the methods of peaceful settlement of disputes concerning the elimination of racial discrimination.

SEE ALSO *Race and Racial Prejudice: Impact of the UNESCO Declaration.*

UNESCO EXECUTIVE BOARD. Established in accordance with article 3 of the UNITED NATIONS EDUCATIONAL, SCIENTIFIC AND CULTURAL ORGANIZATION CONSTITUTION, the Executive Board consists of 51 members, each representing the government of the State of which he is a national, elected by the General Conference from among the delegates appointed by the member states. The president of the General Conference sits on the board *ex officio* in an advisory capacity. The board's composition and functions are set out in detail in the constitution (article 5).

UNESCO GENERAL CONFERENCE. Established in accordance with article 3 of the UNITED NATIONS EDUCATIONAL, SCIENTIFIC AND CULTURAL ORGANIZATION CONSTITUTION, the conference consist of representatives of the States members of the organization. Its main task is to determine the policies and program of work of the organization. Its composition, functions, and procedures are set out in detail in the constitution (article 4).

U

UNESCO INTERNATIONAL CHARTER OF PHYSICAL EDUCATION AND SPORT (1978). The International Charter, adopted by the UNESCO GENERAL CONFERENCE (20th session), held in Paris, on 21 November 1978, declares that the practice of physical education and sport is a fundamental right for all and that physical education and sport form an essential element of lifelong education in the overall education system. It calls for national and international cooperation as a prerequisite for the universal and well-balanced promotion of physical education and sport.

The recommendation that UNESCO develop and promulgate such an international declaration was made by the First International Conference of Ministers and Senior Officials responsible for Physical Education and Sport, which met in Paris in 1976. The text was drafted in 1977 by the Interim Intergovernmental Committee for Physical Education and Sport and won unanimous approval by the General Conference the following year. In 1979, the Intergovernmental Committee called upon UNESCO member States to translate, distribute, publicize, and otherwise disseminate the provisions of the international charter and to apply its provisions in territories under their jurisdiction.

The text of the international charter (*UNESCO's Standard-Setting Instruments,* No. I.C.1) is as follows:

Preamble

The General Conference of the United Nations Educational, Scientific and Cultural Organization, meeting in Paris at its twentieth session, this twenty-first day of November 1978,

Recalling that in the United Nations Charter the peoples proclaimed their faith in fundamental human rights and in the dignity and worth of the human person, and affirmed their determination to promote social progress and better standards of life,

Recalling that by the terms of the Universal Declaration of Human Rights, everyone is entitled to all the rights and freedoms set forth therein without discrimination of any kind as to race, colour, sex, language, religion, political or other opinion, national or social origin, property, birth or other consideration,

Convinced that one of the essential conditions for the effective exercise of human rights is that everyone should be free to develop and preserve his or her physical, intellectual and moral powers, and that access to physical education and sport should consequently be assured and guaranteed for all human beings,

Convinced that to preserve and develop the physical, intellectual and moral powers of the human being improves the quality of life at the national and the international levels,

Believing that physical education and sport should make a more effective contribution to the inculcation of fundamental human values underlying the full development of peoples,

Stressing accordingly that physical education and sport should seek to promote closer communion between peoples and between individuals, together with disinterested emulation, solidarity and fraternity, mutual respect and understanding, and full respect for the integrity and dignity of human beings,

Considering that responsibilities and obligations are incumbent upon the industrialized countries and the developing countries alike for reducing the disparity which continues to exist between them in respect of free and universal access to physical education and sport,

Considering that to integrate physical education and sport in the natural environment is to enrich them and to inspire respect of the earth's resources and a concern to conserve them and use them for the greater good of humanity as a whole,

Taking into account the diversity of the forms of training and education existing in the world, but noting that, notwithstanding the differences between national sports structures, it is clearly evident that physical education and sport are not confined to physical well-being and health but also contribute to the full and well-balanced development of the human being,

Taking into account, furthermore, the enormous efforts that have to be made before the right to physical education and sport can become a reality for all human beings,

Stressing the importance for peace and friendship among peoples of cooperation between the international governmental and non-governmental organizations responsible for physical education and sport,

Proclaims this International Charter for the purpose of placing the development of physical education and sport at the service of human progress, promoting their development, and urging governments, competent non-governmental organizations, educators, families and individuals themselves to be guided thereby, to disseminate it and to put it into practice.

Article 1. The Practice of Physical Education and Sport is a Fundamental Right for All. 1.1. Every human being has a fundamental right of access to physical education and sport, which are essential for the full development of his personality. The freedom to develop physical, intellectual and moral powers through physical education and sport must be guaranteed both within the educational system and in other aspects of social life.

1.2. Everyone must have full opportunities, in accordance with his national tradition of sport, for practising physical education and sport, developing his physical fitness and attaining a level of achievement in sport which corresponds to his gifts.

1.3. Special opportunities must be made available for young people, including children of pre-school age, for the aged and for the handicapped to develop their personalities to the full through physical education and sport programmes suited to their requirements.

Article 2. Physical Education and Sport Form an Essential Element of Lifelong Education in the Overall Education System. 2.1. Physical education and sport, as an essential dimension of education and culture, must develop the abilities, will-power and self-discipline of every human being as a fully integrated member of society. The continuity of physical activity and the practice of sports must be ensured throughout life by means of a global, lifelong and democratized education.

2.2. At the individual level, physical education and sport contribute to the maintenance and improvement of health, provide a wholesome leisure-time occupation and enable man to overcome the drawbacks of modern living. At the community level, they enrich social relations and develop fair play, which is essential not only to sport itself but also to life in society.

2.3. Every overall education system must assign the requisite place and importance to physical education and sport in order to establish a balance and strengthen links between physical activities and other components of education.

Article 3. Physical Education and Sport Programmes Must Meet Individual and Social Needs. 3.1. Physical education and sport programmes must be designed to suit the requirements and personal characteristics of those practising them, as well as the institutional, cultural, socio-economic and climatic conditions of each country. They must give priority to the requirements of disadvantaged groups in society.

3.2. In the process of education in general, physical education and sport programmes must, by virtue of both their content and their timetables, help to create habits and behaviour patterns conducive to full development of the human person.

3.3. Even when it has spectacular features, competitive sport must always aim, in accordance with the Olympic ideal, to serve the purpose of educational sport, of which it represents the crowning epitome. It must in no way be influenced by profit-seeking commercial interests.

Article 4. Teaching, Coaching and Administration of Physical Education and Sport, Should be Performed by Qualified Personnel. 4.1. All personnel who assume professional responsibility for physical education and sport must have appropriate qualifications and training. They must be carefully selected in sufficient numbers and given preliminary as well as further training to ensure that they reach adequate levels of specialization.

4.2. "Voluntary personnel", given appropriate training and supervision, can make an invaluable contribution to the comprehensive development of sport and encourage the participation of the population in the practice and organization of physical and sport activities.

4.3. Appropriate structures must be established for the training of personnel for physical education and sport. Personnel who have received such training must be given a status in keeping with the duties they perform.

Article 5. Adequate Facilities and Equipment are Essential to Physical Education and Sport. 5.1. Adequate and sufficient facilities and equipment must be provided and installed to meet the needs of intensive and safe participation in both in-school and out-of-school programmes concerning physical education and sport.

5.2. It is incumbent on governments, public authorities, schools and appropriate private agencies, at all levels, to join forces and plan together so as to provide and make optimum use of installations, facilities and equipment for physical education and sport.

5.3. It is essential that plans for rural and urban development include provision for long-term needs in the matter of installations, facilities and equipment for physical education and sport, taking into account the opportunities offered by the natural environment.

Article 6. Research and Evaluation are Indispensable Components of the Development of Physical Education and Sport. 6.1. Research and evaluation in physical education and sport should make for the progress of all forms of sport and help to bring about an improvement in the health and safety of participants as well as in training methods and organization and management procedures. The education

system will thereby benefit from innovations calculated to develop better teaching methods and standards of performance.

6.2. Scientific research, whose social implications in this sphere should not be overlooked, must be oriented in such a way that it does not allow of improper applications to physical education and sport.

Article 7. Information and Documentation Help to Promote Physical Education and Sport. 7.1. The collection, provision and dissemination of information and documentation on physical education and sport constitute a major necessity. In particular, there is a need to circulate information on the results of research and evaluation studies concerning programmes, experiments and activities.

Article 8. The Mass Media Should Exert a Positive Influence on Physical Education and Sport. 8.1. Without prejudice to the right of freedom of information, it is essential that everyone involved in the mass media be fully conscious of his responsibilities having regard to the social importance, the humanistic purpose and the moral values embodied in physical education and sport.

8.2. Relations between those involved in the mass media and specialists in physical education and sport must be close and based on mutual confidence in order to exercise a positive influence on physical education and sport and to ensure objective and well-founded information. Training of personnel for the media may include elements relating to physical education and sport.

Article 9. National Institutions Play a Major Role in Physical Education and Sport. 9.1. It is essential that public authorities at all levels and specialized non-governmental bodies encourage those physical education and sport activities whose educational value is most evident. Their action shall consist in enforcing legislation and regulations, providing material assistance and adopting all other measures of encouragement, stimulation and control. The public authorities will also ensure that such fiscal measures are adopted as may encourage these activities.

9.2. It is incumbent on all institutions responsible for physical education and sport to promote a consistent, overall and decentralized plan of action in the framework of lifelong education so as to allow for continuity and coordination between compulsory physical activities and those practised freely and spontaneously.

Article 10. International Co-operation is a Prerequisite for the Universal and Well-balanced Promotion of Physical Education and Sport. 10.1. It is essential that States and those international and regional intergovernmental and non-governmental organizations in which interested countries are represented and which are responsible for physical education and sport give physical education and sport greater prominence in international bilateral and multilateral co-operation.

10.2. International co-operation must be prompted by wholly disinterested motives in order to promote and stimulate endogenous development in this field.

10.3. Through co-operation and the pursuit of mutual interest in the universal language of physical education and sport, all peoples will contribute to the preservation of lasting peace, mutual respect and friendship and will thus create a propitious climate for solving international problems. Close collaboration between all interested national and international governmental and non-governmental agencies, based on respect for the specific competence of each, will necessarily encourage the development of physical education and sport throughout the world.

U

UNESCO INTERNATIONAL CONVENTION FOR THE PROTECTION OF PERFORMERS, PRODUCERS OF PHONOGRAMS AND BROADCASTING ORGANIZATIONS (1961). Known as the "Rome Convention," this instrument was adopted in Rome on 26 October 1961 by the Diplomatic Conference on the International Protection of Performers, Producers of Phonograms, and Broadcasting Organizations, convened by ILO, UNESCO, and the International Union for the Protection of Literary and Artistic Works and entered into force on 18 May 1964. Its purposes are to protect the property rights of performers iin their performances, of recording companies in their recordings, and of broadcasting organizations in their broadcasts. States wishing to accede to the convention must be parties either to the UNIVERSAL COPYRIGHT CONVENTION or to the earlier Berne Convention for the Protection of Literary and Artistic Works.

An intergovernmental committee, with a secretariat provided jointly by ILO, UNESCO, and the WORLD INTELLECTUAL PROPERTY ORGANIZATION, studies questions concerning the application and operation of the convention and collects proposals and prepares documentation relating to its possible revision.

The text of the convention (*UNESCO's Standard-Setting Instruments,* No. V.2.A.3) is as follows:

The Contracting States, moved by the desire to protect the rights of performers, producers of phonograms, and broadcasting organisations,

Have agreed as follows:

Article 1. Protection granted under this Convention shall leave intact and shall in no way affect the protection of copyright in literary and artistic works. Consequently, no provision of this Convention may be interpreted as prejudicing such protection.

Article 2. 1. For the purposes of this Convention, national treatment shall mean the treatment accorded by the domestic law of the Contracting State in which protection is claimed:

(a) to performers who are its nationals, as regards performances taking place, broadcast, or first fixed, on its territory;

(b) to producers of phonograms who are its nationals, as regards phonograms first fixed or first published on its territory;

(c) to broadcasting organisations which have their headquarters on its territory, as regards broadcasts transmitted from transmitters situated on its territory.

2. National treatment shall be subject to the protection specifically guaranteed, and the limitations specifically provided for, in this Convention.

Article 3. For the purpose of this Convention:

(a) "Performers" means actors, singers, musicians, dancers, and other persons who act, sing, deliver, declaim, play in, or otherwise perform literary or artistic works;

(b) "Phonogram" means any exclusively aural fixation of sounds of a performance or of other sounds;

(c) "Producer of phonograms" means the person who,

or the legal entity which, first fixes the sounds of a performance or other sounds;

(d) "Publication" means the offering of copies of a phonogram to the public in reasonable quantity;

(e) "Reproduction" means the making of a copy or copies of a fixation;

(f) "Broadcasting" means the transmission by wireless means for public reception of sounds or of images and sounds;

(g) "Rebroadcasting" means the simultaneous broadcasting by one broadcasting organisation of the broadcast of another broadcasting organisation.

Article 4. Each Contracting State shall grant national treatment to performers if any of the following conditions is met:

(a) the performance takes place in another Contracting State;

(b) the performance is incorporated in a phonogram which is protected under Article 5 of this Convention;

(c) the performance, not being fixed on a phonogram, is carried by a broadcast which is protected by Article 6 of this Convention.

Article 5. 1. Each Contracting State shall grant national treatment to producers of phonograms if any of the following conditions is met:

(a) the producer of the phonogram is a national of another Contracting State (criterion of nationality);

(b) the first fixation of the sound was made in another Contracting State (criterion of fixation);

(c) the phonogram was first published in another Contracting State (criterion of publication).

2. If a phonogram was first published in a non-contracting State but if it was also published, within thirty days of its first publication, in a Contracting State (simultaneous publication), it shall be considered as first published in the Contracting State.

3. By means of a notification deposited with the Secretary-General of the United Nations, any Contracting State may declare that it will not apply the criterion of publication or, alternatively, the criterion of fixation. Such notification may be deposited at the time of ratification, acceptance or accession, or at any time thereafter; in the last case, it shall become effective six months after it has been deposited.

Article 6. 1. Each Contracting State shall grant national treatment to broadcasting organisations if either of the following conditions is met:

(a) the headquarters of the broadcasting organisation is situated in another Contracting State;

(b) the broadcast was transmitted from a transmitter situated in another Contracting State.

2. By means of a notification deposited with the Secretary-General of the United Nations, any Contracting State may declare that it will protect broadcasts only if the headquarters of the broadcasting organisation is situated in another Contracting State and the broadcast was transmitted from a transmitter situated in the same Contracting State. Such notification may be deposited at the time of ratification, acceptance or accession, or at any time thereafter; in the last case, it shall become effective six months after it has been deposited.

Article 7. 1. The protection provided for performers by this Convention shall include the possibility of preventing:

(a) the broadcasting and the communication to the public, without their consent, of their performance, except where the performance used in the broadcasting or the public communication is itself already a broadcast performance or is made from a fixation;

(b) the fixation, without their consent, of their unfixed performance;

(c) the reproduction, without their consent, of a fixation of their performance:

(i) if the original fixation itself was made without their consent;

(ii) if the reproduction is made for purposes different from those for which the performers gave their consent;

(iii) if the original fixation was made in accordance with the provisions of Article 15, and the reproduction is made for purposes different from those referred to in those provisions.

2. (1) If broadcasting was consented to by the performers, it shall be a matter for the domestic law of the Contracting State where protection is claimed to regulate the protection against rebroadcasting, fixation for broadcasting purposes, and the reproduction of such fixation for broadcasting purposes.

(2) The terms and conditions governing the use by broadcasting organisations of fixations made for broadcasting purposes shall be determined in accordance with the domestic law of the Contracting State where protection is claimed.

(3) However, the domestic law referred to in subparagraphs (1) and (2) of this paragraph shall not operate to deprive performers of the ability to control, by contract, their relations with broadcasting organisations.

Article 8. Any Contracting State may, by its domestic laws and regulations, specify the manner in which performers will be represented in connexion with the exercise of their rights if several of them participate in the same performance.

Article 9. Any Contracting State may, by its domestic laws and regulations, extend the protection provided for in this Convention to artistes who do not perform literary or artistic works.

Article 10. Producers of phonograms shall enjoy the right to authorise or prohibit the direct or indirect reproduction of their phonograms.

Article 11. If, as a condition of protecting the rights of producers of phonograms, or of performers, or both, in relation to phonograms, a Contracting State, under its domestic law, requires compliance with formalities, these shall be considered as fulfilled if all the copies in commerce of the published phonogram or their containers bear a notice consisting of the symbol Ⓟ , accompanied by the year date of the first publication, placed in such a manner as to give reasonable notice of claim of protection; and if the copies or their containers do not identify the producer or the licensee of the producer (by carrying his name, trade mark or other appropriate designation), the notice shall also include the name of the owner of the rights of the producer; and, furthermore, if the copies or their containers do not identify the principal performers, the notice shall also include the name of the person who, in the country in which the fixation was effected, owns the rights of such performers.

Article 12. If a phonogram published for commercial purposes, or a reproduction of such phonogram, is used directly for broadcasting or for any communication to the public, a single equitable remuneration shall be paid by the user to the performers, or to the producers of the phonograms, or to both. Domestic law may, in the absence of agreement between these parties, lay down the conditions as to the sharing of this remuneration.

Article 13. Broadcasting organisations shall enjoy the right to authorise or prohibit:

(a) the rebroadcasting of their broadcasts;

(b) the fixation of their broadcasts;

(c) the reproduction:

(i) of fixations, made without their consent, of their broadcasts;

(ii) of fixations, made in accordance with the provisions of Article 15, of their broadcasts, if the reproduction is made for purposes different from those referred to in those provisions;

(d) the communication to the public of their television broadcasts if such communication is made in places accessible to the public against payment of an entrance fee; it shall be a matter for the domestic law of the State where protection of this right is claimed to determine the conditions under which it may be exercised.

Article 14. The term of protection to be granted under this Convention shall last at least until the end of a period of twenty years computed from the end of the year in which:

(a) the fixation was made—for phonograms and for performances incorporated therein;

(b) the performance took place—for performances not incorporated in phonograms;

(c) the broadcast took place—for broadcasts.

Article 15. 1. Any Contracting State may, in its domestic laws and regulations, provide for exceptions to the protection guaranteed by this Convention as regards:

(a) private use;

(b) use of short excerpts in connexion with the reporting of current events;

(c) ephemeral fixation by a broadcasting organisation by means of its own facilities and for its own broadcasts;

(d) use solely for the purposes of teaching or scientific research.

2. Irrespective of paragraph 1 of this Article, any Contracting State may, in its domestic laws and regulations, provide for the same kinds of limitations with regard to the protection of performers, producers of phonograms and broadcasting organisations, as it provides for, in its domestic laws and regulations, in connexion with the protection of copyright in literary and artistic works. However, compulsory licences may be provided for only to the extent to which they are compatible with this Convention.

Article 16. 1. Any State, upon becoming party to this Convention, shall be bound by all the obligations and shall enjoy all the benefits thereof. However, a State may at any time, in a notification deposited with the Secretary-General of the United Nations, declare that:

(a) as regards Article 12:

(i) it will not apply the provisions of that Article;

(ii) it will not apply the provisions of that Article in respect of certain uses;

(iii) as regards phonograms the producer of which is not a national of another Contracting State, it will not apply that Article;

(iv) as regards phonograms the producer of which is a national of another Contracting State, it will limit the protection provided for by that Article to the extent to which, and to the term for which, the latter State grants protection to phonograms first fixed by a national of the State making the declaration; however, the fact that the Contracting State of which the producer is a national does not grant the protection to the same beneficiary or beneficiaries as the

State making the declaration shall not be considered as a difference in the extent of the protection;

(b) as regards Article 13, it will not apply item (d) of that Article; if a Contracting State makes such a declaration, the other Contracting States shall not be obliged to grant the right referred to in Article 13, item (d), to broadcasting organisations whose headquarters are in that State.

2. If the notification referred to in paragraph 1 of this Article is made after the date of the deposit of the instrument of ratification, acceptance or accession, the declaration will become effective six months after it has been deposited.

Article 17. Any State which, on October 26, 1961, grants protection to producers of phonograms solely on the basis of the criterion of fixation may, by a notification deposited with the Secretary-General of the United Nations at the time of ratification, acceptance or accession, declare that it will apply, for the purposes of Article 5, the criterion of fixation alone and, for the purposes of paragraph 1 (a) (iii) and (iv) of Article 16, the criterion of fixation instead of the criterion of nationality.

Article 18. Any State which has deposited a notification under paragraph 3 of Article 5, paragraph 2 of Article 6, paragraph 1 of Article 16 or Article 17, may, by a further notification deposited with the Secretary-General of the United Nations, reduce its scope or withdraw it.

Article 19. Notwithstanding anything in this Convention, once a performer has consented to the incorporation of his performance in a visual or audio-visual fixation, Article 7 shall have no further application.

Article 20. 1. This Convention shall not prejudice rights acquired in any Contracting State before the date of coming into force of this Convention for that State.

2. No Contracting State shall be bound to apply the provisions of this Convention to performances or broadcasts which took place, or to phonograms which were fixed, before the date of coming into force of this Convention for that State.

Article 21. The protection provided for in this Convention shall not prejudice any protection otherwise secured to performers, producers of phonograms and broadcasting organizations.

Article 22. Contracting States reserve the right to enter into special agreements among themselves in so far as such agreements grant to performers, producers of phonograms or broadcasting organisations more extensive rights than those granted by this Convention or contain other provisions not contrary to this Convention.

Article 23. This Convention shall be deposited with the Secretary-General of the United Nations. It shall be open until June 30, 1962 for signature by any State invited to the Diplomatic Conference on the International Protection of Performers, Producers of Phonograms and Broadcasting Organisations which is a party to the Universal Copyright Convention or a member of the International Union for the Protection of Literary and Artistic Works.

Article 24. 1. This Convention shall be subject to ratification or acceptance by the signatory States.

2. This Convention shall be open for accession by any State invited to the Conference referred to in Article 23, and by any State Member of the United Nations, provided that in either case such State is a party to the Universal Copyright Convention or a member of the International Union for the Protection of Literary and Artistic Works.

3. Ratification, acceptance or accession shall be effected by the deposit of an instrument to that effect with the Secretary-General of the United Nations.

Article 25. 1. This Convention shall come into force three months after the date of deposit of the sixth instrument of ratification, acceptance or accession.

2. Subsequently, this Convention shall come into force in respect of each State three months after the date of deposit of its instrument of ratification, acceptance or accession.

Article 26. 1. Each Contracting State undertakes to adopt, in accordance with its Constitution, the measures necessary to ensure the application of this Convention.

2. At the time of deposit of its instrument of ratification, acceptance or accession, each State must be in a position under its domestic law to give effect to the terms of this Convention.

Article 27. 1. Any State may, at the time of ratification, acceptance or accession, or at any time thereafter, declare by notification addressed to the Secretary-General of the United Nations that this Convention shall extend to all or any of the territories for whose international relations it is responsible, provided that the Universal Copyright Convention or the International Convention for the Protection of Literary and Artistic Works applies to the territory or territories concerned. This notification shall take effect three months after the date of its receipt.

2. The notifications referred to in paragraph 3 of Article 5, paragraph 2 of Article 6, paragraph 2 of Article 16 and Articles 17 and 18, may be extended to cover all or any of the territories referred to in paragraph 1 of this Article.

Article 28. 1. Any Contracting State may denounce this Convention, on its own behalf, or on behalf of all or any of the territories referred to in Article 27.

2. The denunciation shall be effected by a notification addressed to the Secretary-General of the United Nations and shall take effect twelve months after the date of receipt of the notification.

3. The right of denunciation shall not be exercised by a Contracting State before the expiry of a period of five years from the date on which the Convention came into force with respect to that State.

4. A Contracting State shall cease to be a party to this Convention from that time when it is neither a party to the Universal Copyright Convention nor a member of the International Union for the Protection of Literary and Artistic Works.

5. This Convention shall cease to apply to any territory referred to in Article 27 from that time when neither the Universal Copyright Convention nor the International Convention for the Protection of Literary and Artistic Works applies to that territory.

Article 29. 1. After this Convention has been in force for five years, any Contracting State may, by notification addressed to the Secretary-General of the United Nations, request that a conference be convened for the purpose of revising the Convention. The Secretary-General shall notify all Contracting States of this request. If, within a period of six months following the date of notification by the Secretary-General of the United Nations, not less than one half of the Contracting States notify him of their concurrence with the request, the Secretary-General shall inform the Director-General of the International Labour Office, the Director-General of the United Nations Educational, Scientific and Cultural Organization and the Director of the Bureau of the International Union for the Protection of Literary and Artistic Works, who shall convene a revision conference in co-operation with the Intergovernmental Committee provided for in Article 32.

2. The adoption of any revision of this Convention shall require an affirmative vote by two-thirds of the States at-

tending the revision conference, provided that this majority includes two-thirds of the States which, at the time of the revision conference, are parties to the Convention.

3. In the event of adoption of a Convention revising this Convention in whole or in part, and unless the revising Convention provides otherwise:

(a) this Convention shall cease to be open to ratification, acceptance or accession as from the date of entry into force of the revising Convention;

(b) this Convention shall remain in force as regards relations between or with Contracting States which have not become parties to the revising Convention.

Article 30. Any dispute which may arise between two or more Contracting States concerning the interpretation or application of this Convention and which is not settled by negotiation shall, at the request of any one of the parties to the dispute, be referred to the International Court of Justice for decision, unless they agree to another mode of settlement.

Article 31. Without prejudice to the provisions of paragraph 3 of Article 5, paragraph 2 of Article 6, paragraph 1 of Article 16 and Article 17, no reservation may be made to this Convention.

Article 32. 1. An Intergovernmental Committee is hereby established with the following duties:

(a) to study questions concerning the application and operation of this Convention; and

(b) to collect proposals and to prepare documentation for possible revision of this Convention.

2. The Committee shall consist of representatives of the Contracting States, chosen with due regard to equitable geographical distribution. The number of members shall be six if there are twelve Contracting States or less, nine if there are thirteen to eighteen Contracting States and twelve if there are more than eighteen Contracting States.

3. The Committee shall be constituted twelve months after the Convention comes into force by an election organised among the Contracting States, each of which shall have one vote, by the Director-General of the International Labour Office, the Director-General of the United Nations Educational, Scientific and Cultural Organization and the Director of the Bureau of the International Union for the Protection of Literary and Artistic Works, in accordance with rules previously approved by a majority of all Contracting States.

4. The Committee shall elect its Chairman and officers. It shall establish its own rules of procedure. These rules shall in particular provide for the future operation of the Committee and for a method of selecting its members for the future in such a way as to ensure rotation among the various Contracting States.

5. Officials of the International Labour Office, the United Nations Educational, Scientific and Cultural Organization and the Bureau of the International Union for the Protection of Literary and Artistic Works, designated by the Directors-General and the Director thereof, shall constitute the Secretariat of the Committee.

6. Meetings of the Committee, which shall be convened whenever a majority of its members deems it necessary, shall be held successively at the headquarters of the International Labour Office, the United Nations Educational, Scientific and Cultural Organization and the Bureau of the International Union for the Protection of Literary and Artistic Works.

7. Expenses of members of the Committee shall be borne by their respective Governments.

Article 33. 1. The present Convention is drawn up in English, French and Spanish, the three texts being equally authentic.

2. In addition, official texts of the present Convention shall be drawn up in German, Italian and Portuguese.

Article 34. 1. The Secretary-General of the United Nations shall notify the States invited to the Conference referred to in Article 23 and every State Member of the United Nations, as well as the Director-General of the International Labour Office, the Director-General of the United Nations Educational, Scientific and Cultural Organization and the Director of the Bureau of the International Union for the Protection of Literary and Artistic Works:

(a) of the deposit of each instrument of ratification, acceptance or accession;

(b) of the date of entry into force of the Convention;

(c) of all notifications, declarations or communications provided for in this Convention;

(d) if any of the situations referred to in paragraphs 4 and 5 of Article 28 arise.

2. The Secretary-General of the United Nations shall also notify the Director-General of the International Labour Office, the Director-General of the United Nations Educational, Scientific and Cultural Organization and the Director of the Bureau of the International Union for the Protection of Literary and Artistic Works of the requests communicated to him in accordance with Article 29, as well as of any communication received from the Contracting States concerning the revision of the Convention.

In faith whereof, the undersigned, being duly authorised thereto, have signed this Convention.

Done at Rome, this twenty-sixth day of October 1961, in a single copy in the English, French and Spanish languages. Certified true copies shall be delivered by the Secretary-General of the United Nations to all the States invited to the Conference referred to in Article 23 and to every State Member of the United Nations, as well as to the Director-General of the International Labour Office, the Director-General of the United Nations Educational, Scientific and Cultural Organization and the Director of the Bureau of the International Union for the Protection of Literary and Artistic Works.

SEE ALSO *UNESCO Recommendation concerning the Status of the Artist; UNESCO Recommendation for the Safeguarding and Preservation of Moving Images.*

UNESCO INTERNATIONAL PROGRAM FOR THE DEVELOPMENT OF COMMUNICATIONS.

The UN General Assembly received at its 1988 session a report by the Director-General of UNESCO (UN Doc.A/ 43/670) on the application of UNESCO's International Program for the Development of Communication (IPDC) and on the social, economic, and cultural effects of the accelerated development of communication technologies.

As regards the international program, the Director-General reported that, in its seven years of operation, IPDC had disbursed more than $23 million to various inter-regional, regional, and national projects; this amount, however, fell far short of the need and indeed was insignificant in comparison with the total turnover of the world's INFORMATION AND COMMUNICATION industries, which in 1986 totalled more than $1 billion. In this connection, the Director-General appealed to the international community to make IPDC one of the outstanding programs which would enable UNESCO to recover its universality.

Regarding communication technologies, the Director-General pointed out that UNESCO's program of collaborative research into the impact of such technologies, initiated at a symposium held in Rome in December 1983, aims, first, at promoting a series of cooperative research studies of the social, economic, and cultural effects of the accelerated development of communication technologies and, later, at preparing and distributing inventories of such research as may be in progress throughout the world. The function of UNESCO in this process is not primarily to conduct research in its own right or to develop a highly structured methodology for comparative research, but rather to act as a catalyst and facilitator, attempting to bring together individual researchers and institutions and to encourage them to pool their efforts, thus extending the comparability of their work.

At the end of 1988, some 30 interdisciplinary studies of various dimensions of the new communication techniques and their impact were in progress in all world regions, coordinated by 10 research institutes or non-governmental organizations. These included studies of the impact of direct broadcasting satellites in the Maghreb region and in various Asian countries; popular media and the new communication technologies in the Caribbean; the impact of new technologies on the endogenous cultures of Africa; state-of-the-art surveys of integrated services digital networks (ISDN) in western European countries; innovative applications of new communication technologies in the socialist countries of Europe; and a comparative international study on the impact of new communication technologies on the consumption of popular music.

The UN General Assembly on 6 December 1988 (resolution 43/60 B) expressed the view that the International Program for the Development of Communications represents a significant step towards the gradual elimination of existing imbalances in the field of information and communications. The assembly reaffirmed its support for UNESCO and its constitution, and endorsed UNESCO's ongoing efforts to encourage a free flow and wider and better-balanced dissemination of information with a view to establishing a new world information and communication order, seen as an evolving and continous process, in accordance with the relevant consensus resolutions of UNESCO's General Conference.

UNESCO RECOMMENDATION CONCERNING EDUCATION FOR INTERNATIONAL UNDERSTANDING, CO-OPERATION AND PEACE AND EDUCATION RELATING TO HUMAN RIGHTS AND FUNDAMENTAL FREEDOMS (1974). This milestone recommendation was adopted by the UNESCO GENERAL CONFERENCE (18th session), held in Paris, on 19 November 1974. Its guiding principle is that all education should be infused with the aims and purposes set forth in the UNITED NATIONS CHARTER, the UNESCO constitution, and the UNIVERSAL DECLARATION OF HUMAN RIGHTS, particularly article 26, para. 2.

The text of the recommendation *(UNESCO's Standard-Setting Instruments,* No. I.B.3) is as follows:

The General Conference of the United Nations Educational, Scientific and Cultural Organization, meeting in Paris from 17 October to 23 November 1974, at its eighteenth session,

Mindful of the responsibility incumbent on States to achieve through education the aims set forth in the Charter of the United Nations, the Constitution of Unesco, the Universal Declaration of Human Rights and the Geneva Conventions for the Protection of Victims of War of 12 August 1949, in order to promote international understanding, co-operation and peace and respect for human rights and fundamental freedoms,

Reaffirming the responsibility which is incumbent on Unesco to encourage and support in Member States any activity designed to ensure the education of all for the advancement of justice, freedom, human rights and peace,

Noting nevertheless that the activity of Unesco and of its Member States sometimes has an impact only on a small minority of the steadily growing numbers of schoolchildren, students, young people and adults continuing their education, and educators, and that the curricula and methods of international education are not always attuned to the needs and aspirations of the participating young people and adults,

Noting moreover that in a number of cases there is still a wide disparity between proclaimed ideals, declared intentions and the actual situation,

Having decided at its seventeenth session, that this education should be the subject of a recommendation to Member States,

Adopts this nineteenth day of November 1974, the present recommendation.

The General Conference recommends that Member States should apply the following provisions by taking whatever legislative or other steps may be required in conformity with the constitutional practice of each State to give effect within their respective territories to the principles set forth in this recommendation.

The General Conference recommends that Member States bring this recommendation to the attention of the authorities, departments or bodies responsible for school education, higher education and out-of-school education, of the various organizations carrying out educational work among young people and adults such as student and youth movements, associations of pupils' parents, teachers' unions and other interested parties.

The General Conference recommends that Member States submit to it, by dates and in the form to be decided upon by the Conference, reports concerning the action taken by them in pursuance of this recommendation.

I. Significance of Terms

1. For the purposes of this recommendation:

(a) The word "education" implies the entire process of social life by means of which individuals and social groups learn to develop consciously within, and for the benefit of, the national and international communities, the whole of their personal capacities, attitudes, aptitudes and knowledge. This process is not limited to any specific activities.

(b) The terms "international understanding", "co-operation" and "peace" are to be considered as an indivisible whole based on the principle of friendly relations between peoples and States having different social and political systems and on the respect for human rights and fundamental freedoms. In the text of this recommendation, the different connotations of these terms are sometimes gathered together in a concise expression, "international education".

(c) "Human rights" and "fundamental freedoms" are those defined in the United Nations Charter, the Universal Declaration of Human Rights and the International Covenants on Economic, Social and Cultural Rights, and on Civil and Political Rights.

II. Scope

2. This recommendation applies to all stages and forms of education.

III. Guiding Principles

3. Education should be infused with the aims and purposes set forth in the Charter of the United Nations, the Constitution of Unesco and the Universal Declaration of Human Rights, particularly Article 26, paragraph 2, of the last-named, which states: "Education shall be directed to the full development of the human personality and to the strengthening of respect for human rights and fundamental freedoms. It shall promote understanding, tolerance and friendship among all nations, racial or religious groups, and shall further the activities of the United Nations for the maintenance of peace."

4. In order to enable every person to contribute actively to the fulfilment of the aims referred to in paragraph 3, and promote international solidarity and co-operation, which are necessary in solving the world problems affecting the individuals' and communities' life and exercise of fundamental rights and freedoms, the following objectives should be regarded as major guiding principles of educational policy:

(a) an international dimension and a global perspective in education at all levels and in all its forms;

(b) understanding and respect for all peoples, their cultures, civilizations, values and ways of life, including domestic ethnic cultures and cultures of other nations;

(c) awareness of the increasing global interdependence between peoples and nations;

(d) abilities to communicate with others;

(e) awareness not only of the rights but also of the duties incumbent upon individuals, social groups and nations towards each other;

(f) understanding of the necessity for international solidarity and cooperation;

(g) readiness on the part of the individual to partici-

pate in solving the problems of his community, his country and the world at large.

5. Combining learning, training, information and action, international education should further the appropriate intellectual and emotional development of the individual. It should develop a sense of social responsibility and of solidarity with less privileged groups and should lead to observance of the principles of equality in everyday conduct. It should also help to develop qualities, aptitudes and abilities which enable the individual to acquire a critical understanding of problems at the national and the international level; to understand and explain facts, opinions and ideas; to work in a group; to accept and participate in free discussions; to observe the elementary rules of procedure applicable to any discussion; and to base value-judgements and decisions on a rational analysis of relevant facts and factors.

6. Education should stress the inadmissibility of recourse to war for purposes of expansion, aggression and domination, or to the use of force and violence for purposes of repression, and should bring every person to understand and assume his or her responsibilities for the maintenance of peace. It should contribute to international understanding and strengthening of world peace and to the activities in the struggle against colonialism and neo-colonialism in all their forms and manifestations, and against all forms and varieties of racialism, fascism, and apartheid as well as other ideologies which breed national and racial hatred and which are contrary to the purposes of this recommendation.

IV. National Policy, Planning and Administration

7. Each Member State should formulate and apply national policies aimed at increasing the efficacy of education in all its forms and strengthening its contribution to international understanding and co-operation, to the maintenance and development of a just peace, to the establishment of social justice, to respect for and application of human rights and fundamental freedoms, and to the eradication of the prejudices, misconceptions, inequalities and all forms of injustice which hinder the achievement of these aims.

8. Member States should in collaboration with the National Commissions take steps to ensure co-operation between ministries and departments and co-ordination of their efforts to plan and carry out concerted programmes of action in international education.

9. Member States should provide, consistent with their constitutional provisions, the financial, administrative, material and moral support necessary to implement this recommendation.

V. Particular Aspects of Learning, Training and Action

Ethical and Civic Aspects. 10. Member States should take appropriate steps to strengthen and develop in the processes of learning and training, attitudes and behaviour based on recognition of the equality and necessary interdependence of nations and peoples.

11. Member States should take steps to ensure that the principles of the Universal Declaration of Human Rights and of the International Convention on the Elimination of All Forms of Racial Discrimination become an integral part of the developing personality of each child, adolescent, young person or adult by applying these principles in the daily conduct of education at each level and in all its forms, thus enabling each individual to contribute personally to

the regeneration and extension of education in the direction indicated.

12. Member States should urge educators, in collaboration with pupils, parents, the organizations concerned and the community, to use methods which appeal to the creative imagination of children and adolescents and to their social activities and thereby to prepare them to exercise their rights and freedoms while recognizing and respecting the rights of others and to perform their social duties.

13. Member States should promote, at every stage of education, an active civic training which will enable every person to gain a knowledge of the method of operation and the work of public institutions, whether local, national or international, to become acquainted with the procedures for solving fundamental problems; and to participate in the cultural life of the community and in public affairs. Wherever possible, this participation should increasingly link education and action to solve problems at the local, national and international levels.

14. Education should include critical analysis of the historical and contemporary factors of an economic and political nature underlying the contradictions and tensions between countries, together with study of ways of overcoming these contradictions, which are the real impediments to understanding, true international co-operation and the development of world peace.

15. Education should emphasize the true interests of peoples and their incompatibility with the interests of monopolistic groups holding economic and political power, which practise exploitation and foment war.

16. Student participation in the organization of studies and of the educational establishment they are attending should itself be considered a factor in civic education and an important element in international education.

Cultural Aspects. 17. Member States should promote, at various stages and in various types of education, study of different cultures, their reciprocal influences, their perspectives and ways of life, in order to encourage mutual appreciation of the differences between them. Such study should, among other things, give due importance to the teaching of foreign languages, civilizations and cultural heritage as a means of promoting international and inter-cultural understanding.

Study of the Major Problems of Mankind. 18. Education should be directed both towards the eradication of conditions which perpetuate and aggravate major problems affecting human survival and well-being—inequality, injustice, international relations based on the use of force—and towards measures of international co-operation likely to help solve them. Education which in this respect must necessarily be of an interdisciplinary nature should relate to such problems as:

(a) equality of rights of peoples, and the right of peoples to self-determination;

(b) the maintenance of peace; different types of war and their causes and effects; disarmament; the inadmissibility of using science and technology for warlike purposes and their use for the purposes of peace and progress; the nature and effect of economic, cultural and political relations between countries and the importance of international law for these relations, particularly for the maintenance of peace;

(c) action to ensure the exercise and observance of human rights, including those of refugees; racialism and its eradication; the fight against discrimination in its various forms;

(d) economic growth and social development and

their relation to social justice; colonialism and decolonization; ways and means of assisting developing countries; the struggle against illiteracy; the campaign against disease and famine; the fight for a better quality of life and the highest attainable standard of health; population growth and related questions;

(e) the use, management and conservation of natural resources, pollution of the environment;

(f) preservation of the cultural heritage of mankind;

(g) the role and methods of action of the United Nations system in efforts to solve such problems and possibilities for strengthening and furthering its action.

19. Steps should be taken to develop the study of those sciences and disciplines which are directly related to the exercise of the increasingly varied duties and responsibilities involved in international relations.

Other Aspects. 20. Member States should encourage educational authorities and educators to give education planned in accordance with this recommendation an interdisciplinary, problem-oriented content adapted to the complexity of the issues involved in the application of human rights and in international co-operation, and in itself illustrating the ideas of reciprocal influence, mutual support and solidarity. Such programmes should be based on adequate research, experimentation and the identification of specific educational objectives.

21. Member States should endeavour to ensure that international educational activity is granted special attention and resources when it is carried out in situations involving particularly delicate or explosive social problems in relations, for example, where there are obvious inequalities in opportunities for access to education.

VI. Action in Various Sectors of Education

22. Increased efforts should be made to develop and infuse an international and inter-cultural dimension at all stages and in all forms of education.

23. Member States should take advantage of the experience of the Associated Schools which carry out, with Unesco's help, programmes of international education. Those concerned with Associated Schools in Member States should strengthen and renew their efforts to extend the programme to other educational institutions and work towards the general application of its results. In other Member States, similar action should be undertaken as soon as possible. The experience of other educational institutions which have carried out successful programmes of international education should also be studied and disseminated.

24. As pre-school education develops, Member States should encourage in it activities which correspond to the purposes of the recommendation because fundamental attitudes, such as, for example, attitudes on race, are often formed in the pre-school years. In this respect, the attitude of parents should be deemed to be an essential factor for the education of children, and the adult education referred to in paragraph 30 should pay special attention to the preparation of parents for their role in pre-school education. The first school should be designed and organized as a social environment having its own character and value, in which various situations, including games, will enable children to become aware of their rights, to assert themselves freely while accepting their responsibilities, and to improve and extend through direct experience their sense of belonging to larger and larger communities—the family,

the school, then the local, national and world communities.

25. Member States should urge the authorities concerned, as well as teachers and students, to re-examine periodically how post-secondary and university education should be improved so that it may contribute more fully to the attainment of the objectives of this recommendation.

26. Higher education should comprise civic training and learning activities for all students that will sharpen their knowledge of the major problems which they should help to solve, provide them with possibilities for direct and continuous action aimed at the solution of those problems, and improve their sense of international co-operation.

27. As post-secondary educational establishments, particularly universities, serve growing numbers of people, they should carry out programmes of international education as part of their broadened function in lifelong education and should in all teaching adopt a global approach. Using all means of communication available to them, they should provide opportunities, facilities for learning and activities adapted to people's real interests, problems and aspirations.

28. In order to develop the study and practice of international co-operation, post-secondary educational establishments should systematically take advantage of the forms of international action inherent in their role, such as visits from foreign professors and students and professional co-operation between professors and research teams in different countries. In particular, studies and experimental work should be carried out on the linguistic, social, emotional and cultural obstacles, tensions, attitudes and actions which affect both foreign students and host establishments.

29. Every stage of specialized vocational training should include training to enable students to understand their role and the role of their professions in developing their society, furthering international co-operation, maintaining and developing peace, and to assume their role actively as early as possible.

30. Whatever the aims and forms of out-of-school education, including adult education, they should be based on the following considerations:

(a) as far as possible a global approach should be applied in all out-of-school education programmes, which should comprise the appropriate moral, civic, cultural, scientific and technical elements of international education;

(b) all the parties concerned should combine efforts to adapt and use the mass media of communication, self-education, and inter-active learning, and such institutions as museums and public libraries to convey relevant knowledge to the individual, to foster in him or her favourable attitudes and a willingness to take positive action, and to spread knowledge and understanding of the educational campaigns and programmes planned in accordance with the objectives of this recommendation;

(c) the parties concerned, whether public or private, should endeavour to take advantage of favourable situations and opportunities, such as the social and cultural activities of youth centres and clubs, cultural centres, community centres or trade unions, youth gatherings and festivals, sporting events, contacts with foreign visitors, students or immigrants and exchanges of persons in general.

31. Steps should be taken to assist the establishment and development of such organizations as student and teacher associations for the United Nations, international relations clubs and Unesco Clubs, which should be associated with the preparation and implementation of co-ordinated programmes of international education.

32. Member States should endeavour to ensure that, at each stage of school and out-of-school education, activities directed towards the objectives of this recommendation be co-ordinated and form a coherent whole within the curricula for the different levels and types of education, learning and training. The principles of co-operation and association which are inherent in this recommendation should be applied in all educational activities.

VII. Teacher Preparation

33. Member States should constantly improve the ways and means of preparing and certifying teachers and other educational personnel for their role in pursuing the objectives of this recommendation and should, to this end:

(a) provide teachers with motivations for their subsequent work; commitment to the ethics of human rights and to the aim of changing society, so that human rights are applied in practice; a grasp of the fundamental unity of mankind; ability to instill appreciation of the riches which the diversity of cultures can bestow on every individual, group or nation;

(b) provide basic interdisciplinary knowledge of world problems and the problems of international co-operation, through, among other means, work to solve these problems;

(c) prepare teachers themselves to take an active part in devising programmes of international education and educational equipment and materials, taking into account the aspirations of pupils and working in close collaboration with them;

(d) comprise experiments in the use of active methods of education and training in at least elementary techniques of evaluation, particularly those applicable to the social behaviour and attitudes of children, adolescents and adults;

(e) develop aptitudes and skills such as a desire and ability to make educational innovations and to continue his or her training; experience in teamwork and in interdisciplinary studies; knowledge of group dynamics; and the ability to create favourable opportunities and take advantage of them;

(f) include the study of experiments in international education, especially innovative experiments carried out in other countries, and provide those concerned, to the fullest possible extent, with opportunities for making direct contact with foreign teachers.

34. Member States should provide those concerned with direction, supervision or guidance—for instance, inspectors, educational advisers, principals of teacher-training colleges and organizers of educational activities for young people and adults—with training, information and advice enabling them to help teachers work towards the objectives of this recommendation, taking into account the aspirations of young people with regard to international problems and new educational methods that are likely to improve prospects for fulfilling these aspirations. For these purposes, seminars or refresher courses relating to international and inter-cultural education should be organized to bring together authorities and teachers; other seminars or courses might permit supervisory personnel and teachers to meet with other groups concerned such as parent, students, and teachers' associations. Since there must be a gradual but profound change in the role of education, the results of experiments for the remodelling of structures

and hierarchical relations in educational establishments should be reflected in training, information and advice.

35. Member States should endeavour to ensure that any programme of further training for teachers in service or for personnel responsible for direction includes components of international education and opportunities to compare the results of their experiences in international education.

36. Member States should encourage and facilitate educational study and refresher courses abroad, particularly by awarding fellowships, and should encourage recognition of such courses as part of the regular process of initial training, appointment, refresher training and promotion of teachers.

37. Member States should organize or assist bilateral exchanges of teachers at all levels of education.

VIII. Educational Equipment and Materials

38. Member States should increase their efforts to facilitate the renewal, production, dissemination and exchange of equipment and materials for international education, giving special consideration to the fact that in many countries pupils and students receive most of their knowledge about international affairs through the mass media outside the school. To meet the needs expressed by those concerned with international education, efforts should be concentrated on overcoming the lack of teaching aids and on improving their quality. Action should be on the following lines:

(a) appropriate and constructive use should be made of the entire range of equipment and aids available, from textbooks to television, and of the new educational technology;

(b) there should be a component of special mass media education in teaching to help the pupils to select and analyse the information conveyed by mass media;

(c) a global approach, comprising the introduction of international components, serving as a framework for presenting local and national aspects of different subjects and illustrating the scientific and cultural history of mankind, should be employed in textbooks and all other aids to learning, with due regard to the value of the visual arts and music as factors conducive to understanding between different cultures;

(d) written and audio-visual materials of an interdisciplinary nature illustrating the major problems confronting mankind and showing in each case the need for international co-operation and its practical form should be prepared in the language or languages of instruction of the country with the aid of information supplied by the United Nations, Unesco and other Specialized Agencies;

(e) documents and other materials illustrating the culture and the way of life of each country, the chief problems with which it is faced, and its participation in activities of world-wide concern should be prepared and communicated to other countries.

39. Member States should promote appropriate measures to ensure that educational aids, especially textbooks, are free from elements liable to give rise to misunderstanding, mistrust, racialist reactions, contempt or hatred with regard to other groups or peoples. Materials should provide a broad background of knowledge which will help learners to evaluate information and ideas disseminated through the mass media that seem to run counter to the aims of this recommendation.

40. According to its needs and possibilities, each Member State should establish or help to establish one or more documentation centres offering written and audio-visual material devised according to the objectives of this recommendation and adapted to the different forms and stages of education. These centres should be designed to foster the reform of international education, especially by developing and disseminating innovative ideas and materials, and should also organize and facilitate exchanges of information with other countries.

IX. Research and Experimentation

41. Member States should stimulate and support research on the foundations, guiding principles, means of implementation and effects of international education and on innovations and experimental activities in this field, such as those taking place in the Associated Schools. This action calls for collaboration by universities, research bodies and centres, teacher-training institutions, adult education training centres and appropriate non-governmental organizations.

42. Member States should take appropriate steps to ensure that teachers and the various authorities concerned build international education on a sound psychological and sociological basis by applying the results of research carried out in each country on the formation and development of favourable or unfavourable attitudes and behaviour, on attitude change, on the interaction of personality development and education and on the positive or negative effects of educational activity. A substantial part of this research should be devoted to the aspirations of young people concerning international problems and relations.

X. International Co-operation

43. Member States should consider international co-operation a responsibility in developing international education. In the implementation of this recommendation they should refrain from intervening in matters which are essentially within the domestic jurisdiction of any State in accordance with the United Nations Charter. By their own actions, they should demonstrate that implementing this recommendation is itself an exercise in international understanding and co-operation. They should, for example, organize, or help the appropriate authorities and non-governmental organizations to organize, an increasing inumber of international meetings and study sessions on international education; strengthen their programmes for the reception of foreign students, research workers, teachers and educators belonging to workers' associations and adult education associations; promote reciprocal visits by schoolchildren, and student and teacher exchanges; extend and intensify exchanges of information on cultures and ways of life; arrange for the translation or adaptation and dissemination of information and suggestions coming from other countries.

44. Member States should encourage the co-operation between their Associated Schools and those of other countries with the help of Unesco in order to promote mutual benefits by expanding their experiences in a wider international perspective.

45. Member States should encourage wider exchanges of textbooks, especially history and geography textbooks, and should, where appropriate, take measures, by concluding, if possible, bilateral and multilateral agreements, for the reciprocal study and revision of textbooks and other educational materials in order to ensure that they are accurate,

balanced, up to date and unprejudiced and will enhance mutual knowledge and understanding between different peoples.

The foregoing is the authentic text of the Recommendation duly adopted by the General Conference of the United Nations Educational, Scientific and Cultural Organization during its eighteenth session, which was held in Paris and declared closed the twenty-third day of November 1974.

In faith whereof we have appended our signatures this twenty-fifth day of November 1974.

SEE ALSO Center for the Study of Human Rights, Columbia University; Education; Harvard Law School Human Rights Program; Human Rights: Teaching; Human Rights Teaching Prize; United Nations Institute for Training and Research; United Nations University.

UNESCO RECOMMENDATION CONCERNING TECHNICAL AND VOCATIONAL EDUCATION, REVISED (1974).

The recommendation, adopted by the UNESCO GENERAL CONFERENCE (18th session), held in Paris, on 19 November 1974, revises the original recommendation on the subject which had been issued by the conference in 1962 by taking into account many new technological and educational developments. Like the earlier text, the 1974 recommendation sets out a series of general principles, goals, and guidelines to be applied by UNESCO's member States, individually and collectively, with a view to ensuring to everyone the right to work and the right to education.

The text of the recommendation *(UNESCO's Standard-Setting Instruments,* No. I.B.4) is as follows:

The General Conference of the United Nations Educational, Scientific and Cultural Organization, meeting in Paris, at its eighteenth session, held from 17 October to 23 November 1974,

Recalling the constitutional responsibilities of the Organization for the promotion of education,

Recognizing that technical and vocational education have to contribute to the maintenance of peace and friendly understanding between the various nations,

Considering that education must now be seen as a lifelong process,

Recognizing that technical and vocational education is a prerequisite for sustaining the complex structure of modern civilization and economic and social development,

Recalling the principles set forth in Articles 23 and 26 of the Universal Declaration of Human Rights guaranteeing all the right to work and to education,

Considering therefore that all have a right to an education enabling full participation in contemporary society,

Taking into account the diversity of education systems throughout the world, as well as the particular and urgent needs of developing countries,

Considering that in spite of this diversity similar goals are pursued and similar questions and problems arise in all countries concerning technical and vocational education and that therefore common standards and measures are called for,

Having adopted for this purpose at its twelfth session the Recommendation concerning Technical and Vocational Education,

Recognizing however that the rapid technological and educational changes of the last decade require new, creative, and efficient efforts in technical and vocational education to improve education as a whole for social, economic and cultural development,

Having decided at its seventeenth session that in view of these changes this Recommendation should be revised in order to better serve Member States,

Noting that the International Labour Conference has adopted, over the years, a number of instruments dealing with various aspects of vocational guidance and vocational training and, in particular, the Vocational Guidance Recommendation, 1949, the Vocational Training (Agriculture) Recommendation, 1956, and the Vocational Training Recommendation, 1962, and that the Conference, at its 59th session, had adopted substantive conclusions with a view to adoption, in 1975, of a new instrument or instruments on vocational guidance and vocational training,

Noting further the close collaboration between Unesco and the International Labour Organisation (ILO) in drawing up their respective instruments so that they pursue harmonious objectives, avoiding duplication and conflict, and with a view to continued collaboration for effective implementation of the two instruments,

Adopts this Recommendation this nineteenth day of November 1974.

The General Conference recommends that when developing and improving technical and vocational education, Member States should apply the following provisions by taking whatever legislative or other steps may be required to give effect, within their respective territories, to the principles set forth in this Recommendation.

The General Conference recommends that Member States should bring this Recommendation to the knowledge of the authorities and bodies concerned with technical and vocational education.

The General Conference recommends that Member States should report to it, at such times and in such manner as shall be determined by it, on the action they have taken to give effect to the Recommendation.

I. Scope

1. This Recommendation applies to all forms and aspects of education which are technical and vocational in nature provided either in educational institutions or under their authority, directly by public authorities, or through other forms of organized education, public or private.

2. For the purposes of this Recommendation: "technical and vocational education" is used as a comprehensive term referring to those aspects of the educational process involving, in addition to general education, the study of technologies and related sciences and the acquisition of practical skills, attitudes, understanding and knowledge relating to occupations in various sectors of economic and social life. Technical and vocational education is further understood to be:

    (a) an integral part of general education;

    (b) a means of preparing for an occupational field;

    (c) an aspect of continuing education.

3. Technical and vocational education, being part of the total education process, is included in the term 'education' as defined in the Convention and Recommendation

against Discrimination in Education adopted by the General Conference of the United Nations Educational, Scientific and Cultural Organization at its eleventh session and the provisions of that Convention and Recommendation are therefore applicable to it.

4. This recommendation should be understood as setting forth general principles, goals and guidelines to be applied by each individual country according to needs and resources. The application of the provisions in their particulars and the timing of the implementation will therefore depend upon the conditions existing in a given country.

II. Technical and Vocational Education in relation to the Educational Process: Objectives

5. Given immense scientific and technological development, either in progress or envisaged, which characterizes the present era, technical and vocational education should be a vital aspect of the educational process and in particular should:

(a) contribute to the achievement of society's goals of greater democratization and social, cultural and economic development, while at the same time developing the potential of individuals for active participation in the establishment and implementation of these goals;

(b) lead to an understanding of the scientific and technological aspects of contemporary civilization in such a way that men comprehend their environment and are capable of acting upon it while taking a critical view of the social, political and environmental implications of scientific and technological change.

6. Given the necessity for new relationships between education, working life, and the community as a whole, technical and vocational education should exist as part of a system of lifelong education adapted to the needs of each particular country. This system should be directed to:

(a) abolishing barriers between levels and areas of education, between education and employment and between school and society through:

(i) the integration of technical and vocational and general education in all educational streams above primary level;

(ii) the creation of open and flexible educational structures;

(iii) the taking into account of individuals' educational needs and of the evolution of occupations and jobs;

(b) improving the quality of life by permitting the individual to expand his intellectual horizons and to acquire and to constantly improve professional skills and knowledge while allowing society to utilize the fruits of economic and technological change for the general welfare.

7. Technical and vocational education should begin with a broad basic vocational education, thus facilitating horizontal and vertical articulation within the education system and between school and employment thus contributing to the elimination of all forms of discrimination and should be designed so that it:

(a) is an integral part of everyone's basic general education in the form of initiation to technology and to the world of work;

(b) may be freely and positively chosen as the means by which one develops talents, interests and skills leading to an occupation in the sectors listed in paragraph 2 or to further education;

(c) allows access to other aspects and areas of education at all levels by being grounded on a solid general edu-

cation and, as a result of the integration mentioned in paragraph 6(a), containing a general education component through all stages of specialization;

(d) allows transfers from one field to another within technical and vocational education;

(e) is readily available to all and for all appropriate types of specialization, within and outside formal education systems, and in conjunction or in parallel with training in order to permit educational, career and job mobility at a minimum age at which the general basic education is considered to have been acquired, according to the education system in force in each country;

(f) is available on the above terms and on a basis of equality to women as well as men;

(g) is available to disadvantaged and handicapped persons in special forms adapted to their needs in order to integrate them more easily into society.

8. In terms of the needs and aspirations of individuals, technical and vocational education should:

(a) permit the harmonious development of personality and character and foster the spiritual and human values, the capacity for understanding, judgment, critical thinking and self-expression;

(b) prepare the individual to learn continuously by developing the necessary mental tools, practical skills and attitudes;

(c) develop capacities for decision-making and the qualities necessary for active and intelligent participation, teamwork and leadership at work and in the community as a whole.

III. Policy, Planning and Administration

9. Policy should be formulated and technical and vocational education administered in support of the general objectives adopted for the educational process as well as for national and, if possible, regional social and economic requirements, and an appropriate legislative and financial framework adopted. Policy should be directed to both the structural and the qualitative improvement of technical and vocational education.

10. Particular attention should be given to planning the development and expansion of technical and vocational education:

(a) high priority should be placed on technical and vocational education in national development plans as well as in plans for educational reform;

(b) planning should be based upon a thorough evaluation of both short-term and long-term needs taking into consideration any variation in needs which may exist within a country;

(c) adequate provision for proper current and future allocation of financial resources should be a major element of planning;

(d) planning should be done by a responsible body or bodies having authority on the national level. This body should have available to it data which have been collated, analysed, synthesized and interpreted by qualified staff provided with adequate research facilities.

11. Planning should be responsive to national and, if possible, regional, economic and social trends, to projected changes in demand for different classes of goods and services, and for different types of skills and knowledge in such a way that technical and vocational education may easily adapt to the evolving situation be it rural or urban. This

planning should also be co-ordinated with current and projected training action and the evolution of employment.

12. While the education authorities should have primary responsibility, the following groups and authorities should be actively associated in policy formulation, and in the planning process. Structures, on both national and local levels, taking the form of public agencies or consultative or advisory bodies, should be created to permit this:

(a) public authorities responsible for planning economic and social policy, labour and employment, and for the various occupational sectors (industry, agriculture, commerce);

(b) representatives of non-governmental organizations within each occupation sector from among employers and workers;

(c) any authority or body, such as a training body or extension services, responsible for out-of-school education and training;

(d) representatives of those responsible—both in public education and in State-recognized private education—for executing educational policy including teachers, examining bodies and administrators;

(e) parent, former pupil, student and youth organizations;

(f) representatives from the community at large.

13. Policies for the structural improvement of technical and vocational education should be established within the framework of broad policies designed to implement the principle of lifelong education through the creation of open, flexible and complementary structures for education, training and educational and vocational guidance, regardless of whether these activities take place within the system of formal education or outside it. In this respect consideration should be given to the following:

(a) multipurpose secondary education offering diversified curricula including work-study programmes;

(b) open tertiary institutions recruiting from a variety of sources and offering programmes ranging from short specialized ones to longer full-time programmes of integrated studies and professional specialization;

(c) establishing a system of equivalencies whereby credit is given for completion of any approved programme and recognition is granted to educational and professional qualifications achieved through various means.

14. Policy should be directed to ensuring high quality in such a way as to exclude the possibility of any judgement which discriminates between the different educational streams, whatever their ultimate goal, In this respect special efforts should be made to ensure that technical and vocational education in rural areas meets the same standards as that offered in urban ones.

15. In order to ensure quality, responsible national authorities should establish certain criteria and standards, subject to periodic review and evaluation, applying in all aspects of technical and vocational education, including to the extent possible non-formal education for:

(a) all forms of recognition of achievement and consequent qualification;

(b) staff qualifications;

(c) ratios of teaching and training staff to learners;

(d) the quality of curricula and teaching materials;

(e) safety precautions for all learning environments;

(f) physical facilities, building, workshop layouts, quality and type of equipment.

16. Policies should be established fostering research related to technical and vocational education, with particular emphasis on its potential within lifelong education, and directed to its improvement. This research should be carried out by competent staff on national and institutional levels as well as through individual initiative. To this end:

(a) special emphasis should be placed on curriculum development, research concerning teaching and learning methods and materials, and where the need exists, on technologies and techniques applied to development problems;

(b) financial resources and physical facilities should be made available through institutions of higher education, specialized research institutions and professional organizations for applying the results of this research on an experimental basis in representatively selected institutions for technical and vocational education;

(c) channels should be created for the widespread dissemination and rapid application of the positive results of research and experimentation;

(d) the effectiveness of technical and vocational education should be evaluated using, among other data, relevant statistics including those concerning part-time enrollments and drop-out rates which are in some cases neglected;

(e) particular attention should be given to all research efforts to humanize working conditions.

17. Provision should be made within administrative structures for evaluation, supervisory and accreditation services, staffed by technical and vocational education specialists, to ensure the rapid application of new research findings and to maintain standards:

(a) evaluation services as a whole should ensure the quality and smooth operation of technical and vocational education by continuous review and action directed to constant improvement of staff, facilities and programmes;

(b) supervisory services for the staff should encourage improvement in the quality of teaching by providing guidance and advice and recommending continuing education;

(c) all programmes of technical and vocational education, in particular, those offered by private bodies, should be subject to approval by the public authorities through some means of accreditation or form of public inspection.

18. Particular attention should be given to the material resources required for technical and vocational education. Priorities should be carefully established with due regard for immediate needs and the probable directions of future expansion and adequate cost controls introduced:

(a) institutional planning should be directed to ensuring maximum efficiency and flexibility in use;

(b) the planning, construction and equipping of facilities should be carried out in collaboration with specialist teachers and educational architects and with due regard for their purpose, prevailing local factors and relevant research;

(c) adequate funds should be allocated for recurrent expenditure for supplies and maintenance and repair of equipment.

IV. Technical and Vocational Aspects of General Education

19. An initiation to technology and to the world of work should be an essential component of general education without which this education is incomplete. An understanding of the technological facet of modern culture in both its positive and negative attributes, and an appreciation of work requiring practical skills should thereby be acquired. This initiation should further be a major concern

in educational reform and change with a view to greater democratization of education. It should be a required element in the curriculum, beginning in primary education and continuing through the early years of secondary education.

20. Opportunities for general technical and vocational initiation should continue to be available to those who wish to avail themselves of it within the educational system and outside it in places of work or community centres.

21. The technical and vocational initiation in the general education of youth should fulfil the educational requirements of all ranges of interest and ability. It should mainly perform three functions:

(a) to enlarge educational horizons by serving as an introduction to the world of work and the world of technology and its products through the exploration of materials, tools, techniques and the process of production, distribution and management as a whole, and to broaden the learning process through practical experience;

(b) to orient those with the interest and ability toward technical and vocational education as preparation for an occupational field or toward training outside the formal education system;

(c) to promote in those who will leave formal education at whatever level but with no specific occupational aims or skills, attitudes of mind and ways of thought likely to enhance their aptitudes and potential, to facilitate the choice of an occupation and access to a first job, and to permit them to continue their vocational training and personal education.

22. Required general technical and vocational studies in the schools having great importance for the orientation and education of youth programmes, should include a proper balance between theoretical and practical work. A properly structured programme of such studies should be drawn up by the competent authorities in collaboration with the professional community and with those responsible for technical and vocational education. These programmes should:

(a) be based upon a problem-solving and experimental approach and involve experience in planning methods and decision-making;

(b) introduce the learner to a broad spectrum of technological fields and at the same time to productive work situations;

(c) develop a certain command of valuable practical skills such as tool use, repair and maintenance and safety procedures, whether applicable to future education, training and employment or to leisure time, and a respect for their value;

(d) develop an appreciation of good design and craftsmanship and the ability to select goods on the basis of their quality;

(e) develop the ability to communicate including the use of graphical means;

(f) develop the ability to measure and calculate accurately;

(g) be closely related to the local environment without, however, being limited to it.

23. The technical and vocational initiation in programmes of general educational enrichment for older youth and adults should be directed to enabling those engaged in working life to:

(a) understand the general implications of technological change, its impact on their professional and private lives, and how man may shape this change;

(b) to use practical skills for improving the home and community environment and thus the quality of life and, in appropriate conditions, for productive leisure-time activities.

V. Technical and Vocational Education as Preparation for an Occupational Field

24. Given disparities that may exist between formal education, whether secondary or tertiary, and the employment and career opportunities available, the highest priority should be given to technical and vocational education which prepares young people to exercise occupations in the sectors covered by this recommendation. Consequently the structure and content of traditional education, whether general or technical and vocational, should be adapted accordingly through:

(a) the diversification of secondary education in the later stages so that it may be pursued in conjunction with employment or training, or may lead to employment or to higher education, thereby offering to all youth educational options corresponding to their needs;

(b) the introduction of new programmes into tertiary education more relevant to the career needs of young adults;

(c) the development of educational structures and programmes on all levels centred on organized and flexible interchange between educational institutions including training institutions and those responsible for employment in the various occupational sectors.

25. Technical and vocational education as preparation for an occupational field should provide the foundation for productive and satisfying careers and should:

(a) lead to the acquisition of broad knowledge and basic skills applicable to a number of occupations within a given field so that the individual is not limited by his education in his freedom of occupational choice, and later transfer from one field to another in the course of working life is facilitated;

(b) at the same time offer a thorough and specialized preparation for initial employment and effective training within employment;

(c) provide the background in terms of skills, knowledge and attitudes, for continuing education at any point in the individual's working life.

26. Premature and narrow specialization should be avoided:

(a) in principle 15 should be considered the lower age limit for beginning specialization;

(b) a period of common studies concerning basic knowledge and skills should be required for each broad occupational sector before a special branch is chosen.

27. Because it is desirable that women seek wider participation in all kinds of occupations outside family and domestic activities, they should have the same educational opportunities available to them as men in order to prepare for an occupation and should be encouraged to take advantage of these through appropriate legislative measures and widespread distribution of information concerning these opportunities.

28. Special provision should be made for out-of-school and unemployed youth and children of migrant workers with the minimum or less of primary education, as well as for those not entering education or training programmes after completion of compulsory schooling, in order that they may acquire employable skills.

29. Given the necessity of integrating the physically and mentally disadvantaged into society and its occupations, the same educational opportunities should be available to them as to the non-handicapped in order that they may achieve qualification for an occupation; special measures or special institutions may be required.

Organization. 30. Technical and vocational education as preparation for an occupational field should be organized on a national or, if possible, regional basis, so as to respond positively to over-all social, economic and educational requirements and to the needs of different groups of the population without discrimination.

31. Several organizational patterns of technical and vocational education, including both full-time and part-time options should exist within each country. The following patterns of organization for example should be considered:

(a) full time including practical training as well as general education, provided in an educational establishment, either comprehensive or specialized;

(b) part-time programmes such as the following in which general education and theoretical and broad practical aspects of the occupational field are given in an educational establishment while specialized practical training is acquired during work in the chosen occupation:

(i) the day-release system providing for young workers and apprentices to attend an educational establishment at least one day a week and preferably two;

(ii) the sandwich system under which periods in an educational institution alternate with training periods in a factory, farm, business establishment or other undertaking;

(iii) the block-release system whereby young workers are released to attend courses for one or two short periods of at least ten to fifteen weeks in total length per year which may be especially adapted to conditions in areas of low population density by provision of boarding facilities.

32. The responsible authorities should encourage part-time education, therefore:

(a) these programmes should be available directly after completion of minimum compulsory or required schooling, and should continue to be available to the highest level of formal education;

(b) the educational qualifications acquired by this means should be equivalent to those acquired by full-time education;

(c) where employers are responsible for the practical training aspect for part-time students, this training should be as broad as possible serving the educational and training needs of the individual, and should meet national standards.

33. In view of the increasing requirement for highly qualified middle-level manpower in all fields, and the increasing numbers completing secondary education or its equivalent, the development of programmes of technical and vocational education corresponding to further qualifying tertiary education should be given high priority. The following patterns of organization should be considered;

(a) a period of from one to two years of guided work experience followed by a part-time or briefer full-time programme of specialization;

(b) part-time programmes;

(c) full-time programmes as an extension of programmes given in specialized secondary institutions or given in tertiary institutions.

34. The high cost of equipment for the practical component of technical and vocational education requires that this be organized so that benefits received are in proportion to the cost. Consideration should be given to the following as a means of achieving this:

(a) centralized workshops, or mobile units, could be used to serve several educational institutions;

(b) workshops attached to educational institutions could be designed so that they are suitable for use by the community at large particularly for continuing education programmes;

(c) although workshops and laboratories in advanced secondary or tertiary institutions should be designed primarily for pedagogical purposes, they might also be equipped and staffed so that equipment for use in technical and vocational studies in general education may be produced.

35. Enterprises should be closely associated in the practical training of those preparing for occupations in their particular sector, and should be encouraged to take responsibility, in co-operation with educational institutions, for the organization of this training.

Programme Content. 36. All programmes of technical and vocational education as preparation for an occupational field should:

(a) aim at providing scientific knowledge, technical versatility and the broad skills and knowledge required for rapid adaptation to new ideas and procedures and for steady career development;

(b) be based on an analysis of broad occupational requirements worked out for the long term between education authorities including organizations representing educational research and administration and employment authorities and occupational organizations concerned;

(c) include a proper balance between general subjects, science and technology, and studies of both the theoretical and practical aspects of the occupational field, with the practical component in all cases related to the theoretical one;

(d) stress developing a sense of professional values and responsibilities from the standpoint of human needs.

37. In particular programmes should:

(a) whenever possible be interdisciplinary in character as many occupations now require knowledge and training in two or more traditional areas of study;

(b) be based on curricula designed around core knowledge and skills;

(c) include studies of the social and economic aspects of the occupational field as a whole;

(d) include the study of at least one foreign language of international use which, while conducive to a higher cultural level, will give special emphasis to the requirements of communication and the acquisition of a scientific and technical vocabulary;

(e) include an introduction to organizational and planning skills;

(f) emphasize instruction in safety procedures relative to the materials and equipment used in a given occupational field and the importance of safe working conditions and the health aspects relative to the occupation as a whole.

38. While based on the above general principles and components, and thus pursuing in all cases broader educational aims, programmes in their practical aspect should be designed taking into account special occupational requirements with regard to the particular executive, organizational, analytical and practical skills required.

39. Technical and vocational education programmes leading to university qualification, while encouraging re-

search and offering high-level specialization, should be developed with particular attention to:

(a) the inclusion of components directed to developing attitudes whereby those with broad responsibilities in technological fields constantly relate their professional tasks to larger human goals;

(b) relating more closely higher technical and vocational education for the industrial and agricultural sectors to the requirements of these sectors. In this regard consideration should be given to creating within tertiary institutions, centres for the testing and certification of industrial and agricultural products, supervised by the public authorities and serving both educational and research purposes.

40. Programmes of technical and vocational education as preparation for occupations within the agricultural sector should be designed in accordance with the over-all social and economic requirements of rural development. Therefore:

(a) both general aspects and the technical and vocational aspects, while adapted in terms of both organization and content to the special requirements of agricultural occupations, should be of the same quality as those for other occupational areas;

(b) programmes should be directed to the development and application of technologies especially suited to rural development through close coordination between education and extension services and between these and research services and institutions;

(c) programmes should be directed to preparing qualified people for all types of occupations and ranges of technical competence necessary for rural development;

(d) programmes should be broadly conceived, including in addition to the special occupational area, an introduction to the commercial aspects of agriculture and the functioning of rural economic institutions.

41. Where lack of resources limits the expansion of technical and vocational education, emphasis in the initial stages should be placed on developing programmes for occupations in areas of critical manpower shortage, and in areas of immediate development potential.

42. Programmes preparing for occupations in small industry, individual farming or the artisan trades, whether urban or rural, and particularly for self-employment, should include commercial studies enabling those engaged in such occupations to take responsibility not only for production, but also for marketing, competent management and the rational organization of the whole enterprise.

43. Programmes leading to occupations in the business and commercial sector should include:

(a) a thorough grounding in the methods and skills developed as a result of the application of technology to business and office management and particularly to the acquisition and processing of information;

(b) training in the organizational and management skills required for the smooth operation of enterprises in all economic sectors;

(c) an introduction to marketing and distribution procedures.

44. Special attention should be given to developing programmes for preparing personnel at all levels for the social services sector (e.g. community and family work, nursing and paramedical occupations, nutrition and food technology, home economics and environmental improvement). Those programmes should:

(a) emphasize the relation of the special occupational field to raising standards of living in terms of food, cloth-

ing, housing, medical services, the quality of family life or that of the environment as the case may be;

(b) be well adapted to the special requirements of local conditions in particular those of climate and geography, materials available and community organization and social patterns.

VI. Technical and Vocational Education as Continuing Education

45. The development and expansion of technical and vocational education as continuing education, both within and outside the formal education system, and within the framework of lifelong education, should be a priority objective of all educational strategies and broad provision should be made for allowing everyone, whatever the educational qualifications achieved prior to employment, to continue both their professional and general education.

46. In addition to permitting adults to make up deficiencies in general education or professional qualifications, which has often been the only objective of continuing education, it should now:

(a) offer possibilities of personal development and professional advancement;

(b) permit the updating and refreshing of knowledge and practical abilities and skills in the occupational field;

(c) enable the individual to adapt to technological changes in his occupation or to enter another occupation if these changes render his particular job obsolete;

(d) be available throughout working life without restriction of age, sex, prior education and training or position;

(e) be broad in scope, including general education elements, and not simply specialized training for one particular job.

47. The appropriate authorities should be encouraged to provide the basic conditions for technical and vocational education as continuing education, including consideration of measures providing for paid educational leave or other forms of financial aid.

48. The technical and vocational aspect of continuing education should actively be encouraged through such means as:

(a) widespread dissemination of information concerning the programmes available, and how one may take advantage of existing opportunities, including full use of mass media to this end;

(b) recognition of successful completion of programmes in terms of remuneration and professional advancement.

49. Those responsible for organizing programmes of continuing technical and vocational education recognized by the public authorities should consider the following forms:

(a) courses given during working hours at the place of work;

(b) fuller part-time courses especially designed for continuing education given in secondary and tertiary institutions, already staffed and equipped for technical and vocational education;

(c) evening and week-end courses given in the above types of institutions or in community centres;

(d) correspondence courses;

(e) courses given on educational television;

(f) periodic seminars;

(g) inter-enterprise programmes;

(h) informal discussion groups created and organized on the initiative of students.

50. The following forms of organization of leave should be considered:

(a) day release;

(b) block release of varying lengths;

(c) release for one or more hours during the working day.

51. Programmes of technical and vocational education as continuing education should:

(a) be designed and taught on the basis of the special requirements of adults, and use teaching methods which take into account the expertise which they have already acquired;

(b) contain a built-in mechanism for rapid adjustment to the needs of particular individuals or groups and to technological change.

52. Special provision should be made for groups with particular requirements:

(a) in the case of women, because of the necessity of periods of absence form the labour force imposed by maternity and family responsibilities, in order to enable them to update their knowledge and to improve their professional skills for re-entry into employment;

(b) to enable older workers to adapt to new occupations;

(c) to provide foreign workers and handicapped workers with specific facilities for pre-training to enable them to adapt to a training programme or to working life;

(d) the resources of continuing education should be used to offer unskilled and semi-skilled workers the opportunity to improve their qualifications.

53. Particular attention should be paid to the development of continuing education programmes suitable in rural areas in terms of content, physical location and time of year offered.

VII. Guidance

54. Guidance should be viewed as a continuous process and a vital element in education, directed to aiding all to make positive educational and occupational choices. It should ensure that the individual be provided with the necessary prerequisites:

(a) to become aware of his interests and abilities and able to set himself precise objectives;

(b) to pursue a course of education, whether preparatory or continuing, commensurate with these;

(c) to make decisions concerning his occupation, both in the initial and later stages, which lead to a satisfying career;

(d) to facilitate transitions between education and employment at whatever level or stage.

55. Guidance services on the national, local and institutional levels should ensure that the paths are kept open between education and initial training and employment, and employment and continuing education and training through:

(a) close liaison and co-ordination with training, counselling, employment and placement services;

(b) ensuring that all necessary information concerning employment and career opportunities is available and actively disseminated;

(c) ensuring that those in employment have access to information concerning opportunities in continuing education and training.

56. While emphasizing the needs of the individual, guidance for young people should be accompanied by information which gives them a realistic view of the opportunities available in a given occupational cluster, including information regarding probable developments in the market and in employment structures, and what may be expected in terms of remuneration, career advancement and possibilities for occupational change.

57. Particular attention should be given to guidance for girls and women:

(a) this guidance should cover the same broad range of education, training and employment opportunities as for boys and men;

(b) it should systematically encourage girls and women to take advantage of the opportunities available to them.

58. Guidance given in the technical and vocational aspects of general education during the observation or orientation cycle of secondary schooling should:

(a) cover a broad range of occupations with supplementary visits to work places and acquaint the student with the eventual necessity of choosing an occupation and the importance of this choice being as rational as possible;

(b) aid students in making a positive choice concerning educational streams or options for those wishing to pursue technical and vocational education as preparation for an occupational field or training programmes outside the educational system, and aid those not continuing their formal education or entering training to find employment, while encouraging them to continue their education at a later date.

59. Guidance in technical and vocational education as preparation for an occupational field should:

(a) inform the student of the various possibilities open in the particular field of interest, the educational background required and the possibilities for later continuing education;

(b) encourage the student to choose an educational programme which will limit his later employment options as little as possible;

(c) follow the progress of the student during the educational programmes;

(d) supplement the later stages of the programmes by short periods of work experience and study of real work situations.

60. Guidance in technical and vocational education as continuing education should:

(a) help the employed adult choose the programme of continuing education most suited to his needs;

(b) enable him to place himself in relation to the various levels of study and afford him the means of making effective choices.

61. Guidance should be given on the basis of:

(a) knowledge of the individual which takes account of the social and family factors influencing his attitudes and expectations;

(b) information obtained from objective evaluation of the results of testing including aptitude tests;

(c) knowledge of his educational achievements and/ or achievements in employment;

(d) knowledge of employment and career opportunities as well as job satisfaction in the occupational sector in which he is interested or engaged and of demands made;

(e) medical records indicating whether the student is physically able to pursue a given occupation.

62. The effectiveness of guidance services should contin-

ually be assessed and statistics kept on both the national and institutional levels through:

(a) the keeping of cumulative records concerning the education of the student as well as follow-up records concerning his employment;

(b) a built-in system of evaluation of both quality of staff performance and the methods used in order to effect change or improvement where needed.

VIII. The Teaching and Learning Processes: Methods and Materials

63. In all aspects of technical and vocational education, the methodology of learning should assume equal importance in the teaching and learning process with the subject-matter itself. All aspects of technical and vocational education should be oriented to the needs of the learner and directed to motivating him, and methods and materials developed accordingly.

64. Theory and practice should form an integrated whole: what is learned in the laboratory, workshop or in enterprises should be directly related to the mathematical and scientific foundations of the particular operation or process, and conversely, technical theory, as well as the mathematics and science sustaining it, should be illustrated through their practical applications.

65. Full use should be made of the resources provided by educational technology, with special emphasis on the methods and materials of self-education, in particular audio-visual aids, including multi-media systems, programmed instruction and the use of mass media.

66. The methods and materials used in technical and vocational education should be carefully adapted to the group to be taught. In this respect:

(a) where the language of instruction differs from the native language, teaching materials should make maximum use of numerical and graphical representation, written material being kept to a minimum;

(b) where materials developed in one country are adapted for use in another, this adaptation should be carefully made with due regard to local factors.

67. Machines and equipment used in workshops in educational institutions should be geared to the level and training of the users. This equipment should be simple and designed expecially for pedagogical purposes without however being obsolete or teaching obsolete procedures. Training using complex equipment may be given more appropriately and efficiently on the job.

Evaluation. 68. Evaluation should be an integral part of the teaching and learning process in technical and vocational education, and its major function should be the development of the particular individual in accordance with his interests and capacities.

69. Although standards of performance should be upheld, evaluation of the student's work should be made on a total basis considering among others his class participation, his interest and attitude, his relative progress, allowance being made for his aptitudes, and examinations and other tests.

70. Students should participate in the evaluation of their own progress and the evaluation of student work should have a system of feedback built into it so that learning problems and their causes may be identified and steps taken to correct them.

71. Continuous evaluation of the teaching process should be made by both teachers and their supervisors, with the participation of students as well, in order to determine the effectiveness of the methods and materials used, and to devise alternatives should the need arise. Continuous evaluation of the teaching-learning process should be undertaken with the participation of representatives from the occupational fields concerned.

IX. Staff

72. To enhance the achievement of the objectives of technical and vocational education, a priority should be given to the recruitment and preparation of adequate numbers of well-qualified and competent teachers, administrators, and guidance staff and to the provision of the necessary training and other facilities to enable them to function effectively in their profession.

73. The emoluments and conditions of service which are offered should compare favourably with those enjoyed by persons with similar qualification and experience in other occupational sectors. In particular, promotions, salaries and pension scales for technical and vocational education staff should take into account any relevant experience acquired in employment outside the educational sector.

Teaching Staff. 74. All teachers in technical and vocational education, including those who teach only practice, should be considered an integral part of the teaching profession and as such should be recognized as having the same status as their colleagues in other fields. In this regard:

(a) the Recommendation concerning the Status of Teachers adopted by the Special Intergovernmental Conference on the Status of Teachers on 5 October 1966 is applicable to them especially as regards the provisions concerning preparation for a profession and continuing education; employment and career; the rights and responsibilities of teachers; conditions for effective teaching and learning; teachers' salaries; social security;

(b) arbitrary distinctions between teachers employed by various types of educational institutions, e.g. specialized technical and vocational institutions and general education institutions should be eliminated.

75. Teachers involved in any aspect of technical and vocational education, whether on a full-time or part-time basis, should possess the personal, ethical, professional and teaching qualities essential for the accomplishment of their work.

76. Teachers of technical and vocational aspects in general education should:

(a) be familiar with a broad range of specialities;

(b) develop the ability to relate these to each other as well as to the larger social, economic and historical and cultural context;

(c) where this aspect of technical and vocational education serves primarily an occupation or educational orientation function, be able to give guidance.

77. Considering technical and vocational education as preparation for an occupational field, teachers in this area should have special qualifications depending on the occupation for which they are preparing students;

(a) if the occupational field requires primarily practical skills the teacher should himself have long employment experience in the exercise of these skills;

(b) if students are to be prepared for technician or middle management positions, teachers should have a thorough knowledge, preferably acquired through appropriate practical experience, of the special requirements of this type of position;

(c) if the occupational field requires research and theoretical analysis, e.g. an engineering field, the teacher should have a university education and be actively engaged in research himself.

78. Considering technical and vocational education as continuing education, teachers in this area should, in addition to the special preparation for teaching adults, have an adequate knowledge of the working environment of their students and have specialized knowledge and skills in their teaching field.

79. Skilled professionals employed in appropriate sectors outside education should be invited to teach, at suitable points in technical and vocational education, certain programmes in schools, universities or other educational institutions in order to link the world of work more closely to the classroom.

80. Teachers of general subjects in institutions which offer technical and vocational education, in addition to the usual qualification, both professional and in their teaching field, should receive a special initiation concerning the objectives and requirements of technical and vocational education.

81. Preparation for technical and vocational teaching should be given as a tertiary programme, thereby requiring completion of secondary education or its equivalent for entrance. All types of programme should be designed with the following objectives in mind:

(a) to maintain standards of education and professional preparation in vigour for the teaching profession as a whole and to contribute to the raising of these over-all standards;

(b) to develop in the future teacher the ability to teach both theoretical and practical aspects of his field;

(c) to ensure that the teacher will be qualified, with minimum further training, to teach other groups than those for which he was prepared initially.

82. Varied and flexible programmes, full time and part time, adapted to the special requirements of a wide variety of recruitment sources as well as to those of the field to be taught and the group or groups to be taught should be available.

83. In those cases where it is difficult for intending technical and vocational teachers to acquire employment experience, consideration should be given to creating units, attached to teacher-training institutions, for the production of equipment and teaching materials for the schools in which intending teaching staff would be required to work for varying lengths of time.

84. The professional preparation of all technical and vocational teachers should include the following elements:

(a) educational theory both in general and as especially applying to technical and vocational education;

(b) educational psychology and sociology as it especially applies to the group or groups for which the future teacher will be responsible;

(c) special teaching methods appropriate to the field of technical and vocational education for which the future teacher is preparing and the groups to be taught, in methods of evaluation of student work and in classroom management;

(d) training in the choice and use of the whole range of modern teaching techniques and aids presupposing the use of up-to-date methods and materials in the programme of professional preparation itself;

(e) training in how to create and produce appropriate teaching materials, of special importance in those cases where technical and vocational teaching materials are in short supply;

(f) a period of supervised practice teaching experience before appointment to a teaching post;

(g) an introduction to educational and occupational guidance methods as well as to educational administration;

(h) a thorough grounding in safety and emphasis on the ability to teach safe working practice and habitually to set a good working example.

85. Staff responsible for the preparation of technical and vocational teachers should have obtained the highest qualifications possible in their field:

(a) teacher-educators responsible for special technical and vocational fields should have qualifications in their field equivalent to those of special subjects staff in other institutions and programmes of higher education, including advanced degrees and employment experience in a related occupational field;

(b) teacher-educators responsible for the pedagogical aspect of teacher preparation should themselves be experienced teachers in technical and vocational education and should possess the highest qualifications in a specialized field of education.

86. Staff responsible for the preparation of technical and vocational teachers should be actively engaged in research in their field and provision should be made for this in terms of a reasonable teaching load and access to appropriate facilities.

87. Teaching staff should be encouraged to continue their education, whatever the field in which they specialize, and should have the necessary means to do so. This continuing education which should be made available in a wide range of facilities, should include:

(a) periodic review and updating of knowledge and skills in the special field;

(b) periodic updating of professional skills and knowledge;

(c) periodic work in the occupational sector relating to the special field.

88. Account should be taken of a teacher's achievements in continuing education when the responsible authorities consider questions of promotion, seniority and status concerning him.

Administrative and Guidance Staff. 89. Administrative responsibilities for technical and vocational education programmes should be entrusted to persons with the following qualifications:

(a) teaching experience in a field of technical and vocational education;

(b) proficiency acquired through study and employment experience in one of the fields taught in the programme;

(c) a broad vision of technical and vocational education as a whole and of the interrelation of the various aspects;

(d) a knowledge of administrative techniques.

90. The heads of establishments in technical and vocational education should receive adequate administrative assistance so that they can devote most of their time to the highly important educational and scientific aspects of their work. Technical and vocational education establishments should have sufficient staff to provide the following services:

(a) advice and guidance for candidates and students;

(b) the preparation, supervision and co-ordination of all practical work and experiments;

(c) the maintenance of instruments, apparatus and tools in workshops and laboratories.

91. Administrators should keep up to date with new administrative techniques and trends through programmes of continuing education. Prospective administrators should receive special training in methods and problems involved in the task. This preparation should include:

(a) management methods appropriate to educational administration;

(b) methods of allocation of available resources given the objectives of the various programmes for which they will be responsible;

(c) planning methods.

92. Guidance staff should receive special preparation for their tasks whether they are specialists or are teachers serving also as guidance staff. This preparation should stress psychology, pedagogy, sociology and economics. Guidance staff should be equipped to make objective assessments of aptitude, interest and motivation and to have at hand up-to-date information concerning career and education opportunities. During this preparation they should acquire a direct knowledge of the economy and the world of work through systemically organized visits to enterprises and periods of time spent in enterprises. Guidance staff should be required and provided with facilities—including the opportunity for practical experience—to keep up with new methods of guidance and information as to new or changed educational training and employment opportunities.

X. International Co-operation

93. Member States should give priority to international co-operation in the field of technical and vocational education.

(a) This co-operation, whether in the framework of bilateral or multilateral agreements, or through international organizations, should be directed to improving the quality of technical and vocational education and developing and expanding it where necessary.

(b) Every effort should be made to co-ordinate within any given country the international assistance activities in the field of technical and vocational education.

94. Member States should take special measures to provide foreigners (in particular migrants and refugees) and their children living within their territory with technical and vocational education. Such measures should take into account the special needs of such persons in the host country as well as in view of their possible return to their country.

95. Provisions should be made at national, regional and international levels for the regular exchange of information, documentation, and materials of international interest obtained from research and development efforts on all levels concerning technical and vocational education, in particular:

(a) publications concerning, among others, comparative education, psychological and pedagogical problems affecting general and technical and vocational education, and current trends;

(b) information and documentation concerning curriculum development, methods and materials, study opportunities abroad, employment opportunities including

manpower requirements, working conditions and social benefits;

(c) teaching materials and equipment;

(d) mass media programmes of an informational or pedagogical character.

96. Regional co-operation among countries having a common cultural heritage and facing common problems in the development or extension of technical and vocational education should be highly encouraged through:

(a) periodic meetings on the ministerial level and the establishment of a standing committee or organization to review policies formulated and actions taken;

(b) the creation of joint facilities for higher level research, the development of prototype materials and equipment, and the preparation of staff for the training of teachers where the costs of such facilities are too high to be sustained by any one country in a given region.

97. The development of both written and audio-visual teaching and learning materials which are suitable for international or regional use should be considered a priority area in international co-operation. These materials should contribute to the progressive establishment of common standards for professional qualifications acquired through technical and vocational education.

98. Member States should encourage the creation of a climate of opinion favourable to international co-operation in the field of technical and vocational education through:

(a) teacher and student fellowships and exchanges;

(b) establishment of sustained contacts between similar institutions in different countries;

(c) provision of employment experience abroad, particularly when opportunities at home are limited.

99. To facilitate international co-operation, Member States should apply within technical and vocational education internationally recommended standards and norms relating in particular to:

(a) systems of measure;

(b) scientific and technical symbols;

(c) occupational qualifications;

(d) information processing;

(e) equivalencies of qualifications acquired through technical and vocational education implying standardization of curricula and testing, including aptitude tests, for some technical fields;

(f) safety and security through testing of materials and products.

100. Internationally recommended standards and norms concerning technical and vocational education should be continuously evaluated through sustained research concerning the effectiveness of their application in the various countries especially in order to facilitate the establishment of equivalence of qualifications and free movement of individuals between the different national systems of education.

The foregoing is the authentic text of the Recommendation duly adopted by the General Conference of the United Nations Educational, Scientific and Cultural Organization during its eighteenth session, which was held in Paris and declared closed the twenty-third day of November 1974.

In faith whereof we have appended our signatures this twenty-fifth day of November 1974.

SEE ALSO UNESCO *Convention on Technical and Vocational Education.*

UNESCO RECOMMENDATION CONCERNING THE PRESERVATION OF CULTURAL PROPERTY ENDANGERED BY PUBLIC OR PRIVATE WORKS (1968). The recommendation defines "cultural property" and calls upon all States members of the United Nations Educational, Scientific and Cultural Organization to ensure that such property is protected and preserved, especially against public or private works likely to damage or destroy it. It was adopted on 19 November 1968, in Paris, by the UNESCO GENERAL CONFERENCE (15th session). The text is as follows:

The General Conference of the United Nations Educational, Scientific and Cultural Organization, meeting in Paris from 15 October to 20 November 1968, at its fifteenth session,

Considering that contemporary civilization and its future evolution rest upon, among other elements, the cultural traditions of the peoples of the world, their creative force and their social and economic development,

Considering that cultural property is the product and witness of the different traditions and of the spiritual achievements of the past and thus is an essential element in the personality of the peoples of the world,

Considering that it is indispensable to preserve it as much as possible, according to its historical and artistic importance, so that the significance and message of cultural property become a part of the spirit of peoples who thereby may gain consciousness of their own dignity,

Considering that preserving cultural property and rendering it accessible constitute, in the spirit of the Declaration of the Principles of International Cultural Co-operation adopted on 4 November 1966 in the course of its fourteenth session, means of encouraging mutual understanding among peoples and thereby serve the cause of peace,

Considering also that the well-being of all peoples depends, *inter alia,* upon the existence of a favourable and stimulating environment and that the preservation of cultural property of all periods of history contributes directly to such an environment,

Recognizing, on the other hand, the role that industrialization, towards which world civilization is moving, plays in the development of peoples and their spiritual and national fulfilment,

Considering, however, that the prehistoric, protohistoric and historic monuments and remains, as well as numerous recent structures having artistic, historic or scientific importance are increasingly threatened by public and private works resulting from industrial development and urbanization,

Considering that it is the duty of governments to ensure the protection and the preservation of the cultural heritage of mankind, as much as to promote social and economic development,

Considering in consequence that it is urgent to harmonize the preservation of the cultural heritage with the changes which follow from social and economic development, making serious efforts to meet both requirements in a broad spirit of understanding, and with reference to appropriate planning,

Considering equally that adequate preservation and accessibility of cultural property constitute a major contribution to the social and economic development of countries and regions which possess such treasures of mankind by means of promoting national and international tourism,

Considering finally that the surest guarantee for the preservation of cultural property rests in the respect and the attachment felt for it by the people themselves, and persuaded that such feelings may be greatly strengthened by adequate measures carried out by Member States,

Having before it proposals concerning the preservation of cultural property endangered by public or private works, which constitute item 16 on the agenda of the session,

Having decided at its thirteenth session that proposals on this item should be the subject of an international instrument in the form of a recommendation to Member States,

Adopts on this nineteenth day of November 1968 this recommendation.

The General Conference recommends that Member States should apply the following provisions by taking whatever legislative or other steps may be required to give effect within their respective territories to the norms and principles set forth in this recommendation.

The General Conference recommends that Member States should bring this recommendation to the attention of the authorities or services responsible for public or private works as well as to the bodies responsible for the conservation and the protection of monuments and historic, artistic, archaeological and scientific sites. It recommends that authorities and bodies which plan programmes for education and the development of tourism be equally informed.

The General Conference recommends that Member States should report to it, on the dates and in a manner to be determined by it, on the action they have taken to give effect to this recommendation.

I. Definition

1. For the purpose of this recommendation, the term "cultural property" applies to:

(a) Immovables, such as archaeological and historic or scientific sites, structures or other features of historic, scientific, artistic or architectural value, whether religious or secular, including groups of traditional structures, historic quarters in urban or rural built-up areas and the ethnological structures of previous cultures still extant in valid form. It applies to such immovables constituting ruins existing above the earth as well as to archaeological or historic remains found within the earth. The term cultural property also includes the setting of such property;

(b) Movable property of cultural importance including that existing in or recovered from immovable property and that concealed in the earth, which may be found in archaeological or historical sites or elsewhere.

2. The term "cultural property" includes not only the established and scheduled architectural, archaeological and historic sites and structures, but also the unscheduled or unclassified vestiges of the past as well as artistically or historically important recent sites and structures.

II. General Principles

3. Measures to preserve cultural property should extend to the whole territory of the State and should not be confined to certain monuments and sites.

4. Protective inventories of important cultural property, whether scheduled or unscheduled, should be maintained.

Where such inventories do not exist, priority should be given in their establishment to the thorough survey of cultural property in areas where such property is endangered by public or private works.

5. Due account should be taken of the relative significance of the cultural property concerned when determining measures required for the:

(a) Preservation of an entire site, structure, or other forms of immovable cultural property from the effects of private or public works;

(b) Salvage or rescue of cultural property if the area in which it is found is to be transformed by public or private works, and the whole or a part of the property in question is to be preserved and removed.

6. Measures should vary according to the character, size and location of the cultural property and the nature of the dangers with which it is threatened.

7. Measures for the preservation or salvage of cultural property should be preventive and corrective.

8. Preventive and corrective measures should be aimed at protecting or saving cultural property from public or private works likely to damage and destroy it, such as:

(a) Urban expansion and renewal projects, although they may retain scheduled monuments while sometimes removing less important structures, with the result that historical relations and the setting of historic quarters are destroyed;

(b) Similar projects in areas where groups of traditional structures having cultural value as a whole risk being destroyed for the lack of a scheduled individual monument;

(c) Injudicious modifications and repair of individual historic buildings;

(d) The construction or alteration of highways which are a particular danger to sites or to historically important structures or groups of structures;

(e) The construction of dams for irrigation, hydroelectric power or flood control;

(f) The construction of pipelines and of power and transmission lines of electricity;

(g) Farming operations including deep ploughing, drainage and irrigation operations, the clearing and levelling of land and afforestation;

(h) Works required by the growth of industry and the technological progress of industrialized societies such as airfields, mining and quarrying operations and dredging and reclamation of channels and harbours.

9. Member States should give due priority to measures required for the preservation *in situ* of cultural property endangered by public or private works in order to preserve historical associations and continuity. When overriding economic or social conditions require that cultural property be transferred, abandoned or destroyed, the salvage or rescue operations should always include careful study of the cultural property involved and the preparations of detailed records.

10. The results of studies having scientific or historic value carried out in connexion with salvage operations, particularly when all or much of the immovable cultural property has been abandoned or destroyed, should be published or otherwise made available for future research.

11. Important structures and other monuments which have been transferred in order to save them from destruction by public or private works should be placed on a site or in a setting which resembles their former position and natural, historic or artistic associations.

12. Important movable cultural property, including representative samples of objects recovered from archaeological excavations, obtained from salvage operations should be preserved for study or placed on exhibition in institutions such as museums, including site museums, or universities.

III. Preservation and Salvage Measures

13. The preservation or salvage of cultural property endangered by public or private works should be ensured through the means mentioned below, the precise measures to be determined by the legislation and organizational system of the State:

(a) Legislation;

(b) Finance;

(c) Administrative measures;

(d) Procedures to preserve and to salvage cultural property;

(e) Penalties;

(f) Repairs;

(g) Awards;

(h) Advice;

(i) Educational programmes.

Legislation. 14. Member States should enact or maintain on the national as well as on the local level the legislative measures necessary to ensure the preservation or salvage of cultural property endangered by public or private works in accordance with the norms and principles embodied in this recommendation.

Finance. 15. Member States should ensure that adequate budgets are available for the preservation or salvage of cultural property endangered by public or private works. Although differences in legal systems and traditions as well as disparity in resources preclude the adoption of uniform measures, the following should be considered:

(a) The national or local authorities responsible for the safeguarding of cultural property should have adequate budgets to undertake the preservation or salvage of cultural property endangered by public or private works; or

(b) The costs of preserving or salvaging cultural property endangered by public or private works, including preliminary archaelogical research, should form part of the budget of construction costs; or

(c) The possibility of combining the two methods mentioned in subparagraphs a and b above should be provided for.

16. In the event of unusual costs due to the size and complexity of the operations required, there should be possibilities of obtaining additional funds through enabling legislation, special subventions, a national fund for monuments or other appropriate means. The services responsible for the safeguarding of cultural property should be empowered to administer or to utilize these extra-budgetary contributions required for the preservation or salvage of cultural property endangered by public or private works.

17. Member States should encourage proprietors of artistically or historically important structures, including structures forming part of a traditional group, or residents in a historic quarter in urban or rural built-up areas to preserve the character and aesthetic qualities of their cultural property, which would otherwise be endangered by public or private works, through:

(a) Favourable tax rates; or

(b) The establishment, through appropriate legislation, of a budget to assist, by grants, loans or other measures, local authorities, institutions and private owners of artistically, architecturally, scientifically or historically important structures including groups of traditional structures to maintain or to adapt them suitably for functions which would meet the needs of contemporary society; or

(c) The possibility of combining the two methods mentioned in subparagraphs a and b above should be provided for.

18. If the cultural property is not scheduled or otherwise protected it should be possible for the owner to request such assistance from the appropriate authorities.

19. National or local authorities, as well as private owners, when budgeting for the preservation of cultural property endangered by public or private works, should take into account the intrinsic value of cultural property and also the contribution it can make to the economy as a tourist attraction.

Administrative Measures 20. Responsibility for the preservation or salvage of cultural property endangered by public or private works should be entrusted to appropriate official bodies. Whenever official bodies or services already exist for the protection of cultural property, these bodies or services should be given responsibility for the preservation of cultural property against the dangers caused by public or private works. If such services do not exist, special bodies or services should be created for the purpose of the preservation of cultural property endangered by public or private works; and although differences of constitutional provisions and traditions preclude the adoption of a uniform system, certain common principles should be adopted.

(a) There should be a co-ordinating or consultative body, composed of representatives of the authorities responsible for the safeguarding of cultural property, for public and private works, for town planning, and of research and educational institutions, which should be competent to advise of the preservation of cultural property endangered by public or private works and, in particular, on conflicts of interest between requirements for public or private works and the preservation or salvage of cultural property.

(b) Provincial, municipal or other forms of local government should also have services responsible for the preservation or salvage of cultural property endangered by public or private works. These services should be able to call upon the assistance of national services or other appropriate bodies in accordance with their capabilities and requirements.

(c) The services responsible for the safeguarding of cultural property should be adequately staffed with the specialists required for the preservation or salvage of cultural property endangered by public or private works, such as architects, urbanists, archaeologists, historians, inspectors and other specialists and technicians.

(d) Administrative measures should be taken to co-ordinate the work of the different services responsible for the safeguarding of cultural property with that of other services responsible for public and private works and that of any other department or service whose responsibilities touch upon the problem of the preservation or salvage of cultural property endangered by public or private works.

(e) Administrative measures should be taken to establish an authority or commission in charge of urban development programmes in all communities having scheduled or unscheduled historic quarters, sites and monuments

which need to be preserved against public and private construction.

21. At the preliminary survey stage of any project involving construction in a locality recognized as being of cultural interest or likely to contain objects of archaelogical or historical importance, several variants of the project should be prepared, at regional or municipal level, before a decision is taken. The choice between these variants should be made on the basis of a comprehensive comparative analysis, in order that the most advantageous solution, both economically and from the point of view of preserving or salvaging cultural property, may be adopted.

Procedures to Preserve and to Salvage Cultural Property. 22. Thorough surveys should be carried out well in advance of any public or private works which might endanger cultural property to determine:

(a) The measures to be taken to preserve important cultural property *in situ;*

(b) The amount of salvage operations which would be required such as the selection of archaeological sites to be excavated, structures to be transferred and movable cultural property salvaged, etc.

23. Measures for the preservation or salvage of cultural property should be carried out well in advance of public or private works. In areas of archaeological or cultural importance, such as historic towns, villages, sites, and districts, which should be protected by the legislation of every country, the starting of new work should be made conditional upon the execution of preliminary archaeological excavations. If necessary, work should be delayed to ensure that adequate measures are taken for the preservation or salvage of the cultural property concerned.

24. Important archaeological sites, and, in particular, prehistoric sites as they are difficult to recognize, historic quarters in urban or rural areas, groups of traditional structures, ethnological structures of previous cultures and other immovable cultural property which would otherwise be endangered by public or private works should be protected by zoning or scheduling:

(a) Archaeological reserves should be zoned or scheduled and, if necessary, immovable property purchased, to permit thorough excavation or the preservation of the ruins found at the site.

(b) Historic quarters in urban or rural centres and groups of traditional structures should be zoned and appropriate regulations adopted to preserve their setting and character, such as the imposition of controls on the degree to which historically or artistically important structures can be renovated and the type and design of new structures which can be introduced. The preservation of monuments should be an absolute requirement of any well-designed plan for urban redevelopment especially in historic cities or districts. Similar regulations should cover the area surrounding a scheduled monument or site and its setting to preserve its association and character. Due allowance should be made for the modification of ordinary regulations applicable to new construction; these should be placed in abeyance when new structures are introduced into an historical zone. Ordinary types of commercial advertising by means of posters and illuminated announcements should be forbidden, but commercial establishments could be allowed to indicate their presence by means of judiciously presented signs.

25. Member States should make it obligatory for persons finding archaeological remains in the course of public or private works to declare them at the earliest possible mo-

ment to the competent service. Careful examination should be carried out by the service concerned and, if the site is important, construction should be deferred to permit thorough excavation, due allowance or compensation being made for the delays incurred.

26. Member States should have provisions for the acquisition, through purchase, by national or local governments and other appropriate bodies of important cultural property endangered by public or private works. When necessary, it should be possible to effect such acquisition through expropriation.

Penalties. 27. Member States should take steps to ensure that offenses, through intent or negligence, against the preservation or salvage of cultural property endangered by public or private works are severely punished by their Penal Code, which should provide for fines or imprisonment or both.

In addition, the following measures could be applied:

(a) Whenever possible, restoration of the site or structure at the expense of those responsible for the damage to it;

(b) In the case of a chance archaeological find, payment of damages to the State when immovable cultural property has been damaged, destroyed or neglected; confiscation without compensation when a movable object has been concealed.

Repairs. 28. Member States should, when the nature of the property so allows, adopt the necessary measures to ensure the repair, restoration or reconstruction of cultural property damaged by public or private works. They should also foresee the possibility of requiring local authorities and private owners of important cultural property to carry out repairs or restorations, with technical and financial assistance if necessary.

Awards. 29. Member States should encourage individuals, associations and municipalities to take part in programmes for the preservation or salvage of cultural property endangered by public or private works. Measures to that effect could include:

(a) *Ex gratia* payments to individuals reporting or surrendering hidden archaeological finds;

(b) Awards of certificates, medals or other forms of recognition to individuals, even if they belong to government service, associations, institutions or municipalities which have carried out outstanding projects for the preservation or salvage of cultural property endangered by public or private works.

Advice. 30. Member States should provide individuals, associations or municipalities lacking the required experience or staff with technical advice or supervision to maintain adequate standards for the preservation or salvage of cultural property endangered by public or private works.

Educational Programmes. 31. In a spirit of international collaboration, Member States should take steps to stimulate and develop among their nationals interest in, and respect for, the cultural heritage of the past of their own and other traditions in order to preserve or to salvage cultural property endangered by public or private works.

32. Specialized publications, articles in the press and radio and television broadcasts should publicize the dangers to cultural property arising from ill-conceived public or private works as well as cases where cultural property has been successfully preserved or salvaged.

33. Educational institutions, historical and cultural associations, public bodies concerned with the tourist industry and associations for popular education should have programmes to publicize the dangers to cultural property arising from short-sighted public or private works, and to underline the fact that projects to preserve cultural property contribute to international understanding.

34. Museums and educational institutions and other interested organizations should prepare special exhibitions on the dangers to cultural property arising from uncontrolled public or private works and on the measures which have been used to preserve or to salvage cultural property which has been endangered.

The foregoing is the authentic text of the recommendation duly adopted by the General Conference of the United Nations Educational, Scientific and Cultural Organization during its fifteenth session, which was held in Paris and declared closed the twentieth day of November 1968.

In faith whereof we have appended our signatures this twenty-second day of November 1968.

UNESCO RECOMMENDATION CONCERNING THE STATUS OF TEACHERS (1966).

The recommendation, adopted in Paris on 5 October 1966 by an intergovernmental conference by UNESCO, sets out a number of general principles, goals, and guidelines applicable to the status of teachers and to educational objectives and policies, and deals extensively with the professional and social conditions affecting teachers.

The intergovernmental conference, at which the INTERNATIONAL LABOR ORGANIZATION was represented by a tripartite delegation of its governing body, proposed the establishment of a joint ILO/UNESCO committee to examine reports submitted by States on the application of the recommendation. Such a committee has met at six-year intervals since 1970 and has submitted reports to the competent organs of the two specialized agencies.

The text of the recommendation (*UNESCO's Standard-Setting Instruments,* No. I.B.2) is as follows:

The Special Intergovernmental Conference on the Status of Teachers,

Recalling that the right to education is a fundamental human right,

Conscious of the responsibility of the States for the provision of proper education for all in fulfilment of Article 26 of the Universal Declaration of Human Rights, of Principles 5, 7 and 10 of the Declaration of the Rights of the Child and of the United Nations Declaration concerning the Promotion among Youth of the Ideals of Peace. Mutual Respect and Understanding between Peoples,

Aware of the need for more extensive and widespread general and technical and vocational education, with a view to making full use of all the talent and intelligence available as an essential contribution to continued moral and cultural progress and economic and social advancement,

Recognizing the essential role of teachers in educational advancement and the importance of their contribution to the development of man and modern society,

Concerned to ensure that teachers enjoy the status commensurate with this role,

Taking into account the great diversity of the laws, regulations and customs which, in different countries, determine the patterns and organization of education,

Taking also into account the diversity of the arrangements which in different countries apply to teaching staff, in particular according to whether the regulations concerning the public service apply to them,

Convinced that in spite of these differences similar questions arise in all countries with regard to the status of teachers and that these questions call for the application of a set of common standards and measures, which it is the purpose of this Recommendation to set out,

Noting the terms of existing international conventions which are applicable to teachers, and in particular of instruments concerned with basic human rights such as the Freedom of Association and Protection of the Right to Organize Convention, 1948, the Right to Organize and Collective Bargaining Convention, 1949, the Equal Remuneration Convention, 1951, and the Discrimination (Employment and Occupation) Convention, 1958, adopted by the General Conference of the International Labour Organisation, and the Convention against Discrimination in Education, 1960, adopted by the General Conference of the United Nations Educational, Scientific and Cultural Organization,

Noting also the recommendations on various aspects of the preparation and the status of teachers in primary and secondary schools adopted by the International Conference on Public Education convened jointly by the United Nations Educational, Scientific and Cultural Organization and the International Bureau of Education, and the Recommendation concerning Technical and Vocational Education, 1962, adopted by the General Conference of the United Nations Educational, Scientific and Cultural Organization,

Desiring to supplement existing standards by provisions relating to problems of peculiar concern to teachers and to remedy the problems of teacher shortage,

Has adopted this Recommendation:

I. Definitions

1. For the purpose of the Recommendation:

(a) the word "teacher" covers all those persons in schools who are responsible for the education of pupils;

(b) the expression "status" as used in relation to teachers means both the standing or regard accorded them, as evidenced by the level of appreciation of the importance of their function and of their competence in performing it, and the working conditions, remuneration and other material benefits accorded them relative to other professional groups.

II. Scope

2. This Recommendation applies to all teachers in both public and private schools up to the completion of the secondary stage of education, whether nursery, kindergarten, primary, intermediate or secondary, including those providing technical, vocational, or art education.

III. Guiding Principles

3. Education from the earliest school years should be directed to the all-round development of the human personality and to the spiritual, moral, social, cultural and economic progress of the community, as well as to the inculcation of deep respect for human rights and funda-

mental freedoms; within the framework of these values the utmost importance should be attached to the contribution to be made by education to peace and to understanding, tolerance and friendship among all nations and among racial or religious groups.

4. It should be recognized that advance in education depends largely on the qualifications and ability of the teaching staff in general and on the human, pedagogical and technical qualities of the individual teachers.

5. The status of teachers should be commensurate with the needs of education as assessed in the light of educational aims and objectives; it should be recognized that the proper status of teachers and due public regard for the profession of teaching are of major importance for the full realization of these aims and objectives.

6. Teaching should be regarded as a profession: it is a form of public service which requires of teachers expert knowledge and specialized skills, acquired and maintained through rigorous and continuing study; it calls also for a sense of personal and corporate responsibility for the education and welfare of the pupils in their charge.

7. All aspects of the preparation and employment of teachers should be free from any form of discrimination on grounds of race, colour, sex, religion, political opinion, national or social origin, or economic condition.

8. Working conditions for teachers should be such as will best promote effective learning and enable teachers to concentrate on their professional tasks.

9. Teachers' organizations should be recognized as a force which can contribute greatly to educational advance and which therefore should be associated with the determination of educational policy.

IV. Educational Objectives and Policies

10. Appropriate measures should be taken in each country to the extent necessary to formulate comprehensive educational policies consistent with the Guiding Principles, drawing on all available resources, human and otherwise. In so doing, the competent authorities should take account of the consequences for teachers of the following principles and objectives:

(a) it is the fundamental right of every child to be provided with the fullest possible educational opportunities; due attention should be paid to children requiring special educational treatment;

(b) all facilities should be made available equally to enable every person to enjoy his right to education without discrimination on grounds of sex, race, colour, religion, political opinion, national or social origin, or economic condition;

(c) since education is a service of fundamental importance in the general public interest, it should be recognized as a responsibility of the State, which should provide an adequate network of schools, free education in these schools and material assistance to needy pupils; this should not be construed so as to interfere with the liberty of the parents and, when applicable, legal guardians to choose for their children schools other than those established by the State, or so as to interfere with the liberty of individuals and bodies to establish and direct educational institutions which conform to such minimum educational standards as may be laid down or approved by the State;

(d) since education is an essential factor in economic growth, educational planning should form an integral part of total economic and social planning undertaken to improve living conditions;

(e) since education is a continuous process the various branches of the teaching service should be so co-ordinated as both to improve the quality of education for all pupils and to enhance the status of teachers;

(f) there should be free access to a flexible system of schools, properly interrelated, so that nothing restricts the opportunities for each child to progress to any level in any type of education;

(g) as an educational objective, no State should be satisfied with mere quantity, but should seek also to improve quality;

(h) in education both long-term and short-term planning and programming are necessary; the efficient integration in the community of today's pupils will depend more on future needs than on present requirements;

(i) all educational planning should include at each stage early provision for the training, and the further training, of sufficient numbers of fully competent and qualified teachers of the country concerned who are familiar with the life of their people and able to teach in the mother tongue;

(j) co-ordinated systematic and continuing research and action in the field of teacher preparation and in-service training are essential, including, at the international level, co-operative projects and the exchange of research findings;

(k) there should be close co-operation between the competent authorities, organizations of teachers, of employers and workers, and of parents as well as cultural organizations and institutions of learning and research, for the purposes of defining educational policy and its precise objectives;

(l) as the achievement of the aims and objectives of education largely depends on the financial means made available to it, high priority should be given, in all countries, to setting aside, within the national budgets, an adequate proportion of the national income for the development of education.

V. Preparation for the Profession

Selection. 11. Policy governing entry into preparation for teaching should rest on the need to provide society with an adequate supply of teachers who possess the necessary moral, intellectual and physical qualities and who have the required professional knowledge and skills.

12. To met this need, educational authorities should provide adequate inducements to prepare for teaching and sufficient places in appropriate institutions.

13. Completion of an approved course in an appropriate teacher-preparation institution should be required of all persons entering the profession.

14. Admission to teacher preparation should be based on the completion of appropriate secondary education, and the evidence of the possession of personal qualities likely to help the persons concerned to become worthy members of the profession.

15. While the general standards for admission to teacher preparation should be maintained, persons who may lack some of the formal academic requirements for admission, but who possess valuable experience, particularly in technical and vocational fields, may be admitted.

16. Adequate grants or financial assistance should be available to students preparing for teaching to enable them to follow the courses provided and to live decently; as far as possible, the competent authorities should seek to establish a system of free teacher-preparation institutions.

17. Information concerning the opportunities and the grants or financial assistance for teacher preparation should be readily available to students and other persons who may wish to prepare for teaching.

18. (1) Fair consideration should be given to the value of teacher-preparation programmes completed in other countries as establishing in whole or in part the right to practise teaching.

(2) Steps should be taken with a view to achieving international recognition of teaching credentials conferring professional status in terms of standards agreed to internationally.

Teacher-Preparation Programmes. 19. The purpose of a teacher-preparation programme should be to develop in each student his general education and personal culture, his ability to teach and educate others, an awareness of the principles which underlie good human relations, within and across national boundaries, and a sense of responsibility to contribute both by teaching and by example to social, cultural and economic progress.

20. Fundamentally a teacher-preparation programme should include:

(a) general studies;

(b) study of the main elements of philosophy, psychology, sociology as applied to education, the theory and history of education, and of comparative education, experimental pedagogy, school administration and methods of teaching the various subjects;

(c) studies related to the student's intended field of teaching;

(d) practice in teaching and in conducting extracurricular activities under the guidance of fully qualified teachers.

21. (1) All teachers should be prepared in general, special and pedagogical subjects in universities, or in institutions on a level comparable to universities, or else in special institutions for the preparation of teachers.

(2) The content of teacher-preparation programmes may reasonably vary according to the tasks the teachers are required to perform in different types of schools, such as establishments for handicapped children or technical and vocational schools. In the latter case, the programmes might include some practical experience to be acquired in industry, commerce or agriculture.

22. A teacher-preparation programme may provide for a professional course either concurrently with or subsequent to a course of personal academic or specialized education or skill cultivation.

23. Education for teaching should normally be full-time; special arrangements may be made for older entrants to the profession and persons in other exceptional categories to undertake all or part of their course on a part-time basis, on condition that the content of such courses and the standards of attainment are on the same level as those of the full-time courses.

24. Consideration should be given to the desirability of providing for the education of different types of teachers, whether primary, secondary, technical, specialist or vocational teachers, in institutions organically related or geographically adjacent to one another.

Teacher-Preparation Institutions. 25. The staff of teacher-preparation institutions should be qualified to teach in their own discipline at a level equivalent to that of higher education. The staff teaching pedagogical subjects should have had experience of teaching in schools and wherever possible should have this experience periodically refreshed by secondment to teaching duties in schools.

26. Research and experimentation in education and in the teaching of particular subjects should be promoted through the provision of research facilities in teacher-preparation institutions and research work by their staff and students. All staff concerned with teacher education should be aware of the findings of research in the field with which they are concerned and endeavour to pass on its results to students.

27. Students as well as staff should have the opportunity of expressing their views on the arrangements governing the life, work and discipline of a teacher-preparation institution.

28. Teacher-preparation institutions should form a focus of development in the education service, both keeping schools abreast of the results of research and methodological progress, and reflecting in their own work the experience of schools and teachers.

29. The teacher-preparation institutions should, either severally or jointly, and in collaboration with another institution of higher education or with the competent education authorities, or not, be responsible for certifying that the student has satisfactorily completed the course.

30. School authorities, in co-operation with teacher-preparation institutions, should take appropriate measures to provide the newly-trained teachers with an employment in keeping with their preparation, and individual wishes and circumstances.

VI. Further Education for Teachers

31. Authorities and teachers should recognize the importance of in-service education designed to secure a systematic improvement of the quality and content of education and of teaching techniques.

32. Authorities, in consultation with teachers' organizations, should promote the establishment of a wide system of in-service education, available free to all teachers. Such a system should provide a variety of arrangements and should involve the participation of teacher-preparation institutions, scientific and cultural institutions, and teachers' organizations. Refresher courses should be provided, especially for teachers returning to teaching after a break in service.

33. (1) Courses and other appropriate facilities should be so designed as to enable teachers to improve their qualifications, to alter or enlarge the scope of their work or seek promotion and to keep up to date with their subject and field of education as regards both content and method.

(2) Measures should be taken to make books and other material available to teachers to improve their general education and professional qualifications.

34. Teachers should be given both the opportunities and the incentives to participate in courses and facilities and should take full advantage of them.

35. School authorities should make every endeavour to ensure that schools can apply relevant research findings both in the subjects of study and in teaching methods.

36. Authorities should encourage and, as far as possible, assist teachers to travel in their own country and abroad, either in groups or individually, with a view to their further education.

37. It would be desirable that measures taken for the preparation and further education of teachers should be developed and supplemented by financial and technical co-operation on an international or regional basis.

VII. Employment and Career

Entry into the Teaching Profession. 38. In collaboration with teachers' organizations, policy governing recruitment into employment should be clearly defined at the appropriate level and rules should be established laying down the teachers' obligations and rights.

39. A probationary period on entry to teaching should be recognized both by teachers and by employers as the opportunity for the encouragement and helpful initiation of the entrant and for the establishment and maintenance of proper professional standards as well as the teacher's own development of his practical teaching proficiency. The normal duration of probation should be known in advance and the conditions for its satisfactory completion should be strictly related to professional competence. If the teacher is failing to complete his probation satisfactorily, he should be informed of the reasons and should have the right to make representations.

Advancement and Promotion. 40. Teachers should be able, subject to their having the necessary qualifications, to move from one type or level of school to another within the education service.

41. The organization and structure of an education service, including that of individual schools, should provide adequate opportunities for and recognition of additional responsibilities to be exercised by individual teachers, on condition that those responsibilities are not detrimental to the quality or regularity of their teaching work.

42. Consideration should be given to the advantages of schools sufficiently large for pupils to have the benefits and staff the opportunities to be derived from a range of responsibilities being carried by different teachers.

43. Posts of responsibility in education, such as that of inspector, educational administrator, director of education or other posts of special responsibility, should be given as far as possible to experienced teachers.

44. Promotion should be based on an objective assessment of the teacher's qualifications for the new post, by reference to strictly professional criteria laid down in consultation with teachers' organizations.

Security of Tenure. 45. Stability of employment and security of tenure in the profession are essential in the interests of education as well as in that of the teacher and should be safeguarded even when changes in the organization of or within a school system are made.

46. Teachers should be adequately protected against arbitrary action affecting their professional standing or career.

Disciplinary Procedures related to Breaches of Professional Conduct. 47. Disciplinary measures applicable to teachers guilty of breaches of professional conduct should be clearly defined. The proceedings and any resulting action should only be made public if the teacher so requests, except where prohibition from teaching is involved or the protection or well-being of the pupils so requires.

48. The authorities or bodies competent to propose or apply sanctions and penalties should be clearly designated.

49. Teachers' organizations should be consulted when the machinery to deal with disciplinary matters is established.

50. Every teacher should enjoy equitable safeguards at each stage of any disciplinary procedure, and in particular:

(a) the right to be informed in writing of the allegations and the grounds for them;

(b) the right to full access to the evidence in the case;

(c) the right to defend himself and to be defended by a representative of his choice, adequate time being given to the teacher for the preparation of his defence;

(d) the right to be informed in writing of the decisions reached and the reasons for them;

(e) the right to appeal to clearly designated competent authorities or bodies.

51. Authorities should recognize that effectiveness of disciplinary safeguards as well as discipline itself would be greatly enhanced if the teachers were judged with the participation of their peers.

52. The provisions of the foregoing paragraphs 47–51 do not in any way affect the procedures normally applicable under national laws or regulations to acts punishable under criminal laws.

Medical Examinations. 53. Teachers should be required to undergo periodical medical examinations, which should be provided free.

Women Teachers with Family Responsibilities. 54. Marriage should not be considered a bar to the appointment or to the continued employment of women teachers, nor should it affect remuneration or other conditions of work.

55. Employers should be prohibited from terminating contracts of service for reasons of pregnancy and maternity leave.

56. Arrangements such as crèches or nurseries should be considered where desirable to take care of the children of teachers with family responsibilities.

57. Measures should be taken to permit women teachers with family responsibilities to obtain teaching posts in the locality of their homes and to enable married couples, both of whom are teachers, to teach in the same general neighbourhood or in one and the same school.

58. In appropriate circumstances women teachers with family responsibilities who have left the profession before retirement age should be encouraged to return to teaching.

Part-time Service. 59. Authorities and schools should recognize the value of part-time service given, in case of need, by qualified teachers who for some reason cannot give full-time service.

60. Teachers employed regularly on a part-time basis should:

(a) receive proportionately the same remuneration and enjoy the same basic conditions of employment as teachers employed on a full-time basis;

(b) be granted rights corresponding to those of teachers employed on a full-time basis as regards holidays with pay, sick leave and maternity leave, subject to the same eligibility requirements; and

(c) be entitled to adequate and appropriate social security protection, including coverage under employers' pension schemes.

VIII. The Rights and Responsibilities of Teachers

Professional Freedom. 61. The teaching profession should enjoy academic freedom in the discharge of professional duties. Since teachers are particularly qualified to judge the teaching aids and methods most suitable for their pupils, they should be given the essential role in the choice and the adaptation of teaching material, the selection of textbooks and the application of teaching methods, within the framework of approved programmes, and with the assistance of the educational authorities.

62. Teachers and their organizations should participate in the development of new courses, textbooks and teaching aids.

63. Any systems of inspection or supervision should be designed to encourage and help teachers in the performance of their professional tasks and should be such as not to diminish the freedom, initiative and responsibility of teachers.

64. (1) Where any kind of direct assessment of the teacher's work is required, such assessment should be objective and should be made known to the teacher.

(2) Teachers should have a right to appeal against assessments which they deem to be unjustified.

65. Teachers should be free to make use of such evaluation techniques as they may deem useful for the appraisal of pupils' progress, but should ensure that no unfairness to individual pupils results.

66. The authorities should give due weight to the recommendations of teachers regarding the suitability of individual pupils for courses and further education of different kinds.

67. Every possible effort should be made to promote close co-operation between teachers and parents in the interests of pupils, but teachers should be protected against unfair or unwarranted interference by parents in matters which are essentially the teacher's professional responsibility.

68. (1) Parents having a complaint against a school or a teacher should be given the opportunity of discussing it in the first instance with the school principal and the teacher concerned. Any complaint subsequently addressed to higher authority should be put in writing and a copy should be supplied to the teacher.

(2) Investigations of complaints should be so conducted that the teachers are given a fair opportunity to defend themselves and that no publicity is given to the proceedings.

69. While teachers should exercise the utmost care to avoid accidents to pupils, employers of teachers should safeguard them against the risk of having damages assessed against them in the event of injury to pupils occurring at school or in school activities away from the school premises or grounds.

Responsibilities of Teachers. 70. Recognizing that the status of their profession depends to a considerable extent upon teachers themselves, all teachers should seek to achieve the highest possible standards in all their professional work.

71. Professional standards relating to teacher performance should be defined and maintained with the participation of the teachers' organizations.

72. Teachers and teachers' organizations should seek to co-operate fully with authorities in the interests of the pupils, of the education service and of society generally.

73. Codes of ethics or of conduct should be established by the teachers' organizations, since such codes greatly contribute to ensuring the prestige of the profession and the exercise of professional duties in accordance with agreed principles.

74. Teachers should be prepared to take their part in extra-curricular activities for the benefit of pupils and adults.

Relations between Teachers and the Education Service as a

Whole. 75. In order that teachers may discharge their responsibilities, authorities should establish and regularly use recognized means of consultation with teachers' organizations on such matters as educational policy, school organization, and new developments in the education service.

76. Authorities and teachers should recognize the importance of the participation of teachers, through their organizations and in other ways, in steps designed to improve the quality of the education service, in educational research, and in the development and dissemination of new improved methods.

77. Authorities should facilitate the establishment and the work of panels designed, within a school or within a broader framework, to promote the co-operation of teachers of the same subject and should take due account of the opinions and suggestions of such panels.

78. Administrative and other staff who are responsible for aspects of the education service should seek to establish good relations with teachers and this approach should be equally reciprocated.

Rights of Teachers. 79. The participation of teachers in social and public life should be encouraged in the interests of the teacher's personal development, of the education service and of society as a whole.

80. Teachers should be free to exercise all civic rights generally enjoyed by citizens and should be eligible for public office.

81. Where the requirements of public office are such that the teacher has to relinquish his teaching duties, he should be retained in the profession for seniority and pension purposes and should be able to return to his previous post or to an equivalent post after his term of public office has expired.

82. Both salaries and working conditions for teachers should be determined through the process of negotiation between teachers' organizations and the employers of teachers.

83. Statutory or voluntary machinery should be established whereby the right of teachers to negotiate through their organizations with their employers, either public or private, is assured.

84. Appropriate joint machinery should be set up to deal with the settlement of disputes between the teachers and their employers arising out of terms and conditions of employment. If the means and procedures established for these purposes should be exhausted or if there should be a breakdown in negotiations between the parties, teachers' organizations should have the right to take such other steps as are normally open to other organizations in the defence of their legitimate interests.

IX. Conditions for Effective Teaching and Learning

85. Since the teacher is a valuable specialist, his work should be so organized and assisted as to avoid waste of his time and energy.

Class Size. 86. Class size should be such as to permit the teacher to give the pupils individual attention. From time to time provision may be made for small group or even individual instruction for such purposes as remedial work, and on occasion, for large group instruction employing audiovisual aids.

Ancillary Staff. 87. With a view to enabling teachers to concentrate on their professional tasks, schools should be provided with ancillary staff to perform non-teaching duties.

Teaching Aids. 88. (1) Authorities should provide teachers and pupils with modern aids to teaching. Such aids should not be regarded as a substitute for the teacher but as a means of improving the quality of teaching and extending to a larger number of pupils the benefits of education.

(2) Authorities should promote research into the use of such aids and encourage teachers to participate actively in such research.

Hours of Work. 89. The hours teachers are required to work per day and per week should be established in consultation with teachers' organizations.

90. In fixing hours of teaching account should be taken of all factors which are relevant to the teacher's work load, such as:

(a) the number of pupils with whom the teacher is required to work per day and per week;

(b) the necessity to provide time for adequate planning and preparation of lessons and for evaluation of work;

(c) the number of different lessons assigned to be taught each day;

(d) the demands upon the time of the teacher imposed by participation in research, in co-curricular and extra-curricular activities, in supervisory duties and in counselling of pupils;

(e) the desirability of providing time in which teachers may report to and consult with parents regarding pupil progress.

91. Teachers should be provided time necessary for taking part in in-service training programmes.

92. Participation of teachers in extra-curricular activities should not constitute an excessive burden and should not interfere with the fulfilment of the main duties of the teacher.

93. Teachers assigned special educational responsibilities in addition to classroom instruction should have their normal hours of teaching reduced correspondingly.

Annual Holidays with Pay. 94. All teachers should enjoy a right to adequate annual vacation with full pay.

Study Leave. 95. (1) Teachers should be granted study leave on full or partial pay at intervals.

(2) The period of study leave should be counted for seniority and pension purposes.

(3) Teachers in areas which are remote from population centres and are recognized as such by the public authorities should be given study leave more frequently.

Special Leave. 96. Leave of absence granted within the framework of bilateral and multilateral cultural exchanges should be considered as service.

97. Teachers attached to technical assistance projects should be granted leave of absence and their seniority, eligibility for promotion and pension rights in the home country should be safeguarded. In addition special arrangements should be made to cover their extraordinary expenses.

98. Foreign guest teachers should similarly be given leave of absence by their home countries and have their seniority and pension rights safeguarded.

99. (1) Teachers should be granted occasional leave of absence with full pay to enable them to participate in the activities of their organizations.

(2) Teachers should have the right to take up office in their organizations; in such case their entitlements should be similar to those of teachers holding public office.

100. Teachers should be granted leave of absence with full pay for adequate personal reasons under arrangements specified in advance of employment.

Sick Leave and Maternity Leave. 101. (1) Teachers should be entitled to sick leave with pay.

(2) In determining the period during which full or partial pay shall be payable, account should be taken of cases in which it is necessary for teachers to be isolated from pupils for long periods.

102. Effect should be given to the standards laid down by the International Labour Organisation in the field of maternity protection, and in particular the Maternity Protection Convention, 1919, and the Maternity Protection Convention (Revised), 1952, as well as to the standards referred to in paragraph 126 of this Recommendation.

103. Women teachers with children should be encouraged to remain in the service by such measures as enabling them, at their request, to take additional unpaid leave of up to one year after childbirth without loss of employment, all rights resulting from employment being fully safeguarded.

Teacher Exchange. 104. Authorities should recognize the value both to the education service and the teachers themselves of professional and cultural exchanges between countries and of travel abroad on the part of teachers; they should seek to extend such opportunities and take account of the experience acquired abroad by individual teachers.

105. Recruitment for such exchanges should be arranged without any discrimination, and the persons concerned should not be considered as representing any particular political view.

106. Teachers who travel in order to study and work abroad should be given adequate facilities to do so and proper safeguards of their posts and status.

107. Teachers should be encouraged to share teaching experience gained abroad with other members of the profession.

School Buildings. 108. School buildings should be safe and attractive in overall design and functional in layout; they should lend themselves to effective teaching, and to use for extra-curricular activities and, especially in rural areas, as a community centre; they should be constructed in accordance with established sanitary standards and with a view to durability, adaptability and easy, economic maintenance.

109. Authorities should ensure that school premises are properly maintained, so as not to threaten in any way the health and safety of pupils and teachers.

110. In the planning of new schools representative teacher opinion should be consulted. In providing new or additional accommodation for an existing school the staff of the school concerned should be consulted.

Special Provisions for Teachers in Rural or Remote Areas. 111. (1) Decent housing, preferably free or at a subsidized rental, should be provided for teachers and their families in areas remote from population centres and recognized as such by the public authorities.

(2) In countries where teachers, in addition to their normal teaching duties, are expected to promote and stimulate community activities, development plans and programmes should include provision for appropriate accommodation for teachers.

112. (1) On appointment or transfer to schools in remote areas, teachers should be paid removal and travel expenses for themselves and their families.

(2) Teachers in such areas should, where necessary, be given special travel facilities to enable them to maintain their professional standards.

(3) Teachers transferred to remote areas should, as an inducement, be reimbursed their travel expenses from their place of work to their home town once a year when they go on leave.

113. Whenever teachers are exposed to particular hardships, they should be compensated by the payment of special hardship allowances which should be included in earnings taken into account for pension purposes.

X. Teachers' Salaries

114. Amongst the various factors which affect the status of teachers, particular importance should be attached to salary, seeing that in present world conditions other factors, such as the standing or regard accorded them and the level of appreciation of the importance of their function, are largely dependent, as in other comparable professions, on the economic position in which they are placed.

115. Teachers' salaries should:

(a) reflect the importance to society of the teaching function and hence the importance of teachers as well as the responsibilities of all kinds which fall upon them from the time of their entry into the service;

(b) compare favourably with salaries paid in other occupations requiring similar or equivalent qualifications;

(c) provide teachers with the means to ensure a reasonable standard of living for themselves and their families as well as to invest in further education or in the pursuit of cultural activities, thus enhancing their professional qualification;

(d) take account of the fact that certain posts require higher qualifications and experience and carry greater responsibilities.

116. Teachers should be paid on the basis of salary scales established in agreement with the teachers' organizations. In no circumstances should qualified teachers during a probationary period or if employed on a temporary basis be paid on a lower salary scale than that laid down for established teachers.

117. The salary structure should be planned so as not to give rise to injustices or anomalies tending to lead to friction between different groups of teachers.

118. Where a maximum number of class contact hours is laid down, a teacher whose regular schedule exceeds the normal maximum should receive additional remuneration on an approved scale.

119. Salary differentials should be based on objective criteria such as levels of qualification, years of experience or degrees of responsibility but the relationship between the lowest and the highest salary should be of a reasonable order.

120. In establishing the placement on a basic salary scale of a teacher of vocational or technical subjects who may have no academic degree, allowance should be made for the value of his practical training and experience.

121. Teachers' salaries should be calculated on an annual basis.

122. (1) Advancements within the grade through salary increments granted at regular, preferably annual, intervals should be provided.

(2) The progression from the minimum to the maximum of the basic salary scale should not extend over a period longer than 10 to 15 years.

(3) Teachers should be granted salary increments for service performed during periods of probationary or temporary appointment.

123. (1) Salary scales for teachers should be reviewed periodically to take into account such factors as a rise in the cost of living, increased productivity leading to higher standards of living in the country or a general upward movement in wage or salary levels.

(2) Where a system of salary adjustments automatically following a cost-of-living index has been adopted, the choice of index should be determined with the participation of the teachers' organizations and any cost-of-living allowance granted should be regarded as an integral part of earnings taken into account for pension purposes.

124. No merit rating system for purposes of salary determination should be introduced or applied without prior consultation with and acceptance by the teachers' organizations concerned.

XI. Social Security

General Provisions. 125. All teachers, regardless of the type of school in which they serve, should enjoy the same or similar social security protection. Protection should be extended to periods of probation and of training for those who are regularly employed as teachers.

126. (1) Teachers should be protected by social security measures in respect of all the contingencies included in the International Labour Organisation Social Security (Minimum Standards) Convention, 1952, namely by medical care, sickness benefit, unemployment benefit, old-age benefit, employment injury benefit, family benefit, maternity benefit, invalidity benefit and survivors' benefit.

(2) The standards of social security provided for teachers should be at least as favourable as those set out in the relevant instruments of the International Labour Organisation and in particular the Social Security (Minimum Standards) Convention, 1952.

(3) Social security benefits for teachers should be granted as a matter of right.

127. The social security protection of teachers should take account of their particular conditions of employment, as indicated in paragraphs 128–140.

Medical Care. 128. In regions where there is a scarcity of medical facilities teachers should be paid travelling expenses necessary to obtain appropriate medical care.

Sickness Benefit. 129. (1) Sickness benefit should be granted throughout any period of incapacity for work involving suspension of earnings.

(2) It should be paid from the first day in each case of suspension of earnings.

(3) Where the duration of sickness benefit is limited to a specified period, provisions should be made for extensions in cases in which it is necessary for teachers to be isolated from pupils.

Employment Injury Benefit. 130. Teachers should be protected against the consequences of injuries suffered not only during teaching at school but also when engaged in school activities away from the school premises or grounds.

131. Certain infectious diseases prevalent among children should be regarded as occupational diseases when contracted by teachers who have been exposed to them by virtue of their contact with pupils.

Old-age Benefit. 132. Pension credits earned by a teacher under any education authority within a country should be portable should the teacher transfer to employment under any other authority within that country.

133. Taking account of national regulations, teachers who, in case of a duly recognized teacher shortage, continue in service after qualifying for a pension should either receive credit in the calculation of the pension for the additional years of service or be able to gain a supplementary pension through an appropriate agency.

134. Old-age benefit should be so related to final earnings that the teacher may continue to maintain an adequate living standard.

Invalidity Benefit. 135. Invalidity benefit should be payable to teachers who are forced to discontinue teaching because of physical or mental disability. Provision should be made for the granting of pensions where the contingency is not covered by extended sickness benefit or other means.

136. Where disability is only partial in that the teacher is able to teach part time, partial invalidity benefit should be payable.

137. (1) Invalidity benefit should be so related to final earnings that the teacher may continue to maintain an adequate living standard.

(2) Provision should be made for medical care and allied benefits with a view to restoring or, where this is not possible, improving the health of disabled teachers, as well as for rehabilitation services designed to prepare disabled teachers, wherever possible, for the resumption of their previous activity.

Survivors' Benefit. 138. The conditions of eligibility for survivors' benefit and the amount of such benefit should be such as to enable survivors to maintain an adequate standard of living and as to secure the welfare and education of surviving dependent children.

Means of Providing Social Security for Teachers. 139. (1) The social security protection of teachers should be assured as far as possible through a general scheme applicable to employed persons in the public sector or in the private sector as appropriate.

(2) Where no general scheme is in existence for one or more of the contingencies to be covered, special schemes, statutory or non-statutory, should be established.

(3) Where the level of benefits under a general scheme is below that provided for in this Recommendation, it should be brought up to the recommended standard by means of supplementary schemes.

140. Consideration should be given to the possibility of associating representatives of teachers' organizations with the administration of special and supplementary schemes, including the investment of their funds.

XII. The Teacher Shortage

141. (1) It should be a guiding principle that any severe supply problem should be dealt with by measures which are recognized as exceptional, which do not detract from or endanger in any way professional standards already established or to be established and which minimize educational loss to pupils.

(2) Recognizing that certain expedients designed to deal with the shortage of teachers, such as over-large classes and the unreasonable extension of hours of teaching duty are incompatible with the aims and objectives of education and are detrimental to the pupils, the competent authorities as a matter of urgency should take steps to render these expedients unnecessary and to discontinue them.

142. In developing countries, where supply considerations may necessitate short-term intensive emergency preparation programmes for teachers, a fully professional, extensive programme should be available in order to pro-

duce corps of professionally prepared teachers competent to guide and direct the educational enterprise.

143. (1) Students admitted to training in short-term, emergency programmes should be selected in terms of the standards applying to admission to the normal professional programme, or even higher ones, to ensure that they will be capable of subsequently completing the requirements of the full programme.

(2) Arrangements and special facilities, including extra study leave on full pay, should enable such students to complete their qualifications in service.

144. (1) As far as possible, unqualified personnel should be required to work under the close supervision and direction of professionally qualified teachers.

(2) As a condition of continued employment such persons should be required to obtain or complete their qualifications.

145. Authorities should recognize that improvements in the social and economic status of teachers, their living and working conditions, their terms of employment and their career prospects are the best means of overcoming any existing shortage of competent and experienced teachers, and of attracting to and retaining in the teaching profession substantial numbers of fully qualified persons.

XIII. Final Provision

146. Where teachers enjoy a status which is, in certain respects, more favourable than that provided for in this Recommendation, its terms should not be invoked to diminish the status already granted.

The foregoing is the authentic text of the Recommendation duly adopted by the Special Intergovernmental Conference on the Status of Teachers, which was held in Paris and declared closed the fifth day of October 1966.

In faith whereof we have appended our signatures this fifth day of October 1966.

UNESCO RECOMMENDATION CONCERNING THE STATUS OF THE ARTIST (1980). The recommendation was adopted by the UNESCO General Conference (21st session), held in Belgrade, on 27 October 1980. It calls upon UNESCO's member States to adopt the measures necessary for the preservation, development, and dissemination of culture with a view to ensuring the full exercise of the rights set out in articles 22, 23, 24, 25, 27, and 28 of the UNIVERSAL DECLARATION OF HUMAN RIGHTS and articles 6 and 15 of the INTERNATIONAL COVENANT ON ECONOMIC, SOCIAL AND CULTURAL RIGHTS.

The text of the Recommendation is as follows:

The General Conference of the United Nations Educational, Scientific and Cultural Organization, meeting in Belgrade from 23 September to 28 October 1980 at its twenty-first session,

Recalling that, under the terms of Article 1 of its Constitution, the purpose of the Organization is to contribute to peace and security by promoting collaboration among the nations through education, science, and culture in order to further universal respect for justice, for the rule of law and for the human rights and fundamental freedoms which are affirmed for the peoples of the world, without distinction of race, sex, language or religion, by the Charter of the United Nations,

Recalling the terms of the Universal Declaration of Human Rights, and particularly Articles 22, 23, 24, 25, 27 and 28 thereof, quoted in the annex to this Recommendation,

Recalling the terms of the United Nations International Covenant on Economic, Social and Cultural Rights, particularly its Articles 6 and 15, quoted in the annex to this Recommendation, and the need to adopt the necessary measures for the preservation, development and dissemination of culture, with a view to ensuring the full exercise of these rights,

Recalling the Declaration of the Principles of International Cultural Co-operation, adopted by the General Conference of Unesco at its fourteenth session, particularly its Articles III and IV, which are quoted in the annex to this Recommendation, as well as the Recommendation on Participation by the People at Large in Cultural Life and their Contribution to it, adopted by the General Conference of Unesco at its nineteenth session,

Recognizing that the arts in their fullest and broadest definitions are and should be an integral part of life and that it is necessary and appropriate for governments to help create and sustain not only a climate encouraging freedom of artistic expression but also the material conditions facilitating the release of this creative talent,

Recognizing that every artist is entitled to benefit effectively from the social security and insurance provisions contained in the basic texts, Declarations, Covenant and Recommendation mentioned above,

Considering that the artist plays an important role in the life and evolution of society and that he should be given the opportunity to contribute to society's development and, as any other citizen, to exercise his responsibilities therein, while preserving his creative inspiration and freedom of expression,

Further recognizing that the cultural, technological, economic, social and political development of society influences the status of the artist and that it is consequently necessary to review his status, taking account of social progress in the world,

Affirming the right of the artist to be considered, if he so wishes, as a person actively engaged in cultural work and consequently to benefit, taking account of the particular conditions of his artistic profession, from all the legal, social and economic advantages pertaining to the status of workers,

Affirming further the need to improve the social security, labour and tax conditions of the artist, whether employed or self-employed, taking into account the contribution to cultural development which the artist makes,

Recalling the importance, universally acknowledged both nationally and internationally, of the preservation and promotion of cultural identity and of the role in this field of artists who perpetuate the practice of traditional arts and also interpret a nation's folklore,

Recognizing that the vigour and vitality of the arts depend, *inter alia*, on the well-being of artists both individually and collectively,

Recalling the conventions and recommendations of the International Labour Organisation (ILO) which have recognized the rights of workers in general and, hence, the rights of artists and, in particular, the conventions and recommendations listed in the appendix to this Recommendation,

Taking note, however, that some of the International Labour Organisation standards allow for derogations or even expressly exclude artists, or certain categories of them, owing to the special conditions in which artistic activity takes place, and that it is consequently necessary to extend their field of application and to supplement them by other standards,

Considering further that this recognition of their status as persons engaged in cultural work should in no way compromise their freedom of creativity, expression and communication but should, on the contrary, confirm their dignity and integrity,

Convinced that action by the public authorities is becoming necessary and urgent in order to remedy the disquieting situation of artists in a large number of Member States, particularly with regard to human rights, economic and social circumstances and their conditions of employment, with a view to providing artists with the conditions necessary for the development and flowering of their talents and appropriate to the role that they are able to play in the planning and implementation of cultural policies and cultural development activities of communities and countries and in the improvement of the quality of life,

Considering that art plays an important part in education and that artists, by their works, may influence the conception of the world held by all people, and particularly by youth,

Considering that artists must be able collectively to consider and, if necessary, defend their common interests, and therefore must have the right to be recognized as a professional category and to constitute trade union or professional organizations,

Considering that the development of the arts, the esteem in which they are held and the promotion of arts education depend in large measure on the creativity of artists.

Aware of the complex nature of artistic activity and of the diverse forms it takes and, in particular, of the importance, for the living conditions and the development of the talents of artists, of the protection of their moral and material rights in their works, or performances, or the use made of them, and of the need to extend and reinforce such protection,

Considering the need to endeavour to take account as far as possible of the opinion both of artists and of the people at large in the formulation and implementation of cultural policies and for that purpose to provide them with the means for effective action,

Considering that contemporary artistic expression is presented in public places and that these should be laid out so as to take account of the opinions of the artists concerned,

Considering therefore that there should be close co-operation between architects, contractors and artists in order to lay down aesthetic guidelines for public places which will respond to the requirements of communication and make an effective contribution to the establishment of new and meaningful relationships between the public and its environment,

Taking into account the diversity of circumstances of artists in different countries and within the communities in which they are expected to develop their talents, and the varying significance attributed to their works by the societies in which they are produced,

Convinced, nevertheless, that despite such differences, questions of similar concern arise in all countries with regard to the status of the artist, and that a common will and inspiration are called for if a solution is to be found and if the status of the artist is to be improved, which is the intention of this Recommendation,

Taking note of the provisions of the international conventions in force relating, more particularly, to literary and artistic property, and in particular of the Universal Convention and the Berne Convention for the Protection of Literary and Artistic Works, and of those relating to the protection of the rights of performers, of the resolutions of the General Conference, of the recommendations made by Unesco's intergovernmental conferences on cultural policies, and of the conventions and recommendations adopted by the International Labour Organisation, listed in the appendix to this Recommendation,

Having before it, as item 31 of the agenda of the session, proposals concerning the status of the artist,

Having decided, at its twentieth session, that this question should be the subject of a recommendation to Member States,

Adopts this Recommendation this twenty-seventh day of October 1980:

The General Conference recommends that Member States implement the following provisions, taking whatever legislative or other steps may be required—in conformity with the constitutional practice of each State and the nature of the questions under consideration—to apply the principles and norms set forth in this Recommendation within their respective territories.

For those States which have a federal or non-unitary constitutional system, the General Conference recommends that, with regard to the provisions of this Recommendation the implementation of which comes under the legal jurisdiction of individual constituent States, countries, provinces, cantons or any other territorial and political subdivisions that are not obliged by the constitutional system of the federation to take legislative measures, the federal government be invited to inform the competent authorities of such States, countries, provinces or cantons of the said provisions, with its recommendation for their adoption.

The General Conference recommends that Member States bring this Recommendation to the attention of authorities, institutions and organizations in a position to contribute to improvement of the status of the artist and to foster the participation of artists in cultural life and development.

The General Conference recommends that Member States report to it, on dates and in a manner to be determined by it, on the action they have taken to give effect to this Recommendation.

1. Definitions. For the purposes of this Recommendation:

1. "Artist" is taken to mean any person who creates or gives creative expression to, or re-creates works of art, who considers his artistic creation to be an essential part of his life, who contributes in this way to the development of art and culture and who is or asks to be recognized as an artist, whether or not he is bound by any relations of employment or association.

2. The word "status" signifies, on the one hand, the regard accorded to artists, defined as above, in a society, on the basis of the importance attributed to the part they are called upon to play therein and, on the other hand, recognition of the liberties and rights, including moral, economic and social rights, with particular reference to income and social security, which artists should enjoy.

2. Scope of Application. This Recommendation applies to all artists as defined in paragraph I.1, irrespective of the discipline or form of art practised by such artists. These include *inter alia* all creative artists and authors within the meaning of the Universal Copyright Convention and the Berne Convention for the Protection of Literary and Artistic Works, as well as performers and interpreters within the meaning of the Rome Convention for the Protection of Performers, Producers of Phonograms and Broadcasting Organizations.

3. Guiding Principles. 1. Member States, recognizing that art reflects, preserves and enriches the cultural identity and spiritual heritage of the various societies, constitutes a universal form of expression and communication and, as a common denominator in ethnic, cultural or religious differences, brings home to everyone the sense of belonging to the human community, should accordingly, and for these purposes, ensure that the population as a whole has access to art.

2. Member States should encourage all activities designed to highlight the action of artists for cultural development, including in particular activities carried out by the mass media and the educational system, and for the employment of leisure and cultural purposes.

3. Member States, recognizing the essential role of art in the life and development of the individual and of society, accordingly have a duty to protect, defend and assist artists and their freedom of creation. For this purpose, they should take all necessary steps to stimulate artistic creativity and the flowering of talent, in particular by adopting measures to secure greater freedom for artists, without which they cannot fulfil their mission, and to improve their status by acknowledging their right to enjoy the fruits of their work. Member States should endeavour by all appropriate means to secure increased participation by artists in decisions concerning the quality of life. By all means at their disposal, Member States should demonstrate and confirm that artistic activities have a part to play in the nations' global development effort to build a juster and more humane society and to live together in circumstances of peace and spiritual enrichment.

4. Member States should ensure, through appropriate legislative means when necessary, that artists have the freedom and the right to establish trade unions and professional organizations of their choosing and to become members of such organizations, if they so wish, and should make it possible for organizations representing artists to participate in the formulation of cultural policies and employment policies, including the professional training of artists, and in the determination of artists' conditions of work.

5. At all appropriate levels of national planning, in general, and of planning in the cultural field, in particular, Member States should make arrangements, by close coordination of their policies relating to culture, education and employment among other things, to define a policy for providing assistance and material and moral support for artists and should ensure that public opinion is informed of the justification and the need for such a policy. To that end, education should place due emphasis on the encouragement of artistic awareness, so as to create a public capable of appreciating the work of the artist. Without prejudice to the rights that should be accorded to them under copyright legislation, including resale rights (*droit de suite*) when this is not part of copyright, and under neighbouring rights legislation, artists should enjoy equitable conditions and their profession should be given the public consideration that it merits. Their conditions of work and of employment should be such as to provide opportunities for artists who so wish to devote themselves fully to their artistic activities.

6. Since freedom of expression and communication is the essential prerequisite for all artistic activities, Member States should see that artists are unequivocally accorded the protection provided for in this respect by international and national legislation concerning human rights.

7. In view of the role of artistic activity and creation in the cultural and overall development of nations, Member States should create conditions enabling artists fully to participate, either individually or through their associations or trade unions, in the life of the communities in which they practise their art. They should associate them in the formulation of local and national cultural policies, thus stressing their important contribution in their own society as well as towards world progress in general.

8. Member States should ensure that all individuals, irrespective of race, colour, sex, language, religion, political or other opinion, national or social origin, economic status or birth, have the same opportunities to acquire and develop the skills necessary for the complete development and exercise of their artistic talents, to obtain employment, and to exercise their profession without discrimination.

4. The Vocation and Training of the Artist. 1. Member States should encourage, at school and from an early age, all measures tending to strengthen respect for artistic creation and the discovery and development of artistic vocations, and should bear in mind that, if it is to be effective, the stimulation of artistic creativity calls for provision of the necessary professional training of talent to produce works of outstanding quality. For this purpose, Member States should:

(a) take the necessary measures to provide an education designed to stimulate artistic talent and vocation;

(b) take all appropriate measures, in association with artists, to ensure that education gives due prominence to the development of artistic sensitivity and so contributes to the training of a public receptive to the expression of art in all its forms;

(c) take all appropriate measures, whenever possible, to institute or develop the teaching of particular artistic disciplines;

(d) seek by means of incentives, such as the granting of fellowships or paid educational leave, to ensure that artists have the opportunity to bring their knowledge up to date in their own discipline or in related specialities and fields, to improve their technical skills, to establish contacts which will stimulate creativity, and to undergo retraining so as to have access to and work in other branches of art; for these purposes, Member States should see that appropriate facilities are provided and that those already existing are, where necessary, improved and developed;

(e) adopt and develop co-ordinated, comprehensive vocational guidance and training policies and programmes, taking into consideration the particular employment situation of artists and enabling them to enter other sectors of activity if necessary;

(f) stimulate artists' participation in the restoration, conservation and use of the cultural heritage in the widest sense of the term, and provide artists with the means of transmitting to future generations the knowledge and artistic skills which they possess;

(g) recognize the importance in arts and craft training of the traditional ways of transmitting knowledge and in particular of the initiation practices of various communities, and take all appropriate measures to protect and encourage them;

(h) recognize that art education should not be separated from the practice of living art, and see that such education is reoriented in such a way that cultural establishments, theatres, art studios, radio and television broadcasting organizations, etc., play an important part in this type of training and apprenticeship;

(i) give particular attention to the development of women's creativity and the encouragement of groups and organizations which seek to promote the role of women in the various branches of artistic activity;

(j) recognize that artistic life and the practice of the arts have an international dimension and accordingly provide those engaged in artistic activities with all the means and, in particular, travel and study grants, likely to enable them to establish lively and far-reaching contacts with other cultures;

(k) take all appropriate steps to promote the free international movement of artists, and not to hinder the freedom of artists to practise their art in the country of their choice, while ensuring that these do not prejudice the development of endogenous talents and the conditions of work and employment of national artists;

(l) give special attention to the needs of traditional artists, in particular by facilitating their travel inside and outside their own country to serve the development of local traditions.

2. As far as possible and without prejudice to the freedom and independence of both artists and educators, Member States should undertake and support initiatives to ensure that artists, during their training, are made aware of their community's cultural identity, including traditional and folk cultures, thereby contributing to the affirmation or revival of that identity and those cultures.

5. *Social Status.* Member States should promote and protect the status of artists by considering artistic activity, including innovation and research, as a service to the community. They should make it possible for them to enjoy the esteem necessary for the full development of their work and provide the economic safeguards to which artists are entitled as people actively engaged in cultural work. Member States should:

1. Grant artists public recognition in the form best suited to their respective cultural environments and establish a system, where it does not already exist or is inadequately designed, to give artists the prestige to which they are entitled.

2. See that the artist benefits from the rights and protection provided for in international and national legislation relating to human rights.

3. Endeavour to take the necessary steps to see that artists enjoy the same rights as are conferred on a comparable group of the active population by national and international legislation in respect of employment and living and working conditions, and see that self-employed artists enjoy, within reasonable limits, protection as regards income and social security.

4. Recognize the importance of international protection of the rights of artists under the terms of existing conventions and in particular of the Berne Convention for the Protection of Literary and Artistic Works, the Universal Copyright Convention, and the Rome Convention for the Protection of Performers, Producers of Phonograms and Broadcasting Organizations, and take all necessary steps to extend the field of application, scope and effectiveness of those instruments, particularly—in the case of Member

States which have not already done so—by considering the possibility of adhering to them.

5. Recognize the right of trade union and professional organizations of artists to represent and defend the interests of their members and give them the opportunity to advise the public authorities on suitable measures for stimulating artistic activity and ensuring its protection and development.

6. *Employment, Working and Living Conditions of the Artist; Professional and Trade Union Organizations.* 1. Being aware of the need to improve the social recognition of artists by according them the moral and material support required to remedy their difficulties, Member States are invited to:

(a) consider measures for supporting artists at the beginning of their careers, in particular during the initial period when they are attempting to devote themselves completely to their art;

(b) promote the employment of artists in their own disciplines, particularly by devoting a proportion of public expenditure to artistic works;

(c) promote artistic activities within the context of development and stimulate public and private demand for the fruits of artistic activity in order to increase opportunities of paid work for artists, *inter alia* by means of subsidies to art institutions, commissions to individual artists, or the organization of artistic events at the local, regional or national levels, and by establishing art funds;

(d) identify remunerative posts which could be given to artists without prejudice to their creativity, vocation and freedom of expression and communication, and in particular:

(i) give artists opportunities in the relevant categories of the educational and social services systems at national and local levels and in libraries, museums, academies and other public institutions;

(ii) increase the participation of poets and writers in the overall effort towards the translation of foreign literature;

(e) encourage the development of the necessary facilities (museums, concert halls, theatres, and other forums) conducive to fostering the dissemination of the arts and the meeting of artists with the public;

(f) study the possibility of establishing, within the framework of employment policies or public employment services, effective machinery to assist artists to find jobs and that of adhering to the Fee-Charging Employment Agencies Convention (revised) (No. 96) of the International Labour Organisation, which is listed in the appendix to this Recommendation.

2. Within the context of a general policy to encourage artistic creativity, cultural development and the promotion and improvement of conditions of employment, Member States are invited, wherever possible, practical and in the interest of the artist, to:

(a) encourage and facilitate the application of the standards adopted for various groups of the active population to artists, and ensure that they enjoy all the rights accorded to the corresponding groups in respect of working conditions;

(b) seek means of extending to artists the legal protection concerning conditions of work and employment defined by the standards of the International Labour Organisation, in particular the standards relating to:

(i) hours of work, weekly rest and paid leave in all fields of activities, more particularly, in the case of performers, taking into consideration the hours spent in travelling and rehearsal as well as those spent in public performance or appearances;

(ii) protection of life, health and the working environment;

(c) take into consideration the particular problems of artists, in respect of the premises where they work, while at the same time ensuring the preservation of the architectural heritage and the environment and upholding regulations pertaining to safety and health, when administering regulations relative to the alteration of artists' premises where this is in the interests of artistic activity;

(d) make provision when necessary for appropriate forms of compensation for artists, preferably in consultation with organizations representing artists and their employers, when, for reasons connected with the nature of the artistic activity undertaken or the artists' employment status, the standards relating to the matters referred to in paragraph 2(b)(i) of this section cannot be observed;

(e) recognize that profit-sharing systems, in the form of deferred salaries or shares in the profits of production, may prejudice artists' rights *via-à-vis* their real incomes and social security entitlement and take appropriate measures in such cases to preserve these rights.

3. With the object of giving specific consideration to the child artist, Member States are invited to take account of the provisions of the United Nations Declaration of the Rights of the Child.

4. Recognizing the part played by professional and trade union organizations in the protection of employment and working conditions, Member States are invited to take appropriate steps to:

(a) observe and secure observance of the standards relating to freedom of association, to the right to organize and to collective bargaining, set forth in the international labour conventions listed in the appendix to this Recommendation and ensure that these standards and the general principles on which they are founded may apply to artists;

(b) encourage the free establishment of such organizations in disciplines where they do not yet exist;

(c) provide opportunities for all such organizations, national or international, without prejudice to the right of freedom of association, to carry out their role to the full.

5. Member States are invited to endeavour within their respective cultural environments to provide the same social protection for employed and self-employed artists as that usually granted respectively to other employed and self-employed groups. Provision should likewise be made for measures to extend appropriate social protection to dependent members of the family. The social security system which Member States may find it well to adopt, improve or supplement should take into consideration the special features of artistic activity, characterized by the intermittent nature of employment and the sharp variations in the incomes of many artists without, however, this entailing a limitation of the artist's freedom to create, publish and disseminate his work. In this context, Member States are invited to consider the adoption of special means of financing social security for artists, for example by resorting to new forms of financial participation either by the public authorities or by the business undertakings which market or which use the services or works of artists.

6. Recognizing in general that national and international legislation concerning the status of artists is lagging behind the general advances in technology, the development of the media of mass communication, the means of mechanical reproduction of works of art and of performances, the education of the public, and the decisive part played by the cultural industries, Member States are invited to take, wherever necessary, appropriate measures to:

(a) ensure that the artist is remunerated for the distribution and commercial exploitation of his work, and provide for the artist to maintain control of his work against unauthorized exploitation, modification or distribution;

(b) provide, to the extent possible, for a system guaranteeing the exclusive moral and material rights of artists in respect of any prejudice connected with the technical development of new communication and reproduction media, and of cultural industries; this means, in particular, establishing rights for performers, including circus and variety artists, and puppeteers; in doing so, it would be appropriate to take account of the provisions of the Rome Convention and, with reference to problems arising from the introduction of cable diffusion and videograms, of the Recommendation adopted by the Intergovernmental Committee of the Rome Convention in 1979;

(c) compensate any prejudice artists might suffer in consequence of the technical development of new communication and reproduction media and of cultural industries by favouring, for example, publicity for and dissemination of their works, and the creation of posts;

(d) ensure that cultural industries benefiting from technological changes, including radio and television organizations and mechanical reproduction undertakings, play their part in the effort to encourage and stimulate artistic creation, for instance by providing new employment opportunities, by publicity, by the dissemination of works, payment of royalties or by any other means judged equitable for artists;

(e) assist artists and organizations of artists to remedy, when they exist, the prejudicial effects on their employment or work opportunities of new technologies.

7. (a) Convinced of the uncertainty of artists' incomes and their sudden fluctuations, of the special features of artistic activity and of the fact that many artistic callings can be followed only for a relatively short period of life, Member States are invited to make provision for pension rights for certain categories of artists according to length of career and not the attainment of a certain age and to take into account in their taxation system the particular conditions of artists' work and activity;

(b) in order to preserve the health and prolong the professional activity of certain categories of artists (for example ballet dancers, dancers, vocalists) Member States are invited to provide them with adequate medical care not only in the event of incapacity for work but also for the purpose of preventing illness, and to consider the possibility of research into the health problems peculiar to artistic professions;

(c) taking into account the fact that a work of art should be considered neither as a consumer good nor as an investment, Member States are invited to consider the possibility of alleviating indirect taxation on works of art and on artistic performances at the time of their creation, dissemination or first sale, and this in the interest of artists or of development of the arts.

8. In view of the growing importance of international exchanges of works of art, and contacts between artists, and the need to encourage them, Member States separately or collectively, without prejudice to the development of national cultures, are invited to:

(a) assist freer circulation of such work by, *inter alia,* flexible customs arrangements and concessions in relation to import duties, particularly as regards temporary importation;

(b) take measures to encourage international travel and exchange by artists, giving due attention to visiting national artists.

7. *Cultural Policies and Participation.* Member States should endeavour, in accordance with paragraphs III.7 and V.5 of this Recommendation, to take appropriate measures to have the opinions of artists and the professional and trade union organizations representing them, as well as of the people at large, in the spirit of Unesco's Recommendation on Participation by the People at Large in Cultural Life and their Contribution to It, taken carefully into account in the formulation and execution of their cultural policies. To this end, they are invited to make the necessary arrangements for artists and their organizations to participate in discussions, decision-making processes and the subsequent implementation of measures aimed, *inter alia,* at:

(a) the enhancement of the status of artists in society, for example measures relating to the employment and working and living conditions of the artist, to the provision of material and moral support for artistic activities by the public authorities, and to the professional training of the artist;

(b) the promotion of culture and art within the community, for example measures relating to cultural development, to the protection and effective presentation of the cultural heritage, including folklore and the other activities of traditional artists, to cultural identity, to relevant aspects of environmental issues and the use of leisure, and to the place of culture and art in education;

(c) the encouragement of international cultural co-operation, for example measures relating to the dissemination and translation of works, to the exchange of works and of persons, and to the organization of regional or international cultural events.

8. *Utilization and Implementation of This Recommendation.* 1. Member States should strive to extend and supplement their own action in respect of the status of the artist by co-operating with all the national or international organizations whose activities are related to the objectives of this Recommendation, in particular with National Commissions for Unesco, national and international artists' organizations, the International Labour Office and the World Intellectual Property Organization.

2. Member States should, by the most appropriate means, support the work of the above-mentioned bodies representing artists and enlist their professional co-operation to enable artists to benefit from the provisions set forth in this Recommendation and to obtain recognition of the status described herein.

9. *Existing Advantages.* Where artists enjoy, in certain respects, a status which is more favourable than that provided for in this Recommendation, its terms shall not in any case be invoked to diminish the advantages already acquired or directly or indirectly to affect them.

SEE ALSO *Universal Copyright Convention and Protocols.*

UNESCO RECOMMENDATION FOR THE SAFE-GUARDING AND PRESERVATION OF MOVING IMAGES (1980). The recommendation was adopted by the UNESCO General Conference (21st session), held in Belgrade, on 27 October 1980. It calls upon governments to take appropriate measures to ensure the safeguarding and preservation of moving images (such as feature films, short films, popular science films, newsreels, documentaries, and animated and educational films) with due regard for freedom of opinion, expression, and information, for the need to strengthen peace and international understandbing, and for the legitimate position of copyright holders and of all the holders of other rights in such images.

The text of the recommendation is as follows:

The General Conference of the United Nations Educational, Scientific and Cultural Organization, meeting in Belgrade from 23 September to 28 October 1980, at its twenty-first session,

Considering that moving images are an expression of the cultural identity of peoples, and because of their educational, cultural, artistic, scientific and historical value, form an integral part of a nation's cultural heritage,

Considering that moving images constitute new forms of expression, particularly characteristic of present-day society, whereby an important and ever-increasing part of contemporary culture is manifested,

Considering that moving images also provide a fundamental means of recording the unfolding of events and, as such, constitute important and often unique testimonies, of a new dimension, to the history, way of life and culture of peoples and to the evolution of the universe,

Noting that moving images have an increasingly important role to play as a means of communication and mutual understanding among all the peoples of the world,

Noting furthermore that, by disseminating knowledge and culture throughout the world, moving images contribute extensively to the education and to the enrichment of each human being,

Considering however that, due to the nature of their material embodiment and the various methods of their fixation, moving images are extremely vulnerable and should be maintained under specific technical conditions,

Noting furthermore that many elements of the moving image heritage have disappeared due to deterioration, accident or unwarranted disposal, which constitutes an irreversible impoverishment of that heritage,

Recognizing the results yielded by the efforts of specialized institutions to save moving images from the dangers to which they are exposed,

Considering that it is necessary for each State to take the appropriate complementary measures to ensure the safeguarding and preservation for posterity of this particularly fragile part of its cultural heritage, just as other forms of cultural property are safeguarded and preserved as a source of enrichment for present and future generations,

Considering at the same time that the appropriate measures to ensure the safeguarding and preservation of moving images should be taken with due regard for freedom of opinion, expression and information, recognized as an essential part of human rights and fundamental freedoms inherent in the dignity of the human being, for the need to strengthen peace and international understanding and for the legitimate position of copyright holders and of all the holders of other rights in moving images,

Recognizing also the rights of States to take appropriate measures for the safeguarding and preservation of moving images, taking into account their obligations under international law,

Considering that moving images created by the peoples of the world also form part of the heritage of mankind as a whole and consequently that closer international co-operation should be promoted to safeguard and preserve these irreplaceable records of human activity and, in particular, for the benefit of those countries with limited resources,

Considering furthermore that, due to increasing international co-operation, imported moving images have an important role in the cultural life of most countries,

Considering that important aspects of the history and culture of certain countries, and, in particular, of those previously colonized, are recorded in the form of moving images which are not always accessible to the countries concerned,

Noting that the General Conference has already adopted international instruments relating to the protection of the movable cultural heritage and, in particular, the Convention for the Protection of Cultural Property in the Event of Armed Conflict (1954), the Recommendation on the Means of Prohibiting and Preventing the Illicit Export, Import and Transfer of Ownership of Cultural Property (1964), the Convention on the Means of Prohibiting and Preventing the Illicit Import, Export and Transfer of Ownership of Cultural Property (1970), the Recommendation of the International Exchange of Cultural Property (1976) and the Recommendation on the Protection of Movable Cultural Property (1978),

Desiring to supplement and extend the application of the standards and principles laid down in these conventions and recommendations,

Bearing in mind the terms of the Universal Copyright Convention, the Berne Convention for the Protection of Literary and Artistic Works and the Convention for the Protection of Performers, Producers of Phonograms and Broadcasting Organizations,

Having before it proposals concerning the safeguarding and preservation of moving images,

Having decided, at its twentieth session, that this question should be the subject of a Recommendation to Member States,

Adopts, this twenty-seventh day of October 1980, the present Recommendation:

The General Conference recommends that Member States apply the following provisions by taking whatever legislative or other steps may be required, in conformity with the constitutional system or practice of each State, to give effect within their respective territories to the principles and norms formulated in this Recommendation.

The General Conference recommends that Member States bring this Recommendation to the attention of the appropriate authorities and bodies.

The General Conference recommends that Member States submit to it, by the dates and in the form which it shall prescribe, reports concerning the action taken by them in pursuance of this Recommendation.

1. Definitions. 1. For the purpose of this Recommendation:

(a) "moving images" shall be taken to mean any series of images recorded on a support (irrespective of the method of recording or of the nature of the support, such as film, tape or disc, used in their initial or subsequent fixation), with or without accompanying sound, which when projected impart an impression of motion and which are intended for communication or distribution to the public or are made for documentation purposes; they shall be taken to include *inter alia* items in the following categories:

(i) cinematographic productions (such as feature films, short films, popular science films, newsreels and documentaries, animated and educational films);

(ii) television productions made by or for broadcasting organizations;

(iii) videographic productions (contained in videograms) other than those referred to under (i) and (ii) above;

(b) "pre-print material" shall be taken to mean the material support for moving images, consisting in the case of a cinematographic film of a negative, internegative or interpositive, and in the case of a videogram of a master, such pre-print material being intended for the procurement of copies;

(c) "projection copy" shall be taken to mean the material support for moving images intended for actual viewing and/or the communication of the images.

2. For the purposes of this Recommendation, "national production" shall be taken to mean moving images, the maker or at least one of the co-makers of which has his headquarters or habitual residence within the territory of the State concerned.

2. General Principles. 3. All moving images of national production should be considered by Member States as an integral part of their 'moving image heritage'. Moving images of original foreign production may also form part of the cultural heritage of a country when they are of particular national importance from the point of view of the culture or history of the country concerned. Should it not be possible for this heritage to be handed down in its entirety to future generations for technical or financial reasons, as large a proportion as possible should be safeguarded and preserved. The necessary arrangements should be made to ensure that concerted action is taken by all the public and private bodies concerned in order to elaborate and apply an active policy to this end.

4. The appropriate measures should be taken to ensure that the moving image heritage is afforded adequate physical protection from the depredations wrought by time and by the environment. Since poor storage conditions accelerate the deterioration process to which the material supports are continuously subject and may even lead to their total destruction, moving images should be preserved in officially recognized film and television archives and processed according to the highest archival standards. Furthermore, research should be specifically directed towards the development of high quality and lasting support-media for the proper safeguarding and preservation of moving images.

5. Measures should be taken to prevent the loss, unwarranted disposal or deterioration of any item of the national production. Means should therefore be instituted in each country whereby pre-print material or archival quality copies of moving images may be systemically acquired, safeguarded and preserved in public or private non-profit-making archival institutions.

6. Access should be made available as far as possible to

the works and information sources represented by moving images which are acquired, safeguarded and preserved by public and private non-profit-making institutions. Their utilization should not prejudice either the legitimate rights or the interests of those involved in the making and exploitation thereof, in accordance with the provisions of the Universal Copyright Convention, the Berne Convention for the Protection of Literary and Artistic Works and the Convention for the Protection of Performers, Producers of Phonograms and Broadcasting Organizations, and national legislation.

7. In order to ensure that a truly effective safeguarding and preservation programme is successfully undertaken, the co-operation of all those involved in the making, distribution, safeguarding and preservation of moving images should be obtained. Public information activities should therefore be organized in particular with a view to instilling in the professional circles concerned a general awareness of the significance of moving images for a country's heritage and the consequent need to safeguard and preserve them as testimonies to the life of contemporary society.

3. Measures Recommended. 8. In accordance with the principles set out above, and in conformity with their normal constitutional practice, Member States are invited to take all the necessary steps, including the provision to officially recognized archives of appropriate resources in terms of staff, equipment and funds, to safeguard and preserve effectively their moving image heritage in accordance with the following guidelines:

Legal and Administrative Measures

9. To ensure that moving images forming part of the cultural heritage of countries are systematically preserved, Member States are invited to take measures whereby officially recognized archives are able to acquire for safeguarding and preservation any part or all of their country's national production. Such measures may include, for example, voluntary arrangements with the holders of rights for the deposit of moving images, acquisition of moving images by purchase or donation or the institution of mandatory deposit systems through appropriate legislation or administrative measures. Such systems should complement and coexist with existing archival arrangements relating to publicly owned moving images. Measures taken should be consistent with the provisions of national legislation and international instruments concerning the protection of human rights, copyright and the protection of performers, producers of phonograms and broadcasting organizations relating to moving images, and should take into account the special conditions provided in favour of developing countries in certain of these instruments. When mandatory deposit systems are adopted, they should provide that:

(a) moving images of national production, whatever the physical characteristics of their support medium or the purpose for which they were created, should be deposited in at least one complete copy of the highest archival quality, preferably in the form of pre-print material;

(b) the material should be deposited by the maker—as defined by national legislation—having his headquarters or habitual residence within the territory of the State concerned, irrespective of any co-production arrangement made with a foreign maker;

(c) the material deposited should be preserved in officially recognized film or television archives; where they do not exist, every effort should be made to establish such in-

stitutions at the national and/or regional level; pending the establishment of officially recognized archives, the material should be provisionally stored in appropriately equipped premises;

(d) the deposit should be made as soon as possible within a maximum time-limit fixed by national regulations;

(e) the depositor should have controlled access to the deposited material whenever further printing is required, on condition that such access does not cause any damage to or deterioration of the material deposited;

(f) the officially recognized archives should be entitled, subject to the relevant provisions of international conventions and of national legislation governing copyright and the protection of performers, producers of phonograms and broadcasting organizations, to:

(i) take all the necessary measures in order to safeguard and preserve the moving image heritage, and, where possible, to enhance the technical quality; where the reproduction of moving images is involved, due regard should be given to all the rights in the images concerned;

(ii) permit the viewing on their premises of a projection copy on a non-profit-making basis by a limited number of viewers for purposes of teaching, scholarship or research, provided that such use does not conflict with the normal exploitation of the work and on condition that no deterioration of or damage to the material deposited is thereby caused;

(g) the material deposited and the copies made therefrom should not be used for any other purposes, nor should their contents be modified;

(h) officially recognized archives should be entitled to request users to make a reasonable contribution to the cost of the services provided.

10. The safeguarding and preservation of all moving images of national production should be regarded as the highest objective. However, until such time as developments in technology make this feasible everywhere, in those cases where it is not possible, for technical reasons of cost or space, to record all publicly broadcast moving images or to safeguard and preserve on a long-term basis all the material deposited, each Member State is invited to establish the principles for determining which images should be recorded and/or deposited for posterity, including 'ephemeral recordings' having an exceptional documentary character. Those moving images which, because of their educational, cultural, artistic, scientific and historical value, form part of a nation's cultural heritage should be retained on a priority basis. Any system introduced to this end should foresee that selection should be based on the broadest possible consensus of informed opinion and should take particular account of the appraisal criteria established by the archival profession. Furthermore, due care should be taken to prevent the elimination of material until sufficient time has elapsed to allow for the necessary perspective. Material eliminated in this way should be returned to the depositor.

11. Foreign producers, and those responsible for the public distribution of moving images made abroad, should be encouraged, in accordance with the spirit of this Recommendation and without prejudice to the free movement of moving images across national borders, to deposit voluntarily in the officially recognized archives of the countries in which they are publicly distributed a copy of moving images of the highest archival quality, subject to all the rights therein. In particular, those responsible for the distribution of moving images, dubbed or subtitled in the language

or languages of the country in which they are publicly distributed, which are regarded as an integral part of the moving image heritage of the country concerned or which are of significant value for the cultural needs of teaching or research, should be urged to deposit the material relating to these images in the spirit of international co-operation. Officially recognized archives should seek establishment of such deposit systems, and furthermore, the acquisition, subject to all the rights therein, of copies of moving images which are of exceptional universal value, even if they have not been publicly distributed in the country concerned. Control of and access to such material should be governed by the provisions of paragraph 9(e), (f), (g) and (h) above.

12. Member States are invited to conduct follow-up studies on the effectiveness of the measures proposed in paragraph 11. If, following a reasonable trial period, the suggested form of voluntary deposit fails to ensure the adequate safeguarding and preservation of adapted moving images that are of particular national importance from the standpoint of the culture or history of a State, it would be for the State concerned, under the provisions of its national legislation, to define such measures as would prevent the disappearance, particularly though destruction, of copies of adapted moving images, due regard being given to the rights of all those holding legitimate rights in such moving images of particular national importance.

13. Member States are invited furthermore to investigate the feasibility of permitting—taking due account of international conventions concerning copyright and the protection of performers, producers of phonograms and broadcasting organizations—officially recognized archives to utilize the deposited material for research and recognized teaching purposes provided that such utilization does not conflict with the normal exploitation of the works.

Technical Measures

14. Member States are invited to pay due attention to the archival standards concerning storage and treatment of moving images recommended by the international organizations competent in the field of the safeguarding and preservation of moving images.

15. Furthermore, Member States are invited to make the necessary arrangements to ensure that the institutions responsible for safeguarding and preserving the moving image heritage take the following measures:

(a) establish and make available national filmographies and catalogues of all categories of moving images and descriptions of their holdings, seeking, where possible, the standardization of cataloguing systems; these documentary materials would together form an inventory of the country's moving image heritage;

(b) collect, preserve and make available for research purposes institutional records, personal papers and other material that document the origin, production, distribution and projection of moving images, subject to the agreement of those concerned;

(c) maintain in good condition the equipment, some of which may no longer be in general use but which may be necessary for the reproduction and projection of material preserved or, should that not prove possible, ensure that the moving images concerned are transferred onto another material support permitting their reproduction and projection;

(d) ensure that the standards applicable to the storage, safeguarding, preservation, restoration and duplication of moving images are rigorously applied;

(e) as far as possible, improve the technical quality of the moving images to be safeguarded and preserved, ensuring that they are in a condition conducive to their long-term and effective storage and use; when treatment involves the reproduction of material, due regard should be given to all the rights in the images concerned.

16. Member States are invited to encourage private bodies and individuals holding moving images to take the necessary steps to ensure the safeguarding and preservation of these images under adequate technical conditions. These bodies and individuals should be encouraged to entrust to officially recognized archives the pre-print material if available or, in default thereof, copies of moving images made before the introduction of the deposit system.

Supplementary Measures

17. Member States are invited to encourage the competent authorities and other bodies concerned with the safeguarding and preservation of moving images to undertake public information activities in order to:

(a) promote among all those involved in the making and distribution of moving images an appreciation of the lasting value of such images from the educational, cultural, artistic, scientific and historical points of view and an awareness of the consequent need to collaborate in their safeguarding and preservation;

(b) draw the attention of the public at large to the educational, cultural, artistic, scientific and historical importance of moving images and to the measures necessary for their safeguarding and preservation.

18. Measures should be taken at the national level in order to co-ordinate research in fields related to the safeguarding and preservation of moving images and to encourage research specifically directed towards their long-term preservation at a reasonable cost. Information on methods and techniques for safeguarding and preserving moving images, including the results of relevant research, should be disseminated to all concerned.

19. Training programmes in the safeguarding and restoration of moving images should be organized, covering the most recent methods and techniques.

4. International Co-operation. 20. Member States are invited to associate their efforts in order to promote the safeguarding and preservation of moving images which form part of the cultural heritage of nations. Such co-operation should be stimulated by the competent international governmental and non-governmental organizations and should comprise the following measures:

(a) participation in international programmes for the establishment of the necessary infrastructure, at the regional or national level, to safeguard and preserve the moving image heritage of countries which do not possess appropriate facilities or adequate resources;

(b) exchange of information on methods and techniques for the safeguarding and preservation of moving images and, in particular, on the findings of recent research;

(c) organization of national or international training courses in related fields in particular for nationals of developing countries;

(d) joint action for the standardization of cataloguing methods specifically intended for archival holdings of moving images;

(e) authorization, subject to the relevant provisions of

international conventions and of national legislation governing copyright and the protection of performers, producers of phonograms and broadcasting organizations, of the lending of copies of moving images to other officially recognized archives exclusively for purposes of teaching, scholarship or research, provided that the consent of the holders of rights and the archives concerned is obtained to such lending and that no deterioration of or damage to the material lent is thereby caused.

21. Technical co-operation should be provided in particular to developing countries, in order to ensure or facilitate the adequate safeguarding and preservation of their moving image heritage.

22. Member States are invited to co-operate for the purpose of enabling any State to gain access to moving images that relate to its history or culture and of which it does not hold either pre-print material or projection copies. To this end each Member State is invited:

(a) to facilitate, in the case of moving images on deposit in officially recognized archives and which relate to the history or culture of another country, the acquisition by the officially recognized archives of that country of either pre-print material or a projection copy thereof;

(b) to encourage private bodies or institutions within its territory which hold such moving images to deposit on a voluntary basis either pre-print material or a projection copy thereof with the officially recognized archives of the country concerned.

Where necessary, the material supplied in accordance with (a) and (b) above should be made available against reimbursement of the cost by the requesting body. However, in view of the cost involved, pre-print material or projection copies of moving images held by Member States as public property and which relate to the history and culture of developing countries should be made available to the officially recognized archives of those countries under especially favourable conditions. Any material provided in accordance with this paragraph should be made available subject to any copyright and any rights of performers, producers of phonograms or broadcasting organizations which may exist therein.

23. When moving images forming part of a country's cultural or historical heritage have been lost by that country, whatever the circumstances, and in particular as a consequence of colonial or foreign occupation, Member States are invited, in connection with requests for such images, to co-operate in the spirit of resolution 5/10.1/1, III, adopted by the General Conference at its twentieth session.

SEE ALSO *Universal Copyright Convention and Protocols.*

UNESCO RECOMMENDATION ON PARTICIPATION BY THE PEOPLE AT LARGE IN CULTURAL LIFE AND THEIR CONTRIBUTION TO IT (1976).

This recommendation, which aims at ensuring the promotion and protection of cultural rights as human rights, was adopted by the UNESCO GENERAL CONFERENCE (19th session), held in Nairobi, Kenya, on 26 November 1976. In scope it concerns, in its own words, "everything that should be done by Member States or the authorities to democratize the means and instruments of cultural activity, so as to enable all individuals to participate freely and fully in cultural creation and its benefits, in accordance with the requirements of social progress."

The text of the recommendation (*UNESCO's Standard-Setting Instruments*, No. IV.B.7) is as follows:

The General Conference of the United Nations Educational, Scientific and Cultural Organization, meeting in Nairobi from 26 October to 30 November 1976, at its nineteenth session.

Recalling that under the terms of Article 27 of the Universal Declaration of Human Rights, "everyone has the right freely to participate in the cultural life of the community, to enjoy the arts and to share in scientific advancement and its benefits",

Recalling that the Constitution of Unesco states, in its Preamble, that the wide diffusion of culture, and the education of humanity for justice and liberty and peace are indispensable to the dignity of man,

Recalling the provisions of the Declaration of the Principles of International Cultural Co-operation adopted by the General Conference of Unesco on 4 November 1966 at its fourteenth session, and in particular Article 1 which states that "each culture has a dignity and value which must be respected and preserved", and Article IV which stipulates that one of the aims of international cultural co-operation is "to enable everyone to have access to knowledge, to enjoy the arts and literature of all peoples, to share in advances made in science in all parts of the world and in the resulting benefits, and to contribute to the enrichment of cultural life", and also the provisions of the Final Act of the Conference on Security and Co-operation in Europe to the effect that the participating States, "desiring to contribute to the strengthening of peace and understanding among peoples and to the spiritual enrichment of the human personality without distinction as to race, sex, language or religion", will set themselves the objective, amongst others, of promoting access by all to their respective cultural achievements,

Considering that cultural development not only complements and regulates general development but is also a true instrument of progress,

Considering:

(a) that culture is an integral part of social life and that a policy for culture must therefore be seen in the broad context of general State policy, and that culture is, in its very essence, a social phenomenon resulting from individuals joining and co-operating in creative activities,

(b) that culture is today becoming an important element in human life and one of the principal factors in the progress of mankind, and that an essential premise for such progress is to ensure the constant growth of society's spiritual potential, based on the full, harmonious development of all its members and the free play of their creative faculties.

(c) that culture is not merely an accumulation of works and knowledge which an èlite produces, collects and conserves in order to place it within reach of all; or that a people rich in its past and its heritage offers to others as a model which their own history has failed to provide for them; that culture is not limited to access to works of art and the humanities, but is at one and the same time the acquisition of knowledge, the demand for a way of life and the need to communicate,

Considering that participation by the greatest possible number of people and associations in a wide variety of cultural activities of their own free choice is essential to the development of the basic human values and dignity of the individual, and that access by the people at large to cultural values can be assured only if social and economic conditions are created that will enable them not only to enjoy the benefits of culture, but also to take an active part in overall cultural life and in the process of cultural development,

Considering that access to culture and participation in cultural life are two complementary aspects of the same thing, as is evident from the way in which one affects the other—access may promote participation in cultural life and participation may broaden access to culture by endowing it with its true meaning—and that without participation, mere access to culture necessarily falls short of the objectives of cultural development,

Noting that cultural action often involves only a minute proportion of the population and that, moreover, existing organizations and the means used do not always meet the needs of those who are in a particularly vulnerable position because of their inadequate education, low standard of living, poor housing conditions and economic and social dependence in general,

Noting that there is often a wide discrepancy between the reality and the proclaimed ideals, declared intentions, programmes or expected results,

Considering that while it is essential and urgent to define objectives, contents and methods for a policy of participation by the people at large in cultural life, the solutions envisaged cannot be identical for all countries, in view of the current differences between the socio-economic and political situations in States,

Reaffirming the principles of respect for the sovereignty of States, non-interference in the internal affairs of other countries, equality of rights and the right of peoples to self-determination,

Aware of the responsibility which devolves upon Member States to implement cultural policies for the purpose of advancing the objectives set forth in the Charter of the United Nations, the Constitution of Unesco, the International Covenant on Economic, Social and Cultural Rights, and the Declaration of the Principles of International Cultural Co-operation,

Bearing in mind that elimination of the economic and social inequality which prevents broad sections of the population from gaining access to knowledge which is the foundation of science and technology, and from becoming aware of their own cultural needs, implies broader participation on their part; that to these obstacles must be added a resistance to change, and barriers of all kinds, whether they are of political or commercial origin or take the form of a reaction by closed communities,

Considering that the problem of access and participation can be solved by collective approaches extending to many sectors and aspects of life; that such approaches should be diversified according to the special characteristics of each community, the whole forming a true design for living calling for basic policy options,

Considering that access to culture and participation in cultural life are essential components of an overall social policy dealing with the condition of the working masses, the organization of labour, leisure time, family life, education and training, town-planning and the environment,

Aware of the important role that can be played in cultural and social life by: young people, whose mission is to contribute to the evolution and progress of society; parents, particularly because of the decisive influence which they exercise on the cultural education of children and the development of their creativity; elderly people who are available to discharge a new social and cultural function; workers, because of the active contribution they make to social changes; artists, as creators and bearers of cultural values; cultural development personnel whose task is to secure the effective participation in cultural life of all sections of the population and to ascertain and express their aspirations, relying for this purpose on the collaboration of the spontaneous leaders of the community,

Considering that access and participation, which should provide everyone with the opportunity not only to receive benefits but also to express himself in all the circumstances of social life, imply the greatest liberty and tolerance in the fields of cultural training and the creation and dissemination of culture,

Considering that participation in cultural life presupposes an affirmation of the personality, its dignity and value, and also the implementation of the fundamental rights and freedoms of man attested by the Charter of the United Nations and international legal instruments concerning human rights, and that the cultural development of the individual is hindered by such phenomena as the policy of aggression, colonialism, neo-colonialism, fascism and racism in all its forms and manifestations, as well as by other causes,

Considering that participation in cultural life takes the form of an assertion of identity, authenticity and dignity; that the integrity of identity is threatened by numerous causes of erosion stemming, in particular, from the prevalence of inappropriate models or of techniques which have not been fully mastered,

Considering that the assertion of cultural identity should not result in the formation of isolated groups but should, on the contrary, go hand in hand with a mutual desire for wide and frequent contacts, and that such contacts are a fundamental requirement without which the objectives of the present recommendation would be unattainable,

Bearing in mind the fundamental part played by general education, cultural education and artistic training, and the use of working time and free time, with a view to full cultural development, in a context of life-long education,

Considering that the mass media can serve as instruments of cultural enrichment, both by opening up unprecedented possibilities of cultural development, in contributing to the liberation of the latent cultural potential of individuals, to the preservation and popularization of traditional forms of culture, and to the creation and dissemination of new forms, and by turning themselves into media for group communication and promoting direct participation by the people,

Considering that the ultimate objective of access and participation is to raise the spiritual and cultural level of society as a whole on the basis of humanistic values and to endow culture with a humanistic and democratic content, and that this in turn implies taking measures against the harmful effect of 'commercial mass culture', which threatens national cultures and the cultural development of mankind, leads to debasement of the personality and exerts a particularly harmful influence on the young generation,

Having before it, as item 28 of the agenda of the session, proposals concerning participation by the people at large in cultural life and their contribution to it,

Having decided at its eighteenth session that this question should be made the subject of an international regulation, to take the form of a recommendation to Member States,

Adopts, this twenty-sixth day of November 1976, the present Recommendation.

The General Conference recommends Member States to implement the following provisions, taking whatever legislative or other steps may be required—in conformity with the constitutional practice of each State and the nature of the question under consideration—to apply the principles and norms formulated in this Recommendation within their respective territories.

The General Conference recommends Member States to bring this Recommendation to the knowledge of authorities, institutions and organizations which can help to ensure participation by the people at large in cultural life and their contribution to it.

The General Conference recommends Member States to submit to it, at such times and in such manner as it shall determine, reports concerning the action they have taken upon this Recommendation.

I. Definitions, and Scope of the Recommendation

1. This Recommendation concerns everything that should be done by Member States or the authorities to democratize the means and instruments of cultural activity, so as to enable all individuals to participate freely and fully in cultural creation and its benefits, in accordance with the requirements of social progress.

2. For the purposes of the Recommendation:

(a) by access to culture is meant the concrete opportunities available to everyone, in particular through the creation of the appropriate socio-economic conditions, for freely obtaining information, training, knowledge and understanding, and for enjoying cultural values and cultural property;

(b) by participation in cultural life is meant the concrete opportunities guaranteed for all—groups or individuals—to express themselves freely, to communicate, act, and engage in creative activities with a view to the full development of their personalities, a harmonious life and the cultural progress of society;

(c) by communication is meant relations between groups or individuals desirous of freely exchanging or pooling information, ideas and knowledge with a view to promoting dialogue, concerted action, understanding and a sense of community while respecting their originality and their differences, in order to strengthen mutual understanding and peace.

3. For the purposes of the Recommendation:

(a) the concept of culture has been broadened to include all forms of creativity and expression of groups or individuals, both in their ways of life and in their artistic activities;

(b) free democratic access to culture of the people at large presupposes the existence of appropriate economic and social policies;

(c) participation in cultural life presupposes involvement of the different social partners in decision-making related to cultural policy as well as in the conduct and evaluation of activities;

(d) free participation in cultural life is related to:

(i) a development policy for economic growth and social justice;

(ii) a policy of life-long education which is geared to the needs and aspirations of all people and makes them aware of their own intellectual potentialities and sensitivity, provides them with cultural education and artistic training, improves their powers of self-expression and stimulates their creativity, thus enabling them more successfully to master social changes and to participate more fully in the community life of society;

(iii) a science and technology policy inspired by the resolve to safeguard the cultural identity of the peoples;

(iv) a social policy directed towards progress and, more precisely, the attenuation—with a view to their elimination—of the inequalities handicapping certain groups and individuals, especially the least privileged, in regard to their living conditions, their opportunities and the fulfilment of their aspirations;

(v) an environment policy designed, through the planned use of space and the protection of nature, to create a background to living conducive to the full development of individuals and societies;

(vi) a communicaton policy designed to strengthen the free exchange of information, ideas and knowledge, in order to promote mutual understanding, and encouraging to this end the use and extension of both modern and traditional media for cultural purposes;

(vii) a policy for international co-operation based on the principle of equality of cultures, mutual respect, understanding and confidence and strengthening of peace.

II. Legislation and Regulations

4. It is recommended that Member States, if they have not already done so, adopt legislation or regulations in conformity with their national constitutional procedures, or otherwise modify existing practices in order to:

(a) guarantee as human rights those rights bearing on access to and participation in cultural life, in the spirit of the Universal Declaration of Human Rights, of the International Covenant on Economic, Social and Cultural Rights and of the International Covenant on Civil and Political Rights and in accordance with the ideals and objectives set forth in the United Nations Charter and in the Constitution of Unesco;

(b) provide effective safeguards for free access to national and world cultures by all members of society without distinction or discrimination based on race, colour, sex, language, religion, political convictions, national or social origin, financial situation or any other consideration and so to encourage free participation by all sections of the population in the process of creating cultural values;

(c) pay special attention to women's full entitlement to access to culture and to effective participation in cultural life;

(d) promote the development and dissemination of national cultures and the development of international co-operation in order to make the cultural achievements of other peoples better known and to strengthen friendship and mutual understanding;

(e) create appropriate conditions enabling the populations to play an increasingly active part in building the future of their society, to assume responsibilities and duties and exercise rights in that process;

(f) guarantee the recognition of the equality of cultures, including the cultures of national minorities and of foreign minorities if they exist, as forming part of the common heritage of all mankind, and ensure that they are promoted at all levels without discrimination; ensure that national minorities and foreign minorities have full opportunities for gaining access to and participating in the cultural life of the countries in which they find themselves in order to enrich it with their specific contributions, while safeguarding their right to preserve their cultural identity;

(g) protect, safeguard and enhance all forms of cultural expression such as national or regional languages, dialects, folk arts and traditions both past and present, and rural cultures as well as cultures of other social groups;

(h) ensure that the handicapped are integrated in cultural life and have opportunities of contributing to it;

(i) ensure equality of access to education;

(j) guarantee freedom of expression and communication serving to strengthen the ideals of humanism;

(k) bring about conditions conducive to creative work and ensure the freedom of creative artists and the protection of their works and rights;

(l) improve the professional status of the various categories of personnel required for the implementation of cultural policies;

(m) ensure that cultural education and artistic training are given their proper place in the curricula of educational and training establishments, and extend enjoyment of the artistic heritage to the population outside the education system;

(n) multiply opportunities for intellectual, manual or gestural creation and encourage artistic training, experience and expression with a view to bringing about the integration of art and life;

(o) provide the mass media with a status ensuring their independence, due attention being paid to the effective participation of creative artists and the public; these media should not threaten the authenticity of cultures or impair their quality; they ought not to act as instruments of cultural domination but serve mutual understanding and peace;

(p) reconcile the duty to protect and enhance everything connected with the cultural heritage, traditions and the past with the need to allow the endeavours of the present and the modern outlook to find expression;

(q) (i) protect and enhance the heritage of the past, and particularly ancient monuments and traditions which may contribute to the essential equilibrium of societies subject to a rapid process of industrialization and urbanization;

(ii) make the public aware of the importance of town-planning and architecture, not only because they are the reflection of cultural and social life, but above all because they condition the very background to living;

(iii) associate the population with the conservation and management of the natural environment both at the national and at the international levels, since the quality of the natural environment is essential to the full development of the human personality;

(r) create, through the appropriate bodies, conditions making it possible for work and leisure, each in its own way, to offer opportunities for cultural creation to each and every one, and lay down conditions governing working and leisure hours and the operational organization of cultural institutions which will enable the greatest possible number of people to gain access to culture and participate in cultural life;

(s) reject concepts which, under the guise of cultural action, are based on violence and aggression, domination, contempt and racial prejudice, as well as on debasing ideas or practices;

(t) strengthen their work in support of peace and international understanding, in accordance with the Declaration of the Principles of International Cultural Co-operation and encourage the dissemination of ideas and cultural goods conducive to the strengthening of peace, security and co-operation.

III. Technical, Administrative, Economic and Financial Measures

5. It is recommended to Member States, if they have not already done so, that they make the necessary technical, administrative and financial resources available to upgrade policies for cultural action from the insignificant position to which they may still be relegated until they reach an operationally effective level enabling them to achieve the goals of life-long education and cultural development and to ensure to the maximum that the people at large have access to culture and participate freely in cultural life. For this purpose Member States should take the following measures:

A. Ways and Means of Cultural Action. Decentralization of Facilities, Activities and Decisions. 6. Member States or the appropriate authorities should:

(a) foster decentralization of activities and encourage the development of local centres, special attention being paid to under-populated peripheral or under-privileged areas;

(b) encourage, extend and strengthen the network of cultural and artistic institutions not only in large towns but also in smaller towns, villages and urban neighbourhoods;

(c) encourage the setting up of facilities best suited to the needs of the users and foster the integration of facilities used for cultural activities with those which are designed for social and educational work and which should be mobile to some extent, in order to make available to the widest possible public all the means needed for the heightening of awareness and for cultural development;

(d) encourage the use for cultural purposes of all public facilities that promote communication among groups and individuals;

(e) encourage inter-regional and inter-community exchanges;

(f) stimulate regional or local initiative, both by providing decision-makers with the necessary resources at appropriate levels and by sharing the decision-making function with the representatives of other parties interested in cultural problems; and to this end develop secondary centres for administrative decision-making;

(g) develop methods for the promotion or artistic creation and cultural activity by the people at large, based upon the people's own organizations, in both residential areas and working places;

(h) apply special measures for certain disadvantaged groups and for environments with a poorly developed cultural life. Special attention should be paid to, e.g., children, the handicapped, people living in hospitals and prisons, and people living in remotely situated areas, as well as those in city slums. Decisions and responsibility should, as much as possible, be left with the group participating in the activities.

Concerted Action. 7. Member States or the appropriate authorities should encourage concerted action and co-operation both as regards the activities themselves and decision-making:

(a) by paying special attention to creative cultural and

artistic non-institutional and non-professional activities and by providing all possible support to amateur activities in all their diversity;

(b) by establishing advisory structures, at the local, regional and national levels, bringing together representatives of the professional and social groups concerned who will participate in determining the objectives and ways and means of cultural action.

Trade Unions and Other Workers' Organizations. 8. Member States or the appropriate authorities should take all such measures as will be of assistance to socio-cultural organizations for the people at large, trade unions and other workers' organizations for wage-earners or the self-employed (farmers, craftsmen, etc.) in freely carrying out their cultural policies or projects so as to enable them to enjoy the whole wealth of cultural values and to take an active part in the cultural life of society.

"Animation." 9. Member States or the appropriate authorities should:

(a) contribute to the training of cultural development personnel, in particular of "animateurs", who should act as information, communication and expression intermediaries, by putting people in contact with each other and serving as a connecting link between the public, the work of art, and the artist, and between the public and cultural institutions;

(b) provide such personnel with means of action enabling them, on the one hand, to give support to the spontaneous "animateurs" of local communities and, on the other hand, to stimulate initiative and participation, using the necessary training methods;

(c) encourage the use of instruments and equipment for communication and expression which have education value and offer a potential for creation, by making them available to cultural centres and institutions such as public libraries, museums, etc.

Artistic Creation. 10. Member States or other appropriate authorities should:

(a) create social, economic and financial conditions which should provide artists, writers and composers of music with the necessary basis for free creative work;

(b) define, for this purpose, in adition to the legal measures connected with copyright and the protection of works of art:

(i) social measures applying to all professional artists and fiscal measures designed to assist not only collective forms of artistic creation (theatre, cinema, etc.) but also individual artists;

(ii) a policy of fellowships, prizes, State commissions, and the engagement of artists, particularly for the construction and decoration of public buildings;

(iii) a policy for the dissemination of culture (exhibitions, performances of musical and theatrical works, etc.);

(iv) a research policy that offers individual artists, groups and institutions the possibility of carrying out experiments and research in multi-purpose workshops, without feeling obliged to produce successful results, in such a way as to foster an artistic and cultural renewal;

(c) consider establishing funds to provide aid for artistic creation;

(d) encourage the endeavours of all who have a vocation for artistic creation and help young people to develop their talents without any discrimination and strengthen specialized institutions providing professional training in all the arts;

(e) promote opportunities for the publication of high-quality reproductions of artistic works, the publication and translation of literary works and the publication and performance of musical compositions;

(f) associate artists at all levels in the formulation and implementation of cultural policies;

(g) ensure the multiplicity of bodies called upon to assess works of art and the regular renewal of their membership, as well as the multiplicity of sources of finance, so as to safeguard the freedom of creative artists;

(h) give technical, administrative and financial assistance to groups of amateur artists and support co-operation between non-professional and professional artists.

Cultural Industries. 11. Member States or the appropriate authorities should make sure that the criterion of profit-making does not exert a decisive influence on cultural activities, and, in drawing up cultural policies, provide for machinery for negotiating with private cultural industries, as well as for supplementary or alternative initiatives.

Dissemination. 12. Member States or the appropriate authorities should:

(a) adopt a policy of granting subsidies and awarding prizes for cultural goods and services, and bring about conditions which will ensure that they are disseminated and become accessible to the broadest possible social categories, particularly in cultural fields neglected by commercial enterprises;

(b) take steps by means of a policy of appropriate subsidies and contracts, to further the development of the activities of cultural associations at the national, regional and local levels;

(c) give prominence to a type of dissemination which is conducive to an active frame of mind in the public rather than to passive consumption of cultural products.

Research. 13. Member States or the appropriate authorities should foster cultural development research projects which aim, *inter alia,* at evaluating current activities as well as stimulating new experiments and studying their impact on the widest possible audiences, with a view to the possible adoption of fresh measures in connexion with cultural policies.

B. Policies Related to Cultural Action. Communication. 14. Member States or the appropriate authorities should:

(a) promote all occasions for communication, such as meetings, debates, public performances, group activities, and festivals, for the purpose of encouraging dialogue and a continuous exchange of ideas between individuals, the public, creative artists, "animateurs" and producers;

(b) develop the opportunities for cultural contact and exchange provided by sports events, nature discovery expeditions, art and aesthetic education, current events and tourism;

(c) encourage the usual social intermediaries (communities, institutions, agencies, trade unions, and other groups) to promote information and free cultural expression for their members on the widest possible scale, in order to increase their awareness of and familiarize them with cultural activities;

(d) supply information that is apt to generate feedback and personal initiative;

(e) facilitate access to written works by arranging for mobile and flexible forms of dissemination, and provide for extension work in places such as libraries or reading rooms;

(f) promote extensive use of audio-visual media in order to bring the best of the culture of both past and present within the reach of large sectors of the population, including, where applicable, oral traditions, in the collection of which the media can assuredly assist;

(g) promote the active participation of audiences by enabling them to have a voice in the selection and production of programmes, by fostering the creation of a permanent flow of ideas between the public, artists and producers and by encouraging the establishment of production centres for use by audiences at local and community levels;

(h) encourage the communication media to increase the number and variety of their programmes in order to offer the widest range of choices, bearing in mind the extreme diversity of audiences, to enhance the cultural quality of programmes intended for the public at large, to select spoken and visual languages accessible to all audiences, to give preference to material which serves the purposes of information and education rather than those of propaganda and publicity and to pay special attention to the protection of national cultures from potentially harmful influences of some types of mass production;

(i) promote comparative studies and research on the reciprocal influence as between the artist, the mass media and society and on the relationship between the production and impact of cultural programmes;

(j) provide, with a view to life-long education, an introduction to audio-visual languages as well as to choosing communication media and programmes with discrimination from an early age;

(k) develop, in a general way, forms of education and training which are adapted to the special characteristics of audiences in order to make them capable of receiving, selecting and grasping the mass of information which is put into circulation in modern societies.

Education. 15. Member States or the appropriate authorities should:

(a) link cultural plans systematically with educational plans within the context of life-long education embracing the family, the school, community life, vocational training, continuing education and cultural activity;

(b) help people at large to gain access to knowledge, bearing in mind the need to create socio-economic conditions such as will allow them to participate in community life, and make whatever changes may be required in educational systems, content and methods;

(c) develop, in a systematic manner, cultural education and artistic training programmes at all levels by inviting contributions from artists and those responsible for cultural action.

Youth. 16. Member States or the appropriate authorities should offer young people a wide range of cultural activities which correspond to their needs and aspirations, encourage them to acquire a sense of social responsibility, awaken their interests in the cultural heritage of their own country and in that of all mankind and, with a view to cultural co-operation in a spirit of friendship, international understanding and peace, promote the ideals of humanism and respect for widely recognized educational and moral principles.

Environment. 17. Member States or the appropriate authorities should:

(a) set up machinery for concerted action allowing the inhabitants or their representatives to be closely associated with the preparation and implementation of town-planning projects and changes to the architectural setting in which they live, and also with the safeguarding of historic quarters, towns and sites and their integration into a modern environment;

(b) take into consideration the international instruments adopted on such issues by intergovernmental organizations.

IV. International Co-operation

18. Member States or the appropriate authorities should:

(a) strengthen bilateral and multilateral, and regional and international cultural co-operation with due regard for the generally recognized principles of international law and the ideals and objectives of the United Nations, sovereignty and independence of States, mutual advantage, and the equality of cultures;

(b) inspire in the people at large respect for other peoples and a refusal to countenance acts of international violence and policies based on force, domination and aggression;

(c) encourage the circulation of ideas and cultural values conducive to better understanding among men;

(d) develop and diversify cultural exchanges with a view to promoting an ever deeper appreciation of the values of each culture and, in particular, draw attention to the cultures of the developing countries as a mark of esteem for their cultural identity;

(e) contribute actively to the implementation of cultural projects and to the production and dissemination of works created by common endeavours, and develop direct contacts and exchanges between institutions and persons active in the cultural field, as well as research on cultural development;

(f) encourage non-governmental organizations, socio-cultural organizations for the people at large, trade unions and social and occupational groups, women's associations, youth movements, co-operatives and other organizations (for instance, artists' associations) to participate in international cultural exchanges and their development;

(g) take account, in exchanges of persons, of the mutual enrichment resulting from co-operation between specialists from different countries;

(h) bear in mind that the need for introductory courses and information on culture is all the greater when the aim is to arouse interest in the civilizations and cultures of other nations in order to open men's minds to the recognition of the plurality and equality of cultures;

(i) ensure that the messages chosen are inserted or reinserted into a universal context so that opportunities for access to culture may have significance for the whole international community;

(j) take account of the important contribution that the press, books, audio-visual media, and in particular television, can make to the mutual understanding of nations and to their knowledge of the cultural achievements of other nations; encourage the use of communication media, including tele-communication satellites, to promote the ideals of peace, human rights and fundamental freedoms, friendship among men and international understanding and co-operation, and thus create the necessary conditions to enable their national cultures to resist ideas of hatred between peoples, war, force and racism, in view of their adverse consequences and their corruptive effect on young people;

(k) provide appropriate financial facilities for activities which aim at promoting international exchanges and cultural co-operation.

V. Federal or Confederate States

19. In the implementation of this Recommendation, Member States with a federal or confederate constitution shall not be bound to carry the provisions of the Recommendation into effect when competence for the latter is constitutionally vested in each of the constituent states, provinces or cantons; in such a case, the sole obligation of the federal or confederate government concerned shall be to inform the states, provinces or cantons of those provisions and to recommend their adoption.

The foregoing is the authentic text of the Recommendation duly adopted by the General Conference of the United Nations Educational, Scientific and Cultural Organization during its nineteenth session, which was held in Nairobi, and declared closed the thirtieth day of November 1976.

In faith whereof we have appended our signatures.

UNESCO RECOMMENDATION ON THE DEVELOPMENT OF ADULT EDUCATION (1976). The recommendation, adopted by the UNESCO GENERAL CONFERENCE (19th session), held in Nairobi, on 26 November 1976, was prepared on recommendation of the Third International Conference on Adult Education, which met in Tokyo from 25 July to 7 August 1972. It calls upon UNESCO's member States to promote the development of adult education, the improvement of its content and methods, and efforts to find new educational strategies; and to put their experience with regard to adult education at the disposal of other member States by providing them with technical assistance and, in appropriate cases, with material or financial assistance.

The text of the recommendation (*UNESCO's Standard-Setting Instruments*, No. I.B.5) is as follows:

The General Conference of the United Nations Educational, Scientific and Cultural Organization, meeting in Nairobi from 26 October to 30 November 1976, at its nineteenth session,

Recalling the principles set forth in Articles 26 and 27 of the Universal Declaration of Human Rights, guaranteeing and specifying the right of everyone to education and to participate freely in cultural, artistic and scientific life and the principles set forth in Articles 13 and 15 of the International Covenant on Economic, Social and Cultural Rights,

Considering that education is inseparable from democracy, the abolition of privilege and the promotion within society as a whole of the ideas of autonomy, responsibility and dialogue,

Considering that the access of adults to education, in the context of life-long education, is a fundamental aspect of the right to education and facilitates the exercise of the right to participate in political, cultural, artistic and scientific life,

Considering that for the full development of the human personality, particularly in view of the rapid pace of scientific, technical, economic and social change, education must be considered on a global basis and as a life-long process,

Considering that the development of adult education, in the context of life-long education, is necessary as a means of achieving a more rational and more equitable distribution of educational resources between young people and adults, and between different social groups, and of ensuring better understanding and more effective collaboration between the generations and greater political, social and economic equality between social groups and between the sexes,

Convinced that adult education as an integral part of life-long education can contribute decisively to economic and cultural development, social progress and world peace as well as to the development of educational systems,

Considering that the experience acquired in adult education must constantly contribute to the renewal of educational methods, as well as to the reform of educational systems as a whole,

Considering the universal concern for literacy as being a crucial factor in political and economic development, in technological progress and in social and cultural change, so that its promotion should therefore form an integral part of any plan for adult education,

Reaffirming that the attainment of this objective entails creating situations in which the adults are able to choose, from among a variety of forms of educational activity the objectives and content of which have been defined with their collaboration, those forms which meet their needs most closely and are most directly related to their interests,

Bearing in mind the diversity of modes of training and education throughout the world and the special problems peculiar to the countries whose education systems are as yet underdeveloped or insufficiently adapted to national needs,

In order to give effect to the conclusions, declarations and recommendations formulated by the second and third international conferences on adult education (Montreal, 1960; Tokyo, 1972) and, as far as the relevant paragraphs are concerned, by the World Conference of the International Women's Year (Mexico, 1975),

Desirous of making a further contribution to putting into effect the principles set forth in the recommendations addressed by the International Conference on Public Education to the Ministries of Education concerning the access of women to education (Recommendation No. 34, 1952), facilities for education in rural areas (Recommendation No. 47, 1958), and literacy and adult education (Recommendation No. 58, 1965), in the Declaration adopted at the International Symposium for Literacy in Persepolis (1975) and in the Recommendation concerning Education for International Understanding, Co-operation and Peace, and Education relating to Human Rights and Fundamental Freedoms adopted by the General Conference at its eighteenth session (1974);

Taking note of the provisions of the Revised Recommendation concerning Technical and Vocational Education adopted by the General Conference at its eighteenth session (1974) and of resolution 3.426 adopted at that same session with a view to the adoption of an international instrument concerning action designed to ensure that the people at large have free democratic access to culture and an opportunity to take an active part in the cultural life of society,

Noting further that the International Labour Conference has adopted a number of instruments concerned with various aspects of adult education, and in particular the recommendation on vocational guidance (1949), the recommendation on vocational training in agriculture (1956), as well as the convention and recommendation concerning paid educational leave (1974), and of human resources development (1975),

Having decided, at its eighteenth session, that adult education would be the subject of a recommendation to Member States,

Adopts this twenty-sixth day of November 1976,the present Recommendation.

The General Conference recommends that Member States apply the following provisions by taking whatever legislative or other steps may be required, and in conformity with the constitutional practice of each State, to give effect to the principles set forth in this Recommendation.

The General Conference recommends that Member States bring this Recommendation to the attention of the authorities, departments or bodies responsible for adult education and also of the various organizations carrying out educational work for the benefit of adults, and of trade union organizations, associations, enterprises, and other interested parties.

The General Conference recommends that Member States report to it, at such dates and in such form as shall be determined by it, on the action taken by them in pursuance of this Recommendation.

I. Definition

1. In this Recommendation:

the term "adult education" denotes the entire body of organized educational processes, whatever the content, level and method, whether formal or otherwise, whether they prolong or replace initial education in schools, colleges and universities as well as in apprenticeship, whereby persons regarded as adult by the society to which they belong develop their abilities, enrich their knowledge, improve their technical or professional qualifications or turn them in a new direction and bring about changes in their attitudes or behaviour in the twofold perspective of full personal development and participation in balanced and independent social, economic and cultural development;

adult education, however, must not be considered as an entity in itself; it is a subdivision, and an integral part of, a global scheme for life-long education and learning;

the term "life-long education and learning", for its part, denotes an overall scheme aimed both at restructuring the existing education system and at developing the entire educational potential outside the education system;

in such a scheme men and women are the agents of their own education, through continual interaction between their thoughts and actions;

education and learning, far from being limited to the period of attendance at school, should extend throughout life, include all skills and branches of knowledge, use all possible means, and give the opportunity to all people for full development of the personality;

the educational and learning processes in which children, young people and adults of all ages are involved in the course of their lives, in whatever form, should be conqsidered as a whole.

II. Objectives and Strategy

2. Generally speaking, the aims of adult education should be to contribute to:

(a) promoting work for peace, international understanding and co-operation;

(b) developing a critical understanding of major con-

temporary problems and social changes and the ability to play an active part in the progress of society with a view to achieving social justice;

(c) promoting increased awareness of the relationship between people and their physical and cultural environment, and fostering the desire to improve the environment and to respect and protect nature, the common heritage and public property;

(d) creating an understanding of and respect for the diversity of customs and cultures, on both the national and the international planes;

(e) promoting increased awareness of, and giving effect to various forms of communication and solidarity at the family, local, national, regional and international levels;

(f) developing the aptitude for acquiring, either individually, in groups or in the context of organized study in educational establishments specially set up for this purpose, new knowledge, qualifications, attitudes or forms of behaviour conducive to the full maturity of the personality;

(g) ensuring the individuals' conscious and effective incorporation into working life by providing men and women with an advanced technical and vocational education and developing the ability to create, either individually or in groups, new material goods and new spiritual or aesthetic values;

(h) developing the ability to grasp adequately the problems involved in the upbringing of children;

(i) developing the aptitude for making creative use of leisure and for acquiring any necessary or desired knowledge;

(j) developing the necessary discernment in using mass communication media, in particular radio, television, cinema and the press, and interpreting the various messages addressed to modern men and women by society;

(k) developing the aptitude for learning to learn.

3. Adult education should be based on the following principles:

(a) it should be based on the needs of the participants and make use of their different experiences in the development of adult education; the most educationally underprivileged groups should be given the highest priority within a perspective of collective advancement;

(b) it should rely on the ability and determination of all human beings to make progress throughout their lives both at the level of their personal development and in relation to their social activity;

(c) it should awaken an interest in reading and develop cultural aspirations;

(d) it should stimulate and sustain the interest of adult learners, appeal to their experience, strengthen their self-reliance, and enlist their active participation at all stages of the educational process in which they are involved;

(e) it should be adapted to the actual conditions of everyday life and work and take into account the personal characteristics of adult learners, their age, family, social, occupational or residential background and the way in which these interrelate;

(f) it should seek the participation of individual adults, groups and communities in decision-making at all levels of the learning process; including determination of needs, curriculum development, programme implementation and evaluation and should plan educational activities with a view to the transformation of the working environment and of the life of adults;

(g) it should be organized and operated flexibly by

taking into account social, cultural, economic and institutional factors of each country and society to which adult learners belong;

(h) it should contribute to the economic and social development of the entire community;

(i) it should recognize as an integral part of the educational process the forms of collective organization established by adults with a view to solving their day-to-day problems;

(j) it should recognize that every adult, by virtue of his or her experience of life, is the vehicle of a culture which enables him or her to play the role of both learner and teacher in the educational process in which he or she participates.

4. Each Member State should:

(a) recognize adult education as a necessary and specific component of its education system and as a permanent element in its social, cultural and economic development policy; it should, consequently, promote the creation of structures, the preparation and implementation of programmes and the application of educational methods which meet the needs and aspirations of all categories of adults, without restriction on grounds of sex, race, geographical origin, age, social status, opinion, belief or prior educational standard;

(b) recognize that although, in a given situation or for a specific period, adult education may play a compensatory role, it is not intended as a substitute for adequate youth education which is a prerequisite for the full success of adult education;

(c) in eliminating the isolation of women from adult education, work towards ensuring equality of access and full participation in the entire range of adult education activities, including those which provide training for qualifications leading to activities or responsibilities which have hitherto been reserved for men;

(d) take measures with a view to promoting participation in adult education and community development programmes by members of the most underprivileged groups, whether rural or urban, settled or nomadic, and in particular illiterates, young people who have been unable to acquire an adequate standard of general education or a qualification, migrant workers and refugees, unemployed workers, members of ethnic minorities, persons suffering from a physical or mental handicap, persons experiencing difficulties of social adjustment and those serving prison sentences. In this context, Member States should associate themselves in the search for educational strategies designed to foster more equitable relations among social groups.

5. The place of adult education in each education system should be defined with a view to achieving:

(a) a rectification of the main inequalities in access to initial education and training, in particular inequalities based on age, sex, social position or social or geographical origin;

(b) the assurance of a scientific basis for life-long education and learning as well as greater flexibility in the way in which people divide their lives between education and work, and, in particular, providing for the alternation of periods of education and work throughout the life span, and facilitating the integration of continuing education into the activity of work itself;

(c) recognition, and increased exploitation, of the actual or potential educational value of the adult's various experiences;

(d) easy transfer from one type or level of education to another;

(e) greater interaction between the education system and its social, cultural and economic setting;

(f) greater efficiency from the point of view of the contribution of educational expenditure to social, cultural and economic development.

6. Consideration should be given to the need for an adult education component, including literacy, in the framing and execution of any development programme.

7. The objectives and goals of adult education policy should be incorporated in national development plans; they should be defined in relation to the overall objectives of education policy and of social, cultural and economic development policies.

Adult education and other forms of education, particularly school and higher education and initial vocational training, should be conceived and organized as equally essential components in a co-ordinated but differentiated education system according to the tenets of life-long education and learning.

8. Measures should be taken to encourage the public authorities, institutions or bodies engaged in education, voluntary associations, workers' and employers' organizations, and those directly participating in adult education, to collaborate in the task of defining further and giving effect to these objectives.

III. Content of Adult Education

9. Adult education activities, viewed as forming part of life-long education and learning, have no theoretical boundaries and should meet the particular situations created by the specific needs of development, of participation in community life and of individual self-fulfilment; they cover all aspects of life and all fields of knowledge and are addressed to all people whatever their level of achievement. In defining the content of adult education activities priority should be given to the specific needs of the educationally most underprivileged groups.

10. Civic, political, trade union and co-operative education activities should be aimed particularly towards developing independent and critical judgement and implanting or enhancing the abilities required by each individual in order to cope with changes affecting living and working conditions, by effective participation in the management of social affairs at every level of the decision-making process.

11. While not excluding approaches intended to achieve a short-term solution in a particular situation, technical and vocational education activities should as a general rule emphasize the acquisition of qualifications which are sufficiently broad to allow of subsequent changes of occupation and a critical understanding of the problems of working life. It is necessary to integrate general and civic education with technical and vocational education.

12. Activities designed to promote cultural development and artistic creation should encourage appreciation of existing cultural and artistic values and works and, at the same time, should aim to promote the creation of new values and new works, by releasing the expressive capabilities inherent in each individual or group.

13. Participation in adult education should not be restricted on grounds of sex, race, geographical origin, culture, age, social status, experience, belief and prior educational standard.

14. With regard to women, adult education activities

should be integrated as far as possible with the whole contemporary social movement directed towards achieving self-determination for women and enabling them to contribute to the life of society as a collective force, and should thus focus specifically on certain aspects, in particular:

(a) the establishment in each society of conditions of equality between men and women;

(b) the emancipation of men and women from the preconceived models imposed on them by society in every field in which they carry responsibility;

(c) civic, occupational, psychological, cultural and economic autonomy for women as a necessary condition for their existence as complete individuals;

(d) knowledge about the status of women, and about women's movements, in various societies, with a view to increased solidarity across frontiers.

15. With regard to settled or nomadic rural populations, adult education activities should be designed in particular to:

(a) enable them to use technical procedures and methods of individual or joint organization likely to improve their standard of living without obliging them to forgo their own values;

(b) put an end to the isolation of individuals or groups;

(c) prepare individuals or groups of individuals who are obliged, despite the efforts made to prevent excessive depopulation of rural areas, to leave agriculture, either to engage in a new occupational activity while remaining in a rural environment, or to leave this environment for a new way of life.

16. With regard to such persons or groups as have remained illiterate or are experiencing difficulty in adjusting to society because of the slenderness of their resources, their limited education or their restricted participation in community life, adult education activities should be designed not only to enable them to acquire basic knowledge (reading, writing, arithmetic, basic understanding of natural and social phenomena), but also to make it easier for them to engage in productive work, to promote their self-awareness and their grasp of the problems of hygiene, health, household management and the upbringing of children, and to enhance their autonomy and increase their participation in community life.

17. With regard to young people who have been unable to acquire an adequate standard of general education or a qualification, adult education activities should, in particular, enable them to acquire additional general education with a view to developing their ability to understand the problems of society and shoulder social responsibilities, and to gaining access to the vocational training and general education which are necessary for the exercise of an occupational activity.

18. If people wish to acquire educational or vocational qualifications which are formally attested by certificates of education or of vocational aptitude and which, for social or economic reasons, they have not been able to obtain earlier, adult education should enable them to obtain the training required for the award of such certificates.

19. With regard to the physically or mentally handicapped, adult education activities should be designed, in particular, to restore or offset the physical or mental capacities which have been impaired or lost as a result of their handicap, and to enable them to acquire the knowledge and skills and, where necessary, the professional qualifica-

tions required for their social life and for the exercise of an occupational activity compatible with their handicap.

20. With regard to migrant workers, refugees, and ethnic minorities, adult education activities should in particular:

(a) enable them to acquire the linguistic and general knowledge as well as the technical or professional qualifications necessary for their temporary or permanent assimilation in the society of the host country and, where appropriate, their reassimilation in the society of their country of origin;

(b) keep them in touch with culture, current developments and social changes in their country of origin.

21. With regard to unemployed persons, including the educated unemployed, adult education activities should be designed, in particular, to adapt or modify their technical or professional qualification with a view to enabling them to find or return to employment and to promote a critical understanding of their socio-economic situation.

22. With regard to ethnic minorities, adult education activities should enable them to express themselves freely, educate themselves and their children in their mother tongues, develop their own cultures and learn languages other than their mother tongues.

23. With regard to the aged, adult education activities should be designed, in particular:

(a) to give all a better understanding of contemporary problems and of the younger generation;

(b) to help acquire leisure skills, promote health and find increased meaning in life;

(c) to provide a grounding in the problems facing retired people and in ways of dealing with such problems, for the benefit of those who are on the point of leaving working life;

(d) to enable those who have left working life to retain their physical and intellectual faculties and to continue to participate in community life and also to give them access to fields of knowledge or types of activity which have not been open to them during their working life.

V. Methods, Means, Research and Evaluation

24. Adult education methods should take account of:

(a) incentives and obstacles to participation and learning specially affecting adults;

(b) the experience gained by adults in the exercise of their family, social and occupational responsibilities;

(c) the family, social or occupational obligations borne by adults and the fatigue and impaired alertness which may result from them;

(d) the ability of adults to assume responsibility for their own learning;

(e) the cultural and pedagogical level of the teaching personnel available;

(f) the psychological characteristics of the learning process;

(g) the existence and characteristics of cognitive interests;

(h) use of leisure time.

25. Adult education activities should normally be planned and executed on the basis of identified needs, problems, wants and resources, as well as defined objectives. Their impact should be evaluated, and reinforced by whatever follow-up activities may be most appropriate to given conditions.

26. Particular emphasis should be placed on adult education activities intended for an entire social or geographical

entity, mobilizing all its inherent energies with a view to the advancement of the group and social progress in a community setting.

27. In order to encourage the broadest possible participation, it may be appropriate in some situations to add, to locally based adult education, methods such as:

(a) remote teaching programmes such as correspondence courses and radio or television broadcasts, the intended recipients of such programmes being invited to form groups with a view to listening or working together (such groups should receive appropriate pedagogical support);

(b) programmes launched by mobile units;

(c) self-teaching programmes;

(d) study circles;

(e) use of voluntary work by teachers, students and other community members.

The various services which public cultural institutions (libraries, museums, record libraries, video-cassette libraries) are able to put at the disposal of adult learners should be developed on a systematic basis, together with new types of institutions specializing in adult education.

28. Participation in an adult education programme should be a voluntary matter. The State and other bodies should strive to promote the desire of individuals and groups for education in the spirit of life-long education and learning.

29. Relations between the adult learner and the adult educator should be established on a basis of mutual respect and co-operation.

30. Participation in an adult education programme should be subject only to the ability to follow the course of training provided and not to any (upper) age limit or any condition concerning the possession of a diploma or qualification; any aptitude tests on the basis of which a selection might be made if necessary should be adapted to the various categories of candidates taking such tests.

31. It should be possible to acquire and accumulate learning, experiences and qualifications through intermittent participation. Rights and qualifications obtained in this way should be equivalent to those granted by the systems of formalized education or of such character as to allow for continued education within this.

32. The methods used in adult education should not appeal to a competitive spirit but should develop in the adult learners a shared sense of purpose and habits of participation, mutual help, collaboration and team work.

33. Adult education programmes for the improvement of technical or professional qualifications should, as far as possible, be organized during working time and, in the case of seasonal work, during the slack season. This should, as a general rule, be applied also to other forms of education, in particular literacy programmes and trade union education.

34. The premises necessary for the development of adult education activities should be provided; depending on the case, these may be premises used exclusively for adult education, with or without residential accommodation, or multi-purpose or integrated facilities or premises generally used or capable of being used for other purposes—in particular, clubs, workshops, school, university and scientific establishments, social, cultural or socio-cultural centres or open air sites.

35. Member States should actively encourage co-operative research in all aspects of adult education and its objectives. Research programmes should have a practical basis. They should be carried out by universities, adult education bodies and research bodies, adopting an interdisciplinary approach. Measures should be taken with a view to disseminating the experience and the results of the research programmes to those concerned at the national and international levels.

36. Systematic evaluation of adult education activities is necessary to secure optimum results from the resources put into them. For evaluation to be effective it should be built into the programmes of adult education at all levels and stages.

V. The Structures of Adult Education

37. Member States should endeavour to ensure the establishment and development of a network of bodies meeting the needs of adult education; this network should be sufficiently flexible to meet the various personal and social situations and their evolution.

38. Measures should be taken in order to:

(a) identify and anticipate educational needs capable of being satisfied through adult education programmes;

(b) make full use of existing educational facilities and create such facilities as may be lacking to meet all defined objectives;

(c) make the necessary long-term investments for the development of adult education; in particular for the professional education of planners, administrators, those who train educators, organizational and training personnel, the preparation of educational strategies and methods suitable for adults, the provision of capital facilities, the production and provision of the necessary basic equipment such as visual aids, apparatus and technical media;

(d) encourage exchanges of experience and compile and disseminate statistical and other information on the strategies, structures, content, methods and results, both quantitative and qualitative, of adult education;

(e) abolish economic and social obstacles to participation in education, and to systematically bring the nature and form of adult education programmes to the attention of all potential beneficiaries, but especially to the most disadvantaged, by using such means as active canvassing by adult education institutions and voluntary organizations, to inform, counsel and encourage possible and often hesitant participants in adult education.

39. In order to achieve these objectives it will be necessary to mobilize organizations and institutions specifically concerned with adult education; and the full range, both public and private of schools, universities, cultural and scientific establishments, libraries and museums, and, in addition, other institutions not primarily concerned with adult education, such as:

(a) mass information bodies: the press, radio and television;

(b) voluntary associations and consortia;

(c) professional, trade union, family and co-operative organizations;

(d) families;

(e) industrial and commercial firms which may contribute to the training of their employees;

(f) educators, technicians or qualified experts working on an individual basis;

(g) any persons or groups who are in a position to make a contribution by virtue of their education, training, experience or professional or social activities and are both willing and able to apply the principles set forth in the Preamble and the objectives and strategy outlined in the Recommendation;

(h) the adult learners themselves.

40. Member States should encourage schools, vocational education establishments, colleges and institutions of higher education to regard adult education programmes as an integral part of their own activities and to participate in action designed to promote the development of such programmes provided by other institutions, in particular by making available their own teaching staff, conducting research and training the necessary personnel.

VI. Training and Status of Persons Engaged in Adult Education Work

41. It should be recognized that adult education calls for special skills, knowledge, understanding and attitudes on the part of those who are involved in providing it, in whatever capacity and for any purpose. It is desirable therefore that they should be recruited with care according to their particular functions and receive initial and in-service training for them according to their needs and those of the work in which they are engaged.

42. Measures should be taken to ensure that the various specialists who have a useful contribution to make to the work of adult education take part in those activities, whatever their nature or purpose.

43. In addition to the employment of full-time professional workers, measures should be taken to enlist the support of anyone capable of making a contribution, regular or occasional, paid or voluntary, to adult education activities, of any kind. Voluntary involvement and participation in all aspects of organizing and teaching are of crucial importance, and people with all kinds of skills are able to contribute to them.

44. Training for adult education should, as far as practicable, include all those aspects of skill, knowledge, understanding and personal attitude which are relevant to the various functions undertaken, taking into account the general background against which adult education takes place. By integrating these aspects with each other, training should itself be a demonstration of sound adult education practice.

45. Conditions of work and remuneration for full-time staff in adult education should be comparable to those of workers in similar posts elsewhere, and those for paid part-time staff should be appropriately regulated, without detriment to their main occupation.

VII. Relations between Adult Education and Youth Education

46. The education of young people should progressively be oriented towards life-long education and learning, taking into account the experience gained in regard to adult education, with a view to preparing young people, whatever their social origins, to take part in adult education or to contribute to providing it.

To this end, measures should be taken with a view to:

(a) making access to all levels of education and training more widely available;

(b) removing the barriers between disciplines and also between types and levels of education;

(c) modifying school and training syllabuses with the aim of maintaining and stimulating intellectual curiosity, and also placing greater emphasis, alongside the acquisition of knowledge, on the development of self-teaching patterns of behaviour, a critical outlook, a reflective attitude and creative abilities;

(d) rendering school institutions of higher education and training establishments increasingly open to their economic and social environment and linking education and work more firmly together;

(e) informing young people at school and young people leaving full-time education or initial training of the opportunities offered by adult education;

(f) bringing together, where desirable, adults and adolescents in the same training programme;

(g) associating youth movements with adult education ventures.

47. In cases where a training course organized as part of adult education leads to the acquisition of a qualification in respect of which a diploma or certificate is awarded when the qualification is acquired through study in school or university, such training should be recognized by the award of a diploma or certificate having equal status. Adult education programmes which do not lead to the acquisition of a qualification similar to those in respect of which a diploma or certificate is awarded should, in appropriate cases, be recognized by an award.

48. Adult education programmes for youth need to be given the highest priority because in most parts of the world the youth form an extremely large segment of society and their education is of the greatest importance for political, economic, social and cultural development of the society in which they live. The programmes of adult education for youth should take account not only of their learning needs, but should enable them to orient themselves for the society of the future.

VIII. The Relations between Adult Education and Work

49. Having regard to the close connection between guaranteeing the right to education and the right to work, and to the need to promote the participation of all, whether wage-earners or not, in adult education programmes, not only by reducing the constraints to which they are subject but also by providing them with the opportunity of using in their work the knowledge, qualifications or aptitudes which adult education programmes are designed to make available to them, and of finding in work a source of personal fulfilment and advancement, and a stimulus to creative activity in both work and social life, measures should be taken:

(a) to ensure that, in the formulation of the curriculum of adult education programmes and activities, the working experience of adults should be taken into account;

(b) to improve the organization and conditions of work and, in particular, to alleviate the arduous character of work and reduce and adjust working hours;

(c) to promote the granting of educational leave during working time, without loss of remuneration or subject to the payment of compensatory remuneration and payments for the purpose of offsetting the cost of the education received and to use any other appropriate aid to facilitate education or updating during working life;

(d) to protect the employment of persons thus assisted;

(e) to offer comparable facilities to housewives and other homemakers and to non-wage-earners, particularly those of limited means.

50. Member States should encourage or facilitate the inclusion in collective labour agreements of clauses bearing on adult education, and in particular clauses stipulating:

(a) the nature of the material possibilities and financial benefits extended to employees, and in particular those employed in sectors where rapid technological change is taking place or those threatened with being laid off, with a view to their participation in adult education programmes;

(b) the manner in which technical or professional qualifications acquired through adult education are taken into account in determining the employment category and in establishing the level of remuneration.

51. Member States should also invite employers:

(a) to anticipate and publicize, by level and type of qualification, their skilled manpower requirements and the methods of recruitment which are envisaged to meet such needs;

(b) to organize or develop a recruitment system such as will encourage their employees to seek to improve their occupational qualifications.

52. In connection with adult training programmes organized by employers for their staff, Member States should encourage them to ensure that:

(a) employees participate in the preparation of the programmes;

(b) those taking part in such programmes are chosen in consultation with the workers' representative bodies;

(c) participants receive a certificate of training or paper qualification on completion of the programme enabling them to satisfy third parties that they have completed a given course or received a given qualification.

53. Measures should be taken with a view to promoting the participation of adults belonging to labouring, agricultural or craft communities in the implementation of adult education programmes intended for such communities; to this end they should be granted special facilities with the aim of enabling the workers to take those decisions which primarily concern them.

IX. Management, Administration, Co-ordination and Financing of Adult Education

54. There should be set up, at all levels, international, regional, national and local:

(a) structures or procedures for consultation and co-ordination between public authorities which are competent in the field of adult education;

(b) structures or procedures for consultation, co-ordination and harmonization between the said public authorities, the representatives of adult learners and the entire range of bodies carrying out adult education programmes or activities designed to promote the development of such programmes.

It should be among the principal functions of these structures, for which resources should be made available, to identify the objectives, to study the obstacles encountered, to propose and, where appropriate, carry out the measures necessary for implementation of the adult education policy and to evaluate the progress made.

55. There should be set up at national level, and, where appropriate, at sub-national level, structures for joint action and co-operation between the public authorities and bodies responsible for adult education on the one hand and the public or private bodies responsible for radio and television on the other.

It should be among the principal functions of these structures to study, propose and, where appropriate, carry out measures designed to:

(a) ensure that the mass media make a substantial contribution to leisure-time occupations and to the education of the people;

(b) guarantee freedom of expression, through the mass media, for all opinions and trends in the field of adult education;

(c) promote the cultural or scientific value and the educational qualities of programmes as a whole;

(d) establish a two-way flow of exchanges between those responsible for or those professionally engaged in educational programmes broadcast by radio or television and the persons for whom the programmes are intended.

56. Member States should ensure that the public authorities, while assuming their own specific responsibilities for the development of adult education:

(a) encourage, by laying down an appropriate legal and financial framework, the creation and development of adult education associations and consortia on a voluntary and administratively independent basis;

(b) provide competent non-governmental bodies participating in adult education programmes, or in action designed to promote such programmes, with technical or financial resources enabling them to carry out their task;

(c) see that such non-governmental bodies enjoy the freedom of opinion and the technical and educational autonomy which are necessary in order to give effect to the principles set forth in paragraph 2 above;

(d) take appropriate measures to ensure the educational and technical efficiency and quality of programmes or action conducted by bodies in receipt of contributions from public funds.

57. The proportion of public funds, and particularly of public funds earmarked for education, allocated to adult education, should match the importance of such education for social, cultural and economic development, as recognized by each Member State within the framework of this Recommendation. The total allocation of funds to adult education should cover at least:

(a) provision of suitable facilities or adaptation of existing facilities;

(b) production of all kinds of learning materials;

(c) remuneration and further training of educators;

(d) research and information expenses;

(e) compensation for loss of earnings;

(f) tuition, and, where necessary and if possible, accommodation and travel costs of trainees.

58. Arrangements should be made to ensure, on a regular basis, the necessary funds for adult education programmes and action designed to promote the development of such programmes; it should be recognized that the public authorities, including local authorities, credit organizations, provident societies and national insurance agencies where they exist, and employers should contribute to these funds to an extent commensurate with their respective responsibilities and resources.

59. The necessary measures should be taken to obtain optimum use of resources made available for adult education. All available resources, both material and human, should be mobilized to this end.

60. For the individual, lack of funds should not be an obstacle to participation in adult education programmes. Member States should ensure that financial assistance for study purposes is available for those who need it to undertake adult education. The participation of members of underprivileged social groups should, as a general rule, be free of charge.

X. International Co-operation

61. Member States should strengthen their co-operation, whether on a bilateral or multilateral basis, with a view to promoting the development of adult education, the improvement of its content and methods, and efforts to find new educational strategies.

To this end, they should endeavour to incorporate specific clauses bearing on adult education in international agreements concerned with co-operation in the fields of education, science and culture, and to promote the development and strengthening of adult education work in Unesco.

62. Member States should put their experience with regard to adult education at the disposal of other Member States by providing them with technical assistance and, in appropriate cases, with material or financial assistance.

They should systematically support adult education activities conducted in countries so wishing, through Unesco and through other international organizations, including non-governmental organizations, with a view to social, cultural and economic development in the countries concerned.

Care should be taken to ensure that international co-operation does not take the form of a mere transfer of structures, curricula, methods and techniques which have originated elsewhere, but consists rather in promoting and stimulating development within the countries concerned, through the establishment of appropriate institutions and well co-ordinated structures adapted to the particular circumstances of those countries.

63. Measures should be taken at national, regional and international level:

(a) with a view to making regular exchanges of information and documentation on the strategies, structures, content, methods and results of adult education and on relevant research;

(b) with a view to training educators capable of working away from their home country, particularly under bilateral or multilateral technical assistance programmes.

These exchanges should be made on a systematic basis, particularly between countries facing the same problems and so placed as to be capable of applying the same solutions; to this end, meetings should be organized, more especially on a regional or sub-regional basis, with a view to publicizing relevant experiments and studying to what extent they are reproducible; similarly, joint machinery should be set up in order to ensure a better return on the research which is undertaken.

Member States should foster agreements on the preparation and adoption of international standards in important fields, such as the teaching of foreign languages and basic studies, with a view to helping create a universally accepted unit-credit system.

64. Measures should be taken with a view to the optimum dissemination and utilization of audio-visual equipment and materials, as well as educational programmes and the material objects in which they are embodied. In particular, it would be appropriate:

(a) to adapt such dissemination and utilization to the various countries' social needs and conditions, bearing in mind their specific cultural characteristics and level of development;

(b) to remove, as far as possible, the obstacles to such dissemination and utilization resulting from the regulations governing commercial or intellectual property.

65. In order to facilitate international co-operation, Member States should apply to adult education the standards recommended at international level, in particular with regard to the presentation of statistical data.

66. Member States should support the action undertaken by Unesco, as the United Nations Specialized Agency competent in this field, in its efforts to develop adult education, particularly in the fields of training, research and evaluation.

67. Member States should regard adult education as a matter of global and universal concern, and should deal with the practical consequences which arise therefrom, furthering the establishment of a new international order, to which Unesco, as an expression of the world community in educational, scientific and cultural matters, is committed.

The foregoing is the authentic text of the Recommendation duly adopted by the General Conference of the United Nations Educational, Scientific and Cultural Organization during its nineteenth session, which was held in Nairobi and declared closed the thirtieth day of November 1976.

In faith whereof we have appended our signatures.

UNESCO RECOMMENDATION ON THE STATUS OF SCIENTIFIC RESEARCHERS (1974). The

recommendation, adopted by the UNESCO GENERAL CONFERENCE (18th session), held in Paris, on 20 November 1974, sets out measures to be taken by UNESCO member States to assist and encourage the development of scientific researchers of integrity and maturity and to enable everyone within its jurisdiction to share in scientific advancement and its benefits.

The text of the recommendation (*UNESCO's Standard-Setting Instruments,* No. II.B.1) is as follows:

The General Conference of the United Nations Educational, Scientific and Cultural Organization (Unesco), meeting in Paris from 17 October to 23 November 1974 at its eighteenth session,

Recalling that, by the terms of the final paragraph of the Preamble to its Constitution, Unesco seeks—by means of promoting (*inter alia*) the scientific relations of the peoples of the world—to advance the objectives of international peace and of the common welfare of mankind for which the United Nations Organization was established and which its Charter proclaims,

Considering the terms of the Universal Declaration of Human Rights adopted by the United Nations General Assembly on 10 December 1948, and in particular Article 27.1 thereof which provides that everyone has the right freely to participate in the cultural life of the community, and to share in scientific advancement and its benefits,

Recognizing that:

(a) scientific discoveries and related technological developments and applications open up vast prospects for progress made possible in particular by the optimum utilization of science and scientific methods for the benefit of mankind and for the preservation of peace and the reduction of international tensions but may, at the same time, entail certain dangers which constitute a threat especially in cases where the results of scientific research are used against mankind's vital interests in order to prepare wars involving destruction on a massive scale or for purposes of the exploitation of one nation by another, and in any event give rise to complex ethical and legal problems;

(b) to face this challenge, Member States should develop or devise machinery for the formulation and execution of adequate science and technology policies, that is to say, policies designed to avoid the possible dangers and fully realize and exploit the positive prospects inherent in such discoveries, technological developments and applications;

Recognizing also:

(a) that a cadre of talented and trained personnel is the cornerstone of an indigenous research and experimental development capability and indispensable for the utilization and exploitation of research carried out elsewhere;

(b) that open communication of the results, hypotheses and opinions—as suggested by the phrase "academic freedom"—lies at the very heart of the scientific process, and provides the strongest guarantee of accuracy and objectivity of scientific results;

(c) the necessity of adequate support and essential equipment for performance of research and experimental development;

Observing that, in all parts of the world, this aspect of policy-making is coming to assume increasing importance for the Member States; having in mind the intergovernmental initiatives set out in the Annex to this recommendation, demonstrating recognition by Member States of the growing value of science and technology for tackling various world problems on a broad international basis, thereby strengthening co-operation among nations as well as promoting the development of individual nations; and confident that these trends predispose Member States to the taking of concrete action for the introduction and pursuit of adequate science and technology policies,

Persuaded that such government action can considerably assist in the creation of those conditions which encourage and assist indigenous capability to perform research and experimental development in an enhanced spirit of responsibility towards man and his environment,

Believing that one of the foremost of these conditions must be to ensure a fair status for those who actually perform research and experimental development in science and technology, taking due account of the responsibilities inherent in and the rights necessary to the performance of that work,

Considering that scientific research activity is carried out in exceptional working conditions and demands a highly responsible attitude on the part of the scientific researchers towards that work, towards their country and towards the international ideals and objectives of the United Nations, and that workers in this profession accordingly need an appropriate status,

Convinced that the current climate of governmental, scientific and public opinion makes the moment opportune for the General Conference to formulate principles for the assistance of member governments desirous of ensuring fair status for the workers concerned,

Recalling that much valuable work in this respect has already been accomplished both in respect of workers generally and in respect of scientific researchers in particular, notably by the international instruments and other texts recalled in this Preamble, and in the annex to this recommendation,

Conscious that the phenomenon frequently known as the "Brain Drain" of scientific researchers has in the past caused widespread anxiety, and that to certain Member States it continues to be a matter of considerable preoccupation; having present in mind, in this respect, the paramount needs of the developing countries; and desiring accordingly to give scientific researchers stronger reasons for serving in countries and areas which stand most in need of their services,

Convinced that similar questions arise in all countries with regard to the status of scientific researchers and that these questions call for the adoption of the common approaches and so far as practicable the application of the common standards and measures which it is the purpose of this recommendation to set out,

However, taking fully into account, in the adoption and application of this Recommendation, the great diversity of the laws, regulations and customs which, in different countries, determine the pattern and organization of research work and experimental development in science and technology,

Desiring for these reasons to complement the standards and recommendations set out in the laws and decrees of every country and sanctioned by its customs and those contained in the international instruments and other documents referred to in this Preamble and in the annex to this recommendation, by provisions relating to questions of central concern to scientific researchers,

Having before it, as item 26 of the agenda of the session, proposals concerning the status of scientific researchers,

Having decided, at its seventeenth session, that these proposals should take the form of a recommendation to Member States,

Adopts this Recommendation this twentieth day of November 1974.

The General Conference recommends that Member States should apply the following provisions by taking whatever legislative or other steps may be required to apply within their respective territories the principles and norms set forth in this recommendation.

The General Conference recommends that Member States should bring this recommendation to the attention of the authorities, institutions and enterprises responsible for the conduct of research and experimental development and the application of its results, and of the various organizations representing or promoting the interests of scientific researchers in association, and other interested parties.

The General Conference recommends that Member States should report to it, on dates and in a manner to be determined by it, on the action they have taken to give effect to this recommendation.

I. Scope of Application

1. For the purposes of this recommendation:

(a) (i) The word "science" signifies the enterprise whereby mankind, acting individually or in small or large groups, makes an organized attempt, by means of the objective study of observed phenomena, to discover and master the chain of causalities; brings together in a co-ordinated form the resultant sub-systems of knowledge by means of systematic reflection and conceptualization, often largely expressed in the symbols of mathematics; and thereby furnishes itself with the opportunity of using, to its own advantage, understanding of the processes and phenomena occurring in nature and society.

(ii) The expression "the sciences" signifies a complex of fact and hypothesis, in which the theoretical element is normally capable of being validated, and to that extent includes the sciences concerned with social facts and phenomena.

(b) the word "technology" signifies such knowledge as relates directly to the production or improvement of goods or services.

(c) (i) The expression "scientific research" signifies those processes of study, experiment, conceptualization and theory-testing involved in the generation of scientific knowledge, as described in paragraphs 1 (a) (i) and 1 (a) (ii) above.

(ii) The expression "experimental development" signifies the processes of adaptation, testing and refinement which lead to the point of practical applicability.

(d) (i) the expression "scientific researchers" signifies those persons responsible for investigating a specific domain in science or technology.

(ii) On the basis of the provisions of this recommendation, each Member State may determine the criteria for inclusion in the category of persons recognized as scientific researchers (such as possession of diplomas, degrees, academic titles or functions), as well as the exceptions to be allowed for.

(e) The word "status" was used in relation to scientific researchers signifies the standing or regard accorded them, as evidenced, first, by the level of appreciation both of the duties and responsibilities inherent in their function and of their competence in performing them, and, secondly, by the rights, working conditions, material assistance and moral support which they enjoy for the accomplishment of their task.

2. This recommendation applies to all scientific researchers, irrespective of:

(a) the legal status of their employer, or the type of organization or establishment in which they work;

(b) their scientific or technological fields of specialization;

(c) the motivation underlying the scientific research and experimental development in which they engage;

(d) the kind of application to which that scientific research and experimental development relates most immediately.

3. In the case of scientific researchers performing scientific research and experimental development on a part-time basis, this recommendation applies to them only at such times and in such contexts as they are engaged upon the activity of scientific research and experimental development.

II. Scientific Researchers in the Context of National Policy-making

4. Each Member State should strive to use scientific and technological knowledge for the enhancement of the cultural and material well-being of its citizens, and to further the United Nations ideals and objectives. To attain this objective each Member State should equip itself with the personnel, institutions and mechanisms necessary for developing and putting into practice national science and technology policies aimed at directing scientific research and experimental development efforts to the achievement of national goals while according a sufficient place to science *per se*. By the policies they adopt in respect of science and technology, by the way in which they use science and technology in policy-making generally, and by their treat-

ment of scientific researchers in particular, Member States should demonstrate that science and technology are not activities to be carried on in isolation but part of the nations' integrated effort to set up a society that will be more humane and really just.

5. At all appropriate stages of their national planning generally, and of their planning in science and technology specifically. Member States should:

(a) treat public funding of scientific research and experimental development as a form of public investment the returns on which are, for the most part, necessarily long term; and

(b) take all appropriate measure to ensure that the justification for, and indeed the indispensability of such expenditure is held constantly before public opinion.

6. Member States should make every effort to translate into terms of international policies and practices, their awareness of the need to apply science and technology in a great variety of specific fields of wider than national concern: namely, such vast and complex problems as the preservation of international peace and the elimination of want and other problems which can only be effectively tackled on an international basis, such as pollution monitoring and control, weather forecasting and earthquake prediction.

7. Member States should cultivate opportunities for scientific researchers to participate in the outlining of national scientific research and experimental development policy. In particular, each Member State should ensure that these processes are supported by appropriate institutional mechanisms enjoying adequate advice and assistance from scientific researchers and their professional organizations.

8. Each Member State should institute procedures adapted to its needs for ensuring that, in the performance of publicly-supported scientific research and experimental development, scientific researchers respect public accountability while at the same time enjoying the degree of autonomy appropriate to their task and to the advancement of science and technology. It should be fully taken into account that creative activities of scientific researchers should be promoted in the national science policy on the basis of utmost respect for the autonomy and freedom of research necessary to scientific progress.

9. With the above ends in view, and with respect for the principle of freedom of movement of scientific researchers, Member States should be concerned to create that general climate, and to provide those specific measures for the moral and material support and encouragement of scientific researchers, as will:

(a) ensure that young people of high calibre find sufficient attraction in the vocation, and sufficient confidence in scientific research and experimental development as a career offering reasonable prospects and a fair degree of security, to maintain a constantly adequate regeneration of the nation's scientific and technological personnel;

(b) facilitate the emergence and stimulate the appropriate growth, among its own citizens, of a body of scientific researchers regarding themselves and regarded by their colleagues throughout the world as worthy members of the international scientific and technological community.

(c) encourage a situation in which the majority of scientific researchers or young people who aspire to become scientific researchers are provided with the necessary incentives to work in the service of their country and to return there if they seek some of their education, training or experience abroad.

III. The Initial Education and Training of Scientific Researchers

10. Member States should have regard for the fact that effective scientific research calls for scientific researchers of integrity and maturity, combining high moral and intellectual qualities.

11. Among the measures which Member States should take to assist the emergence of scientific researchers of this high calibre are:

(a) ensuring that, without discrimination on the basis of race, colour, sex, language, religion, political or other opinion, national or social origin, economic condition or birth, all citizens enjoy equal opportunities for the initial education and training needed to qualify for scientific research work, as well as ensuring that all citizens who succeed in so qualifying enjoy equal access to available employment in scientific research;

(b) encouragement of the spirit of community service as an important element in such education and training for scientific workers.

12. So far as is compatible with the necessary and proper independence of educators, Member States should lend their support to all educational initiatives designed to foster that spirit, such as:

(a) the incorporation or development, in the curricula and courses concerning the natural sciences and technology, of elements of social and environmental sciences;

(b) the development and use of educational techniques for awakening and stimulating such personal qualities and habits of mind as:

(i) disinterestedness and intellectual integrity;

(ii) the ability to review a problem or situation in perspective and in proportion, with all its human implications;

(iii) skill in isolating the civic and ethical implications, in issues involving the search for new knowledge and which may at first sight seem to be of a technical nature only;

(iv) vigilance as to the probable and possible social and ecological consequences of scientific research and experimental development activities;

(v) willingness to communicate with others not only in scientific and technological circles but also outside those circles, which implies willingness to work in a team and in a multi-occupational context.

IV. The Vocation of the Scientific Researcher

13. Member States should bear in mind that the scientific researchers' sense of vocation can be powerfully reinforced if he is encouraged to think of his work in terms of service both to his fellow countrymen and to his fellow human beings in general. Member States should seek, in their treatment of and attitude towards scientific researchers, to express encouragement for scientific research and experimental development performed in this broad spirit of community service.

The Civic and Ethical Aspect of Scientific Research. 14. Member States should seek to encourage conditions in which scientific researchers, with the support of the public authorities, have the responsibility and the right:

(a) to work in a spirit of intellectual freedom to pursue, expound and defend the scientific truth as they see it;

(b) to contribute to the definition of the aims and objectives of the programmes in which they are engaged and to the determination of the methods to be adopted which should be humanely, socially and ecologically responsible;

(c) to express themselves freely on the human, social or ecological value of certain projects and in the last resort withdraw from those projects if their conscience so dictates;

(d) to contribute positively and constructively to the fabric of science, culture and education in their own country, as well as to the achievement of national goals, the enhancement of their fellow citizens' well-being, and the furtherance of the international ideals and objectives of the United Nations;

it being understood that Member States, when acting as employees of scientific researchers, should specify as explicitly and narrowly as possible the cases in which they deem it necessary to depart from the principles set out in paragraphs (a) to (d) above.

15. Member States should take all appropriate steps to urge all other employers of scientific researchers to follow the recommendations contained in paragraph 14.

The International Aspect of Scientific Research. 16. Member States should recognize that scientific researchers encounter with increasing frequency situations in which the scientific research and experimental development on which they are engaged has an international dimension; and should endeavour to assist scientific researchers to exploit such situations in the furtherance of international peace, co-operation and understanding, and the common welfare of mankind.

17. Member States should in particular provide all possible support to the initiatives of scientific researchers undertaken in search of improved understanding of factors involved in the survival and well-being of mankind as a whole.

18. Each Member State should enlist the knowledge, industry and idealism of those of its citizens who are scientific researchers, especially of the younger generation, in the task of furnishing as generous a contribution as its resources can permit to the world's scientific and technological research effort. Member States should welcome all the advice and assistance scientific researchers can provide, in socio-economic development efforts that will contribute to the consolidation of an authentic culture and of national sovereignty.

19. In order that the full potentialities of scientific and technological knowledge be promptly geared to the benefit of all peoples, Member States should urge scientific researchers to keep in mind the principles set out in paragraphs 16, 17 and 18.

V. Conditions for Success on the Part of Scientific Researchers

20. Member States should:

(a) bear in mind that the public interest, as well as that of scientific researchers, requires moral support and material assistance conducive to successful performance in scientific research and experimental development by scientific researchers;

(b) recognize that in this respect they have, as employers of scientific researchers, a leading responsibility and should attempt to set an example to other employers of such researchers;

(c) urge all other employers of scientific researchers to pay close attention to the provision of satisfactory working conditions for scientific researchers, notably in respect of all the provisions of the present Section;

(d) ensure that scientific researchers enjoy the conditions of work and pay commensurate with their status and performance without discrimination on the basis of sex, language, age, religion or national origin.

Adequate Career Development Prospects and Facilities. 21. Member States should draw up, preferably within the framework of a comprehensive national manpower policy, policies in respect of employment which adequately cover the needs of scientific researchers, in particular by:

(a) providing scientific researchers in their direct employment with adequate career development prospects and facilities, though not necessarily exclusively in the fields of scientific research and experimental development; and encouraging non-governmental employers to do likewise;

(b) making every effort to plan scientific research and experimental development in such a way that the scientific researchers concerned are not subjected, merely by the nature of their work, to avoidable hardship;

(c) considering the provision of the necessary funds for facilities for readaptation and redeployment in respect of the scientific researchers in their permanent employ, as an integral part of scientific research and experimental development planning, especially, but not exclusively, in the case of programmes or projects designed as limited duration activities; and where these facilities are not possible, by providing appropriate compensatory arrangements;

(d) offering challenging opportunities for young scientific researchers to do significant scientific research and experimental development, in accordance with their abilities.

Permanent Self Re-education. 22. Member States should seek to encourage that:

(a) like other categories of workers facing similar problems, scientific researchers enjoy opportunities for keeping themselves up to date in their own and in related subjects, by attendance at conferences, by free access to libraries and other sources of information, and by participation in educational or vocational courses; and where necessary, scientific researchers should have the opportunity to undergo further scientific training with a view to transferring to another branch of scientific activity;

(b) appropriate facilities are provided for this purpose.

Mobility in General and the Civil Service in Particular. 23. Member States should take measures to encourage and facilitate, as part of a comprehensive national policy for highly-qualified manpower, the interchange or mobility of scientific researchers as between scientific research and experimental development service in the government and in the higher education and productive enterprise contexts.

24. Member States should also bear in mind that the machinery of government at all levels can benefit from the special skills and insights provided by scientific researchers. All Member States could therefore profitably benefit from a careful comparative examination of the experience gained in those Member States which have introduced salary scale and other conditions of employment specially designed for scientific researchers, with a view to determining to what extent such schemes would help meet their own national needs. Matters which appear to require particular attention in this respect are:

(a) optimum utilization of scientific researchers within the framework of a comprehensive national policy for highly-qualified manpower;

(b) the desirability of providing procedures with all the necessary guarantees allowing for the periodic review of the material conditions of scientific researchers to ensure that they remain equitably comparable with those of other workers having equivalent experience and qualifications and in keeping with the country's standard of living;

(c) the possibility of providing adequate career development prospects in public research bodies; as well as the need to give scientifically or technologically qualified researchers the option of transferring from scientific research and experimental development positions to administrative positions.

25. Member States should furthermore turn to advantage the fact that science and technology can be stimulated by close contact with other spheres of national activity, and vice versa. Member States should accordingly take care not to discourage scientific researchers whose predilections and talents, initially cultivated in the scientific research and experimental development context proper, lead them to progress into cognate activities. Member States should on the contrary be vigilant to encourage those scientific researchers whose original scientific research and experimental development training and subsequently acquired experience reveal potentialities lying in such fields as management of scientific research and experimental development or the broader field of science and technology policies as a whole, to develop to the full their talents in these directions.

Participation in International Scientific and Technological Gatherings. 26. Member States should actively promote the interplay of ideas and information among scientific researchers throughout the world, which is vital to the healthy development of science and technology; and to this end should take all measures necessary to ensure that scientific researchers are enabled, throughout their careers, to participate in international scientific and technological gatherings and to travel abroad.

27. Member States should furthermore see to it that all government or quasi-governmental organizations in which or under whose authority scientific research and experimental development are performed, regularly devote a portion of their budget to financing the participation at such international scientific and technological gatherings, of scientific researchers in their employ.

Access by Scientific Researchers to Positions of Greater Responsibility with Corresponding Rewards. 28. Member States should encourage in practice that decisions as to access by scientific researchers in their employ to positions of greater responsibility and correspondingly higher rewards, are formulated essentially on the basis of fair and realistic appraisal of the capacities of the persons concerned, as evidenced by their current or recent performances, as well as on the basis of formal or academic evidence of knowledge acquired or skills demonstrated by them.

Protection of Health; Social Security. 29. (a) Member States should accept that, as employers of scientific researchers, the onus is on them—in accordance with national regulations, and the international instruments concerned with the protection of workers in general from hostile or dangerous environments—to guarantee so far as is reasonably possible the health and safety of the scientific researchers in their employ, as of all other persons likely to be affected by the scientific research and experimental development in question. They should accordingly ensure that the managements of scientific establishments enforce appropriate safety standards, train all those in their employ in the necessary safety procedures; monitor and safeguard the health of all persons at risk; take due note of warnings of new (or possible new) hazards brought to their attention, in particular by the scientific researchers themselves, and act accordingly; ensure that the working day and rest periods are of reasonable length, the latter to include annual leave on full pay.

(b) Member States should take all appropriate steps to urge like practices on all other employers of scientific researchers.

30. Member States should ensure that provision is made for scientific researchers to enjoy (in common with all other workers) adequate and equitable social security arrangements appropriate to their age, sex, family situation, state of health and to the nature of the work they perform.

Promotion, Appraisal, Expression and Recognition of Creativity. Promotion. 31. Member States should be actively concerned to stimulate creative performance in the field of science and technology by all scientific researchers.

Appraisal. 32. Member States should, as regards scientific researchers in their employ:

(a) take due account, in all procedures for appraisal of the creativity of scientific researchers, of the difficulty inherent in measuring a personal capacity which seldom manifests itself in a constant and unfluctuating form;

(b) enable, and as appropriate encourage scientific researchers in whom it appears this capacity might be profitably stimulated:

(i) either to turn to a new field of science or technology;

(ii) or else to progress from scientific research and experimental development to other occupations in which the experience they have acquired and the other personal qualities of which they have given proof can be put to better use in a new context.

33. Member States should urge like practices upon other employers of scientific researchers.

34. As elements pertinent to appraisal of creativity, Member States should seek to ensure that scientific researchers may:

(a) receive without hindrance the questions, criticisms and suggestions addressed to them by their colleagues throughout the world, as well as the intellectual stimulus afforded by such communications and the exchanges to which they give rise;

(b) enjoy in tranquillity international acclaim warranted by their scientific merit.

Expression by Publication. 35. Member States should encourage and facilitate publication of the results obtained by scientific researchers, with a view to assisting them to acquire the reputation which they merit as well as with a view to promoting the advancement of science and technology, education and culture generally.

36. To this end, Member States should ensure that the scientific and technological writings of scientific researchers enjoy appropriate legal protection, and in particular the protection afforded by copyright law.

37. Member States should, in consultation with scientific researchers' organizations and a matter of standard practice encourage the employers of scientific researchers, and themselves as employers seek:

(a) to regard it as the norm that scientific researchers be at liberty and encouraged to publish the results of their work;

(b) to minimize the restrictions placed upon scientific researchers' right to publish their findings, consistent with public interest and the right of their employers and fellow workers;

(c) to express as clearly as possible in writing in the terms and conditions of their employment the circumstances in which such restrictions are likely to apply;

(d) similarly, to make clear the procedures by which scientific researchers can ascertain whether the restrictions mentioned in this paragraph apply in a particular case and by which he can appeal.

Recognition. 38. Member States should demonstrate that they attach high importance to the scientific researcher's receiving appropriate moral support and material compensation for the creative effort which is shown in his work.

39. Accordingly, Member States should:

(a) bear in mind that:

(i) the degree to which scientific researchers receive credit for and acknowledgement of their proven creativity, may affect their level of perceived job satisfaction;

(ii) job satisfaction is likely to affect performance in scientific research generally, and may affect specifically the creative element in that performance;

(b) adopt, and urge the adoption of, appropriate treatment of scientific researchers with respect to their proven creative effort.

40. Similarly, Member States should adopt, and urge the adoption of, the following standard practices:

(a) written provisions to be included in the terms and conditions of employment of scientific researchers, stating clearly what rights (if any) belong to them (and, where appropriate, other interested parties) in respect of any discovery, invention, or improvement in technical know-how which may arise in the course of the scientific research and experimental development which those researchers undertake:

(b) the attention of scientific researchers to be always drawn by the employer to such written provisions before the scientific researchers enter employment.

Reasonable Flexibility in the Interpretation and Application of Texts Setting out the Terms and Conditions of Employment of Scientific Researchers. 41. Member States should seek to ensure that the performance of scientific research and experimental development be not reduced to pure routine. They should therefore see to it that all texts setting out terms of employment for, or governing the conditions of work of scientific researchers, be framed and interpreted with all the desirable flexibility to meet the requirements of science and technology. This flexibility should not however be invoked in order to impose on scientific researchers conditions that are inferior to those enjoyed by other workers of equivalent qualifications and responsibility.

The Advancement of their Various Interests by Scientific Researchers in Association. 42. Member States should recognize it as wholly legitimate, and indeed desirable, that scientific researchers should associate to protect and promote their individual and collective interests, in bodies such as trade unions, professional associations and learned societies, in accordance with the rights of workers in general and inspired by the principles set out in the international instruments listed in the annex to this recommendation. In all cases where it is necessary to protect the rights of scientific researchers, these organizations should have the right to support the justified claims of such researchers.

VI. Utilization and Exploitation of the Present Recommendation

43. Member States should strive to extend and complement their own action in respect of the status of scientific re-

searchers, by co-operating with all national and international organizations whose activities fall within the scope and objectives of this recommendation, in particular National Commissions for Unesco; international organizations; organizations representing science and technology educators; employers generally; learned societies, professional associations and trade unions of scientific researchiers; associations of science writers; youth organizations.

44. Member States should support the work of the bodies mentioned above by the most appropriate means.

45. Member States should enlist the vigilant and active co-operation of all organizations representing scientific researchers, in ensuring that the latter may, in a spirit of community service, effectively assume the responsibilities, enjoy the rights and obtain the recognition of the status described in this recommendation.

VII. Final Provision

46. Where scientific researchers enjoy a status which is, in certain respects, more favourable than that provided for in this recommendation, its terms should not be invoked to diminish the status already acquired.

UNESCO SECRETARIAT. Established in accordance with article 3 of the UNITED NATIONS EDUCATIONAL, SCIENTIFIC AND CULTURAL ORGANIZATION CONSTITUTION, the Secretariat consists of the Director-General and the staff which he appoints and directs. The responsibilities of the Director-General and of the staff are exclusively international in character and are set out in the constitution (article 6).

UNION OF ARAB JURISTS. An international non-governmental organization in consultative status with the UN Economic and Social Council (Category II) and with UNESCO, the union consists of associations of jurists' associations in 17 countries. Founded in 1975 in Baghdad, its main function is to work for the political and economic liberation of the Arab homeland, to care for the Arab legal heritage, to formulate constitutional and legal frameworks for progressive political and social principles to be applied in the Arab homeland, and to defend human rights by providing legal measures for their realization. The union has also been involved in the preparation of the draft of an "Arab Agreement for Human Rights and Fundamental Freedoms."

UAJ published the bi-annual journal *Al-Huquqi*.

Union of Arab Jurists. Address: Almansor P.O.B. 6026, Baghdad, Iraq. Telephone: 5375820, 5375231. Telex: 21-2661, HUQUQIYN IK. Secretary-General: Shibib Lazim Al-Maliki.

UNION OF SOVIET SOCIALIST REPUBLICS. The largest country in the world, the Union of Soviet Socialist Republics covers one-sixth of the world's land area. Situated partly in eastern Europe and partly in northern Asia, it has borders with Afghanistan, China, Czechoslovakia, Finland, Hungary, Iran, Mongolia, Norway, North Korea, Poland, Romania, and Turkey.

Formerly the Russian Empire, it was proclaimed a republic on 14 September 1917 after the successful insurrection of the Bolsheviks. The new government, elected by the second all-Russian Congress of Soviets, was headed by V. I. Lenin (a pseudonym for Vladimir Ilyich Ulyanov). The constitution of the Russian Soviet Federal Socialist Republic was adopted by the fifth congress on 10 July 1918.

Other Soviet republics, including those set up in the Ukraine, Byelorussia, and Transcaucasia, established treaty relations with the Russian Soviet Federal Socialist Republic and, in 1922, joined it in a Union. The Transcaucasian Republic later split to form the Armenian Soviet Socialist Republic, and Azerbaijan Soviet Socialist Republic, and the Georgian Soviet Socialist Republic, each of which remained within the Union of Soviet Socialist Republics.

Before, during, and after World War II, the Soviet Union acquired additional territories. In August 1940, three independent Balkan countries—Lithuania, Latvia, and Estonia—were annexed and incorporated in the union. A part of East Prussia was transferred to the Union in 1946 in accordance with the Potsdam Declaration of the governments of the United Kingdom, the Soviet Union, and the United States of America. A province which had been ceded to Finland earlier was returned to the union in 1947 by the treaty of peace between the two countries. And the southern portion of the Sakhalin and the Kurile Islands were transferred from Japan to the union after the defeat of Japan, by agreement with the victorious powers.

As a result, the Union of Soviet Socialist Republics comprises the following 15 constituent republics: Russian S.F.S.R., Ukraine, Uzbekistan, Kazakhstan, Byelorussia, Azerbaijan, Georgia, Moldavia, Tadhikistan, Kirgizia, Lithuania, Armenia, Turkmenistan, Latvia, and Estonia.

The population of the union is estimated by the UN (1990) to be 291,822,000. The main ethnic groups are the slavic peoples: Russians, who make up about 52% of the population and are scattered throughout the union; Ukrainians, who make up about 16% and are concentrated in the Ukrainian S.S.R., and Byelorussians, who make up about 4% and are concentrated in the Byelorussian S.S.R. A fourth slavic group, the Poles, comprise less than 1% of the total population and are settled mainly in the western Ukraine. Other ethnic groups include the Jews, about 10,000 of whom live in the Jewish Autonomous District of Eastern Siberia, while the remainder are scattered about the European portion of the country; the Gypsies, who are nomadic; and the Asian peoples of the Caucasus, Soviet Central Asia, and Siberia.

Russian is the official language and the one in common use. Major language groups include the Baltic (Lithuanians and Letts), the Finnish (Mordvinians, Estonians, Udmurts, Mari, Komi, Komi-Permyaks, Kerelians, and Finns), Turkic (Tartars, Chuvash, Bashkirs, and Gagauz), Mongol (Kalmyks), and Romance (Moldavians).

Most citizens of the Union of Soviet Socialist Republics adhere to atheistic or non-religious beliefs. Among the portion of the population that retains religious beliefs (Christians, Muslims, Jews, and Buddhists) the largest religious organization is the Russian Orthodox Church. Under the constitution, the Church is separated from the State and the school from the Church. The teaching of religious dogma is prohibited, and all public education is of a secular nature. Parents or legal guardians may, however, give their children a religious upbringing in accordance with their own beliefs.

The Union of Soviet Socialist Republics is divided into 129 territories and regions, each with its own arrangements for local self-government. There are 20 autonomous Soviet Socialist Republics, eight autonomous regions, and ten autonomous areas.

The Russian Soviet Federal Socialist Republic is the leading and largest political unit; it occupies more than three-quarters of the territory of the union and has the largest percentage—about 83%—of Russians in its population. It includes Moscow, the capital of the U.S.S.R., and Leningrad. Its land is rich in natural resources including iron ore, coal, oil, and precious metals; and it produces about 70% of the industrial and agricultural products of the union.

Sixteen of the 20 autonomous republics lie within the boundaries of the Russian Soviet Federal Socialist Republic; two are in Georgia and one each is in Azerbaijan and Uzbekistan. Five of the autonomous regions are in the RSFSR; one each is in Azerbaijan, Georgia, and Tadzhikistan. All of the autonomous areas are in the RSFSR.

The BYELORUSSIAN S.S.R. and the UKRAINIAN S.S.R., both established in 1919 as constituent republics of the U.S.S.R., are unique in that, in accordance with understandings reached before the preparation of the United Nations Charter, they became members of the United Nations. The Ukrainian S.S.R. was enlarged in 1954, when the Crimea was added.

Under its 1977 constitution, which, in 1990, was in the process of revision, the Union of Soviet Socialist Republics is (art. 70) "an integral, federal, multinational State formed on the principle of socialist federalism as a result of the free self-determination of nations and the voluntary association of equal Soviet Socialist Republics." Each union republic has its own constitution. The right of constituent republics to secede from the union is formally recognized.

Activities in the spheres of war and peace, diplomatic relations, defense, foreign trade, State security, economic planning, education, the basic principles of legislation, and other matters of all-union significance are reserved to the central government.

The Supreme Soviet of the U.S.S.R.—the central legislative branch—consists of two chambers of 750 members each: the Council of the Union and the Council of Nationalities. Members of the Council of the Union are elected by popular vote of constituencies having approximately equal populations (roughly one deputy for every 360,000 people). Members of the Council of Nationalities are elected on the basis of national territorial areas (32 deputies from each union republic, 11 from each autonomous republic, 5 from each autonomous region, and 1 from each autonomous area). The Supreme Soviet convenes twice a year for sessions of two or three days each to consider and adopt or reject the recommendations of the standing commissions of its two chambers.

Candidates for election as deputies are nominated by conferences to which participating organizations send delegates. Up to 1984, such conferences normally proposed only a single nominee for each constituency. Members of the only legal political party, the Communist Party of the Soviet Union, tended to dominate the nominal lists, although in many cases non-party citizens were put forward. Voters were given the choice of endorsing the nominee whose name appeared on the ballot by not deleting it, or refusing to vote for him by striking out his name. Under this procedure, on 4 March 1984, 1,071 members of the Communist Party and 428 non-party deputies were elected to the Supreme Soviet; the vote in favor of the single list of candidates was above 99.9% in the case of each of the two chambers.

Since 1987, however, an increasing number of elections for public office have been conducted with more candidates nominated than posts available, thus providing voters with a certain amount of choice.

Members of the Council of Ministers—the highest executive and administrative body of state authority in the U.S.S.R.—are appointed jointly by the Council of the Union and the Council of Nationalities. The council consists of a chairman and several vice chairmen, ministers of the U.S.S.R., and the chairman of the Union State Committee. In addition, the chairmen of the Councils of Ministers of the Union Republics serve *ex officio* as members of the Union Council of Ministers. The council is directly responsible to the Supreme Soviet and reports to it at regular intervals. However, much of the council's day-to-day operations are delegated to its presidium, which meets at frequent intervals.

The Supreme Soviet also has its presidium, elected by the two chambers meeting in joint session. This group consists of the chairman, the first vice chairman, and 15 vice chairmen (one from each union republic), 21 members, and a secretary (39 members in all). Its function is to convene meetings of the Supreme Soviet; to coordinate the work of its standing commissions; to interpret the laws of the union; to take action accepting or rejecting international treaties; to decide questions relating to citizenship, pardons, amnesties, martial law, and states of emergency; and to appoint the high command of the Soviet armed forces and Soviet diplomatic representatives. It also acts as the supreme authority of the State when the Supreme Soviet is not in session.

The procurator-general of the U.S.S.R., appointed by the Supreme Soviet, supervises the application of the law by the judicial system, and appoints all procurators of the republics, autonomous republics, and autonomous regions. In addition, he participates, in his capacity as State prosecutor, in the most important cases. The prosecutor-general's office is vested with extensive powers to protect the rights of persons detained or arrested; and, under his supervision, all places of detention are inspected at regular intervals by supervisory commissions composed of representatives of trade unions, youth organizations, and local authorities.

In 1988, U.S.S.R. General Secretary Mikhail Gorbachev, addressing the UN General Assembly in New York City, indicated that the entire system of power and administration in his country had been undergoing a profound democratic reform under the process of *perestroika*:

With the recent decisions by the U.S.S.R. Supreme Soviet on amendments to the Constitution and the adoption of the Law on Elections, we have completed the first stage of the process of political reform. Without pausing, we have begun the second stage of this process with the main task of improving the relationship between the center and the republics, harmonizing interethnic relations on the principles of Leninist internationalism that we inherited from the Great Revolution, and, at the same time, reorganizing the local system of Soviet power.

A great deal of work lies ahead. Major mistakes will have to be dealt with concurrently. We are full of confidence. We have a theory and a policy, and also the vanguard force of *perestroika*—the party, which also is restructuring itself in accordance with new tasks and fundamental changes in society as a whole. What is most important is that all our peoples and all generations of citizens of our great country support *perestroika*.

We have become deeply involved in building a socialist State based on the rule of law. Work on a series of new laws has been completed or is nearing completion. Many of them will enter into force as early as 1989, and we expect them to meet the highest standards from the standpoint of ensuring the rights of the individual. Soviet democracy will be placed on a solid normative base. I am referring, in particular, to laws on the freedom of conscience, *glasnost*, public associations and organizations, and many others.

In places of confinement, there are no persons convicted for their political or religious beliefs. Additional guarantees are to be included in the new draft laws that rule out any form of persecution on those grounds. Naturally this does not apply to those who committed actual criminal offenses of state crimes such as espionage, sabotage, terrorism, etc., whatever their political or ideological beliefs.

Draft amendments to the penal code have been prepared and are awaiting their turn. Among the articles being revised are those relating to capital punishment. The problem of exit from and entry to our country, including the question of leaving it for a family reunification, is being dealt with in a humane spirit.

As you know, one of the reasons for refusal to leave is a person's knowledge of secrets. Strictly warranted time limitations on the secrecy rule will now be applied. Every person seeking employment at certain agencies or enterprises will be informed of this rule. In case of disputes, there is a right of appeal under the law.

This removes from the agenda the problem of the so-called "refuseniks."

We intend to expand the Soviet Union's participation in the United Nations and in the Conference of Security and Cooperation in Europe monitoring arrangements. We believe that the jurisdiction of the International Court of Justice at the Hague as regards the interpretation and implementation of agreements of human rights should be binding on all States. We regard as part of the Helsinki process the cessation of jamming of all foreign radio broadcasts beamed at the Soviet Union.

Overall, this is our credo. Political problems must be solved only by political means; human problems, only in a humane way. . . .

For detailed information on changes in the law and practice of the Soviet Union affecting the realization in that country of civil, political, and other human rights and fundamental freedoms, see UNION OF SOVIET SOCIALIST REPUBLICS: IMPLEMENTATION OF THE INTERNATIONAL COVENANT ON CIVIL AND POLITICAL RIGHTS.

UNION OF SOVIET SOCIALIST REPUBLICS: IMPLEMENTATION OF THE INTERNATIONAL COVENANT ON CIVIL AND POLITICAL RIGHTS.

On 26 August 1988, the government of the Union of Soviet Socialist Republics submitted to the UN HUMAN RIGHTS COMMITTEE its third periodic report (UN Doc. CCPR/C/52/Add. 2), in accordance with article 40 of that covenant. On 2 October 1989, it submitted supplementary information for inclusion in the report (UN Doc. CCPR/C/52/Add. 6).

The text of the report, in which the supplementary information has been incorporated, is reproduced below. The paragraph numbers used in the report have been retained; where paragraphs containing supplementary information have been inserted, these have been given numbers followed by letters (i.e., 20A, 20B, etc.).

The report is reproduced in full because it provides precise information about substantial changes in the law and practice of the Soviet Union, which profoundly affect the realization in that country of all human rights and fundamental freedoms and, in particular, civil and political rights.

The report is as follows:

Part I

1. This report supplements the initial and second periodic reports submitted in accordance with the International Covenant on Civil and Political Rights (documents CCPR/C/1/Add.22 of 31 January 1978 and CCPR/C/28/Add.3 of 4 May 1964).

2. The report is submitted pursuant to Article 40 of the Covenant and to the Human Rights Committee's decision on periodicity. Account was taken in compiling the report of the guidelines regarding the form and content of periodic reports, in which it is stressed that "The aim of reports submitted under Article 40, paragraph 1(b), will be to complete the information required by the Committee . . . and bring it up to date" (document CCPR/620 of 19 August 1981). Accordingly, in the second part of the report only those articles are taken into consideration for which new supplementary information is available.

3. The fundamental law of the State is the 1977 Constitution of the USSR, which preserves continuity with the ideas and principles enunciated in the first Soviet Constitution of 1918, the 1924 Constitution of the USSR and the 1936 Constitution of the USSR.

4. It sets forth the foundations of the social structure and policy of the USSR, the rights, freedoms and duties of its citizens and the organizational principles and aims of the socialist State of the whole people.

5. The Union of Soviet Socialist Republics is a socialist State of the whole people, expressing the will and interests of the workers, peasants and intelligentsia and the working people of all nationalities and ethnic groups in the country (Article 1). All power in the USSR belongs to the people. The people exercises State power through Soviets of People's Deputies which constitute the political base of the USSR (Article 2). The organization and activities of the Soviet State are conducted in accordance with the principles of democratic centralism: the elected nature of all State authorities from bottom to top; the accountability of those authorities to the people; and the binding nature of decisions by higher-place authorities for those lower-placed (Article 3). The most important aspects of State activities are put before the whole people for discussion and also for vote (referendum).

6. The Union of Soviet Socialist Republics is a unified federal multinational state formed on the basis of the principle of socialist federalism as a result of the free self-determination of nations and the voluntary union of Soviet Socialist Republics with equal rights (Article 70). The USSR consists of 15 union republics, 20 autonomous republics, 8 autonomous oblasts, 10 autonomous okrugs and 128 krais and oblasts. Over 100 nationalities live in the Soviet Union.

7. The period that has elapsed since the submission of the second periodic report has seen substantial changes in the life of Soviet society. At the present time the development and deepening of Soviet democracy and the improvement of the system of the rights and freedoms of Soviet citizens and of ways and means of giving them effect are based on the policy of restructuring ("perestroika") being carried out under the leadership of the Communist Party of the Soviet Union.

8. The purpose of perestroika is to develop still more fully the humanist nature of Soviet society in all its decisive aspects: economic, social, political and moral. Its aim is to restore the unquestionable priority of man, with his ideals and interests, and to achieve a real consolidation of humanist values in economics, in social and political relationships and in culture. "As a result of perestroika socialism can and must fully realise its potentialities as a system of real humanism serving and enhancing man. It is designed to create a society for people, for the flowering of their creative work, their prosperity, their health, their physical and spiritual development, a society in which man feels himself the master with full rights and really is the master" [M. S. Gorbachev, "October and *Perestroika*—The Revolution continues, 1917–1987," *Politizdat* (Moscow, 1987): 32 (tr. from Russian)].

9. Giving a comprehensive definition of the policy of perestroika at the January 1987 plenum of the Central Committee of the Communist Party of the Soviet Union, M.S. Gorbachev noted in particular that "Perestroika means relying on the vital creativity of the masses; it means the many-sided development of democracy and socialist self-management, the encouragement of initiatives and spontaneous activities, the strengthening of discipline and order, the extension of a policy of openness, criticism and self-criticism in all spheres of public life; it means respect of a high degree for the value and dignity of the person". Perestroika presupposes priority being given to the development of the social sphere and the ever fuller satisfaction of the requirements of Soviet people for good conditions of work, everyday life, leisure, education and medical services; protection of their life, health, dignity and well-being; constant care for the spiritual riches and culture of every individual and of society as a whole; the ability to combine the solving of large-scale key problems in the life of society with the solving of the current problems that worry the people.

10. Thus, perestroika is a democratization of the whole of public life, presupposing further comprehensive development of the whole system of rights and freedoms of Soviet citizens, an improvement in the organizational and legal mechanisms for giving effect to those freedoms and the strengthening of socialist legality.

11. As part of the work being carried out in the USSR for the further democratization of society and the improvement of the legal basis of State and public life the humanist trend in the Soviet system of public law is being deepened and extended, setting in the forefront the rights and lawful interests of man.

12. With a view to developing democracy at work and the consistent application of the principles of true self-

management to the functioning of work collectives, an Act of the USSR was adopted on 30 June 1987 on "State enterprises (unions of enterprises)". In this Act one of the leading trends in perestroika is given practical effect—the trend towards effective utilization of direct democracy.

13. Side by side with the development of direct democracy, measures have also been taken to improve the functioning of representative democracy, and above all of the Soviets of People's Deputies at all levels. Thus, in accordance with a Decree of the Central Committee of the CPSU, the Presidium of the Supreme Soviet of the USSR and the Council of Ministers of the USSR dated 25 July 1986 "Measures for further enhancing the role and strengthening the responsibility of the Soviets of People's Deputies for speeding up social and economic development in the light of the decisions of the twenty-seventh Congress of the CPSU" [*Vedomosti Verkhovnogo Soveta SSSR* 31 [1986]: 593] the powers of the Soviets were substantially extended [*Vedomosti Verkhovnogo Soveta SSSR* 25 [1987] 355].

14. One of the main moving forces in perestroika is the comprehensive development of a policy of openness ("glasnost"). Glasnost presupposes the greatest possible openness in the activities of State and public organizations and the possibility for all workers to voice their opinions on any aspect of public life. With a view to ensuring openness the first legislative measures have already been adopted: an Act of the USSR "Nationwide discussion of important aspects of State activities", an Act of the USSR "Procedure for appealing to the courts in respect of illegal acts by officials that encroach on citizens' rights". These Acts were adopted on 30 June 1987. The Act of the USSR "State enterprises (unions of enterprises)", should also help to strengthen glasnost.

15. The development of glasnost and of the constitutional right to criticize is guaranteed by the embodiment in Soviet legislation of criminal liability for the persecution of citizens for criticism (See, for instance, Article 139 of the Criminal Code of the RSFSR introduced by a decree of the Presidium of the Supreme Soviet of the RSFSR, dated 30 October 1985 [*Vedomosti Verkhovnogo Sovieta RSFSR* 45 (1985).])

16. A whole set of measures has been adopted with a view to strengthening the régime of socialist legality and improving the effectiveness of the work of bodies that protect people's rights. In this connection mention should be made above all of a Decree of the Central Committee of the CPSU dated 20 November 1986 "The further consolidation of socialist legality and order based on due process of law and the strengthening of the protection of citizens' rights and lawful interests"; a Decree of the Central Committee of the CPSU dated 4 June 1987 "Measures to enhance the role of supervision by the procurators in strengthening socialist legality and order based on due process of law and a Decree of the Presidium of the Supreme Soviet of the USSR dated 16 June 1987," "Amendments and additions to the Act of the USSR, The Procurator's Office of the USSR; a Decree of the Presidium of the Supreme Soviet of the USSR "Appeals by citizens to the Supreme Soviet of the USSR" dated 17 February 1987; a Decree of the Presidium of the Supreme Soviet of the USSR dated 24 July 1987 "The work of organs of the judiciary in providing the population with legal services"; a Decree of the Central Committee of the CPSU dated 2 April 1988 "Progress in the control of criminality in the Soviet Union and supplementary measures to prevent infringements of the law", and other statutory instruments.

17. The development of direct and representative de-

mocracy in all spheres of Soviet society and the consolidation of the principle of glasnost as a basis for its further progressive development are indissolubly linked to the extension and strengthening of judicial, organizational and material guarantees for the rights and freedoms of the citizens of the USSR already proclaimed. All the statutory instruments listed above are working towards that end. At the same time, as part of the comprehensive development of the rights of Soviet citizens, legislative measures have already been adopted that are of a concrete, practical nature; the procedure for Soviet citizens to leave and return to the USSR has been substantially simplified. Protection of the right of citizens to life and health has been strengthened. Protection of the interests of the family and children has been widened and measures are being taken in the USSR to guarantee the rights and freedoms not only of Soviet citizens but also of other persons living on the territory of the Soviet Union.

18. The new orientation in the life of Soviet society presupposes the systematic development of the personal initiative of Soviet citizens. In this connection a whole range of legislative measures have already been adopted, in particular an Act of the USSR dated 19 November 1986 "Individual working activity", an Act of the USSR dated 26 May 1988 "Cooperation in the USSR" and a series of Decrees of the Council of Ministers of the USSR aimed at creating the most favourable conditions possible for the functioning of cooperative organizations in the Soviet Union.

19. In this atmosphere of openness and the further democratization of every aspect of public and State life, more favourable conditions are being created for giving effect to the political rights and freedoms enjoyed by the citizens. This is shown in particular by the establishment of a large number of new voluntary public organizations, by the active utilization of political rights, such as the right of peaceful assembly, and by the wide utilization by citizens of their constitutional right to criticize every aspect of State and public life.

[Paragraphs 20A–20U have been interopolated from UN Doc. CCPR/C/52/Add.6.]

20A. The amendments to the Soviet Constitution made in late 1988 and the new USSR Act on the Election of People's Deputies of the USSR adopted on the basis of those amendments on 1 December 1988 marked a new important stage in the democratization of Soviet society.

20B. On the basis of this Act the first genuinely democratic elections for many decades, affording the real possibility of nominating alternative candidates and voting for them, were held in the country in March 1989.

20C. These elections, during which the popular masses had the opportunity to express their wishes freely, led to the formulation of the new supreme bodies of State power—the Congress of People's Deputies of the USSR and the Supreme Soviet of the USSR, which has now in effect become a standing parliament.

20E. The meetings of the Congress of People's Deputies of the USSR, held in May-June 1989, and the first session of the Supreme Soviet of the USSR, which took place from early June until early August, passed a considerable number of decisions of exceptional importance for the democratization of the country. For example, the decree of the Congress of People's Deputies of the USSR entitled "Main orientation of the domestic and foreign policy of the USSR" contains a decision calling for work to begin immediately on the preparation of a new Soviet Constitution. The Decree states that the new Constitution should embody the principles of human, democratic socialism, inalienable human rights and the security and legal protection of the individual. The new Constitution should be the embodiment of an economic, social and State structure that would preclude the emergence of a personality cult or authoritarianism and prevent the continuation of methods of government by administrative fiat.

20F. The Congress stated its determination to uphold the supremacy of law in all areas of State and public life and the equality before the law of all citizens, officials and organizations without exception. All citizens are responsible before the law for their actions. But the State, too, as represented by its organs and officials, should also be accountable to each and every citizen and to the whole of the Soviet people for its actions. The principle that everything is permissible except where prohibited by law should consistently be applied in the political, economic and social activities of citizens, public organizations, co-operatives and enterprises.

20G. The Decree adopted by the Congress goes on to state that the main aspects of the work of State bodies and officials must be strictly governed by law. Unlawful individual or *collegial* acts by officials which infringe citizens' rights can be appealed in the courts. In this connection, it was decided to broaden considerably the sphere of application of the 1988 Act concerning appeals against actions by public officials.

20H. The Decree further states that the law forms the basis of a constitutional State, protects the freedom and equality of citizens and public order and safeguards the principle of social justice.

20I. The Congress proceeds from a recognition of the fact that the inalienable rights to life and freedom, the right to inviolability and safety of the person and the home and the right of peoples to self-determination are immutable and sacred human rights. No infringement of human rights or of the rights of peoples is permissible. The Soviet legislative system, the courts and all law enforcement bodies must consistently and strictly implement and protect these rights. *(Vedemosti Syezda Narodnykh Deputatov SSR i Verkhovnogo Soveta SSSR* 3 [1989]: sect. 52).

20J. The Congress instructed the Supreme Soviet of the USSR to consider the edicts adopted in 1988 by the Presidium of the USSR Supreme Soviet on the procedure for the organization and conduct of meetings and demonstrations and on the duties and rights of the internal forces of the USSR Ministry of Internal Affairs, as regards their consistency with the Soviet Constitution.

20K. These edicts are to be considered and approved at the autumn session of the USSR Supreme Soviet.

20L. The first session of the USSR Supreme Soviet approved an agenda of legislative work for the forthcoming year. This includes legislation to protect the rights and lawful interests of citizens covering the press and other mass information media, and public associations of citizens in the USSR; the rights of Soviet trade unions; youth and State policy concerning youth in the USSR, and freedom of conscience and religious organizations; and the procedure for settlement of collective labour disputes. *(Izvestiya* 20, July 1989).

20M. An important role in ensuring legality and protecting citizens' rights will be played by the House Standing Commissions and the Committees of the USSR Supreme Soviet. The first session of the USSR Supreme Soviet *inter alia* established 14 committees, some of which will deal directly with aspects of the protection of human rights including issues relating to *glasnost,* citizens' rights and appeals lodged by private individuals; issues relating to legislation, the legal system and law and order; the protection of public health; the situation of women and family, maternal and child welfare; matters relating to veterans and the disabled; and youth affairs. (See the decree of the USSR Supreme Soviet of 7 June 1989 in *Vedomosti Syezda Narodnykh Deputatov SSR i Verkhovnogo Soveta SSSR* 1 [1989]: sect. 33.)

20N. An extremely important role in the protection of citizens' rights and freedoms has been assigned to the Constitutional Review Committee of the USSR. This Committee will in particular carry out the following functions:

20O. On its own initiative or on the instructions of the Congress of People's Deputies of the USSR, it will submit conclusions to the Congress of People's Deputies indicating whether draft USSR legislation to be considered by the Congress is consistent with the Soviet Constitution;

20P. On its own initiative, on the instructions of the Congress of People's Deputies or at the suggestion of the Supreme Soviet of the USSR or of the supreme bodies of State power of the union republics, it will submit conclusions to the USSR Supreme Soviet indicating whether acts or draft legislation of the USSR Supreme Soviet or of its houses are consistent with the Soviet Constitution and the laws of the USSR adopted by the Congress of People's Deputies;

20Q. It will monitor consistency with the Soviet Constitution and law of the constitutions and laws of the union republics and of the decrees and ordinances issued by the Council of Ministers of the USSR or by the Councils of Ministers of the union republics;

20R. On its own initiative, on the instructions of the Congress of People's Deputies of the USSR or at the suggestion of the USSR Supreme Soviet or its houses, the Presidium of the USSR Supreme Soviet, the Chairman of the USSR Supreme Soviet, the house standing commissions and the committees of the USSR Supreme Soviet, the Council of Ministers of the USSR or the supreme bodies of State power of the union republics, it will submit conclusions indicating whether the acts of other State bodies or public organizations are consistent with the Soviet Constitution and laws of the USSR.

20S. Where acts or individual provisions thereof are found to conflict with the Soviet Constitution or the laws of the USSR, the Constitutional Review Committee of the USSR will send its conclusion to the body which issued the act for the situation to be remedied. The Soviet Constitution stipulates that the adoption of such a conclusion by the Committee suspends implementation of any acts or individual provisions thereof which conflict with the Soviet Constitution or Soviet law. The Constitutional Review Committee of the USSR has the right to apply to the Congress of People's Deputies of the USSR, the Supreme Soviet or the Council of Ministers of the USSR for the repeal of acts issued by their subordinate bodies or officials which conflict with the Soviet Constitution or Soviet law.

20T. These constitutional provisions should play an important role in protecting citizens' rights and strengthening the rules of law in the country.

20U. The Congress of People's Deputies and the Supreme Soviet of the USSR reaffirmed the need to continue work on the preparation and adoption of a number of other important normative acts governing citizens' rights and freedoms.

21. The task has been set of elaborating in the very near future new criminal, criminal-procedure and corrective-labour legislation more completely in line with the condi-

tions under which Soviet society is developing and more effective in protecting the interests and rights of the citizens. This should lead to a strengthening of discipline and of order based on due process of law. The criminal legislation of the USSR and the union republics is being improved through consistent application of democratic principles, through mandatory punishment for crimes committed, by adhering by the principles of justice and humanism, through a more clearcut delimitation of crimes on the basis of the degree of danger to society which they represent, and through wider sentencing of persons who have committed minor crimes to punishments that do not involve deprivation of liberty (See "In the Politburo of the Central Committee of the CPSU," *Pravda*, 2 February 1988).

22. The effective implementation of the rights and freedoms of Soviet citizens and the strengthening of socialist legality will be promoted by the organization in the Soviet Union of universal education in the law under a unified nationwide programme covering all strata of the population, both at the centre and in the localities. A decision on this was adopted at the February 1988 Plenum of the Central Committee of the CPSU (See "Progress in restructuring secondary and higher educational establishments and the tasks of the Party in carrying out the restructuring" [Decree of the Plenum of the Central Committee of the CPSU, 18 February 1988] *Pravda,* 20 February 1988).

23. At the present moment in the Soviet Union an Act on the rights of trade unions is being prepared. This Act defines the legal basis for the activity of the trade unions of the USSR, extends the possibilities for their participation in the solving of State and public problems and envisages wider guarantees to enable them to carry out their statutory duties.

24. The policy of perestroika being carried out in the USSR, in addition to being concerned with the solving of problems of internal development, is aimed also at consolidating new political thinking in respect of international relationships. By new political thinking is understood the establishment of relations of cooperation, trust and mutual understanding between peoples and assuring for every person a right to peace based on a comprehensive system of international security and disarmament. An important concrete step towards giving practical effect to the new political thinking in international relations was the conclusion of a Treaty between the Union of Soviet Socialist Republics and the United States of America on the Elimination of their Intermediate-Range and Shorter-Range Missiles, dated 8 December 1987 and ratified by both parties in May 1988.

25. Attaching great importance to ensuring human rights and freedoms the Union of Soviet Socialist Republics considers that among all the international agreements and treaties on human rights adopted in the United Nations system in accordance with the United Nations Charter, a special place belongs to the international covenants on human rights, insofar as the States that have signed them have assumed the corresponding obligations in international law. In this context the International Covenant on Civil and Political Rights sets forth in detail the duties of States in those spheres; all the rights and freedoms embodied in the Covenant are interdependent with and indivisible from the rights and freedoms proclaimed in the International Covenant on Economic, Social and Cultural Rights.

26. On 18 October 1973 the Soviet Union ratified the International Covenants on Civil and Political Rights and on Economic, Social and Cultural Rights. It is a party to the covenants aimed at fighting discrimination. Since 2 July 1962 it has been a party to the Convention against Discrimination in Education. Since 22 January 1969 it has been a party to the International Convention on the Elimination of All Forms of Racial Discrimination and since 19 December 1980 to the Convention on the Elimination of All Forms of Discrimination Against Women. The USSR has also ratified the Convention on the Prevention and Punishment of the Crime of Genocide (18 March 1954), the International Convention on the Suppression and Punishment of the Crime of Apartheid (15 October 1975), the Convention on the Political Rights of Women (18 March 1954) and the Supplementary Convention on the Abolition of Slavery, the Slave Trade and Institutions and Practices similar to Slavery (12 April 1957).

27. On 11 March 1969 the USSR ratified a convention on the non-applicability of the statute of limitations to war crimes and crimes against humanity. It is continuing to work actively for the prosecution of Nazi war criminals and is promoting agreements on and support of effective international cooperation in that sphere. Thus, on 30 December 1987 in Moscow a memorandum of understanding and cooperation was signed between the Procurator's Office of the USSR and the Canadian Ministry of Justice on judicial proceedings against Nazi war criminals.

28. The USSR is also a party to a whole series of conventions of the International Labour Organization, such as those on forced labour, the 40–hour working week, the protection of wages, freedom of association and the protection of the right to organize, as well as on other problems.

29. In the period under review the Soviet Union continued to play an active part in international cooperation on human rights, maintaining contacts with the United Nations Human Rights Commission and other United Nations bodies and also with organs set up in connection with agreements on human rights.

30. The USSR has ratified international treaties of great importance for ensuring human rights, such as the Convention against Torture and other Cruel, Inhuman or Degrading Forms of Treatment and Punishment (21 January 1987) and the International Convention Against Apartheid in Sports (7 May 1987).

31. The Soviet Union has also made the necessary efforts to control certain repellent phenomena of modern times that constitute a threat to basic human rights and freedoms, such as international terrorism and drug trafficking. These efforts have included, in addition to measures of an internal nature, active participation in international cooperation on both a bilateral and a multilateral basis. In particular, the USSR became a party to the International Convention against the Taking of Hostages (7 May 1987) and the Convention on Crimes and Other Acts Carried Out on Board Aircraft (4 December 1987). In February 1988 a Memorandum of Understanding was signed between the USSR and the United Kingdom on cooperation in the prevention of the illegal production of, traffic in and abuse of narcotic drugs and psychotropic substances.

32. Soviet participation in international treaties concerned with human rights effectively supplements the internal system for protecting human rights in the USSR itself. Thus in accordance with Article 19 of the Act of the USSR "Procedure for concluding, implementing and denouncing international treaties" the international treaties of the USSR must be unswervingly observed by the Union of Soviet Socialist Republics in accordance with the norms of international law.

33. The Foundations of Civil Procedure of the USSR and the Union Republics, the Foundations of Civil Legislation in the USSR and the Union Republics, the Foundations of Marriage and Family Legislation in the USSR and the Union Republics, the Foundations of Legislation on Education in USSR and the Union Republics and the Foundations of the Health Legislation of the USSR and the Union Republics, provide that if by international treaty rules are established that differ from those enshrined in Soviet legislation, then the rules of the international treaty shall take precedence.

34. In cases where meeting international treaty obligations makes it necessary to promulgate an Act of the USSR or a Decree or Resolution of the Presidium of the Supreme Soviet of the USSR or to take a decision or issue orders in the Council of Ministers of the USSR, the ministries concerned, the State committees and branches of the administration of the USSR and the Ministry of Justice of the USSR, in accordance with established procedure, put forward proposals for the adoption of the necessary legislation (Article 24 of the Act of the USSR on the procedure for concluding, implementing and denouncing international treaties of the USSR).

35. The Soviet Union is in favour of the development of cooperation as part of the Helsinki process, in particular in matters of humanitarian collaboration. At the Vienna meeting of States parties to the CSCE the USSR proposed that an all-European conference be held in Moscow.

36. Information is given below in regard to particular articles of the International Covenant on Civil and Political Rights concerning those new legislative acts of the USSR and the Union Republics that have been adopted since consideration of the second periodic report of the USSR.

Part II

Right to Self-determination (Article 1 of the Covenant). 37. The right to self-determination is guaranteed by the Constitution of the USSR, under which every Union Republic has the right to secede from the USSR if it so wishes. Of great significance for ensuring the further free economic, social and cultural development of all the peoples inhabiting the USSR is the political document which forms the cornerstone of Soviet society—the Programme of the CPSU adopted in a new version in 1986 at the Twenty-seventh Congress of the CPSU. In particular it formulates today's tasks in regard to nation-building and the harmonization of relationships between nationalities. These include:

—constant concern for further enhancing the role of Union and autonomous republics, autonomous oblasts and autonomous okrugs in fulfilling nationwide tasks;

—the active participation of working people of all nationalities in the work of the organs of State power and management;

—an increase in the material and spiritual potential of every republic as part of a unified economic complex;

—the development of a single culture of the Soviet people, taking many different forms according to nationality but internationalist in spirit, based on the best interests and the indigenous progressive traditions of the peoples of the USSR.

As was the case before, Soviet legislation guarantees the free development and utilization of their native languages by all citizens of the USSR on a basis of equal rights; this was particularly stressed in the decision of the February 1988 Plenum of the Central Committee of the CPSU. . .

39. There is surely no need to demonstrate the importance of the socialist foundations for the development of national relationships. It was precisely socialism that put an end to national oppression and inequality of rights and to any encroachment on the rights of individuals on the grounds of nationality and it was precisely socialism that guaranteed the economic and spiritual progress of all peoples and ethnic groups. The successes of Soviet nationality policy are beyond dispute, but regard must also be had to what lies ahead for the development of national relationships. Today, when democracy and self-management are expanding, when there is a swift rise in national consciousness among all peoples and ethnic groups, when the processes of internationalization are being deepened, special importance must be given to the timely and just settlement of any problems that arise on the only possible basis—in the interests of the prosperity of every people and ethnic group, in the interests of their coming still closer together, in the interests of society as a whole. In this connection it must be remembered that in the sphere of national relationships undesirable phenomena and distortions have occurred. There have been cases of overemphasis on local interests, a tendency for peoples to turn in on themselves, attitudes of national arrogance and even clashes. Perestroika in the USSR is particularly aimed at eliminating these phenomena.

40. The task is to ensure that in every national region, economic and social progress is accompanied by spiritual progress based on the cultural identity of peoples and ethnic groups, so that nationalities living outside the borders of their own State territorial structures or not possessing such structures are given every possible opportunity to meet their national cultural aspirations, particularly in regard to education, contacts and national creative work, as well as to the establishment of foci of national culture, the use of the mass media and the satisfaction of religious needs.

41. It is a matter, above all, of extending the rights of union republics and autonomous territorial structures by delimiting the competence of the USSR as a whole and of the Soviet republics, decentralizing, handing over to the localities a number of management functions, strengthening independence and responsibility in economic, social and cultural development, protecting nature and activating those bodies in the political system through which national interests can be determined and agreed upon. In this respect in a number of republics commission for relations between nationalities and international education have been established.

42. All national problems require careful comprehensive approaches based on thorough analysis and objective assessments of each particular situation. They should be settled with calm and the utmost responsibility within the framework of socialist democracy and legality and in the first instance by taking steps to meet one another halfway, taking into account the developing processes of revolutionary renewal, without detriment to the solid unity between the peoples of the USSR.

[Paragraph 42A has been interpolated from UN Doc. CCPR/C/52/Add. 6.]

42A. The establishment of effective legal safeguards against any attempt to practise discrimination on racial or ethnic grounds is the purpose of the Edict of the Presidium of the USSR Supreme Soviet of 8 April 1989 entitled "Amendments and supplements to the USSR Act on Criminal Liability for Offences against the State and to certain other legislative acts of the USSR". This substantially amended the wording of article 11 of the USSR Act on Criminal Liability for Offences against the State (art. 74 of the Criminal Code of the RSFSR), which establishes criminal liability for the violation of national or racial equality of rights. Thus, whereas in the previous version criminal liability was applied to propaganda and agitation with a view to the incitement of racial or national hatred or discord, as well as to the direct or indirect limitation of citizens' rights or the establishment of direct or indirect advantages in respect of racial or ethnic origin, the new version establishes criminal liability for "acts deliberately intended to incite national or racial hatred or discord, or to denigrate national honour and dignity . . ." (thereafter as in the previous version), such acts being punishable by deprivation of liberty for a term of up to three years or by a fine of up to 2,000 roubles (previously the penalty was deprivation of liberty for the same period or banishment for a period of two to five years). In addition the new version of article 11 included two sections which define the aggravating circumstances under which the penalty is considerably greater. These include commission of the above-mentioned acts using force, deceit or threats, the commission of such acts by officials (punishable by deprivation of liberty for up to five years or by a fine of up to 5,000 roubles), or their commission by a group of persons which results in loss of life or other serious consequences (in which case the penalty is deprivation of liberty for a term of up to 10 years).

Equality of Rights and Protection of Rights (Article 2 of the Covenant). 43. In the USSR the equality of rights of citizens is a principle of the Constitution and is given concrete form in all branches of current legislation. During the report period further legislative consolidation of this principle has occurred.

44. The codes in force since 1984–1985 in the Union Republics concerning administrative infringements, contain special articles on the consideration of cases of administrative infringements of the law on the basis of the equality of all citizens. For instance, Article 228 of the RSFSR Code on Administrative Infringements of the Law adopted on 20 June 1984 states: "Consideration of a case of administrative infringement of the law is based on the equality before the law, and before the body considering the case, of all citizens, independently of their origin, social status, property, race, nationality, sex, level of education, language, attitude to religion, nature and form of occupation, place of residence or any other circumstances."

45. The Act of the USSR "Nationwide Discussion of Important Aspects of State Activities" adopted on 30 June 1987 forbids any direct or indirect limitations of the rights of citizens of the USSR to participate in the discussion no matter what their origin, social status, property or other circumstances (Article 6).

46. With a view to improving the means of ensuring legal protection of citizens' rights and particularly protection by the courts, an Act of the USSR was adopted on 30 June 1987 under the title "Procedure for Appealing to the Courts in respect of Illegal Acts by Officials that Encroach on Citizens' Rights". This Act gives concrete form to a citizen's constitutional right to judicial protection and in particular to the provisions of Part II, Article 58 of the Constitution of the USSR.

47. The preamble to the Act stresses the completeness of the social, economic, political and personal rights and freedoms proclaimed and guaranteed by the Constitution of the USSR and by Soviet legislation and enjoyed by Soviet citizens. It states unambiguously that respect for the individual and protection of citizens' rights and freedoms are an obligation for all State bodies, public organizations and officials.

48. According to the Act "A citizen has the right to appeal to the courts if he considers that the acts of an official are encroaching on his rights" (Article 1). The law does not contain an actual list of the actions by officials that may be appealed against. It gives a summarized universal set of characteristics of such acts: "Acts by officials that break the law, with an exceeding of authority encroaching on citizens' rights, include acts as a result of which:

a citizen is illegally deprived of the possibility of fully or partially enjoying a right provided for in the law or other statutory instrument

a duty is illegally laid on a citizen".

49. The Act consolidates a citizen's right to complain to the courts of an action carried out by an official on his own behalf and in his own name or on behalf of the body he represents.

50. The new Act does not annul or amend the laws previously enacted on the judicial protection of personal, property, family, labour, housing or other rights and freedoms of citizens. Those laws remain in force today. The Act extends the possibilities open to citizens of defending their interests by invoking the law.

51. Delimitation of the sphere of application of this Act from those of other Acts on this subject is guaranteed by certain of its provisions stating that the procedure it lays down for lodging a complaint does not apply to the actions of officials covered by a different procedure of complaint (before the courts or through administrative channels) laid down by criminal procedure and civil procedure legislation, legislation on the procedure for considering labour disputes concerning discoveries, inventions and rationalization proposals, administrative infringements of the law, individual working activity or other legislation of the USSR and the Union Republics. Because of considerations relating to the protection of State secrets, the Act of 30 June 1987 does not extend either to complaints against actions connected with ensuring the defensive capacity of the Soviet Union and guaranteeing State security.

52. Thus, the law enshrines the principle that a complaint may be laid before the court in respect of any actions of officials except for those for which a complaint procedure is specifically laid down in other legislation.

53. An Act of the USSR dated 20 October 1987 amends the Act on the procedure for appealing to the courts in respect of illegal acts by officials that encroach on citizens' rights.

54. A complaint about an official's actions may, at the discretion of the complainant, be heard before a court either immediately or after it has been lodged with a higher official or body. The complaint must be laid before a rayon (city) people's court within a month from the day when the citizen becomes aware of the official's illegal acts or from the day he receives a refusal to meet his complaint by a higher official or body, or from the day when the time limit laid down by law for considering the complaint has expired. The citizen may appeal to a court either personally or through a representative. At his request the complaint may be made by an authorized representative of a public organization or work collective.

55. The court must consider a complaint within 10 days as a rule at an open session attended by the complainant and the official complained of. Representatives of public

organizations and work collectives and also officials of higher bodies or their representatives may take part in the court hearing. If the court recognizes that the actions complained of are illegal it will hand down a judgement saying that the complaint is well-founded and ordering the official to eliminate the infringements that have occurred.

56. The court's order for the elimination of the infringement that has occurred is sent to the official against whose actions the complaint was made or to the official or body next higher in rank. The court and the citizen must be informed of the measures taken to implement the court's decision in regard to the complaint no later than one month from the time when the decision was notified. If the decision is not implemented the court takes the measures laid down in the legislation in force. Complaints of citizens in regard to actions by officials are not liable to State tax.

57. An appeal or protest in accordance with the rules of civil procedure can be made against a decision of the court to refuse to accept a complaint and against a court's decision on the complaint itself. Pending the hearing of the appeal or protest execution of the court's order is suspended.

58. The Act makes the proviso that the lodging of a complaint by a citizen for slanderous purposes will render him liable to criminal proceedings in accordance with the legislation in force.

59. Both in spirit and in content the Act of the USSR "Procedure for appealing to the courts in respect of illegal acts by officials that encroach on citizens' rights" is intended to strengthen citizens' protection by the law and to reinforce legality and to extend openness and democracy.

60. The additions and amendments introduced by the Decree of the Presidium of the Supreme Soviet of the USSR dated 16 June 1987 into the Act of the USSR "The Procurator's Office of the USSR" are intended to strengthen legality and order based on due legal process, to enhance the protection of citizens by the law and to delimit public interests more consistently. The new wording of the Act provides in particular that procurators, in using their authority to monitor and supervise, should make sure that State bodies, public organizations and officials act on the basis of socialist legality. In accordance with the rights granted to them and the duties laid upon them the procurators must ensure the protection of law and order, the interests of society and the rights and freedoms of citizens.

61. Orders by procurators to eliminate infringements of the law they detect, issued within the time limit laid down, are binding. Procurators are authorized to issue injunctions on the elimination of infringements of the law, particularly in cases where there has been detriment to the rights and lawful interests of citizens. An injunction must be carried out immediately and the procurator informed of that fact.

62. Measures of legal defence are also provided for in the codes on administrative infringements of the law adopted in the Union Republics in the period 1984–1985. Thus the RSFSR Code on Administrative Infringements states "Observance of legislative requirements in applying measures against administrative infringements of the law is ensured by systematic control on the part of higher bodies and officials, by supervision on the part of the Procurator's Office, by the right of appeal and by other means laid down in the legislation" (Article 8).

63. The codes of the Union Republics on administrative infringements include a special chapter which regulates in detail the procedure for lodging appeals or protests against decisions on cases of administrative infringements. It states, in particular, that an appeal may be sent both to the courts and to the higher administrative level. A citizen has the right to appeal against decisions concerning administrative penalties taken by officials or by collective bodies such as the Executive Committees of the local Soviets, Commissions of the Executive Committee, etc.

64. In 1987, as part of the process of assessing the effectiveness of the activities of bodies for legal protection in defending the interests of citizens, providing the population with legal services and ensuring a proper attitude on the part of State bodies to requests, appeals, critical remarks and declarations by citizens, the Presidium of the Supreme Soviet of the USSR adopted a number of consolidating decrees aimed at ensuring still more consistent application by all competent authorities and officials of the means that have been given to the population for legal protection and satisfaction of its lawful interests.

65. In a decree of the Presidium of the Supreme Soviet of the USSR "Appeals by citizens to the Supreme Soviet of the USSR" dated 17 February 1987, it was noted with satisfaction that citizens had begun to exercise more actively their constitutional right to criticize shortcomings in the activities of Soviet and economic bodies and in the struggle against abuses, bureaucracy, infringements of the law and denial of social justice.

66. The Presidium emphasized that criticism of shortcomings is one of the forms of democracy. Proposals, critical remarks, complaints and expressions of wishes from the working people are an important channel for determining public opinion and a substantial source of the information necessary if Soviets of People's Deputies at all levels are to work effectively. With that in mind, the Presidium of the Supreme Soviet of the USSR decreed that information on appeals by citizens to the Supreme Soviet should be sent to the Presidia of the Supreme Soviets of the Union Republics for consideration and the drawing of practical conclusions, drawing particular attention to the need for consistent meeting of demands for an enhancement of the role and an increase in the responsibility of Soviets of People's Deputies in speeding up socialist economic development in their territories and improving the services offered to the people; in constantly improving the activities of enterprises, establishments and organizations administratively subject to them that are directly connected with the satisfaction of the everyday needs of the people and in settling problems touching on the essential interests of the citizens; in extending openness in the work of the Soviets of People's Deputies; in reacting promptly to cases where insufficient attention had been paid to problems raised in statements and appeals; and in putting a decisive stop to any attempts to clamp down on criticism and to the use of letters for slanderous purposes.

67. The Presidium of the Supreme Soviet of the USSR instructed the Presidia of the Supreme Soviets of the Union and Autonomous Republics and the local Soviets of People's Deputies to adopt additional measures designed to improve the consideration of appeals from citizens and to arrange for citizens wishing to make such appeals to be given a hearing. It proposed that they should carefully analyse and draw conclusions from the proposals and critical remarks made by working people and make fuller use of them in their activities.

68. At the same time the Presidium of the Supreme Soviet of the USSR instructed the editorial boards of the paper *Izvestia Sovetov Narodnykh Deputatov SSSR* and the journal *Sovety Narodnykh Deputatov* to give regular space to

U

matters dealt with in appeals from citizens received by the Soviets of People's Deputies.

69. On 30 July 1987 the Presidium of the Supreme Soviet of the USSR adopted a Decree "The work of organs of the judiciary in providing the population with legal services". The Decree assessed the activities of the Soviets of People's Deputies, the courts, the legal profession and other judicial establishments from the point of view of further strengthening legality and order based on the due process of law and providing still better protection for the rights of the individual. On the basis of a summary of the practices that have grown up, the Presidium instructed the Presidia of the Supreme Soviets and Councils of Ministers of the Union and Autonomous Republics to ensure that all levels of the Soviets of People's Deputies elected in 1987 should work effectively to provide reliable protection of citizens' rights, strengthen their leadership and control over the functioning of bodies administratively subject to them, increase the accountability and liability of staff for unswerving implementation of the law and strengthen their connections with work collectives and the public at large.

70. The Decree especially noted the need, now that the management of the economy is being radically restructured, to enhance the role and responsibility of the legal services in enterprises, establishments and organizations in protecting the rights and lawful interests of workers and employees.

71. The Decree envisaged increased publication of the texts of laws and codes and commentaries on them and also of reference and popular works on the law, the regular publication in newspapers and journals of articles and commentaries explaining the rights and duties of Soviet citizens and an extension of popularization work aimed at making advanced experience in providing legal aid to the population as widely known as possible.

Equality of Rights between Men and Women (Article 3 of the Covenant). 72. Soviet legislation devotes much attention to providing women, and particularly pregnant women and women with small children, with special privileges ensuring their right to work, to promotion and to participation in public life and giving them a possibility equal to that enjoyed by men of making use of those rights. In the 80s, particularly after 1984, the legislation on this subject was further developed. It is quoted in the section on Articles 23 and 24 of the Covenant.

73. Provision is made in the short-term, medium-term and long-term programmes for the socio-economic development of the Soviet Union to make it easier for women to make effective use of their legally recognized rights, equal to those of men, to work, to receive an education and to participate in public, political, cultural and other social activities, by improving their conditions of life and work, by extending help to families with children etc. For example, the Act of the USSR "State plan for the economic and social development of the USSR in 1986–1990" of 19 June 1986 envisages:

—an increase in the duration of partially paid leave for working mothers to look after a child until the age of 18 months and at the same time the right to additional unpaid leave until the child has reached the age of two;

—the duration of antenatal leave for working mothers is to be increased from 56 to 70 calendar days and unpaid leave to look after sick children to 14 days;

—the age of children for whom grants are paid to poor families is to be increased from 8 to 12 years;

—the amounts assigned for board in pre-school estab-

lishments are being increased and children up to 3 years of age are provided free with any medicaments they need;

—newly married couples for the first year of their marriage will not have to pay the tax levied on citizens with small families;

Most of these measures have already been put in effect (see Articles 23–24).

74. The more active involvement of women in the social and political life of the country, and the provision of extended possibilities for them to protect their rights and lawful interests have been promoted by the widespread formation in establishments and in undertakings of such public organizations as the Women's Councils, which have been united in a single system headed by the Soviet Women's Committee.

[Paragraphs 74A–74M have been interpolated from UN Doc. CCPR/C/52/Add. 6.]

State of Emergency (Article 4 of the Covenant). 74A. A curfew, and in some cases, martial law, were introduced in the territory of the USSR in September 1988 and are still in force in some towns and districts of six Union Republics (Azerbaidzhan, Armenia, Uzbekistan, Kazakhstan, Tadzhikistan and Georgia) because of heightened inter-ethnic tensions and with a view to ensuring the proper maintenance of law and order and public safety.

74B. The curfew was generally imposed from 9 or 10 p.m. until 5 or 6 a.m. During this time the movements of individuals and vehicles were restricted and the forces of law and order were authorized where necessary to stop and examine vehicles and persons not carrying special permits, to check internal passports, establish the identity of the persons breaking the curfew and clarify the situation with them.

74C. The martial law measures took the form of the prohibition or restriction of meetings and demonstrations, strikes and public events; restriction of the entry of non-residents into districts under martial law; and prohibition of the storage of firearms, explosives and incendiary materials, together with their confiscation.

74D. These restrictions were necessitated by inter-ethnic confrontations which involved the use of violence, cold steel and firearms, and generally resulted in bodily injury, arson, and damage to homes, industrial and administrative buildings and other property.

74E. Martial law and the curfew were introduced for the first time on 21 September 1988 in the Nagorno-Karabakh autonomous region and in Agdam district of the Azerbaidzhan SSR. This was preceded, in particular, by large-scale confrontations between Armenian and Azerbaidzhani members of the population which resulted in 49 civilian casualties, of whom 17 were hospitalized and one died, and caused about 30 residential and other buildings to be set on fire. Persons with extremist attitudes attacked the local public prosecutor's office and some militia workers were injured.

74F. A curfew was subsequently introduced in Azerbaidzhan in the towns of Baku, Nakhichevan and Kirovobad (on 24 November 1988) and in 17 districts of the Republic (on 5 December 1988).

74G. In Armenia a curfew was imposed on 24 November 1988 in Yerevan and on 5 December 1988 in 16 districts of the Republic.

74H. In Georgia a curfew was imposed from 9 to 14 April 1989 in Tbilisi and certain restrictions were introduced on 18 July 1989 in the Abkhaz Autonomous Republic of the Georgian SSR.

74I. In Uzbekistan a curfew was imposed on 4 June 19-89 in Fergana. A curfew was introduced from 19 June to 24 July in Novy-Uzen in the Gurev region of the Kazakh SSR.

74J. In Tadzhikistan a curfew was imposed on 13 July 1989 in Isfara and in three villages of Leninabad region.

74K. The introduction of the above restrictions by the State authorities is not inconsistent with the provisions of the Soviet Constitution or the International Covenant on Civil and Political Rights. These restrictions are temporary and are designed to prevent dangerous developments in the above-mentioned towns and districts resulting from the incitement of ethnic discord by persons with extremist attitudes.

74L. These measures have helped to prevent groups from disturbing public order and to protect citizens' personal and property rights and the safety of the population as a whole.

74M. The restrictions still in force will be lifted once the situation in these areas has returned to normal.

Right to Life (Article 6 of the Covenant). 75. At the present time the USSR is conducting a comprehensive and active study on the possibility of substantially reducing application of the death penalty by cutting down the number of crimes for which the ultimate sentence can be handed down. An example of extending the possibility of reprieving persons sentenced to death is the Decree of the Presidium of the Supreme Soviet of the USSR dated 23 May 1986 "Supplementing Article 23 of the Foundations of Criminal Legislation of the Union of Socialist Soviet Republics and the Union Republics", which provides that when a death sentence is commuted to a sentence of imprisonment, the term shall be for over 15 years but not more than 20 years.

76. Another aspect of the right to life regulated in detail by Soviet legislation is compensation for harm caused to the life and health of citizens. On 3 July 1984, with a view to strengthening protection of the citizen's right to life and health and reducing accidents at work, Decree No. 690 of the Council of Ministers of the USSR laid down rules for compensation by enterprise, establishments and organizations for damage caused to workers and employees through injury or other impairment of health connected with their performance of their working tasks. A Decree of the State Committee of the USSR on Labour and Social Questions and of the Presidium of the All-Union Central Council of Trades Unions dated 13 February 1985 brought into force instructions for applying those rules. In these instruments the basic principles governing compensation for harm caused to the life and health of citizens were further developed.

77. Workers and employees who fully or partially lose their capacity for work as a result of injury through the fault of the organization for which they work must be fully compensated by that organization for the harm caused. What is envisaged is that the organization must give the victim an amount of compensation, which together with the pension received under the State Social Insurance scheme, fully compensates for the wages he received before the injury to his health. If working capacity is partially lost, sums above the pension and the wage which the victim can earn while still partially able to work are paid in compensation.

78. In addition to compensation for lost wages the victim can also receive compensation for additional expenditure incurred through the damage to his health: expenditure for extra food, the purchase of medicaments, the fitting of prostheses, nursing care, sanatorium and health resort treatment including the fare to the place of treatment and back and where necessary that of the person accompanying the victim, the procurement of special means of conveyance, major repairs to them, the purchase of fuel and some other items.

79. The legislation also protects the rights of those who were materially dependent on the victim. It is provided that in the case of the victim's death the right to compensation for loss applies to persons unable to work who were maintained by the dead person or, at the time of his death, had the right to receive maintenance from him and also to one of the relations, a spouse or other member of a family, if that person does not work and is occupied in looking after children, brothers, sisters or grandchildren of the dead person under the age of 8.

80. The main provisions of the rules for the compensation of loss and of the accompanying instructions apply also in other cases of harm caused as a result of damage to the health of a citizen or his death. For this reason a Decree No. 13 was adopted by the Plenum of the Supreme Court of the USSR, dated 5 September 1986, "Practice of the courts in cases concerning compensation for harm caused by impairment of health".

81. The statutory instruments listed maintain a simplified procedure for paying sums in compensation for loss in connection with damage to health incurred at work. The appropriate compensation is paid to the victim on the instructions of the management of the enterprise, establishment or organization in which he worked and received his injury. At the same time the victim has the right to judicial protection of his interests. If he does not agree with the decision of the management and also of the trade union committee to which he has the right to appeal against the management's decision, he may take the matter before the courts.

[Paragraph 81A has been interpolated from UN Doc. CCPR/C/52/Add. 6.]

81A. The edict of the Presidium of the USSR Supreme Soviet of 29 January 1988 entitled "Procedure governing compensation for harm caused to manual and non-manual workers by the occupational disease of pneumoconiosis" removed the restrictions hitherto applied to compensation for the harm caused by one of the most widespread occupational diseases of miners, geologists, etc. These persons are now entitled to receive full compensation for such harm, where necessary, from their own enterprise.

82. In the years that have elapsed since the adoption of the International Covenant on Civil and Political Rights more comprehensive interpretations of the right to life have been formulated in international law, so that it includes the individual right of every person and the collective right of every people to live in peace, free from the use of armed force and the threat of force, in a world free of the arms race and free of the use of nuclear weapons and other weapons of mass destruction.

83. The Soviet Union believes that the preservation of international peace and the prevention of a nuclear catastrophe are an indispensable condition for implementing both the right to life and the whole complex of political, civil and other human rights. This conviction has been reflected in the most important documents of the Communist Party of the Soviet Union and the Soviet State. It is embodied in practical steps taken by the USSR in the international arena and in concrete initiatives which the Soviet Union has put forward, particularly in the last few years.

84. The new version of the Programme of the Commu-

nist Party of the Soviet Union adopted on 1 March 1986 proclaimed it as the solemn duty of the CPSU "to do all in its power to preserve peaceful conditions for the constructive work of the Soviet people, to make international relations healthier and to stop the arms race that is the scourge of the world, so as to avert the threat of atomic war that hangs over the peoples". The Programme stresses that there is no weapon that the Soviet Union would not be ready to limit or prohibit on a mutual basis under effective supervision. It gives a concrete list of the tasks which the CPSU and the Soviet State will try to accomplish with a view to achieving general and complete disarmament:

—limitation and restriction of the sphere of war preparations, particularly those connected with weapons of mass destruction;

—the achievement, stage by stage by the end of the twentieth century, of the complete elimination of nuclear weapons by stopping the testing and production of all forms of such weapons, by all nuclear powers renouncing first use of such weapons and by the freezing, reduction and destruction of their stocks of them;

—the cessation of production and the elimination of other forms of weapons of mass destruction, including chemical weapons, and a prohibition on the creation of new types of destructive weapons;

—a reduction in the armed forces of States, first of all of the permanent members of the United Nations Security Council and countries linked with them through military agreements;

—a reduction in conventional weapons and a cessation of the creation of new forms of weapons which in their striking power would approximate to weapons of mass destruction; and a reduction in military expenditure;

—the freezing and reduction of armed forces and weapons in the most explosive regions of the world, the elimination of military bases on foreign soil, and the adoption of measures to strengthen mutual trust and reduce the risk of armed conflicts arising, including the risk of them arising by accident.

85. At its 27th Congress in 1986 the Communist Party of the Soviet Union came out in favour of the creation of a comprehensive system of international security. Among the foundations for such a system the Party proposed:

In the military sphere,

—renunciation by the nuclear powers of war, either nuclear or conventional, against one another or against third parties;

—the prohibition of an arms race in space, the cessation of all tests of nuclear weapons and their complete elimination, the prohibition and destruction of chemical weapons and renunciation of the creation of other means of mass destruction;

—a strictly controlled reduction in the level of war potential of States, down to the limits of a reasonable sufficiency;

—the disbanding of military groupings and, as a step towards it, an agreement not to extend existing or form new groupings;

—a proportional and commensurate reduction in military budgets;

In the political sphere,

—unconditional respect in international practice for the right of every people to select, in a sovereign manner, the pathways and forms of its own development;

—a just political regulation of international crises and regional conflicts;

—the development of a set of measures aimed at strengthening trust between States and, the creation of effective guarantees against attack from outside and of the inviolability of their frontiers;

—the development of effective measures for preventing international terrorism, including security in the use of international land, air and sea communications.

In the economic sphere,

—exclusion from international practice of all forms of discrimination;

—renunciation of a policy of economic blockades and sanctions, if they are not directly recommended by the world community;

—a joint search for ways of regulating in a just manner the problems of indebtedness;

—the development of principles for using, to the benefit of the world community, and particularly of the developing countries, part of the resources that will be released as a result of the reduction in military spending:

—the uniting of efforts in the exploration and peaceful utilization of space and the settlement of global problems on which the fate of civilization depends.

In the humanitarian sphere,

—cooperation in the dissemination of the ideas of peace, disarmament and international security;

—increasing the degree to which the peoples are given general objective information about, and can become mutually acquainted with, life in each other's countries, and strengthening the spirit of mutual understanding and concord in relations between them;

—the eradication of genocide, apartheid and the preaching of fascism or any other doctrine of racial, national or religious exclusivity, and elimination of discrimination against people on the basis of such doctrines;

—the extension—while respecting the laws of each individual country—of international cooperation in implementing the political, social and personal rights of man;

—the solving, in a humane and positive spirit, of questions of the reuniting of families, the celebration of marriages and the development of contacts between peoples and organizations;

—the strengthening of and search for new forms of cooperation in the sphere of culture, art, science, education and medicine (Political Report of the Central Committee of the CPSU at its 27th Congress).

86. To develop the main elements in a comprehensive system of international security and guarantee the implementation of the right to life, the Soviet Union is in favour of fighting international terrorism and ensuring security against international terrorist acts. In a Decree of the Presidium of the Supreme Soviet of the USSR dated 10 July 1987 "The adherence of the Union of Soviet Socialist Republics to the International Convention against the Taking of Hostages" special stress is laid on the following "The Union of Soviet Socialist Republics rejects international terrorism, which threatens the life of innocent people, constitutes a menace to their freedom and personal integrity, and destabilizes the international situation, no matter what motives are adduced to explain the terrorist acts. The USSR accordingly considers that paragraph 1 of Article 9 of the Convention should be applied in such a way that it corresponds to the proclaimed aims of the Convention, including the development of international cooperation in the taking of effective measures for the prevention, prosecution and punishment of all acts of hostage-taking as a manifestation of international terrorism, including the

handing-over of the presumed criminals". In fulfillment of its obligations under this Convention the Decree made the taking of hostages a criminal offence. Articles corresponding to this Decree have also been inserted in the criminal codes of the Union Republics.

Prohibition against subjecting People to Torture or to Cruel, Inhuman or Degrading Treatment or Punishment (Article 7 of the Covenant). 87. As stated in the two previous reports, Soviet legislation has consistently consolidated the prohibition against subjecting anybody to torture or to cruel, inhuman or degrading treatment or punishment.

88. In the international arena the Soviet Union has also consistently spoken in favour of active international cooperation designed to put an end to tortures. On 21 January 1987 the Presidium of the Supreme Soviet of the USSR adopted a Decree "Ratification of the Convention against Torture and other Cruel, Inhuman or Degrading Forms of Treatment and Punishment signed on behalf of the Government of the USSR in New York on 10 December 1985".

The Right to Freedom and Security of Person (Article 9). 89. The efforts developed in the Soviet Union since 1985 to put into effect the restructuring policy in connection with the universal confirmation of the principle of social legality and the equality of citizens before the law has made it necessary to develop a set of measures specially designed to improve the effectiveness of the work of bodies for protecting the rights of the citizen. A Decree of the Central Committee of the CPSU dated 20 November 1986 was devoted to this under the title of "Further consolidation of socialist legality and order based on due process of law, and the strengthening of protection of citizens' rights and lawful interests". The unswerving observance of the laws and the further strengthening of guarantees of citizens' rights and lawful interests are considered by the Decree as a necessary condition for the normal functioning of the Soviet political system and as a most important integral aspect of perestroika. Every case in which legality is infringed, the Decree goes on to say, must on principle be sharply assessed and subjected to rigorous analysis and persons guilty of committing actions against the rights of people must be punished with all the severity of the law. The Decree gives guidance on restructuring the work of the courts, the Procurator's Office, the militia and other bodies charged with defending the law so that they reliably guarantee protection of the interests of the State and the rights of the citizens.

90. A logical continuation of this line was the Decree of the Central Committee of the CPSU dated 4 June 1987 under the title of "Measures to enhance the role of supervision by the procurators in strengthening socialist legality and order based on due process of law" in which the key ideas of socialist legality are developed, and also the Decree of the Presidium of the Supreme Soviet of the USSR dated 16 June 1987 under the title of "Amendments and additions to the Act of the USSR 'The Procurator's Office of the USSR' ". The Decree pays special attention to the role of the Procurator's Office in ensuring the rights and lawful interests of Soviet citizens. It contains a wide programme for activity by the Procurator's Office and above all for the improvement of its work in general supervision of the fulfillment of the laws.

91. The amendments and additions introduced into the Act of the USSR "The Procurator's Office of the USSR" by the Decree of 16 June 1987 lay stress on concern for comprehensively guaranteeing the constitutional rights of citizens. In the new wording of Article 3 of the Act, it is stressed that the struggle to prevent infringements of the laws designed to ensure the rights and lawful interests of citizens is an independent sector of the work of the Procurator's Office. Glasnost in the activities of the bodies depending on that Office is intensified. The Decree makes the procurators responsible for informing the Presidia of the Supreme Soviets and Councils of Ministers of the Union and Autonomous Republics, the local Soviets of People's Deputies and work collectives about progress in ensuring observance of the law and respect for the due process of law (some other provisions of the Decree are commented on in the section on Article 2 of the Covenant).

92. In ensuring the right to freedom and security of person a substantial role is played also by a statutory instrument—Order No. 9 of the Procurator General of the USSR dated 19 February 1988 and entitled "The strictest observance of legality in using arrest as a measure for cutting short or prolonging the duration of detention in custody in a preliminary investigation", aimed at ensuring that the Procurator's Office of the USSR takes decisive steps to ensure reliable defence of the constitutional rights and freedoms of Soviet citizens during criminal proceedings.

93. In January 1988 the Presidium of the Supreme Soviet of the USSR in a decree approved "Regulations on the conditions and procedure for providing psychiatric care", in which the procedure for preserving the rights and lawful interests of persons suffering from mental disorders is defined. The Decree lays down the independence of the medical psychiatrist in reaching his decisions and deals with questions of medical confidentiality and the rules concerning primary psychiatric certification. Legal guarantees are provided against possible errors and abuses in providing psychiatric care for the population. The regulations restore the principle of criminal liability if a person known to be healthy is placed in a psychiatric hospital.

[Paragraphs 93A–93D have been interpolated from UN Doc. CCPR/C/52/Add. 6.]

93A. In this connection, at the same time that this decree was adopted, a new article was introduced in the criminal codes of the union republics establishing criminal liability for the placement of a person known to be in sound mental health in a psychiatric hospital. If, before the adoption of the decree, compulsory treatment of persons in this category was being carried out in general and special hospitals, and the patients were under the responsibility of the Soviet Ministry of Internal Affairs, they are now transferred to the care of the Soviet Ministry of Health. The regulations guarantee the right of citizens to appeal to the courts in cases where they do not agree with the decisions of the psychiatrists and psychiatric boards. They are guaranteed legal assistance by a lawyer with a view to ensuring that their rights are upheld.

93B. The Supreme Court consolidated judicial practice concerning compensation for prejudice caused to citizens as a result of the unlawful institution of criminal proceedings against them, and its plenum adopted decree No. 15 of 23 December 1988 on "Certain issues in the judicial application of the edict of the Presidium of the Supreme Soviet of the USSR of 18 May 1981, entitled 'Compensation for prejudice caused to citizens by the unlawful actions of State and social organizations, and also those of officials in the implementation of their official functions' ".

93C. This contains interpretative provisions, which are of mandatory application for the courts, designed to ensure the complete elimination of all adverse consequences for the victims, and including the payment of sums of money and the restoration of labour rights, pension rights or other civil rights.

93D. On 2 March 1989 the Plenum of the Supreme Soviet of the USSR adopted decree No. 2 on the "Judicial application of article 7 of the Basic Principles of Civil Legislation of the USSR and the Union Republics Relating to Protection of the Honour and Dignity of Citizens and Organizations". It provides interpretative provisions designed to extend opportunities for citizens to request the courts to order the rebuttal of items of information defamatory to them which have been published in the press, broadcast on the radio or television or disseminated by means of other mass media, stated in public declarations, communicated to officials, etc. Citizens are granted the right to demand rebuttal of defamatory items of information disseminated regarding the members of their family or other relatives.

The Right of Persons Deprived of Their Liberty to Be Treated with Humanity (Article 10 of the Covenant). 94. A Decree of the Presidium of the Supreme Soviet of the USSR dated 2 April 1985 under the title of "Amendments and additions to the Foundations of Criminal Legislation of the USSR and the Union Republics and the Foundations of Corrective-Labour Legislation of the USSR and the Union Republics" envisages a further humanization of the system for serving criminal sentences. It extends the serving of sentences in colony-settlements instead of in corrective-labour colonies of other types. Under the terms of the Decree, male offenders will serve sentences in corrective-labour colonies as follows:

—if sentenced for the first time to deprivation of liberty for crimes committed by negligence, in colony-settlements for persons who have committed crimes of negligence;

—if sentenced for the first time to deprivation of liberty for a period of not more than five years for deliberate crimes that are not grave offences, in colony-settlements for persons who have committed deliberate crimes;

—if sentenced for the first time to deprivation of liberty for deliberate crimes that are not grave offences, except for those indicated in the law, in general corrective-labour colonies;

—if sentenced for the first time to deprivation of liberty for grave offences, in colonies with stricter conditions;

—if sentenced for particularly dangerous crimes against the State or if they have already served sentences involving deprivation of liberty, in colonies with severe conditions;

—if they are recidivists considered to be particularly dangerous, in colonies with special conditions;

Women sentenced to deprivation of liberty shall serve their sentences in corrective-labour colonies as follows:

—if considered dangerous recidivists, sentenced for particularly dangerous crimes against the State, in colonies with severe conditions;

—if sentenced for the first time to deprivation of liberty for crimes committed by negligence, in colony-settlements for persons who have committed crimes by negligence;

—if sentenced for the first time for deliberate crimes listed in the law, in colony-settlements for persons who have committed deliberate crimes;

—other women condemned to deprivation of liberty shall serve their sentences in general corrective-labour colonies.

The serving of sentences in training labour colonies is designated for:

—male minors, sentenced for the first time to deprivation of liberty and also female minors, the sentences to be served in colonies of the general type;

—male minors, who have already served sentences involving deprivation of liberty, shall serve their new sentences in colonies with stricter conditions.

95. Depending on the nature and degree of danger to the public from the crime committed, the personality of the guilty person and other circumstances of the case, and with a statement of the motives for the decision taken, the court may sentence persons to deprivation of liberty as follows:

—those condemned for the first time for crimes committed by negligence and also for deliberate crimes indicated in the law, to a sentence to be served in corrective labour colonies of the general type;

—other persons condemned to deprivation of liberty but not considered to be particularly dangerous recidivists to sentences to be served in corrective-labour colonies of any type except colonies with special conditions and colony-settlements;

—male minors to sentences to be served in training labour colonies of the general type instead of colonies with stricter conditions.

96. In corrective labour establishments general secondary education is provided for young people serving sentences, and vocational and technical training or in-service vocational training for persons serving sentences who have no profession. At the same time, people over 40 years of age serving sentences are given general education and disabled persons in the first and second groups are also given vocational and technical education or in-service training at work according to their own wishes. To enable them to take examinations the pupils in these establishments are released from work for a certain period. Wages are not paid for those periods, but board and lodging are provided free. The procedure for training set forth above was introduced in an Act of the USSR dated 27 November 1985 "The introduction of amendments to some legislative acts of the USSR in connection with the basic directions of reform in general education and vocational training and adoption of the new version of the Foundations of the Legislation of the USSR and Union Republics in regard to Education".

The Right to Liberty of Movement, including the Right to Leave any Country (Article 12 of the Covenant). 97. During the review period the conditions for departure from and entry to the USSR by Soviet citizens have undergone substantial changes. These changes were introduced by a Decree of the Council of Ministers of the USSR dated 28 August 1986 which added to the regulations concerning entry to the USSR and departure from the USSR of 22 September 1970 a new section "Consideration of applications for entry into the Union of Soviet Socialist Republics or departure from the Union of Soviet Socialist Republics on private business". The provisions of the new section came into effect on 1 January 1987.

98. Under their terms the principle is established that entry into the USSR and departure from the USSR on private business is permitted for citizens of the USSR, foreign citizens and stateless persons, independently of their origin, social status, property, race, nationality, sex, level of education, language and attitude to religion (paragraph 20 of the Regulations).

99. The grounds for entry into the USSR and departure from the USSR on private business are clearly defined (paragraph 21 of the Regulations). These are: reunion with

members of the family, meetings with close relatives, entry into marriage, visits to seriously ill relatives, visits to places where near relatives are buried and settlement of questions of inheritance. This list is not exhaustive. The regulations state that "other important grounds can also serve as a basis for entry or departure".

100. The regulations answer the question of how to interpret reunion with members of the family. Paragraph 24 provides that an application for departure abroad for reunion with members of the family shall be considered when an invitation is presented from a husband, wife, father, mother, son, daughter, brother or sister. On the basis essentially of a wish to help a person on his or her own to found a family if that person so wishes, it is laid down that if a person applying for departure has no family members in the USSR an application for departure can be taken into consideration if an invitation from another relative is presented.

101. Up till 1 January 1987, as a rule departure was not allowed when most of the close relatives remained in the USSR. These limitations have now been abolished.

102. An application to go abroad to be reunited with members of one's family as listed in paragraph 24 of the Regulations, is taken into consideration if notarized attestations are attached from the members of the family remaining in the USSR and also from a former spouse if there are minor children from their joint marriage, declaring that there are no obligations as laid down by the legislation of the USSR which the applicant has not met.

103. Among such obligations are, for example, those arising from Article 66 of the Constitution of the USSR. This states "Citizens of the USSR are obliged to concern themselves with the upbringing of children, to train them for socially useful work and to raise them as worthy members of socialist society. Children are obliged to care for their parents and help them".

104. Soviet citizens may leave the country temporarily on the invitation of any relatives and friends and in their turn may invite them as guests to visit them in the USSR. Until 1 January 1987 departure was permitted only once a year. This limitation has now been abolished.

105. Departure from the USSR for a Soviet citizen is prohibited only in cases clearly defined in paragraph 25 of the Regulations:

—if the person concerned has knowledge of State secrets or there are other reasons touching the security of the State;

—if the departure involves encroachment on the essential rights and lawful interests of other citizens of the USSR;

—if he has unfulfilled obligations to the State or property obligations involving the material or legal interests of State, cooperative or other public organizations;

—if there are legal grounds rendering him liable to criminal prosecution;

—if he has been sentenced for committing a crime.

Each of these grounds has effect for a limited time. Permission to leave the country is given after the circumstance that was an obstacle to obtaining it no longer applies. Permission for departure may be refused if during a previous stay abroad the applicant for departure has committed acts detrimental to the interests of the State or if he has been found guilty of infraction of Customs or currency legislation and also if, when making the application, he has given false information.

106. Entry into the USSR of a Soviet citizen who lives permanently abroad may be temporarily refused only in exceptional circumstances. Such circumstances are clearly listed in paragraph 26 of the Regulations. They include the need to ensure State security, the protection of public order and the health and morality of the population and the protection of the rights and lawful interests of Soviet citizens and other persons.

107. Further to the regulations on entry into and departure from the USSR, time limits for considering applications for entry and departure have been fixed. According to paragraph 28, an application for temporary entry to the USSR and departure from the USSR on private business must be considered as quickly as possible, and as a rule within a month, or if the journey is connected with a serious illness or death of a relative, within three days. An application for entry into the USSR or departure from the USSR for permanent residence must be considered within one month. Where further study is necessary the time limit may be extended but not beyond six months. The results of consideration of an application and, in the event of refusal, the motives for that refusal, must be brought to the attention of the applicant. In the case of a refusal of an application for entry to the USSR or departure from USSR on private business a repeat application on these matters will not be considered as a rule earlier than six months after the first application has been refused.

108. Children under 18 years of age may go abroad only on application by their legal representatives and as a rule only if they are to be accompanied by those representatives.

109. Departure from the USSR to another country for permanent residence by children from 14 to 18 years of age can only be allowed if they agree in writing and their agreement is countersigned by a notary.

110. Among the types of private business that provide a basis for an application for entry to the USSR or departure from the USSR paragraph 21 of the Regulations includes marriage. On 8 May 1987 the Ministry of Justice of the USSR approved "Instructions on the procedure for the registration in the USSR of the marriages of Soviet citizens with foreigners and stateless persons" aimed at preventing any encroachment on the rights and interests of foreigners and Soviet citizens when they enter into marriage or after they have entered into marriage, regardless of their later place of residence.

Equality of All Citizens before the Courts and Tribunals. Right to a Fair Hearing (Article 14 of the Covenant). 111. Of particular significance for the consistent implementation of the provisions of the Soviet law guaranteeing the equality of citizens before the courts and tribunals and the right to a fair and public hearing are the Decree of the Central Committee of the CPSU dated 20 November 1986 under the title "The further consolidation of socialist legality and order based on due process of law and strengthening of protection of citizens' rights and lawful interests", the Decree of the Central Committee of the CPSU dated 4 June 1987 under the title of "Measures to enhance the role of supervision by the procurators in supervising in strengthening Soviet legality and order based on due process of law" and the Decree of the Presidium of the Supreme Soviet of the USSR under the title "The Procurator's Office of the USSR", adopted as part of the implementation of the restructuring policy. These documents are analysed in the section relating to Article 9 of the Covenant.

112. At the present moment the question is being considered of allowing a lawyer to take part in the criminal procedures as a general rule from the time when a charge is filed or at an even earlier stage.

Freedom from Arbitrary Interference in Privacy, Home or Correspondence (Article 17). 113. The aim of strengthening the rule of law with a view to consistently ensuring freedom from arbitrary interference in a citizen's privacy, home or correspondence and protecting him against attacks on his honour and dignity is served by an Act of the USSR adopted by the Supreme Soviet of the USSR on 30 June 1987 under the title "Procedure for appealing to the court in respect of illegal acts by officials that encroach on the rights of citizens" (a detailed description of the Act is given in the section on Article 2 of the Covenant).

Right to Freedom of Thought, Conscience and Religion (Article 18 of the Covenant). 114. Lenin's Decree adopted 70 years ago, separating the church from the State and education from the church, created a new basis for the relations between them. These relations have not always followed a normal course, but life itself and history have united believers and unbelievers as citizens of the Soviet Union as patriots, both in the years of tribulation in the Great Patriotic War and in the foundation of our socialist motherland and the struggle for peace. The attitude to the religious view of the world current in our country as being non-materialistic and unscientific does not excuse any lack of respect for the spiritual world of believers and even less the use of any sort of administrative pressure to consolidate materialist viewpoints.

115. All believers, no matter what religion they profess, are citizens of the USSR with full rights. The overwhelming majority of them are playing an active part in our productive and social life and solving the tasks of perestroika. A bill now being prepared concerning the freedom of conscience is based on Leninist principles and takes into account all modern realities.

[Paragraphs 115A–115E have been interpolated from UN Doc. CCPR/C/52/Add. 6.]

115A. No recent cases have been recorded in which criminal proceedings have been instituted against citizens for violations of legislation on religious worship, and the number of those against whom administrative proceedings have been brought has dropped sharply.

115B. The number of applications from believers for registration of new religious communities is growing. Analysis of these applications shows that most of them are prompted by a wish on the part of believers to make use of the right to form religious associations under current legislation. Churches are once again being transferred to the communities being registered. Practice has shown that the registration of communities and the transfer of buildings to them for religious use reduces situations of conflict between believers and local authorities and helps to reduce the number of unregistered communities and ministers of religion.

115C. Nevertheless, cases of unjustified refusal to register religious communities still occur, running counter to the constitutional principle of freedom of conscience and legislation on religious worship currently in force, and giving believers grounds for dissatisfaction.

115D. It is also noteworthy that, in cases of registration of religious communities, executive committees frequently ignore the time-limits laid down by the law for consideration of citizens' applications, obliging them to complain to Republic-level or urban councils on religious affairs.

115E. On the whole, however, clergy and believers of the various faiths maintain normal relations with local authorities. The communities transfer money to the Fund for Peace and play an active part in a variety of charitable activities.

115F. During the period under review steps were taken on an extensive scale in the USSR to mark the 1000th anniversary of the adoption of Christianity in Rus, the 600th anniversary of the adoption of Catholicism in Lithuania and the 1100th anniversary of the adoption of Islam by the Volga Bulgarians.

The Right to Hold and Express Opinions without Interference (Article 19 of the Covenant). 116. The extension of guarantees and the step-by-step implementation of the right of Soviet citizens to hold and freely express their opinions without interference have become important and effective instruments for putting into effect the perestroika policy being carried out in the USSR. The question of openness ("glasnost") as an essential condition for the practical implementation of the development of democracy was considered in detail at the 27th Congress of the Communist Party of the Soviet Union, where it was stressed that "It is essential for us to extend openness (glasnost). This is a political question. Without openness there is not and cannot be democracy or political creativity on the part of the masses or their participation in management" (Political report of the Central Committee of the CPSU at the 27th Congress).

117. Legal guarantees of the effective exercise by Soviet citizens of the right to hold and express their opinions freely have been strengthened, as was noted in the previous reports, in the Constitution and current legislation of the Soviet Union.

118. Among others, the most widespread ways of exercising the right to free expression of opinions are speeches by citizens at meetings in their places of work or residence and the sending of letters, complaints and proposals to State bodies and public organizations, which are obliged to consider such documents in accordance with procedures laid down and to send proper replies to them. The right to complain of the actions of officials or State and public bodies is among the constitutional rights in the USSR (Article 58 of the Constitution of the USSR). It has been given practical form in the Act of the USSR already mentioned "Procedure for appealing to the courts in respect of illegal acts by officials that encroach on citizens' rights" adopted by the Supreme Soviet of the USSR on 30 June 1987, with the amendments introduced by the Act of the USSR dated 20 October 1987. In the Decree of the Presidium of the Supreme Soviet of the USSR "Appeals by citizens to the Supreme Soviet of the USSR" dated 17 February 1987 such appeals are described as one of the forms of democracy. It is laid down that all organs of State power must react promptly and in accordance with the law to the critical comments made in such appeals (the main postulates of these Acts and this Decree were discussed in the section on Article 2 of the Covenant).

119. A Soviet citizen is also entitled to write to the newspapers and journals with a request to publish letters, notes, appeals and other materials or also simply to send letters or telegrams to any of the organs of the mass media—newspapers, magazines, radio and television. The mass media regularly publish citizens' letters on problems of Soviet and international life or reviews of such letters.

120. Implementation of the policy of perestroika being carried out in the USSR presupposes the further development of openness and its conversion into an effective form of popular control. The political decisions to ensure this were taken at the January 1987 Plenum of the Central Committee of the CPSU. In a Decree dated 28 January 1987

"Perestroika and the staffing policy of the Communist Party," the Plenum made it obligatory for all party committees and party organizations to adopt supplementary measures aimed at extending glasnost and developing criticism and self-criticism, particularly criticism from below, and to use this tried and tested weapon fully for training staff in a spirit of refusal to accept short-comings, healthy insatisfaction with what has been achieved and the elimination of any form of deviation from the norms of socialist morality.

121. The task was set at the Plenum of strengthening the legal basis and guarantees of glasnost. The documentation of the Plenum emphasized that the time had come to begin to develop legal instruments guaranteeing glasnost. These instruments should ensure maximum openness in the activities of State and public organizations and give working people a real possibility of expressing their opinions on any aspect of the life of society (Report to the Plenum of the Secretary-General of the Central Committee of the CPSU, dated 27 January 1987).

122. A concrete step in this direction was the adoption by the Supreme Soviet of the USSR on 30 June 1987 of an Act of the USSR under the title of "Nationwide discussion of important aspects of State activities" (an exposition of this Act is given in the section relating to Article 25 of the Covenant).

[Paragraph 122A has been interpolated from UN Doc. CCPR/C/52/Add. 6.]

122A. An edict of the Presidium of the Supreme Soviet of the USSR dated 8 April 1989, following ratification by the Supreme Soviet in June 1989, abolished criminal liability for anti-Soviet agitation and propaganda as provided for in article 7 of the USSR Act on Criminal Liability for Offences against the State (article 70 of the Criminal Code of the RSFSR). Article 7 has now been completely reworded in accordance with the standards of genuinely democratic States. In its new wording it declares to be criminal acts public appeals for the forcible overthrow or change of the Soviet State and social order enshrined in the Constitution of the USSR, and also the dissemination of material of such content for that purpose. It is quite clear that the scope of the article has been narrowed down, and that it is now more concrete in nature and precludes any arbitrary interpretation. The article clearly indicates that it is not heterodoxy that is regarded as a crime, but very specific actions of incitement to violence, which thereby present a danger both for the State and for citizens. It is also important to point out that the Edict of the Presidium of the Supreme Soviet of the RSFSR of 8 April 1989 on amendments and supplements to the Criminal Code and the Code of Criminal Procedure of the RSFSR deleted from the Criminal Code of the RSFSR article No. 190[1], which laid down criminal liability for the dissemination of fabrications known to be untrue which are defamatory to the Soviet State and social order. This article, and also the above-mentioned article 7 in its former wording, were in practice interpreted fairly broadly, which resulted in their being used to deal with people with unorthodox opinions, those who rightly criticized negative aspects of life in the USSR. Consequently its deletion constitutes an important step towards the fuller realization of one of the most important human rights, the right to the free expression of one's opinion.

The Right of Peaceful Assembly (Article 21 of the Covenant).
123. The holding of assemblies and meetings of citizens to discuss the most varied aspects of the internal and external policy of the Soviet State and of Soviet and international life is widespread in the Soviet Union. Assemblies on the territorial principle are convened in citizens' places of residence also to discuss and decide questions of direct interest to them. For this purpose in the countryside village meetings are regularly convened which represent assemblies of all the adult inhabitants of the village. Citizens' assemblies at their places of work are held to discuss both questions of production and other matters of interest to the workers in the enterprise concerned. With a view to implementing the requirements of Article 50 of the Constitution of the USSR regulations were adopted in 1987 in Moscow, Leningrad, Riga, Tallinn and other cities on the organization and holding of assemblies and meetings, street processions, demonstrations and other events. At the present time the question is being discussed of improving the legal regulation of conditions and procedures for holding peaceful assemblies, processions and demonstrations. In the period of perestroika the citizens of the USSR have made particularly active use of their constitutional right of peaceful assembly. Meanwhile, peaceful assemblies, meetings, processions and demonstrations are being held quite often, including those held by people who do not share official points of view. However, such activities should not be accompanied by infringements of administrative law.

[Paragraphs 123A–123O have been interpolated from UN Doc. CCPR/C/52/Add. 6.]

123A. Research indicates that more than 50 per cent of them are devoted to problems of nationalities, one in four or five to issues related to the development of the State and the Party, one in fourteen to environmental questions and about one in five to other issues: efforts to combat bureaucratism, corruption and the authoritarian and pressure-based mode of operation of the *apparat,* the defence of citizens' social rights and lawful interests, the protection of architectural and artistic treasures, issues of urban construction, and so on—in other words, most of them are conducted in support of *perestroika,* and the realization of the plans and ideas which underlie it.

123B. On 28 July 1988, bearing in mind the provisions of the International Covenant on Civil and Political Rights, and in the interests of a uniform approach to procedures for the organization and conduct of large-scale events of a social and political nature, the Presidium of the Supreme Soviet of the USSR adopted an edict on the "Procedure for the Organization and Conduct of Gatherings, Meetings, Street Processions and Demonstrations in the USSR".

123C. Following the proclamation of the above-mentioned edict of the Presidium of the Supreme Soviet of the USSR, the records of the Soviet Ministry of Internal Affairs alone indicate that during 1988 informal associations in the country held 913 gatherings, meetings, street processions and demonstrations, and a further 1,339 between 1 January and 31 May 1989, in which some 15 million people participated.

123D. Study of the application of this legislation shows that many principles in it are valid and are being put into effect by officials and citizens, and that meetings and demonstrations afford a vast potential for the development of democracy. As they take place, in accordance with the law, a contest occurs between various interests and views on how best to tackle one single problem—that of accelerating the ongoing *perestroika* in the country, and improving the lives of Soviet people.

123E. Regrettably, certain leaders of informal associations who have extremist attitudes, skilfully exploiting temporary difficulties in the supply of food and housing and other problems, are deliberately putting forward unlawful demands. They claim that in the context of *perestroika* it is not necessary to observe the requirements of the Constitution and Soviet laws, and it is no accident that the meetings and demonstrations they have organized without authorization sometimes grow into large-scale disorder, leading to painful consequences. Confirmation of this is offered by the tragic events in Transcaucasia and Central Asia, where unauthorized meetings led to large-scale disorder, injury and death, destruction of property, migration to other regions and so on.

123F. Regrettably, this legislation is not always carefully and unswervingly implemented by individual citizens or even by certain officials of the executive committees of local soviets of people's deputies and law enforcement bodies.

123G. The following are the most typical violations of the established procedures for the organization and holding of gatherings, meetings, street processions and demonstrations:

The holding of unauthorized public events by individual citizens: 56 per cent of the meetings and demonstrations in question were conducted without authorization from the executive committee of the appropriate soviet of people's deputies;

The holding of meetings and demonstrations at a different time and place from that indicated in the decision taken by the executive committee.

Disturbance of public order by the participants in meetings and demonstrations;

Failure by the participants in the meetings and demonstrations to comply with the lawful orders of the staff of the soviet of people's deputies and the militia to cease unauthorized events and to refrain from disturbing public order.

Despite the provisions of article 3 of the edict, which provides that applications for the holding of gatherings, meetings, street processions and demonstrations must be considered and approved by an executive committee, that is in a collegial decision, many such applications have not been submitted to executive committees, and decisions on them have been taken individually by chairmen or their deputies.

Significant numbers of violations of the legislation in question occur in the context of the activities of law enforcement bodies.

The most frequent violations are breaches of legislation concerning administrative infringements of rules relating to the preparation and content of reports of administrative infringements: data confirming the identity of the offender, witnesses and victims are missing, the specific provision of the legislation breached is not indicated, or material proof is not attached to the file. There are cases where records of administrative detention of offenders are completely lacking from the files, even though the period of administrative detention must be taken into account when determining the period of administrative arrest. In the absence of records this cannot be done.

123H. The file contains no information on the degree of premeditation or no proof is provided that the person was aware that no permission had been given for the holding of the event, or recognized the unlawful nature of his or her actions, and foresaw that the breach of public order would have harmful consequences.

123I. Many records contain an indication that the unlawful conduct continued despite an order by a duly authorized person, but these circumstances, which aggravate the responsibility of the offender, are not given proper judicial evaluation. The organizers of unauthorized meetings and other large-scale events giving rise to proceedings under the law are frequently not identified.

123J. Certain members of the militia, when performing their duties, have sometimes exceeded their authority and violated their instructions, for example when taking away still and cine cameras and exposing the film.

123K. There has been more than one case where administrative proceedings have been brought against citizens who were present at the site of the prohibited meetings by chance and did not participate in them.

123L. As regards violation of established procedures for the organization and conduct of gatherings, meetings, street processions and demonstrations, between August 1988 and May 1989 officials of law enforcement bodies prepared 2,670 reports concerning administrative infringements, 2,396 citizens were given a warning that law breaking was unacceptable, 833 persons were fined and 308 were placed under administrative arrest.

123M. The following may be identified as grounds and circumstances conducive to breaches of the procedures for the organization and conduct of large-scale events.

123N. Many gatherings, meetings and demonstrations are carried out without authorizations, but the organizers and participants are not prosecuted. As for members of executive committees, an absolute majority of them bear no responsibility for breaches of the above-mentioned legislation, since the law makes no provision for concrete responsibility for such infringements. An unlawful decision of an executive committee may be appealed against only to the next higher executive and administrative body. Under current legislation such decisions are not reviewed by people's courts. In this way members of the executive committees of soviets of people's deputies cannot in practice be called to account; it is possible only to complain about their actions to a higher body. There is a need for relations between meeting organizers and officials of soviets to be such that not only is the citizen responsible before the State, but in addition the representatives of State authority are accountable to the citizen. This is one of the principles of the socialist constitutional State which is being constructed.

123O. For this problem to be solved there is a need for new approaches on the part of soviets of people's deputies vis-à-vis public organizations and groups which take the initiative to hold meetings and demonstrations, as well as new thinking on the part of elected representatives of the people. Also needed is stronger supervision by soviets of people's deputies at all levels and enhanced monitoring by the procurators of the implementation of legislation concerning meetings and demonstrations.

124. In 1988 the Council of Ministers of the USSR annulled paragraphs 1 and 2 of the Decree of the Council of Peoples' Commissars of the USSR dated 15 May 1935 "The procedure for permitting the holding of congresses, conferences and meetings of trade union organizations". Now such meetings may be held without prior permission.

The Right to Freedom of Association (Article 22 of the Covenant). 125. Under the Constitution of the USSR, the guiding and directing force of Soviet society and the nucleus of its political system and of State and public organizations is the Communist Party of the Soviet Union.

126. On 1 March 1986 a Decree of the 27th Congress of the CPSU on Amendments to the Party statutes approved a new wording of the statutes, which states *inter alia* that the CPSU brings together on a voluntary basis the advanced

and most class-conscious part of the working class, the collective farmers and the intelligentsia of the USSR. In its activities the CPSU is guided by its Programme, which defines the tasks of planned and comprehensive improvement of socialism on the basis of speeding up the social and economic development of the country. It bases its work on the strict observance of Leninist norms of party life, the principles of democratic centralism, a collective leadership, the comprehensive development of democracy inside the party, the creative activity of communists, criticism and self-criticism and widespread glasnost. Any citizen of the Soviet Union who has reached the age of 18 years, accepts the Party Programme and Statutes and takes an active part in the construction of communism, working in a Party organization, carrying out the decisions of the Party and paying his Party dues, can be a member of the Party.

127. On setting out in 1985 to implement the policy of perestroika and the renewal of all aspects of Soviet society, the CPSU at the same time aimed at carrying out restructuring inside the Party. In a Decree of the Plenum of the Central Committee of the CPSU "Perestroika and the staffing policy of the Party" dated 28 January 1987 it was stressed that to deepen perestroika means, above all, to restructure the work of the party itself, and of its cadres at all levels from the Central Committee down to the primary party organizations.

128. The Soviet Union has established the most favourable possible conditions for bringing citizens together in trades unions, which have been granted complete freedom of activity. The trades unions are the public organizations in the USSR with the greatest mass membership.

129. State and economic bodies do not interfere in the work of the trades unions. Moreover, according to the law they are obliged to give every possible support to the active work of the trades unions in every sphere that has to do with satisfying the lawful interests of their members.

130. At the 18th Congress of the Trades Unions of the USSR, held in February/March 1987, a new version of the statutes of the Trades Unions of the USSR was adopted. This version set out the place and role of trades unions in the political system of Soviet society, the development of socialist self-management by the people and the acceleration of the socio-economic development of the country. The rights and duties of trades union members were clarified, as were the tasks of the primary trades union organizations. The statutes were supplemented by provisions aimed at further improving and democratizing the norms of activity inside the trades unions, strengthening the links between union bodies and the masses and extending glasnost. The term of office of trades union committees and workshop committees of trades union organizations with 150 members or more was extended to 2–3 years. Partial changes were made in the structure of trades union organizations in productive enterprises and also in research-and-production combines scattered over great areas. The statutes contained a new section "The trades unions and State and public organizations".

131. The draft bill on the rights of the trades unions of the USSR now being prepared in accordance with a decision of the 18th Congress of the Soviet Trades Unions clearly defines the right of association of the citizens of the USSR, their freedom to organize and operate trades unions and the basic rights of trades unions in their interrelationships with State and economic bodies and with self-management bodies of work collectives.

132. Implementation of perestroika in the USSR has created the preconditions for a sharp activation of cooperatives, youth organizations, associations for friendship with foreign countries, associations for the protection of nature and the protection of historical and cultural monuments, associations of book lovers, creative unions, sports, cultural, technical and scientific societies and all other types of public organization. New public organizations have arisen, including philanthropic societies (the V I Lenin Children's Fund, the Soviet Cultural Fund), artistic associations (Union of Cultural Workers, Union of Theatre Workers, Designers' Union) and others (such as the All-Union Organization of War and Labour Veterans), which have become a widespread phenomenon in the socio-cultural life of the Soviet Union. In the framework of the Soviet Committee for European Security and Cooperation a commission for international cooperation on humanitarian matters and human rights has been established.

133. Work has continued on strengthening the statutory basis for the organization and operation of public organizations. At the present time the procedure for citizens to become associated in various forms of public organization has been laid down in a number of statutory instruments. Thus the Foundations of the Labour Legislation of the USSR and the Union Republics consolidate the rights of workers and employees to come together in trades unions. The regulations concerning voluntary societies regulate the procedure for founding various types of unions of workers—scientific, cultural, technical, sports, etc.

134. In accordance with the Act of the USSR "Individual working activity", adopted on 19 November 1986, individual activity in small trades and crafts and in the provision of everyday services for the population is allowed, as well as other forms of activity based exclusively on the personal labour of citizens and members of their families. The Act of the USSR on "Co-operation in the USSR" adopted on 26 May 1988 defines the overall legal, economic and organizational foundations for the activities of co-operatives in the USSR. . . .

138. An Act of the USSR already mentioned "State enterprises (unions of enterprises)", dated 30 June 1987, helps Soviet citizens to exercise in practice the right of association and consolidates the legal basis for their active enlistment in economic and public activities connected with the socialization and self-expression of individuals with the help of and through the medium of work collectives and public organizations.

139. This Act introduced election of leading staff (as a rule on a competitive basis). The principle of electivity applies to the managers of enterprises, structural units in unions of enterprises, factories, workshops, departments, sectors, farms and sections and also to foremen and team leaders (Article 6). The director of an enterprise or structural unit in a union of enterprises is elected at a general assembly (conference) of the workers by secret or open ballot (depending on the decision of the assembly) for a period of five years and is confirmed in office by the next higher authority. The managers of subdivisions—factories, workshops, departments, sectors, farms and sections and also foremen and team leaders—are elected in secret or open ballot by the groups of workers concerned for a period of five years and are confirmed in office by the director of the enterprise concerned. Elected managers may be relieved of their duties before their time is up by decision of the general assembly of the work collective which elected them to office. When their term of office expires managers released from their duties may be elected again or sent off to other

work. However, they must be given either their former work or duties or work on an equivalent level.

140. The way an enterprise is managed is based on the principle of democratic centralism, combining centralized leadership with socialist self-management by the work collective. The main way in which the authority of the work collective is exercised is through the general assembly (conference). According to paragraph 5 in Article 6 of the Act of the USSR "State enterprises (unions of enterprises)", the general assembly or conference of the work collective:

—elects the leaders of the enterprise and the works council and is given reports on their activities;

—considers and approves plans for the economic and social development of the enterprise and lays down ways of increasing work productivity and profit (income), improving the effectiveness of production and the quality of the goods produced, preserving and increasing the people's property and strengthening the material and technical base of production as a foundation for the work collective's activities;

—approves a collective agreement and authorizes the trades union committee to sign it, together with the management of the enterprise on behalf of the work collective;

—commits itself to socialist obligations and at the suggestion of the management and the trade union committee approves rules for internal work regulations;

—considers other important aspects of the activities of the enterprise concerned.

141. In the period between assemblies or conferences the authority of the work collective is exercised by the works' council of the enterprise or structural unit of a union of enterprise. Paragraph 1 of Article 7 of the Act defined the main powers of the works' council. The works' council:

—watches over the fulfillment of the decisions of general assemblies (conferences) of the work collective and the action taken in response to critical comments and proposals by workers and employees, and informs the work collective of their implementation;

—hears reports from the management on progress in the fulfillment of plans and contractual obligations and the results of productive and economic activity and outlines measures to promote more effective work on the part of the enterprise and the observance of principle of social justice;

—takes decisions on questions of improving the management and organizational structure of the enterprise and ensuring that the pay given to the workers is commensurate with their personal contribution to the work and that social benefits are fairly distributed;

—takes decisions on the utilization of funds for the development of production, research, technology, material incentives and social progress and the assignment of finance for constructing dwellings, children's establishments and canteens, improving working conditions and safety, providing medical, household and cultural services for workers and employees and dealing with other questions connected with the social development of the work collective;

—decides on questions connected with the training and further training of staff and observance of the rules of internal work discipline and of State production and labour discipline; outlines measures to improve matters in those respects;

—exercises control over the provision of privileges and advantages for innovators, advanced producers and war and labour veterans out of the funds for material incentives and social development;

—decides on other questions connected with the development of production and social activities, if they have not been included in the terms of reference of the assembly (conference) of the work collective.

142. Decisions of the works' council, if taken within its terms of reference and in accordance with current legislation, are mandatory on the management and members of the work collective. In the case of disagreement between the management and the works' council, the question at issue is decided at a general assembly (conference) of the work collective.

143. The works' council is elected by the general assembly (conference) of the work collective of the enterprises or structural unit of a union of enterprises by secret or open ballot for a term of two to three years. Workers, team leaders, foremen, specialists, representatives of the management and of the Party, trades unions, young communists and other public organizations can be elected to the works' council. The number of members of the Council is determined by the general assembly (conference) of the work collective. The members representing the management should not exceed one quarter of the total membership of the works' council. In subsequent elections, at least one third of the membership of the council should as a rule come up for election.

144. The members of the works' council carry out their duties as public servants. A member of the council cannot be dismissed or subjected to any other disciplinary penalty without the agreement of the works' council. A member of the council who has not justified the confidence of the work collective can be removed by decision of the general assembly of that collective.

145. The Act emphasized the duty of the management of an enterprise to create the necessary conditions for the works' council to operate effectively (paragraph 3, Article 7).

[Paragraphs 145A–145I have been interpolated from UN Doc. CCPR/C/52/Add. 6.]

145A. In the context of the broadening and deepening of Soviet democracy, and the substantial enhancement of the role of working people, their collectives and their organizations in tackling State and public issues in the country and consolidating the rule of law and the legal order, an important role is played by efforts to mould a socialist constitutional State and further develop the judicial regulation of social relations within this context.

145B. This was the aim of a bill which has been drafted on voluntary societies, independent social bodies and independent public associations, specifying the aims, principles of formation and activities of voluntary societies, independent social bodies and independent public associations.

145C. An important task is that of setting down procedures whereby independent public associations, which will encompass the vast bulk of the existing "informal associations", may be set up not only within institutions of culture and sport, houses and palaces of culture, and so on, but also independently.

145D. It is envisaged that appeals against decisions by the bodies concerned refusing to register the statutes of voluntary societies or terminating their activities may also be heard in people's courts, affording a major guarantee of the protection of citizens' rights.

145E. The bill was drawn up in the light of the Soviet Union's obligations under the International Covenant on Civil and Political Rights.

145F. According to approximate data, there are more than 60,000 voluntary societies currently in the USSR. Many of them fall into the informal category.

145G. A large, realistically minded proportion of the societies favour relations of partnership and equal rights with official organs of authority and members of other societies, and actively participate in the democratic processes under way in the country.

145H. At the same time, the intrinsically positive process of the independent advance of informal associations has drawbacks: a critical interpretation of the recent past, the democratization of public life, and the opening up of areas previously closed to criticism have given rise to various negative trends: leaders have emerged who have an exclusively critical approach, and many of them are notable for a nihilist viewpoint in the legal sphere, a failure to understand that the current process is aimed at extending socialist democracy, and that genuine democracy cannot exist outside the law. The activities of certain informal associations sometimes goes beyond their declared purposes and programmes.

145I. In cases where the actual activities and purposes of informal associations come up against constitutional prohibitions (for example, war propaganda or racial and nationalist chauvinism) or the criminal law, appropriate judicial measures are taken in accordance with the law. At the same time it should be pointed out that the predominant trend in the work of law enforcement bodies places emphasis not on measures of compulsion or prohibition, but on preventive measures.

Protection of the Family and the Child (Article 23 and 24 of the Covenant). 146. The constitutional provisions aimed at ensuring that society and the State protect the family and children have now been developed further and have found practical application in the expansion of aid to young families and the granting of additional privileges to pregnant women and women with children. A Decree of the Presidium of the Supreme Soviet of the USSR "Extension of privileges for working pregnant women and women with minor children" dated 2 September 1987, helps to provide working women with the more favourable working conditions necessary for the harmonious combination of work in social production with bringing up children. In fulfillment of this Decree corresponding amendments were made to the Foundations of Labour Legislation of the USSR and the Union Republics. Those amendments can be summarized as follows.

147. The management of an enterprise, establishment or organization is obliged at the request of women with children under 8 years of age, pregnant women and women looking after a sick member of their family to arrange a shorter working day or shorter working week for them (Article 26 of the Foundations).

148. Pregnant women and women with children up to 2 years of age must not be sent away on mission or be given overtime work, night work or holiday work (Article 69).

149. Women with children under 18 months of age who cannot carry out their former work must be transferred to other work, but will keep the average wages for their former work until the child has reached the age of 18 months (Article 70).

150. At the request of a woman during the time she is on leave to look after a child, she may work an incomplete working week or work at home. Meanwhile she maintains

the right to receive allowances during the period of partially paid leave for looking after the child (Article 71).

151. If a woman with a child under 18 months of age is working, she must be given breaks to feed the child at least every three hours, for at least 30 minutes each time. Such breaks shall be included in the working day and shall be paid (Article 72).

152. The dismissal of pregnant women and mothers with children under 18 months of age on the initiative of the management is not permitted, except where an establishment, enterprise or organization is completely liquidated, in which case they may be dismissed but must be found other work. The management is bound by law to carry out obligatory work placement for pregnant women and women with children up to 18 months of age, even when they are dismissed on completion of a fixed-term labour agreement (Article 73).

[Paragraph 152A has been interpolated from UN Doc. CCPR/C/52/Add. 6.]

152A. The next major step in this direction was a decree adopted in August 1989 by the Council of Ministers of the USSR and the All-Union Central Council of Trades Unions under the title "Increasing the length of leave for women with young children", whereby paid leave on the birth of a child was extended until the child reaches one and a half years of age, and in addition unpaid leave was extended to three years (enterprises have the right to grant the mother full pay for these three years). Additional expenditure by the State on the implementation of this decree totals 1 billion roubles a year. The aim is to create more favourable conditions for the physical development of children at an early age, to create the basis for a healthy body and mind, and to reduce infant mortality.

153. According to Decree No. 117 of the Council of Ministers of the USSR and the All-Union Central Trades Union Council under the title "Increasing the period of paid leave to look after a sick child", dated 20 October 1987, from 1 November 1987 onwards a medical certificate with pay is issued for up to 14 days to enable a working woman to look after a sick child.

154. In Soviet legislation special emphasis is placed on the system of measures for the judicial protection of children in the event of the dissolution of their parents' marriage. A decree of the Council of Ministers of the USSR entitled "Measures to improve the material situation of minors whose parents fail to pay maintenance" adopted on 25 January 1989 extends the range of persons receiving material assistance to cover children, drawing on funds earmarked for the payment of allowances for minor children (the "maintenance fund").

[Paragraph 154A has been interpolated from UN Doc. CCPR/C/52/Add. 6.]

154A. Allowances are currently paid not only during the period when a search is being conducted for parents who have failed to pay maintenance, but also in cases where recovery is impossible for reasons beyond the control of those responsible for paying it (for example, when the person against whom the order to pay maintenance is made is absent in a corrective labour institution in which his or her earnings are insufficient, or when he or she is in a medical institution for treatment without receiving a social insurance allowance). Allowances are also paid for the maintenance of a child when the person responsible for maintenance payments lives permanently on the territory of another State with which the USSR has no treaty covering matters relating to the reciprocal application of judicial decisions. The allowance amounts to 20 roubles a month for each child.

155. The allowances are paid from the total allowances recovered from the defaulting parent that were payable during the period of search, with an additional penalty of ten per cent on those sums and 50% of the State tax for dissolution of a marriage by a court or the civil registry authorities, the minimum amount of which is increased by the Decree of the Council of Ministers of the USSR of 6 February 1984 to 100 roubles. A Decree of the Presidium of the Supreme Soviet of the RSFSR dated 25 April 1984 and similar decrees by the Presidia of the Supreme Soviets of the other Union Republics, introduced the amendments on the size of the State tax into the Marriage and Family Codes and the Civil Procedure Codes of the Union Republics.

156. The judicial procedure for obtaining maintenance for children has been simplified. A Decree of the Presidium of the Supreme Soviet of the USSR dated 1 February 1985 provided that in the absence of dispute between the interested parties an application for the payment of maintenance for minor children is considered individually by the people's court without civil proceedings. Corresponding Decrees have been adopted by the Presidia of the Supreme Soviets of the Union Republics, in particular the RSFSR—a Decree of the Presidium of the Supreme Soviet of the RSFSR, dated 20 February 1985.

157. In connection with the extension of the leave given to mothers for looking after children to 18 months and with a view to protecting the health of mother and child, a Decree of the Presidium of the Supreme Soviet of the USSR dated 19 January 1984, amended Article 13 of the Foundations of Marriage and Family Legislation of the USSR and the Union Republics, extending from 1 year to 18 months the period during which a woman after the birth of a child for whom her husband refuses to provide material support is entitled to ask the courts for alimony for the child's maintenance.

158. A Decree of the Presidium of the Supreme Soviet of the USSR dated 14 October 1986 introduced amendments into Article 22 of the Foundations of Marriage and Family Legislation, which established the amount of alimony payable for children. With a view to ensuring that all children have the necessary vital minimum it is provided that the amount of alimony must be at least 20 roubles per month for each child, with maintenance of the former amount of alimony in proportion to the wages earned by the person paying it. Also established was the right of the court, at the request of the payer of alimony, to reduce both the size of the proportionate parts and the minimum amount of alimony not only in the cases previously set out in the Act but also "for other valid reasons". A Decree of the Council of Ministers of the USSR and the All-Union Central Council of Trades Unions dated 25 September 1986 in cases when the amount of alimony is less than 20 roubles for each child, gave the right to executive committees of rayon or city Soviets of People's Deputies to pay supplements to the alimony from the local budget to poor families in dire need with three or more children being reared by one parent.

159. Special measures are laid down in Soviet legislation so that not a single child is left neglected and so that all children have everything they need for their complete development. For that reason special attention is paid to every type of protection for the rights and interests of children who have been deprived of parental care. This is shown by the Decrees of the Central Committee of the CPSU and the Council of Ministers of the USSR adopted on 24 January 1985 and 31 July 1987 concerning measures aimed at improving the upbringing, education and material care of orphan children and children deprived of parental care in infant homes, children's homes and boarding schools.

160. A Decree of the Council of Ministers of the USSR dated 26 October 1987 established the V. I. Lenin Soviet Children's Fund. The Fund's resources are made up of voluntary contributions, donations and monies allocated by public organizations, unions of creative workers, the work collectives in enterprises and establishments and individual citizens. The Children's Fund does not have to pay taxes, State and Customs duties or other forms of levy. It is concerned with the education, upbringing and material care of children and adolescents, particularly orphans. On 4 May 1988 the Council of Ministers of the USSR adopted a Decree "Participation of the V. I. Lenin Soviet Children's Fund in work to improve the protection of the health of mother and child in various regions of the Soviet Union".

161. These Decrees were aimed in the first place at creating optimum conditions in State children's establishments, for children to live and develop in an all-round way, to train them to an occupation or profession and make them into good citizens on the basis of the social justice that is guaranteed by socialist society.

[Paragraph 161A has been interpolated from UN Doc. CCPR/C/52/Add. 6.]

161A. For the purpose of improving the system of education and social protection for such children, on 17 August 1988 the Council of Ministers of the USSR, on the initiative of the Soviet Children's Fund, adopted a decree concerning the establishment of family-type children's homes in the country. Between 1988 and 1991 it is planned to construct 30 children's villages in 14 of the union republics. The measures laid down in the decree will make it possible to provide more than 12,000 orphan children with a family upbringing in the coming years.

162. Among the series of measures outlined in a Decree by the Central Committee of the CPSU and the Council of Ministers of the USSR dated 19 November 1987 aspects of the protection of motherhood and childhood are given priority. A radical restructuring of the work of outpatient and polyclinic establishments for women and children, nursing homes and children's hospitals is planned, and propaganda for a healthy lifestyle is to be intensified, modern birth control methods are to be introduced, spa and health resort treatment is to be extended and the network of medical genetic counselling centres and "Marriage and the Family" clinics is to be developed further.

Right to Take Part in the Conduct of Public Affairs (Article 25 of the Covenant). 163. As stated in the most important political and legal acts of the CPSU and the Soviet State, the further democratization of Soviet society, the active enlistment of the citizens' energies in the management of public affairs and State matters and the consistent implementation of the citizens' right to participate in the conduct of State affairs are the core of the perestroika policy being carried out in the USSR.

The new version of the Programme of the Communist Party of the Soviet Union adopted by the 27th Congress states that the CPSU considers:

—that at the present stage the strategic line for the development of the political system consists in the improvement of Soviet democracy and the ever fuller exercise of socialist self-management by the people on the basis of active and effective participation of workers and their collectives and organizations in the settlement of matters of State and public importance. The Programme states that the Party will unflinchingly pursue the policy of democratizing management and the process of developing and adopting State decisions, a policy of ensuring the selection of the optimum variants, taking in account and comparing various opinions and proposals by working people. The range of questions which can be decided only after discussion in the work collectives, in the standing committees of the Soviets of People's Deputies and in the trades unions, Young Communist organizations and other public organizations is being extended. The most important draft bills and decisions will be put out for nationwide discussion and voting. It is necessary also to further improve the system of adopting and giving effect to the electors' mandates and citizen's declarations and proposals, studying public opinion and keeping the public well-informed about the decisions taken and the results of implementing them.

164. The documentation of the 27th Congress of the CPSU singles out several main trends in the development of the political system of Soviet society, paving the way towards a still fuller and more consistent exercise by Soviet citizens of their right to participate in the conduct of State affairs. These include an increase in the activity and an improvement in the work of the whole system of representative bodies of socialist democracy from the local Soviets of People's Deputies right up to the Supreme Soviet of the USSR and the Supreme Soviets of the Union and Autonomous Republics; encouragement of initiatives from public organizations and their involvement in the running of the country; the use of all forms of direct democracy, including the direct participation of the popular masses in the elaboration, adoption and implementation of State decisions and an extension of the rights of enterprises and work collectives; and a further deepening of the principles of openness and democracy in the organization and activities of all State bodies and public organizations (Political Report of the Central Committee of the CPSU to the 27th Congress of the CPSU).

165. On 21 June 1987, in all the Union and Autonomous Republics periodic elections were held for the local Soviets of People's Deputies. They demonstrated a high degree of public interest and active participation in establishing higher and local State authorities, which is one of the institutionalized channels for enlisting citizens' energies in the management of the State. The preparation and holding of the elections were in conformity with the Constitution of the USSR and the Constitutions of the Union and Autonomous Republics, wide use being made of the democratic mechanisms laid down in the present legislation on elections to local Soviets of People's Deputies. During the election campaign new approaches to the organization of elections were put into effect.

166. In the pre-election meetings several candidatures were considered as a rule for each electoral district. Decisions on putting forward a candidate to be a deputy were taken under conditions of free and businesslike discussion. Altogether 3480372 candidatures were discussed at pre-election meetings to discuss candidates as deputies.

167. As an experiment, in each of the Union Republics elections were held on the basis of multi-mandate electoral districts. In the RSFSR, for instance, this innovation was tried out on the basis of a Decree of the Presidium of the Supreme Soviet of the RSFSR dated 26 February 1987 under the title of "The experimental conduct of elections to local Soviets of People's Deputies of the RSFSR on the basis of multi-mandate electoral districts". The number of candidates put forward in these districts exceeded the number of mandates. The candidates who at the elections received fewer votes, but enough to be taken into consideration, became reserve deputies, with the right of consultative voice during meetings of the Soviets.

168. Elections were held for 52566 Soviets of People's Deputies including 6 krai, 123 oblast, 8 autonomous republic, 10 autonomous okrug, 3127 rayon, 2164 city, 666 urban rayon, 3863 settlement and 42599 rural Soviets of People's Deputies. As an experiment elections in multi-mandate electoral districts were carried out in 162 rayons for rayon, urban (in cities divided into rayons), settlement and rural Soviets.

169. Elections were carried out with the widest possible participation of the working people. To conduct the elections, 953780 electoral commissions were formed, in the work of which 8577811 representatives of public organizations and work collectives took part.

170. To conduct the elections for local Soviets of People's Deputies 2251273 electoral districts were created, made up of 2160 for elections to krai Soviets, 29817 to oblast Soviets, 1360 to autonomous oblast Soviets, 1165 to autonomous okrug Soviets, 249273 to rayon Soviets (3668 of them multi-mandate districts), 289698 to urban Soviets (1678 of them multi-mandate districts), 148831 to rayon Soviets in cities, 208870 to settlement Soviets (including 2255 multi-mandate electoral districts), and 1325099 to rural Soviets (including 15540 multi-mandate electoral districts). 179589 electoral sectors were created in the country.

171. There were 184425691 voters on the electoral rolls; 183254887 took part in the elections, or 99.37%.

172. 2321766 deputies were elected to local Soviets of People's Deputies; 54.7% of the membership of the Soviets was up for election.

173. In 74 electoral districts for elections to rayon Soviets, 28 for elections to urban Soviets, 5 for elections to urban rayon Soviets, 105 for elections to settlement Soviets and 864 for elections to rural Soviets, the candidates for deputy did not receive over half the votes of the total electorate in the corresponding electoral districts and failed to be elected.

174. As already noted, on 30 June 1987, with a view to developing direct democracy and further extending the practice of enlisting the help of the citizens in the running of State affairs through the medium of public organizations, the Supreme Soviet of the USSR adopted an Act of the USSR under the title of "Nationwide discussion of important aspects of State activities". The Act is called upon to strengthen the legal guarantees for the participation of citizens in taking decisions on important aspects of State and public activities on the basis of glasnost and a comparison and consideration of various opinions and proposals put forward by the working people. The Act defines the procedure for nationwide discussion of important State matters and also the basic postulates for discussion by the population of important questions of local significance.

175. Article 6 of the Act states "Citizens of the USSR have the right to participate freely in the discussion of important aspects of State and public life".

In discussing questions of nationwide, republican or local significance the citizens of the USSR have the right to participate direct or through public organizations, work collectives, meetings in the place of residence, public self-help associations, meetings of men serving in the armed forces and the mass media.

176. The Act prohibits any direct or indirect limitations on the rights of citizens of the USSR to take part in discussions on the basis of their origins, social status, property, race, nationality or other similar circumstances. It envisages the prosecution of officials in State and public bodies who permit infringements of the provisions of the Act and also of persons who hinder citizens of the USSR from freely exercising their right to take part in the discussion.

177. Draft bills and decisions on the main lines of political, economic and social development of the Soviet Union, the implementation of the citizens' constitutional rights, freedoms and duties and other very important aspects of State life under the jurisdiction of the USSR as a whole are put forward for nationwide discussion.

178. Means have been provided for organizing the nationwide discussions and for summing up and taking into consideration proposals and comments by citizens and other participants in the discussion.

179. Among the basic postulates of the Act in regard to the discussion of important matters of local significance is, in particular, an indication that draft decisions of the local Soviets of the People's Deputies and their Executive Committees must be put forward for discussion by the people when they touch on plans for complex economic and social development, the budget, the ensuring of socialist legality, the protection of law and order and the rights of citizens, the work of enterprises, establishments and organizations concerned with providing services for the population, and other important aspects of State, economic and socio-cultural development in the localities.

180. The Act in question serves as a basis for preparing laws in the Union and Autonomous Republics on the procedure for discussing important aspects of State affairs in those Republics and the discussion by the population of important questions of local significance.

181. It has long been the practice in the USSR for wide sections of the public to discuss draft bills and other important decisions of nationwide, Republican and local significance. Thus, during the period between 1962 and 1987, over 30 draft State instruments were put forward for nationwide discussion. The whole of the population discussed the drafts of the Constitution of the USSR, the Foundations of Housing Legislation, the Foundations of Marriage and Family Legislation, legislation on reform of the schools and the protection of nature and historical and cultural monuments and many other subjects. In 1986 a draft bill of the USSR "State enterprises (unions of enterprises)" was put forward for nationwide discussion. The Act of the USSR dated 30 June 1987 under the title "Nationwide discussion of important aspects of State activities" provides a solid legal basis for the further development of this channel for the participation of Soviet citizens in preparing State decisions.

182. Somewhat earlier, decisions had been taken in the Union Republics designed to ensure more active utilization of forms of direct participation of the people in the settlement of questions of local and nationwide significance, such as general assemblies and meetings of citizens in their places of residence. Thus, a Decree adopted on 27 August 1985 by the Presidium of the Supreme Soviet of the RSFSR under the title "Provisions concerning general assemblies and meetings of citizens in their places of residence in the RSFSR" laid down the powers of such assemblies and the procedures for preparing and conducting them.

183. One of the forms of democracy most widely practised in the USSR is the participation of citizens in rectification of the activities of State bodies and public organizations in the shape of proposals, the expression of wishes and critical comments by workers. The Decree "Appeals by citizens to the Supreme Soviet of the USSR", dated 17 February 1987, laid upon other representative bodies in the country the duty of developing more thoughtful, thorough and comprehensive means of considering, summarizing and monitoring ways of meeting the complaints and criticisms of the public (a short exposition of this Decree is given in the section on Article 2 of the Covenant).

184. Soviet citizens are afforded wide opportunities for exercising the right to take part in public and State affairs and for developing self-management under the Act of the USSR entitled "State enterprises (unions of enterprises)" dated 30 June 1987. This Act recognizes the work collective in an enterprise or union of enterprises as the master, utilizing the national property assigned to the enterprise and ensuring a combination of the interests of society, the work collective and each individual worker (paragraph 2, Article 1). It calls for the work collective to be self-managing, thus creating a deep personal interest on the part of each worker in the rational utilization of the nation's property and ensuring his integral participation in the affairs of the work collective and the State (paragraph 3, Article 1). As the master with full rights in the enterprise, the work collective takes independent decisions on questions of production and social development (paragraph 3, Article 2). The enterprise has the right, on its own initiative, to take any decisions it wishes provided that it is not in breach of the existing legislation (paragraph 2, Article 2).

185. Socialist self-management is carried out in a completely open way through the participation of the whole community and its public organizations in reaching the most important decisions and monitoring their implementation and also through the elective nature of the leadership (the procedure for electing leading staff is dealt with in the section on Article 22 of the Covenant).

186. The Act of the USSR "State enterprises (unions of enterprises)" defines the range of activities (economic operations and transactions) for which the director alone has authority. All other questions are determined by the work collective and its general assembly (conference) or by the works council elected by the assembly or conference which acts in the period between assemblies or conferences. All workers in the enterprise or union of enterprises are members with equal rights of the work collective and all participate on an equal basis in the general assemblies and conferences and the taking of decisions.

187. An assembly (conference) of a work collective is convened when necessary, but at least twice a year, and considers particular questions on the initiative of the management, the works council, public or other organizations or individual workers. No limitations in this regard are envisaged.

188. The Act regulates in detail the powers of the general assembly or conference and also of the works council (the powers in question were quoted in the section on Article 22 of the Covenant).

189. Since the second half of the 80s in the USSR a restructuring of the State apparatus has been under way. It is being carried out on the basis of the postulates of the Act just discussed and in accordance with the requirements of glasnost, democratization and the redistribution of functions to the benefit of self-managing production collectives.

190. With a view to democratization and a reduction in the State apparatus joint decrees were adopted by the Cen-

tral Committee of the CPSU and the Council of Ministers of the USSR concerning the improvement of the organization and activities of ministries and branches of the administration. These include a number of decrees dated 17 July 1987: "The restructuring of planning and the enhancement of the role of the State Planning Committee of the USSR under the new conditions of economic management", "Enhancement of the role of the State Committee of the USSR for Science and Technology in managing scientific and technical progress in the Soviet Union", "Restructuring material and technical procurement arrangements and activities of the State Committee for Material Procurement of the USSR under the new conditions of economic management", "Restructuring the financial system and enhancing the role of the Ministry of Finance of the USSR under the new conditions of economic management", "Improvement of the banking system in the USSR and an intensification of its work for improving the effectiveness of the economy", "Measures for a radical improvement in statistical work in the USSR", "Restructuring the activities of the ministries and branches of the administration in the sphere of material production under the new conditions of economic management", "Improvement of the activities of republican organs of management". Also approved was a Decree of the Central Committee of the CPSU, the Council of Ministers of the USSR and the All-Union Central Trades Union Council under the title of "Intensifying work to implement an active social policy and enhance the role of the State Committee of the USSR on Labour and Social Questions". This was dated 17 July 1987.

191. In the same period democratic principles in the activities of public organizations were strengthened. This was reflected most obviously, for example, in the statutes of the unions of creative workers of a new generation—the union of Cultural Workers etc. (aspects of the participation of citizens of the USSR in the activities of public organizations and through public organizations in the conduct of State affairs were dealt with in the section on Article 22 of the Covenant).

Protection against Discrimination (Article 26 of the Covenant).
192. Practically all codifying and other legal instruments in the USSR and the Union Republics touching on the rights and duties of Soviet and foreign citizens include a prohibition on discrimination in some wording or another, and envisage ways of protecting people against discrimination (this is discussed in detail in the sections on Articles 2, 3, 18 and 20 of the Covenant). As an example, reference may be made to the Act of the USSR "Nationwide discussion of important aspects of State activities" dated 30 June 1987. Article 6 of that Act states "any direct or indirect limitation on the rights of citizens of the USSR to take part in discussion on the basis of their origin, race, nationality, sex, level of education, language, attitude to religion, duration of residence in a particular locality, nature and type of occupation etc. is forbidden".

The Rights of Minorities (Article 27 of the Covenant). 193. On 27 November 1985 the Supreme Soviet of the USSR approved a new version of the Foundations of Legislation on Education in the USSR and the Union Republics, inserting amendments and additions in the light of the main directions of reform in general education and professional education. Article 4 of the Foundations, embodying the most important principles of education in the USSR, puts in first place the equality of all citizens of the USSR in their right to receive an education, independently, in particular, of their race, nationality, language and other factors. One of the principles stated was the freedom to choose the language of instruction: instruction in their native language or in the language of another people of the USSR.

194. The principle of the freedom of choice of language of instruction is also laid down in Article 3 of the Foundations, which sets forth the guarantees of the right of citizens of the USSR to education. The content of that principle is discussed in detail in Article 20 of the Foundations: pupils in general schools are given the opportunity of learning in their native language or in the language of another people of the USSR. Their parents or persons in *loco parentis* have the right to choose for the children at their own desire a school with the required language of instruction. In addition to the language in which teaching is conducted, pupils, if they so wish, may study the language of another people of the USSR.

195. In teaching establishments where teaching is carried on in a language other than Russian, the necessary steps have been taken to enable the Russian language to be studied together with the native language, since Russian has been voluntarily adopted by the Soviet people as the means of communication between nationalities.

196. With a view to ensuring wider acquaintance with the culture of the peoples of the world and to extending the opportunities for acquiring more thorough professional knowledge, teaching is also conducted in foreign languages in some teaching establishments.

197. An essential condition for ensuring the unity of the whole of secondary education throughout the USSR is stated in Article 21 of the Foundations, viz. the need to take into comprehensive consideration the special national characteristics of the peoples of the Union Republics.

198. The constitutional principle of non-discrimination on racial, national or any other grounds, is also reflected in the Act of the USSR "Nationwide discussion of important aspects of State activities" (1987), in the Administrative Infringement Codes of the Union Republics (1984–1985) and in other statutory instruments.

UNITED ARAB EMIRATES. A federation of seven coastal States located in western Asia on the Gulf of Oman: Abu Dhabi, Dubai, Sharjah, Ajman, Fujairah, Umm al-Qaiwain, and Ras al-Khaimah, the federation has borders with Oman, Qatar, and Saudi Arabia. It was formed in 1971 and became a member of the United Nations in 1972. Its population is estimated by the UN (1990) to be 1,578,000. Ethnic groups include persons of Arab, Indian, Iranian, and Pakistani descent. Languages commonly used include Arabic (official), Farsi, and English. Religions practiced include Islam (Sunni and Shi'ite) (90%), Christianity (4%), Hinduism (4%), and others (2%). Literacy is estimated at 57%.

The government (1990) took the form of a federation of monarchies, each headed by an emir. Joint policies are adopted only in respect of foreign relations, defense, and development; otherwise, each emirate maintains its own system of government. The Supreme Council of Rulers, made up of the emirs or their representatives, elects the president and prime minister, who act as head of State and of government, respectively. It also appoints a Council of Ministers, which drafts legislation, based primarily upon the Islamic Shar'ia. Drafts of laws are considered by an elected 40-member National Council, which has consultative functions only, consisting of eight members each from Abu Dhabi and Dubai, six members each from Ras al Khaimah and Sharjah, and four each from the other emirates. The jurisdiction of local courts, where rules of Islamic law prevail, extends to all citizens of the United Arab Emirates and to nationals of other Arab and Islamic States. There are no political parties.

UNITED KINGDOM. The United Kingdom of Great Britain and Northern Ireland is a country occupying a large portion of the British Isles, in the Atlantic Ocean and the North Sea off the northwest coast of Europe. It comprises a union of England, Northern Ireland, Scotland, and Wales. England occupies the southeastern three-fifths of the island of Great Britain; Wales occupies the western portion, and Scotland, the northern one-third. Northern Ireland occupies the northeastern tip of the second largest of the British Isles, the larger southern portion being occupied by Ireland. The United Kingdom includes, in addition, a number of colonies and dependencies, among them Anguilla, Bermuda, the British Antarctic Territory, the British Indian Ocean Territory, the British Virgin Islands, the Cayman Islands, the Channel Islands, the Falkland Islands and dependencies, Gibraltar, Hong Kong, the Isle of Man, the Leeward Islands, Montserrat, Pitcairn Island, St. Helena, and the Turks and Caicos Islands.

Created in 1707 when Scotland, England, and Wales were united, the United Kingdom gained a fourth member after a rebellion in Ireland (1916–1921) had divided that country into the Irish Free State and Northern Ireland. It became a member of the United Nations in 1945. Its population is estimated by the UN (1990) to be 56,176,000. Ethnic groups include English, Scottish, Welsh, and Irish, joined in recent years by immigrants from the West Indian islands and Asian and African countries. Languages commonly used include English (official), Irish, Welsh, and Gaelic. The predominant religion is Christianity; Judaism and Islam are also practiced. The Church of England (Protestant Episcopal) is the established church of England; the monarch is its temporal head, with the right to appoint to various Church offices. The Church of Scotland (Presbyterian) is the established church of Scotland. Literacy is estimated at 99%.

The Government (1990) took the form of a monarchy. Under the unwritten constitution, which consists primarily of statutes, common law, and practice, the monarch is head of State. The prime minister, representing the party or coalition given a majority in election of members of the House of Commons, is appointed by the monarch and serves as head of government. The supreme legislative authority, Parliament, consists of the 635-member House of Commons, composed of members (516 for England, 36 for Wales, 71 for Scotland, and 12 for Northern Ireland) elected by popular vote for terms of five years, unless Parliament is dissolved earlier; and the House of Lords, which includes more than 1,000 members (hereditary peers, life peers and peeresses, certain judges, and the bishops and archbishops of the Church of England). Executive power is exercised by the cabinet, headed by the prime minister; all members of the cabinet are members of one of the two houses of Parliament. The main activity of the House of Commons is to consider legislation proposed by the cabinet; the House of Lords may delay certain bills—but not "money bills"—for a maximum of one year. The judiciary includes magistrate's courts, county courts, high courts, and appellate courts and, in certain circumstances, the House of Lords. Political parties include the Conservative Party, the Labour Party, the Social Democrats, the Liberal Party, the Ulster Nationalists and other Northern Irish parties, the Scottish Nationalist Party, and the Welsh Nationalist Party.

Discord between ethnic groups residing in the United Kingdom was first brought to world attention by the Notting Hill riots of 1958, aimed, in part, at ending discrimination against immigrant workers in employment and housing. Legislation aimed at reducing the flow of immigration was adopted in 1962, 1968, and 1971 but did not resolve the problem. After 1964, large numbers of foreign workers began to arrive from former British colonies in Asia, Africa, and the Caribbean, sometimes with the help and encouragement of British industry. Unable to accommodate themselves to British ways of life or to find suitable employment or accommodations, they complained bitterly of discrimination.

The Race Relations Act of 1968 established the Race Relations Board, with little authority, and the Community Relations Commission, which could only coordinate voluntary efforts at reducing racial tensions. It was replaced by the Race Relations Act of 1976, which made direct or indirect racial discrimination unlawful in fields of employment, education, and the provision of goods, services, facilities and premises; and gives individuals a right of direct access to the civil courts and industrial tribunals for legal remedies for unlawful discrimination. The 1976 act also established the independent Commission for Racial Equality, vested with wide powers and the duty to work towards the elimination of discrimination, to promote equality of opportunity and good race relations, and to keep the operation of the act under review. The commission also has discretion to assist individuals who consider that they have been the subject of unlawful discrimination.

In addition, section 5A of the Public Order Act 1936 (which was inserted in the Race Relations Act of 1976) makes it an offence for any person to publish or distribute written matter, or to use words in any public place or at any public meeting, where the matter or words are threatening, abusive, or insulting and likely to stir up hatred against any racial group in Great Britain.

Intolerance and discrimination based on religion or belief have plagued Northern Ireland for many centuries. After numerous rebellions and a threat of civil war, the British Parliament in 1920 separated Catholic southern Ireland from predominantly Protestant northern Ireland, leaving each with its own government and parliament. When Ireland became a dominion in 1921 and gained sovereignty as the Republic of Ireland, Northern Ireland chose to remain as part of the United Kingdom.

From 1921 to 1972, Northern Ireland had a directly elected subordinate parliament and government. In 1972, responsibility for its administration was assumed by the United Kingdom government and parliament. This constitutional arrangement is, however, considered temporary, although it has been in force for approximately 20 years. In the meantime, the British government has preserved Northern Ireland's separate statute book.

The Catholics of Northern Ireland, who make up about one-third of its population, staged massive demonstrations in 1968 and 1969, charging discrimination in housing, employment, and political rights. Elements of the Irish Republican Army (IRA)—a faction committed to ending the partition of the country but which had been outlawed in the Irish Republic—directed acts of violence and terrorism against against members of the Protestant majority, against the police, and eventually against the British troops sent in to quell the disturbances.

Between 1969 and 1989, more than 2,750 persons were killed in Northern Ireland in sporadic waves of violence, and the religious communities came to resemble hostile armed camps. A considerable body of legislation was enacted to deal with the specific problems of religious, cultural and political discrimination, including the Northern Ireland Constitution Act 1973, making it illegal for any public authority to discriminate on grounds of religious belief or politi-

cal opinion and establishing the Standing Advisory Committee on Human Rights to advise the government on the effectiveness of the law; the Fair Employment (Northern Ireland) Act 1976, outlawing discrimination in employment on ground of religious or political belief and setting up the Fair Employment Agency to enforce and promote equality of opportunity in employment; and the Prevention of Incitement to Hatred Act (Northern Ireland) 1970, prohibiting the use of written matter or words likely to provoke hatred based on religious belief, color, race, or ethnic or national origin, against any section of the public.

In addition to anti-discrimination laws, Great Britain has enacted legislation in response to terrorism, particularly on the part of the IRA, which has resulted in curtailing civil liberties in Northern Ireland. Among these statues are the 1974 Prevention of Terrorism Act, as amended in 1976, 1984, and 1985; and the 1973 Northern Ireland Emergency Provisions Act, amended in 1978 and 1987. These acts restrict the activities of organizations connected with terrorism; expand the British criminal code to include terrorism and related activities; curtail the due process protection of suspected terrorists; authorize searches, seizures, and arrests without warrants for suspected terrorists; and allow the Secretary of State of Northern Ireland to detain a suspected terrorist for an unlimited period of time, *inter alia*.

The United Kingdom government considers the problem in Northern Ireland to be based primarily on the political division between those who wish Northern Ireland to remain as part of the United Kingdom and those who do not. In 1984, the Anglo–Irish Agreement was signed, affirming that any change in Northern Ireland's status will come about only with the consent of the majority there.

Territories. The government of Great Britain administers a number of territories, including Anguilla, Bermuda, the British Antarctic Territory, the British Indian Territory, the British Virgin Islands, the Cayman Islands, the Channel Islands, the Falkland Islands and Dependencies, Gibraltar, Hong Kong, the Isle of Man, the Leeward Islands, Montserrat, Pitcairn Island, St. Helena, and the Turks and Caicos Islands.

Of these, the UN General Assembly has repeatedly, in recent years, affirmed the inalienable right of the people of certain of those territories—Anguilla, the Cayman Islands, Montserrat, Bermuda, the Turks and Caicos Islands, and the British Virgin Islands—to SELF-DETERMINATION and independence, and has called upon the United Kingdom government to expedite the process of decolonization in accordance with the expressed wishes of the people of each territory.

In the case of each of these territories, the General Assembly has pointed out that it is the responsibility of the United Kingdom, as the administering power, to create such conditions in the territories as would enable their peoples to exercise freely and without interference, from a well-informed standpoint as to the available options, their inalienable right to self-determination and independence. At the same time, it has made it clear that it it is ultimately for the peoples of the territories themselves to determine freely their future political status.

As regards Gibraltar, which was turned over to Great Britain in accordance with the Treaty of Utrecht in 1713, Spain has never ceased to call for its return. A referendum on the question was held in 1967, but the residents of Gibraltar—nearly all of Spanish, Italian, or Maltese descent—voted overwhelming to remain a British territory. Although Spain blocked Gibraltar's land border from 1969 to 1980, the situation did not change. In 1980, however, the two governments indicated that they would settle the dispute in keeping with a UN resolution which called for the restoration of the territory to Spain at an unspecified future date; and the border was reopened.

As regards Hong Kong, the United Kingdom reached a unique understanding with the People's Republic of China in 1984 under which the crown colony would return to Chinese sovereignty on 30 June 1997 as a special administrative region of the People's Republic but would retain its western social, economic, and legal system as well as its status as a free port. Under the agreement, Hong Kong's basic lifestyle would remain unchanged, its laws would continue in effect, and basic human rights—including freedom of speech, freedom of assembly and association, and freedom of religion or belief—would be guaranteed by the government of China. However, after the events in China in June 1989, when the Chinese government crushed a growing liberal movement toward democratization, residents of Hong Kong are said in media reports to be fearful of the future of their rights.

UNITED NATIONS CHARTER (1945). The Charter of the United Nations was signed on 26 June 1945 at the conclusion of the United Nations Conference on International Organization, San Francisco, and entered into force on 24 October 1945. The INTERNATIONAL COURT OF JUSTICE STATUTE is an integral part of the charter.

The charter defines the purposes of the United Nations, among them:

Article 1. (2). To develop friendly relations among nations based on respect for the principle of equal rights and self-determination of peoples, and to take other appropriate measures to strengthen universal peace;

(3). To achieve international co-operation in solving international problems of an economic, social, cultural, or humanitarian character, and in promoting and encouraging respect for human rights and for fundamental freedoms for all without distinction as to race, sex, language, or religion.

It establishes the obligation of member States to co-operate for the advancement of these purposes in articles 55 and 56. Other provisions which have a direct bearing upon the promotion and protection of human rights are to be found in articles 8, 13, 24, 55, 56, 62, 73, 76, and 87.

Amendments to articles 23, 27, and 61 of the charter were adopted by the UN General Assembly on 17 December 1963 and entered into force on 31 August 1965. A further amendment to article 61 was adopted on 20 December 1971 and entered into force on 24 September 1973. An amendment to article 109, adopted on 20 December 1965, entered into force on 12 June 1968.

The amendment to article 23 enlarged the membership of the Security Council from 11 to 15. Article 27, as amended, provides that decisions of the Security Council on procedural matters shall be made by an affirmative vote of nine members (formerly seven) and on all other matters by an affirmative vote of nine members (formerly seven), including the concurring votes of the five permanent members of the Council. The amendment to article 61, which entered into force on 31 August 1965, enlarged the membership of the Economic and Social Council from 18 to 27. The subsequent amendment to that article, which entered into force on 24 September 1973, further increased the membership of the council to 54. The amendment to article 109, which relates to the first paragraph of that article, provides that a general conference of member States for the purpose of reviewing the charter may be held at a date and place to be fixed by a two-thirds' vote of the members of the General Assembly and by a vote of any nine (formerly seven) members of the Security Council.

The text of the United Nations Charter, as amended, is as follows:

We the peoples of the United Nations determined
to save succeeding generations from the scourge of war, which twice in our lifetime has brought untold sorrow to mankind, and
to reaffirm faith in fundamental human rights, in the dignity and worth of the human person, in the equal rights of men and women and of nations large and small, and
to establish conditions under which justice and respect

for the obligations arising from treaties and other sources of international law can be maintained, and

to promote social progress and better standards of life in larger freedom, and for these ends

to practice tolerance and live together in peace with one another as good neighbours, and

to unite our strength to maintain international peace and security, and

to ensure, by the acceptance of principles and the institution of methods, that armed force shall not be used, save in the common interest, and

to employ international machinery for the promotion of the economic and social advancement of all peoples, have resolved to combine our efforts to accomplish these aims.

Accordingly, our respective Governments, through representatives assembled in the city of San Francisco, who have exhibited their full powers found to be in good and due form, have agreed to the present Charter of the United Nations and do hereby establish an international organization to be known as the United Nations.

Chapter I
Purposes and Principles

Article 1. The Purposes of the United Nations are:

1. To maintain international peace and security, and to that end: to take effective collective measures for the prevention and removal of threats to the peace, and for the suppression of acts of aggression or other breaches of the peace, and to bring about by peaceful means, and in conformity with the principles of justice and international law, adjustment or settlement of international disputes or situations which might lead to a breach of the peace;

2. To develop friendly relations among nations based on respect for the principle of equal rights and self-determination of peoples, and to take other appropriate measures to strengthen universal peace;

3. To achieve international co-operation in solving international problems of an economic, social, cultural, or humanitarian character, and in promoting and encouraging respect for human rights and for fundamental freedoms for all without distinction as to race, sex, language, or religion; and

4. To be a centre for harmonizing the actions of nations in the attainment of these common ends.

Article 2. The Organization and its Members, in pursuit of the Purposes stated in Article 1, shall act in accordance with the following Principles.

1. The Organization is based on the principle of the sovereign equality of all its Members.

2. All Members, in order to ensure to all of them the rights and benefits resulting from membership, shall fulfil in good faith the obligations assumed by them in accordance with the present Charter.

3. All Members shall settle their international disputes by peaceful means in such a manner that international peace and security, and justice, are not endangered.

4. All Members shall refrain in their international relations from the threat or use of force against the territorial integrity or political independence of any state, or in any other manner inconsistent with the Purposes of the United Nations.

5. All Members shall give the United Nations every assistance in any action it takes in accordance with the present Charter, and shall refrain from giving assistance to any state against which the United Nations is taking preventive or enforcement action.

6. The Organization shall ensure that states which are not Members of the United Nations act in accordance with these Principles so far as may be necessary for the maintenance of international peace and security.

7. Nothing contained in the present Charter shall authorize the United Nations to intervene in matters which are essentially within the domestic jurisdiction of any state or shall require the Members to submit such matters to settlement under the present Charter; but this principle shall not prejudice the application of enforcement measures under Chapter VII.

Chapter II
Membership

Article 3. The original Members of the United Nations shall be the states which, having participated in the United Nations Conference on International Organization at San Francisco, or having previously signed the Declaration by United Nations of 1 January 1942, sign the present Charter and ratify it in accordance with Article 110.

Article 4. 1. Membership in the United Nations is open to all other peace-loving states which accept the obligations contained in the present Charter and, in the judgment of the Organization, are able and willing to carry out these obligations.

2. The admission of any such state to membership in the United Nations will be effected by a decision of the General Assembly upon the recommendation of the Security Council.

Article 5. A Member of the United Nations against which preventive or enforcement action has been taken by the Security Council may be suspended from the exercise of the rights and privileges of membership by the General Assembly upon the recommendation of the Security Council. The exercise of these rights and privileges may be restored by the Security Council.

Article 6. A Member of the United Nations which has persistently violated the Principles contained in the present Charter may be expelled from the Organization by the General Assembly upon the recommendation of the Security Council.

Chapter III
Organs

Article 7. 1. There are established as the principal organs of the United Nations: a General Assembly, a Security Council, an Economic and Social Council, a Trusteeship Council, an International Court of Justice, and a Secretariat.

2. Such subsidiary organs as may be found necessary may be established in accordance with the present Charter.

Article 8. The United Nations shall place no restrictions on the eligibility of men and women to participate in any capacity and under conditions of equality in its principal and subsidiary organs.

Chapter IV
The General Assembly

Composition

Article 9. 1. The General Assembly shall consist of all the Members of the United Nations.

2. Each Member shall have not more than five representatives in the General Assembly.

Functions and Powers

Article 10. The General Assembly may discuss any questions or any matters within the scope of the present Charter or relating to the powers and functions of any organs provided for in the present Charter, and, except as provided in Article 12, may make recommendations to the Members of the United Nations or to the Security Council or to both on any such questions or matters.

Article 11. 1. The General Assembly may consider the general principles of co-operation in the maintenance of international peace and security, including the principles governing disarmament and the regulation of armaments, and may make recommendations with regard to such principles to the Members or to the Security Council or to both.

2. The General Assembly may discuss any questions relating to the maintenance of international peace and security brought before it by any Member of the United Nations, or by the Security Council, or by a state which is not a Member of the United Nations in accordance with Article 35, paragraph 2, and, except as provided in Article 12, may make recommendations with regard to any such questions to the state or states concerned or to the Security Council or to both. Any such question on which action is necessary shall be referred to the Security Council by the General Assembly either before or after discussion.

3. The General Assembly may call the attention of the Security Council to situations which are likely to endanger international peace and security.

4. The powers of the General Assembly set forth in this Article shall not limit the general scope of Article 10.

Article 12. 1. While the Security Council is exercising in respect of any dispute or situation the functions assigned to it in the present Charter, the General Assembly shall not make any recommendation with regard to that dispute or situation unless the Security Council so requests.

2. The Security-General, with the consent of the Security Council, shall notify the General Assembly at each session of any matters relative to the maintenance of international peace and security which are being dealt with by the Security Council and shall similarly notify the General Assembly, or the Members of the United Nations if the General Assembly is not in session, immediately the Security Council ceases to deal with such matters.

Article 13. 1. The General Assembly shall initiate studies and make recommendations for the purpose of:

a. promoting international co-operation in the political field and encouraging the progressive development of international law and its codification;

b. promoting international co-operation in the economic, social, cultural, educational, and health fields, and assisting in the realization of human rights and fundamental freedoms for all without distinction as to race, sex, language, or religion.

2. The further responsibilities, functions and powers of the General Assembly with respect to matters mentioned in paragraph 1(b) above are set forth in Chapters IX and X.

Article 14. Subject to the provisions of Article 12, the General Assembly may recommend measures for the peaceful adjustment of any situation, regardless of origin, which it deems likely to impair the general welfare or friendly relations among nations, including situations resulting from a violation of the provisions of the present Charter setting forth the Purposes and Principles of the United Nations.

Article 15. 1. The General Assembly shall receive and consider annual and special reports from the Security Council; these reports shall include an account of the measures that the Security Council has decided upon or taken to maintain international peace and security.

2. The General Assembly shall receive and consider reports from the other organs of the United Nations.

Article 16. The General Assembly shall perform such functions with respect to the international trusteeship system as are assigned to it under Chapters XII and XIII, including the approval of the trusteeship agreements for areas not designated as strategic.

Article 17. 1. The General Assembly shall consider and approve the budget of the Organization.

2. The expenses of the Organization shall be borne by the Members as apportioned by the General Assembly.

3. The General Assembly shall consider and approve any financial and budgetary arrangements with specialized agencies referred to in Article 57 and shall examine the administrative budgets of such specialized agencies with a view to making recommendations to the agencies concerned.

Voting

Article 18. 1. Each member of the General Assembly shall have one vote.

2. Decisions of the General Assembly on important questions shall be made by a two-thirds majority of the members present and voting. These questions shall include: recommendations with respect to the maintenance of international peace and security, the election of the non-permanent members of the Security Council, the election of the members of the Economic and Social Council, the election of members of the Trusteeship Council in accordance with paragraph 1(c) of Article 86, the admission of new Members to the United Nations, the suspension of the rights and privileges of membership, the expulsion of Members, questions relating to the operation of the trusteeship system, and budgetary questions.

3. Decisions on other questions, including the determination of additional categories of questions to be decided by a two-thirds majority, shall be made by a majority of the members present and voting.

Article 19. A Member of the United Nations which is in arrears in the payment of its financial contributions to the Organization shall have no vote in the General Assembly if the amount of its arrears equals or exceeds the amount of the contributions due from it for the preceding two full years. The General Assembly may, nevertheless, permit such a Member to vote if it is satisfied that the failure to pay is due to conditions beyond the control of the Member.

Procedure

Article 20. The General Assembly shall meet in regular annual sessions and in such special sessions as occasion may require. Special sessions shall be convoked by the Secretary-General at the request of the Security Council or of a majority of the Members of the United Nations.

Article 21. The General Assembly shall adopt its own rules of procedure. It shall elect its President for each session.

Article 22. The General Assembly may establish such subsidiary organs as it deems necessary for the performance of its functions.

Chapter V
The Security Council

Composition

Article 23. 1. The Security Council shall consist of fifteen Members of the United Nations. The Republic of China, France, the Union of Soviet Socialist Republics, the United Kingdom of Great Britain and Northern Ireland, and the

United States of America shall be permanent members of the Security Council. The General Assembly shall elect ten other Members of the United Nations to be non-permanent members of the Security Council, due regard being specially paid, in the first instance to the contribution of Members of the United Nations to the maintenance of international peace and security and to the other purposes of the Organization, and also to equitable geographical distribution.

2. The non-permanent members of the Security Council shall be elected for a term of two years. In the first election of the non-permanent members after the increase of the membership of the Security Council from eleven to fifteen, two of the four additional members shall be chosen for a term of one year. A retiring member shall not be eligible for immediate re-election.

3. Each member of the Security Council shall have one representative.

Functions and Powers

Article 24. 1. In order to ensure prompt and effective action by the United Nations, its Members confer on the Security Council primary responsibility for the maintenance of international peace and security, and agree that in carrying out its duties under this responsibility the Security Council acts on their behalf.

2. In discharging these duties the Security Council shall act in accordance with the Purposes and Principles of the United Nations. The specific powers granted to the Security Council for the discharge of these duties are laid down in Chapters VI, VII, VIII, and XII.

3. The Security Council shall submit annual and, when necessary, special reports to the General Assembly for its consideration.

Article 25. The Members of the United Nations agree to accept and carry out the decisions of the Security Council in accordance with the present Charter.

Article 26. In order to promote the establishment and maintenance of international peace and security with the least diversion for armaments of the world's human and economic resources, the Security Council shall be responsible for formulating, with the assistance of the Military Staff Committee referred to in Article 47, plans to be submitted to the Members of the United Nations for the establishment of a system for the regulation of armaments.

Voting

Article 27. 1. Each member of the Security Council shall have one vote.

2. Decisions of the Security Council on procedural matters shall be made by an affirmative vote of nine members.

3. Decisions of the Security Council on all other matters shall be made by an affirmative vote of nine members including the concurring votes of the permanent members; provided that, in decisions under Chapter VI, and under paragraph 3 of Article 52, a party to a dispute shall abstain from voting.

Procedure

Article 28. 1. The Security Council shall be so organized as to be able to function continuously. Each member of the Security Council shall for this purpose be represented at all times at the seat of the Organization.

2. The Security Council shall hold periodic meetings at which each of its members may, if it so desires, be represented by a member of the government or by some other specially designated representative.

3. The Security Council may hold meetings at such places other than the seat of the Organization as in its judgment will best facilitate its work.

Article 29. The Security Council may establish such subsidiary organs as it deems necessary for the performance of its functions.

Article 30. The Security Council shall adopt its own rules of procedure, including the method of selecting its President.

Article 31. Any Member of the United Nations which is not a member of the Security Council may participate, without vote, in the discussion of any question brought before the Security Council whenever the latter considers that the interests of that Member are specially affected.

Article 32. Any Member of the United Nations which is not a member of the Security Council or any state which is not a Member of the United Nations, if it is a party to a dispute under consideration by the Security Council, shall be invited to participate, without vote, in the discussion relating to the dispute. The Security Council shall lay down such conditions as it deems just for the participation of a state which is not a Member of the United Nations.

Chapter VI
Pacific Settlement of Disputes

Article 33. 1. The parties to any dispute, the continuance of which is likely to endanger the maintenance of international peace and security, shall, first of all, seek a solution by negotiation, enquiry, mediation, conciliation, arbitration, judicial settlement, resort to regional agencies or arrangements, or other peaceful means of their own choice.

2. The Security Council shall, when it deems necessary, call upon the parties to settle their dispute by such means.

Article 34. The Security Council may investigate any dispute, or any situation which might lead to international friction or give rise to a dispute, in order to determine whether the continuance of the dispute or situation is likely to endanger the maintenance of international peace and security.

Article 35. 1. Any Member of the United Nations may bring any dispute, or any situation of the nature referred to in Article 34, to the attention of the Security Council or of the General Assembly.

2. A state which is not a Member of the United Nations may bring to the attention of the Security Council or of the General Assembly any dispute to which it is a party if it accepts in advance, for the purposes of the dispute, the obligations of pacific settlement provided in the present Charter.

3. The proceedings of the General Assembly in respect of matters brought to its attention under this Article will be subject to the provisions of Articles 11 and 12.

Article 36. 1. The Security Council may, at any stage of a dispute of the nature referred to in Article 33 or of a situation of like nature, recommend appropriate procedures or methods of adjustment.

2. The Security Council should take into consideration any procedures for the settlement of the dispute which have already been adopted by the parties.

3. In making recommendations under this Article the Security Council should also take into consideration that legal disputes should as a general rule be referred by the parties to the International Court of Justice in accord with the provisions of the Statute of the Court.

Article 37. 1. Should the parties to a dispute of the

referred to in Article 33 fail to settle it by the means indicated in that Article, they shall refer it to the Security Council.

2. If the Security Council deems that the continuance of the dispute is in fact likely to endanger the maintenance of international peace and security, it shall decide whether to take action under Article 36 or to recommend such terms of settlement as it may consider appropriate.

Article 38. Without prejudice to the provisions of Articles 33 to 37, the Security Council may, if all the parties to any dispute so request, make recommendations to the parties with a view to a pacific settlement of the dispute.

Chapter VII
Action with respect to Threats to the Peace, Breaches of the Peace, and Acts of Aggression

Article 39. The Security Council shall determine the existence of any threat to the peace, breach of the peace, or act of aggression and shall make recommendations, or decide what measures shall be taken in accordance with Articles 41 and 42, to maintain or restore international peace and security.

Article 40. In order to prevent an aggravation of the situation, the Security Council may, before making the recommendations or deciding upon the measures provided for in Article 39, call upon the parties concerned to comply with such provisional measures as it deems necessary or desirable. Such provisional measures shall be without prejudice to the rights, claims, or position of the parties concerned. The Security Council shall duly take account of failure to comply with such provisional measures.

Article 41. The Security Council may decide what measures not involving the use of armed force are to be employed to give effect to its decisions, and it may call upon the Members of the United Nations to apply such measures. These may include complete or partial interruption of economic relations and of rail, sea, air, postal, telegraphic, radio, and other means of communication, and the severance of diplomatic relations.

Article 42. Should the Security Council consider that measures provided for in Article 41 would be inadequate or have proved to be inadequate, it may take such action by air, sea, or land forces as may be necessary to maintain or restore international peace and security. Such action may include demonstrations, blockade, and other operations by air, sea, or land forces of Members of the United Nations.

Article 43. 1. All Members of the United Nations, in order to contribute to the maintenance of international peace and security, undertake to make available to the Security Council, on its call and in accordance with a special agreement or agreements, armed forces, assistance, and facilities, including rights of passage, necessary for the purpose of maintaining international peace and security.

2. Such agreement or agreements shall govern the numbers and types of forces, their degree of readiness and general location, and the nature of the facilities and assistance to be provided.

3. The agreement or agreements shall be negotiated as soon as possible on the initiative of the Security Council. They shall be concluded between the Security Council and Members or between the Security Council and groups of Members and shall be subject to ratification by the signatory states in accordance with their respective constitutional processes.

Article 44. When the Security Council has decided to use force it shall, before calling upon a Member not represented on it to provide armed forces in fulfilment of the obligations assumed under Article 43, invite that Member, if the Member so desires, to participate in the decisions of the Security Council concerning the employment of contingents of that Member's armed forces.

Article 45. In order to enable the United Nations to take urgent military measures, Members shall hold immediately available national air-force contingents for combined international enforcement action. The strength and degree of readiness of these contingents and plans for their combined action shall be determined, within the limits laid down in the special agreement or agreements referred to in Article 43, by the Security Council with the assistance of the Military Staff Committee.

Article 46. Plans for the application of armed force shall be made by the Security Council with the assistance of the Military Staff Committee.

Article 47. 1. There shall be established a Military Staff Committee to advise and assist the Security Council on all questions relating to the Security Council's military requirements for the maintenance of international peace and security, the employment and command of forces placed at its disposal, the regulation of armaments, and possible disarmament.

2. The Military Staff Committee shall consist of the Chiefs of Staff of the permanent members of the Security Council or their representatives. Any Member of the United Nations not permanently represented on the Committee shall be invited by the Committee to be associated with it when the efficient discharge of the Committee's responsibilities requires the participation of that Member in its work.

3. The Military Staff Committee shall be responsible under the Security Council for the strategic direction of any armed forces placed at the disposal of the Security Council. Questions relating to the command of such forces shall be worked out subsequently.

4. The Military Staff Committee, with the authorization of the Security Council and after consultation with appropriate regional agencies, may establish regional sub-committees.

Article 48. 1. The action required to carry out the decisions of the Security Council for the maintenance of international peace and security shall be taken by all the Members of the United Nations or by some of them, as the Security Council may determine.

2. Such decisions shall be carried out by the Members of the United Nations directly and through their action in the appropriate international agencies of which they are members.

Article 49. The Members of the United Nations shall join in affording mutual assistance in carrying out the measures decided upon by the Security Council.

Article 50. If preventive or enforcement measures against any state are taken by the Security Council, any other state, whether a Member of the United Nations or not, which finds itself confronted with special economic problems arising from the carrying out of those measures shall have the right to consult the Security Council with regard to a solution of those problems.

Article 51. Nothing in the present Chapter shall impair the inherent right of individual or collective self-defence if an armed attack occurs against a Member of the United Nations, until the Security Council has taken measures necessary to maintain international peace and security. Measures taken by Members in the exercise of this right to self-defence shall be immediately reported to the Security

Council and shall not in any way affect the authority and responsibility of the Security Council under the present Charter to take at any time such action as it deems necessary in order to maintain or restore international peace and security.

Chapter VIII
Regional Arrangements

Article 52. 1. Nothing in the present Charter precludes the existence of regional arrangements or agencies for dealing with such matters relating to the maintenance of international peace and security as are appropriate for regional action, provided that such arrangements or agencies and their activities are consistent with the Purposes and Principles of the United Nations.

2. The Members of the United Nations entering into such arrangements or constituting such agencies shall make every effort to achieve pacific settlement of local disputes through such regional arrangements or by such regional agencies before referring them to the Security Council.

3. The Security Council shall encourage the development of pacific settlement of local disputes through such regional arrangements or by such regional agencies either on the initiative of the states concerned or by reference from the Security Council.

4. This Article in no way impairs the application of Articles 34 and 35.

Article 53. 1. The Security Council shall, where appropriate, utilize such regional arrangements or agencies for enforcement action under its authority. But no enforcement action shall be taken under regional arrangements or by regional agencies without the authorization of the Security Council, with the exception of measures against any enemy state, as defined in paragraph 2 of this Article, provided for pursuant to Article 107 or in regional arrangements directed against renewal of aggressive policy on the part of any such state, until such time as the Organization may, on request of the Governments concerned, be charged with the responsibility for preventing further aggression by such a state.

2. The term enemy state as used in paragraph 1 of this Article applies to any state which during the Second World War has been an enemy of any signatory of the present Charter.

Article 54. The Security Council shall at all times be kept fully informed of activities undertaken or in contemplation under regional arrangements or by regional agencies for the maintenance of international peace and security.

Chapter IX
International Economic and Social Co-operation

Article 55. With a view to the creation of conditions of stability and well-being which are necessary for peaceful and friendly relations among nations based on respect for the principle of equal rights and self-determination of peoples, the United Nations shall promote:

a. higher standards of living, full employment, and conditions of economic and social progress and development;

b. solutions of international economic, social, health, and related problems; and international cultural and educational co-operation; and

c. universal respect for, and observance of, human rights and fundamental freedoms for all without distinction as to race, sex, language, or religion.

Article 56. All Members pledge themselves to take joint and separate action in co-operation with the Organization for the achievement of the purposes set forth in Article 55.

Article 57. 1. The various specialized agencies, established by intergovernmental agreement and having wide international responsibilities, as defined in their basic instruments, in economic, social, cultural, educational, health, and related fields, shall be brought into relationship with the United Nations in accordance with the provisions of Article 63.

2. Such agencies thus brought into relationship with the United Nations are hereinafter referred to as specialized agencies.

Article 58. The Organization shall make recommendations for the co-ordination of the policies and activities of the specialized agencies.

Article 59. The Organization shall, where appropriate, initiate negotiations among the states concerned for the creation of any new specialized agencies required for the accomplishment of the purposes set forth in Article 55.

Article 60. Responsibility for the discharge of the functions of the Organization set forth in this Chapter shall be vested in the General Assembly and, under the authority of the General Assembly, in the Economic and Social Council, which shall have for this purpose the powers set forth in Chapter X.

Chapter X
The Economic and Social Council

Composition

Article 61. 1. The Economic and Social Council shall consist of fifty-four Members of the United Nations elected by the General Assembly.

2. Subject to the provisions of paragraph 3, eighteen members of the Economic and Social Council shall be elected each year for a term of three years. A retiring member shall be eligible for immediate re-election.

3. At the first election after the increase in the membership of the Economic and Social Council from twenty-seven to fifty-four members, in addition to the members elected in place of the nine members whose term of office expires at the end of that year, twenty-seven additional members shall be elected. Of these twenty-seven additional members, the term of office of nine members so elected shall expire at the end of one year, and of nine other members at the end of two years, in accordance with arrangements made by the General Assembly.

4. Each member of the Economic and Social Council shall have one representative.

Functions and Powers

Article 62. 1. The Economic and Social Council may make or initiate studies and reports with respect to international economic, social, cultural, educational, health, and related matters and may make recommendations with respect to any such matters to the General Assembly, to the Members of the United Nations, and to the specialized agencies concerned.

2. It may make recommendations for the purpose of promoting respect for, and observance of, human rights and fundamental freedoms for all.

3. It may prepare draft conventions for submission to the General Assembly, with respect to matters falling within its competence.

4. It may call, in accordance with the rules prescribed by the United Nations, international conferences on matters falling within its competence.

Article 63. 1. The Economic and Social Council may enter into agreements with any of the agencies referred to in Article 57, defining the terms on which the agency concerned shall be brought into relationship with the United Nations. Such agreements shall be subject to approval by the General Assembly.

2. It may co-ordinate the activities of the specialized agencies through consultation with and recommendations to such agencies and through recommendations to the General Assembly and to the Members of the United Nations.

Article 64. 1. The Economic and Social Council may take appropriate steps to obtain regular reports from the specialized agencies. It may make arrangements with the Members of the United Nations and with the specialized agencies to obtain reports on the steps taken to give effect to its own recommendations and to recommendations on matters falling within its competence made by the General Assembly.

2. It may communicate its observations on these reports to the General Assembly.

Article 65. The Economic and Social Council may furnish information to the Security Council and shall assist the Security Council upon its request.

Article 66. 1. The Economic and Social Council shall perform such functions as fall within its competence in connexion with the carrying out of the recommendations of the General Assembly.

2. It may, with the approval of the General Assembly, perform services at the request of Members of the United Nations and at the request of specialized agencies.

3. It shall perform such other functions as are specified elsewhere in the present Charter or as may be assigned to it by the General Assembly.

Voting

Article 67. 1. Each member of the Economic and Social Council shall have one vote.

2. Decisions of the Economic and Social Council shall be made by a majority of the members present and voting.

Procedure

Article 68. The Economic and Social Council shall set up commissions in economic and social fields and for the promotion of human rights, and such other commissions as may be required for the performance of its functions.

Article 69. The Economic and Social Council shall invite any Member of the United Nations to participate, without vote, in its deliberations on any matter of particular concern to that Member.

Article 70. The Economic and Social Council may make arrangements for representatives of the specialized agencies to participate, without vote, in its deliberations and in those of the commissions established by it, and for its representatives to participate in the deliberations of the specialized agencies.

Article 71. The Economic and Social Council may make suitable arrangements for consultation with non-governmental organizations which are concerned with matters within its competence. Such arrangements may be made with international organizations and, where appropriate, with national organizations after consultation with the Member of the United Nations concerned.

Article 72. 1. The Economic and Social Council shall adopt its own rules of procedure, including the method of selecting its President.

2. The Economic and Social Council shall meet as required in accordance with its rules, which shall include provision for the convening of meetings on the request of a majority of its members.

Chapter XI
Declaration regarding Non-self-governing Territories

Article 73. Members of the United Nations which have or assume responsibilities for the administration of territories whose peoples have not yet attained a full measure of self-government recognize the principle that the interests of the inhabitants of these territories are paramount, and accept as a sacred trust the obligation to promote to the utmost, within the system of international peace and security established by the present Charter, the well-being of the inhabitants of these territories, and, to this end:

a. to ensure, with due respect for the culture of the peoples concerned, their political, economic, social, and educational advancement, their just treatment, and their protection against abuses;

b. to develop self-government, to take due account of the political aspirations of the peoples, and to assist them in the progressive development of their free political institutions, according to the particular circumstances of each territory and its peoples and their varying stages of advancement;

c. to further international peace and security;

d. to promote constructive measures of development, to encourage research, and to co-operate with one another and, when and where appropriate, with specialized international bodies with a view to the practical achievement of the social, economic, and scientific purposes set forth in this Article; and

e. to transmit regularly to the Secretary-General for information purposes, subject to such limitation as security and constitutional considerations may require, statistical and other information of a technical nature relating to economic, social, and educational conditions in the territories for which they are respectively responsible other than those territories to which Chapters XII and XIII apply.

Article 74. Members of the United Nations also agree that their policy in respect of the territories to which this Chapter applies, no less than in respect of their metropolitan areas, must be based on the general principle of good-neighbourliness, due account being taken of the interests and well-being of the rest of the world, in social, economic, and commercial matters.

Chapter XII
International Trusteeship System

Article 75. The United Nations shall establish under its authority an international trusteeship system for the administration and supervision of such territories as may be placed there-under by subsequent individual agreements. These territories are hereinafter referred to as trust territories.

Article 76. The basic objectives of the trusteeship system, in accordance with the Purposes of the United Nations laid down in Article 1 of the present Charter, shall be:

a. to further international peace and security;

b. to promote the political, economic, social, and educational advancement of the inhabitants of the trust territories, and their progressive development towards self-government or independence as may be appropriate to the particular circumstances of each territory and its peoples and the freely expressed wishes of the peoples concerned, and as may be provided by the terms of each trusteeship agreement;

c. to encourage respect for human rights and for fundamental freedoms for all without distinction as to race, sex, language, or religion, and to encourage recognition of the interdependence of the peoples of the world; and

d. to ensure equal treatment in social, economic, and commercial matters for all Members of the United Nations and their nationals, and also equal treatment for the latter in the administration of justice, without prejudice to the attainment of the foregoing objectives and subject to the provisions of Article 80.

Article 77. 1. The trusteeship system shall apply to such territories in the following categories as may be placed thereunder by means of trusteeship agreements:

a. territories now held under mandate;

b. territories which may be detached from enemy states as a result of the Second World War; and

c. territories voluntarily placed under the system by states responsible for their administration.

2. It will be a matter for subsequent agreement as to which territories in the foregoing categories will be brought under the trusteeship system and upon what terms.

Article 78. The trusteeship system shall not apply to territories which have become Members of the United Nations, relationship among which shall be based on respect for the principle of sovereign equality.

Article 79. The terms of trusteeship for each territory to be placed under the trusteeship system, including any alteration or amendment, shall be agreed upon by the states directly concerned, including the mandatory power in the case of territories held under mandate by a Member of the United Nations, and shall be approved as provided for in Articles 83 and 85.

Article 80. 1. Except as may be agreed upon in individual trusteeship agreements, made under Articles 77, 79, and 81, placing each territory under the trusteeship system, and until such agreements have been concluded, nothing in this Chapter shall be construed in or of itself to alter in any manner the rights whatsoever of any states or any peoples or the terms of existing international instruments to which Members of the United Nations may respectively be parties.

2. Paragraph 1 of this Article shall not be interpreted as giving grounds for delay or postponement of the negotiation and conclusion of agreements for placing mandated and other territories under the trusteeship system as provided for in Article 77.

Article 81. The trusteeship agreement shall in each case include the terms under which the trust territory will be administered and designate the authority which will exercise the administration of the trust territory. Such authority, hereinafter called the administering authority, may be one or more states or the Organization itself.

Article 82. There may be designated, in any trusteeship agreement, a strategic area or areas which may include part or all of the trust territory to which the agreement applies, without prejudice to any special agreement or agreements made under Article 43.

Article 83. 1. All functions of the United Nations relating to strategic areas, including the approval of the terms of the trusteeship agreements and of their alteration or amendment, shall be exercised by the Security Council.

2. The basic objectives set forth in Article 76 shall be applicable to the people of each strategic area.

3. The Security Council shall, subject to the provisions of the trusteeship agreements and without prejudice to security considerations, avail itself of the assistance of the Trusteeship Council to perform those functions of the United Nations under the trusteeship system relating to political, economic, social, and educational matters in the strategic areas.

Article 84. It shall be the duty of the administering authority to ensure that the trust territory shall play its part in the maintenance of international peace and security. To this end the administering authority may make use of volunteer forces, facilities, and assistance from the trust territory in carrying out the obligations towards the Security Council undertaken in this regard by the administering authority, as well as for local defence and the maintenance of law and order within the trust territory.

Article 85. 1. The functions of the United Nations with regard to trusteeship agreements for all areas not designated as strategic, including the approval of the terms of the trusteeship agreements and of their alteration or amendment, shall be exercised by the General Assembly.

2. The Trusteeship Council, operating under the authority of the General Assembly, shall assist the General Assembly in carrying out these functions.

Chapter XIII
The Trusteeship Council

Composition

Article 86. 1. The Trusteeship Council shall consist of the following Members of the United Nations:

a. those Members administering trust territories;

b. such of those Members mentioned by name in Article 23 as are not administering trust territories; and

c. as many other Members elected for three-year terms by the General Assembly as may be necessary to ensure that the total number of members of the Trusteeship Council is equally divided between those Members of the United Nations which administer trust territories and those which do not.

2. Each member of the Trusteeship Council shall designate one specially qualified person to represent it therein.

Functions and Powers

Article 87. The General Assembly and, under its authority, the Trusteeship Council, in carrying out their functions, may:

a. consider reports submitted by the administering authority;

b. accept petitions and examine them in consultation with the administering authority;

c. provide for periodic visits to the respective trust territories at times agreed upon with the administering authority; and

d. take these and other actions in conformity with the terms of the trusteeship agreements.

Article 88. The Trusteeship Council shall formulate a questionnaire on the political, economic, social, and educational advancement of the inhabitants of each trust territory, and the administering authority for each trust territory within the competence of the General Assembly shall make an annual report to the General Assembly upon the basis of such questionnaire.

Voting

Article 89. 1. Each member of the Trusteeship Council shall have one vote.

2. Decisions of the Trusteeship Council shall be made by a majority of the members present and voting.

Procedure

Article 90. 1. The Trusteeship Council shall adopt its own rules of procedure, including the method of selecting its President.

2. The Trusteeship Council shall meet as required in accordance with its rules, which shall include provision for the convening of meetings on the request of a majority of its members.

Article 91. The Trusteeship Council shall, when appropriate, avail itself of the assistance of the Economic and Social Council and of the specialized agencies in regard to matters with which they are respectively concerned.

Chapter XIV
The International Court of Justice

Article 92. The International Court of Justice shall be the principal judicial organ of the United Nations. It shall function in accordance with the annexed Statute, which is based upon the Statute of the Permanent Court of International Justice and forms an integral part of the present Charter.

Article 93. 1. All Members of the United Nations are *ipso facto* parties to the Statute of the International Court of Justice.

2. A state which is not a Member of the United Nations may become a party to the Statute of the International Court of Justice on conditions to be determined in each case by the General Assembly upon the recommendation of the Security Council.

Article 94. 1. Each Member of the United Nations undertakes to comply with the decision of the International Court of Justice in any case to which it is a party.

2. If any party to a case fails to perform the obligations incumbent upon it under a judgment rendered by the Court, the other party may have recourse to the Security Council, which may, if it deems necessary, make recommendations or decide upon measures to be taken to give effect to the judgment.

Article 95. Nothing in the present Charter shall prevent Members of the United Nations from entrusting the solution of their differences to other tribunals by virtue of agreements already in existence or which may be concluded in the future.

Article 96. 1. The General Assembly or the Security Council may request the International Court of Justice to give an advisory opinion on any legal question.

2. Other organs of the United Nations and specialized agencies, which may at any time be so authorized by the General Assembly, may also request advisory opinions of the Court on legal questions arising within the scope of their activities.

Chapter XV
The Secretariat

Article 97. The Secretariat shall comprise a Secretary-General and such staff as the Organization may require. The Secretary-General shall be appointed by the General Assembly upon the recommendation of the Security Council. He shall be the chief administrative officer of the Organization.

Article 98. The Secretary-General shall act in that capacity in all meetings of the General Assembly, of the Security Council, of the Economic and Social Council, and of the Trusteeship Council, and shall perform such other functions as are entrusted to him by these organs. The Secretary-General shall make an annual report to the General Assembly on the work of the Organization.

Article 99. The Secretary-General may bring to the attention of the Security Council any matter which in his opinion may threaten the maintenance of international peace and security.

Article 100. 1. In the performance of their duties the Secretary-General and the staff shall not seek or receive instructions from any government or from any other authority external to the Organization. They shall refrain from any action which might reflect on their position as international officials responsible only to the Organization.

2. Each Member of the United Nations undertakes to respect the exclusively international character of the responsibilities of the Secretary-General and the staff and not to seek to influence them in the discharge of their responsibilities.

Article 101. 1. The staff shall be appointed by the Secretary-General under regulations established by the General Assembly.

2. Appropriate staffs shall be permanently assigned to the Economic and Social Council, the Trusteeship Council, and, as required, to other organs of the United Nations. These staffs shall form a part of the Secretariat.

3. The paramount consideration in the employment of the staff and in the determination of the conditions of service shall be the necessity of securing the highest standards of efficiency, competence, and integrity. Due regard shall be paid to the importance of recruiting the staff on as wide a geographical basis as possible.

Chapter XVI
Miscellaneous Provisions

Article 102. 1. Every treaty and every international agreement entered into by any Member of the United Nations after the present Charter comes into force shall as soon as possible be registered with the Secretariat and published by it.

2. No party to any such treaty or international agreement which has not been registered in accordance with the provisions of paragraph 1 of this Article may invoked that treaty or agreement before any organ of the United Nations.

Article 103. In the event of a conflict between the obligations of the Members of the United Nations under the present Charter and their obligations under any other international agreement, their obligations under the present Charter shall prevail.

Article 104. The Organization shall enjoy in the territory of each of its Members such legal capacity as may be necessary for the exercise of its functions and the fulfilment of its purposes.

Article 105. 1. The Organization shall enjoy in the territory of each of its Members such privileges and immunities as are necessary for the fulfilment of its purposes.

2. Representatives of the Members of the United Nations and officials of the Organization shall similarly enjoy such privileges and immunities as are necessary for the independent exercise of their functions in connexion with the Organization.

3. The General Assembly may make recommendations with a view to determining the details of the application of

paragraphs 1 and 2 of this Article or may propose conventions to the Members of the United Nations for this purpose.

Chapter XVII
Transitional Security Arrangements

Article 106. Pending the coming into force of such special agreements referred to in Article 43 as in the opinion of the Security Council enable it to begin the exercise of its responsibilities under Article 42, the parties to the Four-Nation Declaration, signed at Moscow, 30 October 1943, and France, shall, in accordance with the provisions of paragraph 5 of that Declaration, consult with one another and as occasion requires with other Members of the United Nations with a view to such joint action on behalf of the Organization as may be necessary for the purpose of maintaining international peace and security.

Article 107. Nothing in the present Charter shall invalidate or preclude action, in relation to any state which during the Second World War has been an enemy of any signatory to the present Charter, taken or authorized as a result of that war by the Governments having responsibility for such action.

Chapter XVIII
Amendments

Article 108. Amendments to the present Charter shall come into force for all Members of the United Nations when they have been adopted by a vote of two thirds of the members of the General Assembly and ratified in accordance with their respective constitutional processes by two thirds of the Members of the United Nations, including all the permanent members of the Security Council.

Article 109. 1. A General Conference of the Members of the United Nations for the purpose of reviewing the present Charter may be held at a date and place to be fixed by a two-thirds vote of the members of the General Assembly and by a vote of any nine members of the Security Council. Each Member of the United Nations shall have one vote in the conference.

2. Any alteration of the present Charter recommended by a two-thirds vote of the conference shall take effect when ratified in accordance with their respective constitutional processes by two thirds of the Members of the United Nations including all the permanent members of the Security Council.

3. If such a conference has not been held before the tenth annual session of the General Assembly following the coming into force of the present Charter, the proposal to call such a conference shall be placed on the agenda of that session of the General Assembly, and the conference shall be held if so decided by a majority vote of the members of the General Assembly and by a vote of any seven members of the Security Council.

Chapter XIX
Ratification and Signature

Article 110. 1. The present Charter shall be ratified by the signatory states in accordance with their respective constitutional processes.

2. The ratifications shall be deposited with the Government of the United States of America, which shall notify all the signatory states of each deposit as well as the Secretary-General of the Organization when he has been appointed.

3. The present Charter shall come into force upon the deposit of ratifications by the Republic of China, France, the Union of Soviet Socialist Republics, the United Kingdom of Great Britain and Northern Ireland, and the United States of America, and by a majority of the other signatory states. A protocol of the ratifications deposited shall thereupon be drawn up by the Government of the United States of America which shall communicate copies thereof to all the signatory states.

4. The states signatory to the present Charter which ratify it after it has come into force will become original Members of the United Nations on the date of the deposit of their respective ratifications.

Article 111. The present Charter, of which the Chinese, French, Russian, English, and Spanish texts are equally authentic, shall remain deposited in the archives of the Government of the United States of America. Duly certified copies thereof shall be transmitted by that Government to the Governments of the other signatory states.

In faith whereof the representatives of the Governments of the United Nations have signed the present Charter.

Done at the city of San Francisco the twenty-sixth day of June, one thousand nine hundred and forty-five.

SEE ALSO *Declaration on the Occasion of the Twenty-Fifth Anniversary of the United Nations.*

UNITED NATIONS CHILDREN'S FUND (UNICEF).

The United Nations International Children's Emergency Fund, established by the General Assembly on 11 December 1946 (resolution 57 [I]), has since been utilized for the benefit of children and adolescents of countries and territories which were victims of aggression. Its assistance is provided on the basis of need, without discrimination on the ground of race, creed, national status, or political belief. In 1953, the assembly decided to continue the fund indefinitely; it changed its title to the United Nations Children's Fund but retained the acronym UNICEF.

From 1956 to 1982, UNICEF was governed by an executive board consisting of 30 members elected by the Economic and Social Council. In April 1982, the General Assembly enlarged the board to 41 members selected with the following geographic distribution: (1) nine seats for African States; (2) nine seats for Asian States; (3) four seats for eastern European States; (4) six seats for Latin American States; (5) 12 seats for western European and other States; and (6) one seat to be rotated among the five regional groups in the following order: (a) African States, (b) Latin American States, (c) Asian States, (d) western European and other States, and (e) eastern European States.

The UNICEF board usually meets once a year, in New York, for approximately ten days. At each session, the board establishes a "Programmer Committee" and a "Committee on Administration and Finance." Its reports are directed through the Economic and Social Council to the General Assembly.

UNITED NATIONS DEVELOPMENT FUND FOR WOMEN. Originally established by the General Assembly on 16 December 1976 as the Voluntary Fund for the United Nations Decade for Women (resolution 31/133), the name and mandate of the fund were changed in 1984 when the General Assembly made it "a separate and identifiable entity in autonomous association with the United Nations Development Programme" (UNDP) and re-titled it the United Nations Development Fund for Women. The fund is used primarily to serve as a catalyst with the goal of ensuring the appropriate involvement of women in mainstream development activities, as often as possible at the pre-investment stages, and secondarily to support innovative and experimental activities benefitting women in line with national and regional priorities.

Whereas the UNDP administrator is accountable for all operations of the fund, he is advised by a consultative committee on all matters of policy. The committee is composed of five member States designated by the president of the General Assembly with due regard for equitable geographical distribution. Members are appointed for a term of three years. The board determines the time and place of its meetings. The board reports to the governing body of the UNDP; its report is also provided to the General Assembly and to the COMMISSION ON THE STATUS OF WOMEN.

At its 1988 session, the General Assembly took note (decision 43/325) of the appointments, by its president, of the German Democratic Republic, India, Mexico, the Netherlands, and Senegal as members of the consultative committee for a three-year term of office beginning on 1 January 1989.

The General Assembly, on 8 December 1988, took note of the report of the administrator of the United Nations Development Program on the activities of the United Nations Development Fund for Women (UN Doc. A/43/643, annex) and reaffirmed the dual priorities of the fund. It expressed its appreciation to governments, non-governmental organizations, and individuals contributing to the fund but noted that the fund's resources had been insufficient to enable it to respond adequately to the increasing requests received.

UNITED NATIONS EDUCATIONAL, SCIENTIFIC AND CULTURAL ORGANIZATION. By its constitution, which entered into force on 4 November 1946, UNESCO was established as an autonomous permanent intergovernmental organization with the basic purpose of contributing to peace and security "by promoting collaboration among the nations through education, science, and culture in order to further universal respect for justice, for the rule of law, and for the human rights and fundamental freedoms which are affirmed for the peoples of the world, without distinction of race, sex, language, or religion, by the Charter of the United Nations."

To realize this goal, UNESCO is mandated to:

(a) collaborate in the work of advancing the mutual knowledge and understanding or peoples, through all means of mass communication and to that end recommend such international agreements as may be necessary to promote the free flow of ideas by word and image;

(b) give fresh impulse to popular education and to the spread of culture:

by collaborating with Members, at their request, in the development of educational activities;

by instituting collaboration among the nations to advance the ideal of equality of educational opportunity without regard to race, sex or any distinctions, economic or social;

by suggesting educational methods best suited to prepare the children of the world for the responsibilities of freedom;

(c) maintain, increase and diffuse knowledge:

by assuring the conservation and protection of the world's inheritance of books, works of art and monuments of history and science, and recommending to the nations concerned the necessary international conventions;

by encouraging co-operation among the nations in all branches of intellectual activity, including the international exchange of persons active in the fields of education, science and culture and the exchange of publications, objects of artistic and scientific interest and other materials of information;

by initiating methods of international co-operation calculated to give the people of all countries access to the printed and published materials produced by any of them. . . .

Under the terms of the agreement between the United Nations and UNESCO, which entered into force on 14 December 1946, UNESCO transmits to the UN regular reports on its activities and complies to the fullest extent practicable with any request which the UN may make for the furnishing of special reports, studies, or information.

A total of 161 States are members of UNESCO; they include all UN member States with the exception of Djibouti, Solomon Islands, South Africa, the United States of America (which withdrew from membership on 31 December 1984), and Vanuatu; and seven non-member States of the UN—the Democratic People's Republic of Korea, the Republic of Korea, Monaco, Namibia (represented by the UN Council for Namibia), San Marino, Switzerland, and Tonga.

All States members of UNESCO are represented in the UNESCO GENERAL CONFERENCE, which determines policies and establishes programs of work for the organization. The UNESCO EXECUTIVE BOARD, which is responsible for the execution of the programs, consists of 51 members elected by the conference from among the delegates appointed by the member States, together with the president of the conference who sits *ex officio* in an advisory capacity. The UNESCO SECRETARIAT is headed by the Director-General, who in his capacity as chief executive officer of the organization appoints and directs its staff.

The ultimate aim in all sectors of UNESCO's activities—education, science, culture, and communication—is to safeguard human rights and peace. Even those activities which are not explicitly designed to develop respect for human rights in general, or to secure the implementation of specific rights or freedoms, serve, nevertheless, to create the material, intellectual, moral, and cultural conditions necessary if human rights are to become a living reality—rather than a aspiration—for everyone.

UNITED NATIONS EDUCATIONAL, SCIENTIFIC AND CULTURAL ORGANIZATION: CONSTITUTION (1945).

UNITED NATIONS EDUCATIONAL, SCIENTIFIC AND CULTURAL ORGANIZATION: CONSTITUTION (1945). The constitution of UNESCO was adopted on 16 November 1945 by the Conference for the Establishment of an Educational, Scientific and Cultural Organization of the United Nations, convened in London by the governments of France and Great Britain, and entered into force on 4 November 1946.

The purpose of UNESCO, a specialized agency of the United Nations, as stated in the constitution (article 1), is "to contribute to peace and security by promoting collaboration among the nations through education, science and culture in order to further universal respect for justice, for the rule of law and for human rights and fundamental freedoms which are affirmed for the peoples of the world, without distinction of race, sex, language or religion, by the Charter of the United Nations."

UNESCO's functions include collaboration in the work of advancing the mutual knowledge and understanding of peoples through all means of mass communication; giving fresh impulse to popular education and to the spread of culture; and maintaining, increasing, and diffusing knowledge through international cooperation.

The text of the constitution (United Nations, *Treaty Series,* vol. 4, p. 275), as amended by the UNESCO GENERAL CONFERENCE at its second, third, fourth, fifth, sixth, seventh, eighth, ninth, tenth, twelfth, fifteenth, seventeenth, nineteenth, twentieth, and twenty-first sessions, is as follows:

The Governments of the States Parties to this Constitution on behalf of their peoples declare:

That since wars begin in the minds of men, it is in the minds of men that the defences of peace must be constructed;

That ignorance of each other's ways and lives has been a common cause, throughout the history of mankind, of that suspicion and mistrust between the peoples of the world through which their differences have all too often broken into war;

That the great and terrible war which has now ended was a war made possible by the denial of the democratic principles of the dignity, equality and mutual respect of men, and by the propagation, in their place, through ignorance and prejudice, of the doctrine of the inequality of men and races;

That the wide diffusion of culture, and the education of humanity for justice and liberty and peace are indispensable to the dignity of man and constitute a sacred duty which all the nations must fulfill in a spirit of mutual assistance and concern;

That a peace based exclusively upon the political and economic arrangements of governments would not be a peace which could secure the unanimous, lasting and sincere support of the peoples of the world, and that the peace must therefore be founded, if it is not to fail, upon the intellectual and moral solidarity of mankind.

For these reasons, the States Parties to this Constitution, believing in full and equal opportunities for education for all, in the unrestricted pursuit of objective truth, and in the free exchange of ideas and knowledge, are agreed and determined to develop and to increase the means of communication between their peoples and to employ these means for the purposes of mutual understanding and a truer and more perfect knowledge of each other's lives;

In consequence whereof they do hereby create the United Nations Educational, Scientific and Cultural Organization for the purpose of advancing, through the educational and scientific and cultural relations of the peoples of the world, the objectives of international peace and of the common welfare of mankind for which the United Nations Organization was established and which its Charter proclaims.

Article 1. Purposes and functions. 1. The purpose of the Organization is to contribute to peace and security by promoting collaboration among the nations through education, science and culture in order to further universal respect for justice, for the rule of law and for the human rights and fundamental freedoms which are affirmed for the peoples of the world, without distinction of race, sex, language or religion, by the Charter of the United Nations.

2. To realize this purpose the Organization will:

(a) Collaborate in the work of advancing the mutual knowledge and understanding of peoples, through all means of mass communication and to that end recommend such international agreements as may be necessary to promote the free flow of ideas by word and image;

(b) Give fresh impulse to popular education and to the spread of culture by collaborating with Members, at their request in the development of educational activities; by instituting collaboration among the nations to advance the ideal of equality of educational opportunity without regard to race, sex or any distinctions, economic or social; [and] by suggesting educational methods best suited to prepare the children of the world for the responsibilities of freedom;

(c) Maintain, increase and diffuse knowledge by assuring the conservation and protection of the world's inheritance of books, works of art and monuments of history and science, and recommending to the nations concerned the necessary international conventions; by encouraging co-operation among the nations in all branches of intellectual activity, including the international exchange of persons active in the fields of education, science and culture and the exchange of publications, objects of artistic and scientific interest and other materials of information; [and] by initiating methods of international co-operation calculated to give the people of all countries access to the printed and published materials produced by any of them.

3. With a view to preserving the independence, integrity and fruitful diversity of the cultures and educational systems of the States Members of the Organization, the Organization is prohibited from intervening in matters which are essentially within their domestic jurisdiction.

Article 2. Membership. 1. Membership of the United Nations Organization shall carry with it the right to membership of the United Nations Educational, Scientific and Cultural Organization.

2. Subject to the conditions of the Agreement between this Organization and the United Nations Organization, approved pursuant to Article 10 of this Constitution, States not Members of the United Nations Organization may be admitted to membership of the Organization, upon recommendation of the Executive Board, by a two-thirds majority vote of the General Conference.

3. Territories or groups of territories which are not responsible for the conduct of their international relations may be admitted as Associate Members by the General Conference by a two-thirds majority of Members present and voting, upon application made on behalf of such territory or group of territories by the Member or other authority having responsibility for their international relations. The nature and extent of the rights and obligations of Associate Members shall be determined by the General Conference.

4. Members of the Organization which are suspended from the exercise of the rights and privileges of membership of the United Nations Organization shall, upon the request of the latter, be suspended from the rights and privileges of this Organization.

5. Members of the Organization which are expelled from the United Nations Organization shall automatically cease to be Members of this Organization.

6. Any Member State or Associate Member of the Organization may withdraw from the Organization by notice addressed to the Director-General. Such notice shall take effect on 31 December of the year following that during which the notice was given. No such withdrawal shall affect the financial obligations owed to the Organization on the date the withdrawal takes effect. Notice of withdrawal by an Associate Member shall be given on its behalf by the Member State or other authority having responsibility for its international relations.

Article 3. Organs. The Organization shall include a General Conference, an Executive Board and a Secretariat.

Article 4. The General Conference.

A. Composition

1. The General Conference shall consist of the representatives of the States Members of the Organization. The Government of each Member State shall appoint not more than five delegates, who shall be selected after consultation with the National Commission, if established, or with educational, scientific and cultural bodies.

B. Functions

2. The General Conference shall determine the policies and the main lines of work of the Organization. It shall take decisions on programmes submitted to it by the Executive Board.

3. The General Conference shall, when it deems desirable and in accordance with the regulations to be made by it, summon international conferences of States on education, the sciences and humanities or the dissemination of knowledge; non-governmental conferences on the same subjects may be summoned by the General Conference or by the Executive Board in accordance with such regulations.

4. The General Conference shall, in adopting proposals for submission to the Member States, distinguish between recommendations and international conventions submitted for their approval. In the former case a majority vote shall suffice; in the latter case a two-thirds majority shall be required. Each of the Member States shall submit recommendations or conventions to its competent authorities within a period of one year from the close of the session of the General Conference at which they were adopted.

5. Subject to the provisions of Article 5, paragraph 5 (c), the General Conference shall advise the United Nations Organization on the educational, scientific and cultural aspects of matters of concern to the latter; in accordance with terms and procedure agreed upon between the appropriate authorities of the two Organizations.

6. The General Conference shall receive and consider the reports sent to the Organization by Member States on the action taken upon the recommendations and conventions referred to in paragraph 4 above or, if it so decides, analytical summaries of these reports.

7. The General Conference shall elect the members of the Executive Board and, on the recommendation of the Board, shall appoint the Director-General.

C. Voting

8. (a) Each Member State shall have one vote in the General Conference. Decisions shall be made by a simple majority except in cases in which a two-thirds majority is required by the provisions of this Constitution, or the Rules of Procedure of the General Conference. A majority shall be a majority of the Members present and voting.

(b) A Member State shall have no vote in the General Conference if the total amount of contributions due from it exceeds the total amount of contributions payable by it for the current year and the immediately preceding calendar year.

(c) The General Conference may nevertheless permit such a Member State to vote, if it is satisfied that failure to pay is due to conditions beyond the control of the Member Nation.

D. Procedure

9. (a) The General Conference shall meet in ordinary session every two years. It may meet in extraordinary session if it decides to do so itself or if summoned by the Executive Board, or on the demand of at least one-third of the Member States.

(b) At each session the location of its next ordinary session shall be designated by the General Conference. The location of an extraordinary session shall be decided by the General Conference if the session is summoned by it, or otherwise by the Executive Board.

10. The General Conference shall adopt its own rules of procedure. It shall at each session elect a President and other officers.

11. The General Conference shall set up special and technical committees and such other subordinate bodies as may be necessary for its purposes.

12. The General Conference shall cause arrangements to

be made for public access to meetings, subject to such regulations as it shall prescribe.

E. Observers

13. The General Conference, on the recommendation of the Executive Board and by a two-thirds majority may, subject to its rules of procedure, invite as observers at specified sessions of the Conference or of its Commissions representatives of international organizations, such as those referred to in Article 11, paragraph 4.

14. When consultative arrangements have been approved by the Executive Board for such international nongovernmental or semi-governmental organizations in the manner provided in Article 11, paragraph 4, those organizations shall be invited to send observers to sessions of the General Conference and its Commissions.

F. Transitional Provision

15. Notwithstanding the provisions of paragraph 9 (a) of this Article, the General Conference shall hold its twenty-second session in the third year following its twenty-first session.

Article 5. Executive Board.

A. Composition

1. The Executive Board shall be elected by the General Conference from among the delegates appointed by the Member States and shall consist of fifty-one members each of whom shall represent the Government of the State of which he is a national. The President of the General Conference shall sit *ex officio* in an advisory capacity on the Executive Board.

2. In electing the members of the Executive Board the General Conference shall endeavour to include persons competent in the arts, the humanities, the sciences, education and the diffusion of ideas, and qualified by their experience and capacity to fulfil the administrative and executive duties of the Board. It shall also have regard to the diversity of cultures and a balanced geographical distribution. Not more than one national of any Member State shall serve on the Board at any one time, the President of the Conference excepted.

3. Members of the Board shall serve from the close of the session of the General Conference which elected them until the close of the second ordinary session of the General Conference following that election. They shall not be immediately eligible for a second term. The General Conference shall, at each of its ordinary sessions, elect the number of members required to fill vacancies occurring at the end of the session.

4. (a) In the event of the death or resignation of a member of the Executive Board, his replacement for the remainder of his term shall be appointed by the Executive Board on the nomination of the Government of the State the former member represented.

(b) The Government making the nomination and the Executive Board shall have regard to the factors set forth in paragraph 2 of this Article.

(c) When exceptional circumstances arise, which, in the considered opinion of the represented State, make it indispensable for its representative to be replaced, even if he does not tender his resignation, measures shall be taken in accordance with the provisions of sub-paragraph (a) above.

B. Functions

5. (a) The Executive Board shall prepare the agenda for the General Conference. It shall examine the programme of work for the Organization and corresponding budget estimates submitted to it by the Director-General in accordance with paragraph 3 of Article 6 and shall submit them with such recommendations as it considers desirable to the General Conference.

(b) The Executive Board, acting under the authority of the General Conference, shall be responsible for the execution of the programme adopted by the Conference. In accordance with the decisions of the General Conference and having regard to circumstances arising between two ordinary sessions, the Executive Board shall take all necessary measures to ensure the effective and rational execution of the programme by the Director-General.

(c) Between ordinary sessions of the General Conference, the Board may discharge the functions of adviser to the United Nations, set forth in Article 4, paragraph 5, whenever the problem upon which advice is sought has already been dealt with in principle by the Conference, or when the solution is implicit in decisions of the Conference.

6. The Executive Board shall recommend to the General Conference the admission of new Members to the Organization.

7. Subject to decisions of the General Conference, the Executive Board shall adopt its own rules of procedure. It shall elect its officers from among its members.

8. The Executive Board shall meet in regular session at least twice a year and may meet in special session if convoked by the Chairman on his own initiative or upon the request of six members of the Board.

9. The Chairman of the Executive Board shall present, on behalf of the Board, to each ordinary session of the General Conference, with or without comments, the reports on the activities of the Organization which the Director-General is required to prepare in accordance with the provisions of Article 6.3(b).

10. The Executive Board shall make all necessary arrangements to consult the representatives of international organizations or qualified persons concerned with questions within its competence.

11. Between sessions of the General Conference, the Executive Board may request advisory opinions from the International Court of Justice on legal questions arising within the field of the Organization's activities.

12. Although the members of the Executive Board are representative of their respective Governments they shall exercise the powers delegated to them by the General Conference on behalf of the Conference as a whole.

C. Transitional Provisions

13. Notwithstanding the provisions of paragraph 3 of this Article,

(a) Members of the Executive Board elected prior to the seventeenth session of the General Conference shall serve until the end of the term for which they were elected.

(b) Members of the Executive Board appointed, prior to the seventeenth session of the General Conference, by the Board in accordance with the provisions of paragraph 4 of this Article to replace members with a four-year term shall be eligible for a second term of four years.

Article 6. Secretariat.

1. The Secretariat shall consist of a Director-General and such staff as may be required.

2. The Director-General shall be nominated by the Executive Board and appointed by the General Conference for a period of six years, under such conditions as the Conference may approve, and shall be eligible for reappointment. He shall be the chief administrative officer of the Organization.

3. (a) The Director-General, or a deputy designated by

him, shall participate, without the right to vote, in all meetings of the General Conference, of the Executive Board, and of the Committees of the Organization. He shall formulate proposals for appropriate action by the Conference and the Board, and shall prepare for submission to the Board a draft programme of work for the Organization with corresponding budget estimates.

(b) The Director-General shall prepare and communicate to Member States and to the Executive Board periodical reports on the activities of the Organization. The General Conference shall determine the periods to be covered by these reports.

4. The Director-General shall appoint the staff of the Secretariat in accordance with staff regulations to be approved by the General Conference. Subject to the paramount consideration of securing the highest standards of integrity, efficiency and technical competence, appointment to the staff shall be on as wide a geographical basis as possible.

5. The responsibilities of the Director-General and of the staff shall be exclusively international in character. In the discharge of their duties they shall not seek or receive instructions from any Government or from any authority external to the Organization. They shall refrain from any action which might prejudice their positions as international officials. Each State Member of the Organization undertakes to respect the international character of the responsibilities of the Director-General and the staff, and not to seek to influence them in the discharge of their duties.

6. Nothing in this Article shall preclude the Organization from entering into special arrangements within the United Nations Organization for common services and staff and for the interchange of personnel.

Transitional Provision

7. Notwithstanding the provisions of paragraph 2 of this Article, the Director-General nominated by the Executive Board and appointed by the General Conference in 1980 shall serve for a term of seven years.

Article 7. National Co-operating Bodies. 1. Each Member State shall make such arrangements as suit its particular conditions for the purpose of associating its principal bodies interested in educational, scientific and cultural matters with the work of the Organization, preferably by the formation of a National Commission broadly representative of the Government and such bodies.

2. National Commission or National Co-operating Bodies, where they exist, shall act in an advisory capacity to their respective delegations to the General Conference and to their Governments in matters relating to the Organization and shall function as agencies of liaison in all matters of interest to it.

3. The Organization may, on the request of a Member State, delegate, either temporarily or permanently, a member of its Secretariat to serve on the National Commission of that State, in order to assist in the development of its work.

Article 8. Reports by Member States. Each Member State shall submit to the Organization, at such times and in such manner as shall be determined by the General Conference, reports on the laws, regulations and statistics relating to its educational, scientific and cultural institutions and activities, and on the action taken upon the recommendations and conventions referred to in Article 4, paragraph 4.

Article 9. Budget. 1. The Budget shall be administered by the Organization.

2. The General Conference shall approve and give final effect to the budget and to the appointment of financial responsibility among the States Members of the Organization subject to such arrangement with the United Nations as may be provided in the agreement to be entered into pursuant to Article 10.

3. The Director-General, with the approval of the Executive Board, may receive gifts, bequests, and subventions directly from Governments, public and private institutions, associations and private persons.

Article 10. Relations with the United Nations Organization. This Organization shall be brought into relation with the United Nations Organization, as soon as practicable, as one of the Specialized Agencies referred to in Article 57 of the Charter of the United Nations. This relationship shall be effected through an agreement with the United Nations Organization under Article 63 of the Charter, which agreement shall be subject to the approval of the General Conference of this Organization. The agreement shall provide for effective co-operation between the two Organizations in the pursuit of their common purposes, and at the same time shall recognize the autonomy of this Organization, within the fields of its competence as defined in this Constitution. Such agreement may, among other matters, provide for the approval and financing of the budget of the Organization by the General Assembly of the United Nations.

Article 11. Relations with Other Specialized International Organizations and Agencies. 1. This Organization may co-operate with other specialized intergovernmental organizations and agencies whose interests and activities are related to its purposes. To this end the Director-General, acting under the general authority of the Executive Board, may establish effective working relationships with such organizations and agencies and establish such joint committees as may be necessary to assure effective co-operation. Any formal arrangements entered into with such organizations or agencies shall be subject to the approval of the Executive Board.

2. Whenever the General Conference of this Organization and the competent authorities of any other specialized intergovernmental organizations or agencies whose purpose and functions lie within the competence of this Organization deem it desirable to effect a transfer of their resources and activities to this Organization, the Director-General, subject to the approval of the Conference, may enter into mutually acceptable arrangements for this purpose.

3. This Organization may make appropriate arrangements with other intergovernmental organizations for reciprocal representation at meetings.

4. The United National Educational, Scientific and Cultural Organization may make suitable arrangements for consultation and co-operation with non-governmental international organizations concerned with matters within its competence, and may invite them to undertake specific tasks. Such co-operation may also include appropriate participation by representatives of such organizations on advisory committees set up by the General Conference.

Article 12. Legal Status of the Organization. The provisions of Articles 104 and 105 of the Charter of the United Nations Organization concerning the legal status of that Organization, its privileges and immunities, shall apply in the same way to this Organization.

Article 13. Amendments. 1. Proposals for amendments to this Constitution shall become effective upon receiving the approval of the General Conference by a two-thirds majority; provided, however, that those amendments which involve fundamental alterations in the aims of the Organization or new obligations for the Member States shall require subsequent acceptance on the part of two-thirds of the Member States before they come into force. The draft texts of proposed amendments shall be communicated by the Director-General to the Member States at least six months in advance of their consideration by the General Conference.

2. The General Conference shall have power to adopt by a two-thirds majority rules of procedure for carrying out the provisions of this Article.

Article 14. Interpretation. 1. The English and French texts of this Constitution shall be regarded as equally authoritative.

2. Any question or dispute concerning the interpretation of this Constitution shall be referred for determination to the International Court of Justice or to an arbitral tribunal, as the General Conference may determine under its rules of procedure.

Article 15. Entry into Force. 1. This constitution shall be subject to acceptance. The instrument of acceptance shall be deposited with the Government of the United Kingdom.

2. This Constitution shall remain open for signature in the archives of the Government of the United Kingdom. Signature may take place either before or after the deposit of the instrument of acceptance. No acceptance shall be valid unless preceded or followed by signature.

3. This Constitution shall come into force when it has been accepted by twenty of its signatories. Subsequent acceptances shall take effect immediately.

4. The Government of the United Kingdom will inform all Members of the United Nations of the receipt of all instruments of acceptance and of the date on which the Constitution comes into force in accordance with the preceding paragraph.

In faith whereof, the undersigned, duly authorized to that effect, have signed this Constitution in the English and French languages, both texts being equally authentic.

Done in London the sixteenth day of November, one thousand nine hundred and forty-five, in a single copy, in the English and French languages, of which certified copies will be communicated by the Government of the United Kingdom to the Governments of all the Members of the United Nations.

UNITED NATIONS ENVIRONMENT PROGRAM (UNEP).

An intergovernmental organization established in 1972 by the UN General Assembly (resolution 2997 [XXVII]) as an outgrowth of the United Nations Conference on the Human Environment, held in Stockholm earlier that year.

UNEP is directed by a Governing Body composed of 58 UN member States, elected by the General Assembly for a three-year term of office. With the assistance of a network of more than 100 stations for monitoring pollution of the atmosphere and at least 10 for recording daily changes in the environment, the program identifies, assesses, and monitors major environmental problems and provides warnings of significant environmental problems, risks, and opportunities to all concerned. Its particular concern is the impact of national and international environmental policies and measures on the developing countries. Among its main areas of activity are desertification, the disposal of potentially toxic wastes, protection of the right of every human being to a clean environment, and the conservation of nature and wildlife in all parts of the world. Among UNEP's priorities is "Earthwatch," a program to identify relevant environmental issues and provide data as a basis for effective environmental management. The three main components of Earthwatch are the Global Environmental Monitoring System (which monitors, measures, and interprets selected environmental variables, such as climate and health), the International Referral System (a worldwide register of sources of environment information), and the International Register of Potentially Toxic Chemicals (which supplies background information on the scientific, socioeconomic, and regulatory aspects of such chemicals).

The program is financed entirely by the voluntary contributions of UN member States. The governing body, which administers the UNEP fund, allocates the available funds on a regional basis. That body also administers smaller trust funds established to protect the environment of particular areas, such as the Regional Trust Fund for the Protection of the Mediterranean Sea and the Regional Trust Fund for the Protection of West and Central Africa.

United Nations Environment Program. Address: P.O. Box 30552, Gigiri, Nairobi, Kenya. Telephone: (254 2) 333930. Cable: UNITERRA NAIROBI. Telex: 22068–22173. Executive Director: Dr. Mostafa K. Tolba.

UNITED NATIONS HIGH COMMISSIONER FOR REFUGEES (UNHCR).

On 14 December 1950, the Un General Assembly adopted the Statute of the Office of the United Nations High Commissioner for Refugees. The office came into existence, as authorized by the statute, on 1 January 1951, originally for a period of three years. The mandate of the office has since been renewed many times, most recently for a period of five years beginning 1 January 1989 (General Assembly resolution 42/108).

Assistance to refugees was first organized under international auspices in 1921 with the appointment of Dr. Fridtjof Nansen, of Norway, as League of Nations High Commissioner for Refugees. During World War II, the United Nations Relief and Rehabilitation Administration (UNRRA) was established in 1943 to assist persons displaced because of the hostilities, many of whom were reluctant or unwilling to be repatriated to their countries of origin. UNRRA was succeeded by the International Refugees Organization (IRO) in

1946; by the time IRO ceased operations in 1952, it has resettled more than a million displaced persons and refugees and had repatriated about 73,000 to their former homelands. On 3 December 1949, the UN General Assembly recognized the continuing responsibility of the United Nations for the international protection of refugees after the termination of IRO and decided to appoint a United Nations High Commissioner for Refugees.

The Statute of the Office of the High Commissioner, adopted by the General Assembly on 14 December 1950 (resolution 428 [V], specifies that the high commissioner's work shall be of an entirely nonpolitical character; that it shall be humanitarian and social; and that it shall relate, as a rule, to groups and categories of refugees. The high commissioner's policy directives are given by the General Assembly or the Economic and Social Council. The high commissioner is mandated to provide for the protection of refugees within the competence of his office by (1) promoting the conclusion and ratification of international conventions for the protection of refugees, supervising their application, and proposing amendments thereto; (2) promoting through special agreements with governments the execution of any measures calculated to improve the situation of refugees and to reduce the number requiring protection; (3) assisting governmental and private efforts to promote voluntary repatriation or assimilation with new national communities; (4) promoting the admission of refugees, not excluding those in the most destitute categories, to the territories of States; (5) endeavoring to obtain permission for refugees to transfer their assets, and especially those necessary for their resettlement; (6) obtaining from governments information concerning the number and conditions of refugees in their territories and the laws and regulations concerning them; (7) keeping in close touch with the governments and intergovernmental organizations concerned; (8) establishing contact in such manner as he may think best with private organizations dealing with refugee questions; and (9) facilitating the coordination of efforts of private organizations concerned with the welfare of refugees.

Refugees in "divided countries" are not a responsibility of the high commissioner, nor is he concerned with refugees for which another UN body has assumed full responsibility, such as the Arab refugees from Palestine, which fall within the mandate of UNRWA. The high commissioner's primary concerns are those persons who, owing to well-founded fear of persecution for reasons of race, religion, nationality, or political opinion, are outside their country of origin and cannot, or do not, owing to such fear, avail themselves of the protection of that country.

In addition to providing international protection to refugees within its mandate, the Office of the UN High Commissioner for Refugees provides them with various forms of assistance until they are settled. On 2 February 1952, the General Assembly authorized the high commissioner to appeal for funds to enable emergency aid to be given to the most needy groups of refugees within his mandate (resolution 538 [VI]); in 1954, this emergency fund was incorporated into a new voluntary UN Refugee Fund.

The high commissioner is elected by the General Assembly on recommendation of the Secretary-General. At its 1989 session, the assembly, on proposal of the Secretary-General, elected Mr. Thorvald Stoltenberg as United Nations High Commissioner for Refugees for a period of four years beginning on 1 January 1990.

The program of the high commissioner is administered by an executive committee composed of representatives of 43 states which are UN members or members of a specialized agency, elected by the Economic and Social Council on the widest geographical basis from those states with a demonstrated interest in, and devotion to, the solution of the refugee problem. Members of the executive committee serve for the duration of the high commissioner's mandate. As at 1 January 1989, they are: Algeria, Argentina, Australia, Austria, Belgium, Brazil, Canada, China, Colombia, Denmark, Finland, France, Federal Republic of Germany, Greece, Holy See, Islamic Republic of Iran, Israel, Italy, Japan, Lebanon, Lesotho, Madagascar, Morocco, Netherlands, Nicaragua, Nigeria, Norway, Pakistan, Somalia, Sudan, Sweden, Switzerland, Thailand, Tunisia, Turkey, Uganda, United Kingdom of Great Britain and Northern Ireland, United Republic of Tanzania, United States of America, Venezuela, Yugoslavia, Zaire, and the United Nations Council for Namibia.

The executive committee holds one session per year, of about ten days' duration, at the United Nations office in Geneva. It has two subsidiary bodies: the Sub-Committee of the Whole on International Protection and the Sub-Committee on Administrative and Financial Matters; these usually meet in Geneva a few days prior to the opening of the session of the executive committee.

The Office of the League of Nations High Commissioner for Refugees was awarded the Nobel Peace Prize in 1938. The Office of the UN High Commissioner for Refugees was awarded that prize in 1954 and again in 1981.

SEE ALSO Refugee entries.

UNITED NATIONS HIGH COMMISSIONER FOR REFUGEES: STATUTE (1950). The statute, adopted by the UN General Assembly on 14 December 1950 (resolution 428 [V]), authorizes the establishment of the Office of the United Nations High Commissioner for Refugees. The text of the statute, annexed to the resolution, is as follows:

Chapter I—General Provisions

1. The United Nations High Commissioner for Refugees, acting under the authority of the General Assembly, shall assume the function of providing international protection, under the auspices of the United Nations, to refugees who fall within the scope of the present Statute and of seeking permanent solutions for the problem of refugees by assisting governments and, subject to the approval of the governments concerned, private organizations to facilitate the voluntary repatriation of such refugees, or their assimilation within new national communities.

In the exercise of his functions, more particularly when difficulties arise, and for instance with regard to any controversy concerning the international status of these persons, the High Commissioner shall request the opinion of an advisory committee on refugees if it is created.

2. The work of the High Commissioner shall be of an entirely non-political character; it shall be humanitarian and social and shall relate, as a rule, to groups and categories of refugees.

3. The High Commissioner shall follow policy directives given him by the General Assembly or the Economic and Social Council.

4. The Economic and Social Council may decide, after hearing the views of the High Commissioner on the subject, to establish an advisory committee on refugees, which shall consist of representatives of States Members and States non-members of the United Nations, to be selected by the Council on the basis of their demonstrated interest in and devotion to the solution of the refugee problem.

5. The General Assembly shall review, not later than at its eighth regular session, the arrangements for the Office of the High Commissioner with a view to determining whether the Office should be continued beyond 31 December 1963.

Chapter II—Functions of the High Commissioner

6. The competence of the High Commissioner shall extend to:

A. (i) Any person who has been considered a refugee under the Arrangements of 12 May 1926 and 30 June 1928 or under the Conventions of 28 October 1933 and 10 February 1938, the Protocol of 14 September 1939 or the Constitution of the International Refugee Organization;

(ii) Any person who, as a result of events occurring before 1 January 1951 and owing to well-founded fear of being persecuted for reasons of race, religion, nationality or political opinion, is outside the country of his nationality and is unable or, owing to such fear or for reasons other than personal convenience, is unwilling to avail himself of the protection of that country; or who, not having a nationality and being outside the country of his former habitual residence, is unable or, owing to such fear or for reasons other than personal convenience, is unwilling to return to it.

Decisions as to eligibility taken by the International Refugee Organization during the period of its activities shall not prevent the status of refugee being accorded to persons who fulfil the conditions of the present paragraph;

The competence of the High Commissioner shall cease to apply to any person defined in section A above if:

(a) He has voluntarily re-availed himself of the protection of the country of his nationality; or

(b) Having lost his nationality, he has voluntarily re-acquired it; or

(c) He has acquired a new nationality, and enjoys the protection of the country of his new nationality; or

(d) He has voluntarily re-established himself in the country which he left or outside which he remained owing to fear of persecution; or

(e) He can no longer, because the circumstances in connexion with which he has been recognized as a refugee have ceased to exist, claim grounds other than those of personal convenience, for continuing to refuse to avail himself of the protection of the country of his nationality. Reasons of a purely economic character may not be invoked; or

(f) Being a person who has no nationality, he can no longer, because the circumstances in connexion with which he has been recognized as a refugee have ceased to exist and he is able to return to the country of his former habitual residence, claim grounds other than those of personal convenience for continuing to refuse to return to that country;

B. Any other person who is outside the country of his nationality or, if he has no nationality, the country of his former habitual residence, because he has or had well-founded fear of persecution by reason of his race, religion, nationality or political opinion and is unable or, because of such fear, is unwilling to avail himself of the protection of the government of the country of his nationality, or, if he has no nationality, to return to the country of his former habitual residence.

7. Provided that the competence of the High Commissioner as defined in paragraph 6 above shall not extend to a person:

(a) Who is a national of more than one country unless he satisfies the provisions of the preceding paragraph in relation to each of the countries of which he is a national; or

(b) Who is recognized by the competent authorities of the country in which he has taken residence as having the rights and obligations which are attached to the possession of the nationality of that country; or

(c) Who continues to receive from other organs or agencies of the United Nations protection or assistance; or

(d) In respect of whom there are serious reasons for considering that he has committed a crime covered by the provisions of treaties of extradition or a crime mentioned in article VI of the London Charter of the International Military Tribunal or by the provisions of article 14, paragraph 2, of the Universal Declaration of Human Rights.

8. The High Commissioner shall provide for the protection of refugees falling under the competence of his Office by:

(a) Promoting the conclusion and ratification of international conventions for the protection of refugees, supervising their application and proposing amendments thereto;

(b) Promoting through special agreements with governments the execution of any measures calculated to improve the situation of refugees and to reduce the number requiring protection;

(c) Assisting governmental and private efforts to promote voluntary repatriation or assimilation within new national communities;

(d) Promoting the admission of refugees, not excluding those in the most destitute categories, to the territories of States;

(e) Endeavouring to obtain permission for refugees to transfer their assets and especially those necessary for their resettlement;

(f) Obtaining from governments information concerning the number and conditions of refugees in their territories and the laws and regulations concerning them;

(g) Keeping in close touch with the governments and inter-governmental organizations concerned;

(h) Establishing contact in such manner as he may think best with private organizations dealing with refugee questions;

(i) Facilitating the co-ordination of the efforts of private organizations concerned with the welfare of refugees.

9. The High Commissioner shall engage in such additional activities, including repatriation and resettlement, as the General Assembly may determine, within the limits of the resources placed at his disposal.

10. The High Commissioner shall administer any funds, public or private, which he receives for assistance to refugees, and shall distribute them among the private and, as appropriate, public agencies which he deems best qualified to administer such assistance.

The High Commissioner may reject any offers which he does not consider appropriate or which cannot be utilized.

The High Commissioner shall not appeal to governments for funds or make a general appeal, without the prior approval of the General Assembly.

The High Commissioner shall include in his annual report a statement of his activities in this field.

11. The High Commissioner shall be entitled to present his views before the General Assembly, the Economic and Social Council and their subsidiary bodies.

The High Commissioner shall report annually to the General Assembly through the Economic and Social Council; his report shall be considered as a separate item on the agenda of the General Assembly.

12. The High Commissioner may invite the co-operation of the various specialized agencies.

Chapter III—Organization and Finances

13. The High Commissioner shall be elected by the General Assembly on the nomination of the Secretary-General. The terms of appointment of the High Commissioner shall be proposed by the Secretary-General and approved by the General Assembly. The High Commissioner shall be elected for a term of three years, from 1 January 1951.

14. The High Commissioner shall appoint, for the same term, a Deputy High Commissioner of a nationality other than his own.

15. (a) Within the limits of the budgetary appropriations provided, the staff of the Office of the High Commissioner shall be appointed by the High Commissioner and shall be responsible to him in the exercise of their functions.

(b) Such staff shall be chosen from persons devoted to the purposes of the Office of the High Commissioner.

(c) Their conditions of employment shall be those provided under the staff regulations adopted by the General Assembly and the rules promulgated thereunder by the Secretary-General.

(d) Provision may also be made to permit the employment of personnel without compensation.

16. The High Commissioner shall consult the governments of the countries of residence of refugees as to the need for appointing representatives therein. In any country recognizing such need, there may be appointed a representative approved by the government of that country. Subject to the foregoing, the same representative may serve in more than one country.

17. The High Commissioner and the Secretary-General shall make appropriate arrangements for liaison and consultation on matters of mutual interest.

18. The Secretary-General shall provide the High Commissioner with all necessary facilities within budgetary limitations.

19. The Office of the High Commissioner shall be located in Geneva, Switzerland.

20. The Office of the High Commissioner shall be financed under the budget of the United Nations. Unless the General Assembly subsequently decides otherwise, no expenditure, other than administrative expenditures relating to the functioning of the Office of the High Commissioner, shall be borne on the budget of the United Nations, and all other expenditures relating to the activities of the High Commissioner shall be financed by voluntary contributions.

21. The administration of the Office of the High Commissioner shall be subject to the Financial Regulations of the United Nations and to the financial rules promulgated thereunder by the Secretary-General.

22. Transactions relating to the High Commissioner's funds shall be subject to audit by the United Nations Board of Auditors, provided that the Board may accept audited accounts from the agencies to which funds have been allocated. Administrative arrangements for the custody of such funds and their allocation shall be agreed between the High Commissioner and the Secretary-General in accordance with the Financial Regulations of the United Nations and rules promulgated thereunder by the Secretary-General.

UNITED NATIONS INSTITUTE FOR TRAINING AND RESEARCH. UNITAR was established in 1965 pursuant to a decision taken by the UN General Assembly at its 1963 session (resolution 1934 [XVIII]) as an autonomous institution within the framework of the United Nations system. Its basic purpose is to enhance the effectiveness of the United Nations in achieving its major objectives—in particular, the maintenance of peace and security and the promotion of economic and social development—through appropriate training and research programs. Its activities include the preparation of studies of UN problems, function, and structures and the organization of training courses for senior officials of the United Nations system and of governments. Although the institute has dealt with human rights problems only occasionally, it participated actively in the observance of the Decade for Action to Combat Racism and Racial Discrimination and published a comprehensive study entitled *Racism and its Elimination,* prepared by one of its special fellows, Sir Rupert John (St. Vincent and the Grenadines) (United Nations publication, Sales No. E.81.15.ST/18).

An international board of trustees, appointed by the UN secretary-general in consultation with the president of the General Assembly and the president of the Economic and Social Council, is the policymaking organ for the institute. The executive director is appointed by the secretary-general after consultation with the board of trustees. Mr. Michel Doo Kingue has served as UNITAR's executive director since 1 January 1983.

In recent years, the institute has experienced difficulty in determining its future role and in establishing long-term financing arrangements. In December 1988, the General Assembly noted with concern (resolution 43/201) that the 1988 UN Pledging Conference for Development Activities had not provided the institute with the level of resources required to maintain a minimum training program and institutional structure. In the resolution, the assembly reaffirmed the continuing validity of the institute's mandate and requested the secretary-general to present to it, in 1990, his recommendations on the future of the institute, together with detailed financial information.

UNITED NATIONS SECRETARIAT. Established in accordance with the UNITED NATIONS CHARTER (article 7) as a principal organ of the United Nations, the UN Secretariat consists of the secretary-general and his staff. As chief administrative officer, the secretary-general performs the functions entrusted to him by the charter and by UN organs and reports annually to the General Assembly on the work of the organization as a whole. In addition, he may, on his own initiative, bring to the attention of the Security Council any matter which, in his opinion, threatens the maintenance of international peace and security.

The secretary-general appoints all other members of the UN Secretariat under regulations established by the General Assembly. The charter forbids him (article 100) from seeking or receiving instructions from any government or from any other authority external to the organization; and each member State undertakes to respect the exclusively international character of the Secretariat's responsibilities and not to seek to influence its members in the discharge of their duties. The charter stipulates (article 101) that the paramount consideration in the employment of the staff and in the determination of conditions of service is the necessity of securing the highest standards of efficiency, competence, and integrity. The staff is recruited on as wide a geographical basis as possible.

The main Secretariat units having responsibilities

in the field of human rights are the CENTER FOR HUMAN RIGHTS and the ADVANCEMENT OF WOMEN BRANCH of the Center for Social Development and Humanitarian Affairs. Other units dealing with particular human rights questions when they arise include the Department of Political and Security Council Affairs; the Department of Political Affairs, Trusteeship and Decolonization; the Department of International Economic and Social Affairs; the Department of Public Information; the Office of Legal Affairs; the Office of the United Nations Children's Fund; the Office of the Special Representative of the Secretary-General for Namibia; and the Secretariat of the UN Committee and Congresses on Crime Prevention and Control, all located in New York; as well as the Office of the United Nations High Commissioner for Refugees, located in Geneva; the Office of the United Nations Environment Program and the Center for Human Settlements, located in Nairobi; and the Office of the World Food Program, located in Rome.

In accordance with the United Nations Charter (article 97), the secretary-general is appointed by the General Assembly upon the recommendation of the Security Council. The rules of procedure of the General Assembly provide (rule 141) that, when the council has submitted its recommendation on the appointment of the secretary-general, the assembly shall consider the recommendation and vote upon it by secret ballot in private meeting. In practice, however, the assembly has never held a private meeting; and, on four occasions, it did not take a vote by secret ballot.

The following persons served as secretary-general in the past: Mr. Trygve Lie, 1 February 1946 to 10 April 1953; Mr. Dag Hammarskjold, 11 April 1953 to 17 September 1962; Mr. U Thant, 3 November 1961 to 31 December 1971; and Mr. Kurt Waldheim, 1 January 1972 to 31 December 1981.

On 15 December 1981, the General Assembly appointed (resolution 36/137) Mr. Javier Pérez de Cuéllar as secretary-general for a term of office beginning on 1 January 1982 and ending on 31 December 1986. On 10 October 1986, it reappointed him (resolution 41/1) secretary-general for a term of office ending on 31 December 1991, expressing its appreciation for the effective and dedicated service he had rendered to the United Nations during his first term of office. Both appointments were by acclamation.

The General Assembly has established two subsidiary bodies to deal with matters relating to the employment of UN staff. (1) The United Nations Administrative Tribunal, established on 9 December 1949 (resolution 351 [IV]) is competent to hear and pass judgment upon applications alleging non-observance of employment contracts of Secretariat staff members or of the terms of appointment of such staff members. The tribunal is composed of seven members, no two of whom may be nationals of the same country. Only three sit in a particular case. The tribunal establishes its own rules and its schedule of meetings. Its decisions are taken by majority vote, and its judgments are final and without appeal. Its competence has been extended to a number of specialized agencies, which have agreed to be bound by its judgments and to pay any compensation awarded by the tribunal in respect of a staff member of the agency.

(2) The International Civil Service Commission, established on 18 December 1974 (resolution 3357 [XXIX]) deals with matters affecting the salary and personnel system of the UN and its related agencies. It is composed of 15 members appointed by the General Assembly "in their personal capacity as individuals of recognized competence who have had substantial experience of executive responsibility in public administration or related fields, particularly in personnel management." The term of office is four years. Recommendations of the commission are communicated to the UN secretary-general and, through him, to the executive heads of other organizations. Decisions taken thereon by the General Assembly are communicated by the secretary-general to the executive heads of the other organizations for action under their constitutional procedures.

UNITED NATIONS STANDARD MINIMUM RULES FOR THE ADMINISTRATION OF JUVENILE JUSTICE ("BEIJING RULES"), (1985).

The Standard Minimum Rules, also known as the Beijing Rules, was drafted by an Interregional Preparatory Meeting held at Beijing, China, from 14 to 18 May 1984, and was recommended for adoption by the Seventh United Nations Congress on the Prevention of Crime and the Treatment of Offenders, held in Milan from 26 August to 6 September 1985. In adopting them on 29 November 1985 (resolution 40/33), the UN General Assembly recognized that the young, owing to their early stage of human development, require particular care and assistance with regard to physical, mental, and social development and require legal protection in conditions of peace, freedom, dignity, and security.

The assembly invited member States to adapt their national legislation, policies, and practices, particularly in the training of juvenile justice personnel, to the Beijing Rules, and to report periodically to the COMMITTEE ON CRIME PREVENTION AND CONTROL on the results of their efforts to put the rules into effect.

The text of the rules (including the commentaries designed to clarify their meaning) annexed to General Assembly resolution 40/33, is as follows:

Part One. General Principles
1. Fundamental Perspectives

1.1 Member States shall seek, in conformity with their respective general interests, to further the well-being of the juvenile and her or his family.

1.2 Member States shall endeavour to develop conditions that will ensure for the juvenile a meaningful life in the community, which, during that period in life when she or he is most susceptible to deviant behaviour, will foster a process of personal development and education that is as free from crime and delinquency as possible.

1.3 Sufficient attention shall be given to positive measures that involve the full mobilization of all possible resources, including the family, volunteers and other community groups, as well as schools and other community institutions, for the purpose of promoting the well-being of the juvenile, with a view to reducing the need for intervention under the law, and of effectively, fairly and humanely dealing with the juvenile in conflict with the law.

1.4 Juvenile justice shall be conceived as an integral part of the national development process of each country, within a comprehensive framework of social justice for all juveniles, thus, at the same time, contributing to the protection of the young and the maintenance of a peaceful order in society.

1.5 These Rules shall be implemented in the context of economic, social and cultural conditions prevailing in each Member State.

1.6 Juvenile justice services shall be systematically developed and co-ordinated with a view to improving and sustaining the competence of personnel involved in the services, including their methods, approaches and attitudes.

Commentary. These broad fundamental perspectives refer to comprehensive social policy in general and aim at promoting juvenile welfare to the greatest possible extent, which will minimize the necessity of intervention by the juvenile justice system, and in turn, will reduce the harm that may be caused by any intervention. Such care measures for the young, before the onset of delinquency, are basic policy requisites designed to obviate the need for the application of the Rules.

Rules 1.1 to 1.3 point to the important role that a constructive social policy for juveniles will play, *inter alia,* in the prevention of juvenile crime and delinquency. Rule 1.4 defines juvenile justice as an integral part of social justice for juveniles, while rule 1.6 refers to the necessity of constantly improving juvenile justice, without falling behind the development of progressive social policy for juveniles in general and bearing in mind the need for consistent improvement of staff services.

Rule 1.5 seeks to take account of existing conditions in Member States which would cause the manner of implementation of particular rules necessarily to be different from the manner adopted in other States.

2. Scope of the Rules and Definitions Used

2.1 The following Standard Minimum Rules shall be applied to juvenile offenders impartially, without distinction of any kind, for example, as to race, colour, sex, language, religion, political or other opinions, national or social origin, property, birth or other status.

2.2 For purposes of these Rules, the following definitions shall be applied by Member States in a manner which is compatible with their respective legal systems and concepts:

(a) A *juvenile* is a child or young person who, under the respective legal systems, may be dealt with for an offence in a manner which is different from an adult;

(b) An *offence* is any behaviour (act or omission) that is punishable by law under the respective legal systems;

(c) A *juvenile offender* is a child or young person who is alleged to have committed or who has been found to have committed an offence.

2.3 Efforts shall be made to establish, in each national jurisdiction, a set of laws, rules and provisions specifically applicable to juvenile offenders and institutions and bodies entrusted with the functions of the administration of juvenile justice and designed:

(a) To meet the varying needs of juvenile offenders, while protecting their basic rights;

(b) To meet the needs of society;

(c) To implement the following rules thoroughly and fairly.

Commentary. The Standard Minimum Rules are deliberately formulated so as to be applicable within different legal systems and, at the same time, to set some minimum standards for the handling of juvenile offenders under any definition of a juvenile and under any system of dealing with juvenile offenders. The Rules are always to be applied impartially and without distinction of any kind.

Rule 2.1 therefore stresses the importance of the Rules always being applied impartially and without distinction of any kind. The rule follows the formulation of principle 2 of the Declaration of the Rights of the Child.

Rule 2.2 defines "juvenile" and "offence" as the components of the notion of the "juvenile offender", who is the main subject of these Standard Minimum Rules (see, however, also rule 3 and 4). It should be noted that age limits will depend on, and are explicitly made dependent on, each respective legal system, thus fully respecting the economic, social, political, cultural and legal systems of Member States. This makes for a wide variety of ages coming under the definition of "juvenile", ranging from 7 years to 18 years or above. Such a variety seems inevitable in view of the different national legal systems and does not diminish the impact of these Standard Minimum Rules.

Rule 2.3 is addressed to the necessity of specific national legislation for the optimal implementation of these Standard Minimum Rules, both legally and practically.

3. Extension of the Rules

3.1 The relevant provisions of the Rules shall be applied not only to juvenile offenders but also to juveniles who may be proceeded against for any specific behaviour that would not be punishable if committed by an adult.

3.2 Efforts shall be made to extend the principles embodied in the Rules to all juveniles who are dealt with in welfare and care proceedings.

3.3 Efforts shall also be made to extend the principles embodied in the Rules to young adult offenders.

Commentary. Rule 3 extends the protection afforded by the Standard Minimum Rules for the Administration of Juvenile Justice to cover:

(a) The so-called "status offences" prescribed in various national legal systems where the range of behaviour considered to be an offence is wider for juveniles than it is for adults (for example, truancy, school and family disobedience, public drunkenness, etc.) (rule 3.1);

(b) Juvenile welfare and care proceedings (rule 3.2);

(c) Proceedings dealing with young adult offenders, depending of course on each given age limit (rule 3.3).

The extension of the Rules to cover these three areas seems to be justified. Rule 3.1 provides minimum guarantees in those fields, and rule 3.2 is considered a desirable step in the direction of more fair, equitable and humane justice for all juveniles in conflict with the law.

4. Age of Criminal Responsibility

4.1 In those legal systems recognizing the concept of the age of criminal responsibility for juveniles, the beginning of that age shall not be fixed at too low an age level, bearing in mind the facts of emotional, mental and intellectual maturity.

Commentary. The minimum age of criminal responsibility differs widely owing to history and culture. The modern approach would be to consider whether a child can live up to the moral and psychological components of criminal responsibility; that is, whether a child, by virtue of her or his individual discernment and understanding, can be held responsible for essentially anti-social behaviour. If the age of criminal responsibility is fixed too low or if there is no lower age limit at all, the notion of responsibility would become meaningless. In general, there is a close relationship between the notion of responsibility for delinquent or criminal behaviour and other social rights and responsibilities (such as marital status, civil majority, etc.).

Efforts should therefore be made to agree on a reasonable lowest age limit that is applicable internationally.

5. Aims of Juvenile Justice

5.1 The juvenile justice system shall emphasize the well-being of the juvenile and shall ensure that any reaction to juvenile offenders shall always be in proportion to the circumstances of both the offenders and the offence.

Commentary. Rule 5 refers to two of the most important objectives of juvenile justice. The first objective is the promotion of the well-being of the juvenile. This is the main focus of those legal systems in which juvenile offenders are dealt with by family courts or administrative authorities, but the well-being of the juvenile should also be emphasized in legal systems that follow the criminal court model, thus contributing to the avoidance of merely punitive sanctions. (See also rule 14.)

The second objective is "the principle of proportionality". This principle is well-known as an instrument for curbing punitive sanctions, mostly expressed in terms of just desert in relation to the gravity of the offence. The response to young offenders should be based on the consideration not only of the gravity of the offence but also of personal circumstances. The individual circumstances of the offender (for example, social status, family situation, the harm caused by the offence or other factors affecting personal circumstances) should influence the proportionality of the reaction (for example, by having regard to the offender's endeavour to indemnify the victim or to her or his willingness to turn to a wholesome and useful life).

By the same token, reactions aiming to ensure the welfare of the young offender may go beyond necessity and therefore infringe upon the fundamental rights of the young individual, as has been observed in some juvenile justice systems. Here, too, the proportionality of the reaction to the circumstances of both the offender and the offence, including the victim, should be safeguarded.

In essence, rule 5 calls for no less and no more than a fair reaction in any given case of juvenile delinquency and crime. The issues combined in the rule may help to stimulate development in both regards: new and innovative types of reactions are as desirable as precautions against any undue widening of the net of formal social control over juveniles.

6. Scope of Discretion

6.1 In view of the varying special needs of juveniles as well as the variety of measures available, appropriate scope for discretion shall be allowed at all stages of proceedings and at the different levels of juvenile justice administration, including investigation, prosecution, adjudication and the follow-up of dispositions.

6.2 Efforts shall be made, however, to ensure sufficient accountability at all stages and levels in the exercise of any such discretion.

6.3 Those who exercise discretion shall be specially qualified or trained to exercise it judiciously and in accordance with their functions and mandates.

Commentary. Rules 6.1, 6.2 and 6.3 combine several important features of effective, fair and humane juvenile justice administration: the need to permit the exercise of discretionary power at all significant levels of processing so that those who make determinations can take the actions deemed to be the most appropriate in each individual case; and the need to provide checks and balances in order to curb any abuses of discretionary power and to safeguard the rights of the young offender. Accountability and professionalism are instruments best apt to curb broad discretion. Thus, professional qualifications and expert training are emphasized here as a valuable means of ensuring the judicious exercise of discretion in matters of juvenile offenders. (See also rules 1.6 and 2.2.) The formulation of specific guidelines on the exercise of discretion and the provision of systems of review, appeal and the like in order to permit scrutiny of decisions and accountability are emphasized in this context. Such mechanisms are not specified here, as they do not easily lend themselves to incorporation into international standard minimum rules, which cannot possibly cover all differences in justice systems.

7. Rights of Juveniles

7.1 Basic procedural safeguards such as the presumption of innocence, the right to be notified of the charges, the right to remain silent, the right to counsel, the right to the presence of a parent or guardian, the right to confront and cross-examine witnesses and the right to appeal to a higher authority shall be guaranteed at all stages of proceedings.

Commentary. Rule 7.1 emphasizes some important points that represent essential elements for a fair and just trial and that are internationally recognized in existing human rights instruments. (See also rule 14.) The presumption of innocence, for instance, is also to be found in article 11 of the Universal Declaration of Human Rights and in article 14, paragraph 2, of the International Covenant on Civil and Political Rights.

Rules 14 *seq.* of these Standard Minimum Rules specify issues that are important for proceedings in juvenile cases, in particular, while rule 7.1 affirms the most basic procedural safeguards in a general way.

8. Protection of Privacy

8.1 The juvenile's right to privacy shall be respected at all stages in order to avoid harm being caused to her or him by undue publicity or by the process of labelling.

8.2 In principle, no information that may lead to the identification of a juvenile offender shall be published.

Commentary. Rule 8 stresses the importance of the protection of the juvenile's right to privacy. Young persons are particularly susceptible to stigmatization. Criminological research into labelling processes has provided evidence of the detrimental effects (of different kinds) resulting from the permanent identification of young persons as "delinquent" or "criminal".

Rule 8 also stresses the importance of protecting the juvenile from the adverse effects that may result from the publication in the mass media of information about the case (for example, the names of young offenders, alleged or convicted). The interest of the individual should be protected and upheld, at least in principle. (The general contents of rule 8 are further specified in rule 21.)

9. Saving Clause

9.1 Nothing in these Rules shall be interpreted as precluding the application of the Standard Minimum Rules for the Treatment of Prisoners adopted by the United Nations and other human rights instruments and standards recognized by the international community that relate to the care and protection of the young.

Commentary. Rule 9 is meant to avoid any misunderstanding in interpreting and implementing the present Rules in conformity with principles contained in relevant existing or emerging international human rights instruments and standards—such as the Universal Declaration of Human Rights; the International Covenant on Economic, Social and Cultural Rights and the International Covenant on Civil and Political Rights; and the Declaration of the Rights of the Child and the draft convention on the rights of the child. It should be understood that the application of the present Rules is without prejudice to any such international instruments which may contain provisions of wider application. (See also rule 27.)

Part Two. Investigation and Prosecution
10. Initial Contact

10.1 Upon the apprehension of a juvenile, her or his parents or guardian shall be immediately notified of such apprehension, and, where such immediate notification is not possible, the parents or guardian shall be notified within the shortest possible time thereafter.

10.2 A judge or other competent official or body shall, without delay, consider the issue of release.

10.3 Contacts between the law enforcement agencies and a juvenile offender shall be managed in such a way as to respect the legal status of the juvenile, promote the well-being of the juvenile and avoid harm to her or him, with due regard to the circumstances of the case.

Commentary. Rule 10.1 is in principle contained in rule 92 of the Standard Minimum Rules for the Treatment of Prisoners.

The question of release (rule 10.2) shall be considered without delay by a judge or other competent official. The latter refers to any person or institution in the broadest sense of the term, including community boards or police authorities having power to release an arrested person.

(See also the International Covenant on Civil and Political Rights, article 9, paragraph 3.)

Rule 10.3 deals with some fundamental aspects of the procedures and behaviour on the part of the police and other law enforcement officials in cases of juvenile crime. To "avoid harm" admittedly is flexible wording and covers many features of possible interaction (for example, the use of harsh language, physical violence or exposure to the environment). Involvement in juvenile justice processes in itself can be "harmful" to juveniles; the term "avoid harm" should be broadly interpreted, therefore, as doing the least harm possible to the juvenile in the first instance, as well as any additional or undue harm. This is especially important in the initial contact with law enforcement agencies, which might profoundly influence the juvenile's attitude towards the State and society. Moreover, the success of any further intervention is largely dependent on such initial contacts. Compassion and kind firmness are important in these situations.

11. Diversion

11.1 Consideration shall be given, wherever appropriate, to dealing with juvenile offenders without resorting to formal trial by the competent authority, referred to in rule 14.1 below.

11.2 The police, the prosecution or other agencies dealing with juvenile cases shall be empowered to dispose of such cases, at their discretion, without recourse to formal hearings, in accordance with the criteria laid down for that purpose in the respective legal system and also in accordance with the principles contained in these Rules.

11.3 Any diversion involving referral to appropriate community or other services shall require the consent of the juvenile, or her or his parents or guardian, provided that such decision to refer a case shall be subject to review by a competent authority, upon application.

11.4 In order to facilitate the discretionary disposition of juvenile cases, efforts shall be made to provide for community programmes, such as temporary supervision and guidance, restitution, and compensation of victims.

Commentary. Diversion, involving removal from criminal justice processing and, frequently, redirection to community support services, is commonly practised on a formal and informal basis in many legal systems. This practice serves to hinder the negative effects of subsequent proceedings in juvenile justice administration (for example, the stigma of conviction and sentence). In many cases, non-intervention would be the best response. Thus, diversion at the outset and without referral to alternative (social) services may be the optimal response. This is especially the case where the offence is of a non-serious nature and where the family, the school or other informal social control institutions have already reacted, or are likely to react, in an appropriate and constructive manner.

As stated in rule 11.2, diversions may be used at any point of decision-making—by the police, the prosecution or other agencies such as the courts, tribunals, boards or councils. It may be exercised by one authority or several or all authorities, according to the rules and policies of the respective systems and in line with the present Rules. It need not necessarily be limited to petty cases, thus rendering diversion an important instrument.

Rule 11.3 stresses the important requirement of securing the consent of the young offender (or the parent or guardian) to the recommended diversionary measure(s). (Diversion to community service without such consent would contradict the Convention concerning the Abolition of Forced Labour.) However, this consent should not be left unchallengeable, since it might sometimes be given out of sheer desperation on the part of the juvenile. The rule underlines that care should be taken to minimize the potential for coercion and intimidation at all levels in the diversion process. Juveniles should not feel pressured (for example, in order to avoid court appearance) or to be pressured into consenting to diversion programmes. Thus, it is advocated that provision should be made for an objective appraisal of the appropriateness of disposition involving young offenders by a "competent authority upon application". (The "competent authority" may be different from that referred to in rule 14.)

Rule 11.4 recommends the provision of viable alternatives to juvenile justice processing in the form of community-based diversion. Programmes that involve settlement by victim restitution and those that seek to avoid future conflict with the law through temporary supervision and guidance are especially commended. The merits of individual cases would make diversion appropriate, even when more serious offences have been committed (for example, first offense, the act having been committed under peer pressure, etc.).

12. Specialization Within the Police

12.1 In order to best fulfil their functions, police officers who frequently or exclusively deal with juveniles or who are primarily engaged in the prevention of juvenile crime shall be specially instructed and trained. In large cities, special police units should be established for that purpose.

Commentary. Rule 12 draws attention to the need for specialized training for all law enforcement officials who are involved in the administration of juvenile justice. As police are the first point of contact with the juvenile justice system, it is most important that they act in an informed and appropriate manner.

While the relationship between urbanization and crime is clearly complex, an increase in juvenile crime has been associated with the growth of large cities, particularly with rapid and unplanned growth. Specialized police units would therefore be indispensable, not only in the interest of implementing specific principles contained in the present instrument (such as rule 1.6) but more generally for improving the prevention and control of juvenile crime and the handling of juvenile offenders.

13. Detention Pending Trial

13.1 Detention pending trial shall be used only as a measure of last resort and for the shortest possible period of time.

13.2 Whenever possible, detention pending trial shall be replaced by alternative measures, such as close supervision, intensive care or placement with a family or in an educational setting or home.

13.3 Juveniles under detention pending trial shall be entitled to all rights and guarantees of the Standard Minimum Rules for the Treatment of Prisoners adopted by the United Nations.

13.4 Juveniles under detention pending trial shall be kept separate from adults and shall be detained in a separate institution or in a separate part of an institution also holding adults.

13.5 While in custody, juveniles shall receive care,

protection and all necessary individual assistance—social, educational, vocational, psychological, medical and physical—that they may require in view of their age, sex and personality.

Commentary. The danger to juveniles of "criminal contamination" while in detention pending trial must not be underestimated. It is therefore important to stress the need for alternative measures. By doing so, rule 13.1 encourages the devising of new and innovative measures to avoid such detention in the interest of the well-being of the juvenile.

Juveniles under detention pending trial are entitled to all the rights and guarantees of the Standard Minimum Rules for the Treatment of Prisoners as well as the International Covenant on Civil and Political Rights, especially article 9 and article 10, paragraphs 2 *(b)* and 3.

Rule 13.4 does not prevent States from taking other measures against the negative influences of adult offenders which are at least as effective as the measures mentioned in the rule.

Different forms of assistance that may become necessary have been enumerated to draw attention to the broad range of particular needs of young detainees to be addressed (for example, females or males, drug addicts, alcoholics, mentally ill juveniles, young persons suffering from the trauma of arrest for example, etc.).

Varying physical and psychological characteristics of young detainees may warrant classification measures by which some are kept separate while in detention pending trial, thus contributing to the avoidance of victimization and rendering more appropriate assistance.

The Sixth United Nations Congress on the Prevention of Crime and the Treatment of Offenders, in its resolution 4 on juvenile justice standards specified that the Rules, *inter alia,* should reflect the basic principle that pre-trial detention should be used only as a last resort, that no minors should be held in a facility where they are vulnerable to the negative influences of adult detainees and that account should always be taken of the needs particular to their stage of development.

Part Three. Adjudication and Disposition
14. Competent Authority to Adjudicate

14.1 Where the case of a juvenile offender has not been diverted (under rule 11), she or he shall be dealt with by the competent authority (court, tribunal, board, council, etc.) according to the principles of a fair and just trial.

14.2 The proceedings shall be conducive to the best interests of the juvenile and shall be conducted in an atmosphere of understanding, which shall allow the juvenile to participate therein and to express herself or himself freely.

Commentary. It is difficult to formulate a definition of the competent body or person that would universally describe an adjudicating authority. "Competent authority" is meant to include those who preside over courts or tribunals (composed of a single judge or of several members), including professional and lay magistrates as well as administrative boards (for example, the Scottish and Scandinavian systems) or other more informal community and conflict resolution agencies of an adjudicatory nature.

The procedure for dealing with juvenile offenders shall in any case follow the minimum standards that are applied almost universally for any criminal defendant under the procedure known as "due process of law". In accordance with due process, a "fair and just trial" included such basic safeguards as the presumption of innocence, the presenta-

tion and examination of witnesses, the common legal defences, the right to remain silent, the right to have the last word in a hearing, the right to appeal, etc. (See also rule 7.1).

15. Legal Counsel, Parents and Guardians

15.1 Throughout the proceedings the juvenile shall have the right to be represented by a legal advisor or to apply for free legal aid where there is provision for such aid in the country.

15.2 The parents or the guardian shall be entitled to participate in the proceedings and may be required by the competent authority to attend them in the interest of the juvenile. They may, however, be denied participation by the competent authority if there are reasons to assume that such exclusion is necessary in the interest of the juvenile.

Commentary. Rule 15.1 uses terminology similar to that found in rule 93 of the Standard Minimum Rules for the Treatment of Prisoners. Whereas legal counsel and free legal aid are needed to assure the juvenile legal assistance, the right of the parents or guardian to participate as stated in rule 15.2 should be viewed as general psychological and emotional assistance to the juvenile—a function extending throughout the procedure.

The competent authority's search for an adequate disposition of the case may profit, in particular, from the cooperation of the legal representatives of the juvenile (or, for that matter, some other personal assistant who the juvenile can and does really trust). Such concern can be thwarted if the presence of parents or guardians at the hearings plays a negative role, for instance, if they display a hostile attitude towards the juvenile; hence, the possibility of their exclusion must be provided for.

16. Social Inquiry Reports

16.1 In all cases except those involving minor offences, before the competent authority renders a final disposition prior to sentencing, the background and circumstances in which the juvenile is living or the conditions under which the offence has been committed shall be properly investigated so as to facilitate judicious adjudication of the case by the competent authority.

Commentary. Social inquiry reports (social reports or presentence reports) are an indispensable aid in most legal proceedings involving juveniles. The competent authority should be informed of relevant facts about the juvenile, such as social and family background, school career, educational experiences, etc. For this purpose, some jurisdictions use special social services or personnel attached to the court or board. Other personnel, including probation officers, may serve the same function. The rule therefore requires that adequate social services should be available to deliver social inquiry reports of a qualified nature.

17. Guiding Principles in Adjudication and Disposition

17.1 The disposition of the competent authority shall be guided by the following principles:

(a) The reaction taken shall always be in proportion not only to the circumstances and the gravity of the offence but also to the circumstances and the needs of the juvenile as well as to the needs of the society;

(b) Restrictions on the personal liberty of the juvenile shall be imposed only after careful consideration and shall be limited to the possible minimum;

(c) Deprivation of personal liberty shall not be imposed unless the juvenile is adjudicated of a serious act involving violence against another person or of persistence in committing other serious offences and unless there is no other appropriate response;

(d) The well-being of the juvenile shall be the guiding factor in the consideration of her or his case.

17.2 Capital punishment shall not be imposed for any crime committed by juveniles.

17.3 Juveniles shall not be subject to corporal punishment.

17.4 The competent authority shall have the power to discontinue the proceedings at any time.

Commentary. The main difficulty in formulating guidelines for the adjudication of young persons stems from the fact that there are unresolved conflicts of a philosophical nature, such as the following:

(a) Rehabilitation versus just desert;

(b) Assistance versus repression and punishment;

(c) Reaction according to the singular merits of an individual case versus reaction according to the protection of society in general;

(d) General deterrence versus individual incapacitation.

The conflict between these approaches is more pronounced in juvenile cases than in adult cases. With the variety of causes and reactions characterizing juvenile cases, these alternatives become intricately interwoven.

It is not the function of Standard Minimum Rules for the Administration of Juvenile Justice to prescribe which approach is to be followed but rather to identify one that is most closely in consonance with internationally accepted principles. Therefore, the essential elements as laid down in rule 17.1, in particular in subparagraphs (a) and (c), are mainly to be understood as practical guidelines that should ensure a common starting point; if heeded by the concerned authorities (see also rule 5), they could contribute considerably to ensuring that the fundamental rights of juvenile offenders are protected, especially the fundamental rights of personal development and education.

Rule 17.1 (b) implies that strictly punitive approaches are not appropriate. Whereas in adult cases, and possibly also in cases of severe offences by juveniles, just desert and retributive sanctions might be considered to have some merit, in juvenile cases such considerations should always be outweighed by the interest of safeguarding the well-being and the future of the young person.

In line with resolution 8 of the Sixth United Nations Congress, it encourages the use of alternatives to institutionalization to the maximum extent possible, bearing in mind the need to respond to the specific requirements of the young. Thus, full use should be made of the range of existing alternative sanctions and new alternative sanctions should be developed, bearing the public safety in mind. Probation should be granted to the greatest possible extent via suspended sentences, conditional sentences, board orders and other dispositions.

Rule 17.1 (c) corresponds to one of the guiding principles in resolution 4 of the Sixth Congress which aims at avoiding incarceration in the case of juveniles unless there is no other appropriate response that will protect the public safety.

The provision prohibiting capital punishment in rule 17.2 is in accordance with article 6, paragraph 5, of the International Covenant on Civil and Political Rights.

The provision against corporal punishment is in line with article 7 of the International Covenant on Civil and

Political Rights and the Declaration on the Protection of All Persons from Being Subjected to Torture and Other Cruel, Inhuman or Degrading Treatment or Punishment as well as the Convention against Torture and Other Cruel, Inhuman or Degrading Treatment or Punishment and the draft convention on the rights of the child.

The power to discontinue the proceedings at any time (rule 17.4) is a characteristic inherent in the handling of juvenile offenders as opposed to adults. At any time, circumstances may become known to the competent authority which would make a complete cessation of the intervention appear to be the best disposition of the case.

18. Various Disposition Measures

18.1 A large variety of disposition measures shall be made available to the competent authority, allowing for flexibility so as to avoid institutionalization to the greatest extent possible. Such measures, some of which may be combined, include:

(a) Care, guidance and supervision orders;

(b) Probation;

(c) Community service orders;

(d) Financial penalties, compensation and restitution;

(e) Intermediate treatment and other treatment orders;

(f) Orders to participate in group counselling and similar activities;

(g) Orders concerning foster care, living communities or other educational settings;

(h) Other relevant orders.

18.2 No juvenile shall be removed from parental supervision, whether partly or entirely, unless the circumstances of her or his case make this necessary.

Commentary. Rule 18.1 attempts to enumerate some of the important reactions and sanctions that have been practised and proved successful thus far, in different legal systems. On the whole they represent promising options that deserve replication and further development. The rule does not enumerate staffing requirements because of possible shortages of adequate staff in some regions; in those regions measures requiring less staff may be tried or developed.

The examples given in rule 18.1 have in common, above all, a reliance on and an appeal to the community for the effective implementation of alternative dispositions. Community-based correction is a traditional measure that has taken on many aspects. On that basis, relevant authorities should be encouraged to offer community-based services.

Rule 18.2 points to the importance of the family which, according to article 10, paragraph 1, of the International Covenant on Economic, Social and Cultural Rights, is "the natural and fundamental group unit of society". Within the family, the parents have not only the right but also the responsibility to care for and supervise their children. Rule 18.2, therefore, requires that the separation of children from their parents is a measure of last resort. It may be resorted to only when the facts of the case clearly warrant this grave step (for example, child abuse).

19. Least Possible Use of Institutionalization

19.1 The placement of a juvenile in an institution shall always be a disposition of last resort and for the minimum necessary period.

Commentary. Progressive criminology advocates the use

of non-institutional over institutional treatment. Little or no difference has been found in terms of the success of institutionalization as compared to non-institutionalization. The many adverse influences on an individual that seem unavoidable within any institutional setting evidently cannot be outbalanced by treatment efforts. This is especially the case for juveniles, who are vulnerable to negative influences. Moreover, the negative effects, not only of loss of liberty but also of separation from the usual social environment, are certainly more acute for juveniles than for adults because of their early stage of development.

Rule 19 aims at restricting institutionalization in two regards: in quantity ("last resort") and in time ("minimum necessary period"). Rule 19 reflects one of the basic guiding principles of resolution 4 of the Sixth United Nations Congress: a juvenile offender should not be incarcerated unless there is no other appropriate response. The rule, therefore, makes the appeal that if a juvenile must be institutionalized, the loss of liberty should be restricted to the least possible degree, with special institutional arrangements for confinement and bearing in mind the differences in kinds of offenders, offences and institutions. In fact, priority should be given to "open" over "closed" institutions. Furthermore, any facility should be of a correctional or educational rather than of a prison type.

Avoidance of Unnecessary Delay

20.1 Each case shall from the outset be handled expeditiously, without any unnecessary delay.

Commentary. The speedy conduct of formal procedures in juvenile cases is a paramount concern. Otherwise, whatever good may be achieved by the procedure and the disposition is at risk. As time passes, the juvenile will find it increasingly difficult, if not impossible, to relate the procedure and disposition to the offence, both intellectually and psychologically.

21. Records

21.1 Records of juvenile offenders shall be kept strictly confidential and closed to third parties. Access to such records shall be limited to persons directly concerned with the disposition of the case at hand or other duly authorized persons.

21.2 Records of juvenile offenders shall not be used in adult proceedings in subsequent cases involving the same offender.

Commentary. The rule attempts to achieve a balance between conflicting interests connected with records or files: those of the police, prosecution and other authorities in improving control versus the interests of the juvenile offender. (See also rule 8.) "Other duly authorized persons" would generally include, among others, researchers.

22. Need for Professionalism and Training

22.1 Professional education, in-service training, refresher courses and other appropriate modes of instruction shall be utilized to establish and maintain the necessary professional competence of all personnel dealing with juvenile cases.

22.2 Juvenile justice personnel shall reflect the diversity of juveniles who come into contact with the juvenile justice system. Efforts shall be made to ensure the fair representation of women and minorities in juvenile justice agencies.

Commentary. The authorities competent for disposition may be persons with very different backgrounds (magis-

trates in the United Kingdom of Great Britain and Northern Ireland and in regions influenced by the common law system; legally trained judges in countries using Roman law and in regions influenced by them; and elsewhere elected or appointed laymen or jurists, members of community-based boards, etc.). For all these authorities, a minimum training in law, sociology, psychology, criminology and behavioural sciences would be required. This is considered as important as the organizational specialization and independence of the competent authority.

For social workers and probation officers, it might not be feasible to require professional specialization as a prerequisite for taking over any function dealing with juvenile offenders. Thus, professional on-the-job instruction would be minimum qualifications.

Professional qualifications are an essential element in ensuring the impartial and effective administration of juvenile justice. Accordingly, it is necessary to improve the recruitment, advancement and professional training of personnel and to provide them with the necessary means to enable them to properly fulfil their functions.

All political, social, sexual, racial, religious, cultural or any other kind of discrimination in the selection, appointment and advancement of juvenile justice personnel should be avoided in order to achieve impartiality in the administration of juvenile justice. This was recommended by the Sixth United Nations Congress. Furthermore, the Sixth Congress called on Member States to ensure the fair and equal treatment for women as criminal justice personnel and recommended that special measures should be taken to recruit, train and facilitate the advancement of female personnel in juvenile justice administration.

Part Four. Non-institutional Treatment
23. Effective Implementation of Disposition

23.1 Appropriate provisions shall be made for the implementation of orders of the competent authority, as referred to in rule 14.1 above, by that authority itself or by some other authority as circumstances may require.

23.2 Such provisions shall include the power to modify the orders as the competent authority may deem necessary from time to time, provided that such modification shall be determined in accordance with the principles contained in these Rules.

Commentary. Disposition in juvenile cases, more so than in adult cases, tends to influence the offender's life for a long period of time. Thus, it is important that the competent authority or an independent body (parole board, probation office, youth welfare institutions or others) with qualifications equal to those of the competent authority that originally disposed of the case should monitor the implementation of the disposition. In some countries a *juge d'exécution des peines* has been installed for this purpose.

The composition, powers and functions of the authority must be flexible; they are described in general terms in rule 23 in order to ensure wide acceptability.

24. Provision of Needed Assistance

24.1 Efforts shall be made to provide juveniles, at all stages of the proceedings, with necessary assistance such as lodging, education or vocational training, employment or any other assistance, helpful and practical, in order to facilitate the rehabilitative process.

Commentary. The promotion of the well-being of the juvenile is of paramount consideration. Thus, rule 24 emphasizes the importance of providing requisite facilities, services and other necessary assistance as may further the best interests of the juvenile throughout the rehabilitative process.

25. Mobilization of Volunteers and Other Community Services

25.1 Volunteers, voluntary organizations, local institutions and other community resources shall be called upon to contribute effectively to the rehabilitation of the juvenile in a community setting and, as far as possible, within the family unit.

Commentary. This rule reflects the need for a rehabilitative orientation of all work with juvenile offenders. Co-operation with the community is indispensable if the directives of the competent authority are to be carried out effectively. Volunteers and voluntary services, in particular, have proved to be valuable resources but are at present underutilized. In some instances, the co-operations of ex-offenders (including ex-addicts) can be of considerable assistance.

Rule 25 emanates from the principles laid down in rules 1.1 to 1.6 and follows the relevant provisions of the International Covenant on Civil and Political Rights.

Part Five. Institutional Treatment
26. Objectives of Institutional Treatment

26.1 The objective of training and treatment of juveniles placed in institutions is to provide care, protection, education and vocational skills, with a view to assisting them to assume socially constructive and productive roles in society.

26.2 Juveniles in institutions shall receive care, protection and all necessary assistance—social, educational, vocational, psychological, medical and physical—that they may require because of their age, sex and personality and in the interest of their wholesome development.

26.3 Juveniles in institutions shall be kept separate from adults and shall be detained in a separate institution or in a separate part of an institution also holding adults.

26.4 Young female offenders placed in an institution deserve special attention as to their personal needs and problems. They shall by no means receive less care, protection, assistance, treatment and training than young male offenders. Their fair treatment shall be ensured.

26.5 In the interest and well-being of the institutionalized juvenile, the parents or guardians shall have a right of access.

26.6 Inter-ministerial and inter-departmental co-operation shall be fostered for the purpose of providing adequate academic or, as appropriate, vocational training to institutionalized juveniles, with a view to ensuring that they do not leave the institution at an educational disadvantage.

Commentary. The objectives of institutional treatment as stipulated in rules 26.1 and 26.2 would be acceptable to any system and culture. However, they have not yet been attained everywhere, and much more has to be done in this respect.

Medical and psychological assistance, in particular, are extremely important for institutionalized drug addicts, violent and mentally ill young persons.

The avoidance of negative influences through adult offenders and the safeguarding of the well-being of juveniles in an institutional setting, as stipulated in rule 26.3, are in line with one of the basic guiding principles of the Rules, as set out by the Sixth Congress in its resolution 4. The rule does not prevent States from taking other measures against the negative influences of adult offenders, which are at least as effective as the measures mentioned in the rule. (See also rule 13.4).

Rule 26.4 addresses the fact the female offenders normally receive less attention than their male counterparts, as pointed out by the Sixth Congress. In particular, resolution 9 of the Sixth Congress calls for the fair treatment of female offenders at every stage of criminal justice processes and for special attention to their particular problems and needs while in custody. Moreover, this rule should also be considered in the light of the Caracas Declaration of the Sixth Congress, which, *inter alia,* calls for equal treatment in criminal justice administration, and against the background of the Declaration on the Elimination of Discrimination against Women and the Convention on the Elimination of All Forms of Discrimination against Women.

The right of access (rule 26.5) follows from the provisions of rules 7.1, 10.1, 15.2 and 18.2. Inter-ministerial and inter-departmental co-operation (rule 26.6) are of particular importance in the interest of generally enhancing the quality of institutional treatment and training.

27. Application of the Standard Minimum Rules for the Treatment of Prisoners Adopted by the United Nations

27.1 The Standard Minimum Rules for the Treatment of Prisoners and related recommendations shall be applicable as far as relevant to the treatment of juvenile offenders in institutions, including those in detention pending adjudication.

27.2 Efforts shall be made to implement the relevant principles laid down in the Standard Minimum Rules for the Treatment of Prisoners to the largest possible extent so as to meet the varying needs of juveniles specific to their age, sex and personality.

Commentary. The Standard Minimum Rules for the Treatment of Prisoners were among the first instruments of this kind to be promulgated by the United Nations. It is generally agreed that they have had a world-wide impact. Although there are still countries where implementation is more an aspiration than a fact, those Standard Minimum Rules continue to be an important influence in the humane and equitable administration of correctional institutions.

Some essential protections covering juvenile offenders in institutions are contained in the Standard Minimum Rules for the Treatment of Prisoners (accommodation, architecture, bedding, clothing, complaints and requests, contact with the outside world, food, medical care, religious service, separation of ages, staffing, work, etc.) as are provisions concerning punishment and discipline, and restraint for dangerous offenders. It would not be appropriate to modify those Standard Minimum Rules according to the particular characteristics of institutions for juvenile offenders within the scope of the Standard Minimum Rules for the Administration of Juvenile Justice.

Rule 27 focuses on the necessary requirements for juveniles in institutions (rule 27.1) as well as on the varying needs specific to their age, sex and personality (rule 27.2). Thus, the objectives and content of the rule interrelates to the relevant provisions of the Standard Minimum Rules for the Treatment of Prisoners.

28. Frequent and Early Recourse to Conditional Release

28.1 Conditional release from an institution shall be used by the appropriate authority to the greatest possible extent, and shall be granted at the earliest possible time.

28.2 Juveniles released conditionally from an institution shall be assisted and supervised by an appropriate authority and shall receive full support by the community.

Commentary. The power to order conditional release may rest with the competent authority, as mentioned in rule 14.1, or with some other authority. In view of this, it is adequate to refer here to the "appropriate" rather than to the "competent" authority.

Circumstances permitting, conditional release shall be preferred to serving a full sentence. Upon evidence of satisfactory progress towards rehabilitation, even offenders who had been deemed dangerous at the time of their institutionalization can be conditionally released whenever feasible. Like probation, such release may be conditional on the satisfactory fulfilment of the requirements specified by the relevant authorities for a period of time established in the decision, for example, relating to "good behaviour" of the offender, attendance in community programmes, residence in half-way houses, etc.

In the case of offenders conditionally released from an institution, assistance and supervision by a probation or other officer (particularly where probation has not yet been adopted) should be provided and community support should be encouraged.

29. Semi-institutional Arrangements

29.1 Efforts shall be made to provide semi-institutional arrangements, such as half-way houses, educational homes, day-time training centres and other such appropriate arrangements that may assist juveniles in their proper reintegration into society.

Commentary. The importance of care following a period of institutionalization should not be underestimated. This rule emphasizes the necessity of forming a net of semi-institutional arrangements.

This rule also emphasized the need for a diverse range of facilities and services designed to meet the different needs of young offenders re-entering the community and to provide guidance and structural support as an important step towards successful reintegration into society.

Part Six. Research, Planning, Policy Formulation and Evaluation
30. Research as a Basis for Planning, Policy Formulation and Evaluation

30.1 Efforts shall be made to organize and promote necessary research as a basis for effective planning and policy formulation.

30.2 Efforts shall be made to review and appraise periodically the trends, problems and causes of juvenile delinquency and crime as well as the varying particular needs of juveniles in custody.

30.3 Efforts shall be made to establish a regular evaluative research mechanism built into the systems of juvenile justice administration and to collect and analyse relevant data and information for appropriate assessment and future improvement and reform of the administration.

30.4 The delivery of services in juvenile justice administration shall be systematically planned and implemented as an integral part of national development efforts.

Commentary. The utilization of research as a basis for an informed juvenile justice policy is widely acknowledged as an important mechanism for keeping practices abreast of advances in knowledge and the continuing development and improvement of the juvenile justice system. The mutual feedback between research and policy is especially important in juvenile justice. The mutual and often drastic changes in the life-styles of the young and in the forms and dimensions of juvenile crime, the societal and justice responses to juvenile crime and delinquency quickly become outmoded and inadequate.

Rule 30 thus establishes standards for integrating research into the process of policy formulation and application in juvenile justice administration. The rule draws particular attention to the need for regular review and evaluation of existing programmes and measures and for planning within the broader context of overall development objectives.

A constant appraisal of the needs of juveniles, as well as the trends and problems of delinquency, is a prerequisite for improving the methods of formulating appropriate policies and establishing adequate interventions, at both formal and informal levels. In this context, research by independent persons and bodies should be facilitated by responsible agencies, and it may be valuable to obtain and to take into account the views of juveniles themselves, not only those who come into contact with the system.

The process of planning must particularly emphasize a more effective and equitable system for the delivery of necessary services. Towards that end, there should be a comprehensive and regular assessment of the wide-ranging, particular needs and problems of juveniles and an identification of clear-cut priorities. In that connection, there should also be a co-ordination in the use of existing resources, including alternatives and community support that would be suitable in setting up specific procedures designed to implement and monitor established programmes.

SEE ALSO *Children: Detention; United States of America: Execution of Juvenile Offenders.*

UNITED NATIONS TRUST FUND FOR PUBLICITY AGAINST *APARTHEID*.

The UN General Assembly decided, on 14 December 1973, that a trust fund should be established (resolution 3151 C [XXVIII]) to ensure wider distribution of its publications against *apartheid* and to assist non-governmental organizations in developing anti-*apartheid* information activities. The United Nations Trust Fund for Publicity against *Apartheid* was accordingly established by the Secretary-General. The fund is financed by voluntary contributions from member States and is administered by the Centre Against Apartheid of the UN Secretariat, in consultation with the SPECIAL COMMITTEE AGAINST APARTHEID.

UNITED NATIONS TRUST FUND FOR SOUTH AFRICA.

The fund was established by the UN General Assembly on 15 December 1965 (resolution 2054 B [XX]). As clarified by the assembly on 2 December

1968 (resolution 2397 [XXIII]), the purpose of the fund is to provide (1) legal assistance to persons persecuted under the repressive and discriminatory legislation of South Africa; (2) relief to such persons and their dependents; (3) education of such persons and their dependents; and (4) relief for refugees from South Africa.

Under resolution 2054 B (XX), the president of the General Assembly nominates five member States, each of which appoints a person to serve on the Committee of Trustees of the Trust Fund. The term of office of these appointees is indeterminate. The committee holds one session per year and reports to the General Assembly through the secretary-general.

In 1988, the General Assembly, having considered the secretary-general's report on the trust fund (UN Doc. A/43/682) and the annexed report of the Committee of Trustees, reaffirmed that increasing humanitarian and legal assistance by the international community to those persecuted under repressive and discriminatory legislation in South Africa and Namibia is more than ever necessary to alleviate their plight and sustain their efforts.

UNITED NATIONS UNIVERSITY. A system of academic institutions established by the UN General Assembly on 11 December 1972 (resolution 2951 [XXVII]), consisting of a programming and coordinating central organ and a decentralized system of affiliated institutions, integrated into the world university economy and devoted to action-oriented research into the pressing global problems of human survival, development, and welfare, as well as to the post-graduate training of young scholars and research workers for the benefit of the world community.

The university center is located in Tokyo, Japan. It unites a global network of institutions and scholars and has established its own research and training centers in various parts of the world. Capital and recurrent costs are met entirely from voluntary contributions by governmental and non-governmental sources and are allocated by the University Council, which is composed of 24 members appointed jointly by the UN Secretary-General and the Director-General of UNESCO for terms of six years. The rector of the university is a member of the council, appointed for a term of five years by the UN Secretary-General in consultation with the Director-General of UNESCO. He is assisted by a university center in planning, coordinating, and administering the overall program.

Between 1977 and 1981, the university focused its attention on problems of global significance: world hunger, human and social development, and the use and management of natural resources. From 1982 onwards, five priority themes have predominated: (1) peace security, conflict resolution, and global transformation; (2) global economy; (3) hunger, poverty, resources, and environment; (4) human and social development and co-existence of peoples, cultures, and social systems; and (5) science and technology and their social and ethical implications. Under the Human Development Project, which examines the impact of development change on the welfare and rights of individuals, families, groups, and communities, the following activities relating to the realization of human rights are under way (UN Doc. A/43/31, para. 90–97):

Perceptions of Desirable Societies in Different Religious and Ethical Systems. The view of religious thinkers on contemporary issues is increasingly influential, and often may provide insights on how development might proceed in harmony with the values deeply held in a society. Three sections of this project dealing with Christianity, Islam and Buddhism have been completed and the resulting collections of papers are being edited for publication. Participants in the study on Hinduism met in Delhi in March to discuss the specific approaches of Hinduism to social issues, including its critique of modernity and the practical idealism represented in such movements as Sarvodaya and Svadhyay. A number of papers were commissioned following the meeting.

Two conferences were held at Tokyo on subjects relating to the project in 1987. In April, a symposium on "The future of mankind and co-operation among religions" discussed the forms and possibilities of inter-religious co-operation. A seminar on "Science, technology and spiritual values: an Asian approach to modernization" took place in May. It provided a reflection on the contribution of religions to the critique of modern societies, from an Asian perspective.

Economic Aspects of Human Development. Research continued on five topics: alternative development experiences; development paradigms and the economy-culture interface; alternative epistemologies and methodologies; foundations of economics and alternative development; and obstacles to development: the case of Argentina (1945–1985). A meeting was held at Geneva in June, where papers on the first three topics were presented and discussed. The project's main ideas and conclusions were presented at the North-South Round-table on "Managing human development" which was sponsored by the United Nations Development Programme (UNDP) at Bucharest in September.

The Global Impact of Human Migration. Data gathered from 400–500 migrant workers from seven Asian countries to the Arab world form the empirical base for this study. The data base has been computerized at the Marga Institute in Sri Lanka, where it is available for further research and retrieval. Country studies derived from this collection were edited and reviewed for publication in 1987. Further analytical and conceptual papers on the political and sociocultural aspects of migration were completed, along with a case study of immigration to France. A survey of research on migration by the United Nations and other international agencies was also prepared, covering three topics: the formulation of international policies, conventions and regulations governing migration; technical assistance for problems of migration, including refugees; and other issues relating to migration.

The United Nations University also acted as an associate executing agency, in co-operation with the International Labour Organisation (ILO), of a research programme on the "Enhancement of household capacity in the post-migration phase". This is a subprogramme of the Asian Regional Programme on International Labour Migration, which is funded by UNDP. A workshop in Bangkok in December brought together researchers from Bangladesh, India, the Republic of Korea, Pakistan, the Philippines, Sri Lanka and Thailand to review final reports of data from each country on approximately 50 households of returned migrant workers. Several manuscripts are also being prepared for publication.

Ethnic Minorities and Human and Social Development. The products of this project include a computerized World Guide to Ethnic Minorities, which is being centralized at El Colegio de México in Mexico City. Data have been collected thus far on more than 800 ethnic groups. Co-operating institutions around the world have provided inputs in return for access to the data bank. The Guide includes items on the principal social, economic and cultural characteristics of each minority, as well as information on major economic and political problems arising from relations with other ethnic groups or with the state. Reference is also included to international dimensions where they exist.

An international seminar on the "New faces of racism", held at Amsterdam in October, dealt with tensions among different ethnic groups in the industrialized countries of Western Europe. It was co-sponsored by the United Nations University, International Alert, the Swedish Ombudsman for Race Relations, and the Mayor of Amsterdam. A second seminar, held at Kampala in September, scrutinized "Ethnic conflicts and human rights in East Africa" and was co-sponsored by International Alert and the Makerere Institute of Social Research with the participation of the United Nations University. Several manuscripts are also being prepared for publication.

Human Rights and Scientific and Technological Development. In 1986, the United Nations Commission on Human Rights invited the United Nations University to conduct a study on the positive and negative effects of scientific and technological developments on human rights and fundamental freedoms. A proposal was drawn up, and research papers were commissioned.

A workshop was convened in July 1989 to agree on a research plan. The final report was expected to be ready in February 1991. The university stated (E/CN.4/1990/29) that it would not, therefore, be possible to provide a report for consideration by the Commission on Human Rights at its 46th session, held in February 1990.

United Nations University. Address: Toho Seimei Building, 15–1 Shibuya-ku, Tokyo 150, Japan. Telephone: (03) 499–2811. Cable: CUNATUNIV TOKYO. Telex: J 25442 UNATUNIV. Rector: Prof. Soedjatmoko.

UNITED NATIONS VOLUNTARY FUND FOR ADVISORY SERVICES AND TECHNICAL ASSISTANCE IN THE FIELD OF HUMAN RIGHTS. The fund was established by the secretary-general of the United Nations in 1987 in accordance with a request by the UN COMMISSION ON HUMAN RIGHTS (resolution 1987/38), in which the commission authorized the secretary-general to receive voluntary contributions to the fund from governments, intergovernmental and non-governmental organizations, and individuals in a position to make such contributions and to solicit contributions or to make such representations or appeals for contributions as he deems appropriate. The objective of the trust fund is to provide additional financial support for practical activities focused on the implementation of international conventions and other international instruments on human rights promulgated by the United Nations, its specialized agencies, and regional organizations.

The commission, in its resolution, requested the secretary-general to bring regularly to the attention of all governments and of the competent human rights organs possibilities that exist under the trust fund to provide advisory services and technical assistance to governments at their request and encouraged governments in need of technical assistance in the field of human rights to avail themselves of the advisory services of experts.

In his report on the fund presented to the 1990 session of the Commission on Human Rights (UN Doc. E/CN.4/1990/43, annex I), the secretary-general indicated that contributions amounting to $US 1,035,404 had been received as of 31 December 1989, and that an additional $US 361,730 had been pledged. Expenditures and commitments entered into in 1988–1989 totalled $US 883,700, leaving an estimated balance of $US 135,000. The balance had been earmarked for previously approved and ongoing projects scheduled for 1990. Actual expenditures included: advisory services of experts, $164,500; provision of reference libraries, $16,500; fellowships, $126,800; training courses and workshops, 568,000; and publications, $7,900.

SEE ALSO Advisory Services in the Field of Human Rights.

UNITED NATIONS VOLUNTARY FUND FOR INDIGENOUS POPULATIONS. The fund was established by the UN General Assembly on 13 December 1985 (resolution 40/130). Its sole purpose is to assist representatives of indigenous communities and organizations to participate in the deliberations of the

WORKING GROUP ON INDIGENOUS POPULATIONS by providing them with financial assistance, funded by means of voluntary contributions from governments, non-governmental organizations, and other private or public entities. The only beneficiaries of the fund are representatives of indigenous peoples' organizations and communities (1) who are so considered by the Board of Trustees of the fund, (2) who would not, in the opinion of that board, be able to attend the sessions of the working group without the assistance provided by the fund, and (3) who would be able to contribute to a deeper knowledge on the part of the working group of the problems affecting indigenous populations and who would secure a broad geographical representation.

The Board of Trustees is composed of five persons having broad experience in dealing with indigenous issues, who serve in their personal capacity. Members are appointed by the secretary-general for a three-year term, which is renewable, in consultation with the chairman of the Sub-Commission on Prevention of Discrimination and Protection of Minorities.

The Board of Trustees held its first session in April 1988 and examined requests for financial assistance for 86 indigenous representatives. In light of the funds available, it recommended the awarding of 27 travel and subsistence grants. The beneficiaries came from 19 countries to attend the sixth session of the working group, which was convened at the European Office of the United Nations in Geneva from 1 to 5 August 1988.

SEE ALSO *ILO Indigenous and Tribal Peoples Convention; Indigenous Populations Convention: ILO Action; Indigenous Populations: Study of the Problem of Discrimination; Indigenous Rights: Draft Universal Declaration.*

UNITED NATIONS VOLUNTARY FUND FOR VICTIMS OF TORTURE. The fund was established in accordance with a decision taken by the UN General Assembly in 1981 (resolution 36/151) by which what was formerly known as the United Nations Trust Fund for Chile was given a broader mandate under a new name and charged with "receiving voluntary contributions for distribution, through established channels of assistance, as humanitarian, legal and financial aid to individuals whose human rights have been severely violated as a result of torture and to relatives of such victims, priority being given to aid to victims of violations by States in which the human rights situation has been the subject of resolutions or decisions adopted either by the Assembly, the Economic and Social Council or the Commission on Human Rights."

The voluntary fund is administered by the Secretary-General, with the advice of a board of trustees composed of a chairman and four members with wide experience in the field of human rights who act in their personal capacity. They are appointed by the Secretary-General with due regard for equitable geographical distribution and in consultation with their governments. The term of office is indeterminate. Members of the board are Mr. Jaap Walkate (Chairman) (Netherlands); Mrs. Elizabeth Odio Benito (Costa Rica); Mr. Waleed Sadi (Jordan); Mr. Ivan Tosevski (Yugoslavia); and Mr. S. Amos Wako (Kenya).

Between 1983 and 1988, the voluntary fund made 131 grants, totalling $3,688,894. The grants went to 67 projects in 32 countries in Africa, America, Asia, and Europe. Many of the projects were implemented in countries such as Argentina, the Philippines, Uganda, and Uruguay, where there have been important political changes in recent years and where persons tortured in the past, under different political conditions, are still urgently in need of help. The focus of the grants is on therapy and rehabilitation projects.

On 15 December 1989, the UN General Assembly took note of the report of the Secretary-General on the work of the board (UN Doc. A/44/708), and expressed (resolution 44/145) its gratitude and appreciation to all who had contributed to the fund, to the board of trustees for their work, and to the Secretary-General for the support given to the board.

UNITED STATES OF AMERICA. A country of the North American continent, lying between the Atlantic Ocean on the east and the Pacific Ocean on the west, the United States includes, in addition to its continental area, the states of Alaska and Hawaii and has borders with Canada to the north and Mexico to the south. It declared its independence from Great Britain on 4 July 1776. In 1945, it became a member of the United Nations and has since acted as host to UN headquarters in New York City.

Its population is estimated by the UN (1990) to be 248,429,000. In addition to the English-speaking white Christian majority, there are more than 25 million black Americans, many descended from slaves transported involuntarily from Africa and the Caribbean before—and even after—the slave trade was prohibited by law in 1807; 7 million Jews, 2 million Puerto Ricans; 2 million indigenous American Indians; and several million immigrants or refugees from such countries as Austria, China, Germany, Ireland, Italy, Japan, Mexico, the Philippines, Poland, and the Soviet Union. The language in common use is English; however, recent immigrants tend to adhere to their national language within their own communities. Christianity (more than 50 million Catholics and 73 million Protestants) and Judaism (more than 7 million) are the predominant religions. Literacy is estimated at 99%.

The government (1990) took the form of a republic. Under the constitution, there are three coordinate branches of government; the executive, the legislative, and the judicial. The powers allocated to each branch are so interlinked that none can function entirely independently of the others. The legislature makes the law, the executive branch enforces it, and the judiciary interprets it through cases and controversies that it is called upon to settle. It is this interrelationship that ensures the enjoyment of the rights laid down in the constitution but also extends them to meet the changing demands of a modern, complex society.

The legislative branch, which makes the law, consists of a bi-cameral congress composed of a 435-member House of Representatives and a 100-member Senate. The number of members from each state in the House is Representatives is proportionate to the population of that state; members are elected by the state's voters for two-year terms of office. The number of members from each state in the Senate is two, regardless of the population of the state; members are elected by the state's voters for six-year terms of office, one-third of the total membership retiring every two years unless re-elected.

The judicial branch, which interprets the law, is independent and its members, appointed by the president with the advice and consent of the Senate, serve for life and cannot be removed except for treason, bribery, or other high crimes. The Supreme Court reviews cases from the lower federal courts and certain cases originating in state courts involving questions of federal law. It has the power to invalidate any federal or state law or executive action which it finds contrary to provisions of the constitution.

There are 12 federal courts of appeal and 89 federal trial courts, each with from 1 to 27 judgeships. There are also special federal courts, such as the U.S. Claims Court, to deal with specialized problems arising under federal statutes. The courts handle civil as well as criminal cases. Persons convicted of penal offenses may be confined in prison or in an institution, fined, or both, or in the case of drug addicts may be committed to hospitals for treatment.

The executive branch, which enforces the law, is headed by the president who functions both as head of State and of government, and also as commander-in-chief of the armed forces. The vice president has no established function other than to serve *ex officio* as president of the Senate but may succeed the presi-

dent in office if the latter dies or is seriously disabled. The president is limited to two four-year terms of office.

Within the executive branch, the Civil Rights Division of the Department of Justice is responsible for enforcing federal civil rights laws that prohibit discrimination on the basis of race, national origin, religion, and, in some cases, sex or handicap, in the areas of voting, education, employment, housing, credit, the use of public facilities and public accommodations, and in the administration of federally assisted programs. Among the congressional standards which it enforces are the Civil Rights Acts of 1957, 1960, 1964, and 1968; the Voting Rights Act of 1965; the Equal Educational Opportunities Act of 1974; the Equal Credit Opportunity Act of 1976; and the Civil Rights of Institutionalized Persons Act of 1980. It also has the obligation to enforce specific criminal statutes, including those concerning willful deprivation of constitutional rights under color of law or through conspiracy, involuntary servitude, and violent interference with federally protected activities. A special section of the division concentrates on protecting the rights of indigenous American Indians while another, the Sex Discrimination Task Force, reviews all federal policies, programs, and procedures with a view to eliminating discrimination against women and obtaining appropriate corrective action.

An independent agency, the Equal Employment Opportunity Commission, established in accordance with the Civil Rights Act of 1964, enforces that act by examining charges and complaints of job discrimination based on race, color, religion, sex, or national origin by private employers, state and local governments, and educational institutions with 15 or more employees, or by the federal government, private and public employment agencies, labor organizations and joint labor-management committees for apprenticeship and training. The commission first endeavors to remedy the unlawful practices through informal methods of conciliation, conference, and persuasion. If it concludes that judicial action is necessary to carry out the purposes of the act, the commission—or the attorney-general in a case involving a governmental agency or political sub-division—may bring an action for appropriate relief pending final disposition of a charge.

A second independent agency, the Commission on Civil Rights, established by the Civil Rights Act of 1957 and re-established by the United States Commission on Civil Rights Act of 1983, collects and studies information on discrimination or denials of equal protection of the laws because of race, color, religion, sex, age, handicap, national origin or in the administration of justice in such areas as voting rights, enforcement of federal civil rights laws, and equality of opportunity in education, employment, and housing. It makes findings of fact but has no enforcement authority. Its findings and recommendations are submitted to the president and to Congress, and many of its recommendations have been enacted either by statute, executive order, or regulation. The commission also evaluates federal laws and the effectiveness of government equal opportunity programs and serves as a clearinghouse for information on civil rights.

Within the Department of State, the Bureau of Human Rights and Humanitarian Affairs is responsible for the formulation and development and—in cooperation with other bureaus—the implementation of U.S. policy relating to the observance of human rights throughout the world. The bureau maintains liaison with non-governmental organizations active in the field of human rights and is principally responsible for the preparation of the annual State Department report on human rights practices in countries that are members of the United Nations or receive U.S. economic or military assistance. In addition, the bureau provides the department's advice to the Immigration and Naturalization Service regarding applications for political asylum by foreign nationals.

These safeguards notwithstanding, human rights and fundamental freedoms are not always enjoyed by everyone residing in the United States of America. For example, during World War II, more than 112,000 Americans of Japanese descent were interned or relocated from their homes in the western part of the country; and it was only in 1988 that the government acknowledged the wrongful act and awarded reparations to those who had suffered from it. Implementation of section 105 of the Civil Liberties Act of 1988, which provides restitution, is in the hands of the Civil Rights Division.

During the "McCarthy era" of the 1950s, thousands of Americans suspected of having ties to the Communist Party were harassed by congressional investigative committees and federal "loyalty boards," and denied employment, the right to leave the country, and other rights on the spurious ground of "guilt by association."

More recently, the U.S. Supreme Court has upheld the use of the death penalty, even against the mentally retarded and immature juveniles, and has moved to review decades of political decisions aimed at protecting freedom of speech, separation of Church and State, and the rights of women including the right to choose an abortion in certain circumstances. However, as indicated above, none of the three coordinate branches of government can function entirely independent of the others; and actions by the judiciary are subject to concurrence or reversal by the execu-

tive or the legislative branches, or by both. Thus, for example, the U.S. Congress in mid-1990 took up a proposed Civil Rights Act of 1990 designed specifically to overturn five 1989 Supreme Court decisions that had made it harder for workers to bring and win employment discrimination cases and easier for employers to challenge court-ordered civil rights actions.

Territories The government of the United States of America retained, or assumed, responsibility for the administration of several non-self-governing territories shortly after the establishment of the United Nations, including the trust territory of the Pacific Islands, American Samoa, Guam, and the United States Virgin Islands. In accordance with the United Nations Charter, it is now in the process of establishing the independence of those territories.

The trust territory of the Pacific Islands consists of three archipelagos: the Marshall Islands, the Carolines, and the Marianas. Although in the Marianas, the island of Guam is not a part of the trust territory.

On 28 May 1986, the UN TRUSTEESHIP COUNCIL adopted resolution 2183 (LIII), by which it noted that the peoples of the Northern Mariana Islands, the Marshall Islands, the Federated States of Micronesia, and Paulau had freely exercised their right to self-determination in plebescites observed by visiting missions of the council. They had chosen free association with the United States in the case of the Marshall Islands, the Federated States of Micronesia, and Paulau, and commonwealth status in the case of the Northern Marianas. The council concluded that the United States government had satisfactorily discharged its obligations under the trusteeship agreement and that the agreement should be terminated.

With regard to Guam, the UN General Assembly on 22 November 1988 reaffirmed (resolution 43/42), as it had on earlier occasions, the inalienable right of its people to SELF-DETERMINATION and independence and called upon the U.S. government to expedite the process of decolonization in accordance with the expressed wishes of the people of the territory.

With regard to American Samoa, the assembly likewise reaffirmed (resolution 43/43) the inalienable right of the people to self-determination and independence and called upon the U.S. government to expedite the process of decolonization. It also reaffirmed the responsibility of the administering power, under the charter, to promote the economic and social development of American Samoa and called upon it to intensify its efforts to strengthen and diversify the economy of the territory. In particular, it urged the administering power and the territorial government to take effective measures to safeguard and guarantee the inalienable right of the people of

American Samoa to own and dispose of the natural resources of the territory, including marine resources, and to establish and maintain control over the future development of those resources.

With regard to the question of the U.S. Virgin Islands, the UN General Assembly on 22 November 1988 welcomed (resolution 43/44) the enactment of legislation, in March 1988, providing for a referendum to be held in November 1989 on options available for the territory's future status, i.e., statehood, independence, free association, incorporated territory, *status quo,* commonwealth, or compact of federal relations. The assembly reaffirmed that it is ultimately for the people of the United States Virgin Islands themselves to determine their future political status in accordance with the relevant provisions of the Charter of the United Nations and the relevant resolutions of the General Assembly; and, in that connection, called upon the administering power, in cooperation with the territorial government, to facilitate programs of political education in the territory in order to foster an awareness among the people of the possibilities open to them in the exercise of their right of self-determination.

Guam, American Samoa, and the U.S. Virgin Islands each has a local legislature, acts of which are subject to modification or annulment by the U.S. Congress.

Puerto Rico has enjoyed limited self-government since 1952, when it attained the status of a commonwealth and its people began to elect their governor and other officials. However, the federal government remains responsible for its foreign relations, and a number of federal agencies continue to operate there.

The right of the people of Puerto Rico to self-determination and independence was considered by the SPECIAL COMMITTEE ON THE SITUATION WITH REGARD TO THE IMPLEMENTATION OF THE DECLARATION ON THE GRANTING OF INDEPENDENCE TO COLONIAL COUNTRIES AND PEOPLES in February 1989, on the basis of a report prepared by its rapporteur (UN Doc. A/AC.109/L.1703). After examining the report and devoting several meetings to hearing delegations, observers, and representatives of more than 50 interested organizations, the special committee on 17 August 1989 adopted a resolution in which it reaffirmed (UN Doc. A/AC.109/L.1703) the inalienable right of the people of Puerto Rico to self-determination and independence, in conformity with General Assembly resolution 1514 (XV), and the full applicability of the fundamental principles of that resolution with respect to Puerto Rico.

The special committee expressed its hope, and that of the international community, that, in any consulta-

tions, the people of Puerto Rico may exercise without hindrance its right to self-determination and independence, with the express recognition of the people's sovereignty and full political equality, in accordance with para. 5 of General Assembly resolution 1514 (XV). It requested its rapporteur to report in 1990 on the implementation of this and other resolutions concerning Puerto Rico and decided to retain the question on its agenda for further consideration.

Later in the year, the UN General Assembly considered the question of the U.S. Virgin Islands. On 11 December 1989, it took note (resolution 44/99) of the statement of the representative of the United States of America, as the administering power, that the participation of the people of the territory in the electoral process demonstrated that they exercised responsibility for local government and local political affairs, and that the policy of the United States was to respond to the wishes of the people regarding their future political status whenever they indicated the direction in which they wished to proceed.

In the resolution, the assembly reaffirmed the inalienable right of the people of the U.S. Virgin Islands to self-determination and independence in conformity with the DECLARATION ON THE GRANTING OF INDEPENDENCE TO COLONIAL COUNTRIES AND PEOPLES, and pointed out that it is the responsibility of the United States of America, as the administering power, to continue to create such conditions in the U.S. Virgin Islands as will enable the people of the territory to exercise that right freely and without interference. It called upon the United States to continue to take all necessary measures, in cooperation with the territorial government, to counter problems related to drug trafficking and to facilitate participation in various international and regional organizations. And it urged member States and organizations of the United Nations system to extend all assistance with a view to rehabilitating and reconstructing the territory devastated by hurricane Hugo.

UNITED STATES OF AMERICA: CONSTITUTION. The Constitution of the United States of America, completed by the Constitutional Convention on 17 September 1787, was ratified by the conventions of a number of states up to 29 May 1790, and entered into force on 4 March 1789. Ten amendments to the constitution, constituting its "Bill of Rights," were proposed by the U.S. Congress on 25 September 1789 and entered into force on 30 December 1791. Fourteen additional amendments were adopted subsequently, of which one—the 18th, adopted in 1919 and prohibiting the manufacture, sale, or transportation of intoxicating liquors—was repealed on 5 December

1933. The texts of the remaining amendments, relating to human rights and fundamental freedoms, are as follows:

Amendment 1. Congress shall make no law respecting an establishment of religion, or prohibiting the free exercise thereof; or abridging the freedom of speech, or of the press; or the right of the people peaceably to assemble, and to petition the Government for a redress of grievances.

Amendment 2. A well regulated Militia, being necessary to the security of a free State, the right of the people to keep and bear Arms, shall not be infringed.

Amendment 3. No Soldier shall, in time of peace, be quartered in any house, without the consent of the Owner, nor in time of war, but in a manner to be prescribed by law.

Amendment 4. The right of the people to be secure in their persons, houses, papers, and effects, against unreasonable searches and seizures, shall not be violated, and no Warrants shall issue, but upon probable cause, supported by Oath or affirmation, and particularly describing the place to be searched and the person or things to be seized.

Amendment 5. No person shall be held to answer for a capital, or otherwise infamous crime, unless on a presentment or indictment of a Grand Jury, except in cases arising in the land or naval forces, or in the Militia, when in actual service in time of War or public danger; nor shall any person be subject for the same offence to be twice put in jeopardy of life or limb; nor shall be compelled in any criminal case to be a witness against himself, nor be deprived of life, liberty, or property, without due process of law; nor shall private property be taken for public use, without just compensation.

Amendment 6. In all criminal prosecutions the accused shall enjoy the right to a speedy and public trial, by an impartial jury of the State and district wherein the crime shall have been committed, which district shall have been previously ascertained by law, and to be informed of the nature and cause of the accusation; to be confronted with the witnesses against him; to have compulsory process for obtaining witnesses in his favor, and to have the Assistance of Counsel for his defence.

Amendment 7. In suits at common law, where the value in controversy shall exceed twenty dollars, the right of trial by jury shall be preserved, and no fact tried by a jury shall be otherwise re-examined in any Court of the United States, than according to the rules of the common law.

Amendment 8. Excessive bail shall not be required, nor excessive fines imposed, nor cruel and unusual punishments inflicted.

Amendment 9. The enumeration in the Constitution, of certain rights shall not be construed to deny or disparage others retained by the people.

Amendment 10. The powers not delegated to the United States by the Constitution, nor prohibited by it to the States, are reserved to the States respectively or to the people.

Amendment 11. The Judicial power of the United States shall not be construed to extend to any suit in law or equity, commenced or prosecuted against one of the United States by Citizens of another State, or by Citizens or Subjects of any Foreign State.

Amendment 12. The Electors shall meet in their respective states, and vote by ballot for President and Vice-President, one of whom, at least, shall not be an inhabitant of the same state with themselves; they shall name in their ballots the person voted for as President, and in distinct ballots the person voted for as Vice-President, and they shall make distinct lists of all persons voted for as President and of all persons voted for as Vice-President, and of the number of votes for each, which lists they shall sign and certify, and transmit sealed to the seat of the government of the United States, directed to the President of the Senate;—The President of the Senate shall, in the presence of the Senate and House of Representatives, open all the certificates and the votes shall then be counted;—The person having the greatest number of votes for President, shall be the President, if such number be a majority of the whole number of Electors appointed; and if no person have such majority, then from the persons having the highest numbers not exceeding three on the list of those voted for as President, the House of Representatives shall choose immediately, by ballot, the President. But in choosing the President the votes shall be taken by states, the representation from each state having one vote; a quorum for this purpose shall consist of a member or members from two-thirds of the states, and a majority of all the states shall be necessary to a choice. And if the House of Representatives shall not choose a President whenever the right of choice shall devolve upon them, before the fourth day of March next following, then the Vice-President shall act as President, as in the case of the death or other constitutional disability of the President.—That person having the greatest number of votes as Vice-President shall be the Vice-President, if such number be a majority of the whole number of Electors appointed, and if no person have a majority, then from the two highest numbers on the list, the Senate shall choose the Vice-President; a quorum for the purpose shall consist of two-thirds of the whole number of Senators, and a majority of the whole number shall be necessary to a choice. But no person constitutionally ineligible to the office of President shall be eligible to that of Vice-President of the United States.

Amendment 13. Section 1. Neither slavery nor involuntary servitude, except as a punishment for crime whereof the party shall have been duly convicted, shall exist within the United States, or any place subject to their jurisdiction.

Section 2. Congress shall have power to enforce this article by appropriate legislation.

Amendment 14. Section 1. All persons born or naturalized in the United States, and subject to the jurisdiction thereof, are citizens of the United States and of the State wherein they reside. No State shall make or enforce any law which shall abridge the privileges or immunities of citizens of the United States; nor shall any State deprive any person of life, liberty, or property, without due process of law; nor deny to any person within its jurisdiction the equal protection of the laws.

Section 2. Representatives shall be apportioned among the several States according to their respective numbers, counting the whole number of persons in each State, excluding Indians not taxed. But when the right to vote at any election for the choice of electors for President and Vice-President of the United States, Representatives in Congress, the Executive and Judicial officers of a State, or the members of the Legislature thereof, is denied to any of the male inhabitants of such State, being twenty-one years of age, and citizens of the United States, or in any way abridged, except for participation in rebellion, or other crime the basis of representation therein shall be reduced in the proportion which the number of such male citizens shall bear to the whole number of male citizens twenty-one years of age in such State.

Section 3. No person shall be a Senator or Representative

in Congress, or elector of President and Vice-President, or hold any office, civil or military, under the United States, or under any State, who, having previously taken an oath as a member of Congress, or as an officer of the United States, or as a member of any State legislature, or as an executive or judicial officer of any State, to support the Constitution of the United States, shall have engaged in insurrection or rebellion against the same, or given aid or comfort to the enemies thereof: But Congress may by a vote of two-thirds of each House, remove such disability.

Section 4. The validity of the public debt of the United States, authorized by law, including debts incurred for payment of pensions and bounties for services in suppressing insurrection or rebellion, shall not be questioned. But neither the United States nor any State shall assume or pay any debt or obligation incurred in aid of insurrection or rebellion against the United States, or any claim for the loss or emancipation of any slave; but all such debts, obligations and claims shall be held illegal and void.

Section 5. The Congress shall have power to enforce, by appropriate legislation, the provisions of this article.

Amendment 15. Section 1. The right of citizens of the United States to vote shall not be denied or abridged by the United States or by any state on account of race, color, or previous condition of servitude.

Section 2. The Congress shall have power to enforce this article by appropriate legislation.

Amendment 16. The Congress shall have power to lay and collect taxes on incomes, from whatever source derived, without apportionment among the several States, and without regard to any census or enumeration.

Amendment 17. The Senate of the United States shall be composed of two Senators from each State, elected by the people thereof, for six years; and each Senator shall have one vote. The electors in each State shall have the qualifications requisite for electors of the most numerous branch of the State legislatures.

When vacancies happen in the representation of any State in the Senate, the executive authority of such State shall issue writs of election to fill such vacancies: *Provided,* That the legislature of any State may empower the executive thereof to make temporary appointments until the people fill the vacancies by election as the legislature may direct.

This amendment shall not be so construed as to affect the election or term of any Senator chosen before it becomes valid as part of the Constitution.

Amendment 18. [Prohibition of manufacture, transportation, or sale of intoxicating Liquors]. Repeal proclaimed 5 December 1933, by amendment 21.

Amendment 19. The right of citizens of the United States to vote shall not be denied or abridged by the United States or by any State on account of sex.

Congress shall have power to enforce this article by appropriate legislation.

Amendment 20. Section 1. The terms of the President and Vice-President shall end at noon on the twentieth day of January, and the terms of Senators and Representatives at noon on the third day of January, of the years in which such terms would have ended if this article had not been ratified; and the terms of their successors shall then begin.

Section 2. The Congress shall assemble at least once in every year, and such meeting shall begin at noon on the third day of January, unless they shall by law appoint a different day.

Section 3. If, at the time fixed for the beginning of the term of the President, the President elect shall have died, the Vice President elect shall become President. If a President shall not have been chosen before the time fixed for the beginning of his term, or if the President elect shall have failed to qualify, then the Vice President elect shall act as President until a President shall have qualified; and the Congress may by law provide for the case wherein neither a President elect nor a Vice President elect shall have qualified, declaring who shall then act as President, or the manner in which one who is to act shall be selected, and such person shall act accordingly until a President or Vice President shall have qualified.

Section 4. The Congress may by law provide for the case of the death of any of the persons from whom the House of Representatives may choose a President whenever the right of choice shall have devolved upon them, and for the case of the death of any of the persons from whom the Senate may choose a Vice President whenever the right of choice shall have devolved upon them.... (Temporary measures omitted).

Amendment 21. Section 1. The eighteenth article of amendment to the Constitution of the United States is hereby repealed.

Section 2. The transportation or importation into any State, Territory, or possession of the United States for delivery or use therein of intoxicating liquors, in violation of the laws thereof, is hereby prohibited.... (Temporary measures omitted).

Amendment 22. Section 1. No person shall be elected to the office of the President more than twice, and no person who has held the office of President, or acted as President, for more than two years of a term to which some other person was elected President shall be elected to the office of the President more than once. But this Article shall not apply to any person holding the office of President when this Article was proposed by the Congress, and shall not prevent any person who may be holding the office of President, or acting as President, during the term within which this Article becomes operative from holding the office of President or acting as President during the remainder of such term.... [Temporary measures [Section 2] omitted].

Amendment 23. The District [of Columbia] constituting the seat of Government of the United States shall appoint in such manner as the Congress may direct:

A number of electors of President and Vice President equal to the whole number of Senators and Representatives in Congress to which the District would be entitled if it were a State, but in no event more than the least populous State; they shall be in addition to those appointed by the States, but they shall be considered, for the purposes of the election of President and Vice President, to be electors appointed by a State; and they shall meet in the District and perform such duties as provided by the twelfth article of amendment.

Section 2. The Congress shall have power to enforce this article by appropriate legislation.

Amendment 24. Section 1. The right of citizens of the United States to vote in any primary or other election for President or Vice President, for electors for President or Vice President, or for Senator or Representative in Congress shall not be denied or abridged by the United States or any State by reason of failure to pay any poll tax or other tax.

Section 2. The Congress shall have power to enforce this article by appropriate legislation.

Amendment 25. Section 1. In case of the removal of the

President from office or of his death or resignation, the Vice President shall become President.

Section 2. Whenever there is a vacancy of Vice President, the President shall nominate a Vice President who shall take office upon confirmation by a majority vote of both houses of Congress.

Section 3. Whenever the President transmits to President pro tempore of the Senate and the Speaker of the House of Representatives his written declaration that he is unable to discharge the powers and duties of his office, and until he transmits to them a written declaration to the contrary, such powers and duties shall be discharged by the Vice President as Acting President.

Section 4. Whenever the Vice President and a majority of either the principal officers of the executive departments or of such other body as Congress may by law provide, transmit to the President pro tempore of the Senate and the Speaker of the House of Representatives their written declaration that the President is unable to discharge the powers and duties of his office, the Vice President shall immediately assume the powers and duties of the office as Acting President.

Thereafter, when the President transmits to the President pro tempore of the Senate and the Speaker of the House of Representatives his written declaration that no inability exists, he shall resume the powers and duties of his office, unless the Vice President and a majority of either the principal officers of the executive departments or such other body as Congress may by law provide transmit within four days to the President pro tempore of the Senate and the Speaker of the House of Representatives their written declaration that the President is unable to discharge the powers and duties of his office. Thereupon, Congress shall decide the issue, assemblying within forty-eight hours for that purpose if not in session. If the Congress, within twenty-one days after the receipt of the latter written declaration, or if Congress is not in session within twenty-one days after Congress is required to assemble, determines, by a two-thirds vote of both houses that the President is unable to discharge the powers and duties of his office, the Vice President shall continue to discharge the same as Acting President; otherwise, the President shall resume the powers and duties of his office.

Amendment 26. Section 1. The right of citizens of the United States who are 18 years of age or older to vote shall not be denied or abridged by the United States or any state on account of age.

Section 2. The Congress shall have the power to enforce this article by appropriate legislation.

UNITED STATES OF AMERICA: DECLARATION OF INDEPENDENCE (1776).

Adopted unanimously by the Representatives of the United States of America, assembled in Congress on 4 July 1776, the declaration inspired many national and international human rights instruments adopted since that date. The text is as follows:

When in the course of human events, it becomes necessary for one people to dissolve the political bands which have connected them with another, and to assume among the powers of the earth the separate and equal station to which the Laws of Nature and of Nature's God entitle them, a decent respect to the opinions of mankind requires that they should declare the causes which impel them to the separation.

We hold these truths to be self-evident, that all men are created equal, that they are endowed by their Creator with certain unalienable Rights, that among these are Life, Liberty, and the pursuit of Happiness. That to secure these rights, Governments are instituted among Men, deriving their just powers from the consent of the governed. That whenever any Form of Government becomes destructive of these ends, it is the Right of the People to alter or to abolish it, and to institute new Government, laying its foundation on such principles and organizing its powers in such form, as to them shall seem most likely to effect their Safety and Happiness. Prudence, indeed, will dictate that Governments long established should not be changed for light and transient causes; and accordingly all experience hath shown, that mankind are more disposed to suffer, while evils are sufferable, than to right themselves by abolishing the forms to which they are accustomed. But when a long train of abuses and usurpations, pursuing invariably the same Object evinces a design to reduce them under absolute Despotism, it is their right, it is their duty, to throw off such Government, and to provide new Guards for their future security. Such has been the patient sufferance of these Colonies; and such is now the necessity which constrains them to alter their former systems of government. The history of the present King of Great Britain is a history of repeated injuries and usurpations, all having in direct object the establishment of an absolute tyranny over these States. To prove this, let facts be submitted to a candid world.

He has refused his assent to laws, the most wholesome and necessary for the public good.

He had forbidden his Governors to pass laws of immediate and pressing importance, unless suspended in their operation till his assent should be obtained; and when so suspended, he has utterly neglected o attend to them.

He has refused to pass other laws for the accommodation of large districts of people, unless those people would relinquish the right of representation in the legislature, a right inestimable to them and formidable to tyrants only.

He has called together legislative bodies at places unusual, uncomfortable, and distant from the depository of their public records, for the sole purpose of fatiguing them into compliance with his measures.

He has dissolved representative houses repeatedly, for opposing with manly firmness his invasion on the rights of the people.

He has refused for a long time, after such dissolutions, to cause others to be elected; whereby the legislative powers, incapable of annihilation, have returned to the people at large for their exercise; the State remaining in the meantime exposed to all the dangers of invasion from without and convulsions within.

He has endeavoured to prevent the population of these States, for that purpose obstructing the laws for naturalization of foreigners; refusing to pass others to encourage their migration hither, and raising the conditions of new appropriations of lands.

He has obstructed the administration of justice, by refusing his assent to laws for establishing judiciary powers.

He has made judges dependent on his will alone, for the tenure of their offices, and the amount and payment of their salaries.

He has erected a multitude of new offices, and sent

hither swarms of officers to harass our people, and eat out their substance.

He has kept among us, in times of peace, standing armies without the consent of our legislatures.

He has affected to render the military independent of and superior to the civil power.

He has combined with others to subject us to a jurisdiction foreign to our constitution, and unacknowledged by our laws; giving his assent to their acts of pretended legislation:

For quartering large bodies of armed troops among us:

For protecting them, by a mock trial, from punishment for any murders which they should commit on the inhabitants of these States:

For cutting off our trade with all parts of the world:

For imposing taxes on us without our consent:

For depriving us in many cases of the benefits of trial by jury:

For transporting us beyond seas to be tried for pretended offences:

For abolishing the free system of English laws in a neighbouring Province, establishing therein an arbitrary government, and enlarging its boundaries so as to render it at once an example and fit instrument for introducing the same absolute rule into these Colonies:

For taking away our Charters, abolishing our most valuable laws, and altering fundamentally the forms of our governments:

For suspending our own Legislatures, and declaring themselves invested with power to legislate for us in all cases whatsoever.

He has abdicated government here, by declaring us out of his protection and waging war against us.

He has plundered our seas, ravaged our coasts, burnt our towns, and destroyed the lives of our people.

He is at this time transporting large armies of foreign mercenaries to compleat the works of death, desolation, and tyranny, already begun with circumstances of cruelty and perfidy scarcely parallelled in the most barbarous ages, and totally unworthy the head of a civilized nation.

He has constrained our fellow citizens taken captive on the high seas to bear arms against their country, to become the executioners of their friends and brethren, or to fall themselves by their hands.

He has excited domestic insurrections amongst us, and had endeavoured to bring on the inhabitants of our frontiers the merciless Indian savages, whose known rule of warfare is an undistinguished destruction of all ages, sexes, and conditions.

In every stage of these oppressions we have petitioned for redress in the most humble terms: our repeated petitions have been answered only by repeated injury. A prince whose character is thus marked by every act which may define a tyrant, is unfit to be the ruler of a free people.

Nor have we been wanting in attention to our British brethren. We have warned them from time to time of attempts by their Legislature to extend an unwarrantable jurisdiction over us. We have reminded them of the circumstances of our emigration and settlement here. We have appealed to their native justice and magnanimity, and we have conjured them by the ties of our common kindred to disavow these usurpations, which would inevitably interrupt our connections and correspondence. They too have been deaf to the voice of justice and of consanguinity. We must, therefore, acquiesce in the necessity, which de-

nounces our separation, and hold them, as we hold the rest of mankind, enemies in war, in peace friends.

We, therefore, the Representatives of the United States of America, in General Congress assembled, appealing to the Supreme Judge of the world for the rectitude of our intentions, do, in the name, and by authority of the good people of these Colonies, solemnly publish and declare, That these United Colonies are, and of right ought to be Free and Independent States; that they are absolved from all allegiance to the British Crown, and that all political connection between them and the State of Great Britain is and ought to be totally dissolved; and that as Free and Independent States they have full power to levy war, conclude peace, contract alliances, establish commerce, and to do all other acts and things which independent States may of right do. And for the support of this declaration, with a firm reliance on the protection of Divine Providence, we mutually pledge to each other our lives, our fortunes and our sacred honor.

UNITED STATES OF AMERICA: EXECUTION OF JUVENILE OFFENDERS.

The INTER-AMERICAN COMMISSION ON HUMAN RIGHTS, in its annual report for 1986–1987 (OAS doc. OEA/Ser.L/V/II.71, doc. 9 rev. 1, chap. III) set out a series of resolutions regarding specific cases presented to it which the commission had processed in accordance with the applicable legal provisions.

Resolution 3/87 relates to case 9647 (United States), in which the government of the United States of America is alleged to have denied the internationally protected right to life to James Terry Roach and Jay Pinkerton by condemning them to death and executing them for crimes committed while they were under the age of eighteen. The issue presented by the case was the following: Does the absence of a federal prohibition on the execution of juvenile offenders within U.S. domestic law violate the human rights standards applicable to the United States under the Inter-American system?

The commission's conclusion was—by five votes to one—that the United States Government had violated article 1 (right to life) and article 2 (right to equality before the law) of the AMERICAN DECLARATION OF THE RIGHTS AND DUTIES OF MAN in executing James Terry Roach and Jay Pinkerton.

Resolution 3/87, and the dissenting opinion of one member of the commission, are as follows (*Ibid.*, pp. 148–183):

I. Introduction

A. Summary of the Facts and the Petitioners' Complaint. 1. The Petitioners are James Terry Roach and Jay Pinkerton who were sentenced to death and executed in the United States for crimes which they were adjudged to have committed, and which they perpetrated before their eighteenth birthdays.

2. The Petitioners are represented by David Weissbrodt

and Mary McClymont. The American Civil Liberties Union and the International Human Rights Law Group have co-sponsored the complaint. Amnesty International also filed a petition with the Commission alleging that the imminent execution of James Terry Roach, while lawful in the United States, is a violation of international law. Eighteen organizations have communicated to the Commission their support of the complaint.

3. James Terry Roach was convicted of the rape and murder of a fourteen year old girl and the murder of her seventeen year old boyfriend. Roach committed these crimes at the age of seventeen and was sentenced to death in the General Session Court, Richland County, South Carolina on 16 December 1977. Roach petitioned the United States Supreme Court for a writ of certiorari on three separate occasions. All petitions were denied. Roach also exhausted all appeals to the state and federal courts, and on 10 January 1986 he was executed.

4. Jay Pinkerton was convicted of murder and attempted rape which he committed at the age of seventeen. The death sentence was appealed to the Texas Supreme Court which affirmed the trial court's decision. The United States Supreme Court denied Pinkerton's writ of certiorari on 7 October 1985. Pinkerton was executed on 15 May 1986.

5. On 23 February 1987, the U.S. Supreme Court announced that it would decide in its next term the case of *Thompson v. Oklahoma*, thereby, for the first time, taking up the issue of the execution of juvenile offenders. The constitutional issue presented is whether the execution of a juvenile offender violates the U.S. Constitution's prohibition on cruel and unusual punishment.

6. In their complaint to the Commission, the petitioners allege that the United States has violated Article I (right to life), Article VII (special protection of children), and Article XXVI (prohibition against cruel, infamous or unusual punishment) of the American Declaration of the Rights and Duties of Man by executing persons for crimes committed before their eighteenth birthday. The Petitioners allege a violation of their right to life guaranteed under the American Declaration, as informed by customary international law, which prohibits the execution of persons who committed crimes under the age of eighteen.

B. Proceedings Before the Commission. 7. The petition on behalf of James Terry Roach was filed with the Commission on 4 December 1985 and registered as Case N° 9647 (United States). Jay Pinkerton's petition was registered with the Commission on 8 May 1986 following the setting of the date for his execution.

8. In both the case of Roach and of Pinkerton, the Commission cabled the United States Secretary of State, George P. Shultz, and the respective Governor of the Petitioner's state, requesting a stay of execution pending the Commission's examination and decision of Case N° 9647. The Commission stated in each telegram that its request for information did not prejudge the admissibility of the case in accordance with Article 34 of the Commission's Regulations.

9. Petitioner Roach had sought provisional relief measures under Article 29 of the Commission's Regulations. On 12 December 1985, the Chairman of the Commission cabled Secretary of State, George P. Shultz, and South Carolina Governor, Richard W. Riley, requesting a stay of execution pending the Commission's examination of the case. The Chairman stated that granting such a stay of execution would "be in the spirit of major human rights instruments and the universal trend favorable to the abolition of the

death penalty." The Commission also requested that the U.S. Government provide information concerning the Petitioner's complaint.

10. On 23 December 1985 the Executive Secretary of the Commission cabled the United States Government with additional information relating to the date of Roach's execution scheduled for 10 January 1986 and stressed the necessity of receiving a response by that date. The Commission also reiterated its previous request to stay the execution of the Petitioner. Another cable was sent to the Secretary of State with a stay of execution request on 6 January 1986.

11. On 9 January 1986 the U.S. State Department replied. It stated that: "Under the circumstances, with respect to the Commission's request that the execution be stayed pending consideration of the case, the United States is constrained to reply that the matter is now in the hands of authorities for the State of South Carolina and, under the U.S. federal system, there are no domestic legal grounds for executive intervention in the implementation of the sentence."

12. On 9 January 1986 the Secretary General of the Organization of American States cabled an appeal to the Governor of South Carolina to "follow the current tendency of almost all the countries in this hemisphere and to stay the execution."

13. On 9 January 1986, Governor Riley of South Carolina responded to the cables requesting a stay of execution by informing the Executive Secretary of his decision not to intervene in the case of James Terry Roach. The Governor stated that he had reviewed the case thoroughly and believed that the case had been "fairly litigated at the trial level and that all of his appeals in the courts have been given full and fair consideration." As a result, he found "no reason to intervene in the judicial process or to grant a request for clemency."

14. On 20 February 1986, the lawyers for the Petitioners filed a brief on Case 9647 with the Commission, setting forth their legal arguments pertaining to the case.

15. On 8 April 1986, the Petitioners requested that additional information compiled by Amnesty International on comparative national laws which proscribe the execution of persons under the age of eighteen around the world be incorporated by reference into the Petitioners' brief.

16. On 26 March 1986, the United States requested an extension of time until 28 August 1986 in order to respond fully to the issues raised by the Petitioners. The Commission at its 67th Session granted the U.S. Government an extension until 1 July 1986 in order to have a draft decision on the case before its next regular session.

17. On 9 May 1986, after having been informed by the Petitioners that Jay Pinkerton was to be executed on 15 May 1986, the Commission cabled the Secretary of State and Governor Mark White of Texas requesting a stay of execution in the case of Jay Pinkerton pending the Commission's examination and decision on Case 9647.

18. The U.S. Government responded on 14 May 1986. It stated that, as in the case of James Terry Roach, "the United States considers that U.S. domestic standards with respect to application of the death penalty are fully consistent with the principles stated in the Declaration," and given the U.S. federal system "there are no domestic legal grounds (. . .) for executive intervention in the implementation of Mr. Pinkerton's sentence." The Governor of Texas did not respond to the Commission's request for a stay of execution.

19. On 15 July 1986, the U.S. Government submitted its brief in response to petitioners' brief.

C. The Final Decision. 20. This final decision was drawn up by the Commission in accordance with Article 53 of the Regulations of the Inter-American Commission on Human Rights. The text of this final decision was adopted by the Commission on 27 March 1987. The following members were present: Gilda Russomano, President; Marco Tulio Bruni Celli; Oliver H. Jackman; Elsa Kelly; and Luis Adolfo Siles.

This final decision is now transmitted to the parties.

Bruce McColm, a U.S. national, chose not to participate in this decision, pursuant to Article 19 of the Commission's Regulations.

Marco Gerardo Monroy Cabra was not present at the Commission on that date.

II. The Facts

21. The facts of the present case are not in dispute between the parties.

22. In the present case, the Petitioners allege that the United States has denied them the internationally protected right to life by condemning them to death and executing them for crimes committed while under the age of eighteen. The issue presented is: Does the absence of a federal prohibition on the execution of juveniles offenders within U.S. domestic law violate the human rights standards applicable to the United States under the inter-American system?

A. James Terry Roach. 23. Petitioner Roach was seventeen Jyears old when he committed the rape and the murder of a fourteen year old girl and the murder of her seventeen year old boyfriend. Evidence revealed that Roach was borderline mentally retarded, with an I.Q. of between 75 and 80 and that he apparently suffered from Huntington's Chorea, an incurable brain disease. The psychological and medical evidence presented at the April 1980 postconviction proceedings suggest Roach actually functioned at the mental age of twelve when the offense was committed. Roach had two codefendants. One was another youth of 16 who turned state's evidence and received life imprisonment. The other was J.C. Shaw, a twenty-two year old adult, who received the death sentence on 11 January 1985. Evidence showed Roach had been under the adult's influence when the offenses were committed.

24. Jurisdiction of the juvenile court in South Carolina is limited to those under seventeen years of age. Therefore, Roach was sentenced to death in adult criminal court in pursuance of South Carolina's death penalty statute which follows the Georgia statute upheld by the Supreme Court in *Gregg v. Georgia,* 428 U.S. 153 (1976). The South Carolina death penalty statute provides for a bifurcated trial which first considers the guilt or innocence of the defendant, and then upon conviction, a separate sentencing proceeding is conducted to determine whether the defendant is to be sentenced to life imprisonment or death. Roach pleaded guilty to the charges. At the sentencing hearing, the judge heard additional mitigating and aggravating evidence. At least one aggravating circumstance must be found beyond a reasonable doubt before the death sentence may be imposed. South Carolina law has seven statutory aggravating circumstances and nine statutory mitigating circumstances. Among the mitigating factors is that, "The defendant was below the age of 18 at the time of the crime." S.C. Code, 16-3-20 (C)(b)(9).

25. In considering the mitigating factors in the Roach case, the sentencing judge found that Roach had been under the domination of an adult during the commission of the crime. The judge also found that Roach's capacity to conform his conduct to the requirements of the law was substantially impaired, and that he was under the influence of extreme mental or emotional disturbance as he and his codefendants were "shooting up" drugs and drinking beer before the offense. Another mitigating factor was that Roach had no significant history of prior criminal activity involving the use of violence against another. Roach's mental retardation, anti-social personality disorder, and the fact that he was below the age of 18 at the time of the crime, were also considered by the judge in Roach's sentencing. *Roach v. Martin,* 757 F.2d 1463, 1468-69 (1985).

26. Nevertheless, the sentencing judge also found beyond a reasonable doubt three statutory aggravating circumstances: murder committed while in the commission of rape, murder committed while in the commission of kidnapping, and murder committed while in the commission of robbery. S.C. Code 16-3-20 (C)(a)(1)(a), (c), (e). The judge found the evidence in the case warranted the imposition of the death penalty after weighing both mitigating and aggravating circumstances.

27. This sentence was upheld on direct appeal by the South Carolina Supreme Court. *State v. Shaw (and Roach),* 255 S.E. 2d 799, (1979). (First capital case reviewed under the current death penalty statutes) South Carolina law provides for a mandatory review in the imposition of the death penalty. Roach was later denied post conviction relief by the state trial court and the appeal of this was denied by the State Supreme Court of South Carolina. *Roach v. State,* Memo Op. N° 81-MO-197 (S.C. July 17, 1981).

28. Petitioner also sought review of his case from the United States Supreme Court. He challenged as unconstitutional, among other issues, the imposition of the death penalty as being grossly disproportionate and offensive to contemporary standards of decency due to, among other factors, his age when the crime was committed. However, the Supreme Court denied the writ of certiorari. *Roach v. State,* 444 U.S. 1026, *reh'g denied* 444 U.S. 1104 (1980). He again raised the same issue of his age, as being one factor which resulted in the unconstitutionality of the imposition of the death penalty, in another petition for certiorari. This was denied on 25 January 1982. *Roach v. South Carolina,* 455 U.S. 927 (1982).

29. Roach brought a petition for a writ of habeas corpus in the U.S. District Court of South Carolina. This request was also denied. *Roach v. Martin,* Civil Action N° 81-1907-14 (May 11, 1984). He appealed this denial, raising again the issue of his age as being a factor prohibiting the imposition of the death penalty. The U.S. Court of Appeals for the Fourth Circuit affirmed the district courts denial of the writ. *Roach v. Martin,* 757 F.2d 1463 (4th Cir. 1983). His final appeal to the United States Supreme Court was denied on 7 October 1985, and the petition for rehearing was denied on 2 December 1985. See, *Roach v. Aiken,* N° 85-6155 (A-531). Petitioner Roach was executed in Columbia, South Carolina on 10 January 1986.

B. Jay Pinkerton. 30. Petitioner Pinkerton was found guilty of murder in the course of burglary with the intent to commit rape. The crime was committed when he was seventeen years old. Petitioner at seventeen was also beyond the age limit of the jurisdiction of Texas juvenile courts (age 17) and was tried as an adult. He was sentenced to death in accordance with the Texas capital punishment statute which had been upheld by the Supreme Court. *Jurek v. Texas,* 428 U.S. 262 (1976).

31. The Texas death penalty statute currently provides for the imposition of the death sentence only for capital murders. A capital murder is the intentional or knowing killing of a person accompanied by one of five listed aggravating factors. These factors focus on the identity of the victim and the dangerousness of the actor's conduct. Pinkerton was convicted of intentionally committing murder in the course of committing burglary which is one of the statutory aggravating factors defining capital murder. Tex. Code Crim. Proc. Ann., art. 19.03 (a)(2).

32. Conviction of capital murder results in either a mandatory death sentence or life imprisonment. The jury at the sentencing hearing must find beyond a reasonable doubt that (1) the actor killed intentionally or knowingly; (2) he will probably commit other crimes of violence if not executed; and (3) the killing was unreasonable in response to the provocation, if any, of the deceased. To warrant the death sentence all twelve jury members must answer each of these issues affirmatively. The Supreme Court of the United States upheld this Texas statute in *Jurek v. Texas,* 428 U.S. 262 (1976), finding that the second question is interpreted to allow the defendant to bring to the jury's attention whatever mitigating circumstances he may be able to show. *Id.* at 272. Therefore, although the statute does not specify age, this may be taken into consideration at the sentencing hearing. Texas law prohibits the imposition of the death penalty on anyone younger than seventeen when the capital felony was committed. Texas C.C.P., 8.07(e).

33. Pinkerton's statutorily provided review was taken to the Court of Criminal Appeals where his conviction and sentence were affirmed. Subsequent federal and state appeals were denied. The United States Supreme Court denied certiorari on 7 October 1985. *Pinkerton v. McCotter,* 88 L.Ed. 2d 158 (1985). Jay Pinkerton was executed by the State of Texas on 15 May 1986.

III. Submissions of the Parties

A. The Petitioners. 34. The Petitioners allege that the imposition of the death penalty on James Terry Roach and Jay Pinkerton by United States courts for crimes committed before their eighteenth birthday violated the American Declaration of the Rights and Duties of Man. Specifically, Petitioners allege violations of Article I (right to life), Article VII (special protection of children), and Article XXVI (cruel, infamous or unusual punishment) of the American Declaration as informed by customary international law which prohibits the imposition of the death penalty for crimes committed by juveniles under eighteen.

35. The Petitioners state that the United States is subject to the jurisdiction of the Commission as a member States of the Organization of American States and is obligated, therefore, to observe the enumerated rights in the American Declaration.

36. The Petitioners' case meets the admissibility requirements of Article 37 of the Commission's Regulations as the Petitioners have exhausted all domestic remedies. United States courts, both federal and state, have failed to address Petitioners' claims that the imposition of the death penalty on juvenile offenders is constitutionally prohibited.

37. The Petitioners' complaint may be summarized as follows:

(a) Imposition of the death penalty on juveniles violates the American Declaration as informed by customary international law.

(b) The United States is legally bound by the American Declaration of the Rights and Duties of Man. The American Declaration should be interpreted according to the canons of the Vienna Convention on the Law of Treaties because the Convention represents a world-wide consensus on how international instruments should be construed.

(c) Articles 31 and 32 of the Vienna Convention set out the principal interpretative norms for treaties and other international instruments. According to Article 31 of the Vienna Convention, the terms of the American Declaration should be interpreted in accordance with their ordinary meaning and in light of the object and purpose of the instrument. Construing Articles I, VII and XXVI together and in accordance with their ordinary meaning, and in light of the object and purpose of the Declaration, these articles should be interpreted to prohibit the execution of persons who committed offenses under the age of 18.

(d) The U.S. Government is incorrect in asserting that the rights in the Declaration "must be interpreted in terms of the intentions of the member states at the time of the adoption of the Declaration, not in terms of changing norms of customary international law." This rigid and static approach to the interpretation of the Declaration is in conflict with the terms of the Declaration, the norms of the Vienna Convention, the normal approach which international bodies take to human rights instruments, the practice of the Commission, and the practice of the United States in its own domestic cases. The preamble to the American Declaration states, "The international protection of the rights of man should be the principal guide of an *evolving* American law. . . ." (Emphasis added).

(e) In construing the terms of the American Declaration in light of its object and purpose, the Commission should pay particular attention to Article XXVI which forbids "cruel, infamous or unusual punishment." This is broader than the United States constitutional prohibition against cruel *and* unusual punishment. Juveniles are recognized as lacking in maturity and are most susceptible to various influences and psychological pressure. Killing a young person who has not had the chance to mature to adulthood is the "ultimate cruel punishment," therefore, Article XXVI should be interpreted as a prohibition against the execution of juveniles. Then, on its ordinary meaning and in light of the object and purpose of these articles, the United States is violating the American Declaration by executing juveniles.

(f) Article 31 of the Vienna Convention also looks to "relevant rules of international law" to help interpret treaties. Therefore, the Commission should take into account the customary international law norm prohibiting the execution of juvenile offenders. This prohibition has obtained the status of customary international law. Pursuant to Article 38(1)(b) of the Statute of the International Court of Justice, "international custom, as evidence of a general practice accepted as law" is one of the sources of international law. Treaties are clearly evidence of State practice, especially if accompanied by *opinio juris,* or claims in the treaty or the *travaux préparatoires* indicating that a treaty provision is a restatement of pre-existing customary laws.

(g) The major human rights instruments such as the American Convention on Human Rights (Article 4(5)), the International Covenant on Civil and Political Rights (Article 6(5)), and the Fourth Geneva Convention prohibit the imposition of the death penalty on persons under eighteen years of age.

Article 4(5) of the American Convention reads: "Capital punishment shall not be imposed upon persons who, at the time the crime was committed, were under 18 years of age or over 70 years of age; nor shall it be applied to pregnant women." The fourth Geneva Convention states in Article 68, in relevant part: "In any case, the death penalty may not be pronounced on a protected person who was under eighteen years of age at the time of the offence."

As of January 1, 1986 there are 162 states parties to this Convention, including the United States. This Convention applies to periods of international armed conflict and Article 68 forbids the execution of civilians and military personnel no longer in combat, who committed offenses prior to the age of 18. If nearly all the nations of the world, including the United States, have agreed to such a norm for periods of international armed conflict, the norm protecting juvenile offenders from execution ought to apply with even greater force for periods of peace.

(h) In addition, approximately two-thirds of the nations of the world have either abolished the death penalty or have prohibited it for juveniles by adhering to these human rights instruments. Whereas the European "Convention for the Protection of Human Rights and Fundamental Freedoms" (1950), in Article 2 allowed the death penalty, an evolving abolitionist philosophy is reflected in Protocol N° 6 which states "the death penalty shall be abolished. No one shall be condemned to such penalty or executed."

Petitioners point out that the *travaux préparatoires* of these Conventions demonstrate that these prohibitions against juvenile executions are in fact codifications of customary international law as can be derived from the debates during the drafting of the provisions of these Conventions.

(i) As further evidence of State practice, in terms of actually carrying out the death sentence, Petitioners submit evidence, compiled by Amnesty International, to the effect that since 1979, although 80 nations of the world have executed over 11,000 persons, only six persons who committed offenses under 18 were executed by four nations, including the United States.

In the United States, the laws of various jurisdictions which permit the use of the death penalty nonetheless recognize the uniqueness of juvenile offenders and at least 21 states set a minimum age for imposition of the death penalty. Therefore, although the data is incomplete, available information shows that national laws, as well as the practice of states not to execute minors, further demonstrate the existence of a customary law norm prohibiting execution of offenders who committed capital crimes as juveniles.

(j) The Commission should not rely on the *travaux préparatoires* of the American Declaration as the U.S. Government argues. The United States relies for support on the deletion of language pertaining to capital punishment from the Inter American Juridical Committee's draft. The original Article I reads as follows: "Every person has the right to life, including the fetus (*'los que están por nacer'*) and the terminally ill, the insane, and mentally retarded. Capital punishment shall only be applied in cases in which pre-existing law has established it for exceptionally grave crimes."

The original second sentence of Article I concerning capital punishment was dropped in the subsequent and final drafts. Like the capital punishment language, the latter half of the first sentence was also deleted in subsequent and final drafts. The present version of Article I reads: "Every human being has the right to life, liberty and the security of his person."

The deletion of the capital punishment language can no more by interpreted to infer that the drafters necessarily meant to authorize widely its use than can the deletion of the clause in the first sentence be interpreted to mean that the insane, terminally ill, or mentally retarded were no longer afforded the right to life. Instead, the deletion of the capital punishment language could be read to mean that the drafters were simply unable or unwilling to delineate each and every instance when capital punishment would be prohibited as they did not want to authorize it necessarily in every context.

(k) Finally, there is a limit on any State's ability to regulate a matter, such as capital punishment, if the result will violate international law. Domestic legislation of member states cannot validate conflict with international obligations; a state cannot invoke its contrary domestic law as justification for its failure to abide by an agreement. The United States argument that at the time of the drafting of the Declaration the death penalty was widely practiced and could not generally be considered cruel or unusual is irrelevant. Petitioners argue that "[H]uman rights instruments. . . are drafted to improve the human rights situation and not certainly to reconfirm any alleged right of nature to continue violating human rights."

(1) The petitioners request that the Commission find that the United States has violated the American Declaration, as interpreted in the light of customary international law, by having executed Petitioners Roach and Pinkerton for offenses they committed while under the age of eighteen. Petitioners also request the Commission to recommend that a moratorium be imposed on the execution of other juvenile offenders in the United States.

B. The Government. 38. The U.S. Government considers that the absence of a prohibition on the execution of juvenile offenders within United States domestic law is not inconsistent with human rights standards applicable to the United States. The Commission must look to the American Declaration for the relevant standards as the United States is not a party to the American Convention. The argument may be summarized as follows:

(a) The American Declaration is *silent* on the issue of capital punishment as Article I simply states, "Every human being has the right to life, liberty and the security of his person." From the drafting history of the Declaration, there is evidence that Article I was not meant to affect the legislative discretion of the American states with respect to capital punishment. A Declaration that does not expressly limit the circumstances under which the death penalty may be imposed may not be interpreted as foreclosing the reasonable discretion of the American states to determine for themselves the minimum age at which imposition of the death penalty is appropriate.

(b) The drafters considered and declined to adopt any specific standards on the issue of capital punishment. The reference to capital punishment prohibiting it except for exceptional crimes was deleted in the final draft. The debate surrounding Article I demonstrates that a standard on capital punishment could not be devised due to the diversity of State legislation in the hemisphere. Therefore, the States are able to legislate within their own discretion on the issue of capital punishment.

(c) Only Article I is at issue because if no standard on capital punishment was incorporated into the American

Declaration, then a prohibition against the execution of juveniles could not be "silently subsumed" within the other rights. Article VII on the special protection and care of women and children was not contemplated to extend to juveniles convicted of serious crimes. There is no official record of the drafters' intentions but the use of the word "children" was not meant to refer to juveniles nearing their eighteenth year.

There is also no official record of the drafters' intentions with regard to the prohibition against "cruel, infamous or unusual punishment" of Article XXVI. However, at the time of the drafting the death penalty was widely practiced and therefore, could not be considered cruel or unusual.

None of the three articles of the Declaration cited by petitioners addresses the death penalty or establishes any particular age of majority. The U.S. Government believes that the Declaration is deliberately silent on the issue of capital punishment. Therefore, there purposely is no limitation on the legislative prerogative of the American States regarding the imposition of the death sentence.

(d) The Vienna Convention should not be relied on to interpret the American Declaration as the Declaration is not a treaty and it is not binding on the United States. The U.S. Government does not agree with the Commission's holding in Case N° 2141 (United States) that the Declaration acquired binding force with the adoption of the revised OAS Charter. Res. 23/81, OAS/Ser. L/V/II.52, Doc. 48., Mar. 6, 1981. The Declaration was not drafted with the intent to create legal obligations, therefore the Commission should take special care "where the intentions of the drafters are manifest with respect to any particular article," not to overturn that meaning.

Even assuming the Vienna Convention could be applied to the Declaration, the Petitioners have not shown the "clear meaning" of Articles I, VII, or XXVI. Each is "ambiguous" with respect to the prohibition of the death penalty on juveniles. Therefore, recourse to the *travaux préparatoires* is necessary.

(e) The petitioners request that the Commission look to the American Convention and other international instruments to "interpret" the Declaration as encompassing the standard of Article 4(5). This requires the Commission to go far beyond its interpretative powers. Specific standards in the American Convention, such as the prohibition against the execution of those who committed crimes under eighteen years of age, are binding only on those parties to the Convention. These standards were not accepted by the United States.

(f) The three human rights instruments mentioned by petitioners are irrelevant to the Commission's consideration of the case. The United States is not a party to the International Covenant nor the American Convention, and standards cannot be imposed by "interpretation" on a State which is not a party. See, Case N° 2141 (United States). In addition, the United States delegate at the drafting of the American Convention pointed out that the United States had problems with Article 4(5)'s arbitrary age limit of 18 conflicting with its federal structure.

(g) Petitioners are also incorrect in stating that Article 4(5) of the American Convention is declaratory of customary international law. The age of majority for purposes of imposing the death penalty is not a matter of uniform state practice. Some countries desired a specific age limit while others wanted reference only to "minors" or "juveniles" during the drafting of the International Covenant's

Article 6(5), demonstrating that they were not codifying an already existing binding norm. Instead, this was a specific standard intended to create uniformity where none existed.

At the same time, there is no evidence of *opinio juris*. Even the states which have enacted prohibitions against the execution of those who committed crimes before their eighteenth birthday did not do so out of any sense of legal obligation. Since the American Convention and the International Covenant have been enacted, any changes in state legislation cannot be viewed as evidence of a generally applicable customary rule of law. "Relevant rules of law" must exist apart from any conventional or treaty standards. "Simply because states in the U.S. or other nations have chosen eighteen as the age of majority does not impose an obligation that other states must choose the exact same age."

(h) The U.S. Government does not acknowledge the existence of a customary international law norm which prohibits the execution of juveniles. To establish a norm of customary law there must be "extensive and virtually uniform" state practice and second, evidence of a belief that this practice is rendered obligatory by the existence of a rule of law requiring it. The rule must be recognized as a legal obligation based on the custom or practice of states. In this case, there is neither the uniformity of state practice, nor the required *opinio juris* to regard the standard as a binding norm of customary international law.

(i) The U.S. Government further maintains that it has dissented from such a standard. It abstained from participating in the debate and vote on the draft International Covenant, and submitted it to the U.S. Senate with reservations. The United States also opposed Article 4(5) of the American Convention, and when President Carter signed the American Convention he proposed the Senate advice and consent to ratification of the treaty be accompanied by a reservation stating that "United States adherence to Article 4 is subject to the Constitution and other law of the United States." *Four Treaties Pertaining to Human Rights, Message from the President of the United States*, S. Doc. N° Exec. C, D, E, 8F, at xii, 95th Cong., 2d Sess (1978).

The U.S. Government concludes its brief by stating that "There is no basis in international law for applying to the United States a standard taken from treaties to which it is not a party and which it has indicated it will not accept when it becomes a treaty."

(j) The U.S. Government requests the Commission to hold that the recent executions are not inconsistent with the American Declaration.

IV. Admissibility

39. In denying Roach's and Pinkerton's appeals for a writ of certiorari, the U.S. Supreme Court deliberately decided not to review the issue of the constitutionality of the execution of juvenile offenders. As pointed out in Petitioners' brief, Justice Brennan in his dissent stated that the Roach case afforded "an opportunity to address the important question whether an accused may . . . be sentenced to death for a capital offense he committed while a juvenile." Since the U.S. Supreme Court chose not to address the question the Commission finds that the Petitioners had no further domestic remedies to exhaust.

40. In spite of the fact that the U.S. Supreme Court has not addressed the issue of the constitutionality of applying the death penalty to juvenile offenders, it has established certain trial and sentencing standards for state death pen-

alty cases. A review of the evolution of these Supreme Court standards is relevant here.

A. The United States Supreme Court and the Death Penalty. 41. In the United States, since the 19th century the courts have moved away from mandatory death sentences, as such a system fails to take into account the individual and his circumstances. However, by 1972 the United States Supreme Court found that the courts had moved so far from a mandatory system that unlimited discretion had been given to the judge or jury to decide who received the death penalty. In *Furman v. Georgia,* 408 U.S. 238 (1972), the Court held that such unguided discretion created arbitrary and capricious imposition of the death penalty in violation of the Eighth Amendment's prohibition against cruel and unusual punishment. While the *Furman* decision did not hold that the death penalty, *per se,* violates the Eighth Amendment, it, in effect, suspended executions and made federal and state death penalty statutes inoperative until new laws were drafted which would comply with the Constitution in light of *Furman v. Georgia.* The execution of Gary Gilmore on January 17, 1977 was the first execution since June 2, 1967. In the decade since Gilmore there have been more than 60 executions. In the decade 1976–1986 over 3,000 people have been sentenced to death in the United States. Between 1963 and 1985 the U.S. did not execute a criminal who was under the age of 18 at the time of the crime. Since then three have been executed.

After *Furman* many states enacted new death penalty statutes. In 1976, the Court began to examine the post-*Furman* statutes and in *Gregg v. Georgia,* 428 U.S. 153 (1976), it addresses the question avoided in *Furman,* namely, is the imposition of the death penalty *per se* unconstitutional? The Court in *Gregg* stated that it was not unconstitutional, and began to set out guidelines for imposition of the death penalty.

(a) The U.S. Supreme Court held in *Gregg v. Georgia* that the Eighth Amendment, which has been interpreted in a flexible manner to accord with "evolving standards of decency," prohibits the death penalty if it is grossly disproportionate to the crime or if it is imposed arbitrarily or capriciously. The Court, however, upheld the Georgia statute in *Gregg* because it was carefully drafted to ensure that the sentencing authority was given adequate information and guidance. The Georgia statute provides for a bifurcated trial in which the jury first determines the defendant's guilt or innocence. At the sentencing hearing, the jury then considers any mitigating and/or aggravating circumstances in the case. Before the death penalty could be imposed the jury had to find that one or more statutory aggravating factors existed beyond a reasonable doubt and that such factors were not outweighed by mitigating factors.

(b) In two companion cases, the Court upheld the death penalty statutes of Florida and Texas which provide that the judge or the jury is given specific and detailed guidance to assist them in deciding whether to impose the death sentence or life imprisonment. *Proffit v. Florida,* 428 U.S. 242 (1976); *Jurek v. Texas,* 428 U.S. 262 (1976). Each statute guides and focuses the sentencing authority's objective consideration of the particular circumstances of the offense and the offender.

(c) The standards necessary to guide the jury or judge in sentencing have focused on the nature and circumstances of the crime and the character and record of the defendant. Aggravating circumstances may include such issues as whether the murder was committed by a convict or if the murder was atrocious or heinous. Special attention

has been given by the Supreme Court to the mitigating factors. In *Lockett v. Ohio,* 438 U.S. 586 (1978), the Court struck down the Ohio death penalty statute which only specified three factors to be considered in the mitigation of the defendant's sentence. The Court found that the Eighth and Fourteenth Amendments require that the sentencer, "not be precluded from considering as a mitigating factor, any aspect of the defendant's record or character and any of the circumstances of the offense. . . ." *Id.* at 604. In that case, the sentencing judge had been precluded by the Ohio statute from considering as mitigating factors: the defendant's lack of a prior criminal record; the fact that she was twenty-one; her lack of specific intent to cause death; and her relatively minor part in the crime.

(d) In *Eddings v. Oklahoma,* 455 U.S. 104 (1982), the Court added that the states must consider the background and mental and emotional development of the defendant as mitigating factors. The defendant in *Eddings* had committed a murder at the age of sixteen. The Court had granted the writ of certiorari on the question of whether, in the light of contemporary standards, the Eighth Amendment forbids the execution of a defendant who was under eighteen at the time of the offense. The Court, however, declined to address that issue. It decided the case instead in light of *Lockett v. Ohio,* vacating the death sentence because it had been imposed without the type of individualized consideration of mitigating factors required by the Constitution. The Court's reversal of the death sentence evidences the importance the Court attaches to mitigating evidence in determining fair and just sentencing. The trial judge had refused to take into account the defendant's unhappy childhood and unique emotional disturbances. The Court's consideration of the mitigating evidence in the case emphasized the defendant's youth, his "serious emotional problems," his severe lack of the "care, concern and paternal attention that children deserve," and his "neglectful, sometimes even violent, family background."

B. The Juvenile Justice System in the United States. 42. The U.S. criminal justice system, since the beginning of the twentieth century, has treated children differently than adults. Reformers in the U.S. wished to abolish the harsh adult procedures and sentences applied to children who had committed crimes. The belief was that children should be treated and rehabilitated and therefore should not be subjected to the "harshness" and "rigidity" of the adult criminal law. (See, *In re Gault,* 387 U.S. 1, 15–16 (1967).)

(a) Every state in the United States has juvenile courts. The maximum age over which a juvenile court has jurisdiction is set by the state legislature. The age limits vary for juvenile jurisdiction, but most states set the limit between sixteen and eighteen. The focus in juvenile court is on the child's condition, not his guilt. Therefore, the purpose of a separate juvenile justice system is to rehabilitate children and to make social services available to help them. Punishment in juvenile court is not stressed; the maximum sentence which can be imposed is institutional confinement until the child reaches twenty-one years of age.

(b) Sometimes a juvenile court may have jurisdiction but it may waive its right to hear a case. The case is then brought before an adult criminal court. In some states the prosecutor may have the discretion of choosing which court to file in, but in most states the juvenile judge has the discretion of deciding whether to transfer a case or not. In some cases the juvenile may benefit from being transferred to criminal court. He is entitled to all the constitutional protections of an adult, such as the right to a jury trial and perhaps the ability to post bond if the jurisdiction provides such measures. Juries may be more sympathetic to a youth in criminal court. Nevertheless, because transfer to criminal court subjects the accused juvenile to adult punishments, the transfer process has been recognized as a critically important stage in juvenile court proceedings. (See, *Kent v. United States,* 383 U.S. 541 (1966).)

(c) There is little statutory guidance as to which children should be transferred for trial in adult criminal court. The juvenile court judge is given a great deal of discretion in determining who stays within the family court's jurisdiction. Since *Kent,* many states have adopted objective criteria by statute to be used in waiving juvenile jurisdiction. The two most common criteria used are the age of the youth and the nature of the offense.

(d) Many states set a minimum age at which a child cannot be transferred out of juvenile court jurisdiction. The exact age limit varies from state to state, from 13 years of age in Mississippi to 16 years in California.

(e) The nature of the alleged offense and the accused's prior history of criminal activity are also often used at a transfer hearing. For extremely serious crimes such as murder, rape and aggravated assault, states will rarely retain juvenile court jurisdiction. Such crimes are often used as objective criteria to determine that the child is not amenable to treatment within the juvenile system. Some states allow only for discretionary transfer if the juvenile is accused of a felony (e.g., Colorado). Other states such as Pennsylvania and Massachusetts have mandatory transfer provisions which are triggered if a child over fourteen years has allegedly committed murder.

(f) Some U.S. states have no death penalty laws in force, others prohibit the death penalty for juveniles. Fourteen states as of 1985, specifically mention age as a mitigating factor in their death penalty statutes. Indiana, however, allows for the transfer of a 10 year old in certain cases to adult criminal court. Indiana does not specify age as a mitigating factor in its death penalty statute, but it may be considered under "any other circumstances appropriate for consideration." Ind. Code Ann. 35-50-2-9. Therefore, in Indiana it is possible that a ten year old could receive the death penalty and be executed.

V. Opinion of the Commission

A. Point at Issue. 43. The question presented by the petitioners in the present case is whether the absence of a federal prohibition within U.S. domestic law on the execution of persons who committed serious crimes under the age of 18 is inconsistent with human rights standards applicable to the United States under the inter-American system.

Crimes in the United States fall under either state or federal jurisdiction. A defendant may be tried in federal court if he is charged with the commission of a crime under federal law, or he may appeal to a federal court from a state court under certain circumstances. A great deal of autonomy has been left to the states in prescribing the appropriate punishment for criminal conduct. However, all punishment must be in conformity with the United States Constitution as interpreted by the Supreme Court.

B. The International Obligation of the United States Under the American Declaration. 44. The American Declaration is silent on the issue of capital punishment. Article I of the American Declaration reads as follows: "Every human being has the right to life, liberty and the security of his person."

45. The American Convention on Human Rights, on the other hand, refers specifically to capital punishment in five of its provisions. Article 4 of the American Convention, which protects the right to life, reads as follows: *"Article 4. Right to Life.* 1. Every person has the right to have his life respected. This right shall be protected by law and, in general, from the moment of conception. No one shall be arbitrarily deprived of his life."

2. In countries that have not abolished the death penalty, it may be imposed only for the most serious crimes and pursuant to a final judgment rendered by a competent court and in accordance with a law establishing such punishment, enacted prior to the commission of the crime. The application of such punishment shall not be extended to crimes to which it does not presently apply.

3. The death penalty shall not be reestablished in states that have abolished it.

4. In no case shall capital punishment be inflicted for political offenses or related common crimes.

5. Capital punishment shall not be imposed upon persons who, at the time the crime was committed, were under 18 years of age or over 70 years of age; nor shall it be applied to pregnant women.

6. Every person condemned to death shall have the right to apply for amnesty, pardon, or commutation of sentence, which may be granted in all cases. Capital punishment shall not be imposed while such a petition is pending decision by the competent authority.

46. The international obligation of the United States of America, as a member of the Organization of American States (OAS), under the jurisdiction of the Inter-American Commission on Human Rights is governed by the Charter of the OAS (Bogotá, 1948), as amended by the Protocol of Buenos Aires on 27 February 1967, ratified by the United States on 23 April 1968.

47. The United States is a member State of the Organization of American States, but is not a State party to the American Convention on Human Rights, and, therefore, cannot be found to be in violation of Article 4(5) of the Convention, since as the Commission stated in *Case 2141* (United States), para. 31: "it would be impossible to impose upon the United States Government or that of any other State member of the OAS, by means of 'interpretation,' an international obligation based upon a treaty that such State has not duly accepted or ratified."

48. As a consequence of articles 3 *j*, 16, 51 *e*, 112 and 150 of the Charter, the provisions of other instruments of the OAS on human rights acquired binding force. Those instruments, approved with the vote of the U.S. Government, are the following: American Declaration of the Rights and Duties of Man (Bogotá, 1948) and the Statute and Regulations of the IACHR

49. The Statute provides that, for the purpose of such instruments, the IACHR is the organ of the OAS entrusted with the competence to promote the observance of and respect for human rights. For the purpose of the Statute, human rights are understood to be the rights set forth in the American Declaration in relation to States not parties to the American Convention on Human Rights (San José, 1969).

C. The Petitioners' Argument. 50. The central violation denounced in the petition concerns a violation of the right to life, Article I of the Declaration, which states: "Every human being has the right to life . . ." Since the Declaration is silent on the issue of capital punishment, Petitioners, in connection with Article I, seek an affirmative response to the question: Is there a norm of customary international law which prohibits the imposition of the death penalty on persons who committed capital crimes before completing eighteen years of age?

51. The elements of a norm of customary international law are the following:

(a) a concordant practice by a number of states with reference to a type of situation falling within the domain of international relations;

(b) a continuation or repetition of the practice over a considerable period of time;

(c) a conception that the practice is required by or consistent with prevailing international law; and

(d) general acquiescence in the practice by other states.

52. The evidence of a customary rule of international law requires evidence of widespread state practice. Article 38 of the Statute of the International Court of Justice (I.C.J.) defines "international custom, as evidence of a general practice accepted as law." The customary rule, however, does not bind States which protest the norm.

In the *Fisheries Case* (United Kingdom v. Norway) the I.C.J. found that although the ". . . ten-mile rule has been adopted by certain States both in their national law and in their treaties and conventions, and although certain arbitral decisions have applied it as between these States, other States have adopted a different limit. Consequently, the ten-mile rule has not acquired the authority of a general rule of law."

How many states need to engage in the state practice for it to acquire the authority of a customary norm has never been definitively established, but it is clear that while a universal practice is not necessary, the practice must be common and widespread.

53. The U.S. Government, in December 1977, transmitted the American Convention on Human Rights, *inter alia,* to the U.S. Senate for advice and consent to ratification subject to specified reservations. As regards the issue in question, the U.S. Government proposed reservations to Articles 4 and 5 which were presented as follows:

Article 4 deals with the right to life generally, and includes provisions on capital punishment. Many of the provisions of Article 4 are not in accord with United States law and policy, or deal with matters in which the law is unsettled. The Senate may wish to enter a reservation as follows: "United States adherence to Article 4 is subject to the Constitution and other law of the United States."

[Article (5)], [p]aragraph 5 requires that minors subject to criminal proceedings are to be separated from adults and brought before specialized tribunals as speedily as possible. (. . .) With respect to paragraph (5), the law reserves the right to try minors as adults in certain cases and there is no present intent to revise these laws. The following statement is recommended: "The United States (. . .) with respect to paragraph (5), reserves the right in appropriate cases to subject minors to procedures and penalties applicable to adults."

54. Since the United States has protested the norm, it would not be applicable to the United States should it be held to exist. For a norm of customary international law to be binding on a State which has protested the norm, it must have acquired the status of *jus cogens*. Petitioners do not argue that a rule prohibiting the execution of juvenile offenders has acquired the authority of *jus cogens*, a peremptory norm of international law from which no derogation is permitted. The Commission, however, is not a judicial body

and is not limited to considering only the submissions presented by the parties to a dispute.

D. General Principles applicable to the Present Case. 55. The concept of *jus cogens* is derived from ancient law concepts of a "superior order" of legal norms, which the laws of man or nations may not contravene. The norms of *jus cogens* have been described by publicists as comprising "international public policy." They are "rules which have been accepted, either expressly by treaty or tacitly by custom, as being necessary to protect the public interest of the society of States or to maintain the standards of public morality recognized by them."

According to Ian Brownlie, the major distinguishing feature of rules of *jus cogens* is their "relative indelibility." Brownlie suggests certain examples of *jus cogens* such as: "the prohibition of aggressive war, the law of genocide, the principle of racial non-discrimination, crimes against humanity, and the rules prohibiting trade in slaves and piracy."

Since the acceptance of norms of *jus cogens* is still subject to some debate in some sectors, it might be argued that the International Court of Justice did not consider the prohibition against genocide, for example, to be a norm of *jus cogens*. It has been argued, however, that the World Court has made "indirect references" to the concept of *jus cogens*, without actually calling it such by name, in the advisory opinion on the *Reservations to the Genocide Convention* case, in which the Court stated: ". . . that the principles underlying the Convention are principles which are recognized by civilized nations as binding on States, even without any conventional obligation."

The rule prohibiting genocide would be binding on States not parties to the Genocide Convention, even if derived only from customary international law, without having acquired the status of *jus cogens*, but it achieves the status of *jus cogens* precisely because it is the kind of rule that it would shock the conscience of mankind and the standards of public morality for a State to protest.

The International Court of Justice, in a later case, categorized the prohibition of genocide as an obligation *erga omnes*. Whereas the ICJ does not make reference to the concept *jus cogens*, it has been suggested that the examples given of obligations *erga omnes* are examples of what the ICJ would consider to be norms of *jus cogens*. The following distinction between obligations of a State vis-à-vis the international community *(erga omnes)* and vis-à-vis another State is taken from the judgment in the *Barcelona Traction* case:

"In these circumstances it is logical that the Court should first address itself to what was originally presented as the subject-matter of the third preliminary objection: namely the question of the right of Belgium to exercise diplomatic protection of Belgian shareholders in a company which is a juristic entity incorporated in Canada, the measures complained of having been taken in relation not to any Belgian national but to the company itself.

"When a State admits into its territory foreign investments or foreign nationals, whether natural or juristic persons, it is bound to extend to them the protection of the law and assumes obligations concerning the treatment to be afforded them. These obligations, however, are neither absolute nor unqualified. In particular, an essential distinction should be drawn between the obligations of a State towards the international community as a whole, and those arising vis-à-vis another State in the field of diplomatic protection. By their very nature the former are the concern of all States. In view of the importance of the rights involved, all States can be held to have a legal interest in their protection; they are obligations *erga omnes*.

"Such obligations derive, for example, in contemporary international law, from the outlawing of acts of aggression, and of genocide, as also from the principles and rules concerning the basic rights of the human person, including protection from slavery and racial discrimination. Some of the corresponding rights of protection have entered into the body of general international law *(Reservations to the Convention on the Prevention and Punishment of the Crime of Genocide,* Advisory Opinion, I.C.J. Reports 1951, p. 23); others are conferred by international instruments of a universal or quasi-universal character.

"Obligations the performance of which is the subject of diplomatic protection are not of the same category."

As to whether "the principles and rules concerning the basic rights of the human person" is intended to mean that all codified human rights provisions contained in international treaties are embraced by the concept of *jus cogens* is an issue that is both controversial and beyond the scope of the matter presented for the Commission to decide.

56. The Commission finds that in the member States of the OAS there is recognized a norm of *jus cogens* which prohibits the State execution of children. This norm is accepted by all the States of the inter-American system, including the United States. The response of the U.S. Government to the petition in this case affirms that "[A]ll states, moreover, have juvenile justice systems; none permits its juvenile courts to impose the death penalty."

57. The Commission finds that this case arises, not because of doubt concerning the existence of an international norm as to the prohibition of the execution of children but because the United States disputes the allegation that there exists consensus as regards the age of majority. Specifically, what needs to be examined is the United States law and practice, as adopted by different states, to transfer adolescents charged with heinous crimes to adult criminal courts where they are tried and may be sentenced as adults.

58. Since the federal Government of the United States has not preempted this issue, under the U.S. constitutional system the individual states are free to exercise their discretion as to whether or not to allow capital punishment in their states and to determine the minimum age at which a juvenile may be transferred to an adult criminal court where the death penalty may be imposed. Thirteen states and the U.S. capital have abolished the death penalty entirely. As regards the other states which have enacted death penalty statutes since the *Furman* decision, these states have adopted death penalty statutes which either 1) prohibit the execution of persons who committed capital crimes under the age of eighteen, or 2) allow for juveniles to be transferred to adult criminal courts where they may be sentenced to the death penalty. It is the discretion and practice of this second group of states which has become the subject of our analysis. Whereas approximately ten retentionist states have now enacted legislation barring the execution of under-18 offenders, a hodge-podge of legislation characterizes the other states which allow transfer of juvenile offenders to adult courts from age 17 to as young as age 10, and some states have no specific minimum age. The Indiana state statute *(supra)* which allows a ten year old to be judged before an adult criminal court and potentially sentenced to death shocks this Commission.

59. The juvenile justice system was established in the United States at the turn of the century as a result of reformist efforts to mitigate the harshness of the adult criminal justice system. Under common law, children under the age of seven were conclusively presumed to have no criminal capacity and for children from age seven to fourteen, the presumption was rebuttable and the child could be convicted of a crime and executed. By a long series of statutory changes this age has been steadily increased, and the age of criminal incapacity is now set at 14 in most states. Consequently a child below the statutory age may be prosecuted by an adult criminal court but would not be adjudged responsible for a crime, the child would be adjudged a juvenile delinquent.

60. The Commission is convinced by the U.S. Government's argument that there does not now exist a norm of customary international law establishing 18 to be the minimum age for imposition of the death penalty. Nonetheless, in light of the increasing numbers of States which are ratifying the American Convention on Human Rights and the United Nations Covenant on Civil and Political Rights, and modifying their domestic legislation in conformity with these instruments, the norm is emerging. As mentioned above, thirteen states and the U.S. capital have abolished the death penalty entirely and nine retentionist states have abolished it for offenders under the age of 18.

61. The Commission, however, does not find the age question dispositive of the issue before it, which is whether the absence of a federal prohibition within U.S. domestic law on the execution of juveniles, who committed serious crimes under the age of 18, is in violation of the American Declaration.

62. The Commission finds that the diversity of state practice in the U.S.—reflected in the fact that some states have abolished the death penalty, while others allow a potential threshold limit of applicability as low as 10 years of age—results in very different sentences for the commission of the same crime. The deprivation by the State of an offender's life should not be made subject to the fortuitous element of where the crime took place. Under the present system of laws in the United States, a hypothetical sixteen year old who commits a capital offense in Virginia may potentially be subject to the death penalty, whereas if the same individual commits the same offense on the other side of the Memorial Bridge, in Washington, D.C., where the death penalty has been abolished for adults as well as for juveniles, the sentence will not be death.

63. For the federal Government of the United States to leave the issue of the application of the death penalty to juveniles to the discretion of state officials results in a patchwork scheme of legislation which makes the severity of the punishment dependent not, primarily, on the nature of the crime committed, but on the location where it was committed. Ceding to state legislatures the determination of whether a juvenile may be executed is not of the same category as granting states the discretion to determine the age of majority for purposes of purchasing alcoholic beverages or consenting to matrimony. The failure of the federal government to preempt the states as regards this most fundamental right—the right to life—results in a pattern of legislative arbitrariness throughout the United States which results in the arbitrary deprivation of life and inequality before the law, contrary to Articles I and II of the American Declaration of the Rights and Duties of Man, respectively.

Conclusion

64. The Commission concludes, by 5 votes to 1, that the United States Government violated Article I (right to life) of the American Declaration of the Rights and Duties of Man in executing James Terry Roach and Jay Pinkerton.

65. The Commission concludes, by 5 votes to 1 that the United States Government violated Article II (right to equality before the law) of the American Declaration of the Rights and Duties of Man in executing James Terry Roach and Jay Pinkerton.

Dissenting Opinion of Dr. Marco Gerardo Monroy Cabra, Member of the Inter-American Commission on Human Rights

Before explaining the reasons for my dissenting opinion, I must first make some general observations. In this Case N° 9647, there is no discussion as regards the facts that are accepted by the United States Government, and which are that James Terry Roach and Jay Pinkerton were sentenced to death and executed in the United States for crimes for which they were tried and which they committed before the age of 18. However, since the United States is not a State Party to the American Convention on Human Rights, Article 20 of the Statute of the Inter-American Commission on Human Rights, approved through Resolution N° 447, applies. That resolution, which was adopted by the OAS General Assembly on October 31, 1979, establishes the following as falling within the competence of the Commission: "b) to examine communications submitted to it and any other available information, to address the government of any member state not a Party to the Convention for information deemed pertinent by this Commission, and to make recommendations to it, when it finds this appropriate, in order to bring about more effective observance of fundamental human rights." With regard to the principle of human rights that should be applied: "2. For the purposes of the present Statute, human rights are understood to be: (a) The rights set forth in the American Convention on Human Rights, in relation to the States parties thereto; (b) *The rights set forth in the American Declaration of the Rights and Duties of Man,* in relation to the other member states." This means that since the United States is not a State Party to the American Convention, the question of whether or not a human rights violation has occurred with respect to the petitioners must be examined in the light of the American Declaration of the Rights and Duties of Man. I should also note that this case was processed in accordance with Chapter III "Petitions concerning States that are not Parties to the American Convention on Human Rights" (Art. 48 through 50) of the current Regulations of the Inter-American Commission on Human Rights, approved by the Commission at its meeting on April 8, 1980 during the 49th regular session.

The task therefore is to determine whether the sentences handed down by the United States courts violated articles 1 and 2 of the American Declaration of the Rights and Duties of Man by imposing the death penalty on persons who committed capital crimes while under 18 years of age. To interpret the 1948 American Declaration of the Rights and Duties of Man, the Inter-American Commission on Human Rights referred, in its majority decision, to customary international law and to *jus cogens.* I must therefore refer to these aspects.

It must, however, be made clear that the aim is not to use this case to determine generally whether or not U.S. laws on the death penalty violate customary international law, since the Commission is not empowered to issue advisory opinions; rather it must only interpret the American Declaration of the Rights and Duties of Man, for which it can refer to general international law. The Commission has said that in this case "the only point at issue is whether the absence of a federal prohibition within U.S. domestic law on the execution of juveniles who committed serious crimes under the age of 18 is inconsistent with human rights standards applicable to the United States under the inter-American system"?. In my view, this is not the problem. The case consists of examining whether or not the human rights of petitioners James Terry Roach and Jay Pinkerton were violated, under the terms of the 1948 American Declaration of the Rights and Duties of Man. This is an individual case that was processed by the Commission according to the Regulations in effect for States not Parties to the American Convention on Human Rights, and therefore, there is no reason to address the matter of compatibility between U.S. federal or state legislation and general international law. This aspect does not lie within the sphere of competence of the Commission, which could not make general observations and recommendations when ruling on a case, especially since it does not have judicial functions.

In light of the foregoing, I wish to explain the legal reasons that influenced my decision not to join in the Commission's majority decision:

1. The U.S. Application of the Death Penalty to Juveniles Does Not Violate the American Declaration of the Rights and Duties of Man. Article 1 of the American Declaration of the Rights and Duties of Man approved by the IX International Conference of American States held in Bogota from March 30 through May 2, 1948, and included in the Final Act of the Conference states: "Every human being has the right to life, liberty and the security of his person." This article makes no reference, either explicitly or implicitly, to prohibition of the death penalty with respect to minors. The draft of the Inter-American Juridical Committee included the following as Article 1: "Every person has the right to life. This right extends to the right to life of incurables, imbeciles and the insane."

"Capital punishment may only be applied in cases in which it has been prescribed by pre-existing law for crimes of exceptional gravity." After discussion, the IX Conference decided to omit any reference to the death penalty and to change the wording proposed by the Inter-American Juridical Committee. Article 1, therefore, was drafted in its present form, making no reference to the death penalty. A close look at the preparatory work leads to the unmistakable conclusion that the States participating in the IX International Conference of American States in Bogota in 1948 did not wish to preclude the death penalty since, otherwise, they would have agreed on its prohibition and, consequently, approved the text by the Inter-American Juridical Committee, which confined its application to crimes of exceptional gravity. An interpretation of Article 1 in the light of its current meaning, while taking into account the preparatory work recorded in the Proceedings of the Conference, the specific deletion of the provision concerning the death penalty would allow one to conclude that the American Declaration of the Rights and Duties of Man did not regulate the matter of the death penalty, and of course, far less did it include any provision on the general or specific proscription of its application in the case of juveniles. One might therefore conclude, with regard to this first aspect, that if the American Declaration of the Rights and Duties of

Man remained silent on the death penalty and did not approve the draft that included it, the United States can establish the death penalty without violating Article 1 or any other standard in the aforecited American Declaration of the Rights and Duties of Man.

2. In this case, it is not possible to apply treaties not in effect for the United States. The United States is a member of the Organization of American States (OAS) since it ratified the OAS Charter amended by the 1967 Protocol of Buenos Aires when it deposited the instrument of ratification on April 23, 1968. As the Charter establishes, the Inter-American Commission on Human Rights is an organ of the OAS. The United States is bound by the Statute and the Regulations of the Inter-American Commission on Human Rights. The United States is also bound by the American Declaration of the Rights and Duties of Man, which as has been seen, does not prohibit the death penalty and remains silent on this matter. But the United States has not ratified the 1969 American Convention on Human Rights, "Pact of San José, Costa Rica", and therefore, is not bound by Article 4.5, which states: "Capital punishment shall not be imposed upon persons who, at the time the crime was committed, were under 18 years of age or over 70 years of age; nor shall it be applied to pregnant women."

In December of 1977, the United States Government sent the American Convention on Human Rights to the Senate for its approval and subsequent ratification. At the same time, it suggested making certain "reservations". With regard to Articles 4 and 5, it proposed the following reservations. "Article 4 deals with the right to life generally, and includes provisions on capital punishment. Many of the provisions of Article 4 are not in accord with United States law and policy, or deal with matters in which the law is still unsettled. The Senate may wish to enter a reservation as follows: 'United States adherence to Article 4 is subject to the Constitution and other law of the United States.' "

Article 5, "[P]aragraph (5) requires that minors subject to criminal proceedings are to be separated from adults and brought before specialized tribunals as speedily as possible." "With respect to paragraph 5, the law reserves the right to try minors as adults in certain cases and there is no present intent to revise these laws. The following statement is recommended: 'The United States . . . with respect to paragraph 5, reserves the right in appropriate cases to subject minors to procedures and penalties applicable to adults' " (United States State Department, publication 8961, General Foreign Policy Series 310, November 1978). This means that articles 4 and 5 cannot be applied to the United States, since it has stated specifically that even if it ratified the Convention, it would make reservations on those provisions.

Treaties do not engender obligations for third states without their consent. The United States Government is therefore not obliged to comply with the provisions of Article 4.5 of the American Convention on Human Rights. Also, the United States has not ratified the International Covenant on Civil and Political Rights, adopted and opened for signature, ratification and accession by the United Nations General Assembly on December 16, 1966 in its resolution 2200 A (XXI), and which entered into effect on March 23, 1976. Under these conditions, the United States is not obliged to comply with the provisions of Article 6.5 of that Covenant, which states: "Sentence of death shall not be imposed for crimes committed by persons below eighteen years of age and shall not be carried out on pregnant women."

The United States is only bound by the Fourth Geneva Convention, which states in its Article 68: "In any case, the death penalty may not be pronounced on a protected person who was under eighteen years of age at the time of the offence." However, this treaty applies only in international conflicts, and therefore, cannot be applied for the execution of juveniles in the United States in times of normalcy and in the absence of an international conflict.

In conclusion, Neither the American Convention on Human Rights (Article 4 [5]), nor the International Covenant on Civil and Political Rights (Art 6 [5]), nor the Fourth Geneva Convention (Art. 68) is applicable to the pronouncement of the death penalty with respect to minors under 18 in the United States.

3. There is no existing rule in customary international law prohibiting the imposition of the death penalty with respect to juveniles. Article 38 of the Statute of the International Court of Justice lists as a source of international law: "(b) international custom, as evidence of a general practice accepted as law". Max Sorensen states the following (Manual of Public International Law, St. Martin's Press, New York, 1968, page 130): "This formula has been criticized often because it reverses the logical order of events; in practice, in order to prove the existence of a customary rule, it is necessary to show that there exists a 'general practice' which conforms to the rule and which is 'accepted as law'. Custom is the direct product of the necessities of international life. It arises when states acquire the habit of adopting, with respect to a given situation, and whenever that situation recurs, a given attitude to which legal significance is attributed."

Ch. Rousseau, Professor of international law (Derecho Internacional Público Profundizado, La Ley, Buenos Aires, 1966, pages 96–97) lists three characteristics of custom: "a) It is above all the expression of a common practice, resulting from precedents, in other words, from the repetition of conclusive acts; b) Second, custom presents itself as an obligatory practice, that is to say, it must be accepted as law, as corresponding to a legal need. In the absence of this psychological element, there would be no customary rule but rather a purely nonbinding custom or practice of international courtesy; c) Finally, international custom is a practice that evolves".

A generalized and uniform practice does not suffice; of vital importance is the *opinio juris*. In the judgment on the North Sea Continental Shelf Case, the International Court of Justice said the following on the requirement of the subjective element and *opinio juris:* "Not only must the acts concerned amount to a settled practice, but they must also be such, or be carried out in such a way, as to be evidence of a belief that this practice is rendered obligatory by the existence of a rule of law requiring it. The need for such a belief, i.e., the existence of a subjective element, is implicit in the very notion of the *opinio juris sive necessitatis*. The States concerned must therefore feel that they are conforming to what amounts to a legal obligation. The frequency, or even habitual character of the acts is not in itself enough. There are many international acts, e.g., in the field of ceremonial and protocol, which are performed almost invariably, but which are motivated only by considerations of courtesy, convenience or tradition, and not by any sense of legal duty." ((I.C.J. Reports, 1969, page 44). According to Professor of international law, Eduardo Jiménez de Arechaga, (El Derecho Internacional Contemporáneo, Publishers: Tecnos, Madrid, 1980, pages 19 et seq), customary law, which finds its expression in treaties, can operate in three different ways: the text of the treaty can simply declare a customary rule that existed previously; it can give concrete expression to a rule that is developing in *statu nascendi;* or, the provision of a treaty can convert *de lege ferenda* to a subsequent state practice after a process of consolidation whereupon it converts to custom. In other cases, the custom can derive from the consensus of states in adopting United Nations General Assembly resolutions, as in the case of the 1970 Declaration on Principles of International Law concerning Friendly Relations and Cooperation among States in accordance with the Charter of the United Nations, or the 1963 Declaration of Legal Principles Governing the Activities of States in the Exploration and Use of Outer Space, or Resolution 1514 on the Granting of Independence to Colonial Countries and Peoples, etc.

According to Sorensen (op cit. p. 133), it is not possible to speak of a custom as general if its observance is confined to a particular group of states. This means that an essential requirement concerning custom is that it should derive from the community of States as a whole. Sorensen notes that: "A custom cannot be transformed into a rule of law if it encounters opposition of a proportion of the states comprising the international community or, as the case may be, the region or group within which it is in operation. For in such a case the requisite is not forthcoming" (op cit p. 135). This implies that the opposition of a number of states thwarts the formation of a general customary rule.

The application of the foregoing principles to Case 9647 shows, in my view, the nonexistence of a general rule of customary law prohibiting the application of the death penalty on persons who committed capital crimes under 18 years of age. This conclusion is drawn from the following analysis:

The fact that prohibition of the death penalty with respect to juveniles under 18 years of age appears in the American Convention on Human Rights (Article 4.5), in the International Covenant on Civilian and Political Rights (Article 6.5) and in the Fourth Geneva Convention (Art. 68) does not mean that these treaties have declared an existing custom or have crystalized or reflected a custom. The only thing that can be accepted is the generating effect *de lege ferenda,* which can lead to the development of the custom if state practice in the matter is consolidated. With regard to the prohibition of the death penalty, there is no uniformity in the laws of states, since some allow it and others prohibit it; further, some prohibit the death penalty in the case of minors, and others accept it or remain silent on the subject. It is possible that with time, the practice of States will lead to the emergence of the custom in the instant case, but at present, it is not an international custom.

The practice and the laws of states with regard to the death penalty in general and in relation to minors show variations and discrepancies. Ultimately, one sees a lack of continuity, and contrary to the Commission's mistaken view, it is not possible to find standard and constant application of it practiced with the intent of producing legal effects. There is no proof to the effect that all states worldwide feel bound by an obligatory rule of customary law prohibiting the death penalty with respect to juveniles under 18 years of age given the fact that the laws of the states are not even uniform as regards the age at which an individual is punishable.

In fact, there is no evidence of *opinio juris,* that is to say, demonstration of state practice that has led to nonapplication of the death penalty with respect to minors under 18 years of age, or that this has been a practice for a long time.

Moreover, one must bear in mind that not only has the United States not given its consent to the development of the so-called custom; but rather it has not been proven that uniformity exists, not even with respect to the abolition of the death penalty. In the matter of the Barcelona Traction case, the International Court of Justice said that "a body of rules could only have developed with the consent of the parties concerned. The difficulties encountered have been reflected in the evolution of the law on the subject." (I.C.J. Reports, 1970, page 48, par. 89). Nor can one speak in terms of local American custom, since the American Convention on Human Rights has only been ratified by 19 of the 32 states in the Americas, an indication that there is no standard practice in the Americas regarding the prohibition of the death penalty, and even less so with regard to juveniles. The International Covenant on Civil and Political Rights has not yet been ratified by all states worldwide, and the Fourth Geneva Convention (art. 68), which has received 162 ratifications, only applies to international armed conflicts, and consequently, cannot be considered to be a demonstration of a custom in time of peace.

In conclusion, it was not proven that a widespread and uniform practice exists on the part of states, or the *opinio juris* or conviction that that practice has become obligatory because of the existence of a norm prohibiting the death penalty with respect to minors under 18 years of age. This custom does not derive from state practice, or from the provisions of public treaties that have not been ratified by all states. One cannot therefore consider that there is consensus on this matter.

4. Prohibition of the death penalty with respect to minors under 18 years of age is not a norm of Jus Cogens. Article 53 of the Vienna Convention on the Law of Treaties defines *jus cogens* as a "norm accepted and recognized by the international community of States as a whole as a norm from which no derogation is permitted and which can be modified only by a subsequent norm of general international law having the same character."

In its reference to reservations on genocide (May 28, 1951), the I.C.J. said that "the principles underlying the Convention are principles which are recognized by civilized nations as binding on States, even without any conventional obligation." The Shucking opinion in 1934 relies on *jus cogens* (C.D.L. Report, 80).

The following appeared as examples of *jus cogens* at the Vienna Conference on the Law of Treaties: a) Treaty concerning a case of the illegitimate use of force in violation of the principles of the Charter; b) Treaty concerning the perpetration of any other criminal act in international law; and c) Treaty to prohibit the perpetration or tolerance of such acts as the slave trade, piracy and genocide in the supression of which every State is obliged to cooperate. While human rights standards constitute principles of *jus cogens,* as we have said in our publication on human rights (*'Los Derechos Humanos,* Marco Gerardo Monroy Cabra, Edit. Temis, 1980), the prohibition of the death penalty with respect to juveniles under 18 years of age is not in the nature of a norm of *jus cogens.* Indeed, it has not been proven that uniformity exists, since not all states prohibit the death penalty and not all States prohibit the pronouncement of it with respect to minors under 18 years of age. While there is undoubtedly a tendency towards abolishing the death penalty, it cannot be said that the prohibition of the death penalty for minors under 18 years of age is a norm that has been accepted by the international community as a whole, and consequently, a norm of *jus cogens* has not been created. The prohibition of the death penalty with respect to minors under 18 years of age cannot be compared with the cases cited at the Vienna Conference, such as the prohibition of piracy or slavery or the white slave trade or racial discrimination or the prohibition of genocide, since in all these cases, all states prohibit them. Such is not the case here. The death penalty is still recognized by a considerable number of States. One cannot speak in terms of the existence of a norm of *jus cogens* in effect for the OAS member States since the American Convention on Human Rights, which prohibits the execution of minors under 18 years of age, has only been ratified by 19 States. Also, there are reservations on the matter of the death penalty and it is not a norm that has been accepted by the 32 American states, and far less by all states worldwide. By virtue of this fact, it is therefore not a general imperative norm. One need hardly point out that there can be no "American *jus cogens*" or "Africani *jus cogens*", etc. Rather, one must be in the presence of an imperative norm that has gained acceptance in the international community "as a whole", as the Vienna Convention on the Law of Treaties states in its Article 53.

Not even in the United States is there a rule setting age 18 as the minimum age for imposition of the death penalty, and to date, the Supreme Court of Justice has not declared such application unconstitutional. The punishable age is not uniform among states since some set it at age 16, others at 17, and others at 18. This means that there is no standard legislation among states as regards the minimum punishable age or the minimum age for imposition of the death penalty.

In conclusion, it cannot be inferred from either the practice of states, or from international jurisprudence, or from doctrine, or from the laws of the states that a norm of *jus cogens* prohibiting the imposition of the death penalty with respect to minors under 18 years age of age has come into existence. While human rights standards are of *jus cogens,* specifically the prohibition of the death penalty and its application to minors under 18 years of age do not constitute an imperative norm of general international law since it has not been accepted by all states that make up the international legal community.

5. There has been no violation of article 2 of the American Declaration of the Rights and Duties of Man. Article 2 of the American Declaration of the Rights and Duties of Man states: "All persons are equal before the law and have the rights and duties established in this Declaration, without distinction as to race, sex, language, creed or any other factor."

I do not consider the imposition of the death penalty with respect to minors under 18 years of age to constitute a violation of Article 2 of the American Declaration of the Rights and Duties of Man, because there is no federal law in the United States establishing such a prohibition and the laws of the States are not uniform in this matter. We are not discussing here the arbitrary deprivation of life because there is no federal law in the United States setting the death penalty for minors under 18 years of age; neither is there any prohibition in conventional international law applicable to the United States, nor in customary international either, as previously demonstrated.

6. Interpretation of the American Declaration of the Rights and Duties of Man done by the Inter-American Commission on Human Rights. The Commission used the Vienna Convention on the Law of Treaties in order to interpret the American Declaration of the Rights and Duties of Man, which is a mistake since the Declaration is not a public treaty, not having gone through the necessary stages for the adoption, authentication, manifestation of consent to abide by the treaty, entry into force, registry and publication of any international treaty. Also, in interpreting the Declaration, the Commission did not attribute any value to the preparatory work leading up to the American Declaration of the Rights and Duties of Man contained in the Proceedings of the IX International Conference of American States held in Bogota in 1948. If this background had been taken into account, it would have concluded that there was a consensus to delete any reference to the death penalty from Article 1 in view of the differences that existed among the States on this matter.

The Commission interpreted Article XXVI of the Declaration prohibiting the imposition of "cruel, infamous or unusual punishment," as though this provision prohibited the execution of minors, when this conclusion cannot be drawn from the background and discussions concerning the American Declaration of the Rights and Duties of Man recorded in the Proceedings of the IX International Conference of American States in Bogota. Furthermore, given the fact that some American states applied the death penalty in 1948, it cannot be said that at that time it was considered cruel, infamous or unusual punishment.

To interpret the 1948 American Declaration of the Rights and Duties of Man, the Commission resorted to an analysis of customary international law, but it has already been ascertained that the petitioners have not proven that such a custom exists.

The American Declaration of the Rights and Duties of Man cannot be interpreted in the light of the provisions of the American Convention on Human Rights, the International Covenant on Civil and Political Rights and other treaties on human rights because these treaties are subsequent to the aforecited Declaration and are only binding for States Parties to them.

The erroneous interpretation of the 1948 American Declaration of the Rights and Duties of Man led the Commission to conclude that the Declaration prohibits the death penalty with respect to minors under 18 years of age when this conclusion cannot be drawn from either the letter or spirit of the Declaration.

In interpreting the American Declaration of the Rights and Duties of Man issued in 1948, the Commission could hardly use the practice of states as it stands in 1987, customary international law in effect today, the current notion of *jus cogens,* when the truth is that when drafting that Declaration, the States were not in agreement on prohibiting the death penalty as is apparent from the fact that the pertinent reference was deleted from the Inter-American Juridical Committee's draft. The only point that the Commission should have studied was whether the rights of James Terry Roach and Jay Pinkerton had been disregarded, under the terms of the American Declaration of the Rights and Duties of Man. It was not relevant to analyze whether or not the absence of a federal law in the United States establishing that prohibition of the death penalty with respect to minors violated customary international law, because the Commission is not an international tribunal, or whether U.S. legislation is in conflict with with *jus cogens,* because this was not requested by the petitioners and is beyond the purview of the Commission. In this case, it could only apply the American Declaration of the Rights and Duties of Man because it is the sole international human rights instrument that is binding on the United States.

But even if one were to accept that the Commission could resort to customary international law or to *jus cogens* to interpret the Declaration, one cannot conclude that the United States violated articles 1 and 2 of that Declaration or any norm of general customary international law, since no violation in this regard has been proven in this case.

7. *Conclusions* The following conclusions can be drawn from the foregoing: a) the imposition of the death penalty by state courts in the United States with respect to minors under 18 years of age does not violate articles 1 and 2 of the American Declaration of the Rights and Duties of Man; b) the imposition of the death penalty with respect to minors under 18 years of age does not violate customary international law since there is no custom in this matter, and c) the prohibition of the death penalty with respect to minors under 18 years of age is not a norm of *jus cogens* since it has not been accepted by the international community as a whole.

In accordance with the foregoing, the Inter-American Commission on Human Rights should have exonerated the United States from the charges levied against it by the petitioners.

It is thus that I substantiate my dissenting vote as regards the decision adopted by the Inter-American Commission on Human Rights.

The United States requested reconsideration of Case N° 9647. During the 71st period of sessions, the commission received the request for reconsideration, which it granted, and by a majority vote, decided not to modify its decision. In a separate publication, the commission presented the text of the U.S. government's request for reconsideration, the observations of the petitioners, the reasons of the commission for not modifying its decision, and the separate opinion of Dr. Monroy Cabra. Ambassador Elsa D. Kelly did not participate at this meeting. Mr. Bruce McColm, pursuant to Article 19 of the commission's regulations, did not participate in this matter.

SEE ALSO *American Convention on Human Rights: Additional Protocol on the Death Penalty; Capital Punishment: World Survey; Death Penalty: Applications to Persons under the Age of 18.*

UNIVERSAL COPYRIGHT CONVENTION, REVISED (1971). The Universal Copyright Convention, originally adopted at Geneva on 6 September 1952, was revised by the Conference for the Revision of the Universal Copyright Convention, convened by UNESCO, and adopted by that conference, in Paris, on 24 July 1971. The revised convention entered into force on 10 July 1974.

One purpose of the revision was to introduce a preferential system to benefit the developing countries (articles 5*bis*, 5*ter*, and 5*quater*). Another was to establish standard periods and provisions of copyright protection in all the contracting States.

The revised convention covers not only the authors of literary works but also the originators of musical, dramatic and cinematographic productions, paintings, engravings, and sculpture. Article 4*bis* extends the overall protection of the convention to include the basic rights ensuring the author's economic interests, including the exclusive right to authorize reproduction by any means, public performance, and broadcasting.

Two protocols are annexed to the Universal Copyright Convention as revised at Paris on 24 July 1971. **UNIVERSAL COPYRIGHT CONVENTION: PROTOCOL 1** concerns the application of the convention to works of stateless persons and refugees; **UNIVERSAL COPYRIGHT CONVENTION: PROTOCOL 2** concerns the application of the convention to the works of certain international organizations.

The text of the convention (*UNESCO's Standard-Setting Instruments*, No. V.2.A.2) is as follows:

The Contracting States,

Moved by the desire to ensure in all countries copyright protection of literary, scientific and artistic works,

Convinced that a system of copyright protection appropriate to all nations of the world and expressed in a universal convention, additional to, and without impairing international systems already in force, will ensure respect for the rights of the individual and encourage the development of literature, the sciences and the arts.

Persuaded that such a universal copyright system will facilitate a wider dissemination of works of the human mind and increase international understanding,

Have resolved to revise the Universal Copyright Convention as signed at Geneva on 6 September 1952 (hereinafter called 'the 1952 Convention'), and consequently,

Have agreed as follows:

Article 1. Each Contracting State undertakes to provide for the adequate and effective protection of the rights of authors and other copyright proprietors in literary, scientific and artistic works, including writings, musical, dramatic and cinematographic works, and paintings, engravings, and sculpture.

Article 2. 1. Published works of nationals of any Contracting State and works first published in that State shall enjoy in each other Contracting State the same protection as that other State accords to works of its nationals first published in its own territory, as well as the protection specially granted by this Convention.

2. Unpublished works of nationals of each Contracting State shall enjoy in each other Contracting State the same protection as that other State accords to unpublished works of its own nationals, as well as the protection specially granted by this Convention.

3. For the purpose of this Convention any Contracting State may, by domestic legislation, assimilate to its own nationals any person domiciled in that State.

Article 3. 1. Any Contracting State which, under its domestic law, requires as a condition of copyright, compliance with formalities such as deposit, registration, notice, notarial certificates, payment of fees or manufacture or publication in that Contracting State, shall regard these requirements as satisfied with respect to all works protected in accordance with this Convention and first published outside its territory and the author of which is not one of its nationals, if from the time of the first publication all the copies of the work published with the authority of the author or other copyright proprietor bear the symbol © accompanied by the name of the copyright proprietor and the year of first publication placed in such manner and location as to give reasonable notice of claim of copyright.

2. The provisions of paragraph 1 shall not preclude any Contracting State from requiring formalities or other conditions for the acquisition and enjoyment of copyright in respect of works first published in its territory or works of its nationals wherever published.

3. The provisions of paragraph 1 shall not preclude any Contracting State from providing that a person seeking judicial relief must, in bringing the action, comply with procedural requirements, such as that the complainant must appear through domestic counsel or that the complainant must deposit with the court or an administrative office, or both, a copy of the work involved in the litigation; provided that failure to comply with such requirements shall not affect the validity of the copyright, nor shall any such requirement be imposed upon a national of another Contracting State if such a requirement is not imposed on nationals of the State in which protection is claimed.

4. In each Contracting State there shall be legal means of protecting without formalities the unpublished works of nationals of other Contracting States.

5. If a Contracting State grants protection for more than one term of copyright and the first term is for a period longer than one of the minimum periods prescribed in Article 4, such State shall not be required to comply with the provisions of paragraph 1 of this Article in respect of the second or any subsequent term of copyright.

Article 4. 1. The duration of protection of a work shall be governed, in accordance with the provisions of Article 2 and this Article, by the law of the Contracting State in which protection is claimed.

2. (a) The term of protection for works protected under this Convention shall not be less than the life of the author and twenty-five years after his death. However, any Contracting State which, on the effective date of this Convention in that State, has limited this term for certain classes of works to a period computed from the first publication of the work, shall be entitled to maintain these exceptions and to extend them to other classes of works. For all these classes the term of protection shall not be less than twenty-five years from the date of first publication.

(b) Any Contracting State which, upon the effective date of this Convention in that State, does not compute the term of protection upon the basis of the life of the author, shall be entitled to compute the term of protection from the date of the first publication of the work or from its registration prior to publication, as the case may be, provided the term of protection shall not be less than twenty-five years from the date of first publication or from its registration prior to publication, as the case may be.

(c) If the legislation of a Contracting State grants two or more successive terms of protection, the duration of the first term shall not be less than one of the minimum periods specified in sub-paragraphs (a) and (b).

3. The provisions of paragraph 2 shall not apply to photographic works or to works of applied art; provided, however, that the term of protection in those Contracting States which protect photographic works, or works of applied art in so far as they are protected as artistic works, shall not be less than ten years for each of said classes of works.

4. (a) No Contracting State shall be obliged to grant protection to a work for a period longer than that fixed for the class of works to which the work in question belongs, in the case of unpublished works by the law of the Contracting State of which the author is a national, and in the case of published works by the law of the Contracting State in which the work has been first published.

(b) For the purposes of the application of subparagraph (a), if the law of any Contracting State grants two or more successive terms of protection, the period of protection of that State shall be considered to be the aggregate of those terms. However, if a specified work is not protected by such State during the second or any subsequent term for any reason, the other Contracting State shall not be obliged to protect it during the second or any subsequent term.

5. For the purposes of the application of paragraph 4, the work of a national of a Contracting State, first published in a non-Contracting State, shall be treated as though first published in the Contracting State of which the author is a national.

6. For the purposes of the application of paragraph 4, in case of simultaneous publication in two or more Contracting States, the work shall be treated as though first published in the State which affords the shortest term; any work published in two or more Contracting States within thirty days of its first publication shall be considered as having been published simultaneously in said Contracting States.

Article 4bis. 1. The rights referred to in Article 1 shall include the basic rights ensuring the author's economic interests, including the exclusive right to authorize reproduction by any means, public performance and broadcasting. The provisions of this Article shall extend to works protected under this Convention either in their original form or in any form recognizably derived from the original.

2. However, any Contracting State may, by its domestic legislation, make exceptions that do not conflict with the spirit and provisions of this Convention, to the rights mentioned in paragraph 1 of this Article. Any State whose legislation so provides, shall nevertheless accord a reasonable degree of effective protection to each of the rights to which exception has been made.

Article 5. 1. The rights referred to in Article 1 shall include the exclusive right of the author to make, publish and authorize the making and publication of translations of works protected under this Convention.

2. However, any Contracting State may, by its domestic legislation, restrict the right of translation of writings, but only subject to the following provisions:

(a) If, after the expiration of a period of seven years from the date of the first publication of a writing, a translation of such writing has not been published in a language in general use in the Contracting State, by the owner of the right of translation or with his authorization, any national of such Contracting State may obtain a non-exclusive licence from the competent authority thereof to translate the work into that language and publish the work so translated.

(b) Such national shall in accordance with the procedure of the State concerned, establish either that he has requested, and been denied, authorization by the proprietor of the right to make and publish the translation, or that, after due diligence on his part, he was unable to find the owner of the right. A licence may also be granted on the same conditions if all previous editions of a translation in a language in general use in the Contracting State are out of print.

(c) If the owner of the right of translation cannot be found, then the applicant for a licence shall send copies of

U

his application to the publisher whose name appears on the work and, if the nationality of the owner of the right of translation is known, to the diplomatic or consular representative of the State of which such owner is a national, or to the organization which may have been designated by the government of that State. The licence shall not be granted before the expiration of a period of two months from the date of the dispatch of the copies of the application.

(d) Due provision shall be made by domestic legislation to ensure to the owner of the right of translation a compensation which is just and conforms to international standards, to ensure payment and transmittal of such compensation, and to ensure a correct translation of the work.

(e) The original title and the name of the author of the work shall be printed on all copies of the published translation. The licence shall be valid only for publication of the translation in the territory of the Contracting State where it has been applied for. Copies so published may be imported and sold in another Contracting State if a language in general use in such other State is the same language as that into which the work has been so translated, and if the domestic law in such other State makes provision for such licences and does not prohibit such importation and sale. Where the foregoing conditions do not exist, the importation and sale of such copies in a Contracting State shall be governed by its domestic law and its agreements. The licence shall not be transferred by the licensee.

(f) The licence shall not be granted when the author has withdrawn from circulation all copies of the work.

Article 5 bis. 1. Any Contracting State regarded as a developing country in conformity with the established practice of the General Assembly of the United Nations may, by a notification deposited with the Director-General of the United Nations Educational, Scientific and Cultural Organization (hereinafter called "the Director-General") at the time of this ratification, acceptance or accession or thereafter, avail itself of any or all of the exceptions provided for in Articles 5*ter* and 5*quater.*

2. Any such notification shall be effective for ten years from the date of coming into force of this Convention, or for such part of that ten-year period as remains at the date of deposit of the notification, and may be renewed in whole or in part for further periods of ten years each if, not more than fifteen or less than three months before the expiration of the relevant ten-year period, the Contracting State deposits a further notification with the Director-General. Initial notifications may also be made during these further periods of ten years in accordance with the provisions of this Article.

3. Notwithstanding the provisions of paragraph 2, a Contracting State that has ceased to be regarded as a developing country as referred to in paragraph 1 shall no longer be entitled to renew its notification made under the provisions of paragraph 1 or 2, and whether or not it formally withdraws the notification such State shall be precluded from availing itself of the exceptions provided for in Articles 5*ter* and 5*quater* at the end of the current ten-year period, or at the end of three years after it has ceased to be regarded as a developing country, whichever period expires later.

4. Any copies of a work already made under the exceptions provided for in Articles 5*ter* and 5*quater* may continue to be distributed after the expiration of the period for which notifications under this Article were effective until their stock is exhausted.

5. Any Contracting State that has deposited a notification in accordance with Article 13 with respect to the appli-

cation of this Convention to a particular country or territory, the situation of which can be regarded as analogous to that of the States referred to in paragraph 1 of this Article, may also deposit notifications and renew them in accordance with the provisions of this Article with respect to any such country or territory. During the effective period of such notifications, the provisions of Articles 5*ter* and 5*quater* may be applied with respect to such country or territory. The sending of copies from the country or territory to the Contracting State shall be considered as export within the meaning of Articles 5*ter* and 5*quater.*

Article 5ter. 1. (a) Any Contracting State to which Article 5*bis*(1) applies may substitute for the period of seven years provided for in Article 5 (2) a period of three years or any longer period prescribed by its legislation. However, in the case of a translation into a language not in general use in one or more developed countries that are party to this Convention or only the 1952 Convention, the period shall be one year instead of three.

(b) A Contracting State to which Article 5*bis* (1) applies may, with the unanimous agreement of the developed countries party to this Convention or only the 1952 Convention and in which the same language is in general use, substitute, in the case of translation into that language, for the period of three years provided for in sub-paragraph (a) another period as determined by such agreement but not shorter than one year. However, this sub-paragraph shall not apply where the language in question is English, French or Spanish. Notification of any such agreement shall be made to the Director-General.

(c) The licence may only be granted if the applicant, in accordance with the procedure of the State concerned, establishes either that he has requested, and been denied, authorization by the owner of the right of translation, or that, after due diligence on his part, he was unable to find the owner of the right. At the same time as he makes his request he shall inform either the International Copyright Information Centre established by the United Nations Educational, Scientific and Cultural Organization or any national or regional information centre which may have been designated in a notification to that effect deposited with the Director-General by the government of the State in which the publisher is believed to have his principal place of business.

(d) If the owner of the right of translation cannot be found, the applicant for a licence shall send, by registered airmail, copies of this application to the publisher whose name appears on the work and to any national or regional information centre as mentioned in sub-paragraph (c). If no such centre is notified he shall also send a copy to the international copyright information centre established by the United Nations Educational, Scientific and Cultural Organization.

2. (a) Licences obtainable after three years shall not be granted under this Article until a further period of six months has elapsed and licences obtainable after one year until a further period of nine months has elapsed. The further period shall begin either from the date of the request for permission to translate mentioned in paragraph 1 (c) or, if the identity or address of the owner of the right of translation is not known, from the date of dispatch of the copies of the application for a licence mentioned in paragraph 1 (d).

(b) Licences shall not be granted if a translation has been published by the owner of the right of translation or with his authorization during the said period of six or nine months.

3. Any licence under this Article shall be granted only for the purpose of teaching, scholarship or research.

4. (a) Any licence granted under this Article shall not extend to the export of copies and shall be valid only for publication in the territory of the Contracting State where it has been applied for.

(b) Any copy published in accordance with a licence granted under this Article shall bear a notice in the appropriate language stating that the copy is available for distribution only in the Contracting State granting the licence. If the writing bears the notice specified in Article 3 (1) the copies shall bear the same notice.

(c) The prohibition of export provided for in sub-paragraph (a) shall not apply where a governmental or other public entity of a State which has granted a licence under this Article to translate a work into a language other than English, French or Spanish sends copies of a translation prepared under such licence to another country if:

(i) the recipients are individuals who are nationals of the Contracting State granting the licence, or organizations grouping such individuals;

(ii) the copies are to be used only for the purpose of teaching, scholarship or research;

(iii) the sending of the copies and their subsequent distribution to recipients is without the object of commercial purpose; and

(iv) the country to which the copies have been sent has agreed with the Contracting State to allow the receipt, distribution or both and the Director-General has been notified of such agreement by any one of the governments which have concluded it.

5. Due provision shall be made at the national level to ensure:

(a) that the licence provides for just compensation that is consistent with standards of royalties normally operating in the case of licences freely negotiated between persons in the two countries concerned; and

(b) payment and transmittal of the compensation; however, should national currency regulations intervene, the competent authority shall make all efforts, by the use of international machinery, to ensure transmittal in internationally convertible currency or its equivalent.

6. Any licence granted by a Contracting State under this Article shall terminate if a translation of the work in the same language with substantially the same content as the edition in respect of which the licence was granted is published in the said State by the owner of the right of translation or with his authorization, at a price reasonably related to that normally charged in the same State for comparable works. Any copies already made before the licence is terminated may continue to be distributed until their stock is exhausted.

7. For works which are composed mainly of illustrations a licence to translate the text and to reproduce the illustrations may be granted only if the conditions of Article 5*quater* are also fulfilled.

8. (a) A licence to translate a work protected under this Convention, published in printed or analogous forms of reproduction, may also be granted to a broadcasting organization having its headquarters in a Contracting State to which Article 5*bis* (1) applies, upon an application made in that State by the said organization under the following conditions:

(i) the translation is made from a copy made and acquired in accordance with the laws of the Contracting State;

(ii) the translation is for use only in broadcasts intended exclusively for teaching or for the dissemination of the results of specialized technical or scientific research to experts in a particular profession;

(iii) the translation is used exclusively for the purposes set out in condition (ii), through broadcasts lawfully made which are intended for recipients on the territory of the Contracting State, including broadcasts made through the medium of sound or visual recordings lawfully and exclusively made for the purpose of such broadcasts;

(iv) sound or visual recordings of the translation may be exchanged only between broadcasting organizations having their headquarters in the Contracting State granting the licence; and

(v) all uses made of the translation are without any commercial purpose.

(b) Provided all of the criteria and conditions set out in sub-paragraph (a) are met, a licence may also be granted to a broadcasting organization to translate any text incorporated in an audio-visual fixation which was itself prepared and published for the sole purpose of being used in connexion with systematic instructional activities.

(c) Subject to sub-paragraphs (a) and (b), the other provisions of this Article shall apply to the grant and exercise of the licence.

9. Subject to the provisions of this Article, any licence granted under this Article shall be governed by the provisions of Article 5, and shall continue to be governed by the provisions of Article 5 and of this Article, even after the seven-year period provided for in Article 5 (2) has expired. However, after the said period has expired, the licensee shall be free to request that the said licence be replaced by a new licence governed exclusively by the provisions of Article 5.

Article 5quater. 1. Any Contracting State to which Article 5*bis* (1) applies may adopt the following provisions:

(a) If, after the expiration of (i) the relevant period specified in sub-paragraph (c) commencing from the date of first publication of a particular edition of a literary, scientific or artistic work referred to in paragraph 3, or (ii) any longer period determined by national legislation of the State, copies of such edition have not been distributed in that State to the general public or in connexion with systematic instructional activities at a price reasonably related to that normally charged in the State for comparable works, by the owner of the right of reproduction or with his authorization, any national of such State may obtain a non-exclusive licence from the competent authority to publish such edition at that or a lower price for use in connexion with systematic instructional activities. The licence may only be granted if such national, in accordance with the procedure of the State concerned, establishes either that he has requested, and been denied, authorization by the proprietor of the right to publish such work, or that, after due diligence on his part, he was unable to find the owner of the right. At the same time as he makes his request he shall inform either the international copyright information centre established by the United Nations Educational, Scientific and Cultural Organization or any national or regional information centre referred to in sub-paragraph (d).

(b) A licence may also be granted on the same conditions if, for a period of six months, no authorized copies of the edition in question have been on sale in the State concerned to the general public or in connexion with system-

1651

atic instructional activities at a price reasonably related to that normally charged in the State for comparable works.

(c) The period referred to in sub-paragraph (a) shall be five years except that:

(i) for works of the natural and physical sciences, including mathematics, and of technology, the period shall be three years;

(ii) for works of fiction, poetry, drama and music, and for art books, the period shall be seven years.

(d) If the owner of the right of reproduction cannot be found, the applicant for a licence shall send, by registered air mail, copies of his application to the publisher whose name appears on the work and to any national or regional information centre identified as such in a notification deposited with the Director-General by the State in which the publisher is believed to have his principal place of business. In the absence of any such notification, he shall also send a copy to the international copyright information centre established by the United Nations Educational, Scientific and Cultural Organization. The licence shall not be granted before the expiration of a period of three months from the date of dispatch of the copies of the application.

(e) Licences obtainable after three years shall not be granted under this Article:

(i) until a period of six months has elapsed from the date of the request for permission referred to in sub-paragraph (a) or, if the identity or address of the owner of the right of reproduction is unknown, from the date of the dispatch of the copies of the application for a licence referred to in sub-paragraph (d);

(ii) if any such distribution of copies of the edition as is mentioned in sub-paragraph (a) has taken place during that period.

(f) The name of the author and the title of the particular edition of the work shall be printed on all copies of the published reproduction. The licence shall not extend to the export of copies and shall be valid only for publication in the territory of the Contracting State where it has been applied for. The licence shall not be transferable by the licensee.

(g) Due provisions shall be made by domestic legislation to ensure an accurate reproduction of the particular edition in question.

(h) A licence to reproduce and publish a translation of a work shall not be granted under this Article in the following cases:

(i) where the translation was not published by the owner of the right of translation or with his authorization;

(ii) where the translation is not in a language in general use in the State with power to grant the licence.

2. The exceptions provided for in paragraph 1 are subject to the following additional provisions:

(a) Any copy published in accordance with a licence granted under this Article shall bear a notice in the appropriate language stating that the copy is available for distribution only in the Contracting State to which the said licence applies. If the edition bears the notice specified in Article 3 (1), the copies shall bear the same notice.

(b) Due provision shall be made at the national level to ensure:

(i) that the licence provides for just compensation that is consistent with standards of royalties normally operating in the case of licences freely negotiated between persons in the two countries concerned; and

(ii) payment and transmittal of the compensation; however, should national currency regulations intervene, the competent authority shall make all efforts, by the use of international machinery, to ensure transmittal in internationally convertible currency or its equivalent.

(c) Whenever copies of an edition of a work are distributed in the Contracting State to the general public or in connexion with systematic instructional activities, by the owner of the right of reproduction or with his authorization, at a price reasonably related to that normally charged in the State for comparable works, any licence granted under this Article shall terminate if such edition is in the same language and is substantially the same in content as the edition published under the licence. Any copies already made before the licence is terminated may continue to be distributed until their stock is exhausted.

(d) No licence shall be granted when the author has withdrawn from circulation all copies of the edition in question.

3. (a) Subject to sub-paragraph (b), the literary, scientific or artistic works to which this Article applies shall be limited to works published in printed or analogous forms of reproduction.

(b) The provisions of this Article shall also apply to reproduction in audio-visual form of lawfully made audio-visual fixations including any protected works incorporated therein and to the translation of any incorporated text into a language in general use in the State with power to grant the licence; always provided that the audio-visual fixations in question were prepared and published for the sole purpose of being used in connexion with systematic instructional activities.

Article 6. "Publication", as used in this Convention, means the reproduction in tangible form and the general distribution to the public of copies of a work from which it can be read or otherwise visually perceived.

Article 7. This Convention shall not apply to works or rights in works which, at the effective date of this Convention in a Contracting State where protection is claimed, are permanently in the public domain in the said Contracting State.

Article 8. 1. This Convention, which shall bear the date of 24 July 1971, shall be deposited with the Director-General and shall remain open for signature by all States party to the 1952 Convention for a period of 120 days after the date of this Convention. It shall be subject to ratification or acceptance by the signatory States.

2. Any State which has not signed this Convention may accede thereto.

3. Ratification, acceptance or accession shall be effected by the deposit of an instrument to that effect with the Director-General.

Article 9. 1. This Convention shall come into force three months after the deposit of twelve instruments of ratification, acceptance or accession.

2. Subsequently, this Convention shall come into force in respect of each State three months after that State has deposited its instrument of ratification, acceptance or accession.

3. Accession to this Convention by a State not party to the 1952 Convention shall also constitute accession to that Convention; however, if its instrument of accession is deposited before this Convention comes into force, such State may make its accession to the 1952 Convention conditional upon the coming into force of this Convention. After the coming into force of this Convention, no State may accede solely to the 1952 Convention.

4. Relations between States party to this Convention and

States that are party only to the 1952 Convention, shall be governed by the 1952 Convention. However, any State party only to the 1952 Convention may, by a notification deposited with the Director-General, declare that it will admit the application of the 1971 Convention to works of its nationals or works first published in its territory by all States party to this Convention.

Article 10. 1. Each Contracting State undertakes to adopt, in accordance with its Constitution, such measures as are necessary to ensure the application of this Convention.

2. It is understood that at the date this Convention comes into force in respect of any State, that State must be in a position under its domestic law to give effect to the terms of this Convention.

Article 11. 1. An Intergovernmental Committee is hereby established with the following duties:

(a) to study the problems concerning the application and operation of the Universal Copyright Convention;

(b) to make preparation for periodic revisions of this Convention;

(c) to study any other problems concerning the international protection of copyright, in co-operation with the various interested international organizations, such as the United Nations Educational, Scientific and Cultural Organization, the International Union for the Protection of Literary and Artistic Works and the Organization of American States;

(d) to inform States party to the Universal Copyright Convention as to its activities.

2. The Committee shall consist of the representatives of eighteen States party to this Convention or only to the 1952 Convention.

3. The Committee shall be selected with due consideration to a fair balance of national interests on the basis of geographical location, population, languages and stage of development.

4. The Director-General of the United Nations Educational, Scientific and Cultural Organization, the Director-General of the World Intellectual Property Organization and the Secretary-General of the Organization of American States, or their representatives, may attend meetings of the Committee in an advisory capacity.

Article 12. The Intergovernmental Committee shall convene a conference for revision whenever it deems necessary, or at the request of at least ten States party to this Convention.

Article 13. 1. Any Contracting State may, at the time of deposit of its instrument of ratification, acceptance or accession, or at any time thereafter, declare by notification addressed to the Director-General that this Convention shall apply to all or any of the countries or territories for the international relations of which it is responsible and this Convention shall thereupon apply to the countries or territories named in such notification after the expiration of the term of three months provided for in Article 9. In the absence of such notification, this Convention shall not apply to any such country or territory.

2. However, nothing in this Article shall be understood as implying the recognition or tacit acceptance by a Contracting State of the factual situation concerning a country or territory to which this Convention is made applicable by another Contracting State in accordance with the provisions of this Article.

Article 14. 1. Any Contracting State may denounce this Convention in its own name or on behalf of all or any of the countries or territories with respect to which a notification

has been given under Articles 13. The denunciation shall be made by notification addressed to the Director-General. Such denunciation shall also constitute denunciation of the 1952 Convention.

2. Such denunciation shall operate only in respect of the State or of the country or territory on whose behalf it was made and shall not take effect until twelve months after the date of receipt of the notification.

Article 15. A dispute between two or more Contracting States concerning the interpretation or application of this Convention, not settled by negotiation, shall, unless the States concerned agree on some other method of settlement, be brought before the International Court of Justice for determination by it.

Article 16. 1. This Convention shall be established in English, French and Spanish. The three texts shall be signed and shall be equally authoritative.

2. Official texts of this Convention shall be established by the Director-General, after consultation with the governments concerned, in Arabic, German, Italian and Portuguese.

3. Any Contracting State or group of Contracting States shall be entitled to have established by the Director-General other texts in the language of its choice by arrangement with the Director-General.

4. All such texts shall be annexed to the signed texts of this Convention.

Article 17. 1. This Convention shall not in any way affect the provisions of the Berne Convention for the Protection of Literary and Artistic Works or membership in the Union created by that Convention.

2. In application of the foregoing paragraph, a declaration has been annexed to the present Article. This declaration is an integral part of this Convention for the States bound by the Berne Convention on 1 January 1951, or which have or may become bound to it at a later date. The signature of this Convention by such States shall also constitute signature of the said declaration, and ratification, acceptance or accession by such States shall include the declaration, as well as this Convention.

Article 18. This Convention shall not abrogate multilateral or bilateral copyright conventions or arrangements that are or may be in effect exclusively between two or more American Republics. In the event of any difference either between the provisions of such existing conventions or arrangements and the provisions of this Convention, or between the provisions of this Convention and those of any new convention or arrangement which may be formulated between two or more American Republics after this Convention comes into force, the convention or arrangement most recently formulated shall prevail between the parties thereto. Rights in works acquired in any Contracting State under existing conventions or arrangements before the date this Convention comes into force in such State shall not be affected.

Article 19. This Convention shall not abrogate multilateral or bilateral conventions or arrangements in effect between two or more Contracting States. In the event of any difference between the provisions of such existing conventions or arrangements and the provisions of this Convention, the provisions of this Convention shall prevail. Rights in works acquired in any Contracting State under existing conventions or arrangements before the date on which this Convention comes into force in such State shall not be affected. Nothing in this Article shall affect the provisions of Articles 17 and 18.

Article 20. Reservations to this Convention shall not be permitted.

Article 21. 1. The Director-General shall send duly certified copies of this Convention to the States interested and to the Secretary-General of the United Nations for registration by him.

2. He shall also inform all interested States of the ratifications, acceptances and accessions which have been deposited, the date on which this Convention comes into force, the notification under this Convention and denunciations under Article 14.

Appendix Declaration relating to Article 17. The States which are members of the International Union for the Protection of Literary and Artistic Works (hereinafter called "the Berne Union") and which are signatories to this Convention,

Desiring to reinforce their mutual relations on the basis of the said Union and to avoid any conflict which might result from the co-existence of the Berne Convention and the Universal Copyright Convention,

Recognizing the temporary need of some States to adjust their level of copyright protection in accordance with their stage of cultural, social and economic development,

Have, by common agreement, accepted the terms of the following declaration:

(a) Except as provided by paragraph (b), works which, according to the Berne Convention, have as their country of origin a country which has withdrawn from the Berne Union after 1 January 1951, shall not be protected by the Universal Copyright Convention in the countries of the Berne Union;

(b) Where a Contracting State is regarded as a developing country in conformity with the established practice of the General Assembly of the United Nations, and has deposited with the Director-General of the United Nations Educational, Scientific and Cultural Organization, at the time of its withdrawal from the Berne Union, a notification to the effect that it regards itself as a developing country, the provisions of paragraph (a) shall not be applicable as long as such State may avail itself of the exceptions provided for by this Convention in accordance with Article 5*bis*;

(c) The Universal Copyright Convention shall not be applicable to the relationships among countries of the Berne Union in so far as it relates to the protection of works having as their country of origin, within the meaning of the Berne Convention, a country of the Berne Union.

Resolution concerning Article 11. The Conference for Revision of the Universal Copyright Convention,

Having considered the problems relating to the Intergovernmental Committee provided for in Article 11 of this Convention, to which this resolution is annexed,

Resolves that:

1. At its inception, the Committee shall include representatives of the twelve States members of the Intergovernmental Committee established under Article 11 of the 1952 Convention and the resolution annexed to it, and, in addition, representatives of the following States: Algeria, Australia, Japan, Mexico, Senegal and Yugoslavia.

2. Any States that are not party to the 1952 Convention and have not acceded to this Convention before the first ordinary session of the Committee following the entry into force of this Convention shall be replaced by other States to be selected by the Committee at its first ordinary session in conformity with the provisions of Article 11 (2) and (3).

3. As soon as this Convention comes into force the Committee as provided for in paragraph 1 shall be deemed to be constituted in accordance with Article 11 of this Convention.

4. A session of the Committee shall take place within one year after the coming into force of this Convention; thereafter the Committee shall meet in ordinary session at intervals of not more than two years.

5. The Committee shall elect its Chairman and two Vice-Chairmen. It shall establish its Rules of Procedures having regard to the following principles:

(a) The normal duration of the term of office of the members represented on the Committee shall be six years with one-third retiring every two years, it being however understood that, of the original terms of office, one-third shall expire at the end of the Committee's second ordinary session which will follow the entry into force of this Convention, a further third at the end of its third ordinary session, and the remaining third at the end of its fourth ordinary session.

(b) The rules governing the procedure whereby the Committee shall fill vacancies, the order in which terms of membership expire, eligibility for re-election, and election procedures, shall be based upon a balancing of the needs for continuity of membership and rotation of representation, as well as the considerations set out in Article 11 (3).

Expresses the wish that the United Nations Educational, Scientific and Cultural Organization provide its Secretariat.

In faith whereof the undersigned, having deposited their respective full powers, have signed this Convention.

Done at Paris, this twenty-fourth day of July 1971, in a single copy.

UNIVERSAL COPYRIGHT CONVENTION, REVISED (1971): PROTOCOL 1.

The protocol provides for application of the convention to the works of stateless persons and refugees. It was adopted by the Conference for the Revision of the Universal Copyright Convention, in Paris, on 24 July 1971, and entered into force on 10 July 1974. It is subject to ratification, acceptance, or accession by States parties to the UNIVERSAL COPYRIGHT CONVENTION (REVISED).

The text of the protocol (*UNESCO's Standard-Setting Instruments,* No. V.2.A.2) is as follows:

The States party hereto, being also party to the Universal Copyright Convention as revised at Paris on 24 July 1971 (hereinafter called "the 1971 Convention").

Have accepted the following provisions:

1. Stateless persons and refugees who have their habitual residence in a State party to this Protocol shall, for the purposes of the 1971 Convention, be assimilated to the nationals of that State.

2. (a) This Protocol shall be signed and shall be subject to ratification or acceptance, or may be acceded to, as if the provisions of Article 8 of the 1971 Convention applied hereto.

(b) This Protocol shall enter into force in respect of each State, on the date of deposit of the instrument of ratification, acceptance or accession of the State concerned or on the date of entry into force of the 1971 Convention with respect to such State, whichever is the later.

(c) On the entry into force of this Protocol in respect of a State not party to Protocol 1 annexed to the 1951 Convention, the latter Protocol shall be deemed to enter into force in respect of such State.

In faith whereof the undersigned, being duly authorized thereto, have signed this Protocol.

Done at Paris this twenty-fourth day of July 1971, in the English, French and Spanish languages, the three texts being equally authoritative, in a single copy which shall be deposited with the Director-General of the United Nations Educational, Scientific and Cultural Organization. The Director-General shall send certified copies to the signatory States, and to the Secretary-General of the United Nations for registration.

UNIVERSAL COPYRIGHT CONVENTION, REVISED (1971): PROTOCOL 2.

The protocol provides for application of the convention to the works of certain international organizations, in particular to works published for the first time by the United Nations, by the specialized agencies in relationship therewith, or by the ORGANIZATION OF AMERICAN STATES. It was adopted by the Conference for the Revision of the Universal Copyright Convention, in Paris, on 24 July 1971, and entered into force on 10 July 1974. It is subject to ratification, acceptance, or accession by States parties to the UNIVERSAL COPYRIGHT CONVENTION (REVISED).

The text of the protocol (*UNESCO's Standard-Setting Instruments,* No. V.2.A.2) is as follows:

The States party hereto, being also party to the Universal Copyright Convention as revised at Paris on 24 July 1971 (hereinafter called "the 1971 Convention"),

Have accepted the following provisions:

1. (a) The protection provided for in Article 2 (1) of the 1971 Convention shall apply to works published for the first time by the United Nations, by the Specialized Agencies in relationship therewith, or by the Organization of American States.

(b) Similarly, Article 2 (2) of the 1971 Convention shall apply to the said organization or agencies.

2. (a) This Protocol shall be signed and shall be subject to ratification or acceptance, or may be acceded to, as if the provisions of Article 8 of the 1971 Convention applied hereto.

(b) This Protocol shall enter into force for each State on the date of deposit of the instrument of ratification, acceptance or accession of the State concerned or on the date of entry into force of the 1971 Convention with respect to such State, whichever is the later.

In faith whereof the undersigned, being duly authorized thereto, have signed this Protocol.

Done at Paris, this twenty-fourth day of July 1971, in the English, French and Spanish languages, the three texts being equally authoritative, in a single copy which shall be deposited with the Director-General of the United Nations Educational, Scientific and Cultural Organization. The Director-General shall send certified copies to the signatory States, and to the Secretary-General of the United Nations for registration.

UNIVERSAL DECLARATION OF HUMAN RIGHTS (1948).

The declaration, universally accepted as establishing "a common standard of achievement for all peoples and all nations," sets out the basic principles upon which the human rights activities of the United Nations system are based. Since its adoption, it has exercised incalculable influence upon governments and peoples everywhere; has made the men and women of every land conscious of the rights and freedoms to which they are entitled and inspired them to have these rights and freedoms recognized and respected; and promoted and protected not only the rights of individuals but also of peoples of different races, cultures, languages, religions, and social backgrounds. Fittingly, its anniversary is observed each year in nearly every country and territory of the world on 10 December: Human Rights Day.

The declaration was adopted and proclaimed on 10 December 1948 by the UN General Assembly (resolution 217 [III]). The text, annexed to that resolution, is as follows:

Preamble

Whereas recognition of the inherent dignity and of the equal and inalienable rights of all members of the human family is the foundation of freedom, justice and peace in the world,

Whereas disregard and contempt for human rights have resulted in barbarous acts which have outraged the conscience of mankind, and the advent of a world in which human beings shall enjoy freedom of speech and belief and freedom from fear and want has been proclaimed as the highest aspiration of the common people,

Whereas it is essential, if man is not to be compelled to have recourse, as a last resort, to rebellion against tyranny and oppression, that human rights should be protected by the rule of law,

Whereas it is essential to promote the development of friendly relations between nations,

Whereas the peoples of the United Nations have in the Charter reaffirmed their faith in fundamental human rights, in the dignity and worth of the human person and in the equal rights of men and women and have determined to promote social progress and better standards of life in larger freedom,

Whereas Member States have pledged themselves to achieve, in co-operation with the United Nations, the promotion of universal respect for and observance of human rights and fundamental freedoms,

Whereas a common understanding of these rights and freedoms is of the greatest importance for the full realization of this pledge,

Now, therefore,

The General Assembly

Proclaims this Universal Declaration of Human Rights as a common standard of achievement for all peoples and all nations, to the end that every individual and every organ of society, keeping this Declaration constantly in mind, shall strive by teaching and education to promote respect for these rights and freedoms and by progressive measures, national and international, to secure their universal and effective recognition and observance, both among the peoples of Member States themselves and among the peoples of territories under their jurisdiction.

Article 1. All human beings are born free and equal in dignity and rights. They are endowed with reason and conscience and should act towards one another in a spirit of brotherhood.

Article 2. Everyone is entitled to all the rights and freedoms set forth in this Declaration, without distinction of any kind, such as race, colour, sex, language, religion, political or other opinion, national or social origin, property, birth or other status.

Furthermore, no distinction shall be made on the basis of the political, jurisdictional or international status of the country or territory to which a person belongs, whether it be independent, trust, non-self-governing or under any other limitation of sovereignty.

Article 3. Everyone has the right to life, liberty and security of person.

Article 4. No one shall be held in slavery or servitude; slaver and the slave trade shall be prohibited in all their forms.

Article 5. No one shall be subjected to torture or to cruel, inhuman or degrading treatment or punishment.

Article 6. Everyone has the right to recognition everywhere as a person before the law.

Article 7. All are equal before the law and are entitled without any discrimination to equal protection of the law. All are entitled to equal protections against any discrimination in violation of this Declaration and against any incitement to such discrimination.

Article 8. Everyone has the right to an effective remedy by the competent national tribunals for acts violating the fundamental rights granted him by the constitution or by law.

Article 9. No one shall be subjected to arbitrary arrest, detention or exile.

Article 10. Everyone is entitled in full equality to a fair and public hearing by an independent and impartial tribunal, in the determination of his rights and obligations and of any criminal charge against him.

Article 11. 1. Everyone charged with a penal offence has the right to be presumed innocent until proven guilty according to law in a public trial at which he has had all the guarantees necessary for his defence.

2. No one shall be held guilty of any penal offence on account of any act or omission which did not constitute a penal offence, under national or international law, at the time when it was commited. Nor shall a heavier penalty be imposed than the one that was applicable at the time the penal offence was committed.

Article 12. No one shall be subjected to arbitrary interference with his privacy, family, home, or correspondence, nor to attacks upon his honour and reputation. Everyone has the right to the protection of the law against such interference or attacks.

Article 13. 1. Everyone has the right to freedom of movement and residence within the borders of each State.

2. Everyone has the right to leave any country, including his own, and to return to his country.

Article 14. 1. Everyone has the right to seek and to enjoy in other countries asylum from persecution.

2. This right may not be invoked in the case of prosecutions genuinely arising from non-political crimes or from acts contrary to the purposes and principles of the United Nations.

Article 15. 1. Everyone has the right to a nationality.

2. No one shall be arbitrarily deprived of his nationality nor denied the right to change his nationality.

Article 16. 1. Men and women of full age, without any limitation due to race, nationality or religion, have the right to marry and to found a family. They are entitled to equal rights as to marriage, during marriage and at its dissolution.

2. Marriage shall be entered into only with the free and full consent of the intending spouses.

3. The family is the natural and fundamental group unit of society and is entitled to protection by society and the State.

Article 17. 1. Everyone has the right to own property alone as well as in association with others.

2. No one shall be arbitrarily deprived of his property.

Article 18. Everyone has the right to freedom of thought, conscience and religion; this right includes freedom to change his religion or belief, and freedom, either alone or in community with others and in public or private, to manifest his religion or belief in teaching, practice, worship and observance.

Article 19. Everyone has the right to freedom of opinion and expression; this right includes freedom to hold opinions without interference and to seek, receive and impart information and ideas through any media and regardless of frontiers.

Article 20. 1. Everyone has the right to freedom of peaceful assembly and association.

2. No one may be compelled to belong to an association.

Article 21. 1. Everyone has the right to take part in the government of his country, directly of through freely chosen representatives.

2. Everyone has the right of equal access to public service in his country.

3. The will of the people shall be the basis of the authority of government; this will shall be expressed in periodic and genuine elections which shall be by universal and equal suffrage and shall be held by secret vote or by equivalent free voting procedures.

Article 22. Everyone, as a member of society, has the right to social security and is entitled to realization, through national effort and international co-operation and in accordance with the organization and resources of each State, of the economic, social and cultural rights indispensable for his dignity and the free development of his personality.

Article 23. 1. Everyone has the right to work, to free choice of employment, to just and favourable conditions of work and to protection against unemployment.

2. Everyone, without any discrimination, has the right to equal pay for equal work.

3. Everyone who works has the right to just and favourable remuneration ensuring for himself and his family an existence worthy of human dignity, and supplemented, if necessary, by other means of social protection.

4. Everyone has the right to form and to join trade unions for the protection of his interests.

Article 24. Everyone has the right to rest and leisure, including reasonable limitation of working hours and periodic holidays with pay.

Article 25. 1. Everyone has the right to a standard of living adequate for the health and well-being of himself and of his family, including food, clothing, housing and medical care and necessary social services, and the right to security in the event of unemployment, sickness, disability, widowhood, old age or other lack of livelihood in circumstances beyond his control.

2. Motherhood and childhood are entitled to special care and assistance. All children, whether born in or out of wedlock, shall enjoy the same social protection.

Article 26. 1. Everyone has the right to education. Education shall be free, at least in the elementary and fundamental stages. Elementary education shall be compulsory. Technical and professional education shall be made generally available and higher education shall be equally accessible to all on the basis of merit.

2. Education shall be directed to the full development of human personality and to the strengthening of respect for human rights and fundamental freedoms. It shall promote understanding, tolerance and friendship among all nations, racial or religious groups, and shall further the activities of the United Nations for the maintenance of peace.

3. Parents have a prior right to choose the kind of education that shall be given to their children.

Article 27. 1. Everyone has the right freely to participate in the cultural life of the community, to enjoy the arts and to share in scientific advancement and its benefits.

2. Everyone has the right to the protection of the moral and material interests resulting from any scientific, literary or artistic production of which he is the author.

Article 28. Everyone is entitled to a social and international order in which the rights and freedoms set forth in this Declaration can be fully realized.

Article 29. 1. Everyone has duties to the community in which alone the free and full development of his personality is possible.

2. In the exercise of his rights and freedoms, everyone shall be subject only to such limitations as are determined by law solely for the purpose of securing due recognition and respect for the rights and freedoms of others and of meeting the just requirements of morality, public order and the general welfare in a democratic society.

3. These rights and freedoms may in no case be exercised contrary to the purposes and principles of the United Nations.

Article 30. Nothing in this Declaration may be interpreted as implying for any State, group or person any right to engage in any activity or to perform any act aimed at the destruction of any of the rights and freedoms set forth herein.

SEE ALSO *African Charter on Human and Peoples' Rights; American Convention on Human Rights and Protocol; American Declaration on the Rights and Duties of Man; European Convention on Human Rights and Protocols I-VIII; European Social Charter and Protocol; Helsinki Accord: Final Act of the Conference on Security and Cooperation in Europe; Inter-American Charter of Social Guarantees; International Bill of Human Rights; International Covenant on Civil and Political Rights and Protocols; International Covenant on Economic, Social and Cultural Rights; United Nations Charter.*

UNIVERSAL DECLARATION ON THE ERADICATION OF HUNGER AND MALNUTRITION (1974).

The World Food Conference, convened at Rome from 5 to 16 November 1974 by the UN General Assembly (resolution 3180 [XXVIII]), sought to develop ways and means whereby the international community as a whole could act to resolve the world's food problem. The declaration, charting a course for future work, also served to remind the world that "every man, woman and child had the inalienable right to be free from hunger and malnutrition in order to develop fully and maintain their physical and mental faculties."

The text of the declaration (*Report of the World Food Conference,* United Nations publication, Sales No. E.75.II.A.3, chap. I), adopted by the conference on 16 November 1974 and endorsed by the General Assembly on 17 December 1974 (resolution 3348 [XXIX]), is as follows:

The World Food Conference,
Recognizing that:

(a) The grave food crisis that is afflicting the peoples of the developing countries where most of the world's hungry and ill-nourished live and where more than two thirds of the world's population produce about one third of the world's food—an imbalance which threatens to increase in the next 10 years—is not only fraught with grave economic and social implications, but also acutely jeopardizes the most fundamental principles and values associated with the right to life and human dignity as enshrined in the Universal Declaration of Human Rights;

(b) The elimination of hunger and malnutrition, included as one of the objectives in the United Nations Declaration on Social Progress and Development, and the elimination of the causes that determine this situation are the common objectives of all nations;

(c) The situation of the peoples afflicted by hunger and malnutrition arises from their historical circumstances, especially social inequalities, including in many cases alien and colonial domination, foreign occupation, racial discrimination, *apartheid* and neo-colonialism in all its forms, which continue to be among the greatest obstacles to the full emancipation and progress of the developing countries and all the peoples involved;

(d) This situation has been aggravated in recent years by a series of crises to which the world economy has been subjected, such as the deterioration in the international monetary system, the inflationary increase in import costs, the heavy burdens imposed by external debt on the balance of payments of many developing countries, a rising food demand partly due to demographic pressure, speculation, and a shortage of, and increased costs for, essential agricultural inputs;

(e) These phenomena should be considered within the framework of the on-going negotiations on the Charter of Economic Rights and Duties of States, and the General Assembly of the United Nations should be urged unanimously to agree upon, and to adopt, a Charter that will be an effective instrument for the establishment of new international economic relations based on principles of equity and justice;

(f) All countries, big or small, rich or poor, are equal. All countries have the full right to participate in the decisions on the food problem;

(g) The well-being of the peoples of the world largely depends on the adequate production and distribution of food as well as the establishment of a world food security system which would ensure adequate availability of, and reasonable prices for, food at all times, irrespective of periodic fluctuations and vagaries of weather and free of political and economic pressures, and should thus facilitate, amongst other things, the development process of developing countries;

(h) Peace and justice encompass an economic dimension helping the solution of the world economic problems, the liquidation of under-development, offering a lasting and definitive solution of the food problem for all peoples and guaranteeing to all countries the right to implement freely and effectively their development programmes. To this effect, it is necessary to eliminate threats and resort to force and to promote peaceful co-operation between States to the fullest extent possible, to apply the principles of non-interference in the internal affairs of other States, full equality of rights and respect of national independence and sovereignty, as well as to encourage the peaceful co-operation between all States, irrespective of their political, social and economic systems. The further improvement of international relations will create better conditions for international co-operation in all fields which should make possible large financial and material resources to be used, *inter alia,* for developing agricultural production and substantially improving world food security;

(i) For a lasting solution of the food problem all efforts should be made to eliminate the widening gaps which today separate developed and developing countries and to bring about a new international economic order. It should be possible for all countries to participate actively and effectively in the new international economic relations by the establishment of suitable international systems, where appropriate, capable of producing adequate action in order to establish just and equitable relations in international economic co-operation;

(j) Developing countries reaffirm their belief that the primary responsibility for ensuring their own rapid development rests with themselves. They declare, therefore, their readiness to continue to intensify their individual and collective efforts with a view to expanding their mutual co-operation in the field of agricultural development and food production, including the eradication of hunger and malnutrition;

(k) Since, for various reasons, many developing countries are not yet always able to meet their own food needs, urgent and effective international action should be taken to assist them, free of political pressures,

Consistent with the aims and objectives of the Declaration on the Establishment of a New International Economic Order and the Programme of Action adopted by the General Assembly at its sixth special session,

The Conference consequently solemnly proclaims:

1. Every man, woman and child has the inalienable right to be free from hunger and malnutrition in order to develop fully and maintain their physical and mental faculties. Society today already possesses sufficient resources, organizational ability and technology and hence the competence to achieve this objective. Accordingly, the eradication of hunger is a common objective of all the countries of the international community, especially of the developed countries and others in a position to help.

2. It is a fundamental responsibility of Governments to work together for higher food production and a more equitable and efficient distribution of food between countries and within countries. Governments should initiate immediately a greater concerted attack on chronic malnutrition and deficiency diseases among the vulnerable and lower income groups. In order to ensure adequate nutrition for all, Governments should formulate appropriate food and nutrition policies integrated in over-all socio-economic and agricultural development plans based on adequate knowledge of available as well as potential food resources. The importance of human milk in this connexion should be stressed on nutritional grounds.

3. Food problems must be tackled during the preparation and implementation of national plans and programmes for economic and social development, with emphasis on their humanitarian aspects.

4. It is a responsibility of each State concerned, in accordance with its sovereign judgement and internal legislation, to remove the obstacles to food production and to provide proper incentives to agricultural producers. Of prime importance for the attainment of these objectives are effective measures of socio-economic transformation by agrarian, tax, credit and investment policy reform and the reorganization of rural structures, such as the reform of the conditions of ownership, the encouragement of producer and consumer co-operatives, the mobilization of the full potential of human resources, both male and female, in the developing countries for an integrated rural development and the involvement of small farmers, fishermen and landless workers in attaining the required food production and employment targets. Moreover, it is necessary to recognize the key role of women in agricultural production and rural economy in many countries, and to ensure that appropriate education, extension programmes and financial facilities are made available to women on equal terms with men.

5. Marine and inland water resources are today becoming more important than ever as a source of food and economic prosperity. Accordingly, action should be taken to promote a rational exploitation of these resources, preferably for direct human consumption, in order to contribute to meeting the food requirements of all peoples.

6. The efforts to increase food production should be complemented by every endeavour to prevent wastage of food in all its forms.

7. To give impetus to food production in developing countries and in particular in the least developed and most seriously affected among them, urgent and effective international action should be taken, by the developed countries and other countries in a position to do so, to provide them with sustained additional technical and financial assistance on favourable terms and in a volume sufficient to their needs on the basis of bilateral and multilateral arrangements. This assistance must be free of conditions inconsistent with the sovereignty of the receiving States.

8. All countries, and primarily the highly industrialized countries, should promote the advancement of food production technology and should make all efforts to promote the transfer, adaptation and dissemination of appropriate food production technology for the benefit of the developing countries and, to that end, they should *inter alia* make all efforts to disseminate the results of their research work to Governments and scientific institutions of developing countries in order to enable them to promote a sustained agricultural development.

9. To assure the proper conservation of natural resources being utilized, or which might be utilized, for food production, all countries must collaborate in order to facilitate the preservation of the environment, including the marine environment.

10. All developed countries and others able to do so should collaborate technically and financially with the developing countries in their efforts to expand land and water

resources for agricultural production and to assure a rapid increase in the availability, at fair costs, of agricultural inputs such as fertilizers and other chemicals, high-quality seeds, credit and technology. Co-operation among developing countries, in this connexion, is also important.

11. All States should strive to the utmost to readjust, where appropriate, their agricultural policies to give priority to food production, recognizing, in this connexion the interrelationship between the world food problem and international trade. In the determination of attitudes towards farm support programmes for domestic food production, developed countries should take into account, as far as possible, the interest of the food-exporting developing countries, in order to avoid detrimental effect on their exports. Moreover, all countries should co-operate to devise effective steps to deal with the problem of stabilizing world markets and promoting equitable and remunerative prices, where appropriate through international arrangements, to improve access to markets through reduction or elimination of tariff and non-tariff barriers on the products of interest to the developing countries, to substantially increase the export earnings of these countries, to contribute to the diversification of their exports, and apply to them, in the multilateral trade negotiations, the principles as agreed upon in the Tokyo Declaration, including the concept of non-reciprocity and more favourable treatment.

12. As it is common responsibility of the entire international community to ensure the availability at all times of adequate world supplies of basic food-stuffs by way of appropriate reserves, including emergency reserves, all countries should co-operate in the establishment of an effective system of world food security by:

Participating in and supporting the operation of the Global Information and Early Warning System on Food and Agriculture;

Adhering to the objectives, policies and guidelines of the proposed International Undertaking on World Food Security as endorsed by the World Food Conference;

Earmarking, where possible, stocks or funds for meeting international emergency food requirements as envisaged in the proposed International Undertaking on World Food Security and developing international guidelines to provide for the co-ordination and the utilization of such stocks;

Co-operating in the provision of food aid for meeting emergency and nutritional needs as well as for stimulating rural employment through development projects.

All donor countries should accept and implement the concept of forward planning of food aid and make all efforts to provide commodities and/or financial assistance that will ensure adequate quantities of grains and other food commodities.

Time is short. Urgent and sustained action is vital. The Conference, therefore, calls upon all peoples expressing their will as individuals, and through their Governments and non-governmental organizations, to work together to bring about the end of the age-old scourge of hunger.

The Conference affirms:

The determination of the participating States to make full use of the United Nations system in the implementation of this Declaration and the other decisions adopted by the Conference.

SEE ALSO *Food; Hunger and Malnutrition; Standard of Living; World Food Council.*

URUGUAY. The Oriental Republic of Uruguay is a country in temperate South America, on the Atlantic Ocean. It has borders with Argentina and Brazil and achieved independence in 1828 as a buffer between those two countries. It became a member of the United Nations in 1945. Its population is estimated by the UN (1990) to be 3,128,000. Ethnic groups include persons of European (mainly Spanish, Italian, and Portuguese) descent, and mestizos (descendents of Amerindians absorbed into the Spanish and Portuguese populations). The language commonly used is Spanish (official). Christianity (Roman Catholic, 66%; Protestant denominations, 2%) is the predominant religion; Judaism is the religion of about 3%, and the remainder profess other faiths or none at all. Literacy is estimated at 94%.

The government (1990) took the form of a republic. Under the 1967 constitution, the president, elected by universal suffrage for a term of five years, is head of State and of government. Legislation is prepared by a bicameral General Assembly, consisting of a 99-member Chamber of Deputies and a 30-member Senate, all elected by popular vote. The independent judiciary is headed by the Supreme Court of Justice. Political parties include the Colorado Party, the Blanco Party, and the Broad Front Coalition.

The military regime which governed the country between 1973 and 1985 was accused of gross violations of human rights while in office, including widespread torture, "disappearances" and mistreatment of tens of thousands of persons. In turning the government over to civilian rule in March 1985, it demanded total amnesty for all such abuses. The amnesty was approved after acrimonious debate in both houses of the General Assembly, and signed on 22 December 1986 by President Julio Maria Sanguinetti as a step necessary to attain national reconciliation. The amnesty law barred judicial prosecution of military and police officials accused of human rights violations that took place prior to 1985. The office of the president retained the power to investigate cases of persons who "disappeared" during the period of military rule.

The **WORKING GROUP ON ENFORCED OR INVOLUNTARY DISAPPEARANCES** of the UN Commission on Human Rights informed the Commission at its 1987 session that it had transmitted 64 cases to the government and that seven of those cases had been clarified by the government's responses and one by a non-governmental source, leaving 56 cases outstanding.

In this connection, the working group was informed by the permanent representative of Uruguay to the United Nations Office at Geneva that, since a new democratic government had come into power in

Uruguay, disappearances had ceased and would not occur in the future provided democracy was preserved. The new government had taken several measures to put an end to human rights violations, such as an amnesty law covering all political offenses, which had permitted the release of political prisoners, the return of exiles, and the reintegration of former officials to their posts. Concerning cases of disappearances, a parliamentary commission had been established in which all Uruguayan political parties participated. According to the findings of the commission, a total of 164 Uruguayan nationals had disappeared while military governments were in power; only 32 of them had disappeared in Uruguay, whereas 127 had disappeared in Argentina, three in Chile, and two in Paraguay. The report of the commission had been transmitted to the judiciary to initiate proceedings.

In November 1989, Luis Alberto Lacalle, of the centrist National Party, was elected president of Uruguay, replacing President Sanguinetti of the Colorado Party, who was not eligible to stand for re-election. He promised an efficient, productive government that would substitute private enterprise for state control and reduce inflation which had been running at more than 80% per year.

V

VANCOUVER DECLARATION ON HUMAN SETTLEMENTS (1976).

VANCOUVER DECLARATION ON HUMAN SETTLEMENTS (1976). The declaration was adopted on 11 June 1976 by HABITAT, the United Nations Conference on Human Settlements, convened at Vancouver from 31 May to 11 June 1976 with the mandate (a) to stimulate innovation, serve as a means for the exchange of experience, and ensure the widest possible dissemination of new ideas and technologies in the field of human settlements; (b) to formulate and make recommendations for an international program in this field which will assist governments; and (c) to stimulate interest in developing appropriate financial systems and institutions for human settlements among those making financial resources available and those in a position to use such resources, considering that the most appropriate and effective action for dealing with human settlements problems is action at the national level, but that such action will require assistance and cooperation between and among all states.

The UN General Assembly on 16 December 1976 took note (resolution 31/109) of the report of the conference (United Nations publication, Sales No. E.76. IV.7), including the Vancouver Declaration (chap. I), and urged all governments to take the recommendations contained therein into account when reviewing their existing policies and strategies in the field of human settlements. The text of the declaration is as follows:

HABITAT: United Nations Conference on Human Settlements,

Aware that the Conference was convened following recommendation of the United Nations Conference on the Human Environment and subsequent resolutions of the General Assembly, particularly resolution 3128 (XXVIII) by which the nations of the world expressed their concern over the extremely serious condition of human settlements, particularly that which prevails in developing countries,

Recognizing that international co-operation, based on the principles of the United Nations Charter, has to be developed and strengthened in order to provide solutions for world problems and to create an international community based on equity, justice and solidarity,

Recalling the decisions of the United Nations Conference on the Human Environment, as well as the recommendations of the World Population Conference, the United Nations World Food Conference, the Second General Conference of the United Nations Industrial Development Organization, the World Conference of the International Women's Year; the Declaration and Programme of Action adopted by the sixth special session of the General Assembly of the United Nations and the Charter of Economic Rights and Duties of States that establish the basis of the New International Economic Order,

Noting that the condition of human settlements largely determines the quality of life, the improvement of which is a prerequisite for the full satisfaction of basic needs, such as employment, housing, health services, education and recreation,

Recognizing that the problems of human settlements are not isolated from the social and economic development of countries and that they cannot be set apart from existing unjust international economic relations,

Being deeply concerned with the increasing difficulties facing the world in satisfying the basic needs and aspirations of peoples consistent with principles of human dignity,

Recognizing that the circumstances of life for vast numbers of people in human settlements are unacceptable, particularly in developing countries, and that, unless positive and concrete action is taken at national and international levels to find and implement solutions, these conditions are likely to be further aggravated, as a result of:

Inequitable economic growth, reflected in the wide disparities in wealth which now exist between countries and between human beings and which condemn millions of people to a life of poverty, without satisfying the basic requirements for food, educations, health services, shelter, environmental hygiene, water and energy;

Social, economic, ecological and environmental deterioration which are exemplified at the national and international levels by inequalities in living conditions, social segregation, racial discrimination, acute unemployment, illiteracy, disease and poverty, the breakdown of social relationships and traditional cultural values and the increasing degradation of life-supporting resources of air, water and land;

World population growth trends which indicate that numbers of mankind in the next 25 years would double, thereby more than doubling the need for food, shelter and all other requirements for life and human dignity which are at the present inadequately met;

Uncontrolled urbanization and consequent conditions of overcrowding, pollution, deterioration and psychological tensions in metropolitan regions;

Rural backwardness which compels a large majority of

mankind to live at the lowest standards of living and contribute to uncontrolled urban growth;

Rural dispersion exemplified by small scattered settlements and isolated homesteads which inhibit the provision of infrastructure and services, particularly those relating to water, health and education;

Involuntary migration, politically, racially, and economically motivated, relocation and expulsion of people from their national homeland,

Recognizing also that the establishment of a just and equitable world economic order through necessary changes in the areas of international trade, monetary systems, industrialization, transfer of resources, transfer of technology, and the consumption of world resources, is essential for socio-economic development and improvement of human settlement, particularly in developing countries,

Recognizing further that these problems pose a formidable challenge to human understanding, imagination, ingenuity and resolve, and that new priorities to promote the qualitative dimensions to economic development, as well as a new political commitment to find solutions resulting in the practical implementation of the New International Economic Order, become imperative:

I. Opportunities and Solutions. 1. Mankind must not be daunted by the scale of the task ahead. There is need for awareness of and responsibility for increased activity of the national Governments and international community, aimed at mobilization of economic resources, institutional changes and international solidarity by:

(a) Adopting bold, meaningful and effective human settlement policies and spatial planning strategies realistically adapted to local conditions;

(b) Creating more livable, attractive and efficient settlements which recognize human scale, the heritage and culture of people and the special needs of disadvantaged groups especially children, women and the infirm in order to ensure the provision of health, services, education, food and employment within a framework of social justice;

(c) Creating possibilities for effective participation by all people in the planning, building and management of their human settlements;

(d) Developing innovative approaches in formulating and implementing settlement programmes through more appropriate use of science and technology and adequate national and international financing;

(e) Utilizing the most effective means of communications for the exchange of knowledge and experience in the field of human settlements;

(f) Strengthening bonds of international co-operation both regionally and globally;

(g) Creating economic opportunities conducive to full employment where, under healthy, safe conditions, women and men will be fairly compensated for their labour in monetary, health and other personal benefits.

2. In meeting this challenge, human settlements must be seen as an instrument and object of development. The goals of settlement policies are inseparable from the goals of every sector of social and economic life. The solutions to the problems of human settlements must therefore be conceived as an integral part of the development process of individual nations and the world community.

3. With these opportunities and considerations in mind, and being agreed on the necessity of finding common principles that will guide Governments and the world community in solving the problems of human settlements, the Conference proclaims the following general principles and guidelines for action.

II. General Principles. 1. The improvement of the quality of life of human beings is the first and most important objective of every human settlement policy. These policies must facilitate the rapid and continuous improvement in the quality of life of all people, beginning with the satisfaction of the basic needs of food, shelter, clean water, employment, health, education, training, social security without any discrimination as to race, colour, sex, language, religion, ideology, national or social origin or other cause, in a frame of freedom, dignity and social justice.

2. In striving to achieve this objective, priority must be given to the needs of the most disadvantaged people.

3. Economic development should lead to the satisfaction of human needs and is a necessary means towards achieving a better quality of life, provided that it contributes to a more equitable distribution of its benefits among people and nations. In this context particular attention should be paid to the accelerated transition in developing countries from primary development to secondary development activities, and particularly to industrial development.

4. Human dignity and the exercise of free choice consistent with over-all public welfare are basic rights which must be assured in every society. It is therefore the duty of all people and Governments to join the struggle against any form of colonialism, foreign aggression and occupation, domination, *apartheid* and all forms of racism and racial discrimination referred to in the resolutions as adopted by the General Assembly of the United Nations.

5. The establishment of settlements in territories occupied by force is illegal. It is condemned by the international community. However, action still remains to be taken against the establishment of such settlements.

6. The right of free movement and the right of each individual to choose the place of settlement within the domain of his own country should be recognized and safeguarded.

7. Every State has the sovereign and inalienable right to choose its economic system, as well as its political, social and cultural system, in accordance with the will of its people, without interference, coercion or external threat of any kind.

8. Every State has the right to exercise full and permanent sovereignty over its wealth, natural resources and economic activities, adopting the necessary measures for the planning and management of its resources, providing for the protection, preservation and enhancement of the environment.

9. Every country should have the right to be a sovereign inheritor of its own cultural values created throughout its history, and has the duty to preserve them as an integral part of the cultural heritage of mankind.

10. Land is one of the fundamental elements in human settlements. Every State has the right to take the necessary steps to maintain under public control the use, possession, disposal and reservation of land. Every State has the right to plan and regulate use of land, which is one of its most important resources, in such a way that the growth of population centres both urban and rural are based on a comprehensive land use plan. Such measures must assure the attainment of basic goals of social and economic reform for every country, in conformity with its national and land tenure system and legislation.

11. The nations must avoid the pollution of the biosphere and the oceans and should join in the effort to end irrational exploitation of all environmental resources,

whether non-renewable or renewable in the long term. The environment is the common heritage of mankind and its protection is the responsibility of the whole international community. All acts by nations and people should therefore be inspired by a deep respect for the protection of the environmental resources upon which life itself depends.

12. The waste and misuse of resources in war and armaments should be prevented. All countries should make a firm commitment to promote general and complete disarmament under strict and effective international control, in particular in the field of nuclear disarmament. Part of the resources thus released should be utilized so as to achieve a better quality of life for humanity and particularly the peoples of developing countries.

13. All persons have the right and the duty to participate, individually and collectively in the elaboration and implementation of policies and programmes of their human settlements.

14. To achieve universal progress in the quality of life, a fair and balanced structure of the economic relations between States has to be promoted. It is therefore essential to implement urgently the New International Economic Order, based on the Declaration and Programme of Action approved by the General Assembly in its sixth special session, and on the Charter of Economic Rights and Duties of States.

15. The highest priority should be placed on the rehabilitation of expelled and homeless people who have been displaced by natural or man-made catastrophes, and especially by the act of foreign aggression. In the latter case, all countries have the duty to fully co-operate in order to guarantee that the parties involved allow the return of displaced persons to their homes and to give them the right to possess and enjoy their properties and belongings without interference.

16. Historical settlements, monuments and other items of national heritage, including religious heritage, should be safeguarded against any acts of aggression or abuse by the occupying Power.

17. Every State has the sovereign right to rule and exercise effective control over foreign investments, including the transnational corporations—within its national jurisdiction, which affect directly or indirectly the human settlements programmes.

18. All countries, particularly developing countries, must create conditions which make possible the full integration of women and youth in political, economic and social activities, particularly in the planning and implementation of human settlement proposals and in all the associated activities, on the basis of equal rights, in order to achieve an efficient and full utilization of available human resources, bearing in mind that women constitute half of the world population.

19. International co-operation is an objective and a common duty of all States, and necessary efforts must therefore be made to accelerate the social and economic development of developing countries, within the framework of favourable external conditions, which are compatible with their needs and aspirations and which contains the due respect for the sovereign equality of all States.

III. Guidelines for Action. 1. It is recommended that Governments and international organizations should make every effort to take urgent action as set out in the following guidelines:

2. It is the responsibility of Governments to prepare spatial strategy plans and adopt human settlement policies to guide the socio-economic development efforts. Such policies must be an essential component of an over-all development strategy, linking and harmonizing them with policies on industrialization, agriculture, social welfare, and environmental and cultural preservation so that each supports the other in a progressive improvement in well-being of all mankind.

3. A human settlement policy must seek harmonious integration or co-ordination of a wide variety of components, including, for example, population growth and distribution, employment, shelter, land use, infrastructure and services. Governments must create mechanisms and institutions to develop and implement such a policy.

4. It is of paramount importance that national and international efforts give priority to improving the rural habitat. In this context, efforts should be made towards the reduction of disparities between rural and urban areas, as needed between regions and within urban areas themselves, for a harmonious development of human settlements.

5. The demographic, natural and economic characteristics of many countries, require policies on growth and distribution of population, land tenure and localization of productive activities to ensure orderly processes of urbanization and arrange for rational occupation of rural space.

6. Human settlement policies and programmes should define and strive for progressive minimum standards for an acceptable quality of life. These standards will vary within and between countries, as well as over periods of time, and therefore must be subject to change in accordance with conditions and possibilities. Some standards are most appropriately defined in quantitative terms, thus providing precisely defined targets at the local and national levels. Others must be qualitative, with their achievement subject to felt need. At the same time, social justice and a fair sharing of resources demand the discouragement of excessive consumptions.

7. Attention must also be drawn to the detrimental effects of transposing standards and criteria that can only be adopted by minorities and could heighten inequalities, the misuse of resources and the social, cultural and ecological deterioration of the developing countries.

8. Adequate shelter and services are a basic human right which places an obligation on Governments to ensure their attainment by all people, beginning with direct assistance to the least advantaged through guided programmes of self-help and community action. Governments should endeavour to remove all impediments hindering attainments of these goals. Of special importance is the elimination of social and racial segregation, *inter alia,* through the creation of better balanced communities, which blend different social groups, occupation, housing and amenities.

9. Health is an essential element in the development of the individual and one of the goals of human settlement policies should be to improve environmental health conditions and basic health services.

10. Basic human dignity is the right of people, individually and collectively, to participate directly in shaping the policies and programmes affecting their lives. The process of choosing and carrying out a given course of action for human settlement improvement should be designed expressly to fulfil that right. Effective human settlement policies require a continuous co-operative relationship between a Government and its people at all levels. It is recommended that national governments promote programmes that will en-

courage and assist local authorities to participate to a greater extent in national development.

11. Since a genuine human settlement policy requires the effective participation of the entire population, recourse must therefore be made at all times to technical arrangements permitting the use of all human resources, both skilled and unskilled. The equal participation of women must be guaranteed. These goals must be associated with a global training programme to facilitate the introduction and use of technologies that maximize productive employment.

12. International and national institutions should promote and institute education programmes and courses in the subject of "human settlements".

13. Land is an essential element in development of both urban and rural settlements. The use and tenure of land should be subject to public control because of its limited supply through appropriate measures and legislation including agrarian reform policies—as an essential basis for integrated rural development—that will facilitate the transfer of economic resources to the agricultural sector and the promotion of the agro-industrial effort, so as to improve the integration and organization of human settlements, in accordance with national development plans and programmes. The increase in the value of land as a result of public decision and investment should be recaptured for the benefit of society as a whole. Governments should also ensure that prime agricultural land is destined to its most vital use.

14. Human settlements are characterized by significant disparities in living standards and opportunities. Harmonious development of human settlements requires the reduction of disparities between rural and urban areas, between regions and within regions themselves. Governments should adopt policies which aim at decreasing the differences between living standards and opportunities in urban and non-urban areas. Such policies at the national level should be supplemented by policies designed to reduce disparities between countries within the framework of the New International Economic Order.

15. In achieving the socio-economic and environmental objectives of the development of human settlements, high priority should be given to the actual design and physical planning processes which have as their main tasks the synthesis of various planning approaches and the transformation of broad and general goals into specific design solutions. The sensitive and comprehensive design methodologies related to the particular circumstances of time and space, and based on consideration of the human scale should be pursued and encouraged.

16. The design of human settlements should aim at providing a living environment in which identities of individuals, families and societies are preserved and adequate means for maintaining privacy, the possibility of face-to-face interactions and public participation in the decision-making process are provided.

17. A human settlement is more than a grouping of people, shelter and work places. Diversity in the characteristics of human settlements reflecting cultural and aesthetic values must be respected and encouraged and areas of historical, religious or archaelogical importance and nature areas of special interest preserved for posterity. Places of worship, especially in areas of expanding human settlements, should be provided and recognized in order to sat-

isfy the spiritual and religious needs of different groups in accordance with freedom of religious expression.

18. Governments and the international community should facilitate the transfer of relevant technology and experience and should encourage and assist the creation of endogenous technology better suited to the socio-cultural characteristics and patterns of population by means of bilateral or multilateral agreements having regard to the sovereignty and interest of the participating States. The knowledge and experience accumulated on the subject of human settlements should be available to all countries. Research and academic institutions should contribute more fully to this effort by giving greater attention to human settlements problems.

19. Access should be granted, on more favourable terms, to modern technology, which should be adapted, as necessary, to the specific economic, social and ecological conditions and to the different stages of development of the developing countries. Efforts must be made to ensure that the commercial practices governing the transfer of technology are adapted to the needs of the developing countries and to ensure that buyers' rights are not abused.

20. International, technical and financial co-operation by the developed countries with the developing countries must be conducted on the basis of respect for national sovereignty and national development plans and programmes and designed to solve problems relating to projects, under human settlement programmes, aimed at enhancing the quality of life of the inhabitants.

21. Due attention should be given to implementation of conservation and recycling technologies.

22. In the planning and management of human settlements, Governments should take into consideration all pertinent recommendations on human settlements planning which have emerged from earlier conferences dealing with the quality of life and development problems which affect it, starting with the high global priority represented by the transformation of the economic order at the national and international levels (sixth and seventh special sessions), the environmental impact of human settlements (Stockholm Conference on the Human Environment), the housing and sanitary ramifications of population growth (World Population Conference, Bucharest), rural development and the need to increase food supply (World Food Conference, Rome) and the effect on women of housing and urban development (International Women's Conference, Mexico City).

23. While planning new human settlements of restructuring existing ones, a high priority should be given to the promotion of optimal and creative conditions of human coexistence. This implies the creation of a well-structured urban space on a human scale, the close interconnexion of the different urban functions, the relief of urban man from intolerable psychological tensions due to overcrowding and chaos, the creation of chances of human encounters and the elimination of urban concepts leading to human isolation.

24. Guided by the foregoing principles, the international community must exercise its responsibility to support national efforts to meet the human settlements challenges facing them. Since resources of Governments are inadequate to meet all needs, the international community should provide the necessary financial and technical assistance, evolve appropriate institutional arrangements and

seek new effective ways to promote them. In the meantime, assistance to developing countries must at least reach the percentage targets set in the International Development Strategy for the Second United Nations Development Decade.

SEE ALSO Declaration of the United Nations Conference on the Human Environment; Environment; Homelessness; Housing; Shelter.

VANUATU. The Republic of Vanuatu is a country occupying an archipelago consisting of about 80 islands in the South Pacific Ocean, between New Caledonia and Fiji. The largest islands are Efate, Espiritu Santo, Malekula, Malo, Pentecost, and Tanna. Formerly known as the New Hebrides, an Anglo–French condominium, Vanuatu achieved independence from Great Britain and France in 1980 and became a member of the United Nations in 1981. Its population is estimated by the UN (1990) to be 164,000. The people are predominantly of Melanesian descent. Languages used commonly include Malaysian, French, and English. Religions practiced include Christianity (Presbyterian 37%, Anglican 15%, other Protestant denominations 24%, Roman Catholic 15%), and Animism (9%).

The government (1990) took the form of a republic and member of the Commonwealth of Nations, of which the British monarch is the symbolic head. Under the 1980 constitution, the president, elected by an electoral college for a term of five years, is head of State. The prime minister, representing the party or coalition given an elective majority, is head of government. Legislation is prepared by a 39-member Parliament, elected by popular vote. The Vanuaaku Party is the predominant political group.

VENEZUELA. The Republic of Venezuela is a country in tropical South America, on the Caribbean Sea; it includes 72 offshore islands. It has borders with Brazil, Colombia, and Guyana. It achieved independence from Spain in 1821 and became a member of the United Nations in 1945. Its population is estimated by the UN (1990) to be 19,735,000. Although Venezuela does not classify or characterize its population by ethnic origin, it can be said that most of its people are of mestizo (mixed white and Amerindian) descent. There is an indigenous population of some 140,645 persons in rural, forest, and frontier areas: more than 20,000 families organized into some 1,595 indigenous communities, forming culturally and linguistically coherent, stable, and cohesive communities representing over 30 distinctive ethnic minorities. Languages commonly used include Spanish,

Portuguese, Arabic, German, and a number of Amerindian vernaculars. Christianity (Roman Catholic, 96%; Protestant denominations, 1%) is the predominant religion; others total 3%. Literacy is estimated at 86%.

The government (1990) took the form of a federal republic, with 20 states, two federal territories, and a dependency (the offshore islands). Each state is autonomous and has its own governor and legislature. The president is elected by universal and compulsory suffrage for a term of four years; he is not eligible for re-election until ten years after the end of his term. Assisted by a 24-member Council of Ministers, he serves as head of State and of government. There is a bicameral Congress, including the 200-member Chamber of Deputies and the 47-member Senate, all members of which are elected by popular vote for terms of five years. The judiciary is independent and headed by a Supreme Court of 18 members. Political parties include the Democratic Action Party, the Social Christian Party, the People's Electoral Movement, and the Democratic Republican Union.

Carlos Andres Perez, who stepped down in 1979 after serving four years as president of Venezuela, was re-elected in January 1988—the first Venezuelan president to win re-election. He succeeded President Jaime Lusinchi on 2 February 1989.

As regards Venezuela's indigenous populations, the government stated, in a report presented to the **COMMITTEE ON THE ELIMINATION OF RACIAL DISCRIMINATION** on 25 September 1986, that (UN Doc. CERD/C/148/Add. 18, para. 19–20):

Article 77 of the Constitution prescribes that the law shall establish the special régime required for the protection of the indigenous communities and for their gradual incorporation into national life. In other words, in regulating matters of concern to the indigenous communities, the Venezuelan State must be guided by the fact that they need special and more extensive protection than that enjoyed by the other inhabitants of the country and that the indigenous peoples must be incorporated gradually into national life, as far as the various institutions and mechanisms are concerned that regulate the life or circumstances of the other inhabitants of Venezuela.

In conformity with the provisions of article 61 of the Constitution, the Venezuelan State assumes the obligation not to permit discrimination based on race, sex, creed or social status. It follows that the members of indigenous communities have the individual, social, economic and political rights which the Venezuelan State recognizes to all inhabitants of the Republic, including the right to life; liberty and security of person; inviolability of the home and correspondence; freedom of movement throughout the national territory; to profess one's religious faith and to worship, in private or public; to express one's opinion, either orally or in writing; to address petitions to any public entity or official; to use the organs for the administration of justice for the defence of one's rights and interests; to freedom of association, for lawful ends; to meet, either in public or private, without prior permission; to protection of health and to education; to work and to social security; to engage freely in a remunerative activity of one's choice; to vote or to hold public office and, finally, all those rights granted or bestowed by the Constitution and the laws, treaties or conventions on the protection of human rights, to most of which Venezuela is a party.

VIET NAM. The Socialist Republic of Viet Nam is a country in southeastern Asia, occupying the eastern and southern part of the Indochinese Peninsula, on the South China Sea. It achieved independence in 1976 through the formal unification of North and South Viet Nam after the capitulation of the former Republic of Viet Nam and became a member of the United Nations in 1977. Its population is estimated by the UN (1990) to be 66,153,000. Apart from the majority Vietnamese (Kinh), who comprise more than 84% of the population, there are more than 50 ethnic minorities, including Tay, Thai, Muong, Nung, Kho-me, Gia-rai, Ede, Cham, and Coho. Each of these communities has its own written and spoken language and its own manners and customs. Languages commonly used include Vietnamese (official), French, Chinese, Khmer, and the minority vernaculars. Religions practiced include Buddhism, Christianity, Animism, Islam, and Taoism. Literacy is estimated at 78%.

The government (1990) took the form of a republic. Under the 1980 constitution, the Communist Party is the ruling political party. Executive authority is exercised by the State Council and Council of Ministers, with "people's committees" governing in local jurisdictions. National legislation is prepared by the National Assembly; local legislation, by people's councils. The judiciary is headed by the Supreme People's Court. At an election held in April 1981, 829 candidates participated after being nominated at public meetings and 496 were elected. In addition to the Communist Party, two political parties—the Socialist Party and the Democratic Party—participated.

Between April 1975 and August 1984 more than 550,000 "boat people" from Viet Nam found refuge abroad; and, in 1985, it was estimated that they continued to leave at the rate of 1,000 per month. Arrangements introduced by the United Nations High Commissioner for Refugees increased significantly the rescue of asylum-seekers in distress at sea, and international preventive measures resulted in a sharp decline in the number of refugee boats attacked by pirates.

As regards the treatment of its ethnic minorities, the government of Viet Nam, in a report submitted on 22 December 1983 to the COMMITTEE ON THE ELIMINATION OF RACIAL DISCRIMINATION, indicated that the basic laws of the Vietnamese state stipulate, *inter alia,* the following principles: (a) solidarity, unity, and equality among the nationalities; elimination of national divisiveness and marks of contempt; and removal of the discrepancy in economic, cultural, and social development levels among the various ethnic groups; and (b) guaranteeing the rights and fundamental freedoms of citizens without any discrimination. In order to implement these principles, the government took steps to ensure the development of the minorities, among them "encouraging the development of production in the highlands, encouraging the ethnic groups to make use of their own spoken and written languages, establishing communal dispensaries in the highlands, establishing five universities and training colleges essentially for the children of the ethnic minorities, and granting priority access for young people from the ethnic minorities to the country's other universities."

The Commission on Ethnic Affairs was established in 1955 to monitor the application of the minorities policies. The commission was converted in 1958 into the Central Committee of Nationalities, an organ with ministerial powers whose chairman is a member of the Council of Ministers.

Vietnamese military expansion into Laos and Cambodia have given rise to allegations of violations of the human rights of the peoples of those countries and to charges that their right to self-determination has been denied.

W

WAR CRIMES FILES. On 31 August 1987, the UN SUB-COMMISSION ON PREVENTION OF DISCRIMINATION AND PROTECTION OF MINORITIES pointed out (resolution 1987/2) that the files of the War Crimes Commission, of which the United Nations is the custodian, were at that time accessible only to UN member States by virtue of rules which had been established by the UN SECRETARIAT. Considering that these files might contain important sources of information concerning violations of human rights and fundamental freedoms during the Nazi regime, the sub-commission welcomed the prospect of a decision to broaden access to them.

Having been informed that the secretary-general had determined that at least a majority of the 17 States that had been members of the commission were willing for the rules of access to be relaxed, under considerations to be determined jointly, the sub-commission recommended that the Commission on Human Rights encourage the secretary-general to pursue these efforts and to suggest to him that the sub-commission advise him with regard to the drafting of guidelines concerning who, other than member States, should have access to the files and under what circumstances.

Before the commission met for its 1988 session, however, access to the files of the War Crimes Commission had been broadened by the secretary-general, in agreement with the States which had been members of the commission, as a result of a meeting convened by the secretary-general in September 1987.

WAR CRIMINALS: PROSECUTION AND PUNISHMENT. In one of its earliest decisions, the UN General Assembly on 13 February 1946 called (resolution 3 [I]) for the development of international cooperation to secure the punishment, in the countries where their deeds were committed, of war criminals and persons who had committed crimes against mankind.

At its 1987 session, the SUB-COMMISSION ON PREVENTION OF DISCRIMINATION AND PROTECTION OF MINORITIES noted that such cooperation had been established

and was continuing but that, nevertheless, a large number of war criminals and persons guilty of crimes against mankind continued to live in territories of UN member States. It called for further international cooperation in this field to prosecute and punish them.

The UN COMMISSION ON HUMAN RIGHTS, at its 1988 session, commended (resolution 1988/47) the cooperation among various UN member States which had resulted in the fair trial and just punishment of important war criminals, including the Nazi war criminal Klaus Barbie, for their crimes against humanity; and noted the spirit of cooperation shown by several member States in facilitating the extradition of war criminals who, in the aftermath of the World War II, had attempted to elude responsibility for their deeds by taking refuge in other countries. At the same time, it recognized that, according to consistent and well-documented reports, a large number of persons alleged to have committed war crimes and crimes against humanity live in the territories of member States. It urged all States to take the necessary measures, in accordance with their national constitutional systems, to ensure full international cooperation for the purpose of securing, preferably in the place where they committed their deeds, the prosecution and punishment of all those who have committed war crimes and crimes against humanity.

SEE ALSO Convention on the Non-Applicability of Statutory Limitations to War Crimes and Crimes against Humanity; European Convention on the Non-Applicability of Statutory Limitations on Crimes against Humanity and War Crimes; Principles of International Law. . . Charter of the Nurmberg Tribunal. . . .

WAR RESISTERS' INTERNATIONAL. An international non-governmental organization in consultative status with the Economic and Social Council (Category II) and with UNESCO, the War Resisters League has sections in 18 countries and associate organizations in 18 countries.

Founded in 1921 in the Netherlands as *Paco,* the organization moved to London and changed its name in 1923. It endeavors to help pacifists and their national organizations to wage the struggle for peace on a world-wide scale, to provide legal and financial assistance to conscientious objectors, and to work for disarmament and the abolition of conscription. It provides a link between peace organizations in all parts of the world, and actively seeks legal recognition of conscientious objection to military service. It offers training sessions in non-violent direct action and promotes this form of social change.

WRI publishes *The Broken Rifle* six times a year, in English, French, and German; in addition, the *WRI Newsletter* is also published six times a year (alternately with *The Broken Rifle*). The news release service "Newsline" provides updates on WRI activities in English, French, and German.

War Resisters International. Address: 55 Dawes Street, London SE 17 1EL, UK. Telephone: (44-1) 703-7189. Chairperson: Narayan Desai.

Yearbook of International Organizations 1989/90 (K.G. Saur).

WOMEN AND PEACE. In 1982, the General Assembly adopted and proclaimed (resolution 37/63) the DECLARATION ON THE PARTICIPATION OF WOMEN IN PROMOTING INTERNATIONAL PEACE AND CO-OPERATION, in which it recognized that women and men have an equal and vital interest in contributing to international peace and cooperation and that, to this end, women must be enabled to exercise their right to participate in the economic, social, cultural, civil, and political affairs of society on an equal footing with men.

In May 1988, the Economic and Social Council, wishing to encourage the active participation of women in promoting international peace, security, and cooperation and the elimination of violence against women within the family and society appealed (resolution 1988/28) to all governments to take practical institutional, educational, and organizational measures to facilitate women's participation on an equal footing with men in activities related to peace, disarmament negotiations, and the resolution of conflicts and to inform the Secretary-General of the activities undertaken. The Secretary-General was requested to report on such activities to the third special session of the General Assembly devoted to disarmament and peace.

SEE ALSO *Declaration of Mexico on the Equality of Women and Their Contribution to Development and Peace.*

WOMEN IN THE UN SECRETARIAT. At a time when the United Nations faces an expanding role in world affairs, it becomes increasingly important that both men and women participate actively and visibly at all levels in the work of the organization, under conditions of full equality, in accordance with article 8 of the charter of the United Nations.

In 1985, the General Assembly approved (resolution 40/258 B) a detailed action program (UN Doc. A/C.5/40/30) designed to address the obstacles to the improvement of the status of women in the United Nations Secretariat. In a progress report to the Assembly, dated 12 October 1988 (UN Doc. A/C.5/43/14), the Secretary-General indicated that, within the secretariat, the Office of Human Resources Management is responsible for implementing the action program, while the Steering Committee for the Improvement of the Status of Women in the Secretariat—a high-level advisory group of senior women and men appointed by the Secretary-General, monitors the progress made and provides guidance through regular reports to the Secretary-General.

During the first months of 1988, according to the progress report, the steering committee identified a number of major achievements of the action program, including the following:

(a) The percentage of women in posts subject to geographical distribution had risen from 22.9 per cent in March 1985 to 26.2 per cent at 31 March 1988;

(b) Since March 1985, several women had been appointed to high-level posts, including three to the post of Under-Secretary-General;

(c) Nine women who had served on a succession of short-term contracts had been subsequently recruited, after a special review;

(d) The guidelines on cumulative seniority had contributed to the women's rate of advancement in the Professional category;

(e) In recruiting at entry levels for Professional staff, the percentage of women had risen, particularly through increased publicity on the principle of equality in Member States participating in national examinations;

(f) An effort was being made to redress inconsistencies in the classification standards for the secretarial occupation;

(g) Supervisory training had been strengthened and inter-agency co-operation in that area had been initiated;

(h) Inequities adversely affecting former General Service staff from other duty stations had been removed from the recruitment standards for that category for New York;

(i) Conditions for maternity leave had been improved;

(j) Inter-agency consultations had started on improved arrangements for child-care and adoption leave;

(k) The structure of the appeals process had been strengthened;

(l) Training modules had been prepared that addressed sexual harassment and gender discrimination.

The steering committee identified a number of priorities for the improvement of the status of women in the secretariat, including further recruitment, assignment, and promotion of women at senior levels; the establishment of a career development system for the general service and related categories; and the strengthening of training programs and human resources planning systems within the organization. The Secretary-General accepted these recommendations and indicated that implementation of the action program will be pursued to the extent possible, taking into account the prevailing restraints on recruitment.

In October 1989, the Secretary-General submitted a report on the subject to the General Assembly (UN Doc. A/44/604), in which he stated that, of the 24 undersecretary-general positions, 22 were held by men and only two were held by women (8.3%); that 17 assistant-secretary-general positions were held by men and none by women; that, of the 85 D-2 positions, 78 were held by men and seven by women (8.2%); and that, of the 235 D-1 positions, 220 were held by men and 15 by women (6.4%).

Noting the report, and noting also that a senior-level officer had been deployed as the focal point for women, in the Office of the Assistant Secretary-General for Human Resources Management of the Secretariat responsible for all aspects of the action program for the improvement of the status of women in the secretariat, the assembly requested the Secretary-General (resolution 44/75) to intensify his efforts to increase the number of women employed throughout the United Nations system, particularly in senior policy-level and decisionmaking posts, in order to achieve an overall participation rate by women of 30% by 1990. It also requested him to make renewed efforts to ensure more equitable representation of women from developing countries in posts subject to geographical distribution, subject to article 101 of the UNITED NATIONS CHARTER.

WOMEN'S INTERNATIONAL DEMOCRATIC FEDERATION.

An international organization in consultative status with the UN Economic and Social Council (Category I) and with ILO, UNESCO, and UNICEF, the federation brings together 138 national organizations located in 124 countries and territories.

Founded at the International Congress of Women in Paris in 1945, WIDF has worked since that time to unite women regardless of race, nationality, religion, or political opinion with a view to implementing and defending their rights as mothers, workers, and citizens. It devotes particular attention to the rights of women in society and the family, including the right to work, the right to equal pay for equal work, and the right to education at all levels. It also has a special concern for the rights of children, including their right to education, health care, and adequate nutrition and their right to a happy childhood in a harmonious family.

WIDF was active in initiating the observance of IN-TERNATIONAL WOMEN'S YEAR (1975) and contributed to the drafting of the DECLARATION OF THE RIGHTS OF THE CHILD. From time to time, it has joined with other organizations in publicizing gross violations of the human rights of women and children under foreign domination or occupation or under repressive regimes.

WIDF publishes the quarterly review *Women of the World* in English, French, Spanish, German, Russian, and Arabic; produces a *Newsletter;* and issues numerous brochures, leaflets, and reports.

Women's International Democratic Federation. Address: 13 Unter den Linden, 1080 Berlin, GDR. Telephone: 200 03 31. Cable: FEDEINTFEM BERLIN. Telex: 115080 WIDF DD. General Secretary: Mirjam Vire-Tuominen.

WOMEN'S INTERNATIONAL LEAGUE FOR PEACE AND FREEDOM.

An international non-governmental organization in consultative status with the UN Economic and Social Council (Category II) and with ILO, UNESCO, and FAO.

Since it was founded by the International Women's Congress, convened at The Hague in 1915 under the chairmanship of Jane Addams, the league has endeavored to unite women of all countries to oppose war, exploitation, and oppression. It stands for the equality of all people in a world free of racism and sexism, for the building of a constructive peace through world disarmament, and for the changing of government priorities with a view to meeting human needs. It promotes and defends civil and political rights and is particularly interested in the elimination of all forms of discrimination, the protection of minorities, the elimination of slavery in all its forms, the abolition of capital punishment, and the advancement of women.

The league's principal publications are *Peace and Freedom, Pax et Libertas,* the *Legislative Bulletin,* and *Program and Action Bulletin,* and *Building Peace.*

Women's International League for Peace and Freedom. Address: 1 rue de Varembé, P.O. 28, CH-1211, Geneva 20, Switzerland. Telephone: (41-22) 33-61-75. Secretary-General: Edith Ballantyne.

W

WOMEN'S INTERNATIONAL NETWORK. A nonprofit participatory network founded in 1975 to provide a worldwide communication system by, for, and about women of all ages, national or social origins, backgrounds, and beliefs, the network, with the assistance of organizations and individuals in many countries, collects and disseminates problems facing women in all parts of the world, concentrating on areas of prejudice and discrimination on the ground of sex and various forms of cruel, inhuman, or degrading treatment. It publishes the *Women's International Network News* periodically, and issues reports from time to time.

Women's International Network. Address: 187 Grant Street, Lexington, Maine 02173, U.S.A. Telephone: (617) 862–9431. Coordinator: Fran P. Hosken.

WOMEN'S INTERNATIONAL ZIONIST ORGANIZATION. An international non-governmental organization in consultative status with the UN Economic and Social Council (Category II), WIZO's affiliated federations, in 52 countries and territories, include about 260,000 individual members.

The organization provides constructive social welfare and educational facilities to women, senior citizens, and children in Israel and conducts educational research and programs on the status of women, child welfare, citizenship, education and professional training. It maintains 650 institutions and services in Israel, serving all segments of the population.

WIZO publishes *WIZO News-Bulletin* (monthly), *Bamat Hai-sha* (six times a year), *Inside WIZO* (six times a year), *WIZO Review* (six times a year), and *Menorah* (annually).

Women's International Zionist Organization. Address: Blvd. David Hamelech 38, P.O. Box 33159, Tel Aviv 61331, Israel. Telephone: 257321. Cable: ISRAWIZO TELAVIV. Secretary-General: Dolly Faitelson.

Yearbook of International Organizations 1989/90 (K. G. Saur).

WOMEN WORKERS: ILO PLAN OF ACTION ON EQUALITY OF OPPORTUNITY AND TREATMENT OF MEN AND WOMEN IN EMPLOYMENT. The action taken by the International Labor Organization to promote equal opportunities and equal treatment for men and women during 1987 and 1988 is described in a memorandum (UN Doc. E/CN.4/Sub.2/1988/3 para. 13–19), submitted to the Sub-Commission on Prevention of Discrimination and Protection of Minorities by the ILO Director-General, as follows:

In 1987, the ILO Governing Body approved a Plan of Action on Equality of Opportunity and Treatment of Men and Women in Employment. This Plan of Action is intended to provide the main framework for ILO activities to follow up on its 1985 Conference resolution on equal opportunities and equal treatment for men and women in employment and the Forward-Looking Strategies for the Advancement of Women adopted by the World Conference to Review and Appraise the Achievements of the United Nations Decade for Women: Equality, Development and Peace (Nairobi, July 1985). The overriding objective of the Plan is to ensure the full integration of women's needs and concerns into all ILO activities in order to strengthen the ILO's capacity to respond to the needs of Governments, employers and workers in their efforts to improve the situation of women workers and translate into practice the principles embodied in relevant decisions and international labour standards. The Plan of Action identifies a wide range of activities to be implemented in the coming years.

During 1987 an interdepartmental committee composed of department heads was established by the Director-General to keep the Governing Body regularly informed of progress in the implementation of the Plan of Action. Currently, a report, to be submitted to the ILO Governing Body in November 1988, is being prepared on the progress made thus far in implementing the Plan.

During the last year, the ILO continued to strengthen its promotional activities in respect to equality of opportunity and treatment between men and women in employment. Technical advisory services provided to member States were stepped up. Further efforts were undertaken to ensure that women's concerns were adequately reflected in ILO technical co-operation projects. Collection of data and dissemination of information on women's access to employment and working conditions continued to be of priority.

In regard to the possible need for the revision of existing standards or for additional standards on equality of opportunity and treatment, law and practice reports were prepared on the working and employment conditions of part-time workers and night work for women for consideration as possible future agenda items for the International Labour Conference. The November 1987 session of the Governing Body decided to place the question of night work in general on the agenda of the seventy-sixth (1989) session of the International Labour Conference.

Vocational training activities to promote equality of opportunity for women were multi-faceted in approach and activities included: case studies in France, India, Ireland, the Philippines and Sweden on the implications of information technology for the training requirements of women; projects in Bangladesh and India to strengthen the capacity of NGOs to assist poor rural and urban women in improving their income-generating activities through management training programmes, materials and methodologies appropriate to women with low levels of literacy; projects in Botswana, Lesotho and Zimbabwe to devise innovative approaches and methods for promoting women entrepreneurs; in the Middle East national and regional vocational rehabilitation projects were designed and implemented to develop administrative and legislative measures to integrate disabled women in income-generating activities; as part of the UNDP-sponsored regional programme to improve the performance of training initiatives in Africa, the ILO collaborated with the World Bank in setting up a programme on women in management.

In regard to ILO efforts to improve the situation of rural women, the main emphasis has been on improving women's access to land and productive resources. Activities included: the completion of studies on women's access to land in India, Malaysia, Nigeria and Zimbabwe, on home-based workers in Latin America; two reports were published on grass-roots women's initiatives in Tanzania and on the experiences of a project for women refugees in Somalia; the India component of a regional South Asia project on employment opportunities for rural women through organization was completed and an expanded follow-up project on wasteland development was initiated; the second phase of a regional project on assistance to female-headed households was started in Bangladesh, India and Nepal and a new South-East Asian regional project on the provision of research and assistance to rural women workers in the new putting-out system was initiated; under an energy and rural women's work project, three studies were published on fuel availabilities in central Mexico, store programmes in Latin America and afforestation in India, as well as a report on cooking efficiency programme planning in Ethiopia; projects for poor rural women were initiated in five African countries: Guinea, Mali, Niger, Tanzania and Zimbabwe, as well as a project with women settlers in Upper Egypt.

Other areas in which the ILO intensified its research and technical co-operation activities in favour of women workers in the last year included: enhancing women's role in co-operative development and their participation in co-operative initiatives; increasing the capacity of trade unions to act effectively on behalf of women workers; improving women's access to science and technology; and analysing the role of women in the informal sector of developing countries.

SEE ALSO *ILO Discrimination (Employment and Occupation) Convention; ILO Equal Remuneration Convention; ILO Equality of Treatment (Social Security) Convention; ILO Maternity Protection Benefits; ILO Night Work (Women) Convention; Nairobi Forward-looking Strategies for the Advancement of Women.*

WORK. The right of everyone to work is proclaimed in the UNIVERSAL DECLARATION OF HUMAN RIGHTS in the following terms:

Article 23. 1. Everyone has the right to work, to free choice of employment, to just and favourable conditions of work and to protection against unemployment.

2. Everyone, without any discrimination, has the right to equal pay for equal work.

3. Everyone who works has the right to just and favourable remuneration ensuring for himself and his family an existence worthy of human dignity, and supplemented, if necessary, by other means of social protection.

4. Everyone has the right to form and to join trade unions for the protection of his interests.

The INTERNATIONAL COVENANT ON ECONOMIC, SOCIAL AND CULTURAL RIGHTS contains the following provisions:

Article 6. 1. The States Parties to the present Covenant recognize the right to work, which includes the right of everyone to the opportunity to gain his living by work which he freely chooses or accepts, and will take appropriate steps to safeguard this right.

2. The steps to be taken by a State Party to the present Covenant to achieve the full realization of this right shall include technical and vocational guidance and training programmes, policies and techniques to achieve steady economic, social and cultural development and full and productive employment under conditions safeguarding fundamental political and economic freedoms to the individual.

Article 7. The States Parties to the present Covenant recognize the right of everyone to the enjoyment of just and favourable conditions of work which ensure, in particular:

(a) Remuneration which provides all workers, as a minimum, with:

(i) Fair wages and equal remuneration for work of equal value without distinction of any kind, in particular women being guaranteed conditions of work not inferior to those enjoyed by men, with equal pay for equal work;

(ii) A decent living for themselves and their families in accordance with the provisions of the present Covenant;

(b) Safe and healthy working conditions;

(c) Equal opportunity for everyone to be promoted in his employment to an appropriate higher level, subject to no considerations other than those of seniority and competence;

(d) Rest, leisure and reasonable limitation of working hours and periodic holidays with pay, as well as remuneration for public holidays.

The INTERNATIONAL CONVENTION ON THE ELIMINATION OF ALL FORMS OF RACIAL DISCRIMINATION provides for non-discrimination on racial grounds in respect of the right, as follows:

Article 5. In compliance with the fundamental obligations laid down in article 2 of this Convention, States Parties undertake to prohibit and to eliminate racial discrimination in all its forms and to guarantee the right of everyone, without distinction as to race, colour, or national or ethnic origin, to equality before the law, notably in the enjoyment of the following rights:. . . .

(e) Economic, social and cultural rights, in particular:

(i) the rights to work, free choice of employment, just and favourable conditions of work, protection against unemployment, equal pay for equal work, just and favourable remuneration. . . .

The CONVENTION ON THE ELIMINATION OF ALL FORMS OF DISCRIMINATION AGAINST WOMEN provides for non-discrimination in the ground of sex in respect of the right, as follows:

Article 11. 1. States Parties shall take all appropriate measures to eliminate discrimination against women in the field of employment in order to ensure, on a basis of equality of men and women, the same rights, in particular:

(a) The right to work as an inalienable right of all human beings;

(b) The right to the same employment opportunities,

including the application of the same criteria for selection in matters of employment;

(c) The right to free choice of profession and employment, the right to promotion, job security and all benefits and conditions of service and the right to receive vocational training and retraining, including apprenticeships, advanced vocational training and recurrent training;

(d) The right to equal remuneration, including benefits, and to equal treatment in respect of work of equal value, as well as equality of treatment in the evaluation of the quality of work;

(e) The right to social security, particularly in cases of retirement, unemployment, sickness, invalidity and old age and other incapacity to work, as well as the right to paid leave;

(f) The right to protection of health and to safety in working conditions, including the safeguarding of the function of reproduction.

2. In order to prevent discrimination against women on the grounds of marriage or maternity and to ensure their effective right to work, States Parties shall take appropriate measures:

(a) To prohibit, subject to the imposition of sanctions, dismissal on the grounds of pregnancy or of maternity leave and discrimination in dismissals on the basis of marital status;

(b) To introduce maternity leave with pay or with comparable social benefits without loss of former employment, seniority or social allowances;

(c) To encourage the provision of the necessary supporting social services to enable parents to combine family obligations with work responsibilities and participation in public life, in particular through promoting the establishment and development of a network of child-care facilities;

(d) To provide special protection to women during pregnancy in types of work proved to be harmful to them.

3. Protective legislation relating to matters covered in this article shall be reviewed periodically in the light of scientific and technological knowledge and shall be revised, repealed or extended as necessary.

The **AFRICAN CHARTER OF HUMAN AND PEOPLE'S RIGHTS,** open for acceptance by member States of the **ORGANIZATION OF AFRICAN UNITY,** contains the following provision:

Article 15. Every individual shall have the right to work under equitable and satisfactory conditions and shall receive equal pay for equal work.

Article 6 of the International Covenant on Economic, Social and Cultural Rights is unique in that its second paragraph, rather than providing that all States parties shall "ensure" or "guarantee" enjoyment of the right, instead prescribes a series of specific steps to be taken by them for this purpose. Paragraph 1 of the article is so worded as not to permit the introduction of forced labor by a State party, and paragraph 2 appears to cover both the right to be provided with work and the right not to be prevented from working.

Within the United Nations system, primary respon-

sibility for the preparation and supervision of international measures relating to the right to work lies with the **INTERNATIONAL LABOR ORGANIZATION.** Its basic instruments in this endeavor are the **ILO DISCRIMINATION (EMPLOYMENT AND OCCUPATION) CONVENTION,** adopted by the International Labor Conference in 1958, and the **ILO EMPLOYMENT CONVENTION,** adopted by the conference in 1964.

The Convention Concerning Discrimination in Respect of Employment and Occupation, also known as the Discrimination (Employment and Occupation) Convention, 1958 (ILO Convention No. 111), provides that States parties undertake "to declare and pursue a national policy designed to promote, by methods appropriate to national conditions and practice, equality of opportunity and treatment in respect of employment and occupation, with a view to eliminating any discrimination in respect thereof." They further undertake "to seek the co-operation of employers' and workers' organizations and other appropriate bodies in promoting the acceptance and observance of this policy" and "to repeal any statutory provisions and to modify any administrative instructions or practices which are inconsistent with the policy." In respect of employment under the direct control of the national authority, States parties undertake to pursue the policy of equality of opportunity and treatment.

The Convention Concerning Employment Policy, also known as the Employment Policy Convention, 1964 (ILO Convention NO. 122) provides, in article 1, that:

1. With a view to stimulating economic growth and development, raising levels of living, meeting manpower requirements and overcoming unemployment and underemployment, each Member shall declare and pursue, as a major goal, an active policy designed to promote full, productive and freely chosen employment.

2. The said policy should aim at ensuring that:

(a) There is work for all who are available for and seeking work;

(b) Such work is as productive as possible;

(c) There is freedom of choice of employment and the fullest possible opportunity for each worker to qualify for, and to use his skills and endowments in, a job for which he is well suited, irrespective of race, color, sex, religion, political opinion, national extraction or social origin;

(3) The said policy shall take due account of the stage and level or economic development and the mutual relationships between employment objectives and other economic and social objectives, and shall be pursued by methods that are appropriate to national conditions and practices.

Both conventions are supervised by international machinery established by the International Labor Conference in 1926, consisting of two components:

on the one hand, a committee of independent experts responsible for examining the reports received from governments on measures they have taken to give effect to such instruments, and, on the other hand, the establishment, at each session of the conference, of a committee responsible for examining the question of the application of the conventions. The government reports are required, annually, under article 22 of the ILO constitution.

In accordance with the procedures for the implementation of the International Covenant on Economic, Social and Cultural Rights, adopted by the Economic and Social Council on 11 May 1976 (resolution 1988 [LX]), the ILO submits to the council at regular intervals reports on the progress made in achieving the observance of the provisions of that document falling within the scope of its activities, as provided under article 18 of the covenant. The ILO's tenth report, issued on 31 December 1987 (UN Doc. E/1988/6) contains information on such progress with reference to the provisions of articles 6, 7, 8, 9, and 10, all of which deal with aspects of the right to work. It also contains a list of the principal relevant ILO conventions, reproduced below.

Preparation of such reports is entrusted to the ILO COMMITTEE OF EXPERTS ON THE APPLICATION OF CONVENTIONS AND RECOMMENDATIONS. In the ninth such report, in 1987, the Committee of Experts noted that the Economic and Social Council had decided (resolution 1985/17) to set up a COMMITTEE ON ECONOMIC, SOCIAL AND CULTURAL RIGHTS. Following the creation of the new committee, the Committee of Experts re-examined the manner in which the ILO could best submit its reports in accordance with article 18 of the covenant. The ILO committee recommended that the ILO should no longer seek to evaluate separately the extent to which the covenant was implemented, but that it should inform the new committee of the results of the operation of the various ILO supervisory procedures in the fields covered by the covenant. It would remain open to the Committee of Experts to report on particular situations whenever it deemed this desirable or when specifically requested to do so by the new committee. The ILO Governing Body, in May 1987, approved this recommendation.

The tenth report accordingly had been drawn up in accordance with the arrangements approved by the ILO Governing Body. In addition to information on the situation concerning articles 6 to 9 of the covenant in a number of countries and the list of relevant ILO conventions mentioned above, it included the following general considerations (E/1988/6, para. 7–12):

In previous reports, the Committee of Experts has commented on several occasions on the relationship between the provisions of the Covenant and the standards laid down in international labour Conventions, the nature of the obligations resulting from them and the way in which the Committee of Experts consequently presented its comments on the implementation of the Covenant. Upon the completion of the first cycle of the reporting programme on the Covenant, the Committee of Experts, in its sixth report (E/1983/40), recalled these general observations which it hoped could be of use to the States Parties and would be of interest to the Economic and Social Council and its Sessional Working Group responsible for examining the implementation of the Covenant. It would therefore appear appropriate to recall briefly the main points of these observations.

The Committee of Experts noted that the provisions of Article 2, paragraph 1, of the Covenant, and the nature of a number of the rights recognized in the Covenant, rather than implying an immediate obligation to achieve a fixed standard, require continuing action for the mobilization of available resources in order to progressively implement and improve the exercise of these rights. This is the case, for example, with the right to work, the right to the enjoyment of just and favourable conditions of work and the right to social security, which the States Parties undertake to recognize in accordance with Articles 6, 7 and 9 respectively of the Covenant. However, in respect of trade union rights, the States Parties undertake in accordance with Article 8 of the Covenant, not only to recognize, but also to ensure the rights in question. The nature of obligations under Article 8 of the Covenant is therefore similar to those under corresponding ILO Conventions. The Committee of Experts also noted that the achievement of union rights is not dependent on the availability of resources, but should represent an important contribution not only to a basic freedom but also to the effective participation of the productive forces in society in the development process.

With regard to the subjects dealt with in the various Articles of the Covenant, those covered by Articles 6–9 are all within the competence of the ILO. In respect of Articles 10–12, only two questions dealt with in paragraphs 2 and 3 of Article 10 fall directly within the scope of the ILO, namely maternity protection and the protection of children and young persons in relation to employment and work. However, of the matters dealt with within the framework of the application of Articles 6–9 of the Covenant, those in the fields of training and employment, remuneration and social security, affect the right to an adequate standard of living, within the meaning of Article 11. Similarly, questions concerning occupational safety and health and the provision of health care within the framework of social security also affect the right to health within the meaning of Article 12. Articles 13–15 deal with questions which fall principally within the scope of organizations other than the ILO.

Article 23 of the Covenant includes among the methods of international action for the achievement of the rights recognized in the Pact, the conclusion of Conventions and the adoption of Recommendations. In this respect, ILO standards that are relevant to Articles 6–10 of the Covenant, even if they have not been ratified, may provide a useful source of reference and guidance in the fields under consideration.

Mention may be made in this connection of the general surveys of the Committee of Experts that are undertaken each year on the application of instruments selected by the Governing Body of the ILO as the subject of reports on unratified Conventions and Recommendations and under article 19 of the Constitution of the International Labour

Organisation. These general surveys in recent years have dealt with questions directly linked to the rights provided for under Articles 6–10 of the Covenant: abolition of forced labour (1979), minimum age (1981), freedom of association and collective bargaining (1983), working time (1984), equal remuneration (1986), protection of the working environment (1987). In 1988, the general survey of the Committee of Experts will be on the Discrimination (Employment and Occupation) Convention (No. 111) and Recommendation (No. 111), 1958. In 1989, the survey will deal with social security standards concerning old-age benefits.

In addition to standard-setting activities, other ILO activities may be of interest in view of their relevance to questions having a general influence on the recognition and achievement of the human rights provided for in the Covenant. Reference may be made by way of illustration to the High-Level Meeting on Employment and Structural Adjustment (Geneva, 23–25 November 1987), attended by representatives of the principal international institutions concerned, which examined the consequences of international trade and financial and monetary practices on employment and poverty. These questions are closely related to issues of the current international economic situation in respect of which the Committee on Economic, Social and Cultural Rights has expressed its deep concern (Report on the First Session of the Committee, paragraph 302). Similarly, a number of the subjects discussed at the International Labour Conference or examined by the various bodies of the Governing Body of the ILO would be of interest within the framework of the international measures likely to contribute to the effective implementation of the Covenant referred to under its Articles 22 and 23.

Principal ILO Conventions relevant to Articles 6–10 of the Covenant. The following is a list, for each of articles 6–10 of the International Covenant on Economic, Social and Cultural Rights, of the principal relevant ILO conventions.

Article 6 of the Covenant

Unemployment Convention, 1919 (No. 2); Forced Labour Convention, 1930 (No. 29); Fee-Charging Employment Agencies Convention, 1933 (No. 34); Employment Service Convention, 1948 (No. 88); Fee-Charging Employment Agencies Convention (Revised), 1949 (No. 96); Abolition of Forced Labour Convention, 1957 (No. 105); Discrimination (Employment and Occupation) Convention, 1958 (No. 111); Social Policy (Basic Aims and Standards) Convention, 1962 (No. 117); Employment Policy Convention, 1964 (No. 122); Paid Educational Leave Convention, 1974 (No. 140); Human Resources Development Convention, 1975 (No. 142); Workers with Family Responsibilities Convention, 1981 (No. 156); Termination of Employment Convention, 1982 (No. 158); Vocational Rehabilitation and Employment (Disabled Persons) Convention, 1983 (No. 159).

Article 7 of the Covenant

Remuneration. Minimum Wage-Fixing Machinery Convention, 1928 (No. 26); Minimum Wage-Fixing Machinery (Agriculture) Convention, 1951 (No. 99); Minimum Wage-Fixing Convention, 1970 (No. 131).

Equal Remuneration. Equal Remuneration Convention, 1951 (No. 100).

Rest, Limitation of Working Hours and Holidays with Pay.

Hours of Work (Industry) Convention, 1919 (No. 1); Weekly Rest (Industry) Convention, 1921 (No. 14); Hours of Work (Commerce and Offices) Convention, 1930 (No. 30); Forty-Hour Week Convention, 1935 (No. 47); Holidays with Pay Convention, 1936 (No. 52); Holidays with Pay (Agriculture) Convention, 1952 (No. 101); Weekly Rest (Commerce and Offices) Convention, 1957 (No. 106); Holidays with Pay Convention (Revised), 1970 (No. 132).

Safe and Healthy Working Conditions. White Lead (Painting) Convention, 1921 (No. 13); Marking of Weight (Packages Transported by Vessels) Convention, 1929 (No. 27); Protection against Accidents (Dockers) Convention, 1929 (No. 28); Protection against Accidents (Dockers) Convention (Revised), 1932 (No. 32); Safety Provisions (Building) Convention, 1937 (No. 62); Labour Inspection Convention, 1947 (No. 81); Radiation Protection Convention, 1960 (No. 115); Guarding of Machinery Convention, 1963 (No. 119); Hygiene (Commerce and Offices) Convention, 1964 (No. 120); Maximum Weight Convention, 1967 (No. 127); Labour Inspection (Agriculture) Convention, 1969 (No. 129); Benzene Convention, 1971 (No. 136); Occupational Cancer Convention, 1974 (No. 139); Working Environment (Air Pollution, Noise and Vibration) Convention, 1977 (No. 148); Occupational Safety and Health (Dock Work) Convention, 1979 (No. 152); Occupational Safety and Health Convention, 1981 (No. 155); Occupational Health Services Convention, 1985 (No. 161); Asbestos Convention, 1986 (No. 162).

Article 8 of the Covenant

Right of Association (Agriculture) Convention, 1921 (No. 11); Freedom of Association and Protection of the Right to Organise Convention, 1948 (No. 87); Right to Organise and Collective Bargaining Convention, 1949 (No. 98); Workers' Representatives Convention, 1971 (No. 135); Rural Workers' Organisations Convention, 1975 (No. 141); Labour Relations (Public Service) Convention, 1978 (No. 151); Collective Bargaining Convention, 1981 (No. 154).

Article 9 of the Covenant

Workmen's Compensation (Agriculture) Convention, 1921 (No. 12); Workmen's Compensation (Accidents) Convention, 1925 (No. 17); Workmen's Compensation (Occupational Diseases) Convention, 1925 (No. 18); Equality of Treatment (Accident Compensation) Convention, 1925 (No. 19); Sickness Insurance (Industry) Convention, 1927 (No. 24); Sickness Insurance (Agriculture) Convention, 1927 (No. 25); Old-Age Insurance (Industry, etc.) Convention, 1933 (No. 35); Old-Age Insurance (Agriculture) Convention, 1933 (No. 36); Invalidity Insurance (Industry, etc.) Convention, 1933 (No. 37); Invalidity Insurance (Agriculture) Convention, 1933 (No. 38); Survivors' Insurance (Industry, etc.) Convention, 1933 (No. 39); Survivors' Insurance (Agriculture) Convention, 1933 (No. 40); Workmen's Compensation (Occupational Diseases) Convention (Revised), 1934 (No. 42); Unemployment Provisions Convention, 1934 (No. 44); Maintenance of Migrants' Pension Rights Convention, 1935 (No. 48); Social Security (Minimum Standards) Convention, 1952 (No. 102); Equality of Treatment (Social Security) Convention, 1962 (No. 118); Employment Injury Benefits Convention, 1964 (No. 121); Invalidity, Old-Age and Survivors' Benefits Convention, 1967 (No. 128); Medical Care and Sickness Benefits Convention, 1969 (No. 130); Maintenance of Social Security Rights Convention, 1982 (No. 157).

Article 10 of the Covenant

Maternity Protection. Maternity Protection Convention, 1919 (No. 3); Maternity Protection Convention, (Revised), 1952, (No. 103).

Protection of Children and Young Persons in Relation to Employment and Work. Minimum Age (Industry) Convention, 1919 (No. 5); Minimum Age (Sea) Convention, 1920 (No. 7); Minimum Age (Agriculture) Convention, 1921 (No. 10); Minimum Age (Trimmers and Stokers) Convention, 1921 (No. 15); Minimum Age (Non-Industrial Employment) Convention, 1932 (No. 33); Minimum Age (Sea) Convention (Revised), 1936 (No. 58); Minimum Age (Industry) Convention (Revised), 1937 (No. 59); Minimum Age (Non-Industrial Employment) Convention (Revised), 1937 (No. 60); Minimum Age (Fishermen) Convention, 1959 (No. 112); Social Policy (Basic Aims and Standards) Convention, 1952 (No. 117); Minimum Age (Underground Work) Convention, 1965 (No. 123); Minimum Age Convention, 1973 (No. 138); Night Work of Young Persons (Industry) Convention, 1919 (No. 6); Night Work (Bakeries) Convention, 1925 (No. 20); Night Work of Young Persons (Non-Industrial Occupations) Convention, 1946 (No. 79); Night Work of Young Persons (Industry) Convention (Revised), 1948 (No. 90); White Lead (Painting) Convention, 1921 (No. 13) (Article 3); Radiation Protection Convention, 1960 (No. 115) (Article 7); Maximum Weight Convention, 1967 (No. 127) (Article 7); Benzene Convention, 1971 (No. 136) (Article 11); Medical Examination of Young Persons (Sea) Convention, 1921 (No. 16); Medical Examination (Seafarers) Convention, 1946 (No. 73); Medical Examination of Young Persons (Industry) Convention, 1946 (No. 77); Medical Examination of Young Persons (Non-Industrial Occupations) Convention, 1946 (No. 78); Medical Examination (Fishermen) Convention, 1959 (No. 113); Medical Examination of Young Persons (Underground Work) Convention, 1965 (No. 124).

SEE ALSO *Declaration of Principles and Program of Action of the Tripartite Conference on Employment; Employment: Anti-Discrimination Agencies; Unemployment; Youth: Education and Work.*

WORKING GROUP OF GOVERNMENTAL EXPERTS ON THE RIGHT TO DEVELOPMENT.

The working group was established by the UN Commission on Human Rights on 11 March 1981 (resolution 35 [XXXVII]), originally to study the scope and contents of the RIGHT TO DEVELOPMENT and the most effective means to ensure the realization, in all countries, of the economic, social, and cultural rights set out in various international instruments, paying particular attention to the obstacles encountered by developing countries in their efforts to ensure the enjoyment of those rights.

The working group consists of 15 experts nominated by their governments and appointed by the chairman of the Commission on Human Rights for an indeterminate term of office. It normally convenes for a session of approximately three weeks, before or during the annual session of the commission, at the United Nations office in Geneva.

For several years after its establishment, the working group concentrated on the preparation of the DECLARATION ON THE RIGHT TO DEVELOPMENT. This phase of its work culminated, in December 1986, in the adoption and proclamation of the declaration by the UN General Assembly on 4 December 1986 (resolution 41/128).

At that time, the assembly and the commission were in agreement that the working group should be continued to consider matters relating to the implementation of the provisions of the declaration. Under this new mandate, the group has since held annual open-ended sessions in which all members of the commission may participate.

WORKING GROUP ON A DRAFT DECLARATION ON THE RIGHT AND RESPONSIBILITY TO PROMOTE AND PROTECT HUMAN RIGHTS.

On 16 March 1984, the UN Commission on Human Rights established (decision 1984/116) the Working Group to Draft a Declaration on the Right and Responsibility of Individuals, Groups, and Organs of Society to Promote and Protect Universally Recognized Human Rights and Fundamental Freedoms. The sessional working group, open to all members of the commission, held its first meeting prior to the 1985 session of the commission and was later convened annually for periods of from six-to-eight days prior to subsequent sessions of the commission.

On 1 March 1990, the working group reported to the commission (UN Doc. E/CN.4/1990/47) that it had not been able to complete the drafting of the declaration and asked that it be authorized to meet for eight working days prior to the commission's 1991 session. The report included an account of the discussions in the working group and a series of "Texts Provisionally Adopted by the Working Group at First Reading" (Annex 1 of the report), reproduced below:

Chapter I

A. No one shall participate in violating the [universally recognized] human rights and fundamental freedoms of others, and no one shall be subject to punishment or adverse action of any kind for refusing, [individually or in association with others], to violate or otherwise be associated with violations of [universally recognized] human rights and fundamental freedoms.

B. Each State has a prime responsibility and duty to promote and protect [universally recognized] human rights and fundamental freedoms, *inter alia,* by adopting such legislative, administrative and other steps as may be necessary to create the social and political conditions and legal guarantees required to ensure that all persons, individually and in association with others, are able to enjoy these rights and freedoms in practice.

Everyone has the right, individually and in association with others, to promote and to strive for the protection and realization of [universally recognized] human rights and fundamental freedoms at the national and international levels. Each State shall adopt such legislative, administrative and other steps as may be necessary to give effect to this right.

[Language to be added reflecting the role of national and international law as well as other modalities, to be formulated when discussing issues assigned to Chapter V.]

Chapter II

Title. The rights to know, to be informed about, and to impart to others knowledge of universally recognized human rights and fundamental freedoms.

Paragraph 1. All persons have the right to know, and, individually as well as together with others, to be informed about, and to make known [their] universally recognized human rights and fundamental freedoms.

Paragraph 2. Everyone has the right, individually as well as together with others

(a) to seek, obtain, receive and hold information about these rights and freedoms, [including access to information on the means by which these rights and freedoms are given effect in domestic legislative, judicial or administrative systems];

(b) to publish, impart or disseminate freely to others views, information and knowledge of universally recognized human rights and fundamental freedoms. . . .

Paragraph 5. Everyone has the right to develop and discuss new human rights ideas and principles, and to advocate their universal acceptance.

Paragraph 6. 1. The State has the responsibility to take legislative, judicial, administrative or other appropriate measures to promote the understanding by all persons under its jurisdiction of their civil, political, economic, social and cultural rights.

2. Such measures shall include:

(a) the publication and widespread distribution of national laws and regulations and of basic international human rights instruments;

(b) full and equal access to international documents in the field of human rights, including the State's periodic reports to the bodies established by the international human rights treaties to which it is a party, as well as the official report of these bodies.

3. The State has the responsibility to promote and improve the teaching of human rights and fundamental freedoms at all levels of education, and to encourage all those responsible for training lawyers, law enforcement officers, the personnel of the armed forces and public officials to include appropriate elements of human rights teaching in their training programmes.

Chapter III

Article 1. For the purpose of promoting and protecting [universally recognized] human rights and fundamental freedoms, everyone has the right, individually and in association with others, at the national and international levels:

(a) to meet or assemble peacefully;

(b) to form, join, and participate in non-governmental organizations, associations, or where relevant groups;

(c) to communicate with non-governmental or intergovernmental organizations.

Article 2. Everyone has the right, individually and in association with others, to have effective access, on a nondiscriminatory basis, to participation in the government of his country and in the conduct of public affairs. This includes, *inter alia,* the right, individually and in association with others, to submit to governmental bodies and agencies and organizations concerned with public affairs criticism and proposals for improving their functioning and to draw attention to any aspect of their work which may hinder or impede the promotion, protection and realization of human rights and fundamental freedoms.

Article 3. Everyone has the right, individually and in association with others, to participate in peaceful activities directed against violations of human rights and fundamental freedoms.

Chapter IV

Article 1. In the exercise of the right to promote and protect the human rights referred to in the present declaration, as well as in the exercise of other [universally recognized] human rights and fundamental freedoms, everyone has the right to protection and recourse to effective remedies in the event of violations of those rights.

Article 2. To this end, everyone has the right, *inter alia,* to:

(a) draw public attention to violations of human rights and to complain about the policies and actions of individual officials and governmental bodies by petitions or other means to competent national judicial, administrative, legislative authorities or any other competent authority provided for by the legal system of the State, as well as to any relevant competent international bodies;

(b) complain to and have that complaint promptly reviewed in a public hearing and decided by an independent, impartial and competent judicial or other authority established by law;

(c) obtain a just decision and award providing redress, including any compensation due as well as enforcement of the decision and award, all without undue delay;

(d) attend such relevant hearings or proceedings or, as the case may be, trials to assess their fairness and compliance with national and international standards;

(e) offer and provide assistance, including professionally qualified legal assistance, in defending [universally recognized] human rights and fundamental freedoms;

(f) seek and accept such assistance of his own free choice in order to enjoy effectively the measures of protection referred to in this Chapter;

(g) unhindered access to and communication with international bodies with general or special competence to receive and consider communications on matters of human rights in accordance with applicable international instruments and procedures.

Article 3. To the same end, each State shall, *inter alia:*

(a) ensure the protection by the competent authorities of everyone, individually or in association with others, against any violence, threats, retaliation, *de facto* or *de jure* adverse discrimination, pressure or any other arbitrary action as a consequence of their legitimate exercise of the rights referred to in this declaration.

WORKING GROUP ON COMMUNICATIONS. This working group was established in accordance with resolution 1503 (XLVIII) of the UN Economic and Social Council, which authorized the Sub-Commission on Prevention of Discrimination and Protection of Minorities "to consider all communications, including replies of governments thereon, received by the Secretary-General under Council resolution 728 F (XXVIII) of 30 July 1959, with a view to bringing to the attention of the Sub-Commission those communications, together with the replies of governments if any, which appear to reveal a consistent pattern of gross and reliably-attested violations of human rights and fundamental freedoms within the terms of reference of the Sub-Commission."

The working group consists of five members of the sub-commission, one from each of the following regional groups: Africa, Asia, Latin America, eastern Europe, and western Europe and others. At each annual session, the sub-commission approves the composition of the working group for the following year.

The working group meets in closed sessions, generally for a period of two weeks prior to each session of the sub-commission. The results of its work are communicated to the sub-commission confidentially. The sub-commission, after examining its report and deciding to refer particular situations to the UN Commission on Human Rights, invites the governments concerned to submit written observations on those situations direct to the commission. The commission, after studying the situations and the comments of the government concerned thereon and after hearing from the chairman/rapporteur of the working group if he wishes to take the floor, reaches a decision as to the action required to deal with the situation.

SEE ALSO Complaints and Other Communications concerning Human Rights.

WORKING GROUP ON CONTEMPORARY FORMS OF SLAVERY. This working group, originally established as the Working Group on Slavery by the SUB-COMMISSION ON PREVENTION OF DISCRIMINATION AND PROTECTION OF MINORITIES on 17 May 1974 (decisions 16 and 17 [LVI]), was renamed the Working Group on Contemporary Forms of Slavery by the UN COMMISSION ON HUMAN RIGHTS in 1988 (resolution 1988/42). The working group meets at the European office of the United Nations in Geneva for a period of three working days immediately prior to each annual session of the sub-commission and reviews developments in the field of slavery and the slave trade as defined in the SLAVERY CONVENTION, the SUPPLEMENTARY CONVENTION ON THE ABOLITION OF SLAVERY, THE SLAVE TRADE, AND INSTITUTIONS AND PRACTICES SIMILAR TO SLAVERY, and the CONVENTION FOR THE SUPPRESSION OF THE TRAFFIC IN PERSONS AND OF THE EXPLOITATION OF THE PROSTITUTION OF OTHERS.

The working group consists of five members of the sub-commission, one from each of the following regional groups: Africa, Asia, Latin America, eastern Europe, and western Europe and others.

At its 1988 session, the working group reviewed recent developments relating to contemporary forms of slavery and the slave trade, including the exploitation of CHILD LABOR and the sale of children, DEBT BONDAGE, TRAFFIC IN PERSONS AND EXPLOITATION OF THE PROSTITUTION OF OTHERS, and certain SLAVERY-LIKE PRACTICES OF APARTHEID AND COLONIALISM; and formulated a program of work for the period 1989 to 1991.

At its 1989 session, it again reviewed developments in those fields, concentrating on those relating to the sale of children, child prostitution, and child pornography. In its report, it included (UN Doc. E/CN.4/Sub.2/1989/39, chap. VII) a number of proposals for dealing with these problems for consideration by its parent bodies. It also included the draft of a "Program of Action for Prevention of Sale of Children, Child Prostitution and Child Pornography" (see CHILDREN: SALE AND TRAFFICKING).

WORKING GROUP ON DETENTION. In 1974, the UN Sub-Commission on Prevention of Discrimination and Protection of Minorities decided (resolution 7 [XXVII]) to review annually developments concerning the human rights of persons subjected to any form of detention or imprisonment. At its 1981 session, the sub-commission set up a sessional working group to assist it in this task. Similar working groups have been established at each subsequent session of the sub-commission.

The working group meets for five or six days each year immediately before the sub-commission's session, normally at the United Nations office in Geneva. It consists of one member of the sub-commission from each of five regional groups: one from an African State, one from an Asian State, one from a Latin American State, one from an eastern European State, and one from a western Europe or other State. Members are nominated by the regional groups and appointed by the sub-commission.

At its 1989 session, the Working Group on Detention conducted its annual review of developments concerning the human rights of persons subjected to any form of DETENTION or IMPRISONMENT and devoted particular attention to questions relating to such matters as the privatization of prisons and the execution of young offenders. In addition, it made progress in preparing a draft declaration on the protection of all persons against enforced or involuntary disappearances and authorized its chairman to prepare a revised draft, on the basis of informal discussions in the working group, for consideration at its 1990 session.

SEE ALSO *Death Penalty: Application to Persons under the Age of 18; Disappearances: UN Draft Declaration; Prisons:Privatization*

WORKING GROUP ON ENFORCED OR INVOLUNTARY DISAPPEARANCES.

This working group of the UN COMMISSION ON HUMAN RIGHTS was first established by the commission on 29 February 1980 (resolution 20 [XXXVI]). Its mandate was extended annually until 1986. In 1986, and again in 1988 (resolutions 1986 /55 and 1988/34), its mandate was extended for two years so as to enable the group to take into consideration all information communicated to it on the cases brought to its attention, while maintaining its annual reporting cycle.

The working group is composed of five members of the commission, serving as experts in their individual capacities. They are appointed by the chairman of the commission and serve for indeterminate terms. As of 1 January 1990, the members were: Mr. Ivan Tosevski (Yugoslavia), chairman/rapporteur; Mr. Toine van Dongen (Netherlands); Mr. Jonas K.D. Foli (Ghana); Mr. Agha Hilaly (Pakistan); and Mr. Diego Garcia-Sayan (Peru).

The Working Group's activities are summarized under the heading DISAPPEARANCE OF PERSONS. Its methods of work, as described by the working group in the report which it presented to the 1988 session of the Commission on Human Rights, are as follows (UN Doc. E/CN.4/1988/19, para. 16–30):

The Working Group's methods of work are based on its mandate as stipulated in Commission on Human Rights resolution 20 (XXXVI) and are specifically geared to its main objective. That objective is to assist families in determining the fate and whereabouts of their missing relatives who, having disappeared, are placed outside the protective precinct of the law. To this end, the Working Group endeavours to establish a channel of communication between the families and the Governments concerned, with a view to ensuring that sufficiently documented and clearly identified individual cases which the families, directly or indirectly, have brought to the Group's attention, are investigated and the whereabouts of the missing person clarified. The Group's role ends when the fate and whereabouts of the missing person have been clearly established as a result of investigations by the Government or the search by the family, irrespective of whether that person is alive or dead. The Group's approach is strictly non-accusatory. It does not concern itself with the question of determining responsibility for specific cases of disappearance or for other human rights violations which may have occurred in the course of disappearances. In sum, the Group's activity is humanitarian in nature.

A typical example of enforced or involuntary disappearance may be described in general terms as follows: a clearly identified person is detained against his will by officials of any branch or level of government or by organized groups or private individuals allegedly acting on behalf or with the support, permission or acquiescence of the Government. These forces then conceal the whereabouts of that person or refuse to disclose his fate or to acknowledge that the person was detained.

The Working Group does not deal with situations of international armed conflict, in view of the competence of the International Committee of the Red Cross (ICRC) in such situations, as established by the Geneva Conventions of 12 August 1949 and the Protocols additional thereto.

In transmitting cases of disappearances, the Working Group deals exclusively with Governments, basing itself on the principle that Governments must assume responsibility for any violation of human rights on their territory. If, however, disappearances are attributed to terrorist or insurgent movements fighting the Government on its own territory, the Working Group has refrained from processing them. The Group considers that, as a matter of principle, such groups may not be approached with a view to investigating or clarifying disappearances for which they are held responsible.

Reports on disappearances are considered admissible by the Working Group when they originate from the family or friends of the missing person. Such reports may, however, be channelled to the Working Group through representatives of the family, Governments, intergovernmental organizations, humanitarian organizations and other reliable sources. They must be submitted in writing with a clear indication of the identity of the sender.

In order to enable Governments to carry out meaningful investigations, the Working Group provides them with information containing at least a minimum of basic data. In addition, the Working Group constantly urges the sources of reports to furnish as many details as possible on the identity of the missing person (if available, identity card numbers) and the circumstances of the disappearance. The Group requires the following minimum elements:

(a) Full name of the missing person;

(b) Date of disappearance, i.e., day, month and year of arrest or abduction or day, month and year when the missing person was last seen. When the missing person was last seen in a detention centre, an approximate indication is sufficient (i.e. March or spring 1980);

(c) Place of arrest or abduction or where the missing person was last seen (at least indication of town or village);

(d) Parties presumed to have carried out the arrest or abduction or to hold the missing person in unacknowledged detention;

(e) Steps taken to determine the fate or whereabouts of the missing person or at least an indication that efforts to resort to domestic remedies were frustrated or have otherwise been inconclusive.

Reported cases of disappearances are placed before the Working Group for detailed examination during its sessions. Those which fulfil the requirements as outlined above are transmitted, upon the Group's specific authorization, to the Governments concerned requesting them to carry out investigations and to inform the Group about their results. The reported cases are communicated by letter from the Group's Chairman to the Government concerned through the Permanent Representative to the United Nations.

Cases that occurred within the three months preceding receipt of the report by the Group are transmitted directly to the Ministers for Foreign Affairs by means of a cable. Their transmission can be authorized by the Chairman on the basis of a specific delegation of power given to him by the Group. Cases which occurred prior to the three-month limit but not more than one year before the date of their receipt by the Secretariat, provided that they had some connection with a case which occurred within the three-month period, can be transmitted between sessions by letter upon authorization by the Chairman.

At least once a year the Working Group reminds every Government concerned of the cases which have not yet been clarified. Furthermore, at any time during the year, any Government may request the summaries of the outstanding and/or clarified cases which the Working Group has transmitted to it.

All replies received from Governments on reports of disappearances are examined by the Working Group and summarized in the Group's annual report to the Commission on Human Rights. The number of cases on which a Government has provided one or several specific replies are listed in the statistical summary concerning each country in the annual report. Any information given on specific cases is forwarded to the sources of those reports who are invited to make observations thereon or to provide additional details on the cases.

If the reply clearly indicates where the missing person is (whether alive or dead) and if that information is sufficiently definite for the family to be reasonably expected to accept it, the Working Group considers the case clarified at the session following the receipt of that information. The case is accordingly listed under the heading "Cases clarified by the Government's responses" in the statistical summary of the annual report.

If the reply provides definite information on the missing person's fate after the reported date of disappearance, but does not unambiguously specify the person's present whereabouts (for instance that the person was released from prison some time ago or that he is free without stating where), a reply from the source has to be awaited. If the source does not respond within six months of the date on which the Government's reply was communicated to it, the case is considered clarified. If the source contests the Government's information on reasonable grounds, the Government is so informed and invited to comment.

If the sources provide well-documented information that a case has erroneously been considered clarified, because the Government's reply referred to a different person, does not correspond to the reported situation or has not reached the source within the six-month period described above, the Working Group transmits the case to the Government anew requesting it to comment. In such instances the respective case is again listed among the outstanding cases and a specific explanation is given in the Group's report to the Commission on Human Rights, describing the above-mentioned errors or discrepancies.

Any substantive additional information which the sources submit on an outstanding case is placed before the Working Group and, following its approval, transmitted to the Government concerned. If the additional information received amounts to a clarification of the case, the Government is informed immediately without awaiting the Group's next session. Clarifications by the sources are summarized in the Group's annual report and listed in the statistical summary under the heading "Cases clarified by non-governmental sources."

The Working Group retains cases on its files as long as the exact whereabouts of the missing persons have not been determined, in accordance with the criteria outlined in paras. 16, 26 and 27. This principle is not affected by changes of Government in a given country. However, the Working Group accepts the closure of a case on its files when the competent authority specified in the relevant national law pronounces, with the concurrence of the relatives and other interested parties, on the presumption of death of a person reported missing.

The following supplementary rules were added by the working group in the course of its meetings in 1988 (UN Doc. E/CN.4/1989/18, para 23):

(a) Reports on a disappearance indicating that officials from more than one country were directly responsible for or involved in a disappearance would be communicated to both the Government of the country where the disappearance occurred and the Government of the country whose officials or agents were alleged to have participated in the arrest or the abduction of the missing person. However, the case would only be counted in the statistics of the country in which the person was reportedly held in detention or last seen;

(b) In the case of the disappearance of a pregnant woman, the child presumed to have been born during the mother's captivity would be mentioned in the description of the case of the mother. The child would be treated as a separate case when witnesses reported that the mother had actually given birth to a child during detention.

In its report to the 1990 session of the Commission on Human Rights, the working group included the following observations on its work during the ten-year period from February 1980 to February 1990 (UN Doc. E/CN.4/1990/13, chap. V, para. 337–365):

Already a full decade ago, numerous reports of widespread disappearances had been perturbing world public opinion. In 1980—at the prompting of the General Assembly, the Economic and Social Council and the Sub-Commission—the Commission on Human Rights responded to these reports by setting up the Working Group on Enforced or Involuntary Disappearances. The present report to the Commission is therefore the Group's tenth. At this juncture, a brief review of its activities to date seems warranted. Such an examination will permit the Commission to remind itself of the Group's evolution over the years, and it may help to indicate new directions for the Group to take. The Group has chosen to do this by highlighting a number of aspects of disappearances, both as regards the problem itself, and as regards the approach taken by the Group. Some of these have already been discussed in previous reports to the Commission.

In different terms, the Working Group has consistently expressed the view that enforced or involuntary disappearances constitute the most comprehensive denial of human rights of our time. They are a gruesome form of human rights violation which, the Group believes, continue to warrant the unstinting attention of the international community and in particular that of the Commission on Human Rights.

In its first two reports, the Working Group specifically dwelt on the question of which human rights and fundamental freedoms are violated as a result of a disappearance. It pointed out that practically all basic human rights of a disappeared person are infringed in one way or another following an abduction. The same holds true, in a greater or lesser extent, for all economic, social and cultural rights guaranteed by the various international instruments. Likewise, the Working Group has drawn attention to the wide circle of victims caused by a disappearance. Family members and other relatives or dependents suffer the immediate consequences of a disappearance. Not only are they subjected to agonizing uncertainty about what happened to their parent, child or spouse, but in many cases economic hardship and social alienation may be part of their sorry lot. The psychological effects on children are found to be severe, even devastating at times. Children born during the captivity of their disappeared mothers constitute a category all by themselves.

Making people disappear seems to be a convenient tactic for suppressing insurgence or stifling dissent, for it takes the victim out of the protective precinct of the law. People regarded as too militant in their quest for social justice or political reform may not be easily silenced by the process of law. The same may be true for people suspected of subversive activities. Yet, regardless of how sophisticated the protection of the individual citizen against abuse by his own Government provided by the law, all legal guarantees and procedural safeguards come to grinding halt once a person is reported missing. Disappearances continue to manifest themselves in may ways. Yet, whatever form they take, the result is almost invariably the same: once the authorities disclaim any responsibility or knowledge of a particular case, prospects for finding the person alive become increasiingly grim.

Several features may be emphasized which, in the Working Group's experience, are either contributing factors or corollaries to the incidence of disappearances. One striking relationship is that between states of emergency and serious social or political turmoil or subversive activity. Situations such as these are common and often lead to human rights violations, including disappearances. One of the reasons is that the powers of the civil authorities are being curtailed and the military operations are no longer or too little subject to ordinary democratic control or political guidance. This may be the result of the prevailing balance of power among the various branches of government, or of a deliberate policy of *laissez-aller*. In the most extreme form, of course, the military and security personnel can be consciously used by civilian or military Government as a instrument of repression.

In many cases, paramilitary groups carry out disappearances. It is difficult in some situations to identify a direct link between those groups and certain military authorities or other branches of the executive; whilst in other situations the relationship may be all too clear, as evidenced by the absence of any real obstacles to or consequences of their operations.

Harassment of witnesses and of relatives is a profoundly disturbing consequence of disappearances. The increasing number of reports on incidents of this nature have prompted the Working Group to draw the Commission's attention to this issue. It is a practice which essentially adds insult to injury because it is directed at a group which is already vulnerable. The Working Group intends to intensify its contacts with Governments on this matter. The Commission, for its part, should continue to keep a close eye on developments in this regard.

Perhaps the single most important factor contributing to the phenomenon of disappearances may be that of impunity. The Working Group's experience over the past 10 years has confirmed the age-old adage that impunity breeds contempt for the law. Perpetrators of human rights violations, whether civilian or military, will become all the more brazen when they are not held to account before a court of law. Impunity can also induce victims of these practices to resort to a form of self-help and take the law into their own hands, which in turn exacerbates the spiral of violence.

Military courts contribute significantly to impunity, in the Working Group's experience. A recurrent theme in times of internal crisis or under the doctrine of national security is that military personnel attested to have engaged in gross misconduct are almost invariably acquitted or given sentences that are disproportionate to the crime committed. Subsequent promotions are even commonplace.

One other cause of impunity, apart from the conduct induced by the State, is often institutional paralysis of the judicial system, in particular, the virtual or total lack of implementation of *habeas corpus*. Paralysis may be due either to overburdening of the judicial system on top of a longstanding lack of resources, or to assassination or systematic intimidation of judicial officers and other magistrates. Paralysis may also occur through lack of co-operation by the executive branch. *Habeas corpus*, for instance, is potentially one of the most powerful legal tools for unearthing the fate or wherabouts of a disappeared person. The most sophisticated rules governing this institution, however, are rendered inoperative in a situation where co-operation stops at the barrack's gate. In certain countries, *habeas corpus* laws have purposefully been subjected to severe restrictions.

On the question of impunity and responsibility, the Working Group's position, though clear and consistent from the very beginning, seems worth restating. In line with its non-accusatory approach, the Group does not engage in the attribution of responsibility of individual officers or agents of the State for individual cases of disappearances. More generally, the Group remains of the view that those responsible for disappearances should be prosecuted to the full extent of the law, a task that falls on the State. This concern was shared very early on by the General Assembly in resolution 33/173, which is one of the bases for the Group's mandate. The Group is primarily interested in the matter of responsibility from the perspective of prevention of disappearances.

Essentially, the mandate of the Working Group as described in Commission on Human Rights resolution 20 (XXXVI) is "to examine questions enforced or involuntary disappearances". (The distinction between enforced and involuntary, incidentally, is one of historical value only and no longer plays any role in practice.) On the basis of its terms of reference, the Working Group has from its early days operated on three different levels. First of all, and for the most part, the Group has been concerned with individual cases, trying to assist relatives to ascertain the fate and wherabouts of their loved ones. On a second level, the Group has studied situations of disappearances in individual countries; it has recorded its observations in its general reports as in special reports following visits to certain countries. Thirdly, it has devoted attention to the phenomenon of disappearances *per se*, its dynamics and dimensions. This is evident from the conclusions and recommendations in each of its reports to the Commission, as well as from chapters on specific aspects of the problem.

It has been argued that the Working Group's approach to individual cases represents at the same time the strongest and the weakest point in its endeavors. Strong, in the sense that the Group opened a window—unique at the time—into the United Nations system, allowing private individuals whose rights have been violated to address the pertinent human rights body swiftly and directly. Weak, in the sense that the Group seeks to clarify cases of disappearanes through co-operation with Governments which probably were responsible for them in the first place and who have little, if anything, to gain by strenous investigations. Be that as it may, the Working Group has insisted repeatedly that its humanitarian approach, perhaps imperfect, is the only real option available to it, and that only through co-operation and dialogue with States can its primary objective—the elimination of disappearances—be achieved. That is still the Group's view today.

It is a matter of satisfaction to the Working Group that, through patient and persistent efforts over the years, it has been able increasingly to move Governments towards a more responsive attitude. Indeed, there are only a few countries that have never given substantive replies to the Group's communications. On the other hand, when examining the substantive content of the co-operation received, one is struck by significant differences. Whereas some Governments have made efforts to comply with the Group's request by providing as much information as possible— Colombia is a case in point—others have, through written submissions and oral presentations and often by high-level delegations, tried to inform the Working Group about the political and other circumstances affecting the phenomenon in their countries or of the various problems encountered in the process of investigation. In the past year, this was the case for Argentina, Mexico, the Philippines, and Sri Lanka. Although it is difficult to establish clear categories in this regard, the Working Group has attempted to reflect in each country subsection the degree of co-operation it is currently receiving from the government concerned.

Very soon after its creation, the Working Group began to develop a mechanism to deal with the influx of a great many cases of disappearances in a matter that would allow a dynamic response to the needs of people looking for missing relatives and friends. Part of that mechanism was the so-called urgent action procedure, which requires the Chairman in between sessions of the Group to process cases submitted within three months after their alleged disappearance. Even though the overall clarification rate against all outstanding cases is not considerable—it hovers around 7 per cent—clarifications under the urgent action procedure are as high as 25 per cent. This suggests that when acting swiftly, the Group may in effect help to prevent irreparable damage. The urgent procedure was subsequently emulated by other thematic mechanisms of the Commission.

Almost from the beginning, the Working Group has relied on visits as a preferred option for assessing the overall situation of disappearances in a given country. Not only does a visit provide an opportunity to obtain first-hand information on the matter, it also puts the Group in direct contact with family members, witnesses and non-governmental groups, as well as with the competent authorities at different levels. Working relationships established

in the course of a visit usually continue afterwards. A visit also enables the Group to get the views of people from different segments of society, in order to analyse properly the context of disappearances. In 1982, visits were made to Mexico and Cyprus. In 1984, the Group addressed a letter to eight Governments, requesting them to consider the possibility of such a visit. A similar request to five Governments was sent in 1988. The Group's first visit to a country where the phenomenon was still developing occurred in 1985, when two members of the Group went to Peru, following an invitation of the Government. Similar visits took place to Peru in 1986, Guatemala in 1987 and Colombia in 1988. At the moment, the Group has three invitations outstanding to visit El Salvador, Sri Lanka and the Philippines.

Since 1985, following reports on its various visits, the Working Group has been able to make headway in the further development of its methods of work. Two features are worth mentioning. The first one relates to the format of its reports: its account of the visit was published as a separate addendum to the main report, so that it might circulate independently. The second more important one, had to do with the manner in which the Working Group expresses a position. As a rule, the Group never submits an evaluation of any given situation of disappearances. Under the various country sections of its general reports, the Group describes to the Commission what action it has taken, and gives a brief summary of the viewpoints submitted by both governmental and non-governmental sources. The conclusions and recommendations in its 10 general reports do not pertain to the situation in any country in particular, at least not explicitly so. In the four reports on its various countries, however, the Group felt it was in a better position to offer its own analysis of the situation and provide specific recommendations.

On the question of country-specific recommendations, the Commission, in resolution 1989/27, asked Governments to give all necessary attention to them. Unfortunately, the Working Group has no information to present on the extent to which any follow-up is indeed being given to these recommendations. This is all the more disturbing as most recommendations are geared to such issues as guaranteeing the right to *habeas corpus*, setting up tracing mechanisms, strengthening the judicial system and improving the security of non-governmental organizations and human rights activists. Perhaps the Commission should henceforth take a more critical look at this matter and accord it due priority at its forty-sixth session.

As to the format of its reports, the Group soon found a form of presentation which seemed to command the approval of the Commission. The introduction of statistical summaries, further refined in successive reports, as well as graphs, not only provided possibilities for easy reference, but also constituted unique features in human rights reporting. Of course, these cannot take away a basic drawback, namely that the figures presented by the Group are based entirely on submissions from external sources, processed according to the Group's criteria. Consequently, they do not necessarily reflect the true dimensions of a given situation of disappearances, which in many cases may be considerably larger; nor do they allow for any comparison between countries or geographical regions.

Over the past 10 years, the Working Group has transmitted some 19,000 cases to a total of 41 Governments. It must be remembered that only those cases are being forwarded which conform to the criteria established by the Group. Therefore, the total number of cases examined by the

Group, including the ones that did not qualify for transmission, is at least 50,000. Most Governments to which cases had been sent, have made oral presentations to the Group at one time or another. Scores of non-governmental organizations, *ad-hoc* groups as well as individual witnesses have provided the group with pertinent information during its 29 meetings and its several missions. Some 20 Governments maintain more or less regular contact with the Group. A list of the non-governmental organizations that have addressed themselves to the Group over the years, is contained in annex I of the report.

In 1989, the Working Group dealt with some 700 cases said to have occurred in that very same year. This represents an alarming increase since 1988, when the corresponding number of cases totalled some 400. The Group is concerned about this development, in particular over the sharp rise in disappearances in certain countries, as reflected by the statistical summaries in the preceding pages.

For a number of years the Group has been stressing the importance of greater awareness of its aims and purpose as well as its *modus operandi*. Such awareness could, in its view, avoid erroneus ideas about what the Group was set up to do, prevent false expectations about what it could reasonably achieve and dispel misgivings about how it pursues its mandate. In the light of this, the Centre for Human Rights has recently published an information leaflet on the Working Group in its fact sheet series. Also, and more important for the Commission itself, the Working Group, in 1988, presented for the first time a comprehensive account of the methods of work it had developed over the previous eight years of operation. Since then it has continued to reflect on the development of its methods of work and kept the Commission informed accordingly.

The Working Group hopes that enhanced publicity may prompt organizations that have hitherto been unaware of the Group's existence to seek a working relationship with it. This, in turn, may lead to a more diversified flow of information, particularly from those corners of the world where human rights infrastructure—in terms of grass-root organizations, national commissions and the like—is as yet rather frail.

In 1988, for the first time in history, an international judicial body rendered a judgement on cases of disappearances. The Inter-American Court of Human Rights, in deciding three cases that took place in Honduras, made a number of important observations which have a direct bearing on the Working Group's activities and methods of work. First, the Court made a detailed analysis of the internationally recognized principle of the State's responsibility for the human rights violations committed within its territory and its obligations to prevent such violations or to investigate them where they have occurred. It declared that such responsibility continued to exist, for as long as uncertainty remained concerning the ultimate fate of the disappeared person.

These considerations have in different words been retained also by the Human Rights Committee in recent views expressed on cases brought before it under the Optional Protocol. These views are of direct relevance for the Working Group and reinforce the positions it has consistently taken. For in its dialogue with certain Governments arguments had been advanced first of all that cases stemming from a previous political period should not be ascribed to the Government in office and, hence, dropped from the Group's dossier. Secondly, it had been suggested rather strongly that the Working Group should declare inadmissable cases reported to it long after the alleged date of occurrence.

The Group, for its part, has always taken the view that a situation of disappearance does not come to an end once no new cases have been reported over a certain period of time. Under its terms of reference, the Group will continue to deal with cases as long as they have not been clarified. It believes that the need to insist on investigation of all cases of disappearances lies at the heart of its mandate. It does so bearing in mind the interest of those who will suffer anguish and bitterness as long as they cannot be assured of the fate or whereabouts of their loved ones. Furthermore, the Group has repeatedly stated that the advent of democracy or civil Government does not, in itself, imply that no new cases of disappearance will occur.

On three different occaisions, the Working Group has recommended that the Commission on Human Rights, in one form or another, take action on the idea of an international instrument against disappearances. The Group feels gratified that the Sub-Commission is now in the process of elaborating a draft declaration on the subject, generously supported by a number of non-governmental organizations, and has offered some constructive comments. Hopefully, the Sub-Commission will pursue this exercise with all the necessary vigour.

The Working Group would like to commend the members of the Secretariat, whose unwavering dedication has allowed the Group to develop its methods of work and to deal with its case load. Particularly in the initial period, when the Group had to find its way through uncharted territory under sometimes trying circumstances, but also up to the present, innovative thinking as well as common sense have been the hallmarks of the Centre's support unit. Sifting through the thousands of communications, entering them into the computer, cross-checking data, correspondence with sources and governments, preparing documentation, all of this is so labour-intensive that without the Secretariat, the Group would have been utterly helpless. Unfortunately, the Centre for Human Rights has, for several years already, been contending with a chronic shortage in financial and human resources. If immediate remedies are not applied, the level of service to the Working Group will no longer be sustainable. This will inevitably result in backlogs that would not be fair to the families concerned, nor to the respective Governments, for that matter. The Commission would be well-advised to give this question its most serious consideration; its agenda gives it ample occasion to do so.

Finally, the Working Group wishes to reiterate that the advisory services system, would be of considerable benefit for many countries where the problem of disappearances has been epidemic. It hopes that more and more Governments will avail themselves of the possibilities offered by the United Nations in this regard. As it is in the minds of people that human rights violations are conceived, it is in their minds, and hearts, that consciousness about the inherent dignity of the human person must be instilled. Failing that, it will be quite impossible to end disappearances for all time. In any event, given the difficulties, the road ahead will be long and ardous.

After examining the report of the working group, the Commission on Human Rights, on 2 March 1990, expressed its concern (resolution 1990/30) that the practice of enforced or involuntary disappearances continued in various regions of the world, and at the growing number of reports concerning harassment of witnesses of disappearances, or relatives of disappeared persons. It reminded the working group of the obligation to discharge its mandate in a discreet and conscientious manner, and of the need to observe, in its humanitarian task, United Nations standards and practices regarding the receipt of communications, their consideration, their evaluation, the transmittal to governments of all communications received and the consideration of government replies. The commission also noted with concern that some governments had never provided substantive replies concerning disappearances alleged to have occurred in their country. It urged all governments concerned to cooperate with and assist the working group, and to take steps to protect the families of disappeared persons against any intimidation or ill-treatment to which they might be subject.

The commission extended for two years the term of the mandate of the working group, while maintaining its annual reporting procedure.

SEE ALSO Argentina: Disappearance of Children; Disappearances entries; Honduras entries; Impunity: NGO Reaction; Peru: Disappearances.

WORKING GROUP ON INDIGENOUS POPULA-TIONS. Creation of the working group was first proposed by the UN SUB-COMMISSION ON PREVENTION OF DISCRIMINATION AND PROTECTION OF MINORITIES in 1982 (resolution 2 [XXXIV]). The proposal was endorsed by the COMMISSION ON HUMAN RIGHTS (resolution 1982/19) and the ECONOMIC AND SOCIAL COUNCIL (resolution 1982/34). The council thereby authorized the sub-commission to establish annually a Working Group on Indigenous Populations to meet for up to five working days before the sub-commission's sessions in order to (a) review developments pertaining to the promotion and protection of human rights and fundamental freedoms of indigenous populations, including information obtained by the Secretary-General from governments, specialized agencies, regional intergovernmental organizations, and non-governmental organizations in consultative status, particularly those of indigenous peoples, and to analyze such materials and to submit its conclusions to the sub-commission; and (b) give special attention to the evolution of standards concerning the rights of indigenous populations, taking account of both the similarities and the differences in the situations and aspirations of indigenous populations throughout the world.

The working group meets for five working days each year immediately before each annual session of the sub-commission, normally at the United Nations office in Geneva. It consists of one member of the sub-commission from each of five regional groups: one from an African State, one from an Asian State, one from a Latin American State, one from an eastern European State, and one from a western European or other State. Before the close of each sub-commission session, its chairman, after consulting with the regional groups, designates five members to constitute the working group for the next year.

More than 350 experts took part in the 1989 session of the working group, including observers from more than 32 UN member States and the Holy See, representatives of the ILO, observers from more than 30 non-governmental organizations in consultative status, and representatives of several hundred indigenous peoples' organizations and other interested groups.

The working group, at that session, held a general review of the situation and developments pertaining to the promotion and protection of the human rights and fundamental freedoms of indigenous peoples and heard reports highlighting some of the most important issues confronting them. In the course of the discussion, a number of proposals and recommendations were put forward, including general calls for greater consultation between governments and indigenous peoples, for the demilitarization of areas occupied by indigenous peoples, and for the resettlement of people brought into indigenous areas to change artificially the ethnic consistency of the area. There were also specific calls for:

(a) a special rapporteur or member of the working group to be mandated to witness and investigate human rights abuses to indigenous people;

(b) an international recourse procedure to be established for the use of indigenous people who had suffered human rights violations, e.g., a high commissioner or an international ombudsman;

(c) a permanent institution to be set up to monitor the deaths of indigenous people while in the custody of government authorities;

(d) a special committee of 24 to investigate the situation of indigenous peoples, as far as their decolonization mandate allows;

(e) elections for indigenous peoples to be conducted under the aegis of the United Nations;

(f) debt relief for economically disadvantaged countries, when provided, to be allocated to the assistance of indigenous peoples;

(g) the forthcoming United Nations Global Consultation on Development to take into account indigenous peoples and an international conference to be convened to examine the experience of indigenous peoples in their attempts at self-development;

(h) the United Nations to extend technical assistance to indigenous peoples and communities in their attempts at self-development;

(i) the United Nations Center on Transnational Corporations to monitor the work of transnational corporations and international institutions on projects which may affect the life and conditions of indigenous peoples; and

(j) a proclamation by the United Nations of an "International Year for Indigenous Rights," with an explicit focus on the development process for indigenous peoples.

The working group also considered the first revised text of a proposed draft "Universal Declaration on the Rights of Indigenous Peoples" which had been prepared at its requests by its chairman-rapporteur, Mrs. Erica-Irene A. Daes (Greece) (UN Doc. E/CN.4/Sub.2/1989/33) and suggested amendments and additions to it. It recommended that Ms. Daes be entrusted with the task of preparing a second revised text of the draft declaration based on the comments received in writing by members of the group as well as those made at sessions of the group. The sub-commission later endorsed (resolution 1989/34) the recommendations of the working group and requested the Secretary-General to transmit the working group's report to governments, indigenous peoples, and intergovernmental and non-governmental organizations for specific comments and proposals for the further elaboration of the revised text of the draft declaration.

SEE ALSO Indigenous Populations: Study of the Problem of Discrimination; Indigenous Rights: Draft Universal Declaration.

WORKING GROUP ON THE DRAFT BODY OF PRINCIPLES AND GUARANTEES FOR THE PROTECTION OF MENTALLY-ILL PERSONS AND FOR THE IMPROVEMENT OF MENTAL HEALTH CARE.

At its 1989 session, the UN Commission on Human Rights established an open-ended working group to examine, revise, and simplify as necessary the "Draft Body of Principles and Guarantees for the Protection of Mentally-ill Persons and for the Improvement of Mental Health Care" which had been prepared by the SUB-COMMISSION ON PREVENTION OF DISCRIMINATION AND PROTECTION OF MINORITIES after consideration of a report on the subject (UN Doc. E/CN.4/Sub.2/1984/16) prepared by the sub-commission's special rapporteur, Mrs. Erica-Irene A. Daes (Greece).

The working group, open to all members of the commission, held its first session at the United Nations office in Geneva, from 8 to 19 January 1990. For the texts adopted provisionally at that session, see MENTALLY ILL PERSONS: DRAFT PRINCIPLES FOR THEIR PROTECTION.

The working group will resume its work at a second session to be held in January 1991.

WORKING GROUP ON THE RIGHTS OF PERSONS BELONGING TO NATIONAL, ETHNIC, RELIGIOUS AND LINGUISTIC MINORITIES.

At its 1978 session, the UN COMMISSION ON HUMAN RIGHTS set up a working group, open to all members of the commission, to consider the drafting of a declaration on the rights of members of minorities, within the framework of the principles set forth in article 27 of the INTERNATIONAL COVENANT ON CIVIL AND POLITICAL RIGHTS. A draft declaration on the rights of persons belonging to national, ethnic, religious, and linguistic minorities was submitted by Yugoslavia (Un Doc. E/CN.4/L.1367/Rev. 1) and submitted to the working group to serve as a basis for discussion.

Open-ended working groups have been established at each subsequent session of the commission to continue the drafting of the declaration. In 1981, a revised and consolidated text was prepared by the working group's chairman/rapporteur; this revised text has since served as the basis for discussions in the working group. In its report to the commission's 1989 session (UN Doc. E/CN.4/1989/38), the working group indicated that, as of 7 March 1989, it had provisionally adopted the title, the preamble, and articles 1 to 4 of the draft declaration. These texts, set out in an annex to the report, are reproduced below.

The commission decided (resolution 1989/61) that it would establish another open-ended working group at its 1990 session to continue consideration of the revised draft declaration proposed by Yugoslavia.

Draft Declaration on the Rights of Persons Belonging to National or Ethnic, Religious or Linguistic Minorities (Texts on Which Preliminary Agreement Has Been Reached)

The General Assembly,

Reaffirming that one of the basic aims of the United Nations, as proclaimed in its Charter, is to promote and encourage respect for human rights and for fundamental freedoms for all, without distinction as to race, sex, language or religion.

[Reaffirming] [Reiterating] [Declaring] faith in fundamental human rights, in the dignity and worth of the human person, in the equal rights of men and women and of nations large and small,

Desiring to promote the realization of the principles [concerning the rights of] [persons belonging to] [minorities] which form the basis of the Charter of the United Nations, the Universal Declaration of Human Rights, the Convention on the Prevention and Punishment of the Crime of Genocide and the International Convention on the Elimination of All Forms of Racial Discrimination as well as other relevant international instruments [that have been adopted at the universal or regional level and those concluded between individual States Members of the United Nations],

Inspired by [Based on] the provisions of article 27 of the International Covenant on Civil and Political Rights concerning the rights of persons belonging to ethnic, religious or linguistic minorities,

Considering that the promotion and protection of the rights of persons belonging to [national or] ethnic, religious or linguistic minorities contribute to the political and social stability of States in which they live,

Confirming that friendly relations and co-operation among States, which take place in the spirit of the Declaration on Principles of International Law concerning Friendly Relations and Co-operation among States in accordance with the Charter of the United Nations, contribute to international peace and security and to the creation of more favourable conditons for the realization and promotion of human rights, including the rights of [persons belonging to] [national or], ethnic, linguistic and religious minorities,

Emphasizing that the constant promotion and realization of the rights of persons belonging to minorities, as an integral part of the development of society as a whole and within the constitutional framework, would in turn contribute to the strengthening of friendship and co-operation among peoples and States,

Bearing in mind the work done so far within the United Nations system, in particular the Commission on Human Rights, the Sub-Commission on Prevention of Discrimination and Protection of Minorities as well as the bodies established pursuant to the International Covenants on Human Rights and other relevant international human rights instruments on promoting and protecting the rights of persons belonging to [national or] ethnic, religious or linguistic minorities,

Recognizing the need to ensure even more effective implementation of international human rights instruments relating to the rights of persons belonging to [national or] ethnic, religious or linguistic minorities,

Proclaim this Declaration on the Rights of Persons Belonging to [National or] Ethnic, Religious or Linguistic Minorities;

Article 1. 1. [Persons belonging to] [national or] ethnic, linguistic and religious minorities (hereinafter referred to as minorities) have the right to respect for, and the promotion of, their ethnic, cultural, linguistic and religious identity without any discrimination.

2. [Persons belonging to] minorities have the right to life, liberty and security of person and all other human rights and freedoms without discrimination.

Article 2. 1. In accordance with the Charter of the United Nations and other relevant international instruments, [persons belonging to] minorities have the right to be protected against any activity, including propaganda, [directed against minorities] which:

(i) may threaten their existence [or identity]

(ii) [interferes with their freedom of expression or association] [or the development of their own characteristics]; or

(iii) otherwise prevents their full enjoyment and exer-

cise of universally recognized human rights and fundamental freedoms.

2. In accordance with their respective constitutional processes [and in accordance with the relevant international treaties to which they are parties], all States shall undertake to adopt legislative or other appropriate measures to prevent and combat such activities, with due regard to the principles embodied in this Declaration and in the Universal Declaration of Human Rights.

Article 3. 1. [Persons belonging to] minorities have the right, individually or in community with the other members of their group, to enjoy their own culture, to profess and practice their own religion, and to use their own language, freely and without interference or any form of discrimination.

2. All states [which have not yet done so] shall [take measures to create favourable conditions to enable [persons belonging to] minorities to freely]/[ensure that [persons belonging to] minorities are freely able to] express their characteristics, to develop their [education,] culture, language, religion, traditions and customs, and to participate on an equitable basis in the cultural, religious, social, economic and political life in the country where they live.

3. To the same ends, persons belonging to minorities shall enjoy, without any discrimination, the right to establish and maintain contacts with other members of their group [and with other minorities], expecially by exercise of residence within the borders of each State, and the right to leave any country, including their own, and to return to their countries. [This right shall be exercised in accordance with national legislation and relevant international human rights instruments.]

Article 4. 1. All States shall take legislative or other appropriate and effective measures, especially in the fields of teaching, education, culture and information, to promote and protect the human rights and fundamental freedoms of [persons belonging to] minorities.

2. Such measures shall include facilitation of the enjoyment by [persons belonging to] minorities of their freedom to seek, receive and impart information and ideas of all kinds, regardless of frontiers, in particular through utilization of all forms of communication [This freedom shall be exercised in accordance with national legislation and relevant international human rights instruments.]

3. Such measures should also include the exchange of information [and experience] among States in the aforementioned fields, with a view to strengthening mutual understanding, tolerance and friendship among all people, including [persons belonging to] minorities, [as well as to develop further friendly relations and cooperation among States in accordance with the Charter of the United Nations.]/[as well as to develop further international cooperation in the spirit of the Declaration on Principles of International Law concerning Friendly Relations and Cooperation among States in accordance with the Charter of the United Nations].

WORKING GROUP TO EXAMINE SITUATIONS WHICH APPEAR TO REVEAL A CONSISTENT PATTERN OF GROSS VIOLATIONS OF HUMAN RIGHTS. The working group, established by the UN COMMISSION ON HUMAN RIGHTS at its 1974 session (decision 3 [XXX]), examines the particular situations re-

ferred to the commission under resolution 1503 (XLVIII) of the UN Economic and Social Council, including those transmitted by confidential resolution of the SUB-COMMISSION ON PREVENTION OF DISCRIMINATION AND PROTECTION OF MINORITIES.

The working group first met prior to the commission's 1975 session and submitted its recommendations confidentially to the commission. A similar working group was set up each year since then. Meetings of the working group are closed to the public. They are normally held during the one-week period immediately prior to the commission's annual session. The working group's reports are communicated confidentially to the commission.

In 1974, the commission decided (decision 3 [XXX]) that the governments concerned should thenceforth be invited to submit written observations relating to the particular situations which had been referred to the commission. In 1978, it decided (decision 5 [XXXIV]) to issue invitations, during the first week of each session, to the States directly concerned, asking them to send representatives to address the commission and to answer any questions put to them by its members. In 1979, it decided (decision 14 [XXXV]) to authorize its working groups in future to communicate the text of the relevant recommendations as soon as possible to the governments directly concerned in order to facilitate their participation in the examination of the situations concerning their countries. In 1980, it decided (decision 9 [XXXVI]) that the States invited to attend the closed meetings of the commission under council resolution 1503 (XLVIII) should have the right to attend and to participate in the entire discussion of the situation concerning them and to be present during the adoption of the final decision taken in regard to that situation.

The working group consists of five members of the commission, one from an African State, one from an Asian State, one from a Latin American State, one from an eastern European State, and one from a western Europe or other State. Before the end of each session of the commission, its chairman announces, after consultations with the regional groups, the names of the members designated to serve in their personal capacity on the working group at the forthcoming session.

WORLD ALLIANCE OF REFORMED CHURCHES.

An international non-governmental organization in consultative status (Roster) with the UN Economic and Social Council, WARC has 166 affiliated member churches in 80 countries.

The current World Alliance of Reformed Churches emerged in 1970 from the merger of the World Presbyterian Alliance and International Congregational Council. WARC seeks to foster an ecumenical movement among Christian churches and to further the work of evangelism, mission, and stewardship. It is also committed to helping member churches which are weak or persecuted and to promoting and defending religious and civil liberties wherever they are threatened. WARC has undertaken the causes of individual member churches in Korea, Taiwan, South Africa, and Romania, among others. In 1976, it issued a booklet "Theological Basis of Human Rights," which concluded that Christian churches, congregations, and ecumenical organizations should represent the unassailable dignity of human beings and the unity of their human rights and duties and should press for the restoration of particular rights which have become neglected, weakened, or repressed.

WARC publishes *Reformed World* (quarterly) and *Reformed Press Service* (irregularly).

World Alliance of Reformed Churches. Address: 150 route de Ferney, 1211 Geneva 20, Switzerland. Telephone: 022–916238. Cable: WARC Geneva. Telex: 23423 OIK (WARC) Geneva. Fax: (41-22) 91-03-61 WARC Reformierter Weltbund. Secretary-General: Rev. Dr. Edmond Perret.

WORLD ASSOCIATION FOR THE SCHOOL AS AN INSTRUMENT OF PEACE.

An international non-governmental organization in consultative status with the UN Economic and Social Council (Roster) and with UNESCO and the Council of Europe, the association includes national sections in 17 countries and organizations, individuals, and schools in more than 70 countries.

Founded in Geneva in 1967, the World Association promotes universal principles of civic education and endeavors to unite mankind through the teaching of human rights and peace to children in school. It also works to open the door to mutual understanding for children throughout the world, to teach respect for life and for man, and to help the child to understand that progress requires the active collaboration of all. The association publishes the quarterly *Ecole et paix.*

World Association for the School as an Instrument of Peace. Address: Rue du Simplon 5–7, CH–1207 Geneva, Switzerland. Telephone: (022) 35–24–22 and (022) 36–44–52. President: Jacques Mühlethaler.

Yearbook of International Organizations 1989/90 (K. G. Saur).

WORLD ASSOCIATION OF WORLD FEDERAL-ISTS. An international non-governmental organization in consultative status with the UN Economic and Social Council (Category II) and with UNESCO, the association brings together 40 national and associated organizations, with a total membership of more than 25,000.

Founded in Luxembourg in 1946, WAWF coordinates policies and activities directed toward the creation of a world federation having a defined sphere of jurisdiction, functioning through a legislature to make world law, a judiciary to interpret that law, and an executive with adequate powers to enforce it upon individuals, associations and states. In this connection, it studies the possibilities for revision of the UNITED NATIONS CHARTER that would give the UN limited powers to prevent war and to increase the well being of people everywhere, without interfering with internal sovereignties of member States. It assists in the establishment of new national organizations to achieve these purposes, organizes conferences on peace action, and promotes the exchange of relevant political and educational information.

WAWF publishes two quarterlies, *Transnational Perspectives* and *World Federalist News,* and issues special reports from time to time.

World Association of World Federalists. Address: Leliegracht 21, 1016 GR Amsterdam, Netherlands. Telephone: (31–20) 227502. Executive Director: Ron J. Rutherglen.

Yearbook of International Organizations 1989/90 (K. G. Saur).

WORLD CONFEDERATION OF LABOR. An international organization in consultative status with the UN Economic and Social Council (Category I) and with ILO, UNESCO, and FAO, WCL's membership includes national organizations and professional federations in more 95 countries and territories, representing a total individual membership of about 15 million workers.

Founded at the Hague in 1920 as the International Federation of Christian Trade Unions, the organization changed its name to World Confederation of Labor in1968 and revised its organizational structure in 1969 to reflect the increasing role of third world workers' organizations. WCL's current principal functions are to promote human and trade union rights, to ensure the exercise of those rights by all workers, to give moral and material support to its affiliated organizations, and to promote the exchange of information between them. In a larger sense, it works for peace, disarmament, and the solidarity of workers and peoples.

WCL publishes the monthly review *Labor,* the fortnightly bulletin *Flash,* and the bi-annual journal *Events,* in English, French, Spanish, German, and Dutch.

World Confederation of Labor. Address: Rue de Treves 33, B-1040 Brussels, Belgium. Telephone: (32-2) 230-62-95. Cable: MUNDOLABOR. Telex: 26-966 CMTWEL B. Fax: (32-2) 230-87-22. Secretary-General: Jan Kulakowski.

WORLD CONFEDERATION OF ORGANIZATIONS OF THE TEACHING PROFESSION. An international non-governmental organization in consultative status with the UN Economic and Social Council (Category II), and with ILO, UNESCO, OAS, and the Council of Europe, the confederation includes 160 national teachers' organizations and has a total individual membership of more than 11 million.

The confederation was founded in 1952 by a merger of three major international federations: The World Organization of the Teaching Profession (WOTP), The International Federation of Teachers' Associations (IFTA), and the International Federation of Secondary Teachers (known by its French acronym FIPESO). IFTA and FIPESO remain in being as constituent federations of WCOTP.

The World Confederation exerts independent political influence on behalf of teachers and works for equality of opportunity through education and for improvement of the quality of education. It asserts and defends the individual and collective rights of teachers and strives for the advancement of their status and the improvement of their working conditions. It maintains that the professional and trade union interests of teachers are inseparable and in the preparation and promotion of the ILO/UNESCO RECOMMENDATION CONCERNING THE STATUS OF TEACHERS.

WCOTP publishes *echo,* a quarterly newsletter (in English, French, Spanish, Chinese, German, and Japanese); a biennial report on activities and programs (in English, French, and Spanish); a handbook; reports of conferences, seminars, studies, and investigations; and service publications on various aspects of education, trade union operations, welfare services, and international affairs.

World Confederation of Organisations of the Teaching Profession. Address: 5 avenue du Moulin, 1110 Morges, Switzerland. Telephone: 801-74-67. Cable: TEACHING 1110 Morges. Telex: 458 219 WCTP CH. Fax: (41-21) 801-74-69. Secretary General: Robert Harris.

WORLD CONFERENCE ON HUMAN RIGHTS. The UN General Assembly, at its 1989 session, noted (resolution 44/156) the progress made by the United Nations over the past 20 years towards achieving its goal of promoting respect for human rights and fundamental freedoms for all, without distinction as to race, sex, language, or religion but noted also that there are still areas in which further progress could be made towards this goal.

Considering that, in view of the progress made and the new challenges that lie ahead, it would be appropriate to conduct a review of what has been accomplished through the human rights program and what remains to be done, it requested the Secretary-General to seek the views of governments, specialized agencies, non-governmental organizations, and United Nations bodies concerned with human rights regarding the desirability of convening a world conference on human rights for the purpose of dealing with the questions facing the United Nations in connection with the promotion and protection of human rights. The Secretary-General's report is to be presented to the General Assembly at its 1990 session.

WORLD CONFERENCE ON RELIGION AND PEACE. An international non-governmental organization in consultative status with the UN Economic and Social Council (Category II) and with UNESCO, the World Conference includes 20 national affiliates and individual members in 34 countries.

In 1968, the World Conference on Religion and Peace International was founded to promote common actions for peace and justice by believers of all traditional world religions. The first World Conference on Religion and Peace was convened in Kyoto on the initiative of American and Japanese religious leaders. World assemblies have since been held in Louvain, Belgium (1974), Princeton, New Jersey, U.S.A. (1979) and Nairobi, Kenya (1984).

WCRP's main function is to promote inter-religious cooperation and understanding. It works for the establishment of world peace and the realization by everyone of human rights and fundamental freedoms and consistently champions the rights of members of religious and ethnic minorities. In addition, it conducts humanitarian projects on an interreligious basis.

The conference publishes the proceedings of its conferences and the quarterly newsletter *Religion for Peace.*

World Conference on Religion and Peace International. Address: Chateau Pictet, 14 CH Auguste Vil-bert, Grand Saconnex, CH 1218 Geneva, Switzerland. Telephone: (41-22) 798-51-62. Cable: RELPEACE GENEVA. Fax: (22) 91-00-34. Secretary-General: Dr. John B. Taylor.

WORLD COUNCIL OF INDIGENOUS PEOPLES. An international non-governmental organization in consultative status with the UN Economic and Social Council (Category II) and with UNESCO, the council was founded in 1975 at the International Conference of Indian Peoples held in Port Alberni, Canada, a conference which brought together 52 delegates from indigenous organizations in 19 countries; it has since grown to include individuals and organizations in 29 countries.

Under the WCIP charter, the council's main functions are to protect the rights, further the interests, and ensure unity of indigenous peoples in accordance with their own cultures; to contribute in all ways to abolish the possibility of physical and cultural genocide and ethnocide; to participate in combating racism; to ensure political, economic, and social justice to indigenous peoples; and to promote and support the principle of equality among indigenous peoples and the people of nations who may surround them. It supports and finances indigenous organizations and encourages them to work together to achieve common goals.

The council issues the WCIP *Newsletter* from time to time.

World Council of Indigenous Peoples. Address: 555 King Edward Avenue, 0N K1N 6N5, Ottawa, Canada. Telephone: (613) 230-9030. Fax: (613) 564-5952. Telex: 0533338. President: Donald Rojas Maroto.

WORLD FEDERATION FOR MENTAL HEALTH. An international non-governmental organization in consultative status with the UN Economic and Social Council (Category II) and with ILO, UNESCO, and WHO, the federation has approximately 120 member associations (national and international organizations working to enhance and maintain mental health resources) and approximately 100 national affiliates (organizations supporting WFMH's goals but not directly involved in its work).

The federation was founded in London in 1948, during the Third International Congress on Mental Health, as the successor to the *Comite international d'hygiene mentale,* which had been established in 1931. It endeavors to promote among peoples and nations everywhere the highest possible standard of mental health, as defined in the broadest biological, medical, educational, social, and cultural terms. It collaborates with the United Nations and other international agencies to improve mental health services in their member States. Through international, regional, and national projects, WFMH works to overcome the stigma attached to mental illness, to increase the number and effectiveness of trained mental health workers, to protect the rights of patients suffering from mental ill-health, and to stimulate the creation of national and regional mental health associations. It also serves as an international clearing house for information on mental health issues.

WFMH publishes the WFMH *Newsletter* five times a year and issues the proceedings of its World Conferences on Mental Health (held every two years). In addition, it produces monographs on particular aspects of its work.

World Federation for Mental Health. Address: 1021 Prince Street, Alexandria, Virginia (U.S.A.) 22314-2971. Telephone: (703) 684-7722. Cable: MENSANTE. Secretary-General: Dr. Eugene B. Brody.

Yearbook of International Organizations 1989/90 (K. G. Saur).

WORLD FEDERATION OF DEMOCRATIC YOUTH.

An international non-governmental organization in consultative status with the UN Economic and Social Council (Category I) and with ILO, UNESCO, and FAO, WFDY has more than 270 affiliated and observer organizations in 112 countries and territories.

The World Federation of Democratic Youth was founded in London in 1945. It works to promote the active participation of youth in economic, social, cultural, and political life by acting against all restriction and discrimination connected with age, sex, methods of education, domicile, property, social status, religion, political convictions, color, and race. The federation supports the struggle of world youth for higher living standards; better conditions of education, work, and leisure; and the development of cultural, educational, and sports activities for young people to ensure optimal human development. To accomplish these goals, WFDY conducts seminars and establishes voluntary work camps. It also has established a voluntary international aid fund.

The federation publishes *WFDY News* and *World Youth* monthly in English, French, and Spanish.

World Federation of Democratic Youth. Address: P.O. Box 147, Ady Endre útca 19, H-1389 Budapest, Hungary. Telephone: (36-1) 154-095. Cable: DIVSZ Budapest. Telex: 22-7197 DIVSZ H. Fax: (36-1) 352-746. Secretary-General: Ryörgy Szabö.

Yearbook of International Organizations 1989/90 (K. G. Saur).

WORLD FEDERATION OF METHODIST WOMEN.

An international non-governmental organization in consultative status (Category II) with the UN Economic and Social Council, WFMW has national units in 71 countries.

Founded in 1939 in Pasadena, California (USA), the federation works to build a Christian community through evangelism, ministries, education, and social services. Its work is carried out in eight main areas: social justice; health; family life; the changing role of women; instability in the home; child abuse; drug and alcohol abuse; and cross-cultural programs. WFMW conducts local and regional seminars for leadership training and Bible study and holds a quinquennial assembly.

The federation publishes the quarterly *Tree of Life* and the *WFMW Newsletter,* as well as the *WFMW Handbook* and *Methodist Women: A World Sisterhood.*

World Federation of Methodist Women. Address: 7100 Grey Oaks Drive, New Orleans, LA (USA). Telephone: (504) 246-6562. President: Edith Ming.

Yearbook of International Organizations 1989/90 (K. G. Saur).

WORLD FEDERATION OF TRADE UNIONS.

An international non-governmental organization in consultative status with the UN Economic and Social Council (Categroy I) and with ILO, UNESCO, and FAO, WFTU is composed of 92 affiliated organizations in 76 countries, representing approximately 214 million members.

Established in 1945 as an international trade union organization affiliating national trade union centers, the World Federation of Trade Unions has as one of its aims, as stated in its constitution, "the achievement of economic and political democracy, the development of workers' rights and freedoms, respect for human rights and the implementation of the Universal Declaration of Trade Union Rights." Its principle concern is to coordinate the activities of affiliated national centers in promoting international solidarity in defense of trade union rights and human rights and to organize support for these struggles in various countries.

Among WFTU's regular publications are the weekly "Flashes" (issued in Arabic, English, French, Russian, and Spanish) and the monthly *World Trade Union Movement* (issued in Arabic, English, French, German, Japanese, Romanian, Russian, and Spanish).

World Federation of Trade Unions. Address: Vinohradska 10, 12147 Prague 2, Czechoslovakia. Telephone: 235-35-65. Cable: FESYMOND. Telex: 121525 WFTU C. Fax: (42-2) 26-43-80. General Secretary: Ibrahim Zakaria.

WORLD FEDERATION OF UNITED NATIONS ASSOCIATIONS.

An international non-governmental organization in consultative status with the UN Economic and Social Council (Category I) and with ILO, UNESCO and FAO, the federation has 68 national affiliates.

WFUNA was founded in 1946, in Luxembourg, to mobilize support for the purposes and principles set out in the United Nations Charter and to stimulate public awareness and understanding of the activities of the United Nations and its agencies. It conducts worldwide educational programs, projects, conferences, and seminars and uses all media of information to disseminate knowledge of the United Nations. It issues periodic reports on its projects and the quarterly *WFUNA Bulletin*.

World Federation of United Nations Associations. Address: Palais des Nations, CH 1211 Geneva 10, Switzerland. Telephone: 330730. Cable: WORFEDUNA Geneva. Fax: 339879. Telex: 289696. Secretary-General: Marek Hagmajer.

WORLD FOOD COUNCIL.

The council, established by the UN General Assembly on 17 December 1974 (resolution 3348 [XXIX]), was set up "at the ministerial or plenipotentiary level to function as an organ of the United Nations." It mandate, as had been proposed to the assembly by the World Food Conference on 16 November 1974 (resolution XXII), includes the following tasks:

(c) The Council should review periodically major problems and policy issues affecting the world food situation, and the steps being proposed or taken to resolve them by Governments, by the United Nations system and by its regional organizations, and should further recommend remedial action as appropriate. The scope of the Council's review should extend to all aspects of world food problems in order to adopt an integrated approach towards their solution;

(d) The Council should establish its own programme of action for co-ordination of relevant United Nations bodies and agencies. While doing so, it should give special attention to the problems of the least developed countries and the countries most seriously affected;

(e) The Council should maintain contacts with, receive reports from, give advice to, and make recommendations to United Nations bodies and agencies with regard to the formulation and follow-up of world food policies;

(f) The Council should work in full co-operation with regional bodies to formulate and follow up policies approved by the Council. Committees to be established by these regional bodies should be serviced by existing United Nations of FAO bodies in the region concerned.

The council consists of 36 members nominated by the Economic and Social Council and elected by the General Assembly "taking into consideration balanced geographical distribution, with one-third of the members retiring every year and the retiring members being eligible for re-election." The members of the council are elected according to the following pattern: nine members from African States, eight members from Asian States, seven members from Latin American States, four members from socialist States of eastern Europe, and eight members from western European and other States. The term of office is three years.

The council normally meets in ministerial sessions once a year; special sessions are held when the need arises. Sessions are usually held in Rome, but the council has also met in other places, including the Philippines, Mexico, and Canada. The council reports to the General Assembly through the Economic and Social Council.

WORLD HEALTH ORGANIZATION (WHO).

By its constitution of 1946, the World Health Organization was established as an autonomous permanent intergovernmental organization dedicated to the premise that the enjoyment of the highest attainable standard of health is one of the fundamental rights of every human being without distinction as to race, religion, political belief, economic, or social condition. Over the years, WHO has specialized in carrying out worldwide campaigns to combat communicable diseases. In developing countries, in particular, it has wiped out smallpox, checked the spread of cholera, and immunized millions of children against the diseases of childhood: diptheria, tetanus, whooping cough, poliomylitis, measles, and tuberculosis. It has also developed, through biomedical research, efficient techniques to combat tropical diseases such as malaria, schistosomiasis, filariasis, trepanosomiasis, leprosy, and leishmaniasis. Its international health regulations provide for epidemiological disease surveillance on a worldwide scale, promote the development of national surveillance services, and improve cooperation among countries in this field. WHO also carried out an extensive technical assistance program covering many aspects of public health, in which the teaching and training of health personnel are emphasized.

A total of 165 States are members of the World Health Organization; they include all States members of the United Nations with only two exceptions (Brunei and St. Christopher and Nevis), and Cook Islands, North Korea, South Korea, Morocco, Namibia (formerly represented by the United Nations Council for Namibia), San Marino, Switzerland, and Tonga. WHO's main organs are the World Health Assembly, composed of representatives of each member State;

the executive board, consisting of 30 persons technically qualified in the field of health who are elected by the assembly on the basis of nominations by member States; and the Secretariat, headed by the Director-General, who is appointed by the assembly on the nomination of the executive board.

The World Health Assembly meets annually for a period of about two weeks, usually at ILO headquarters in Geneva during the month of May. The executive board meets twice a year, one session of about three weeks' duration in January and a second of about two days' duration in May, also at WHO headquarters in Geneva.

Many of the activities of WHO have been decentralized to six regional organizations, each maintaining a regional office and a regional committee composed of States within the region. These offices are in New Delhi, for southeast Asia; Alexandria, for the eastern Mediterranean; Manila, for the western Pacific; Washington, for the Americas (Pan American Sanitary Bureau); Brazzaville, for Africa; and Copenhagen, for Europe. The International Agency for Cancer Research, located in Lyon, France, is an autonomous body within the framework of the WHO.

Under the terms of its agreement with the United Nations, the World Health Organization transmits reports to UN organs on its activities and complies with requests from those organs for special reports, studies, or information. In 1985, for example, WHO was represented on the Working Group on Traditional Practices Affecting the Health of Women and Children, which prepared a comprehensive report on this subject at the request of the UN Economic and Social Council (resolution 1984/34).

WORLD HEALTH ORGANIZATION: CONSTITUTION (1946).

The constitution of WHO was adopted on 22 July 1946 by the World Health Conference, convened in New York by the United Nations, and entered into force on 7 April 1948.

The objective of WHO, a specialized agency of the United Nations, as stated in the constitution (article 1), is "the attainment by all peoples of the highest possible level of health." WHO is authorized to take all necessary action to attain that objective. The long list of its functions, set out in article 2 of the constitution, is supplemented from time to time by new mandates added by the UN General Assembly.

The text of the constitution (United Nations, *Treaty Series*, vol. 14, p. 185), as amended by the 20th, 26th, and 29th World Health Assemblies, is as follows:

The states parties to this Constitution declare, in conformity with the Charter of the United Nations, that the following principles are basic to the happiness, harmonious relations and security of all peoples:

Health is a state of complete physical, mental and social well-being and not merely the absence of disease or infirmity.

The enjoyment of the highest attainable standard of health is one of the fundamental rights of every human being without distinction of race, religion, political belief, economic or social condition.

The health of all peoples is fundamental to the attainment of peace and security and is dependent upon the fullest co-operation of individuals and States.

The achievement of any State in the promotion and protection of health is of value to all.

Unequal development in different countries in the promotion of health and control of disease, especially communicable disease, is a common danger.

Healthy development of the child is of basic importance; the ability to live harmoniously in a changing total environment is essential to such development.

The extension to all peoples of the benefits of medical, psychological and related knowledge is essential to the fullest attainment of health.

Informed opinion and active co-operation on the part of the public are of the utmost importance in the improvement of the health of the people.

Governments have a responsibility for the health of their peoples which can be fulfilled only by the provision of adequate health and social measures.

Accepting these principles, and for the purpose of co-operation among themselves and with others to promote and protect the health of all peoples, the Contracting Parties agree to the present Constitution and hereby establish the World Health Organization as a specialized agency within the terms of Article 57 of the Charter of the United Nations.

Chapter I—Objective

Article 1. The objective of the World Health Organization (hereinafter called the Organization) shall be the attainment by all peoples of the highest possible level of health.

Chapter II—Functions

Article 2. In order to achieve its objective, the functions of the Organization shall be:

(a) to act as the directing and co-ordinating authority on international health work;

(b) to establish and maintain effective collaboration with the United Nations, specialized agencies, governmental health administrations, professional groups and such other organizations as may be deemed appropriate;

(c) to assist Governments, upon request, in strengthening health services;

(d) to furnish appropriate technical assistance and, in emergencies, necessary aid upon the request or acceptance of Governments;

(e) to provide or assist in providing, upon the request of the United Nations, health services and facilities to special groups, such as the peoples of trust territories;

(f) to establish and maintain such administrative and technical services as may be required, including epidemiological and statistical services;

(g) to stimulate and advance work to eradicate epidemic, endemic and other diseases;

(h) to promote, in co-operation with other specialized

agencies where necessary, the prevention of accidental injuries;

(i) to promote, in co-operation with other specialized agencies where necessary, the improvement of nutrition, housing, sanitation, recreation, economic or working conditions and other aspects of environmental hygiene;

(j) to promote co-operation among scientific and professional groups which contribute to the advancement of health;

(k) to propose conventions, agreements and regulations, and make recommendations with respect to international health matters and to perform such duties as may be assigned thereby to the Organization and are consistent with its objective;

(l) to promote maternal and child health and welfare and to foster the ability to live harmoniously in a changing total environment;

(m) to foster activities in the field of mental health, especially those affecting the harmony of human relations;

(n) to promote and conduct research in the field of health;

(o) to promote improved standards of teaching and training in the health, medical and related professions;

(p) to study and report on, in co-operation with other specialized agencies where necessary, administrative and social techniques affecting public health and medical care from preventive and curative points of view, including hospital services and social security;

(q) to provide information, counsel and assistance in the field of health;

(r) to assist in developing an informed public opinion among all peoples on matters of health;

(s) to establish and revise as necessary international nomenclatures of diseases, of causes of death and of public health practices;

(t) to standardize diagnostic procedures as necessary;

(u) to develop, establish and promote international standards with respect to food, biological, pharmaceutical and similar products;

(v) generally to take all necessary action to attain the objective of the Organization.

Chapter III—Membership and Associate Membership

Article 3. Membership in the Organization shall be open to all States.

Article 4. Members of the United Nations may become Members of the Organization by signing or otherwise accepting this Constitution in accordance with the provisions of Chapter XIX and in accordance with their constitutional processes.

Article 5. The States whose Governments have been invited to send observers to the International Health Conference held in New York, 1946, may become Members by signing or otherwise accepting this Constitution in accordance with the provisions of Chapter XIX and in accordance with their constitutional processes provided that such signature or acceptance shall be completed before the first session of the Health Assembly.

Article 6. Subject to the conditions of any agreement between the United Nations and the Organization, approved pursuant to Chapter XVI, States which do not become Members in accordance with Articles 4 and 5 may apply to become Members and shall be admitted as Members when their application has been approved by a simple majority vote of the Health Assembly.

Article 7. If a Member fails to meet its financial obligations to the Organization or in other exceptional circumstances, the Health Assembly may, on such conditions as it thinks proper, suspend the voting privileges and services to which a Member is entitled. The Health Assembly shall have the authority to restore such voting privileges and services.

Article 8. Territories or groups of territories which are not responsible for the conduct of their international relations may be admitted as Associate Members by the Health Assembly upon application made on behalf of such territory or group of terrorists by the Member or other authority having responsibility for their international relations. Representatives of Associate Members to the Health Assembly should be qualified by their technical competence in the field of health and should be chosen from the native population. The nature and extent of the rights and obligations of Associate Members shall be determined by the Health Assembly.

Chapter IV—Organs

Article 9. The work of the Organization shall be carried out by:

(a) The World Health Assembly (herein called the Health Assembly);

(b) The Executive Board (hereinafter called the Board);

(c) The Secretariat.

Chapter V—The World Health Assembly

Article 10. The Health Assembly shall be composed of delegates representing Members.

Article 11. Each Member shall be represented by not more than three delegates, one of whom shall be designated by the Member as chief delegate. These delegates should be chosen from among persons most qualified by their technical competence in the field of health, preferably representing the national health administration of the Member.

Article 12. Alternates and advisers may accompany delegates.

Article 13. The Health Assembly shall meet in regular annual session and in such special sessions as may be necessary. Special sessions shall be convened at the request of the Board or of a majority of the Members.

Article 14. The Health Assembly, at each annual session, shall select the country or region in which the next annual session shall be held, the Board subsequently fixing the place. The Board shall determine the place where a special session shall be held.

Article 15. The Board, after consultation with the Secretary-General of the United Nations, shall determine the date of each annual and special session.

Article 16. The Health Assembly shall elect its President and other officers at the beginning of each annual session. They shall hold office until their successors are elected.

Article 17. The Health Assembly shall adopt its own rules of procedure.

Article 18. The functions of the Health Assembly shall be:

(a) to determine the policies of the Organization;

(b) to name the Members entitled to designate a person to serve on the Board;

(c) to appoint the Director-General;

(d) to review and approve reports and activities of the Board and of the Director-General and to instruct the

Board in regard to matters upon which action, study, investigation or report may be considered desirable;

(e) to establish such committees as may be considered necessary for the work of the Organization;

(f) to supervise the financial policies of the Organization and to review and approve the budget;

(g) to instruct the Board and the Director-General to bring to the attention of Members and of international organizations, governmental or non-governmental, any matter with regard to health which the Health Assembly may consider appropriate;

(h) to invite any organization, international or national, governmental or non-governmental, which has responsibilities related to those of the Organization, to appoint representatives to participate, without right of vote, in its meetings or in those of the committees and conferences convened under its authority, on conditions prescribed by the Health Assembly; but in the case of national organizations, invitations shall be issued only with the consent of the Government concerned;

(i) to consider recommendations bearing on health made by the General Assembly, the Economic and Social Council, the Security Council or Trusteeship Council of the United Nations, and to report to them on the steps taken by the Organization to give effect to such recommendations;

(j) to report to the Economic and Social Council in accordance with any agreement between the Organization and the United Nations;

(k) to promote and conduct research in the field of health by the personnel of the Organization, by the establishment of its own institutions or by co-operation with official or non-official institutions of any Member with the consent of its Government;

(l) to establish such other institutions as it may consider desirable;

(m) to take any other appropriate action to further the objective of the Organization.

Article 19. The Health Assembly shall have authority to adopt conventions or agreements with respect to any matter within the competence of the Organization. A two-thirds vote of the Health Assembly shall be required for the adoption of such conventions or agreements, which shall come into force for each Member when accepted by it in accordance with its constitutional processes.

Article 20. Each Member undertakes that it will, within eighteen months after the adoption by the Health Assembly of a convention or agreement, take action relative to the acceptance of such convention or agreement. Each Member shall notify the Director-General of the action taken, and if it does not accept such convention or agreement within the time limit, it will furnish a statement of the reasons for non-acceptance. In case of acceptance, each Member agrees to make an annual report to the Director-General in accordance with Chapter XIV.

Article 21. The Health Assembly shall have authority to adopt regulations concerning:

(a) sanitary and quarantine requirements and other procedures designed to prevent the international spread of disease;

(b) nomenclatures with respect to diseases, causes of death and public health practices;

(c) standards with respect to diagnostic procedures for international use;

(d) standards with respect to the safety, purity and po-

tency of biological, pharmaceutical and similar products moving in international commerce;

(e) advertising and labelling of biological, pharmaceutical and similar products moving in international commerce.

Article 22. Regulations adopted pursuant to Article 21 shall come into force for all Members after due notice has been given of their adoption by the Health Assembly except for such Members as may notify the Director-General of rejection or reservations within the period stated in the notice.

Article 23. The Health Assembly shall have authority to make recommendations to Members with respect to any matter within the competence of the Organization.

Chapter VI—The Executive Board

Article 24. The Board shall consist of thirty-one persons designated by as many Members. The Health Assembly, taking into account an equitable geographical distribution, shall elect the Members entitled to designate a person to serve on the Board, provided that, of such Members, not less than three shall be elected from each of the regional organizations established pursuant to Article 44. Each of these Members should appoint to the Board a person technically qualified in the field of health, who may be accompanied by alternates and advisers.

Article 25. These Members shall be elected for three years and may be reelected, provided that of the eleven members elected at the first session of the Health Assembly held after the coming into force of the amendment to this Constitution increasing the membership of the Board from thirty to thirty-one the term of office of the additional Member elected shall, insofar as may be necessary, be of such lesser duration as shall facilitate the election of at least one Member from each regional organization in each year.

Article 26. The Board shall meet at least twice a year and shall determine the place of each meeting.

Article 27. The Board shall elect its Chairman from among its members and shall adopt its own rules of procedure.

Article 28. The functions of the Board shall be:

(a) to give effect to the decisions and policies of the Health Assembly;

(b) to act as the executive organ of the Health Assembly;

(c) to perform any other functions entrusted to it by the Health Assembly;

(d) to advise the Health Assembly on questions referred to it by that body and on matters assigned to the Organization by conventions, agreements and regulations;

(e) to submit advice or proposals to the Health Assembly on its own initiative;

(f) to prepare the agenda of meetings of the Health Assembly;

(g) to submit to the Health Assembly for consideration and approval a general programme of work covering a specific period;

(h) to study all questions within its competence;

(i) to take emergency measures within the functions and financial resources of the Organization to deal with events requiring immediate action. In particular it may authorize the Director-General to take the necessary steps to combat epidemics, to participate in the organization of health relief to victims of a calamity and to undertake studies and research the urgency of which has been drawn to the attention of the Board by any Member or by the Director-General.

Article 29. The Board shall exercise on behalf of the whole Health Assembly the powers delegated to it by that body.

Chapter VII—The Secretariat

Article 30. The Secretariat shall comprise the Director-General and such technical and administrative staff as the Organization may require.

Article 31. The Director-General shall be appointed by the Health Assembly on the nomination of the Board on such terms as the Health Assembly may determine. The Director-General, subject to the authority of the Board, shall be the chief technical and administrative officer of the Organization.

Article 32. The Director-General shall be *ex-officio* Secretary of the Health Assembly, of the Board, of all commissions and committees of the Organization and of conferences convened by it. He may delegate these functions.

Article 33. The Director-General or his representative may establish a procedure by agreement with Members, permitting him, for the purpose of discharging his duties, to have direct access to their various departments, especially to their health administrations and to national health organizations, governmental or non-governmental. He may also establish direct relations with international organizations whose activities come within the competence of the Organization. He shall keep regional offices informed on all matters involving their respective areas.

Article 34. The Director-General shall prepare and submit to the Board the financial statements and budget estimates of the Organization.

Article 35. The Director-General shall appoint the staff of the Secretariat in accordance with staff regulations established by the Health Assembly. The paramount consideration in the employment of the staff shall be to assure that the efficiency, integrity and internationally representative character of the Secretariat shall be maintained at the highest level. Due regard shall be paid also to the importance of recruiting the staff on as wide a geographical basis as possible.

Article 36. The conditions of service of the staff of the Organization shall conform as far as possible with those of other United Nations organizations.

Article 37. In the performance of their duties the Director-General and the staff shall not seek or receive instructions from any government or from any authority external to the Organization. They shall refrain from any action which might reflect o their position as international officers. Each member of the Organization on its part undertakes to respect the exclusively international character of the Director-General and the staff and not to seek to influence them.

Chapter VIII—Committees

Article 38. The Board shall establish such committees as the Health Assembly may direct and, on its own initiative or on the proposal of the Director-General, may establish any other committees considered desirable to serve any purpose within the competence of the Organization.

Article 39. The Board, from time to time and in any event annually, shall review the necessity for continuing each committee.

Article 40. The Board may provide for the creation of or the participation by the Organization in joint or mixed committees with other organizations and for the representation of the Organization in committees established by such other organizations.

Chapter IX—Conferences

Article 41. The Health Assembly or the Board may convene local, general, technical or other special conferences to consider any matter within the competence of the Organization and may provide for the representation at such conferences of international organizations and, with the consent of the Government concerned, of national organizations, governmental or non-governmental. The manner of such representation shall be determined by the Health Assembly or the Board.

Article 42. The Board may provide for representation of the Organization at conferences in which the Board considers that the Organization has an interest.

Chapter X—Headquarters

Article 43. The location of the headquarters of the Organization shall be determined by the Health Assembly after consultation with the United Nations.

Chapter XI—Regional Arrangements

Article 44. (a) The Health Assembly shall from time to time define the geographical areas in which it is desirable to establish a regional organization.

(b) The Health Assembly may, with the consent of a majority of the Members situated within each area so defined, establish a regional organization to meet the special needs of such area. There shall not be more than one regional organization in each area.

Article 45. Each regional organization shall be an integral part of the Organization in accordance with this Constitution.

Article 46. Each regional organization shall consist of a regional committee and a regional office.

Article 47. Regional committees shall be composed of representatives of the Member States and Associate Members in the region concerned. Territories or groups of territories within the region, which are not responsible for the conduct of their international relations and which are not Associate Members, shall have the right to be represented and to participate in regional committees. The nature and extent of the rights and obligations of these territories or groups of territories in regional committees shall be determined by the Health Assembly in consultation with the Member or other authority having responsibility for the international relations of these territories and with the Member States in the region.

Article 48. Regional committees shall meet as often as necessary and shall determine the place of each meeting.

Article 49. Regional committees shall adopt their own rules of procedure.

Article 50. The functions of the regional committee shall be:

(a) to formulate policies governing matters of an exclusively regional character;

(b) to supervise the activities of the regional office;

(c) to suggest to the regional office the calling of technical conferences and such additional work or investigation in health matters as in the opinion of the regional committee would promote the objective of the Organization within the region;

(d) to co-operate with the respective regional committees of the United Nations and with those of other specialized agencies and with other regional international organizations having interests in common with the Organization;

(e) to tender advice, through the Director-General, to the Organization on international health matters which have wider than regional significance;

(f) to recommend additional regional appropriations by the Governments of the respective regions if the proportion of the central budget of the Organization allotted to that region is insufficient for the carrying-out of the regional functions;

(g) such other functions as may be delegated to the regional committee by the Health Assembly, the Board or the Director-General.

Article 51. Subject to the general authority of the Director-General of the Organization, the regional office shall be the administrative organ of the regional committee. It shall, in addition, carry out within the region the decisions of the Health Assembly and of the Board.

Article 52. The head of the regional office shall be the Regional Director appointed by the Board in agreement with the regional committee.

Article 53. The staff of the regional office shall be appointed in a manner to be determined by agreement between the Director-General and the Regional Director.

Article 54. The Pan American Sanitary Organization [renamed Pan American Health Organization in 1958] represented by the Pan American Sanitary Bureau and the Pan American Sanitary Conferences, and all other intergovernmental regional health organizations in existence prior to the date of signature of this Constitution, shall in due course be integrated with the Organization. This integration shall be effected as soon as practicable through common action based on mutual consent of the competent authorities expressed through the organizations concerned.

Chapter XII—Budget and Expenses

Article 55. The Director-General shall prepare and submit to the Board the budget estimates of the Organization. The Board shall consider and submit to the Health Assembly such budget estimates together with any recommendations the Board may deem advisable.

Article 56. Subject to any agreement between the Organization and the United Nations, the Health Assembly shall review and approve the budget estimates and shall apportion the expenses among the Members in accordance with a scale to be fixed by the Health Assembly.

Article 57. The Health Assembly or the Board acting on behalf of the Health Assembly may accept and administer gifts and bequests made to the Organization provided that the conditions attached to such gifts or bequests are acceptable to the Health Assembly or the Board and are consistent with the objective and policies of the Organization.

Article 58. A special fund to be used at the discretion of the Board shall be established to meet emergencies and unforeseen contingencies.

Chapter XIII—Voting

Article 59. Each Member shall have one vote in the Health Assembly.

Article 60. (a) Decisions of the Health Assembly on im-portant questions shall be made by a two-thirds majority of the Members present and voting. These questions shall include: the adoption of conventions or agreements; the approval of agreements bringing the Organization into relation with the United Nations and inter-governmental organizations and agencies in accordance with Articles 69, 70 and 72; amendments to this Constitution.

(b) Decisions on other questions, including the determination of additional categories of questions to be decided by a two-thirds majority, shall be made by a majority of the Members present and voting.

(c) Voting on analogous matters in the Board and in committees of the Organization shall be made in accordance with paragraphs (a) and (b) of this Article.

Chapter XIV—Reports Submitted by States

Article 61. Each Member shall report annually to the Organization on the action taken and progress achieved in improving the health of its people.

Article 62. Each Member shall report annually on the action taken with respect to recommendations made to it by the Organization and with respect to convention, agreements and regulations.

Article 63. Each Member shall communicate promptly to the Organization important laws, regulations, official reports and statistics pertaining to health which have been published in the State concerned.

Article 64. Each Member shall provide statistical and epidemiological reports in a manner to be determined by the Health Assembly.

Article 65. Each Member shall transmit upon the request of the Board such additional information pertaining to health as may be practicable.

Chapter XV—Legal Capacity, Privileges and Immunities

Article 66. The Organization shall enjoy in the territory of each Member such legal capacity as may be necessary for the fulfilment of its objective and for the exercise of its functions.

Article 67. (a) The Organization shall enjoy in the territory of each Member such privileges and immunities as may be necessary for the fulfilment of its objective and for the exercise of its functions.

(b) Representatives of Members, persons designated to serve on the Board and technical and administrative personnel of the Organization shall similarly enjoy such privileges and immunities as are necessary for the independent exercise of their functions in connexion with the Organization.

Article 68. Such legal capacity, privileges and immunities shall be defined in a separate agreement to be prepared by the Organization in consultation with the Secretary-General of the United Nations and concluded between the Members.

Chapter XVI—Relations With Other Organizations

Article 69. The Organization shall be brought into relation with the United Nations as one of the specialized agencies referred to in Article 57 of the Charter of the United Nations. The agreement or agreements bringing the Organization into relation with the United Nations shall be subject to approval by a two-thirds vote of the Health Assembly.

Article 70. The Organization shall establish effective relations and co-operate closely with such other inter-governmental organizations as may be desirable. Any formal agreement entered into with such organizations shall be subject to approval by a two-thirds vote of the Health Assembly.

Article 71. The Organization may, on matters within its competence, make suitable arrangements for consultation and co-operation with non-governmental international organizations and, with the consent of the Government concerned, with national organizations, governmental or non-governmental.

Article 72. Subject to the approval by a two-thirds vote of the Health Assembly, the Organization may take over from any other international organization or agency whose purpose and activities lie within the field of competence of the Organization such functions, resources and obligations as may be conferred upon the Organization by international agreement or by mutually acceptable arrangements entered into between the competent authorities of the respective organizations.

Chapter XVII—Amendments

Article 73. Texts of proposed amendments to this Constitution shall be communicated by the Director-General to Members at least six months in advance of their consideration by the Health Assembly. Amendments shall come into force for all Members when adopted by a two-thirds vote of the Health Assembly and accepted by two-thirds of the Members in accordance with their respective constitutional processes.

Chapter XVIII—Interpretation

Article 74. The Chinese, English, French, Russian and Spanish texts of this Constitution shall be regarded as equally authentic.

Article 75. Any question or dispute concerning the interpretation or application of this Constitution which is not settled by negotiation or by the Health Assembly shall be referred to the International Court of Justice in conformity with the Statute of the Court, unless the parties concerned agree on another mode of settlement.

Article 76. Upon authorization by the General Assembly of the United Nations or upon authorization in accordance with any agreement between the Organization and the United Nations, the Organization may request the International Court of Justice for an advisory opinion on any legal question arising within the competence of the Organization.

Article 77. The Director-General may appear before the Court on behalf of the Organization in connexion with any proceedings arising out of any such request for an advisory opinion. He shall make arrangements for the presentation of the case before the Court, including arrangements for the argument of different views on the question.

Chapter XIX—Entry-into-Force

Article 78. Subject to the provisions of Chapter III, this Constitution shall remain open to all States for signature or acceptance.

Article 79. (a) States may become parties to this Constitution by

  (i) signature without reservation as to approval;

  (ii) signature subject to approval followed by acceptance; or

  (iii) acceptance.

(b) Acceptance shall be effected by the deposit of a formal instrument with the Secretary-General of the United Nations.

Article 80. This Constitution shall come into force when twenty-six Members of the United Nations have become parties to it in accordance with the provisions of Article 79.

Article 81. In accordance with Article 102 of the Charter of the United Nations, the Secretary-General of the United Nations will register this Constitution when it has been signed without reservation as to approval on behalf of one State or upon deposit of the first instrument of acceptance.

Article 82. The Secretary-General of the United Nations will inform States parties to this Constitution of the date when it has come into force. He will also inform them of the dates when other States have become parties to this Constitution.

In faith whereof the undersigned representatives, having been duly authorized for that purpose, sign this Constitution.

Done in the City of New York this twenty-second day of July 1946, in a single copy in the Chinese, English, French, Russian and Spanish languages, each text being equally authentic. The original texts shall be deposited in the archives of the United Nations. The Secretary-General of the United Nations will send certified copies to each of the Governments represented at the Conference.

WORLD INTELLECTUAL PROPERTY ORGANIZATION. Established in accordance with the Convention Establishing the World Intellectual Property Organization, signed at Stockholm on 14 July 1967, WIPO became a specialized agency of the United Nations in December 1974. Its basic function is to promote the protection of intellectual property, including patented inventions and copyrighted artistic works, and to administer a number of international treaties for this purpose.

The organization, which has its headquarters in Geneva and a membership of more than 125 States, is governed by a General Assembly and a conference, each consisting of all its member States. Its activities are coordinated by the International Bureau, which centralizes information of all kinds relating to the protection of intellectual property and maintains international registers of patents, trademarks, industrial designs, and appellations of origin.

The term "intellectual property" is defined in the convention (art. 2) as including the rights relating to "literary, artistic and scientific works; performances of performing artists, phonograms, and broadcasts; inventions in all fields of human endeavor; scientific discoveries; industrial designs; trademarks, service marks, and commercial names and designations; protection against unfair competition; and all other rights resulting from intellectual activity in the industrial, scientific, literary or artistic fields."

The objectives of the organization are (art. 3) "(1) to promote the protection of intellectual property throughout the world through cooperation among

States and, where appropriate, in collaboration with any other international organization; and (2) to ensure administrative cooperation among the Unions." The term "Unions" in this context refers to the Paris Union, established by the Convention for the Protection of Industrial Property, signed in Paris on 20 March 1883; the Berne Union, established by the Convention for the Protection of Literary and Artistic Works, signed in Berne on 9 September 1886; and similar groups established by any other international agreement the administration of which is assumed by WIPO.

SEE ALSO UNESCO Recommendation concerning the Status of the Artist; UNESCO Recommendation for the Safeguarding and Preservation of Moving Images; Universal Copyright Convention and Protocols.

WORLD JEWISH CONGRESS. An international non-governmental organization in consultative status with the UN Economic and Social Council (Category II) and with UNESCO, WJC is affiliated with Jewish communities and representative organizations in approximately 70 countries.

Founded in Geneva in 1936 as the successor to the Committee of Jewish Delegations, the congress fosters the unity of Jewish people and seeks to ensure the continuity and development of Jewish religious, spiritual, cultural, and social heritage. In addition to supporting Jewish solidarity throughout the world and intensifying the bonds of world Jewry with the State of Israel, WJC works to secure the rights, status, and interest of Jews and Jewish communities and defends these rights wherever by are denied, violated, or threatened.

WJC has an international publication program. The Congress publishes *News and Views* (New York); *Gesher* (Jerusalem); *Boletin Informativo OJI* (Buenos Aires), *Coloquio* (Buenos Aires), *Patterns of Prejudice* and *Christian Jewish Relations* (London), and *Batfutsot* (Jerusalem).

World Jewish Congress. Address: 501 Madison Avenue, New York, NY 10022 (USA). Telephone: (212) 775-5770. Telex: 236129 WJC UR. Fax: (1-212) 755-5883. Secretary-Treasurer: Israel Singer.

Yearbook of International Organizations 1989/90 (K. G. Saur).

WORLD MOVEMENT OF MOTHERS. An international non-governmental organization in consultative status with the UN Economic and Social Council (Category II) and with UNESCO and FAO, also known by its French title, *Mouvement Mondial des Mères*

(MMM), it has 45 national affiliates and individual members in an additional 32 countries.

Founded in 1947, in Paris, as an apolitical organization devoted to defining and defending the principal role of the mother in the life of the family, as well as in the educational development of the child, the World Movement prepares surveys and studies and organizes symposia and conferences to promote national, regional, and international recognition of the rights of mothers and their children and of families in distress. It has conducted research on such subjects as slavery, fetus commerce, respect for specific cultures, philosophic and religious liberty, and the rights of children.

MMM publishes bulletins and reports on its work and issues the periodical *Nouvelles et documents du MMM.*

World Movement of Mothers. Address: 56 rue de Passy, 75016 Paris, France. Telephone: 45-20-55-80. President: Marie-Laure Beck.

WORLD MUSLIM CONGRESS. An international non-governmental organization in consultative status (Category I) with the UN Economic and Social Council, WMC has branches and affiliates in 67 countries.

Founded in 1926 in Mecca, the congress works for greater fellowship, unity, and cooperation among Muslims and for the social and cultural solidarity of all mankind. It conducts study groups, public seminars, symposia, and cultural exhibitions. It also publishes the weekly *Muslim World* in English and the *World Muslim Gazetter.*

World Muslim Congress. Address: 9/A Block 7, Gulshan e-Iqbal, University Road, Karachi 47, Pakistan. Telephone: (92-1) 460712. Cable: 'AHBAB' Karachi. Telex: 24318 UMMAT PK. Secretary-General: Dr. Khalid Khan.

Yearbook of International Organizations 1989/90 (K. G. Saur).

WORLD PEACE COUNCIL. An international non-governmental organization in consultative status with the UN Economic and Social Council (Roster) and with UNESCO, WPC has national committees in 139 countries and territories.

Founded in Warsaw in 1950, the council works for the prohibition of all weapons of mass destruction and the end of the arms race; for the abolition of foreign military bases; for disarmament; for the elimination of all forms of colonialism and racial discrimination; for the right of peoples to sovereignty and independence; for non-interference in the internal affairs of nations; and for peaceful co-existence between States. WPC has standing commissions devoted to disarmament, development, human rights, racial discrimination, and environmental issues. It also campaigns for nuclear weapon-free zones.

WPC publishes the monthly *Peace Courier* and the bi-monthly journals *Disarmament Forum* and *New Perspectives,* all in English, French, German, and Spanish. It also publishes the quarterly *International Mobilization Against Apartheid and for the Liberation of Southern Africa* in English and French and the periodical *Indo-China Newsletter.*

World Peace Council. Address: Lönnrotinkatu 25A 6 krs, SF-00180 Helsinki, Finland. Telephone: (358-0) 693-10-44. Cable: Worldpax. Telex: 12-1680. Secretary-General: Romesh Chandra.

Yearbook of International Organizations 1989/90 (K. G. Saur).

WORLD UNION FOR PROGRESSIVE JUDAISM.

An international non-governmental organization in consultative status with the UN Economic and Social Council (Roster) and with UNESCO, WUPJ has over 1.5 million constituent, associate, and honorary members in 23 countries.

The World Union for Progressive Judaism encourages the formation of progressive Jewish religious communities or congregations in different countries and stimulates and encourages the study of Judaism and its adaptation to modern life.

The union issues reports of its annual conferences and has published *The First Twenty-five Years 1925–1951,* reviewing its activities since it was established in London.

World Union for Progressive Judaism. Address: 838 Fifth Avenue, New York, NY 10021 (USA). Telephone: (212) 249-0100. Executive Director: Rabbi Richard G. Hirsch.

Yearbook of International Organizations 1989/90 (K. G. Saur).

WORLD UNION OF CATHOLIC WOMEN'S ORGANIZATIONS.

An international non-governmental organization in consultative status with the UN Economic and Social Council (Category II) and with ILO, UNESCO, FAO, and the Council of Europe, WUCWO has 90 affiliated and corresponding organizations in 44 countries.

Founded in Brussels in 1910 and originally called the "International Union of Catholic Women's Leagues," the union supports the building of a more just and fraternal human community, fosters the advancement of women, and promotes the collaboration of women in fashioning society and in the mission of the Church. It has developed educational activities on all continents and holds a quadrenniel Congress. It publishes the *WUCWO Newsletter* (six times a year) in English, French, German, and Spanish.

World Union of Catholic Women's Organizations. Address: 20 rue Notre-Dame des Champs, F-75006 Paris, France. Telephone: (33-1) 45-44-27-65. Secretary-General: Geraldine MacCarthy.

Yearbook of International Organizations 1989/90 (K. G. Saur).

WORLD UNIVERSITY SERVICE.

An international non-governmental organization in consultative status with the UN Economic and Social Council (Category II) and with UNESCO and FAO, WUS has national committees in 44 countries.

Founded in 1920—as an outgrowth of the World Student Christian Federation and under the name of "European Student Relief"—to publicize and relieve the needs of students and academies who suffered from the effects of World War I, the programs and self-help projects of the World University Service were extended during the 1930s into the fields of student health, cooperative work, and research into problems of higher education. In 1970, following a decision of its General Assembly, WUS moved away from its university welfare role into its present role of promoting social welfare through university action. WUS' programs are action-oriented and fall into six broad categories: (1) defense of human rights; (2) development education; (3) anti-discrimination programs; (4) scholarships; (5) social action; and (6) community development. National WUS chapters are actively engaged in similar programs financed out of resources available in the individual countries.

WUS publishes the monthly *WUS News* and the annual *WUS Action.*

World University Service. Address: Chemin des Iris 5, CH-1216 Geneva COINTRIN, Switzerland. Telephone: (41-22) 798-87-11. Cable: INTERSTUD GENEVA. Telex: 27273 WUS CH. Secretary-General: Nigel Hartley.

Yearbook of International Organizations 1989/90 (K. G. Saur).

WORLD VETERANS FEDERATION.

An international non-governmental organization in consultative status with the UN Economic and Social Council

(Category I) and with the Council of Europe, WVF is composed of associations of war veterans, former resistants, deportees, prisoners of war, and war victims, totalling more than 20 million members in 52 countries.

Founded in 1950 in Paris as the "International Federation of War Veterans' Organizations," the federation works for international peace and security by application, in letter and spirit, of the UN Charter and the implementation of the Universal Declaration of Human Rights and defends the spiritual and material interests of war veterans and victims by legal and constitutional means. It sponsors and encourages surveys and research on rehabilitation of handicapped persons, and legislation concerning war veterans and protection of human rights. It also supports disarmament and peace-keeping missions. The creation of the International Sports Organization for the Disabled in 1961 was a WVF initiative. Of particular concern to the federation is the problem of accessibility of the man-made environment—housing, public transportation, streets, work-places—and, with that in view, it created an international information and stimulation center, INTER ACCENT.

WVF publishes periodicals and reports on international cooperation in areas such as rehabilitation,veterans legislation, economic development, disarmament, and human rights.

World Veterans Federation. Address: Rue Hamelin 16, F-75116 Paris, France. Telephone: (33-1) 47-04-33-00. Cable: WORLDVET Paris. Telex: FMACWVF 643253 F. FMAC. Secretary-General: Serge Wourgaft.

Yearbook of International Organizations 1989/90 (K. G. Saur).

WORLD YOUNG WOMEN'S CHRISTIAN ASSOCIATION. An international non-governmental organization in consultative status with the UN Economic and Social Council (Category II) and with UNESCO, the Young Women's Christian Association is an international voluntary women's organization which began as a prayer and service circle in Great Britain in 1955. At present, the World YWCA unites women and girls in 75 national YWCA's. Current issues of concern in the YWCA movement include the denial of political, social, and legal rights to women; violence against women and children in the family and society; unfair labor practices against women workers; exploitation of women as sex objects; neglect of indigenous people's rights; apartheid, detention, and denial of the right of self-determination in Southern Africa, the Middle East, and Central America.

Among its publications, the World YWCA issues a networkletter (bi-annually) and action alerts.

World Young Women's Christian Association. Address: 37 Quai Wilson, CH-1201 Geneva, Switzerland. Telephone: (022) 32-31-00. Cable: SOROMUNDI, GENEVA. General Secretary: Elaine Hesse Greif.

Y

YEMEN. The Yemeni Republic is an Arab country occupying the southwestern portion of the Arabian Peninsula, established on 22 May 1990 by the merger of the countries formerly known as the Yemen Arab Republic (North Yemen) and the People's Democratic Republic of Yemen (South Yemen). It has borders with Oman and Saudi Arabia and fronts on the Red Sea and the Gulf of Aden. North Yemen achieved independence from Turkey in 1934 and became a member of the United Nations in 1947. South Yemen achieved independence from Great Britain in 1967 and became a member of the United Nations the same year. The combined population of the unified country is estimated by the United Nations (1990) to be 13,000,000, almost all of Arab origin. Arabic is the only language in common use; English and Mahri are used in some business transactions. The predominant religion is Islam. Literacy is estimated at 20%.

The government (1990) took the form of a republic. Its capital is Aden, formerly capital of South Yemen. Its president, elected by the parliaments of North and South Yemen, is Ali Abdullah Saleh, former president of North Yemen; its vice president, also elected by the two parliaments, is Ali Salem al-Baidh, former secretary-general of South Yemen's ruling Socialist Party. Three men, elected in the same way, join them to form the five-member ruling Council: Salem Saleh Mohammed, Mr. Baidh's former deputy; Abdel Karim al-Arshi, former speaker of the parliament of North Yemen; and Abdel-Aziz Abdulghani, former prime minister of North Yemen.

Popular elections are scheduled to be held in 1992.

YOUTH: EDUCATION AND WORK. At its 1981 session, the UN General Assembly, in the course of preparing for the observance of 1985 as International Youth Year: Participation, Development, Peace, recognized (resolution 36/29) the profound importance of the role of youth for all-around development of each country and expressed its view that further action was needed to codify and implement the rights of youth, with special regard for the right to work, stipulated as a fundamental human right in article 6 of the INTERNA-

TIONAL COVENANT ON ECONOMIC, SOCIAL AND CULTURAL RIGHTS.

In the resolution, the Assembly indicated its awareness of the fact that the unemployment of youth is a hindrance to the full participation of young people in the socio-economic life of their country, limits their ability to participate in the development process and is, furthermore, a source of increased social ills; and, in this regard, emphasized the importance of the secondary and higher education of youth as well as of its access to appropriate technical, vocational guidance, and training programs. It considered it necessary that states and international organizations should examine in a more comprehensive, systematic, and effective manner, ways, and means to secure human rights, particularly the right to education and to work, aimed at solving the problem of youth employment.

Accordingly the Assembly called upon all States to adopt appropriate legislative, administrative, and other measures for the implementation and the enjoyment by youth of human rights and appealed to governmental and non-governmental organizations to pay increased attention to the securing and realization of the basic right of young people to education and vocational training and to work.

At its 1988 session, the Assembly, after considering again the question of youth, expressed its conviction (resolution 43/94) that it is necessary to ensure full enjoyment by youth of the rights stipulated in the UNIVERSAL DECLARATION OF HUMAN RIGHTS, the international covenant on economic, social and cultural rights and the INTERNATIONAL COVENANT ON CIVIL AND POLITICAL RIGHTS; invited national coordinating bodies and bodies implementing policies and programs in the field of youth to give priority to human rights activities to be undertaken after 1985, particularly the right of young people to education and to work; stressed the importance for youth and youth organizations of the freedom of association so as to enable their active and direct participation in policies, projects, and activities organized on their behalf; and stressed the need to intensify the efforts for educating youth in accordance with national experience, conditions, and priorities and to act effectively as channels of communication.

Finally, the Assembly emphasized that providing education and employment to each young person is a worthy goal for all States and should serve the full development of the human being, which can best be ensured by countries that respect the fundamental rights and freedoms of everyone.

SEE ALSO *Declaration on the Promotion among Youth of the Ideals of Peace, Mutual Respect and Understanding among Peoples; Human Rights and Youth.*

YUGOSLAVIA. The Socialist Federal Republic of Yugoslavia is a country in southern Europe, on the Adriatic Sea. It has borders with Albania, Austria, Bulgaria, Greece, Hungary, Italy, and Romania. As the kingdom of the Serbs, Croats, and Slovenes, Yugoslavia achieved independence in 1918 and became a member of the United Nations in 1945. Its population is estimated by the UN (1990) to be 23,895,000. Ethnic groups include Serbs (36.2%), Croats (19.7%), Bosnian Muslims (8.9%), Slovenes (7.8%), Albanians (7.7%), Macedonians (5.9%), Yugoslavs (5.4%), Montenegrins (2.5%), Hungarians (1.9%), Gypsies (0.7%), Turks (0.5%), Slovaks (0.4%), Romanians (0.2%), Ruthenians/Ukrainians (0.2%), and others (0.2%). Languages commonly used include Serbo–Croatian, Slovenian, Macedonian (all official), Albanian, Hungarian, and Italian. Among those who practice a religion, Christianity predominates (Eastern Orthodox, 41%, and Roman Catholic, 32%); however, atheistic beliefs are held by a large proportion of the population. Literacy is estimated at 85%.

The government (1990) took the form of a republic, in which were federated the Socialist Republic of Bosnia and Herzegovinia, the Socialist Republic of Croatia, the Socialist Republic of Macedonia, the Socialist Republic of Montenegro, the Socialist Republic of Serbia, and the Socialist Republic of Slovenia. Within the Socialist Republic of Serbia, there are two autonomous provinces: the Socialist Autonomous Province of Kosovo and the Socialist Autonomous Republic of Vojvodina.

Under the 1974 constitution of Yugoslavia, the State presidency, elected every five years, has nine members: eight represent the republics and autonomous provinces, while the ninth is the president of the presidium of the League of Communists, serving *ex officio*. The members of the presidency take turns in serving for one year each as president of the republic and head of State.

There is also a Federal Executive Council, composed of 29 ministers elected on a basis providing proportional representation for the republics and autonomous provinces. The president of the council, elected by the legislature on nomination of the presidency, serves as prime minister and head of government. The legislative body, known as the Chambers of Assembly, consists of the Federal Chamber, composed of 30 delegates of self-managing organizations, communities, and socio-political organizations from each republic and 20 from each autonomous province; and the Chamber of Republics and Provinces, composed of 12 delegates from each republican assembly and eight from each provincial assembly. The League of Communists and the Social Alliance of the Working People are active as political parties.

Invaded on 6 April 1941 by the German Army assisted by forces from Bulgaria, Hungary, and Italy, Yugoslavia was divided among the invading powers; and, for a long period, fearful atrocities were committed by the occupation forces. However, contingents of Yugoslav troops resisted fiercely from their mountain strongholds under the leadership of Draja Mikhailovich; and, in 1942, a separate "Army of National Liberation," organized by Josip Broz Tito with the support of the Soviet Union, entered the struggle. For a short time, the two liberation forces fought each other, but eventually they turned against the common foe. Helped by the surrender of Italy in 1943, they expelled the invaders from Yugoslavia.

By November 1944, Tito's Council of Liberation had become the only effective governing force in the country. It was merged with the remnants of the monarchy headed by Peter II; but, in national elections held in 1945, Tito won broad support—the monarchists boycotted the election—and emerged as premier. Under his guidance, Yugoslavia remained in harmony with other eastern European countries for some years, pursuing a vigorous policy of socialization, reconstruction, and industrialization. In 1946, the trial and conviction of Archbishop Stepinac and the execution of Mikhailovich—who was charged with collaboration with the Axis and treason because his guerrillas had fought Tito's forces—provoked great indignation throughout the non-communist world.

In 1948, a breach developed between Russia and Yugoslavia. Tito announced that Yugoslavia intended to pursue its "independent way to socialism" and charged that the Soviet Union was seeking to control his country; and was, in turn, accused of being hostile to the Soviet Union and of deviating from the program of the Communist Party. After 1948, Yugoslavia maintained its independence only with economic and military assistance supplied by the United States and its western allies. An eastern economic blockade which lasted from 1949 to 1953 forced Yugoslavia to seek new contacts in the West. It has since identified itself as a leader of the non-aligned nations.

As regards human rights, modern Yugoslavia under its rotating presidency recognizes and protects certain civil and political rights which the international community considers to be of primary importance: citizens are permitted to work abroad and to emigrate to other countries if they wish, churches are open and function without State interference, the right to own private property is respected, and private participation in business ventures is permitted.

The peoples of Yugoslavia, however, tend to regard themselves not as Yugoslavians but as Serbians, Croatians, Montenegrins, Bosnians, Slovenians, or ethnic Albanians; and tension between these groups erupts into violence from time to time. Serbia, for example, has experienced great difficulty in controlling the population of its autonomous province of Kosovo, in which ethnic Albanians constitute more than 80% of the population. Ethnic Albanians have also provoked confrontations in Montenegro and Macedonia, which, like Kosovo, share borders with Albania. And in central Bosnia–Herzegovina, where the Islamic faith is widely practiced, waves of religious nationalism have from time to time produced intolerance and discrimination.

Intermittant strife between the six republics, and between ethnic groups as such, escalated in 1989 when other European countries moved more rapidly towards pluralism. Fierce arguments developed on the pace of political change but went unresolved because the system of rotating presidencies and chairmanships limited the ability of local and national governments to make decisions and to act upon them.

However, in January 1990, the Yugoslav Communist Party, after a long and bitter debate, renounced its constitutionally guaranteed "leading role in society" and called upon Parliament to enact "political pluralism, including a multi-party system." And in April, the first free multi-party elections since Tito assumed power were held in Croatia after its Communist Party had expressed readiness "to compete in elections with other political programs." In those elections, the conservative and nationalist Croatian Democratic Union won a solid majority and called upon its leader, Franjo Tudjman—a former communist who had been jailed in 1972 for supporting Croatian nationalism and in 1981 for criticizing Yugoslavia's one-party system—to form a government that would guarantee the enjoyment of human rights to everyone in Croatia, including members of minorities, while contributing to the unity and stability of Yugoslavia.

Provisions of the constitution which relate to human rights appear under the heading YUGOSLAVIA: CONSTITUTION.

In addition, as the government of Yugoslavia pointed out in a report presented to the Human Rights Committee on 28 February 1978 (UN Doc. CCPR/C/1/Add. 23, sec. 30):

. . . . In the Socialist Federal Republic of Yugoslavia, in addition to civil and political rights guaranteed by the International Covenant (on Civil and Political Rights), working people and citizens are also guaranteed the right to self-management, on the basis of which every working man decides, on an equal footing with other working people, on his own labour, on the conditions and results of labour, on his own and common interests and on the guidance of social development, and exercises power and manages other social affairs (Constitution of the SFRY, Basic Principles, section II).

The basic elements of the right to self-management were already laid down in the 1963 Constitution, particularly as the right and duty of working people to:

Manage the work organization directly or through management bodies which they elect themselves;

Organize production or other activities, concern themselves with the development of the working organization and adopt plans and programmes of work and development;

Decide on the exchange of products and services and on other matters relating to the business of the working organization;

Decide on the use of social resources and on their allocation, and put them to economically advantageous use with a view to attaining the best business effects for the working organization and the social community;

Distribute the income of the working organization and ensure the development of the material base of their labour; distribute income to workers; meet the obligations of the work organizations towards the social community.

Decide on recruitment of workers for the work organization, on the termination of their work in the work organization and on other mutual labour relationships; fix the work hours in the work organization in accordance with general conditions for work; regulate other matters of common interest; ensure internal control and the public nature of work;

Determine and promote their working conditions; organize safety at work, and vacations; secure conditions for their education and the raising of their personal and social standard of living;

Decide on the detachment of part of the organization and its constituting as a separate organization and on the fusion and association of the work organization with other working organizations.

The Law on Associated Labour, passed at the end of 1976, stipulates in article 1 that workers in realizing their status in associated labour manage their own and overall social labour in basic and other organizations of associated labour, in other self-managing organizations and communities, and in society as a whole. Socialist self-management socio-economic relations in associated labour ensure that workers manage, in their own as well as in the collective and general interest, their labour and the conditions and results of their labour.

Workers take part in the regulation of general conditions of work and in co-ordination, direction and social planning in associated labour also through their delegations and delegates in the assemblies of socio-political communities.

YUGOSLAVIA: CONSTITUTION.

The constitution of the Socialist Federal Republic of Yugoslavia includes the following provisions (articles 153–203) specifically relating to human rights and fundamental freedoms:

Chapter III
The Freedoms, Rights, and Duties of Man and Citizen

Article 153. The freedoms and rights of man and citizen, spelled out by the present Constitution, shall be realized through solidarity among people and through the fulfillment of duties and responsibilities of everyone towards all and all towards everyone.

The freedoms of man and citizen shall only be restricted by the equal freedoms and rights of others and by the constitutionally specified interests of the socialist community.

Each shall be bound to respect the freedoms and rights of others and shall be responsible therefor.

Article 154. Citizens shall be equal in their rights and duties regardless of nationality, race, sex, language, religion, education, or social status.

All shall be equal before the law.

Article 155. Working people and citizens shall have the inalienable right to self-management which enables each individual to decide on his personal and common interests in an organization of associated labor, local community, self-managing community of interest, other self-managing organization or community, socio-political community—and in all other forms of their self-management integration and mutual linkage.

Each individual shall be responsible for self-management decision-making and the implementation of decisions.

Article 156. All citizens who have reached the age of eighteen years shall have the right to elect and be elected members of delegations in basic self-managing organizations and communities and to elect and be elected delegates to the assemblies of the socio-political communities.

Workers in organizations of associated labor and working people in all forms of labor and resource pooling, regardless of age, shall have the right to elect and be elected to delegations to the assemblies of the socio-political communities and to elect delegates to the assemblies of these communities.

Workers in organizations of associated labor and working people in all forms of labor and resource pooling shall, regardless of age, have the right to elect and be elected members of or delegates in managing bodies of these organizations.

Article 157. Citizens shall have the right to submit petitions and proposals to the bodies and agencies of the socio-political communities and other competent bodies and organizations, to receive an answer thereto, and to take political and other kinds of initiative of general concern.

Article 158. Everyone shall be bound conscientiously and in the interest of socialist society based on self-management to exercise self-management, public, and other social functions vested in him.

Article 159. The right to work shall be guaranteed.

Rights acquired on account of labor shall be inalienable.

All those who manage or dispose of social resources and socio-political communities shall be bound to create increasing favorable conditions for the realization of the right to work.

The social community shall create conditions for the vocational rehabilitation of citizens who are not fully able to work and for their adequate employment.

The right to relief during temporary unemployment shall be guaranteed subject to conditions spelled out by statute.

A worker may be dismissed from his job against his will only under conditions and in a way specified by statute.

Whoever will not work, although fit for work, shall not enjoy the rights and protection due to him on account of labor.

Article 160. Freedom to work is guaranteed.

Everyone shall be free to choose his occupation and job.

Every citizen shall have access, on equal terms, to every job and every function in society.

Forced labor is prohibited.

Article 161. Working people shall have the right to such working conditions as ensure their physical and moral integrity and security.

Article 162. Workers shall be entitled to limited working hours.

Workers shall not work more than 42 hours a week. In certain activities and in certain cases, it may be provided by statute that the working time can, for a limited period, exceed 42 hours a week, if so required by the nature of the work or exceptional circumstances.

Conditions for still shorter working hours may be laid down by statute.

Workers shall be entitled to daily and weekly rest and to an annual holiday with pay of not less than eighteen working days.

Workers shall have the right to health, other types of care, and personal security in work.

Young people, women, and disabled persons shall enjoy special consideration.

Article 163. The right of workers to social security shall be ensured through obligatory insurance based on the principles of reciprocity and solidarity, on past labor in self-managing communities of interest, and on the basis of contributions collected from workers' personal incomes and contributions collected from income of organizations of associated labor or contributions collected on resources of other organizations or communities in which they work. On the basis of this insurance, the workers shall have, in conformity with statute, the right to health care and other benefits in the case of illness, childbirth benefits, benefits in the case of diminution or loss of working capacity and unemployment. They shall also enjoy old age and other social security benefits, and, for their dependents, the right to health care, survivors' pensions, and other social security benefits.

Social security benefits for working people and citizens who are not covered by the compulsory social insurance scheme shall be regulated by statute on the principles of reciprocity and solidarity.

Article 164. Citizens shall be guaranteed the right to acquire a tenancy title to a dwelling in social ownership, which ensures him permanent occupancy, under conditions specified by statute of a socially owned dwelling for the satisfaction of his personal and family housing needs.

The right of citizens to a dwelling subject to the right of ownership shall be regulated by statute.

Article 165. Elementary education lasting at least eight years shall be obligatory.

Economic and other conditions for the establishment and operation of schools and other institutions for the education of citizens and the promotion of their activities shall be ensured through self-managing communities of interest, on the principles of reciprocity and solidarity among working people, organizations of associated labor, and other self-managing organizations and communities and socio-political communities in conformity with statute.

Citizens shall be entitled, under equal conditions specified by statute, to acquire knowledge and vocational training at all levels of education in all schools and other institutions of education.

Article 166. Freedom of thought and choice shall be guaranteed.

Article 167. Freedom of the press and other media of information and public expression, freedom of association, freedom of speech and public expression, and freedom of gathering and public assembly shall be guaranteed.

Citizens shall have the right to express and publish their opinions through information media.

Citizens, organizations, and citizens' associations may, under conditions specified by statute, publish newspapers and other publications and disseminate information through other information media.

Article 168. Citizens shall be guaranteed the right to be informed of events in the country and in the world which are of concern to their life and work as well as of questions of concern to the community.

The press, radio, television, and other media of information shall be bound to inform the public truthfully and objectively and to make public the opinions of and information about bodies, organizations, and citizens of concern to the public.

The right to correct published information that has violated the rights and interests of an individual, organization, or body shall be guaranteed.

Article 169. Scientific, scholarly, and artistic creative activity shall be free.

Creators of scientific, scholarly, and artistic works and of scientific discoveries and technical inventions shall have moral and material rights to their achievements. The rights of creators to their works may not be used in a way contrary to society's interest in new scientific achievements and technical inventions being applied.

The volume, duration, restriction, termination, and protection of the rights of creators to their works and the rights of the organizations of associated labor in which these works were created as a result of the labor and resource pooling shall be laid down by statute.

Article 170. Citizens shall be guaranteed the right to opt for a nation or nationality, to express their national culture, and to use their language and alphabet freely.

No citizen shall be obliged to state to which nation or nationality he belongs nor to opt for any one nation or nationality.

Propagating or practicing national inequality and any incitement of national, racial, or religious hatred and intolerance shall be unconstitutional and punishable.

Article 171. Members of nationalities shall, in conformity with the constitution and statute, have the right to use their language and alphabet in the exercise of their rights and duties and in proceedings before state agencies and organizations exercising public powers.

Members of the nations and nationalities of Yugoslavia shall, on the territory of each Republic and/or Autonomous Province, have the right to instruction in their own language in conformity with statute.

Article 172. The defense of the country shall be the inviolable and inalienable right and the supreme duty and honor of every citizen.

Article 173. Citizens shall have the right and duty to take part in social self-defense.

Article 174. Profession of religion shall be free and shall be an individual's private affair.

Religious communities shall be separate from the state and shall be free to conduct their religious affairs and religious services.

Religious communities may found religious schools only for the training of the clergy.

Abuse of religion and religious activities for political purposes shall be unconstitutional.

The social community may provide financial help to religious communities.

Religious communities may have the right to own real property within specific limits determined by statute.

Article 175. A man's life is inviolate.

The death penalty may be provided by federal statute and invoked only in exceptional cases of grave criminal offense.

Article 176. The inviolability of the integrity of the human personality, personal and family life, and other human rights shall be guaranteed.

Any extortion of a confession or statement shall be forbidden and punishable.

Article 177. Man's freedom shall be inviolable.

No one may be deprived of liberty except in cases and by the procedure specified by statute.

Deprivation of liberty may last only as long as there are statutory grounds therefor.

Any unlawful deprivation of liberty shall be punishable.

Article 178. A person for whom there are grounds for suspicion that he has committed a criminal offense may be detained and held in detention only when this is indispensable for the conduct of criminal proceedings or for reasons of public safety. Detention shall be ordered by a court of law. Only, exceptionally, under conditions spelled out by statute, may detention be ordered by another statutorily empowered authority—but for no longer than three days.

A written order with a statement of grounds must be served on a person detained at the moment of detention or not later than 24 hours thereafter. The person detained may lodge an appeal against this order which must be decided upon by the court within 48 hours.

The duration of detention shall be kept to the shortest, necessary period of time.

Detention ordered by a court of first instance may not last more than three months. Exceptionally, the Supreme Court may extend this time limit for another three months. If upon the expiry of these time limits no charge sheet has been filed, the prisoner shall be released.

Article 179. Respect for the human personality and human dignity shall be guaranteed in criminal proceedings, in any other proceedings in the case of deprivation or restriction of liberty, and during the enforcement of a penalty.

Article 180. Every person shall be entitled to equal protection of his rights in proceedings before a court of law, state agencies, and other bodies and organizations which make decisions concerning his rights, obligations, and interests.

Everyone shall be guaranteed the right of appeal or other legal remedy against decisions of courts of law, state agencies, and other bodies and organizations which make decisions concerning his rights or interests founded on statute.

Legal aid shall be provided through the Bar as an independent social service as well as through other forms of legal assistance.

Article 181. No one shall be punished for any act which before its commission was not defined as a punishable offense by statute or a legal provision based on statute or for which no penalty has been established.

Criminal offenses and criminal law sanctions may only be established by statute.

Sanctions for criminal offenses shall be imposed by a competent court in proceedings regulated by statute.

No one may be considered guilty of a criminal offense until so proven by a final judgment of a court of law.

Any person who has been unjustifiably convicted of a criminal offense or who has been deprived of liberty without cause shall be entitled to rehabilitation and compensation for damage by society and to other statutorily established rights.

Article 182. The right to defend oneself against charges shall be guaranteed.

No one accessible to the court or another agency authorized to conduct proceedings may be sentenced without prior examination in the forms specified by statute or without being afforded an opportunity to defend himself.

In criminal proceedings, the accused shall be entitled to counsel who shall be enabled, in conformity with statute, to defend and protect the rights and interests of the accused. Statutory provisions shall regulate when the accused must have defense counsel.

Article 183. Citizens shall be guaranteed freedom of movement and residence.

Restriction of freedom of movement or residence may be provided for by law, but only in order to ensure the conduct of criminal proceedings, to prevent the spread of contagious diseases, to protect public order, or when so required by the defense interests of the country.

Article 184. Homes shall be inviolable.

No one may enter any dwelling or premises of another or search them against the will of their tenant without a warrant.

The person whose dwelling or other premises are being searched shall have the right to have a member of his family or his representative present during the search.

A search may only be carried in the presence of two witnesses.

Subject to conditions spelled out by statute, a person in an official capacity may enter a dwelling or premises of others without a warrant from the competent authority and carry out a search in the absence of witnesses, if this is indispensable to the immediate arrest of the perpetrator of a criminal offense, to protect the safety of life and property, or if it appears obvious that evidence in criminal proceedings could not be secured otherwise.

Any illegal entry into and search of a dwelling or premises of another shall be prohibited and punishable.

Article 185. Secrecy of mail and of other means of communication shall be inviolable.

Provisions to depart from the principle of inviolability of secrecy of mail and of other means of communication, pursuant to an order by a competent authority, may only be made by statute if this is indispensable to the conduct of criminal proceedings or to the security of the country.

Article 186. Everyone shall be entitled to health care.

Cases in which uninsured citizens are entitled to health care using social resources shall be spelled out by statute.

Article 187. Veterans, disabled veterans, and survivors of fallen veterans shall be guaranteed rights which ensure their social security, as well as special rights as spelled out by statute.

Disabled veterans shall be entitled to vocational rehabilitation, disability benefits, and other forms of care.

Article 188. Mothers and children shall enjoy special social protection.

Minors deprived of parental care and other persons unable to take care of themselves or their rights and interests shall enjoy special social protection.

Article 189. Citizens who are not able to work and have no necessary means of support shall be entitled to assistance by the social community.

Article 190. The family shall enjoy social protection. Marriage and marital and family legal relations shall be regulated by statute.

A marriage shall be validly contracted before a competent agency by free consent of the prospective spouses.

Parents shall have the right and duty to raise and educate their children. Children shall be bound to care for their parents in need of assistance.

Children born out of wedlock shall have the same rights and duties as children born in wedlock.

Article 191. It is a human right to decide freely on family planning.

This right may only be restricted for reasons of health.

Article 192. Man shall have the right to a healthy environment.

Conditions for the realization of this right shall be ensured by the social community.

Article 193. Anyone who utilizes land, water, or other natural goods shall be bound to do so in a way which ensures conditions for man's work and life in a healthy environment.

Everyone shall be bound to preserve nature and its goods, natural landmarks, and rarities and cultural monuments.

Article 194. The right of inheritance shall be guaranteed.

Inheritance shall be regulated by statute.

No one may retain ownership of real property and the means of labor on grounds of inheritance in excess of the limits laid down by the constitution or statute.

Inheritance of the property of a person who enjoyed social or other kinds of assistance from the social community may be restricted by statute.

Article 195. Everyone shall be bound to contribute, under equal conditions and proportionate to his economic possibilities, to the satisfaction of general social needs.

Article 196. Everyone shall be bound to help other persons in danger and on the basis of solidarity to participate with others in combating any general danger.

Article 197. Everyone shall be bound to abide by the constitution and law.

Those conditions under which failure to discharge duties established by the constitution and statute are punishable shall be spelled out by statute.

Article 198. Any arbitrary act which violates or restricts the rights of man shall be unconstitutional and punishable regardless of who has committed the act.

No one shall use coercion or restrict the right of another, except in cases and in proceedings regulated by statute.

Article 199. Everyone shall be entitled to damages for any loss caused to him in connection with the performance of an office or other activity in a state agency and/or organization in charge of affairs of public concern, or through any illegal or wrongful activity by an individual or body in charge of such an office or activity.

The damages shall be paid by the socio-political community or organization in which this office or activity is performed. The party wronged shall also be entitled, in conformity with statute, to claim damages directly from the tort-feasor for the loss he has caused.

Article 200. Every citizen of the Socialist Federal Republic of Yugoslavia when abroad shall enjoy the protection of the Socialist Federal Republic of Yugoslavia.

No citizens of the Socialist Federal Republic of Yugoslavia may be deprived of citizenship, banished, or extradited.

A citizen of the Socialist Federal Republic of Yugoslavia who is absent from the country and who also has another citizenship may, exceptionally upon authority of federal statute, be deprived of the citizenship of the Socialist Federal Republic of Yugoslavia only if by his activities he causes harm to international and other interests of Yugoslavia or if he refuses to perform his citizen's duties.

Article 201. Aliens in Yugoslavia shall enjoy the freedoms and rights of man spelled out by the present Constitution and shall have other rights and duties specified by statute and international treaties.

Article 202. Foreign citizens and stateless persons who are persecuted for supporting democratic views and movements, social and national emancipation, the freedoms and rights of the human personality, or the freedom of scientific and artistic creative endeavor shall be guaranteed the right of asylum.

Article 203. The freedoms and rights guaranteed by the present Constitution may not be restricted.

No one may use the freedoms and rights established by the present Constitution in order to: disrupt the foundations of the socialist self-management, democratic order established by the present Constitution; endanger the independence of the country; violate the freedoms and rights of man and citizen guaranteed by the present Constitution; endanger peace and equality in international cooperation; foster national, racial, or religious hatred or intolerance; or abet the commission of criminal offenses— nor may these freedoms be used in a way which offends public morals. It shall be specified by statute in which cases and under what conditions the use of these freedoms in a way contrary to the present Constitution will entail a restriction or a ban on their use.

These freedoms and rights shall be realized and duties performed pursuant to the present Constitution. The mode of realization of individual freedoms and rights may be regulated only by statute and only when so provided by the present Constitution or when this is indispensable to their realization.

The freedoms and rights guaranteed by the present Constitution shall enjoy judicial protection.

Z

ZAIRE. The Republic of Zaire is a country in middle Africa, on the Atlantic Ocean. It has borders with Angola, Burundi, Central African Republic, Congo, Rwanda, Sudan, Uganda, and Zambia. Formerly known as the Belgian Congo, it achieved independence from Belgium in 1960 as the Democratic Republic of the Congo and became a member of the United Nations the same year. Its name was changed to Zaire in 1971. Its population is estimated by the UN (1990) to be 33,797,000. Ethnic groups include the Bantu, who comprise the majority, and minorities of Sudanese, Nilotes, Pygmies, and Hamites. In addition, 329,000 refugees were living in Zaire in 1985, including 265,000 from Angola. Languages commonly used include French (official), Lingala (a *lingua franca*), Kiswahili, Tshiluba, Kikongo, and about 200 regional vernaculars. Religions practiced include Christianity (Roman Catholic, 50%; Protestant denominations, 20%), Islam (10%), Animism, (10%) and Kimbanguist (10%). Literacy is estimated at 55%.

The government (1990) took the form of a republic. Under the 1978 constitution, as amended in 1980, supreme power is vested in the sole political party, the *Mouvement Populaire de la Revoluntion* (MPR), whose leader is automatically president and head of State, although this is confirmed in a popular election. Members of the unicameral National Legislative Council are elected (one per 100,000 inhabitants) from a list prepared by the MPR and serve for five-year terms. The judiciary includes the Justice Department, the Supreme Court, nine courts of appeal, and 32 courts of first instance.

Belgium recognized the Republic of the Congo as an independent nation on 30 June 1960; but, within a week, a mutiny broke out in the Congolese army and grave acts of violence were committed against Belgian officers and civilians. On 10 July, Belgian troops intervened and occupied the principal cities. These disorders led to a mass exodus of Belgians, resulting in the breakdown of essential services in many parts of the country.

On 12 July 1960, Joseph Kasavubu and Patrice Lumumba, president and prime minister, respectively, of the new republic, called upon the United Na-

tions to protect the national territory against external aggression by Belgium. The UN Security Council on 14 July called upon Belgium to withdraw its troops and arranged for them to be replaced by contingents from neutral countries under United Nations command. These contingents were initially ordered to use force only in self-defense; later they were permitted to use force as a last resort if necessary to prevent civil war.

The United Nations force restored order as the Belgian troops withdrew and eventually reached a maximum strength of about 20,000. However, serious differences about their functions soon arose between Prime Minister Lumumba and UN Secretary-General Dag Hammarskjold. Lumumba maintained that they should be used to subdue the rebel government of Katanga Province, headed by Moishe Tshombe, while Hammarskjold stated that this was outside the mandate given them by the Security Council.

In September 1960, President Kasavubu dismissed Lumumba. Later that year, Lumumba, after several months of confinement to his residence under United Nations guard, left the house and was apprehended with several colleagues by Congolese troops. Taken to Katanga Province, he was killed on 17 January 1961. Later, on 17 September 1961, UN Secretary-General Dag Hammarskjold died in a plane crash en route to a peace conference in Katanga Province.

After long negotiations punctuated by sporadic outbreaks of violence, the Katangese secession ended on 14 January 1963. However, the United Nations force remained in the country to assist in maintaining law and order. The United Nations also provided the government with the technical assistance necessary to ensure the continued operation of essential services and to supply necessary food and medical supplies. Both the military and the civilian operations were discontinued in June 1964.

In 1965, Col. Joseph Mobutu, chief of staff of the army, seized power from President Kasavubu. After a period of military rule, Mobutu was elected president for a seven-year term in 1970 and re-elected in 1977. Mobutu's policy of soliciting international investment to replace Belgian interests won wide support abroad. However, his arrangement which permitted Zairians—including army officers and government officials—to take over and operate businesses which had been established by some 40,000 expatriate Portuguese, Greeks, Belgians, French, and Pakistanis, created havoc in trade circles and disrupted the flow of many necessities of life.

Invaders from neighboring Angola attacked Katanga (now known as Shaba) Province in 1977 and again in 1978. They were turned back in 1977 by 1,500 Moroccan troops airlifted from France and, in 1978, by 1,750 Belgian soldiers and Foreign Legion paratroopers flown to the area by the U.S. Air Force. Later Zaire and Angola signed an agreement not to support rebels in each other's country.

Non-governmental organizations, including AMNESTY INTERNATIONAL and the INTERNATIONAL LEAGUE FOR THE RIGHTS AND LIBERATION OF PEOPLES, have repeatedly drawn the attention of the Commission on Human Rights to the situation prevailing in Zaire. In particular, they have pointed out that the country, once self-sufficient in food, has become almost wholly dependent upon outside sources to feed its population; that more than 50% of the population suffers from the effects of bacteriological, viral, and parasitical diseases; and that infant mortality is catastrophic.

A representative of Zaire, Mr. Lwamba-Katansi, provided information concerning the human rights situation in his country at a meeting of the HUMAN RIGHTS COMMITTEE held at Geneva on 10 July 1987. He referred in particular to the Department of Rights and Freedoms of the Citizens, which had been established on 31 October 1986, to which he was personally attached. The department's function, he said, (UN Doc. CCPR/C/Sr. 738, para. 20)

was to receive complaints from all citizens who considered that they had been wronged by judicial or administrative decisions, acts of violence, etc. It was headed by a Political Office, composed of the Minister in charge of the Department and his advisers. Below there were several legal services specializing in various kinds of case: a service dealing with judicial proceedings, another with administrative actions, another with political matters and another for international issues (he was personally attached to the last named service). At the bottom level, there were offices, each composed of three persons including a principal delegate, chosen in the commune or neighbourhood for his high reputation, and not necessarily a lawyer, and was therefore assisted by two lawyers. In Kinshasa, there was an office for each commune, 24 in all, and also two offices which dealt specifically with complaints from firms, one for the west side of the town and the other for the east side. When a complaint was submitted to an office, the latter examined it and if it considered the complainant to be justified, it transmitted the complaint to the central administration of the Department. If, however, the delegation considered that the complaint did not fulfil the necessary

conditions, it advised the complainant about other remedies, for example, through official channels. When a complaint was referred to the central administration, the latter considered it and on the basis of that examination, the Minister took the decision he deemed appropriate to restore the rights of the complainant. In the event a decision thus taken not being implemented by any body or individual, the Department could make representation to the Permanent Disciplinary Commission appointed by the Central Committee of the People's Movement for the Revolution or to the President of the Republic himself.

The committee had handled about 500 complaints, he added, and its functions had been widely publicized through the information media.

Visit of Special Rapporteur to Zaire. From 13 to 20 January 1990, Mr. Peter Koojmans (Netherlands), special rapporteur of the UN Commission on Human Rights on the question of the human rights of all persons subjected to any form of detention or imprisonment, torture, or other cruel, inhuman, or degrading treatment or punishment, visited Zaire on invitation of the government. Prepared and organized by the Department of Rights and Freedoms of the Citizens, the visit enabled the special rapporteur to hold discussions with many high officials and to visit two offices of the department. His evaluation of the human rights situation in Zaire, and his recommendations, were set out in his report to the commission as follows (UN Doc. E/CN.4/1990/17Add. 1, para. 33–51):

As stated before, the human rights situation in Zaire has considerably improved during the recent years. The Government has taken some meaningful steps to strengthen the existing mechanisms guaranteeing the respect of human rights by introducing new ones. The creation of a separate Department of Rights and Freedoms of the Citizen is, in itself, quite unique and has undoubtedly contributed to a greater awareness of the importance of human rights both with the population and with the authorities. The department has only been operational for two and a half years and to a certain extent is still in the formation period; it is therefore too early to give a conclusive evaluation of its efficiency. Informing the people about their rights by the dissemination of material which is understandable to everyone is one of the most important requisites for the rule of law. The President of the Bar Association told the Special Rapporteur that although detained persons were entitled to legal assistance as from the moment of their arrest, in actual practice, and due to lack of information, people hardly ever resorted to a lawyer until the moment their case came before a court. Nor was it generally known that a person who did not have the necessary means to employ a lawyer could address the judge or the President of the Bar Association who then had to ask the Bar to designate a lawyer.

It is equally important to inform the law-enforcing authorities about the detainee's rights and to instruct them to respect the detainee's inherent dignity. The introduction of training courses for the personnel of the law-enforcement forces is, therefore, of great significance. Such courses should not only be focused on mentality training but also on the teaching of how to conduct interrogations in a manner which recognizes and respects the detainee's rights and dignity.

The competence of the Department of Rights and Freedoms of the Citizen to visit and inspect all places of detention concurrently with the legally prescribed periodic visits by magistrates of the Public Prosecutor's office may be an effective preventive measure against illegal arrests and detention. These, in turn, may—and in fact often did in the past—lead to torture and maltreatment. The Special Rapporteur was informed that in all cases when a detainee was not duly registered with the Public Prosecutor's office, the Department could have him released immediately. He was also informed that in all other cases where the legal provisions had seemingly not been complied with, it was left to the Public Prosecutor's office to decide on the lawfulness of the detention. Moreover, the Department itself could, on its own initiative, table such cases during the meetings with the Judicial Council which were provided for on a monthly basis in the protocol of co-ordination concluded with that body.

In view of the fact that the number of alleged cases of illegal or arbitrary arrest or detention is still relatively high, the Special Rapporteur feels that the Public Prosecutor's office should thoroughly scrutinize the legality of all arrests, not only at the moment when they are registered (after the 48-hour term), but also when requests for the renewal of a remand order are made.

Of equal importance for the strict compliance with the legal rules is the presentation of the detainee *in persona* to the competent judge within five days after his arrest since this enables the detainee to inform the judge about the circumstances under which he was arrested and to provide him with all other relevant information. There again, the Special Rapporteur feels that the prevalent rules should be applied more strictly. It has come to his knowledge that in numerous cases detainees were not presented to a judge within the period prescribed by the law, or were not presented to a judge at all, although a remand order was issued.

Useful as the competences of the Department are, in essence they are corrective measures which—apart from cases of manifestly illegal detention—would not have been necessary if the Public Prosecutor's office and the judiciary had carried out their mandate satisfactorily.

Article 9, paragraph 4, of the International Covenant on Civil and Political Rights states that anyone who is deprived of his liberty by arrest or detention shall be entitled to take proceedings before a court, in order that that court may decide without delay on the lawfulness of his detention and order his release if the detention is not lawful. It has not become clear to the Special Rapporteur whether the Code of Criminal Procedure explicitly gives a detained person such right to take, on his own initiative or through his lawyer, such proceedings before a court. In view of the fact that the report submitted by the Government of Zaire under article 40 of the International Covenant on Civil and Political Rights makes no mention of such legal provisions (while being very elaborate on other issues), the Special Rapporteur feels entitled to assume that such a provision does not exist. An amendment to the Code of Criminal Procedure to bring it in conformity with article 9, paragraph 4, of the International Covenant on Civil and Political Rights would be an important step to suppress and prevent illegal or arbitrary arrest or detention.

All law-enforcement forces have their own places of detention (*cachots*). As stated before, in the case of common crimes, the suspect is usually transferred to a general prison relatively soon after his arrest. Persons, however, who are suspected of having committed offences against the security of the State or of the armed forces are usually kept in the detention place of the security agency concerned until the investigation has been completed. The Administrateur-Général of Agence Nationale de Documentation told the Special Rapporteur that in such cases it was impossible to transfer the suspect to the place where accused persons awaiting trial were normally kept in view of the fact that such places of detention were relatively open and the régime for visitors was relatively liberal. In sensitive cases, therefore, the suspect had to be detained at the agency's detention place until the investigation was finalized. The magistrates of the Public Prosecutor's office were, nevertheless, informed and once the inquiry was finished, the suspect was transferred to the Judiciary.

In general, the Special Rapporteur feels that it is rather undesirable if suspects are held in places run by the agency which is at the same time the investigating authority. Such a situation may easily lead to undue influence or even duress since living conditions and conditions of detention may be made subservient to the course of the investigation.

The Special Rapporteur feels that it would be useful to establish central detention facilities in the main cities for persons suspected of having committed security offences and who would consequently be tried by the Cour de Sûreté de l'Etat. Such detention centres should be placed under the supervision of the Judicial Council just like ordinary prisons. The various detention places of the law-enforcement and security agencies should only be used as a provisional lock-up until the arrest has been legalized. Evidence obtained from the suspect outside such central detention facilities and not confirmed by him during his stay there should not be admitted in court.

The Special Rapporteur was informed that a number of secret places of detention which had not been registered with the President of the Judicial Council, as required by the law, had recently been closed, and that those who had run these places of detention would be prosecuted. The Special Rapporteur is of the opinion that severe punishment of persons who exploit illegal places of detention is a highly effective preventive measure. Evidence collected in such places should not be accepted as legally obtained evidence.

During his mission, the Special Rapporteur visited the Central Prison of Kinshasa (Makala Prison) and two detention places (*cachots*) of the Service d'Action et de Renseignements Militaires and of the Agence Nationale de Documentation respectively. He was able to talk to a number of detainees in private. None of them claimed to have been subjected to torture or maltreatment in the places where they were presently kept, although a number of persons who were serving prison sentences in Makala Prison after having been tried by the Cour de Sûreté de l'Etat said they had been tortured during their preventive detention in 1984–85. The two persons kept in the AND detention place were both foreigners awaiting a decision to expel or extradite them. One of them had been kept there for about eight months, the other for about two months. Although according to the papers shown, they had been registered with the Public Prosecutor's office, they said they had never been presented to a judge. The eight persons kept in the SARM detention place had all been arrested or kept in custody (four Angolan soldiers awaiting a decision on their return to Angola) quite recently.

Those parts of Makala Prison shown to the Special Rapporteur were clean and well-kept. Living conditions seemed to be acceptable and medical care to be adequate. There is one pavilion for female detainees which is not separated from the other pavilions. Accused persons were not separated from convicted persons, as required by article 10, paragraph 2 (a), of the International Covenant on Civil and Political Rights. They, however, are not required to work whereas for convicted prisoners work is obligatory. According to the prison authorities, juveniles were kept in other detention places. The Special Rapporteur feels that the establishment of a separate detention centre for accused persons, part of which could be reserved, as a separate unit, for persons suspected of having committed security-related offences, as recommended in paragraph 42, above, would be a commendable measure.

As regards the question of administrative detention, the Special Rapporteur feels that the Government should clarify its position on this issue. As long as it is practised, the conditions under which a person may be temporarily detained should be laid down and should be subjected to judicial control by the Supreme Court.

The fact that the Department of Rights and Freedoms of the Citizen is authorized to receive complaints from citizens who claim that their fundamental rights have been violated is another indication that meaningful steps have been taken to strengthen the rule of law in Zaire. The Special Rapporteur visited two of the Department's local offices in Kinshasa and talked with the main delegates of these offices. The main delegate is a person who is chosen from people who have a good reputation and authority in society and is assisted by two lawyers and an administrative staff. The local offices are easily accessible to the public. The Special Rapporteur was impressed by the commitment of the persons he met. He was informed that sometimes the authorities to whom the complaint referred were uncooperative and were obviously not yet used to the new developments, he was also informed that members of some of the law-enforcement forces still tended to be rather indifferent to the rights of the citizens who often fell victims to harassment. It could, therefore, be recommendable to strengthen the position of the local offices in order to enable them to take corrective measures on the spot.

The Special Rapporteur could not avoid noting that the resources of the local offices were minimal. No means of transport was available and there was no telephone. Under such circumstances, work was extremely difficult and was certainly less effective than if it was done in more adequate conditions. In view of the priority given to human rights issues by the Government, it may be recommended that the local offices be provided with appropriate equipment in order to enable them to carry out satisfactorily their highly important task.

In conclusion, it can be said that until recent years, the legal and institutional framework in principle guaranteed the respect for human rights quite satisfactorily, but that in actual practice the system did not work properly. The result was that in a considerable number of cases even the most basic human rights, like the right to physical and mental integrity, were violated. The creation of DDLC can be seen as a remarkably bold effort to revitalize the long-neglected system of checks and balances. The Zairian Government must be commended since it decided to approach the question in a comprehensive way, reflected in the Department's

work programme: consciousness-building, training and formation, co-ordination between the various Government organs and redress. It is precisely this comprehensive character which makes the creation of the DDLC a unique experiment. As stated earlier, it is still too early to evaluate the outcome of the experiment. But it can only be successful if all branches of Government are fully prepared to strictly comply with the rules.

It has to be recognized that the authorities are hampered in carrying out their programme by the fact that the existing infrastructure is badly deficient and as a developing country Zaire will face tremendous difficulties in improving this infrastructure. As the Special Rapporteur said in previous reports: everyone should be aware of the fact that respect for civil and political rights depends not only on political will—indispensable as that may be—but often also requires costly investments. It is in particular with regard to this second element that international solidarity can play a decisive role.

The phenomenon of torture has considerably decreased in Zaire. Satisfactory as this may be, no government should be content with that statement of fact. It is as important to strengthen the structure which may prevent its recurrence. It is a well-known fact that illegal or arbitrary arrests and detentions may easily lead to situations where torture is likely to be practised. It is therefore only logical that the DDLC has made the extinction of such illegal arrests one of its main objectives. The following recommendations should be seen in that context:

(a) The procedure for the ratification of the United Nations Convention against Torture and Other Cruel, Inhuman or Degrading Treatment or Punishment should be completed at the earliest possible date;

(b) The training of law-enforcement personnel on human rights issues should get high priority;

(c) The provisions of the law with regard to arrest or deprivation of liberty should be strictly complied with. The Public Prosecutor's office should in each case carefully scrutinize the conditions under which the arrest is made and the grounds on which it is made. No person should be remanded in custody until he is seen by the competent judge;

(d) As long as administrative detention is still practised, it should only be applied under independent judicial control by the Supreme Court;

(e) The Code of Criminal Procedure should be amended to give a detained person the right to bring proceedings before a court in order to have the lawfulness of his detention decided upon without delay;

(f) All officials who have not complied with the legal provisions for arrest or detention should be either disciplined or prosecuted, without delay; if they have abused their authority by seriously violating basic human rights, including torture, they should be severely punished;

(g) Special detention centres under the supervision of the Judicial Council should be established for people who are accused of having committed crimes against the security of the State or the armed forces;

(h) Only evidence obtained under interrogation in such detention centres should be admitted in court;

(i) All possible efforts should be made to provide the local offices of the DDLC with the equipment necessary for the effective exercise of their tasks;

(j) The competences of the officials of the DDLC to take corrective measures in cases of abuse of authority by law-enforcement personnel against individuals should be strengthened.

ZAMBIA. The Republic of Zambia is a landlocked country in eastern Africa. It has borders with Angola, Botswana, Malawi, Mozambique, Namibia, Tanzania, Zaire, and Zimbabwe. Formerly known as Northern Rhodesia, it achieved independence from Great Britain in 1964 and became a member of the United Nations the same year. Its population is estimated by the UN (1990) to be 7,912,000. Ethnic groups include numerous Bantu and other tribal communities. Languages in common use include English (official) and about 70 tribal vernaculars. Religions practiced include Christianity, Animism, Hinduism, and Islam. Literacy is estimated at 54%.

The government (1990) took the form of a republic and member of the Commonwealth of Nations, of which the British monarch is the symbolic head. Under the 1973 constitution, the sole candidate for the presidency of Zambia is the person selected to be the president of the United National Independence Party (UNIP)—the only legal political party—by that party's General Conference; voters may say "yes" or "no" to his candidacy. Dr. Kenneth Kaunda, first elected for a five-year term in 1973, was re-elected in 1978 and 1983. The second-ranking government official is the secretary-general of the UNIP, appointed by the president of that party from the membership of the party's Central Committee.

National policy is formulated by the 25-member Central Committee. Legislation is prepared by a National Assembly composed of up to 136 members—125 elected by popular vote for terms of five years and the remainder appointed by the president to reflect appropriate geographical and tribal representation. There is also an advisory House of Chiefs, on which the country's traditional tribal authorities are represented.

The area in south central Africa occupied by Zambia was not penetrated by Europeans until the latter half of the 19th century, when David Livingstone reached Victoria Falls (1855) and Cecil Rhodes obtained the first mineral concessions from local chiefs (1888). Northern Rhodesia was proclaimed a British sphere of influence and became a protectorate administered by the British Colonial Office. In 1953, it joined with Southern Rhodesia (now Zimbabwe) and Nyasaland (now Malawi) to form the Federation of Rhodesia and Nyasaland. The federation, however, was dissolved ten years later, its unity destroyed by inability to reconcile African demands for greater participation in government and European fears for their future under an African majority regime.

On 24 October 1964, Northern Rhodesia achieved independence as the Republic of Zambia, and a new nation comprising 73 ethnic tribes found itself at the center of the liberation struggle in southern Africa. After some indecision, the 1964 constitution was abrogated in 1873 for a new one designed to achieve a "one-party participatory democracy."

As the arms struggles in its neighboring countries intensified, Zambia became host to thousands of refugees from those countries who were fighting for independence. Because some of them were suspected of being enemy agents sent to destabilize Zambia, a "state of emergency" was maintained for several years, under which the government could detain people, seize their property, and amend or suspend any law by administrative fiat.

In April 1990, Zambia experienced its second cholera epidemic in three months, reflecting the deep poverty of most of its township-dwelling population and the disintegration of such public services as garbage collection, water purification, and sanitation.

ZIMBABWE. A landlocked country in eastern Africa, Zimbabwe has borders with Botswana, Mozambique, South Africa, and Zambia. Formerly known as Southern Rhodesia, it achieved independence from Great Britain in 1980 and became a member of the United Nations the same year. Its population is estimated by the UN (1990) to be 10,511,000. Ethnic groups include descendents of the Mashona, Matabele, and other indigenous tribes; Asians, Europeans, and persons of mixed ancestry. Languages commonly used include English (official), Shona, Sindebele, and many regional vernaculars. Religions practiced include Syncretism (mixtures of Christianity and traditional African faiths), 49%; Christianity (Anglicans, Presbyterians, Methodists, Roman Catholics, and others), 25%; Animism, 24%; Hinduism, 1%; and Islam, 1%. Literacy is estimated at 55%.

The government (1990) took the form of a republic and member of the Commonwealth of Nations, of which the British sovereign is the symbolic head. Under the 1979 constitution, the president was to be elected by Parliament for a term of six years and to serve as head of State. However, the constitution was amended in 1987 to create the position of executive president: a president who is also prime minister. As the sole candidate, Prime Minister Robert Mugabe, president of the Zimbabwe African National Union (ZANU) Party, was elected to this post.

Up to late 1987, Parliament consisted of a 100-member House of Assembly and a 40-member

Senate. The House of Assembly is composed of 80 members elected by the country's 8.5 million blacks and 20 elected by the white population of about 100,000, and the Senate consists of 30 members elected by the black members of the House of Assembly and 10 by the white members of that house. However, on 21 August 1987, Parliament abolished the practice of reserving seats for the white minority.

Zimbabwe's judicial system is independent of other branches of the government and, in appropriate cases, applies African customary law. Village courts and community courts have been established to replace the tribal courts and district commissioner's courts of colonial days.

A British colony from 1890 until 1980, Zimbabwe (then Southern Rhodesia) was never directly administered from London; it was rather internally self-governing with its own legislature, civil service, armed forces, and police. From 1953 to 1963, it was joined in the Federation of Northern Rhodesia and Nyasaland (now Zambia and Malawi). When the federation was dissolved, the United Kingdom refused to grant independence to Southern Rhodesia until it demonstrated its intention to move towards eventual majority rule. White Rhodesians, led by Prime Minister Ian Smith, would not take this step. Instead Smith issued a Unilateral Declaration of Independence from the United Kingdom on 11 November 1965.

Although the British government considered the declaration to be illegal, it did not use force to end the rebellion; instead, it imposed unilateral economic sanctions on Rhodesia and requested other countries to do the same. The United Nations Security Council, on 16 December 1966, imposed mandatory economic sanctions for the first time on a State. On 29 May 1968, the Security Council broadened these sanctions by imposing an almost total embargo on all trade with the country.

During the early 1970s, Southern Rhodesia was the target of frequent guerrilla activity which resulted in widespread destruction and economic dislocation, as well as a sharp drop in white morale. The pressure intensified in 1974 after shifts in power in Mozambique and Angola occurred as a result of the change of government in Portugal, and by the formation of a "patriotic front" by the two major African groups, the Zimbabwe African National Union (ZANU), led by Robert Mugabe, and the Zimbabwe African People's Union (ZAPU), led by Joshua Nkomo.

In 1976, the Ian Smith government met with these and other black leaders in Geneva but failed to reach agreement on steps to be taken to resolve the situation. However, in 1977, an "interim settlement" was signed in Salisbury calling for qualified majority rule and elections with universal suffrage. Elections held in April 1979 returned Bishop Abel Muzorewa, chairman of the United National African Council, as the country's first black prime minister. However, unrest in the country and conflict between various factions continued in many areas.

A new round of consultations between the parties and other black-ruled States was initiated by the British government at Lancaster House, London, on 10 September 1979, and resulted after three months of bargaining with an agreement signed on 21 December calling for a ceasefire, new elections, a transition period under British rule, and a new constitution which would implement majority rule while protecting minority rights.

Under the agreement, Rhodesia reverted temporarily to the status of a British colony. A new constitution was adopted and elections were held. Robert Mugabe, leader of the victorious ZANU Party, formed the first government of the new country, called Zimbabwe, which was granted independence by the British government on 18 April 1980.

Since independence, the government has sought national reconciliation but has refused to share power with the minority political party, ZAPU. Emphasis has been placed upon reconstruction, integration of the armed forces, reestablishment of education and social services, and resettlement of approximately one million refugees, and displaced persons. Some progress has also been achieved in reversing past discriminatory practices in employment, wages, and land distribution.

However, destabilizing guerrilla activity has continued in some parts of the country, blamed sometimes on neighboring South Africa and sometimes on the Ndebele tribesmen who are the main followers of ZAPU's Joshua Nkomo. In 1983 and 1984, the government sent troops into parts of Matabeleland to suppress such guerrilla activity; these "security forces" were widely reported to have used undue violence in accomplishing their assignment. More recently dissident guerrillas have been charged with the murder of a number of white farmers and of tourists and with attacks upon government installations and personnel. In addition, the Mozambique National Resistance, which is fighting the Marxist government of neighboring Mozambique, has declared war against Zimbabwe because of its military support for Mozambique and has conducted hit-and-run raids across the frontier.

In the 1985 election, the Zimbabwe African National Union increased its majority in the House of Assembly but failed to win the 70 seats Mugabe had sought with a view to ensuring eventual one-party rule. In the 1990 election, the Zimbabwe Unity Movement (ZUM) won considerable support for its stand in favor of capitalism and multi-party democracy and against increasing unemployment and disintegration of the transport services. But, although his calls for a one-party State won him few supporters, President Robert Mugabe was re-elected by wide margins on both occasions.

The elections, on 31 March–1 April 1990, involved five political parties, contesting 119 parliamentary seats. All parties campaigned freely, held rallies throughout the country, and had access to the news media. The voting was by secret ballot. Mr. Mugabe won 78% of the total vote, and his party won 116 of the 119 seats in the parliament.

ZONTA INTERNATIONAL. An international non-governmental organization in consultative status with the UN Economic and Social Council (Category I) and with UNESCO, UNICEF, and the Council of Europe, Zonta International unites about 1000 clubs, totalling 35,000 individual members, in 50 countries.

Founded in 1919 in Buffalo, New York, and formally entitled Zonta International—International Service Organization of Executive and Professional Women—ZI endeavors to improve the legal, political, economic, and professional status of women and to encourage their entry into business and the professions. In the United States, it annually awards 6,000 Amelia Earhart fellowships to women for graduate work in aerospace sciences. It sponsors programs to improve international relations and supports projects for the advancement of women. It publishes the quarterly magazine *The Zontian.*

Zonta International. Address: 557 W. Randolph St., Suite 2040, Chicago, IL., 60606-2284 (U.S.A.) Telephone: (312) 930-5848. Fax: (1-312) 930-0951. Executive Director: Valerie F. Levitan.

Yearbook of International Organizations, 1989/90 (K.G. Saur)

APPENDIX A

SELECTED BIBLIOGRAPHY

The selected bibliography below is divided into two parts. Part I contains references relating to human rights conditions in individual countries, while Part II refers to general subject headings.

The bibliography has been prepared by Laura Reiner and Hap Pitkin of Human Rights Internet (HRI), respectively, associate editor and former research associate of HRI, under the direction of Laurie S. Wiseberg, Internet's executive director.

The bibliography, which is a selection of the entries in HRI's bibliographic database, covers the years 1985–1989, although it may also include some earlier citations, especially those published in the first half of the 1980s. It is largely of works published in English, supplemented by material in French, Spanish, Portuguese, and German. The references are primarily to reports of non-governmental organizations (NGOs) and occasionally to pamphlets or press releases issued by these organizations. The bibliography includes scholarly studies (monographs and articles from periodical literature), though no attempt has been made to do a systematic review of the scholarly literature. Some governmental and intergovernmental reports are listed; but, by and large, United Nations documentation and that of other intergovernmental organizations have not been included because this material is often referred to in the main entries of this encyclopedia.

In selecting material for inclusion in this bibliography, every effort was made to choose serious and representative studies of the material received and regularly abstracted by Human Rights Internet. To augment this selected reference, the reader may refer to the quarterly issues of the *HRI Reporter*, and to the directories published periodically by Internet: North America (1984); Latin America, Africa, and Asia (1981); Western Europe (1982); Eastern Europe (1987); Africa (1989); and Latin America and the Caribbean (1990, in English and Spanish). Because of the range of material, some of the information listed may be not available in standard libraries. In such cases, the reader may contact the publisher directly (the addresses of many governmental and non-governmental organizations will be found in this book or in Internet's "Master List of Organizations"). In addition, HRI's documentation center can supply copies of specific documents that are difficult to obtain elsewhere.

Finally, the number of entries under any heading is not intended to reflect the extent or degree of human rights problems in an individual country or on a specific topic. Rather, the number and kind of references reflect the availability of information and the specific concerns of the agency conducting the study.

PART I: COUNTRIES

Afghanistan

Afghan Refugee Information Network. *ARIN Newsletter* 23 (Winter 1986): 1–32. NGO newsletter, in English.

Amnesty International. *Afghanistan: Torture of Political Prisoners.* London: 1986. NGO report, in English.

——————. *Afghanistan: Unlawful Killings and Torture.* London: 1988. NGO report, in English.

Association Amitie Franco-Afghane (Franco-Afghan Friendship Association). "Les Refugies Afghans" (The Afghan Refugees). *Les Nouvelles D'Afghanistan* 35–36 (December 1987). NGO special issue, in French.

Center on War and the Child. *Afghanistan: The War against Children, a Summary Report.* Eureka Springs, AR: 1987. NGO report, in English.

Centre de Recherches et d'Etudes Documentaires sur l'Afghanistan (Center for Research and Documentary Studies on Afghanistan). *Buletin du CEREDAF* 44 (October 1988). NGO newsletter devoted to Afghanistan, in French.

Ermacora, Felix. "Afghanistan and the Conscience of the World." *SIM Newsletter* 17 (March 1987): 3–12. NGO article, in English.

Federation Internationale des Droits de l'Homme (International Federation of Human Rights). *Rapport de Mission: Afghanistan, Sept/Oct/Nov*

1985: Enquete sur le Depeuplement du Pays (Mission Report: Afghanistan, Sept/Oct/Nov 1985: Inquiry on Depopulation). *La Lettre de la FIDH* 64 (1985). NGO special issue, in French.

Heinz, Wolfgang S. *Ursachen und Folgen von Menschenrechtsverletzungen in der Dritten Welt* (Causes and Consequences of Human Rights Violations in Third World Countries). Saarbrucken, FRG: Verlag Breitenbach, 1986. Scholarly monograph, in German; bibliography on Afghanistan, pp. 357–360. Also, 20 pages of bibliography on human rights and development at end of volume.

Human Rights Internet. "From Passion to Conciliation." *Human Rights Internet Reporter* 12, no. 2 (Winter 1988): 61. Journal article, in English.

International Humanitarian Enquiry Commission on Displaced Persons in Afghanistan. *Mission to Afghanistan and Pakistan: September/October/November 1985.* Paris: Bureau International Afghanistan, 1986. NGO mission report, in English.

International League for Human Rights. *Report on the Status of Human Rights in Afghanistan.* New York: 1985. NGO report submitted to the UN Human Rights Committee in conjunction with the first periodic review of the initial report of Afghanistan under Article 40 of the International Covenant on Civil and Political Rights, in English.

Rubin, B. B. *To Die in Afghanistan.* New York: Asia Watch Committee, 1985. NGO mission report, in English.

U.N. Commission on Human Rights. *Report on the Situation of Human Rights in Afghanistan.* Prepared by Special Rapporteur Felix Ermacora, E/ CN.4/ 1987/22. 1987.

——————. *Report on the Situation of Human Rights in Afghanistan.* Prepared by Special Rapporteur Felix Ermacora, E/CN.4/1986/24. 1986.

U.S. Helsinki Watch Committee and Asia Watch. *By all Parties to the Conflict: Violations of the Laws of War in Afghanistan.* New York: 1988. NGO report, in English.

——————. *Tears, Blood and Cries: Human Rights in Afghanistan since the Invasion, 1979–1984.* New York: 1984. NGO report, in English.

——————. *To Win the Children: Afghanistan's Other War.* New York: 1986. NGO report, in English.

Wirsing, Robert. *The Baluchis and Pathans.* London: Minority Rights Group, 1987. NGO report, in English.

Algeria

Amnesty International. "Algeria: Death Penalty." *Urgent Action Letter.* London: 16 July 1986. NGO bulletin, in English.

——————. *The Imprisonment of Prisoners of Conscience in Algeria.* London: August 1986. NGO background paper, in English.

——————. "Killings, Torture: AI Seeks Inquiry." *Amnesty International Newsletter* 18, no. 12 (December 1988): 1. NGO article, in English.

Bekhechi, M. A. "Human Rights in Algeria: A Legal Analysis." Paper presented at the Workshop on Human Rights Documentation, Maseru, Lesotho, 24–28 August 1987. Scholarly conference paper, in French.

——————. "Souverainete, developpement et Droits de l'homme dans la Constitution algerienne et en Droit International" (Sovereignty, Development and Human Rights in the Algerian Constitution and International Law). Paper delivered at a colloquium on "The Constitution and Constitutionalism in Algeria," University of Annaba, 26–28 April 1987. Scholarly conference paper, in French.

Bouvier, Phillipe. "Rapport de Mission sur les Conditions d'Incarceration des Detenus de la Ligue Algerienne des Droits de l'Homme a Lambese: Algerie" (Mission Report on the Prison Conditions of Members of the Algerian League for Human Rights Detained at Lambese, Algeria). *Lettre de la FIDH* 146 (11 February 1986): 3–10. NGO mission report, in French.

Charfi, Mohamed. "Report on a Mission to Medea, Algeria." *ICJ Newsletter* 28 (January–March 1986): 29–36. NGO mission report, in English.

Federation Internationale de Droits de l'Homme (FIDH). "Algeria: La liberte d'association sous surveillance" (Algeria: Liberty of Association uner Surveillance). *Lettre de la FIDH* 214 (22 September 1987): 4. NGO article, in French.

Ramadane, Saeed. "Algeria's Perestroika—Without Glasnost." *Writers and Scholars International* 18, no. 1 (January 1989): 17–18. NGO article, in English.

Senghor, Jean-Gabriel. *Algerie: Proces de la Ligue de Droits de l'Homme (Medea)* (Algeria: Trial of the League for Human Rights ([Medea]). Paris: FIDH, 1986. NGO mission report, in French.

——————. *Rapport de Mission: Algerie: Ligue de Droits de l'Homme (Ali Yahia)* (Mission Report: Algeria: League for Human Rights [Me. Abdennour Ali Yahia]). Paris: FIDH, 1985. NGO mission report, in French.

Sivan, Emmanuel. "The Kabyls: An Oppressed Minority in North Africa." In *Case Studies on Human Rights and Fundamental Freedoms: A World Survey,* Vol 1, edited by Willem A. Veenhoven, 261–279. The Hague: Martinus Nijhoff, 1975. Edited collection, in English.

Angola

Amnesty International. *People's Republic of Angola: Background Briefing on Amnesty International's Concerns.* London: 1982. NGO report, in English.

——————. *Political Imprisonment in the People's Republic of Angola.* London 1984. NGO report, in English.

Brennan, T. O. *Uprooted Angolans: From Crisis to Catastrophe.* Washington, D.C.: U.S. Committee for Refugees, 1987. NGO report, in English.

Brooke, James. "The Yearning of Refugees: Angola Unity." *New York Times,* 6 October 1988. News article, in English.

Davis, Jennifer. *Report on a Visit to Angola: February 1–10, 1981.* New York: American Committee on Africa (ACOA), 1981. NGO report, in English.

Gqubule, Thandeka. "Eyewitness Tales of Abuses in Angola." *Johannesburg Weekly Mail,* 5 August 1988. News article, in English.

Kramer, Reed. "Children Caught in Long-lasting War." *Africa News* 28, no. 7 (December 1987): 9–10. News article, in English.

Morna, C. L. "Women and Children on the Frontline." *Africa Report* 33, no. 4 (July–August 1988): 33–36. NGO article, in English.

Pierson-Mathy, P., R. Schware, and R. Harvey. *IADL Fact-Finding Mission to Southern Africa.* Brussels: International Association of Democratic Lawyers (IADL), 1978. NGO mission report, in English.

Waters, Cherri. *Destabilizing Angola: South Africa's War and U. S. Policy: A Background Resource.* Washington, D. C.: Washington Office on Africa (WOA) and Center for International Policy (CIP), 1986. NGO background paper, in English.

Argentina

Abuelas de Plaza de Mayo (Grandmothers of Plaza de Mayo). *Information* 10 (September 1986): 1–15. NGO bulletin, in Spanish.

Academia de Humanismo Cristiano (Academy of Christian Humanism). "Violacion de Derechos Humanos y Democratization en Argentina" (Violation of Human Rights and Democratization in Argentina). *Chilean Review of Human Rights* 2, no. 4 (1985): 14–27. Journal article, in Spanish.

Action des Chretiens pour l'Abolition de la Torture (Christian Action for the Abolition of Torture). "Les Enfants Disparus en Argentine" (The Disappeared Children in Argentina). *Courrier de l'ACAT* 59 (November 1985): 10–16. NGO article, in French.

Agosin, Majorie. "A Visit to the Mothers of the Plaza de Mayo." *Human Rights Quarterly* 9, no. 3 (August 1987): 426–435. Scholarly article, in English.

Americas Watch Committee. *Truth and Partial Justice in Argentina.* New York: 1987. NGO report, in English.

Amnesty International. *Argentina: The Military Juntas and Human Rights, Report of the Trial of the Former Junta Members.* London: 1987. NGO report, in English.

——————. *The Missing Children of Argentina: A Report of Current Investigations.* London: 1985. NGO report, in English.

Asamblea Permanente por los Derechos Humanos (Permanent Assembly for Human Rights). "Presos politicos: historia sin final . . ." (Political Prisoners: Story Without End . . .) *Derechos Humanos* 3, no. 13 (April 1988): 13. NGO article, in Spanish.

——————. *Violencia Policial en la Argentina y los Medios Legales para Combatirla* (Police Violence in Argentina and Legal Methods to Combat It). Buenos Aires: 1986, NGO report, in Spanish.

Comision Nacional sobre la Desaparicion de Personas (National Commission on the Disappeared). *Nunca Mas: The Report of the Argentine National Commission on the Disappeared.* New York: Farrar Straus Giroux and Index on Censorship, 1986. Government report, in English.

Garro, A. M., and H. Dahl. "Legal Accountability for Human Rights Violations in Argentina: One Step Forward and Two Steps Back." *Human Rights Law Journal* 8, pts. 2–4 (1987): 283–344. Scholarly article, in English.

Oficina de Solidaridad para Exiliados Argentinos (Office of Solidarity for Argentine Exiles). *Reencuentro.* Buenos Aires: 1986. NGO bulletin, in Spanish.

Partnoy, Alicia. *The Little School: Tales of Disappearance and Survival in Argentina.* Pittsburgh, PA: Cleis Press, 1986. Collection of essays, in English.

Poneman, Daniel. *Argentina: Democracy on Trial.* New York: Paragon House, 1987. Scholarly monograph, in English.

Servicio Paz y Justicia—Argentina (Service for Peace and Justice—Argentina). *The Argentine Military Crisis: A Preliminary Balance.* Buenos Aires: 1988. NGO report, in English.

Simpson, John, and Jana Bennett. *The Disappeared and the Mothers of the Plaza.* New York: St. Martin's Press, 1985. Scholarly monograph, in English.

Washington Office on Latin America. "Argentina Curbs Prosecution of Military." *Latin America Update* 12, no. 1 (January–February 1987): 1–6. NGO article, in English.

Westerveen, Gert. "Return to Democracy in Argentina and Uruguay: Some Outstanding Human

Rights Problems." *SIM Newsletter* 11 (July 1985): 9–16. NGO article, in English.

Australia

Asian Bureau Australia. "Mining Company Threatens." *Asian Bureau Australial Newsletter* 91 (Winter 1988): 1–2. NGO article, in English.

Bailey, Peter. "The Australian Human Rights Commission." Paper presented at the LAWASIA Conference on . . . South Pacific, 12–14 April 1985. Conference paper, in English.

Castles, S., B. Cope, M. Kalantzis, and M. Morrissey. "The Bicentenary and the Failure of Australian Nationalism." *Race and Class* 29, no. 3 (Winter 1988): 69–85. NGO article, in English.

Edwards, Judy. *Prostitution and Human Rights: A Western Australian Case Study.* Discussion Paper No. 8. Canberra: Human Rights Commission (Australia), 1986. NGO occasional paper, in English.

Einfeld, Marcus. *Bicentennial Oration: Human Rights and Constitutional Entrenchment, Statement by . . . President of the Australian Human Rights and Equal Opportunity Commission on the Presentation of the Report of the Commission's Inquiry into the Social and Material Needs of the Residents of Toomelah, Boggabilla and Goondiwindi.* Syndey: 1988. Collection of speeches, in English.

Freedom of Information and Expression in Australia. Commentaries on Freedom of Information and Expression No. 11. London: Article 19, 1988. NGO report, in English.

Human Rights Commission: Annual Report 1984–85. Canberra: 1986. Government report, in English.

Human Rights Commission. *Teaching, Enacting and Sticking Up for Human Rights.* Occasional Paper No. 9. Canberra: 1985. Government monograph, in English.

Indochina Refugee Association. *Refugees' Experience of Anti-Asian Sentiments in the Brisbane Area.* Discussion Paper No. 9. Canberra: Human Rights Commission, 1986. NGO occasional paper, in English.

International Work Group for Indigenous Affairs. *Land Rights Now: The Aboriginal Fight for Land in Australia.* IWGIA Document 54. Copenhagen: 1985. NGO report, in English.

Law Association for Asia and the Pacific (LAWASIA). "Aboriginal Deaths in Custody." *Human Rights Newsletter* 1, no. 6 (April–July 1987): 1–22. NGO newsletter, in English.

Nettheim, Garth. "Indigenous Rights, Human Rights with Reference to Australia." Paper presented at a seminar on "The Rights of Indigenous Peoples," organized by the Australian National Com-

mission for UNESCO, 1 May 1986. Conference paper, in English.

——————. "The Aborigine in Comparative Law." Paper presented at the 12th International Congress on Comparative Law, Sydney, 19 August 1986. Conference paper, in English.

Survival International. "Sympathy Abroad, Backlash at Home." *Survival International News* 21 (1988): 6. NGO article, in English.

Suter, K. D. "Australian Aborigines: The Continuing Crisis." *Human Rights Internet* 13, no. 1 (1989). Commentary, in English.

Tay, Alice Erh-Soon. *Human Rights for Australia.* Discussion Paper No. 1. Canberra: Human Rights Commission (Australia), 1986. Bibliography, in English.

Witton, Ron. "Australia: Post-War Immigration and the Development of Legal Rights." *Human Rights Forum* 1, no. 5 (January–March 1986): 3–9. NGO article, in English.

Austria

Nowak, Manfred. *Politische Grundrechte* (Political Rights). Vienna: Springer Verlag, 1988. Scholarly monograph, in German; bibliography on pp. 542–572.

Nowak, M., D. Steurer, and H. Tretter, eds. *Fortschritt im Bewustsein der Grund—und Menschenrechte: Festschrift fur Felix Ermacora* (Progress in the Spirit of Human Rights: Essays in Honor of Felix Ermacora). Kehl am Rhein, FRG: N.P. Engel Verlag, 1988. Scholarly edited collection, in English and German.

World Jewish Congress, Commission on the Holocaust and Crimes of the Nazis. *Waldheim's Nazi Past: The Dossier.* Geneva: 1988. NGO report, in English.

Bahamas

Grand Bahama Human Rights Association. *Bahama Watch.* 1 (1989): 1–10. NGO newspaper, in English.

Bahrain

Amnesty International. "Bahrain: Torture of Prisoners." *Amnesty International Newsletter* 16, no. 11 (November 1986): 7. NGO newsletter article, in English.

——————. *Bahrain: Concerns in the State of Bahrain.* London: 1989. NGO report, in English.

——————. *Bahrain: Conviction of Nine Political Prisoners.* London: 1988. NGO report, in English.

——————. *Bahrain: Incommunicado Detention and Unfair Trial.* London: 1988. NGO report, in English.

——————. *Reports of Torture of Political Prisoners in Bahrain.* London: 1986. NGO report, in English.

Committee for the Defence of Human Rights in Bahrain. "Statement on the Bahraini Government Repressive Acts." Damascus, Syria: 8 October 1988. NGO urgent action statement, in English.

Committee for the Defence of Political Prisoners in Bahrain. "Slow Death or Permanent Adversity for the Detainees prior to Release." London: 26 May 1987. NGO appeal, in English.

Federation Internationale des Droits de l'Homme (International Federation of Human Rights). "Bahrein: Greve de la faim des prisonniers politique" (Bahrain: Hunger Strike by Political Prisoners). *Lettre de la FIDH* 214 (22 September 1987): 2. NGO article, in French.

Index on Censorship. "Eighteen Women Arrested in Bahrain." *Briefing Paper* 249 (14 July 1986): 1. NGO bulletin, in English.

Institute for Women's Studies in the Arab World. "Women of Bahrain." *AL-RAIDA* 8, no. 37 (1 August 1986): 1–16. NGO bulletin, in English.

Bangladesh

Amnesty International. *Bangladesh: Detention Without Trial of Opposition Members.* London: 17 November 1987. NGO issue paper, in English.

——————. *Bangladesh: Large-Scale Detention without Trial of Opposition Members, July 1987–February 1988.* London: 1988. NGO report, in English.

——————. "File on Torture: Bangladesh." *Amnesty International Bulletin* (Ottawa, Canada) 13, no. 5 (July–August 1986): 9–10. NGO bulletin article, in English.

Andreassen, Bard-Anders, and Asbjorn Eide, eds. *Human Rights in Developing Countries 1987/88: A Yearbook on Human Rights in Countries Receiving Nordic Aid.* Copenhagen: Christian Michelsen Institute, 1988. NGO report, in English; bibliography, classified by country, pp. 357–372.

Child Workers in Asia Support Group. "Child Labour in Bangladesh." *Child Workers in Asia* 3, no. 1 (January–March 1987): 3–4. NGO article, in English.

Commission for Justice and Peace of the Catholic Bishops' Conference. "All BAVS Clinics Closed after Forced Sterilization Incident." *Hotline Newsletter* 10 (August–September 1987): 8. NGO news article, in English.

——————. "CCHRB Expresses Concern over Land-Grabbing." *Hotline Newsletter* 26 (January 1987): 3. NGO article, in English.

——————. "Child Labour." *Hotline Newsletter* 25 (November 1986): 5. NGO article, in English.

——————. "Hardship Encourages Sterilization: A Survey of 950 Sterilized Persons in Bangladesh." *Hotline Newsletter* 22 (May 1986): 1, 4–5. NGO article, in English.

Index on Censorship. "Bangladesh Detains Opposition Leaders and Censors the Press." *Briefing Paper* 289 (18 November 1987): 1. NGO briefing paper, in English.

International Work Group for Indigenous Affairs. "Bangladesh: Garo Lands Taken with Government Support." *IWGIA Newsletter* 50 (July 1987): 33–34. NGO article, in English.

——————. "Bangladesh: Three Massacres in the Chittagong Hill Tracts and Violent Attacks on Tribal Peoples in Dighinala." *IWGIA Newsletter* 47 (October 1986): 7–11. NGO article, in English.

Liberty International. *Human Rights Report on Bangladesh (January 1985–July 1985).* Mymensingh, Bangladesh: 1985. NGO bulletin, in English.

Martuza, Ghulam, and M. A. Momen. *Trade Unionism and Trade Union Laws in Bangladesh.* Dhaka, Bangladesh: Bangladesh Society for the Enforcement of Human Rights, 1986. NGO monograph, in English.

Mey, Wolfgang. *Wir Wollen Nicht Euch—Wir Wollen Eurer Land* (We Don't Want You—We Want Your Land). Goettingen, FRG: Gesellschaft fur Bedrohte Volker (Society for Endangered Peoples), 1988. NGO report, in German.

Rahman, Anisur. "Laws Affecting Journalism in Bangladesh." *Hotline Newsletter* 17 (July 1985): 1–6. NGO article, in English.

Ram, Mohan. "Bangladesh: The Tribal Turmoil." *Far Eastern Economic Review* (26 June 1986): 21–22. Journal article, in English.

Shamin, Ishrat. *Trafficking of Asian Women: A Case Study of Bangladesh,* July 1987. Scholarly conference paper, in English, bibliography, p. 12.

Survival International. "Bangladesh: Chittagong Hill Tracts: More Refugees." London: June 1986. NGO urgent action bulletin, in English.

——————. *Bangladesh: Genocide in the Chittagong Hill Tracts—New Evidence.* London: 2 May 1985. NGO bulletin, in English.

U.S. Committee for Refugees. *From Isolation to Exile: Refugees from the Chittagong Hill Tracts of Bangladesh.* Washington, D.C.: 1988. NGO report, in English.

Barbados

Barrow, Christine. "Caribbean Women Being Exploited: Low Pay, Job Insecurity, No Unionisation in Barbados." *Caribbean Contact* 14, no. 6 (November 1986): 9. NGO newspaper article, in English.

Belgium

Index on Censorship. "Censorship in Belgium." *Index on Censorship* 16, no. 3 (March 1987): 39. NGO article, in English.

Minority Rights Group. *Co-Existence in Some Plural European Societies*. London: 1986. NGO report, in English.

Belize

"Belize." *Mesoamerica* 6, no. 12 (December 1987): 2–3. News article, in English.

Benin

Amnesty International. "Benin: Fear of Torture/Legal Concern." *Urgent Action* (15 November 1985): 1. NGO bulletin, in English.
——————. *Benin: Human Rights Violations*. London: 1987. NGO report, in English.
——————. *Benin: Political Imprisonment and Torture*. London: 1988. NGO report, in English.
——————. *Benin: Recent Arrest of Students and other Individuals*. London: 1985. NGO report, in English.

Bolivia

Asamblea Permanente de Derechos Humanos de Bolivia (Permanent Assembly for Human Rights in Bolivia). "APDHB Condena Violencia Policial" (APDHB Condemns Police Violence). *Asamblea Permanente de Derechos Humanos de Bolivia Boletin* 8 (January–June 1987): 5. NGO article, in Spanish.
——————. "Los Derechos Humanos y Juventud [sic]" (Human Rights and Youth). *Asamblea Permanente de Derechos Humanos de Bolivia Boletin* 1, no. 3 (June 1985): 1–2. NGO article, in Spanish.

Asociation de Familiares de Detenidos, Desaparecidos y Martires por la Liberacion Nacional (Association of Relatives of the Detained, Disappeared, and Martyrs of National Liberation). "Logros de ASOFAMD" (Achievements of ASOFAMD). *Boletin* 2, no. 10 (1985): 3–5. NGO bulletin, in Spanish.
——————. *Parotani: Informe sobre la Represion a los Campesinos* (Parotani: Report on the Repression of Peasants). La Paz, Bolivia: 1987. NGO mission report, in Spanish.

Centro de Documentacion e Informacion-Bolivia (Documentation and Information Center-Bolivia). "Juicio de Responsabilidades: Dichos y Hechos del Ex-General" (Trial of Responsibility: Words and Deeds of the Ex-General). *INFORME "R"* 117 (July 1986): 9–12. NGO article, in Spanish.
——————. "La Huelga contra el hambre" (The Hunger Strike). *Informe "R"* 7, no. 125 (April 1987): 10–12. NGO article, in Spanish.
——————. "La Mujer en Bolivia: Discriminacion, Lucha y Participacion" (Women in Bolivia: Discrimination, Struggle, and Participation) *Informe "R"* 5 (July 1985): 9–10. NGO article, in Spanish.
——————. "Reconquista de las Libertades" (Reconquest of Liberties). *Informe "R"* 5 (June 1985): 9–10. NGO article, in Spanish.
——————. "Strategies for Survival." *Bolivia Bulletin* 2, no. 4 (September 1986): 2. NGO article, in English.

"Collapse of Bolivian Mining Drives Idle Workers to Cities," *Latinamerica Press,* 12 February 1987. New article, in English.

Council on Hemispheric Affairs. "No Peace in La Paz: Protests against Austerity and U.S. Presence Lead to State of Siege." *Washington Report on the Hemisphere* 6, no. 24 (September 1986): 1, 6. NGO article, in English.

Del Granado, Juan. *Juicio a la Dictadura de Luis Garcia Meza: Contra la Impunidad* (Bring Luis Garcia Meza's Dictatorship to Justice: Against Impunity). La Paz, Bolivia: Asamblea Permanente de los Derechos Humanos de Bolivia, 1987. NGO report, in Spanish.

Botswana

Amoah, P.K.A. "The Independence of the judiciary in Botswana, Lesotho and Swaziland." *CIJL Bulletin* no. 19–20 (April–October 1987): 16–32. NGO article, in Enlgish.

Andreassen, Bard-Anders, and Asjborn Eide, eds. "Botswana." In *Human Rights in Developing Countries 1987–88: A Yearbook on Human Rights in Countries Receiving Nordic Aid,* 26–39. Copenhagen: Akademisk Forlag, 1988. NGO report, in English; bibliography, pp. 357–358.

Laurin, Yves. *La Situation des Refugies Sud-Africains au Lesotho et au Botswana: Mission d'Enquete Effectue au Mois de Juin 1983* (The Situation of South African Refugees in Lesotho and Botswana: Mission of Inquiry Undertaken in June 1983). Paris: Federation Internationale des Droits de l'Homme, 1983. NGO mission report, in French.

Maope, K. A. *Human Rights in Botswana, Lesotho and Swaziland: A Survey of the BOLESWA Countries,* Human and People's Rights Monograph Series No.1. Roma, Lesotho: Institute of Southern African Studies, 1986. NGO scholarly monograph, in English.

Neff, Stephen C. "Human Rights in Africa: Thoughts on the African Charter on Human and Peoples' Rights in the Light of Case Law from Botswana, Lesotho, and Swaziland." *International and Comparative Law Quarterly* 33 (1984): 331–347. Scholarly article, in English.

——————. *Human Rights in Botswana, Lesotho and Swaziland: Implications of Adherence to International Human Rights Treaties.* Human and Peoples' Rights Monograph Series No. 2. Roma, Lesotho: Institute of Southern African Studies, 1986. Scholarly monograph, in English.

Stephen, David. *The San of the Kalahari.* London: Minority Rights Group, 1982. NGO report, in English; selective bibliography, p. 16.

Southall, R. J. "Botswana as a Host Country for Refugees." *Journal of Commonwealth and Comparative Politics* 12, no. 2 (1984): 151–179. Scholarly article, in English.

Brazil

Americas Watch Committee. *Police Abuse in Brazil.* New York: 1987. NGO report, in English.

Amnesty International. *Brazil: Authorized Violence in Rural Areas.* London: 1988. NGO report, in English.

Archdiocese of Sao Paulo. *Brazil: Nunca Mais* (Brazil: Never Again). 3d edition. Petropolis, Brazil: Editora Vozes, Ltda., 1985. Research project report, in Portuguese.

Barros Laraia, Roque de. *New Trends in Brazilian Indian Affairs.* London: International Organisation for the Elimination of All Forms of Racial Discrimination, 1985. NGO report, in English.

Branford, Sue, and Oriel Glock. *The Last Frontier: Fighting over Land in the Amazon.* London: Zed Press, 1985. Scholarly monograph, in English.

Bridel, Renee, and Jean-Paul Collomp. *The Sexual Exploitation and Abuse of Children in Brazil: 13 November– 2 December 1986.* Paris: Federation Internationale des Droits de l'Homme, 1987. NGO mission report, in English.

Caldeira, Cesar. "Human Rights and the Brazilian Constitution of 1988." *Human Rights Internet Reporter* 13, no. 1 (Spring 1989).

Catholic Institute for International Relations. *Liberate the Land: A Statement by the Bishops of Brazil.* Third World Theology Series. London: 1986. NGO monograph, in English.

Centre for the Independence of Judges and Lawyers. "Report of the Human Rights Committee of the Federal Council of the Order of Advocates of Brazil." *CIJL Bulletin* 15 (April 1985): 42–46. NGO article, in English.

Comissao Pastoral da Terra (Pastoral Commission for Land). "Conflitos de Terra no Brasil" (Land Conflicts in Brazil). *Cadernos Do CEAS* 98 (July– August 1985): 16–26. NGO article, in Portuguese.

——————. "Conflictos de Terra no Brasil—1985: A Violenca na Luta Pela Terra" (Land Conflicts in Brazil—1985: Violence in the Struggle over Land). *Cadernos Do CEAS* 104 (July–August 1986): 42–51. NGO article, in Portuguese.

Comissao Pro-Indio de Sao Paulo (Pro-Indian Commission of Sao Paulo). *A Questao da Mineracao em Terra Indigena* (The Issue of Mining on Indian Land). Sao Paulo: 1985. NGO monograph, in Portuguese.

Defence for Children International. "Traffic in Brazilian Babies: Adoption (Un)Limited." *International Children's Rights Monitor* 3, no. 3 (1986): 11 NGO article, in English.

de Souza Martins, Jose. "A Escravidao Hoje no Brazil" (Slavery Today in Brazil). *Cadernos Do CEAS* 104 (July–August 1986): 52–54. NGO article, in Portuguese.

Humphrey, John. "Ford in Brazil: Management Plays Tough." *International Labour Reports* 19 (January– February 1987): 24–25. NGO article, in English.

Junqueira, Carmen, and Betty Mindlin. *The Aripuana Park and the Polonoroeste Programme.* Translated by Sheila Aikman. Cophenhagen: International Work Group for Indigenous Affairs, 1987. NGO monograph, in English.

Pope, Clara Amanda. *Human Rights and the Catholic Church in Brazil, 1970–1983: The Pontifical Justice and Peace Commission of the Sao Paulo Archdiocese—A Case Study.* 25 March 1984. Unpublished scholarly paper, in English.

Sakek, M. T., and J. A. Borges. *Educacion y Ciudadnia: La Exclusion Politica de los Analfabetos en el Brazil* (Education and Citizenship: The Political Exclusion of Illiterates in Brazil). San Jose, Costa Rica: Instituto Interamericano de Derechos Humanos, Centro de Asesoria y Promocion Electoral, Inter-American Institute of Human Rights, and Center for Electoral Counseling and Promotion, 1985. IGO monograph, in Spanish.

Wechsler, Lawrence. "A Reporter at Large: A Miracle, a Universe." Parts 1 and 2 *The New Yorker* (25 May and 1 June 1987): 69–85; 72–93. Magazine article, in English.

World Council of Churches, Commission on the Churches' Participation in Development. *The Debt Crisis and Brazil: A Case Study.* Geneva: 1987. NGO monograph, in English; bibliography, p.45.

Brunei Darussalam

Amnesty International. *Administrative Detention.* London: 1988. NGO report, in English.

──────. *Southeast Asia: Human Rights Violations in Brunei, Indonesia, Malaysia, Philippines.* London: 1987. NGO report, in English.

Malaysia-Singapore-Brunei Studies Group. *Berita* 12, no. 3 (Fall 1986): 1–17. NGO articles, in English.

Bulgaria

Amnesty International. *Bulgaria: Continuing Human Rights Abuses against Ethnic Turks.* London: 1987. NGO report, in English.

"Bulgaria—No Relaxation for Muslims." *Impact International* 16, no. 20 (November 1986): 2. NGO article, in English.

"Bulgaria's Turks Tell of Terror in Forced Assimilation Drive." *Washington Post,* 8 April 1986. In English.

Commission on Security and Cooperation in Europe. *Basket I—Implementation of the Final Act of the Conference on Security and Cooperation in Europe: Findings Eleven Years after Helsinki.* Washington, D.C.: GPO, 1987. Government report, 1987, in English.

──────. *National Minorities in Eastern Europe: The Turkish Minority in Bulgaria.* Washington, D.C.: GPO, 1987. Government report, in English.

Eviatar, Daphne. *Violations of the Helsinki Accords: Bulgaria.* New York: U.S. Helsinki Watch Committee, 1986. NGO report, in English.

"The Experience of Being Bulgarized." *The Economist,* 14 December 1985. Magazine article, in English.

International Commission of Jurists. "Bulgaria/Turkey." *The ICJ Review* 38 (June 1987): 1–3. NGO article, in English.

Internationale Gesellschaft fur Menschenrechte (International Society for Human Rights). *CSCE and Human Rights: Divided Families and the Denial of Freedom of Movement (Documentation).* Frankfurt/Main, FRG: 1987. NGO document collection, in English.

Korkud, Refik. *Bulgaria Carries on Chauvinistic Policies.* Ankara, Turkey: Turkiye Fikir Ajansi, 1986. Situation report, in English.

"The Position of the Turks in Bulgaria." *Review of International Affairs* 36, no. 837 (February 1985). Journal article, in English.

Research Center for Religion and Human Rights in Closed Societies. *Bulgaria: Imprisonment of Ethnic Turks: Human Rights Abuses during the Forced Assimilation of the Ethnic Turkish Minority.* London: 1988. NGO report, in English.

Seytmuratova, Ayshe, and Ibrahim Tuna. "Bulgaria: Genocide Bulgarian-Style." *RCDA—Religion in Communist-Dominated Areas* 23, no. 7–9 (1984): 125, 127. NGO article, in English.

Tuna, Ibrahim. "The Persecution of the Turkish Minority in Bulgaria." *RCDA—Religion in Communist-Dominated Areas* 26, no. 2 (Spring 1987): 1–2. NGO article, in English.

U.S. Helsinki Watch Committee. "Bulgaria." In *Ten Years Later: Violations of the Helsinki Accords,* 1–5. New York: 1985. NGO report, in English.

──────. *Destroying Ethnic Identity: The Turks of Bulgaria.* New York: 1986. NGO mission report, in English.

Burkina Faso

Action des Chretiens pour l'Ablotion de la Torture (Christian Action for the Abolition of Torture). "Burkina Faso." *Courrier de l'ACAT* no. 70–71 (December 1986): 25. NGO article, in French.

Amnesty International. *Burkina Faso: Legal Concern/Torture.* London: 1988. NGO bulletin, in English.

──────. *Burkina Faso: Political Imprisonment and the Use of Torture from 1983 to 1988.* London: 1988. NGO report, in English.

Jaudel, Etienne. *Rapport de Mission: Burkina Faso* (Mission Report: Burkina Faso). Paris: Federation Internationale des Droits de l'Homme, 1988. NGO report, in French.

Miaille, Michel. "Burkina Faso: Compte-Rendu de Mission: Proces CEAO contre Diawara et Autres (Burkina Faso: Mission Report on the CEAO Trial of Diawara and others). *Lettre de la FIDH* 157 (27 May 1986): 5–8. NGO mission report, in French.

Women's International Network. "Female Circumcision: Genital and Sexual Mutilation." *WIN News* 14, no. 3 (Summer 1988): 24–27; 14, no. 4 (Autumn 1988): 21–26; 15, no. 1 (Winter 1989): 28–29. NGO edited collection, in English.

Burundi

Amnesty International. "Burundi." *Weekly Update Service,* 12 September 1985. NGO bulletin, in English.

──────. "Burundi." *Weekly Update Service,* 19 December 1985. NGO bulletin, in English.

——————. "Burundi." *Weekly Update Service*, 24 September 1988. NGO bulletin, in English.

——————. *Burundi: Killings of Children by Government Troops.* London: 1988. NGO report, in English.

——————. "Campaigns for Prisoners of the Month: Burundi." *Amnesty International Newsletter* 16, no. 9 (September 1986): 2. NGO article, in English.

——————. *Religious Intolerance.* London: 1986. NGO report, in English.

Breytenbach, W.J. "Inter-Ethnic Conflict in Africa." In *Case Studies on Human Rights and Fundamental Freedoms: A World Survey,* vol. 1, edited by W. A. Veenhoven, 309–331. The Hague: Martinus Nijhoff: 1975. Collection of articles, in English.

"Burundi Sentence." *Impact International* 16. no. 21 (November 1986): 4. Magazine article, in English.

U.S. Department of State. *Country Reports on Human Rights Practices for 1988.* Washington, D.C.: GPO, 1989. Government report, in English.

Cambodia

Abrams, F., D. Orentlicher, and S. Heder. *Kampuchea: After the Worst.* New York: Lawyers Committee for Human Rights, 1985. NGO mission report, in English.

Amnesty International. *Kampuchea: Political Imprisonment and Torture.* London: 1987. NGO report, in English.

——————. *Kampuchea: Officially Reported Political Arrests and Allegations of Torture and Arbitrary Detention.* London: 1988. NGO report, in English.

Cambodia Documentation Commission. *The Khmer Rouge Genocide: Accountability and Response.* New York: 1987. NGO report, in English.

Chanda, Nayan. *Brother Enemy: The War after the War.* Harcourt Brace Jovanovich: 1986. Scholarly monograph, in English.

Fischer, Elise. "Regard sur . . . le Cambodge" (Focus on . . . Kampuchea). *Courrier de l'ACAT* 66 (June 1986): 2–4. NGO article, in French.

Hannum, Hurst. "International Law and Cambodian Genocide: The Sounds of Silence." *Human Rights Quarterly* 11, no. 1 (February 1989): 82–138. Scholarly article, in English.

Hannum, H., and D. Hawk. *The Case against the Standing Committee of the Communist Party of Kampuchea.* New York: Cambodia Documentation Commission, 1986. NGO legal brief (draft), in English.

Indochina Policy Forum. *Recommendation for the New Administration on U.S. Policy toward Indochina.* Queenstown, MD: Aspen Institute, 1988. NGO report, in English.

Kiernan, Ben. *Cambodia: The Eastern Zone Massacres.* New York: Center for the Study of Human Rights, Columbia University, 1987. Scholarly study, in English.

U.S. Committee for Refugees. "Cambodia: Peace at Last or the Return of Pol Pot?" *Refugee Reports* 9, no. 7 (15 July 1988): 1–8. NGO article, in English.

Cameroon

Amnesty International. *Cameroon: Amnesty International's Concerns Arising from the April 1984 Coup Attempt.* London: 1987. NGO report, in English.

——————. *Cameroon: The Imprisonment of Jehovah's Witnesses.* London: 1985. NGO report, in English.

——————. *Religious Intolerance.* London: 1986. NGO report, in English.

——————. *Summary Trials and Secret Executions in the Republic of Cameroon.* London: 1984. NGO report, in English.

Ankomah, Baffour. "Cameroon's Forbidden Topics." *Index on Censorship* 17, no. 2 (February 1988): 22–24. NGO article, in English.

Baudelot, Yves, and Alfred Pognon. *Rapport de Mission d'Observation Judiciare: Proces de Monsier Ahidjo et de ses Deux Aides de Camp* (Trial Observer Mission Report: The Trial of Mr Ahidjo and his Two Aides). Paris: Federation Internationale des Droits de l'Homme, 1984. NGO mission report, in French.

Baudouin, Patrick. "Intervention de la FIDH au Cameroun." (FIDH Intervention in Cameroon). *La Lettre de la FIDH* 173 (25 November 1986): 3–4. NGO case note, in French.

Beti, Mongo. "Biya or Botha—What's the Difference?" *Index on Censorship* 16, no. 9 (October 1987): 40, 42. NGO article, in English.

Bipoun-Woum, Joseph-Marie. "Cameroon." In *Individual Rights and the State in Foreign Affairs,* edited by Elihu Lauterpacht and J. G. Collier, 77–93. New York: Praeger, 1977. Collection of scholarly articles, in English.

"Cameroon: Fon Gorji Kinka Arrested." *West Africa,* 10 June 1985. Magazine article, in English.

"Cameroon: Tightening the Grip." *Index on Censorship* 15, no. 5 (May 1986): 30–31, 37. NGO article, in English.

Committee for Human Rights in Cameroon. *Cameroon Monitor.* NGO monthly newsletter, in English.

Hodges, Tony. *Jehovah's Witnesses in Africa.* London: Minority Rights Group, 1985. NGO report, in English; bibliography, p. 14.

Index on Censorship. "Cameroon: French Publisher Protests." *Index on Censorship* 14, no. 5 (October 1985): 24–25. NGO article, in English.

Nwosu, Humphrey N. "The Concepts of Nationalism and Right in Self-Determination: Cameroon as a Case Study." *Africa Quarterly* 16, no. 2 (1976): 256–273. NGO article, in English.

Canada

Baker, David. "An Overview of Human Rights for Disabled People in Canada." Paper presented at the International Experts Meeting on Ways and Means to Ensure Effective Exercise of Human Rights by Disadvantaged Groups, Quebec, Canada, 18 September 1985. In English.

Bayefsky, A. F., and M. Eberts, eds. *Equality Rights and the Canadian Charter of Rights and Freedoms*. Canadian Legal Classic Series. Toronto: Carswell, 1985. Scholarly edited collection, in English.

Boldt, M., and J. A. Long, eds. *The Quest for Justice: Aboriginal Peoples and Aboriginal Rights*. Toronto: University of Toronto Press, 1985. Scholarly edited collection, in English.

British Columbia Council of Human Rights. *Human Rights: A Responsibility We All Share*. Vancouver, Canada: 1986. Government bulletin, in English.

Canada (Government of). *Implementation of the International Covenant on Economic, Social and Cultural Rights, Initial Reports . . . Concerning Rights Covered by Articles 13 to 15 . . . Canada*, 7 May 1985, E/1982/3/Add 34. IGO document, in English.

Canadian Charter of Rights: Annotated. Aurora, Ontario: Canada Law Book, 1987. Reference book, in English and French.

Canadian Council on Social Development, Court Challenges Program. *A Guide to the Charter for Equality-Seeking Groups*. Ottawa, Canada: 1987. Government manual, in English and French.

Federation Internationale des Droits de l'Homme. *Labrador and Northeastern Quebec*. Paris: 1986. NGO mission report, in English.

Gesellschaft fur Bedrohte Volker (Association for Endangered Peoples). "Inuit in Kanada." *Pogrom* 119 (16 January 1986): 46–56. NGO article, in German.

Jones, Camille. "Toward Equal Rights and Amendment of Section 12(1)(b) of the Indian Act: A Postscript to Lovelace v. Canada." *Harvard Women's Law Journal* 8 (Spring 1985): 195–213. Scholarly article, in English.

Latin American Working Group. *An Anti-Intervention Handbook: Canadians and the Crisis in Central America*. Toronto: 1985. Handbook, in English.

Matas, David. *Domestic Implementation of International Human Rights Agreements*. 12 January 1987. Unpublished scholarly article, in English.

Mathews, R., and C. Pratt. "Human Rights and Foreign Policy: Principles and Canadian Practice." *Human Rights Quarterly* 7, no. 2 (May 1985): 159–188. Scholarly article, in English.

Nolan, C. J. "The Influence of Parliament on Human Rights in Canadian Foreign Policy." *Human Rights Quarterly* 7, no. 3 (August 1985): 373–390. Scholarly article, in English.

Refugee Documentation Project (York University). "Beyond the Plaut Report: Toward a Truly Humanitarian Refugee Policy for Canada." *Refuge* 5, no. 1 (October 1985): 6–9. NGO article, in English.

Schelew, Michael. "The New Refugee Measures—The End of Canada's Humanitarian Tradition." *Amnesty International Bulletin* 13, no. 5 (July–August 1986): 14–15. NGO article, in English.

Smith, James G. E. "Canada—The Lubicon Lake Cree." *Cultural Survival Quartrly* 11, no. 3 (1987): 61–62. NGO article, in English.

Turpel, M. E., R. Jones, and P. File "Aboriginal Peoples: A Human Rights Perspective." *Rights and Freedoms* 59 (February 1987): 3–4. NGO article, in English.

Central African Republic

Amnesty International. *Arrests and Cases of Political Imprisonment Reported to Amnesty International in the Central African Republic during the First Half of 1985*. London: 1985. NGO bulletin, in English.

——————. "Disappearances." *Urgent Action*, 22 May 1985. NGO bulletin, in English.

Azonga, Tikum Mbah. "Central African Republic: Kolingba's Promises." *West Africa*, 30 June 1986, 1356–1357. Magazine article, in English.

"CAR: Clemency for Political Detainees." *West Africa*, 15 September 1986, 1947. Magazine article, in English.

Demafouth, Jean-Jacques. "Landlocked and Uninformed." *Index on Censorship* 14, no. 5 (October 1985): 22–24. NGO article, in English.

Chad

Amnesty International. *Chad: Arrests of Members of the Hadjerai Ethnic Group* London: 1988. NGO report, in English.

——————. *Chad: Imprisonment of Suspected Opponents of the Government in the Abeche Region—Information Provided by Governmental Authorities during an Amnesty International Mission to the Republic of Chad.* London: 1985. NGO mission report, in English.

————. *Republic of Chad: Political Arrests in June and July 1988*. London: 1988. NGO report, in English.

————. *Republique du Tchad: "Disparitions," Executions, Extrajudiciares et Detention Secrete* (Republic of Chad: "Disappearances," Extrajudicial Executions and Secret Detention). London: 1987. NGO report, in French.

Whiteman, Kaye. *Chad*. London: Minority Rights Group, 1988. NGO report, in English.

Chile

American Association for the Advancement of Science, Committee on Scientific Freedom and Responsibility. *The Open Secret: Torture and the Medical Profession in Chile*. Washington, D.C.: 1987. NGO report, in English.

Americas Watch Committee. *Chile: Human Rights and the Plebiscite*. New York: 1988. NGO report, in English.

Amnesty International. *Chile Briefing*. London: 1988. NGO briefing, in English.

Ampuero, R., M. Calamai, V. Murillo, and R. Sandri, eds. *Cile: Fra Dittatura E Democrazia* (Chile: Dictatorship and Democracy). Milan: Franco Angeli Libri, 1985. Collection of scholarly articles, in Italian.

Anderson, F. R., W. W. Falsgraf, F. S. Moran, Jr., R. J. Woolsey, and A. Young. *Chile at the Crossroads: A Report of the Delegation of the American Bar Association to Chile, April 18–22, 1988*. Chicago, IL: American Bar Association, 1988. NGO mission report, in English.

Comision Chilena de Derechos Humanos (Chilean Commission for Human Rights). *Informe de la Comision Chilena de Derechos Humanos Sobre la Situation de los Derechos Humanos en Chile Durante 1986* (Chilean Commission for Human Rights Report on the 1986 Human Rights Situation in Chile). Santiago, Chile: 1987. NGO report, in Spanish.

Detzner, J. A. *Tribunales Chilenos y Derecho Internacional de Derechos Humanos: La Recepcion del Derecho Internacional de Derechos Humanos en el Derecho Interno Chileno* (Chilean Courts and International Human Rights Law: The Reception of International Human Rights Law in Chilean National Law). Santiago, Chile: Comision Chilena de Derechos Humanos, 1988. NGO monograph, in Spanish; bibliography, pp 161–182.

Deutsche Kommission Justitia et Pax (German Justice and Peace Commission). *Ley Justicia y Represion en Chile* (Law, Justice and Repression in Chile). Bonn, FRG: 1987. Mission report, in Spanish.

Freedom, House. *A Mission to Chile*. New York: 1988. NGO mission report, in English.

Fruhling, Hugo. *Nonprofit Organization as Opposition to Authoritarian Rule: The Case of Human Rights Organizations and Private Research Centers in Chile*. New Haven, CT: Program on Non-Profit Organizations and Institute for Social and Policy Studies (Yale University), n.d. Scholarly research paper, in English.

————, ed. *Represion Politica y Defensa de los Derechos Humanos (Political Repression and the Defense of Human Rights)*. Santiago, Chile: Centro de Estudios Sociales, 1986. NGO edited collection, in Spanish.

Inter-American Commission on Human Rights. *Report on the Situation of Human Rights in Chile*. Doc. 17. Washington, D. C.: 1985. IGO mission report, in English.

Medina Quiroga, Cecilia. *The Battle of Human Rights: Gross, Systematic Violations and the Inter-American System*. Dordrecht, Netherlands: Martinus Nijhoff, 1986. Scholarly monograph, in English.

Orellana, P. V. *Algunos Aspectos Cuantitativos de la Situacion de los Presos Politicos en Chile* (Some Quantitative Aspects of the Political Prisoner Situation in Chile). Santiago, Chile: Fundacion de Ayuda Social de las Iglesias Cristianas, 1988. Scholarly monograph, in Spanish.

Physicians for Human Rights. *Sowing Fear: The Uses of Torture and Psychological Abuse in Chile*. Somerville, MA: 1988. NGO report, in English.

U.N. Commission on Human Rights. *Question of Human Rights in Chile: Report. . . .* Prepared by Special Rapporteur F. V. Jimenez, E/CN 4/1987/7. 1987. IGO document, in English.

————. *Question of Human Rights in Chile*. Prepared by Special Rapporteur F.V. Jimenez, E/CN 4/1986/2. 1986. IGO document, in English.

U.S. House of Representatives, Subcommittee on Human Rights and International Relations and Subcommittee on Western Hemisphere Relations. *US Policy, Human Rights and the Prospects for Democracy in Chile*. Washington, D.C.: GPO, 1988. Government hearings, in English.

Vicaria de la Solidaridad (Vicariate of Solidarity). *Vicaria de la Solidaridad Duodecimo Ano de Labor 1987* (Vicariate of Solidarity 1987, 12th Year of Activity). Santiago, Chile: 1988. NGO report (issued annually), in Spanish.

Washington Office on Latin America. *Chile, the Multilateral Development Banks and U.S. Human Rights Law: A Delegation Report*. Washington, D.C.: 1986. NGO mission report, in English.

Zabel, W. D., D. Orentlicher, and D. E. Nachman. *Human Rights and the Administration of Justice in Chile:*

Report of a Delegation of the Association of the Bar of the City of New York and of the International Bar Association. London: International Bar Association, 1987. NGO mission report, in English.

China

Amnesty International. *People's Republic of China: Summary of Amnesty International's Concerns, January 1987–April 1988.* London: 1988. NGO report, in English.

————. *China: Prisoners of Conscience in the People's Republic of China.* London: 1987. NGO report, in English.

————. *China: Torture and Ill-Treatment of Prisoners.* London: 1987. NGO report, in English.

Asia Watch. *Human Rights in Tibet.* Washington, D. C.: 1988. NGO report, in English.

Cohen, Roberta. "China: Anyone Interested?" *Index on Censorship* 17, no. 1 (January 1988): 19–25. NGO article, in English.

————. "People's Republic of China: The Human Rights Exception." *Human Rights Quarterly* 9, no. 4 (November 1987): 447–549. Scholarly article, in English.

Crothall, Geoffrey. "China Spring." *Index on Censorship* 17, no. 6 (June 1988): 7–10. NGO article, in English.

Donnelly, J., and R. E. Howard, eds. *International Handbook on Human Rights.* Westport, CT: Greenwood Press, 1987. Scholarly edited collection, in English.

Edwards, R. R., L. Henkin, and A. J. Nathan. *Human Rights in Contemporary China.* New York: Columbia University Press, 1986. Scholarly essays, in English.

Fleming, P., and I. Zuloaga. "The Catholic Church in China: A New Chapter." *Religion in Communist Lands* 14, no. 2 (Summer 1986): 124–133. NGO article, in English.

Gesellschaft fur Bedrohte Volker und Verein der Tibetaner in Deutschland (Association for Endangered Peoples and Association of Tibetans in Germany). *Tibet: Traum oder Trauma?* (Tibet: Dream or Trauma?). Gottingen, FRG: 1987. NGO report, in German.

Hsiung, James C. *Human Rights in East Asia: A Cultural Perspective.* New York: Pergamon House, 1985. Scholarly edited collection, in English.

Ledger, W. P. *The Chinese and Human Rights in Tibet.* London: Parliamentary Human Rights Group, 1988. NGO report, in English.

Ross, L., and M. Silk. "The Individual in China." *Index on Censorship* 17, no. 2 (February 1988): 28–31. NGO article, in English.

Van Walt van Praag, M. C. *Population Transfer and the Survival of the Tibetan Identity.* New York: U.S. Tibet Committee, 1986. NGO monograph, in English.

————. *The Status of Tibet: History, Rights, and Prospects in International Law.* Boulder, CO: Westview Press, 1987. Scholarly monograph, in English.

Wing-yue, Leung. *Smashing the Iron Rice Pot: Workers and Unions in China's Market Socialism.* Kowloon, Hong Kong: Asia Monitor Resource Center, 1988. NGO report, in English.

Wu, Y., F. Michael, J. F. Copper, T. Lee, M. Hsia Chang, and A. J. Gregor. *Human Rights in the People's Republic of China.* Boulder, CO: Westview Press, 1988. Scholarly study, in English.

Zuckerman, Laurence. "China's Leading Journalist is Victim of Crackdown-Again." *CPJ Update* 28 (March–April 1987): 1, 4. NGO article, in English.

Colombia

Americas Watch. *The Central Americanization of Colombia? Human Rights and the Peace Process.* New York: 1986. NGO report, in English.

————. *Human Rights in Colombia as President Barco Begins.* New York: 1986. NGO report, in English.

Amnesty International. *Colombia Briefing.* New York: 1988. NGO briefing, in English.

Asociacion de Familiares de Detenidos Desaparecidos (Association of Families of the Detained-Disappeared). *Informe Colombiano* (Colombian Report). Bogota: 1987. NGO report, in Spanish.

Colectivo de Abogados Jose Alvear Restrepo (Jose Alvear Restrepo Lawyers' Collective). *El Camino de la Niebla: La Desaparicion Forzada en Colombia y su Impunidad* (The Foggy Road: Forced Disappearance and Impunity in Colombia). Bogota: 1988. NGO report, in Spanish.

Comision Andina de Juristas (Andean Commission of Jurists). *Colombia: El Derecho a la Justicia* (Colombia: The Right to Justice). Lima, Peru: 1988. NGO report, in Spanish.

————. "Colombia: Violencia y Democracia" (Colombia: Violence and Democracy) *Boletin* 16 (November 1987): 2–28. NGO article, in Spanish.

Comite Permanente por la Defensa de los Derechos Humanos (Permanent Committee for the Defense of Human Rights). *Itinerario de la Represion y la Violencia Institucionalizadas: Colombia 1986* (Itinerary of Institutionalized Violence and Repression: Colombia 1986). Bogota: 1988. NGO report, in Spanish.

——————. "La Justicia Colombiana Condena la Utilizacion de la Tortura en los Interrogatorios Judiciales" (The Colombian Judiciary Condemns the Use of Torture in Judicial Inquests). *Boletin de Prensa* (10 July 1985). NGO bulletin, in Spanish.

——————. *Relacion de Victimas de Desaparicion Forzada en Colombia* (Account of Victims of Forced Disappearances in Colombia). Bogota: 1987. NGO report, in Spanish.

Giraldo, Javier. *Algunos Rasgos de la Situation de Violencia que Vive Hoy Colombia* (Some Features of Violence in Colombia Today). Bogota: Centro de Investigacion y Educacion Popular, 1987. NGO report, in Spanish.

Index on Censorship. "Colombia: Violence and the Media." *Index on Censorship* 17, no. 1 (January 1988): 32–35. NGO article, in English.

International Work Group for Indigenous Affairs. "Colombia: Massacre of Embera Indians Causes International Outcry." *IWGIA Newsletter* 50 (July 1987): 82–86. NGO article, in English.

Mendex Madrigal, Luis, ed. *Derechos Humanos y Servicios Legales en el Campo: Colombia 1988* (Human Rights and Legal Services in the Countryside: Colombia 1988). Bogota: Instituto Latinoamericano de Servicios Legales Alternativos, Comision Andina de Juristas, and International Commission of Jurists, 1988. NGO conference proceedings, in Spanish.

Sanchez G., and D. Meertens. *Bandoleros, Gamonales y Campesinos: El Caso de la Violencia en Colombia* (Bandits, Landowners and Peasants: The Case of Violence in Colombia). 3d edition. Bogota: El Ancora Editores, 1985. NGO report, in Spanish; bibliography, pp. 246–255.

Umana Luna, Eduardo. *Hacia la Peace? (Los Ilicitos y los Presos Politicos: Las Amnistias y los Indultos* (Towards Peace? [Illicit Behavior and Political Prisoners: Amnesties and Pardons]) Bogota: Comite de Solidaridad con los Presos Politicos, 1985. Scholarly monograph, in Spanish.

——————. *La Tramoya Colombiana (Praxis y Derechos Humanos* (The Colombian "Entanglement" [Practice and Human Rights]) Bogota: Corporacion Colectivo de Abogados, 1988. Scholarly monograph, in Spanish.

Varon, Miguel. "Colombia: New Government Fails to Halt Multiple Killings." *Latinamerica Press* 18, no. 35 (25 September 1986): 1–2. NGO newsletter article, in English.

Vervaele, John. "Criminal Law and the Protection of Human Rights in Colombia." *SIM Newsletter: Neth-erlands Quarterly of Human Rights* 6, no.3 (October 1988): 5–27. Scholarly article, in English.

Comoros

Amnesty International. "Campaign for Prisoners of the Month: Comoros." *Amnesty International Newsletter* 16, no. 7 (July 1986): 2. NGO article, in English.

——————. *Comoros: The Detention without Trial and Allegations of Torture of Suspected Opponents of the Government.* London: 1985. NGO report, in English.

——————. *Comoros: Prisoners of Conscience.* London: 1985. NGO report, in English.

Fagart, Thierry. *Rapport de Mission (4 au 8 mai 1985): La Situation des Droits de l'Homme en Republique Islamique des Comores* (Mission Report [May 4–8 1985]: The Human Rights Situation in the Islamic Republic of the Comoros). Paris: Federation Internationale des Droits de l'Homme, 1985. NGO mission report, in French.

Congo

Amnesty International. *Congo: Background to Political Arrests in 1987 and 1988.* London: 1988. NGO report, in English.

——————. *Reports of Torture in the People's Republic of the Congo.* London: 1985. NGO report, in English.

Federation Internationale des Droits de l'Homme (International Federation of Human Rights). *Congo: 3 au 7 Aout 1986, Me. Henri Choukroun, Proces de Brazzaville* (Congo: August 3–17, 1986, Me. Henri Choukroun, Trial in Brazzaville). Paris: 1986. NGO mission report, in French.

Freedom of Information and Expression in the Congo: A Commentary by Article 19 on the Report Submitted to the United Nations Human Rights Committee by the Government of the Congo. London: Article 19, 1987. NGO report, in English.

Menga, Roger-Julien. *La Charte Africaine des Droits de l'Homme et des Peuples et l'Ordre Juridique Congolais* (The African Charter of Human And Peoples' Rights and the Congolese Juridical Order). Geneva: Institut Universitaire de Hautes Etudes Internationales, 1984. Scholarly monograph, in French; bibliography, pp. 148–158.

Tchibinda, J. F., and N. Mayetela. "The Rights of the Child in the People's Republic of the Congo." In *Law and the Status of the Child,* vol. 1, edited by Anna Mamalakis Papas, 183–220. New York: United Nations Institute for Training and Research (UNITAR), 1983. Collection of scholarly articles, in English.

Costa Rica

Bourgois, Philippe. *Ethnic Diversity on a Corporate Plantation: Guaymi Labor on a United Fruit Brands Subsidiary in Bocas del Toro, Panama, and Talamanca, Costa Rica.* Cambridge, MA: Cultural Survival, 1985. NGO special paper, in English.

Centro de Derechos Humanos. "Fray Francisco de Vitoria, O.P." (Center for Human Rights "Fr. Francisco de Vitoria, O.P.") "Costa Rica." *Justicia y Paz* 2, no. 1 (November 1986): 54–55. NGO article, in Spanish.

Comision Costarricense de Derechos Humanos (Costa Rican Commission for Human Rights). "CODEHU Ante la Situacion de los Reclusos" (CODEHU and the Conditions of Prisoners). *Informativo* 4 (March–April 1986): 16. NGO article, in Spanish.

——————. *Consideraciones en Torno a los Derechos Humanos en Costa Rica* (Considerations concerning Human Rights in Costa Rica). San Jose, Costa Rica: 1987. NGO report, in Spanish.

——————. *Informe sobre la Situation de los Derechos Humanos en Costa Rica* (Report on the Human Rights Situation in Costa Rica). San Jose, Costa Rica: 1987. NGO report, in Spanish.

——————. *Informe sobre la Situacion de los Derechos Humanos en Costa Rica* (Report on the Human Rights Situation in Costa Rica). San Jose, Costa Rica: 1988. NGO report, in Spanish.

Comision para la Defensa de los Derechos Humanos (Central American Committee for Defense of Human Rights). *Informe sobre la Situacion de los Derechos Humanos en Centroamerica, 1986* (Report on the Human Rights Situation in Central America, 1986). San Jose, Costa Rica: 1987. NGO monograph, in English.

"Costa Rica: More Strife on Fruit Farms." *Central America Report* 14, no. 5 (6 February 1987): 38. News article, in English.

Fernandez, G., and L. Narvaez "Refugees and Human Rights in Costa Rica: The Mariel Cubans." *International Migration Review* 21 (Summer 1987): 406–415. Scholarly research note, in English.

Hernadez Valle, Ruben. *Costa Rica: Elecciones de 1986 Analisis de los Resultados* (Costa Rica: 1986 Elections Analysis of the Results). San Jose, Costa Rica: Instituto Interamericano de Derechos Humanos, Centro de Asesoria y Promocion Electoral/Inter-American Institute of Human Rights, and Center for Electoral Counseling and Promotion, 1986. Research paper, in Spanish.

McColm R Bruce. *To License a Journalist? A Landmark Decision in the Schmidt Case. The Opinion of the Inter-American Court of Human Rights.* New York: Freedom House, 1986. NGO report, in English.

Cuba

Amnesty International. *Cuba: Recent Developments affecting the Situation of Political Prisoners and the Use of the Death Penalty—An Update.* London: 1989. NGO report, in English.

Association Internationale Contre la Torture (International Association against Torture). *Mission to Cuba: Report.* Milan: 1988. NGO mission report, in Spanish, French, and English.

Bengelsdorf, Carollee. "On the Problem of Studying Women in Cuba." *Race and Class* 27, no. 2 (Autumn 1985): 35–50. Scholarly article, in English.

Bofill Pages, Ricardo, comp. *Cuba 1988: La Situacion de los Derechos Humanos* (Cuba 1988: The Human Rights Situation). Miami, FLA: Comite Cubano Pro Derechos Humanos, 1989. NGO report, in Spanish.

Cuban-American Committee. "Moving Towards Reconciliation: Church-State Relations in Cuba." *Cuban-American Bulletin* 3, no. 3 (December 1985): 1–3. NGO bulletin, in English.

Donnelly, J., and R. E. Howard, eds. *International Handbook on Human Rights.* Westport, CT: Greenwood Press, 1987. Scholarly edited collection, in English.

Evenson, Debra. "Cuba's Prisons." *Cuba Update* 7, nos. 3–4 (Fall 1986): 1–3. Journal article, in English.

Henkin, A. H., M. J. Camejo, R. J. Hiller, M. H. Posner, S. Ritchin, and K. Roth. *Human Rights in Cuba: Report of a Delegation of the Association of the Bar of the City of New York.* New York: Association of the Bar of the City of New York, 1988. NGO mission report, in English.

Institute for Policy Studies. "Cuban Prisons: A Preliminary Report." *Cuba Update* (June 1988): 25–29. NGO article, in English.

National Lawyers Guild. "Criminal Justice in Cuba." *Cuba Update* (June 1988): 22–24. NGO article on fact-finding mission, in English.

Organization of American States. *Informe Anual de la Comision Interamericana de Derechos Humanos 1985–1986* (Annual Report of the Inter-American Commission of Human Rights 1985–1986). Washington, D. C.: 1986. IGO annual report, in Spanish.

Pedraza-Bailey, Sylvia. "Cuba's Exiles: Portrait of a Refugee Migration." *International Migrations Review* 19, no. 1 (Spring 1985): 4–34. Scholarly article, in English; bibliography, pp. 31–34.

Ruether, Rosemary R. "Towards a Post-Revolutionary Church—Christians and Cubans: A Renewal of Faith." *Christianity and Crisis* 45, no. 13 (26 August 1985): 329–333. Magazine article, in English.

UN Commission on Human Rights. *Consideration of the Report of the Mission which Took Place in Cuba in Accordance with Commission Decision 1988/106.* 21 February 1989. 11 bis. IGO document, in English.

U. S. Department of State, Bureau of Human Rights and Humanitarian Affairs. *Human Rights in Castro's Cuba.* Washington, D. C.: GPO, 1986. Government report, in English and Spanish.

Cyprus

Amnesty International. "Amnesty International Concerns in Western Europe—October 1986–March 1987." *External Report* (April 1987). NGO report, in English.

Commission on Security and Cooperation in Europe. *Human Rights Abuses in Cyprus* Washington, D. C.: GPO, 1985. Government hearings, in English.

Friends of Cyprus. *The Cyprus Observer* 6, no. 4 (August 1988). Series of NGO articles, in English.

Czechoslovakia

Aurednik, Tomas. "Judicial Repression in Czechoslovakia." *East European Reporter* 1, no. 2 (Summer 1985): 47–49. NGO article, in English.

Bugajski, Janusz. *Czechoslovakia: Charter 77's Decade of Dissent.* New York: Praeger and the Center for Strategic and International Studies, 1987. Scholarly monograph, in English.

Charter 77. "Let the People Breathe." *East European Reporter* 2, no. 4 (1987): 15–20. NGO document collection, in English.

Church in Distress Charity/Aid to Eastern Priests. *Kirche I Not: Kirche, Nation, Frieden* (Church in Distress: Church, Nation, Peace). Konigstein, FRG: 1985. Edited collection of past conference proceedings, in German.

Commission on Security and Cooperation in Europe. *Basket I—Implementation of the Final Act of the Conference on Security and Cooperation in Europe: Findings Eleven Years after Helsinki.* Washington, D. C.: GPO, 1987. Government report, in English.

——————. *Human Rights in Czechoslovakia: The Documents of Charter 77 (1982–1987).* Washington, D. C.: GPO, 1988. Government document collection, in English.

Entr'aide et Action/Help and Action Coordination Committee. "Events in Czechoslovakia." *Help and Action Newsletter* 10, no. 50 (Spring 1988): 18–26. NGO bulletin, in English.

Heneka, A., F. Janouch, V. Precan, and J. Vladislav, eds. *Besieged Culture: Czechoslovakia Ten Years after Helsinki.* Stockholm: Charter 77 Foundation and the International Helsinki Federation for Human Rights, 1985. NGO edited collection, in English.

International League for Human Rights. *Human Rights in Czechoslovakia: Comments on the Czechoslovak Government's Official Report to the Committee on the Elimination of Racial Discrimination.* New York: 1987. NGO report, in English.

Kavan, Jan. "Repression in Czechoslovakia." *East European Reporter* (Spring 1985): 20–22. Magazine article, in English.

Martin, P., J. Obrman, V. Kusin, M. Hajek, B. Janat, and S. Devaty. "Situation Report: Czechoslovakia." *Radio Free Europe Research* 13, no. 35 (2 September 1988): 1–28. Government report, in English; bibliography, p. 9, 12, 17.

Pehe, Jiri. "The Prague Spring—in 1988." *Freedom at Issue* 102 (May–June 1988): 17–23. NGO article, in English.

Radio Free Europe/Radio Liberty. "Charter 77." *Radio Free Europe Research* Special Report No. 1 (17 January 1987): 1–21. Government report, in English.

——————. "Charter 77 Document on Conditions in Prisons." *Radio Free Europe Research* 12, no. 36 (11 September 1987): 31–33. Government article, in English.

——————. "Charter 77 on the Federal Assembly Elections." *Radio Free Europe Research* 11, no. 23 (6 June 1986): 21. Government report, in English.

——————. "Eastern Europe in 1988." *Radio Free Europe Research* 13, no. 52 (30 December 1988): 1–53. Government background paper, in English.

——————. "Protestant Churches in Czechoslovakia: Less than Complete Loyalty." *Radio Free Europe Research* 11, no. 29 (18 July 1986): 1–8. Government bulletin, in English.

U.S. Helsinki Watch Committee. *A Decade of Dedication.* New York: 1987. NGO book on Charter 77, in English.

——————. *From Below: Independent Peace and Environmental Movements in Eastern Europe and the USSR.* New York: 1987. NGO report, in English.

U.S. Helsinki Watch Committee/Physicians for Human Rights. *Medical Mission to Czechoslovakia.* New York: 1988. NGO report, in English.

U.S. Helsinki Watch Committee. *Ten Years of Charter 77.* New York: 1986. NGO book, in English.

——————. *Violations of the Helsinki Accords: Czechoslovakia.* New York: 1986. NGO report, in English.

Ward, Ann. "New Wave of Religious Persecution in Czechoslovakia." *East European Reporter* 1, no. 4 (Winter 1986): 41–42. NGO article, in English.

Denmark

Amnesty International. *Amnesty International Concerns in Western Europe, March 1986–September 1986.* London: 1986. NGO report, in English.

Monggaard, Paul. "Danish Working Week Cut." *Free Labour World* 3 (28 February 1987): 2. NGO article, in English.

Djibouti

Arab Organization for Human Rights. *Report: Human Rights in the Arab World.* Cairo: 1987. NGO report, in Arabic and English.

Gesellschaft fur Bedrohte Volker (Association for Endangered Peoples). "Horn von Afrika: Nationalitatenkonflikte in Athiopien, Somalia, und Djibouti" (The Horn of Africa: Nationality Conflict in Ethiopia, Somalia, and Djibouti). *Pogrom* 127–128 (February 1987): 13–84. NGO article, in German.

Dominica

Thompson, Robert. *Green Gold: Bananas and Dependency in the Eastern Caribbean.* London: Latin American Bureau, 1987. NGO monograph, in English.

Dominican Republic

Amnesty International. *Dominican Republic: Daniel Valdez de la Rosa, Charles Henry Tejada Jackson.* London: 1986. NGO report, in English.

Brea Franco, J., V. Butten, J. Campillo Perez, and J. A. Silie Gaton. *Legislacion Electoral de la Republica Dominicana* (Dominican Republic Electoral Legislation). San Jose, Costa Rica: Instituto Interamericano de Derechos Humanos, Centro de Asesoria y Promocion Electoral/Inter-American Institute of Human Rights, and Center for Electoral Counseling and Promotion, 1986. Research paper, in Spanish.

Centro de Investigacion y Accion Social de la Compania de Jesus (Jesuit Center for Research and Social Action). *Estudios Sociales* 19, no. 63 (January–March 1986). Journal issue devoted to Dominican Republic, in Spanish.

Centro de Planificacion y Accion Ecumenica (Ecumenical Action and Planning Center). "Seminario Nacional Sobre Metodologias y Tecnicas de Educacion con Mujeres Rurales" (National Seminar on Methods and Techniques of Rural Education for Women). *CEPAE* 30–31 (June–October 1985): 1–52. NGO journal devoted to conference proceedings, in Spanish.

Council on Hemispheric Affairs. "Chaotic Elections in the Dominican Republic." *Washington Report on the Hemisphere* 6, no. 18 (11 June 1986): 4. NGO article, in English.

Latin American Documentation. *The Churches in the Caribbean.* Lima, Peru: 1986. NGO document collection, in English.

"Neoslavery in the Cane Fields: Haitians in the Dominican Republic." *Caribbean Review* 14, no. 4 (1985): 18–20. Journal article, in English.

Plant, Roger. *Sugar and Modern Slavery: A Tale of Two Countries.* London: Zed Press, 1987. Scholarly monograph, in English.

Proyecto Caribeno de Justicia y Paz (Caribbean Project for Justice and Peace). *Republica Dominicana: Sangre y Fuego en Protestas por el Alza de Precios* (Dominican Republic: Blood and Fire in Protests over Price Increases). Rio Piedras, Puerto Rico: 1986. NGO report, in Spanish.

Ecuador

Americas Watch Committee and Andean Commission of Jurists. *Human Rights in Ecuador.* New York: 1988. NGO report, in English.

Asociacion Latinoamericana para los Derechos Humanos (Latin American Association for Human Rights). *Violencia y Derechos Humanos en el Ecuador 1985* (Violence and Human Rights in Ecuador 1985). Guayaquil, Ecuador: 1985. NGO report, in Spanish.

Carrasco, Victoria. "Discriminacion Racial en el Ecuador." *Derechos del Pueblo* 33 (May 1986): 3–4. NGO article, in Spanish.

Comision de Derechos Humanos del Parlamento Latinoamericano (Human Rights Commission of the Latin American Parliament). *Informe del Ecuador* (Report on Ecuador). Quito, Ecuador: 1987. IGO report, in Spanish.

Comision Ecumenica de Derechos Humanos (Ecumenical Commission for Human Rights). "Continua Violacion de Derechos Humanos" (Human Rights Violations Continue) *Derechos del Pueblo* 34 (July 1986): 6–8. NGO article, in Spanish.

——————. "Derecho a la Tierra" (The Right to Land). *Derechos del Pueblo* 43 (January 1988): 1–12. NGO article, in Spanish.

——————. "1986 en lo Economico: Graves Efectos Sociales" (1986, the Economy: Grave Social Effects). *Derechos del Pueblo* 37 (January 1987): 10–11. NGO article, in Spanish.

——————. "Situacion Carcelaria" (Prison Conditions). *Derechos del Pueblo* 37 (January 1987): 1–9. NGO article, in Spanish.

——————. 'Situation Carcelaria" (Prison Conditions). *Derechos del Pueblo* 43 (January 1988): 1–10. NGO article, in Spanish.

Comision por la Defensa de los Derechos Humanos (Commission for the Defense of Human Rights). "Amedrentamiento y Terrorismo Estatal" (Intimidation and State Terrorism). *Testimonio* 2, no. 8 (July 1987): 12–14. NGO article, in Spanish.

Comite de Familiares de Presos y Perseguidos Politicos del Ecuador (Committee of Relatives of Political Prisoners and Persecuted of Ecuador). "Presos Politicos de Guayaquil: Un Ano Tres Meses Enjaulados" (Guayaquil Political Prisoners: One Year and Three Months in Prison). *COFPPE* 2 (April 1987): 14–16. NGO article, in Spanish.

Corkill, D., and D. Cubitt. *Ecuador: Fragile Democracy.* London: Latin American Bureau, 1988. NGO report, in English; bibliography of books in English on Ecuador, 1978–1988, p. 113.

Inter-Church Committee on Human Rights in Latin America. *ICCHRLA 1987 Annual Reports: General Concerns and Brief Country Reports.* Toronto, Canada: 1988. NGO report, in English.

International Work Group for Indigenous Affairs. *IWGIA Newsletter* 51–52 (October–December 1987). NGO journal issue devoted to conference report, in English.

Egypt

Amin, Mustafa. "If it Makes the President Happy." *Index on Censorship* 14, no. 5 (October 1985): 18–21. NGO article, in English.

An-Na'im, Abdullahi Ahmed. "Religious Freedom in Egypt: Under the Shadow of the Islamic 'Dhiman' System." In *Religious Liberty and Human Rights in Nations and in Religion,* edited by Leonard Swindler, 43–59. 1986. Conference paper in edited collection, in English.

Arab Organization for Human Rights. *Report: Human Rights in the Arab World.* Cairo: 1987. NGO report, in Arabic.

Dudley, James. "Human Rights Practices in the Arab States: The Modern Impact of Shari'a Values." *George Journal of International and Comparative Laws* 12 (1982): 55–93. Scholarly article, in English.

El-Kharboutly, A., and A. Hussein. "Law and the States of Women in the Arab Republic of Egypt." *Columbia Human Rights Law Review* 8, no. 1 (Spring–Summer 1976): 35–50. Scholarly article, in English.

International League for Human Rights. *Human Rights in the Arab Republic of Egypt.* New York: 1985. NGO report, in English.

Karas, Shawky F. *The Copts since the Arab Invasion: Strangers in Their Land.* Jersey City, NJ: American, Canadian and Australian Coptic Association, 1986. NGO report, in English.

National Spiritual Assembly of the Baha'is of the U.S. *Egyptian Baha'is Appeal Convictions on Religious Charges.* Washington, D C: 1988. NGO press release, in English.

El Salvador

Americas Watch Committee. *The Civilian Toll 1986–1987: Ninth Supplement to the Report on Human Rights in El Salvador.* New York: 1987. NGO report, in English.

——————. *Labor Rights in El Salvador.* New York: 1988. NGO report, in English.

——————. *Land Mines in El Salvador and Nicaragua: The Civilian Victims.* New York: 1986. NGO report, in English.

——————. *Managing the Facts: How the Administration Deals with Reports of Human Rights Abuses in El Salvador.* New York: 1985. NGO report, in English.

——————. *Nightmare Revisited 1987–88.* New York: 1988. NGO report, in English.

——————. *Settling into Routine: Human Rights Abuses in Duarte's Second Year: Eighth Supplement to the Report on Human Rights in El Salvador.* New York: 1986. NGO report, in English.

Amnesty International. *El Salvador: "Death Squads"—A Government Strategy.* London: 1988. NGO report, in English.

Comision Arquidiocesana de Justicia y Paz, Oficina de Tutela Legal del Arzobispado (Justice and Peace Commission of the Archdiocese, Legal Aid Office of the Archbishop). *Informe Mensual de la Oficina de Tutela Legal del Arzobispado* (Monthly Report of the Legal Aid Office of the Archbishop) 47 (March 1986). NGO monthly report, in Spanish.

Comision de Derechos Humanos de El Salvador (Human Rights Commission of El Salvador). *Human Rights in El Salvador.* San Salvador, El Salvador: 1987. NGO report, in English.

——————. *Report on Human Rights in El Salvador from August to December 1987.* San Salvador: 1987. NGO report, in English.

——————. *Situacion de los Derechos Humanos y las Libertades Fundamentales en El Salvador* (The Situation of Human Rights and Fundamental Liberties in El Salvador). San Salvador: 1987. NGO report, in Spanish.

──────. *Torture in El Salvador.* San Salvador: 1986. NGO report, in English.

Comision para la Defensa de los Derechos Humanos (Central American Committee for the Defense of Human Rights). *Informe sobre la Situacion de los Derechos Humanos en Centroamerica, 1986* (Report on the Human Rights Situation in Central America, 1986). San Jose, Costa Rica: 1987. NGO monograph, in Spanish.

El Rescate, Human Rights Department, Unitarian Universalist Service Committee. *El Salvador Update: Counterterrorism in Action.* Los Angeles, CA: 1987. NGO report, in English.

──────. *El Salvador Update: Labor under Siege.* Los Angeles: 1985. NGO report, in English.

El Salvador Committee for Human Rights. *Prolonging the Agony: The Human Cost of Low Intensity Warfare in El Salvador.* London: 1987. NGO report, in English.

Federacion de Comites de Madres y Familiares de Presos-Desaparecidos y Asesinados Politicos de El Salvador (Federation of Committees of Mothers and Families of Political Prisoners-Disappeared and Assassinated in El Salvador). *Report on Human Rights Violations in El Salvador.* San Salvador: 1987. NGO report, in Spanish.

Instituto de Derechos Humanos, Universidad Centroamericana "Jose Simeon Canas" (Human Rights Institute, Central American University "Jose Simeon Canas"). *Los Derechos Humanos en El Salvador en 1986* (Human Rights in El Salvador 1986). San Salvador: 1987. NGO report, in Spanish.

──────. *Los Derechos Humanos en El Salvador en 1987* (Human Rights in El Salvador in 1987.) San Salvador: 1988. NGO report, in Spanish.

──────. *Los Derechos Humanos y el Decreto 50* (Human Rights and Decree 50). San Salvador: 1986. NGO report, in Spanish.

──────. *Report on Repression against the Salvadoran Labor and Cooperative Movements September 1966–August 1987.* San Salvador: 1987. NGO report, in English.

Lawyers Committee for Human Rights. *From the Ashes: A Report on Justice in El Salvador.* New York: 1987. NGO report, in English.

──────. *El Salvador: Human Rights Dismissed—A Report on 16 Unresolved Cases.* New York: 1986. NGO report, in English.

Montes, S., F. Melendez, and E. Palacios. *Los Derechos Economicos, Sociales y Culturales en El Salvador* (Economic, Social and Cultural Rights in El Salvador). San Salvador: Instituto de Derechos

Humanos Universidad Centroamericana "Jose Simeon Canas", 1988. NGO report, in Spanish.

Organizacion Regional Interamericana de Trabajadores (Regional Interamerican Organization of Workers). *Los Derechos Sindicales en Centroamerica* (The Rights of Trade Unions in Central America). Mexico City, Mexico: 1988. NGO report, in Spanish.

Organization of American States. *Annual Report of the Inter-American Commission on Human Rights 1986–87.* Washington, D.C.: 1987. IGO annual report, in English.

Socorro Juridico Cristiano "Arzobispo Oscar Romero" (Christian Legal Aid "Archbishop Oscar Romero"). *Human Rights in El Salvador: Report for the Period January–December 1986.* San Salvador: 1987. NGO report, in English.

──────. *Informe Trimestral sobre la Situacion de los Derechos Humanos en El Salvador Abril–Junio 1988* (Quarterly Report on the Human Rights Situation in El Salvador April–June 1988). San Salvador: 1988. NGO report, in Spanish.

U.N. Commission on Human Rights. *Final Report on the Situation of Human Rights in El Salvador.* Prepared by Special Rapporteur Jose Antonio Pastor Ridruejo. 3 February 1986. IGO document, in English.

──────. *Final Report on the Situation of Human Rights in El Salvador.* Prepared by Special Rapporteur Jose Antonio Pastor Ridruejo, E/CN 4/1987/21. 2 February 1987. IGO report, in English.

Equatorial Guinea

Amnesty International. *Military Trials and the Use of the Death Penalty in Equatorial Guinea.* London: 1987. NGO briefing paper, in English.

Heinz, Wolfgang S. *Ursachen und Folgen von Menschenrechtsverletzungen in der Dritten Welt* (Causes and Consequences of Human Rights Violations in Third World Countries). Saarbrucken, FGR: Verlag Breitenbach, 1986. Scholarly monograph, in German; bibliography on Equatorial Guinea, pp. 217–218.

Liniger-Goumaz, Max. "No Change." *Index on Censorship* 16, no 4 (April 1987): 31–32. NGO article, in English.

Radda Barnen, International Commission of Jurists (Swedish Section). *UN Assistance for Human Rights.* Stockholm: 1988. NGO report, in English.

SOS Torture. *Equatorial Guinea: Arrests and Court Martials.* Geneva: 1988. NGO urgent action bulletin, in English and French.

Ethiopia

Amnesty International. *Ethiopia: "Disappearances"*. London: 1987. NGO report, in English.

——————. *Ethiopia: Political Imprisonment and Torture*. London: 1986. NGO report, in English.

Clay, Jason W. "Refugees Flee Ethiopian Collectivization." *Cultural Survival Quarterly* 10, no. 2 (1986): 80–85. Research report, in English.

Clay, J. W., and B. K. Holcomb. *Politics and the Ethiopian Famine 1984–1985*. Cambridge, MA: Cultural Survival, 1985. NGO report, in English; bibliography, pp. 247–250.

Clay, J. W., S. Steingraber, and P. Niggli. *The Spoils of Famine: Ethiopian Famine Policy and Peasant Agriculture*. Cambridge, MA: Cultural Survival, 1988. NGO report, in English.

Colchester, M., and V. Luling, eds. *Ethiopia's Bitter Medicine: Settling for Disaster: An Evaluation of the Ethiopian Government's Resettlement Programme*. London: Survival International, 1986. NGO report, in English.

Dqulos, Mikael. "Christians in Marxist Ethiopia." *Religion in Communist Lands* 14, no. 2 (Summer 1986): 134–147. Scholarly article, in English.

Eritrean People's Liberation Front. "Appeal to the Commission of Human Rights." *Adulis* 5, no. 3 (April 1988): 10. ARM article, in English.

Federation Internationale des Droits de l'Homme (International Federation of Human Rights). "Extrait du Rapport sur la Situation de 195 Refugies Politiques Delivres de la Prison de Mekele (Ethiopie)" (Extract of the Report on the Situation of 195 Political Refugees Released from the Prison at Mekele [Ethiopia]). *La Lettre de la FIDH* 170–171 (11 November 1986): 3–9. NGO article, in French.

Gesellschaft fur Bedrohte Volker (Association for Endangered Peoples). "Horn von Afrika: Nationalitatenkonflikte in Athiopien, Somalia, und Djibouti" (The Horn of Africa: Nationality Conflict in Ethiopia, Somalia, and Djibouti). *Pogrom* 127–128 (February 1987): 13–84. NGO article, in German.

——————. "Fragwurdige Methoden sur Bekamfpung der Hungersnot: Athiopien—Deportationer und Zwangsarbeitslager" (Questionable Methods of Fighting the Hunger Emergency: Ethiopia—Deportation and Forced Labor). *Pogrom* 25/85 (May 1985): 1–80. NGO article, in German.

Heinz, Wolfgang S. *Ursachen und Folgen von Menschenrechtsverletzungen in der Dritten Welt* (Causes and Consequences of Human Rights Violations in Third World Countries). Saarbrucken, FRG: Verlag Breitenbach, 1986. Scholarly monograph, in German; bibliography on Ethiopia, pp. 273–275.

Kibreab, Gaim. *Refugees and Development in Africa: The Case of Eritrea*. Trenton, NJ: Red Sea Press, 1987. Monograph, in English; bibliography, pp. 293–305.

Korn, David A. *Ethiopia: The United States and the Soviet Union*. Carbondale, IL: Southern Illinois University Press, 1986. Scholarly monograph, in English; bibliography, pp. 190–191.

Luling, Virginia. "Ethiopia: Resettlement, Villagisation and the Ethiopian Peoples." *IWGIA Newsletter* 47 (October 1986): 27–39. NGO article, in English.

Lyon, A., M. McColgan, C. Rostoker, and D. Malapel. "Torture and the Violation of Human Rights in Tigray, Ethiopia—Mission Report." *La Lettre de la FIDH* (February 1986). NGO special issue, mission report, in English.

Kessler, D., and T. Parfitt. *The Falashas: The Jews of Ethiopia*. London: Minority Rights Group, 1985. NGO report, in English.

Relief Society of Tigray. *Report on Interviews Conducted in Damazin Camp in the Blue Nile Province of Sudan with Tigrayan Refugees who have Escaped from Resettlement Camps in South-West Ethiopia*. Washington, D.C.: 1986. NGO report, in English.

Ruiz, Hiram A. *Beyond the Headlines: Refugees in the Horn of Africa*. Washington, D.C.: United States Committee for Refugees, 1988. NGO issue paper, in English; selective bibliography, p. 44.

Tiquet, Margaret. "Ethiopia: "Destroy the Muslims."" *Index on Censorship* 16, no. 4 (April 1987): 33–34. NGO article, in English.

U.S. House of Representatives, Subcommittee on Africa and Subcommittee on Human Rights and International Organizations. *Human Rights and Food in Ethiopia*. Washington, D.C.: GPO, 1985. Government hearings, in English.

U.S. House of Representatives, Subcommittee on Human Rights and International Organizations, Subcommittee on International Economic Policy and Trade, and Subcommittee on Africa. *Human Rights in Ethiopia*. Washington, D.C.: GPO, 1988. Government hearings, in English.

White, Peter. "A Little Humanity amid the Horrors of War." *National Geographic* 170, no. 5 (November 1986): 647–679. Magazine article, in English.

U.N. Commission on Human Rights. *Equatorial Guinea: Provision of Expert Assistance in the Field of Human Rights* . . . Prepared by Special Rapporteur Fernando Volio Jimenez. 16 January 1985. IGO report, in English and Spanish.

Zentrale Dokumentationsstelle der Freien Wohlfahrtspflege fur Fluchtling. *Arbeitsmaterialien fur den Unterricht: Die Weltfluchtlingsproblematik und ihre Auswirkungen in der Bundesrepublik Deutschland* (Study Materials: The World Refugee Problem and its Consequences in the Federal Republic of Germany). Bonn, FRG: 1987. NGO edited collection, in German.

Fiji

Amnesty International. *Fiji: Arrests under a New Internal Security Decree.* London: 1988. NGO report, in English.

──────────. *Fiji: Restrictions on Fundamental Rights.* London: 1987. NGO report, in English.

Scott-Murphy, J., D. Dunstan, and N. Khan. *Human Rights in Melanesia: The Report of the Evatt Foundation Delegation.* Sydney, Australia: H. V. Evatt Memorial Foundation, 1988. NGO report, in English.

Tinker, H., N. Duraiswamy, Y. Ghai, and M. Ennals. *Fiji.* London: Minority Rights Group, 1987. NGO report, in English.

Finland

Amnesty International. *Amnesty International Concerns in Western Europe March 1986—September 1986.* London: 1986. NGO report, in English.

──────────. *Conscientious Objection to Military Service.* London: 1988. NGO report, in English.

──────────. *Finland: Protection of Refugees.* London: 1987. NGO report, in English.

Beach, Hugh. *The Saami of Lapland.* London: Minority Rights Group, 1988. NGO report, in English; bibliography, p. 16.

Center for Women Policy Studies. "Responses to Wife Abuse in Four Western Countries." *Response* 8, no. 2 (Spring 1985): 15–18. NGO article, in English.

International Work Group for Indigenous Affairs. *Self-Determination and Indigenous Peoples: Sami Rights and Northern Perspectives.* Copenhagen: 1987. NGO conference proceedings, in English.

Korsmo, Fae L. "Nordic Security and the Saami Minority: Territorial Rights in Northern Fennoscandia." *Human Rights Quarterly* 10, no. 4 (November 1988): 509–524. Scholarly article, in English.

France

Amnesty International. *Amnesty International Concerns in Western Europe March 1986—September 1986.* London: 1986. NGO report, in English.

──────────. *Amnesty International Concerns in Western Europe October 1986—March 1987.* London: 1987. NGO report, in English.

──────────. *Conscientious Objection to Military Service.* London: 1988. NGO report, in English.

──────────. "France (New Caledonia): Statement to the United Nations Special Committee on Decolonization," August 1988. NGO statement, in English.

──────────. "Statement on New Caledonia to the UN Special Committee on Decolonization," 14 August 1987. NGO statement, in English.

Baudelot, Yves. *Situation des 101 Mailens Expules de France* (The Situation of 101 Malians Expelled from France). *Lettre de la FIDH* 73 (December 1986): 1–8. NGO mission report, in English.

Freedom of Information and Expression in France. London: Article 19, 1989. NGO report, in English.

Ligue des Droits de l'Homme (League for Human Rights). "Une Declaration sur la Situation en Nouvelle Caledonie" (A Declaration on the Situation in New Caledonia). Paris: 1987. NGO statement, in French.

Mastny, Vojtech. *Helsinki, Human Rights and European Security.* Durham, NC: Duke University Press, 1986. Scholarly monograph, in English.

Ruzie, Davie. "Klaus Barbie and the French Legal Process." *Patterns of Prejudice* 20, no. 3 (July 1986): 27–33. NGO article, in English.

Texier, Philippe. "1987: 'The Year of the Judges' in France?" *CIJL Bulletin* 21 (April 1988): 19–22. NGO article, in English.

Tubiana, Michel. "Droit d'Asile en Europe, des Principes a la Reality" (The Right to Asylum in Europe, from the Principles to the Reality). *Homme et Liberte* 47 (May–June 1987): 15–21. NGO article, in French.

"Visa Clampdown," *West Africa,* 1 December 1986. News article, in English.

French Guiana

Federation Internationale des Droits de L'Homme (International Federation of Human Rights). "Texte du communique de Press." *Lettre de la FIDH* 194 (April 1987): 2. NGO press release, in French.

Federal Republic of Germany

Amnesty International. *Amnesty International Concerns in Western Europe October 1986—March 1987.* London: 1987. NGO report, in English.

──────────. *Conscientious Objection to Military Service.* London: 1988. NGO report, in English.

——————. *West Berlin: The Anti-IMF/World Bank Protests of September 1988*. London: 1989. NGO report, in English.

Bergmann, Warner. "Public Beliefs about Anti-Jewish Attitudes in West Germany: A Case of Pluralistic Ignorance." *Patterns of Prejudice* 22, no. 3 (Autumn 1988): 15–21. Scholarly article, in English.

Burgerrechte und Polizei (Civil Liberties and Police). Berlin, FRG: Civil Liberties and Police, 1986. Collection of NGO articles, in German.

Kaldor, Pierre. "Political Blacklisting in West Germany: The Verdict of the ILO." *International Review of Contemporary Law* 1988-1 (1988): 79–88. NGO article, in English.

Internationale Gesellschaft fur Menschenrechte (International Society for Human Rights). *Ist die Versammlungsfreiheit in der Bundesrepublik Deutschland Noch Gewahrleistet?* (Is Freedom of Assembly Still Guaranteed in the Federal Republic of Germany?). Frankfurt, FRG: 1987. NGO report, in German.

Komitee fur Grundrechte und Demokratie (Committee for Basic Rights and Democracy). *Auswirkungen des Auslanderrechts auf die Situation der Migrantinen, Inbesondere Turkischer Frauen* (Consequences of Laws concerning Aliens on the Situation of Migrants, Especially Turkish Women). Senbachstal, FRG: 1987. NGO report, in German.

——————. *Der Prozess: Justiz in der Bundesrepublik Deutschland. Am Beispiel Peter-Jurgen Boock, 1983–84 at Stuttgard-Stammheim* (The Trial of Justice in the Federal Republic of Germany. A Case Study of Peter-Jurgen Boock, 1983–84, at Stuttgart-Stammheim). Sensbachtal, FRG: 1985. NGO report, in German.

——————. *Frauenhauser: Bestandaufnahme* (Women's Shelters: A Stocktaking). Sensbachtal, FRG: 1987. NGO report, in German.

——————. *Gewalt Verhaltnisse* (Circumstances of Sexual Abuse). Sensbachtal, FRG: 1987. NGO report, in German.

——————. *Jahrbuch '86* (Yearbook '86). Sensbachtal, FRG: 1987. NGO edited collection, in German.

Samson, Klaus. *Federal Republic of Germany: Political Discrimination in Public Employment—Findings of an ILO Inquiry*. Scholarly study, in English.

Schnapp, F. E. "Individual Rights under German Constitutional Law: A First Glance at the Basic Law of the Federal Republic of Germany." *Saint Louis University Press Law Forum* 5 (1986): 113–124. Journal article, in English.

Sigler, Jay A., ed. *International Handbook on Race and Race Relations*. 1st ed. Westport, CT: Greenwood Press, 1987. Scholarly edited collection, in English; bibliography, pp. 449–454.

Tubiana, Michel. "Droit d'Asile en Europe, des Principes a la Realitie" (The Right to Asylum in Europe, from the Principles to the Reality). *Homme et Liberte* 47 (May–June 1987): 15–21. NGO article, in English.

Wallraff, Gunter. "Lowest of the Low: The Turkish Worker in West Germany." *Race and Class* 28, no. 2 (August 1986): 45–58. Journal article, in English.

Zentrale Dokumentationsstelle der Freien Wohlfahrtspflege fur Fluchtlinge. *Arbeitsmaterialien fur den Unterricht: Die Weltfluchtlingsproblematik und ihre Auswirkungen in der Bundesrepublik Deutschland* (Study Materials: The World Refugee Problem and its Consequences in the Federal Republic of Germany). Bonn, FRG: 1987. NGO edited collection, in German.

Gabon

Agbabiaka, Tunde. "Gabon: 25 Years After," *West Africa*, 9 September 1985. News article, in English.

"Gabon: Opponents Granted Clemency," *West Africa*, 30 June 1986. News article, in English.

German Democratic Republic

Amnesty International. *Conscientious Objection to Military Service*. London: 1988. NGO report, in English.

——————. "GDR Announces Amnesty and Abolishes Death Penalty," 24 July 1987. NGO press release, in English.

——————. *German Democratic Republic: Recent Developments*. London: 1988. NGO report, in English.

——————. *The Imprisonment of Persons Seeking to Leave a Country or to Return to their own Country*. London: 1986. NGO report, in English.

Boyse, Matthew. "East German Lutheran Synod Calls for Human Rights Improvements." *Radio Free Europe Research* 10, no. 4 (October 1985): 1–5. Government report, in English.

——————. "The GDR and Third World Refugees to Western Europe." *Radio Free Europe Research* 10, no. 38 (September 1985: 1–5. Government report, in English.

Buchholz, Erich. "Abolition of the Death Penalty in the GDR." *GDR Committee for Human Rights Bulletin* 13, no. 2/87 (1987): 140–146. NGO article, in English.

Commission on Security and Cooperation in Europe. *Basket I—Implementation of the Final Act of the Conference on Security and Cooperation in Europe: Findings Eleven Years after Helsinki*. Washington, D.C.: GPO, 1987. Government report, in English.

Church in Distress Charity/Aid to Eastern Priests. *Kirche I Not: Kirche, Nation, Frieden* (Church in Distress: Church, Nation, Peace). Konigstein, FRG: 1985. Edited collection of past conference proceedings, in German.

Donovan, Barbara. "East German Leaders Continue to Crack Down on the Church." *Radio Free Europe Research* 13, no. 42 (October 1988): 1–3. NGO report, in English; bibliography, p. 3.

————. "Emigration and Dissent in the GDR." *Radio Free Europe Research* 13 no. 7 (February 1988): 1–3. NGO article, in English.

Internationale Gesellschaft fur Menschenrechte (International Society for Human Rights). *CSCE and Human Rights: Divided Families and the Denial of Freedom of Movement (Documentation)*. Frankfurt, FRG: 1987. NGO document collection, in English.

————. *Menschenrechte in der DDR und Ost-Berlin* (Human Rights in the GDR and East Berlin). Frankfurt, FRG: 1986. NGO report, in German.

Klippenstein, Lawrence. "Exercising a Free Conscience: The Conscientious Objectors of the Soviet Union and the German Democratic Republic." *Religion in Communist Lands* 13, no. 3 (Winter, 1985): 282–291. Scholarly article, in English.

Kusin, Vladimir V. "Overview of Dissent in Eastern Europe." *Radio Free Europe Research* (December 1987): 1–5. NGO report, in English.

Poppe, Ulrike. "Menschenrechtsdiskussion in der DDR: Neue Wege?" (Discussion of Human Rights in the GDR: New Directions?). *Grenzfall* 11/12 (December 1987): 14–15. NGO article, in German.

Radio Free Europe/Radio Liberty. "Eastern Europe in 1988." *Radio Free Europe Research* 13, no. 52 (December 1988): 1–53. Government background paper, in English.

Ramet, Pedro. "East Germany: Strategies of Church-State Coexistence." *Religion in Communist-Dominated Areas* 24, no. 2 (Spring 1985): 37–41. NGO article, in English.

U.S. Helsinki Watch Committee. *From Below: Independent Peace and Environmental Movements in Eastern Europe and the USSR*. New York: 1987. NGO report, in English.

————. "East Germany." In *Ten Years Later: Violation of the Helsinki Accords*, 31–53. York: 1985. NGO report, in English.

————. *Violations of the Helsinki Accords: East Germany*. New York: 1986. NGO report, in English.

Ghana

Amnesty International. *The Death Penalty in Ghana*. London: 1985. NGO report, in English.

Blay-Amihere, Kabral. "Ghana's *Free Press.*" *Index on Censorship* 16, no. 1 (January 1987): 21–22. NGO article, in English.

Flinterman, Cees. "The Administration of Justice in Ghana." *CIJL Bulletin* 15 (April 1985): 26–41. NGO article, in English.

"Ghana: Ben Ephson Still Held," *West Africa*, 18 January 1988. News article, in English.

"Ghana: Women in Distress," *West Africa*, 2 September 1986. News article, in English.

Graft-Johnson, K.E.de. *Measures Taken in Ghana to Ensure the Effective Exercise of Human Rights for Disadvantaged Social Groups*. Paper presented at International Experts Meeting on Ways and Means to Ensure Effective Exercise of Human Rights by Disadvantaged Groups, Quebec, Canada, 29 November 1985 Conference paper, in English.

Head, Ivan L. "International Standards of Civil Procedure: The Aliens in the Courts of Ghana." *St. Louis University Law Journal* 12, no. 3 (Spring 1986): 392–417. Scholarly article, in English.

Greece

Amnesty International. *Amnesty International Concerns in Western Europe—October 1986–March 1987*. London: 1987. NGO report, in English.

————. *Conscientious Objection to Military Service*. London: 1988. NGO report, in English.

————. *Greece: Conscientious Objection*. London: 1988. NGO report, in English.

————. "Greek CO's End Second Hunger Strike," 4 July 1988. NGO press release, in English.

Pollis, Adamantia. "The State, the Law and Human Rights in Modern Greece." *Human Rights Quarterly* 9, no. 4 (November 1987): 587–614. Scholarly article, in English.

Grenada

Committee for Human Rights in Granada. *Newsletter of the Committee for Human Rights in Grenada*. NGO bi-annual newsletter, in English.

Ramshaw, P., and Steers T. *Intervention on Trial: The New York War Crimes Tribunal on Central America and the Caribbean*. New York: Praeger Publishers and National Lawyers Guild, 1987. Scholarly study, in English.

Sandford, Gregory. *The New Jewel Movement: Granada's Revolution, 1979–1983*. Washington, D.C.: U.S.

Department of State, Foreign Service Institute, 1985. Government monograph, in English.

Thompson, Robert. *Green Gold: Bananas and Dependency in the Eastern Caribbean.* London: Latin American Bureau, 1987. NGO monograph, in English.

Guatemala

American Association for the Advancement of Science. *Guatemala: Case Reports 1980–1985.* Washington, D.C.: 1986. NGO report, in English.

American Association for the International Commission of Jurists. *Guatemala: A New Beginning.* New York: 1987. NGO report, in English.

Americas Watch Committee. *Civil Patrols in Guatemala.* New York: 1986. NGO report, in English.

————. *Guatemala Revised: How the Reagan Administration Finds "Improvements" in Human Rights in Guatemala.* New York: 1985. NGO report, in English.

————. *Guatemala: The Group for Mutual Support, 1984–1985.* Washington, D.C.: 1985. NGO report, in English.

————. *Human Rights in Guatemala: During Cerezo's First Year.* New York: 1987. NGO report, in English.

Amnesty International. *Guatemala: The Human Rights Record.* London: 1987. NGO report, in English.

Asociacion Centroamericana de Familiares de Detenidos-Desaparecidos (Central American Association of Families of the Detained and Disappeared). *La Practica de la Desaparicion Forzada de Personas en Guatemala* (The Practice of Forced Disappearance of Persons in guatemala). San Jose, Costa Rica: 1988. NGO report, in Spanish; bibliography (annotated by key words), pp. 297–304.

Ciencia y Tecnologia para Guatemala (Science and Technology for Guatemala). *Tortura y Legalidad en Guatemala* (Torture and Legality in Guatemala). Mexico City, Mexico: 1986. NGO monograph, in Spanish.

Comision de Derechos Humanos de Guatemala (Guatemala Human Rights Commission). *El Nino Guatemalteco en la Coyuntura Actual* (Guatemalan Children in the Current Coyuntura Actual). Mexico City, Mexico: 1986. NGO report, in Spanish.

————. *Regarding the Status of Human Rights for the Indigenous Population of Guatemala.* Geneva: 1985. NGO bulletin, in English.

Comision para la Defensa de los Derechos Humanos (Commission for the Defense of Human Rights). *Informe sobre la Situacion de la Derechos Humanos en Centro-america, 1986* (Report on the Human Rights Situation in Central American, 1986). San Jose, Costa Rica: 1987. NGO monograph, in English.

Comite Pro-Justicia y Paz de Guatemala (Justice and Peace Committee of Guatemala). *Human rights in Guatemala.* Mexico City, Mexico: 1987. NGO report, in English.

Guatemala Human Rights Commission (USA). *Report on the Situation of Human Rights in Guatemala.* Washington, D.C.: 1986. NGO report, in English.

Heinz, Wolfgang S. *Ursachen und Folgen von Menschenrechtsverletzungen in der Dritten Welt* (Causes and Consequences of Human Rights Violations in Third World Countries). Saarbrucken, FRG: Verlag Breitenbach, 1986. Scholarly monograph, in German; bibliography on Guatemala, pp. 529–530.

Inter-Church Committee on Human Rights in Latin America. *1986 Annual Report on the Human Rights Situation in Guatemala.* Toronto, Canada: 1987. NGO report, in English.

————. *1987 Annual Report on the Human Rights Situation in Guatemala.* Toronto: 1987. NGO report, in English.

International Human Rights Law Group and Washington Office on Latin America. *Political Transition and the Rule of Law in Guatemala.* Washington, D.C.: 1988. NGO mission report, in English.

Krueger, C., and K. Enge. *Security and Development Conditions in the Guatemalan Highlands.* Washington, D.C.: Washington Office on Latin America, 1985. NGO mission report, in English; bibliography, p.68.

Manz, Beatriz. *Refugees of a Hidden War: The Aftermath of Counterinsurgency in Guatemala.* Albany, NY: State University of New York Press, 1988. Scholarly monograph, in English.

Minnesota Lawyers International Human Rights Committee. *Expectations Denied: Habeas Corpus and the Search for Guatemala's Disappeared.* Minneapolis, MN: 1988. NGO report, in English.

Organization of American States. *Annual Report of the Inter-American Commission on Human Rights 1986–1987.* Washington, D.C.: 1987. IGO annual report, in English.

Painter, John. *Guatemala: False Hope, False Freedom.* London: Latin America Bureau and Catholic Institute for International Relations, 1987. NGO monograph, in English.

Rouquette, R., A. Garapon, and A. Breton. *Guatemala: Sur la Situation Generale et Notamment Celle des Droits de l'Homme* (Guatemala: The General Situation and Current Status of Human Rights). Paris: Federation Internationale des Droits de l'Homme, 1985. NGO mission report, in French.

Simon, Jean-Marie. *Guatemala: Eternal Spring—Eternal Tyranny.* New York: W. W. Norton, 1987. Monograph, in English.

U.N. Commission on Human Rights. *Report on the Situation of Human Rights in Guatemala.* Prepared by Special Rapporteur Viscount Colville of Culross. 13 February 1986. IGO document, in English.

————. *Report . . . on the Situation of Human Rights in Guatamala.* Prepared by Special Rapporteur Viscount Colville of Culross, E/Cn.4/1987/24. 5 December 1986. IGO document, in English.

Guinea

Amnesty International. *A Summary of Amnesty International's Concerns in the Republic of Guinea.* London: 1986. NGO report, in English.

Freedom of Information and Expression in Guinea. London: Article 19, 1989. NGO report, in English.

"Guinea: Conte Falters on Reforms." *Africa News* 29, no. 3 (8 February 1988): 4. NGO article, in English.

Ligue Francaise pour la Defense des Droits de l'Homme et du Citoyen (French League for the Defense of Human Rights and the Citizen). "Un Communique de la Ligue des Droits de l'Homme sur les Declarations Recentes des Dirigeants Guineens" (Communique of the League for the Defense of Human Rights on the Recent Declarations of the Guinean Authorities), 24 July 1985. NGO press release, in French.

Radda Barnen, International Commission of Jurists (Swedish Section). *UN Assistance for Human Rights.* Stockholm: 1988. NGO report, in English.

"Toxic Terrorism," *West Africa,* 20 June 1988. News article, in English.

Guinea Bissau

Amnesty International. "Guinea Bissau: Death Penalty," 14 July 1986. NGO urgent action bulletin, in English.

"Toxic Terrorism," *West Africa,* 20 June 1988. News article, in English.

Guyana

Americas Watch Committee and Parliamentary Human Rights Group. *Political Freedom in Guyana.* New York: 1985. NGO mission report, in English.

Amnesty International. "Death Penalty: Guyana," 1 July 1986. NGO urgent action bulletin, in English.

Guyana Human Rights Association. *Brief on Police Violence.* Georgetown, Guyana: 1988. NGO report, in English.

————. *Guyana Human Rights Report 1988.* Georgetown, Guyana: 1988. NGO annual report, in English.

Guyanese Council for Democracy. "Another Electoral Fraud: Burnham Style?," 2 November 1985. NGO press release, in English.

Latin America Documentation. "Guyana: Attacks on Church Leaders Prompt Caribbean Protest." *LADOC* 16, no. 6 (July-August 1986): 38–39. NGO article, in English.

SOS: Human Rights for Guyana. "Changes in Guyana are Cosmetic, Says Tennasee." *SOS Guyana* 7 (Fall 1986): 1, 3–4. NGO article, in English.

————. "Government Ruthless Says Observer Team." *SOS Guyana* 2 (July 1985): 1, 5. NGO article on mission report, in English.

Haiti

American Friends Service Committee. *Haiti: Background to the Elections, January 17, 1988.* Philadelphia, PA: 1988. NGO report, in English.

Americas Watch Committee and National Coalition for Haitian Refugees. *Haiti: Terror and the 1987 Elections.* New York: 1987. NGO mission report, in English.

Amnesty International. *Haiti: Deaths in Detention, Torture and Inhuman Prison Conditions.* London: 1987. NGO report, in English.

Bajeaux, J.C., J.M. Garcia Laguardia, C.J. Gutierrez, and C. Urcuyo Fournier. *Elecciones y Proceso de Democratizacion en Haiti* (Elections and Democratization in Haiti). San Jose, Costa Rica: Instituto Interamericano de Derechos Humanos, Centro de Asesoria y Promocion Electoral/Inter-American Institute of Human Rights, and Center for Electoral Counseling and Promotion, 1986. IGO monograph, in Spanish.

Catholic Institute for International Relations. *Comment: Haiti.* London: 1988. NGO background paper, in English.

Centre Haitien de Defense des Libertes Publiques (Haitian Center for the Defense of Public Liberties). *Expose sur la Situation Generale et les Droits de l'Homme, 1er Janvier 1987–30 Juin 1987* (Report on the General Situation and Human Rights, January 1–June 30, 1987). Port-au-Prince, Haiti: 1987. NGO report, in French.

Chamberlain, G., and M.S. Hooper. "Haiti: Plus Ca Change." *NACLA Report on the Americas* 21, no. 3 (May–June 1987): 14–39. NGO article, in English.

Comite Haitiano-Venezolano de Defensa de los Derechos Humanos (Haitian-Venezuela Committee for the Defense of Human Rights). "Mujeres de Haiti" (Haitian Women). *Bambu, Voz de la Libertad* 9 (January–March 1985). NGO special issue, in Spanish.

Conference des Eglises de la Caraibe (Caribbean Conference of Churches). *Rapport Officiel de la CEC: Portant sur une mission d'enquete et de bonne volonte en Haiti* (CEC Oficial Report: Concerning a Mission of Inquiry and Goodwill to Haiti). Barbados: 1987. NGO mission report, in French.

Federation Internationale des Droits de l'Homme (International Federation of Human Rights). *Rapport de Mission: Haiti* (Mission Report: Haiti). Paris, 1987. NGO mission report, in French.

Inter-American Commission on Human Rights. *Report on the Situation of Human Rights in Haiti.* Washington, D.C.: 1988. IGO report, in English.

Latin American Bureau. *Haiti: Family Business.* London: 1985. Monograph, in English; bibliography, pp. 83–84.

Ligue des Anciens Prisonniers Politiqes Haitiens, des Amis et Parents des Disparus (League of Former Political Prisoners, Friends and Relatives of the Disappeared). "Droits de l'homme 1987." *Le Militant* 4 (January 1988): 2–5. NGO article, in French.

National Coalition for Haitian Refugees and Americas Watch Committee. *Duvalierism since Duvalier.* New York: 1986. NGO report, in English.

————. *Haiti 1987 Election Watch.* New York: 1987. NGO document collection, in English.

Organization of American States *Annual Report of the Inter-American Commission on Human Rights 1986–1987.* Washington, D.C.: 1987. IGO annual report, in English.

————. *Informe Anual de la Comision Interamericana de Derechos Humanos 1985–1986* (Annual Report of the Inter-American Commission on Human Rights 1985–1986). Washington, D.C.: 1986. IGO annual report, in Spanish.

Plant, Roger. *Sugar and Modern Slavery: A Tale of Two Countries.* London: Zed Press, 1987. Scholarly monograph, in English.

U.S. Congress, Subcommittee on Human Rights and International Organizations. *Human rights in Haiti: Hearings before the . . . 99th Congress, First Session.* Washington, D.C.: GPO, 1985. Government hearings, in English.

Washington Office on Haiti. *The Government of Haiti: Noncompliance with the Criteria for U.S. Foreign Assistance—Report to Congress.* Vol. 1 and 2. Washington, D.C.: 1985. NGO report, in English.

————. *Haiti: Barriers to Justice and Democracy.* Washington, D.C.: 1986. NGO mission report, in English.

Honduras

Altrows, L., and D. Racicot. *CCIC Observer Mission to El Salvador and Honduras, April 21–May 14, 1985.* Ottawa, Canada: Canadian Council for International Co-operation, 1985. NGO mission report, in English.

Americas Watch Committee. *Human Rights in Honduras: Central America's "Sideshow."* New York: 1987. NGO report, in English.

————. *The Sumus in Nicaragua and Honduras: An Endangered People.* New York: 1987. NGO report, in English.

Amnesty International. *Honduras: Civilian Authority Military Power: Human Rights Violations in the 1980s.* London: 1988. NGO report, in English.

Asociacion Centroamericana de Familiares de Detenidos-Desaparecidos (Central American Association of Families of the Detained-Disappeared). *Honduras Desaparecidos, Juicio v Condena* (Honduras: Disappearances, Trial and Sentence). San Jose, Costa Rica: 1989. NGO report, in Spanish.

Centro de Documentacion de Honduras (Honduras Documentation Center). *Balance Semestral de la Situacion de los Derechos Humanos en Honduras* (Human Rights Situation in Honduras: Semi-Annual Report). Tegucigalpa, Honduras: 1985. NGO bulletin, in Spanish.

————. *Honduras: Realidad Nacional y Crisis Regional* (Honduras: National Reality and Regional Crisis). Tegucigalpa, Honduras: 1986. NGO edited collection/conference proceedings, in Spanish.

————. *La Contra in Honduras* (The Contras in Honduras). Tegucigalpa, Honduras: 1987. NGO report, in Spanish.

————. *La Tortura en Honduras* (Torture in Honduras). Tegucigalpa: 1987. NGO report, in Spanish.

Comision para la Defensa de los Derechos Humanos (Commission for the Defense of Human Rights). *Informe sobre la Situacion de los Derechos Humanos en Centro-america, 1986* (Report on the Human Rights Situation in Central America). San Jose, Costa Rica: 1987. NGO monograph, in Spanish.

Comite para la Defensa de los Derechos Humanos en Honduras (Committee to Defend Human Rights in Honduras). *Human Rights in Honduras.* Somerville, MA: Honduras Information Center, 1988. NGO report, in English.

————. *Situacion de Derechos Humanos en Honduras: Informe Anual* (Human Rights Situation in Honduras: Annual Report). Tegucigalpa, Honduras: 1986. NGO report, in Spanish.

—————. *The Situation of Human Rights in Honduras 1987.* Somerville, MA: Honduras Information Center, 1988. NGO report, in English.

Corte Interamerica de Derechos Humanos (Inter-American Court of Human Rights). *Corte Interamericana de Derechos Humanos: Caso Godinez Cruz, Sentencia del 20 de Enero de 1989* (Inter-American Court of Human rights: Godinez Cruz Case, January 20, 1989, Decision). San Jose, Costa Rica, 1989. IGO document, in Spanish.

Federation Internationale de Droits de l'Homme (International Federation of Human Rights). *Rapport de Mission: Honduras, 1 au 10 Fevrier, 1986* (Mission Report: Honduras, 1–10 February 1986). Paris: 1986. NGO mission report (special issue of *La Lettre de FIDH* 66), in French.

Honduras Information Center. "The Human Rights Situation in Honduras, 1986." *Honduras Update* 1 (May 1987). NGO report in special issue, in English.

Instituto de Investigaciones Socio-Economicas de Honduras (Honduran Institute for Socio-Economic research). *Honduras: Fuerzas Armadas 1988, Contrainurgencia Interna y Disuasion Regional* (Honduras: Armed Forces 1988, Internal Counterinsurgency and Regional Dissuasion). Mexico City, Mexico: 1988. NGO report, in Spanish.

Inter-Church Committee on Human Rights in Latin America. *ICCHRLA 1987 Annual Report: General Concerns and Brief Country Reports.* Toronto, Canada: 1988. NGO report, in English.

Meza, V., M. Benjamin, and P. L. Shepherd. "The War Comes Home." *NACLA Report on the Americas* (January-February 1988): 13–40. NGO article, in English.

Organization of American States. *Informe Anual de la Corte Interamericana de Derechos Humanos* (Annual Report of the Inter-American Court of Human Rights). Washington, D.C.: 1988. IGO annual report, in Spanish.

Peckenham, N., and A. Street, eds. *Honduras: Portrait of a Captive Nation.* New York: Praeger Publishers, 1985. Edited collection, in English.

Rosenberg, M.B., and P. L. Shepherd, eds. *Honduras Confronts its Future.* Boulder CO: Lynne Rienner Publishers, 1986. Document collection, in English.

Tillet, Rebecca. *Investigacion sobre el Habeas Corpus en la Corte Suprema de Justicia Honduras, C A, 1980–1985* (Investigation of Habeas Corpus Practice and Procedure in the Honduran Supreme Court, 1980–1985). Tegucigalpa, Honduras: Comite para la Defensa de los Derechos Humanos en Honduras, 1986. NGO report, in Spanish.

Hong Kong

Amnesty International. *Hong Kong: Memorandum on the Draft Basic Law of the Hong Kong Special Administrative Region.* London: 1988. NGO report, in English.

Cerquone, J., and V. Hamilton, eds. *Uncertain Harbors: The Plight of Vietnamese Boat People.* Washington, D.C.: U.S. Committee for Refugees, 1987. NGO issue paper, in English.

Hong Kong Christian Council. "Basic Law and Religious Freedom." *News and Views* (April 1987): 3–22. NGO article, in English.

—————. "Emigration Hits Hong Kong." *News and Views* (December 1987): 3–19. NGO article, in English.

Morgan, S. M., and E. Colson, eds. *People in Upheaval.* Staten Island, NY: Center for Migration Studies of New York, 1987. NGO document collection, in English.

Society for Community Organization. *Growth of People's Power.* Hong Kong: 1987. NGO report, in English and Chinese.

World Press Freedom Committee. *Report of World Press Freedom Committee Delegation to Hong Kong and Singapore.* Washington, D.C.: 1987. NGO mission report, in English.

Worssam, Richard. "A Refugee's Home is his Prison." *News and Views* (July 1987): 17–18. NGO article, in English.

Hungary

Bency, Gyorgy. *Censored and Alternative Modes of Cultural Expression in Hungary.* New York: U.S. Helsinki Watch Committee, 1985. NGO report, in English.

Commission on Security and Cooperation in Europe. *Basket I—Implementation of the Final Act of the Conference on Security and Cooperation in Europe: Findings Eleven Years after Helsinki.* Washington, D.C.: GPO, 1987. Government report, in English.

"Eastern Europe in 1988." *Radio Free Europe Research* 13, no. 52 (30 December 1988). Government backgroup paper, in special issue, in English.

Fleischman, Janet. *Violations of the Helsinki Accords: Hungary.* New York: U.S. Helsinki Watch Committee, 1986. NGO report, in English.

Fox, John P. "The Situation of the Hungarian Catholic Church." *Religion in communist-Dominated Areas* 24, no. 3 (Summer 1985): 84–85. NGO article, in English.

Markos, Edith. "Restrictions on Foreign Travel to be Eased." *Radio Free Europe Research* 12, no. 48 (28 November 1987): 47–51. NGO article, in English.

————. "The Government Promises the Church More Religious Freedom." *Radio Free Europe Research* 13, no. 38 (23 September 198): 13–17. NGO report, in English; bibliography, p. 17.

"Social and Economic Rights in the Soviet Bloc." *Survey: A Journal of East and West Studies* 29, no. 4 (August 1987). NGO special issue, in English.

U.S. Helsinki Watch Committee. *From Below: Independent Peace and Environmental Movements in Eastern Europe and the USSR.* New York: 1987. NGO report, in English.

————. "Hungary." In *Ten Years Later: Violation of the Helsinki Accords,* 55–68. New York: 1985. NGO report, in English.

India

Agarwal, A., J. Merrifield, and R. Tandon. *No Place to Run: Local Realities and Global Issues of the Bhopal Disaster.* New Market, TN: Highlander Research and Education Center and Society for Participatory Research in Asia, 1985. NGO report, in English.

Amnesty International. *India: Allegations of Extrajudicial Killings by the Provincial Armed Constabulary in and around Meerut, 22–23 May 1987.* London: 1987. NGO report, in English.

————. *The Need to Review Cases against 324 Sikhs Held for More Than Four Years in Jodhpur Jail, Rajasthan.* London: 1988. NGO issue paper, in English.

Andreassen, B.A., and A. Eide, eds. *Human Rights in Developing Countries 1987/88: A Yearbook on Human Rights in Countries Receiving Nordic Aid.* Copenhagen: Christian Michelsen Institute, 1988. NGO report, in English; bibliography, pp. 357–372.

Bhargava, Ashok. "The Bhopal Incident and Union Carbide: Ramifications of an Industrial Accident." *Bulletin of Concerned Asian Scholars* 18, no. 4 (October–December 1986): 2–19. NGO article, in English.

Bhopal: Industrial Genocide? A Unique Compilation of Documents from Indian Publications. Hong Kong: Asian Regional Exchange for New Alternatives, 1985. Edited collection, in English.

Cultural Survival. "Mountain Peoples." *Cultural Survival Quarterly* 10, no. 3 (1986). Edited collection, in special issue, in English.

Donnelly, J., and R. E. Howard, eds. *International Handbook on Human Rights.* Westport, CN: Greenwood Press, 1987. Scholarly edited collection, in English.

Guttal, G. H. "Human Rights: The Indian Law." *Indian Journal of International Law* 26, no. 1 and 2 (January-June 1986): 53–71. Scholarly article, in English.

"Inde: Pays Riche, Peuple Pauvre." *Bulletin CRIDEV* 53 (November 1985). NGO special issue bulletin, in French.

International Commission of Jurists. *The Independence of Judges and Lawyers in South Asia.* Geneva: 1988. NGO conference report, in English.

————. "India: Situation in the State of Punjab." *The Review* 36 (June 1986): 7–12. NGO article, in English.

International Work Group for Indigenous Affairs. *The Naga Nation and its Struggle against Genocide.* Copenhagen: 1986. NGO report, in English.

Joshi, Barbara R., ed. *Untouchable! Voices of the Dalit Liberation Movement.* London: Minority Rights Group, 1986. Edited collection, in English.

Kothari, Smithu. "Ecology vs. Survival: The Struggle for Survival in India." In *The International Context of Rural Poverty in the Third World: Issues for Research and Action by Grassroots Organizations and Legal Activists,* 203–224. Center for Law in Development, 1986. NGO monograph, in English.

Liddle, J., and R. Joshi. *Daughters of Independence: Gender, Caste, and Class in India.* London: Zed Books, 1986. Scholarly monograph, in English.

"The Politics of Human Rights." *Lokayan Bulletin* 5, no. 4/5 (1987). Collection of scholarly articles in special issue, in English.

Reddy, O. Chinnappa. "Human Rights Movement in India." *Socio-Legal Concern Newsletter* 2, no. 6 (June 1986): 2–10. NGO article, in English.

————. *The Indian Legal System and Human Rights.* Madras, India: Centre for Socio-Legal Research and Documentation Service, 1987. Speech, in English.

"Safeguards to Human Rights under the Indian Constitution." *Socio-Legal Concern Newsletter* 4, no. 11 and 12 (November-December 1988): 8–23. NGO article, in English.

Sangari, K., and S. Said. "Sati in Modern India: A Report." *Economic and Political Weekly* (1 August 1981): 1284–1288. Journal article, in English.

Sigler, Jay A., ed. *International Handbook on Race and Race Relations.* Westport, CN: Greenwood Press, 1987. Scholarly edited collection, in English; bibliography, pp. 449–454.

Singh, R., B. Joshi, and S. Singh, ed. *The Turning Point—India's Future Direction?* Syracuse, NY: 1985. Edited collection, in English.

U.S. Committee for Refugees. *From Isolation to Exile: Refugees from the Chittagong Hill Tracts of Bangladesh.* Washington, D.C.: 1988. NGO report, in English.

Vigil India Movement. "Cultural Rights vs. Human Rights." *Vigil India* 44 (February 1988). NGO bulletin special issue, in English.

Indonesia

Amnesty International. *East Timor Violations of Human Rights: Extrajudicial Executions, "Disappearances," Torture and Political Imprisonment.* London: 1985. NGO report, in English.

————. *Indonesia: The Appliation of the Death Penalty.* London: 1987. NGO report, in English.

Asia Watch. *Testimony by the Asia Watch Committee before the U.S. Trade Representative concerning Labor Rights in Indonesia.* Washington, D.C.: 1987. NGO statement, in English.

Association de Solidarite avec Timor Oriental (Association in Solidarity with East Timor). *Timor Informations* no. 41–42 (March-April 1988). NGO articles in special issue, in French.

Bizot, Jack. *The Forgotten Cause: East Timor's Right to Self-Determination.* London: Parliamentary Human Rights Group, 1988. NGO report, in English.

Canada-Asia Working Group. "Human Rights in Asia: Submission Prepared for the 44th Session of the United Nations Commission on Human Rights." *Currents* 10, no. 1 (February 1988): 1–55. NGO report, in English.

Catholic Institute for International Relations. *East Timor: A Christian Reflection.* London: 1987. NGO statement, in English and French.

Eldridge, Philip. *Aid, Basic Needs and the Politics of Reform in Indonesia.* Clayton, Australia: Monash University, Centre of Southeast Asian Studies, 1980. Scholarly monograph, in English.

Federation Internationale des Droits de l'Homme (International Federation of Human Rights). *Indonesie: Dossier sur la Situation des Droits de l'Homme* (Indonesia: Dossier on the Human Rights Situation). Paris: 1987. NGO report, in French.

Heinz, Wolfgang S. *Ursachen und Folgen von Menschenrechtsverletzungen in der Dritten Welt* (Causes and Consequences of Human Rights Violations in Third World Countries). Saarbrucken, FRG: Verlag Breitenbach, 1986. Scholarly monograph, in German; bibliography on Indonesia, pp. 400–402.

Hiorth, F. *Timor Past and Present.* Townsville, Australia: James Cook University of North Queensland, Centre for Southeast Asian Studies, 1985. Scholarly monograph, in English.

Human Rights Council of Australia. *Irian Jaya and Human Rights: A Working Group Report.* Canberra, Australia: 1986. NGO report, in English.

Human Rights in South and Southeast Asia. Papers presented at the State University of New York at Buffalo, NY 25–26 May 1988. Conference proceedings, in English.

Indonesian Documentation and Information Centre. *Indonesian Workers and their Right to Organise: Developments 1987–88.* Leiden, Netherlands: 1988. NGO report, in English.

Lev, Daniel S. *Legal Aid in Indonesia.* (Department of Political Science, University of Washington, Seattle, WA 98195). Unpublished scholarly paper, in English.

Meagher, J. Patrick. *Reflections on the Human Rights Situation in Indonesia.* Jakarta: Institute for Development Studies, 1987. Research paper, in English.

Morgan, S., and E. Colson, ed. *People in Upheaval.* Staten Island, NY: Center for Migration Studies of New York, 1987. NGO document collection, in English.

Nietschmann, Bernard. "Economic Development by Invasion of Indigenous Nations: Cases of Indonesia and Bangladesh." *Cultural Survival Quarterly* 10, no. 2 (1986): 2–12. NGO article, in English.

Otten, Mariel. *Transmigrasi: Myths and Realities—Indonesian Resettlement Policy, 1965–1985.* Copenhagen: International Work Group for Indigenous Affairs, 1986. NGO monograph, in English.

Ramos-Horta, J. *Funu: The Unfinished Saga of East Timor.* Trenton, NJ: Red Sea Press, 1987. Scholarly monograph, in English.

Sasono, Adi. "The Role of NGOs in Promoting Human Rights: Some Notes on Indonesian Experiences." *Human Rights Forum* 1, no. 1 (1985): 15–18. NGO article, in English.

TAPOL, British Campaign for the Defence of Political Prisoners and Human Rights in Indonesia. *Indonesia: Muslims on Trial.* London: 1987. NGO report, in English.

Taswell, Ruth, ed. *Southeast Asian Tribal Groups and Ethnic Minorities.* Cambridge, MA: Cultural Survival, 1987. NGO conference proceedings, in English.

Thoolen, Hans, ed. *Indonesia and the Rule of Law: Twenty Years of "New Order" Government.* London: Frances Pinter Publishers for the International Commission of Jurists and the Netherlands Institute of Human Rights, 1987. Scholarly monograph, in English.

Witjes, Ben. *The Indonesian Law on Social Organizations.* (Nijmegen, Netherlands). Unpublished research paper, in English.

Iran

Amnesty International. *Evidence of Torture in Iran.* London: 1984. NGO report, in English.

————. *Iran: Persistent Violations of Human Rights.* London: 1988. NGO report, in English.

—————. *Religious Intolerance.* London: 1986. NGO report, in English.

Bakhas, Shaul. *The Reign of the Ayatollahs.* New York: Basic Books, 1984. Scholarly monograph, in English.

Bashiriyeh, Hossein. *The State and Revolution in Iran.* New York: St. Martin's Press, 1984. Scholarly monograph, in English.

Benard, C., and Z. Khalilzad. *"The Government of God:" Iran's Islamic Republic.* New York: Columbia University Press, 1984. Scholarly monograph, in English.

Elahi, Maryam. "The Rights of the Child under Islamic Law: Prohibition of the Child Soldier." *Columbia Human Rights Law Review* 19, no. 2 (Spring 1988): 259–279. Scholarly article, in English.

Federation Internationale des Droits de l'Homme (International Federation of Human Rights). "Le Martyr du Peuple Kurde" (The Martyrdom of the Kurdish People). *Lettre de la FIDH* 241 (22 March 1988). NGo newsletter, in French.

Femmes sous Lois Musulmanes (Women Living under Muslim Laws). *Dossier No. 1.* Montpellier, France: 1986. NGO document collection, in French and English.

International Gesellschaft fur Menschenrechte (International Society for Human Rights). *Menschenrechte in der Islamischen Republik Iran* (Human Rights in the Islamic Republic of Iran). Frankfurt, FRG: 1987. NGO report, in German.

McDowall, David. *The Kurds.* Rev. ed. London: 1985. NGO report, in English; bibliography, p. 31.

Meron, Theodor. "Iran's Challenge to the International Law of Human Rights." *Human rights Internet* 13, no. 1 (Spring 1989). NGO article, in English.

Parliamentary Human Rights Group. *The Abuse of Human Rights in Iran.* London: 1986. NGO report, in English.

U.N. Commission on Human Rights. *Report of the Human Rights Situation in the Islamic Republic of Iran.* . . . Prepared by Special Rapporteur Reynaldo Galindo Pohl, E/CN.4/1987/23. 28 January 1987. IGO report, in English.

U.N. Security Council. *Report of the Mission Dispatched by the Secretary-General on the Situation of Prisoners of War in the Islamic Republic of Iran and Iraq.* 24 August 1988. IGO mission report, in English.

Iraq

Amnesty International. "Amnesty International Calls on Iraqi Government to Investigate Reports of Security Forces' Use of Thallium Poisoning against Political Opponents," 13 January 1988. NGO press release, in English.

—————. *Amnesty International's Concerns in Iraq.* London: 1987. NGO statement, in English.

—————. *The Death Penalty in Iraq: Introduction and Background.* London: 1987. NGO background paper, in English.

—————. *Executions in Iraq.* London: 1988. NGO briefing paper, in English.

—————. "Iraqi Children Victims of Brutal Abuse by Security Forces, Amnesty International Charges," 28 February 1989. NGO press release, in English.

Arab Organization for Human Rights. *Report: Human Rights in the Arab World.* Cairo: 1987. NGO report, in Arabic and English.

Committee against Repression and for Democratic Rights in Iraq. "Chemical Weapons: UN Report Brands Iraq as a Violator of the 1925 Geneva Protocol," March 1986. NGO flier, in English.

—————. "Cyanide Massacre at Halabja." *Iraq Solidarity Voice* 19 (April 1988): 1–8. NGO article, in English.

—————. *Facts about Abu Graib, the Notorious Prison in Iraq.* London: 1987. NGO report, in English.

—————. *Saddam's Iraq: Revolution or Reaction?* 2d ed. London: Zed Books, 1989. NGO edited collection, in English.

Dudley, James. "Human Rights Practices in the Arab States: The Modern Impact of Shari'a Values." *Georgia Journal of International and Comparative Law* 12 (1982): 55–93. Scholarly article, in English.

Federation Internationale des Droits de l'Homme (International Federation of Human Rights). *The Human Rights Situation in Iraq.* Paris: 1986. NGO report, in French.

—————. "Le Martyr du Peuple Kurde" (The Martyrdom of the Kurdish People). *Lettre de la FIDH* 241 (22 March 1988). NGO newsletter, in French.

Freedom of Information and Expression in Iraq: A Commentary by Article 19 on the Report Submitted to the United Nations Committee by the Government of Iraq. London: Article 19, 1987. NGO report, in English.

Isis-Women's International Cross-Cultural Exchange. "Iraq: Detained and Disappeared Women." *Women's World* 14 (June 1987): 24. NGO article, in English.

"Kurdistan: A Homeland Besieged." *Toward Freedom: Report on Non-Alignment in the Developing Countries* 37, no.5 (October-November 1988): 57, 60. NGO news article, in English.

McDowall, David. *The Kurds.* 4th rev. ed. London: Minority Rights Group, 1985. NGO report, in English; bibliography, p. 31.

Physicians for Human Rights. *Winds of Death: Iraq's Use of Poison Gas against its Kurdish Population.* Somerville, MA: 1989. NGO report, in English.

Research Group for Middle East and Mediterranean Affairs. "Four Nations Oppress the Kurds." *Memo: Middle East and Mediterranean Outlook* 37 (February 1987): 2. NGO article, in English.

Ireland

Fitzgerald, Eithne. "Irish Women Today." *America* 158, no. 10 (12 March 1988): 266–268. NGO article, in English.

Robbins, T., and R. Robertson, eds. *Church-State Relations: Tensions and Transitions.* New Brunswick, NJ: Transaction Books, 1987. Scholarly edited collection, in English.

Israel and Occupied Territories

Amnesty International. *Conscientious Objection to Military Service.* London: 1988. NGO report, in English.

——————. *Excessive Force: Beatings to Maintain Law and Order.* London: 1988. NGO report, in English.

——————. *Israel and the Occupied Territories: Prisoner Cases—September 1987 to February 1988.* London: 1988. NGO report, in English.

Aronson, Geoffrey. *Creating Facts: Israel, Palestinians and the West Bank.* Washington, D.C.: Institute for Palestine Studies, 1987. Scholarly monograph, in English.

Ashmore, Robert B. "Palestinian Universities under Israeli Occupation—A Human Rights Analysis." *American-Arab Affairs* 16 (Spring 1986): 79–92. NGO journal article and mission report, in English.

Association for Civil Rights in Israel. *The Legal and Administrative System.* Jerusalem: 1985. NGO monograph, in English.

Averick, Sara M. *A Human Rights Comparison: Israel Versus the Arab States.* Washington, D.C.: American Israel Public Affairs Committee, 1988. Political report, in English.

Beinin, Joel. "From Land Day to Equality Day." *MERIP Middle East Report* 150 (January-February 1988): 24–27. NGO article, in English.

Berliner, Marilyn J. "Palestinian Arab Self-Determination and Israeli Settlements on the West Bank: An Analysis of Their Legality Under International Law." *Loyola of Los Angeles International and Comparative Law Journal* 8, no. 3 (1985–1986): 551–52. Scholarly article, in English.

Blanchard, Francis. *Report on the Situation of Workers of the Occupied Arab Territories.* Vol. 2. Geneva: ILO, 1988. IGO report, in English.

Cohen, Esther Rosalind. *Human Rights in the Israeli-Occupied Territories, 1967–1982.* Manchester, England: Manchester University Press, 1985. Scholarly monograph, in English.

Cossali, P., and C. Robson. *Stateless in Gaza.* London: Zed Books, 1986. Documentary, in English.

Database Project on Palestinian Human Rights. *Uprising Update: December 8, 1988—Human Rights at the End of Year One of the Palestinian Uprising.* Chicago, IL: 1988. NGO document collection, in English.

Dinstein, Yoram, ed. *Israel Yearbook on Human Rights.* Tel Aviv: Alpha Press, 1985. Scholarly yearbook, in English.

——————. *Israel Yearbook on Human Rights.* Tel Aviv: Alpha Press, 1986. Scholarly yearbook, in English.

Donnelly, J., and R. E. Howard, ed. *International Handbook on Human Rights.* Westport, CT: Greenwood Press, 1987. Scholarly edited collection, in English.

Falloon, Virgil. *Excessive Secrecy, Lack of Guidelines: A Report on Military Censorship in the West Bank.* Ramallah, Occupied Territories: Law in the Service of Man/Al-Haq, 1986. NGO report, in English.

Federation Internationale des Droits de l'Homme (International Federation of Human Rights). "Israel: Droits de l'Homme dans les Territoires Occupes" (Israel: Human Rights in the Occupied Territories). *La Lettre de la FIDH 169 (28 October 1986):* 5–11. NGO report, in French.

Hunt, Paul. *Justice? The Military Court System in the Israeli-Occupied Territories.* Ramallah, Occupied Territories: Law in the Service of Man/Al-Haq and Gaza Centre for Rights and the Law, 1987. NGO report, in English.

Institute for Palestine Studies. *United Nations Resolutions on Palestine and the Arab-Israeli Conflict.* Washington, D.C.: 1988. NGO document collection, in English.

International Standing Committee of Lawyers on the Question of Palestine and Peace in the Middle East and International Association of Democratic Lawyers. *Palestine and Law.* Brussels: 1988. NGO articles/fact-finding missions, in English and French *(Palestine et Droit)*.

Israeli League for Human and Civil Rights. *Report on the Violations of Human Rights in the Territories during the Uprising, 1988.* Tel Aviv: 1988. NGO report, in English.

Law in the Service of Man/Al-Haq. *Punishing a Nation: Human Rights Violations during the Palestinian Uprising, December 1987-December 1988*. Ramallah, Occupied Territories: 1988. NGO report, in English.

Physicians for Human Rights. *Casualties of Conflict: Medical Care and Human Rights in the West Bank and Gaza Strip*. Somerville, MA: 1988. NGO mission report, in English.

Playfair, Emma. *Administrative Detention in the Occupied West Bank*. Ramallah, Occupied Territories: Law in the Service of Man/Al-Haq, 1986. NGO study, in English.

——————. *Demolition and Sealing of Houses as a Punitive Measure in the Israeli-Occupied West Bank*. Ramallah, Occupied Territories: Law in the Service of Man/Al-Haq, 1987. NGO report, in English.

Pressberg, Gail. "The Uprising: Causes and Consequences." *Journal of Palestine Studies* 18, no. 3 (Spring 1988): 38–50. Scholarly article, in English.

Shahak, Israel. "A Summary of the System of Legal Apartheid which is in Force in the Occupied Territories." *Palestine Human Rights Newsletter* 6, no. 6 (November-December 1986): 9. NGO article, in English.

Shalev, Carmel. *The Price of Insurgency: Civil Rights in the Occupied Territories*. Jerusalem: West Bank Database Project, 1988. NGO report, in English.

Shehadeh, Raja. "Occupier's Law and the Uprising." *Journal of Palestine Studies* 18, no. 3 (Spring 1988): 24–37. Scholarly article, in English.

Vermund, S. H., S. G. Miller, and S. P. Cohen. *Health Status and Services in the West Bank and Gaza Strip—Report of "Cooperation for Development: A Community-Based Health Project."* New York: Institute for Middle East Peace and Development, 1985. NGO report, in English.

Vitullo, Anita. *Ansar 2: Detention, Humiliation, and Intimidation*. Chicago, IL: Palestine Human Rights Information Center and Human Rights Research and Education Foundation/Database Project, 1987. NGO report, in English.

Italy

Amnesty International. *Amnesty International Concerns in Western Europe: October 1986–March 1987*. London: 1987. NGO report, in English.

——————. *Conscientious Objection to Military Service*. London: 1988. NGO report, in English.

Cavallari, Vincenzo. "The Universal Declaration of Human Rights and the Italian System of Penal Protection." *Review of Contemporary Law* 15, no. 2 (1988): 53–56. Scholarly article, in English.

Zagrebelsky, Vladimiro. "Measures Taken in Italy to Ensure the Effective Exercise of Human Rights by Migrants and the Unemployed." Paper presented at the International Experts Meeting on Ways and Means to Ensure Effective Exercise of Human Rights by Disadvantaged Groups, Quebec, Canada, 14 November 1985. Unpublished conference paper, in English.

Ivory Coast

Amnesty International. *Cote D'Ivoire: Forcible Conscription of Trade Unionists*. London: 1988. NGO report, in English.

International Commission of Jurists. *Les Services Juridiques en Milieu Rural (Afrique de l'Ouest)* (Legal Services in Rural Areas [West Africa]). Geneva: 1987. NGO report, in French.

Kannyo, Edward. *Human Rights in Africa: Report of a Visit to Nigeria, Ghana, Ivory Coast, Senegal and Upper Volta*. New York: International League for Human Rights, 1981. NGO report, in English.

Jamaica

Amnesty International. *Jamaica: The Death Penalty*. London: 1989. NGO report, in English.

Chevigny, P., and L. Whitman. *Human Rights in Jamaica*. New York: Americas Watch Committee, 1986. NGO mission report, in English.

Daly, Denis. *Human Rights Situation in Jamaica and the Prospects for a CARICOM Human Rights Charter*. Georgetown, Guyana: Guyana Human Rights Association, 1986. NGO bulletin, in English.

Donnelly, J., and R. E. Howard, eds. *International Handbook on Human Rights*. Westport, CT: Greenwood Press, 1987. Scholarly edited collection, in English.

Organization of American States. *Annual Report of the Inter-American Commission on Human Rights 1986–87*. Washington, D.C.: 1987. IGO annual report, in English.

Thompson, Robert. *Green Gold: Bananas and Dependency in the Eastern Caribbean*. London: Latin American Bureau, 1987. NGO monograph, in English.

Japan

Ando, Isamu, SJ. "Human Rights in Japan." *Social and Pastoral Bulletin* 27 (15 October 1988): 7–11. NGO article, in English translated from Japanese.

Buraku Liberation Research Institute. *Discrimination against Buraku Today.* Osaka: 1986. NGO book, in English.

Canada-Asia Working Group. "Human Rights in Asia: Submission Prepared for the 45th Session of the U.N. Commission on Human Rights, Geneva, February 1989." *Currents* 11, no. 1 (February 1989). NGO report, in English.

——————. "Human Rights in Asia: Submission Prepared for the 44th Session of the U.N. Commission on Human Rights." *Currents* 10, no. 1 (February 1988). NGO report, in English.

Donnelly, J., and R. E. Howard, eds. *International Handbook on Human Rights.* Westport, CT: Greenwood Press, 1987. Scholarly edited collection, in English.

Good, Martha H. "Freedom of Expression in Comparative Perspective: Japan's Quiet Revolution." *Human Rights Quarterly* 7, no. 3 August 1985): 429–445. Scholarly article, in English.

Hsiung, James C. *Human Rights in East Asia: A Cultural Perspective.* New York: Pergamon Publishers, 1985. Scholarly edited collection, in English.

International Commission of Jurists. *Human Rights and Mental patients in Japan.* Geneva: 1985. NGO report, in English.

Iwasawa, Yuji. *Legal Treatment of Koreans in Japan: The Impact of International Human Rights Law on Japanese Law.* Washington, D.C.: International Human Rights Law Group, 1986. NGO mission report, in English.

Japan Civil Liberties Union. *Report Concerning Present Status of Human Rights in Japan.* Tokyo: 1988. NGO report, in English.

Kajimura, Hideki. "Confronting Japanese Racism: Toward a Korean Identity." *AMPO: Japan-Asia Quarterly Review* 20, no. 1 and 2 (1988): 35–41. NGO article, in English.

Pacific-Asia Resources Center. "Japan's Human Imports." *AMPO: Japan-Asia Quarterly Review* 19, no. 4 (1988): 2–37. NGO articles, in English.

Parker, K., and E. Jaudel. *Police Cell Detention in Japan: The Kaiyo Kangoku System.* Paris: Federation Internationale des Droits de l'Homme and Association of Humanitarian Lawyers, 1989. NGO mission report, in English and French.

Sigler, Jay A., ed. *International Handbook on Race and Race Relations.* Westport, CT: Greenwood Press, 1987. Scholarly edited collection, in English; bibliography, pp. 449–454.

Sjoberg, Katarina. "Japan: The Ainu—A Fourth World Population." *IWGIA Newsletter* 48 (December 1986): 42–66. NGO article, in English.

Wessels, D. *Advancing Human Rights: Japan, East Asia, and the World.* Tokyo: Institute of International Relations for Advanced Studies on Peace and Development in Asia, Sophia University, 1986. Scholarly research report, in English.

Jordan

Amnesty International. "Jordan: Detention without Trial," 30 November 1988. NGO urgent action bulletin, in English.

——————. "Jordan: Fear of Ill-Treatment," 14 December 1988. NGO urgent action bulletin, in English.

Arab Organization for Human Rights. "Jordan: AOHR Receives a Reply from the Jordanian Minister of Information." *AOHR Newsletter* 18–19 (December 1988): 8. NGO article, in English and Arabic.

——————. "Jordan: Political Prisoners Complain." *AOHR Newsletter* 7–8 (May 1987). NGO article, in English and Arabic.

——————. *Human Rights in the Arab World.* Cairo: 1987. NGO report, in English and Arabic.

Goldstein, Eric. "Jordan's King Ends Crackdown, but Press Freedom Still Elusive." *CPJ Update* 25 (August–September 1986): 3. NGO article, in English.

Kenya

Amnesty International. *Human Rights in Kenya—An Update.* London: 1988. NGO report, in English.

——————. *Kenya: Torture, Political Detention and Unfair Trial.* London: 1987. NGO report, in English.

Andreassen, B. A., and A. Eide, eds. "Kenya." *Human Rights in Developing Countries 1987/88: A Yearbook on Human Rights in Countries Receiving Nordic Aid,* 40–69. Copenhagen: Akademisk Forlag, 1988. NGO report, in English: bibliography, pp. 358–360.

Hilsum, Lindsey. "The Dynamics of Discontent." *Africa Report* 33, no. 1 (January 1988): 22–26. NGO article, in English.

International Commission of Jurists. "Kenya." *ICJ Review* 39 (December 1987): 12–15. NGO article, in English.

Jutterstrom, Christina. "Country Reports: Kenya." *IPI Report* 35, no. 7 (July 1986): 17–18. NGO article, in English.

Kirschner, R. H., and K. Hannibal. *Kenya: Medicolegal Aspects of the Inquests into the Death of Peter Njenga Karanja.* New York: American Association for the Advancement of Science, Committee on Scientific Freedom and Responsibility, and Physicians for Human Rights, 1988. NGO report, in English.

Mazrui, Ali A. "Human Rights in Kenya." *African Journal of International Law* 1, no. 1 (Summer 1988): 92–98. Scholarly article, in English.

McLean S., and S. E. Graham, ed. *Female Circumcision, Excision and Infibulation: The Facts and Proposals for Change.* 2d rev. ed. London: Minority Rights Group, 1985. NGO report, in English; bibliography.

Norwegian Human Rights Project, Christian Michelsen Institute. *Human Rights in Developing Countries 1986.* Oslo: Universitetsforlaget, 1986. Government annual report, in English; bibliography, classified by country.

Ringera, A. G. "Kenya: A Review of Human Rights during the Period May 1982 to April 1985." Unpublished conference paper, in English.

Tomasevski, Katarina. "Case Study of Kenya." *Foreign Aid and Human Rights* (1988): 70–142. NGO report, in English.

Wamwere, Koigi wa. *Conscience on Trial.* Trenton, NJ: Africa World Press, 1988. NGO report, in English.

Korea, North

Asia Watch. *1987 Annual Report.* Washington, D.C.: 1987. NGO annual report, in English.

Canada-Asia Working Group. "Report of the Canadian Council of Churches Delegation to the Democratic Republic of Korea, 4–13 November 1988." *Currents* 10, no. 4 (December 1988). NGO mission report, in English; bibliography.

Korea, South

Amnesty International. *Political Imprisonment in the Republic of Korea.* London: 1987. NGO report, in English.

——————. *South Korea: Human Rights Developments, January–March 1988.* London: 1988. NGO report, in English.

——————. *South Korea Violations of Human Rights.* London: 1986. NGO mission report, in English.

Asia Watch. *Assessing Reform in South Korea.* Washington, D.C.: 1988. NGO mission report, in English.

——————. *A Stern, Steady Crackdown: Legal Process and Human Rights in South Korea.* New York: 1987. NGO report, in English.

Canada-Asia Working Group. "Human Rights in Asia, Submission Prepared for the 45th Session of the United Nations Commission on Human Rights, Geneva, February 1989." *Currents* 11, no. 1 (February 1989). NGO report, in English.

——————. *"Human Rights in Asia, Submission to the 43d Session of the United Nations Commission on Human Rights."* Currents (1987). NGO report, in English.

Hsiung, James C. *Human Rights in East Asia: A Cultural Perspective.* New York: Pergamon Publishers, 1985. Scholarly edited collection, in English.

International Human Rights Law Group. *The 1987 Korean Presidential Election.* Washington, D.C.: 1988. NGO mission report, in English.

——————. *To the Precipice and Beyond: A Review of Political Developments in the Republic of Korea, January 1986–July 1987.* Washington, D.C.: 1987. NGO report, in English.

International Labor Movement Institute, *How the Mass Media are Controlled in South Korea—Pre-Censorship by "Instructions to the Press."* Tokyo: 1986. NGO report, in English.

International League for Human Rights. *Human Rights in the Republic of Korea: Trade Unions and Workers Rights.* New York: 1987. NGO report, in English.

Joint Christian Committee of the National Coalition for Democracy. *Election Watch: A Documentation of Cases of Election Fraud.* Seoul: 1987. NGO election observer report, in English.

North American Coalition for Human Rights in Korea. "Election Watch." *Korea/Update* 85 (December 1987): 3–55. NGO report, in English.

——————. *Labor Rights Violations in the Republic of Korea.* Washington, D.C.: 1985. NGO report, in English.

——————. "Peace and the Reunification of Korea." *Korea/Update* (1987). NGO report in special issue, in English.

Oxman, S. A., O. Triffterer, and F. B. Cruz. *South Korea: Human Rights in the Emerging Politics—Report on an ICJ Mission from 25 March to 12 April 1987.* Geneva: International Commission of Jurists, 1987. NGO mission report, in English.

Physicians for Human Rights. *The Use of Tear Gas in the Republic of Korea: A Report by Health Professionals.* Somerville, MA: 1987. NGO mission report, in English.

U. S. House of Representatives, Subcommittee on Human Rights and International Organizations and Subcommittee on Asian and Pacific Affairs. *Assessing the Prospects for Democratization in Korea.* Washington, D.C.: GPO, 1988. Government hearings, in English.

——————. *Political Developments and Human Rights in the Republic of Korea: Hearings and Markup,* 99th Congress, 2d Session. Washington, D.C.: 1986. Government hearings, in English.

Wessels, D. *Advancing Human Rights: Japan, East Asia, and the World.* Tokyo: Institute of International Relations for Advanced Studies on Peace and Development in Asia, Sophia University, 1986. Scholarly research report, in English.

West, J. M., and E. J. Baker. "The 1987 Constitutional Reform in South Korea: Electoral Process and Judicial Independence." *Harvard Human Rights Yearbook* 1 (1988): 135–177. Scholarly article, in English.

World Council of Church. *Behind the Mask: Human Rights in Asia and Latin America, an Inter-Regional Encounter.* Geneva: 1988. NGO report, in English.

Kuwait

Arab Organization for Human Rights. *Human Rights in the Arab World.* Cairo: 1987. NGO report, in English and Arabic.

Birks, J. S., and C. A. Sinclair. *Nature and Process of Labor Importing: The African in the Gulf States, Kuwait, Bahrain, Qatar, and the United Arab Emirates.* Geneva: ILO, 1978. IGO report, in English.

Centre d'Etudes et de Recherches sur l'Orient Chretien (Middle East Christian Research Center). "Kuwait: The Rights of Women." *Plus* 1, no. 1 (1985): 4–5. NGO article, in English.

Ismael, Jacqueline S. "The Conditions of Egyptian Labor in the Gulf: A Profile of Kuwait." *Arab Studies Quarterly* 8, no. 4 (Fall 1986): 390–403. Scholarly journal article, in English; bibliography, p. 403.

"Kuwait Imposes Censorship of the Press." *IPI Report* 7 (July 1986): 20. NGO report, in English.

Media Analysis Center. "Kuwait: Facing Terrorist Challenges and Internal Entanglements." *Contemporary Mideast Backgrounder* 246 (May 1988): 1–9. NGO report, in English.

Laos

Amnesty International. *Laos: Recent Information on "Re-education" in Attapeu Province.* London: 1988. NGO report, in English.

Cultural Survival. "Militarization and Indigenous Peoples: Part I—The Americas and the Pacific." *Cultural Survival Quarterly* 11, no. 3 (1987). NGO special issue, in English.

Morgan, S. M., and E. Colson, ed. *People in Upheaval.* Staten Island, NY: Center for Migration Studies of New York, 1987. NGO document collection, in English.

Lebanon

Amnesty International. *Arrests in Syria and Lebanon by Syrian Forces.* London: 1986. NGO report, in English.

——————. "Lebanon: Arrests by South Lebanon Army," 23 July 1987. NGO urgent action bulletin, in English.

Arab Organization for Human Rights. *Human Rights in the Arab World.* Cairo: 1987. NGO report, in English and Arabic.

Donnelly, J., and R. E. Howard, ed. *International Handbook on Human Rights.* Westport, CT: Greenwood Press, 1987. Scholarly edited collection, in English.

Haddad, William W. "International Opinion and the Second Israel War in Lebanon." *Arab Studies Quarterly* 7, no. 4 (Fall 1985): 102–110. Book review article, in English.

MacDowall, David. *Lebanon: A Conflict of Minorities.* London: Minority Rights Group, 1986. NGO report, in English.

"Occupation Watch: Lebanon/Palestinians." *Israel and Palestine Political Report* 115 (May–June 1985): 18–24. NGO article, in English.

Office of the United Nations Disaster Relief Coordinator (UNDRO). "Lebanon: Mission Assesses Relief Needs." *UNDRO News* (November–December 1985): 14–15. IGO article, in English.

Lesotho

Amoah, P.K.A. "The Independence of the Judiciary in Botswana, Lesotho and Swaziland." *CIJL Bulletin* 19–20 (April–October 1987): 16–32. NGO article, in English.

Cooper, Dave. "Unions in Botswana: Comparisons with Lesotho." *South African Labour Bulletin* 10, no. 8 (July–August 1985): 103–114. Journal article, in English.

Maope, K. A. *Human Rights in Botswana, Lesotho and Swaziland: A Survey of the BOLESWA Countries.* Roma, Lesotho: Institute of Southern African Studies, 1986. NGO report, in English.

Neff, Stephen C. "Human Rights in Africa: Thoughts on the African Charter on Human and Peoples' Rights in the Light of Case Law from Botswana, Lesotho, and Swaziland." *International and Comparative Law Quarterly* 33 (1984): 331–347. Scholarly article, in English.

——————. *Human Rights in Botswana, Lesotho and Swaziland: Implications of Adherence to International Human Rights Treaties.* Roma, Lesotho: Institute of Southern African Studies, 1986. Scholarly study, in English.

Okullu, H., A. Wako, and N. Koshy. *Report of the AAC-WCC Delegation to Lesotho.* Geneva: AAC-WCC, 1985. NGO report, in English.

Liberia

Committee to Protect Journalists. "Liberian Journalists Face Bleak Future." *CPJ Update* 20 (September–October 1985): 1–2. NGO article, in English.

Fund for Free Expression. *Best Friends: Violations of Human Rights in Liberia, America's Closest Ally in Africa.* New York: 1986. NGO mission report, in English.

Hayden, Thomas. *Report on Liberia: Human Rights Issues.* Washington, D.C.: Society of African Misions, 1985. NGO report, in English.

International Commission of Jurists. "Liberia." *ICJ Review* 36 (June 1986): 13–16. NGO article, in English.

Lawyers Committee for Human Rights. *Liberia: A Promise Betrayed, a Report on Human Rights.* New York: 1986. NGO report, in English.

"Liberia: 'Free and Fair' or Foul?," *West Africa,* 5 August 1985. News article, in English.

Liberia Research and Information Project. "Neither Free nor Fair: October 1985 Election Report." *Liberia Alert* (January 1986). NGO special issue, in English.

Liebenow, J. Gus. *Liberia: The Quest for Democracy.* Bloomington, IN: Indiana University Press, 1987. Scholarly monograph, in English.

Massing, Michael. "Threats Silence Liberia's Press." *CPJ Update* 24 (May–June 1986): 5. NGO article, in English.

Schneebaum, S. M., L. Garber, and J. Whalen. *Recent Developments in Liberia: The Need for Congressional Response.* Washington, D.C.: International Human Rights Law Group, 1986. NGO comment, in English.

Schneebaum, S. M., and J. Whalen. *Human Rights in Liberia: A Preliminary Report Based on Two Trial Observer Missions (February–March and May 1986).* Washington, D.C.: International Human Rights Law Group, 1986. NGO mission report, in English.

U. S. House of Representatives, Subcommittee on Human Rights and International Organizations and Subcommittee on Africa. *Liberia: Recent Developments and United States Foreign Policy,* 99th Cong., 2d sess. Washington, D.C.: GPO, 1986. Government hearings, in English.

Libya

African-American Institute. "The Press and Africa." *Africa Report* 32, no. 2 (March–April 1987). NGO special issue, in English.

Amnesty International. *Libya: Summary of Amnesty International's Prisoner Concerns in the Great Socialist People's Libyan Arab Jamahiriya.* London: 1987. NGO report, in English.

Arab Organization for Human Rights. "Libya: Assassination of Opponents Continue." *AOHR Newsletter* 12–13 (December 1987): 1. NGO article, in English.

Centre d'Etudes et de Recherches sur l'Orient Chretien (Middle East Christian Research Center). "Libya: Mass Expulsion of Foreign Workers." *Plus* 1, no. 1 (1985): 14, 22–23, 26. NGO article, in English.

Madagascar

Action des Chretiens pour l'Abolition de la Torture (Christian Action for the Abolition of Torture). "Madagascar: des Faits et des Rumeurs" (Madagascar: The Facts and the Rumors). *Courrier de l'ACAT* 70–71 (December 1986): 2–5. NGO article, in French.

Malawi

Amnesty International. *Malawi.* London: 1986. NGO report, in English.

————. "Malawi Imprisonment of Political Opponents," November 1986. NGO briefing paper, in English.

Gibbs, James. "Singing in the Dark Rain." *Index on Censorship* 17, no. 2 (February 1988): 18–22. NGO article, in English.

Malaysia

Aliran Kesedaran Negara. "Aliran is 10." *Aliran Monthly* 7, no. 7 (July–August 1987): 2–16. NGO article, in English.

————. "ISA Detentions: The Struggle Goes On." *Aliran Monthly* 7, no. 11 (November–December 1987): 2–8. NGO interview, in English.

————. "The 2M Today: The Muzzled Media." *Aliran Monthly* 8, no. 3 (1988): 2–14. NGO article, in English.

Amnesty International. *Malaysia: "Operation Lallang:" Detention without Trial under the Internal Security Act.* London: 1988. NGO report, in English.

————. *Southeast Asia: Human Rights Violations in Brunei, Indonesia, Malaysia, Philippines, Singapore and Thailand.* London: 1987. NGO report, in English.

Canada-Asia Working Group. "Human Rights in Asia, Submission Prepared for the 44th Session of the United Nations Commission on Human Rights." *Currents* 11, no. 1 (February 1988). NGO special issue, in English.

————. "Human Rights in Asia, Submission prepared for the 44th Session of the United Nations Commission on Human Rights." *Currents* 10, no. 1 (February 1988). NGO special issue, in English.

Consumers' Association of Penang. *Rape in Malaysia: The Victims and the Rapists—The Myths and the Realities*. Penang, Malaysia: 1988. NGO study, in English.

Duthie, Stephen. "Malaysia is Stiffening Press Restrictions." *Human Rights Forum* 12 (October–December 1987): 10–13. NGO article, in English.

Kirby, Justice. "Malaysia—the Judiciary and the Rule of Law." *ICJ Review* 41 (December 1988): 40–43. NGO article, in English.

Regional Council on Human Rights in Asia. *The Law and Practice of Preventive Detention in the ASEAN Region*. Manila, Philippines: 1988. NGO report, in English.

Robertson, Geoffrey. "Malaysia: Justice Hangs in the Balance." *CIJL Bulletin* 22 (October 1988): 8–12. NGO article, in English.

Sigler, Jay A., ed. *International Handbook on Race and Race Relations*. Westport, CT: Greenwood Press, 1987. Scholarly edited collection, in English; bibliography, pp. 449–454.

Taswell, Ruth, ed. *Southeast Asian Tribal Groups and Ethnic Minorities*. Cambridge, MA: Cultural Survival, 1987. NGO conference proceedings, in English.

U. S. House of Representatives, Subcommittee on Human Rights and International Organizations. *Recent Developments in Malaysia and Singapore, 1988*, 100th Cong., 2d sess. Washington, D.C.: GPO, 1988. Government hearings, in English.

Mali

Amnesty International. "Mali: Taoudenit Prison Closed," 7 November 1988. NGO urgent action bulletin, in English.

International Commission of Jurists. *Les Services Juridiques en Milieu Rural (Afrique de l'Ouest)* (Legal Services in Rural Areas [West Africa]). Geneva: 1987. NGO report, in French.

Women's International Network. "Female Circumcision: Genital and Sexual Mutilation." *WIN News* 14, no. 3 (Summer 1988): 24–27; 14, no. 4 (Autumn 1988): 21–26; 15, no. 1 (Winter 1989): 28–29. NGO edited collection, in English.

Malta

Amnesty International. *Amnesty International Concerns in Western Europe—October 1986–March 1987*. London: 1987. NGO report, in English.

——————. *Amnesty International Concerns in Western Europe—March 1986–September 1986*. London: 1986. NGO report, in English.

International Helsinki Federation for Human Rights. *Human Rights in Malta*. Vienna: 1985. NGO mission report, in English.

Mauritania

Federation Internationale des Droits de l'Homme (International Federation of Human Rights). "Mauritanie: La Mort de Tene Youssouf Gueye" (Mauritania: The Death of Tene Youssouf Gueye). *Lettre de la FIDH* 269 (3 October 1988): 3. NGO article, in French.

——————. "Mauritanie: Rapport sur l'Affaire des Baa'thistes" (Report on the Baa'th Affair). *Lettre de la FIDH* 270 (10 October 1988): 2–5. NGO article, in French.

——————. *Rapport de Mission: Mauritanie Avril–Decembre 1987* (Mission Report: Mauritania, April–December 1987). Paris: 1987. NGO mission report, in French.

Lawless, R., and L. Monahan, eds. *War and Refugees: The Western Sahara Conflict*. London: Refugee Studies Programme, Queen Elizabeth House, 1987. Scholarly edited collection, in English.

Mauritius

Ecumenical Coalition on Third World Tourism. *Third World People and Tourism: Approaches to a Dialogue*. Bangkok: 1986. NGO conference proceedings, in English.

Mexico

Academia Mexicana de Derechos Humanos (Mexican Academy of Human Rights). *Informe de Actividades de la Academia Mexicana de Derechos Humanos, A.C. Junio 1986–Junio 1987* (Report on the Activities of the Mexican Academy of Human Rights June 1986–June 1987). Mexico City: 1987. NGO report, in Spanish.

Alvarez Icaza, Jose. *Donde y Como se Reprimio la Prensa en Mexico: 1984–1986* (Repression of the Mexican Press: 1984–1986). Mexico City: 1987. Scholarly study, in Spanish.

Amnesty International. *Mexico: Exchange of Communications on Reported Violations of Human Rights in Huitzilan de Serdan, Puebla*. London: 1987. NGO report, in English.

——————. *Mexico: Exchange of Correspondence with the Mexican Government on Human Rights Violations in the States of Oaxaca and Chiapas*. London: 1987. NGO report, in English.

——————. *Mexico Human Rights in Rural Areas: Exchange of Documents with the Mexican Government on*

Human Rights Violations in Oaxaca and Chiapas. London: 1986. NGO mission report, in English.

—————. "Mexico: Peasant and Indian Victims of Abuses." *Amnesty International Newsletter* 16, no. 8 (June 1986): 8. NGO article, in English.

"Behind Bars: Repression and Protest in Chiapas." *The Other Side of Mexico* 4 (January–March 1988): 4, 6, 8. News article, in English.

Committee to Protect Journalists. "Drugs and Corruption Deadly Beat for Mexican Press." *CPJ Update* 27 (January–February 1987): 1, 5. NGO article, in English.

Cultural Survival. "Mountain Peoples." *Cultural Survival Quarterly* 10, no. 3 (1986). NGO special issue, in English.

Durand Aleantara, Carlos Humberto. *Minorias Nacionales y Derechos Humanos: El Caso de los Triques de Oaxaca, Mexico* (National Minorities and Human Rights: The Case of the Triquis of Oaxaca, Mexico). Chapingo, Mexico: Asociacion Americana de Juristas, 1987. NGO report, in Spanish.

Federation Internationale des Droits de l'Homme (International Federation of Human Rights). *Mexique: Situation des Droits de l'Homme* (Mexico: Human Rights Situation). Paris: 1985. NGO report, in French.

—————. *Rapport sur la Situation des Refugies du Guatemala au Mexique* (Report on the Status of Guatemalan Refugees in Mexico). Paris: 1985. NGO mission report, in French.

Ferris, Elizabeth G. *The Central American Refugees.* New York: Praeger Publishers, 1987. Scholarly study, in English.

Reding, Andrew. "Mexico at a Crossroads." *World Policy Journal* 5, no. 4 (Fall 1988): 615–650. Scholarly article, in English.

Stavenhagen, Rodolfo. "Mexico y los Derechos Humanos" (Mexico and Human Rights). *Justicia y Paz* 5, no. 1 (November 1988): 15–21. NGO article, in Spanish.

U.N. High Commission for Refugees. "Asylum in Mexico: A Proud Tradition." *Refugees* 34 (October 1986): 19–31. IGO magazine article, in English.

Morocco

Amnesty International. *Torture in Morocco.* New York: 1986. NGO report, in English.

Anti-Slavery Society. *Child Labour in Morocco's Carpet Industry.* London: 1978. NGO report, in English.

Arab Organization for Human Rights. *Human Rights in the Arab World.* Cairo: 1987. NGO report, in English or Arabic.

Bendourou, Omar. "The Exercise of Political Freedoms in Morocco." *ICJ Review* 40 (June 1988): 31–41. NGO article, in English.

Chaoui, Abdelkader. "Blindfold Justice." *Index on Censorship* 18, no. 1 (January 1989): 20–22. NGO article, in English.

Henderson, George. "How Morocco Treats its Dissidents." *Index on Censorship* 13, no. 6 (December 1984): 30–31. NGO article, in English.

Lawless, R., and L. Monahan, ed. *War and Refugees: The Western Sahara Conflict.* London: Refugee Studies Programme, Queen Elizabeth House, 1987. Scholarly edited collection, in English.

Lederman, N., and A. Weber. *Rapport de Mission: Maroc, Proces de Casablanca, Affaire de Baha'is* (Mission Report: Morocco, Trial of Baha'is in Casablanca) Paris: Federation International des Droits d l'Homme, 1984. NGO mission report, in French.

Minkowski, A., and C. Rostoker. *Rapport de Mission: La Situation des Grevistes de la Faim de Marrakech (28 Julliet–1 Aout)* (Mission Report: The Situation of the Hunger Strikers of Marrakech [July 28–August 1]). Paris: Federation Internationale des Droits de l'Homme, 1985. NGO mission report, in French.

Sivan, Emmanuel. "The Kabyls: An Oppressed Minority in North Africa." In *Case Studies on Human Rights and Fundamental Freedoms: A World Survey,* vol. 1, edited by W. A. Veenhoven, 261–279. The Hague: Martinus Nijhoff, 1975. Edited collection, in English.

Smith, Theresa K. "Human Rights and the Western Sahara War." *Association of Concerned Africa Scholars Bulletin* 23 (Spring 1988): 10–17. Scholarly article, in English.

Weber, Alain. "Morcco: L'Affaire des Baha'is du Maroc devant la Cour Supreme de Rabat" (Morocco: The Trial of Baha'is before the Supreme Court of Rabat) *Lettre de la FIDH* 225 (1 December 1987): 3–4. NGO article, in French.

Mozambique

Andreassen, B. A., and A. Eide, eds. "Mozambique." In *Human Rights in Developing Countries 1987/88: A Yearbook on Human Rights in Countries Receiving Nordic Aid,* 70–89. Copenhagen: Atademiskforlag, 1988. NGO report, in English; bibliography, pp. 350–361.

Berman, Nina. "Project Launched in Mozambique to Aid Children 'Instrumentalized' by War." *Action for Children* 3, no. 4 (1988): 1, 8. NGO article, in English.

Gersony, Robert. *Summary of Mozambican Refugee Accounts of Principally Conflict-Related Experience in*

Mozambique. Washington, D.C.: U.S. Department of State, 1988. Government report, in English.

Magaia, Lina. *Dumba Nengue: Run for your Life.* Trans. from Portuguese by Michael Wolfers. Trenton, NJ: Africa World Press, 1988. Report, in English.

Marshall, Judith. " 'What has Ruined our Lives Is the War': Voices from Nampula." *Southern Africa Report* 4, no. 2 (October 1988): 15–18. NGO article, in English.

Norwegian Human Rights Project, Christian Michelsen Institute. *Human Rights in Developing Countries 1986.* Oslo: Universitetsforlaget, 1986. Government annual report, in English; bibliography, classified by country.

Southern African Research and Documentation Centre. *Mozambique: The Victims of Apartheid.* Harare, Zimbabwe: 1987. NGO report, in English.

U.S. Committee for Refugees. *Refugees from Mozambique: Shattered Land, Fragile Asylum.* Washington, D.C.: 1986. NGO report, in English.

──────────. *World Refugee Survey—1987 Review.* Washington, D.C.: 1988. NGO special issue, in English; bibliography, pp. 81–84.

"War and Hunger: Mozambique, What Kind of War?," *Africa News,* 21 December 1987. News article, in English.

Myanmar

Amnesty International. *Burma: Extrajudicial Execution, Torture and Political Imprisonment of Members of the Shan and other Ethnic Minorities.* London: 1988. NGO report, in English.

──────────. *Burma: Extrajudicial Execution and Torture of Members of Ethnic Minorities.* London: 1988. NGO report, in English.

──────────. *Burma: The 18 September 1988 Military Takeover and its Aftermath.* London: 1988. NGO report, in English.

Gesellschaft fur Bedrohte Volker (Association for Endangered Peoples). *Pogrom: Zeitschrift fur Bedrohte Volker* (Pogrom: Journal for Endangered Peoples) 137 (December 1987). NGO article collection, in German.

International Work Group for Indigenous Affairs. *The Naga Nation and its Struggle against Genocide.* Copenhagen: 1986. NGO report, in English.

Szteinbok, Maria. "Burma 1988." *Human Rights Newsletter* (December 1988): 1–28. NGO report, in English.

Taswell, Ruth, ed. *Southeast Asian Tribal Groups and Ethnic Minorities.* Cambridge, MA: Cultural Survival, 1987. NGO conference proceedings, in English.

Walker, J. "Boy Soldiers in a Grown-up's War." *Child Workers in Asia* 3, no. 1 (January–March 1987): 1–2. NGO article, in English.

Namibia

Amnesty International. *Namibia: Torture and Ill-Treatment of Prisoners.* London: 1987. NGO report, in English.

──────────. *Statement by Amnesty International to the Ad Hoc Working Group of Experts on Southern Africa.* Geneva: 1985. NGO testimony, in English.

Boggio, Alice. "La Namibie ou le Rapt d'un Vaste Pays" (Namibia or the Rape of a Vast Country) *Courrier de l'ACAT* 85 (May 1988): 2–4. NGO article, in French.

Centre for the Independence of Judges and Lawyers. "Namibia: Economic Harassment Threatens Independence of Lawyers." *CIJL Bulletin* 15 (April 1985): 3–5. NGO article, in English.

Clearly, Sean. "The Utility of Bills of Rights in Culturally Heterogeneous Societies: A Preliminary Examination of the Namibia Model." *South Africa International* 16, no. 4 (April 1986): 175–190. Scholarly article, in English.

Cosslett, Christopher E. "International 'Illegality' and Anomalous Natural Resources Development: The Case of Namibia, 1966–1986." *Lesotho Law Journal* 3, no. 1 (1987): 223–258. Scholarly article, in English.

Fraenkel, P., P. Murray, and K. Stearman. *The Namibians.* 3d ed. London: Minority Rights Group, 1985. NGO study, in English; selective bibliography, p. 31.

Katjavivi, Peter H. *A History of Resistance in Namibia.* Paris: UNESCO, 1988. Scholarly monograph, in English.

Landis, Elizabeth S. "Namibia: A Transatlantic View." *South African Journal on Human Rights* 3 (November 1987): 347–366. Scholarly article, in English.

Lawyers' Committee for Civil Rights under Law. *South Africa 1987: Choking Internal Resistance.* Washington, D.C.: 1988. NGO annual report, in English.

McDougall, Gay J. "International Law, Human Rights, and Namibian Independence." *Human Rights Quarterly* 8, no. 3 (August 1986): 443–470. Scholarly article, in English.

──────────. *Statement Read to U.N. Fourth Committee Hearings on Namibia.* Washington, D.C.: Lawyers' Committee for Civil Rights under Law, 1986. NGO speech, in English.

Schoombee, Hannes. "An Important Human Rights Decision in Nambia: Katofa v. Administrator-General for SWA 1985 (4) SA 211 (SWA)." *South African Journal on Human Rights* 2, no. 1 (March 1986): 74–79. Scholarly article, in English.

TransAfrica Forum. "Namibia: Occupation, Apartheid and Quest for Freedom." *TransAfrica Issue Brief* 5, no. 3 (June–July 1986): 1–16. NGO article, in English; selective bibliography.

U.N. Commission on Human Rights. *Report of the AD Hoc Working Group of Experts . . . [to Investigate and Study, during the Period 1985–1986, the Policies and Practices which Violated Human Rights in South Africa and Namibia]*, E/CN.4/AC.22/1987/1. Geneva: 1987. IGO document, in English.

Nepal

Amnesty International. "Journalists Prosecuted." *Amnesty International Newsletter* 26, no. 5 (May 1987): 8. NGO news article, in English.

——————. *Nepal: A Pattern of Human Rights Violations.* London: 1987. NGO report, in English.

——————. *Religious Intolerance.* London: 1986. NGO report, in English.

"Child Labor in Nepal: The Facts behind the Himalayas." *Child Workers in Asia* 1, no. 1 (July–Sept. 1985): 3–5. NGO bulletin article, in English.

Index on Censorship. "Bannings and Arrests in Nepal," 18 December 1986. NGO briefing paper, in English.

International Commission of Jurists. *The Independence of Judges and Lawyers in South Asia.* Geneva: 1988. NGO conference report, in English.

Kumar, Ram Narayan. "Sentenced to Servitude: Continuing Repression in Nepal." *Inside Asia* 10 (Nov.–Dec. 1986): 50–52. Magazine article, in English.

Netherlands

Advies Commissie Mensenrechten (Dutch Human Rights and Foreign Policy Advisory Committee). *Development Cooperation and Human Rights.* The Hague: 1987. Government commission report, in English.

Breum, M., and A. Hendriks, eds. *AIDS and Human Rights: An International Perspective.* Copenhagen: Danish Center of Human Rights, 1988. Edited collection, in English.

Grunfeld, Fred. *Human Rights: The International Protection and Promotion of Human Rights and its Significance for British and Netherlands' Domestic Law.* Course offered at the Faculty of Law, University of Limburg, Netherlands, 1987–1988. Syllabus/university course outline, in English.

Heringa, Aalt Willem. "Recent Dutch Cases Invalidating Discriminatory Social Security Laws." *SIM Newsletter: Netherlands Quarterly of Human Rights* 6, no. 1 (1988): 19–26. NGO article, in English.

Pettman, Ralph. *Incitement to Racial Hatred: The International Experience.* Canberra, Australia: Human Rights Commission, 1982. Government monograph, in English.

Sigler, Jay A., ed. *International Handbook on Race and Race Relations.* Westport, CT: Greenwood Press, 1987. Scholarly edited collection, in English; bibliography, pp.449–454.

New Zealand

Center for Women Policy Studies. "Responses to Wife Abuse in Four Western Countries." *Response* 8, no. 2 (Spring 1985): 15–18. NGO article, in English.

Hucker, Bruce. "Immigration Bill Still Discriminates." *Accent* 1, no. 7 (December 1986): 24–25. News article, in English.

International Work Group for Indigenous Affairs. "Aoteraoa (New Zealand): The Struggle for Self-Determination." *IWGIA Newsletter* 50 (July 1987): 15–24. NGO article, in English.

"Justice and Waitangi." *Accent* 2, no.2 (March 1987): 6–22. News article, in English.

Sigler, Jay A., ed. *International Handbook on Race and Race Relations.* Westport, CT: Greenwood Press, 1987. Scholarly edited collection, in English; bibliography, pp. 449–454.

Stover, Sue. "Stumbling towards Aotearoa: Race Relations in New Zealand." *National Outlook* 8, no. 5 (June 1986): 11–13. Magazine article, in English.

Tarnopolsky, Walter S. "Race Relations Commissions in Canada, Australia, New Zealand, the United Kingdom and the United States." *Human Rights Law Journal* 6, parts 2–4 (1985): 145–178. Scholarly article, in English.

United Nations Commission on Human Rights. *Implementation of the Declaration on the Elimination of All Forms of Intolerance and of Discrimination based on Religion or Belief.* Prepared by Special Rapporteur Angelo Vidal d'Almeida Ribero, E/CN.4/1987/35. 1986. IGO document, in English.

Nicaragua

Americas Watch Committee. *Human Rights in Nicaragua 1986.* New York: 1987. NGO report, in English.

——————. *Human Rights in Nicaragua: August 1987 to August 1988.* New York: 1988. NGO report, in English.

——————. *Land Mines in El Salvador and Nicaragua: The Civilian Victims.* New York: 1986. NGO report, in English.

——————. *The Sumus in Nicaragua and Honduras: An Endangered People.* New York: 1987. NGO report, in English.

Andreassen, B. A., and A. Eide, eds. "Nicaragua." In *Human Rights in Developing Countries 1987/88: A Yearbook on Human Rights in Countries Receiving Nordic Aid.* Copenhagen: Christian Michelsen Institute, 1988. NGO report, in English; bibliography, pp. 357–372, classified by country.

Asociacion Nicaraguense Pro-Derechos Humanos (Nicaraguan Association for Human Rights). *Violation of Human Rights by the Government of Nicaragua.* San Jose, Costa Rica: 1987. NGO report, in English.

Bourgois, Philippe. "Nicaragua: The Miskitu Conflict on the Atlantic Coast." *IWGIA Newsletter* 49 (April 1987): 69–89. NGO article/conference paper, in English; bibliography, pp. 88–89.

Catholic Institute for International Relations. *Right to Survive: Human Rights in Nicaragua.* London: 1987. NGO study, in English.

Comision Nacional de Promocion y Proteccion de los Derechos Humanos (National Commission for the Promotion and Protection of Human Rights). *Derechos Humanos en Nicaragua* (Human Rights in Nicaragua). Managua: 1987. Government report in Spanish and English.

——————. *Discussion and Analysis of the Americas Watch Report, "Human Rights in Nicaragua, 1985–86."* Managua: 1986. Government report, in English.

Diskin, M., T. Bossert, S. Nahmad, and S. Varese. *Peace and Autonomy on the Atlantic Coast of Nicaragua.* Pittsburgh, PA: Latin American Studies Association, 1986. Scholarly study, in English.

Donnelly, J., and R. E. Howard. *International Handbook on Human Rights.* Westport, CT: Greenwood Press, 1987. Scholarly edited collection, in English.

Gallo, Jeanne. *Responding to the Rights of the Poor: Nicaragua, the Church and the U.S.* Boston, MA: Gritare, 1985. Monograph, in English.

International League for Human Rights. *Report on Human Rights Defenders in Nicaragua.* New York: 1986. NGO report, in English.

Medina Quiroga, Cecilia. *The Battle of Human Rights: Gross, Systematic Violations and the Inter-American System.* Dordrecht, the Netherlands: Martinus Nijhoff, 1988. Scholarly monograph, in English.

National Lawyers Guild. *Freedom of Expression in Nicaragua.* New York: 1986. NGO mission report, in English.

Organization of American States. *Inter-American Yearbook on Human Rights 1986.* Dordrecht, the Netherlands: Martinus Nijhoff, 1988. IGO annual report, in Spanish and English.

Payne, Douglas W. *The Democratic Mask.* New York: Freedom House, 1985. Monograph, in English.

Walker, Thomas W., ed. *Nicaragua: The First Five Years.* New York: Praeger Publishers, 1985. Edited collection, in English.

Washington Office on Latin America. *Nicaragua: Violations of the Laws of War by Both Sides, First Supplement, January-March 1986.* Washington, D.C.: 1986. NGO report, in English.

Niger

Hosken, Fran. "Women, Health and Development in East and West Africa: A Personal View." *WIN News* 9, no. 2 (April 1983): 1–12. NGO report, in English.

International Commission of Jurists. *Les Services Juridiques en Milieu Rural (Afrique de l'Ouest)* (Legal Services in Rural Areas [West Africa]). Geneva: 1987. NGO report, in French.

Nigeria

Africa-American Institute. "The Press and Africa." *Africa Report* 32, no. 2 (March–April 1987). NGO special issue, in English.

Aguda, T. *The Challenge of the Nigerian Nation: An Examination of its Legal Development, 1969–1985.* Lagos: Nigerian Institute of Advanced Legal Studies, 1985. Scholarly monograph, in English.

Amnesty International. *The Use of the Death Penalty in Nigeria.* London: 1985. NGO report, in English.

Chhangani, R. C. "Recent Development in the Extradition Law of Nigeria." *Indian Journal of International Law* 26, nos. 2–3 (July–December 1986): 483–500. Scholarly article, in English.

Civil Liberties Organisation. *Annual Report 1988: Violations of Human Rights in Nigeria.* Lagos: 1988. NGO report, in English.

——————. *Human Rights Conditions in Nigeria: Mid-Year Report* (November 1987–May 1988. Lagos: 1988. NGO report, in English.

——————. *Prison Study No. 1: A Preliminary Survey of Conditions of Inmates in the Prisons.* Lagos: 1988. NGO report, in English.

Femmes sous Lois Musulmanes (Women Living under Muslim Laws). *Dossier No. 1.* Montpellier, France: 1986. NGO document collection, in English.

Hayward, Fred M., ed. *Elections in Independent Africa.* Boulder, CO: Westview Press, 1987. Scholarly study, in English.

McLean S., and S. E. Graham, eds. *Female Circumcision, Excision and Infibulation: The Facts and Proposals for Change.* 2d rev. ed. London: Minority Rights Group, 1985. NGO report, in English.

"Nigeria: 25 Years, Part I." *West Africa,* 30 September 1985, 2019–2048; "Nigeria: 25 Years, Part II."

West Africa, 7 October 1985, 2089–2114. News article, in English.

Obadina, Tunde. "How Free is our Press?" *Index on Censorship* 17, no. 9 (October 1988): 31–34. NGO article, in English.

Obe, Ad'Obe. "Nigeria: Control of Human Rights." *West Africa,* 16 June 1986. News article, in English.

Women's International Network. "Female Circumcision: Genital and Sexual Mutilation." *WIN News* 14, no. 3 (Summer 1988): 24–27; 14 no. 4 (Autumn 1988): 21–26; 15, no. 1 (Winter 1989): 28–29. NGO edited collection, in English.

Norway

Amnesty International. *Amnesty International Concerns in Western Europe, March 1986–September 1986.* London: 1986. NGO report, in English.

——————. *Amnesty International Concerns in Western Europe, October 1986–March 1987.* London: 1987. NGO report, in English.

——————. *Conscientious Objection to Military Service.* London: 1988. NGO report, in English.

"Art on the Frontlines." *Africa News,* 7 December 1987. News article, in English.

Beach, Hugh. *The Saami of Lapland.* London: Minority Rights Group, 1988. NGO report, in English.

Breum, M., and A. Hendriks, eds. *AIDS and Human Rights: An International Perspective.* Copenhagen: Danish Center of Human Rights, 1988. Edited collection, in English.

Brostad, J., J. Dahl, A.Gray, H. C. Gullov, G. Henriksen, J. B. Jorgensen, and I. Kleivan, eds. *Native Power: The Quest for Autonomy and Nationhood of Indigenous Peoples.* Oslo: International Work Group for Indigenous Affairs and Universitetsforlaget, 1985. Scholarly edited collection, in English.

International Work Group for Indigenous Affairs. *Self-Determination and Indigenous Peoples: Sami Rights and Northern Perspectives.* Copenhagen: 1987. NGO conference proceedings, in English.

Isis International. "Legal Battle in Norway over Sextours to Thailand." *Women in Action* no. 88/2 (June 1988). NGO article, in English.

Korsmo, Fae L. "Nordic Security and the Saami Minority:' Terroritorial Rights in Northern Fennoscandia." *Human Rights Quarterly* 10, no. 4 (November 1988): 509–524. Scholarly article, in English.

Whitaker, Alan. "Radiation in Lappland." *Anti-Slavery Newsletter* 2, no. 7 (1986): 1. NGO article, in English.

Oman

Arab Organization for Human Rights. *Report: Human Rights in the Arab World.* Cairo: 1987. NGO report, in Arabic or English.

——————. "Sultanat of Oman: Torture and Ill-treatment." *AOHR Newsletter* 11 (August 1987): 4. NGO article, in English.

Pacific Islands

Clark, Roger S. *Free Association: A Critical View.* Paper presented to the Conference on the Future Political Status of the U.S. Virgin Islands, 26–27 February 1988, St. Thomas Campus, University of the Virgin Islands. Scholarly unpublished paper, in English.

——————. *Petition concerning the Trust Territory of the Pacific Islands: Presented to the United Nations Trusteeship Council.* New York: International League for Human Rights, 1987. Petition, in English.

Clark, R., and S. R. Roff. *Micronesia: The Problem of Palau.* Rev. ed. London: Minority Rights Group, 1987. NGO report, in English.

Cultural Survival. "Militarization and Indigenous Preoples: Part I - The Americas and the Pacific." *Cultural Survival Quarterly* 11, no. 3 (1987). NGO special issue, in English.

Fawcett, J. T., and B. V. Carino., eds. *Pacific Bridges: The New Migration from Asia and the Pacific Islands.* Staten Island, NY: Center for Migration Studies of New York, 1987. NGO document collection, in English.

International League for Human Rights. *Report of the International Observer Mission, Palau Referendum, December 1986.* New York: 1987. NGO mission report, in English.

Pakistan

Americas Watch, Asia Watch, U. S. Helsinki Watch, and Lawyers Committee for Human Rights. *Critique: Review of the Department of State's Country Reports on Human Rights Practices for 1985.* New York: 1986. NGO report, in English.

Amnesty International. *Children: The Youngest Victims.* London: 1987. NGO report, in English.

——————. *Pakistan: The Death Penalty.* London: 1988. NGO report, in English.

——————. *Pakistan: Political Prisoners Convicted in Unfair Trials during the Martial Law Period.* London: 1987. NGO statement, in English.

Andreassen, B. A., and A. Eide, eds. "Pakistan." In *Human Rights in Developing Countries 1987/88: A Yearbook on Human Rights in Countries Receiving*

Nordic Aid. Copenhagen: Christian Michelsen Institute, 1988. NGO report, in English; bibliography, pp. 357–372, classified by country.

Association Amitie Franco-Afghane (Franco-Afghan Friendship Association). "Les Refugies Afghans" (The Afghan Refugees). *Les Nouvelles d'Afghanistan* no. 35–36 (December 1987). NGO special issue, in French.

Federation Internationale des Droits de l'Homme (International Federation of Human Rights). *Rapport de Mission: Afghanistan, Sept./Oct./Nov. 1985: Enquete sur le Depeuplement du Pays* (Mission Report: Afghanistan . . .: Inquiry on Depopulation). *La Lettre de la FIDH* 64 (Winter 1985). NGO mission report, in French; bibliography of publications on human rights violations, situation of civilian populations, and the problems of refugees in Afghanistan (1976–1985), pp. 9–10.

Femmes sous Lois Musulmanes (Women Living under Muslim Laws). *Dossier No. 2* Montpellier, France: 1986. NGO document collection, in English.

Human Rights in South and Southeast Asia. Papers presented at the State University of New York at Buffalo, 25–26 May 1988. Conference proceedings, in English.

Human Rights Commission of Pakistan. *Bonded Labour in Brick Kiln Industry of Pakistan.* Lahore, Pakistan: 1988. NGO mission report, in English.

————. *One-Day Seminar on the United Nations Convention on the Elimination of All Forms of Discrimination against Women, October 30, 1987.* Lahore: 1988. NGO conference report, in English.

Idara-e-Aman-o-Insaf (Christian Conference of Asia). *Pakistan: Struggle for Human Rights.* Kowloon, Hong Kong: 1986. NGO edited collection, in English.

Information, Freedom and Censorship: The ARTICLE 19 World Report 1988. London: ARTICLE 19, 1988. NGO report, in English; bibliography on suggested further reading, pp. 324–326.

International Catholic Child Bureau. *Children and Drug Abuse.* Geneva:1988. NGO manual, in English.

International Commission of Jurists. *The Independence of Judges and Lawyers in South Asia.* Geneva: 1988. NGO conference report, in English.

Isis International. *Women in Action.* Rome: 1987. NGO directory, in English.

Lawyers Committee for Human Rights. *Zia's Law: Human Rights under Military Rule in Pakistan.* New York: 1985. NGO mission report, in English.

Newberg, Paula. "Pakistan's Troubled Landscape." *World Policy Journal* 4, no. 2 (Spring 1987): 313–331. Scholarly article, in English.

Norwegian Human Rights Project, Christian Michelsen Institute. *Human Rights in Developing Countries 1986.* Oslo: Universitetsforlaget, 1986. Government annual report, in English.

Refugee Studies Programme. *The Crisis of Migration from Afghanistan: Domestic and Foreign Implications.* Oxford, UK: 1987. Conference proceedings, in English.

U. S. Helsinki Watch Committee, Asia Watch. *By All Parties to the Conflict: Violations of the Laws of War in Afghanistan.* New York: 1988. NGO report, in English.

Wirsing, Robert. *The Baluchis and Pathans.* Rev. ed. London: 1987. NGO report, in English.

Panama

Americas Watch Committee. *Human Rights in Panama.* New York: 1988. NGO mission report, in English.

Amnesty International. *Panama: Assault on Human Rights.* London: 1988. NGO report, in English.

Centro de Asesoria y Promocion Electoral, Instituto Interamericano de Derechos Humanos, instituto de Investigaciones Juridicas, Universidad Nacional Autonoma de Mexico (Center for Electoral Counseling and Promotion, Inter-American Institute for Human Rights, and the Institute of Legal Research, National Autonomous University of Mexico). *Legislacion Electoral Comparada: Colombia, Mexico, Panama, Venezuela y Centroamerica* (Electoral Legislation Compared: Colombia, Mexico, Panama, Venezuela, and Central America). San Jose, Costa Rica: 1986. Research paper, in Spanish.

Centro de Capacitacion Social (Center for Social Training). "El Sistema Penitenciario: Rehabilitacion o Purgatorio?" (Prison System: Rehabilitation or Purgatory?). *Dialogo Social* 20, no. 201 (June 1987): 56. NGO article, in Spanish.

Centro de Capacitacion Social y Comision Nacional de Derechos Humanos en Panama (Center for Social Training and National Human Rights Commission of Panama). *Informe sobre los Derechos Humanos en Panama a la X Asamblea de CODEHUCA* (Report on the Human Rights Situation in Panama Presented to the Tenth CODEHUCA Assembly). Panama City: 1988. NGO report, in Spanish.

Centro de Investigacion de los Derechos Humanos y Socorro Juridico de Panama (Human Rights Research Center and Legal Aid of Panama). *Resumen Anual 1986* (Annual Report 1986). Panama: 1987. NGO report, in Spanish.

——————. *La Ley 20 y Los Derechos Humanos* (Law 20 and Human Rights). Panama City: 1987. NGO report, in Spanish.

Comision de Derechos Humanos de la Provincia de Chirique (Human Rights Commission of Chiriqui Province). *Informe sobre Violaciones de los Derechos Humanos en la Provincia de Chiriqui, Rep. de Panama* (Report on Human Rights Violations in Chiriqui Province, Republic of Panama: 1987. NGO report, in Spanish.

Comision para la Defensa de los Derechos Humanos en Centroamerica (Commission for the Defense of Human Rights in Central America). "Informe—Analisis sobre la Situacion de los Derechos Humanos en Panama" (Report—Analysis on the Human Rights Situation in Panama). *Brecha* (Sept.–Oct. 1988): 14–21. NGO article, in Spanish.

Latin American Documentation. *The Church and Native Peoples.* Lima, Peru: 1986. NGO document collection, in English.

Panamanian Committee for Human Rights. *The Human Rights Report: Review of 1985.* Washington, D. C.: 1986. NGO report, in English.

——————. *The Struggle of an Independent Newspaper.* 1986. Unpublished paper, in English.

Physicians for Human Rights. *Panama 1987: Health Consequences of Police and Military Actions.* Somerville, MA: 1988. NGO mission report, in English.

Papua New Guinea

Committee Against Repression in the Pacific and Asia. "Harassment of Papuan Refugees Continues." *Asia Pacific Solidarity* 20 (June 1985): 14–16. NGO article, in English.

Human Rights Council of Australia. *Irian Jaya and Human Rights: A Working Group Report.* Canberra: 1986. NGO report, in English.

International Commission of Jurists, Australian Section. *Refuji: Report of the 1986 Mission to Papua New Guinea.* Sydney: 1986. NGO mission report, in English.

Refugees Studies Programme, Queen Elizabeth House. *Refugee Participation Network Newsletter* 3 (Nov. 1988). NGO articles, in English.

Scott-Murphy, J., D. Dunstan, and N. Khan. *Human Rights in Melanesia: The Report of the Evatt Foundation Delegation.* Sydney, Australia: H.V. Evatt Memorial Foundation, 1988. NGO report, in English.

Paraguay

Alegre Ortiz, Heriberto. *La Sociedad Cautiva* (The Captive Society). Asuncion, Paraguay: Comision de Defensa de los Derechos Humanos del Paraguay, 1987. NGO monograph, in Spanish.

American Watch Committee. *Paraguay: Latin America's Oldest Dictatorship under Pressure.* New York: 1986. NGO mission report, in English.

——————. *Paraguay: Repression in the Countryside.* New York: 1988. NGO report, in English.

Amnesty International. *Human Rights Violations in Paraguay.* London: 1985. NGO report, in English.

Bouvier, V. M. *Decline of the Dictator: Paraguay at a Crossroads.* Washington, D. C.: Washington Office on Latin America, 1988. NGO report, in English.

Comite de Iglesias para Ayundas de Emergencia (Committee of the Churches for Emergency Assistance). "Expulsion de Familias Campesinas" (Eviction of Peasant Families). *Notas Trimestrales* 4 (Jan.–March 1987): 21–22. NGO article, in Spanish.

——————. "Sindicalistas Detenidos" (Labor Leaders Arrested). *Notas Trimestrales* 4 (Jan.–March 1987): 25–27. NGO article, in Spanish.

Davis, Shelton H. *Land Rights and Indigenous Peoples: The Role of the Inter-American Commission on Human Rights.* Cambridge, MA: Cultural Survival, 1988. NGO report, in English.

Informe sobre el Desalojo de Campesinos Sin Tierras por Fuerzas Combinadas del Ejercito y la Policia en la Zona de Juan E. O'Leary (Report of the Eviction of Landless Peasants by Combined Forces of the Army and the Police in the Juan E. O'Leary Zone). Asuncion, Paraguay: Washington Office on Latin America, 1986. NGO mission report, in Spanish.

Inter-American Commission on Human Rights. *Report of the Situation of Human Rights in Paraguay,* OEA/Serv. L/V/II.71, Doc. 19, rev. 1. Washington, D. C.: 1987. IGO report, in English.

Inter-Church Committee on Human Rights in Latin America. *ICCHRLA 1987 Annual Report: General Concerns and Brief Country Reports.* Toronto, Canada: 1988. NGO report, in English.

Lawyers Committee for Human Rights. *The Human Rights Price of "Pax Stroessniana": A Report to the United Nations Commission on Human Rights Pursuant to ECOSOC Resolution 1503.* New York: 1985. NGO report, in English.

Organization of American States. *Informe Anual de la Comision Interamericana de Derechos Humanos 1985–1986* (Annual Report of the Inter-American Commission on Human Rights 1985–1986). Washington, D. C.: 1986. IGO annual report, in Spanish.

——————. *Inter-American Yearbook on Human Rights 1986*. Dordrecht, the Netherlands: Martinus Nijhoff, 1988. IGO annual report, in Spanish.

"Paraguay: Arrests Increase as Social Movements Challenge Stroessner Rule." *Latin-America Press*, 1 January 1987, 3–4.

Secretariado Internacional de Juristas por la Amnistia y la Democracia en Paraguay (International Secretariat of Lawyers for Amnesty and Democracy in Paraguay). *Paraguay un Desafio a la Responsabilidad Internacional* (Paraguay: A Challenge to International Responsibility). Montevideo, Uruguay: 1986. Conference proceedings, in Spanish.

U. S. House of Representatives, Subcommittee on Human Rights and International Organizations. *Status of U. S. Human Rights Policy, 1987*. Washington, D. C.: GPO, 1987. Government hearings, in English.

Peru

Americas Watch Committee. *A Certain Passivity: Failing to Curb Human Rights Abuses in Peru*. New York: 1987. NGO report, in English.

——————. *Human Rights in Peru after President Garcia's First Year*. New York: 1986. NGO report, in English.

——————. *New Opportunity for Democratic Authority—Human Rights in Peru*. New York: 1985. NGO mission report, in English and Spanish.

——————. *Tolerating Abuses: Violations of Human Rights in Peru*. New York: 1986. NGO report, in English.

Amnesty International. *States of Emergency: Torture and Violations of the Right to Life under States of Emergency*. London: 1988. NGO report in English.

Bequele, A., and J. Boyden, eds. *Combating Child Labour*. Geneva: ILO, 1988. IGO monograph, in English.

Burneo Labrin, Jose. *Derechos de la Persona ante el Juez, la Policia y en la Carcel* (Rights of the Individual before the Judge, the Police, and while in Prison). Lima: Comision Episcopal de Accion Social, 1985. Research paper, in Spanish.

Centro de Estudios y Publicaciones. "A Proposito de la Violencia: Lo que Esta en Juego en el Pais" (About Violence: What is at Stake in the Country). *Paginas* 91 (June 1988): 43–51. NGO article, in Spanish.

Chipoco, C. C., and P. T. De Valdez. *Derechos Humanos: El Pasado no Fue Diferente* (Human Rights: The Past was no Different). Lima: Instituto de Defensa Legal, 1986. NGO report, in Spanish.

Cultural Survival. "Mountain People." *Cultural Survival Quarterly* 10, no. 3 (1986). NGO edited collection, in English.

Escuela de Derechos Humanos. *La Protection Legal de los Derechos Humanos en el Peru* (The Legal Protection of Human Rights in Peru). Lima: 1986. Scholarly document collection, in English.

Farnsworth, Elizabeth. "Peru: A Nation in Crisis." *World Policy Journal* 5, no. 4 (Fall 1988): 725–746. Scholarly article, in English.

Federation Internationale des Droits de l'Homme (International Federation of Human Rights). *Rapport de Mission—Perou* (Mission Report—Peru). Paris: 1985. NGO mission report, in French.

Garcia Belaunde, Domingo. *Una Democracia en Transicion (Las Elecciones Peruanas de 1985)* (Democracy in Transition: 1985 Peruvian Elections). San Jose, Costa Rica: Instituto Interamericano de Derechos Humanos, Centro de Asesoria y Promocion Electoral, Inter-American Institute of Human Rights, and Center for Electoral Counseling and Promotion, 1986. Research paper, in Spanish.

Garcia-Sayan, Diego. *Habeas Corpus y Estados de Emergencia* (Habeas Corpus and States of Emergency). Lima: Comision Andina de Juristas and the Friedrich Naumann Foundation, 1988. NGO report, in Spanish.

Gray, Andrew. *And After the Gold Rush. . .? Human Rights and Self-Development among the Amarakaeri of Southeastern Peru*. Copenhagen: International Work Group for Indigenous Affairs, 1985. NGO conference report, in English.

Instituto de Defensa Legal (Institute for Legal Defense). *Los Sucesos de los Penales: Nueva Abdicacion de la Autoridad Democratica. Un Enfoque Juridico* (A New Abdication of Democratic Authority in Peru: A Legal Analysis . . . Recent Events in the Prisons). Lima: 1986. NGO report, in Spanish.

Inter-Church Committee on Human Rights in Latin America. *1986 Annual Report on the Human Rights Situation in Peru*. Toronto, Canada: 1987. NGO report, in English.

Isis International *Rural Women in Latin America*. Rome: 1987. NGO monograph, in English.

Latin American Documentation. *The Church and Native Peoples*. Lima: 1986. NGO document collection, in English.

Overseas Development Council and Washington Office on Latin America. *Peru: Democratic Elections and Economic Crisis 1985*. Washington, D. C.: 1985. NGO conference report, in English.

United Nations Commission on Human Rights. *Report of the Working Group on Enforced or Involuntary*

Disappearances: Report on a Second Visit to Peru by Two Members of the Working Group. . . , E/CN.4/1987/15/Add. 1. 1986. IGO mission, in English.

U. S. House of Representatives. Subcommittee on Human Rights and International Organizations. *Human Rights in Peru . . . ,* 99th Cong., 1st sess., 1985. Government hearings, in English.

Washington Office on Latin America. *Peru in Peril: The Economy and Human Rights 1985–1987.* Washington, D. C.: 1987. NGO report, in English.

Washington Office on Latin America and Ecumenical Committee on the Andes. *A Conference on Peru.* Washington, D. C.: 1987. NGO conference report, in English; bibliography on publications and audiovisuals, pp. 30–31.

The Philippines

Amnesty International. *Philippines: Incommunicado Detention, Ill-treatment and Torture during 1988.* London: 1988. NGO report, in English.

——————. "Philippines: The Killing and Intimidation of Human Rights Lawyers." *CIJL Bulletin* 22 (October 1988): 40–57. NGO report, in English.

——————. *Philippines: Unlawful Killings by Military and Paramilitary Forces.* London: 1988. NGO report, in English.

Asian Human Rights Commission. *Report of the Asian Human Rights Commission Study Mission to the Philippines.* Hong Kong: 1988. NGO report, in English.

Bello, Walden. *U. S.-Sponsored Low-Intensity Conflict in the Philippines.* San Francisco: Institute for Food and Development Policy, 1987. NGO report, in English.

Canlas, M., M. Miranda, and J. Putzel. *Land Poverty and Politics in the Philippines.* London: Catholic Institute for International Relations, 1988. NGO conference paper, in English.

Catholic Institute for International Relations. *The Labour Trade: Filipino Migrant Workers around the World.* London: 1987. NGO report, in English.

Christian Conference of Asia. "United States Military Presence in Asia." *Asian Issues* 2, no. 10 (April 1987). NGO edited collection, in English.

Claude, R., E. Stover, and J. Lopez. *Health Professionals and Human Rights in the Philippines.* Washington, D. C.: American Association for the Advancement of Science and Clearinghouse on Science and Human Rights, 1987. NGO report, in English.

Cull, H. A., and D. W. Allen. *Human Rights Advocacy in the Philipines: Report on a Mission to the Philippines, August 1985.* Geneva: International Commission of Jurists, 1987. NGO mission report, in English.

Delacruz, E., A. Jordan, and J. Emmanuel. *Death Squads in the Philippines.* San Francisco: Alliance for Philippine Concerns, 1987. NGO report, in English.

Donnelly, J., and R. E. Howard. *International Handbook on Human Rights.* Westport, CT: Greenwood Press, 1987. Scholarly edited collection, in English.

Eagle, Julian. *A Smouldering Land: Lessons from the Philippines.* London: Catholic Institute for International Relations and Christian Aid, 1987. NGO report, in English.

Ecumenical Commission for Displaced Families and Communities. *Primer: Displacement in the Philippines—Nature, Causes, Effects, Extent, Limits, Remedies and Victims' Rights.* Quezon City, Philippines: 1987. NGO manual, in English.

Ecumenical Movement for Justice and Peace. *Mission Reports (February–June 1987): Compilation of Reports from Fact-Finding Missions Organized and Participated in by the Ecumenical Movement for Justice and Peace.* Quezon City: Philippines: 1987. NGO mission report, in English.

Episcopal Commission on Tribal Filipinos. "Who Owns the Land?" *Tribal Forum* 8, no. 2 (March–April 1987). NGO special issue, in English.

Fay, Chip. *Counter-Insurgency and Tribal Peoples in the Philippines.* Washington, D. C.: Survival International USA, 1987. NGO report, in English.

General Assembly Binding Women for Reforms, Integrity, Equality, Leadership and Action. *Let's Work Together for the Protection of Human Rights of Filipino Women: A Documentation Report on the Human Rights Situation of Filipino Women.* Quezon City, Philippines: 1988. NGO report, in English.

Heinz, Wolfgang S. *Ursachen und Folgen von Menschenrechtsverletzungen in der Dritten Welt* (Causes and Consequences of Human Rights Violations in Third World Countries). Saarbrucken, FRG: Verlag Breitenbach, 1986. Scholarly monograph, in German; bibliography on the Philippines, pp. 447–449.

Lawyers Committee for Human Rights. *"Salvaging" Democracy: Human Rights in the Philippines.* New York: 1985. NGO report, in English.

——————. *Vigilantes in the Philippines: A Threat to Democratic Rule.* New York: 1988. NGO report, in English.

Lawyers Committee for Human Rights and Asia Watch. *Lawyers under Fire: Attacks on Human Rights Attorneys in the Philippines.* New York: 1988. NGO report, in English.

Leary, V., A. A. Ellis, and K. Madlener. *The Philippines: Human Rights after Martial Law.* Geneva: International Commission of Jurists, 1984. NGO mission report, in English.

Maglipon, Jo-Ann. *The Mendiola Tragedy, January 23, 1987: A Smouldering Land*. Manila: National Council of Churches in the Philippines and Forum for Rural Concerns, 1987. NGO report, in English.

National Federation of Sugar Workers—Food and General Trades. *Documentation Report: Trade Union Repression and Human Rights Violations*. Bacolod City, Philippines: 1988. NGO report in English.

Pablo, L., J. Sayo, E. Mondez, C. Garcia, and N. Garde. *Primer on Militarization*. Quezon City, Philippines: Ecumenical Movement for Justice and Peace, 1988. NGO issue paper, in English.

Philippine Alliance of Human Rights Advocates. *Right-wing Vigilantes and U. S. Involvement: Report of a U.S.-Philippine Fact-Finding Mission to the Philippines, May 20–30, 1987*. Manila: 1987. NGO mission report, in English.

Philippine Senate Commission on Justice and Human Rights. *Report on Vigilante Groups*. Quezon City, Philippines: 1988. Government report, in English.

Presidential Committee on Human Rights. *Annual Report for 1986*. Manila: 1987. Government commission annual report, in English.

Protestant Association for World Mission. *The Pain Will Go on until Justice Is Done: What Can We Do to Enforce Human Rights in the Philippines?* Manila: 1986. NGO edited collection, in English.

Starner, F. L. *The Rising Sun and Tangled Roots: A Philippine Profile*. Hong Kong: Christian Conference on Asia, 1986. NGO report, in English.

Taswell, Ruth, ed. *Southeast Asian Tribal Groups and Ethnic Minorities*. Cambridge, MA: Cultural Survival, 1987. NGO conference proceedings, in English.

Wiseberg, L. S., and L. Ocampo. "The Philippines Revisited: Plus ca change, Plus ca reste la meme. Excerpts from a report by the International League for Human Rights." *Human Rights Internet* 13, no. 1 (Spring 1989). NGO report, in English.

Poland

Bartoszewski, W. T, *Polish-Jewish Relations: A Current Debate among Polish Catholics*. London: Institute of Jewish Affairs, 1987. NGO report, in English.

Commission on Security and Cooperation in Europe. *Basket I—Implementation of the Final Act of the Conference on Security and Cooperation in Europe: Findings Eleven Years after Helsinki*. Washington, D. C.: GPO, 1987. Government report, in English.

Committee in Support of Solidarity. *Repression in Poland, September 1986–October 1987: A List of 810 Victims*. New York: 1987. NGO report, in English.

—————. "Solidarity and Human Rights: Five Years Later." *Committee in Support of Solidarity Reports* 35 (31 August 1985): 16–31. NGO article, in English.

—————. *The Use of Political Imprisonment in the Polish People's Republic: A Partial List of Political Prisoners*. New York: 1986. NGO report, in English.

Davies, Gareth. "Conscientious Objection and the Freedom and Peace Movement in Poland." *Religion in Communist Lands* 16, no. 1 (Spring 1988): 4–20. NGO article, in English.

Donnelly, J., and R. E. Howard, eds. *International Handbook on Human Rights*. Westport, CT: Greenwood Press, 1987. Scholarly edited collection, in English.

Freedom of Information and Expression in Poland: A Commentary by ARTICLE 19 on the Report Submitted to the United Nations' Human Rights Committee by the Government of the Polish People's Republic. London: ARTICLE 19, 1987. NGO report, in English.

Information Centre for Polish Affairs. "The Helsinki Committee in Poland: Violations of Basic Freedoms in the Polish People's Republic from 1 November 1986 to 30 April 1987." *Uncensored Poland News Bulletin* 13 (June 1987). NGO report, in English.

—————. "Human Rights in Poland: An Expert View." *Uncensored Poland News Bulletin* 22 (Nov. 1987): 17–20. NGO article, in English.

—————. *Polonia en 1985* (Poland in 1985). Panama City: Comite Interamericano de Derechos Humanos y Sindicales, 1986. NGO background paper, in Spanish.

—————. "Reprisals Against Freedom and Peace Activists." *Uncensored Poland News Bulletin* 23 (Nov. 1987): 25–28. NGO article, in English.

International League for Human Rights. *Human Rights in Poland: Comments on the Second Periodic Report of the Government of Poland to the Human Rights Committee under the International Covenant on Civil and Political Rights*. New York: 1987. NGO report, in English.

Kedzia, Zdzislaw. "Interpretation and Protection of the Constitutional Rights and Freedoms in Poland." *SIM Newsletter: Netherlands Quarterly of Human Rights*. 6, no. 1 (1988): 38–53. Scholarly article, in English.

Korba, Irena. "Five Years Underground: The Opposition and the Church in Poland since Martial Law." *Religion in Communist Lands* 15, no. 2 (Summer 1987): 167–181. NGO article, in English.

Moody, J., and R. Boyes. *The Priest and the Policeman: The Courageous Life and Cruel Murder of Father Jerzy Popieluszko.* New York: Summit Books, 1987. Scholarly monograph, in English.

Polish Helsinki Committee. *Human Rights Violations in Poland 1983–1986.* London: Information for Polish Affairs, 1986. NGO report, in English.

Polish Helsinki Watch Committee and U. S. Helsinki Watch Committee. *Human Rights in Poland since December 1981: A Report by the Polish Helsinki Committee to the Human Rights Experts Meeting in Ottawa, May 1985.* Warsaw and New York: 1985. NGO report, in Polish and English.

Radio Free Europe/Radio Liberty. "Situation Report on Poland." *Radio Free Europe Research* 13, no. 18 (6 May 1988): 3–38. Government report, in English.

Robbins, T., and R. Robertson, eds. *Church-State Relations: Tensions and Transitions.* New Brunswick, NJ: Transaction Books, 1987. Scholarly edited collection, in English.

Roth, Kenneth. *Repression Disguised as Law: Human Rights in Poland.* New York: Lawyers Committee for Human Rights, 1987. NGO report, in English.

"Social and Economic Rights in the Soviet Bloc." *Survey: A Journal of East & West Studies* 29, no. 4 (August 1987). NGO special issue, in English.

U. S. Helsinki Watch Committee. *From Below: Independent Peace and Environmental Movements in Eastern Europe and the USSR.* New York: 1987. NGO report, in English.

U. S. Helsinki Watch Committee. "Poland." In *Ten Years Later: Violations of the Helsinki Accords,* 69–103. New York: 1985. NGO report, in English.

—————. *Reinventing Civil Society: Poland's Quiet Revolution, 1981–1986.* New York: 1986. NGO report, in English.

—————. *Violations of the Helsinki Accords: Poland.* New York: 1986. NGO report, in English.

Vinton, L., J. B. de Weydenthal, and A. Pomian. "Situation Report Poland." *Radio Free Europe Research* 13, no. 34 (26 August 1988): 3–24. NGO report, in English; bibliography, p. 5, 10, 15, and 24.

Qatar

Arab Organization for Human Rights. *Report: Human Rights in the Arab World.* Cairo: 1987. NGO report, in Arabic or English.

Birks, J. S., and C. A. Sinclair. *Nature and Process of Labor Importing: The African in the Gulf States, Kuwait, Bahrain, Qatar, and the United Arab Emirates.* Geneva: ILO, 1978. IGO study, in English.

Romania

Amnesty International. *Conscientious Objection to Military Service.* London: 1988. NGO report, in English.

—————. *The Imprisonment of Persons Seeking to Leave a Country or to Return to their Own Country.* London: 1986. NGO report, in English.

Commission on Security and Cooperation in Europe. *Basket I—Implementation of the Final Act of the Conference on Security and Cooperation in Europe: Findings Eleven Years after Helsinki.* Washington, D. C.: GPO, 1987. Government report, in English.

Funnemark, Bjorn Cato. *SOS Transylvania: A Report on the Suppression of the Hungarian Minority in Romania.* Vienna: International Helsinki Federation for Human Rights, 1988. NGO report, in English; bibliography, pp. 59–60.

International Confederation of Free Trade Unions. *Violations by the Government of the Socialist Republic of Romania of the Rights to Freedom of Association and Collective Bargaining.* Brussels: 1989. NGO report, in English.

International Federation for the Protection of the Rights of Ethnic, Religious, Linguistic and other Minorities. *The State of Religious and Human Rights in Albania and Romania.* New York: 1988. NGO report, in English.

International League for Human Rights. *Romania's Human Rights Record: Comments on the Government of Romania's Official Report to the Human Rights Committee.* New York: 1987. NGO report, in English.

Internationale Gesellschaft fur Menschenrechte (International Society for Human Rights). *CSCE and Human Rights: Divided Families and the Denial of Freedom of Movement (Documentation).* Frankfurt/Main, FRG: 1987. NGO document collection, in English.

Radio Free Europe/Radio Liberty. "Eastern Europe in 1988." *Radio Free Europe Research* 13, no. 52 (30 December 1988). Government background paper, in English.

—————. "Romania's Human Rights Record at the Vienna Conference." *Radio Free Europe Research* 11, no. 53 (30 December 1986): 3–7. Government article, in English.

Shafir, M., and D. Ionescu. "Rural Resettlement: Situation Report Romania." *Radio Free Europe Research* 13, no. 34 (23 August 1988): 3–22. NGO report, in English.

Socor, Vladimir. "Known Prisoners of Conscience in Romania: An Annotated Checklist." *Radio Free Europe Research* (7 August 1987). Government report, in English.

Solso, Christine K. *Ioan Ruta: A Cast Study of Human Rights in Romania.* Minneapolis, MN: Minnesota Lawyers International Human Rights Committee, 1988. NGO report, in English.

U. S. Helsinki Watch Committee. "Romania." In *Ten Years Later: Violations of the Helsinki Accords,* 105–128. New York: 1985. NGO report, in English.

——————. *Violations of the Helsinki Accords: Romania.* New York: 1986. NGO report, in English.

Rwanda

Clark, Lance. "Post-Emergency Assistance for Refugees in Eastern and Southern Africa." *Migration News* no. 3–4 (July–December 1987): 3–24. NGO research paper, in English.

Freedom of Information and Expression in Rwanda: A Commentary by ARTICLE 19 on the Report Submitted to the U.N. Human Rights Committee by the Government of Rwanda. London: ARTICLE 19, 1988. NGO report, in English.

"Rwanda: The Right to Choose." *Africa News,* 8 August 1988, 6–7. News article, in English.

St. Vincent and Grenadines

Caribbean Conference of Churches. "Focus on Caribbean Human Rights." *Caribbean Contact* 16, no. 1 (June 1988): 8–9. NGO article, in English.

Organization of American States. *Annual Report of the Inter-American Commission on Human Rights 1986–1987.* Washington, D. C.: 1987. IGO annual report, in English.

Sao Tome and Principe

African-American Institute. "Sao Tome Snuffs out Attempted Coup." *Africa Report* 33, no. 3 (May–June 1988): 9. NGO article, in English.

Saudi Arabia

Arab Organization for Human Rights. "Human Rights in the Arab World: Saudi Arabia." *AOHR Newsletter* no. 14–15 (February 1988): 7–8. NGO article, in English.

——————. *Report: Human Rights in the Arab World.* Cairo: 1987. NGO report, in Arabic or English.

Assaf, George. "A Constitution for Saudi Arabia: King Fahd's Plan for 'Democracy.'" *Plus* 1, no. 1 (1985): 35–43. NGO article, in English.

Peroncel-Huugoz, Jean-Pierre. "Arabie Seoudite: Les Travailleurs Immigres Devant l'Intolerance Religieuse" (Saudi Arabia: Migrant Workers Face Religious Intolerance). *Lettre de la FIDH* 257 (12 July 1988): 3–6. NGO article, in French.

Senegal

Donnelly, J., and R. E. Howard, eds. *International Handbook on Human Rights.* Westport, CT: Greenwood Press, 1987. Scholarly edited collection, in English.

Freedom of Information and Expression in Senegal: A Commentary by ARTICLE 19 on the Report Submitted to the U.N. Human Rights Committee by the Government of the Republic of Senegal. London: 1987. NGO report, in English; bibliography of sources, p. 30.

Hayward, Fred M. *Elections in Independent Africa.* Boulder, CO: Westview Press, 1987. Scholarly study, in English.

International Commission of Jurists. *Les Services Juridiques en Milieu Rural (Afrique de l'Ouest)* (Legal Services in Rural Areas [West Africa]). Geneva: 1987. NGO report, in French.

Kannyo, Edward. *Human Rights in Africa: Report of a Visit to Nigeria, Ghana, Ivory Coast, Senegal and Upper Volta.* New York: International League for Human Rights, 1981. NGO report, in English.

McLean, S., and S. E. Graham, eds. *Female Circumcision, Excision and Infibulation: The Facts and Proposals for Change.* 2d rev. ed. London: Minority Rights Groups, 1985. NGO report, in English.

Seychelles

Amnesty International. *Seychelles: Political Imprisonment and Allegations regarding the "Disappearance" or Extrajudicial Execution of Suspected Opponents of the Government.* London: 1985. NGO report, in English.

Sierra Leone

"Sierra Leone: Lawyers Call for Reform." *West Africa,* 27 May 1985. News article, in English.

South Africa

Amnesty International. *South Africa: Detention and Torture of Trade Unionists.* London: 1986. NGO report, in English.

Andreassen, B. A., and A. Eide, eds. *Human Rights in Developing Countries 1987/88: A Yearbook on Human Rights in Countries Receiving Nordic Aid.* Copenhagen: Christian Michelsen Institute, 1988. NGO report, in English.

Black Sash. *"Greenflies": Municipal Police in the Eastern Cape.* Mowbray, South Africa: 1987. NGO report, in English.

——————. *Memorandum on the Suffering of Children in South Africa.* Johannesburg: 1986. NGO report, in English.

Catholic Institute for International Relations. *Now Everyone is Afraid: The Changing Face of Policing in South Africa.* Cape Town: 1988. NGO report, in English.

Cole, Josette. *Crossroads: The Politics of Reform and Repression 1976–1986.* Johannesburg: Raven Press, 1987. Scholarly monograph, in English; bibliography, pp. 165–169.

Cook, Helena. *The War against Children: South Africa's Younger Victims.* New York: Lawyers Committee for Human Rights, 1986. NGO mission report, in English.

Cowling, M. G. "Judges and the Protection of Human Rights in South Africa: Articulating the Inarticulate Premise." *South African Journal on Human Rights* 3 (July 1987): 177–201. Scholarly article, in English.

Detainees' Parents Support Committee. *A Memorandum on Children under Repression.* Johannesburg: 1986. NGO report, in English.

Donnelly, J., and R. E. Howard, eds. *International Handbook on Human Rights.* Westport, CT: Greenwood Press, 1987. Scholarly edited collection, in English.

Foster, Don. *Detention and Torture in South Africa: Psychological, Legal and Historical Studies.* Cape Town: David Philip, 1987. Scholarly monograph, in English; bibliography, pp. 238–246.

Foster, D., and D. Sandler. *A Study of Detention and Torture in South Africa: Preliminary Report.* Cape Town: 1985. NGO report, in English.

Hanlon, Joseph. *Beggar Your Neighbours: Apartheid Power in Southern Africa.* London: Catholic Institute for International Relations, 1986. NGO report, in English.

Haysom, Nicholas. "Licence to Kill, Part II: A Comparative Survey of the Law in the United Kingdom, United States of America and South Africa." *South African Journal on Human Rights* 3 (July 1987): 202–222. Scholarly article, in English.

——————. *Mabangalala: The Rise of Right Wing Vigilantes in South Africa.* London: Catholic Institute for International Relations, 1986. NGO report, in English.

Haysom, N., and G. Marcus. " 'Undesirability' and Criminal Liability under the Publications Act 42 of 1974." *South African Journal on Human Rights* 1 (May 1985). Scholarly article, in English.

International Defence and Aid Fund for Southern Africa. *Apartheid's Violence against Children.* London: 1988. NGO report, in English.

Jupp, Michael. *Children under Apartheid.* Brooklyn, NY: Defense for Children International-USA, 1987. NGO report, in English; bibliography, pp. 187–191.

"Laissez-Faire": Mining in South Africa and Private Enterprise." *South African Journal on Human Rights* 3 (July 1987): 167–176. Scholarly article, in English.

Lawyer's Committee for Human Rights. *Crisis in Crossroads: A Report on Human Rights.* New York: 1988. NGO report, in English.

Moffett, M. R. *Government Restrictions on the Press in South Africa.* Washington, D. C.: International Human Rights Law Group, 1987. NGO report, in English.

Platzky, L., and C. Walker. *The Surplus People: Forced Removals in South Africa.* Johannesburg: Ravan Press, 1985. NGO report, in English.

Rayner, Mary. *Turning a Blind Eye: Medical Accountability and the Prevention of Torture in South Africa.* Washington, D. C.: American Association for the Advancement of Science and Committee on Scientific Freedom and Responsibility, 1987. NGO report, in English.

South African Council of Churches. *Rural Poverty Challenges the Church.* Johannesburg: 1984. NGO conference report, in English; bibliography, pp. 169–172.

Thompson, Leonard. *The Political Mythology of Apartheid.* New Haven, CT: Yale University Press, 1985. Scholarly study, in English; extensive footnotes.

Transvaal Rural Action Committee. *Kwandebele—The Struggle against "Independence.".* Johannesburg: 1986. NGO report, in English.

U.N. Sub-Commission on Prevention of Discrimination and Protection of Minorities. *Adverse Consequences for the Enjoyment of Human Rights of Political, Military, Economic and other Forms of Assistance Given to the Racist and Colonialist Regime of South Africa.* Report of Special Rapporteur Mr. Ahmad M. Khalifa, E/CN.4/Sub.2/1987/8/Rev. 1. 1987. IGO report, in English.

Unterhalter, Elaine. *Forced Removals: The Division Segregation and Control of the People of South Africa.* London: International Defence and Aid Fund for Southern Africa, 1987. NGO report, in English.

van Es, A., and M. van Grup. *Health Professionals and Human Rights in South Africa.* Leiden, the Netherlands: Johannes Wier Foundation/ Dutch Foundation for Health and Human Rights, 1987. NGO mission report, in English.

van Zyl Smit, Dirk. " 'Normal' Prisons in an 'Abnormal' Society? A Comparative Perspective on South African Prison Law and Practice." *South frican Journal on Human Rights* 3 (July 1987): 147–165. Scholarly article, in English.

Spain

Amnesty International. *Amnesty International Concerns in Western Europe, October 1986–March 1987.* London: 1987. NGO report, in English.

———————. *Conscientious Objection to Military Service.* London: 1988. NGO report, in English.

Asociacion Pro Derechos Humanos de Espana (Spanish Human Rights Association). *Informe Anual Derechos Humanos en Espana 1987* (Annual Report on Human Rights in Spain 1987). Madrid: 1987. NGO annual report, in Spanish.

———————. *Informe Sobre la Carcel de Ocana I* (Report on the Ocana I Prison). Madrid: 1985. NGO mission report, in Spanish.

Donnelly, J., and R. E. Howard, eds. *International Handbook on Human Rights.* Westport, CT: Greenwood Press, 1987. Scholarly edited collection, in English.

Jacoby, Daniel M. *Espane: Proces d'Un Militant Basque* (Spain: Trial of a Basque Militant). Paris: Federation Internationale des Droits de l'Homme, 1985. NGO mission report, in French.

Jurgies, Wolfgang. "Gernika 1937 and 1987" (Guernica 1937 and 1987). *Pogrom* 133 (June 1987): 14–16. NGO article, in German.

Korn, David. "State Terrorism: A Spanish Watergate?" *Freedom at Issue* 105 (Nov.–Dec. 1988). Scholarly article, in English.

Pulver, Bernhad. "Els Paisos Catalans" (The Catalonian Countries). *Pogrom* 133 (June 1987): 17–21. NGO article, in German.

Rodriguez Guerrero, L. F. "La Ley Antiterrorista Rompe el Sistema Constitucional" (Antiterrorist Law Breaks the Constitutional System). *Derechos Humanos* 9 (February–March 1985): 9–11. NGO article, in Spanish.

Sri Lanka

Amnesty International. *Sri Lanka: Extrajudicial Executions and "Disappearances" in May 1985.* London: 1985. NGO report, in English.

———————. *Sri Lanka: Recent Reports of Disappearances and Torture.* London: 1987. NGO report, in English.

———————. *Sri Lanka: What Has Happened to the "Disappeared"?* London: 1988. NGO report, in English.

———————. *States of Emergency: Torture and Violations of the Right to Life under States of Emergency.* London: 1988. NGO report, in English.

Andreassen, B. A., and A. Eide, eds. "Sri Lanka." In *Human Rights in Developing Countries 1987/88: A Yearbook on Human Rights in Countries Receiving Nordic Aid.* Copenhagen: Christian Michelsen Institute, 1988. NGO report, in English, bibliography, classified by country, pp. 357–372.

Canada-Asia Working Group. "Human Rights in Asia: Submission Prepared for the 45th Session of the U.N. Commission on Human Rights." *Currents* 11, no. 1 (February 1989). NGO report, in English.

———————. "Human Rights in Asia: Submission Prepared for the 44th Session of the U. N. Commission on Human Rights." *Currents* 10, no. 1 (February 1988). NGO report, in English.

Centre for Society and Religion. "Women Against Militarisation, Racism and Violence." *Logos* 27, no. 1 (March 1988). NGO special issue, in English.

Civil Rights Movement of Sri Lanka. *Death in Custody.* Colombo, Sri Lanka: 1988. NGO report, in English.

Hyndman, Patricia. "Human Rights, the Rule of Law and the Situation in Sri Lanka." *University of New South Wales Law Journal* 8, no. 2 (1985): 337–361. Scholarly article, in English.

———————. "The 1951 Convention Definition of Refugee: An Appraisal with Particular Reference to the Case of Sri Lanka Tamil Applicants." *Human Rights Quarterly* 9, no. 1 (February 1987): 49–73. Scholarly article, in English.

Jayawardena, K., and J. Uyangoda, eds. "Special Issue on the National Question in Sri Lanka." *South Asia Bulletin* 6, no. 2 (Fall 1986). Scholarly special issue, in English.

Norwegian Human Rights Project, Christian Michelsen Institute. *Human Rights in Developing Countries 1986* Oslo: Universitetsforlaget, 1986. Government annual report, in English; bibliography, classified by country.

Rajanayagam, P. *Sri Lanka: Human Rights Violations—Extrajudicial and Arbitrary Killings.* London: Human Rights Council and Tamil Information Centre, 1987. NGO monograph, in English.

Rubin, Barnett R. *Cycles of Violence: Human Rights in Sri Lanka since the Indo-Sri Lanka Agreement.* Washington, D. C.: Asia Watch, 1987. NGO report, in English.

Social Scientists Association. *Ethnicity and Social Change in Sri Lanka.* Colombo, Sri Lanka: 1985. Scholarly edited collection, in English.

Sri Lanka Project, British Refugee Council. "Jaffna—The Aftermath." *Sri Lanka Monitor* 1 (February 1988): 2. NGO article, in English.

Vije, Mayan. *Where Serfdom Thrives: The Plantation Tamils of Sri Lanka.* Madras, India: Tamil Information and Research Unit, 1987. NGO report, in English.

Wynne, Alison. *Lament for Lanka*. Kowloon, Hong Kong: Christian Conference of Asia, 1988. NGO mission report, in English.

Sudan

Aguda, A., and O. Aguda. "Judicial Protection of Some Fundamental Rights in Nigeria and in the Sudan before and during Military Rule." *Journal of African Law* 16, no. 2 (Summer 1982): 130–144. Scholarly article, in English.

Amnesty International. *Religious Intolerance*. London: 1986. NGO report, in English.

——————. *Sudan: Human Rights Developments since 1985*. London: 1988. NGO statement, in English.

An-Na'im, A. A. "Detention without Trial in the Sudan: The Use and Abuse of Legal Powers." *Columbia Human Rights Law Review* 17, no. 2 (Spring-Summer 1986): 159–187. Scholarly article, in English.

Arab Organization for Human Rights. "Grave Violations in the Coper Prison." *AOHR Newsletter* 11 (August 1987): 3. NGO article, in English.

——————. *Report: Human Rights in the Arab World*. Cairo: 1987. NGO report, in Arabic or English.

Davis, Joseph E. "The Islamization of the Sudan." *The First Freedom* 1, no. 3 (Oct. 1988): 3–5. NGO article, in English.

Lesch, Ann. "Sudan." In *International Handbook on Race and Race Relations*, ed. J. Sigler, 263–281. Westport, CT: Greenwood Press, 1987. Scholarly book chapter, in English; bibliography, pp. 279–280.

McLean, S., and S. Graham, eds. *Female Circumcision, Excision and Infibulation: The Facts and Proposals for Change*. 2d rev. ed. London: Minority Rights Group, 1985. NGO report, in English.

Rogge, John R. *Too Many, Too Long: Sudan's Twenty-Year Refugee Dilemma*. Totowa, NJ: Rowman and Allanheid, 1985. Scholarly monograph, in English; bibliography, pp. 185–190.

Survival International. "1,000 Massacred." *Survival International News* 19 (1988): 3. NGO article, in English.

——————. "War Wastes Sudan Tribes." *Survival International News* 22 (1988): 1–2. NGO article, in English.

U.N. High Commissioner for Refugees. "Sudan under Stress." *Refugees* (April 1988): 15–35. IGO article, in English.

Suriname

Amnesty International. *Suriname: Violations of Human Rights*. London: 1987. NGO report, in English.

Caribbean Rights. *The Old Shoe, It Fits?: Report of General Election in Suriname, November 25, 1987.* Georgetown, Guyana: 1988. NGO report, in English.

Council on Hemispheric Affairs. "Brunswijk Brings Battle to Bouterse: Surinamese Government Accused of Civilian Killings." *Washington Report on the Hemisphere* 7, no. 7 (24 December 1986): 1, 7. NGO article, in English.

Inter-American Commission on Human Rights. *Second Report on the Human Rights Situation in Suriname*. Washington, D. C.: 1985. IGO report, in English.

International Alert. *Suriname: An International Alert Report*. London: 1988. NGO report, in English; bibliography, pp. 37–38.

International Work Group for Indigenous Affairs. "Suriname—Call for Support for Indian Peoples." *IWGIA Newsletter* 49 (April 1987): 105–112. NGO article, in English.

Organization of American States. *Annual Report of the Inter-American Commission on Human Rights 1986–1987*. Washington, D.C.: 1987. IGO annual report, in English.

——————. *Informe Anual de la Comision Interamericana de Derechos Humanos 1985–1986* (Annual Report of the Inter-American Commission on Human Rights 1985–1986). Washington, D.C.: 1986. IGO annual report, in Spanish.

——————. *Inter-American Yearbook on Human Rights 1986*. Dordrecht, the Netherlands: Martinus Nijhoff, 1988. IGO annual report, in Spanish.

U.S. Committee for Refugees. *Flight from Suriname: Refugees in French Guiana*. Washington, D.C.: 1987. NGO report, in English.

Zwart, T. "Consideration of Human Rights Violations by International Organs: The Case of Suriname." *SIM Newsletter* 12 (Oct. 1985): 34–43. NGO article, in English.

Swaziland

Amnesty International. *Swaziland: Detentions under the 60-Day Law*. London: 1985. NGO report, in English.

Amoah, P.K.A. "Independence of the Judiciary in Botswana, Lesotho and Swaziland." *CIJL Bulletin* nos. 10 and 11 (April–October 1987): 16–32. NGO article, in English.

——————. "Swaziland: Human Rights Situation since May 1982." September 1985. Unpublished conference paper, in English.

Armstrong, Alice, ed. *Women and Law in Southern Africa*. Harare, Zimbabwe: Zimbabwe Publishing House, 1987. Scholarly edited collection, in English.

Maope, K. A. *Human Rights in Botswana, Lesotho and Swaziland: A Survey of the BOLESWA Countries.* Roma, Lesotho: Institute of Southern African Studies, 1986. NGO report, in English.

Neff, Stephen C. "Human Rights in Africa: Thoughts on the African Charter on Human and Peoples' Rights in the Light of Case Law from Botswana, Lesotho, and Swaziland." *International and Comparative Law Quarterly* 33 (1984): 331–347. Scholarly article, in English.

——————. *Human Rights in Botswana, Lesotho and Swaziland: Implications of Adherence to International Human Rights Treaties.* Roma, Lesotho: Institute of Southern Africa Studies, 1986. Scholarly study, in English.

Sweden

Amnesty International. *Conscientious Objection to Military Service.* London: 1988. NGO report, in English.

Beach, Hugh. *The Saami of Lapland.* London: Minority Rights Groups, 1988. NGO report, in English.

Brostad, J., J. Dahl, A. Gray, et al, eds. *Native Power: The Quest for Autonomy and Nationhood of Indigenous Peoples.* Oslo, Norway: International Work Group for Indigenous Affairs and Universitetsforlaget, 1985. Scholarly edited collection, in English.

Davey, Sheila. *Children and Pornography: A Survey of the Protection of Minors against Pornography.* Geneva: International Catholic Child Bureau, 1988. NGO report, in English.

International Work Group for Indigenous Affairs. *Self-Determination and Indigenous Peoples: Saami Rights and Northern Perspectives.* Copenhagen: 1987. NGO conference proceedings, in English.

Korsmo, Fae L. "Nordic Security and the Saami Minority: Territorial Rights in Northern Fennoscandia." *Human Rights Quarterly* 10, no. 4 (Nov. 1988): 509–524. Scholarly article, in English.

Minority Rights Group. *Co-existence in Some Plural European Societies.* London: 1986. NGO report, in English.

Whitaker, Alan. "Radiation in Lappland." *Anti-Slavery Newsletter* 2, no. 7 (1986): 1. NGO article, in English.

Zentrale Dokumentatiensstelle der Freien Wohlfahrtspflege fur Fluchtlinge and European Legal Network on Asylum. *European Lawyers Workshop on Detention, Choice of Residence and Freedom of Movement of Asylum Seekers and Refugees.* Bonn, FRG: 1987. NGO conference report, in English.

Switzerland

Amnesty International. *Amnesty International Concerns in Western Europe—October 1986–March 1987.* London: 1987. NGO report, in English.

——————. *Conscientious Objection to Military Service.* London: 1988. NGO report, in English.

——————. "Switzerland: Refoulement," 2 January 1987. NGO urgent action bulletin, in English.

Minority Rights Group. *Co-existence in Some Plural European Societies.* London: 1986. NGO report, in English.

Sigler, Jay A., ed. *International Handbook on Race and Race Relations.* Westport, CT: Greenwood Press, 1987. Scholarly edited collection, in English; bibliography, pp. 449–454.

Syria

Amnesty International. *Arrests in Syria and Lebanon by Syrian Forces.* London: 1986. NGO report, in English.

——————. "Syria: Torture, Health, Legal Concern," 14 July 1988; and "Further Information on UA 186/88," 1 December 1988. NGO urgent action bulletins, in English.

Arab Organization for Human Rights. *Report: Human Rights in the Arab World.* Cairo: 1987. NGO report, in Arabic or English.

Centre for the Independence of Judges and Lawyers. "Syria: Continued Detention of Lawyers." *CIJL Bulletin* 15 (April 1985): 6–8. NGO bulletin article, in English.

Federation Internationale des Droits de l'Homme (International Federation of Human Rights). "Le Martyr du Peuple Kurde" (The Martyrdom of the Kurdish People). *Lettre de la FIDH* 241 (22 March 1988). NGO article, in French.

International Commission for the Defence of Human Rights in Syria. *Bulletin of the International Commission for the Defence of Human Rights in Syria* (January 1988). NGO newsletter, in English.

McDowall, David. *The Kurds.* 4th rev. ed. London: Minority Rights Group: 1985. NGO report, in English.

Taiwan

Amnesty International. *Republic of China (Taiwan): Political Imprisonment in Taiwan.* London: 1986. NGO report, in English.

——————. "Taiwan: Amnesty of 22 April 1988," 24 March 1988. NGO urgent action bulletin, in English.

——————. *Taiwan: The Death Penalty*. London: 1988. NGO report, in English.

——————. *Trial of Two Prisoners of Conscience*. London: 1988. NGO report, in English.

Asia Resource Center and Formosan Association for Human Rights. *Martial Law in Taiwan*. Washington, D. C.: 1985. NGO report, in English.

Canada-Asia Working Group. "Human Rights in Asia: Submission to the 43d Session of the U.N. Commission on Human Rights." *Currents* (January 1987). NGO report in English.

——————. "Human Rights in Asia: Submission Prepared for the 44th Session of the U.N. Commission on Human Rights." *Currents* 10, no. 1 (February 1988). NGO report, in English.

——————.Human Rights in Asia: Submission prepared for the 45th Session of the U. N. Commission on Human Rights." *Currents* 11, no. 1 (February 1989). NGO report in English.

Christian Conference of Asia. "Aboriginal Minorities in Taiwan and the Philippines." *CCA News* 22, no. 1 (15 January 1987): 6. NGO article, in English.

Committee to Protect Journalists. "New Measures Taken against Taiwan's Opposition Press," 5 June 1986. NGO press release, in English.

Formosan Association for Public Affairs and Formosan Association for Human Rights. *The Taiwan Confrontation Crisis*. Washington, D.C.: 1985. NGO report, in English.

Hsiung, James. C. *Human Rights in East Asia: A Cultural Perspective*. New York: Pergamon House Publishers, 1985. Scholarly edited collection, in English.

Index on Censorship. "Publishers and Editors Jailed in Taiwan," 19 June 1986. NGO briefing paper, in English.

International Committee for Human Rights in Taiwan. "Eight Political Prisoners Remain Imprisoned." *Taiwan Communique* 34 (28 May 1988): 16–19. NGO article, in English.

——————. "Freedom of the Press?" *Taiwan Communique* 26 (15 August 1986): 15–21. NGO article, in English.

——————. "Imprisoned Taiwanese Opposition Leaders on Hunger Strike." *Taiwan Communique* 20 (18 June 1985): 1–5. NGO article, in English.

——————. "Taiwan Ends Martial Law after 38 Years." *Taiwan Communique* 31 (10 September 1987): 1, 6. NGO article, in English.

——————. "Taiwan's New National Security Law Still Highly Restrictive," 26 January 1987. NGO press release, in English.

——————. "Torture Common in Taiwan's Prisons." *Taiwan Communique* 26 (15 August 1986): 14–15. NGO article, in English.

Luce, D., and R. Rumpf. *Martial Law in Taiwan*. Washington, D.C.: Asia Resource Center and Formosan Association for Human Rights, 1985. NGO monograph, in English.

Morgan, S. M., and E. Colson, eds. *People in Upheaval*. Staten Island, NY: Center for Migration Studies of New York, 1987. NGO document collection, in English.

Society for the Protection of East Asians' Human Rights. "Secret Police Cracks Down on Taiwan Opposition," 2 May 1986. NGO bulletin, in English.

Taiwan Church News. "Issues of Taiwan's Aborigines." *Occasional Bulletin* 5, no. 1 (Dec. 1987–Jan. 1988): 7–12. NGO article, in English.

World Council of Churches. *Behind the Mask: Human Rights in Asia and Latin America, An Inter-Regional Encounter.* Geneva: 1988. NGO report, in English.

Tanzania

Andreassen, B.A., and E. Asjborn, eds. "Tanzania." In *Human Rights in Developing Countries 1987/88: A Yearbook on Human Rights in Countries Receiving Nordic Aid*, 90–109. Copenhagen: Christian Michelsen Institute, 1988. NGO report in English; bibliography, pp. 361–362.

Kumar, Umesh. "Some Preliminary Observations on the Administration of Justice in a One-Party State: The Tanzanian Experience." *Lesotho Law Journal* 2, no. 1 (1986): 119–154. Scholarly article, in English.

Nyange, Herbert. *An Independent Judiciary and the Protection of Human Rights: An Examination of the Attitude of the Executive in the Phase One Government of Tanzania toward the Judiciary in Situations of its Complicity to Violations of Human Rights*. Toronto, Canada: AHRA, 1986. NGO report, in English.

——————. "Legislative and Judicial Implementation of the Norm against Torture: The Case of Tanzania." *Indian Journal of International Law* 27, no 2–3 (April–Sept. 1987): 208–227. Scholarly article, in English.

Norwegian Human Rights Project, Christian Michelsen Institute. *Human Rights in Developing Countries 1986*. Oslo: Universitetsforlaget, 1986. Government annual report, in English; bibliography, classified by country.

Skelton, James W., Jr. "Standards of Procedural Due Process under International Law vs. Preventive Detention in Selected African States." *Houston Journal of International Law* 2 (Spring 1980): 307–331. Scholarly article, in English.

Thailand

American Council for Nationalities Service. "Resettlement Hopes Fade for Cambodians in Thailand." *Refugee Reports* 7, no. 7 (11 July 1986): 1–9. NGO article, in English.

Amnesty International. "Slum Dwellers: The Less Privileged Segment of Urban Population: A Case of Bangkok Slum and Squatter Settlements." *Human Rights Forum* 1, no. 4 (Oct.–Dec. 1985): 9–16. NGO article, in English.

——————. *Thailand: Extrajudicial Executions of Kampuchean Refugees.* London: 1988. NGO report, in English.

Cerquone, J., and V. Hamilton. *Uncertain Harbors: The Plight of Vietnamese Boat People.* Washington, D.C.: U. S. Committee for Refugees, 1987. NGO issue paper, in English.

Coordinating Group for Religion in Society. "Facing up to Child Labor Abuse." *Human Rights in Thailand Report* 9, no. 1 (Jan.–March 1985): 12–13. NGO conference report, in English.

Gallagher, Dennis. *The Refugee Situation in Thailand.* Washington, D. C.: Refugee Policy Group, 1985. NGO report, in English.

Kriyurawond, Sayamol. "Land Problems in the Highlands in the Far North." *UCL Newsletter* (July–Sept. 1987): 16–19. NGO article, in English.

Lawyers Committee for Human Rights. *Seeking Shelter: Cambodians in Thailand.* New York: 1987. NGO mission report, in English.

Mameechai, K., and S. Isrowuthakul. "Human Rights and the Environment." *UCL Newsletter* (July–Sept. 1987): 12–15. NGO article, in English.

Pruksakasemsuk, Somyot. "Thai Workers' Struggle Continues." *UCL Newsletter* (Oct. 1988): 27–29. NGO article, in English.

Robinson, Court. "Refugees in Thailand: 'Is the Glass Half Full or Half Empty?' " *Refugee Reports* 8, no. 9 (11 Sept. 1987): 1–8. NGO article, in English.

——————. "Vietnamese Refugees in Thailand Face First-Asylum Crisis." *Refugee Reports* 9, no. 2 (26 Feb. 1988): 1–7. NGO article, in English.

Robinson, C., and A. Wallenstein. *Unfulfilled Hopes: The Humanitarian Parole/Immigrant Visa Program for Border Cambodians.* Washington, D. C.: U. S. Committee for Refugees, 1988. NGO issue paper, in English.

Sigler, Jay A., ed. *International Handbook on Race and Race Relations.* Westport, CT: Greenwood Press, 1987. Scholarly edited collection, in English; bibliography, pp. 449–454.

Soontorn, J. B., S. Kaiyoorawongs, and S. Chaykert. "Hill Tribes and Human Rights." *UCL Newsletter* (Oct. 1988): 16–19. NGO report, in English.

Survival International. "Thailand: Tribal Villages Torched." *Survival International News* 19 (1988): 2. NGO article, in English.

Tanchainan, Sucheela. "Sexual Violence against Women and the Women's Movement in Thailand." *Thai Development Newsletter* 3, no. 4 (1st quarter 1986): 3–5. NGO article, in English.

Tapp, Nicholas. *The Hmong of Thailand: Opium People of the Golden Triangle.* London: Anti-Slavery Society for the Protection of Human Rights and Cultural Survival, 1986. NGO monograph, in English.

Taswell, Ruth, ed. *Southeast Asian Tribal Groups and Ethnic Minorities.* Cambridge, MA: Cultural Survival, 1987. NGO conference proceedings, in English.

Thai Development Support Committee. "Tourism Promotion and its Effects on Thai Women." *Thai Development Newsletter* 4, no. 1 (June 1986): 10–14. NGO article, in English.

——————. "Background to Human Rights Situation in Thailand." *Thai Development Newsletter* 12 (Dec. 1986): 13–19. NGO article, in English.

Thongpao, Thongbai. "The State of Human Rights in Thailand in 1985." *Thai Development Newsletter* 3, no. 4 (1st quarter 1986): 11–14. NGO article, in English.

U. S. Committee for Refugees. *Refugees from Laos: In Harm's Way.* Washington, D.C.: 1986. NGO issue paper, in English.

Tibet

Asia Watch. *Human Rights in Tibet.* Washington, D. C.: 1988. NGO report, in English.

Gesellschaft fur Bedrohte Volker und Verein der Tibetaner in Deutschland (Association for Endangered Peoples and Association of Tibetans in Germany). *Tibet: Traum oder Trauma?* (Tibet: Dream or Trauma?). Gottingen, FRG: 1987. NGO report, in German.

Ledger, W. P. *The Chinese and Human Rights in Tibet.* London: Parliamentary Human Rights Group, 1988. NGO report, in English.

Van Walt van Praag, M. C. *Population Transfer and the Survival of the Tibetan Identity.* New York: U. S. Tibet Committee, 1986. NGO monograph, in English.

——————. *The Status of Tibet: History, Rights, and Prospects in International Law.* Boulder, CO: Westview Press, 1987. Scholarly monograph, in English.

Togo

Action des Chretiens pour l'Abolition de la Torture (Christian Action for the Abolition of Torture). "Regard sur . . . le Togo" (Focus on Togo). *Courrier de l'ACAT* 77 (July–Aug. 1987): 2–4. NGO article, in French.

Africa News Service. "Togo: Rights Spotlighted." *African News* 30, no. 12 (13 Dec. 1988): 6–7. NGO article, in English.

Amnesty International. *Togo: Political Imprisonment and Torture.* London: 1986. NGO report, in English.

International Commission of Jurists. *Les Services Juridiques en Milieu Rural (Afrique d l'Ouest)* (Legal Services in Rural Areas [West Africa]). Geneva: 1987. NGO report, in French.

"Togo Accused of Violations." *West Africa,* 15 December 1986, 2628. Magazine article, in English.

Trinidad and Tobago

Freedom of Information and Expression in Trinidad and Tobago. London: ARTICLE 19, 1988. NGO report, in English.

Organization of American States. *Annual Report of the Inter-American Commission on Human Rights 1986–1987.* Washington, D.C.: 1987. IGO annual report, in English.

Sigler, Jay A., ed. *International Handbook on Race and Race Relations.* Westport, CT: Greenwood Press, 1987. Scholarly edited collection, in English; bibliography, pp. 449–454.

Trinidad and Tobago Bureau on Human Rights. *Report on Human Rights in Trinidad and Tobago.* San Fernando, Trinidad: 1986. NGO report, in English.

——————. *Report on the Administration of Justice in Trinidad and Tobago.* San Fernando, Trinidad: 1987. NGO report, in English.

Tunisia

Arab Organization for Human Rights. *Report: Human Rights in the Arab World.* Cairo: 1987. NGO report, in Arabic or English.

Federation Internationale des Droits de L'Homme (International Federation of Human Rights). "Tunisia: Judicial Observation Mission." *FIDH Letter* (7–10 July 1986). NGO article, in French.

——————. *Tunisie: Proces d'Islamiste Tunisiens devant la Cour de Surete de l'Etat* (Tunisia: Trial of Islamic Tunisians before the State Security Court). Paris: 1987. NGO report, in French.

Freedom of Information and Expression in Tunisia: A Commentary by ARTICLE 19 on the Report Submitted to the U. N. Human Rights Committee by the Government of the Republic of Tunisia. London: ARTICLE 19, 1987. NGO report, in English.

Institute for Women's Studies in the Arab World. "Tunisian Women Speak." *Al-Raida* 8, no. 33 (1 Aug. 1985). NGO article, in English.

International League for Human Rights. *Tunisia's Human Rights Record: A Critique of the Government's Official Report to the U. N. Human Rights Committee.* New York: 1986. NGO report, in English.

Ligue tunisienne pour la defense des Droits de l'Homme (Tunisian League for the Defense of Human Rights). *Dossier: Plaidoyer pour la Ligue* (Documents: The Case for the League). Tunisia: 1987. NGO document collection, in French or Arabic.

Marzouki, Moncef. *L'Arrache Corps* (The Body Broken). Paris: Editions Alternative et Paralleles, 1979. Scholarly monograph, in French; bibliography, pp. 255–257.

——————. "Winning Freedom." *Index on Censorship* 18, no. 1 (Jan. 1989): 23–35. NGO article, in English.

Minnesota Lawyers International Human Rights Committee. *Tunisia: Human Rights Crisis of 1987.* Minneapolis, MN: 1988. NGO report, in English, bibliography, pp. 69–70.

Sidem-Poulain, Odile. "Proces de M. Ahmed Mestiri—Secretaire General du Movement des Democrates Socialistes" (The trial of Mr. Ahmed Mestiri—General Secretary of the Socialist Democrat Movement). *La Lettre de la FIDH* 70 (4 June 1986). NGO mission report, in French.

——————. *Rapport de Mission: Tunisie* (Mission Report: Tunisia). Paris: Federation Internationale des Droits de l'Homme, 1987. NGO report, in French.

Turkey

Amnesty International. *Turkey: An Unsafe Country of Waiting for Iranian Refugees.* London: 1988. NGO report, in English.

——————. *Turkey: Brutal and Systematic Abuse of Human Rights.* London: 1989. NGO report, in English.

——————. *Turkey: The Death Penalty—Recent Developments and Some Examples.* London: 1988. NGO report, in English.

——————. *Turkey: Torture and Medical Neglect of Prisoners.* London: 1988. NGO report, in English.

Balian, Hrair. *Turkey: Continued Violations of International human Rights and Humanitarian Law.* Berkeley, CA: Human Rights Advocates, 1987. NGO report, in English.

Commission on Security and Cooperation in Europe. *Human Rights Abuses in Cyprus.* Washington, D.C.: 1985. Government hearing, in English.

—————. *The State of Human Rights in Turkey (An Update): Report Submitted to the Congress of the United States.* Washington, D.C.: 1988. Government report, in English.

Committee for Defence of Democratic Rights in Turkey. "Kurdistan Refugees—Out of the Frying Pan into the Fire." *Turkey Newsletter* 84 (Nov.–Dec. 1988): 8–9. NGO article in English.

Defence for Children International. *Children in Prison in Turkey.* Geneva: 1988. NGO report, in English.

Dikerdem, Mehmet Ali. "A Turkish Tug-of-War." *Index on Censorship* 16, no. 6 (June 1987): 15–19. NGO article, in English.

Federation Internationale des Droits de l'Homme (International Federation of Human Rights). "Le Martyr du Peuple Kurde" (The Martyrdom of the Kurdish People). *Lettre de la FIDH* 241 (22 March 1988). NGO article, in French.

—————. "Turquie: Depuis 1981, 33 Morts dans la Prison de Diyarbakir" (Turkey: Since 1981, 33 Deaths in the Diyarbakir Prison). *Lettre de la FIDH* 158 (3 June 1986): 3. NGO article, in French.

Laber, J., and L. Whitman. *State of Flux: Human Rights in Turkey.* New York: U.S. Helsinki Watch Committee, 1987. NGO report, in English.

Lang, D. M., and C.J. Walker. *The Armenians.* London: Minority Rights Group, 1987. NGO report, in English.

McDowall, David. *The Kurds.* 4th rev. ed. London: Minority Rights Group, 1985. NGO report, in English.

Peeters, Yvo J. D. "The Rights of Minorities in Present-day Turkey." *Europa Ethnica* 44, no. 3 (1987): 131–137. News article, in English.

Salmon, Mireille. *Rapport de Mission en Turquie* (Report of the Human Rights Mission to Turkey). Brussels, Belgium: International Association of Democratic Lawyers, 1986. NGO mission report, in French.

Siesby, Erik. *The Framework for Democracy and Human Rights in Turkish Law.* Vienna, Austria: International Helsinki Federation for Human Rights, 1988. NGO report, in English.

U. S. Helsinki Watch Committee. *Destroying Ethnic Identity: The Kurds of Turkey—An Update.* New York: 1988. NGO report, in English.

—————. *Freedom and Fear: Human Rights in Turkey.* New York: 1986. NGO report, in English.

—————. "Turkey." In *Ten Years Later: Violation of the Helsinki Accords,* 129–149. New York: 1986. NGO report, in English.

—————. *Violations of the Helsinki Accords: Turkey.* New York: 1986. NGO report, in English.

Uganda

Amnesty International. *Administrative Detention.* London: 1988. NGO report, in English.

—————. *Aide-Memoire: Summary of Amnesty International's Concerns in the Republic of Uganda.* London: 1987. NGO report, in English.

—————. *Uganda: Criminal Charges against Critical Journalists.* London: 1988. NGO report, in English.

—————. *Uganda: Evidence of Torture.* New York: 1985. NGO report, in English.

—————. *Violations of Human Rights in the Republic of Uganda.* London: 1985. NGO report, in English.

"Censorship in Uganda." *Index on Censorship* 16, no. 3 (March 1987): 40. NGO article, in English.

Center on War and the Child. *Uganda: Land of the Child Soldier, a Summary Report.* Eureka Springs, AR: 1987. NGO report, in English.

Clark, Lance. "Post-Emergency Assistance for Refugees in Eastern and Southern Africa." *Migration News* no. 3–4 (July–Dec. 1987): 3–24. NGO research paper, in English.

Donnelly, J., and R. E. Howard, eds. *International Handbook on Human Rights.* Westport, CT: Greenwood Press, 1987. Scholarly edited collection, in English.

Heinz, Wolfgang S. *Ursachen und Folgen von Menschenrechtsverletzungen in der Dritten Welt* (Causes and Consequences of Human Rights Violations in Third World Countries). Saarbrucken, FGR: Verlag Breitenbach, 1986. Scholarly monograph, in German; bibliography on Uganda, pp. 315–318.

International Alert. *Uganda: International Seminar on Internal Conflict.* London: 1987. NGO conference report, in English.

International League for Human Rights. *Uganda after Amin: A Case of Displacement and Discrimination against the Banyarwanda Population.* New York: 1985. NGO report, in English.

NGO Committee on UNICEF and UNICEF. "Child Soldiers of Uganda." *Action for Children* 1, no. 5 (1986): 6. IGO article, in English.

Radda Barnen, International Commission of Jurists (Swedish Section). *U.N. Assistance for Human Rights.* Stockholm: 1988. NGO report, in English.

Rusk, John D. "Uganda: Breaking out of the Mold?" *Africa Today* no. 2–3 (15 June 1987): 91–101. News article, in English.

Uganda Human Rights Activists. *Report on Human Rights in Uganda*. Kampala, Uganda: 1987. NGO report, in English.

U. S. Committee for Refugees. *Human Rights in Uganda: The Reasons for Refugees*. Washington, D.C.: 1985. NGO report, in English.

Union of Soviet Socialist Republics

Alexeyeva, Ludmilla. *U.S. Broadcasting to the Soviet Union*. New York: U.S. Helsinki Watch Committee, 1986. NGO report, in English.

American Association for the Advancement of Science, Committee on Scientific Freedom and Responsibility. *Scientists Imprisoned in the Soviet Union in Violation of the Helsinki Final Act of 1975*. Washington, D. C.: 1987. NGO report, in English.

Amnesty international. *USSR: Review of Punitive Psychiatry since January 1987*. London: 1988. NGO report, in English.

Artz, Donna E. *Denial of Due Process: Soviet Failure to Provide for Appeal of Emigration Refusals*. Huntington, NY: Soviet Jewry Law Project, 1988. NGO report, in English.

Barist, J., O.C. Pell, E. Oshman, and M.E. Hamel. *Who May Leave: A Review of Soviet Practice Restricting Emigration on Grounds of Knowledge of "State Secrets" in Comparison with Standards of International Law and the Policies of Other States*. New York: National Conference on Soviet Jewry and White & Case, 1987. NGO report, in English.

Commission on Security and Cooperation in Europe. *Basket I—Implementation of the Final Act of the Conference on Security and Cooperation in Europe: Findings Eleven Years after Helsinki*. Washington, D. C.: GPO, 1987. Government report, in English.

——————. *Documents of the Helsinki Monitoring Groups in the USSR and Lithuania (1976–1986)*. Vol. 3. Washington, D.C.: 1987. Government document collection, in English.

——————. "Reform and Human Rights: The Gorbachev Record." *Report Submitted to the Congress of the United States*. Washington, D.C.: GPO, 1988. Government report, in English.

Das Land und die Welt. *List of Political Prisoners in the USSR*. Munich, FRG: 1988. NGO report, in English.

Donnelly, J., and R. E. Howard, eds. *International Handbook on Human Rights*. Westport, CT: Greenwood Press, 1987. Scholarly edited collection, in English.

Field, Francis. "Nagorno-Karabakh: A Constitutional Conundrum." *Radio Liberty Research Bulletin* 30 (15 July 1988). NGO report, in English.

Fitzpatrick, Catherine A. *Soviet Abuse of Psychiatry for Political Purposes*. New York: U.S. Helsinki Watch Committee, 1987. NGO report, in English.

Internationale Gesellschaft fur Menschenrechte (International Society for Human Rights). *CSCE and Human Rights: Divided Families and the Denial of Freedom of Movement*. Vols. 1 and 2. Frankfurt, FRG: 1986. NGO report, in English.

International Helsinki Federation for Human Rights. *On Speaking Terms: An Unprecedented Human Rights Mission to the Soviet Union*. Vienna, Austria: 1988. NGO report, in English.

International League for Human Rights. *Civil and Political Rights in the Mongolian People's Republic*. New York: 1986. NGO report, in English.

Jhabvala, Farrokh. "The Soviet Bloc's View of the Implementation of Human Rights Accords." *Human Rights Quarterly* 7, no. 4 (Nov. 1985):461–491. Scholarly article, in English.

Korey, William. "Helsinki, Human Rights and the Gorbachev Style." *Ethics and International Affairs* 1 (1987): 113–133. Scholarly article, in English.

Lang, D. M., and C. J. Walker. *The Armenians*. Rev. ed. London: Minority Rights Group, 1987. NGO report, in English.

Mazeika, Rasa, ed. *Violations of Human Rights in Soviet Occupied Lithuania: A Report for 1983–1986*. Philadelphia, PA: Lithuanian American Community, 1988. NGO report, in English.

Parchomenko, Walter. *Soviet Images of Dissidents and Nonconformists*. New York: Praeger, 1986. Monograph, in English.

Sigler, Jay A., ed. *International Handbook on Race and Race Relations*. Westport, CT: Greenwood Press, 1987. Scholarly edited collection, in English; bibliography, pp. 449–454.

"Social and Economic Rights in the Soviet Bloc." *Survey: A Journal of East and West Studies* 29, no. 4 (Aug. 1987). NGO special issue, in English.

Tolz, Vera. "Informal Groups in the USSR in 1988." *Radio Liberty Research Bulletin* 46 (30 Oct. 1988). NGO report, in English.

U.S. Congress, Subcommittee on Human Rights and International Organizations and Subcommittee on Europe and the Middle East. *Religious Persecution in the Soviet Union, Part I: Soviet Jewry*, 99th Cong., 1st sess., 1985. Government hearings, in English.

U.S. Helsinki Watch Committee, Asia Watch. *By All Parties to the Conflict: Violations of the Laws of War in Afghanistan*. New York: 1988. NGO report, in English.

——————. *From Below: Independent Peace and Environmental Movements in Eastern Europe and the USSR*. New York: 1987. NGO report, in English.

————. *Violations of the Helsinki Accords: USSR.* New York: 1986. NGO report, in English.

World Federation of Free Latvians. *Latvian Dissent.* Rockville, MD: 1985. NGO report, in English.

Wrobel, Brian. *Glasnost and Soviet Criminal Trials: A Report by the Parliamentary Human Rights Group.* London: Parliamentary Human Rights Group, 1987. NGO report, in English.

United Kingdom

American Protestants for Truth about Ireland. *Documents concerning Summary Executions by the British Army and the Royal Ulster Constabulary.* Gwynedd, PA: 1988. NGO brief, in English.

Amnesty International. *Amnesty International Concerns in Western Europe, March 1986–September 1986.* London: 1986. NGO report, in English.

————. *United Kingdom: Alleged Forced Admissions during Incommunicado Detention.* London: 1988. NGO report, in English.

————. *United Kingdom-Northern Ireland: Killings by Security Forces and "Supergrass" Trials.* London: 1988. NGO report, in English.

Bailey, Sidney, ed. *Human Rights and Responsibilities in Britain and Ireland: A Christian Perspective.* London: Macmillan, 1988. Scholarly study, in English.

Bonnechere, Michele. *Rapport Preliminarie sur la Mission d'Observation du Proces Concernant Gerard Kelly et Brendan McFarlane . . .* (Preliminary Report on the Observer Mission to the Trial of Gerard Kelly and Brendan McFarlane . . .). Brussels, Belgium: International Association of Democratic Lawyers, 1987. NGO report, in French.

Gordon, P., and A. Newnham. *Different Worlds: Racism and Discrimination in Britain.* 2d rev. ed. London: The Runnymede Trust, 1986. NGO report, in English.

Haysom, Nicholas. "Licence to Kill, Part II: A Comparative Survey of the Law in the United Kingdom, United States of America and South Africa." *South African Journal on Human Rights* 3, pt. 2 (July 1987): 202–222. Scholarly article, in English.

Independent Commission on International Humanitarian Issues. *Refugees: Dynamics of Displacement.* London: Zed Books, 1986. NGO monograph, in English.

Index on Censorship 17, no. 8 (Sept. 1988). NGO special issue on the United Kingdom, in English.

Irish American Unity Conference, Human Rights Committee. *Report on Human Rights in Northern Ireland.* Whitestone, NY: 1985. NGO report, in English.

National Council for Civil Liberties. *Identity Cards and the Threat to Civil Liberties.* London: 1988. NGO briefing paper, in English.

Pettman, Ralph. *Incitement to Racial Hatred: The International Experience.* Canberra, Australia: Human Rights Commission, 1982. Government monograph, in English.

Sieghart, Paul, ed. *Human Rights in the United Kingdom.* London: Human Rights Network, 1988. NGO monograph, in English; footnotes to article contain substantial bibliographic references.

Sigler, Jay A., ed. *International Handbook on Race and Race Relations.* Westport, CT: Greenwood Press, 1987. Scholarly edited collection, in English; bibliography, pp. 449–454.

Tarnopolsky, Walter S. "Race Relations Commissions in Canada, Australia, New Zealand, the United Kingdom and the United States." *Human Rights Law Journal* 6, pt. 2–4 (1985): 145–178. Scholarly article, in English.

United States of America

American Friends Service Committee, Criminal Justice Program. *The Lessons of Marion: The Failure of a Maximum Security Prison-A History and Analysis, with Voices of Prisoners.* Philadelphia, PA: 1985. NGO report, in English.

Amnesty International. *Allegations of Ill-Treatment in Marion Prison, Illinois, USA.* London: 1987. NGO report, in English.

————. *United States of America: The Death Penalty.* London: 1987. NGO report, in English.

Anti-Defamation League of B'nai B'rith. *1987 Audit of Anti-Semitic Incidents.* New York: 1987. NGO report, in English.

————. *Hate Groups in America: A Record of Bigotry and Violence.* Rev. ed. New York: 1988. NGO report, in English; bibliography, pp. 91–96.

Bermann, Karl. *Under the Big Stick.* Boston, MA: South End Press, 1986. Scholarly monograph, in English.

Brandit, James R. "Reconciling Free Speech and Equality: What Justifies Censorship?" *Harvard Journal of Law and Public Policy* 9, no. 2 (Spring 1986): 429–460. Scholarly article, in English.

Breum, M., and A. Hendriks, eds. *AIDS and Human Rights: An International Perspective.* Copenhagen: Danish Center of Human Rights, 1988. Edited collection, in English.

Brostad, J., J. Dahl, A. Gray, et al. *Native Power: The Quest for Autonomy and Nationhood of Indigenous Peoples.* Oslo, Norway: International Work Group for Indigenous Affairs and Universitetsforlaget, 1985. Scholarly edited collection, in English.

Carleton, D., and M. Stohl. "The Foreign Policy of Human Rights: Rhetoric and Reality from Jimmy Carter to Ronald Reagan." *Human Rights Quarterly* 7, no. 2 (May 1985): 205–229. Scholarly article, in English.

Champagne, Duane. *Strategies and Conditions of Political and Cultural Survival in American Indian Societies.* Cambridge, MA: Cultural Survival, 1985. NGO occasional paper, in English.

Donnelly, J., and R. E. Howard, eds. *International Handbook on Human Rights.* Westport, CT: Greenwood Press, 1987. Scholarly edited collection, in English.

Edelman, M. W., and J. D. Weill. "Status of Children in the 1980s." *Columbia Human Rights Law Review* 17, no. 2 (Spring–Summer 1986): 139–158. Scholarly article, in English.

Fawcett, J. T., and B. V. Carino, eds. *Pacific Bridges: The New Migration from Asia and the Pacific Islands.* Staten Island, NY: Center for Migration Studies of New York, 1987. NGO document collection, in English.

Finn, J., and L. R. Sussman, eds. *Today's American: How Free?* New York: Freedom House, 1986. Edited collection, in English.

Forbes, Susan S. *Adaptation and Integration of Recent Refugees to the United States.* Washington, D.C.: Refugee Policy Group, 1985. NGO report, in English.

Forsythe, David P. "Congress and Human Rights in U.S. Foreign Policy: The Fate of General Legislation." *Human Rights Quarterly* 9, no. 3 (Aug. 1987): 382–404. Scholarly article, in English.

————. *Human Rights and U.S. Foreign Policy: Congress Reconsidered.* Gainesville, FL: University Presses of Florida, 1988. Scholarly study, in English.

Gibney, Mark. "A 'Well-founded Fear' of Persecution." *Human Rights Quarterly* 10, no. 1 (Feb. 1988): 109–121. Scholarly article, in English.

Kozol, Jonathan. *Rachel and her Children: Homeless Families in America.* New York: Crown Publishers, 1988. Scholarly monograph, in English; bibliography, pp. 249–252.

Leibowitz, Arnold H. "Comparative Analysis of Immigration in Key Developed Countries in Relation to Immigration Reforms and Control Legislation in the United States." *Human Rights Law Journal* 7, no. 1 (1986): 1–73. Scholarly article, in English.

Lutz, Chris, comp. *They Don't All Wear Sheets: A Chronology of Racist and Far Right Violence—1980–1986.* New York: Center for Democratic Renewal and National Council of Churches, 1987. NGO report, in English.

Mower, A. Glenn, Jr. *Human Rights and American Foreign Policy: The Carter and Reagan Experiences.* Westport, CT: Greenwood Press, 1987. Scholarly monograph, in English; bibliography, pp. 159–163.

Pacific Northwest Research Center, Africa Fund. *Unified List of U.S. Companies with Investments or Loans in South Africa and Namibia.* New York: Updated periodically. NGO report, in English.

Pettman, Ralph. *Incitement to Racial Hatred: The International Experience.* Canberra, Australia: Human Rights Commission, 1982. Government monograph, in English.

Presidential Commission on the Human Immunodeficiency Virus Epidemic. *Report of the Commission.* Washington, D.C.: 1988. Government report, in English.

Rowles, James P. "Nicaragua vs. the United States: Issues of Law and Policy." *The International Lawyer* 20, no. 4 (Fall 1986): 1245–1288. Scholarly article, in English.

Shilts, Randy. *And the Band Played on: Politics, People and the AIDS Epidemic.* New York: St. Martin's Press, 1987. Journalistic monograph, in English.

Sigler, Jay, A., ed. *International Handbook on Race and Race Relations.* Westport, CT: Greenwood Press, 1987. Scholarly edited collection, in English; bibliography, pp. 449–454.

Streib, Victor L. *Death Penalty for Juveniles.* Bloomington, IN: Indiana University Press, 1987. Scholarly report, in English; bibliography, pp. 237–250.

Tarnopolsky, Walter S. "Race Relations Commissions in Canada, Australia, New Zealand, the United Kingdom and the United States." *Human Rights Law Journal* 6, pt. 2–4 (1985): 145–178. Scholarly article, in English.

Washington Council of Lawyers. "Reagan Civil Rights: The First Twenty Months." *New York Law School Human Rights Annual* 1 (1983): 99–171. Scholarly article in yearbook, in English.

Watch Committees, Lawyers Committee for Human Rights. *The Reagan Administration's Record on Human Rights in 1987.* New York: 1987. NGO report, in English.

Uruguay

Bloche, Maxwell Gregg. *Uruguay's Military Physicians: Cogs in a System of State Terror.* Washington, D.C.: American Association for the Advancement of Science, Committee on Scientific Freedom and Responsibility, 1987. NGO report, in English.

Centro de Informacion, Investigacion y Documentacion del Uruguay (Center for Information, Research and Documentation of Uruguay). "La

Mujer en Uruguay" (Women in Uruguay). *Boletin Sercom* 2 (1985): 2–15. NGO article, in Spanish.

"El Plebiscito Va: Hazana de Pueblo" (The Plebiscite Result: The People's Triumph). *Brecha* 4, no. 162 (23 Dec. 1988). News article, in Spanish.

Fruhling, Hugo, ed. *Represion Politica y Defensa de los Derechos Humanos* (Political Repression and the Defense of Human Rights). Santiago, Chile: Academia de Humanismo Cristiano and Ediciones Chile y America, 1986. NGO edited collection, in Spanish.

Heinz, Wolfgang S. *Ursachen und Folgen von Menschenrechtsverletzungen in der Dritten Welt* (Causes and Consequences of Human Rights Violations in Third World Countries). Saarbrucken, FGR: Verlag Breitenbach, 1986. Scholarly monograph, in German; bibliography on Uruguay, pp. 571–572.

Instituto Interamericano de Derechos Humanos (Inter-American Institute of Human Rights). *Revista IIDH* 5 (Jan.–June 1987). IGO document collection, in English.

Inter-Church Committee on Human Rights in Latin America. *ICCHRLA 1987 Annual Report: General Concerns and Brief Country Reports.* Toronto, Canada: 1988. NGO report, in English.

Madres y Familiares de Detenidos y Desaparecidos (Mothers and Relatives of the Detained-Disappeared). *Situation concerning the Investigation of Prisoners and Disappeared in Uruguay.* Montevideo, Uruguay: 1985. NGO report, in Spanish.

Perez Aquirre, Luis. *Derechos Humanos: Un Relato Militante de Su Defensa y Promocion en el Uruguay* (Human Rights: A Participatory Account of their Defense and Promotion in Uruguay). Montevideo: Servicio Paz y Justicia, 1986. NGO report, in Spanish.

Secretariat International des Juristes pour l'Amnistie en Uruguay (International Secretariat of Lawyers for Amnesty in Uruguay). *Situacion de las Personas Desapapecidas y los Hechos que la Motivaron* (Situation of the Disappeared Persons and the Motivation behind It). Paris: 1985. NGO report, in Spanish.

Servicio Paz y Justicia (Service for Peace and Justice). *Informe: Derechos Humanos en Uruguay/1988* (Report: Human Rights in Uruguay 1988). Montevideo, Uruguay: 1988. NGO annual report, in Spanish.

——————. "La Condicion de la Mujer" (The Condition of Women). *Paz y Justicia 1*, no. 6 (June–July 1986): 20–41. NGO article, in Spanish.

——————. "Uruguay: Paz vs. Crisis" (Uruguay: Peace vs. Crisis). *Pax y Justicia 1*, no. 7 (Aug.–Sept. 1986): 29–34. NGO article, in Spanish.

Varela, Carlos. "The Referendum Campaign in Uruguay: An Unprecendented Challenge to Impunity." *Human Rights Internet* 13, no. 1 (Spring 1989). Commentary, in English.

Westerveen, Gert. "Return to Democracy in Argentina and Uruguay: Some Outstanding Human Rights Problems." *SIM Newsletter* 11 (July 1985): 9–16. NGO article, in English.

Vanuatu

International Confederation of Free Trade Unions. "Strikes on Vanuatu." *Free Labour World* 8/88 (31 May 1988): 3. NGO article, in English.

Scott-Murphy, J., D. Dunstan, and N. Khan. *Human Rights in Melanesia: The Report of the Evatt Foundation Delegation.* Sydney, Australia: H.V. Evatt Memorial Foundation, 1988. NGO report, in English.

Venezuela

Branch, Hilary. "Death Well Revelations, Muzzle on Press Shocks Venezuelans." *Latinamerica Press* 16, no. 21 (5 June 1986): 1–2. News service article, in English.

Colchester, Marcus, ed. *The Health and Survival of the Venezuelan Yanoama.* London: Anthropology Resource Center, Survival International, and International Work Group for Indigenous Affairs. Scholarly articles, in English.

Federation Internationale des Droits de l'Homme (International Federation of Human Rights). "Venezuela: Un Nouvel Etat Concerne par les Disparitions Forcees des Personnes?" (Venezuela: A New State Affected by Forced Disappearances of People?) *Lettre de la FIDH* 164 (16 Sept. 1986): 1–21. NGO bulletin article, in French.

Latin American Documentation. *The Church and Native Peoples.* Lima, Peru: 1986. NGO document collection, in English.

——————. "Venezuela: The Church Speaks for the Unemployed." *LADOC* no. 6 (July–Aug. 1986): 1–9. NGO bulletin article, in English.

Molina, Jose Enrique. *Democracia Representative y Participacion Politica en Venezuela* (Representative Democracy and Political Participation in Venezuela). San Jose, Costa Rica: Instituto Interamericano de Derechos Humanos and Centro de Asesoria y Promocion Electoral, 1986. IGO monograph, in Spanish.

Pocaterra, Noeli. "Venezuela: Education and Indigenous Women." *IWGIA Newsletter* 55–56 (Oct.–Dec. 1988): 105–115. NGO article, in English.

Programa Venezolano de Educacion-Accion en Derechos Humanos (Venezuelan Program of Human

Rights Education and Action). *Los Detenidos de Agosto (Resumen Cronologico de la Informacion de Prensa)* (August Detainees [Chronological Summary of Press Information]). Caracas: 1988. NGO report, in Spanish.

Survival International. *An End to Laughter? Tribal Peoples and Economic Development.* London: 1985. NGO report, in English.

Vietnam

Amnesty International. *Religious Intolerance.* London: 1986. NGO report, in English.

—————. *Socialist Republic of Viet Nam: Possible Continued Detention in "Re-education Camps" Causes Concern.* London: 1988. NGO report, in English.

—————. *The Imprisonment of Persons Seeking to Leave a Country or to Return to Their Own Country.* London: 1986. NGO report, in English.

—————. *Viet Nam: Thousands Released in National Day Amnesty.* London: 1987. NGO report, in English.

Asia Watch. *1987 Annual Report.* Washington, D.C.: 1987. NGO annual report, in English.

—————. *Still Confined: Journalists in "Re-education" Camps and Prisons in Vietnam.* New York: 1987. NGO report, in English.

—————. "Trial of Writers, Postal Worker in Vietnam," 16 June 1988. NGO urgent action bulletin, in English.

Chanda, Nayan. *Brother Enemy: The War after the War.* New York: Harcourt Brace Jovanovich, 1986. Scholarly monograph, in English.

Lithuanian Catholic Religious Aid. "Violations of Human and Trade Union Rights in the Socialist Republic of Vietnam." *Economic and Social Bulletin* 34, no. 1 (Jan.–March 1986): 7–9. NGO article, in English.

Marr, David, G. "Church and State in Vietnam." *Indochina Issues* 74 (April 1987): 1–10. NGO issue paper, in English.

Que Me, Vietnam Committee on Human Rights. *Vietnam 1987: Human Rights Revelations by Top C.P.V. Officials and Hanoi Press.* Genevilliers, France: 1987. NGO report, in English.

Robinson, Court. "Southeast Asian Refugees: Critical Mass?" *Indochina Issues* 77 (Dec. 1987): 1–7. NGO article, in English.

Zentrale Dokumentationsstelle der Freien Wohlfahrtspflege fur Fluchtlinge. *Arbeitsmaterialien fur den Unterricht: Die Weltfluchtlingsproblematik und ihre Auswirkungen in der Bundesrepublik Deutschland* (Study Materials: The World Refugee Problem and its Consequences in the Federal Republic of Germany). Bonn, FRG: 1987. NGO edited collection, in German.

Western Sahara

Comite Suisse de Soutien au Peuple Sahraoui (Swiss Committee for Support of the Saharan People). "Commission des Droits de l'Homme de l'ONU: Nouvelle Resolution sur le Sahara Occidental" (UN Commission on Human Rights: New Resolution on Western Sahara). *Nouvelles Sahraouis* 36 (June 1985): 5–6. NGO article, in French.

Hodges, Tony. *The Western Saharans.* London: Minority Rights Group, 1984. NGO report, in English; selective bibliography, pp. 19–20.

Lawless, R., and L. Monahan, eds. *War and Refugees: The Western Sahara Conflict.* London: Refugee Studies Programme, Queen Elizabeth House, 1987. Scholarly edited collection, in English.

Smith, Theresa K. "Human Rights and the Western Sahara War." *Association of Concerned Africa Scholars Bulletin* 23 (Spring 1988): 10–17. Scholarly article, in English.

Yemen

Amnesty International. *Yemen: Incommunicado Detention and Unfair Trial.* London: 1988. NGO report, in English.

Arab Organization for Human Rights. *Report: Human Rights in the Arab World.* Cairo: 1987. NGO report, in English or Arabic.

Yugoslavia

Amnesty International. *Conscientious Objection to Military Service.* London: 1988. NGO report, in English.

Camejo, M. J., and C. Fitzpatrick. *Violations of the Helsinki Accords: Yugoslavia.* New York: U.S. Helsinki Watch Committee, 1988. NGO report, in English.

Cavoski, Kosta. "Why There is More Free Speech in Belgrade than in Zagreb." *Index on Censorship* 15, no. 8 (Aug. 1986): 22–24. NGO article, in English.

Centre for the Independence of Judges and Lawyers. "Yugoslavia: Detention of Lawyer Vladimir Seks." *CIJL Bulletin* 15 (April 1985): 13–14. NGO article, in English.

"Communist Decline Conjures up the Bogey of Islamic Revival." *Impact International* 16, no. 13 (11–24 July 1986): 9–10. Magazine article, in English.

"Conscientious Objection: The Situation in Yugoslavia." *Religion in Communist Lands* 15, no. 3

(Winter 1987): 332–335. NGO article, in English.

Dimitrijevic, Vojin. "Human Rights Today." *Studies* (1988). Scholarly articles, in English, French, and Spanish.

"Eastern Europe in 1988." *Radio Free Europe Research* 13, no. 52 (30 December 1988). Government background paper, in English.

Marjanovic, S., R. Marjanovic, and N. Novakovic. "Measures Taken in Yugoslavia to Ensure the Effective Exercise of Human Rights by Handicapped People." Paper presented at the Conference of International Experts Meeting on Ways and Means to Ensure Effective Exercise of Human Rights by Disadvantaged Groups, Quebec, Canada, 20 Nov. 1985. Unpublished conference paper, in English.

Matas, David. "Human Rights in Yugoslavia." *IHR Newsletter* 8 (Summer 1988). NGO article, in English.

Stankovic, Sobodan. "Political Prisoners." *Radio Free Europe Research* 12, no. 26 (29 June 1987). Government report, in English.

——————. "Slovenia's Intellectuals Become Restless." *Radio Free Europe Research* 11, no. 35, pt. 1 (29 Aug. 1986): 13–16. Government article, in English.

——————. "Yugoslavia's Turks Complain about Their Position." *Radio Free Europe Research* 11, no. 35, pt. 1 (29 Aug. 1986): 17–19. Government article, in English.

U.S. Helsinki Watch Committee. *From Below: Independent Peace and Environmental Movements in Eastern Europe and the USSR.* New York: 1987. NGO report, in English.

——————. "Yugoslavia." In *Ten Years Later: Violations of the Helsinki Accords,* 301–326. New York: 1986. NGO report, in English.

Zaire

Africa News Service. "In Focus: Zaire, Parts 1–4." *Africa News* 29, nos. 1, 3, 5, and 7 (8 Feb.–4 April 1988). NGO articles, in English.

Amnesty International. *Prisoners of Conscience Restricted under the Terms of Administrative Banishment Orders in the Republic of Zaire.* London: 1985. NGO report, in English.

——————. *Republic of Zaire: Amnesty International's Concerns between January 1987 and January 1988.* London: 1988. NGO report, in English.

——————. *Torture in Zaire—The Pattern and Individual Cases.* London: 1986. NGO report, in English.

——————. *Zaire: Reports of Torture and Killings Committed by the Armed Forces in the Shaba Region.* London: 1986. NGO report, in English.

Crisis in Zaire: Myths and Realities. Trenton, NJ: Africa World Press, 1986. Scholarly collection, in English.

Federation Internationale des Droits de l'Homme (International Federation of Human Rights). "Zaire: Le Comite des Droits de l'Homme de l'ONU Constate les Violations Dont ont ete Victims des Parlementaires de l'Opposition" (Zaire: The United Nations Committee on Human Rights Verifies Violations against Opposition Members of Parliament). *La Lettre de la FIDH* 159 (17 June 1986): 3. NGO article, in French.

Freedom of Information and Expression in Zaire: Commentary by ARTICLE 19 on the Report Submitted to the U.N. Human Rights Committee by the Government of Zaire. London: ARTICLE 19, 1987. NGO report, in English; bibliography of sources, pp. 44–45.

International League for Human Rights. *Zaire's Human Rights Record: Comments on the Government of Zaire's Official Report to the Human Rights Committee.* New York: 1987. NGO report, in English.

Posner, Michael. "Zaire under Mobutu." *Index on Censorship* 16, no. 9 (Oct. 1987): 24–25, 40. NGO article/testimony, in English.

Zambia

Amnesty International. *Amnesty International's Concerns in the Republic of Zambia.* London: 1987. NGO report, in English.

Andreassen, B.A., and A. Eide, eds. "Zambia." In *Human Rights in Developing Countries 1987/88: A Yearbook on Human Rights in Countries Receiving Nordic Aid,* 110–127. Copenhagen, Denmark: Christian Michelsen Institute, 1988. NGO report, in English. Bibliography on Zambia, pp. 362–363.

Armstrong, Alice, ed. *Women and Law in Southern Africa.* Harare, Zimbabwe: Zimbabwe Publishing House, 1987. Scholarly edited collection, in English.

Freedom of Information and Expression in Zambia. London: ARTICLE 19, 1988. NGO report, in English.

Freund, P.J., and K. Kalumba. "Spontaneously Settled Refugees in Northwestern Province, Zambia." *International Migration Review* 20, no. 2 (Summer 1986): 299–312. NGO article, in English.

Hamalengwa, Munyonzwe. "The Legal System of Zambia." *AHRA Working Paper* 19 (1986). Research paper, in English.

Mubako, S. V. "Fundamental Rights and Judicial Review: The Zambian Experience." *Zimbabwe Law*

Review 1–2 (1983–1984): 97–132. Scholarly article, in English.

Ndulo, M., and K. Turner. *Civil Liberties Cases in Zambia.* Oxford, UK: African Law Reports, 1984. Legal monograph/collection, in English.

Parker, Collins. "Control of Executive Discretion and Preventive Detention in Zambia." *Comparative and International Law Journal of Southern Africa* 13, no. 2 (July 1980): 159–176. Scholarly article, in English.

Tramberg Hanson, Karen. "Urban Women and Work in Africa: A Zambian Case." *TransAfrica Forum* 4, no. 3 (Spring 1987): 9–23. NGO article, in English.

U.N. High Commissioner for Refugees. "Zambia under Threat." *Refugees* 31 (July 1986): 11–13. IGO journal article, in English.

Zimba, L. S. *The Zambian Bill of Rights: An Historical and Comparative Study of Human Rights in Commonwealth Africa.* Nairobi: East African Publishing House, 1984. Scholarly study, in English.

Zimbabwe

Amnesty International. *Detention without Trial of Political Prisoners in Zimbabwe.* London: 1985. NGO report, in English.

——————. *Zimbabwe: Detention without Trial of Seven Opposition Politicians.* London: 1985. NGO report, in English.

Andreassen, B.A., and A. Eide, eds. "Zimbabwe." In *Human Rights in Developing Countries 1987/88: A Yearbook on Human Rights in Countries Receiving Nordic Aid,* 128–160. Copenhagen, Denmark: Christian Michelsen Institute, 1988. NGO report, in English; bibliography on Zimbabwe, pp. 363–365.

Armstrong, Alice, ed. *Women and Law in Southern Africa.* Harare, Zimbabwe: Zimbabwe Publishing House, 1987. Scholarly edited collection, in English.

Arnold, M. W., L. Garber, and B. Wrobel. *Zimbabwe: Report on the 1985 General Elections: Based on a Mission of the Election Observer Project of the International Human Rights Law Group.* Washington, D.C.: International Human Rights Law Group, 1986. NGO mission report, in English.

Berkeley, B., and E. Schrage. *Zimbabwe: Wages of War—A Report on Human Rights.* New York: Lawyers Committee for Human Rights, 1986. NGO mission report, in English.

Catholic Commission for Justice and Peace in Zimbabwe. "The Labour Relations Act." *Catholic Commission for Justice and Peace in Zimbabwe Bulletin* 7 (April 1986): 2–3. NGO article, in English.

Hatchard, John. "The Institution of the Ombudsman in Africa with Special Reference to Zimbabwe." *International and Comparative Law Quarterly* 35, pt. 2 (April 1986): 255–270. Scholarly article, in English.

Women's Action Group. *Speak Out/Taurai/Khulumani.* Harare, Zimbabwe: 1989. NGO articles, in English and African languages.

PART II: GENERAL SUBJECTS

Abortion

Frankowski, S. J., and G. F. Cole. *Abortion and Protection of the Human Fetus.* Dordrecht, the Netherlands: Martinus Nijhoff Publishers, 1987. Scholarly collection, in English; bibliography, pp. 332–334.

Harvard Women's Law Journal 10 (Spring 1987). Scholarly articles in special issue, in English.

Miskiewicz, Sophia. "Demographic Policies and Abortion in Eastern Europe." *Radio Free Europe Research* (8 December 1986). Government report, in English.

Sheeran, Patrick J. *Women, Society, the State, and Abortion: A Structuralist Analysis.* New York: Praeger, 1987. Scholarly monograph, in English.

Szumski, Bonnie, ed. *Abortion: Opposing Viewpoints.* St. Paul, MN: Greenhaven Press, 1986. Edited collection, in English; bibliography, pp. 49, 81, 106, 145, 169, and 200 (for periodical literature) and an annotated list of monographs, pp. 207–210.

Women's International Network. "The Status of Women in the USA 1988." *WIN News* 14, no. 1 (Winter 1988): 1–16. NGO article, in English.

Accused

Black Sash. *Memorandum on the Suffering of Children in South Africa.* Johannesburg, South Africa: 1986. NGO report, in English.

Criminal Justice. St. Paul, MN: Greenhaven Press, 1985. Edited collection, in English; bibliography, B 1–2

Paridaens, Desiree. "Negative Effects of Foreign Criminal Judgments in Europe." *SIM Newsletter: Netherlands Quarterly of Human Rights* 6, no. 3 (October 1988): 35–42. Scholarly article, in English.

Aggression

Bendremer, Jutta. *Aggression, Suppression, Holocaust.* Course offered by the Dept. of English, University of Akron, OH, Summer 1987. Syllabus/university course outline, in English.

Friedlander, Robert A. "The Enforcement of International Criminal Law: Fact or Fiction." *Case Western Reserve Journal of International Law* 17, no. 1 (Winter 1985): 79–90. Scholarly article, in English.

Paust, Jordan J. "Aggression against Authority: The Crime of Oppression, Politicide and other Crimes against Human Rights." *Case Western Reserve Journal of International Law* 18, no. 2 (Spring 1986): 283–306. Scholarly article, in English.

Servicio Paz y Justicia, Argentina (Srevice for Peace and Justice, Argentina). *Centroamerica: Efectos de Una Agresion Regional* (Central America: Effects of a Regional Aggression). Buenos Aires, Argentina: 1987. NGO report, in Spanish.

AIDS

AIDS in South Africa." *Critical Health* 22 (April 1988). NGO report, in English.

Bacon, Lisa. "Lessons of AIDS: Racism, Homophobia are the Real Epidemic." *Listen Real Loud* 8, no. 2 (Fall 1987): 1, 6. NGO article, in English; bibliography, pp. 151–165.

Breum, M., and A. Hendriks, eds. *AIDS and Human Rights: An International Perspective.* Copenhagen: Danish Center of Human Rights, 1988. Edited collection, in English.

Gostin, L., and W. J. Curran, guest eds. "AIDS, Law and Policy." *Law, Medicine and Health Care* 15, no. 1–2 (Summer 1987). Scholarly article, in English; bibliography, organized by such headings as "antidiscrimination," "criminal law," "education," "employment," "homosexuals," "immigration," "insurance," "law and policy," "prison," and "privacy," pp. 86–89.

——————. "AIDS, Science and Epidemiology." *Law, Medicine and Health Care* 14, no. 5–6 (Dec. 1986). Scholarly article, in English.

Guest, Iain. "Special Report: The World Health Organization and AIDS." *UN Watch* 2 (Spring/Summer 1988): 2–11. IGO report, in English.

ISIS-Women's International Cross-Cultural Exchange. *Women's World* 18 (June 1988). NGO articles in special issue on AIDS, in English.

McCormick, Richard A. "AIDS: The Shape of the Ethical Challenge." *America* 158, no. 6 (13 Feb. 1988): 147–154. NGO article, in English.

Noticias Aliadas. "Cuba Continues Massive AIDS Testing Program." *Latinamerica Press* 19, no. 33 (17 Sept. 1987): 1–2. News article, in English.

Panos Institute. *AIDS and the Third World.* 2d ed. London: 1987. NGO report, in English.

"Realism on AIDS." *The Nation* 246, no. 6 (13 Feb. 1988): 1. Editorial, in English.

Sabatier, Renee. *Blaming Others: Prejudice, Race and Worldwide AIDS.* London: Panos Institute and the Norwegian Red Cross, 1988. Monograph, in English.

Shilts, Randy. *And the Band Played on: Politics, People and the AIDS Epidemic.* New York: St. Martin's Press, 1987. Journalistic monograph, in English.

Sullivan, K. M., and M. A. Field. "AIDS and the Coercive Power of the State." *Harvard Civil Rights-Civil Liberties Law Review* 23, no. 1 (Winter 1988): 139–197. Scholarly article, in English.

Tinker, Jon. "AIDS in the Developing Countries." *Issues in Science and Technology* (Winter 1988): 43–48. Scholarly article, in English.

Aliens

Adepoju, Aderanti. "Illegals and Expulsion in Africa: The Nigerian Experience." *International Migration Review* 18, no. 3 (Fall 1984): 426–436. Journal article, in English.

Bauman, Christopher P. "An International Standard of Partial Compensation upon the Expropriation of an Alien's Property." *Case Western Reserve Journal of International Law* 19, no. 1 (Winter 1987): 103–119. Scholarly article, in English.

Billard, Annick. "Immigration Law: Sanctions Take Effect." *Refugees* 48 (Dec. 1987): 40. IGO article, in English.

Center for Migration Studies. "Dateline Update: The Sanctuary Movement in the U.S.: A Chronicle of Recent Developments - Part IV." *Migration Today* 8, no. 3 (1985): 4. NGO article, in English.

———. "Women in Migration." *International Migration Review* 18, no. 4 (Winter 1984). Scholarly articles in a special issue, in English.

Council of Europe, Directorate of Human Rights. *Human Rights of Aliens in Europe*. Dordrecht, the Netherlands: Martinus Nijhoff, 1985. IGO conference proceedings, in English.

Komitee fur Grundrechte und Demokratie (Committee for Basic Rights and Democracy). *Auswirkingen des Auslanderrechts auf die Situation der Migrantinen, Inbesondere Turkischer Frauen* (Consequences of Laws concerning Aliens on the Situation of Migrants, especially Turkish Women). Senbachstal, FRG: 1987. NGO report, in German.

Fagen, P. W., and S. Aguayo. *Central Americans in Mexico and the United States: Unilateral, Bilateral, and Regional Perspectives*. Washington, D. C.: Center for Immigration Policy and Refugee Assistance, 1988. NGO study, in English.

Ferris, Elizabeth G. *The Central American Refugees*. New York: Praeger Publishers, 1987. Scholarly report, in English.

Frelick, Bill. *The Back of the Hand: Bias and Restrictionism towards Central American Asylum Seekers in North America*. Washington, D. C.: U.S. Committee for Refugees, 1988. NGO monograph, in English.

Gibney, Mark. *Strangers or Friends*. Westport, CT: Greenwood Press, 1986. Scholarly monograph, in English.

Hull, Elizabeth. *Without Justice for All: The Constitutional Rights of Aliens*. Westport, CT: Greenwood Press, 1985. Scholarly monograph, in English.

Human Rights Commission. *Human Rights and the Migration Act 1958*. Canberra, Australia: 1985. Government report, in English.

International Committee for the Revision of Japan's Alien Registration Law. Letter and appeal, 27 May 1986. NGO appeal, in English.

International Helsinki Federation for Human Rights. *Asylum Policy and Family Reunification Policy in Ten European Countries*. Vienna, Austria: 1985. NGO report, in English.

"Irregular Migration: An International Perspective." *International Migration Review* 18, no. 3 (Fall 1984). Scholarly articles in a special issue, in English.

Leibowitz, Arnold H. "Comparative Analysis of Immigration in Key Developed Countries in Relation to Immigration Reform and Control Legislation in the United States." *Human Rights Law Journal* 7, no. 1 (1986): 1–73. Scholarly article, in English.

Melady, T. P., and M. Melady. *Uganda: The Asian Exiles*. Maryknoll, NY: Orbis Books, 1976. Scholarly monograph, in English.

Minnesota Lawyers International Human Rights Committee. *Oakdale Detention Center: The First Year of Operation*. Minneapolis, MN: 1987. NGO report, in English.

Paatii Ofosu-Amaah, W. "Restriction of Aliens in Business in Ghana and Kenya." *International Lawyer* 8, no. 3 (July 1974): 452–477. Scholarly article, in English.

Plender, Richard, ed. *International Migration Law*. Rev. 2d ed. Dordrecht, the Netherlands: Martinus Nijhoff, 1988. Scholarly edited collection, in English.

Refugee Documentation Project. "Asylum in North America: Crisis." *Refuge* 7, no. 1 (Sept. 1987). NGO article, in English.

Rosenberg, Lory D. "Asylum Practice: Winning Strategies after Cardoza-Fonseca." *CARDF Newsletter* (June 1987): 12–13. NGO article, in English.

Triantafillou, Patty. "Legalization of Illegal Aliens: A Humanitarian Approach Long Overdue." *Syracuse Journal of International Law and Commerce* 12, no. 3 (Spring 1986): 572–584. Scholarly article, in English.

United Nations Commission on Human Rights. *Further Promotion and Encouragement of Human Rights and Fundamental Freedoms . . . National Institutions for the Protection of Human Rights: Report of the Secre-*

tary General, E/CN.4/1987/37. 1986. IGO document, in English.

Yothment, Nivita Riley. *The Undocumented: Victims of Oppression*. Tucson, AZ: ACCORD, 1979. NGO report, in English; bibliography, pp. 28–29.

SEE ALSO *Immigration, Refugees*

Amnesty

Amnesty International. *Argentina: The Military Juntas and Human Rights—Report of the Trial of the Former Junta Members*. London: 1987. NGO report, in English.

—————. "GDR Announces Amnesty and Abolishes Death Penalty," 24 July 1987. NGO press release, in English.

—————. "Taiwan: Amnesty of 22 April 1988," 24 March 1988. NGO urgent action bulletin, in English.

—————. *Viet Nam: Thousands Released in National Day Amnesty*. London: 1987. NGO report, in English.

"An Amnesty Hedged with Conditions." *Radio Free Europe Research* 11, no. 34, pt. 2 (22 August 1986): 3–8. Government bulletin article, in English.

Aspen Institute for Humanistic Studies. *State Crimes: Punishment or Pardon*. Aspen, CO: 1988. NGO conference papers, in English.

Comision Andina de Juristas (Andean Commission of Jurists). "Chile: La Justicia Subordinata" (Chile: Justice Subordinated). *Boletin Comision Andina de Juristas* 13 (Dec. 1986): 7–8. NGO article, in Spanish.

"El referendum contra la impunidad se pone en marcha" (Uruguayan Human Rights Referendum Campaign Gets underway). *Brecha* 2, no. 66 (30 Jan. 1987): 2. News article, in Spanish.

Esponda, Jaime. *La Dimension Educative del Hacer Justicia en la Transicion Democratica* (The Educative Dimension of Doing Justice in the Democratic Tradition). Montevideo, Uruguay: Consejo de Education de Adultos de America Latina, 1986. NGO monograph, in Spanish.

Gamarra, Jorge. "Crisis institucional, ley de impuniday y referendum (Institutional Crisis, Amnesty and Referendum) *Brecha* 2, no. 66 (30 Jan. 1987): 16–17. News article, in Spanish.

Garro, A. M., and H. Dahl. "Legal Accountability for Human Rights Violations in Argentina: One Step Forward and Two Steps Back." *Human Rights Law Journal* 8, pts. 2–4 (1987): 283–344. Scholarly article, in English.

"Human Rights Update: December." *Latinamerica Press* 19, no. 2 (22 Jan. 1987): 7. News article, in English.

"Los ministros de la Corte son funcionarios sujetos a responsabilidades politicas" (Court Ministers are Functionaries Subjected to Political Responsibilities). *Brecha* 3, no. 120 (26 Feb. 1986): 15. News article, in Spanish.

Poland Watch Center. "Political Prisoners Released." *Poland Watch Digest* 7–8 (Aug.–Sept. 1986): 1–5. NGO article, in English.

"Referendum: En Agosto Podria Llegarse al Total de Firmas Exigidos" (Referendum: Collection of Needed Signatures Could Be Completed in August). *Brecha* 2, no. 84 (12 June 1987): 2. News article, in Spanish.

Umana Luna, Eduardo. *Hacia La Paz? (Los Ilicitos y Los Presos Policos: Las Amnistias y los Indultos)* (Towards Peace? [Illicit Behavior and Political Prisoners: Amnesties and Pardons]). Bogota, Colombia: Comite de Solidaridad con los Presos Politicos, 1985. Monograph, in Spanish.

Washington Office on Latin America. "Argentina Curbs Prosecution of Military." *Latin America Update* 12, no. 1 (Jan.–Feb. 1987): 1–6. NGO article, in English.

Westerveen, Gert. "Return to Democracy in Argentina and Uruguay: Some Outstanding Human Rights Problems." *SIM Newsletter* 11 (July 1985): 9–16. NGO scholarly article, in English.

Bonded Labor

Bonnet, Michel. "Child Slavery: The Kharkar Camps of Pakistan." *International Children's Rights Monitor* 5, no. 2–3 (1988): 4–5. NGO article, in English.

Centre for Socio-Legal Research and Documentation Service. "Public Interest Litigation." *Socio-Legal Concern* 2, no. 1 (Jan. 1986): 3–21. NGO article, in English.

—————. "The Human Rights Situation in India—A Socio-Legal Contrast." *Socio-Legal Concern Newsletter* 1, no. 12 (Dec. 1985): 3–14. NGO article, in English.

Centro Ecumenico de Documentacao e Informacao (Ecumenical Center for Documentation and Information). "Terra e Mais que um Pedaco de Chao" (Land is More Than a Piece of Soil). *Tempo e Presenca* 211 (Aug. 1986): 3–28. NGO article, in Portuguese.

Dalit Sahitya Akademy. "Violation of Human Rights in India: Bonded Labor." *Dalit Voice* 7, no. 8 (1–15 March 1988): 16. NGO article, in English.

de Souza Martina, Jose. "A Escravidao Hoje no Brazil" (Slavery Today in Brazil). *Cadernos do CEAS* 104 (July–Aug. 1986): 52–54. NGO article, in Portuguese.

Gopinath, Deepti. "In Bondage—Kolse Bhatti Kamgars." *The Lawyers Collective* 1, no. 9 (Sept. 1986): 14–15. NGO article, in English.

Human Rights Commission of Pakistan. *Bonded Labour in Brick Kiln Industry of Pakistan.* Lahore, Pakistan: 1988. NGO mission report, in English.

International Commission of Jurists. "Judicial Application of the Rule of Law: Bandhua Mukti Morcha (Bonded Labour Liberation Front) vs. Union of India and Others." *The Review* 15 (June 1986). NGO article, in English.

Joshi, Barbara R., ed. *Untouchable! Voices of the Dalit Liberation Movement.* London: Minority Rights Group, 1986. Edited collection, in English.

Rajpipla Social Service Society. "Ways in which the Effective Exercise of Human Rights is Ensured by the Poor in India." Paper presented at the International Experts Meeting on Ways and Means to Ensure Effective Exercise of Human Rights by Disadvantaged Groups, Quebec, Canada, 6 Aug. 1985. Unpublished conference paper, in English.

Social Impact Foundation. "India: Agnivesh Deplores Bihar Government Apathy towards Bonded Labor." *Impact: Asian Magazine for Human Transformation* 22, no. 8 (Aug. 1987): 6–7. NGO article, in English.

Third World Foundation for Social and Economic Studies. *Third World Affairs 1986.* London: 1986. Yearbook, in English.

Vigil India Movement. "A Recapitulation of Some Events." *Vigil India* 42 (June 1987): 2–5. NGO article, in English.

SEE ALSO *Debt Bondage.*

Caste

Bajwa, Kishan. "Anti-Reservation Violence in Gujarat Reaches a New Peak: Over 100 People Killed in Last Two Months." *India Now* 8, no. 7–9 (July–Sept. 1985): 20. Magazine article, in English.

Centre for Socio-Legal Research and Documentation Service. "Constitutional Provisions relating to Caste." *Socio-Legal Concern Newsletter* 2, no. 10 (Oct. 1986): 12–19. NGO article, in English.

—————. "Salient Features of the Protection of Civil Rights Act, 1955." *Socio-Legal Concern Newsletter* 2, no. 10 (Oct. 1986): 9–11. NGO article, in English.

—————. "Why Reservations for SCs, STs and OBCs?" *Socio-Legal Concern Newsletter* 2, no. 10 (Oct. 1986): 3–4. NGO article, in English.

Chunakara, Mathews George. "Growing Caste Frenzy and the Anti-Reservation Movement." *The Other Side* (Aug. 1985): 37–41. Magazine article, in English.

"Crisis and Mobilization: Politics in South Asia." *South Asia Bulletin* 7, nos. 1 and 2 (Fall 1987): 50–122. Scholarly articles/edited collection, in English.

Dalit Sahitya Akademy. "Amnesty Probe of SC/ST Human Rights Violations." *Dalit Voice* 7, no. 10 (1–15 April 1988): 14. NGO article, in English.

—————. "Bihar Heading for Major Upheaval." *Dalit Voice* 6, no. 1 (16–30 Nov. 1986): 7. NGO book review, in English.

Downing, T., and G. Kushner, eds. *Human Rights and Anthropology.* Cambridge, MA: Cultural Survival, 1988. Edited collection, in English.

Joshi, Barbara R., ed. *Untouchable! Voices of the Dalit Liberation Movement.* London: Minority Rights Group, 1986. Edited collection, in English.

Lapierre, Dominique. *The City of Joy.* Trans. Kathryn Spink. Garden City, NY: Doubleday & Co., 1985); originally published in French as *La Cite de la Joie* (Paris: Editions Robert Laffont). Novel, in English.

Liddle, J., and R. Joshi. *Daughters of Independence: Gender, Caste and Class in India.* London: (Zed Books, 1986), Monograph, in English.

Lokayan. "The Golana Massacre: A Report from Gujarat Lokayan." *Lokayan Bulletin* 4, no. 3–4 (May–Aug. 1986): 74–78. NGO article, in English.

"Rs. 100 Crore Fund to Launch Anti-Reservation War." *Dalit Voice* 4, no. 16 (1–15 June 1985): 11–12. NGO article, in English.

Surendra, Lawrence, comp. "India - The Ahmadabad Barbecue." *Impact International* 16, no. 14 (25 July–7 Aug. 1986): 8–9. Magazine article, in English.

Vigil India Movement. "A Recapitulation of Some Events." *Vigil India* 42 (June 1987): 2–5. NGO article, in English.

Yalman, Hur. "On the Purity of Women in the Castes of Ceylon and Malabar." *Royal Anthropology Institute* 93, no. 1 (Jan.–June 1983): 25–58. Scholarly article, in English.

Chemical Weapons

Committee against Repression and for Democratic Rights in Iraq. "Chemical Weapons: UN Report

Brands Iraq as a Violator of the 1925 Geneva Protocol," March 1986. NGO flier, in English.

——————. "Cyanide Massacre at Halabja." *Iraq Solidarity Voice* 19 (April 1988). NGO article, in English.

"Corporate Crime and Violence." *Multinational Monitor* 8, no. 4 (April 1987): 4–25. Article in special issue, in English.

Cultural Survival. "Militarization and Indigenous Peoples: Part I—The Americas and the Pacific." *Cultural Survival Quarterly* 11, no. 3 (1987). NGO special issue, in English.

Ermacora, Felix. "Afghanistan and the Conscience of the World." *SIM Newsletter* 17 (March 1987): 3–12. NGO article, in English.

Federation Internationale des Droits de l'Homme (International Federation of Human Rights). "Le Martyr du Peuple Kurde" (The Martyrdom of the Kurdish People). *La Lettre de la FIDH* 241 (22 March 1988). NGO newsletter, in French.

"Fumigaciones e incendios: efectos devastadores" (Chemical Fumigations and Forest Fires: Devastating Effects). *Noticias de Guatemala* 9, no. 142 (July 1987): 3–6. News article, in Spanish.

International Association of Political Scientists for the United Nations. *United Nations Middle East Brief.* Vienna, Austria: 1988. NGO document collection, in English.

International Working Group for Indigenous Affairs. "Burma: Human Rights in Burma." *IWGIA Newsletter* 50 (July 1987): 35–45. NGO article, in English.

"Kurdistan: A Homeland Besieged." *Toward Freedom: Report on Non-Alignment in the Developing Countries* 37, no. 5 (Oct.–Nov. 1988): 57, 60. News article, in English.

Physicians for Human Rights. *Winds of Death: Iraq's Use of Poison Gas against its Kurdish Population.* Somerville, MA: 1989. NGO report, in English.

Ramshaw, P., and T. Steers. *Intervention on Trial: The New York War Crimes Tribunal on Central America and the Caribbean.* New York: Praeger Publishers and National Lawyers Guild, 1987. NGO study, in English.

Robinson, J., J. Guillemin, and M. Meselson. "Yellow Rain: The Story Collapses." *Foreign Policy* 68 (Fall 1987): 100–117. Scholarly article, in English.

Saeedpour, Vera Beaudin. *Information Packet.* New York: Kurdish Program, Cultural Survival, 1988. NGO press release, in English.

Children

A. Child Labor

Agnelli, Susanna. *Street Children: A Growing Urban Tragedy.* London: Independent Commission on International Humanitarian Issues and Weidenfield and Nicolson, 1986. NGO monograph, in English.

Albright, J., M. Kunstel, and R. McKay. *Stolen Childhood: A Global Report on the Exploitation of Children.* New York: Defense for Children International-USA, 1987. News articles and photographs, in English.

Anti-Slavery Society. *Child Labour in Morocco's Carpet Industry.* London: 1978. NGO report, in English.

Balai. "Working Children in Asia: Facts and Fantasies." *Balai Asian Journal* 14 (1986). NGO journal, in English.

Bequele, A., and J. Boyden, eds. *Combating Child Labour.* Geneva: International Labor Office, 1988. IGO monograph, in English.

Bonnet, Michel. "Child Slavery: The Kharkar Camps of Pakistan." *International Children's Rights Monitor* 5, no. 2–3 (1988): 4–5. NGO article, in English. (The journal *International Children's Rights Monitor,* published in Geneva, Switzerland, focuses entirely on children's rights and is an excellent source for all children's issues).

Centre for Socio-Legal Research and Documentation Service. "Shocking Facts and Figures about Child Labour in India." *Socio-Legal Concern Newsletter* 3, no. 4 (April 1987): 2–3. NGO article, in English.

——————. "The Children (Pledging of Labour) Act, 1933." *Socio-Legal Concern Newsletter* 2, no. 3 (March 1986): 7–8. NGO article, in English.

Child Workers in Asia Support Group. *Child Workers in Asia* 1–5 (1985–1989). (This NGO journal, published in Bangkok, Thailand, deals entirely with child labor and is an excellent source of information.

Coordinating Group for Religion in Society. "Facing up to Child Labor Abuse." *Human Rights in Thailand Report* 9, no. 1 (Jan.–March 1985): 12–13. NGO article/conference report, in English.

Costa, Roseline. "Child Labour." *Hotline Newsletter* 25 (Nov. 1986): 5. NGO article, in English.

Defence for Children International. *1987 Activity Report of the International Secretariat of DCI.* Geneva: 1988. NGO annual report, in English.

Defense for Children International-USA. *Database on the Rights of the Child.* New York: 1987. Abstracts, in English.

Faculty of Law, Chulalongkorn University. *Alternative Human Rights Materials for Thai Youth.* Bangkok, Thailand: 1986. NGO report, in English.

"Kinderarbeit und Kinderelend in Nordostbrasilien" (Child Labor and Poverty in Northeast Brazil). *Brasilien Nachrichten* 87 (1985): 2–9. NGO article, in German.

Lapierre, Dominique. *The City of Joy.* Trans. Kathryn Spink. Garden City, NY: Doubleday & Company, 1985. Novel, in English; originally published in French as *La Cite de la Joie* (Paris: Editions Robert Laffont).

Schellinski, Kristina. "The Cave Children of Sekota." *Action for Children* 1, no. 4 (1986): 4. NGO article, in English. (The journal *Action for Children,* published in New York by NGO Committee on UNICEF and UNICEF, is an excellent source of information on children's rights.)

UNICEF. "Children in Especially Difficult Circumstances." *UNICEF Development Education Resource Bulletin* 1 (1987). IGO special issue bulletin, in English; bibliography.

B. Child Soldiers

Berman, Nina. "Project Launched in Mozambique to Aid Children 'Instrumentalized' by War." *Action for Children* 3, no. 4 (1988): 1, 8. NGO article, in English.

Center on War and the Child. *Uganda: Land of the Child Soldier—A Summary Report.* Eureka Springs, AR: 1987. NGO report, in English.

Cohen, Cynthia Price. "Commission Approves Final Text of Children's Convention." *Human Rights Internet* 13, no. 1 (Spring 1989). News article, in English.

Cultural Survival. "Children: The Battleground of Change." *Cultural Survival Quarterly* 10, no. 4 (1986). NGO article, in English.

Elahi, Maryam. "The Rights of the Child under Islamic Law: Prohibition of the Child Soldier." *Columbia Human Rights Law Review* 19, no. 2 (Spring 1988): 259–279. Scholarly article, in English.

Ennew, Judith. "Child Soldiers: Serving or Working?" *International Children's Rights Monitor* 2, no. 2 (2d quarter 1985): 18–19. NGO article, in English.

NGO Committee on UNICEF and UNICEF. "Child Soldiers of Uganda." *Action for Children* 1, no. 5 (1986): 6. IGO article, in English.

Pompey, Carmen. "The Military Training of the Young." *Radio Free Europe Research* 11, no. 46 (14 November 1986): 25–26. Government bulletin article, in English.

Radda Barnen and Swedish Save the Children. *A Humanitarian Appeal for Children in Armed Conflicts.* Stockholm: 1987. NGO appeal, in English.

U.S. Helsinki Watch Committee and Asia Watch Committee. *To Win the Children: Afghanistan's Other War.* New York: 1986. NGO report, in English.

Wlaker, J. "Boy Soldiers in a Grown-up's War." *Child Workers in Asia* 3, no. 1 (Jan.–March 1987): 1–2. NGO article, in English.

C. Children in Adult Prisons

African National Congress, Women's Section. "Children in Jails: Prison-Visit Doctors Warn of 'Chilling Prospect.'" *Women and Children under Apartheid* 3 (June–July 1986): 1–2. NGO article, in English.

American-Arab Anti-Discrimination Committee. *Children of the Stones.* Washington, D.C.: 1988. NGO report, in English.

Amnesty International. *Children: The Youngest Victims.* London: 1987. NGO report, in English.

Cook, Helena. *The War against Children: South Africa's Younger Victims.* New York: Lawyers Committee for Human Rights, 1986. NGO mission report, in English.

Defense for Children International. "Apartheid's Children." *International Children's Rights Monitor* 4, no. 2 (2d quarter 1987). NGO article, in English.

—————. *Children in Prison in Turkey.* Geneva: 1988. NGO report, in English.

Detainees' Parents Support Committee. *A Memorandum on Children under Repression.* Johannesburg, South Africa: 1986. NGO report, in English.

Jupp, Michael. *Children under Apartheid.* Brooklyn, NY: Defense for Children International-USA, 1987. NGO report, in English; bibliography, pp. 187–191.

Prisoners' Friends Association in Israel. "Treatment of Child Offenders," 7 December 1987. NGO background paper, in English.

Sopher, Sharon. *Witness to Apartheid.* San Francisco, CA: Southern Africa Media Center/California Newsreel, 1986. Documentary film, in English.

Streib, Victor L. *Death Penalty for Juveniles.* Bloomington, IN: Indiana University Press, 1987. Scholarly report, in English; classified bibliography, pp. 237–250.

Tomasevski, Katarina. *Children in Adult Prisons: An International Perspective.* New York: St. Martin's Press, 1986. NGO report, in English.

—————. "The Placement of Children in Institutions: Deprivation of Liberty . . . or Not?" *International Children's Rights Monitor* 3, no. 3 (Nov. 1986): 7–10. NGO article, in English.

Civilians

Americas Watch Committee. *Land Mines in El Salvador and Nicaragua: The Civilian Victims.* New York: 1986. NGO report, in English.

—————. *The Civilian Toll 1986–1987: Ninth Supplement to the Report on Human Rights in El Salvador.* New York: 1987. NGO report, in English.

Amnesty International. *Aide-Memoire: Summary of Amnesty International's Concerns in the Republic of Uganda.* London: 1987. NGO report, in English.

—————. *Panama: Assault on Human Rights.* London: 1988. NGO report, in English.

—————. *Suriname: Violations of Human Rights.* London: 1987. NGO report, in English.

—————. *Uganda: Detention of Alleged Political Opponents by the National Resistance Army.* London: 1987. NGO report, in English.

Andean Commission of Jurists. "Peru: New Denunciation of Extra-Judicial Killings." *Andean Newsletter* 2 (3 Dec. 1986): 5–6. NGO article, in English.

Asamblea Permanente por los Derechos Humanos (Permanent Assembly for Human Rights). *Violencia Policial en al Argentina y los Medios Legales para Combatirla* (Police Violence in Argentina and Legal Methods to Combat it). Buenos Aires: 1986. NGO report, in Spanish.

Asociacion Nicarguense Pro-Derechos Humanos (Nicaraguan Association for Human Rights). *Second Six-Month Report on Human Rights in the Nicaraguan Resistance.* San Jose, Costa Rica: 1988. NGO report, in English.

Centro de Documentacion de Honduras (Honduras Documentation Center). *La Tortura en Honduras* (Torture in Honduras). Tegucigalpa, Honduras: 1987. NGO report, in Spanish.

Civil Rights Movement of Sri Lanka. "The Ordeal of the People of Jaffna," 18 Nov. 1987. NGO statement, in English.

Collins, Frank. *Nonviolence and Death at Bir Zeit University: An Investigative Report.* Database Project on Palestinian Human Rights, 1987. NGO report, in English.

Comision de Derechos Humanos de El Salvador (Human Rights Commission of El Salvador). *Human Rights in El Salvador.* San Salvador: 1987. NGO report, in English.

Comision Nacional de Promocion y Proteccion de los Derechos Humanos (National Commission for the Promotion and Protection of Human Rights). "Contra Violence." *Derechos Humanos* 2 (March–April 1988): 23–25. Government article, in Spanish and English.

Comision Nacional sobre la Desaparicion de Personas (National Commission on the Disappeared).

Nunca Mas: The Report of the Argentine National Commission on the Disappeared. New York: Farrar Straus Giroux and Index on Censorship, 1986. Government report, in English.

Comite Pro-Justicia y Paz de Guatemala (Justice and Peace Committee of Guatemala). *Violaciones a los Derechos Humanos en Guatemala: Junio de 1987* (Human Rights Violations in Guatemala: June 1987). Mexico City, Mexico: 1987. NGO report, in Spanish.

Eritrean Relief Committee. "Ethiopian Military Escalates Violences against Eritreans," 26 May 1988. NGO press release, in English.

Fay, Chip. *Counter-Insurgency and Tribal Peoples in the Philippines.* Washington, D.C.: Survival International-USA, 1987. NGO report, in English.

Frente Farabundo Marti para la Liberacion Nacional-Frente Democratico Revolucionario (Farabundo Marti National Liberation Front-Revolutionary Democratic Front). *Human Rights and Peace: Principal Human Rights Violations and Prospects for a Political Solution in El Salvador.* San Salvador: 1986. Opposition forces report, in English.

Federacion Latinoamericana de Asociaciones de Familiares de Detenidos Desaparecidos (Latin American Federation of Associations of Families of the Detained-Disappeared). *Hasta Encontrarlos!* 7, no. 32 (Jan.–Feb. 1988). NGO newsletter, in Spanish.

Henry Dunant Institute. *International Dimensions of Humanitarian Law.* Dordrecht, the Netherlands: Martinus Nijhoff and UNESCO, 1988. Edited collection, in English; bibliography, pp. 301–313.

Inter-Church Committee on Human Rights in Latin America. *1987 Annual Report on the Human Rights Situation in Guatemala.* Toronto, Canada: 1987. NGO report, in English.

—————. *ICCHRLA 1987 Annual Reports: General Concerns and Brief Country Reports.* Toronto, Canada: 1988. NGO report, in English.

Liga Mexicana por la Defensa de los Derechos Humanos (Mexican League for the Defense of Human Rights). "Oaxaca Demands Justice." *Boletin de la LIMEDDH* 1, no. 2 (June 1987). NGO article, in Spanish.

Montex, Segundo. *La Situacion de los Derechos Humanos en El Salvador en 1987* (The Human Rights Situation in El Salvador). San Salvador: Instituto de Derechos Humanos, Universidad Centroamericana "Jose Simeon Canas," 1987. NGO report, in Spanish.

Physicians for Human Rights. *Panama 1987: Health Consequences of Police and Military Actions.* Somerville, MA: 1988. NGO mission report, in English.

Task Force Detainees of the Philippines. "Human Rights after the First 100 Days of the Aquino Administration." *Philippine Human Rights Update* 1, no. 7 (15 March–14 July 1986): 12–17. NGO article, in English.

Tribuna por la Vida (Tribune for Life). *Testimonios Tribuna por la Vida* (Tribune for Life Testimonies). Bogota, Colombia: 1987. Conference report/testimonies, in Spanish.

Watch Committees, Lawyers Committee for Human Rights. *The Reagan Administration's Record on Human Rights in 1987.* New York: 1987. NGO report, in English.

Witness for Peace. *What We Have Seen and Heard in Nicaragua.* Washington, D.C.: 1987. NGO report, in English.

Colonialism

Ait-Ahmed, Honcine. "Frantz Fanon et les Droits e l'Homme" (Frantz Fanon and Human Rights). *Geneve-Afrique* 25, no. 2 (1987): 123–128. Scholarly article, in French.

Bruckner, Pascal. *The Tears of the White Man: Compassion as Contempt.* Trans. William R. Beer. New York: Free Press, 1986. Scholarly monograph, in English.

Christian Conference of Asia. *Nuclear Free Nation.* Kowloon, Hong Kong: 1988. NGO report, in English.

Clark, R., and S.R. Roff. *Micronesia: The Problem of Palau.* Rev. ed. London: Minority Rights Group, 1987. NGO report, in English.

El-Ayouty, Yassin. *The United Nations and Decolonisation: The Role of Afro-Asia.* The Hague, Netherlands: Martinus Nijhoff, 1971. Scholarly monograph, in English.

Falk, Richard. "The Algiers Declaration of the Rights of People and the Struggle for Human Rights." In *Human Rights and State Sovereignty,* ed. R. Falk, 185–194. New York: Holmes & Meier, 1980. Scholarly study, in English.

Faulwetter, Helmut. "The Brain Drain and Human Rights." *GDR Committee for Human Rights Bulletin* 12, no. 3 (1986): 151–163. Government article, in English.

Gesellschaft fur Bedrohte Volker und Verein der Tibetaner in Deutschland (Association for Endangered Peoples and Association of Tibetians in Germany). *Tibet: Traum oder Trauma?* (Tibet: Dream or Trauma?). Gottingen, FRG: 1987. NGO report, in German.

Giglio, Carlo. "Cause e Fattori della Decolonizzazione dell'Africa" (Causes and Factors in the Decolonization of Africa). *Politico: Revista Italiana di Scienze Politiche* 31, no. 4 (Dec. 1966): 619–637. Scholarly article, in Italian.

Haas, Ernst. B. "The Attempt to Terminate Colonialism: Acceptance of the United Nations Trusteeship System." In *The United Nations Political Systems,* ed. David A. Kay, 281–301. New York: Wiley, 1967. Scholarly study, in English.

"International Assistance and Support to Peoples and Movements Struggling against Colonialism, Racism, Racial Discrimination, and Apartheid." UN Seminar held in Yaounde, Cameroon, 28 April–9 May 1986. Conference write-up, in English.

Jayawardena, K., and J. Uyangoda, eds. "Special Issue on the National Question in Sri Lanka." *South Asia Bulletin* 6, no. 2 (Fall 1986). Scholarly special issue, in English.

Johnson, Penny. "The Routine of Repression." *MERIP Middle East Report* 150 (Jan.–Feb. 1988): 3–7, 10–11. NGO article, in English.

Katjavivi, Peter H. *A History of Resistance in Namibia.* Paris: UNESCO, 1988. Scholarly monograph, in English.

Lawless, R., and L. Monahan, eds. *War and Refugees: The Western Sahara Conflict.* London: Refugee Studies Programme, Queen Elizabeth House, 1987. Scholarly edited collection, in English.

Ligue des Droits de l'Homme (League for Human Rights). "Une Declaration sur la Siutation en Nouvelle Caledonie" (A Declaration of the Situation in New Caledonia), 27 February 1987. NGO statement, in French.

Montano, German. "Teologia de la Liberacion o Indianidad Liberadora?" (Theology of Liberation or Liberating 'Indianness'?). *Boletin Chitakolla* 32/33 (May–June 1986): 8–14. NGO article, in Spanish.

Schirmer, D. B., and S. R. Shalom, eds. *The Philippines Reader: A History of Colonialism, Neocolonialism, Dictatorship and Resistance.* Boston, MA: South End Press, 1987. Scholarly edited collection, in English.

Shepherd, George W., Jr. *The Trampled Grass: Tributary States and Self-Reliance in the Indian Ocean Zone of Peace.* New York: Praeger, 1987. Scholarly study, in English; bibliography, pp. 159–170.

Weinstein, W., L. Jones, and F. McCoy. *African Perspectives on Human Rights: Unpublished Paper Prepared for the U.S. Department of State.* Washington, D.C.: Council for Policy and Social Research, 1980. Unpublished paper, in English.

Conscientious Objection

Amnesty International. *Adoption of Prisoner of Conscience-Switzerland.* London: 1986. NGO appeal, in English.

——————. *Amnesty International Concerns in Western Europe—October 1986–March 1987.* London: 1987. NGO report, in English.

——————. *Amnesty International Concerns in Western Europe—March 1986–September 1986.* London: 1986. NGO report, in English.

——————. *Conscientious Objection to Military Service.* London: 1988. NGO report, in English.

——————. *Greece: Conscientious Objection.* London: 1988. NGO report, in English.

——————. "Greek CO's End Second Hunger Strike," 4 July 1988. NGO press release, in English.

Bacon, Margaret Hope. *The Quiet Rebels: The Story of the Quakers in America.* Philadelphia, PA: New Society Publishers, 1985. Scholarly monograph, in English; bibliography, pp. 221–224.

Catholic Institute for International Relations. *Country and Conscience: South African Conscientious Objectors.* London: 1988. NGO report, in English.

Committee in Support of Solidarity. "On Freedom and Peace." *Committee in Support of Solidarity Reports* (17 Dec. 1986): 24–30. NGO article, in English.

Davies, Gareth. "Conscientious Objection and the Freedom and Peace Movement in Poland." *Religion in Communist Lands* 16, no. 1 (Spring 1988): 4–20. NGO article, in English.

East European Cultural Foundation. "Freedom and Peace International Seminar." *East European Reporter* 2, no. 4 (1987): 56–59. NGO article, in English.

——————. " 'Freedom and Peace'—Poland's Independent Peace Movement." *East European Reporter* 2, no. 1 (Spring 1986): 44–49. NGO article, in English.

Freedom and Peace Movement. *Documents from the Independent Seminar: "International Peace and the Helsinki Agreements".* Warsaw, Poland: 1987. NGO document collection, in English.

Human Awareness Programme. *Militarisation Dossier.* Johannesburg, South Africa: 1986. NGO dossier, in English.

Information Centre for Polish Affairs. "Keston College on Jehovah's Witnesses Imprisoned for Refusing Military Service." *Uncensored Poland News Bulletin* 5/87 (6 March 1987): 18–19. NGO article, in English.

——————. "Reprisals against Freedom and Peace Activists." *Uncensored Poland News Bulletin* 23 (30 Nov. 1987): 25–28. NGO article, in English.

Keston College. "Conscientious Objection: The Situation in Yugoslavia." *Religion in Communist Lands* 15, no. 3 (Winter 1987): 332–335. NGO article, in English.

Klein, Yossi. " 'Refuseniks' Grow among Ranks in Israeli Army." *In These Times* 12, no. 26 (25 May–June 7 1988): 11. News article, in English.

Klippenstein, Lawrence. "Exercising a Free Conscience: The Conscientious Objectors of the Soviet Union and the German Democratic Republic." *Religion in Communist Lands* 13, no. 3 (Winter 1985): 282–291. Scholarly article, in English.

KOS/Committee for Social Resistance. "Poland—Underground Journal KOS Addresses Congress of Intellectuals." *East European Reporter* 1, no. 4 (Winter 1986): 13–20. Journal article/past conference, in English.

Lithuanian Information Center. "New Underground Publication Appears in Lithuanian," 24 Sept. 1985. NGO bulletin, in English.

Michalski, Franek. " 'Freedom and Peace' Movement Emerges in Poland." *Peace and Democracy News* 2, no. 2 (Summer–Fall 1986): 3–4. NGO article, in English.

Musalo, Karen. "Conscientious Objection to Military Service Accepted as Valid Basis for Claim to Political Asylum for Salvadoran Men." *Immigration Newsletter* 16, no. 3 (May–June 1987): 3–7. NGO article, in English.

Niemczyk, Piotr. "The 'Softies' Do Not Join the Forces." *Uncensored Poland News Bulletin* 4/88 (19 Feb. 1988): 19–20. NGO article, in English.

"Pushing on Apartheid's Pillars." *Sojourners* 17, no. 5 (May 1988): 28–31. NGO article, in English.

Radio Free Europe/Radio Liberty. "Conscientious Objectors May Be Allowed Alternative to Military Service." *Radio Free Europe Research* 13, no. 6 (12 Feb. 1988). Government article, in English.

Southern African Catholic Bishops' Conference. *The Things that Make for Peace.* Pretoria, South Africa: 1985. NGO report, in English.

U.S. Helsinki Watch Committee. "Eastern European Appeal on Conscientious Objective," March 1988. NGO press release, in English.

——————. *Fron Below: Independent Peace and Environmental Movements in Eastern Europe and the USSR.* New York: 1987. NGO report, in English.

Crimes Against Humanity

Asamblea Permanente por los Derechos Humanos (Permanent Assembly for Human Rights). "Obediencia Debida: Desde Donde y Hasta Cuando?" (Due Obedience: From Where and Until When?). *Derechos Humanos* 2, no. 10 (May 1987): 3–4. NGO article, in Spanish.

—————. "Tribunal Etico de la Salud contra la Impunidad" (Health Workers' Ethical Tribunal against Impunity). *Derechos Humanos* 3, no. 13 (April 1988): 16–18. NGO article, in Spanish.

Bassiouni, Cherif. "Nuremberg Forty Years after: An Introduction." *Case Western Reserve Journal of International Law* 18, no. 2 (Spring 1986): 261–266. Scholarly article, in English.

"Cuales son y Como Deben Prevenirse los Delitos de Lesa Humanidad" (What Are Crimes against Humanity, and How Should They Be Prevented?). *Brecha* 2, no. 85 (18 June 1987): 4. News article, in Spanish.

Hamalengwa, Munyonzwe. *The Case for the Prosecution of Apartheid Criminals in Canada.* North York, Canada: 1988. NGO report, in English.

Hannum, Hurst. "International Law and Cambodian Genocide: The Sounds of Silence." *Human Rights Quarterly* 11, no. 1 (Feb. 1989): 82–138. Scholarly article, in English.

Hannum, H., and D. Hawk. *The Case against the Standing Committee of the Communist Party of Kampuchea.* New York: Cambodia Documentation Commission, 1986. NGO legal brief (draft), in English.

Lifton, Robert J. *The Nazi Doctors: Medical Killing and the Psychology of Genocide.* New York: Basic Books, 1986. Scholarly monograph, in English.

Lippman, Matthew. "The Denaturalization of Nazi War Criminals in the United States: Is Justice Being Served?" *Houston Journal of International Law* 7, no. 2 (Spring 1985): 169–214. Scholarly article, in English.

Paust, Jordan J. "Aggression against Authority: The Crime of Oppression, Politicide and Other Crimes against Human Rights." *Case Western Reserve Journal of International Law* 18, no. 2 (Spring 1986): 283–306. Scholarly article, in English.

Ruzie, Davie. "Klaus Barbie and the French Legal Process." *Patterns of Prejudice* 20, no. 3 (July 1986): 27–33. NGO article, in English.

United Nations Centre for Human Rights. *Human Rights: A Compilation of International Instruments.* New York: 1988. Document collection, in English.

Wallimann, I., and M. N. Dobkowski, eds. *Genocide and the Modern Age: Etiology and Case Studies of Mass Death.* Westport, CT: Greenwood Press, 1987. Scholarly edited collection, in English.

World Jewish Congress, Commission on the Holocaust and Crimes of the Nazis. *Waldheim's Nazi Past: The Dossier.* Geneva: 1988. NGO report, in English.

Criminal Justice

American Friends Service Committee, Criminal Justice Program. *The Lessons of Marion: The Failure of a Maximum Security Prison - A History and Analysis, with Voices of Prisoners.* Philadelphia, PA: 1985. NGO report, in English.

Asamblea Permanente por los Derechos Humanos (Permanent Assembly for Human Rights). "Obediencia Debida: Desde Donde y Hasta Cuando?" (Due Obedience: From Where and until When?) *Derechos Humanos* 2, no. 10 (May 1987): 3–4. NGO article, in Spanish.

Asia Watch. *A Stern, Steady Crackdown: Legal Process and Human Rights in South Korea.* New York: 1987. NGO report, in English.

"Carceles de Provincia, Centros de Degradacion" (Provincial Prisons, Degradation Centers). *Proceso* 551 (25 May 1987): 22–25. News article, in Spanish.

Center for Constitutional Rights. *Docket Report 1988–1989.* New York: 1988. NGO report, in English.

Centro de Capacitacion Social (Center for Social Training). "El Sistema Penitenciario: Rehabilitacion o Purgatorio?" (Prison System: Rehabilitation or Purgatory?). *Dialogo Social* 20, no. 201 (June 1987). NGO article, in Spanish.

Civil Liberties Organisation. *Annual Report 1988: Violations of Human Rights in Nigeria.* Lagos, Nigeria: 1988. NGO report, in English.

Colvin, Greg. "Report on the Seventh United Nations Congress on the Prevention of Crime and the Treatment of Offenders." *Crime and Social Justice* 25 (1986). Scholarly article/conference report, in English.

Comision Andina de Juristas (Andean Commission of Jurists). "Colombia: Violencia y Democracia" (Colombia: Violence and Democracy). *Boletin* 16 (Nov. 1987): 2–28. NGO article, in Spanish.

Committee for the Defence of Human Rights in Bahrain. "A Statement on the Latest Saudi Legislation," 9 Oct. 1988. NGO urgent action appeal, in English.

Criminal Justice. St. Paul MN: Greenhaven Press, 1985. Edited collection, in English; bibliography, p. B 1–2.

Currin, Brian. *Rehabilitation of the Real Offender.* Pretoria, South Africa: Lawyers for Human Rights, 1988. NGO speech, in English.

Esponda, Jaime. "Justicia Penal y Derechos Humanos en Chile" (Criminal Justice and Human Rights in

Chile). *Revista Chilena de Derechos Humanos* 2, no. 1 (3d quarter 1985): 23–39. Scholarly article, in Spanish.

Instituto de Defensa Legal (Institute for Legal Defense). *Los Sucesos de los Penales: Nueva Abdicacion de la Autoridad Democratica, un Enfoque Juridico* (A New Abdication of Democratic Authority in Peru: A Legal Analysis . . . Recent Events in the Prisons). Lima, Peru: 1986. NGO report, in Spanish.

Instituto Historico Centroamericano (Central American Historical Institute). "Jails and Justice in Nicaragua." *Envio* 5, no. 64 (Oct. 1985): 14–28. NGO article/past conference, in English.

National Lawyers Guild. "Criminal Justice in Cuba." *Cuba Update* (June 1988): 22–24. NGO article on fact-finding mission, in English.

Paduano, A., and C. A. Stafford Smith. "Deathly Errors: Juror Misperceptions concerning Parole in the Imposition of the Death Penalty." *Columbia Human Rights Law Review* 18, no. 2 (Spring 1987): 211–257. NGO article, in English.

Seventh UN Congress on the Prevention of Crime and the Treatment of Offenders. *Selected Documents.* Milan: 1985. IGO documents/conference papers, in English.

Tillet, Rebecca. *Investigacion sobre el Habeas Corpus en La Corte Suprema de Justicia Honduras, C.A. 1980–1985* (Investigation of Habeas Corpus Practice and Procedure in the Honduran Supreme Court, 1980–1985). Tegucigalpa, Honduras: Comite para la Defensa de los Derechos Humanos en Honduras, 1986. NGO report in Spanish.

Wishnevsky, Julia. "Abuse of Law on 'Malicious Disobedience' in Soviet Camps." *Radio Liberty Research Bulletin* 30, no. 36 (3 Sept. 1986). Government research paper, in English.

Wrobel, Brian. *Glasnost and Soviet Criminal Trials: A Report by the Parliamentary Human Rights Group,* 1987. London: Parliamentary Rights Group, 1987. NGO report, in English.

Cultural Rights

Acosta-Belen, E., and B. R. Sjostrom, eds. *The Hispanic Experience in the United States: Contemporary Issues and Perspectives.* New York: Praeger, 1988. Scholarly collection, in English; bibliography, pp. 243–254.

Amnesty International. *Bulgaria: Continuing Human Rights Abuses against Ethnic Turks.* London: 1987. NGO report, in English.

Asia Watch. *Human Rights in Tibet: An Asia Watch Report.* Washington, D.C.: 1988. NGO report, in English.

Avedon, John F. "Tibet Today." *Utne Reader* 32 (March–April 1989): 34–41. News article/book excerpt, in English.

Barry, Hugh R. *A Representation to the International Labor Organization on behalf of Soviet Jewish Hebrew Teachers.* Waltham, MA: Soviet Jewry Legal Advocacy Center, 1985. International petition, in English.

Bence, Gyorgy. *Censored and Alternative Modes of Cultural Expression in Hungary.* Vienna, Austria: International Helsinki Federation for Human Rights, 1985. NGO report, in English.

Catholic Institute for International Relations. *East Timor: A Christian Reflection.* London: 1987. NGO statement, in English and French.

Central Tibetan Secretariat. *From Liberation to Liberalisation: Views on 'Liberated' Tibet.* Dharamsala, India: 1982. Scholarly monograph, in English.

Churchill, Ward, ed. *Critical Issues in Native North America.* Copenhagen, Denmark: International Work Group for Indigenous Affairs, 1988. NGO monograph.

Comision Chilena de Derechos Humanos (Chilean Commission for Human Rights. *Encuentro Internacional del Arte, la Ciencia y la Cultura por la Democracia en Chile* (International Conference on Art, Science and Culture for Democracy in Chile). Santiago, Chile: 1988. NGO conference report/ scholarly articles, in Spanish.

Commission of Culture of Underground Solidarity, International Helsinki Federation for Human Rights. *Culture in Poland.* Trans. Bohdan and Elizabeth Wasiutynski. Vienna: 1985. NGO report, in English.

Ermacora, Felix. *Menschenrechte in der Sich Wandelinden Welt: II Band, Theorie und Praxis: Die Verwirklichung der Menschenrechte in Afrika und im Nahen Osten* (Human Rights in the Changing World: Vol. 2, Theory and Practice: The Realization of Human Rights in Africa and the Near East). Vienna: Verlag der Osterreichische Akademie der Wissenschaften, 1983. Scholarly study, in German.

Federation Internationale des Droits de l'Homme (International Federation of Human Rights). "Le Martyr du Peuple Kurde" (The Martyrdom of the Kurdish People). *Lettre de la FIDH* 241 (22 March 1988). NGO newsletter, in French.

Funnemark, Bjorn Cato. *SOS Transylvania: A Report on Suppression of the Hungarian Minority in Romania.* Vienna: International Helsinki Federation for

Human Rights, 1988. NGO report, in English; bibliography, pp. 59–60.

Gesellschaft fur Bedrohte Volker (Association for Endangered Peoples). "Inuit in Kanada" (Inuit in Canada). *Pogrom* 119 (16 Jan. 1985): 46–56. NGO article, in German.

Hitchens, C., and D. Stephen. *Inequalities in Zimbabwe.* Rev. ed. London: Minority Rights Group, 1981. NGO report, in English; selective bibliography, p. 20.

Implementation of the International Covenant on Economic, Social and Cultural Report, Initial Reports . . . concerning Rights covered by Articles 13 to 15 . . . Canada. New York: UN Economic and Social Council, 1985. Government report/IGO document, in English.

Institute of Jewish Affairs. "Jewish Culture in the USSR Today." *Research Report* 10 (Dec. 1985). NGO bulletin, in English.

Kordud, Refik. *Bulgaria Carries on Chauvinistic Policies.* Ankara, Turkey: Turkiye Fikir Anjansi, 1986. Situtation report, in English.

Lizarralde, R., S. Beckermann, and P. Elsass. *Indigenous Survival among the Bari and Arhuaco: Strategies and Perspectives.* Copenhagen, Denmark: International Work Group for Indigenous Affairs, 1987. NGO document, in English.

Mazeika, Rasa, ed. *Violations of Human Rights in Soviet-Occupied Lithuania: A Report for 1983–1986.* Philadelphia, PA: Lithuanian American Community, 1988. NGO report, in English.

Nahaylo, Bohdan. "Independent Group to Promote Culture Formed in Ukraine." *The Ukrainian Backgrounder* 2/88 (1 Feb. 1988). NGO article, in English.

"Nationalities Policy in the USSR: Discrimination against Ethnic Groups." *The Ukrainian Weekly,* 9 June 1985: 7, 12–13. Newspaper article, in English.

Norwegian Human Rights Project, Christian Michelsen Institute. *Human Rights in Developing Countries 1986.* Oslo: Universitetsforlaget, 1986. Government annual report, in English; bibliography, classified by country.

Radio Free Europe/Radio Liberty. "Charter 77 Addresses Budapest Forum." *Radio Free Europe Research* 10, no. 42 (18 Oct. 1985): 3–7. Government report, in English.

Rossel, Pierre, ed. *Tourism: Manufacturing the Exotic.* Copenhagen, Denmark: International Work Group for Indigenous Affairs, 1988. NGO report, in English.

Shafir, M., and D. Ionescu. "Rural Resettlement: Situation Report Romania." *Radio Free Europe Research* 13, no. 34 (23 Aug. 1988): 3–22. NGO report, in English.

Social Scientists Association. *Ethnicity and Social Change in Sri Lanka.* Colombo, Sri Lanka: 1985. Scholarly edited collection, in English.

Survival International. "The New Eldorado Threat to Indians in Brazil and Venezuela." *Survival International Newsletter* 20 (1988): 1–3. NGO article, in English.

Taswell, Ruth, ed. *Southeast Asian Tribal Groups and Ethnic Minorities.* Cambridge, MA: Cultural Survival, 1987. NGO conference proceedings, in English.

Thornberry, Patrick. *Minorities and Human Rights Laws.* London: Minority Rights Group, 1987. NGO report, in English.

U.S. Helsinki Watch Committee. *Destroying Ethnic Identity: The Kurds of Turkey—An Update.* New York: 1988. NGO report, in English.

Vigil India Movement. "Cultural Rights vs. Human Rights." *Vigil India* 44 (Feb. 1988). NGO special issue, in English.

Zanga, Louis. "Albanian Demands for Better Cultural Standards." *Radio Free Europe Research* 10, no. 52 (27 Dec. 1985). Government report, in English.

Death Penalty

A. General

Amnesty International. *Cuba: Recent Developments Affecting the Situation of Political Prisoners and the Use of the Death Penalty—An Update.* London: 1989. NGO report, in English.

——————. "GDR Announces Amnesty and Abolishes Death Penalty," 24 July 1987. NGO press release, in English.

——————. *Indonesia: The Application of the Death Penalty.* London: 1987. NGO report, in English.

——————. *Jamaica: The Death Penalty.* London: 1989. NGO report, in English.

——————. *Military Trials and the Use of the Death Penalty in Equatorial Guinea.* London: 1987. NGO briefing paper, in English.

——————. *Pakistan: The Death Penalty.* London: 1988. NGO report, in English.

——————. *Taiwan: The Death Penalty.* London: 1988. NGO report, in English.

——————. *The Death Penalty in Ghana.* London: 1985. NGO report, in English.

——————. *The Death Penalty in Iraq: Introduction and Background.* London: 1987. NGO background paper, in English.

——————. *The Death Penalty in the People's Republic of China: Sentencing Rallies and Executions.* London: 1986. NGO report, in English.

——————. "The Death Penalty in South Africa." *Amnesty International Newsletter* 18, no. 12 (Dec. 1988): 3–6. NGO article, in English.

——————. *The Use of the Death Penalty in Nigeria.* London: 1985. NGO report, in English.

——————. *Turkey: The Death Penalty—Recent Developments and Some Examples.* London: 1988. NGO report, in English.

——————. *United States of America: The Death Penalty.* London: 1987. NGO report, in English.

——————. *USSR: New Death Penalty Laws May Soon Be Made Public.* London: 1988. NGO report, in English.

——————. *USSR: The Death Penalty Debate.* London: 1987. NGO report, in English.

Buchholz, Erich. "Abolition of the Death Penalty in the GDR." *GDR Committee for Human Rights Bulletin* 13, no. 2/87 (1987): 140–146. NGO article, in English.

Konovalov, Valerii. "The Death Penalty in the USSR, 1987." *Radio Liberty Research Bulletin* 5 (25 Jan. 1988) Government article, in English.

Laulie, Max. "La Pena de Muerte Debe Ser Abolida" (The Death Penalty Must Be Abolished). *Boletin Internacional* 91 (June 1988). NGO conference report, in Spanish.

Paduano, A., and C.A. Stafford Smith. "Deathly Errors: Juror Misperceptions concerning Parole in the Imposition of the Death Penalty." *Columbia Human Rights Law Review* 18, no. 2 (Spring 1987): 211–257. NGO article, in English.

Reoch, Richard. *Human Rights and the Death Penalty.* London: Amnesty International, 1970. Lecture, in English.

Szumski, B., L. Hall, and S. Bursell, eds. *The Death Penalty: Opposing Viewpoints.* St. Paul, MN: Greenhaven Press, 1986. Edited collection, in English; bibliography, pp. 94, 129, and 167 (for periodical literature) and 169–170 (for monographs).

"The Death Penalty and the Judiciary." *Crime and Social Justice* 25 (1986): 67–113. Scholarly article, in English.

B. Juveniles

Amnesty International. *USA: The Death Penalty—Developments in 1988.* London: 1989. NGO report, in English.

Inter-American Commission on Human Rights. "Application of Death Penalty on Juveniles in the U.S./Violation of Human Rights Obligation under the Inter-American System." *Human Rights Law Journal* 8, Pts. 2–4 (1987): 345–361. IGO decision/IGO resolution, in English.

Streib, Victor L. *Death Penalty for Juveniles.* Bloomington, IN: Indiana University Press, 1987. Scholarly report, in English; classified bibliography, pp. 237–250.

Debt Bondage

Brass, Tom. "Debt Bondage in India." In *Third World Affairs 1986,* 290–304. London: Third World Foundation for Social and Economic Studies, 1986. Yearbook, in English.

SEE ALSO *Bonded Labor.*

Detention

A. Administrative

Amnesty International. *Administrative Detention.* London: 1988. NGO report, in English.

——————. *South Korea: Administrative Detention.* London: 1989. NGO report, in English.

——————. *Swaziland: Detentions under the 60-Day Law.* London: 1985. NGO report, in English.

Birzeit University, Public Relations Office. *The Twentieth Year: A Report on the Status of Academic Freedom and Human Rights at Birzeit University in the Twentieth Year of Israeli Military Occupation.* Jerusalem, Occupied Territories: 1988. Conference report, in English.

Law in the Service of Man/Al-Haq. *Administrative Detention in the Occupied West Bank.* Ramalleh, Occupied Territories: 1986. NGO report, in English.

——————. *Ansar 3: A Case for Closure.* Ramallah, Occupied Territories: 1988. NGO mission report, in English.

——————. *Briefing Papers on Twenty Years of Israeli Occupation of the West Bank and Gaza.* Ramallah, Occupied Territories: 1987. NGO briefing paper collection, in English.

——————. *Punishing a Nation: Human Rights Violations during the Palestinian Uprising, Dec. 1987–Dec. 1988.* Ramallah, Occupied Territories: 1988. NGO report, in English.

Playfair, Emma. *Administrative Detention in the Occupied West Bank.* Ramallah, Occupied Territories: Law in the Service of Man/Al-Haq, 1986. NGO occasional paper, in English.

Shalev, Carmel. *The Price of Insurgency: Civil Rights in the Occupied Territories.* Jerusalem, Israel: West Bank Database Project, 1988. NGO report, in English.

Vitullo, Anita. *Ansar 2: Detention, Humiliation, and Intimidation.* Chicago, IL: Palestine Human Rights Information Center and Human Rights Research and Education Foundation/Database Project, 1987. NGO report, in English.

Zucker, Dedi. "Droits de l'Homme et Repression de l'Intifada" (Human Rights and Repression of the Intifadah). *Revue d'Etudes Palestiniennes* 29 (Oct. 1988): 75–91. NGO article, in French.

B. General

Aliran Kesedaran Negara. "Preventive Detention in Malaysia." *Human Rights Forum* 1, no. 3 (July–Sept. 1985): 3–6. NGO article, in English.

Amnesty International. *Bangladesh: Large-Scale Detention without Trial of Opposition Members, July 1987–Feb. 1988.* London: 1988. NGO report, in English.

————. *Comoros. The Detention without Trial and Allegations of Torture of Suspected Opponents of the Government.* London: 1985. NGO report, in English.

————. *Detention of Journalists in Uganda.* London: 1984. NGO report, in English.

————. *Detention without Trial of Political Prisoners in Zimbabwe.* London: 1985. NGO report, in English.

————. *Haiti: Deaths in Detention, Torture and Inhumane Prison Conditions.* London: 1987. NGO report, in English.

————. *Kampuchea: Officially Reported Political Arrests and Allegations of Torture and Arbitrary Detention.* London: 1988. NGO report, in English.

————. Kenya: Torture, Political Detention and Unfair Trials. London: 1987. NGO report, in English.

————. *Malaysia: "Operation Lalang": Detention without Trial under the Internal Security Act.* London: 1988. NGO report, in English.

————. *Philippines: Incommunicado Detention, Ill-Treatment and Torture during 1988.* London: 1988. NGO report, in English.

————. *Socialist Republic of Viet Nam: Possible Continued Detention in "Reeducation Camps" Causes Concern.* London: 1988. NGO report, in English.

————. *South Africa: Detention and Torture of Trade Unionists.* London: 1986. NGO report, in English.

————. *South Africa: Detention under the State of Emergency.* London: 1985. NGO report, in English.

————. *The Ill-Treatment and Torture of Political Prisoners at Detention Centers in Kinshasa.* London: 1980. NGO report, in English.

————. *Uganda: Detention of Alleged Political Opponents by the National Resistance Army.* London: 1987. NGO report, in English.

————. *United Kingdom: Alleged Forced Admissions during Incommunicado Detention.* London: 1988. NGO report, in English.

An-Na'im, Adbullahi Ahmed. "Detention without Trial in the Sudan: The Use and Abuse of Legal Powers." *Columbia Human Rights Law Review* 17, no. 2 (Spring–Summer 1986): 159–187. Scholarly article, in English.

Arab Organization for Human Rights. "Syria: A Special Committee to Investigate Detention of Palestinians." *AOHR Newsletter* 12–13 (Dec. 1987): 2. NGO article, in English.

Berkan, Judith. "Preventive Detention." *Puerto Rico Libre* (Fall 1985): 11, 30. NGO bulletin article, in English.

Budlender, G. "Children in Detention—An Update." *South African Outlook* 177, no. 1394 (Aug. 1987): 84–85. NGO article, in English.

Central American Refugee Defense Fund. "Oakdale Detention Center." *Central American Refugee Defense Fund Newsletter* (June 1986): 1, 7. NGO newsletter article, in English.

Centre for Socio-Legal Research and Documentation Service. "Editorial: Law of Preventive Detention." *Socio-Legal Concern Newsletter* 3, no. 7 (July 1987): 1. NGO editorial, in English.

Conboy, Kevin. "Detention without Trial in Kenya." *The Georgia Journal of International and Comparative Law* 8, no. 2 (1987): 441–461. Scholarly article, in English.

Foster, Don. *Detention and Torture in South Africa: Psychological, Legal and Historical Studies.* Cape Town, South Africa: David Philip, 1987. Scholarly monograph, in English; bibliography, pp. 238–246.

"Free South Africa's Children: A Symposium on Children in Detention." *Human Rights Quarterly* 10, no. 1 (Feb. 1988): 10–108. Conference proceedings, in English.

Hamad, Saida. "Attorney's Report Details Appalling Conditions in Detention Camp." *Al-Fajr* 9, no. 408 (13 March 1988): 1, 13. News article, in English.

Julien-Laferriere, F., and B. Tayon. *Rapport de Mission: Chili, sur les Conditions de Detention apres les Incidents du 18/10* (Mission Report: Chile, on the Conditions of Detention after the Events of Oct. 18). Paris: Federation Internationale des Droits de l'Homme, 1985. NGO mission report, in French.

Minnesota Lawyers International Human Rights Committee. *Oakdale Detention Center: The First Year of Operation.* Minneapolis, MN: 1987. NGO report, in English.

"New Detention Legislation." *ANC News Brief* 10, no. 22 (1 June 1986): 11–12. NGO bulletin article, in English.

Parker, Collins. "Control of Executive Discretion and Preventive Detention in Zambia." *Comparative and International Law Journal of Southern Africa* 13, no. 2 (July 1980): 159–176. Scholarly article, in English.

Parker, K., and E. Jaudel. *Police Cell Detention in Japan: The Kaiyo Kangoku System.* Paris: Federation Internationale des Droits de l'Homme and Association of Humanitarian Lawyers, 1989. NGO mission report, in English and French.

Regional Council on Human Rights in Asia. *The Law and Practice of Preventive Detention in the ASEAN Region.* Manila, Philippines: 1988. NGO report, in English

Skelton, James W., Jr. "Standards of Procedural Due Process under International Law vs. Preventive Detention in Selected African States." *Houston Journal of International Law* 2, no. 2 (Spring 1980): 307–331. Scholarly article, in English.

Sri Lanka Project, British Refugee Council. "Detention without Charge." *Sri Lanka Monitor* 1 (Feb. 1988): 3. NGO article, in English.

United Nations Commission on Human Rights. *Question of the Human Rights of all Persons subjected to any Form of Detention or Imprisonment, Torture and Other Cruel, Inhuman or Degrading Treatment or Punishment.* Prepared by Special Rapporteur P. Kooijmans, E/CN.4/1987/13. 9 Jan. 1987. IGO report, in English.

United Nations Commission on Human Rights, Working Group on Enforced or Involuntary Disappearances. *Questions of the Human Rights of all Persons subjected to any Form of Detention or Imprisonment, in Particular: Question of Enforced or Involuntary Disappearances: Addendum: Report on a Visit to Peru (17–22 June 1985).* E/CN.4/1986/18/Add 1. 8 Jan. 1986. IGO document, in English.

Zentrale Dokumentationsstelle der Freinen Wohlfahrtspflege fur Fluchtlinge (European Legal Network on Asylum). *European Lawyers Workshop on Detention, Choice or Residence and Freedom of Movement of Asylum Seekers and Refugees.* Bonn, FRG: 1987. NGO conference report, in English.

Development

Alston, Philip. "Making Space for New Human Rights: The Case of the Right to Development." *Harvard Human Rights Yearbook* 1 (1988): 3–40. Scholarly article, in English.

Association Senegalaise d'Etudes et de Recherches Juridiques (Senegalese Association for Juridical Study and Research). *Revue Senegalaise de Droit: Numero Special Relatif au Colloque de Dakar sur le Developpement et les Droits de l'Homme* (Senegalese Law Review: Special Issue on the Dakar Colloquium on Development and Human Rights) 11, no. 22 (Dec. 1977). NGO conference report, in French.

Bedjaoui, Mohammed. "The Right to Development and the *Jus Cogens.*" *Lesotho Law Journal* 2, no. 2 (1986): 93–129. Scholarly article, in English.

Bekhechi, Mohammed Abdelwahab. "Souverainete, Developpement et Droits de l'homme dans la Constitution algerienne et en Droit International" (Sovereignty, Development and Human Rights in the Algerian Constitution and International Law). Paper delivered at a colloquium on "The Constitution and Constitutionalism in Algeria," Universite de Annaba, 26–28 April 1987, Oran, Algeria. Scholarly conference paper, in French.

Boatman, J. "China: The Long March to Development." *Multinational Monitor* 8 no. 3 (March 1987). NGO article, in English.

Cook, Rebecca. "Human Rights and Development: Are Women Still Separate and Unequal." *Proceedings of the 1986 Conference of the Canadian Council on International Law on "International Law and Development,"* 315–347. Ottawa, Ontario: 1987. Scholarly article, in English.

Dimitrijevic, Vojin. *Development as a Right.* Paper presented at the African Seminar on Human Rights and Development, 24–28 May 1982, Gaborone, Botswana. Conference paper, in English.

Ecumenical Coalition on Third World Tourism and Center for Development Education. *Tourism, Prostitution, Development.* Rev. ed. Bangkok, Thailand: 1984. NGO report, in German and English.

Espiritu, A.C. "Law, Development and Human Rights in the ASEAN." *Human Rights Forum* 1, no. 2 (1985): 1–9. NGO magazine article, in English.

Howard, Rhoda. "Law and Economic Rights in Commonwealth Africa." *California Western International Law Journal* 15, no. 3 (Summer 1985): 607–632. Scholarly article, in English.

International Commission of Jurists. *Development, Human Rights and the Rule of Law.* New York: Pergamon Press, 1981. NGO report, in English.

Kibola, H. S. *Some Conceptual Aspects of Human Rights: The Basis for the Right to Development in Africa.* Paper presented at a seminar on "Law and Human Rights in Development," Gaborone, Botswana, 24–28 May 1982. Unpublished paper, in English.

Kunig, Philip. "The 'Inner Dimension' of the Right to Development: Considerations concerning the Responsibility of Developing Countries." *Law and State* 36 (1987): 46–64. Scholarly article, in English.

M'Baye, Keba. "Le Droit au Developpement." In *Le Droit au Development au Plan International, Colloque, La Haye, 16–18 Octobre, 1979* (The Right to Development at the International Level, Collloquium, The Hague, 16–18 Oct. 1979), ed. Rene-Jean Dupuy. The Hague: Alphen aan den Rijn, Sijthoff and Noordhoff for Academie de Droit International de la Haye and Universite des Nations Unies, 1980. Chapter in conference proceedings, in French.

——————. "Le Droit au Developpement comme un Droit de l'Homme" (The Right to Development as a Human Right). *Revue des Droits de l'Homme: Droit International et Compare* 5, no. 2–3 (1972): 505–534. Scholarly article/lecture, in French.

——————. "Le Developpement et les Droits de l'Homme: Rapport Introductif—Dakar Colloquium, 1978" (Development and Human Rights: Introductory Report, Dakar Colloquium, 1978). *Revue Senegalaise de Droit* 11, no. 22 (Sept. 1978): 19–51. Scholarly article, in French.

Ngcongco, L. D., T. T. Fako, and S. Bakwena, eds. *Human Rights and Development in Africa.* Selected proceedings of a workshop on Human Rights and Development in Africa, Institute of Development Management, Gaborone, Botswana, 1–3 April 1985. Unpublished conference proceedings, in English.

Nietschmann, Bernard. "Economic Development by Invasion of Indigenous Nations: Cases of Indonesia and Bangladesh." *Cultural Survival Quarterly* 10, no. 2 (1986): 2–12. NGO magazine article, in English.

Paul, James C. N. *The World Bank, Human Rights and Development: Some Obligations of the Bank.* Paper prepared for the annual meeting of the Canadian Association of African Studies, Edmonton, 7–9 May 1987. Unpublished scholarly paper, in English.

Rose, Leslie. "Bargaining with Beijing." *Multinational Monitor* 8, no. 3 (March 1987). NGO article, in English.

Shephard, G. W., Jr., and V. Nanda, eds. *Human Rights and Third World Development.* Westport, CT (USA): Greenwood Press, 1985. Scholarly study, in English.

Soedjatmoko, A. *The Primacy of Freedom in Development.* University Press of America, 1985. Scholarly study, in English.

Stewart, Frances. *Basic Needs in Development Countries.* Baltimore, MD (USA): Johns Hopkins University Press, 1985. Scholarly study, in English.

Steif, William. "China: The Long March to Development." *Multinational Monitor* 8, no. 3 (March 1987). NGO article, in English.

Subbian, Adaikkalam. *Bibliography on Human Rights and Development—Third World Countries.* Annamalainagar, Tamil Nadu, India: Annamalai University, Department of History, 1985. Bibliography, in English.

United Nations. "Assembly adopts Declaration on Right to Development, Acts on Wide Range of Issues Related to Human Rights." *UN Chronicle* 24, no. 1 (Feb. 1987): 119. IGO article, in English.

——————. *Report of the World Conference to Review and Appraise the Achievements of the United Nations Decade for Women: Equality, Development and Peace, Nairobi, 15–26 July 1985.* A/CONF.116/28/Rev. 1. 1986. IGO conference report, in English.

United Nations Commission on Human Rights. *Problems related to the Right to Enjoy an Adequate Standard of Living: The Right to Development (Report of the Working Group of Governmental Experts on the Right to Development).* E/CN.4/1987/10. 29 Jan. 1987. IGO report, in English.

United Nations Non-Governmental Liaison Service. *Directory of Development Education Periodicals.* Geneva: 1986. Directory/bibliography, in English.

Washington Office on Latin America. *Chile: The Multilateral Development Banks and U.S. Human Rights Law: A Delegation Report.* Washington, D.C.: 1986. NGO mission report, in English.

World Bank. *World Development Report.* Oxford (UK): Oxford University Press, published annually. Annual report, in English.

Disabled Persons

Baker, David. "An Overview of Human Rights for Disabled People in Canada." Paper presented at International Experts Meeting on Ways and Means to Ensure Effective Exercise of Human Rights by Disadvantaged Groups, Quebec, Canada,18 Sept. 1985. Unpublished conference paper, in English.

Bayefsky, A. F., and M. Eberts, eds. *Equality Rights and the Canadian Charter of Rights and Freedoms.* Toronto, Canada: Carswell, 1985. Edited collection, in English.

"Bibliography for Central America." *One in Ten* 5, nos. 1/2 (1986): 10–12. Bibliography, in English.

Canadian Council on Social Development, Court Challenges Program. *A Guide to the Charter for Equality-Seeking Groups.* Ottawa, Canada: 1987. Government manual, in English and French.

Committee for Public Justice. "Civil Wrongs and the Handicapped." *Justice Watch* 6, no. 1 (March

1986): 1–3, 6–7. NGO newsletter article, in English.

Evans, T., P. Molan, and P. Burgess. *The Treatment of Disabled Persons in Social Security and Taxation Law.* Canberra, Australia: Human Rights Commission, 1986. Government monograph, in English.

Graft-Johnson, K. E. de. "Measures Taken in Ghana to Ensure the Effective Exercise of Human Rights for Disadvantaged Social Groups." Paper presented at International Experts Meeting on Ways and Means to Ensure Effective Exercise of Human Rights by Disadvantaged Groups, Quebec, Canada, 18 Sept. 1985. Unpublished conference paper, in English.

Marjanovic, S., R. Marjanovic, and N. Novakovic. "Measures Taken in Yugoslavia to Ensure the Effective Exercise of Human Rights by Handicapped People." Paper presented at International Experts Meeting on Ways and Means to Ensure Effective Exercise of Human Rights by Disadvantaged Groups, Quebec, Canada, 18 Sept. 1985. Unpublished conference paper, in English.

Sheehan, R., and J. Jardine. *Epilepsy and Human Rights.* Canberra, Australia: Human Rights Commission, 1984. Government monograph, in English.

Taiwan Church News. "The Continuing Struggle for Rights of the Disabled." *Occasional Bulletin* 5, no. 1 (Dec. 1987–Jan. 1988): 3. NGO article, in English.

Ware, Helen. *Legal and Ethical Aspects of the Management of Newborns with Severe Disabilities.* Canberra, Australia: Human Rights Commission, 1985. Government monograph, in English.

Disappearances

Action des Chretiens pour l'Abolition de la Torture (Christian Action for the Abolition of Torture). "Les Enfants Disparus en Argentine (The Disappeared Children in Argentina). *Courrier de l'ACAT* 59 (Nov. 1985): 10–16. NGO bulletin article, in French.

American Association for the Advancement of Science, Clearinghouse on Science and Human Rights. *Guatemala: Case Reports 1980–1985.* Washington, D.C.: 1986. NGO report, in English.

Americas Watch Committee. *Settling into Routine: Human Rights Abuses in Duarte's Second Year: Eighth Supplement to the Report on Human Rights in El Salvador.* New York: 1986. NGO report, in English.

——————. *The Central-Americanization of Colombia? Human Rights and the Peace Process.* New York: 1986. NGO report, in English.

Amnesty International. *East Timor Violations of Human Rights: Extrajudicial Executions, 'Disappearance,' Torture and Political Imprisonment.* London: 1985. NGO report, in English.

——————. *Recent Developments in the Investigations into "Disappearances" in Argentina.* London: 1985. NGO report, in English.

——————. *Sri Lanka: Extrajudicial Executions and "Disappearances" in May 1985.* London: 1985. NGO statement, in English.

——————. *Sri Lanka: What Has Happened to the "Disappeared"?* London: 1988. NGO report, in English.

——————. *The Missing Children of Argentina: A Report of Current Investigations.* London: 1985. NGO report, in English.

Asociacion Centroamericana de Familiares de Detenidos-Desaparecidos (Central American Association of Families of the Detained-Disappeared). *Honduras: Desaparecidos, Juicio y Condena* (Honduras: Disappearances, Trial and Sentence). San Jose, Costa Rica: 1989. NGO report, in Spanish.

——————. "La Practica de la Desaparicion Forzada de Personas" (The Practice of Forced Disappearances of Persons), July 1985. NGO Statement, in Spanish.

——————. *La Practica de la Desaparicion Forzada de Personas en Guatemala* (The Practice of Forced Disappearance of Persons in Guatemala). San Jose, Costa Rica: 1988. NGO report, in Spanish; bibliography, annotated by key words, 297–304.

Chile Committee for Human Rights. "The Disappeared—Confessions of a Secret Agent." *Chile Update* 59/60 (April 1985): 5. NGO bulletin article, in English.

Ecumenical Forum of Canada. "Human Rights, the Disappeared and the Church in Argentina." *Nunca Mas* 12, no. 4 (Sept. 1985): 1–7. NGO bulletin article, in English.

Guatamala News and Information Bureau. "Disappeared: GAM Demands Cerezo Take a Stand." *Guatemala!* 7, no. 3 (May–June 1986): 1, 8. Newsletter article, in English.

Liga Colombiana por los Derechos y la Liberacion de los Pueblos y Colectivo de Abogados Jose Alvear Restrepo (Colombian League for the Rights and Liberation of Peoples and Jose Alvear Restrepo Lawyers' Collective). *El Camino de la Niebla: La Desaparicion Forzada en Colombia y su Impunidad* (The Foggy Road: Forced Disappearance and Impunity in Colombia). Bogota, Colombia: 1988. NGO report in Spanish.

Minnesota Lawyers International Human Rights Committee. *Expectations Denied: Habeas Corpus and the*

Search for Guatemala's Disappeared. Minneapolis, MN: 1988. NGO report, in English.

Rodley, Nigel S. "UN Action Procedures against 'Disappearances,' Summary or Arbitrary Executions, and Torture." *Human Rights Quarterly* 8, no. 4 (Nov. 1986): 700–730. Scholarly article, in English.

Secretariat International des Juristes pour l'Amnistie en Uruguay (International Secretariat of Lawyers for Amnesty in Uruguay). *Situacion de las Personas Desaparecidas y los Hechos que la Motivaron* (Situation of the Disappeared Persons and the Motivation behind It). Paris: 1985. NGO report, in Spanish.

Simpson, J., and J. Bennett. *The Disappeared and the Mothers of the Plaza.* New York: St. Martin's Press, 1985. Scholarly study, in English.

Wiseberg, L. S., and L. Ocampo. "The Philippines Revisited: Plus ca change, Plus ca reste la meme. Excerpts from a Report by the International League for Human Rights." *Human Rights Internet* 13, no. 1 (Spring 1989). Commentary, NGO report, in English.

Discrimination

Ahooja-Patel, K. "United Nations in Africa: International Year for Action to Combat Racism and Racial Discrimination." *Genve-Afrique* 10, no. 1 (1971): 74–75. Scholarly article, in English.

Anti-Defamation League of B'nai B'rith. *Hate Groups in America: A Record of Bigotry and Violence.* Rev. ed. New York: 1988. NGO report, in English; bibliography, pp. 91–96.

Armstrong, Alice, ed. *Women and Law in Southern Africa.* Harare, Zimbabwe: Zimbabwe Publishing House, 1987. Scholarly edited collection, in English.

Bacon, Lisa. "Lessons of AIDS: Racism, Homophobia are the Real Epidemic." *Listen Real Loud* 8, no. 2 (Fall 1987): 1, 6. NGO article, in English; bibliography: extensive references pp. 151–165.

Currin, Brian. "Human Rights and the Group Areas Act." NGO statement issued by Lawyers for Human Rights (Pretoria, S.A.), 22 June 1988.

DeLeon, David. *Everything is Changing: Contemporary U.S. Movements in Historical Perspective.* New York: Praeger Publishers, 1988. Scholarly monograph, in English.

Femmes sous Lois Musulmanes (Women Living under Muslim Laws). *Dossier No. 1.* Montpellier, France: 1986. NGO document collection, in French.

——————. *Dossier No. 2.* Montpellier, France: 1986. NGO document collection, in English.

Garver, C., and D. Raizman. *Race Relations: A Feature and Documentary Filmography.* New York: Center for the Study of Human Rights, Columbia University, 1987. Filmography, in English.

Gordon, Paul. *Anti-Racist Materials for Adult and Community Education.* London: Runnymede Trust, 1986. NGO bibliography, with comprehensive references on racism with a focus on the United Kingdom, in English.

Human Awareness Programme. *Changing Attitudes in a Changing South Africa: Can It Be Done?* Johannesburg, South Africa: 1987. NGO manual, in English.

Hunter, Jane. *Undercutting Sanctions: Israel, the U.S. and South Africa.* Washington, D. C.: Washington Middle East Associates, 1986. NGO report, in English.

Isis International. *Rural Women in Latin America.* Rome: 1987. NGO monograph, in English.

Lacob, Mirian. "Standing up for the Voiceless." *Africa Report,* 33, no. 3 (May–June 1988): 65–67. NGO article, in English.

LeBoeuf, Denise. "Psychiatric Malpractice: Exploitation of Women Patients." *Harvard Women's Law Journal* 11 (Spring 1988): 83–116. Scholarly article, in English.

Lutz, Chris, comp. *They Don't All Wear Sheets: A Chronology of Racist and Far Right Violence—1980–1986.* New York: Center for Democratic Renewal and National Council of Churches, 1987. NGO report, in English.

Maope, K.A. *Human Rights in Botswana, Lesotho and Swaziland: A Survey of the BOLESWA Countries.* Roma, Lesotho: Institute of Southern African Studies, 1986. NGO report, in English.

Mernissi, Fatima. *Beyond the Veil: Male-Female Dynamic in Modern Muslim Society.* Bloomington, IN: Indiana University Press, 1987. Scholarly report, in English.

Norgren, J., and S. Nanda. *American Cultural Pluralism and Law.* New York: Praeger, 1988. Scholarly monograph, in English; selected bibliography, p. 5.

Nowak, M., D. Steurer, and H. Tretter, eds. *Fortschritt im Bewusstsein der Grund- und Menschenrechte: Festschrift fur Felix Ermacora* (Progress in the Spirit of Human Rights: Essays in Honor of Felix Ermcora). Kehl am Rhein, FRG: N.P. Engel Verlag, 1988. Scholarly edited collection, in English and German.

Sigler, Jay A., ed. *International Handbook on Race and Race Relations.* Westport, CT: Greenwood Press, 1987. Scholarly edited collection, in English; bibliography, pp. 449–454.

Suter, Keith D. "Australian Aborigines: The Continuing Crisis." *Human Rights Internet* 13, no. 1 (Spring 1989). Commentary, in English.

Transformation Resource Centre. "Role of Women in Free South Africa." *Work for Justice* 13 (Jan. 1987): 4–5. NGO article, in English.

Disinvestment

American Committee on Africa. *Public Investment and South Africa.* New York: 1986. NGO report, in English.

Crisfield, Judea. *For Freedom in South Africa.* Davis, CA: Crisfield Films and Video, 1986. Documentary, in English.

"End Loans to Southern Africa." *Embargo Newsletter* 1 (Autumn 1986). NGO newsletter, in English.

Ethical Investment Research and Information Service. *UK Companies: South African Pay and Conditions.* London: 1986. NGO report, in English.

Hunter, Jane. *Undercutting Sanctions: Israel, the U.S. and South Africa.* Washington, D.C.: Washington Middle East Associates, 1986. NGO report, in English.

International Confederation of Free Trade Unions. *Investment in Apartheid.* Brussels, Belgium: 1988. NGO report, in English.

Kaempfer, W.H., J.A. Lehman, and A.D. Lowenberg. "Divestment, Investment Sanctions, and Disinvestment: An Evaluation of Anti-Apartheid Policy Instruments." *International Organization* 41, no. 3 (Summer 1987): 457–473. Scholarly article, in English.

Khan, Haider Ali. "Measuring and Analyzing the Economic Effects of Trade Sanctions against South Africa: A New Approach." *Africa Today* 33, nos. 2, 3 (15 June 1987): 5–25. Scholarly article, in English.

Lawyers Committee for Human Rights. *United States Policy toward South Africa.* New York: 1989. NGO report, in English.

Leonard, Richard. "International Business Machines in South Africa: Time to Withdraw." *The Corporate Examiner* 15, no. 4 (1986): 3A–3D. NGO bulletin article, in English.

National Council of Churches. *South Africa: A Guide to Campus Involvement and Activity.* New York: n.d. NGO booklet, with bibliography of resources, in English.

Pacific Northwest Research Center, Africa Fund. *Unified List of U.S. Companies with Investments of Loans in South Africa and Namibia.* New York: Updated periodically. NGO report, in English.

Schmidt, Elizabeth. *One Step in the Wrong Direction: An Analysis of the Sullivan Principles.* New York: Epis-

copal Churchpeople for a Free Southern Africa, 1985. NGO report, in English.

Schoeman, Elna. *South African Sanctions Directory: 1946–1988: Actions by Governments, Banks, Churches, Trade Unions, Universities, International and Regional Organizations.* Braamfontein, South Africa: South African Institute of International Affairs, 1989. Bibliography, in English.

Shipping Research Bureau. *Newsletter on the Oil Embargo against South Africa* 5 (Sept. 1986). Newsletter, with list of Shipping Research Bureau publications, in English.

"Small Print of the U.S.' Sanctions Law." *Southscan* 4 (7 Oct. 1986): 5. Bulletin article, in English.

Sutcliff, M., and P. Wellings. "Disinvestment and Black Worker 'Attitudes, in South Africa: A Critical Comment." *IDOC Internazionale* 16, no. 5 (Oct. 1985): 18–26. NGO bulletin article, in English.

Thomas, Franklin A. *South Africa: Time Running Out.* New York: Ford Foundation, 1985. Speech, in English.

Toronto Committee for the Liberation of Southern Africa. *Southern Africa Report* 2 no. 6 (Oct. 1986). NGO newsletter, in English; bibliography, list of resources on sanctions and divestment, p. 29.

Transnational Information Exchange. "Meeting the Corporate Challenge: A Handbook on Corporate Campaigns." *TIE Report* 18–19 (Feb. 1985). NGO Report, special issue, in English.

Wright, Sanford. "Comprehensive International Sanctions against South Africa: An Evaluation of Costs and Effectiveness." *Africa Today* 33, nos. 2, 3 (15 June 1987): 47–59. Scholarly article, in English.

Economic, Social and Cultural Rights

Alston, Philip. "Out of the Abyss: The Challenges Confronting the New UN Committee on Economic, Social and Cultural Rights." *Human Rights Quarterly* 9, no. 3 (Aug. 1987): 332–381. Scholarly article, in English.

Ganji, Manouchehr. *A Study on the Realization of Economic, Social, and Cultural Rights—Question of the Realization of the Economic, Social, and Cultural Rights Contained in the Universal Declaration of Human Rights and in the International Covenant on Economic, Social and Cultural Rights in Developing Countries: The Widening Gap.* New York: United Nations, 1974. IGO report, in English.

Gros Espiel, Hector. *Los Derechos Economicos, Sociales y Culturales en el Sistema Interamericano (Economic, Social and Cultural Rights in the Interamerican*

System). San Jose, Costa Rica: Libro Libre, 1986. Monograph, in Spanish.

"Symposium on 'The implementation of the International Covenant on Economic, Social and Cultural Rights.'" *Human Rights Quarterly* 9, no. 2 (May 1987). Special issue with scholarly articles, in English.

Education

Aji, Mallam Umaru. *The Right to Education in Rural Communities: The Nigerian Experience.* Paper presented at the International Conference on Human Rights Education in Rural Environments, organized by UNESCO and the Ford Foundation, University of Lagos, Nigeria, 26–29 Nov. 1985. Unpublished conference paper, in English.

Christie, Pam. *The Right to Learn: The Struggle for Education in South Africa.* Braamfontein, South Africa: Ravan Press, 1985. Research study, in English; bibliography at end of each chapter.

Davies, John. "United States Foreign Policy and the Education of Black South Africans." *Africa Perspective* 26 (1985): 61–79. Student publication article, in English.

Dorjee, Ngawang. "Treating Unequals as Equals." *Tibetan Review* 21, no. 5 (May 1986): 12–13, 21. Magazine article, in English.

Drinan, Robert F., ed. *The Right to be Educated.* Washington, D.C.: Corpus, 1968. Edited collection, in English.

Gordon, P., and A. Newnham. *Different Worlds: Racism and Discrimination in Britain.* 2d rev. ed. London: The Runnymede Trust, 1986. NGO report, in English.

"Guatemala: The Statistics Say It All." *This Week: Central America and Panama* 10, no. 1 (5 Jan. 1987): 2–4. News article, in English.

Latin America Documentation. "Haiti: National Priorities according to the Bishops Conference." *LADOC* 17, no. 1 (Sept.–Oct. 1986): 4–8. Journal article, in English.

Law in the Service of Man/Al-Haq. "Al-Haq's Action to Defend the Right to Education." *Law in the Service of Man Newsletter* 13 (May–June 1986): 1. NGO newsletter article.

National Coalition of Advocates for Students. *New Voices: Immigrant Students in U.S. Public Schools.* Boston, MA: 1988. NGO report, in English.

Nuseiben, Reem. "Israel Closes All Palestinian Academic Institutions." *Al-Fajr* 9, no. 403 (7 Feb. 1988): 1. News article, in English.

Robinson, Cedric J. "Education Is for All or Isn't It?" *NASSA News* 23, no. 6 (June 1986): 12–16. Journal article, in English.

Samara, Maha. "Education is the Key to Increase Gulf Women's Contribution in Economic Development." *Al-Raida* 8, no. 41 (1 Aug. 1987): 10–11. NGO article, in English.

Subbian, A. "Education—A Human Right or a Privilege to Indian Children." *Journal of Annamalai University* (Aug. 1987): 161–170. Scholarly speech, in English.

UNESCO Regional Office for Education in Africa. *Colloque Regional sur l'Exercise du Droit a l'Education, Dakar 1980* (Regional Colloquium on the Exercise of the Right to Education). Dakar, Senegal: 1980. Conference proceedings, in English.

Environment

Clad, James. "Pollution affecting Fishing Villages in Kampung Kuala Juru." *Human Rights Forum* 1, no. 2 (1985): 23–24. NGO magazine, in English.

Comision para la Defensa de los Derechos Humanos en Centroamerica (Central American Commission for the Defense of Human Rights). "La Protection du Milieu Ambiant" (Protection of the Environment). *Caminando! (En Marche)* 9, no. 2 (May 1988): 13–16. NGO article, in French.

"Corporate Crime and Violence." *Multinational Monitor* 8, no. 4 (April 1987): 4–25. Special issue, in English.

Jacobson, Jodi L. *Environmental Refugees: A Yardstick of Habitability.* Washington, D. C.: Worldwatch Institute, 1988. NGO monograph, in English.

National Council of Churches in the Philippines. "Technology from the Underside." *Tugon* 6, no.1 (1986). NGO article/conference proceedings, in English.

Peng, Khor Kok. "Industrial Pollution in Cisalak Village." *Human Rights Forum* 1, no. 4 (Oct.–Dec. 1985): 17–20. NGO magazine, in English.

Rao, M., and G. Singh, eds. *The Environmental Activists' Handbook: Environmental Act, Important Judgments, Strategies.* Puntamba, Maharashtra, India: Asha Kendra Documentation Centre, n. d. NGO report, in English.

Sahabat Alam Malaysia. "Award for Paraquat Sprayers who Retired Early." *Suara Sam* 3, no. 5 (Aug. 1986): 2. NGO newsletter article, in English.

————. "Ban Killer Pesticides." *Suara Sam* 3, no. 4 (July 1986): 6–9. NGO newsletter article, in English.

Third World Network. *Report on Toxic Waste Dumping in Third World Countries.* Penang, Malaysia: 1988. NGO report, in English.

" 'Toxic Terrorism,' " *West Africa,* 20 June 1988, 1108–1109, 1144. News article, in English.

Equality

Castles, S., B. Cope, M. Kalantzis, and M. Morrissey. "The Bicentenary and the Failure of Australian Nationalism." *Race and Class* 29, no. 3 (Winter 1988): 69–85. NGO article, in English.

Dalit Sahitya Akademy. "Amnesty Probe of SC/St Human Rights Violations." *Dalit Voice* 7, no. 10 (1–15 April 1988): 14. NGO article, in English.

Downing, T. E., and G. Kushner, eds. *Human Rights and Anthropology.* Cambridge, MA: Cultural Survival, 1988. Edited collection/bibliography, in English.

Dryden, Phyllis Kay. "Annotated Bibliography of Political Rights of African Women." *African Law Studies* 7 (Dec. 1972): 27–61. Bibliography, in English.

Fraser, Arvonne. "For Women, the Whole World is Still the 'Developing World.' " *Human Rights Internet* (Spring 1989). Commentary, in English.

Femmes sous Lois Musulmanes (Women Living under Muslim Laws). *Dossier No. 1.* Montpellier, France: 1986. NGO document collection, in English.

Hady, Maher Abdel. "Note on the Rights of Israeli Palestinians in Respect to Equality." Paper presented at 2d International Conference on Peoples Rights, Center for International Legal and Economic Studies, Zagazig University, Cairo, Egypt, 25–28 Nov. 1985. Unpublished conference paper, in Arabic.

Inter-Parliamentary Union. *Participation des Femmes a la Vie Politique et au Processus de Prise de Decision* (Participation of Women in Political Life and the Process of Decisionmaking). Geneva, Switzerland: 1988. NGO report, in French.

Movement for Inter-Racial Justice and Equality. "The PTA: How It Affects You." *Justice and Equality* (1985): 5–6. NGO newsletter article, in English.

Nettheim, Ron. "The Aborigine in Comparative Law." Paper presented at the 12th International Congress on Comparative Law, Sydney, Australia, 19 Aug. 1986. Conference paper, in English.

Tarnopolsky, W. S. "Race Relations Commissions in Canada, Australia, New Zealand, the United Kingdom and the United States." *Human Rights Law Journal* 6, pts. 2–4 (1985): 145–178. Scholarly article, in English.

Ethnic Conflicts

Ahmed, Feroz. "Ethnicity and Politics: The Rise of Muhajir Separatism." *South Asia Bulletin* 8, nos. 1,

2 (Spring–Fall 1988): 33–45. Scholarly article, in English.

Asiwaju, A., ed. *Partitioned Africans: Ethnic Relations across Africa's International Boundaries.* Lagos, Nigeria: University of Lagos Press, 1976. Scholarly edited collection, in English.

Comite Intermouvements aupres des Evacues, Institut Oecumenique pour le Developpement des Peuples, et Mouvement Internationale N'Krumah (Joint Committee for Refugees, Ecumenical Institute for the Development of Peoples, and the International Nkrumah Movement). *Africa's Refugee Crisis.* Trans. (from French) Michael John. London: Zed Books, 1986. NGO monograph, in English.

Engineer, A. A. "Hindu-Muslim, Hindu-Sikh Problem— A Comparative View." *India Now* 8, no. 6 (June 1985): 5–8. Magazine article, in English.

Field, Francis. "Nagorno-Karabakh: A Constitutional Conundrum." *Radio Liberty Research Bulletin* 30 (3495) (15 July 1988). NGO report, in English.

Gesellschaft fur Bedrohte Volker (Association for Endangered Peoples). "Horn von Afrika: Nationalitatenkonflikte in Athiopien, Somalia, und Djibouti" (The Horn of Africa: Nationality Conflict in Ethiopia, Somalia, and Djibouti). *Pogrom* 127–128 (Feb. 1987): 13–84. NGO article, in German.

Israeli League for Human and Civil Rights. *Report on the Violations of Human Rights in the Territories during the Uprising, 1988.* Tel Aviv, Israel: 1988. NGO report, in English.

Korkud, Refik. *Bulgaria Carries on Chauvinistic Policies.* Ankara, Turkey: Turkiye Fikir Ajansi, 1986. Situation report, in English.

Kuper, Leo. *The Prevention of Genocide.* New Haven, CT (USA): Yale University Press, 1985. Scholarly monograph, in English; bibliography, 255–278.

Lemarchand, Rene. *Rwanda and Burundi.* New York: Praeger, 1970). Scholarly monograph, in English.

Lemarchand, R., and D. Martin. *Selective Genocide in Burundi.* London: Minority Rights Group, 1974. NGO report, in English.

Naidu, Arjuna. "The Protection of Human Rights in Sri Lanka: Some Lessons for South Africa?" *South African Journal of Human Rights* 1 (March 1987): 52–65. Scholarly article, in English.

Norwegian Human Rights Project, Christian Michelsen Institute. *Human Rights in Developing Countries 1986.* Oslo, Norway: Universitetsforlaget, 1986). Government annual report, in English; bibliography, classified by country.

"Roots of Ethnic Violence." *Justice* 1, no. 4 (July–Aug. 1985): 21. Magazine article, in English.

Ruiz, Hiram A. *Detained in Exile: Ethiopians in Somalia's Shalembod Camp.* Washington, D.C.: U.S. Committee for Refugees, 1987. NGO issue paper, in English.

Shalev, Carmel. *The Price of Insurgency: Civil Rights in the Occupied Territories.* Jerusalem, Israel: West Bank Database Project, 1988. NGO report, in English.

Sigler, Jay A., ed. *International Handbook on Race and Race Relations.* Westport, CT (USA): Greenwood Press, 1987. Scholarly edited collection, in English; bibliography, 449–454.

Sikh Human Rights Group. *Conference: Delhi Riots/Massacres of Sikhs.* London: 1987. NGO conference report, in English.

Social Scientists Association. *Ethnicity and Social Change in Sri Lanka.* Colombo, Sri Lanka: 1985. Scholarly edited collection, in English.

Stichting Mensenrechten Groningen (Human Rights Foundation of Groningen). "Politieke Crisis in Somalie" (Political Crisis in Somalia). *Bulletin* 7 (Jan. 1987): 7–11. NGO article, in Dutch.

Studie-en Informatiencentrum Mensenrechten (Netherlands Institute of Human Rights). *Ethnic Violence, Development and Human Rights. Final Report of the 2d Consultation, Utrecht, Feb. 1–3 1985.* Utrecht, Netherlands: 1985. NGO conference report, in English; bibliography on ethnic conflict in Sri Lanka, 135–137.

Thornberry, Patrick. *Minorities and Human Rights Law.* London: Minority Rights Group, 1987. NGO report, in English.

U.S. House of Representatives, Subcommittee on Human Rights and International Organizations, Subcommittee on Africa, and Committee on Foreign Affairs. *Recent Violence in Burundi: What Should be the U.S. Response?* Washington, D.C.: USGPO, 1988. Government hearings, in English.

Vincent, Jack. "Freedom and International Conflict: Another Look." *International Studies Quarterly* 31, no. 1 (March 1987): 103–112. Scholarly journal article, in English.

Wynne, Alison. *Lament for Lanka.* Kowloon, Hong Kong: Christian Conference of Asia, 1988. NGO mission report, in English.

Food

Brownlie, Ian. *The Human Right to Food.* London: Commonwealth Secretariat, 1987. IGO study, in English.

Centro Ecumenico de Documentacao e Informacao (Ecumenical Center for Documentation and Information). "Os que Vivem do Lixo" (The Ones Who Live on Garbage). *Tempo E Presenca* 215 (Dec. 1986): 8–9. NGO journal article, in Portuguese.

Clark, John. *For Richer for Poorer: An Oxfam Report on Western Connections with World Hunger.* Oxford, UK: Oxfam, 1986. NGO report and scholarly monograph, in English.

Eritrean People's Liberation Front. *The Ethiopian Prisoners of War: The Prisoners on Nobody's Conscience.* Brussels, Belgium: 1987. NGO report, in English.

Ecumenical Committee on the Andes. "Peru: Hunger, Poverty and Economic Crisis." *Andean Focus* 4, no. 1 (Feb. 1987): 1–4. NGO article, in English.

Fenton, T.P., and M.J. Heffon. *Food, Hunger, Agribusiness: A Directory of Resources.* Maryknoll, NY (USA): Orbis Books, 1987. Directory/bibliography, in English.

Guyana Human Rights Association. *Guyana Human Rights Report 1986,* Georgetown, Guyana: 1986. NGO report, in English.

"Human Rights Issues in United States Foreign Policy." *Harvard Human Rights Yearbook* 1 (1988). Scholarly article, in English.

Independent Commission on International Humanitarian Issues. *Famine: A Man-Made Disaster?* New York: Vintage Books, 1985. NGO report, in English.

Lappe, F. M., and J. Collins. *World Hunger: Twelve Myths.* New York: Grove Press, for Institute for Food and Development Policy, 1986. NGO monograph, in English.

Lappe, F.M., R. Schurman, and K. Danaher. *Betraying the National Interest.* New York: Grove Press for the Institute for Food and Development Policy, 1987. NGO monograph, in English.

Marks, S. P. "Emerging Human Rights: A New Generation for the 1980's?" *Rutgers Law Review* 33, no. 2 (Winter 1981): 435–452. Scholarly article, in English.

Noorani, A.G. "The Right to Food." *Economic and Political Weekly* (22 Aug. 1987): 1426. Magazine article, in English.

Operation Hunger. *Hunger Bulletin, Updates and Statistics.* Braamfontein, South Africa: 1986. NGO report, in English.

UNICEF and NGO Committe for UNICEF. "Colonial Past and Contemporary Economy Trap Negros Islanders in Bitter Harvest of Hunger." *Action for Children* 1, no. 6 (1986): 1–4. NGO/IGO article, in English.

U.S. House of Representatives, Subcommittee on Africa and Subcommittee on Human Rights and International Organizations. *Human Rights and Food in Ethiopia,* 99th cong., 2d sess. Washington, D.C.: USGPO, 1985. Government hearings, in English.

U.S. House of Representatives, Subcommittee on Human Rights and International Organizations, Subcommittee on International Economic Policy and Trade, and Subcommittee on Africa. *Human Rights in Ethiopia.* Washington, D.C.: 1988. Government hearings, in English.

SEE ALSO Hunger.

Forced Labor

American Latvian Association. "Chernobyl Cleanup—No Protective Clothing." *Latvian News Digest* 11, no. 1 (Feb. 1987): 2. NGO article, in English.

Amnesty International. *Laos: Recent Information on "Re-education" in Attapeu Province.* London: 1988. NGO report, in English.

——————. "Mali: Taoudenit Prison Closed," 7 Nov. 1988. NGO urgent action bulletin, in English.

Bonnet, Michel. "Child Slavery: The Kharkar Camps of Pakistan." *International Children's Rights Monitor* 5, no. 2–3 (1988): 4–5. NGO article, in English.

Center for the Progress of Peoples. "Forced Labour for the 'Bamboo Wall.' " 23 Feb. 1987. NGO urgent action bulletin, in English.

Commission on Security and Cooperation in Europe. *Soviet Forced Labor Practices.* Washington, D.C.: 1986. Government hearings, in English.

Committee against Repression and for Democratic Rights in Iraq. *Facts about Abu Graib, the Notorious Prison in Iraq.* London: 1987. NGO report, in English.

Cronje, Suzanne. *Equatorial Guinea—The Forgotten Dictatorship. Forced Labour and Political Murder in Central Africa.* London: Anti-Slavery Society, 1976. NGO report, in English.

Gopinath, Deepti. "In Bondage—Kolse Bhatti Kamgara." *The Lawyers Collective* 1, no. 9 (Sept. 1986): 14–15. NGO article, in English.

"Haitian Workers Abused." *Latinamerica Press* 19, no. 3 (29 Jan. 1987): 5. News article, in English.

Hovet, T. *International Protection of Human Rights.* Course offered in Political Science at the University of Oregon, Eugene, OR, (USA), Winter 1988. Syllabus/course outline, in English.

Ilves, Toomas. "Additional Information on Estonians at Chernobyl." *Radio Free Europe Research* 11, no. 45 (7 Nov. 1986): 3–4. Government bulletin article, in English.

Law in the Service of Man/Al-Haq. *Dahriyyeh: Centre for Punishment.* Ramallah, Occupied Territories: May 1988. NGO report, in English.

Lithuanian Catholic Religious Aid. "Violations of Human and Trade Union Rights in the Socialist Republic of Vietnam." *Economic and Social Bulletin* 34, no. 1 (Jan.–March 1986): 7–9. NGO bulletin article, in English.

Lithuanian National Foundation. "The Shadow of Chernobyl." *Elta Information Bulletin* 10 (Oct. 1986): 7–10. NGO bulletin article, in English.

Marples, D.R. "Chernobyl: Past and Future." *Freedom at Issue* 99 (Nov.–Dec. 1987): 22–27. NGO article, in English.

M'Baye, Keba. "Les Realities du Monde Noir et les Droits de l'Homme" (The Realities of the Black World and Human Rights). *Revue des Droits de l'Homme: Droit International et Droit Compare* 2, no. 3 (1969): 382–394. Scholarly article, in English.

Nathan, F. S., Jr. "Apartheid and Black Labor in South Africa: Applying Section 307 of the Smoot-Hawley Tariff Act to Goods produced by Black South Africans." *Case Western Reserve Journal of International Law* 19, no. 3 (Summer 1987): 441–439. Scholarly article, in English.

Plant, Roger. *Sugar and Modern Slavery: A Tale of Two Countries.* London: Zed Press, 1987. Scholarly monograph, in English.

Radio Free Europe. "New Campaign on the Employment of Idle Youth." *Radio Free Europe Research* 10, no. 42 (18 Oct. 1985): 11–14. Government report, in English.

——————. "Samizdat Periodical on Forced Labor and Shirkers." *Radio Free Europe Research* 10, no. 37 (13 Sept. 1985): 29–31. Government report, in English.

Sathyaraj, Ranjit. "Human Rights Violations in the Northeast." Bangalore, India: 1987. Unpublished scholarly paper, in English.

Survival International. "Ethiopia—Anuak Uprooted." *Survival International News* 19 (1988): 1. NGO article, in English.

U. S. Helsinki Watch Committee. *Violations of the Helsinki Accords: USSR.* New York: 1986. NGO report, in English.

Freedoms and Rights

A. Freedom of Association

Amnesty International. *Program of Action for Banned People in South Africa 1985–86: South Africa Banning and Banishment.* London: 1985. NGO report, in English.

——————. *Tunisia: Imprisonment of Trade Unionists in 1978.* London: 1979. NGO report, in English.

Federation Internationale des Droits de l'Homme (International Federation of Human Rights). "Algerie: La Liberte d'Association sous Surveillance" (Algeria: Liberty of Association under

Surveillance). *Lettre de la FIDH* 214 (22 Sept. 1987): 4. NGO article, in French.

International Confederation of Free Trade Unions. *Annual Survey of Violations of Trade Union Rights 1988*. Brussels, Belgium: 1988. NGO report, in English.

——————. *Violations by the Government of the Socialist Republic of Romania of the Rights to Freedom of Association and Collective Bargaining*. Brussels, Belgium: 1989. NGO report, in English.

Nahaylo, Bohdan. "Independent Groups in the Ukraine under Attack." *Radio Liberty Research Bulletin* 39 (12 Sept. 1988). NGO report, in English.

Organizacion Regional Interamericana de Trabajadores (Regional Interamerican Organization of Workers). *Los Derechos Sindicales en Centroamerica* (The Rights of Trade Unions in Central America). Mexico City, Mexico: 1988. NGO report, in Spanish.

"Palestinian Trade Unions and Workers under Occupation, Part 1," *Al-Fajr: Jerusalem Palestinian Weekly*, 2 Oct. 1988. News article, in English.

"Palestinian Trade Unions and Workers under Occupation, Part 2," *Al-Fajr: Jerusalem Palestinian Weekly*, 11 Oct. 1988. News article, in English.

Pruksakasemsuk, Somyot. "Thai Workers' Struggle Continues." *UCL Newsletter* (Oct. 1988): 27–29. NGO article, in English.

Reisch, Alfred. "First Step Taken toward Resurrecting a Multiparty System." *Radio Free Europe Research* 17, no. 46 (17 Nov. 1988): 3–6. NGO report, in English; bibliography, 6.

Scoble, H. M., and L. S. Wiseberg. *Freedom of Association for Human Rights Organizations*. Washington, D.C.: Human Rights Internet, 1981. Unpublished monograph, in English.

Sedler, R. A. "The Constitutional Protection of Freedom of Religion, Expression, and Association in Canada and the United States: A Comparative Analysis." *Case Western Reserve Journal of International Law* 20, no. 2 (Summer 1988): 577–621. Scholarly article, in English.

Welch, C. E., Jr. "The Right of Asociation in Ghana and Tanzania." *Journal of Modern African Studies* 16, no. 4 (Dec. 1978): 639–656. Scholarly article, in English.

B. Freedom of Information

ARTICLE 19. *Freedom of Information and Expression in Australia*. London: 1988. NGO report, in English.

——————. *Freedom of Information and Expression in France*. London: 1989. NGO report, in English.

——————. *Freedom of Information and Expression in Rwanda*. London: 1988. NGO report, in English.

——————. *Freedom of Information and Expression in Trinidad and Tobago*. London: 1988. NGO report, in English.

——————. *Freedom of Information and Expression in Zambia*. London: 1988. NGO report, in English.

"Cameroon: Tightening the Grip." *Index on Censorship* 15, no. 5 (May 1986): 30–31. News article, in English.

Commission on Security and Cooperation in Europe. *Reform and Human Rights: The Gorbachev Record: Report submitted to the Congress of the United States*. Washington, D.C.: USGPO, 1988. Government report, in English.

Goldstein, Eric. "As Palestinian Uprising Continues, Israel Gets Tough with Journalists." *CPJ Update* 33 (June 1988): 1. NGO article, in English.

International Parliamentary Group for Human Rights in the USSR. *Report on Current Human Rights Abuses in the USSR*. Washington, D.C.: 1985. NGO report, in English.

Kleinwachgter, Wolfgang. "Freedom of Information and Peaceful Coexistence: On the Legal Basis of a New International Information and Communication Order (NIIO)." *GDR Committee for Human Rights Bulletin* 11, no. 3 (1985): 147–166. NGO article, in English.

Maier, A., et al. "The Ceaucescu Era—An Era of Restrictions." *Radio Free Europe Research* 10, no. 27 (5 July 1985): 41–48. Government report, in English.

"Mahdi Government Clamps Down on Dissent as Economy Disintegrates." *Africa Report* 32, no. 5 (Sept.–Oct. 1987): 10–11. News article, in English.

Sieghart, Paul, ed. *Human Rights in the United Kingdom*. London: Human Rights Network, 1988. NGO monograph, in English; footnotes to the articles contain substantial bibliographic references.

Sussman, L. R. "News Flows Suffer when Journalists Become Victims." *Freedom at Issue* 106 (Jan.–Feb. 1989): 39–45. NGO article, in English.

C. Freedom of Movement and Residence

Americas Watch Committee. *A Certain Passivity: Failing to Curb Human Rights Abuses in Peru*. New York: 1987. NGO report, in English.

Amnesty International. *The Imprisonment of Persons Seeking to Leave a Country or to Return to Their Own Country*. London: 1986. NGO report, in English.

——————. *Prisoners of Conscience Restricted under the Terms of Administrative Banishment Orders in the*

Republic of Zaire. London: 1985. NGO report, in English.

——————. *Program of Action for Banned People in South Africa 1985–86: South Africa Banning and Banishment*. London: 1985. NGO report, in English.

Barist, J. O., C. Pell, E. Oshman, and M. E. Hamel. *Who May Leave: A Review of Soviet Practice Restricting Emigration on Grounds of Knowledge of "State Secrets" in Comparison with Standards of International Law and the Policies of Other States*. New York: National Conference on Soviet Jewry and White & Case, 1987. NGO report, in English.

Bohr, Ann. "A Belated Step in the Repatriation of the Chechen and Ingush." *Radio Liberty Research Bulletin* 18 (4 May 1988). Government article, in English.

Catholic Institute for International Relations. *East Timor: A Christian Reflection*. London: 1987. NGO statement, in English and French.

Cohen, Robin. *Endgame in South Africa?* London and Paris: James Currey and UNESCO, 1986. Scholarly monograph, in English; bibliography and reading guide, 97–105.

Cultural Survival. "Counterinsurgency and the Development Pole Strategy in Guatemala." *Cultural Survival Quarterly* 12, no. 3 (1988): 11–17. NGO article, in English.

Drinnon, Richard. *Keeper of Concentration Camps: Dillion S. Myer and American Racism*. Berkeley, CA (USA): University of California Press, 1987. Scholarly monograph, in English.

Ecumenical Commission for Displaced Families and Communities. *Primer: Displacement in the Philippines—Nature, Causes, Effects, Extent, Limits, Remedies and Victims' Rights*. Quezon City, Philippines: 1987. NGO manual, in English.

Funnemark, B. C. *SOS Transylvania: A Report on Suppression of the Hungarian Minority in Romania*. Vienna, Austria: International Helsinki Federation for Human Rights, 1988. NGO report, in English; bibliography, 59–60.

Grahamstown Rural Committee. "Orderly Urbanisation: The Reality." *GRC Newsletter* 4 (July 1986). NGO article, in English.

International League for Human Rights. *Uganda after Amin: A Case of Displacement and Discrimination against the Banyarwanda Population*. New York: 1985. NGO report, in English.

International Gesellschaft fur Menschenrechte (International Society for Human (Rights). *CSCE and Human Rights: Divided Families and the Denial of Freedom of Movement (Documentation)*. Frankfurt/Main, FRG: 1987. NGO document collection, in English.

Markos, Edith. "Restrictions on Foreign Travel to be Eased." *Radio Free Europe Research* 12, no. 48 (28 Nov. 1987): 47–51. Government article, in English.

Plender, Richard, ed. *International Migration Law*. 2d rev. ed. Dordrecht, Netherlands: Martinus Nijhoff, 1988. Scholarly edited collection, in English.

Shafir, M., and D. Ionescu. "Rural Resettlement: Situation Report Romania." *Radio Free Europe Research* 13, no. 34 (23 Aug. 1988): 3–22. NGO report, in English.

Shapiro, J. B. *Info '85: A Folder of Facts and Figures on South Africa*. Grant Park, South Africa: Human Awareness Programme, 1985. NGO report, in English.

Survival International. "Ethiopia—Anuak Uprooted." *Survival International News* 19 (1988): 1. NGO article, in English.

——————. "Ethiopia's Brave New Villages." *Survival International News* 22 (1988): 2–3. NGO article, in English.

U. S. Helsinki Watch Committee. *Destroying Ethnic Identity: The Kurds of Turkey—An Update*. New York: 1988. NGO report, in English.

——————. *Ten Years Later: Violation of the Helsinki Accords*. New York: 1985. NGO report, in English.

D. Freedom of Thought (Conscience and Religion)

Amnesty International. *Romania: Cases of Religious and Political Imprisonment*. London: 1985. NGO bulletin, in English.

Asia Watch. "Trial of Writers, Postal Worker in Vietnam." New York: 1988. NGO urgent action bulletin, in English.

Catholic Institute for International Relations. *Country and Conscience: South African Conscientious Objectors*. London: 1988. NGO report, in English.

"Conscientious Objection: The Situation in Yugoslavia." *Religion in Communist Lands* 15, no. 3 (Winter 1987): 332–335. NGO article, in English.

International League for Human Rights. *Romania's Human Rights Record: Comments on the Government of Romania's Official Report to the Human Rights Commission* New York: 1987. NGO report, in English.

Klein, Yossi. " 'Refusniks' Grow among Ranks in Israeli Army." *In These Times* 12, no. 26 (25 May–7 June 1988): 11. News article, in English.

Klippenstein, Lawrence. "Exercising a Free Conscience: The Conscientious Objectors of the Soviet Union and the German Democratic Republic." *Religion in*

Communist Lands 13, no. 3 (Winter 1985): 282–291. Scholarly article, in English.

Lithuanian Catholic Religious Aid. "News from the Dioceses." *Chronicle of the Catholic Church in Lithuania* 72 (8 Jan. 1988): 40–50. NGO article/petition, in English.

Polish Helsinki Watch Committee. *Violations of Human Rights in Poland, 1984–85 (Fourth Report)*. Trans. Agnieszka Kolakowska. New York: Committee in Support of Solidarity, 1985. NGO report, in English.

Skryba, Adam. *Human Rights in Eastern Europe: A Syllabus*. New York: Center for the Study of Human Rights, Columbia University, 1987. Course syllabus, in English; extensive bibliography for each session.

Task Force Detainees of the Philippines. "The Violations Defended by TFDF and the Violations It Documents." *Philippine Human Rights Update* 2, no. 11 (Sept. 1987): 10–13, 22. NGO article, in English.

E. Right to Life

Amnesty International. *States of Emergency: Torture and Violations of the Right to Life under States of Emergency*. London: 1988. NGO report, in English.

Frankowski, S.J., and G. F. Cole. *Abortion and Protection of the Human Fetus*. Dordrecht, Netherlands: Martinus Nijhoff Publishers, 1987. Scholarly collection, in English; bibliography, 332–334.

Grant, J. P. *The State of the World's Children 1988*. New York: UNICEF, 1989. IGO report, in English.

Haysom, Nicholas. "Licence to Kill, Part I: The South African Police and the Use of Deadly Force." *South African Journal on Human Rights* 3, no. 1 (March 1987): 3–27. Scholarly article, in English.

——————. "Licence to Kill, Part II: A Comparative Survey of the Law in the United Kingdom, United States of America and South Africa." *South African Journal on Human Rights* 3, no. 2 (July 1987): 202–222. Scholarly article, in English.

Inter-American Commission on Human Rights. *Report on the Situation of Human Rights in Haiti*. Washington, D.C.: 1988. IGO report, in English.

Kuper, Leo. *The Prevention of Genocide*. New Haven, CT (USA): Yale University Press, 1985. Scholarly monograph, in English; bibliography, 255–278.

Medical Action Group. "Report on the Ongoing MAG Survey on Cases of Violations of Medical Neutrality and Rights of Health Professionals and Workers from Jan. 1987 to June 1988." *Progress Notes* 2, no. 7 (Aug. 1988): 6–8. NGO article, in English.

Premont, Daniel, gen. ed. *Essais sur le Concept de "Droits de Vivre"—Essays on the Concept of a "Right to Live"*. Brussels, Belgium: Bruylant, for Association de Consultants Internationaux en Droits de l'Homme, 1988. Scholarly edited collection, in English and French.

Shehadeh, Raja. *Occupier's Law: Israel and the West Bank*. Washington, D.C.: Institute for Palestine Studies and Law in the Service of Man/Al-Haq, 1985. NGO report, in English.

F. Right to Organize

Americas Watch Committee. *Labor Rights in El Salvador*. New York: 1988. NGO report, in English.

Amnesty international. *Cote D'Ivoire: Forcible Conscription of Trade Unionists*. London: 1988. NGO report, in English.

Arab Organization for Human Rights. *Report: Human Rights in the Arab World*. Cairo, Egypt, 1987. NGO report, in Arabic or English.

Bunting, Brian. *The Rise of the South African Reich*. 3d ed. London: International Defence and Aid Fund for Southern Africa, 1986. NGO study, in English.

Comite Europeen pour la Defense des Refugies et Immigres (European Committee for the Defense of Refugees and Immigrants). *Land and Liberty: The Struggle of Agricultural Workers of Andalusia*. Forcalquier, France: 1985. NGO report, in English.

International Confederation of Free Trade Unions. *Annual Survey of Violations of Trade Union Rights 1988*. Brussels, Belgium: 1988. NGO report, in English.

——————. "Indonesia: Workers' Rights Denied." *Free Labour World* 2/88 (29 Jan. 1988): 2. NGO article, in English.

——————. "Nicaragua: Sandinistas to Open Investigation on Union Right Abuses." *Free Labour World* 6/88 (29 April 1988): 1, 3. NGO article, in English.

——————. "South Korean Trade Unions State Their Claims." *Free Labour World* 8/88 (31 May 1988): 2. NGO article, in English.

——————. "Union Freedoms under Threat in Tunisia." *Free Labour World* 15/85 (15 Nov. 1985): 1. NGO mission report, in English.

——————. *Violations by the Government of the Socialist Republic of Romania of the Rights to Freedom of Association and Collective Bargaining*. Brussels, Belgium: 1989. NGO report, in English.

International Defence and Aid Fund for Southern Africa. "New Unions Formed." *Focus on Repression in Southern Africa* 69 (Feb. 1987): 11. NGO article, in English.

International League for Human Rights. *Tunisia's Human Rights Record: A Critique of the Government's Official Report to the United Nations Human Rights Committee.* New York: 1986. NGO report, in English.

Labrador, Virgilio S. "Blood and Fruits: Human Rights Violations in Banana and Pineapple Plantations." *Alternative* 2, no. 1 (1987): 34–40. NGO article, in English.

Organizacion Regional Interamericana de Trabajadores (Regional Interamerican Organiation of Workers). *Los Derechos Sindicales en Centroamerica* (The Rights of Trade Unions in Central America). Mexico City, Mexico: 1988. NGO report, in Spanish.

"Palestinian Trade Unions and Workers under Occupation, Part 1." *Al-Fajr: Jerusalem Palestinian Weekly* 9, nos. 437 (2 Oct. 1988). News article, in English.

"Palestinian Trade Unions and Workers under Occupation, Part 2." *Al-Fajr: Jerusalem Palestinian Weekly* 9, nos. 438 (11 Oct. 1988). News article, in English.

Pruksakasemsuk, Somyot. "Thai Workers' Struggle Continues." *UCL Newsletter* (Oct. 1988): 27–29. NGO article, in English.

Wing-yue, Leung. *Smashing the Iron Rice Pot: Workers and Unions in China's Market Socialism.* Kowloon, Hong Kong: Asia Monitor Resource Center, 1988. NGO report, in English.

G. Right of Peaceful Assembly

Alekseeva, Lyudmila. "Public Unrest in the USSR." *Radio Liberty Research Bulletin* 29, no. 38 (18 Sept. 1985). Government report, in English.

Amnesty International. *Indonesia: Arrests of Muslim Activists relating to the Tanjung Priok Incident of 12 Sept. 1984.* London: 1985. NGO report, in English.

Asia Watch. *Human Rights in Tibet: An Asia Watch Report.* Washington, D.C.: 1988. NGO report, in English.

Berkeley, B., and E. Schrage. *Zimbabwe: Wages of War—A Report on Human Rights.* New York: Lawyers Committee for Human Rights, 1986. NGO mission report, in English.

Detainees' Parents Support Committee. *Fourth Special Report on State of Emergency.* Johannesburg, South Africa: 1986. NGO report, in English.

Fuller, Elizabeth. "Georgian Official Explains New Restrictions on Meetings and Demonstrations."

Radio Liberty Research Bulletin 32, no. 16 (8 April 1988). Government article, in English.

Handley, Robin. *The Right of Peaceful Assembly in the A.C.T.* Canberra, Australia: Human Rights Commission, 1985. Government monograph, in English.

Information Centre for Polish Affairs. "Reprisals against Participants of May Demonstrations." *Uncensored Poland News Bulletin* 14/88 (30 July 1988): 9–11. NGO article, in English.

International Human Rights Law Group. *To the Precipice and Beyond: A Review of Political Developments in the Republic of Korea, Jan. 1986–July 1987.* Washington, D.C.: 1987. NGO report, in English.

International League for Human Rights. *Tunisia's Human Rights Record: A Critique of the Government's Official Report to the UN Human Rights Committee.* New York: 1986. NGO report, in English.

Levin, L., P. Benjamin, and D. Smuts. "Human Rights Index." *South African Journal on Human Rights* 4, no. 1 (March 1988): 110–138. Index, in English.

Obe, Ad'Obe. "Nigeria: Control of Human Rights." *West Africa* 3589 (16 June 1986): 1250. Magazine article, in English.

U. S. House of Representatives, Subcommittee on Human Rights and International Organizations. *Recent Developments in Malaysia and Singapore, 1988,* 100th Cong., 2d sess. Washington, D.C.: USGPO, 1988. Government hearings, in English.

Washington Office on Latin America. "Crackdown on Opposition Marks Paraguayan Electoral Climate," 5 Feb. 1988. NGO press release, in English.

H. Right to Vote

American Friends Service Committee. *Haiti: Background to the Elections, 17 Jan. 1988.* Philadelphia, PA (USA): 1988. NGO report, in English.

Americas Watch Committee. *Chile: Human Rights and the Plebiscite.* New York: 1988. NGO report, in English.

Freedom House. *A Mission to Chile.* New York: 1988. NGO mission report, in English.

International League for Human Rights. *Report of the International Observer Mission, Palau Referendum, Dec. 1986.* New York: 1987. NGO mission report, in English.

Inter-Parliamentary Union. *Participation des Femmes a la Vie Politique et au Processes de Prise de Decision* (Participation of Women in Political Life and the Process of Decisionmaking). Geneva, Switzerland: Centre International de Documentation Parlementaire, 1988. NGO report.

Nowak, Manfred,. *Politische Grundrechte* (Political Rights). Vienna, Austria: Springer Verlag, 1988.

Scholarly monograph, in German; bibliography, 542–572.

Perez, Alberto. "Con el Referendum el Pueblo Uruguayo Recupera la Plenitud de la Democracia" (With the Referendum, the Uruguayan People Recover a Full Democracy). *Revista de IELSUR* 2 (July 1988): 31–40. NGO article, in Spanish.

Pollack, A. J. "The South West Africa Cases and the Jurisprudence of International Law." *International Organiation* 23, no. 4 (Autumn 1969): 767–787. Scholarly article, in English.

Steiner, H. J. "Political Participation as a Human Right." *Harvard Human Rights Yearbook* 1 (1988): 77–134. Scholarly article, in English.

Third World Network. *Belauans Struggle to Stay Nuclear Free and to Protect Their Sovereignty.* Penang, Malaysia: 1988. NGO report, in English.

Ungor, Beraet Z. "Women in the Middle East and North Africa and Universal Suffrage." *The Annals* 375 (Jan. 1968): 72–81. Scholarly article, in English.

U. S. House of Representatives, Subcommittee on Human Rights and International Organizations and Subcommittee on Africa. *Liberia: Recent Developments and U.S. Foreign Policy,* 99th cong. 2d sess. Washington, D.C.: USGPO, 1986. Government hearings, in English.

U. S. House of Representatives, Subcommittee on Human Rights and International Relations and Subcommittee on Western Hemisphere Relations. *U.S. Policy, Human Rights and the Prospects for Democracy in Chile.* Washington, D.C.: USGPO, 1988. Government hearings, in English.

Washington Office on Latin America. "Crackdown on Opposition Marks Paraguayan Electoral Climate," 5 Feb. 1988. NGO press release, in English.

Washington Office on Latin America and Catholic Institute for International Relations. *Conditions for Chile's Plebiscite on Pinochet.* Washington, D.C.: 1988. NGO mission report, in English.

Health

Abraham, Martin. *The Lessons of Bhopal: A Community Action Resource Manual on Hazardous Technologies.* Penang, Malaysia: International Organization of Consumers Unions, 1985. NGO report, in English.

Agarwal, A., J. Merrifield, and R. Tandon. *No Place to Run: Local Realities and Global Issues of the Bhopal Disaster.* New Market, TN (USA): Highlander Research and Education Center and Society for Participatory Research in Asia, 1985. NGO report, in English.

Bhopal: Industrial Genocide? A Unique Compilation of Documents from Indian Publications. Hong Kong: Asian Regional Exchange for New Alternatives, 1985. Edited collection, in English.

Breum, M., and A. Hendriks, eds. *AIDS and Human Rights: An International Perspective.* Copenhagen, Denmark: Danish Center of Human Rights, 1988. Edited collection, in English.

Claude, R., E. Stover, and J. Lopez. *Health Professionals and Human Rights in the Philippines.* Washington, D.C.: American Association for the Advancement of Science, 1987. NGO report, in English.

Coordinating Committee for Primary Health Care of Thai NGOs. *Proceedings of International Conference on Primary Health Care and People's Movement, Cholburi, Thailand, 23–28 Feb. 1986.* Bangkok, Thailand: 1986. NGO conference proceedings, in English.

Evers, T., P. Molan, and P. Burgess. *The Treatment of Disabled Persons in Social Security and Taxation Law.* Canberra, Australia: Human Rights Commission, 1986. Government monograph, in English.

"Female Circumcision Endangers 75 Million." *Canadian Human Rights Advocate* 2, no. 6 (June 1986): 12–13. NGO bulletin article, in English.

Human Rights Commission of Pakistan. *Bonded Labour in Brick Kiln Industry of Pakistan.* Lahore, Pakistan: 1988. NGO mission report, in English.

International Commission of Health Professions. *Health and Human Rights.* Geneva, Switzerland: 1986. NGO document collection, in English, French, and Spanish.

Jaising, Indira. *The Bhopal Tragedy: What Really Happened and What It Means for American Workers and Communities at Risk.* New York; Council on International and Public Affairs, 1986. Background report, in English.

"Organizing for Health." *Critical Health* 21 (Dec. 1987). NGO bulletin article, in English.

Panos Institute. *AIDS and the Third World.* 2d ed. London: 1987. NGO report, in English.

Physicians for Human Rights. *Casualties of Conflict: Medical Care and Human Rights in the West Bank and Gaza Strip: Report of a Medical Fact-Finding Mission by Physicians for Human Rights.* Somerville, MA (USA): 1988. NGO mission report, in English.

Sabatier, Renee. *Blaming Others: Prejudice, Race and Worldwide AIDS.* London: Panos Institute and the Norwegian Red Cross, 1988. Monograph, in English.

Sheehan, R., and J. Jardine. *Epilepsy and Human Rights.* Canberra, Australia: Human Rights Commission, 1984. Government monograph, in English.

Shilts, Randy. *And the Band Played on: Politics, People and the AIDS Epidemic.* New York: St. Martin's Press, 1987. Journalistic monograph, in English.

van Es, A. and M. van Grup. *Health Professionals and Human Rights in South Africa.* Leiden, Netherlands: Johannes Wier Foundation/Dutch Foundation for Health and Human Rights, 1987. NGO mission report, in English.

Varma, Daya. "First Major Medical Survey on Bhopal Gas Victims: 80% of Residents within 2km of Carbide Plant Sick." *India Now* 8, no. 6 (June 1985): 13. Magazine article, in English.

Vermund, S.H., S.G. Miller, and S.P. Cohen. *Health Status and Services in the West Bank and Gaza Strip—Report of "Cooperation for Development: A Community-based Health Project".* New York: Institute for Middle East Peace and Development, 1985. NGO report, in English.

Ware, Helen. *Legal and Ethical Aspects of the Management of Newborns with Severe Disabilities.* Canberra, Australia: Human Rights Commission, 1985. Government monograph, in English.

Health Workers (Physicians)

American Association for the Advancement of Science, Committee on Scientific Freedom and Responsibility. *The Open Secret: Torture and the Medical Profession in Chile.* Washington, D.C.: 1987. NGO report, in English.

American Committee for Human Rights. *Medical Fact-Finding Mission to Chile.* Somerville, MA (USA): 1986. NGO mission report, in English.

Amnesty International. *Human Rights in Chile: The Role of the Medical Profession.* London: 1986. NGO report, in English.

Asamblea Permanente por los Derechos Humanos (Permanent Assembly for Human Rights) "Tribunal Etico de la Salud contra la Impunidad" (Health Workers' Ethical Tribunal against Impunity). *Derechos Humanos* 3, no. 13 (April 1988): 16–18. NGO article, in Spanish.

Bloche, M. G. *Uruguay's Military Physicians: Cogs in a System of State Terror.* Washington, D.C.: American Association for the Advancement of Science, Committee on Scientific Freedom and Responsibility, 1987. NGO report, in English.

Claude, R., E. Stover, and J. Lopez. *Health Professionals and Human Rights in the Philippines.* Washington, D.C.: American Association for the Advancement of Science, Clearinghouse on Science and Human Rights, 1987. NGO report, in English.

Committee for Health Rights in Central America and Fr. Moriarty Central American Refugee Program. *Political Asylum: A Handbook for Legal and Mental Health Workers.* San Francisco, CA: 1987. NGO manual, in English.

"Doctors, Ethics, and Torture." *Danish Medical Bulletin* (Aug. 1987): 185–216. Conference proceedings, in English.

Fitzpatrick, C.A. *Soviet Abuse of Psychiatry for Political Purposes.* New York: U.S. Helsinki Watch Committee, 1987. NGO report, in English.

Jyde, Charles. "Psychiatry: A New Form of Repression." *SOS Torture* 3 (June 1986): 26–27. NGO magazine article, in English and French.

Lery, N., H. Chambaz, and J.-F. Labarthe. "Health Personnel Confronted with Torture and Inhuman, Cruel and Degrading Treatment." *SOS Torture* 3 (June 1986): 31–34. NGO magazine article, in English and French.

Lifton, R. J. *The Nazi Doctors: Medical Killing and the Psychology of Genocide.* New York: Basic Books, 1986. Scholarly monograph, in English.

National Academy of Sciences. *Science and Human Rights.* Washington, D.C.: National Academy Press, 1988. NGO conference papers, in English.

Nightingale, E. O., and E. Stover. "A Question of Conscience: Physicians in Defense of Human Rights." *Journal of the American Medical Associations* 255, no. 20 (23–30 May 1986): 2794–2797. Scholarly article, in English.

Orr, Wendy, et al. *Affidavit before the Supreme Court of South Africa.* Port Elizabeth, South Africa: National Medical and Dental Association, 1985. Legal affadavit, in English.

Palestine Committee for Non-Governmental Organizations. "Gaza Medical Relief Committee under Fire." *Jerusalem* 18 (Aug.-Sept. 1986): 14. NGO magazine article, in English.

People's Mojahedin of Iran. "Widespread Protest by Iranian Physicians: Regime Dissolves Iranian Medical Association, Arrests and Tortures Doctors in Extensive Crackdown." *Iran Liberation* 2 (21 July 1986): 1. Opposition movement article, in English.

Physicians for Human Rights. *Sowing Fear: The Use of Torture and Psychological Abuse in Chile.* Somerville, MA (USA): 1988. NGO report, in English.

Rayner, Mary. *Turning a Blind Eye: Medical Accountability and the Prevention of Torture in South Africa.* Washington, D.C.: American Association for the Advancement of Science and Committee on Scientific Freedom and Responsibility, 1987. NGO report, in English.

Trabajamos para la Vida: Consecuencias de la Represion en el Cono Sur, el Medico los Derechos Humanos (We Work for Life: Consequences of Repression in the Southern Cone, Physicians and Human Rights). Montevideo, Uruguay: Universidad de la Republica, Facultad de Medicina, 1987. Conference proceedings, in Spanish.

SEE ALSO Medical Ethics

Homeless

Agnelli, Susanna. *Street Children: A Growing Urban Tragedy.* London: Independent Commission on International Humanitarian Issues and Weidenfield and Nicolson, 1986. NGO monograph, in English.

Conroy, J.D. *Shelter for the Homeless: Asian-Pacific Needs and Australian Responses.* Canberra, Australia: Australian Council for Overseas Aid, 1987. NGO report, in English.

Defense for Children International-USA. *Database on the Rights of the Child.* New York: 1987; bibliography, in English.

—————. *The Children's Guardian: Computerized Database on the Violations of the Rights of the Child, Abstracts and Index by Topic and Geography.* New York: 1986. Bibliography, in English.

Einfield, Marcus. *Bicentennial Oration—Human Rights and Constitutional Entrenchment, Statement by . . . President of the Australian Human Rights and Equal Opportunity Commission on the Presentation of the Report of the Commission's Inquiry into the Social and Material Needs of the Residents of Toomelah, Boggabilla and Goondiwindi.* Sydney, Australia: Australian Commission on Human Rights, 1988. Speeches, in English.

Gomez, Terence. "Struggle for Shelter: The Plight of the Kampung Jaya Squatters." *Aliran Monthly* 7, no. 9 (Sept.-Oct. 1987): 13–15. NGO article, in English.

Kaufman M.S. " 'Crazy' Until Proven Innocent? Civil Commitment of the Mentally Ill Homeless." *Columbia Human Rights Law Review* 19, no. 2 (Spring 1988): 333–367. Scholarly article, in English.

Kozol, Jonathan. *Rachel and Her Children: Homeless Families in America.* New York: Crown Publishers, 1988. Scholarly monograph, in English; bibliography, 249–252.

Lapierre, Dominique. *The City of Joy.* Trans. Kathryn Spink. Garden City, NY (USA): Doubleday & Co., 1985. Novel; originally published in French as *La Cite de la Joie* (Editions Robert Laffont).

Lawyer's Committee for Human Rights. *Crisis in Crossroads: A Report on Human Rights.* New York: 1988. NGO report, in English.

Playfair, Emma. *Demolition and Sealing of Houses as a Punitive Measure in the Israeli-Occupied West Bank.*

Ramallah, Occupied Territories: Law in the Service of Man/Al-Haq, 1987. NGO report, in English.

Pontifical Commission "Justicia et Pax." *What Have You Done to Your Homeless Brother? The Church and the Housing Problem.* Vatican City: 1985. Church statement, in English.

Silver, H. M. "Voluntary Admission to New York Hospitals: The Rights of the Mentally Ill Homeless." *Columbia Human Rights Law Review* 19, no. 2 (Spring 1988): 333–367. Scholarly article, in English.

Trehub, Aaron. "Social and Economic Rights in the Soviet Union: Work, Health Care, Social Security, and Housing." *Radio Liberty Research Bulletin* 3/86 (29 Dec. 1986). Government bulletin article, in English.

United Nations Department of Public Information. *Building for the Homeless.* New York: 1987. IGO report, in English.

Vigil India Movement. "Humanity in Harmony: A Report on the Tenth Anniversary National Conference of the Vigil India Movement." *Vigil India* 43 (Aug. 1987): 4–5. NGO article/conference report, in English.

Hostages

Americas Watch Committee. *Human Rights in Colombia as President Barco Begins.* New York: 1986. NGO mission report, in English.

Amnesty International. "Amnesty International's Concerns in Iraq," 19 June 1987. NGO statement, in English.

—————. *The Death Penalty in Iraq: Introduction and Background.* London: 1987. NGO background paper.

Comision Andina de Juristas (Andean Commission of Jurists). "Colombia: Palacio de Justicia: Un ano Despues" (Colombia: Palace of Justice: One Year Later). *Boletin Comision Andina de Juristas* 13 (Dec. 1986): 5–6. NGO bulletin article, in Spanish.

Hovet, T. *International Protection of Human Rights.* Course offered in Political Science at the University of Oregon, Eugene, (OR, USA), Winter 1988. Syllabus/university course outline, in English.

Labarthe, Jean-Francoise. "Activities of the ICRC: For Political Detainees; against Torture." *SOS Torture* 3 (June 1986): 28–30. NGO magazine article, in English and French.

Max Planck Institute for Comparative Public and International Law. *Encyclopedia of Public International Law, Vol 8: Human Rights and the Individual in International Law—International Economic Relations.* Amsterdam, NY (USA): Oxford, North Holland, 1985. Encyclopedia, in English.

Rubin, Barnett R. *Cycles of Violence: Human Rights in Sri Lanka since the Indo-Sri Lanka Agreement.* Washington, D. C.: Asia Watch, 1987. NGO report, in English.

"The Middle East: Fighting, Booby-trapped Cars, Hostages: Ten Years of War in Lebanon." *The ICRC Worldwide 1985* (1986): 13–16. NGO annual report article, in English.

Housing

Al-Ghazali, Said. "Israeli Army Seals Homes, Rooms." *Al Fajr,* 29 Aug. 1986. Newspaper article, in English.

Aliran Kesedaran Negara. "Eviction: The Moral Aspects." *Aliran Monthly* 6, no. 9 (Sept.-Oct. 1986): 11–13. NGO article, in English.

Amnesty International. "Slum Dwellers: The Less Privileged Segment of Urban Population: A Case of Bangkok Slum and Squatter Settlements." *Human Rights Forum* 1, no. 4 (Oct.-Dec. 1985): 9–16. NGO magazine article, in English.

Center for the Progress of Peoples. "Pakistan: Demolition of Squatter Houses," 28 Oct. 1987. NGO urgent action letter, in English.

Committee on the Right to Housing. *Slum and Pavement Dwellers Eviction: The Human Face.* Bombay, India: 1986. NGO pamphlet, in English.

Conroy, J. *Shelter for the Homeless: Asian-Pacific Needs and Australian Responses.* Canberra, Australia: Australian Council for Overseas Aid, 1987. NGO report, in English.

Cortese, Michele. "Property Rights and Human Values: A Right of Access to Private Property for Tenant Organizers." *Columbia Human Rights Law Review* 17, no. 2 (Spring-Summer 1986): 257–282. Scholarly article, in English.

Das, P.K., and C. Gonsalves. *The Struggle for Housing: A Peoples' Manifesto.* Bombay, India: Nivara Hakk Suraksha Samit, 1987. NGO report, in English; bibliography: basic statistics on Bombay, plus information on housing, social services, and slum population.

Database Project on Palestinian Human Rights. *Uprising Update: Dec. 8, 1988: Human Rights at the End of Year One of the Palestinian Uprising.* Chicago, IL (USA): 1988. NGO document collection, in English.

Gomez, Terence. "Struggle for Shelter: The Plight of the Kampung Jaya Squatters." *Aliran Monthly* 7, no. 9 (Sept.-Oct. 1987): 13–15. NGO article, in English.

Gordon, P., and D. A. Newnham. *Different Worlds: Racism and Discrimination in Britain.* 2d rev. ed. London: The Runnymede Trust, 1986. NGO report, in English.

Kruger, Franz. "Community Opposes New Style Removal." *Work in Progress* 46 (Feb. 1987): 30–33. NGO article, in English.

Law in the Service of Man/Al-Haq. "House Demolition and Sealing." *Law in the Service of Man Newsletter* 14 (July-Aug. 1986): 1. NGO article, in English.

——————. *Punishing a Nation: Human Rights Violations during the Palestinian Uprising, Dec. 1987-Dec. 1988.* Ramallah, Occupied Territories: 1988. NGO report, in English.

Metcalf, G. R. *Fair Housing Comes of Age.* Westport, CT (USA): Greenwood Press, 1988. Scholarly monograph, in English.

Miskiewicz, Sophia. "Housing in Eastern Europe: A 'Social Right' Abandoned." *Radio Free Europe Research* 11, no. 25 (20 June 1986). Government report, in English.

Playfair, Emma. *Demolition and Sealing of Houses as a Punitive Measure in the Israeli-Occupied West Bank.* Ramallah, Occupied Territories: Law in the Service of Man/Al-Haq, 1987. NGO report, in English.

People's Union for Democratic Rights. "India: Children Jailed for Want of Homes." *International Children's Rights Monitor* 3, no. 3 (3d quarter 1986): 16. NGO article, in English.

Pontifical Commission "Justicia et Pax." *What Have You Done to Your Homeless Brother? The Church and the Housing Problem.* Vatican City: 1985. Church statement, in English.

Shafir, M., and D. Ionescu. "Rural Resettlement: Situation Report Romania." *Radio Free Europe Research* 13, no. 34 (23 Aug. 1988): 3–22. NGO report, in English.

Shapiro, J. B. *Info '85: A Folder of Facts and Figures on South Africa.* Grant Park, South Africa: Human Awareness Programme, 1985. NGO report, in English.

Trehub, Aaron. "Social and Economic Rights in the Soviet Union: Work, Health Care, Social Security, and Housing." *Radio Liberty Research Bulletin* (29 Dec. 1986). Government bulletin article, in English.

SEE ALSO *Homeless*

Human Rights (General)

Amnesty International. *Amnesty International Report 19—.* NGO annual report, in English, French, Spanish, and Arabic. London.

——————. *Amnesty International USA Legal Support Network Newsletter.* NGO semi-annual newsletter, in English; published mainly for lawyers who are members of AI-USA. New York.

ARTICLE 19. *Information, Freedom and Censorship: The ARTICLE 19 World Report 19—*. NGO annual report, in English; bibliography included. Essex (UK): Longman Group.

Commission on the Independence of Judges and Lawyers. *ICJL Bulletin*. NGO bi-annual newsletter. Geneva, Switzerland.

Federational International des Droits de l'Homme (International Federation of Human Rights). *La Lettre de la FIDH*. NGO weekly, in French. Paris.

Freedom House. *Freedom at Issue*. NGO bi-monthly journal, in English; January/February issue contains Freedom House's annual survey of freedom around the world. New York.

Gastil, Raymond D. *Freedom in the World: Political Rights and Civil Liberties*. Westport, CT (USA): Greenwood Press, published annually. Yearbook, in English; from 1978–1981 published by Freedom House (NY).

Human Rights in Developing Countries. Kehl, Strasbourg, and Arlington: N.P. Engel, published annually. Yearbook; joint project of Norwegian Institute of Human Rights (Oslo), Christian Michelsen Institute (Bergen, Norway), Danish Center of Human Rights (Copenhagen), Abo Akademi Institute of Human Rights (Abo/Turku, Finland), Netherlands Institute of Human Rights (Utrecht), and Human Rights Research Education Centre (Ottawa, Canada). Concentrates on 13 developing countries which are major partner countries receiving aid from the Nordic countries, the Netherlands, and Canada.

Human Rights Watch. *Human Rights Watch*. Joint newsletter of the Watch committees (Americas Watch, Asia Watch, U.S. Helsinki Watch), in English. New York.

—————. *The Persecution of Human Rights Monitors: A Worldwide Survey*. Annual report, in English. New York.

Human Rights Watch and Lawyers Committee for Human Rights. *Critique: Review of the U.S. Department of State's Country Reports on Human Rights Practices*. NGO yearbook, in English; published jointly from 1983–1989, but solely by Lawyers Committee for Human Rights since 1990. New York.

—————. *The Reagan/Bush Administration's Record in Human Rights in 19—*. NGO annual report, in English; published jointly from 1986–1989, but solely by Human Rights Watch since 1990. New York.

Index on Censorship. "Annual Report." *Index on Censorship*. NGO article published annually in quarterly journal; in English. London.

International Commission of Jurists. *ICJ Newsletter*. NGO quarterly journal, in English. Geneva, Switzerland.

International Committee of the Red Cross. *Bulletin*. NGO monthly. Geneva, Switzerland.

UN Centre for Human Rights. *Human Rights Newsletter*. IGO bi-annual publication. Geneva, Switzerland.

U.S. Department of State. *Country Reports on Human Rights Practices*. Governmental annual report (usually issued in February), in English. Washington, D.C. (USA).

Hunger

Ardanaz, Jose. "Democracias Debiles y Dictaduras Criminales en America Latina: Por Luchar Contra el Hambre y la Represion Hay Millones de Personas Represaliadas" (Weak Democracies and Criminal Dictatorships in Latin America: Thousands Repressed for Their Involvement in the Struggle against Hunger and Oppression). *Madres de Plaza de Mayo* 2, no. 19 (June 1986): 10–11. NGO newspaper article, in English.

Brennan, T. O. *Uprooted Angolana: From Crisis to Catastrophe*. Washington, D.C.: U.S. Committee for Refugees, 1987. NGO report, in English.

Centro Ecumenico de Documentacao e Informacao (Ecumenical Center for Documentation and Information). "CMI Denuncia Fome e Divida Externa" (WCC World Council of Churches Denounces Hunger and External Debt). *Tempo e Presenca* 201 (Sept. 1985): 14–15. NGO magazine article, in Portuguese.

—————. "O Problema da Fome no Brazil" (The Hunger Problem in Brazil). *Tempo e Presenca* 200 (Aug. 1985): 6–8. NGO magazine article, in Portuguese.

Clark, John. *For Richer for Poorer: An Oxfam Report on Western Connections with World Hunger*. Oxford, UK: Oxfam, 1986. NGO report/scholarly monograph, in English.

Clay, J.W., S. Steingraber, and P. Niggli. *The Spoils of Famine: Ethiopian Famine Policy and Peasant Agriculture*. Cambridge, MA (USA): Cultural Survival, 1988. NGO report, in English.

Defense for Children International-USA. *Database on the Rights of the Child*. New York: 1987. NGO bibliography, in English.

Ecumenical Committee on the Andes. "Peru: Hunger, Poverty and Economic Crisis." *Andean Focus* 4, no. 1 (Feb. 1987): 1–4. NGO article, in English.

Edelman, M. W., and J. D. Weill. "Status of Children in the 1980s." *Columbia Human Rights Law Review* 17, no. 2 (Spring-Summer 1986): 139–158. Scholarly article, in English.

Fenton, T. P., and M. J. Heffon. *Food, Hunger, Agribusiness: A Directory of Resources.* Maryknoll, NY (USA): Orbis Books, 1987. Directory/bibliography, in English.

Gesellschaft fur Bedrohte Volker (Association for Endangered Peoples). "Menschenrechtesverletzungen in Athiopien 1974 bis 1985" (Human Rights Violations in Ethiopia 1974 to 1985). *Pogrom* 115 (June 1985): 1–16. NGO magazine article, in German.

——————. "Fragwurdige Methoden sur Bekamfpung der Hungersnot: Athiopien—Deportationer und Zwangsarbeitslager" (Questionable Methods of Fighting the Hunger Emergency: Ethiopia Deportation and Forced Labor). *Pogrom* 25/85 (28 May 1985): 1–80. NGO bulletin article, in German.

Hopkins, Raymond F. "Ending Hunger in Africa." *Issue: A Journal of Africanist Opinion* 16, no. 2 (1988): 36–44. Scholarly article, in English.

International Committee of the Red Cross. "The Beirut Delegation Appeals." *ICRC Bulletin* 133 (Feb. 1987): 1. NGO article, in English.

Internationale Gesellschaft fur Menschenrechte (International Society for Human Rights). "Terror, Mord, und Hunger in Uganda" (Terror, Death and Hunger in Uganda). *Menschenrechte* (March-April 1987). NGO article, in German.

Kibola, H. S. *Some Conceptual Aspects of Human Rights: The Basis for the Right to Development in Africa.* Paper presented at a seminar on "Law and Human Rights in Development," 24–28 May 1982, Gaborone, Botswana. Unpublished paper, in English.

Kutzner, P., and N. Lagoudakis. *Who's Involved with Hunger: An Organization Guide for Education and Advocacy.* 4th ed. Washington, D.C.: World Hunger Education Service, 1985. Directory, in English.

Lappe, F. M., and J. Collins. *World Hunger: Twelve Myths.* New York: Grove Press, for Institute for Food and Development Policy, 1986. NGO monograph, in English.

Operation Hunger. *Hunger Bulletin, Updates and Statistics.* Braamfontein, South Africa: 1986. NGO report, in English.

South African Council of Churches. *Rural Poverty Challenges the Church.* Johannesburg, South Africa: 1984. NGO conference report, in English; bibliography, 169–172.

United Nations Children's Fund. *Children on the Front Line: The Impact of Apartheid, Destabilization and Warfare on Children in Southern and South Africa.* Geneva, Switzerland: 1987. IGO report, in English; bibliography: 35, 65.

United Nations Children's Fund, NGO Committee for UNICEF. "Colonial Past and Contemporary Economy Trap Negros Islanders in Bitter Harvest of Hunger." *Action for Children* 1, no. 6 (1986): 1–4. NGO/IGO article, in English.

Vicaria de la Solidaridad, Arzobispado de Santiago (Vicariate of Solidarity, Archbishop of Santiago). "Hambre: Mucho mas de lo que se Confiesa" (Much More Hunger than Admitted). *Solidaridad, Compromiso con la Verdad* 214 (14 Dec. 1985): 12–15. NGO newspaper article, in Spanish.

Wallace, Tina. "Refugees and Hunger in Eastern Sudan." *Review of African Political Economy* 33 (Aug. 1985): 64–68. Scholarly article, in English.

"War and Hunger: Mozambique—What Kind of War?" *Africa News* 28, no. 8 (21 Dec. 1987): 5–6, 10. News article, in English.

SEE ALSO Food

Illiteracy

American Friends Service Committee. "Leah Tutu: Literacy First Goal of Domestic Workers in South Africa." *Listen Real Loud* 7, no. 1/2 (Winter-Spring 1986): 1, 12. NGO journal article, in English.

ARTICLE 19. *Information, Freedom and Censorship: The ARTICLE 19 World Report 1988.* London: Longman Group, 1988. NGO report, in English; bibliography: suggested further reading, 324–326.

Association for World Education. "Dayemi Complex Bangladesh." *Journal of World Education* 17, no. 4 (Oct. 1986): 1. NGO bulletin article, in English.

Centro de Documentacion e Informacion-Bolivia (Center for Information and Documentation-Bolivia). "La Mujer en Bolivia: Discriminacion, Lucha y Participacion" (Women in Bolivia: Discrimination, Struggle and Participation). *Informe "T"* 5 (July 1985): 9–10. NGO bulletin, in Spanish.

DeLeon, Pedro. "Reality del Campesino Dominicano" (Reality of the Dominican Peasant). *ALAI* 11, no. 85 (Nov. 1986): 10–11. NGO journal article, in Spanish.

Grant, J. P. *The State of the World's Children 1988.* New York: UNICEF, 1989. IGO report, in English.

Indian Cultural Development Centre. *Programme for Support of Indigenous Conflict Resolution and Village Self-Reliance. . . .* Madras, India: 1988. NGO report, in English.

International Commission of Jurists. *Report of Seminars on Legal Services for the Rural Poor and Other*

Disadvantaged Groups. Geneva, Switzerland: 1988. NGO report, in English.

Kahn, Nighat Said. *Women in Pakistan: A New Era?* London: Change International Reports, Women and Society, 1985. NGO report, in English.

Korn, David A. *Ethiopia: The United States and the Soviet Union.* Carbondale, IL (USA): Southern Illinois University Press, 1986. Scholarly monograph, in English; bibliography, 190–191.

Latin America Documentation. "Haiti: National Priorities according to the Bishops Conference." *LADOC* 17, no. 1 (Sept.-Oct. 1986): 4–8. NGO journal article, in English.

Manz, Beatriz. *Refugees of a Hidden War: The Aftermath of Counterinsurgency in Guatemala.* Albany, NY (USA): State University of New York Press, 1988. Scholarly monograph, in English.

Markos, Edith. "The Fast-Growing Gypsy Minority and Its Problems." *Radio Free Europe Research* (15 June 1987): 13–16. Government report, in English.

"Nucleos de Educacion Femenina: Organizacion Popular Autogestionaria" (Women's Education Centers: Self-Managing Popular Organization). *Informe "R"* 6, no. 119 (Oct. 1986): 15. NGO bulletin article, in Spanish.

Richmond, Kyle. "Picking up the Pieces: Literacy Campaign Leads Church Initiatives in Haiti." *Sojourners* 16, no. 8 (Aug./Sept. 1987): 9–10. NGO article, in English.

Samara, Maha. "Education is the Key to Increase Gulf Women's Contribution in Economic Development." *Al-Raida* 8, no. 41 (1 Aug. 1987): 10–11. NGO article, in English.

Sheehan, G., and M. Hopkins. "Meeting Basic Needs: An Examination of the World Situation in 1970." *International Labour Review* 117, no. 5 (Sept.-Oct. 1978): 523–542. Article, in English.

UNICEF. *Children on the Front Line: The Impact of Apartheid, Destabilization and Warfare on Children in Southern and South Africa.* Geneva, Switzerland: 1987. IGO report, in English; bibliography: 35, 65.

Vije, Mayan. *Where Serfdom Thrives: The Plantation Tamils of Sri Lanka.* Madras, India: Tamil Information and Research Unit, 1987. NGO report, in English.

Washington Office on Haiti. *Haiti: Barriers to Justice and Democracy.* Washington, D.C.: 1986. NGO mission report, in English.

Immigration

American Civil Liberties Union. *Salvadorans in the United States: The Case for Extended Voluntary Departure.* Washington, D.C.: 1983. NGO report, in English.

Anker, Deborah. "U.S. Immigration and Asylum Policy: A Brief Historical Perspective." *Harvard Law Bulletin* 38, no. 4 (Summer 1987): 4–8. Scholarly article, in English.

Bentz, Thomas. *New Immigrants: Portraits in Passage.* New York: Pilgrim Press, 1981. Scholarly monograph, in English.

Fagen, P. W., and S. Aguayo. *Central Americans in Mexico and the United States: Unilateral, Bilateral, and Regional Perspectives.* Washington, D.C.: Center for Immigration Policy and Refugee Assistance, 1988. NGO study, in English.

Fawcett, J. T., and B. V. Carino, eds. *Pacific Bridges: The New Migration from Asia and the Pacific Islands.* Staten Island, NY (USA): Center for Migration Studies of New York, 1987. NGO document collection, in English.

Ferris, E. G. *The Central American Refugees.* New York: Praeger Publishers, 1987. Scholarly report, in English.

Frelick, Bill. *The Back of the Hand: Bias and Restrictionism towards Central American Asylum Seekers in North America.* Washington, D.C.: U.S. Committee for Refugees, 1988. NGO monograph, in English.

Kritz, M. M., ed. *U.S. Immigration and Refugee Policy: Global and Domestic Issues.* Lexington, MA (USA): Lexington Books, 1982. Scholarly edited collection; each chapter is followed by a list of references.

Morgan, S. M., and E. Colson, eds. *People in Upheaval.* Staten Island, NY (USA): Center for Migration Studies of New York, 1987. NGO document collection, in English.

National Coalition of Advocates for Students. *New Voices: Immigrant Students in U.S. Public Schools.* Boston, MA (USA): 1988. NGO report, in English.

Plender, Richard, ed. *International Migration Law.* 2d rev. ed. Dordrecht, Netherlands: Martinus Nijhoff, 1988. Scholarly edited collection, in English.

Robinson, C., and A. Wallenstein. *Unfulfilled Hopes: The Humanitarian Parole/Immigrant Visa Program for Border Cambodians.* Washington, D.C.: U.S. Committee for Refugees, 1988. NGO issue paper, in English.

Torrealba, R., and F. Urrea, eds. *Migraciones Internacionales en las Americas* (International Migrations in the Americas). Caracas, Venezuela: Centro de Estudios de Pastoral y Asistencia Migratoria, 1987. NGO document collection/conference proceedings, in Spanish.

SEE ALSO *Aliens, Refugees*

Indigenous Peoples

American Friends Service Committee, Latin America and Caribbean Programs. *Struggle over Autonomy: A Report on the Atlantic Coast of Nicaragua.* Philadelphia, PA (USA): 1987. NGO report, in English.

Americas Watch Committee. *Human Rights in Nicaragua 1986.* New York: 1987. NGO report, in English.

Amnesty International. "Amnesty International Reports Killings and Torture in Colombia," 17 July 1986. NGO press release, in English.

————. *Brazil: Cases of Killings and Ill-Treatment of Indigenous People.* London: 1988. NGO report, in English.

————. *Guatemala: The Human Rights Record.* London: 1987. NGO report, in English.

————. *Mexico Human Rights in Rural Areas: Exchange of Documents with the Mexican Government on Human Rights Violations in Oaxaca and Chiapas.* London: 1986. NGO mission report, in English.

Branford, S., and O. Glock. *The Last Frontier: Fighting over Land in the Amazon.* London: Zed Press, 1985. Scholarly monograph, in English.

Comite de Solidaridad con los Presos Politicos (Committee of Solidarity with Political Prisoners). *"Que Gran Pais Tenemos"* ("What a Great Country We Have"). Bogota, Colombia: 1985. Edited collection, in Spanish.

Comite para la Defensa de los Derechos Humanos en Honduras (Committee for the Defense of Human Rights in Honduras). *Situacion de Derechos Humanos en Honduras: Informe Anual* (Human Rights Situation in Honduras: Annual Report). Tegucigalpa, Honduras: 1986. NGO report, in Spanish.

Corkill, D., and D. Cubitt. *Ecuador: Fragile Democracy.* London: Latin American Bureau, 1988. NGO report, in English; bibliography: books in English on Ecuador, 1978–1988, p. 113.

Durand, A., and H. Carolos. *Minorias Nacionales y Derechos Humanos: El Caso de los Triquis de Oaxaca, Mexico* (National Minorities and Human Rights: The Case of the Triquis of Oaxaca, Mexico). Chapingo, Mexico: Asociacion American de Juristas, 1987. NGO report, in Spanish.

Einfeld, Marcus. *Bicentennial Oration: Human Rights and Constitutional Entrenchment, Statement by . . . President of the Australian Human Rights and Equal Opportunity Commission on the Presentation of the Report of the Commission's Inquiry into the Social and Material Needs of the Residents of Toomelah, Boggabilla and Goondiwindi.* Sydney, Australia: Australian Human Rights and Equal Opportunity Commission, 1988. Speeches, in English.

Gray, Andrew, comp. *IWGIA Yearbook 1987: Indigenous Peoples and Development.* Copenhagen, Denmark: International Work Group for Indigenous Affairs, 1987. NGO report, in English.

Guyana Human Rights Association. *Guyana Human Rights Report 1988.* Georgetown, Guyana: 1988. NGO annual report, in English.

Heinz, W. S. *Indigenous Populations, Ethnic Minorities and Human Rights.* Berlin, FRG: Quorum Verlag, 1988. Scholarly monograph, in English.

Ligue des Droits de l'Homme (League for Human Rights). "Une Declaration sur la Situation en Nouvelle Caledonie" (A Declaration on the Situation in New Caledonia), 27 Feb. 1987. NGO statement, in French.

Mey, Wolfgang. *Wir Wollen Nicht Euch—Wir Wollen Eurer Land* (We Don't Want You—We Want Your Land). Goettingen, FRG: Gesellschaft fur Bedrohte Volker, 1988. NGO report, in German.

Ortiz, R.D. *The Miskito Indians of Nicaragua.* London: Minority Rights Group, 1988. NGO monograph, in English; bibliography, 16–19.

People's Union for Civil Liberties, Committee for the Protection of Democratic Rights, and People's Union for Democratic Rights. *Bastar—An Investigation into an "Encounter".* Delhi, India: Vikas Printing Service, 1985. NGO mission report, in English.

Secretariado Internacional de Juristas por las Amnistia y la Democracia en Paraguay (International Secretariat of Lawyers for Amnesty and Democracy in Paraguay) [and] Secretariado Internacional de Juristas por la Amnistia en Uruguay (International Secretariat of Lawyers for Amnesty in Uruguay). *Paraguay un Desafio a la Responsabilidad Internacional* (Paraguay: A Challenge to International Responsibility). Montevideo, Uruguay: 1988. Conference proceedings, in Spanish.

Simon, Jean-Marie. *Guatemala: Eternal Spring—Eternal Tyranny.* New York: W.W. Norton, 1987. Scholarly monograph, in English.

U. S. Committee for Refugees. *From Isolation to Exile: Refugees from the Chittagong Hill Tracts of Bangladesh.* Washington, D.C.: 1988. NGO report, in English.

SEE ALSO Minorities

Judiciary

Americas Watch Committee. *Human Rights in Colombia as President Barco Begins.* New York: 1986. NGO mission report, in English.

——————. *Human Rights in Peru after President Garcia's First Year.* New York: 1986. NGO mission report, in English.

——————. *Paraguay: Repression in the Countryside.* New York: 1988. NGO report, in English.

Amnesty International. *The Role of the Judiciary and the Legal Profession in the Protection of Human Rights in Chile.* London: 1986. NGO report, in English.

Chevigny, P., L. Whitman, and B. Chevigny. *Human Rights in Jamaica.* New York: Americas Watch Committee, 1986. NGO mission report, in English.

Civil Rights Movement of Sri Lanka. "The Nallanayagam Case and after," 1 Oct. 1986. NGO press release, in English.

Cowling, M.G. "Judges and the Protection of Human Rights in South Africa: Articulating the Inarticulate Premise." *South African Journal on Human Rights* 3, pt. 2 (July 1987): 177–201. Scholarly article, in English.

Comision Alemana Justicia y Paz (German Justice and Peace Commission). *Ley Justicia y Represion en Chile* (Law, Justice and Repression in Chile). Bonn, FRG: 1987. NGO mission report, in Spanish.

Elias, T. O. "Organisation and Development of the Legal Profession in Africa, in Particular, the Ability of the Bar and Judiciary to Uphold the Rights of Both the Citizen and the State." *African Journal of International Law* 1, no 1 (Summer 1988): 11–30. Scholarly article, in English.

Franck, T. M. *Human Rights in Third World Perspective.* 3 vols. Dobbs Ferry, NY (USA): Oceana Publications, 1982. Compilation of comments and case studies, in English.

Free Legal Assistance Group. *Towards an Independent Competent and Honest Judiciary.* Manila, Philippines, 1986. NGO position paper, in English.

Garcia-Sayan, Diego. *Habeas Corpus y Estados de Emergencia* (Habeas Corpus and States of Emergency). Lima, Peru: Comision Andina de Juristas and the Friedrich Naumann Foundation, 1988. NGO report, in Spanish.

Hunt, Paul. *Justice? The Military Court System in the Israeli-Occupied Territories.* Ramallah, Occupied Territories: Law in the Service of Man (Al-Haq) and Gaza Centre for Rights and Law, 1987. NGO report, in English.

International Commission of Jurista. *The Independence of Judges and Lawyers in South Asia.* Geneva, Switzerland: 1988. NGO conference report, in English.

——————. *The Independence of the Judiciary and the Legal Profession in English-Speaking Africa. A Report of Seminars Held in Lusaka from 10–14 Nov. 1986 and in Banjul from 6–10 April 1987, Convened Jointly by the Centre for the Independence of Judges and Lawyers, African Bar Association, and International Commission of Jurists.* Geneva, Switzerland: 1988. NGO conference report, in English.

Lawyers Committee for Human Rights. *Zia's Law: Human Rights under Military Rule in Pakistan.* New York: 1985. NGO mission report, in English.

National Coalition for Haitian Refugees and Americas Watch Committee. *Duvalierism since Duvalier.* New York: 1986. NGO mission report, in English.

Nwabueze B. O. *Judicialism in Commonwealth Africa: The Role of the Courts in Government.* New York: St. Martin's Press, 1977. Scholarly study, in English.

Phillips, Fred. "The Judges Demonstrate Their Independence Leading Commonwealth Caribbean Constitutional Cases." In *West Indian Constitutions: Post-Independence Reform,* 205–241. Dobbs Ferry, NY (USA): Oceana Publications, 1985. Scholarly study, in English.

Thoolen, Hans, ed. *Indonesia and the Rule of law: Twenty Years of "New Order" Government.* London: Frances Pinter Publishers for the International Commission of Jurists and the Netherlands Institute of Human Rights, 1987. NGO report/scholarly study, in English.

Trinidad and Tobago Bureau on Human Rights. *Report on the Administration of Justice in Trinidad and Tobago.* San Fernando, Trinidad: 1987. NGO report, in English.

——————. *Struggle for Justice: State Authorised Corruption of the Police Service in Trinidad and Tobago.* 3 vols. Trinidad, West Indies: 1986. NGO report, in English.

Wrobel, Brian. *Glasnost and Soviet Criminal Trials: A Report by the Parliamentary Human Rights Group.* London: Parliamentary Human Rights Group, 1987. NGO report, in English.

Zabel, W. D., D. Orenlicher, and D. E. Nachman. *Human Rights and the Administration of Justice in Chile: Report of a Delegation of the Association of the Bar of the City of New York and of the International Bar Association.* London: International Bar Association, 1987. NGO mission report, in English.

Labor

Asia Monitor Resource Center. *Asia Labour Monitor.* NGO journal, in English. Hong Kong.

Benson, Miriam. "Equal Pay for Work of Equal Value." In *Israel Yearbook on Human Rights,* 66–87. Tel Aviv, Israel: Alpha Press, 1986. Scholarly article, in English.

International Confederation of Free Trade Unions. *Annual Survey of Violations of Trade Union Rights.* NGO yearbook, in English. Brussels, Belgium.

International Labour Organisation. *International Labour Reports.* IGO annual report, in English. London.

Joyce, James Avery. *World Labour Rights and Their Protection.* London: Croom Helm, 1980. Scholarly study, in English.

Martuza, G., and M. A. Momen. *Trade Unionism and Trade Union Laws in Bangladesh.* Dhaka, Bangladesh: Bangladesh Society for the Enforcement of Human Rights, 1986. NGO monograph, in English; bibliography on trade unions and trade union laws in Bangladesh.

Miskiewicz, Sophia. "The Right to Work in Eastern Europe." *Radio Free Europe Research* 12, no. 24 (16 June 1987). Government report, in English.

Organzacion Regional Interamericana de Trabajadores (Regional Interamerican Organization of Workers). *Los Derechos Sindicales en Centroamerica (The Rights of Trade Unions in Central America).* Mexico City, Mexico: 1988. NGO report, in Spanish.

Souza Lobo, E., L. Gitahy, and M. Rosa. "Lotte Operaie e Lotte dele Operaie" (Workers' Struggle and Women Workers' Struggle). *IDOC Internazionale* 16, no. 4 (Aug. 1985): 56–63. Magazine article, in English and Italian.

Wing-yue, Leung. *Smashing the Iron Rice Pot: Workers and Unions in China's Market Socialism.* Kowloon, Hong Kong: Asia Monitor Resource Center, 1988. NGO report, in English.

Marriage

Armstrong, Alice, ed. *Women and Law in Southern Africa.* Harare, Zimbabwe: Zimbabwe Publishing House, 1987. Scholarly edited collection, in English.

Bayefsky, A.F., and M. Eberts, eds. *Equality Rights and the Canadian Charter of Rights and Freedoms.* Toronto, Canada: Carswell, 1985. Edited collection, in English.

Centre d'Etudes et de Recherches sur l'Orient Chretien (Middle East Christian Research Center). "Kuwait: The Rights of Women." *Plus* 1, no. 1 (1985): 4–5. NGO magazine article, in English.

Comite Democratique des Femmes d'Iran (Democratic Committee of Iranian Women). "La Situation des Femmes Iraniennes" (The Situation of Iranian Women). Paris: Ligue des Droits de l'Homme, 1986. NGO letter, in English.

Cook, Rebecca. "Human Rights and Development: Are Women Still Separate and Unequal?" *Proceedings of the 1986 Conference of the Canadian Council on International Law on "International Law and Development,"* 315–347. Ottawa, Ontario: Canadian

Council on International Law, 1987. Scholarly article, in English.

European Commission of Human Rights. *Stock-taking on the European Convention on Human Rights: A Periodic Note on the Concrete Results Achieved under the Convention, Supplement 1987.* Strasbourg, France: Publications and Documents Divisions, Council of Europe, 1988. IGO report, in English.

Femmes sous Lois Musulmanes (Women Living under Muslim Laws). *Dossier No. 1.* Montpellier, France: 1986. NGO document collection, in English.

————. *Dossier No. 2.* Montpellier, France: 1986. NGO document collection, in English.

Fraser, Arvonne. "For Women, the Whole World is Still the 'Developing World.' " *Human Rights Internet* (Spring 1989). Commentary, in English.

Ivan-Smith, E., N. Tandom, and J. Connors. *Women in Sub-Saharan Africa.* London: Minority Rights Group, 1988. NGO report, in English.

Kearney, R.N., and B. D. Miller. "The Spiral of Suicide and Social Change in Sri Lanka." *Marga* 8, no. 3 (1986): 1–29. Journal article, in English.

Riftin, Naomi. "Women Beseiged." *Viewpoint* 2 (Nov. 1986): 6. NGO article, in English.

SEE ALSO *Women*

Martial Law

Archdiocese of Sao Paulo. *Brasil: Nunca Mais* (Brazil: Never Again). 3d ed. Petropolis, Brazil: Editora Vozes, Ltda, 1985. Scholarly monograph/research project report, in Portuguese.

Asia Resource Center and Formosan Association for Human Rights. *Martial Law in Taiwan.* Washington, D.C.: 1985. NGO report, in English.

Asian Legal Resource Centre. *Use of Emergency Regulations in Peacetime in the Region. Workshop Papers, Kuala Lumpur, 5–8 Oct. 1987.* Kowloon, Hong Kong: 1987. NGO conference papers, in English.

Federation Internationale des Droits de l'Homme (International Federation of Human Rights). *Rapport de Mission—Perou* (Mission Report—Peru). Paris: 1985. NGO mission report, in French.

Lawyers Committee for Human Rights. *Zia's Law: Human Rights under Military Rule in Pakistan.* New York: 1985. NGO mission report, in English.

Leary, V., A. A. Ellis, and K. Madlener. *The Philippines: Human Rights after Martial Law.* Geneva, Switzerland: International Commission of Jurists, 1984. NGO mission report, in English.

Lobsack-Fullgraf, Lilli. "State of Emergency and Human Rights." *Alternative* 2, no. 1 (1987): 8–13. NGO article, in English.

Patel, Dorab. "Martial Law and Human Rights in Pakistan." *Towards International Cooperation for Human Rights in Asia* (Fall 1985): 1–3. NGO journal article, in English.

Schirmer, D. B., and S. R. Shalom, eds. *The Philippines Reader: A History of Colonialism, Neocolonialism, Dictatorship and Resistance.* Boston, MA (USA): South End Press, 1987. Scholarly edited collection, in English.

U.S. Helsinki Watch Committee. *Reinventing Civil Society—Poland's Quiet Revolution, 1981–1986.* New York: 1986. NGO report, in English.

Yap, T. H. "Indonesia: Military Rule and the Law." *Towards International Cooperation for Human Rights in Asia* (Fall 1985): 4–6. NGO journal article, in English.

SEE ALSO State of Emergency

Medical Ethics

American Association for the Advancement of Science, Committee on Scientific Freedom and Responsibility. *The Open Secret: Torture and the Medical Profession in Chile.* Washington, D. C.: 1987. NGO report, in English.

Amnesty International. *Human Rights in Chile: The Role of the Medical Profession.* London: 1986. NGO report, in English.

Asamblea Permanente de Derechos Humanos de Bolivia (Permanent Assembly for Human Rights in Bolivia). "Primera Mesa Redonda sobre Etica Medica en la Represion" (First Round Table on Medical Ethics with Reference to Repression). *Boletin* 1, no. 5 (Aug. 1985). NGO bulletin supplement, in Spanish.

————. "Tribunal Etico de la Salud contra la Impunidad" (Health Workers' Ethical Tribunal against Impunity). *Derechos Humanos* 3, no. 13 (April 1988): 16–18. NGO article, in Spanish.

Bernstein, Hilda. *No. 46-Steve Biko.* London: International Defence and Aid Fund for Southern Africa, 1978. NGO study, in English.

Bloche, M. G. *Uruguay's Military Physicians: Cogs in a System of State Terror.* Washington, D.C.: American Association for the Advancement of Science, Committee on Scientific Freedom and Responsibility, 1987. Report, in English.

Claude, R., E. Stover, and J. Lopez. *Health Professionals and Human Rights in the Philippines.* Washington, D.C.: American Association for the Advancement of Science, Clearinghouse on Science and Human Rights, 1987. NGO report, in English.

"Doctors, Ethics, and Torture." *Danish Medical Bulletin* (Aug. 1987): 185–216. Conference proceedings, in English.

Fitzpatrick, C. A. *Soviet Abuse of Psychiatry for Political Purposes.* New York: U.S. Helsinki Watch Committee, 1987. NGO report, in English.

Lery, N., H. Chambaz, and J.-F. Labarthe. "Health Personnel Confronted with Torture and Inhuman, Cruel and Degrading Treatment." *SOS Torture* 3 (June 1986): 31–34. NGO journal article, in English and French.

Lifton, R. J. *The Nazi Doctors: Medical Killing and the Psychology of Genocide.* New York: Basic Books, 1986. Scholarly monograph, in English.

National Academy of Sciences. *Science and Human Rights.* Washington, D.C.: National Academy Press, 1988. NGO conference papers, in English.

Nightingale, E. O., and E. Stover. "A Question of Conscience: Physicians in Defense of Human Rights." *Journal of the American Medical Association* 255, no. 20 (23–30 May 1986): 2794–2797. Journal article, in English.

Rayner, Mary. *Turning a Blind Eye: Medical Accountability and the Prevention of Torture in South Africa.* Washington, D.C.: American Association for the Advancement of Science, Committee on Scientific Freedom and Responsibility, 1987. NGO report, in English.

Szumski, Bonnie, ed. *Death/Dying 1985 Supplement.* St. Paul, MN (USA): Greenhaven Press, 1985. Edited collection, in English; bibliography.

Trabajamos para la Vida: Consecuencias de la Represion en el Cono Sur, el Medico y los Derechos Humanos (We Work for Life: Consequences of Repression in the Southern Cone, Physicians and Human Rights). Montevideo, Uruguay: Universidad de la Republica, Facultad de Medicina, 1987. Conference proceedings, in Spanish.

van Es, A., and M. van Grup. *Health Professionals and Human Rights in South Africa.* Leiden, Netherlands: Johannes Wier Foundation and Dutch Foundation for Health and Human Rights, 1987. NGO mission report, in English.

SEE ALSO Health Workers

Mentally Ill Rights

Bayefsky, A.F., and M. Eberts, eds. *Equality Rights and the Canadian Charter of Rights and Freedoms.* Toronto, Canada: Carswell, 1985. Edited collection, in English.

Canadian Human Rights Advocate. "Treatment at Psychiatric Hospital Challenged, Reports of Abuse Trigger Inquiry at Institution." *Canadian*

Human Rights Advocate 1, no. 8 (July 1985): 1–4. NGO newsletter article, in English.

Carney, T., and P. Singer. *Ethical and Legal Issues in Guardianship Options for Intellectually Disadvantaged People.* Canberra, Australia: Human Rights Commission, 1986. Government research paper, in English.

Chalidze, Lisa. "A Comparison of Norms—Rights of the Mentally Ill and Allegedly Mentally Ill." *New York Law School Human Rights Annual* 1 (1983): 75–97. Scholarly article, in English.

Heginbotham, Chris. *The Rights of Mentally Ill People.* London: Minority Rights Group, 1987. NGO report, in English.

Herr, Stanley S. *Issues in Human Rights: A Guide for Parents, Professionals, Policymakers and All Those who Are Concerned about the Rights of the Mentally Retarded and Developmentally Disabled People.* New York: 1984. Guidebook, in English.

International Commission of Jurists. *Human Rights and Mental Patients in Japan.* Geneva, Switzerland: 1985. NGO mission report, in English.

Japan Civil Liberties Union. *Report concerning Present Status of Human Rights in Japan.* Tokyo, Japan: 1988. NGO report, in English.

Sieghart, Paul, ed. *Human Rights in the United Kingdom.* London: Human Rights Network, 1988. NGO monograph, in English; footnotes to articles contain substantial bibliographic references.

Silver, Hedy M. "Voluntary Admission to New York Hospitals: The Rights of the Mentally Ill Homeless." *Columbia Human Rights Law Review* 19, no. 2 (Spring 1988): 333–367. Scholarly article, in English.

Mercenaries

Danaher, Kevin, ed. *South Africa and the United States: An Annotated Bibliography.* Washington, D.C.: Institute of Policy Studies, 1980. Bibliography, in English.

Weissbrodt, David. "Country-Related and Thematic Developments at the 1988 Session of the UN Commission on Human Rights." *Human Rights Quarterly* 10, no. 4 (Nov. 1988): 544–558. Scholarly article, in English.

Migrant Workers

Birks, J.S., and C.A. Sinclair. *Nature and Process of Labor Importing: The African in the Gulf States, Kuwait, Bahrain, Qatar, and the United Arab Emirates.* Geneva, Switzerland: International Labour Office, 1978. IGO study, in English.

Catholic Institute for International Relations. *The Labour Trade: Filipino Migrant Workers around the World.* London: 1987. NGO report, in English.

Comite Europeen pour la Defense des Refugies et Immigres (European Committee for the Defense of Refugees and Immigrants). *Land and Liberty: The Struggle of Agricultural Workers of Andalusia.* Forcalquier, France: 1985. NGO report, in English.

Downing, T.E., and G. Kushner, eds. *Human Rights and Anthropology.* Cambridge, MA (USA): Cultural Survival, 1988. Edited collection/bibliography, in English.

Fawcett, J.T., and B. V. Carino, eds. *Pacific Bridges: The New Migration from Asia and the Pacific Islands.* Staten Island, NY (USA): Center for Migration Studies of New York, 1987. NGO document collection, in English.

Goldman, Chris. *Human Rights and the Migratory Labour System.* Roma, Lesotho: Institute of Southern African Studies, 1987. Scholarly study, in English.

International Migration Review 20, no. 4 (Winter 1986). Special issue with scholarly articles on "Temporary Worker Programs: Mechanism, Conditions, Consequences," in English.

Isis International. *Rural Women in Latin America.* Rome: 1987. NGO monograph, in English.

Keyter, Carl, comp. and ed. *Report of Proceedings of the Second Consultation on Migration and Development.* Organized by the Agency for Industrial Mission and the Transformation Resource Centre, held at the National University of Lesotho, Roma, 1–5 June 1986. Maseru, Lesotho: Transformation of Resource Centre, 1986. Conference proceedings, in English.

Lurie, Peter. "AIDS and Labour Policy." *South African Labour Bulletin* 12, no. 8 (Oct. 1987): 80–88. NGO article, in English; bibliography, pp. 86–88.

Lye, William F. "Three Views of the Migrant Labor System in South Africa." *Africa Today* 31, no. 4 (4th quarter 1984): 35–38. Book review article, in English.

Plender, Richard, ed. *International Migration Law.* Rev. 2d ed. Dordrecht, Netherlands: Martinus Nijhoff, 1988. Scholarly edited collection, in English.

Quaker Office at the United Nations. *Drafting an International Convention on the Protection of the Rights of All Migrant Workers and Their Families.* New York: 1987. NGO conference report, in English.

Rugege, S. *Legal Aspects of Labor Migration from Lesotho to the Southern African Mines.* Geneva: International Labor Office, 1979. IGO study, in English.

Shapiro, J.B. *Info '85: A Folder of Facts and Figures on South Africa.* Grant Park, South Africa: Human Awareness Programme, 1985. NGO report, in English.

Torrealba, R., and F. Urrea, eds. *Migraciones Internacionales en las Americas* (International Migrations in the Americas). Caracas, Venezuela: Centro de Estudios de Pastoral y Asistencia Migratoria, 1987. NGO document collection/conference proceedings, in Spanish.

Transformation Resource Centre. *Report of a Conference on Successful Small Rural Development Projects.* Conference held at Marakabei, Lesotho, 17–20 Nov. 1988. Marakabei, Lesotho: 1988. NGO conference proceedings, in English.

Whiteside, A., and C. Patel. *Black Migrant Workers' Rights in South Africa.* Geneva, Switzerland: International Labour Office, 1986. IGO manual, in English.

Minorities

Amnesty Intenational. *Protecting Human Rights: International Procedures and How to Use Them.* London: 1987. NGO manual, in English.

Burger, Julian. *Report from the Frontier: The State of the World's Indigenous Peoples.* Cambridge, MA (USA) and London: Cultural Survival and Zed Books, 1987. Scholarly study, in English.

Chaliand, Gerard, ed. *Minority Peoples in the Age of Nation-States.* London: Minority Rights Group, 1989. Scholarly report, in English; originally published in French.

Cultural Survival. *Cultural Survival Quarterly.* NGO quarterly journal, in English. Cambridge, MA (USA).

—————. *Cultural Survival Reports.* NGO series of major reports and books on indigenous peoples, in English. Cambridge, MA (USA).

Davies, Peter, ed. *Human Rights.* London: Minority Rights Group, 1988. Collection of essays, in English.

Downing, T.E., and G. Kushner, eds. *Human Rights and Anthropology.* Cambridge, MA (USA): Cultural Survival, 1988. Scholarly study, in English.

Garber, Larry. *Guidelines for International Election Observing.* Washington, D.C. (USA): International Human Rights Law Group, 1984. Manual, in English.

Gesellschaft fur bedrohte Volker (Society for Endangered Peoples). *Pogrom.* Journal and book-length reports issued as special issues ("Reihe Pogrom") in German. Gottingen, FRG.

—————. *Vierte Welt Aktuell.* Posters and urgent action bulletins, in German. Gottingen, FRG.

Groupement pour les Droits des Minorities (Minority Rights Group -France). *Les Minorities dans les Balkans* (Minorities in the Balkans). Paris: 1987. NGO report, in French.

Hannum, Hurst, ed. *Guide to International Human Rights Practice.* Philadelphia, PA (USA): University of Pennsylvania Press, 1984. Scholarly study, in English.

Heinz, Wolfgang S. *Indigenous Populations, Ethnic Minorities and Human Rights.* Berlin, FRG: Quorum Verlag, 1988. Scholarly study, in English.

Indian Law Resource Center. *Indian Rights—Human Rights: Handbook for Indians on International Human Rights Complaints Procedures.* Washington, D.C. (USA): 1984. NGO manual, in English.

International Work Group for Indigenous Affairs. *IWGIA Documents.* NGO series of special reports, in English. Copenhagen, Denmark.

—————. *IWGIA Newsletter.* NGO irregularly issued report, in English. Copenhagen, Denmark.

—————. *IWGIA Yearbook.* NGO annual report, in English. Copenhagen, Denmark.

—————. *Native Power: The Quest for Autonomy and Nationhood of Indigenous Peoples.* Copenhagen: Universitetsforlaget, 1985. NGO study, in English.

Joshi, Barbara, ed. *Untouchable! Voices of the Dalit Liberation Movement.* London: Minority Rights Group, 1986. NGO report, in English.

Kubota, Yo, ed. *Peoples for Human Rights: IMADR Yearbook 1988* 1, no. 1 (1989). Special issue on international efforts to eliminate discrimination, in English.

Minority Rights Group. *MRG Reports.* NGO series of reports on status of ethnic, religious, or racial minorities in countries throughout the world, in English; up to 1990, 80 reports have been published.

Moody, Roger, ed. *The Indigenous Voice: Visions and Realities.* 2 vols. Copenhagen, Denmark, and London: International Work Group for Indigenous Affairs and Zed Books, 1988. Scholarly study, in English.

Sieghart, Paul, ed. *Human Rights in the UK.* London: Minority Rights Group, 1988. Collection of essays, in English.

Sigler, J.A., ed. *International Handbook on Race and Race Relations.* Westport, CT (USA): Greenwood Press, 1987. Collection, in English.

—————. *Minority Rights: A Comparative Analysis.* Westport, CT (USA): Greenwood Press, 1983. Scholarly study, in English.

Staples, Lee. *Roots to Power: A Manual for Grassroots Organizing.* New York: Praeger Publishers, 1984. Manual, in English.

Stormorken, Bjorn, *HURIDOCS Standard Formats for Recording and Exchange of Information on Human Rights.* Kluwer Academic, 1985. Manual, in English.

Survival International. *Survival International News.* NGO quarterly, in English. London and New York.

Thornberry, Patrick. *Minorities and Human Rights Law.* London: Minority Rights Group, 1987. NGO report, in English.

Van Dyke, Vernon. *Human Rights, Ethnicity, and Discrimination.* Westport, CT (USA): Greenwood Press, 1985. Scholarly study, in English.

Whitaker, Ben, ed. *Minorities: A Question of Human Rights?* London: Minority Rights Group, 1984. Collection of essays, in English.

Yacoub, Joseph. *Les Assyro-Chaldeens: Un Peuple Oublie de l'Histoire* (The Assyro-Chaldeens: A People outside of History). London: Minority Rights Group, 1987, in French.

SEE ALSO *Indigenous Peoples, Self-Determination*

Nationality

Amnesty International. *The Imprisonment of Persons Seeking to Leave a Country or to Return to Their Own Country.* London: 1986. NGO report, in English.

Info-Turk. *Black Book on the Militarist "Domocracy" in Turkey.* Brussels, Belgium: 1986. NGO report, in English.

International League for Human Rights. *Romania's Human Right Record: Comments on the Government of Romania's Official Report to the Human Rights Committee.* New York: 1987. NGO report, in English.

——————. *Uganda after Amin: A Case of Displacement and Discrimination against the Banyarwanda Population.* New York: 1985. NGO report, in English.

Japan Civil Liberties Union. *Report concerning Present Status of Human Rights in Japan.* Tokyo: 1988. NGO report, in English.

Max Planck Institute for Comparative Public and International Law. *Encyclopedia of Public Inernational Law, Vol. 8: Human Rights and the Individual in International Law—International Economic Relations.* New York: North-Holland, 1985. Encyclopedia, in English.

"Nationalities Policy in the USSR: Discrimination against Ethnic Groups," *The Ukrainian Weekly,* 9 July 1985. Newspaper article, in English.

Nietschmann, Bernard. "Economic Development by Invasion of Indigenous Nations: Cases of Indone-

sia and Bangladesh." *Cultural Survival Quarterly* 10, no. 2 (1986): 2–12. NGO article, in English.

Plender, Richard, ed. *International Migration Law.* Rev. 2d ed. Dordrecht, Netherlands: Martinus Nijhoff, 1988. Scholarly edited collection, in English.

Radio Free Europe/Radio Liberty. "The Kosovo Conflict: Situation Report Yugoslavia." *Radio Free Europe Research* 13, no. 38 (23 Sept. 1988). Government report, in English; bibliography, pp. 5, 10, 14, 18–19.

Sheehy, Ann. "Gorbachev Comments on Nationality Relations." *Radio Liberty Research* (28 Jan. 1987): 1–4. Government article, in English.

Social Scientists Association. *Ethnicity and Social Change in Sri Lanka.* Colombo, Sri Lanka: 1985. Scholarly edited collection, in English.

U.S. Helsinki Watch Committee. "USSR." In *Ten Years Later: Violations of the Helsinki Accords,* 151–299. New York: 1985. NGO report, in English.

Non-governmental Organizations

Artucio, Alejandro. "Los Derechos Humanos y las Organizaciones no Gubernamentales" (Human Rights and Non-Governmental Organizations). *Revista de IELSUR* 2 (July 1988): 13–22. NGO article, in Spanish.

Blaser, Arthur W. "Human Rights in the Third World and Development of International Nongovernmental Organizations." In *Human Rights and Third World Development,* ed. G. W. Shephard and V. Nanda, 273–285. Westport, CT (USA): Greenwood Press, 1985. Chapter in scholarly study, in English.

Boler, Jean. "The Mothers Committee of El Salvador: National Human Rights Activists." *Human Rights Quarterly* 7, no. 4 (Nov. 1985): 541–556. Scholarly article, in English.

Drzemczewski, Andrew. "The Role of NGOs in Human Rights Matters in the Council of Europe." *Human Rights Law Journal* 8, pts. 2–4 (1987): 273–282. Scholarly article, in English.

Fenton, T. P., and M. J. Heffron, comp. and ed. *Human Rights: A Directory of Resources.* Maryknoll, NY (USA): Orbis Books, 1989. Directory, in English.

Fruhling, Hugo. "Nonprofit Organizations as Opposition to Authoritarian Rule: The Case of Human Rights Organizations and Private Research Centers in Chile." Research paper available from Program on Non-Profit Organizations and Institute for Social Studies, Yale University, New Haven, CT (USA); in English.

Fruhling, H., G. Alberti, and F. Portales. *Organizaciones de Derechos Humanos de America del Sur* (Human Rights Organizations in South America). San Jose, Costa Rica: Instituto Interamericano de Derechos Humanos, 1989. Directory, in Spanish.

Human Rights Internet. *Africa: Human Rights Directory and Bibliography.* Cambridge, MA (USA): 1989. Directory, in English.

——————. *Directorio de Organizaciones de Derechos Humanos: America Latina y El Caribe* (Human Rights Directory: Latin America and the Caribbean). Cambridge, MA (USA): 1990. Directory, in English and Spanish.

——————. *Human Rights Directory Eastern Europe and the USSR.* Cambridge, MA (USA): 1987. Directory, in English.

——————. *Human Rights Directory: Latin America, Africa, Asia.* Cambridge, MA (USA): 1981. Directory, in English.

——————. *Human Rights Directory Western Europe.* Cambridge, MA (USA): 1982. Directory, in English.

——————. *North American Human Rights Directory.* 3d ed. Cambridge, MA (USA): 1984. Directory, in English.

Humphrey Institute of Public Affairs: Women, Public Policy, and Development Project. *Women's Organizations and Changes in Public Policy: Bellagio Discussion Report.* Minneapolis, MN (USA): 1985. Conference report, in English.

International Commission of Jurists. *Report of Seminars on Legal Services for the Rural Poor and Other Disadvantaged Groups (South-East Asia, Jakarta, 11–16 Jan. 1987: South-Asia, Rajpipla, 27–31 Dec. 1987).* Geneva, Switzerland: 1988. NGO report, in English.

International Peace Research Institute, Oslo. "Special Issue: Humanitarian Organization-Building in the Third World." *Bulletin of Peace Proposals* 18, no. 2 (1987). Scholarly article, in English.

Livezey, L. W. *Nongovernmental Organizations and the Idea of Human Rights.* Princeton, NJ (USA): Center of International Studies, 1988. Scholarly monograph, in English; bibliography, pp. 166–196.

Mignone, E. F. "Las Organizaciones de Derechos Humanos en las Democracias en Transicion" (Human Rights Organizations in Democracies in Transition). *Revista de IELSUR* 2 (July 1988): 23–29. NGO article, in Spanish.

Miserez, Diana, ed. *Refugees—The Trauma of Exile: The Humanitarian Role of Red Cross and Red Crescent.* Dordrecht, Netherlands: Martinus Nijhoff Publishers, 1988. Scholarly edited collection, in English.

NGOs and Africa: A Strategy Workshop. Geneva, Switzerland: UN Non-Governmental Liaison Service, 1985. NGO conference report, in English.

Rodley, N. S. "Monitoring Human Rights by the UN System and Non-Governmental Organizations." In *Human Rights and American Foreign Policy,* ed. D. P. Kommers and G. D. Loescher, 157–178. Notre Dame, IN (USA): Notre Dame University Press, 1979. Scholarly article, in English.

Sasono, Adi. "The Role of NGOs in Promoting Human Rights: Some Notes on Indonesian Experiences." *Human Rights Forum* 1, no. 1 (1985): 15–18. NGO journal article, in English.

Schirmer, J. G. "Those Who Die for Life Cannot be Called Dead: Women and Human Rights Protest in Latin America." *Harvard Human Rights Yearbook* 1 (1988): 41–76. Scholarly article, in English.

UNESCO. *World Directory of Human Rights Teaching and Research Institutions.* Paris: 1988. Directory, in English, Spanish, and French.

Verzola, Robert. "Human Rights Information Networking." *Sarilakas-Grassroots Development* 3, no. 2 (2d quarter 1988): 13–15, 20. NGO article, in English.

Weingartner, Erich. *Human Rights: Solidarities, Networks and the Ecumenical Movement.* Quezon City, Philippines: National Council of Churches in the Philippines–Human Rights Desk, 1988. NGO occasional paper, in English.

Wiseberg, L.S., and H. M. Scoble. "Monitoring Human Rights Violations: The Role of Non-Governmental Human Rights Organizations." In *Human Rights and American Foreign Policy,* ed. D. P. Kommers and G. D. Loescher, 179–208. Scholarly article, in English.

Nuclear Issues

American Latvian Association. "Chernobyl Cleanup—No Protective Clothing." *Latvian News Digest* 11, no. 1 (Feb. 1987): 2. NGO article, in English.

Christian Conference of Asia. *HEIWA: Life for the People.* Kowloon, Hong Kong: 1985. NGO conference proceedings, in English.

——————. *Nuclear Free Nation.* Kowloon, Hong Kong: 1988. NGO report, in English.

Clark, R., and S. R. Roof. *Micronesia: The Problem of Palau.* Rev. ed. London: Minority Rights Group, 1987. NGO report, in English.

Cultural Survival Quarterly 11, no. 3 (1987). NGO special issue on "Militarization and Indigenous Peoples: Part I—The Americas and the Pacific," in English.

Donn, Gari, ed. *Missiles, Reactors, and Civil Liberties: Against the Nuclear State.* Glasgow, Scotland: Scottish Council for Civil Liberties, 1981. NGO edited collection, in English.

Gesellschaft fur bedrohte Volker (Association for Endangered Peoples). "Solange radioaktive Flusse fliessen: Uranium Abbau in den Black Hills" (As Long as Radioactive Rivers Flow: Uranium Processing in the Black Hills). *Pogrom* 135 (Aug. 1987): 20–28. NGO article, in German.

International League for Human Rights. *Report of the International Observer Mission: Palau Referendum, Dec. 1986.* New York: 1987. NGO mission report, in English.

Kuper, Leo. *The Prevention of Genocide.* New Haven, CT (USA): Yale University Press, 1985. Scholarly monograph, in English; bibliography, pp. 255–278.

Southern African Catholic Bishops' Conference. *The Things that Make for Peace.* Pretoria, South Africa: 1985. NGO report, in English.

Stankovic, Slobodan. "Ecological Concerns." *Radio Free Europe Research* (20 Nov. 1986): 31–32. Government article, in English.

Third World Network. *Belauans Struggle to Stay Nuclear Free and to Protect Their Sovereignty.* Penang, Malaysia: 1988. NGO report, in English.

U.S. Helsinki Watch Committee. *From Below: Independent Peace and Environment Movements in Eastern Europe and the USSR.* New York: 1987. NGO report, in English.

What is Hiroshima, Mommy? Vision of a Thousand Cranes: A Guide to the 20 Best Films, Videotapes, and Slide Shows for Hiroshima and Nagasaki Days. New York: Alternative Media Information Center, n.d. Audio-visuals directory, in English.

Whitaker, Alan. "Radiation in Lappland." *Anti-Slavery Newsletter* 2, no. 7 (1986): 1. NGO article, in English.

Prisoners of War

Arab Organization for Human Rights. "Plight of Iraqi Prisoners of War in Iran." *AOHR Newsletter* 11 (Aug. 1987): 1. NGO article, in English.

Ashoor, Yadh ben. "Islam and International Humanitarian Law." *International Review of the Red Cross* 62, no. 722 (March-April 1980): 59–60. Scholarly article, in English.

Djurovic, Gradimir. *The Central Tracing Agency of the International Committee of the Red Cross.* Trans. from French by M. Monkhouse and D. Cornwell. Geneva, Switzerland: Henry Dunant Institute, 1968. Scholarly monograph, in English; bibliography—classified into unpublished and published sources; ICRC documents and conferences; and other international conferences, books, and articles.

Eritrean People's Liberation Front. *The Ethiopian Prisoners of War: The Prisoners on Nobody's Conscience.* Brussels, Belgium: 1987. NGO report, in English.

Murray, Christiana. "The 1977 Geneva Protocols and Conflict in Southern Africa." *International and Comparative Law Quarterly* 33 (1984): 462–470. Scholarly article, in English.

People's Mojahedin Organization of Iran. *Khomeini: The Enemy of Peace and Freedom.* Paris: 1986. Political report, in English.

United Nations Security Council. *Report of the Mission Dispatched by the Secretary-General on the Situation of Prisoners of War in the Islamic Republic of Iran and Iraq.* IGO mission report, in English.

U. S. Helsinki Committee and Asia Watch. *By All Parties to the Conflict: Violations of the Laws of War in Afghanistan.* New York: 1988. NGO report, in English.

Prisoners' Rights

American Friends Service Committee, Criminal Justice Program. *The Lessons of Marion: The Failure of a Maximum Security Prison—A History and Analysis, with Voices of Prisoners.* Philadelphia, PA (USA): 1985. NGO report, in English.

Amnesty International. *Haiti: Deaths in Detention, Torture, and Inhuman Prison Conditions.* London: 1987. NGO report, in English.

——————. *India: A Review of Human Rights Violations.* London: 1988. NGO issue paper, in English.

——————. *South Africa: Human Rights Violations under the National State of Emergency.* London: 1986. NGO bulletin, in English.

British Campaign for the Defence of Political Prisoners and Human Rights in Indonesia. "Indonesia's Concentration Camps." *TAPOL Bulletin* 70 (July 1985): 13. NGO bulletin article, in English.

Burneo Labrin, Jose. *Derechos de la Persona ante el Juez, la Policia y en la Carcel* (Rights of the Individual before the Judge, the Police, and while in Prison). Lima, Peru: Comision Episcopal de Accion Social: 1985. Research paper, in Spanish.

Centro Ecumenico de Documentacao e Informacao (Ecumenical Center for Documentation and Information). "O Preso no Brasil de Hoje" (Prisoners in Brazil Today). *Tempo e Presenca* 215 (Dec. 1986): 10–11. NGO journal article, in Portuguese.

Comision Costarricense de Derechos Humanos (Costa Rican Commission for Human Rights). "CODEHU ante la Situacion de los Recluso" (CODEHU and the Conditions of Prisoners). *Informativo* 4 (March-April 1988): 16. NGO article, in Spanish.

Comision Ecumenica de Derechos Humanos (Ecumenical Commission for Human Rights). "Situacion

Carcelaria" (Prison Situation). *Derechos del Pueblo* 37 (Jan. 1987): 9. NGO article, in Spanish.

Comite de Iglesias (Committee of Churches). "Condiciones Inhumanas y Maltrato de Presos Origina Violencia en el Penal" (Inhuman Conditions and Ill-treatment of Prisoners Lead to Violence). *Noticias Complementarias* (7 Aug. 1986): 5–9. NGO newsletter article, in Spanish.

Committee against Repression and for Democratic Rights in Iraq. *The Great Massacre: First Hand Account of the Great Massacre of Abu-Ghraib Prisoners by an Official of the Iraqi Abu-Ghraib Prison.* London: 1985. NGO report, in English.

Defence for Children International. *Children in Prison in Turkey.* Geneva, Switzerland: 1988. NGO report, in English.

Detainees' Parents Support Committee. *Fourth Special Report on State of Emergency.* Johannesburg, South Africa: 1986. NGO report, in English.

——————. *Review of 1987.* Johannesburg, South Africa: 1988. NGO report, in English.

Gonsalves, C., M. Desai, and J. Cox. *Leading Cases on Prisoners' Rights.* Bombay, India: Legal Resource Centre, Youth for Unity and Voluntary Action, 1989. NGO study, in English.

"Ill-treatment of Punjab Detenus." India Now 8, no. 7–9 (July-Sept. 1985): 18–19. Magazine article, in English.

Instituto de Defensa Legal (Institute for Legal Defense). *Los Sucesos de los Penales: Nueva Abdicacion de la Autoridad Democratica, un Enfoque Juridico* (A New Abdication of Democratic Authority in Peru: A Legal Analysis . . . Recent Events in the Prisons). Lima, Peru: 1986. NGO report, in Spanish.

Instituto Historico Centroamericano (Central American Historical Institute). "Jails and Justice in Nicaragua." *Envio* 5, no. 64 (Oct. 1985): 14–28. Journal article/past conference, in English.

Lawyers' Comittee for Civil Rights under Law, Southern Africa Project. *South Africa 1986: A Permanent State of Emergency.* Washington, D.C.: 1987. NGO annual report, in English.

Popkin, Maggie. *Waiting for Justice: Treatment of Political Prisoners under El Salvador's Decree 50.* Washington, D.C.: International Human Rights Law Group, 1987. NGO report, in English.

Roth, Kenneth. *Repression Disguised as Law: Human Rights in Poland.* New York: Lawyers Committee for Human Rights, 1987. NGO report, in English.

Shalev, Carmel. *The Price of Insurgency: Civil Rights in the Occupied Territories.* Jerusalem, Israel: West Bank Database Project, 1988. NGO report, in English.

Sieghart, Paul, ed. *Human Rights in the United Kingdom.* London: Human Rights Network, 1988. NGO monograph, in English; footnotes to the articles contain substantial bibliographic references.

Solso, Christine K. *Ioan Ruta: A Case Study of Human Rights in Romania.* Minneapolis, MN (USA): Minnesota Lawyers International Human Rights Committee, 1988. NGO report, in English.

van Zyl Smit, Dirk. " 'Normal' Prisons in an 'Abnormal' Society? A Comparative Perspective on South African Prison Law and Practice." *South African Journal on Human Rights* 3, pt. 2 (July 1987): 147–165. Scholarly article, in English.

Refugees

A. Annual Reports

U.S. Committee for Refugees. *World Refugee Survey— 19— Review.* Washington, D.C. This annual review contains a bibliography; in English.

B. Bibliographies

Center for Documentation on Refugees and Save the Children Alliance. *A Selected and Annotated Bibliography on Refugee Children.* Geneva, Switzerland: 1988. In English.

Central America Resource Center. *Sourcebook on Central American Refugee Policy: A Bibliography with Subject and Country Index.* Austin, TX (USA): Lyndon B. Johnson School of Public Affairs, University of Texas at Austin, 1985. In English and Spanish.

Institut Africaine pour le Developpement Economique (African Institute for Economic Development). *Les Refugies en Afrique: Bibliographie Commentee* (Refugees in Africa: Annotated Bibliography). Abidjan, Ivory Coast: 1986. In French.

International Refugee Integration Resource Centre. *International Bibliography of Refugee Literature.* Geneva, Switzerland: 1985. In English.

United Nations High Commissioner for Refugees, Refugee Documentation Center. *Refugee Abstracts.* Geneva, Switzerland. Quarterly journal, in English; some abstracts may be in French, German, or Spanish.

United Nations High Commissioner for Refugees and Refugee Policy Group. *A Selected and Annotated Bibliography on Refugee Women.* Geneva, Switzerland: 1985. In English.

Williams, C. L. *An Annotated Bibliography on Refugee Mental Health.* Minneapolis, MN (USA): Refugee Assistance Program, Mental Health-Technical Assistance Center, University of Minnesota, 1987. In English.

C. Directories and Handbooks

European Consultation on Refugees and Exiles. *Asylum in Europe: A Handbook for Agencies Assisting Refugees*. 3d ed. The Hague, Netherlands: 1983. In English.

Refugee Studies Programme, Queen Elizabeth House. *The Directory of Current Research on Refugees and Other Forced Migrants*. 2d ed. Oxford, UK: 1988. In English.

Zimmerman, D., N. Avrin, and O. D. Cava, comps. *A Directory of International Migration Study Centers, Research Programs and Library Resources*. Staten Island, NY (USA): Center for Migration Studies of New York, 1987. In English.

D. General Monographs

American Association for the Advancement of Science. *Scientists in Exile: Issues and Perspectives on the Refugee Experience*. Washington, D. C.: 1988. NGO report, in English.

Baker, Ron, ed. *The Psycholosocial Problems of Refugees*. London: British Refugee Council and European Consultation on Refugees and Exiles, 1983. Scholarly edited collection, in English.

Gordenker, Leon. *Refugees in International Politics*. New York: Columbia University Press, 1987. Scholarly report, in English; bibliography, pp. 215–220.

Grahl-Madsen, Atle. *Territorial Asylum*. Stockholm, Sweden: Almqvist and Wiksell International, in collaboration with Oceana Publications, 1980. Scholarly monograph, in English.

Hull, Elizabeth. *Without Justice for All: The Constitutional Rights of Aliens*. Westport, CT (USA): Greenwood Press, 1985. Scholarly monograph, in English.

Jacobson, J. L. *Environmental Refugees: A Yardstick of Habitability*. Washington, D.C.: Worldwatch Institute, 1988. NGO monograph, in English.

Martin, D. A., ed. *The New Asylum Seekers: Refugee Law in the 1980s*. Dordrecht, Netherlands: Martinus Nijhoff, 1988. Scholarly edited collection, in English.

Morgan, S. M., and E. Colson, eds. *People in Upheaval*. Staten Island, NY (USA): Center for Migration Studies of New York, 1987. NGO document collection in English.

Nanda, Ved P., ed. *Refugee Law and Policy: International and U.S. Responses*. Westport, CT (USA): Greenwood Press, 1989. Scholarly edited collection, in English.

Plender, Richard, ed. *Basic Documents on International Migration Law*. Dordrecht, Netherlands: Martinus Nijhoff, 1988. Scholarly document collection, in English.

—————. *International Migration Law*. Rev. 2d ed. Dordrecht, Netherlands: Martinus Nijhoff, 1988. Scholarly edited collection, in English.

Tomasi, Lydio F., ed. *In Defense of the Alien*. Vol 5, *Refugees and Asylum*. New York: Center for Migration Studies, 1983. Conference proceedings, in English.

—————. *In Defense of the Alien*. Vol. 6, *Immigration and Refugee Policy*. New York: Center for Migration Studies, 1984. Conference proceedings, in English.

E. Journals

American Council for Nationalities Service. *Refugee Reports*. Washington, D.C. NGO journal, in English.

Center for Migration Studies. *Migration World*. New York. NGO journal, in English; prior to 1986, *Migration Today*.

New Francophone Summary of Information on Refugees and Asylum. *Documentation Refugies*. NGO documentation, in French.

Oxford University. *International Journal of Refugee Law*. Oxford University Press, UK. Quarterly scholarly journal, in English.

—————. *Journal of Refugee Studies*. Oxford University Press, UK. Scholarly document collection, in English.

F. Region/Country Specific Studies

Aiboni, S. A. *Protection of Refugees in Africa*. Uppsala, Sweden: Scandinavian Institute of African Studies and Svenska Institutet for Internationell Ratt, 1978. Scholarly study, in English; bibliography, pp. 151–155.

American Civil Liberties Union. *Salvadorans in the United States: The Case for Extended Voluntary Departure*. Washington, D.C.: 1983. NGO report, in English; appendices.

Anker, D. E. "Discretionary Asylum: A Protection Remedy for Refugees under the Refugee Act of 1980." *Virginia Journal of International Law* 28, no.1 (Fall 1987): 1–72. Scholarly article, in English.

—————. "U.S. Immigration and Asylum Policy: A Brief Historical Perspective." *Harvard Law Bulletin* 38, no. 4 (Summer 1987): 4–8. Scholarly article, in English.

Brennan, T. O. *Uprooted Angolans: From Crisis to Catastrophe*. Washington, D.C.: U. S. Committee for Refugees, 1987. NGO report, in English.

British Refugee Council. *Uprooted: The Displaced of Central America*. London: 1986. NGO report, in English.

Clay, J.W., and B. K. Holcomb. *Politics and the Ethiopian Famine 1984–1985.* Cambridge, MA (USA): Cultural Survival, 1985. NGO report, in English; bibliography: pp. 247–250.

Colchester, M., and V. Luling, eds. *Ethiopia's Bitter Medicine: Settling for Disaster—An Evaluation of the Ethiopian Government's Resettlement Programme.* London: Survival International, 1986. NGO report, in English.

Comite Intermouvements aupres des Evacues, Institut Oecumenique pour le Developpement des Peuples, et Mouvement International N'Krumah (Joint Committee for Refugees, Ecumenical Institute for the Development of Peoples, and the International Nkrumah Movement). *Africa's Refugee Crisis.* Trans. Michael John. London: Zed Books, 1986. NGO monograph, in English; originally available in French.

Fagen, P. W., and S. Aguayo. *Central Americans in Mexico and the United States: Unilateral, Bilateral, and Regional Perspectives.* Washington, D.C.: Center for Immigration Policy and Refugee Assistance, 1988. NGO study, in English.

Ferris, E. G. *The Central American Refugees.* New York: Praeger Publishers, 1987. Scholarly report, in English.

Kibreab, Gaim. *African Refugees.* Trenton, NJ (USA): Africa World Press, 1985. Scholarly study, in English.

Lawless, R., and L. Monahan, eds. *War and Refugees: The Western Sahara Conflict.* London: Refugee Studies Programme, Queen Elizabeth House, 1987. Scholarly edited collection, in English.

Ohaegbulom, F. U. "Human Rights and the Refugee Situation in Africa." In *Human Rights and Third World Development,* ed. G. W. Shephard, Jr., and V. Nanda, 197–230. Westport, CT (USA): Greenwood Press, 1985. Chapter in scholarly collection, in English.

Nanda, V. P. "The African Refugee Dilemma: A Challenge for International Law and Policy." *Africa Today* 32, nos. 1 and 2 (1st and 2d quarters 1985): 61–75. Conference proceedings in scholarly journal, in English.

Refugee Studies Programme, Queen Elizabeth House. *The Crisis of Migration from Afghanistan: Domestic and Foreign Implications—A Summary of the Proceedings of an International Symposium, 29 March–2 April 1987.* NGO conference proceedings, Oxford, UK: 1988. NGO conference proceedings, in English.

——————. *Implementation of the OAU/UN Conventions and Domestic Legislation concerning the Rights and Obligations of Refugees in Africa, 14–28 September 1986: Final Report.* Oxford, UK: 1988. NGO conference proceedings, in English.

Robinson, C., and A. Wallenstein. *Unfulfilled Hopes: The Humanitarian Parole/Immigrant Visa Program for Border Cambodians.* Washington, D.C.: U.S. Committee for Refugees, 1988. NGO issue paper, in English.

Rogge, J. R. *Too Many, Too Long: Sudan's Twenty-Year Refugee Dilemma.* Totowa, NJ (USA): Rowman and Allanheld, 1985. Scholarly monograph, in English; bibliography, pp. 185–190.

Ruiz, H.A. *Beyond the Headlines: Refugees in the Horn of Africa.* Washington, D.C.: U.S. Committee for Refugees, 1988. NGO issue paper, in English; selected bibliography.

U.S. Committee for Refugees. *From Isolation to Exile: Refugees from the Chittagong Hill Tracts of Bangladesh.* Washington, D.C.: 1988. NGO report, in English.

——————. *Refugees from Mozambique: Shattered Land, Fragile Asylum.* Washington, D.C.: 1986. NGO report, in English.

Yundt, Keith W. *Latin American States and Political Refugees.* New York: Praeger Publishers, 1989. Scholarly monograph, in English.

Remedy

Alston, P., and M. Rodriguez-Bustelo. *Taking Stock of the United Nations Human Rights Procedures: Report of a January 1988 Workshop at Lake Mohonk, NY.* Medford, MA (USA): Fletcher School of Law and Diplomacy, Tufts University, 1988. Conference report, in English.

Amnesty International. *The Human Rights Committee.* 3 Parts. London: 1986. NGO report, in English; bibliographies in parts 1 and 2 list official documents, books, pamphlets, and articles on the Human Rights Committee (part 1) and resources (part 2).

——————. *The Human Rights Committee—Protecting Human Rights: International Procedures and How to Use Them.* London: 1987. NGO background paper, in English, French, and Spanish; bibliography.

Bailey, Sidney, ed. *Human Rights and Responsibility in Britain and Ireland: A Christian Perspective.* London: Macmillan, for the Project of the Churches on Human Rights and Responsibilities in the United Kingdom and the Republic of Ireland, 1988. Scholarly study, in English.

Cancado Trindade, A. A. "O Esgotamento dos Recursos Internos e a Evolucao da Nocao de 'Vitima' no Direito Internacional dos Direitos Humanos" (The Exhaustion of Internal Resources and the Notion of "Victim" in International Human Rights

Law). *Revista IIDH* 3 (Jan.-June 1986): 5–78. NGO scholarly article, in Portuguese.

Comision Para la Defensa de los Derechos Humanos en Centroamerica (Central American Commission for the Defense of Human Rights in Central America). *Elementos para la Defensa de los Derechos Humanos* (Materials for the Defense of Human Rights). San Jose, Costa Rica: 1987. NGO conference proceedings, in Spanish.

International Women's Rights Action Watch. *Assessing the Status of Women: A Guide to Using the Convention on the Elimination of All Forms of Discrimination against Women.* New York and Minneapolis, MN (USA): 1988. NGO manual, in English.

SOS Torture. *Practical Guide to the International Procedures relative to Complaint and Appeals against Acts of Torture, Disappearances and Other Inhuman or Degrading Treatment.* Geneva, Switzerland: 1988. NGO manual, in English.

Zwart, T. "Consideration of Human Rights Violations by International Organs: The Case of Suriname." *SIM Newsletter* 12 (Oct. 1985): 34–43. NGO article, in English.

Science and Technology

Comittee in Support of Solidarity. "In Defense of Academic Freedom: A Half Year's Struggle." *Committee in Support of Solidarity Reports* 36 (5 Oct. 1985); 19–26. NGO bulletin, in English.

Development Cooperation Information Department of the Ministry of Foreign Affairs. *Development Cooperation and the World Economy.* Cooperation between the Netherlands and Developing Countries No. 16. The Hague: n.d. Government report, in English.

Premont, D., M. Tom, and P. Mayenzet. *Essais sur le Concept de "Droits de Vivre"* (Essays on the Concept of a "Right to Live"). Brussels, Belgium: Bruylant, for the Association de Consultants Internationaux en Droits de l'Homme, 1988. Scholarly edited collection, in English and French.

Tinker, Jon. "AIDS in the Developing Countries." *Issues in Science and Technology* (Winter 1988): 43–48. Scholarly article, in English.

Self-Determination

Bizot, Jack. *The Forgotten Cause: East Timor's Right to Self-Determination.* London: Parliamentary Human Rights Group, 1988. NGO report, in English.

Boldt, M., and J. A. Long, eds. *The Quest for Justice: Aboriginal Peoples and Aboriginal Rights.* Toronto, Canada: University of Toronto Press, 1985. Edited collection, in English.

Brostad, J., J. Dahl, A. Gray, et al, eds. *Native Power: The Quest for Autonomy and Nationhood of Indigenous Peoples.* Oslo, Norway: International Work Group for Indigenous Affairs and Universitetsforlaget, 1985. Scholarly edited collection, in English; bibliography, on the works of Helge Kleivan, pp. 342–348.

Burger, Julian. *Report from the Frontier: The State of the World's Indigenous Peoples.* London (UK) and Cambridge, MA (USA): Zed Books and Cultural Survival, 1987. NGO monograph, in English; bibliography, pp. 293–300.

Christian Conference of Asia: *HEIWA: Life for the People.* Kowloon, Hong Kong: 1985. NGO conference proceedings, in English.

Cassese, A., and E. Jouve, eds. *Pour un Droit des Peuples: Essais sur la Declaration d'Alger* (For the Right of Peoples: Essays on the Algiers Declaration). Paris: Berger-Levrault, 1978. Edited collection, in French.

El Salhi, Abderachmen. "The Right to Self-Determination." Paper presented at the Second International Conference on Peoples Rights, Cairo, Egypt, Center for International Legal and Economic Studies, Zagazig University, 25–28 Nov. 1985. Unpublished conference paper, in Arabic.

Gibson, Richard. *African Liberation Movements: Contemporary Struggles against White Minority Rule.* London: Oxford University Press, for the Institute of Race Relations, 1972. Scholarly study, in English; bibliography, pp. 333–336.

Gray, Andrew, comp. *IWGIA Yearbook 1987: Indigenous Peoples and Development.* Copenhagen, Denmark: International Work Group for Indigenous Affairs, 1987. NGO report, in English.

Gretton, John. *Western Sahara—The Fight for Self-Determination.* London: Anti-Slavery Society, 1976. NGO report, in English.

Hannum, Hurst. *Autonomy, Sovereignty and Self-Determination: The Accommodation of Conflicting Rights.* Philadelphia, PA (USA): University of Pennsylvania Press, 1990. Scholarly study, in English.

International Committee of the Red Cross. *Annual Report 19—.* Geneva, Switzerland. NGO annual report, in English and French.

International Work Group for Indigenous Affairs. *IWGIA Yearbook 19—: Indigenous Peoples and Human Rights.* Copenhagen, Denmark. NGO yearbook, in English.

————. *Self-Determination and Indigenous Peoples: Sami Rights and Northern Perspectives.* Copenhagen, Denmark, 1987. NGO conference proceedings, in English.

Julien, Pierre. "Droits de l'Homme et Droit a l'Auto-determination" (Human Rights and the Right to

Self-Determination). Paper presented at the Second International Conference on Peoples Rights, Cairo, Egypt, Center for International Legal and Economic Studies, Zagazig University, 25–28 Nov. 1985. Unpublished conference paper, in French.

Kircher, Ingrid A. *The Kanaks of New Caldonia*. London: Minority Rights Group, 1986. NGO report, in English; bibliography, classified into books, articles, newspapers, journals, bulletins, and documents.

Kiss, Alexandre. "The Peoples' Right to Self-Determination." *Human Rights Law Journal* 7, no. 2–4 (1986): 165–175. Scholarly article, in English.

Mazzawi, Musa. "Salf-Determination in International Law: A Study of the Rhodesian Case." *Poly Law Review* 1, no. 1 (Summer 1975): 15–23. Scholarly article, in English.

Nwosu, Humphrey N. "The Concepts of Nationalism and Right to Self-Determination: Cameroon as a Case Study." *Africa Quarterly* 2 (1976): 256–273. Scholarly article, in English.

Ortiz, R. D. *Indians of the Americas: Human Rights and Self-Determination*. London: Zed Books, 1984. Scholarly monograph, in English; bibliography, pp. 281–305.

Paust, J. J. "Aggression against Authority: The Crime of Oppression, Politicide and Other Crimes against Human Rights." *Case Western Reserve Journal of International Law* 18, no. 2 (Spring 1986): 283–306. Scholarly article, in English.

Roach, Charles. "Righteous Ambiguity: International Law and the Indigenous Peoples." *Without Prejudice: The EAFORD International Review of Racial Discrimination* 1, no. 1 (Fall 1987): 30–47. NGO article, in English.

Thompson, Ruth, ed. *The Rights of Indigenous Peoples in International Law: Selected Essays on Self-Determination*. Saskatoon, Saskatchewan (Canada): Native Law Centre, University of Saskatchewan, 1987. NGO conference proceedings, in English.

Thornberry, Patrick. *Minorities and Human Rights Law*. London: Minority Rights Group, 1987. NGO report, in English.

Thurer, Daniel. "The Rights of Self-Determination." *Law and State* 35 (1987): 22–39. Scholarly article, in English.

United Nations Commission on Human Rights. *The Right of Peoples to Self-Determination and its Application to Peoples under Colonial or Alien Domination or Foreign Occupation: Report of the Secretary-General*, E/CN.4/1987/12 and Add. 1. Geneva, Switzerland: 1986, 1987. IGO document, in English.

SEE ALSO *Minorities*

Slavery

Ashoor, Yadh ben. "Islam and International Humanitarian Law." *International Review of the Red Cross* 62, no. 722 (March-April 1980): 59–69. Scholarly article, in English.

Averick, Sara M. *A Human Rights Comparison: Israel Vs. the Arab States*. Washington, D.C.: American Israel Public Affairs Committee, 1988. NGO report, in English.

Davis, D. B. *Slavery and Human Progress*. New Haven, CT (USA): Yale University Press, 1984. Scholarly study, in English.

de Souza Martins, Jose. "A Escravidae Hoje no Brazil" (Slavery Today in Brazil). *Cadernos do CEAS* 104 (July-Aug. 1986): 52–54. NGO journal article, in Portuguese.

Downing, T.E., and G. Kushner, eds. *Human Rights and Anthropology*. Cambridge, MA (USA): Cultural Survival, 1988. Edited collection/bibliography, in English.

Hancock, Ian. *The Pariah Syndrome: An Account of Gypsy Slavery and Persecution*. Ann Arbor, MI (USA): Karoma Publishers, 1987. Scholarly monograph, in English; bibliography, pp. 163–175.

International Centre for the Legal Protection of Human Rights. *Life, Liberty and Security of Person: Selected International Human Rights Instruments*. London: 1986. Document collection, in English.

Lovejoy, Paul. *Transformations in Slavery*. Cambridge, MA (USA): Cultural Survival, 1988. Scholarly study, in English.

M'Baye, Keba. "Les Realites du Monde Noir et les Droits de l'Homme" (The Realities of the Black World and Human Rights). *Revue des Droits de l'Homme: Droit International et Droit Compare* 2, no.3 (1969): 382–394. Scholarly article, in French.

Mercer, John. *Slavery in Mauritania Today*. Edinburgh, Scotland: Human Rights Group, 1982. NGO report, in English.

Miers, S., and I. Kopytoff, eds. *Slavery in Africa: Historical and Anthropological Perspectives*. Madison, WI (USA): University of Wisconsin Press, 1977. Scholarly edited collection, in English.

Nowak, M., D. Steurer, and H. Tretter, eds. *Fortschritt im Bewusstsein der Grund- und Menschenrechte: Festschrift fur Feli Ermacora* (Progress in the Spirit of Human Rights: Essays in Honor of Felix Ermacora). Kehl am Rhein, FRG: N.P. Engel Verlag, 1988. Scholarly edited collection, in English and German.

Plant, Roger. *Sugar and Modern Slavery: A Tale of Two Countries*. London: Zed Press, 1987. Scholarly monograph, in English; annotated suggestions for further reading, pp. 168–172.

Umozurike, U. O. "The African Slave Trade and the Attitudes of International Law towards It." *Howard Law Journal* 16, no. 2 (1971): 334–349. Scholarly article, in English.

Social Security

Comite Pro Justicia y Paz de Guatemala (Justice and Peace Committee of Guatemala). *Human Rights in Guatemala: Summary of the Report on the Human Rights Situation in Guatemala (Nov. 1984–Oct. 1985).* Report presented to the UN Commission on Human Rights, 42d sess. Trans. from Spanish by the World Council of Churches. Guatemala: 1986. NGO report, in English.

Evers, T., P. Molan, and P. Burgess. *The Treatment of Disabled Persons in Social Security and Taxation Law.* Canberra, Australia: Human Rights Commission, 1986. Government monograph, in English.

Health and Welfare Rights, Social Policy and the Needs of Women and Children: A Human Rights Research Agenda—Report on a Conference. New York: Center for the Study of Human Rights, Columbia University, n.d. Preliminary draft of an NGO conference report, in English.

Heringa, Aalt Willem. "Recent Dutch Cases Invalidating Discriminatory Social Security Laws." *SIM Newsletter: Netherlands Quarterly of Human Rights* 6, no. 1 (1988): 19–26. NGO article, in English.

Honduras Information Center. "The Human Rights Situation in Honduras, 1986." *Honduras Update* 1 (May 1987). NGO special issue, in English.

International Social Security Association. *Current Research in Social Security.* Geneva, Switzerland: 1986. Research abstracts; in English, French, German, and Spanish.

Kaufman, Otto. "International Aspects of Social Security in the French-speaking Countries South of the Sahara." *Law and State* 34 (1986): 106–119. Scholarly article, in English.

Organizacion Regional Interamericana de Trabajadores (Regional Interamerican Organization of Workers). *Los Derechos Sindicales en Centroamerica* (The Rights of Trade Unions in Central America). Mexico City, Mexico: 1988. NGO report, in Spanish.

Sheehan, R., and J. Jardine. *Epilepsy and Human Rights.* Canberra, Australia: Human Rights Commission, 1984. Government monograph, in English.

Statelessness

Africa News Service. "Rwanda: The Right to Choose." *Africa News* 30, no. 3 (8 Aug. 1988): 6–7. NGO article, in English.

British Refugee Council. "Citizenship Crisis Solved for Plantation Tamils." *Sri Lanka Monitor* 8 (Oct. 1988). NGO article, in English.

Touman, Khalil. "The Human Side of Family Reunification." *Al-Fajr* 8, no. 351 (6 Feb. 1987): 8. News article, in English.

Vije, Mayan. *Where Serfdom Thrives: The Plantation Tamils of Sri Lanka.* Madras, India: Tamil Information and Research Unit, 1987. NGO report, in English.

State of Emergency

Americas Watch Committee. *Human Rights in Panama.* New York: 1988. NGO mission report, in English.

Amnesty International. *Human Rights Violations in Paraguay.* London: 1985. NGO report, in English.

——————. *South Africa: Detention under the State of Emergency.* London: 1985. NGO report, in English.

——————. *States of Emergency: Torture and Violations of the Right to Life under States of Emergency.* London: 1988. NGO report, in English.

Asian Legal Resource Centre. *Use of Emergency Regulations in Peacetime in the Region, Workshop Papers, Kuala Lumpur, 5–8 Oct. 1987.* Kowloon, Hong Kong: 1987. NGO conference papers, in English.

Basson, Dion. "Judicial Activism in a State of Emergency: An Examination of Recent Decisions of the South African Courts." *South African Journal on Human Rights* 3, pt. 1 (March 1987): 28–43. Scholarly article, in English.

Berkeley, B., and E. Schrage. *Zimbabwe: Wages of War—A Report of Human Rights.* New York: Lawyers Committee for Human Rights, 1986. NGO mission report, in English.

Chadha, Amit Singh. *Terrorism in the Punjab.* Cambridge, MA (USA): 1986. Unpublished student paper, in English; bibliography.

Comision de Derechos Humanos de El Salvador (Human Rights Commission of El Salvador). *Situacion de los Derechos Humanos y las Libertades Fundamentales en El Salvador* (The Situation of Human Rights and Fundamental Liberties in El Salvador). San Salvador, El Salvador: 1987. NGO report, in Spanish.

Comision para la Defensa de los Derechos Humanos en Centroamerica (Central American Commission for the Defense of Human Rights). *Human Rights in Central America: Summary of the Prevailing Situation in Guatemala, El Salvador, and Honduras.* San Jose, Costa Rica: 1986. NGO report, in English.

Comite para la Defensa de los Derechos Humanos en Honduras (Committee to Defend Human Rights in Honduras). *Human Rights in Honduras.* Somerville, MA (USA): Honduras Information Center, 1988. NGO report, in English.

Detainees' Parents Support Committee. *Review of 1987.* Johanesburg, South Africa: 1988. NGO report, in English.

Garcia-Sayan, Diego. *Habeas Corpus y Estados de Emergencia* (Habeas Corpus and States of Emergency). Lima, Peru: Comision Andina de Juristas and the Friedrich Nauman Foundation, 1988. NGO report, in Spanish.

Himwiingwa, Paulsen Afro. *Emergency Powers in Zambia.* Zambia: University of Zambia, 1984. LLM dissertation, in English.

Human Awareness Programme. *Militarisation Dossier.* Johannesburg, South Africa: 1986. NGO dossier, in English.

Info-Turk. *Black Book on the Militarist "Democracy" in Turkey.* Brussels, Belgium: 1986. NGO report, in English.

Inter-American Commission on Human Rights. *Report of the Situation of Human Rights in Chile.* Washington, D.C.: 1985. IGO mission report, in English.

International Commission of Jurists. *States of Emergency: Their Impact on Human Rights.* Geneva, Switzerland: 1983. NGO report, in English.

International League for Human Rights. "Human Rights during the State of Siege: The Real Situation, Nov. 6, 1984–June 16, 1985." *News from the Chilean Commission for Human Rights.* Trans. from Spanish by ILHR. New York: 1985. Occasional series, in English.

——————. *Tunisia's Human Rights Record: A Critique of the Government's Official Report to the UN Human Rights Committee.* New York: 1986. NGO report, in English.

Koshy, Ninan. "The Erosion of the Rule of Law in Asia." *Human Rights Forum* (March 1988): 1–8. NGO article, in English.

Luce, D., and R. Rumpf. *Martial Law in Taiwan.* Washington, D.C.: Asia Resource Center and Formosan Association for Human Rights, 1985. Monograph, in English; bibliography lists resources and organizations.

Melendez, Florentin. *La Suspension de los Derechos Fundamentales en El Derecho Internacional Convencional* (Suspension of Fundamental Rights in International Conventional Law). San Salvador, El Salvador: Instituto de Derechos Humanos, Universidad Centroamericana "Jose Simeon Canas," 1987. Scholarly monograph, in Spanish.

Regional Council on Human Rights in Asia. *The Law and Practice of Preventive Detention in the ASEAN Region.* Manila, Philippines: 1988. NGO report, in English.

Shraga, Daphna. "Human Rights in Emergency Situations under the European Convention on Human Rights." In *Israel Yearbook on Human Rights,* 217–242. Jerusalem, Israel: Alpha Press, 1986. Scholarly article, in English.

U.S. Helsinki Watch Committee. *Violations of the Helsinki Accords: Poland.* New York: 1986. NGO report, in English.

SEE ALSO *Martial Law*

State Terrorism

Aspen Institute for Humanistic Studies. *State Crimes: Punishment or Pardon.* Aspen, CO (USA): 1988. NGO conference papers, in English.

Bowen, Gordon L. "The Political Economy of State Terrorism: Barrier to Human Rights in Guatemala." In *Human Rights and Third World Development,* ed. G.W. Shephard, Jr., and V. Nanda, 83–124. Westport, CT (USA): Greenwood Press, 1985. Scholarly study, in English.

Committee against Repression and for Democratic Rights in Iraq. *Saddam's Iraq: Revolution or Reaction?* 2d ed. London: Zed Books, 1989. Edited collection, in English; bibliography.

Conquest, Robert. *The Harvest of Sorrow: Soviet Collectivization and the Terror—Famine.* New York: Oxford University Press, 1986. Scholarly monograph, in English; bibliography, pp. 394–396 (this selected bibliography includes collected individual testimonies and documents, accounts by former party activists, and Soviet fictional accounts.

Database Project on Palestinian Human Rights. *Uprising Update: Dec. 8, 1988—Human Rights at the End of Year One of the Palestinian Uprising.* Chicago, IL (USA): 1988. NGO document collection, in English.

Giraldo, Javier. *Algunos Rasgos de la Situation de Violencia que Vive Hoy Colombia* (Some Features of Violence in Colombia Today). Bogota, Colombia: Centro de Investigacion y Educacion Popular, 1987. NGO report, in Spanish.

Independent Commission on International Humanitarian Issues. *Disappeared! Technique of Terror.* London: 1986. NGO report/study, in English.

Info-Turk. *Black Book on the Militarist "Democracy" in Turkey.* Brussels, Belgium: 1986. NGO report, in English.

Institut des Etudes Palestiniennes. "Le terrorisme d'Etat israelien en mer" (Israeli State Terrorism at Sea). *Revue d'Etudes Palestiniennes* 26 (Winter 1988): 71–88. Scholarly article, in French.

Instituto de Derechos Humanos, Universidad Centroamericana "Jose Simeon Canas" (Human Rights Institute, Central American University "Jose Simeon Canas") and Center for International Affairs, Harvard University. *La resistencia no violenta ante los regimens salvadorenos que han utilizade el terror institucionlizado en el periodo 1972–1987* (Nonviolent Resistance toward Salvadoran Regimes Using Institutionalized Terror, 1972–1987). San Salvador, El Salvador: 1988. Research paper, in Spanish.

Lewellen, Ted C. "Structures of Terror: A Systems Analysis of Repression in El Salvador." In *Human Rights and Third World Development*, ed. G. W. Shephard, Jr., and V. Nanda, 59–81. Scholarly article, in English; bibliography, 79–81.

Luce, D., and R. Rumpf. *Martial Law in Taiwan*. Washington, D.C.: Asia Resource Center and Formosan Association for Human Rights, 1985. Monograph, in English; bibliography lists resources and organizations.

Martinez, Victoria, comp. *Terrorismo de Estado: Efectos Psicologicos en los Ninos (State Terrorism: Psychological Effects on Children)*. Buenos Aires, Argentina: Movimiento Solidario de Salud Mental, 1987. NGO monograph, in Spanish; classified bibliography, 166–167.

National Lawyers Guild, Lawyers Committee against U.S. Intervention in Central America. *Counterinsurgency as Terrorism: Human Rights Violations in Guatemala*. Boston, MA (USA): National Immigration Project, 1983. NGO report, in English.

People's Union for Democratic Rights. *Behind the Killings in Bihar: A Report on Patna, Gaya and Singhbum*. New Delhi, India: 1986. NGO mission report, in English.

—————————. *Communal Terrorism in the Punjab*. New Delhi, India: 1987. NGO issue paper, in English.

Singh, Devinderrjit. *Sikhs, Arms and Terrorism*. Cambridge (UK): Cambridge University Sikh Society, 1986. Monograph, in English.

Stohl, M., and G. A. Lopez, ed. *Government Violence and Repression: An Agenda for Research*. Westport, CT (USA): Greenwood Press, 1986. Scholarly edited collection, in English; bibliographic note.

—————————. *Terrible beyond Endurance? The Foreign Policy of State Terrorism*. Westport, CT (USA): Greenwood Press, 1988. Scholarly edited collection, in English; bibliography, in essay form, pp. 337–342.

Van Der Vyver, J. D. "State-Sponsored Terror Violence." *South African Journal on Human Rights* 4, no. 1 (March 1988): 55–75. Scholarly article, in English.

Territorial Rights

Adar, Korwa Gombe. "The Principles of Self-Determination and Territorial Integrity Make Strange Litigants in International Relations: A Recapitulation." *Indian Journal of international Law* 26, no. 2–3 (July–Dec. 1986): 425–477. Scholarly article, in English.

Hough, W.J.H., III. "The Annexation of the Baltic States and its Effect on the Development of Law Prohibiting Forcible Seizure of Territory." *New York Law School Journal of International and Comparative Law* 6, no. 2 (Winter 1985). NGO article journal, in English.

Korsmo, Fae L. "Nordic Security and the Saami Minority: Territorial Rights in Northern Fennoscandia." *Human Rights Quarterly* 10, no. 4 (Nov. 1988): 509–524. Scholarly article, in English.

Terrorism and Other International Crimes

Americas Watch Committee. *The Continuing Terror: Seventh Supplement to the Report on Human Rights in El Salvador*. New York: 1985. NGO report, in English.

Aspen Institute for Humanistic Studies. *State Crimes: Punishment or Pardon*. Aspen, CO (USA): 1986. NGO conference papers, in English.

Baunach, P. J. "The U.S.-U.K. Supplementary Extradition Treaty: Justice for Terrorists or Terror for Justice?" *Connecticut Journal of International Law* 2, no. 2 (Spring 1987): 463–498. Scholarly article, in English.

Comision Andina de Juristas (Andean Commission of Jurists). "Peru: Tribunales Especiales y Terrorismo" Peru: Specialized Tribunals and Terrorism). *Boletin Comision Andina de Juristas* 13 (Dec. 1986): 12–14. NGO bulletin article, in Spanish.

Gersony, Robert. *Summary of Mozambican Refugee Accounts of Principally Conflict-Related Experience in Mozambique*. Washington, D.C.: U. S. Department of State, 1988. Government report, in English.

Giraldo, Javier. *Algunos Rasgos de la Situation de Violencia que Vive Hoy Colombia (Some Features of Violence in Colombia Today)*. Bogota, Colombia: Centro de Investigacion y Educacion Popular, 1987. NGO report, in Spanish.

Institut des Etudes Palestiniennes (Institute of Palestine Studies). "Le Terrorisme d'Etat Israelien en Mer" (Israeli State Terrorism at Sea). *Revue d'Etudes Palestiniennes* 26 (Winter 1988): 71–88. Scholarly article, in French.

Media Analysis Center. "Kuwait: Facing Terrorist Challenges and Internal Entanglements." *Contemporary Mideast Backgrounder* 246 (May 1988). NGO paper, in English.

National Lawyers Guild and Lawyers Committee against U. S. Intervention in Central America. *Counterinsurgency as Terrorism: Human Rights Violations in Guatemala.* Boston, MA (USA): National Immigration Project, 1983. NGO report in English.

Patrnogic, J., and Z. Meriboute. *Terrorism and International Law.* San Remo, Italy: International Institute of Humanitarian Law, 1987. Scholarly article, in English.

People's Union for Democratic Rights. *Communal Terrorism in Punjab.* New Delhi, India: 1987. NGO report, in English.

Pyle, C. H. "Defining Terrorism." *Foreign Policy* 64 (Fall 1986): 63–78. Scholarly article, in English.

Rubin, B. R. *Cycles of Violence: Human Rights in Sri Lanka since the Indo-Sri Lanka Agreement.* Washington, D.C.: Asia Watch, 1987. NGO report, in English.

Schmid, A. P. *Political Terrorism: A Research Guide to Concepts, Theories, Data Bases and Literature.* New Brunswick, NJ (USA): Transaction Books, 1986. Research guide, in English.

Schmid, A.P., A. J. Jongman, et al. *Political Terrorism: A New Guide to Actors, Authors, Concepts, Data Bases, Theories and Literature.* 2d ed. New Brunswick, NJ (USA): Transaction Books, 1988. Handbook/directory/bibliography, in English.

Singh, D. *Sikhs, Arms and Terrorism* Cambridge, UK: Cambridge University Sikh Society, 1986. Scholarly monograph, in English.

Washington Office on Africa Educational Fund and Mozambique Support Network. *Apartheid's Contras: Rural Terrorism and Mozambique's Struggle for Survival.* Washington, D.C.: 1988. NGO report, in English.

Torture

American Association for the Advancement of Science, Committee on Scientific Freedom and Responsibility. *The Open Secret: Torture and the Medical Profession in Chile.* Washington, D.C.: 1987. NGO report, in English.

Amnesty International. *File on Torture.* London: 1984. NGO report, in English.

──────. *Human Rights in Chile: The Role of the Medical Profession.* London: 1986. NGO report, in English.

──────. *States of Emergency: Torture and Violations of the Right to Life under States of Emergency.* London: 1988. NGO report, in English.

──────. *Torture in the Eighties.* London: 1984. NGO report, in English.

Christensen, Jan. "Amnesty International's Work for Children." *International Treatment and Rehabilitation of Torture Victims* 1, no. 2–3 (Jan. 1989): 3–5. NGO article, in English.

Claude, R., E. Stover, and J. Lopez. *Health Professionals and Human Rights in the Philippines.* Washington, D.C.: American Association for the Advancement of Science, Clearinghouse on Science and Human Rights: 1987. NGO report, in English.

"Doctors, Ethics, and Torture." *Danish Medical Bulletin* (Aug. 1987): 185–216. Conference proceedings, in English.

Lifton, Robert J. *The Nazi Doctors: Medical Killing and the Psychology of Genocide.* New York: Basic Books, 1986. Scholarly monograph, in English.

Marzouki, Moncef. *L'Arrache Corps* (The Broken Body). Paris: Editions Alternative et Paralleles, 1979. Scholarly monograph, in French; bibliography, pp. 255–257.

National Academy of Sciences. *Science and Human Rights.* Washington, D.C.: National Academy Press, 1988. NGO conference papers, in English.

Physicians for Human Rights. *Sowing Fear: The Uses of Torture and Psychological Abuse in Chile.* Somerville, MA (USA): 1988. NGO report, in English.

Ramshaw, P., and T. Steers. *Intervention on Trial: The New York War Crimes Tribunal on Central America and the Caribbean.* New York: Praeger Publishers and National Lawyers Guild, 1987. NGO report, in English.

Rayner, Mary. *Turning a Blind Eye: Medical Accountability and the Prevention of Torture in South Africa.* Washington, D.C.: American Association for the Advancement of Science, Committee on Scientific Freedom and Responsibility, 1987. NGO report, in English.

Rehabiliterings Center for Torturofre (Rehabilitation Centre for Torture Victims). *Annual Report 19──.* Copenhagen, Denmark. NGO annual report, in English.

SOS Torture. *Practical Guide to the International Procedures Relative to Complaint and Appeals against Acts of Torture, Disappearances and Other Inhuman or Degrading Treatment.* Geneva, Switzerland, 1988. Manual, in English.

Sottas, Eric. "Some Salient Features of the Convention against Torture and Other Cruel, Inhuman or Degrading Treatment or Punishment." *SOS Torture* 4 (Sept. 1986): 35–39. NGO journal article, in English and French.

──────. "The Role of NGOs in the Defence and Promotion of Human Rights, Especially in Relation to the Question of Torture." *SOS Torture* 6

(Jan. 1987): 28–35. NGO editorial, in English and French.

Stover, E., and E. Nightingale, eds. *The Breaking of Bodies and Minds: Torture, Psychiatric Abuse, and the Health Professionals.* New York: American Association for the Advancement of Science, 1985. Collection of essays, in English.

Trabajamos para la Vida: Consecuencias de la Represion en el Cono Sur, el Medico y los Derechos Humanos (We Work for Life: Consequences of Repression in the Southern Cone, Physicians and Human Rights). Montevideo, Uruguay: Universidad de la Republica, Facultad de Medicina, 1987. Conference proceedings, in Spanish.

United Nations Commission on Human Rights. *Question of the Human Rights of All Persons Subjected to any Form of Detention or Imprisonment, Torture and Other Cruel, Inhuman or Degrading Treatment or Punishment.* Report by Special Rapporteur P. Kooijmans, E/CN.4/1987/13, 43d sess. Geneva, Switzerland: 1987. IGO report, in English.

War Crimes

Aspen Institute for Humanistic Studies. *State Crimes: Punishment or Pardon.* Aspen, CO (USA): 1988. NGO conference papers, in English.

Bassiouni, Cherif. "Nuremberg Forty Years After: An Introduction." *Case Western Reserve Journal of International Law* 18, no. 2 (Spring 1986); 261–266. Scholarly article, in English.

Cotler, Irwin. Nazi War Crimes—An International Legal Responsibility." *Patterns of Prejudice* 20, no. 4 (Oct. 1986): 31–41. NGO journal article, in English.

Hamalengwa, Munyonzwe. *The Case for the Prosecution of Apartheid Criminals in Canada.* North York, Canada: 1988. NGO report, in English.

Lippman, Matthew. "The Denaturalization of Nazi War Criminals in the United States: Is Justice Being Served?" *Houston Journal of International Law* 7, no. 2 (Spring 1985); 169–214. Scholarly article, in English.

Max Planck Institute for Comparative Public and International Law. *Encyclopedia of Public International, Vol. 8: Human Rights and the Individual in International Law—International Economic Relations.* New York: North-Holland, 1985. Encyclopedia, in English; bibliography after each article.

Perez Esquivel, Adolfo. "El Juicio Debe Ir Mas Alla de las Juntas y Alcanzar a los Represores" (The Judgment Must Go beyond the Juntas and Reach Those Who Carried out the Repression). *Reencuentro* 1, no. 5 (June 1985): 11. NGO bulletin article, in Spanish.

Ramshaw, P., and T. Steers. *Intervention on Trial: The New York War Crimes Tribunal on Central America and the Caribbean.* New York: Praeger Publishers and the National Lawyers Guild, 1987. NGO study, in English.

Ruzie, Davie. "Klaus Barbie and the French Legal Process." *Patterns of Prejudice* 20, no. 3 (July 1986): 27–33. NGO article, in English.

Wieland, G. "40th Anniversary of the Nuremberg Trial of German Major War Criminals: The GDRs Contribution to Punishing Nazi Crimes." *GDR Committee for Human Rights Bulletin* 11, no. 3 (1985): 167–179. NGO bulletin article, in English.

World Jewish Congress, Commission on the Holocaust and Crimes of the Nazis. *Waldheim's Nazi Past: The Dossier.* Geneva, Switzerland: 1988. NGO report, in English.

Women

Change. *Thinkbook.* A series of reports and handbooks, including G. Ashworth, *Of Violence and Violation: Women and Human Rights* (London: 1986).

Femmes sous Lois Musulmanes (Women Living under Muslim Laws). *Dossier.* Journal published quarterly. Montpellier, France.

Flanz, Gisbert H. *Comparative Women's Rights and Political Participation in Europe.* Transnational Publishers, 1983. Scholarly study, in English.

Fraser, Arvonne S. *The UN Decade for Women: Documents and Dialog.* Boulder, CO (USA): Westview Press, 1987. Collection, in English.

Hevener, N. K. *International Law and the Status of Women.* Boulder, CO (USA): Westview Press, 1983. Scholarly study, in English.

Khushalani, Y. *Dignity and Honour of Women as Basic and Fundamental Human Rights.* Kluwer Academic, 1983. Scholarly study, in English; special focus of widespread rape of Bangladeshi women by Pakistanis in 1971.

Liddle, J., and R. Joshi. *Daughters of Independence: Gender, Caste and Class in India.* London: Zed Books, 1986. Scholarly study, in English.

International Women's Rights Action Watch. *Assessing the Status of Women: A Guide to Reporting Using the Convention on the Elimination of All Forms of Discrimination against Women.* New York: 1988. NGO report, in English.

—————. *The Women's Watch.* Quarterly newsletter, in English, published in Minneapolis, MN (USA) and New York.

International Women's Tribune Centre. *Rights of Women: A Workbook of International Conventions re-*

lating to Women's Issues and Concerns. New York: 1983. NGO workbook, in English.

──────. The Tribune: A Women and Development Quarterly. Newsletter, in English, published in New York.

Isis International. Powerful Images: A Women's Guide to Audiovisual Resources. Rome: 1986. Resource, in English.

──────. Rural Women in Latin America: Experiences from Ecuador, Peru and Chile. Santiago, Chile: 1987. NGO study, in English and Spanish.

──────. Women and Media: Analysis, Alternatives and Action. Rome: 1984. NGO study, in English.

──────. Women in Action. Quarterly journal, in English; also published in Spanish as Mujeres en Accion.

Isis: Women's International Cross-Cultural Exchange. Women's World. Quarterly newsletter, in English. Geneva, Switzerland.

Shreir, Sally, ed. Women's Movements of the World: An International Directory. London: Longman Group, 1988. Directory, in English.

United Nations. Report of the World Conference to Review and Appraise the Achievements of the United Nations Decade for Women: Equality, Development and Peace, Nairobi, 15–26 July 1985. New York: 1986. IGO conference report, in English.

Women's International Network. Female Sexual Mutilations: The Facts and Proposals for Action. Lexington, MA (USA): 1980.

──────. Win News. Quarterly journal, in English. Lexington, MA (USA).

SEE ALSO: Marriage.

Youth

Americas Watch Committee. Paraguay: Latin America's Oldest Dictatorship under Pressure. New York: 1986. NGO mission report, in English.

Amnesty International. China: Prisoners of Conscience in the People's Republic of China. London: 1987. NGO report, in English.

──────. Students Convicted in April 1983 by the Revolutionary Military Tribunal in the People's Republic of Mozambique. London: 1984. NGO report, in English.

Asamblea Permanente de Derechos Humanos de Bolivia (Permanent Assembly for Human Rights in Bolivia). "Los Derechos Humanos y Juventud (sic)" (Human Rights and Youth). Boletin 1, no. 3 (June 1985): 1–2. NGO bulletin, in Spanish.

Bir Zeit University. "An Urgent Appeal From Bir Zeit University," 15 April 1987. Urgent action bulletin, in English.

Bouvier, Virginia M. Decline of the Dictator: Paraguay at a Crossroads. Washington, D.C.: Washington Office on Latin America, 1988. NGO report, in English.

Bugajski, Janusz. Czechoslovakia: Charter 77's Decade of Dissent. New York and London: Praeger and the Center for Strategic and International Studies, 1987. Scholarly monograph, in English; bibliography summarizes 23 selected Charter 77 documents, presented in chronological order, pp. 104–114.

Centre for Socio-Legal Research and Documentation Service. "Young Persons Harmful Publications Act No. 93 of 1956." Socio-Legal Concern Newsletter 2, no. 5 (May 1986): 9–11. NGO bulletin article, in English.

Civil Liberties Organisation. Human Rights Condition in Nigeria: Mid-Year Report (Nov. 1987-May 1988). Lagos, Nigeria: 1988. NGO report, in English.

Collins, Frank. Non-Violence and Death at Bir Zeit University: An Investigative Report. Jerusalem: Database Project on Palestinian Human Rights, 1987. NGO report, in English.

East European Cultural Foundation. "Demonstration in Budapest." East European Reporter 2, no. 1 (Spring 1986): 2–3. NGO journal article, in English.

Idara-e-Aman-o-Insaf, Christian Conference of Asia. Pakistan: Struggle for Human Rights. Kowloon, Hong Kong: 1986. NGO edited collection, in English.

Index on Censorship. "Students and Trade Unionists Jailed in Tunisia." Briefing Paper 248 (14 July 1986): 1. NGO bulletin, in English.

"Iran's Universities Preyed upon by War and Repression," Iran Liberation, 10 June 1986. Newspaper narticle, in English.

Lawyers Committee for Human Rights. Liberia: A Promise Betrayed, a Report on Human Rights. New York: 1986. NGO report, in English.

Meagher, J. Patrick. Reflections on the Human Rights Situation in Indonesia. Jakarta, Indonesia: Institute for Development Studies, 1987. Research paper, in English.

North American Coalition for Human Rights in Korea. "Concentration Camps for Students Threatened in New 'Campus Stabilization Law.'" Korea Update 74 (15 Aug. 1985): 1–2. NGO newsletter article, in English.

Oxman, S. A., O. Triffterer, and F. B. Cruz. South Korea: Human Rights in the Emerging Politics—Report of an ICJ Mission from 25 March to 12 April 1987. Geneva, Switzerland: International Commission of Jurists, 1987. NGO mission report, in English.

"Problems of Contemporary Soviet Youth: Interview with Vasily Semenov, Former Sailor in the Soviet Fishing Fleet." *Samizdat Bulletin* 146 (June 1985). NGO bulletin, in English.

Radio Free Europe/Radio Liberty. "Independent Students' Association Demands Legalization." *Radio Free Europe Research* 13, no. 8 (26 Feb. 1988). Government article, in English.

Shehadeh, Raja. *Occupier's Law: Israel and the West Bank.* Washington, D.C.: Institute for Palestine Studies and Law in the Service of Man, 1985. NGO report, in English.

Stevens-Arroyo, A. M. "Human Rights in Puerto Rico: 1985," 17 March 1985. Scholarly unpublished paper, in English.

Thoolen, Hans, ed. *Indonesia and the Rule of Law: Twenty Years of "New Order" Government.* London: Francis Pinter Publishers, for the International Commission of Jurists and the Netherlands Institute of Human Rights, 1987. Scholarly NGO report, in English.

APPENDIX B

GLOSSARY

ABROGATION. Annulment, cancellation, or repeal of a law or rule by legislative or other constitutional authority or by usage that invalidates it.

ABUSE OF RIGHTS. Excessive or unreasonable invocation of rights contrary to limitations or restrictions legitimately placed upon them.

ACCEPTANCE. The act by which a State establishes definitively its consent to be bound by the terms of a particular treaty or other bilateral or multilateral agreement. Acceptance may be by ratification, by accession, or by succession. Signature of a treaty or agreement normally constitutes only a preliminary to acceptance.

AD HOC. (L). "For a special purpose." In the international community, an *ad hoc* committee or commission is one created to perform a single mandate and ceases to exist after it has fulfilled its mandate.

ALIEN. An individual who is not a national of the State in which he or she is present.

AMNESTY. The abolition or overlooking an offence of a political nature, such as treason or rebellion—by a government, frequently on condition that the offender resume his duties as a citizen within a prescribed time.

APARTHEID. A system of institutionalized racial segregation and discrimination for the purpose of establishing and maintaining domination by one racial group of persons over another racial group of persons and systematically oppressing them, such as that pursued in South Africa.

APARTHEID **IN SPORTS.** Application of the policies and practices of *apartheid* in sports activities, whether organized on a professional or an amateur basis.

ASYLUM. The principle that everyone has the right to seek and enjoy freedom from persecution in other countries, embodied in the Universal Declaration of Human Rights. Territorial asylum refers to the right of States to admit into their territory, or to refuse to extradite, persons persecuted elsewhere for political reasons. Diplomatic asylum refers to the right of States to offer refuge in their legations to persons persecuted for political reasons in countries where the legations are located.

BIOLOGICAL WEAPONS. Living organisms—whatever their nature or the infective material derived from them—which are intended to cause disease or death in man, animals, or plants; and which depend for their effects on their ability to multiply in the person, animal, or plant attacked.

CHEMICAL WEAPONS. Weapons which employ chemical sustances, whether gaseous, liquid, or solid, because of their direct toxic effects on man, animals, or plants.

COLLECTIVE BARGAINING. All negotiations which take place between an employer, a group of employers or one or more employers' organizations, on the one hand, and one or more workers' organizations, on the other, for (1) determining working conditions and terms of employment; and/or (2) regulating relations between employers and workers; and/or (3) regulating relations between employers or their organizations and a workers' organization.

CONCILIATION. Settlement of a dispute between two parties by a third party acting as mediator, with a view to reaching an amicable settlement.

CONSENT. Agreement of the parties legally concerned.

CONTRACTING STATE. One which has consented to be bound by a treaty, whether or not the treaty has entered into force.

CONVENTION. A term, in UN usuage, which indicates a treaty concluded between two or among more

States. Human rights conventions are international agreements containing provisions to promote or protect one or more human rights or fundamental freedoms. Such conventions are normally prepared by a body within the UN system or by a special conference convened for that purpose and are open for signature and ratification by the States specified in the convention. A convention enters into force only after it has been ratified by the number of States specified in one of its articles and is legally binding only upon those States which have ratified it.

CONVENTIONAL WEAPONS. Military armament or all kinds, except nuclear, chemical, or biological weapons.

COPYRIGHT. The exclusive legal right to reproduce, publish, and sell the matter and form of any produced work. Under various conventions, copyright protection extends to the rights of authors, organizations, and other proprietors in literary, scientific, and artistic works, including writings; musical, dramatic, and cinematographic works; paintings, engravings, and sculpture; published and unpublished works; and translations, among others.

CORPUS JURIS CIVILIS. (L) The body of civil law.

COUP D'ETAT. (Fr) A sudden, decisive exercise of force in politics, usually involving the violent overthrow of a government by a group of conspirators.

COVENANT. A treaty of exceptional importance, concluded between two or more States.

CRIMES AGAINST HUMANITY. Actions punishable as crimes under international law and encompassing murder, extermination, enslavement, deportation and other inhuman acts done against any civilian population, or persecutions on political, racial, or religious grounds, when such acts are done or such persecutions are carried on or in execution of or in connection with any crime against peace or any war crime.

CRIMES AGAINST PEACE. Actions punishable as crimes under international law and encompassing (1) the planning, preparation, initiation, or waging of a war of aggression or a war in violation of international treaties, agreements, or assurances; or (2) participation in a common plan or conspiracy for the accomplishment of any of the acts mentioned in (1).

DECLARATION. A formal and solemn instrument, setting our principles of great and lasting

importance. As contrasted with conventions, declarations adopted by United Nations organs are morally but not legally binding upon all member States; they set out international principles and standards with which all States are expected to comply.

DECOLONIZATION. The process by which a trust or non-self-governing territory or a territory subjected to alien subjugation, domination, or exploitation achieves independence and self-government.

DEROGATION. Refusal or failure of a State party to a treaty to fulfill an obligation that it has accepted under the treaty.

DEVELOPMENT. Participation in, contribution to, and enjoyment by every human being and all peoples of cultural, social, economic, and political objectives.

DISABLED PERSON. A person unable to ensure by him- or herself, wholly or partly, the necessities of a normal individual and/or social life, as a result of deficiency, either congenital or not, in his or her physical or mental capabilities.

DISCRIMINATION. Any distinction, exclusion, limitation, or preference which, being based on race, color, sex, language, religion, political or other opinion, national or social origin, economic condition, property, or birth, has the purpose or effect of nullifying or impairing equality of treatment.

DISINFORMATION. Purposeful release and dissemination of false or distorted information.

DISINVESMTENT. Withdrawal of assets or invested funds, or cancellation of financial aid or subsidies, as a protest against a national public policy which is internationally unacceptable.

EQUALITY OF STATES. The principle that every independent State enjoys full equality with all other independent States, regardless of discrepancies of power.

EXTRADITION. The delivery of a suspected or convicted person by the State in which the person is located to the State in the jurisdiction of which the offense was committed or the person convicted.

FORCED OR COMPULSORY LABOR. Work or service which is exacted from any person for any penalty and for which the person has not offered himself voluntarily.

GENOCIDE. Any of the following acts committed with intent to destroy, in whole or in part, a national, ethnical, racial, or religious group as such: (1) killing members of the group; (2) causing serious bodily or mental harm to members of the group; (3) deliberately inflicting on the group conditions of life calculated to bring about its physical destruction in whole or in part; (4) imposing measures intended to prevent births within the group; and (5) forcibly transferring children of the group to another group.

GOOD OFFICES. An endeavor by an impartial third party (usually a high-ranking national or international official or a commission composed of such officials) to bring together States involved in a dispute with a view to persuading them to reach an amicable settlement.

HABEAS CORPUS. (L) An order requiring that a detained person be brought before a judge or court within a specified time for investigation of the legality of his detention.

HEGEMONY. Predominant political, economic, or other influence exercised by one State over another, or over a group of States.

HOSTAGE. A person seized, detained, or threatened with death or injury in order to compel a third party—such as a State, an intergovernmental organization, a natural or juridical person, or a group of persons—to do or abstain from doing any act as an explicit or implicit condition for his release.

INCENDIARY WEAPON. A shell, bomb, or grenade containing a substance that burns with an intense heat.

INDIGENOUS PEOPLES. A term applied to (a) tribal peoples in independent countries whose social, cultural and economic conditions distinguish them from other sections of the national community, and whose status is regulated wholly or partially by their own traditions or by special laws or regulations; (b) peoples in independent countries who are descendents of the populations which inhabited the country, or a geographical region to which the country belongs, at the time of conquest or colonization or the establishment of present State boundaries and who, irrespective of their legal status, retain some or all of their own social, economic, cultural, and political institutions. Self-identification as tribal or native is regarded as a fundamental criterion for determining whether a people is to be regarded as indigenous.

INTERNATIONAL ORGANIZATION. An organization composed of States.

JUS COGENS. (L) A peremptory norm of general international law, i.e., a standard accepted and recognized by the international community of States as a whole as one from which no derogation is permitted and one which can be modified only by a subsequent norm of general international law having the same character. If a new peremptory norm of general international law should emerge, any existing treaty in conflict with that norm becomes void and ends.

LAW ENFORCEMENT OFFICIALS. All officers of the law, whether appointed or elected, who exercise police powers, especially the powers of arrest or detention. In countries where police powers are exercised by military authorities, whether uniformed or not, or by State security forces, officers of such services are regarded as law enforcement officials.

LIMITATIONS. Restrictions on the exercise or full enjoyment of rights or freedoms.

MARTIAL LAW. Government or control by military forces over civilians or civilian authorities in domestic territory. Also a wartime system of government or control established or administered in hostile territory under which existing civil laws and the normal administration of justice are replaced by a system dependent solely on the will of the military commander.

MERCENARY. Any person who (a) is specially recruited locally or abroad to fight in an armed conflict; (b) is motivated to take part in the hostilities essentially by the desire for private gain and, in fact, is promised, by or on behalf of a party to the conflict, material compensation substantially in excess of that promised or paid to combatants of similar rank and functions in the armed forces of that party; (c) is neither a national of a party to the conflict nor a resident of territory controlled by a party to the conflict; (d) is not a member of the armed forces of a party to the conflict; and (e) has not been sent by a State which is not a party to the conflict on official duty as a member of its armed forces. Also any person who, in any other situation, (a) is specially recruited locally or abroad for the purpose of participating in a concerted act of violence aimed at: (i) overthrowing a government or otherwise undermining the constitutional order of a State; or (ii) undermining the territorial integrity of a State; (b) is motivated to take part therein essentially by the desire for significant private gain and is prompted by the promise or payment of material compensation; (c) is neither a national nor a resident of the State against which such an act is directed; (d) has not been sent by a State on official duty; and (e) is not a member of the armed forces of the State on whose territory the act is undertaken.

MIGRANT WORKER. Any person who leaves a country in which he is a citizen and travels to another country, otherwise than on his own account, with a view to being employed. The term *excludes* frontier workers; artists and members of liberal professions who have entered the country on a short-term basis; seamen; persons coming specifically for training or education; and employees of organizations and States who have travelled to that country at the request of their employer to undertake specific duties or assignments, for a limited and defined period of time, and who are required to leave that country on the completion of their assigment.

NEGOTIATING STATE. A State that participated in the drawing up of a treaty.

NEO-COLONIALISM. The *de facto* exercise of economic or political dominance by a strong nation over a weak nation or group of nations without reducing them *de jure* to colonial status.

NON BIS IN IDEM. (L) The principle that no one should be tried twice for the same crime.

NON-INTERVENTION. The principle that no State or group of States has the right to interfere, directly or indirectly, for any reason, in matters that are essentially within the domestic jurisdiction of another State. This principle does not however, prejudice the application by the United Nations of enforcement measures under article 7 of the UN Charter.

NON-REFOULEMENT. (Fr) The principle that no one should be rejected at a frontier, expelled, or returned to a country where he will be subject to persecution.

NULLUM POENA SINE LEGE. (L) The principle that no act is punishable without a pre-existing legal prohibition.

PACTA SUNT SERVANDA. (L) The principle that every treaty in force is binding upon all parties to it and must be performed by them in good faith.

PROTOCOL. A treaty revising or adding to the provisions of an earlier treaty.

RATIFICATION. The international act by which a State establishes its consent to be bound by the terms of a treaty.

REMEDY. The means by which a right is enforced or its violation is prevented, redressed, or compensated.

REPATRIATION. The right of any refugee, if he so wishes, to leave his country of asylum and to return to the country of his nationality. The Statute of the United Nations High Commissioner for Refugees requires the High Commissioner to facilitate and promote the voluntary repatriation of refugees. For such an action to be "voluntary" presupposes the elimination, or at least the substantial removal, of the cause of the fear or danger which had led the refugee to depart from the country of his nationality; it also presupposes, in many cases, the willingness of the country of origin to re-admit the refugee and to cooperate with the country of asylum in arranging for his safe return.

RESERVATION. A unilateral statement, however phrased or named, made by a State when ratifying or otherwise consenting to be bound by the terms of a treaty, purporting to exclude or to modify the legal effect of certain provisions of the treaty in their application to that State.

RES NULLIUS. (L) A territory not claimed by any State.

SELF-DETERMINATION. The right of all peoples freely to determine their political status and freely to pursue their economic, social, and cultural development. They may, for their own ends, freely dispose of their natural wealth and resources without prejudice to any obligations arising out of international economic cooperation, based upon the principle of mutual benefit, and international law. In no case may a people be deprived of its own means of subsistence.

SOVEREIGNTY. The absolute power of an independent State to do whatever may be necessary to maintain its independence and to regulate its internal affairs without interference from, or accountability to, any external authority.

STATE. A body of people occupying a fixed territory, politically organized under one government, exercising sovereignty over all persons and things within its boundaries, capable of making war and peace and of entering into international relations with other such entities.

STATELESS PERSON. A person who is not considered a national by any State under the operation of its law.

STATE PARTY. A State which has expressed, on the international plane, by an act of ratification (acceptance, approval, or accession) or by a notification of succession, its consent to be bound by the terms of a treaty, and for which the treaty is in force.

STATE TERRORISM. Government recognition of and support to terrorist groups. Support may be given by supplying arms, aiding and abetting in the terrorists' plans, providing financial aid, assisting in training or supplying training facilities, providing housing, and any other means that provides succor to a terrorist group.

STATUTORY LIMITATION. A legal provision to the effect that no suit shall be maintained, nor any criminal charge be made, unless initiated within a specified period of time.

SUCCESSION OF STATES. Replacement of one State by another in the responsibility for the international relations of a country or territory.

TREATY. An international agreement concluded between two or more States in written form and governed by international law, whether embodied in a single instrument or in two or more instruments, and whatever its particular designation (agreement, convention, covenant, etc.).

VICTIMS OF ABUSE OF POWER. Persons who, individually or collectively, have suffered harm, including physical or mental injury, emotional suffering, economic loss, or substantial impairment of their fundamental rights, through acts or omissions that do not yet constitute violations of national criminal laws but of internationally recognized norms relating to human rights.

WAR CRIMES. Actions punishable as crimes under international law, including violations of the law of customs of war, which include—but are not limited to—murder, ill-treatment, or deportation to slave-labor or for any other purpose of the civilian population of or in occupied territory; murder or ill-treatment of prisoners of war or persons on the seas; killing of hostages; plunder of public or private property; and wanton destruction of cities, towns, or villages, or devastation not justified by military necessity.

APPENDIX C

STATUS OF INTERNATIONAL HUMAN RIGHTS CONVENTIONS

The status of a number of important human rights conventions, as of the date mentioned in each case, is indicated in the paragraphs below. For this purpose, the conventions are divided into (1) those concluded under the auspices of the United Nations, (2) those concluded by diplomatic conferences, (3) those concluded under the auspices of the International Labor Organization, (4) those concluded under the auspices of the United Nations Educational, Scientific and Cultural Organization, (5) those concluded under the auspices of the Council of Europe, (6) those concluded under the auspices of the Organization of African Unity and (7) those concluded under the auspices of the Organization of American States.

Within each grouping, the conventions on which information is available are arranged in alphabetical order.

1. Conventions Concluded under the Auspices of the United Nations

A. Convention against Torture and Other Cruel, Inhuman or Degrading Treatment or Punishment

Up to 1 June 1990, the following States have become parties to the convention by ratification or accession: Afghanistan, Algeria, Argentina, Australia, Austria, Belize, Brazil, Bulgaria, Byelorussian S.S.R., Cameroon, Canada, Chile, China, Colombia, Czechoslovakia, Denmark, Ecuador, Egypt, Finland, France, German Democratic Republic, Greece, Guatemala, Guinea, Guyana, Hungary, Italy, Libya, Luxembourg, Mexico, Netherlands, New Zealand, Norway, Panama, Paraguay, Peru, Philippines, Poland, Portugal, Senegal, Somalia, Spain, Sweden, Switzerland, Togo, Tunisia, Turkey, Uganda, Ukrainian S.S.R., Union of Soviet Socialist Republics, United Kingdom of Great Britain and Northern Ireland, and Uruguay.

The following States have signed the convention: Belgium, Bolivia, Costa Rica, Cuba, Cyprus, Dominican Republic, Gabon, Gambia, Federal Republic of Germany, Iceland, Indonesia, Israel, Liechtenstein, Morocco, Nicaragua, Nigeria, Sierra Leone, Sudan, United States of America, Venezuela, and Yugoslavia.

The following States have made the declaration recognizing the competence of the Committee Against Torture under articles 21 and 22 of the Convention: Argentina, Austria, Denmark, Ecuador, Finland, France, Greece, Luxembourg, Netherlands, Norway, Portugal, Spain, Sweden, Switzerland, Togo, Tunisia, Turkey, United Kingdom of Great Britain and Northern Ireland, and Uruguay. The provisions of articles 21 and 22

entered into force on 26 June 1987 in accordance with article 21 (para. 2) and article 22 (para. 8).

B. Convention for the Suppression of the Traffic in Persons and of the Exploitation of the Prostitution of Others

Up to 1 June 1990, the following States have become parties to the Convention by ratification or accession: Afghanistan, Albania, Algeria, Argentina, Bangladesh, Belgium, Bolivia, Brazil, Bulgaria, Burkina Faso, Byelorussian S.S.R., Cameroon, Central African Republic, Congo, Cuba, Cyprus, Czech and Slovak Federal Republic, Djibouti, Ecuador, Egypt, Ethiopia, Finland, France, German Democratic Republic, Guinea, Haiti, Hungary, India, Iraq, Israel, Italy, Japan, Jordan, Kuwait, Laos, Libya, Luxembourg, Malawi, Mali, Mauritania, Mexico, Morocco, Niger, Norway, Pakistan, Philippines, Poland, Republic of Korea, Romania, Senegal, Singapore, South Africa, Spain, Sri Lanka, Syria, Ukrainian S.S.R., Union of Soviet Socialist Republics, Venezuela, Yemen, and Yugoslavia.

The convention has been signed by Myanmar, Denmark, Honduras, Iran, and Liberia.

C. Convention on Consent to Marriage, Minimum Age for Marriage, and Registration of Marriages

Up to 1 March 1990, the following States have become parties to the convention by ratification or accession: Antigua and Barbuda, Argentina, Austria, Barbados, Benin, Brazil, Burkina Faso, Cuba, Czechoslovakia, Denmark, Dominican Republic, Fiji, Finland, German Democratic Republic, Federal Republic of Germany,

Guatemala, Guinea, Hungary, Iceland, Mali, Mexico, Netherlands, New Zealand, Niger, Norway, Philippines, Poland, Samoa, Spain, Sweden, Trinidad and Tobago, Tunisia, United Kingdom of Great Britain and Northern Ireland, Venezuela, Yemen, and Yugoslavia.

The Convention has been signed by France, Greece, Israel, Italy, Romania, Sri Lanka, and the United States of America.

D. Convention on the Elimination of All Forms of Discrimination against Women

Up to 1 June 1990, the following States have become parties to the convention by ratification or accession: Angola, Antigua and Barbuda, Argentina, Australia, Austria, Bahamas, Bangladesh, Barbados, Belgium, Belize, Bhutan, Brazil, Bulgaria, Burkina Faso, Byelorussian S.S.R., Canada, Cape Verde, China, Colombia, Congo, Costa Rica, Cuba, Cyprus, Czechoslovakia, Denmark, Dominica, Dominican Republic, Ecuador, Egypt, El Salvador, Equatorial Guinea, Ethiopia, Finland, France, Gabon, German Democratic Republic, Federal Republic of Germany, Ghana, Greece, Guatemala, Guinea, Guinea Bissau, Guyana, Haiti, Honduras, Hungary, Iceland, Indonesia, Iraq, Ireland, Italy, Jamaica, Japan, Kenya, Laos, Liberia, Libya, Liechtenstein, Luxembourg, Madagascar, Malawi, Mali, Mauritius, Mexico, Mongolia, New Zealand, Nicaragua, Nigeria, Norway, Peru, Philippines, Poland, Portugal, Republic of Korea, Romania, Rwanda, St. Kitts and Nevis, St. Lucia, St. Vincent and the Grenadines, Senegal, Sierra Leone, Spain, Sri Lanka, Sweden, Tanzania, Thailand, Togo, Trinidad and Tobago, Tunisia, Turkey, Uganda, Ukrainian S.S.R., Union of Soviet Socialist Republics, United Kingdom of Great Britain and Northern Ireland, Uruguay, Venezuela, Viet Nam, Yemen, Yugoslavia, Zaire, and Zambia.

The convention has been signed by Afghanistan, Benin, Bolivia, Burundi, Cambodia, Cameroon, Chile, Cote d'Ivoire (Ivory Coast), Gambia, Grenada, India, Israel, Jordan, Lesotho, Netherlands, Switzerland and the United States of America.

E. Convention on the Nationality of Married Women

Up to 1 March 1990, the following States have become parties to the convention by ratification or accession: Albania, Antigua and Barbuda, Argentina, Australia, Austria, Bahamas, Barbados, Brazil, Bulgaria, Byelorussian S.S.R., Canada, Cuba, Cyprus, Czechoslovakia, Denmark, Dominican Republic, Ecuador, Fiji, Finland, German Democratic Republic,

Federal Republic of Germany, Ghana, Guatemala, Hungary, Iceland, Ireland, Israel, Jamaica, Lesotho, Libya, Luxembourg, Malawi, Malaysia, Mali, Malta, Mauritius, Mexico, Netherlands, New Zealand, Nicaragua, Norway, Poland, Romania, Sierra Leone, Singapore, Sri Lanka, Swaziland, Sweden, Tanzania, Trinidad and Tobago, Tunisia, Uganda, Ukrainian S.S.R., Union of Soviet Socialist Republics, Venezuela, Yugoslavia, and Zambia.

The convention has been signed by Belgium, Chile, Colombia, Guinea, India, Pakistan, Portugal, and Uruguay.

F. Convention on the Non-Applicability of Statutory Limitations to War Crimes and Crimes against Humanity

Up to 1 March 1990, the following States have become parties to the convention by ratification or accession: Cuba, Czechoslovakia, Democratic People's Republic of Korea, Gambia, German Democratic Republic, Hungary, India, Kenya, Laos, Libya, Mongolia, Nicaragua, Nigeria, Philippines, Poland, Romania, Rwanda, St. Vincent and the Grenadines, Tunisia, Ukrainian S.S.R., Union of Soviet Socialist Republics, Viet Nam, Yemen, and Yugoslavia.

The convention has been signed by Mexico.

G. Convention on the Political Rights of Women

Up to 1 March 1990, the following States have become parties to the convention by ratification or accession: Afghanistan, Albania, Angola, Antigua and Barbuda, Argentina, Australia, Austria, Bahamas, Barbados, Belgium, Bolivia, Brazil, Bulgaria, Byelorussian S.S.R., Canada, Central African Republic, Chile, Colombia, Congo, Costa Rica, Cuba, Cyprus, Czechoslovakia, Denmark, Dominican Republic, Ecuador, Egypt, Ethiopia, Fiji, Finland, France, Gabon, German Democratic Republic, Federal Republic of Germany, Ghana, Greece, Guatemala, Guinea, Haiti, Hungary, Iceland, India, Ireland, Israel, Italy, Indonesia, Jamaica, Japan, Laos, Lebanon, Lesotho, Libya, Luxembourg, Madagascar, Malawi, Mali, Malta, Mauritania, Mauritius, Mexico, Mongolia, Morocco, Nepal, Netherlands, New Zealand, Nicaragua, Niger, Nigeria, Norway, Pakistan, Papua New Guinea, Paraguay, Peru, Philippines, Poland, Republic of Korea, Romania, Senegal, Sierra Leone, Solomon Islands, Spain, Swaziland, Sweden, Tanzania, Thailand, Trinidad and Tobago, Tunisia, Turkey, Ukrainian S.S.R., Union of Soviet Socialist Republics, United Kingdom of Great Britain and Northern Ireland, United States of America, Venezuela, Yemen, Yugoslavia, Zaire, and Zambia.

The convention has been signed by El Salvador, Liberia, Myanmar, and Uruguay.

H. Convention on the Prevention and Punishment of the Crime of Genocide

Up to 1 June 1990, the following States have become parties to the convention by ratification or accession: Afghanistan, Albania, Algeria, Antigua and Barbuda, Argentina, Australia, Austria, Bahamas, Bahrain, Barbados, Belgium, Brazil, Bulgaria, Burkina Faso, Byelorussian S.S.R., Cambodia, Canada, Chile, China, Colombia, Costa Rica, Cuba, Cyprus, Czechoslovakia, Democratic People's Republic of Korea, Denmark, Ecuador, Egypt, El Salvador, Ethiopia, Fiji, Finland, France, Gabon, Gambia, German Democratic Republic, Federal Republic of Germany, Ghana, Greece, Guatemala, Haiti, Honduras, Hungary, Iceland, India, Iran, Iraq, Ireland, Israel, Italy, Jamaica, Jordan, Laos, Lebanon, Lesotho, Liberia, Libya, Luxembourg, Maldives, Mali, Mexico, Monoco, Mongolia, Morocco, Mozambique, Myanmar, Nepal, Netherlands, New Zealand, Nicaragua, Norway, Pakistan, Panama, Papua New Guinea, Peru, Philippines, Poland, Republic of Korea, Romania, Rwanda, St. Vincent and the Grenadines, Saudi Arabia, Senegal, Spain, Sri Lanka, Sweden, Syria, Tanzania, Togo, Tonga, Tunisia, Turkey, Ukrainian S.S.R., Union of Soviet Socialist Republics, United Kingdom of Great Britain and Northern Ireland, United States of America, Uruguay, Venezuela, Viet Nam, Yemen, Yugoslavia, and Zaire.

The convention has been signed by Bolivia, Dominican Republic, and Paraguay.

I. International Convention Against Apartheid *in Sports*

Up to 1 March 1990, the following States have become parties to the convention by ratification or accession: Algeria, Antigua and Barbuda, Bahamas, Bolivia, Bulgaria, Burkina Faso, Byelorussian S.S.R., Czechoslovakia, Equatorial Guinea, Ethiopia, German Democratic Republic, Ghana, Guinea, Guyana, Iran, Iraq, Jamaica, Jordan, Libya, Mali, Mauritania, Mexico, Mongolia, Nepal, Niger, Nigeria, Peru, Philippines, Poland, Qatar, St. Kitts and Nevis, Senegal, Syria, Tanzania, Togo, Tunisia, Uganda, Ukrainian S.S.R., Union of Soviet Socialist Republics, Uruguay, Venezuela, Yugoslavia, Zambia, and Zimbabwe.

The convention has been signed by Benin, Burundi, Cameroon, Cape Verde, Central African Republic, China, Colombia, Cuba, Cyprus, Ecuador, Egypt, Gabon, Guinea-Bissau, Haiti, Hungary, Indonesia, Kenya, Lebanon, Liberia, Madagascar, Malaysia, Maldives, Morocco, Nicaragua, Panama, Rwanda, Saint Lucia, Sierra Leone, Somalia, Sudan, Trinidad and Tobago, Yemen, and Zaire.

J. International Convention against the Taking of Hostages

Up to 1 March 1990, the following States have become parties to the convention by ratification or accession: Antigua and Barbuda, Austria, Bahamas, Barbados, Bhutan, Brunei Darussalam, Bulgaria, Byelorussian S.S.R., Cameroon, Canada, Chile, Czechoslovakia, Denmark, Dominica, Ecuador, Egypt, El Salvador, Federal Republic of Germany, Finland, German Democratic Republic, Ghana, Greece, Guatemala, Honduras, Hungary, Iceland, Italy, Japan, Jordan, Kenya, Kuwait, Lesotho, Malawi, Mauritius, Mexico, Netherlands, New Zealand, Norway, Oman, Panama, Philippines, Portugal, Republic of Korea, Senegal, Spain, Suriname, Sweden, Switzerland, Trinidad and Tobago, Ukrainian S.S.R., Union of Soviet Socialist Republics, United Kingdom of Great Britain and Northern Ireland, Venezuela, and Yugoslavia.

The following States have signed the convention: Belgium, Bolivia, Canada, Dominican Republic, Gabon, Greece, Haiti, Iraq, Israel, Jamaica, Liberia, Luxembourg, New Zealand, Uganda, and Zaire.

K. International Convention on the Elimination of All Forms of Racial Discrimination

Up to 1 June 1990, the following States have become parties to the convention by ratification or accession: Afghanistan, Algeria, Antigua and Barbuda, Argentina, Australia, Austria, Bahamas, Bahrain, Bangladesh, Barbados, Belgium, Bolivia, Botswana, Brazil, Bulgaria, Burkina Faso, Burundi, Byelorussian S.S.R., Cambodia, Cameroon, Canada, Cape Verde, Central African Republic, Chad, Chile, China, Colombia, Congo, Costa Rica, Cote d'Ivoire (Ivory Coast), Cuba, Cyprus, Czechoslovakia, Denmark, Dominican Republic, Ecuador, Egypt, El Salvador, Ethiopia, Federal Republic of Germany, Fiji, Finland, France, Gabon, Gambia, German Democratic Republic, Ghana, Greece, Guatemala, Guinea, Guyana, Haiti, Holy See, Hungary, Iceland, India, Iran, Iraq, Israel, Italy, Jamaica, Jordan, Kuwait, Laos, Lebanon, Lesotho, Liberia, Libya, Luxembourg, Madagascar, Maldives, Mali, Malta, Mauritania, Mauritius, Mexico, Mongolia, Morocco, Mozambique, Namibia, Nepal, Netherlands, New Zealand, Nicaragua, Niger, Nigeria, Norway, Pakistan, Panama, Papua New Guinea, Peru, Philippines, Poland, Portugal, Qatar, Republic of Korea, Romania, Rwanda, Saint Lucia, St. Vincent and the Grenadines, Senegal, Seychelles, Sierra Leone, Solomon Islands, Somalia, Spain, Sri Lanka, Sudan, Suriname, Swaziland, Sweden, Syria, Tanzania, Togo, Tonga, Trinidad and Tobago, Tunisia, Uganda, Ukrainian S.S.R., Union of Soviet Socialist Republics, United Arab Emirates, United Kingdom of Great Britain and Northern Ireland, Uruguay, Venezuela, Viet Nam, Yemen, Yugoslavia, Zaire, and Zambia.

The convention has been signed by Benin, Bhutan, Grenada, Ireland, Turkey, and the United States of America.

The following States have made the declaration recognizing the competence of the Committee on the Elimination of Racial Discrimination under article 14 of the convention: Costa Rica, Denmark, Ecuador, France, Iceland, Netherlands, Norway, Peru, Senegal, Sweden, and Uruguay.

L. International Convention on the Suppression and Punishment of the Crime of Apartheid

Up to 1 June 1990, the following States have become parties to the convention by ratification or accession: Afghanistan, Algeria, Antigua and Barbuda, Argentina, Bahamas, Bahrain, Bangladesh, Barbados, Benin, Bolivia, Bulgaria, Burkina Faso, Burundi, Byelorussian S.S.R., Cambodia, Cameroon, Cape Verde, Central African Republic, Chad, China, Colombia, Congo, Costa Rica, Cuba, Czechoslovakia, Ecuador, Egypt, El Salvador, Ethiopia, Gabon, Gambia, German Democratic Republic, Ghana, Guinea, Guyana, Haiti, Hungary, India, Iran, Iraq, Jamaica, Kuwait, Laos, Lesotho, Liberia, Libya, Madagascar, Maldives, Mali, Mauritania, Mexico, Mongolia, Mozambique, Namibia, Nepal, Nicaragua, Niger, Nigeria, Pakistan, Panama, Peru, Philippines, Poland, Qatar, Romania, Rwanda, St. Vincent and the Grenadines, Sao Tome and Principe, Senegal, Seychelles, Somalia, Sri Lanka, Sudan, Suriname, Syria, Tanzania, Togo, Trinidad and Tobago, Tunisia, Uganda, Ukrainian S.S.R., Union of Soviet Socialist Republics, United Arab Emirates, Venezuela, Viet Nam, Yemen, Yugoslavia, Zaire, and Zambia.

The convention has been signed by Jordan, Kenya, and Oman.

M. International Covenant on Civil and Political Rights

Up to 1 June 1990, the following States have become parties to the covenant by ratification or accession: Afghanistan, Algeria, Argentina, Australia, Austria, Barbados, Belgium, Bolivia, Bulgaria, Burundi, Byelorussian S.S.R., Cameroon, Canada, Central African Republic, Chile, Colombia, Congo, Costa Rica, Cyprus, Czechoslovakia, Democratic People's Republic of Korea, Denmark, Dominican Republic, Ecuador, Egypt, El Salvador, Equatorial Guinea, Federal Republic of Germany, Finland, France, Gabon, Gambia, German Democratic Republic, Republic of Germany, Guinea, Guyana, Hungary, Iceland, India, Iran, Iraq, Ireland, Italy, Jamaica, Japan, Jordan, Kenya, Lebanon, Libya, Luxembourg, Madagascar, Mali, Mauri-

tius, Mexico, Mongolia, Morocco, Netherlands, New Zealand, Nicaragua, Niger, Norway, Panama, Peru, Philippines, Poland, Portugal, Republic of Korea, Romania, Rwanda, St. Vincent and the Grenadines, San Marino, Senegal, Somalia, Spain, Sri Lanka, Sudan, Suriname, Sweden, Syria, Tanzania, Togo, Trinidad and Tobago, Tunisia, Ukrainian S.S.R., Union of Soviet Socialist Republics, United Kingdom of Great Britain and Northern Ireland, Uruguay, Venezuela, Viet Nam, Yemen, Yugoslavia, Zaire, and Zambia.

The covenant has been signed by Cambodia, Honduras, Israel, Liberia, and the United States of America.

The following States have made the declaration recognizing the competence of the Human Rights Committee under article 41 of the covenant: Argentina, Austria, Belgium, Canada, Congo, Denmark, Ecuador, Federal Republic of Germany, Finland, Gambia, Hungary, Iceland, Italy, Luxembourg, Netherlands, New Zealand, Norway, Peru, Philippines, Senegal, Spain, Sri Lanka, Sweden, and the United Kingdom of Great Britain and Northern Ireland.

N. International Covenant on Civil and Political Rights: Optional Protocol

Up to 1 June 1990, the following States have become parties to the optional protocol by ratification or accession: Algeria, Argentina, Austria, Barbados, Bolivia, Cameroon, Canada, Central African Republic, Colombia, Congo, Costa Rica, Denmark, Dominican Republic, Ecuador, Equatorial Guinea, Finland, France, Gambia, Hungary, Iceland, Ireland, Italy, Jamaica, Libya, Luxembourg, Madagascar, Mauritius, Netherlands, New Zealand, Nicaragua, Niger, Norway, Panama, Peru, Philippines, Portugal, Republic of Korea, St. Vincent and the Grenadines, San Marino, Senegal, Somalia, Spain, Suriname, Sweden, Togo, Trinidad and Tobago, Uruguay, Venezuela, Zaire, and Zambia.

The optional protocol has been signed by Cyprus, El Salvador, Guinea, and Honduras.

O. International Covenant on Economic, Social and Cultural Rights

Up to 1 June 1990, the following States have become parties to the covenant by ratification or accession: Afghanistan, Algeria, Argentina, Australia, Austria, Barbados, Belgium, Bolivia, Bulgaria, Burundi, Byelorussian S.S.R., Cameroon, Canada, Central African Republic, Chile, Colombia, Congo, Costa Rica, Cyprus, Czechoslovakia, Democratic People's Republic of Korea, Denmark, Dominican Republic, Ecuador, Egypt, El Salvador, Equatorial Guinea, Federal Republic of Germany, Finland, France, Gabon, Gambia,

German Democratic Republic, Greece, Guatemala, Guinea, Guyana, Honduras, Hungary, Iceland, India, Iran, Iraq, Ireland, Italy, Jamaica, Japan, Jordan, Kenya, Lebanon, Libya, Luxembourg, Madagascar, Mali, Mauritius, Mexico, Mongolia, Morocco, Netherlands, New Zealand, Nicaragua, Niger, Norway, Panama, Peru, Philippines, Poland, Portugal, Republic of Korea, Romania, Rwanda, St. Vincent and the Grenadines, San Marino, Senegal, Solomon Islands, Somalia, Spain, Sri Lanka, Sudan, Suriname, Sweden, Syria, Tanzania, Togo, Trinidad and Tobago, Tunisia, Uganda, Ukrainian S.S.R., Union of Soviet Socialist Republics, United Kingdom of Great Britain and Northern Ireland, Uruguay, Venezuela, Viet Nam, Yemen, Yugoslavia, Zaire, and Zambia.

The covenant has been signed by Cambodia, Israel, Liberia, Malta, and the United States of America.

P. Slavery Convention Signed at Geneva on 25 September 1925, as amended by 1953 Protocol

Up to 1 June 1990, the following States have become parties to the convention, as amended, by ratification or accession: Afghanistan, Albania, Algeria, Antigua and Barbuda, Australia, Austria, Bahamas, Bangladesh, Barbados, Belgium, Bolivia, Cameroon, Canada, Cuba, Cyprus, Denmark, Ecuador, Egypt, Ethiopia, Federal Republic of Germany, Fiji, Finland, France, Gambia, German Democratic Republic, Greece, Guatemala, Guinea, Hungary, India, Iraq, Ireland, Israel, Italy, Jamaica, Jordan, Kuwait, Lesotho, Liberia, Libya, Madagascar, Malawi, Mali, Malta, Mauritania, Mauritius, Mexico, Monaco, Mongolia, Morocco, Myanmar, Nepal, Netherlands, New Zealand, Nicaragua, Niger, Nigeria, Norway, Pakistan, Papua New Guinea, Philippines, Romania, Saint Lucia, St. Vincent and the Grenadines, Saudi Arabia, Sierra Leone, Solomon Islands, South Africa, Spain, Sri Lanka, Sudan, Sweden, Switzerland, Syria, Tanzania, Trinidad and Tobago, Tunisia, Turkey, Uganda, Ukrainian S.S.R., Union of Soviet Socialist Republics, United Kingdom of Great Britain and Northern Ireland, United States of America, Yemen, Yugoslavia, and Zambia.

2. Conventions Concluded by Special Diplomatic Conferences

A. Convention on the Reduction of Statelessness

Up to 1 March 1990, the following States have become parties to the Convention on the Reduction of Statelessness by ratification or accession: Australia, Austria, Bolivia, Canada, Costa Rica, Denmark, Federal Republic of Germany, Ireland, Kiribati, Libya,

Netherlands, Niger, Norway, Sweden, United Kingdom of Great Britain and Northern Ireland, Yugoslavia, and Zambia.

The convention has been signed by the Dominican Republic, France, and Israel.

B. Convention relating to the Status of Refugees

Up to 1 March 1990, the following 102 States have become parties to the convention by ratification or accession: Algeria, Angola, Argentina, Australia, Austria, Belgium, Benin, Bolivia, Botswana, Brazil, Burkina Faso, Burundi, Cameroon, Canada, Central African Republic, Chad, Chile, China, Colombia, Congo, Costa Rica, Cote d'Ivoire (Ivory Coast), Cyprus, Denmark, Djibouti, Dominican Republic, Ecuador, Egypt, El Salvador, Equatorial Guinea, Ethiopia, Federal Republic of Germany, Fiji, Finland, France, Gabon, Gambia, Ghana, Greece, Guatemala, Guinea, Guinea-Bissau, Haiti, Holy See, Hungary, Iceland, Iran, Ireland, Israel, Italy, Jamaica, Japan, Kenya, Lesotho, Liberia, Liechtenstein, Luxembourg, Madagascar, Malawi, Mali, Malta, Mauritania, Morocco, Mozambique, Netherlands, New Zealand, Nicaragua, Niger, Nigeria, Norway, Panama, Papua New Guinea, Paraguay, Peru, Philippines, Portugal, Rwanda, Samoa, Sao Tome and Principe, Senegal, Seychelles, Sierra Leone, Somalia, Spain, Sudan, Suriname, Sweden, Switzerland, Tanzania, Togo, Tunisia, Turkey, Tuvalu, Uganda, United Kingdom of Great Britain and Northern Ireland, Uruguay, Yemen, Yugoslavia, Zaire, Zambia, and Zimbabwe.

C. Convention relating to the Status of Refugees: Protocol

Up to 1 March 1990, the following States have become parties to the protocol by ratification or accession: Algeria, Angola, Argentina, Australia, Austria, Belgium, Benin, Bolivia, Botswana, Brazil, Burkina Faso, Burundi, Cameroon, Canada, Cape Verde, Central African Republic, Chad, Chile, China, Colombia, Congo, Costa Rica, Cote d'Ivoire (Ivory Coast), Cyprus, Denmark, Djibouti, Dominican Republic, Ecuador, Egypt, El Salvador, Equatorial Guinea, Ethiopia, Federal Republic of Germany, Fiji, Finland, France, Gabon, Gambia, Ghana, Greece, Guatemala, Guinea, Guinea-Bissau, Haiti, Holy See, Hungary, Iceland, India, Indonesia, Ireland, Israel, Italy, Jamaica, Japan, Kenya, Lesotho, Liberia, Liechtenstein, Luxembourg, Malawi, Mali, Malta, Mauritania, Morocco, Mozambique, Netherlands, New Zealand, Nicaragua, Niger, Nigeria, Norway, Panama, Papua New Guinea, Paraguay, Peru, Philippines, Portugal, Rwanda, Sao Tome and Principe, Senegal, Seychelles, Sierra Leone, Somalia, Spain, Sudan, Suriname, Swaziland, Sweden, Switzerland, Tanzania, Togo, Tunisia, Turkey, Tuvalu, Uganda, United Kingdom of Great Britain and Northern Ireland, United States of America, Uruguay, Venezuela, Yemen, Yugoslavia, Zaire, Zambia, and Zimbabwe.

D. Convention relating to the Status of Stateless Persons

Up to 1 March 1990, the following States have become parties to the convention by ratification or accession: Algeria, Antigua and Barbuda, Argentina, Australia, Barbados, Belgium, Bolivia, Botswana, Costa Rica, Denmark, Ecuador, Federal Republic of Germany, Fiji, Finland, France, Greece, Guinea, Ireland, Israel, Italy, Kiribati, Lesotho, Liberia, Libya, Luxembourg, Netherlands, Norway, Republic of Korea, Sweden, Switzerland, Trinidad and Tobago, Tunisia, Uganda, United Kingdom of Great Britain and Northern Ireland, Yugoslavia, and Zambia.

The convention has been signed by Brazil, Colombia, El Salvador, Guatemala, Holy See, Honduras, Liechtenstein, and the Philippines.

E. Geneva Conventions: Protocols I and II

Up to 1 June 1990, the following States have become parties to the protocols by ratification or accession: Algeria, Angola (Protocol I only), Antigua and Barbuda, Argentina, Austria, Bahamas, Bangladesh, Bahrain, Barbados, Belgium, Belize, Benin, Bolivia, Botswana, Bulgaria, Burkina Faso, Byelorussian S.S.R., Cameroon, Central African Republic, China, Comoros, Congo, Costa Rica, Cote d'Ivoire (Ivory Coast), Cuba (Protocol I only), Cyprus, Czech and Slovak Federal Republic, Democratic People's Republic of Korea, Denmark, Ecuador, El Salvador, Equatorial Guinea, Finland, France (Protocol II only), Gabon, Gambia, Ghana, Greece, Guatemala, Guyana, Guinea, Guinea-Bissau, Holy See, Hungary, Iceland, Italy, Jamaica, Jordan, Kuwait, Laos, Libya, Liberia, Liechtenstein, Luxembourg, Mali, Malta, Mauritania, Maritius, Mexico (Protocol I only), Mozambique (Protocol I only), Namibia, Netherlands, New Zealand, Niger, Nigeria, Norway, Oman, Peru, Philippines (Protocol II only), Qatar (Protocol I only), Republic of Korea, Rwanda, St. Kitts and Nevis, Saint Lucia, Saint Vincent and the Grenadines, Samoa, Saudi Arabia (Protocol I only), Senegal, Seychelles, Sierra Leone, Solomon Islands, Spain, Suriname, Sweden, Switzerland, Syria, (Protocol I only), Tanzania, Togo, Tunisia, Ukrainian S.S.R., Union of Soviet Socialist Republics, United Arab Emirates, Uruguay, Vanuatu, Viet Nam (Protocol I only), Yemen, Yugoslavia, and Zaire (Protocol I only).

F. Supplementary Convention on the Abolition of Slavery, the Slave Trade, and Institutions and Practices Similar to Slavery

Up to 1 June 1990, the following States have become parties to the supplementary convention by ratification or accession: Afghanistan, Albania, Algeria, Antigua and Barbuda, Argentina, Australia, Austria, Bahamas, Bahrain, Bangladesh, Barbados, Belgium, Bolivia, Brazil, Bulgaria, Byelorussian Soviet Socialist Republic, Cambodia, Cameroon, Canada, Central African Republic, Congo, Côte d'Ivoire, Cuba, Cyprus, Czech and Slovak Federal Republic, Denmark, Djibouti, Dominican Republic, Ecuador, Egypt, Ethiopia, Federal Republic of Germany, Ghana, Greece, Guatemala, Guinea, Haiti, Hungary, Iceland, India, Iran, Iraq, Ireland, Israel, Italy, Jamaica, Jordan, Kuwait, Laos, Lesotho, Libya, Luxembourg, Madagascar, Malawi, Malaysia, Mali, Malta, Mauritania, Mauritius, Mexico, Mongolia, Morocco, Nepal, Netherlands, New Zealand, Nicargua, Niger, Nigeria, Norway, Pakistan, Philippines, Poland, Portugal, Romania, Saint Lucia, Saint Vincent and the Grenadines, San Marino, Saudi Arabia, Senegal, Sierra Leone, Singapore, Solomon Islands, Spain, Sri Lanka, Sudan, Suriname, Sweden, Switzerland, Syria, Tanzania, Togo, Trinidad and Tobago, Tunisia, Turkey, Uganda, Ukrainian S.S.R., Union of Soviet Socialist Republics, United Kingdom of Great Britain and Northern Ireland, United States of America, Yugoslavia, Zaire, and Zambia.

The supplementary convention has been signed by El Salvador, Liberia, and Peru.

G. Universal Copyright Convention (Revised)

Up to 1 January 1990, the following States have become parties, by ratification or accession, to the convention as revised: Algeria, Andorra, Argentina, Australia, Austria, Bahamas, Bangladesh, Barbados, Belgium, Belize, Brazil, Bulgaria, Cameroon, Canada, Chile, Colombia, Costa Rica, Cuba, Czechoslovakia, Denmark, Dominican Republic, Ecuador, El Salvador, Federal Republic of Germany, Fiji, Finland, France, German Democratic Republic, Ghana, Greece, Guatemala, Guinea, Haiti, Holy See, Hungary, Iceland, India, Ireland, Israel, Italy, Japan, Kenya, Laos, Lebanon, Liberia, Liechtenstein, Luxembourg, Malawi, Malta, Mauritius, Mexico, Monaco, Morocco, Netherlands, New Zealand, Nicaragua, Nigeria, Pakistan, Panama, Paraguay, Peru, Poland, Portugal, Republic of Korea, St. Vincent and the Grenadines, Senegal, Spain, Sri Lanka, Sweden, Switzerland, Trinidad and Tobago, Tunisia, Union of Soviet Socialist Republics, Venezuela, Yugoslavia, and Zambia.

The following States have signed the convention: Honduras, San Marino, and Uruguay.

3. Conventions Prepared Under the Auspices of the International Labor Organization

A. *ILO Abolition of Forced Labor Convention, 1957 (No. 105)*

Up to 1 June 1990, the convention had been ratified or acceded to by the following States: Afghanistan, Algeria, Angola, Antigua and Barbuda, Argentina, Australia, Austria, Bahamas, Bangladesh, Barbados, Belgium, Belize, Benin, Brazil, Burundi, Cameroon, Canada, Cape Verde, Central African Republic, Chad, Colombia, Comoros, Costa Rica, Cote d'Ivoire (Ivory Coast), Cuba, Cyprus, Denmark, Djibouti, Dominica, Dominican Republic, Ecuador, Egypt, El Salvador, Federal Republic of Germany, Fiji, Finland, France, Ghana, Greece, Grenada, Guatemala, Guinea, Guinea-Bissau, Guyana, Haiti, Honduras, Iceland, Iran, Iraq, Israel, Italy, Jamaica, Jordan, Kenya, Kuwait, Lebanon, Liberia, Libya, Luxembourg, Malaysia, Mali, Malta, Mauritius, Mexico, Morocco, Mozambique, Netherlands, New Zealand, Nicaragua, Niger, Nigeria, Norway, Pakistan, Panama, Papua New Guinea, Paraguay, Peru, Philippines, Poland, Portugal, Rwanda, Saint Lucia, Saudi Arabia, Senegal, Seychelles, Sierra Leone, Somalia, Spain, Sudan, Suriname, Swaziland, Sweden, Switzerland, Syria, Tanzania, Thailand, Tunisia, Turkey, Uganda, United Kingdom, Uruguay, Venezuela, Yemen, and Zimbabwe.

B. *ILO Collective Bargaining Convention, 1981 (No. 154)*

Up to 1 June 1990, the convention has been ratified or acceded to by the following States: Belgium, Cyprus, Finland, Gabon, Niger, Nigeria, Spain, Sweden, Switzerland, Uganda, Uruguay, and Zambia.

C. *ILO Discrimination (Employment and Occupation) Convention, 1958 (No. 111)*

Up to 1 June 1990, the convention has been ratified or acceded to by the following States: Afghanistan, Algeria, Angola, Antigua and Barbuda, Argentina, Australia, Austria, Bangladesh, Barbados, Belgium, Benin, Bolivia, Brazil, Bulgaria, Burkina Faso, Cameroon, Canada, Cape Verde, Central African Republic, Chad, Chile, Colombia, Costa Rica, Cote d'Ivoire (Ivory Coast), Cuba, Cyprus, Czechoslovakia, Denmark, Dominica, Dominican Republic, Ecuador, Egypt, Ethiopia, Federal Republic of Germany, Finland, France, Gabon, German Democratic Republic, Ghana, Greece, Guatemala, Guinea, Guinea-Bissau, Guyana, Haiti, Honduras, Hungary, Iceland, India, Iran,

Iraq, Israel, Italy, Jamaica, Jordan, Kuwait, Lebanon, Lesotho, Liberia, Madagascar, Malawi, Mali, Malta, Mauritania, Mexico, Mongolia, Morocco, Mozambique, Nepal, Netherlands, New Zealand, Nicaragua, Niger, Norway, Pakistan, Panama, Paraguay, Peru, Philippines, Poland, Portugal, Qatar, Romania, Rwanda, Saint Lucia, San Marino, Sao Tome and Principe, Saudi Arabia, Senegal, Sierra Leone, Somalia, Spain, Sudan, Swaziland, Sweden, Switzerland, Syria, Togo, Trinidad and Tobago, Tunisia, Turkey, Ukrainian S.S.R., Union of Soviet Socialist Republics, Uruguay, Venezuela, Viet Nam, Yemen, Yugoslavia, and Zambia.

D. *ILO Equal Remuneration Convention, 1951 (No. 100)*

Up to 1 June 1990, the convention has been ratified or acceded to by the following states: Afghanistan, Albania, Algeria, Angola, Argentina, Australia, Austria, Barbados, Belgium, Benin, Bolivia, Brazil, Bulgaria, Burkina Faso, Byelorussian S.S.R., Cameroon, Canada, Cape Verde, Central African Republic, Chad, Chile, Colombia, Comoros, Costa Rica, Cote d'Ivoire (Ivory Coast), Cuba, Cyprus, Czechoslovakia, Denmark, Djibouti, Dominica, Dominican Republic, Ecuador, Egypt, Equatorial Guinea, Federal Republic of Germany, Finland, France, Gabon, German Democratic Republic, Ghana, Greece, Guatemala, Guinea, Guinea-Bissau, Guyana, Haiti, Honduras, Hungary, Iceland, India, Indonesia, Iran, Iraq, Ireland, Israel, Italy, Jamaica, Japan, Jordan, Lebanon, Libya, Luxembourg, Madagascar, Malawi, Mali, Malta, Mexico, Mongolia, Morocco, Mozambique, Nepal, Netherlands, New Zealand, Nicaragua, Niger, Nigeria, Norway, Panama, Paraguay, Peru, Philippines, Poland, Portugal, Romania, Rwanda, Saint Lucia, San Marino, Sao Tome and Principe, Saudi Arabia, Senegal, Sierra Leone, Spain, Sudan, Swaziland, Sweden, Switzerland, Syria, Togo, Tunisia, Turkey, Ukrainian S.S.R., Union of Soviet Socialist Republics, United Kingdom, Venezuela, Yemen, Yugoslavia, Zaire, Zambia, and Zimbabwe.

E. *ILO Equality of Treatment (Social Security) Convention, 1962 (No. 118)*

Up to 1 June 1990, the convention has been ratified or acceded to by the following States: Bangladesh, Barbados, Bolivia, Brazil, Cape Verde, Central African Republic, Denmark, Ecuador, Federal Republic of Germany, Finland, France, Guatemala, Guinea, India, Iran, Iraq, Ireland, Israel, Italy, Jordan, Kenya, Libya, Madagascar, Mauritania, Mexico, Netherlands, Norway, Pakistan, Rwanda, Suriname, Sweden, Syria, Tunisia, Turkey, Uruguay, Venezuela, Viet Nam, and Zaire.

F. ILO Right to Organize and Collective Bargaining Convention, 1949 (No. 98)

Up to 1 June 1990, the convention has been ratified or acceded to by the following States: Afghanistan, Albania, Algeria, Angola, Antigua and Barbuda, Argentina, Australia, Austria, Bahamas, Bangladesh, Barbados, Belgium, Belize, Benin, Bolivia, Botswana, Brazil, Bulgaria, Burkina Faso, Byelorussian S.S.R., Cameroon, Cape Verde, Central African Republic, Chad, Colombia, Comoros, Costa Rica, Cote d'Ivoire (Ivory Coast), Cuba, Cyprus, Czechoslovakia, Denmark, Djibouti, Dominica, Dominican Republic, Ecuador, Egypt, Ethiopia, Federal Republic of Germany, Fiji, Finland, France, Gabon, German Democratic Republic, Ghana, Greece, Grenada, Guatemala, Guinea, Guinea-Bissau, Guyana, Haiti, Honduras, Hungary, Iceland, Indonesia, Iran, Iraq, Ireland, Israel, Italy, Jamaica, Jordan, Kenya, Lebanon, Lesotho, Liberia, Libya, Luxembourg, Malawi, Malaysia, Mali, Malta, Mauritius, Mongolia, Morocco, Nigeria, Norway, Pakistan, Panama, Papua New Guinea, Paraguay, Peru, Philippines, Poland, Portugal, Romania, Rwanda, Saint Lucia, San Marino, Senegal, Sierra Leone, Singapore, Spain, Sri Lanka, Sudan, Swaziland, Sweden, Syria, Tanzania, Togo, Trinidad and Tobago, Tunisia, Turkey, Uganda, Ukrainian S.S.R., Union of Soviet Socialist Republics, United Arab Emirates, United Kingdom, Uruguay, Venezuela, Viet Nam, Yemen, Yugoslavia, and Zaire.

G. ILO Social Security (Minimum Standards) Convention, 1952 (No. 102)

Up to 1 June 1990, the convention has been ratified or acceded to by the following States: Bahamas, Barbados, Belgium, Bolivia, Costa Rica, Czechoslovakia, Denmark, Ecuador, Federal Republic of Germany, France, Greece, Iceland, Ireland, Israel, Italy, Japan, Libya, Luxembourg, Mauritania, Mexico, Netherlands, Niger, Norway, Peru, Senegal, Spain, Sweden, Switzerland, Tanzania, Turkey, United Kingdom, Venezuela, Yugoslavia, and Zaire.

H. ILO Working Environment (Air Pollution, Noise and Vibration) Convention, 1977 (No. 148)

Up to 1 June 1990, the convention has been ratified or acceded to by the following states: Brazil, Costa Rica, Cuba, Czechoslovakia, Denmark, Ecuador, Egypt, Finland, France, Ghana, Guinea, Iraq, Italy, Malta, Norway, Portugal, San Marino, Spain, Sweden, Tanzania, Union of Soviet Socialist Republics, United Kingdom, Uruguay, Yugoslavia, and Zambia.

4. Conventions Prepared under the Auspices of UNESCO

A. UNESCO Convention against Discrimination in Education

Up to 1 January 1990, the following States have become parties to the convention by ratification or accession: Albania, Algeria, Argentina, Australia, Barbados, Belize, Benin, Brazil, Brunei Darussalam, Bulgaria, Byelorussian S.S.R., Central African Republic, Chile, Congo, Costa Rica, Cuba, Cyprus, Czechoslovakia, Denmark, Dominica, Dominican Republic, Ecuador, Egypt, Federal Republic of Germany, Finland, France, German Democratic Republic, Guatemala, Guinea, Hungary, Indonesia, Iran, Iraq, Israel, Italy, Jordan, Kuwait, Lebanon, Liberia, Libya, Luxembourg, Madagascar, Malta, Mauritius, Mongolia, Morocco, Netherlands, New Zealand, Nicaragua, Niger, Nigeria, Norway, Panama, Peru, Philippines, Poland, Portugal, Romania, St. Vincent and the Grenadines, Saudi Arabia, Senegal, Sierra Leone, Solomon Islands, Spain, Sri Lanka, Swaziland, Sweden, Tanzania, Tunisia, Uganda, Ukrainian S.S.R., Union of Soviet Socialist Republics, United Kingdom of Great Britain and Northern Ireland, Venezuela, Viet Nam, and Yugoslavia.

The following States have also become parties to the 1962 protocol instituting a Conciliation and Good Offices Commission to be responsible for seeking a settlement of any disputes which may arise between States parties to the Convention against Discrimination in Education: Argentina, Australia, Brunei Darussalam, Costa Rica, Cyprus, Denmark, Dominica, Egypt, Federal Republic of Germany, France, Guatemala, Israel, Italy, Libya, Madagascar, Malta, Morocco, Niger, Norway, Panama, Philippines, Portugal, St. Vincent and the Grenadines, Senegal, Solomon Islands, United Kingdom of Great Britain and Northern Ireland, and Viet Nam.

B. UNESCO Convention for the Protection of Cultural Property in the Event of Armed Conflict

Up to 1 January 1990, the following States have become parties to the convention by ratification or accession: Albania, Australia, Austria, Belgium, Brazil, Bulgaria, Burkina Faso, Byelorussian S.S.R., Cameroon, Cote d'Ivoire (Ivory Coast), Cuba, Cyprus, Czechoslovakia, Dominican Republic, Ecuador, Egypt, Federal Republic of Germany, France, Gabon, German Democratic Republic, Ghana, Greece, Guatemala, Guinea, Holy See, Hungary, India, Indonesia, Iran, Iraq, Israel, Italy, Jordan, Kuwait, Lebanon,

Libya, Liechtenstein, Luxembourg, Madagascar, Malaysia, Mali, Mexico, Monaco, Mongolia, Morocco, Myanmar, Netherlands, Nicaragua, Niger, Nigeria, Norway, Oman, Pakistan, Panama, Poland, Qatar, Romania, San Marino, Saudi Arabia, Senegal, Spain, Sudan, Sweden, Switzerland, Syria, Tanzania, Thailand, Tunisia, Turkey, Ukrainian S.S.R., Union of Soviet Socialist Republics, Yemen, Yugoslavia, and Zaire.

The following States have signed the convention: Andorra, Denmark, El Salvador, Japan, New Zealand, Philippines, Portugal, United Kingdom of Great Britain and Northern Ireland, United States of America, and Uruguay.

C. UNESCO Convention on the Means of Prohibiting and Preventing the Illicit Import, Export and Transfer of Ownership of Cultural Property

Up to 1 January 1990, the convention has been ratified or acceded to by the following States: Algeria, Argentina, Bangladesh, Bolivia, Brazil, Bulgaria, Burkina Faso, Byelorussian S.S.R., Cambodia, Cameroon, Canada, Central African Republic, Colombia, Cuba, Cyprus, Czechoslovakia, Democratic People's Republic of Korea, Dominican Republic, Ecuador, Egypt, El Salvador, German Democratic Republic, Greece, Guatemala, Guinea, Honduras, Hungary, India, Iran, Iraq, Italy, Jordan, Kuwait, Libya, Madagascar, Mali, Mauritania, Mauritius, Mexico, Nepal, Nicaragua, Niger, Nigeria, Oman, Pakistan, Panama, Peru, Poland, Portugal, Qatar, Republic of Korea, Saudi Arabia, Senegal, Spain, Sri Lanka, Syria, Tanzania, Tunisia, Turkey, Ukrainian S.S.R., United States of America, Uruguay, Union of Soviet Socialist Republics, Yugoslavia, Zaire, and Zambia.

D. UNESCO International Convention for the Protection of Performers, Producers of Phonograms and Broadcasting Organizations

Up to 1 January 1990, the following States have become parties to the convention by ratification or accession: Austria, Barbados, Brazil, Burkina Faso, Chile, Colombia, Congo, Costa Rica, Czechoslovakia, Denmark, Dominican Republic, Ecuador, El Salvador, Federal Republic of Germany, Fiji, Finland, France, Guatemala, Ireland, Italy, Luxembourg, Mexico, Monaco, Niger, Norway, Panama, Paraguay, Peru, Philippines, Sweden, United Kingdom of Great Britain and Northern Ireland, and Uruguay.

The following States have signed the convention: Belgium, Cambodia, Iceland, India, Israel, Lebanon, Spain, and Yugoslavia.

5. Conventions Prepared under the Auspices of the Council of Europe

A. European Agreement relating to Persons Participating in Proceedings of the European Commission and of the Court of Human Rights

Up to 1 February 1990, the agreement has been ratified by the following States: Austria, Belgium, Cyprus, Denmark, Federal Republic of Germany, France, Ireland, Italy, Liechtenstein, Luxembourg, Malta, Netherlands, Norway, Portugal, San Marino, Spain, Sweden, Switzerland, and the United Kingdom of Great Britain and Northern Ireland.

B. European Convention for the Prevention of Torture

Up to 1 February 1990, the convention has been ratified by the following States: Austria, Cyprus, Denmark, France, Ireland, Italy, Luxembourg, Malta, Netherlands, Norway, Spain, Sweden, Switzerland, Turkey, and the United Kingdom of Great Britain and Northern Ireland.

C. European Convention on Human Rights

Up to 1 February 1990, the following States have become parties to the European Convention on Human Rights by ratification or accession: Austria, Belgium, Cyprus, Denmark, Federal Republic of Germany, France, Greece, Iceland, Ireland, Italy, Liechtenstein, Luxembourg, Malta, Netherlands, Norway, Portugal, San Marino, Spain, Sweden, Switzerland, Turkey, and the United Kingdom of Great Britain and Northern Ireland. Finland, which acceded to the council on 5 May 1989, has not become a party to the Convention.

All of the States parties to the convention have made a declaration under article 25 thereof recognizing for three years the competence of the European Commission on Human Rights to receive individual petitions.

All of the States parties to the convention, except Turkey, have made a declaration under article 46 thereof recognizing the compulsory jurisdiction of the European Court of Human Rights.

D. European Convention on Human Rights: Protocols

Up to 1 February 1990, Protocol I has been ratified by all the States parties to the convention except Liechtenstein, Spain, and Switzerland.

Protocol II has been ratified by all the States parties to the convention.

Protocol IV is in force among the following States: Austria, Belgium, Denmark, Federal Republic of Germany, France, Iceland, Ireland, Italy, Luxembourg, Netherlands, Norway, Portugal, San Marino, and Sweden.

Protocol VI has been ratified by the following States: Austria, Denmark, Federal Republic of Germany, France, Iceland, Italy, Luxembourg, Netherlands, Norway, Portugal, San Marino, Spain, Sweden, and Switzerland. It entered into force on 1 March 1985.

Protocol VII has been ratified by the following States: Austria, Denmark, France, Greece, Iceland, Luxembourg, Norway, San Marino, Spain, Sweden, and Switzerland. It entered into force on 1 November 1988.

Protocol VIII has been ratified by all States parties to the convention. It entered into force on 1 January 1990.

E. *European Convention on Social Security*

Up to 1 January 1990, the following States have become parties to the convention by ratification or accession: Austria, Luxembourg, Netherlands, Portugal, and Turkey.

The following States have signed the convention: Belgium, France, Greece, Ireland, and Italy.

F. *European Convention on the Suppression of Terrorism*

Up to 1 January 1990, the following States have become parties to the convention by ratification or accession: Austria, Belgium, Cyprus, Denmark, Federal Republic of Germany, France, Greece, Iceland, Italy, Liechtenstein, Luxembourg, Netherlands, Norway, Portugal, Spain, Sweden, Switzerland, Turkey, and the United Kingdom of Great Britain and Northern Ireland.

Ireland and Malta have signed the convention.

G. *European Social Charter*

Up to 1 January 1990, the following States have become parties to the charter by ratification or accession: Austria, Cyprus, Denmark, Federal Republic of Germany, France, Greece, Iceland, Ireland, Italy, Malta, Netherlands, Norway, Spain, Sweden, and United Kingdom of Great Britain and Northern Ireland.

The following States have signed the charter: Belgium, Luxembourg, Portugal, Switzerland, and Turkey.

6. Conventions Prepared under the Auspices of the Organization of African Unity

A. *African Charter on Human and Peoples' Rights*

Up to 1 January 1990, the following States have become parties to the African Convention on Human and People's Rights by ratification or accession: Algeria, Benin, Botswana, Burkina Faso, Cape Verde, Central African Republic, Chad, Congo, Comoros, Egypt, Equatorial Guinea, Gabon, Gambia, Ghana, Guinea, Guinea-Bissau, Liberia, Libya, Mali, Mauritania, Niger, Nigeria, Rwanda, Sao Tome and Principe, Senegal, Sierra Leone, Somalia, Sudan, Tanzania, Togo, Tunisia, Uganda, Zaire, Zambia, and Zimbabwe.

B. *African Convention governing the Specific Aspects of Refugee Problems in Africa*

Up to 1 January 1990, the following States have become parties to the convention by ratification or accession: Algeria, Angola, Benin, Burkina Faso, Burundi, Cameroon, Cape Verde, Central African Republic, Chad, Congo, Egypt, Equatorial Guinea, Ethiopia, Gabon, Gambia, Ghana, Guinea, Lesotho, Liberia, Libya, Malawi, Mali, Mauritania, Morocco, Niger, Nigeria, Rwanda, Senegal, Seychelles, Sierra Leone, Sudan, Swaziland, Tanzania, Togo, Uganda, Zaire, Zambia, and Zimbabwe.

7. Conventions Prepared under the Auspices of the Organization of American States

A. *American Convention on Human Rights*

Up to 1 January 1990, the following States have become parties to the convention by ratification or accession: Argentina, Barbados, Bolivia, Colombia, Costa Rica, Dominican Republic, Ecuador, El Salvador, Grenada, Guatemala, Haiti, Honduras, Jamaica, Mexico, Nicaragua, Panama, Peru, Suriname, Uruguay, and Venezuela.

The following States have signed the convention: Chile and Paraguay.

The following States have accepted the competence of the Inter-American Commission on Human Rights to hear petitions brought by one State party against another: Argentina, Colombia, Costa Rica, Ecuador, Jamaica, Peru, Uruguay, and Venezuela.

The following States have accepted the competence of the Inter-American Court of Human Rights: Argentina, Colombia, Costa Rica, Ecuador, Guatemala, Honduras, Peru, Suriname, Uruguay, and Venezuela.

*B. Inter-American Convention on Conflict of Laws
concerning the Adoption of Minors*

Up to 1 June 1990, the following countries have become parties to the convention by ratification or accession: Colombia and Mexico.

The convention has been signed by Bolivia, Brazil, Chile, Dominican Republic, Ecuador, Haiti, Uruguay, and Venezuela.

APPENDIX D

CHRONOLOGICAL LIST OF INTERNATIONAL INSTRUMENTS CONCERNED WITH HUMAN RIGHTS

The following is a listing in chronological order of the international instruments concerning the realization of human rights which can be found in this encyclopedia:

Document Title	*Date of Adoption*
ILO Right of Association (Agriculture) Convention	12 November 1921
Protocol for the Prohibition of the Use in War of Asphyxiating, Poisonous or Other Gases, or of Bacteriological Methods of Warfare	17 June 1925
Slavery Convention signed at Geneva, as Amended	25 September 1926
ILO Forced Labor Convention	28 June 1930
Atlantic Charter	14 August 1941
Declaration by United Nations	1 January 1942
International Labor Organization Constitution	10 May 1944
United Nations Charter	26 June 1945
United Nations Educational, Scientific and Cultural Organization Charter	16 November 1945
World Health Organization Charter	22 July 1946
ILO Labor Inspection Convention	11 July 1947
Organization of American States Charter	30 April 1948
Inter-American Charter of Social Guarantees	2 May 1948
Inter-American Convention on the Granting of Political Rights to Women	2 May 1948
Inter-American Convention on the Granting of Civil Rights to Women	2 May 1948
American Declaration on the Rights and Duties of Man	2 May 1948
ILO Freedom of Association and Protection of the Right to Organize Convention	9 July 1948
ILO Night Work (Women) Convention, revised	9 July 1948
Convention on the Prevention and Punishment of the Crime of Genocide	9 December 1948
Universal Declaration of Human Rights	10 December 1948
Council of Europe Statute	5 May 1949
ILO Migration for Employment Convention, revised	1 July 1949
ILO Protection of Wages Convention	1 July 1949
ILO Right to Organize and Collective Bargaining Convention	1 July 1949
Geneva Convention Relative to the Treatment of Prisoners of War	12 August 1949
Geneva Convention Relative to the Protection of Civilian Persons in Time of War	12 August 1949
Declaration concerning the Essentials of Peace	1 December 1949
Convention for the Suppression of the Traffic in Persons and of the Exploitation of the Prostitution of Others	2 December 1949

Document Title	*Date of Adoption*
European Convention on Human Rights	4 November 1950
UNESCO Agreement on the Importation of Educational, Scientific and Cultural Materials, and annexed Protocol	22 November 1950
ILO Equal Remuneration Convention	29 June 1951
Convention relating to the Status of Refugees	28 July 1951
European Convention on Human Rights: Protocol I	20 March 1952
ILO Maternity Protection Convention, revised	28 June 1952
ILO Social Security (Minimum Standards) Convention	28 June 1952
Universal Copyright Convention, revised, and Protocols	6 September 1952
Convention on the International Right of Correction	16 December 1952
Convention on the Political Rights of Women	20 December 1952
Protocol amending the Slavery Convention Signed at Geneva on 25 September 1926	23 October 1953
Inter-American Convention on Diplomatic Asylum	28 March 1954
Inter-American Convention on Territorial Asylum	28 March 1954
UNESCO Convention for the Protection of Cultural Property in the Event of Armed Conflict	14 May 1954
Convention relating to the Status of Stateless Persons	28 September 1954
Standard Minimum Rules for the Treatment of Prisoners	30 August 1955
European Convention on Establishment and Protocol	13 December 1955
Supplementary Convention on the Abolition of Slavery, the Slave Trade, and Institutions and Practices Similar to Slavery	13 December 1956
Convention on the Nationality of Married Women	29 January 1957
ILO Abolition of Forced Labor Convention	25 June 1957
European Agreement on Regulations governing the Movement of Persons between Member States of the Council of Europe	13 December 1957
European Convention on Extradition	13 December 1957
Convention on the High Seas	28 April 1958
ILO Discrimination (Employment and Occupation) Convention	25 June 1958
Declaration of the Rights of the Child	20 November 1959
UNESCO Convention against Discrimination in Education	14 December 1960
Declaration on the Granting of Independence to Colonial Countries and Peoples	14 December 1960
Convention on the Reduction of Statelessness	30 August 1961
European Social Charter	18 October 1961
UNESCO International Convention for the Protection of Performers, Producers of Phonograms and Broadcasting Organizations	26 October 1961
ILO Social Policy (Basic Aims and Standards) Convention	23 June 1962
ILO Equality of Treatment (Social Security) Convention	28 June 1962
Convention on Consent to Marriage, Minimum Age for Marriage and Registration of Marriages	7 November 1962
UNESCO Convention against Discrimination in Education: Protocol	10 December 1962
Declaration on Permanent Sovereignty over Natural Resources	14 December 1962
European Convention on Human Rights: Protocol II	6 May 1963
European Convention on Human Rights: Protocol III	6 May 1963
European Convention on Human Rights: Protocol IV	6 May 1963
Organization of African Unity Charter	25 May 1963
Declaration on the Elimination of All Forms of Racial Discrimination	20 November 1963
European Code on Social Security and Protocol	16 April 1964
ILO Employment Policy Convention	9 July 1964
Protocol to the Charter of the Organization of African Unity, Establishing the Commission of Mediation, Conciliation and Arbitration	21 July 1964
Cairo Declaration: Program for Peace and International Cooperation	10 October 1964

Document Title	*Date of Adoption*
Recommendation on Consent to Marriage, Minimum Age for Marriage and Registration of Marriages	1 November 1965
Inter-American Declaration on Racial Integration in the Americas	30 November 1965
Declaration on the Promotion among Youth of the Ideals of Peace, Mutual Respect and Understanding among Peoples	7 December 1965
International Convention on the Elimination of All Forms of Racial Discrimination	21 December 1965
European Convention on Human Rights: Protocol V	20 January 1966
UNESCO Declaration on the Principles of International Cultural Co-operation	4 November 1966
UNESCO Recommendation concerning the Status of Teachers	5 November 1966
European Convention on the Adoption of Children	24 April 1967
Declaration on the Elimination of All Forms of Discrimination against Women	7 November 1967
Declaration on Territorial Asylum	14 December 1967
Proclamation of Teheran	13 May 1968
Convention on the Non-Applicability of Statutory Limitations to War Crimes and Crimes against Humanity	26 November 1968
European Agreement relating to Persons Participating in Proceedings of the European Commission and Court of Human Rights	6 May 1969
ILO Medical Care and Sickness Benefits Convention	25 June 1969
African Convention governing the Specific Aspects of Refugee Problems in Africa	10 September 1969
American Convention on Human Rights	22 November 1969
Declaration on Social Progress and Development	11 December 1969
European Declaration on Mass Communication Media and Human Rights	23 January 1970
European Convention on the Repatriation of Minors	28 May 1970
ILO Minimum Wage Fixing Convention	22 June 1970
ILO Holidays with Pay Convention, revised	24 June 1970
Declaration on Principles of International law concerning Friendly Relations and Cooperation among States in Accordance with the Charter of the United Nations	24 October 1970
Declaration on the Occasion of the 25th Anniversary of the United Nations	24 October 1970
Convention on the Means of Prohibiting and Preventing the Illicit Import, Export and Transfer of Ownership of Cultural Property	14 November 1970
Basic Principles for the Protection of Civilian Populations in Armed Conflicts	9 December 1970
Convention for the Suppression of Unlawful Seizure of Aircraft	16 December 1970
ILO Workers' Representatives Convention	23 June 1971
Universal Copyright Convention and Protocols I and II, revised	24 July 1971
Convention for the Suppression of Unlawful Acts against the Safety of Civil Aviation	23 September 1971
Convention on the Prohibition of the Development, Production and Stockpiling of Bacteriological (Biological) and Toxic Weapons and on their Destruction	10 April 1972
European Convention on the Transfer of Proceedings in Criminal Matters	15 May 1972
Declaration of the United Nations Conference on the Human Environment	16 June 1972
UNESCO Declaration of Guiding Principles on the Use of Satellite Broadcasting for the Free Flow of Information, the Spread of Education and Greater Cultural Exchange	15 November 1972

Document Title	*Date of Adoption*
UNESCO Convention concerning the Protection of the World Cultural Heritage	16 November 1972
European Convention on Social Security	14 December 1972
ILO Minimum Age Convention	26 June 1973
International Convention on the Suppression and Punishment of the Crime of *Apartheid*	30 November 1972
Principles of International Cooperation in the Detection, Arrest, Extradition and Punishment of Persons Guilty of War Crimes and Crimes against Humanity	3 December 1973
Basic Principles of the Legal Status of the Combatants struggling against Colonial and Alien Domination and Racist Regimes	12 December 1972
Convention on the Prevention and Punishment of Crimes against Internationally Protected Persons, including Diplomatic Agents	14 December 1973
European Convention on the Non-Applicability of Statutory Limitation to Crimes against Humanity and War Crimes	25 January 1974
ILO Paid Educational Leave Convention	24 June 1974
Universal Declaration on the Eradication of Hunger and Malnutrition	16 November 1974
UNESCO Recommendation concerning Education for International Understanding, Cooperation and Peace and Education relating to Human Rights and Fundamental Freedoms	19 November 1974
UNESCO Recommendation concerning Technical and Vocational Education, revised	19 November 1974
UNESCO Recommendation on the Status of Scientific Researchers	20 November 1974
Declaration on the Protection of Women and Children in Emergency and Armed Conflict	11 December 1974
ILO Human Resources Development Convention	23 June 1975
ILO Rural Workers' Organizations Conventions	23 June 1975
ILO Migrant Workers (Supplementary Provisions) Convention	23 June 1975
Declaration of Mexico on the Equality of Women and Their Contribution to Development and Peace	2 July 1975
Helsinki Accord: Final Act of the Conference on Security and Cooperation in Europe	1 August 1975
European Convention on Extradition	15 October 1975
European Agreement on the Legal Status of Children Born Out of Wedlock	15 October 1975
Declaration on the Use of Scientific and Technological Progress in the Interests of Peace and for the Benefit of Mankind	10 November 1975
Declaration on the Protection of All Persons from Being Subjected to Torture and Other Cruel, Inhuman or Degrading Treatment or Punishment	9 December 1975
Declaration on the Rights of Disabled Persons	9 December 1975
Vancouver Declaration on Human Settlements	11 June 1976
Declaration of Principles and Program of Action of the Tripartite World Conference on Employment	14 June 1976
Declaration of Abijan	9 July 1976
UNESCO Agreement on the Importation of Educational, Scientific and Cultural Materials: Protocol	26 November 1976
UNESCO Recommendation on the Development of Adult Education	26 November 1976
UNESCO Recommendation on Participation by the People at Large in Cultural Life and Their Contribution to It	26 November 1976
European Convention on the Suppression of Terrorism	27 January 1977
Geneva Conventions: Protocols I and II	9 June 1977
ILO Working Environment (Air Pollution, Noise and Vibration) Convention	20 June 1977

Document Title	*Date of Adoption*
Lagos Declaration against *Apartheid*	2 August 1977
Declaration on the Rights of Deaf-Blind Persons	16 September 1977
European Convention on the Legal Status of Migrant Workers	24 November 1977
International Declaration against *Apartheid* in Sports	14 December 1977
European Convention on Extradition: Second Additional Protocol	17 March 1978
Charter of Rights for Migrant Workers in Southern Africa	7 April 1978
ILO Labor Relations (Public Service) Convention	27 June 1978
Declaration of Alma Ata	12 September 1978
UNESCO International Charter of Physical Education and Sport	21 November 1978
UNESCO Declaration on Race and Racial Prejudice	27 November 1978
UNESCO Declaration on Fundamental Principles concerning the Contribution of the Mass Media to Strengthening Peace and International Understanding, to the Promotion of Human Rights and to Countering Racialism, *Apartheid,* and Incitement to War	28 November 1978
Declaration on the Preparation of Societies for Life in Peace	15 December 1978
Code of Conduct for Law Enforcement Officials	17 December 1979
International Convention against the Taking of Hostages	17 December 1979
Convention on the Elimination of all Forms of Discrimination against Women	18 December 1979
European Convention on Recognition and Enforcement of Decisions concerning Custody of Children and on Restoration of Custody of Children	28 May 1980
European Convention for the Protection of Individuals with Regard to Automatic Processing of Personal Data	28 January 1981
Inter-American Convention on Extradition	25 February 1981
Convention on Prohibitions or Restrictions on the Use of Certain Conventional Weapons Which May be Deemed Excessively Injurious or to Have Indiscriminate Effects, and Protocols	10 April 1981
ILO Collective Bargaining Convention	19 June 1981
ILO Occupational Safety and Health Convention	22 June 1981
ILO Workers with Family Responsibilities Convention	23 June 1981
African Charter on Human and Peoples' Rights	28 June 1981
Declaration on the Elimination of All Forms of Intolerance and of Discrimination Based on Religion or Belief	25 November 1981
Declaration on the Inadmissibility of Intervention and Interference in the Internal Affairs of States	9 December 1981
Declaration on the Prevention of Nuclear Catastrophe	9 December 1981
European Recommendation concerning International Co-operation in the Prosecution and Punishment of Terrorism	15 January 1982
European Declaration on Freedom of Expression and Information	29 April 1982
Declaration on the Participation of Women in Promoting International Peace and Co-operation	3 December 1982
Principles governing the Use by States of Artificial Earth Satellites for International Direct Television Broadcasting	10 December 1982
Principles of Medical Ethics Relevant to the Role of Health Personnel, particularly Physicians, in the Protection of Prisoners and Detainees against Torture and Other Cruel, Inhuman or Degrading Treatment or Punishment	18 December 1982
European Convention on Human Rights: Protocol VI	28 April 1983
Declaration of the Second World Conference to Combat Racism and Racial Discrimination	12 August 1983
Geneva Declaration on Palestine	7 September 1983
Convention on International Civil Aircraft	10 May 1984

Document Title	*Date of Adoption*
Inter-American Convention on Conflict of Laws concerning the Adoption of Minors	24 May 1984
Safeguards Guaranteeing the Protection of the Rights of Those Facing the Death Penalty	25 May 1984
Nairobi Forward-looking Strategies for the Advancement of Women	26 July 1984
Declaration on the Right of Peoples to Peace	12 November 1984
European Convention on Human Rights: Protocol VII	22 November 1984
Convention against Torture and Other Cruel, Inhuman or Degrading Treatment or Punishment	10 December 1984
Declaration on the Control of Drug Trafficking and Drug Abuse	14 December 1984
European Convention on Human Rights: Protocol VIII	19 March 1985
Proclamation of the International Year of Peace	24 October 1985
Basic Principles of the Independence of the Judiciary	29 November 1985
Declaration of Basic Principles for Victims of Crime and Abuse of Power	29 November 1985
United Nations Standard Minimum Rules for the Administration of Juvenile Justice (Beijing Rules)	29 November 1985
Inter-American Convention to Prevent and Punish Torture	9 December 1985
International Convention against *Apartheid* in Sports	10 December 1985
Declaration on the Human Rights of Individuals who are not Nationals of the Country in Which They Live	13 December 1985
Declaration on Social and Legal Principles relating to the Protection and Welfare of Children, with Special Reference to Foster Placement and Adoption Nationally and Internationally	3 December 1986
Declaration on the Right to Development	4 December 1986
European Convention for the Prevention of Torture and Inhuman or Degrading Treatment or Punishment	26 June 1987
European Social Charter: Protocol	26 November 1987
Khartoum Declaration	8 March 1988
Apartheid: ILO Declaration and Program of Action	16 June 1988
American Convention on Human Rights: Additional Protocol with Regard to Economic, Social and Cultural Rights	17 November 1988
Body of Principles for the Protection of All Persons under any Form of Detention or Imprisonment	9 December 1988
European Convention on Transfrontier Television	5 May 1989
Principles on the Effective Prevention and Investigation of Extra-legal, Arbitrary and Summary Executions	24 May 1989
ILO Indigenous and Tribal Peoples Convention	27 June 1989
Tallinn Guidelines for Action on Human Resources Development in the Field of Disability	22 August 1989
Convention on the Rights of the Child	20 November 1989
International Convention against the Recruitment, Use, Financing and Training of Mercenaries	4 December 1989
Declaration on *Apartheid* and its Destructive Consequences in South Africa	14 December 1989
International Covenant on Civil and Political Rights: Second Optional Protocol, Aiming at Abolition of the Death Penalty	15 December 1989

APPENDIX E

INTERNATIONAL LABOR CODE

Every international convention adopted by the International Labor Conference has a bearing—however slight—upon the realization of human rights and fundamental freedoms. While, for reasons of space, those reproduced in the encyclopedia are limited to those most directly concerned with the subject and most effectively implemented by the machinery developed by the International Labor Organization, there are many others of importance.

A complete list of the conventions adopted by the conference in the 70-year period between 1919 and 1989 is reproduced below. As a group, these instruments are sometimes referred to as the "International Labor Code."

No. 1. Hours of Work (Industry) Convention, 1919
No. 2. Unemployment Convention, 1919
No. 3. Maternity Protection Convention, 1919
No. 4. Night Work (Women) Convention, 1919
No. 5. Minimum Age (Industry) Convention, 1919
No. 6. Night Work of Young Persons (Industry) Convention, 1919
No. 7. Minimum Age (Sea) Convention, 1920
No. 8. Unemployment Indemnity (Shipwreck) Convention, 1920
No. 9. Placing of Seamen Convention, 1920
No. 10. Minimum Age (Agriculture) Convention, 1921
No. 11. Right of Association (Agriculture) Convention, 1921
No. 12. Workmen's Compensation (Agriculture) Convention, 1921
No. 13. White Lead (Painting) Convention, 1921
No. 14. Weekly Rest (Industry) Convention, 1921
No. 15. Minimum Age (Trimmers and Stokers) Convention, 1921
No. 16. Medical Examination of Young Persons (Sea) Convention, 1921
No. 17. Workmen's Compensation (Accidents) Convention, 1925
No. 18. Workmen's Compensation (Occupational Diseases) Convention, 1925
No. 19. Equality of Treatment (Accident Compensation) Convention, 1925
No. 20. Night Work (Bakeries) Convention, 1925
No. 21. Inspection of Emigrants Convention, 1926
No. 22. Seamen's Articles of Agreement Convention, 1926
No. 23. Repatriation of Seamen Convention, 1926

No. 24. Sickness Insurance (Industry) Convention, 1927
No. 25. Sickness Insurance (Agriculture) Convention, 1927
No. 26. Minimum Wage-Fixing Machinery Convention, 1928
No. 27. Marking of Weight (Packages Transported by Vessels) Convention, 1929
No. 28. Protection against Accidents (Dockers) Convention, 1929
No. 29. Forced Labour Convention, 1930
No. 30. Hours of Work (Commerce and Offices) Convention, 1930
No. 31. Hours of Work (Coal Mines) Convention, 1931
No. 32. Protection against Accidents (Dockers) Convention (Revised), 1932
No. 33. Minimum Age (Non-Industrial Employment) Convention, 1932
No. 34. Fee-Charging Employment Agencies Convention, 1933
No. 35. Old-Age Insurance (Industry, etc.) Convention, 1933
No. 36. Old-Age Insurance (Agriculture) Convention, 1933
No. 37. Invalidity Insurance (Industry, etc.) Convention, 1933
No. 38. Invalidity Insurance (Agriculture) Convention, 1933
No. 39. Survivors' Insurance (Industry, etc.) Convention, 1933
No. 40. Survivors' Insurance (Agriculture) Convention, 1933
No. 41. Night Work (Women) Convention (Revised), 1934

No. 42.   Workmen's Compensation (Occupational Diseases) Convention (Revised), 1934

No. 43.   Sheet-Glass Works Convention, 1934

No. 44.   Unemployment Provision Convention, 1934

No. 45.   Underground Work (Women) Convention, 1935

No. 46.   ˙ Hours of Work (Coal Mines) Convention (Revised), 1935

No. 47.   Forty-Hour Week Convention, 1935

No. 48.   Maintenance of Migrants' Pension Rights Convention, 1935

No. 49.   Reduction of Hours of Work (Glass-Bottle Works) Convention, 1935

No. 50.   Recruiting of Indigenous Workers Convention, 1936

No. 51.   Reduction of Hours of Work (Public Works) Convention, 1936

No. 52.   Holidays with Pay Convention, 1936

No. 53.   Officers' Competency Certificates Convention, 1936

No. 54.   Holidays with Pay (Sea) Convention, 1936

No. 55.   Shipowners' Liability (Sick and Injured Seamen) Convention, 1936

No. 56.   Sickness Insurance (Sea) Convention, 1936

No. 57.   Hours of Work and Manning (Sea) Convention, 1936

No. 58.   Minimum Age (Sea) Convention (Revised), 1936

No. 59.   Minimum Age (Industry) Convention (Revised), 1937

No. 60.   Minimum Age (Non-Industrial Employment) Convention (Revised), 1937

No. 61.   Reduction of Hours of Work (Textiles) Convention, 1937

No. 62.   Safety Provisions (Building) Convention, 1937

No. 63.   Convention concerning Statistics of Wages and Hours of Work, 1938

No. 64.   Contracts of Employment (Indigenous Workers) Convention, 1939

No. 65.   Penal Sanctions (Indigenous Workers) Convention, 1939

No. 66.   Migration for Employment Convention, 1939

No. 67.   Hours of Work and Rest Periods (Road Transport) Convention, 1939

No. 68.   Food and Catering (Ships' Crews) Convention, 1946

No. 69.   Certification of Ships' Cooks Convention, 1946

No. 70.   Social Security (Seafarers) Convention, 1946

No. 71.   Seafarers' Pensions Convention, 1946

No. 72.   Paid Vacations (Seafarers) Convention, 1946

No. 73.   Medical Examination (Seafarers) Convention, 1946

No. 74.   Certification of Able Seamen Convention, 1946

No. 75.   Accommodation of Crews Convention, 1946

No. 76.   Wages, Hours of Work and Manning (Sea) Convention, 1946

No. 77.   Medical Examination of Young Persons (Industry) Convention, 1946

No. 78.   Medical Examination of Young Persons (Non-Industrial Occupations) Convention, 1946

No. 79.   Night Work of Young Persons (Non-Industrial Occupations) Convention, 1946

No. 80.   Final Articles Revision Convention, 1946

No. 81.   Labour Inspection Convention, 1947

No. 82.   Social Policy (Non-Metropolitan Territories) Convention, 1947

No. 83.   Labour Standards (Non-Metropolitan Territories) Convention, 1947

No. 84.   Right of Association (Non-Metropolitan Territories) Convention, 1947

No. 85.   Labour Inspectorates (Non-Metropolitan Territories) Convention, 1947

No. 86.   Contracts of Employment (Indigenous Workers) Convention, 1947

No. 87.   Freedom of Association and Protection of the Right to Organise Convention, 1948

No. 88.   Employment Service Convention, 1948

No. 89.   Night Work (Women) Convention (Revised), 1948

No. 90.   Night Work of Young Persons (Industry) Convention (Revised), 1948

No. 91.   Paid Vacations (Seafarers) Convention (Revised), 1949

No. 92.   Accommodation of Crews Convention (Revised), 1949

No. 93.   Wages, Hours of Work and Manning (Sea) Convention (Revised), 1949

No. 94.   Labour Clauses (Public Contracts) Convention, 1949

No. 95.   Protection of Wages Convention, 1949

No. 96.   Fee-Charging Employment Agencies Convention (Revised), 1949

No. 97.   Migration for Employment Convention (Revised), 1949

No. 98.   Right to Organise and Collective Bargaining Convention, 1949

No. 99.   Minimum Wage Fixing Machinery (Agriculture) Convention, 1951

No. 162. Asbestos Convention, 1986

No. 163. Seafarers' Welfare Convention, 1987

No. 164. Health Protection and Medical Care (Seafarers) Convention, 1987

No. 165. Social Security (Seafarers) Convention (Revised), 1987

No. 166. Repatriation of Seafarers Convention (Revised), 1987

No. 167. Safety and Health in Construction Convention, 1988

No. 168. Employment Promotion and Protection against Unemployment Convention, 1988

No. 169. Indigenous and Tribal Peoples Convention, 1989

APPENDIX F

UNITED NATIONS CENTRE FOR HUMAN RIGHTS: ORGANIGRAM

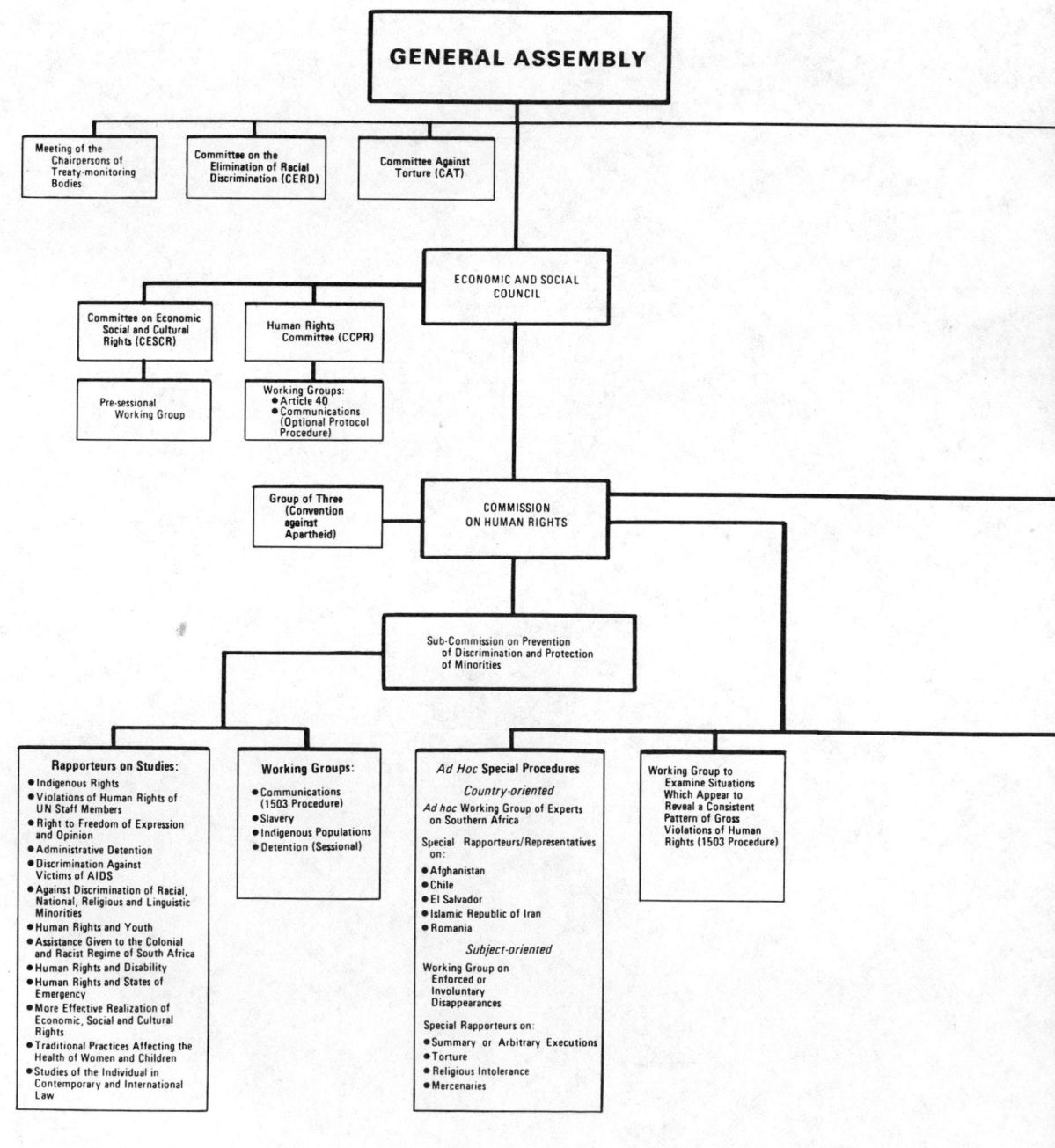

GENERAL ASSEMBLY

Meeting of the
Chairpersons of
Treaty-monitoring
Bodies

Committee on the
Elimination of Racial
Discrimination (CERD)

Committee Against
Torture (CAT)

ECONOMIC AND SOCIAL
COUNCIL

Committee on Economic
Social and Cultural
Rights (CESCR)

Human Rights
Committee (CCPR)

Pre-sessional
Working Group

Working Groups:
● Article 40
● Communications
(Optional Protocol
Procedure)

Group of Three
(Convention
against
Apartheid)

COMMISSION
ON HUMAN RIGHTS

Sub-Commission on Prevention
of Discrimination and Protection
of Minorities

Rapporteurs on Studies:
● Indigenous Rights
● Violations of Human Rights of
UN Staff Members
● Right to Freedom of Expression
and Opinion
● Administrative Detention
● Discrimination Against
Victims of AIDS
● Against Discrimination of Racial,
National, Religious and Linguistic
Minorities
● Human Rights and Youth
● Assistance Given to the Colonial
and Racist Regime of South Africa
● Human Rights and Disability
● Human Rights and States of
Emergency
● More Effective Realization of
Economic, Social and Cultural
Rights
● Traditional Practices Affecting the
Health of Women and Children
● Studies of the Individual in
Contemporary and International
Law

Working Groups:
● Communications
(1503 Procedure)
● Slavery
● Indigenous Populations
● Detention (Sessional)

Ad Hoc **Special Procedures**

Country-oriented
Ad hoc Working Group of Experts
on Southern Africa

Special Rapporteurs/Representatives
on:
● Afghanistan
● Chile
● El Salvador
● Islamic Republic of Iran
● Romania

Subject-oriented
Working Group on
Enforced or
Involuntary
Disappearances

Special Rapporteurs on:
● Summary or Arbitrary Executions
● Torture
● Religious Intolerance
● Mercenaries

Working Group to
Examine Situations
Which Appear to
Reveal a Consistent
Pattern of Gross
Violations of Human
Rights (1503 Procedure)

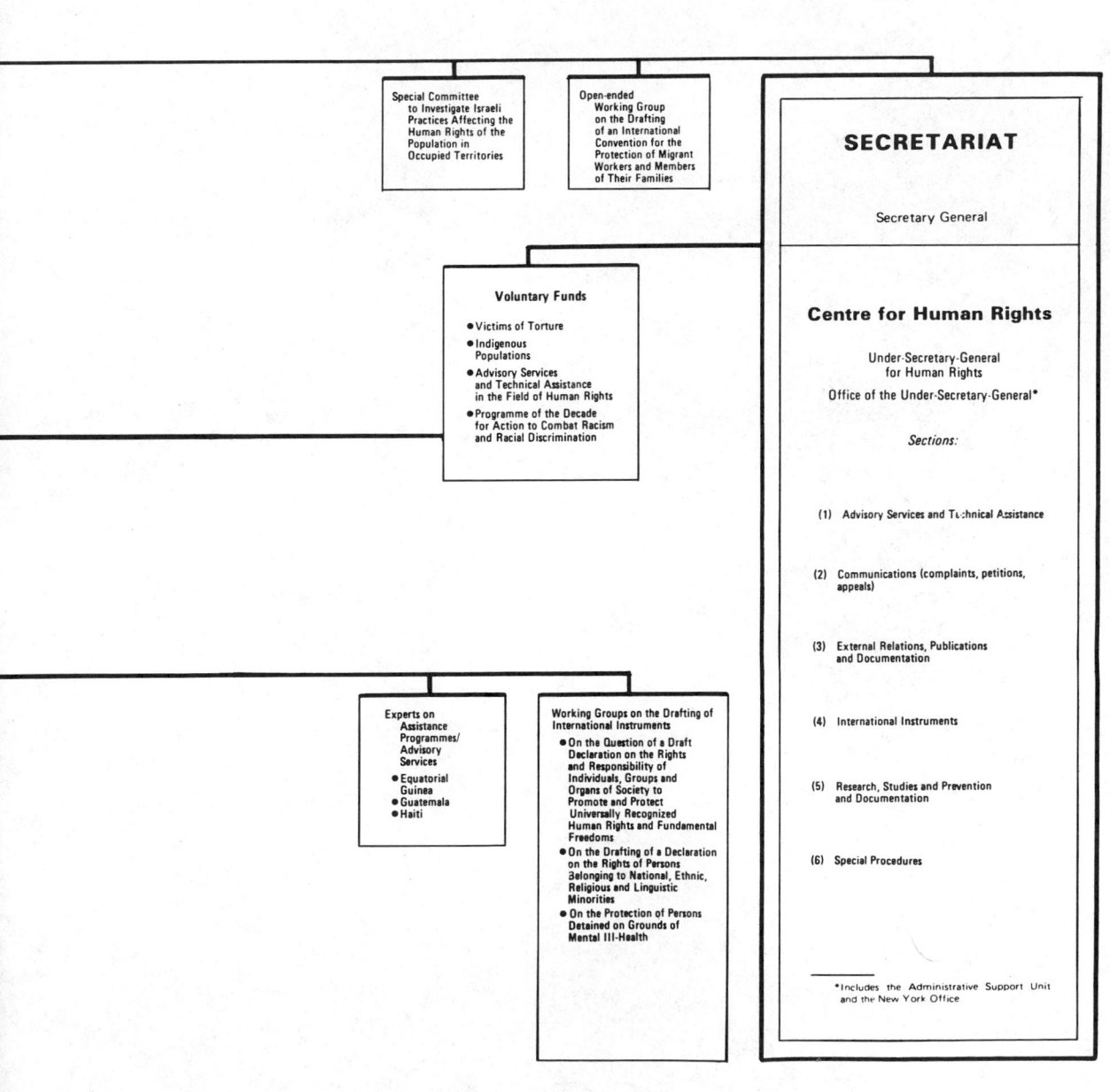

Special Committee to Investigate Israeli Practices Affecting the Human Rights of the Population in Occupied Territories

Open-ended Working Group on the Drafting of an International Convention for the Protection of Migrant Workers and Members of Their Families

SECRETARIAT

Secretary General

Centre for Human Rights

Under-Secretary-General for Human Rights

Office of the Under-Secretary-General*

Sections:

(1) Advisory Services and Technical Assistance

(2) Communications (complaints, petitions, appeals)

(3) External Relations, Publications and Documentation

(4) International Instruments

(5) Research, Studies and Prevention and Documentation

(6) Special Procedures

*Includes the Administrative Support Unit and the New York Office

Voluntary Funds

- Victims of Torture
- Indigenous Populations
- Advisory Services and Technical Assistance in the Field of Human Rights
- Programme of the Decade for Action to Combat Racism and Racial Discrimination

Experts on Assistance Programmes/ Advisory Services

- Equatorial Guinea
- Guatemala
- Haiti

Working Groups on the Drafting of International Instruments

- On the Question of a Draft Declaration on the Rights and Responsibility of Individuals, Groups and Organs of Society to Promote and Protect Universally Recognized Human Rights and Fundamental Freedoms
- On the Drafting of a Declaration on the Rights of Persons Belonging to National, Ethnic, Religious and Linguistic Minorities
- On the Protection of Persons Detained on Grounds of Mental Ill-Health

APPENDIX G

UNITED NATIONS STUDIES AND REPORTS ON HUMAN RIGHTS ISSUES

In response to a request by the Sub-Commission on Prevention of Discrimination and Protection of Minorities, the UN secretary-general submitted to that organ at its 1990 session a list of studies and reports on particular human rights issues which had been prepared for, or mandated by, United Nations bodies concerned with human rights.

The list, reproduced below, includes (a) studies and reports prepared for the General Assembly, (b) studies and reports prepared for the Economic and Social Council, (c) studies and reports prepared for the Commission on Human Rights, (d) studies and reports prepared for the sub-commission itself, and (e) studies and reports under preparation by special rapporteurs or experts of the sub-commission. It does not, however, include studies or reports which review developments in situations of human rights in particular countries or areas, nor does it include studies or reports prepared for, or mandated by, other functional commissions of the Economic and Social Council, such as the Commission on the Status of Women or the Commission on Social Development.

The list provides the title of the study or report, its author, the year when its final version was considered, and the document symbol. If the study or report was issued as a United Nations publication, its sales number is also indicated.

The list is as follows (UN Doc. E/CN.4/Sub.2/1990/2):

A. Studies and Reports Prepared for the UN General Assembly

1. *Report on Respect for Human Rights in Armed Conflicts*, prepared by the Secretary-General, 1977 (A/32/144 and Add.1).

2. *Report on Protection of Broad Sectors of the Population against Social and Material Inequalities, as well as Other Harmful Effects Which May Arrive from the Use of Scientific and Technological Developments*, prepared by the Secretary-General, 1975 (A/10/146).

B. Studies and Reports Prepared for the UN Economic and Social Council

1. *Freedom of Information, 1953*, report submitted by Mr. Salvador P. López, Rapporteur, 1954 (E/2426 and Add.1–5).

2. *Report on Developments in the Field of Freedom of Information since 1954*, prepared by Mr. Hilding Eek (Sweden), consultant appointed by the Secretary-General at the request of the Council, 1961 (E/3443).

3. *Concise Summary of Information on Slavery*, report prepared by Mr. Hans Engen (Norway), Rapporteur appointed by the Council, 1955 (E/2673 and Add.1–4).

4. *The Problem of Protecting Sources of Information of News Personnel*, study by the Secretary-General, 1955 (E/2693 and Add.1–3).

5. *Legal Aspects of the Rights and Responsibilities of Media of Information*, study by the Secretary-General, 1955 (E/2698 and Add.1).

6. *Study on Capital Punishment*, prepared by Mr. Marc Ancel (France), consultant of the Secretary-General, 1961 (ST/SOA/SD9; Sales No. 1962.IV.2).

7. *Report on Slavery*, prepared by Mr. Mohammed Awad (Egypt), Special Rapporteur appointed by the Secretary-General, at the request of the Council, 1966 (E/4168/Rev.1; Sales No. 67.XIV.2).

8. *Report on the Suppression of the Traffic in Persons and the Exploitation of the Prostitution of Others*, prepared by Mr. Jean Fernant-Laurent, Special Rapporteur appointed by the Secretary-General, at the request of the Council, 1983 (E/1983/7).

C. Studies and Reports Prepared for the UN Commission on Human Rights

1. *Study of the Legal Validity of the Undertaking concerning Minorities*, prepared by the Secretary-General, 1950 (E/CN.4/367 and Add.1 and Corr.1).

2. *Activities of the United Nations and of the Specialized Agencies in the Field of Economic, Social and Cultural Rights,* report of the Secretary-General, 1952 (E/CN.4/364/Rev.1; Sales No. 1952.IV.4).

3. *Right of Asylum,* memorandum by the Secretary-General, 1957 (E/CN.4/738 and Corr.1 and 2).

4. *Freedom of Information,* special report of the *Ad hoc* Committee on Freedom of Information established by Commission on Human Rights resolution IX (XIII), 1957 (E/CN.4/762 and Corr.1).

5. *Study of the Right of Everyone to be Free from Arbitrary Arrest, Detention and Exile,* prepared by the Committee on the Right of Everyone to be Free from Arbitrary Arrest, Detention and Exile, consisting of four members of the Commission on Human Rights, elected by the Commission, 1962 (E/CN.4/826/Rev.1; Sales No. 65.XIV.2).

6. *Economic and Social Consequences of Racial Discrimination,* report of the Executive-Secretary of the Economic Commission for Africa, 1962 (Sales No. E.63.II.K.1).

7. *Question of the Applicability of Statutory Limitation to War Crimes and Crimes against Humanity,* study of the Secretary-General, 1966 (E/CN.4/906).

8. *Capital Punishment: Developments 1961–1965,* study prepared by Professor Norval Morris (Australia), consultant appointed by the Secretary-General, 1968 (Sales No. E.67.IV.15, part II).

9. *Study of the Right of Arrested Persons to Communicate with Those Whom It Is Necessary for Them to Consult in Order to Ensure Their Defence Or to Protect Their Essential Interests,* prepared by the Committee on the Right of Everyone to be Free from Arbitrary Arrest, Detention and Exile, 1969 (E/CN.4/996).

10. *Study of Apartheid and Racial Discrimination in Southern Africa,* prepared by Mr. Manouchehr Ganji (Iran), Special Rapporteur, 1968 (E/CN.4/979 and Add.1–8).

11. *The Realization of Economic, Social and Cultural Rights: Problems, Policies, Progress,* report prepared by Mr. Manouchehr Ganji (Iran), Special Rapporteur, 1974 (E/CN.4/1131; Sales No. 75.XIV.2).

12. *Study concerning the Question of Apartheid from the Point of View of International Penal Law,* prepared by the *Ad hoc* Working Group of Experts on Southern Africa, 1972 (E/CN.4/1075).

13. *Study on Ways and Means of Ensuring the Implementation of International Instruments such as the International Convention on the Suppression and Punishment of the Crime of Apartheid, including the Establishment of the International Jurisdiction Envisaged by the Convention,* prepared by the *Ad hoc* Working Group of Experts on Southern Africa, 1980 (E/CN.4/1426).

14. *Report on Certain Aspects of Human Rights and Technological Developments,* prepared by the Secretary-General, 1970 (E/CN.4/1028 and Add.1–3).

15. *Respect for the Privacy of Individuals and the Integrity and Sovereignty of Nations in the Light of Advances in Recording and Other Techniques,* report of the Secretary-General, 1974 (E/CN.4/1116 and Add.1–3).

16. *Use of Electronics Which May Affect the Rights of the Person and the Limits Which Should Be Placed on Such Use in a Democratic Society,* report of the Secretary-General, 1975 (E/CN.4/1142 and Add.1–2).

17. *Protection of the Human Personality and Its Physical and Intellectual Integrity, in the Light of Advances in Biology, Medicine and Biochemistry,* report of the Secretary-General, 1975 (E/CN.4/1172 and Add.1–3).

18. *The Balance Which Should Be Established between Scientific and Technological Progress and the Intellectual, Spiritual, Cultural and Moral Advancement of Humanity,* report of the Secretary-General, 1976 (E/CN.4/1199 and Add.1).

19. *The Human Rights Implications of the Genetic Manipulation of Microbes,* report of the Secretary-General, 1977 (E/CN.4/1236).

20. *The Impact of Scientific and Technological Developments on Economic, Social and Cultural Rights,* reports of the Secretary-General submitted in 1972, 1973, 1974 and 1976 (E/CN.4/1084; E/CN.4/1115; E/CN.4/1141 and E/CN.4/1198).

21. *The International Dimensions of the Right to Development as a Human Right in Relation with Other Human Rights Based on International Co-operation including the Right to Peace, Taking into Account the Requirements of the New International Economic Order and the Fundamental Human Needs,* report of the Secretary-General, 1979 (E/CN.4/1334).

22. *The Regional and National Dimensions of the Right to Development as a Human Right,* study by the Secretary-General, 1981 (E/CN.4/1421 and 1488).

23. *Human Rights and Mass Exoduses,* study prepared by Mr. Sadruddin Aga Khan, Special Rapporteur, 1982 (E/CN.4/1503).

24. *Study on the Effects of the Policy of Apartheid on Black Women and Children,* prepared by the *Ad hoc* Working Group of Experts on Southern Africa, 1982 and 1983 (E/CN.4/1497 and E/CN.4/1983/38).

25. *Study on the Criminal Effects of Apartheid,* prepared by the *Ad hoc* Working Group of Experts on Southern Africa, 1987 (E/CN.4/1985/14).

26. *Traditional Practices Affecting the Health of Women and Children,* report of the Working Group on Traditional Practices Affecting the Health of Women and Children, established by the Commission on Human Rights in 1984 (E/CN.4/1986/42).

D. Studies and Reports Prepared for the UN Sub-Commission on Prevention of Discrimination and Protection of Minorities

1. *Report on the Prevention of Discrimination,* prepared by the Secretary-General, 1949 (E/CN.4/Sub.2/40).

2. *The Main Types and Causes of Discrimination,* memorandum of the Secretary-General, 1949 (E/CN.4/Sub.2/40/Rev.1; Sales No. 1949, XIV.3).

3. *Definition and Classification of Minorities,* memorandum of the Secretary-General, 1949 (E/CN.4/Sub.2/85).

4. *Memorandum on the Population of the Aaland Islands,* prepared by Mr. Eric Einar Ekstrand (Sweden) at the request of the Sub-Commission, 1950 (E/CN.4/Sub.2/101).

5. *Memorandum on the German Minority in Denmark,* prepared by Mr. Eric Einar Ekstrand (Sweden) at the request of the Sub-Commission, 1950 (E/CN.4/Sub.2/102).

6. *Prevention of Discrimination and Denial of Fundamental Freedoms in Respect of Political Groups,* memorandum of the Secretary-General, 1951 (E/CN.4/Sub.2/129).

7. *Preliminary Report on the Proposed Study on Discrimination in the Matter of Religious Rights and Practices,* prepared by Mr. Philip Halperan (United States of America), 1954 (E/CN.4/Sub.2/162).

8. *Preliminary Study of Discrimination in the Matter of Emigration, Immigration and Travel,* prepared by Mr. José D. Inglés (Philippines), 1955 (E/CN.4/Sub.2/167).

9. *Measures for the Cessation of National, Racial or Religious Hostility,* report by the Secretary-General, 1956 (E/CN.4/Sub.2/172).

10. *Study of Discrimination in Education,* prepared by Mr. Charles D. Ammoun (Lebanon), Special Rapporteur, 1956 (E/CN.4/Sub.2/181/Rev.1; Sales No. E.57.XIV.3).

11. *Study of Discrimination in the Matter of Religious Rights and Practices,* prepared by Mr. Arcot Krishnaswami (India), Special Rapporteur, 1959 (E/CN.4/Sub.2/200/Rev.1; Sales No. E.60.XIV.2).

12. *Study of Discrimination in the Matter of Political Rights,* prepared by Mr. Hernán Santa Cruz (Chile), Special Rapporteur, 1962 and 1973 (E/CN.4/Sub.2/213/Rev.1; Sales No. E.63.XIV.2).

13. *Study of Discrimination in Respect of the Right of Everyone to Leave any Country, Including his Own, and to Return to his Country,* prepared by Mr. José D. Inglés (Philippines), Special Rapporteur, 1963 (E/CN.4/Sub.2/299/Rev.1; Sales No. E.64.XIV.2).

14. *Study of Discrimination Against Persons Born out of Wedlock,* prepared by Mr. Vieno Voitto Saario (Finland), Special Rapporteur, 1965 (E/CN.4/Sub.2/265/Rev.1; Sales No. E.68.XIV.3).

15. *Study of Equality in the Administration of Justice,* prepared by Mr. Mohammed Ahmed Abu Rannat (Sudan), Special Rapporteur, 1969 (E/CN.4/Sub.2/296/Rev.1; Sales No. E.71.XIV.3).

16. *Special Study of Racial Discrimination in the Political, Economic and Cultural Spheres,* prepared by Mr. Hernán Santa Cruz (Chile), Special Rapporteur, 1970 (E/CN.4/Sub.2/307/Rev.1). The study was published under the title *Racial Discrimination* in 1971 as a United Nations Publication, Sales No. E.71.XIV.2. A revised and updated version of the study was published in 1976 as a United Nations Publication, Sales No. E.76.XIV.2.

17. *Study of the Rights of Persons Belonging to Ethnic, Religious and Linguistic Minorities,* prepared by Mr. Francesco Capotorti (Italy), Special Rapporteur, 1978 (E/CN.4/Sub.2/384/Rev.1; Sales No. E.78.XIV.1).

18. *Study of the Question of the Prevention and Punishment of the Crime of Genocide,* prepared by Mr. Nicodème Ruhashyankiko (Rwanda) Special Rapporteur, 1978 (E/CN.4/Sub.2/416).

19. *Study of the Exploitation of Labour through Illicit and Clandestine Trafficking,* prepared by Mrs. Halima Embarek Warzazi (Morocco), Special Rapporteur, 1975 (E/CN.4/Sub.2/L.640; Sales No. E.86.XIV.1).

20. *Study of the Adverse Consequences for the Enjoyment of Human Rights of Political, Military, Economic and Other Assistance Given to the Colonialist and Racist Régimes in Southern Africa,* prepared by Mr. Ahmed M. Khalifa (Egypt), Special Rapporteur, 1978 (E/CN.4/Sub.2/383/Rev.2; Sales No. E.79/XIV.3). Since then the Special Rapporteur has submitted annual updated reports on the subject.

21. *Study of International Provisions Protecting the Human Rights of Non-Citizens,* prepared by Baroness Elles (United Kingdom), Special Rapporteur, 1977 (E/CN.4/Sub.2/392/Rev.1; Sales No. 80.XIV.2).

22. *Study of the Implementation of United Nations Resolutions Relating to the Right of Peoples under Colonial and Alien Domination to Self-Determination,* prepared by Mr. Hector Gros Espiell (Uruguay), Special Rapporteur, 1978 (E/CN.4/Sub.2/405/Rev.1; Sales No. E. 79. XIV.5).

23. *Study on the Impact of Foreign Economic Aid and Assistance on Respect for Human Rights in Chile,* prepared by Mr. Antonio Cassese (Italy), 1978 (E/CN.4/Sub.2/412 [Vol. I–IV]).

24. *Study of the Individual's Duties to the Community and the Limitations on Human Rights and Freedoms under Article 29 of the Universal Declaration of Human Rights: A Contribution to the Freedom of the Individual under Law,* prepared by Mrs. Erica-Irene A. Daes (Greece), Special Rapporteur, 1980 (E/CN.4/Sub.2/432/Rev.1; Sales No. E.82.XIV.1).

25. *Study of the Historical and Current Development of the Right to Self-Determination on the Basis of the Charter of the United Nations and Other Instruments Adopted by United Nations Organs, with Particular Reference to the Promotion and Protection of Human Rights and Fundamental Freedoms,* prepared by Mr. Aureliu Cristescu (Romania), Special Rapporteur, 1978 (E/CN.4/Sub.2/404; Sales No. E.80.XIV.3).

26. *Study of the Implications for Human Rights of Recent Developments concerning Situations Known as State of Siege or Emergency,* prepared by Mrs. Nicole Questiaux (France), Special Rapporteur, 1982 (E/CN.4/Sub.2/1982/15).

27. *Updating of the Report on Slavery,* prepared by Mr. Benjamin Whitaker (United Kingdom), Special Rapporteur (E/CN.4/Sub.2/1982/20/Rev.1; Sales No. 84.XIV.1).

28. *Study on Discriminatory Treatment against Members of Racial, Ethnic, Religious or Linguistic Groups at the Various Levels in the Administration of Criminal Justice Proceedings, Such as Police, Military, Administrative and Judicial Investigations, Arrest, Detention, Trial and Execution of Sentences, Including the Ideologies or Beliefs Which Contribute or Lead to All Forms of Racism in the Administration of Criminal Justice,* prepared by Mr. Justice Abu Sayeed Chowdhury (Bangladesh), Special Rapporteur, 1982 (E/CN.4/Sub.2/1982/7).

29. *Study on the Exploitation of Child Labour,* prepared by Mr. A. Bouhdiba (Tunisia), Special Rapporteur, 1981 (E/CN.4/Sub.2/479/Rev.1; Sales No. E.82.XIV.2).

30. *Study of the New International Economic Order and the Promotion of Human Rights,* prepared by Mr. Raul Ferrero (Peru), Special Rapporteur, 1983 (E/CN.4/Sub.2/1983/24 and Add.1–2; Sales No. E.85.XIV.6.).

31. *Study on Guidelines, Principles and Guarantees for the Protection of Persons Suffering from Mental Disorder,* prepared by Mrs. Erica-Irene A. Daes (Greece), Special Rapporteur, 1983 (E/CN.4/Sub.2/1983/17/Rev.1; Sales No. E.85.XIV.9).

32. *Study of the Problem of Discrimination against Indigenous Populations,* prepared by Mr. José Martinez Cobo (Ecuador), Special Rapporteur, 1981, 1982, 1983 and 1984 (E/CN.4/Sub.2/1986/7 and Add.1–4; Sales No. E.86.XIV.3 [contains only chapter XXI of the final report: conclusions, proposals and recommendations]).

33. *Study of the Question of Conscientious Objection to Military Service,* prepared by Mr. Asbjørn Eide (Norway) and Mr. L.C. Mubanga-Chipoya (Zambia), Special Rapporteurs, 1983 (E/CN.4/Sub.2/1983/30).

34. *Study on Relevant Guidelines in the Field of Computerized Personal Files, Particularly as They Affect the Privacy of the Individual,* Mrs. Nicole Questiaux (France), Special Rapporteur, completed by Mr. Louis Joinet (France), 1983 (E/CN.4/Sub.2/1983/18).

35. *Revised and Updated Report on the Question of the Prevention and Punishment of the Crime of Genocide,* prepared by Mr. Benjamin Whitaker (United Kingdom), Special Rapporteur, 1985 (E/CN.4/Sub.2/1985/6 and Corr.1).

36. *Draft Body of Principles and Guidelines on the Right and Responsibility of Individuals, Groups and Organs of Society to Promote and Protect Human Rights and Fundamental Freedoms,* prepared by Mrs. Erica-Irene A. Daes (Greece), Special Rapporteur, 1985 (E/CN.4/Sub.2/1985/30 and Add.1).

37. *Proposal concerning a Definition of the Term "Minority,"* submitted by Mr. Jules Deschênes (Canada), 1985 (E/CN.4/Sub.2/1985/31 and Corr.1).

38. *Study on Amnesty Laws and Their Role in the Safeguard and Promotion of Human Rights,* prepared by Mr. Louis Joinet (France), Special Rapporteur, 1985 (E/CN.4/Sub.2/1985/16).

39. *Annual Reports and List of States Which, since 1 January 1985, Have Proclaimed, Extended or Terminated a State of Emergency,* presented by Mr. Leandro Despouy (Argentina), Special Rapporteur (E/CN.4/Sub.2/1987/19; E/CN.4/Sub.2/1988/18 and Add.1; E/CN.4/Sub.2/1989/30 and Add.1 and Add.2/Rev.1).

40. *Analysis concerning the Proposition to Elaborate a Second Optional Protocol to the International Covenant on Civil and Political Rights Aiming at the Abolition of the Death Penalty,* prepared by Mr. Marc J. Bossuyt (Belgium), Special Rapporteur, 1987 and 1988 (E/CN.4/Sub.2/1987/20).

41. *Report on the Right to Adequate Food as a Human Right,* submitted by Mr. Asbjørn Eide (Norway), Special Rapporteur, 1987 (E/CN.4/Sub.2/1987/23; Sales No. E.89.XIV.2; Studies Series, Human Rights, No. 1).

42. *Reports on the Mission to Mauritania,* prepared by Mr. Marc J. Bossuyt (Belgium), Expert of the Sub-Commission, 1984, 1985 and 1987 (E/CN.4/Sub.2/1984/23, E/CN.4/Sub.2/1985/26 and E/CN.4/Sub.2/1987/27).

43. *Current Dimensions of the Problems of Intolerance and of Discrimination on Grounds of Religion or Belief,* study prepared by Mrs. Elizabeth Odio-Benito (Costa Rica), Special Rapporteur, 1987 (E/CN.4/Sub.2/1987/26; Sales No. E.89.XIV.3; Studies Series, Human Rights, No. 2).

44. *International Peace and Security as an Essential Condition for the Enjoyment of Human Rights, Above All the Right to Life,* report of the Secretary-General, 1988 (E/CN.4/Sub.2/1988/2).

45. *Prevention of the Disappearances of Children in Argentina,* report prepared by Mr. Theo van Boven (Netherlands), 1988 (E/CN.4/Sub.2/1988/19).

46. *Study on the Independence and Impartiality of the Judiciary, Jurors and Assessors and the Independence of Lawyers,* prepared by Mr. L.M. Singhvi (India), Special Rapporteur, 1985 and 1988 (E/CN.4/Sub.2/1985/18 and Add.1–6; E/CN.4/Sub.2/1988/20 and Add.1 and Add.1/Corr.1).

47. *Draft Guidelines for the Regulation of Computerized Personal Data Files,* prepared by Mr. Louis Joinet (France), Special Rapporteur, 1988 (E/CN.4/Sub.2/1988/22).

48. *Study on the Legal and Social Problems of Sexual Minorities,* prepared by Mr. Jean Fernand-Laurent (France) pursuant to Economic and Social Council resolution 1983/30; 1988 (E/CN.4/Sub.2/1988/31).

49. *Analysis of Current Trends and Developments in Respect of the Right of Everyone to Leave any Country, including His Own, and to Return to His Country, And to Have the Possibility to Enter Other Countries, without Discrimination or Hindrance, Especially of the Right to Employment,* Mr. Mubanga-Chipoya (Zambia), Special Rapporteur, 1988 and 1989 (E/CN.4/Sub.2/1988/35 and Add.1 and Add.1/Corr.1).

50. *Respect for the Right to Life: Elimination of Chemical Weapons,* report of the Secretary-General, 1989 (E/CN/4/Sub.2/1989/4).

51. *Study on the Achievements Made and Obstacles Encountered during the Decades to Combat Racism and Racial Discrimination,* prepared by Mr. Asbjørn Eide (Norway), 1989 (E/CN.4/Sub.2/1989/8 and Add.1).

52. *Hopi-Navajo Relocation,* summary of information submitted by Mrs. Erica-Irene A. Daes (Greece) and Mr. John Carey (United States of America), 1989 (E/CN/4/Sub.2/1989/35 [Part I and Part II; and Add.1]).

53. *Study on Ways and Means for Establishing an Effective Mechanism for the Implementation of the Slavery Conventions,* prepared by the Secretary-General, 1989 (E/CN.4/Sub.2/1989/37).

54. *Status of the Individual and Contemporary International Law,* report prepared by Mrs. Erica-Irene A. Daes (Greece), Special Rapporteur, 1989 (E/CN.4/Sub.2/1989/40).

E. Studies and Reports Now under Preparation by Special Rapporteurs of the Sub-Commission

1. *Report on the Right to a Fair Trial,* Mr. Stanislaw Chernichenko (USSR) and Mr. William Treat (United States of America).

2. *Report on Human Rights of Detained Juveniles,* Mrs. Mary Bautista (Philippines).

3. *Report on Administrative Detention without Charge or Trial,* Mr. Louis Joinet (France).

4. *Human Rights and Disability,* Mr. Leandro Despouy (Argentina).

5. *Study on Recent Developments with Regard to Traditional Practices affecting the Health of Women and Children,* Mrs. Halima E. Warzazi (Morocco).

6. *Annual Updated Report and List of Banks, Transnational Corporations and Other Organizations Assisting South Africa,* Mr. Ahmed Khalifa (Egypt).

7. *Study on the Realization of Economic, Social and Cultural Rights,* Mr. Danilo Türk (Yugoslavia).

8. *Annual Reports and List of Countries Which Have Proclaimed, Extended or Terminated a State of Emergency,* Mr. Leandro Despouy (Argentina).

9. *Report on Violations of Human Rights of Staff Members of the United Nations System,* Mrs. Mary Bautista (Philippines).

10. *Study on Treaties, Agreements and Other Constructive Agreements Concluded between States and Indigenous Peoples,* Mr. Miguel Alfonso Martinez (Cuba).

11. *Human Rights and Youth,* Mr. Dimitru Mazilu (Romania).

12. *Report on the Right to Restitution, Compensation and Rehabilitation for Victims of Gross Violations of Human Rights,* Mr. Theo van Boven (Netherlands).

13. *Study on the Right to Freedom of Opinion and Expression,* Mr. Louis Joinet (France) and Mr. Danilo Türk (Yugoslavia).

14. *Study on Problems and Causes of Discrimination against HIV-infected People or People with AIDS,* Mr. Luis Varela Quiros (Costa Rica).

15. *Study on Possible Ways and Means of Facilitating the Peaceful Solution of Problems involving Minorities,* Mr. Asbjørn Eide (Norway).

APPENDIX H

MEMBERSHIP OF INTER-GOVERNMENTAL ORGANIZATIONS CONCERNED WITH HUMAN RIGHTS

1. Arab League

Up to 30 June 1990, the following 21 States were members of the Arab League: Algeria, Bahrain, Djibouti, Egypt, Iraq, Jordan, Kuwait, Lebanon, Libya, Mauritania, Morocco, Oman, Palestine, Qatar, Saudi Arabia, Somalia, Sudan, Syria, Tunisia, the United Arab Emirates, and Yemen. (*N.B.* North and South Yemen, both members, merged in May 1990.)

2. Commonwealth of Nations

Up to 30 June 1990, the following 47 States were members of the Commonwealth of Nations: Antigua, Australia, Bahamas, Bangladesh, Barbados, Belize, Botswana, Brunei, Canada, Cyprus, Dominica, Gambia, Ghana, Grenada, Guyana, India, Jamaica, Kenya, Kiribati, Lesotho, Malawi, Malaysia, Maldives, Malta, Mauritius, Namibia, New Zealand, Nigeria, Papua New Guinea, St. Kitts and Nevis, Saint Lucia, St. Vincent and the Grenadines, Seychelles, Sierra Leone, Singapore, Solomon Islands, Sri Lanka, Swaziland, Tanzania, Tonga, Trinidad, Uganda, United Kingdom of Great Britain and Northern Ireland, Vanuatu, Western Samoa, Zambia, and Zimbabwe. There are two "special members:" Nauru and Tuvalu.

3. Conference on Security and Co-Operation in Europe

Up to 30 June 1990, the following 34 States were members of the Conference on Security and Co-operation in Europe (CSCE) (the Helsinki Agreement): Austria, Belgium, Bulgaria, Canada, Cyprus, Czechoslovakia, Denmark, Germany, Finland, France, Great Britain, Greece, Hungary, Iceland, Ireland, Italy, Liechtenstein, Luxembourg, Malta, Monaco, Netherlands, Norway, Poland, Portugal, Romania, San Marino, Spain, Sweden, Switz-erland, Turkey, United States of America, Union of Soviet Socialist Republics, the Vatican, and Yugoslavia. (*N. B.* East and West Germany, both members, merged in Oct. 1990.)

4. Non-Aligned Movement ("Group of 77")

Up to 15 February 1990, the following 101 States were members of the Non-Aligned Movement: Afghanistan, Algeria, Angola, Argentina, Bahamas, Bahrain, Bangladesh, Barbados, Belize, Benin, Bhutan, Bolivia, Botswana, Burkina Faso, Burundi, Cambodia, Cameroon, Cape Verde, Central African Republic, Chad, Colombia, Comoros, Congo, Cuba, Cyprus, Djibouti, Ecuador, Egypt, Equatorial Guinea, Ethiopia, Gabon, Gambia, Ghana, Grenada, Guinea, Guinea-Bissau, Guyana, India, Indonesia, Iran, Iraq, Ivory Coast, Jamaica, Jordan, Kenya, Kuwait, Laos, Lebanon, Lesotho, Liberia, Libya, Madagascar, Malawi, Malaysia, Maldives, Mali, Malta, Mauritania, Mauritius, Morocco, Mozambique, Namibia, Nepal, Nicaragua, Niger, Nigeria, North Korea, Oman, Pakistan, Palestine Liberation Organization, Panama, Peru, Qatar, Rwanda, St. Lucia, Sao Tome and Principe, Saudi Arabia, Senegal, Seychelles, Sierra Leone, Singapore, Somalia, Sri Lanka, Sudan, Suriname, Swaziland, Syria, Tanzania, Togo, Trinidad and Tobago, Tunisia, Uganda, United Arab Emirates, Vanuatu, Venezuela, Vietnam, Yemen, Yugoslavia, Zaire, Zambia, and Zimbabwe. (*N. B.* North and South Yemen, both members, merged in May 1990.)

5. North Atlantic Treaty Organization

Up to 30 June 1990, the following 16 States were members of the North Atlantic Treaty Organization (NATO): Belgium, Canada, Denmark, France, Greece, Iceland, Italy, Luxembourg, Netherlands, Norway, Portugal, Spain, Turkey, the United Kingdom of Great Britain and Northern Ireland, the United States of America, and West Germany. (*N. B.* As of Oct. 1990, East and West Germany merged. Germany remains a NATO member.)

6. Organization of African Unity

Up to 30 June 1990, the following 50 States were members of the Organization of African Unity (OAU): Algeria, Angola, Benin, Botswana, Burkina Faso, Burundi, Cameroon, Cape Verde, Central African Republic, Chad, Comoros, Congo, Djibouti, Egypt, Equatorial Guinea, Ethiopia, Gabon, Gambia, Ghana, Guinea, Guinea-Bissau, Ivory Coast, Kenya, Lesotho, Liberia, Libya, Madagascar, Malawi, Mali, Mauritania, Mauritius, Morocco, Mozambique, Niger, Nigeria, Rwanda, Sao Tome, Senegal, Seychelles, Sierra Leone, Somalia, Sudan, Swaziland, Tanzania, Togo, Tunisia, Uganda, Zaire, Zambia, and Zimbabwe.

7. Organization of American States

Up to 30 June 1990, the following 31 States were members of the Organization of American States (OAS): Antigua, Argentina, Bahamas, Barbados, Bolivia, Brazil, Chile, Colombia, Costa Rica, Cuba, Dominica, Dominican Republic, Ecuador, El Salvador, Grenada, Haiti, Honduras, Jamaica, Mexico, Nicaragua, Panama, Paraguay, Peru, St. Kitts and Nevis, St. Lucia, St. Vincent and the Grenadines, Suriname, Trinidad, the United States of America, Uruguay, and Venezuela.

8. Organization of the Islamic Conference

Up to 15 February 1990, the following 41 States were members of the Organization of the Islamic Conference: Afghanistan, Algeria, Bahrain, Bangladesh, Burkina Faso, Cameroon, Chad, Comoros, Cyprus, Djibouti, Egypt, Gabon, Gambia, Guinea, Guinea-Bissau, Indonesia, Iran, Jordan, Kuwait, Lebanon, Libya, Malaysia, Mali, Mauritania, Morocco, Niger, Oman, Pakistan, Palestine Liberation Organization, Qatar, Saudi Arabia, Senegal, Sierra Leone, Somalia, Sudan, Syria, Tunisia, Turkey, Uganda, United Arab Emirates, and Yemen. (*N. B.* North and South Yemen, both members, merged in May 1990.)

9. Organization of Petroleum-Exporting Countries

Up to 30 June 1990, the following 13 States were members of the Organization of Petroleum-Exporting Countries (OPEC): Algeria, Ecuador, Gabon, Indonesia, Iran, Iraq, Kuwait, Libya, Nigeria, Qatar, Saudi Arabia, United Arab Emirates, and Venezuela.

10. Warsaw Pact

Up to the close of 1990, the following six States were members of the Warsaw Pact: Bulgaria, Czechoslovakia, Hungary, Poland, Romania, and the Union of Soviet Socialist Republics. East Germany was a member of the Warsaw Pact until it merged with West Germany in Oct. 1990. The re-united Germany is a member of NATO.

APPENDIX I

LIST OF NATIONAL INSTITUTIONS CONCERNED WITH HUMAN RIGHTS

This list of national institutions for the promotion and protection of human rights is established in accordance with the information submitted by governments. The list is as follows (E/CN.4/1989/47:36–47):

I. Legislative Organs established to Examine the Constitutionality of Laws

A. *Legislative Organs*

Ad hoc Commission (Spain, United States)

Advisory Commission (or investigatory commission) (Barbados)

Bureau for Petitions and Appeals (Yugoslavia)

Civil Liberty Protection Unit (Thailand)

Commission Consultative des Droits de l'Homme (France)

Commission for Information and Guidance regarding Human Rights (Suriname)

Commission générale de Pétitions (Spain)

Commission législative constitutionnelle et de Justice (Spain)

Committee Deals (Finland)

Committee of Petitions (India, United Kingdom)

Commission permanente constitutionnelle (Spain)

Commission permanente de Pétitions (Spain)

Direito e Justica (Portugal)

House of Commons (United Kingdom)

House of Congress (United States)

Human Rights Commission (El Salvador)

Litigation Expeditions Unit (Thailand)

Ligue pour la Défense et la Promotion des Droits de l'Homme (Madagascar)

Lower House (Finland)

Parliament (Finland, France, New Zealand, Poland)

Parliament Committee for Constitutional Law (Finland)

Presidium of the Supreme Soviet (USSR)

Privacy Commissioner (New Zealand)

Public Petitions Committee (New Zealand)

Select Committee on Statutory Instruments (United Kingdom)

Senate Select Committee (United States)

Standing Commission (Byelorussian SSR, Ukrainian SSR and USSR)

Standing Commission on Petitions (Spain)

Supreme Court (Poland)

Surate Legal Committee (Zimbabwe)

Wanganiu Computer Centre Privacy Commission (New Zealand)

B. *Organs established to Examine the Constitutionality of Laws*

Constitutional Council (Hungary)

II. Judicial Organs

A. *Courts of General Jurisdiction*

Appeal Court (Finland, France, Singapore, United Kingdom)

Assize Court (France)

Chancellor of Justice (Finland)

Chamber of Appeal (Chambre de Recours) (France)

Circuit Courts of Appeals (United States)

Common Courts (Poland)

Consejero de Estado (Venezuela)

Constitutional Council (France)

Constitutional Court (Canada, El Salvador, Federal Republic of Germany, Guatemala, India, Panama, Spain)

Constitutional Guarantees (Ecuador)

Constitutional Tribunal (Thailand)

Council of State (France)

County Courts (United Kingdom)

Courts of Criminal Appeal (Singapore)

Crown Court (United Kingdom)

Defender of the People (Defensor de Pueblo) (Spain)

District Courts (Singapore)

Federal Constitutional Court (Federal Republic of Germany)

Federal Courts (Canada, United States)

High Court, (Argentina, Barbados, Colombia, El Salvador, India, Nigeria, Panama, Singapore, Spain, United Kingdom, Venezuela)

House of Lords (United Kingdom)

Magistrates' Courts (Singapore, United Kingdom)

Parliamentary Ombudsman (Finland)

Supreme Court (Canada, Cyprus, Ecuador, El Salvador, Finland, Federal Republic of Germany, India, Nigeria, Papua New Guinea, Panama, Poland, Singapore, Spain, Sri Lanka, United States, USSR)

Supreme Court of Appeal (France)

B. Constitutional Courts

Acción Popular de Inconstitucionalidad (El Salvador, Panama, Venezuela)

Constitutional Court (Canada, El Salvador, Federal Republic of Germany, India, Panama, Spain)

Constitutional Guarantees Court (Ecuador)

Executive Collegiate Bodies of the Autonomous Communities (Spain)

High Court (Spain)

People's Advocate (Spain)

Supreme Court (Spain)

Supreme Electoral Court (Ecuador)

C. Special Courts and Tribunals

1. Labor Courts

Arbeidsretten (Norway)

Central Labour Court (Thailand)

Conseils de Prud-hommes (France, Tunisia)

Council of State (Belgium, Finland, France, Greece)

Defensor del Pueblo (Spain)

Insurance Court (Finland)

Labour Court (Barbados, Finland, Federal Republic of Germany, India, Kenya, Papua New Guinea, Thailand)

Labour Relations Board (Canada)

Self-Management Court (Yugoslavia)

Special Court (France, Netherlands)

Supreme Administrative Court (Finland, Poland)

Workers' Mediatory Commissions (Poland)

2. Juvenile and Children's Courts

Assize Court for Minors (France)

Children and Young Persons' Courts (New Zealand)

Children's Board (New Zealand)

Children's Courts (Australia)

Juvenile and Children's Courts (Australia, France, Thailand)

Juvenile Assize (France)

Juvenile Court (Barbados, El Salvador, France)

Minors' Penal Court (Tunisia)

Special Juvenile Court (Italy)

3. Other Specialized Courts

Broadcasting Tribunal (New Zealand)

Deportation Review Tribunal (New Zealand)

Family Courts (Australia)

Indecent Publication Tribunal (New Zealand)

Maori Appellate Court (New Zealand)

Maori Land Court (New Zealand)

Ministerio Fiscal (Spain)

Social Insurance Court (Norway)

D. Administrative Courts and Tribunals

Administrative Courts (Austria, Belgium, France, Greece, Netherlands, Tunisia)

Conseil d'Etat (France)

Cour de Cassation (France)

Supreme Administrative Court (Finland)

E. Other Organs established within the Framework of the Judicial System

1. Ombudsman and Similar Institutions

Ad Hoc Arbitrator (Fiji)

Assemblies of Socio-Political Communities (Yugoslavia)

Children's Ombudsman (Norway)

Civil Ombudsman's Protection against Arbitrariness in Public Administration (Norway)

Commission of Counter Corruption (Thailand)

Commission of Investigation (Tanzania)

Commission for Self-Management Workers Supervision (Yugoslavia)

Equal Opportunities Commissioner (Norway)

Equal Opportunities Council (Norway)

Médiateur (France)

Ministerio Público (Colombia, Ecuador, Guatemala, Portugal, Venezuela)

Nigerian Public Complaints Commission (Nigeria)

Ombudsman (Australia, Austria, Barbados, Canada, Denmark, Fiji, Finland, France, Federal Republic of Germany, Ghana, Guatemala, Guyana, India, Jamaica, Japan, Mauritius, New Zealand, Nigeria, Norway, Portugal, Spain, Sudan, Sweden, Tanzania, Trinidad and Tobago, United Kingdom, United States, Zambia, Zimbabwe)

Supreme Court of Justice (Organic Law) (Venezuela)

Permanent Arbitrator (Fiji)

Permanent Commission of Enquiry (Tanzania)

Prokuratura (Albania, Bulgaria, Byelorussian SSR,

Czechoslovakia, Democratic Republic of Germany, Hungary, Poland, Romania, Ukrainian SSR, USSR, Yugoslavia)

Prosecutor's (Finland)

Provedor de Justica (Portugal)

Public Complaints Commission (Nigeria)

Servicio du Provedor de Justica (Portugal)

Social Attorney of Self-Management (Yugoslavia)

Social Mediatory Commissions (Poland)

Wanganiu Computer Centre Privacy Commission (New Zealand)

Volksanwaltschaft (Austria)

Workers' Councils in Undertaking (Yugoslavia)

Works' Mediatory Commissions (Poland)

2. Legal Assistance Services

Bureau of Civil Liberty and Public Interest Protection (Thailand)

Citizens Legal Assistance Office (Philippines)

Colleges of Attorneys (Byelorussian SSR, Ukrainian SSR, USSR)

Community Legal Services (Barbados)

Legal Aid Association (Japan)

Legal Aid Board (Finland)

Legal Aid Council Office (Nigeria)

Legal Aid Regulation of the Public Prosecution (Thailand)

Legal Aid Service Regulation Issued by the Public Prosecution Department (Thailand)

Legal Aid Unit (Thailand)

Maluganik Tukisiiniakvit Legal Service Centre (Canada)

Native Courtworkers' Association (Canada)

Public Defender Office (United States)

Public Legal Aid (United States)

III. Administrative Organs

A. Human Rights Commissions and Similar Public Bodies Expressly Entrusted with Overall Responsibilities in the Field of Human Rights

Advisory Body of the Commission for Human Rights of the Federal Secretariat for Foreign Affairs (Yugoslavia)

Australian Commission of Jurists (Australia)

Board's Membership (Canada)

Canadian Human Rights Commission (Canada)

Canadian Human Rights Act (Canada)

Central Civil Liberties Bureau of the Ministry of Justice (Japan)

Civil Liberties Bureau (Japan)

Civil Liberties Protection Unit (Thailand)

Commission des Droits de l'Homme de l'Ordre des Avocats (Portugal)

Commission for Fundamental Rights (New Zealand)

Commission for Information and Guidance regarding Human Rights (Suriname)

Commissioner for Community Relations (Australia)

Committees of Minors (USSR)

Committees of the International Covenant on Economic, Social and Cultural Rights (Iraq)

Committees on the International Covenant on Civil and Political Rights (Iraq)

Computer-based Information Centre (New Zealand)

Council for the Protection of Human Rights (Brazil)

Danish Human Rights Division (Denmark)

Department of the Secretary of State (Canada)

Directorate of Human Rights of the Department of State (Canada)

District Minority Committees (Pakistan)

Federal Human Rights Commission (Canada)

Federal-Provincial Committee of Officials responsible for Human Rights (Canada)

Federal-Provincial-Territorial Committees (Canada)

Foreign and Public Relations Unit (Thailand)

Human Rights Commission (Australia)

Human Rights Division (Israel)

Human Rights Society (Pakistan)

Human Rights Tribunal (Canada)

Italian Interministerial Committee on Human Rights (Italy)

Iraq National Human Rights Commission (Iraq)

National Commission for the Promotion and Protection of Human Rights (Nicaragua)

National Human Rights Committee (Iraq)

National Institutions for the Promotion and Protection of Human Rights (Suriname)

New Zealand Human Rights Commission (New Zealand)

Norwegian Human Rights Committee (Norway)

Police Complaints Board (United Kingdom)

Provincial Human Rights Commissions (Canada)

Provincial Minister of Justice (Canada)

Sami Committee (Finland)

Senate Legal Committee (Zimbabwe)

Standing Advisory Commission on Human Rights (Northern Ireland)

Supervisory Committees (USSR)

United States Civil Rights Commission (United States)

United States Equal Employment Opportunity Commissions (United States)

Voluntary Crime Prevention Boards (USSR)

Voluntary People's Militia (Byelorussian SSR, Ukrainian SSR, USSR)

B. Agencies for the Protection of Specific Groups

  1. Agencies for the Protection of Persons belonging to Ethnic, Linguistic and Religious Minorities

Advisory Board for Gypsy Affairs (Finland)
Advisory Committee (Pakistan)
Australian Federal Chancellery (Australia)
Australian Institute of Multicultural Affairs (Australia)
Central Council of German Sinti and Rom (Federal Republic of Germany)
Commission consultative pour les Refugiés (Portugal)
Commission to Promote the Principle of Equality and Collective Rights (Yugoslavia)
Commission for Lappish Affairs (Finland)
Commission for Racial Equality (United Kingdom)
Commission interministérielle d'Appui aux Refugiés et Apatrides (Portugal)
Commission of Minors (Ukrainian SSR)
Commission on Civil Rights (United States)
Commissioner for Linguistic Minorities (India)
Commissioner for Scheduled Castes and Tribes (India)
Committee for Refugee Matters (Finland)
Committee for the Slovene-speaking and Croatian-speaking Minorities (Austria)
Committee of Inquiry into the Education of Children (United Kingdom)
Committee on Migration Affairs (Finland)
Counsellor for Aliens (Finland)
Cuban Institute of Friendship (Cuba)
Ethnic and Religious Committees (Canada)
District Minority Committees (Pakistan)
Fair Employment Agency (Northern Ireland)
Human Rights Society (Pakistan)
Indian Minority Commission (India)
Mexican Commission for Assistance to Refugees (Mexico)
National Board of Social Welfare (Finland)
National Committees (Czechoslovakia)
Office of the Commissioner for Community Relations (Australia)
Office of Race Relations Conciliator (New Zealand)
Permanent Commission of Enquiry (Tanzania)
Presidential Council for Minority Rights (Singapore)
Public Complaints Commission of Nigeria (Nigeria)
Sami Committee (Finland)
Social Welfare Services (Cyprus)
Standing Advisory Commission on Human Rights (Northern Ireland)
Tunisian League of Human Rights (Tunisia)
Research Centre for Domestic Languages (Finland)

2. Agencies for the Protection of Indigenous Populations
Committee for Refugee Matters (Finland)

Department of Maori and Island Affairs (New Zealand)
Finnish Commission for Lappish Affairs (Finland)
Instituto Nacional Indigenista de Mexico (Mexico)
Norwegian Lapp Council (Norway)
Swedish Commission on Sami Affairs (Sweden)

3. Agencies for the Protection of Aliens, Migrants, and Immigrants
Aliens Advisory Commission (Belgium)
Australian Ethnic Affairs Council (Australia)
Commission on Ethnic Prejudice and Discrimination (Sweden)
Committee on Migration Affairs (Finland)
Directorate for Aliens and Refugee Board (Denmark)
Multi-Cultural Resource Centres (Australia)
Norwegian Foreign Workers' Association (Norway)

4. Agencies for the Protection and Promotion of Children and Minors
Child Care Board (Barbados)
Children's Ombudsman (Norway)
Chinese People's National Committee for the Defence of Children (China)
Commission on Children's Rights (Sweden)
Council for Family Affairs (Poland)
Egyptian Supreme Council for the Child (Egypt)
Federal Inter-agency Committee for Children and Youth (United States)
Indian National Children's Board (India)
Juvenile Welfare Board (Norway)
Maternity and Child Welfare (USSR)
Minor's Association (Mexico)
National Children's Board (India)
National Commission for the Year (Algeria)
National Council for the Child (Dominican Republic)
National Council for Children's Affairs (Bangladesh)
National Directorate for Children and Family (Panama)
National Policy for the Children (India)
Orphans' Housing Aid Society (Poland)
Polish Pathfinders' Union (Poland)
Polish Students' Association (Poland)
Rural Youth Union (Poland)
Social Welfare Board (Finland)
Society of the Friends for Children (Poland)
Standing Commission on Women's Working and Living Conditions, Maternity and Child Welfare (Byelorussian SSR)
Supreme Council for the Child (Egypt)
Union of Socialist Polish Youth (Poland)

5. Agencies for the Protection of Women

Australian National Women's Advisory Council (Australia)

Commission of Supreme Soviet on Women's Working and Living Conditions (USSR)

Commission on Women's Rights (Barbados)

Committee on the Status of Women (India)

National Committee on Women (India)

Office of Women's Affairs (Australia)

C. Equal Employment Agencies

Danish Equality Council (Denmark)

Department of Employment and Employment Promotion of the Ministry of Labour and Social Services (Zimbabwe)

Employment Departments at the Local People's Councils (Poland)

Employment Division (Barbados)

Equal Council (Denmark)

Equal Employment Opportunity Commission (United States)

Equality Ombudsman (Finland)

Equality of Treatment Committee (Austria)

French Supreme Council for Professional Equality between Men and Women (France)

General Division (Barbados)

National and Local Employment Discrimination Committees (Australia)

National and State Committees on Discrimination in Employment and Occupation (Australia)

Portuguese Commission on Women's Rights (Portugal)

Tax and Valuation Division of Appeal Tribunal (Barbados)

Tripartite Advisory Committee (India)

Vigilance Committee (India)

D. Institutions for the Dissemination of Information, in Particular Information on Human Rights

Australian National Commission for UNESCO (Australia)

Civil Liberties Bureaux (Japan)

Civil Liberties Commissioners (Japan)

Commission for Information and Guidance regarding Human Rights (Suriname)

Committees for the Defence of Human Rights (Venezuela)

Committee on Human Rights (German Democratic Republic)

Council for the Protection of Human Rights (Brazil)

Human Rights Commission (Nicaragua)

Human Rights Permanent Commission on the Right to *Amparo* (Ecuador)

Marangopoulos Foundation for Human Rights (Greece)

Nigerian Institute of International Affairs Services (Nigeria)

People's Councils (Poland)

People's Universities in the USSR (USSR)

Polish Institute for International Affairs (Poland)

Polish Red Cross Society (Poland)

Scholarly Research and Information on Human Rights (Poland)

Society for the Popularization of Culture and Science (Poland)

Society of Friends of the United Nations (Poland)

Yermouth University of Jordan (Jordan)

E. Educational Institutions

Academy of Social Sciences (Poland)

Canadian Foundation for Human Rights (Canada)

Canadian Human Rights Commission (Canada)

Central Committee of the Polish United Workers' Party (Poland)

Child Care Board (Barbados)

Civil Liberties Bureaux (Japan)

Civil Liberties Commissioners (Japan)

Committee of Inquiry into the Education of Children (United Kingdom)

Commission for Educational Planning and Research Promotion (Federal Republic of Germany)

International Institute of Human Rights (France)

Judicial Office (Spain)

Legal Education of the Population in the Field of Human Rights (Ukrainian SSR)

National Commission on the Role of the Filipino (Philippines)

Nigerian Institute of International Affairs (Nigeria)

Norwegian Human Rights Committee (Norway)

Swedish National Educational Board (Sweden)

F. Health Care Systems

Aboriginal Health Programme (Australia)

Association of Catholics "Caritas" (Poland)

Directorate of Epidemic Disease (Senegal)

Community Health Programme (Austria)

Departments of Health and Social Welfare (Poland)

Environmental Health Units (Iraq)

Family Planning Association (New Zealand)

Health Service Commissioner (United Kingdom)

National Commission for Disabled Persons (Philippines)

National Family Planning and Populations Bureau (Tunisia)

Occupational Health Safety and Compensation Department (Zimbabwe)

Polish Committee for Social Aid (Poland)

Polish Red Cross (Poland)
Population Control and Family Planning Division of the Ministry of Health (Bangladesh)
Provincial People's Acting Councils (Poland)
Rural Health Centres (Cyprus)
Swedish National Board (Sweden)
Swedish National Board of Health and Welfare (Sweden)
Village Health Committees (India)

G. Society Security and Social Welfare Schemes

Central Social Welfare Board (India)
Co-operative Insurance Institutions (Poland)
Department of Social Services of Ministry of Labour and Social Services (Zimbabwe)
Housing Corporation (Bahamas)
Insurance Units (Poland)
National Commission for Integral Family Development (Mexico)
National Insurance Board (Barbados)
Nigerian Ministry of Social Development (Nigeria)
Ministry of Social Services and Development (Philippines)
Social Security Division (Barbados)
State-controlled Social Insurance Institution (Poland)
Youth, Sports and Culture (Niger)

IV. Non-Governmental Organizations

Amnesty International, Finnish Section (Finland)
Amicale des Femmes Juristes (Senegal)
Anti-Racism Movement (Canada)
Association for the Protection of Human Rights against Encroachments of Psychiatry (Austria)
Association of the Friends of Human Rights (Egypt)
Association sénégalaise de Recherche et d'Etudes juridiques (Senegal)
Association sénégalaise pour les Nations Unies (Senegal)
Australian Section of Amnesty International (Australia)
Catholic Church (Dominican Republic)
Central Union for Child Welfare (Finland)
Comité sénégalaise des Droits de l'Homme (Senegal)

Committee for Human Rights of the Lawyers' Association (Portugal)
Commission de la Condition féminine (Portugal)
Commission portugaise Pro-Amnesty International (Portugal)
Commission nationale des Droits de la Femme sénégalaise (Senegal)
Conseil supérieur de l'Egalité professionnelle entre les Femmes et les Hommes (France)
Dominican Human Rights Committee (Dominican Republic)
Egyptian Association for Human Rights (Egypt)
Ethnic and Religious Committees (Canada)
Federation of Iraqi Jurists (Iraq)
Fondation pour les Droits de l'Homme (Greece)
Finnish Gypsy Association (Finland)
Finnish Red Cross (Finland)
Francisco Ulises Espaillat Foundation (Dominican Republic)
General Federation of Iraqi Women (Iraq)
Ihmisoikenspuristit (Finland)
Indian (India)
Indonesian Institute for the Defence of Human Rights (Indonesia)
Iraqi Human Rights Society (Iraq)
Innuit and Native Organization (Canada)
Lawyers' Association (Iraq)
League for Human Rights (Austria)
Ligue portugaise des Droits de l'Homme (Portugal)
Mediatory Commission of the Labour Courts at District Courts (Poland)
Organization for Disabled Groups (Canada)
Provincial Civil Liberties Associations (Canada)
Section grecque de l'Amnesty International (Greece)
Section nationale des Juristes démocrates (Senegal)
Section sénégalaise de l'Association des Barreaux africains (Senegal)
Unión Dominicana para la Defensa de los Derechos Humanos (Dominican Republic)
Union pour les Droits de l'Homme et des Citoyens (Greece)
Unioni Women's Rights Union (Finland)
Women's Rights Organization (Canada)
Workers' Unions (USSR)
Works Mediatory Commissions (Poland)

SUBJECT INDEX

Arms
  Arms Sales and Human Rights, 100
  Convention on Prohibitions or Restrictions on the Use of
    Certain Conventional Weapons which may be
    Deemed to be Excessively Injurious or to Have
    Indiscriminate Effects and Protocols, 262
  See also: Biological Weapons; Chemical Weapons; Civil-
    ians; Nuclear Weapons
Arrest
  Arbitrary Arrest, Detention or Exile, 92
  Arrest, Detention, and Abduction of International Civil
    Servants, 100
  Arrested Person's Right to Communicate, 104
  Legal Aid, 1029
  See also: Prisoners
Artists
  UNESCO International Convention for the Protection of
    Performers, Producers of Phonograms and Broad-
    casting Organizations, 1510
  UNESCO Recommendation concerning the Status of the
    Artist, 1540
  UNESCO Recommendation for the Safeguarding and
    Preservation of Moving Images, 1545
  See also: Copyright
Assembly and Association, 105
  ILO Collective Bargaining Convention, 795
  ILO Freedom of Association and Protection of the Right
    to Organize Convention, 805
  ILO Freedom of Association Committee of the Govern-
    ing Body, 806
  ILO Freedom of Association Fact-finding and Concilia-
    tion Commission, 806
  ILO Labor Relations (Public Service) Convention, 823
  ILO Right of Association (Agriculture) Convention, 847
  ILO Right to Organize and Collective Bargaining Con-
    vention, 847
  ILO Rural Workers' Organizations Convention, 848
  ILO Workers' Representatives Convention, 860
  State of Emergency: Freedom of Association, 1410
  Thought, Conscience and Religion, 1430
  Appendix A (Freedom of Association), 1800
  Appendix A (Right to Organize), 1803
  Appendix A (Right of Peaceful Assembly), 1804
  See also: Expression; Freedoms and Rights
Assistance
  See: Advisory Services; Economic Assistance; Legal Aid;
    Victims
Associations
  See: NGOs
Asylum
  Declaration on Territorial Asylum, 365
  Inter-American Convention on Diplomatic Asylum,
    895
  Inter-American Convention on Territorial Asylum, 900
  See also: Immunity
Australia, 110
  Australia: Constitution, 116
  Appendix A, 1718
Austria, 117
  Austria: Constitution, 118
  Appendix A, 1718
Authoritarianism
  See: Totalitarianism
Authority
  See: Immunity; Impunity; Judiciary; Law Enforcement;
    Medical Ethics

Authors
  See: Artists; Copyright; Journalists
Awards
  European Human Rights Prize, 562
  Human Rights Teaching Prize, 788
Azania, 119
  Pan Africanist Congress of Azania, 1190

Bahamas, 120
  Appendix A, 1718
Bahrain, 120
  Appendix A, 1718
Bail
  See: Arrest
Bangladesh, 121
  Appendix A, 1719
Banjul Charter
  African Charter on Human and Peoples' Rights, 12
Bantustans
  See: Apartheid; South Africa
Bar associations
  See: NGOs
Barbados, 122
  Appendix A, 1720
Bargaining
  See: Workers
Battered Women
  See: Domestic Violence; Women
Beijing Rules
  United Nations Standard Minimum Rules for the Ad-
    ministration of Juvenile Justice, 1616
Belgium, 127
  Belgium: Constitution, 128
Belief
  See: Thought, Conscience and Religion
Belize, 130
  Appendix A, 1720
Benin, 130
  Appendix A, 1720
Bhutan, 131
Bibliography
  Appendix A—Countries, 1715
  Appendix A—General Subjects, 1778
Bi-culturalism
  See: Culture; Discrimination, cultural
Bill of Rights
  See: International Bill of Human Rights; National Law
Bioethics
  See: Medical Ethics; Science and Technology
Biological Weapons
  Convention on the Prohibition of the Development, Pro-
    duction and Stockpiling of Bacteriological (Biologi-
    cal) and Toxin Weapons and on Their Destruction,
    282
  Protocol for the Prohibition of the Use of Asphyxiating,
    Poisonous or Other Gases and of Bacteriological
    Methods of Warfare, 1244
  See also: Chemical Weapons; Nuclear Weapons
Birth
  Abortion, 1
  Convention on the Reduction of Statelessness, 284
  European Convention on the Legal Status of Children
    born out of Wedlock, 536
  ILO Maternity Protection Convention, 824
  Marriage and the Family, 1045